THE CAMBRIDGE ANNOTATED STUDY BIBLE

New Revised Standard Version

THE CAMBRIDGE ANNOTATED STUDY BIBLE

New Revised Standard Version

NOTES
AND REFERENCES BY
HOWARD CLARK KEE

Published by the Press Syndicate of the University of Cambridge
The Pitt Building, Trumpington Street, Cambridge CB2 1RP
40 West 20th Street, New York, NY 10011-4211, USA
10 Stamford Road, Oakleigh, Melbourne 3166, Australia

Printed in Great Britain at
the University Press, Cambridge

ISBN 0 521 50777 4 hardback

CONTENTS

PREFACE TO THE NEW REVISED STANDARD VERSION

This preface is addressed to you by the Committee of translators, who wish to explain, as briefly as possible, the origin and character of our work. The publication of our revision is yet another step in the long, continual process of making the Bible available in the form of the English language that is most widely current in our day. To summarize in a single sentence: the New Revised Standard Version of the Bible is an authorized revision of the Revised Standard Version, published in 1952, which was a revision of the American Standard Version, published in 1901, which, in turn, embodied earlier revisions of the King James Version, published in 1611.

In the course of time, the King James Version came to be regarded as "the Authorized Version." With good reason it has been termed "the noblest monument of English prose," and it has entered, as no other book has, into the making of the personal character and the public institutions of the English-speaking peoples. We owe to it an incalculable debt.

Yet the King James Version has serious defects. By the middle of the nineteenth century, the development of biblical studies and the discovery of many biblical manuscripts more ancient than those on which the King James Version was based made it apparent that these defects were so many as to call for revision. The task was begun, by authority of the Church of England, in 1870. The (British) Revised Version of the Bible was published in 1881-1885; and the American Standard Version, its variant embodying the preferences of the American scholars associated with the work, was published, as was mentioned above, in 1901. In 1928 the copyright of the latter was acquired by the International Council of Religious Education and thus passed into the ownership of the churches of the United States and Canada that were associated in this Council through their boards of education and publication.

The Council appointed a committee of scholars to have charge of the text of the American Standard Version and to undertake inquiry concerning the need for further revision. After studying the questions whether or not revision should be undertaken, and if so, what its nature and extent should be, in 1937 the Council authorized a revision. The scholars who served as members of the Committee worked in two sections, one dealing with the Old Testament and one with the New Testament. In 1946 the Revised Standard Version of the New Testament was published. The publication of the Revised Standard Version of the Bible, containing the Old and New Testaments, took place on September 30, 1952. A translation of the Apocryphal/Deuterocanonical Books of the Old Testament followed in 1957. In 1977 this collection was issued in an expanded edition, containing three additional texts received by Eastern Orthodox communions (3 and 4 Maccabees and Psalm 151). Thereafter the Revised Standard Version gained the distinction of being officially authorized for use by all major Christian churches: Protestant, Anglican, Roman Catholic, and Eastern Orthodox.

The Revised Standard Version Bible Committee is a continuing body, comprising about thirty members, both men and women. Ecumenical in representation, it includes scholars affiliated with various Protestant denominations, as well as several Roman Catholic members, an Eastern Orthodox member, and a Jewish member who serves in the Old Testament section. For a period of time the Committee included several members from Canada and from England.

Because no translation of the Bible is perfect or is acceptable to all groups of readers, and because discoveries of older manuscripts and further investigation of linguistic features of the text continue to become available, renderings of the Bible have proliferated. During the years following the publication of the Revised Standard Version, twenty-six other English translations and revisions of the Bible were produced by committees and by individual scholars—not to mention twenty-five other translations and revisions of the New Testament alone. One of the latter was the second edition of the RSV New Testament, issued in 1971, twenty-five years after its initial publication.

Following the publication of the RSV Old Testament in 1952, significant advances were made in the discovery and interpretation of documents in Semitic languages related to Hebrew. In addition to the information that had become available in the late 1940s from the Dead Sea texts of Isaiah and Habakkuk, subsequent acquisitions from the same area brought to light many other early copies of all the books of the Hebrew Scriptures (except Esther), though most of these copies are fragmentary. During the same period early Greek manuscript copies of books of the New Testament also became available.

In order to take these discoveries into account, along with recent studies of documents in Semitic languages related to Hebrew, in 1974 the

Policies Committee of the Revised Standard Version, which is a standing committee of the National Council of the Churches of Christ in the U.S.A., authorized the preparation of a revision of the entire RSV Bible.

For the Old Testament the Committee has made use of the *Biblia Hebraica Stuttgartensia* (1977; ed. sec. emendata, 1983). This is an edition of the Hebrew and Aramaic text as current early in the Christian era and fixed by Jewish scholars (the "Masoretes") of the sixth to the ninth centuries. The vowel signs, which were added by the Masoretes, are accepted in the main, but where a more probable and convincing reading can be obtained by assuming different vowels, this has been done. No notes are given in such cases, because the vowel points are less ancient and reliable than the consonants. When an alternative reading given by the Masoretes is translated in a footnote, this is identified by the words "Another reading is."

Departures from the consonantal text of the best manuscripts have been made only where it seems clear that errors in copying had been made before the text was standardized. Most of the corrections adopted are based on the ancient versions (translations into Greek, Aramaic, Syriac, and Latin), which were made prior to the time of the work of the Masoretes and which therefore may reflect earlier forms of the Hebrew text. In such instances a footnote specifies the version or versions from which the correction has been derived and also gives a translation of the Masoretic Text. Where it was deemed appropriate to do so, information is supplied in footnotes from subsidiary Jewish traditions concerning other textual readings (the *Tiqqune Sopherim*, "emendations of the scribes"). These are identified in the footnotes as "Ancient Heb tradition."

Occasionally it is evident that the text has suffered in transmission and that none of the versions provides a satisfactory restoration. Here we can only follow the best judgment of competent scholars as to the most probable reconstruction of the original text. Such reconstructions are indicated in footnotes by the abbreviation Cn ("Correction"), and a translation of the Masoretic Text is added.

For the New Testament the Committee has based its work on the most recent edition of *The Greek New Testament*, prepared by an interconfessional and international committee and published by the United Bible Societies (1966; 3rd ed. corrected, 1983; information concerning changes to be introduced into the critical apparatus of the forthcoming 4th edition was available to the Committee). As in that edition, double brackets are used to enclose a few passages that are generally regarded to be later additions to the text, but which we have retained because of their evident antiquity and their importance in the textual tradition. Only in very rare instances have we replaced the text or the punctuation of the Bible Societies' edition by an alternative that seemed to us to be superior. Here and there in the footnotes the phrase, "Other ancient authorities read," identifies alternative readings preserved by Greek manuscripts and early versions. In both Testaments, alternative renderings of the text are indicated by the word "Or."

As for the style of English adopted for the present revision, among the mandates given to the Committee in 1980 by the Division of Education and Ministry of the National Council of Churches of Christ (which now holds the copyright of the RSV Bible) was the directive to continue in the tradition of the King James Bible, but to introduce such changes as are warranted on the basis of accuracy, clarity, euphony, and current English usage. Within the constraints set by the original texts and by the mandates of the Division, the Committee has followed the maxim, "As literal as possible, as free as necessary." As a consequence, the New Revised Standard Version (NRSV) remains essentially a literal translation. Paraphrastic renderings have been adopted only sparingly, and then chiefly to compensate for a deficiency in the English language—the lack of a common gender third person singular pronoun.

During the almost half a century since the publication of the RSV, many in the churches have become sensitive to the danger of linguistic sexism arising from the inherent bias of the English language towards the masculine gender, a bias that in the case of the Bible has often restricted or obscured the meaning of the original text. The mandates from the Division specified that, in references to men and women, masculine-oriented language should be eliminated as far as this can be done without altering passages that reflect the historical situation of ancient patriarchal culture. As can be appreciated, more than once the Committee found that the several mandates stood in tension and even in conflict. The various concerns had to be balanced case by case in order to provide a faithful and acceptable rendering without using contrived English. Only very occasionally has the pronoun "he" or "him" been retained in passages where the reference may have been to a woman as well as to a man; for example, in several legal texts in Leviticus and Deuteronomy. In such instances of formal, legal language, the options of either putting the passage in the plural or of introducing additional nouns to avoid masculine pronouns in English seemed to the Committee to obscure the historic structure and literary character of the original. In the vast majority of cases, however, inclusiveness has been attained by simple rephrasing or by introducing plural forms when this does not distort the meaning of the passage. Of course, in narrative and in parable no attempt was made to generalize the sex of individual persons.

Another aspect of style will be detected by readers who compare the more stately English rendering of the Old Testament with the less formal rendering adopted for the New Testament. For example, the traditional distinction between *shall* and *will* in English has been retained in the Old Testament as appropriate in rendering a document that embodies what may be termed the classic form of Hebrew, while in the New Testament the abandonment of such distinctions in the usage of the future tense in English reflects the more colloquial nature of the koine Greek used by most New Testament authors except when they are quoting the Old Testament.

Careful readers will notice that here and there in the Old Testament the word LORD (or in certain cases GOD) is printed in capital letters. This represents the traditional manner in English versions of rendering the Divine Name, the "Tetragrammaton" (see the notes on Exodus 3.14, 15), following the precedent of the ancient Greek and Latin translators and the long established practice in the reading of the Hebrew Scriptures in the synagogue. While it is almost if not quite certain that the Name was originally pronounced "Yahweh," this pronunciation was not indicated when the Masoretes added vowel sounds to the consonantal Hebrew text. To the four consonants YHWH of the Name, which had come to be regarded as too sacred to be pronounced, they attached vowel signs indicating that in its place should be read the Hebrew word *Adonai* meaning "Lord" (or *Elohim* meaning "God"). Ancient Greek translators employed the word *Kyrios* ("Lord") for the Name. The Vulgate likewise used the Latin word *Dominus* ("Lord"). The form "Jehovah" is of late medieval origin; it is a combination of the consonants of the Divine Name and the vowels attached to it by the Masoretes but belonging to an entirely different word. Although the American Standard Version (1901) had used "Jehovah" to render the Tetragrammaton (the sound of Y being represented by J and the sound of W by V, as in Latin), for two reasons the Committees that produced the RSV and the NRSV returned to the more familiar usage of the King James Version. (1) The word "Jehovah" does not accurately represent any form of the Name ever used in Hebrew. (2) The use of any proper name for the one and only God, as though there were other gods from whom the true God had to be distinguished, began to be discontinued in

Judaism before the Christian era and is inappropriate for the universal faith of the Christian Church.

It will be seen that in the Psalms and in other prayers addressed to God the archaic second person singular pronouns (*thee, thou, thine*) and verb forms (*art, hast, hadst*) are no longer used. Although some readers may regret this change, it should be pointed out that in the original languages neither the Old Testament nor the New makes any linguistic distinction between addressing a human being and addressing the Deity. Furthermore, in the tradition of the King James Version one will not expect to find the use of capital letters for pronouns that refer to the Deity—such capitalization is an unnecessary innovation that has only recently been introduced into a few English translations of the Bible. Finally, we have left to the discretion of the licensed publishers such matters as section headings, cross-references, and clues to the pronunciation of proper names.

This new version seeks to preserve all that is best in the English Bible as it has been known and used through the years. It is intended for use in public reading and congregational worship, as well as in private study, instruction, and meditation. We have resisted the temptation to introduce terms and phrases that merely reflect current moods, and have tried to put the message of the Scriptures in simple, enduring words and expressions that are worthy to stand in the great tradition of the King James Bible and its predecessors.

In traditional Judaism and Christianity, the Bible has been more than a historical document to be preserved or a classic of literature to be cherished and admired; it is recognized as the unique record of God's dealings with people over the ages. The Old Testament sets forth the call of a special people to enter into covenant relation with the God of justice and steadfast love and to bring God's law to the nations. The New Testament records the life and work of Jesus Christ, the one in whom "the Word became flesh," as well as describes the rise and spread of the early Christian Church. The Bible carries its full message, not to those who regard it simply as a noble literary heritage of the past or who wish to use it to enhance political purposes and advance otherwise desirable goals, but to all persons and communities who read it so that they may discern and understand what God is saying to them. That message must not be disguised in phrases that are no longer clear, or hidden under words that have changed or lost their meaning; it must be presented in language that is direct and plain and meaningful to people today. It is the hope and prayer of the translators that this version of the Bible may continue to hold a large place in congregational life and to speak to all readers, young and old alike, helping them to understand and believe and respond to its message.

For the Committee,
BRUCE M. METZGER

Names and Order of the Books of the

OLD AND NEW TESTAMENTS

THE OLD TESTAMENT

THE NEW TESTAMENT

ABBREVIATIONS

The following abbreviations are used for the books of the Bible:

OLD TESTAMENT

Gen	Genesis	2 Chr	2 Chronicles	Dan	Daniel
Ex	Exodus	Ezra	Ezra	Hos	Hosea
Lev	Leviticus	Neh	Nehemiah	Joel	Joel
Num	Numbers	Esth	Esther	Am	Amos
Deut	Deuteronomy	Job	Job	Ob	Obadiah
Josh	Joshua	Ps	Psalms	Jon	Jonah
Judg	Judges	Prov	Proverbs	Mic	Micah
Ruth	Ruth	Eccl	Ecclesiastes	Nah	Nahum
1 Sam	1 Samuel	Song	Song of Solomon	Hab	Habakkuk
2 Sam	2 Samuel	Isa	Isaiah	Zeph	Zephaniah
1 Kings	1 Kings	Jer	Jeremiah	Hag	Haggai
2 Kings	2 Kings	Lam	Lamentations	Zech	Zechariah
1 Chr	1 Chronicles	Ezek	Ezekiel	Mal	Malachi

NEW TESTAMENT

Mt	Matthew	Eph	Ephesians	Jas	James
Mk	Mark	Phil	Philippians	1 Pet	1 Peter
Lk	Luke	Col	Colossians	2 Pet	2 Peter
Jn	John	1 Thess	1 Thessalonians	1 Jn	1 John
Acts	Acts of the Apostles	2 Thess	2 Thessalonians	2 Jn	2 John
		1 Tim	1 Timothy	3 Jn	3 John
Rom	Romans	2 Tim	2 Timothy	Jude	Jude
1 Cor	1 Corinthians	Titus	Titus	Rev	Revelation
2 Cor	2 Corinthians	Philem	Philemon		
Gal	Galatians	Heb	Hebrews		

OTHER ABBREVIATIONS

Ant.	Josephus, *Antiquities of the Jews*
Aram	Aramaic
BCE	Before Common Era
CE	Common Era
Ch, chs	Chapter, chapters
Cn	Correction; made where the text has suffered in transmission and the versions provide no satisfactory restoration but where the Standard Bible Committee agrees with the judgment of competent scholars as to the most probable reconstruction of the original text.
Gk	Septuagint, Greek version of the Old Testament
Heb	Hebrew of the consonantal Masoretic Text of the Old Testament
Josephus	Flavius Josephus (Jewish historian, about 37–100 CE)
Macc.	The book(s) of the Maccabees
Ms(s)	Manuscript(s)
MT	The Hebrew of the pointed Masoretic Text of the Old Testament
OL	Old Latin
QsMs(s)	Manuscript(s) found at Qumran by the Dead Sea
Sam	Samaritan Hebrew text of the Old Testament
Syr	Syriac Version of the Old Testament
Syr H	Syriac Version of Origen's Hexapla
Tg	Targum
Vg	Vulgate, Latin Version of the Bible

APOCRYPHAL
OR DEUTEROCANONICAL BOOKS

Tob	Tobit	Song of Thr	Prayer of Azariah and the Song of the Three Jews
Jdt	Judith	Sus	Susanna
Add Esth	Additions to Esther	Bel	Bel and the Dragon
Wis	Wisdom	1 Macc	1 Maccabees
Sir	Sirach (Ecclesiasticus)	2 Macc	2 Maccabees
Bar	Baruch	3 Macc	3 Maccabees
1 Esd	1 Esdras	4 Macc	4 Maccabees
2 Esd	2 Esdras	Pr Man	Prayer of Manasseh
Let Jer	Letter of Jeremiah		

THE STORY OF THE BIBLE

The Bible is the cumulative record of response to God's disclosure of himself among those who believe that he has called them to be his people. This call to special relationship results in a covenant between God and his people. The Hebrew and Greek words meaning "covenant" lie behind the familiar terms, "Old Testament" and "New Testament," since Christians claim that Jesus established the New Covenant which fulfilled and supplanted the Old Covenant with Israel (cf. Jer 31.31-34; 1 Cor 11.25). The ground of the covenantal relationship is mediated through the leaders and prophets of Israel, and through Jesus of Nazareth, whose followers acclaim him as the chosen and empowered agent of God (Messiah, Christ, "anointed") and Lord.

Inevitably, throughout the biblical period the responses to God's calling his people were heard and reported in ways which were influenced by the social and cultural context of those who responded. The language, the imagery, the issues reflect the setting in which God's address was heard. This is true for ancient Israel, for later Jewish groups, and for the early Christians in the variety of their backgrounds. The Bible is the net result of these responses to God's self-revelation. Its writings vary widely in form: story, history, law, prophecy, poetry, visions of the future. Through the centuries when the traditions were transmitted orally and when the written records were copied and edited, modifications and updating took place in the form of editing and supplementing in order to heighten the relevance of these ancient materials for the changing situations of those who saw themselves as God's people. Even after basic decisions were made about which copies were to be considered authoritative by the respective religious communities, the scribes who copied the documents made minor alterations. Ancient translations introduced still other types of variations, and there were differing opinions as to which of the documents were to be considered authoritative for the communities. Yet the astounding fact is that, in spite of these human factors in the recording, transmission and preservation processes, recently discovered ancient copies of parts of the Bible show how faithfully the text has been preserved throughout two millennia, or even longer in the case of the records of the law and the prophets of Israel. In what follows we shall trace briefly the processes of writing, collecting and transmitting these traditions which serve as the ground of the claims of covenant relationship with God. The study aids throughout this Bible include introductions to the individual books of the Bible and detailed information to assist the reader to understand more precisely the language, concepts and culture in which the message of the Bible is expressed.

THE GROWTH AND STRUCTURE OF THE OLD TESTAMENT

What Christians call the Old Testament is a collection of the writings which developed over centuries, beginning in ancient Israel and continuing until the second and first centuries BCE when Jews were dominated by Greek and Roman rulers of the eastern Mediterranean region. Over this period of time, the early traditions were freshly appropriated and edited in order to make them available and to show their relevance for the Jewish people in the changing circumstances in which they found themselves.

The Five Books of the Law

The basic core of these writings is the first five books: Genesis, Exodus, Leviticus, Numbers and Deuteronomy. Although they include very ancient traditions which go back to the days of the founders of Israel – Abraham, Isaac, and Jacob – the whole collection of narrative and legal material was edited and arranged in its present form after the return of the Jews from their captivity in Babylon (beginning about 538 BCE). Encouraged by Cyrus, the Persian ruler who conquered the Babylonians, the returning Jews re-established their worship of God in their land over the next century and a half by rebuilding the temple and through receiving instruction in their traditions from the priests. The consolidation and reworking of the ancient traditions may have begun in Babylon, but it was made available in its finished form in the early fifth century BCE to the people of Israel, once again living in their land. Moses, whose role in the establishment of the covenant with God and the receiving of the law was so central in these traditions, was given credit for having produced the whole of the five books, which came to be referred to as "the Law of Moses." The dominant effect of the priestly editing of the material is apparent, however, in the heavy weight placed on purity and priestly requirements in these books. Included in this complex said to come from Moses are (1) ancient stories of the wandering tribes and their patriarchal leaders, as depicted in Genesis; (2) narratives of the period of residence and enslavement in Egypt, culminating in God's actions in behalf of his people to enable them to gain freedom and the subsequent founding of the covenant agreement at Sinai; (3) the reaffirmation and expansion of the law and the covenantal obligations in the book of Deuteronomy (which means, second giving of the law). In its edited form, this body of material served as the basis for the reconstituting of Jewish existence in the land of Palestine from the fifth century BCE on, and was concerned chiefly with the renewal of the worship of God in the central shrine in Jerusalem. Known as Torah (the Hebrew term for instruction), or Pentateuch (the Greek term for "five volumes"), or the Law of Moses, these books are the basic element in both the Jewish and the Christian Bibles.

The Historical Writings

At about the same time that the "Law of Moses" was being edited and freshly appropriated, the historical writings of Israel were being reworked and expanded as well. The book of Judges describes the struggles of the ancient Israelites settling in the land of Canaan or Palestine, as it came to be called because the Philistines dominated it before and after the return of Israel from the sojourn in Egypt. After a period in which various rulers ("judges") arose in response to local needs or tribal crises, a monarchy was established, which gave way to two kingdoms – one in the north of Israel and one in the south, each with its own monarch and with temples in Samaria and Jerusalem respectively. These developments are described in Judges, 1 and 2 Samuel, 1 and 2 Kings. The story is retold from a strongly priestly perspective in 1 and 2 Chronicles, which were probably produced by the same priestly writers who edited the Law of Moses in the form that we now have. The accounts of the priestly leaders in making available the law and instructing the people in it are given in the books of Ezra and Nehemiah, which describe the situation in Palestine after the return of Israel from the Babylonian exile.

In the second century BCE, members of the priestly family launched a successful revolt against the pagan king of Syria, Antiochus IV, who was trying to force his Jewish subjects to perform divine honors in his behalf, since he claimed to be a manifestation of the gods (in Greek, *Epiphanes*). Their efforts resulted in the establishment of an independent Jewish state, dominated by the Hasmonean family. Judah (or Judas), one of the leaders of the independence movement, had the nickname Maccabaeus (meaning hammer), which led to its being called the Maccabean revolt. In this period of priestly-dominated independence – 165-63 BCE –

several historical works were produced: 1 Esdras, which describes the exile of the Jews to Babylon and their return; 1 and 2 Maccabees, which in different ways and styles recount the restoration of the Jewish monarchy and the purification of the temple. These writings were not included in the Hebrew Bible, but appear in the Greek version of the Jewish scriptures that was widely used by Jews and Christians alike (see below).

Poetic and Narrative Writings

Although there are both poetic and narrative features in some of the wisdom writings of the Bible (discussed below, Section D), two types of biblical literature are characterized chiefly by their poetic and narrative form: (1) Poetic throughout are the Psalms, which were intended for use in worship, both corporate and private. Traditionally associated with David, some of the psalms may go back to his time, but in the present arrangement the psalms (many of which date from the time of the Babylonian exile or after the return to the land) have been grouped into five books, presumably on the model of the five-fold Law of Moses: Psalms 1-41; 42-71; 72-89; 90-106; 107-150. The themes in the psalms include praise, confession, lament, and commitment to God's law.

(2) Also from the post-exilic period is the Song of Solomon (or Song of Songs) which may have originated as a secular love poem, but which seems to have been interpreted by Jews and Christians in antiquity as a symbolic depiction of God's love for his covenant people. Lamentations, a poetic work traditionally linked with Jeremiah, was probably written after his time, and calls for sustained trust in God even in the face of national tragedy. Poetic in form is Ecclesiastes, which is a solemn warning about the limitations of human understanding. It was probably written in the fourth or third century after Israel had come under the spell of the philosophical learning of the Greeks. Similarly pessimistic about the extent and depth of human understanding is the Book of Job, the central part of which consists of poetic dialogues regarding the meaning of human suffering (3.1-31.40). The work as we find it concludes with God's challenge to Job, and the latter's calm acceptance of the inscrutable wisdom of God concerning human suffering (38.1-42.6).

Two narratives concerning women and their insights into the purpose and methods of God are the books of Ruth and Esther. The former may have been written before the Babylonian exile, and attests God's fidelity in preserving the family line, involving those outside the tribal limits of Israel. Esther, on the other hand, dramatizes God's work in delivering his people from the dominance of foreign powers. Although the book describes a situation in Persia, it was likely written after the return of Israel to Palestine in the fifth century BCE. Two other stories that are not found in the Hebrew Bible but which have been regarded as scripture by many Jews and Christians are Judith and Tobit, both written in the later second century BCE. Judith is a gruesome murder story in which a brave Jewish woman entices and decapitates a Babylonian general. It is intended not merely to entertain but also to demonstrate courage in opposing pagan rulers who presently dominate God's people. Tobit is a compelling story, set in the capital of Assyria during the captivity of the northern tribes of Israel (eighth century BCE). It combines reports of acts of piety on the part of the blind Jewish hero with descriptions of angelic and demonic forces over which God's purpose for his people triumphs.

Wisdom Literature

Proverbs includes wisdom sayings which may go back to Solomon (mid-tenth century BCE), the prototype of the wise man, to whom the work as a whole is attributed. But the present collection is probably from the fifth century BCE. It offers guides for the individual to a happy, fulfilled life at a time when hope for political or social renewal is low. Ecclesiastes (in Hebrew, *Koheleth*), on the other hand, represents a critique of human wisdom, which the author thinks cannot offer a satisfactory explanation of the ways of God with his people. Job is basically a set of dialogues concerning the meaning of human suffering, concluding with God's challenge to Job and the latter's sober, humble reply. The work may have been written during the first part of Israel's exile in Babylon. Three other wisdom writings which do not appear in the Hebrew Bible, but which were honored as scripture by many Jews and early Christians are (1) the Wisdom of Sirach (also known as Ecclesiasticus, and Ben Sira), (2) the Wisdom of Solomon, and (3) Baruch. Sirach makes the credible claim to have been written by a professional Jewish teacher, who offers a compend of his teaching with the aim of showing that Israel, its history and its traditional beliefs and laws are from God: in them lies true wisdom. The Wisdom of Solomon is written in sophisticated Greek and uses technical terms deriving from Greek philosophy. Although it could not have been written by Solomon, the author wants to honor the tradition of wisdom connected with the name of Israel's wise king, and makes a case for the basic compatibility of Greek philosophy and the Jewish understanding of God and his purpose in the world. The author was probably writing in mid-first century Alexandria, where other Jewish writers were at work synthesizing pagan learning and their own ancient tradition of divinely revealed wisdom. Baruch purports to have been written by the secretary of Jeremiah, the prophet (Jer 45.1), but it comes from the first century BCE and uses the story of Israel's exile in Babylon and return to give promise of the liberation of Jerusalem and its people in the age to come. The wisdom lies in the lesson that beyond the people's time of testing comes divine deliverance.

Prophetic and Apocalyptic Literature

The books of prophecy in the Old Testament may be grouped in three categories: (1) the major prophets; (2) the minor prophets; (3) the apocalyptic literature. In the first category are the books of Isaiah, Jeremiah and Ezekiel; in the second are the twelve short works: Hosea, Joel, Amos, Obadiah, Jonah, Micah, Nahum, Habbakkuk, Zephaniah, Haggai, Zechariah, Malachi. The only complete work in the third category, apocalyptic, is Daniel, but portions of Isaiah and Zechariah are so classified. Apocalyptic (which comes from the Greek word for "revelation") means a special disclosure by God to a chosen person or group. What is revealed is God's purpose for his people in the trials of the present and the vindication that he is soon to achieve for them in the future. Often this revelation is conveyed through visions, dreams, or symbolic events, the meaning of which is reserved for the in-group of God's people. In the ancient Greek translation of the Jewish Bible (see below) there are other apocalyptic writings: supplements to Daniel (Song of the Three Young Men, Susanna, Bel and the Dragon) and 2 Esdras, in which the prediction of the fall of Babylon is a symbolic representation of the fall of Rome, the new enemy of the people of God. Christians have revised this writing attributed to Ezra (Esdras) by adding two opening and two closing chapters (1-2; 15-16).

In contrast to these apocalyptic writers, the prophets are concerned with insight rather than foresight. They seek to interpret to God's people what his purpose for them is in the present, including the difficulties they are experiencing, and to call them to obedience to the divine will, the fulfillment of which the prophet expects in the future through the renewal of the covenant between God and his people. As with the legal and historical traditions of Israel, the records of the oracles of the prophets were modified and supplemented by later generations. For example, Isaiah 1-40 consists of prophetic pronouncements on the eve of northern Israel's being taken off to captivity in Assyria (late eighth/early seventh century BCE), but inserted into these prophecies are four chapters of apocalyptic pronouncements (Isa 24-27). Isa 40-66 comes from a later century, when – following the exile – the nation returned to its land. Similar later inserts may be found in Zechariah, for example. What has happened in the expansion of these prophetic writings is not deceit or forgery, but demonstration that the word of God to the prophet continues to have direct relevance in the altered circumstances of the covenant people. We shall note below how new translations and additions to the biblical literature continued and developed with this aim of making the scriptures relevant for the new situations in which the people of God found themselves.

THE GROWTH AND STRUCTURE OF THE NEW TESTAMENT

In the message of Jesus and in nearly all the writings we now call the New Testament, references to "the scriptures" mean the Jewish Bible, or the Old Testament. But within a generation after the lifetime of Jesus, certain early Christian writings began to be circulated, to be used for instruction and adjudication of disputes, and to take their place as the distinctive Christian scriptures. Four types of writing are to be found in what came to be called the New Testament: (1) gospels; (2) letters; (3) epistles or treatises; (4) apocalypses.

Gospels

As in the case of the Jewish scriptures, the traditions concerning the life and message of Jesus were circulated orally for decades following his crucifixion. It is to these reports that Luke refers in his gospel (1.2) when he mentions what had been transmitted by those who from the launching of Jesus' career had been "eyewitnesses." Down into the second century there were those who claimed to be transmitting orally these reports from the first followers of Jesus. At times they confirm, at times supplement, and on occasion disagree with what is now found in the four gospels included in the New Testament.

As for written records about Jesus, the earliest seems to have been one which consisted chiefly of the sayings of Jesus. Known as Q (from the German word for source, *Quelle*), it was used as a source by Matthew and Luke, although each adapted and arranged freely the material he drew from it. The first narrative account of Jesus was Mark, the opening line of which "the beginning of the gospel of Jesus Christ" provided the term by which this type of writing came to be known. The Greek original word, *euangelion*, which means "good news," was used to refer to the narrative itself. Mark's gospel was probably written in the late 60s just before the fall of Jerusalem to the Roman army (see below). It was used as the basic source and structure for the Gospels of Matthew and Luke, and in a general way by John, although all three of these gospels represent significant adaptation and supplementation of Mark's structure and content through the special sources and in the service of the distinctive interests of each writer.

All the gospels are anonymous, but each of them came to be identified with one of the apostles or with a close associate of an apostle: Matthew is one of the twelve disciples (Mt 10.3); Mark is the companion of Peter (1 Pet 5.13); Luke is mentioned in the Pauline letters (Philem 24; Col 4.14); John has been identified as the disciple who had a special relationship to Jesus (Jn 13.23), and in a letter attributed to John there is mention of his role as direct witness (1 Jn 1.1). Each of the gospels reflects the distinctive circumstances of the author and the community that is being addressed: Mark writes with a sense of urgency that the divine judgment that is about to fall on Jerusalem and its temple is a sign of the soon coming of the end of the age (Mk 13.1-2) and the necessity to preach the gospel as widely as possible (13.30). Matthew was writing in the later first century when the break between Judaism and Christianity was taking place in an environment of growing conflict and competition: what God promised and commanded in the law and the prophets is finding its fulfillment in Jesus and his people (Mt 5.17-20). The promises to historic Israel will be bestowed on a new "nation," the people of the new covenant (Mt 21.43). Luke is writing his gospel as volume one of a two part work which will describe the progress of the gospel from its basis in the Jewish scriptures through its fulfillment in the life of Jesus (Lk 4.21), in his death and resurrection (Lk 24.27), and in the spread of the gospel from Jerusalem to the ends of the earth (Acts 1.8; 2.17). John presents the gospel of Jesus as intended for all who will respond in faith (Jn 1.12-13). His words and deeds disclose his glory to his faithful followers (Jn 2.11; 20.30-31). Other gospels have survived from the second and subsequent centuries which attribute additional teachings to Jesus or recount stories of his birth and childhood, but only these four have been recognized by the church at large as authoritative.

Letters

The oldest writings included in the New Testament are the letters of Paul. These may be divided into two groups: (1) those certainly by Paul, and (2) those written by a later generation in his name. In the first group are 1 and 2 Thessalonians, Galatians, 1 and 2 Corinthians, Romans, Philippians and Philemon. The pseudonymous letters written in Paul's name are Colossians, Ephesians, 1 and 2 Timothy and Titus. The differences between the two types of communication are clear. The authentic letters of Paul set the pattern for this mode of communication between the churches and their regional leaders. The apostles claimed to have been chosen and commissioned by the risen Christ to proclaim the gospel throughout the civilized world. They were to give guidance to the Christian communities whose members had responded in faith to the gospel and who now stood in need of counsel as to what they were to do as they awaited the end of the age. The community needs included both internal responsibilities and relationships as well as their role with respect to those outside the communities. Paul's relationship with the churches to whom the letters are written is based on past and prospective first-hand involvement with them. His authority rests on his having been commissioned by the Risen Lord. The influence of his former life in Judaism is apparent, in that as a Pharisee he had been concerned with formation of faithful communities for whom the relevance of scripture was primary. But as one exposed to Greek philosophy, which had influenced Jewish thought in this period, he was also able to incorporate its concepts into his ethical system, as is evident in his inclusion of Stoic virtues among the fruits of the Spirit (Gal 5.22) and his employing the Stoic teaching about the human conscience (Rom 2.12-16). At the same time, his expectations about human history are shaped by the Jewish apocalyptic world-view.

(2) The later letters attributed to Paul serve a significantly different function. With the passing of time and the non-fulfillment of the earlier expectation of Christ's soon triumphant return, it became essential for them to have guidance in the responsibility for leadership, for the classification of members as to role and rights, and to provide a sense of continuity and stability with regard to the tradition in which they stood and which they sought to preserve. The churches had to prepare for a long period of stability and survival while maintaining ties with the tradition from which they had emerged.

Epistles or Treatises

Once the pattern had been set by the authentic letters of Paul for that mode of communication and for the exercize of authority between the apostolic leader and the community under apostolic supervision, other writers sought to demonstrate their authority and to serve the needs of communities more broadly for the church as a whole. This role was fulfilled by writing in the name of an apostle or by claiming to stand in the apostolic tradition. 1 and 2 Peter were written to a post-apostolic generation in the name of Peter, but they address issues and offer solutions which would not have been foreseen by the first apostolic leaders. James implicitly claims continuity with James the brother of Jesus, although the style and the issues addressed in this treatise reflect a later phase of the church's life. Jude (or Judah) makes a similar claim to convey the apostolic insights in relation to problems that are emerging in the second or subsequent generation of the life of the Christian communities. Other anonymous documents echo the style and vocabulary of an earlier writing – as does the Gospel of John – but adapt that tradition to serve the changed needs of the communities addressed. Hebrews is anonymous and seems to be speaking to the needs of the church at large, although the concluding counsel and personal messages (Heb 13) echo the methods of Paul in speaking to the needs of his readers. The authentic Pauline letters have evidently become the model for pastoral communication on the part of second generation church leadership.

Apocalypse

There is only a single writing included in the New Testament which conforms to the literary and conceptual mode of communication known as an apocalypse. This is the Revelation to John. The style and point of view of this John are basically different from those of the authors of the Gospel and Letters of John. As in the Old Testament apocalypses, the writer is conveying to his readers God-given insights concerning the time of testing through which the faithful community is passing and articulating the hopes for triumph over the powers of evil and for the vindication of his people which God is soon to achieve. The mix of vision and symbolic modes of communication, which is characteristic of Jewish apocalypses, has been adapted by the author to serve the needs of the communities addressed. Apocalyptic style and outlook are found in segments of other New Testament writings as well: (1) in the Gospel of Mark (Mk 13, and especially the parallel in Matt 24-25), where God's judgment on the wicked and vindication of the faithful are depicted; (2) in the letters of Paul, particularly in 1 Thess 4 and 1 Cor 15, where he is describing the return of Christ in triumph and the renewal of God's people. Characteristic of this apocalyptic point of view are Paul's declaration in 1 Cor 15.51, "Listen, I will tell you a mystery!" and Jesus' promise in Mk 4.11, "To you has been given the secret of the kingdom of God."

THE CANON OF SCRIPTURE

By the first century BCE there was a growing number of writings which claimed to be reliable legal, prophetic, wisdom and narrative traditions concerning the history and religion of Israel. Rather than allow the list to grow without limit, it was deemed necessary to make some decisions as to which documents were to be regarded as authoritative for the religious community. This need was intensified by the emergence of Christianity, which claimed to have the true understanding of the biblical tradition and whose scholars were modifying some of the Jewish texts to confirm the Christian claims about God's activity among them. Within the Christian community by the second century there was not only an array of Jewish documents but also an ever-increasing number of gospels, acts, and epistles vying for acceptance as the basic scriptures for Christians. To determine which of these literary candidates were to be accepted as authoritative and normative for their respective communities required that a standard list be drawn up. The name scholars have given to this list is *canon*, from the Greek word which means "rule" or "norm."

The Old Testament Canon

For the Jewish community there was a long-established standard body of authoritative scripture, which had achieved normative status about 400 BCE: the Five Books of Moses. In the intervening years a second cluster was edited and put in official form, which came to be given the designation, the Former Prophets: Joshua, Judges, Samuel and Kings. Subsequently, the prophetic writings were grouped, led by the three major figures (Isaiah, Jeremiah and Ezekiel), followed by the twelve minor prophets. By the early second century BCE these groupings of the Jewish scriptures were widely recognized as authoritative by many Jews, as is apparent from the reference to them in the prologue to the Greek translation of the Wisdom of Sirach which was produced about the turn of that century. Yet which books should be included in what became the third section of the Jewish scriptures, the Writings, was a fluid question for centuries to come. By the first century CE, for example, Josephus, the Jewish historian, mentions only four books which contain hymns and offer guidelines for human life, but by the second century CE, the author of 4 Esdras mentions 24 sacred books which are to be made available to the public, plus 70 others which are to be kept secret. This reference to secrecy gave rise to the designation of writings on the fringe of the canon as *apocrypha*, which means "hidden." Later Jewish tradition has affirmed that a group of scholars met at Jamnia (Yavneh) on the Mediterranean coast of Palestine in the late first century CE who drew up the definitive list of the Jewish scriptures. No copy or record of such a list has been preserved, however. It is probable that the list which determined what would be included in the Hebrew Bible was developed in the second and subsequent centuries CE by the leaders of the emergent rabbinic movement (see below).

Complicating the selection of the normative list were the linguistic changes that had come among Jews over the course of the seven centuries since their ancestors were taken off to captivity in Babylon. Over the centuries the Jews living there shifted from speaking Hebrew to Aramaic, a kindred semitic language. Paraphrases of the scripture in Aramaic have been found at the site of the Dead Sea community; known as *targum*, this adaptation of the scripture into Aramaic continued to be used for several subsequent centuries until Hebrew became once again more widely used. From the fourth century BCE on, however, Jews in Palestine and Egypt – and throughout the Mediterranean world – came under the influence of the Greek language and culture which were aggressively imposed on subject peoples by Alexander and his successors. In the intellectual center, Alexandria, Jews used a Greek version of the Bible and wrote about it in the same language. It was there that the basic Greek translation was made which came to be known as the Septuagint (meaning, "seventy"), a term derived from a legendary Letter of Aristeas, which claimed that 72 Jewish translators from Jerusalem had finished the work simultaneously and that the results matched in every detail. The LXX, as scholars designate this version begun probably in the second century BCE, was expanded to include more recent writings, some of which were originally in Greek (such as the Wisdom of Solomon), as well as additions to books found in the Hebrew scriptures (Additions to Daniel and Esther). That a Greek translation was also used among Palestinian Jews in this period is demonstrated by the discovery of fragments of Greek versions of Exodus, Leviticus and Numbers, Tobit and Sirach among the scrolls found in the Dead Sea Caves. The LXX must have undergone continuing revision in Palestine in the coming centuries.

The determination of the authoritative list of Jewish scriptures was a protracted process, but the need for it was stimulated by the Christians' claim to have their own list and their own crucial interpretive supplement: the New Testament. The Jews developed their own equivalent interpretive tool: the Mishnah and Talmud (one in Palestine and one in

Babylon), which took shape from the second to the sixth centuries CE and which provided the guidelines for Jewish use of scripture that have dominated down to the present day.

The Christians in the latter part of the second century CE began to draw up lists of canonical Old Testament scriptures. The oldest surviving list is that of Melito of Sardis (ca. 175), who included all the books now identified as the Old Testament, with the exception of Esther. In the third century Origen of Alexandria asserted that the Christians should have all 22 books that the Jews have in their canon, a conviction echoed by Athanasius (also from Alexandria) a century later. Jerome (340?-420), though he produced the basic Latin version of the Bible, insisted that the church in the west should use the Hebrew Bible. Yet the dominant version continued to be the LXX, with its more extensive canon. It remains the normative Bible for most of the eastern churches, and its canon is the basis of the Roman Catholic Vulgate (common Latin), as was affirmed by the sixteenth century Catholic Council of Trent. The Protestant Reformers, however, adopted as their canon the Hebrew Bible as developed in the rabbinic period, which remains the standard list and text of the Jewish Bible.

The New Testament Canon

The basic documents of Judaism were from the beginning of Christianity appealed to as providing the foundation for its claim to be the fulfillment through Jesus of God's covenant promises. Paul asserts that the gospel was "promised by God in the holy scriptures" (Rom 1.2), and that Christ's death "for our sins" was "in accordance with the scriptures" (1 Cor 15.3). In Mark 12.24 (cf. Mt 22.29) Jesus is quoted as rebuking his Jewish critics because they know "neither the scriptures nor the power of God." For the Christians, however, it was not enough simply to possess or read the Jewish scriptures: the framework and criteria for understanding these scriptures were the message and meaning of Jesus Christ. What was essential was to have the records of what he had said and done, as well as accurate interpretations of Jesus by those he had called to be his earliest followers and messengers. These documents, in addition to some later interpretations, comprise what we know as the New Testament.

Surprisingly, none of the early Christian writings seems to have come from Judea, and there is little evidence about the apostolic circle there, apart from references in Paul's letters and Acts to the church in Jerusalem. Probably the Christians there were forced to flee the city during the Roman attack in 66-70. Scholars have often assigned the

Gospel of Mark to Rome (in association with Peter), Matthew to Antioch in Syria, while Paul's letters, the Gospel of John, Luke-Acts and Revelation have been located in cities of Greece and Asia Minor. For the early church what was essential was to link each writing with an apostolic figure in order to ensure its reliability and authority. By the middle of the second century the gospels and letters were being read in Christian worship, along with the Old Testament, as Justin Martyr (100-165) reports.

1. The Pauline Letters. The first group of Christian writings to be brought together was a collection of the letters of Paul – both those now considered to be by him and those written later in his name and with features of his style. To write in his name was not regarded in first-century culture as a form of deceit but as a way of honoring him and identifying with his tradition and insights in a changed situation. Those presumably by Paul include 1 and 2 Thessalonians, 1 and 2 Corinthians, Galatians, Philippians, Romans and Philemon. Those which identify with his tradition but seem to have been written for a later generation include Colossians, Ephesians, 1 and 2 Timothy, and Titus. So crucial for the church of the second century were the letters of Paul that Marcion of Sinope in Asia Minor, who wanted a radical break between Christianity and Judaism, insisted on limiting the Christian scriptures to ten letters of Paul, in addition to a version of the Gospel of Luke from which all favorable references to Judaism had been removed. The letters of Paul and those written in his name came to share apostolic authority, thereby forming a vital third of the developing New Testament.

2. Gospels. Although the gospels originated in different places and each was intended for a distinctive purpose, they were all considered to be linked directly or indirectly with an apostle. The attempt by Tatian in the late second century to combine the four into a single consecutive narrative, the *Diatessaron* (which means, "composed of four"), was not accepted widely or for long. Justin Martyr (100-165) wrote that, just as there were four elements in the universe and four directions on the face of the earth, so it was divinely intended that there be four gospels. Available from the second century, however, are other gospels (such as the Gospel of Thomas and the Gospel of Peter) which seemingly were produced to supplement or reinterpret the Jesus tradition. But the church stood firm with the basic four.

3. Other Writings. The authority of the other books that came to be included in the New Testament also rested on their being linked with an apostle. Acts served multiple purposes: justifying the spread of

Christianity to the Gentile world; engaging that world by combining the narrative style of popular literature of the period with the repeated claims that through Jesus and the apostles the scripture was being fulfilled. Yet essential for its authority are the figures of Paul and others in the apostolic circle based in Jerusalem. The link with apostolic authority is implicit in the imitation of Paul's style in the letters written in his name and in anonymous writings in epistolary style: Hebrews and the three Letters of John. Other writings of this general type were written in the name of an apostle (1 and 2 Peter), or in the name of one of Jesus' kinsmen (Jude, James). The Revelation of John likewise claims apostolic origin, although its apocalyptic style and outlook raised questions about its origins and value for the first three or four centuries when the church was looking for a firm establishment rather than for the end of the age. Another apocalypse, attributed to Peter, was first widely read and then ultimately rejected as spurious.

Important for conveying the developing sense of the authority of these New Testament writings is the passage in what is probably the latest of these books, 2 Peter 3.15-16, where the author describes the letters of Paul as a part of the "other scriptures" which it is the church's task to wrestle with and to understand. Like the people of God's covenant with Israel, the members of the community of the New Covenant see themselves as engaged in the interpretation and appropriation of a body of authoritative writings: the canon of scripture.

THE PRESERVATION OF THE TEXT OF THE BIBLE

The Old Testament

The oldest known copies of any parts of the Hebrew Bible were found in caves near the Dead Sea, beginning in the late nineteen-forties. They were written on scrolls made from leather or papyrus (formed by pressing into sheets a certain type of reed). The complete scroll of Isaiah from these caves shows what most biblical scrolls looked like: strips of leather sewn together side by side to form a continuous scroll measuring 25 feet in length and about 10 inches in height. The writing was in columns of about 30 lines each. The reader unrolled the scroll from one hand to the other from right to left, since that is the way Hebrew writing runs. The oldest copy from the Dead Sea caves goes back to the third century BCE, and contains part of the book of Exodus.

Scholars compared these biblical texts with those in the complete editions of the Hebrew Bible based on medieval copies, which has for centuries been the standard edition for Jewish and Christian scholars. It was evident that some variants in these new scrolls corresponded to the Hebrew text which lay behind the LXX and other such ancient versions of the Bible as the one preserved by the Samaritans in Palestine. The differences in the legal sections were often merely explanatory of otherwise puzzling passages or they offered cross-references to other biblical writings, which suggests that the copyist was maintaining a balance between faithful preservation of the tradition and concern for clarity of understanding. The fragments from the historical books were fewer in number, and showed links with the LXX as well. The full text of Isaiah, as well as copies of sections of this prophet, indicate that there had been a standardized version of this book by the second century BCE. On the other hand, the text of Jeremiah suggests that the Hebrew version must have existed in a shorter form, as is attested by the translation in the LXX. The Psalms scrolls from the Dead Sea finds include additional passages, some of which are found elsewhere in the Hebrew Bible or Jewish writings, but some were not known at all prior to these discoveries. Fragments of some books long known only from the Greek translation in LXX were found in the Hebrew or Aramaic original, such as Sirach and Tobit, and appear in a longer form.

In caves south of the site of the center for the Dead Sea community and dating from as late as the early second century CE there were also found fragments or sections of biblical writings, including another manuscript of Sirach in Hebrew. The text of these biblical copies more nearly matches that of the LXX. Similarly, an ancient version of the Pentateuch preserved at Nablus by the Samaritans – which they claim is an original copy of the law from the time of Joshua, but which is actually a compilation of late medieval manuscripts from their sect – on the whole resembles the standardized text of the Hebrew Bible which seems to have been used by the LXX translators.

In medieval times there was an effort on the part of Jewish scholars to assist those who read the Hebrew Bible in public by adding vowel markings to the older text, which consisted solely of the consonants, as is evident from the more ancient copies described above. That this had long been a problem is apparent in an edition of the Old Testament prepared by Origen of Alexandria who placed in six parallel columns the Hebrew and Greek texts, including a system of transliteration of the Hebrew into Greek. The most important of the Jewish medieval manuscripts of this edition of the Bible with its aids for reading date from the ninth to the eleventh centuries, and served as the basis for a standard edition produced in the sixteenth century (known as the Textus Receptus). It combined with the basic consonantal text the following: vowel markings, variants, paraphrases and scholarly comments from medieval rabbis. In the present century (1929-1937) R. Kittel and Paul E. Kahle prepared for the Bible Society in Stuttgart what has become the standard critical edition of the Hebrew Bible: the Biblia Hebraica Stuttgartensia (1977). This edition of the text was used extensively by the scholars preparing the New Revised Standard Version and the Revised English Bible (see below). In process at the Hebrew University in Jerusalem and at the Pontifical Biblical Commission in Rome are critical editions of the Hebrew Bible which take into account more fully the evidence from all available sources for the analysis and reconstruction of the text of the Hebrew Bible.

Text of the New Testament

Until the Renaissance, Christians seem to have been content to use the New Testament in the form in which it was available in their own particular linguistic tradition: in Greek or in ancient translations into Latin, Syriac, Coptic, Ethiopic or Armenian. (See below, Translations of the Bible.) In the early sixteenth century, however, the surge of intellectual inquiry concerning ancient sources led to the attempt to reconstruct the original form of the New Testament. Up until the invention of printing in the fifteenth century, books – including the New Testament – were available only through hand-written copies. Earlier, Greek was written in large separate letters (uncials); later a smoother flowing style was used (cursives or minuscules). After 800, the easier style of writing was used in copying the New Testament, with the result that surviving copies of minuscules outnumber the uncials by ten to one. It was these late manuscripts, and only a few of them, that the Dutch scholar, Erasmus, used as the basis for his first printed edition of the Greek New Testament in 1546. He and other scholars made subsequent improvements, however, and this set the pattern for the ensuing centuries in what is designated to the present day as the Textus Receptus.

In the eighteenth and nineteenth centuries, however, scholars found and began to use much earlier copies of the New Testament, dating back to the fourth and fifth centuries. Careful analysis of these manuscripts showed that there had been textual traditions different from those included in the Textus Receptus. Publication of the New Testament text from a fourth-century Bible found in 1844 at St. Catherine's Monastery at Mt. Sinai (which became known as the Codex Sinaiticus), together with a fresh appraisal of another equally ancient manuscript (Codex Vaticanus) which had lain little noticed in the Vatican Library since the fifteenth century, led to the defining of different types of textual tradition. Proposals by B.F. Westscott and F.J.A. Hort in their 1882 edition of the Greek New Testament, subsequently modified by B.H. Streeter in his 1924 work, *The Four Gospels: A Study of Origins*, identified the following types:

(1) "Alexandrian," which seems to be closest to the original text, while displaying some features of alteration in language and style.

(2) "Western," which is a tradition that alters and adds, especially in the gospels and Acts, but which was by no means limited to the western Mediterranean region as the name implied.

(3) "Caesarean," which was a mode of textual development identified first in the work of Origen after he moved from Alexandria to Caesarea, but which now seems to have been used earlier in Egypt.

(4) "Byzantine," which has been linked with Syria and Antioch, was thought to represent late modifications, but which now is seen to include some fine ancient readings as well.

The chief value of this descriptive system is not to classify types of texts by place of origin but to alert the reader who is analyzing the texts as to what were the tendencies for modification that were operative among the scribes who were making the copies of the New Testament or that were dominant in their locality. Fresh material and altered perspectives have been introduced through the discovery in the late nineteenth and early twentieth centuries of copies of parts of the New Testament on papyrus. Some of these date back to early in the Common Era. A fragment of the Gospel of John now in the John Rylands Library in Manchester was written early in the first half of the second century CE. Ancient versions of the New Testament (see below) and quotations from it in Christian writers of the second and third centuries provide additional material and insight concerning the precise content, the preservation and the modification of the New Testament text. What is remarkable is that, by comparison with ancient copies of literature from the culture of ancient Greece and Rome, there are so many copies available for analysis and that their disagreements concern relatively minor issues.

TRANSLATIONS OF THE BIBLE

Ancient Translations of the Hebrew Bible

The translation of the Hebrew Bible most influential and most widely used by Jews and early Christians was the version that began as early as the second century BCE and came to be known as the Septuagint (LXX). We have noted earlier the legend recorded in the Letter of Aristeas, which was developed to prove the divine activity involved in the translation process. Originally developed in Alexandria, the Greek version underwent revisions in Palestine on down into the first century CE, as the portions found in the Dead Sea caves show conclusively. Later translations in the second century CE made adjustments for the changes that were taking place in the spoken Greek language. Those of Aquila and Symmachus have survived only in fragments, but they seem to have replaced the LXX, which Christians had taken over as their edition of what they called the Old Testament. Theodotion (first or second century CE) included in his Greek translation material which filled in parts of books which were present in abbreviated forms in the LXX, but he also supplied additional passages in Job and Jeremiah which went beyond what had become the standard Hebrew text. Christian scholars such as Origen, Lucian of Antioch and Jerome offer details which demonstrate how analysis of the versions of the LXX was being carried on in the attempt to discover if possible the original. Copies of the LXX on papyrus have survived as well, but the chief sources for modern scholarship to pursue this analysis and reconstruction of LXX are the great ancient copies of the Greek Bible, especially Codex Vaticanus and Codex Sinaiticus. Printed editions of the LXX first appeared in the sixteenth century, and in the current scene the most important editions are the ones produced at Cambridge University (1906-1940) and at Goettingen (still in process).

In the early centuries CE in Babylon and in Palestine, paraphrases of the Hebrew Bible were prepared in Aramaic, the dominant native language of the Middle East in this period. Called Targums (or *targumim*), they continued to be produced down into the middle ages. The Christians, on the other hand, developed in the first and second centuries CE their own translations of the Old Testament into an Aramaic dialect, Syriac. In subsequent centuries other Syriac versions were produced, of which the Peshitta (fourth/fifth century CE) had the widest and most enduring use.

Early translations into Latin are described by Jerome about 400 CE as highly diverse, although the Latin-speaking church fathers, Tertullian and Cyprian, quote extensively both the Old and New Testaments in Latin. About that time Jerome began to produce his own fresh translation of the Old Testament, as he had earlier done for the New Testament. From this beginning developed the common Latin translation known as the Vulgate. Efforts over the centuries to recover the original wording of the Vulgate and more recently to produce a critical edition of it have been frustrated for lack of ancient evidence. Translations of the Bible for Coptic and Ethiopian Christians in Africa were based on the Greek text, even though Ethiopic is a semitic language.

Early Translations of the New Testament

In the previous section we noted how many translations of the Bible were developed in the early church during the early years of its existence. These included, of course, the New Testament, but some distinctive features or contemporary significance of some of the ancient translations of the New Testament may be noted. By the end of the second century CE translations of the New Testament into Syriac and Latin were completed. Especially influential in the Syriac church, however, was the *Diatessaron* of Tatian (fl. 160-180), in which he interwove the material from the four gospels, with the result that copies of the New Testament from then on tended to harmonize the differences among the gospel accounts. Interest in the Coptic versions of the New Testament has been stimulated by the discovery in 1945 of a library of Coptic writings in Upper Egypt. The evident importance of the Gospel of Thomas there has led a few scholars to suggest that this gospel, or the tradition which it contains, antedates our four canonical gospels. By the fifth century there were translations of the New Testament into Armenian and Georgian as Christianity spread into southern Russia. The Arabic version is considerably later, and closely related to the older semitic-language version, which was in Syriac.

English Versions of the Bible

As Christianity began to spread across England through the work of Augustine (in 600 CE) and other Christian leaders in subsequent centuries, paraphrases and translations of parts of the Bible appeared in Anglo-Saxon. The first complete translation of the Bible into English was by John Wycliffe (1330-84) and his associates; it was based on the Vulgate. With the rise of the Reformation in sixteenth-century Germany, William Tyndale (1490-1536) had completed by the time of his martyrdom a fresh translation of the New Testament from the Greek, and was at work on a translation of the Hebrew Old Testament. In the subsequent struggles for power between Catholics and Protestants there were various editions produced, some based on German translations (Coverdale Bible, 1535) and some on the work of Tyndale and Latin translations: the Great Bible (1539-41); the Geneva Bible produced by Protestant exiles in 1560 during the reign of the Catholic queen, Mary Tudor; the Bishops' Bible in 1568.

What became the dominant translation, however, was prepared by a group of university scholars under the auspices of James I and was completed in 1611: the King James Version, or Authorized Version. Its elegant style influenced English language and literature for centuries. It was revised by a group of English Protestant scholars in 1881-85 (Revised Version), and then more thoroughly by an American committee of scholars as the Revised Standard Version (1946-51), which has in turn been reworked as the New Revised Standard (1990). This translation is the basis for this present Cambridge Study Bible. Other widely-used recent translations include the New American Standard Version (1971) and the New International Version (1978).

Freer translations into contemporary English have been prepared by various groups and individuals: *The Bible: an American Translation* in 1931; J.B. Phillips' *New Testament in Modern English* in 1958; *The New English Bible* (1961-70), which has undergone a thorough revision: *The Revised English Bible* (1989); *The Good News Bible*, or *Today's English Version*, which is widely used throughout the English-speaking world, and is based on sophisticated linguistic insights with the aim of producing in modern English the "dynamic equivalent" of the original language.

Roman Catholic translations into English based on the Vulgate include the Douay-Rheims (1582-1609), *The Confraternity Revision of the New Testament* (1941), Ronald Knox's Bible (1944-50), *The New American Bible* (1952-70), which shared the aims and methods of the RSV. Most recently there has been an English translation of a French edition prepared in Jerusalem by Dominican scholars, and hence known as *The Jerusalem Bible*. This readable and accurate translation has understandably gained wide use.

THE JEWS FROM THE EXILE TO THE RABBINIC ERA

In order to understand the developments within Judaism that led to the formation of the Bible and that took such diverse forms that from it emerged various Jewish groups – and early Christianity – it is essential to trace the outlines of Jewish history in the period after Jews were permitted by the Persian rulers to return to their land from their exile in Babylon. The first stages of this process took place over nearly two centuries, beginning with the Persian king Cyrus in 539 BCE, and continuing through the reign of Artaxerxes II (404-358). The books of Nehemiah and Ezra describe how these two priestly figures were empowered by the Persian kings to re-establish the temple worship in Jerusalem and to encourage and then to enforce obedience to the law, which was edited and expanded by priests during and following the exile (Ezra 7.25; Neh 10.15-39). A system of local magistrates was set up to require conformity to the law, with power of imprisonment or death, confiscation of property or banishment for the violators. The ideological hold of covenantal separatism on the Jews was reinforced by Persian policy.

When the young Macedonian venturer, Alexander the Great, conquered this part of the world, which he did by defeating the Persian ruler Darius III in 331, his goal was very different from that of the Persians: he sought to unify the culture of the world on the Greek model (that is, to *hellenize*) by uniting peoples of various ethnic, religious and cultural origins. This was symbolized by a forced marriage of 10,000 Greeks with 10,000 Persian women. In these circumstances, when Alexander conquered the territory from Syria south into Egypt, the Jews were a small city-state in and around Jerusalem, at first little affected by the hellenization policy. Other cities in the area were rebuilt on the hellenistic model, including Samaria and its temple on Mt. Gerizim. After Alexander's death and the struggle between the generals who became his successors as rulers of the conquered territories – the Ptolemies in Egypt and the Seleucids in Syria – non-Jewish settlements developed along the seacoast, and cooperative arrangements were made with non-Jewish rulers east of the Jordan. The basic pattern of administration was the toparchy: a city and the land around it were governed in local affairs by a regional council, called a *synedrion*, but the whole region was militarily controlled by the central hellenistic government. In Judea the council was composed of priests and local power figures; by 198 the Seleucid ruler Antiochus II was firmly in control. This policy was continued by the Romans down into the Common Era. Two major groups vying for dominance in the council through the post of highpriest were the descendants of the first high priest of the restored temple, Onias, and the priestly partisans of Tobias, who were more open to the hellenization process.

Meanwhile Rome had risen to power in the Mediterranean world, first by defeating the Carthaginians in the west, followed by overcoming the Macedonians, and then by invading Asia Minor, from which point they began to influence the Seleucids and the Ptolemies through virtual power of appointment of their rulers. When Antiochus IV, who had spent years as a hostage in Rome, came to power in Syria, he issued a decree prohibiting local sacrifical practices and forbidding conformity to local religious law, including the Jewish temple cult and law (1 Macc 1.41-58). Not only was the decree enforced, but pagan sacrifices in honor of the king were offered on the temple altar (1.59) and Jews as a whole were forced to offer public sacrifice in his behalf. In 168 Mattathias, a priest, and his sons defied the decree and instigated a revolt which spread rapidly among the Jews. As noted above, military leadership was assumed by one of the sons of Mattathias, Judas, whose nickname was "the hammer" (Maccabeus), and who was able to defeat the Syrian army, thereby regaining control over Judea and rededicating the temple in 165.

After a century of intra-Jewish disputes, of intervention by the Seleucids, the Ptolemies and the Romans, and of involvement of the Maccabees in alliances with anti-Roman forces in the area, the Romans invaded and took over the land in 63 BCE. Many Jews had become alienated by the increasing secularization and brutalization of the Maccabean rulers, including intra-family murders, and by their violation of priestly and marital law. When Pompey came with the Roman troops, the Jews lost political autonomy, and later failed again in efforts at political revolt in 67-70 and 132-135 CE. In 37 BCE the Romans designated as king of the Jews a man from the land of the Nabateans, which lay east of the Jordan: Herod. He built the city and temple of Jerusalem, as well as a hellenistic-style villa near Jericho and a coastal city named Caesarea, which was complete with theaters, baths, aqueduct, and gymnasia. Real power remained with the Roman governor and his troops based in Syria.

Religiously, however, the temple and the priesthood were dominant social factors. A steady flow of Jewish pilgrims from east and west were the major contributors to the local economy, through their spending for food, lodging, and sacrifices and fees for changing money into temple coinage. In this period the Pharisees sought to personalize religious commitment through informal gatherings in homes for reading and study of the law and the prophetic heritage of the Jews, and through table fellowship in which they adapted the laws for temple ritual purity to their shared meals. The scribes (interpreters of the law) had developed at the time of the instructional program on the return from exile (Neh 8.2), and had become an important feature of religious life as more and more sought to appropriate the law for their daily lives (Sir 38.24-39.14). The Essenes – in home-gatherings and in the monastic community they established overlooking the Dead Sea – emphasized their distinctiveness as God's true covenant people, and believed that God had granted them special revelation into the interpretation of scripture and concerning the fulfillment of the divine plan which would place them in power instead of the priestly group in Jerusalem, whom they regarded as hopelessly corrupt and impure. Other Jews emphasized wisdom, and sought to develop a synthesis of their law and the philosophical principles that had arisen among the Greeks. In terms of wealth and power, the dominant segment of the Jews, however, consisted of the priests. Their chief supporters were called the Sadducees. In spite of the variety of answers among these various Jewish groups, the universal question was, What is required for participation in the covenant which God has over the centuries sought to establish with his people?

The Romans developed a series of administrative arrangements in Palestine after the death of Herod, including having his son, Archelaus, as local ruler for a time (4 BCE - 6 CE), with other descendants of Herod controlling Galilee, the Syrian coast and the region east of the Jordan. Herod Antipas, for example, was in power from 4 BCE until 49 CE. Judea and Galilee were reasonably prosperous, with the latter region profiting from developing cities, commercial transit from the east to the coast, and fishing and agriculture. Yet the growing gap between rich and poor, the severity of taxation, and the secular values of the puppet ruler led to widespread unrest. The public protest against Roman expropriation of temple funds in 66 evoked a violent response from the Roman troops. A Jewish nationalist movement erupted, which was quickly joined by sympathizers in Judea and Galilee, even though the priestly groups remained content with the Roman system which kept them in power. The revolutionaries attacked palaces and fortresses, and gained control of Jerusalem. The initial attempt of Syrian-based Roman troops to repress the revolt failed, but major forces were sent in under Vespasian by order of the emperor Nero (54-68). As the Jewish groups gained control, they began fighting among themselves, with the result that popular support dwindled. By late 67, the Romans were in control of Galilee; in 68-69 they dominated the coastal regions, Samaria, the Jordan Valley, and Judea. In early 70 Titus (Vespasian having returned to Rome as emperor) successfully laid siege to Jerusalem, although a few fortresses held out. Masada by the Dead Sea, which is best-known from recent excavations, fell in 73. The temple was destroyed, as was the Dead Sea community center. Priests, Sadducees, Essenes vanished. Only the Pharisees offered a viable option for post-revolutionary Judaism.

Dropping the designation "Pharisee," this group began to organize a system for study, worship and above all for the maintenance of group identity that could triumph over political or cultural aggression and change. The leaders, who took to themselves the title of *rabbi* (which meant "great man," but which came to mean "teacher" or "authoritative interpreter"), seem to have met at Yavneh (Jamnia) on the seacoast in the decades after 70 to develop a pattern of common life based on the appropriation of the scriptures. That strategy and process continued to mature in the second to the sixth centuries CE long after the Pharisees had disappeared. It produced the mass of legal and anecdotal material that became the Mishnah and the Talmud. Throughout this period the informal beginnings of gatherings in households (which is what *synagogue* was initially) became increasingly institutionalized and developed formalized synagogue worship and study.

The aggressive program of Hadrian (117-138) to impose Greco-Roman culture on the land of the Jews included a plan to convert Jerusalem and its temple into a model pagan city, and according to one source he forbade Jews to circumcize. Coupled with injustice on the part of rich land-owners, in 132 a second revolt arose, led by a man who came to be known as Bar Kochba, "son of the star," a messianic designation to indicate his liberation of Israel from pagan control. His guerrilla tactics were initially effective, but the Roman commanders pursued him and his forces to their hideouts at the southern end of the Dead Sea, where the last efforts came to an end in 135. Hadrian followed through with his plan: Jerusalem became Aelia Capitolina and the temple was transformed and dedicated to Zeus.

Under Antoninus Pius (138-161) some degree of autonomy was restored to the Jews, and the synagogue-based movement flourished. They developed theories (1) that the oral law was as old as the written and went back to Moses, (2) that there had been a great assembly to adjudicate religious matters as far back as Ezra (which they called Sanhedrin, derived from the Greek, *synedrion*), and (3) that the institutionalized patterns of synagogue instruction and worship were not recent innovations but ancient. Simultaneously, Christianity was developing its interpretation of scripture, its patterns of worship, and its structures of leadership, as is evident from the later books of the New Testament.

THE CHURCH IN THE APOSTOLIC AGE

Beginning with Jesus, the early Christians shared with their Jewish contemporaries the following issues: How were they to reclaim the heritage of God's covenant with his people? What was the basis for sharing in that covenant? How is God at work for and through his people to achieve his purpose for them and for creation?

Jesus' answers to these issues are apparent in the oldest layers of the gospel tradition. In response to the question from John the Baptist as to whether he is God's agent of renewal ("the one who is to come": Lk 7.19-23) Jesus calls attention to his healing of the blind, the deaf, his cleansing the lepers, his raising the dead, and his preaching good news to the poor. These actions are all announced in the prophets as signs of God's establishing the new age (Isa 29.18-19; 35.5-6; 61.1). In his words and acts of calling men and women to prepare for the coming Rule of God in the world, Jesus sets aside such factors as ritual purity, ethnic origin, occupation, as well as physical and even moral condition. Those who respond to him in faith are lepers, Gentiles, tax-collectors, sinners. That this open invitation to participation is central to his role is apparent when he quotes without dispute his opponents' characterization of him as "a friend of tax-collectors and sinners" (Lk 7.34). The same pattern of open relationships pervades our oldest gospel, Mark, and is justified by Jesus in debate with the religious leaders. It is his suffering and death which provide the ground of acceptance with God (Mk 10.45), not flawless moral and ritual performance. His followers saw God's vindication of this understanding of God's purpose for his people in Jesus' having been raised from the dead. It is this message and this defining of God's people that Jesus charged his followers to proclaim. It is these deprived and excluded people that they are to reach with God's message, and these modes of human renewal that they are to practise (Mk 3.13-19). They celebrated their life together as God's people in the same way other Jewish fellowships of that period did: in a meal of bread and wine. But for Jesus and his followers, this meal recalled his death and looked forward to the fulfillment of God's purpose for and through them (Mk 14.22-25).

Within a year or two after the death of Jesus, Paul the Pharisee learned that in Damascus there were groups consisting of Jews, Gentiles, and the ritually impure which were meeting in homes for prayer and fellowship, claiming to be God's people and announcing that Jesus was God's agent to establish his kingdom on earth. Damascus was one of the ten hellenized cities (Decapolis) in a region through which Jesus had passed and preached (Mk 7.31). Paul's Pharisaic convictions about the ethnic and ritual requirements for participation in the covenant moved him to set about destroying this movement, as he later acknowledged (Gal 1.13-14). His encounter with the risen Christ transformed him and his estimate of the community of the new covenant (1 Cor 11.25), so that he now saw Jesus as God's agent to reconcile the world to himself. He also perceived that God had called him to proclaim that message to the whole world (2 Cor 5.19-20). This new understanding was seen not as in conflict with the Jewish scriptures but as God's intended fulfillment of them. This conviction is effectively summarized in the opening lines of Paul's letter to the Romans: God appointed him to his apostolic role for the sake of "the gospel of God which he promised beforehand through his prophets in the holy scriptures," a message which concerns God's Son, through whom Paul has been commissioned to "bring about the obedience of faith among all the Gentiles for the sake of his name" (Rom 1.1-5).

Paul's letters also show at many points his grasp of basic concepts from the philosophy which was spread throughout the Roman world of his time, with its concept of an inherent law of nature which every human being is capable of recognizing and obeying through conscience. All humanity will be judged in the last day by the degree of obedience to that law. Paul uses that argument in Rom 2.12-16, just as he sees certain Stoic virtues to be produced by the Spirit within the lives of Christians (Gal 5.22-23). His ability to combine his Pharisaic insights and knowledge of scripture with his grasp of pagan language and philosophy made him uniquely well-suited to give leadership for the community's outreach to the Roman world.

The leaders among the Jerusalem-based apostles were less clear in their understanding of how God's covenant people were to relate to the Jewish heritage and how non-Jews should be included in the membership. Peter, who is pictured in the gospel accounts as impetuous and ambivalent, continued that manner of life when, according to Paul (Gal 2), he initially joined in table fellowship with Gentile Christians and then refused to do so. The division of labor agreed upon by the apostles, whereby Peter should concentrate on a mission to Jews and Paul on the Gentile mission, did not negate the basic conviction derived from Jesus that Jews and Gentiles alike were potential members of the new community. Yet the continuing ambiguity of the Jerusalem leaders on that issue is indicated in Acts 15, where James (Jesus' brother) decrees that Gentiles must observe certain minimal dietary laws ("abstain...from whatever has been strangled and from blood" [15.20]). This account probably comes from the later first or early second century, but it indicates the degree to which Old Testament law as understood in first-century Judaism was still considered in some Christian quarters to be binding on members of the covenant people of both Jewish and Gentile origins. As we have noted, in the second century some Christians (chiefly Marcion) went to the extreme of repudiating all the Old Testament and removing all Jewish elements from the New Testament. That view was rejected by the mainstream of the church, which recognized in the Jewish scriptures and especially in the covenantal promises the ground of its being and its hope.

Paul had called Christians to be obedient to the secular political powers of the day, which he saw as divinely established for the maintenance of order in society (Rom 13.1-3). In the later part of the first century, however, Roman authorities began to oppress the Christians, especially as it became apparent that they were not merely a sub-group within Judaism. The issue of the legality of Christianity came to a head in the early second century when Trajan (98-117) decided that Christians who refused to offer the required sacrifices in behalf of the emperor were to be executed. Even after persecution of Christians had begun, the leaders counselled subjection to the political authorities (1 Pet 2.13-17), although it might lead to suffering "as a Christian" (1 Pet 4.12-19).

Christians in the late first and early second century responded to the political and cultural pressures of Roman society in a variety of ways. Some undertook a synthesis of insights from scripture, from the gospel, and from intellectual concepts of the day. The Letter of James, for example, redefines moral obligation in terms of law which combines features of the Law of Moses and Stoic ethics. The Letter to the Hebrews unites the scriptural view of history as the arena in which God works out his purpose for his people with the philosophical concept of the ideal world (in which forms and models of reality exist forever) and the material world (in which imperfect, decaying copies of the ideals are found). The result in Hebrews is that Jesus is the ideal of sacrifice and access to God, while Jewish history and cult are time-bound, transitory copies of the real. The Gospel of John shifts major interest from the age to come (as in Mark and Paul) to the mystical realities in which God's people may even now participate. John does so by using organic images of Christ – shepherd and flock, vine and branches, water of life – and calling his readers to share in the light and renewal of life that Jesus makes possible. The style and language were well suited to engage those Jews and Gentiles in the first two centuries who were seeking religious fulfillment through mystical participation in the divine: "I am in my Father, and you in me, and I in you" (Jn 14.20). Jesus' relationship to God is affirmed by the statement – simple in form but complex in implications – "The Father and I are one" (Jn 10.30). On a more pragmatic level, by the end of the first century when persecution seemed inevitable, other Christians looked to direct divine intervention to defeat the Roman official opposition and to vindicate the faithful. The Revelation of John is evidence of this point of view in the apostolic period.

Perhaps the most important development for the church in the long view was the emergence in the later decades of the first century and on down into the second century of patterns of official responsibilities within the local congregations and in regions. The formation of these ecclesiastical roles is hinted at in the letters of Paul, but becomes explicit in the later letters written in his name, where deacons, presbyters and bishops are given specific roles. Similarly, the obligations of members are outlined in these later New Testament writings as well. The development of all these lines – community definition in relation to Judaism, synthesis with contemporary religious and philosophical aspirations, confronting the political challenge from Rome, organizing the Christians for an ongoing enterprise – are the themes which are addressed in the post-apostolic writings of Christianity.

INTRODUCTIONS TO THE INDIVIDUAL BOOKS OF THE OLD TESTAMENT

The First Five Books

GENESIS, EXODUS, LEVITICUS, NUMBERS, DEUTERONOMY

Variously designated as the Books of Moses, the Law of Moses, the Pentateuch (meaning "five books"), and Torah (Hebrew for "Teaching"), these writings have been the introductory core of the Bible for Jews and Christians since the first century of our era. They are the end-product of a process of oral transmission, and of combining and editing local and national traditions that stretch back over many centuries before the Common Era. Some of the material consists of local lore that was associated with peoples who lived in the land of Canaan long before the confederation of the tribes of Israel, and some of it is linked with the various shrines where the tribes of Israel worshipped before the establishment of the temple in Jerusalem. Accordingly there are passages which reflect the special interests or convictions of the northern or southern tribes of Israel at Shechem and Hebron respectively. Some traditions show kinship with stories of creation, of divine blessing and punishment that are found among the remains of other nations of the ancient Near East, although the Israelite traditions bear the stamp of the distinctive convictions of this people: that the God of Israel is Lord of history and the one who has called this group of tribes to special privilege and responsibility. The four dominant themes in these five books attributed to Moses are (1) how God was manifested to the leaders of his people; (2) the nature of the promise involved in the covenant relationship betwen God and Israel, as well as (3) the nature of the covenantal obligations, moral and cultic, on the part of the Israelite tribes; (4) the pilgrim experience of Israel as it came into and took over the promised land where God dwelt among his people.

Since the nineteenth century archaeologists have recovered vast numbers of documents from the ancient Near East, including official records, public inscriptions, works of literature, religious liturgies and personal communications. Parallels in language, modes of expression, literary forms are remarkable. In these ancient writings there is occasionally mention of personal or tribal names which are found in the Bible as well. For example, in correspondence between kings in Babylonia and their local puppet rulers in Syria and Palestine in the fourteenth century found in Egypt at Amarna, there is frequent mention of semi-nomadic people in Canaan who are known as Hapiru or Habiru – which is a self-reference (=Hebrews) for the people of Abraham (Gen 14.13) and is used of the Israelites frequently in Exodus (from 1.15-21.2), in the historical books (1 Sam 4.6-9; 13.3; 29.3) and the prophets (Jer 34.9,14).

Embedded at various points in the extended narrative of the books of the Pentateuch as they now exist are small items of ancient tradition which probably go back to the period of oral transmission or to documents which predate the Bible as we know it. These include three types: (1) sayings, such as the consequences of murder in Gen 9.6; the pronouncements when the ark of the covenant was moved, in Num 10.35-36; (2) songs, such as the Song of Miriam in Ex 15.21 and the Song of the Well in Num 21.17-18; (3) narrative episodes, such as Abraham's offering of his son Isaac in Gen 22.

The oldest items in the tradition go back to the epoch of the patriarchs: Abraham, Isaac and Jacob. The earliest collection of this material, which was edited in light of the subsequent establishment of the central shrine in Jerusalem, dates from the time of David and Solomon. Some of these stories and sayings reflect their place of origin in that some use the name of God preferred in the north (*Elohim*) while others show preference for the name, *Yahweh*, which was used by the southern tribes. A major and quite thorough organization of the tradition, with heavy emphasis on the responsibilities of the tribes of Israel under the covenant with God called for a fresh commitment on the part of the people, and hence came to be known as the Deuteronomic reform, from the Greek term for "second giving of the Law." This probably took place in the late sixth century BCE under King Josiah (2 Kings 22-23; 2 Chronicles 34-35).

During Israel's exile in Babylon the tradition was reworked anew under the influence of the priestly leaders who looked forward to assuming leadership for the people in the event of their liberation and return to their land. This restoration to the land and the re-establishment of the temple worship took place in the sixth century BCE, at which time the priestly leaders, Ezra and Nehemiah, carefully instructed the people in the revised version of the traditions, laws and cultic regulations. It is likely that modification and expansion of the priestly requirements continued in the years after the return of Israel to the land. Similar editing and inclusion of Deuteronomic and priestly concerns are evident in the Book of Joshua as well.

It was the final edited form of these Five Books that from the fourth century BCE on provided the Jewish people with the norms for understanding their history, their special relationship with God, and the resultant moral and cultic responsibilities, and which came to serve as the introduction to the sacred scriptures for both Jews and Christians.

GENESIS

The first eleven chapters of Genesis (which means "origin") consist mostly of stories about how the universe began: the origins of the world, the human race, human sin, languages. They are told in much the same style of epic narrative as may be found in other ancient Near Eastern cultures. Archaeologists have discovered literatures of other nations from this part of the world which include stories that quite closely resemble those in the Bible. What is distinctive about the Genesis stories, however, is that they are told as evidence of the overarching purpose of Israel's God for his people, so that one learns through them about God's hopes for humanity, about human responsibility and failure, about divine judgment and provision for continuity of God's purpose in spite of human sin and mortality (Gen 5.1-9.28). The first four chapters present two different accounts of creation: the first (1.1-2.3) emphasizes divine order and human responsibility, as evident in the need to obey the sabbath law of rest on the seventh day; the second account includes the saga of the disobedience of humans and the divine provision for sustaining the covenant through generations of offspring. Genealogies demonstrate this continuity of covenant relationship: Gen 5, 10, 11, 36. The persistence of God's purpose stands in spite of human pride and the resultant divine judgment, as in the stories of the flood (Gen 6) and the Tower of Babel (Gen 11).

Central throughout the book from Gen 11 on are the twin themes of (1) God's initiative in establishing a covenant relationship with his people through Abraham and his posterity, and (2) God's guidance of his people through historical experiences which involve pagan people and their rulers, as well as conflicts within and failures among the covenant people. The essential mode of conveying the divine purpose is through visions of God that are granted to Abraham (12.1-7; 15.1-21; 17.1-22;

18.1-21; 22.1-19), Isaac (26.23-25) and Jacob (28.10-17; 32.24-32; 35.9-15; 46.2-4). God tests the depth of Abraham's commitment to the divine purpose by calling for the sacrifice of his son (Gen 22). In the subsequent events of Israel's history, God is at work triumphing over human failure, deceit and opposition as he works to accomplish his goal for the covenant people.

The fact that God as well as human leading characters in Genesis are reported with different names – God, Lord; Abram, Abraham; Jacob, Israel – is an indication of the multiple sources which have been woven together to form Genesis as we have it. Important elements later included in the law given at Sinai as reported in the Pentateuch are already present in the pre-Mosaic accounts, such as the priestly requirements of sabbath observance (Gen 2.1-3) and the rite of circumcision (17.9-14) show. The series of events that takes Jacob and his family to Egypt prepares the way for the great divine disclosures that are to shape the subsequent history of Israel: the deliverance of the people from slavery, and the establishment of the law and covenant at Sinai through Moses. Genesis makes clear that God has been in control of the destiny of his people ever since the creation of the world. The form and content of this book show that it is the end result of a process of editing that went on over centuries and was influenced by Israel's changing historical and cultural circumstances. Following the priestly version of the creation story in 1.1-2.4a, Genesis 2.4b-11.32 presents the traditions about the origins of the world and of humanity; 12.1-50.26 describes the family origins of God's people.

EXODUS

The name of this book comes from the Old Greek translation (the Septuagint) and means "The Way Out" (i.e., out of slavery in Egypt). The composite nature of Exodus is evident as the account moves from narratives to the recitation of community obligations and priestly regulations. As in Genesis, God works to accomplish his purpose through human responses of trust as well as through failures and opposition. Certain central figures – in this book, Moses and Aaron – are chosen by God for the leading roles in the renewal and enrichment of the covenant relationship, and their designation is confirmed through their experiences of visions and appearances of God. Concrete confirmation of the covenant promise is given through the genealogies which demonstrate the preservation of the covenant family. 1 Kings 6.1 dates the escape of

Israel from Egypt to 480 years before the time of Solomon, which began about 960 BCE. The events described in Exodus, however, fit best in the period of transition of the XIXth Egyptian dynasty, when the capital was moved from Thebes to the Nile delta, which would be just after 1300. The figure 480 is probably only a round figure for a dozen successive generations.

The events in which God is seen as triumphing over human opposition include actions against Pharaoh and the Egyptians in the form of the plagues (Ex 7-10), the defense against the hostile Amalekites (Ex 17), and God's judgment on Israel when the people reverted to pagan idolatrous rites (Ex 32). On the positive side God's works in behalf of his people are evident in the crossing of the Red Sea (Ex 13-14) and in the divine provision of food and drink in the desert of Sinai (Ex 16). The primary acts of God's self-disclosure in Exodus are the dramatic accompaniments of the revelation to Moses on Mt. Sinai (Ex 19-31) through which the covenant is elaborated, confirmed, and communicated by Moses to the people.

Woven into this vivid narrative are two elements which give substance and continuity to the covenantal relationship: (1) the legal and (2) the liturgical traditions of Israel. The core of the law is given as the Ten Commandments in Ex 20, which appear in a different form in Deut 5. The sacred number "ten" is confirmed in Ex 34.28; Deut 4.13; 10.4. This basic legal tradition is greatly expanded in Ex 21-31, and even more extensively in Leviticus and Deuteronomy, with the priestly requirements elaborated and intensified, since these came to be regarded as the essential means of gaining and maintaining the special identity of Israel as God's people. The liturgical aspects of the developing tradition are apparent in the songs of Miriam and Moses found in Ex 15, which celebrate God's deliverance of his people, and in the Passover ceremony in which are recalled his acts of liberation of Israel from slavery (Ex 12.14-20). The priestly expansion of these features of the older tradition included in Exodus shows that central to participation in the ongoing life of the covenant people were (1) the periodic historical recollections of what God had done to establish Israel as the covenant people, (2) the recommitment of each generation of Israelites to that past and the divine acts, and (3) the obedience to the rules which were now seen to be essential for maintenance of good standing within that community. Significantly, the book ends with two essential features: (1) the preparations of the tribes for transit to the land of Canaan where they are to settle as God's people, and where God will dwell among them in the central shrine (Ex 33-40.33); and (2) the final divine self-disclosure which confirms the covenant and focuses on Israel's destiny and obligations as God's people (40.34-38).

LEVITICUS

Leviticus is the major product of the post-exilic editing and expansion of the older legal and cultic traditions of Israel. In it are described in detail how the priests – sons of Aaron – are to preside over the ceremonies performed in the temple in order to maintain the divinely-intended relationship of obedience and purity between God and his people Israel. In spite of the traditional name for this book, Leviticus, the Levites are mentioned only a few times (Lev 25), and it is the Aaronic priests who have the dominant role of mediating between God and the people. They are the agents of purification (Lev 8-9), and as such have received divine confirmation (9.23-24). Detailed instructions are given for their consecration and for the purification of their offerings (Lev 11, 21-22). The specific acts which require the offerings are both voluntary and involuntary violations of personal or community purity. Details of the process of preparation of the offerings are also provided here (Lev 1-7). The forms of impurity include acts of sin, ceremonial defilement, polluting types of sickness (Lev 12-15), for which the appropriate modes of cleansing and restoration of standing within the community are described. Emphasis is placed on intra-community responsibility, both moral and ritual, including the command to love one's neighbor (Lev 19.18). On the other hand, there are solemn warnings about the judgment that will fall on those who fail to avail themselves of the divinely-provided remedy for human sin (Lev 10, 24, 26). The feasts which are to be celebrated in order to confirm the experience of community, historically and in the present, are described in detail (Lev 16, 23). The combination of God's grace and demand toward his people is reflected in Lev 25, where the provision is made for the extension of the weekly sabbath to times of rest in the seventh year and the fiftieth year (7 x 7 + 1), and in the outline of blessings that are promised in return for obedience and punishment for disobedience (Lev 26). The integrity of one's word is essential for the experience of community (Lev 27). All these demands and promises are linked with Moses and the law given at Sinai (27.34).

NUMBERS

The designation of this book as Numbers derives from the accounts of a census of the male Israelites for military purposes at the beginning (Num 1.3) and near the end (Num 26). Significantly, the Levites are excluded from military service, since they must prepare the ongoing ceremonies for the worship of God in the central shrine (1.48-53). There are five major concerns that run throughout the book: (1) The maintenance of the covenant community through ritual purity from physical and from social acts which threaten its integrity (Num 5; 18-19). This purity is represented in a heightened form by certain persons who take special vows of purity: the Nazirites (Num 6). (2) Akin to this is the provision for continuity of covenant renewal through ceremonies in the central sanctuary (Num 7-9), especially the prescribed offerings and feasts which recall God's dealings with his people in the past (Num 28-29). That God is present with them is attested by the sacred voice (7.89) and the luminous cloud (9.15-23). (3) There are repeated reminders that God's leading is operative in preparing the people for the transition from nomadic existence in the desert to a settled mode of life in the land of Canaan, which has been promised them (Num 10-17). Even a pagan soothsayer affirms what the God of Israel has in store for his people (Num 22). (4) Joshua is to lead them into the land (Num 27), and assurance of their ultimate military success in the invasion is given through the defeat of the Midianites (Num 31). Details of the Exodus journey as well as of settlement in the land are also presented (Num 33-35). (5) At the same time there are solemn warnings and concrete demonstrations of what will result from Israel's disobedience of the covenant obligations (Num 12, 14, 16, 25), as well as evidence of the effectiveness of intercession with God by the faithful majority (Num 21). Two of the tribes decide to settle in the land east of the Jordan: Reuben and Gad (Num 32), leaving the other ten to prepare for the difficult but divinely supported entrance into the promised land.

Numbers serves to show how God cared for the covenant people in the past, as the priestly editor perceives it from his perspective following the exile (fifth century BCE). It is especially significant in that historical setting, since once again Israel was returning to this land and had to reestablish the central shrine where the covenant relationship would be celebrated while maintaining its moral and ritual integrity.

The book is divided into three main sections: 1.1-10.10, The Divine Ordering of Israel at Sinai; 10.11-20.13, Israel in the Wilderness; 20.14-36.13, From Kadesh to Moab: Preparing to Enter the Promised Land.

DEUTERONOMY

The name of this book derives from the report in 10.1-2 that Moses gave the law to the people for a second time, after the original copy given him by God was smashed in reponse to their idolatry (9.15-17). The Old Latin translation rendered this as *deuteronomium*.

The overall structure of Deuteronomy in its present form resembles that of treaty agreements between major ancient near eastern political powers and vassal states that have been recovered by archaeologists. Here the dependent nation in the covenant agreement is Israel, and the great power is Yahweh. The book is divided, like the ancient covenants, into (1) an historical prologue (Deut 1-4); (2) the basic principles of the covenant (Deut 5-11); (3) the specifics of the people's obligation in order to maintain the covenant relationship (Deut 12-16); (4) curses and blessing, linked with the degree to which the people meet or fail to meet their obligations (Deut 17-30); (5) instructions about preserving and publicly proclaiming the covenant agreement (Deut 31-34).

According to 2 Kings 22-23, a copy of the law was rediscovered in the temple during the reign of King Josiah in 621 BCE. The document thus found is almost certainly the central section of this book of Deuteronomy, written earlier in the seventh century. In it are set forth the responsibilities and obligations of those who call themselves God's people, with a dual emphasis on living by these standards and instructing one's children by them. The basic themes include the single, central sanctuary in the Jerusalem temple, the avoidance of idolatry, the distinction between clean and unclean animals; the observance of the seventh year of grace (sabbatical), tithing (15), the administration of justice and the rule of the king (17), the support of priests (18), and how purity and integrity are to be maintained among the covenant people (23-25), and how instruction of children is essential for perpetuating the covenant relationship. Especially important passages for the subsequent development of Judaism include the promise that a prophet like Moses will come (18.14-22) and the annual observance of the feasts which recall Israel's founding experiences and constitute her ongoing renewal as God's people (16). The basis for the covenant relationship in God's actions historically in behalf of his people is offered in 26.6-9. The major section of Deuteronomy (12-26) was likely written in the northern district of Israel, although it may incorporate older legal tradition which was subsequently transferred to the central shrine of the southern tribes in Jerusalem.

Probably during the exile, when hopes were building for the resumption of the worship of God in the temple in Jerusalem (28), this older document was expanded and edited so as to reflect the experience of the exile and the return of Israel to the land under priestly guidance and instruction. The renewal ceremony in Deut 27 may come from the ancient tradition used at the shrine in Shechem before the Jerusalem temple was built, for example. But the present book of Deuteronomy comes from a situation where restoration to the land is in process, and where legitimacy for the calamity of the exile and the strict regulations for purity of God's people are sought by this retelling of Yahweh's activity in the founding of Israel. The concluding summary of the law – both promises and warnings – is given in Deut 28, with a repetition of the themes of God's call to Israel, the warning of judgment for disobedience and the promise of renewal in Deut 29-30. Also added to the older material are an account of Moses' final instructions to Joshua, his successor, who will lead Israel into the land of promise. In Deut 32-33 there are two ancient songs attributed to Moses, in which he celebrates what God has done for his people and offers promises for the future of the tribes of Israel. The book in its present form comes to a close with an account of the death of Moses (34), an acclaim of the new leader Joshua, and praise of Moses as unique in his direct-experience of God and in the wonderful works that God did through him in behalf of Israel.

The Historical Books

The historical books of the Old Testament may be seen as representing three different types of writings: (1) The books of Joshua, Judges, 1 and 2 Samuel, 1 and 2 Kings are designated in the Hebrew Bible as "the Former Prophets." Although these books include older material, in their present form they demonstrate the view to be found in the Book of Deuteronomy, which is that the successes and failures of the tribes of Israel are demonstrations of God's power: he upholds the tribes when they are obedient, and punishes them when they fail to obey. The term "Latter Prophets" is used for the writings in which the actions and pronouncements of the prophets of Israel are reported.

(2) A second group of historical writings includes 1 and 2 Chronicles, Ezra and Nehemiah. These are written from the perspective of the priestly leaders, who believed that Israel's conformity to the ritual requirements set forth in the law was essential to the people's survival. Prepared during and

after the return of the Israelite tribes from exile in Babylon (sixth-fifth centuries BCE), they describe Israel's adjustment to living in the land of Palestine. Similar perspectives are evident in later writings included in the Old Testament Apocrypha: 1 and 2 Maccabees, and 1 and 2 Esdras. (These last two books are known as 3 and 4 Esdras in the Latin canon of scripture.) The books of Maccabees describe the successful revolt of the Jews under the leadership of a priestly family during the reign of the hellenistic king, Antiochus IV Epiphanes, who had tried to force Jews to participate in a cult honoring him as divine. 4 Esdras, which was written about the year 100 CE, includes veiled predictions of the destruction of the heathen power controlling the Jews and their land: the Romans. The issue in these later historical writings is how Israel is to preserve its integrity as the people of God while dominated by pagan political and cultural powers.

(3) A third group of historical writings recounts history in more personal terms, by showing how the actions of a brave individual had important results for the preservation of God's people. This type might be designated as edifying historical narratives. The style is more like that of a short story than what might be considered history. Three such writings included in the Hebrew canon are Ruth, Esther, and Jonah. Later works of this type which were included in the Old Testament Apocrypha are Tobit, Judith, Susanna (which is one of a group of later additions to Daniel), and Additions to Esther.

The three biographical narratives in the Hebrew Old Testament canon offer vivid narrative accounts of how God's purpose is disclosed through dramatic experiences, difficulties, and direct divine intervention. Ruth and Esther have been placed among the historical books, while Jonah was given a place among the Minor Prophets. All these writings could be classified as historical novels, in that they mix (sometimes anachronistically) known historical figures and situations with otherwise unknown events and persons in such a way as to demonstrate the direct activity of God in human affairs. The aim is not to portray the past objectively, but to use these vivid stories as a means of encouragement and instruction for readers in the writer's own time. Examples of this approach include Ruth, which shows how God can work through a faithful individual – even though she is a woman in a male-dominated society and a non-Israelite – in order to preserve the royal line of Israel and thereby to prepare for the coming of the ideal king, David. Esther mingles features that derive from a variety of historical circumstances from the sixth to the second century BCE to demonstrate how God preserves his people when they stand firm in their convictions, in spite of pressure from a pagan ruler. Jonah's aim is to describe God's direct action in history and his potential sovereignty over all the peoples of the world.

The historical value of all three of these types of book is great, not only for the periods they describe and the ancient sources which the authors at times incorporate, but also for what the editing of the sources and the re-working of the historical evidence reveal about the times and circumstances of the community at the time of the final editor. Even for the Jews and the Christians who have accepted as scripture only the books in the Hebrew canon, works from all three types still come into consideration. In the larger canon accepted by Jews in ancient times and by many Christians today (especially those in the eastern churches), as well as by scholars interested in the wider background of early Judaism and Christianity, all three kinds of historical writings are of great value.

JOSHUA

The book of Joshua is a history of Israel's transition from life in the desert of Sinai to settlement in the land of Palestine. The understanding of God and his relation to his people of the final editor of this body of historical material – including Joshua, Judges, 1 and 2 Samuel and 1 and 2 Kings, which covers the period from Joshua to the exile of Israel to Babylon – is that of the author of Deuteronomy. The rise and fall of the tribes of Israel is a sign of God's power, not of his weakness or lack of concern. The economic and political conditions of Israel reflect directly the degree of the people's obedience or disobedience to their covenantal obligations to Yahweh, their God. It is this outlook which is expressed in Joshua 1 and elaborated in Joshua 23.

The book may be divided into three major sections: (1) How the land was conquered by the twelve tribes (Josh 2-12); (2) How the land was divided among the twelve tribes (Josh 13-21); (3) How the people of Israel assembled before God at the central shrine in Shechem (Josh 23-24). Some scholars regard Joshua as so closely linked in style and intent to the Pentateuch (the five so-called books of Moses, Genesis through Deuteronomy) that they think of Joshua as the final book in a Hexateuch. Whatever the literary and editorial links may be, Joshua surely shares the basic outlook and strategy of the first five books.

JUDGES

The name of this book comes from the usual translation of a Hebrew word, *shaphat*, which might better be rendered as "ruler." It implies one who settles disputes and assigns responsibilities, and is used when the role of Yahweh as sovereign over his people is depicted in the Psalms (Ps 96.13; 98.9). The book includes three sections of unequal length: (1) accounts of the military expeditions of Israelite tribes into adjacent territories north and south of their land (1.1-2.5); (2) reports of the role of the "judges," or divinely designated leaders (2.5-16.31); (3) the conquest of the territory to the north by the tribe of Dan (17-21).

Although the book as a whole gives evidence of having been edited from the Deuteronomic point of view, the closing chapters (17-21) do not seem to share that perspective. Incorporated into the book is an ancient poem, the Song of Deborah (Judg 5), which describes vividly how a Canaanite king was tricked and murdered. The unsettled and diverse state of the Israelite tribes is apparent from the reports of civil war between tribes (Judg 19-21) and the use by Israelites of elements from non-Israelite religions, such as images (Judg 17.4-6), the veneration of sacred trees, human sacrifice, and killing someone for vengeance. Some of the judges had authority over the whole of Israel (Othniel, Ehud, Gideon, Samson, Deborah, and Barak), while others functioned in only certain designated areas (Tola and Jair, Ibzan, Elon, Abdon). Other leaders (Shamgar, Abimelech) are not designated as judges. The places described as centers for the worship of Yahweh include Bethel, Shechem, Shiloh in the north, and Bethlehem and Hebron in the south. Thus the range of sources and the changing circumstances of the Israelites are reflected in this book.

The central section of Judges (2.6-16.31), however, builds on the themes of the sins of the people, how they were punished by defeats at the hands of neighboring tribes (such as the Midianites) (6.1-10) and the expulsion of false claimants to leadership (9.1-57). But it also shows how God raised up leaders to accomplish his purpose for his people and how they displayed human frailties (Gideon and Samson), and how obedience to Yahweh can bring defeat of Israel's enemies (the Philistines).

RUTH

Although the Book of Ruth purports to come from the time of the Judges (Ruth 1.1), it reflects a very different social and political situation from the moral and leadership chaos of the Book of Judges. Instead, it presents an idealized picture of life among God's people when ethnic and religious issues arise as a result of the devotion of a non-Israelite woman to the family and God of her deceased husband. The centrality of the issue of inclusiveness within the people of God reflects the time after the return of Israel from her period of captivity in Babylon and the problem that Jews faced about whether they should marry non-Israelites or allow them to share in the life of God's covenant people. The linguistic influence of the exile in Babylon (sixth-fifth century BCE) is evident in the traces of Aramaic forms of speech (which was spoken by northern semitic peoples in Syria and parts of Mesopotamia). Ruth 4.7 refers to a legal restriction of a type documented only in the post-exilic code included in Deut 25.9 about Israelite intermarriage.

The book of Ruth reflects the major issue that confronted Israelites on their return from exile: Is ethnic origin within Israel essential for participation in the life of God's people? Could a non-Israelite share in God's people and purpose? Ruth was from Moab, east of the Jordan. Negative answers are given to these questions in other documents from that period: Ezra 9 and 10; Nehemiah 13. In Ruth, however, non-Israelites can choose to participate, and God can give them an essential place in his purpose for Israel. The child born to the widowed Ruth by Boaz was the grandfather of David, Israel's ideal king. Also, in a male-dominated culture like that of Israel, the faith and fidelity of women play a crucial role in the accomplishment of God's purposes for his people.

1 and 2 SAMUEL

The large body of historical material that is regularly divided into four blocks (1 and 2 Samuel, 1 and 2 Kings) was almost certainly originally prepared as a single consecutive narrative of the history of Israel from the founding of the monarchy until its destruction in the sixth century when the people were exiled to Babylon. The divisions of the text are somewhat arbitrary, as when the account of the death of David could have brought 2 Samuel to a close, but is now located at 1 Kings 2. Variant versions of incidents are reported, such as the procedure for choosing Saul to be king, as well as the reasons for his subsequent rejection from that role, or the basis of personal relations between Saul and David, including whether David first appeared as a musician or a warrior. The editor seems to have transmitted the traditions from different sources (or tribes) without trying to harmonize them.

The beginning of the process of assembling these accounts may have taken place through court archivists in the time of David and Solomon, but all was edited in the post-exilic time from the Deuteronomic point of view. The aim was to show that the rise or fall of God's people is correlated directly with the degree of obedience or disobedience to Yahweh on the part of their leader. The historical account was extended beyond the time of Solomon, the epoch of Israel's greatest power, to report the fall of Jerusalem and the exile. Also evident in these accounts is the prophetic point of view, which seems hostile to the monarchy and condemns the Israelites' use of pagan names, as when in 2 Sam 2-4 the king is named Ishbaal (from the name of the Canaanite god, Baal), but is called Ishbosheth (from *bosheth*, which means "shame"). On the one hand, Israel's desire to have a king is condemned, on the ground that God alone should rule his people (1 Sam 8), but David is honored as the ideal king, even though his personal failings are pictured in detail, including his self-serving ruthlessness.

The structure of 1 and 2 Samuel is as follows:

1 Sam 1-7 - The early years of Samuel as God's messenger.

1 Sam 8-15 - The relationships between Samuel and Saul.

1 Sam 16-31 - The struggles between Saul and David, culminating in Saul's death.

2 Sam 1-4 - David's initial struggle to become king.

2 Sam 5-8 - David becomes king, establishes his capital in Jerusalem, and controls the territories east of the Jordan.

2 Sam 9-24 - David's problems with his family, and with the claims to royal power from the descendants of Saul.

1 and 2 KINGS

The First and Second Books of Kings include information about the course of the Israelite monarchy from the close of David's reign until Jerusalem and the land of Judah came under control of the Babylonians and the inhabitants were exiled to Babylon (587 BCE). The fifth century BCE editor included features which indicate his reasons for preparing this document: (1) the repeated references to ancient sources (the Book of the Acts of Solomon; the Book of the Chronicles of the Kings of Judah); (2) the editorial comments concerning how successive kings obeyed or failed to obey the will of the God of Israel. Examples are Asa, who did what was right in the eyes of the Lord (1 Kings 15.11), and Baasha, who did what was evil (1 Kings 15.34). The claim to historical documentation and the references to divine judgment show the hand of the Deuteronomic editor, as in Joshua and Judges. Highest praise is reserved for Josiah (2 Kings 22-23), who attempted a reform of God's people, and Hezekiah (2 Kings 19-20), who obeyed the voice of God's prophet, Isaiah. In addition to unnamed prophets (1 Kings 13), two well-known prophets who called the kings and the people to obey God were Elijah (1 Kings 17- 2 Kings 1) and Elisha (2 Kings 3-9).

The books may be divided into four main sections:

1 Kings 1-2, which brings to a close the account of David's reign and the succession of Solomon.

1 Kings 3-11 describes the reign of Solomon, the construction of the temple, and the establishment of the priestly system there. Also described are his taking many wives and God's action against him.

1 Kings 12-2 Kings 16 reports the division of the kingdom into the Israelite monarchy based in the north at Shechem, and the Jerusalem-based monarchy and priesthood of Judah.

2 Kings 17-25 describes the fall of the Israelite monarchy to the Assyrians in 722, and the seizure of Jerusalem by the Babylonians in 587, despite reforms under Hezekiah (2 Kings 18) and Josiah (2 Kings 22-23). Most Jews were exiled to Babylon, but some fled to Egypt (2 Kings 24-25). Although Omri is denounced as a wicked king of Israel (1 Kings 16), the effectiveness of his reign politically and militarily is attested in Assyrian archives, where the tribes of Israel are called "the house of Omri."

These documents refer to the official records of the monarchies, but are running critical commentaries on Israel's leadership in this period. The aim is to show God's control of events, not his failure to uphold his people.

1 and 2 CHRONICLES

These two books, together with Ezra and Nehemiah, form a comprehensive account of the origins and destiny of God's people, written from the perspective of the priestly leaders and emphasizing the centrality of the temple and its ritual for the welfare of Israel. The documents build on the tradition of the law given through Moses, but refer to it in its final form, which was edited by those who held the priestly point of view. The worship in the temple is regarded as the primary basis of Israel's relationship with God. Accordingly, the genealogies which open the series (1 Chr 1-9) give special attention to the Levites, priests and functionaries in the temple cultus, including psalmists and singers. David's chief role is to prepare the place and the materials for the building of the temple (1 Chr 10-29).

The climax of the work comes in 2 Chr 1-9, where Solomon's building and dedication of the temple are detailed. The last section (2 Chr 10-36) recounts the split of Israel into the northern and southern kingdoms, and the carrying off of the population into exile. More space than in the books of Samuel or Kings is devoted to the work of the reforming kings: Jehoshaphat, Hezekiah, and Josiah. By contrast, none of the rulers of the northern kingdom (which worshipped God on Mt Gerizim, near Shechem) is ever depicted in Chronicles in a favorable light. The proper rule of Israel is guided by obedience to God as his will was set forth in the Law of Moses, which was given to Israel. But it was David and Solomon through whom these priestly norms were put into effective operation, and thus under whom true peace was for a time experienced by Israel. 2 Chronicles ends with a declaration of hope for the return of Israel from captivity and for the restoration of the temple cult, and thereby of the peace of Israel. This material (2 Chr 36) is repeated in Ezra 1 (see under Ezra).

The naming of eight generations of descendants of King Zerubbabel in 1 Chr 3.19-24 suggests that these writings date from long after his time, and hence no earlier than the fourth century BCE. The absence of reference to Alexander the Great or the effort by him and his successors to impose hellenistic culture on the peoples subject to them – including Israel – suggests a mid-fourth century date. Indication of the influence of Persian dualistic concepts on Israel's religious views is to be found in the assigning to Satan (rather than to God) of responsibility for David's having intruded into a divine secret by conducting a census of Israel (cf. 2 Sam 24.1 with 1 Chr 21.1).

This development of the priestly perspective on the history of Israel is also evident in two later works written in this tradition: Ezra and Nehemiah.

EZRA and NEHEMIAH

These two books should be read as offering a sequential account of the rebuilding of the temple in Jerusalem and then of the walls of the city. Ezra 1-6 describes the temple construction and resumption of the worship of God there. Ezra 7-10 includes a decree of the Persian king, encouraging the Israelites to return to their historic land. It is written in imperial Aramaic, which would have been the official language of the

Persian court in its dealings with subject peoples throughout the Middle East in this era (4.6-6.18). In both Ezra and Nehemiah there are lists of the returnees and of the temple officials, together with a report of the commitment by the people to obey the temple regulations and carry out faithfully there the worship of the God of Israel.

Since this return and the renewal of temple worship led by Ezra are dated to the seventh year of king Ahasuerus (Ezra 7.7), who reigned from 464-423, these events would have taken place before Nehemiah's return to Jerusalem, which is dated to the twentieth year of Artaxerxes. It is more likely, however, that Ezra's work actually began under Artaxerxes II (404-358 BCE), which would indicate that the Israelites returned to Judah in stages over a period of more than a century and a half, beginning in the reign of Cyrus (around 538). The rebuilding of the temple took place under Zerubbabel at the turn of the fifth/fourth centuries BCE, with walls rebuilt under Nehemiah in the later fifth century.

Ezra's work was to consolidate the resumption of the temple worship and to establish a program of instruction so that the legal and ritual traditions would be passed down through successive generations of repatriated Jews. Crucial for this undertaking was the final form of the law, in which the priestly editors made the temple cult the central instrument of group identity for God's people. This concept was reinforced by appending these two books to 1 and 2 Chronicles, which recounted God's guidance of Israel's history, highlighting the central shrine in Jerusalem, and dismissing the competitive temple in Samaria. David and Solomon receive special honor as the ones who established this cultic center and its priestly order as the primary ground of Israel's relationship to God.

ESTHER

The book of Esther represents the category of edifying historical narrative, along with Ruth and Jonah. The leading figure at the outset is King Ahasuerus (better known to historians as Xerxes), who reigned over the Persian Empire from 484 to 465. In this story there is a major figure among the Jews of Susa (the Persian capital): Mordecai, who had been exiled from Palestine under the Babylonian ruler, Nebuchadnezzar (2.5-6). This exile is known from reliable historical sources to have taken place in 598. This chronological difficulty combines with the symbolic links of the names of the major characters of the story with Babylonian deities – Mordecai = Marduk; Esther = Ishtar – to suggest that this narrative is a mixture of historical recollections and imaginative expansions written down at a considerably later time than the events that are being described. A major aim of the book is to offer Jews guidelines for their relationships with and attitudes toward pagan peoples among whom they must live. It is possible that this story was written in the second century BCE, when a pagan ruler (the hellenistic king of Syria, Antiochus IV Epiphanes) who had tried to pervert Israel's worship of God was prevented from doing so by divine intervention: the Maccabean revolt and the establishment of the independent Jewish state. This story of the days of Jewish captivity in the eastern regions confirms that God takes care of his own in unexpected ways. Curiously, the name of God is never mentioned in Esther, although there is indirect evidence of divine relief: "deliverance will arise from another quarter" (4.14).

In addition to the general theme of divine help for the faithful people, the book explains the origins of the Feast of Purim. *Pur* is neither a Hebrew nor a Persian word, but comes from Akkadian, the language of ancient Babylonia. It means "lot," and is used in the story when Haman, the enemy of God's people, chooses by lot the day on which he will put them all to death. But by God's workings, that becomes the day when the champion of the Jews, Mordecai, is exalted and the king grants them freedom to slaughter their Persian opponents. Ahasuerus exalts the two faithful Jews, Esther and Mordecai, and executes their enemy. This positive view of a Persian ruler fits well with the acclaim of Cyrus in Isa 45.1 as "the Lord's anointed," because he gave permission for the Jews to return from exile in Babylon to their land.

Among some later Jews there was dissatisfaction with the Esther story, especially with its lack of mention of God. Accordingly, additions were made to it in which God is named, the details of his miraculous intervention in behalf of his people are increased, and God's purpose is more explicitly revealed through dreams and interpretations of them. These supplements are available in the additions to Esther, found in the Apocrypha.

Wisdom and Poetical Writings

Approximately half of the Old Testament canon consists of documents which depict the past and future of God's people and their responsibilities in terms of the history of Israel and the developing guidelines for that relationship as they were given by God and appropriated by his people in the changing circumstances of their historical existence. These comprise the first five books, or Torah (Instruction), traditionally credited to Moses (Genesis through Deuteronomy), and the historical books which follow (from Joshua through Esther) which cover the period from the settlement in the land of Canaan under Joshua to the reconstitution of Israel after the return from captivity in Babylon in the later sixth century BCE and subsequently. The other half of the Old Testament canon, however, includes writings which perceive the relationship between God and his people in significantly different ways.

Beginning with Job, that relationship is presented in ways that depart wholly from the legal and historical emphases of the books noted above. These writings include a questing, personal struggle to understand and affirm God's workings in human life, and in some cases the effort to discern basic principles of divine action and human response. Intensely personal versions of this seeking for meaning behind the seeming chaos of human existence are the books of Job and Ecclesiastes. The effort to prescribe basic patterns for human behavior in response to the purpose of God is evident in the book of Proverbs. The celebration of human love is dramatically expressed in the Song of Solomon. Another extended collection of materials is intended to enable groups of Israelites and individuals to share in the worship of God, ranging from lament and confession to praise and commitment: the Psalms and Lamentations (with psalm-like features in other writings as well). Much of this material is in poetry, including Proverbs, the Psalms, Song of Solomon, Lamentations, most of Job and parts of Ecclesiastes.

The issues and style of communication in the poetic and wisdom materials were powerfully influenced by Israel's wide and extended exposure during and following the exile in Babylon (sixth century BCE and subsequently) to the advanced cultures of Babylonia and Persia, and still later (after the mid-fourth century) to that of the Greeks. This cultural and intellectual impact is manifest in the continuing search within this literature for theoretical principles underlying God's action among his people – past and present – and for a direct experience of God. It is these themes which find expression in the poetic and wisdom literature produced in this period. These writings have parallels in the literature of other societies in the ancient Near East over many centuries, especially Egyptian and Mesopotamian cultures.

JOB

Job was a figure in Jewish tradition known for his righteous way of life, as Ezekiel testifies (Ezek 14.12-20). According to the book that bears his name, he was from Uz, a region south and east of Palestine, as were his friends who visited him to offer advice (Job 2.11). Thus his relation to the God of Israel is implied in terms of his faith relationship rather than his ethnic origins. In the prose introduction (Job 1-2) and conclusion (42.7-17) to the book, the name of God used is Yahweh, while other names for God appear in the major part, which is poetic. Further, in the prose parts (which may have been adapted from an ancient story), the issue raised by a kind of royal prosecutor ("the Satan" = the adversary) is whether Job would remain as faithful and obedient to God if he were to be deprived of his wealth, family and the high regard of his community. The epilogue describes him as regaining what he lost, with his trust as well as his prosperity as high as they were before.

The poetic center of Job, however, pictures his struggle about suffering and the will of God in a much more complex way. It seems clear that the series of dialogues which make up the main part of the book have been expanded and adapted in order to soften the radical criticisms of God that Job utters at points. Job's lament at the misery of his existence and the expressed wish that he was dead (Job 3) evoke a series of responses from his friends, Eliphaz (Job 4-5), Bildad (Job 8), and Zophar (Job 11). In turn, Job replies to their criticisms (Job 6-7, 9-10, 12-14). A second series of criticisms by these three (Job 15, 18, 20) is similarly responded to by Job (Job 16-17, 19, 21). The third series of debates has probably been altered in the process of transmission of the text: the critics speak in Job 22, 24-27, but Job's defensive statements are mingled with the criticisms. A chapter about the nature of true wisdom (Job 28) leads to Job's final defense before his human critics in Job 29-31. Then the poetic section concludes with a dialogue in which God challenges Job and his complaints (Job 38-39, 41), which is followed by brief, contrite acceptances by Job (40.1-5; 42.1-6).

Throughout the debates, Job places the blame on God for his sufferings and deprivation (Job 19), for the divine lack of concern for the poor or for punishment of the wicked (Job 24). He does affirm, however, that God is omnipotent over the whole realm of nature (Job 26) and that the seeming prosperity of the wicked is only temporary (Job 27). His statements and his condition are greeted with scorn by his contemporaries (Job 29-30), although he has always been law-abiding and generous

(Job 31). His critics resume the traditional theme that if Job is suffering, he must have disobeyed God. They insist that the wisdom and justice of God are beyond human comprehension, so human beings must simply accept what he does in the universe (Job 35-36). God's own response is in the form of two sets of challenging questions as to what Job could possibly know about the power and purpose of God in creating the geological, astronomical and wildlife features of the world. Following each, Job feels chastened for having questioned the wisdom and purposes of God (40.1-5), and rejoices that at last he has seen God in direct encounter (42.1-6).

The dates which scholars have assigned to the document vary widely, but the emphasis on the order of the natural world, including the signs of the zodiac (38.31-32) may indicate that it was written before the issue of national identity became as important as it did in the second-century Maccabean period, but while there was already intellectual impact on Jewish thinking from the Greek philosophical world, with its concern for cosmic order. Fourth or third century would be a likely period for the composition of Job in its present form, which is framed by the older prose story, with the possibility of later modifications to make Job appear less radical.

PSALMS

"Psalm" is a term derived from the Greek word *psalmos* (which is a translation of the Hebrew word *mizmor*), meaning "song," and is used in the title of many of the psalms. Although not all these poems may have been written to be sung, they have been read and sung in worship for more than two millennia, first in Jewish and then in Christian assemblies. These poetic works have been traditionally attributed to David, but although some may come from his time (tenth century BCE), others date from after the return of Israel from exile in Babylon (fifth century), and some are as late as the second century, which seems to be the time when they were collected and edited in their present form. Like the so-called Law of Moses (Genesis to Deuteronomy), the psalms were arranged in five books: 1-41; 42-72; 73-89; 90-106; 107-150. Each section ends in a doxology, with Ps 150 serving as the hymnic conclusion to the entire collection. Some scholars have sought to identify earlier groups of psalms, based on instructions given to the singers or leaders of the worshippers using the psalms (for example, Korahites in Ps 42-49, 84-85, 87-88; or Asaph in Ps 73-83). Other psalm-like passages in the Old Testament include Gen 49, Ex 15, Deut 32-33, Judges 5. A basic factor in the origin of these writings was the religious poetry of other Near Eastern cultures, since both the poetic style and the function of the latter in worship of the ancient gods are reflected in the psalms. What differentiates the psalms of Israel from the pagan poems, however, is the central importance in the psalms of God's activity in the history and preservation of his covenant people.

Although the categories overlap in some cases, the following distinctions may be made among the psalms. On the basis of literary pattern, there are (with some examples of each type): (1) Hymns of Praise: Ps 40, 92, 116, 138; (2) Laments, some as confessions, Ps 32, 38, 51, 102; some as invoking God's judgment on the enemies, Ps 35, 59, 70, 137, 140; (3) Affirmations of Gratitude and Trust in the LORD, some from the community (15, 67, 100, 118, 133, 146) and some from individuals (9, 18, 23, 30, 40, 92, 103, 121, 139); (4) Enthronement Celebrations and Renewal of the Covenant, which marked the initial ascent to the throne of the ruler of Israel, or in an annual ceremony called the people to renewal of their covenant with God (enthronement: 2, 20, 45, 72, 110; covenant renewal: 50, 76, 89, 105, 114); (5) The Law and the Wisdom of God, in which God's disclosure of his purpose for his people is celebrated, through the prophetic word and through scripture (1, 25, 34, 37, 49, 58, 101, 112, 119).

The themes which recur in the psalms include the triumph of God over the powers of evil (Ps 29), God's deliverance of Israel from slavery (Ps 68), the presence of God in the temple (Ps 48), the destruction of Jerusalem (Ps 79), the exile in Babylon (Ps 137), and the rebuilding of the city after the return from exile (Ps 51). In the psalms the major indications of God's special relationship with Israel are the establishment of the Davidic monarchy, God's continuing presence in the temple, his power in the creation of the world and in his control of Israel's history, and the communication of wisdom to his people through the law. Some are written in the first person, but may express the concerns and devotion of the wider community (Ps 23, 51, 54, 59, 69, 71, 102, 116, 130). The psalms are both witness and instrument of Israel's response to what God has done for his covenant people.

Probably in the period after the return of Israel from exile in Babylon, editing of the psalms for transmission and use in worship led to the inclusion of introductory phrases which suggest authorship (*David*) and give instructions about the public singing and musical accompaniment of the psalms. Many of the terms used in this connection can no longer be translated with certainty.

PROVERBS

In its present form, the book of Proverbs is attributed to Solomon, just as the books of the law are assigned to Moses and the Psalms to David. Careful analysis of the book shows, however, that the tradition here has been expanded and adapted over the centuries. It was appropriate to link this material with Solomon, since in the historical tradition of Israel (1 Kings 10.1-10) he is reported to have been famous throughout the Middle East for his wisdom, as evidenced by the coming to him of the Queen of Sheba. Discoveries in the past century have shown the close parallels between parts of Proverbs and wisdom tradition from Egypt (22.17-25.7) and from Ugaritic sources (25.2-7).

Scholars have noted seven stages in the development of Proverbs: (1) 1-9; (2) 10-22.16; (3) 22.17-24.34; (4) 25-29; (5) 30; (6) 31.1-9; (7) 31.10-31. Section (1) is thought to be the latest; parts of (3), (5) and (6) give the best evidence of ties with other Middle Eastern wisdom traditions. (4) may go back to Solomonic tradition as preserved in the eighth century BCE.

The wisdom in Proverbs includes all manner of advice for personal and social behavior, with the aim of maintaining purity of individual and common life. Those features are shared with other literatures of the Middle East, but there are three features of Proverbs which display important links with the older traditions of Israel. (1) Wisdom comes through knowledge of Yahweh, the God of Israel, rather than through shrewd observation of the world and how it might work more smoothly. (2) Order in society is maintained by God, who discloses his purpose through wisdom which perceptive humans are able to attain. (3) Order in the created world is depicted as the work of God's companion, Wisdom, through whom the world was made (8.22-31). There are also explicit links between wisdom and covenant (2.17) as well as the law of the covenant (28.4-9; 29.18). Thus Proverbs as we have it has used and adapted wisdom tradition from a range of perspectives while making claims for the distinctive role of wisdom in Israel.

ECCLESIASTES

The title of this book in the Hebrew original is Koheleth, which means one who addresses the community. He is identified (1.1) as "son of David" and "king," but the point of view expressed fits better with the hellenistic period than with the time of Solomon. While building on the tradition of the latter as a man of wisdom, what is being explored here is the basic structure and meaning of human existence in a mode which reflects the philosophies of the third and second centuries with their effort to discern patterns and inherent order in the world and in human experience. The work opens on a note of futility: there is no overarching meaning or purpose to be discovered: "all is vanity" (1.2-11). The only thing sure is that death will come (9.3-5). Society is filled with inequities and injustices (9.11; 10), "all is vanity" (12.8), and no human being can figure out what is going on (7.23; 8.17). The one positive possibility for humans is to enjoy life while they can (3.13; 6.3; 8.15; 9.7-10). This sounds like the philosophy of the Epicureans, for whom present modest pleasures were the best that life offered.

But Koheleth also declares that wisdom enables one to know in one's heart what should be done and when (8.5). This sounds like the Stoic philosophers' understanding of the conscience as the innate human capacity to know and obey the divine order of the universe. Such wisdom is said to make its possessor immensely strong (7.19). This perception takes specific form when one learns to "fear God, and keep his commandments" (12.13), which is a way of life to be followed from youth (11.9-10). Such obedience gives new significance to participation in the formal worship of God in the temple (5.1). With those who follow this way of life all will be well (8.12). Ecclesiastes reflects the conceptual struggle of those who are discouraged by the lack of meaning and injustice of routine existence, but who seek to see behind this discouraging outlook the continuing and rewarding relationship of the individual with the traditional God of Israel.

SONG OF SOLOMON

Also known as the Song of Songs (1.1). The great king of Israel is mentioned by name in this writing (3.9, 11; 8.11), although there are no details about him here as an historical figure. The major theme throughout is the experience of love. The work may be a dramatic dialogue between bride and bridegroom, with comments by the chorus of companions. Some scholars regard it as a ritual adapted from a pagan cult in which the sexual union of a male and a female deity is the central feature. Other scholars think it is simply a loose collection of more than two dozen love songs.

The references to Solomon and the identification of the bride as a woman from Shulam (or Shunem; 6.13) provided links with the traditions about the songs which Solomon composed (1 Kings 4.32), and the coming of a Shunammite woman to care for David in his old age (1 Kings 1.1-4) helped support the ancient theory that this work was by Solomon (late tenth century BCE). The occurrence of Persian and Greek words in the poems (4.8; 8.5) suggests a much later date, however – the fifth or fourth century. It was in this period that the ancient Near Eastern myth of the sexual union of Ishtar and Tammuz was matched by the hellenistic myths of Venus and Adonis, and of Isis and Osiris in Egypt. The imagery of a wedding between Yahweh and his people had an important precedent in the book of the prophet Hosea, who pictures Israel's infidelity to her God under this image. It was these precedents in the religious thinking of Israel and her neighbors which led to the allegorical interpretation of the Song of Songs as symbolic of the relationship of God and Israel, and later of Christ and the church. Without this symbolic interpretation, the book shows that in biblical tradition sexual union was good and blessed of God.

Prophetic Writings

The Hebrew word for prophet, *nabi*, seems to have meant originally someone who is seized by superhuman power and utters threats, predictions, or brings curses on enemies. Prophets of this sort appear in traditions describing Israel's exodus from Egypt through the territory east of the Jordan toward the land of Canaan (Num 11.27). Such prophets were available for hire, as is evident in the story of Balaam the prophet who refused to curse Israel (Num 22-24). From ancient Near Eastern documents there is evidence that prophets were frequently attached to royal establishments and to sanctuaries as advisors and prognosticators in behalf of the priestly or royal establishments. It is in this capacity that Samuel offers advice to the people of Israel (1 Sam 3.19-4.1), and anoints Saul to be Israel's leader (1 Sam 9-10). Similarly, it is Nathan the prophet who anoints David to be king (2 Sam 7), and who rebukes him for his abuse of royal power in having a man killed in order to gain the widow as his wife (2 Sam 11-12). In the ninth century BCE, the prophets Elijah (1 Kings 17 ff.) and Elisha (2 Kings 2-9) bring critical messages and actions from God to challenge the rulers and the people of their day.

It is in the eighth century, however, that the prophets appear, collections of whose oracles were preserved in the biblical books known as the Prophets. They functioned as critics of the rulers and the leaders of the people in both the northern kingdom of Israel and the southern kingdom of Judah around 750, which was the time of the great surge of power of the Assyrians, who swept across the Near East from Mesopotamia, establishing a vast empire and dominating the Israelite people. Amos and Hosea were prophets in the northern territory in this period, and Isaiah was active in the south. They spoke at a time of profound threat to the existence of these states, when there were two rival sanctuaries (one in Samaria, and one in Jerusalem), and when the freedom and integrity of the covenant relationship between God and his people were in jeopardy. The prophets call the leaders and the people to renew and to take with new seriousness their covenant obligation to Yahweh their God. The crisis was a continuing one, since the Israelites never regained political independence and had, therefore, to rethink what the guidelines were to be for the social, political, and moral structure of the nation.

In 722, many from the northern tribes were forced to migrate to Assyria, where they seem to have been settled in the northern districts of Mesopotamia. Then in 597 and 587, the southern tribes were deported to Babylon, but with the defeat of the Babylonians by the Persians in 550, a new imperial policy which encouraged captive peoples to return to their native territories enabled the tribes of Judah to go back to Jerusalem and its vicinity. In the later fourth century the Persians in turn were overcome by Alexander the Great, whose successors (the Ptolemies and the Seleucids) controlled the Jews in Palestine until they were able to achieve an autonomous state under the Maccabees for just over a century from 168 to 63 BCE when the Romans took over the eastern Mediterranean lands. In this series of changing political and cultural situations, the Jews were struggling with the basic questions about their identity as a people, and about the trustworthiness of the covenant agreement between Yahweh and Israel as his people. How was their tradition to be understood, and what was their future as God's people? It was the prophets who addressed these issues and sought to give direction to the religious and political leaders of the people.

In the effort to give critical guidance in these continuing struggles, there was a deep need to re-examine and reappropriate the older traditions of Israel. This was the case with the historical traditions, which were reworked in the sixth century (in either Babylon or Palestine) by a person or group known to modern scholars as the Deuteronomist ("second giver of the law"), whose edition of the law is almost certainly the one reported in 2 Kings 22.3-20 and 2 Chr 34.8-33 to have been found in the temple in Jerusalem during the reign of Josiah (640-609). It was given its final form during the exile in Babylon, however (587-539 BCE). In Deuteronomy 18.15-19 Moses is pictured as in the tradition of the prophets, since he is the one through whom God's purpose for and expectations from his people have been disclosed. The editing of the Mosaic tradition was an essential way of bringing that tradition up to date for Israel in its radically changed circumstances. This passage in Deut 18 announces that there will be other prophets who will carry forward that role of renewing God's people in the future. The further updating and editing of the legal tradition which took place later in the sixth century had the aim of showing the continuing relevance and the specific cultic requirements of the priestly traditions of Israel. The Deuteronomic editing also produced the historical books known as Samuel and Kings, while the priestly editors shaped 1 and 2 Chronicles. What is laid out for Israel in these updated documents is the history and political traditions, as well as the social and cultic obligations of those who consider themselves God's covenant people. The prophets are the ones who address the present situation in the light of these experiences and obligations, and call the people to account before Yahweh their God.

The central issues in this process are, Who is to rule God's people and how? How is Israel to honor and obey Yahweh? What are the means and the criteria for group identity of those who call themselves God's people? Answering these questions was complicated by the lack of political autonomy even after the temple was rebuilt (520-515) and the people were rallied in Jerusalem to hear and obey the revised law of Moses under Ezra and Nehemiah in the mid-fifth century. Also, the traditions connected with the prophets of Israel were edited and expanded in order to speak relevantly to the altered circumstances. The conflict and regional chaos that characterized the end of the Persian rule and the subsequent struggles for power among Alexander's successors gave rise to messianic hopes that God would commission and empower an agent or agents to set matters right with his people, and to liberate the oppressed and the exploited in Israel. The prophets addressed these situations at first in hope of nationwide renewal, but as chaos grew, they addressed their messages to the faithful minority to whom they believed God was disclosing his purpose and whom God would save and vindicate in the future. The basic documents were eventually arranged in four groups: Isaiah, Jeremiah, Ezekiel, and the Twelve Prophets. During the second century BCE when the Jewish tribes were caught in a battle between the Greek rulers of Syria and Egypt, one prophetic figure, Daniel, announced the end of all earthly political powers and the gift by

God of a kingdom of righteousness to the faithful remnant of his people. The conflict in which Israel was involved was depicted as led by forces which were not merely political and human, but cosmic, so that God's direct action alone could bring ultimate victory.

It is these diverse themes, strategies and circumstances that are apparent in the rich prophetic traditions of Israel. Each of the books attributed to the prophets must be examined individually in order to see how these concerns, challenges and expectations are formulated in the changing conditions of the original prophets themselves as well as those of the later editors and adapters of this material.

ISAIAH

The book of Isaiah, which is the longest in the entire Bible, includes material which reflects the changing circumstances of the people of Israel from the eighth century down to the fifth century BCE. Major insights and themes concerning the relationship of God and his people recur with significant variations throughout the changing social and political conditions of this extended period. The basic early core consists of prophetic oracles spoken by Isaiah in Jerusalem over a period of about forty years: from 740 to 722 (prior to the fall of the northern Kingdom of Israel to the Assyrians) and two decades afterward (722-701), when Judah had become a vassal kingdom of Assyria. This core has been supplemented and edited by later generations of those who stood in the prophetic tradition of Isaiah, and whose oracles reflect the changing circumstances of the life of God's people before and during their exile in Babylon and at their return to Jerusalem, which began in the last third of the sixth century BCE.

The changing political conditions in Palestine and the regions to the east (Syria and Mesopotamia) which shaped the life of Israel from the time of Isaiah onward may be summarized (with dates) as follows:

Expansion of Assyria: siege of Damascus (732) and Samaria (722); invasion of Palestine (701) and Egypt (671).

Rise of Babylonia (605); first deportation of Jews to Babylon (597); fall of Jerusalem and second deportation (587).

Rise of Persia (550) and fall of Babylon (539); return of Jewish exiles and rebuilding of Jerusalem temple (520-515).

Rise of Alexander the Great (336-323); Egyptian-based Ptolemies control Palestine (323-200); Syrian-based Seleucids control Palestine

(200-168); Maccabees establish a Jewish priestly monarchy (168-63); Romans take over Palestine (63 BCE).

The Isaiah material and its characteristic motifs were developed over the extended period of time and changing conditions from the rise of Assyria to the triumph of the Medo-Persians in the last half of the sixth century. The basic themes throughout are: (1) that the affairs of nations are the concern of God and the arena of his action within the world and in relation to his people Israel. (2) The people – both Israelites and Judahites – are to trust God and to fulfill their obligations to him cultically (in the temple: the proper shrine and with the proper worship) and ethically (with respect to the welfare of all God's people). (3) The immediate threat to God's people is of judgment – on the pagan nations as well as on Israel. The goal is "peace" (*shalom*) which will result in the accomplishment of God's purpose for the faithful remnant of his people and for the whole of the creation. In the later stages of development of this material, the prophetic oracles are closely akin to apocalyptic style and content, with the emphasis on the conflict that must precede the final resolution of the difficulties faced by the people, and the special relationship to God enjoyed by the faithful group to whom God's purpose has been revealed.

Detailed analysis of the material now included in what has been traditionally known as Isaiah shows that it may be grouped as follows:

1. Isaiah 1-12. The crisis resulting from Assyria's taking over the land, and the encouraging outcome of Hezekiah's accession to the throne of Judah in 715.
2. Isaiah 13-23. The relations of Israel and Judah to the neighboring powers in the eighth century. Later elements (sixth century) in Isa 13-14.
3. Isaiah 24-27. Prophecies from the later sixth century.
4. Isaiah 28-33. Reaction to Judah's rebellion from Assyria (mostly from Isaiah of Jerusalem).
5. Isaiah 34-35. Apocalyptic material, late sixth century.
6. Isaiah 36-39. Narrative of the political events in the reign of Hezekiah. Cf. 2 Kings 18.13-20.19.
7. Isaiah 40-55. Addressed to Judean exiles in Babylon.
8. Isaiah 56-66. Revised expectations about restoration in the land and of the people of God, probably dating from after the return had begun, but before the reforms were launched by Ezra and Nehemiah in the fifth century BCE.

JEREMIAH

This book describes how God's people should respond to the changing political conditions in Judah and the neighboring nations, as well as the changing circumstances of the prophet Jeremiah, in the period from 617 to 586 BCE. His prophetic role was carried out during the reigns of five kings of Judah, of whom the most significant were Josiah (640-609), Jehoiakim (609-598) and Zedekiah (597-587). The latter was designated by the Babylonians as a regent while the true king, Jehoiachin, was in exile in Babylon (598-97; cf. 2 Kings 24). The contents are a mixture of literary types: oracles in prose and poetry, prose narratives, biographical narratives, sermons. These materials are intermingled, probably as the result of subsequent editing and expanding of the authentic material from Jeremiah under the enduring influence of the Deuteronomic reform which had been launched by Josiah (2 Kings 22.3-20; 2 Chr 34.1-33) and which subsequently resulted in the editing of the legal and historical writings (especially Deuteronomy and the books of Samuel and Kings). During the prophetic career of Jeremiah, Judah became for a time (609-605) a vassal of Egypt, and attempted an unsuccessful revolt against the Babylonians who controlled the country after 597 (Jer 27-28), which resulted in Zedekiah's being taken captive to Babylon in 587. Jeremiah's basic theme is that because Israel and its leaders in both the northern and southern kingdoms have failed to meet their covenantal obligations to God, the people are subject to the inescapable judgment of God.

The book may be divided as follows on the basis of different literary forms and content:

1. Poetic oracles (Jer 1-6). Includes the call of the prophet and recalls Israel's failures under Moses' leadership (2.6-8).
2. Sermons, confessions and interpretations of oracles (Jer 7-24). The links with Deuteronomy are more explicit here: failure to fulfill the covenant has brought upon Israel divine judgment, and now it will come upon Judah as well.
3. Narratives and Oracles of Conflict (Jer 25-45). God's controversy with the rulers of Judah and with the false prophets who promise peace and quick renewal of the nation, and who fail to see God's hand at work in the fall of the nation and the exile in Babylon. Also present are themes of ultimate renewal of the covenant (Jer 30-32), for which Christians claim fulfillment (31.31-34; Heb 8.8-12).
4. Oracles concerning the Nations (Jer 46-51). Pronouncements of God's judgment on Egypt and the other nations that surrounded Israel

and Judah, with a final prophecy of the doom of Babylon (Jer 50-51), ending with the last words of Jeremiah (51.64).

5. Narrative of the Destruction of Jerusalem and the temple (Jer 52). The contents are a variant of the account of these events in 2 Kings 24.18-25.30.

The prose sermons which appear throughout Jeremiah in its present form seek to show that the fall of Jerusalem and the exile of the people of Israel are the direct consequence of their failure to fulfill their obligations to God in proper worship and in just dealings with each other. Only those Israelites who were taken captive to Babylon will share in the restoration which is to follow this time of punishment by God. In the latter half of Jeremiah there is a recurrent theme that the failures of the people are the reverse of the qualities that are to characterize the nation when God restores and renews it. In the prose sections there are recurrent hints to the reader as to how the overall purpose of God is to be discerned in the judgment that has occurred and the renewal of the covenant that is to follow. These clues to the divine purpose may come from later editors of the Jeremiah traditions.

LAMENTATIONS

Two factors combined to assign these poems of lament to Jeremiah: (1) historically, he was fulfilling his prophetic role at the time of the fall of Jerusalem to the Babylonians, which is described so movingly in Lamentations, and (2) in 2 Chronicles 35.25 there is a reference to a lament which he uttered for Josiah, the king of Judah whose efforts at reform did not turn aside what was regarded as the divine judgment on the disobedient people of God in the tragic years 597-587 (2 Kings 22-24; 2 Chronicles 34-35). The Lamentations are anonymous, however, though they were likely written in the years just before or after the final deportation of the Jews to Babylon in 587.

There are five laments, the first and last of which sound the note of sorrow and astonishment at the punishment God has brought upon his people (Lam 1, 5). All of the social and religious structures of the life of God's people have been shattered. Lamentations 2 emphasizes that it is God who has brought about this destruction of both the temple and the monarchy. Chapter 4 continues the picture of disaster, noting that even the religious leaders and rulers have been sinful and have therefore been set aside by God. The depth of the corruption of the people is evident in the repeated report of mothers devouring their own children (2.20; 4.10). The central chapter (Lam 3) is different in strategy, since the nation under divine judgment is now portrayed as a person. It is also different in outlook, since it calls for repentance and renewal, while holding out the hope that God will punish those nations which are persecuting God's people (3.55-66). The extent of the judgment on the community is apparent in the acknowledgement that their land is now lost to them, and all of the Jewish religious and social patterns have been destroyed (Lam 5). The work ends on a note affirming God's sovereignty, while imploring him to return and renew his people. Later Jews and Christians saw in these laments predictions respectively of the fall of Jerusalem to the Romans in 70 CE and of the crucifixion of Jesus.

EZEKIEL

The opening lines of Ezekiel provide the reader with specific time and place for the prophet's activity: at the Chebar river (or canal) in Mesopotamia, in the fifth year of the exile of Jehoiachin, king of Judah (=593). Since concern for the temple and the priestly cult dominate the prophecies of Ezekiel, it is possible that he was of priestly descent and that the phrase "thirtieth year" (1.1) refers to the time when he would have begun his priestly activity (Num 4.23). Although he is reported to have been transported in prophetic visions to Jerusalem, his career as prophet seems to have been carried out entirely in Babylonian territory among other exiles from Judea (3.15).

Ezekiel's prophetic activity takes at least five different forms: (1) visions, as when he sees the corruption of the temple and the departure from it of God's presence (Ezek 8-10); (2) ecstatic experiences, as when he was enabled to see the throne of God (Ezek 1) and when he was transported to Jerusalem and projected into the future to see the restoration of the temple (Ezek 40-48); (3) symbolic actions, as when he is told to lie on his side for 390 days, which serves as a symbol of the protracted siege of Jerusalem; (4) personal experiences, which become the medium for prophetic insight, as in the death of his wife, which symbolizes the loss of Jerusalem and its temple (24.15-27). Similarly, Ezekiel himself is depicted as the sentinel who announces the impending judgment of God on the disobedient nation. (5) The majority of his prophetic pronouncements are in the form of oracles, however. In the present book of Ezekiel these are grouped, together with the visions and reports of the prophet's symbolic experiences, in three sections: (1) The oracles against Israel and Jerusalem (Ezek 1-24); (2) the oracles against the surrounding nations (Ezek 25-32), and (3) the oracles of restoration of the city and temple in Jerusalem (Ezek 33-48). Since there was no temple where the people of Israel might gather in Babylon, the elders of the people gathered in the house of Ezekiel to hear his counsel and prophetic expectations (8.1; 20.1) – a social development which anticipates the later emergence of synagogues among the Jews dispersed throughout the Mediterranean world and ultimately in Palestine itself.

A recurrent theme in Ezekiel's prophetic message is God's covenant with Israel – both the failure of the people to meet their covenantal obligations and the assurance that God will renew the covenant with them (Ezek 16; 17; 20; 34; 37; 44). The major emphasis in this relationship between God and his people is holiness, and the present loss of that quality. Here the book of Ezekiel displays a close connection with the developments in exilic and post-exilic Israel which led to the reworking of both the legal and historical traditions along priestly lines, as evident in the priestly additions to the Mosaic laws and the retelling of Israel's history from the priestly perspective in 1 and 2 Chronicles. This contrasts with Jeremiah, where the links with the legal and historical traditions are primarily with Moses and the legal tradition, especially with the Deuteronomic editing of the law as well as the retelling of Israel's history from that perspective.

Throughout Ezekiel the primary interest is in the purity of Israel's worship of God, and the present loss of that quality in part through the failure of the priestly leadership (Ezek 7). God will bring Israel back into right covenantal relationship, and the people will live in obedience (20.33-44) under what is called a covenant of peace (37.26). Blame for the failure to meet those obligations in the past is to be accepted by individuals, however, not merely assigned to irresponsible leaders, royal and priestly in the past or present (Ezek 18). Unlike parts of Isaiah, where participation in the covenant renewal will include Gentiles and those on the periphery of the community of Israel, in Ezekiel there is no expectation of universal or broadly representative sharing in the benefits of the covenant. Judah will repent and enjoy the new relationship (16.59-63), but access to the covenant is restricted to the authentic people of Israel (34.30; 44.1-14).

DANIEL

The first six chapters of Daniel, written in the third person, describe Daniel and his companions in their challenges and struggles with the ruling powers in Babylon. Chapters 7-12, written in the first person, report the visions which Daniel was enabled by God to see concerning the changing leadership in the world, culminating in the final establishment of God's rule through and in behalf of his people. The narrative of Daniel locates him in the setting of events which had led to the exile of Jews in Babylon. Described in 2 Kings 24-25, these date from the turn of the sixth century BCE. Daniel 1-6 recounts the experiences of Daniel and his associates which show a mixture of admiration and hatred toward them from their pagan captors. The pressure which these faithful ones endure is the result of efforts by the ruling culture to force them to abandon their distinctive ways and to conform to the pattern of non-Israelite life and religion. The fidelity displayed by Daniel and the revelations of the divine purpose granted to him by God are major characteristics of apocalyptic literature, of which Daniel is the oldest complete example. The name, Daniel, resembles that of certain wise individuals who appear in other literatures of the ancient Near East, as well as in Ezekiel 14.14, 20 and 28.3, where there is a condemnation of the proud prince of Tyre.

Although the author writes as though he were living in the days of the Babylonian empire (605-539 BCE), the historical persons he describes in his symbolic way and such linguistic details as the use of Greek names for three of the musical instruments he names in Dan 3.5, indicate that the book took its final form only in the second century BCE. The mixture of Hebrew (1.1-2.4a and 8.1-12.13) and Aramaic (2.4b-7.28) and the range of other materials included in various ancient versions of Daniel (Bel and the Dragon, Song of the Three Young Men, Susanna) show that the book of Daniel underwent a long and complicated process of expansion and translation. The most common form of the book probably took shape in the mid-second century BCE, after initial hopes of renewal of Israel through the Maccabean rulers and priests began to fade. The fact that the semitic-language version of Daniel begins and ends in Hebrew may indicate that it was originally all in Aramaic, but was later edited with a Hebrew beginning and ending to encourage its acceptance into the Hebrew canon.

Ch. 1 describes the superior physical and intellectual abilities of Daniel and his friends, which lead the king to try to educate them and incorporate them into the life of the royal court. Their refusal to partake of the royal food, because it was not ritually pure, is vindicated by the divine care they experience. In Ch. 2 Daniel interprets the dream of the king, showing the divine plan for successive world empires and God's control of human history. In Ch. 3, the refusal of Daniel and friends to participate in the ceremonies of divine honors for the king leads to their preservation by God and to judgment on their opponents. Daniel's interpretation of the vision of the hand writing a message on the wall of the king's banquet hall in Ch. 5 once more announces the overthrow of the Babylonian rule by the Persians and God's sovereignty over history. The king's decree prohibiting prayer to anyone but the monarch himself (Ch.6) is defied by Daniel, who is preserved by God from being devoured by the lions into whose den he has been thrown. The stories show God's control of human affairs, his sovereignty over all earthly rulers, and his preservation of those who remain faithful to him and his laws.

Chapters 7-12 consist of four visions of Daniel concerning history and the fulfillment of God's purpose for his people. In 7.3-17 are described four beasts which emerged from the sea. On the basis of the predictions of such specific details as the desecration of the temple in Dan 8 and 10-12 it can be inferred that they represent four successive empires in the Middle East: the lion = Babylon; the bear = Media; the leopard = Persia; the fourth with the multiple horns depicts the hellenistic empires following Alexander the Great. The changing sequence of these world empires within the book itself (see notes on the text) confirm the conclusion that the book underwent extensive revision. The "little horn" is Antiochus IV Epiphanes (175-163), who polluted the temple by placing there a statue of himself as a divine figure (1 Macc 1.54-61). This event triggered the Jewish revolt led by the Maccabees in 168-165. The final shift of authority in 7.13 to "one like a son of man" (that is, a human being in contrast to these weird animals) is clarified in 7.18 as God's placing in power the faithful community: "the saints of the Most High." The calculations of days and years until the fulfillment of these promises (Dan 8-9), as in the new interpretation of Jeremiah's prediction of the seventy years until God's purpose will be achieved (25.11-12; 29.10), are typical of apocalyptic writing. The figurative description of the end of the renewal process becomes vague, which suggests that the book was written shortly after the Maccabean revolt's initial successes in establishing an independent Jewish state. Daniel's way of interpreting history and the theme of the importance of fidelity to God on the part of his people were powerfully influential within Judaism down to the time of Christ. The basic themes are (1) that God is master of history, (2) that sovereignty over the world will be given to the faithful core of his people, and (3) that this future has been disclosed to them.

HOSEA

Hosea, whose name means "[God] has saved," declares that God is going to bring judgment on his people – especially on the northern tribes of Israel – because of their failure to fulfill their obligations under the covenant agreement with God. He does look beyond the experience of judgment to the renewal of Israel and Judah that will follow the period of punishment. The present introductory lines (1.1) imply that he was carrying on his prophetic work during the long period from the reign of Uzziah the king of Judah (783-742) to the reign of Hezekiah (715-687). The best clue is the reference to the reign of the king of the northern tribes, Jeroboam II (786-746), which suggests that Hosea was active in the middle years of the eighth century. He seems to have uttered his prophetic oracles before the fall of the northern kingdom to the Assyrians in 722 BCE.

It is clear that his own personal experience with an unfaithful wife is the symbolic and deeply-felt basis of his prophetic attack on Israel and Judah for their failure to fulfill their responsibilities to Yahweh, the god of the covenant who chose them as his people. The symbolism of the infidelity of the people permeates the first three chapters of Hosea, pointing to the corruption of the worship of God by the importation of pagan rites, probably including the use of cult prostitutes, as in the worship of Baal (2.1-13; 4.12-19). There follows a series of solemn warnings of the judgment that is to fall on the people because of their betrayal of the covenant (4.1-11.11). By their repudiation of the special relationship to God and their corruption of worship in the temple, the priestly system has been effectively abandoned (4.1-10). If they are truly repentant and change their way of life, God will open the way for restoration of the nation and of the Davidic kingship, under which the northern and southern tribes had earlier been united. The leaders continue to depend for security on treaties with the rulers of the powerful neighboring pagan states – Syria, Assyria, and Egypt – instead of on their God. Their unfaithlessness to the covenant is also evident in the social injustice that characterizes the leaders, including the exploitation of the poor (6.4-7.16; 8.1-14). Just as Hosea's faithless wife ruined the lives of their children, so whore-like Israel has violated the covenant, forsaken the Lord, corrupted the sanctuary, left the people warped and deformed by God's judgment and soon to be carried off into exile (9.1-17). Israel's independent existence will end with the exile to Assyria and the cessation of the kingly rule among the northern tribes (10.1-15). Yet even in the midst of these dire prophecies of doom, Hosea reminds his hearers of God's ultimate restoration and renewal of his people (11.1-11).

The last oracles continue the themes of judgment and renewal (12.1-14.9), but recall God's deliverance of his people in the past from slavery in Egypt (12.9; 13.4-6). Yet judgment is now inescapable (13.7-16). Even so, there is a call to repentance (14.1-3) and another warning against foolish reliance on Assyria for guaranteeing the future. God will restore the nation in his own way and in his own time (14.4-8). The prophecies end with a wisdom-type saying that the wise will understand God's ways and the truly upright will walk in them (14.9). The overarching theme of God's love for his people is vividly expressed in 11.1-6, where God's care for his people in the past is the model for their loving, obedient reliance upon him in the perilous present situation.

JOEL

The book of Joel opens without any indication of the time or place of the prophet's activity, and with no explicit reference to his prophetic role. This work falls into two sections: 1.2-2.27, and 2.28-3.21. "The word of the LORD" has come to the prophet in relation to the plague of locusts which has devastated the land (1.1-12). It came at a time of tranquility and hence of complacency for Israel under beneficent Persian rule. Now Joel calls for Israel to repent of its evil ways even while he beseeches God to help his people (1.13-20), since the catastrophe that has come is seen as a foretaste of the coming Day of the Lord, when the army of God will devastate the land and the cities because of the peoples' unfaithfulness to God and to their covenantal obligations (2.1-11).

At 2.18-29, the focus shifts from the immediate crisis caused by the plague to the renewal of God's people and the outpouring of judgment on the hostile nations, depicted with apocalyptic language and imagery. The Spirit of God is to be poured out on the whole human race (2.28-29), although only the faithful within Israel will repent and share in the age of renewal that is to follow. The solemn signals of cosmic judgment will lead some to call on the Lord, and they will be delivered (2.30-32). All the nations of the earth will be brought to the scene of God's judgment and will be condemned for their having contributed to the dispersion of Israel from Jerusalem and the land (3.1-8). Since one of the nations to which Israelites have been sold in slavery is that of the Greeks (3.6), this second section of Joel probably comes from the fourth century when commerce between Greece and the cities of Tyre and Sidon was flourishing. The results of this mistreatment of God's people will be war and not peace. International conflict will characterize these times which lead to the triumph of God's purpose for his people, as is indicated by the reversal in 3.10 of the advice in Isa 2.4 and Mic 4.8 to convert weapons into farm tools. The nations are to be punished by God; Israel and Jerusalem will be vindicated and renewed in the end time (3.11-21).

AMOS

From the opening lines of this book and from a short biographical section (7.10-17) can be drawn the only information we have about the origins and life of Amos. Although he carried out his prophetic role in the north of Israel after the northern and southern tribes divided into separate kingdoms following the death of Solomon (922 BCE), he was originally from a small city south of Jerusalem, Tekoah (1.1). His public activity as a prophet was during the reigns of the northern king, Jeroboam II (786-746) and of the southern king, Uzziah (783-742). At times Amos uses the term Israel to refer to the northern tribes, but he also uses it to refer to the historic experiences of the full twelve tribes, especially when considering their exodus from Egypt and their original settling in the land of Canaan. Probably Amos was active as prophet around 750. His denial that he is a prophet (7.14) shows that he is not one of the official prophets connected with the temple or the royal establishment. Instead, he maintains his independence from the established powers while relying solely on what he is persuaded God has told him to declare. His major concerns are (1) that the rich and powerful leaders of Israel exploit the poor and seize their lands, and (2) that they keep up a show of honoring the God of Israel while engaging in immoral acts and even pagan forms of worship. His primary theme is that this betrayal of the special relationship between God and Israel will result in divine punishment and the destruction of the nation.

The book consists of two main parts: the words of Amos (1.3-6.14) and the visions of Amos (7.1-9.10). After predicting that God will bring under judgment the nations surrounding Israel (Damascus, 1.3-5; Gaza, 1.6-8; Tyre, 1.9-10; Edom, 1.11-12; Ammon, 1.13-15; Moab, 2.1-3; and even the southern tribes of Judah, 2.4-5), Amos announces the doom of Israel itself (2.6-16). The reason for this judgment is the leaders' injustice to the poor (2.6-7a), the immorality of their personal behavior (2.7b), and their gross self-indulgence (2.8). He recalls all that God has done in the past for Israel and how they have rejected these ancient models of responsibility (2.9-12). Now they can only await Yahweh's judgment that is soon to fall (2.13-16). God remains in control of the history of Israel and the nations, and he will punish the faithless people (3.1-8). The other nations will know of their weakness and exploit it (3.9-12). It will result in the destruction of the costly homes of the rich (3.13-15). Judgment will fall and they will be scattered in spite of their vain show of religiosity (4.1-5). They have shown in the past that God's judgment does not bring them to repentance (4.6-13), and they will surely experience punishment for their injustice and immorality (5.1-17). The day of the Lord will bring destruction, not deliverance, and will result in their being exiled to a land beyond Damascus (5.18-27). This doom will fall on the selfish, ruthless rulers and the rich who have abandoned God and concern for his people (6.1-14).

The visions of Amos (7.1-9.10) present the same themes of the certainty of God's judgment of Israel which will fall because he holds them accountable for their misdeeds (8.1-9.10). There are only two brief notes of hope in these prophetic oracles: 5.15 and 9.8, where there is a prediction that a remnant of Israel will be delivered by God from this fearsome punishment. The final oracle of promise of the restoration of David's kingdom probably comes from the period after the exile of Israel to Babylon (in 722) and the return of some of the Israelites in the late sixth to mid-fifth centuries BCE. The report of the complaint of Amaziah the priest against Amos (7.10-17) may be later as well. Scholars have also noted what may be fragments of hymns that are now included in the prophetic oracles: 1.2; 4.13; 5.8-9; 9.5-6, although these could be elements of the actual prophetic style of Amos.

OBADIAH

Obadiah, the shortest of the Old Testament books, begins with the oracle against Edom. Doom is predicted as compensation for the pride and cruelty of this nation, and especially for its having shared in the pillaging and massacre of the population of Jerusalem by the Babylonians in 587 under Nebuchadnezzar. The distinctive feature of this prophetic book is that Edom (or Esau) has betrayed the special familial relationship with Israel (or Jacob), and has therefore wholly violated the covenant God made with his people. The coming day of Yahweh will destroy all God's enemies, including Edom, and will place in power Judah, which will rule all the lands of Israel and the regions east of the Jordan (vv.19-20). Through Judah, God's rule in the world will be forever established (v. 20). There are clear literary links between Obadiah and Jeremiah 49 (as well as less direct ties with Joel 1-3). Perhaps these later prophets drew on the Obadiah tradition in shaping their own messages.

JONAH

Jonah, whose mission to the pagan city of Nineveh is described in this book, is mentioned in 2 Kings 14.25 as being sent to the king, Jeroboam II (786-746), to reassure him that his restoration of his realm to the borders it had in the time of David was evidence that God had a future purpose for Israel. In the Book of Jonah, however, both the tone and intent of the message are very different. What God communicates to the prophet through his extraordinary adventures is that he is concerned for people of other nations, just as he is for the covenant community. The book dates from long after the time of Jeroboam, but mention of the Twelve Prophets (which includes Jonah) in Jewish writings from the early second century BCE (Tobit 14.4-8) provides the lower limit for this writing. The free shifting of the name of God between Elohim and Yahweh (which earlier represented two different traditions) and the need to detail the size and splendor of Nineveh confirm the proposal for a late date for this little book. It was probably written in the third century when the Jews were in the contested middle region between the hellenistic realms of Egypt and Syria, which were competing for control of the eastern Mediterranean world. The question was, Should their understanding of God and his ways with humanity go out to non-Jews?

Jonah's psalm-like hymn (2.1-10) recalls the imagery of older biblical writings which depict God's gaining control of the hostile waters (Gen 1.1-13; Ps 104.5-9). The precedent for outreach to Gentiles is provided in the story of Elisha (2 Kings 5), who heals a leper sent to him by a pagan ruler. Jonah's personal struggle over this issue is like that of Elijah, who asked God to let him die rather than require him to carry out his witness (1 Kings 19.4-8). Jonah learns about the inclusiveness of God's purpose in hard ways: by the subterranean voyage he takes when, sent to Nineveh, he took ship in the opposite direction (Jonah 1); when God rebukes him for being concerned about a dying plant but indifferent about a threatened city full of human beings (4.10-11). Reluctantly,

Jonah proclaims his message of repentance (3.4). God spares the city (3.10) and Jonah is perplexed, just as many Jews of that period would have been by this portrayal of God and his messengers as concerned for humans apart from their ethnic or cultic state.

MICAH

The name Micah is a shortened form of Micaiah, which means "Who is like Yahweh?," and implies that no one is like the God of Israel. The introductory lines (1.1) state that his prophetic activity was during the reigns of the following kings of Judah: Jotham (742-735), Ahaz (735-715) and Hezekiah (715-687). Jeremiah 26.18 confirms his activity in the time of Hezekiah. The fall of the northern kingdom of Israel (in 722) and the Assyrian invasion of the southern kingdom of Judah (in 701) are reflected in the prophetic oracles, and possibly the later return of Israel from exile in Babylon. The oracles fall into four groups which alternate between judgment and promise. (1) Samaria (Israel) is challenged in 1.2-7 and Judah in 1.8-2.11, followed by a promise of renewal of God's people (2.12-13). Then follows a severe indictment of the rulers of Israel, the heads of families and the professional priests who say what their masters want to hear (3.1-12). (2) The prophet promises that there will be universal participation in the worship of the God of Israel (4.1-5), when the nation is restored following the exile (4.6-5.1), and a new king in the line of David (5.2-6) rules over the faithful remnant of the people in a land purged of the magical and idolatrous practices and the cruel use of force that exists within Israel (5.7-15).

(3) The third group of oracles (6.1-16) presents God's challenge to Israel as a people who have forgotten their historic origins when God led them out of slavery in Egypt, as well as their obligations for social and moral justice and for faithful, exclusive worship of Yahweh in the way prescribed in the law. As a result, they are characterized by infidelity (7.1-7) both to their God and to one another, and even within families. (4) The final section (7.8-20) includes a call to the people to repent, with assurance that God will vindicate the faithful, that the city of Jerusalem will be restored, and that other nations will acknowledge God's triumph in behalf of his people. The new relationship will be based solely on God's love and fidelity to his people Israel.

NAHUM

Like Obadiah, this brief book offers prophetic oracles against nations regarded as enemies of Israel: Assyria, which was a major power in the Middle East for nearly a century and a half (745-609); and Edom, a small people located south and east of the Jordan, whose origins were linked with Esau, brother and antagonist of Jacob (Gen 25.19-33). The oracles of Nahum are directed against Nineveh, the huge, powerful, wealthy capital of Assyria. Regarded as impregnable, the city was taken following a siege by the Medes in 625, and by the Medes and Babylonians in 612, with the destruction of its power base in 609. There are six oracles, in which the themes alternate between the assured destruction of Nineveh by God's action and the certain deliverance and liberation of Judah that is to follow: 1.2-11; 1.12-15; 2.1-13; 3.1-7; 3.8-13; 3.14-19. Promises of renewal of Judah appear in 1.15; 2.2. Throughout there are vivid poetic images of God's overwhelming of the proud, cruel city.

HABAKKUK

The prophet who utters these oracles is identified as Habakkuk (1.1), which is a semitic name for a common garden plant. From details of the pronouncements it can be inferred that he was active around the end of the sixth century BCE when the Babylonians were striving successfully to dominate the Middle East. The book consists of a debate between the prophet and God (1.2-2.20), with an extended hymn of praise at the conclusion (3.1-19). The prophet asks why God does not act in response to the injustice and disobedience which characterize his people (1.2-4). God announces that he is acting, and that he will use the Chaldeans (the Babylonians) to crush Israel and to expose the folly of its military preparations that have given it a false sense of security (1.5-11). This section may be dated after 605 when the Egyptians were defeated by the Babylonians in Syria. The prophet then asks why God allows his people to be treated like fish caught helplessly in a net. Is he intent only on destroying them (1.12-17)? God replies that the sole ground for relationship between Yahweh and his people is their trust in him and his purpose for them (2.1-5). The appeal to those who see themselves as righteous to live by faith (2.4) is quoted in its Greek version by Paul (Rom 1.17; Gal 3.11) and Hebrews (10.38-39). The final prophetic oracle (2.6-20) indicts the wicked who exploit other people, seizing property and committing violent crimes.

They will experience similar treatment at the hands of God's agents, and they are fools to trust in idols which are made by human hands.

The book ends with the extended hymn (3.1-19) in which the prophet sings the praise of God who will come in the future as in the past to manifest his power and purpose for his people by controlling the created world and its inhabitants. Now he will defeat the enemies of his people. The hymn concludes with the prophet's expression of awe before the majesty of God and his confidence that in spite of seeming setbacks, his purpose will triumph. The last lines indicate the use of the hymn in worship.

ZEPHANIAH

Zephaniah opens with the claim that the word of the Lord came to him during the reign of Josiah, king of Judah (640-609). Although Judah was at that time still subject to Assyria, the growing power of Egypt and the mounting threat to Assyria in its own territory from the Babylonians resulted in relaxation of external pressures and a degree of peace and freedom for Judah under Josiah. The oracles of Zephaniah come from two stages in the reign of Josiah: Zeph 1-2 from the beginning of his rule, and Zeph 3 after 612 when Josiah's attempt at reform (removal of all shrines except the temple in Jerusalem; renewal of commitment to the law of Moses; 2 Kings 23) had largely failed. Zeph 3.20 probably dates from a much later time, following the return of Jews from the exile in Babylon.

The theme of the first two chapters is God's universal judgment on his covenant people and on all the nations. The major sins of the people are idolatry (1.4-6), adopting foreign ways (1.8), unethical actions among the people of God (1.9), and widespread indifference and unbelief (1.12). There will be a holy war: not God against the enemies of Judah, but his contest with his own disobedient people. The war will begin in Jerusalem (1.10-11) and spread to the neighboring nations in every direction (1.12-2.15). God's call of his people to repentance (2.3) has been refused by the leaders of Judah in Jerusalem who reject the word of God, as recovered in the newly-found copy of the law (3.2-4). But God's call will go out to all the nations (3.8-10). A remnant of Israel will trust in God and will be preserved by him (3.11-13). The oracles end with the promise of the restoration of the people, including the weak and the despised, and the defeat of their enemies (3.14-19). The last verse (3.20) was probably added after the return of the people to the land of Judah following their release from exile in Babylon.

HAGGAI

The book of the prophet Haggai, whose name means "festal," begins with dates and details that link him with the beginning of the restoration of Israel to their land in the period following the defeat of the Babylonians by the Persians in 539. Named in addition to the Persian ruler, Darius (522-486) are the governor of Judah, Zerubbabel, and the chief priest, Joshua (1.1, 12; 2.2, 21, 23). Both political and religious leadership are essential for the stability of the restored people of God. Haggai is mentioned along with the prophet Zechariah in the historical account of the return to the land in Ezra 5.1; 6.14, where we learn that an altar was built, priests and Levites were appointed (Ezra 3-4).

The book opens with an instruction to rebuild the temple (1.2-11), with an explanation that the lack of the proper worship of God is the cause of the poverty of the people and the failure of their flocks and crops. In 1.12-15 the leaders agree to carry out the rebuilding task. 2.1-9 cautions the faithful not to be disappointed with the smaller and less impressive rebuilt temple in Jerusalem, since it will be an essential step toward the prosperity of the land and the construction of a more splendid temple. 2.10-19 deals with issues of ritual purity in relation to the temple worship, with reminders that failure to honor God properly will result in an unproductive land and the poverty of its people. The section ends with assurance of future blessings on land and people. The book closes (2.20-23) with promises that God's purpose will be fulfilled through Zerubabbel (whose name means "shoot of Babylon"), so that in spite of his pagan name and his having been appointed by the Persians as governor of Judah, he will be the instrument of renewal.

ZECHARIAH

Like Haggai, the book of Zechariah (meaning "Yahweh remembers") is linked with the reign of Darius (522-486) and the leadership of the returned exiles through Zerubbabel, the governor of Judah appointed by the Persians (4.6-10), and Joshua, the chief priest (3.1-10). The book may be divided into two major sections, following the initial call to repentance for the renewal of God's People (1.2-6): Visions (1.7-6.15) and Oracles (7.1-14.21). Portions of the oracles may come from as late as the fourth century, as in 9.13 where the ascendancy of Greece (which occurred under Alexander the Great) is mentioned. Most of the details fit well with the events of the sixth and early fifth century, however.

Visions: (1) The Horsemen (1.7-17), who symbolize God's action to restore Judah and Jerusalem, to rebuild the temple, and to allow the prosperity of the land. (2) The Horns and the Blacksmiths (1.18-21), who represent the opponents of Judah whom God will enable them to overcome. (3) The Man with the Measuring Line (2.1-5), who is a symbol of Jerusalem which will be rebuilt and restored to prosperity. In 2.6-13 there is an interlude in which the prophet appeals to Israel to return to the land, with the promise that God will dwell in their midst. (4) Joshua and Satan (3.1-10) anticipate the imminent purification, robing and installation of Joshua as priest in the renewed sanctuary in Jerusalem. (5) The Lampstand and the Olive Trees (4.1-14) stand for the king and the high priest whose roles and efforts unite to restore the temple, the pattern of worship there, and the people. They are the two Anointed Ones: Joshua and Zerubbabel. (6) The Flying Scroll (5.1-4) communicates the divine judgment on those who violate the law of Moses. (7) The Woman in a Basket (5.5-11) symbolizes the wickedness that is to be removed from the land. (8) The Four Chariots (6.1-8) represent the instruments which will extend God's sovereignty over the whole of the earth. The visions conclude (6.9-15) with the portrayal of the two ruling figures – king and priest – as signs of assurance that God's will and purpose for his people will be achieved and sustained.

A series of oracles occupies the second half of the book of Zechariah. (7.1-7) The pious acts of the people are not aimed at obedience to God but are performed to make them feel that they are being religious. (7.8-14) It is neglect of God's law which has led to the scattering of Israel among the nations of the world. (8.1-23) God promises to return and to dwell in the sanctuary in Jerusalem. The result will be peace and prosperity, truth, justice and mutual concern among the people of God. Their gatherings will be festivals rather than fasts, and people of other nations will seek the God of Israel. At this point the oracles shift from expectations of soon historical and political renewal to future and even cosmic settings, in which the present order of existence is replaced and transformed. (9.1-17) The model for change becomes the divine warrior figure who defeats his cosmic enemies and renews the sanctuary, as in Ex 15 and the Song of Deborah (Judg 5). God will punish the neighboring nations which cause difficulties for Israel and renew the people and the land. He will come in humility, bringing peace and with an ever-widening area of his rule. He will protect his people and judge their antagonists. (10.1-12) God's wrath is poured out against the irresponsible leaders of the people (shepherds). The faithful remnant of Judah and Israel will be gathered from among the nations and restored. Similarly, in 11.1-17 those who exploit or mishandle the leadership of Israel will be called to account by God, not in historical circumstances but in cosmic renewal. (12.1-13.6) Jerusalem will be preserved against attack by other nations, and the Davidic ruler will be restored to power. God will have compassion on the people of Jerusalem and the members of the royal family for the losses they have suffered in the past. The persecuted agent of God will be vindicated, while the idolatry of the people and the activity of false prophets are denounced. (13.7-9) God's striking the sheep and the shepherd represent the chastisement of Israel and its leaders with the aim of recalling to obedience the faithful remnant of the people. (14.1-21) God's defeat of the nations that ravaged the holy city is to be matched by the geological and topographical changes in Jerusalem and vicinity. The survivors acknowledge and honor the God of Israel, but those who refuse to do so will be punished. The temple and the city will be a wholly renewed context of holiness for God's people. The cosmic setting of this conflict and the rejection of earthly religious and political leadership evidence the shift of the prophetic tradition toward the apocalyptic view of history and of God's people. A similar transformation appears also in Isa 24-25 and 34-35, but is more fully developed in Daniel.

MALACHI

The name given to this book, Malachi (1.1), which means "my messenger," derives from the mention of God's messenger in 3.1. Whoever the author was, he was active as a prophet in the first half of the fifth century. Profound disillusionment had set in among the people within a few decades of the rebuilding of the temple and the establishment of the worship of God there after 520. The prophetic pronouncements alternate between the themes of judgment and promise. 1.2-5 reminds the readers that God's warnings to humanity are certain of fulfillment, and that his power to visit judgment is not limited to Israel: he denounced Esau (Edom), the brother of Jacob (Gen 25.24-30; 36.1) and the predictions were carried out. 1.6-2.9 contrasts the perversion of the worship of God that is being carried out by the priests in the rebuilt temple in Jerusalem with the faithful devotion to God that is to be found among the nations of the world. A curse is pronounced on the priests who have violated God's covenant with Levi and his offspring for them to serve God in the sanctuary. 2.10-17 depicts Judah's violation of the covenant by the practice of divorcing Jewish wives in order to marry women of wealthy and influential Gentile families.

3.1-7 describes the coming messenger and agent of God who will purify the priesthood. God will judge the powerful in Israel for their injustice to the poor and weak of their people. The unchanging God calls them to change their ways. 3.8-18 includes warnings concerning the failure of the people to tithe and to meet their obligations to God. When they do so, God will shower blessings upon them, rewarding those who obey the covenant. 4.1-6 promises defeat of the oppressors of God's people and the coming of an agent of God to lead, to heal and to bless the nation. The primary obligation of Israel is to obey the law of Moses (as formulated and expanded during and subsequent to their exile in Babylon; the process is operative behind the accounts in Ezra and Nehemiah). The book ends with the promise of the return of Elijah the prophet to call the people to repent in order to prepare them for God's impending visit to bring them under judgement.

INTRODUCTIONS TO THE INDIVIDUAL BOOKS OF THE NEW TESTAMENT

The Gospels and Acts

MATTHEW

Since the early centuries of the church, our first gospel has been attributed to Matthew, the tax-collector named in Mt 9.9; 10.3. But the writer's use of Greek sources concerning Jesus (including the Gospel of Mark) and the evidence that it was written after the Fall of Jerusalem in 70 CE suggest that it was not the work of one of Jesus' disciples, but was written by an unknown author late in the first century. The structure of the gospel is clear: the first two chapters describe the birth and youth of Jesus (Mt 1-2); the last three chapters depict his encounter with the authorities in Jerusalem, his death, resurrection and the commissioning of his followers (Mt 26-28). The most important structural feature, however, is that the main body of the gospel is divided into five major sections, each of which ends in a variant of the phrase, "When Jesus had finished ..." Each section includes two sub-sections (a series of narratives and then an extended discourse):

(1) Preparation and Program for Ministry (Mt 3-7) – Narrative (3.1-4.25); Discourse: Sermon on the Mount (Mt 5-7).

(2) The Authority of Jesus (Mt 8-10) – Narrative (8.1-9.38); Discourse: Sending of the Twelve Disciples (Mt 10.1-42).

(3) The Kingdom and its Coming (Mt 11-13) – Narrative (11.1-12.50); Discourse: The Parables of the Kingdom (Mt 13).

(4) The Life of the New Community (Mt 14-18) – Narrative (Mt 14-17); Discourse: Regulations for the Common Life (Mt 18).

(5) The End of the Age (Mt 19-22; 24-25) – Narrative (Mt 19-22); Discourse: The Coming of the End of the Age (Mt 24-25). Mt 23 has been inserted in this scheme, probably at a later time, when the conflict between the two emergent movements – Christianity and rabbinic Judaism – was becoming more intense. Evidence in Matthew of the more formal development of Christianity in the later first century appears in the use of "church," in the authority given to the

apostles to build it (Mt 16.18), in the regulations for settling disputes within the church (Mt 18), and in the formalization of prayers, instruction and the rite of baptism (6.9-13; 28.18-20). The result of the structure and the incorporation of these features into Matthew is that from the early centuries on it has served as a kind of constitution for the church, and was accordingly placed first in the New Testament canon.

MARK

The second gospel in the traditional New Testament order is actually the earliest gospel, and very likely the pioneer work in that literary form. Although it has some features of a biography, it is a document written to convey to the early Christian community the following: (1) the identity and intentions of its founder, Jesus; (2) the aims and authority which he transmitted to his earliest followers; (3) the significance of the seeming defeat and tragedy of his death; (4) the promise of God's future action in the world to complete the defeat of the powers of evil and to vindicate Jesus' followers; (5) guidelines as to how his followers are to carry forward his work and how they are to live as the faithful people of God. Jesus' healings and exorcisms are described as evidence that God is already overcoming evil in human experience, and Jesus' pronouncements of forgiveness and open attitude are extended to those whose birth, occupation, or ritual condition excluded them from the traditional covenant people (Gentiles, and those whose diseases or occupations made them ritually impure by Jewish standards). There is an element of urgency in Mark, which is heightened by the frequent use of "immediately" and by run-on sentences beginning simply with "And," as well as by direct predictions of the soon coming of the Son of Man in triumph (9.1; 13.30). The impending destruction of the temple will prepare for the gathering of God's new people (13.1-27). Meanwhile, the readers are to spread the message of the gospel, to manifest the power by which evil is being defeated, and to await the end of the age when God's kingdom comes in fulness.

There is no story in Mark of Jesus' birth (as in Matthew and Luke), but the gospel begins with the preparation through John the Baptist (1.1-11) for Jesus' public work of announcing the coming of God's Rule and performing healings which point to its coming (1.14-8.30). Although both these kinds of activity continue throughout this gospel, at 8.31-38 Jesus begins to tell his followers of his suffering and death. At the same time he predicts that God will vindicate him within their lifetime, and as a sign of divine confirmation of that promise he is transformed in the presence of some of his disciples (9.1-8). Jesus also is pictured as taking issue with the dominant ways that his Jewish contemporaries understood God's requirements of his people (Mk 7; 10-12). In parables (Mk 4) and prophetic predictions (Mk 13) he tells his followers what the outcome will be for their activity in proclaiming the kingdom of God and what the fate of the temple and its holy city will be (Mk 13). The final chapters describe his seizure by the authorities, his trial and execution by the Romans. Throughout there are promises that beyond his death will be God's vindication of him and them.

The work is anonymous and written in crude Greek, although with a vivid and compelling style. Probably because Peter figures importantly in this gospel, it came to be associated with Mark, who is mentioned in the letters of Paul and Acts as a co-worker of the apostolic leaders. In 1 Peter 5.13 he is identified as Peter's "son," which implies a close working relationship between them. Whoever the author was, Mark was probably written shortly before the Roman destruction of Jerusalem in 70 CE (Mk 13.1-2).

LUKE

Detailed analysis of Luke shows that the author had three major sources on which he drew: (1) Mark; (2) a source also shared with Matthew (known as Q, which consisted almost wholly of sayings), and (3) a special source otherwise unknown. Luke's style is the most literarily sophisticated of all the gospels: his prologue, and that of Acts (which is the second volume of his account of the origins of Christianity), display the literary conventions of historians of his time. In the opening sections, his narratives and poetry (hymns) are modelled after the Old Testament. There are features throughout Luke and Acts which resemble the writings of Greco-Roman historians and biographers of the period. The work was intended for a more sophisticated readership than Mark, for example.

The structure of Luke's gospel is a blend of geographical and conceptual features. (1) In 1.5-4.13, the preparation for the birth and career of Jesus takes place chiefly in the vicinity of Jerusalem. (2) His ministry is launched in Galilee (4.14-9.50). (3) The preparation of his followers for his death and resurrection and for their mission takes place on the way to Jerusalem (9.51-19.27; note 13.33). (4) The crucial events of his challenge to Judaism, the preparation of his disciples for his death, his arrest and execution, and his appearances to his followers – all take place in Jerusalem (19.28-24.53). It is there they are to remain until they are empowered by God for their work in his name. His presence will be with them in the breaking of bread and in the interpretation of the scriptures (24.35, 45).

By the middle of the second century, this work (and its sequel, the Acts of the Apostles) were assigned to Luke, who was a companion and co-worker of Paul (Philemon 24; Col 4.14). But there is no firm evidence of special medical knowledge or of close kinship with the thought of Paul. The author was probably a Gentile, although he is eager throughout the gospel and Acts to show continuities between Judaism and Christianity. But he makes his case in such a way as to show that God had always intended that Gentiles would share in the life of his people. He wrote after the destruction of Jerusalem, as his detailed references to the Roman capture of the city show (Lk 19.43 ff.), probably around the end of the first century.

JOHN

The fourth gospel resembles the others in a general way, but it has several important features which set it apart from the other three. (1) It is introduced by a prologue which depicts Jesus as the incarnation of God's wisdom (in Greek, *logos*), thereby portraying him as the embodiment of the divine purpose to create the world and to call together an obedient people of God. As the agent of renewal of God's people, Jesus is contrasted with John the Baptist, who recognizes that Jesus' place in God's purpose is superior to his own (John 1.1-18). (2) In reporting the miracles of Jesus, this gospel specifies that his mighty deeds are manifestations of the glory of God (2.11), and that those who read these accounts are invited to trust in him as God's Son (20.30-31). (3) Jesus' teachings are reported by John in the form of extended discourses, rather than as collections of individual sayings, as is true of most of the teachings of Jesus in the other gospels. Most of them highlight who Jesus is in the purpose of God: for example, the bread of life (6.35); the light of the world (8.12); the good shepherd (10.11); the resurrection and the life (11.25); the way, the truth, the life (14.6); the true vine (15.1). (4) Events reported in the other gospels are assigned to a different place in Jesus' career, such as the cleansing of the temple (2.13-21) and other accounts of his confrontations with the Jewish authorities in Jerusalem, which come early in John. Both the teachings of Jesus and his miracles are presented in John as indicators that participation in God's new people is a possibility in the present: in the wedding feast (2.1-11); the participation by non-Israelites in the true worship of God (4.1-26); the miraculous feeding of the covenant people in the desert (6.25-59); the true flock of God (10.1-18); sharing in the fruitfulness of God's people (15.1-11). At the same time, the mounting hostility between Jews and Jesus' followers is reflected in John (9.22). The ground of relationship within this new community is love, as is indicated through Jesus' last meal with his disciples (13.34-35; 15.9), which has none of the features of the eucharist.

Like the other gospels, this work gives no indication as to who wrote it. By the end of the second century, there was a widespread theory that its author was John, the son of Zebedee, who was identified as "the other disciple" (18.15-16) or "the disciple whom Jesus loved" (19.26-27; 20.2-4). But there is no evidence that this assumption is accurate. John 21 is almost certainly a later addition to the original gospel, in which the responsibilities of the disciples are given more specific form than in the rest of this gospel. The work as a whole seems more concerned with the symbolic meaning of Jesus than with merely providing information about his career.

ACTS

Acts as the sequel to the Gospel of Luke is indicated by the reference in Acts 1.1 to "the first book," and is confirmed by the similarity between them in style and point of view. Acts was probably written in the early second century at a time when two major issues confronted the early church: (1) As Christianity spread throughout the Roman world, how was it to come to terms with Roman culture and politics? (2) How were Christians to make good their claim that they were the true heirs of the promises that God made to his people in the biblical tradition? In order to address these needs, the author employs three literary strategies of his time: (1) He uses the conventions of historical writing in this period, with its emphasis on the overall purpose and meaning which are to be seen behind and through the succession of reported events. (2) A vivid narrative style used by writers to propagandize for a religious tradition, emphasizing miraculous manifestations of the divine in both public and private events, has been adopted for his own ends by the author. (3) Since the Roman authorities tolerated Judaism because its writings and practices were ancient – so long as its adherents avoided moves toward political independence – the Christians stressed that Jesus and the movement he launched represented the true intent of the Jewish scriptures.

The author and the community for which he spoke were persuaded that what Jesus had begun was in process of coming to fulfillment. Just as in Luke's gospel there is an emphasis on Jesus' having reached out to non-Israelites, so the outpouring of the Spirit (which he promised, Acts 1.8) had launched a movement that was to reach from Jerusalem to the ends of the earth, with representatives of all nations gathered there on the day of Pentecost (Acts 2.5-11). Acts pictures the stages in the progress of this divine activity: at Jerusalem, where Jews and Gentile converts respond by the thousands to the message about Jesus (Acts 2); the designation of representatives of Greek culture to serve the community and to preach to those on the outer boundaries of Judaism (Acts 6); the coming to faith of such outsiders (from the Jewish point of view) as Samaritans (Acts 7), an Ethiopian eunuch (Acts 8), and a Roman military officer (Acts 10). Peter is the one who launches this outreach to the Roman world (Acts 10), but Paul is pictured as the one chosen by God to develop the geographical spread of Christianity to Syria, Cyprus, Asia Minor, Greece – including Athenian intellectuals (Acts 17) – and finally Rome itself. Yet it is clear that when Paul arrived there were already Jews open to Christianity in such places as Corinth (Acts 18.1) and Rome (Acts 28). Principles must be worked out for bringing Jews and Gentiles into the fellowship of these new communities (Acts 15). But above all, the Christians must make clear that they are not political subversives. The final section of Acts reports that this conclusion was reached by the various public officials before whom Paul was brought to trial (Acts 21-28). In conveying his message, the author of Acts uses literary methods of his time, ranging from sermons and speeches to vivid narrative of travel and of human interchange. It provides precedent, strategy and rationale for the outreach of Christianity to the wider Roman world.

The Letters of Paul

ROMANS

This, the most systematic of Paul's letters, was written to a church that he had not founded or visited. The origins of the church in Rome are unknown, but the first Christians there were probably of Jewish origin, since some of them were expelled from the city by the action of the emperor Claudius (Acts 18.1-4). This incident is also mentioned by the

Roman historian, Suetonius. These reports indicate that as early as 49-50 there was a Christian community in Rome. Paul writes to introduce himself to them, since he intends to pass through Rome on his way to Spain (15.28). The main issue which he addresses in this letter is one that would be central for a church of members from both Jewish and Gentile backgrounds: What are the qualifications for participating in the people of God?

After the formal greeting, into which Paul inserts a credal formula about Christ (1.1-7), he introduces himself and describes his long-standing interest in the church in Rome (1.8-15). From this he launches into an extended statement of his main concern: the definition of the covenant people. In 1.16-5.20 he describes the human condition before God: alienated, self-centered, disobedient. God has acted in Jesus Christ to set his people in right relationship to himself, which is attained through trust in what God has done and not as a reward for moral or ritual performance. 6.1-8.17 outlines the consequences and the potential of this new relationship: through baptism, the faithful are linked to the new humanity, which has symbolically died, been buried, and raised to enter a new life (6.1-12). The actual behavior of those in this relationship ranges from continuing enslavement to sin to renewal and fulfillment of life through God's Spirit. Yet it is only in the future that God's purpose will achieve its full goal through and for his people, when all are finally conformed to the image of God's wholly obedient Son.

In setting out this picture of the reconstituted people of God, Paul describes the origin and destiny of historic Israel, and how that has led to the announcement and promise of the fulfillment of God's plan for the New Israel (9.1-11.36). The members of this new community have God-given resources and responsibilities toward one another (12.1-15.13) but also toward the Roman state (13.1-7). The letter concludes with extended personal remarks by Paul in which he appraises his own work and indicates his plans for the future. These include a circuit of the churches in Greece and Asia Minor to collect a relief fund for the Jerusalem Christians, and the journey through Rome to his proposed new field of mission in Spain. Because of the high mobility of merchants and craftsmen in the Roman world, Paul has already met many who are now part of the church in Rome. To them he sends greetings, as well as advice about dealing with troublemakers in their midst (16.1-23). The letter concludes with praise to God (16.15-17).

1 CORINTHIANS

Writing from Ephesus (16.8-9), Paul announces his intention to return to Corinth for an extended stay (16.5), but meanwhile he wants to respond to the matters about which the Corinthians have written him (7.1). His earlier letter to them is mentioned in 5.9. Since then other issues have been reported to Paul through unidentified sources. Accordingly, this letter follows a kind of checklist of his concerns and theirs. In between these topics Paul has inserted remarks on matters which he thinks are relevant to the problems and needs of this divided and somewhat irresponsible Christian community. Located on the narrow isthmus which joins mainland Greece with the Peloponnese peninsula to the south, Corinth – with its two seaports on the east and west and its long tradition of sensual devotion to the love goddess, Aphrodite – was a culturally diverse and worldly city. Paul deals with the issues there in topical fashion, although some scholars have tried to discover pieces of other letters in this writing.

The advice which Paul offers in dealing with these issues includes a contrast between human and divine wisdom (2.6-16); the need to settle disputes within the Christian community (6.1-11); the precedent from ancient Israel for the uncertainty of the life of God's people (10.1-13); the true nature of Christian love (13.1-13). The problems of which he has heard concern conflicts within the church as a result of the members' identifying themselves with one of their apostolic leaders over against another, or of their too high estimate of human learning (1.10-4.21). What is essential is God's wisdom as it has been disclosed through Christ, not human ideas or capabilities.

The questions raised by the Corinthians which Paul addresses include how to handle members who exercize sexual freedom, including incest (5.1-13) and relationships with prostitutes (6.12-20). The issue as to whether it is better for Christians to marry or to remain single is also discussed (7.1-40). Then Paul turns to more explicitly religious issues: whether it is permissible for Christians to eat food which has been offered as a sacrifice to idols (8.1-12; 10.1-22); how the members of the community are to behave and to assume roles in their corporate life and worship, with special attention to the roles of women (11.1-14.40); how important, how credible is the belief in the resurrection of the dead (15.1-58). Paul's approach to all these problems stresses three factors: the corporate unity of God's people; the power of the Holy Spirit to energize and enable the members; the experience and authority of the apostles as those commissioned by Christ to carry forward the life and work of the church. The letter concludes with general advice to the community, information about Paul's travel plans, and personal greetings. 1 Corinthians gives the reader the clearest insight into the life and working of a Christian community in that part of the early church so powerfully influenced by Paul.

2 CORINTHIANS

What is known as Second Corinthians probably comprises two letters of Paul to the church in Corinth, following a "tearful letter" he had sent them, according to 2 Cor 2.3-4. His fourth communication to them consists of 2 Cor 1-9, followed by the final preserved letter, 2 Cor 10-13. It is possible that 6.14-7.1 is a misplaced fragment of yet another letter of Paul, since it seems to interrupt the flow of thought from 6.11-13 to 7.2. The style and vocabulary confirm that all the parts originated with Paul.

None of these letters is as systematic as 1 Cor, but all deal with intensely personal issues: the relationship of Paul with the Corinthian Christians; their accusations against him and their critical assessment of his apostolic role. His detractors included some who visited the church in Corinth, claiming authority and insights superior to his (2 Cor 11). In the course of replying to his critics and defending himself, Paul wrote some of the most compelling passages in his letters: the contrast between God's dealings with his people in the old and the new covenant (3.7-18); the nature of the new creation which God is accomplishing (5.17-21); Jesus' acceptance of poverty so that he could bring riches to his people (8.9); Paul's own transforming experience of being taken up into the presence of God (12.1-9). In the concluding section he tells the Corinthians twice (12.14; 13.1) that he plans to visit them again. He urges them to prepare a contribution for the Jerusalem church (8.1-15), which he will come to collect on his way to present this offering from the Gentile churches to the primary community of faith.

GALATIANS

Paul's letter to the Galatians departs from the formal style found in his other letters and shows a sense of urgency to the point of incomplete sentences in a few places. In 1.1-2 the customary giving of thanks for the addressees is missing, and his intensity of feeling results in awkward syntax at 2.4-5. Writing to Christians living in central Asia Minor, where the populace was primarily Celtic (called Galatian in Greek), Paul has heard that Christians of Jewish origin have insisted that members must accept circumcision and take on the obligation to obey the Law of Moses in order to share in the covenant community. He reminds his readers that the message of grace which he preached to them came from God (1.6-12) and that it has been confirmed through his personal encounter with the risen Christ (1.13-17), as well as through the effectiveness of his preaching to the Gentiles (1.18-22). Further, his outreach to Gentiles has been approved by the Jerusalem-based apostles (2.1-10).

When Peter had retreated from this understanding of freedom from the law, he had been rebuked by Paul (2.11-21), who reminded him and now informs the Galatians that participation in God's people has always been a divine gift to be accepted through trust in God's promise, not a human achievement (3.1-22). Life in the new community is open across all ethnic, sexual and social boundaries (3.23-4.7). Paul regrets that the Galatian Christians seem inclined to accept these legalistic regulations as imposed by the false teachers, and he appeals to biblical precedent for the freedom which he proclaims (4.8-5.1). The rich resource for the life of faith is the Spirit which God provides for his people, rather than reliance on corrupt human instincts and urges (5.2-26). This power can renew and sustain the Christian community (6.1-10). The letter concludes with a warning against these inappropriate rules and requirements that some have sought to impose on the Galatians.

The visit of Paul to the Jerusalem church leaders described in Gal 1-2 is probably the same as the one that is recounted in Acts 15, although the latter report differs as to the circumstances and the outcome. Galatians probably dates from the fifties, and could have been written from one of several cities in Syria or Greece.

EPHESIANS

Although many ancient manuscripts of this letter indicate that it was addressed to "the saints who are in Ephesus," the oldest and best copies do not name the addressees. This has led some scholars to conclude that Paul wrote this as a general letter to all the churches. Careful analysis raises the further question as to whether this book was written by Paul. Although it resembles the Letter to the Colossians in some details of form and content, it differs from his letters in typical vocabulary, style and structure. Instead of a theological introduction and a highly personal conclusion, as in Paul's letters, this writing consists of an extended formal introduction ending in a long prayer (1.3-3.21) followed by a series of recommendations about how the readers should live (4.1-6.24).

There is no discussion of local issues within a specific church. Emphasis falls on the present exalted state of Christ and the church (1.7-12, 20-23; 2.1-10), rather than on the struggle and ultimate vindication of which Paul writes in his letters. Instead of dealing with the problem of divisions within the church over the issue of requiring members to obey the Jewish law (as in Galatians and Romans), this letter declares the new unity of God's people (2.11-18), and depicts the church as an established structure in which God dwells (2.19-22) and which is characterized by its unity and clear assignment of responsibilities (4.1-16). Similarly, there are to be well-defined ranks within the communities, with specific modes of obligation for husbands and wives, children and parents, servants and masters (5.22-6.9). At the end of the letter (6.19-22), the writer imitates the style of Paul with reference to his own condition ("in chains") and to one of his co-workers, "Tychicus." Written about the year 100, the work was quoted by Ignatius of Antioch and others early in the second century because it served effectively as a guideline for the developing Gentile institutional churches.

PHILIPPIANS

Paul wrote this letter to the Christian community in Philippi, a city of Macedonia in northeastern Greece located on the main Roman highway which led from the Aegean Sea to the Adriatic Sea, where commercial and military elements crossed to and from Italy. According to Acts 16.11-12, Philippi was Paul's first center of missionary activity on the mainland of Europe.

Following the opening greetings (1.1-2), Paul offers thanks for the Philippian Christians' support of his work (1.3-7), and expresses confidence that his present imprisonment is part of God's purpose and that they will be rewarded for their blameless, fruitful lives (1.8-10). The Roman guards who hold him in prison and others who know of his condition have recognized that he is there because of his testimony for Christ, and thus members of the community where he is imprisoned have taken courage to join him in proclaiming the word of God. His being in prison and even the possibility of his martyrdom are providing him opportunity for proclaiming the gospel of Christ, although he still hopes that he may be released and visit the Philippians once more (1.19-30). He urges them to show humility and concern for others, as Christ accepted his suffering and death in behalf of others, which he describes by quoting an ancient Christian hymn (2.6-11). Just as God exalted the obedient Christ, so He will reward the Philippians for their fidelity and commitment to God's work. Meanwhile, Paul will try to maintain communication with them through his fellow-workers (2.19-30). In commenting on the false teachers who promote an ascetic way of life as being essential for Christians, Paul offers a brief autobiography in which he is seen as transformed from a devout Pharisee, obsessed with observing the law, into one who sees himself as accepted by God solely on the basis of the death and resurrection of Christ (3.1-4.1). He now strives to live a disciplined way of life in response to God's call, and urges his readers to follow his example. The letter ends with prayers, exhortations and thanks for their continued personal support for him and his work (4.2-23).

Scholars have debated whether the letter was written from prison in Caesarea in Palestine (Acts 23-26), from Rome, or from some city closer to Philippi, such as Ephesus. Since military units of the Praetorian Guard (1.13) were stationed in major cities throughout the empire, the place of origin cannot be determined. Since he is facing possible martyrdom, the letter probably comes from near the end of his career, possibly around 60.

COLOSSIANS

Colossae, a small inland city in Asia Minor, was located about 100 miles east of Ephesus, not far from Laodicea. Exchange of letters and personnel among these three cities is noted in the Letter to the Colossians. Following greetings (1.1-2) and the expression of thanks for the faith and love and fruitful work of the community there (1.3-8), there is a prayer for increase in knowledge among the members and in their power to endure, so that they may share in the kingdom of God's Son (1.9-14). There is a detailed description of Christ as God's agent for renewal of the world, as head of the church, and as instrument of divine reconciliation (1.15-23). The author describes his own sufferings in behalf of the community and his commitment to increase their understanding of Christ and their maturity as God's people (1.34-2.7). Then the focus shifts to warnings against false teachings and explanations of the role of Christ in human renewal (2.8-3.17). The writer informs his readers that Christ, in whom the fulness of God dwells (2.9), has freed them from cosmic powers as well as from religious regulations to which some people are trying to force them to conform. The members are told that they have already been raised into the presence of Christ (3.1-3), and that they should therefore live the appropriate life of peace and purity which reflects the image of God in which they have been created anew (3.5-17). In 3.18-4.1 are listed responsibilities assigned to various types of people within the community: wives and husbands, fathers and children, slaves and masters. The letter ends with requests for prayer in behalf of Paul and his co-workers, and an exchange of messages among those joined in his mission (4.2-18).

Because this letter emphasizes what God has already done for his people, in contrast to Paul's usual message about what God is going to do in the future, and because it gives detailed descriptions of false teachings and wrong rules which were being promulgated in the churches, some scholars doubt that Paul wrote it, dating it to the later first century. The practice of producing documents in the name of a known thinker or leader was common in the ancient world, and regarded as an honor rather than a dishonesty. If Paul did write this letter, it is evidence of a shift from his earlier sense of the imminence of the end of the age and from his earlier willingness to work with those with whom he disagreed, as evident in his earlier letters. This letter claims to have been written from prison (4.3, 10, 18), which could be from Ephesus, Caesarea or Rome. Mention of Onesimus, the runaway slave (4.10-14), also named in Philemon 8-14, suggests a close link between this letter and the Pauline tradition. If the letter is from an eastern city, the date could be in the mid-fifties; if from Rome, closer to 60.

1 THESSALONIANS

Written about the year 50, this is probably the oldest preserved letter of Paul. Thessalonica was a major port on the Aegean Sea, through which passed the Via Egnatia, the major Roman road across the Balkan peninsula, ending at Philippi to the east. The dominant religion in this Thessalonica was the worship of Cabirus, a Greek god who had died but was expected to return and defeat the enemies of his followers. After fleeing to this city from Philippi, Paul enjoyed a warm response to him and his message about Christ as the deliverer of his people. After leaving this city (3.1-5), Paul had sent Timothy back to see how the community was doing, and now his favorable report of their courage and fidelity (3.6-10) made him eager to return in spite of present difficulties (2.17-20).

Urging them to continue to live holy lives, in contrast to the immorality of the devotees of the local deity (4.1-8), he gave them assurance that those of their members who had died would have a share in the fulfillment of God's purpose when Christ returns in triumph to gather all his people (4.13-5.11). Meanwhile, they are to be morally responsible, obedient to their community leaders, and caring for the needy among them (5.12-14). There are no hints of organization within the church, but they are to live in constant expectation of the end of the age, meeting obligations within their fellowship.

2 THESSALONIANS

Written soon after 1 Thessalonians, this brief letter addresses the false claim of some in the community that Christ had already returned. Paul tells them what will take place when Christ does reappear: the wicked and the unbelievers will be punished; the faithful will be delivered from their enemies and rewarded by God for their faithful service (1.3-12). But before this happens, there will be an unprecedented outpouring of Satan's activity, and many people will be taken in by these spectacular events (2.1-12). But God by his Spirit is already at work, renewing the lives of his people in preparation for the final triumph. Paul asks for their prayers that he will be preserved from the schemes of the wicked powers, and warns those who do not heed his instructions (3.1-18). Some scholars have thought that Paul could not have foretold the soon coming of Christ, as in 1 Thess, and then have described events which would precede that coming (2 Thess). But both these features are present in Jewish apocalyptic writings: promises and warnings. Both letters exhibit Paul's characteristic style and vocabulary, and fit well with the stage of his career which centered in Corinth and the cities of Greece.

1 TIMOTHY

1 and 2 Timothy and Titus are called by scholars the Pastorals, since in them the writer addresses the needs and responsibilities of those in charge of the Christian communities. The style and themes of these books are so similar as to indicate a common author. In all of them the concerns are for (1) the appointment and supervision of those in leadership roles, and (2) proper content for the instruction given in the churches in matters of doctrine and behavior. The author adopts the name of Paul and concludes each letter with references to his associates, as Paul does in his authentic letters. But the structure of the church and

the specific content of its teaching indicate a generation or two later than the time of the historical Paul.

1 Timothy begins with warnings against false teachings, emphasizing correct beliefs rather than trust in God (1.3-7). Jesus is called "God and Savior," with no reference to his suffering and death. The economic level of the members of the community addressed seems high, with some women showing off their wealth (2.9; 6.17-19). The requirements for leadership are specific: bishops (3.1-7), deacons (3.8-13) and elders (5.17-22). Correct doctrine and true piety are essential for the members (4.1-16). Slaves must obey their masters (6.1-2). The term used for the coming of Christ, *epiphaneia*, is not found in Paul's letters but is used in Greek writings for disclosures of the gods to humans. The moral requirements are stated in the common vocabulary of Greek ethical writings of the period. This is another example of a later generation honoring an earlier leader by writing a work in his name.

2 TIMOTHY

For the general features of this and the other Pastoral Letters, see the Introduction to 1 Timothy. As in that writing, the vocabulary and style, as well as the circumstances of the church, reflect a generation later than that of Paul. The reader is called to stand firm "in the faith" which has been handed down through successive generations of believers (1.5-13), and is to be transmitted through instruction by reliable teachers (2.2-15). Disputes over belief and behavior plague the community (2.20-26), and society as a whole is becoming corrupt and degenerate (3.1-13; 4.3-4), so believers are advised to cling to correct faith and practice as taught in the scriptures (3.14-16). Absent are references to the cross and resurrection of Jesus, and the coming of Christ is not expected in the near future, but is a kind of ultimate hope and promise of reward for fidelity in faith and action. The main task of the leaders is to train the members so that what they believe and how they behave is correct, rather than to convert unbelievers. The writing probably dates from the early second century, one or two generations after Paul.

TITUS

Like the other Pastorals (see Introduction to 1 Timothy), Titus is written in the name of Paul and includes greetings from those linked with Paul in his letters and in the book of Acts. But the content, vocabulary, style and circumstances indicate that this book is from a later period. Emphasis falls on knowledge of the truth (1.1) and on soundness of faith, which now means correct doctrine (1.13). This will show itself in proper behavior (*eusebeia*), a common term in Greek literature of this period, but never found in the authentic letters of Paul. The elders and bishops are to give instruction in sound doctrine and right living, and to refute those who promote erroneous teaching (1.5-9; 2.1-8). The churches are plagued by irreligion (2.12) and torn by dissension and controversy (3.9-11). Slaves are to obey masters (2.9) and Christians are to submit to earthly rulers (3.1). Reborn by the Holy Spirit through baptism (3.5) they await in the unspecified future (2.12; 3.4) God's final disclosure of his purpose for them and his reward for their fidelity. There are suggestions in 1.12 and 3.12 that the letter was written in Crete, which Acts 27.8 reports that Paul visited on his final journey to Rome.

PHILEMON

This is the shortest of the Pauline letters, and the only surviving one that was written to an individual by Paul. Its style matches well the prevailing form and flavor of personal letters in the Roman world of this period. Persons mentioned in this letter are among those referred to in the Letter to the Colossians: Onesimus (Col 4.7-9), the runaway slave, and Archippus (Col 4.17). Paul's plea is for Philemon to forgive and accept as a "beloved brother" this slave (Onesimus) who had run away and had become an important helper of Paul, who was in prison. This may have been in Ephesus, but mention of Luke and Mark as his companions (Philem 23; Col 4.10, 14) suggests that the setting is Rome, where Paul was under house arrest but freely accessible to visitors (Acts 28.16-31). In Col 4.7-9 Onesimus is reported to be returning to Colossae along with Tychicus. Presumably the personal letter to Philemon and the letter to the church as a whole (Colossians) were written at about the same time.

The aim of Paul's letter is that the runaway slave, who is now a member of the new community (Philem 16), will be graciously received by his owner, rather than being punished as the law would have permitted. There is no indication that he is to be freed, however, since Paul elsewhere accepts the status of slaves as a given feature of society (1 Cor 7.20) and calls only for obedience by slaves to their masters (Col 3.21-22). Paul will compensate Philemon for any losses caused by Onesimus, whose name means "Helpful."

Epistles or Treatises

HEBREWS

Hebrews is a sophisticated and elaborate discourse on the continuities and contrasts between the ground of the relationship of God to the historic covenant people, Israel, and that of the new Christian community which has been established through Jesus. The contrasts the author makes are not merely between past and present, but (building on Greek philosophical tradition) between the temporal, repeated and passing features of human history and the eternal, unchanging and final realities disclosed through Christ. This is the import of the contrasts in Hebrews between the one and the many, the shadow and the substance (10.1), the old and the new (8.13), the earthly and the heavenly (9.8-12), the imperfect copy and the eternal ideal (9.23-24). Jesus is described in terms drawn from Jewish wisdom tradition, which was itself influenced by Greek philosophy (compare 11.1 with Wisdom of Solomon 7.26).

Hebrews is a skillful discourse, rather than a letter. Apart from a few personal remarks at the end (13.22-25), the writing consists of alternating theological affirmations about Jesus as the instrument of God's revelation and redemption and exhortations to the community. The latter appear in 2.1-4; 3.7-4.16; 5.11-6.12; 10.19-39; 12.1-29. The rest of the work is divided into five major sections:

(1) 1.1-14 – Jesus as primary agent of God's self-disclosure to humanity and God's rule over the universe. He has already accomplished the purification of his people, and demonstrated his superiority to the angels. (2) 2.5-3.6 – Jesus' cleansing of God's people is superior to the method of purification instituted by Moses. (3) 5.1-10 – Jesus is superior to the High Priest of Israel as the effective representative of God's people. (4) 6.13-10.18 – Jesus is the fulfillment of the covenant promise to Abraham; he transcends the Levitical priestly system and mediates a superior covenant eternally in the heavenly sanctuary. (5) 11.1-40 – Throughout the history of God's dealing with his covenant people, the sole effective ground of relationship has been that of trust in the promise of God. What faith looked for earlier has now been revealed in Jesus, the one who began and who will bring to completion God's purpose for the community of faith (12.2).

Since the references to the Israelite sanctuary and priesthood are based on the Jewish scriptures, one need not assume that the Jerusalem temple was still standing at the time this letter was written. The intellectual level of the writing and the theoretical way in which the contrast with Jesus' sacrifice is developed suggest that the anonymous author was writing in the late first or early second century.

JAMES

After the letter-like opening lines (1.1), this work reads like a moral exhortation on the model of philosophical ethical treatises of the early second century. The major emphases on self-discipline, perseverance and the warnings of judgment for moral behavior conform to the Stoic style of this period. The address to "the twelve tribes of the dispersion" does not signify that the primary readers were Jews, but that the Christians now see themselves as the true heirs of the promises to Israel, and the obligations which that relationship carries.

The issues addressed in the book give a clear picture of the nature of the Christian community involved. Faith is seen as a matter of correct beliefs, rather than as primarily trust in God. The contents of the true doctrine are not indicated, but the author's major concern is for proper behavior on the part of those who belong to this religion, the Greek term for which is used in a positive sense only here in the New Testament (1.26-27). The central issues for James are (1) preferential treatment of the rich (2.14-26), (2) the problem of pride in what some teachers suppose to be wisdom (3.13-18), (3) greed and ambition as sources of conflict within the community (4.1-4), and (4) the divisive effect of the wealth of some of the members (5.1-6). What is called for is an approach to life that includes control of one's tongue (3.1-5), humility, submissiveness, and contrition (4.5-10), the avoidance of boasting (4.13-17). The work ends with an appeal for patience in view of the coming of Christ, which is expected soon (5.7-9). Taking oaths is to be avoided (5.12). Prayers are to be offered for the sick and for erring members of the community (5.12-20), and Elijah is cited as an example of one whose prayers were effective (1 Kings 18.42-45).

Jesus is mentioned only with reference to his formal titles (1.1; 2.1), and the only quotation from his teaching (2.8) is itself a quotation from Leviticus 19.18. There is no mention of Jesus' healing activity, or of his death and resurrection. His coming is expected as judge (5.9), and the basis for judgment will be the degree to which one has obeyed the law (2.8-13). The writing conveys the sense that it originated in a segment of the early church which was more concerned about morals than doctrine, and which saw itself as the true Israel. It is especially appropriate, therefore, to have this book written in the name of the father of the twelve tribes of Israel: James (in Greek, *Iakobos* = Jacob). This was a common name among Jews and early Christians, so the identity of the author cannot be determined, but the strongly Greek orientation of the ethics here set forth seems to rule out either the disciple James or James the brother of Jesus. A late first century date seems likely.

1 PETER

Addressed to the churches in the Roman provinces that stretch across the northern half of Asia Minor and written in a style which in general resembles the later letters attributed to Paul (especially Ephesians), this writing claims to be from Peter. The author alludes to his having seen the sufferings and glory of Jesus (5.1), and includes greetings from those associated with Peter in Acts 12-15: Silvanus and Mark. Yet the fluent style of the Greek and the kinship of its theological outlook with that of Paul suggest that it is not by Peter, but a pseudonymous work from the generation after the apostles. Apart from the introductory greetings (1.1-2) and the concluding remarks (5.12-14) there is no clear structure in the letter, but it revolves around five recurrent themes: (1) What God has done in Christ to constitute his new people (1.3-25; 3.18-22); (2) relationships within the community, which include growth (2.1-2) and acceptance of responsibility in the new structure of God's people (2.4-10; 4.7-11; 5.1-5), the avoidance of a sensual manner of life (4.2-5), and the fulfillment of obligations on the part of wives and husbands (3.1-7). (3) Relationships to the rest of the world involve being morally and legally responsible, even to giving due honor to the emperor (2.16-17), and being prepared to offer a public defense of one's position as a Christian, while carefully avoiding any violation of public law or private conscience (3.15-17). (4) Yet Christians must be prepared to suffer precisely because they are Christians (3.13-14; 4.1, 12-19; 5.6-11). This new factor reflects the changed attitude of the Roman authorities toward Christians, who until the reign of Domitian (81-96) seem to have been tolerated as a sub-group among the Jews, but when the Jewish and Christian movements separated, the Romans began to seek out and punish the Christians for their refusal to offer sacrifices to the emperor as divine.

Other distinctive features of 1 Peter include the claim that Jesus had gone to preach to the spirits of the dead who would not have had an opportunity to hear the gospel (3.18-20) and the belief that baptism not only symbolizes rebirth into God's people but in some way accomplishes salvation (3.19-22). It was in the provinces of Asia Minor in the second century that the issue of Christians' refusal to participate in divine honors to the emperor became a serious matter of public policy, as we know from the letters exchanged between Pliny (the local governor) and the emperor Trajan. 1 Peter was probably written in the name of Peter, who tradition reports was martyred under Nero (before 68) in Rome. That city is probably referred to cryptically as "Babylon" (5.13), the place where historically God's people had been mistreated by a pagan power.

2 PETER

Peter is identified as the writer of this letter in the opening lines (1.1-2), and reference is made to his having seen the transfiguration of Jesus (1.17-18; cf. Mk 9.2-8; Mt 17.1-9; Lk 9.28-36). Two important factors show, however, that Peter did not write this letter: (1) a part of it is directly dependent on the book of Jude (cf. 2.1-8 with Jude 4-16). (2) The writer uses many philosophical abstractions (piety, superior knowledge, virtue; 1.3-4) and describes the Christian life in terms borrowed from Stoic and Neoplatonic philosophy (the string of virtues named in 1.5-7; the reference to becoming partakers of the divine nature, 1.4). Faith is understood to mean correct doctrine, and the goal of the readers is to become established in the truth (1.8-14). The ground of Christian faith is the apostolic witness (1.16-19), although there is a warning against false witnesses and false claims (1.20-2.3). God will reward the faithful and punish the wicked as he did in the days of ancient Israel (2.4-22).

Two distinctive features of this writing (3.1-17) are (1) in contrast to other New Testament writings where there are expectations of the nearness of the end of the present age, the author asserts that no human can predict when Christ will return; and (2) the writer's commendation of the wisdom to be found in the letters of Paul, which he says are to be included with "the other scriptures" (2 Pet 3.15-16). Elsewhere in the New Testament, "scriptures" is used by Christians to refer to the Jewish sacred writings, which Christians came to call the Old Testament. That these writings of Paul should have received such authoritative status as scripture is a further indication of the late date of this writing, probably in the early decades of the second century. The author and place of origin are unknown, but clearly it is from a segment of the church where the traditional authority of Peter was highly regarded.

1 JOHN

This anonymous message of instruction and exhortation has none of the typical features of a letter, but its portrayal of Jesus as the Word of God in human form and the emphasis on love of one another within the community echo the Gospel of John. The opening section (1.1-2.17) recalls the human sphere in which Jesus lived and was observed by his followers, but by its light/dark imagery, it warns the readers that error is encroaching on the community which he established. His present role of advocate in behalf of his people matches the redemptive role which led to his death for the benefit of the world into which he came. His commandment to love and the other responsibilities of the people of God stand in contrast to the love of the present world-order which is evident among some professed members. The anti-Christ figure is represented by the false teachers who deny that Jesus is in truth the Christ (2.18-26). The result of this conflict is that there are two types of Christians within the community: those who obey God's commandments, and those who do the will of the Devil. The issue is, Which spirit will be followed? The children of God will follow his Spirit; the children of the devil will obey his spirit (4.1-6). God's true people accept the gifts of God: his Son, the Spirit, the love which he pours out (4.7-5.18). In turn they are assured and confident in the day of judgment about the power of love which enables them to obey God, about eternal life, about God's answer to their prayers, and of his preservation of them from sin. Though all the human structure of society is under the power of the evil one, they may be confident in the relationship with God that Christ has opened for them (5.19-20). The writing ends with a warning against idolatry.

Although there are no indications of place or specific time of writing, 1 John reflects a change from the Gospel of John in that the community has been penetrated by those who deny the full humanity of Jesus and who do not consider his death as expiation for human sins. A likely date for this document is the first quarter of the second century when Christians were exposed to – and some accepted – the dualistic philosophy which regarded the material world as basically evil. Some of its adherents thought they should show their liberation from the material world by living amorally. The existence of such a movement can be documented in the second-century writings discovered in Egypt earlier in this century which claim superior knowledge: Gnosis. 1 John may come from a situation in which the Gnostic movement was taking shape.

2 and 3 JOHN

The formal openings and the concluding greetings, as well as the contents, show that these are authentic letters. The author, who identifies himself simply as "the elder" (*presbyteros*), writes that he wants to visit the community to whom his letters are addressed. In 2 John, the central issue is the denial that Jesus came in fully human form (2 Jn 7; see Introduction to 1 John). To reject the doctrine of Jesus as God's Word become flesh (cf. John 1.14) is to disqualify oneself from participation in the community of faith. The "elect lady" to whom the letter is written refers to the community: "lady" (*kyria*) is a pun on Lord (*kyrios*), whose people constitute the community addressed.

In 3 John, the elder commends the hospitality and support that members have provided for travelling Christians who have visited them. He condemns Diotrophes, who has refused to accept the authority of the elder. This factor shows that the Johannine community has shifted from the earlier state of full mutuality among the members (as is evident in John 13) to a hierarchical structure in which the decisions of certain officials are to be obeyed. The elder is now a figure of authority in the region on matters of doctrine and correct behavior of the members, not merely a local leader. Like 1 and 2 John, this writing probably comes from the early second century.

JUDE

The writer of this brief work is identified as Jude (Judah), the brother of James (Jacob). In Mk 6.3 and Mt 13.55 these two are listed as the brothers of Jesus. The style and content of the letter and the conditions within Christianity that are depicted come from a much later stage in the life of the church than that of the first generation of Jesus' followers. Faith is now seen as a fixed body of truth delivered to Christians and is to be preserved at all costs (3). Irreligious persons have infiltrated the community and are corrupting it through moral misdeeds and theological untruths (4). The letter offers assurance that God will judge these unworthy people just as he did in the time of Lot and of Moses, and as he banished from heaven the disobedient angels (5-7, 11). In a series of vivid, mixed images the writer depicts the waywardness, the fruitlessness and the impending doom of these moral and theological deviants (12-13). Their downfall was predicted by Enoch (14-17), and their perversions were foreseen by the apostles (17-19). The true believers are encouraged to build themselves up in the faith, to remain in the love of God, and to wait for Christ's coming in triumph. A liturgical blessing brings the work to a close. Noteworthy is the fact that there are here references to two documents from Jewish apocalyptic literature: the Assumption of Moses (9) and the Apocalypse of Enoch (1 Enoch 1.9); these quotations show that some Christians were supporting their convictions by appeal to writings which did not find their way into the Jewish or Christian canons of scripture. Jude was used as a basic source by the author of 2 Peter (see above).

Apocalypse

REVELATION

The Revelation claims to have been written by John in exile on the island of Patmos in the Aegean Sea. The revelation (in Greek, *apokalypsis*) which he receives is about Jesus Christ and is transmitted through him (1.1-3). The work as a whole is the only complete apocalypse in the New Testament. It is to be read, heeded and kept – that is, its warnings and counsel are to be observed. Though addressed to the seven churches of Asia Minor, where the issue of Christian refusal to take part in the imperial Roman cult is first clearly documented, its message of what God is about to do to achieve his purpose is relevant for all the churches in the whole of the Roman world (1.4-20). Each church (2.1-3.19) is given a variant of the themes of commendation for faithfulness, of warning about expelling the false teachers and those who misbehave, with a promise of ultimate vindication by God. The churches of Sardis and Laodicea are rebuked for their lack of commitment, while Philadelphia is praised for its fidelity. An essential clue to the circumstances for writing Revelation is given in 2.13, where there is a cryptic reference to the center of the imperial cult, which was in fact located in Pergamum. All persons subject to Rome were required by the end of the first century to offer prayers or sacrifice in the name of the emperor, who was to be regarded as divine. Christians refused to comply; the penalty was death.

4.1-16.21 gives a series of interlocking visions of the process by which God accomplishes his purpose in defeating the powers of evil and establishing his universal rule over the creation. The divine throne is depicted (4.2-11) and the scroll on which is written the divine plan is unrolled, prior to fulfillment. The seven seals on the scroll (6.1-8.5) and the seven trumpets (8.6-11.15) represent the judgment of God on rebellious humanity, and especially on the human political power which stands opposed to God's purpose and threatens his people. The defeat of the evil powers is accomplished by a mixture of human and angelic forces (15.1-16.17). The seventh bowl of divine wrath is poured out on imperial Rome, "the great city," whose destruction is pictured in the next major section (17.1-18.24). The harlot and the beast are images of the idolatrous imperial cult, which is promoted as a means of retaining political power and social control. Babylon is the symbolic name of the proud city that seeks to thwart God's purpose for his people (18.1), but it is destroyed in a great and tragic cataclysm. In sharp contrast there appears the City of God, which symbolizes the structure of human society that fulfills God's intention for the human race (19.1-22.5). The evil powers are overcome, symbolized by the beast, the dragon and Satan. The ensuing triumph of God is accompanied by the renewal of heaven and earth and by the appearance on earth of the New Jerusalem, where God is directly present and accessible to his people (21.1-27). The public sign of this consummation of God's purpose will be the coming of Christ (22.6-21). Hence the repeated prayer, "Come!"

There is no way of determining which of the many early Christians who bore the name of John produced this dramatic work. The differences between Revelation and the other writings attributed to John (the gospel and the three letters) in matters of literary style and imagery are so great as to preclude their having been produced by the same author. Here the emphasis is on judgment, social and political conflict, and the return of Christ as a signal of universal renewal. Probably Revelation was written after the beginnings of persecution of Christians by the Roman state – perhaps as early as the time of Domitian (81-96), or more likely during the reign of Trajan (98-117), who formulated the policy requiring universal participation in the cult of the emperor.

NRSV

THE HEBREW SCRIPTURES
COMMONLY CALLED
THE OLD TESTAMENT

New Revised Standard Version

ALPHABETICAL LIST OF BOOKS OF THE OLD TESTAMENT

GENESIS

See the Introductions, pp. 2, 30, and 32-33 above.

Six Days of Creation and the Sabbath

1 In the beginning when God created[a]
the heavens and the earth, 2 the earth
was a formless void and darkness covered
the face of the deep, while a wind from God[b]
swept over the face of the waters. 3 Then
God said, "Let there be light"; and there was
light. 4 And God saw that the light was
good; and God separated the light from the
darkness. 5 God called the light Day, and the
darkness he called Night. And there was
evening and there was morning, the first
day.
6 And God said, "Let there be a dome in
the midst of the waters, and let it separate
the waters from the waters." 7 So God made
the dome and separated the waters that
were under the dome from the waters that
were above the dome. And it was so. 8 God
called the dome Sky. And there was evening
and there was morning, the second day.
9 And God said, "Let the waters under
the sky be gathered together into one place,
and let the dry land appear." And it was so.
10 God called the dry land Earth, and the
waters that were gathered together he called
Seas. And God saw that it was good. 11 Then
God said, "Let the earth put forth vegetation: plants yielding seed, and fruit trees of
every kind on earth that bear fruit with the
seed in it." And it was so. 12 The earth
brought forth vegetation: plants yielding
seed of every kind, and trees of every kind
bearing fruit with the seed in it. And God
saw that it was good. 13 And there was
evening and there was morning, the third
day.
14 And God said, "Let there be lights in
the dome of the sky to separate the day
from the night; and let them be for signs
and for seasons and for days and years,
15 and let them be lights in the dome of the
sky to give light upon the earth." And it
was so. 16 God made the two great lights—
the greater light to rule the day and the
lesser light to rule the night—and the stars.
17 God set them in the dome of the sky to
give light upon the earth, 18 to rule over the
day and over the night, and to separate the
light from the darkness. And God saw that
it was good. 19 And there was evening and
there was morning, the fourth day.
20 And God said, "Let the waters bring
forth swarms of living creatures, and let
birds fly above the earth across the dome of
the sky." 21 So God created the great sea
monsters and every living creature that
moves, of every kind, with which the waters swarm, and every winged bird of every
kind. And God saw that it was good. 22 God
blessed them, saying, "Be fruitful and multiply and fill the waters in the seas, and let
birds multiply on the earth." 23 And there
was evening and there was morning, the
fifth day.
24 And God said, "Let the earth bring
forth living creatures of every kind: cattle
and creeping things and wild animals of the
earth of every kind." And it was so. 25 God
made the wild animals of the earth of every
kind, and the cattle of every kind, and
everything that creeps upon the ground of
every kind. And God saw that it was
good.
26 Then God said, "Let us make humankind[c] in our image, according to our likeness; and let them have dominion over the
fish of the sea, and over the birds of the air,
and over the cattle, and over all the wild
animals of the earth,[d] and over every creeping thing that creeps upon the earth."
27 So God created humankind[d] in his image,
in the image of God he created them;[e]
male and female he created them.
28 God blessed them, and God said to them,
"Be fruitful and multiply, and fill the earth
and subdue it; and have dominion over the
fish of the sea and over the birds of the air
and over every living thing that moves
upon the earth." 29 God said, "See, I have
given you every plant yielding seed that is
upon the face of all the earth, and every
tree with seed in its fruit; you shall have
them for food. 30 And to every beast of the
earth, and to every bird of the air, and to
everything that creeps on the earth, everything that has the breath of life, I have
given every green plant for food." And it
was so. 31 God saw everything that he had
made, and indeed, it was very good. And
there was evening and there was morning,
the sixth day.

[a] Or *when God began to create* or *In the beginning God created* [b] Or *while the spirit of God* or *while a mighty wind* [c] Heb *adam* [d] Syr: Heb *and over all the earth* [e] Heb *him*

1.1-2.4a The Priestly Account of the Creation. The emphasis falls on the sovereignty of God and the orderliness of the process of creation. Throughout this section, God is given the name *elohim* in the Hebrew original.
1.2 *The earth was a formless void.* God forms and orders the world out of existing, chaotic matter. *The deep...the waters.* In the mythology of Canaan and Mesopotamia the waters were the symbols of chaos which the more powerful beneficent deities had to bring under control.
1.3 *God said.* The power of God to achieve his purpose is evident when he speaks his intention and it is accomplished.
1.4 *God separated the light from the darkness.* The ordering of light and darkness establishes the rhythm of time, with evening followed by morning, which is the principle of Israelite days beginning at sundown.
1.6-10 *God...separated the waters...the waters that were gathered together.* God's ordering of the world results in the separation of sky and earth, of sea and dry land.
1.14-19 The ordering of day and night is accomplished by the positioning of the sun, moon and stars.
1.26-28 *Let us make humankind in our image.* The Hebrew word for man is *adam*, which serves as the name of the first human being in these creation stories. Essential to the role of humans created in God's image is their exercise of authority over the earth and all living things upon it.

1.1 Jn 1.1,2; Ps 8.3; Isa 44.24; 42.5; 45.18
1.2 Jer 4.23; Ps 104.30
1.3 Ps 33.6,9; 2 Cor 4.6
1.4 Isa 45.7
1.5 Ps 74.16
1.6 Jer 10.12
1.7 Prov 8.28; Ps 148.4
1.9 Job 26.10; Prov 8.29; Jer 5.22; 2 Pet 3.5
1.10 Ps 33.7
1.11 Lk 6.44
1.14 Ps 74.16; 104.19
1.16 Ps 136.8,9; Job 38.7
1.18 Jer 31.35
1.21 Ps 104.25,26
1.22 Gen 8.17
1.25 Jer 27.5
1.26 Ps 100.3; Acts 17.26; Col 3.10
1.27 1 Cor 11.7; Gen 5.2; Mt 19.4
1.28 Gen 9.1,7; Lev 26.9
1.29 Ps 104.14,15; 136.25
1.30 Ps 145.15; Job 38.41
1.31 Ps 104.24

2 Thus the heavens and the earth were
finished, and all their multitude. 2 And
on the seventh day God finished the work
that he had done, and he rested on the
seventh day from all the work that he had
done. 3 So God blessed the seventh day and
hallowed it, because on it God rested from
all the work that he had done in creation.
4 These are the generations of the heavens and the earth when they were created.

Another Account of the Creation

In the day that the LORD God made the
earth and the heavens, 5 when no plant of
the field was yet in the earth and no herb
of the field had yet sprung up—for the LORD
God had not caused it to rain upon the
earth, and there was no one to till the
ground; 6 but a stream would rise from the
earth, and water the whole face of the
ground— 7 then the LORD God formed man
from the dust of the ground,[f] and breathed
into his nostrils the breath of life; and the
man became a living being. 8 And the LORD
God planted a garden in Eden, in the east;
and there he put the man whom he had
formed. 9 Out of the ground the LORD God
made to grow every tree that is pleasant to
the sight and good for food, the tree of life
also in the midst of the garden, and the tree
of the knowledge of good and evil.
10 A river flows out of Eden to water the
garden, and from there it divides and becomes four branches. 11 The name of the
first is Pishon; it is the one that flows
around the whole land of Havilah, where
there is gold; 12 and the gold of that land is
good; bdellium and onyx stone are there.
13 The name of the second river is Gihon; it
is the one that flows around the whole land
of Cush. 14 The name of the third river is
Tigris, which flows east of Assyria. And the
fourth river is the Euphrates.
15 The LORD God took the man and put
him in the garden of Eden to till it and keep
it. 16 And the LORD God commanded the
man, "You may freely eat of every tree of
the garden; 17 but of the tree of the knowledge of good and evil you shall not eat, for
in the day that you eat of it you shall die."
18 Then the LORD God said, "It is not
good that the man should be alone; I will
make him a helper as his partner." 19 So out
of the ground the LORD God formed every
animal of the field and every bird of the air,
and brought them to the man to see what
he would call them; and whatever the man
called every living creature, that was its
name. 20 The man gave names to all cattle,
and to the birds of the air, and to every
animal of the field; but for the man[g] there
was not found a helper as his partner. 21 So
the LORD God caused a deep sleep to fall
upon the man, and he slept; then he took
one of his ribs and closed up its place with
flesh. 22 And the rib that the LORD God had
taken from the man he made into a woman
and brought her to the man. 23 Then the
man said,
"This at last is bone of my bones
and flesh of my flesh;
this one shall be called Woman,[h]
for out of Man[i] this one was taken."
24 Therefore a man leaves his father and his
mother and clings to his wife, and they
become one flesh. 25 And the man and his
wife were both naked, and were not
ashamed.

The First Sin and Its Punishment

3 Now the serpent was more crafty than
any other wild animal that the LORD
God had made. He said to the woman, "Did
God say, 'You shall not eat from any tree
in the garden'?" 2 The woman said to the
serpent, "We may eat of the fruit of the
trees in the garden; 3 but God said, 'You
shall not eat of the fruit of the tree that is
in the middle of the garden, nor shall you
touch it, or you shall die.' " 4 But the serpent
said to the woman, "You will not die; 5 for
God knows that when you eat of it your
eyes will be opened, and you will be like
God,[j] knowing good and evil." 6 So when the
woman saw that the tree was good for food,
and that it was a delight to the eyes, and
that the tree was to be desired to make one
wise, she took of its fruit and ate; and she
also gave some to her husband, who was
with her, and he ate. 7 Then the eyes of both
were opened, and they knew that they were
naked; and they sewed fig leaves together
and made loincloths for themselves.
8 They heard the sound of the LORD God
walking in the garden at the time of the
evening breeze, and the man and his wife
hid themselves from the presence of the
LORD God among the trees of the garden.
9 But the Lord God called to the man, and

[f] Or *formed a man* (Heb *adam*) *of dust from the ground* (Heb *adamah*) [g] Or *for Adam* [h] Heb *ishshah* [i] Heb *ish* [j] Or *gods*

2.3 *God blessed the seventh day and hallowed it.* God's rest is the model for the priestly rule that all humanity shall rest on the seventh day (Ex 31.12-17).
2.4a *generations.* A term often used of successive human generations here implies God's plan and ordering of creation.
2.4b-3.24 The Earlier Tradition about Creation. As in the priestly tradition, the earth exists but is now shaped and ordered by Yahweh. Humans are created as males first, then plants and animals, and finally a woman.
2.4b *the LORD God.* The Hebrew text combines with the more general name of God used by Semitic people throughout the Middle East and preferred by the northern tribes of Israel, *elohim*, the special name of God preferred among the southern tribes of Judah: *Yahweh*, which means, "He who causes to be [all that is]."
2.5-6 As is still the case in much of the Middle East today, the fertility of the earth was made possible by water from streams rather than by falling rain.
2.8 *a garden in Eden. Eden* in Hebrew means luxury or pleasure. Variants of the Eden story appear in the prophets: in Ezek 28.11-19, Eden is the garden or mountain dwelling of God; in Isa 51.3, Ezek 36.35 and Joel 2.3 it is the symbol of the renewal of the land for God's people.
2.10-14 *A river flows out of Eden and becomes four branches.* A geographical parenthesis in the Eden story. Except for the Tigris and Euphrates in what is now Iraq, these rivers cannot be identified. Pishon may be the Persian Gulf, and Gihon is probably an unknown stream in lower Mesopotamia, unless Cush is Ethiopia here, in which case the river is the Nile. Havilah may be northeastern Arabia, as in Gen 25.18. The prominence of places in Mesopotamia suggests that the Eden story may have originated there, in the ancestral land of Abraham (Gen 11.31).
2.9 *the tree of life...the tree of knowledge.* These are symbols of the means by which human life is sustained and human understanding is attained. The Semitic terms for knowledge mean not merely information but participation. Hence the prohibition of eating the fruit of the tree of knowledge in 2.17, since those who eat may perform evil as well as good deeds.
2.19-20 *out of the ground.* The Hebrew word for ground, *adamah*, sounds like the word for and name of the first human, Adam. For a human to give names to the animals is an indication of human control of, and responsibility for, other forms of life in the created order.
2.21-24 *flesh.* Flesh means the softer parts of the human body and the sexual organs, but it also represents the weaker and more vulnerable dimensions of human existence.
3.1 *the serpent.* In Semitic mythology, the serpent is pictured as a creature from the sea that opposes the purposes of the good deity. A variant of that is found here, where the sly aim of the serpent is to estrange humans from the creator by urging them to exploit and pervert the special role they have in the purpose of God.
3.5-7 The serpent promises, *You will be like God,* but what results from the eating of the fruit of knowledge is that man and woman are aware of sexual urges and inherent limitations.
3.9-13 The negative effect of partaking of the fruit of knowledge is evident in the human effort to shift blame for disobedience to the serpent and to God.

2.1 Ps 33.6
2.2 Ex 20.11; Heb 4.4
2.3 Isa 58.13
2.5 Gen 1.12; Job 38.26-28
2.7 Gen 3.19; Ps 103.14; Job 33.4; Acts 17.25; 1 Cor 15.45
2.8 Isa 51.3; Gen 3.24; 4.16
2.9 Ezek 31.8; Gen 3.22; Rev 2.7; 22.2,14
2.12 Num 11.7
2.14 Dan 10.4
2.17 Deut 30.15,19,20; Rom 6.23; Jas 1.15
2.18 1 Cor 11.9
2.19 Gen 1.20,24; Ps 8.6
2.21 1 Sam 26.12
2.23 Eph 5.30; 1 Cor 11.8
2.24 Mt 19.5; Mk 10.7,8; 1 Cor 6.16; Eph 5.31
2.25 Gen 3.7,10,11
3.1 2 Cor 11.3; Rev 12.9; 20.2
3.3 2 Cor 11.3
3.4 Jn 8.44
3.6 1 Tim 2.14
3.8 Job 31.33; Jer 23.24

said to him, "Where are you?" [10]He said, "I heard the sound of you in the garden, and I was afraid, because I was naked; and I hid myself." [11]He said, "Who told you that you were naked? Have you eaten from the tree of which I commanded you not to eat?" [12]The man said, "The woman whom you gave to be with me, she gave me fruit from the tree, and I ate." [13]Then the LORD God said to the woman, "What is this that you have done?" The woman said, "The serpent tricked me, and I ate." [14]The LORD God said to the serpent,

"Because you have done this,
cursed are you among all animals
and among all wild creatures;
upon your belly you shall go,
and dust you shall eat
all the days of your life.
[15] I will put enmity between you and the woman,
and between your offspring and hers;
he will strike your head,
and you will strike his heel."
[16] To the woman he said,
"I will greatly increase your pangs in childbearing;
in pain you shall bring forth children,
yet your desire shall be for your husband,
and he shall rule over you."
[17]And to the man[k] he said,
"Because you have listened to the voice of your wife,
and have eaten of the tree
about which I commanded you,
'You shall not eat of it,'
cursed is the ground because of you;
in toil you shall eat of it all the days of your life;
[18] thorns and thistles it shall bring forth for you;
and you shall eat the plants of the field.
[19] By the sweat of your face
you shall eat bread
until you return to the ground,
for out of it you were taken;
you are dust,
and to dust you shall return."

20 The man named his wife Eve,[l] because she was the mother of all living. [21]And the LORD God made garments of skins for the man[m] and for his wife, and clothed them.

22 Then the LORD God said, "See, the man has become like one of us, knowing good and evil; and now, he might reach out his hand and take also from the tree of life, and eat, and live forever"— [23]therefore the LORD God sent him forth from the garden of Eden, to till the ground from which he was taken. [24]He drove out the man; and at the east of the garden of Eden he placed the cherubim, and a sword flaming and turning to guard the way to the tree of life.

Cain Murders Abel

4 Now the man knew his wife Eve, and she conceived and bore Cain, saying, "I have produced[n] a man with the help of the LORD." [2]Next she bore his brother Abel. Now Abel was a keeper of sheep, and Cain a tiller of the ground. [3]In the course of time Cain brought to the LORD an offering of the fruit of the ground, [4]and Abel for his part brought of the firstlings of his flock, their fat portions. And the LORD had regard for Abel and his offering, [5]but for Cain and his offering he had no regard. So Cain was very angry, and his countenance fell. [6]The LORD said to Cain, "Why are you angry, and why has your countenance fallen? [7]If you do well, will you not be accepted? And if you do not do well, sin is lurking at the door; its desire is for you, but you must master it."

8 Cain said to his brother Abel, "Let us go out to the field."[o] And when they were in the field, Cain rose up against his brother Abel, and killed him. [9]Then the LORD said to Cain, "Where is your brother Abel?" He said, "I do not know; am I my brother's keeper?" [10]And the LORD said, "What have you done? Listen; your brother's blood is crying out to me from the ground! [11]And now you are cursed from the ground, which has opened its mouth to receive your brother's blood from your hand. [12]When you till the ground, it will no longer yield to you its strength; you will be a fugitive and a wanderer on the earth." [13]Cain said to the LORD, "My punishment is greater than I can bear! [14]Today you have driven me away from the soil, and I shall be hidden from your face; I shall be a fugitive and a wanderer on the earth, and anyone who meets me may kill me." [15]Then the LORD said to

[k] Or *to Adam* [l] In Heb *Eve* resembles the word for *living* [m] Or *for Adam* [n] The verb in Heb resembles the word for *Cain* [o] Sam Gk Syr Compare Vg: MT lacks *Let us go out to the field*

3.10 1 Jn 3.20
3.12 Prov 28.13
3.13 2 Cor 11.3; 1 Tim 2.14
3.14 Isa 65.25; Mic 7.17
3.15 Jn 8.44; Acts 13.10; 1 Jn 3.8; Isa 7.14; Mt 1.23; Rom 16.20; Rev 12.7
3.16 Isa 13.8; Gen 4.7; 1 Cor 11.3; Eph 5.22
3.17 1 Sam 15.23; Gen 2.17; Rom 8.20-22
3.18 Ps 104.14
3.19 Gen 2.7; Ps 90.3; 104.29; Eccl 12.7
3.22 Rev 22.2
3.23 Gen 4.2
3.24 Gen 2.8,9
4.2 Lk 11.50,51
4.3 Num 18.12
4.4 Num 18.17; Lev 3.16; Heb 11.4
4.5 Isa 3.9; Jude 11
4.8 Mt 23.35; 1 Jn 3.12
4.10 Heb 12.24; Rev 6.10
4.12 ver 14
4.14 Ps 51.11; Gen 9.6; Num 35.19, 21,27
4.15 Ps 79.12; Ezek 9.4,6

3.14-19 In a series of poetic pronouncements God brings judgments which explain unhappy aspects of human existence: the hostility between humans and snakes; the pains of women in childbirth and the subservience of women to men; the necessity for men to toil in order to produce crops and to face inevitable death.
3.21 *the LORD God made garments of skins.* Even in their disobedient condition, God provides the basic needs for the chief of his creatures.
3.22-23 *tree of life.* Having disobeyed God and thereby ruined the peaceful conditions of original creation, humans are delivered from an endless existence in sorrow and suffering by being denied access to the fruits of this tree.
4.1-26 Cain as Symbol of Human Alienation from God.
4.1 *Cain.* The name is a pun on the word for "I have given birth."
4.2 *Abel.* The name means "breath, vapor," symbolizing the brevity and frailty of human existence.
4.3 *Cain brought to the LORD an offering.* This is the first instance of an offering being presented to God, and is depicted as a means of approaching the deity in order to gain acceptance. *the firstlings of the flock... fat portions.* Details of the appropriate offerings to God are given in Lev 1.8-9.24. The sanctity of the firstborn of any species is set forth in Ex 13.2,12, 15, including firstborn sons (Ex 22.29). Also in Lev 27.26; Num 3.12.
4.10 *your brother's blood is crying out to me.* The life of animals and humans is understood to be located in the blood (Lev 17.11, 14).
4.14 Having murdered his brother out of envy, Cain is the symbol of human alienation and fear-ridden mobility.
4.15 *the LORD put a mark on Cain.* This special sign of Cain and his posterity is an indication of tribal blood vengeance common among primitive people; the penalty for killing anyone in Cain's tribe is especially severe.

4.17-25 The progeny of Cain indicate by name and role the complexity of civilization. *Enoch* (17) is probably from the Hebrew word meaning "dedicated"; he had a special relationship of closeness with God, as Gen 5.24 indicates. *Tubal-cain* means "metal-worker"; *Jabal* is "leader" of flocks; *Jubal* means "trumpet," and he is the prototype of musicians. Two of the names include as a final syllable a reference to God = el: Mehujael, Methusael.
4.24 *seven...seventy-sevenfold.* As this poetic warning declares, the vengeance promised to Cain against any who attacked him (4.15) is now greatly multiplied.
4.26 *Enosh.* Adam's grandson is fittingly called "human being." *To invoke the name of the* LORD. Even though the special name of God, *Yahweh*, is said to have been revealed much later to Israel through Moses (Ex 3.14), the Yahwist editor of this tradition reports it as in use very early.
5.1-32 This ten-stage genealogy, which extends the list from Adam to Noah and includes the number of years each one lived, probably derives from the priestly editors for whom the continuity of family line was of major importance. The gradual decrease in length of human life may be the priestly equivalent of the fall of humanity and the imposition of death as a punishment for sin in the J tradition of human origins and early existence.
5.24 Unlike the other descendants of Adam who die after lives of many centuries in length, Enoch, who has *walked with God*, leaves the earth because *God took him.* Enoch is linked in the biblical tradition with others like Moses and Elijah who were believed to have been taken up to God when their earthly lives ended (Deut 34.6; 2 Kings 2.11; Heb 11.5).
5.29 *Noah.* The name derives from the Hebrew word for "comfort" or "consolation," which in this context refers to the deliverance from extinction of a group of human beings as well as the partial relief that Noah brings for working the soil after God cursed it (Gen 3.17-19).

him, "Not so![p] Whoever kills Cain will suffer
a sevenfold vengeance." And the LORD put
a mark on Cain, so that no one who came
upon him would kill him. [16]Then Cain went
away from the presence of the LORD, and
settled in the land of Nod,[q] east of Eden.

Beginnings of Civilization

17 Cain knew his wife, and she conceived and bore Enoch; and he built a city,
and named it Enoch after his son Enoch.
[18]To Enoch was born Irad; and Irad was the
father of Mehujael, and Mehujael the father
of Methushael, and Methushael the father
of Lamech. [19]Lamech took two wives; the
name of the one was Adah, and the name
of the other Zillah. [20]Adah bore Jabal; he
was the ancestor of those who live in tents
and have livestock. [21]His brother's name
was Jubal; he was the ancestor of all those
who play the lyre and pipe. [22]Zillah bore
Tubal-cain, who made all kinds of bronze
and iron tools. The sister of Tubal-cain was
Naamah.

23 Lamech said to his wives:
"Adah and Zillah, hear my voice;
you wives of Lamech, listen to what I
say:
I have killed a man for wounding me,
a young man for striking me.
24 If Cain is avenged sevenfold,
truly Lamech seventy-sevenfold."

25 Adam knew his wife again, and she
bore a son and named him Seth, for she
said, "God has appointed[r] for me another
child instead of Abel, because Cain killed
him." [26]To Seth also a son was born, and
he named him Enosh. At that time people
began to invoke the name of the LORD.

Adam's Descendants to Noah and His Sons

5 This is the list of the descendants of
Adam. When God created humankind,[s]
he made them[t] in the likeness of God. [2]Male
and female he created them, and he blessed
them and named them "Humankind"[s] when
they were created.

3 When Adam had lived one hundred
thirty years, he became the father of a son
in his likeness, according to his image, and
named him Seth. [4]The days of Adam after
he became the father of Seth were eight
hundred years; and he had other sons and
daughters. [5]Thus all the days that Adam
lived were nine hundred thirty years; and
he died.

6 When Seth had lived one hundred five
years, he became the father of Enosh. [7]Seth
lived after the birth of Enosh eight hundred
seven years, and had other sons and daughters. [8]Thus all the days of Seth were nine
hundred twelve years; and he died.

9 When Enosh had lived ninety years, he
became the father of Kenan. [10]Enosh lived
after the birth of Kenan eight hundred fifteen
years, and had other sons and daughters.
[11]Thus all the days of Enosh were nine
hundred five years; and he died.

12 When Kenan had lived seventy years,
he became the father of Mahalalel. [13]Kenan
lived after the birth of Mahalalel eight
hundred and forty years, and had other
sons and daughters. [14]Thus all the days of
Kenan were nine hundred and ten years;
and he died.

15 When Mahalalel had lived sixty-five
years, he became the father of Jared.
[16]Mahalalel lived after the birth of Jared
eight hundred thirty years, and had other
sons and daughters. [17]Thus all the days of
Mahalalel were eight hundred ninety-five
years; and he died.

18 When Jared had lived one hundred
sixty-two years he became the father of
Enoch. [19]Jared lived after the birth of Enoch
eight hundred years, and had other sons
and daughters. [20]Thus all the days of Jared
were nine hundred sixty-two years; and he
died.

21 When Enoch had lived sixty-five years,
he became the father of Methuselah. [22]Enoch
walked with God after the birth of
Methuselah three hundred years, and had
other sons and daughters. [23]Thus all the
days of Enoch were three hundred sixty-five
years. [24]Enoch walked with God; then he
was no more, because God took him.

25 When Methuselah had lived one
hundred eighty-seven years, he became the
father of Lamech. [26]Methuselah lived after
the birth of Lamech seven hundred eighty-
two years, and had other sons and daughters. [27]Thus all the days of Methuselah were
nine hundred sixty-nine years; and he died.

28 When Lamech had lived one hundred
eighty-two years, he became the father of a
son; [29]he named him Noah, saying, "Out of
the ground that the LORD has cursed this

[p] Gk Syr Vg: Heb *Therefore* [q] That is *Wandering* [r] The verb in Heb resembles the word for *Seth* [s] Heb *adam* [t] Heb *him*

4.17 Ps 49.11
4.18 Gen 5.25,28,30
4.23 Ex 20.13; Lev 19.18; Deut 32.35; Lk 3.36; ver 18
4.24 ver 15
4.25 Gen 5.3; 4.8
4.26 1 Kings 18.24; Ps 116.17; Joel 2.32; Zeph 3.9; 1 Cor 1.2
5.1 Gen 1.26; Eph 4.24; Col 3.10
5.2 Gen 1.27
5.3 Gen 4.25
5.5 Gen 3.19; Heb 9.27
5.6 Gen 4.26
5.7 Lk 3.38
5.11 1 Chr 1.1
5.12 1 Chr 1.2
5.15 1 Chr 1.2
5.18 Jude 14,15
5.21 1 Chr 1.3; Lk 3.37; Jude 14
5.24 2 Kings 2.11; Heb 11.5
5.26 Lk 3.36
5.29 Gen 3.17-19

5.32 Gen 6.10; 10.21
6.1 Gen 1.28
6.2 Deut 7.1-4
6.3 1 Pet 3.19; Ps 78.39
6.5 Gen 8.21
6.6 1 Sam 15.11,29; 2 Sam 24.16; Mal 3.6; Jas 1.17; Isa 63.10
6.8 Gen 19.19; Ex 33.12; Lk 1.30; Acts 7.46
6.9 Gen 7.1; Ezek 14.14,20; Heb 11.7; 2 Pet 2.5; Gen 5.22
6.10 Gen 5.32
6.12 Ps 14.1-3
6.13 Ezek 7.2,3; ver 17
6.14 Heb 11.7; 1 Pet 3.20
6.17 Gen 7.4,21-23
6.18 Gen 7.1,7,13; 1 Pet 3.20; 2 Pet 2.5
6.19 Gen 7.8,9,15,16
6.20 Gen 7.9,15
6.22 Heb 11.7; Gen 7.5
7.1 Mt 24.38; Lk 17.26
7.2 Lev 11; 10.10; Ezek 44.23
7.7 Gen 6.22; ver 1

one shall bring us relief from our work and from the toil of our hands." [30]Lamech lived after the birth of Noah five hundred ninety-five years, and had other sons and daughters. [31]Thus all the days of Lamech were seven hundred seventy-seven years; and he died.[t]

32 After Noah was five hundred years old, Noah became the father of Shem, Ham, and Japheth.

The Wickedness of Humankind

6 When people began to multiply on the face of the ground, and daughters were born to them, [2]the sons of God saw that they were fair; and they took wives for themselves of all that they chose. [3]Then the LORD said, "My spirit shall not abide[u] in mortals forever, for they are flesh; their days shall be one hundred twenty years." [4]The Nephilim were on the earth in those days—and also afterward—when the sons of God went in to the daughters of humans, who bore children to them. These were the heroes that were of old, warriors of renown.

5 The LORD saw that the wickedness of humankind was great in the earth, and that every inclination of the thoughts of their hearts was only evil continually. [6]And the LORD was sorry that he had made humankind on the earth, and it grieved him to his heart. [7]So the LORD said, "I will blot out from the earth the human beings I have created—people together with animals and creeping things and birds of the air, for I am sorry that I have made them." [8]But Noah found favor in the sight of the LORD.

Noah Pleases God

9 These are the descendants of Noah. Noah was a righteous man, blameless in his generation; Noah walked with God. [10]And Noah had three sons, Shem, Ham, and Japheth.

11 Now the earth was corrupt in God's sight, and the earth was filled with violence. [12]And God saw that the earth was corrupt; for all flesh had corrupted its ways upon the earth. [13]And God said to Noah, "I have determined to make an end of all flesh, for the earth is filled with violence because of them; now I am going to destroy them along with the earth. [14]Make yourself an ark of cypress[u] wood; make rooms in the ark, and cover it inside and out with pitch. [15]This is how you are to make it: the length of the ark three hundred cubits, its width fifty cubits, and its height thirty cubits. [16]Make a roof[v] for the ark, and finish it to a cubit above; and put the door of the ark in its side; make it with lower, second, and third decks. [17]For my part, I am going to bring a flood of waters on the earth, to destroy from under heaven all flesh in which is the breath of life; everything that is on the earth shall die. [18]But I will establish my covenant with you; and you shall come into the ark, you, your sons, your wife, and your sons' wives with you. [19]And of every living thing, of all flesh, you shall bring two of every kind into the ark, to keep them alive with you; they shall be male and female. [20]Of the birds according to their kinds, and of the animals according to their kinds, of every creeping thing of the ground according to its kind, two of every kind shall come in to you, to keep them alive. [21]Also take with you every kind of food that is eaten, and store it up; and it shall serve as food for you and for them." [22]Noah did this; he did all that God commanded him.

The Great Flood

7 Then the LORD said to Noah, "Go into the ark, you and all your household, for I have seen that you alone are righteous before me in this generation. [2]Take with you seven pairs of all clean animals, the male and its mate; and a pair of the animals that are not clean, the male and its mate; [3]and seven pairs of the birds of the air also, male and female, to keep their kind alive on the face of all the earth. [4]For in seven days I will send rain on the earth for forty days and forty nights; and every living thing that I have made I will blot out from the face of the ground." [5]And Noah did all that the LORD had commanded him.

6 Noah was six hundred years old when the flood of waters came on the earth. [7]And Noah with his sons and his wife and his sons' wives went into the ark to escape the waters of the flood. [8]Of clean animals, and of animals that are not clean, and of birds, and of everything that creeps on the ground, [9]two and two, male and female, went into the ark with Noah, as God had commanded Noah. [10]And after seven days the waters of

6.1-8 This second story of human defiance of God's ordering the creation includes the divine provision for the rescue of the small faithful community from the universal judgment. *Sons of God* refers to heavenly beings who should have restricted their associations to those of their own kind, but who marry human women. From now on, the human lifespan is severely limited – to no more than *one hundred twenty years*. The offspring of these wrongful sexual unions were *Nephilim*, from a word which means "fallen ones." They may be similar to other giant figures who appear in the narratives of Deut 2.10-11; 3.11; 9.2. God intends to obliterate virtually the whole creation; Noah and his family alone escape this divine wrath.
6.9-8.19 The Flood. The present version of this story, which has close parallels in the ancient Akkadian Epic of Gilgamesh (dating back to about 2000 BCE), is composite, incorporating features of the Yahwistic and priestly traditions.
6.17 *a flood...to destroy all flesh.* The judgment of God falls on both human beings and the forms of life for which God gave humans responsibility.
6.18 *I will establish my covenant with you.* This is the first instance of the covenantal agreements into which God enters with his people through chosen leaders. Other major figures include Abra[ha]m (Gen 15.18), Moses (Ex 34.10), Joshua (Josh 24.25), David (2 Sam 23.5). A new covenant is promised through Jeremiah (Jer 31.31) and is seen to be fulfilled through Jesus (1 Cor 11.25).
6.19 *two of every kind...male and female.* Representatives of both sexes are essential for the renewal of the life of the earth after the flood.
7.1 *You alone are righteous.* Noah alone of all the human race has been obedient to God and his purpose for the world.
7.2 *Seven pairs of all clean animals.* The priestly tradition is evident here in the detail that ritually pure animals are to be included in pairs up to the sacred number seven, rather than merely two of each species of all kinds.

[u] Meaning of Heb uncertain [v] Or *window*

7.11-12 *The fountains of the great deep burst forth...the rain fell on the earth forty days.* The flood waters come from the clouds above as well as from the waters gathered under the earth (Gen 1.7), since there is a temporary reversal of God's establishment of order in the creation (7.17-24). As the ordering once led to life for all creatures, so now the chaos leads to death for all but those preserved in the vessel of safety prescribed by God.
8.4 *The ark came to rest on the mountains of Ararat.* Ararat, or Urartu, is a mountainous region in what is now northeastern Turkey. It served as a natural barrier which prevented the Assyrians from extending their territory north and west from the Tigris-Euphrates valley, and was thought by them to include the world's highest mountains.
8.20-22 Noah's offering of ritually pure birds and animals is in the priestly tradition. God's response is to rule out any repetition of the universal judgment on earthly forms of life and to promise unceasing continuity of seasons, of sowings and harvests. Yet with the declaration that *the inclination of the human heart is evil from youth,* the universality of human evil is pronounced. The *heart* is the seat of human decision-making, not merely of the emotions.

the flood came on the earth.
11 In the six hundredth year of Noah's
life, in the second month, on the seventeenth day of the month, on that day all the
fountains of the great deep burst forth, and
the windows of the heavens were opened.
12The rain fell on the earth forty days and
forty nights. 13On the very same day Noah
with his sons, Shem and Ham and Japheth,
and Noah's wife and the three wives of his
sons entered the ark, 14they and every wild
animal of every kind, and all domestic
animals of every kind, and every creeping
thing that creeps on the earth, and every
bird of every kind—every bird, every winged
creature. 15They went into the ark with
Noah, two and two of all flesh in which
there was the breath of life. 16And those
that entered, male and female of all flesh,
went in as God had commanded him; and
the LORD shut him in.
17 The flood continued forty days on the
earth; and the waters increased, and bore
up the ark, and it rose high above the earth.
18The waters swelled and increased greatly
on the earth; and the ark floated on the face
of the waters. 19The waters swelled so mightily on the earth that all the high mountains
under the whole heaven were covered; 20the
waters swelled above the mountains, covering them fifteen cubits deep. 21And all flesh
died that moved on the earth, birds, domestic animals, wild animals, all swarming
creatures that swarm on the earth, and all
human beings; 22everything on dry land in
whose nostrils was the breath of life died.
23He blotted out every living thing that was
on the face of the ground, human beings
and animals and creeping things and birds
of the air; they were blotted out from the
earth. Only Noah was left, and those that
were with him in the ark. 24And the waters
swelled on the earth for one hundred fifty
days.

The Flood Subsides

8 But God remembered Noah and all
the wild animals and all the domestic
animals that were with him in the ark. And
God made a wind blow over the earth, and
the waters subsided; 2the fountains of the
deep and the windows of the heavens were
closed, the rain from the heavens was restrained, 3and the waters gradually receded
from the earth. At the end of one hundred
fifty days the waters had abated; 4and in the
seventh month, on the seventeenth day of
the month, the ark came to rest on the
mountains of Ararat. 5The waters continued to abate until the tenth month; in the
tenth month, on the first day of the month,
the tops of the mountains appeared.
6 At the end of forty days Noah opened
the window of the ark that he had made
7and sent out the raven; and it went to and
fro until the waters were dried up from the
earth. 8Then he sent out the dove from him,
to see if the waters had subsided from the
face of the ground; 9but the dove found no
place to set its foot, and it returned to him
to the ark, for the waters were still on the
face of the whole earth. So he put out his
hand and took it and brought it into the ark
with him. 10He waited another seven days,
and again he sent out the dove from the
ark; 11and the dove came back to him in the
evening, and there in its beak was a freshly
plucked olive leaf; so Noah knew that the
waters had subsided from the earth. 12Then
he waited another seven days, and sent out
the dove; and it did not return to him any
more.
13 In the six hundred first year, in the
first month, the first day of the month, the
waters were dried up from the earth; and
Noah removed the covering of the ark, and
looked, and saw that the face of the ground
was drying. 14In the second month, on the
twenty-seventh day of the month, the earth
was dry. 15Then God said to Noah, 16"Go
out of the ark, you and your wife, and your
sons and your sons' wives with you. 17Bring
out with you every living thing that is with
you of all flesh—birds and animals and
every creeping thing that creeps on the
earth—so that they may abound on the
earth, and be fruitful and multiply on the
earth." 18So Noah went out with his sons
and his wife and his sons' wives. 19And
every animal, every creeping thing, and
every bird, everything that moves on the
earth, went out of the ark by families.

God's Promise to Noah

20 Then Noah built an altar to the LORD,
and took of every clean animal and of every
clean bird, and offered burnt offerings on
the altar. 21And when the LORD smelled the
pleasing odor, the LORD said in his heart, "I
will never again curse the ground because
of humankind, for the inclination of the
human heart is evil from youth; nor will I

7.11 Gen 8.2; Prov 8.28; Ezek 26.19
7.12 ver 4.17
7.13 ver 1,7; 6.18
7.15 Gen 6.20
7.16 ver 2,3
7.17 ver 4,12
7.18 Ps 104.26
7.21 Gen 6.13,17
7.22 Gen 2.7
7.23 1 Pet 3.20; 2 Pet 2.5
7.24 Gen 8.3
8.1 Gen 19.29; Ex 2.24; 1 Sam 1.19; Ex 14.21; Job 12.15; Ps 29.10; Isa 44.27; Nah 1.4
8.2 Gen 7.11; Job 38.37
8.3 Gen 7.24
8.4 Jer 51.27
8.6 2 Pet 2.5
8.7 1 Kings 17.4,6
8.11 Mt 10.16
8.13 2 Pet 3.5,6
8.16 Gen 7.13
8.17 Gen 1.22
8.20 Gen 12.7,8; 13.18; 22.9; 7.2; 22.2; Ex 10.25
8.21 Lev 1.9; 2 Cor 2.15; Gen 3.17; 6.17; 9.11,15

ever again destroy every living creature as
I have done.
22 As long as the earth endures,
seedtime and harvest, cold and heat,
summer and winter, day and night,
shall not cease."

The Covenant with Noah

9 God blessed Noah and his sons, and
said to them, "Be fruitful and multiply, and fill the earth. 2The fear and dread
of you shall rest on every animal of the
earth, and on every bird of the air, on
everything that creeps on the ground, and
on all the fish of the sea; into your hand
they are delivered. 3Every moving thing
that lives shall be food for you; and just as
I gave you the green plants, I give you
everything. 4Only, you shall not eat flesh
with its life, that is, its blood. 5For your own
lifeblood I will surely require a reckoning:
from every animal I will require it and from
human beings, each one for the blood of
another, I will require a reckoning for human
life.
6 Whoever sheds the blood of a human,
by a human shall that person's blood
be shed;
for in his own image
God made humankind.
7And you, be fruitful and multiply, abound
on the earth and multiply in it."
8 Then God said to Noah and to his sons
with him, 9"As for me, I am establishing my
covenant with you and your descendants
after you, 10and with every living creature
that is with you, the birds, the domestic
animals, and every animal of the earth with
you, as many as came out of the ark.[w] 11I
establish my covenant with you, that never
again shall all flesh be cut off by the waters
of a flood, and never again shall there be
a flood to destroy the earth." 12God said,
"This is the sign of the covenant that I
make between me and you and every living
creature that is with you, for all future
generations: 13I have set my bow in the
clouds, and it shall be a sign of the covenant between me and the earth. 14When
I bring clouds over the earth and the bow
is seen in the clouds, 15I will remember my
covenant that is between me and you and
every living creature of all flesh; and the
waters shall never again become a flood to
destroy all flesh. 16When the bow is in the
clouds, I will see it and remember the everlasting covenant between God and every
living creature of all flesh that is on the
earth." 17God said to Noah, "This is the sign
of the covenant that I have established
between me and all flesh that is on the
earth."

Noah and His Sons

18 The sons of Noah who went out of
the ark were Shem, Ham, and Japheth.
Ham was the father of Canaan. 19These
three were the sons of Noah; and from these
the whole earth was peopled.
20 Noah, a man of the soil, was the first
to plant a vineyard. 21He drank some of the
wine and became drunk, and he lay uncovered in his tent. 22And Ham, the father of
Canaan, saw the nakedness of his father,
and told his two brothers outside. 23Then
Shem and Japheth took a garment, laid it
on both their shoulders, and walked backward and covered the nakedness of their
father; their faces were turned away, and
they did not see their father's nakedness.
24When Noah awoke from his wine and
knew what his youngest son had done to
him, 25he said,
"Cursed be Canaan;
lowest of slaves shall he be to his
brothers."
26He also said,
"Blessed by the LORD my God be Shem;
and let Canaan be his slave.
27 May God make space for[x] Japheth,
and let him live in the tents of Shem;
and let Canaan be his slave."
28 After the flood Noah lived three hundred fifty years. 29All the days of Noah were
nine hundred fifty years; and he died.

Nations Descended from Noah

10 These are the descendants of Noah's
sons, Shem, Ham, and Japheth;
children were born to them after the flood.
2 The descendants of Japheth: Gomer,
Magog, Madai, Javan, Tubal, Meshech, and
Tiras. 3The descendants of Gomer: Ashkenaz,
Riphath, and Togarmah. 4The descendants
of Javan: Elishah, Tarshish, Kittim, and
Rodanim.[y] 5From these the coastland peoples spread. These are the descendants of

[w] Gk: Heb adds *every animal of the earth* [x] Heb *yapht*, a play on *Japheth* [y] Heb Mss Sam Gk See 1 Chr 1.7: MT *Dodanim*

8.22 Isa 54.9; Jer 33.20,25
9.1 ver 7; Gen 1.28
9.3 Deut 12.15; Gen 1.29
9.4 Lev 17.10-16; Deut 12.23; 1 Sam 14.33
9.5 Ex 21.28; Gen 4.9,10
9.6 Ex 21.12,14; Lev 24.17; Mt 26.52; Gen 1.27
9.7 ver 1,19
9.9 Gen 6.18; Isa 54.9
9.10 Ps 149.9
9.11 Isa 54.9
9.12 Gen 17.11
9.13 Ezek 1.28; Rev 4.3
9.15 Lev 26.42,45; Deut 7.9
9.16 Gen 17.13,19
9.18 Gen 10.6
9.19 Gen 5.32
9.23 Ex 20.12
9.25 Deut 27.16
9.26 Ps 144.15
9.27 Eph 2.13,14; 3.6
10.2 1 Chr 1.5-7
10.5 Gen 5.32

9.1-17 The provisions by God and the responsibility of humans under the covenant are outlined, including human responsibility for and sovereignty over other forms of life on the earth, and the sanctity of human life itself, since it is created in the divine image. The promise is repeated that there will not be another universal judgment on the earth and its inhabitants.
9.18-28 These stories, with cursings and blessings, describe the repopulation of the earth after the flood, but they also account for the differing status before God of the three major groups of people with whom the biblical accounts are concerned: Shem,ancestor of the tribes of Israel; Ham, father of Canaan, whose descendants inhabited the land when Abraham came there from Mesopotamia and later when the Israelites came from Egypt in the time of Moses; Japheth, who in 10.2-5 is described as the progenitor of many tribes and peoples throughout the Middle East and eastern Mediterranean regions.
9.21 *He drank some of the wine and became drunk.* Here wine is a symptom of human depravity. Elsewhere in the Old Testament wine is a symbol of productivity and prosperity (Deut 7.13; Amos 9.13-14).
9.22 *Ham...saw the nakedness of his father.* Both the severity of Ham's punishment and the note about *what [Noah's] youngest son had done to him* suggest a sexual assault.
10.1-32 A detailed genealogy of the sons of Noah follows. *The descendants of Ham* include many of the nations of Africa and Mesopotamia; Canaan's descendants populate what is later known as Syria and Palestine, with *their [own family of] languages* akin to but distinct from Hebrew (10.20). The descendants of Shem are closest linguistically and ethnically to the Semitic people of Israel. In compact form, this account depicts the spread of population, language and culture of the entire Middle East.

Japheth[z] in their lands, with their own language, by their families, in their nations.

6 The descendants of Ham: Cush, Egypt, Put, and Canaan. 7 The descendants of Cush: Seba, Havilah, Sabtah, Raamah, and Sabteca. The descendants of Raamah: Sheba and Dedan. 8 Cush became the father of Nimrod; he was the first on earth to become a mighty warrior. 9 He was a mighty hunter before the LORD; therefore it is said, "Like Nimrod a mighty hunter before the LORD." 10 The beginning of his kingdom was Babel, Erech, and Accad, all of them in the land of Shinar. 11 From that land he went into Assyria, and built Nineveh, Rehoboth-ir, Calah, and 12 Resen between Nineveh and Calah; that is the great city. 13 Egypt became the father of Ludim, Anamim, Lehabim, Naphtuhim, 14 Pathrusim, Casluhim, and Caphtorim, from which the Philistines come.[a]

15 Canaan became the father of Sidon his firstborn, and Heth, 16 and the Jebusites, the Amorites, the Girgashites, 17 the Hivites, the Arkites, the Sinites, 18 the Arvadites, the Zemarites, and the Hamathites. Afterward the families of the Canaanites spread abroad. 19 And the territory of the Canaanites extended from Sidon, in the direction of Gerar, as far as Gaza, and in the direction of Sodom, Gomorrah, Admah, and Zeboiim, as far as Lasha. 20 These are the descendants of Ham, by their families, their languages, their lands, and their nations.

21 To Shem also, the father of all the children of Eber, the elder brother of Japheth, children were born. 22 The descendants of Shem: Elam, Asshur, Arpachshad, Lud, and Aram. 23 The descendants of Aram: Uz, Hul, Gether, and Mash. 24 Arpachshad became the father of Shelah; and Shelah became the father of Eber. 25 To Eber were born two sons: the name of the one was Peleg,[b] for in his days the earth was divided, and his brother's name was Joktan. 26 Joktan became the father of Almodad, Sheleph, Hazarmaveth, Jerah, 27 Hadoram, Uzal, Diklah, 28 Obal, Abimael, Sheba, 29 Ophir, Havilah, and Jobab; all these were the descendants of Joktan. 30 The territory in which they lived extended from Mesha in the direction of Sephar, the hill country of the east. 31 These are the descendants of Shem, by their families, their languages, their lands, and their nations.

32 These are the families of Noah's sons, according to their genealogies, in their nations; and from these the nations spread abroad on the earth after the flood.

The Tower of Babel

11 Now the whole earth had one language and the same words. 2 And as they migrated from the east,[c] they came upon a plain in the land of Shinar and settled there. 3 And they said to one another, "Come, let us make bricks, and burn them thoroughly." And they had brick for stone, and bitumen for mortar. 4 Then they said, "Come, let us build ourselves a city, and a tower with its top in the heavens, and let us make a name for ourselves; otherwise we shall be scattered abroad upon the face of the whole earth." 5 The LORD came down to see the city and the tower, which mortals had built. 6 And the LORD said, "Look, they are one people, and they have all one language; and this is only the beginning of what they will do; nothing that they propose to do will now be impossible for them. 7 Come, let us go down, and confuse their language there, so that they will not understand one another's speech." 8 So the LORD scattered them abroad from there over the face of all the earth, and they left off building the city. 9 Therefore it was called Babel, because there the LORD confused[d] the language of all the earth; and from there the LORD scattered them abroad over the face of all the earth.

Descendants of Shem

10 These are the descendants of Shem. When Shem was one hundred years old, he became the father of Arpachshad two years after the flood; 11 and Shem lived after the birth of Arpachshad five hundred years, and had other sons and daughters.

12 When Arpachshad had lived thirty-five years, he became the father of Shelah; 13 and Arpachshad lived after the birth of Shelah four hundred three years, and had other sons and daughters.

14 When Shelah had lived thirty years, he became the father of Eber; 15 and Shelah lived after the birth of Eber four hundred three years, and had other sons and daughters.

16 When Eber had lived thirty-four years,

[z] Compare verses 20, 31. Heb lacks *These are the descendants of Japheth* [a] Cn: Heb *Casluhim, from which the Philistines come, and Caphtorim* [b] That is *Division* [c] Or *migrated eastward* [d] Heb *balal*, meaning *to confuse*

11.1 *The whole earth had one language.* This statement is in tension with the preceding description of ethnic and linguistic differences among the inhabitants of the region.
11.1-9 Another story of human pride and self-will, which traits result in humans being visited by divine judgment. Here the punishment is the mixture of human languages, so that there cannot be a unified humanity or a universal scheme of independence from God. The event takes place on *the plain of Shinar*, which is the location of the city of Babylon. Human arrogance leads to the erection of *a tower with its top in the heavens* which is a ziggurat, a typical sacred pyramid of this period in Mesopotamia. Calling the city *Babel* is a complex pun, since the word actually means "Gate of god," but is here traced to the Hebrew term for "confusion."
11.10-32 This genealogy links Shem, son of Noah, with Abram, who is to be the crucial figure in the establishment of God's covenant with his people. Haran is the name of a brother of Abram as well as of a city in northern Mesopotamia.

10.6 1 Chr 1.8-10
10.9 Mic 5.6
10.10 Mic 5.6
10.13 1 Chr 1.8,11
10.15 1 Chr 1.13
10.18 1 Chr 1.16; 18.3
10.19 Num 34.2-12
10.22 1 Chr 1.17; Gen 14.1,9; 2 Kings 15.29; Gen 11.10; Isa 66.19
10.23 Job 1.1
10.24 Gen 11.12; Lk 3.35
10.25 1 Chr 1.19
10.26-29 1 Chr 1.20-23
10.32 ver 1
11.2 Ex 1.11,14; 5.7-19
11.4 Deut 1.28
11.5 Gen 18.21
11.6 Acts 17.26; Gen 9.19
11.7 Gen 1.26; 42.23; Ex 4.11; 1 Cor 14.2,11
11.8 Lk 1.51; Gen 10.25,32
11.9 Gen 10.10
11.10 Gen 10.22; 1 Chr 1.17

he became the father of Peleg; [17]and Eber lived after the birth of Peleg four hundred thirty years, and had other sons and daughters.

18 When Peleg had lived thirty years, he became the father of Reu; [19]and Peleg lived after the birth of Reu two hundred nine years, and had other sons and daughters.

20 When Reu had lived thirty-two years, he became the father of Serug; [21]and Reu lived after the birth of Serug two hundred seven years, and had other sons and daughters.

22 When Serug had lived thirty years, he became the father of Nahor; [23]and Serug lived after the birth of Nahor two hundred years, and had other sons and daughters.

24 When Nahor had lived twenty-nine years, he became the father of Terah; [25]and Nahor lived after the birth of Terah one hundred nineteen years, and had other sons and daughters.

26 When Terah had lived seventy years, he became the father of Abram, Nahor, and Haran.

Descendants of Terah

27 Now these are the descendants of Terah. Terah was the father of Abram, Nahor, and Haran; and Haran was the father of Lot. [28]Haran died before his father Terah in the land of his birth, in Ur of the Chaldeans. [29]Abram and Nahor took wives; the name of Abram's wife was Sarai, and the name of Nahor's wife was Milcah. She was the daughter of Haran the father of Milcah and Iscah. [30]Now Sarai was barren; she had no child.

31 Terah took his son Abram and his grandson Lot son of Haran, and his daughter-in-law Sarai, his son Abram's wife, and they went out together from Ur of the Chaldeans to go into the land of Canaan; but when they came to Haran, they settled there. [32]The days of Terah were two hundred five years; and Terah died in Haran.

The Call of Abram

12 Now the LORD said to Abram, "Go from your country and your kindred and your father's house to the land that I will show you. [2]I will make of you a great nation, and I will bless you, and make your name great, so that you will be a blessing. [3]I will bless those who bless you, and the one who curses you I will curse; and in you all the families of the earth shall be blessed."[e]

4 So Abram went, as the LORD had told him; and Lot went with him. Abram was seventy-five years old when he departed from Haran. [5]Abram took his wife Sarai and his brother's son Lot, and all the possessions that they had gathered, and the persons whom they had acquired in Haran; and they set forth to go to the land of Canaan. When they had come to the land of Canaan, [6]Abram passed through the land to the place at Shechem, to the oak[f] of Moreh. At that time the Canaanites were in the land. [7]Then the LORD appeared to Abram, and said, "To your offspring[g] I will give this land." So he built there an altar to the LORD, who had appeared to him. [8]From there he moved on to the hill country on the east of Bethel, and pitched his tent, with Bethel on the west and Ai on the east; and there he built an altar to the LORD and invoked the name of the LORD. [9]And Abram journeyed on by stages toward the Negeb.

Abram and Sarai in Egypt

10 Now there was a famine in the land. So Abram went down to Egypt to reside there as an alien, for the famine was severe in the land. [11]When he was about to enter Egypt, he said to his wife Sarai, "I know well that you are a woman beautiful in appearance; [12]and when the Egyptians see you, they will say, 'This is his wife'; then they will kill me, but they will let you live. [13]Say you are my sister, so that it may go well with me because of you, and that my life may be spared on your account." [14]When Abram entered Egypt the Egyptians saw that the woman was very beautiful. [15]When the officials of Pharaoh saw her, they praised her to Pharaoh. And the woman was taken into Pharaoh's house. [16]And for her sake he dealt well with Abram; and he had sheep, oxen, male donkeys, male and female slaves, female donkeys, and camels.

17 But the LORD afflicted Pharaoh and his house with great plagues because of Sarai, Abram's wife. [18]So Pharaoh called Abram, and said, "What is this you have done to me? Why did you not tell me that she was your wife? [19]Why did you say, 'She is my sister,' so that I took her for my wife?

[e] Or *by you all the families of the earth shall bless themselves* [f] Or *terebinth* [g] Heb *seed*

11.30 Gen 16.1
11.31 Gen 15.7; Neh 9.7; Acts 7.4
12.1 Acts 7.3; Heb 11.8
12.2 Gen 15.5; 17.4,5; 18.18; 22.17; 28.14; 32.12; 35.11; 46.3
12.3 Gen 27.29; Ex 23.33; Num 24.9; Gen 18.18; 22.18; 26.4; Acts 3.25; Gal 3.8
12.4 Gen 11.27,31
12.5 Gen 14.14; 11,31
12.6 Heb 11.9; Deut 11.30; Gen 10.18,19
12.7 Gen 17.1; 13.15; 17.8; Ps 105.9; Gen 13.4
12.8 Gen 13.4
12.12 Gen 20.11
12.13 Gen 20.5,13
12.15 Gen 20.2
12.16 Gen 20.14
12.17 Gen 20.18; 1 Chr 16.21; Ps 105.14
12.18 Gen 20.9,10

11.28 *in Ur of the Chaldeans.* Excavations at this site show the city to have been settled as early as 5500 BCE and to have become a major urban cultural and religious center in the period from 3000-2350 BCE. From that epoch were recovered the most impressive architectural and artistic remains. Ur continued to rise and fall under successive dynasties, including the Old Babylonian period from 2000 to 1740, which is probably the time of Abraham. Names and customs mentioned in the biblical narratives of this period match those reported in documents from Ur and other Mesopotamian sites in this period. Ur did not adopt the designation "of the Chaldees" until the sixth century BCE when the Chaldeans took over the former Babylonian empire. It was in this period and in Babylonia that Genesis received its major editing.
12.1 *Abram.* This form of the patriarch's name means "exalted father"; later (17.5) his name is reportedly changed to Abraham, "ancestor of a multitude." The instruction to him to *go from your country and your kindred* fits with other writings from Mesopotamia in this period which reflect the high mobility of tribes and peoples that is implied here.
12.2-3 *I will make of you a great nation.* This is the covenantal promise which the LORD now makes to Abraham. The blessings of this new relationship and new people are not the privileged possession of the family itself: they reach out to *all the families of the earth.*
12.6-9 Abram's route follows the main highways of commerce between Mesopotamia, Syria, Palestine and Egypt. Two of his stopping points figure importantly in the subsequent history of Israel: Shechem and Bethel. The former site forty miles north of Jerusalem is the place where the covenant with Yahweh was renewed when the tribes of Israel came out of Egypt into the land of promise (Josh 24). Bethel was the center of the worship of the God of Israel in the time of Jacob (Gen 28.19), of the judges (Judg 20.18), and of Amos (Amos 7.12-13). *To your offspring I will give this land.* For Abram and his posterity to enter the covenant relationship with God requires them to end their nomadic life. They are ultimately to settle in the land, and at Ai Abram builds a sanctuary to honor the LORD. The people's migratory existence is not yet over, however, since Abram is now to go to Egypt. In Josh 8, Ai is among the places captured by the tribes of Israel as they enter the land on their return from Egypt.
12.9 *Negeb* means the dry semi-desert area south and west of the Dead Sea which forms a bridge between southern Israel, Sinai and Egypt. Ancient trade routes crossed it, some following the Mediterranean on the west and others the Gulf of Aqabah on the east.

13.1-14 As Abram and Lot return to Palestine with their families, flocks and possessions acquired in Egypt, they decide to divide the land between them. Lot chooses the area to the east, including the fertile valley of the Jordan and the regions along the deep cleft of the Dead Sea. There is a warning about the subsequent wickedness of Sodom. Abram settles in Canaan on the hills and plains west of the Jordan river. God promises him *offspring like the dust of the earth* and possession of the land forever. Abram settles *by the oaks of Mamre, which are at Hebron,* a city located about twenty miles south of Jerusalem on a high mountain ridge but with an abundant supply of water for flocks and crops.
14.1-16 The coalition of rulers of regions in Mesopotamia attacks and pillages the city-states in the valley of the Dead Sea. Shinar, which is Babylon, and Elam, which was a prosperous district east of the Tigris-Euphrates valley, are the only certainly identifiable nations in this list of attackers. Among those carried off with the loot is Lot, the nephew of Abram. The latter is identified here as *the Hebrew,* a term found in many ancient texts from the region which refers to wanderers who disrupted the lives of the settled communities. Abram rallies a group of local allies who pursue the raiders beyond Damascus, recovering the loot and the captives they have taken.

Now then, here is your wife, take her, and
be gone." [20]And Pharaoh gave his men
orders concerning him; and they set him on
the way, with his wife and all that he had.

Abram and Lot Separate

13 So Abram went up from Egypt, he
and his wife, and all that he had,
and Lot with him, into the Negeb.
2 Now Abram was very rich in livestock,
in silver, and in gold. [3]He journeyed on by
stages from the Negeb as far as Bethel, to
the place where his tent had been at the
beginning, between Bethel and Ai, [4]to the
place where he had made an altar at the
first; and there Abram called on the name
of the LORD. [5]Now Lot, who went with
Abram, also had flocks and herds and tents,
[6]so that the land could not support both of
them living together; for their possessions
were so great that they could not live together, [7]and there was strife between the
herders of Abram's livestock and the herders of Lot's livestock. At that time the
Canaanites and the Perizzites lived in the
land.
8 Then Abram said to Lot, "Let there be
no strife between you and me, and between
your herders and my herders; for we are
kindred. [9]Is not the whole land before you?
Separate yourself from me. If you take the
left hand, then I will go to the right; or if
you take the right hand, then I will go to
the left." [10]Lot looked about him, and saw
that the plain of the Jordan was well watered everywhere like the garden of the
LORD, like the land of Egypt, in the direction
of Zoar; this was before the LORD had destroyed Sodom and Gomorrah. [11]So Lot chose
for himself all the plain of the Jordan, and
Lot journeyed eastward; thus they separated from each other. [12]Abram settled in
the land of Canaan, while Lot settled among
the cities of the Plain and moved his tent
as far as Sodom. [13]Now the people of Sodom
were wicked, great sinners against the LORD.
14 The LORD said to Abram, after Lot had
separated from him, "Raise your eyes now,
and look from the place where you are,
northward and southward and eastward
and westward; [15]for all the land that you
see I will give to you and to your offspring[h]
forever. [16]I will make your offspring like the
dust of the earth; so that if one can count
the dust of the earth, your offspring also
can be counted. [17]Rise up, walk through the
length and the breadth of the land, for I will
give it to you." [18]So Abram moved his tent,
and came and settled by the oaks[i] of Mamre,
which are at Hebron; and there he built an
altar to the LORD.

Lot's Captivity and Rescue

14 In the days of King Amraphel of
Shinar, King Arioch of Ellasar, King
Chedorlaomer of Elam, and King Tidal of
Goiim, [2]these kings made war with King
Bera of Sodom, King Birsha of Gomorrah,
King Shinab of Admah, King Shemeber of
Zeboiim, and the king of Bela (that is, Zoar).
[3]All these joined forces in the Valley of
Siddim (that is, the Dead Sea).[j] [4]Twelve
years they had served Chedorlaomer, but in
the thirteenth year they rebelled. [5]In the
fourteenth year Chedorlaomer and the kings
who were with him came and subdued the
Rephaim in Ashteroth-karnaim, the Zuzim
in Ham, the Emim in Shaveh-kiriathaim,
[6]and the Horites in the hill country of Seir
as far as El-paran on the edge of the wilderness; [7]then they turned back and came
to En-mishpat (that is, Kadesh), and subdued all the country of the Amalekites, and
also the Amorites who lived in Hazazon-
tamar. [8]Then the king of Sodom, the king
of Gomorrah, the king of Admah, the king
of Zeboiim, and the king of Bela (that is,
Zoar) went out, and they joined battle in
the Valley of Siddim [9]with King Chedorlaomer of Elam, King Tidal of Goiim, King
Amraphel of Shinar, and King Arioch of
Ellasar, four kings against five. [10]Now the
Valley of Siddim was full of bitumen pits;
and as the kings of Sodom and Gomorrah
fled, some fell into them, and the rest fled
to the hill country. [11]So the enemy took all
the goods of Sodom and Gomorrah, and all
their provisions, and went their way; [12]they
also took Lot, the son of Abram's brother,
who lived in Sodom, and his goods, and
departed.
13 Then one who had escaped came and
told Abram the Hebrew, who was living by
the oaks[i] of Mamre the Amorite, brother of
Eshcol and of Aner; these were allies of
Abram. [14]When Abram heard that his
nephew had been taken captive, he led
forth his trained men, born in his house,
three hundred eighteen of them, and went
in pursuit as far as Dan. [15]He divided his

12.20 Prov 21.1
13.1 Gen 12.9
13.3 Gen 12.8,9
13.4 Gen 12.7,8
13.7 Gen 26.20
13.8 Prov 15.18; 20.3
13.10 Gen 19.17-29; Deut 2.8; 47.6; 14.8
13.12 Gen 19.29
13.13 Gen 18.20; 2 Pet 2.7,8
13.14 Gen 28.14; Deut 3.27
13.15 Gen 12.7; 17.8; Deut 34.3; Acts 7.5; 2 Chr 20.7
13.16 Gen 16.10; 28.14
13.17 Num 13.17-24
13.18 Gen 14.13; 35.27
14.1 Isa 11.11; Dan 8.2
14.2 Gen 10.19; Deut 29.23; Gen 13.10
14.3 Num 34.12; Deut 3.17; Josh 3.16
14.5 Gen 15.20; Deut 2.20
14.6 Deut 2.12,22
14.7 2 Chr 20.2
14.11 ver 16,21
14.12 Gen 12.5; 13.12
14.13 Gen 13.18; ver 24
14.14 Gen 13.8; 15.3

[h] Heb *seed* [i] Or *terebinths* [j] Heb *Salt Sea*

forces against them by night, he and his servants, and routed them and pursued them to Hobah, north of Damascus. [16]Then he brought back all the goods, and also brought back his nephew Lot with his goods, and the women and the people.

Abram Blessed by Melchizedek

17 After his return from the defeat of Chedorlaomer and the kings who were with him, the king of Sodom went out to meet him at the Valley of Shaveh (that is, the King's Valley). [18]And King Melchizedek of Salem brought out bread and wine; he was priest of God Most High.[k] [19]He blessed him and said,

"Blessed be Abram by God Most High,[k]
maker of heaven and earth;
[20] and blessed be God Most High,[k]
who has delivered your enemies into your hand!"

And Abram gave him one tenth of everything. [21]Then the king of Sodom said to Abram, "Give me the persons, but take the goods for yourself." [22]But Abram said to the king of Sodom, "I have sworn to the LORD, God Most High,[k] maker of heaven and earth, [23]that I would not take a thread or a sandal-thong or anything that is yours, so that you might not say, 'I have made Abram rich.' [24]I will take nothing but what the young men have eaten, and the share of the men who went with me—Aner, Eshcol, and Mamre. Let them take their share."

God's Covenant with Abram

15 After these things the word of the LORD came to Abram in a vision, "Do not be afraid, Abram, I am your shield; your reward shall be very great." [2]But Abram said, "O LORD GOD, what will you give me, for I continue childless, and the heir of my house is Eliezer of Damascus?"[l] [3]And Abram said, "You have given me no offspring, and so a slave born in my house is to be my heir." [4]But the word of the LORD came to him, "This man shall not be your heir; no one but your very own issue shall be your heir." [5]He brought him outside and said, "Look toward heaven and count the stars, if you are able to count them." Then he said to him, "So shall your descendants be." [6]And he believed the LORD; and the LORD[m] reckoned it to him as righteousness.

7 Then he said to him, "I am the LORD who brought you from Ur of the Chaldeans, to give you this land to possess." [8]But he said, "O LORD GOD, how am I to know that I shall possess it?" [9]He said to him, "Bring me a heifer three years old, a female goat three years old, a ram three years old, a turtledove, and a young pigeon." [10]He brought him all these and cut them in two, laying each half over against the other; but he did not cut the birds in two. [11]And when birds of prey came down on the carcasses, Abram drove them away.

12 As the sun was going down, a deep sleep fell upon Abram, and a deep and terrifying darkness descended upon him. [13]Then the LORD[m] said to Abram, "Know this for certain, that your offspring shall be aliens in a land that is not theirs, and shall be slaves there, and they shall be oppressed for four hundred years; [14]but I will bring judgment on the nation that they serve, and afterward they shall come out with great possessions. [15]As for yourself, you shall go to your ancestors in peace; you shall be buried in a good old age. [16]And they shall come back here in the fourth generation; for the iniquity of the Amorites is not yet complete."

17 When the sun had gone down and it was dark, a smoking fire pot and a flaming torch passed between these pieces. [18]On that day the LORD made a covenant with Abram, saying, "To your descendants I give this land, from the river of Egypt to the great river, the river Euphrates, [19]the land of the Kenites, the Kenizzites, the Kadmonites, [20]the Hittites, the Perizzites, the Rephaim, [21]the Amorites, the Canaanites, the Girgashites, and the Jebusites."

The Birth of Ishmael

16 Now Sarai, Abram's wife, bore him no children. She had an Egyptian slave-girl whose name was Hagar, [2]and Sarai said to Abram, "You see that the LORD has prevented me from bearing children; go in to my slave-girl; it may be that I shall obtain children by her." And Abram listened to the voice of Sarai. [3]So, after Abram had lived ten years in the land of Canaan, Sarai, Abram's wife, took Hagar the Egyptian, her slave-girl, and gave her to her husband Abram as a wife. [4]He went in to Hagar, and she conceived; and when she

[k] Heb *El Elyon* [l] Meaning of Heb uncertain [m] Heb *he*

14.16 ver 11,12
14.17 1 Sam 18.6,18
14.18 Heb 7.1; Ps 110.4; Heb 5.6,10
14.19 ver 22; Mt 11.25
14.20 Gen 24.27; Heb 7.4
14.22 Dan 12.7; ver 19
14.23 2 Kings 5.16
15.1 Dan 10.1; Gen 21.17; 26.24; Deut 33.29; Prov 11.8
15.2 Acts 7.5
15.3 Gen 14.14
15.4 Gal 4.28
15.5 Ps 147.4; Jer 33.22; Gen 22.17; Rom 4.18; Heb 11.12
15.7 Gen 11.31; 13.15,17
15.8 Lk 1.18
15.10 Jer 34.18; Lev 1.17
15.12 Gen 2.21
15.13 Acts 7.6; Ex 12.40
15.14 Ex 12.36
15.15 Gen 25.8
15.16 1 Kings 21.26
15.17 Jer 34.18,19
15.18 Gen 24.7; 12.7; Ex 23.31; Num 34.3; Deut 11.24; Josh 1.4
16.1 Gen 11.30; 21.9; Gal 4.24
16.2 Gen 30.3,4,9,10
16.3 Gen 12.5

14.17-24 The local rulers of southern Palestine are both grateful to Abram and impressed by what they perceive to be divine support for his counter-attack. Melchizedek, whose name means "king of righteousness" and who is king of Salem (=Jerusalem), conveys to Abram the blessing of *God Most High*. As both king and priest, he is identified in Hebrews 7 as the prototype of the ultimate agent of God's covenant with his people. Abram honors the local deity by paying a tithe – *one tenth of everything* – of what he has recovered. He further strengthens his reputation with the local rulers by his declaration that he *would not take...anything* of the possessions of these people which he has regained from their attackers.
15.1-18 *The word of the LORD came to Abram. Word* connotes far more than merely a message; it is the promise and purpose of God for his people, which are regarded by the writer as certain of fulfillment. Since Abram has no male heir, he cannot understand how the covenant hope will be achieved. Instead, it looks as though his chief servant, Eliezer, will be his heir. God promises him innumerable offspring, and Abram's trust in this assurance (*he believed the LORD*) results in God's setting him in right relationship with him, in the certainty that he will have an heir and that his posterity will possess the land which God has given. Visible evidence that God will fulfill the covenant promise is provided when Abram has *brought him all these [sacrificial animals] and cut them in two*. This practice is referred to in Jer 34.18-19, where contracting parties passed between the halves of the sacrificial victims. Here, however, the fidelity to the covenant rests on God alone, as symbolized by the *smoking fire pot and [the] flaming torch*.
15.12-16 Some scholars regard as a later insertion the warning to Abram that his posterity will experience four hundred years of slavery. This prediction refers to the experience in Egypt, which is said to have lasted about that long (Ex 12.40). The vast extent of the land promised to Abraham – *from the river of Egypt to...the river Euphrates* (15.18-21) – would include the territory of Israel's two great oppressors: the Egyptians and the Babylonians. Historically, Israel never controlled the expanse from the Nile to what is modern Iraq or dominated the peoples here listed.
16.1-15 The misguided attempt of Sarai and Abram to help God fulfill his covenant promise by providing an heir. Sarai's proposal to Abram to *go in to my slave girl* to provide a child for the barren mistress is in keeping with custom amply documented from ancient sources in the region.

saw that she had conceived, she looked with contempt on her mistress. 5Then Sarai said to Abram, "May the wrong done to me be on you! I gave my slave-girl to your embrace, and when she saw that she had conceived, she looked on me with contempt. May the LORD judge between you and me!" 6But Abram said to Sarai, "Your slave-girl is in your power; do to her as you please." Then Sarai dealt harshly with her, and she ran away from her.

7 The angel of the LORD found her by a spring of water in the wilderness, the spring on the way to Shur. 8And he said, "Hagar, slave-girl of Sarai, where have you come from and where are you going?" She said, "I am running away from my mistress Sarai." 9The angel of the LORD said to her, "Return to your mistress, and submit to her." 10The angel of the LORD also said to her, "I will so greatly multiply your offspring that they cannot be counted for multitude." 11And the angel of the LORD said to her,

"Now you have conceived and shall bear
 a son;
you shall call him Ishmael,[n]
 for the LORD has given heed to your
 affliction.
12 He shall be a wild ass of a man,
 with his hand against everyone,
 and everyone's hand against him;
 and he shall live at odds with all his kin."

13So she named the LORD who spoke to her, "You are El-roi";[o] for she said, "Have I really seen God and remained alive after seeing him?"[p] 14Therefore the well was called Beer-lahai-roi;[q] it lies between Kadesh and Bered.

15 Hagar bore Abram a son; and Abram named his son, whom Hagar bore, Ishmael. 16Abram was eighty-six years old when Hagar bore him[r] Ishmael.

The Sign of the Covenant

17 When Abram was ninety-nine years old, the LORD appeared to Abram, and said to him, "I am God Almighty;[s] walk before me, and be blameless. 2And I will make my covenant between me and you, and will make you exceedingly numerous." 3Then Abram fell on his face; and God said to him, 4"As for me, this is my covenant with you: You shall be the ancestor of a multitude of nations. 5No longer shall your name be Abram,[t] but your name shall be Abraham;[u] for I have made you the ancestor of a multitude of nations. 6I will make you exceedingly fruitful; and I will make nations of you, and kings shall come from you. 7I will establish my covenant between me and you, and your offspring after you throughout their generations, for an everlasting covenant, to be God to you and to your offspring[v] after you. 8And I will give to you, and to your offspring after you, the land where you are now an alien, all the land of Canaan, for a perpetual holding; and I will be their God."

9 God said to Abraham, "As for you, you shall keep my covenant, you and your offspring after you throughout their generations. 10This is my covenant, which you shall keep, between me and you and your offspring after you: Every male among you shall be circumcised. 11You shall circumcise the flesh of your foreskins, and it shall be a sign of the covenant between me and you. 12Throughout your generations every male among you shall be circumcised when he is eight days old, including the slave born in your house and the one bought with your money from any foreigner who is not of your offspring. 13Both the slave born in your house and the one bought with your money must be circumcised. So shall my covenant be in your flesh an everlasting covenant. 14Any uncircumcised male who is not circumcised in the flesh of his foreskin shall be cut off from his people; he has broken my covenant."

15 God said to Abraham, "As for Sarai your wife, you shall not call her Sarai, but Sarah shall be her name. 16I will bless her, and moreover I will give you a son by her. I will bless her, and she shall give rise to nations; kings of peoples shall come from her." 17Then Abraham fell on his face and laughed, and said to himself, "Can a child be born to a man who is a hundred years old? Can Sarah, who is ninety years old, bear a child?" 18And Abraham said to God, "O that Ishmael might live in your sight!" 19God said, "No, but your wife Sarah shall bear you a son, and you shall name him Isaac.[w] I will establish my covenant with him as an everlasting covenant for his offspring after him. 20As for Ishmael, I have

[n] That is *God hears* [o] Perhaps *God of seeing* or *God who sees* [p] Meaning of Heb uncertain [q] That is *the Well of the Living One who sees me* [r] Heb *Abram* [s] Traditional rendering of Heb *El Shaddai* [t] That is *exalted ancestor* [u] Here taken to mean *ancestor of a multitude* [v] Heb *seed* [w] That is *he laughs*

16.7-10 The angel of the LORD halts Hagar's attempt to escape the harsh treatment she receives from Sarai, which would have resulted in the loss of Abram's son. The statement, *I will so greatly multiply your offspring,* shows that it is the LORD who is speaking to Hagar.
16.12 *A wild ass of a man.* Ishmael is the ancestor of the Canaanite semi-nomadic people who were troublesome neighbors of Israel.
16.14 Kadesh and Bered were located in the southern Negeb on the route to Sinai and Egypt.
17.1-14 A priestly account of God's covenant with Abraham. The primary response called for is the circumcision of males as a visible sign of participation in the covenant. This parallels the institution of the sabbath in the covenant with Adam (2.1-3) and the prohibition of eating blood in the covenant with Noah (9.4-7). As the change of his name implies, Abraham is to be the ancestor of *a multitude of nations,* not merely of the nation Israel, so that its benefits are to reach out to all peoples. The covenant is to be *everlasting,* and is to result in Abraham's settlement in *all the land of Canaan for a perpetual holding.*
17.15-16 The change of name from Sarai to Sarah makes no difference in basic meaning, but it implies a change in status and parallels the change in Abraham's name.
17.17-21 Abraham responds to God's promise of an heir born to Sarah with a mixture of hilarious disbelief and an attempt at a substitute solution: Ishmael. God responds with an order to give the son a name that will be a constant reminder of disbelief – Isaac (= "he laughs") – and promises of blessing for Ishmael, but also assurances of the covenant to be established with Isaac.

16.5 Gen 31.53
16.7 Gen 21.17,18; 22.11,15; 31.11; 20.1
16.10 Gen 17.20
16.11 Ex 3.7,9
16.12 Gen 25.18
16.13 Gen 32.30
16.15 Gal 4.22
17.1 Gen 28.3; Ex 6.3; Deut 18.13
17.2 Gen 15.18
17.4 Gen 35.11; 48.19
17.5 Neh 9.7; Rom 4.17
17.6 Gen 35.11; Mt 1.6
17.7 Gal 3.17; Gen 26.24; 28.13; Rom 9.8
17.8 Gen 12.7; Ps 105.9,11; Gen 23.4; 28.4; Ex 6.7; Lev 26.12
17.10 Acts 7.8
17.11 Ex 12.48; Deut 10.16; Rom 4.11
17.12 Lev 12.3; Lk 2.21
17.14 Ex 4.24
17.16 Gen 18.10; 35.11; Gal 4.31
17.17 Gen 18.12; 21.6
17.19 Gen 18.10; 21.2; 26.2-5
17.20 Gen 16.10; 25.12,16

heard you; I will bless him and make him
fruitful and exceedingly numerous; he shall
be the father of twelve princes, and I will
make him a great nation. [21]But my covenant I will establish with Isaac, whom
Sarah shall bear to you at this season next
year." [22]And when he had finished talking
with him, God went up from Abraham.
23 Then Abraham took his son Ishmael
and all the slaves born in his house or
bought with his money, every male among
the men of Abraham's house, and he circumcised the flesh of their foreskins that
very day, as God had said to him. [24]Abraham
was ninety-nine years old when he was
circumcised in the flesh of his foreskin.
[25]And his son Ishmael was thirteen years
old when he was circumcised in the flesh
of his foreskin. [26]That very day Abraham
and his son Ishmael were circumcised; [27]and
all the men of his house, slaves born in the
house and those bought with money from
a foreigner, were circumcised with him.

A Son Promised to Abraham and Sarah

18 The LORD appeared to Abraham[x]
by the oaks[y] of Mamre, as he sat
at the entrance of his tent in the heat of the
day. [2]He looked up and saw three men
standing near him. When he saw them, he
ran from the tent entrance to meet them,
and bowed down to the ground. [3]He said,
"My lord, if I find favor with you, do not
pass by your servant. [4]Let a little water be
brought, and wash your feet, and rest yourselves under the tree. [5]Let me bring a little
bread, that you may refresh yourselves, and
after that you may pass on—since you have
come to your servant." So they said, "Do as
you have said." [6]And Abraham hastened
into the tent to Sarah, and said, "Make
ready quickly three measures[z] of choice
flour, knead it, and make cakes." [7]Abraham
ran to the herd, and took a calf, tender and
good, and gave it to the servant, who
hastened to prepare it. [8]Then he took curds
and milk and the calf that he had prepared,
and set it before them; and he stood by
them under the tree while they ate.
9 They said to him, "Where is your wife
Sarah?" And he said, "There, in the tent."
[10]Then one said, "I will surely return to you
in due season, and your wife Sarah shall
have a son." And Sarah was listening at the
tent entrance behind him. [11]Now Abraham
and Sarah were old, advanced in age; it had
ceased to be with Sarah after the manner
of women. [12]So Sarah laughed to herself,
saying, "After I have grown old, and my
husband is old, shall I have pleasure?" [13]The
LORD said to Abraham, "Why did Sarah
laugh, and say, 'Shall I indeed bear a child,
now that I am old?' [14]Is anything too
wonderful for the LORD? At the set time I will
return to you, in due season, and Sarah
shall have a son." [15]But Sarah denied, saying, "I did not laugh"; for she was afraid.
He said, "Oh yes, you did laugh."

Judgment Pronounced on Sodom

16 Then the men set out from there, and
they looked toward Sodom; and Abraham
went with them to set them on their way.
[17]The LORD said, "Shall I hide from Abraham
what I am about to do, [18]seeing that
Abraham shall become a great and mighty
nation, and all the nations of the earth shall
be blessed in him?[a] [19]No, for I have chosen[b]
him, that he may charge his children and
his household after him to keep the way of
the LORD by doing righteousness and justice;
so that the LORD may bring about for
Abraham what he has promised him."
[20]Then the LORD said, "How great is the
outcry against Sodom and Gomorrah and
how very grave their sin! [21]I must go down
and see whether they have done altogether
according to the outcry that has come to
me; and if not, I will know."
22 So the men turned from there, and
went toward Sodom, while Abraham remained standing before the LORD.[c] [23]Then
Abraham came near and said, "Will you
indeed sweep away the righteous with the
wicked? [24]Suppose there are fifty righteous
within the city; will you then sweep away
the place and not forgive it for the fifty
righteous who are in it? [25]Far be it from you
to do such a thing, to slay the righteous
with the wicked, so that the righteous fare
as the wicked! Far be that from you! Shall
not the Judge of all the earth do what is
just?" [26]And the LORD said, "If I find at
Sodom fifty righteous in the city, I will
forgive the whole place for their sake."
[27]Abraham answered, "Let me take it upon
myself to speak to the Lord, I who am but
dust and ashes. [28]Suppose five of the fifty

[x] Heb *him* [y] Or *terebinths* [z] Heb *seahs* [a] Or *and all the nations of the earth shall bless themselves by him* [b] Heb *known* [c] Another ancient tradition reads *while the LORD remained standing before Abraham*

18.1-15 This Yahwist (J) version of God's promise of a son to Abraham and Sarah includes vivid contrasts between the reception of the divine visitors by Abraham and by the residents of Sodom and Gomorrah (Gen 19). The *three men* who come to Abraham's tent seem to be the LORD and two companions, although the narrative details are not always clear. They are welcomed with typical Middle Eastern hospitality and offered food. The promise of a son elicits laughter from Sarah in this account, although she later protests, *I did not laugh.*
18.16-33 The LORD decides not to withhold from Abraham the judgment that is to fall on Sodom. The promises of abundant posterity and blessings through him to all nations are affirmed as in the priestly version (Gen 17.5-6), and he and his children are to manifest *righteousness and justice.* This contrasts sharply with the moral conditions in the city where Lot lives, which God is about to destroy. Abraham's sense of justice leads him to intercede in behalf of the righteous minority that may dwell in these doomed places. The divine action of mass destruction is at variance with modern views of individual responsibility but fits ancient views of corporate identity.

17.23 Gen 14.14
17.24 Rom 4.11
18.1 Gen 13.18; 14.13
18.2 ver 16,22; Gen 32.24; Josh 5.13; Judg 13.6-11
18.4 Gen 19.2; 43.24
18.5 Judg 6.18,19; 13.15,16
18.8 Gen 19.3
18.10 Rom 9.9
18.11 Gen 17.17; Rom 4.19
18.12 1 Pet 3.6
18.14 Jer 32.17,27; Zech 8.6; Mt 3.9; Lk 1.37
18.18 Gal 3.8
18.19 Deut 4.9,10; 6.7; Josh 24.15; Eph 6.4
18.20 Gen 19.13; Ezek 16.49,50
18.21 Gen 11.5
18.22 Gen 19.1
18.23 Heb 10.22; Num 16.22
18.24 Jer 5.1
18.25 Job 8.20; Isa 3.10,11; Rom 3.6
18.27 Gen 3.19; Job 4.19; 30.19; 42.6; 2 Cor 5.1

19.1-29 In contrast with the obedience and compassion of Abraham in the previous chapter, some men in Sodom want to commit homosexual rape on the visitors. Lot's offer of his daughters as sexual partners is morally ambiguous, but the divine judgment begins when the would-be attackers are struck blind. God and his agents advise Lot to flee before doom falls on the cities, the results of which Abraham sees from a distance, where he remains under the special care of God.

righteous are lacking? Will you destroy the whole city for lack of five?" And he said, "I will not destroy it if I find forty-five there." [29]Again he spoke to him, "Suppose forty are found there." He answered, "For the sake of forty I will not do it." [30]Then he said, "Oh do not let the Lord be angry if I speak. Suppose thirty are found there." He answered, "I will not do it, if I find thirty there." [31]He said, "Let me take it upon myself to speak to the Lord. Suppose twenty are found there." He answered, "For the sake of twenty I will not destroy it." [32]Then he said, "Oh do not let the Lord be angry if I speak just once more. Suppose ten are found there." He answered, "For the sake of ten I will not destroy it." [33]And the LORD went his way, when he had finished speaking to Abraham; and Abraham returned to his place.

The Depravity of Sodom

19 The two angels came to Sodom in the evening, and Lot was sitting in the gateway of Sodom. When Lot saw them, he rose to meet them, and bowed down with his face to the ground. [2]He said, "Please, my lords, turn aside to your servant's house and spend the night, and wash your feet; then you can rise early and go on your way." They said, "No; we will spend the night in the square." [3]But he urged them strongly; so they turned aside to him and entered his house; and he made them a feast, and baked unleavened bread, and they ate. [4]But before they lay down, the men of the city, the men of Sodom, both young and old, all the people to the last man, surrounded the house; [5]and they called to Lot, "Where are the men who came to you tonight? Bring them out to us, so that we may know them." [6]Lot went out of the door to the men, shut the door after him, [7]and said, "I beg you, my brothers, do not act so wickedly. [8]Look, I have two daughters who have not known a man; let me bring them out to you, and do to them as you please; only do nothing to these men, for they have come under the shelter of my roof." [9]But they replied, "Stand back!" And they said, "This fellow came here as an alien, and he would play the judge! Now we will deal worse with you than with them." Then they pressed hard against the man Lot, and came near the door to break it down. [10]But the men inside reached out their hands and brought Lot into the house with them, and shut the door. [11]And they struck with blindness the men who were at the door of the house, both small and great, so that they were unable to find the door.

Sodom and Gomorrah Destroyed

12 Then the men said to Lot, "Have you anyone else here? Sons-in-law, sons, daughters, or anyone you have in the city—bring them out of the place. [13]For we are about to destroy this place, because the outcry against its people has become great before the LORD, and the LORD has sent us to destroy it." [14]So Lot went out and said to his sons-in-law, who were to marry his daughters, "Up, get out of this place; for the LORD is about to destroy the city." But he seemed to his sons-in-law to be jesting.

15 When morning dawned, the angels urged Lot, saying, "Get up, take your wife and your two daughters who are here, or else you will be consumed in the punishment of the city." [16]But he lingered; so the men seized him and his wife and his two daughters by the hand, the LORD being merciful to him, and they brought him out and left him outside the city. [17]When they had brought them outside, they[d] said, "Flee for your life; do not look back or stop anywhere in the Plain; flee to the hills, or else you will be consumed." [18]And Lot said to them, "Oh, no, my lords; [19]your servant has found favor with you, and you have shown me great kindness in saving my life; but I cannot flee to the hills, for fear the disaster will overtake me and I die. [20]Look, that city is near enough to flee to, and it is a little one. Let me escape there—is it not a little one?—and my life will be saved!" [21]He said to him, "Very well, I grant you this favor too, and will not overthrow the city of which you have spoken. [22]Hurry, escape there, for I can do nothing until you arrive there." Therefore the city was called Zoar.[e] [23]The sun had risen on the earth when Lot came to Zoar.

24 Then the LORD rained on Sodom and Gomorrah sulfur and fire from the LORD out of heaven; [25]and he overthrew those cities, and all the Plain, and all the inhabitants of the cities, and what grew on the ground. [26]But Lot's wife, behind him, looked back, and she became a pillar of salt.

[d] Gk Syr Vg: Heb *he* [e] That is *Little*

18.32 Judg 6.39; Jas 5.16

19.1 Gen 18.22; 18.1ff

19.2 Heb 13.2; Gen 18.4

19.3 Gen 18.8

19.5 Isa 3.9; Judg 19.22; Rom 1.24

19.6 Judg 19.23

19.8 see Judg 19.24

19.9 2 Pet 2.7,8; Ex 2.14

19.11 see 2 Kings 6.18; Acts 13.11

19.12 Gen 7.1; 2 Pet 2.7,9

19.13 Gen 18.20; 1 Chr 21.15

19.14 Num 16.21; Ex 9.21; Lk 17.28

19.15 Num 16.24,26; Rev 18.4

19.16 Lk 18.13; Ps 34.22

19.17 1 Kings 19.3; Jer 48.6; ver 26

19.21 Job 42.8,9; Ps 145.9

19.24 Deut 29.23; Isa 13.19; Lk 17.29; Jude 7

19.25 Ps 107.34

19.26 Lk 17.32

27 Abraham went early in the morning to the place where he had stood before the Lord; [28]and he looked down toward Sodom and Gomorrah and toward all the land of the Plain and saw the smoke of the land going up like the smoke of a furnace.

29 So it was that, when God destroyed the cities of the Plain, God remembered Abraham, and sent Lot out of the midst of the overthrow, when he overthrew the cities in which Lot had settled.

The Shameful Origin of Moab and Ammon

30 Now Lot went up out of Zoar and settled in the hills with his two daughters, for he was afraid to stay in Zoar; so he lived in a cave with his two daughters. [31]And the firstborn said to the younger, "Our father is old, and there is not a man on earth to come in to us after the manner of all the world. [32]Come, let us make our father drink wine, and we will lie with him, so that we may preserve offspring through our father." [33]So they made their father drink wine that night; and the firstborn went in, and lay with her father; he did not know when she lay down or when she rose. [34]On the next day, the firstborn said to the younger, "Look, I lay last night with my father; let us make him drink wine tonight also; then you go in and lie with him, so that we may preserve offspring through our father." [35]So they made their father drink wine that night also; and the younger rose, and lay with him; and he did not know when she lay down or when she rose. [36]Thus both the daughters of Lot became pregnant by their father. [37]The firstborn bore a son, and named him Moab; he is the ancestor of the Moabites to this day. [38]The younger also bore a son and named him Ben-ammi; he is the ancestor of the Ammonites to this day.

Abraham and Sarah at Gerar

20 From there Abraham journeyed toward the region of the Negeb, and settled between Kadesh and Shur. While residing in Gerar as an alien, [2]Abraham said of his wife Sarah, "She is my sister." And King Abimelech of Gerar sent and took Sarah. [3]But God came to Abimelech in a dream by night, and said to him, "You are about to die because of the woman whom you have taken; for she is a married woman." [4]Now Abimelech had not approached her; so he said, "Lord, will you destroy an innocent people? [5]Did he not himself say to me, 'She is my sister'? And she herself said, 'He is my brother.' I did this in the integrity of my heart and the innocence of my hands." [6]Then God said to him in the dream, "Yes, I know that you did this in the integrity of your heart; furthermore it was I who kept you from sinning against me. Therefore I did not let you touch her. [7]Now then, return the man's wife; for he is a prophet, and he will pray for you and you shall live. But if you do not restore her, know that you shall surely die, you and all that are yours."

8 So Abimelech rose early in the morning, and called all his servants and told them all these things; and the men were very much afraid. [9]Then Abimelech called Abraham, and said to him, "What have you done to us? How have I sinned against you, that you have brought such great guilt on me and my kingdom? You have done things to me that ought not to be done." [10]And Abimelech said to Abraham, "What were you thinking of, that you did this thing?" [11]Abraham said, "I did it because I thought, There is no fear of God at all in this place, and they will kill me because of my wife. [12]Besides, she is indeed my sister, the daughter of my father but not the daughter of my mother; and she became my wife. [13]And when God caused me to wander from my father's house, I said to her, 'This is the kindness you must do me: at every place to which we come, say of me, He is my brother.' " [14]Then Abimelech took sheep and oxen, and male and female slaves, and gave them to Abraham, and restored his wife Sarah to him. [15]Abimelech said, "My land is before you; settle where it pleases you." [16]To Sarah he said, "Look, I have given your brother a thousand pieces of silver; it is your exoneration before all who are with you; you are completely vindicated." [17]Then Abraham prayed to God; and God healed Abimelech, and also healed his wife and female slaves so that they bore children. [18]For the Lord had closed fast all the wombs of the house of Abimelech because of Sarah, Abraham's wife.

The Birth of Isaac

21 The Lord dealt with Sarah as he had said, and the Lord did for Sarah as he had promised. [2]Sarah conceived and bore Abraham a son in his old age, at

19.27 Gen 18.22
19.28 Rev 9.2; 18.9
19.29 2 Pet 2.7
19.31 Gen 38.8,9; Deut 25.5
19.32 Mk 12.19
19.38 Deut 2.19
20.1 Gen 18.1; 16.7,14; 26.6
20.2 ver 12; Gen 12.13,15
20.3 Ps 105.14; Job 33.15; Gen 26.11
20.5 1 Kings 9.4; 2 Kings 20.3
20.7 1 Sam 7.5; Job 42.8
20.9 Gen 26.10; Ex 32.21; Josh 7.25; Gen 34.7
20.11 Ps 36.1; Gen 12.12; 26.7
20.13 ver 5
20.14 Gen 12.16
20.15 Gen 13.9
20.17 Num 12.13; Job 42.9
20.18 Gen 12.17
21.1 1 Sam 2.21; Gen 17.16,21; Gal 4.23
21.2 Acts 7.8; Gal 4.22; Heb 11.11; Gen 17.21

19.30-38 In the manner of the moral depravity of these doomed cities, Lot's daughters commit acts of incest with their drunken father. From this came the progenitors of two Semitic tribes that lived east of the Jordan and the Dead Sea during the time of Israel's entrance and occupation of the land: the Moabites and the Ammonites.
20.1a Abraham continues his semi-nomadic existence, living in the arid southern area, the Negeb.
20.1b This story recalls Abraham's deceptive behavior in Egypt (Gen 12.10-20) and anticipates that of Isaac (26.6-11).
20.3-18 God's appearing *in a dream* to convey messages is a common feature of Genesis from this point on. Abimelech's *integrity of heart* is acknowledged by God, and Abraham not only acknowledges that he was trying to protect himself but claims a half-truth: he and Sarah have a common father. Abimelech pays handsomely to exonerate Sarah – who is still pure to bear Isaac – and the fertility of Abimelech and his wives and concubines is restored.
21.1-7 Sarah gives birth to Isaac in fulfillment of the promises made to her and Abraham (17.15-21; 18.9-15). As Abraham's age is one hundred it is clear that the son is a gift of God, not an ordinary human achievement. The reason for Isaac's name is not that Abraham and Sarah laughed cynically, as in the earlier stories (17.17; 18.12), but because *God has brought laughter.*

21.8-19 Although Ishmael is not named in this section, when Sarah sees him playing with her *infant* son Isaac (when Hagar's son would have been about fifteen [17.25]), she fears that he will overshadow Isaac, and demands that he and his mother be expelled. Abraham agrees, but God continues to protect the mother and child. The role of each child is different (21.12): Isaac will be the one through whom the line of the covenant people will continue, while Ishmael will be the progenitor of *a great nation* (21.18).
21.20-21 Ishmael takes up life as a nomadic hunter in a section of the southern desert adjacent to Egypt.
21.22-34 The covenant between Abraham and Abimelech, which is confirmed by an *oath* and gifts, takes place at Beer-sheba, a well which Abraham claims to have dug, and the name of which means either "Well of the Oath" or "Well of the Seven," referring to the seven ewes given by Abraham. Implicit is that he will not settle there, but will accept his status as an *alien*, or temporary resident.
21.32-34 References to the residence of Abimelech and Abraham in *the land of the Philistines* is anachronistic, since these people migrated from the region by the Aegean Sea to the southern coastal area west of Jerusalem only in the twelfth century BCE. They were important economic and military competition for the Israelites down to the Babylonian exile in the sixth century, so that mention of them reflects the time when the Genesis traditions were being edited in their present form.
22.1-14 This incident is said to have occurred in *the land of Moriah*, a place which cannot be identified with certainty but which in later tradition was located at Jerusalem (2 Chr 3.1). In substance and literary style this is the most dramatic of the stories of God's direct dealings with Abraham. There is an advance notice to the reader that God did not insist on the death of Isaac but *tested Abraham* to see how great his faith was. The narrative includes considerable dialogue between father and son, God and Abraham. The answer to Isaac's question about the victim for the burnt offering is that *God himself will provide the lamb*, which is actually *a ram caught in a thicket*. For Abraham to *fear God* is an indication, not of fright or terror, but of profound respect and full obedience. The name which Abraham assigns to the place, *the Lord will provide*, accurately describes God's fidelity in enabling Abraham to meet the covenantal obligations.

the time of which God had spoken to him.
3Abraham gave the name Isaac to his son
whom Sarah bore him. 4And Abraham circumcised his son Isaac when he was eight
days old, as God had commanded him.
5Abraham was a hundred years old when
his son Isaac was born to him. 6Now Sarah
said, "God has brought laughter for me;
everyone who hears will laugh with me."
7And she said, "Who would ever have said
to Abraham that Sarah would nurse children? Yet I have borne him a son in his old
age."

Hagar and Ishmael Sent Away

8 The child grew, and was weaned; and
Abraham made a great feast on the day
that Isaac was weaned. 9But Sarah saw the
son of Hagar the Egyptian, whom she had
borne to Abraham, playing with her son
Isaac.[f] 10So she said to Abraham, "Cast out
this slave woman with her son; for the son
of this slave woman shall not inherit along
with my son Isaac." 11The matter was very
distressing to Abraham on account of his
son. 12But God said to Abraham, "Do not be
distressed because of the boy and because
of your slave woman; whatever Sarah says
to you, do as she tells you, for it is through
Isaac that offspring shall be named for you.
13As for the son of the slave woman, I will
make a nation of him also, because he is
your offspring." 14So Abraham rose early in
the morning, and took bread and a skin of
water, and gave it to Hagar, putting it on
her shoulder, along with the child, and sent
her away. And she departed, and wandered
about in the wilderness of Beer-sheba.
15 When the water in the skin was gone,
she cast the child under one of the bushes.
16Then she went and sat down opposite him
a good way off, about the distance of a
bowshot; for she said, "Do not let me look
on the death of the child." And as she sat
opposite him, she lifted up her voice and
wept. 17And God heard the voice of the boy;
and the angel of God called to Hagar from
heaven, and said to her, "What troubles
you, Hagar? Do not be afraid; for God has
heard the voice of the boy where he is.
18Come, lift up the boy and hold him fast
with your hand, for I will make a great
nation of him." 19Then God opened her eyes
and she saw a well of water. She went, and
filled the skin with water, and gave the boy
a drink.
20 God was with the boy, and he grew
up; he lived in the wilderness, and became
an expert with the bow. 21He lived in the
wilderness of Paran; and his mother got a
wife for him from the land of Egypt.

Abraham and Abimelech Make a Covenant

22 At that time Abimelech, with Phicol
the commander of his army, said to
Abraham, "God is with you in all that you
do; 23now therefore swear to me here by
God that you will not deal falsely with me
or with my offspring or with my posterity,
but as I have dealt loyally with you, you
will deal with me and with the land where
you have resided as an alien." 24And
Abraham said, "I swear it."
25 When Abraham complained to
Abimelech about a well of water that
Abimelech's servants had seized, 26Abimelech
said, "I do not know who has done this; you
did not tell me, and I have not heard of it
until today." 27So Abraham took sheep and
oxen and gave them to Abimelech, and the
two men made a covenant. 28Abraham set
apart seven ewe lambs of the flock. 29And
Abimelech said to Abraham, "What is the
meaning of these seven ewe lambs that you
have set apart?" 30He said, "These seven
ewe lambs you shall accept from my hand,
in order that you may be a witness for me
that I dug this well." 31Therefore that place
was called Beer-sheba;[g] because there both
of them swore an oath. 32When they had
made a covenant at Beer-sheba, Abimelech,
with Phicol the commander of his army, left
and returned to the land of the Philistines.
33Abraham[h] planted a tamarisk tree in Beer-
sheba, and called there on the name of the
LORD, the Everlasting God.[i] 34And Abraham
resided as an alien many days in the land
of the Philistines.

The Command to Sacrifice Isaac

22 After these things God tested
Abraham. He said to him, "Abraham!" And he said, "Here I am." 2He said,
"Take your son, your only son Isaac, whom
you love, and go to the land of Moriah, and
offer him there as a burnt offering on one
of the mountains that I shall show you."

[f] Gk Vg: Heb lacks *with her son Isaac* [g] That is *Well of seven* or *Well of the oath* [h] Heb *He* [i] Or *the* LORD, *El Olam*

21.3 Gen 17.19
21.4 Gen 17.12; Acts 7.8
21.5 Gen 17.17
21.6 Ps 126.2; Isa 54.1
21.9 Gen 16.15; Gal 4.29
21.10 Gal 4.30
21.11 Gen 17.18
21.12 Rom 9.7; Heb 11.18
21.13 ver 18; Gen 16.10; 17.20
21.17 Ex 3.7
21.18 ver 13
21.19 Num 22.31
21.20 Gen 28.15; 39.2,3,21
21.21 Gen 24.4
21.22 Gen 20.2; 26.26,28
21.25 Gen 26.15,18,20-22
21.27 Gen 26.31
21.30 Gen 31.48,52
21.31 Gen 26.33
21.33 Gen 4.26; Deut 33.27
22.2 Heb 11.17; 2 Chr 3.1

22.6 Jn 19.17
22.7 Jn 1.29,36; Rev 13.8
22.9 Heb 11.17-19
22.12 Gen 26.5; 1 Sam 15.22
22.16 Heb 6.13,14
22.17 Gen 15.5; 26.4; 32.12; 24.60
22.18 Gal 3.8,16; Acts 3.25; Gen 18.19
22.23 Gen 24.15
23.2 Josh 14.15; ver 19; Gen 13.18
23.4 1 Chr 29.15; Ps 105.12; Heb 11.9,13
23.6 Gen 14.14; 24.35
23.8 Gen 25.9
23.10 Gen 24.20,24; Ruth 4.4
23.11 see 2 Sam 24.21-24

3So Abraham rose early in the morning, saddled his donkey, and took two of his young men with him, and his son Isaac; he cut the wood for the burnt offering, and set out and went to the place in the distance that God had shown him. 4On the third day Abraham looked up and saw the place far away. 5Then Abraham said to his young men, "Stay here with the donkey; the boy and I will go over there; we will worship, and then we will come back to you." 6Abraham took the wood of the burnt offering and laid it on his son Isaac, and he himself carried the fire and the knife. So the two of them walked on together. 7Isaac said to his father Abraham, "Father!" And he said, "Here I am, my son." He said, "The fire and the wood are here, but where is the lamb for a burnt offering?" 8Abraham said, "God himself will provide the lamb for a burnt offering, my son." So the two of them walked on together.

9 When they came to the place that God had shown him, Abraham built an altar there and laid the wood in order. He bound his son Isaac, and laid him on the altar, on top of the wood. 10Then Abraham reached out his hand and took the knife to kill[j] his son. 11But the angel of the LORD called to him from heaven, and said, "Abraham, Abraham!" And he said, "Here I am." 12He said, "Do not lay your hand on the boy or do anything to him; for now I know that you fear God, since you have not withheld your son, your only son, from me." 13And Abraham looked up and saw a ram, caught in a thicket by its horns. Abraham went and took the ram and offered it up as a burnt offering instead of his son. 14So Abraham called that place "The LORD will provide";[k] as it is said to this day, "On the mount of the LORD it shall be provided."[l]

15 The angel of the LORD called to Abraham a second time from heaven, 16and said, "By myself I have sworn, says the LORD: Because you have done this, and have not withheld your son, your only son, 17I will indeed bless you, and I will make your offspring as numerous as the stars of heaven and as the sand that is on the seashore. And your offspring shall possess the gate of their enemies, 18and by your offspring shall all the nations of the earth gain blessing for themselves, because you have obeyed my voice." 19So Abraham returned to his young men, and they arose and went together to Beer-sheba; and Abraham lived at Beer-sheba.

The Children of Nahor

20 Now after these things it was told Abraham, "Milcah also has borne children, to your brother Nahor: 21Uz the firstborn, Buz his brother, Kemuel the father of Aram, 22Chesed, Hazo, Pildash, Jidlaph, and Bethuel." 23Bethuel became the father of Rebekah. These eight Milcah bore to Nahor, Abraham's brother. 24Moreover, his concubine, whose name was Reumah, bore Tebah, Gaham, Tahash, and Maacah.

Sarah's Death and Burial

23 Sarah lived one hundred twenty-seven years; this was the length of Sarah's life. 2And Sarah died at Kiriath-arba (that is, Hebron) in the land of Canaan; and Abraham went in to mourn for Sarah and to weep for her. 3Abraham rose up from beside his dead, and said to the Hittites, 4"I am a stranger and an alien residing among you; give me property among you for a burying place, so that I may bury my dead out of my sight." 5The Hittites answered Abraham, 6"Hear us, my lord; you are a mighty prince among us. Bury your dead in the choicest of our burial places; none of us will withhold from you any burial ground for burying your dead." 7Abraham rose and bowed to the Hittites, the people of the land. 8He said to them, "If you are willing that I should bury my dead out of my sight, hear me, and entreat for me Ephron son of Zohar, 9so that he may give me the cave of Machpelah, which he owns; it is at the end of his field. For the full price let him give it to me in your presence as a possession for a burying place." 10Now Ephron was sitting among the Hittites; and Ephron the Hittite answered Abraham in the hearing of the Hittites, of all who went in at the gate of his city, 11"No, my lord, hear me; I give you the field, and I give you the cave that is in it; in the presence of my people I give it to you; bury your dead." 12Then Abraham bowed down before the people of the land. 13He said to Ephron in the hearing of the people of the land, "If you only will listen to me! I will give the price of the field; accept it from me, so that I may bury my dead there." 14Ephron answered Abraham,

22.15-19 The account of the second confirmatory vision of Abraham uses only Yahweh as the name of God, and may come from the J source. Abraham's willingness to sacrifice the son for whom he had waited so long and in whose birth he had believed in the face of all human doubts is honored by God. In addition to the huge numbers of his posterity (*numerous as the stars...and the sand*), they will enjoy political and military power over their enemies. And through them divine benefits will come to *all the nations of the earth*. Once more Abraham returns to his semi-nomadic residence at Beer-sheba, "well of the oath," the name of which is a reminder of the covenant with God.
22.20-24 The names of Abraham's nephews which are identifiable correspond to place names in the area east of modern Lebanon and Jordan bordering the Arabian desert.
23.1-20 The death of Sarah is the occasion for Abraham to arrange a family burial site and to obtain possession of a piece of the promised land. The place he wants belongs to the Hittites, a term originally for tribes who migrated to Syria and Palestine from Anatolia beginning in the seventeenth century BCE, but which by the twelfth century came to be used by the Assyrians and later by the Babylonians for Canaanite peoples. The location is identified with Kiriath-arba, which is apparently the older name for Hebron, but also with Mamre. The burial site is referred to as *cave* and *field of Machpelah* (the meaning of which is unknown). The traditional site near Hebron is marked by an impressive structure built by Herod and subsequently modified, which now contains a synagogue and a mosque, since in Islam Ibrahim is a major figure. Abraham's concern to *bury my dead out of my sight* indicates his concern to have safe, secure burial places for his family. The purchase of the site is carried out in typical Middle Eastern fashion, with the parties being courteous and deferential, indicating indirectly what the price is, meeting the demands, and all occurring in the presence of abundant witnesses. Most important is that Abraham now has a *possession* in the land of promise.

[j] Or *to slaughter* [k] Or *will see*; Heb traditionally transliterated *Jehovah Jireh* [l] Or *he shall be seen*

24.1-67 Securing a Bride for Isaac from Abraham's Family. The instruction to *put your hand under my thigh* is a euphemism for swear by the genital organs, which here emphasizes the seriousness of the promise and symbolizes the importance of continuity of the line of Abraham. The instruction to *go to my country and my kindred* is a sign of the necessity that marriage be within the tribal unit. Isaac is not to be taken there, lest he become absorbed in his ancestral culture, but instead he must be on location for the fulfillment of the covenant promise in the new land. The abundant gifts for the family of the bride include *camels*, which are probably anachronistic, since they were not domesticated in this region until the end of the second millennium BCE. *Aram-naharaim* was in the northwestern region of Mesopotamia, and the *city of Nahor* may have been Haran (Gen 11.31; 12.4). (24.14) The purpose of God through Isaac combines two crucial factors: the choice of his wife is *appointed* by God, and the result will manifest God's *steadfast love.* Abraham is the uncle of Rebekah's father, Nahor. Her gracious act toward the servant and his camels leads him to give her expensive gifts. A gold shekel was worth the cost of an ox or two tons of grain. (24.29-32) Typical regional hospitality is offered the travelers by Rebekah's brother, Laban. The servant recounts his experience and the purpose of his journey in vivid detail, culminating in his insistence on an immediate answer about Rebekah as bride for Isaac. Otherwise, he must *turn* to other options. With the agreement of Rebekah and her family, the farewell blessing on her echoes the promises to Abraham and Isaac of many *offspring* and success over *foes.* On arrival in the Negeb, Rebekah chastely covers herself in preparation for meeting her husband, and he indicates her place of honor as matriarch of the family by taking her *into his mother Sarah's tent.*

15"My lord, listen to me; a piece of land
worth four hundred shekels of silver—what
is that between you and me? Bury your
dead." 16Abraham agreed with Ephron; and
Abraham weighed out for Ephron the silver
that he had named in the hearing of the
Hittites, four hundred shekels of silver, according to the weights current among the
merchants.

17 So the field of Ephron in Machpelah,
which was to the east of Mamre, the field
with the cave that was in it and all the trees
that were in the field, throughout its whole
area, passed 18to Abraham as a possession
in the presence of the Hittites, in the presence of all who went in at the gate of his
city. 19After this, Abraham buried Sarah his
wife in the cave of the field of Machpelah
facing Mamre (that is, Hebron) in the land
of Canaan. 20The field and the cave that is
in it passed from the Hittites into Abraham's
possession as a burying place.

The Marriage of Isaac and Rebekah

24 Now Abraham was old, well advanced in years; and the LORD had
blessed Abraham in all things. 2Abraham
said to his servant, the oldest of his house,
who had charge of all that he had, "Put
your hand under my thigh 3and I will make
you swear by the LORD, the God of heaven
and earth, that you will not get a wife for
my son from the daughters of the Canaanites,
among whom I live, 4but will go to my
country and to my kindred and get a wife
for my son Isaac." 5The servant said to him,
"Perhaps the woman may not be willing to
follow me to this land; must I then take
your son back to the land from which you
came?" 6Abraham said to him, "See to it
that you do not take my son back there.
7The LORD, the God of heaven, who took me
from my father's house and from the land
of my birth, and who spoke to me and
swore to me, 'To your offspring I will give
this land,' he will send his angel before you,
and you shall take a wife for my son from
there. 8But if the woman is not willing to
follow you, then you will be free from this
oath of mine; only you must not take my
son back there." 9So the servant put his
hand under the thigh of Abraham his master
and swore to him concerning this matter.

10 Then the servant took ten of his
master's camels and departed, taking all
kinds of choice gifts from his master; and he
set out and went to Aram-naharaim, to the
city of Nahor. 11He made the camels kneel
down outside the city by the well of water;
it was toward evening, the time when
women go out to draw water. 12And he
said, "O LORD, God of my master Abraham,
please grant me success today and show
steadfast love to my master Abraham. 13I
am standing here by the spring of water,
and the daughters of the townspeople are
coming out to draw water. 14Let the girl to
whom I shall say, 'Please offer your jar that
I may drink,' and who shall say, 'Drink, and
I will water your camels'—let her be the
one whom you have appointed for your
servant Isaac. By this I shall know that you
have shown steadfast love to my master."

15 Before he had finished speaking, there
was Rebekah, who was born to Bethuel son
of Milcah, the wife of Nahor, Abraham's
brother, coming out with her water jar on
her shoulder. 16The girl was very fair to look
upon, a virgin, whom no man had known.
She went down to the spring, filled her jar,
and came up. 17Then the servant ran to
meet her and said, "Please let me sip a little
water from your jar." 18"Drink, my lord,"
she said, and quickly lowered her jar upon
her hand and gave him a drink. 19When she
had finished giving him a drink, she said,
"I will draw for your camels also, until they
have finished drinking." 20So she quickly
emptied her jar into the trough and ran
again to the well to draw, and she drew for
all his camels. 21The man gazed at her in
silence to learn whether or not the LORD had
made his journey successful.

22 When the camels had finished drinking, the man took a gold nose-ring weighing a half shekel, and two bracelets for her
arms weighing ten gold shekels, 23and said,
"Tell me whose daughter you are. Is there
room in your father's house for us to spend
the night?" 24She said to him, "I am the
daughter of Bethuel son of Milcah, whom
she bore to Nahor." 25She added, "We have
plenty of straw and fodder and a place to
spend the night." 26The man bowed his
head and worshiped the LORD 27and said,
"Blessed be the LORD, the God of my master
Abraham, who has not forsaken his steadfast love and his faithfulness toward my
master. As for me, the LORD has led me on
the way to the house of my master's kin."

28 Then the girl ran and told her mother's household about these things. 29Rebekah
had a brother whose name was Laban; and

23.15 Ex 30.13; Ezek 45.12
23.16 Jer 32.9; Zech 11.12
23.17 Gen 25.9; 49.30-32; 50.13; Acts 7.16
24.1 ver 35; Gen 13.2
24.2 Gen 47.29
24.3 Gen 14.22; 10.1,19; 26.34,35; 28.1,2,8
24.4 Gen 28.2; 12.1
24.7 Gen 12.7; 13.15; 15.18; Ex 23.20,23
24.9 ver 2
24.10 Gen 11.31,32; 27.43
24.11 1 Sam 9.11
24.12 ver 27; Gen 26.24; Ex 3.6
24.13 ver 43
24.14 see Judg 6.17,37; 1 Sam 6.7
24.15 ver 45; Gen 22.20,23
24.16 Gen 26.7
24.18 ver 14,16
24.19 ver 14
24.21 ver 12-14; 56
24.22 ver 27
24.24 ver 15
24.26 ver 48,52
24.27 ver 42,48,21
24.29 Gen 29.5,13

Laban ran out to the man, to the spring.
30 As soon as he had seen the nose-ring, and
the bracelets on his sister's arms, and when
he heard the words of his sister Rebekah,
"Thus the man spoke to me," he went to
the man; and there he was, standing by the
camels at the spring. 31 He said, "Come in,
O blessed of the LORD. Why do you stand
outside when I have prepared the house
and a place for the camels?" 32 So the man
came into the house; and Laban unloaded
the camels, and gave him straw and fodder
for the camels, and water to wash his feet
and the feet of the men who were with him.
33 Then food was set before him to eat; but
he said, "I will not eat until I have told my
errand." He said, "Speak on."
34 So he said, "I am Abraham's servant.
35 The LORD has greatly blessed my master,
and he has become wealthy; he has given
him flocks and herds, silver and gold, male
and female slaves, camels and donkeys. 36 And
Sarah my master's wife bore a son to my
master when she was old; and he has given
him all that he has. 37 My master made me
swear, saying, 'You shall not take a wife for
my son from the daughters of the Canaanites,
in whose land I live; 38 but you shall go to
my father's house, to my kindred, and get
a wife for my son.' 39 I said to my master,
'Perhaps the woman will not follow me.'
40 But he said to me, 'The LORD, before whom
I walk, will send his angel with you and
make your way successful. You shall get a
wife for my son from my kindred, from my
father's house. 41 Then you will be free from
my oath, when you come to my kindred;
even if they will not give her to you, you
will be free from my oath.'
42 "I came today to the spring, and said,
'O LORD, the God of my master Abraham, if
now you will only make successful the way
I am going! 43 I am standing here by the
spring of water; let the young woman who
comes out to draw, to whom I shall say,
"Please give me a little water from your jar
to drink," 44 and who will say to me, "Drink,
and I will draw for your camels also"—let
her be the woman whom the LORD has
appointed for my master's son.'
45 "Before I had finished speaking in my
heart, there was Rebekah coming out with
her water jar on her shoulder; and she went
down to the spring, and drew. I said to her,
'Please let me drink.' 46 She quickly let down
her jar from her shoulder, and said, 'Drink,
and I will also water your camels.' So I
drank, and she also watered the camels.
47 Then I asked her, 'Whose daughter are
you?' She said, 'The daughter of Bethuel,
Nahor's son, whom Milcah bore to him.' So
I put the ring on her nose, and the bracelets
on her arms. 48 Then I bowed my head and
worshiped the LORD, and blessed the LORD,
the God of my master Abraham, who had
led me by the right way to obtain the
daughter of my master's kinsman for his
son. 49 Now then, if you will deal loyally and
truly with my master, tell me; and if not,
tell me, so that I may turn either to the
right hand or to the left."
50 Then Laban and Bethuel answered,
"The thing comes from the LORD; we cannot
speak to you anything bad or good. 51 Look,
Rebekah is before you, take her and go, and
let her be the wife of your master's son, as
the LORD has spoken."
52 When Abraham's servant heard their
words, he bowed himself to the ground
before the LORD. 53 And the servant brought
out jewelry of silver and of gold, and garments, and gave them to Rebekah; he also
gave to her brother and to her mother
costly ornaments. 54 Then he and the men
who were with him ate and drank, and
they spent the night there. When they rose
in the morning, he said, "Send me back to
my master." 55 Her brother and her mother
said, "Let the girl remain with us a while,
at least ten days; after that she may go."
56 But he said to them, "Do not delay me,
since the LORD has made my journey successful; let me go that I may go to my
master." 57 They said, "We will call the girl,
and ask her." 58 And they called Rebekah,
and said to her, "Will you go with this
man?" She said, "I will." 59 So they sent
away their sister Rebekah and her nurse
along with Abraham's servant and his men.
60 And they blessed Rebekah and said to her,

"May you, our sister, become
  thousands of myriads;
may your offspring gain possession
  of the gates of their foes."

61 Then Rebekah and her maids rose up,
mounted the camels, and followed the man;
thus the servant took Rebekah, and went
his way.
62 Now Isaac had come from[m] Beer-
lahai-roi, and was settled in the Negeb.
63 Isaac went out in the evening to walk[n] in
the field; and looking up, he saw camels

[m] Syr Tg: Heb *from coming to* [n] Meaning of Heb word is uncertain

24.31 Gen 26.29
24.32 Gen 43.24; Judg 19.21
24.35 ver 1; Gen 13.2
24.36 Gen 21.2,10; 25.5
24.38 ver 4
24.39 ver 5
24.40 ver 7
24.41 ver 8
24.42 ver 11,12
24.43 ver 13,14
24.45 ver 15,17; 1 Sam 1.13
24.46 ver 18
24.47 ver 23,24
24.48 ver 26,27
24.49 Gen 47.29; Josh 2.14
24.50 Ps 118.23; Gen 31.24
24.52 ver 26
24.53 ver 10,22
24.54 ver 56,59
24.59 Gen 35.8
24.60 Gen 17.16; 22.17
24.62 Gen 16.14; 25.11; 20.1
24.63 Ps 1.2; 77.12; 119.15; 143.5; 145.5

25.1-6 Although according to this tradition Abraham has many children, only Isaac is *his son.* The others are sent to live in the eastern regions. The best-known of these is Midian, whose descendants figure importantly in the subsequent history of God's people (Gen 37; Ex 2-3; Judg 6-8).
25.11 Isaac has taken up residence at one of the wells in the Negeb, Beer-lahai-roi (Gen 16.14).
25.12-18 Ishmael's descendants maintain connection with his mother's native Egypt while their territory reaches to northwest Arabia. He has twelve sons, as later will Jacob and Esau.
25.29-35.29 Although this major section begins with the designation of *the descendants of Isaac,* the central figure throughout is Jacob. In the vivid narratives there is a blend of two themes: the sovereign freedom of God in fulfilling his covenant promises in spite of hostile human efforts, and the clever, amoral schemes of Jacob and Rebekah which move him into a position of wealth and power. Scholars have sought to identify passages from the Elohist (E), Yahwistic (J), and priestly (P) sources, but the present text as edited in the post-exilic period weaves together the older separate traditions.
25.19-20 Rebekah's native city is identified as Paddan-aram, in northwest Mesopotamia. Isaac's son Jacob is identified in Deut 26.5 as *a wandering Aramean.*
25.21-27 Pregnant with twins, Rebekah seeks and receives an oracle from God which predicts the dominance of the second son over the first. The characteristics of the first, *red* and *hairy,* are Hebrew words for the regions where his descendants lived: Edom and Seir. In contrast to Esau's life as hunter and farmer, Jacob is a nomadic herdsman. His name and initial act in process of emergence from the womb – *gripping Esau's heel* – symbolize his aggressive nature.
25.29-34 Impetuous Esau sells his favored status as oldest son to his greedy brother in exchange for a serving of stew.

coming. 64 And Rebekah looked up, and when she saw Isaac, she slipped quickly from the camel, 65 and said to the servant, "Who is the man over there, walking in the field to meet us?" The servant said, "It is my master." So she took her veil and covered herself. 66 And the servant told Isaac all the things that he had done. 67 Then Isaac brought her into his mother Sarah's tent. He took Rebekah, and she became his wife; and he loved her. So Isaac was comforted after his mother's death.

Abraham Marries Keturah

25 Abraham took another wife, whose name was Keturah. 2 She bore him Zimran, Jokshan, Medan, Midian, Ishbak, and Shuah. 3 Jokshan was the father of Sheba and Dedan. The sons of Dedan were Asshurim, Letushim, and Leummim. 4 The sons of Midian were Ephah, Epher, Hanoch, Abida, and Eldaah. All these were the children of Keturah. 5 Abraham gave all he had to Isaac. 6 But to the sons of his concubines Abraham gave gifts, while he was still living, and he sent them away from his son Isaac, eastward to the east country.

The Death of Abraham

7 This is the length of Abraham's life, one hundred seventy-five years. 8 Abraham breathed his last and died in a good old age, an old man and full of years, and was gathered to his people. 9 His sons Isaac and Ishmael buried him in the cave of Machpelah, in the field of Ephron son of Zohar the Hittite, east of Mamre, 10 the field that Abraham purchased from the Hittites. There Abraham was buried, with his wife Sarah. 11 After the death of Abraham God blessed his son Isaac. And Isaac settled at Beer-lahai-roi.

Ishmael's Descendants

12 These are the descendants of Ishmael, Abraham's son, whom Hagar the Egyptian, Sarah's slave-girl, bore to Abraham. 13 These are the names of the sons of Ishmael, named in the order of their birth: Nebaioth, the firstborn of Ishmael; and Kedar, Adbeel, Mibsam, 14 Mishma, Dumah, Massa, 15 Hadad, Tema, Jetur, Naphish, and Kedemah. 16 These are the sons of Ishmael and these are their names, by their villages and by their encampments, twelve princes according to their tribes. 17 (This is the length of the life of Ishmael, one hundred thirty-seven years; he breathed his last and died, and was gathered to his people.) 18 They settled from Havilah to Shur, which is opposite Egypt in the direction of Assyria; he settled down[o] alongside of[p] all his people.

The Birth and Youth of Esau and Jacob

19 These are the descendants of Isaac, Abraham's son: Abraham was the father of Isaac, 20 and Isaac was forty years old when he married Rebekah, daughter of Bethuel the Aramean of Paddan-aram, sister of Laban the Aramean. 21 Isaac prayed to the LORD for his wife, because she was barren; and the LORD granted his prayer, and his wife Rebekah conceived. 22 The children struggled together within her; and she said, "If it is to be this way, why do I live?"[q] So she went to inquire of the LORD. 23 And the LORD said to her,

"Two nations are in your womb,
and two peoples born of you shall be divided;
the one shall be stronger than the other,
the elder shall serve the younger."

24 When her time to give birth was at hand, there were twins in her womb. 25 The first came out red, all his body like a hairy mantle; so they named him Esau. 26 Afterward his brother came out, with his hand gripping Esau's heel; so he was named Jacob.[r] Isaac was sixty years old when she bore them.

27 When the boys grew up, Esau was a skillful hunter, a man of the field, while Jacob was a quiet man, living in tents. 28 Isaac loved Esau, because he was fond of game; but Rebekah loved Jacob.

Esau Sells His Birthright

29 Once when Jacob was cooking a stew, Esau came in from the field, and he was famished. 30 Esau said to Jacob, "Let me eat some of that red stuff, for I am famished!" (Therefore he was called Edom.[s]) 31 Jacob said, "First sell me your birthright." 32 Esau said, "I am about to die; of what use is a birthright to me?" 33 Jacob said, "Swear to me first."[t] So he swore to him, and sold his

[o] Heb *he fell* [p] Or *down in opposition to* [q] Syr: Meaning of Heb uncertain [r] That is *He takes by the heel* or *He supplants* [s] That is *Red* [t] Heb *today*

24.67 Gen 29.18; 23.1,2; 25.20
25.2 1 Chr 1.32,33
25.5 Gen 24.35,36
25.8 Gen 15.15; 35.29; 49.29,33
25.10 Gen 23.16
25.11 Gen 24.62
25.12 Gen 16.15
25.13 1 Chr 1.29-31
25.16 Gen 17.20
25.18 Gen 16.12
25.20 Gen 24.15,19
25.21 1 Sam 1.17; Ps 127.3
25.23 Gen 17.16; Num 20.14; Gen 27.29; Mal 1.3; Rom 9.12
25.25 Gen 27.11
25.26 Hos 12.3; Gen 27.36
25.27 Gen 27.3,5
25.33 Heb 12.16

26.1 Gen 12.10; 20.1,2
26.2 Gen 12.7; 17.1; 18.1; 12.1
26.3 Gen 20.1; 12.2,7; 13.15; 15.18; 22.16-18
26.4 Gen 15.5; 22.17; Ex 32.15; Gen 12.3; 22.18; Gal 3.8
26.7 Gen 12.13; 20.2,12,13
26.10 Gen 20.9
26.12 ver 3
26.14 Gen 24.35; 37.11
26.15 Gen 21.25,30
26.18 Gen 21.31
26.22 Gen 17.6
26.24 Gen 17.7; 24.12; Ex 3.6
26.25 Gen 12.7,8; 13.4,18; Ps 116.17
26.26 Gen 21.22
26.27 ver 16
26.28 Gen 21.22,23
26.31 Gen 21.31
26.33 Gen 21.31

birthright to Jacob. 34 Then Jacob gave Esau
bread and lentil stew, and he ate and drank,
and rose and went his way. Thus Esau
despised his birthright.

Isaac and Abimelech

26 Now there was a famine in the
land, besides the former famine
that had occurred in the days of Abraham.
And Isaac went to Gerar, to King Abimelech
of the Philistines. 2 The LORD appeared to
Isaac[u] and said, "Do not go down to Egypt;
settle in the land that I shall show you.
3 Reside in this land as an alien, and I will
be with you, and will bless you; for to you
and to your descendants I will give all these
lands, and I will fulfill the oath that I swore
to your father Abraham. 4 I will make your
offspring as numerous as the stars of heaven,
and will give to your offspring all these
lands; and all the nations of the earth shall
gain blessing for themselves through your
offspring, 5 because Abraham obeyed my voice
and kept my charge, my commandments,
my statutes, and my laws."
6 So Isaac settled in Gerar. 7 When the
men of the place asked him about his wife,
he said, "She is my sister"; for he was afraid
to say, "My wife," thinking, "or else the
men of the place might kill me for the sake
of Rebekah, because she is attractive in
appearance." 8 When Isaac had been there
a long time, King Abimelech of the Philistines
looked out of a window and saw him fondling his wife Rebekah. 9 So Abimelech called
for Isaac, and said, "So she is your wife!
Why then did you say, 'She is my sister'?"
Isaac said to him, "Because I thought I
might die because of her." 10 Abimelech said,
"What is this you have done to us? One of
the people might easily have lain with your
wife, and you would have brought guilt
upon us." 11 So Abimelech warned all the
people, saying, "Whoever touches this man
or his wife shall be put to death."
12 Isaac sowed seed in that land, and in
the same year reaped a hundredfold. The
LORD blessed him, 13 and the man became
rich; he prospered more and more until he
became very wealthy. 14 He had possessions
of flocks and herds, and a great household,
so that the Philistines envied him. 15 (Now
the Philistines had stopped up and filled
with earth all the wells that his father's
servants had dug in the days of his father
Abraham.) 16 And Abimelech said to Isaac,
"Go away from us; you have become too
powerful for us."
17 So Isaac departed from there and
camped in the valley of Gerar and settled
there. 18 Isaac dug again the wells of water
that had been dug in the days of his father
Abraham; for the Philistines had stopped
them up after the death of Abraham; and
he gave them the names that his father had
given them. 19 But when Isaac's servants
dug in the valley and found there a well of
spring water, 20 the herders of Gerar quarreled
with Isaac's herders, saying, "The water is
ours." So he called the well Esek,[v] because
they contended with him. 21 Then they dug
another well, and they quarreled over that
one also; so he called it Sitnah.[w] 22 He moved
from there and dug another well, and they
did not quarrel over it; so he called it
Rehoboth,[x] saying, "Now the LORD has made
room for us, and we shall be fruitful in the
land."
23 From there he went up to Beer-sheba.
24 And that very night the LORD appeared to
him and said, "I am the God of your father
Abraham; do not be afraid, for I am with
you and will bless you and make your
offspring numerous for my servant
Abraham's sake." 25 So he built an altar
there, called on the name of the LORD, and
pitched his tent there. And there Isaac's
servants dug a well.
26 Then Abimelech went to him from
Gerar, with Ahuzzath his adviser and Phicol
the commander of his army. 27 Isaac said to
them, "Why have you come to me, seeing
that you hate me and have sent me away
from you?" 28 They said, "We see plainly
that the LORD has been with you; so we say,
let there be an oath between you and us,
and let us make a covenant with you 29 so
that you will do us no harm, just as we
have not touched you and have done to
you nothing but good and have sent you
away in peace. You are now the blessed of
the LORD." 30 So he made them a feast, and
they ate and drank. 31 In the morning they
rose early and exchanged oaths; and Isaac
set them on their way, and they departed
from him in peace. 32 That same day Isaac's
servants came and told him about the well
that they had dug, and said to him, "We
have found water!" 33 He called it Shibah;[y]

[u] Heb *him* [v] That is *Contention* [w] That is *Enmity* [x] That is *Broad places* or *Room* [y] A word resembling the word for *oath*

26.1 The *former famine* is mentioned in 12.10.
26.2-16 Isaac's extended stay in the realm of Abimelech and his claim that Rebekah is his sister parallel the stories of Abraham in 12.10-16 and 20.1-18. The advice of the LORD, *Do not go down to Egypt*, contrasts with the instruction to Jacob (Israel) in 45.3-4 to go there and that God will be with him. The covenantal promises are given to Isaac here (26.3-5) as they were to Abraham in 12.2-7; 15.7; 22.17, but a new feature which reflects the later period in which Genesis was finally edited is the inclusion of obedience to *my commandments, my statutes, and my laws*. Combining agriculture with developing *flocks and herds* was a typical pattern for semi-nomads at this time in this area. The enormous productivity of the crops and the flocks was evidence that *The LORD blessed him*, but led the king to drive him away.
26.17-35 *Gerar* is an unknown place in the Negeb. Isaac's reopening of the wells and the digging of new water sources – with their symbolic names – leads the local people to allow him to reside at various places in the region, culminating in the mutual agreement reached with Abimelech like the earlier one with Abraham (21.22-34). The report that Esau's taking wives from among the local people caused conflicts within his family has its sequel in 28.8-9, where he marries the daughter of his uncle Ishmael.

27.1-40 Rebekah deceives Isaac into blessing Jacob. The preparation and eating of food were regarded as essential to the completion of covenant agreements. At issue is the utterance of a blessing which will guarantee the prosperity of the son and his first place in the family hierarchy. It is not a wish but a prophetic pronouncement which is irrevocable and inevitable in its effect. The secondary role for Esau is now determined, and he is assigned to nomadic, marginal existence in endless struggle for survival, though with ultimate independence from Jacob.

therefore the name of the city is Beer-sheba[z] to this day.

Esau's Hittite Wives

34 When Esau was forty years old, he married Judith daughter of Beeri the Hittite, and Basemath daughter of Elon the Hittite; [35]and they made life bitter for Isaac and Rebekah.

Isaac Blesses Jacob

27 When Isaac was old and his eyes were dim so that he could not see, he called his elder son Esau and said to him, "My son"; and he answered, "Here I am." [2]He said, "See, I am old; I do not know the day of my death. [3]Now then, take your weapons, your quiver and your bow, and go out to the field, and hunt game for me. [4]Then prepare for me savory food, such as I like, and bring it to me to eat, so that I may bless you before I die."

5 Now Rebekah was listening when Isaac spoke to his son Esau. So when Esau went to the field to hunt for game and bring it, [6]Rebekah said to her son Jacob, "I heard your father say to your brother Esau, [7]'Bring me game, and prepare for me savory food to eat, that I may bless you before the LORD before I die.' [8]Now therefore, my son, obey my word as I command you. [9]Go to the flock, and get me two choice kids, so that I may prepare from them savory food for your father, such as he likes; [10]and you shall take it to your father to eat, so that he may bless you before he dies." [11]But Jacob said to his mother Rebekah, "Look, my brother Esau is a hairy man, and I am a man of smooth skin. [12]Perhaps my father will feel me, and I shall seem to be mocking him, and bring a curse on myself and not a blessing." [13]His mother said to him, "Let your curse be on me, my son; only obey my word, and go, get them for me." [14]So he went and got them and brought them to his mother; and his mother prepared savory food, such as his father loved. [15]Then Rebekah took the best garments of her elder son Esau, which were with her in the house, and put them on her younger son Jacob; [16]and she put the skins of the kids on his hands and on the smooth part of his neck. [17]Then she handed the savory food, and the bread that she had prepared, to her son Jacob.

18 So he went in to his father, and said, "My father"; and he said, "Here I am; who are you, my son?" [19]Jacob said to his father, "I am Esau your firstborn. I have done as you told me; now sit up and eat of my game, so that you may bless me." [20]But Isaac said to his son, "How is it that you have found it so quickly, my son?" He answered, "Because the LORD your God granted me success." [21]Then Isaac said to Jacob, "Come near, that I may feel you, my son, to know whether you are really my son Esau or not." [22]So Jacob went up to his father Isaac, who felt him and said, "The voice is Jacob's voice, but the hands are the hands of Esau." [23]He did not recognize him, because his hands were hairy like his brother Esau's hands; so he blessed him. [24]He said, "Are you really my son Esau?" He answered, "I am." [25]Then he said, "Bring it to me, that I may eat of my son's game and bless you." So he brought it to him, and he ate; and he brought him wine, and he drank. [26]Then his father Isaac said to him, "Come near and kiss me, my son." [27]So he came near and kissed him; and he smelled the smell of his garments, and blessed him, and said,

"Ah, the smell of my son
is like the smell of a field that the LORD
has blessed.
[28] May God give you of the dew of heaven,
and of the fatness of the earth,
and plenty of grain and wine.
[29] Let peoples serve you,
and nations bow down to you.
Be lord over your brothers,
and may your mother's sons bow down
to you.
Cursed be everyone who curses you,
and blessed be everyone who blesses
you!"

Esau's Lost Blessing

30 As soon as Isaac had finished blessing Jacob, when Jacob had scarcely gone out from the presence of his father Isaac, his brother Esau came in from his hunting. [31]He also prepared savory food, and brought it to his father. And he said to his father, "Let my father sit up and eat of his son's game, so that you may bless me." [32]His father Isaac said to him, "Who are you?" He answered, "I am your firstborn son, Esau." [33]Then Isaac trembled violently, and said,

[z] That is *Well of the oath* or *Well of seven*

26.34 Gen 28.8; 36.2

26.35 Gen 27.46

27.2 Gen 47.29

27.3 Gen 25.27,28

27.4 ver 27; Gen 48.9,15; 49.28

27.8 ver 13

27.11 Gen 25.25

27.12 ver 21,22

27.13 ver 8; Mt 27.25

27.15 ver 27

27.19 ver 4

27.21 ver 12

27.23 ver 16

27.25 ver 4,10,19,31

27.27 Heb 11.20; Song 4.11

27.28 Deut 33.13,28; Gen 45.18

27.29 Gen 9.25; 25.23; 49.8; 12.3; Num 24.9; Zeph 2.8

27.31 ver 4

27.32 ver 18

27.33 Gen 28.3,4; Rom 11.29

27.34 Heb 12.17
27.36 Gen 25.26,32-34
27.37 ver 28.29
27.38 Heb 12.17
27.39 ver 28
27.40 Gen 25.23; 2 Kings 8.20-22
27.41 Gen 32.3-11
27.43 ver 8,13; Gen 24.29
27.46 Gen 26.34,35
28.1 Gen 24.3,4
28.2 Gen 25.20
28.3 Gen 17.1,6
28.4 Gen 12.2; 17.8
28.6 ver 1
28.8 Gen 24.3; 26.35
28.9 Gen 36.3
28.12 Jn 1.51
28.13 Gen 35.1; 48.3; 26.24; 13.15; 35.12
28.14 Gen 13.14-16; 22.17; 12.3; 18.18; 22.18; 26.4

"Who was it then that hunted game and
brought it to me, and I ate it all[a] before you
came, and I have blessed him?—yes, and
blessed he shall be!" 34When Esau heard his
father's words, he cried out with an exceedingly great and bitter cry, and said to his
father, "Bless me, me also, father!" 35But he
said, "Your brother came deceitfully, and he
has taken away your blessing." 36Esau said,
"Is he not rightly named Jacob?[b] For he has
supplanted me these two times. He took
away my birthright; and look, now he has
taken away my blessing." Then he said,
"Have you not reserved a blessing for me?"
37Isaac answered Esau, "I have already made
him your lord, and I have given him all his
brothers as servants, and with grain and
wine I have sustained him. What then can
I do for you, my son?" 38Esau said to his
father, "Have you only one blessing, father?
Bless me, me also, father!" And Esau lifted
up his voice and wept.

39 Then his father Isaac answered him:
"See, away from[c] the fatness of the earth
shall your home be,
and away from[d] the dew of heaven on
high.
40 By your sword you shall live,
and you shall serve your brother;
but when you break loose,[e]
you shall break his yoke from your
neck."

Jacob Escapes Esau's Fury

41 Now Esau hated Jacob because of the
blessing with which his father had blessed
him, and Esau said to himself, "The days of
mourning for my father are approaching;
then I will kill my brother Jacob." 42But the
words of her elder son Esau were told to
Rebekah; so she sent and called her younger
son Jacob and said to him, "Your brother
Esau is consoling himself by planning to kill
you. 43Now therefore, my son, obey my
voice; flee at once to my brother Laban in
Haran, 44and stay with him a while, until
your brother's fury turns away— 45until
your brother's anger against you turns away,
and he forgets what you have done to him;
then I will send, and bring you back from
there. Why should I lose both of you in one
day?"

46 Then Rebekah said to Isaac, "I am
weary of my life because of the Hittite
women. If Jacob marries one of the Hittite
women such as these, one of the women of
the land, what good will my life be to me?"

28 Then Isaac called Jacob and blessed
him, and charged him, "You shall
not marry one of the Canaanite women.
2Go at once to Paddan-aram to the house
of Bethuel, your mother's father; and take
as wife from there one of the daughters of
Laban, your mother's brother. 3May God
Almighty[f] bless you and make you fruitful
and numerous, that you may become a
company of peoples. 4May he give to you
the blessing of Abraham, to you and to
your offspring with you, so that you may
take possession of the land where you now
live as an alien—land that God gave to
Abraham." 5Thus Isaac sent Jacob away;
and he went to Paddan-aram, to Laban son
of Bethuel the Aramean, the brother of
Rebekah, Jacob's and Esau's mother.

Esau Marries Ishmael's Daughter

6 Now Esau saw that Isaac had blessed
Jacob and sent him away to Paddan-aram
to take a wife from there, and that as he
blessed him he charged him, "You shall not
marry one of the Canaanite women," 7and
that Jacob had obeyed his father and his
mother and gone to Paddan-aram. 8So when
Esau saw that the Canaanite women did
not please his father Isaac, 9Esau went to
Ishmael and took Mahalath daughter of
Abraham's son Ishmael, and sister of
Nebaioth, to be his wife in addition to the
wives he had.

Jacob's Dream at Bethel

10 Jacob left Beer-sheba and went toward Haran. 11He came to a certain place
and stayed there for the night, because the
sun had set. Taking one of the stones of the
place, he put it under his head and lay
down in that place. 12And he dreamed that
there was a ladder[g] set up on the earth, the
top of it reaching to heaven; and the angels
of God were ascending and descending on
it. 13And the LORD stood beside him[h] and
said, "I am the LORD, the God of Abraham
your father and the God of Isaac; the land
on which you lie I will give to you and to
your offspring; 14and your offspring shall be
like the dust of the earth, and you shall

[a] Cn: Heb *of all* [b] That is *He supplants* or *He takes by the heel* [c] Or *See, of* [d] Or *and of* [e] Meaning of Heb uncertain [f] Traditional rendering of Heb *El Shaddai* [g] Or *stairway* or *ramp* [h] Or *stood above it*

27.41-28.5 Esau's plot to kill Jacob is the occasion for the latter to marry within his tribe. Like Isaac (Gen 24), he goes to the ancestral center, Padan-aram, to procure a wife from Laban, Rebekah's brother.
28.6-9 Esau approximates his brother's strategy by marrying his uncle Ishmael's daughter. Polygamy is the norm, and endogamy is preferred.
28.10-22 Jacob's goal, Haran, in northern Mesopotamia, is the city where Abram's father went after leaving Ur of the Chaldees (Gen 11.31-32) and where he died, and from where Abram by God's instruction migrated to the land of Canaan (Gen 12). Isaac's wife was from there (Gen 24.10). The *ladder* in Jacob's dream probably refers to the step-like pyramids, called ziggurats, which in Mesopotamian religions were thought to provide access to the gods above. The voice of the LORD renews the promises made to Abraham, though now with the addition of two generations of offspring. Once again, possession of the land of Canaan and sharing by *all the families of the earth* in the benefits of the covenant are pronounced. That this is a place of meeting of God and humans is attested in the name *Bethel,* the house of God. In the days of Israel's first king, Saul, Bethel is a place where worshippers are reported as *going up to God* (1 Sam 10.3). The stone *pillar* which Jacob had the strength to set up alone is an example of sacred columns found among many people of the ancient Middle East, often seen as sexual symbols of union with the deities. In later Israelite law, they were prohibited (Ex 23.24; Deut 7.5; Lev 26.1) and they were also denounced by the prophets (Hos 3.4; Mic 5.13). He promises to erect *God's house* on the site, a project which is described in Gen 35.

29.1-14 Jacob meets Rachel and Laban. The fact that *the stone* had to be *rolled from the mouth of the well* shows that it was a cistern rather than a spring, with a massive stone cover that was to be removed only when all users were present. Jacob showed his strength and special favor for Rachel when he *rolled the stone* singlehandedly. Then he showed his affection for his mother's family when he *kissed Rachel and wept*, identifying his relationship to her and her family.
29.15-30.24 Lacking the tangible resources to pay the price for the bride of his choice, Rachel, he agrees to work for her father for seven years. In a reversal of Jacob's string of tricks played on his relatives to gain his personal ends, Laban keeps him in his service for fourteen years by insisting on giving him first his older daughter, Leah ("cow"), and then, seven years later, Rachel ("ewe"). The term *week* used here refers to a cycle of seven – in this case, seven years. Like Sarah, *Rachel was barren*. It is only after a series of sons are born to Leah (Reuben, Simeon, Levi and Judah), to Rachel's maid (Dan and Naphtali) and to Leah's maid (Gad and Asher), then again to Leah when she uses a type of the nightshade plant known as mandrake to enhance her fertility (Issachar and Zebulun, in addition to a daughter, Dinah) that *God heeded* Rachel's prayer and she bears Jacob a son (Joseph).

spread abroad to the west and to the east
and to the north and to the south; and all
the families of the earth shall be blessed[i] in
you and in your offspring. 15Know that I am
with you and will keep you wherever you
go, and will bring you back to this land; for
I will not leave you until I have done what
I have promised you." 16Then Jacob woke
from his sleep and said, "Surely the LORD is
in this place—and I did not know it!" 17And
he was afraid, and said, "How awesome is
this place! This is none other than the
house of God, and this is the gate of heaven."
18 So Jacob rose early in the morning,
and he took the stone that he had put
under his head and set it up for a pillar and
poured oil on the top of it. 19He called that
place Bethel;[j] but the name of the city was
Luz at the first. 20Then Jacob made a vow,
saying, "If God will be with me, and will
keep me in this way that I go, and will give
me bread to eat and clothing to wear, 21so
that I come again to my father's house in
peace, then the LORD shall be my God, 22and
this stone, which I have set up for a pillar,
shall be God's house; and of all that you
give me I will surely give one tenth to you."

Jacob Meets Rachel

29 Then Jacob went on his journey,
and came to the land of the people
of the east. 2As he looked, he saw a well in
the field and three flocks of sheep lying
there beside it; for out of that well the flocks
were watered. The stone on the well's mouth
was large, 3and when all the flocks were
gathered there, the shepherds would roll
the stone from the mouth of the well, and
water the sheep, and put the stone back in
its place on the mouth of the well.
4 Jacob said to them, "My brothers, where
do you come from?" They said, "We are
from Haran." 5He said to them, "Do you
know Laban son of Nahor?" They said, "We
do." 6He said to them, "Is it well with him?"
"Yes," they replied, "and here is his daughter Rachel, coming with the sheep." 7He
said, "Look, it is still broad daylight; it is not
time for the animals to be gathered together. Water the sheep, and go, pasture
them." 8But they said, "We cannot until all
the flocks are gathered together, and the
stone is rolled from the mouth of the well;
then we water the sheep."
9 While he was still speaking with them,
Rachel came with her father's sheep; for she
kept them. 10Now when Jacob saw Rachel,
the daughter of his mother's brother Laban,
and the sheep of his mother's brother Laban,
Jacob went up and rolled the stone from the
well's mouth, and watered the flock of his
mother's brother Laban. 11Then Jacob kissed
Rachel, and wept aloud. 12And Jacob told
Rachel that he was her father's kinsman,
and that he was Rebekah's son; and she ran
and told her father.
13 When Laban heard the news about
his sister's son Jacob, he ran to meet him;
he embraced him and kissed him, and
brought him to his house. Jacob[k] told Laban
all these things, 14and Laban said to him,
"Surely you are my bone and my flesh!"
And he stayed with him a month.

Jacob Marries Laban's Daughters

15 Then Laban said to Jacob, "Because
you are my kinsman, should you therefore
serve me for nothing? Tell me, what shall
your wages be?" 16Now Laban had two
daughters; the name of the elder was Leah,
and the name of the younger was Rachel.
17Leah's eyes were lovely,[l] and Rachel was
graceful and beautiful. 18Jacob loved Rachel;
so he said, "I will serve you seven years for
your younger daughter Rachel." 19Laban
said, "It is better that I give her to you than
that I should give her to any other man;
stay with me." 20So Jacob served seven
years for Rachel, and they seemed to him
but a few days because of the love he had
for her.
21 Then Jacob said to Laban, "Give me
my wife that I may go in to her, for my time
is completed." 22So Laban gathered together
all the people of the place, and made a feast.
23But in the evening he took his daughter
Leah and brought her to Jacob; and he
went in to her. 24(Laban gave his maid
Zilpah to his daughter Leah to be her maid.)
25When morning came, it was Leah! And
Jacob said to Laban, "What is this you have
done to me? Did I not serve with you for
Rachel? Why then have you deceived me?"
26Laban said, "This is not done in our country—giving the younger before the firstborn.
27Complete the week of this one, and we
will give you the other also in return for
serving me another seven years." 28Jacob
did so, and completed her week; then Laban
gave him his daughter Rachel as a wife.

[i] Or *shall bless themselves* [j] That is *House of God* [k] Heb *He* [l] Meaning of Heb uncertain

28.15 Gen 26.3; Num 6.24; Ps 121.7,8; Gen 48.21; Deut 31.6,8
28.16 Ex 3.5; Josh 5.15
28.18 Gen 35.14; Lev 8.10-12
28.19 Judg 1.23,26; Hos 4.15
28.20 Gen 31.13; ver 15; 1 Tim 6.8
28.21 Judg 11.31; 2 Sam 19.24,30; Deut 26.17; 2 Sam 15.8
28.22 Gen 35.7,14; Lev 27.30
29.1 Judg 6.3,33
29.4 Gen 28.10
29.5 Gen 24.24,29
29.6 Gen 43.27
29.9 Ex 2.16
29.10 Ex 2.17
29.12 Gen 13.8; 14.14,16; 24.28
29.13 Gen 24.29,31; 33.4
29.14 Judg 9.2
29.18 Hos 12.12
29.21 Judg 15.1
29.22 Judg 14.10; Jn 2.1,2
29.27 Judg 14.12

29.30 ver 17,18
29.31 Ps 127.3; Gen 30.1
29.32 Gen 16.11; 31.42
29.34 Gen 49.5
29.35 Gen 49.8; Mt 1.2
30.1 1 Sam 1.5,6
30.2 Gen 20.18; 29.31
30.3 Gen 16.2
30.4 Gen 16.3,4
30.6 Lam 3.59
30.8 Mt 4.13
30.9 ver 4
30.13 Prov 31.28
30.14 Gen 25.30
30.15 Num 16.9,13
30.20 Mt 4.13
30.22 1 Sam 1.19,20; Gen 29.31
30.23 Isa 4.1; Lk 1.25
30.24 Gen 35.17
30.25 Gen 24.54,56
30.27 Gen 39.3,5
30.28 Gen 29.15
30.29 Gen 31.38-40
30.30 1 Tim 5.8
30.32 Gen 31.8

29(Laban gave his maid Bilhah to his daughter Rachel to be her maid.) 30So Jacob went
in to Rachel also, and he loved Rachel more
than Leah. He served Laban[m] for another
seven years.
31 When the LORD saw that Leah was
unloved, he opened her womb; but Rachel
was barren. 32Leah conceived and bore a
son, and she named him Reuben;[n] for she
said, "Because the LORD has looked on my
affliction; surely now my husband will love
me." 33She conceived again and bore a son,
and said, "Because the LORD has heard[o] that
I am hated, he has given me this son also";
and she named him Simeon. 34Again she
conceived and bore a son, and said, "Now
this time my husband will be joined[p] to me,
because I have borne him three sons";
therefore he was named Levi. 35She conceived again and bore a son, and said, "This
time I will praise[q] the LORD"; therefore she
named him Judah; then she ceased bearing.
30 When Rachel saw that she bore
Jacob no children, she envied her
sister; and she said to Jacob, "Give me
children, or I shall die!" 2Jacob became very
angry with Rachel and said, "Am I in the
place of God, who has withheld from you
the fruit of the womb?" 3Then she said,
"Here is my maid Bilhah; go in to her, that
she may bear upon my knees and that I too
may have children through her." 4So she
gave him her maid Bilhah as a wife; and
Jacob went in to her. 5And Bilhah conceived
and bore Jacob a son. 6Then Rachel said,
"God has judged me, and has also heard my
voice and given me a son"; therefore she
named him Dan.[r] 7Rachel's maid Bilhah
conceived again and bore Jacob a second
son. 8Then Rachel said, "With mighty
wrestlings I have wrestled[s] with my sister,
and have prevailed"; so she named him
Naphtali.
9 When Leah saw that she had ceased
bearing children, she took her maid Zilpah
and gave her to Jacob as a wife. 10Then
Leah's maid Zilpah bore Jacob a son. 11And
Leah said, "Good fortune!" so she named
him Gad.[t] 12Leah's maid Zilpah bore Jacob
a second son. 13And Leah said, "Happy am
I! For the women will call me happy"; so
she named him Asher.[u]
14 In the days of wheat harvest Reuben
went and found mandrakes in the field, and
brought them to his mother Leah. Then
Rachel said to Leah, "Please give me some
of your son's mandrakes." 15But she said to
her, "Is it a small matter that you have
taken away my husband? Would you take
away my son's mandrakes also?" Rachel
said, "Then he may lie with you tonight for
your son's mandrakes." 16When Jacob came
from the field in the evening, Leah went out
to meet him, and said, "You must come in
to me; for I have hired you with my son's
mandrakes." So he lay with her that night.
17And God heeded Leah, and she conceived
and bore Jacob a fifth son. 18Leah said, "God
has given me my hire[v] because I gave my
maid to my husband"; so she named him
Issachar. 19And Leah conceived again, and
she bore Jacob a sixth son. 20Then Leah
said, "God has endowed me with a good
dowry; now my husband will honor[w] me,
because I have borne him six sons"; so she
named him Zebulun. 21Afterwards she bore
a daughter, and named her Dinah.
22 Then God remembered Rachel, and
God heeded her and opened her womb.
23She conceived and bore a son, and said,
"God has taken away my reproach"; 24and
she named him Joseph,[x] saying, "May the
LORD add to me another son!"

Jacob Prospers at Laban's Expense

25 When Rachel had borne Joseph, Jacob
said to Laban, "Send me away, that I may
go to my own home and country. 26Give me
my wives and my children for whom I have
served you, and let me go; for you know
very well the service I have given you."
27But Laban said to him, "If you will allow
me to say so, I have learned by divination
that the LORD has blessed me because of
you; 28name your wages, and I will give it."
29Jacob said to him, "You yourself know
how I have served you, and how your cattle
have fared with me. 30For you had little
before I came, and it has increased abundantly; and the LORD has blessed you wherever I turned. But now when shall I provide
for my own household also?" 31He said,
"What shall I give you?" Jacob said, "You
shall not give me anything; if you will do
this for me, I will again feed your flock and
keep it: 32let me pass through all your flock
today, removing from it every speckled and

30.25-43 When Laban agrees with Jacob to divide the flocks as a way of paying him for his services, Jacob engages in a form of imitative magic which stimulates the reproduction of the striped, spotted and black sheep that were to become his as he left. It is with irony that he notes *"My honesty will answer for me later."*

[m] Heb *him* [n] That is *See, a son* [o] Heb *shama* [p] Heb *lawah* [q] Heb *hodah* [r] That is *He judged* [s] Heb *niphtal* [t] That is *Fortune* [u] That is *Happy* [v] Heb *sakar* [w] Heb *zabal* [x] That is *He adds*

31.1-32.2 Having discovered how Jacob's scheme has robbed him of his resources and that the family gods have been stolen as well, Laban pursues him. Jacob, having become *exceedingly rich* through his accumulation of flocks, camels, donkeys, and male and female slaves, has set out for his home territory in Canaan. When Laban overtakes them, Rachel tricks her father to prevent his finding the household gods she is sitting on, and Jacob defends his actions in gaining such an abundance of flocks and other possessions on the grounds that the God of his ancestors has enabled him to prosper. Implicit here is the impotence of the household gods as contrasted with the God of Abraham. Another name for this God is the Fear of Isaac, or "the God whom Isaac fears," because of his limitless power. The *covenant* with the LORD into which Laban and Jacob enter is sealed by shared meals and marked by a sacred *pillar*, which is to remind both that God will be keeping watch on their respective behavior even when they cannot watch one another. Laban's choice (31.47) of an Aramaic name for the place, Jegar-sadutha, and Jacob's assigning to it a Hebrew name, Galeed, indicate the mixed cultural and ethnic circumstances and resultant tensions under which these traditions arose. Mahanaim, the name which Jacob later gives to the place of the covenant, probably means that he regards it as God's military-like encampment, where he fights on Jacob's side.

spotted sheep and every black lamb, and the
spotted and speckled among the goats; and
such shall be my wages. 33So my honesty
will answer for me later, when you come
to look into my wages with you. Every one
that is not speckled and spotted among the
goats and black among the lambs, if found
with me, shall be counted stolen." 34Laban
said, "Good! Let it be as you have said."
35But that day Laban removed the male
goats that were striped and spotted, and all
the female goats that were speckled and
spotted, every one that had white on it, and
every lamb that was black, and put them
in charge of his sons; 36and he set a distance
of three days' journey between himself and
Jacob, while Jacob was pasturing the rest of
Laban's flock.
37 Then Jacob took fresh rods of poplar
and almond and plane, and peeled white
streaks in them, exposing the white of the
rods. 38He set the rods that he had peeled
in front of the flocks in the troughs, that is,
the watering places, where the flocks came
to drink. And since they bred when they
came to drink, 39the flocks bred in front of
the rods, and so the flocks produced young
that were striped, speckled, and spotted.
40Jacob separated the lambs, and set the
faces of the flocks toward the striped and
the completely black animals in the flock of
Laban; and he put his own droves apart,
and did not put them with Laban's flock.
41Whenever the stronger of the flock were
breeding, Jacob laid the rods in the troughs
before the eyes of the flock, that they might
breed among the rods, 42but for the feebler
of the flock he did not lay them there; so
the feebler were Laban's, and the stronger
Jacob's. 43Thus the man grew exceedingly
rich, and had large flocks, and male and
female slaves, and camels and donkeys.

Jacob Flees with Family and Flocks

31 Now Jacob heard that the sons of
Laban were saying, "Jacob has taken
all that was our father's; he has gained all
this wealth from what belonged to our
father." 2And Jacob saw that Laban did not
regard him as favorably as he did before.
3Then the LORD said to Jacob, "Return to the
land of your ancestors and to your kindred,
and I will be with you." 4So Jacob sent and
called Rachel and Leah into the field where
his flock was, 5and said to them, "I see that
your father does not regard me as favorably
as he did before. But the God of my father
has been with me. 6You know that I have
served your father with all my strength;
7yet your father has cheated me and changed
my wages ten times, but God did not permit
him to harm me. 8If he said, 'The speckled
shall be your wages,' then all the flock bore
speckled; and if he said, 'The striped shall
be your wages,' then all the flock bore
striped. 9Thus God has taken away the
livestock of your father, and given them to
me.
10 During the mating of the flock I once
had a dream in which I looked up and saw
that the male goats that leaped upon the
flock were striped, speckled, and mottled.
11Then the angel of God said to me in the
dream, 'Jacob,' and I said, 'Here I am!'
12And he said, 'Look up and see that all the
goats that leap on the flock are striped,
speckled, and mottled; for I have seen all
that Laban is doing to you. 13I am the God
of Bethel,[y] where you anointed a pillar and
made a vow to me. Now leave this land at
once and return to the land of your birth.'
" 14Then Rachel and Leah answered him,
"Is there any portion or inheritance left to
us in our father's house? 15Are we not
regarded by him as foreigners? For he has
sold us, and he has been using up the
money given for us. 16All the property that
God has taken away from our father belongs to us and to our children; now then,
do whatever God has said to you."
17 So Jacob arose, and set his children
and his wives on camels; 18and he drove
away all his livestock, all the property that
he had gained, the livestock in his possession that he had acquired in Paddan-aram,
to go to his father Isaac in the land of
Canaan.
19 Now Laban had gone to shear his
sheep, and Rachel stole her father's household gods. 20And Jacob deceived Laban the
Aramean, in that he did not tell him that
he intended to flee. 21So he fled with all that
he had; starting out he crossed the
Euphrates,[z] and set his face toward the hill
country of Gilead.

Laban Overtakes Jacob

22 On the third day Laban was told that
Jacob had fled. 23So he took his kinsfolk
with him and pursued him for seven days

[y] Cn: Meaning of Heb uncertain [z] Heb *the river*

30.33 Ps 37.6
30.37 Gen 31.9-12
30.43 Gen 12.16; 13.2; 24.35; 26.13,14
31.3 Gen 28.15,20,21; 32.9
31.5 ver 3,42; Gen 48.15
31.7 ver 41; Job 19.3; Ps 37.28; 105.14
31.8 Gen 30.32
31.11 Gen 48.16
31.13 Gen 28.13,18,20
31.14 Gen 29.15,27
31.19 ver 30.34; Judg 17.5; 1 Sam 19.13; Hos 3.4
31.21 Gen 37.25
31.23 Gen 13.8

31.24 Gen 20.3; Job 33.15; Gen 24.50
31.26 1 Sam 30.2
31.27 ver 55; Ruth 1.9,14; Acts 20.37
31.29 ver 53,24
31.30 ver 19
31.32 Gen 44.9
31.35 Ex 20.12; Lev 19.32
31.39 Ex 22.10-13
31.41 Gen 29.27,30; ver 7
31.42 Ps 124.1,2; ver 53; Isa 8.13; Gen 29.32; 1 Chr 12.17
31.44 Gen 21.27,32; 26.28; Josh 24.27
31.45 Gen 28.18
31.48 Josh 24.27
31.49 Judg 11.29; 1 Sam 7.5
31.53 Gen 16.5; 21.23; 28.13; ver 42

until he caught up with him in the hill country of Gilead. [24]But God came to Laban the Aramean in a dream by night, and said to him, "Take heed that you say not a word to Jacob, either good or bad."

25 Laban overtook Jacob. Now Jacob had pitched his tent in the hill country, and Laban with his kinsfolk camped in the hill country of Gilead. [26]Laban said to Jacob, "What have you done? You have deceived me, and carried away my daughters like captives of the sword. [27]Why did you flee secretly and deceive me and not tell me? I would have sent you away with mirth and songs, with tambourine and lyre. [28]And why did you not permit me to kiss my sons and my daughters farewell? What you have done is foolish. [29]It is in my power to do you harm; but the God of your father spoke to me last night, saying, 'Take heed that you speak to Jacob neither good nor bad.' [30]Even though you had to go because you longed greatly for your father's house, why did you steal my gods?" [31]Jacob answered Laban, "Because I was afraid, for I thought that you would take your daughters from me by force. [32]But anyone with whom you find your gods shall not live. In the presence of our kinsfolk, point out what I have that is yours, and take it." Now Jacob did not know that Rachel had stolen the gods.[a]

33 So Laban went into Jacob's tent, and into Leah's tent, and into the tent of the two maids, but he did not find them. And he went out of Leah's tent, and entered Rachel's. [34]Now Rachel had taken the household gods and put them in the camel's saddle, and sat on them. Laban felt all about in the tent, but did not find them. [35]And she said to her father, "Let not my lord be angry that I cannot rise before you, for the way of women is upon me." So he searched, but did not find the household gods.

36 Then Jacob became angry, and upbraided Laban. Jacob said to Laban, "What is my offense? What is my sin, that you have hotly pursued me? [37]Although you have felt about through all my goods, what have you found of all your household goods? Set it here before my kinsfolk and your kinsfolk, so that they may decide between us two. [38]These twenty years I have been with you; your ewes and your female goats have not miscarried, and I have not eaten the rams of your flocks. [39]That which was torn by wild beasts I did not bring to you; I bore the loss of it myself; of my hand you required it, whether stolen by day or stolen by night. [40]It was like this with me: by day the heat consumed me, and the cold by night, and my sleep fled from my eyes. [41]These twenty years I have been in your house; I served you fourteen years for your two daughters, and six years for your flock, and you have changed my wages ten times. [42]If the God of my father, the God of Abraham and the Fear[b] of Isaac, had not been on my side, surely now you would have sent me away empty-handed. God saw my affliction and the labor of my hands, and rebuked you last night."

Laban and Jacob Make a Covenant

43 Then Laban answered and said to Jacob, "The daughters are my daughters, the children are my children, the flocks are my flocks, and all that you see is mine. But what can I do today about these daughters of mine, or about their children whom they have borne? [44]Come now, let us make a covenant, you and I; and let it be a witness between you and me." [45]So Jacob took a stone, and set it up as a pillar. [46]And Jacob said to his kinsfolk, "Gather stones," and they took stones, and made a heap; and they ate there by the heap. [47]Laban called it Jegar-sahadutha:[c] but Jacob called it Galeed.[d] [48]Laban said, "This heap is a witness between you and me today." Therefore he called it Galeed, [49]and the pillar[e] Mizpah,[f] for he said, "The LORD watch between you and me, when we are absent one from the other. [50]If you ill-treat my daughters, or if you take wives in addition to my daughters, though no one else is with us, remember that God is witness between you and me."

51 Then Laban said to Jacob, "See this heap and see the pillar, which I have set between you and me. [52]This heap is a witness, and the pillar is a witness, that I will not pass beyond this heap to you, and you will not pass beyond this heap and this pillar to me, for harm. [53]May the God of Abraham and the God of Nahor"—the God of their father—"judge between us." So Jacob swore by the Fear[b] of his father Isaac, [54]and Jacob offered a sacrifice on the height and

[a] Heb *them* [b] Meaning of Heb uncertain [c] In Aramaic *The heap of witness* [d] In Hebrew *The heap of witness* [e] Compare Sam: MT lacks *the pillar* [f] That is *Watchpost*

32.3-21 Jacob's Plan to Appease Esau. When the messengers sent by Jacob to Esau to tell him that his brother is returning a wealthy man from his extended stay *with Laban as an alien* report that Esau is coming with *four hundred men*, he can only assume that it is for purposes of attack, seizure and slaughter. His scheme is to ingratiate himself in advance of the meeting by sending ahead batches of livestock which are to be given in sequence to Esau, whom he deferentially refers to as *my lord*.

32.22-32 As a parenthesis in the story of Jacob's tense dealings with his brother comes the story of his struggle with God, who comes in the form of a *man* who is a powerful wrestling partner but is unable to defeat him. Jacob's name is accordingly changed to Israel, just as his original name was given when he grasped his brother's heel (25.26). The setting for this contest with God is called Penuel, although its designation as *Peniel* makes more explicit its significance as the place where Jacob saw "the face of God." The explanation of why pious Israelites avoid the *thigh muscle* is a reminder that these traditions were edited in their present form at a much later time, although this dietary restriction is not included in the biblical laws.

called his kinsfolk to eat bread; and they ate bread and tarried all night in the hill country.

55[h] Early in the morning Laban rose up, and kissed his grandchildren and his daughters and blessed them; then he departed and returned home.

32 Jacob went on his way and the angels of God met him; 2and when Jacob saw them he said, "This is God's camp!" So he called that place Mahanaim.[h]

Jacob Sends Presents to Appease Esau

3 Jacob sent messengers before him to his brother Esau in the land of Seir, the country of Edom, 4instructing them, "Thus you shall say to my lord Esau: Thus says your servant Jacob, 'I have lived with Laban as an alien, and stayed until now; 5and I have oxen, donkeys, flocks, male and female slaves; and I have sent to tell my lord, in order that I may find favor in your sight.'"

6 The messengers returned to Jacob, saying, "We came to your brother Esau, and he is coming to meet you, and four hundred men are with him." 7Then Jacob was greatly afraid and distressed; and he divided the people that were with him, and the flocks and herds and camels, into two companies, 8thinking, "If Esau comes to the one company and destroys it, then the company that is left will escape."

9 And Jacob said, "O God of my father Abraham and God of my father Isaac, O LORD who said to me, 'Return to your country and to your kindred, and I will do you good,' 10I am not worthy of the least of all the steadfast love and all the faithfulness that you have shown to your servant, for with only my staff I crossed this Jordan; and now I have become two companies. 11Deliver me, please, from the hand of my brother, from the hand of Esau, for I am afraid of him; he may come and kill us all, the mothers with the children. 12Yet you have said, 'I will surely do you good, and make your offspring as the sand of the sea, which cannot be counted because of their number.'"

13 So he spent that night there, and from what he had with him he took a present for his brother Esau, 14two hundred female goats and twenty male goats, two hundred ewes and twenty rams, 15thirty milch camels and their colts, forty cows and ten bulls, twenty female donkeys and ten male donkeys. 16These he delivered into the hand of his servants, every drove by itself, and said to his servants, "Pass on ahead of me, and put a space between drove and drove." 17He instructed the foremost, "When Esau my brother meets you, and asks you, 'To whom do you belong? Where are you going? And whose are these ahead of you?' 18then you shall say, 'They belong to your servant Jacob; they are a present sent to my lord Esau; and moreover he is behind us.'" 19He likewise instructed the second and the third and all who followed the droves, "You shall say the same thing to Esau when you meet him, 20and you shall say, 'Moreover your servant Jacob is behind us.'" For he thought, "I may appease him with the present that goes ahead of me, and afterwards I shall see his face; perhaps he will accept me." 21So the present passed on ahead of him; and he himself spent that night in the camp.

Jacob Wrestles at Peniel

22 The same night he got up and took his two wives, his two maids, and his eleven children, and crossed the ford of the Jabbok. 23He took them and sent them across the stream, and likewise everything that he had. 24Jacob was left alone; and a man wrestled with him until daybreak. 25When the man saw that he did not prevail against Jacob, he struck him on the hip socket; and Jacob's hip was put out of joint as he wrestled with him. 26Then he said, "Let me go, for the day is breaking." But Jacob said, "I will not let you go, unless you bless me." 27So he said to him, "What is your name?" And he said, "Jacob." 28Then the man[i] said, "You shall no longer be called Jacob, but Israel,[j] for you have striven with God and with humans,[k] and have prevailed." 29Then Jacob asked him, "Please tell me your name." But he said, "Why is it that you ask my name?" And there he blessed him. 30So Jacob called the place Peniel,[l] saying, "For I have seen God face to face, and yet my life is preserved." 31The sun rose upon him as he passed Penuel, limping because of his

31.55 Gen 18.33; 30.25
32.2 Ps 103.21
32.3 Gen 33.14,16; 25.30; 36.8,9
32.4 Prov 15.1
32.5 Gen 30.43; 33.8,15
32.6 Gen 33.1
32.7 ver 11
32.9 Gen 31.42; 28.15; 31.13
32.10 Gen 24.27; Job 8.7
32.11 Gen 27.41,42; 33.4
32.12 Gen 28.13-15
32.13 Gen 43.11; Prov 18.16
32.20 Prov 21.14
32.22 Deut 3.16; Josh 12.2
32.24 Hos 12.3,4
32.26 Hos 12.4
32.28 Gen 35.10; 1 Kings 18.31
32.29 Judg 13.17,18
32.30 Gen 16.13; Ex 24.11; Num 12.8; Judg 6.22; 13.22

[g] Ch 32.1 in Heb [h] Here taken to mean *Two camps* [i] Heb *he* [j] That is *The one who strives with God* or *God strives* [k] Or *with divine and human beings* [l] That is *The face of God*

hip. [32]Therefore to this day the Israelites do not eat the thigh muscle that is on the hip socket, because he struck Jacob on the hip socket at the thigh muscle.

Jacob and Esau Meet

33 Now Jacob looked up and saw Esau coming, and four hundred men with him. So he divided the children among Leah and Rachel and the two maids. [2]He put the maids with their children in front, then Leah with her children, and Rachel and Joseph last of all. [3]He himself went on ahead of them, bowing himself to the ground seven times, until he came near his brother.

4 But Esau ran to meet him, and embraced him, and fell on his neck and kissed him, and they wept. [5]When Esau looked up and saw the women and children, he said, "Who are these with you?" Jacob said, "The children whom God has graciously given your servant." [6]Then the maids drew near, they and their children, and bowed down; [7]Leah likewise and her children drew near and bowed down; and finally Joseph and Rachel drew near, and they bowed down. [8]Esau said, "What do you mean by all this company that I met?" Jacob answered, "To find favor with my lord." [9]But Esau said, "I have enough, my brother; keep what you have for yourself." [10]Jacob said, "No, please; if I find favor with you, then accept my present from my hand; for truly to see your face is like seeing the face of God—since you have received me with such favor. [11]Please accept my gift that is brought to you, because God has dealt graciously with me, and because I have everything I want." So he urged him, and he took it.

12 Then Esau said, "Let us journey on our way, and I will go alongside you." [13]But Jacob said to him, "My lord knows that the children are frail and that the flocks and herds, which are nursing, are a care to me; and if they are overdriven for one day, all the flocks will die. [14]Let my lord pass on ahead of his servant, and I will lead on slowly, according to the pace of the cattle that are before me and according to the pace of the children, until I come to my lord in Seir."

15 So Esau said, "Let me leave with you some of the people who are with me." But he said, "Why should my lord be so kind to me?" [16]So Esau returned that day on his way to Seir. [17]But Jacob journeyed to Succoth,[m] and built himself a house, and made booths for his cattle; therefore the place is called Succoth.

Jacob Reaches Shechem

18 Jacob came safely to the city of Shechem, which is in the land of Canaan, on his way from Paddan-aram; and he camped before the city. [19]And from the sons of Hamor, Shechem's father, he bought for one hundred pieces of money[n] the plot of land on which he had pitched his tent. [20]There he erected an altar and called it El-Elohe-Israel.[o]

The Rape of Dinah

34 Now Dinah the daughter of Leah, whom she had borne to Jacob, went out to visit the women of the region. [2]When Shechem son of Hamor the Hivite, prince of the region, saw her, he seized her and lay with her by force. [3]And his soul was drawn to Dinah daughter of Jacob; he loved the girl, and spoke tenderly to her. [4]So Shechem spoke to his father Hamor, saying, "Get me this girl to be my wife."

5 Now Jacob heard that Shechem[p] had defiled his daughter Dinah; but his sons were with his cattle in the field, so Jacob held his peace until they came. [6]And Hamor the father of Shechem went out to Jacob to speak with him, [7]just as the sons of Jacob came in from the field. When they heard of it, the men were indignant and very angry, because he had committed an outrage in Israel by lying with Jacob's daughter, for such a thing ought not to be done.

8 But Hamor spoke with them, saying, "The heart of my son Shechem longs for your daughter; please give her to him in marriage. [9]Make marriages with us; give your daughters to us, and take our daughters for yourselves. [10]You shall live with us; and the land shall be open to you; live and trade in it, and get property in it." [11]Shechem also said to her father and to her brothers, "Let me find favor with you, and whatever you say to me I will give. [12]Put the marriage present and gift as high as you like, and I will give whatever you ask me; only give

33.1 Gen 32.6
33.3 Gen 18.2; 42.6
33.4 Gen 45.14,15
33.5 Gen 48.9; Ps 127.3; Isa 8.18
33.8 Gen 32.14-16
33.10 Gen 43.3; 2 Sam 3.13
33.11 1 Sam 25.27
33.14 Gen 32.3
33.15 Gen 34.11; 47.25; Ruth 2.13
33.17 Judg 8.5,14; Ps 60.6
33.18 Josh 24.1; Judg 9.1; Gen 25.20; 28.2
33.19 Josh 24.32; Jn 4.5
34.1 Gen 30.21
34.4 Judg 14.2
34.7 Deut 22.21; Josh 7.15; Judg 20.6; 2 Sam 13.12
34.10 Gen 13.9; 20.15
34.12 Ex 22.16; Deut 22.29; 1 Sam 18.25

[m] That is *Booths* [n] Heb *one hundred qesitah* [o] That is *God, the God of Israel* [p] Heb *he*

33.1-20 When Jacob and Esau meet, the latter is overwhelmed with affection. Jacob in turn compares the meeting with his having seen *the face of God,* who has confirmed the covenantal promises. After polite debate, Esau accepts the gifts offered by his brother, but Jacob shrewdly uses his concern for his flocks and family to avoid returning with him to the southern regions of Seir. After a period of residence at Succoth on the bank of the Jabbok, east of the Jordan, Jacob crosses west of the Jordan and goes south to *the city of Shechem.* There he bought a *plot of land,* as Abraham had done (Gen 23), and *erected an altar* as had Abraham (12.7). Both actions symbolized the acquisition of the whole of Canaan by the descendants of these patriarchs and the fact that Shechem was to be the central meeting place of God and his people when the tribes of Israel returned from their time of slavery in Egypt (Josh 24).
34.1-31 This violent story of conflict with other tribes resident in Canaan and between the families of the sons of Jacob is composite in nature and only later reached its final form. The slaughter of the men of Shechem by Simeon and Levi fits well their description in Gen 49.5-7 as angry and murderous, and they are denied a share of a portion of the land distributed among Jacob's sons. The refusal to allow Dinah to marry a local ruler is an indication of the threat to the integrity of God's people that was represented by marriage with the local tribes.

35.1-15 In preparation for meeting God again at Bethel Jacob engages in both cultural and ritual purification by ridding himself of the symbols of Mesopotamian religion and social status. The powerful presence of God protects him as he goes. At the site his new name and the covenant promises are renewed; the altar and the sacred pillar are re-established (Gen 28.10-22).

me the girl to be my wife."

13 The sons of Jacob answered Shechem and his father Hamor deceitfully, because he had defiled their sister Dinah. [14]They said to them, "We cannot do this thing, to give our sister to one who is uncircumcised, for that would be a disgrace to us. [15]Only on this condition will we consent to you: that you will become as we are and every male among you be circumcised. [16]Then we will give our daughters to you, and we will take your daughters for ourselves, and we will live among you and become one people. [17]But if you will not listen to us and be circumcised, then we will take our daughter and be gone."

18 Their words pleased Hamor and Hamor's son Shechem. [19]And the young man did not delay to do the thing, because he was delighted with Jacob's daughter. Now he was the most honored of all his family. [20]So Hamor and his son Shechem came to the gate of their city and spoke to the men of their city, saying, [21]"These people are friendly with us; let them live in the land and trade in it, for the land is large enough for them; let us take their daughters in marriage, and let us give them our daughters. [22]Only on this condition will they agree to live among us, to become one people: that every male among us be circumcised as they are circumcised. [23]Will not their livestock, their property, and all their animals be ours? Only let us agree with them, and they will live among us." [24]And all who went out of the city gate heeded Hamor and his son Shechem; and every male was circumcised, all who went out of the gate of his city.

Dinah's Brothers Avenge Their Sister

25 On the third day, when they were still in pain, two of the sons of Jacob, Simeon and Levi, Dinah's brothers, took their swords and came against the city unawares, and killed all the males. [26]They killed Hamor and his son Shechem with the sword, and took Dinah out of Shechem's house, and went away. [27]And the other sons of Jacob came upon the slain, and plundered the city, because their sister had been defiled. [28]They took their flocks and their herds, their donkeys, and whatever was in the city and in the field. [29]All their wealth, all their little ones and their wives, all that was in the houses, they captured and made their prey. [30]Then Jacob said to Simeon and Levi, "You have brought trouble on me by making me odious to the inhabitants of the land, the Canaanites and the Perizzites; my numbers are few, and if they gather themselves against me and attack me, I shall be destroyed, both I and my household." [31]But they said, "Should our sister be treated like a whore?"

Jacob Returns to Bethel

35 God said to Jacob, "Arise, go up to Bethel, and settle there. Make an altar there to the God who appeared to you when you fled from your brother Esau." [2]So Jacob said to his household and to all who were with him, "Put away the foreign gods that are among you, and purify yourselves, and change your clothes; [3]then come, let us go up to Bethel, that I may make an altar there to the God who answered me in the day of my distress and has been with me wherever I have gone." [4]So they gave to Jacob all the foreign gods that they had, and the rings that were in their ears; and Jacob hid them under the oak that was near Shechem.

5 As they journeyed, a terror from God fell upon the cities all around them, so that no one pursued them. [6]Jacob came to Luz (that is, Bethel), which is in the land of Canaan, he and all the people who were with him, [7]and there he built an altar and called the place El-bethel,[q] because it was there that God had revealed himself to him when he fled from his brother. [8]And Deborah, Rebekah's nurse, died, and she was buried under an oak below Bethel. So it was called Allon-bacuth.[r]

9 God appeared to Jacob again when he came from Paddan-aram, and he blessed him. [10]God said to him, "Your name is Jacob; no longer shall you be called Jacob, but Israel shall be your name." So he was called Israel. [11]God said to him, "I am God Almighty:[s] be fruitful and multiply; a nation and a company of nations shall come from you, and kings shall spring from you. [12]The land that I gave to Abraham and Isaac I will give to you, and I will give the land to your offspring after you." [13]Then God went up from him at the place where he had spoken with him. [14]Jacob set up a pillar in the place where he had spoken with him,

[q] That is *God of Bethel* [r] That is *Oak of weeping* [s] Traditional rendering of Heb *El Shaddai*

34.14 Gen 17.14

34.19 1 Chr 4.9

34.24 Gen 23.10

34.25 Gen 49.5-7

34.30 Gen 49.6; Ex 5.21; Gen 36.26,27

35.1 Gen 28.13,19; 27.43

35.2 Gen 31.19; Ex 19.10,14

35.3 Gen 32.7,24; 28.20-22; 28.15

35.4 Hos 2.13; Josh 24.26

35.5 Ex 15.16; Deut 2.25; 11.25

35.6 Gen 28.19; 48.3

35.7 Gen 28.13

35.8 Gen 24.59

35.9 Hos 12.4; Gen 32.29

35.10 Gen 32.28

35.11 Gen 17.1; 28.3; 48.4; 17.6,16; 36.31

35.12 Gen 13.15; 26.3; 28.13

35.13 Gen 17.22

35.14 Gen 28.18

a pillar of stone; and he poured out a drink offering on it, and poured oil on it. [15]So Jacob called the place where God had spoken with him Bethel.

The Birth of Benjamin and the Death of Rachel

16 Then they journeyed from Bethel; and when they were still some distance from Ephrath, Rachel was in childbirth, and she had hard labor. [17]When she was in her hard labor, the midwife said to her, "Do not be afraid; for now you will have another son." [18]As her soul was departing (for she died), she named him Ben-oni;[t] but his father called him Benjamin.[u] [19]So Rachel died, and she was buried on the way to Ephrath (that is, Bethlehem), [20]and Jacob set up a pillar at her grave; it is the pillar of Rachel's tomb, which is there to this day. [21]Israel journeyed on, and pitched his tent beyond the tower of Eder.

22 While Israel lived in that land, Reuben went and lay with Bilhah his father's concubine; and Israel heard of it.

Now the sons of Jacob were twelve. [23]The sons of Leah: Reuben (Jacob's firstborn), Simeon, Levi, Judah, Issachar, and Zebulun. [24]The sons of Rachel: Joseph and Benjamin. [25]The sons of Bilhah, Rachel's maid: Dan and Naphtali. [26]The sons of Zilpah, Leah's maid: Gad and Asher. These were the sons of Jacob who were born to him in Paddan-aram.

The Death of Isaac

27 Jacob came to his father Isaac at Mamre, or Kiriath-arba (that is, Hebron), where Abraham and Isaac had resided as aliens. [28]Now the days of Isaac were one hundred eighty years. [29]And Isaac breathed his last; he died and was gathered to his people, old and full of days; and his sons Esau and Jacob buried him.

Esau's Descendants

36 These are the descendants of Esau (that is, Edom). [2]Esau took his wives from the Canaanites: Adah daughter of Elon the Hittite, Oholibamah daughter of Anah son[v] of Zibeon the Hivite, [3]and Basemath, Ishmael's daughter, sister of Nebaioth. [4]Adah bore Eliphaz to Esau; Basemath bore Reuel; [5]and Oholibamah bore Jeush, Jalam, and Korah. These are the sons of Esau who were born to him in the land of Canaan.

6 Then Esau took his wives, his sons, his daughters, and all the members of his household, his cattle, all his livestock, and all the property he had acquired in the land of Canaan; and he moved to a land some distance from his brother Jacob. [7]For their possessions were too great for them to live together; the land where they were staying could not support them because of their livestock. [8]So Esau settled in the hill country of Seir; Esau is Edom.

9 These are the descendants of Esau, ancestor of the Edomites, in the hill country of Seir. [10]These are the names of Esau's sons: Eliphaz son of Adah the wife of Esau; Reuel, the son of Esau's wife Basemath. [11]The sons of Eliphaz were Teman, Omar, Zepho, Gatam, and Kenaz. [12](Timna was a concubine of Eliphaz, Esau's son; she bore Amalek to Eliphaz.) These were the sons of Adah, Esau's wife. [13]These were the sons of Reuel: Nahath, Zerah, Shammah, and Mizzah. These were the sons of Esau's wife, Basemath. [14]These were the sons of Esau's wife Oholibamah, daughter of Anah son[w] of Zibeon: she bore to Esau Jeush, Jalam, and Korah.

Clans and Kings of Edom

15 These are the clans[x] of the sons of Esau. The sons of Eliphaz the firstborn of Esau: the clans[x] Teman, Omar, Zepho, Kenaz, [16]Korah, Gatam, and Amalek; these are the clans[x] of Eliphaz in the land of Edom; they are the sons of Adah. [17]These are the sons of Esau's son Reuel: the clans[x] Nahath, Zerah, Shammah, and Mizzah; these are the clans[x] of Reuel in the land of Edom; they are the sons of Esau's wife Basemath. [18]These are the sons of Esau's wife Oholibamah: the clans[x] Jeush, Jalam, and Korah; these are the clans[x] born of Esau's wife Oholibamah, the daughter of Anah. [19]These are the sons of Esau (that is, Edom), and these are their clans.[x]

20 These are the sons of Seir the Horite, the inhabitants of the land: Lotan, Shobal, Zibeon, Anah, [21]Dishon, Ezer, and Dishan; these are the clans[x] of the Horites, the sons of Seir in the land of Edom. [22]The sons of

[t] That is *Son of my sorrow* [u] That is *Son of the right hand* or *Son of the South* [v] Sam Gk Syr: Heb *daughter* [w] Gk Syr: Heb *daughter* [x] Or *chiefs*

35.15 Gen 28.19
35.17 Gen 30.24
35.19 Gen 48.7; Ruth 1.2; Mic 5.2; Mt 2.6
35.20 1 Sam 10.2
35.22 Gen 49.2; 1 Chr 5.1; 1 Cor 5.1
35.27 Gen 18.1; 23.9
35.29 Gen 25.8; 15.15
36.1 Gen 25.30
36.2 Gen 26.34; 28.9
36.6 Gen 12.5
36.7 Gen 13.6,11; 17.8; 28.4
36.8 Gen 32.3
36.10 1 Chr 1.35
36.12 Ex 17.8,14
36.15 1 Chr 1.34
36.17 1 Chr 1.35,37
36.18 ver 25; 1 Chr 1.52
36.20 Gen 14.6; Deut 2.12,22; 1 Chr 1.38

35.16-29 The last of Jacob's sons, Benjamin, was born to Rachel just before her death. The location of neither Ephrath nor Eder is known with certainty, but tradition associates them here with Bethlehem. In earlier accounts in Genesis, the sons of Jacob were reportedly born in various places, but here the symbolic move (like that of Abraham) is from northern Mesopotamia to the promised land, where the patriarchs, Abraham and Isaac, had *resided as aliens.* Just as the two hostile brothers, Isaac and Ishmael, buried Abraham, so Jacob and Esau bury Isaac.
36.1-40 Just as the genealogies of Esau and Isaac serve as a transition to the stories of Jacob, so the genealogy of Esau and the lists of territories controlled by his descendants, *the kings who reigned in the land of Edom,* prepare for the next major series of stories, which concerns Joseph and his brothers (Gen 37-50). The Esau tradition represents a compilation of old sources.

37.1-50.26 Joseph and his Brothers.
37.1-11 Although the introductory lines call this *the story of the family of Jacob*, the major focus is on Joseph, whose two sons, Ephraim and Manasseh, effectively kept the number of the tribes of Jacob at twelve after the descendants of Levi disappeared (perhaps becoming identified as the priestly group [Deut 18]). While still a *helper* of his brothers, Joseph was given a distinctive honor by his father in the form of a *long robe with sleeves*, a garment which set him apart as a non-laborer and a member of the ruling class. His brothers *hated him* because of this favored status and because of the dreams of himself in a position of power.
37.12-36 His brothers, pasturing the flock at Shechem, where Jacob had bought land (33.18-20), decide *Let us kill him*. Reuben and then Judah intervene to keep him alive, but he is sold to some distant relatives – Midianite traders, whose ancestor, Midian, was a son of Abraham (Gen 25.2). They sell him as a slave to *Potiphar...the captain of the guard* of Pharaoh, the ruler of Egypt.

Lotan were Hori and Heman; and Lotan's sister was Timna. 23 These are the sons of Shobal: Alvan, Manahath, Ebal, Shepho, and Onam. 24 These are the sons of Zibeon: Aiah and Anah; he is the Anah who found the springs[y] in the wilderness, as he pastured the donkeys of his father Zibeon. 25 These are the children of Anah: Dishon and Oholibamah daughter of Anah. 26 These are the sons of Dishon: Hemdan, Eshban, Ithran, and Cheran. 27 These are the sons of Ezer: Bilhan, Zaavan, and Akan. 28 These are the sons of Dishan: Uz and Aran. 29 These are the clans[z] of the Horites: the clans[z] Lotan, Shobal, Zibeon, Anah, 30 Dishon, Ezer, and Dishan; these are the clans[z] of the Horites, clan by clan[a] in the land of Seir.

31 These are the kings who reigned in the land of Edom, before any king reigned over the Israelites. 32 Bela son of Beor reigned in Edom, the name of his city being Dinhabah. 33 Bela died, and Jobab son of Zerah of Bozrah succeeded him as king. 34 Jobab died, and Husham of the land of the Temanites succeeded him as king. 35 Husham died, and Hadad son of Bedad, who defeated Midian in the country of Moab, succeeded him as king, the name of his city being Avith. 36 Hadad died, and Samlah of Masrekah succeeded him as king. 37 Samlah died, and Shaul of Rehoboth on the Euphrates succeeded him as king. 38 Shaul died, and Baal-hanan son of Achbor succeeded him as king. 39 Baal-hanan son of Achbor died, and Hadar succeeded him as king, the name of his city being Pau; his wife's name was Mehetabel, the daughter of Matred, daughter of Me-zahab.

40 These are the names of the clans[z] of Esau, according to their families and their localities by their names: the clans[z] Timna, Alvah, Jetheth, 41 Oholibamah, Elah, Pinon, 42 Kenaz, Teman, Mibzar, 43 Magdiel, and Iram; these are the clans[z] of Edom (that is, Esau, the father of Edom), according to their settlements in the land that they held.

Joseph Dreams of Greatness

37 Jacob settled in the land where his father had lived as an alien, the land of Canaan. 2 This is the story of the family of Jacob.

Joseph, being seventeen years old, was shepherding the flock with his brothers; he was a helper to the sons of Bilhah and Zilpah, his father's wives; and Joseph brought a bad report of them to their father. 3 Now Israel loved Joseph more than any other of his children, because he was the son of his old age; and he had made him a long robe with sleeves.[b] 4 But when his brothers saw that their father loved him more than all his brothers, they hated him, and could not speak peaceably to him.

5 Once Joseph had a dream, and when he told it to his brothers, they hated him even more. 6 He said to them, "Listen to this dream that I dreamed. 7 There we were, binding sheaves in the field. Suddenly my sheaf rose and stood upright; then your sheaves gathered around it, and bowed down to my sheaf." 8 His brothers said to him, "Are you indeed to reign over us? Are you indeed to have dominion over us?" So they hated him even more because of his dreams and his words.

9 He had another dream, and told it to his brothers, saying, "Look, I have had another dream: the sun, the moon, and eleven stars were bowing down to me." 10 But when he told it to his father and to his brothers, his father rebuked him, and said to him, "What kind of dream is this that you have had? Shall we indeed come, I and your mother and your brothers, and bow to the ground before you?" 11 So his brothers were jealous of him, but his father kept the matter in mind.

Joseph Is Sold by His Brothers

12 Now his brothers went to pasture their father's flock near Shechem. 13 And Israel said to Joseph, "Are not your brothers pasturing the flock at Shechem? Come, I will send you to them." He answered, "Here I am." 14 So he said to him, "Go now, see if it is well with your brothers and with the flock; and bring word back to me." So he sent him from the valley of Hebron.

He came to Shechem, 15 and a man found him wandering in the fields; the man asked him, "What are you seeking?" 16 "I am seeking my brothers," he said; "tell me, please, where they are pasturing the flock." 17 The man said, "They have gone away, for I heard them say, 'Let us go to Dothan.' " So

[y] Meaning of Heb uncertain [z] Or *chiefs* [a] Or *chief by chief* [b] Traditional rendering (compare Gk): *a coat of many colors*; Meaning of Heb uncertain

36.25 ver 18; 1 Chr 1.52
36.27 1 Chr 1.42
36.31 1 Chr 1.43
36.39 1 Chr 1.50
36.40 1 Chr 1.51
37.1 Gen 17.8; 28.4
37.3 Gen 44.20
37.4 Gen 27.41; 49.22,23
37.7 Gen 42.6,9; 43.26; 44.14
37.8 Gen 49.26
37.10 Gen 27.29
37.11 Acts 7.9
37.14 Gen 35.27
37.17 2 Kings 6.13

Joseph went after his brothers, and found them at Dothan. 18 They saw him from a distance, and before he came near to them, they conspired to kill him. 19 They said to one another, "Here comes this dreamer. 20 Come now, let us kill him and throw him into one of the pits; then we shall say that a wild animal has devoured him, and we shall see what will become of his dreams." 21 But when Reuben heard it, he delivered him out of their hands, saying, "Let us not take his life." 22 Reuben said to them, "Shed no blood; throw him into this pit here in the wilderness, but lay no hand on him"—that he might rescue him out of their hand and restore him to his father. 23 So when Joseph came to his brothers, they stripped him of his robe, the long robe with sleeves[c] that he wore; 24 and they took him and threw him into a pit. The pit was empty; there was no water in it.

25 Then they sat down to eat; and looking up they saw a caravan of Ishmaelites coming from Gilead, with their camels carrying gum, balm, and resin, on their way to carry it down to Egypt. 26 Then Judah said to his brothers, "What profit is it if we kill our brother and conceal his blood? 27 Come, let us sell him to the Ishmaelites, and not lay our hands on him, for he is our brother, our own flesh." And his brothers agreed. 28 When some Midianite traders passed by, they drew Joseph up, lifting him out of the pit, and sold him to the Ishmaelites for twenty pieces of silver. And they took Joseph to Egypt.

29 When Reuben returned to the pit and saw that Joseph was not in the pit, he tore his clothes. 30 He returned to his brothers, and said, "The boy is gone; and I, where can I turn?" 31 Then they took Joseph's robe, slaughtered a goat, and dipped the robe in the blood. 32 They had the long robe with sleeves[c] taken to their father, and they said, "This we have found; see now whether it is your son's robe or not." 33 He recognized it, and said, "It is my son's robe! A wild animal has devoured him; Joseph is without doubt torn to pieces." 34 Then Jacob tore his garments, and put sackcloth on his loins, and mourned for his son many days. 35 All his sons and all his daughters sought to comfort him; but he refused to be comforted, and said, "No, I shall go down to Sheol to my son, mourning." Thus his father bewailed him. 36 Meanwhile the Midianites had sold him in Egypt to Potiphar, one of Pharaoh's officials, the captain of the guard.

Judah and Tamar

38 It happened at that time that Judah went down from his brothers and settled near a certain Adullamite whose name was Hirah. 2 There Judah saw the daughter of a certain Canaanite whose name was Shua; he married her and went in to her. 3 She conceived and bore a son; and he named him Er. 4 Again she conceived and bore a son whom she named Onan. 5 Yet again she bore a son, and she named him Shelah. She[d] was in Chezib when she bore him. 6 Judah took a wife for Er his firstborn; her name was Tamar. 7 But Er, Judah's firstborn, was wicked in the sight of the LORD, and the LORD put him to death. 8 Then Judah said to Onan, "Go in to your brother's wife and perform the duty of a brother-in-law to her; raise up offspring for your brother." 9 But since Onan knew that the offspring would not be his, he spilled his semen on the ground whenever he went in to his brother's wife, so that he would not give offspring to his brother. 10 What he did was displeasing in the sight of the LORD, and he put him to death also. 11 Then Judah said to his daughter-in-law Tamar, "Remain a widow in your father's house until my son Shelah grows up"—for he feared that he too would die, like his brothers. So Tamar went to live in her father's house.

12 In course of time the wife of Judah, Shua's daughter, died; when Judah's time of mourning was over,[e] he went up to Timnah to his sheepshearers, he and his friend Hirah the Adullamite. 13 When Tamar was told, "Your father-in-law is going up to Timnah to shear his sheep," 14 she put off her widow's garments, put on a veil, wrapped herself up, and sat down at the entrance to Enaim, which is on the road to Timnah. She saw that Shelah was grown up, yet she had not been given to him in marriage. 15 When Judah saw her, he thought her to be a prostitute, for she had covered her face. 16 He went over to her at the road side, and said, "Come, let me come in to you," for he did not know that she was his daughter-in-law. She said, "What will you give me, that you may come in to me?" 17 He answered, "I will send you a kid from the flock." And

[c] See note on 37.3 [d] Gk: Heb *He* [e] Heb *when Judah was comforted*

37.18 1 Sam 19.1; Mt 27.1; Acts 23.12
37.21 Gen 42.22
37.25 ver 28,36; Gen 43.11; Jer 8.22
37.26 ver 20; Gen 4.10; Job 16.18
37.27 Gen 42.21
37.28 Judg 6.3; Gen 45.4,5; Acts 7.9; Gen 39.1
37.29 Gen 44.13
37.30 Gen 42.13,36
37.31 ver 3,23
37.33 ver 20; Gen 44.28
37.34 ver 29; 2 Sam 3.31
37.35 2 Sam 12.17; Gen 42.38; 44.29,31
37.36 Gen 39.1
38.3 Gen 46.12; Num 26.19
38.7 1 Chr 2.3
38.8 Deut 25.5; Mt 22.24
38.9 Deut 25.6
38.11 Ruth 1.12,13
38.12 Josh 15.10,57
38.14 ver 11,26
38.17 Ezek 16.33; ver 20

38.1-30 recounts the story of Judah, whose descendants in the time of David become the dominant tribe and are based in the Jerusalem area. Here he is trying to ensure that he will have a continuing family line after the LORD puts to death his two wicked sons. *His daughter-in-law Tamar* is determined to have a child and, having dressed herself as a prostitute, entices Judah to have intercourse with her. She gives birth to twins who are vying for position before birth, as Jacob and Esau were (Gen 25.24-26). The temple prostitute was an important person in the Canaanite religion, where fertility of the crops was assured by sexual union with the cult prostitutes. Perez and Zerah figure importantly in the later history of Judah (Num 26.19-22).

39.1-23 resumes the story of Joseph, which consists mostly of vivid, straightforward narrative through 48.22.
39.2-5 That the LORD is the moving force behind these events is made explicit, and is said to have been discernible even to Potiphar, so that *the blessing of the LORD was on all that he had.*
39.14 After Joseph refuses to have sexual intercourse with Potiphar's wife, she denounces him as a *Hebrew* who has tried to rape her. The term Hebrew may have been used as a derogatory form for someone of low social status, although it is a patronymic of Abram (Gen 14.13), and took on ethnic (Deut 15.12) and national (1 Sam 13.3-7; Jon 1.9) connotations.

she said, "Only if you give me a pledge,
until you send it." [18]He said, "What pledge
shall I give you?" She replied, "Your signet
and your cord, and the staff that is in your
hand." So he gave them to her, and went
in to her, and she conceived by him. [19]Then
she got up and went away, and taking off
her veil she put on the garments of her
widowhood.
20 When Judah sent the kid by his friend
the Adullamite, to recover the pledge from
the woman, he could not find her. [21]He
asked the townspeople, "Where is the temple prostitute who was at Enaim by the
wayside?" But they said, "No prostitute has
been here." [22]So he returned to Judah, and
said, "I have not found her; moreover the
townspeople said, 'No prostitute has been
here.' " [23]Judah replied, "Let her keep the
things as her own, otherwise we will be
laughed at; you see, I sent this kid, and you
could not find her."
24 About three months later Judah was
told, "Your daughter-in-law Tamar has
played the whore; moreover she is pregnant
as a result of whoredom." And Judah said,
"Bring her out, and let her be burned." [25]As
she was being brought out, she sent word
to her father-in-law, "It was the owner of
these who made me pregnant." And she
said, "Take note, please, whose these are,
the signet and the cord and the staff."
[26]Then Judah acknowledged them and said,
"She is more in the right than I, since I did
not give her to my son Shelah." And he did
not lie with her again.
27 When the time of her delivery came,
there were twins in her womb. [28]While she
was in labor, one put out a hand; and the
midwife took and bound on his hand a
crimson thread, saying, "This one came out
first." [29]But just then he drew back his
hand, and out came his brother; and she
said, "What a breach you have made for
yourself!" Therefore he was named Perez.[f]
[30]Afterward his brother came out with the
crimson thread on his hand; and he was
named Zerah.[g]

Joseph and Potiphar's Wife

39 Now Joseph was taken down to
Egypt, and Potiphar, an officer of
Pharaoh, the captain of the guard, an Egyptian, bought him from the Ishmaelites who
had brought him down there. [2]The LORD
was with Joseph, and he became a successful man; he was in the house of his Egyptian master. [3]His master saw that the LORD
was with him, and that the LORD caused all
that he did to prosper in his hands. [4]So
Joseph found favor in his sight and attended
him; he made him overseer of his house and
put him in charge of all that he had. [5]From
the time that he made him overseer in his
house and over all that he had, the LORD
blessed the Egyptian's house for Joseph's
sake; the blessing of the LORD was on all that
he had, in house and field. [6]So he left all
that he had in Joseph's charge; and, with
him there, he had no concern for anything
but the food that he ate.
Now Joseph was handsome and good-
looking. [7]And after a time his master's wife
cast her eyes on Joseph and said, "Lie with
me." [8]But he refused and said to his master's wife, "Look, with me here, my master
has no concern about anything in the house,
and he has put everything that he has in
my hand. [9]He is not greater in this house
than I am, nor has he kept back anything
from me except yourself, because you are
his wife. How then could I do this great
wickedness, and sin against God?" [10]And
although she spoke to Joseph day after day,
he would not consent to lie beside her or
to be with her. [11]One day, however, when
he went into the house to do his work, and
while no one else was in the house, [12]she
caught hold of his garment, saying, "Lie
with me!" But he left his garment in her
hand, and fled and ran outside. [13]When she
saw that he had left his garment in her
hand and had fled outside, [14]she called out
to the members of her household and said
to them, "See, my husband[h] has brought
among us a Hebrew to insult us! He came
in to me to lie with me, and I cried out with
a loud voice; [15]and when he heard me raise
my voice and cry out, he left his garment
beside me, and fled outside." [16]Then she
kept his garment by her until his master
came home, [17]and she told him the same
story, saying, "The Hebrew servant, whom
you have brought among us, came in to me
to insult me; [18]but as soon as I raised my
voice and cried out, he left his garment
beside me, and fled outside."
19 When his master heard the words
that his wife spoke to him, saying, "This is

38.18 ver 25
38.19 ver 14
38.24 Lev 21.9; Deut 22.21
38.25 ver 18
38.26 1 Sam 24.17; ver 14
38.29 Gen 46.12; Num 26.20; Mt 1.3
39.1 Gen 37.28,36; Ps 105.17
39.2 ver 3,21,23
39.3 Gen 21.22; 26.28; Acts 7.9
39.4 ver 8,22
39.5 Gen 30.27
39.7 2 Sam 13.11; Prov 7.15-20
39.9 Gen 20.6; 42.18; 2 Sam 12.13
39.12 Prov 7.13-25
39.17 Ex 23.1; Ps 120.3
39.19 Prov 6.34,35

[f] That is *A breach* [g] That is *Brightness*; perhaps alluding to the crimson thread [h] Heb *he*

39.20 Ps 105.18
39.21 ver 21; Ps 105.19; Ex 3.21; Dan 1.9
39.22 ver 4
39.23 ver 2,3,8
40.1 ver 11,13
40.3 Gen 39.20,23
40.8 Gen 41.16; Dan 2.27,28
40.12 Gen 41.12,25; Dan 2.36; 4.19
40.14 Lk 23.42; Josh 2.12
40.15 Gen 37.26-28
40.18 ver 12
40.19 ver 13
40.20 ver 13,19
40.21 ver 13
40.22 ver 19
41.8 Dan 2.1,3,27; 4.5,7,19; Ex 7.11,22
41.10 Gen 40.2,3

the way your servant treated me," he became enraged. [20]And Joseph's master took
him and put him into the prison, the place
where the king's prisoners were confined;
he remained there in prison. [21]But the LORD
was with Joseph and showed him steadfast
love; he gave him favor in the sight of the
chief jailer. [22]The chief jailer committed to
Joseph's care all the prisoners who were in
the prison, and whatever was done there,
he was the one who did it. [23]The chief jailer
paid no heed to anything that was in Joseph's
care, because the LORD was with him; and
whatever he did, the LORD made it prosper.

The Dreams of Two Prisoners

40 Some time after this, the cupbearer
of the king of Egypt and his baker
offended their lord the king of Egypt. [2]Phar-
aoh was angry with his two officers, the
chief cupbearer and the chief baker, [3]and he
put them in custody in the house of the
captain of the guard, in the prison where
Joseph was confined. [4]The captain of the
guard charged Joseph with them, and he
waited on them; and they continued for
some time in custody. [5]One night they both
dreamed—the cupbearer and the baker of
the king of Egypt, who were confined in the
prison—each his own dream, and each
dream with its own meaning. [6]When Joseph
came to them in the morning, he saw that
they were troubled. [7]So he asked Pharaoh's
officers, who were with him in custody in
his master's house, "Why are your faces
downcast today?" [8]They said to him, "We
have had dreams, and there is no one to
interpret them." And Joseph said to them,
"Do not interpretations belong to God? Please
tell them to me."
9 So the chief cupbearer told his dream
to Joseph, and said to him, "In my dream
there was a vine before me, [10]and on the
vine there were three branches. As soon as
it budded, its blossoms came out and the
clusters ripened into grapes. [11]Pharaoh's cup
was in my hand; and I took the grapes and
pressed them into Pharaoh's cup, and placed
the cup in Pharaoh's hand." [12]Then Joseph
said to him, "This is its interpretation: the
three branches are three days; [13]within three
days Pharaoh will lift up your head and
restore you to your office; and you shall
place Pharaoh's cup in his hand, just as you
used to do when you were his cupbearer.
[14]But remember me when it is well with
you; please do me the kindness to make
mention of me to Pharaoh, and so get me
out of this place. [15]For in fact I was stolen
out of the land of the Hebrews; and here
also I have done nothing that they should
have put me into the dungeon."
16 When the chief baker saw that the
interpretation was favorable, he said to
Joseph, "I also had a dream: there were
three cake baskets on my head, [17]and in the
uppermost basket there were all sorts of
baked food for Pharaoh, but the birds were
eating it out of the basket on my head."
[18]And Joseph answered, "This is its interpretation: the three baskets are three days;
[19]within three days Pharaoh will lift up
your head—from you!—and hang you on
a pole; and the birds will eat the flesh from
you."
20 On the third day, which was Pharaoh's birthday, he made a feast for all his
servants, and lifted up the head of the chief
cupbearer and the head of the chief baker
among his servants. [21]He restored the chief
cupbearer to his cupbearing, and he placed
the cup in Pharaoh's hand; [22]but the chief
baker he hanged, just as Joseph had interpreted to them. [23]Yet the chief cupbearer did
not remember Joseph, but forgot him.

Joseph Interprets Pharaoh's Dream

41 After two whole years, Pharaoh
dreamed that he was standing by
the Nile, [2]and there came up out of the Nile
seven sleek and fat cows, and they grazed
in the reed grass. [3]Then seven other cows,
ugly and thin, came up out of the Nile after
them, and stood by the other cows on the
bank of the Nile. [4]The ugly and thin cows
ate up the seven sleek and fat cows. And
Pharaoh awoke. [5]Then he fell asleep and
dreamed a second time; seven ears of grain,
plump and good, were growing on one
stalk. [6]Then seven ears, thin and blighted
by the east wind, sprouted after them. [7]The
thin ears swallowed up the seven plump
and full ears. Pharaoh awoke, and it was
a dream. [8]In the morning his spirit was
troubled; so he sent and called for all the
magicians of Egypt and all its wise men.
Pharaoh told them his dreams, but there
was no one who could interpret them to
Pharaoh.
9 Then the chief cupbearer said to Pharaoh, "I remember my faults today. [10]Once
Pharaoh was angry with his servants, and

40.1-20 As with Joseph's dreams, what Pharaoh's *chief cupbearer* and *chief baker* see is not a vision of God but a symbolic indication of their own future. It is the *interpretations* of these dreams which *belong to God,* as Joseph makes clear.

41.1-36 Similarly, Pharaoh's dream is a disclosure to him of what God *is about to do.* Not only is the prospect of seven years of abundance followed by seven years of famine revealed, but the remedy for the crisis as well, including the gathering of *one fifth of the produce of the land* to be stored up in preparation for the period of want. Everything has been *fixed by God.*

41.37-57 Pharaoh declares that it is God who *has shown...all this* to Joseph, and that this is the source of his wisdom (Ps 105.16-22). Joseph is assigned authority by Pharaoh over the royal household and the affairs of the people, in token of which he is given the *signet ring* which is the prime symbol of royal power. In addition to the other perquisites, he is given absolute control over preparations for the storing of food during the years of plenty. He has children by the daughter of the priest of On, whose vast temple near what is now Cairo was dedicated to the sun god. The two sons, Manasseh and especially Ephraim, figure importantly in the subsequent history of Israel (Josh 16-17; 20-21). Ephraim becomes a designation for the whole northern kingdom of Israel in Hosea and Isaiah.

put me and the chief baker in custody in the house of the captain of the guard. 11We dreamed on the same night, he and I, each having a dream with its own meaning. 12A young Hebrew was there with us, a servant of the captain of the guard. When we told him, he interpreted our dreams to us, giving an interpretation to each according to his dream. 13As he interpreted to us, so it turned out; I was restored to my office, and the baker was hanged."

14 Then Pharaoh sent for Joseph, and he was hurriedly brought out of the dungeon. When he had shaved himself and changed his clothes, he came in before Pharaoh. 15And Pharaoh said to Joseph, "I have had a dream, and there is no one who can interpret it. I have heard it said of you that when you hear a dream you can interpret it." 16Joseph answered Pharaoh, "It is not I; God will give Pharaoh a favorable answer." 17Then Pharaoh said to Joseph, "In my dream I was standing on the banks of the Nile; 18and seven cows, fat and sleek, came up out of the Nile and fed in the reed grass. 19Then seven other cows came up after them, poor, very ugly, and thin. Never had I seen such ugly ones in all the land of Egypt. 20The thin and ugly cows ate up the first seven fat cows, 21but when they had eaten them no one would have known that they had done so, for they were still as ugly as before. Then I awoke. 22I fell asleep a second time[i] and I saw in my dream seven ears of grain, full and good, growing on one stalk, 23and seven ears, withered, thin, and blighted by the east wind, sprouting after them; 24and the thin ears swallowed up the seven good ears. But when I told it to the magicians, there was no one who could explain it to me."

25 Then Joseph said to Pharaoh, "Pharaoh's dreams are one and the same; God has revealed to Pharaoh what he is about to do. 26The seven good cows are seven years, and the seven good ears are seven years; the dreams are one. 27The seven lean and ugly cows that came up after them are seven years, as are the seven empty ears blighted by the east wind. They are seven years of famine. 28It is as I told Pharaoh; God has shown to Pharaoh what he is about to do. 29There will come seven years of great plenty throughout all the land of Egypt. 30After them there will arise seven years of famine, and all the plenty will be forgotten in the land of Egypt; the famine will consume the land. 31The plenty will no longer be known in the land because of the famine that will follow, for it will be very grievous. 32And the doubling of Pharaoh's dream means that the thing is fixed by God, and God will shortly bring it about. 33Now therefore let Pharaoh select a man who is discerning and wise, and set him over the land of Egypt. 34Let Pharaoh proceed to appoint overseers over the land, and take one-fifth of the produce of the land of Egypt during the seven plenteous years. 35Let them gather all the food of these good years that are coming, and lay up grain under the authority of Pharaoh for food in the cities, and let them keep it. 36That food shall be a reserve for the land against the seven years of famine that are to befall the land of Egypt, so that the land may not perish through the famine."

Joseph's Rise to Power

37 The proposal pleased Pharaoh and all his servants. 38Pharaoh said to his servants, "Can we find anyone else like this—one in whom is the spirit of God?" 39So Pharaoh said to Joseph, "Since God has shown you all this, there is no one so discerning and wise as you. 40You shall be over my house, and all my people shall order themselves as you command; only with regard to the throne will I be greater than you." 41And Pharaoh said to Joseph, "See, I have set you over all the land of Egypt." 42Removing his signet ring from his hand, Pharaoh put it on Joseph's hand; he arrayed him in garments of fine linen, and put a gold chain around his neck. 43He had him ride in the chariot of his second-in-command; and they cried out in front of him, "Bow the knee!"[j] Thus he set him over all the land of Egypt. 44Moreover Pharaoh said to Joseph, "I am Pharaoh, and without your consent no one shall lift up hand or foot in all the land of Egypt." 45Pharaoh gave Joseph the name Zaphenath-paneah; and he gave him Asenath daughter of Potiphera, priest of On, as his wife. Thus Joseph gained authority over the land of Egypt.

46 Joseph was thirty years old when he entered the service of Pharaoh king of Egypt. And Joseph went out from the presence of

[i] Gk Syr Vg: Heb lacks *I fell asleep a second time* [j] *Abrek*, apparently an Egyptian word similar in sound to the Hebrew word meaning *to kneel*

41.11 Gen 40.5

41.12 Gen 40.12ff

41.13 Gen 40.21,22

41.14 Ps 105.20; Dan 2.25; Ps 113.7,8

41.15 ver 12

41.16 Dan 2.30; Acts 3.12; 2 Cor 3.5; Gen 40.8

41.24 ver 8

41.25 ver 28,32

41.27 2 Kings 8.1

41.28 ver 25,32

41.29 ver 47

41.30 ver 54,56; Gen 47.13

41.32 Num 23.19; Isa 46.10,11

41.35 ver 48

41.38 Num 27.18; Dan 4.8,18

41.40 Ps 105.21,22; Acts 7.10

41.41 Gen 42.6

41.42 Esth 3.10; Dan 5.7,16,29

41.43 Esth 6.9

41.44 Ps 105.22

41.46 Gen 37.2

41.50 Gen 46.20
41.52 Gen 17.6; 28.3; 49.22
41.54 ver 30; Ps 105.16; Acts 7.11
41.56 Gen 42.6
42.1 Acts 7.12
42.2 Gen 43.8
42.4 Gen 35.24
42.5 Gen 41.57; Acts 7.11
42.6 Gen 41.41,55; 37.7
42.7 ver 30
42.9 Gen 37.6-9
42.13 Gen 43.7; 37.30
42.18 Lev 25.43
42.20 ver 34
42.21 Hos 5.15; Prov 21.13
42.22 Gen 37.22; 9.5.6

Pharaoh, and went through all the land of Egypt. 47 During the seven plenteous years the earth produced abundantly. 48 He gathered up all the food of the seven years when there was plenty[k] in the land of Egypt, and stored up food in the cities; he stored up in every city the food from the fields around it. 49 So Joseph stored up grain in such abundance—like the sand of the sea—that he stopped measuring it; it was beyond measure.

50 Before the years of famine came, Joseph had two sons, whom Asenath daughter of Potiphera, priest of On, bore to him. 51 Joseph named the firstborn Manasseh,[l] "For," he said, "God has made me forget all my hardship and all my father's house." 52 The second he named Ephraim,[m] "For God has made me fruitful in the land of my misfortunes."

53 The seven years of plenty that prevailed in the land of Egypt came to an end; 54 and the seven years of famine began to come, just as Joseph had said. There was famine in every country, but throughout the land of Egypt there was bread. 55 When all the land of Egypt was famished, the people cried to Pharaoh for bread. Pharaoh said to all the Egyptians, "Go to Joseph; what he says to you, do." 56 And since the famine had spread over all the land, Joseph opened all the storehouses,[n] and sold to the Egyptians, for the famine was severe in the land of Egypt. 57 Moreover, all the world came to Joseph in Egypt to buy grain, because the famine became severe throughout the world.

Joseph's Brothers Go to Egypt

42 When Jacob learned that there was grain in Egypt, he said to his sons, "Why do you keep looking at one another? 2 I have heard," he said, "that there is grain in Egypt; go down and buy grain for us there, that we may live and not die." 3 So ten of Joseph's brothers went down to buy grain in Egypt. 4 But Jacob did not send Joseph's brother Benjamin with his brothers, for he feared that harm might come to him. 5 Thus the sons of Israel were among the other people who came to buy grain, for the famine had reached the land of Canaan.

6 Now Joseph was governor over the land; it was he who sold to all the people of the land. And Joseph's brothers came and bowed themselves before him with their faces to the ground. 7 When Joseph saw his brothers, he recognized them, but he treated them like strangers and spoke harshly to them. "Where do you come from?" he said. They said, "From the land of Canaan, to buy food." 8 Although Joseph had recognized his brothers, they did not recognize him. 9 Joseph also remembered the dreams that he had dreamed about them. He said to them, "You are spies; you have come to see the nakedness of the land!" 10 They said to him, "No, my lord; your servants have come to buy food. 11 We are all sons of one man; we are honest men; your servants have never been spies." 12 But he said to them, "No, you have come to see the nakedness of the land!" 13 They said, "We, your servants, are twelve brothers, the sons of a certain man in the land of Canaan; the youngest, however, is now with our father, and one is no more." 14 But Joseph said to them, "It is just as I have said to you; you are spies! 15 Here is how you shall be tested: as Pharaoh lives, you shall not leave this place unless your youngest brother comes here! 16 Let one of you go and bring your brother, while the rest of you remain in prison, in order that your words may be tested, whether there is truth in you; or else, as Pharaoh lives, surely you are spies." 17 And he put them all together in prison for three days.

18 On the third day Joseph said to them, "Do this and you will live, for I fear God: 19 if you are honest men, let one of your brothers stay here where you are imprisoned. The rest of you shall go and carry grain for the famine of your households, 20 and bring your youngest brother to me. Thus your words will be verified, and you shall not die." And they agreed to do so. 21 They said to one another, "Alas, we are paying the penalty for what we did to our brother; we saw his anguish when he pleaded with us, but we would not listen. That is why this anguish has come upon us." 22 Then Reuben answered them, "Did I not tell you not to wrong the boy? But you would not listen. So now there comes a reckoning for his blood." 23 They did not know that Joseph understood them, since he spoke with them

[k] Sam Gk: MT *the seven years that were* [l] That is *Making to forget* [m] From a Hebrew word meaning *to be fruitful* [n] Gk Vg Compare Syr: Heb *opened all that was in* (or, *among*) *them*

42.4 Benjamin is Jacob's youngest son, whose birth to the aged Rachel resulted in her death.

through an interpreter. 24He turned away
from them and wept; then he returned and
spoke to them. And he picked out Simeon
and had him bound before their eyes.
25Joseph then gave orders to fill their bags
with grain, to return every man's money to
his sack, and to give them provisions for
their journey. This was done for them.

Joseph's Brothers Return to Canaan

26 They loaded their donkeys with their
grain, and departed. 27When one of them
opened his sack to give his donkey fodder
at the lodging place, he saw his money at
the top of the sack. 28He said to his brothers,
"My money has been put back; here it is in
my sack!" At this they lost heart and turned
trembling to one another, saying, "What is
this that God has done to us?"

29 When they came to their father Jacob
in the land of Canaan, they told him all that
had happened to them, saying, 30"The man,
the lord of the land, spoke harshly to us,
and charged us with spying on the land.
31But we said to him, 'We are honest men,
we are not spies. 32We are twelve brothers,
sons of our father; one is no more, and the
youngest is now with our father in the land
of Canaan.' 33Then the man, the lord of the
land, said to us, 'By this I shall know that
you are honest men: leave one of your
brothers with me, take grain for the famine
of your households, and go your way. 34Bring
your youngest brother to me, and I shall
know that you are not spies but honest
men. Then I will release your brother to
you, and you may trade in the land.'"

35 As they were emptying their sacks,
there in each one's sack was his bag of
money. When they and their father saw
their bundles of money, they were dismayed.
36And their father Jacob said to them, "I am
the one you have bereaved of children:
Joseph is no more, and Simeon is no more,
and now you would take Benjamin. All this
has happened to me!" 37Then Reuben said
to his father, "You may kill my two sons if
I do not bring him back to you. Put him
in my hands, and I will bring him back to
you." 38But he said, "My son shall not go
down with you, for his brother is dead, and
he alone is left. If harm should come to him
on the journey that you are to make, you
would bring down my gray hairs with sorrow
to Sheol."

The Brothers Come Again, Bringing Benjamin

43 Now the famine was severe in the
land. 2And when they had eaten
up the grain that they had brought from
Egypt, their father said to them, "Go again,
buy us a little more food." 3But Judah said
to him, "The man solemnly warned us,
saying, 'You shall not see my face unless
your brother is with you.' 4If you will send
our brother with us, we will go down and
buy you food; 5but if you will not send him,
we will not go down, for the man said to
us, 'You shall not see my face, unless your
brother is with you.'" 6Israel said, "Why did
you treat me so badly as to tell the man
that you had another brother?" 7They replied, "The man questioned us carefully
about ourselves and our kindred, saying, 'Is
your father still alive? Have you another
brother?' What we told him was in answer
to these questions. Could we in any way
know that he would say, 'Bring your brother
down'?" 8Then Judah said to his father
Israel, "Send the boy with me, and let us
be on our way, so that we may live and not
die—you and we and also our little ones.
9I myself will be surety for him; you can
hold me accountable for him. If I do not
bring him back to you and set him before
you, then let me bear the blame forever. 10If
we had not delayed, we would now have
returned twice."

11 Then their father Israel said to them,
"If it must be so, then do this: take some
of the choice fruits of the land in your bags,
and carry them down as a present to the
man—a little balm and a little honey, gum,
resin, pistachio nuts, and almonds. 12Take
double the money with you. Carry back
with you the money that was returned in
the top of your sacks; perhaps it was an
oversight. 13Take your brother also, and be
on your way again to the man; 14may God
Almighty[o] grant you mercy before the man,
so that he may send back your other brother
and Benjamin. As for me, if I am bereaved
of my children, I am bereaved." 15So the
men took the present, and they took double
the money with them, as well as Benjamin.
Then they went on their way down to
Egypt, and stood before Joseph.

16 When Joseph saw Benjamin with
them, he said to the steward of his house,
"Bring the men into the house, and slaughter an animal and make ready, for the men

42.24 Gen 43.30; 45.14,15; 43.14,23

42.25 Gen 44.1; Rom 12.17,20,21

42.26 Gen 37.31-35

42.30 ver 7

42.31 ver 11

42.33 Gen 15.19,20

42.35 Gen 43.12,15

42.36 Gen 43.14

42.38 Gen 37.33,35; 44.31

43.1 Gen 41.56,57

43.3 Gen 42.20; 44.23

43.7 ver 27; Gen 42.13

43.9 Gen 42.37; 44.32; Philem 18,19

43.11 Gen 32.20; Prov 18.16; Gen 37.25; Jer 8.22

43.12 Gen 42.35; ver 21,22

43.14 Gen 17.1; 28.3; 35.11; Ps 106.46; Gen 42.24

43.16 Gen 44.1

[o] Traditional rendering of Heb *El Shaddai*

are to dine with me at noon." [17]The man
did as Joseph said, and brought the men to
Joseph's house. [18]Now the men were afraid
because they were brought to Joseph's house,
and they said, "It is because of the money,
replaced in our sacks the first time, that we
have been brought in, so that he may have
an opportunity to fall upon us, to make
slaves of us and take our donkeys." [19]So
they went up to the steward of Joseph's
house and spoke with him at the entrance
to the house. [20]They said, "Oh, my lord, we
came down the first time to buy food; [21]and
when we came to the lodging place we
opened our sacks, and there was each one's
money in the top of his sack, our money in
full weight. So we have brought it back
with us. [22]Moreover we have brought down
with us additional money to buy food. We
do not know who put our money in our
sacks." [23]He replied, "Rest assured, do not
be afraid; your God and the God of your
father must have put treasure in your sacks
for you; I received your money." Then he
brought Simeon out to them. [24]When the
steward[p] had brought the men into Joseph's
house, and given them water, and they had
washed their feet, and when he had given
their donkeys fodder, [25]they made the present
ready for Joseph's coming at noon, for they
had heard that they would dine there.
26 When Joseph came home, they
brought him the present that they had
carried into the house, and bowed to the
ground before him. [27]He inquired about
their welfare, and said, "Is your father well,
the old man of whom you spoke? Is he still
alive?" [28]They said, "Your servant our father is well; he is still alive." And they
bowed their heads and did obeisance. [29]Then
he looked up and saw his brother Benjamin,
his mother's son, and said, "Is this your
youngest brother, of whom you spoke to
me? God be gracious to you, my son!"
[30]With that, Joseph hurried out, because he
was overcome with affection for his brother,
and he was about to weep. So he went into
a private room and wept there. [31]Then he
washed his face and came out; and controlling himself he said, "Serve the meal." [32]They
served him by himself, and them by themselves, and the Egyptians who ate with him
by themselves, because the Egyptians could
not eat with the Hebrews, for that is an
abomination to the Egyptians. [33]When they
were seated before him, the firstborn according to his birthright and the youngest
according to his youth, the men looked at
one another in amazement. [34]Portions were
taken to them from Joseph's table, but
Benjamin's portion was five times as much
as any of theirs. So they drank and were
merry with him.

Joseph Detains Benjamin

44 Then he commanded the steward
of his house, "Fill the men's sacks
with food, as much as they can carry, and
put each man's money in the top of his
sack. [2]Put my cup, the silver cup, in the top
of the sack of the youngest, with his money
for the grain." And he did as Joseph told
him. [3]As soon as the morning was light, the
men were sent away with their donkeys.
[4]When they had gone only a short distance
from the city, Joseph said to his steward,
"Go, follow after the men; and when you
overtake them, say to them, 'Why have you
returned evil for good? Why have you stolen my silver cup?[q] [5]Is it not from this that
my lord drinks? Does he not indeed use it
for divination? You have done wrong in
doing this.' "
6 When he overtook them, he repeated
these words to them. [7]They said to him,
"Why does my lord speak such words as
these? Far be it from your servants that they
should do such a thing! [8]Look, the money
that we found at the top of our sacks, we
brought back to you from the land of Canaan;
why then would we steal silver or gold from
your lord's house? [9]Should it be found with
any one of your servants, let him die;
moreover the rest of us will become my
lord's slaves." [10]He said, "Even so; in accordance with your words, let it be: he with
whom it is found shall become my slave,
but the rest of you shall go free." [11]Then
each one quickly lowered his sack to the
ground, and each opened his sack. [12]He
searched, beginning with the eldest and
ending with the youngest; and the cup was
found in Benjamin's sack. [13]At this they
tore their clothes. Then each one loaded his
donkey, and they returned to the city.
14 Judah and his brothers came to
Joseph's house while he was still there; and
they fell to the ground before him. [15]Joseph
said to them, "What deed is this that you
have done? Do you not know that one such
as I can practice divination?" [16]And Judah

[p] Heb *the man* [q] Gk Compare Vg: Heb lacks *Why have you stolen my silver cup?*

43.20 Gen 42.3,10
43.21 Gen 42.35; ver 12,15
43.23 Gen 42.24
43.24 Gen 18.4; 19.2; 24.32
43.26 Gen 37.7,10
43.27 ver 7; Gen 45.3
43.28 Gen 3.7,10
43.29 Gen 35.17,18; 42.13; Num 6.25; Ps 67.1
43.30 Gen 42.24; 45.2,14,15; 46.29
43.31 Gen 45.1
43.32 Gen 46.34
43.34 Gen 45.22
44.1 Gen 42.25
44.5 ver 15; Lev 19.26; Deut 18.10-14
44.8 Gen 43.21
44.9 Gen 31.32
44.13 Gen 37.29,34; Num 14.6
44.14 Gen 37.7,10
44.15 ver 5
44.16 ver 9

43.21 *In full weight* implies that there were regional standards of weight, and hence of value, operative for precious metals.
43.32 An important cultural feature of life in the Middle East in this period was the rule insisting that food be shared only with members of one's own tribe or people.
44.1-17 To use a cup *for divination* could involve interpreting the movement of liquid mixtures or the effects of the liquid on objects placed in the cup. The diviner could determine by such a method the answer to prior questions. Joseph identifies himself as one who *practices divination*, and orders the enslavement of Benjamin, the one who has apparently stolen the cup.
44.14,18-34 It is Judah who intercedes in behalf of Benjamin on the ground that his failure to return to Canaan would be a fatal blow to Jacob. Judah and Benjamin become the major tribes in the southern part of Israel from the time of David on.

said, "What can we say to my lord? What can we speak? How can we clear ourselves? God has found out the guilt of your servants; here we are then, my lord's slaves, both we and also the one in whose possession the cup has been found." [17]But he said, "Far be it from me that I should do so! Only the one in whose possession the cup was found shall be my slave; but as for you, go up in peace to your father."

Judah Pleads for Benjamin's Release

18 Then Judah stepped up to him and said, "O my lord, let your servant please speak a word in my lord's ears, and do not be angry with your servant; for you are like Pharaoh himself. [19]My lord asked his servants, saying, 'Have you a father or a brother?' [20]And we said to my lord, 'We have a father, an old man, and a young brother, the child of his old age. His brother is dead; he alone is left of his mother's children, and his father loves him.' [21]Then you said to your servants, 'Bring him down to me, so that I may set my eyes on him.' [22]We said to my lord, 'The boy cannot leave his father, for if he should leave his father, his father would die.' [23]Then you said to your servants, 'Unless your youngest brother comes down with you, you shall see my face no more.' [24]When we went back to your servant my father we told him the words of my lord. [25]And when our father said, 'Go again, buy us a little food,' [26]we said, 'We cannot go down. Only if our youngest brother goes with us, will we go down; for we cannot see the man's face unless our youngest brother is with us.' [27]Then your servant my father said to us, 'You know that my wife bore me two sons; [28]one left me, and I said, Surely he has been torn to pieces; and I have never seen him since. [29]If you take this one also from me, and harm comes to him, you will bring down my gray hairs in sorrow to Sheol.' [30]Now therefore, when I come to your servant my father and the boy is not with us, then, as his life is bound up in the boy's life, [31]when he sees that the boy is not with us, he will die; and your servants will bring down the gray hairs of your servant our father with sorrow to Sheol. [32]For your servant became surety for the boy to my father, saying, 'If I do not bring him back to you, then I will bear the blame in the sight of my father all my life.' [33]Now therefore, please let your servant remain as a slave to my lord in place of the boy; and let the boy go back with his brothers. [34]For how can I go back to my father if the boy is not with me? I fear to see the suffering that would come upon my father."

Joseph Reveals Himself to His Brothers

45 Then Joseph could no longer control himself before all those who stood by him, and he cried out, "Send everyone away from me." So no one stayed with him when Joseph made himself known to his brothers. [2]And he wept so loudly that the Egyptians heard it, and the household of Pharaoh heard it. [3]Joseph said to his brothers, "I am Joseph. Is my father still alive?" But his brothers could not answer him, so dismayed were they at his presence.

4 Then Joseph said to his brothers, "Come closer to me." And they came closer. He said, "I am your brother, Joseph, whom you sold into Egypt. [5]And now do not be distressed, or angry with yourselves, because you sold me here; for God sent me before you to preserve life. [6]For the famine has been in the land these two years; and there are five more years in which there will be neither plowing nor harvest. [7]God sent me before you to preserve for you a remnant on earth, and to keep alive for you many survivors. [8]So it was not you who sent me here, but God; he has made me a father to Pharaoh, and lord of all his house and ruler over all the land of Egypt. [9]Hurry and go up to my father and say to him, 'Thus says your son Joseph, God has made me lord of all Egypt; come down to me, do not delay. [10]You shall settle in the land of Goshen, and you shall be near me, you and your children and your children's children, as well as your flocks, your herds, and all that you have. [11]I will provide for you there—since there are five more years of famine to come—so that you and your household, and all that you have, will not come to poverty.' [12]And now your eyes and the eyes of my brother Benjamin see that it is my own mouth that speaks to you. [13]You must tell my father how greatly I am honored in Egypt, and all that you have seen. Hurry and bring my father down here." [14]Then he fell upon his brother Benjamin's neck and wept, while Benjamin wept upon his neck. [15]And he kissed all his brothers and wept upon them; and after that

45.5-8 In revealing himself to his brothers, Joseph places no blame on them but asserts instead that *God sent [him] ...to preserve a remnant* of God's people, and that God has sent them to him. What has occurred is God's action, not human failing.

45.10 *The land of Goshen* where Jacob and his sons are to reside is the well-watered and fertile northeastern part of the Nile delta, adjacent to what is now the entrance to the Suez Canal.

44.18 Gen 37.7,8; 41.40-44

44.20 ver 30; Gen 43.8; 37.33; 42.13,38

44.23 Gen 43.3

44.28 Gen 37.31-35

44.29 Gen 42.36,38

44.32 Gen 43.9

45.1 Acts 7.13

45.2 ver 14,15; Gen 46.29

45.3 Gen 43.27

45.4 Gen 37.28

45.5 Isa 40.2; Gen 37.28; 44.20; 50.20

45.8 Gen 41.43

45.10 Gen 46.28,34; 47.1

45.13 Acts 7.14

his brothers talked with him.

16 When the report was heard in Pharaoh's house, "Joseph's brothers have come," Pharaoh and his servants were pleased. [17]Pharaoh said to Joseph, "Say to your brothers, 'Do this: load your animals and go back to the land of Canaan. [18]Take your father and your households and come to me, so that I may give you the best of the land of Egypt, and you may enjoy the fat of the land.' [19]You are further charged to say, 'Do this: take wagons from the land of Egypt for your little ones and for your wives, and bring your father, and come. [20]Give no thought to your possessions, for the best of all the land of Egypt is yours.'"

21 The sons of Israel did so. Joseph gave them wagons according to the instruction of Pharaoh, and he gave them provisions for the journey. [22]To each one of them he gave a set of garments; but to Benjamin he gave three hundred pieces of silver and five sets of garments. [23]To his father he sent the following: ten donkeys loaded with the good things of Egypt, and ten female donkeys loaded with grain, bread, and provision for his father on the journey. [24]Then he sent his brothers on their way, and as they were leaving he said to them, "Do not quarrel[r] along the way."

25 So they went up out of Egypt and came to their father Jacob in the land of Canaan. [26]And they told him, "Joseph is still alive! He is even ruler over all the land of Egypt." He was stunned; he could not believe them. [27]But when they told him all the words of Joseph that he had said to them, and when he saw the wagons that Joseph had sent to carry him, the spirit of their father Jacob revived. [28]Israel said, "Enough! My son Joseph is still alive. I must go and see him before I die."

Jacob Brings His Whole Family to Egypt

46 When Israel set out on his journey with all that he had and came to Beer-sheba, he offered sacrifices to the God of his father Isaac. [2]God spoke to Israel in visions of the night, and said, "Jacob, Jacob." And he said, "Here I am." [3]Then he said, "I am God,[s] the God of your father; do not be afraid to go down to Egypt, for I will make of you a great nation there. [4]I myself will go down with you to Egypt, and I will also bring you up again; and Joseph's own hand shall close your eyes."

5 Then Jacob set out from Beer-sheba; and the sons of Israel carried their father Jacob, their little ones, and their wives, in the wagons that Pharaoh had sent to carry him. [6]They also took their livestock and the goods that they had acquired in the land of Canaan, and they came into Egypt, Jacob and all his offspring with him, [7]his sons, and his sons' sons with him, his daughters, and his sons' daughters; all his offspring he brought with him into Egypt.

8 Now these are the names of the Israelites, Jacob and his offspring, who came to Egypt. Reuben, Jacob's firstborn, [9]and the children of Reuben: Hanoch, Pallu, Hezron, and Carmi. [10]The children of Simeon: Jemuel, Jamin, Ohad, Jachin, Zohar, and Shaul,[t] the son of a Canaanite woman. [11]The children of Levi: Gershon, Kohath, and Merari. [12]The children of Judah: Er, Onan, Shelah, Perez, and Zerah (but Er and Onan died in the land of Canaan); and the children of Perez were Hezron and Hamul. [13]The children of Issachar: Tola, Puvah, Jashub,[u] and Shimron. [14]The children of Zebulun: Sered, Elon, and Jahleel [15](these are the sons of Leah, whom she bore to Jacob in Paddan-aram, together with his daughter Dinah; in all his sons and his daughters numbered thirty-three). [16]The children of Gad: Ziphion, Haggi, Shuni, Ezbon, Eri, Arodi, and Areli. [17]The children of Asher: Imnah, Ishvah, Ishvi, Beriah, and their sister Serah. The children of Beriah: Heber and Malchiel [18](these are the children of Zilpah, whom Laban gave to his daughter Leah; and these she bore to Jacob—sixteen persons). [19]The children of Jacob's wife Rachel: Joseph and Benjamin. [20]To Joseph in the land of Egypt were born Manasseh and Ephraim, whom Asenath daughter of Potiphera, priest of On, bore to him. [21]The children of Benjamin: Bela, Becher, Ashbel, Gera, Naaman, Ehi, Rosh, Muppim, Huppim, and Ard [22](these are the children of Rachel, who were born to Jacob—fourteen persons in all). [23]The children of Dan: Hashum.[v] [24]The children of Naphtali: Jahzeel, Guni, Jezer, and Shillem [25](these are the children of Bilhah, whom Laban gave to his daughter Rachel, and these she bore to Jacob—seven persons in all). [26]All the persons belonging to Jacob who came into Egypt, who were his own offspring, not

[r] Or *be agitated* [s] Heb *the God* [t] Or *Saul* [u] Compare Sam Gk Num 26.24; 1 Chr 7.1: MT *Iob* [v] Gk: Heb *Hushim*

46.1-7 Jacob's assembling of his sons, their families and their possessions at Beersheba is in the tradition of covenant promise and fulfillment that began there with Abraham (21.22-32) and continued with Isaac (26.5).

46.8-27 The narrative is interrupted by the genealogy of Jacob, which brings the full number of his household to the symbolic number of completeness, 70, which is reaffirmed in Ex 1.5 and Deut 10.22. The repetition of the historically dubious tradition that all Jacob's sons were born in Padan-aram emphasizes the importance of linking the tribes of Israel with their origins in northwestern Mesopotamia (Gen 35.26). The reason that *all shepherds are abhorrent to the Egyptians* may be that they represented the semi-nomadic peoples who penetrated the land of Egypt periodically from the northeast and were regarded as crude and intrusive in the stable culture of that land.

45.18 Gen 27.28; Num 18.12,29
45.22 Gen 43.34
46.1 Gen 28.10; 26.24; 28.13
46.2 Job 33.14,15; Gen 22.11; 31.11
46.3 Gen 28.13; 12.2
46.4 Gen 28.15; 50.13,24,25; Ex 3.8; Gen 50.1
46.5 Gen 45.19,21
46.6 Acts 7.15; Deut 26.5; Josh 24.4; Ps 105.23; Isa 52.4
46.8 Ex 1.1
46.10 Ex 6.15
46.11 1 Chr 6.1,16
46.12 1 Chr 2.3; 4.21; 38.3,7,10,29
46.17 1 Chr 7.30
46.18 Gen 30.10; 29.24
46.19 Gen 44.27
46.20 Gen 41.50
46.21 1 Chr 7.6; 8.1
46.23 1 Chr 7.12
46.24 1 Chr 7.13
46.25 Gen 30.5,7; 29.29
46.26 Ex 1.5

including the wives of his sons, were sixty-
six persons in all. 27 The children of Joseph,
who were born to him in Egypt, were two;
all the persons of the house of Jacob who
came into Egypt were seventy.

Jacob Settles in Goshen

28 Israel[w] sent Judah ahead to Joseph to
lead the way before him into Goshen. When
they came to the land of Goshen, 29 Joseph
made ready his chariot and went up to
meet his father Israel in Goshen. He presented himself to him, fell on his neck, and
wept on his neck a good while. 30 Israel said
to Joseph, "I can die now, having seen for
myself that you are still alive." 31 Joseph said
to his brothers and to his father's household, "I will go up and tell Pharaoh, and
will say to him, 'My brothers and my father's household, who were in the land of
Canaan, have come to me. 32 The men are
shepherds, for they have been keepers of
livestock; and they have brought their flocks,
and their herds, and all that they have.'
33 When Pharaoh calls you, and says, 'What
is your occupation?' 34 you shall say, 'Your
servants have been keepers of livestock from
our youth even until now, both we and our
ancestors'—in order that you may settle in
the land of Goshen, because all shepherds
are abhorrent to the Egyptians."

47 So Joseph went and told Pharaoh,
"My father and my brothers, with
their flocks and herds and all that they
possess, have come from the land of Canaan;
they are now in the land of Goshen." 2 From
among his brothers he took five men and
presented them to Pharaoh. 3 Pharaoh said
to his brothers, "What is your occupation?"
And they said to Pharaoh, "Your servants
are shepherds, as our ancestors were." 4 They
said to Pharaoh, "We have come to reside
as aliens in the land; for there is no pasture
for your servants' flocks because the famine
is severe in the land of Canaan. Now, we
ask you, let your servants settle in the land
of Goshen." 5 Then Pharaoh said to Joseph,
"Your father and your brothers have come
to you. 6 The land of Egypt is before you;
settle your father and your brothers in the
best part of the land; let them live in the
land of Goshen; and if you know that there
are capable men among them, put them in
charge of my livestock."

7 Then Joseph brought in his father Jacob,
and presented him before Pharaoh, and
Jacob blessed Pharaoh. 8 Pharaoh said to
Jacob, "How many are the years of your
life?" 9 Jacob said to Pharaoh, "The years of
my earthly sojourn are one hundred thirty;
few and hard have been the years of my life.
They do not compare with the years of the
life of my ancestors during their long sojourn." 10 Then Jacob blessed Pharaoh, and
went out from the presence of Pharaoh.
11 Joseph settled his father and his brothers,
and granted them a holding in the land of
Egypt, in the best part of the land, in the
land of Rameses, as Pharaoh had instructed.
12 And Joseph provided his father, his brothers, and all his father's household with food,
according to the number of their dependents.

The Famine in Egypt

13 Now there was no food in all the
land, for the famine was very severe. The
land of Egypt and the land of Canaan languished because of the famine. 14 Joseph
collected all the money to be found in the
land of Egypt and in the land of Canaan, in
exchange for the grain that they bought;
and Joseph brought the money into Pharaoh's house. 15 When the money from the
land of Egypt and from the land of Canaan
was spent, all the Egyptians came to Joseph,
and said, "Give us food! Why should we die
before your eyes? For our money is gone."
16 And Joseph answered, "Give me your livestock, and I will give you food in exchange
for your livestock, if your money is gone."
17 So they brought their livestock to Joseph;
and Joseph gave them food in exchange for
the horses, the flocks, the herds, and the
donkeys. That year he supplied them with
food in exchange for all their livestock.
18 When that year was ended, they came to
him the following year, and said to him,
"We can not hide from my lord that our
money is all spent; and the herds of cattle
are my lord's. There is nothing left in the
sight of my lord but our bodies and our
lands. 19 Shall we die before your eyes, both
we and our land? Buy us and our land in
exchange for food. We with our land will
become slaves to Pharaoh; just give us seed,
so that we may live and not die, and that
the land may not become desolate."

20 So Joseph bought all the land of Egypt
for Pharaoh. All the Egyptians sold their
fields, because the famine was severe upon

[w] Heb *He*

47.1-12 Jacob and his sons do not intend to become permanent dwellers in Goshen but to *reside as aliens* there, just as Abraham and Isaac had in the land of Canaan. The mention of *the land of Rameses* may be anachronistic, since it was only later under Rameses II (1290-1144) that the vast building program began in that region through the use of Hebrew slaves (Ex 1.8-14). The editor has woven together here different versions of this incident of the settlement of the tribes in Goshen.
47.13-26 In the process of preparing supplies adequate to survive the famine, Joseph acquires all the land and all the people as property of Pharaoh. One fifth of all the produce goes to Pharaoh; only the priests are exempt and are supported by *a fixed allowance from Pharaoh.*

46.27 Deut 10.22; Acts 7.14
46.28 Gen 47.1
46.29 Gen 45.14,15
46.31 Gen 47.1
46.33 Gen 47.2,3
46.34 Gen 13.7,8; 26.20; 37.2; 45.10,18; Ex 8.26
47.1 Gen 46.31
47.3 Gen 46.33,34
47.4 Gen 15.13; Deut 26.5; Gen 43.1; 46.34
47.6 ver 11; Gen 45.10,18
47.8 Ps 39.12; Heb 11.9,13; Job 14.1; Gen 25.7; 35.28
47.10 ver 7
47.11 Ex 1.11; 12.37; ver 6.27
47.13 Gen 41.30; Acts 7.11
47.14 Gen 41.56
47.15 ver 19

47.22 Ezra 7.24
47.24 Gen 41.34
47.25 Gen 33.15
47.26 ver 22
47.27 ver 11; Gen 46.3; Ex 1.7
47.29 Deut 31.14; Gen 24.2,49
47.30 Gen 49.29; 50.5,13
47.31 Gen 21.23,24; 24.3; 31.53; 50.25
48.3 Gen 35.9,12; 28.19; 35.6
48.4 Gen 18.8
48.5 Gen 46.20; Josh 13.7; 14.4
48.7 Gen 33.18; 35.19,20
48.9 Gen 33.5
48.10 Gen 27.1,27
48.11 Gen 45.26
48.14 ver 19
48.15 Gen 17.1; Heb 11.21
48.16 Gen 28.25; 31.11,13,24; 28.14; 46.3
48.17 ver 14

them; and the land became Pharaoh's. [21]As
for the people, he made slaves of them[x] from
one end of Egypt to the other. [22]Only the
land of the priests he did not buy; for the
priests had a fixed allowance from Pharaoh,
and lived on the allowance that Pharaoh
gave them; therefore they did not sell their
land. [23]Then Joseph said to the people, "Now
that I have this day bought you and your
land for Pharaoh, here is seed for you; sow
the land. [24]And at the harvests you shall
give one-fifth to Pharaoh, and four-fifths
shall be your own, as seed for the field and
as food for yourselves and your households,
and as food for your little ones." [25]They
said, "You have saved our lives; may it
please my lord, we will be slaves to Pharaoh."
[26]So Joseph made it a statute concerning
the land of Egypt, and it stands to this
day, that Pharaoh should have the fifth.
The land of the priests alone did not become
Pharaoh's.

The Last Days of Jacob

27 Thus Israel settled in the land of Egypt,
in the region of Goshen; and they gained
possessions in it, and were fruitful and
multiplied exceedingly. [28]Jacob lived in the
land of Egypt seventeen years; so the days
of Jacob, the years of his life, were one
hundred forty-seven years.
29 When the time of Israel's death drew
near, he called his son Joseph and said to
him, "If I have found favor with you, put
your hand under my thigh and promise to
deal loyally and truly with me. Do not bury
me in Egypt. [30]When I lie down with my
ancestors, carry me out of Egypt and bury
me in their burial place." He answered, "I
will do as you have said." [31]And he said,
"Swear to me"; and he swore to him. Then
Israel bowed himself on the head of his bed.

Jacob Blesses Joseph's Sons

48 After this Joseph was told, "Your
father is ill." So he took with him
his two sons, Manasseh and Ephraim. [2]When
Jacob was told, "Your son Joseph has come
to you," he[y] summoned his strength and sat
up in bed. [3]And Jacob said to Joseph, "God
Almighty[z] appeared to me at Luz in the
land of Canaan, and he blessed me, [4]and
said to me, 'I am going to make you fruitful
and increase your numbers; I will make of
you a company of peoples, and will give this
land to your offspring after you for a perpetual
holding.' [5]Therefore your two sons,
who were born to you in the land of Egypt
before I came to you in Egypt, are now
mine; Ephraim and Manasseh shall be mine,
just as Reuben and Simeon are. [6]As for the
offspring born to you after them, they shall
be yours. They shall be recorded under the
names of their brothers with regard to their
inheritance. [7]For when I came from Paddan,
Rachel, alas, died in the land of Canaan on
the way, while there was still some distance
to go to Ephrath; and I buried her there on
the way to Ephrath" (that is, Bethlehem).
8 When Israel saw Joseph's sons, he said,
"Who are these?" [9]Joseph said to his father,
"They are my sons, whom God has given
me here." And he said, "Bring them to me,
please, that I may bless them." [10]Now the
eyes of Israel were dim with age, and he
could not see well. So Joseph brought them
near him; and he kissed them and embraced
them. [11]Israel said to Joseph, "I did
not expect to see your face; and here God
has let me see your children also." [12]Then
Joseph removed them from his father's knees,[a]
and he bowed himself with his face to the
earth. [13]Joseph took them both, Ephraim in
his right hand toward Israel's left, and
Manasseh in his left hand toward Israel's
right, and brought them near him. [14]But
Israel stretched out his right hand and laid
it on the head of Ephraim, who was the
younger, and his left hand on the head of
Manasseh, crossing his hands, for Manasseh
was the firstborn. [15]He blessed Joseph, and
said,

"The God before whom my ancestors
Abraham and Isaac walked,
the God who has been my shepherd all
my life to this day,
16 the angel who has redeemed me from all
harm, bless the boys;
and in them let my name be perpetuated,
and the name of my ancestors
Abraham and Isaac;
and let them grow into a multitude on
the earth."

17 When Joseph saw that his father laid
his right hand on the head of Ephraim, it
displeased him; so he took his father's hand,
to remove it from Ephraim's head to
Manasseh's head. [18]Joseph said to his father,

[x] Sam Gk Compare Vg: MT *He removed them to the cities* [y] Heb *Israel* [z] Traditional rendering of Heb *El Shaddai* [a] Heb *from his knees*

47.27-31 Joseph agrees to make the symbolically important transfer of the body of Jacob back to the land promised to him and his *ancestors.*
48.1-22 Jacob's last recorded act is the adoption of Ephraim and Manasseh, sons of Joseph, as his own, and the pronouncement of special blessing on Ephraim. The firstborn, Manasseh, is assigned a secondary role, as was the case with Jacob and Esau (Gen 25-27). To Joseph is granted a special *portion,* which involves a multiple pun on Shechem, located between the mountains Ebal and Gerizim, where the northern tribes located the central shrine of Yahweh. It was near Shechem that Jacob bought the sole piece of land that he owned (Gen 33.18-19).

"Not so, my father! Since this one is the
firstborn, put your right hand on his head."
19 But his father refused, and said, "I know,
my son, I know; he also shall become a
people, and he also shall be great. Nevertheless his younger brother shall be greater
than he, and his offspring shall become a
multitude of nations." 20 So he blessed them
that day, saying,

"By you[b] Israel will invoke blessings,
saying,
'God make you[b] like Ephraim and like
Manasseh.' "

So he put Ephraim ahead of Manasseh.
21 Then Israel said to Joseph, "I am about to
die, but God will be with you and will bring
you again to the land of your ancestors. 22 I
now give to you one portion[c] more than to
your brothers, the portion[c] that I took from
the hand of the Amorites with my sword
and with my bow."

Jacob's Last Words to His Sons

49 Then Jacob called his sons, and
said: "Gather around, that I may
tell you what will happen to you in days to
come.

2 Assemble and hear, O sons of Jacob;
listen to Israel your father.

3 Reuben, you are my firstborn,
my might and the first fruits of my vigor,
excelling in rank and excelling in power.
4 Unstable as water, you shall no longer excel
because you went up onto your father's bed;
then you defiled it—you[d] went up onto my couch!

5 Simeon and Levi are brothers;
weapons of violence are their swords.
6 May I never come into their council;
may I not be joined to their company—
for in their anger they killed men,
and at their whim they hamstrung oxen.
7 Cursed be their anger, for it is fierce,
and their wrath, for it is cruel!
I will divide them in Jacob,
and scatter them in Israel.

8 Judah, your brothers shall praise you;
your hand shall be on the neck of your enemies;
your father's sons shall bow down before you.
9 Judah is a lion's whelp;
from the prey, my son, you have gone up.
He crouches down, he stretches out like a lion,
like a lioness—who dares rouse him up?
10 The scepter shall not depart from Judah,
nor the ruler's staff from between his feet,
until tribute comes to him;[e]
and the obedience of the peoples is his.
11 Binding his foal to the vine
and his donkey's colt to the choice vine,
he washes his garments in wine
and his robe in the blood of grapes;
12 his eyes are darker than wine,
and his teeth whiter than milk.

13 Zebulun shall settle at the shore of the sea;
he shall be a haven for ships,
and his border shall be at Sidon.

14 Issachar is a strong donkey,
lying down between the sheepfolds;
15 he saw that a resting place was good,
and that the land was pleasant;
so he bowed his shoulder to the burden,
and became a slave at forced labor.

16 Dan shall judge his people
as one of the tribes of Israel.
17 Dan shall be a snake by the roadside,
a viper along the path,
that bites the horse's heels
so that its rider falls backward.

18 I wait for your salvation, O LORD.

19 Gad shall be raided by raiders,
but he shall raid at their heels.

20 Asher's[f] food shall be rich,
and he shall provide royal delicacies.

21 Naphtali is a doe let loose
that bears lovely fawns.[g]

[b] *you* here is singular in Heb [c] Or *mountain slope* (Heb *shekem*, a play on the name of the town and district of Shechem) [d] Gk Syr Tg: Heb *he* [e] Or *until Shiloh comes* or *until he comes to Shiloh* or (with Syr) *until he comes to whom it belongs* [f] Gk Vg Syr: Heb *From Asher* [g] Or *that gives beautiful words*

49.1-28 The narrative which leads to the stories of the deaths of Jacob and Joseph is interrupted to report the farewell prophecies of Jacob, which in their present form reflect the subsequent history of the tribes of Israel.
49.1 *What will happen to you in the days to come* indicates the two dimensions of the pronouncements attributed to Jacob here: (1) the certainty that what he announces will occur; (2) the conviction that the future of God's people is determined by God.
49.3-4 *Reuben* is condemned, in spite of his superior gifts and powers, because of his incestuous relationship with his father's concubine (Gen 35.22). The Reuben tribe remained in the east of the Jordan region (Josh 13.15-23) and was soon greatly reduced in numbers (Deut 33.6).
49.5-6 *Simeon and Levi* lose their places within Israel. Simeon was apparently absorbed by Judah (Josh 15.1-63; 19.1-9), while Levi disappears, unless the tribe of Levi was replaced by the cultic functionaries, the Levites (Deut 33.8-11).
49.8-12 *Judah* is promised a role of special honor, triumphing over enemies and attaining the sovereign rule. The phrase variously translated as *until tribute comes to him*, or *until Shiloh comes*, or *until he comes to Shiloh* has been interpreted as a prophecy of the coming of a messiah, but probably refers to the dominant role of Judah before the monarchy is established. Then the kings will be of the tribe of Judah (2 Sam 2.4-11), and it is from Judah that the prophets expect the king to arise who will be renowned to the ends of the earth (Mic 5.2-4). The flourishing vine is the symbol of the prosperity that Judah will enjoy.
49.13 *Zebulun* is to be oriented toward the sea in the northern region adjacent to Tyre and Sidon.
49.14-15 *Issachar* is strong but lazy, and becomes a slave at forced labor under the neighboring Canaanites. Issachar's territory is described in Josh 19.17-23.
49.16-17 *Dan* is a small tribe that seems to have been located in various places (Judg 1.34; 5.18; 18.1-31; Josh 19.47-48), but to have been slyly effective in its dealings with others.
49.18 is a comment at the mid-point in the poetic sequence of prophetic pronouncements.
49.19 *Gad* was engaged in marauding attacks.
49.20 *Asher* is characterized by wealth and indulgence (Deut 33.23).
49.21 *Naphtali* is gentle, uttering beautiful words as though giving birth to *lovely fawns*. The tribe was located adjacent to the Sea of Galilee (Deut 33.23).

48.19 ver 14; Num 1.33,35
48.21 Gen 26.3; 28.15; 46.4; 50.24
48.22 Josh 24.32; Jn 4.5
49.1 Num 24.14
49.3 Gen 29.32; Deut 21.17
49.4 Gen 35.22; Deut 27.20
49.5 Gen 34.25-30
49.6 Prov 1.15; Eph 5.11; Gen 34.26
49.7 Josh 19.1,9; 21.1-42
49.8 Deut 33.7; 1 Chr 5.2
49.9 Ezek 19.5-7; Mic 5.8
49.10 Num 24.17; Ps 60.7; Lk 1.32; Isa 2.2; 11.1
49.13 Deut 33.18,19; Josh 19.10,11
49.16 Deut 33.22; Judg 18.1,2
49.17 Judg 18.26,27
49.18 Ex 15.2; Ps 25.5; 119.166, 174; Isa 25.9; Mic 7.7
49.19 Deut 33.20; 1 Chr 5.18
49.20 Deut 33.24,25; Josh 19.24
49.21 Deut 33.23

49.22 Deut 33.13-17
49.23 Gen 37.4,24,28
49.24 Ps 18.34; Isa 41.10; Ps 132.2,5; Isa 1.24; Ps 23.1; Isa 28.16; 1 Pet 2.6-8
49.25 Gen 28.3,13; 32.9; 48.3; 27.28
49.26 Deut 33.15,16
49.28 Gen 23.16-20
49.29 Gen 25.8; 47.30
49.30 Gen 23.16
49.31 Gen 23.19; 25.9; 35.29
49.33 Gen 25.8; Acts 7.15; ver 29
50.1 Gen 46.4
50.2 ver 26
50.3 ver 10; Num 20.29; Deut 34.8
50.5 Gen 47.29-31
50.8 Ex 8.22
50.10 2 Sam 1.17; 1 Sam 31.13; Job 2.13
50.13 Gen 49.29,30; 23.16
50.15 Gen 37.28; 42.21,22

[22] Joseph is a fruitful bough,
a fruitful bough by a spring;
his branches run over the wall.[h]
[23] The archers fiercely attacked him;
they shot at him and pressed him hard.
[24] Yet his bow remained taut,
and his arms[i] were made agile
by the hands of the Mighty One of Jacob,
by the name of the Shepherd, the Rock of Israel,
[25] by the God of your father, who will help you,
by the Almighty[j] who will bless you
with blessings of heaven above,
blessings of the deep that lies beneath,
blessings of the breasts and of the womb.
[26] The blessings of your father
are stronger than the blessings of the eternal mountains,
the bounties[k] of the everlasting hills;
may they be on the head of Joseph,
on the brow of him who was set apart from his brothers.

[27] Benjamin is a ravenous wolf,
in the morning devouring the prey,
and at evening dividing the spoil."

28 All these are the twelve tribes of Israel, and this is what their father said to them when he blessed them, blessing each one of them with a suitable blessing.

Jacob's Death and Burial

29 Then he charged them, saying to them, "I am about to be gathered to my people. Bury me with my ancestors—in the cave in the field of Ephron the Hittite, [30]in the cave in the field at Machpelah, near Mamre, in the land of Canaan, in the field that Abraham bought from Ephron the Hittite as a burial site. [31]There Abraham and his wife Sarah were buried; there Isaac and his wife Rebekah were buried; and there I buried Leah— [32]the field and the cave that is in it were purchased from the Hittites." [33]When Jacob ended his charge to his sons, he drew up his feet into the bed, breathed his last, and was gathered to his people.

50 Then Joseph threw himself on his father's face and wept over him and kissed him. [2]Joseph commanded the physicians in his service to embalm his father. So the physicians embalmed Israel; [3]they spent forty days in doing this, for that is the time required for embalming. And the Egyptians wept for him seventy days.

4 When the days of weeping for him were past, Joseph addressed the household of Pharaoh, "If now I have found favor with you, please speak to Pharaoh as follows: [5]My father made me swear an oath; he said, 'I am about to die. In the tomb that I hewed out for myself in the land of Canaan, there you shall bury me.' Now therefore let me go up, so that I may bury my father; then I will return." [6]Pharaoh answered, "Go up, and bury your father, as he made you swear to do."

7 So Joseph went up to bury his father. With him went up all the servants of Pharaoh, the elders of his household, and all the elders of the land of Egypt, [8]as well as all the household of Joseph, his brothers, and his father's household. Only their children, their flocks, and their herds were left in the land of Goshen. [9]Both chariots and charioteers went up with him. It was a very great company. [10]When they came to the threshing floor of Atad, which is beyond the Jordan, they held there a very great and sorrowful lamentation; and he observed a time of mourning for his father seven days. [11]When the Canaanite inhabitants of the land saw the mourning on the threshing floor of Atad, they said, "This is a grievous mourning on the part of the Egyptians." Therefore the place was named Abel-mizraim;[l] it is beyond the Jordan. [12]Thus his sons did for him as he had instructed them. [13]They carried him to the land of Canaan and buried him in the cave of the field at Machpelah, the field near Mamre, which Abraham bought as a burial site from Ephron the Hittite. [14]After he had buried his father, Joseph returned to Egypt with his brothers and all who had gone up with him to bury his father.

Joseph Forgives His Brothers

15 Realizing that their father was dead, Joseph's brothers said, "What if Joseph still bears a grudge against us and pays us back in full for all the wrong that we did to him?"

49.22-26 Joseph is to be productive and effective in defense, because strengthened and protected by God, for whom five metaphoric names are uttered here: *Mighty One, Shepherd, Rock, God of your father, El Shaddai,* which may mean the God who dwells on the mountain: Sinai, Gerizim (overlooking Shechem), Moriah (in Jerusalem, 2 Chr 3.1). It is appropriate that Joseph, whose tribe was to be the dominant factor in the northern region of Israel, receives these special blessings from Jacob. **49.27** *Benjamin* is pictured as ravenous and greedy (Josh 20.16). **49.20-50.24** The narrative resumes, culminating in the reports of the deaths of Jacob and Joseph. Jacob asks to be united in death *with my ancestors* – with Abraham and Sarah, with Isaac and Rebekah, and with Leah, in continuity with the origins of the covenant people. Joseph orders the embalming of his father's corpse, a custom which fits the Egyptian belief in preparing for a life after death. Following the traditional period of mourning, which lasts *seventy days,* a great retinue from the royal establishment accompanies Joseph to perform the burial. The brief account of the mourning ceremony at Atad, east of the Jordan (50.10-12), may represent a different tradition about the interment of Jacob than the one described at the traditional patriarchal site *at Machpelah near Mamre,* which Abraham bought. On returning to Egypt, Joseph forgives his brothers for their plot to be rid of him, since what they have done with intention to do harm has been God's instrument for preserving the family of the covenant people (50.20). Facing his own death, Joseph asks that his embalmed body be taken back to the land promised to Abraham, Isaac and Jacob (Ex 13.19). This was done, and he was buried at Shechem in the ground that Jacob bought as his first possession of the promised land (Josh 24.32).

[h] Meaning of Heb uncertain [i] Heb *the arms of his hands* [j] Traditional rendering of Heb *Shaddai* [k] Cn Compare Gk: Heb *of my progenitors to the boundaries* [l] That is *mourning* (or *meadow*) *of Egypt*

16So they approached[m] Joseph, saying, "Your
father gave this instruction before he died,
17'Say to Joseph: I beg you, forgive the
crime of your brothers and the wrong they
did in harming you.' Now therefore please
forgive the crime of the servants of the God
of your father." Joseph wept when they
spoke to him. 18Then his brothers also wept,[n]
fell down before him, and said, "We are
here as your slaves." 19But Joseph said to
them, "Do not be afraid! Am I in the place
of God? 20Even though you intended to do
harm to me, God intended it for good, in
order to preserve a numerous people, as he
is doing today. 21So have no fear; I myself
will provide for you and your little ones."
In this way he reassured them, speaking
kindly to them.

Joseph's Last Days and Death

22 So Joseph remained in Egypt, he and
his father's household; and Joseph lived one
hundred ten years. 23Joseph saw Ephraim's
children of the third generation; the children of Machir son of Manasseh were also
born on Joseph's knees.
24 Then Joseph said to his brothers, "I
am about to die; but God will surely come
to you, and bring you up out of this land
to the land that he swore to Abraham, to
Isaac, and to Jacob." 25So Joseph made the
Israelites swear, saying, "When God comes
to you, you shall carry up my bones from
here." 26And Joseph died, being one hundred ten years old; he was embalmed and
placed in a coffin in Egypt.

[m] Gk Syr: Heb *they commanded* [n] Cn: Heb *also came*

50.18 Gen 37.7,10; 41.43
50.19 Gen 45.5; Deut 32.35; Rom 12.19; Heb 10.30
50.20 Gen 37.26,27; 45.5,7
50.21 Gen 45.11; 47.12
50.24 Gen 48.21; Heb 11.22; Gen 13.15,17; 17.7,8; 26.3; 28.13; 35.12

EXODUS

See the Introductions, pp. 2, 30, and 33-35 above.

1.1-7 The opening section serves as a transition from Genesis, prepared by a later editor. To say that *the land was filled with* the offspring of the twelve sons of Jacob is an exaggerated way of describing their rapid growth in numbers in the Nile delta area.
1.8-14 The ruler of Egypt when Jacob and his sons arrived was probably the last Pharaoh of the 18th dynasty, who was replaced in 1305 by Seti I, the new king. The capital, earlier located at Thebes in upper Egypt, was now in the lower Nile delta. It was in this enormous rebuilding project that the Israelites were forced to serve.
1.15-22 The unsuccessful effort to destroy the Israelites by killing off all the male infants at birth anticipates the act of God's judgment in killing all the first-born children of the Egyptians (Ex 11.4-5).

1 These are the names of the sons of
Israel who came to Egypt with Jacob,
each with his household: 2Reuben, Simeon,
Levi, and Judah, 3Issachar, Zebulun, and
Benjamin, 4Dan and Naphtali, Gad and
Asher. 5The total number of people born to
Jacob was seventy. Joseph was already in
Egypt. 6Then Joseph died, and all his broth-
ers, and that whole generation. 7But the
Israelites were fruitful and prolific; they
multiplied and grew exceedingly strong, so
that the land was filled with them.

The Israelites Are Oppressed

8 Now a new king arose over Egypt, who
did not know Joseph. 9He said to his people,
"Look, the Israelite people are more numerous and more powerful than we. 10Come, let
us deal shrewdly with them, or they will
increase and, in the event of war, join our
enemies and fight against us and escape
from the land." 11Therefore they set taskmasters over them to oppress them with
forced labor. They built supply cities, Pithom
and Rameses, for Pharaoh. 12But the more
they were oppressed, the more they multiplied and spread, so that the Egyptians came
to dread the Israelites. 13The Egyptians became ruthless in imposing tasks on the
Israelites, 14and made their lives bitter with
hard service in mortar and brick and in
every kind of field labor. They were ruthless
in all the tasks that they imposed on them.
15 The king of Egypt said to the Hebrew
midwives, one of whom was named Shiphrah
and the other Puah, 16"When you act as
midwives to the Hebrew women, and see
them on the birthstool, if it is a boy, kill
him; but if it is a girl, she shall live." 17But
the midwives feared God; they did not do as
the king of Egypt commanded them, but
they let the boys live. 18So the king of Egypt
summoned the midwives and said to them,
"Why have you done this, and allowed the
boys to live?" 19The midwives said to Pharaoh, "Because the Hebrew women are not
like the Egyptian women; for they are vigorous and give birth before the midwife
comes to them." 20So God dealt well with
the midwives; and the people multiplied and
became very strong. 21And because the

1.1 Gen 46.8-27
1.5 Gen 46.27
1.6 Gen 50.26
1.7 Gen 46.3; 47.27; Acts 7.17
1.8 Acts 7.18,19
1.9 Ps 105.24,25
1.11 Ex 3.7; 5.6
1.14 Ps 81.6
1.16 Acts 7.19
1.17 ver 21
1.20 ver 12; Isa 3.10
1.21 1 Sam 2.35

1.22 Acts 7.19
2.1 Ex 6.19,20
2.2 Acts 7.20; Heb 11.23
2.4 Ex 15.20; Num 26.59
2.10 Acts 7.21
2.11 Acts 7.23,24; Heb 11.24-26
2.13 Acts 7.26-28
2.14 Gen 19.9; Acts 7.27
2.15 Acts 7.29; Gen 24.11; 29.2
2.17 Gen 29.3,10
2.18 Ex 3.1; Num 10.29
2.20 Gen 31.54
2.21 Acts 7.29; Gen 4.25; 18.2
2.22 Ex 18.3; Heb 11.13,14
2.23 Acts 7.30; Deut 26.7; Ex 3.9; Jas 5.4
2.24 Ex 6.5; Ps 105.8,42; Gen 22.16-18
2.25 Ex 4.31; 3.7
3.1 Ex 2.18; 4.27; 18.5
3.2 Deut 33.16; Mk 12.26
3.3 Acts 7.31
3.5 Josh 5.15; Acts 7.33
3.6 Mt 22.31,32; Mk 12.26; Lk 20.37; Acts 7.32
3.7 Ex 2.25; Neh 9.9; Acts 7.34

midwives feared God, he gave them families.
22Then Pharaoh commanded all his people,
"Every boy that is born to the Hebrews[a] you
shall throw into the Nile, but you shall let
every girl live."

Birth and Youth of Moses

2 Now a man from the house of Levi
went and married a Levite woman.
2The woman conceived and bore a son; and
when she saw that he was a fine baby, she
hid him three months. 3When she could
hide him no longer she got a papyrus basket for him, and plastered it with bitumen
and pitch; she put the child in it and placed
it among the reeds on the bank of the river.
4His sister stood at a distance, to see what
would happen to him.
5 The daughter of Pharaoh came down
to bathe at the river, while her attendants
walked beside the river. She saw the basket
among the reeds and sent her maid to bring
it. 6When she opened it, she saw the child.
He was crying, and she took pity on him,
"This must be one of the Hebrews' children," she said. 7Then his sister said to
Pharaoh's daughter, "Shall I go and get you
a nurse from the Hebrew women to nurse
the child for you?" 8Pharaoh's daughter
said to her, "Yes." So the girl went and
called the child's mother. 9Pharaoh's daughter said to her, "Take this child and nurse
it for me, and I will give you your wages."
So the woman took the child and nursed it.
10When the child grew up, she brought him
to Pharaoh's daughter, and she took him as
her son. She named him Moses,[b] "because,"
she said, "I drew him out[c] of the water."

Moses Flees to Midian

11 One day, after Moses had grown up,
he went out to his people and saw their
forced labor. He saw an Egyptian beating a
Hebrew, one of his kinsfolk. 12He looked this
way and that, and seeing no one he killed
the Egyptian and hid him in the sand.
13When he went out the next day, he saw
two Hebrews fighting; and he said to the
one who was in the wrong, "Why do you
strike your fellow Hebrew?" 14He answered,
"Who made you a ruler and judge over us?
Do you mean to kill me as you killed the
Egyptian?" Then Moses was afraid and
thought, "Surely the thing is known."
15When Pharaoh heard of it, he sought to
kill Moses.
But Moses fled from Pharaoh. He settled
in the land of Midian, and sat down by a
well. 16The priest of Midian had seven daughters. They came to draw water, and filled
the troughs to water their father's flock.
17But some shepherds came and drove them
away. Moses got up and came to their
defense and watered their flock. 18When
they returned to their father Reuel, he said,
"How is it that you have come back so soon
today?" 19They said, "An Egyptian helped us
against the shepherds; he even drew water
for us and watered the flock." 20He said to
his daughters, "Where is he? Why did you
leave the man? Invite him to break bread."
21Moses agreed to stay with the man, and
he gave Moses his daughter Zipporah in
marriage. 22She bore a son, and he named
him Gershom; for he said, "I have been an
alien[d] residing in a foreign land."
23 After a long time the king of Egypt
died. The Israelites groaned under their slavery, and cried out. Out of the slavery their
cry for help rose up to God. 24God heard
their groaning, and God remembered his
covenant with Abraham, Isaac, and Jacob.
25God looked upon the Israelites, and God
took notice of them.

Moses at the Burning Bush

3 Moses was keeping the flock of his
father-in-law Jethro, the priest of
Midian; he led his flock beyond the wilderness, and came to Horeb, the mountain of
God. 2There the angel of the LORD appeared
to him in a flame of fire out of a bush; he
looked, and the bush was blazing, yet it was
not consumed. 3Then Moses said, "I must
turn aside and look at this great sight, and
see why the bush is not burned up." 4When
the LORD saw that he had turned aside to
see, God called to him out of the bush,
"Moses, Moses!" And he said, "Here I am."
5Then he said, "Come no closer! Remove the
sandals from your feet, for the place on
which you are standing is holy ground."
6He said further, "I am the God of your
father, the God of Abraham, the God of
Isaac, and the God of Jacob." And Moses hid
his face, for he was afraid to look at God.
7 Then the LORD said, "I have observed
the misery of my people who are in Egypt;
I have heard their cry on account of their

[a] Sam Gk Tg: Heb lacks *to the Hebrews* [b] Heb *Mosheh* [c] Heb *mashah* [d] Heb *ger*

2.1-10 Both the parents of Moses are from the tribe of Levi, which disappears in later Israelite history, where the Levites are the priestly functionaries. The story of his being concealed in a *papyrus basket* which is placed *among the reeds on the bank of the river* closely resembles the Legend of Sargon, which dates from 1000 years earlier in Mesopotamia. Adopted by *Pharaoh's daughter...as her son*, he is given an Egyptian name meaning "son," as in Thutmose (son of Thut, the god). At this point, Moses' brother Aaron and sister Miriam are not mentioned, which may indicate a different literary tradition.
2.11-22 Forced to flee because of his violent intervention in behalf of an abused Hebrew, Moses lives as *an alien*, helps water flocks and thereby finds a wife among another Semitic tribe, the Midianites, near the Gulf of Aqabah, just as Jacob did among the Arameans (Gen 29.1-12). Indicating the diversity of traditions being drawn upon in the Pentateuch, Moses' father-in-law is here named Reuel, while in 3.1 he is called Jethro and in Judg 1.16 he is Hobab.
2.23-25 The successor as king of Egypt was Rameses II, who expanded the building projects in the Land of Goshen, and built a new capital city named for himself. Pointing up God's continuing concern for his covenant people, he is said to have *heard, remembered, looked upon*, and taken *notice of them*.
3.1-12 God Confronts Moses on the Holy Mountain. Called Horeb here, the mountain is later named Sinai (Ex 19). Now identified as the high peak in the southern part of the Sinai peninsula; some scholars have proposed that it may actually have been a mountain in the northeastern section. Although the messenger is first identified as *the angel of the LORD*, it is in fact *the LORD* himself who addresses Moses. Many sources indicate that Israel shared with the Midianites a holy place of God in the desert: Judg 1.16; 4.17-22; 1 Sam 15.6. That Moses *was afraid to look at God* fits with the prohibitions against seeing him uttered later in this book: Ex 19.21; 33.20. Initially God identifies himself with the God of the patriarchs Abraham, Isaac and Jacob (3.6), following this with the promise of his deliverance of his people from slavery into the promised land now occupied by other Semitic peoples (3.7). Moses asks what qualifications he has for leading such an undertaking (3.11), to which God responds with the assurance that after the people have escaped from Egypt through Moses' leadership, they will encounter God on this mountain.

3.13-22 God Discloses his Name to Moses and Repeats his Purpose for his People. Moses wants to know who the God is that is commissioning him for this role (3.13). The answer can be variously translated, as indicated in the notes; another possibility is "He who causes to be what is." Moses is to lead his people out into the desert to meet their God. His authority from the God of Israel will be demonstrated by the punitive signs he will give to force the king to allow the people to leave, but the popular response to the wonders he performs will include generous gifts to the Israelites on the part of the Egyptians, so that the tribes *will not go empty-handed.*

4.1-9 Moses' Request for Signs of God's Authorization of Him. He is given three miraculous capabilities: to convert his staff – a symbol of power – into a snake, which was a Canaanite symbol of fertility (4.2-5); to catch and then to cure a dread skin disease (4.6-8); to convert the water from the Nile into blood (4.9), which was understood to be the bearer of life (Lev. 17.11).

4.10-20 Moses' protest that he cannot fulfill this role because he is not eloquent evokes the LORD's anger, and is countered by God's preparing his articulate brother Aaron to be the spokesman for Moses. The instrument of power, *the staff,* is to remain in Moses' hand, however, and on his return to Egypt with wife and family, he carries it.

taskmasters. Indeed, I know their sufferings, [8]and I have come down to deliver them from the Egyptians, and to bring them up out of that land to a good and broad land, a land flowing with milk and honey, to the country of the Canaanites, the Hittites, the Amorites, the Perizzites, the Hivites, and the Jebusites. [9]The cry of the Israelites has now come to me; I have also seen how the Egyptians oppress them. [10]So come, I will send you to Pharaoh to bring my people, the Israelites, out of Egypt." [11]But Moses said to God, "Who am I that I should go to Pharaoh, and bring the Israelites out of Egypt?" [12]He said, "I will be with you; and this shall be the sign for you that it is I who sent you: when you have brought the people out of Egypt, you shall worship God on this mountain."

The Divine Name Revealed

13 But Moses said to God, "If I come to the Israelites and say to them, 'The God of your ancestors has sent me to you,' and they ask me, 'What is his name?' what shall I say to them?" [14]God said to Moses, "I AM WHO I AM."[e] He said further, "Thus you shall say to the Israelites, 'I AM has sent me to you.' " [15]God also said to Moses, "Thus you shall say to the Israelites, 'The LORD,[f] the God of your ancestors, the God of Abraham, the God of Isaac, and the God of Jacob, has sent me to you':

This is my name forever,
and this my title for all generations.

[16]Go and assemble the elders of Israel, and say to them, 'The LORD, the God of your ancestors, the God of Abraham, of Isaac, and of Jacob, has appeared to me, saying: I have given heed to you and to what has been done to you in Egypt. [17]I declare that I will bring you up out of the misery of Egypt, to the land of the Canaanites, the Hittites, the Amorites, the Perizzites, the Hivites, and the Jebusites, a land flowing with milk and honey.' [18]They will listen to your voice; and you and the elders of Israel shall go to the king of Egypt and say to him, 'The LORD, the God of the Hebrews, has met with us; let us now go a three days' journey into the wilderness, so that we may sacrifice to the LORD our God.' [19]I know, however, that the king of Egypt will not let you go unless compelled by a mighty hand.[g] [20]So I will stretch out my hand and strike Egypt with all my wonders that I will perform in it; after that he will let you go. [21]I will bring this people into such favor with the Egyptians that, when you go, you will not go empty-handed; [22]each woman shall ask her neighbor and any woman living in the neighbor's house for jewelry of silver and of gold, and clothing, and you shall put them on your sons and on your daughters; and so you shall plunder the Egyptians."

Moses' Miraculous Power

4 Then Moses answered, "But suppose they do not believe me or listen to me, but say, 'The LORD did not appear to you.' " [2]The LORD said to him, "What is that in your hand?" He said, "A staff." [3]And he said, "Throw it on the ground." So he threw the staff on the ground, and it became a snake; and Moses drew back from it. [4]Then the LORD said to Moses, "Reach out your hand, and seize it by the tail"—so he reached out his hand and grasped it, and it became a staff in his hand— [5]"so that they may believe that the LORD, the God of their ancestors, the God of Abraham, the God of Isaac, and the God of Jacob, has appeared to you."

6 Again, the LORD said to him, "Put your hand inside your cloak." He put his hand into his cloak; and when he took it out, his hand was leprous,[h] as white as snow. [7]Then God said, "Put your hand back into your cloak"—so he put his hand back into his cloak, and when he took it out, it was restored like the rest of his body— [8]"If they will not believe you or heed the first sign, they may believe the second sign. [9]If they will not believe even these two signs or heed you, you shall take some water from the Nile and pour it on the dry ground; and the water that you shall take from the Nile will become blood on the dry ground."

10 But Moses said to the LORD, "O my Lord, I have never been eloquent, neither in the past nor even now that you have spoken to your servant; but I am slow of speech and slow of tongue." [11]Then the LORD said to him, "Who gives speech to mortals? Who makes them mute or deaf, seeing or blind? Is it not I, the LORD? [12]Now

[e] Or *I am what I* AM OR *I* WILL BE WHAT *I* WILL BE [f] The word "LORD" when spelled with capital letters stands for the divine name, *YHWH*, which is here connected with the verb *hayah*, "to be" [g] Gk Vg: Heb *no, not by a mighty hand* [h] A term for several skin diseases; precise meaning uncertain

3.8 Gen 50.24,25; ver 17; Josh 24.11
3.9 Ex 2.23; 1.13,14
3.10 Mic 6.4
3.12 Gen 31.3; Josh 1.5
3.14 Ex 6.3; Jn 8.58; Heb 13.8
3.15 Ps 135.13; Hos 12.5
3.17 Gen 15.14,16; Josh 24.11
3.18 Ex 4.31; 5.13
3.19 Ex 5.2; 6.1
3.20 Ex 6.6; 9.15; Deut 6.22; Neh 9.10; Ex 12.31
3.21 Ex 11.3; 12.36
3.22 Ex 11.2,3; 12.35,36
4.1 Ex 3.18; 6.30
4.2 ver 17.20
4.6 Num 12.10; 2 Kings 5.27
4.7 Num 12.13,14; Deut 32.39; 2 Kings 5.14; Mt 8.3
4.9 Ex 7.19
4.10 Ex 6.12; Jer 1.6
4.11 Ps 94.9; Mt 11.5
4.12 Isa 50.4; Jer 1.9; Mt 10.19; Mk 13.11; Lk 12.11,12; 21.14,15

go, and I will be with your mouth and
teach you what you are to speak." 13But he
said, "O my Lord, please send someone
else." 14Then the anger of the LORD was
kindled against Moses and he said, "What
of your brother Aaron, the Levite? I know
that he can speak fluently; even now he is
coming out to meet you, and when he sees
you his heart will be glad. 15You shall speak
to him and put the words in his mouth; and
I will be with your mouth and with his
mouth, and will teach you what you shall
do. 16He indeed shall speak for you to the
people; he shall serve as a mouth for you,
and you shall serve as God for him. 17Take
in your hand this staff, with which you
shall perform the signs."

Moses Returns to Egypt

18 Moses went back to his father-in-law
Jethro and said to him, "Please let me go
back to my kindred in Egypt and see whether
they are still living." And Jethro said to
Moses, "Go in peace." 19The LORD said to
Moses in Midian, "Go back to Egypt; for all
those who were seeking your life are dead."
20So Moses took his wife and his sons, put
them on a donkey and went back to the
land of Egypt; and Moses carried the staff of
God in his hand.
21 And the LORD said to Moses, "When
you go back to Egypt, see that you perform
before Pharaoh all the wonders that I have
put in your power; but I will harden his
heart, so that he will not let the people go.
22Then you shall say to Pharaoh, 'Thus says
the LORD: Israel is my firstborn son. 23I said
to you, "Let my son go that he may worship
me." But you refused to let him go; now I
will kill your firstborn son.' "
24 On the way, at a place where they
spent the night, the LORD met him and tried
to kill him. 25But Zipporah took a flint and
cut off her son's foreskin, and touched Moses'[i]
feet with it, and said, "Truly you are a
bridegroom of blood to me!" 26So he let him
alone. It was then she said, "A bridegroom
of blood by circumcision."
27 The LORD said to Aaron, "Go into the
wilderness to meet Moses." So he went; and
he met him at the mountain of God and
kissed him. 28Moses told Aaron all the words
of the LORD with which he had sent him,
and all the signs with which he had charged
him. 29Then Moses and Aaron went and
assembled all the elders of the Israelites.
30Aaron spoke all the words that the LORD
had spoken to Moses, and performed the
signs in the sight of the people. 31The people
believed; and when they heard that the
LORD had given heed to the Israelites and
that he had seen their misery, they bowed
down and worshiped.

Bricks without Straw

5 Afterward Moses and Aaron went to
Pharaoh and said, "Thus says the
LORD, the God of Israel, 'Let my people go,
so that they may celebrate a festival to me
in the wilderness.' " 2But Pharaoh said, "Who
is the LORD, that I should heed him and let
Israel go? I do not know the LORD, and I will
not let Israel go." 3Then they said, "The God
of the Hebrews has revealed himself to us;
let us go a three days' journey into the
wilderness to sacrifice to the LORD our God,
or he will fall upon us with pestilence or
sword." 4But the king of Egypt said to them,
"Moses and Aaron, why are you taking the
people away from their work? Get to your
labors!" 5Pharaoh continued, "Now they
are more numerous than the people of the
land[j] and yet you want them to stop working!" 6That same day Pharaoh commanded
the taskmasters of the people, as well as
their supervisors, 7"You shall no longer give
the people straw to make bricks, as before;
let them go and gather straw for themselves. 8But you shall require of them the
same quantity of bricks as they have made
previously; do not diminish it, for they are
lazy; that is why they cry, 'Let us go and
offer sacrifice to our God.' 9Let heavier work
be laid on them; then they will labor at it
and pay no attention to deceptive words."
10 So the taskmasters and the supervisors of the people went out and said to the
people, "Thus says Pharaoh, 'I will not give
you straw. 11Go and get straw yourselves,
wherever you can find it; but your work
will not be lessened in the least.' " 12So the
people scattered throughout the land of
Egypt, to gather stubble for straw. 13The
taskmasters were urgent, saying, "Complete
your work, the same daily assignment as
when you were given straw." 14And the
supervisors of the Israelites, whom Pharaoh's taskmasters had set over them, were
beaten, and were asked, "Why did you
not finish the required quantity of bricks

[i] Heb *his* [j] Sam: Heb *The people of the land are now many*

4.14 ver 27 **4.15** Ex 7.1,2; Num 23.5,12,16; Deut 5.13 **4.17** ver 2; Ex 7.9-20 **4.19** Ex 2.15,23 **4.20** Ex 17.9; Num 20.8 **4.21** Ex 7.3,13; 9.12,35; 10.1; 14.8; Deut 2.30; Jn 12.40; Rom 19.18 **4.22** Isa 63.16; 64.8; Hos 11.1; Rom 9.4; Jer 31.9 **4.23** Ex 5.1; 6.11; 7.16; 12.29 **4.24** Num 22.22; Gen 7.14 **4.25** Josh 5.2,3 **4.27** ver 14; Ex 3.1 **4.28** ver 15,16; 8,9 **4.29** Ex 3.16 **4.30** ver 16 **4.31** ver 8,9; Ex 3.18; 2.25; 3.7; 12.27

5.1 Ex 3.18; 4.23; 10.9 **5.2** Job 21.15; Ex 3.19 **5.3** Ex 3.18 **5.4** Ex 1.11; 2.11; 6.6,7 **5.5** Ex 1.7,9 **5.6** Ex 1.11; 3.7 **5.8** ver 17 **5.10** ver 6 **5.14** ver 6; Isa 10.24

4.21 Moses is told that he is to perform his signs to persuade Pharaoh that God is with Israel, but is at the same time informed that the king will not agree to let them go.
4.22-23 God's people are here called by the LORD *my firstborn son,* a title which is repeated by the prophet Hosea (11.1).
4.24-26 The requirement that all males in the covenant people were to be circumcised is reported in Gen 17.9-12, which is probably from the priestly source. Exodus reports no circumcision of Moses, a lack which from the later priestly viewpoint would have disqualified him from leadership of God's people. God's anger can be understood on this basis, as can the remedy provided by Zipporah, who circumcises their child and touches with the foreskin Moses' genitals, for which the phrase *Moses' feet* is a euphemism.
4.27-31 Together Moses and Aaron communicate God's purpose to the *elders:* that is, to the mature males with responsibility for the group. *The words of the LORD* are both verbal communications and visible actions (signs) which convey the purpose and promise of God to the covenant people. They trusted that God was now ready to deliver them from their *misery,* and they accordingly *bowed down and worshiped.*
5.1-23 The LORD's instruction to his people to withdraw to the wilderness to join in group worship of him evokes a range of responses. Pharaoh thinks it is a ruse to enable them to avoid their building projects, so he increases their load by requiring them to find their own *straw,* which served as a binder for making bricks. He declares (5.5) that they are more numerous than the Egyptians, which goes beyond the statement of their growing numbers in 1.7-12. The *supervisors* blame Moses and Aaron for having caused the difficulty, spoiling Pharaoh's esteem of them (5.21, *brought us into bad odor)* and threatening their lives (*put a sword in their* [the Egyptian officials'] *hand.* Moses *turned to the LORD* in order to shift the blame to God for his apparent failure *to deliver your people* (5.23).

6.1-7.13 Serves as a transition into the next major narrative section, in which are described the plagues that fall on the Egyptians and lead to the release of the Israelites (7.13-12.30). This interim section is priestly tradition, as is apparent from the prominent place given to the descendants of Levi and to the role of Aaron, and from the use of El Shaddai, the special name of God in the priestly version of the covenant with Abraham in Gen 17.1. The encounter with God (3.2-8) is a variant of Ex 3.1-4.17, which derives largely from the J tradition.
6.9 *Their broken spirit* refers to the Israelites' crushed will and purpose as a result of their suffering as slaves.
6.10-13 The assignment to convey instructions to Pharaoh is given in this tradition to both Moses and Aaron, the latter embodying the priestly tradition.
6.14-25 The genealogy begins with the two older sons of Jacob, Reuben and Simeon, but concentrates on Levi and his offspring, which includes both Aaron and Moses. This passage resembles Num 3, where the order of the priestly family and the assigning of ranks are detailed. The last names in this list, Putiel and Phinehas, are both Egyptian. The latter figures importantly in other Old Testament books for his role in safeguarding the marital and genealogical purity of God's people, as in Num 25; 31.6; Josh 22.30-34; Judg 20.27-28. He is also the ancestor of Ezra (Ezra 8.2), who in his priestly role instructs those Israelites who return to the land from their exile in Babylon.
6.26-7.13 The twin roles of Moses and Aaron in effecting the deliverance of Israel from Egypt are made explicit here. Aaron is not merely speaking in Moses' behalf but is now his *prophet*. Aaron's staff which *became a snake* outperforms that of Moses (4.2-5) by devouring the snakes of *the magicians of Egypt* (7.8-13). Yet Pharaoh's heart (which in ancient Semitic thought was the seat of the will, not of the emotions) remains *hardened*, and he refuses to hear Yahweh's instruction to free his people.

yesterday and today, as you did before?"
15 Then the Israelite supervisors came to
Pharaoh and cried, "Why do you treat your
servants like this? 16No straw is given to
your servants, yet they say to us, 'Make
bricks!' Look how your servants are beaten!
You are unjust to your own people."[k] 17He
said, "You are lazy, lazy; that is why you
say, 'Let us go and sacrifice to the LORD.'
18Go now, and work; for no straw shall be
given you, but you shall still deliver the
same number of bricks." 19The Israelite
supervisors saw that they were in trouble
when they were told, "You shall not lessen
your daily number of bricks." 20As they left
Pharaoh, they came upon Moses and Aaron
who were waiting to meet them. 21They
said to them, "The LORD look upon you and
judge! You have brought us into bad odor
with Pharaoh and his officials, and have
put a sword in their hand to kill us."
22 Then Moses turned again to the LORD
and said, "O LORD, why have you mistreated
this people? Why did you ever send me?
23Since I first came to Pharaoh to speak in
your name, he has mistreated this people,
and you have done nothing at all to deliver
your people."

Israel's Deliverance Assured

6 Then the LORD said to Moses, "Now
you shall see what I will do to Pharaoh: Indeed, by a mighty hand he will let
them go; by a mighty hand he will drive
them out of his land."
2 God also spoke to Moses and said to
him: "I am the LORD. 3I appeared to Abraham,
Isaac, and Jacob as God Almighty,[l] but by
my name 'The LORD'[m] I did not make myself
known to them. 4I also established my
covenant with them, to give them the land
of Canaan, the land in which they resided
as aliens. 5I have also heard the groaning
of the Israelites whom the Egyptians are
holding as slaves, and I have remembered
my covenant. 6Say therefore to the Israelites, 'I am the LORD, and I will free you from
the burdens of the Egyptians and deliver
you from slavery to them. I will redeem you
with an outstretched arm and with mighty
acts of judgment. 7I will take you as my
people, and I will be your God. You shall
know that I am the LORD your God, who has
freed you from the burdens of the Egyptians.
8I will bring you into the land that I swore
to give to Abraham, Isaac, and Jacob; I will
give it to you for a possession. I am the
LORD.' " 9Moses told this to the Israelites; but
they would not listen to Moses, because of
their broken spirit and their cruel slavery.
10 Then the LORD spoke to Moses, 11"Go
and tell Pharaoh king of Egypt to let the
Israelites go out of his land." 12But Moses
spoke to the LORD, "The Israelites have not
listened to me; how then shall Pharaoh
listen to me, poor speaker that I am?"[n]
13Thus the LORD spoke to Moses and Aaron,
and gave them orders regarding the Israelites and Pharaoh king of Egypt, charging
them to free the Israelites from the land of
Egypt.

The Genealogy of Moses and Aaron

14 The following are the heads of their
ancestral houses: the sons of Reuben, the
firstborn of Israel: Hanoch, Pallu, Hezron,
and Carmi; these are the families of Reuben.
15The sons of Simeon: Jemuel, Jamin, Ohad,
Jachin, Zohar, and Shaul,[o] the son of a
Canaanite woman; these are the families of
Simeon. 16The following are the names of
the sons of Levi according to their
genealogies: Gershon,[p] Kohath, and Merari,
and the length of Levi's life was one hundred thirty-seven years. 17The sons of
Gershon:[p] Libni and Shimei, by their families. 18The sons of Kohath: Amram, Izhar,
Hebron, and Uzziel, and the length of
Kohath's life was one hundred thirty-three
years. 19The sons of Merari: Mahli and Mushi.
These are the families of the Levites according to their genealogies. 20Amram married
Jochebed his father's sister and she bore
him Aaron and Moses, and the length of
Amram's life was one hundred thirty-seven
years. 21The sons of Izhar: Korah, Nepheg,
and Zichri. 22The sons of Uzziel: Mishael,
Elzaphan, and Sithri. 23Aaron married
Elisheba, daughter of Amminadab and sister
of Nahshon, and she bore him Nadab, Abihu,
Eleazar, and Ithamar. 24The sons of Korah:
Assir, Elkanah, and Abiasaph; these are the
families of the Korahites. 25Aaron's son
Eleazar married one of the daughters of
Putiel, and she bore him Phinehas. These
are the heads of the ancestral houses of the
Levites by their families.
26 It was this same Aaron and Moses to

[k] Gk Compare Syr Vg: Heb *beaten, and the sin of your people* [l] Traditional rendering of Heb *El Shaddai* [m] Heb *YHWH*; see note at 3.15 [n] Heb *me? I am uncircumcised of lips* [o] Or *Saul* [p] Also spelled *Gershom*; see 2.22

5.17 ver 8
5.21 Ex 14.11; 15.24; Gen 16.5; 34.30
5.22 Num 11.11; Jer 4.10
5.23 Ex 3.8
6.1 Ex 3.19,20; 7.4,5; 12.31,33,39
6.3 Ps 68.4; 83.18; Isa 52.6; Jer 16.21; Ezek 37.6,13
6.4 Gen 15.18; 28.4
6.5 Ex 2.24
6.6 Deut 26.8
6.7 Deut 4.20; 26.8; Ps 81.6; Ex 16.12; Isa 41.20
6.8 Gen 15.18
6.14 Gen 46.9; Num 26.5-11
6.15 Gen 46.10; 1 Chr 4.24
6.16 Gen 46.11; Num 3.17
6.17 1 Chr 6.17
6.18 1 Chr 6.2,18
6.19 1 Chr 6.19
6.20 Ex 2.1,2; Num 26.59
6.21 Num 16.1; 1 Chr 6.37,38
6.22 Lev 10.4; Num 3.30
6.24 Num 26.11
6.25 Josh 24.33; Num 25.7-11; Ps 106.30

whom the LORD said, "Bring the Israelites out of the land of Egypt, company by company." [27]It was they who spoke to Pharaoh king of Egypt to bring the Israelites out of Egypt, the same Moses and Aaron.

Moses and Aaron Obey God's Commands

28 On the day when the LORD spoke to Moses in the land of Egypt, [29]he said to him, "I am the LORD; tell Pharaoh king of Egypt all that I am speaking to you." [30]But Moses said in the LORD's presence, "Since I am a poor speaker,[q] why would Pharaoh listen to me?"

7 The LORD said to Moses, "See, I have made you like God to Pharaoh, and your brother Aaron shall be your prophet. [2]You shall speak all that I command you, and your brother Aaron shall tell Pharaoh to let the Israelites go out of his land. [3]But I will harden Pharaoh's heart, and I will multiply my signs and wonders in the land of Egypt. [4]When Pharaoh does not listen to you, I will lay my hand upon Egypt and bring my people the Israelites, company by company, out of the land of Egypt by great acts of judgment. [5]The Egyptians shall know that I am the LORD, when I stretch out my hand against Egypt and bring the Israelites out from among them." [6]Moses and Aaron did so; they did just as the LORD commanded them. [7]Moses was eighty years old and Aaron eighty-three when they spoke to Pharaoh.

Aaron's Miraculous Rod

8 The LORD said to Moses and Aaron, [9]"When Pharaoh says to you, 'Perform a wonder,' then you shall say to Aaron, 'Take your staff and throw it down before Pharaoh, and it will become a snake.'" [10]So Moses and Aaron went to Pharaoh and did as the LORD had commanded; Aaron threw down his staff before Pharaoh and his officials, and it became a snake. [11]Then Pharaoh summoned the wise men and the sorcerers; and they also, the magicians of Egypt, did the same by their secret arts. [12]Each one threw down his staff, and they became snakes; but Aaron's staff swallowed up theirs. [13]Still Pharaoh's heart was hardened, and he would not listen to them, as the LORD had said.

The First Plague: Water Turned to Blood

14 Then the LORD said to Moses, "Pharaoh's heart is hardened; he refuses to let the people go. [15]Go to Pharaoh in the morning, as he is going out to the water; stand by at the river bank to meet him, and take in your hand the staff that was turned into a snake. [16]Say to him, 'The LORD, the God of the Hebrews, sent me to you to say, "Let my people go, so that they may worship me in the wilderness." But until now you have not listened.' [17]Thus says the LORD, "By this you shall know that I am the LORD." See, with the staff that is in my hand I will strike the water that is in the Nile, and it shall be turned to blood. [18]The fish in the river shall die, the river itself shall stink, and the Egyptians shall be unable to drink water from the Nile.'" [19]The LORD said to Moses, "Say to Aaron, 'Take your staff and stretch out your hand over the waters of Egypt—over its rivers, its canals, and its ponds, and all its pools of water—so that they may become blood; and there shall be blood throughout the whole land of Egypt, even in vessels of wood and in vessels of stone.'"

20 Moses and Aaron did just as the LORD commanded. In the sight of Pharaoh and of his officials he lifted up the staff and struck the water in the river, and all the water in the river was turned into blood, [21]and the fish in the river died. The river stank so that the Egyptians could not drink its water, and there was blood throughout the whole land of Egypt. [22]But the magicians of Egypt did the same by their secret arts; so Pharaoh's heart remained hardened, and he would not listen to them; as the LORD had said. [23]Pharaoh turned and went into his house, and he did not take even this to heart. [24]And all the Egyptians had to dig along the Nile for water to drink, for they could not drink the water of the river.

25 Seven days passed after the LORD had struck the Nile.

The Second Plague: Frogs

8[r] Then the LORD said to Moses, "Go to Pharaoh and say to him, 'Thus says the LORD: Let my people go, so that they may worship me. [2]If you refuse to let them go, I will plague your whole country with frogs. [3]The river shall swarm with frogs; they shall come up into your palace, into

[q] Heb *am uncircumcised of lips;* see 6.12 [r] Ch 7.26 in Heb

6.29 ver 11; Ex 7.2
6.30 ver 12; Ex 4.10
7.1 Ex 4.16
7.2 Ex 4.15
7.3 Ex 4.21; 11.9
7.4 Ex 3.19,20; 10.1; 11.9; 12.51; 13.3,9; 6.6
7.5 ver 17; Ex 8.19; 3.20
7.6 ver 2
7.7 Deut 34.7; Acts 7.23,30
7.9 Isa 7.11; Jn 2.18; Ex 4.2,17
7.10 ver 9; Ex 4.3
7.11 Gen 41.8; ver 22; Ex 8.7,18
7.13 ver 4; Ex 4.21
7.14 Ex 8.15; 10.1,20,27
7.15 ver 10; Ex 4.2,3
7.16 Ex 3.12,18; 5.1,3
7.17 ver 5; Ex 5.2; 4.9; Rev 11.6; 16.4,6
7.18 ver 21,24
7.19 Ex 8.5,6,16; 9.22; 10.12,21; 14.21,26
7.20 Ps 78.44; 105.29
7.21 ver 18
7.22 ver 11; Ex 8.7
8.1 Ex 3.12,18
8.3 Ps 105.30

7.14-12.36 The Plagues Prepare for Israel's Escape from Egypt. The account of the plagues that Yahweh sent to persuade Pharaoh to liberate the people of Israel is composite, with elements from the J and E as well as the priestly traditions. In the J strand, Yahweh is the operator, while in the E material, Moses is the agent. In the priestly material, Aaron is the chief actor. Some scholars have proposed that what happens in these plagues is an extreme form of natural occurrences in Egypt: flood waters of red mud, various kinds of natural disorder, and outbreaks of pestilences. But the stories portray God at work in each of these catastrophes, seeking to convey his will to an obstinate pagan ruler. Two themes that run through these stories are the varying abilities of the Egyptian magicians to duplicate the miracles, and the rising, reluctant willingness of Pharaoh to release the enslaved Israelites.
7.14-24 The First Plague: Water becomes Blood. It is ironic that what for Israel symbolized life – blood – becomes an instrument of death. Aaron's special role is introduced in 7.19-20, 22. The magicians can match this miracle (7.22), and Pharaoh is unyielding.
8.1-15 The Second Plague: Frogs. Clearly this invasion of *land* and *houses* by frogs goes far beyond a natural occurrence, although the magicians have similar powers (8.7). Aaron's role is depicted in 8.5-6,8,12. When Moses *cried out to the LORD* and *there was a respite* from the frogs, Pharaoh once again refused to free the people.

8.16-19 The Third Plague: Gnats. This is depicted as entirely the work of Aaron, and the magicians cannot match it (8.18). Instead, they attribute the power to *the finger of God*, a phrase which is used of the law which God has prescribed for his people (Ex.31.18; Deut 9.10) and of the creation itself (Ps 8.3). It is also used by Jesus in defining the source of power for his exorcisms (Lk 11.20).

8.20-32 The Fourth Plague: Flies. The term used here in the ancient Greek translation specifies "dog-flies." Only the Land of Goshen, *where my people live*, will be protected by the LORD from these pests. Once more, Pharaoh at first relents and then resumes his negative stand (8.29-32).

your bedchamber and your bed, and into the houses of your officials and of your people,[s] and into your ovens and your kneading bowls. 4The frogs shall come up on you and on your people and on all your officials.' " 5[t]And the LORD said to Moses, "Say to Aaron, 'Stretch out your hand with your staff over the rivers, the canals, and the pools, and make frogs come up on the land of Egypt.' " 6So Aaron stretched out his hand over the waters of Egypt; and the frogs came up and covered the land of Egypt. 7But the magicians did the same by their secret arts, and brought frogs up on the land of Egypt.

8 Then Pharaoh called Moses and Aaron, and said, "Pray to the LORD to take away the frogs from me and my people, and I will let the people go to sacrifice to the LORD." 9Moses said to Pharaoh, "Kindly tell me when I am to pray for you and for your officials and for your people, that the frogs may be removed from you and your houses and be left only in the Nile." 10And he said, "Tomorrow." Moses said, "As you say! So that you may know that there is no one like the LORD our God, 11the frogs shall leave you and your houses and your officials and your people; they shall be left only in the Nile." 12Then Moses and Aaron went out from Pharaoh; and Moses cried out to the LORD concerning the frogs that he had brought upon Pharaoh.[u] 13And the LORD did as Moses requested: the frogs died in the houses, the courtyards, and the fields. 14And they gathered them together in heaps, and the land stank. 15But when Pharaoh saw that there was a respite, he hardened his heart, and would not listen to them, just as the LORD had said.

The Third Plague: Gnats

16 Then the LORD said to Moses, "Say to Aaron, 'Stretch out your staff and strike the dust of the earth, so that it may become gnats throughout the whole land of Egypt.' " 17And they did so; Aaron stretched out his hand with his staff and struck the dust of the earth, and gnats came on humans and animals alike; all the dust of the earth turned into gnats throughout the whole land of Egypt. 18The magicians tried to produce gnats by their secret arts, but they could not. There were gnats on both humans and animals. 19And the magicians said to Pharaoh, "This is the finger of God!" But Pharaoh's heart was hardened, and he would not listen to them, just as the LORD had said.

The Fourth Plague: Flies

20 Then the LORD said to Moses, "Rise early in the morning and present yourself before Pharaoh, as he goes out to the water, and say to him, 'Thus says the LORD: Let my people go, so that they may worship me. 21For if you will not let my people go, I will send swarms of flies on you, your officials, and your people, and into your houses; and the houses of the Egyptians shall be filled with swarms of flies; so also the land where they live. 22But on that day I will set apart the land of Goshen, where my people live, so that no swarms of flies shall be there, that you may know that I the LORD am in this land. 23Thus I will make a distinction[v] between my people and your people. This sign shall appear tomorrow.' " 24The LORD did so, and great swarms of flies came into the house of Pharaoh and into his officials' houses; in all of Egypt the land was ruined because of the flies.

25 Then Pharaoh summoned Moses and Aaron, and said, "Go, sacrifice to your God within the land." 26But Moses said, "It would not be right to do so; for the sacrifices that we offer to the LORD our God are offensive to the Egyptians. If we offer in the sight of the Egyptians sacrifices that are offensive to them, will they not stone us? 27We must go a three days' journey into the wilderness and sacrifice to the LORD our God as he commands us." 28So Pharaoh said, "I will let you go to sacrifice to the LORD your God in the wilderness, provided you do not go very far away. Pray for me." 29Then Moses said, "As soon as I leave you, I will pray to the LORD that the swarms of flies may depart tomorrow from Pharaoh, from his officials, and from his people; only do not let Pharaoh again deal falsely by not letting the people go to sacrifice to the LORD."

30 So Moses went out from Pharaoh and prayed to the LORD. 31And the LORD did as Moses asked: he removed the swarms of flies from Pharaoh, from his officials, and from his people; not one remained. 32But Pharaoh hardened his heart this time also, and would not let the people go.

[s] Gk: Heb *upon your people* [t] Ch 8.1 in Heb [u] Or *frogs, as he had agreed with Pharaoh* [v] Gk Vg: Heb *will set redemption*

8.5 Ex 7.19

8.6 Ps 78.45; 105.30

8.7 Ex 7.11

8.8 ver 25,28; Ex 9.27,28; 10.17

8.10 Ex 9.14; Deut 33.26; Ps 86.8; Isa 46.9; Jer 10.6,7

8.12 ver 30; Ex 9.33; 10.18

8.15 Ex 7.4

8.17 Ps 105.31

8.18 Ex 7.11

8.19 Ex 7.5; 10.7

8.20 Ex 9.13; 7.15; ver 1

8.22 Ex 9.4,6,26; 10.23; 11.6,7

8.24 Ps 78.45; 105.31

8.27 Ex 3.18; 5.3

8.28 ver 8,15,29

8.29 ver 8,15

8.32 ver 8,15; Ex 4.21

The Fifth Plague: Livestock Diseased

9 Then the LORD said to Moses, "Go to Pharaoh, and say to him, 'Thus says the LORD, the God of the Hebrews: Let my people go, so that they may worship me. 2 For if you refuse to let them go and still hold them, 3 the hand of the LORD will strike with a deadly pestilence your livestock in the field: the horses, the donkeys, the camels, the herds, and the flocks. 4 But the LORD will make a distinction between the livestock of Israel and the livestock of Egypt, so that nothing shall die of all that belongs to the Israelites.' " 5 The LORD set a time, saying, "Tomorrow the LORD will do this thing in the land." 6 And on the next day the LORD did so; all the livestock of the Egyptians died, but of the livestock of the Israelites not one died. 7 Pharaoh inquired and found that not one of the livestock of the Israelites was dead. But the heart of Pharaoh was hardened, and he would not let the people go.

The Sixth Plague: Boils

8 Then the LORD said to Moses and Aaron, "Take handfuls of soot from the kiln, and let Moses throw it in the air in the sight of Pharaoh. 9 It shall become fine dust all over the land of Egypt, and shall cause festering boils on humans and animals throughout the whole land of Egypt." 10 So they took soot from the kiln, and stood before Pharaoh, and Moses threw it in the air, and it caused festering boils on humans and animals. 11 The magicians could not stand before Moses because of the boils, for the boils afflicted the magicians as well as all the Egyptians. 12 But the LORD hardened the heart of Pharaoh, and he would not listen to them, just as the LORD had spoken to Moses.

The Seventh Plague: Thunder and Hail

13 Then the LORD said to Moses, "Rise up early in the morning and present yourself before Pharaoh, and say to him, 'Thus says the LORD, the God of the Hebrews: Let my people go, so that they may worship me. 14 For this time I will send all my plagues upon you yourself, and upon your officials, and upon your people, so that you may know that there is no one like me in all the earth. 15 For by now I could have stretched out my hand and struck you and your people with pestilence, and you would have been cut off from the earth. 16 But this is why I have let you live: to show you my power, and to make my name resound through all the earth. 17 You are still exalting yourself against my people, and will not let them go. 18 Tomorrow at this time I will cause the heaviest hail to fall that has ever fallen in Egypt from the day it was founded until now. 19 Send, therefore, and have your livestock and everything that you have in the open field brought to a secure place; every human or animal that is in the open field and is not brought under shelter will die when the hail comes down upon them.' " 20 Those officials of Pharaoh who feared the word of the LORD hurried their slaves and livestock off to a secure place. 21 Those who did not regard the word of the LORD left their slaves and livestock in the open field.

22 The LORD said to Moses, "Stretch out your hand toward heaven so that hail may fall on the whole land of Egypt, on humans and animals and all the plants of the field in the land of Egypt." 23 Then Moses stretched out his staff toward heaven, and the LORD sent thunder and hail, and fire came down on the earth. And the LORD rained hail on the land of Egypt; 24 there was hail with fire flashing continually in the midst of it, such heavy hail as had never fallen in all the land of Egypt since it became a nation. 25 The hail struck down everything that was in the open field throughout all the land of Egypt, both human and animal; the hail also struck down all the plants of the field, and shattered every tree in the field. 26 Only in the land of Goshen, where the Israelites were, there was no hail.

27 Then Pharaoh summoned Moses and Aaron, and said to them, "This time I have sinned; the LORD is in the right, and I and my people are in the wrong. 28 Pray to the LORD! Enough of God's thunder and hail! I will let you go; you need stay no longer." 29 Moses said to him, "As soon as I have gone out of the city, I will stretch out my hands to the LORD; the thunder will cease, and there will be no more hail, so that you may know that the earth is the LORD's. 30 But as for you and your officials, I know that you do not yet fear the LORD God." 31 (Now the flax and the barley were ruined, for the barley was in the ear and the flax was in bud. 32 But the wheat and the spelt were not ruined, for they are late in coming up.) 33 So Moses left Pharaoh, went out of the city, and stretched out his hands to the LORD; then the thunder and the hail ceased, and

9.1 Ex 8.1
9.2 Ex 8.2
9.4 Ex 8.22
9.6 Ex 11.5; ver 4
9.7 Ex 7.14; 8.32
9.9 Rev 16.2
9.12 Ex 4.21
9.13 Ex 8.20
9.14 Ex 8.10
9.15 Ex 3.20
9.16 Rom 9.17
9.18 ver 23,24
9.20 Prov 13.13
9.22 Rev 16.21
9.23 Gen 19.24; Josh 10.11; Ps 78.47; Isa 30.30; Ezek 38.22; Rev 8.7
9.25 ver 19; Ps 78.47; 105.32,33
9.26 Ex 8.22; 9.4,6; 10.23; 11.7; 12.13
9.27 Ex 8.8; 10.16,17; 2 Chr 12.6; Ps 129.4
9.28 Ex 8.8; 10.17
9.29 1 Kings 8.22; Ps 143.6; Ex 8.22; 19.5; 20.11; Ps 24.1

9.1-7 The Fifth Plague: Livestock Diseased. Again the plague falls on the livestock of the Egyptians, but of the animals *of the Israelites not one died*. Possibly inclusion of *camels* among those stricken is anachronistic, since they were probably not domesticated until around 1100.
9.8-12 The Sixth Plague: Boils. Here the major role is that of Aaron. The magicians cannot perform this and suffer along with the other Egyptians. Pharaoh continues to be unrelenting.
9.13-35 The Seventh Plague: Thunder and Hail. While these weather phenomena are rare in Egypt, they do occur occasionally. What intensifies the miraculous aspects of this story is that the disaster has no effect on the Israelites, their lands or their flocks. Again, Pharaoh first promises to let the people go (9.28), but then he reverses himself once *the rain and the hail and the thunder had ceased.*

10.1-20 The Eighth Plague: Locusts. The description of this plague is preceded by a brief editorial passage (10.1-2) indicating God's intention to convey a message to later generations of Israelites: how he has worked through the follies of hostile powers to achieve his purpose for his people. Unlike the earlier accounts of the plagues, this one includes the report that the Egyptian officials try to persuade Pharaoh to release the Israelites. He refuses when he learns from Moses that adults, children and livestock are to leave in order to *celebrate...the LORD's festival.* Sensing that they have no intention to return to their servile life, he refuses to allow them to go.

10.21-29 The Ninth Plague: Darkness. Although some scholars link this story with the common phenomenon of thick, dark clouds that occasionally move across the eastern Mediterranean world, the symbolism is clear: the Egyptians are in the dark as to God's role and purpose in the world, while *all the Israelites had light where they lived.* This time Pharaoh's offer of partial release (excluding the livestock) is refused by Moses, since the animals were essential for the sacrifices that were to be instituted in the Sinai experience of receiving God's law for his people.

the rain no longer poured down on the earth. 34But when Pharaoh saw that the rain and the hail and the thunder had ceased, he sinned once more and hardened his heart, he and his officials. 35So the heart of Pharaoh was hardened, and he would not let the Israelites go, just as the LORD had spoken through Moses.

The Eighth Plague: Locusts

10 Then the LORD said to Moses, "Go to Pharaoh; for I have hardened his heart and the heart of his officials, in order that I may show these signs of mine among them, 2and that you may tell your children and grandchildren how I have made fools of the Egyptians and what signs I have done among them—so that you may know that I am the LORD."

3 So Moses and Aaron went to Pharaoh, and said to him, "Thus says the LORD, the God of the Hebrews, 'How long will you refuse to humble yourself before me? Let my people go, so that they may worship me. 4For if you refuse to let my people go, tomorrow I will bring locusts into your country. 5They shall cover the surface of the land, so that no one will be able to see the land. They shall devour the last remnant left you after the hail, and they shall devour every tree of yours that grows in the field. 6They shall fill your houses, and the houses of all your officials and of all the Egyptians—something that neither your parents nor your grandparents have seen, from the day they came on earth to this day.' " Then he turned and went out from Pharaoh.

7 Pharaoh's officials said to him, "How long shall this fellow be a snare to us? Let the people go, so that they may worship the LORD their God; do you not yet understand that Egypt is ruined?" 8So Moses and Aaron were brought back to Pharaoh, and he said to them, "Go, worship the LORD your God! But which ones are to go?" 9Moses said, "We will go with our young and our old; we will go with our sons and daughters and with our flocks and herds, because we have the LORD's festival to celebrate." 10He said to them, "The LORD indeed will be with you, if ever I let your little ones go with you! Plainly, you have some evil purpose in mind. 11No, never! Your men may go and worship the LORD, for that is what you are asking." And they were driven out from Pharaoh's presence.

12 Then the LORD said to Moses, "Stretch out your hand over the land of Egypt, so that the locusts may come upon it and eat every plant in the land, all that the hail has left." 13So Moses stretched out his staff over the land of Egypt, and the LORD brought an east wind upon the land all that day and all that night; when morning came, the east wind had brought the locusts. 14The locusts came upon all the land of Egypt and settled on the whole country of Egypt, such a dense swarm of locusts as had never been before, nor ever shall be again. 15They covered the surface of the whole land, so that the land was black; and they ate all the plants in the land and all the fruit of the trees that the hail had left; nothing green was left, no tree, no plant in the field, in all the land of Egypt. 16Pharaoh hurriedly summoned Moses and Aaron and said, "I have sinned against the LORD your God, and against you. 17Do forgive my sin just this once, and pray to the LORD your God that at the least he remove this deadly thing from me." 18So he went out from Pharaoh and prayed to the LORD. 19The LORD changed the wind into a very strong west wind, which lifted the locusts and drove them into the Red Sea;[w] not a single locust was left in all the country of Egypt. 20But the LORD hardened Pharaoh's heart, and he would not let the Israelites go.

The Ninth Plague: Darkness

21 Then the LORD said to Moses, "Stretch out your hand toward heaven so that there may be darkness over the land of Egypt, a darkness that can be felt." 22So Moses stretched out his hand toward heaven, and there was dense darkness in all the land of Egypt for three days. 23People could not see one another, and for three days they could not move from where they were; but all the Israelites had light where they lived. 24Then Pharaoh summoned Moses, and said, "Go, worship the LORD. Only your flocks and your herds shall remain behind. Even your children may go with you." 25But Moses said, "You must also let us have sacrifices and burnt offerings to sacrifice to the LORD our God. 26Our livestock also must go with us; not a hoof shall be left behind, for we must choose some of them for the worship of the LORD our God, and we will not know what

9.35 Ex 4.21
10.1 Ex 4.21; 7.14
10.2 Ex 12.26,27; 13.8,14,15; Deut 4.9; Ps 44.1; Ex 7.5,15
10.3 Jas 4.10; 1 Pet 5.6; Ex 4.23
10.4 Rev 9.3
10.5 Ex 9.32; Joel 1.4; 2.25
10.6 Ex 8.3,31
10.7 Ex 7.5; 8.19; 12.33
10.8 Ex 8.8,25
10.9 Ex 12.37,38; ver 26; Ex 5.1
10.11 ver 28
10.12 Eccl 7.19; ver 4,5
10.14 Ps 78.46; 105.34; Joel 2.1-11
10.15 ver 5; Ps 105.35
10.16 Ex 9.27
10.17 Ex 8.8,29
10.20 Ex 4.21; 11.10
10.21 Deut 28.29
10.22 Ps 105.28
10.24 ver 8,10
10.26 ver 9

[w] Or *Sea of Reeds*

10.27 ver 20
10.28 ver 11
10.29 Heb 11.27
11.1 Ex 12.31,33,39
11.2 Ex 3.22; 12.35,36
11.3 Ex 3.21; 12.36; Deut 34.10-12
11.4 Ex 12.29
11.5 Ex 12.12,29; Ps 78.51; 105.36; 135.8; 136.10
11.6 Ex 12.30
11.7 Ex 8.22
11.8 Ex 12.31-33
11.9 Ex 7.3,4
11.10 Ex 4.21; 10.20,27
12.2 Ex 13.4; Deut 16.1
12.5 Lev 22.18-20
12.6 Lev 23.5; Num 9.3; Deut 16.1,6
12.8 Ex 34.25; Num 9.11,12; Deut 16.7
12.10 Ex 23.18; 34.25
12.11 ver 27
12.12 Ex 11.4,5; Num 33.4
12.14 ver 6; Ex 13.9; ver 17; Ex 13.10
12.15 Ex 23.15; 34.18; Lev 23.5,6; Deut 16.3; ver 19; Num 9.13
12.16 Lev 23.7,8
12.17 ver 41; Ex 13.3
12.18 ver 2; Lev 23.5-8; Num 28.16-25

to use to worship the LORD until we arrive there." [27]But the LORD hardened Pharaoh's heart, and he was unwilling to let them go. [28]Then Pharaoh said to him, "Get away from me! Take care that you do not see my face again, for on the day you see my face you shall die." [29]Moses said, "Just as you say! I will never see your face again."

Warning of the Final Plague

11 The LORD said to Moses, "I will bring one more plague upon Pharaoh and upon Egypt; afterwards he will let you go from here; indeed, when he lets you go, he will drive you away. [2]Tell the people that every man is to ask his neighbor and every woman is to ask her neighbor for objects of silver and gold." [3]The LORD gave the people favor in the sight of the Egyptians. Moreover, Moses himself was a man of great importance in the land of Egypt, in the sight of Pharaoh's officials and in the sight of the people.

4 Moses said, "Thus says the LORD: About midnight I will go out through Egypt. [5]Every firstborn in the land of Egypt shall die, from the firstborn of Pharaoh who sits on his throne to the firstborn of the female slave who is behind the handmill, and all the firstborn of the livestock. [6]Then there will be a loud cry throughout the whole land of Egypt, such as has never been or will ever be again. [7]But not a dog shall growl at any of the Israelites—not at people, not at animals—so that you may know that the LORD makes a distinction between Egypt and Israel. [8]Then all these officials of yours shall come down to me, and bow low to me, saying, 'Leave us, you and all the people who follow you.' After that I will leave." And in hot anger he left Pharaoh.

9 The LORD said to Moses, "Pharaoh will not listen to you, in order that my wonders may be multiplied in the land of Egypt." [10]Moses and Aaron performed all these wonders before Pharaoh; but the LORD hardened Pharaoh's heart, and he did not let the people of Israel go out of his land.

The First Passover Instituted

12 The LORD said to Moses and Aaron in the land of Egypt: [2]This month shall mark for you the beginning of months; it shall be the first month of the year for you. [3]Tell the whole congregation of Israel that on the tenth of this month they are to take a lamb for each family, a lamb for each household. [4]If a household is too small for a whole lamb, it shall join its closest neighbor in obtaining one; the lamb shall be divided in proportion to the number of people who eat of it. [5]Your lamb shall be without blemish, a year-old male; you may take it from the sheep or from the goats. [6]You shall keep it until the fourteenth day of this month; then the whole assembled congregation of Israel shall slaughter it at twilight. [7]They shall take some of the blood and put it on the two doorposts and the lintel of the houses in which they eat it. [8]They shall eat the lamb that same night; they shall eat it roasted over the fire with unleavened bread and bitter herbs. [9]Do not eat any of it raw or boiled in water, but roasted over the fire, with its head, legs, and inner organs. [10]You shall let none of it remain until the morning; anything that remains until the morning you shall burn. [11]This is how you shall eat it: your loins girded, your sandals on your feet, and your staff in your hand; and you shall eat it hurriedly. It is the passover of the LORD. [12]For I will pass through the land of Egypt that night, and I will strike down every firstborn in the land of Egypt, both human beings and animals; on all the gods of Egypt I will execute judgments: I am the LORD. [13]The blood shall be a sign for you on the houses where you live: when I see the blood, I will pass over you, and no plague shall destroy you when I strike the land of Egypt.

14 This day shall be a day of remembrance for you. You shall celebrate it as a festival to the LORD; throughout your generations you shall observe it as a perpetual ordinance. [15]Seven days you shall eat unleavened bread; on the first day you shall remove leaven from your houses, for whoever eats leavened bread from the first day until the seventh day shall be cut off from Israel. [16]On the first day you shall hold a solemn assembly, and on the seventh day a solemn assembly; no work shall be done on those days; only what everyone must eat, that alone may be prepared by you. [17]You shall observe the festival of unleavened bread, for on this very day I brought your companies out of the land of Egypt: you shall observe this day throughout your generations as a perpetual ordinance. [18]In the first month, from the evening of the fourteenth day until the evening of the

11.1-10 Warning of the Final Plague: the Death of the Firstborn. Although the death in the night of all the firstborn children of the Egyptians is not described until 12.29-30, it is predicted in detail here. The fact that *not a dog shall growl at any of the Israelites* means that the divine judgment will pass them by, and they will finally be given permission by the Egyptian authorities to leave the land of their enslavement. The priestly editorial impact is seen (11.12) in the linking of Aaron with Moses in relation to the *wonder before Pharaoh* by which the Egyptians are shown the power of Israel's God.

12.1-28 God's Provision of a Remedy to Deliver Humanity from Divine Judgment: the Passover. This account of the origin of the Passover to be celebrated by *the whole congregation of Israel* is composite and represents the end product of a complex of cultural and literary traditions. Yet the event to which it is here related – the move of the Israelites from Egypt to the land of Canaan – has remained central for the identity of the covenant people from the time of its historical occurrence, probably in the thirteenth century BCE. Elements of later priestly regulations have been woven into the narrative and instructions. Two types of group ceremonies have been combined: (1) those of nomadic peoples, relating to the annual cycle of the seasons, and (2) those of agricultural people, relating to the harvest cycle and the birth of lambs in the flocks. They have been integrated with the historical experience of Israel's liberation from slavery in Egypt (as in Josh 5.10-12) and later with the annual pilgrimages to the central shrines of Israel to renew the covenantal commitment (as in 2 Kings 23.21-23).

12.2 *The first month of the year* was in the autumn among nomadic people, but was moved to the spring when Israel became a settled people.

12.3-5 The participation in the feast by households shows that the benefits are a group heritage and that to partake is an expression of commitment to the group. For the lamb to be *without blemish*, combined with the other requirements for preparation and eating, shows that ritual purity is to characterize the life of the community as defined in the priestly tradition. The *unleavened bread and bitter herb* which are eaten are a typical nomadic diet and remind the partakers of the origins of this people as landless semi-nomads.

12.7-10 *The blood...on the... doorposts* symbolizes both the dedication to God of the household and the protective function of the blood against evil powers. See 12.23, where it is *the destroyer* who is kept away by the blood. Although the origin is uncertain, *Passover* may be a pun on the verb translated *"pass over,"* which means to skip or leap, implying that the plague as instrument of divine judgment simply leapt over the Israelites and their homes.

12.14-20 The more elaborate details for preparing and eating the sacred meal derive from the priestly tradition, and clearly imply that the celebration is a longstanding tradition, *a perpetual ordinance.*

12.21-27 Repeats the instructions in simpler form, probably from an older J tradition. **12.29-30** Before continuing with instructions for the Passover and related ceremonies, the narrative resumes with a report of the doom that falls on the firstborn of Egyptians, both human and livestock, and the realization of it by Pharaoh, his officials and all the Egyptians. **12.31-42** The Exodus Begins. Pharaoh and the Egyptians now urge Moses and the people of Israel *to hasten their departure.* The earlier proposal that the Israelites ask for precious metals and jewelry (3.22) is put into effective action, so that they *plundered the Egyptians.* The route of the Exodus led first *to Succoth,* which is probably a town on the Egyptian border, and has no connection with the Feast of Booths (Succoth) in Neh 8.13-18. The number of adult males reported as setting out, 600,000, in addition to women, children and the *mixed crowd,* would amount to 3,000,000, which is an overstatement. Perhaps the Hebrew word for "thousand" should be translated here as "section of a tribe." The report of their taking *unleavened bread* may be historical, but serves as legitimation for its sacred use. The claim that the Israelites had been in Egypt for *four hundred thirty years* is not accurate unless one dates Israel's original migration to Egypt to the period of the Hyksos (Asiatics who ruled Egypt from about 1670 to 1560). **12.43-51** Priestly Additions to the Passover Instructions. Aaron is associated with Moses and the ritual features are emphasized: exclusion of any *foreigner* or *uncircumcised;* inclusion of any *circumcised...slave;* use of only perfect sacrificial animals.

twenty-first day, you shall eat unleavened
bread. [19]For seven days no leaven shall be
found in your houses; for whoever eats
what is leavened shall be cut off from the
congregation of Israel, whether an alien or
a native of the land. [20]You shall eat nothing
leavened; in all your settlements you shall
eat unleavened bread.

21 Then Moses called all the elders of
Israel and said to them, "Go, select lambs
for your families, and slaughter the passover
lamb. [22]Take a bunch of hyssop, dip it in the
blood that is in the basin, and touch the
lintel and the two doorposts with the blood
in the basin. None of you shall go outside
the door of your house until morning. [23]For
the LORD will pass through to strike down
the Egyptians; when he sees the blood on
the lintel and on the two doorposts, the
LORD will pass over that door and will not
allow the destroyer to enter your houses to
strike you down. [24]You shall observe this
rite as a perpetual ordinance for you and
your children. [25]When you come to the
land that the LORD will give you, as he has
promised, you shall keep this observance.
[26]And when your children ask you, 'What
do you mean by this observance?' [27]you
shall say, 'It is the passover sacrifice to the
LORD, for he passed over the houses of the
Israelites in Egypt, when he struck down
the Egyptians but spared our houses.' " And
the people bowed down and worshiped.

28 The Israelites went and did just as the
LORD had commanded Moses and Aaron.

The Tenth Plague: Death of the Firstborn

29 At midnight the LORD struck down all
the firstborn in the land of Egypt, from the
firstborn of Pharaoh who sat on his throne
to the firstborn of the prisoner who was in
the dungeon, and all the firstborn of the
livestock. [30]Pharaoh arose in the night, he
and all his officials and all the Egyptians;
and there was a loud cry in Egypt, for there
was not a house without someone dead.
[31]Then he summoned Moses and Aaron in
the night, and said, "Rise up, go away from
my people, both you and the Israelites! Go,
worship the LORD, as you said. [32]Take your
flocks and your herds, as you said, and be
gone. And bring a blessing on me too!"

The Exodus: From Rameses to Succoth

33 The Egyptians urged the people to
hasten their departure from the land, for
they said, "We shall all be dead." [34]So the
people took their dough before it was leavened, with their kneading bowls wrapped
up in their cloaks on their shoulders. [35]The
Israelites had done as Moses told them; they
had asked the Egyptians for jewelry of silver
and gold, and for clothing, [36]and the LORD
had given the people favor in the sight of
the Egyptians, so that they let them have
what they asked. And so they plundered the
Egyptians.

37 The Israelites journeyed from Rameses
to Succoth, about six hundred thousand
men on foot, besides children. [38]A mixed
crowd also went up with them, and livestock in great numbers, both flocks and
herds. [39]They baked unleavened cakes of
the dough that they had brought out of
Egypt; it was not leavened, because they
were driven out of Egypt and could not
wait, nor had they prepared any provisions
for themselves.

40 The time that the Israelites had lived
in Egypt was four hundred thirty years. [41]At
the end of four hundred thirty years, on
that very day, all the companies of the LORD
went out from the land of Egypt. [42]That was
for the LORD a night of vigil, to bring them
out of the land of Egypt. That same night
is a vigil to be kept for the LORD by all the
Israelites throughout their generations.

Directions for the Passover

43 The LORD said to Moses and Aaron:
This is the ordinance for the passover: no
foreigner shall eat of it, [44]but any slave who
has been purchased may eat of it after he
has been circumcised; [45]no bound or hired
servant may eat of it. [46]It shall be eaten in
one house; you shall not take any of the
animal outside the house, and you shall not
break any of its bones. [47]The whole congregation of Israel shall celebrate it. [48]If an
alien who resides with you wants to celebrate the passover to the LORD, all his
males shall be circumcised; then he may
draw near to celebrate it; he shall be
regarded as a native of the land. But no
uncircumcised person shall eat of it; [49]there
shall be one law for the native and for the
alien who resides among you.

50 All the Israelites did just as the LORD
had commanded Moses and Aaron. [51]That
very day the LORD brought the Israelites out
of the land of Egypt, company by company.

12.19 ver 15
12.21 Heb 11.28; ver 11; Num 9.4
12.22 ver 7
12.23 ver 12,13
12.24 Ex 13.5,10
12.26 Ex 13.14,15; Josh 4.6
12.27 ver 11; Ex 4.31
12.29 Ex 11.4; 4.23; 9.6; Ps 78.51; 105.36
12.30 Ex 11.6
12.31 Ex 8.8,25
12.32 Ex 10.9,26
12.33 ver 39; Ex 10.7; 11.1; Ps 105.38
12.35 Ex 3.21,22; 11.2,3
12.36 Ex 3.22
12.37 Num 33.3,4; Ex 38.26; Num 1.46; 11.21
12.38 Num 11.4; Ex 17.3
12.39 ver 31-33; Ex 11.1
12.40 Gen 15.13; Acts 7.6; Gal 3.17
12.41 ver 17; Ex 3.8,10; 6.6
12.42 Ex 13.10; Deut 16.1
12.46 Num 9.12; Jn 19.33,36
12.47 Num 9.13,14
12.49 Num 15.15,16; Gal 3.28
12.51 ver 41

13 The Lord said to Moses: [2]Consecrate to me all the firstborn; whatever is the first to open the womb among the Israelites, of human beings and animals, is mine.

The Festival of Unleavened Bread

3 Moses said to the people, "Remember this day on which you came out of Egypt, out of the house of slavery, because the Lord brought you out from there by strength of hand; no leavened bread shall be eaten. [4]Today, in the month of Abib, you are going out. [5]When the Lord brings you into the land of the Canaanites, the Hittites, the Amorites, the Hivites, and the Jebusites, which he swore to your ancestors to give you, a land flowing with milk and honey, you shall keep this observance in this month. [6]Seven days you shall eat unleavened bread, and on the seventh day there shall be a festival to the Lord. [7]Unleavened bread shall be eaten for seven days; no leavened bread shall be seen in your possession, and no leaven shall be seen among you in all your territory. [8]You shall tell your child on that day, 'It is because of what the Lord did for me when I came out of Egypt.' [9]It shall serve for you as a sign on your hand and as a reminder on your forehead, so that the teaching of the Lord may be on your lips; for with a strong hand the Lord brought you out of Egypt. [10]You shall keep this ordinance at its proper time from year to year.

The Consecration of the Firstborn

11 "When the Lord has brought you into the land of the Canaanites, as he swore to you and your ancestors, and has given it to you, [12]you shall set apart to the Lord all that first opens the womb. All the firstborn of your livestock that are males shall be the Lord's. [13]But every firstborn donkey you shall redeem with a sheep; if you do not redeem it, you must break its neck. Every firstborn male among your children you shall redeem. [14]When in the future your child asks you, 'What does this mean?' you shall answer, 'By strength of hand the Lord brought us out of Egypt, from the house of slavery. [15]When Pharaoh stubbornly refused to let us go, the Lord killed all the firstborn in the land of Egypt, from human firstborn to the firstborn of animals. Therefore I sacrifice to the Lord every male that first opens the womb, but every firstborn of my sons I redeem.' [16]It shall serve as a sign on your hand and as an emblem[x] on your forehead that by strength of hand the Lord brought us out of Egypt."

The Pillars of Cloud and Fire

17 When Pharaoh let the people go, God did not lead them by way of the land of the Philistines, although that was nearer; for God thought, "If the people face war, they may change their minds and return to Egypt." [18]So God led the people by the roundabout way of the wilderness toward the Red Sea.[y] The Israelites went up out of the land of Egypt prepared for battle. [19]And Moses took with him the bones of Joseph who had required a solemn oath of the Israelites, saying, "God will surely take notice of you, and then you must carry my bones with you from here." [20]They set out from Succoth, and camped at Etham, on the edge of the wilderness. [21]The Lord went in front of them in a pillar of cloud by day, to lead them along the way, and in a pillar of fire by night, to give them light, so that they might travel by day and by night. [22]Neither the pillar of cloud by day nor the pillar of fire by night left its place in front of the people.

Crossing the Red Sea

14 Then the Lord said to Moses: [2]Tell the Israelites to turn back and camp in front of Pi-hahiroth, between Migdol and the sea, in front of Baal-zephon; you shall camp opposite it, by the sea. [3]Pharaoh will say of the Israelites, 'They are wandering aimlessly in the land; the wilderness has closed in on them.' [4]I will harden Pharaoh's heart, and he will pursue them, so that I will gain glory for myself over Pharaoh and all his army; and the Egyptians shall know that I am the Lord. And they did so.

5 When the king of Egypt was told that the people had fled, the minds of Pharaoh and his officials were changed toward the people, and they said, "What have we done, letting Israel leave our service?" [6]So he had his chariot made ready, and took his army with him; [7]he took six hundred picked chariots and all the other chariots of Egypt

[x] Or *as a frontlet*; Meaning of Heb uncertain [y] Or *Sea of Reeds*

13.2 ver 12.13,15; Ex 22.29; Lk 2.23
13.3 Ex 3.20; 6.1; 12.19
13.5 Ex 3.8; 12.25,26
13.6 Ex 12.15-20
13.8 ver 14; Ex 10.2
13.9 ver 16; Ex 12.14; Deut 6.8; 11.18
13.10 Ex 12.24,25
13.12 ver 2; Ex 22.29; 34.19
13.13 Ex 34.20; Num 18.15,16
13.14 Ex 12.26,27; Deut 6.20; ver 3,9
13.15 Ex 12.29
13.16 ver 9
13.17 Ex 14.11,12; Num 14.1-4; Deut 17.16
13.19 Gen 50.25,26; Josh 24.32; Acts 7.16
13.20 Num 33.6-8
13.21 Ex 14.19,24; 33.9,10; Ps 78.14; 105.39; 1 Cor 10.1
14.2 Num 33.7,8
14.4 ver 17; Ex 4.21; 7.5

13.1-2 Consecration of the Firstborn. This brief instruction recalls God's designation of Israel as *firstborn son* (4.22) and the death of the firstborn among the Egyptians in the tenth plague, announced in 4.23 and carried out in 12.29-30. The Festival of the Firstborn is elaborated in Lev 27.26-27, and in Num 3; 8; 18. Its original significance was to ensure and celebrate the fertility of families and flocks. Here it is given an historical point of reference.
13.3-10 The Festival of Unleavened Bread. Written in the light of developing tradition; the rules of the feast are specified and elaborated, and clearly anticipate Israel's life after settling in the land of Canaan. The instruction of the children in the meaning of this experience recalls 6.4-9 and 12.14-20 The *sign on...hand and...forehead* were probably a kind of tattoo, but became associated by the second or first century BCE with the practice of wearing a small box (phylactery) which contained a parchment on which verses of scripture were written. Found in the remains of the Dead Sea community, they are mentioned in Mt 23.5 and in rabbinic literature of the second century CE and later.
13.11-16 The Consecration of the Firstborn. The meaning and the details of this ceremony are repeated from a J tradition, with clear anticipation that it will be practiced for a long time in the future. Every firstborn male is to be sacrificed to the Lord as an act of dedication and gratitude, but *every firstborn of my sons* is to be freed from this decree through a ritually pure sacrifice offered in his stead.
13.17-14.30 The Exodus Continues: Israel Crosses the Red Sea. Various traditions have been woven together in this passage reporting the events which were crucial and formative for the subsequent history of God's people Israel.
13.17 The route to the land of Canaan avoided by the Israelites is *the way of the land of the Philistines*, which was the shorter, well-travelled highway along the Mediterranean coast, since there would have been Egyptian guards and army units on this commercial route. This would have caused the Israelites to *face war*. The Philistines did not settle in this coastal region until at least a century later, but the editor knows the highway by this name.
13.18 The Hebrew word for *sea [yam]* can also mean "lake." The Red Sea, or Sea of Reeds, probably means one of the marshy lakes in the eastern Nile delta area, bordering on the wilderness of Sinai, rather than the Gulf of Suez farther south. That the Israelites were *prepared for battle* cannot be meant literally, since with families and livestock they were involved in complex migration. The battle is the Lord's.
13.19 The promise to take *the bones of Joseph* when Israel goes to the land of Canaan is reported in Gen 50.25-26.
13.22 *The pillar of cloud* and *the pillar of fire* are the visible evidence of the Lord's presence, his leadership of the people, and his purpose for them.
14.1-2 That these cities in the northeastern region of the Nile delta are named confirms the theory that the crossing of the sea was in the marshy lake region rather than in the Gulf itself. *Baal-Zephon* is the name of a Canaanite deity, indicating the mixed cultural situation in this delta region bordering the land of Canaan.
14.3-4 God's triumph over the Egyptians will persuade the people of Israel as well as the Egyptians of the sovereignty of the Lord.
14.5-9 The entire army, including the cavalry with 600 specially chosen chariots, is on the march to overtake and capture the fleeing Israelites. The repetition of some details in 14.8-9 shows the composite nature of this account.

with officers over all of them. [8]The LORD
hardened the heart of Pharaoh king of Egypt
and he pursued the Israelites, who were
going out boldly. [9]The Egyptians pursued
them, all Pharaoh's horses and chariots, his
chariot drivers and his army; they overtook
them camped by the sea, by Pi-hahiroth, in
front of Baal-zephon.
10 As Pharaoh drew near, the Israelites
looked back, and there were the Egyptians
advancing on them. In great fear the Israelites cried out to the LORD. [11]They said to
Moses, "Was it because there were no graves
in Egypt that you have taken us away to
die in the wilderness? What have you done
to us, bringing us out of Egypt? [12]Is this not
the very thing we told you in Egypt, 'Let us
alone and let us serve the Egyptians'? For
it would have been better for us to serve the
Egyptians than to die in the wilderness."
[13]But Moses said to the people, "Do not be
afraid, stand firm, and see the deliverance
that the LORD will accomplish for you today;
for the Egyptians whom you see today you
shall never see again. [14]The LORD will fight
for you, and you have only to keep still."
15 Then the LORD said to Moses, "Why
do you cry out to me? Tell the Israelites to
go forward. [16]But you lift up your staff, and
stretch out your hand over the sea and
divide it, that the Israelites may go into the
sea on dry ground. [17]Then I will harden the
hearts of the Egyptians so that they will go
in after them; and so I will gain glory for
myself over Pharaoh and all his army, his
chariots, and his chariot drivers. [18]And the
Egyptians shall know that I am the LORD,
when I have gained glory for myself over
Pharaoh, his chariots, and his chariot drivers."
19 The angel of God who was going
before the Israelite army moved and went
behind them; and the pillar of cloud moved
from in front of them and took its place
behind them. [20]It came between the army
of Egypt and the army of Israel. And so the
cloud was there with the darkness, and it
lit up the night; one did not come near the
other all night.
21 Then Moses stretched out his hand
over the sea. The LORD drove the sea back
by a strong east wind all night, and turned
the sea into dry land; and the waters were
divided. [22]The Israelites went into the sea on
dry ground, the waters forming a wall for
them on their right and on their left. [23]The
Egyptians pursued, and went into the sea
after them, all of Pharaoh's horses, chariots,
and chariot drivers. [24]At the morning watch
the LORD in the pillar of fire and cloud
looked down upon the Egyptian army, and
threw the Egyptian army into panic. [25]He
clogged[z] their chariot wheels so that they
turned with difficulty. The Egyptians said,
"Let us flee from the Israelites, for the LORD
is fighting for them against Egypt."

The Pursuers Drowned

26 Then the LORD said to Moses, "Stretch
out your hand over the sea, so that the
water may come back upon the Egyptians,
upon their chariots and chariot drivers."
[27]So Moses stretched out his hand over the
sea, and at dawn the sea returned to its
normal depth. As the Egyptians fled before
it, the LORD tossed the Egyptians into the
sea. [28]The waters returned and covered the
chariots and the chariot drivers, the entire
army of Pharaoh that had followed them
into the sea; not one of them remained.
[29]But the Israelites walked on dry ground
through the sea, the waters forming a wall
for them on their right and on their left.
30 Thus the LORD saved Israel that day
from the Egyptians; and Israel saw the
Egyptians dead on the seashore. [31]Israel saw
the great work that the LORD did against the
Egyptians. So the people feared the LORD and
believed in the LORD and in his servant
Moses.

The Song of Moses

15 Then Moses and the Israelites sang
this song to the LORD:

"I will sing to the LORD, for he has
triumphed gloriously;
horse and rider he has thrown into
the sea.
2 The LORD is my strength and my
might,[a]
and he has become my salvation;
this is my God, and I will praise him,
my father's God, and I will exalt
him.
3 The LORD is a warrior;
the LORD is his name.

4 "Pharaoh's chariots and his army he
cast into the sea;
his picked officers were sunk in the
Red Sea.[b]

[z] Sam Gk Syr: MT *removed* [a] Or *song* [b] Or *Sea of Reeds*

14.10-13 A major factor in this crisis is the disbelief of the Israelites, who blame Moses for the difficulties they now face. Moses reaffirms to the fearful people that the victory is the LORD's.
14.15-25 The three manifestations of God's power here are through Moses' *stretched out hand, the angel of God,* and the direct action of *the LORD.* These reflect the different sources which underlie the present account. The pillar of cloud takes on a new function: to confuse the Egyptians and to obscure from them the passage of the Israelites, while the pillar of fire continues to lead the Israelites. God's action is described as at work through a natural phenomenon: *a strong east wind,* which by *forming a wall* of the lake water enabled the Israelites to cross as on *dry land.* When the Egyptians followed in pursuit, the LORD first clogged their chariot wheels, and then ordered Moses to make the waters return so that *the sea returned to its normal depth.* The entire army of Pharaoh that had entered the sea was drowned in the waters. Their recognition that *the LORD is fighting for [Israel] against Egypt* was too late for them to survive.
14.30-31 At last the people of Israel recognize *the great work of the LORD,* and come to trust both *the LORD* and *his servant Moses.*
15.1-18 The Song of Moses. The poetic style of this hymn and the imagery of its celebration of the triumph of Yahweh show clear affinity with sacred poems found by archaeologists at sites in the Near East dating from this epoch, especially at Ugarit in Syria. The portrait of God controlling the waters of the sea recalls the creation story of Genesis 1, and is echoed in the Psalms (74.12-15; 93.3-4). It is a sign of God's authority in both the cosmic and historical spheres. The overall picture is of God's strength and effectiveness in achieving *salvation,* which means victory for his people, establishing and maintaining them in their special relationship to him. None of *the gods* of the neighboring peoples can match Yahweh's power, and none is his equal in *holiness,* which is his majestic, pure and powerful nature. His *steadfast love* is evident in his fidelity to the covenant he has made with his people, as shown when he *redeemed* them by liberating them from slavery in Egypt. The defeat by Israel of the nations named here – Philistia, Edom, Moab – did not occur until centuries later, nor did the establishment in the mountain in Jerusalem of God's *abode, the sanctuary,* take place until centuries later, which indicates that the hymn achieved its present form no earlier than the time of David or Solomon when the temple was built there. Yet the divine act of deliverance at the Red Sea remains central for Israel's covenant relationship with Yahweh.

14.8 ver 4; Num 33.3; Acts 13.17
14.9 Ex 15.9
14.10 Neh 9.9
14.11 Ps 106.7,8
14.13 Gen 15.1; ver 30; Ex 15.2
14.14 Ex 15.3; Deut 1.30; 3.22; Isa 30.15
14.16 Ex 4.17; Num 20.8,9,11; Isa 10.26
14.17 ver 4
14.18 ver 25
14.19 Ex 13.21,22
14.21 ver 16; Ps 106.9; 114.3,5; Isa 63.12,13
14.22 Ex 15.19; Neh 9.11; Heb 11.29
14.24 Ex 13.21
14.25 ver 4,18
14.27 Ex 15.1,7
14.28 Ps 78.53; 106.11
14.29 Ex 15.19; Neh 9.11; Heb 11.29
14.30 Ps 106.8
14.31 Ps 106.12
15.1 Ps 106.12; Rev 15.3
15.2 Ps 59.17; Ex 3.15,16
15.3 Ps 24.8; 83.18
15.4 Ex 14.6,7,17,28

15.5 ver 10; Neh 9.11
15.6 Ps 118.15
15.7 Ex 14.27; Ps 78.49,50
15.8 Ex 14.22,29; Ps 78.13
15.9 Ex 14.5
15.10 Ex 14.28
15.11 Ex 8.10; Deut 3.24; Isa 6.3; Rev 4.8; Ps 22.23; 72.18
15.13 Neh 9.12; Ps 77.15; 78.54
15.14 Deut 2.25; Hab 3.7
15.15 Gen 36.15; Num 22.3; Josh 5.1
15.16 Ex 23.27; 1 Sam 25.37; Ps 74.2
15.17 Ps 44.2; 78.54
15.18 Ps 10.16
15.19 Ex 14.23,28
15.20 Judg 4.4; Num 26.59; 1 Sam 18.6; Ps 30.11; 150.4
15.21 ver 1
15.22 Ps 77.20; Num 33.8
15.23 Num 33.8
15.24 Ex 14.11; Ps 106.13
15.25 Ex 14.10; Ps 50.15
15.26 Deut 7.12; 28.27
15.27 Num 33.9,10

5 The floods covered them;
they went down into the depths like a stone.
6 Your right hand, O LORD, glorious in power—
your right hand, O LORD, shattered the enemy.
7 In the greatness of your majesty you overthrew your adversaries;
you sent out your fury, it consumed them like stubble.
8 At the blast of your nostrils the waters piled up,
the floods stood up in a heap;
the deeps congealed in the heart of the sea.
9 The enemy said, 'I will pursue, I will overtake,
I will divide the spoil, my desire shall have its fill of them.
I will draw my sword, my hand shall destroy them.'
10 You blew with your wind, the sea covered them;
they sank like lead in the mighty waters.

11 "Who is like you, O LORD, among the gods?
Who is like you, majestic in holiness,
awesome in splendor, doing wonders?
12 You stretched out your right hand,
the earth swallowed them.

13 "In your steadfast love you led the people whom you redeemed;
you guided them by your strength to your holy abode.
14 The peoples heard, they trembled;
pangs seized the inhabitants of Philistia.
15 Then the chiefs of Edom were dismayed;
trembling seized the leaders of Moab;
all the inhabitants of Canaan melted away.
16 Terror and dread fell upon them;
by the might of your arm, they became still as a stone
until your people, O LORD, passed by,
until the people whom you acquired passed by.
17 You brought them in and planted them on the mountain of your own possession,
the place, O LORD, that you made your abode,
the sanctuary, O LORD, that your hands have established.
18 The LORD will reign forever and ever."
19 When the horses of Pharaoh with his
chariots and his chariot drivers went into
the sea, the LORD brought back the waters
of the sea upon them; but the Israelites
walked through the sea on dry ground.

The Song of Miriam

20 Then the prophet Miriam, Aaron's
sister, took a tambourine in her hand; and
all the women went out after her with
tambourines and with dancing. 21 And
Miriam sang to them:
"Sing to the LORD, for he has triumphed gloriously;
horse and rider he has thrown into the sea."

Bitter Water Made Sweet

22 Then Moses ordered Israel to set out
from the Red Sea,[c] and they went into the
wilderness of Shur. They went three days in
the wilderness and found no water. 23 When
they came to Marah, they could not drink
the water of Marah because it was bitter.
That is why it was called Marah.[d] 24 And the
people complained against Moses, saying,
"What shall we drink?" 25 He cried out to
the LORD; and the LORD showed him a piece
of wood;[e] he threw it into the water, and
the water became sweet.
There the LORD[f] made for them a statute
and an ordinance and there he put them to
the test. 26 He said, "If you will listen carefully to the voice of the LORD your God, and
do what is right in his sight, and give heed
to his commandments and keep all his statutes, I will not bring upon you any of the
diseases that I brought upon the Egyptians;
for I am the LORD who heals you."
27 Then they came to Elim, where there
were twelve springs of water and seventy
palm trees; and they camped there by the
water.

15.19-21 A brief prose summary of God's defeat of the Egyptians and deliverance of his people prepares for resuming the narrative at 15.22. But first comes another celebration of God's triumph, attributed to Moses' sister Miriam, here portrayed as an ecstatic prophetess like Deborah (Judg 4-5). The *tambourines and...dancing* anticipate the celebrations at the crowning of Israel's kings – 1 Sam 10.19 (Saul) and 1 Sam 18.6-7 (David) – and more broadly in praise of God (Ps 87,149,150).
15.22-17.7 God Provides Basic Necessities: Water and Food.
15.22-27 Initial entrance into the wilderness of Sinai is at Shur, which was probably located east or southeast of what is now the Suez Canal. The location of Marah cannot be determined, but the experience of the bitter water made potable signifies the combination of God's testing his people and providing for their needs which characterizes the Exodus experience as a whole. Anticipating the giving of the law at Sinai, which in its final edited and elaborated form extends from Ex 18 to Num 10, is the report of Yahweh's giving his people *commandments* and *statutes* which they are to obey if they want to experience God as one who *heals* rather than as one who judges and destroys. Like most of the other places named in these accounts, the oasis of Elim is not identifiable.

[c] Or *Sea of Reeds* [d] That is *Bitterness* [e] Or *a tree* [f] Heb *he*

16.1-36 God Provides Bread and Meat.
16.1 *The wilderness of Sin* is probably the western part of the Sinai peninsula. Sinai as a whole consists of a coastal strip on the perimeter, about ten to fifteen miles wide, and a high plateau in the central part, sloping upward to mountains in the south which reach an elevation of more than 8,000 feet. One of these peaks has been identified since early Christian times as Mt. Sinai, or Horeb, as it is also known (Ex 3.1; 17.6).
16.2-3 Once again Moses and Aaron are blamed for the difficulties in which the Israelites find themselves.
16.4-12 God will provide bread that will fall from heaven like the dew and meat in the form of migratory birds. Quail annually cross Sinai between Asia and Africa. The special provision for a double supply on *the sixth day* anticipates the establishment of the sabbath law.
16.13-36 The *quails* arrive in the evening, and the *fine flaky substance* appears in the mornings. The Hebrew name for it – manna – is a pun on the Israelites' question, *What is it?*, when they first saw it. The importance of the event as confirming the sabbath is evident in the specific instructions (16.27-30) and in the retelling of the story of God's providing it (16.31-36). The present account has been shaped by the later legal developments in Israel, with the added historical note that Israel was in the wilderness for *forty years*.

Bread from Heaven

16 The whole congregation of the Israelites set out from Elim; and Israel came to the wilderness of Sin, which is between Elim and Sinai, on the fifteenth day of the second month after they had departed from the land of Egypt. 2 The whole congregation of the Israelites complained against Moses and Aaron in the wilderness. 3 The Israelites said to them, "If only we had died by the hand of the LORD in the land of Egypt, when we sat by the fleshpots and ate our fill of bread; for you have brought us out into this wilderness to kill this whole assembly with hunger."

4 Then the LORD said to Moses, "I am going to rain bread from heaven for you, and each day the people shall go out and gather enough for that day. In that way I will test them, whether they will follow my instruction or not. 5 On the sixth day, when they prepare what they bring in, it will be twice as much as they gather on other days." 6 So Moses and Aaron said to all the Israelites, "In the evening you shall know that it was the LORD who brought you out of the land of Egypt, 7 and in the morning you shall see the glory of the LORD, because he has heard your complaining against the LORD. For what are we, that you complain against us?" 8 And Moses said, "When the LORD gives you meat to eat in the evening and your fill of bread in the morning, because the LORD has heard the complaining that you utter against him—what are we? Your complaining is not against us but against the LORD."

9 Then Moses said to Aaron, "Say to the whole congregation of the Israelites, 'Draw near to the LORD, for he has heard your complaining.' " 10 And as Aaron spoke to the whole congregation of the Israelites, they looked toward the wilderness, and the glory of the LORD appeared in the cloud. 11 The LORD spoke to Moses and said, 12 "I have heard the complaining of the Israelites; say to them, 'At twilight you shall eat meat, and in the morning you shall have your fill of bread; then you shall know that I am the LORD your God.' "

13 In the evening quails came up and covered the camp; and in the morning there was a layer of dew around the camp. 14 When the layer of dew lifted, there on the surface of the wilderness was a fine flaky substance, as fine as frost on the ground. 15 When the Israelites saw it, they said to one another, "What is it?"[g] For they did not know what it was. Moses said to them, "It is the bread that the LORD has given you to eat. 16 This is what the LORD has commanded: 'Gather as much of it as each of you needs, an omer to a person according to the number of persons, all providing for those in their own tents.' " 17 The Israelites did so, some gathering more, some less. 18 But when they measured it with an omer, those who gathered much had nothing over, and those who gathered little had no shortage; they gathered as much as each of them needed. 19 And Moses said to them, "Let no one leave any of it over until morning." 20 But they did not listen to Moses; some left part of it until morning, and it bred worms and became foul. And Moses was angry with them. 21 Morning by morning they gathered it, as much as each needed; but when the sun grew hot, it melted.

22 On the sixth day they gathered twice as much food, two omers apiece. When all the leaders of the congregation came and told Moses, 23 he said to them, "This is what the LORD has commanded: 'Tomorrow is a day of solemn rest, a holy sabbath to the LORD; bake what you want to bake and boil what you want to boil, and all that is left over put aside to be kept until morning.' " 24 So they put it aside until morning, as Moses commanded them; and it did not become foul, and there were no worms in it. 25 Moses said, "Eat it today, for today is a sabbath to the LORD; today you will not find it in the field. 26 Six days you shall gather it; but on the seventh day, which is a sabbath, there will be none."

27 On the seventh day some of the people went out to gather, and they found none. 28 The LORD said to Moses, "How long will you refuse to keep my commandments and instructions? 29 See! The LORD has given you the sabbath, therefore on the sixth day he gives you food for two days; each of you stay where you are; do not leave your place on the seventh day." 30 So the people rested on the seventh day.

31 The house of Israel called it manna; it was like coriander seed, white, and the taste of it was like wafers made with honey. 32 Moses said, "This is what the LORD has commanded: 'Let an omer of it be kept throughout your generations, in order that they may see the food with which I fed you

[g] Or *"It is manna"* (Heb *man hu*, see verse 31)

16.1 Num 33.11,12
16.2 Ex 14.11; 1 Cor 10.10
16.3 Ex 17.3; Num 11.4,5
16.4 Jn 6.31; 1 Cor 10.3; Deut 8.2,16
16.5 ver 22
16.7 ver 12; Num 14.27; 16.11
16.9 Num 16.16
16.10 ver 7; Num 16.19
16.13 Num 11.31; Ps 78.27,28; 105.40
16.14 Num 11.7-9; ver 31
16.15 ver 4
16.18 2 Cor 8.15
16.19 ver 23; Ex 12.10; 23.18
16.22 ver 5; Ex 34.31
16.23 Ex 20.8; 23.12
16.24 ver 20
16.28 Ps 78.10
16.31 Num 11.6-9

16.33 Heb 9.4
16.34 Ex 25.16,21
16.35 Josh 5.12; Neh 9.20,21
17.1 Ex 16.1
17.2 Num 20.3; Deut 6.16; 1 Cor 10.9
17.3 Ex 16.2,3
17.4 Ex 14.15; Num 14.10; 1 Sam 30.6
17.5 Ex 3.16,18; 7.20
17.6 Num 20.10; Ps 114.8; 1 Cor 10.4
17.7 Ps 81.7
17.8 Num 24.20; Deut 25.17-19
17.9 Ex 4.20
17.14 Ex 34.27; Num 24.20; Deut 29.19
18.1 Ex 2.16; 3.1
18.2 Ex 4.25
18.3 Acts 7.29; Ex 2.22
18.5 Ex 3.1,12
18.7 Gen 43.26-28
18.8 Ps 81.7
18.10 Ps 68.19,20
18.11 Ex 12.12; 15.11; 1 Sam 2.3

in the wilderness, when I brought you out of the land of Egypt.' " 33 And Moses said to Aaron, "Take a jar, and put an omer of manna in it, and place it before the LORD, to be kept throughout your generations." 34 As the LORD commanded Moses, so Aaron placed it before the covenant,[h] for safekeeping. 35 The Israelites ate manna forty years, until they came to a habitable land; they ate manna, until they came to the border of the land of Canaan. 36 An omer is a tenth of an ephah.

Water from the Rock

17 From the wilderness of Sin the whole congregation of the Israelites journeyed by stages, as the LORD commanded. They camped at Rephidim, but there was no water for the people to drink. 2 The people quarreled with Moses, and said, "Give us water to drink." Moses said to them, "Why do you quarrel with me? Why do you test the LORD?" 3 But the people thirsted there for water; and the people complained against Moses and said, "Why did you bring us out of Egypt, to kill us and our children and livestock with thirst?" 4 So Moses cried out to the LORD, "What shall I do with this people? They are almost ready to stone me." 5 The LORD said to Moses, "Go on ahead of the people, and take some of the elders of Israel with you; take in your hand the staff with which you struck the Nile, and go. 6 I will be standing there in front of you on the rock at Horeb. Strike the rock, and water will come out of it, so that the people may drink." Moses did so, in the sight of the elders of Israel. 7 He called the place Massah[i] and Meribah,[j] because the Israelites quarreled and tested the LORD, saying, "Is the LORD among us or not?"

Amalek Attacks Israel and Is Defeated

8 Then Amalek came and fought with Israel at Rephidim. 9 Moses said to Joshua, "Choose some men for us and go out, fight with Amalek. Tomorrow I will stand on the top of the hill with the staff of God in my hand." 10 So Joshua did as Moses told him, and fought with Amalek, while Moses, Aaron, and Hur went up to the top of the hill. 11 Whenever Moses held up his hand, Israel prevailed; and whenever he lowered his hand, Amalek prevailed. 12 But Moses' hands grew weary; so they took a stone and put it under him, and he sat on it. Aaron and Hur held up his hands, one on one side, and the other on the other side; so his hands were steady until the sun set. 13 And Joshua defeated Amalek and his people with the sword.

14 Then the LORD said to Moses, "Write this as a reminder in a book and recite it in the hearing of Joshua: I will utterly blot out the remembrance of Amalek from under heaven." 15 And Moses built an altar and called it, The LORD is my banner. 16 He said, "A hand upon the banner of the LORD![k] The LORD will have war with Amalek from generation to generation."

Jethro's Advice

18 Jethro, the priest of Midian, Moses' father-in-law, heard of all that God had done for Moses and for his people Israel, how the LORD had brought Israel out of Egypt. 2 After Moses had sent away his wife Zipporah, his father-in-law Jethro took her back, 3 along with her two sons. The name of the one was Gershom (for he said, "I have been an alien[l] in a foreign land"), 4 and the name of the other, Eliezer[m] (for he said, "The God of my father was my help, and delivered me from the sword of Pharaoh"). 5 Jethro, Moses' father-in-law, came into the wilderness where Moses was encamped at the mountain of God, bringing Moses' sons and wife to him. 6 He sent word to Moses, "I, your father-in-law Jethro, am coming to you, with your wife and her two sons." 7 Moses went out to meet his father-in-law; he bowed down and kissed him; each asked after the other's welfare, and they went into the tent. 8 Then Moses told his father-in-law all that the LORD had done to Pharaoh and to the Egyptians for Israel's sake, all the hardship that had beset them on the way, and how the LORD had delivered them. 9 Jethro rejoiced for all the good that the LORD had done to Israel, in delivering them from the Egyptians.

10 Jethro said, "Blessed be the LORD, who has delivered you from the Egyptians and from Pharaoh. 11 Now I know that the LORD is greater than all gods, because he delivered the people from the Egyptians,[n] when they dealt arrogantly with them." 12 And

[h] Or *treaty* or *testimony*; Heb *eduth* [i] That is *Test* [j] That is *Quarrel* [k] Cn: Meaning of Heb uncertain [l] Heb *ger* [m] Heb *Eli*, my God; *ezer*, help [n] The clause *because . . . Egyptians* has been transposed from verse 10

17.1-7 Another example of God's special provision for the needs of his people is offered in the account of the water that flows from the rock in response to the complaint of the people to Moses for having led them out into this desert land. Once more, the instrument of Moses' beneficent authority is his *staff*, just as it was used for judgmental purpose when he turned the water of the Nile into blood (Ex 7.17-19). The names of the place, *Massah and Meribah*, are symbolic of the "testing" and "conflict" which characterize the life of the people. Their question, *Is the Lord among us or not?*, receives a vivid answer in what follows.
17.8-18.27 Anticipations of Hostility and Acceptance that Israel will Experience on Entering the Land of Promise.
17.8-16 The name Amalek, grandson of Esau (Gen 36.15-16), was given to this semi-nomadic tribe which lived on the edge of the desert east of Sinai and Jordan, and periodically raided Israel (Judg 6.1-6; 1 Sam 30.1-20). Two statements stand in tension here: that Amalek's name will be blotted out (vs.14), and that there will be continuing wars with Amalek (vs.16). The incident anticipates similar conflicts with other Semitic tribes that Israel engaged in during the settlement in and occupancy of the land of Canaan. There is also an anticipation of the role that Joshua will have when Israel moves into the land (33.1). The *banner* is a standard or ornamented pole which symbolizes and embodies Yahweh's power and purpose.
18.1-27 Jethro's Honoring of Yahweh and Advice to Moses.
18.2 There is no indication why Moses sent away his wife, Zipporah, and their sons, but the arrival of *Jethro* in friendship shows that there was no conflict involved.
18.5 Evidence of the later editing of this material is given by the note that Moses was encamped at *the mountain of God*. According to 19.1-2, this event does not take place until later.
18.10-12 The reports of God's mighty acts in behalf of Israel persuade Jethro that Yahweh *is* greater than all gods, which is less than a fully monotheistic affirmation. His sharing of a ceremonial meal *in the presence of God* is a sign of his seeking to share in the covenant relationship with Yahweh.

18.13-26 Jethro's recommendations to Moses for administering justice and settling disputes within the Israelite community – including grouping them by tens, hundreds, and thousands, and assigning lesser *officers* – reflects much later developments in Israel, probably during the initial years of settlement in the land under the leadership of the judges (see Judg).
18.27 Although Jethro departs, Moses will have a continuing relationship with his father-in-law under the name of Hobab (Num 10.29-36).
19.1-9 God Speaks to his Covenant People from Sinai.
19.4-5 God tells the people through Moses that he has acted to free them, and that they now must obey God's *voice* and keep his *covenant* if they are to enjoy the special relationship with him as *a priestly kingdom and a holy nation.*
19.8 Speaking for the community, *the elders of the people* commit themselves to full obedience to the LORD.
19.9-25 Holy God and Consecrated People. God's holiness has not only moral and religious but also physical dimensions, so that the people cannot touch the mountain, nor are they allowed to see God when he descends *upon Mount Sinai.* These solemn instructions prepare the people to receive the guidelines for their lives and for their special relationship to God.

Jethro, Moses' father-in-law, brought a burnt offering and sacrifices to God; and Aaron came with all the elders of Israel to eat bread with Moses' father-in-law in the presence of God.

13 The next day Moses sat as judge for the people, while the people stood around him from morning until evening. [14]When Moses' father-in-law saw all that he was doing for the people, he said, "What is this that you are doing for the people? Why do you sit alone, while all the people stand around you from morning until evening?" [15]Moses said to his father-in-law, "Because the people come to me to inquire of God. [16]When they have a dispute, they come to me and I decide between one person and another, and I make known to them the statutes and instructions of God." [17]Moses' father-in-law said to him, "What you are doing is not good. [18]You will surely wear yourself out, both you and these people with you. For the task is too heavy for you; you cannot do it alone. [19]Now listen to me. I will give you counsel, and God be with you! You should represent the people before God, and you should bring their cases before God; [20]teach them the statutes and instructions and make known to them the way they are to go and the things they are to do. [21]You should also look for able men among all the people, men who fear God, are trustworthy, and hate dishonest gain; set such men over them as officers over thousands, hundreds, fifties and tens. [22]Let them sit as judges for the people at all times; let them bring every important case to you, but decide every minor case themselves. So it will be easier for you, and they will bear the burden with you. [23]If you do this, and God so commands you, then you will be able to endure, and all these people will go to their home in peace."

24 So Moses listened to his father-in-law and did all that he had said. [25]Moses chose able men from all Israel and appointed them as heads over the people, as officers over thousands, hundreds, fifties, and tens. [26]And they judged the people at all times; hard cases they brought to Moses, but any minor case they decided themselves. [27]Then Moses let his father-in-law depart, and he went off to his own country.

The Israelites Reach Mount Sinai

19 On the third new moon after the Israelites had gone out of the land of Egypt, on that very day, they came into the wilderness of Sinai. [2]They had journeyed from Rephidim, entered the wilderness of Sinai, and camped in the wilderness; Israel camped there in front of the mountain. [3]Then Moses went up to God; the LORD called to him from the mountain, saying, "Thus you shall say to the house of Jacob, and tell the Israelites: [4]You have seen what I did to the Egyptians, and how I bore you on eagles' wings and brought you to myself. [5]Now therefore, if you obey my voice and keep my covenant, you shall be my treasured possession out of all the peoples. Indeed, the whole earth is mine, [6]but you shall be for me a priestly kingdom and a holy nation. These are the words that you shall speak to the Israelites."

7 So Moses came, summoned the elders of the people, and set before them all these words that the LORD had commanded him. [8]The people all answered as one: "Everything that the LORD has spoken we will do." Moses reported the words of the people to the LORD. [9]Then the LORD said to Moses, "I am going to come to you in a dense cloud, in order that the people may hear when I speak with you and so trust you ever after."

The People Consecrated

When Moses had told the words of the people to the LORD, [10]the LORD said to Moses: "Go to the people and consecrate them today and tomorrow. Have them wash their clothes [11]and prepare for the third day, because on the third day the LORD will come down upon Mount Sinai in the sight of all the people. [12]You shall set limits for the people all around, saying, 'Be careful not to go up the mountain or to touch the edge of it. Any who touch the mountain shall be put to death. [13]No hand shall touch them, but they shall be stoned or shot with arrows;[o] whether animal or human being, they shall not live.' When the trumpet sounds a long blast, they may go up on the mountain." [14]So Moses went down from the mountain to the people. He consecrated the people, and they washed their clothes. [15]And he

[o] Heb lacks *with arrows*

18.15 Num 9.8; Deut 17.8-13
18.18 Num 11.14,17
18.19 Ex 3.12; Num 27.5
18.20 Deut 1.18
18.21 ver 25; Deut 1.13,15
18.22 Deut 1.17,18; Num 11.17
18.25 Deut 1.15
18.26 ver 22
18.27 Num 10.29,30
19.2 Ex 17.1; 18.5
19.3 Ex 20.21; Acts 7.38
19.4 Deut 29.2; Isa 63.9
19.5 Deut 5.2; 7.6; 10.14
19.6 1 Pet 2.5; Rev 1.6; 5.10; Deut 14.21; 26.19
19.8 Ex 24.3,7
19.9 ver 16; Ex 24.15
19.10 Lev 11.44,45; Heb 10.22; Gen 35.2; Num 8.7; 19.19
19.11 ver 16
19.12 Heb 12.20
19.13 ver 17

said to the people, "Prepare for the third
day; do not go near a woman."
16 On the morning of the third day there
was thunder and lightning, as well as a
thick cloud on the mountain, and a blast of
a trumpet so loud that all the people who
were in the camp trembled. 17 Moses brought
the people out of the camp to meet God.
They took their stand at the foot of the
mountain. 18 Now Mount Sinai was wrapped
in smoke, because the LORD had descended
upon it in fire; the smoke went up like the
smoke of a kiln, while the whole mountain
shook violently. 19 As the blast of the trumpet grew louder and louder, Moses would
speak and God would answer him in thunder. 20 When the LORD descended upon Mount
Sinai, to the top of the mountain, the LORD
summoned Moses to the top of the mountain, and Moses went up. 21 Then the LORD
said to Moses, "Go down and warn the
people not to break through to the LORD to
look; otherwise many of them will perish.
22 Even the priests who approach the LORD
must consecrate themselves or the LORD will
break out against them." 23 Moses said to the
LORD, "The people are not permitted to come
up to Mount Sinai; for you yourself warned
us, saying, 'Set limits around the mountain
and keep it holy.' " 24 The LORD said to him,
"Go down, and come up bringing Aaron
with you; but do not let either the priests
or the people break through to come up to
the LORD; otherwise he will break out against
them." 25 So Moses went down to the people
and told them.

The Ten Commandments

20 Then God spoke all these words:
2 I am the LORD your God, who
brought you out of the land of Egypt, out
of the house of slavery; 3 you shall have no
other gods before[p] me.
4 You shall not make for yourself an idol,
whether in the form of anything that is in
heaven above, or that is on the earth beneath, or that is in the water under the
earth. 5 You shall not bow down to them or
worship them; for I the LORD your God am
a jealous God, punishing children for the
iniquity of parents, to the third and the
fourth generation of those who reject me,
6 but showing steadfast love to the thousandth generation[q] of those who love me
and keep my commandments.
7 You shall not make wrongful use of
the name of the LORD your God, for the LORD
will not acquit anyone who misuses his
name.
8 Remember the sabbath day, and keep
it holy. 9 Six days you shall labor and do all
your work. 10 But the seventh day is a sabbath
to the LORD your God; you shall not do any
work—you, your son or your daughter,
your male or female slave, your livestock,
or the alien resident in your towns. 11 For in
six days the LORD made heaven and earth,
the sea, and all that is in them, but rested
the seventh day; therefore the LORD blessed
the sabbath day and consecrated it.
12 Honor your father and your mother,
so that your days may be long in the land
that the LORD your God is giving you.
13 You shall not murder.[r]
14 You shall not commit adultery.
15 You shall not steal.
16 You shall not bear false witness against
your neighbor.
17 You shall not covet your neighbor's
house; you shall not covet your neighbor's
wife, or male or female slave, or ox, or
donkey, or anything that belongs to your
neighbor.
18 When all the people witnessed the
thunder and lightning, the sound of the
trumpet, and the mountain smoking, they
were afraid[s] and trembled and stood at a
distance, 19 and said to Moses, "You speak to
us, and we will listen; but do not let God
speak to us, or we will die." 20 Moses said to
the people, "Do not be afraid; for God has
come only to test you and to put the fear
of him upon you so that you do not sin."
21 Then the people stood at a distance, while
Moses drew near to the thick darkness where
God was.

The Law concerning the Altar

22 The LORD said to Moses: Thus you
shall say to the Israelites: "You have seen
for yourselves that I spoke with you from
heaven. 23 You shall not make gods of silver
alongside me, nor shall you make for yourselves gods of gold. 24 You need make for me
only an altar of earth and sacrifice on it
your burnt offerings and your offerings of
well-being, your sheep and your oxen; in
every place where I cause my name to be
remembered I will come to you and bless
you. 25 But if you make for me an altar of

[p] Or *besides* [q] Or *to thousands* [r] Or *kill* [s] Sam Gk Syr Vg: MT *they saw*

20.1-23.19 The Law of the LORD from Sinai.
20.2 As preface to the rules for God's people there is a brief reminder of his crucial act of liberation in their behalf. Then follow the Ten Commandments.
20.3 The first commandment insists on God's primary position over all other gods, rather than a monotheistic claim.
20.4-6 The second commandment prohibits the use of material images to represent God or as the focus of worship. Love is the basis of the reciprocal relationship between God and his people.
20.7 The third commandment asserts the sanctity of the divine name, which is not to be used for any unworthy purposes. The name is not only who God is, but it also serves as the instrument of his power, which is evident in the report of its disclosure to Moses (3.13-20).
20.8-11 The fourth commandment, the holiness of the sabbath, is to be observed by Israelites and by all who dwell in their land. It is here said to be modelled on Yahweh's rest after six days of creation, although the priestly account of creation (Gen 2.1-3) probably justifies the sabbath rule by this report of God's day of rest.
20.12 The fifth commandment demands equal honor for mothers with fathers, which is an unusual feature in the wider society of the Middle East, where women were primarily instruments of male procreation and expendable slaves.
20.13 The sixth commandment – prohibition against killing – seems to apply only among members of the covenant community, since holy war is allowed for Israel (Deut 19.11-13; Num 35.6-21). Unpremeditated killing is tolerated, however (Ex 21.12-17).
20.14 The seventh commandment against adultery means violation of the marital rights of another man through intercourse with a married or betrothed woman (Deut 22.22-27).
20.15 The eighth commandment, which is against stealing, may mean theft in general, but the term is used of kidnapping Joseph in Gen 40.15.
20.16 The ninth commandment prohibits false evidence or perjury, presumably against another member of the covenant community.
20.17 The tenth commandment denounces the desire to obtain what belongs to a neighbor, which would mean another Israelite.
20.18-21 The awesome appearance of Yahweh to Moses shows that the relationship of God to his people is through an intermediary, and that this is for them a time of testing and *fear*.
20.22-23.19 The Book of the Covenant. This term is used in 24.7. The rules for the community which are given here deal with the members' relationship with God as well as with other members.
20.22-26 Concerning the Altar. Israel in its nomadic life will meet God at simple altars of earth or unhewn stones, free of images, carvings or stairs, ascending which might cause indecent exposure of the worshippers to onlookers.

19.16 Heb 12.18,19; Ex 40.34
19.18 Ps 104.32; Heb 12.18; Gen 19.28; Ps 68.7,8
19.19 Heb 12.21; Ps 81.7
19.21 Ex 3.5
19.22 Lev 10.3; 2 Sam 6.7
19.23 ver 12
20.1 Deut 5.22
20.2 Deut 5.6,7,8
20.3 Jer 35.15
20.4 Lev 26.1; Deut 4.15-19; Ps 97.7
20.5 Isa 44.15,19; Deut 4.24; Jer 32.18
20.6 Deut 7.9
20.7 Lev 19.12; Mt 5.33
20.8 Ex 23.12; 31.15
20.9 Ex 34.21; Lk 13.14
20.11 Gen 2.2,3
20.12 Lev 19.3; Mt 15.4; Mk 7.10; Eph 6.2
20.13 Rom 13.9
20.14 Mt 19.18
20.15 Mt 19.18
20.16 Ex 23.1; Mt 19.18
20.17 Rom 7.7; 13.9
20.18 Heb 12.18; Ex 19.18
20.19 Deut 5.23-27
20.20 Ex 14.13; 15.25; Deut 4.10
20.21 Deut 5.22
20.22 Neh 9.13
20.23 ver 3; Ex 32.1,2,4
20.24 Lev 1.2; Deut 12.5; Gen 12.2
20.25 Deut 27.5,6

21.1-11 Concerning Slaves. Hebrew slaves are to be granted freedom after seven years, as are their wives, except those given to a slave by the master. Yet the slave can voluntarily maintain the relationship for life, having his ear pierced as a sign of this commitment (Ps 40.6-7). The rights of women sold into slavery are firmly maintained.
21.12-17 Concerning Violence. Premeditated murder is punishable by death; anyone who commits an unpremeditated killing is to be allowed to flee to a city of refuge. Punishments are specified not only for various forms of physical attack but even for cursing one's father or mother. On the whole, retaliation is to be equivalent to the harm suffered by the victim : *eye for eye, tooth for tooth.*
21.33-22.15 Concerning Damage to Property and Restitution. Owners of livestock are responsible for death caused by the animals if they have been warned of the danger their livestock might cause, just as they are obligated to pay for harm done to other animals as a result of negligence. These regulations presuppose a more settled existence in the land, rather than nomadic life, as do the rules about harm to others done by housebreakers (22.2,7) or damage done to fields and vineyards (22.5-6).

stone, do not build it of hewn stones; for if
you use a chisel upon it you profane it.
26You shall not go up by steps to my altar,
so that your nakedness may not be exposed
on it."

The Law concerning Slaves

21 These are the ordinances that you
shall set before them:
2 When you buy a male Hebrew slave,
he shall serve six years, but in the seventh
he shall go out a free person, without debt.
3If he comes in single, he shall go out single;
if he comes in married, then his wife shall
go out with him. 4If his master gives him
a wife and she bears him sons or daughters,
the wife and her children shall be her
master's and he shall go out alone. 5But if
the slave declares, "I love my master, my
wife, and my children; I will not go out a
free person," 6then his master shall bring
him before God.[t] He shall be brought to the
door or the doorpost; and his master shall
pierce his ear with an awl; and he shall
serve him for life.
7 When a man sells his daughter as a
slave, she shall not go out as the male
slaves do. 8If she does not please her master,
who designated her for himself, then he
shall let her be redeemed; he shall have no
right to sell her to a foreign people, since
he has dealt unfairly with her. 9If he designates her for his son, he shall deal with
her as with a daughter. 10If he takes another wife to himself, he shall not diminish
the food, clothing, or marital rights of the
first wife.[u] 11And if he does not do these
three things for her, she shall go out without debt, without payment of money.

The Law concerning Violence

12 Whoever strikes a person mortally
shall be put to death. 13If it was not premeditated, but came about by an act of God,
then I will appoint for you a place to which
the killer may flee. 14But if someone willfully
attacks and kills another by treachery, you
shall take the killer from my altar for execution.
15 Whoever strikes father or mother shall
be put to death.
16 Whoever kidnaps a person, whether
that person has been sold or is still held in
possession, shall be put to death.
17 Whoever curses father or mother shall
be put to death.
18 When individuals quarrel and one
strikes the other with a stone or fist so that
the injured party, though not dead, is confined to bed, 19but recovers and walks around
outside with the help of a staff, then the
assailant shall be free of liability, except to
pay for the loss of time, and to arrange for
full recovery.
20 When a slaveowner strikes a male or
female slave with a rod and the slave dies
immediately, the owner shall be punished.
21But if the slave survives a day or two,
there is no punishment; for the slave is the
owner's property.
22 When people who are fighting injure
a pregnant woman so that there is a miscarriage, and yet no further harm follows,
the one responsible shall be fined what the
woman's husband demands, paying as much
as the judges determine. 23If any harm follows, then you shall give life for life, 24eye
for eye, tooth for tooth, hand for hand, foot
for foot, 25burn for burn, wound for wound,
stripe for stripe.
26 When a slaveowner strikes the eye of
a male or female slave, destroying it, the
owner shall let the slave go, a free person,
to compensate for the eye. 27If the owner
knocks out a tooth of a male or female
slave, the slave shall be let go, a free person,
to compensate for the tooth.

Laws concerning Property

28 When an ox gores a man or a woman
to death, the ox shall be stoned, and its flesh
shall not be eaten; but the owner of the ox
shall not be liable. 29If the ox has been
accustomed to gore in the past, and its
owner has been warned but has not restrained it, and it kills a man or a woman,
the ox shall be stoned, and its owner also
shall be put to death. 30If a ransom is
imposed on the owner, then the owner shall
pay whatever is imposed for the redemption
of the victim's life. 31If it gores a boy or a
girl, the owner shall be dealt with according
to this same rule. 32If the ox gores a male
or female slave, the owner shall pay to the
slaveowner thirty shekels of silver, and the
ox shall be stoned.
33 If someone leaves a pit open, or digs
a pit and does not cover it, and an ox or
a donkey falls into it, 34the owner of the pit

[t] Or *to the judges* [u] Heb *of her*

21.1 Deut 4.14
21.2 Lev 25.39-41; Deut 15.12-18
21.6 Ex 22.8,9,28
21.7 Neh 5.5; ver 2,3
21.10 1 Cor 7.3,5
21.12 Gen 9.6; Lev 24.17
21.13 Num 35.22; Deut 19.4,5
21.14 Deut 19.11,12; Heb 10.26; 1 Kings 2.28-34
21.16 Deut 24.7
21.17 Lev 20.9; Mt 15.4; Mk 7.10
21.21 Lev 25.45,46
21.23 Lev 24.19
21.24 Mt 5.38
21.28 Gen 9.5
21.30 ver 22
21.32 see Zech 11.12,13; Mt 26.15
21.33 Lk 14.5

22.1 2 Sam 12.6
22.2 Mt 24.43; Num 35.27
22.3 Ex 21.2
22.7 ver 4
22.8 ver 28; Ex 21.6; Deut 17.8,9; 19.17
22.9 ver 8,28
22.11 Heb 6.16
22.12 Gen 31.39
22.16 Deut 22.28,29
22.18 Lev 20.27; Deut 18.10
22.19 Lev 18.23; Deut 27.21
22.20 Deut 17.2,3,5
22.21 Lev 19.33; Deut 10.19
22.22 Deut 24.17,18
22.23 Deut 15.9; Lk 18.7; Ps 18.6
22.24 Ps 69.24; 109.9
22.25 Lev 25.35-37; Deut 23.19,20
22.28 Lev 24.15,16; Acts 23.5
22.29 Ex 23.16; 13.2,12

shall make restitution, giving money to its
owner, but keeping the dead animal.
35 If someone's ox hurts the ox of another, so that it dies, then they shall sell the
live ox and divide the price of it; and the
dead animal they shall also divide. 36But if
it was known that the ox was accustomed
to gore in the past, and its owner has not
restrained it, the owner shall restore ox for
ox, but keep the dead animal.

Laws of Restitution

22[v] When someone steals an ox or a
sheep, and slaughters it or sells it,
the thief shall pay five oxen for an ox, and
four sheep for a sheep.[w] The thief shall make
restitution, but if unable to do so, shall be
sold for the theft. 4When the animal, whether
ox or donkey or sheep, is found alive in the
thief's possession, the thief shall pay double.
2[x] If a thief is found breaking in, and is
beaten to death, no bloodguilt is incurred;
3but if it happens after sunrise, bloodguilt is
incurred.
5 When someone causes a field or vineyard to be grazed over, or lets livestock loose
to graze in someone else's field, restitution
shall be made from the best in the owner's
field or vineyard.
6 When fire breaks out and catches in
thorns so that the stacked grain or the
standing grain or the field is consumed, the
one who started the fire shall make full
restitution.
7 When someone delivers to a neighbor
money or goods for safekeeping, and they
are stolen from the neighbor's house, then
the thief, if caught, shall pay double. 8If the
thief is not caught, the owner of the house
shall be brought before God,[y] to determine
whether or not the owner had laid hands
on the neighbor's goods.
9 In any case of disputed ownership involving ox, donkey, sheep, clothing, or any
other loss, of which one party says, "This
is mine," the case of both parties shall come
before God;[y] the one whom God condemns[z]
shall pay double to the other.
10 When someone delivers to another a
donkey, ox, sheep, or any other animal for
safekeeping, and it dies or is injured or is
carried off, without anyone seeing it, 11an
oath before the LORD shall decide between
the two of them that the one has not laid
hands on the property of the other; the
owner shall accept the oath, and no restitution shall be made. 12But if it was stolen,
restitution shall be made to its owner. 13If
it was mangled by beasts, let it be brought
as evidence; restitution shall not be made
for the mangled remains.
14 When someone borrows an animal
from another and it is injured or dies, the
owner not being present, full restitution
shall be made. 15If the owner was present,
there shall be no restitution; if it was hired,
only the hiring fee is due.

Social and Religious Laws

16 When a man seduces a virgin who is
not engaged to be married, and lies with
her, he shall give the bride-price for her and
make her his wife. 17But if her father refuses
to give her to him, he shall pay an amount
equal to the bride-price for virgins.
18 You shall not permit a female sorcerer to live.
19 Whoever lies with an animal shall be
put to death.
20 Whoever sacrifices to any god, other
than the LORD alone, shall be devoted to
destruction.
21 You shall not wrong or oppress a
resident alien, for you were aliens in the
land of Egypt. 22You shall not abuse any
widow or orphan. 23If you do abuse them,
when they cry out to me, I will surely heed
their cry; 24my wrath will burn, and I will
kill you with the sword, and your wives
shall become widows and your children
orphans.
25 If you lend money to my people, to
the poor among you, you shall not deal
with them as a creditor; you shall not exact
interest from them. 26If you take your
neighbor's cloak in pawn, you shall restore
it before the sun goes down; 27for it may be
your neighbor's only clothing to use as
cover; in what else shall that person sleep?
And if your neighbor cries out to me, I will
listen, for I am compassionate.
28 You shall not revile God, or curse a
leader of your people.
29 You shall not delay to make offerings
from the fullness of your harvest and from
the outflow of your presses.[a]
The firstborn of your sons you shall give
to me. 30You shall do the same with your

[v] Ch 21.37 in Heb [w] Verses 2, 3, and 4 rearranged thus: 3b, 4, 2, 3a [x] Ch 22.1 in Heb [y] Or *before the judges* [z] Or *the judges condemn* [a] Meaning of Heb uncertain

22.16-23.19 Concerning Social Relationships and Religious Rules. Respect for the rights of others in the community leads to punishment for sexual abuse of virgins, and for exploitation of resident aliens, of a widow or orphan, or of the poor.
The compassion of God is extended to any member of the community who calls to God for help. On the other hand, the death penalty is decreed for the *female sorcerer*, for anyone who has sexual relations with an animal, and for those who make sacrifices to a god other than Yahweh. Neither God nor the leader he chooses for his people is to be denounced. Instead, offerings from the harvests are to be presented to God, as are the symbolically important firstborn sons, and the firstborn of the flocks and herds. The people as a whole are to be holy and dedicated to God, so that impure meat is to be discarded by them.

23.1-9 Justice and compassion are to characterize all one's dealings within the community, including response to the guilty, the poor, the powerful, resident aliens, and even to animals. **23.10-19** Detailed instructions are given for observing the sabbaths and the annual festivals, including the feasts of unleavened bread and the harvest. The cycle of crops anticipates Israel's life settled in the land. The forbidden practice of boiling *a kid in its mother's milk* is known to have been used by the Canaanites as part of their fertility rites. **23.20-33** Reaffirming the Promise that Israel will Enter the Land. Preceding Israel on its entrance into the land and providing counsel on the authority of God's *name* will be an *angel* as God's messenger and agent to defeat all *enemies*. These will include several Semitic tribes, but also the Hittites, Indo-European people from Asia Minor who dominated Syria and Canaan at the peak of their power from 1300-1200 BCE. The process of Israel's occupation of the land will be slow, but the ultimate extent of territory they control will be bounded by the Red Sea and the Sinai desert to the south, the Mediterranean (sea of the Philistines) to the west, and the Euphrates to the northeast. Only in the time of David and Solomon was Israelite control so extensive.

oxen and with your sheep: seven days it shall remain with its mother; on the eighth day you shall give it to me.

31 You shall be people consecrated to me; therefore you shall not eat any meat that is mangled by beasts in the field; you shall throw it to the dogs.

Justice for All

23 You shall not spread a false report. You shall not join hands with the wicked to act as a malicious witness. 2 You shall not follow a majority in wrongdoing; when you bear witness in a lawsuit, you shall not side with the majority so as to pervert justice; 3 nor shall you be partial to the poor in a lawsuit.

4 When you come upon your enemy's ox or donkey going astray, you shall bring it back.

5 When you see the donkey of one who hates you lying under its burden and you would hold back from setting it free, you must help to set it free.[b]

6 You shall not pervert the justice due to your poor in their lawsuits. 7 Keep far from a false charge, and do not kill the innocent and those in the right, for I will not acquit the guilty. 8 You shall take no bribe, for a bribe blinds the officials, and subverts the cause of those who are in the right.

9 You shall not oppress a resident alien; you know the heart of an alien, for you were aliens in the land of Egypt.

Sabbatical Year and Sabbath

10 For six years you shall sow your land and gather in its yield; 11 but the seventh year you shall let it rest and lie fallow, so that the poor of your people may eat; and what they leave the wild animals may eat. You shall do the same with your vineyard, and with your olive orchard.

12 Six days you shall do your work, but on the seventh day you shall rest, so that your ox and your donkey may have relief, and your homeborn slave and the resident alien may be refreshed. 13 Be attentive to all that I have said to you. Do not invoke the names of other gods; do not let them be heard on your lips.

The Annual Festivals

14 Three times in the year you shall hold a festival for me. 15 You shall observe the festival of unleavened bread; as I commanded you, you shall eat unleavened bread for seven days at the appointed time in the month of Abib, for in it you came out of Egypt.

No one shall appear before me empty-handed.

16 You shall observe the festival of harvest, of the first fruits of your labor, of what you sow in the field. You shall observe the festival of ingathering at the end of the year, when you gather in from the field the fruit of your labor. 17 Three times in the year all your males shall appear before the Lord GOD.

18 You shall not offer the blood of my sacrifice with anything leavened, or let the fat of my festival remain until the morning.

19 The choicest of the first fruits of your ground you shall bring into the house of the LORD your God.

You shall not boil a kid in its mother's milk.

The Conquest of Canaan Promised

20 I am going to send an angel in front of you, to guard you on the way and to bring you to the place that I have prepared. 21 Be attentive to him and listen to his voice; do not rebel against him, for he will not pardon your transgression; for my name is in him.

22 But if you listen attentively to his voice and do all that I say, then I will be an enemy to your enemies and a foe to your foes.

23 When my angel goes in front of you, and brings you to the Amorites, the Hittites, the Perizzites, the Canaanites, the Hivites, and the Jebusites, and I blot them out, 24 you shall not bow down to their gods, or worship them, or follow their practices, but you shall utterly demolish them and break their pillars in pieces. 25 You shall worship the LORD your God, and I[c] will bless your bread and your water; and I will take sickness away from among you. 26 No one shall miscarry or be barren in your land; I will fulfill the number of your days. 27 I will send

[b] Meaning of Heb uncertain [c] Gk Vg: Heb *he*

22.30 Deut 15.19; Lev 22.27
22.31 Lev 19.6; 22.8
23.1 Ex 20.16; Ps 35.11
23.2 Deut 16.19
23.4 Deut 22.1
23.5 Deut 22.4
23.6 ver 2,3
23.7 Rom 1.18
23.8 Deut 10.17; 16.19
23.9 Ex 22.21
23.10 Lev 25.3
23.12 Ex 20.8-11
23.15 Ex 12.15; 34.20
23.16 Ex 34.22; Deut 16.13
23.19 Ex 22.29; Deut 14.21
23.20 Ex 32.34; 15.16,17
23.21 Num 14.11; Ps 78.40,56; Num 14.35
23.22 Gen 12.2
23.23 Josh 24.8,11
23.24 Ex 20.5; Lev 18.3; Ex 34.13
23.25 Deut 6.13; Mt 4.10; Deut 28.5; Ex 15.26
23.26 Deut 7.14; Mal 3.11; Job 5.26; Ex 15.14,16; Deut 7.23

23.28 Deut 7.20; Josh 24.12
23.29 Deut 7.22
23.31 Gen 15.18; Josh 21.44; 24.12,18
23.32 Deut 7.2; ver 13,24
23.33 Deut 7.1-5,16
24.1 Lev 10.1,2; Num 11.16
24.3 ver 7; Ex 19.8
24.4 Deut 31.9; Gen 28.18
24.6 Heb 9.18
24.7 Heb 9.19; ver 3
24.8 Heb 9.20; 1 Pet 1.2
24.9 ver 1
24.10 Ezek 1.26; Rev 4.3; Mt 17.2
24.15 Ex 19.9
24.16 Ex 16.10
24.17 Ex 3.2; Deut 4.36; Heb 12.18,29
24.18 Ex 34.28; Deut 9.9
25.2 Ex 35.5,21; 2 Cor 8.12; 9.7
25.6 Ex 27.20; 30.23,34
25.7 Ex 28.4,6,15
25.8 Ex 36.1,3,4; Heb 9.1,2; Ex 29.45; Rev 21.3
25.9 ver 40; Acts 7.44; Heb 8.2,5

my terror in front of you, and will throw
into confusion all the people against whom
you shall come, and I will make all your
enemies turn their backs to you. 28And I
will send the pestilence[d] in front of you,
which shall drive out the Hivites, the
Canaanites, and the Hittites from before
you. 29I will not drive them out from before
you in one year, or the land would become
desolate and the wild animals would multiply against you. 30Little by little I will drive
them out from before you, until you have
increased and possess the land. 31I will set
your borders from the Red Sea[e] to the sea
of the Philistines, and from the wilderness
to the Euphrates; for I will hand over to you
the inhabitants of the land, and you shall
drive them out before you. 32You shall make
no covenant with them and their gods.
33They shall not live in your land, or they
will make you sin against me; for if you
worship their gods, it will surely be a snare
to you.

The Blood of the Covenant

24 Then he said to Moses, "Come up
to the LORD, you and Aaron, Nadab,
and Abihu, and seventy of the elders of
Israel, and worship at a distance. 2Moses
alone shall come near the LORD; but the
others shall not come near, and the people
shall not come up with him."
3 Moses came and told the people all the
words of the LORD and all the ordinances;
and all the people answered with one voice,
and said, "All the words that the LORD has
spoken we will do." 4And Moses wrote down
all the words of the LORD. He rose early in
the morning, and built an altar at the foot
of the mountain, and set up twelve pillars,
corresponding to the twelve tribes of Israel.
5He sent young men of the people of Israel,
who offered burnt offerings and sacrificed
oxen as offerings of well-being to the LORD.
6Moses took half of the blood and put it in
basins, and half of the blood he dashed
against the altar. 7Then he took the book
of the covenant, and read it in the hearing
of the people; and they said, "All that the
LORD has spoken we will do, and we will be
obedient." 8Moses took the blood and dashed
it on the people, and said, "See the blood
of the covenant that the LORD has made
with you in accordance with all these words."

On the Mountain with God

9 Then Moses and Aaron, Nadab, and
Abihu, and seventy of the elders of Israel
went up, 10and they saw the God of Israel.
Under his feet there was something like a
pavement of sapphire stone, like the very
heaven for clearness. 11God[f] did not lay his
hand on the chief men of the people of
Israel; also they beheld God, and they ate
and drank.
12 The LORD said to Moses, "Come up to
me on the mountain, and wait there; and
I will give you the tablets of stone, with the
law and the commandment, which I have
written for their instruction." 13So Moses set
out with his assistant Joshua, and Moses
went up into the mountain of God. 14To the
elders he had said, "Wait here for us, until
we come to you again; for Aaron and Hur
are with you; whoever has a dispute may
go to them."
15 Then Moses went up on the mountain, and the cloud covered the mountain.
16The glory of the LORD settled on Mount
Sinai, and the cloud covered it for six days;
on the seventh day he called to Moses out
of the cloud. 17Now the appearance of the
glory of the LORD was like a devouring fire
on the top of the mountain in the sight of
the people of Israel. 18Moses entered the
cloud, and went up on the mountain. Moses
was on the mountain for forty days and
forty nights.

Offerings for the Tabernacle

25 The LORD said to Moses: 2Tell the
Israelites to take for me an offering; from all whose hearts prompt them to
give you shall receive the offering for me.
3This is the offering that you shall receive
from them: gold, silver, and bronze, 4blue,
purple, and crimson yarns and fine linen,
goats' hair, 5tanned rams' skins, fine leather,[g]
acacia wood, 6oil for the lamps, spices for
the anointing oil and for the fragrant incense, 7onyx stones and gems to be set in
the ephod and for the breastpiece. 8And
have them make me a sanctuary, so that
I may dwell among them. 9In accordance
with all that I show you concerning the
pattern of the tabernacle and of all its furniture, so you shall make it.

24.1-8 The Blood of the Covenant. This account is composite, with the people kept at a distance in vs.1 and all of them involved in the ceremony in vv. 3-8. The 70 elders are the representatives of the people as a whole, and the 12 pillars symbolize the 12 tribes of Israel. *The book of the covenant* is read, and the people agree to obey it. The blood is the symbolic factor binding God (symbolized by *the altar)* and the people in *the covenant.*
24.9-18 God is Revealed to Israel's Leadership on Sinai. Nadab and Abihu, sons of Aaron (Ex 6.23) are killed by the unholy fire they kindled on God's altar (Lev 10.1-2). All the representatives *saw the God of Israel.* The specifics of God's instructions for his people are given to Moses inscribed on *tablets of stone.* The presence of God is compared with a radiant, fiery cloud of *glory,* a visible, awesome sign of his power in the midst of his people. Moses' stay on the mountain lasts *forty days and nights,* which is the same as the period when Noah is in the ark (Gen 7.4) and when the land of Canaan is spied out before the people enter (Num 14.34).
25.1-31.18 Regulations for Building and Operating the Sanctuary of God in the Midst of his People.
25.1-9 The people are to contribute the precious metals, jewels, fabrics, animal skins and kinds of wood that will be required to prepare the mobile sanctuary in which will be housed the sacred box containing the tablets of the covenant. The description combines features which may go back to early times with many which developed as late as after the exile when the temple was rebuilt in the sixth century after Israel's return from exile in Babylon. The cost of the materials in this description seems impossible for the fleeing Israelites, so that these expensive features must come from a later situation. The details of the *pattern* for the construction are said to come from God.

[d] Or *hornets*: Meaning of Heb uncertain [e] Or *Sea of Reeds* [f] Heb *He* [g] Meaning of Heb uncertain

25.10-22 The *ark* or sacred container for the covenant measured a little over four feet square and two feet in height, and had rings to make possible its being carried on poles. The top was to have a cover of gold (often translated as *mercy seat*) with two winged sphinxes (*cherubim*) mounted above it, facing each other, to symbolize the invisible presence of God there between them. It is here that God *will meet with* the representative of his people to convey *all my commands for the Israelites*. In Num 10.35-36, Moses speaks to the ark as though it were God going before his people.
25.23-30 Another symbol of God's being in the midst of his people is the table for *the bread of the Presence*. Also made to be portable, the food and drink upon it represent the continuing fellowship of God with his covenant people.
25.31-40 The seven-branched lampstand not only illuminates the interior of the sacred tent but also symbolizes the light of knowledge of God's purpose for his people. A later version of this lampstand is depicted on the Arch of Titus in Rome, where the treasures taken from the temple of Herod in 70 CE are on display.
26.1-37 The sacred tent consists of linen curtains on the sides, decorated with colors, and sheets of fabric made from goats' hair on the top, the whole bound together with golden and bronze clasps. On the outside are *coverings of rams' skins...*and *fine leather*. Like the table for the bread, the framework to support the complex tent is made of *acacia wood*, and is overlaid with gold. The inner sanctuary for the ark of the covenant is separated off by an elaborately woven curtain from *the holy place*, where the table and the lampstand are located.

The Ark of the Covenant

10 They shall make an ark of acacia wood; it shall be two and a half cubits long, a cubit and a half wide, and a cubit and a half high. 11 You shall overlay it with pure gold, inside and outside you shall overlay it, and you shall make a molding of gold upon it all around. 12 You shall cast four rings of gold for it and put them on its four feet, two rings on the one side of it, and two rings on the other side. 13 You shall make poles of acacia wood, and overlay them with gold. 14 And you shall put the poles into the rings on the sides of the ark, by which to carry the ark. 15 The poles shall remain in the rings of the ark; they shall not be taken from it. 16 You shall put into the ark the covenant[h] that I shall give you.

17 Then you shall make a mercy seat[i] of pure gold; two cubits and a half shall be its length, and a cubit and a half its width. 18 You shall make two cherubim of gold; you shall make them of hammered work, at the two ends of the mercy seat.[j] 19 Make one cherub at the one end, and one cherub at the other; of one piece with the mercy seat[j] you shall make the cherubim at its two ends. 20 The cherubim shall spread out their wings above, overshadowing the mercy seat[j] with their wings. They shall face one to another; the faces of the cherubim shall be turned toward the mercy seat.[j] 21 You shall put the mercy seat[j] on the top of the ark; and in the ark you shall put the covenant[h] that I shall give you. 22 There I will meet with you, and from above the mercy seat,[j] from between the two cherubim that are on the ark of the covenant,[h] I will deliver to you all my commands for the Israelites.

The Table for the Bread of the Presence

23 You shall make a table of acacia wood, two cubits long, one cubit wide, and a cubit and a half high. 24 You shall overlay it with pure gold, and make a molding of gold around it. 25 You shall make around it a rim a handbreadth wide, and a molding of gold around the rim. 26 You shall make for it four rings of gold, and fasten the rings to the four corners at its four legs. 27 The rings that hold the poles used for carrying the table shall be close to the rim. 28 You shall make the poles of acacia wood, and overlay them with gold, and the table shall be carried with these. 29 You shall make its plates and dishes for incense, and its flagons and bowls with which to pour drink offerings; you shall make them of pure gold. 30 And you shall set the bread of the Presence on the table before me always.

The Lampstand

31 You shall make a lampstand of pure gold. The base and the shaft of the lampstand shall be made of hammered work; its cups, its calyxes, and its petals shall be of one piece with it; 32 and there shall be six branches going out of its sides, three branches of the lampstand out of one side of it and three branches of the lampstand out of the other side of it; 33 three cups shaped like almond blossoms, each with calyx and petals, on one branch, and three cups shaped like almond blossoms, each with calyx and petals, on the other branch—so for the six branches going out of the lampstand. 34 On the lampstand itself there shall be four cups shaped like almond blossoms, each with its calyxes and petals. 35 There shall be a calyx of one piece with it under the first pair of branches, a calyx of one piece with it under the next pair of branches, and a calyx of one piece with it under the last pair of branches—so for the six branches that go out of the lampstand. 36 Their calyxes and their branches shall be of one piece with it, the whole of it one hammered piece of pure gold. 37 You shall make the seven lamps for it; and the lamps shall be set up so as to give light on the space in front of it. 38 Its snuffers and trays shall be of pure gold. 39 It, and all these utensils, shall be made from a talent of pure gold. 40 And see that you make them according to the pattern for them, which is being shown you on the mountain.

The Tabernacle

26 Moreover you shall make the tabernacle with ten curtains of fine twisted linen, and blue, purple, and crimson yarns; you shall make them with cherubim skillfully worked into them. 2 The length of each curtain shall be twenty-eight cubits, and the width of each curtain four cubits; all the curtains shall be of the same size. 3 Five curtains shall be joined to one another; and the other five curtains shall be joined to one another. 4 You shall make

[h] Or *treaty*, or *testimony*; Heb *eduth* [i] Or *a cover* [j] Or *the cover*

25.10 Ex 37.1-9
25.16 Deut 31.26; Heb 9.4
25.17 Ex 37.6; Rom 3.25; Heb 9.5
25.20 1 Kings 8.7; Heb 9.5
25.21 Ex 26.34; ver 16
25.22 Ex 29.42,43; 30.6,36; Ps 80.1
25.23 Ex 37.10-16; Heb 9.2
25.29 Ex 37.16; Num 4.7
25.30 Lev 24.5-9
25.31 Ex 37.17; Heb 9.2; Rev 1.12
25.32 Ex 38.18
25.34 Ex 37.20
25.37 Ex 27.21; Lev 24.3,4
25.40 Ex 26.30; Acts 7.44; Heb 8.5
26.1 Ex 36.8
26.3 Ex 36.10

26.5 Ex 36.12
26.7 Ex 36.14
26.11 Ex 36.18
26.14 Ex 36.19
26.15 Ex 36.20
26.20 Ex 36.23
26.25 Ex 36.30
26.30 Ex 25.9,40; 27.8; Acts 7.44; Heb 8.5
26.31 Ex 36.35; Mt 27.51; Heb 9.3
26.33 Ex 25.16; 40.21; Lev 16.2; Heb 9.2,3
26.34 Ex 25.21; 40.20; Heb 9.5
26.35 Ex 40.22,24; Heb 9.2
26.36 Ex 36.37
26.37 Ex 36.38

loops of blue on the edge of the outermost curtain in the first set; and likewise you shall make loops on the edge of the outermost curtain in the second set. 5You shall make fifty loops on the one curtain, and you shall make fifty loops on the edge of the curtain that is in the second set; the loops shall be opposite one another. 6You shall make fifty clasps of gold, and join the curtains to one another with the clasps, so that the tabernacle may be one whole.

7 You shall also make curtains of goats' hair for a tent over the tabernacle; you shall make eleven curtains. 8The length of each curtain shall be thirty cubits, and the width of each curtain four cubits; the eleven curtains shall be of the same size. 9You shall join five curtains by themselves, and six curtains by themselves, and the sixth curtain you shall double over at the front of the tent. 10You shall make fifty loops on the edge of the curtain that is outermost in one set, and fifty loops on the edge of the curtain that is outermost in the second set.

11 You shall make fifty clasps of bronze, and put the clasps into the loops, and join the tent together, so that it may be one whole. 12The part that remains of the curtains of the tent, the half curtain that remains, shall hang over the back of the tabernacle. 13The cubit on the one side, and the cubit on the other side, of what remains in the length of the curtains of the tent, shall hang over the sides of the tabernacle, on this side and that side, to cover it. 14You shall make for the tent a covering of tanned rams' skins and an outer covering of fine leather.[k]

The Framework

15 You shall make upright frames of acacia wood for the tabernacle. 16Ten cubits shall be the length of a frame, and a cubit and a half the width of each frame. 17There shall be two pegs in each frame to fit the frames together; you shall make these for all the frames of the tabernacle. 18You shall make the frames for the tabernacle: twenty frames for the south side; 19and you shall make forty bases of silver under the twenty frames, two bases under the first frame for its two pegs, and two bases under the next frame for its two pegs; 20and for the second side of the tabernacle, on the north side twenty frames, 21and their forty bases of silver, two bases under the first frame, and two bases under the next frame; 22and for the rear of the tabernacle westward you shall make six frames. 23You shall make two frames for corners of the tabernacle in the rear; 24they shall be separate beneath, but joined at the top, at the first ring; it shall be the same with both of them; they shall form the two corners. 25And so there shall be eight frames, with their bases of silver, sixteen bases; two bases under the first frame, and two bases under the next frame.

26 You shall make bars of acacia wood, five for the frames of the one side of the tabernacle, 27and five bars for the frames of the other side of the tabernacle, and five bars for the frames of the side of the tabernacle at the rear westward. 28The middle bar, halfway up the frames, shall pass through from end to end. 29You shall overlay the frames with gold, and shall make their rings of gold to hold the bars; and you shall overlay the bars with gold. 30Then you shall erect the tabernacle according to the plan for it that you were shown on the mountain.

The Curtain

31 You shall make a curtain of blue, purple, and crimson yarns, and of fine twisted linen; it shall be made with cherubim skillfully worked into it. 32You shall hang it on four pillars of acacia overlaid with gold, which have hooks of gold and rest on four bases of silver. 33You shall hang the curtain under the clasps, and bring the ark of the covenant[l] in there, within the curtain; and the curtain shall separate for you the holy place from the most holy. 34You shall put the mercy seat[m] on the ark of the covenant[l] in the most holy place. 35You shall set the table outside the curtain, and the lampstand on the south side of the tabernacle opposite the table; and you shall put the table on the north side.

36 You shall make a screen for the entrance of the tent, of blue, purple, and crimson yarns, and of fine twisted linen, embroidered with needlework. 37You shall make for the screen five pillars of acacia, and overlay them with gold; their hooks shall be of gold, and you shall cast five bases of bronze for them.

[k] Meaning of Heb uncertain [l] Or *treaty*, or *testimony*; Heb *eduth* [m] Or *the cover*

27.1-21 The courtyard surrounding the tent consists of hangings suspended from *pillars*, and (assuming the cubit to be about a foot and a half) is approximately 75 feet by 150 feet. The altar of burnt offering is built of acacia wood with *a grating of bronze*, and implements of bronze as well. The *horns on its four corners* probably symbolized the possibility of making direct contact with God's power, as in the attainment of asylum by grasping the horn according to 1 Kings 1.50-51. The altar is also equipped with *rings* in order to be portable. A lamp burning olive oil is to be lighted all night every night, as a sign of God's continuing presence with his people.
28.1-43 The attire of the priests – identified here as *Aaron and his sons* – is to include *a breastpiece, an ephod, a robe, a checkered tunic, a turban, and a sash*. Details are given for the ephod and the breastpiece, both of which are made of fine textiles with colorful and expensive decorations of colored thread and precious stones. The ephod was originally a loincloth, but here is described as an elaborate undergarment, with stones at the shoulders carved with the names of the twelve tribes. The breastpiece is not a form of armor but a fancy tunic decorated with gold and precious stones, also representing the twelve tribes, among whom Aaron and the priests are to serve as judges. Essential to their decision-making role is the device known as *Urim and Thummim*, which was a kind of sacred lot by which the bearer could determine God's will on a yes/no basis. The turban worn by the priest was to bear a jewelled pin with the engraved words *Holy to the Lord*, thereby symbolizing the special role and relationship of the priest as mediator between God and members of the community. The priests' genitals (*naked flesh*) are to be covered with a special linen garment, lest they expose themselves while serving at the altar and thereby bring death on themselves as divine judgment.

The Altar of Burnt Offering

27 You shall make the altar of acacia wood, five cubits long and five cubits wide; the altar shall be square, and it shall be three cubits high. [2]You shall make horns for it on its four corners; its horns shall be of one piece with it, and you shall overlay it with bronze. [3]You shall make pots for it to receive its ashes, and shovels and basins and forks and firepans; you shall make all its utensils of bronze. [4]You shall also make for it a grating, a network of bronze; and on the net you shall make four bronze rings at its four corners. [5]You shall set it under the ledge of the altar so that the net shall extend halfway down the altar. [6]You shall make poles for the altar, poles of acacia wood, and overlay them with bronze; [7]the poles shall be put through the rings, so that the poles shall be on the two sides of the altar when it is carried. [8]You shall make it hollow, with boards. They shall be made just as you were shown on the mountain.

The Court and Its Hangings

9 You shall make the court of the tabernacle. On the south side the court shall have hangings of fine twisted linen one hundred cubits long for that side; [10]its twenty pillars and their twenty bases shall be of bronze, but the hooks of the pillars and their bands shall be of silver. [11]Likewise for its length on the north side there shall be hangings one hundred cubits long, their pillars twenty and their bases twenty, of bronze, but the hooks of the pillars and their bands shall be of silver. [12]For the width of the court on the west side there shall be fifty cubits of hangings, with ten pillars and ten bases. [13]The width of the court on the front to the east shall be fifty cubits. [14]There shall be fifteen cubits of hangings on the one side, with three pillars and three bases. [15]There shall be fifteen cubits of hangings on the other side, with three pillars and three bases. [16]For the gate of the court there shall be a screen twenty cubits long, of blue, purple, and crimson yarns, and of fine twisted linen, embroidered with needlework; it shall have four pillars and with them four bases. [17]All the pillars around the court shall be banded with silver; their hooks shall be of silver, and their bases of bronze. [18]The length of the court shall be one hundred cubits, the width fifty, and the height five cubits, with hangings of fine twisted linen and bases of bronze. [19]All the utensils of the tabernacle for every use, and all its pegs and all the pegs of the court, shall be of bronze.

The Oil for the Lamp

20 You shall further command the Israelites to bring you pure oil of beaten olives for the light, so that a lamp may be set up to burn regularly. [21]In the tent of meeting, outside the curtain that is before the covenant,[n] Aaron and his sons shall tend it from evening to morning before the Lord. It shall be a perpetual ordinance to be observed throughout their generations by the Israelites.

Vestments for the Priesthood

28 Then bring near to you your brother Aaron, and his sons with him, from among the Israelites, to serve me as priests—Aaron and Aaron's sons, Nadab and Abihu, Eleazar and Ithamar. [2]You shall make sacred vestments for the glorious adornment of your brother Aaron. [3]And you shall speak to all who have ability, whom I have endowed with skill, that they make Aaron's vestments to consecrate him for my priesthood. [4]These are the vestments that they shall make: a breastpiece, an ephod, a robe, a checkered tunic, a turban, and a sash. When they make these sacred vestments for your brother Aaron and his sons to serve me as priests, [5]they shall use gold, blue, purple, and crimson yarns, and fine linen.

The Ephod

6 They shall make the ephod of gold, of blue, purple, and crimson yarns, and of fine twisted linen, skillfully worked. [7]It shall have two shoulder-pieces attached to its two edges, so that it may be joined together. [8]The decorated band on it shall be of the same workmanship and materials, of gold, of blue, purple, and crimson yarns, and of fine twisted linen. [9]You shall take two onyx stones, and engrave on them the names of the sons of Israel, [10]six of their names on the one stone, and the names of the remaining six on the other stone, in the order of their birth. [11]As a gem-cutter engraves signets, so you shall

27.1 Ex 38.1; Ezek 43.13
27.3 Num 4.14
27.8 Ex 25.40; 26.30
27.9 Ex 38.9
27.10 Ex 38.17
27.14 Ex 38.15
27.16 Ex 36.37
27.20 Lev 24.2
27.21 Ex 26.31,33; 30.8; 28.43; Lev 3.17; 16.34
28.1 Num 18.7; Heb 5.1; 4
28.2 Ex 29.5,29; 31.10
28.3 Ex 31.3,6
28.4 see ver 15,6,31,39
28.6 Ex 39.2
28.9 1 Chr 29.2

[n] Or *treaty*, or *testimony*; Heb *eduth*

28.12 ver 29; Ex 39.7
28.15 Ex 39.8
28.17 Ex 39.10ff
28.21 Ex 39.14
28.24 Ex 39.17
28.26 Ex 39.17
28.29 ver 12
28.30 Lev 8.8; Num 27.21
28.31 Ex 39.22
28.36 Ex 39.30,31
28.38 ver 43; Lev 10.17; Num 18.1; Heb 9.28; 1 Pet 2.24
28.40 ver 4; Ex 39.27-29
28.41 Ex 29.7-9; 30.30; Lev 8; Heb 7.28
28.42 Ex 39.28
28.43 Ex 20.26; Lev 20.19,20; Ex 27.21; Lev 17.7

engrave the two stones with the names of
the sons of Israel; you shall mount them in
settings of gold filigree. 12You shall set the
two stones on the shoulder-pieces of the
ephod, as stones of remembrance for the
sons of Israel; and Aaron shall bear their
names before the LORD on his two shoulders
for remembrance. 13You shall make settings
of gold filigree, 14and two chains of pure
gold, twisted like cords; and you shall attach
the corded chains to the settings.

The Breastplate

15 You shall make a breastpiece of judgment, in skilled work; you shall make it in
the style of the ephod; of gold, of blue and
purple and crimson yarns, and of fine twisted
linen you shall make it. 16It shall be square
and doubled, a span in length and a span
in width. 17You shall set in it four rows of
stones. A row of carnelian,[o] chrysolite, and
emerald shall be the first row; 18and the
second row a turquoise, a sapphire[p] and a
moonstone; 19and the third row a jacinth,
an agate, and an amethyst; 20and the fourth
row a beryl, an onyx, and a jasper; they
shall be set in gold filigree. 21There shall be
twelve stones with names corresponding to
the names of the sons of Israel; they shall
be like signets, each engraved with its name,
for the twelve tribes. 22You shall make for
the breastpiece chains of pure gold, twisted
like cords; 23and you shall make for the
breastpiece two rings of gold, and put the
two rings on the two edges of the breastpiece.
24You shall put the two cords of gold in the
two rings at the edges of the breastpiece;
25the two ends of the two cords you shall
attach to the two settings, and so attach it
in front to the shoulder-pieces of the ephod.
26You shall make two rings of gold, and put
them at the two ends of the breastpiece, on
its inside edge next to the ephod. 27You shall
make two rings of gold, and attach them in
front to the lower part of the two shoulder-
pieces of the ephod, at its joining above the
decorated band of the ephod. 28The
breastpiece shall be bound by its rings to the
rings of the ephod with a blue cord, so that
it may lie on the decorated band of the
ephod, and so that the breastpiece shall not
come loose from the ephod. 29So Aaron
shall bear the names of the sons of Israel
in the breastpiece of judgment on his heart
when he goes into the holy place, for a
continual remembrance before the LORD. 30In
the breastpiece of judgment you shall put
the Urim and the Thummim, and they shall
be on Aaron's heart when he goes in before
the LORD; thus Aaron shall bear the judgment of the Israelites on his heart before the
LORD continually.

Other Priestly Vestments

31 You shall make the robe of the ephod
all of blue. 32It shall have an opening for the
head in the middle of it, with a woven
binding around the opening, like the opening in a coat of mail,[q] so that it may not
be torn. 33On its lower hem you shall make
pomegranates of blue, purple, and crimson
yarns, all around the lower hem, with bells
of gold between them all around—34a golden
bell and a pomegranate alternating all
around the lower hem of the robe. 35Aaron
shall wear it when he ministers, and its
sound shall be heard when he goes into the
holy place before the LORD, and when he
comes out, so that he may not die.
36 You shall make a rosette of pure gold,
and engrave on it, like the engraving of a
signet, "Holy to the LORD." 37You shall fasten it on the turban with a blue cord; it
shall be on the front of the turban. 38It shall
be on Aaron's forehead, and Aaron shall
take on himself any guilt incurred in the
holy offering that the Israelites consecrate
as their sacred donations; it shall always be
on his forehead, in order that they may find
favor before the LORD.
39 You shall make the checkered tunic
of fine linen, and you shall make a turban
of fine linen, and you shall make a sash
embroidered with needlework.
40 For Aaron's sons you shall make tunics
and sashes and headdresses; you shall make
them for their glorious adornment. 41You
shall put them on your brother Aaron, and
on his sons with him, and shall anoint
them and ordain them and consecrate them,
so that they may serve me as priests. 42You
shall make for them linen undergarments to
cover their naked flesh; they shall reach
from the hips to the thighs; 43Aaron and his
sons shall wear them when they go into the
tent of meeting, or when they come near
the altar to minister in the holy place; or
they will bring guilt on themselves and die.
This shall be a perpetual ordinance for him
and for his descendants after him.

[o] The identity of several of these stones is uncertain [p] Or *lapis lazuli* [q] Meaning of Heb uncertain

29.1-37 The ceremony of ordination of the priests lasts for *seven days*, and involves the sacrifice of *a young bull* and *two rams without blemish*. For the priests to lay their hands on the sacrificial animals is a sign of their offering of themselves completely to God's service in behalf of his people. The smoke of the sacrifices goes up to the LORD as *a pleasing odor*. Total commitment is further symbolized by the sprinkling of the priests with blood and *anointing oil*. That they *eat the food* which comes from the sacrificial ram is yet another symbol of participation in the common life of the covenant people.

The Ordination of the Priests

29 Now this is what you shall do to
them to consecrate them, so that
they may serve me as priests. Take one
young bull and two rams without blemish,
[2]and unleavened bread, unleavened cakes
mixed with oil, and unleavened wafers spread
with oil. You shall make them of choice
wheat flour. [3]You shall put them in one
basket and bring them in the basket, and
bring the bull and the two rams. [4]You shall
bring Aaron and his sons to the entrance
of the tent of meeting, and wash them with
water. [5]Then you shall take the vestments,
and put on Aaron the tunic and the robe
of the ephod, and the ephod, and the
breastpiece, and gird him with the decorated band of the ephod; [6]and you shall set
the turban on his head, and put the holy
diadem on the turban. [7]You shall take the
anointing oil, and pour it on his head and
anoint him. [8]Then you shall bring his sons,
and put tunics on them, [9]and you shall gird
them with sashes[r] and tie headdresses on
them; and the priesthood shall be theirs by
a perpetual ordinance. You shall then ordain Aaron and his sons.
10 You shall bring the bull in front of the
tent of meeting. Aaron and his sons shall
lay their hands on the head of the bull,
[11]and you shall slaughter the bull before the
LORD, at the entrance of the tent of meeting,
[12]and shall take some of the blood of the
bull and put it on the horns of the altar
with your finger, and all the rest of the
blood you shall pour out at the base of the
altar. [13]You shall take all the fat that covers
the entrails, and the appendage of the liver,
and the two kidneys with the fat that is on
them, and turn them into smoke on the
altar. [14]But the flesh of the bull, and its skin,
and its dung, you shall burn with fire outside
the camp; it is a sin offering.
15 Then you shall take one of the rams,
and Aaron and his sons shall lay their
hands on the head of the ram, [16]and you
shall slaughter the ram, and shall take its
blood and dash it against all sides of the
altar. [17]Then you shall cut the ram into its
parts, and wash its entrails and its legs, and
put them with its parts and its head, [18]and
turn the whole ram into smoke on the altar;
it is a burnt offering to the LORD; it is a
pleasing odor, an offering by fire to the
LORD.
19 You shall take the other ram; and
Aaron and his sons shall lay their hands on
the head of the ram, [20]and you shall slaughter the ram, and take some of its blood and
put it on the lobe of Aaron's right ear and
on the lobes of the right ears of his sons,
and on the thumbs of their right hands, and
on the big toes of their right feet, and dash
the rest of the blood against all sides of the
altar. [21]Then you shall take some of the
blood that is on the altar, and some of the
anointing oil, and sprinkle it on Aaron and
his vestments and on his sons and his sons'
vestments with him; then he and his vestments shall be holy, as well as his sons and
his sons' vestments.
22 You shall also take the fat of the ram,
the fat tail, the fat that covers the entrails,
the appendage of the liver, the two kidneys
with the fat that is on them, and the right
thigh (for it is a ram of ordination), [23]and
one loaf of bread, one cake of bread made
with oil, and one wafer, out of the basket
of unleavened bread that is before the LORD;
[24]and you shall place all these on the palms
of Aaron and on the palms of his sons, and
raise them as an elevation offering before
the LORD. [25]Then you shall take them from
their hands, and turn them into smoke on
the altar on top of the burnt offering of
pleasing odor before the LORD; it is an offering by fire to the LORD.
26 You shall take the breast of the ram
of Aaron's ordination and raise it as an
elevation offering before the LORD; and it
shall be your portion. [27]You shall consecrate the breast that was raised as an elevation offering and the thigh that was raised
as an elevation offering from the ram of
ordination, from that which belonged to
Aaron and his sons. [28]These things shall be
a perpetual ordinance for Aaron and his
sons from the Israelites, for this is an offering; and it shall be an offering by the
Israelites from their sacrifice of offerings of
well-being, their offering to the LORD.
29 The sacred vestments of Aaron shall
be passed on to his sons after him; they
shall be anointed in them and ordained in
them. [30]The son who is priest in his place
shall wear them seven days, when he comes
into the tent of meeting to minister in the
holy place.
31 You shall take the ram of ordination,
and boil its flesh in a holy place; [32]and
Aaron and his sons shall eat the flesh of the
ram and the bread that is in the basket, at

[r] Gk: Heb *sashes, Aaron and his sons*

29.1 Lev 8.2
29.2 Lev 6.19-23
29.4 Ex 40.12; Heb 10.22
29.5 Ex 28.2,8
29.6 Lev 8.9
29.7 Lev 8.12
29.8 Lev 8.13
29.9 Num 18.7; Ex 28.41
29.10 Lev 1.4; 8.14
29.12 Lev 8.15; Ex 27.2
29.13 Lev 3.3
29.14 Lev 4.11,12,21
29.15 Lev 8.18; 1.4-9
29.18 Gen 8.21
29.21 Ex 30.25,31; ver 1; Heb 9.22
29.23 Lev 8.26
29.24 Lev 7.30
29.25 Lev 8.28
29.26 Lev 8.29
29.27 Lev 7.31,34; Deut 18.3
29.28 Lev 10.15
29.29 Num 20.26,28; 18.8
29.30 Num 20.28; Lev 8.35; 9.1,8
29.31 Lev 8.31
29.32 Mt 12.4

the entrance of the tent of meeting. 33They themselves shall eat the food by which atonement is made, to ordain and consecrate them, but no one else shall eat of them, because they are holy. 34If any of the flesh for the ordination, or of the bread, remains until the morning, then you shall burn the remainder with fire; it shall not be eaten, because it is holy.

35 Thus you shall do to Aaron and to his sons, just as I have commanded you; through seven days you shall ordain them. 36Also every day you shall offer a bull as a sin offering for atonement. Also you shall offer a sin offering for the altar, when you make atonement for it, and shall anoint it, to consecrate it. 37Seven days you shall make atonement for the altar, and consecrate it, and the altar shall be most holy; whatever touches the altar shall become holy.

The Daily Offerings

38 Now this is what you shall offer on the altar: two lambs a year old regularly each day. 39One lamb you shall offer in the morning, and the other lamb you shall offer in the evening; 40and with the first lamb one-tenth of a measure of choice flour mixed with one-fourth of a hin of beaten oil, and one-fourth of a hin of wine for a drink offering. 41And the other lamb you shall offer in the evening, and shall offer with it a grain offering and its drink offering, as in the morning, for a pleasing odor, an offering by fire to the LORD. 42It shall be a regular burnt offering throughout your generations at the entrance of the tent of meeting before the LORD, where I will meet with you, to speak to you there. 43I will meet with the Israelites there, and it shall be sanctified by my glory; 44I will consecrate the tent of meeting and the altar; Aaron also and his sons I will consecrate, to serve me as priests. 45I will dwell among the Israelites, and I will be their God. 46And they shall know that I am the LORD their God, who brought them out of the land of Egypt that I might dwell among them; I am the LORD their God.

The Altar of Incense

30 You shall make an altar on which to offer incense; you shall make it of acacia wood. 2It shall be one cubit long, and one cubit wide; it shall be square, and shall be two cubits high; its horns shall be of one piece with it. 3You shall overlay it with pure gold, its top, and its sides all around and its horns; and you shall make for it a molding of gold all around. 4And you shall make two golden rings for it; under its molding on two opposite sides of it you shall make them, and they shall hold the poles with which to carry it. 5You shall make the poles of acacia wood, and overlay them with gold. 6You shall place it in front of the curtain that is above the ark of the covenant,[s] in front of the mercy seat[t] that is over the covenant,[s] where I will meet with you. 7Aaron shall offer fragrant incense on it; every morning when he dresses the lamps he shall offer it, 8and when Aaron sets up the lamps in the evening, he shall offer it, a regular incense offering before the LORD throughout your generations. 9You shall not offer unholy incense on it, or a burnt offering, or a grain offering; and you shall not pour a drink offering on it. 10Once a year Aaron shall perform the rite of atonement on its horns. Throughout your generations he shall perform the atonement for it once a year with the blood of the atoning sin offering. It is most holy to the LORD.

The Half Shekel for the Sanctuary

11 The LORD spoke to Moses: 12When you take a census of the Israelites to register them, at registration all of them shall give a ransom for their lives to the LORD, so that no plague may come upon them for being registered. 13This is what each one who is registered shall give: half a shekel according to the shekel of the sanctuary (the shekel is twenty gerahs), half a shekel as an offering to the LORD. 14Each one who is registered, from twenty years old and upward, shall give the LORD's offering. 15The rich shall not give more, and the poor shall not give less, than the half shekel, when you bring this offering to the LORD to make atonement for your lives. 16You shall take the atonement money from the Israelites and shall designate it for the service of the tent of meeting; before the LORD it will be a reminder to the Israelites of the ransom given for your lives.

The Bronze Basin

17 The LORD spoke to Moses: 18You shall make a bronze basin with a bronze stand

[s] Or *treaty*, or *testimony*; Heb *eduth* [t] Or *the cover*

29.33 Lev 10.14,15,17; 22.10
29.34 Lev 8.32
29.35 Lev 8.33
29.36 Heb 10.11; Ex 40.10
29.37 Ex 40.10; Mt 23.19
29.38 Num 28.3
29.42 Ex 30.8
29.43 1 Kings 8.11
29.44 Lev 21.15
29.45 Ex 25.8; Lev 26.12; Rev 21.3
29.46 Ex 20.2
30.1 Ex 37.25
30.6 Ex 25.21,22
30.7 ver 34,35; Ex 27.21
30.9 Lev 10.1
30.10 Lev 16.18
30.12 Num 1.2,5; 31.50; Mt 20.28; 2 Sam 24.15
30.13 Mt 17.24
30.15 Prov 22.2
30.16 Ex 38.25; Num 16.40

29.38-46 The continuing expression of the special relationship of Israel to the LORD is given by the daily offering of *two lambs* at the altar. Through this ongoing practice are guaranteed the enduring presence of God with his people and their knowledge of his work in establishing and guiding them.
30.1-10 The altar of incense appears to be a later addition, since it is not mentioned in the earlier detailed descriptions of the tent and its equipment. The incense symbolizes the continuing presence of the people before God through prayers. The altar is to be purified annually through an atoning sacrifice.
30.11-16 As a means of conducting a census and assuring that all Israelites give monetary support for the sanctuary, everyone over the age of 20 is to pay a half-shekel into the treasury annually, as a form of atoning sacrifice.
30.17-38 Preparing the Priests to Serve in the Tent. For Aaron and his sons to *wash with water* in *a bronze basin*, both *hands and feet*, is essential to guarantee their purity whenever they enter the sanctuary. The exceedingly costly ingredients of the *sacred anointing oil* and the *incense* reflect a later epoch in Israel's history than the wilderness journey. The oil is essential for consecrating the sacred vessels as well as the priests who use them, and anyone who uses them for secular purposes will be expelled from the covenant community: *cut off from the people*. Similarly, the incense is to be used to honor the LORD alone, and not *as perfume*.

31.1-11 The Divinely Endowed Artisans who Construct the Tent and its Furnishings. Bezalel and Oholiab are *filled with divine spirit*, or with the Spirit of God, which provides them with the intelligence and skills to carry out the demanding tasks of preparing the sanctuary and the garments to be worn by the priests.
31.12-17 The Sabbath laws are given in a somewhat briefer form than the priestly version in 16.22-30. Here God's rest on the seventh day of creation is noted.

for washing. You shall put it between the tent of meeting and the altar, and you shall put water in it; [19]with the water[u] Aaron and his sons shall wash their hands and their feet. [20]When they go into the tent of meeting, or when they come near the altar to minister, to make an offering by fire to the LORD, they shall wash with water, so that they may not die. [21]They shall wash their hands and their feet, so that they may not die: it shall be a perpetual ordinance for them, for him and for his descendants throughout their generations.

The Anointing Oil and Incense

22 The LORD spoke to Moses: [23]Take the finest spices: of liquid myrrh five hundred shekels, and of sweet-smelling cinnamon half as much, that is, two hundred fifty, and two hundred fifty of aromatic cane, [24]and five hundred of cassia—measured by the sanctuary shekel—and a hin of olive oil; [25]and you shall make of these a sacred anointing oil blended as by the perfumer; it shall be a holy anointing oil. [26]With it you shall anoint the tent of meeting and the ark of the covenant,[v] [27]and the table and all its utensils, and the lampstand and its utensils, and the altar of incense, [28]and the altar of burnt offering with all its utensils, and the basin with its stand; [29]you shall consecrate them, so that they may be most holy; whatever touches them will become holy. [30]You shall anoint Aaron and his sons, and consecrate them, in order that they may serve me as priests. [31]You shall say to the Israelites, "This shall be my holy anointing oil throughout your generations. [32]It shall not be used in any ordinary anointing of the body, and you shall make no other like it in composition; it is holy, and it shall be holy to you. [33]Whoever compounds any like it or whoever puts any of it on an unqualified person shall be cut off from the people."

34 The LORD said to Moses: Take sweet spices, stacte, and onycha, and galbanum, sweet spices with pure frankincense (an equal part of each), [35]and make an incense blended as by the perfumer, seasoned with salt, pure and holy; [36]and you shall beat some of it into powder, and put part of it before the covenant[v] in the tent of meeting where I shall meet with you; it shall be for you most holy. [37]When you make incense according to this composition, you shall not make it for yourselves; it shall be regarded by you as holy to the LORD. [38]Whoever makes any like it to use as perfume shall be cut off from the people.

Bezalel and Oholiab

31 The LORD spoke to Moses: [2]See, I have called by name Bezalel son of Uri son of Hur, of the tribe of Judah: [3]and I have filled him with divine spirit,[w] with ability, intelligence, and knowledge in every kind of craft, [4]to devise artistic designs, to work in gold, silver, and bronze, [5]in cutting stones for setting, and in carving wood, in every kind of craft. [6]Moreover, I have appointed with him Oholiab son of Ahisamach, of the tribe of Dan; and I have given skill to all the skillful, so that they may make all that I have commanded you: [7]the tent of meeting, and the ark of the covenant,[v] and the mercy seat[x] that is on it, and all the furnishings of the tent, [8]the table and its utensils, and the pure lampstand with all its utensils, and the altar of incense, [9]and the altar of burnt offering with all its utensils, and the basin with its stand, [10]and the finely worked vestments, the holy vestments for the priest Aaron and the vestments of his sons, for their service as priests, [11]and the anointing oil and the fragrant incense for the holy place. They shall do just as I have commanded you.

The Sabbath Law

12 The LORD said to Moses: [13]You yourself are to speak to the Israelites: "You shall keep my sabbaths, for this is a sign between me and you throughout your generations, given in order that you may know that I, the LORD, sanctify you. [14]You shall keep the sabbath, because it is holy for you; everyone who profanes it shall be put to death; whoever does any work on it shall be cut off from among the people. [15]Six days shall work be done, but the seventh day is a sabbath of solemn rest, holy to the LORD; whoever does any work on the sabbath day shall be put to death. [16]Therefore the Israelites shall keep the sabbath, observing the sabbath throughout their generations, as a perpetual covenant. [17]It is a sign forever between me and the people of Israel that in six days the LORD made heaven and earth, and on the seventh day he rested, and was refreshed."

[u] Heb *it* [v] Or *treaty*, or *testimony*; Heb *eduth* [w] Or *with the spirit of God* [x] Or *the cover*

30.18 Ex 38.8; 40.7,30
30.19 Ex 40.31,32
30.21 Ex 28.43
30.25 Ex 37.29; 40.9
30.26 Lev 8.10
30.29 Ex 29.37
30.30 Lev 8.12,30
30.32 ver 25,37
30.33 ver 38; Ex 12.15
30.35 ver 25
30.36 Ex 29.42; Lev 16.2; ver 32; Ex 29.37; Lev 2.3
31.2 Ex 35.30-36.1
31.6 Ex 35.34
31.7 Ex 36.8; 37.1,6
31.8 Ex 37.10,17
31.11 Ex 30.25,31; 37.29; 30.34
31.13 Lev 19.3,30; Ezek 20.12,20
31.14 Ex 35.2; Num 15.32,35
31.15 Ex 16.23; 20.9,10
31.17 ver 13; Gen 2.2,3

The Two Tablets of the Covenant

18 When God[y] finished speaking with Moses on Mount Sinai, he gave him the two tablets of the covenant,[z] tablets of stone, written with the finger of God.

The Golden Calf

32 When the people saw that Moses delayed to come down from the mountain, the people gathered around Aaron, and said to him, "Come, make gods for us, who shall go before us; as for this Moses, the man who brought us up out of the land of Egypt, we do not know what has become of him." [2]Aaron said to them, "Take off the gold rings that are on the ears of your wives, your sons, and your daughters, and bring them to me." [3]So all the people took off the gold rings from their ears, and brought them to Aaron. [4]He took the gold from them, formed it in a mold,[a] and cast an image of a calf; and they said, "These are your gods, O Israel, who brought you up out of the land of Egypt!" [5]When Aaron saw this, he built an altar before it; and Aaron made proclamation and said, "Tomorrow shall be a festival to the LORD." [6]They rose early the next day, and offered burnt offerings and brought sacrifices of well-being; and the people sat down to eat and drink, and rose up to revel.

7 The LORD said to Moses, "Go down at once! Your people, whom you brought up out of the land of Egypt, have acted perversely; [8]they have been quick to turn aside from the way that I commanded them; they have cast for themselves an image of a calf, and have worshiped it and sacrificed to it, and said, 'These are your gods, O Israel, who brought you up out of the land of Egypt!' " [9]The LORD said to Moses, "I have seen this people, how stiff-necked they are. [10]Now let me alone, so that my wrath may burn hot against them and I may consume them; and of you I will make a great nation."

11 But Moses implored the LORD his God, and said, "O LORD, why does your wrath burn hot against your people, whom you brought out of the land of Egypt with great power and with a mighty hand? [12]Why should the Egyptians say, 'It was with evil intent that he brought them out to kill them in the mountains, and to consume them from the face of the earth'? Turn from your fierce wrath; change your mind and do not bring disaster on your people. [13]Remember Abraham, Isaac, and Israel, your servants, how you swore to them by your own self, saying to them, 'I will multiply your descendants like the stars of heaven, and all this land that I have promised I will give to your descendants, and they shall inherit it forever.' " [14]And the LORD changed his mind about the disaster that he planned to bring on his people.

15 Then Moses turned and went down from the mountain, carrying the two tablets of the covenant[b] in his hands, tablets that were written on both sides, written on the front and on the back. [16]The tablets were the work of God, and the writing was the writing of God, engraved upon the tablets. [17]When Joshua heard the noise of the people as they shouted, he said to Moses, "There is a noise of war in the camp." [18]But he said,

"It is not the sound made by victors,
or the sound made by losers;
it is the sound of revelers that I hear."

[19]As soon as he came near the camp and saw the calf and the dancing, Moses' anger burned hot, and he threw the tablets from his hands and broke them at the foot of the mountain. [20]He took the calf that they had made, burned it with fire, ground it to powder, scattered it on the water, and made the Israelites drink it.

21 Moses said to Aaron, "What did this people do to you that you have brought so great a sin upon them?" [22]And Aaron said, "Do not let the anger of my lord burn hot; you know the people, that they are bent on evil. [23]They said to me, 'Make us gods, who shall go before us; as for this Moses, the man who brought us up out of the land of Egypt, we do not know what has become of him.' [24]So I said to them, 'Whoever has gold, take it off'; so they gave it to me, and I threw it into the fire, and out came this calf!"

25 When Moses saw that the people were running wild (for Aaron had let them run wild, to the derision of their enemies), [26]then Moses stood in the gate of the camp, and said, "Who is on the LORD's side? Come to me!" And all the sons of Levi gathered around him. [27]He said to them, "Thus says the LORD, the God of Israel, 'Put your sword on your side, each of you! Go back and forth from gate to gate throughout the

[y] Heb *he* [z] Or *treaty*, or *testimony*; Heb *eduth* [a] Or *fashioned it with a graving tool*; Meaning of Heb uncertain

31.18 Ex 24.12; 32.15,16; 34.1,28
32.1 Ex 24.18; Deut 9.9; Acts 7.40; Ex 13.21
32.2 Ex 35.22
32.4 Deut 9.16; Acts 7.41
32.6 1 Cor 10.7
32.7 Deut 9.12; Dan 9.24; Gen 6.11,12
32.8 Ex 20.3,4,23; 1 Kings 12.28
32.9 Num 14.11-20; Ex 33.3,5; 34.9; Acts 7.31
32.10 Deut 9.14; Num 14.12
32.11 Deut 9.18
32.12 Num 14.13; Deut 9.28; ver 14
32.13 Gen 22.16; Heb 6.13; Gen 12.7; 13.15; Ex 13.5
32.14 Ps 106.45
32.15 Deut 9.15
32.16 Ex 31.18
32.19 Deut 9.16,17
32.20 Deut 9.21
32.21 Gen 26.10
32.22 Deut 9.24
32.23 ver 1
32.24 ver 4
32.27 Num 25.7-13

31.18, with its mention of *the two tablets of the covenant*, prepares for resumption of the narrative. The writing on these stone slabs is by *the finger of God*, to which the magicians attributed the plagues in Egypt (8.19).
32.1-35 The Israelites Lapse into Idolatry. The *image of a calf*, which Aaron makes for the people during Moses' absence on the holy mountain, resembles the fertility gods worshiped by the Canaanites in the region. To the calf the people give credit for their having escaped from slavery in *the land of Egypt* and so they erect an altar to worship this deity. God is ready to destroy them, but Moses talks him out of it (32.11-14). On his return, when Moses finds the people engaged in some kind of pagan revelry, he smashes the stone tablets and calls Aaron to account. Aaron's excuse is that when he threw the people's gold into the fire, the calf image emerged spontaneously. Moses has two remedies: the milder one is to force the people to drink water mixed with ground gold, but the second requires the Levites to slaughter 3000 of the people in a single day (32.26-29). God's final mode of punishment is to send *a plague on the people*. When Moses asks God to forgive them, and is instructed to lead them *to the place about which I have spoken*, he is warned that they will still undergo *punishment...for their sin*, which was brought about by Aaron. God's threat to blot out of the book the names of the sinners is a reference to the belief that God keeps an official list of his people (Ps 69.28; Dan 12.1; Mal 3.16). This theme occurs frequently in Revelation (for example, 3.5; 13.8; 21.27).

camp, and each of you kill your brother,
your friend, and your neighbor.' " [28]The
sons of Levi did as Moses commanded, and
about three thousand of the people fell on
that day. [29]Moses said, "Today you have
ordained yourselves[b] for the service of the
LORD, each one at the cost of a son or a
brother, and so have brought a blessing on
yourselves this day."
30 On the next day Moses said to the
people, "You have sinned a great sin. But
now I will go up to the LORD; perhaps I can
make atonement for your sin." [31]So Moses
returned to the LORD and said, "Alas, this
people has sinned a great sin; they have
made for themselves gods of gold. [32]But
now, if you will only forgive their sin—but
if not, blot me out of the book that you have
written." [33]But the LORD said to Moses,
"Whoever has sinned against me I will blot
out of my book. [34]But now go, lead the
people to the place about which I have
spoken to you; see, my angel shall go in
front of you. Nevertheless, when the day
comes for punishment, I will punish them
for their sin."
35 Then the LORD sent a plague on the
people, because they made the calf—the
one that Aaron made.

The Command to Leave Sinai

33 The LORD said to Moses, "Go, leave
this place, you and the people
whom you have brought up out of the land
of Egypt, and go to the land of which I
swore to Abraham, Isaac, and Jacob, saying, 'To your descendants I will give it.' [2]I
will send an angel before you, and I will
drive out the Canaanites, the Amorites, the
Hittites, the Perizzites, the Hivites, and the
Jebusites. [3]Go up to a land flowing with
milk and honey; but I will not go up among
you, or I would consume you on the way,
for you are a stiff-necked people."
4 When the people heard these harsh
words, they mourned, and no one put on
ornaments. [5]For the LORD had said to Moses,
"Say to the Israelites, 'You are a stiff-necked
people; if for a single moment I should go
up among you, I would consume you. So
now take off your ornaments, and I will
decide what to do to you.' " [6]Therefore the
Israelites stripped themselves of their ornaments, from Mount Horeb onward.

The Tent outside the Camp

7 Now Moses used to take the tent and
pitch it outside the camp, far off from the
camp; he called it the tent of meeting. And
everyone who sought the LORD would go
out to the tent of meeting, which was
outside the camp. [8]Whenever Moses went
out to the tent, all the people would rise and
stand, each of them, at the entrance of their
tents and watch Moses until he had gone
into the tent. [9]When Moses entered the
tent, the pillar of cloud would descend and
stand at the entrance of the tent, and the
LORD would speak with Moses. [10]When all
the people saw the pillar of cloud standing
at the entrance of the tent, all the people
would rise and bow down, all of them, at
the entrance of their tent. [11]Thus the LORD
used to speak to Moses face to face, as one
speaks to a friend. Then he would return to
the camp; but his young assistant, Joshua
son of Nun, would not leave the tent.

Moses' Intercession

12 Moses said to the LORD, "See, you
have said to me, 'Bring up this people'; but
you have not let me know whom you will
send with me. Yet you have said, 'I know
you by name, and you have also found
favor in my sight.' [13]Now if I have found
favor in your sight, show me your ways, so
that I may know you and find favor in your
sight. Consider too that this nation is your
people." [14]He said, "My presence will go
with you, and I will give you rest." [15]And
he said to him, "If your presence will not
go, do not carry us up from here. [16]For how
shall it be known that I have found favor
in your sight, I and your people, unless you
go with us? In this way, we shall be distinct,
I and your people, from every people on the
face of the earth."
17 The LORD said to Moses, "I will do the
very thing that you have asked; for you
have found favor in my sight, and I know
you by name." [18]Moses said, "Show me
your glory, I pray." [19]And he said, "I will
make all my goodness pass before you, and
will proclaim before you the name, 'The
LORD';[c] and I will be gracious to whom I will
be gracious, and will show mercy on whom
I will show mercy. [20]But," he said, "you
cannot see my face; for no one shall see me
and live." [21]And the LORD continued, "See,

[b] Gk Vg Compare Tg: Heb *Today ordain yourselves* [c] Heb *YHWH*; see note at 3.15

33.1-6 Preparations to Leave Sinai. The earlier promise that God would clear the land of its present inhabitants (23.23-33) is now about to be fulfilled: Israel is to leave the land where the covenant with God was confirmed. The LORD characterizes the people as *stiff-necked,* and orders them to rid themselves of all ornaments which might involve them in local idolatrous practices.
33.7-11 This description of *the tent of meeting* differs in detail from other accounts of the portable sanctuary: it is located *outside the camp,* instead of in the center of Israel's encampment, and Joshua instead of Aaron and his sons presides over the tent. The passage represents a separate tradition about the origins of Israel's worship center: in this one the LORD talks to Moses *face to face.* In the second set of descriptions of the sanctuary from this point on in Exodus, the word for tent (*ohel*) is replaced predominantly by the word for dwelling or tabernacle (*mishkan*).
33.12-23 Different from this is a tradition about Moses' encounter with God which appears in the following passage. As Moses earlier sought to learn Yahweh's name (3.13-15), so now he seeks to see his face, just as Jacob is reported to have done (Gen 32.30). Instead, he is allowed to see God's back as he passes *the cleft of the rock* in which God placed him. Yet another tradition about seeing God is given in 34.27-35.

32.30 1 Sam 12.20,23; 2 Sam 16.12; Num 25.13
32.31 Deut 9.18; Ex 20.23
32.32 Ps 69.28; Rom 9.3; Dan 12.1; Rev 3.5; 13.8; 17.8; 21.27
32.33 Deut 29.20; Ps 9.5
32.34 Ex 3.17; 23.20; Ps 99.8
32.35 ver 4,24,28
33.1 Ex 2.7,13; Gen 12.7
33.2 Ex 32.34; 23.27-31
33.3 Ex 3.8,17; 32.9,10
33.4 Num 14.1,39
33.7 Ex 29.42,43; Deut 4.29
33.8 Num 16.27
33.9 Ex 25.22; 31.18; Ps 99.7
33.11 Num 12.8; Deut 34.10; Ex 24.13
33.12 Ex 32.34; ver 17; Jer 1.5; Jn 10.14,15; 2 Tim 2.19
33.13 Ex 34.9; Ps 25.4; Deut 9.26,29
33.14 Isa 63.9; Josh 22.4
33.16 Num 14.14; Ex 34.10
33.17 ver 12
33.19 Rom 9.15,16,18
33.20 Gen 32.20; Isa 6.5

there is a place by me where you shall
stand on the rock; 22 and while my glory
passes by I will put you in a cleft of the
rock, and I will cover you with my hand
until I have passed by; 23 then I will take
away my hand, and you shall see my back;
but my face shall not be seen."

Moses Makes New Tablets

34 The LORD said to Moses, "Cut two
tablets of stone like the former
ones, and I will write on the tablets the
words that were on the former tablets, which
you broke. 2 Be ready in the morning, and
come up in the morning to Mount Sinai and
present yourself there to me, on the top of
the mountain. 3 No one shall come up with
you, and do not let anyone be seen throughout all the mountain; and do not let flocks
or herds graze in front of that mountain."
4 So Moses cut two tablets of stone like the
former ones; and he rose early in the morning
and went up on Mount Sinai, as the LORD
had commanded him, and took in his hand
the two tablets of stone. 5 The LORD descended in the cloud and stood with him
there, and proclaimed the name, "The LORD."[d]
6 The LORD passed before him, and proclaimed,

"The LORD, the LORD,
a God merciful and gracious,
slow to anger,
and abounding in steadfast love and faithfulness,
7 keeping steadfast love for the thousandth generation,[e]
forgiving iniquity and transgression and sin,
yet by no means clearing the guilty,
but visiting the iniquity of the parents
upon the children
and the children's children,
to the third and the fourth generation."

8 And Moses quickly bowed his head toward
the earth, and worshiped. 9 He said, "If now
I have found favor in your sight, O Lord, I
pray, let the Lord go with us. Although this
is a stiff-necked people, pardon our iniquity
and our sin, and take us for your inheritance."

The Covenant Renewed

10 He said: I hereby make a covenant.
Before all your people I will perform marvels, such as have not been performed in all
the earth or in any nation; and all the
people among whom you live shall see the
work of the LORD; for it is an awesome thing
that I will do with you.

11 Observe what I command you today.
See, I will drive out before you the Amorites,
the Canaanites, the Hittites, the Perizzites,
the Hivites, and the Jebusites. 12 Take care
not to make a covenant with the inhabitants of the land to which you are going, or
it will become a snare among you. 13 You
shall tear down their altars, break their
pillars, and cut down their sacred poles[f]
14 (for you shall worship no other god, because the LORD, whose name is Jealous, is
a jealous God). 15 You shall not make a
covenant with the inhabitants of the land,
for when they prostitute themselves to their
gods and sacrifice to their gods, someone
among them will invite you, and you will
eat of the sacrifice. 16 And you will take
wives from among their daughters for your
sons, and their daughters who prostitute
themselves to their gods will make your
sons also prostitute themselves to their gods.

17 You shall not make cast idols.

18 You shall keep the festival of
unleavened bread. Seven days you shall eat
unleavened bread, as I commanded you, at
the time appointed in the month of Abib; for
in the month of Abib you came out from
Egypt.

19 All that first opens the womb is mine,
all your male[g] livestock, the firstborn of cow
and sheep. 20 The firstborn of a donkey you
shall redeem with a lamb, or if you will not
redeem it you shall break its neck. All the
firstborn of your sons you shall redeem.

No one shall appear before me empty-
handed.

21 Six days you shall work, but on the
seventh day you shall rest; even in plowing
time and in harvest time you shall rest.
22 You shall observe the festival of weeks, the
first fruits of wheat harvest, and the festival
of ingathering at the turn of the year. 23 Three
times in the year all your males shall appear
before the LORD God, the God of Israel. 24 For
I will cast out nations before you, and
enlarge your borders; no one shall covet
your land when you go up to appear before
the LORD your God three times in the year.

25 You shall not offer the blood of my

[d] Heb *YHWH*; see note at 3.15 [e] Or *for thousands* [f] Heb *Asherim* [g] Gk Theodotion Vg Tg: Meaning of Heb uncertain

33.23 Jn 1.18
34.1 Ex 32.16,19; ver 28
34.2 Ex 19.20
34.3 Ex 19.12,13,21
34.5 Ex 33.19
34.6 Num 14.18; Neh 9.17; Ps 86.15; 103.8
34.7 Ex 20.6,7; Ps 103.3; Dan 9.9; Eph 4.32
34.8 Ex 4.31
34.9 Ex 33.3,15,16
34.10 Deut 5.2; 4.32
34.11 Deut 6.3; Ex 33.2
34.12 Ex 23.32,33
34.13 Ex 23.24; 2 Kings 18.4
34.14 Ex 20.3,5; Deut 4.24
34.15 Judg 2.17; Num 25.2; 1 Cor 8.4,7.10
34.16 Deut 7.3; Num 25.1
34.17 Ex 32.8
34.18 Ex 12.2,15-17; 13.4
34.19 Ex 13.2; 22.29
34.20 Ex 13.13; 23.15
34.21 Ex 20.9; Lk 13.14
34.22 Ex 23.16
34.23 Ex 23.14-17
34.25 Ex 23.18; 12.10

34.1-29 Renewal of the Covenant. The report of Moses' making new *tablets of stone* to replace those destroyed by him in his wrath serves the editor of Exodus as an opportunity to repeat another version of much of the law and covenant which occupies most of the rest of the book of Exodus. There is a return to Sinai, and God writes the law on the stones, and in hymnic form describes his mercy and fidelity to the covenant (vv.6-7). Moses renews his plea to God for pardon for the disobedient people. All the symbols and structures of Canaanite worship are to be destroyed when Israel enters the land, and there is to be no social or sexual intercourse with the pagan inhabitants. These solemn warnings are followed by a repetition of some of the basic laws: avoidance of idolatry; observance of the cycle of feasts, including those related to the fertility of crops and flocks; dedication of the firstborn and of *the first fruits* of the harvests to God; observance of the sabbath rest. The prohibition of boiling *a kid in its mother's milk* and the 40-day period of Moses' stay on Sinai are repeated from earlier accounts (*cf.* 23.19; 24.18) Once again God writes on the tablets *the words of the covenant.*

sacrifice with leaven, and the sacrifice of the festival of the passover shall not be left until the morning.

26 The best of the first fruits of your ground you shall bring to the house of the LORD your God.

You shall not boil a kid in its mother's milk.

27 The LORD said to Moses: Write these words; in accordance with these words I have made a covenant with you and with Israel. 28 He was there with the LORD forty days and forty nights; he neither ate bread nor drank water. And he wrote on the tablets the words of the covenant, the ten commandments.[h]

The Shining Face of Moses

29 Moses came down from Mount Sinai. As he came down from the mountain with the two tablets of the covenant[i] in his hand, Moses did not know that the skin of his face shone because he had been talking with God. 30 When Aaron and all the Israelites saw Moses, the skin of his face was shining, and they were afraid to come near him. 31 But Moses called to them; and Aaron and all the leaders of the congregation returned to him, and Moses spoke with them. 32 Afterward all the Israelites came near, and he gave them in commandment all that the LORD had spoken with him on Mount Sinai. 33 When Moses had finished speaking with them, he put a veil on his face; 34 but whenever Moses went in before the LORD to speak with him, he would take the veil off, until he came out; and when he came out, and told the Israelites what he had been commanded, 35 the Israelites would see the face of Moses, that the skin of his face was shining; and Moses would put the veil on his face again, until he went in to speak with him.

Sabbath Regulations

35 Moses assembled all the congregation of the Israelites and said to them: These are the things that the LORD has commanded you to do:

2 Six days shall work be done, but on the seventh day you shall have a holy sabbath of solemn rest to the LORD; whoever does any work on it shall be put to death. 3 You shall kindle no fire in all your dwellings on the sabbath day.

Preparations for Making the Tabernacle

4 Moses said to all the congregation of the Israelites: This is the thing that the LORD has commanded: 5 Take from among you an offering to the LORD; let whoever is of a generous heart bring the LORD's offering: gold, silver, and bronze; 6 blue, purple, and crimson yarns, and fine linen; goats' hair, 7 tanned rams' skins, and fine leather;[j] acacia wood, 8 oil for the light, spices for the anointing oil and for the fragrant incense, 9 and onyx stones and gems to be set in the ephod and the breastpiece.

10 All who are skillful among you shall come and make all that the LORD has commanded: the tabernacle, 11 its tent and its covering, its clasps and its frames, its bars, its pillars, and its bases; 12 the ark with its poles, the mercy seat,[k] and the curtain for the screen; 13 the table with its poles and all its utensils, and the bread of the Presence; 14 the lampstand also for the light, with its utensils and its lamps, and the oil for the light; 15 and the altar of incense, with its poles, and the anointing oil and the fragrant incense, and the screen for the entrance, the entrance of the tabernacle; 16 the altar of burnt offering, with its grating of bronze, its poles, and all its utensils, the basin with its stand; 17 the hangings of the court, its pillars and its bases, and the screen for the gate of the court; 18 the pegs of the tabernacle and the pegs of the court, and their cords; 19 the finely worked vestments for ministering in the holy place, the holy vestments for the priest Aaron, and the vestments of his sons, for their service as priests.

Offerings for the Tabernacle

20 Then all the congregation of the Israelites withdrew from the presence of Moses. 21 And they came, everyone whose heart was stirred, and everyone whose spirit was willing, and brought the LORD's offering to be used for the tent of meeting, and for all its service, and for the sacred vestments. 22 So they came, both men and women; all who were of a willing heart brought brooches and earrings and signet rings and pendants, all sorts of gold objects, everyone bringing an offering of gold to the LORD. 23 And everyone who possessed blue or purple or crimson yarn or fine linen or goats' hair or

34.29-35 On his descent from Sinai, and *whenever he went in before the LORD*, Moses' face was luminous with the radiant glory of Yahweh. This confirmed that what he told the people *had been commanded* by God, but he placed a *veil on his face* to avoid overwhelming his hearers with the reflected glory.
35.1-39.31 Repeated Instructions. This repetition of the sabbath law includes the unique prohibition against kindling a fire. More extensive instructions are given for preparing the portable sanctuary and for collecting contributions from the people (*cf.* 25.1-9). The commissioning of the artisans to erect the shrine parallels 31.1-11, as do the descriptions of the process of construction, with variations in detail: 36.8-38, Bezalel and Oholiab, the construction of the tabernacle (*cf.* 26.1-37); 37.1-9, making the ark of the covenant (*cf.* 25.10-22); 37.10-16, making the table for the bread of the Presence (*cf.* 25.23-30); 37.17-24, making the lampstand (cf.25.31-40); 37.25-28, making the altar of incense (*cf.* 30.1-10); 37.29, the anointing oil and the incense (*cf.* 30.22-38); 38.1-7, the altar of burnt offering (*cf.* 27.1-8); 38.8, the bronze basin (*cf.* 30.17-21); 38.9-20, the court of the tabernacle (*cf.* 27.9-19); 39.1-31, the vestments for the priesthood (*cf.* 28.1-43). 38.21-31, with its report of the value of the precious metals used and the census, reflects later developments of economic prosperity in Israel, and the specifics of leadership recounted here match those reported in Numbers 1-4, with Ithamar as head of the Levites, who are established as part of the priestly institution.

34.26 Ex 23.19
34.27 Ex 17.14; 24.4
34.28 Ex 24.18; 31.18; 34.1; Deut 4.13; 10.4
34.29 Ex 32.15; Mt 17.2; 2 Cor 3.7,13
34.32 Ex 24.3
34.33 2 Cor 3.13
34.34 2 Cor 3.16
35.1 Ex 34.32
35.2 Ex 31.15
35.3 Ex 16.23
35.4 Ex 25.1-9
35.10 Ex 31.6
35.11 Ex 26.1,2ff
35.13 Ex 25.23,30; Lev 24.5,6
35.15 Ex 30.1
35.19 Ex 31.10
35.21 Ex 25.2
35.23 1 Chr 29.8

[h] Heb *words* [i] Or *treaty*, or *testimony*; Heb *eduth* [j] Meaning of Heb uncertain [k] Or *the cover*

35.25 Ex 28.3
35.27 1 Chr 29.6; Ezra 2.68
35.28 Ex 30.23
35.29 ver 21
35.30 Ex 31.1-6
35.35 ver 31
36.1 Ex 25.8
36.2 Ex 35.21,26; 1 Chr 29.5
36.3 Ex 35.27
36.5 2 Chr 24.14; 31.6-10; 2 Cor 8.23
36.8 Ex 26.1-14
36.12 Ex 26.5
36.14 Ex 26.7
36.19 Ex 26.14
36.20 Ex 26.15-29

tanned rams' skins or fine leather,[l] brought them. [24]Everyone who could make an offering of silver or bronze brought it as the LORD's offering; and everyone who possessed acacia wood of any use in the work, brought it. [25]All the skillful women spun with their hands, and brought what they had spun in blue and purple and crimson yarns and fine linen; [26]all the women whose hearts moved them to use their skill spun the goats' hair. [27]And the leaders brought onyx stones and gems to be set in the ephod and the breastpiece, [28]and spices and oil for the light, and for the anointing oil, and for the fragrant incense. [29]All the Israelite men and women whose hearts made them willing to bring anything for the work that the LORD had commanded by Moses to be done, brought it as a freewill offering to the LORD.

Bezalel and Oholiab

30 Then Moses said to the Israelites: See, the LORD has called by name Bezalel son of Uri son of Hur, of the tribe of Judah; [31]he has filled him with divine spirit,[m] with skill, intelligence, and knowledge in every kind of craft, [32]to devise artistic designs, to work in gold, silver, and bronze, [33]in cutting stones for setting, and in carving wood, in every kind of craft. [34]And he has inspired him to teach, both him and Oholiab son of Ahisamach, of the tribe of Dan. [35]He has filled them with skill to do every kind of work done by an artisan or by a designer or by an embroiderer in blue, purple, and crimson yarns, and in fine linen, or by a weaver—by any sort of artisan or skilled designer.

36 Bezalel and Oholiab and every skillful one to whom the LORD has given skill and understanding to know how to do any work in the construction of the sanctuary shall work in accordance with all that the LORD has commanded.

2 Moses then called Bezalel and Oholiab and every skillful one to whom the LORD had given skill, everyone whose heart was stirred to come to do the work; [3]and they received from Moses all the freewill offerings that the Israelites had brought for doing the work on the sanctuary. They still kept bringing him freewill offerings every morning, [4]so that all the artisans who were doing every sort of task on the sanctuary came, each from the task being performed, [5]and said to Moses, "The people are bringing much more than enough for doing the work that the LORD has commanded us to do." [6]So Moses gave command, and word was proclaimed throughout the camp: "No man or woman is to make anything else as an offering for the sanctuary." So the people were restrained from bringing; [7]for what they had already brought was more than enough to do all the work.

Construction of the Tabernacle

8 All those with skill among the workers made the tabernacle with ten curtains; they were made of fine twisted linen, and blue, purple, and crimson yarns, with cherubim skillfully worked into them. [9]The length of each curtain was twenty-eight cubits, and the width of each curtain four cubits; all the curtains were of the same size.

10 He joined five curtains to one another, and the other five curtains he joined to one another. [11]He made loops of blue on the edge of the outermost curtain of the first set; likewise he made them on the edge of the outermost curtain of the second set; [12]he made fifty loops on the one curtain, and he made fifty loops on the edge of the curtain that was in the second set; the loops were opposite one another. [13]And he made fifty clasps of gold, and joined the curtains one to the other with clasps; so the tabernacle was one whole.

14 He also made curtains of goats' hair for a tent over the tabernacle; he made eleven curtains. [15]The length of each curtain was thirty cubits, and the width of each curtain four cubits; the eleven curtains were of the same size. [16]He joined five curtains by themselves, and six curtains by themselves. [17]He made fifty loops on the edge of the outermost curtain of the one set, and fifty loops on the edge of the other connecting curtain. [18]He made fifty clasps of bronze to join the tent together so that it might be one whole. [19]And he made for the tent a covering of tanned rams' skins and an outer covering of fine leather.[l]

20 Then he made the upright frames for the tabernacle of acacia wood. [21]Ten cubits was the length of a frame, and a cubit and a half the width of each frame. [22]Each frame had two pegs for fitting together; he did this for all the frames of the tabernacle. [23]The frames for the tabernacle he made in this

[l] Meaning of Heb uncertain [m] Or *the spirit of God*

way: twenty frames for the south side; 24and he made forty bases of silver under the twenty frames, two bases under the first frame for its two pegs, and two bases under the next frame for its two pegs. 25For the second side of the tabernacle, on the north side, he made twenty frames 26and their forty bases of silver, two bases under the first frame and two bases under the next frame. 27For the rear of the tabernacle westward he made six frames. 28He made two frames for corners of the tabernacle in the rear. 29They were separate beneath, but joined at the top, at the first ring; he made two of them in this way, for the two corners. 30There were eight frames with their bases of silver: sixteen bases, under every frame two bases.

31 He made bars of acacia wood, five for the frames of the one side of the tabernacle, 32and five bars for the frames of the other side of the tabernacle, and five bars for the frames of the tabernacle at the rear westward. 33He made the middle bar to pass through from end to end halfway up the frames. 34And he overlaid the frames with gold, and made rings of gold for them to hold the bars, and overlaid the bars with gold.

35 He made the curtain of blue, purple, and crimson yarns, and fine twisted linen, with cherubim skillfully worked into it. 36For it he made four pillars of acacia, and overlaid them with gold; their hooks were of gold, and he cast for them four bases of silver. 37He also made a screen for the entrance to the tent, of blue, purple, and crimson yarns, and fine twisted linen, embroidered with needlework; 38and its five pillars with their hooks. He overlaid their capitals and their bases with gold, but their five bases were of bronze.

Making the Ark of the Covenant

37 Bezalel made the ark of acacia wood; it was two and a half cubits long, a cubit and a half wide, and a cubit and a half high. 2He overlaid it with pure gold inside and outside, and made a molding of gold around it. 3He cast for it four rings of gold for its four feet, two rings on its one side and two rings on its other side. 4He made poles of acacia wood, and overlaid them with gold, 5and put the poles into the rings on the sides of the ark, to carry the ark. 6He made a mercy seat[n] of pure gold; two cubits and a half was its length, and a cubit and a half its width. 7He made two cherubim of hammered gold; at the two ends of the mercy seat[o] he made them, 8one cherub at the one end, and one cherub at the other end; of one piece with the mercy seat[o] he made the cherubim at its two ends. 9The cherubim spread out their wings above, overshadowing the mercy seat[o] with their wings. They faced one another; the faces of the cherubim were turned toward the mercy seat.[o]

Making the Table for the Bread of the Presence

10 He also made the table of acacia wood, two cubits long, one cubit wide, and a cubit and a half high. 11He overlaid it with pure gold, and made a molding of gold around it. 12He made around it a rim a handbreadth wide, and made a molding of gold around the rim. 13He cast for it four rings of gold, and fastened the rings to the four corners at its four legs. 14The rings that held the poles used for carrying the table were close to the rim. 15He made the poles of acacia wood to carry the table, and overlaid them with gold. 16And he made the vessels of pure gold that were to be on the table, its plates and dishes for incense, and its bowls and flagons with which to pour drink offerings.

Making the Lampstand

17 He also made the lampstand of pure gold. The base and the shaft of the lampstand were made of hammered work; its cups, its calyxes, and its petals were of one piece with it. 18There were six branches going out of its sides, three branches of the lampstand out of one side of it and three branches of the lampstand out of the other side of it; 19three cups shaped like almond blossoms, each with calyx and petals, on one branch, and three cups shaped like almond blossoms, each with calyx and petals, on the other branch—so for the six branches going out of the lampstand. 20On the lampstand itself there were four cups shaped like almond blossoms, each with its calyxes and petals. 21There was a calyx of one piece with it under the first pair of branches, a calyx of one piece with it under the next pair of

36.24 Ex 26.21
36.27 Ex 26.22
36.31 Ex 26.26
36.35 Ex 26.31-37
37.1 Ex 25.10-20
37.3 Ex 25.12
37.6 Ex 25.17
37.10 Ex 25.23-29
37.16 Ex 25.29
37.17 Ex 25.31-39
37.19 Ex 25.33
37.21 Ex 25.35

[n] Or *a cover* [o] Or *the cover*

37.25 Ex 30.1-5
37.29 Ex 30.23,34
38.1 Ex 27.1-8
38.8 Ex 30.18
38.9 Ex 27.9-19
38.11 Ex 27.11
38.14 Ex 27.14
38.18 Ex 27.16
38.21 Num 4.28,33
38.22 Ex 31.2,6
38.24 Ex 30.13

branches, and a calyx of one piece with it
under the last pair of branches. 22Their
calyxes and their branches were of one
piece with it, the whole of it one hammered
piece of pure gold. 23He made its seven
lamps and its snuffers and its trays of pure
gold. 24He made it and all its utensils of a
talent of pure gold.

Making the Altar of Incense

25 He made the altar of incense of acacia
wood, one cubit long, and one cubit wide;
it was square, and was two cubits high; its
horns were of one piece with it. 26He overlaid it with pure gold, its top, and its sides
all around, and its horns; and he made for
it a molding of gold all around, 27and made
two golden rings for it under its molding,
on two opposite sides of it, to hold the poles
with which to carry it. 28And he made the
poles of acacia wood, and overlaid them
with gold.

Making the Anointing Oil and the Incense

29 He made the holy anointing oil also,
and the pure fragrant incense, blended as
by the perfumer.

Making the Altar of Burnt Offering

38 He made the altar of burnt offering
also of acacia wood; it was five
cubits long, and five cubits wide; it was
square, and three cubits high. 2He made
horns for it on its four corners; its horns
were of one piece with it, and he overlaid
it with bronze. 3He made all the utensils of
the altar, the pots, the shovels, the basins,
the forks, and the firepans: all its utensils he
made of bronze. 4He made for the altar a
grating, a network of bronze, under its
ledge, extending halfway down. 5He cast
four rings on the four corners of the bronze
grating to hold the poles; 6he made the
poles of acacia wood, and overlaid them
with bronze. 7And he put the poles through
the rings on the sides of the altar, to carry
it with them; he made it hollow, with boards.

8 He made the basin of bronze with its
stand of bronze, from the mirrors of the
women who served at the entrance to the
tent of meeting.

Making the Court of the Tabernacle

9 He made the court; for the south side
the hangings of the court were of fine twisted
linen, one hundred cubits long; 10its twenty
pillars and their twenty bases were of bronze,
but the hooks of the pillars and their bands
were of silver. 11For the north side there
were hangings one hundred cubits long; its
twenty pillars and their twenty bases were
of bronze, but the hooks of the pillars and
their bands were of silver. 12For the west
side there were hangings fifty cubits long,
with ten pillars and ten bases; the hooks of
the pillars and their bands were of silver.
13And for the front to the east, fifty cubits.
14The hangings for one side of the gate were
fifteen cubits, with three pillars and three
bases. 15And so for the other side; on each
side of the gate of the court were hangings
of fifteen cubits, with three pillars and three
bases. 16All the hangings around the court
were of fine twisted linen. 17The bases for
the pillars were of bronze, but the hooks of
the pillars and their bands were of silver;
the overlaying of their capitals was also of
silver, and all the pillars of the court were
banded with silver. 18The screen for the
entrance to the court was embroidered with
needlework in blue, purple, and crimson
yarns and fine twisted linen. It was twenty
cubits long and, along the width of it, five
cubits high, corresponding to the hangings
of the court. 19There were four pillars; their
four bases were of bronze, their hooks of
silver, and the overlaying of their capitals
and their bands of silver. 20All the pegs for
the tabernacle and for the court all around
were of bronze.

Materials of the Tabernacle

21 These are the records of the tabernacle, the tabernacle of the covenant,[p] which
were drawn up at the commandment of
Moses, the work of the Levites being under
the direction of Ithamar son of the priest
Aaron. 22Bezalel son of Uri son of Hur, of
the tribe of Judah, made all that the LORD
commanded Moses; 23and with him was
Oholiab son of Ahisamach, of the tribe of
Dan, engraver, designer, and embroiderer in
blue, purple, and crimson yarns, and in fine
linen.

24 All the gold that was used for the

[p] Or *treaty*, or *testimony*; Heb *eduth*

work, in all the construction of the sanctuary, the gold from the offering, was twenty-
nine talents and seven hundred thirty
shekels, measured by the sanctuary shekel.
[25]The silver from those of the congregation
who were counted was one hundred talents
and one thousand seven hundred seventy-
five shekels, measured by the sanctuary
shekel; [26]a beka a head (that is, half a
shekel, measured by the sanctuary shekel),
for everyone who was counted in the
census, from twenty years old and upward,
for six hundred three thousand, five hundred fifty men. [27]The hundred talents of
silver were for casting the bases of the
sanctuary, and the bases of the curtain; one
hundred bases for the hundred talents, a
talent for a base. [28]Of the thousand seven
hundred seventy-five shekels he made hooks
for the pillars, and overlaid their capitals
and made bands for them. [29]The bronze
that was contributed was seventy talents,
and two thousand four hundred shekels;
[30]with it he made the bases for the entrance
of the tent of meeting, the bronze altar and
the bronze grating for it and all the utensils
of the altar, [31]the bases all around the court,
and the bases of the gate of the court, all
the pegs of the tabernacle, and all the pegs
around the court.

Making the Vestments for the Priesthood

39 Of the blue, purple, and crimson
yarns they made finely worked
vestments, for ministering in the holy place;
they made the sacred vestments for Aaron;
as the LORD had commanded Moses.

2 He made the ephod of gold, of blue,
purple, and crimson yarns, and of fine twisted
linen. [3]Gold leaf was hammered out and cut
into threads to work into the blue, purple,
and crimson yarns and into the fine twisted
linen, in skilled design. [4]They made for the
ephod shoulder-pieces, joined to it at its two
edges. [5]The decorated band on it was of the
same materials and workmanship, of gold,
of blue, purple, and crimson yarns, and of
fine twisted linen; as the LORD had commanded Moses.

6 The onyx stones were prepared, enclosed in settings of gold filigree and
engraved like the engravings of a signet,
according to the names of the sons of Israel.
[7]He set them on the shoulder-pieces of the
ephod, to be stones of remembrance for the
sons of Israel; as the LORD had commanded
Moses.

8 He made the breastpiece, in skilled work,
like the work of the ephod, of gold, of blue,
purple, and crimson yarns, and of fine twisted
linen. [9]It was square; the breastpiece was
made double, a span in length and a span
in width when doubled. [10]They set in it four
rows of stones. A row of carnelian,[q] chrysolite, and emerald was the first row; [11]and
the second row, a turquoise, a sapphire,[r]
and a moonstone; [12]and the third row, a
jacinth, an agate, and an amethyst; [13]and
the fourth row, a beryl, an onyx, and a
jasper; they were enclosed in settings of gold
filigree. [14]There were twelve stones with
names corresponding to the names of the
sons of Israel; they were like signets, each
engraved with its name, for the twelve
tribes. [15]They made on the breastpiece chains
of pure gold, twisted like cords; [16]and they
made two settings of gold filigree and two
gold rings, and put the two rings on the two
edges of the breastpiece; [17]and they put the
two cords of gold in the two rings at the
edges of the breastpiece. [18]Two ends of the
two cords they had attached to the two
settings of filigree; in this way they attached
it in front to the shoulder-pieces of the
ephod. [19]Then they made two rings of gold,
and put them at the two ends of the
breastpiece, on its inside edge next to the
ephod. [20]They made two rings of gold, and
attached them in front to the lower part of
the two shoulder-pieces of the ephod, at its
joining above the decorated band of the
ephod. [21]They bound the breastpiece by its
rings to the rings of the ephod with a blue
cord, so that it should lie on the decorated
band of the ephod, and that the breastpiece
should not come loose from the ephod; as
the LORD had commanded Moses.

22 He also made the robe of the ephod
woven all of blue yarn; [23]and the opening
of the robe in the middle of it was like the
opening in a coat of mail,[s] with a binding
around the opening, so that it might not be
torn. [24]On the lower hem of the robe they
made pomegranates of blue, purple, and
crimson yarns, and of fine twisted linen.
[25]They also made bells of pure gold, and put
the bells between the pomegranates on the
lower hem of the robe all around, between
the pomegranates; [26]a bell and a pomegranate, a bell and a pomegranate all around on
the lower hem of the robe for ministering;

38.25 Ex 30.11-16
38.26 Ex 30.13,15; Num 1.46
38.27 Ex 26.19,21,25, 32
39.1 Ex 35.23; 28.4
39.2 Ex 28.6-12
39.6 Ex 28.9
39.7 Ex 28.12
39.8 Ex 28.15-28
39.11 Ex 28.18
39.14 Ex 28.21
39.16 Ex 28.24
39.19 Ex 28.26
39.22 Ex 28.31-34

[q] The identification of several of these stones is uncertain [r] Or *lapis lazuli* [s] Meaning of Heb uncertain

39.27 Ex 28.39,40.42
39.30 Ex 28.36,37
39.32 ver 42,43; Ex 25.40
39.35 Ex 25.16; 30.6
39.41 Ex 26.33
39.43 Lev 9.22,23
40.2 Ex 12.2; 13.4; ver 17
40.3 ver 21-30
40.9 Ex 30.26
40.10 Ex 29.36,37
40.12 Lev 8.1-13
40.13 Ex 28.41
40.15 Num 25.13
40.20 Ex 25.16
40.21 Ex 26.33; 35.12
40.22 Ex 26.35
40.23 ver 4

as the LORD had commanded Moses.

27 They also made the tunics, woven of fine linen, for Aaron and his sons, [28]and the turban of fine linen, and the headdresses of fine linen, and the linen undergarments of fine twisted linen, [29]and the sash of fine twisted linen, and of blue, purple, and crimson yarns, embroidered with needlework; as the LORD had commanded Moses.

30 They made the rosette of the holy diadem of pure gold, and wrote on it an inscription, like the engraving of a signet, "Holy to the LORD." [31]They tied to it a blue cord, to fasten it on the turban above; as the LORD had commanded Moses.

The Work Completed

32 In this way all the work of the tabernacle of the tent of meeting was finished; the Israelites had done everything just as the LORD had commanded Moses. [33]Then they brought the tabernacle to Moses, the tent and all its utensils, its hooks, its frames, its bars, its pillars, and its bases; [34]the covering of tanned rams' skins and the covering of fine leather,[t] and the curtain for the screen; [35]the ark of the covenant[u] with its poles and the mercy seat;[v] [36]the table with all its utensils, and the bread of the Presence; [37]the pure lampstand with its lamps set on it and all its utensils, and the oil for the light; [38]the golden altar, the anointing oil and the fragrant incense, and the screen for the entrance of the tent; [39]the bronze altar, and its grating of bronze, its poles, and all its utensils; the basin with its stand; [40]the hangings of the court, its pillars, and its bases, and the screen for the gate of the court, its cords, and its pegs; and all the utensils for the service of the tabernacle, for the tent of meeting; [41]the finely worked vestments for ministering in the holy place, the sacred vestments for the priest Aaron, and the vestments of his sons to serve as priests. [42]The Israelites had done all of the work just as the LORD had commanded Moses. [43]When Moses saw that they had done all the work just as the LORD had commanded, he blessed them.

The Tabernacle Erected and Its Equipment Installed

40 The LORD spoke to Moses: [2]On the first day of the first month you shall set up the tabernacle of the tent of meeting. [3]You shall put in it the ark of the covenant,[u] and you shall screen the ark with the curtain. [4]You shall bring in the table, and arrange its setting; and you shall bring in the lampstand, and set up its lamps. [5]You shall put the golden altar for incense before the ark of the covenant,[u] and set up the screen for the entrance of the tabernacle. [6]You shall set the altar of burnt offering before the entrance of the tabernacle of the tent of meeting, [7]and place the basin between the tent of meeting and the altar, and put water in it. [8]You shall set up the court all around, and hang up the screen for the gate of the court. [9]Then you shall take the anointing oil, and anoint the tabernacle and all that is in it, and consecrate it and all its furniture, so that it shall become holy. [10]You shall also anoint the altar of burnt offering and all its utensils, and consecrate the altar, so that the altar shall be most holy. [11]You shall also anoint the basin with its stand, and consecrate it. [12]Then you shall bring Aaron and his sons to the entrance of the tent of meeting, and shall wash them with water, [13]and put on Aaron the sacred vestments, and you shall anoint him and consecrate him, so that he may serve me as priest. [14]You shall bring his sons also and put tunics on them, [15]and anoint them, as you anointed their father, that they may serve me as priests: and their anointing shall admit them to a perpetual priesthood throughout all generations to come.

16 Moses did everything just as the LORD had commanded him. [17]In the first month in the second year, on the first day of the month, the tabernacle was set up. [18]Moses set up the tabernacle; he laid its bases, and set up its frames, and put in its poles, and raised up its pillars; [19]and he spread the tent over the tabernacle, and put the covering of the tent over it; as the LORD had commanded Moses. [20]He took the covenant[u] and put it into the ark, and put the poles on the ark, and set the mercy seat[v] above the ark; [21]and he brought the ark into the tabernacle, and set up the curtain for screening, and screened the ark of the covenant;[u] as the LORD had commanded Moses. [22]He put the table in the tent of meeting, on the north side of the tabernacle, outside the curtain, [23]and set the bread in order on it before the LORD; as the LORD had commanded Moses. [24]He put the lampstand in the tent

39.32-40.38 The Sanctuary Completed: God Appears Within. **39.32-43** presents a list of all the items mentioned in the preparatory instructions: all are now on hand *just as the LORD had commanded.* **40.1-33** describes the process of erecting the sanctuary, which is here identified by a combination of the terms, *tent* and *tabernacle*, reflecting the combination of two originally distinct traditions: (1) the simple, portable *tent of meeting*, as in 33.7-11; (2) the elaborate tabernacle, which the post-exilic priestly tradition describes in terms of the temple as it was erected and functioned during the Israelite monarchy. Strange details result from this combination of traditions, such as the mention of the spreading of *the tent over the tabernacle* (vs. 19), or the placing of *the table in the tent of meeting, on the north side of the tabernacle* (vs.22), or the mention in 36.14 of *the tent over the tabernacle.* Yet orderly process of construction is emphasized here: Moses is the one who carries out the details of erecting and arranging the equipment in this account, *as the LORD had commanded.* The conclusion is appropriate: *So Moses finished the work.*

[t] Meaning of Heb uncertain [u] Or *treaty*, or *testimony*; Heb *eduth* [v] Or *the cover*

40.34-38 God's Presence in the Sanctuary. Here also the two traditions are evident, in that the radiant cloud giving proof of God's presence covered the tent of meeting, while the glory of the LORD filled the tabernacle. Inconvenient and awkward as it would actually have been to move from place to place such a complex structure, Exodus in its final edited form reports that it is this tabernacle which is to move with the Israelites as they start the journey from Sinai. It was there that the details of the covenant promises and responsibilities had been given them by God through Moses; it is from there that they set out for the land where the promises are to be fulfilled.

of meeting, opposite the table on the south side of the tabernacle, [25]and set up the lamps before the LORD; as the LORD had commanded Moses. [26]He put the golden altar in the tent of meeting before the curtain, [27]and offered fragrant incense on it; as the LORD had commanded Moses. [28]He also put in place the screen for the entrance of the tabernacle. [29]He set the altar of burnt offering at the entrance of the tabernacle of the tent of meeting, and offered on it the burnt offering and the grain offering as the LORD had commanded Moses. [30]He set the basin between the tent of meeting and the altar, and put water in it for washing, [31]with which Moses and Aaron and his sons washed their hands and their feet. [32]When they went into the tent of meeting, and when they approached the altar, they washed; as the LORD had commanded Moses. [33]He set up the court around the tabernacle and the altar, and put up the screen at the gate of the court. So Moses finished the work.

The Cloud and the Glory

34 Then the cloud covered the tent of meeting, and the glory of the LORD filled the tabernacle. [35]Moses was not able to enter the tent of meeting because the cloud settled upon it, and the glory of the LORD filled the tabernacle. [36]Whenever the cloud was taken up from the tabernacle, the Israelites would set out on each stage of their journey; [37]but if the cloud was not taken up, then they did not set out until the day that it was taken up. [38]For the cloud of the LORD was on the tabernacle by day, and fire was in the cloud[w] by night, before the eyes of all the house of Israel at each stage of their journey.

[w] Heb *it*

40.25 Ex 25.37
40.26 ver 5
40.28 Ex 26.36
40.30 ver 7
40.32 Ex 30.19,20
40.34 Num 9.15-23
40.36 Num 9.17; 10.11; Neh 9.19
40.38 Ex 13.21; Num 9.15

LEVITICUS

See the Introductions, pp. 2, 30, and 35 above.

1.1-2 Instructions concerning offerings to be presented in the sanctuary are divided into two major sections following this introduction: (1) 1.3-6.7 is a handbook for the people; (2) 6.8-7.38 is a handbook for the priests. Included are offerings of gratitude and those intended to provide expiation of sins and restoration of relationship with God and his people.
1.3-17 *The burnt offering* is an expression of thanks to God, symbolized by the fact that the smoke of the sacrifice ascends as a *pleasing odor to the LORD* (1.9,13, 17). The placing of hands on the *head of the burnt offering* indicates the self-identification of the sacrificer with the sacrifice (1.4). The economic status of those offering it is taken into account, since the sacrifice may be a sheep, a goat or birds (1.10-17). These kinds of offering likely arose among pastoral people.

The Burnt Offering

1 The LORD summoned Moses and spoke to him from the tent of meeting, saying: [2]Speak to the people of Israel and say to them: When any of you bring an offering of livestock to the LORD, you shall bring your offering from the herd or from the flock.

3 If the offering is a burnt offering from the herd, you shall offer a male without blemish; you shall bring it to the entrance of the tent of meeting, for acceptance in your behalf before the LORD. [4]You shall lay your hand on the head of the burnt offering, and it shall be acceptable in your behalf as atonement for you. [5]The bull shall be slaughtered before the LORD; and Aaron's sons the priests shall offer the blood, dashing the blood against all sides of the altar that is at the entrance of the tent of meeting. [6]The burnt offering shall be flayed and cut up into its parts. [7]The sons of the priest Aaron shall put fire on the altar and arrange wood on the fire. [8]Aaron's sons the priests shall arrange the parts, with the head and the suet, on the wood that is on the fire on the altar; [9]but its entrails and its legs shall be washed with water. Then the priest shall turn the whole into smoke on the altar as a burnt offering, an offering by fire of pleasing odor to the LORD.

10 If your gift for a burnt offering is from the flock, from the sheep or goats, your offering shall be a male without blemish. [11]It shall be slaughtered on the north side of the altar before the LORD, and Aaron's sons the priests shall dash its blood against all sides of the altar. [12]It shall be cut up into its parts, with its head and its suet, and the priest shall arrange them on the wood that is on the fire on the altar; [13]but the entrails and the legs shall be washed with water. Then the priest shall offer the whole and

1.1 Num 7.89
1.2 Lev 22.18,19
1.3 Deut 15.21; Heb 9.14; 1 Pet 1.19
1.4 Ex 29.10; Lev 9.7; Num 15.25
1.5 Ex 29.11; Heb 10.11; 12.24; 1 Pet 1.2
1.7 Lev 6.8-13
1.9 Num 15.8-10
1.11 ver 5

turn it into smoke on the altar; it is a burnt offering, an offering by fire of pleasing odor to the LORD.

14 If your offering to the LORD is a burnt offering of birds, you shall choose your offering from turtledoves or pigeons. [15]The priest shall bring it to the altar and wring off its head, and turn it into smoke on the altar; and its blood shall be drained out against the side of the altar. [16]He shall remove its crop with its contents[a] and throw it at the east side of the altar, in the place for ashes. [17]He shall tear it open by its wings without severing it. Then the priest shall turn it into smoke on the altar, on the wood that is on the fire; it is a burnt offering, an offering by fire of pleasing odor to the LORD.

Grain Offerings

2 When anyone presents a grain offering to the LORD, the offering shall be of choice flour; the worshiper shall pour oil on it, and put frankincense on it, [2]and bring it to Aaron's sons the priests. After taking from it a handful of the choice flour and oil, with all its frankincense, the priest shall turn this token portion into smoke on the altar, an offering by fire of pleasing odor to the LORD. [3]And what is left of the grain offering shall be for Aaron and his sons, a most holy part of the offerings by fire to the LORD.

4 When you present a grain offering baked in the oven, it shall be of choice flour: unleavened cakes mixed with oil, or unleavened wafers spread with oil. [5]If your offering is grain prepared on a griddle, it shall be of choice flour mixed with oil, unleavened; [6]break it in pieces, and pour oil on it; it is a grain offering. [7]If your offering is grain prepared in a pan, it shall be made of choice flour in oil. [8]You shall bring to the LORD the grain offering that is prepared in any of these ways; and when it is presented to the priest, he shall take it to the altar. [9]The priest shall remove from the grain offering its token portion and turn this into smoke on the altar, an offering by fire of pleasing odor to the LORD. [10]And what is left of the grain offering shall be for Aaron and his sons; it is a most holy part of the offerings by fire to the LORD.

11 No grain offering that you bring to the LORD shall be made with leaven, for you must not turn any leaven or honey into smoke as an offering by fire to the LORD. [12]You may bring them to the LORD as an offering of choice products, but they shall not be offered on the altar for a pleasing odor. [13]You shall not omit from your grain offerings the salt of the covenant with your God; with all your offerings you shall offer salt.

14 If you bring a grain offering of first fruits to the LORD, you shall bring as the grain offering of your first fruits coarse new grain from fresh ears, parched with fire. [15]You shall add oil to it and lay frankincense on it; it is a grain offering. [16]And the priest shall turn a token portion of it into smoke—some of the coarse grain and oil with all its frankincense; it is an offering by fire to the LORD.

Offerings of Well-Being

3 If the offering is a sacrifice of well-being, if you offer an animal of the herd, whether male or female, you shall offer one without blemish before the LORD. [2]You shall lay your hand on the head of the offering and slaughter it at the entrance of the tent of meeting; and Aaron's sons the priests shall dash the blood against all sides of the altar. [3]You shall offer from the sacrifice of well-being, as an offering by fire to the LORD, the fat that covers the entrails and all the fat that is around the entrails; [4]the two kidneys with the fat that is on them at the loins, and the appendage of the liver, which he shall remove with the kidneys. [5]Then Aaron's sons shall turn these into smoke on the altar, with the burnt offering that is on the wood on the fire, as an offering by fire of pleasing odor to the LORD.

6 If your offering for a sacrifice of well-being to the LORD is from the flock, male or female, you shall offer one without blemish. [7]If you present a sheep as your offering, you shall bring it before the LORD [8]and lay your hand on the head of the offering. It shall be slaughtered before the tent of meeting, and Aaron's sons shall dash its blood against all sides of the altar. [9]You shall present its fat from the sacrifice of well-being, as an offering by fire to the LORD: the whole broad tail, which shall be removed close to the backbone, the fat that covers the entrails, and all the fat that is around the entrails; [10]the two kidneys with the fat that is on them at the loins, and the appendage of the liver,

[a] Meaning of Heb uncertain

1.14 Lev 5.7
1.15 Lev 5.9
1.16 Lev 6.10
1.17 Lev 5.8; Gen 15.10
2.1 Lev 6.14
2.2 ver 9,16; Lev 5.12; 6.15; Acts 10.4
2.3 Lev 6.16; 10.12,13
2.9 ver 2; Ex 29.18
2.10 ver 3
2.11 Lev 6.16,17; Ex 23.18; 34.25
2.12 Lev 7.13; 23.10,11
2.13 Mk 9.49; Num 18.19
2.14 Lev 23.10,14
2.16 ver 2
3.1 Lev 7.11,19; 22.21
3.2 Lev 1.4; Ex 29.11,16,20
3.3 Ex 29.13,22
3.5 Lev 7.28-34; Ex 29.13
3.6 ver 1
3.7 Lev 17.8,9
3.8 Lev 1.4,5; ver 2
3.10 ver 4

2.1-15 Offering grain and *first fruits* developed among agricultural people. Both serve in the culture of the ancient Near East as forms of tribute to a superior. Here the burnt offerings are a *pleasing odor to the LORD* (2.2,9). What is left of the grain offering goes to the priests (2.10). The salt of the covenant (2.13) is the symbol of mutuality in a common meal or a shared relationship (Num 18.19; 2 Chr 13.5).

3.1-17 The *sacrifice of well-being* is a celebration of the relationship between God and his covenant people, with the meal as a mode of communion. The animal to be eaten must be *without blemish* (3.1,6), and the participants must abstain from eating *any fat or any blood* (3.17), since these were regarded as the bearers of life and therefore as belonging to the LORD, the source of all life.

4.1-5.13 The offerings for unintentional violations of God's law are to be made by any individual Israelites (4.1-2, 27-35), by priests (4.3-12), by the people as a whole (4.13-21), and by the rulers (4.22-26). It is in connection with the priest's sin offering that details are first given concerning the ritual process at the altar of God. The guilty one's identification with the sacrificial *bull* or *goat* – male for the sinning priest and female for the ordinary sinner – as well as the killing of it are to take place at the entrance to the sanctuary of God, here referred to as *the tent of meeting* (4.1). The sprinkling of blood and the anointing with blood of the horns of the altar which symbolize God's presence and power, as well as the pouring out of the rest at the foot of the altar, show that these actions represent the purification of the life of the offender as well as the divine judgment against the offense. The result of the priest's making atonement on behalf of the guilty one is that forgiveness is granted by God (4.21,26,35). The non-priestly offenders are to bring as their sin offering a less costly victim: a female goat (4.28) or sheep (4.32).

which you shall remove with the kidneys.
11 Then the priest shall turn these into smoke
on the altar as a food offering by fire to the
LORD.
12 If your offering is a goat, you shall
bring it before the LORD 13 and lay your hand
on its head; it shall be slaughtered before
the tent of meeting; and the sons of Aaron
shall dash its blood against all sides of the
altar. 14 You shall present as your offering
from it, as an offering by fire to the LORD,
the fat that covers the entrails, and all the
fat that is around the entrails; 15 the two
kidneys with the fat that is on them at the
loins, and the appendage of the liver, which
you shall remove with the kidneys. 16 Then
the priest shall turn these into smoke on the
altar as a food offering by fire for a pleasing
odor.
All fat is the LORD's. 17 It shall be a perpetual statute throughout your generations,
in all your settlements: you must not eat
any fat or any blood.

Sin Offerings

4 The LORD spoke to Moses, saying,
2 Speak to the people of Israel, saying:
When anyone sins unintentionally in any
of the LORD's commandments about things
not to be done, and does any one of them:
3 If it is the anointed priest who sins,
thus bringing guilt on the people, he shall
offer for the sin that he has committed a
bull of the herd without blemish as a sin
offering to the LORD. 4 He shall bring the bull
to the entrance of the tent of meeting before
the LORD and lay his hand on the head of
the bull; the bull shall be slaughtered before
the LORD. 5 The anointed priest shall take
some of the blood of the bull and bring it
into the tent of meeting. 6 The priest shall
dip his finger in the blood and sprinkle some
of the blood seven times before the LORD in
front of the curtain of the sanctuary. 7 The
priest shall put some of the blood on the
horns of the altar of fragrant incense that
is in the tent of meeting before the LORD; and
the rest of the blood of the bull he shall pour
out at the base of the altar of burnt offering,
which is at the entrance of the tent of
meeting. 8 He shall remove all the fat from
the bull of sin offering: the fat that covers
the entrails and all the fat that is around
the entrails; 9 the two kidneys with the fat
that is on them at the loins; and the appendage of the liver, which he shall remove
with the kidneys, 10 just as these are removed from the ox of the sacrifice of well-
being. The priest shall turn them into smoke
upon the altar of burnt offering. 11 But the
skin of the bull and all its flesh, as well as
its head, its legs, its entrails, and its dung—
12 all the rest of the bull—he shall carry out
to a clean place outside the camp, to the
ash heap, and shall burn it on a wood fire;
at the ash heap it shall be burned.
13 If the whole congregation of Israel
errs unintentionally and the matter escapes
the notice of the assembly, and they do any
one of the things that by the LORD's commandments ought not to be done and incur
guilt; 14 when the sin that they have committed becomes known, the assembly shall
offer a bull of the herd for a sin offering and
bring it before the tent of meeting. 15 The
elders of the congregation shall lay their
hands on the head of the bull before the
LORD, and the bull shall be slaughtered before
the LORD. 16 The anointed priest shall bring
some of the blood of the bull into the tent
of meeting, 17 and the priest shall dip his
finger in the blood and sprinkle it seven
times before the LORD, in front of the curtain. 18 He shall put some of the blood on the
horns of the altar that is before the LORD in
the tent of meeting; and the rest of the
blood he shall pour out at the base of the
altar of burnt offering that is at the entrance of the tent of meeting. 19 He shall
remove all its fat and turn it into smoke on
the altar. 20 He shall do with the bull just as
is done with the bull of sin offering; he shall
do the same with this. The priest shall make
atonement for them, and they shall be forgiven. 21 He shall carry the bull outside the
camp, and burn it as he burned the first
bull; it is the sin offering for the assembly.
22 When a ruler sins, doing unintentionally any one of all the things that by commandments of the LORD his God ought not
to be done and incurs guilt, 23 once the sin
that he has committed is made known to
him, he shall bring as his offering a male
goat without blemish. 24 He shall lay his
hand on the head of the goat; it shall be
slaughtered at the spot where the burnt
offering is slaughtered before the LORD; it is
a sin offering. 25 The priest shall take some
of the blood of the sin offering with his
finger and put it on the horns of the altar
of burnt offering, and pour out the rest of
its blood at the base of the altar of burnt
offering. 26 All its fat he shall turn into smoke

3.11 ver 5,16; Lev 21.6,8,17

3.16 Lev 7.23-25

3.17 Gen 9.4; Lev 17.10,14; Deut 12.16

4.2 Lev 5.15-18; Ps 19.12

4.3 ver 14,23,28

4.4 Lev 1.4

4.5 Lev 16.14

4.7 Lev 8.15; 9.9; Lev 5.9

4.8 Lev 3.3-5

4.12 Lev 6.11; Heb 13.11

4.13 Num 15.24-26; Lev 5.2-4,17

4.14 ver 3,23,28

4.15 Lev 1.4

4.17 ver 6

4.20 Rom 5.11; Heb 2.17; 10.10-12

4.22 ver 2,13

4.23 ver 14

4.25 ver 7,18,30,34

4.26 ver 19,20

on the altar, like the fat of the sacrifice of well-being. Thus the priest shall make atonement on his behalf for his sin, and he shall be forgiven.

27 If anyone of the ordinary people among you sins unintentionally in doing any one of the things that by the LORD's commandments ought not to be done and incurs guilt, 28 when the sin that you have committed is made known to you, you shall bring a female goat without blemish as your offering, for the sin that you have committed. 29 You shall lay your hand on the head of the sin offering; and the sin offering shall be slaughtered at the place of the burnt offering. 30 The priest shall take some of its blood with his finger and put it on the horns of the altar of burnt offering, and he shall pour out the rest of its blood at the base of the altar. 31 He shall remove all its fat, as the fat is removed from the offering of well-being, and the priest shall turn it into smoke on the altar for a pleasing odor to the LORD. Thus the priest shall make atonement on your behalf, and you shall be forgiven.

32 If the offering you bring as a sin offering is a sheep, you shall bring a female without blemish. 33 You shall lay your hand on the head of the sin offering; and it shall be slaughtered as a sin offering at the spot where the burnt offering is slaughtered. 34 The priest shall take some of the blood of the sin offering with his finger and put it on the horns of the altar of burnt offering, and pour out the rest of its blood at the base of the altar. 35 You shall remove all its fat, as the fat of the sheep is removed from the sacrifice of well-being, and the priest shall turn it into smoke on the altar, with the offerings by fire to the LORD. Thus the priest shall make atonement on your behalf for the sin that you have committed, and you shall be forgiven.

5 When any of you sin in that you have heard a public adjuration to testify and—though able to testify as one who has seen or learned of the matter—does not speak up, you are subject to punishment. 2 Or when any of you touch any unclean thing—whether the carcass of an unclean beast or the carcass of unclean livestock or the carcass of an unclean swarming thing—and are unaware of it, you have become unclean, and are guilty. 3 Or when you touch human uncleanness—any uncleanness by which one can become unclean—and are unaware of it, when you come to know it, you shall be guilty. 4 Or when any of you utter aloud a rash oath for a bad or a good purpose, whatever people utter in an oath, and are unaware of it, when you come to know it, you shall in any of these be guilty. 5 When you realize your guilt in any of these, you shall confess the sin that you have committed. 6 And you shall bring to the LORD, as your penalty for the sin that you have committed, a female from the flock, a sheep or a goat, as a sin offering; and the priest shall make atonement on your behalf for your sin.

7 But if you cannot afford a sheep, you shall bring to the LORD, as your penalty for the sin that you have committed, two turtledoves or two pigeons, one for a sin offering and the other for a burnt offering. 8 You shall bring them to the priest, who shall offer first the one for the sin offering, wringing its head at the nape without severing it. 9 He shall sprinkle some of the blood of the sin offering on the side of the altar, while the rest of the blood shall be drained out at the base of the altar; it is a sin offering. 10 And the second he shall offer for a burnt offering according to the regulation. Thus the priest shall make atonement on your behalf for the sin that you have committed, and you shall be forgiven.

11 But if you cannot afford two turtledoves or two pigeons, you shall bring as your offering for the sin that you have committed one-tenth of an ephah of choice flour for a sin offering; you shall not put oil on it or lay frankincense on it, for it is a sin offering. 12 You shall bring it to the priest, and the priest shall scoop up a handful of it as its memorial portion, and turn this into smoke on the altar, with the offerings by fire to the LORD; it is a sin offering. 13 Thus the priest shall make atonement on your behalf for whichever of these sins you have committed, and you shall be forgiven. Like the grain offering, the rest shall be for the priest.

Offerings with Restitution

14 The LORD spoke to Moses, saying: 15 When any of you commit a trespass and sin unintentionally in any of the holy things of the LORD, you shall bring, as your guilt offering to the LORD, a ram without blemish from the flock, convertible into silver by the sanctuary shekel; it is a guilt offering. 16 And you shall make restitution for the holy thing

4.27 ver 2
4.28 ver 23
4.29 Lev 1.4,5
4.32 ver 28
4.35 Lev 3.5; ver 26,31
5.1 Prov 29.24; ver 17
5.2 Lev 11.24-39; Num 19.11-16
5.5 Lev 16.21; 26.40; Num 5.7; Prov 28.13
5.7 Lev 12.8; 14.21
5.8 Lev 1.15,17
5.9 Lev 4.7,18,30,34
5.10 Lev 1.14-17
5.11 Lev 2.1,2
5.13 Lev 4.26; 2.3
5.14 Lev 22.14; 7.1-10; Ex 30.13
5.16 Lev 6.5; 22.14; Num 5.7,8; Lev 4.26

5.1-13 How to obtain forgiveness for various violations of the law: failure to bear public testimony in a public legal dispute (5.1); contact with a ritually unclean substance (5.2) or an unclean person (5.3); uttering aloud a rash oath (5.4). Awareness of having done such acts requires an act of public *confession* and bringing as an offering to the LORD *a female from the flock...as a sin offering*. If one cannot afford a larger sacrificial animal, birds or even a small amount of *fine flour* may be offered (5.7-12). The flour which remains after the portion has been burned is *for the priest* (5.13).

in which you were remiss, and shall add one-fifth to it and give it to the priest. The priest shall make atonement on your behalf with the ram of the guilt offering, and you shall be forgiven.

17 If any of you sin without knowing it, doing any of the things that by the LORD's commandments ought not to be done, you have incurred guilt, and are subject to punishment. 18 You shall bring to the priest a ram without blemish from the flock, or the equivalent, as a guilt offering; and the priest shall make atonement on your behalf for the error that you committed unintentionally, and you shall be forgiven. 19 It is a guilt offering; you have incurred guilt before the LORD.

6 [b] The LORD spoke to Moses, saying: 2 When any of you sin and commit a trespass against the LORD by deceiving a neighbor in a matter of a deposit or a pledge, or by robbery, or if you have defrauded a neighbor, 3 or have found something lost and lied about it—if you swear falsely regarding any of the various things that one may do and sin thereby— 4 when you have sinned and realize your guilt, and would restore what you took by robbery or by fraud or the deposit that was committed to you, or the lost thing that you found, 5 or anything else about which you have sworn falsely, you shall repay the principal amount and shall add one-fifth to it. You shall pay it to its owner when you realize your guilt. 6 And you shall bring to the priest, as your guilt offering to the LORD, a ram without blemish from the flock, or its equivalent, for a guilt offering. 7 The priest shall make atonement on your behalf before the LORD, and you shall be forgiven for any of the things that one may do and incur guilt thereby.

Instructions concerning Sacrifices

8 [c] The LORD spoke to Moses, saying: 9 Command Aaron and his sons, saying: This is the ritual of the burnt offering. The burnt offering itself shall remain on the hearth upon the altar all night until the morning, while the fire on the altar shall be kept burning. 10 The priest shall put on his linen vestments after putting on his linen undergarments next to his body; and he shall take up the ashes to which the fire has reduced the burnt offering on the altar, and place them beside the altar. 11 Then he shall take off his vestments and put on other garments, and carry the ashes out to a clean place outside the camp. 12 The fire on the altar shall be kept burning; it shall not go out. Every morning the priest shall add wood to it, lay out the burnt offering on it, and turn into smoke the fat pieces of the offerings of well-being. 13 A perpetual fire shall be kept burning on the altar; it shall not go out.

14 This is the ritual of the grain offering: The sons of Aaron shall offer it before the LORD, in front of the altar. 15 They shall take from it a handful of the choice flour and oil of the grain offering, with all the frankincense that is on the offering, and they shall turn its memorial portion into smoke on the altar as a pleasing odor to the LORD. 16 Aaron and his sons shall eat what is left of it; it shall be eaten as unleavened cakes in a holy place; in the court of the tent of meeting they shall eat it. 17 It shall not be baked with leaven. I have given it as their portion of my offerings by fire; it is most holy, like the sin offering and the guilt offering. 18 Every male among the descendants of Aaron shall eat of it, as their perpetual due throughout your generations, from the LORD's offerings by fire; anything that touches them shall become holy.

19 The LORD spoke to Moses, saying: 20 This is the offering that Aaron and his sons shall offer to the LORD on the day when he is anointed: one-tenth of an ephah of choice flour as a regular offering, half of it in the morning and half in the evening. 21 It shall be made with oil on a griddle; you shall bring it well soaked, as a grain offering of baked[d] pieces, and you shall present it as a pleasing odor to the LORD. 22 And so the priest, anointed from among Aaron's descendants as a successor, shall prepare it; it is the LORD's—a perpetual due—to be turned entirely into smoke. 23 Every grain offering of a priest shall be wholly burned; it shall not be eaten.

24 The LORD spoke to Moses, saying: 25 Speak to Aaron and his sons, saying: This is the ritual of the sin offering. The sin offering shall be slaughtered before the LORD at the spot where the burnt offering is slaughtered; it is most holy. 26 The priest who offers it as a sin offering shall eat of it; it shall be eaten in a holy place, in the court of the tent of meeting. 27 Whatever touches its flesh shall become holy; and

[b] Ch 5.20 in Heb [c] Ch 6.1 in Heb [d] Meaning of Heb uncertain

5.14-19; 6.1-7 Compensation required for misuse of *holy things* and the defrauding of a *neighbor*. The *holy things* were the funds and supplies of such necessities as grain, oil, and wine, which were to be set aside by the people of Israel as gifts for the priests (Num 18.8-32). Inadvertent misuse of these commodities was to be paid for in kind or by money in the coinage of the *sanctuary shekel*, which was about twice the value of the shekels in ordinary commercial use. There are no indications of blood sacrifice, but the gift effects removal of guilt from the offending party. To have *defrauded a neighbor* was to *commit a trespass against the LORD* (6.2), since covenantal relationship with God was the basis of his people's identity. Restitution is to be made for the funds taken (6.6-7), and a *ram without blemish...or its [monetary] equivalent* is to be offered to the priest in order to effect atonement.

6.8-7.38 Instructions to the Priests concerning Sacrifices. All the sacrifices are gifts to God, and all result in expiation of the sins of the offenders. The sacrifices also have an intrinsic value, which goes to the priests for their upkeep. The regulations brought together here may have come from various sanctuaries in Palestine, but seem to have been combined by priests of the Jerusalem temple tradition. The instructions parallel those offered in Lev 1-5, but there are differences in details of the garb of the priests and the procedures in the sacrifices, reflecting the different origins of the traditions. In the later sources, the Jerusalem priesthood is limited to the sons of Zadok, one of Aaron's younger sons. He is mentioned as a priest in the time of David (1 Kings 1.26), and appears in the genealogies of Aaron in 1 Chr 6.1-15,50-53. Both Aaron and Moses are said to be from the tribe of Levi. In 1 Chr 29.22, Zadok is anointed priest when Solomon is anointed to be prince/king for the second time. According to Ezek 44.13-15 it is the Levites who serve as priests, while in 1 Chr 6.49-53 a descendant of any of the sons of Aaron may fulfill the priestly office.

6.14-23 The Grain Offering. The *perpetual fire* (6.13) on the altar is convenient in an era when kindling a fire was difficult, and to keep it burning was symbolic of enduring access to forgiveness through the cultic system. The baked grain serves as food for the priests (6.18). A similar offering of grain is to be made by each priest as he enters his cultic office *on the day when he is anointed*, but the priestly version is to be completely burned, since *it is the LORD's* (6.22).

6.24-30 The Sin Offering. Since the priests are holy, they may eat the sin offering within the outer court of the sanctuary (6.27). The sacred quality may be transmitted to garments or the vessels in which the sacrifice was prepared. There is also a prohibition against eating flesh from which blood has been used for *atonement in the holy place*.

5.17 ver 15; 4.2,13,22,27
5.18 ver 15-17
6.2 Num 5.6; Acts 5.4; Col 3.9; Ex 22.7,10; Prov 24.28
6.3 Deut 22.1-3
6.5 Lev 5.16; Num 5.7,8
6.6 Lev 5.15
6.7 Lev 4.26
6.10 Ex 28.39-41,43; 39.27,28
6.14 Lev 2.1,2
6.16 Lev 2.3
6.17 Lev 2.11; ver 26,29,30
6.18 ver 29; Num 18.10; ver 27
6.20 Ex 29.1,2
6.21 Lev 2.5
6.25 Lev 4.2,24,29,33; 1.3,5,11
6.26 Lev 10.17,18
6.27 Ex 29.37

6.28 Ex 11.33; 15.12
6.29 ver 18,25
6.30 Lev 4.1,7,11,12, 18,21
7.1 Lev 5.14-6.7
7.2 Lev 1.11
7.4 Lev 3.4
7.6 Lev 6.16-18; 2.3
7.7 Lev 6.25,26
7.9 Lev 2.3,10
7.14 Num 18.8,11,19
7.15 Lev 22.30
7.16 Lev 19.6-8
7.18 Lev 19.7; Num 18.27
7.20 Lev 22.3
7.21 Lev 11.24,28
7.23 Lev 3.17
7.26 Lev 17.10-14
7.29 Lev 3.1
7.31 ver 34
7.34 Num 18.18,19

when any of its blood is spattered on a
garment, you shall wash the bespattered
part in a holy place. [28]An earthen vessel in
which it was boiled shall be broken; but if
it is boiled in a bronze vessel, that shall be
scoured and rinsed in water. [29]Every male
among the priests shall eat of it; it is most
holy. [30]But no sin offering shall be eaten
from which any blood is brought into the
tent of meeting for atonement in the holy
place; it shall be burned with fire.

7 This is the ritual of the guilt offering.
It is most holy; [2]at the spot where the
burnt offering is slaughtered, they shall
slaughter the guilt offering, and its blood
shall be dashed against all sides of the altar.
[3]All its fat shall be offered: the broad tail,
the fat that covers the entrails, [4]the two
kidneys with the fat that is on them at the
loins, and the appendage of the liver, which
shall be removed with the kidneys. [5]The
priest shall turn them into smoke on the
altar as an offering by fire to the LORD; it is
a guilt offering. [6]Every male among the
priests shall eat of it; it shall be eaten in a
holy place; it is most holy.

7 The guilt offering is like the sin offering, there is the same ritual for them; the
priest who makes atonement with it shall
have it. [8]So, too, the priest who offers anyone's burnt offering shall keep the skin of
the burnt offering that he has offered. [9]And
every grain offering baked in the oven, and
all that is prepared in a pan or on a griddle,
shall belong to the priest who offers it. [10]But
every other grain offering, mixed with oil or
dry, shall belong to all the sons of Aaron
equally.

Further Instructions

11 This is the ritual of the sacrifice of the
offering of well-being that one may offer to
the LORD. [12]If you offer it for thanksgiving,
you shall offer with the thank offering
unleavened cakes mixed with oil, unleavened
wafers spread with oil, and cakes of choice
flour well soaked in oil. [13]With your thanksgiving sacrifice of well-being you shall bring
your offering with cakes of leavened bread.
[14]From this you shall offer one cake from
each offering, as a gift to the LORD; it shall
belong to the priest who dashes the blood
of the offering of well-being. [15]And the flesh
of your thanksgiving sacrifice of well-being
shall be eaten on the day it is offered; you
shall not leave any of it until morning.
[16]But if the sacrifice you offer is a votive
offering or a freewill offering, it shall be
eaten on the day that you offer your sacrifice, and what is left of it shall be eaten
the next day; [17]but what is left of the flesh
of the sacrifice shall be burned up on the
third day. [18]If any of the flesh of your
sacrifice of well-being is eaten on the third
day, it shall not be acceptable, nor shall it
be credited to the one who offers it; it shall
be an abomination, and the one who eats
of it shall incur guilt.

19 Flesh that touches any unclean thing
shall not be eaten; it shall be burned up. As
for other flesh, all who are clean may eat
such flesh. [20]But those who eat flesh from
the LORD's sacrifice of well-being while in a
state of uncleanness shall be cut off from
their kin. [21]When any one of you touches
any unclean thing—human uncleanness or
an unclean animal or any unclean creature—and then eats flesh from the LORD's
sacrifice of well-being, you shall be cut off
from your kin.

22 The LORD spoke to Moses, saying:
[23]Speak to the people of Israel, saying: You
shall eat no fat of ox or sheep or goat. [24]The
fat of an animal that died or was torn by
wild animals may be put to any use, but
you must not eat it. [25]If any one of you eats
the fat from an animal of which an offering
by fire may be made to the LORD, you who
eat it shall be cut off from your kin. [26]You
must not eat any blood whatever, either of
bird or of animal, in any of your settlements. [27]Any one of you who eats any
blood shall be cut off from your kin.

28 The LORD spoke to Moses, saying:
[29]Speak to the people of Israel, saying: Any
one of you who would offer to the LORD your
sacrifice of well-being must yourself bring to
the LORD your offering from your sacrifice of
well-being. [30]Your own hands shall bring
the LORD's offering by fire; you shall bring
the fat with the breast, so that the breast
may be raised as an elevation offering before the LORD. [31]The priest shall turn the fat
into smoke on the altar, but the breast shall
belong to Aaron and his sons. [32]And the
right thigh from your sacrifices of well-
being you shall give to the priest as an
offering; [33]the one among the sons of Aaron
who offers the blood and fat of the offering
of well-being shall have the right thigh for
a portion. [34]For I have taken the breast of
the elevation offering, and the thigh that is
offered, from the people of Israel, from their

7.1-10 The Guilt Offering. The procedures and rules closely resemble those linked with the guilt offering, in that the priests may eat parts of it. But in addition, the priest may keep both the *skin of the burnt offering*, which would have both practical and monetary value, and the grain from that offering.
7.11-36 Instructions concerning various offerings. *The offering of well-being* includes not only the sacrificial animal but also *cakes of leavened bread*, some of which are given *to the LORD*, and some eaten by the priest. The *flesh of [the] thanksgiving sacrifice* is to be eaten within two days by the one making the offering, since the *third day* was regarded as the day when decomposition of a corpse began (7.11-18). The basic rule for participation in cultic meals (7.19-21) is that the meat must be ritually clean, and so must be those who share the holy food. Violators of this law are to be cut off from participation in God's covenant people. Also prohibited for the people of God (7.22-27) are eating the *fat of ox or sheep or goat* or *any blood*. Those who do so lose their family connections and identity. (7.28-36) The worshipper is to bring *the fat with the breast* of the sacrificial animal to the altar as a symbol that the meal is shared with *the LORD*, to whom it is sent up by the priest, who burns the fat on the altar. This contrasts with older tradition, in which the worshippers ate the sacrificial meals *in the presence of God* (Ex 18.12). The right thigh goes to the priest, in accordance with a provision in perpetuity for support of the priesthood.

sacrifices of well-being, and have given them to Aaron the priest and to his sons, as a perpetual due from the people of Israel. [35]This is the portion allotted to Aaron and to his sons from the offerings made by fire to the LORD, once they have been brought forward to serve the LORD as priests; [36]these the LORD commanded to be given them, when he anointed them, as a perpetual due from the people of Israel throughout their generations.

37 This is the ritual of the burnt offering, the grain offering, the sin offering, the guilt offering, the offering of ordination, and the sacrifice of well-being, [38]which the LORD commanded Moses on Mount Sinai, when he commanded the people of Israel to bring their offerings to the LORD, in the wilderness of Sinai.

The Rites of Ordination

8 The LORD spoke to Moses, saying: [2]Take Aaron and his sons with him, the vestments, the anointing oil, the bull of sin offering, the two rams, and the basket of unleavened bread; [3]and assemble the whole congregation at the entrance of the tent of meeting. [4]And Moses did as the LORD commanded him. When the congregation was assembled at the entrance of the tent of meeting, [5]Moses said to the congregation, "This is what the LORD has commanded to be done."

6 Then Moses brought Aaron and his sons forward, and washed them with water. [7]He put the tunic on him, fastened the sash around him, clothed him with the robe, and put the ephod on him. He then put the decorated band of the ephod around him, tying the ephod to him with it. [8]He placed the breastpiece on him, and in the breastpiece he put the Urim and the Thummim. [9]And he set the turban on his head, and on the turban, in front, he set the golden ornament, the holy crown, as the LORD commanded Moses.

10 Then Moses took the anointing oil and anointed the tabernacle and all that was in it, and consecrated them. [11]He sprinkled some of it on the altar seven times, and anointed the altar and all its utensils, and the basin and its base, to consecrate them. [12]He poured some of the anointing oil on Aaron's head and anointed him, to consecrate him. [13]And Moses brought forward Aaron's sons, and clothed them with tunics, and fastened sashes around them, and tied headdresses on them, as the LORD commanded Moses.

14 He led forward the bull of sin offering; and Aaron and his sons laid their hands upon the head of the bull of sin offering, [15]and it was slaughtered. Moses took the blood and with his finger put some on each of the horns of the altar, purifying the altar; then he poured out the blood at the base of the altar. Thus he consecrated it, to make atonement for it. [16]Moses took all the fat that was around the entrails, and the appendage of the liver, and the two kidneys with their fat, and turned them into smoke on the altar. [17]But the bull itself, its skin and flesh and its dung, he burned with fire outside the camp, as the LORD commanded Moses.

18 Then he brought forward the ram of burnt offering. Aaron and his sons laid their hands on the head of the ram, [19]and it was slaughtered. Moses dashed the blood against all sides of the altar. [20]The ram was cut into its parts, and Moses turned into smoke the head and the parts and the suet. [21]And after the entrails and the legs were washed with water, Moses turned into smoke the whole ram on the altar; it was a burnt offering for a pleasing odor, an offering by fire to the LORD, as the LORD commanded Moses.

22 Then he brought forward the second ram, the ram of ordination. Aaron and his sons laid their hands on the head of the ram, [23]and it was slaughtered. Moses took some of its blood and put it on the lobe of Aaron's right ear and on the thumb of his right hand and on the big toe of his right foot. [24]After Aaron's sons were brought forward, Moses put some of the blood on the lobes of their right ears and on the thumbs of their right hands and on the big toes of their right feet; and Moses dashed the rest of the blood against all sides of the altar. [25]He took the fat—the broad tail, all the fat that was around the entrails, the appendage of the liver, and the two kidneys with their fat—and the right thigh. [26]From the basket of unleavened bread that was before the LORD, he took one cake of unleavened bread, one cake of bread with oil, and one wafer, and placed them on the fat and on the right thigh. [27]He placed all these on the palms of Aaron and on the palms of his sons, and raised them as an elevation offering before the LORD. [28]Then Moses took them from their hands and

7.37-38 The editorial origin of this summary of ritual instructions is apparent, since they are reportedly given to Israel at Sinai, which would have been prior to the time of erection of *the tent of meeting* which is mentioned in Lev 1.1. What follows (Lev 8-10) is set out as a description of the first sacrifices offered at Sinai.
8.1-9.24 The Ordination of the Priesthood. At this point the narrative of Ex 29.35 is resumed and the ordination proceeds. This tradition of priesthood is different from others which appear in various Old Testament writings: (1) The patriarchs of Israel who functioned as priests (Gen 14.18), including Moses (Ex 19.14); (2) the kings who offered sacrifices (David [2 Sam 24.25]; Solomon [1 Kings 3.15]); (3) Levites, who were earlier a tribe like others (Gen 34.25) and later become the priestly tribe (Deut 33.8-11); (4) the Zadokites, who claim to be the only true priestly heirs of Aaron (Num 25.13; 1 Kings 1.34-40; 1 Chr 24.3-4, where Zadok is linked with Phinehas, Aaron's grandson). See note on 6.8-7.38.
8.1-5 Preparation of the tent, the equipment and the people for the ordination of the priests. The priestly garb (8.6-9) consists of *tunic, sash, robe and...ephod.* The latter is used for linen undergarments, as well as for robes worn on special occasions, as in 1 Sam 23.9, when David needed to learn about Saul's secret plot against him. Here *the ephod* is an apron of the high priest worn above and below the waist, with a special pocket for the *Urim and Thummim,* which served as a sacred lot for determining God's will on any issue, as in Ex 28.30. The answers were "Yes," "No," and "No answer." The turban (probably borrowed from royal Persian custom) and the *holy crown* were symbols of authority bestowed by God. (8.10-13) *The anointing* of the altar and of Aaron and sons are rites by which they are publicly commissioned and empowered for their God-given roles, which are symbolized by their being clothed with the sacred garb.
8.14-36 Aaron and sons are the first to take part in the cultic ceremonies (sin offering; burnt offering) which reach a climax in *the ram of ordination* ceremony by which they are now commissioned to minister to the people as a whole. The final preparation is a waiting period of *seven days* before they can enter the presence of the LORD. Their total obedience to *all the things that the* LORD *commanded through Moses* is noted.

7.37 Lev 6.9,14,20,25; ver 1,11
7.38 Lev 1.1,2
8.2 Ex 29.1-3; 28.2,4; 30.24,25
8.6 Ex 29.4-6
8.8 Ex 28.30
8.9 Ex 28.36,37
8.10 ver 2
8.12 Ex 30.30; Ps 133.2
8.13 Ex 29.8,9
8.14 Ex 29.10; Lev 4.4
8.15 Lev 4.7; Heb 9.22
8.16 Lev 4.8
8.17 Lev 4.11,12
8.18 Ex 29.15
8.21 Ex 29.18
8.22 Ex 29.19,31
8.25 Ex 29.22
8.26 Ex 29.23
8.28 Ex 29.25

8.29 Ex 29.26
8.30 Ex 30.30; Num 3.3
8.31 Ex 29.31,32
8.32 Ex 29.34
8.33 Ex 29.30,35
8.34 Heb 7.16
9.2 Lev 8.18; Ex 29.1
9.3 Lev 4.23
9.6 ver 23
9.7 Heb 5.1,3
9.8 Lev 4.1-12
9.9 ver 12,18
9.11 Lev 4.11; 8.17
9.15 Lev 4.27-31
9.16 Lev 1.3,10
9.17 Lev 2.1,2; 3.5
9.18 Lev 3.1-11
9.21 Lev 7.30-34
9.23 ver 6; Num 14.10

turned them into smoke on the altar with the burnt offering. This was an ordination offering for a pleasing odor, an offering by fire to the LORD. [29]Moses took the breast and raised it as an elevation offering before the LORD; it was Moses' portion of the ram of ordination, as the LORD commanded Moses.

30 Then Moses took some of the anointing oil and some of the blood that was on the altar and sprinkled them on Aaron and his vestments, and also on his sons and their vestments. Thus he consecrated Aaron and his vestments, and also his sons and their vestments.

31 And Moses said to Aaron and his sons, "Boil the flesh at the entrance of the tent of meeting, and eat it there with the bread that is in the basket of ordination offerings, as I was commanded, 'Aaron and his sons shall eat it'; [32]and what remains of the flesh and the bread you shall burn with fire. [33]You shall not go outside the entrance of the tent of meeting for seven days, until the day when your period of ordination is completed. For it will take seven days to ordain you; [34]as has been done today, the LORD has commanded to be done to make atonement for you. [35]You shall remain at the entrance of the tent of meeting day and night for seven days, keeping the LORD's charge so that you do not die; for so I am commanded." [36]Aaron and his sons did all the things that the LORD commanded through Moses.

Aaron's Priesthood Inaugurated

9 On the eighth day Moses summoned Aaron and his sons and the elders of Israel. [2]He said to Aaron, "Take a bull calf for a sin offering and a ram for a burnt offering, without blemish, and offer them before the LORD. [3]And say to the people of Israel, 'Take a male goat for a sin offering; a calf and a lamb, yearlings without blemish, for a burnt offering; [4]and an ox and a ram for an offering of well-being to sacrifice before the LORD; and a grain offering mixed with oil. For today the LORD will appear to you.' " [5]They brought what Moses commanded to the front of the tent of meeting; and the whole congregation drew near and stood before the LORD. [6]And Moses said, "This is the thing that the LORD commanded you to do, so that the glory of the LORD may appear to you." [7]Then Moses said to Aaron, "Draw near to the altar and sacrifice your sin offering and your burnt offering, and make atonement for yourself and for the people; and sacrifice the offering of the people, and make atonement for them; as the LORD has commanded."

8 Aaron drew near to the altar, and slaughtered the calf of the sin offering, which was for himself. [9]The sons of Aaron presented the blood to him, and he dipped his finger in the blood and put it on the horns of the altar; and the rest of the blood he poured out at the base of the altar. [10]But the fat, the kidneys, and the appendage of the liver from the sin offering he turned into smoke on the altar, as the LORD commanded Moses; [11]and the flesh and the skin he burned with fire outside the camp.

12 Then he slaughtered the burnt offering. Aaron's sons brought him the blood, and he dashed it against all sides of the altar. [13]And they brought him the burnt offering piece by piece, and the head, which he turned into smoke on the altar. [14]He washed the entrails and the legs and, with the burnt offering, turned them into smoke on the altar.

15 Next he presented the people's offering. He took the goat of the sin offering that was for the people, and slaughtered it, and presented it as a sin offering like the first one. [16]He presented the burnt offering, and sacrificed it according to regulation. [17]He presented the grain offering, and, taking a handful of it, he turned it into smoke on the altar, in addition to the burnt offering of the morning.

18 He slaughtered the ox and the ram as a sacrifice of well-being for the people. Aaron's sons brought him the blood, which he dashed against all sides of the altar, [19]and the fat of the ox and of the ram—the broad tail, the fat that covers the entrails, the two kidneys and the fat on them,[e] and the appendage of the liver. [20]They first laid the fat on the breasts, and the fat was turned into smoke on the altar; [21]and the breasts and the right thigh Aaron raised as an elevation offering before the LORD, as Moses had commanded.

22 Aaron lifted his hands toward the people and blessed them; and he came down after sacrificing the sin offering, the burnt offering, and the offering of well-being. [23]Moses and Aaron entered the tent of meeting, and then came out and blessed the people;

9.1-24 The inauguration of the pattern of sacrifices is described: sin offering (8-11); burnt offering (12-14); the offering for the people as a whole (15-17); the peace offering (18-21). Visible confirmation of the propriety of the priestly services is promised (9.4,6), and is provided publicly as Aaron completes the sacrifices and, joined by Moses, blesses the people: *the glory of the LORD appeared to all the people.* Through the instructions given by Moses and the cultic process carried out by the priests, God is with his people.

[e] Gk: Heb *the broad tail, and that which covers, and the kidneys*

and the glory of the LORD appeared to all the people. [24]Fire came out from the LORD and consumed the burnt offering and the fat on the altar; and when all the people saw it, they shouted and fell on their faces.

Nadab and Abihu

10 Now Aaron's sons, Nadab and Abihu, each took his censer, put fire in it, and laid incense on it; and they offered unholy fire before the LORD, such as he had not commanded them. [2]And fire came out from the presence of the LORD and consumed them, and they died before the LORD. [3]Then Moses said to Aaron, "This is what the LORD meant when he said,

'Through those who are near me
 I will show myself holy,
and before all the people
 I will be glorified.' "

And Aaron was silent.

4 Moses summoned Mishael and Elzaphan, sons of Uzziel the uncle of Aaron, and said to them, "Come forward, and carry your kinsmen away from the front of the sanctuary to a place outside the camp." [5]They came forward and carried them by their tunics out of the camp, as Moses had ordered. [6]And Moses said to Aaron and to his sons Eleazar and Ithamar, "Do not dishevel your hair, and do not tear your vestments, or you will die and wrath will strike all the congregation; but your kindred, the whole house of Israel, may mourn the burning that the LORD has sent. [7]You shall not go outside the entrance of the tent of meeting, or you will die; for the anointing oil of the LORD is on you." And they did as Moses had ordered.

8 And the LORD spoke to Aaron: [9]Drink no wine or strong drink, neither you nor your sons, when you enter the tent of meeting, that you may not die; it is a statute forever throughout your generations. [10]You are to distinguish between the holy and the common, and between the unclean and the clean; [11]and you are to teach the people of Israel all the statutes that the LORD has spoken to them through Moses.

12 Moses spoke to Aaron and to his remaining sons, Eleazar and Ithamar: Take the grain offering that is left from the LORD's offerings by fire, and eat it unleavened beside the altar, for it is most holy; [13]you shall eat it in a holy place, because it is your due and your sons' due, from the offerings by fire to the LORD; for so I am commanded. [14]But the breast that is elevated and the thigh that is raised, you and your sons and daughters as well may eat in any clean place; for they have been assigned to you and your children from the sacrifices of the offerings of well-being of the people of Israel. [15]The thigh that is raised and the breast that is elevated they shall bring, together with the offerings by fire of the fat, to raise for an elevation offering before the LORD; they are to be your due and that of your children forever, as the LORD has commanded.

16 Then Moses made inquiry about the goat of the sin offering, and—it had already been burned! He was angry with Eleazar and Ithamar, Aaron's remaining sons, and said, [17]"Why did you not eat the sin offering in the sacred area? For it is most holy, and God[f] has given it to you that you may remove the guilt of the congregation, to make atonement on their behalf before the LORD. [18]Its blood was not brought into the inner part of the sanctuary. You should certainly have eaten it in the sanctuary, as I commanded." [19]And Aaron spoke to Moses, "See, today they offered their sin offering and their burnt offering before the LORD; and yet such things as these have befallen me! If I had eaten the sin offering today, would it have been agreeable to the LORD?" [20]And when Moses heard that, he agreed.

Clean and Unclean Foods

11 The LORD spoke to Moses and Aaron, saying to them: [2]Speak to the people of Israel, saying:

From among all the land animals, these are the creatures that you may eat. [3]Any animal that has divided hoofs and is cleft-footed and chews the cud—such you may eat. [4]But among those that chew the cud or have divided hoofs, you shall not eat the following: the camel, for even though it chews the cud, it does not have divided hoofs; it is unclean for you. [5]The rock badger, for even though it chews the cud, it does not have divided hoofs; it is unclean for you. [6]The hare, for even though it chews the cud, it does not have divided hoofs; it is unclean for you. [7]The pig, for even though it has divided hoofs and is cleft-footed, it

[f] Heb *he*

10.1-7 God's presence as judgment on the disobedient. Nadab and Abihu, linked with Moses and the elders of Israel when they are granted access to the LORD at Sinai according to Ex 24.1,9-11, here are seen as assuming priestly roles for which they are not authorized, symbolized by the *unholy fire* they brought to the altar. The word translated *unholy* appears in Lev 22.12 and Num 16.40 with reference to those not authorized to share in priestly roles. The immediate destruction of Nathan and Abihu by God is an enduring solemn warning to all Israelites not to violate divinely established roles and procedures. The assignment to Aaron's sons, Eleazar and Ithamar, of responsibility for disposing of their corpses shows that only certain of the heirs of Aaron were divinely chosen for the priestly role.
10.8-20 Further instructions to the priests. In addition to a warning against the use of strong drink by priests on duty (10.8-9), there are reminders of the need to differentiate sharply between clean and unclean (10.10-11), and some complicated rules about what to do with the remains of *the grain offering* and of the *goat of the sin offering*. 10.19 reports Aaron's reflection on the consequences of failure to fulfill the cultic laws.
11.1-16.34 Rites and Practices of Purity for God's People.
11.1-47 Ritually pure food. The list of foods which may and may not be eaten is given in somewhat briefer form in Deut 14.3-20. The categories of food classified according to ritual purity are land animals (11.2-8), fish (11.9-12), birds (11.13-19), winged insects (11.20-23). The features which qualify items for human diet include those of animals which have cloven hoofs and chew the cud, fish with both fins and scales, and insects which have four feet and move by leaping. Excluded are those animals which fail to possess these features, but also birds of prey, which may eat unclean items. Detailed are ways in which defiling contact may be made with these unclean creatures (11.20-43). The rationale offered for avoiding such impure food is that as the people of *the LORD your God*, whom he brought *up from the land of Egypt*, they are to be *holy* as he is.

9.24 1 Kings 18.38,39
10.1 Num 3.3,4; Lev 16.12; Ex 30.9
10.2 Num 3.4; 26.61
10.3 Ex 19.22; 30.30; Lev 21.6
10.4 Ex 6.18,22; Acts 5.6,9,10
10.6 Lev 21.1,10; Num 16.22,46; Josh 7.1; 22.18-20
10.7 Lev 21.12
10.9 Ezek 44.21
10.10 Lev 11.47; 20.25; Ezek 22.26
10.11 Deut 24.8; Mal 2.7
10.12 Lev 6.14-18; 21.22
10.14 Ex 29.24,26,27
10.15 Lev 7.29,30,34
10.17 Lev 6.24-30
10.19 Lev 9.8,12
11.2 Deut 14.3-21
11.7 Isa 65.4; 66.3,17
11.8 Isa 52.11; Heb 9.10

11.9 Deut 14.9
11.10 Lev 7.18; Deut 14.3
11.22 Mt 3.4; Mk 1.6
11.25 ver 40
11.29 Isa 66.17
11.32 Lev 15.12
11.33 Lev 6.28; 15.12
11.40 Lev 17.15; 22.8
11.41 ver 29
11.43 Lev 20.25
11.44 Ex 6.7; 19.6; Lev 19.2; 1 Pet 1.15,16

does not chew the cud; it is unclean for you.
[8]Of their flesh you shall not eat, and their
carcasses you shall not touch; they are
unclean for you.
9 These you may eat, of all that are in
the waters. Everything in the waters that
has fins and scales, whether in the seas or
in the streams—such you may eat. [10]But
anything in the seas or the streams that
does not have fins and scales, of the swarming creatures in the waters and among all
the other living creatures that are in the
waters—they are detestable to you [11]and
detestable they shall remain. Of their flesh
you shall not eat, and their carcasses you
shall regard as detestable. [12]Everything in
the waters that does not have fins and
scales is detestable to you.
13 These you shall regard as detestable
among the birds. They shall not be eaten;
they are an abomination: the eagle, the
vulture, the osprey, [14]the buzzard, the kite
of any kind; [15]every raven of any kind; [16]the
ostrich, the nighthawk, the sea gull, the
hawk of any kind; [17]the little owl, the cormorant, the great owl, [18]the water hen, the
desert owl,[g] the carrion vulture, [19]the stork,
the heron of any kind, the hoopoe, and the
bat.[h]
20 All winged insects that walk upon all
fours are detestable to you. [21]But among the
winged insects that walk on all fours you
may eat those that have jointed legs above
their feet, with which to leap on the ground.
[22]Of them you may eat: the locust according
to its kind, the bald locust according to its
kind, the cricket according to its kind, and
the grasshopper according to its kind. [23]But
all other winged insects that have four feet
are detestable to you.

Unclean Animals

24 By these you shall become unclean;
whoever touches the carcass of any of them
shall be unclean until the evening, [25]and
whoever carries any part of the carcass of
any of them shall wash his clothes and be
unclean until the evening. [26]Every animal
that has divided hoofs but is not cleft-footed
or does not chew the cud is unclean for
you; everyone who touches one of them
shall be unclean. [27]All that walk on their
paws, among the animals that walk on all
fours, are unclean for you; whoever touches
the carcass of any of them shall be unclean
until the evening, [28]and the one who carries
the carcass shall wash his clothes and be
unclean until the evening; they are unclean
for you.
29 These are unclean for you among the
creatures that swarm upon the earth: the
weasel, the mouse, the great lizard according to its kind, [30]the gecko, the land crocodile, the lizard, the sand lizard, and the
chameleon. [31]These are unclean for you
among all that swarm; whoever touches
one of them when they are dead shall be
unclean until the evening. [32]And anything
upon which any of them falls when they
are dead shall be unclean, whether an article
of wood or cloth or skin or sacking, any
article that is used for any purpose; it shall
be dipped into water, and it shall be unclean until the evening, and then it shall be
clean. [33]And if any of them falls into any
earthen vessel, all that is in it shall be
unclean, and you shall break the vessel.
[34]Any food that could be eaten shall be
unclean if water from any such vessel comes
upon it; and any liquid that could be drunk
shall be unclean if it was in any such vessel.
[35]Everything on which any part of the carcass
falls shall be unclean; whether an oven or
stove, it shall be broken in pieces; they are
unclean, and shall remain unclean for you.
[36]But a spring or a cistern holding water
shall be clean, while whatever touches the
carcass in it shall be unclean. [37]If any part
of their carcass falls upon any seed set aside
for sowing, it is clean; [38]but if water is put
on the seed and any part of their carcass
falls on it, it is unclean for you.
39 If an animal of which you may eat
dies, anyone who touches its carcass shall
be unclean until the evening. [40]Those who
eat of its carcass shall wash their clothes
and be unclean until the evening; and those
who carry the carcass shall wash their
clothes and be unclean until the evening.
41 All creatures that swarm upon the
earth are detestable; they shall not be eaten.
[42]Whatever moves on its belly, and whatever moves on all fours, or whatever has
many feet, all the creatures that swarm
upon the earth, you shall not eat; for they
are detestable. [43]You shall not make yourselves detestable with any creature that
swarms; you shall not defile yourselves with
them, and so become unclean. [44]For I am
the LORD your God; sanctify yourselves therefore, and be holy, for I am holy. You shall

[g] Or *pelican* [h] Identification of several of the birds in verses 13–19 is uncertain

12.1-8 Purification of women after childbirth. Giving birth to a child, with the attendant loss of blood and body fluid, is as defiling as *menstruation*. *A male child* is to be circumcised *on the eighth day*. The period before cleanness can be regained by the mother is twice as long when the child is female as for a male birth. Both *burnt offering* and *sin offering* are required for purification, with provision for birds to replace the more costly sheep as the sacrificial animal.

13.1-59 Defilement tests for skin diseases. The specific nature of the diseases here described is difficult to determine, but the conditions which signify uncleanness are specified: raw flesh (13.10,14); penetration of the skin by the infection (13.18-27); yellow hairs on the head or beard in the affected area (13.29-37); reddish-white spots in association with baldness (13.42). The person afflicted with such a defiling skin disease is to signal the public by displaying *torn clothes*... and disheveled hair, by shouting out "Unclean," and by living withdrawn from society (13.45). Rules are offered for detecting such skin diseases in garments formerly worn by victims of these defiling ailments (13.47-59).

not defile yourselves with any swarming creature that moves on the earth. 45For I am the LORD who brought you up from the land of Egypt, to be your God; you shall be holy, for I am holy.

46 This is the law pertaining to land animal and bird and every living creature that moves through the waters and every creature that swarms upon the earth, 47to make a distinction between the unclean and the clean, and between the living creature that may be eaten and the living creature that may not be eaten.

Purification of Women after Childbirth

12 The LORD spoke to Moses, saying: 2Speak to the people of Israel, saying:

If a woman conceives and bears a male child, she shall be ceremonially unclean seven days; as at the time of her menstruation, she shall be unclean. 3On the eighth day the flesh of his foreskin shall be circumcised. 4Her time of blood purification shall be thirty-three days; she shall not touch any holy thing, or come into the sanctuary, until the days of her purification are completed. 5If she bears a female child, she shall be unclean two weeks, as in her menstruation; her time of blood purification shall be sixty-six days.

6 When the days of her purification are completed, whether for a son or for a daughter, she shall bring to the priest at the entrance of the tent of meeting a lamb in its first year for a burnt offering, and a pigeon or a turtledove for a sin offering. 7He shall offer it before the LORD, and make atonement on her behalf; then she shall be clean from her flow of blood. This is the law for her who bears a child, male or female. 8If she cannot afford a sheep, she shall take two turtledoves or two pigeons, one for a burnt offering and the other for a sin offering; and the priest shall make atonement on her behalf, and she shall be clean.

Leprosy, Varieties and Symptoms

13 The LORD spoke to Moses and Aaron, saying:

2 When a person has on the skin of his body a swelling or an eruption or a spot, and it turns into a leprous[l] disease on the skin of his body, he shall be brought to Aaron the priest or to one of his sons the priests. 3The priest shall examine the disease on the skin of his body, and if the hair in the diseased area has turned white and the disease appears to be deeper than the skin of his body, it is a leprous[l] disease; after the priest has examined him he shall pronounce him ceremonially unclean. 4But if the spot is white in the skin of his body, and appears no deeper than the skin, and the hair in it has not turned white, the priest shall confine the diseased person for seven days. 5The priest shall examine him on the seventh day, and if he sees that the disease is checked and the disease has not spread in the skin, then the priest shall confine him seven days more. 6The priest shall examine him again on the seventh day, and if the disease has abated and the disease has not spread in the skin, the priest shall pronounce him clean; it is only an eruption; and he shall wash his clothes, and be clean. 7But if the eruption spreads in the skin after he has shown himself to the priest for his cleansing, he shall appear again before the priest. 8The priest shall make an examination, and if the eruption has spread in the skin, the priest shall pronounce him unclean; it is a leprous[l] disease.

9 When a person contracts a leprous[l] disease, he shall be brought to the priest. 10The priest shall make an examination, and if there is a white swelling in the skin that has turned the hair white, and there is quick raw flesh in the swelling, 11it is a chronic leprous[l] disease in the skin of his body. The priest shall pronounce him unclean; he shall not confine him, for he is unclean. 12But if the disease breaks out in the skin, so that it covers all the skin of the diseased person from head to foot, so far as the priest can see, 13then the priest shall make an examination, and if the disease has covered all his body, he shall pronounce him clean of the disease; since it has all turned white, he is clean. 14But if raw flesh ever appears on him, he shall be unclean; 15the priest shall examine the raw flesh and pronounce him unclean. Raw flesh is unclean, for it is a leprous[l] disease. 16But if the raw flesh again turns white, he shall come to the priest; 17the priest shall examine him, and if the disease has turned white, the priest shall pronounce the diseased person clean. He is clean.

18 When there is on the skin of one's

11.45 Ex 6.7
11.47 Lev 10.10
12.2 Lev 15.19; 18.19
12.3 Gen 17.12
12.6 Lk 2.22
12.8 Lk 2.22-24; Lev 5.7; 4.26
13.2 Deut 24.8
13.4 ver 21
13.6 Lev 11.25; 14.8
13.7 Lk 5.14
13.10 Num 12.10; 2 Kings 5.27; 2 Chr 26.20
13.12 Lk 5.12
13.15 Mt 8.3
13.18 Ex 9.9

[l] A term for several skin diseases; precise meaning uncertain

13.19 ver 43
13.21 Num 12.14,15
13.25 ver 15
13.27 ver 5
13.29 ver 44
13.32 ver 5
13.34 Lev 14.8
13.36 ver 30
13.40 Ezek 29.18
13.44 ver 29
13.46 Num 5.2; 12.14; 2 Kings 7.3; 15.5; Lk 17.12
13.51 Lev 14.44

body a boil that has healed, [19]and in the
place of the boil there appears a white
swelling or a reddish-white spot, it shall be
shown to the priest. [20]The priest shall make
an examination, and if it appears deeper
than the skin and its hair has turned white,
the priest shall pronounce him unclean; this
is a leprous[j] disease, broken out in the boil.
[21]But if the priest examines it and the hair
on it is not white, nor is it deeper than the
skin but has abated, the priest shall confine
him seven days. [22]If it spreads in the skin,
the priest shall pronounce him unclean; it
is diseased. [23]But if the spot remains in one
place and does not spread, it is the scar of
the boil; the priest shall pronounce him
clean.
24 Or, when the body has a burn on the
skin and the raw flesh of the burn becomes
a spot, reddish-white or white, [25]the priest
shall examine it. If the hair in the spot has
turned white and it appears deeper than the
skin, it is a leprous[j] disease; it has broken
out in the burn, and the priest shall pronounce him unclean. This is a leprous[j]
disease. [26]But if the priest examines it and
the hair in the spot is not white, and it is
no deeper than the skin but has abated, the
priest shall confine him seven days. [27]The
priest shall examine him the seventh day;
if it is spreading in the skin, the priest shall
pronounce him unclean. This is a leprous[j]
disease. [28]But if the spot remains in one
place and does not spread in the skin but
has abated, it is a swelling from the burn,
and the priest shall pronounce him clean;
for it is the scar of the burn.
29 When a man or woman has a disease
on the head or in the beard, [30]the priest
shall examine the disease. If it appears deeper
than the skin and the hair in it is yellow
and thin, the priest shall pronounce him
unclean; it is an itch, a leprous[j] disease of
the head or the beard. [31]If the priest examines the itching disease, and it appears no
deeper than the skin and there is no black
hair in it, the priest shall confine the person
with the itching disease for seven days. [32]On
the seventh day the priest shall examine the
itch; if the itch has not spread, and there
is no yellow hair in it, and the itch appears
to be no deeper than the skin, [33]he shall
shave, but the itch he shall not shave. The
priest shall confine the person with the itch
for seven days more. [34]On the seventh day
the priest shall examine the itch; if the itch
has not spread in the skin and it appears
to be no deeper than the skin, the priest
shall pronounce him clean. He shall wash
his clothes and be clean. [35]But if the itch
spreads in the skin after he was pronounced
clean, [36]the priest shall examine him. If the
itch has spread in the skin, the priest need
not seek for the yellow hair; he is unclean.
[37]But if in his eyes the itch is checked, and
black hair has grown in it, the itch is
healed, he is clean; and the priest shall
pronounce him clean.
38 When a man or a woman has spots
on the skin of the body, white spots, [39]the
priest shall make an examination, and if the
spots on the skin of the body are of a dull
white, it is a rash that has broken out on
the skin; he is clean.
40 If anyone loses the hair from his head,
he is bald but he is clean. [41]If he loses the
hair from his forehead and temples, he has
baldness of the forehead but he is clean.
[42]But if there is on the bald head or the bald
forehead a reddish-white diseased spot, it is
a leprous[j] disease breaking out on his bald
head or his bald forehead. [43]The priest shall
examine him; if the diseased swelling is
reddish-white on his bald head or on his
bald forehead, which resembles a leprous[j]
disease in the skin of the body, [44]he is
leprous,[j] he is unclean. The priest shall
pronounce him unclean; the disease is on
his head.
45 The person who has the leprous[j]
disease shall wear torn clothes and let the
hair of his head be disheveled; and he shall
cover his upper lip and cry out, "Unclean,
unclean." [46]He shall remain unclean as long
as he has the disease; he is unclean. He
shall live alone; his dwelling shall be outside
the camp.
47 Concerning clothing: when a leprous[j]
disease appears in it, in woolen or linen
cloth, [48]in warp or woof of linen or wool,
or in a skin or in anything made of skin,
[49]if the disease shows greenish or reddish in
the garment, whether in warp or woof or
in skin or in anything made of skin, it is a
leprous[j] disease and shall be shown to the
priest. [50]The priest shall examine the disease, and put the diseased article aside for
seven days. [51]He shall examine the disease
on the seventh day. If the disease has spread
in the cloth, in warp or woof, or in the skin,
whatever be the use of the skin, this is a
spreading leprous[j] disease; it is unclean.

[j] A term for several skin diseases; precise meaning uncertain

14.1-32 How those cured of these skin diseases are to be made ritually pure. The process combines the use of cleansing material with such symbolic actions as the release of a bird and shaving the affected area (14.4,9). The body is to be anointed with oil (14.15), and sacrificial lambs are offered to purge the uncleanness (14.10-14). The prescribed offerings include those used for more general purposes: sin offering, burnt offering, and cereal offering (14.17-20), with provision for the use of doves or pigeons in the case of the poor (14.21-22). Detailed is the priestly procedure for ritual cleansing of those with skin diseases (14.23-32) and for purifying the houses of those thus infected (14.33-53).

52 He shall burn the clothing, whether diseased in warp or woof, woolen or linen, or anything of skin, for it is a spreading leprous[k] disease; it shall be burned in fire.

53 If the priest makes an examination, and the disease has not spread in the clothing, in warp or woof or in anything of skin, 54 the priest shall command them to wash the article in which the disease appears, and he shall put it aside seven days more. 55 The priest shall examine the diseased article after it has been washed. If the diseased spot has not changed color, though the disease has not spread, it is unclean; you shall burn it in fire, whether the leprous[k] spot is on the inside or on the outside.

56 If the priest makes an examination, and the disease has abated after it is washed, he shall tear the spot out of the cloth, in warp or woof, or out of skin. 57 If it appears again in the garment, in warp or woof, or in anything of skin, it is spreading; you shall burn with fire that in which the disease appears. 58 But the cloth, warp or woof, or anything of skin from which the disease disappears when you have washed it, shall then be washed a second time, and it shall be clean.

59 This is the ritual for a leprous[k] disease in a cloth of wool or linen, either in warp or woof, or in anything of skin, to decide whether it is clean or unclean.

Purification of Lepers and Leprous Houses

14 The Lord spoke to Moses, saying: 2 This shall be the ritual for the leprous[k] person at the time of his cleansing:

He shall be brought to the priest; 3 the priest shall go out of the camp, and the priest shall make an examination. If the disease is healed in the leprous[k] person, 4 the priest shall command that two living clean birds and cedarwood and crimson yarn and hyssop be brought for the one who is to be cleansed. 5 The priest shall command that one of the birds be slaughtered over fresh water in an earthen vessel. 6 He shall take the living bird with the cedarwood and the crimson yarn and the hyssop, and dip them and the living bird in the blood of the bird that was slaughtered over the fresh water. 7 He shall sprinkle it seven times upon the one who is to be cleansed of the leprous[k] disease; then he shall pronounce him clean, and he shall let the living bird go into the open field. 8 The one who is to be cleansed shall wash his clothes, and shave off all his hair, and bathe himself in water, and he shall be clean. After that he shall come into the camp, but shall live outside his tent seven days. 9 On the seventh day he shall shave all his hair: of head, beard, eyebrows; he shall shave all his hair. Then he shall wash his clothes, and bathe his body in water, and he shall be clean.

10 On the eighth day he shall take two male lambs without blemish, and one ewe lamb in its first year without blemish, and a grain offering of three-tenths of an ephah of choice flour mixed with oil, and one log[l] of oil. 11 The priest who cleanses shall set the person to be cleansed, along with these things, before the Lord, at the entrance of the tent of meeting. 12 The priest shall take one of the lambs, and offer it as a guilt offering, along with the log[l] of oil, and raise them as an elevation offering before the Lord. 13 He shall slaughter the lamb in the place where the sin offering and the burnt offering are slaughtered in the holy place; for the guilt offering, like the sin offering, belongs to the priest: it is most holy. 14 The priest shall take some of the blood of the guilt offering and put it on the lobe of the right ear of the one to be cleansed, and on the thumb of the right hand, and on the big toe of the right foot. 15 The priest shall take some of the log[l] of oil and pour it into the palm of his own left hand, 16 and dip his right finger in the oil that is in his left hand and sprinkle some oil with his finger seven times before the Lord. 17 Some of the oil that remains in his hand the priest shall put on the lobe of the right ear of the one to be cleansed, and on the thumb of the right hand, and on the big toe of the right foot, on top of the blood of the guilt offering. 18 The rest of the oil that is in the priest's hand he shall put on the head of the one to be cleansed. Then the priest shall make atonement on his behalf before the Lord: 19 the priest shall offer the sin offering, to make atonement for the one to be cleansed from his uncleanness. Afterward he shall slaughter the burnt offering; 20 and the priest shall offer the burnt offering and the grain offering on the altar. Thus the priest shall make atonement on his behalf and he shall be clean.

21 But if he is poor and cannot afford so much, he shall take one male lamb for a

[k] A term for several skin diseases; precise meaning uncertain [l] A liquid measure

13.52 Lev 14.44

13.54 ver 4

13.56 Lev 14.8

14.2 Mt 8.2,4; Mk 1.40,44; Lk 5.12,14; 17.14

14.4 ver 6,49,51,52; Num 19.6

14.7 2 Kings 5.10,14

14.8 Lev 13.6; Num 8.7

14.10 Mt 8.4; Mk 1.44; Lk 5.14

14.12 Lev 5.2,8; 6.6,7; Ex 29.24

14.13 Lev 1.5,11; 6.24-30; 2.3; 7.6

14.14 Lev 8.23

14.18 Lev 4.26

14.19 ver 12

14.21 Lev 5.7,11; 12.8; ver 22

14.22 Lev 12.8; 15.14,15
14.23 ver 10,11
14.24 ver 12
14.25 ver 14
14.28 Lev 5.6
14.30 ver 22; Lev 15.15
14.31 Lev 5.7
14.34 Gen 17.8; Num 32.22; Deut 7.1
14.35 Ps 91.10; Prov 3.33
14.38 Num 12.15
14.40 ver 45
14.44 Lev 13.51
14.49 ver 4
14.51 Ps 51.7
14.53 ver 20
14.54 Lev 13.30

guilt offering to be elevated, to make atonement on his behalf, and one-tenth of an
ephah of choice flour mixed with oil for a
grain offering and a log[m] of oil; 22also two
turtledoves or two pigeons, such as he can
afford, one for a sin offering and the other
for a burnt offering. 23On the eighth day he
shall bring them for his cleansing to the
priest, to the entrance of the tent of meeting, before the LORD; 24and the priest shall
take the lamb of the guilt offering and the
log[m] of oil, and the priest shall raise them
as an elevation offering before the LORD.
25The priest shall slaughter the lamb of the
guilt offering and shall take some of the
blood of the guilt offering, and put it on the
lobe of the right ear of the one to be
cleansed, and on the thumb of the right
hand, and on the big toe of the right foot.
26The priest shall pour some of the oil into
the palm of his own left hand, 27and shall
sprinkle with his right finger some of the oil
that is in his left hand seven times before
the LORD. 28The priest shall put some of the
oil that is in his hand on the lobe of the
right ear of the one to be cleansed, and on
the thumb of the right hand, and the big
toe of the right foot, where the blood of the
guilt offering was placed. 29The rest of the
oil that is in the priest's hand he shall put
on the head of the one to be cleansed, to
make atonement on his behalf before the
LORD. 30And he shall offer, of the turtledoves
or pigeons such as he can afford, 31one[n] for
a sin offering and the other for a burnt
offering, along with a grain offering; and
the priest shall make atonement before the
LORD on behalf of the one being cleansed.
32This is the ritual for the one who has
a leprous[o] disease, who cannot afford the
offerings for his cleansing.

33 The LORD spoke to Moses and Aaron,
saying:

34 When you come into the land of
Canaan, which I give you for a possession,
and I put a leprous[o] disease in a house in
the land of your possession, 35the owner of
the house shall come and tell the priest,
saying, "There seems to me to be some sort
of disease in my house." 36The priest shall
command that they empty the house before
the priest goes to examine the disease, or all
that is in the house will become unclean;
and afterward the priest shall go in to
inspect the house. 37He shall examine the
disease; if the disease is in the walls of the
house with greenish or reddish spots, and
if it appears to be deeper than the surface,
38the priest shall go outside to the door of
the house and shut up the house seven
days. 39The priest shall come again on the
seventh day and make an inspection; if the
disease has spread in the walls of the house,
40the priest shall command that the stones
in which the disease appears be taken out
and thrown into an unclean place outside
the city. 41He shall have the inside of the
house scraped thoroughly, and the plaster
that is scraped off shall be dumped in an
unclean place outside the city. 42They shall
take other stones and put them in the place
of those stones, and take other plaster and
plaster the house.

43 If the disease breaks out again in the
house, after he has taken out the stones and
scraped the house and plastered it, 44the
priest shall go and make inspection; if the
disease has spread in the house, it is a
spreading leprous[o] disease in the house; it
is unclean. 45He shall have the house torn
down, its stones and timber and all the
plaster of the house, and taken outside the
city to an unclean place. 46All who enter
the house while it is shut up shall be unclean until the evening; 47and all who sleep
in the house shall wash their clothes; and
all who eat in the house shall wash their
clothes.

48 If the priest comes and makes an
inspection, and the disease has not spread
in the house after the house was plastered,
the priest shall pronounce the house clean;
the disease is healed. 49For the cleansing of
the house he shall take two birds, with
cedarwood and crimson yarn and hyssop,
50and shall slaughter one of the birds over
fresh water in an earthen vessel, 51and shall
take the cedarwood and the hyssop and the
crimson yarn, along with the living bird,
and dip them in the blood of the slaughtered bird and the fresh water, and sprinkle
the house seven times. 52Thus he shall
cleanse the house with the blood of the bird,
and with the fresh water, and with the
living bird, and with the cedarwood and
hyssop and crimson yarn; 53and he shall let
the living bird go out of the city into the
open field; so he shall make atonement for
the house, and it shall be clean.

54 This is the ritual for any leprous[o]

[m] A liquid measure [n] Gk Syr: Heb *afford,* [31]*such as he can afford, one* [o] A term for several skin diseases; precise meaning uncertain

15.1-33 Unclean discharges from males and females. The *member* from which the male discharge flows is the sexual organ, with the defilement transmitted to the bed, clothing, spittle, saddle, and any vessels used routinely (15.1-11). The *discharge from the member* (15.16) may refer to the results of contracting a venereal disease. The sacrifice of birds, together with ceremonial washing, serves to effect purification. Purification is also required for normal discharge of semen (15.16-18) and for menstruation (15.19-24), as well as for protracted *discharge of blood* (15.25-30), and the less expensive sacrifice of birds is prescribed. The justification for these ritual procedures (15.31) is that the purity of God's people and of the tent of God's presence among them must be preserved.

disease: for an itch, 55for leprous[p] diseases in clothing and houses, 56and for a swelling or an eruption or a spot, 57to determine when it is unclean and when it is clean. This is the ritual for leprous[p] diseases.

Concerning Bodily Discharges

15 The LORD spoke to Moses and Aaron, saying: 2Speak to the people of Israel and say to them:

When any man has a discharge from his member,[q] his discharge makes him ceremonially unclean. 3The uncleanness of his discharge is this: whether his member[q] flows with his discharge, or his member[q] is stopped from discharging, it is uncleanness for him. 4Every bed on which the one with the discharge lies shall be unclean; and everything on which he sits shall be unclean. 5Anyone who touches his bed shall wash his clothes, and bathe in water, and be unclean until the evening. 6All who sit on anything on which the one with the discharge has sat shall wash their clothes, and bathe in water, and be unclean until the evening. 7All who touch the body of the one with the discharge shall wash their clothes, and bathe in water, and be unclean until the evening. 8If the one with the discharge spits on persons who are clean, then they shall wash their clothes, and bathe in water, and be unclean until the evening. 9Any saddle on which the one with the discharge rides shall be unclean. 10All who touch anything that was under him shall be unclean until the evening, and all who carry such a thing shall wash their clothes, and bathe in water, and be unclean until the evening. 11All those whom the one with the discharge touches without his having rinsed his hands in water shall wash their clothes, and bathe in water, and be unclean until the evening. 12Any earthen vessel that the one with the discharge touches shall be broken; and every vessel of wood shall be rinsed in water.

13 When the one with a discharge is cleansed of his discharge, he shall count seven days for his cleansing; he shall wash his clothes and bathe his body in fresh water, and he shall be clean. 14On the eighth day he shall take two turtledoves or two pigeons and come before the LORD to the entrance of the tent of meeting and give them to the priest. 15The priest shall offer them, one for a sin offering and the other for a burnt offering; and the priest shall make atonement on his behalf before the LORD for his discharge.

16 If a man has an emission of semen, he shall bathe his whole body in water, and be unclean until the evening. 17Everything made of cloth or of skin on which the semen falls shall be washed with water, and be unclean until the evening. 18If a man lies with a woman and has an emission of semen, both of them shall bathe in water, and be unclean until the evening.

19 When a woman has a discharge of blood that is her regular discharge from her body, she shall be in her impurity for seven days, and whoever touches her shall be unclean until the evening. 20Everything upon which she lies during her impurity shall be unclean; everything also upon which she sits shall be unclean. 21Whoever touches her bed shall wash his clothes, and bathe in water, and be unclean until the evening. 22Whoever touches anything upon which she sits shall wash his clothes, and bathe in water, and be unclean until the evening; 23whether it is the bed or anything upon which she sits, when he touches it he shall be unclean until the evening. 24If any man lies with her, and her impurity falls on him, he shall be unclean seven days; and every bed on which he lies shall be unclean.

25 If a woman has a discharge of blood for many days, not at the time of her impurity, or if she has a discharge beyond the time of her impurity, all the days of the discharge she shall continue in uncleanness; as in the days of her impurity, she shall be unclean. 26Every bed on which she lies during all the days of her discharge shall be treated as the bed of her impurity; and everything on which she sits shall be unclean, as in the uncleanness of her impurity. 27Whoever touches these things shall be unclean, and shall wash his clothes, and bathe in water, and be unclean until the evening. 28If she is cleansed of her discharge, she shall count seven days, and after that she shall be clean. 29On the eighth day she shall take two turtledoves or two pigeons and bring them to the priest to the entrance of the tent of meeting. 30The priest shall offer one for a sin offering and the other for a burnt offering; and the priest shall make atonement on her behalf before the LORD for her unclean discharge.

[p] A term for several skin diseases; precise meaning uncertain [q] Heb *flesh*

14.56 Lev 13.2

15.2 Lev 22.4; Num 5.2; 2 Sam 3.29; Mt 9.20

15.7 Num 19.19

15.10 Num 19.10

15.12 Lev 6.28; 11.32,33

15.13 ver 28

15.14 Lev 14.22,23

15.15 Lev 14.30,31

15.16 Lev 22.4; Deut 23.10

15.18 1 Sam 21.4

15.19 Lev 12.2

15.21 ver 27

15.24 Lev 20.18

15.25 Mt 9.20; Mk 5.25; Lk 8.43

15.27 ver 21

15.29 Gen 15.9

31 Thus you shall keep the people of
Israel separate from their uncleanness, so
that they do not die in their uncleanness by
defiling my tabernacle that is in their midst.
32 This is the ritual for those who have
a discharge: for him who has an emission
of semen, becoming unclean thereby, 33 for
her who is in the infirmity of her period, for
anyone, male or female, who has a discharge, and for the man who lies with a
woman who is unclean.

The Day of Atonement

16 The LORD spoke to Moses after the
death of the two sons of Aaron,
when they drew near before the LORD and
died. 2 The LORD said to Moses:
Tell your brother Aaron not to come just
at any time into the sanctuary inside the
curtain before the mercy seat[r] that is upon
the ark, or he will die; for I appear in the
cloud upon the mercy seat.[r] 3 Thus shall
Aaron come into the holy place: with a
young bull for a sin offering and a ram for
a burnt offering. 4 He shall put on the holy
linen tunic, and shall have the linen undergarments next to his body, fasten the linen
sash, and wear the linen turban; these are
the holy vestments. He shall bathe his body
in water, and then put them on. 5 He shall
take from the congregation of the people of
Israel two male goats for a sin offering, and
one ram for a burnt offering.
6 Aaron shall offer the bull as a sin
offering for himself, and shall make atonement for himself and for his house. 7 He shall
take the two goats and set them before the
LORD at the entrance of the tent of meeting;
8 and Aaron shall cast lots on the two goats,
one lot for the LORD and the other lot for
Azazel.[s] 9 Aaron shall present the goat on
which the lot fell for the LORD, and offer it
as a sin offering; 10 but the goat on which
the lot fell for Azazel[s] shall be presented
alive before the LORD to make atonement
over it, that it may be sent away into the
wilderness to Azazel.[s]
11 Aaron shall present the bull as a sin
offering for himself, and shall make atonement for himself and for his house; he shall
slaughter the bull as a sin offering for himself. 12 He shall take a censer full of coals of
fire from the altar before the LORD, and two
handfuls of crushed sweet incense, and he
shall bring it inside the curtain 13 and put
the incense on the fire before the LORD, that
the cloud of the incense may cover the
mercy seat[r] that is upon the covenant,[t] or
he will die. 14 He shall take some of the blood
of the bull, and sprinkle it with his finger
on the front of the mercy seat,[r] and before
the mercy seat[r] he shall sprinkle the blood
with his finger seven times.
15 He shall slaughter the goat of the sin
offering that is for the people and bring its
blood inside the curtain, and do with its
blood as he did with the blood of the bull,
sprinkling it upon the mercy seat[r] and before the mercy seat.[r] 16 Thus he shall make
atonement for the sanctuary, because of the
uncleannesses of the people of Israel, and
because of their transgressions, all their
sins; and so he shall do for the tent of
meeting, which remains with them in the
midst of their uncleannesses. 17 No one shall
be in the tent of meeting from the time he
enters to make atonement in the sanctuary
until he comes out and has made atonement for himself and for his house and for
all the assembly of Israel. 18 Then he shall
go out to the altar that is before the LORD
and make atonement on its behalf, and
shall take some of the blood of the bull and
of the blood of the goat, and put it on each
of the horns of the altar. 19 He shall sprinkle
some of the blood on it with his finger seven
times, and cleanse it and hallow it from the
uncleannesses of the people of Israel.
20 When he has finished atoning for the
holy place and the tent of meeting and the
altar, he shall present the live goat. 21 Then
Aaron shall lay both his hands on the head
of the live goat, and confess over it all the
iniquities of the people of Israel, and all their
transgressions, all their sins, putting them
on the head of the goat, and sending it
away into the wilderness by means of someone designated for the task.[u] 22 The goat
shall bear on itself all their iniquities to a
barren region; and the goat shall be set free
in the wilderness.
23 Then Aaron shall enter the tent of
meeting, and shall take off the linen vestments that he put on when he went into
the holy place, and shall leave them there.
24 He shall bathe his body in water in a holy
place, and put on his vestments; then he
shall come out and offer his burnt offering
and the burnt offering of the people, making

[r] Or *the cover* [s] Traditionally rendered *a scapegoat* [t] Or *treaty*, or *testimony*; Heb *eduth* [u] Meaning of Heb uncertain

15.31 Ezek 44.23; Num 5.3; 19.13,20; Ezek 5.11; 23.38
15.32 ver 2,16
15.33 ver 19,24,25
16.1 Lev 10.1,2
16.2 Ex 30.10; Heb 9.7; 10.19; Ex 25.21,22
16.3 Heb 9.7,12,24,25; Lev 4.3
16.4 Ex 28.39; 42.43; ver 24
16.5 Lev 4.13-21
16.6 Lev 9.7; Heb 5.2; 7.27,28; 9.7
16.11 Heb 7.27; 9.7
16.12 Lev 10.1; Ex 30.34
16.13 Lev 22.9
16.14 Heb 9.13,25; Lev 4.6,17
16.15 Heb 9.3,7,12
16.16 Ex 29.36; Heb 2.17
16.18 Lev 4.25; Ezek 43.20,22
16.19 ver 14
16.21 Isa 53.6
16.22 Isa 53.11,12
16.23 ver 4; Ezek 42.14; 44.19
16.24 ver 3-5

16.1-32 The Day of Atonement. This designation of the day and the prescribed ritual appears only in Lev 23.27, although the details are given here. The instruction is given through Moses to Aaron following the death of his sons (10.1-3). Access to the interior of *the sanctuary*, designated here as *the holy place*, is granted to Aaron not just at any time, but only on this special day each year. This contrasts with the account of Moses' frequent visits with Yahweh in the tent of meeting, reported in Ex 33.9-11. The Day of Atonement is not listed with the annual feasts in Ex 23.14-17, however, nor does it appear in the festivals described by Ezekiel in his prophetic portrayal of the renewal of the temple and Israel's worship of God (Ezek 40-47). In the list of appointed festivals in Lev 23, the Day of Atonement is linked with the harvest festivals that marked the end of the old year and the beginning of the new. The institution of this festival must have developed only after the return of Israel from exile in Babylon.
16.2 *The mercy seat.* The Hebrew word refers to the cover over the sacred box in which were preserved the tablets inscribed with the laws given by God to Moses at Sinai. Over that cover, the numinous cloud hovered which was the visible presence of God. The word also means "to cover" sin, in the sense of remove it as a barrier to human relationships with God.
16.3-28 By providing the sacrificial animals, by purifying himself and by donning the priestly garb, Aaron prepares for carrying out the ceremonies. The bull sacrificed is *a sin offering for himself* (16.11). The smoke from the incense serves to shield him from direct vision of God's sacred cloud, which would be fatal (16.13). Of the two goats, one is offered *for the people*, but the sacrifice also effects the purification of the sanctuary, which would otherwise be polluted by the sins of the people represented by the animals offered in their behalf (16.16). To *the live goat*, however, Aaron transmits *all the iniquities of the people of Israel*, and it is driven out into the wilderness (16.20-22). Its designation *for Azazel* (16.8) may indicate a place, but more probably it is the name of an evil spirit or demon thought to dwell in the desert to whom the sins of the people are consigned. The benefits of this atoning work include the welfare of the people as a whole (16.18-19), the transfer of their sin to the condemned goat (16.20-22), the purification of the priests and attendants (16.23-28), and the destruction of all the material used to achieve expiation of the corporate guilt of Israel (16.27).

atonement for himself and for the people.
25 The fat of the sin offering he shall turn
into smoke on the altar. 26 The one who sets
the goat free for Azazel[v] shall wash his
clothes and bathe his body in water, and
afterward may come into the camp. 27 The
bull of the sin offering and the goat of the
sin offering, whose blood was brought in to
make atonement in the holy place, shall be
taken outside the camp; their skin and their
flesh and their dung shall be consumed in
fire. 28 The one who burns them shall wash
his clothes and bathe his body in water, and
afterward may come into the camp.
29 This shall be a statute to you forever:
In the seventh month, on the tenth day of
the month, you shall deny yourselves,[w] and
shall do no work, neither the citizen nor the
alien who resides among you. 30 For on this
day atonement shall be made for you, to
cleanse you; from all your sins you shall be
clean before the LORD. 31 It is a sabbath of
complete rest to you, and you shall deny
yourselves;[w] it is a statute forever. 32 The
priest who is anointed and consecrated as
priest in his father's place shall make atonement, wearing the linen vestments, the holy
vestments. 33 He shall make atonement for
the sanctuary, and he shall make atonement for the tent of meeting and for the
altar, and he shall make atonement for the
priests and for all the people of the assembly. 34 This shall be an everlasting statute for
you, to make atonement for the people of
Israel once in the year for all their sins. And
Moses did as the LORD had commanded him.

The Slaughtering of Animals

17 The LORD spoke to Moses:
2 Speak to Aaron and his sons
and to all the people of Israel and say to
them: This is what the LORD has commanded.
3 If anyone of the house of Israel slaughters
an ox or a lamb or a goat in the camp, or
slaughters it outside the camp, 4 and does
not bring it to the entrance of the tent of
meeting, to present it as an offering to the
LORD before the tabernacle of the LORD, he
shall be held guilty of bloodshed; he has
shed blood, and he shall be cut off from the
people. 5 This is in order that the people of
Israel may bring their sacrifices that they
offer in the open field, that they may bring
them to the LORD, to the priest at the entrance of the tent of meeting, and offer them
as sacrifices of well-being to the LORD. 6 The
priest shall dash the blood against the altar
of the LORD at the entrance of the tent of
meeting, and turn the fat into smoke as a
pleasing odor to the LORD, 7 so that they may
no longer offer their sacrifices for goat-
demons, to whom they prostitute themselves. This shall be a statute forever to
them throughout their generations.
8 And say to them further: Anyone of
the house of Israel or of the aliens who
reside among them who offers a burnt offering or sacrifice, 9 and does not bring it to
the entrance of the tent of meeting, to
sacrifice it to the LORD, shall be cut off from
the people.

Eating Blood Prohibited

10 If anyone of the house of Israel or of
the aliens who reside among them eats any
blood, I will set my face against that person
who eats blood, and will cut that person off
from the people. 11 For the life of the flesh
is in the blood; and I have given it to you
for making atonement for your lives on the
altar; for, as life, it is the blood that makes
atonement. 12 Therefore I have said to the
people of Israel: No person among you shall
eat blood, nor shall any alien who resides
among you eat blood. 13 And anyone of the
people of Israel, or of the aliens who reside
among them, who hunts down an animal
or bird that may be eaten shall pour out its
blood and cover it with earth.
14 For the life of every creature—its blood
is its life; therefore I have said to the people
of Israel: You shall not eat the blood of any
creature, for the life of every creature is its
blood; whoever eats it shall be cut off. 15 All
persons, citizens or aliens, who eat what
dies of itself or what has been torn by wild
animals, shall wash their clothes, and bathe
themselves in water, and be unclean until
the evening; then they shall be clean. 16 But
if they do not wash themselves or bathe
their body, they shall bear their guilt.

Sexual Relations

18 The LORD spoke to Moses, saying:
2 Speak to the people of Israel
and say to them: I am the LORD your God.
3 You shall not do as they do in the land of
Egypt, where you lived, and you shall not
do as they do in the land of Canaan, to

[v] Traditionally rendered *a scapegoat* [w] Or *shall fast*

16.27 Lev 4.12,21; 6.30
16.29 Lev 23.27; Num 29.7
16.31 Lev 23.32; Isa 58.3,5
16.32 ver 4; Num 20.26,28
16.33 ver 6,16-18
16.34 Heb 9.7,25
17.4 Deut 12.5-21; Rom 5.13
17.6 Lev 3.2; Num 18.17
17.7 Ex 22.20; 32.8; 34.15; Deut 32.17; 2 Chr 11.15
17.9 ver 4
17.10 Lev 3.17; Deut 12.16,23
17.11 ver 14; Gen 9.4; Heb 9.22
17.13 Lev 7.26; Deut 12.16
17.14 ver 11
17.15 Ex 22.31; Deut 14.21
18.2 Ex 6.7; Lev 11.44
18.3 Ezek 20.7,8; Ex 23.24; Lev 20.23

17.1-26.46 The Law of Holiness. A distinctive feature of this concluding section of Leviticus is the repeated declaration (with variations), "You shall be holy, for I am holy": 19.2; 20.7,8,26; 21.6, 8,15,23; 22.9,16,32. Holiness is the unique purity of God, and is to be emulated by the separate, pure life of his people through their obedience to his commandments (20.24,26; also 18.4-5; 19.19,37; 20.8,22; 22.31; 26.3,14). The priestly role in making atonement is less prominent here than in the earlier section of Leviticus, with emphasis in this section on the temple and the cultic participation there as central to Israel's achieving and maintaining holiness. There is more exhortation than instruction in the Holiness Code, and the appeals are direct: "You shall...you shall not," with emphasis on the death penalty for failure to conform (17.9,14; 18.29; 19.8; 20.2-21, 27; 21.9; 24.16). Although pre-exilic traditions from Jerusalem (and possibly from other shrines in Palestine) have been incorporated in the Law of Holiness, it has been reworked in the light of (1) the priestly dominance in Israel after the return from exile, (2) the conviction that the exile was a divine punishment rather than a sign of God's impotence to safeguard his people, and (3) the consequent insistence on the uniqueness of God and on the necessity that Israel avoid any contamination from worship of alien deities. *Cf.* Jer 44.2-3,16-19; Ezek 8.6-18; Isa 57.3-10; 65.3-5. Yahweh alone is God; his people must give undivided loyalty and obedience to him.
17.1-9 Rules for eating meat. All slaughtering of animals is to be linked with the central sanctuary, in order to avoid sacrifices or offerings to local deities. The rule against the eating of blood (17.10-16), which is the locus of life and the basis of atonement for human sin, is applied to all Israelites but also to resident aliens. Anything that died of itself or was killed by another animal may not be eaten: this is a precaution against eating blood or impurity of any kind. Violators must be washed in order to restore purity.
18.1-30 Rules for Purity in Sexual Relations. Israel's special relationship as God's people requires that the people follow his commands rather than the practices of her pagan neighbors (18.1-5). Prohibited are all forms of incest (18.6-18). All forms of sexual impurity or irregularity are to be avoided (18.19-23), including intercourse with a woman during menstruation, homosexual relations or sex with animals. Forbidden is the sacrificing of one's children to a deity, as was common in Canaanite religion. The conclusion is drawn that it was such violations of the divine order that led to the expulsion of the Canaanites from this land (18.24-27), and will bring about the exile of Israel (18.28). This warning is written as though addressed to the future, but is in fact an analysis of what happened in the past. For Israel to commit such acts is to abdicate the people's status as God's own (18.29-30).

which I am bringing you. You shall not follow their statutes. 4 My ordinances you shall observe and my statutes you shall keep, following them: I am the LORD your God. 5 You shall keep my statutes and my ordinances; by doing so one shall live: I am the LORD.

6 None of you shall approach anyone near of kin to uncover nakedness: I am the LORD. 7 You shall not uncover the nakedness of your father, which is the nakedness of your mother; she is your mother, you shall not uncover her nakedness. 8 You shall not uncover the nakedness of your father's wife; it is the nakedness of your father. 9 You shall not uncover the nakedness of your sister, your father's daughter or your mother's daughter, whether born at home or born abroad. 10 You shall not uncover the nakedness of your son's daughter or of your daughter's daughter, for their nakedness is your own nakedness. 11 You shall not uncover the nakedness of your father's wife's daughter, begotten by your father, since she is your sister. 12 You shall not uncover the nakedness of your father's sister; she is your father's flesh. 13 You shall not uncover the nakedness of your mother's sister, for she is your mother's flesh. 14 You shall not uncover the nakedness of your father's brother, that is, you shall not approach his wife; she is your aunt. 15 You shall not uncover the nakedness of your daughter-in-law: she is your son's wife; you shall not uncover her nakedness. 16 You shall not uncover the nakedness of your brother's wife; it is your brother's nakedness. 17 You shall not uncover the nakedness of a woman and her daughter, and you shall not take[x] her son's daughter or her daughter's daughter to uncover her nakedness; they are your[y] flesh; it is depravity. 18 And you shall not take[x] a woman as a rival to her sister, uncovering her nakedness while her sister is still alive.

19 You shall not approach a woman to uncover her nakedness while she is in her menstrual uncleanness. 20 You shall not have sexual relations with your kinsman's wife, and defile yourself with her. 21 You shall not give any of your offspring to sacrifice them[z] to Molech, and so profane the name of your God: I am the LORD. 22 You shall not lie with a male as with a woman; it is an abomination. 23 You shall not have sexual relations with any animal and defile yourself with it, nor shall any woman give herself to an animal to have sexual relations with it: it is perversion.

24 Do not defile yourselves in any of these ways, for by all these practices the nations I am casting out before you have defiled themselves. 25 Thus the land became defiled; and I punished it for its iniquity, and the land vomited out its inhabitants. 26 But you shall keep my statutes and my ordinances and commit none of these abominations, either the citizen or the alien who resides among you 27 (for the inhabitants of the land, who were before you, committed all of these abominations, and the land became defiled); 28 otherwise the land will vomit you out for defiling it, as it vomited out the nation that was before you. 29 For whoever commits any of these abominations shall be cut off from their people. 30 So keep my charge not to commit any of these abominations that were done before you, and not to defile yourselves by them: I am the LORD your God.

Ritual and Moral Holiness

19 The LORD spoke to Moses, saying: 2 Speak to all the congregation of the people of Israel and say to them: You shall be holy, for I the LORD your God am holy. 3 You shall each revere your mother and father, and you shall keep my sabbaths: I am the LORD your God. 4 Do not turn to idols or make cast images for yourselves: I am the LORD your God.

5 When you offer a sacrifice of well-being to the LORD, offer it in such a way that it is acceptable on your behalf. 6 It shall be eaten on the same day you offer it, or on the next day; and anything left over until the third day shall be consumed in fire. 7 If it is eaten at all on the third day, it is an abomination; it will not be acceptable. 8 All who eat it shall be subject to punishment, because they have profaned what is holy to the LORD; and any such person shall be cut off from the people.

9 When you reap the harvest of your land, you shall not reap to the very edges of your field, or gather the gleanings of your harvest. 10 You shall not strip your vineyard bare, or gather the fallen grapes of your vineyard; you shall leave them for the poor and the alien: I am the LORD your God.

11 You shall not steal; you shall not deal falsely; and you shall not lie to one another.

[x] Or *marry* [y] Gk: Heb lacks *your* [z] Heb *to pass them over*

18.5 Ezek 20.11; Lk 10.28; Rom 10.5; Gal 3.12

18.7 Lev 20.11

18.9 Lev 20.17

18.12 Lev 20.19

18.14 Lev 20.20

18.15 Lev 20.12

18.16 Lev 20.21

18.17 Lev 20.14

18.19 Lev 15.24; 20.18

18.20 Lev 20.10; Ex 20.14; Prov 6.32; Mt 5.27

18.21 Lev 20.2-5; 19.12; 21.6

18.22 Lev 20.13; Rom 1.27

18.23 Ex 22.19; Lev 20.15; Deut 27.21

18.24 ver 3; Lev 20.23

18.25 Lev 20.23; Deut 9.5; 18.12; ver 28

18.30 Lev 22.9; Deut 11.1; ver 2

19.2 1 Pet 1.16

19.3 Ex 20.8,12; Lev 11.44

19.4 Lev 26.1; Ps 96.5; Ex 20.23; 34.17

19.9 Lev 23.22; Deut 24.20-22

19.11 Ex 20.15; Lev 6.2; Eph 4.25; Col 3.9

19.1-36 The priestly equivalent of the Ten Commandments. Although in form and content these injunctions resemble the giving of the Ten Commandments in Ex 20.1-20, the range of social and moral demands here is more extensive. After a repeated reminder of the unique relationship of God and his people as the basis of his moral and cultic demands (19.1-2), the injunctions begin: honor one's parents; keep the sabbath (19.3); avoid contact with idols or image-making (19.4); take care to eat the sacrifice of well-being within two days (19.5-8); leave part of the crops in the fields and the grapes in the vineyards in order to provide food for the poor and the aliens in the land (19.9-10); avoid stealing, lying and false testimony (19.11-12); be fair in all dealings with neighbors and employees (19.13); show kindness to the deaf and blind (19.14); act in all dealings with integrity and honesty (19.15-16); act in love toward family and neighbors, including reproof of an erring neighbor (19.17-18); observe proper order and distinctions in breeding animals and in sowing crops (19.19); deal fairly with slave women and provide for guilt offering when one is violated (19.20-22); wait four years before eating the fruit of trees planted in the land, to allow for maturity of growth (23-25); avoid all practices connected with pagan religions: eating blood, participating in witchcraft, trimming hair or beard or tattooing one's body as worshippers of other gods do (19.26-28); show due deference to the aged and consideration for aliens in the land (19.32-33); act honestly in all business transactions (19.35). The closing words, *I am the LORD*, echo the theme of the Holiness law.

20.1-27 Violations of God's law punishable by death. The practice of sacrificing a child to a pagan deity, mentioned in 18.21, is now discussed more fully. To give one's *offspring to Molech* (20.2-5) may be a reference to the personal name of a Semitic deity (1 Kings 11.7), or to the widespread Near Eastern practice of sacrificing children, which was carried out near Jerusalem in the late seventh century BCE during the reign of Josiah (2 Kings 23.10) and was revived in the time of Jeremiah (Jer 32.35; also mentioned in Deut 18.10; Ezek 20.31). The rule against consulting wizards or mediums (19.6) is underscored in 20.27, where the death penalty is prescribed for men or women who perform such services. The basic theme of the Holiness Code – Be holy because Yahweh is holy – is repeated in 20.7-8. Denounced are violators of the divinely established order (20.9-21), who curse parents or perform acts of sexual promiscuity. By contrast (20.22-26), to keep the commandments of Yahweh sustains the divinely intended order of life for God's people. Continued life of this people in the land depends on their obedience; earlier occupants were expelled for violations of these rules. As the pure, separate people of God, Israel must observe faithfully the divinely established distinctions in human life within the creation.

12 And you shall not swear falsely by my name, profaning the name of your God: I am the LORD.

13 You shall not defraud your neighbor; you shall not steal; and you shall not keep for yourself the wages of a laborer until morning. 14 You shall not revile the deaf or put a stumbling block before the blind; you shall fear your God: I am the LORD.

15 You shall not render an unjust judgment; you shall not be partial to the poor or defer to the great: with justice you shall judge your neighbor. 16 You shall not go around as a slanderer[a] among your people, and you shall not profit by the blood[b] of your neighbor: I am the LORD.

17 You shall not hate in your heart anyone of your kin; you shall reprove your neighbor, or you will incur guilt yourself. 18 You shall not take vengeance or bear a grudge against any of your people, but you shall love your neighbor as yourself: I am the LORD.

19 You shall keep my statutes. You shall not let your animals breed with a different kind; you shall not sow your field with two kinds of seed; nor shall you put on a garment made of two different materials.

20 If a man has sexual relations with a woman who is a slave, designated for another man but not ransomed or given her freedom, an inquiry shall be held. They shall not be put to death, since she has not been freed; 21 but he shall bring a guilt offering for himself to the LORD, at the entrance of the tent of meeting, a ram as guilt offering. 22 And the priest shall make atonement for him with the ram of guilt offering before the LORD for his sin that he committed; and the sin he committed shall be forgiven him.

23 When you come into the land and plant all kinds of trees for food, then you shall regard their fruit as forbidden;[c] three years it shall be forbidden[d] to you, it must not be eaten. 24 In the fourth year all their fruit shall be set apart for rejoicing in the LORD. 25 But in the fifth year you may eat of their fruit, that their yield may be increased for you: I am the LORD your God.

26 You shall not eat anything with its blood. You shall not practice augury or witchcraft. 27 You shall not round off the hair on your temples or mar the edges of your beard. 28 You shall not make any gashes in your flesh for the dead or tattoo any marks upon you: I am the LORD.

29 Do not profane your daughter by making her a prostitute, that the land not become prostituted and full of depravity. 30 You shall keep my sabbaths and reverence my sanctuary: I am the LORD.

31 Do not turn to mediums or wizards; do not seek them out, to be defiled by them: I am the LORD your God.

32 You shall rise before the aged, and defer to the old; and you shall fear your God: I am the LORD.

33 When an alien resides with you in your land, you shall not oppress the alien. 34 The alien who resides with you shall be to you as the citizen among you; you shall love the alien as yourself, for you were aliens in the land of Egypt: I am the LORD your God.

35 You shall not cheat in measuring length, weight, or quantity. 36 You shall have honest balances, honest weights, an honest ephah, and an honest hin: I am the LORD your God, who brought you out of the land of Egypt. 37 You shall keep all my statutes and all my ordinances, and observe them: I am the LORD.

Penalties for Violations of Holiness

20 The LORD spoke to Moses, saying: 2 Say further to the people of Israel:

Any of the people of Israel, or of the aliens who reside in Israel, who give any of their offspring to Molech shall be put to death; the people of the land shall stone them to death. 3 I myself will set my face against them, and will cut them off from the people, because they have given of their offspring to Molech, defiling my sanctuary and profaning my holy name. 4 And if the people of the land should ever close their eyes to them, when they give of their offspring to Molech, and do not put them to death, 5 I myself will set my face against them and against their family, and will cut them off from among their people, them and all who follow them in prostituting themselves to Molech.

6 If any turn to mediums and wizards, prostituting themselves to them, I will set my face against them, and will cut them off from the people. 7 Consecrate yourselves therefore, and be holy; for I am the LORD your God. 8 Keep my statutes, and observe them; I am the LORD; I sanctify you. 9 All

[a] Meaning of Heb uncertain [b] Heb *stand against the blood* [c] Heb *as their uncircumcision* [d] Heb *uncircumcision*

19.12 Ex 20.7; Lev 18.21
19.13 Ex 22.7-15; 21-27; Deut 24.15; Jas 5.4
19.14 Deut 27.18
19.15 Ex 23.6; Deut 1.17
19.16 Ps 15.3; Ezek 22.9; Ex 23.7
19.17 1 Jn 2.9,11; 3.15; Lk 17.3; Gal 6.1
19.18 Rom 12.19; Ps 103.9; Mt 19.19; Mk 12.31; Rom 13.9
19.19 Deut 22.9,11
19.21 Lev 5.15
19.24 Deut 12.17,18; Prov 3.9
19.26 Lev 17.10; Deut 18.10
19.27 Lev 21.5
19.28 Lev 21.5
19.29 Deut 23.17
19.30 ver 3; Lev 26.2
19.31 Lev 20.6,27; Deut 18.10,11
19.33 Ex 22.21
19.34 Ex 12.48,49; Deut 10.19
20.2 Lev 18.21
20.3 Lev 15.31; 18.21
20.4 Deut 17.2,3,5
20.6 Lev 19.31
20.7 1 Pet 1.16
20.8 Lev 19.37; Ex 31.13
20.9 Ex 21.17; Deut 27.16

20.10 Lev 18.20; Deut 22.22
20.11 Lev 18.7,8
20.12 Lev 18.15
20.13 Lev 18.22
20.14 Deut 27.23
20.15 Lev 18.23
20.17 Lev 18.9
20.18 Lev 18.19
20.19 Lev 18.12,13
20.20 Lev 18.14
20.21 Lev 18.16
20.22 Lev 18.25,26,28
20.23 Lev 18.3,24, 27,30
20.24 Ex 13.5; 33.3,16; ver 26
20.25 Lev 11.1-47; Deut 14.3-21
20.26 ver 24
20.27 Lev 19.31
21.1 Lev 19.28; Ezek 44.25
21.5 Deut 14.1; Ezek 44.20; Lev 19.27
21.6 Lev 18.21; 3.11
21.7 ver 13.14
21.10 Lev 16.32; 10.6.7
21.11 Lev 19.28
21.12 Lev 10.7; Ex 29.6.7

who curse father or mother shall be put to death; having cursed father or mother, their blood is upon them.

10 If a man commits adultery with the wife of[e] his neighbor, both the adulterer and the adulteress shall be put to death. [11]The man who lies with his father's wife has uncovered his father's nakedness; both of them shall be put to death; their blood is upon them. [12]If a man lies with his daughter-in-law, both of them shall be put to death; they have committed perversion, their blood is upon them. [13]If a man lies with a male as with a woman, both of them have committed an abomination; they shall be put to death; their blood is upon them. [14]If a man takes a wife and her mother also, it is depravity; they shall be burned to death, both he and they, that there may be no depravity among you. [15]If a man has sexual relations with an animal, he shall be put to death; and you shall kill the animal. [16]If a woman approaches any animal and has sexual relations with it, you shall kill the woman and the animal; they shall be put to death, their blood is upon them.

17 If a man takes his sister, a daughter of his father or a daughter of his mother, and sees her nakedness, and she sees his nakedness, it is a disgrace, and they shall be cut off in the sight of their people; he has uncovered his sister's nakedness, he shall be subject to punishment. [18]If a man lies with a woman having her sickness and uncovers her nakedness, he has laid bare her flow and she has laid bare her flow of blood; both of them shall be cut off from their people. [19]You shall not uncover the nakedness of your mother's sister or of your father's sister, for that is to lay bare one's own flesh; they shall be subject to punishment. [20]If a man lies with his uncle's wife, he has uncovered his uncle's nakedness; they shall be subject to punishment; they shall die childless. [21]If a man takes his brother's wife, it is impurity; he has uncovered his brother's nakedness; they shall be childless.

22 You shall keep all my statutes and all my ordinances, and observe them, so that the land to which I bring you to settle in may not vomit you out. [23]You shall not follow the practices of the nation that I am driving out before you. Because they did all these things, I abhorred them. [24]But I have said to you: You shall inherit their land, and I will give it to you to possess, a land flowing with milk and honey. I am the LORD your God; I have separated you from the peoples. [25]You shall therefore make a distinction between the clean animal and the unclean, and between the unclean bird and the clean; you shall not bring abomination on yourselves by animal or by bird or by anything with which the ground teems, which I have set apart for you to hold unclean. [26]You shall be holy to me; for I the LORD am holy, and I have separated you from the other peoples to be mine.

27 A man or a woman who is a medium or a wizard shall be put to death; they shall be stoned to death, their blood is upon them.

The Holiness of Priests

21 The LORD said to Moses: Speak to the priests, the sons of Aaron, and say to them:

No one shall defile himself for a dead person among his relatives, [2]except for his nearest kin: his mother, his father, his son, his daughter, his brother; [3]likewise, for a virgin sister, close to him because she has had no husband, he may defile himself for her. [4]But he shall not defile himself as a husband among his people and so profane himself. [5]They shall not make bald spots upon their heads, or shave off the edges of their beards, or make any gashes in their flesh. [6]They shall be holy to their God, and not profane the name of their God; for they offer the LORD's offerings by fire, the food of their God; therefore they shall be holy. [7]They shall not marry a prostitute or a woman who has been defiled; neither shall they marry a woman divorced from her husband. For they are holy to their God, [8]and you shall treat them as holy, since they offer the food of your God; they shall be holy to you, for I the LORD, I who sanctify you, am holy. [9]When the daughter of a priest profanes herself through prostitution, she profanes her father; she shall be burned to death.

10 The priest who is exalted above his fellows, on whose head the anointing oil has been poured and who has been consecrated to wear the vestments, shall not dishevel his hair, nor tear his vestments. [11]He shall not go where there is a dead body; he shall not defile himself even for his father or mother. [12]He shall not go outside

[e] Heb repeats *if a man commits adultery with the wife of*

21.1-24 Rules for the Priests to Maintain Holiness. To be avoided are contact with corpses, except the bodies of close relatives (21.1-4); participation in rites to appease evil spirits when someone has died (21.5); marrying a former prostitute or divorcee (21.7); allowing a daughter to live who has become a prostitute (21.9). The purity of the priest is essential because he provides *the food of...God* (21.6,8). In connection with the burial of the dead, the priest is not to jeopardize his holiness by approaching a dead body – even that of his parent – or engaging in the usual mourning rites *(dishevel his hair, tear his vestments*: 21.10-11), nor leave the *sanctuary* to attend the burial ceremony (21.12). The special requirements for priestly purity in marriage (21.13-14) expand on 21.7, emphasizing the necessity of maintaining purity in one's lineage in order to serve as the one who approaches the holy LORD (21.15). Similarly, the physical condition of the priest may disqualify him from serving (21.17-24), because he approaches the LORD when he brings food to God. In spite of his defect, he may eat the special food set aside for the priests, but may not *come near the curtain* [of the inner sanctuary] *or approach the altar*. That is where the LORD dwells.

22.1-16 Preserving the Holiness of the Gifts to the Altar. In order to preserve the holiness of the *sacred donations* offered to the LORD and to the priests (22.2), the latter must take care that the gifts are not touched by any persons who are unclean (22.4-5), and a defiled priest may not take part in the offering of the *donations* to God until he has been purified (22.6-9). The priest's portion of the holy food may be shared only with qualified members of his household (22.10-16). Anyone who *unintentionally* violates these rules may make monetary payment by way of compensation (22.14). Offerings acceptable to the LORD (22.17-30) include various forms of *sacrifice of well-being to the LORD* (22.21) by which the right relationship with God is maintained: the sacrificial animals must be free of blemish (22.20-22, 24-25), although the purity requirements are relaxed in the case of a *freewill offering*. The same rules as those for the sanctity of a newborn child (Lev 12.2-3) apply to newborn sacrificial animals (22.26-30).

the sanctuary and thus profane the sanctuary of his God; for the consecration of the anointing oil of his God is upon him: I am the LORD. 13 He shall marry only a woman who is a virgin. 14 A widow, or a divorced woman, or a woman who has been defiled, a prostitute, these he shall not marry. He shall marry a virgin of his own kin, 15 that he may not profane his offspring among his kin; for I am the LORD; I sanctify him.

16 The LORD spoke to Moses, saying: 17 Speak to Aaron and say: No one of your offspring throughout their generations who has a blemish may approach to offer the food of his God. 18 For no one who has a blemish shall draw near, one who is blind or lame, or one who has a mutilated face or a limb too long, 19 or one who has a broken foot or a broken hand, 20 or a hunchback, or a dwarf, or a man with a blemish in his eyes or an itching disease or scabs or crushed testicles. 21 No descendant of Aaron the priest who has a blemish shall come near to offer the LORD's offerings by fire; since he has a blemish, he shall not come near to offer the food of his God. 22 He may eat the food of his God, of the most holy as well as of the holy. 23 But he shall not come near the curtain or approach the altar, because he has a blemish, that he may not profane my sanctuaries; for I am the LORD; I sanctify them. 24 Thus Moses spoke to Aaron and to his sons and to all the people of Israel.

The Use of Holy Offerings

22 The LORD spoke to Moses, saying: 2 Direct Aaron and his sons to deal carefully with the sacred donations of the people of Israel, which they dedicate to me, so that they may not profane my holy name; I am the LORD. 3 Say to them: If anyone among all your offspring throughout your generations comes near the sacred donations, which the people of Israel dedicate to the LORD, while he is in a state of uncleanness, that person shall be cut off from my presence: I am the LORD. 4 No one of Aaron's offspring who has a leprous[f] disease or suffers a discharge may eat of the sacred donations until he is clean. Whoever touches anything made unclean by a corpse or a man who has had an emission of semen, 5 and whoever touches any swarming thing by which he may be made unclean or any human being by whom he may be made unclean—whatever his uncleanness may be— 6 the person who touches any such shall be unclean until evening and shall not eat of the sacred donations unless he has washed his body in water. 7 When the sun sets he shall be clean; and afterward he may eat of the sacred donations, for they are his food. 8 That which died or was torn by wild animals he shall not eat, becoming unclean by it: I am the LORD. 9 They shall keep my charge, so that they may not incur guilt and die in the sanctuary[g] for having profaned it: I am the LORD; I sanctify them.

10 No lay person shall eat of the sacred donations. No bound or hired servant of the priest shall eat of the sacred donations; 11 but if a priest acquires anyone by purchase, the person may eat of them; and those that are born in his house may eat of his food. 12 If a priest's daughter marries a layman, she shall not eat of the offering of the sacred donations; 13 but if a priest's daughter is widowed or divorced, without offspring, and returns to her father's house, as in her youth, she may eat of her father's food. No lay person shall eat of it. 14 If a man eats of the sacred donation unintentionally, he shall add one-fifth of its value to it, and give the sacred donation to the priest. 15 No one shall profane the sacred donations of the people of Israel, which they offer to the LORD, 16 causing them to bear guilt requiring a guilt offering, by eating their sacred donations: for I am the LORD; I sanctify them.

Acceptable Offerings

17 The LORD spoke to Moses, saying: 18 Speak to Aaron and his sons and all the people of Israel and say to them: When anyone of the house of Israel or of the aliens residing in Israel presents an offering, whether in payment of a vow or as a freewill offering that is offered to the LORD as a burnt offering, 19 to be acceptable in your behalf it shall be a male without blemish, of the cattle or the sheep or the goats. 20 You shall not offer anything that has a blemish, for it will not be acceptable in your behalf.

21 When anyone offers a sacrifice of well-being to the LORD, in fulfillment of a vow or as a freewill offering, from the herd or from the flock, to be acceptable it must be perfect;

[f] A term for several skin diseases; precise meaning uncertain [g] Vg: Heb *incur guilt for it and die in it*

21.13 ver 7; Ezek 44.22
21.17 ver 6
21.18 Lev 22.23
21.20 Deut 23.1
21.21 ver 6
21.23 ver 12
22.2 Lev 18.21
22.3 Lev 7.20
22.4 Lev 14.1-32; Num 19.11,12; 15.16,17
22.5 Lev 11.24,43,44; 15.7,19
22.8 Ex 22.31; Lev 17.15
22.9 Lev 18.30; ver 16
22.10 ver 13
22.13 ver 10
22.14 Lev 5.15,16
22.16 ver 9
22.19 Lev 1.3
22.20 Deut 15.21; 17.1; Heb 9.14; 1 Pet 1.19
22.21 Lev 3.1,6

22.25 Lev 21.6,17
22.27 Ex 22.30
22.28 Deut 22.6,7
22.29 Lev 7.12
22.30 Lev 7.15
22.31 Lev 19.37
22.32 Lev 18.21; 10.3
22.33 Ex 6.7; Lev 11.45
23.2 ver 4,37,44; Num 29.39
23.3 Lev 19.3; Ex 31.13-17; Deut 5.13
23.4 ver 2
23.5 Ex 12.18,19; Num 28.16,17
23.8 ver 8,21,25, 35,36
23.10 Ex 23.16,19; 34.22,26
23.13 Lev 2.14-16
23.15 Deut 16.9
23.16 Num 28.26
23.17 Lev 2.12; 7.13

there shall be no blemish in it. [22]Anything blind, or injured, or maimed, or having a discharge or an itch or scabs—these you shall not offer to the LORD or put any of them on the altar as offerings by fire to the LORD. [23]An ox or a lamb that has a limb too long or too short you may present for a freewill offering; but it will not be accepted for a vow. [24]Any animal that has its testicles bruised or crushed or torn or cut, you shall not offer to the LORD; such you shall not do within your land, [25]nor shall you accept any such animals from a foreigner to offer as food to your God; since they are mutilated, with a blemish in them, they shall not be accepted in your behalf.

26 The LORD spoke to Moses, saying: [27]When an ox or a sheep or a goat is born, it shall remain seven days with its mother, and from the eighth day on it shall be acceptable as the LORD's offering by fire. [28]But you shall not slaughter, from the herd or the flock, an animal with its young on the same day. [29]When you sacrifice a thanksgiving offering to the LORD, you shall sacrifice it so that it may be acceptable in your behalf. [30]It shall be eaten on the same day; you shall not leave any of it until morning: I am the LORD.

31 Thus you shall keep my commandments and observe them: I am the LORD. [32]You shall not profane my holy name, that I may be sanctified among the people of Israel: I am the LORD; I sanctify you, [33]I who brought you out of the land of Egypt to be your God: I am the LORD.

Appointed Festivals

23 The LORD spoke to Moses, saying: [2]Speak to the people of Israel and say to them: These are the appointed festivals of the LORD that you shall proclaim as holy convocations, my appointed festivals.

The Sabbath, Passover, and Unleavened Bread

3 Six days shall work be done; but the seventh day is a sabbath of complete rest, a holy convocation; you shall do no work: it is a sabbath to the LORD throughout your settlements.

4 These are the appointed festivals of the LORD, the holy convocations, which you shall celebrate at the time appointed for them. [5]In the first month, on the fourteenth day of the month, at twilight,[h] there shall be a passover offering to the LORD, [6]and on the fifteenth day of the same month is the festival of unleavened bread to the LORD; seven days you shall eat unleavened bread. [7]On the first day you shall have a holy convocation; you shall not work at your occupations. [8]For seven days you shall present the LORD's offerings by fire; on the seventh day there shall be a holy convocation: you shall not work at your occupations.

The Offering of First Fruits

9 The LORD spoke to Moses: [10]Speak to the people of Israel and say to them: When you enter the land that I am giving you and you reap its harvest, you shall bring the sheaf of the first fruits of your harvest to the priest. [11]He shall raise the sheaf before the LORD, that you may find acceptance; on the day after the sabbath the priest shall raise it. [12]On the day when you raise the sheaf, you shall offer a lamb a year old, without blemish, as a burnt offering to the LORD. [13]And the grain offering with it shall be two-tenths of an ephah of choice flour mixed with oil, an offering by fire of pleasing odor to the LORD; and the drink offering with it shall be of wine, one-fourth of a hin. [14]You shall eat no bread or parched grain or fresh ears until that very day, until you have brought the offering of your God: it is a statute forever throughout your generations in all your settlements.

The Festival of Weeks

15 And from the day after the sabbath, from the day on which you bring the sheaf of the elevation offering, you shall count off seven weeks; they shall be complete. [16]You shall count until the day after the seventh sabbath, fifty days; then you shall present an offering of new grain to the LORD. [17]You shall bring from your settlements two loaves of bread as an elevation offering, each made of two-tenths of an ephah; they shall be of choice flour, baked with leaven, as first fruits to the LORD. [18]You shall present with the bread seven lambs a year old without blemish, one young bull, and two rams; they shall be a burnt offering to the LORD, along with their grain offering and their

[h] Heb *between the two evenings*

22.31-33 The holiness formula rounds out this section with its affirmation of the correlative holiness of the LORD and his faithful people.
23.1-25.55 Sacred Time: Festivals and the Sacred Calendar. God's ordering of the creation concerns not only its origins but also the operation of all of life – human, animal, agricultural – within it. The specifics of this divine pattern are linked with the agricultural cycles (which echo those of other ancient Near Eastern cultures) but also major events in the past. Dependent on honoring this pattern are prosperity in the land and the continuing renewal of the covenant relationship between God and his people. Some of the precise dates of the festivals are linked with the temple; others, which are less predictable, are based on the agricultural cycle (*cf.* Ex 23.15-16). The calculation of sacred days, as in Ezek 45.21-25, is related to the sowing of crops in the spring and their harvest in the autumn. But the dating is complicated by the incompatibility of the solar and lunar cycles, and by the shift to the Babylonian calendar by Israelites during their exile in Babylon. In the Holiness Code, following the exile, the features are combined and a uniformity has been imposed for observing the sacred times and seasons (23.1-2).
23.3 The Sabbath. Although the cycle of seven days was important for culture throughout the ancient near east, there is no evidence of formal observance of the seventh day of rest prior to the exile. In the post-exilic prophets it has become a basic obligation for Israel (Isa 56.2-7; 58.13-14). The priestly editor of Genesis reports that God observes the sabbath (Gen 2.3). And it has become a capital crime to violate the sabbath day of rest (Ex 31.14; Num 15.32-36).
23.4-8 Passover and Unleavened Bread. Passover was originally a spring festival to assure the fertility of the flocks, and was celebrated in their homes by herdsmen. Its date was in the spring, separated by six months from the agricultural harvest. It became linked with Israel's deliverance from slavery in Egypt, and in Deuteronomy the celebration was moved to the central sanctuary (Deut 16.6). Following the exile, it was also understood as a symbol of future deliverance from domination by Gentile powers and of the renewal of Israel. The feast of unleavened bread, which follows the Passover, provides a link with the annual cycle of fertility for the grain crops, which are dedicated in advance to the LORD.
23.9-14 The Offering of the First Fruits. Here the pastoral and agricultural bases of Israel's life in the land are brought together through the offering of lambs, grain and wine, for which gratitude to God and the continuation of his blessing are symbolized in the rite.
23.15-22 The Festival of Weeks. The end of the harvest season is celebrated, beginning with the *elevation offering*, by which the success of the crops and the thanks to God are expressed. The elaborate calculation of the sacred season compounds the sacred numbers: 7 x 7 + 1 = the fiftieth day. Its rites include the burnt offering, the grain offering, the sin offering, and the elevation offering (assigned to the LORD and the priest). Here also the rule is given for leaving part of the crops in the fields and vineyards for the benefit of the poor and the aliens (23.22).

drink offerings, an offering by fire of pleasing odor to the LORD. [19]You shall also offer one male goat for a sin offering, and two male lambs a year old as a sacrifice of well-being. [20]The priest shall raise them with the bread of the first fruits as an elevation offering before the LORD, together with the two lambs; they shall be holy to the LORD for the priest. [21]On that same day you shall make proclamation; you shall hold a holy convocation; you shall not work at your occupations. This is a statute forever in all your settlements throughout your generations.

22 When you reap the harvest of your land, you shall not reap to the very edges of your field, or gather the gleanings of your harvest; you shall leave them for the poor and for the alien: I am the LORD your God.

The Festival of Trumpets

23 The LORD spoke to Moses, saying: [24]Speak to the people of Israel, saying: In the seventh month, on the first day of the month, you shall observe a day of complete rest, a holy convocation commemorated with trumpet blasts. [25]You shall not work at your occupations; and you shall present the LORD's offering by fire.

The Day of Atonement

26 The LORD spoke to Moses, saying: [27]Now, the tenth day of this seventh month is the day of atonement; it shall be a holy convocation for you: you shall deny yourselves[i] and present the LORD's offering by fire; [28]and you shall do no work during that entire day; for it is a day of atonement, to make atonement on your behalf before the LORD your God. [29]For anyone who does not practice self-denial[j] during that entire day shall be cut off from the people. [30]And anyone who does any work during that entire day, such a one I will destroy from the midst of the people. [31]You shall do no work: it is a statute forever throughout your generations in all your settlements. [32]It shall be to you a sabbath of complete rest, and you shall deny yourselves;[i] on the ninth day of the month at evening, from evening to evening you shall keep your sabbath.

The Festival of Booths

33 The LORD spoke to Moses, saying: [34]Speak to the people of Israel, saying: On the fifteenth day of this seventh month, and lasting seven days, there shall be the festival of booths[k] to the LORD. [35]The first day shall be a holy convocation; you shall not work at your occupations. [36]Seven days you shall present the LORD's offerings by fire; on the eighth day you shall observe a holy convocation and present the LORD's offerings by fire; it is a solemn assembly; you shall not work at your occupations.

37 These are the appointed festivals of the LORD, which you shall celebrate as times of holy convocation, for presenting to the LORD offerings by fire—burnt offerings and grain offerings, sacrifices and drink offerings, each on its proper day— [38]apart from the sabbaths of the LORD, and apart from your gifts, and apart from all your votive offerings, and apart from all your freewill offerings, which you give to the LORD.

39 Now, the fifteenth day of the seventh month, when you have gathered in the produce of the land, you shall keep the festival of the LORD, lasting seven days; a complete rest on the first day, and a complete rest on the eighth day. [40]On the first day you shall take the fruit of majestic[l] trees, branches of palm trees, boughs of leafy trees, and willows of the brook; and you shall rejoice before the LORD your God for seven days. [41]You shall keep it as a festival to the LORD seven days in the year; you shall keep it in the seventh month as a statute forever throughout your generations. [42]You shall live in booths for seven days; all that are citizens in Israel shall live in booths, [43]so that your generations may know that I made the people of Israel live in booths when I brought them out of the land of Egypt: I am the LORD your God.

44 Thus Moses declared to the people of Israel the appointed festivals of the LORD.

The Lamp

24 The LORD spoke to Moses, saying: [2]Command the people of Israel to bring you pure oil of beaten olives for the lamp, that a light may be kept burning regularly. [3]Aaron shall set it up in the tent

23.19 Num 28.30; Lev 3.1
23.21 ver 7
23.22 Lev 19.9
23.24 Num 29.1; Lev 25.9
23.27 Lev 16.29,30
23.29 Gen 17.14
23.30 Lev 20.3,5,6
23.34 Ex 23.16; Num 29.12; ver 42,43
23.36 Num 29.12-38
23.37 ver 2,4
23.39 Ex 23.16; Deut 16.13
23.40 Neh 8.15; Deut 16.14,15
23.42 Neh 8.14-16
23.44 ver 2,37
24.2 Ex 27.20,21

[i] Or *shall fast* [j] Or *does not fast* [k] Or *tabernacles*: Heb *succoth* [l] Meaning of Heb uncertain

of meeting, outside the curtain of the covenant,[m] to burn from evening to morning before the LORD regularly; it shall be a statute forever throughout your generations. 4He shall set up the lamps on the lampstand of pure gold[n] before the LORD regularly.

The Bread for the Tabernacle

5 You shall take choice flour, and bake twelve loaves of it; two-tenths of an ephah shall be in each loaf. 6You shall place them in two rows, six in a row, on the table of pure gold.[o] 7You shall put pure frankincense with each row, to be a token offering for the bread, as an offering by fire to the LORD. 8Every sabbath day Aaron shall set them in order before the LORD regularly as a commitment of the people of Israel, as a covenant forever. 9They shall be for Aaron and his descendants, who shall eat them in a holy place, for they are most holy portions for him from the offerings by fire to the LORD, a perpetual due.

Blasphemy and Its Punishment

10 A man whose mother was an Israelite and whose father was an Egyptian came out among the people of Israel; and the Israelite woman's son and a certain Israelite began fighting in the camp. 11The Israelite woman's son blasphemed the Name in a curse. And they brought him to Moses—now his mother's name was Shelomith, daughter of Dibri, of the tribe of Dan—12and they put him in custody, until the decision of the LORD should be made clear to them.

13 The LORD said to Moses, saying: 14Take the blasphemer outside the camp; and let all who were within hearing lay their hands on his head, and let the whole congregation stone him. 15And speak to the people of Israel, saying: Anyone who curses God shall bear the sin. 16One who blasphemes the name of the LORD shall be put to death; the whole congregation shall stone the blasphemer. Aliens as well as citizens, when they blaspheme the Name, shall be put to death. 17Anyone who kills a human being shall be put to death. 18Anyone who kills an animal shall make restitution for it, life for life. 19Anyone who maims another shall suffer the same injury in return: 20fracture for fracture, eye for eye, tooth for tooth; the injury inflicted is the injury to be suffered. 21One who kills an animal shall make restitution for it; but one who kills a human being shall be put to death. 22You shall have one law for the alien and for the citizen: for I am the LORD your God. 23Moses spoke thus to the people of Israel; and they took the blasphemer outside the camp, and stoned him to death. The people of Israel did as the LORD had commanded Moses.

The Sabbatical Year

25 The LORD spoke to Moses on Mount Sinai, saying: 2Speak to the people of Israel and say to them: When you enter the land that I am giving you, the land shall observe a sabbath for the LORD. 3Six years you shall sow your field, and six years you shall prune your vineyard, and gather in their yield; 4but in the seventh year there shall be a sabbath of complete rest for the land, a sabbath for the LORD: you shall not sow your field or prune your vineyard. 5You shall not reap the aftergrowth of your harvest or gather the grapes of your unpruned vine: it shall be a year of complete rest for the land. 6You may eat what the land yields during its sabbath—you, your male and female slaves, your hired and your bound laborers who live with you; 7for your livestock also, and for the wild animals in your land all its yield shall be for food.

The Year of Jubilee

8 You shall count off seven weeks[p] of years, seven times seven years, so that the period of seven weeks of years gives forty-nine years. 9Then you shall have the trumpet sounded loud; on the tenth day of the seventh month—on the day of atonement—you shall have the trumpet sounded throughout all your land. 10And you shall hallow the fiftieth year and you shall proclaim liberty throughout the land to all its inhabitants. It shall be a jubilee for you: you shall return, every one of you, to your property and every one of you to your family. 11That fiftieth year shall be a jubilee for you: you shall not sow, or reap the aftergrowth, or harvest the unpruned vines. 12For it is a jubilee; it shall be holy to you: you shall eat only what the field itself produces.

13 In this year of jubilee you shall return, every one of you, to your property.

[m] Or *treaty*, or *testimony*; Heb *eduth* [n] Heb *pure lampstand* [o] Heb *pure table* [p] Or *sabbaths*

24.4 Ex 31.8; 39.37
24.5 Ex 25.30
24.6 Ex 25.24; 1 Kings 7.48
24.8 Num 4.7; 1 Chr 9.32; 2 Chr 2.4
24.9 Mt 12.4; Mk 2.26; Lk 6.4; Lev 8.31
24.11 ver 16
24.12 Num 15.34; Ex 18.15,16
24.14 Deut 13.9; 17.7; Lev 20.2,27; Deut 21.21
24.16 1 Kings 21.10,13; Mt 12.31; Mk 3.28
24.17 Ex 21.12; Num 35.30,31; Deut 19.11,12
24.18 ver 21
24.20 Ex 21.23,24; Deut 19.21; Mt 5.38
24.21 ver 17,18
24.22 Ex 12.49; Num 15.16
25.2 Ex 23.10,11
25.6 ver 20,21
25.9 Lev 23.24,27
25.10 ver 13,28,54
25.13 ver 10

24.10-23 How Violators of the Law are to be Punished.
24.10-12 The son of an Israelite woman by an Egyptian *blasphemed the Name* of YHWH (= Yahweh), which means that he pronounced the name of Israel's God, which by post-exilic times was regarded as so sacred that no human being should utter it. Down to the present, pious Jews when reading the Hebrew Bible substitute God's title, Lord (*adonai*) when the text is *YHWH*, which means "I am" (see Ex 3.14). The penalty for this violation of the divine name is death, with the entire *congregation* participating in the execution (24.13-16), and this was then carried out (24.23). Other offenses are punished by death (24.17), but for several the culprit must pay some form of monetary compensation (24.18-21). The same laws apply to Israelites and those of other ethnic origins living in the land (24.22).
25.1-55 Description of Sacred Time is Resumed.
25.1-7 The Sabbatical Year. Here the description of the seventh year of sacred rest amplifies the account in Ex 23.10-11. The specifics of what is to happen in that year match with other passages in the law and the prophets: cancelling of debts (Ex 21.2); reversion of property to ancestral owners (Deut 15.1-15); freeing of slaves (Jer 34.13-16). The land is to rest just as humans are called to do on the sabbath. All that the land produces belongs to God, is holy, and is to be left fallow.
25.8-34 The Year of Jubilee. Compounding the seventh day of rest and the seventh year of rest is the fiftieth year (7x7+1), which is the year of rest for the land and the people, and the time of rectification and restoration of the way God first established his people in the land. The description of this year is found only here and in Num 36.4. The year begins with the *Day of Atonement* (25.9) and is marked by the sounding of *the trumpet*, which in Ex 19.13 and Josh 6.5 is a *yobel*; hence Jubilee. Rules for the sabbath year are extended to the year of Jubilee (25.11-12), including the return of the land to hereditary owners (25.13-17). Payment is to be made to the present owners on the basis of the number of years until Jubilee, when the title of the property will revert to the ancestral owners. In the exchange of property, God will see to it that the lands will produce even in the years when they are not sown (25.18-24). Other specific provisions are made for transfer of property in anticipation of, or at the time of, the year of Jubilee (25.25-34). Generosity is to characterize dealings with poor relatives, other dependents, and resident aliens (25.35-55), for whom facilities, money and basic needs are to be provided. If any have been sold into slavery, they are to be freed in the Jubilee year (25.54).

[14]When you make a sale to your neighbor or buy from your neighbor, you shall not cheat one another. [15]When you buy from your neighbor, you shall pay only for the number of years since the jubilee; the seller shall charge you only for the remaining crop years. [16]If the years are more, you shall increase the price, and if the years are fewer, you shall diminish the price; for it is a certain number of harvests that are being sold to you. [17]You shall not cheat one another, but you shall fear your God; for I am the LORD your God.

18 You shall observe my statutes and faithfully keep my ordinances, so that you may live on the land securely. [19]The land will yield its fruit, and you will eat your fill and live on it securely. [20]Should you ask, What shall we eat in the seventh year, if we may not sow or gather in our crop? [21]I will order my blessing for you in the sixth year, so that it will yield a crop for three years. [22]When you sow in the eighth year, you will be eating from the old crop; until the ninth year, when its produce comes in, you shall eat the old. [23]The land shall not be sold in perpetuity, for the land is mine; with me you are but aliens and tenants. [24]Throughout the land that you hold, you shall provide for the redemption of the land.

25 If anyone of your kin falls into difficulty and sells a piece of property, then the next of kin shall come and redeem what the relative has sold. [26]If the person has no one to redeem it, but then prospers and finds sufficient means to do so, [27]the years since its sale shall be computed and the difference shall be refunded to the person to whom it was sold, and the property shall be returned. [28]But if there is not sufficient means to recover it, what was sold shall remain with the purchaser until the year of jubilee; in the jubilee it shall be released, and the property shall be returned.

29 If anyone sells a dwelling house in a walled city, it may be redeemed until a year has elapsed since its sale; the right of redemption shall be one year. [30]If it is not redeemed before a full year has elapsed, a house that is in a walled city shall pass in perpetuity to the purchaser, throughout the generations; it shall not be released in the jubilee. [31]But houses in villages that have no walls around them shall be classed as open country; they may be redeemed, and they shall be released in the jubilee. [32]As for the cities of the Levites, the Levites shall forever have the right of redemption of the houses in the cities belonging to them. [33]Such property as may be redeemed from the Levites—houses sold in a city belonging to them—shall be released in the jubilee; because the houses in the cities of the Levites are their possession among the people of Israel. [34]But the open land around their cities may not be sold; for that is their possession for all time.

35 If any of your kin fall into difficulty and become dependent on you,[q] you shall support them; they shall live with you as though resident aliens. [36]Do not take interest in advance or otherwise make a profit from them, but fear your God; let them live with you. [37]You shall not lend them your money at interest taken in advance, or provide them food at a profit. [38]I am the LORD your God, who brought you out of the land of Egypt, to give you the land of Canaan, to be your God.

39 If any who are dependent on you become so impoverished that they sell themselves to you, you shall not make them serve as slaves. [40]They shall remain with you as hired or bound laborers. They shall serve with you until the year of the jubilee. [41]Then they and their children with them shall be free from your authority; they shall go back to their own family and return to their ancestral property. [42]For they are my servants, whom I brought out of the land of Egypt; they shall not be sold as slaves are sold. [43]You shall not rule over them with harshness, but shall fear your God. [44]As for the male and female slaves whom you may have, it is from the nations around you that you may acquire male and female slaves. [45]You may also acquire them from among the aliens residing with you, and from their families that are with you, who have been born in your land; and they may be your property. [46]You may keep them as a possession for your children after you, for them to inherit as property. These you may treat as slaves, but as for your fellow Israelites, no one shall rule over the other with harshness.

47 If resident aliens among you prosper, and if any of your kin fall into difficulty with one of them and sell themselves to an alien, or to a branch of the alien's family, [48]after they have sold themselves they shall have the right of redemption; one of their

[q] Meaning of Heb uncertain

25.14 Lev 19.13; 1 Sam 12.3,4; 1 Cor 6.8
25.15 Lev 27.18,23
25.17 ver 14; Lev 19.14,32
25.18 Lev 19.37; 26.4,5
25.20 ver 4,5
25.22 Lev 26.10
25.23 Ex 19.5; Gen 23.4; 1 Cor 29.15; Ps 39.12
25.25 Ruth 2.20; 4.4,6
25.27 ver 50-52
25.28 ver 13
25.32 Num 35.1-8
25.35 Deut 15.7-11; Ps 37.26; Lk 6.35
25.36 Ex 22.25; Deut 23.19,20
25.38 Lev 11.45
25.39 Ex 21.2; Deut 15.12; 1 Kings 9.22
25.41 Ex 21.3; ver 28
25.43 ver 46,53; Ex 1.13,14
25.45 Isa 56.3,6
25.46 ver 43
25.48 Neh 5.5

brothers may redeem them, 49or their uncle
or their uncle's son may redeem them, or
anyone of their family who is of their own
flesh may redeem them; or if they prosper
they may redeem themselves. 50They shall
compute with the purchaser the total from
the year when they sold themselves to the
alien until the jubilee year; the price of the
sale shall be applied to the number of years:
the time they were with the owner shall be
rated as the time of a hired laborer. 51If
many years remain, they shall pay for their
redemption in proportion to the purchase
price; 52and if few years remain until the
jubilee year, they shall compute thus: according to the years involved they shall
make payment for their redemption. 53As a
laborer hired by the year they shall be
under the alien's authority, who shall not,
however, rule with harshness over them in
your sight. 54And if they have not been
redeemed in any of these ways, they and
their children with them shall go free in the
jubilee year. 55For to me the people of Israel
are servants; they are my servants whom
I brought out from the land of Egypt: I am
the LORD your God.

Rewards for Obedience

26 You shall make for yourselves no
idols and erect no carved images
or pillars, and you shall not place figured
stones in your land, to worship at them; for
I am the LORD your God. 2You shall keep my
sabbaths and reverence my sanctuary: I am
the LORD.

3 If you follow my statutes and keep my
commandments and observe them faithfully, 4I will give you your rains in their
season, and the land shall yield its produce,
and the trees of the field shall yield their
fruit. 5Your threshing shall overtake the
vintage, and the vintage shall overtake the
sowing; you shall eat your bread to the full,
and live securely in your land. 6And I will
grant peace in the land, and you shall lie
down, and no one shall make you afraid;
I will remove dangerous animals from the
land, and no sword shall go through your
land. 7You shall give chase to your enemies,
and they shall fall before you by the sword.
8Five of you shall give chase to a hundred,
and a hundred of you shall give chase to
ten thousand; your enemies shall fall before
you by the sword. 9I will look with favor
upon you and make you fruitful and
multiply you; and I will maintain my covenant with you. 10You shall eat old grain
long stored, and you shall have to clear out
the old to make way for the new. 11I will
place my dwelling in your midst, and I shall
not abhor you. 12And I will walk among
you, and will be your God, and you shall
be my people. 13I am the LORD your God
who brought you out of the land of Egypt,
to be their slaves no more; I have broken
the bars of your yoke and made you walk
erect.

Penalties for Disobedience

14 But if you will not obey me, and do
not observe all these commandments, 15if
you spurn my statutes, and abhor my ordinances, so that you will not observe all
my commandments, and you break my
covenant, 16I in turn will do this to you: I
will bring terror on you; consumption and
fever that waste the eyes and cause life to
pine away. You shall sow your seed in vain,
for your enemies shall eat it. 17I will set my
face against you, and you shall be struck
down by your enemies; your foes shall rule
over you, and you shall flee though no one
pursues you. 18And if in spite of this you
will not obey me, I will continue to punish
you sevenfold for your sins. 19I will break
your proud glory, and I will make your sky
like iron and your earth like copper. 20Your
strength shall be spent to no purpose: your
land shall not yield its produce, and the
trees of the land shall not yield their fruit.

21 If you continue hostile to me, and will
not obey me, I will continue to plague you
sevenfold for your sins. 22I will let loose wild
animals against you, and they shall bereave
you of your children and destroy your livestock; they shall make you few in number,
and your roads shall be deserted.

23 If in spite of these punishments you
have not turned back to me, but continue
hostile to me, 24then I too will continue
hostile to you: I myself will strike you sevenfold for your sins. 25I will bring the sword
against you, executing vengeance for the
covenant; and if you withdraw within your
cities, I will send pestilence among you, and
you shall be delivered into enemy hands.
26When I break your staff of bread, ten
women shall bake your bread in a single
oven, and they shall dole out your bread by
weight; and though you eat, you shall not
be satisfied.

26.1-13 Rewards for Obedience. Keeping the commandments of God includes avoidance of idolatry (26.1), observing the sabbath, and honoring the sanctuary (26.2). The rewards will be abundant rains, flourishing crops, peace in the land, freedom from beasts and victory over human enemies (26.3-8). God will confirm the covenant with them, live among them, and they shall be his free and obedient people (26.9-13).

26.14-45 Penalties for Disobedience. These will include terror, defeat and cruel oppression by enemies, loss of children and cattle, widespread resorting to cannibalism, destruction of God's altars, devastation of the land and the scattering of God's people among the nations. If, however, they repent and acknowledge the disobedience practiced by them and their ancestors (26.40-45), after a period of punishment during which the land will enjoy a sabbath rest, the covenant relationship will be renewed. Expressed as a prediction, this passage serves as a justification for what happened in the exile and an interpretation of what was occurring following the return to the land and the subsequent renewal there.

25.49 ver 26
25.50 Job 7.1; Isa 16.14; 21.16
25.51 Jer 32.7
25.54 ver 10,13,28
26.1 Ex 20.4,5; Lev 19.4; Deut 5.8
26.2 Lev 19.30
26.3 Deut 28.1
26.5 Am 9.13; Lev 25.18,19
26.6 Ps 29.11; 147.14; Zeph 3.13; ver 22,25
26.8 Deut 32.30; Josh 23.10
26.9 Gen 17.6,7; 22.17; Neh 9.23
26.10 Lev 25.22
26.11 Ex 25.8; Ps 76.2
26.12 2 Cor 6.16
26.14 Deut 28.15; Mal 2.2
26.16 Deut 28.22; 1 Sam 2.33; Deut 28.35,51
26.17 Lev 17.10; Deut 28.25; Ps 106.41; 53.5; ver 36,37
26.18 ver 21,24,28
26.19 Isa 25.11; Deut 28.23
26.20 Isa 17.10,11; Deut 11.17
26.21 ver 18,24
26.22 Deut 32.24
26.23 Jer 2.30; 5.3
26.24 ver 21,28,41
26.25 Ezek 5.17; Num 14.12
26.26 Ps 105.16; Isa 3.1; Mic 6.14

26.46 The Law of Holiness concludes with a summary declaration that these laws form the basis of the relationship between the LORD and his people, and asserts that they were given through Moses at Sinai. Details show, however, that the laws took on their present form in the period following Israel's return from exile in Babylon and the subsequent establishment of the people in the land under the leadership of the priests.
27.1-34 Offerings Belong to the Lord. This appendix to Leviticus offers details for handling the ancient practice of the *vow*, or votive offering, by which an object or a person was dedicated to God. In earlier times this required that the inhabitants of a captured city should be put to death (Num 21.2; Josh 6; Judg 1.17). On the positive side, a dedicated person might become a permanent slave of the sanctuary, as in the case of Samuel (1 Sam 1.28; 2.18). In both the law (Deut 20.10-18; 25.17-19) and the prophets (Isa 11.15; 33.10-12; 34.1-15; Dan 11.44) it is announced that those nations opposed to Israel will be *devoted to destruction* by God (27.28). Here the term for vow is used in connection with the monetary compensation which must be paid to the priests for buying back objects which have been devoted to the LORD (27.30-33). In addition to the basic cost, the priest is given a 20% fee (27.13,19,27), and payment is to be made in the full-value coinage, *the sanctuary shekel* (27.25).

27 But if, despite this, you disobey me,
and continue hostile to me, [28]I will continue
hostile to you in fury; I in turn will punish
you myself sevenfold for your sins. [29]You
shall eat the flesh of your sons, and you
shall eat the flesh of your daughters. [30]I will
destroy your high places and cut down
your incense altars; I will heap your carcasses on the carcasses of your idols. I will
abhor you. [31]I will lay your cities waste, will
make your sanctuaries desolate, and I will
not smell your pleasing odors. [32]I will devastate the land, so that your enemies who
come to settle in it shall be appalled at it.
[33]And you I will scatter among the nations,
and I will unsheathe the sword against you;
your land shall be a desolation, and your
cities a waste.
34 Then the land shall enjoy[r] its sabbath
years as long as it lies desolate, while you
are in the land of your enemies; then the
land shall rest, and enjoy[r] its sabbath years.
[35]As long as it lies desolate, it shall have the
rest it did not have on your sabbaths when
you were living on it. [36]And as for those of
you who survive, I will send faintness into
their hearts in the lands of their enemies;
the sound of a driven leaf shall put them to
flight, and they shall flee as one flees from
the sword, and they shall fall though no
one pursues. [37]They shall stumble over one
another, as if to escape a sword, though no
one pursues; and you shall have no power
to stand against your enemies. [38]You shall
perish among the nations, and the land of
your enemies shall devour you. [39]And those
of you who survive shall languish in the
land of your enemies because of their iniquities; also they shall languish because of
the iniquities of their ancestors.
40 But if they confess their iniquity and
the iniquity of their ancestors, in that they
committed treachery against me and, moreover, that they continued hostile to me—
[41]so that I, in turn, continued hostile to
them and brought them into the land of
their enemies; if then their uncircumcised
heart is humbled and they make amends for
their iniquity, [42]then will I remember my
covenant with Jacob; I will remember also
my covenant with Isaac and also my covenant with Abraham, and I will remember
the land. [43]For the land shall be deserted by
them, and enjoy[r] its sabbath years by lying
desolate without them, while they shall
make amends for their iniquity, because
they dared to spurn my ordinances, and
they abhorred my statutes. [44]Yet for all that,
when they are in the land of their enemies,
I will not spurn them, or abhor them so as
to destroy them utterly and break my covenant with them; for I am the LORD their
God; [45]but I will remember in their favor the
covenant with their ancestors whom I
brought out of the land of Egypt in the sight
of the nations, to be their God: I am the
LORD.
46 These are the statutes and ordinances
and laws that the LORD established between
himself and the people of Israel on Mount
Sinai through Moses.

Votive Offerings

27 The LORD spoke to Moses, saying:
[2]Speak to the people of Israel and
say to them: When a person makes an
explicit vow to the LORD concerning the
equivalent for a human being, [3]the equivalent for a male shall be: from twenty to sixty
years of age the equivalent shall be fifty
shekels of silver by the sanctuary shekel. [4]If
the person is a female, the equivalent is
thirty shekels. [5]If the age is from five to
twenty years of age, the equivalent is twenty
shekels for a male and ten shekels for a
female. [6]If the age is from one month to five
years, the equivalent for a male is five
shekels of silver, and for a female the equivalent is three shekels of silver. [7]And if the
person is sixty years old or over, then the
equivalent for a male is fifteen shekels, and
for a female ten shekels. [8]If any cannot
afford the equivalent, they shall be brought
before the priest and the priest shall assess
them; the priest shall assess them according
to what each one making a vow can afford.
9 If it concerns an animal that may be
brought as an offering to the LORD, any such
that may be given to the LORD shall be holy.
[10]Another shall not be exchanged or substituted for it, either good for bad or bad for
good; and if one animal is substituted for
another, both that one and its substitute
shall be holy. [11]If it concerns any unclean
animal that may not be brought as an
offering to the LORD, the animal shall be
presented before the priest. [12]The priest shall
assess it: whether good or bad, according to
the assessment of the priest, so it shall be.
[13]But if it is to be redeemed, one-fifth must
be added to the assessment.

[r] Or *make up for*

26.28 ver 24,41
26.29 Deut 28.53
26.30 2 Chr 34.3; Ezek 6.3-6,13
26.31 Ps 74.7; Isa 63.18
26.32 Jer 9.11; 19.18
26.33 Deut 4.27; Ezek 12.15
26.34 ver 43; 2 Chr 36.21
26.36 Ezek 21.7
26.37 Josh 7.12,13
26.38 Deut 4.26
26.39 Deut 4.27; Ezek 4.17
26.40 Jer 3.12-15; Lk 15.18; 1 Jn 1.9
26.41 Ezek 44.9; 2 Chr 12.6,7
26.42 Gen 28.13-15; 26.2-5; 22.15-18
26.43 ver 34,35,15
26.44 Deut 4.31; Rom 11.2
26.45 Ex 6.6-8; Lev 25.38; Gen 17.7
26.46 Lev 7.38; 27.34; 25.1
27.3 Ex 30.13
27.6 Num 18.16
27.8 ver 12
27.12 ver 8
27.13 ver 15,19

27.15 ver 20
27.18 Lev 25.15,16
27.21 Lev 25.10, 28,31; Num 18.14
27.23 ver 18
27.24 Lev 25.28
27.25 Ex 30.13
27.26 Ex 13.2,12
27.27 ver 11,12
27.28 Josh 6.17-19
27.30 Gen 28.22; Mal 3.8,10
27.31 ver 13
27.33 ver 10
27.34 Lev 26.46; Deut 4.5

14 If a person consecrates a house to the LORD, the priest shall assess it: whether good or bad, as the priest assesses it, so it shall stand. 15 And if the one who consecrates the house wishes to redeem it, one-fifth shall be added to its assessed value, and it shall revert to the original owner.

16 If a person consecrates to the LORD any inherited landholding, its assessment shall be in accordance with its seed requirements: fifty shekels of silver to a homer of barley seed. 17 If the person consecrates the field as of the year of jubilee, that assessment shall stand; 18 but if the field is consecrated after the jubilee, the priest shall compute the price for it according to the years that remain until the year of jubilee, and the assessment shall be reduced. 19 And if the one who consecrates the field wishes to redeem it, then one-fifth shall be added to its assessed value, and it shall revert to the original owner; 20 but if the field is not redeemed, or if it has been sold to someone else, it shall no longer be redeemable. 21 But when the field is released in the jubilee, it shall be holy to the LORD as a devoted field; it becomes the priest's holding. 22 If someone consecrates to the LORD a field that has been purchased, which is not a part of the inherited landholding, 23 the priest shall compute for it the proportionate assessment up to the year of jubilee, and the assessment shall be paid as of that day, a sacred donation to the LORD. 24 In the year of jubilee the field shall return to the one from whom it was bought, whose holding the land is. 25 All assessments shall be by the sanctuary shekel: twenty gerahs shall make a shekel.

26 A firstling of animals, however, which as a firstling belongs to the LORD, cannot be consecrated by anyone; whether ox or sheep, it is the LORD's. 27 If it is an unclean animal, it shall be ransomed at its assessment, with one-fifth added; if it is not redeemed, it shall be sold at its assessment.

28 Nothing that a person owns that has been devoted to destruction for the LORD, be it human or animal, or inherited landholding, may be sold or redeemed; every devoted thing is most holy to the LORD. 29 No human beings who have been devoted to destruction can be ransomed; they shall be put to death.

30 All tithes from the land, whether the seed from the ground or the fruit from the tree, are the LORD's; they are holy to the LORD. 31 If persons wish to redeem any of their tithes, they must add one-fifth to them. 32 All tithes of herd and flock, every tenth one that passes under the shepherd's staff, shall be holy to the LORD. 33 Let no one inquire whether it is good or bad, or make substitution for it; if one makes substitution for it, then both it and the substitute shall be holy and cannot be redeemed.

34 These are the commandments that the LORD gave to Moses for the people of Israel on Mount Sinai.

27.34 All these regulations are attributed to the law which Moses received from the LORD at Sinai, although the details of alteration of tradition reveal their late origin.

NUMBERS

1.1 Ex 19.1; 40.2,17
1.2 Ex 38.26; Num 26.2
1.4 ver 16

The First Census of Israel

1 The LORD spoke to Moses in the wilderness of Sinai, in the tent of meeting, on the first day of the second month, in the second year after they had come out of the land of Egypt, saying: 2 Take a census of the whole congregation of Israelites, in their clans, by ancestral houses, according to the number of names, every male individually; 3 from twenty years old and upward, everyone in Israel able to go to war. You and Aaron shall enroll them, company by company. 4 A man from each tribe shall be with you, each man the head of his ancestral house. 5 These are the names of the men who shall assist you:

From Reuben, Elizur son of Shedeur.
6 From Simeon, Shelumiel son of Zurishaddai.
7 From Judah, Nahshon son of Amminadab.
8 From Issachar, Nethanel son of Zuar.
9 From Zebulun, Eliab son of Helon.
10 From the sons of Joseph:
from Ephraim, Elishama son of Ammihud;
from Manasseh, Gamaliel son of Pedahzur.

See the Introductions, pp. 2, 30, and 36 above.

1.1-10.10 The Divine Ordering of Israel at Sinai.
1.1 The name of the book, which is found in the ancient Greek translation (the Septuagint), derives from the census-taking process and the numerical results which are reported in the first four chapters of the book. The Hebrew title, *In the wilderness*, comes from the opening line. Although these instructions are reported as being conveyed by *the LORD...to Moses* at *Sinai...in the second year after they had come out of the land [of Egypt]* and may include some old material, in its present form Numbers represents a recounting of the events and a restating of the commandments from a priestly perspective after the return of Israel from the exile (fifth century BCE).
1.2 The instruction from *the LORD* to Moses and Aaron to take a census of the people of Israel contrasts with the judgment of God on David for counting the people of Israel and Judah (2 Sam 24).
1.5-47 The list of the sons of Jacob and their sons omits the names of Levi and Joseph, but includes the names of Joseph's two sons, Ephraim and Manasseh, to bring the number of the tribes of Israel to twelve. The special treatment of the offspring of Levi is noted in 1.47-53 and 2.33 with a census, and their roles are described more fully in Num 3-4. In 1.46 the number of adult males suitable for military service from the twelve tribes of Israel is given as 603,550. On this basis, a reasonable estimate of the total population (including older and younger men, women and children) would bring the total of the Israelites to more than 2,000,000, which is inaccurate historically for the actual time of Moses.

[11] From Benjamin, Abidan son of Gideoni.
[12] From Dan, Ahiezer son of Ammishaddai.
[13] From Asher, Pagiel son of Ochran.
[14] From Gad, Eliasaph son of Deuel.
[15] From Naphtali, Ahira son of Enan.

[16]These were the ones chosen from the congregation, the leaders of their ancestral tribes, the heads of the divisions of Israel.

17 Moses and Aaron took these men who had been designated by name, [18]and on the first day of the second month they assembled the whole congregation together. They registered themselves in their clans, by their ancestral houses, according to the number of names from twenty years old and upward, individually, [19]as the LORD commanded Moses. So he enrolled them in the wilderness of Sinai.

20 The descendants of Reuben, Israel's firstborn, their lineage, in their clans, by their ancestral houses, according to the number of names, individually, every male from twenty years old and upward, everyone able to go to war: [21]those enrolled of the tribe of Reuben were forty-six thousand five hundred.

22 The descendants of Simeon, their lineage, in their clans, by their ancestral houses, those of them that were numbered, according to the number of names, individually, every male from twenty years old and upward, everyone able to go to war: [23]those enrolled of the tribe of Simeon were fifty-nine thousand three hundred.

24 The descendants of Gad, their lineage, in their clans, by their ancestral houses, according to the number of the names, from twenty years old and upward, everyone able to go to war: [25]those enrolled of the tribe of Gad were forty-five thousand six hundred fifty.

26 The descendants of Judah, their lineage, in their clans, by their ancestral houses, according to the number of names, from twenty years old and upward, everyone able to go to war: [27]those enrolled of the tribe of Judah were seventy-four thousand six hundred.

28 The descendants of Issachar, their lineage, in their clans, by their ancestral houses, according to the number of names, from twenty years old and upward, everyone able to go to war: [29]those enrolled of the tribe of Issachar were fifty-four thousand four hundred.

30 The descendants of Zebulun, their lineage, in their clans, by their ancestral houses, according to the number of names, from twenty years old and upward, everyone able to go to war: [31]those enrolled of the tribe of Zebulun were fifty-seven thousand four hundred.

32 The descendants of Joseph, namely, the descendants of Ephraim, their lineage, in their clans, by their ancestral houses, according to the number of names, from twenty years old and upward, everyone able to go to war: [33]those enrolled of the tribe of Ephraim were forty thousand five hundred.

34 The descendants of Manasseh, their lineage, in their clans, by their ancestral houses, according to the number of names, from twenty years old and upward, everyone able to go to war: [35]those enrolled of the tribe of Manasseh were thirty-two thousand two hundred.

36 The descendants of Benjamin, their lineage, in their clans, by their ancestral houses, according to the number of names, from twenty years old and upward, everyone able to go to war: [37]those enrolled of the tribe of Benjamin were thirty-five thousand four hundred.

38 The descendants of Dan, their lineage, in their clans, by their ancestral houses, according to the number of names, from twenty years old and upward, everyone able to go to war: [39]those enrolled of the tribe of Dan were sixty-two thousand seven hundred.

40 The descendants of Asher, their lineage, in their clans, by their ancestral houses, according to the number of names, from twenty years old and upward, everyone able to go to war: [41]those enrolled of the tribe of Asher were forty-one thousand five hundred.

42 The descendants of Naphtali, their lineage, in their clans, by their ancestral houses, according to the number of names, from twenty years old and upward, everyone able to go to war: [43]those enrolled of the tribe of Naphtali were fifty-three thousand four hundred.

44 These are those who were enrolled, whom Moses and Aaron enrolled with the help of the leaders of Israel, twelve men, each representing his ancestral house. [45]So the whole number of the Israelites, by their ancestral houses, from twenty years old and upward, everyone able to go to war in

1.14 Num 2.14
1.16 Num 16.2; 26.9
1.20 Num 26.5-11
1.22 Num 26.12-14
1.24 Num 26.15-18
1.26 Num 26.19-22
1.28 Num 26.23-25
1.30 Num 26.26,27
1.32 Num 26.35-37
1.34 Num 26.28-34
1.36 Num 26.38-41
1.38 Num 26.42,43
1.40 Num 26.44-47
1.42 Num 26.48-50
1.44 Num 26.64

Israel— 46their whole number was six hundred three thousand five hundred fifty. 47The Levites, however, were not numbered by their ancestral tribe along with them.

48 The LORD had said to Moses: 49Only the tribe of Levi you shall not enroll, and you shall not take a census of them with the other Israelites. 50Rather you shall appoint the Levites over the tabernacle of the covenant,[a] and over all its equipment, and over all that belongs to it; they are to carry the tabernacle and all its equipment, and they shall tend it, and shall camp around the tabernacle. 51When the tabernacle is to set out, the Levites shall take it down; and when the tabernacle is to be pitched, the Levites shall set it up. And any outsider who comes near shall be put to death. 52The other Israelites shall camp in their respective regimental camps, by companies; 53but the Levites shall camp around the tabernacle of the covenant,[a] that there may be no wrath on the congregation of the Israelites; and the Levites shall perform the guard duty of the tabernacle of the covenant.[a] 54The Israelites did so; they did just as the LORD commanded Moses.

The Order of Encampment and Marching

2 The LORD spoke to Moses and Aaron, saying: 2The Israelites shall camp each in their respective regiments, under ensigns by their ancestral houses; they shall camp facing the tent of meeting on every side. 3Those to camp on the east side toward the sunrise shall be of the regimental encampment of Judah by companies. The leader of the people of Judah shall be Nahshon son of Amminadab, 4with a company as enrolled of seventy-four thousand six hundred. 5Those to camp next to him shall be the tribe of Issachar. The leader of the Issacharites shall be Nethanel son of Zuar, 6with a company as enrolled of fifty-four thousand four hundred. 7Then the tribe of Zebulun: The leader of the Zebulunites shall be Eliab son of Helon, 8with a company as enrolled of fifty-seven thousand four hundred. 9The total enrollment of the camp of Judah, by companies, is one hundred eighty-six thousand four hundred. They shall set out first on the march.

10 On the south side shall be the regimental encampment of Reuben by companies. The leader of the Reubenites shall be Elizur son of Shedeur, 11with a company as enrolled of forty-six thousand five hundred. 12And those to camp next to him shall be the tribe of Simeon. The leader of the Simeonites shall be Shelumiel son of Zurishaddai, 13with a company as enrolled of fifty-nine thousand three hundred. 14Then the tribe of Gad: The leader of the Gadites shall be Eliasaph son of Reuel, 15with a company as enrolled of forty-five thousand six hundred fifty. 16The total enrollment of the camp of Reuben, by companies, is one hundred fifty-one thousand four hundred fifty. They shall set out second.

17 The tent of meeting, with the camp of the Levites, shall set out in the center of the camps; they shall set out just as they camp, each in position, by their regiments.

18 On the west side shall be the regimental encampment of Ephraim by companies. The leader of the people of Ephraim shall be Elishama son of Ammihud, 19with a company as enrolled of forty thousand five hundred. 20Next to him shall be the tribe of Manasseh. The leader of the people of Manasseh shall be Gamaliel son of Pedahzur, 21with a company as enrolled of thirty-two thousand two hundred. 22Then the tribe of Benjamin: The leader of the Benjaminites shall be Abidan son of Gideoni, 23with a company as enrolled of thirty-five thousand four hundred. 24The total enrollment of the camp of Ephraim, by companies, is one hundred eight thousand one hundred. They shall set out third on the march.

25 On the north side shall be the regimental encampment of Dan by companies. The leader of the Danites shall be Ahiezer son of Ammishaddai, 26with a company as enrolled of sixty-two thousand seven hundred. 27Those to camp next to him shall be the tribe of Asher. The leader of the Asherites shall be Pagiel son of Ochran, 28with a company as enrolled of forty-one thousand five hundred. 29Then the tribe of Naphtali: The leader of the Naphtalites shall be Ahira son of Enan, 30with a company as enrolled of fifty-three thousand four hundred. 31The total enrollment of the camp of Dan is one hundred fifty-seven thousand six hundred. They shall set out last, by companies.[b]

32 This was the enrollment of the Israelites by their ancestral houses; the total enrollment in the camps by their companies was six hundred three thousand five hundred fifty. 33Just as the LORD had commanded

[a] Or *treaty*, or *testimony*; Heb *eduth* [b] Compare verses 9, 16, 24: Heb *by their regiments*

1.46 Num 2.32; 26.51; Ex 12.37; 38.26
1.47 Num 2.33; 3; 4; 26.57
1.50 Num 3.25-37
1.51 Num 4.1-33
1.52 Num 2.2
1.53 ver 50
2.2 Num 1.52
2.3 Num 10.14
2.5 Num 1.8
2.9 Num 10.14
2.10 Num 1.5
2.12 Num 1.6
2.14 Num 1.14
2.17 Num 1.53
2.20 Num 1.10
2.24 Num 10.22
2.25 Num 1.12
2.27 Num 1.13
2.31 Num 10.25
2.32 Num 1.46; Ex 38.26
2.33 Num 1.47

1.48-54 The Ordering of Responsibility for the Tabernacle. The Levites are assigned the obligation *to carry the tabernacle and all its equipment*, and to set it up, to take it down, and to guard it as the tribes continue their journey through the wilderness toward the promised land (1.48-53).

2.1-34 The Orderly Encampment of the Tribes of Israel. The leaders of the twelve tribes are named and the position of the camps of each tribe is specified, together with the number in each. At *the center of the camps* is located *the tent of meeting*. When the tribes break camp, the order of their march is specified as well.

Moses, the Levites were not enrolled among the other Israelites.

34 The Israelites did just as the LORD had commanded Moses: They camped by regiments, and they set out the same way, everyone by clans, according to ancestral houses.

The Sons of Aaron

3 This is the lineage of Aaron and Moses at the time when the LORD spoke with Moses on Mount Sinai. 2These are the names of the sons of Aaron: Nadab the firstborn, and Abihu, Eleazar, and Ithamar; 3these are the names of the sons of Aaron, the anointed priests, whom he ordained to minister as priests. 4Nadab and Abihu died before the LORD when they offered illicit fire before the LORD in the wilderness of Sinai, and they had no children. Eleazar and Ithamar served as priests in the lifetime of their father Aaron.

The Duties of the Levites

5 Then the LORD spoke to Moses, saying: 6Bring the tribe of Levi near, and set them before Aaron the priest, so that they may assist him. 7They shall perform duties for him and for the whole congregation in front of the tent of meeting, doing service at the tabernacle; 8they shall be in charge of all the furnishings of the tent of meeting, and attend to the duties for the Israelites as they do service at the tabernacle. 9You shall give the Levites to Aaron and his descendants; they are unreservedly given to him from among the Israelites. 10But you shall make a register of Aaron and his descendants; it is they who shall attend to the priesthood, and any outsider who comes near shall be put to death.

11 Then the LORD spoke to Moses, saying: 12I hereby accept the Levites from among the Israelites as substitutes for all the firstborn that open the womb among the Israelites. The Levites shall be mine, 13for all the firstborn are mine; when I killed all the firstborn in the land of Egypt, I consecrated for my own all the firstborn in Israel, both human and animal; they shall be mine. I am the LORD.

A Census of the Levites

14 Then the LORD spoke to Moses in the wilderness of Sinai, saying: 15Enroll the Levites by ancestral houses and by clans. You shall enroll every male from a month old and upward. 16So Moses enrolled them according to the word of the LORD, as he was commanded. 17The following were the sons of Levi, by their names: Gershon, Kohath, and Merari. 18These are the names of the sons of Gershon by their clans: Libni and Shimei. 19The sons of Kohath by their clans: Amram, Izhar, Hebron, and Uzziel. 20The sons of Merari by their clans: Mahli and Mushi. These are the clans of the Levites, by their ancestral houses.

21 To Gershon belonged the clan of the Libnites and the clan of the Shimeites; these were the clans of the Gershonites. 22Their enrollment, counting all the males from a month old and upward, was seven thousand five hundred. 23The clans of the Gershonites were to camp behind the tabernacle on the west, 24with Eliasaph son of Lael as head of the ancestral house of the Gershonites. 25The responsibility of the sons of Gershon in the tent of meeting was to be the tabernacle, the tent with its covering, the screen for the entrance of the tent of meeting, 26the hangings of the court, the screen for the entrance of the court that is around the tabernacle and the altar, and its cords—all the service pertaining to these.

27 To Kohath belonged the clan of the Amramites, the clan of the Izharites, the clan of the Hebronites, and the clan of the Uzzielites; these are the clans of the Kohathites. 28Counting all the males, from a month old and upward, there were eight thousand six hundred, attending to the duties of the sanctuary. 29The clans of the Kohathites were to camp on the south side of the tabernacle, 30with Elizaphan son of Uzziel as head of the ancestral house of the clans of the Kohathites. 31Their responsibility was to be the ark, the table, the lampstand, the altars, the vessels of the sanctuary with which the priests minister, and the screen—all the service pertaining to these. 32Eleazar son of Aaron the priest was to be chief over the leaders of the Levites, and to have oversight of those who had charge of the sanctuary.

33 To Merari belonged the clan of the Mahlites and the clan of the Mushites: these are the clans of Merari. 34Their enrollment, counting all the males from a month old and upward, was six thousand two hundred. 35The head of the ancestral house of the clans of Merari was Zuriel son of Abihail;

3.1-39 The Assignment of Responsibilities to the Levites.
3.1-4 *The sons of Aaron* are those to whom alone the priestly role is granted. Among these descendants are mentioned Nadab and Abihu, with a brief note of their death for having corrupted their priestly trust (Lev 10.1-7).
3.5-13 It is the sons of Levi who are to *assist* Aaron, to *perform duties for him and for the whole congregation* in order to facilitate the actual ritual functions carried out by the priests in the tabernacle. Here the priestly editor of Numbers has placed side by side two Hebrew words for God's dwelling place among his people: one for *tent*, which emphasizes the mobile, changing location of Israel in the older semi-nomadic period; the other for *tabernacle*, which means "dwelling place," and indicates the continuing presence of God in the midst of Israel. Historically, God was understood to be present in the portable tent in the time of Moses (Ex 33.7-11), which was replaced by a more permanent structure, with tent-like features, at Shiloh as Israel settled in the land of Canaan (Josh 22.9-12,19; Judg 18.31), and then by the tent which David brought to Jerusalem (2 Sam 6.17; 1 Kings 1-2). From the perspective after the exile, it is this mobile sanctuary which is the model for the locus of God's presence, rather than the fixed structure of the temple. Only the descendants of Aaron can carry out the priestly functions (3.10), but the Levites stand in the same special position of favor with God as do the firstborn of all creatures: they are especially holy and serve as mediators of God's grace and forgiveness to his covenant people. Hence in a special way, the Levites who make the ritual system possible by their assistance to the priests are God's own (3.11-13).
3.14-39 A Census of the Levites. Like the other twelve tribes, the Levites are here divided up according to their *ancestral houses and clans*. Each male child, from one month of age upward, is to be enrolled as a Levite (3.15,39). The total comes to 22,000. Each group descended from one of the sons of Levi has a different set of responsibilities, which are described in greater detail in Num 4: the Gershonites are assigned care of the tent, and the screen and hangings that partition it; the Kohathites are in charge of the ark, table, altar and other *vessels of the sanctuary*; the sons of Merari handle the frames, rods, pillars and bases which support the tent.

3.2 Num 26.60
3.4 Num 26.61
3.6 Num 8.6-22; 18.1-7
3.9 Num 18.6
3.10 Ex 29.9; Num 1.51
3.12 ver 41; Num 8.16; 18.6
3.13 Ex 13.2,12,15; Num 8.17
3.15 ver 39
3.17 Ex 6.16-22
3.20 Gen 46.11
3.21 Ex 6.17
3.25 Num 4.24-26; Ex 25.9
3.27 1 Chr 26.23
3.29 Ex 6.18
3.33 Ex 6.19

3.36 Num 4.29-32
3.38 Num 18.5; ver 7,8,10
3.39 Num 26.62
3.41 ver 12,45
3.43 ver 39
3.45 ver 12,41
3.46 Ex 13.13; Num 18.15
3.47 Ex 30.13
3.50 ver 46-48
4.3 Num 8.24; ver 23,30,35
4.6 ver 25
4.7 Ex 25.23; 29,30; Lev 24.5-9
4.9 Ex 25.31,37,38
4.11 Ex 30.1,3
4.15 Num 7.9; 2 Sam 6.6,7

they were to camp on the north side of the tabernacle. [36]The responsibility assigned to the sons of Merari was to be the frames of the tabernacle, the bars, the pillars, the bases, and all their accessories—all the service pertaining to these; [37]also the pillars of the court all around, with their bases and pegs and cords.

38 Those who were to camp in front of the tabernacle on the east—in front of the tent of meeting toward the east—were Moses and Aaron and Aaron's sons, having charge of the rites within the sanctuary, whatever had to be done for the Israelites; and any outsider who came near was to be put to death. [39]The total enrollment of the Levites whom Moses and Aaron enrolled at the commandment of the LORD, by their clans, all the males from a month old and upward, was twenty-two thousand.

The Redemption of the Firstborn

40 Then the LORD said to Moses: Enroll all the firstborn males of the Israelites, from a month old and upward, and count their names. [41]But you shall accept the Levites for me—I am the LORD—as substitutes for all the firstborn among the Israelites, and the livestock of the Levites as substitutes for all the firstborn among the livestock of the Israelites. [42]So Moses enrolled all the firstborn among the Israelites, as the LORD commanded him. [43]The total enrollment, all the firstborn males from a month old and upward, counting the number of names, was twenty-two thousand two hundred seventy-three.

44 Then the LORD spoke to Moses, saying: [45]Accept the Levites as substitutes for all the firstborn among the Israelites, and the livestock of the Levites as substitutes for their livestock; and the Levites shall be mine. I am the LORD. [46]As the price of redemption of the two hundred seventy-three of the firstborn of the Israelites, over and above the number of the Levites, [47]you shall accept five shekels apiece, reckoning by the shekel of the sanctuary, a shekel of twenty gerahs. [48]Give to Aaron and his sons the money by which the excess number of them is redeemed. [49]So Moses took the redemption money from those who were over and above those redeemed by the Levites; [50]from the firstborn of the Israelites he took the money, one thousand three hundred sixty-five shekels, reckoned by the shekel of the sanctuary; [51]and Moses gave the redemption money to Aaron and his sons, according to the word of the LORD, as the LORD had commanded Moses.

The Kohathites

4 The LORD spoke to Moses and Aaron, saying: [2]Take a census of the Kohathites separate from the other Levites, by their clans and their ancestral houses, [3]from thirty years old up to fifty years old, all who qualify to do work relating to the tent of meeting. [4]The service of the Kohathites relating to the tent of meeting concerns the most holy things.

5 When the camp is to set out, Aaron and his sons shall go in and take down the screening curtain, and cover the ark of the covenant[c] with it; [6]then they shall put on it a covering of fine leather,[d] and spread over that a cloth all of blue, and shall put its poles in place. [7]Over the table of the bread of the Presence they shall spread a blue cloth, and put on it the plates, the dishes for incense, the bowls, and the flagons for the drink offering; the regular bread also shall be on it; [8]then they shall spread over them a crimson cloth, and cover it with a covering of fine leather,[d] and shall put its poles in place. [9]They shall take a blue cloth, and cover the lampstand for the light, with its lamps, its snuffers, its trays, and all the vessels for oil with which it is supplied; [10]and they shall put it with all its utensils in a covering of fine leather,[d] and put it on the carrying frame. [11]Over the golden altar they shall spread a blue cloth, and cover it with a covering of fine leather,[d] and shall put its poles in place; [12]and they shall take all the utensils of the service that are used in the sanctuary, and put them in a blue cloth, and cover them with a covering of fine leather,[d] and put them on the carrying frame. [13]They shall take away the ashes from the altar, and spread a purple cloth over it; [14]and they shall put on it all the utensils of the altar, which are used for the service there, the firepans, the forks, the shovels, and the basins, all the utensils of the altar; and they shall spread on it a covering of fine leather,[d] and shall put its poles in place. [15]When Aaron and his sons have finished covering the sanctuary and all the furnishings of the sanctuary, as the camp sets out, after that the Kohathites

3.40-51 The Levites and the Firstborn of Israel. In principle all the firstborn humans and cattle belonged to the LORD, but Moses is told by the LORD that he will consider the Levites and their cattle as replacement for the firstborn of the rest of Israel. The census showed that there were 273 fewer Levites than all the firstborn of Israel, so provision is made for monetary payment to the LORD in place of the firstborn for whom there is no Levite substitute. The fee is five shekels for each, the money to be paid *to Aaron and his sons*.

4.1-33 The Responsibilities of the Levites.

4.1-20 The Kohathites are to transport the contents and equipment of the inner sanctuary, once it has been properly wrapped, packed and delivered into their hands by the priests. The Kohathites dare not enter the sanctuary once it has been erected, and must wait until it has been dismantled.

[c] Or *treaty*, or *testimony*; Heb *eduth* [d] Meaning of Heb uncertain

4.21-28 The Gershonites are to carry the tent of meeting itself, including the curtains, the cords and the outer layer *of fine leather*.
4.29-33 The Merarites are to carry everything necessary for holding in place both the tent and the court that surrounded it: frames, bars, pillars, bases, pegs, cords.
4.34-49 The Census of the Levites. Like the men of the other tribes designated for military service, only the Levites between certain ages are to be enrolled, but the ages are 30 to 50. Their total number is given as 8580, who were *appointed to their several tasks of serving or carrying* the components of the tent and its equipment (4.49).

shall come to carry these, but they must not touch the holy things, or they will die. These are the things of the tent of meeting that the Kohathites are to carry.

16 Eleazar son of Aaron the priest shall have charge of the oil for the light, the fragrant incense, the regular grain offering, and the anointing oil, the oversight of all the tabernacle and all that is in it, in the sanctuary and in its utensils.

17 Then the LORD spoke to Moses and Aaron, saying: [18]You must not let the tribe of the clans of the Kohathites be destroyed from among the Levites. [19]This is how you must deal with them in order that they may live and not die when they come near to the most holy things: Aaron and his sons shall go in and assign each to a particular task or burden. [20]But the Kohathites[e] must not go in to look on the holy things even for a moment; otherwise they will die.

The Gershonites and Merarites

21 Then the LORD spoke to Moses, saying: [22]Take a census of the Gershonites also, by their ancestral houses and by their clans; [23]from thirty years old up to fifty years old you shall enroll them, all who qualify to do work in the tent of meeting. [24]This is the service of the clans of the Gershonites, in serving and bearing burdens: [25]They shall carry the curtains of the tabernacle, and the tent of meeting with its covering, and the outer covering of fine leather[f] that is on top of it, and the screen for the entrance of the tent of meeting, [26]and the hangings of the court, and the screen for the entrance of the gate of the court that is around the tabernacle and the altar, and their cords, and all the equipment for their service; and they shall do all that needs to be done with regard to them. [27]All the service of the Gershonites shall be at the command of Aaron and his sons, in all that they are to carry, and in all that they have to do; and you shall assign to their charge all that they are to carry. [28]This is the service of the clans of the Gershonites relating to the tent of meeting, and their responsibilities are to be under the oversight of Ithamar son of Aaron the priest.

29 As for the Merarites, you shall enroll them by their clans and their ancestral houses; [30]from thirty years old up to fifty years old you shall enroll them, everyone who qualifies to do the work of the tent of meeting. [31]This is what they are charged to carry, as the whole of their service in the tent of meeting: the frames of the tabernacle, with its bars, pillars, and bases, [32]and the pillars of the court all around with their bases, pegs, and cords, with all their equipment and all their related service; and you shall assign by name the objects that they are required to carry. [33]This is the service of the clans of the Merarites, the whole of their service relating to the tent of meeting, under the hand of Ithamar son of Aaron the priest.

Census of the Levites

34 So Moses and Aaron and the leaders of the congregation enrolled the Kohathites, by their clans and their ancestral houses, [35]from thirty years old up to fifty years old, everyone who qualified for work relating to the tent of meeting; [36]and their enrollment by clans was two thousand seven hundred fifty. [37]This was the enrollment of the clans of the Kohathites, all who served at the tent of meeting, whom Moses and Aaron enrolled according to the commandment of the LORD by Moses.

38 The enrollment of the Gershonites, by their clans and their ancestral houses, [39]from thirty years old up to fifty years old, everyone who qualified for work relating to the tent of meeting— [40]their enrollment by their clans and their ancestral houses was two thousand six hundred thirty. [41]This was the enrollment of the clans of the Gershonites, all who served at the tent of meeting, whom Moses and Aaron enrolled according to the commandment of the LORD.

42 The enrollment of the clans of the Merarites, by their clans and their ancestral houses, [43]from thirty years old up to fifty years old, everyone who qualified for work relating to the tent of meeting— [44]their enrollment by their clans was three thousand two hundred. [45]This is the enrollment of the clans of the Merarites, whom Moses and Aaron enrolled according to the commandment of the LORD by Moses.

46 All those who were enrolled of the Levites, whom Moses and Aaron and the leaders of Israel enrolled, by their clans and their ancestral houses, [47]from thirty years old up to fifty years old, everyone who qualified to do the work of service and the

4.16 Lev 24.1-3; Ex 30.34; 29.40; 30.23
4.19 ver 4.15
4.23 ver 3
4.25 Num 3.25,26
4.27 Num 3.21
4.30 ver 3
4.31 Num 3.36,37
4.33 ver 28
4.34 ver 2
4.37 Num 3.27
4.38 Gen 46.11
4.41 ver 22
4.45 ver 29
4.47 ver 3,23,30

[e] Heb *they* [f] Meaning of Heb uncertain

5.2 Lev 13.3,46; 15.2; Num 19.11
5.3 Lev 26.11,12; 2 Cor 6.16
5.6 Lev 6.2,3
5.7 Lev 5.5; 26.40; 6.5
5.8 Lev 6.6,7; 7.7
5.9 Lev 6.17,18,26; 7.6-14
5.10 Lev 10.13
5.12 Ex 20.14
5.13 Lev 18.20
5.15 Ezek 29.16
5.18 1 Cor 11.6
5.21 Josh 6.26; 1 Sam 14.24; Neh 10.29
5.22 Deut 27.15; Ps 109.18
5.25 Lev 8.27
5.27 Jer 29.18; 42.18; Zech 8.13

work of bearing burdens relating to the tent
of meeting, [48]their enrollment was eight
thousand five hundred eighty. [49]According
to the commandment of the LORD through
Moses they were appointed to their several
tasks of serving or carrying; thus they were
enrolled by him, as the LORD commanded
Moses.

Unclean Persons

5 The LORD spoke to Moses, saying: [2]Com-
mand the Israelites to put out of the
camp everyone who is leprous,[g] or has a
discharge, and everyone who is unclean
through contact with a corpse; [3]you shall
put out both male and female, putting them
outside the camp; they must not defile their
camp, where I dwell among them. [4]The
Israelites did so, putting them outside the
camp; as the LORD had spoken to Moses, so
the Israelites did.

Confession and Restitution

5 The LORD spoke to Moses, saying: [6]Speak
to the Israelites: When a man or a woman
wrongs another, breaking faith with the
LORD, that person incurs guilt [7]and shall
confess the sin that has been committed.
The person shall make full restitution for
the wrong, adding one fifth to it, and giving
it to the one who was wronged. [8]If the
injured party has no next of kin to whom
restitution may be made for the wrong, the
restitution for wrong shall go to the LORD for
the priest, in addition to the ram of atonement with which atonement is made for the
guilty party. [9]Among all the sacred donations of the Israelites, every gift that they
bring to the priest shall be his. [10]The sacred
donations of all are their own; whatever
anyone gives to the priest shall be his.

Concerning an Unfaithful Wife

11 The LORD spoke to Moses, saying:
[12]Speak to the Israelites and say to them: If
any man's wife goes astray and is unfaithful
to him, [13]if a man has had intercourse with
her but it is hidden from her husband, so
that she is undetected though she has defiled herself, and there is no witness against
her since she was not caught in the act; [14]if
a spirit of jealousy comes on him, and he
is jealous of his wife who has defiled herself;
or if a spirit of jealousy comes on him, and
he is jealous of his wife, though she has not
defiled herself; [15]then the man shall bring
his wife to the priest. And he shall bring the
offering required for her, one-tenth of an
ephah of barley flour. He shall pour no oil
on it and put no frankincense on it, for it
is a grain offering of jealousy, a grain offering of remembrance, bringing iniquity to
remembrance.
16 Then the priest shall bring her near,
and set her before the LORD; [17]the priest shall
take holy water in an earthen vessel, and
take some of the dust that is on the floor
of the tabernacle and put it into the water.
[18]The priest shall set the woman before the
LORD, dishevel the woman's hair, and place
in her hands the grain offering of remembrance, which is the grain offering of jealousy. In his own hand the priest shall have
the water of bitterness that brings the curse.
[19]Then the priest shall make her take an
oath, saying, "If no man has lain with you,
if you have not turned aside to uncleanness
while under your husband's authority, be
immune to this water of bitterness that
brings the curse. [20]But if you have gone
astray while under your husband's authority, if you have defiled yourself and some
man other than your husband has had
intercourse with you," [21]—let the priest
make the woman take the oath of the curse
and say to the woman—"the LORD make
you an execration and an oath among your
people, when the LORD makes your uterus
drop, your womb discharge; [22]now may this
water that brings the curse enter your bowels
and make your womb discharge, your uterus
drop!" And the woman shall say, "Amen.
Amen."
23 Then the priest shall put these curses
in writing, and wash them off into the
water of bitterness. [24]He shall make the
woman drink the water of bitterness that
brings the curse, and the water that brings
the curse shall enter her and cause bitter
pain. [25]The priest shall take the grain offering of jealousy out of the woman's hand,
and shall elevate the grain offering before
the LORD and bring it to the altar; [26]and the
priest shall take a handful of the grain
offering, as its memorial portion, and turn
it into smoke on the altar, and afterward
shall make the woman drink the water.
[27]When he has made her drink the water,
then, if she has defiled herself and has been

[g] A term for several skin diseases; precise meaning uncertain

5.1-31 Maintaining the Purity of the People of Israel.
5.1-4 Those to be driven *out of the camp* are those whose modes of defilement are described in detail in Lev 12-14: the leprous, those with a *discharge*, those who have contacted a corpse.
5.5-10 repeats the provisions for restitution given in Lev 6.1-7, but adds the rule that when the wronged person has died and there is *no next of kin* (male survivor: brother, uncle, cousin; *cf.* Ruth 3-4), the payment of restitution is to go to the priest, with an added fee of 20%.
5.11-31 When a woman is suspected of infidelity to her husband, her guilt or innocence is determined through an elaborate set of tests. The accusing husband brings his wife to the priest, with *a grain offering of jealousy* and *a grain offering of remembrance*. Unlike the other grain offerings, which ascend to God in expression of thanks, the first symbolizes the husband's suspicions and the second is a means to establish a recollection of what actually happened. The *holy water* which the priest gives the woman to drink, mixed with *dust from the floor of the tabernacle*, has a determinative effect: if it causes her no harm, she is innocent. If she is guilty, it will cause a premature birth. Her *uterus [will] drop*, which will cause her to be regarded as *an execration* among her people. A summary of the process concludes the discussion of the infidelity issue (5.29-31).

6.1-21 The Nazirites. The status of *nazirite* is here described as voluntary and temporary, but for Samson (Judg 13.3-7) it was decided by his parents on the advice of the angel and was lifelong in effect. The qualifications for Nazirites include abstinence from wine and anything connected with grapes (6.3), cessation of cutting hair or – even though women may take the vow – trimming the beard (6.5; *cf.* Samson in Judg 13.5; 16.17); and avoidance of contact with the dead (6.6-8; *cf.* Lev 21.1-11). The offerings required are many and costly (6.13-17). The shaving of the head and the burning of the hair with *the sacrifice of well-being* symbolizes the distinctive form of consecration to God that the vow involves. Portions of the sacrifices go to the priest (6.20), and additional contributions to the priest are encouraged by those who can afford them (6.21).
6.22-27 The Priestly Benediction. Liturgical in form (*cf.* Ps 67 and traditional Jewish and Christian usage), this promise of God's blessing is addressed to the individual (*you* is singular), but speaks to the whole of God's people, promising them God's continuing concern and favor, and above all *peace*. This term connotes not only freedom from internal or external conflict, but experience of the completeness of God's purpose and the overcoming of struggle or disappointment. God publicly identifies himself with his covenant people when he *puts [his] name on* them and blesses them.

unfaithful to her husband, the water that
brings the curse shall enter into her and
cause bitter pain, and her womb shall discharge, her uterus drop, and the woman
shall become an execration among her
people. 28But if the woman has not defiled
herself and is clean, then she shall be immune and be able to conceive children.
29 This is the law in cases of jealousy,
when a wife, while under her husband's
authority, goes astray and defiles herself,
30or when a spirit of jealousy comes on a
man and he is jealous of his wife; then he
shall set the woman before the LORD, and
the priest shall apply this entire law to her.
31The man shall be free from iniquity, but
the woman shall bear her iniquity.

The Nazirites

6 The LORD spoke to Moses, saying:
2Speak to the Israelites and say to
them: When either men or women make a
special vow, the vow of a nazirite,[h] to separate themselves to the LORD, 3they shall
separate themselves from wine and strong
drink; they shall drink no wine vinegar or
other vinegar, and shall not drink any grape
juice or eat grapes, fresh or dried. 4All their
days as nazirites[i] they shall eat nothing that
is produced by the grapevine, not even the
seeds or the skins.
5 All the days of their nazirite vow no
razor shall come upon the head; until the
time is completed for which they separate
themselves to the LORD, they shall be holy;
they shall let the locks of the head grow
long.
6 All the days that they separate themselves to the LORD they shall not go near a
corpse. 7Even if their father or mother,
brother or sister, should die, they may not
defile themselves; because their consecration to God is upon the head. 8All their days
as nazirites[i] they are holy to the LORD.
9 If someone dies very suddenly nearby,
defiling the consecrated head, then they
shall shave the head on the day of their
cleansing; on the seventh day they shall
shave it. 10On the eighth day they shall
bring two turtledoves or two young pigeons
to the priest at the entrance of the tent of
meeting, 11and the priest shall offer one as
a sin offering and the other as a burnt
offering, and make atonement for them,
because they incurred guilt by reason of the
corpse. They shall sanctify the head that
same day, 12and separate themselves to the
LORD for their days as nazirites,[i] and bring
a male lamb a year old as a guilt offering.
The former time shall be void, because the
consecrated head was defiled.
13 This is the law for the nazirites[i] when
the time of their consecration has been
completed: they shall be brought to the
entrance of the tent of meeting, 14and they
shall offer their gift to the LORD, one male
lamb a year old without blemish as a burnt
offering, one ewe lamb a year old without
blemish as a sin offering, one ram without
blemish as an offering of well-being, 15and
a basket of unleavened bread, cakes of choice
flour mixed with oil and unleavened wafers
spread with oil, with their grain offering
and their drink offerings. 16The priest shall
present them before the LORD and offer their
sin offering and burnt offering, 17and shall
offer the ram as a sacrifice of well-being to
the LORD, with the basket of unleavened
bread; the priest also shall make the accompanying grain offering and drink offering.
18Then the nazirites[i] shall shave the consecrated head at the entrance of the tent of
meeting, and shall take the hair from the
consecrated head and put it on the fire
under the sacrifice of well-being. 19The priest
shall take the shoulder of the ram, when it
is boiled, and one unleavened cake out of
the basket, and one unleavened wafer, and
shall put them in the palms of the nazirites,[i]
after they have shaved the consecrated head.
20Then the priest shall elevate them as an
elevation offering before the LORD; they are
a holy portion for the priest, together with
the breast that is elevated and the thigh
that is offered. After that the nazirites[i] may
drink wine.
21 This is the law for the nazirites[i] who
take a vow. Their offering to the LORD must
be in accordance with the nazirite[h] vow,
apart from what else they can afford. In
accordance with whatever vow they take,
so they shall do, following the law for their
consecration.

The Priestly Benediction

22 The LORD spoke to Moses, saying:
23Speak to Aaron and his sons, saying, Thus
you shall bless the Israelites: You shall say
to them,
24 The LORD bless you and keep you;

5.29 ver 12,19
6.2 Judg 13.5; 16.17; Am 2.11,12
6.5 1 Sam 1.11
6.6 Lev 19.11-22; 21.1-3
6.10 Lev 5.7
6.12 Lev 5.6
6.13 Acts 21.26
6.14 Num 15.27; Lev 14.10
6.15 Num 15.1-7
6.18 ver 9; Acts 21.24
6.23 1 Chr 23.13
6.24 Deut 28.3-6

[h] That is *one separated* or *one consecrated* [i] That is *those separated* or *those consecrated*

6.25 Ps 80.3,7,19; 119.135; Gen 43.29
6.26 Ps 4.6; 44.3; Jn 14.27
6.27 Deut 28.10; 2 Chr 7.14
7.1 Ex 40.18
7.2 Num 1.5-16
7.7 Num 4.25
7.8 Num 4.28,31,33
7.9 Num 4.5-15
7.10 2 Chr 7.9
7.13 Num 3.47
7.14 Ex 30.34
7.17 Lev 3.1
7.18 Num 1.8
7.23 ver 18
7.24 Num 1.9
7.29 Lev 7.32
7.30 Num 1.5
7.34 Heb 10.7
7.36 Num 1.6

25 the LORD make his face to shine upon
you, and be gracious to you;
26 the LORD lift up his countenance upon
you, and give you peace.
27 So they shall put my name on the
Israelites, and I will bless them.

Offerings of the Leaders

7 On the day when Moses had finished
setting up the tabernacle, and had
anointed and consecrated it with all its
furnishings, and had anointed and consecrated the altar with all its utensils, 2 the
leaders of Israel, heads of their ancestral
houses, the leaders of the tribes, who were
over those who were enrolled, made offerings. 3 They brought their offerings before
the LORD, six covered wagons and twelve
oxen, a wagon for every two of the leaders,
and for each one an ox; they presented
them before the tabernacle. 4 Then the LORD
said to Moses: 5 Accept these from them,
that they may be used in doing the service
of the tent of meeting, and give them to the
Levites, to each according to his service. 6 So
Moses took the wagons and the oxen, and
gave them to the Levites. 7 Two wagons and
four oxen he gave to the Gershonites, according to their service; 8 and four wagons
and eight oxen he gave to the Merarites,
according to their service, under the direction of Ithamar son of Aaron the priest. 9 But
to the Kohathites he gave none, because
they were charged with the care of the holy
things that had to be carried on the shoulders.
10 The leaders also presented offerings
for the dedication of the altar at the time
when it was anointed; the leaders presented
their offering before the altar. 11 The LORD
said to Moses: They shall present their offerings, one leader each day, for the dedication of the altar.
12 The one who presented his offering
the first day was Nahshon son of
Amminadab, of the tribe of Judah; 13 his
offering was one silver plate weighing one
hundred thirty shekels, one silver basin
weighing seventy shekels, according to the
shekel of the sanctuary, both of them full
of choice flour mixed with oil for a grain
offering; 14 one golden dish weighing ten
shekels, full of incense; 15 one young bull,
one ram, one male lamb a year old, for a
burnt offering; 16 one male goat for a sin
offering; 17 and for the sacrifice of well-being,
two oxen, five rams, five male goats, and
five male lambs a year old. This was the
offering of Nahshon son of Amminadab.
18 On the second day Nethanel son of
Zuar, the leader of Issachar, presented an
offering; 19 he presented for his offering one
silver plate weighing one hundred thirty
shekels, one silver basin weighing seventy
shekels, according to the shekel of the sanctuary, both of them full of choice flour
mixed with oil for a grain offering; 20 one
golden dish weighing ten shekels, full of
incense; 21 one young bull, one ram, one
male lamb a year old, as a burnt offering;
22 one male goat as a sin offering; 23 and for
the sacrifice of well-being, two oxen, five
rams, five male goats, and five male lambs
a year old. This was the offering of Nethanel
son of Zuar.
24 On the third day Eliab son of Helon,
the leader of the Zebulunites: 25 his offering
was one silver plate weighing one hundred
thirty shekels, one silver basin weighing
seventy shekels, according to the shekel of
the sanctuary, both of them full of choice
flour mixed with oil for a grain offering;
26 one golden dish weighing ten shekels, full
of incense; 27 one young bull, one ram, one
male lamb a year old, for a burnt offering;
28 one male goat for a sin offering; 29 and for
the sacrifice of well-being, two oxen, five
rams, five male goats, and five male lambs
a year old. This was the offering of Eliab son
of Helon.
30 On the fourth day Elizur son of
Shedeur, the leader of the Reubenites: 31 his
offering was one silver plate weighing one
hundred thirty shekels, one silver basin
weighing seventy shekels, according to the
shekel of the sanctuary, both of them full
of choice flour mixed with oil for a grain
offering; 32 one golden dish weighing ten
shekels, full of incense; 33 one young bull,
one ram, one male lamb a year old, for a
burnt offering; 34 one male goat for a sin
offering; 35 and for the sacrifice of well-being,
two oxen, five rams, five male goats, and
five male lambs a year old. This was the
offering of Elizur son of Shedeur.
36 On the fifth day Shelumiel son of
Zurishaddai, the leader of the Simeonites:
37 his offering was one silver plate weighing
one hundred thirty shekels, one silver basin
weighing seventy shekels, according to the
shekel of the sanctuary, both of them full
of choice flour mixed with oil for a grain
offering; 38 one golden dish weighing ten

7.1-88 The Offerings of the Leaders of Israel. This account is stylized in its repetition of detail, and the whole process is precisely ordered. Though events are described as occurring at the first erection of the tabernacle by Moses (7.1), the opening lines of Numbers (1.1) describe conditions at a later time in the wilderness journey. Further, the huge amounts of equipment and large sums of money said to have been provided by the tribal leaders are inconceivable as historically available among refugees who had escaped from slavery in Egypt and lived for an extended time in the wilderness of Sinai. The symmetry of the gifts, in addition to the report that each set of them was brought each day for twelve days, confirms the impression that the text here is a stylized, idealized construct from a much later time: after the exile. The equipment from the tent and sanctuary (*holy things*) is said to have been carried on the shoulders of the Levites (7.9), rather than on a cart as in 2 Sam 6.3.

shekels, full of incense; [39]one young bull,
one ram, one male lamb a year old, for a
burnt offering; [40]one male goat for a sin
offering; [41]and for the sacrifice of well-being,
two oxen, five rams, five male goats, and
five male lambs a year old. This was the
offering of Shelumiel son of Zurishaddai.
42 On the sixth day Eliasaph son of Deuel,
the leader of the Gadites: [43]his offering was
one silver plate weighing one hundred thirty
shekels, one silver basin weighing seventy
shekels, according to the shekel of the sanctuary, both of them full of choice flour
mixed with oil for a grain offering; [44]one
golden dish weighing ten shekels, full of
incense; [45]one young bull, one ram, one
male lamb a year old, for a burnt offering;
[46]one male goat for a sin offering; [47]and for
the sacrifice of well-being, two oxen, five
rams, five male goats, and five male lambs
a year old. This was the offering of Eliasaph
son of Deuel.
48 On the seventh day Elishama son of
Ammihud, the leader of the Ephraimites:
[49]his offering was one silver plate weighing
one hundred thirty shekels, one silver basin
weighing seventy shekels, according to the
shekel of the sanctuary, both of them full
of choice flour mixed with oil for a grain
offering; [50]one golden dish weighing ten
shekels, full of incense; [51]one young bull,
one ram, one male lamb a year old, for a
burnt offering; [52]one male goat for a sin
offering; [53]and for the sacrifice of well-being,
two oxen, five rams, five male goats, and
five male lambs a year old. This was the
offering of Elishama son of Ammihud.
54 On the eighth day Gamaliel son of
Pedahzur, the leader of the Manassites: [55]his
offering was one silver plate weighing one
hundred thirty shekels, one silver basin
weighing seventy shekels, according to the
shekel of the sanctuary, both of them full
of choice flour mixed with oil for a grain
offering; [56]one golden dish weighing ten
shekels, full of incense; [57]one young bull,
one ram, one male lamb a year old, for a
burnt offering; [58]one male goat for a sin
offering; [59]and for the sacrifice of well-being,
two oxen, five rams, five male goats, and
five male lambs a year old. This was the
offering of Gamaliel son of Pedahzur.
60 On the ninth day Abidan son of
Gideoni, the leader of the Benjaminites: [61]his
offering was one silver plate weighing one
hundred thirty shekels, one silver basin
weighing seventy shekels, according to the
shekel of the sanctuary, both of them full
of choice flour mixed with oil for a grain
offering; [62]one golden dish weighing ten
shekels, full of incense; [63]one young bull,
one ram, one male lamb a year old, for a
burnt offering; [64]one male goat for a sin
offering; [65]and for the sacrifice of well-being,
two oxen, five rams, five male goats, and
five male lambs a year old. This was the
offering of Abidan son of Gideoni.
66 On the tenth day Ahiezer son of
Ammishaddai, the leader of the Danites:
[67]his offering was one silver plate weighing
one hundred thirty shekels, one silver basin
weighing seventy shekels, according to the
shekel of the sanctuary, both of them full
of choice flour mixed with oil for a grain
offering; [68]one golden dish weighing ten
shekels, full of incense; [69]one young bull,
one ram, one male lamb a year old, for a
burnt offering; [70]one male goat for a sin
offering; [71]and for the sacrifice of well-being,
two oxen, five rams, five male goats, and
five male lambs a year old. This was the
offering of Ahiezer son of Ammishaddai.
72 On the eleventh day Pagiel son of
Ochran, the leader of the Asherites: [73]his
offering was one silver plate weighing one
hundred thirty shekels, one silver basin
weighing seventy shekels, according to the
shekel of the sanctuary, both of them full
of choice flour mixed with oil for a grain
offering; [74]one golden dish weighing ten
shekels, full of incense; [75]one young bull,
one ram, one male lamb a year old, for a
burnt offering; [76]one male goat for a sin
offering; [77]and for the sacrifice of well-being,
two oxen, five rams, five male goats, and
five male lambs a year old. This was the
offering of Pagiel son of Ochran.
78 On the twelfth day Ahira son of Enan,
the leader of the Naphtalites: [79]his offering
was one silver plate weighing one hundred
thirty shekels, one silver basin weighing
seventy shekels, according to the shekel of
the sanctuary, both of them full of choice
flour mixed with oil for a grain offering;
[80]one golden dish weighing ten shekels, full
of incense; [81]one young bull, one ram, one
male lamb a year old, for a burnt offering;
[82]one male goat for a sin offering; [83]and for
the sacrifice of well-being, two oxen, five
rams, five male goats, and five male lambs
a year old. This was the offering of Ahira
son of Enan.
84 This was the dedication offering for
the altar, at the time when it was anointed,

7.40 ver 34
7.42 Num 1.14
7.46 ver 34
7.48 Num 1.10
7.52 Heb 10.4
7.54 Num 1.10
7.58 ver 52
7.60 Num 1.11
7.64 ver 52
7.66 Num 1.12
7.70 Heb 10.4
7.72 Num 1.13
7.76 ver 70
7.78 Num 1.15
7.82 ver 70
7.84 ver 1.10

from the leaders of Israel: twelve silver plates,
twelve silver basins, twelve golden dishes,
85each silver plate weighing one hundred
thirty shekels and each basin seventy, all
the silver of the vessels two thousand four
hundred shekels according to the shekel of
the sanctuary, 86the twelve golden dishes,
full of incense, weighing ten shekels apiece
according to the shekel of the sanctuary, all
the gold of the dishes being one hundred
twenty shekels; 87all the livestock for the
burnt offering twelve bulls, twelve rams,
twelve male lambs a year old, with their
grain offering; and twelve male goats for a
sin offering; 88and all the livestock for the
sacrifice of well-being twenty-four bulls, the
rams sixty, the male goats sixty, the male
lambs a year old sixty. This was the dedication offering for the altar, after it was
anointed.
89 When Moses went into the tent of
meeting to speak with the LORD,[j] he would
hear the voice speaking to him from above
the mercy seat[k] that was on the ark of the
covenant[l] from between the two cherubim;
thus it spoke to him.

The Seven Lamps

8 The LORD spoke to Moses, saying:
2Speak to Aaron and say to him: When
you set up the lamps, the seven lamps shall
give light in front of the lampstand. 3Aaron
did so; he set up its lamps to give light in
front of the lampstand, as the LORD had
commanded Moses. 4Now this was how the
lampstand was made, out of hammered
work of gold. From its base to its flowers,
it was hammered work; according to the
pattern that the LORD had shown Moses, so
he made the lampstand.

Consecration and Service of the Levites

5 The LORD spoke to Moses, saying: 6Take
the Levites from among the Israelites and
cleanse them. 7Thus you shall do to them,
to cleanse them: sprinkle the water of purification on them, have them shave their
whole body with a razor and wash their
clothes, and so cleanse themselves. 8Then
let them take a young bull and its grain
offering of choice flour mixed with oil, and
you shall take another young bull for a sin
offering. 9You shall bring the Levites before
the tent of meeting, and assemble the whole
congregation of the Israelites. 10When you
bring the Levites before the LORD, the Israelites shall lay their hands on the Levites,
11and Aaron shall present the Levites before
the LORD as an elevation offering from the
Israelites, that they may do the service of
the LORD. 12The Levites shall lay their hands
on the heads of the bulls, and he shall offer
the one for a sin offering and the other for
a burnt offering to the LORD, to make atonement for the Levites. 13Then you shall have
the Levites stand before Aaron and his sons,
and you shall present them as an elevation
offering to the LORD.
14 Thus you shall separate the Levites
from among the other Israelites, and the
Levites shall be mine. 15Thereafter the Levites
may go in to do service at the tent of
meeting, once you have cleansed them and
presented them as an elevation offering.
16For they are unreservedly given to me
from among the Israelites; I have taken
them for myself, in place of all that open the
womb, the firstborn of all the Israelites.
17For all the firstborn among the Israelites
are mine, both human and animal. On the
day that I struck down all the firstborn in
the land of Egypt I consecrated them for
myself, 18but I have taken the Levites in
place of all the firstborn among the Israelites. 19Moreover, I have given the Levites as
a gift to Aaron and his sons from among
the Israelites, to do the service for the Israelites at the tent of meeting, and to make
atonement for the Israelites, in order that
there may be no plague among the Israelites for coming too close to the sanctuary.
20 Moses and Aaron and the whole
congregation of the Israelites did with the
Levites accordingly; the Israelites did with
the Levites just as the LORD had commanded
Moses concerning them. 21The Levites purified themselves from sin and washed their
clothes; then Aaron presented them as an
elevation offering before the LORD, and Aaron
made atonement for them to cleanse them.
22Thereafter the Levites went in to do their
service in the tent of meeting in attendance
on Aaron and his sons. As the LORD had
commanded Moses concerning the Levites,
so they did with them.
23 The LORD spoke to Moses, saying: 24This
applies to the Levites: from twenty-five years
old and upward they shall begin to do duty
in the service of the tent of meeting; 25and
from the age of fifty years they shall retire

[j] Heb *him* [k] Or *the cover* [l] Or *treaty*, or *testimony*; Heb *eduth*

7.87 Gen 8.20
7.89 Ex 33.9,11; 25.21,22
8.2 Ex 25.37; Lev 24.2,4
8.4 Ex 25.31-40; 25.18
8.7 Num 19.9,17,18; Lev 14.8,9; ver 21
8.8 Lev 2.1
8.9 Lev 8.3
8.12 Ex 29.10
8.14 Num 3.12,45
8.15 ver 11,13
8.16 Num 3.12,45
8.19 Num 1.53
8.21 ver 7,11,12
8.24 Num 4.3

7.89-8.23 Further Instructions about Administering the Sanctuary of God. The specific location of God's presence in the sanctuary is given here: above the cover which closed the box in which were kept the tables of the law, and between *the two cherubim*, which were small winged figures on each side of the cover, rather than the two huge sacred statues in the temple of Solomon referred to in 1 Kings 6.23. It is from here that Moses is said to hear the voice of God.
8.1-4 The Seven Lamps at the Altar of God. The description of the lamps and the lampstand is much simpler here than in Ex 25.31-40 and 37.17-24. The tradition of a lamp in the sanctuary as the sign and symbol of God's illuminating presence there is old, as is shown by the mention of *the lamp of God* at Shiloh (1 Sam 3.3). In certain periods it was lit only at night (Ex 30.8; Lev 24.1-3), but in later times it burned continuously.
8.5-26 Consecration of the Levites and Assignment of Duties.
8.6-7 The ceremonial cleansing and purifying takes the form of washing, shaving entire bodies, and the washing of clothes.
8.8-10 The sacrifices required include whole offerings, grain offerings and sin offerings, which purify them and effect their new relationship with the God of Israel. When *the Israelites lay their hands on the Levites* it is a public sign that the latter are the chosen, qualified representatives of the people for this special role of assisting the priests in the maintenance of right relationship with God. The *son of Aaron* confirms this by presenting the Levites to the LORD with the appropriate offerings. Their distinctive place within the people of God and in relation to God is affirmed explicitly (8.14-19). With the completion of these rituals, the ritual system is instituted, and both priests and Levites are carrying out their assigned roles in it (8.20-22). The final set of rules about the years of service of the Levites (from 30 years) is probably a later adjustment, as comparison with Num 4.3 (from 25 years) and 1 Chron 23.24 (from 20 years) suggests.

9.1-14 Regulations for Observing the Passover. The basic regulations for celebrating the Passover are found in Ex 12.1-20. The date indicated here (12.1-6, *the fourteenth day of the month*, is intended as a link with the *first day of the second month*, given in Num 1.1, as a way of showing the primary nature of this festival. The chief issue here is whether those who are ritually unclean at the time of the Passover feast can participate in it later. The answer is, they may do so *in the second month on the fourteenth day* (9.11), a policy which is also operative in 2 Chr 30. On the other hand, those who are ritually clean and not on a journey, but who fail to take part in the Passover, will forfeit their place in God's people (9.13). Yet *any alien residing among* the people may share in the feast according to the same regulations as apply to the Israelites.
9.15-23 God's Continuing Presence with his People. Visible evidence of God's presence in the midst of his people was given in the glowing cloud which hovered over the tent of meeting. When it lifted up from the tent, that was a sign that the people were to move on (9.17). The length of stay in any place and the signal to continue the journey toward the promised land were determined by the movement of the cloud (9.22-23).
10.1-10 The Trumpets as Signals to God's People. In addition to the visible signal from the cloud, audible signals were given to the people by the blowing of trumpets: the sound of two being blown indicated that all the people were to assemble, but a single trumpet sounding was a summons to the leaders to gather. In case of war, an *alarm* is to be sounded (10.5, 9). Whether this was a special kind of trumpet sound, a shout or some other way of getting the attention of the people cannot be determined. The happier occasions for assembling included festivals and special days of rejoicing (10.10).

from the duty of the service and serve no more. 26 They may assist their brothers in the tent of meeting in carrying out their duties, but they shall perform no service. Thus you shall do with the Levites in assigning their duties.

The Passover at Sinai

9 The LORD spoke to Moses in the wilderness of Sinai, in the first month of the second year after they had come out of the land of Egypt, saying: 2 Let the Israelites keep the passover at its appointed time. 3 On the fourteenth day of this month, at twilight,[m] you shall keep it at its appointed time; according to all its statutes and all its regulations you shall keep it. 4 So Moses told the Israelites that they should keep the passover. 5 They kept the passover in the first month, on the fourteenth day of the month, at twilight,[m] in the wilderness of Sinai. Just as the LORD had commanded Moses, so the Israelites did. 6 Now there were certain people who were unclean through touching a corpse, so that they could not keep the passover on that day. They came before Moses and Aaron on that day, 7 and said to him, "Although we are unclean through touching a corpse, why must we be kept from presenting the LORD's offering at its appointed time among the Israelites?" 8 Moses spoke to them, "Wait, so that I may hear what the LORD will command concerning you."

9 The LORD spoke to Moses, saying: 10 Speak to the Israelites, saying: Anyone of you or your descendants who is unclean through touching a corpse, or is away on a journey, shall still keep the passover to the LORD. 11 In the second month on the fourteenth day, at twilight,[m] they shall keep it; they shall eat it with unleavened bread and bitter herbs. 12 They shall leave none of it until morning, nor break a bone of it; according to all the statute for the passover they shall keep it. 13 But anyone who is clean and is not on a journey, and yet refrains from keeping the passover, shall be cut off from the people for not presenting the LORD's offering at its appointed time; such a one shall bear the consequences for the sin. 14 Any alien residing among you who wishes to keep the passover to the LORD shall do so according to the statute of the passover and according to its regulation; you shall have one statute for both the resident alien and the native.

The Cloud and the Fire

15 On the day the tabernacle was set up, the cloud covered the tabernacle, the tent of the covenant;[n] and from evening until morning it was over the tabernacle, having the appearance of fire. 16 It was always so: the cloud covered it by day[o] and the appearance of fire by night. 17 Whenever the cloud lifted from over the tent, then the Israelites would set out; and in the place where the cloud settled down, there the Israelites would camp. 18 At the command of the LORD the Israelites would set out, and at the command of the LORD they would camp. As long as the cloud rested over the tabernacle, they would remain in camp. 19 Even when the cloud continued over the tabernacle many days, the Israelites would keep the charge of the LORD, and would not set out. 20 Sometimes the cloud would remain a few days over the tabernacle, and according to the command of the LORD they would remain in camp; then according to the command of the LORD they would set out. 21 Sometimes the cloud would remain from evening until morning; and when the cloud lifted in the morning, they would set out, or if it continued for a day and a night, when the cloud lifted they would set out. 22 Whether it was two days, or a month, or a longer time, that the cloud continued over the tabernacle, resting upon it, the Israelites would remain in camp and would not set out; but when it lifted they would set out. 23 At the command of the LORD they would camp, and at the command of the LORD they would set out. They kept the charge of the LORD, at the command of the LORD by Moses.

The Silver Trumpets

10 The LORD spoke to Moses, saying: 2 Make two silver trumpets; you shall make them of hammered work; and you shall use them for summoning the congregation, and for breaking camp. 3 When both are blown, the whole congregation shall assemble before you at the entrance of the tent of meeting. 4 But if only one is blown, then the leaders, the heads of the tribes of Israel, shall assemble before you. 5 When you blow an alarm, the camps on the east side shall set out; 6 when you blow a second alarm, the camps on the south side shall set out. An alarm is to be blown whenever they are to set out. 7 But when

9.1 Num 1.1
9.2 Ex 12.6
9.5 Josh 5.10
9.6 Num 19.11-22
9.8 Ex 18.15; Num 27.5
9.11 Ex 12.8
9.12 Ex 12.10,43,46; Jn 19.36
9.13 ver 7; Ex 12.15
9.14 Ex 12.48,49
9.15 Ex 40.34; Neh 9.12,19; Ps 78.4; Ex 13.21; 40.38
9.17 Num 10.11,12; Ex 40.36-38
9.18 1 Cor 10.1
9.19 Num 1.53; 3.8
9.22 Ex 40.36,37
10.3 Jer 4.5
10.5 ver 14
10.6 ver 18

[m] Heb *between the two evenings* [n] Or *treaty*, or *testimony*; Heb *eduth* [o] Gk Syr Vg: Heb lacks *by day*

10.8 the assembly is to be gathered, you shall
Num 31.6 blow, but you shall not sound an alarm.
10.9 [8]The sons of Aaron, the priests, shall blow
Num 31.6; the trumpets; this shall be a perpetual in-
Judg 2.18; stitution for you throughout your genera-
Ps 106.4 tions. [9]When you go to war in your land
10.10 against the adversary who oppresses you,
Num 29.1; you shall sound an alarm with the trum-
Lev 23.24; pets, so that you may be remembered before
Ps 81.3-5 the LORD your God and be saved from your
10.11 enemies. [10]Also on your days of rejoicing, at
Num 9.17 your appointed festivals, and at the begin-
nings of your months, you shall blow the
10.13 trumpets over your burnt offerings and over
Deut 1.6 your sacrifices of well-being; they shall serve
10.14 as a reminder on your behalf before the
Num 2.3-9 LORD your God: I am the LORD your God.

10.17
Num 4.21-32

Departure from Sinai

10.18 11 In the second year, in the second
Num 2.10-16 month, on the twentieth day of the month,
10.21 the cloud lifted from over the tabernacle of
Num 4.4-20 the covenant.[p] [12]Then the Israelites set out
by stages from the wilderness of Sinai, and
10.22 the cloud settled down in the wilderness of
Num 2.18-24 Paran. [13]They set out for the first time at
10.25 the command of the LORD by Moses. [14]The
Num 2.25- standard of the camp of Judah set out first,
31; Josh company by company, and over the whole
6.9.13 company was Nahshon son of Amminadab.
10.29 [15]Over the company of the tribe of Issachar
Judg 4.11; Ex was Nethanel son of Zuar; [16]and over the
2.18; Gen company of the tribe of Zebulun was Eliab
12.7; 32.12; son of Helon.
Ex 3.8 17 Then the tabernacle was taken down,
10.32 and the Gershonites and the Merarites, who
Ps 22.27-31; carried the tabernacle, set out. [18]Next the
Lev 19.34 standard of the camp of Reuben set out,
10.33 company by company; and over the whole
ver 11; Deut company was Elizur son of Shedeur. [19]Over
1.33; Isa the company of the tribe of Simeon was
11.10 Shelumiel son of Zurishaddai, [20]and over
10.34 the company of the tribe of Gad was Eliasaph
Num 9.15-23 son of Deuel.
21 Then the Kohathites, who carried the
10.35 holy things, set out; and the tabernacle was
Ps 68.1,2; set up before their arrival. [22]Next the stand-
Deut 7.10; ard of the Ephraimite camp set out, com-
32.41 pany by company, and over the whole
company was Elishama son of Ammihud.
11.1 [23]Over the company of the tribe of Manasseh
Num 14.2; was Gamaliel son of Pedahzur, [24]and over
16.11; 17.5; the company of the tribe of Benjamin was
16.35; Abidan son of Gideoni.
Lev 10.2 25 Then the standard of the camp of
Dan, acting as the rear guard of all the
camps, set out, company by company, and
over the whole company was Ahiezer son
of Ammishaddai. [26]Over the company of the
tribe of Asher was Pagiel son of Ochran,
[27]and over the company of the tribe of
Naphtali was Ahira son of Enan. [28]This was
the order of march of the Israelites, company by company, when they set out.
29 Moses said to Hobab son of Reuel the
Midianite, Moses' father-in-law, "We are
setting out for the place of which the LORD
said, 'I will give it to you'; come with us,
and we will treat you well; for the LORD has
promised good to Israel." [30]But he said to
him, "I will not go, but I will go back to
my own land and to my kindred." [31]He said,
"Do not leave us, for you know where we
should camp in the wilderness, and you will
serve as eyes for us. [32]Moreover, if you go
with us, whatever good the LORD does for
us, the same we will do for you."
33 So they set out from the mount of the
LORD three days' journey with the ark of the
covenant of the LORD going before them
three days' journey, to seek out a resting
place for them, [34]the cloud of the LORD being
over them by day when they set out from
the camp.
35 Whenever the ark set out, Moses
would say,

"Arise, O LORD, let your enemies be
scattered,
and your foes flee before you."

[36]And whenever it came to rest, he would
say,

"Return, O LORD of the ten thousand
thousands of Israel."[q]

Complaining in the Desert

11 Now when the people complained
in the hearing of the LORD about
their misfortunes, the LORD heard it and his
anger was kindled. Then the fire of the LORD
burned against them, and consumed some
outlying parts of the camp. [2]But the people
cried out to Moses; and Moses prayed to the
LORD, and the fire abated. [3]So that place was
called Taberah,[r] because the fire of the LORD
burned against them.
4 The rabble among them had a strong
craving; and the Israelites also wept again,
and said, "If only we had meat to eat! [5]We
remember the fish we used to eat in Egypt
for nothing, the cucumbers, the melons, the

10.11-36 Leaving Sinai for the Promised Land.
10.11 The departure is dated a year and a month after God's giving of the law to Moses at Sinai. The route is northward *by stages* (10.12) from the central section of the Sinai peninsula through the *wilderness of Paran*, southwest of the great valley of the Jordan and the Dead Sea. First place in the long line of itinerant Israelites is assigned to the tribe of Judah (10.14), with the tribe of Dan at the rear (10.25), which seems to reflect the relative importance of the tribes in the subsequent history of Israel. Included in the line of march are the Levites, carrying the tabernacle and its equipment (10.17-21) Moses' brother-in-law, Hobab the Midianite (Ex 2.15-22), is reluctant to join the march to the promised land, but Moses encourages him to do so. They all depart led by *the cloud of the LORD*, with Moses' militant songs to Yahweh to mark their arrivals and departures at each stage of the journey (10.35-36).
11.1-12.16 The Discontent of Israel in the Wilderness. A series of stories depicts the pattern of Israel's rebellion against the LORD and his subsequent punishments or pronouncements of forgiveness.
11.1-3 God's anger over the complaints of the people leads to his judgment on them by fire, which consumes the outer edges of the camp as a warning to the rest.
11.4-9 *The rabble among them*, together with *the Israelites*, are weary of the uniform diet of the food that God provided for them in such abundance: the *manna* (*cf.* Ex 16.14-21).

11.2
Num 21.7

[p] Or *treaty*, or *testimony*; Heb *eduth* [q] Meaning of Heb uncertain [r] That is *Burning*

11.4
Ex 12.38;
Ps 78.18; 1
Cor 10.6

11.5
Ex 16.3

11.10-15 When Moses complained bitterly to the LORD because of the intolerable burden of responsibility for caring for the rebellious people, and asked that God would end his life, God's answer took a variety of forms.
11.16-25 *Seventy of the elders of Israel* are designated to serve as agents and mediators between Moses and the people, and are given *some of the spirit that was on* Moses to enable them to fulfill their roles (11.25). The people are surfeited with meat over a period of a month to silence their complaints about having only manna to eat (11.18-20). In addition, quails in great numbers are provided for them to eat. Twice each year, quail migrate in large numbers across the Sinai peninsula. In the midst of this plenty, a plague strikes and many people die (11.31-34). Leaving the place named, to remind them of their inordinate craving for meat and divine punishment, *Kirboth-hattavah* (Graves of craving), they go on to *Hazeroth*, which means "encampments."

leeks, the onions, and the garlic; [6]but now our strength is dried up, and there is nothing at all but this manna to look at."

7 Now the manna was like coriander seed, and its color was like the color of gum resin. [8]The people went around and gathered it, ground it in mills or beat it in mortars, then boiled it in pots and made cakes of it; and the taste of it was like the taste of cakes baked with oil. [9]When the dew fell on the camp in the night, the manna would fall with it.

10 Moses heard the people weeping throughout their families, all at the entrances of their tents. Then the LORD became very angry, and Moses was displeased. [11]So Moses said to the LORD, "Why have you treated your servant so badly? Why have I not found favor in your sight, that you lay the burden of all this people on me? [12]Did I conceive all this people? Did I give birth to them, that you should say to me, 'Carry them in your bosom, as a nurse carries a sucking child,' to the land that you promised on oath to their ancestors? [13]Where am I to get meat to give to all this people? For they come weeping to me and say, 'Give us meat to eat!' [14]I am not able to carry all this people alone, for they are too heavy for me. [15]If this is the way you are going to treat me, put me to death at once—if I have found favor in your sight—and do not let me see my misery."

The Seventy Elders

16 So the LORD said to Moses, "Gather for me seventy of the elders of Israel, whom you know to be the elders of the people and officers over them; bring them to the tent of meeting, and have them take their place there with you. [17]I will come down and talk with you there; and I will take some of the spirit that is on you and put it on them; and they shall bear the burden of the people along with you so that you will not bear it all by yourself. [18]And say to the people: Consecrate yourselves for tomorrow, and you shall eat meat; for you have wailed in the hearing of the LORD, saying, 'If only we had meat to eat! Surely it was better for us in Egypt.' Therefore the LORD will give you meat, and you shall eat. [19]You shall eat not only one day, or two days, or five days, or ten days, or twenty days, [20]but for a whole month—until it comes out of your nostrils and becomes loathsome to you—because you have rejected the LORD who is among you, and have wailed before him, saying, 'Why did we ever leave Egypt?' " [21]But Moses said, "The people I am with number six hundred thousand on foot; and you say, 'I will give them meat, that they may eat for a whole month'! [22]Are there enough flocks and herds to slaughter for them? Are there enough fish in the sea to catch for them?" [23]The LORD said to Moses, "Is the LORD's power limited?[s] Now you shall see whether my word will come true for you or not."

24 So Moses went out and told the people the words of the LORD; and he gathered seventy elders of the people, and placed them all around the tent. [25]Then the LORD came down in the cloud and spoke to him, and took some of the spirit that was on him and put it on the seventy elders; and when the spirit rested upon them, they prophesied. But they did not do so again.

26 Two men remained in the camp, one named Eldad, and the other named Medad, and the spirit rested on them; they were among those registered, but they had not gone out to the tent, and so they prophesied in the camp. [27]And a young man ran and told Moses, "Eldad and Medad are prophesying in the camp." [28]And Joshua son of Nun, the assistant of Moses, one of his chosen men,[t] said, "My lord Moses, stop them!" [29]But Moses said to him, "Are you jealous for my sake? Would that all the LORD's people were prophets, and that the LORD would put his spirit on them!" [30]And Moses and the elders of Israel returned to the camp.

The Quails

31 Then a wind went out from the LORD, and it brought quails from the sea and let them fall beside the camp, about a day's journey on this side and a day's journey on the other side, all around the camp, about two cubits deep on the ground. [32]So the people worked all that day and night and all the next day, gathering the quails; the least anyone gathered was ten homers; and they spread them out for themselves all around the camp. [33]But while the meat was still between their teeth, before it was consumed, the anger of the LORD was kindled against the people, and the LORD struck the people with a very great plague. [34]So that

11.6 Lev 21.5
11.7 Ex 16.14,31
11.9 Ex 16.13,14
11.10 Ps 78.21
11.12 Isa 40.11; 49.23; Gen 26.3; Ex 13.5
11.13 ver 21,22; Jn 6.5-9
11.14 Ex 18.18
11.15 1 Kings 19.4; Jon 4.3
11.16 Ex 24.1,9; Deut 16.18
11.17 ver 25; Ex 19.20; 1 Sam 10.6; 2 Kings 2.15
11.18 Ex 19.10; 16.7; ver 5; Acts 7.39
11.19 Ps 78.29; 106.15; Num 21.5
11.22 Mt 15.33
11.23 Isa 50.2; 59.1; Num 23.19
11.24 ver 16
11.25 ver 17; Num 12.5; 1 Sam 10.5,6,10; Acts 2.17,18
11.26 1 Sam 10.6; 20.26
11.28 Mk 9.38-40
11.29 1 Cor 14.5
11.31 Ex 16.13; Ps 78.26-28; 105.40
11.33 Ps 78.30,31; 106.15
11.34 Deut 9.22

[s] Heb *LORD's hand too short?* [t] Or *of Moses from his youth*

11.35 Num 33.17
12.1 Ex 2.21
12.2 Num 16.3
12.3 Mt 11.29
12.5 Num 11.25; 16.19
12.6 Gen 46.2; 31.10,11; 1 Kings 3.5
12.7 Ps 105.26; Heb 3.2,5
12.8 Ex 33.11; Deut 34.10; Ex 33.19
12.10 Deut 24.9; 2 Kings 5.27; 15.5
12.11 2 Sam 9.19; 24.10
12.14 Lev 13.46; Lev 5.2,3
13.2 Deut 1.22
13.8 ver 16
13.16 ver 8
13.17 ver 21
13.20 Deut 1.24,25; 31.6,23
13.22 Josh 15.13,14; ver 28,33; Ps 78.12

place was called Kibroth-hattaavah,[u] because there they buried the people who had the craving. 35 From Kibroth-hattaavah the people journeyed to Hazeroth.

Aaron and Miriam Jealous of Moses

12 While they were at Hazeroth, Miriam and Aaron spoke against Moses because of the Cushite woman whom he had married (for he had indeed married a Cushite woman); 2 and they said, "Has the LORD spoken only through Moses? Has he not spoken through us also?" And the LORD heard it. 3 Now the man Moses was very humble,[v] more so than anyone else on the face of the earth. 4 Suddenly the LORD said to Moses, Aaron, and Miriam, "Come out, you three, to the tent of meeting." So the three of them came out. 5 Then the LORD came down in a pillar of cloud, and stood at the entrance of the tent, and called Aaron and Miriam; and they both came forward. 6 And he said, "Hear my words:

When there are prophets among you,
  I the LORD make myself known to them in visions;
  I speak to them in dreams.
7 Not so with my servant Moses;
  he is entrusted with all my house.
8 With him I speak face to face—
  clearly, not in riddles;
  and he beholds the form of the LORD.

Why then were you not afraid to speak against my servant Moses?" 9 And the anger of the LORD was kindled against them, and he departed.

10 When the cloud went away from over the tent, Miriam had become leprous,[w] as white as snow. And Aaron turned towards Miriam and saw that she was leprous. 11 Then Aaron said to Moses, "Oh, my lord, do not punish us[x] for a sin that we have so foolishly committed. 12 Do not let her be like one stillborn, whose flesh is half consumed when it comes out of its mother's womb." 13 And Moses cried to the LORD, "O God, please heal her." 14 But the LORD said to Moses, "If her father had but spit in her face, would she not bear her shame for seven days? Let her be shut out of the camp for seven days, and after that she may be brought in again." 15 So Miriam was shut out of the camp for seven days; and the people did not set out on the march until Miriam had been brought in again. 16 After that the people set out from Hazeroth, and camped in the wilderness of Paran.

Spies Sent into Canaan

13 The LORD said to Moses, 2 "Send men to spy out the land of Canaan, which I am giving to the Israelites; from each of their ancestral tribes you shall send a man, every one a leader among them." 3 So Moses sent them from the wilderness of Paran, according to the command of the LORD, all of them leading men among the Israelites. 4 These were their names: From the tribe of Reuben, Shammua son of Zaccur; 5 from the tribe of Simeon, Shaphat son of Hori; 6 from the tribe of Judah, Caleb son of Jephunneh; 7 from the tribe of Issachar, Igal son of Joseph; 8 from the tribe of Ephraim, Hoshea son of Nun; 9 from the tribe of Benjamin, Palti son of Raphu; 10 from the tribe of Zebulun, Gaddiel son of Sodi; 11 from the tribe of Joseph (that is, from the tribe of Manasseh), Gaddi son of Susi; 12 from the tribe of Dan, Ammiel son of Gemalli; 13 from the tribe of Asher, Sethur son of Michael; 14 from the tribe of Naphtali, Nahbi son of Vophsi; 15 from the tribe of Gad, Geuel son of Machi. 16 These were the names of the men whom Moses sent to spy out the land. And Moses changed the name of Hoshea son of Nun to Joshua.

17 Moses sent them to spy out the land of Canaan, and said to them, "Go up there into the Negeb, and go up into the hill country, 18 and see what the land is like, and whether the people who live in it are strong or weak, whether they are few or many, 19 and whether the land they live in is good or bad, and whether the towns that they live in are unwalled or fortified, 20 and whether the land is rich or poor, and whether there are trees in it or not. Be bold, and bring some of the fruit of the land." Now it was the season of the first ripe grapes.

21 So they went up and spied out the land from the wilderness of Zin to Rehob, near Lebo-hamath. 22 They went up into the Negeb, and came to Hebron; and Ahiman, Sheshai, and Talmai, the Anakites, were there. (Hebron was built seven years before Zoan in Egypt.) 23 And they came to the Wadi Eshcol, and cut down from there a

[u] That is *Graves of craving* [v] Or *devout* [w] A term for several skin diseases; precise meaning uncertain [x] Heb *do not lay sin upon us*

12.1-15 *Miriam and Aaron* seize the occasion of Moses' having taken a *Cushite* [Ethiopian] *woman* as his wife to call into question his unique role as leader and spokesman for the LORD. Addressing the three antagonists in the *tent of meeting*, the LORD differentiates between his occasional messages to prophets in visions and dreams and his ongoing conversations with Moses *face to face* (11.8), and warns them of the dangers of speaking *against my servant Moses.* Miriam is thereupon stricken with a leprous disease, and the progress of the journey to the new land is delayed until she recovers (12.15). The subsequent encampment in the *wilderness of Paran* was in the region northwest of the present Gulf of Aqabah and south of Beersheba.

13.1-24 Spying Out the Land of Canaan. This land, inhabited by Semitic peoples among whom Abraham and the patriarchs of Israel lived prior to the period of enslavement in Egypt, has been promised to the twelve tribes of Jacob's sons: God is *giving [it] to the Israelites.* Those sent to inspect the land include representatives from each of the twelve tribes, which here omits Levi and includes Ephraim and Manasseh, the two sons of Joseph (11.3-15). Special mention is made of Hoshea, whose name is reported to have been changed by Moses to *Joshua*, or *Yehohsuah*, thereby including in his name a direct reference to Yahweh, the God who made the covenant with Israel. Also noted (13.6) is Caleb, who represents the tribe of Judah and who is the only one of the spies directly quoted on their return (13.30). Joshua is to have a major role in the ultimate entrance of Israel into the land of Canaan, and Caleb's tribe, Judah, will be the dominant group in the southern part of the land, including Hebron and Jerusalem.

branch with a single cluster of grapes, and they carried it on a pole between two of them. They also brought some pomegranates and figs. [24]That place was called the Wadi Eshcol,[y] because of the cluster that the Israelites cut down from there.

The Report of the Spies

25 At the end of forty days they returned from spying out the land. [26]And they came to Moses and Aaron and to all the congregation of the Israelites in the wilderness of Paran, at Kadesh; they brought back word to them and to all the congregation, and showed them the fruit of the land. [27]And they told him, "We came to the land to which you sent us; it flows with milk and honey, and this is its fruit. [28]Yet the people who live in the land are strong, and the towns are fortified and very large; and besides, we saw the descendants of Anak there. [29]The Amalekites live in the land of the Negeb; the Hittites, the Jebusites, and the Amorites live in the hill country; and the Canaanites live by the sea, and along the Jordan."

30 But Caleb quieted the people before Moses, and said, "Let us go up at once and occupy it, for we are well able to overcome it." [31]Then the men who had gone up with him said, "We are not able to go up against this people, for they are stronger than we." [32]So they brought to the Israelites an unfavorable report of the land that they had spied out, saying, "The land that we have gone through as spies is a land that devours its inhabitants; and all the people that we saw in it are of great size. [33]There we saw the Nephilim (the Anakites come from the Nephilim); and to ourselves we seemed like grasshoppers, and so we seemed to them."

The People Rebel

14 Then all the congregation raised a loud cry, and the people wept that night. [2]And all the Israelites complained against Moses and Aaron; the whole congregation said to them, "Would that we had died in the land of Egypt! Or would that we had died in this wilderness! [3]Why is the LORD bringing us into this land to fall by the sword? Our wives and our little ones will become booty; would it not be better for us to go back to Egypt?" [4]So they said to one another, "Let us choose a captain, and go back to Egypt."

5 Then Moses and Aaron fell on their faces before all the assembly of the congregation of the Israelites. [6]And Joshua son of Nun and Caleb son of Jephunneh, who were among those who had spied out the land, tore their clothes [7]and said to all the congregation of the Israelites, "The land that we went through as spies is an exceedingly good land. [8]If the LORD is pleased with us, he will bring us into this land and give it to us, a land that flows with milk and honey. [9]Only, do not rebel against the LORD; and do not fear the people of the land, for they are no more than bread for us; their protection is removed from them, and the LORD is with us; do not fear them." [10]But the whole congregation threatened to stone them.

Then the glory of the LORD appeared at the tent of meeting to all the Israelites. [11]And the LORD said to Moses, "How long will this people despise me? And how long will they refuse to believe in me, in spite of all the signs that I have done among them? [12]I will strike them with pestilence and disinherit them, and I will make of you a nation greater and mightier than they."

Moses Intercedes for the People

13 But Moses said to the LORD, "Then the Egyptians will hear of it, for in your might you brought up this people from among them, [14]and they will tell the inhabitants of this land. They have heard that you, O LORD, are in the midst of this people; for you, O LORD, are seen face to face, and your cloud stands over them and you go in front of them, in a pillar of cloud by day and in a pillar of fire by night. [15]Now if you kill this people all at one time, then the nations who have heard about you will say, [16]'It is because the LORD was not able to bring this people into the land he swore to give them that he has slaughtered them in the wilderness.' [17]And now, therefore, let the power of the LORD be great in the way that you promised when you spoke, saying,

[18] 'The LORD is slow to anger,
and abounding in steadfast love,
forgiving iniquity and transgression,
but by no means clearing the guilty,
visiting the iniquity of the parents
upon the children

[y] That is *Cluster*

13.17 The spies' route takes them through the level arid area to the south of central Palestine (*Negeb*) into *the hill country*, which rises from near the sea coast eastward to the high ridge which overlooks the cleft of the Jordan and the Dead Sea, and from the *wilderness of Zin* (southwest of the Dead Sea) to *Lebo-hamath*, which is on the Syrian border west of Mt. Hermon at the extreme north of Palestine. On the way they visit Hebron, where the patriarchs and their wives were buried, and the Wadi Eshcol, which is probably near Hebron, and which is said to be older than the important residence city of the Egyptian pharaohs, Zoan, which flourished from the eighteenth to the thirteenth centuries BCE (13.23-24). As evidence of the abundance of the crops in the land, the spies bring back several kinds of fruit. Their report to Moses and the people is given at Kadesh (13.26), which was about 50 miles south of Beersheba in southern Israel. Among the tribes and peoples mentioned in this account are the Anakites (13.22), who were reported to be giants in stature (*cf.*13.33 and 2 Sam 21.18-22); the Amalekites (13.29), a confederacy of semi-nomadic tribes based in the Negeb, who attacked Israel early in the Exodus (Ex 17.8-16); the Hittites, a people whose empire arose in southeastern Asia Minor and who in the sixteenth century dominated the Near East across Syria and into Mesopotamia (*cf.* the promise of God to Joshua about possessing *all the land of the Hittites* in Josh 1.4), and are linked with Abraham (Gen 23.10; 25.9; 49.29-30; 50.13) as well as David and Solomon (2 Sam 11-12; 1 Kings 10.29); the Jebusites, a Semitic tribe resident in the vicinity of Jerusalem (Judg 1.21); the Amorites, a Semitic tribe originally from Mesopotamia that lived in the hill country of Palestine, in eastern Syria and western Mesopotamia, whose extensive literature has been found by modern archaeologists, and who here occupy an area north and east of the upper end of the Dead Sea; and the Canaanites, who were settled in the lower hills, the Jordan Valley and the Mediterranean coastal regions of Palestine, whose ethnic and linguistic ties were with the Phoenicians along the coast of what is now Lebanon and Syria, and who were absorbed by the occupying peoples of Israel.
13.25-33 The Spies Report to the People. After reporting the fertility of the land and showing the fruit (13.26-27), the majority of the spies warn of the great military power and the strong fortifications of the cities, which make invasion impossible (13.28). Caleb's minority proposal is that Israel should *go up at once and occupy it*. The fear of the power of the inhabitants prevails, however.
14.1-10 The People Rebel at the Delay in Entering the Land of Promise. Expressing fear that their *wives and little ones* will be taken captive by the inhabitants of the land, they regret having left Egypt and plan to return. Moses, Joshua and Caleb try to persuade them that God wants them to enter the land and will protect them as they do (14.5-9), but *the whole congregation* rejects the proposal.
14.11-25 God's Threat to Destroy the People and Moses' Intercession in their Behalf. God proposes to *strike [the people] with pestilence*, and then to reconstitute a new covenant people with Moses at the head of it. Moses reminds God that his fidelity and power to fulfill his promises are at stake, and appeals to his love and forgiveness (14.13-19). God forgives Israel and announces his purpose that *all the earth shall be filled with the glory of the LORD*, but that none of the current generation will live to see the fulfillment of God's promise, except Caleb, who urged the people to enter the land (14.20-24). Meanwhile, the people are to remain in *the wilderness [near] the Red Sea* (Deut 1.40).

13.26 ver 3; Num 20.1,16; 32.8
13.27 Ex 3.8; Deut 1.25
13.28 Deut 1.28
13.29 Num 14.43
13.30 Num 14.6,24
13.31 Deut 1.28
13.32 Num 14.36; Ps 106.24; Am 2.9
13.33 Deut 1.28; 9.2
14.2 Num 11.1,5
14.5 Num 16.4,22
14.7 Num 13.27; Deut 1.25
14.8 Deut 10.15; Num 13.27
14.9 Deut 9.7,23,24; 7.18; 20.1,3,4
14.10 Ex 17.4; 16.10; Lev 9.23
14.11 Deut 9.7,8; Ps 78.22; 106.24
14.12 Ex 32.10
14.13 Ps 106.23
14.14 Ex 15.14; Josh 2.9,10; Ex 13.21
14.16 Deut 9.28
14.18 Ex 34.6,7; Ps 103.8; Ex 20.5

to the third and the fourth
generation.'

19 Forgive the iniquity of this people according to the greatness of your steadfast love, just as you have pardoned this people, from Egypt even until now."

20 Then the LORD said, "I do forgive, just as you have asked; 21 nevertheless—as I live, and as all the earth shall be filled with the glory of the LORD— 22 none of the people who have seen my glory and the signs that I did in Egypt and in the wilderness, and yet have tested me these ten times and have not obeyed my voice, 23 shall see the land that I swore to give to their ancestors; none of those who despised me shall see it. 24 But my servant Caleb, because he has a different spirit and has followed me wholeheartedly, I will bring into the land into which he went, and his descendants shall possess it. 25 Now, since the Amalekites and the Canaanites live in the valleys, turn tomorrow and set out for the wilderness by the way to the Red Sea."[z]

An Attempted Invasion is Repulsed

26 And the LORD spoke to Moses and to Aaron, saying: 27 How long shall this wicked congregation complain against me? I have heard the complaints of the Israelites, which they complain against me. 28 Say to them, "As I live," says the LORD, "I will do to you the very things I heard you say: 29 your dead bodies shall fall in this very wilderness; and of all your number, included in the census, from twenty years old and upward, who have complained against me, 30 not one of you shall come into the land in which I swore to settle you, except Caleb son of Jephunneh and Joshua son of Nun. 31 But your little ones, who you said would become booty, I will bring in, and they shall know the land that you have despised. 32 But as for you, your dead bodies shall fall in this wilderness. 33 And your children shall be shepherds in the wilderness for forty years, and shall suffer for your faithlessness, until the last of your dead bodies lies in the wilderness. 34 According to the number of the days in which you spied out the land, forty days, for every day a year, you shall bear your iniquity, forty years, and you shall know my displeasure." 35 I the LORD have spoken; surely I will do thus to all this wicked congregation gathered together against me: in this wilderness they shall come to a full end, and there they shall die.

36 And the men whom Moses sent to spy out the land, who returned and made all the congregation complain against him by bringing a bad report about the land— 37 the men who brought an unfavorable report about the land died by a plague before the LORD. 38 But Joshua son of Nun and Caleb son of Jephunneh alone remained alive, of those men who went to spy out the land.

39 When Moses told these words to all the Israelites, the people mourned greatly. 40 They rose early in the morning and went up to the heights of the hill country, saying, "Here we are. We will go up to the place that the LORD has promised, for we have sinned." 41 But Moses said, "Why do you continue to transgress the command of the LORD? That will not succeed. 42 Do not go up, for the LORD is not with you; do not let yourselves be struck down before your enemies. 43 For the Amalekites and the Canaanites will confront you there, and you shall fall by the sword; because you have turned back from following the LORD, the LORD will not be with you." 44 But they presumed to go up to the heights of the hill country, even though the ark of the covenant of the LORD, and Moses, had not left the camp. 45 Then the Amalekites and the Canaanites who lived in that hill country came down and defeated them, pursuing them as far as Hormah.

Various Offerings

15 The LORD spoke to Moses, saying: 2 Speak to the Israelites and say to them: When you come into the land you are to inhabit, which I am giving you, 3 and you make an offering by fire to the LORD from the herd or from the flock—whether a burnt offering or a sacrifice, to fulfill a vow or as a freewill offering or at your appointed festivals—to make a pleasing odor for the LORD, 4 then whoever presents such an offering to the LORD shall present also a grain offering, one-tenth of an ephah of choice flour, mixed with one-fourth of a hin of oil. 5 Moreover, you shall offer one-fourth of a hin of wine as a drink offering with the burnt offering or the sacrifice, for each lamb. 6 For a ram, you shall offer a grain offering, two-tenths of an ephah of choice flour mixed

[z] Or *Sea of Reeds*

14.19 Ex 34.9; Ps 106.45; 78.38
14.20 Ps 106.23
14.21 Ps 72.19
14.24 ver 7-9; Num 32.12; Josh 14.6-15
14.25 Deut 1.40
14.27 Num 11.1; Ex 16.12
14.28 ver 21; Deut 1.35; see ver 2
14.29 Num 1.45; 26.64
14.30 ver 24; Deut 1.36
14.31 Deut 1.39; Ps 106.24
14.32 1 Cor 10.5
14.33 Num 32.13; Ps 107.40
14.34 Num 13.25; Ps 95.10
14.35 Num 23.19; 26.65
14.36 Num 13.32
14.38 Josh 14.6
14.39 Ex 33.4
14.40 Deut 1.41
14.42 Deut 1.42
14.44 Deut 1.43
14.45 Deut 1.44; Num 21.3
15.2 ver 18
15.3 Lev 23.1-44
15.4 Lev 2.1; 6.14; Ex 29.40; Lev 23.13; 14.10; Num 28.5
15.5 Num 28.7,14
15.6 Num 28.12,14

14.26-45 The Attempted Invasion of the Land is Repulsed. In reponse to the continuing complaints of the Israelites, the LORD announces that he will fulfill these rebels' own predictions and that all of them will die in the wilderness *except Caleb...and Joshua* (14.30,38). The children of the present generation will survive to enter the land, but the period before that occurs will last *forty years* as punishment for the forty days the spies spent in the land (14.34), only to produce such a pessimistic report about Israel's taking the land. The obstinate people thereupon decide to attack the land in spite of God's warning and Moses' reinforcement of it (14.40-43), with the result that they are *defeated* (14.45).

15.1-21 Offerings to the LORD from Israelites and Aliens. After a summary of the types of offerings which are to be made (food offerings, whole offerings, grain offerings, wine offerings), the purposes they serve are sketched: a pleasant odor to the LORD; food and drink for the priests; the fulfillment of obligations to God that individuals have assumed. They are as appropriate and essential for the aliens living in the land as they are for the Israelites. (15.14-16) One law is applicable to all.

with one-third of a hin of oil; [7]and as a drink offering you shall offer one-third of a hin of wine, a pleasing odor to the LORD. [8]When you offer a bull as a burnt offering or a sacrifice, to fulfill a vow or as an offering of well-being to the LORD, [9]then you shall present with the bull a grain offering, three-tenths of an ephah of choice flour, mixed with half a hin of oil, [10]and you shall present as a drink offering half a hin of wine, as an offering by fire, a pleasing odor to the LORD.

11 Thus it shall be done for each ox or ram, or for each of the male lambs or the kids. [12]According to the number that you offer, so you shall do with each and every one. [13]Every native Israelite shall do these things in this way, in presenting an offering by fire, a pleasing odor to the LORD. [14]An alien who lives with you, or who takes up permanent residence among you, and wishes to offer an offering by fire, a pleasing odor to the LORD, shall do as you do. [15]As for the assembly, there shall be for both you and the resident alien a single statute, a perpetual statute throughout your generations; you and the alien shall be alike before the LORD. [16]You and the alien who resides with you shall have the same law and the same ordinance.

17 The LORD spoke to Moses, saying: [18]Speak to the Israelites and say to them: After you come into the land to which I am bringing you, [19]whenever you eat of the bread of the land, you shall present a donation to the LORD. [20]From your first batch of dough you shall present a loaf as a donation; you shall present it just as you present a donation from the threshing floor. [21]Throughout your generations you shall give to the LORD a donation from the first of your batch of dough.

22 But if you unintentionally fail to observe all these commandments that the LORD has spoken to Moses— [23]everything that the LORD has commanded you by Moses, from the day the LORD gave commandment and thereafter, throughout your generations— [24]then if it was done unintentionally without the knowledge of the congregation, the whole congregation shall offer one young bull for a burnt offering, a pleasing odor to the LORD, together with its grain offering and its drink offering, according to the ordinance, and one male goat for a sin offering. [25]The priest shall make atonement for all the congregation of the Israelites, and they shall be forgiven; it was unintentional, and they have brought their offering, an offering by fire to the LORD, and their sin offering before the LORD, for their error. [26]All the congregation of the Israelites shall be forgiven, as well as the aliens residing among them, because the whole people was involved in the error.

27 An individual who sins unintentionally shall present a female goat a year old for a sin offering. [28]And the priest shall make atonement before the LORD for the one who commits an error, when it is unintentional, to make atonement for the person, who then shall be forgiven. [29]For both the native among the Israelites and the alien residing among them—you shall have the same law for anyone who acts in error. [30]But whoever acts high-handedly, whether a native or an alien, affronts the LORD, and shall be cut off from among the people. [31]Because of having despised the word of the LORD and broken his commandment, such a person shall be utterly cut off and bear the guilt.

Penalty for Violating the Sabbath

32 When the Israelites were in the wilderness, they found a man gathering sticks on the sabbath day. [33]Those who found him gathering sticks brought him to Moses, Aaron, and to the whole congregation. [34]They put him in custody, because it was not clear what should be done to him. [35]Then the LORD said to Moses, "The man shall be put to death; all the congregation shall stone him outside the camp." [36]The whole congregation brought him outside the camp and stoned him to death, just as the LORD had commanded Moses.

Fringes on Garments

37 The LORD said to Moses: [38]Speak to the Israelites, and tell them to make fringes on the corners of their garments throughout their generations and to put a blue cord on the fringe at each corner. [39]You have the fringe so that, when you see it, you will remember all the commandments of the LORD and do them, and not follow the lust of your own heart and your own eyes. [40]So you shall remember and do all my commandments, and you shall be holy to your God. [41]I am the LORD your God, who brought you out of the land of Egypt, to be your God: I am the LORD your God.

15.22-31 How to Deal with Unintentional Failure to Fulfill God's Commands. When Israel enters the land, a portion of all bread and dough is to be given to the priests. Inadvertent failure to obey God's commands is to be compensated for by a series of offerings: whole offering, grain offering, drink offering, plus a sin offering (15.22-26). Both native Israelites and resident aliens have cultic provisions to compensate for their failures, but those who disobey knowingly are to *be cut off from among the people,* since they *despised the word of the LORD.* This is now illustrated in the incident which follows.

15.32-36 The Penalty for Violating the Law against Work on the Sabbath. Ex 35.3 prohibits lighting a fire on the sabbath, but this violator of the commandment goes so far as to collect his firewood on that holy day. The death penalty by stoning is carried out by *the whole congregation.*

15.37-41 Fringes on Garments as Reminders of God's Commands. By taking care to attach these colored fringes and threads to their garments, the people of Israel are reminded of the law of God by which they are marked off from all other humanity as those who are holy, consecrated to the LORD. The instruction recalls Deut 22.12, where there are to be twisted tassels at each of the four corners of a cloak. The section ends (15.41) with a declaration of God like those in the Holiness Code concerning his historic deliverance of Israel from Egypt and the special relationship which has resulted.

15.8 Lev 7.11
15.9 Num 28.12,14
15.15 ver 29; Num 9.14
15.18 ver 2
15.19 Josh 5.11,12
15.20 Deut 26.2,10; Lev 2.14
15.22 Lev 4.2
15.24 Lev 4.13; ver 8-10
15.25 Lev 4.20
15.27 Lev 4.27,28
15.28 Lev 4.35
15.29 ver 15
15.31 2 Sam 12.9; Lev 5.1; Ezek 18.20
15.32 Ex 31.14,15; 35.2,3
15.34 Lev 24.12
15.35 Ex 31.14,15; Lev 24.14; Acts 7.58
15.38 Deut 22.12; Mt 23.5
15.39 Deut 4.23; Ps 73.27
15.40 Lev 11.44; Rom 12.1; Col 1.22; 1 Pet 1.15,16

16.1 Ex 6.21; Jude 11
16.2 Num 26.9
16.3 Ps 106.16; Ex 19.6; Num 14.14
16.4 Num 14.5
16.5 Lev 10.3; Ps 65.4; Num 17.5,8
16.9 Num 3.6,9; 8.14
16.11 Ex 16.7,8; 1 Cor 10.10
16.13 Num 11.4-6; Ex 2.14; Acts 7.27,35
16.14 Lev 20.24
16.15 Gen 4.4,5; 1 Sam 12.3
16.16 ver 6,7
16.19 ver 42; Num 14.10; Ex 16.7,10; Lev 9.6,23
16.21 ver 45; Ex 32.10,12
16.22 ver 45; Num 14.5
16.26 Gen 19.12,14
16.28 Ex 3.12; Jn 5.36; Num 24.13; Jn 6.38
16.30 ver 33; Ps 55.15
16.31 Num 26.10
16.32 Num 26.11

Revolt of Korah, Dathan, and Abiram

16 Now Korah son of Izhar son of Kohath son of Levi, along with Dathan and Abiram sons of Eliab, and On son of Peleth—descendants of Reuben—took 2two hundred fifty Israelite men, leaders of the congregation, chosen from the assembly, well-known men,[a] and they confronted Moses. 3They assembled against Moses and against Aaron, and said to them, "You have gone too far! All the congregation are holy, every one of them, and the LORD is among them. So why then do you exalt yourselves above the assembly of the LORD?" 4When Moses heard it, he fell on his face. 5Then he said to Korah and all his company, "In the morning the LORD will make known who is his, and who is holy, and who will be allowed to approach him; the one whom he will choose he will allow to approach him. 6Do this: take censers, Korah and all your[b] company, 7and tomorrow put fire in them, and lay incense on them before the LORD; and the man whom the LORD chooses shall be the holy one. You Levites have gone too far!" 8Then Moses said to Korah, "Hear now, you Levites! 9Is it too little for you that the God of Israel has separated you from the congregation of Israel, to allow you to approach him in order to perform the duties of the LORD's tabernacle, and to stand before the congregation and serve them? 10He has allowed you to approach him, and all your brother Levites with you; yet you seek the priesthood as well! 11Therefore you and all your company have gathered together against the LORD. What is Aaron that you rail against him?"

12 Moses sent for Dathan and Abiram sons of Eliab; but they said, "We will not come! 13Is it too little that you have brought us up out of a land flowing with milk and honey to kill us in the wilderness, that you must also lord it over us? 14It is clear you have not brought us into a land flowing with milk and honey, or given us an inheritance of fields and vineyards. Would you put out the eyes of these men? We will not come!"

15 Moses was very angry and said to the LORD, "Pay no attention to their offering. I have not taken one donkey from them, and I have not harmed any one of them." 16And Moses said to Korah, "As for you and all your company, be present tomorrow before the LORD, you and they and Aaron; 17and let each one of you take his censer, and put incense on it, and each one of you present his censer before the LORD, two hundred fifty censers; you also, and Aaron, each his censer." 18So each man took his censer, and they put fire in the censers and laid incense on them, and they stood at the entrance of the tent of meeting with Moses and Aaron. 19Then Korah assembled the whole congregation against them at the entrance of the tent of meeting. And the glory of the LORD appeared to the whole congregation.

20 Then the LORD spoke to Moses and to Aaron, saying: 21Separate yourselves from this congregation, so that I may consume them in a moment. 22They fell on their faces, and said, "O God, the God of the spirits of all flesh, shall one person sin and you become angry with the whole congregation?"

23 And the LORD spoke to Moses, saying: 24Say to the congregation: Get away from the dwellings of Korah, Dathan, and Abiram. 25So Moses got up and went to Dathan and Abiram; the elders of Israel followed him. 26He said to the congregation, "Turn away from the tents of these wicked men, and touch nothing of theirs, or you will be swept away for all their sins." 27So they got away from the dwellings of Korah, Dathan, and Abiram; and Dathan and Abiram came out and stood at the entrance of their tents, together with their wives, their children, and their little ones. 28And Moses said, "This is how you shall know that the LORD has sent me to do all these works; it has not been of my own accord: 29If these people die a natural death, or if a natural fate comes on them, then the LORD has not sent me. 30But if the LORD creates something new, and the ground opens its mouth and swallows them up, with all that belongs to them, and they go down alive into Sheol, then you shall know that these men have despised the LORD."

31 As soon as he finished speaking all these words, the ground under them was split apart. 32The earth opened its mouth and swallowed them up, along with their households—everyone who belonged to Korah and all their goods. 33So they with all that belonged to them went down alive into Sheol; the earth closed over them, and they perished from the midst of the assembly. 34All Israel around them fled at their outcry, for they said, "The earth will

[a] Cn: Heb *and they confronted Moses, and two hundred fifty men ... well-known men* [b] Heb *his*

16.1-50 The Revolt of the Sons of Levi and Reuben. This story may be a combination of two traditions: one concerning Korah and one about Dathan and Abiram (who are mentioned in Ps 106.17 without Korah). These rebels denounce Moses for what they regard as his failed leadership role over Israel, and assert the holiness of the entire congregation. Moses declares that God will give evidence in the morning of his choice for leadership of his people. Not content with their secondary role as aides in the sanctuary, the Levites now want to function as priests (16.4-11). They respond by charging Moses with failure to fulfill his promise of taking them to an abundant land of their own (16.12-14). Moses' critics are instructed to bring a censer and incense the next day, in order to have a public demonstration of God's choice for leader. Moses and Aaron warn the people as a whole to distance themselves from the wicked rebels (16.23-27). Following Moses' prediction of their doom (16.27-30), the ground opens around them and the rebels, their families and their tents all disappear *alive into Sheol,* the unseen place below the surface of the earth where the dead dwell in perpetual darkness. Fire *from the LORD* destroys the 250 who supported the rebels. The censers which they brought to the test scene are said to have been made *holy* by the sacred fire that covered them, and hence are converted into metal covers for the altar of Yahweh (16.31-40). When the congregation assembles on the next day, God's presence is evident in the radiant cloud, and Moses urges Aaron to proceed to appease God's wrath before the whole of the people is destroyed by a plague that has struck them (16.41-50). 14,700 are reported to have been lost.

17.1-13 The Budding of Aaron's Staff Shows God's Approval of Him.
17.2-3 In spite of the sharp division of responsibility between the priests and the Levites, Aaron and his staff are here seen as representing the tribe of Levi. Of all the staffs of the *ancestral houses*, it is Aaron's alone which goes through the whole vegetation cycle: buds, blossoms, produces *ripe almonds* (17.8). The threat of death to any rebels fills the people with despair, since they regard the tabernacle as unsafe for them to approach (17.12-13).
18.1-22 God's Provision for the Priests and the Levites.
18.1-5 The priesthood is the exclusive role of Aaron and his sons. They alone are allowed to enter the *tent of the covenant*.

swallow us too!" 35And fire came out from
the LORD and consumed the two hundred
fifty men offering the incense.
36[c] Then the LORD spoke to Moses, saying:
37Tell Eleazar son of Aaron the priest to take
the censers out of the blaze; then scatter the
fire far and wide. 38For the censers of these
sinners have become holy at the cost of
their lives. Make them into hammered plates
as a covering for the altar, for they presented them before the LORD and they became holy. Thus they shall be a sign to the
Israelites. 39So Eleazar the priest took the
bronze censers that had been presented by
those who were burned; and they were
hammered out as a covering for the altar—
40a reminder to the Israelites that no outsider, who is not of the descendants of
Aaron, shall approach to offer incense before the LORD, so as not to become like
Korah and his company—just as the LORD
had said to him through Moses.
41 On the next day, however, the whole
congregation of the Israelites rebelled against
Moses and against Aaron, saying, "You
have killed the people of the LORD." 42And
when the congregation had assembled
against them, Moses and Aaron turned
toward the tent of meeting; the cloud had
covered it and the glory of the LORD appeared. 43Then Moses and Aaron came to
the front of the tent of meeting, 44and the
LORD spoke to Moses, saying, 45"Get away
from this congregation, so that I may consume them in a moment." And they fell on
their faces. 46Moses said to Aaron, "Take
your censer, put fire on it from the altar and
lay incense on it, and carry it quickly to the
congregation and make atonement for them.
For wrath has gone out from the LORD; the
plague has begun." 47So Aaron took it as
Moses had ordered, and ran into the middle
of the assembly, where the plague had already begun among the people. He put on
the incense, and made atonement for the
people. 48He stood between the dead and the
living; and the plague was stopped. 49Those
who died by the plague were fourteen thousand seven hundred, besides those who died
in the affair of Korah. 50When the plague
was stopped, Aaron returned to Moses at
the entrance of the tent of meeting.

The Budding of Aaron's Rod

17[d] The LORD spoke to Moses and
Aaron, saying: 2Speak to the Israelites, and get twelve staffs from them, one
for each ancestral house, from all the leaders of their ancestral houses. Write each
man's name on his staff, 3and write Aaron's
name on the staff of Levi. For there shall be
one staff for the head of each ancestral
house. 4Place them in the tent of meeting
before the covenant,[e] where I meet with
you. 5And the staff of the man whom I
choose shall sprout; thus I will put a stop
to the complaints of the Israelites that they
continually make against you. 6Moses spoke
to the Israelites; and all their leaders gave
him staffs, one for each leader, according to
their ancestral houses, twelve staffs; and the
staff of Aaron was among theirs. 7So Moses
placed the staffs before the LORD in the tent
of the covenant.[e]
8 When Moses went into the tent of the
covenant[e] on the next day, the staff of
Aaron for the house of Levi had sprouted.
It put forth buds, produced blossoms, and
bore ripe almonds. 9Then Moses brought
out all the staffs from before the LORD to all
the Israelites; and they looked, and each
man took his staff. 10And the LORD said to
Moses, "Put back the staff of Aaron before
the covenant,[e] to be kept as a warning to
rebels, so that you may make an end of
their complaints against me, or else they
will die." 11Moses did so; just as the LORD
commanded him, so he did.
12 The Israelites said to Moses, "We are
perishing; we are lost, all of us are lost!
13Everyone who approaches the tabernacle
of the LORD will die. Are we all to perish?"

Responsibility of Priests and Levites

18 The LORD said to Aaron: You and
your sons and your ancestral house
with you shall bear responsibility for offenses
connected with the sanctuary, while you
and your sons alone shall bear responsibility for offenses connected with the priesthood. 2So bring with you also your brothers
of the tribe of Levi, your ancestral tribe, in
order that they may be joined to you, and
serve you while you and your sons with

16.35 Num 11.1-3; 26.10
16.38 Prov 20.2; Num 26.10
16.40 Num 3.10; 2 Chr 26.18
16.41 ver 3
16.42 Ex 40.34; ver 19; Num 20.6
16.45 ver 21,24
16.46 Num 8.19; Ps 106.29
16.47 Num 25.7,8,13
16.48 Ps 106.30
16.49 ver 32,35
17.4 Ex 25.22; 29.42,43
17.5 Num 16.5,11
17.7 Num 18.2; Acts 7.44
17.10 Heb 9.4; ver 5
17.13 Num 1.51,53
18.1 Ex 28.38
18.2 Num 3.5-10

[c] Ch 17.1 in Heb [d] Ch 17.16 in Heb [e] Or *treaty*, or *testimony*; Heb *eduth*

you are in front of the tent of the covenant.[f]
3They shall perform duties for you and for
the whole tent. But they must not approach
either the utensils of the sanctuary or the
altar, otherwise both they and you will die.
4They are attached to you in order to perform the duties of the tent of meeting, for
all the service of the tent; no outsider shall
approach you. 5You yourselves shall perform the duties of the sanctuary and the
duties of the altar, so that wrath may never
again come upon the Israelites. 6It is I who
now take your brother Levites from among
the Israelites; they are now yours as a gift,
dedicated to the LORD, to perform the service
of the tent of meeting. 7But you and your
sons with you shall diligently perform your
priestly duties in all that concerns the altar
and the area behind the curtain. I give your
priesthood as a gift;[g] any outsider who
approaches shall be put to death.

The Priest's Portion

8 The LORD spoke to Aaron: I have given
you charge of the offerings made to me, all
the holy gifts of the Israelites; I have given
them to you and your sons as a priestly
portion due you in perpetuity. 9This shall be
yours from the most holy things, reserved
from the fire: every offering of theirs that
they render to me as a most holy thing,
whether grain offering, sin offering, or guilt
offering, shall belong to you and your sons.
10As a most holy thing you shall eat it;
every male may eat it; it shall be holy to
you. 11This also is yours: I have given to
you, together with your sons and daughters, as a perpetual due whatever is set aside
from the gifts of all the elevation offerings
of the Israelites; everyone who is clean in
your house may eat them. 12All the best of
the oil and all the best of the wine and of
the grain, the choice produce that they give
to the LORD, I have given to you. 13The first
fruits of all that is in their land, which they
bring to the LORD, shall be yours; everyone
who is clean in your house may eat of it.
14Every devoted thing in Israel shall be yours.
15The first issue of the womb of all creatures, human and animal, which is offered
to the LORD, shall be yours; but the firstborn
of human beings you shall redeem, and the
firstborn of unclean animals you shall redeem. 16Their redemption price, reckoned
from one month of age, you shall fix at five
shekels of silver, according to the shekel of
the sanctuary (that is, twenty gerahs). 17But
the firstborn of a cow, or the firstborn of a
sheep, or the firstborn of a goat, you shall
not redeem; they are holy. You shall dash
their blood on the altar, and shall turn their
fat into smoke as an offering by fire for a
pleasing odor to the LORD; 18but their flesh
shall be yours, just as the breast that is
elevated and as the right thigh are yours.
19All the holy offerings that the Israelites
present to the LORD I have given to you,
together with your sons and daughters, as
a perpetual due; it is a covenant of salt
forever before the LORD for you and your
descendants as well. 20Then the LORD said to
Aaron: You shall have no allotment in their
land, nor shall you have any share among
them; I am your share and your possession
among the Israelites.

21 To the Levites I have given every
tithe in Israel for a possession in return for
the service that they perform, the service in
the tent of meeting. 22From now on the
Israelites shall no longer approach the tent
of meeting, or else they will incur guilt and
die. 23But the Levites shall perform the service of the tent of meeting, and they shall
bear responsibility for their own offenses; it
shall be a perpetual statute throughout your
generations. But among the Israelites they
shall have no allotment, 24because I have
given to the Levites as their portion the
tithe of the Israelites, which they set apart
as an offering to the LORD. Therefore I have
said of them that they shall have no allotment among the Israelites.

25 Then the LORD spoke to Moses, saying:
26You shall speak to the Levites, saying:
When you receive from the Israelites the
tithe that I have given you from them for
your portion, you shall set apart an offering
from it to the LORD, a tithe of the tithe. 27It
shall be reckoned to you as your gift, the
same as the grain of the threshing floor and
the fullness of the wine press. 28Thus you
also shall set apart an offering to the LORD
from all the tithes that you receive from the
Israelites; and from them you shall give the
LORD's offering to the priest Aaron. 29Out of
all the gifts to you, you shall set apart every
offering due to the LORD; the best of all of
them is the part to be consecrated. 30Say
also to them: When you have set apart the
best of it, then the rest shall be reckoned to
the Levites as produce of the threshing floor,

[f] Or *treaty*, or *testimony*; Heb *eduth* [g] Heb *as a service of gift*

18.3 Num 3.25; 31.36; 4.15
18.4 Num 3.10
18.5 Num 16.46
18.6 Num 3.9,12,45
18.7 Num 3.10; Heb 9.3,6
18.8 Lev 6.16,18; 7.6,32; Ex 29.29; 40.13,15
18.9 Lev 2.2,3; 10.12,13; 6.25,26; 7.7
18.10 Lev 6.16,26
18.11 Ex 29.27; Lev 22.1-16
18.12 Ex 23.19; Deut 18.4; Neh 10.35; Ex 22.29
18.13 Ex 22.29; 23.19; 34.26
18.14 Lev 27.28
18.15 Ex 13.2; Lev 27.26; Ex 13.13
18.16 Lev 27.6
18.17 Lev 3.2,5
18.19 ver 11; 2 Chr 13.5
18.20 Deut 10.9; 12.12; 14.27,29; Josh 13.33; Ezek 44.28
18.21 Lev 27.30-33
18.22 Num 1.51
18.23 Num 3.7; ver 1,20
18.26 Neh 10.38
18.28 Ex 29.27

18.6 The Levites are the aides of the priests, and are given to the latter *as a gift*, to fulfill a servant role in the tent. But they are forbidden under penalty of death to enter the inner part of the sanctuary *behind the curtain*.
18.8-20 All offerings not consumed by burning are to go to the priests and their families, including the monetary payments made to redeem firstborn animals and humans. Of the burnt offerings, the blood and the fat go up to God *for a pleasing odor to the LORD*, but the flesh, breasts and right thighs go to the priests. They do not, however, receive the right to own land or to share in its possession (but see Num 35.1-8).
18.21-31 Only Levites may serve in the tent of meeting. While they also are forbidden to possess land, they receive the tithe paid by all Israelites to the sanctuary, on which they must pay a tithe and from which they must make offerings to be presented to the priests.

19.1-22 Laws for Ritual Purification. The process is carried out in two stages: (1) the preparation of the water of purification (19.1-10) and (2) effecting purification by proper use of the water (19.11-20). The *red* color of the heifer or cow recalls blood with its cleansing effect (Lev 4.3-12). The sacrifice is burnt entirely, but *outside the camp* rather than on the altar. The wood, spice and cloth are mentioned in Lev 14.6-7. Ritual cleansing is accomplished by mixing the ashes of the sacrifice with water; the circumstances under which it is needed are outlined (19.9-22). The one who prepares the cleansing fluid remains unclean throughout the day, however (19.21).
20.1-13 The Waters of Meribah. The next round of bitter complaints against Moses concerns the shortage of water for people and livestock. God's word to Moses and Aaron was to *command the rock...to yield its water*. But Moses in anger strikes the rock *twice with his staff*. Although the water comes out in abundance, the LORD informs Moses and Aaron that their lack of *trust* will result in their being denied the opportunity to lead the people into the land God has given them.

and as produce of the wine press. 31 You may eat it in any place, you and your households; for it is your payment for your service in the tent of meeting. 32 You shall incur no guilt by reason of it, when you have offered the best of it. But you shall not profane the holy gifts of the Israelites, on pain of death.

Ceremony of the Red Heifer

19 The LORD spoke to Moses and Aaron, saying: 2 This is a statute of the law that the LORD has commanded: Tell the Israelites to bring you a red heifer without defect, in which there is no blemish and on which no yoke has been laid. 3 You shall give it to the priest Eleazar, and it shall be taken outside the camp and slaughtered in his presence. 4 The priest Eleazar shall take some of its blood with his finger and sprinkle it seven times towards the front of the tent of meeting. 5 Then the heifer shall be burned in his sight; its skin, its flesh, and its blood, with its dung, shall be burned. 6 The priest shall take cedarwood, hyssop, and crimson material, and throw them into the fire in which the heifer is burning. 7 Then the priest shall wash his clothes and bathe his body in water, and afterwards he may come into the camp; but the priest shall remain unclean until evening. 8 The one who burns the heifer[h] shall wash his clothes in water and bathe his body in water; he shall remain unclean until evening. 9 Then someone who is clean shall gather up the ashes of the heifer, and deposit them outside the camp in a clean place; and they shall be kept for the congregation of the Israelites for the water for cleansing. It is a purification offering. 10 The one who gathers the ashes of the heifer shall wash his clothes and be unclean until evening.

This shall be a perpetual statute for the Israelites and for the alien residing among them. 11 Those who touch the dead body of any human being shall be unclean seven days. 12 They shall purify themselves with the water on the third day and on the seventh day, and so be clean; but if they do not purify themselves on the third day and on the seventh day, they will not become clean. 13 All who touch a corpse, the body of a human being who has died, and do not purify themselves, defile the tabernacle of the LORD; such persons shall be cut off from Israel. Since water for cleansing was not dashed on them, they remain unclean; their uncleanness is still on them.

14 This is the law when someone dies in a tent: everyone who comes into the tent, and everyone who is in the tent, shall be unclean seven days. 15 And every open vessel with no cover fastened on it is unclean. 16 Whoever in the open field touches one who has been killed by a sword, or who has died naturally,[i] or a human bone, or a grave, shall be unclean seven days. 17 For the unclean they shall take some ashes of the burnt purification offering, and running water shall be added in a vessel; 18 then a clean person shall take hyssop, dip it in the water, and sprinkle it on the tent, on all the furnishings, on the persons who were there, and on whoever touched the bone, the slain, the corpse, or the grave. 19 The clean person shall sprinkle the unclean ones on the third day and on the seventh day, thus purifying them on the seventh day. Then they shall wash their clothes and bathe themselves in water, and at evening they shall be clean. 20 Any who are unclean but do not purify themselves, those persons shall be cut off from the assembly, for they have defiled the sanctuary of the LORD. Since the water for cleansing has not been dashed on them, they are unclean.

21 It shall be a perpetual statute for them. The one who sprinkles the water for cleansing shall wash his clothes, and whoever touches the water for cleansing shall be unclean until evening. 22 Whatever the unclean person touches shall be unclean, and anyone who touches it shall be unclean until evening.

The Waters of Meribah

20 The Israelites, the whole congregation, came into the wilderness of Zin in the first month, and the people stayed in Kadesh. Miriam died there, and was buried there.

2 Now there was no water for the congregation; so they gathered together against Moses and against Aaron. 3 The people quarreled with Moses and said, "Would that we had died when our kindred died before the LORD! 4 Why have you brought the assembly of the LORD into this wilderness for us and our livestock to die here? 5 Why have you brought us up out of Egypt, to bring us

[h] Heb *it* [i] Heb lacks *naturally*

18.32 Lev 19.8; 22.2,15,16
19.2 Deut 21.3
19.3 Lev 4.12,21; 16.27
19.4 Lev 4.6; Heb 9.13
19.6 Lev 15.4,6,49
19.7 Lev 11.25; 16.26,28; 22.6
19.9 Heb 9.13; ver 13,20,21
19.11 Num 5.2; Lev 21.1; Acts 21.26,27
19.12 ver 19; Num 31.19
19.13 ver 20; Lev 15.31; ver 9; Num 8.7; Lev 7.20; 22.3
19.16 ver 11
19.17 ver 9
19.19 Ezek 26.25; Heb 10.22
19.20 ver 13
19.22 Hag 2.13,14
20.1 Num 33.36
20.2 Ex 17.1
20.3 Ex 17.2; Num 14.2,3; 16.31-35
20.4 Ex 17.3

20.6 Num 14.5,10
20.8 Ex 17.5; Neh 9.15; Isa 43.20; 48.21
20.10 Ps 106.32,33
20.11 Ps 78.16; Isa 48.21; 1 Cor 10.14
20.12 Num 27.14; Deut 1.37; 3.26,27; Lev 10.3
20.13 Deut 33.8; Ps 95.8
20.14 Deut 2.4
20.15 Gen 46.6; Acts 7.15,19; Ex 12.40; Deut 26.6
20.16 Ex 2.23; 14.19
20.19 Deut 2.6,28
20.21 Judg 11.17; Deut 2.8
20.22 Num 33.37; 21.4
20.24 Gen 25.8; ver 12
20.25 Num 33.38; Deut 32.50
20.28 Num 33.38; Deut 10.6
21.1 Num 33.40; Judg 1.16; Num 13.21
21.4 Num 20.22
21.5 Ps 78.19; Ex 16.3; 17.3; Num 11.6

to this wretched place? It is no place for
grain, or figs, or vines, or pomegranates;
and there is no water to drink." [6]Then
Moses and Aaron went away from the
assembly to the entrance of the tent of
meeting; they fell on their faces, and the
glory of the LORD appeared to them. [7]The
LORD spoke to Moses, saying: [8]Take the staff,
and assemble the congregation, you and
your brother Aaron, and command the rock
before their eyes to yield its water. Thus you
shall bring water out of the rock for them;
thus you shall provide drink for the congregation and their livestock.
9 So Moses took the staff from before
the LORD, as he had commanded him. [10]Mo-
ses and Aaron gathered the assembly together before the rock, and he said to them,
"Listen, you rebels, shall we bring water for
you out of this rock?" [11]Then Moses lifted
up his hand and struck the rock twice with
his staff; water came out abundantly, and
the congregation and their livestock drank.
[12]But the LORD said to Moses and Aaron,
"Because you did not trust in me, to show
my holiness before the eyes of the Israelites,
therefore you shall not bring this assembly
into the land that I have given them."
[13]These are the waters of Meribah,[j] where
the people of Israel quarreled with the LORD,
and by which he showed his holiness.

Passage through Edom Refused

14 Moses sent messengers from Kadesh
to the king of Edom, "Thus says your brother
Israel: You know all the adversity that has
befallen us: [15]how our ancestors went down
to Egypt, and we lived in Egypt a long time;
and the Egyptians oppressed us and our
ancestors; [16]and when we cried to the LORD,
he heard our voice, and sent an angel and
brought us out of Egypt; and here we are
in Kadesh, a town on the edge of your
territory. [17]Now let us pass through your
land. We will not pass through field or
vineyard, or drink water from any well; we
will go along the King's Highway, not turning aside to the right hand or to the left
until we have passed through your territory."
18 But Edom said to him, "You shall not
pass through, or we will come out with the
sword against you." [19]The Israelites said to
him, "We will stay on the highway; and if
we drink of your water, we and our livestock, then we will pay for it. It is only a
small matter; just let us pass through on
foot." [20]But he said, "You shall not pass
through." And Edom came out against them
with a large force, heavily armed. [21]Thus
Edom refused to give Israel passage through
their territory; so Israel turned away from
them.

The Death of Aaron

22 They set out from Kadesh, and the
Israelites, the whole congregation, came to
Mount Hor. [23]Then the LORD said to Moses
and Aaron at Mount Hor, on the border of
the land of Edom, [24]"Let Aaron be gathered
to his people. For he shall not enter the land
that I have given to the Israelites, because
you rebelled against my command at the
waters of Meribah. [25]Take Aaron and his
son Eleazar, and bring them up Mount Hor;
[26]strip Aaron of his vestments, and put
them on his son Eleazar. But Aaron shall be
gathered to his people,[k] and shall die there."
[27]Moses did as the LORD had commanded;
they went up Mount Hor in the sight of the
whole congregation. [28]Moses stripped Aaron
of his vestments, and put them on his son
Eleazar; and Aaron died there on the top of
the mountain. Moses and Eleazar came down
from the mountain. [29]When all the congregation saw that Aaron had died, all the
house of Israel mourned for Aaron thirty
days.

The Bronze Serpent

21 When the Canaanite, the king of
Arad, who lived in the Negeb, heard
that Israel was coming by the way of
Atharim, he fought against Israel and took
some of them captive. [2]Then Israel made a
vow to the LORD and said, "If you will indeed
give this people into our hands, then we
will utterly destroy their towns." [3]The LORD
listened to the voice of Israel, and handed
over the Canaanites; and they utterly destroyed them and their towns; so the place
was called Hormah.[l]
4 From Mount Hor they set out by the
way to the Red Sea,[m] to go around the land
of Edom; but the people became impatient
on the way. [5]The people spoke against God
and against Moses, "Why have you brought
us up out of Egypt to die in the wilderness?
For there is no food and no water, and we

[j] That is *Quarrel* [k] Heb lacks *to his people* [l] Heb *Destruction* [m] Or *Sea of Reeds*

20.14-21 Israel's Request for Passage through Edom Refused. **20.14** From their temporary stopping place at Kadesh, which is midway between the Mediterranean coast and the northern end of the Gulf of Aqabah, Moses sent to the king of Edom, asking permission to cross his territory on their way to the major caravan route, *the King's Highway*, which follows the valley northward from Aqabah into what is now modern Jordan. Edom is another name for Esau, the brother of Jacob, whose other name is Israel (Gen 25.23-26). The *angel* who brought the people out of Egypt is the agent and symbol of the divine leadership and protection that they enjoyed while escaping from slavery (Ex 23.20). The denial of the request for crossing the land is reinforced by a military presence (20.18-21). **20.22-29** The Death of Aaron. Since Mt. Hor must be a mountain west of the Dead Sea (although some would locate it east of the Jordan), the prospect of entering *the land* by this route may indicate that there were two traditions about Israel's coming into the land of Canaan: one possible route leading from the south across the Negeb, and the other from the east across the Jordan. At his death Aaron is symbolically stripped of his vestments; he dies because of his failure to trust the LORD fully. Instead of the customary seven-day period of mourning, for Aaron it lasts thirty days, as it does for Moses (Deut 34.8). **21.1-3** Further resistance to Israel's passage northward to the land comes from the king of Arad, which is eight miles south of Hebron. The Canaanite attackers are destroyed, as indicated by the name given to the place, *Hormah*, which means "destruction." **21.4-9** The route for entering the land now leads west of the district of Edom with the aim of crossing to the east of the Jordan rift just below the Dead Sea. Complaints about the food are met by God's sending *poisonous serpents* among the people, with the result that many Israelites die. But God also provides a remedy in the form of a bronze serpent placed on a pole, to which anyone bitten need only look in order to recover. The snake was originally a Canaanite fertility symbol, but later came to be viewed as a device for warding off evil. This imagery is used of Jesus in Jn 3.14-15.

21.10-20 The Journey through Moab to Mt. Pisgah. Moab was the territory east of the Dead Sea from its upper end south to the Arnon, a perennial stream which flows through a deep canyon from the eastern mountains into the Dead Sea. The territory of the Amorites was north of Moab, and included mountains – one of which is named Pisgah – from which one can look across the cleft of the Jordan to Jericho and the barren cliffs and valleys west of the Jordan (called here *the wasteland*). Other reports of views into the promised land are given in Deut 3.27; 34.1. *The Book of the Wars of the Lord* is mentioned only here, but must have been a collection of war and victory songs. The other song here, celebrating *the well*, recalls the Song of the Sea (Ex 15.1-18) in which the Lord is praised for delivering Israel from Egypt by the miraculous passage through the sea.
21.21-35 Continuing Resistance to Israel's Entering the Land. The land of the Amorites extended northward from the upper end of the Dead Sea between the Jordan River and the mountains to the east. The Ammonites (21.24) lived farther east in territory reaching out to the Arabian desert and including modern Amman. The Israelites defeated the Amorites and settled into their towns and villages. The song quoted here (21.27-30) sees in the defeat of the Amorites the undoing of their god, Chemosh. Farther up the Jordan valley to the north, the king of Bashan was overcome and the region also occupied by the Israelites.

detest this miserable food." [6]Then the Lord sent poisonous[n] serpents among the people, and they bit the people, so that many Israelites died. [7]The people came to Moses and said, "We have sinned by speaking against the Lord and against you; pray to the Lord to take away the serpents from us." So Moses prayed for the people. [8]And the Lord said to Moses, "Make a poisonous[o] serpent, and set it on a pole; and everyone who is bitten shall look at it and live." [9]So Moses made a serpent of bronze, and put it upon a pole; and whenever a serpent bit someone, that person would look at the serpent of bronze and live.

The Journey to Moab

10 The Israelites set out, and camped in Oboth. [11]They set out from Oboth, and camped at Iye-abarim, in the wilderness bordering Moab toward the sunrise. [12]From there they set out, and camped in the Wadi Zered. [13]From there they set out, and camped on the other side of the Arnon, in[p] the wilderness that extends from the boundary of the Amorites; for the Arnon is the boundary of Moab, between Moab and the Amorites. [14]Wherefore it is said in the Book of the Wars of the Lord,

"Waheb in Suphah and the wadis.
The Arnon [15]and the slopes of the
wadis
that extend to the seat of Ar,
and lie along the border of Moab."[q]

16 From there they continued to Beer;[r] that is the well of which the Lord said to Moses, "Gather the people together, and I will give them water." [17]Then Israel sang this song:

"Spring up, O well!—Sing to it!—
18 the well that the leaders sank,
that the nobles of the people dug,
with the scepter, with the staff."

From the wilderness to Mattanah, [19]from Mattanah to Nahaliel, from Nahaliel to Bamoth, [20]and from Bamoth to the valley lying in the region of Moab by the top of Pisgah that overlooks the wasteland.[s]

King Sihon Defeated

21 Then Israel sent messengers to King Sihon of the Amorites, saying, [22]"Let me pass through your land; we will not turn aside into field or vineyard; we will not drink the water of any well; we will go by the King's Highway until we have passed through your territory." [23]But Sihon would not allow Israel to pass through his territory. Sihon gathered all his people together, and went out against Israel to the wilderness; he came to Jahaz, and fought against Israel. [24]Israel put him to the sword, and took possession of his land from the Arnon to the Jabbok, as far as to the Ammonites; for the boundary of the Ammonites was strong. [25]Israel took all these towns, and Israel settled in all the towns of the Amorites, in Heshbon, and in all its villages. [26]For Heshbon was the city of King Sihon of the Amorites, who had fought against the former king of Moab and captured all his land as far as the Arnon. [27]Therefore the ballad singers say,

"Come to Heshbon, let it be built;
let the city of Sihon be established.
28 For fire came out from Heshbon,
flame from the city of Sihon.
It devoured Ar of Moab,
and swallowed up[t] the heights of
the Arnon.
29 Woe to you, O Moab!
You are undone, O people of
Chemosh!
He has made his sons fugitives,
and his daughters captives,
to an Amorite king, Sihon.
30 So their posterity perished
from Heshbon[u] to Dibon,
and we laid waste until fire spread
to Medeba."[v]

31 Thus Israel settled in the land of the Amorites. [32]Moses sent to spy out Jazer; and they captured its villages, and dispossessed the Amorites who were there.

King Og Defeated

33 Then they turned and went up the road to Bashan; and King Og of Bashan came out against them, he and all his people, to battle at Edrei. [34]But the Lord said to Moses, "Do not be afraid of him; for I have given him into your hand, with all his people, and all his land. You shall do to him as you did to King Sihon of the Amorites, who ruled in Heshbon." [35]So they killed

[n] Or *fiery*; Heb *seraphim* [o] Or *fiery*; Heb *seraph* [p] Gk: Heb *which is in* [q] Meaning of Heb uncertain [r] That is *Well* [s] Or *Jeshimon* [t] Gk: Heb *and the lords of* [u] Gk: Heb *we have shot at them; Heshbon has perished* [v] Compare Sam Gk: Meaning of MT uncertain

21.6 Deut 8.15; 1 Cor 10.9
21.7 Ps 78.34
21.9 2 Kings 18.4; Jn 3.14,15
21.10 Num 33.43
21.11 Num 33.44
21.12 Deut 2.13
21.15 ver 28; Deut 2.18,29
21.21 Deut 2.26,27
21.22 Num 20.16,17
21.23 Num 20.21; Deut 2.32
21.24 Deut 2.33; Josh 12.1,2; Ps 135.10,11
21.28 Jer 48.45,46; Deut 2.9,18; Isa 15.1
21.29 Judg 11.24; 1 Kings 11.7,33; 2 Kings 23.13; Jer 48.7,13
21.30 Num 32.3,34; Jer 48.18,22
21.32 Num 32.1; Jer 48.32
21.33 Deut 3.1-7; Josh 13.12
21.34 Deut 3.2; ver 24

him, his sons, and all his people, until there was no survivor left; and they took possession of his land.

Balak Summons Balaam to Curse Israel

22 The Israelites set out, and camped in the plains of Moab across the Jordan from Jericho. [2]Now Balak son of Zippor saw all that Israel had done to the Amorites. [3]Moab was in great dread of the people, because they were so numerous; Moab was overcome with fear of the people of Israel. [4]And Moab said to the elders of Midian, "This horde will now lick up all that is around us, as an ox licks up the grass of the field." Now Balak son of Zippor was king of Moab at that time. [5]He sent messengers to Balaam son of Beor at Pethor, which is on the Euphrates, in the land of Amaw,[w] to summon him, saying, "A people has come out of Egypt; they have spread over the face of the earth, and they have settled next to me. [6]Come now, curse this people for me, since they are stronger than I; perhaps I shall be able to defeat them and drive them from the land; for I know that whomever you bless is blessed, and whomever you curse is cursed."

7 So the elders of Moab and the elders of Midian departed with the fees for divination in their hand; and they came to Balaam, and gave him Balak's message. [8]He said to them, "Stay here tonight, and I will bring back word to you, just as the LORD speaks to me"; so the officials of Moab stayed with Balaam. [9]God came to Balaam and said, "Who are these men with you?" [10]Balaam said to God, "King Balak son of Zippor of Moab, has sent me this message: [11]'A people has come out of Egypt and has spread over the face of the earth; now come, curse them for me; perhaps I shall be able to fight against them and drive them out.'" [12]God said to Balaam, "You shall not go with them; you shall not curse the people, for they are blessed." [13]So Balaam rose in the morning, and said to the officials of Balak, "Go to your own land, for the LORD has refused to let me go with you." [14]So the officials of Moab rose and went to Balak, and said, "Balaam refuses to come with us."

15 Once again Balak sent officials, more numerous and more distinguished than these. [16]They came to Balaam and said to him, "Thus says Balak son of Zippor: 'Do not let anything hinder you from coming to me; [17]for I will surely do you great honor, and whatever you say to me I will do; come, curse this people for me.'" [18]But Balaam replied to the servants of Balak, "Although Balak were to give me his house full of silver and gold, I could not go beyond the command of the LORD my God, to do less or more. [19]You remain here, as the others did, so that I may learn what more the LORD may say to me." [20]That night God came to Balaam and said to him, "If the men have come to summon you, get up and go with them; but do only what I tell you to do." [21]So Balaam got up in the morning, saddled his donkey, and went with the officials of Moab.

Balaam, the Donkey, and the Angel

22 God's anger was kindled because he was going, and the angel of the LORD took his stand in the road as his adversary. Now he was riding on the donkey, and his two servants were with him. [23]The donkey saw the angel of the LORD standing in the road, with a drawn sword in his hand; so the donkey turned off the road, and went into the field; and Balaam struck the donkey, to turn it back onto the road. [24]Then the angel of the LORD stood in a narrow path between the vineyards, with a wall on either side. [25]When the donkey saw the angel of the LORD, it scraped against the wall, and scraped Balaam's foot against the wall; so he struck it again. [26]Then the angel of the LORD went ahead, and stood in a narrow place, where there was no way to turn either to the right or to the left. [27]When the donkey saw the angel of the LORD, it lay down under Balaam; and Balaam's anger was kindled, and he struck the donkey with his staff. [28]Then the LORD opened the mouth of the donkey, and it said to Balaam, "What have I done to you, that you have struck me these three times?" [29]Balaam said to the donkey, "Because you have made a fool of me! I wish I had a sword in my hand! I would kill you right now!" [30]But the donkey said to Balaam, "Am I not your donkey, which you have ridden all your life to this day? Have I been in the habit of treating you this way?" And he said, "No."

31 Then the LORD opened the eyes of Balaam, and he saw the angel of the LORD standing in the road, with his drawn sword

[w] Or *land of his kinsfolk*

22.1 Num 33.48
22.3 Ex 15.15
22.4 Num 31.1-3,8
22.5 Num 23.7; Josh 24.9; Deut 23.4
22.6 ver 17; Num 23.7
22.7 Num 23.23; 24.1
22.8 ver 19
22.12 Num 23.20
22.17 ver 6
22.18 Num 24.13; 1 Kings 22.14; 2 Chr 18.13
22.20 ver 35; Num 23.12,26; 24.13
22.21 2 Pet 2.15
22.23 2 Pet 2.16
22.24 Judg 6.12
22.28 2 Pet 2.16
22.29 Prov 12.10
22.30 2 Pet 2.16
22.31 Josh 5.13-15

22.1-24.25 Balak King of Moab Hires Balaam to Curse Israel. In this series of colorful and amusing stories is depicted the impossibility of defeating the purpose of God for his people. Balaam, a diviner and prophet, was probably linked with the shrine of Baal, the Semitic god (Num 23.28; 31.16), and may have come originally from Mesopotamia, as mention of him at Pethor on the Euphrates suggests (22.5). Balak is fearful that the invaders who have come from Egypt will strip the land *as an ox licks up the grass of the field* (22.4), and wants Balaam to bring a curse on Israel. After having received messages from the LORD, Balaam refuses to accompany the king's agents (23.7-14), but after a warning from God, he does go with them to Moab (23.15-21). On the way, *the angel of the LORD* appears to Balaam repeatedly to discourage him from going, but his donkey has to speak to him before he understands the message (22.23-35). The warning is repeated to Balaam as to what he is to say to the king, as he notifies Balak (22.36-39). The first oracle, which comes to him after altars and sacrifices have been prepared (22.41-23.12) simply declares that this invading people, Israel, is favored of the LORD, and that Balaam cannot denounce them or practice magic in order to harm them (23.23). The second oracle, uttered from Mt. Pisgah, reaffirms Israel's special place in the purpose of God (23.13-26). The third oracle, after describing the experience of hearing *the words of God* and seeing *the vision of the Almighty*, repeats God's blessings on this people, much to the annoyance of the Moabite king (24.10-14). The fourth oracle (24.15-24) predicts triumph over the region by *a star come out of Jacob*, and mentions by name the other Semitic peoples in the region that will be crushed by Israel. The king's scheme to bring a curse on God's people having failed, he and Balaam go their separate ways (24.25).

in his hand; and he bowed down, falling on his face. 32 The angel of the LORD said to him, "Why have you struck your donkey these three times? I have come out as an adversary, because your way is perverse[x] before me. 33 The donkey saw me, and turned away from me these three times. If it had not turned away from me, surely just now I would have killed you and let it live." 34 Then Balaam said to the angel of the LORD, "I have sinned, for I did not know that you were standing in the road to oppose me. Now therefore, if it is displeasing to you, I will return home." 35 The angel of the LORD said to Balaam, "Go with the men; but speak only what I tell you to speak." So Balaam went on with the officials of Balak.

36 When Balak heard that Balaam had come, he went out to meet him at Irmoab, on the boundary formed by the Arnon, at the farthest point of the boundary. 37 Balak said to Balaam, "Did I not send to summon you? Why did you not come to me? Am I not able to honor you?" 38 Balaam said to Balak, "I have come to you now, but do I have power to say just anything? The word God puts in my mouth, that is what I must say." 39 Then Balaam went with Balak, and they came to Kiriath-huzoth. 40 Balak sacrificed oxen and sheep, and sent them to Balaam and to the officials who were with him.

Balaam's First Oracle

41 On the next day Balak took Balaam and brought him up to Bamothbaal; and from there he could see part of the people of Israel.[y]

23 1 Then Balaam said to Balak, "Build me seven altars here, and prepare seven bulls and seven rams for me." 2 Balak did as Balaam had said; and Balak and Balaam offered a bull and a ram on each altar. 3 Then Balaam said to Balak, "Stay here beside your burnt offerings while I go aside. Perhaps the LORD will come to meet me. Whatever he shows me I will tell you." And he went to a bare height.

4 Then God met Balaam; and Balaam said to him, "I have arranged the seven altars, and have offered a bull and a ram on each altar." 5 The LORD put a word in Balaam's mouth, and said, "Return to Balak, and this is what you must say." 6 So he returned to Balak,[z] who was standing beside his burnt offerings with all the officials of Moab. 7 Then Balaam[a] uttered his oracle, saying:

"Balak has brought me from Aram,
the king of Moab from the eastern mountains:
'Come, curse Jacob for me;
Come, denounce Israel!'
8 How can I curse whom God has not cursed?
How can I denounce those whom the LORD has not denounced?
9 For from the top of the crags I see him,
from the hills I behold him;
Here is a people living alone,
and not reckoning itself among the nations!
10 Who can count the dust of Jacob,
or number the dust-cloud[b] of Israel?
Let me die the death of the upright,
and let my end be like his!"

11 Then Balak said to Balaam, "What have you done to me? I brought you to curse my enemies, but now you have done nothing but bless them." 12 He answered, "Must I not take care to say what the LORD puts into my mouth?"

Balaam's Second Oracle

13 So Balak said to him, "Come with me to another place from which you may see them; you shall see only part of them, and shall not see them all; then curse them for me from there." 14 So he took him to the field of Zophim, to the top of Pisgah. He built seven altars, and offered a bull and a ram on each altar. 15 Balaam said to Balak, "Stand here beside your burnt offerings, while I meet the LORD over there." 16 The LORD met Balaam, put a word into his mouth, and said, "Return to Balak, and this is what you shall say." 17 When he came to him, he was standing beside his burnt offerings with the officials of Moab. Balak said to him, "What has the LORD said?" 18 Then Balaam uttered his oracle, saying:

"Rise, Balak, and hear;
listen to me, O son of Zippor:
19 God is not a human being, that he should lie,
or a mortal, that he should change his mind.
Has he promised, and will he not do it?
Has he spoken, and will he not fulfill it?

[x] Meaning of Heb uncertain [y] Heb lacks *of Israel* [z] Heb *him* [a] Heb *he* [b] Or *fourth part*

22.34 Num 14.40; 1 Sam 15.24,30; 2 Sam 12.13
22.35 ver 20
22.37 ver 17; Num 24.11
22.38 ver 18; Num 23.26; 24.13
22.41 Deut 12.2
23.1 ver 29
23.2 ver 14,30
23.3 ver 15
23.4 ver 16
23.5 ver 16; Num 22.35; Deut 18.18; Jer 1.9
23.7 ver 18; Num 24.3,15,23; Job 27.1; 29.1; Ps 78.2; Num 22.6
23.8 Num 22.12
23.9 Ex 33.16; Deut 32.8; 33.28
23.10 Gen 13.16; Ps 116.15
23.11 Num 24.10
23.12 Num 22.20,38
23.14 ver 1,2
23.16 Num 22.20
23.19 1 Sam 15.29; Mal 3.6; Rom 11.29; Titus 1.2; Jas 1.17

20 See, I received a command to bless;
he has blessed, and I cannot revoke it.
21 He has not beheld misfortune in Jacob;
nor has he seen trouble in Israel.
The LORD their God is with them,
acclaimed as a king among them.
22 God, who brings them out of Egypt,
is like the horns of a wild ox for them.
23 Surely there is no enchantment against Jacob,
no divination against Israel;
now it shall be said of Jacob and Israel,
'See what God has done!'
24 Look, a people rising up like a lioness,
and rousing itself like a lion!
It does not lie down until it has eaten the prey
and drunk the blood of the slain."

25 Then Balak said to Balaam, "Do not
curse them at all, and do not bless them at
all." [26]But Balaam answered Balak, "Did I
not tell you, 'Whatever the LORD says, that
is what I must do'?"
27 So Balak said to Balaam, "Come now,
I will take you to another place; perhaps it
will please God that you may curse them for
me from there." [28]So Balak took Balaam to
the top of Peor, which overlooks the
wasteland.[c] [29]Balaam said to Balak, "Build
me seven altars here, and prepare seven
bulls and seven rams for me." [30]So Balak did
as Balaam had said, and offered a bull and
a ram on each altar.

Balaam's Third Oracle

24 Now Balaam saw that it pleased
the LORD to bless Israel, so he did
not go, as at other times, to look for omens,
but set his face toward the wilderness.
[2]Balaam looked up and saw Israel camping
tribe by tribe. Then the spirit of God came
upon him, [3]and he uttered his oracle, saying:

"The oracle of Balaam son of Beor,
the oracle of the man whose eye is clear,[d]
4 the oracle of one who hears the words of God,
who sees the vision of the Almighty,[e]
who falls down, but with eyes uncovered:
5 how fair are your tents, O Jacob,
your encampments, O Israel!
6 Like palm groves that stretch far away,
like gardens beside a river,
like aloes that the LORD has planted,
like cedar trees beside the waters.
7 Water shall flow from his buckets,
and his seed shall have abundant water,
his king shall be higher than Agag,
and his kingdom shall be exalted.
8 God who brings him out of Egypt,
is like the horns of a wild ox for him;
he shall devour the nations that are his foes
and break their bones.
He shall strike with his arrows.[f]
9 He crouched, he lay down like a lion,
and like a lioness; who will rouse him up?
Blessed is everyone who blesses you,
and cursed is everyone who curses you."

10 Then Balak's anger was kindled
against Balaam, and he struck his hands
together. Balak said to Balaam, "I summoned
you to curse my enemies, but instead
you have blessed them these three
times. [11]Now be off with you! Go home! I
said, 'I will reward you richly,' but the LORD
has denied you any reward." [12]And Balaam
said to Balak, "Did I not tell your messengers
whom you sent to me, [13]'If Balak
should give me his house full of silver and
gold, I would not be able to go beyond the
word of the LORD, to do either good or bad
of my own will; what the LORD says, that
is what I will say'? [14]So now, I am going
to my people; let me advise you what this
people will do to your people in days to
come."

Balaam's Fourth Oracle

15 So he uttered his oracle, saying:
"The oracle of Balaam son of Beor,
the oracle of the man whose eye is clear,[d]
16 the oracle of one who hears the words of God,
and knows the knowledge of the Most High,[g]
who sees the vision of the Almighty,[e]

23.20 Isa 43.13
23.21 Ps 32.2,5; Rom 4.7,8; Isa 40.2; Ex 29.45,46; Ps 89.15
23.22 Num 24.8
23.24 Gen 49.9,27
23.26 ver 12; Num 22.38
23.27 ver 13
23.29 ver 1
24.1 Num 23.3,15
24.2 Num 11.25,26; 1 Sam 10.10; 2 Chr 15.1
24.3 Num 23.7,18
24.4 Num 22.20; 12.6
24.6 Ps 1.3; 104.16
24.7 ver 20; 1 Sam 15.8,9; 2 Sam 5.12; 1 Chr 14.2
24.8 Num 23.22,24; Ps 2.9; 45.5; Jer 50.9,17
24.9 Gen 49.9; 12.3; 27.29
24.11 Num 22.17,37
24.13 Num 22.18,20
24.14 Gen 49.1; Dan 2.28; Mic 6.5

[c] Or *overlooks Jeshimon* [d] Or *closed or open* [e] Traditional rendering of Heb *Shaddai* [f] Meaning of Heb uncertain [g] Or *of Elyon*

26.1-65 Census of the Israelites as they prepare to enter the land. Taken by the order of the LORD, the instructions for the process are conveyed to the people at a symbolically important place: *by the Jordan opposite Jericho*. The same pattern prevails for numbering each tribe. The Joseph tribe is divided into Ephraim and Manasseh (26.28-37). The total number of males over 20 in Israel is 601,730, which is slightly fewer than the number given in the earlier census in the wilderness (Num 1.46), but the figures are probably inflated, since historically it is unlikely that there could have been 2,000,000 people making this transition to the land of Canaan. The land is to be distributed on the basis of the relative size of each tribe.

who falls down, but with his eyes
uncovered:
17 I see him, but not now;
I behold him, but not near—
a star shall come out of Jacob,
and a scepter shall rise out of Israel;
it shall crush the borderlands[h] of
Moab,
and the territory[i] of all the
Shethites.
18 Edom will become a possession,
Seir a possession of its enemies,[j]
while Israel does valiantly.
19 One out of Jacob shall rule,
and destroy the survivors of Ir."
20 Then he looked on Amalek, and
uttered his oracle, saying:
"First among the nations was Amalek,
but its end is to perish forever."
21 Then he looked on the Kenite, and
uttered his oracle, saying:
"Enduring is your dwelling place,
and your nest is set in the rock;
22 yet Kain is destined for burning.
How long shall Asshur take you
away captive?"
23 Again he uttered his oracle, saying:
"Alas, who shall live when God does
this?
24 But ships shall come from Kittim
and shall afflict Asshur and Eber;
and he also shall perish forever."
25 Then Balaam got up and went back
to his place, and Balak also went his way.

Worship of Baal of Peor

25 While Israel was staying at Shittim,
the people began to have sexual
relations with the women of Moab. 2 These
invited the people to the sacrifices of their
gods, and the people ate and bowed down
to their gods. 3 Thus Israel yoked itself to the
Baal of Peor, and the LORD's anger was
kindled against Israel. 4 The LORD said to
Moses, "Take all the chiefs of the people and
impale them in the sun before the LORD, in
order that the fierce anger of the LORD may
turn away from Israel." 5 And Moses said to
the judges of Israel, "Each of you shall kill
any of your people who have yoked themselves to the Baal of Peor."
6 Just then one of the Israelites came and
brought a Midianite woman into his family,
in the sight of Moses and in the sight of the
whole congregation of the Israelites, while
they were weeping at the entrance of the
tent of meeting. 7 When Phinehas son of
Eleazar, son of Aaron the priest, saw it, he
got up and left the congregation. Taking a
spear in his hand, 8 he went after the Israelite man into the tent, and pierced the two
of them, the Israelite and the woman,
through the belly. So the plague was stopped
among the people of Israel. 9 Nevertheless
those that died by the plague were twenty-
four thousand.
10 The LORD spoke to Moses, saying:
11 "Phinehas son of Eleazar, son of Aaron
the priest, has turned back my wrath from
the Israelites by manifesting such zeal among
them on my behalf that in my jealousy I did
not consume the Israelites. 12 Therefore say,
'I hereby grant him my covenant of peace.
13 It shall be for him and for his descendants
after him a covenant of perpetual priesthood, because he was zealous for his God,
and made atonement for the Israelites.'"
14 The name of the slain Israelite man,
who was killed with the Midianite woman,
was Zimri son of Salu, head of an ancestral
house belonging to the Simeonites. 15 The
name of the Midianite woman who was
killed was Cozbi daughter of Zur, who was
the head of a clan, an ancestral house in
Midian.
16 The LORD said to Moses, 17 "Harass the
Midianites, and defeat them; 18 for they have
harassed you by the trickery with which
they deceived you in the affair of Peor, and
in the affair of Cozbi, the daughter of a
leader of Midian, their sister; she was killed
on the day of the plague that resulted from
Peor."

A Census of the New Generation

26 After the plague the LORD said to
Moses and to Eleazar son of Aaron
the priest, 2 "Take a census of the whole
congregation of the Israelites, from twenty
years old and upward, by their ancestral
houses, everyone in Israel able to go to war."
3 Moses and Eleazar the priest spoke with
them in the plains of Moab by the Jordan
opposite Jericho, saying, 4 "Take a census of
the people,[k] from twenty years old and
upward," as the LORD commanded Moses.
The Israelites, who came out of the land
of Egypt, were:

[h] Or *forehead* [i] Some Mss read *skull* [j] Heb *Seir, its enemies, a possession* [k] Heb lacks *take a census of the people*: Compare verse 2

24.17 Rev 1.7; Mt 2.2; Gen 49.10
24.18 2 Sam 8.14
24.19 Gen 49.10; Mic 5.2
24.20 Ex 17.8,14,16
24.24 Gen 10.4,21; ver 20
24.25 Num 31.8
25.1 Mic 6.5; Num 31.16; 1 Cor 10.8; Rev 2.14
25.2 Ex 34.15; 20.5; 1 Cor 10.20
25.3 Ps 106.28,29; Hos 9.10
25.4 Deut 4.3
25.7 Ps 106.30
25.9 Deut 4.3; 1 Cor 10.8
25.11 Ps 106.30; Ex 20.5; Deut 32.16,21
25.12 Isa 54.10; Mal 2.4,5
25.13 Ex 40.15; Num 16.46; Heb 2.17
25.15 Num 31.8
25.17 Num 31.2
25.18 Num 31.16
26.2 Ex 30.12; 38.25,26; Num 1.2

5 Reuben, the firstborn of Israel. The
descendants of Reuben: of Hanoch, the clan
of the Hanochites; of Pallu, the clan of the
Palluites; [6]of Hezron, the clan of the
Hezronites; of Carmi, the clan of the Carmites.
[7]These are the clans of the Reubenites; the
number of those enrolled was forty-three
thousand seven hundred thirty. [8]And the
descendants of Pallu: Eliab. [9]The descendants of Eliab: Nemuel, Dathan, and Abiram.
These are the same Dathan and Abiram,
chosen from the congregation, who rebelled
against Moses and Aaron in the company
of Korah, when they rebelled against the
LORD, [10]and the earth opened its mouth and
swallowed them up along with Korah, when
that company died, when the fire devoured
two hundred fifty men; and they became a
warning. [11]Notwithstanding, the sons of
Korah did not die.
12 The descendants of Simeon by their
clans: of Nemuel, the clan of the Nemuelites;
of Jamin, the clan of the Jaminites; of Jachin,
the clan of the Jachinites; [13]of Zerah,
the clan of the Zerahites; of Shaul, the
clan of Shaulites.[l] [14]These are the clans of
the Simeonites, twenty-two thousand two
hundred.
15 The children of Gad by their clans: of
Zephon, the clan of the Zephonites; of Haggi,
the clan of the Haggites; of Shuni, the clan
of the Shunites; [16]Of Ozni, the clan of the
Oznites; of Eri, the clan of the Erites; [17]of
Arod, the clan of the Arodites; of Areli, the
clan of the Arelites. [18]These are the clans of
the Gadites: the number of those enrolled
was forty thousand five hundred.
19 The sons of Judah: Er and Onan; Er
and Onan died in the land of Canaan. [20]The
descendants of Judah by their clans were:
of Shelah, the clan of the Shelanites; of
Perez, the clan of the Perezites; of Zerah, the
clan of the Zerahites. [21]The descendants of
Perez were: of Hezron, the clan of the
Hezronites; of Hamul, the clan of the
Hamulites. [22]These are the clans of Judah:
the number of those enrolled was seventy-
six thousand five hundred.
23 The descendants of Issachar by their
clans: of Tola, the clan of the Tolaites; of
Puvah, the clan of the Punites; [24]of Jashub,
the clan of the Jashubites; of Shimron, the
clan of the Shimronites. [25]These are the
clans of Issachar: sixty-four thousand three
hundred enrolled.
26 The descendants of Zebulun by their
clans: of Sered, the clan of the Seredites; of
Elon, the clan of the Elonites; of Jahleel, the
clan of the Jahleelites. [27]These are the clans
of the Zebulunites; the number of those
enrolled was sixty thousand five hundred.
28 The sons of Joseph by their clans:
Manasseh and Ephraim. [29]The descendants
of Manasseh: of Machir, the clan of the
Machirites; and Machir was the father of
Gilead; of Gilead, the clan of the Gileadites.
[30]These are the descendants of Gilead: of
Iezer, the clan of the Iezerites; of Helek,
the clan of the Helekites; [31]and of Asriel, the
clan of the Asrielites; and of Shechem,
the clan of the Shechemites; [32]and of
Shemida, the clan of the Shemidaites; and
of Hepher, the clan of the Hepherites. [33]Now
Zelophehad son of Hepher had no sons, but
daughters: and the names of the daughters
of Zelophehad were Mahlah, Noah, Hoglah,
Milcah, and Tirzah. [34]These are the clans of
Manasseh; the number of those enrolled
was fifty-two thousand seven hundred.
[35]These are the descendants of Ephraim
according to their clans: of Shuthelah, the
clan of the Shuthelahites; of Becher, the
clan of the Becherites; of Tahan, the clan of
the Tahanites. [36]And these are the descendants of Shuthelah: of Eran, the clan of the
Eranites. [37]These are the clans of the
Ephraimites: the number of those enrolled
was thirty-two thousand five hundred. These
are the descendants of Joseph by their clans.
38 The descendants of Benjamin by their
clans: of Bela, the clan of the Belaites; of
Ashbel, the clan of the Ashbelites; of Ahiram,
the clan of the Ahiramites; [39]of Shephupham,
the clan of the Shuphamites; of Hupham,
the clan of the Huphamites. [40]And the sons
of Bela were Ard and Naaman: of Ard, the
clan of the Ardites; of Naaman, the clan of
the Naamites. [41]These are the descendants
of Benjamin by their clans; the number of
those enrolled was forty-five thousand six
hundred.
42 These are the descendants of Dan by
their clans: of Shuham, the clan of the
Shuhamites. These are the clans of Dan by
their clans. [43]All the clans of the Shuhamites:
sixty-four thousand four hundred enrolled.
44 The descendants of Asher by their
families: of Imnah, the clan of the Imnites;
of Ishvi, the clan of the Ishvites; of Beriah,
the clan of the Beriites. [45]Of the descendants
of Beriah: of Heber, the clan of the Heberites;
of Malchiel, the clan of the Malchielites.

26.5 Ex 6.14
26.9 Num 16.1,2
26.10 Num 16.32,35,38
26.11 Deut 24.16
26.14 Gen 46.10
26.15 Gen 46.16
26.18 Num 1.25
26.22 Num 1.27
26.24 Gen 46.13
26.25 Gen 30.18
26.27 Num 1.31
26.30 Num 27.1; 36.1; Josh 17.2
26.35 1 Chr 7.20
26.37 Num 1.33
26.38 Gen 46.21
26.39 Gen 46.21
26.40 1 Chr 8.3
26.41 Num 1.37
26.42 Gen 46.23
26.43 Num 1.39

[l] Or *Saul . . . Saulites*

26.50 The male Levites *from one month old and up* number 23,000. No land is to be assigned to them, although certain towns are to be assigned to the Levites (Num 35.1-8). *Not one of those enrolled by Moses and Aaron* earlier will survive to enter the land, except Caleb and Joshua (26.64-65).
27.1-11 Request of the Daughters of Zelophehad. Because their father died without male heirs, the daughters of Zelophehad request that they be given a share in the inheritance of their tribe when settlement in the land occurs. This incident serves to set the pattern in Israel for passing on property to daughters, brothers or uncles when there are no male heirs.
27.12-23 Moses Views the Promised Land and Joshua is Designated as his Successor. From the top of a mountain east of the Jordan Moses is able to *see the land that I have given to the Israelites.* Moses is reminded of his failure to show God's *holiness* when he struck the rock at Meribah rather than speaking to it to produce the water needed by the people (Num 20.1-13). As a result, he will not enter the land, but will be replaced by the new leader, Joshua, who is presented to *Eleazar the priest and the whole congregation...and commissioned* by Moses *as the LORD had directed.*

[46]And the name of the daughter of Asher
was Serah. [47]These are the clans of the
Asherites: the number of those enrolled was
fifty-three thousand four hundred. [48]The
descendants of Naphtali by their clans: of
Jahzeel, the clan of the Jahzeelites; of Guni,
the clan of the Gunites; [49]of Jezer, the clan
of the Jezerites; of Shillem, the clan of the
Shillemites. [50]These are the Naphtalites[m] by
their clans: the number of those enrolled
was forty-five thousand four hundred.
51 This was the number of the Israelites
enrolled: six hundred and one thousand
seven hundred thirty.
52 The LORD spoke to Moses, saying: [53]To
these the land shall be apportioned for inheritance according to the number of names.
[54]To a large tribe you shall give a large
inheritance and to a small tribe you shall
give a small inheritance; every tribe shall be
given its inheritance according to its
enrollment. [55]But the land shall be apportioned by lot; according to the names of
their ancestral tribes they shall inherit.
[56]Their inheritance shall be apportioned
according to lot between the larger and the
smaller.
57 This is the enrollment of the Levites
by their clans: of Gershon, the clan of
the Gershonites; of Kohath, the clan of
the Kohathites; of Merari, the clan of the
Merarites. [58]These are the clans of Levi:
the clan of the Libnites, the clan of the
Hebronites, the clan of the Mahlites, the
clan of the Mushites, the clan of the
Korahites. Now Kohath was the father of
Amram. [59]The name of Amram's wife was
Jochebed daughter of Levi, who was born
to Levi in Egypt; and she bore to Amram:
Aaron, Moses, and their sister Miriam. [60]To
Aaron were born Nadab, Abihu, Eleazar,
and Ithamar. [61]But Nadab and Abihu died
when they offered illicit fire before the LORD.
[62]The number of those enrolled was twenty-
three thousand, every male one month old
and up; for they were not enrolled among
the Israelites because there was no allotment given to them among the Israelites.
63 These were those enrolled by Moses
and Eleazar the priest, who enrolled the
Israelites in the plains of Moab by the Jordan opposite Jericho. [64]Among these there
was not one of those enrolled by Moses and
Aaron the priest, who had enrolled the
Israelites in the wilderness of Sinai. [65]For
the LORD had said of them, "They shall die
in the wilderness." Not one of them was left,
except Caleb son of Jephunneh and Joshua
son of Nun.

The Daughters of Zelophehad

27 Then the daughters of Zelophehad
came forward. Zelophehad was son
of Hepher son of Gilead son of Machir son
of Manasseh son of Joseph, a member of the
Manassite clans. The names of his daughters were: Mahlah, Noah, Hoglah, Milcah,
and Tirzah. [2]They stood before Moses, Eleazar
the priest, the leaders, and all the congregation, at the entrance of the tent of meeting, and they said, [3]"Our father died in the
wilderness; he was not among the company
of those who gathered themselves together
against the LORD in the company of Korah,
but died for his own sin; and he had no
sons. [4]Why should the name of our father
be taken away from his clan because he
had no son? Give to us a possession among
our father's brothers."
5 Moses brought their case before the
LORD. [6]And the LORD spoke to Moses, saying:
[7]The daughters of Zelophehad are right in
what they are saying; you shall indeed let
them possess an inheritance among their
father's brothers and pass the inheritance of
their father on to them. [8]You shall also say
to the Israelites, "If a man dies, and has no
son, then you shall pass his inheritance on
to his daughter. [9]If he has no daughter,
then you shall give his inheritance to his
brothers. [10]If he has no brothers, then you
shall give his inheritance to his father's
brothers. [11]And if his father has no brothers,
then you shall give his inheritance to the
nearest kinsman of his clan, and he shall
possess it. It shall be for the Israelites a
statute and ordinance, as the LORD commanded Moses."

Joshua Appointed Moses' Successor

12 The LORD said to Moses, "Go up this
mountain of the Abarim range, and see the
land that I have given to the Israelites.
[13]When you have seen it, you also shall be
gathered to your people, as your brother
Aaron was, [14]because you rebelled against
my word in the wilderness of Zin when the
congregation quarreled with me.[n] You did
not show my holiness before their eyes at
the waters." (These are the waters of

[m] Heb *clans of Naphtali* [n] Heb lacks *with me*

26.47 Num 1.41
26.50 Num 1.43
26.53 Josh 11.23; 14.1
26.54 Num 33.54
26.55 Num 33.54; 34.13
26.59 Ex 6.20
26.60 Num 3.2
26.61 Lev 10.1,2; Num 3.4
26.62 Num 1.47; 18.20,23,24
26.64 Deut 2.14,15
26.65 Num 14.28,29; 1 Cor 10.5,6; Num 14.30
27.1 Num 26.33; 36.1
27.3 Num 26.64,65; 26.33; 16.1,2
27.4 Josh 17.4
27.5 Num 9.8
27.6 Num 36.2
27.12 Num 33.47; Deut 32.49
27.13 Num 31.2
27.14 Num 20.12; Ex 17.7

Meribath-Kadesh in the wilderness of Zin.)
15Moses spoke to the LORD, saying, 16"Let the
LORD, the God of the spirits of all flesh,
appoint someone over the congregation
17who shall go out before them and come
in before them, who shall lead them out
and bring them in, so that the congregation
of the LORD may not be like sheep without
a shepherd." 18So the LORD said to Moses,
"Take Joshua son of Nun, a man in whom
is the spirit, and lay your hand upon him;
19have him stand before Eleazar the priest
and all the congregation, and commission
him in their sight. 20You shall give him
some of your authority, so that all the
congregation of the Israelites may obey.
21But he shall stand before Eleazar the priest,
who shall inquire for him by the decision
of the Urim before the LORD; at his word
they shall go out, and at his word they shall
come in, both he and all the Israelites with
him, the whole congregation." 22So Moses
did as the LORD commanded him. He took
Joshua and had him stand before Eleazar
the priest and the whole congregation; 23he
laid his hands on him and commissioned
him—as the LORD had directed through
Moses.

Daily Offerings

28 The LORD spoke to Moses, saying:
2Command the Israelites, and say
to them: My offering, the food for my offerings by fire, my pleasing odor, you shall
take care to offer to me at its appointed
time. 3And you shall say to them, This is
the offering by fire that you shall offer to the
LORD: two male lambs a year old without
blemish, daily, as a regular offering. 4One
lamb you shall offer in the morning, and
the other lamb you shall offer at twilight[o]
5also one-tenth of an ephah of choice flour
for a grain offering, mixed with one-fourth
of a hin of beaten oil. 6It is a regular burnt
offering, ordained at Mount Sinai for a pleasing odor, an offering by fire to the LORD. 7Its
drink offering shall be one-fourth of a hin
for each lamb; in the sanctuary you shall
pour out a drink offering of strong drink to
the LORD. 8The other lamb you shall offer at
twilight[o] with a grain offering and a drink
offering like the one in the morning; you
shall offer it as an offering by fire, a pleasing
odor to the LORD.

Sabbath Offerings

9 On the sabbath day: two male lambs a
year old without blemish, and two-tenths of
an ephah of choice flour for a grain offering,
mixed with oil, and its drink offering—
10this is the burnt offering for every sabbath,
in addition to the regular burnt offering and
its drink offering.

Monthly Offerings

11 At the beginnings of your months
you shall offer a burnt offering to the LORD:
two young bulls, one ram, seven male lambs
a year old without blemish; 12also three-
tenths of an ephah of choice flour for a
grain offering, mixed with oil, for each bull;
and two-tenths of choice flour for a grain
offering, mixed with oil, for the one ram;
13and one-tenth of choice flour mixed with
oil as a grain offering for every lamb—a
burnt offering of pleasing odor, an offering
by fire to the LORD. 14Their drink offerings
shall be half a hin of wine for a bull, one-
third of a hin for a ram, and one-fourth of
a hin for a lamb. This is the burnt offering
of every month throughout the months of
the year. 15And there shall be one male goat
for a sin offering to the LORD; it shall be
offered in addition to the regular burnt
offering and its drink offering.

Offerings at Passover

16 On the fourteenth day of the first
month there shall be a passover offering to
the LORD. 17And on the fifteenth day of this
month is a festival; seven days shall
unleavened bread be eaten. 18On the first
day there shall be a holy convocation. You
shall not work at your occupations. 19You
shall offer an offering by fire, a burnt offering to the LORD: two young bulls, one ram,
and seven male lambs a year old; see that
they are without blemish. 20Their grain
offering shall be of choice flour mixed with
oil: three-tenths of an ephah shall you offer
for a bull, and two-tenths for a ram; 21one-
tenth shall you offer for each of the seven
lambs; 22also one male goat for a sin offering, to make atonement for you. 23You shall
offer these in addition to the burnt offering
of the morning, which belongs to the regular burnt offering. 24In the same way you
shall offer daily, for seven days, the food of

[o] Heb *between the two evenings*

27.16 Num 16.22
27.17 Deut 31.2; Mt 9.36; Mk 6.34
27.18 Num 11.25-29; Deut 34.9
27.19 Deut 31.3,7,8,23
27.20 Josh 1.16,17
27.21 Ex 28.30
28.2 Lev 3.11
28.3 Ex 29.38
28.7 Ex 29.42
28.10 ver 3
28.11 Num 10.10; Ezek 45.17; 46.6
28.12 Num 15.4-12
28.15 ver 3
28.16 Ex 12.6,18; Lev 23.5; Deut 16.1
28.17 Lev 23.6
28.18 Ex 12.16; Lev 23.7
28.23 ver 3

28.1-29.40 Offerings to be Presented by the Israelites.
28.1-8 The daily offerings are described – lambs, grain and wine – which are *a pleasing odor to the LORD.*
28.9-10 The burnt offerings are indicated which are to be presented on the sabbath in addition to the regular daily sacrifices.
28.11-15 Still more is to be added to the daily requirements for sacrifices in each of the categories: *at the beginnings of your months,* one male goat for a sin offering.
28.16-25 The instructions for the Passover are repeated in compact form (9.1-14; see also Ex 12.1-20).
28.26-31 Other prescribed offerings are those for the Festival of Weeks (Deut 16.10), also known as *the day of the first fruits* (Ex 34.22), and *the Festival of Harvest* (Ex 23.16). These festivals are an expression of gratitude to God for the produce of fields and flocks.

29.1-6 *Festival of Trumpets* (see Lev 23.23-25). The way to manufacture and use the trumpets is described in Num 10.1-10. This celebration is to be marked by a complete cessation of work. In addition to the usual daily offerings, sacrifices should include a young bull, a ram and suitable grain.
29.7-11 Day of Atonement. This is a briefer version of the instructions for the day offered in Lev 16.1-33; 23.26-32. The beginning of this special day may have been the New Year's festival, but it became the annual ceremony of purification and renewal of God's people.
29.12-38 The Festival of Booths. This joyous eight-day-long celebration rejoiced in both the harvest and God's deliverance of his people from slavery in Egypt. A somewhat different account is given in Lev 23.33-43. Omitted here is the feature of requiring the people to prepare booths and dwell in them as a reminder of the experience of the journey from Egypt.

an offering by fire, a pleasing odor to the LORD; it shall be offered in addition to the regular burnt offering and its drink offering. [25]And on the seventh day you shall have a holy convocation; you shall not work at your occupations.

Offerings of the Festival of Weeks

26 On the day of the first fruits, when you offer a grain offering of new grain to the LORD at your festival of weeks, you shall have a holy convocation; you shall not work at your occupations. [27]You shall offer a burnt offering, a pleasing odor to the LORD: two young bulls, one ram, seven male lambs a year old. [28]Their grain offering shall be of choice flour mixed with oil, three-tenths of an ephah for each bull, two-tenths for one ram, [29]one-tenth for each of the seven lambs; [30]with one male goat to make atonement for you. [31]In addition to the regular burnt offering with its grain offering, you shall offer them and their drink offering. They shall be without blemish.

Offerings at the Festival of Trumpets

29 On the first day of the seventh month you shall have a holy convocation; you shall not work at your occupations. It is a day for you to blow the trumpets, [2]and you shall offer a burnt offering, a pleasing odor to the LORD: one young bull, one ram, seven male lambs a year old without blemish. [3]Their grain offering shall be of choice flour mixed with oil, three-tenths of one ephah for the bull, two-tenths for the ram, [4]and one-tenth for each of the seven lambs; [5]with one male goat for a sin offering, to make atonement for you. [6]These are in addition to the burnt offering of the new moon and its grain offering, and the regular burnt offering and its grain offering, and their drink offerings, according to the ordinance for them, a pleasing odor, an offering by fire to the LORD.

Offerings on the Day of Atonement

7 On the tenth day of this seventh month you shall have a holy convocation, and deny yourselves;[p] you shall do no work. [8]You shall offer a burnt offering to the LORD, a pleasing odor: one young bull, one ram, seven male lambs a year old. They shall be without blemish. [9]Their grain offering shall be of choice flour mixed with oil, three-tenths of an ephah for the bull, two-tenths for the one ram, [10]one-tenth for each of the seven lambs; [11]with one male goat for a sin offering, in addition to the sin offering of atonement, and the regular burnt offering and its grain offering, and their drink offerings.

Offerings at the Festival of Booths

12 On the fifteenth day of the seventh month you shall have a holy convocation; you shall not work at your occupations. You shall celebrate a festival to the LORD seven days. [13]You shall offer a burnt offering, an offering by fire, a pleasing odor to the LORD: thirteen young bulls, two rams, fourteen male lambs a year old. They shall be without blemish. [14]Their grain offering shall be of choice flour mixed with oil, three-tenths of an ephah for each of the thirteen bulls, two-tenths for each of the two rams, [15]and one-tenth for each of the fourteen lambs; [16]also one male goat for a sin offering, in addition to the regular burnt offering, its grain offering and its drink offering.

17 On the second day: twelve young bulls, two rams, fourteen male lambs a year old without blemish, [18]with the grain offering and the drink offerings for the bulls, for the rams, and for the lambs, as prescribed in accordance with their number; [19]also one male goat for a sin offering, in addition to the regular burnt offering and its grain offering, and their drink offerings.

20 On the third day: eleven bulls, two rams, fourteen male lambs a year old without blemish, [21]with the grain offering and the drink offerings for the bulls, for the rams, and for the lambs, as prescribed in accordance with their number; [22]also one male goat for a sin offering, in addition to the regular burnt offering and its grain offering and its drink offering.

23 On the fourth day: ten bulls, two rams, fourteen male lambs a year old without blemish, [24]with the grain offering and the drink offerings for the bulls, for the rams, and for the lambs, as prescribed in accordance with their number; [25]also one male goat for a sin offering, in addition to the regular burnt offering, its grain offering and its drink offering.

26 On the fifth day: nine bulls, two rams,

[p] Or *and fast*

28.25 Ex 12.16
28.26 Ex 23.16; 34.22; Lev 23.10,15; Deut 16.10
28.31 ver 3,19
29.1 Ex 23.16; 34.22; Lev 23.24
29.6 Num 28.3,11
29.7 Lev 16.29-34; 23.26-32
29.11 Lev 16.3,5; Num 28.3
29.12 Lev 23.33-35
29.16 ver 11
29.18 ver 3,4,9,10; Num 15.12; 28.7,14
29.22 Num 28.15

29.28 Num 15.24
29.31 ver 22; Gen 8.20
29.35 Lev 23.36
29.39 Lev 23.2; 1 Chr 23.31; 2 Chr 31.3; Lev 7.11,16
30.2 Deut 23.21; Mt 5.23
30.5 Eccl 5.4
30.6 Ps 56.12
30.8 Gen 3.16
30.12 Eph 5.22
30.15 Col 3.18
30.16 Ex 15.26

fourteen male lambs a year old without blemish, [27]with the grain offering and the drink offerings for the bulls, for the rams, and for the lambs, as prescribed in accordance with their number; [28]also one male goat for a sin offering, in addition to the regular burnt offering and its grain offering and its drink offering.

29 On the sixth day: eight bulls, two rams, fourteen male lambs a year old without blemish, [30]with the grain offering and the drink offerings for the bulls, for the rams, and for the lambs, as prescribed in accordance with their number; [31]also one male goat for a sin offering, in addition to the regular burnt offering, its grain offering, and its drink offerings.

32 On the seventh day: seven bulls, two rams, fourteen male lambs a year old without blemish, [33]with the grain offering and the drink offerings for the bulls, for the rams, and for the lambs, as prescribed in accordance with their number; [34]also one male goat for a sin offering, besides the regular burnt offering, its grain offering, and its drink offering. [35]On the eighth day you shall have a solemn assembly; you shall not work at your occupations. [36]You shall offer a burnt offering, an offering by fire, a pleasing odor to the LORD: one bull, one ram, seven male lambs a year old without blemish, [37]and the grain offering and the drink offerings for the bull, for the ram, and for the lambs, as prescribed in accordance with their number; [38]also one male goat for a sin offering, in addition to the regular burnt offering and its grain offering and its drink offering.

39 These you shall offer to the LORD at your appointed festivals, in addition to your votive offerings and your free-will offerings, as your burnt offerings, your grain offerings, your drink offerings, and your offerings of well-being.

40[q] So Moses told the Israelites everything just as the LORD had commanded Moses.

Vows Made by Women

30 Then Moses said to the heads of the tribes of the Israelites: This is what the LORD has commanded. [2]When a man makes a vow to the LORD, or swears an oath to bind himself by a pledge, he shall not break his word; he shall do according to all that proceeds out of his mouth. [3]When a woman makes a vow to the LORD, or binds herself by a pledge, while within her father's house, in her youth, [4]and her father hears of her vow or her pledge by which she has bound herself, and says nothing to her; then all her vows shall stand, and any pledge by which she has bound herself shall stand. [5]But if her father expresses disapproval to her at the time that he hears of it, no vow of hers, and no pledge by which she has bound herself, shall stand; and the LORD will forgive her, because her father had expressed to her his disapproval.

6 If she marries, while obligated by her vows or any thoughtless utterance of her lips by which she has bound herself, [7]and her husband hears of it and says nothing to her at the time that he hears, then her vows shall stand, and her pledges by which she has bound herself shall stand. [8]But if, at the time that her husband hears of it, he expresses disapproval to her, then he shall nullify the vow by which she was obligated, or the thoughtless utterance of her lips, by which she bound herself; and the LORD will forgive her. [9](But every vow of a widow or of a divorced woman, by which she has bound herself, shall be binding upon her.) [10]And if she made a vow in her husband's house, or bound herself by a pledge with an oath, [11]and her husband heard it and said nothing to her, and did not express disapproval to her, then all her vows shall stand, and any pledge by which she bound herself shall stand. [12]But if her husband nullifies them at the time that he hears them, then whatever proceeds out of her lips concerning her vows, or concerning her pledge of herself, shall not stand. Her husband has nullified them, and the LORD will forgive her. [13]Any vow or any binding oath to deny herself,[r] her husband may allow to stand, or her husband may nullify. [14]But if her husband says nothing to her from day to day,[s] then he validates all her vows, or all her pledges, by which she is obligated; he has validated them, because he said nothing to her at the time that he heard of them. [15]But if he nullifies them some time after he has heard of them, then he shall bear her guilt.

16 These are the statutes that the LORD commanded Moses concerning a husband and his wife, and a father and his daughter while she is still young and in her father's house.

[q] Ch 30.1 in Heb [r] Or *to fast* [s] Or *from that day to the next*

29.39-40 This section closes with a summary of the intent of these instructions about offerings and festivals.
30.1-16 Vows Made by Women. Unlike the enduring binding force of vows or pledges made by men, those made by women are subject to nullification by a father or a husband. If the responsible male is silent, however, the vow is binding, as is the vow or pledge made by a widowed or divorced woman.

31.1-54 Israel's Revenge against the Midianites.
31.1-12 After a military attack on the Midianites, which resulted in the killing of all the males, including the king and Balaam the prophet (31.8), the women were taken captive, and the cattle, the flocks and the contents of the towns were seized *as booty*. All the settlements were burned.
31.13-20 Moses orders the execution of all women who have had sexual intercourse and all male children. Young girls are to be kept for service as servants, concubines and wives. The booty taken is to be purified, as are any of the returning troops whose contact with the dead and the impure defiled them.
31.25-54 The booty is to be divided, with preference going to those who took part in the defeat of the Midianites, but with provision for portions to go to the priests. God's protection of the warriors of Israel is evident in that *not one of [them] is missing* (31.49). The abundant gold and jewelry seized are to be offered *to the Lord*, and to be taken *into the tent of meeting*.

War against Midian

31 The Lord spoke to Moses, saying,
2“Avenge the Israelites on the
Midianites; afterward you shall be gathered
to your people.” 3So Moses said to the people, “Arm some of your number for the war,
so that they may go against Midian, to
execute the Lord's vengeance on Midian.
4You shall send a thousand from each of the
tribes of Israel to the war.” 5So out of the
thousands of Israel, a thousand from each
tribe were conscripted, twelve thousand
armed for battle. 6Moses sent them to the
war, a thousand from each tribe, along
with Phinehas son of Eleazar the priest,[f]
with the vessels of the sanctuary and the
trumpets for sounding the alarm in his
hand. 7They did battle against Midian, as
the Lord had commanded Moses, and killed
every male. 8They killed the kings of Midian:
Evi, Rekem, Zur, Hur, and Reba, the five
kings of Midian, in addition to others who
were slain by them; and they also killed
Balaam son of Beor with the sword. 9The
Israelites took the women of Midian and
their little ones captive; and they took all
their cattle, their flocks, and all their goods
as booty. 10All their towns where they had
settled, and all their encampments, they
burned, 11but they took all the spoil and all
the booty, both people and animals. 12Then
they brought the captives and the booty
and the spoil to Moses, to Eleazar the priest,
and to the congregation of the Israelites, at
the camp on the plains of Moab by the
Jordan at Jericho.

Return from the War

13 Moses, Eleazar the priest, and all the
leaders of the congregation went to meet
them outside the camp. 14Moses became
angry with the officers of the army, the
commanders of thousands and the commanders of hundreds, who had come from
service in the war. 15Moses said to them,
“Have you allowed all the women to live?
16These women here, on Balaam's advice,
made the Israelites act treacherously against
the Lord in the affair of Peor, so that the
plague came among the congregation of the
Lord. 17Now therefore, kill every male among
the little ones, and kill every woman who
has known a man by sleeping with him.
18But all the young girls who have not
known a man by sleeping with him, keep
alive for yourselves. 19Camp outside the camp
seven days; whoever of you has killed any
person or touched a corpse, purify yourselves and your captives on the third and
on the seventh day. 20You shall purify every
garment, every article of skin, everything
made of goats' hair, and every article of
wood.”
21 Eleazar the priest said to the troops
who had gone to battle: “This is the statute
of the law that the Lord has commanded
Moses: 22gold, silver, bronze, iron, tin, and
lead— 23everything that can withstand fire,
shall be passed through fire, and it shall be
clean. Nevertheless it shall also be purified
with the water for purification; and whatever cannot withstand fire, shall be passed
through the water. 24You must wash your
clothes on the seventh day, and you shall
be clean; afterward you may come into the
camp.”

Disposition of Captives and Booty

25 The Lord spoke to Moses, saying,
26“You and Eleazar the priest and the heads
of the ancestral houses of the congregation
make an inventory of the booty captured,
both human and animal. 27Divide the booty
into two parts, between the warriors who
went out to battle and all the congregation.
28From the share of the warriors who went
out to battle, set aside as tribute for the
Lord, one item out of every five hundred,
whether persons, oxen, donkeys, sheep, or
goats. 29Take it from their half and give it
to Eleazar the priest as an offering to the
Lord. 30But from the Israelites' half you shall
take one out of every fifty, whether persons,
oxen, donkeys, sheep, or goats—all the
animals—and give them to the Levites who
have charge of the tabernacle of the Lord.”
31 Then Moses and Eleazar the priest did
as the Lord had commanded Moses:
32 The booty remaining from the spoil
that the troops had taken totaled six hundred seventy-five thousand sheep, 33seventy-
two thousand oxen, 34sixty-one thousand
donkeys, 35and thirty-two thousand persons
in all, women who had not known a man
by sleeping with him.
36 The half-share, the portion of those
who had gone out to war, was in number
three hundred thirty-seven thousand five
hundred sheep and goats, 37and the Lord's
tribute of sheep and goats was six hundred

[f] Gk: Heb adds *to the war*

31.2 Num 25.1,16,17; 27.13
31.6 Num 10.9
31.8 Josh 13.21,22; ver 16
31.11 Deut 20.14
31.16 Num 25.1-9; 24.14; 2 Pet 2.15; Rev 2.14
31.17 Judg 21.11
31.23 Num 19.9,17
31.24 Lev 11.25
31.28 Num 18.21-30
31.30 Num 3.7; 8.25; 18.3,4
31.32 Gen 49.27; Ex 15.9
31.37 ver 38,41

31.41 Num 5.9; ver 21,28
31.47 ver 30
31.50 Ex 30.12,16
31.53 ver 32; Deut 20.14
31.54 Ex 30.16
32.1 Ex 12.38; Num 21.32; ver 36
32.7 Num 13.27-14.4
32.8 Num 13.3,26
32.10 Num 14.11,21; Deut 1.34
32.11 Num 14.28-30; Deut 1.35
32.12 Num 14.24; Deut 1.36
32.13 Num 14.33-35; 26.64,65
32.15 Deut 30.17,18
32.17 Josh 4.12,13
32.18 Josh 22.1-4
32.19 ver 33
32.20 Deut 3.18

seventy-five. [38]The oxen were thirty-six thousand, of which the LORD's tribute was seventy-two. [39]The donkeys were thirty thousand five hundred, of which the LORD's tribute was sixty-one. [40]The persons were sixteen thousand, of which the LORD's tribute was thirty-two persons. [41]Moses gave the tribute, the offering for the LORD, to Eleazar the priest, as the LORD had commanded Moses.

42 As for the Israelites' half, which Moses separated from that of the troops, [43]the congregation's half was three hundred thirty-seven thousand five hundred sheep and goats, [44]thirty-six thousand oxen, [45]thirty thousand five hundred donkeys, [46]and sixteen thousand persons. [47]From the Israelites' half Moses took one of every fifty, both of persons and of animals, and gave them to the Levites who had charge of the tabernacle of the LORD; as the LORD had commanded Moses.

48 Then the officers who were over the thousands of the army, the commanders of thousands and the commanders of hundreds, approached Moses, [49]and said to Moses, "Your servants have counted the warriors who are under our command, and not one of us is missing. [50]And we have brought the LORD's offering, what each of us found, articles of gold, armlets and bracelets, signet rings, earrings, and pendants, to make atonement for ourselves before the LORD." [51]Moses and Eleazar the priest received the gold from them, all in the form of crafted articles. [52]And all the gold of the offering that they offered to the LORD, from the commanders of thousands and the commanders of hundreds, was sixteen thousand seven hundred fifty shekels. [53](The troops had all taken plunder for themselves.) [54]So Moses and Eleazar the priest received the gold from the commanders of thousands and of hundreds, and brought it into the tent of meeting as a memorial for the Israelites before the LORD.

Conquest and Division of Transjordan

32 Now the Reubenites and the Gadites owned a very great number of cattle. When they saw that the land of Jazer and the land of Gilead was a good place for cattle, [2]the Gadites and the Reubenites came and spoke to Moses, to Eleazar the priest, and to the leaders of the congregation, saying, [3]"Ataroth, Dibon, Jazer, Nimrah, Heshbon, Elealeh, Sebam, Nebo, and Beon— [4]the land that the LORD subdued before the congregation of Israel—is a land for cattle; and your servants have cattle." [5]They continued, "If we have found favor in your sight, let this land be given to your servants for a possession; do not make us cross the Jordan."

6 But Moses said to the Gadites and to the Reubenites, "Shall your brothers go to war while you sit here? [7]Why will you discourage the hearts of the Israelites from going over into the land that the LORD has given them? [8]Your fathers did this, when I sent them from Kadesh-barnea to see the land. [9]When they went up to the Wadi Eshcol and saw the land, they discouraged the hearts of the Israelites from going into the land that the LORD had given them. [10]The LORD's anger was kindled on that day and he swore, saying, [11]'Surely none of the people who came up out of Egypt, from twenty years old and upward, shall see the land that I swore to give to Abraham, to Isaac, and to Jacob, because they have not unreservedly followed me— [12]none except Caleb son of Jephunneh the Kenizzite and Joshua son of Nun, for they have unreservedly followed the LORD.' [13]And the LORD's anger was kindled against Israel, and he made them wander in the wilderness for forty years, until all the generation that had done evil in the sight of the LORD had disappeared. [14]And now you, a brood of sinners, have risen in place of your fathers, to increase the LORD's fierce anger against Israel! [15]If you turn away from following him, he will again abandon them in the wilderness; and you will destroy all this people."

16 Then they came up to him and said, "We will build sheepfolds here for our flocks, and towns for our little ones, [17]but we will take up arms as a vanguard[u] before the Israelites, until we have brought them to their place. Meanwhile our little ones will stay in the fortified towns because of the inhabitants of the land. [18]We will not return to our homes until all the Israelites have obtained their inheritance. [19]We will not inherit with them on the other side of the Jordan and beyond, because our inheritance has come to us on this side of the Jordan to the east."

20 So Moses said to them, "If you do this—if you take up arms to go before the

32.1-42 Conquest and Division of the Region East of the Jordan.
32.1-5 The tribes of Reuben and Gad, recognizing the great potential for crops and flocks on the lands east of the Jordan River, propose to settle there. Moses insists that for them to fail to participate in Israel's taking over the land of Canaan west of the Jordan will jeopardize the fulfillment of God's promise to the people. Reuben and Gad compromise by saying that they will build sheepfolds in this land east of the river, but will also aid in the conquest of Canaan. Moses agrees to this proposal, and these tribes are granted the former lands of the Amorites, on which they then begin to build their own cities.

[u] Ch: Heb *hurrying*

33.1-48 Summary of the Stages in Israel's Journey from Egypt to the Border of the Promised Land. Details vary from the list given in 21.10-20, including the omission of Meribah and Taberah. Reference to *the Red Sea* must mean the Gulf of Suez. Mention of Ezion-geber is helpful to the modern reader, since its location at the upper end of the Gulf of Aqabah on the east of the Sinai Peninsula is certain. In addition to the list of places where the people camped, Aaron's death is noted once more (33.38-39).

LORD for the war, 21 and all those of you who
bear arms cross the Jordan before the LORD,
until he has driven out his enemies from
before him 22 and the land is subdued before
the LORD—then after that you may return
and be free of obligation to the LORD and to
Israel, and this land shall be your possession
before the LORD. 23 But if you do not do this,
you have sinned against the LORD; and be
sure your sin will find you out. 24 Build
towns for your little ones, and folds for your
flocks; but do what you have promised."
25 Then the Gadites and the Reubenites
said to Moses, "Your servants will do as my
lord commands. 26 Our little ones, our wives,
our flocks, and all our livestock shall remain
there in the towns of Gilead; 27 but your
servants will cross over, everyone armed for
war, to do battle for the LORD, just as my
lord orders."
28 So Moses gave command concerning
them to Eleazar the priest, to Joshua son of
Nun, and to the heads of the ancestral
houses of the Israelite tribes. 29 And Moses
said to them, "If the Gadites and the
Reubenites, everyone armed for battle before the LORD, will cross over the Jordan
with you and the land shall be subdued
before you, then you shall give them the
land of Gilead for a possession; 30 but if they
will not cross over with you armed, they
shall have possessions among you in the
land of Canaan." 31 The Gadites and the
Reubenites answered, "As the LORD has
spoken to your servants, so we will do. 32 We
will cross over armed before the LORD into
the land of Canaan, but the possession of
our inheritance shall remain with us on this
side of[v] the Jordan."
33 Moses gave to them—to the Gadites
and to the Reubenites and to the half-tribe
of Manasseh son of Joseph—the kingdom of
King Sihon of the Amorites and the kingdom of King Og of Bashan, the land and its
towns, with the territories of the surrounding towns. 34 And the Gadites rebuilt Dibon,
Ataroth, Aroer, 35 Atroth-sophan, Jazer,
Jogbehah, 36 Beth-nimrah, and Beth-haran,
fortified cities, and folds for sheep. 37 And the
Reubenites rebuilt Heshbon, Elealeh,
Kiriathaim, 38 Nebo, and Baal-meon (some
names being changed), and Sibmah; and
they gave names to the towns that they
rebuilt. 39 The descendants of Machir son of
Manasseh went to Gilead, captured it, and
dispossessed the Amorites who were there;
40 so Moses gave Gilead to Machir son of
Manasseh, and he settled there. 41 Jair son of
Manasseh went and captured their villages,
and renamed them Havvoth-jair.[w] 42 And
Nobah went and captured Kenath and its
villages, and renamed it Nobah after himself.

The Stages of Israel's Journey from Egypt

33 These are the stages by which the
Israelites went out of the land of
Egypt in military formation under the leadership of Moses and Aaron. 2 Moses wrote
down their starting points, stage by stage,
by command of the LORD; and these are
their stages according to their starting places.
3 They set out from Rameses in the first
month, on the fifteenth day of the first
month; on the day after the passover the
Israelites went out boldly in the sight of all
the Egyptians, 4 while the Egyptians were
burying all their firstborn, whom the LORD
had struck down among them. The LORD
executed judgments even against their gods.
5 So the Israelites set out from Rameses,
and camped at Succoth. 6 They set out from
Succoth, and camped at Etham, which is on
the edge of the wilderness. 7 They set out
from Etham, and turned back to Pi-hahiroth,
which faces Baal-zephon; and they camped
before Migdol. 8 They set out from Pi-hahiroth,
passed through the sea into the wilderness,
went a three days' journey in the wilderness of Etham, and camped at Marah. 9 They
set out from Marah and came to Elim; at
Elim there were twelve springs of water and
seventy palm trees, and they camped there.
10 They set out from Elim and camped by the
Red Sea.[x] 11 They set out from the Red Sea[x]
and camped in the wilderness of Sin. 12 They
set out from the wilderness of Sin and
camped at Dophkah. 13 They set out from
Dophkah and camped at Alush. 14 They set
out from Alush and camped at Rephidim,
where there was no water for the people to
drink. 15 They set out from Rephidim and
camped in the wilderness of Sinai. 16 They
set out from the wilderness of Sinai and
camped at Kibroth-hattaavah. 17 They set
out from Kibrothhattaavah and camped at
Hazeroth. 18 They set out from Hazeroth and
camped at Rithmah. 19 They set out from
Rithmah and camped at Rimmon-perez.
20 They set out from Rimmon-perez and
camped at Libnah. 21 They set out from

[v] Heb *beyond* [w] That is *the villages of Jair* [x] Or *Sea of Reeds*

32.22 Deut 3.12-20
32.24 ver 16,34
32.26 Josh 1.14
32.27 Josh 4.12
32.28 Josh 1.13
32.29 ver 1
32.33 Deut 3.12-17; Josh 12.1-6; Num 21.24,33,35
32.41 Judg 10.4
33.1 Ps 77.20; Mic 6.4
33.3 Ex 12.37; 14.8
33.4 Ex 12.12
33.6 Ex 13.20
33.7 Ex 14.2,9
33.8 Ex 14.22
33.9 Ex 15.27
33.11 Ex 16.1
33.14 Ex 17.1
33.15 Ex 19.1
33.16 Num 11.34
33.17 Num 11.35
33.20 see Josh 10.29

Libnah and camped at Rissah. 22They set
out from Rissah and camped at Kehelathah.
23They set out from Kehelathah and camped
at Mount Shepher. 24They set out from
Mount Shepher and camped at Haradah.
25They set out from Haradah and camped
at Makheloth. 26They set out from Makheloth
and camped at Tahath. 27They set out from
Tahath and camped at Terah. 28They set
out from Terah and camped at Mithkah.
29They set out from Mithkah and camped at
Hashmonah. 30They set out from Hashmonah and camped at Moseroth. 31They set
out from Moseroth and camped at Bene-
jaakan. 32They set out from Bene-jaakan
and camped at Hor-haggidgad. 33They set
out from Hor-haggidgad and camped at
Jotbathah. 34They set out from Jotbathah
and camped at Abronah. 35They set out
from Abronah and camped at Ezion-geber.
36They set out from Ezion-geber and camped
in the wilderness of Zin (that is, Kadesh).
37They set out from Kadesh and camped at
Mount Hor, on the edge of the land of
Edom.
38 Aaron the priest went up Mount Hor
at the command of the LORD and died there
in the fortieth year after the Israelites had
come out of the land of Egypt, on the first
day of the fifth month. 39Aaron was one
hundred twenty-three years old when he
died on Mount Hor.
40 The Canaanite, the king of Arad, who
lived in the Negeb in the land of Canaan,
heard of the coming of the Israelites.
41 They set out from Mount Hor and
camped at Zalmonah. 42They set out from
Zalmonah and camped at Punon. 43They set
out from Punon and camped at Oboth.
44They set out from Oboth and camped at
Iyeabarim, in the territory of Moab. 45They
set out from Iyim and camped at Dibon-gad.
46They set out from Dibon-gad and camped
at Almon-diblathaim. 47They set out from
Almon-diblathaim and camped in the mountains of Abarim, before Nebo. 48They set out
from the mountains of Abarim and camped
in the plains of Moab by the Jordan and
Jericho; 49they camped by the Jordan from
Beth-jeshimoth as far as Abel-shittim in the
plains of Moab.

Directions for the Conquest of Canaan

50 In the plains of Moab by the Jordan
at Jericho, the LORD spoke to Moses, saying:
51Speak to the Israelites, and say to them:
When you cross over the Jordan into the
land of Canaan, 52you shall drive out all the
inhabitants of the land from before you,
destroy all their figured stones, destroy all
their cast images, and demolish all their
high places. 53You shall take possession of
the land and settle in it, for I have given
you the land to possess. 54You shall apportion the land by lot according to your clans;
to a large one you shall give a large inheritance, and to a small one you shall give a
small inheritance; the inheritance shall
belong to the person on whom the lot falls;
according to your ancestral tribes you shall
inherit. 55But if you do not drive out the
inhabitants of the land from before you,
then those whom you let remain shall be
as barbs in your eyes and thorns in your
sides; they shall trouble you in the land
where you are settling. 56And I will do to
you as I thought to do to them.

The Boundaries of the Land

34 The LORD spoke to Moses, saying:
2Command the Israelites, and say
to them: When you enter the land of Canaan
(this is the land that shall fall to you for an
inheritance, the land of Canaan, defined by
its boundaries), 3your south sector shall
extend from the wilderness of Zin along the
side of Edom. Your southern boundary shall
begin from the end of the Dead Sea[y] on the
east; 4your boundary shall turn south of the
ascent of Akrabbim, and cross to Zin, and
its outer limit shall be south of Kadesh-
barnea; then it shall go on to Hazar-addar,
and cross to Azmon; 5the boundary shall
turn from Azmon to the Wadi of Egypt, and
its termination shall be at the Sea.
6 For the western boundary, you shall
have the Great Sea and its[z] coast; this shall
be your western boundary.
7 This shall be your northern boundary:
from the Great Sea you shall mark out your
line to Mount Hor; 8from Mount Hor you
shall mark it out to Lebo-hamath, and the
outer limit of the boundary shall be at
Zedad; 9then the boundary shall extend to
Ziphron, and its end shall be at Hazar-enan;
this shall be your northern boundary.
10 You shall mark out your eastern
boundary from Hazar-enan to Shepham;
11and the boundary shall continue down
from Shepham to Riblah on the east side of

[y] Heb *Salt Sea* [z] Syr: Heb lacks *its*

33.30 Deut 10.6
33.33 Deut 10.7
33.35 Deut 2.8
33.36 Num 20.1
33.37 Num 20.16,22; 21.4
33.38 Num 20.25,28; Deut 10.6
33.40 Num 21.1
33.43 Num 21.10
33.44 Num 21.11
33.47 Num 27.12
33.48 Num 22.1
33.49 Num 25.1
33.52 Ex 23.24,33; 34.13; Deut 7.2,5; 12.3; Josh 11.12
33.54 Num 26.53-55
33.55 Josh 23.13; Ps 106.34,36
34.2 Gen 17.8; Deut 1.7; Ps 78.55; Ezek 47.15
34.3 Josh 15.1-3
34.5 Gen 15.18; Josh 15.4,47
34.7 Ezek 47.15-17
34.8 Num 13.21
34.11 2 Kings 23.33; Deut 3.17; Josh 11.2

33.50-56 How the Israelites are to Take Control of the Land. In addition to driving out the current inhabitants and occupying the lands west of the Jordan, the people are to destroy all features of idolatrous worship there (33.52). The land is to be divided up among the tribes, with the assignments made by a combination of factors: according to the relative size of each tribe and with confirmation by the sacred lot.
34.1-35.15 Settling in the New Land.
34.1-15 The boundaries of the land on both sides of the Jordan are specified, although in some cases uncertainty as to actual locations of the cities and mountains named makes the extent of the land impossible to determine. The *northern boundary* which is defined by *Mount Hor...Lebo-Hamath* on the Orontes River and Zedad would include large sections of Syria far north of the Sea of Galilee and therefore territory which Israel never controlled historically.

34.16-29 The leaders of each of the tribes are designated by Moses. **35.1-8** Although earlier Levites were said not to be granted an allotment of lands (26.62), provision is here made for them to be given certain towns and the lands surrounding them for the pasturing of flocks. **35.9-11** In addition, the Levites are to be in charge of the six cities of refuge that are to be established where anyone who has unintentionally killed somebody may find safety. Three of these cities are to be east of the Jordan and three on the west bank. **35.16-34** How to Deal with Murder and Blood Revenge. What constitutes murder is defined, and how such a death is to be avenged is specified. Also described are forms of death caused accidentally and the ways in which the community should protect those who have killed someone inadvertently. But since blood pollutes the land (Gen 4.10), the killer cannot return to his home until the special rites have been performed for the installation of a new high priest, the sacrifices for which effect purification of the land and the people as a whole (35.32).

Ain; and the boundary shall go down, and reach the eastern slope of the sea of Chinnereth; [12]and the boundary shall go down to the Jordan, and its end shall be at the Dead Sea.[a] This shall be your land with its boundaries all around.

13 Moses commanded the Israelites, saying: This is the land that you shall inherit by lot, which the LORD has commanded to give to the nine tribes and to the half-tribe; [14]for the tribe of the Reubenites by their ancestral houses and the tribe of the Gadites by their ancestral houses have taken their inheritance, and also the half-tribe of Manasseh; [15]the two tribes and the half-tribe have taken their inheritance beyond the Jordan at Jericho eastward, toward the sunrise.

Tribal Leaders

16 The LORD spoke to Moses, saying: [17]These are the names of the men who shall apportion the land to you for inheritance: the priest Eleazar and Joshua son of Nun. [18]You shall take one leader of every tribe to apportion the land for inheritance. [19]These are the names of the men: Of the tribe of Judah, Calbe son of Jephunneh. [20]Of the tribe of the Simeonites, Shemuel son of Ammihud. [21]Of the tribe of Benjamin, Elidad son of Chislon. [22]Of the tribe of the Danites a leader, Bukki son of Jogli. [23]Of the Josephites: of the tribe of the Manassites a leader, Hanniel son of Ephod, [24]and of the tribe of the Ephraimites a leader, Kemuel son of Shiphtan. [25]Of the tribe of the Zebulunites a leader, Eli-zaphan son of Parnach. [26]Of the tribe of the Issacharites a leader, Paltiel son of Azzan. [27]And of the tribe of the Asherites a leader, Ahihud son of Shelomi. [28]Of the tribe of the Naphtalites a leader, Pedahel son of Ammihud. [29]These were the ones whom the LORD commanded to apportion the inheritance for the Israelites in the land of Canaan.

Cities for the Levites

35 In the plains of Moab by the Jordan at Jericho, the LORD spoke to Moses, saying: [2]Command the Israelites to give, from the inheritance that they possess, towns for the Levites to live in; you shall also give to the Levites pasture lands surrounding the towns. [3]The towns shall be theirs to live in, and their pasture lands shall be for their cattle, for their livestock, and for all their animals. [4]The pasture lands of the towns, which you shall give to the Levites, shall reach from the wall of the town outward a thousand cubits all around. [5]You shall measure, outside the town, for the east side two thousand cubits, for the south side two thousand cubits, for the west side two thousand cubits, and for the north side two thousand cubits, with the town in the middle; this shall belong to them as pasture land for their towns.

6 The towns that you give to the Levites shall include the six cities of refuge, where you shall permit a slayer to flee, and in addition to them you shall give forty-two towns. [7]The towns that you give to the Levites shall total forty-eight, with their pasture lands. [8]And as for the towns that you shall give from the possession of the Israelites, from the larger tribes you shall take many, and from the smaller tribes you shall take few; each, in proportion to the inheritance that it obtains, shall give of its towns to the Levites.

Cities of Refuge

9 The LORD spoke to Moses, saying: [10]Speak to the Israelites, and say to them: When you cross the Jordan into the land of Canaan, [11]then you shall select cities to be cities of refuge for you, so that a slayer who kills a person without intent may flee there. [12]The cities shall be for you a refuge from the avenger, so that the slayer may not die until there is a trial before the congregation.

13 The cities that you designate shall be six cities of refuge for you: [14]you shall designate three cities beyond the Jordan, and three cities in the land of Canaan, to be cities of refuge. [15]These six cities shall serve as refuge for the Israelites, for the resident or transient alien among them, so that anyone who kills a person without intent may flee there.

Concerning Murder and Blood Revenge

16 But anyone who strikes another with an iron object, and death ensues, is a murderer; the murderer shall be put to death. [17]Or anyone who strikes another with a stone in hand that could cause death, and death ensues, is a murderer; the

[a] Heb *Salt Sea*

34.13 Josh 14.1,2
34.14 Num 32.33; Josh 14.2,3
34.17 Josh 14.1
34.18 Num 1.4,16
35.2 Lev 25.32-34; Josh 14.3,4
35.6 Josh 20.7-9; 21.3,13,21, 27,32,36,38
35.8 Num 26.54; Lev 25.32-34; Josh 21.1-42
35.11 Deut 19.1-13; Ex 21.13
35.12 Josh 20.2-6
35.15 ver 11
35.16 Ex 21.12,14; Lev 24.17

35.19 ver 21,24,27
35.22 ver 11; Ex 21.13
35.24 ver 12
35.30 ver 16; Deut 17.6; 19.15; Mt 18.16; 2 Cor 13.1; Heb 10.28
35.33 Ps 106.38; Gen 9.6
35.34 Lev 18.25; Ex 29.45,46
36.1 Num 26.29; 27.1
36.2 Num 26.55; 33.54; 27.1,7
36.4 Lev 25.10
36.6 ver 12
36.8 1 Chr 23.22
36.11 Num 27.1

murderer shall be put to death. [18]Or anyone
who strikes another with a weapon of wood
in hand that could cause death, and death
ensues, is a murderer; the murderer shall be
put to death. [19]The avenger of blood is the
one who shall put the murderer to death;
when they meet, the avenger of blood shall
execute the sentence. [20]Likewise, if someone
pushes another from hatred, or hurls something at another, lying in wait, and death
ensues, [21]or in enmity strikes another with
the hand, and death ensues, then the one
who struck the blow shall be put to death;
that person is a murderer; the avenger of
blood shall put the murderer to death, when
they meet.
22 But if someone pushes another suddenly without enmity, or hurls any object
without lying in wait, [23]or, while handling
any stone that could cause death, unintentionally[b] drops it on another and death
ensues, though they were not enemies, and
no harm was intended, [24]then the congregation shall judge between the slayer and
the avenger of blood, in accordance with
these ordinances; [25]and the congregation
shall rescue the slayer from the avenger of
blood. Then the congregation shall send the
slayer back to the original city of refuge.
The slayer shall live in it until the death of
the high priest who was anointed with the
holy oil. [26]But if the slayer shall at any time
go outside the bounds of the original city of
refuge, [27]and is found by the avenger of
blood outside the bounds of the city of
refuge, and is killed by the avenger, no
bloodguilt shall be incurred. [28]For the slayer
must remain in the city of refuge until the
death of the high priest; but after the death
of the high priest the slayer may return
home.
29 These things shall be a statute and
ordinance for you throughout your generations wherever you live.
30 If anyone kills another, the murderer
shall be put to death on the evidence of
witnesses; but no one shall be put to death
on the testimony of a single witness. [31]More-
over you shall accept no ransom for the life
of a murderer who is subject to the death
penalty; a murderer must be put to death.
[32]Nor shall you accept ransom for one who
has fled to a city of refuge, enabling the
fugitive to return to live in the land before
the death of the high priest. [33]You shall not
pollute the land in which you live; for blood
pollutes the land, and no expiation can be
made for the land, for the blood that is shed
in it, except by the blood of the one who
shed it. [34]You shall not defile the land in
which you live, in which I also dwell; for
I the LORD dwell among the Israelites.

Marriage of Female Heirs

36 The heads of the ancestral houses
of the clans of the descendants of
Gilead son of Machir son of Manasseh, of
the Josephite clans, came forward and spoke
in the presence of Moses and the leaders,
the heads of the ancestral houses of the
Israelites; [2]they said, "The LORD commanded
my lord to give the land for inheritance by
lot to the Israelites; and my lord was commanded by the LORD to give the inheritance
of our brother Zelophehad to his daughters.
[3]But if they are married into another Israelite tribe, then their inheritance will be
taken from the inheritance of our ancestors
and added to the inheritance of the tribe
into which they marry; so it will be taken
away from the allotted portion of our inheritance. [4]And when the jubilee of the Israelites comes, then their inheritance will
be added to the inheritance of the tribe into
which they have married; and their inheritance will be taken from the inheritance of
our ancestral tribe."
5 Then Moses commanded the Israelites
according to the word of the LORD, saying,
"The descendants of the tribe of Joseph are
right in what they are saying. [6]This is what
the LORD commands concerning the daughters of Zelophehad, 'Let them marry whom
they think best; only it must be into a clan
of their father's tribe that they are married,
[7]so that no inheritance of the Israelites shall
be transferred from one tribe to another; for
all Israelites shall retain the inheritance of
their ancestral tribes. [8]Every daughter who
possesses an inheritance in any tribe of the
Israelites shall marry one from the clan of
her father's tribe, so that all Israelites may
continue to possess their ancestral inheritance. [9]No inheritance shall be transferred
from one tribe to another; for each of the
tribes of the Israelites shall retain its own
inheritance.'"
10 The daughters of Zelophehad did as
the LORD had commanded Moses. [11]Mahlah,
Tirzah, Hoglah, Milcah, and Noah, the
daughters of Zelophehad, married sons of

36.1-12 Female Heirs must Marry within their Tribe. The special provision for the daughters of Zelophehad to inherit family property (Num 27.1-11), which was normally a prerogative for males only, is now established as a norm: women heirs must marry within their tribe, in order to preserve the tribal inheritance for the present, and to ease the process in the year of jubilee when all property that has changed ownership reverts to its original ancestral tribe (Lev 25.8-55).

[b] Heb *without seeing*

36.13 Conclusion. These instructions have been given by Moses to the Israelites just across the Jordan from Jericho, where, under new leadership – Joshua's – they are soon to begin the invasion of the land of Canaan.

their father's brothers. 12They were married into the clans of the descendants of Manasseh son of Joseph, and their inheritance remained in the tribe of their father's clan.

13 These are the commandments and the ordinances that the LORD commanded through Moses to the Israelites in the plains of Moab by the Jordan at Jericho.

36.13 Num 22.1; Lev 26.46; 27.34

DEUTERONOMY

See the Introductions, pp. 2, 30, and 37-38 above.

1-3 God Leads his People to the Border of the Promised Land.
1.1-8 Introduction. *Horeb* is used in place of Sinai throughout Deuteronomy and three times in Exodus, never in Leviticus or Numbers, while Sinai appears only once in Deuteronomy (33.2). Moses' *words* are spoken *to all Israel*, which is used here without distinction between northern and southern tribes (Judah). The conflicts of Israel on entering the area east of Jordan are sketched, with fuller descriptions in 2.16-3.11 (see Num 21.21-35). Many of the place names used here are unknown, but the term *Amorites* indicates the Semitic tribes in the hill country, east and west of the Jordan, while *Canaanites* refers to the inhabitants of the coastal plain of Palestine. (1.7) The territory to be conquered by Israel is said to extend as far north as the river Euphrates, north and east of the borders of Syria, and it has been promised not only to Abraham (Gen 15) but to all three of the patriarchs.
1.9-18 Appointment of Tribal Leaders and Judges. *Cf.* Num 11.14-17; Ex 18.13-27. In response to Moses' complaint that he cannot *bear the heavy burden of [the people's] disputes* all by himself, the LORD agrees to the appointment of *wise and reputable* leaders by rank, some in charge of groups of thousands, hundreds, fifties and tens, and other *officials* whose responsibilities were record-keeping and interpreting the laws. Such officials later came to be designated as scribes.
1.19-45 Israel's Refusal to Enter the Land and God's Subsequent Punishment of Them. In summary of Num 13-20, Moses reminds the people that *although the LORD has given the land to you* (1.21), they have refused to *take possession* of it, and have ignored the glowing reports of the spies about the fruitfulness of the land out of fear of the inhabitants (1.26-28), forgetting their experience of God's power in his deliverance of them from slavery in Egypt (1.30-33).

Events at Horeb Recalled

1 These are the words that Moses spoke to all Israel beyond the Jordan—in the wilderness, on the plain opposite Suph, between Paran and Tophel, Laban, Hazeroth, and Di-zahab. 2(By the way of Mount Seir it takes eleven days to reach Kadesh-barnea from Horeb.) 3In the fortieth year, on the first day of the eleventh month, Moses spoke to the Israelites just as the LORD had commanded him to speak to them. 4This was after he had defeated King Sihon of the Amorites, who reigned in Heshbon, and King Og of Bashan, who reigned in Ashtaroth and[a] in Edrei. 5Beyond the Jordan in the land of Moab, Moses undertook to expound this law as follows:

6 The LORD our God spoke to us at Horeb, saying, "You have stayed long enough at this mountain. 7Resume your journey, and go into the hill country of the Amorites as well as into the neighboring regions—the Arabah, the hill country, the Shephelah, the Negeb, and the seacoast—the land of the Canaanites and the Lebanon, as far as the great river, the river Euphrates. 8See, I have set the land before you; go in and take possession of the land that I[b] swore to your ancestors, to Abraham, to Isaac, and to Jacob, to give to them and to their descendants after them."

Appointment of Tribal Leaders

9 At that time I said to you, "I am unable by myself to bear you. 10The LORD your God has multiplied you, so that today you are as numerous as the stars of heaven. 11May the LORD, the God of your ancestors, increase you a thousand times more and bless you, as he has promised you! 12But how can I bear the heavy burden of your disputes all by myself? 13Choose for each of your tribes individuals who are wise, discerning, and reputable to be your leaders." 14You answered me, "The plan you have proposed is a good one." 15So I took the leaders of your tribes, wise and reputable individuals, and installed them as leaders over you, commanders of thousands, commanders of hundreds, commanders of fifties, commanders of tens, and officials, throughout your tribes. 16I charged your judges at that time: "Give the members of your community a fair hearing, and judge rightly between one person and another, whether citizen or resident alien. 17You must not be partial in judging: hear out the small and the great alike; you shall not be intimidated by anyone, for the judgment is God's. Any case that is too hard for you, bring to me, and I will hear it." 18So I charged you at that time with all the things that you should do.

Israel's Refusal to Enter the Land

19 Then, just as the LORD our God had ordered us, we set out from Horeb and went through all that great and terrible wilderness that you saw, on the way to the hill country of the Amorites, until we reached Kadesh-barnea. 20I said to you, "You have reached the hill country of the Amorites, which the LORD our God is giving us. 21See, the LORD your God has given the land to you; go up, take possession, as the LORD, the God of your ancestors, has promised you; do not fear or be dismayed."

22 All of you came to me and said, "Let us send men ahead of us to explore the land for us and bring back a report to us regard-

[a] Gk Syr Vg Compare Josh 12.4: Heb lacks *and* [b] Sam Gk: MT *the LORD*

1.3 Num 33.38

1.4 Num 21.24,33

1.6 Ex 3.1; Num 10.11-13

1.8 Gen 12.7; 15.18; 17.7,8; 26.4; 28.13

1.9 Ex 18.18

1.10 Gen 15.5; Deut 10.22

1.11 Gen 22.17; Ex 32.13

1.13 Ex 18.21

1.15 Ex 18.25

1.16 Deut 16.18; Lev 24.22

1.17 Lev 19.15; Jas 2.1; Ex 18.19-26

1.19 ver 2; Deut 8.15; Num 13.26

1.21 Josh 1.9

ing the route by which we should go up and the cities we will come to." [23]The plan seemed good to me, and I selected twelve of you, one from each tribe. [24]They set out and went up into the hill country, and when they reached the Valley of Eshcol they spied it out [25]and gathered some of the land's produce, which they brought down to us. They brought back a report to us, and said, "It is a good land that the LORD our God is giving us."

26 But you were unwilling to go up. You rebelled against the command of the LORD your God; [27]you grumbled in your tents and said, "It is because the LORD hates us that he has brought us out of the land of Egypt, to hand us over to the Amorites to destroy us. [28]Where are we headed? Our kindred have made our hearts melt by reporting, 'The people are stronger and taller than we; the cities are large and fortified up to heaven! We actually saw there the offspring of the Anakim!' " [29]I said to you, "Have no dread or fear of them. [30]The LORD your God, who goes before you, is the one who will fight for you, just as he did for you in Egypt before your very eyes, [31]and in the wilderness, where you saw how the LORD your God carried you, just as one carries a child, all the way that you traveled until you reached this place. [32]But in spite of this, you have no trust in the LORD your God, [33]who goes before you on the way to seek out a place for you to camp, in fire by night, and in the cloud by day, to show you the route you should take."

The Penalty for Israel's Rebellion

34 When the LORD heard your words, he was wrathful and swore: [35]"Not one of these—not one of this evil generation—shall see the good land that I swore to give to your ancestors, [36]except Caleb son of Jephunneh. He shall see it, and to him and to his descendants I will give the land on which he set foot, because of his complete fidelity to the LORD." [37]Even with me the LORD was angry on your account, saying, "You also shall not enter there. [38]Joshua son of Nun, your assistant, shall enter there; encourage him, for he is the one who will secure Israel's possession of it. [39]And as for your little ones, who you thought would become booty, your children, who today do not yet know right from wrong, they shall enter there; to them I will give it, and they shall take possession of it. [40]But as for you, journey back into the wilderness, in the direction of the Red Sea."[c]

41 You answered me, "We have sinned against the LORD! We are ready to go up and fight, just as the LORD our God commanded us." So all of you strapped on your battle gear, and thought it easy to go up into the hill country. [42]The LORD said to me, "Say to them, 'Do not go up and do not fight, for I am not in the midst of you; otherwise you will be defeated by your enemies.' " [43]Although I told you, you would not listen. You rebelled against the command of the LORD and presumptuously went up into the hill country. [44]The Amorites who lived in that hill country then came out against you and chased you as bees do. They beat you down in Seir as far as Hormah. [45]When you returned and wept before the LORD, the LORD would neither heed your voice nor pay you any attention.

The Desert Years

46 After you had stayed at Kadesh as **2** many days as you did, [1]we journeyed back into the wilderness, in the direction of the Red Sea,[c] as the LORD had told me and skirted Mount Seir for many days. [2]Then the LORD said to me: [3]"You have been skirting this hill country long enough. Head north, [4]and charge the people as follows: You are about to pass through the territory of your kindred, the descendants of Esau, who live in Seir. They will be afraid of you, so, be very careful [5]not to engage in battle with them, for I will not give you even so much as a foot's length of their land, since I have given Mount Seir to Esau as a possession. [6]You shall purchase food from them for money, so that you may eat; and you shall also buy water from them for money, so that you may drink. [7]Surely the LORD your God has blessed you in all your undertakings; he knows your going through this great wilderness. These forty years the LORD your God has been with you; you have lacked nothing." [8]So we passed by our kin, the descendants of Esau who live in Seir, leaving behind the route of the Arabah, and leaving behind Elath and Ezion-geber.

When we had headed out along the route of the wilderness of Moab, [9]the LORD said to me: "Do not harass Moab or engage them

[c] Or *Sea of Reeds*

1.23 Num 13.1-3
1.24 Num 13.22-24
1.25 Num 13.27
1.26 Num 14.1-4
1.27 Deut 9.28; Ps 106.25
1.28 Num 13.28, 31-33; Deut 9.1,2
1.30 Ex 14.14; Deut 3.22
1.31 Deut 32.11,12; Acts 13.18
1.32 Ps 106.24
1.33 Ex 13.21; Num 10.33
1.34 Num 14.22-30
1.37 Num 20.12; Deut 3.26; Ps 106.32
1.38 Num 14.30; Deut 3.28; 31.7
1.39 Num 14.3,31
1.40 Num 14.25
1.41 Num 14.40
1.42 Num 14.42
1.43 Num 14.44,45
1.44 Ps 118.12
2.1 Num 21.4
2.4 Num 20.14
2.5 Josh 24.4
2.7 Deut 8.2-4
2.8 Judg 11.18
2.9 ver 18; Num 21.28; Gen 19.36,37

1.34-45 The Penalty for Israel's Rebellion. Summarizing the events described in Num 13-14, Joshua is identified as Moses' *assistant* (1.38), who will achieve *Israel's possession* of the land. As a result of Israel's lack of trust, the attempt to take the land is futile, and it is noted that Yahweh paid no *attention* to the belated penitence of the people.
1.46-2.25 The Journey through Edom, Moab and Ammon. Although Num 20-21 is paralleled here, there is no mention of Edom's refusal to let Israel pass through her territory. Additional notes mention other peoples encountered on the way: the Emim, who are connected with Esau (2.8,10-12) and the Moabites, who are seen as *descendants of Lot* (2.9; Gen 19.30-38).
2.7-14 The broad designation of a period of forty years (=one full generation) is modified to *thirty-eight years* to indicate the initial span of time for God's activity and the inappropriate response of Israel.

2.26-3.22 The Defeat of the Local Kings and the Capture of the East Jordan Lands. The triumphs over King Sihon and King Og included the extermination of the entire populace of their realms (2.34; 3.3,6). In Deut 20.13-14 the command of God is that only males are to be killed when a people is conquered, but the holy war policy here indicated fits with the roughly contemporary inscription by Mesha, king of Moab, which reports his having ordered the killing of all the inhabitants of an Israelite city, Nebo. Throughout this section is repeated the claim that the LORD gave all this to his people, including all the land east of the Jordan as far north as Gilead and Mt. Hermon (2.36; 3.8). The extraordinary size of some of the people conquered is indicated dramatically by King Og's *iron bed,* or stone coffin, which measured 13 feet by 6 feet (3.11).

in battle, for I will not give you any of its land as a possession, since I have given Ar as a possession to the descendants of Lot." 10(The Emim—a large and numerous people, as tall as the Anakim—had formerly inhabited it. 11Like the Anakim, they are usually reckoned as Rephaim, though the Moabites call them Emim. 12Moreover, the Horim had formerly inhabited Seir, but the descendants of Esau dispossessed them, destroying them and settling in their place, as Israel has done in the land that the LORD gave them as a possession.) 13"Now then, proceed to cross over the Wadi Zered."

So we crossed over the Wadi Zered. 14And the length of time we had traveled from Kadesh-barnea until we crossed the Wadi Zered was thirty-eight years, until the entire generation of warriors had perished from the camp, as the LORD had sworn concerning them. 15Indeed, the LORD's own hand was against them, to root them out from the camp, until all had perished.

16 Just as soon as all the warriors had died off from among the people, 17the LORD spoke to me, saying, 18"Today you are going to cross the boundary of Moab at Ar. 19When you approach the frontier of the Ammonites, do not harass them or engage them in battle, for I will not give the land of the Ammonites to you as a possession, because I have given it to the descendants of Lot." 20(It also is usually reckoned as a land of Rephaim. Rephaim formerly inhabited it, though the Ammonites call them Zamzummim, 21a strong and numerous people, as tall as the Anakim. But the LORD destroyed them from before the Ammonites so that they could dispossess them and settle in their place. 22He did the same for the descendants of Esau, who live in Seir, by destroying the Horim before them so that they could dispossess them and settle in their place even to this day. 23As for the Avvim, who had lived in settlements in the vicinity of Gaza, the Caphtorim, who came from Caphtor, destroyed them and settled in their place.) 24"Proceed on your journey and cross the Wadi Arnon. See, I have handed over to you King Sihon the Amorite of Heshbon, and his land. Begin to take possession by engaging him in battle. 25This day I will begin to put the dread and fear of you upon the peoples everywhere under heaven; when they hear report of you, they will tremble and be in anguish because of you."

Defeat of King Sihon

26 So I sent messengers from the wilderness of Kedemoth to King Sihon of Heshbon with the following terms of peace: 27"If you let me pass through your land, I will travel only along the road; I will turn aside neither to the right nor to the left. 28You shall sell me food for money, so that I may eat, and supply me water for money, so that I may drink. Only allow me to pass through on foot— 29just as the descendants of Esau who live in Seir have done for me and likewise the Moabites who live in Ar—until I cross the Jordan into the land that the LORD our God is giving us." 30But King Sihon of Heshbon was not willing to let us pass through, for the LORD your God had hardened his spirit and made his heart defiant in order to hand him over to you, as he has now done.

31 The LORD said to me, "See, I have begun to give Sihon and his land over to you. Begin now to take possession of his land." 32So when Sihon came out against us, he and all his people for battle at Jahaz, 33the LORD our God gave him over to us; and we struck him down, along with his offspring and all his people. 34At that time we captured all his towns, and in each town we utterly destroyed men, women, and children. We left not a single survivor. 35Only the livestock we kept as spoil for ourselves, as well as the plunder of the towns that we had captured. 36From Aroer on the edge of the Wadi Arnon (including the town that is in the wadi itself) as far as Gilead, there was no citadel too high for us. The LORD our God gave everything to us. 37You did not encroach, however, on the land of the Ammonites, avoiding the whole upper region of the Wadi Jabbok as well as the towns of the hill country, just as[d] the LORD our God had charged.

Defeat of King Og

3 When we headed up the road to Bashan, King Og of Bashan came out against us, he and all his people, for battle at Edrei. 2The LORD said to me, "Do not fear him, for I have handed him over to you, along with his people and his land. Do to him as you did to King Sihon of the Amorites, who reigned in Heshbon." 3So the LORD our God also handed over to us King Og of Bashan and all his people. We struck him

2.10 Gen 14.5; Num 13.22,33
2.12 ver 22
2.14 Num 13.26; 14.29-35
2.15 Ps 106.26
2.19 ver 9
2.21 ver 10
2.22 Gen 36.8; ver 12
2.23 Josh 13.2; Gen 10.14; Am 9.7
2.24 Judg 11.18
2.25 Ex 15.14,15; Deut 11.25; Josh 2.9,10
2.26 Deut 20.10
2.27 Num 21.21,22
2.28 Num 20.19
2.30 Num 21.23
2.31 Deut 1.8
2.32 Num 21.23,24; Deut 7.2; 20.16
2.34 Deut 3.6
2.36 Deut 3.12; 4.48; Ps 44.3
2.37 Num 21.24
3.1 Num 21.33-35
3.2 Num 21.34
3.3 Num 21.35

[d] Gk Tg: Heb *and all*

3.4 1 Kings 4.13
3.6 Deut 2.24,34
3.9 Ps 29.6
3.11 Am 2.9; Gen 14.5; 2 Sam 12.26; Jer 49.2
3.12 Deut 2.36; Num 32.32-38; Josh 13.8-13
3.14 Num 32.41; 1 Chr 2.22
3.15 Num 32.39
3.17 Num 34.11; Josh 13.27
3.18 Num 32.20
3.20 Josh 22.4
3.22 Deut 1.30
3.24 Ex 15.11; Ps 86.8
3.26 Deut 1.37; 31.2
3.27 Num 27.12
3.28 Num 27.18,23; Deut 31.3,7
3.29 Deut 4.46; 34.6
4.1 Deut 5.33; 8.1; 16.20; 30.16,19
4.2 Deut 12.32; Josh 1.7; Rev 22.18,19
4.3 Num 25.4; Ps 106.28,29

down until not a single survivor was left. [4]At that time we captured all his towns; there was no citadel that we did not take from them—sixty towns, the whole region of Argob, the kingdom of Og in Bashan. [5]All these were fortress towns with high walls, double gates, and bars, besides a great many villages. [6]And we utterly destroyed them, as we had done to King Sihon of Heshbon, in each city utterly destroying men, women, and children. [7]But all the livestock and the plunder of the towns we kept as spoil for ourselves.

8 So at that time we took from the two kings of the Amorites the land beyond the Jordan, from the Wadi Arnon to Mount Hermon [9](the Sidonians call Hermon Sirion, while the Amorites call it Senir), [10]all the towns of the tableland, the whole of Gilead, and all of Bashan, as far as Salecah and Edrei, towns of Og's kingdom in Bashan. [11](Now only King Og of Bashan was left of the remnant of the Rephaim. In fact his bed, an iron bed, can still be seen in Rabbah of the Ammonites. By the common cubit it is nine cubits long and four cubits wide.) [12]As for the land that we took possession of at that time, I gave to the Reubenites and Gadites the territory north of Aroer,[e] that is on the edge of the Wadi Arnon, as well as half the hill country of Gilead with its towns, [13]and I gave to the half-tribe of Manasseh the rest of Gilead and all of Bashan, Og's kingdom. (The whole region of Argob: all that portion of Bashan used to be called a land of Rephaim; [14]Jair the Manassite acquired the whole region of Argob as far as the border of the Geshurites and the Maacathites, and he named them—that is, Bashan—after himself, Havvoth-jair,[f] as it is to this day.) [15]To Machir I gave Gilead. [16]And to the Reubenites and the Gadites I gave the territory from Gilead as far as the Wadi Arnon, with the middle of the wadi as a boundary, and up to the Jabbok, the wadi being boundary of the Ammonites; [17]the Arabah also, with the Jordan and its banks, from Chinnereth down to the sea of the Arabah, the Dead Sea,[g] with the lower slopes of Pisgah on the east.

18 At that time, I charged you as follows: "Although the LORD your God has given you this land to occupy, all your troops shall cross over armed as the vanguard of your Israelite kin. [19]Only your wives, your children, and your livestock—I know that you have much livestock—shall stay behind in the towns that I have given to you. [20]When the LORD gives rest to your kindred, as to you, and they too have occupied the land that the LORD your God is giving them beyond the Jordan, then each of you may return to the property that I have given to you." [21]And I charged Joshua as well at that time, saying: "Your own eyes have seen everything that the LORD your God has done to these two kings; so the LORD will do to all the kingdoms into which you are about to cross. [22]Do not fear them, for it is the LORD your God who fights for you."

Moses Views Canaan from Pisgah

23 At that time, too, I entreated the LORD, saying: [24]"O Lord GOD, you have only begun to show your servant your greatness and your might; what god in heaven or on earth can perform deeds and mighty acts like yours! [25]Let me cross over to see the good land beyond the Jordan, that good hill country and the Lebanon." [26]But the LORD was angry with me on your account and would not heed me. The LORD said to me, "Enough from you! Never speak to me of this matter again! [27]Go up to the top of Pisgah and look around you to the west, to the north, to the south, and to the east. Look well, for you shall not cross over this Jordan. [28]But charge Joshua, and encourage and strengthen him, because it is he who shall cross over at the head of this people and who shall secure their possession of the land that you will see." [29]So we remained in the valley opposite Beth-peor.

Moses Commands Obedience

4 So now, Israel, give heed to the statutes and ordinances that I am teaching you to observe, so that you may live to enter and occupy the land that the LORD, the God of your ancestors, is giving you. [2]You must neither add anything to what I command you nor take away anything from it, but keep the commandments of the LORD your God with which I am charging you. [3]You have seen for yourselves what the LORD did with regard to the Baal of Peor—how the LORD your God destroyed from among you everyone who followed the Baal of Peor, [4]while those of you who held fast

[e] Heb *territory from Aroer* [f] That is *Settlement of Jair* [g] Heb *Salt Sea*

3.12-22 In this shorter version of Israel's takeover of the East Jordan lands (*cf.* Num 32; Josh 13.8-31), what is seized is assigned to the descendants of Reuben, Gad and Manasseh, extending from the area east of the Dead Sea north to Gilead. Only the wives, children and livestock of these Israelite tribes are to settle in these lands, however, while the adult males join the other tribes in the conquest of Canaan, in which their success will match their triumphs over the kings in east Jordan.
3.23-29 Moses' Prayer and God's Response.
3.23-24 Offering praise to God in the form of rhetorical questions is characteristic of Deuteronomy.
3.25-28 Moses' request to cross over into the land of Canaan is met with anger from the LORD. Instead, he can only look across the valley from *Pisgah*, which is another name for Nebo (see 34.1). Moses is told that it is *Joshua* who will lead the people to take *possession of the land you will see.*
4.1-43 The First of Moses' Farewell Addresses to Israel. Here and throughout Deuteronomy, the emphasis is on instruction in the commandments of God: *the statutes and ordinances that I am teaching you to observe* (4.1), and the instruction to the people to teach *your children and your children's children* (4.9-10). For present and future generations to obey them is essential if Israel is *to enter and occupy the land that the LORD is giving you* (4.5).
4.2-4 All the commandments as given by God through Moses are binding: none is to be added or subtracted. To violate any of them is to invite destruction like that which fell on those of Israel who lapsed into idolatry when they followed the Baal at Peor (Num 25).

to the LORD your God are all alive today.
5 See, just as the LORD my God has charged
me, I now teach you statutes and ordinances for you to observe in the land that
you are about to enter and occupy. [6]You
must observe them diligently, for this will
show your wisdom and discernment to the
peoples, who, when they hear all these
statutes, will say, "Surely this great nation
is a wise and discerning people!" [7]For what
other great nation has a god so near to it
as the LORD our God is whenever we call to
him? [8]And what other great nation has
statutes and ordinances as just as this entire
law that I am setting before you today?
9 But take care and watch yourselves
closely, so as neither to forget the things
that your eyes have seen nor to let them
slip from your mind all the days of your life;
make them known to your children and
your children's children— [10]how you once
stood before the LORD your God at Horeb,
when the LORD said to me, "Assemble the
people for me, and I will let them hear my
words, so that they may learn to fear me
as long as they live on the earth, and may
teach their children so"; [11]you approached
and stood at the foot of the mountain while
the mountain was blazing up to the very
heavens, shrouded in dark clouds. [12]Then
the LORD spoke to you out of the fire. You
heard the sound of words but saw no form;
there was only a voice. [13]He declared to you
his covenant, which he charged you to
observe, that is, the ten commandments;[h]
and he wrote them on two stone tablets.
[14]And the LORD charged me at that time to
teach you statutes and ordinances for you
to observe in the land that you are about
to cross into and occupy.
15 Since you saw no form when the
LORD spoke to you at Horeb out of the fire,
take care and watch yourselves closely, [16]so
that you do not act corruptly by making an
idol for yourselves, in the form of any figure—
the likeness of male or female, [17]the likeness
of any animal that is on the earth, the
likeness of any winged bird that flies in the
air, [18]the likeness of anything that creeps on
the ground, the likeness of any fish that is
in the water under the earth. [19]And when
you look up to the heavens and see the sun,
the moon, and the stars, all the host of
heaven, do not be led astray and bow down
to them and serve them, things that the
LORD your God has allotted to all the peoples
everywhere under heaven. [20]But the LORD
has taken you and brought you out of the
iron-smelter, out of Egypt, to become a
people of his very own possession, as you
are now.
21 The LORD was angry with me because
of you, and he vowed that I should not
cross the Jordan and that I should not enter
the good land that the LORD your God is
giving for your possession. [22]For I am going
to die in this land without crossing over the
Jordan, but you are going to cross over to
take possession of that good land. [23]So be
careful not to forget the covenant that the
LORD your God made with you, and not to
make for yourselves an idol in the form of
anything that the LORD your God has forbidden you. [24]For the LORD your God is a
devouring fire, a jealous God.
25 When you have had children and
children's children, and become complacent
in the land, if you act corruptly by making
an idol in the form of anything, thus doing
what is evil in the sight of the LORD your
God, and provoking him to anger, [26]I call
heaven and earth to witness against you
today that you will soon utterly perish from
the land that you are crossing the Jordan
to occupy; you will not live long on it, but
will be utterly destroyed. [27]The LORD will
scatter you among the peoples; only a few
of you will be left among the nations where
the LORD will lead you. [28]There you will
serve other gods made by human hands,
objects of wood and stone that neither see,
nor hear, nor eat, nor smell. [29]From there
you will seek the LORD your God, and you
will find him if you search after him with
all your heart and soul. [30]In your distress,
when all these things have happened to you
in time to come, you will return to the LORD
your God and heed him. [31]Because the LORD
your God is a merciful God, he will neither
abandon you nor destroy you; he will not
forget the covenant with your ancestors
that he swore to them.
32 For ask now about former ages, long
before your own, ever since the day that
God created human beings on the earth;
ask from one end of heaven to the other:
has anything so great as this ever happened
or has its like ever been heard of? [33]Has any
people ever heard the voice of a god speaking out of a fire, as you have heard, and
lived? [34]Or has any god ever attempted to
go and take a nation for himself from the

[h] Heb *the ten words*

4.5-7 The people's observing the law will bear testimony to other nations concerning the wisdom and discernment of Israel, as well as to God's special work in having created them as a nation. His nearness to them will be evident in the answers he will give to their prayers.
4.9-14 Moses describes again the process at Horeb by which the people were convened to see the fiery signs of God's presence among them and to hear *the covenant* and its obligations summarized in the *ten commandments* inscribed on the *two stone tablets.* See Ex 20.1; 34.10-27.
4.15-20 The fact that the LORD does not appear in any visible form in the fire at Horeb should not lead them to compensate by representing him in the form of any earthly or celestial object. The central evidence of his existence and power is his action in having brought them *out of the iron-smelter* which was their experience in Egypt.
4.21-23 Moses' own experience of the anger of God and God's denial to him of the opportunity to enter the land of promise serve as warnings to Israel against carelessness or defiance in fulfilling their obligations under the *covenant.*
4.25-31 Negligence in obeying the commandments will provoke the anger of the LORD and will result in the destruction of his people. Written as a prophecy but reflecting actual historical developments, there is a reference to the exile and the dispersion of Israel, which began in the sixth century BCE. Moses tells them that *the LORD will scatter* them *among the peoples.* Their numbers will be greatly reduced and many will turn to idolatry, *serving other gods made with human hands.* In these calamitous circumstances they will turn back to *the LORD,* who *is a merciful God* and *will not forget the covenant ...that he swore to keep* with their *ancestors.* It was the return from the exile which led to the editing of these traditions in the so-called five books of Moses, Gen-Deut.
4.32-40 God's uniqueness is evident in his having *created human beings on earth,* in his having spoken directly to his people *out of a fire,* and in his having formed the nation of Israel through the process of their deliverance from Egypt. The only appropriate response to his action and the only way to sustain this special relationship is for them to *keep his statutes and commandments.*

4.6 Deut 30.19,20; 32.46,47
4.7 2 Sam 7.23; Ps 46.1; Isa 55.6
4.9 Prov 4.23; Gen 18.19; Deut 6.7; 11.19; Ps 78.5,6; Eph 6.4
4.10 Ex 19.9,16
4.11 Ex 19.18; Heb 12.18,19
4.12 Deut 5.4,22; Ex 20.22
4.13 Deut 9.9,11; Ex 34.28; 24.12; 31.18
4.16 Ex 32.7; 20.4,5; Deut 5.8
4.19 Deut 17.3; 2 Kings 17.16; Rom 1.25
4.20 1 Kings 8.51; Jer 11.4; Deut 9.29
4.21 Deut 1.37
4.22 Deut 3.25,26
4.23 ver 9,16; Ex 20.4,5
4.24 Ex 24.17; Deut 9.3; Heb 12.29; Deut 6.15
4.25 ver 16,23; 2 Kings 17.17
4.26 Deut 30.18,19
4.27 Deut 28.62,64
4.28 Deut 28.64; 1 Sam 26.19; Ps 115.4,5
4.29 Deut 30.1-3; 2 Chr 15.4; Isa 55.6,7; Jer 29.12-14
4.31 2 Chr 30.9; Ps 116.5
4.32 Deut 32.7; Gen 1.27; Deut 28.64
4.33 Ex 20.22; Deut 5.24,26
4.34 Deut 7.19; Ex 7.3; 13.3; 6.6; Deut 26.8; 34.12

4.35 Deut 32.39; 1 Sam 2.2; Isa 45.5,18; Mk 12.29
4.36 Ex 19.9,19; Heb 12.18
4.37 Deut 10.15; Ex 13.3,9,14
4.38 Deut 7.1; 9.1,4,5
4.39 ver 35; Josh 2.11
4.40 Lev 22.31; Deut 5.16,29,33; Eph 6.2,3
4.41 Num 35.6
4.46 Deut 3.29; Num 21.21-25
4.48 Deut 2.36; 3.12
5.2 Ex 19.5
5.4 Ex 19.9,19; Deut 4.33,36
5.5 Ex 20.18,21
5.6 Ex 20.2-17
5.9 Ex 34.7
5.10 Jer 32.18
5.14 Gen 2.2; Ex 16.29,30
5.15 Deut 15.16; 4.34,37

midst of another nation, by trials, by signs
and wonders, by war, by a mighty hand
and an outstretched arm, and by terrifying
displays of power, as the LORD your God did
for you in Egypt before your very eyes? [35]To
you it was shown so that you would acknowledge that the LORD is God; there is no
other besides him. [36]From heaven he made
you hear his voice to discipline you. On
earth he showed you his great fire, while
you heard his words coming out of the fire.
[37]And because he loved your ancestors, he
chose their descendants after them. He
brought you out of Egypt with his own
presence, by his great power, [38]driving out
before you nations greater and mightier
than yourselves, to bring you in, giving you
their land for a possession, as it is still today.
[39]So acknowledge today and take to heart
that the LORD is God in heaven above and
on the earth beneath; there is no other.
[40]Keep his statutes and his commandments,
which I am commanding you today for
your own well-being and that of your descendants after you, so that you may long
remain in the land that the LORD your God
is giving you for all time.

Cities of Refuge East of the Jordan

41 Then Moses set apart on the east side
of the Jordan three cities [42]to which a
homicide could flee, someone who unintentionally kills another person, the two not
having been at enmity before; the homicide
could flee to one of these cities and live:
[43]Bezer in the wilderness on the tableland
belonging to the Reubenites, Ramoth in
Gilead belonging to the Gadites, and Golan
in Bashan belonging to the Manassites.

Transition to the Second Address

44 This is the law that Moses set before
the Israelites. [45]These are the decrees and
the statutes and ordinances that Moses spoke
to the Israelites when they had come out of
Egypt, [46]beyond the Jordan in the valley
opposite Beth-peor, in the land of King Sihon
of the Amorites, who reigned at Heshbon,
whom Moses and the Israelites defeated
when they came out of Egypt. [47]They occupied his land and the land of King Og of
Bashan, the two kings of the Amorites on
the eastern side of the Jordan: [48]from Aroer,
which is on the edge of the Wadi Arnon,
as far as Mount Sirion[i] (that is, Hermon),
[49]together with all the Arabah on the east
side of the Jordan as far as the Sea of the
Arabah, under the slopes of Pisgah.

The Ten Commandments

5 Moses convened all Israel, and said to
them:
Hear, O Israel, the statutes and ordinances that I am addressing to you today;
you shall learn them and observe them
diligently. [2]The LORD our God made a covenant with us at Horeb. [3]Not with our
ancestors did the LORD make this covenant,
but with us, who are all of us here alive
today. [4]The LORD spoke with you face to face
at the mountain, out of the fire. [5](At that
time I was standing between the LORD and
you to declare to you the words[j] of the LORD;
for you were afraid because of the fire and
did not go up the mountain.) And he said:
6 I am the LORD your God, who brought
you out of the land of Egypt, out of the
house of slavery; [7]you shall have no other
gods before[k] me.
8 You shall not make for yourself an idol,
whether in the form of anything that is in
heaven above, or that is on the earth beneath, or that is in the water under the
earth. [9]You shall not bow down to them or
worship them; for I the LORD your God am
a jealous God, punishing children for the
iniquity of parents, to the third and fourth
generation of those who reject me, [10]but
showing steadfast love to the thousandth
generation[l] of those who love me and keep
my commandments.
11 You shall not make wrongful use of
the name of the LORD your God, for the LORD
will not acquit anyone who misuses his
name.
12 Observe the sabbath day and keep it
holy, as the LORD your God commanded
you. [13]Six days you shall labor and do all
your work. [14]But the seventh day is a sabbath
to the LORD your God; you shall not do any
work—you, or your son or your daughter,
or your male or female slave, or your ox or
your donkey, or any of your livestock, or
the resident alien in your towns, so that
your male and female slave may rest as well
as you. [15]Remember that you were a slave
in the land of Egypt, and the LORD your God
brought you out from there with a mighty
hand and an outstretched arm; therefore

[i] Syr: Heb *Sion* [j] Q Mss Sam Gk Syr Vg Tg: MT *word* [k] Or *besides* [l] Or *to thousands*

4.41-43 A Parenthesis on the Cities of Refuge East of the Jordan. Based on tradition found also in Num 35.9-15 and Josh 20, Israel is to provide refuge for those who have killed someone accidentally. That such a role for cities of refuge may have been established earlier than the time of the editing of Deuteronomy is suggested by the mention of two of them (Gilead, east of the Jordan, and Shechem, west of the Jordan) in the eighth century BCE prophet Hosea (Hos 6.8-9).
4.44-11.32 The Basic Principles of the Covenant.
4.44-49 Introduction to the Law. This opening section, which summarizes briefly the experience of Israel from its escape out of Egypt to the period of waiting in the region east of the Jordan in anticipation of invasion of the land of Canaan, may have been the opening section of an earlier edition of the Book of Deuteronomy. The boundaries of the promised land, which extend only as far north as Mt. Hermon on the southern border of Syria, are given here in more modest dimensions than the extension of Israel's territory to the Euphrates, as in 1.7; 11.24 (see Gen 15.18; Josh 1.4). The only explicit claim that Israel ever controlled land so far into Syria and Mesopotamia is in 1 Kings 4.24, which on other grounds is recognized as an idealized picture from after the return of Israel from the Babylonian exile in the sixth century.
5.1-21 The Deuteronomic Version of the Ten Commandments.
5.1 The principles of God's law are to be not merely preserved but learned and observed diligently.
5.2-5 The covenant is said to have been made *with us* rather than with *our ancestors*, although it was given first at Horeb forty years ago (Deut 1.3) to those who will not be allowed to enter the land. The focus on the present generation is not an historical reference to the time when the law was given, but refers to its continuing relevance and binding quality on each successive generation. The promises and obligations of the covenant are valid in perpetuity, as indicated by the promise of God's love extended *to the thousandth generation* if love and obedience are returned (5.10).
5.6-7 The first commandment is prefaced by the declaration by the LORD of who he is and what he has done, thereby establishing the special relationship between God and his people which only their obedience to the commandments will preserve. For Israel there is to be devotion to no other deity, and especially objectionable would be devotion to the Canaanite deities, male and female, who were thought to make possible the fertility of the world. Also ruled out would be alliances with other nations, which would involve acknowledgement of their deities.
5.8-9 There are to be no visible or tangible representations of the deity, since an image or an idol implies localization and control of the gods.
5.10-11 God alone upholds the covenant with his people: Israel is not to exploit the relationship by unwarranted use of God's powerful name, which is not an arbitrary title but an expression of his basic identity (Ex 3.13-15). The name possesses an inherent power, which is not to be misused or exploited, as by magicians.
5.12-15 Observance of the sabbath includes not only refraining from work – which here applies to slaves, in recollection of Israel's having been freed from slavery in Egypt – but also honoring God's holiness. (See Ex 20.8).
5.12-21 The remainder of the commandments approximate those given in Ex 20.12-17. To *honor your father and your mother* (5.16) means not merely to show respect or affection but to remain within the social and religious norms and traditions in which you were reared. *Murder* means to kill someone within the covenant community, since killing outsiders is not regarded as sinful (5.17). *Adultery* involves intercourse with a married or engaged Israelite woman, which would violate the family line and transmission of property (5.18). To *steal* probably refers to seizure of a person to be sold into slavery or held as a hostage, rather than merely taking property (5.19). *False witness* refers to giving false testimony against a fellow-Israelite (= *neighbor*). Unlike the version of this commandment in Ex 20.17, where the primary emphasis is on coveting tangible property (*house*; Ex 20.17), here the rights of women are highlighted (5.21), as elsewhere in Deuteronomy (12.12,18; 16.11, 14; 29.11). What is presented is not full equality of women with men, but a higher valuing of them, as well as holding them responsible in legal disputes (7.3; 13.6; 15.12; 17.2-5; 22.22). To *covet* involves both greedy attitude and action.

5.22-33 Moses' Role as Mediator and Instructor in the Law. Highlighted again is Moses' unique role as the one with access to God's presence. The people promise to listen, and are enjoined to *follow exactly and completely* the commandments of God if they are to enjoy long life in the land.
6.1-8 Expanding on the tradition in Ex 20.18-21, there is emphasis here on the importance of instructing children – now and in successive generations – in God's commands if the people are to survive and flourish in the land. These instructions are followed by a liturgical formula enjoining total love and obedience (6.5-6), and are to be reinforced by reciting and discussing them with offspring, and by symbolic display of these documents on hands (instruments of work and activity), on the forehead (instrument of thought and vision), and on doorposts and gates (symbols of daily movement in and out of one's house). How this symbolism was initially carried out cannot be determined (Ex 13.4-16), but in the late post-exilic period these instructions were taken literally in the form of containers with verses of scripture written on bits of parchment (Deut 6.4-9; 11.13-21) affixed to foreheads and doorposts known in later times as phylacteries (Mt 23.5) and *mezuzoth*.
6.10-25 Here a warning is given against allowing the affluence of the new land to cause God's people to forget how God has delivered them from slavery in order to *give* them the land with its resources that they did not develop, and thus to be lured into worshiping the local deities and so inviting destruction. Instead as they *occupy the good land* they are to recall their origins and tell about them to their children, as well as to convey to them what God's expectations are of his people, if they are to *be in the right* with the LORD their God.

the LORD your God commanded you to keep the sabbath day.

16 Honor your father and your mother, as the LORD your God commanded you, so that your days may be long and that it may go well with you in the land that the LORD your God is giving you.

17 You shall not murder.[m]

18 Neither shall you commit adultery.

19 Neither shall you steal.

20 Neither shall you bear false witness against your neighbor.

21 Neither shall you covet your neighbor's wife.

Neither shall you desire your neighbor's house, or field, or male or female slave, or ox, or donkey, or anything that belongs to your neighbor.

Moses the Mediator of God's Will

22 These words the LORD spoke with a loud voice to your whole assembly at the mountain, out of the fire, the cloud, and the thick darkness, and he added no more. He wrote them on two stone tablets, and gave them to me. [23]When you heard the voice out of the darkness, while the mountain was burning with fire, you approached me, all the heads of your tribes and your elders; [24]and you said, "Look, the LORD our God has shown us his glory and greatness, and we have heard his voice out of the fire. Today we have seen that God may speak to someone and the person may still live. [25]So now why should we die? For this great fire will consume us; if we hear the voice of the LORD our God any longer, we shall die. [26]For who is there of all flesh that has heard the voice of the living God speaking out of fire, as we have, and remained alive? [27]Go near, you yourself, and hear all that the LORD our God will say. Then tell us everything that the LORD our God tells you, and we will listen and do it."

28 The LORD heard your words when you spoke to me, and the LORD said to me: "I have heard the words of this people, which they have spoken to you; they are right in all that they have spoken. [29]If only they had such a mind as this, to fear me and to keep all my commandments always, so that it might go well with them and with their children forever! [30]Go say to them, 'Return to your tents.' [31]But you, stand here by me, and I will tell you all the commandments, the statutes and the ordinances, that you shall teach them, so that they may do them in the land that I am giving them to possess." [32]You must therefore be careful to do as the LORD your God has commanded you; you shall not turn to the right or to the left. [33]You must follow exactly the path that the LORD your God has commanded you, so that you may live, and that it may go well with you, and that you may live long in the land that you are to possess.

The Great Commandment

6 Now this is the commandment—the statutes and the ordinances—that the LORD your God charged me to teach you to observe in the land that you are about to cross into and occupy, [2]so that you and your children and your children's children may fear the LORD your God all the days of your life, and keep all his decrees and his commandments that I am commanding you, so that your days may be long. [3]Hear therefore, O Israel, and observe them diligently, so that it may go well with you, and so that you may multiply greatly in a land flowing with milk and honey, as the LORD, the God of your ancestors, has promised you.

4 Hear, O Israel: The LORD is our God, the LORD alone.[n] [5]You shall love the LORD your God with all your heart, and with all your soul, and with all your might. [6]Keep these words that I am commanding you today in your heart. [7]Recite them to your children and talk about them when you are at home and when you are away, when you lie down and when you rise. [8]Bind them as a sign on your hand, fix them as an emblem[o] on your forehead, [9]and write them on the doorposts of your house and on your gates.

Caution against Disobedience

10 When the LORD your God has brought you into the land that he swore to your ancestors, to Abraham, to Isaac, and to Jacob, to give you—a land with fine, large cities that you did not build, [11]houses filled with all sorts of goods that you did not fill, hewn cisterns that you did not hew, vineyards and olive groves that you did not plant—and when you have eaten your fill, [12]take care that you do not forget the LORD,

[m] Or *kill* [n] Or *The LORD our God is one LORD,* or *The LORD our God, the LORD is one,* or *The LORD is our God, the LORD is one* [o] Or *as a frontlet*

5.21 Rom 7.7; 13.9
5.22 Ex 31.18; Deut 4.13
5.24 Ex 19.19
5.25 Deut 18.16
5.26 Deut 4.33
5.28 Deut 18.17
5.29 Ps 81.13; Isa 48.18; Deut 4.40
5.31 Ex 24.12
5.32 Deut 17.20; 28.14; Josh 1.7; 23.6
5.33 Deut 4.40
6.2 Ex 20.20; Deut 10.12,13
6.3 Deut 5.33; Gen 15.5; Ex 3.8
6.4 Mk 12.29,32; Jn 17.3; 1 Cor 8.4,6
6.5 Deut 10.12; Mt 22.37; Lk 10.27
6.7 Deut 4.9; Eph 6.4
6.8 Ex 13.9,16; Deut 11.18
6.9 Deut 11.20
6.10 Deut 9.1; Josh 24.13
6.11 Deut 8.10

who brought you out of the land of Egypt, out of the house of slavery. [13]The LORD your God you shall fear; him you shall serve, and by his name alone you shall swear. [14]Do not follow other gods, any of the gods of the peoples who are all around you, [15]because the LORD your God, who is present with you, is a jealous God. The anger of the LORD your God would be kindled against you and he would destroy you from the face of the earth.

16 Do not put the LORD your God to the test, as you tested him at Massah. [17]You must diligently keep the commandments of the LORD your God, and his decrees, and his statutes that he has commanded you. [18]Do what is right and good in the sight of the LORD, so that it may go well with you, and so that you may go in and occupy the good land that the LORD swore to your ancestors to give you, [19]thrusting out all your enemies from before you, as the LORD has promised.

20 When your children ask you in time to come, "What is the meaning of the decrees and the statutes and the ordinances that the LORD our God has commanded you?" [21]then you shall say to your children, "We were Pharaoh's slaves in Egypt, but the LORD brought us out of Egypt with a mighty hand. [22]The LORD displayed before our eyes great and awesome signs and wonders against Egypt, against Pharaoh and all his household. [23]He brought us out from there in order to bring us in, to give us the land that he promised on oath to our ancestors. [24]Then the LORD commanded us to observe all these statutes, to fear the LORD our God, for our lasting good, so as to keep us alive, as is now the case. [25]If we diligently observe this entire commandment before the LORD our God, as he has commanded us, we will be in the right."

A Chosen People

7 When the LORD your God brings you into the land that you are about to enter and occupy, and he clears away many nations before you—the Hittites, the Girgashites, the Amorites, the Canaanites, the Perizzites, the Hivites, and the Jebusites, seven nations mightier and more numerous than you— [2]and when the LORD your God gives them over to you and you defeat them, then you must utterly destroy them. Make no covenant with them and show them no mercy. [3]Do not intermarry with them, giving your daughters to their sons or taking their daughters for your sons, [4]for that would turn away your children from following me, to serve other gods. Then the anger of the LORD would be kindled against you, and he would destroy you quickly. [5]But this is how you must deal with them: break down their altars, smash their pillars, hew down their sacred poles,[p] and burn their idols with fire. [6]For you are a people holy to the LORD your God; the LORD your God has chosen you out of all the peoples on earth to be his people, his treasured possession.

7 It was not because you were more numerous than any other people that the LORD set his heart on you and chose you—for you were the fewest of all peoples. [8]It was because the LORD loved you and kept the oath that he swore to your ancestors, that the LORD has brought you out with a mighty hand, and redeemed you from the house of slavery, from the hand of Pharaoh king of Egypt. [9]Know therefore that the LORD your God is God, the faithful God who maintains covenant loyalty with those who love him and keep his commandments, to a thousand generations, [10]and who repays in their own person those who reject him. He does not delay but repays in their own person those who reject him. [11]Therefore, observe diligently the commandment—the statutes, and the ordinances—that I am commanding you today.

Blessings for Obedience

12 If you heed these ordinances, by diligently observing them, the LORD your God will maintain with you the covenant loyalty that he swore to your ancestors; [13]he will love you, bless you, and multiply you; he will bless the fruit of your womb and the fruit of your ground, your grain and your wine and your oil, the increase of your cattle and the issue of your flock, in the land that he swore to your ancestors to give you. [14]You shall be the most blessed of peoples, with neither sterility nor barrenness among you or your livestock. [15]The LORD will turn away from you every illness; all the dread diseases of Egypt that you experienced, he will not inflict on you, but he will lay them on all who hate you. [16]You shall devour all the peoples that the LORD

[p] Heb *Asherim*

6.13 Deut 10.20
6.15 Deut 4.24
6.16 Mt 4.7; Ex 17.2,7
6.17 Deut 11.22
6.18 Deut 4.40
6.20 Ex 13.14
6.24 Deut 10.12
6.25 Deut 24.13
7.1 Deut 31.3; Acts 13.19
7.2 Ex 23.32; Deut 13.8
7.3 Ex 34.15,16
7.4 Deut 6.15
7.5 Ex 23.24
7.6 Ex 19.5,6; Deut 14.2
7.7 Deut 10.22
7.8 Deut 10.15; Ex 32.13; 13.3,14
7.9 Deut 4.35,39; Neh 1.5
7.12 Lev 26.3; Deut 28.1; Ps 105.8,9
7.13 Deut 28.4
7.14 Ex 23.26
7.15 Ex 15.26
7.16 ver 2; Ex 23.33

7.1-11.32 The Unique Relationship of Israel with her God: the Consequences of Obedience and Disobedience.
7.1-6 On entering the land, Israel is to destroy *utterly* those living there, avoiding any covenantal or marital connections. They are to *smash* all traces of idolatrous worship, including the sacred pillars (symbols of male fertility) and the centers of worship of the local fertility deities. God's people alone are *holy...chosen...treasured* in God's sight.
7.7-11 This new people's place of special favor with God is based on his having *loved* them and *kept the oath* that he made with their *ancestors*, a love manifest in his having brought them up out of Egypt. The only appropriate response to these actions and to his maintenance of *covenant loyalty* is for them to *keep his commandments* and to do so throughout *a thousand [successive] generations*.
7.12-26 The Consequence of Obedience. Obeying the ordinances will lead to God's continued prospering of them, multiplying their offspring, guarding them from illness, and bringing disaster on their enemies. The pace of these beneficial changes will not be too fast, lest the *wild animals* should multiply too fast when their human predators are gone (8.22). But pestilence will overtake the present occupants of the land, and in warfare they will be defeated and their idolatrous images destroyed. All contact with these religious objects is to be avoided.

8.1-20 The Consequences of Disobedience. After God has brought Israel through the wilderness, *feeding* them *with manna* and safeguarding them, they should not forget him when they enter these prosperous lands that he promised to give them, where they *will lack nothing.* Care must be taken continually to obey God's commands, so that he will *confirm his covenant that he swore to their ancestors.* Otherwise they will perish, just like the nations that God destroyed before them as he prepared them to enter the land.

your God is giving over to you, showing them no pity; you shall not serve their gods, for that would be a snare to you.

17 If you say to yourself, "These nations are more numerous than I; how can I dispossess them?" [18]do not be afraid of them. Just remember what the LORD your God did to Pharaoh and to all Egypt, [19]the great trials that your eyes saw, the signs and wonders, the mighty hand and the outstretched arm by which the LORD your God brought you out. The LORD your God will do the same to all the peoples of whom you are afraid. [20]Moreover, the LORD your God will send the pestilence[q] against them, until even the survivors and the fugitives are destroyed. [21]Have no dread of them, for the LORD your God, who is present with you, is a great and awesome God. [22]The LORD your God will clear away these nations before you little by little; you will not be able to make a quick end of them, otherwise the wild animals would become too numerous for you. [23]But the LORD your God will give them over to you, and throw them into great panic, until they are destroyed. [24]He will hand their kings over to you and you shall blot out their name from under heaven; no one will be able to stand against you, until you have destroyed them. [25]The images of their gods you shall burn with fire. Do not covet the silver or the gold that is on them and take it for yourself, because you could be ensnared by it; for it is abhorrent to the LORD your God. [26]Do not bring an abhorrent thing into your house, or you will be set apart for destruction like it. You must utterly detest and abhor it, for it is set apart for destruction.

A Warning Not to Forget God in Prosperity

8 This entire commandment that I command you today you must diligently observe, so that you may live and increase, and go in and occupy the land that the LORD promised on oath to your ancestors. [2]Remember the long way that the LORD your God has led you these forty years in the wilderness, in order to humble you, testing you to know what was in your heart, whether or not you would keep his commandments. [3]He humbled you by letting you hunger, then by feeding you with manna, with which neither you nor your ancestors were acquainted, in order to make you understand that one does not live by bread alone, but by every word that comes from the mouth of the LORD.[r] [4]The clothes on your back did not wear out and your feet did not swell these forty years. [5]Know then in your heart that as a parent disciplines a child so the LORD your God disciplines you. [6]Therefore keep the commandments of the LORD your God, by walking in his ways and by fearing him. [7]For the LORD your God is bringing you into a good land, a land with flowing streams, with springs and underground waters welling up in valleys and hills, [8]a land of wheat and barley, of vines and fig trees and pomegranates, a land of olive trees and honey, [9]a land where you may eat bread without scarcity, where you will lack nothing, a land whose stones are iron and from whose hills you may mine copper. [10]You shall eat your fill and bless the LORD your God for the good land that he has given you.

11 Take care that you do not forget the LORD your God, by failing to keep his commandments, his ordinances, and his statutes, which I am commanding you today. [12]When you have eaten your fill and have built fine houses and live in them, [13]and when your herds and flocks have multiplied, and your silver and gold is multiplied, and all that you have is multiplied, [14]then do not exalt yourself, forgetting the LORD your God, who brought you out of the land of Egypt, out of the house of slavery, [15]who led you through the great and terrible wilderness, an arid wasteland with poisonous[s] snakes and scorpions. He made water flow for you from flint rock, [16]and fed you in the wilderness with manna that your ancestors did not know, to humble you and to test you, and in the end to do you good. [17]Do not say to yourself, "My power and the might of my own hand have gotten me this wealth." [18]But remember the LORD your God, for it is he who gives you power to get wealth, so that he may confirm his covenant that he swore to your ancestors, as he is doing today. [19]If you do forget the LORD your God and follow other gods to serve and worship them, I solemnly warn you today that you shall surely perish. [20]Like the nations that the LORD is destroying before you, so shall you perish, because you would not obey the voice of the LORD your God.

[q] Or *hornets*: Meaning of Heb uncertain [r] Or *by anything that the LORD decrees* [s] Or *fiery*; Heb *seraph*

7.18 Deut 31.6
7.19 Deut 4.34
7.20 Ex 23.28; Josh 24.12
7.21 Deut 10.17
7.22 Ex 23.29,30
7.24 ver 16
7.25 1 Chr 14.12; Josh 7.1,21; Judg 8.27
8.1 Deut 4.1
8.2 Deut 29.5; 13.3
8.3 Ex 16.2,3,12,14, 35; Mt 4.4; Lk 4.7
8.4 Deut 29.5
8.5 Prov 3.12; Heb 12.5,6
8.6 Deut 5.33
8.7 Deut 11.10-12
8.10 Deut 6.11,12
8.14 Ps 106.21
8.15 Num 21.6; 20.11; Ps 78.15; 114.8
8.16 ver 2,3; Ex 16.15
8.18 Prov 10.22; Hos 2.8
8.19 Deut 4.26; 30.18

The Consequences of Rebelling against God

9 Hear, O Israel! You are about to cross
the Jordan today, to go in and dispossess nations larger and mightier than you,
great cities, fortified to the heavens, [2]a strong
and tall people, the offspring of the Anakim,
whom you know. You have heard it said of
them, "Who can stand up to the Anakim?"
[3]Know then today that the LORD your God
is the one who crosses over before you as
a devouring fire; he will defeat them and
subdue them before you, so that you may
dispossess and destroy them quickly, as the
LORD has promised you.
4 When the LORD your God thrusts them
out before you, do not say to yourself, "It
is because of my righteousness that the LORD
has brought me in to occupy this land"; it
is rather because of the wickedness of these
nations that the LORD is dispossessing them
before you. [5]It is not because of your righteousness or the uprightness of your heart
that you are going in to occupy their land;
but because of the wickedness of these
nations the LORD your God is dispossessing
them before you, in order to fulfill the promise that the LORD made on oath to your
ancestors, to Abraham, to Isaac, and to
Jacob.
6 Know, then, that the LORD your God is
not giving you this good land to occupy
because of your righteousness; for you are
a stubborn people. [7]Remember and do not
forget how you provoked the LORD your God
to wrath in the wilderness; you have been
rebellious against the LORD from the day you
came out of the land of Egypt until you
came to this place.
8 Even at Horeb you provoked the LORD
to wrath, and the LORD was so angry with
you that he was ready to destroy you.
[9]When I went up the mountain to receive
the stone tablets, the tablets of the covenant
that the LORD made with you, I remained on
the mountain forty days and forty nights;
I neither ate bread nor drank water. [10]And
the LORD gave me the two stone tablets
written with the finger of God; on them
were all the words that the LORD had spoken
to you at the mountain out of the fire on
the day of the assembly. [11]At the end of
forty days and forty nights the LORD gave
me the two stone tablets, the tablets of the
covenant. [12]Then the LORD said to me, "Get
up, go down quickly from here, for your
people whom you have brought from Egypt
have acted corruptly. They have been quick
to turn from the way that I commanded
them; they have cast an image for themselves." [13]Furthermore the LORD said to me,
"I have seen that this people is indeed a
stubborn people. [14]Let me alone that I may
destroy them and blot out their name from
under heaven; and I will make of you a
nation mightier and more numerous than
they."
15 So I turned and went down from the
mountain, while the mountain was ablaze;
the two tablets of the covenant were in my
two hands. [16]Then I saw that you had
indeed sinned against the LORD your God, by
casting for yourselves an image of a calf;
you had been quick to turn from the way
that the LORD had commanded you. [17]So I
took hold of the two tablets and flung them
from my two hands, smashing them before
your eyes. [18]Then I lay prostrate before the
LORD as before, forty days and forty nights;
I neither ate bread nor drank water, because of all the sin you had committed,
provoking the LORD by doing what was evil
in his sight. [19]For I was afraid that the
anger that the LORD bore against you was
so fierce that he would destroy you. But the
LORD listened to me that time also. [20]The
LORD was so angry with Aaron that he was
ready to destroy him, but I interceded also
on behalf of Aaron at that same time. [21]Then
I took the sinful thing you had made, the
calf, and burned it with fire and crushed it,
grinding it thoroughly, until it was reduced
to dust; and I threw the dust of it into the
stream that runs down the mountain.
22 At Taberah also, and at Massah, and
at Kibroth-hattaavah, you provoked the LORD
to wrath. [23]And when the LORD sent you
from Kadesh-barnea, saying, "Go up and
occupy the land that I have given you," you
rebelled against the command of the LORD
your God, neither trusting him nor obeying
him. [24]You have been rebellious against the
LORD as long as he has[t] known you.
25 Throughout the forty days and forty
nights that I lay prostrate before the LORD
when the LORD intended to destroy you, [26]I
prayed to the LORD and said, "Lord GOD, do
not destroy the people who are your very
own possession, whom you redeemed in
your greatness, whom you brought out of
Egypt with a mighty hand. [27]Remember
your servants, Abraham, Isaac, and Jacob;
pay no attention to the stubbornness of this

[t] Sam Gk: MT *I have*

9.1 Deut 11.31
9.2 Num 13.22,28,32, 33
9.3 Deut 31.3; 4.24; 7.23,24
9.4 Deut 8.17; 18.12; Lev 18.24,25
9.5 Gen 12.7
9.6 ver 13; Ex 32.9; Deut 31.27
9.8 Ex 32.7-10
9.9 Ex 24.12,15,18
9.10 Ex 31.18; Deut 4.13
9.12 Ex 32.7,8; Deut 31.29
9.13 Ex 32.9; ver 6
9.14 Ex 32.10; Deut 29.20; Num 14.12
9.15 Ex 32.15-19; 19.18
9.16 Ex 32.19
9.18 Ex 34.28
9.19 Ex 32.10-14
9.21 Ex 32.20
9.22 Num 11.3,34; Ex 17.7
9.24 ver 7; Deut 31.27
9.25 ver 18
9.26 Ex 32.11-13

9.1-10.5 The Earlier Pattern of Disobedience. Here is rehearsed again what God did in bringing the people to the edge of the land, combined with a warning against the assumption that their new status will be the result of their own *uprightness of heart* (9.5). Moses recalls the series of rebellions against God from Horeb to Kadesh-Barnea, and how it was his own intercession with the LORD and his destruction of the *image of a calf* that preserved them from destruction. Again, when they were on the way to the promised land and had become rebellious yet once more, Moses reminded God of his promises to the patriarchs, *Abraham, Isaac and Jacob*, and of the bad reputation the LORD would gain among other nations for his seeming failure to fulfill his promise to Israel (9.13-28). He described them to the LORD as *the people of your very own possession*, with the result that God gave Israel a second chance to live as his people by preparing for them a second copy of the basic laws written on the *tablets of stone*, which were then placed *in the ark*.

10.6-9 The Role of the Levites. With the death of Aaron and the accession of his son Eleazar to the office of high priest, the Levites assume the full priestly role, which contrasts with their limited functions *(chores)* described in Ezek 44.10-14.
10.10-11 Moses is instructed to resume his task of instructing the people so that they will be ready to *go in and occupy the land.*
10.12-11.31 A Summary of the Covenant Relationship. This section seems to reflect a later stage of editing of Deuteronomy, with repetitions and additions throughout. The basic themes are that God is owner and controller of the universe (10.14), and that Israel is to serve him and keep his commandments. Emphasis is on divine love as well as divine power (10.17-19), to which the appropriate human response is love, compassion and obedience (10.20).
11.1-32 Love and obedience to his commands are the way to show gratitude for God's actions in defeating Israel's enemies and in delivering his people from Egypt (11.1-7). Keeping his commandments will result in his prospering their crops (11.8-13), but if they serve other gods, his anger will result in the closing of the heavens and the failure of their crops (11.16-17). The instructions are expanded from 6.8 about wearing visible signs of obedience to God's commandments (11.18-20). Observing God's laws will result in his expulsion of the nations from the promised land and the extension of their borders in the north from the Euphrates to the Mediterranean (*Western Sea*), which is a territory never actually controlled by Israel. Worship of God in the new land will center on *Mount Gerizim*, which rises above Shechem and is across the valley from *Mount Ebal* (11.26). Lack of reference to the Jerusalem temple suggests that the editor of Deuteronomy is here drawing on a northern tradition which located the center of the worship of Yahweh there in Shechem, as in Josh 24. The section closes with another appeal to obey the commandments on entering the land (11.31-32).

people, their wickedness and their sin, 28otherwise the land from which you have brought us might say, 'Because the LORD was not able to bring them into the land that he promised them, and because he hated them, he has brought them out to let them die in the wilderness.' 29For they are the people of your very own possession, whom you brought out by your great power and by your outstretched arm."

The Second Pair of Tablets

10 At that time the LORD said to me, "Carve out two tablets of stone like the former ones, and come up to me on the mountain, and make an ark of wood. 2I will write on the tablets the words that were on the former tablets, which you smashed, and you shall put them in the ark." 3So I made an ark of acacia wood, cut two tablets of stone like the former ones, and went up the mountain with the two tablets in my hand. 4Then he wrote on the tablets the same words as before, the ten commandments[u] that the LORD had spoken to you on the mountain out of the fire on the day of the assembly; and the LORD gave them to me. 5So I turned and came down from the mountain, and put the tablets in the ark that I had made; and there they are, as the LORD commanded me.

6 (The Israelites journeyed from Beeroth-bene-jaakan[v] to Moserah. There Aaron died, and there he was buried; his son Eleazar succeeded him as priest. 7From there they journeyed to Gudgodah, and from Gudgodah to Jotbathah, a land with flowing streams. 8At that time the LORD set apart the tribe of Levi to carry the ark of the covenant of the LORD, to stand before the LORD to minister to him, and to bless in his name, to this day. 9Therefore Levi has no allotment or inheritance with his kindred; the LORD is his inheritance, as the LORD your God promised him.)

10 I stayed on the mountain forty days and forty nights, as I had done the first time. And once again the LORD listened to me. The LORD was unwilling to destroy you. 11The LORD said to me, "Get up, go on your journey at the head of the people, that they may go in and occupy the land that I swore to their ancestors to give them."

The Essence of the Law

12 So now, O Israel, what does the LORD your God require of you? Only to fear the LORD your God, to walk in all his ways, to love him, to serve the LORD your God with all your heart and with all your soul, 13and to keep the commandments of the LORD your God[w] and his decrees that I am commanding you today, for your own well-being. 14Although heaven and the heaven of heavens belong to the LORD your God, the earth with all that is in it, 15yet the LORD set his heart in love on your ancestors alone and chose you, their descendants after them, out of all the peoples, as it is today. 16Circumcise, then, the foreskin of your heart, and do not be stubborn any longer. 17For the LORD your God is God of gods and Lord of lords, the great God, mighty and awesome, who is not partial and takes no bribe, 18who executes justice for the orphan and the widow, and who loves the strangers, providing them food and clothing. 19You shall also love the stranger, for you were strangers in the land of Egypt. 20You shall fear the LORD your God; him alone you shall worship; to him you shall hold fast, and by his name you shall swear. 21He is your praise; he is your God, who has done for you these great and awesome things that your own eyes have seen. 22Your ancestors went down to Egypt seventy persons; and now the LORD your God has made you as numerous as the stars in heaven.

Rewards for Obedience

11 You shall love the LORD your God, therefore, and keep his charge, his decrees, his ordinances, and his commandments always. 2Remember today that it was not your children (who have not known or seen the discipline of the LORD your God), but it is you who must acknowledge his greatness, his mighty hand and his outstretched arm, 3his signs and his deeds that he did in Egypt to Pharaoh, the king of Egypt, and to all his land; 4what he did to the Egyptian army, to their horses and chariots, how he made the water of the Red Sea[x] flow over them as they pursued you, so that the LORD has destroyed them to this day; 5what he did to you in the wilderness, until you came to this place; 6and what he

[u] Heb *the ten words* [v] Or *the wells of the Bene-jaakan* [w] Q Ms Gk Syr: MT lacks *your God* [x] Or *Sea of Reeds*

9.29 Deut 4.34
10.1 Ex 34.1,2; 25.10
10.2 Deut 4.13; Ex 25.16,21
10.3 Ex 37.1; 34.4
10.4 Ex 20.1
10.5 Ex 40.20
10.6 Num 33.30,31,38
10.7 Num 33.32-34
10.8 Num 3.6; 4.15; Deut 18.5; 21.5
10.9 Num 18.20,24
10.10 Deut 9.18,25; Ex 33.17
10.12 Mic 6.8; Deut 6.13; 5.33; 6.5
10.14 1 Kings 8.27; Ex 19.5
10.15 Deut 4.37
10.16 Jer 4.4; Deut 9.6
10.17 Josh 22.22; Rev 19.16; Acts 10.34
10.18 Ps 68.5
10.19 Lev 19.34
10.20 Mt 4.10; Deut 11.22; Ps 63.11
10.21 Ex 15.2; Ps 106.21,22
10.22 Gen 46.27; Deut 1.10
11.1 Deut 10.12; Zech 3.7
11.2 Deut 8.5; 5.24
11.4 Ex 14.27,28
11.6 Num 16.31-33

did to Dathan and Abiram, sons of Eliab son of Reuben, how in the midst of all Israel the earth opened its mouth and swallowed them up, along with their households, their tents, and every living being in their company; [7]for it is your own eyes that have seen every great deed that the LORD did.

8 Keep, then, this entire commandment that I am commanding you today, so that you may have strength to go in and occupy the land that you are crossing over to occupy, [9]and so that you may live long in the land that the LORD swore to your ancestors to give them and to their descendants, a land flowing with milk and honey. [10]For the land that you are about to enter to occupy is not like the land of Egypt, from which you have come, where you sow your seed and irrigate by foot like a vegetable garden. [11]But the land that you are crossing over to occupy is a land of hills and valleys, watered by rain from the sky, [12]a land that the LORD your God looks after. The eyes of the LORD your God are always on it, from the beginning of the year to the end of the year.

13 If you will only heed his every commandment[y] that I am commanding you today—loving the LORD your God, and serving him with all your heart and with all your soul— [14]then he[z] will give the rain for your land in its season, the early rain and the later rain, and you will gather in your grain, your wine, and your oil; [15]and he[z] will give grass in your fields for your livestock, and you will eat your fill. [16]Take care, or you will be seduced into turning away, serving other gods and worshiping them, [17]for then the anger of the LORD will be kindled against you and he will shut up the heavens, so that there will be no rain and the land will yield no fruit; then you will perish quickly off the good land that the LORD is giving you.

18 You shall put these words of mine in your heart and soul, and you shall bind them as a sign on your hand, and fix them as an emblem[a] on your forehead. [19]Teach them to your children, talking about them when you are at home and when you are away, when you lie down and when you rise. [20]Write them on the doorposts of your house and on your gates, [21]so that your days and the days of your children may be multiplied in the land that the LORD swore to your ancestors to give them, as long as the heavens are above the earth.

22 If you will diligently observe this entire commandment that I am commanding you, loving the LORD your God, walking in all his ways, and holding fast to him, [23]then the LORD will drive out all these nations before you, and you will dispossess nations larger and mightier than yourselves. [24]Every place on which you set foot shall be yours; your territory shall extend from the wilderness to the Lebanon and from the River, the river Euphrates, to the Western Sea. [25]No one will be able to stand against you; the LORD your God will put the fear and dread of you on all the land on which you set foot, as he promised you.

26 See, I am setting before you today a blessing and a curse: [27]the blessing, if you obey the commandments of the LORD your God that I am commanding you today; [28]and the curse, if you do not obey the commandments of the LORD your God, but turn from the way that I am commanding you today, to follow other gods that you have not known.

29 When the LORD your God has brought you into the land that you are entering to occupy, you shall set the blessing on Mount Gerizim and the curse on Mount Ebal. [30]As you know, they are beyond the Jordan, some distance to the west, in the land of the Canaanites who live in the Arabah, opposite Gilgal, beside the oak[b] of Moreh.

31 When you cross the Jordan to go in to occupy the land that the LORD your God is giving you, and when you occupy it and live in it, [32]you must diligently observe all the statutes and ordinances that I am setting before you today.

Pagan Shrines to Be Destroyed

12 These are the statutes and ordinances that you must diligently observe in the land that the LORD, the God of your ancestors, has given you to occupy all the days that you live on the earth.

2 You must demolish completely all the places where the nations whom you are about to dispossess served their gods, on the mountain heights, on the hills, and under every leafy tree. [3]Break down their altars, smash their pillars, burn their sacred poles[c] with fire, and hew down the idols of their

[y] Compare Gk: Heb *my commandments* [z] Sam Gk Vg: MT *I* [a] Or *as a frontlet* [b] Gk Syr: Compare Gen 12.6; Heb *oaks* or *terebinths* [c] Heb *Asherim*

11.8 Josh 1.6,7
11.9 Deut 4.40; 9.5; Ex 3.8
11.11 Deut 8.7
11.13 ver 22; Deut 6.17; 10.12
11.14 Deut 28.12; Joel 2.23
11.15 Deut 6.11
11.16 Deut 29.18; 8.19
11.17 Deut 6.15; 1 Kings 8.35; Deut 4.26
11.18 Deut 6.6,8
11.19 Deut 4.9,10; 6.7
11.20 Deut 6.9
11.22 Deut 6.17; 10.20
11.23 Deut 9.1,5
11.24 Josh 1.3; Gen 15.18; Ex 23.31
11.25 Deut 7.24; Ex 23.27
11.26 Deut 30.1,19
11.27 Deut 28.3
11.28 Deut 28.15
11.29 Deut 27.12; Josh 8.33
11.30 Josh 4.19; Gen 12.6
11.31 Deut 9.1; Josh 1.11
12.1 Deut 4.9,10
12.3 Deut 7.5

12.1-26.15 The Main Body of Deuteronomic Law.
12.1 The enduring force of God's commandments introduces the detailed instructions for a variety of situations.
12.2-28 Worship is to Be Only at the Central Shrine. The existence in the land of multiple pagan shrines, altars, idols, and other objects devoted to the local deities is not to be tolerated: they must be utterly destroyed (12.2-4). Instead, God will choose one place for the presentation of offerings and gifts and for eating special sacred meals in the presence of the LORD.

12.12 Full participation in these joyous ceremonies is open to both male and female members of the wider community. The emphasis here is on the gathering of the worshippers rather than on the priestly functions, as in Leviticus and Numbers. Details for the presentation of offerings and the eating of the special meals are given (12.13-27), but it is specified that regular meals may be eaten anywhere, so long as there is avoidance of contact with the blood. These instructions are to be passed on to successive generations of children (12.28).
12.29-14.2 Warnings against Enticement to Participate in Pagan Worship. The first warning is against imitating the present occupants of the land in their worship of the local gods, and especially in their offering their children as human sacrifices (12.29-32).

gods, and thus blot out their name from their places. 4 You shall not worship the LORD your God in such ways. 5 But you shall seek the place that the LORD your God will choose out of all your tribes as his habitation to put his name there. You shall go there, 6 bringing there your burnt offerings and your sacrifices, your tithes and your donations, your votive gifts, your freewill offerings, and the firstlings of your herds and flocks. 7 And you shall eat there in the presence of the LORD your God, you and your households together, rejoicing in all the undertakings in which the LORD your God has blessed you.

8 You shall not act as we are acting here today, all of us according to our own desires, 9 for you have not yet come into the rest and the possession that the LORD your God is giving you. 10 When you cross over the Jordan and live in the land that the LORD your God is allotting to you, and when he gives you rest from your enemies all around so that you live in safety, 11 then you shall bring everything that I command you to the place that the LORD your God will choose as a dwelling for his name: your burnt offerings and your sacrifices, your tithes and your donations, and all your choice votive gifts that you vow to the LORD. 12 And you shall rejoice before the LORD your God, you together with your sons and your daughters, your male and female slaves, and the Levites who reside in your towns (since they have no allotment or inheritance with you).

A Prescribed Place of Worship

13 Take care that you do not offer your burnt offerings at any place you happen to see. 14 But only at the place that the LORD will choose in one of your tribes—there you shall offer your burnt offerings and there you shall do everything I command you.

15 Yet whenever you desire you may slaughter and eat meat within any of your towns, according to the blessing that the LORD your God has given you; the unclean and the clean may eat of it, as they would of gazelle or deer. 16 The blood, however, you must not eat; you shall pour it out on the ground like water. 17 Nor may you eat within your towns the tithe of your grain, your wine, and your oil, the firstlings of your herds and your flocks, any of your votive gifts that you vow, your freewill offerings, or your donations; 18 these you shall eat in the presence of the LORD your God at the place that the LORD your God will choose, you together with your son and your daughter, your male and female slaves, and the Levites resident in your towns, rejoicing in the presence of the LORD your God in all your undertakings. 19 Take care that you do not neglect the Levite as long as you live in your land.

20 When the LORD your God enlarges your territory, as he has promised you, and you say, "I am going to eat some meat," because you wish to eat meat, you may eat meat whenever you have the desire. 21 If the place where the LORD your God will choose to put his name is too far from you, and you slaughter as I have commanded you any of your herd or flock that the LORD has given you, then you may eat within your towns whenever you desire. 22 Indeed, just as gazelle or deer is eaten, so you may eat it; the unclean and the clean alike may eat it. 23 Only be sure that you do not eat the blood; for the blood is the life, and you shall not eat the life with the meat. 24 Do not eat it; you shall pour it out on the ground like water. 25 Do not eat it, so that all may go well with you and your children after you, because you do what is right in the sight of the LORD. 26 But the sacred donations that are due from you, and your votive gifts, you shall bring to the place that the LORD will choose. 27 You shall present your burnt offerings, both the meat and the blood, on the altar of the LORD your God; the blood of your other sacrifices shall be poured out beside[d] the altar of the LORD your God, but the meat you may eat.

28 Be careful to obey all these words that I command you today,[e] so that it may go well with you and with your children after you forever, because you will be doing what is good and right in the sight of the LORD your God.

Warning against Idolatry

29 When the LORD your God has cut off before you the nations whom you are about to enter to dispossess them, when you have dispossessed them and live in their land, 30 take care that you are not snared into imitating them, after they have been destroyed before you: do not inquire concern-

12.5 ver 11
12.7 Deut 14.26; ver 12.18
12.10 Deut 11.31
12.11 ver 5
12.12 ver 7; Deut 10.9
12.14 ver 11
12.15 ver 20-23; Deut 14.5
12.16 Lev 17.10-12
12.18 ver 5,7,12
12.19 Deut 14.27
12.20 Gen 15.18
12.22 ver 15
12.23 ver 16; Lev 17.11,14
12.25 Deut 4.40; 13.18
12.26 ver 17
12.28 ver 25; Deut 4.40

[d] Or *on* [e] Gk Sam Syr: MT lacks *today*

12.31 Deut 9.5; 18.10
12.32 Deut 4.32
13.1 Mt 24.24; Mk 13.22
13.2 ver 6,13
13.3 Deut 8.2,16
13.4 2 Kings 23.3; Deut 10.20
13.5 Deut 18.20; 17.7
13.6 Deut 17.2-7; 29.18
13.9 Deut 17.5,7
13.11 Deut 19.20
13.13 ver 2,6; see 1 Jn 2.19
13.15 Ex 22.20
13.16 Josh 6.24; 8.28
13.17 Num 25.4; Deut 30.3; 7.13
13.18 Deut 12.28
14.1 Rom 8.16; Lev 21.5
14.2 Deut 7.6
14.4 Lev 11.2-45; Acts 10.14
14.8 Lev 11.26,27
14.9 Lev 11.9

ing their gods, saying, "How did these nations worship their gods? I also want to do the same." [31]You must not do the same for the LORD your God, because every abhorrent thing that the LORD hates they have done for their gods. They would even burn their sons and their daughters in the fire to their gods. [32][f]You must diligently observe everything that I command you; do not add to it or take anything from it.

13 [g]If prophets or those who divine by dreams appear among you and promise you omens or portents, [2]and the omens or the portents declared by them take place, and they say, "Let us follow other gods" (whom you have not known) "and let us serve them," [3]you must not heed the words of those prophets or those who divine by dreams; for the LORD your God is testing you, to know whether you indeed love the LORD your God with all your heart and soul. [4]The LORD your God you shall follow, him alone you shall fear, his commandments you shall keep, his voice you shall obey, him you shall serve, and to him you shall hold fast. [5]But those prophets or those who divine by dreams shall be put to death for having spoken treason against the LORD your God—who brought you out of the land of Egypt and redeemed you from the house of slavery—to turn you from the way in which the LORD your God commanded you to walk. So you shall purge the evil from your midst.

6 If anyone secretly entices you—even if it is your brother, your father's son or[h] your mother's son, or your own son or daughter, or the wife you embrace, or your most intimate friend—saying, "Let us go worship other gods," whom neither you nor your ancestors have known, [7]any of the gods of the peoples that are around you, whether near you or far away from you, from one end of the earth to the other, [8]you must not yield to or heed any such persons. Show them no pity or compassion and do not shield them. [9]But you shall surely kill them; your own hand shall be first against them to execute them, and afterwards the hand of all the people. [10]Stone them to death for trying to turn you away from the LORD your God, who brought you out of the land of Egypt, out of the house of slavery. [11]Then all Israel shall hear and be afraid, and never again do any such wickedness.

12 If you hear it said about one of the towns that the LORD your God is giving you to live in, [13]that scoundrels from among you have gone out and led the inhabitants of the town astray, saying, "Let us go and worship other gods," whom you have not known, [14]then you shall inquire and make a thorough investigation. If the charge is established that such an abhorrent thing has been done among you, [15]you shall put the inhabitants of that town to the sword, utterly destroying it and everything in it—even putting its livestock to the sword. [16]All of its spoil you shall gather into its public square; then burn the town and all its spoil with fire, as a whole burnt offering to the LORD your God. It shall remain a perpetual ruin, never to be rebuilt. [17]Do not let anything devoted to destruction stick to your hand, so that the LORD may turn from his fierce anger and show you compassion, and in his compassion multiply you, as he swore to your ancestors, [18]if you obey the voice of the LORD your God by keeping all his commandments that I am commanding you today, doing what is right in the sight of the LORD your God.

Pagan Practices Forbidden

14 You are children of the LORD your God. You must not lacerate yourselves or shave your forelocks for the dead. [2]For you are a people holy to the LORD your God; it is you the LORD has chosen out of all the peoples on earth to be his people, his treasured possession.

Clean and Unclean Foods

3 You shall not eat any abhorrent thing. [4]These are the animals you may eat: the ox, the sheep, the goat, [5]the deer, the gazelle, the roebuck, the wild goat, the ibex, the antelope, and the mountain-sheep. [6]Any animal that divides the hoof and has the hoof cleft in two, and chews the cud, among the animals, you may eat. [7]Yet of those that chew the cud or have the hoof cleft you shall not eat these: the camel, the hare, and the rock badger, because they chew the cud but do not divide the hoof; they are unclean for you. [8]And the pig, because it divides the hoof but does not chew the cud, is unclean for you. You shall not eat their meat, and you shall not touch their carcasses.

9 Of all that live in water you may eat

[f] Ch 13.1 in Heb [g] Ch 13.2 in Heb [h] Sam Gk Compare Tg: MT lacks *your father's son or*

13.1-5 Instead of following the advice of local prophets and diviners who try to entice Israel into honoring other gods, these agents of the false deities are to be put to death. If close relatives try to involve the Israelites in such worship of pagan deities, God's order is to *kill them*, to *stone them to death*, as a solemn warning to others among God's people (13.6-11). If any traitors from Israel, after careful investigation, are found guilty of encouraging idolatry among the inhabitants of towns in the new land, the entire population is to be killed, and the towns and all their contents are to be burned. Nothing from them is to be kept by the Israelites, whose sole concern is to obey the commands of *the LORD* (13.12-18). Also to be avoided is the practice which was widespread among Israelites (Isa 15.2; Am 8.10; Jer 16.6; Ezek 7.18) and others of lacerating oneself or shaving the forehead as a sign of mourning for the dead. Some Israelites may have been imitating these pagan practices when their pagan neighbors died.

14.3-21 The holiness of God's people precludes any of its members from taking as food any unclean animal, fish, bird, or insect (see Lev 11.2-23). Ritually clean winged creatures are said in Lev 11.21-22 to include locusts, crickets and grasshoppers. An animal that dies of itself cannot be eaten because its blood would not have been drained at the time of death (12.16). The compassion and humane concerns of Deuteronomy are evident in the provision that such food can be given to resident aliens or sold to foreigners, who are not bound by the laws or holiness (14.21). The prohibition against boiling *a kid in its mother's milk* (see Ex 23.19; 34.26) points to a fertility ritual recorded in an ancient text from Ugarit in Syria.

14.22-16.27 The Prescribed Schedule of Religious Duties.
14.22-29 The first cycle of religious obligations is annual: the *tithe* or tenth part of produce from field and flocks, which is to be presented to *the LORD* as an expression of thanks. Unlike the regulation in Num 18.21-32, the tithed commodities may be exchanged for money when one is living at too great a distance from the central shrine in Jerusalem to take the materials there conveniently. In addition, every third year a special tithe is to be offered for the support of the *Levites* as well as for others resident in the area who may lack adequate food or support: *aliens, orphans, widows.*
15.1-18 The next cycle occurs every seventh year: the sabbatical year (15.1-3) when debts are remitted to fellow-Israelites (the rule does not apply for foreigners), including cancellation of all monetary debts and restoration to liberty of those who have been taken as slaves in exchange for a debt. The effect of this law will be to eliminate poverty by freeing the poor from the burden of debt (15.4-5), although 15.11 indicates that the problem will not wholly disappear. Loans may be made to non-Israelites, but borrowing is to be from within God's people only (15.6). The poor are to be dealt with generously, without calculating what will happen to debts at the end of the seven-year period (15.7-11). Setting slaves *free* (15.12-17) is to be accompanied by giving generously to them so that they may begin a new life. The slave-owner is to recall Israel's condition of slavery in Egypt and be compassionate (15.15). Yet the slave may choose to remain for life with the master (15.16-17), in token of which the slave's ear is to be pierced, as in Ex 21.5-6, but the ceremony here is done at home rather than in the sanctuary.

these: whatever has fins and scales you
may eat. [10]And whatever does not have fins
and scales you shall not eat; it is unclean
for you.
11 You may eat any clean birds. [12]But
these are the ones that you shall not eat:
the eagle, the vulture, the osprey, [13]the
buzzard, the kite, of any kind; [14]every raven
of any kind; [15]the ostrich, the nighthawk,
the sea gull, the hawk, of any kind; [16]the
little owl and the great owl, the water hen
[17]and the desert owl,[i] the carrion vulture
and the cormorant, [18]the stork, the heron,
of any kind; the hoopoe and the bat.[j] [19]And
all winged insects are unclean for you; they
shall not be eaten. [20]You may eat any clean
winged creature.
21 You shall not eat anything that dies
of itself; you may give it to aliens residing
in your towns for them to eat, or you may
sell it to a foreigner. For you are a people
holy to the LORD your God.
You shall not boil a kid in its mother's
milk.

Regulations concerning Tithes

22 Set apart a tithe of all the yield of
your seed that is brought in yearly from the
field. [23]In the presence of the LORD your God,
in the place that he will choose as a dwelling for his name, you shall eat the tithe of
your grain, your wine, and your oil, as well
as the firstlings of your herd and flock, so
that you may learn to fear the LORD your
God always. [24]But if, when the LORD your
God has blessed you, the distance is so great
that you are unable to transport it, because
the place where the LORD your God will
choose to set his name is too far away from
you, [25]then you may turn it into money.
With the money secure in hand, go to the
place that the LORD your God will choose;
[26]spend the money for whatever you wish—
oxen, sheep, wine, strong drink, or whatever you desire. And you shall eat there in
the presence of the LORD your God, you and
your household rejoicing together. [27]As for
the Levites resident in your towns, do not
neglect them, because they have no allotment or inheritance with you.
28 Every third year you shall bring out
the full tithe of your produce for that year,
and store it within your towns; [29]the Levites,
because they have no allotment or inheritance with you, as well as the resident aliens, the orphans, and the widows in your
towns, may come and eat their fill so that
the LORD your God may bless you in all the
work that you undertake.

Laws concerning the Sabbatical Year

15 Every seventh year you shall grant
a remission of debts. [2]And this is
the manner of the remission: every creditor
shall remit the claim that is held against a
neighbor, not exacting it of a neighbor who
is a member of the community, because the
LORD's remission has been proclaimed. [3]Of a
foreigner you may exact it, but you must
remit your claim on whatever any member
of your community owes you. [4]There will,
however, be no one in need among you,
because the LORD is sure to bless you in the
land that the LORD your God is giving you
as a possession to occupy, [5]if only you will
obey the LORD your God by diligently observing this entire commandment that I command you today. [6]When the LORD your God
has blessed you, as he promised you, you
will lend to many nations, but you will not
borrow; you will rule over many nations,
but they will not rule over you.
7 If there is among you anyone in need,
a member of your community in any of
your towns within the land that the LORD
your God is giving you, do not be hard-
hearted or tight-fisted toward your needy
neighbor. [8]You should rather open your
hand, willingly lending enough to meet the
need, whatever it may be. [9]Be careful that
you do not entertain a mean thought, thinking, "The seventh year, the year of remission, is near," and therefore view your needy
neighbor with hostility and give nothing;
your neighbor might cry to the LORD against
you, and you would incur guilt. [10]Give
liberally and be ungrudging when you do
so, for on this account the LORD your God
will bless you in all your work and in all
that you undertake. [11]Since there will never
cease to be some in need on the earth, I
therefore command you, "Open your hand
to the poor and needy neighbor in your
land."
12 If a member of your community,
whether a Hebrew man or a Hebrew woman,
is sold[k] to you and works for you six years,
in the seventh year you shall set that person

14.12 Lev 11.3
14.19 Lev 11.20
14.21 Lev 17.15; ver 2; Ex 29.19; 34.26
14.22 Lev 27.30
14.23 Deut 12.5-7; 4.10
14.24 Deut 12.5,21
14.26 Deut 12.7,18
14.27 Deut 12.12; Num 18.20
14.28 Deut 26.12
14.29 Deut 26.12; ver 27; Deut 15.10
15.1 Deut 31.10
15.5 Deut 28.1
15.6 Deut 28.12,13
15.7 1 Jn 3.17
15.8 Lev 25.35
15.9 ver 1; Deut 24.15
15.10 2 Cor 9.5,7; Deut 24.19
15.11 Mt 26.11; Mk 14.7; Jn 12.8
15.12 Ex 21.2; Lev 25.39

[i] Or *pelican* [j] Identification of several of the birds in verses 12–18 is uncertain [k] Or *sells himself or herself*

free. 13 And when you send a male slave[l] out from you a free person, you shall not send him out empty-handed. 14 Provide liberally out of your flock, your threshing floor, and your wine press, thus giving to him some of the bounty with which the LORD your God has blessed you. 15 Remember that you were a slave in the land of Egypt, and the LORD your God redeemed you; for this reason I lay this command upon you today. 16 But if he says to you, "I will not go out from you," because he loves you and your household, since he is well off with you, 17 then you shall take an awl and thrust it through his earlobe into the door, and he shall be your slave[m] forever.

You shall do the same with regard to your female slave.[n]

18 Do not consider it a hardship when you send them out from you free persons, because for six years they have given you services worth the wages of hired laborers; and the LORD your God will bless you in all that you do.

The Firstborn of Livestock

19 Every firstling male born of your herd and flock you shall consecrate to the LORD your God; you shall not do work with your firstling ox nor shear the firstling of your flock. 20 You shall eat it, you together with your household, in the presence of the LORD your God year by year at the place that the LORD will choose. 21 But if it has any defect—any serious defect, such as lameness or blindness—you shall not sacrifice it to the LORD your God; 22 within your towns you may eat it, the unclean and the clean alike, as you would a gazelle or deer. 23 Its blood, however, you must not eat; you shall pour it out on the ground like water.

The Passover Reviewed

16 Observe the month[o] of Abib by keeping the passover for the LORD your God, for in the month of Abib the LORD your God brought you out of Egypt by night. 2 You shall offer the passover sacrifice for the LORD your God, from the flock and the herd, at the place that the LORD will choose as a dwelling for his name. 3 You must not eat with it anything leavened. For seven days you shall eat unleavened bread with it—the bread of affliction—because you came out of the land of Egypt in great haste, so that all the days of your life you may remember the day of your departure from the land of Egypt. 4 No leaven shall be seen with you in all your territory for seven days; and none of the meat of what you slaughter on the evening of the first day shall remain until morning. 5 You are not permitted to offer the passover sacrifice within any of your towns that the LORD your God is giving you. 6 But at the place that the LORD your God will choose as a dwelling for his name, only there shall you offer the passover sacrifice, in the evening at sunset, the time of day when you departed from Egypt. 7 You shall cook it and eat it at the place that the LORD your God will choose; the next morning you may go back to your tents. 8 For six days you shall continue to eat unleavened bread, and on the seventh day there shall be a solemn assembly for the LORD your God, when you shall do no work.

The Festival of Weeks Reviewed

9 You shall count seven weeks; begin to count the seven weeks from the time the sickle is first put to the standing grain. 10 Then you shall keep the festival of weeks for the LORD your God, contributing a freewill offering in proportion to the blessing that you have received from the LORD your God. 11 Rejoice before the LORD your God—you and your sons and your daughters, your male and female slaves, the Levites resident in your towns, as well as the strangers, the orphans, and the widows who are among you—at the place that the LORD your God will choose as a dwelling for his name. 12 Remember that you were a slave in Egypt, and diligently observe these statutes.

The Festival of Booths Reviewed

13 You shall keep the festival of booths[p] for seven days, when you have gathered in the produce from your threshing floor and your wine press. 14 Rejoice during your festival, you and your sons and your daughters, your male and female slaves, as well as the Levites, the strangers, the orphans, and the widows resident in your towns. 15 Seven days you shall keep the festival for the LORD your God at the place that the LORD will choose; for the LORD your God will bless you in all your produce and in all your

[l] Heb *him* [m] Or *bondman* [n] Or *bondwoman* [o] Or *new moon* [p] Or *tabernacles*; Heb *succoth*

15.15 Deut 5.15; 16.12
15.16 Ex 21.5,6
15.19 Ex 13.2
15.20 Deut 12.5-7,17
15.21 Lev 22.19-25
15.22 Deut 12.15,22
15.23 Deut 12.16
16.1 Ex 12.2,29,42; 13.4
16.2 Deut 12.5,26
16.3 Ex 12.8,15
16.4 Ex 13.7; 12.10
16.6 Deut 12.5; Ex 12.6
16.7 Ex 12.8,9
16.8 Ex 12.16
16.9 Ex 23.16; 34.22; Lev 23.15; Num 28.26
16.11 Deut 12.7,12
16.12 Deut 15.15
16.13 Ex 23.16; Lev 23.34
16.14 ver 11
16.15 Lev 23.39

15.19-23 Annual Dedication of the Firstborn of Herds and Flocks. Unlike the procedure outlined in Ex 22.30, this expression of gratitude to God for the fertility of lands and herds need not be done in the first seven days, since allowance is now made for more distant travel to the one central sanctuary.
16.1-17 Annual Cycle of Festivals. Evident in this list of festival regulations is the way in which these ceremonies have taken on multiple meanings, combining significance derived originally from the fertility cycles of the land and its religious traditions with elements from the historical experiences of Israel in Egypt and the wilderness wanderings.
16.1-8 The Passover. Originally associated with the movement of semi-nomadic peoples to new pasture lands for their herds, the festival was linked with God's deliverance of Israel from Egypt. Later the Feast of Unleavened Bread was joined with the Passover in recognition of the fertility of the crops at the first cutting of the grain. After earlier being celebrated in homes (Ex 12.2-4,22-23), it was moved to the central sanctuary. The instruction to return to the *tents* (16.7) is now symbolic of going back from the sanctuary to one's dwelling-place (2 Chr 7.10). Also linked with this feast is the promise of sabbath rest (16.8).
16.9-12 The Feast of Weeks. Marking the end of the cereal harvest, it takes place after seven weeks of cutting grain (Ex 23.16). Characteristic of Deuteronomy is the inclusive list of participants in the feast: family, slaves, Levites, strangers, orphans, widows. Like the Passover, this takes place at the central shrine rather than in the home.
16.13-15 The Feast of Tabernacles. This feast is associated with the harvest of the vineyards as well as of the grain (16.13-15), and like the Passover involves a wide range of participants (16.14; *cf.* 16.11). In Lev 23.43 this festival is understood in connection with the wandering of Israel in the wilderness.

16.16-17 Summary. Three times each year, on the occasion of these three great feasts, all males are to go to the central sanctuary to bring gifts for its support (see Ex 23.17).
16.18-18.22 Establishing Officers and Procedures for Administering Justice. The definitions of official roles here are interspersed with warnings about the consequences of the worship of other gods.
16.18-20 Justice in the life of the people is to be maintained through the official functions of judges and those described as *officials*, whose personal integrity and impartiality will enable them to make the right decisions as disputes arise among the *tribes* and in the *towns*.
16.21-17.7 Planting sacred trees or erecting sacred pillars – both of which are part of the worship of local Canaanite gods – are strictly forbidden. After a brief warning against offering as a sacrifice any animal with a physical defect (although they may be eaten as food; 15.21), additional injunctions are issued against participation in the worship of other gods, including the sun, moon or stars (17.2-7). Conviction of such acts carries a mandatory death sentence, and execution is performed by the community as a whole stoning to death the offender.
17.8-13 The Roles of Priests and Judges. A judicial decision which cannot be decided locally is to be appealed to the central court in Jerusalem, which consists of *levitical priests* and is presided over by a *judge*. The judges rotate in this important office (17.9), so that there is no single supreme judicial figure. The death penalty is to be exacted for refusal to accept the decisions of this court (17.12). Further description of the process is offered in Deut 19.16-21.
17.14-20 Royal Rulers: Rights and Limitations. Describing the establishment of the monarchy as though it were still in the future, Israel is to have a king. This office is simply accepted here, although in 1 Sam 8-15 it is pictured as achieved in defiance of God's purpose for his people. The rules are set down (17.15-17) that the king must be an Israelite by birth, and that his ownership of horses must be limited (which may reflect unfavorably on Solomon's vast holdings in horses; 1 Kings 10), as well as the number of his wives (again in criticism of Solomon's enormous harem; 1 Kings 11.1-8). The king is bound to obey the law as it is interpreted by the levitical priests (17.19), avoiding an autocratic and self-serving rule, if his reign is to endure (17.20).

undertakings, and you shall surely celebrate.

16 Three times a year all your males shall appear before the LORD your God at the place that he will choose: at the festival of unleavened bread, at the festival of weeks, and at the festival of booths.[q] They shall not appear before the LORD empty-handed; [17]all shall give as they are able, according to the blessing of the LORD your God that he has given you.

Municipal Judges and Officers

18 You shall appoint judges and officials throughout your tribes, in all your towns that the LORD your God is giving you, and they shall render just decisions for the people. [19]You must not distort justice; you must not show partiality; and you must not accept bribes, for a bribe blinds the eyes of the wise and subverts the cause of those who are in the right. [20]Justice, and only justice, you shall pursue, so that you may live and occupy the land that the LORD your God is giving you.

Forbidden Forms of Worship

21 You shall not plant any tree as a sacred pole[r] beside the altar that you make for the LORD your God; [22]nor shall you set up a stone pillar—things that the LORD your God hates.

17 You must not sacrifice to the LORD your God an ox or a sheep that has a defect, anything seriously wrong; for that is abhorrent to the LORD your God.

2 If there is found among you, in one of your towns that the LORD your God is giving you, a man or woman who does what is evil in the sight of the LORD your God, and transgresses his covenant [3]by going to serve other gods and worshiping them—whether the sun or the moon or any of the host of heaven, which I have forbidden— [4]and if it is reported to you or you hear of it, and you make a thorough inquiry, and the charge is proved true that such an abhorrent thing has occurred in Israel, [5]then you shall bring out to your gates that man or that woman who has committed this crime and you shall stone the man or woman to death. [6]On the evidence of two or three witnesses the death sentence shall be executed; a person must not be put to death on the evidence of only one witness. [7]The hands of the witnesses shall be the first raised against the person to execute the death penalty, and afterward the hands of all the people. So you shall purge the evil from your midst.

Legal Decisions by Priests and Judges

8 If a judicial decision is too difficult for you to make between one kind of bloodshed and another, one kind of legal right and another, or one kind of assault and another—any such matters of dispute in your towns—then you shall immediately go up to the place that the LORD your God will choose, [9]where you shall consult with the levitical priests and the judge who is in office in those days; they shall announce to you the decision in the case. [10]Carry out exactly the decision that they announce to you from the place that the LORD will choose, diligently observing everything they instruct you. [11]You must carry out fully the law that they interpret for you or the ruling that they announce to you; do not turn aside from the decision that they announce to you, either to the right or to the left. [12]As for anyone who presumes to disobey the priest appointed to minister there to the LORD your God, or the judge, that person shall die. So you shall purge the evil from Israel. [13]All the people will hear and be afraid, and will not act presumptuously again.

Limitations of Royal Authority

14 When you have come into the land that the LORD your God is giving you, and have taken possession of it and settled in it, and you say, "I will set a king over me, like all the nations that are around me," [15]you may indeed set over you a king whom the LORD your God will choose. One of your own community you may set as king over you; you are not permitted to put a foreigner over you, who is not of your own community. [16]Even so, he must not acquire many horses for himself, or return the people to Egypt in order to acquire more horses, since the LORD has said to you, "You must never return that way again." [17]And he must not acquire many wives for himself, or else his heart will turn away; also silver and gold he must not acquire in great quantity for himself. [18]When he has taken the throne of his kingdom, he shall have a copy of this

16.16 Ex 23.14-17; 34.20,23
16.18 Deut 1.16
16.19 Deut 1.17; Ex 23.8
16.21 Ex 34.13; Deut 7.5
17.1 Deut 15.21; Mal 1.8,13
17.2 Deut 13.6
17.4 Deut 13.12,14
17.6 Num 35.30; Deut 19.15; Mt 18.16
17.7 Deut 13.5,9
17.8 Deut 12.5
17.9 Deut 19.17; Ezek 44.24
17.11 Deut 25.1
17.13 Deut 13.11; 19.20
17.14 Deut 11.31; 1 Sam 8.5,19,20
17.15 Jer 30.21
17.16 1 Kings 4.26; 10.26,28; Isa 31.1; Ezek 17.15
17.17 *cf.* 1 Kings 11.3,4
17.18 Deut 31.24-26

[q] Or *tabernacles*; Heb *succoth* [r] Heb *Asherah*

17.19 Josh 1.8
17.20 Deut 5.32
18.1 Deut 10.9; 1 Cor 9.13
18.3 Lev 7.30-34
18.4 Ezra 22.29; Num 18.12
18.5 Ezra 28.1; Deut 10.8
18.8 Neh 12.44,47
18.9 Deut 12.29-31
18.10 Deut 12.31; Lev 19.26,31
18.12 Deut 9.4
18.15 Jn 1.21; Acts 3.22; 7.37
18.16 Deut 5.23-27; Ex 20.19
18.17 Deut 5.28
18.18 ver 15; Isa 51.16; Jn 4.25,26
18.19 Acts 3.23
18.20 Deut 13.1,2,5
18.22 Jer 28.9; ver 20
19.1 Deut 12.29
19.2 Num 35.10,14

law written for him in the presence of the levitical priests. 19It shall remain with him and he shall read in it all the days of his life, so that he may learn to fear the LORD his God, diligently observing all the words of this law and these statutes, 20neither exalting himself above other members of the community nor turning aside from the commandment, either to the right or to the left, so that he and his descendants may reign long over his kingdom in Israel.

Privileges of Priests and Levites

18 The levitical priests, the whole tribe of Levi, shall have no allotment or inheritance within Israel. They may eat the sacrifices that are the LORD's portion[s] 2but they shall have no inheritance among the other members of the community; the LORD is their inheritance, as he promised them.

3 This shall be the priests' due from the people, from those offering a sacrifice, whether an ox or a sheep: they shall give to the priest the shoulder, the two jowls, and the stomach. 4The first fruits of your grain, your wine, and your oil, as well as the first of the fleece of your sheep, you shall give him. 5For the LORD your God has chosen Levi[t] out of all your tribes, to stand and minister in the name of the LORD, him and his sons for all time.

6 If a Levite leaves any of your towns, from wherever he has been residing in Israel, and comes to the place that the LORD will choose (and he may come whenever he wishes), 7then he may minister in the name of the LORD his God, like all his fellow-Levites who stand to minister there before the LORD. 8They shall have equal portions to eat, even though they have income from the sale of family possessions.[s]

Child-Sacrifice, Divination, and Magic Prohibited

9 When you come into the land that the LORD your God is giving you, you must not learn to imitate the abhorrent practices of those nations. 10No one shall be found among you who makes a son or daughter pass through fire, or who practices divination, or is a soothsayer, or an augur, or a sorcerer, 11or one who casts spells, or who consults ghosts or spirits, or who seeks oracles from the dead. 12For whoever does these things is abhorrent to the LORD; it is because of such abhorrent practices that the LORD your God is driving them out before you. 13You must remain completely loyal to the LORD your God. 14Although these nations that you are about to dispossess do give heed to soothsayers and diviners, as for you, the LORD your God does not permit you to do so.

A New Prophet Like Moses

15 The LORD your God will raise up for you a prophet[u] like me from among your own people; you shall heed such a prophet.[v] 16This is what you requested of the LORD your God at Horeb on the day of the assembly when you said: "If I hear the voice of the LORD my God any more, or ever again see this great fire, I will die." 17Then the LORD replied to me: "They are right in what they have said. 18I will raise up for them a prophet[u] like you from among their own people; I will put my words in the mouth of the prophet,[w] who shall speak to them everything that I command. 19Anyone who does not heed the words that the prophet[x] shall speak in my name, I myself will hold accountable. 20But any prophet who speaks in the name of other gods, or who presumes to speak in my name a word that I have not commanded the prophet to speak—that prophet shall die." 21You may say to yourself, "How can we recognize a word that the LORD has not spoken?" 22If a prophet speaks in the name of the LORD but the thing does not take place or prove true, it is a word that the LORD has not spoken. The prophet has spoken it presumptuously; do not be frightened by it.

Laws concerning the Cities of Refuge

19 When the LORD your God has cut off the nations whose land the LORD your God is giving you, and you have dispossessed them and settled in their towns and in their houses, 2you shall set apart three cities in the land that the LORD your God is giving you to possess. 3You shall calculate the distances[y] and divide into three regions the land that the LORD your God gives you as a possession, so that any homicide can flee to one of them.

[s] Meaning of Heb uncertain [t] Heb *him* [u] Or *prophets* [v] Or *such prophets* [w] Or *mouths of the prophets* [x] Heb *he* [y] Or *prepare roads to them*

18.1-8 Roles of the Levitical Priests. They are to have no personal possessions, living instead from the gifts presented by worshipers to the sanctuary, with specifics indicated as to what they will receive in meat, wine, oil and grain. They are to be resident throughout the land among the other tribes, and to go to Jerusalem to serve God in the sanctuary on occasion (18.6-7). Mention in 17.8 of income from the sale of family possessions seems to contradict the rule against Levites' owning property in 18.1, but this may refer to the practice indicated in Lev 27.21, by which consecrated land passed to the priest, and became *the priest's holding.*

18.9-14 Forbidden Practices and Roles. Utterly rejected for God's people are such practices as child sacrifice, as well as to serve as, or use the services of, a diviner, soothsayer, augur, sorcerer, exorcist or spiritualist (who consults with ghosts and conveys oracles from the dead). The sole reliance of God's people concerning the future, their preservation from harm, and facing death is to be on the LORD, not on these evil skills and powers that pervade the pagan religions.

18.15-22 True and False Prophets. God continues to provide messengers who convey his will and purpose to his people – *a prophet like [Moses]* – and will do so in the future (18.18). The people gathered at Horeb had sensed that for them to hear from God directly would result in their destruction, but God has provided an intermediary: his prophet. False prophets will be recognized by the facts that they speak *in the name of other gods* and their predictions prove false, while God's own prophet will be known because what he predicts actually takes place.

19.1-13 The Cities of Refuge. The new land is to be divided into three districts, each of which will include a city of refuge to which those who accidentally kill someone can flee for safety from *the avenger of blood,* who is out to kill the one who chanced to cause the death. The larger the territory of Israel, the more cities of refuge it will need to protect the innocent. Anyone who violates the sanctity of these cities is to be put to death by *the elders of the city.* This responsibility recalls the role of the earlier patriarchal leaders who represented the whole people (Ex 3.16; 4.29), who were assembled by Moses for instruction (Num 11.16), and who represented the people at Sinai (Ex 24.1,9). In the period of the Judges, the elders made important decisions (1 Sam 4.3; 8.4) but here their role is secondary to those of the judges and officials (Deut 16.18-20).

4 Now this is the case of a homicide who might flee there and live, that is, someone who has killed another person unintentionally when the two had not been at enmity before: [5]Suppose someone goes into the forest with another to cut wood, and when one of them swings the ax to cut down a tree, the head slips from the handle and strikes the other person who then dies; the killer may flee to one of these cities and live. [6]But if the distance is too great, the avenger of blood in hot anger might pursue and overtake and put the killer to death, although a death sentence was not deserved, since the two had not been at enmity before. [7]Therefore I command you: You shall set apart three cities.

8 If the LORD your God enlarges your territory, as he swore to your ancestors—and he will give you all the land that he promised your ancestors to give you, [9]provided you diligently observe this entire commandment that I command you today, by loving the LORD your God and walking always in his ways—then you shall add three more cities to these three, [10]so that the blood of an innocent person may not be shed in the land that the LORD your God is giving you as an inheritance, thereby bringing bloodguilt upon you.

11 But if someone at enmity with another lies in wait and attacks and takes the life of that person, and flees into one of these cities, [12]then the elders of the killer's city shall send to have the culprit taken from there and handed over to the avenger of blood to be put to death. [13]Show no pity; you shall purge the guilt of innocent blood from Israel, so that it may go well with you.

Property Boundaries

14 You must not move your neighbor's boundary marker, set up by former generations, on the property that will be allotted to you in the land that the LORD your God is giving you to possess.

Law concerning Witnesses

15 A single witness shall not suffice to convict a person of any crime or wrongdoing in connection with any offense that may be committed. Only on the evidence of two or three witnesses shall a charge be sustained. [16]If a malicious witness comes forward to accuse someone of wrongdoing, [17]then both parties to the dispute shall appear before the LORD, before the priests and the judges who are in office in those days, [18]and the judges shall make a thorough inquiry. If the witness is a false witness, having testified falsely against another, [19]then you shall do to the false witness just as the false witness had meant to do to the other. So you shall purge the evil from your midst. [20]The rest shall hear and be afraid, and a crime such as this shall never again be committed among you. [21]Show no pity: life for life, eye for eye, tooth for tooth, hand for hand, foot for foot.

Rules of Warfare

20 When you go out to war against your enemies, and see horses and chariots, an army larger than your own, you shall not be afraid of them; for the LORD your God is with you, who brought you up from the land of Egypt. [2]Before you engage in battle, the priest shall come forward and speak to the troops, [3]and shall say to them: "Hear, O Israel! Today you are drawing near to do battle against your enemies. Do not lose heart, or be afraid, or panic, or be in dread of them; [4]for it is the LORD your God who goes with you, to fight for you against your enemies, to give you victory." [5]Then the officials shall address the troops, saying, "Has anyone built a new house but not dedicated it? He should go back to his house, or he might die in the battle and another dedicate it. [6]Has anyone planted a vineyard but not yet enjoyed its fruit? He should go back to his house, or he might die in the battle and another be first to enjoy its fruit. [7]Has anyone become engaged to a woman but not yet married her? He should go back to his house, or he might die in the battle and another marry her." [8]The officials shall continue to address the troops, saying, "Is anyone afraid or disheartened? He should go back to his house, or he might cause the heart of his comrades to melt like his own." [9]When the officials have finished addressing the troops, then the commanders shall take charge of them.

10 When you draw near to a town to fight against it, offer it terms of peace. [11]If it accepts your terms of peace and surrenders to you, then all the people in it shall serve you at forced labor. [12]If it does not submit to you peacefully, but makes war against you, then you shall besiege it; [13]and

19.15-21 Witnesses and the Judicial Process. Testimony from two or three witnesses is essential for deciding charges made against anyone in the community. False witnesses are to receive the same punishment they tried to bring upon others. There is a solemn warning that any injustice will be punished by an equivalent penalty.
20.1-21.14 Rules in Time of War.
20.1-9 Since the victory of God's people over their enemies is assured by God's fighting for them, it is essential in time of war to maintain the stability of the social community. Accordingly, the following are to be excused from military service: those with a new house that is to be dedicated, those who have not yet harvested vineyards, those who are engaged to be married, and anyone whose fears of battle may lower the morale of his colleagues.
20.10-18 Before attacking a town, peace is to be offered. If it is declined, all the males are to be killed, while women, children, livestock and contents of the town are to be taken as booty, with everything remaining destroyed. Trees of the fruit-bearing variety are to be preserved, however (20.19-20).

19.4 Num 35.13
19.6 Num 35.12
19.9 Josh 20.7,8
19.10 Deut 21.1-9; Num 35.33
19.13 Deut 7.2
19.14 Deut 27.17
19.15 Num 35.30; Deut 17.6; Mt 18.16; 2 Cor 13.1
19.16 Ex 23.1; Ps 27.12
19.17 Deut 17.9
19.19 Prov 19.5,9
19.21 ver 13; Ex 21.23; Lev 24.20; Mt 5.38
20.1 Deut 13.6,8
20.3 ver 1; Josh 23.10
20.4 Deut 1.30
20.6 1 Cor 9.7
20.7 Deut 24.5
20.8 Judg 7.3
20.10 Lk 14.31

20.14 Josh 8.2; 22.8
20.16 Deut 7.1,2; Josh 11.14
20.18 Ex 23.33
21.1 Josh 1.6
21.5 Deut 17.8-11
21.8 Jon 1.8
21.9 Deut 19.13
21.12 Lev 14.8,9; Num 6.9
21.16 1 Chr 26.10
21.17 Gen 49.3
21.18 Isa 30.1

when the LORD your God gives it into your hand, you shall put all its males to the sword. [14]You may, however, take as your booty the women, the children, livestock, and everything else in the town, all its spoil. You may enjoy the spoil of your enemies, which the LORD your God has given you. [15]Thus you shall treat all the towns that are very far from you, which are not towns of the nations here. [16]But as for the towns of these peoples that the LORD your God is giving you as an inheritance, you must not let anything that breathes remain alive. [17]You shall annihilate them—the Hittites and the Amorites, the Canaanites and the Perizzites, the Hivites and the Jebusites—just as the LORD your God has commanded, [18]so that they may not teach you to do all the abhorrent things that they do for their gods, and you thus sin against the LORD your God.

19 If you besiege a town for a long time, making war against it in order to take it, you must not destroy its trees by wielding an ax against them. Although you may take food from them, you must not cut them down. Are trees in the field human beings that they should come under siege from you? [20]You may destroy only the trees that you know do not produce food; you may cut them down for use in building siegeworks against the town that makes war with you, until it falls.

Law concerning Murder by Persons Unknown

21 If, in the land that the LORD your God is giving you to possess, a body is found lying in open country, and it is not known who struck the person down, [2]then your elders and your judges shall come out to measure the distances to the towns that are near the body. [3]The elders of the town nearest the body shall take a heifer that has never been worked, one that has not pulled in the yoke; [4]the elders of that town shall bring the heifer down to a wadi with running water, which is neither plowed nor sown, and shall break the heifer's neck there in the wadi. [5]Then the priests, the sons of Levi, shall come forward, for the LORD your God has chosen them to minister to him and to pronounce blessings in the name of the LORD, and by their decision all cases of dispute and assault shall be settled. [6]All the elders of that town nearest the body shall wash their hands over the heifer whose neck was broken in the wadi, [7]and they shall declare: "Our hands did not shed this blood, nor were we witnesses to it. [8]Absolve, O LORD, your people Israel, whom you redeemed; do not let the guilt of innocent blood remain in the midst of your people Israel." Then they will be absolved of bloodguilt. [9]So you shall purge the guilt of innocent blood from your midst, because you must do what is right in the sight of the LORD.

Female Captives

10 When you go out to war against your enemies, and the LORD your God hands them over to you and you take them captive, [11]suppose you see among the captives a beautiful woman whom you desire and want to marry, [12]and so you bring her home to your house: she shall shave her head, pare her nails, [13]discard her captive's garb, and shall remain in your house a full month, mourning for her father and mother; after that you may go in to her and be her husband, and she shall be your wife. [14]But if you are not satisfied with her, you shall let her go free and not sell her for money. You must not treat her as a slave, since you have dishonored her.

The Right of the Firstborn

15 If a man has two wives, one of them loved and the other disliked, and if both the loved and the disliked have borne him sons, the firstborn being the son of the one who is disliked, [16]then on the day when he wills his possessions to his sons, he is not permitted to treat the son of the loved as the firstborn in preference to the son of the disliked, who is the firstborn. [17]He must acknowledge as firstborn the son of the one who is disliked, giving him a double portion[z] of all that he has; since he is the first issue of his virility, the right of the firstborn is his.

Rebellious Children

18 If someone has a stubborn and rebellious son who will not obey his father and mother, who does not heed them when they discipline him, [19]then his father and his mother shall take hold of him and bring

21.1-23.1 Various Laws.
21.1-9 On finding a corpse in conquered territory, *the elders...and judges* are to kill a heifer by breaking its neck (thus avoiding contact with its blood) to purge the land of blood-guilt. Beautiful women captives may be taken as wives on a trial basis (21.10-14). The firstborn son is to receive a double portion of his father's inheritance, even if he is the son of the wife less well-liked by the deceased (21.15-17). Parents are to denounce their rebellious son as a *glutton and drunkard* and turn him over to the men of the town for stoning (see Prov 23.20-21; Lk 7.33-34). The body of an executed criminal must not remain overnight on a tree where it was left hanging. To do so defiles the land.

[z] Heb *two-thirds*

22.1-4 Care must be taken to preserve the integrity of the neighbor's property, whether he is present or not. The established orders of life and culture are to be maintained (22.5,9-11) on such matters as differences between the sexes as to attire, growing only vines in a vineyard, pairing only similar draught animals, and mixing different fibers in a textile. Humane concerns require release of a mother bird when her eggs or young are seized and building a protective parapet around the roof of one's house. The visible signs of piety to be displayed on one's cloak (22.12) recall Num 15.37-40.
22.13-30 Laws Concerning Sexual Relations. Claims of, or challenges to, a woman's virginity are to be formally tested by *the elders at the city gate*, with vindication of the innocent and punishment of false accusers carried out. When extra-marital sex acts occur (22.22), both guilty parties are to be put to death. (22.23-29) If a virgin, engaged or not, is raped in town and does not call out for help, she and her attacker are to die. If she was attacked in the country, she is presumed innocent, since no one would be at hand to help her. If she is not engaged, her father is to be paid generous compensation and the man is required to marry her and may not divorce her. Under no circumstances may a man marry one of his father's wives (22.30).

him out to the elders of his town at the gate
of that place. [20]They shall say to the elders
of his town, "This son of ours is stubborn
and rebellious. He will not obey us. He is
a glutton and a drunkard." [21]Then all the
men of the town shall stone him to death.
So you shall purge the evil from your midst;
and all Israel will hear, and be afraid.

Miscellaneous Laws

22 When someone is convicted of a crime
punishable by death and is executed, and
you hang him on a tree, [23]his corpse must
not remain all night upon the tree; you
shall bury him that same day, for anyone
hung on a tree is under God's curse. You
must not defile the land that the LORD your
God is giving you for possession.

22 You shall not watch your neighbor's ox or sheep straying away
and ignore them; you shall take them back
to their owner. [2]If the owner does not reside
near you or you do not know who the
owner is, you shall bring it to your own
house, and it shall remain with you until
the owner claims it; then you shall return
it. [3]You shall do the same with a neighbor's
donkey; you shall do the same with a
neighbor's garment; and you shall do the
same with anything else that your neighbor
loses and you find. You may not withhold
your help.

4 You shall not see your neighbor's donkey or ox fallen on the road and ignore it;
you shall help to lift it up.

5 A woman shall not wear a man's
apparel, nor shall a man put on a woman's
garment; for whoever does such things is
abhorrent to the LORD your God.

6 If you come on a bird's nest, in any
tree or on the ground, with fledglings or
eggs, with the mother sitting on the fledglings
or on the eggs, you shall not take the
mother with the young. [7]Let the mother go,
taking only the young for yourself, in order
that it may go well with you and you may
live long.

8 When you build a new house, you
shall make a parapet for your roof; otherwise you might have bloodguilt on your
house, if anyone should fall from it.

9 You shall not sow your vineyard with
a second kind of seed, or the whole yield
will have to be forfeited, both the crop that
you have sown and the yield of the vineyard itself.

10 You shall not plow with an ox and
a donkey yoked together.

11 You shall not wear clothes made of
wool and linen woven together.

12 You shall make tassels on the four
corners of the cloak with which you cover
yourself.

Laws concerning Sexual Relations

13 Suppose a man marries a woman,
but after going in to her, he dislikes her
[14]and makes up charges against her, slandering her by saying, "I married this woman;
but when I lay with her, I did not find
evidence of her virginity." [15]The father of
the young woman and her mother shall
then submit the evidence of the young
woman's virginity to the elders of the city
at the gate. [16]The father of the young woman
shall say to the elders: "I gave my daughter
in marriage to this man but he dislikes her;
[17]now he has made up charges against her,
saying, 'I did not find evidence of your
daughter's virginity.' But here is the evidence of my daughter's virginity." Then
they shall spread out the cloth before the
elders of the town. [18]The elders of that town
shall take the man and punish him; [19]they
shall fine him one hundred shekels of silver
(which they shall give to the young woman's father) because he has slandered a
virgin of Israel. She shall remain his wife;
he shall not be permitted to divorce her as
long as he lives.

20 If, however, this charge is true, that
evidence of the young woman's virginity
was not found, [21]then they shall bring the
young woman out to the entrance of her
father's house and the men of her town
shall stone her to death, because she committed a disgraceful act in Israel by prostituting herself in her father's house. So you
shall purge the evil from your midst.

22 If a man is caught lying with the wife
of another man, both of them shall die, the
man who lay with the woman as well as
the woman. So you shall purge the evil
from Israel.

23 If there is a young woman, a virgin
already engaged to be married, and a man
meets her in the town and lies with her,
[24]you shall bring both of them to the gate
of that town and stone them to death, the
young woman because she did not cry for
help in the town and the man because he
violated his neighbor's wife. So you shall

21.21 Deut 13.5,11
21.23 Josh 8.29; 10.26,27; Jn 19.31; Gal 3.13
22.1 Ex 23.4
22.4 Ex 23.5
22.6 Lev 22.28
22.7 Deut 4.40
22.9 Lev 19.19
22.11 Lev 19.19
22.12 Num 15.37-41; Mt 23.5
22.13 Deut 24.1
22.15 ver 23ff
22.21 Deut 23.17,18; 13.5
22.22 Lev 20.10; Jn 8.5
22.24 ver 21,22

purge the evil from your midst.

25 But if the man meets the engaged woman in the open country, and the man seizes her and lies with her, then only the man who lay with her shall die. [26]You shall do nothing to the young woman; the young woman has not committed an offense punishable by death, because this case is like that of someone who attacks and murders a neighbor. [27]Since he found her in the open country, the engaged woman may have cried for help, but there was no one to rescue her.

28 If a man meets a virgin who is not engaged, and seizes her and lies with her, and they are caught in the act, [29]the man who lay with her shall give fifty shekels of silver to the young woman's father, and she shall become his wife. Because he violated her he shall not be permitted to divorce her as long as he lives.

30[a] A man shall not marry his father's wife, thereby violating his father's rights.[b]

Those Excluded from the Assembly

23 No one whose testicles are crushed or whose penis is cut off shall be admitted to the assembly of the LORD.

2 Those born of an illicit union shall not be admitted to the assembly of the LORD. Even to the tenth generation, none of their descendants shall be admitted to the assembly of the LORD.

3 No Ammonite or Moabite shall be admitted to the assembly of the LORD. Even to the tenth generation, none of their descendants shall be admitted to the assembly of the LORD, [4]because they did not meet you with food and water on your journey out of Egypt, and because they hired against you Balaam son of Beor, from Pethor of Mesopotamia, to curse you. [5](Yet the LORD your God refused to heed Balaam; the LORD your God turned the curse into a blessing for you, because the LORD your God loved you.) [6]You shall never promote their welfare or their prosperity as long as you live.

7 You shall not abhor any of the Edomites, for they are your kin. You shall not abhor any of the Egyptians, because you were an alien residing in their land. [8]The children of the third generation that are born to them may be admitted to the assembly of the LORD.

Sanitary, Ritual, and Humanitarian Precepts

9 When you are encamped against your enemies you shall guard against any impropriety.

10 If one of you becomes unclean because of a nocturnal emission, then he shall go outside the camp; he must not come within the camp. [11]When evening comes, he shall wash himself with water, and when the sun has set, he may come back into the camp.

12 You shall have a designated area outside the camp to which you shall go. [13]With your utensils you shall have a trowel; when you relieve yourself outside, you shall dig a hole with it and then cover up your excrement. [14]Because the LORD your God travels along with your camp, to save you and to hand over your enemies to you, therefore your camp must be holy, so that he may not see anything indecent among you and turn away from you.

15 Slaves who have escaped to you from their owners shall not be given back to them. [16]They shall reside with you, in your midst, in any place they choose in any one of your towns, wherever they please; you shall not oppress them.

17 None of the daughters of Israel shall be a temple prostitute; none of the sons of Israel shall be a temple prostitute. [18]You shall not bring the fee of a prostitute or the wages of a male prostitute[c] into the house of the LORD your God in payment for any vow, for both of these are abhorrent to the LORD your God.

19 You shall not charge interest on loans to another Israelite, interest on money, interest on provisions, interest on anything that is lent. [20]On loans to a foreigner you may charge interest, but on loans to another Israelite you may not charge interest, so that the LORD your God may bless you in all your undertakings in the land that you are about to enter and possess.

21 If you make a vow to the LORD your God, do not postpone fulfilling it; for the LORD your God will surely require it of you, and you would incur guilt. [22]But if you refrain from vowing, you will not incur guilt. [23]Whatever your lips utter you must diligently perform, just as you have freely vowed to the LORD your God with your own mouth.

[a] Ch 23.1 in Heb [b] Heb *uncovering his father's skirt* [c] Heb *a dog*

22.25 Jn 8.1-11
22.28 Ex 22.16,17
22.30 Deut 27.20
23.17 Deut 22.21
23.19 Ex 22.25; Lev 25.36,37
23.20 Deut 28.12
23.21 Num 30.2; Mt 5.33

23.1-6 Those to be excluded from participation in God's people: males whose sex organs are severely injured; illegitimate children; Ammonites and Moabites, because they hindered Israel's passage through the east Jordan territory.
23.7-8 In contrast with this attitude is the call to Israel to recognize the Edomites as kinfolk (descended from Esau, brother of Jacob) and to respect the Egyptians as those among whom the sons of Jacob resided. Purity is to be maintained in military encampments against nocturnal emissions or excrement (23.9-14). Refuge is to be provided for runaway slaves (23.15-16). The income obtained by female or male prostitutes is not to be included in offerings to the LORD (23.17-18). Interest is not to be charged on loans to other Israelites, but may be taken from *foreigners* (23.19-20). All vows taken are to be fulfilled promptly (23.21-22). Those who pass through a neighbor's field or vineyard may help themselves there, but may not take anything with them (23.24-25).

24.1-6 Laws concerning Marriage and Divorce. A woman who is twice married and twice divorced may not remarry her first husband. A newly-married man is to be given a year free of other duties in order to become well-acquainted with his wife (24.5). Miscellaneous Laws (24.6-25.10). To take a millstone in pledge for a loan is to deprive one's neighbor of an essential resource for preparing daily food (24.6). Kidnapping another Israelite is a capital crime (24.7). Levitical rules and procedures are to be observed in order to prevent the spread of leprous diseases (24.8-9). In making a loan, the privacy of the borrower is not to be violated nor is such essential equipment as his cloak to be seized (24.10-13). The poor are to receive their wages daily, since otherwise they may not survive (24.14-15). Responsibility for crimes lies with the performer, and may not be shifted to parents or children (24.16). Justice is to be shown to resident aliens and to children (24.17-18). In accord with the humane concerns of Deuteronomy, portions of grain and grapes are to be purposely left behind for the benefit of the poor, the aliens, widows and orphans (24.19-22). The punishment for misdeeds is to be proportionate to the crime, not excessive (25.1-3). A tethered draught animal is to be allowed to eat as he works (25.4). The Laws of Levirate Marriage (25.5-10). These laws are aimed at preserving the continuity of family lines within the tribal structure of Israel. The widow seeking to preserve the family line when her husband dies can appeal to *the elders at the gate* to bring pressure on her brother-in-law to follow through his family duty of raising a son in place of the deceased husband. If he refuses, her removal of the sandal and spitting in the face of the irresponsible brother not only constitutes a public insult, but also indicates the loss to his family of property rights.

24 If you go into your neighbor's vineyard, you may eat your fill of grapes, as many as you wish, but you shall not put any in a container.

25 If you go into your neighbor's standing grain, you may pluck the ears with your hand, but you shall not put a sickle to your neighbor's standing grain.

Laws concerning Marriage and Divorce

24 Suppose a man enters into marriage with a woman, but she does not please him because he finds something objectionable about her, and so he writes her a certificate of divorce, puts it in her hand, and sends her out of his house; she then leaves his house [2]and goes off to become another man's wife. [3]Then suppose the second man dislikes her, writes her a bill of divorce, puts it in her hand, and sends her out of his house (or the second man who married her dies); [4]her first husband, who sent her away, is not permitted to take her again to be his wife after she has been defiled; for that would be abhorrent to the LORD, and you shall not bring guilt on the land that the LORD your God is giving you as a possession.

Miscellaneous Laws

5 When a man is newly married, he shall not go out with the army or be charged with any related duty. He shall be free at home one year, to be happy with the wife whom he has married.

6 No one shall take a mill or an upper millstone in pledge, for that would be taking a life in pledge.

7 If someone is caught kidnaping another Israelite, enslaving or selling the Israelite, then that kidnaper shall die. So you shall purge the evil from your midst.

8 Guard against an outbreak of a leprous[d] skin disease by being very careful; you shall carefully observe whatever the levitical priests instruct you, just as I have commanded them. [9]Remember what the LORD your God did to Miriam on your journey out of Egypt.

10 When you make your neighbor a loan of any kind, you shall not go into the house to take the pledge. [11]You shall wait outside, while the person to whom you are making the loan brings the pledge out to you. [12]If the person is poor, you shall not sleep in the garment given you as[e] the pledge. [13]You shall give the pledge back by sunset, so that your neighbor may sleep in the cloak and bless you; and it will be to your credit before the LORD your God.

14 You shall not withhold the wages of poor and needy laborers, whether other Israelites or aliens who reside in your land in one of your towns. [15]You shall pay them their wages daily before sunset, because they are poor and their livelihood depends on them; otherwise they might cry to the LORD against you, and you would incur guilt.

16 Parents shall not be put to death for their children, nor shall children be put to death for their parents; only for their own crimes may persons be put to death.

17 You shall not deprive a resident alien or an orphan of justice; you shall not take a widow's garment in pledge. [18]Remember that you were a slave in Egypt and the LORD your God redeemed you from there; therefore I command you to do this.

19 When you reap your harvest in your field and forget a sheaf in the field, you shall not go back to get it; it shall be left for the alien, the orphan, and the widow, so that the LORD your God may bless you in all your undertakings. [20]When you beat your olive trees, do not strip what is left; it shall be for the alien, the orphan, and the widow.

21 When you gather the grapes of your vineyard, do not glean what is left; it shall be for the alien, the orphan, and the widow. [22]Remember that you were a slave in the land of Egypt; therefore I am commanding you to do this.

25 Suppose two persons have a dispute and enter into litigation, and the judges decide between them, declaring one to be in the right and the other to be in the wrong. [2]If the one in the wrong deserves to be flogged, the judge shall make that person lie down and be beaten in his presence with the number of lashes proportionate to the offense. [3]Forty lashes may be given but not more; if more lashes than these are given, your neighbor will be degraded in your sight.

4 You shall not muzzle an ox while it is treading out the grain.

Levirate Marriage

5 When brothers reside together, and one of them dies and has no son, the wife of the

[d] A term for several skin diseases; precise meaning uncertain [e] Heb lacks *the garment given you as*

23.25 Mt 12.1; Mk 2.23; Lk 6.1

24.1 Deut 22.13-21; Mt 5.31; 19.7; Mk 10.4

24.4 Jer 3.1

24.5 Deut 20.7

24.7 Ex 21.16

24.8 Lev 13.2; 14.2

24.9 Num 12.10

24.13 Ex 22.26; Deut 6.25

24.14 Lev 25.35-43; Deut 15.7-18

24.15 Lev 19.13; Jas 5.4; Deut 15.9

24.16 2 Kings 14.6; 2 Chr 25.4; Jer 31.29,30; Ezek 18.20

24.17 Deut 1.17; 10.17; 16.19

24.18 Deut 16.12

24.19 Lev 19.9.10; 23.22

24.20 Lev 19.10

24.22 ver 18

25.1 Deut 19.17; 1.16,17

25.3 2 Cor 11.24

25.4 1 Cor 9.9; 1 Tim 5.18

25.5 Mt 22.24; Mk 12.19; Lk 20.28

deceased shall not be married outside the
family to a stranger. Her husband's brother
shall go in to her, taking her in marriage,
and performing the duty of a husband's
brother to her, [6]and the firstborn whom she
bears shall succeed to the name of the
deceased brother, so that his name may not
be blotted out of Israel. [7]But if the man has
no desire to marry his brother's widow,
then his brother's widow shall go up to the
elders at the gate and say, "My husband's
brother refuses to perpetuate his brother's
name in Israel; he will not perform the duty
of a husband's brother to me." [8]Then the
elders of his town shall summon him and
speak to him. If he persists, saying, "I have
no desire to marry her," [9]then his brother's
wife shall go up to him in the presence of
the elders, pull his sandal off his foot, spit
in his face, and declare, "This is what is
done to the man who does not build up his
brother's house." [10]Throughout Israel his
family shall be known as "the house of him
whose sandal was pulled off."

Various Commands

11 If men get into a fight with one
another, and the wife of one intervenes to
rescue her husband from the grip of his
opponent by reaching out and seizing his
genitals, [12]you shall cut off her hand; show
no pity.
13 You shall not have in your bag two
kinds of weights, large and small. [14]You
shall not have in your house two kinds of
measures, large and small. [15]You shall have
only a full and honest weight; you shall
have only a full and honest measure, so
that your days may be long in the land that
the LORD your God is giving you. [16]For all
who do such things, all who act dishon-
estly, are abhorrent to the LORD your God.
17 Remember what Amalek did to you
on your journey out of Egypt, [18]how he
attacked you on the way, when you were
faint and weary, and struck down all who
lagged behind you; he did not fear God.
[19]Therefore when the LORD your God has
given you rest from all your enemies on
every hand, in the land that the LORD your
God is giving you as an inheritance to
possess, you shall blot out the remembrance
of Amalek from under heaven; do not forget.

First Fruits and Tithes

26 When you have come into the
land that the LORD your God is
giving you as an inheritance to possess, and
you possess it, and settle in it, [2]you shall
take some of the first of all the fruit of the
ground, which you harvest from the land
that the LORD your God is giving you, and
you shall put it in a basket and go to the
place that the LORD your God will choose as
a dwelling for his name. [3]You shall go to
the priest who is in office at that time, and
say to him, "Today I declare to the LORD
your God that I have come into the land
that the LORD swore to our ancestors to give
us." [4]When the priest takes the basket from
your hand and sets it down before the altar
of the LORD your God, [5]you shall make this
response before the LORD your God: "A
wandering Aramean was my ancestor; he
went down into Egypt and lived there as an
alien, few in number, and there he became
a great nation, mighty and populous. [6]When
the Egyptians treated us harshly and afflicted us, by imposing hard labor on us,
[7]we cried to the LORD, the God of our ancestors; the LORD heard our voice and saw
our affliction, our toil, and our oppression.
[8]The LORD brought us out of Egypt with a
mighty hand and an outstretched arm, with
a terrifying display of power, and with signs
and wonders; [9]and he brought us into this
place and gave us this land, a land flowing
with milk and honey. [10]So now I bring the
first of the fruit of the ground that you, O
LORD, have given me." You shall set it down
before the LORD your God and bow down
before the LORD your God. [11]Then you, together with the Levites and the aliens who
reside among you, shall celebrate with all
the bounty that the LORD your God has
given to you and to your house.
12 When you have finished paying all
the tithe of your produce in the third year
(which is the year of the tithe), giving it to
the Levites, the aliens, the orphans, and the
widows, so that they may eat their fill
within your towns, [13]then you shall say
before the LORD your God: "I have removed
the sacred portion from the house, and I
have given it to the Levites, the resident
aliens, the orphans, and the widows, in
accordance with your entire commandment
that you commanded me; I have neither

25.6 Gen 38.9; Ruth 4.10
25.7 Ruth 4.1,2
25.8 Ruth 4.6
25.9 Ruth 4.7,11
25.13 Lev 19.35-37
25.16 Prov 11.1
25.17 Ex 17.8
25.19 1 Sam 15.2,3
26.2 Ex 22.29; 23.16,19; Num 18.13
26.5 Hos 12.12; Gen 43.1,2; 45.7,11; 46.27; Deut 10.22
26.6 Ex 1.11,14
26.7 Ex 2.23-25
26.8 Deut 4.34
26.9 Ex 3.8
26.11 Deut 12.7
26.12 Deut 14.28,29; Heb 7.5,9,10
26.13 Ps 119.141, 153,176

25.11-12 Wives are forbidden to have physical contact with men other than their husbands, under penalty of cruel punishment.
25.13-16 Honest weights are to be used in all business dealings, both buying and selling.
25.17-19 God's judgment on the Amalekites is enduring for their hostility toward God's people (Ex 17.8-13).
26.1-11 Offering of the Firstfruits. Originally an agricultural ceremony, to show gratitude to God for the crops (Ex 23.19; 36.26), the festival is now linked with the escape from slavery in Egypt and the entrance of Israel into the land. Included is a liturgical-sounding recital of the brief history of Israel from the days of Abraham (*a wandering Aramaean was my father)* through the experiences of prosperity and then enslavement in Egypt, followed by God's great acts of deliverance, culminating in Israel's entrance into the land of promise (vv. 6-9). There is no mention here of Sinai and the law. Instead, the emphasis is on God's gift of the land and its fruitfulness. The *Levites* participate in the ceremony, but are not pictured here as its leaders (26.11). Also sharing are the *aliens.*
26.12-15 As in 14.28, every three years the tithe is not to be taken to the sanctuary in Jerusalem (which may be at a considerable distance) but is to be given to the local people who are in special need: Levites, resident aliens, orphans, widows.

26.16-19 The exhortation to obey God's commandments carries with it the promise of special relationship to the LORD and the exaltation of Israel as a holy people *above all nations*.
27.1-28.69 Final Instructions Concerning the Law.
The setting for Israel's commitment to the law is to be Shechem and its two mountain peaks, Ebal and Gerizim, with those tribes which are viewed positively in the tradition on Gerizim and the rest on Ebal (27.11-13). Gerizim became the sacred mountain of the Samaritans, where their temple was erected. The law is stated negatively: who is to be cursed for disobeying the commandments of God. The prohibitions are against making idols (vs. 15), dishonoring parents (vs. 16), cheating on property lines (vs. 17), misleading someone who is blind (vs. 18), denying justice to the weak (aliens, widows, orphans; vs. 19), committing incest, bestiality or any other sexual irregularity within the family (vv. 20-23), committing murder or taking a bribe to assassinate someone (vv. 24-25). A final curse is on those who fail to obey the law. The response of the people in each case is *Amen*, which expresses confidence in the truth of what has been uttered.

transgressed nor forgotten any of your commandments: [14]I have not eaten of it while
in mourning; I have not removed any of it
while I was unclean; and I have not offered
any of it to the dead. I have obeyed the LORD
my God, doing just as you commanded me.
[15]Look down from your holy habitation,
from heaven, and bless your people Israel
and the ground that you have given us, as
you swore to our ancestors—a land flowing
with milk and honey."

Concluding Exhortation

16 This very day the LORD your God is
commanding you to observe these statutes
and ordinances; so observe them diligently
with all your heart and with all your soul.
[17]Today you have obtained the LORD's agreement: to be your God; and for you to walk
in his ways, to keep his statutes, his commandments, and his ordinances, and to
obey him. [18]Today the LORD has obtained
your agreement: to be his treasured people,
as he promised you, and to keep his commandments; [19]for him to set you high above
all nations that he has made, in praise and
in fame and in honor; and for you to be a
people holy to the LORD your God, as he
promised.

The Inscribed Stones and Altar on Mount Ebal

27 Then Moses and the elders of Israel
charged all the people as follows:
Keep the entire commandment that I am
commanding you today. [2]On the day that
you cross over the Jordan into the land that
the LORD your God is giving you, you shall
set up large stones and cover them with
plaster. [3]You shall write on them all the
words of this law when you have crossed
over, to enter the land that the LORD your
God is giving you, a land flowing with milk
and honey, as the LORD, the God of your
ancestors, promised you. [4]So when you have
crossed over the Jordan, you shall set up
these stones, about which I am commanding you today, on Mount Ebal, and you
shall cover them with plaster. [5]And you
shall build an altar there to the LORD your
God, an altar of stones on which you have
not used an iron tool. [6]You must build the
altar of the LORD your God of unhewn[f]
stones. Then offer up burnt offerings on it
to the LORD your God, [7]make sacrifices of
well-being, and eat them there, rejoicing
before the LORD your God. [8]You shall write
on the stones all the words of this law very
clearly.

9 Then Moses and the levitical priests
spoke to all Israel, saying: Keep silence and
hear, O Israel! This very day you have become the people of the LORD your God.
[10]Therefore obey the LORD your God, observing his commandments and his statutes
that I am commanding you today.

Twelve Curses

11 The same day Moses charged the
people as follows: [12]When you have crossed
over the Jordan, these shall stand on Mount
Gerizim for the blessing of the people: Simeon,
Levi, Judah, Issachar, Joseph, and Benjamin.
[13]And these shall stand on Mount Ebal for
the curse: Reuben, Gad, Asher, Zebulun,
Dan, and Naphtali. [14]Then the Levites shall
declare in a loud voice to all the Israelites:

15 "Cursed be anyone who makes an
idol or casts an image, anything abhorrent
to the LORD, the work of an artisan, and sets
it up in secret." All the people shall respond,
saying, "Amen!"

16 "Cursed be anyone who dishonors
father or mother." All the people shall say,
"Amen!"

17 "Cursed be anyone who moves a
neighbor's boundary marker." All the people shall say, "Amen!"

18 "Cursed be anyone who misleads a
blind person on the road." All the people
shall say, "Amen!"

19 "Cursed be anyone who deprives the
alien, the orphan, and the widow of justice." All the people shall say, "Amen!"

20 "Cursed be anyone who lies with his
father's wife, because he has violated his
father's rights."[g] All the people shall say,
"Amen!"

21 "Cursed be anyone who lies with any
animal." All the people shall say, "Amen!"

22 "Cursed be anyone who lies with his
sister, whether the daughter of his father or
the daughter of his mother." All the people
shall say, "Amen!"

23 "Cursed be anyone who lies with his
mother-in-law." All the people shall say,
"Amen!"

24 "Cursed be anyone who strikes down
a neighbor in secret." All the people shall
say, "Amen!"

26.14 Lev 7.20; Hos 9.4
26.16 Deut 4.29
26.18 Deut 7.6
26.19 Deut 28.1; Ps 148.14; Deut 7.6
27.2 Josh 8.30-32
27.3 Deut 26.9
27.5 Ex 20.25; Jos 8.31
27.9 Deut 26.18
27.12 Josh 8.33-35
27.15 Ex 20.4,23; 34.17
27.16 Ex 21.17; Lev 20.9
27.17 Lev 19.14
27.18 Lev 19.14
27.19 Deut 10.18; 24.17
27.20 Lev 18.8; Deut 22.30
27.21 Lev 18.23
27.22 Lev 18.9; 20.17
27.23 Lev 20.14
27.24 Lev 24.17; Num 35.31

[f] Heb *whole* [g] Heb *uncovered his father's skirt*

27.25 Ex 23.7,8
27.26 Deut 28.15; Gal 3.10
28.1 Deut 7.12-26; 26.19
28.3 Gen 39.5; Ps 128.14
28.4 Gen 49.25; Ps 107.38; Prov 10.22
28.7 Lev 26.7,8
28.9 Deut 7.6
28.10 2 Chr 7.14
28.11 Deut 30.9
28.12 Lev 26.4; Deut 15.6
28.14 Deut 5.32
28.15 Lev 26.14; Josh 23.15; Mal 2.2
28.20 Deut 4.26
28.21 Lev 26.25; Jer 24.10
28.22 Lev 26.16; Am 4.9
28.23 Lev 26.19
28.25 Lev 26.17,37; Jer 15.4
28.26 Jer 7.33; 16.4; 34.20
28.27 ver 60,61
28.29 Job 5.14; Isa 59.10
28.30 Jer 8.10; 12.13; Am 5.11

25 "Cursed be anyone who takes a bribe
to shed innocent blood." All the people shall
say, "Amen!"
26 "Cursed be anyone who does not
uphold the words of this law by observing
them." All the people shall say, "Amen!"

Blessings for Obedience

28 If you will only obey the LORD your
God, by diligently observing all his
commandments that I am commanding you
today, the LORD your God will set you high
above all the nations of the earth; 2all these
blessings shall come upon you and overtake
you, if you obey the LORD your God:
3 Blessed shall you be in the city, and
blessed shall you be in the field.
4 Blessed shall be the fruit of your womb,
the fruit of your ground, and the fruit of
your livestock, both the increase of your
cattle and the issue of your flock.
5 Blessed shall be your basket and your
kneading bowl.
6 Blessed shall you be when you come
in, and blessed shall you be when you go
out.
7 The LORD will cause your enemies who
rise against you to be defeated before you;
they shall come out against you one way,
and flee before you seven ways. 8The LORD
will command the blessing upon you in
your barns, and in all that you undertake;
he will bless you in the land that the LORD
your God is giving you. 9The LORD will
establish you as his holy people, as he has
sworn to you, if you keep the commandments of the LORD your God and walk in his
ways. 10All the peoples of the earth shall see
that you are called by the name of the LORD,
and they shall be afraid of you. 11The LORD
will make you abound in prosperity, in the
fruit of your womb, in the fruit of your
livestock, and in the fruit of your ground in
the land that the LORD swore to your ancestors to give you. 12The LORD will open for
you his rich storehouse, the heavens, to
give the rain of your land in its season and
to bless all your undertakings. You will lend
to many nations, but you will not borrow.
13The LORD will make you the head, and not
the tail; you shall be only at the top, and
not at the bottom—if you obey the commandments of the LORD your God, which I
am commanding you today, by diligently
observing them, 14and if you do not turn
aside from any of the words that I am
commanding you today, either to the right
or to the left, following other gods to serve
them.

Warnings against Disobedience

15 But if you will not obey the LORD your
God by diligently observing all his commandments and decrees, which I am commanding you today, then all these curses
shall come upon you and overtake you:
16 Cursed shall you be in the city, and
cursed shall you be in the field.
17 Cursed shall be your basket and your
kneading bowl.
18 Cursed shall be the fruit of your womb,
the fruit of your ground, the increase of
your cattle and the issue of your flock.
19 Cursed shall you be when you come
in, and cursed shall you be when you go
out.
20 The LORD will send upon you disaster,
panic, and frustration in everything you
attempt to do, until you are destroyed and
perish quickly, on account of the evil of
your deeds, because you have forsaken me.
21The LORD will make the pestilence cling to
you until it has consumed you off the land
that you are entering to possess. 22The LORD
will afflict you with consumption, fever,
inflammation, with fiery heat and drought,
and with blight and mildew; they shall
pursue you until you perish. 23The sky over
your head shall be bronze, and the earth
under you iron. 24The LORD will change the
rain of your land into powder, and only
dust shall come down upon you from the
sky until you are destroyed.
25 The LORD will cause you to be defeated before your enemies; you shall go out
against them one way and flee before them
seven ways. You shall become an object of
horror to all the kingdoms of the earth.
26Your corpses shall be food for every bird
of the air and animal of the earth, and there
shall be no one to frighten them away.
27The LORD will afflict you with the boils of
Egypt, with ulcers, scurvy, and itch, of which
you cannot be healed. 28The LORD will afflict
you with madness, blindness, and confusion
of mind; 29you shall grope about at noon as
blind people grope in darkness, but you
shall be unable to find your way; and you
shall be continually abused and robbed,
without anyone to help. 30You shall become
engaged to a woman, but another man
shall lie with her. You shall build a house,

28.1-68 Blessings and Curses. This material derives from several sources. The first set of curses for disobedience to the law appears in 27.11-26, which resembles the Holiness Code in its emphases (Lev 17-26). The second, in 28.1-68, comes from a later period, and reflects the actual experiences of Israel in captivity in Babylon and in dispersion throughout the world. The promised blessings are those found in earlier lists: fruitfulness of the land, prosperity, and defeat of enemies, which will leave Israel *at the top, not at the bottom*. Everything is contingent upon full obedience to God's law. The curses (28.15-68) include lack of crops and human offspring (vv. 16-19), disaster, panic, frustration (vs. 20), disease, plague, drought, military defeat, plundering of possessions, enslavement, captivity (vs. 36), and domination by aliens. All this will happen because of the people's failure to obey the commandments. Another nation with another language than Hebrew will seize them, which was Babylon (vs. 49). There will be sieges so severe that Israelites will practice cannibalism, eating their own children and female afterbirth, and refusing to share even such food with their families. Again the explanation for these catastrophes (vs. 55) is the people's refusal to obey God. There will be for Israel ruin, destruction and dispersion *among all peoples* (vs. 64), and a lapse into idolatry. There is no ground of assurance of survival of the nation, and no guarantee against a return to slavery (vv. 66-68).

but not live in it. You shall plant a vineyard, but not enjoy its fruit. [31]Your ox shall
be butchered before your eyes, but you shall
not eat of it. Your donkey shall be stolen in
front of you, and shall not be restored to
you. Your sheep shall be given to your
enemies, without anyone to help you. [32]Your
sons and daughters shall be given to another people, while you look on; you will
strain your eyes looking for them all day
but be powerless to do anything. [33]A people
whom you do not know shall eat up the
fruit of your ground and of all your labors;
you shall be continually abused and crushed,
[34]and driven mad by the sight that your
eyes shall see. [35]The LORD will strike you on
the knees and on the legs with grievous
boils of which you cannot be healed, from
the sole of your foot to the crown of your
head. [36]The LORD will bring you, and the
king whom you set over you, to a nation
that neither you nor your ancestors have
known, where you shall serve other gods,
of wood and stone. [37]You shall become an
object of horror, a proverb, and a byword
among all the peoples where the LORD will
lead you.

38 You shall carry much seed into the
field but shall gather little in, for the locust
shall consume it. [39]You shall plant vineyards and dress them, but you shall neither
drink the wine nor gather the grapes, for
the worm shall eat them. [40]You shall have
olive trees throughout all your territory, but
you shall not anoint yourself with the oil,
for your olives shall drop off. [41]You shall
have sons and daughters, but they shall not
remain yours, for they shall go into captivity. [42]All your trees and the fruit of your
ground the cicada shall take over. [43]Aliens
residing among you shall ascend above you
higher and higher, while you shall descend
lower and lower. [44]They shall lend to you
but you shall not lend to them; they shall
be the head and you shall be the tail.

45 All these curses shall come upon you,
pursuing and overtaking you until you are
destroyed, because you did not obey the
LORD your God, by observing the commandments and the decrees that he commanded
you. [46]They shall be among you and your
descendants as a sign and a portent forever.

47 Because you did not serve the LORD
your God joyfully and with gladness of
heart for the abundance of everything,
[48]therefore you shall serve your enemies
whom the LORD will send against you, in
hunger and thirst, in nakedness and lack of
everything. He will put an iron yoke on
your neck until he has destroyed you. [49]The
LORD will bring a nation from far away,
from the end of the earth, to swoop down
on you like an eagle, a nation whose language you do not understand, [50]a grim-
faced nation showing no respect to the old
or favor to the young. [51]It shall consume
the fruit of your livestock and the fruit of
your ground until you are destroyed, leaving you neither grain, wine, and oil, nor the
increase of your cattle and the issue of your
flock, until it has made you perish. [52]It shall
besiege you in all your towns until your
high and fortified walls, in which you trusted,
come down throughout your land; it shall
besiege you in all your towns throughout
the land that the LORD your God has given
you. [53]In the desperate straits to which the
enemy siege reduces you, you will eat the
fruit of your womb, the flesh of your own
sons and daughters whom the LORD your
God has given you. [54]Even the most refined
and gentle of men among you will begrudge
food to his own brother, to the wife whom
he embraces, and to the last of his remaining children, [55]giving to none of them any
of the flesh of his children whom he is
eating, because nothing else remains to him,
in the desperate straits to which the enemy
siege will reduce you in all your towns.
[56]She who is the most refined and gentle
among you, so gentle and refined that she
does not venture to set the sole of her foot
on the ground, will begrudge food to the
husband whom she embraces, to her own
son, and to her own daughter, [57]begrudging
even the afterbirth that comes out from
between her thighs, and the children that
she bears, because she is eating them in
secret for lack of anything else, in the desperate straits to which the enemy siege will
reduce you in your towns.

58 If you do not diligently observe all the
words of this law that are written in this
book, fearing this glorious and awesome
name, the LORD your God, [59]then the LORD
will overwhelm both you and your offspring
with severe and lasting afflictions and grievous and lasting maladies. [60]He will bring
back upon you all the diseases of Egypt, of
which you were in dread, and they shall
cling to you. [61]Every other malady and
affliction, even though not recorded in the
book of this law, the LORD will inflict on you
until you are destroyed. [62]Although once

28.32 ver 41
28.33 Jer 5.17
28.35 ver 27
28.36 2 Kings 17.4,6; 24.12,14; 25.7,11; Deut 4.28
28.37 Jer 24.9; Ps 44.14
28.38 Mic 6.15
28.41 ver 32
28.42 ver 38
28.43 ver 13
28.44 ver 12,13
28.45 ver 15
28.47 Deut 32.15
28.48 Jer 28.13,14
28.49 Jer 5.15
28.51 ver 33
28.52 Jer 10.17,18; Zeph 1.15,16
28.53 Lev 26.29; Jer 19.9; Lam 2.20
28.56 ver 54
28.58 Ex 6.3
28.60 ver 27
28.61 Deut 4.25,26
28.62 Deut 4.27; 10.22

28.63 Jer 12.14; 45.4
28.64 Deut 4.27,28
28.65 Lev 26.16,36
28.67 ver 34
29.1 Deut 5.2,3
29.2 Ex 19.4
29.4 Isa 6.9,10; Acts 28.26,27; Eph 4.18
29.5 Deut 8.4
29.6 Deut 8.3
29.7 Num 21.21-24,33-35; Deut 2.32; 3.1
29.8 Num 32.33; Deut 3.12,13
29.9 Deut 4.6; Josh 1.7
29.11 Josh 9.21,23,27
29.13 Deut 28.9; Ex 6.7; Gen 17.7
29.17 Deut 28.26
29.18 Deut 11.16; Heb 12.15
29.20 Ps 74.1; 79.5; Deut 9.14; Ex 32.33
29.21 Mt 24.51
29.22 Jer 19.8

you were as numerous as the stars in heaven, you shall be left few in number, because you did not obey the LORD your God. 63And just as the LORD took delight in making you prosperous and numerous, so the LORD will take delight in bringing you to ruin and destruction; you shall be plucked off the land that you are entering to possess. 64The LORD will scatter you among all peoples, from one end of the earth to the other; and there you shall serve other gods, of wood and stone, which neither you nor your ancestors have known. 65Among those nations you shall find no ease, no resting place for the sole of your foot. There the LORD will give you a trembling heart, failing eyes, and a languishing spirit. 66Your life shall hang in doubt before you; night and day you shall be in dread, with no assurance of your life. 67In the morning you shall say, "If only it were evening!" and at evening you shall say, "If only it were morning!"—because of the dread that your heart shall feel and the sights that your eyes shall see. 68The LORD will bring you back in ships to Egypt, by a route that I promised you would never see again; and there you shall offer yourselves for sale to your enemies as male and female slaves, but there will be no buyer.

29[h] These are the words of the covenant that the LORD commanded Moses to make with the Israelites in the land of Moab, in addition to the covenant that he had made with them at Horeb.

The Covenant Renewed in Moab

2[i] Moses summoned all Israel and said to them: You have seen all that the LORD did before your eyes in the land of Egypt, to Pharaoh and to all his servants and to all his land, 3the great trials that your eyes saw, the signs, and those great wonders. 4But to this day the LORD has not given you a mind to understand, or eyes to see, or ears to hear. 5I have led you forty years in the wilderness. The clothes on your back have not worn out, and the sandals on your feet have not worn out; 6you have not eaten bread, and you have not drunk wine or strong drink—so that you may know that I am the LORD your God. 7When you came to this place, King Sihon of Heshbon and King Og of Bashan came out against us for battle, but we defeated them. 8We took their land and gave it as an inheritance to the Reubenites, the Gadites, and the half-tribe of Manasseh. 9Therefore diligently observe the words of this covenant, in order that you may succeed[j] in everything that you do.

10 You stand assembled today, all of you, before the LORD your God—the leaders of your tribes,[k] your elders, and your officials, all the men of Israel, 11your children, your women, and the aliens who are in your camp, both those who cut your wood and those who draw your water— 12to enter into the covenant of the LORD your God, sworn by an oath, which the LORD your God is making with you today; 13in order that he may establish you today as his people, and that he may be your God, as he promised you and as he swore to your ancestors, to Abraham, to Isaac, and to Jacob. 14I am making this covenant, sworn by an oath, not only with you who stand here with us today before the LORD our God, 15but also with those who are not here with us today. 16You know how we lived in the land of Egypt, and how we came through the midst of the nations through which you passed. 17You have seen their detestable things, the filthy idols of wood and stone, of silver and gold, that were among them. 18It may be that there is among you a man or woman, or a family or tribe, whose heart is already turning away from the LORD our God to serve the gods of those nations. It may be that there is among you a root sprouting poisonous and bitter growth. 19All who hear the words of this oath and bless themselves, thinking in their hearts, "We are safe even though we go our own stubborn ways" (thus bringing disaster on moist and dry alike)[l]— 20the LORD will be unwilling to pardon them, for the LORD's anger and passion will smoke against them. All the curses written in this book will descend on them, and the LORD will blot out their names from under heaven. 21The LORD will single them out from all the tribes of Israel for calamity, in accordance with all the curses of the covenant written in this book of the law. 22The next generation, your children who rise up after you, as well as the foreigner who comes from a distant country, will see the devastation of that land and the afflictions with which the LORD

[h] Ch 28.69 in Heb [i] Ch 29.1 in Heb [j] Or *deal wisely* [k] Gk Syr: Heb *your leaders, your tribes* [l] Meaning of Heb uncertain

29.1 This conclusion of *the words of the covenant* on this solemn, warning note is said to be what was given at Moab, and *in addition* to the law as it was given at Horeb. It actually represents an expansion of the legal tradition after the exile to account for the sufferings and despair of that experience.
29.2-30.20 The Renewal of the Covenant in Moab. This is seen as added to the covenant God made *at Horeb*, and repeats the basic themes of Deuteronomy. The people are to learn from the miraculous events that accompanied their escape from Egypt – in forty years their clothes and shoes did not wear out! (29.5) – and from their victory over their foes that God has called them and that he wants them to obey the rules of the covenant (29.7-8). Non-Israelite *aliens* are to share in the covenant as well, which God promised to their *ancestors*. Those already inclined to idolatry and disobedience will be judged by *the LORD's* anger and passion, and the disasters that beset the nation are the result of their disobedience (29.22-29).

30.1-10 The Possibility of Restoration. When Israel is in exile or dispersed among the nations, only obedience to God's commands will bring about restoration to the land and to God's favor. They will exceed their ancestors in prosperity and in numbers (30.5). Circumcision is here of the *heart*, rather than the physical ritual act, and will bring them back under God's blessing (30.6). The commandments are no longer to be thought of as carved on the stone tablets only, but as located in the *mouth*, where they will control speaking, and in the *heart*, where they will influence the will. The choice is up to the people: God has provided the alternatives and the resources for an obedient, rewarding life in the land, as promised to the ancestors (30.19-20).

has afflicted it— 23all its soil burned out by sulfur and salt, nothing planted, nothing sprouting, unable to support any vegetation, like the destruction of Sodom and Gomorrah, Admah and Zeboiim, which the LORD destroyed in his fierce anger— 24they and indeed all the nations will wonder, "Why has the LORD done thus to this land? What caused this great display of anger?" 25They will conclude, "It is because they abandoned the covenant of the LORD, the God of their ancestors, which he made with them when he brought them out of the land of Egypt. 26They turned and served other gods, worshiping them, gods whom they had not known and whom he had not allotted to them; 27so the anger of the LORD was kindled against that land, bringing on it every curse written in this book. 28The LORD uprooted them from their land in anger, fury, and great wrath, and cast them into another land, as is now the case." 29The secret things belong to the LORD our God, but the revealed things belong to us and to our children forever, to observe all the words of this law.

God's Fidelity Assured

30 When all these things have happened to you, the blessings and the curses that I have set before you, if you call them to mind among all the nations where the LORD your God has driven you, 2and return to the LORD your God, and you and your children obey him with all your heart and with all your soul, just as I am commanding you today, 3then the LORD your God will restore your fortunes and have compassion on you, gathering you again from all the peoples among whom the LORD your God has scattered you. 4Even if you are exiled to the ends of the world,[m] from there the LORD your God will gather you, and from there he will bring you back. 5The LORD your God will bring you into the land that your ancestors possessed, and you will possess it; he will make you more prosperous and numerous than your ancestors.

6 Moreover, the LORD your God will circumcise your heart and the heart of your descendants, so that you will love the LORD your God with all your heart and with all your soul, in order that you may live. 7The LORD your God will put all these curses on your enemies and on the adversaries who took advantage of you. 8Then you shall again obey the LORD, observing all his commandments that I am commanding you today, 9and the LORD your God will make you abundantly prosperous in all your undertakings, in the fruit of your body, in the fruit of your livestock, and in the fruit of your soil. For the LORD will again take delight in prospering you, just as he delighted in prospering your ancestors, 10when you obey the LORD your God by observing his commandments and decrees that are written in this book of the law, because you turn to the LORD your God with all your heart and with all your soul.

Exhortation to Choose Life

11 Surely, this commandment that I am commanding you today is not too hard for you, nor is it too far away. 12It is not in heaven, that you should say, "Who will go up to heaven for us, and get it for us so that we may hear it and observe it?" 13Neither is it beyond the sea, that you should say, "Who will cross to the other side of the sea for us, and get it for us so that we may hear it and observe it?" 14No, the word is very near to you; it is in your mouth and in your heart for you to observe.

15 See, I have set before you today life and prosperity, death and adversity. 16If you obey the commandments of the LORD your God[n] that I am commanding you today, by loving the LORD your God, walking in his ways, and observing his commandments, decrees, and ordinances, then you shall live and become numerous, and the LORD your God will bless you in the land that you are entering to possess. 17But if your heart turns away and you do not hear, but are led astray to bow down to other gods and serve them, 18I declare to you today that you shall perish; you shall not live long in the land that you are crossing the Jordan to enter and possess. 19I call heaven and earth to witness against you today that I have set before you life and death, blessings and curses. Choose life so that you and your descendants may live, 20loving the LORD your God, obeying him, and holding fast to him; for that means life to you and length of days, so that you may live in the land that the LORD swore to give to your ancestors, to Abraham, to Isaac, and to Jacob.

29.23 Gen 19.24; Isa 34.9; Jer 20.16
29.24 Jer 22.8,9
29.28 1 Kings 14.15; 2 Chr 7.20
30.1 ver 15,19; Deut 11.26; 28.64; 29.28
30.2 Deut 4.29,30
30.3 Jer 29.14; 32.37
30.4 Neh 1.9; Isa 43.6
30.6 Jer 32.39
30.9 Deut 28.11; Jer 32.41
30.11 Isa 45.19
30.12 Rom 10.6-8
30.15 ver 1,19
30.18 Deut 4.26
30.19 Deut 4.26; ver 1
30.20 Deut 6.5; 10.20; Ps 27.1; Jn 11.25

[m] Heb *of heaven* [n] Gk: Heb lacks *If you obey the commandments of the* LORD *your God*

Joshua Becomes Moses' Successor

31 When Moses had finished speaking all[o] these words to all Israel, 2he said to them: "I am now one hundred twenty years old. I am no longer able to get about, and the LORD has told me, 'You shall not cross over this Jordan.' 3The LORD your God himself will cross over before you. He will destroy these nations before you, and you shall dispossess them. Joshua also will cross over before you, as the LORD promised. 4The LORD will do to them as he did to Sihon and Og, the kings of the Amorites, and to their land, when he destroyed them. 5The LORD will give them over to you and you shall deal with them in full accord with the command that I have given to you. 6Be strong and bold; have no fear or dread of them, because it is the LORD your God who goes with you; he will not fail you or forsake you."

7 Then Moses summoned Joshua and said to him in the sight of all Israel: "Be strong and bold, for you are the one who will go with this people into the land that the LORD has sworn to their ancestors to give them; and you will put them in possession of it. 8It is the LORD who goes before you. He will be with you; he will not fail you or forsake you. Do not fear or be dismayed."

The Law to Be Read Every Seventh Year

9 Then Moses wrote down this law, and gave it to the priests, the sons of Levi, who carried the ark of the covenant of the LORD, and to all the elders of Israel. 10Moses commanded them: "Every seventh year, in the scheduled year of remission, during the festival of booths,[p] 11when all Israel comes to appear before the LORD your God at the place that he will choose, you shall read this law before all Israel in their hearing. 12Assemble the people—men, women, and children, as well as the aliens residing in your towns—so that they may hear and learn to fear the LORD your God and to observe diligently all the words of this law, 13and so that their children, who have not known it, may hear and learn to fear the LORD your God, as long as you live in the land that you are crossing over the Jordan to possess."

Moses and Joshua Receive God's Charge

14 The LORD said to Moses, "Your time to die is near; call Joshua and present yourselves in the tent of meeting, so that I may commission him." So Moses and Joshua went and presented themselves in the tent of meeting, 15and the LORD appeared at the tent in a pillar of cloud; the pillar of cloud stood at the entrance to the tent.

16 The LORD said to Moses, "Soon you will lie down with your ancestors. Then this people will begin to prostitute themselves to the foreign gods in their midst, the gods of the land into which they are going; they will forsake me, breaking my covenant that I have made with them. 17My anger will be kindled against them in that day. I will forsake them and hide my face from them; they will become easy prey, and many terrible troubles will come upon them. In that day they will say, 'Have not these troubles come upon us because our God is not in our midst?' 18On that day I will surely hide my face on account of all the evil they have done by turning to other gods. 19Now therefore write this song, and teach it to the Israelites; put it in their mouths, in order that this song may be a witness for me against the Israelites. 20For when I have brought them into the land flowing with milk and honey, which I promised on oath to their ancestors, and they have eaten their fill and grown fat, they will turn to other gods and serve them, despising me and breaking my covenant. 21And when many terrible troubles come upon them, this song will confront them as a witness, because it will not be lost from the mouths of their descendants. For I know what they are inclined to do even now, before I have brought them into the land that I promised them on oath." 22That very day Moses wrote this song and taught it to the Israelites.

23 Then the LORD commissioned Joshua son of Nun and said, "Be strong and bold, for you shall bring the Israelites into the land that I promised them; I will be with you."

24 When Moses had finished writing down in a book the words of this law to the very end, 25Moses commanded the Levites who carried the ark of the covenant of the LORD, saying, 26"Take this book of the law

[o] Q Ms Gk: MT *Moses went and spoke* [p] Or *tabernacles*; Heb *succoth*

31.2 Deut 34.7; 3.27
31.3 Deut 9.3; 3.28
31.5 Deut 7.2
31.6 Josh 10.25; Deut 1.29; 20.4; Heb 13.5
31.7 Deut 1.38; 3.28
31.8 ver 6
31.9 ver 25; Num 4.15
31.10 Deut 15.1; Lev 23.34
31.11 Deut 16.16; Josh 8.34,35
31.12 Deut 4.10
31.13 Deut 11.2; Ps 78.6,7
31.14 Deut 32.49,50; ver 23
31.15 Ex 33.9
31.16 Judg 2.11,12; 10.6,13
31.17 Judg 2.14; 6.13; Deut 32.20; Num 14.42
31.20 Deut 10.6-12; 32.15-17; ver 16
31.21 ver 17; Hos 5.3
31.22 ver 19
31.23 ver 7; Josh 1.6
31.25 ver 9
31.26 ver 19

31.1-34.12 Moses' Last Will and Testament.
31.1-2 Because of his great age (rather than because of his failure to trust God [Deut 32.51; Num 20.1-13]), Moses will not cross to the promised land. But the LORD himself will. There he will destroy the inhabitants and enable his people to occupy the land (31.4-5). They will be led by Joshua (31.7-8), but the law will be given to the *priests* and *elders* of Israel for the institution of the cycle of feasts and for the continuing instruction of the people (31.9-13).

31.30-32.44 The Song of Moses. Appearing to Moses and Joshua in *the tent of meeting*, the LORD announces Moses' death and the apostasy of the people after they enter the land. Moses is to compose a *song*, which is to be taught to the people as a continuing witness to God's purpose for them and their responsibility toward the LORD. After Joshua is commissioned as their leader (31.23), the tribes are assembled to hear the song, which they are to *take to heart* (32.46). **32.1-3** Moses' message is presented in terms which resemble wisdom teaching (see Prov 7.1-3) as well as images used in the Psalms of God, such as the *Rock* (32.4, 15; see Ps 18.2; 28.1; 144.1). God's purposes may be seen at work throughout the ages (32.7), back to the beginnings of human history when peoples were assigned to the control of various gods, and it was the LORD whose *allotted share* was Israel (32.9). Vivid images of the movements of wildlife and birds are used to depict Israel's entrance into the promised land (32.10-14), where they now find themselves in a situation of plenty which has lured them into devotion to the local pagan fertility deities (32.10-15). This will evoke God's judgment on his disobedient and ungrateful people (32.19-25), but he will not utterly destroy them, lest their adversaries think they are responsible for Israel's defeat rather than that it occurred through the judgment of God. They could not have been defeated by their enemies unless God had been at work through and behind these pagan powers, which are corrupt and worthless, used by God to punish his people (32.28-35). Yet God will restore his people when they recognize that power is his alone and that the false gods they worship are futile (32.36-42). The song ends with a summons to Israel to praise God, to recognize how their enemies have been overcome, and to purify the land where they now dwell (32.43).

and put it beside the ark of the covenant of
the LORD your God; let it remain there as a
witness against you. [27]For I know well how
rebellious and stubborn you are. If you
already have been so rebellious toward the
LORD while I am still alive among you, how
much more after my death! [28]Assemble to
me all the elders of your tribes and your
officials, so that I may recite these words in
their hearing and call heaven and earth to
witness against them. [29]For I know that
after my death you will surely act corruptly,
turning aside from the way that I have
commanded you. In time to come trouble
will befall you, because you will do what is
evil in the sight of the LORD, provoking him
to anger through the work of your hands."

The Song of Moses

30 Then Moses recited the words of this
song, to the very end, in the hearing of the
whole assembly of Israel:

32 Give ear, O heavens, and I will speak;
let the earth hear the words of my mouth.
2 May my teaching drop like the rain,
my speech condense like the dew;
like gentle rain on grass,
like showers on new growth.
3 For I will proclaim the name of the LORD;
ascribe greatness to our God!

4 The Rock, his work is perfect,
and all his ways are just.
A faithful God, without deceit,
just and upright is he;
5 yet his degenerate children have dealt falsely with him,[q]
a perverse and crooked generation.
6 Do you thus repay the LORD,
O foolish and senseless people?
Is not he your father, who created you,
who made you and established you?
7 Remember the days of old,
consider the years long past;
ask your father, and he will inform you;
your elders, and they will tell you.
8 When the Most High[r] apportioned the nations,
when he divided humankind,
he fixed the boundaries of the peoples
according to the number of the gods;[s]
9 the LORD's own portion was his people,
Jacob his allotted share.

10 He sustained[t] him in a desert land,
in a howling wilderness waste;
he shielded him, cared for him,
guarded him as the apple of his eye.
11 As an eagle stirs up its nest,
and hovers over its young;
as it spreads its wings, takes them up,
and bears them aloft on its pinions,
12 the LORD alone guided him;
no foreign god was with him.
13 He set him atop the heights of the land,
and fed him with[u] produce of the field;
he nursed him with honey from the crags,
with oil from flinty rock;
14 curds from the herd, and milk from the flock,
with fat of lambs and rams;
Bashan bulls and goats,
together with the choicest wheat—
you drank fine wine from the blood of grapes.
15 Jacob ate his fill;[v]
Jeshurun grew fat, and kicked.
You grew fat, bloated, and gorged!
He abandoned God who made him,
and scoffed at the Rock of his salvation.
16 They made him jealous with strange gods,
with abhorrent things they provoked him.
17 They sacrificed to demons, not God,
to deities they had never known,
to new ones recently arrived,
whom your ancestors had not feared.
18 You were unmindful of the Rock that bore you;[w]
you forgot the God who gave you birth.

19 The LORD saw it, and was jealous[x]
he spurned[y] his sons and daughters.
20 He said: I will hide my face from them,
I will see what their end will be;
for they are a perverse generation,
children in whom there is no faithfulness.
21 They made me jealous with what is no god,
provoked me with their idols.

31.27 Deut 9.6,24
31.28 Deut 4.26
31.29 Deut 32.5; 28.15
32.1 Isa 1.2
32.2 Isa 55.10,11
32.3 Ex 33.19; Deut 3.24
32.4 ver 15,18,30; Deut 7.9; Ps 92.15
32.5 Deut 31.29; Lk 9.41
32.6 Deut 1.31
32.7 Ex 13.14
32.8 Gen 11.8; Acts 17.26
32.9 1 Kings 8.51,53; Jer 10.16
32.10 Jer 2.6; Zech 2.8
32.11 Ex 19.4; Isa 31.5
32.12 ver 39
32.13 Isa 58.14; Job 29.6
32.14 Ps 147.14
32.15 Deut 33.5,26; Isa 1.4
32.16 Ps 78.58; 1 Cor 10.22
32.17 Ps 106.37; Deut 28.64; Judg 5.8
32.18 Isa 17.10; Ps 106.21
32.19 Ps 106.40; Jer 44.21-23
32.20 Deut 31.17,29; ver 5
32.21 ver 16; Rom 10.19

[q] Meaning of Heb uncertain [r] Traditional rendering of Heb *Elyon* [s] Q Ms Compare Gk Tg: MT *the Israelites* [t] Sam Gk Compare Tg: MT *found* [u] Sam Gk Syr Tg: MT *he ate* [v] Q Mss Sam Gk: MT lacks *Jacob ate his fill* [w] Or *that begot you* [x] Q Mss Gk: MT lacks *was jealous* [y] Cn: Heb *he spurned because of provocation*

32.22 Jer 15.14
32.23 Deut 29.21; Ezek 5.16
32.24 Deut 28.22; Lev 26.22; ver 33
32.25 Ezek 7.15; 2 Chr 36.17
32.26 Deut 4.27; Ps 34.16
32.27 Deut 9.26-28; Isa 10.13
32.29 Ps 81.13
32.30 Lev 26.7,8; ver 4
32.31 1 Sam 2.2; 4.8
32.33 Ps 58.4
32.34 Hos 13.12
32.35 Rom 12.19; Heb 10.30
32.36 Ps 135.14; 106.45; Judg 2.18; Joel 2.14
32.37 Jer 2.28
32.39 Isa 41.4; Ps 50.22
32.41 Ezek 21.9,10
32.42 Jer 46.10
32.43 Rom 15.10; Rev 19.2; Ps 85.1
32.46 Deut 6.6; Ezek 40.4
32.47 Deut 30.20

So I will make them jealous with what is no people,
provoke them with a foolish nation.
22 For a fire is kindled by my anger,
and burns to the depths of Sheol;
it devours the earth and its increase,
and sets on fire the foundations of the mountains.
23 I will heap disasters upon them,
spend my arrows against them:
24 wasting hunger,
burning consumption,
bitter pestilence.
The teeth of beasts I will send against them,
with venom of things crawling in the dust.
25 In the street the sword shall bereave,
and in the chambers terror,
for young man and woman alike,
nursing child and old gray head.
26 I thought to scatter them[z]
and blot out the memory of them from humankind;
27 but I feared provocation by the enemy,
for their adversaries might misunderstand
and say, "Our hand is triumphant;
it was not the LORD who did all this."

28 They are a nation void of sense;
there is no understanding in them.
29 If they were wise, they would understand this;
they would discern what the end would be.
30 How could one have routed a thousand,
and two put a myriad to flight,
unless their Rock had sold them,
the LORD had given them up?
31 Indeed their rock is not like our Rock;
our enemies are fools.[z]
32 Their vine comes from the vinestock of Sodom,
from the vineyards of Gomorrah;
their grapes are grapes of poison,
their clusters are bitter;
33 their wine is the poison of serpents,
the cruel venom of asps.

34 Is not this laid up in store with me,
sealed up in my treasuries?
35 Vengeance is mine, and recompense,
for the time when their foot shall slip;
because the day of their calamity is at hand,
their doom comes swiftly.

36 Indeed the LORD will vindicate his people,
have compassion on his servants,
when he sees that their power is gone,
neither bond nor free remaining.
37 Then he will say: Where are their gods,
the rock in which they took refuge,
38 who ate the fat of their sacrifices,
and drank the wine of their libations?
Let them rise up and help you,
let them be your protection!

39 See now that I, even I, am he;
there is no god besides me.
I kill and I make alive;
I wound and I heal;
and no one can deliver from my hand.
40 For I lift up my hand to heaven,
and swear: As I live forever,
41 when I whet my flashing sword,
and my hand takes hold on judgment;
I will take vengeance on my adversaries,
and will repay those who hate me.
42 I will make my arrows drunk with blood,
and my sword shall devour flesh—
with the blood of the slain and the captives,
from the long-haired enemy.

43 Praise, O heavens,[a] his people,
worship him, all you gods![b]
For he will avenge the blood of his children,[c]
and take vengeance on his adversaries;
he will repay those who hate him,[d]
and cleanse the land for his people.[e]

44 Moses came and recited all the words
of this song in the hearing of the people, he
and Joshua[f] son of Nun. 45 When Moses had
finished reciting all these words to all Israel,
46 he said to them: "Take to heart all the
words that I am giving in witness against
you today; give them as a command to
your children, so that they may diligently
observe all the words of this law. 47 This is
no trifling matter for you, but rather your
very life; through it you may live long in
the land that you are crossing over the
Jordan to possess."

[z] Gk: Meaning of Heb uncertain [a] Q Ms Gk: MT *nations* [b] Q Ms Gk: MT lacks this line [c] Q Ms Gk: MT *his servants* [d] Q Ms Gk: MT lacks this line [e] Q Ms Sam Gk Vg: MT *his land his people* [f] Sam Gk Syr Vg: MT *Hoshea*

32.44-47 Moses' message in song is to be taught to children so that the commandments may be observed. Only in this way can Israel *live long in the land.*

32.48-52 Moses' Preparations for Death. The language and terms here show links with Num 20.22-29 (Aaron's death; Moses' successor named, 27.12). Recalled is Moses' and Aaron's disbelief of God at Meribah (Num 20.1-13). The passage probably was joined with what is now Deut 34.1,7-9 before Deut 33 was inserted.
33.1-29 Moses' Final Blessings. This follows the pattern and style of the farewell addresses of the patriarchs Isaac (Gen 27) and Jacob (Gen 49). There are different destinies for each of the twelve tribes in God's plan. Israel is identified as *Jeshurun*, which means "upright" and which is only occasionally appropriate for Israel as here depicted. The unique priestly roles of Levi, in spite of occasional failures (33.8-9) include instruction and leadership in sacrificial offerings (33.10). The other tribes are described in terms of geographical location, economic level or other distinctive advantages. The presence of the LORD with Benjamin probably refers to the sanctuary of God in that territory at Bethel (Gen 12.8; Judg 20.18). The tribes of Joseph (Ephraim and Manasseh) are characterized by prosperity and abundance as signs of God's special favor (33.13-17). Zebulun and Naphtali prosper as a result of their location astride major trade routes that crossed from the Lake of Galilee to the Mediterranean ports (33.18-19). Although Gad *chose the best for himself* in the territory east of the Jordan, he also *executed justice* by aiding the other tribes in the conquest of Canaan (33.20-21). Dan was notorious for attacking caravans as they passed through that territory from Syria to the Mediterranean Sea north of Lake Huleh (33.22). Naphtali flourished in the fertile land west of the Sea of Galilee (33.23), as did Asher adjacent to the commerce and industry on the coast of Tyre and Sidon (33.24-25). The address ends with praise to God, who delivered Israel from her enemies and who continues to subdue the powers of evil (33.26-29).

Moses' Death Foretold

48 On that very day the LORD addressed
Moses as follows: 49"Ascend this mountain
of the Abarim, Mount Nebo, which is in the
land of Moab, across from Jericho, and view
the land of Canaan, which I am giving to
the Israelites for a possession; 50you shall die
there on the mountain that you ascend and
shall be gathered to your kin, as your brother
Aaron died on Mount Hor and was gathered to his kin; 51because both of you broke
faith with me among the Israelites at the
waters of Meribath-kadesh in the wilderness
of Zin, by failing to maintain my holiness
among the Israelites. 52Although you may
view the land from a distance, you shall not
enter it—the land that I am giving to the
Israelites."

Moses' Final Blessing on Israel

33 This is the blessing with which
Moses, the man of God, blessed the
Israelites before his death. 2He said:
The LORD came from Sinai,
and dawned from Seir upon us;[g]
he shone forth from Mount Paran.
With him were myriads of holy ones;[h]
at his right, a host of his own.[i]
3 Indeed, O favorite among[j] peoples,
all his holy ones were in your charge;
they marched at your heels,
accepted direction from you.
4 Moses charged us with the law,
as a possession for the assembly of Jacob.
5 There arose a king in Jeshurun,
when the leaders of the people assembled—
the united tribes of Israel.

6 May Reuben live, and not die out,
even though his numbers are few.

7And this he said of Judah:
O LORD, give heed to Judah,
and bring him to his people;
strengthen his hands for him,[k]
and be a help against his adversaries.

8And of Levi he said:
Give to Levi[l] your Thummim,
and your Urim to your loyal one,
whom you tested at Massah,
with whom you contended at the waters of Meribah;
9 who said of his father and mother,
"I regard them not";
he ignored his kin,
and did not acknowledge his children.
For they observed your word,
and kept your covenant.
10 They teach Jacob your ordinances,
and Israel your law;
they place incense before you,
and whole burnt offerings on your altar.
11 Bless, O LORD, his substance,
and accept the work of his hands;
crush the loins of his adversaries,
of those that hate him, so that they do not rise again.

12Of Benjamin he said:
The beloved of the LORD rests in safety—
the High God[m] surrounds him all day long—
the beloved[n] rests between his shoulders.

13And of Joseph he said:
Blessed by the LORD be his land,
with the choice gifts of heaven above,
and of the deep that lies beneath;
14 with the choice fruits of the sun,
and the rich yield of the months;
15 with the finest produce of the ancient mountains,
and the abundance of the everlasting hills;
16 with the choice gifts of the earth and its fullness,
and the favor of the one who dwells on Sinai.[o]
Let these come on the head of Joseph,
on the brow of the prince among his brothers.
17 A firstborn[p] bull—majesty is his!
His horns are the horns of a wild ox;
with them he gores the peoples,
driving them to[q] the ends of the earth;

32.49 Num 27.12-14

32.51 Num 20.11-13; 27.14

32.52 Deut 34.1-3; 1.37

33.1 Josh 14.6

33.2 Hab 3.3; Dan 7.10; Acts 7.53; Gal 3.19; Rev 5.11

33.3 Hos 11.1; Deut 14.2

33.4 Jn 1.17; Ps 119.111

33.7 Gen 49.8-12

33.8 Ex 28.30; 17.7

33.9 Ex 32.26-29

33.10 Deut 31.9-13; Ex 30.7,8; Ps 51.19

33.11 2 Sam 24.23; Ps 20.3

33.13 Gen 49.25; 27.28

33.15 Gen 49.26

33.16 Ex 3.2,4; Acts 7.30,35

33.17 Num 23.22; Ps 44.5

[g] Gk Syr Vg Compare Tg: Heb *upon them* [h] Cn Compare Gk Sam Syr Vg: MT *He came from Ribeboth-kodesh,* [i] Cn Compare Gk: meaning of Heb uncertain [j] Or *O lover of the* [k] Cn: Heb *with his hands he contended* [l] Q Ms Gk: MT lacks *Give to Levi* [m] Heb *above him* [n] Heb *he* [o] Cn: Heb *in the bush* [p] Q Ms Gk Syr Vg: MT *His firstborn* [q] Cn: Heb *the peoples, together*

such are the myriads of Ephraim,
such the thousands of Manasseh.

18 And of Zebulun he said:
Rejoice, Zebulun, in your going out;
and Issachar, in your tents.
19 They call peoples to the mountain;
there they offer the right sacrifices;
for they suck the affluence of the seas
and the hidden treasures of the sand.

20 And of Gad he said:
Blessed be the enlargement of Gad!
Gad lives like a lion;
he tears at arm and scalp.
21 He chose the best for himself,
for there a commander's allotment
was reserved;
he came at the head of the people,
he executed the justice of the LORD,
and his ordinances for Israel.

22 And of Dan he said:
Dan is a lion's whelp
that leaps forth from Bashan.

23 And of Naphtali he said:
O Naphtali, sated with favor,
full of the blessing of the LORD,
possess the west and the south.

24 And of Asher he said:
Most blessed of sons be Asher;
may he be the favorite of his brothers,
and may he dip his foot in oil.
25 Your bars are iron and bronze;
and as your days, so is your strength.

26 There is none like God, O Jeshurun,
who rides through the heavens to
your help,
majestic through the skies.
27 He subdues the ancient gods,[r]
shatters[s] the forces of old;[t]
he drove out the enemy before you,
and said, "Destroy!"
28 So Israel lives in safety,
untroubled is Jacob's abode[u]
in a land of grain and wine,
where the heavens drop down dew.
29 Happy are you, O Israel! Who is like you,
a people saved by the LORD,
the shield of your help,
and the sword of your triumph!
Your enemies shall come fawning to
you,
and you shall tread on their backs.

Moses Dies and Is Buried in the Land of Moab

34 Then Moses went up from the
plains of Moab to Mount Nebo, to
the top of Pisgah, which is opposite Jericho,
and the LORD showed him the whole land:
Gilead as far as Dan, 2 all Naphtali, the land
of Ephraim and Manasseh, all the land of
Judah as far as the Western Sea, 3 the Negeb,
and the Plain—that is, the valley of Jericho,
the city of palm trees—as far as Zoar. 4 The
LORD said to him, "This is the land of which
I swore to Abraham, to Isaac, and to Jacob,
saying, 'I will give it to your descendants';
I have let you see it with your eyes, but you
shall not cross over there." 5 Then Moses,
the servant of the LORD, died there in the
land of Moab, at the LORD's command. 6 He
was buried in a valley in the land of Moab,
opposite Beth-peor, but no one knows his
burial place to this day. 7 Moses was one
hundred twenty years old when he died; his
sight was unimpaired and his vigor had not
abated. 8 The Israelites wept for Moses in the
plains of Moab thirty days; then the period
of mourning for Moses was ended.
9 Joshua son of Nun was full of the spirit
of wisdom, because Moses had laid his hands
on him; and the Israelites obeyed him, doing
as the LORD had commanded Moses.
10 Never since has there arisen a prophet
in Israel like Moses, whom the LORD knew
face to face. 11 He was unequaled for all the
signs and wonders that the LORD sent him
to perform in the land of Egypt, against
Pharaoh and all his servants and his entire
land, 12 and for all the mighty deeds and all
the terrifying displays of power that Moses
performed in the sight of all Israel.

[r] Or *The eternal God is a dwelling place* [s] Cn: Heb *from underneath* [t] Or *the everlasting arms* [u] Or *fountain*

33.18 Gen 49.13-15
33.19 Isa 2.3; Ps 4.5
33.20 Gen 49.19
33.21 Num 32.1-5; 31,32; Josh 4.12; 22.1-3
33.22 Gen 49.16
33.23 Gen 49.21
33.24 Gen 49.20; Job 29.6
33.25 Deut 4.40; 32.49
33.26 Ex 15.11; Ps 68.33,34
33.27 Ps 90.1,2; Josh 24.18
33.28 Num 23.9; Gen 27.28
33.29 Ps 144.15; 2 Sam 7.23; Ps 18.14; Deut 32.13
34.1 Deut 34.49,52
34.4 Gen 12.7; 28.13
34.5 Deut 34.50; Josh 1.1,2
34.7 Deut 31.2
34.9 Isa 11.2; Num 27.18,23
34.10 Num 12.6,8
34.11 Deut 4.34

34.1-12 The Death of Moses and the Conclusion of Torah. There is an earlier version of Moses' death in Num 27.12-23, which takes place on *Pisgah* rather than *Nebo* (Deut 32.49). The fact that his burial place is unknown *to this day* shows that the account was written long after the events described. Joshua is prepared for effective leadership by *the spirit of wisdom*, which he received through Moses having laid hands upon him (34.9). The book ends with praise of Moses' unique role as *prophet*, and as worker of *signs and wonders* – both capabilities which derived from his special access to the LORD. Perhaps this final note of the editor of Deuteronomy intends to show the superiority of Moses and the legal tradition attributed to him over the prophets and their tradition.

JOSHUA

See the Introductions, pp. 3, 38, and 40 above.

God's Commission to Joshua

1 After the death of Moses the servant of the LORD, the LORD spoke to Joshua son of Nun, Moses' assistant, saying, 2"My servant Moses is dead. Now proceed to cross the Jordan, you and all this people, into the land that I am giving to them, to the Israelites. 3Every place that the sole of your foot will tread upon I have given to you, as I promised to Moses. 4From the wilderness and the Lebanon as far as the great river, the river Euphrates, all the land of the Hittites, to the Great Sea in the west shall be your territory. 5No one shall be able to stand against you all the days of your life. As I was with Moses, so I will be with you; I will not fail you or forsake you. 6Be strong and courageous; for you shall put this people in possession of the land that I swore to their ancestors to give them. 7Only be strong and very courageous, being careful to act in accordance with all the law that my servant Moses commanded you; do not turn from it to the right hand or to the left, so that you may be successful wherever you go. 8This book of the law shall not depart out of your mouth; you shall meditate on it day and night, so that you may be careful to act in accordance with all that is written in it. For then you shall make your way prosperous, and then you shall be successful. 9I hereby command you: Be strong and courageous; do not be frightened or dismayed, for the LORD your God is with you wherever you go."

Preparations for the Invasion

10 Then Joshua commanded the officers of the people, 11"Pass through the camp, and command the people: 'Prepare your provisions; for in three days you are to cross over the Jordan, to go in to take possession of the land that the LORD your God gives you to possess.' "

12 To the Reubenites, the Gadites, and the half-tribe of Manasseh Joshua said, 13"Remember the word that Moses the servant of the LORD commanded you, saying, 'The LORD your God is providing you a place of rest, and will give you this land.' 14Your wives, your little ones, and your livestock shall remain in the land that Moses gave you beyond the Jordan. But all the warriors among you shall cross over armed before your kindred and shall help them, 15until the LORD gives rest to your kindred as well as to you, and they too take possession of the land that the LORD your God is giving them. Then you shall return to your own land and take possession of it, the land that Moses the servant of the LORD gave you beyond the Jordan to the east."

16 They answered Joshua: "All that you have commanded us we will do, and wherever you send us we will go. 17Just as we obeyed Moses in all things, so we will obey you. Only may the LORD your God be with you, as he was with Moses! 18Whoever rebels against your orders and disobeys your words, whatever you command, shall be put to death. Only be strong and courageous."

Spies Sent to Jericho

2 Then Joshua son of Nun sent two men secretly from Shittim as spies, saying, "Go, view the land, especially Jericho." So they went, and entered the house of a prostitute whose name was Rahab, and spent the night there. 2The king of Jericho was told, "Some Israelites have come here tonight to search out the land." 3Then the king of Jericho sent orders to Rahab, "Bring out the men who have come to you, who entered your house, for they have come only to search out the whole land." 4But the woman took the two men and hid them. Then she said, "True, the men came to me, but I did not know where they came from. 5And when it was time to close the gate at dark, the men went out. Where the men went I do not know. Pursue them quickly, for you can overtake them." 6She had, however, brought them up to the roof and hidden them with the stalks of flax that she had laid out on the roof. 7So the men pursued them on the way to the Jordan as far as the fords. As soon as the pursuers had gone out, the gate was shut.

8 Before they went to sleep, she came up to them on the roof 9and said to the men: "I know that the LORD has given you the land, and that dread of you has fallen on us, and that all the inhabitants of the land

1.1-9 Introduction. *Joshua* means "Yahweh is salvation" or "May Yahweh save!" In his role as *Moses' assistant* he is mentioned in Ex 24.13; 33.11; Num 11.28, and was sent out as one of the spies to survey the land of Canaan (Num 13-14). Now he is to serve as successor to Moses (Num 27.15-23; Deut 3.21,28).
1.4 The land to be conquered is described (as in Deut 11.24) as far more than Israel ever controlled historically, extending as it does from the *wilderness* area in the southeast of Transjordan to *the Euphrates* in northeastern Syria and westward to the Mediterranean (*Great Sea*).
1.5-9 The promises and responsibilities expressed in Deuteronomy are repeated here, including total obedience to *all the law*, which is to be the focus of the people's thinking *day and night*. Only by this discipline can the people survive and be assured of God's presence *wherever [they] go*.
1.10-18 Preparations for invasion and takeover of the hill country west of the Jordan Valley. To demonstrate the solidarity of the twelve tribes, the two-and-one-half tribes that were to settle east of the Jordan take part in the invasion of the land of Canaan, while their wives and children remain in what was to be their tribal territory.
1.16-18 These tribes express for all Israel their pledge of obedience to Joshua and their confidence that God's presence with him ensures the success of the conquest of the land of Canaan.
2.1-24 Spies Sent to Jericho. As in the days of Moses, spies survey the land where invasion is contemplated (Num 13). Jericho, the chief city at the southern end of the Jordan Valley, was inhabited from the Stone Age onward, as excavations have shown. Since the walls were built of mud brick and the city was probably quite small at the time of the invasion by the Israelites, no clear evidence of its destruction in the thirteenth century has been found. Some scholars think this story dates from an earlier epoch, but was included here by a later historian. Shittim was a city east of the Jordan, mentioned in Num 25.1.
2.2 To designate the chief in Jericho as *king* was to give him the title common to the rulers of independent cities throughout the land of Canaan. To call Rahab *a prostitute* may mean that she was a professional harlot or that she was a cult prostitute attached to the shrine of a local fertility deity.
2.6 The flat roofs of houses were used for multiple purposes, including drying out crops such as flax.
2.8-11 Here is the first of repeated testimonies by the natives of the land about what they know concerning the power of the God of Israel and the fear that this reputation evokes; *cf.* 5.1.

1.2 Num 12.7; Deut 34.5; ver 11
1.3 Deut 11.24
1.4 Gen 15.18
1.5 Deut 7.24; 31.6-8
1.7 Deut 5.32; 28.14
1.8 Deut 17.8,9; Ps 1.1-3
1.9 Deut 31.7,8,23; Jer 1.8
1.11 Joel 3.2
1.12 Num 32.20-22
1.13 Deut 3.18-20
1.15 Josh 22.1-4
1.17 ver 5,9
2.1 Num 25.1; Heb 11.31; Jas 2.25
2.6 Jas 2.25
2.9 Ex 23.27; Deut 2.25

2.10 Ex 14.21; Num 21.24,34,35
2.11 Ex 15.14,15; Josh 5.1; Deut 4.39
2.12 ver 18
2.14 Judg 1.24
2.16 Jas 2.25
2.17 Gen 24.8
2.18 ver 12; Josh 6.23
2.19 Ezek 33.4
2.24 ver 9; Josh 6.2
3.1 Josh 2.1
3.2 Josh 1.11
3.3 Deut 31.9
3.5 Ex 19.10,14; Josh 7.13
3.7 Josh 4.7; 1.5
3.8 ver 3.17
3.10 Deut 7.1
3.12 Josh 4.2
3.13 Ex 15.8; Ps 78.13

melt in fear before you. 10For we have heard how the LORD dried up the water of the Red Sea[a] before you when you came out of Egypt, and what you did to the two kings of the Amorites that were beyond the Jordan, to Sihon and Og, whom you utterly destroyed. 11As soon as we heard it, our hearts melted, and there was no courage left in any of us because of you. The LORD your God is indeed God in heaven above and on earth below. 12Now then, since I have dealt kindly with you, swear to me by the LORD that you in turn will deal kindly with my family. Give me a sign of good faith 13that you will spare my father and mother, my brothers and sisters, and all who belong to them, and deliver our lives from death." 14The men said to her, "Our life for yours! If you do not tell this business of ours, then we will deal kindly and faithfully with you when the LORD gives us the land."

15 Then she let them down by a rope through the window, for her house was on the outer side of the city wall and she resided within the wall itself. 16She said to them, "Go toward the hill country, so that the pursuers may not come upon you. Hide yourselves there three days, until the pursuers have returned; then afterward you may go your way." 17The men said to her, "We will be released from this oath that you have made us swear to you 18if we invade the land and you do not tie this crimson cord in the window through which you let us down, and you do not gather into your house your father and mother, your brothers, and all your family. 19If any of you go out of the doors of your house into the street, they shall be responsible for their own death, and we shall be innocent; but if a hand is laid upon any who are with you in the house, we shall bear the responsibility for their death. 20But if you tell this business of ours, then we shall be released from this oath that you made us swear to you." 21She said, "According to your words, so be it." She sent them away and they departed. Then she tied the crimson cord in the window.

22 They departed and went into the hill country and stayed there three days, until the pursuers returned. The pursuers had searched all along the way and found nothing. 23Then the two men came down again from the hill country. They crossed over, came to Joshua son of Nun, and told him all that had happened to them. 24They said to Joshua, "Truly the LORD has given all the land into our hands; moreover all the inhabitants of the land melt in fear before us."

Israel Crosses the Jordan

3 Early in the morning Joshua rose and set out from Shittim with all the Israelites, and they came to the Jordan. They camped there before crossing over. 2At the end of three days the officers went through the camp 3and commanded the people, "When you see the ark of the covenant of the LORD your God being carried by the levitical priests, then you shall set out from your place. Follow it, 4so that you may know the way you should go, for you have not passed this way before. Yet there shall be a space between you and it, a distance of about two thousand cubits; do not come any nearer to it." 5Then Joshua said to the people, "Sanctify yourselves; for tomorrow the LORD will do wonders among you." 6To the priests Joshua said, "Take up the ark of the covenant, and pass on in front of the people." So they took up the ark of the covenant and went in front of the people.

7 The LORD said to Joshua, "This day I will begin to exalt you in the sight of all Israel, so that they may know that I will be with you as I was with Moses. 8You are the one who shall command the priests who bear the ark of the covenant, 'When you come to the edge of the waters of the Jordan, you shall stand still in the Jordan.' " 9Joshua then said to the Israelites, "Draw near and hear the words of the LORD your God." 10Joshua said, "By this you shall know that among you is the living God who without fail will drive out from before you the Canaanites, Hittites, Hivites, Perizzites, Girgashites, Amorites, and Jebusites: 11the ark of the covenant of the Lord of all the earth is going to pass before you into the Jordan. 12So now select twelve men from the tribes of Israel, one from each tribe. 13When the soles of the feet of the priests who bear the ark of the LORD, the Lord of all the earth, rest in the waters of the Jordan, the waters of the Jordan flowing from above shall be cut off; they shall stand in a single heap."

14 When the people set out from their tents to cross over the Jordan, the priests bearing the ark of the covenant were in

[a] Or *Sea of Reeds*

2.12-14 The promise to spare the tribe of Rahab is fulfilled in 6.22-25. The explanation of her posterity's survival in Israel may have been the original aim in preserving this tale.
2.16 *The hill country* refers to the ridge of highlands west of the Jordan Valley, the eastern slopes of which were arid and sparsely populated.
2.18-21 The *crimson cord* which Rahab hangs from her window in the wall of Jericho is the visible sign of her fidelity to the agreement with the spies.
2.24 The recurrent theme is that the inhabitants of the land know that God has given this region to his people Israel.
3.1-17 God holds back the waters of the Jordan for Israel to cross over into the land of promise. Although the details of the story are not neatly consistent, its importance for Israel's subsequent worship is indicated in Ps 114.
3.2-4 The *ark of the covenant* is the tangible symbol of God's invisible, powerful presence among his people as they enter the land. The role of the priests (here specified as *levitical)* in carrying the ark is crucial, as is their initial stepping into the river (3.2), which results in the stopping of its flow (3.13) until all the people have crossed (3.17).
3.10 The lists of the tribes to be driven out before the Israelites resemble those in Ex 34.11; Deut 7.1; 20.17, which announce the utter destruction of the inhabitants of the land. Lists of the tribes to be replaced are also given in Josh 1.4; 9.1; 11.3; 12.8; 24.11.

4.1-24 The covenant renewal at Gilgal as Israel enters the land. The *twelve stones* taken from the *middle of the Jordan* symbolize the twelve tribes of Israel, all of whom now cross over the Jordan.
4.7-9 Although the twelve stones are to be set up as *a memorial forever*, this shrine was later denounced by the prophet Amos (Am 4.4; 5.5), along with others where the God of Israel was worshipped (Bethel, Shechem, Gerizim). These were condemned when the temple in Jerusalem came to be considered the sole legitimate dwelling of Yahweh.
4.19-23 *Those twelve stones* are to serve as an enduring reminder of God's two great acts in behalf of his people: the crossing of the Jordan and the crossing of the Red Sea.
4.24 As throughout Deuteronomy, knowledge of God's acts in behalf of his people is to go out *to all the peoples of the earth.* Instruction is central to maintaining the covenant.
5.1 The Amorites are mentioned in documents from the ancient Near East as a powerful people living in parts of Syria and Palestine. Among those with whom they are said to have fought for control of the land are the Habiru (= Hebrews, or Israel), with special mention of the tribe of Benjamin. *The Canaanites,* who are named in Gen 9.18 as sons of Ham (son of Noah), appear in ancient non-biblical writings as a Semitic people inhabiting Palestine, especially the region near the Mediterranean, where their social structure was that of small city-states, each dominated politically and economically by a local *king.*

front of the people. [15]Now the Jordan overflows all its banks throughout the time of harvest. So when those who bore the ark had come to the Jordan, and the feet of the priests bearing the ark were dipped in the edge of the water, [16]the waters flowing from above stood still, rising up in a single heap far off at Adam, the city that is beside Zarethan, while those flowing toward the sea of the Arabah, the Dead Sea,[b] were wholly cut off. Then the people crossed over opposite Jericho. [17]While all Israel were crossing over on dry ground, the priests who bore the ark of the covenant of the LORD stood on dry ground in the middle of the Jordan, until the entire nation finished crossing over the Jordan.

Twelve Stones Set Up at Gilgal

4 When the entire nation had finished crossing over the Jordan, the LORD said to Joshua: [2]"Select twelve men from the people, one from each tribe, [3]and command them, 'Take twelve stones from here out of the middle of the Jordan, from the place where the priests' feet stood, carry them over with you, and lay them down in the place where you camp tonight.' " [4]Then Joshua summoned the twelve men from the Israelites, whom he had appointed, one from each tribe. [5]Joshua said to them, "Pass on before the ark of the LORD your God into the middle of the Jordan, and each of you take up a stone on his shoulder, one for each of the tribes of the Israelites, [6]so that this may be a sign among you. When your children ask in time to come, 'What do those stones mean to you?' [7]then you shall tell them that the waters of the Jordan were cut off in front of the ark of the covenant of the LORD. When it crossed over the Jordan, the waters of the Jordan were cut off. So these stones shall be to the Israelites a memorial forever."

8 The Israelites did as Joshua commanded. They took up twelve stones out of the middle of the Jordan, according to the number of the tribes of the Israelites, as the LORD told Joshua, carried them over with them to the place where they camped, and laid them down there. [9](Joshua set up twelve stones in the middle of the Jordan, in the place where the feet of the priests bearing the ark of the covenant had stood; and they are there to this day.)

10 The priests who bore the ark remained standing in the middle of the Jordan, until everything was finished that the LORD commanded Joshua to tell the people, according to all that Moses had commanded Joshua. The people crossed over in haste. [11]As soon as all the people had finished crossing over, the ark of the LORD, and the priests, crossed over in front of the people. [12]The Reubenites, the Gadites, and the half-tribe of Manasseh crossed over armed before the Israelites, as Moses had ordered them. [13]About forty thousand armed for war crossed over before the LORD to the plains of Jericho for battle.

14 On that day the LORD exalted Joshua in the sight of all Israel; and they stood in awe of him, as they had stood in awe of Moses, all the days of his life.

15 The LORD said to Joshua, [16]"Command the priests who bear the ark of the covenant,[c] to come up out of the Jordan." [17]Joshua therefore commanded the priests, "Come up out of the Jordan." [18]When the priests bearing the ark of the covenant of the LORD came up from the middle of the Jordan, and the soles of the priests' feet touched dry ground, the waters of the Jordan returned to their place and overflowed all its banks, as before.

19 The people came up out of the Jordan on the tenth day of the first month, and they camped in Gilgal on the east border of Jericho. [20]Those twelve stones, which they had taken out of the Jordan, Joshua set up in Gilgal, [21]saying to the Israelites, "When your children ask their parents in time to come, 'What do these stones mean?' [22]then you shall let your children know, 'Israel crossed over the Jordan here on dry ground.' [23]For the LORD your God dried up the waters of the Jordan for you until you crossed over, as the LORD your God did to the Red Sea,[d] which he dried up for us until we crossed over, [24]so that all the peoples of the earth may know that the hand of the LORD is mighty, and so that you may fear the LORD your God forever."

The New Generation Circumcised

5 When all the kings of the Amorites beyond the Jordan to the west, and all the kings of the Canaanites by the sea, heard that the LORD had dried up the waters of the Jordan for the Israelites until they had crossed over, their hearts melted, and

3.15 Josh 4.18
3.16 Ps 66.6; 74.15; ver 13
3.17 Ex 14.29
4.2 Josh 3.12
4.3 ver 19,20
4.6 ver 21; Ex 12.26; 13.14
4.7 Josh 3.13
4.8 ver 19,20
4.9 Ex 28.21
4.12 Num 32.17
4.14 Josh 3.7
4.18 Josh 3.15
4.19 Josh 5.9
4.20 ver 3,8
4.21 ver 6
4.22 Josh 3.17
4.23 Ex 14.21
4.24 1 Kings 8.42,43; Ps 89.13; Ex 14.31
5.1 Num 13.29; Josh 2.9-11

[b] Heb *Salt Sea* [c] Or *treaty,* or *testimony;* Heb *eduth* [d] Or *Sea of Reeds*

5.2 Ex 4.25
5.4 Deut 2.16
5.6 Deut 2.7,14; Num 14.23
5.10 Ex 12.6,8
5.12 Ex 16.35
5.13 Gen 18.2; 32.24; Num 22.31
5.14 Gen 17.3
5.15 Ex 3.5
6.2 Josh 2.9,24; Deut 7.24
6.4 Num 10.8
6.5 Lev 25.9
6.7 Ex 14.15
6.9 ver 13; Isa 52.12
6.13 ver 4,9

there was no longer any spirit in them,
because of the Israelites.
2 At that time the LORD said to Joshua,
"Make flint knives and circumcise the Israelites a second time." 3 So Joshua made flint
knives, and circumcised the Israelites at
Gibeath-haaraloth.[e] 4 This is the reason why
Joshua circumcised them: all the males of
the people who came out of Egypt, all the
warriors, had died during the journey
through the wilderness after they had come
out of Egypt. 5 Although all the people who
came out had been circumcised, yet all the
people born on the journey through the
wilderness after they had come out of Egypt
had not been circumcised. 6 For the Israelites
traveled forty years in the wilderness, until
all the nation, the warriors who came out
of Egypt, perished, not having listened to
the voice of the LORD. To them the LORD
swore that he would not let them see the
land that he had sworn to their ancestors
to give us, a land flowing with milk and
honey. 7 So it was their children, whom he
raised up in their place, that Joshua circumcised; for they were uncircumcised, because
they had not been circumcised on the way.
8 When the circumcising of all the nation was done, they remained in their places
in the camp until they were healed. 9 The
LORD said to Joshua, "Today I have rolled
away from you the disgrace of Egypt." And
so that place is called Gilgal[f] to this day.

The Passover at Gilgal

10 While the Israelites were camped in
Gilgal they kept the passover in the evening
on the fourteenth day of the month in the
plains of Jericho. 11 On the day after the
passover, on that very day, they ate the
produce of the land, unleavened cakes and
parched grain. 12 The manna ceased on the
day they ate the produce of the land, and
the Israelites no longer had manna; they
ate the crops of the land of Canaan that
year.

Joshua's Vision

13 Once when Joshua was by Jericho, he
looked up and saw a man standing before
him with a drawn sword in his hand. Joshua
went to him and said to him, "Are you one
of us, or one of our adversaries?" 14 He
replied, "Neither; but as commander of the
army of the LORD I have now come." And
Joshua fell on his face to the earth and
worshiped, and he said to him, "What do
you command your servant, my lord?" 15 The
commander of the army of the LORD said to
Joshua, "Remove the sandals from your
feet, for the place where you stand is holy."
And Joshua did so.

Jericho Taken and Destroyed

6 Now Jericho was shut up inside and
out because of the Israelites; no one
came out and no one went in. 2 The LORD
said to Joshua, "See, I have handed Jericho
over to you, along with its king and soldiers. 3 You shall march around the city, all
the warriors circling the city once. Thus
you shall do for six days, 4 with seven priests
bearing seven trumpets of rams' horns before
the ark. On the seventh day you shall march
around the city seven times, the priests
blowing the trumpets. 5 When they make a
long blast with the ram's horn, as soon as
you hear the sound of the trumpet, then all
the people shall shout with a great shout;
and the wall of the city will fall down flat,
and all the people shall charge straight
ahead." 6 So Joshua son of Nun summoned
the priests and said to them, "Take up the
ark of the covenant, and have seven priests
carry seven trumpets of rams' horns in
front of the ark of the LORD." 7 To the people
he said, "Go forward and march around the
city; have the armed men pass on before the
ark of the LORD."
8 As Joshua had commanded the people,
the seven priests carrying the seven trumpets of rams' horns before the LORD went
forward, blowing the trumpets, with the ark
of the covenant of the LORD following them.
9 And the armed men went before the priests
who blew the trumpets; the rear guard
came after the ark, while the trumpets blew
continually. 10 To the people Joshua gave
this command: "You shall not shout or let
your voice be heard, nor shall you utter a
word, until the day I tell you to shout. Then
you shall shout." 11 So the ark of the LORD
went around the city, circling it once; and
they came into the camp, and spent the
night in the camp.
12 Then Joshua rose early in the morning, and the priests took up the ark of the
LORD. 13 The seven priests carrying the seven
trumpets of rams' horns before the ark of

[e] That is *the Hill of the Foreskins* [f] Related to Heb *galal* to roll

5.2-7 The use of *flint knives* when the rite of circumcision is reintroduced recalls Moses' wife Zipporah's circumcising her son (Ex 4.25-26), and apparently intends to recall usage dating back to ancient Stone Age times, since metal instruments would ordinarily have been used in Joshua's time. The result of the ceremony is vividly indicated in the name of the place: *Gibeath-haaraloth*, meaning, "Hill of Foreskins." In Genesis the rite is said to date back to the time of Abraham (Gen 17.1-14), where it is declared to be the essential seal of participation in the covenant. Although the requirement of circumcision is not mentioned in the older legal codes of Israel, it is assumed to be in effect in Gen 34.13-24. It is used as a metaphor for committed obedience to God in Deut 10.16; 30.6, and had become obligatory by the time of the priestly code (Lev 12.3). The rite may have assumed special importance during Israel's exile in Babylon, and was then given a prominent place in this history, which was written in post-exilic times. There it is described as making up for *forty years* of neglect of the practice during the *journey through the wilderness*.

5.8-9 The name Gilgal is assigned to the place where the rite of circumcision was performed. Its location is not known, but it must lie between Jericho and the Jordan River.

5.10-12 The second rite renewed on entering the land is *the Passover*. With access to *the produce of the land*, the manna was said to be no longer needed for daily food. Now they are to carry out this celebration of crops and flocks which are seen as given by God.

5.13-15 Joshua's vision of *the army of the LORD* near Jericho is an indication of the holy war in which Israel is to be engaged, and a reminder that they must *annihilate* every person and living thing in the land, so that nothing *that breathes remains alive* (Deut 20.16-17).

6.1-26 The successful outcome is foreseen from the beginning: the *LORD handed Jericho over to you*. The account of the destruction of Jericho draws on different ancient sources, so that not all the details match. Excavations of the ancient mound of Jericho have revealed no evidence of a major attack on the city at the probable date of Israel's conquest of Canaan (mid-thirteenth century), but the use of mud-brick in the city walls and the small size of the city at that time may have obscured the remains. The description of the attack follows the pattern of the holy war (Deut 20): religious rites preceding the attack; the fighting carried out by instructions through the sound of trumpets; the ark of the covenant at the head of the troops symbolizing God's presence and power in the operation; everything seized belongs to the LORD. Non-durable items, as well as all the inhabitants and their livestock (6.20-21) are to be destroyed; silver, gold, and metal objects are to be devoted to God (6.19,24).

6.22-25 The sole survivors of the destruction of Jericho are *Rahab* and *her family*, who are said to have *lived in Israel ever since*.
6.26 A curse is pronounced on the site of Jericho, including the loss of the firstborn child by any who attempt to rebuild it.
6.27 The report of the powerful presence of the LORD with Joshua precedes him as he prepares to lead Israel's further conquest of the land.
7.1-16 This chapter, together with Josh 8, presents a two-sided picture of the consequences for Israel of its disobedience (Josh 7) or obedience (Josh 8) to the people's covenant obligations. The former response brings defeat; the latter brings victory and reward, as promised in Deut 7.9-10.
7.1 *The devoted things* were those that belonged to the LORD and were to be turned over to the priests, in contrast to items which were to be *devoted to destruction* (Josh 6.18).
7.2 Men are sent *from Jericho to Ai, to spy out the land*, as in Josh 2.1 and Num 13. Archaeologists have identified Ai (which means "ruin" or "heap") with the ancient mound of Et-Tell, north of Jerusalem and south of Bethel on the ridge of the hill country. But the excavations provide no evidence of occupation during this period, which may mean that Ai was elsewhere or that a story of earlier Israelite experience has been woven into this narrative. *Bethel* figures importantly in the experience of Jacob and his encounters with God (Gen 28.10-22; 35.1-15), although it came to be a controversial place of worship under Jeroboam (reigned 922-901) according to 1 Kings 12.
7.5 *The slope* refers to the steep eastern side of the hill country, cut by many deep ravines leading down into the Jordan Valley.
7.6 Tearing *clothes*, falling on one's *face*, and putting *dust* on one's head were all expressions of sorrow and penitence.
7.8-9 The reputations of both Israel and the LORD are at stake if God's promise of the land for his people is not fulfilled.
7.11 The cause of the seeming failure of the promise to Israel is that one of its number, Achan, *transgressed my covenant* by taking what belonged to the LORD.

the LORD passed on, blowing the trumpets continually. The armed men went before them, and the rear guard came after the ark of the LORD, while the trumpets blew continually. [14]On the second day they marched around the city once and then returned to the camp. They did this for six days.

15 On the seventh day they rose early, at dawn, and marched around the city in the same manner seven times. It was only on that day that they marched around the city seven times. [16]And at the seventh time, when the priests had blown the trumpets, Joshua said to the people, "Shout! For the LORD has given you the city. [17]The city and all that is in it shall be devoted to the LORD for destruction. Only Rahab the prostitute and all who are with her in her house shall live because she hid the messengers we sent. [18]As for you, keep away from the things devoted to destruction, so as not to covet[g] and take any of the devoted things and make the camp of Israel an object for destruction, bringing trouble upon it. [19]But all silver and gold, and vessels of bronze and iron, are sacred to the LORD; they shall go into the treasury of the LORD." [20]So the people shouted, and the trumpets were blown. As soon as the people heard the sound of the trumpets, they raised a great shout, and the wall fell down flat; so the people charged straight ahead into the city and captured it. [21]Then they devoted to destruction by the edge of the sword all in the city, both men and women, young and old, oxen, sheep, and donkeys.

22 Joshua said to the two men who had spied out the land, "Go into the prostitute's house, and bring the woman out of it and all who belong to her, as you swore to her." [23]So the young men who had been spies went in and brought Rahab out, along with her father, her mother, her brothers, and all who belonged to her—they brought all her kindred out—and set them outside the camp of Israel. [24]They burned down the city, and everything in it; only the silver and gold, and the vessels of bronze and iron, they put into the treasury of the house of the LORD. [25]But Rahab the prostitute, with her family and all who belonged to her, Joshua spared. Her family[h] has lived in Israel ever since. For she hid the messengers whom Joshua sent to spy out Jericho.

26 Joshua then pronounced this oath, saying,

"Cursed before the LORD be anyone
who tries
to build this city—this Jericho!
At the cost of his firstborn he shall
lay its foundation,
and at the cost of his youngest he
shall set up its gates!"

27 So the LORD was with Joshua; and his fame was in all the land.

The Sin of Achan and Its Punishment

7 But the Israelites broke faith in regard to the devoted things: Achan son of Carmi son of Zabdi son of Zerah, of the tribe of Judah, took some of the devoted things; and the anger of the LORD burned against the Israelites.

2 Joshua sent men from Jericho to Ai, which is near Beth-aven, east of Bethel, and said to them, "Go up and spy out the land." And the men went up and spied out Ai. [3]Then they returned to Joshua and said to him, "Not all the people need go up; about two or three thousand men should go up and attack Ai. Since they are so few, do not make the whole people toil up there." [4]So about three thousand of the people went up there; and they fled before the men of Ai. [5]The men of Ai killed about thirty-six of them, chasing them from outside the gate as far as Shebarim and killing them on the slope. The hearts of the people melted and turned to water.

6 Then Joshua tore his clothes, and fell to the ground on his face before the ark of the LORD until the evening, he and the elders of Israel; and they put dust on their heads. [7]Joshua said, "Ah, Lord GOD! Why have you brought this people across the Jordan at all, to hand us over to the Amorites so as to destroy us? Would that we had been content to settle beyond the Jordan! [8]O Lord, what can I say, now that Israel has turned their backs to their enemies! [9]The Canaanites and all the inhabitants of the land will hear of it, and surround us, and cut off our name from the earth. Then what will you do for your great name?"

10 The LORD said to Joshua, "Stand up! Why have you fallen upon your face? [11]Israel has sinned; they have transgressed my covenant that I imposed on them. They have taken some of the devoted things; they have stolen, they have acted deceitfully, and they have put them among their own

6.17 Lev 27.28; Josh 2.4
6.18 Josh 7.1,25
6.20 ver 5; Heb 11.30
6.21 Deut 7.2; 20.16
6.22 Josh 2.14; Heb 11.31
6.23 Josh 2.13
6.24 ver 19
6.25 Heb 11.31
6.26 1 Kings 16.34
6.27 Josh 1.5; 9.1,3
7.1 Josh 6.17-19
7.4 Lev 26.17; 28.25
7.6 Job 2.12; Rev 18.19
7.7 Ex 5.22
7.9 Ex 32.12; Deut 9.28
7.11 ver 1; Josh 6.18,19; see Acts 5.1,2

[g] Gk: Heb *devote to destruction* Compare 7.21 [h] Heb *She*

belongings. 12Therefore the Israelites are unable to stand before their enemies; they turn their backs to their enemies, because they have become a thing devoted for destruction themselves. I will be with you no more, unless you destroy the devoted things from among you. 13Proceed to sanctify the people, and say, 'Sanctify yourselves for tomorrow; for thus says the LORD, the God of Israel, "There are devoted things among you, O Israel; you will be unable to stand before your enemies until you take away the devoted things from among you." 14In the morning therefore you shall come forward tribe by tribe. The tribe that the LORD takes shall come near by clans, the clan that the LORD takes shall come near by households, and the household that the LORD takes shall come near one by one. 15And the one who is taken as having the devoted things shall be burned with fire, together with all that he has, for having transgressed the covenant of the LORD, and for having done an outrageous thing in Israel.' "

16 So Joshua rose early in the morning, and brought Israel near tribe by tribe, and the tribe of Judah was taken. 17He brought near the clans of Judah, and the clan of the Zerahites was taken; and he brought near the clan of the Zerahites, family by family,[i] and Zabdi was taken. 18And he brought near his household one by one, and Achan son of Carmi son of Zabdi son of Zerah, of the tribe of Judah, was taken. 19Then Joshua said to Achan, "My son, give glory to the LORD God of Israel and make confession to him. Tell me now what you have done; do not hide it from me." 20And Achan answered Joshua, "It is true; I am the one who sinned against the LORD God of Israel. This is what I did: 21when I saw among the spoil a beautiful mantle from Shinar, and two hundred shekels of silver, and a bar of gold weighing fifty shekels, then I coveted them and took them. They now lie hidden in the ground inside my tent, with the silver underneath."

22 So Joshua sent messengers, and they ran to the tent; and there it was, hidden in his tent with the silver underneath. 23They took them out of the tent and brought them to Joshua and all the Israelites; and they spread them out before the LORD. 24Then Joshua and all Israel with him took Achan son of Zerah, with the silver, the mantle, and the bar of gold, with his sons and daughters, with his oxen, donkeys, and sheep, and his tent and all that he had; and they brought them up to the Valley of Achor. 25Joshua said, "Why did you bring trouble on us? The LORD is bringing trouble on you today." And all Israel stoned him to death; they burned them with fire, cast stones on them, 26and raised over him a great heap of stones that remains to this day. Then the LORD turned from his burning anger. Therefore that place to this day is called the Valley of Achor.[j]

Ai Captured by a Stratagem and Destroyed

8 Then the LORD said to Joshua, "Do not fear or be dismayed; take all the fighting men with you, and go up now to Ai. See, I have handed over to you the king of Ai with his people, his city, and his land. 2You shall do to Ai and its king as you did to Jericho and its king; only its spoil and its livestock you may take as booty for yourselves. Set an ambush against the city, behind it."

3 So Joshua and all the fighting men set out to go up against Ai. Joshua chose thirty thousand warriors and sent them out by night 4with the command, "You shall lie in ambush against the city, behind it; do not go very far from the city, but all of you stay alert. 5I and all the people who are with me will approach the city. When they come out against us, as before, we shall flee from them. 6They will come out after us until we have drawn them away from the city; for they will say, 'They are fleeing from us, as before.' While we flee from them, 7you shall rise up from the ambush and seize the city; for the LORD your God will give it into your hand. 8And when you have taken the city, you shall set the city on fire, doing as the LORD has ordered; see, I have commanded you." 9So Joshua sent them out; and they went to the place of ambush, and lay between Bethel and Ai, to the west of Ai; but Joshua spent that night in the camp.[k]

10 In the morning Joshua rose early and mustered the people, and went up, with the elders of Israel, before the people to Ai. 11All the fighting men who were with him went up, and drew near before the city, and camped on the north side of Ai, with a ravine between them and Ai. 12Taking about five thousand men, he set them in ambush

[i] Mss Syr: MT *man by man* [j] That is *Trouble* [k] Heb *among the people*

7.13 Josh 3.5; 6.18
7.15 ver 11
7.17 Num 26.20
7.19 Jer 13.16; Jn 9.24; Num 5.6,7; 1 Sam 14.43
7.20 Josh 22.20; 1 Chr 2.7
7.24 Josh 15.7
7.25 Josh 6.18; Deut 17.5
7.26 Deut 13.17; Isa 65.10; Hos 2.15
8.1 Deut 1.21; 7.18; Josh 1.9; 6.2
8.2 ver 27; Deut 20.14
8.4 see Judg 20.20-32
8.8 ver 2
8.10 ver 33

7.12 Here is a bitter irony: what should have been *devoted* to the LORD now is the cause for the offender and his family to be *devoted to destruction*, which means to be condemned to death.
7.13 To *sanctify the people* is to purify them so that they may regain their promised status as God's special people.
7.14-15 One individual is guilty, but the whole covenant people is held accountable. The guilty one is to be identified by sacred lot, as the people come *before the LORD* by tribe, clan and household, so that God may *take* the violator who *transgressed the covenant*.
7.20 The guilty man is Achan, whose tribe is Judah, which occupied the area just south of the territory of Benjamin where Ai was located, extending down the slope to Jericho in the Jordan Valley.
7.21 The *mantle from Shinar* came from Babylonia (Gen 10.10; Isa 11.11; Dan 1.2).
7.24-25 The punishment for covenant violation included the destruction of Achan and his children, together with all their livestock and possessions. All were stoned, burned, and covered under a *great heap of stones*. Mention that the heap *remains to this day* shows that the account was written long after the events described.
7.26 *The Valley of Achor*, the Valley of Trouble, is to be transformed into a door of hope, according to Hos 2.15.
8.1-19 The Reversal of the Defeat at Ai.
8.1-2 The LORD's promise is the total takeover of Ai: king, people, city and land. The Israelites may keep *its spoil and its livestock*, however.
8.9 The ambush of Israelite troops *west of Ai* is described in slightly different terms in 8.11-13.
8.10-14 Joshua leads the main body of the people to the east side of the city, and it is there that the king of Ai – unaware of the ambush – prepares to confront them, where the hills slope steeply down into *the Arabah*, or valley of the Jordan.

between Bethel and Ai, to the west of the city. 13 So they stationed the forces, the main encampment that was north of the city and its rear guard west of the city. But Joshua spent that night in the valley. 14 When the king of Ai saw this, he and all his people, the inhabitants of the city, hurried out early in the morning to the meeting place facing the Arabah to meet Israel in battle; but he did not know that there was an ambush against him behind the city. 15 And Joshua and all Israel made a pretense of being beaten before them, and fled in the direction of the wilderness. 16 So all the people who were in the city were called together to pursue them, and as they pursued Joshua they were drawn away from the city. 17 There was not a man left in Ai or Bethel who did not go out after Israel; they left the city open, and pursued Israel.

18 Then the LORD said to Joshua, "Stretch out the sword that is in your hand toward Ai; for I will give it into your hand." And Joshua stretched out the sword that was in his hand toward the city. 19 As soon as he stretched out his hand, the troops in ambush rose quickly out of their place and rushed forward. They entered the city, took it, and at once set the city on fire. 20 So when the men of Ai looked back, the smoke of the city was rising to the sky. They had no power to flee this way or that, for the people who fled to the wilderness turned back against the pursuers. 21 When Joshua and all Israel saw that the ambush had taken the city and that the smoke of the city was rising, then they turned back and struck down the men of Ai. 22 And the others came out from the city against them; so they were surrounded by Israelites, some on one side, and some on the other; and Israel struck them down until no one was left who survived or escaped. 23 But the king of Ai was taken alive and brought to Joshua.

24 When Israel had finished slaughtering all the inhabitants of Ai in the open wilderness where they pursued them, and when all of them to the very last had fallen by the edge of the sword, all Israel returned to Ai, and attacked it with the edge of the sword. 25 The total of those who fell that day, both men and women, was twelve thousand—all the people of Ai. 26 For Joshua did not draw back his hand, with which he stretched out the sword, until he had utterly destroyed all the inhabitants of Ai. 27 Only the livestock and the spoil of that city Israel took as their booty, according to the word of the LORD that he had issued to Joshua. 28 So Joshua burned Ai, and made it forever a heap of ruins, as it is to this day. 29 And he hanged the king of Ai on a tree until evening; and at sunset Joshua commanded, and they took his body down from the tree, threw it down at the entrance of the gate of the city, and raised over it a great heap of stones, which stands there to this day.

Joshua Renews the Covenant

30 Then Joshua built on Mount Ebal an altar to the LORD, the God of Israel, 31 just as Moses the servant of the LORD had commanded the Israelites, as it is written in the book of the law of Moses, "an altar of unhewn[l] stones, on which no iron tool has been used"; and they offered on it burnt offerings to the LORD, and sacrificed offerings of well-being. 32 And there, in the presence of the Israelites, Joshua[m] wrote on the stones a copy of the law of Moses, which he had written. 33 All Israel, alien as well as citizen, with their elders and officers and their judges, stood on opposite sides of the ark in front of the levitical priests who carried the ark of the covenant of the LORD, half of them in front of Mount Gerizim and half of them in front of Mount Ebal, as Moses the servant of the LORD had commanded at the first, that they should bless the people of Israel. 34 And afterward he read all the words of the law, blessings and curses, according to all that is written in the book of the law. 35 There was not a word of all that Moses commanded that Joshua did not read before all the assembly of Israel, and the women, and the little ones, and the aliens who resided among them.

The Gibeonites Save Themselves by Trickery

9 Now when all the kings who were beyond the Jordan in the hill country and in the lowland all along the coast of the Great Sea toward Lebanon—the Hittites, the Amorites, the Canaanites, the Perizzites, the Hivites, and the Jebusites—heard of this, 2 they gathered together with one accord to fight Joshua and Israel.

3 But when the inhabitants of Gibeon heard what Joshua had done to Jericho and

[l] Heb *whole* [m] Heb *he*

8.16-17 The city is emptied of *all its people* in order to pursue the supposedly fleeing Israelites.
8.18-26 At the signal from Joshua, which was *the sword...stretched out*, the concealed force seizes the city and slaughters the entire population.
8.27-29 After taking the livestock, as permitted (8.2), the city is converted into a heap of ruins, and its king is *hanged*. Care is taken to obey the command in Deut 21.22-23 to bury his body before nightfall in order to avoid pollution of the surrounding land.
8.30-35 Covenant Renewal. This time the erection of the *altar of unhewn stones* and the offering of the appropriate sacrifices is described as carried out far to the north on *Mount Ebal*, which with Mt. Gerizim forms the valley in which Shechem is located. There Jacob built an altar to the God of Israel (Gen 33.18-20), and there Joshua was later to renew the covenant yet again (Josh 24). In some traditions, Ebal was associated with curses on the wicked and disobedient, while Gerizim was the place of blessings (Deut 11.29). The construction of the altar, the installation of the priests, and the location of the ark mark the establishment of the covenant in the new land. *The law of Moses* is not only written down, but is read in its entirety to all the people, including men, *women*, and *little ones*, not only to Israelites but also to *the aliens who resided among them*.
9.1-2 The kings of the Semitic peoples long resident in *the hill country* and *along the coast* of the Mediterranean Sea form a coalition to destroy Israel.
9.3-27 The Gibeonites, also known as *Hivites* (9.7) and related to the Horites from east of the Jordan (Gen 36.2,20,29), are successful in their ruse to avoid an attack by the Israelites through their pretense that they have come from a long distance, drawn by the reputed power of Israel's God.

8.14 Josh 3.16; Judg 20.34
8.18 ver 26; Ex 14.16; 17.9-13
8.19 ver 8
8.22 Deut 7.2
8.25 Deut 20.16-18
8.26 Ex 17.11,12
8.27 ver 2; Num 31.22
8.28 Deut 13.16
8.29 Deut 21.22,23
8.30 Deut 27.2-8
8.31 Ex 20.24,25; Deut 27.5,6
8.32 Deut 27.2,8
8.33 Deut 31.9,12; 27.11-14
8.34 Deut 31.11; Josh 1.8
8.35 Deut 31.12
9.1 Josh 3.10
9.3 Josh 10.2; 6.27

to Ai, 4 they on their part acted with cunning: they went and prepared provisions,[n] and took worn-out sacks for their donkeys, and wineskins, worn-out and torn and mended, 5 with worn-out, patched sandals on their feet, and worn-out clothes; and all their provisions were dry and moldy. 6 They went to Joshua in the camp at Gilgal, and said to him and to the Israelites, "We have come from a far country; so now make a treaty with us." 7 But the Israelites said to the Hivites, "Perhaps you live among us; then how can we make a treaty with you?" 8 They said to Joshua, "We are your servants." And Joshua said to them, "Who are you? And where do you come from?" 9 They said to him, "Your servants have come from a very far country, because of the name of the LORD your God; for we have heard a report of him, of all that he did in Egypt, 10 and of all that he did to the two kings of the Amorites who were beyond the Jordan, King Sihon of Heshbon, and King Og of Bashan who lived in Ashtaroth. 11 So our elders and all the inhabitants of our country said to us, 'Take provisions in your hand for the journey; go to meet them, and say to them, "We are your servants; come now, make a treaty with us." ' 12 Here is our bread; it was still warm when we took it from our houses as our food for the journey, on the day we set out to come to you, but now, see, it is dry and moldy; 13 these wineskins were new when we filled them, and see, they are burst; and these garments and sandals of ours are worn out from the very long journey." 14 So the leaders[o] partook of their provisions, and did not ask direction from the LORD. 15 And Joshua made peace with them, guaranteeing their lives by a treaty; and the leaders of the congregation swore an oath to them.

16 But when three days had passed after they had made a treaty with them, they heard that they were their neighbors and were living among them. 17 So the Israelites set out and reached their cities on the third day. Now their cities were Gibeon, Chephirah, Beeroth, and Kiriath-jearim. 18 But the Israelites did not attack them, because the leaders of the congregation had sworn to them by the LORD, the God of Israel. Then all the congregation murmured against the leaders. 19 But all the leaders said to all the congregation, "We have sworn to them by the LORD, the God of Israel, and now we must not touch them. 20 This is what we will do to them: We will let them live, so that wrath may not come upon us, because of the oath that we swore to them." 21 The leaders said to them, "Let them live." So they became hewers of wood and drawers of water for all the congregation, as the leaders had decided concerning them.

22 Joshua summoned them, and said to them, "Why did you deceive us, saying, 'We are very far from you,' while in fact you are living among us? 23 Now therefore you are cursed, and some of you shall always be slaves, hewers of wood and drawers of water for the house of my God." 24 They answered Joshua, "Because it was told to your servants for a certainty that the LORD your God had commanded his servant Moses to give you all the land, and to destroy all the inhabitants of the land before you; so we were in great fear for our lives because of you, and did this thing. 25 And now we are in your hand: do as it seems good and right in your sight to do to us." 26 This is what he did for them: he saved them from the Israelites; and they did not kill them. 27 But on that day Joshua made them hewers of wood and drawers of water for the congregation and for the altar of the LORD, to continue to this day, in the place that he should choose.

The Sun Stands Still

10 When King Adoni-zedek of Jerusalem heard how Joshua had taken Ai, and had utterly destroyed it, doing to Ai and its king as he had done to Jericho and its king, and how the inhabitants of Gibeon had made peace with Israel and were among them, 2 he[p] became greatly frightened, because Gibeon was a large city, like one of the royal cities, and was larger than Ai, and all its men were warriors. 3 So King Adoni-zedek of Jerusalem sent a message to King Hoham of Hebron, to King Piram of Jarmuth, to King Japhia of Lachish, and to King Debir of Eglon, saying, 4 "Come up and help me, and let us attack Gibeon; for it has made peace with Joshua and with the Israelites." 5 Then the five kings of the Amorites—the king of Jerusalem, the king of Hebron, the king of Jarmuth, the king of Lachish, and the king of Eglon—gathered their forces, and went up with all their armies and camped against Gibeon, and made war against it.

[n] Cn: Meaning of Heb uncertain [o] Gk: Heb *men* [p] Heb *they*

9.6 Josh 5.10
9.7 ver 2; Josh 11.19; Ex 23.32
9.8 Deut 20.11
9.9 Deut 20.15; ver 16,17,24; Josh 2.9,10
9.10 Num 21.24,33
9.14 Num 27.21
9.15 Ex 23.32
9.17 Josh 18.25-28; Ezra 2.25
9.18 Ps 15.4; Eccl 5.2
9.21 ver 15
9.22 ver 6,9,16,17
9.23 Gen 9.25; ver 21.27
9.24 Deut 7.1,2
9.25 Gen 16.6
9.27 ver 21,23; Deut 12.5
10.1 Josh 6.21; 8.22,26,28; 9.15
10.4 ver 1
10.5 Josh 9.2

9.11-15 *A treaty,* or covenant between the Gibeonites and the *leaders of the congregation* guarantees their lives and that Israel will be at *peace with them,* which is a technical term for the ratification of a covenant between this people and Israel. This story, like that of the saving of Rahab in Jericho (6.22-23), serves to explain why not all the inhabitants of the land were killed in spite of the divine order that all the inhabitants were to be slaughtered, as in Jericho (6.20-21).
9.3 Gibeon was a small city a few miles north of Jerusalem.
9.17 Nearby *Kirjath-jearim,* the best known of the Gibeonite cities, was famed for its water supply (Josh 18.12). All the cities were located in the area bordering on the territories assigned to Judah, Benjamin and Dan (Josh 18.14).
9.22-27 Once they had gained protection through the treaty, the Gibeonites were assigned the menial role of *hewers of wood and drawers of water,* which they continued to perform centuries later in the time of David (2 Sam 21.1-11).
10.1-11 The Defeat of a Coalition of Southern Kings who Attacked Israel.
10.1 The name of the leader of the coalition, *Adoni-zedek,* may mean "My Lord is righteous," or "My Lord is Zedek," which could be the name of the local deity; it is given in a language seemingly identical with Hebrew.
10.3 *Jerusalem* is called by its more ancient name, Jebus (Josh 15.8; 18.28) and is also known as Salim in other documents from the ancient Near East (Egyptian and Syrian). Elsewhere in the Bible it is designated *Salem,* in Gen 14.18; Ps 76.2. Occupied from the early Stone Age, it was the site of an ancient sanctuary which was accessible to a spring. Here the temple of Yahweh was later built by Solomon.
10.5 The other cities whose *kings* join Adoni-Zedek to attack the Israelites are important and well-known ancient centers in the hill country south and west of Jerusalem: *Hebron, Jarmuth, Lachish, Eglon.* All are said to be inhabited by Amorites, Semitic peoples whose major centers were south and east of the Jordan Valley.

10.7-10 Joshua is depicted as maintaining his base of operations at Gilgal in the Jordan Valley, from which forays are made into the hill country of Canaan, including this response to the threat from the Amorite troops. *Beth-horon, Azekah and Makkedah* were located on routes that led westward up from the valley of the Jordan to the hill country.
10.11 Additional evidence of God's support for Israel is provided in the form of the *huge stones* which fall and crush the enemy and which are identified as *hail stones*.
10.12-14 The Sun and Moon Stand Still. Deriving from an ancient account of this victory over the enemies of Israel, the Book of Jashar, the cessation of the movement of the heavenly bodies is seen as God's way of providing additional daylight, thereby enabling his people to complete their defeat of their Amorite opponents.
10.15 It is to *Gilgal* that Joshua returns once more after the divinely-guided victory.
10.16-43 This is the first of an extended series of stylized descriptions of the defeat of the area kings and the total destruction of the cities and their populace. Depicted is the triumph of God over Israel's enemies through Joshua and the seizure of cities and regions in the southern districts of Palestine, ending with Joshua's return to Gilgal.

6 And the Gibeonites sent to Joshua at the camp in Gilgal, saying, "Do not abandon your servants; come up to us quickly, and save us, and help us; for all the kings of the Amorites who live in the hill country are gathered against us." 7So Joshua went up from Gilgal, he and all the fighting force with him, all the mighty warriors. 8The Lord said to Joshua, "Do not fear them, for I have handed them over to you; not one of them shall stand before you." 9So Joshua came upon them suddenly, having marched up all night from Gilgal. 10And the Lord threw them into a panic before Israel, who inflicted a great slaughter on them at Gibeon, chased them by the way of the ascent of Beth-horon, and struck them down as far as Azekah and Makkedah. 11As they fled before Israel, while they were going down the slope of Beth-horon, the Lord threw down huge stones from heaven on them as far as Azekah, and they died; there were more who died because of the hailstones than the Israelites killed with the sword.

12 On the day when the Lord gave the Amorites over to the Israelites, Joshua spoke to the Lord; and he said in the sight of Israel,

"Sun, stand still at Gibeon,
and Moon, in the valley of Aijalon."
13 And the sun stood still, and the moon stopped,
until the nation took vengeance on their enemies.

Is this not written in the Book of Jashar? The sun stopped in midheaven, and did not hurry to set for about a whole day. 14There has been no day like it before or since, when the Lord heeded a human voice; for the Lord fought for Israel.

15 Then Joshua returned, and all Israel with him, to the camp at Gilgal.

Five Kings Defeated

16 Meanwhile, these five kings fled and hid themselves in the cave at Makkedah. 17And it was told Joshua, "The five kings have been found, hidden in the cave at Makkedah." 18Joshua said, "Roll large stones against the mouth of the cave, and set men by it to guard them; 19but do not stay there yourselves; pursue your enemies, and attack them from the rear. Do not let them enter their towns, for the Lord your God has given them into your hand." 20When Joshua and the Israelites had finished inflicting a very great slaughter on them, until they were wiped out, and when the survivors had entered into the fortified towns, 21all the people returned safe to Joshua in the camp at Makkedah; no one dared to speak[q] against any of the Israelites.

22 Then Joshua said, "Open the mouth of the cave, and bring those five kings out to me from the cave." 23They did so, and brought the five kings out to him from the cave, the king of Jerusalem, the king of Hebron, the king of Jarmuth, the king of Lachish, and the king of Eglon. 24When they brought the kings out to Joshua, Joshua summoned all the Israelites, and said to the chiefs of the warriors who had gone with him, "Come near, put your feet on the necks of these kings." Then they came near and put their feet on their necks. 25And Joshua said to them, "Do not be afraid or dismayed; be strong and courageous; for thus the Lord will do to all the enemies against whom you fight." 26Afterward Joshua struck them down and put them to death, and he hung them on five trees. And they hung on the trees until evening. 27At sunset Joshua commanded, and they took them down from the trees and threw them into the cave where they had hidden themselves; they set large stones against the mouth of the cave, which remain to this very day.

28 Joshua took Makkedah on that day, and struck it and its king with the edge of the sword; he utterly destroyed every person in it; he left no one remaining. And he did to the king of Makkedah as he had done to the king of Jericho.

29 Then Joshua passed on from Makkedah, and all Israel with him, to Libnah, and fought against Libnah. 30The Lord gave it also and its king into the hand of Israel; and he struck it with the edge of the sword, and every person in it; he left no one remaining in it; and he did to its king as he had done to the king of Jericho.

31 Next Joshua passed on from Libnah, and all Israel with him, to Lachish, and laid siege to it, and assaulted it. 32The Lord gave Lachish into the hand of Israel, and he took it on the second day, and struck it with the edge of the sword, and every person in it, as he had done to Libnah.

33 Then King Horam of Gezer came up to help Lachish; and Joshua struck him and his people, leaving him no survivors.

10.8 Josh 1.5,9; 11.6
10.10 Deut 7.23
10.11 Ps 18.13,14; Isa 30.30
10.12 Hab 3.11
10.13 2 Sam 1.18; Isa 38.8
10.14 ver 42
10.15 ver 43
10.16 ver 5
10.20 Deut 20.16
10.21 Ex 11.7
10.22 Deut 7.24
10.24 Ps 110.5; Isa 26.5,6; Mal 4.3
10.25 ver 8
10.26 Josh 8.29
10.27 Deut 21.23; Josh 8.9
10.28 Deut 20.16; Josh 6.21
10.29 1 Chr 6.57
10.31 2 Kings 14.19

[q] Heb *moved his tongue*

34 From Lachish Joshua passed on with
all Israel to Eglon; and they laid siege to it,
and assaulted it; 35 and they took it that day,
and struck it with the edge of the sword;
and every person in it he utterly destroyed
that day, as he had done to Lachish.
36 Then Joshua went up with all Israel
from Eglon to Hebron; they assaulted it,
37 and took it, and struck it with the edge
of the sword, and its king and its towns,
and every person in it; he left no one
remaining, just as he had done to Eglon,
and utterly destroyed it with every person
in it.
38 Then Joshua, with all Israel, turned
back to Debir and assaulted it, 39 and he took
it with its king and all its towns; they struck
them with the edge of the sword, and utterly destroyed every person in it; he left no
one remaining; just as he had done to
Hebron, and, as he had done to Libnah and
its king, so he did to Debir and its king.
40 So Joshua defeated the whole land,
the hill country and the Negeb and the
lowland and the slopes, and all their kings;
he left no one remaining, but utterly destroyed all that breathed, as the LORD God
of Israel commanded. 41 And Joshua defeated
them from Kadesh-barnea to Gaza, and all
the country of Goshen, as far as Gibeon.
42 Joshua took all these kings and their land
at one time, because the LORD God of Israel
fought for Israel. 43 Then Joshua returned,
and all Israel with him, to the camp at
Gilgal.

The United Kings of Northern Canaan Defeated

11 When King Jabin of Hazor heard
of this, he sent to King Jobab of
Madon, to the king of Shimron, to the king
of Achshaph, 2 and to the kings who were
in the northern hill country, and in the
Arabah south of Chinneroth, and in the
lowland, and in Naphoth-dor on the west,
3 to the Canaanites in the east and the west,
the Amorites, the Hittites, the Perizzites,
and the Jebusites in the hill country, and
the Hivites under Hermon in the land of
Mizpah. 4 They came out, with all their troops,
a great army, in number like the sand on
the seashore, with very many horses and
chariots. 5 All these kings joined their forces,
and came and camped together at the waters
of Merom, to fight with Israel.
6 And the LORD said to Joshua, "Do not
be afraid of them, for tomorrow at this time
I will hand over all of them, slain, to Israel;
you shall hamstring their horses, and burn
their chariots with fire." 7 So Joshua came
suddenly upon them with all his fighting
force, by the waters of Merom, and fell upon
them. 8 And the LORD handed them over to
Israel, who attacked them and chased them
as far as Great Sidon and Misrephoth-maim,
and eastward as far as the valley of Mizpeh.
They struck them down, until they had left
no one remaining. 9 And Joshua did to them
as the LORD commanded him; he hamstrung
their horses, and burned their chariots with
fire.
10 Joshua turned back at that time, and
took Hazor, and struck its king down with
the sword. Before that time Hazor was the
head of all those kingdoms. 11 And they put
to the sword all who were in it, utterly
destroying them; there was no one left who
breathed, and he burned Hazor with fire.
12 And all the towns of those kings, and all
their kings, Joshua took, and struck them
with the edge of the sword, utterly destroying them, as Moses the servant of the LORD
had commanded. 13 But Israel burned none
of the towns that stood on mounds except
Hazor, which Joshua did burn. 14 All the
spoil of these towns, and the livestock, the
Israelites took for their booty; but all the
people they struck down with the edge of
the sword, until they had destroyed them,
and they did not leave any who breathed.
15 As the LORD had commanded his servant
Moses, so Moses commanded Joshua, and so
Joshua did; he left nothing undone of all
that the LORD had commanded Moses.

Summary of Joshua's Conquests

16 So Joshua took all that land: the hill
country and all the Negeb and all the land
of Goshen and the lowland and the Arabah
and the hill country of Israel and its lowland, 17 from Mount Halak, which rises toward Seir, as far as Baal-gad in the valley
of Lebanon below Mount Hermon. He took
all their kings, struck them down, and put
them to death. 18 Joshua made war a long
time with all those kings. 19 There was not
a town that made peace with the Israelites,
except the Hivites, the inhabitants of Gibeon;
all were taken in battle. 20 For it was the
LORD's doing to harden their hearts so that
they would come against Israel in battle, in
order that they might be utterly destroyed,

10.36 Josh 14.13; 15.13; Judg 1.10
10.38 Josh 15.15; Judg 1.11
10.40 Deut 1.7; 7.24; 20.16,17
10.41 Josh 11.16; 15.51
10.42 ver 14
11.1 ver 10
11.2 Josh 12.3ff
11.4 Judg 7.12
11.6 Josh 10.8; 2 Sam 8.4
11.8 Josh 13.6
11.9 ver 6
11.11 Deut 20.16,17
11.14 Num 31.11,12
11.15 Ex 34.11,12; Deut 7.2; Josh 1.7
11.16 Josh 10.40,41; ver 2
11.17 Josh 12.7; Deut 7.24
11.19 Josh 9.3,7
11.20 Deut 2.30; Rom 9.18; Deut 20.16,17

11.1-15 The Summary of the Defeat of the Northern Kings. In this summary account, diverse geographical regions and ethnic groups are represented as having been defeated and displaced by the Israelites.
11.1 *Hazor*, a large city about five miles southwest of Lake Huleh, which is formed by the Jordan south of Mt. Hermon. Excavations have shown Hazor's size and strength to have been appropriate for it to serve as *head of all those kingdoms* (11.10).
11.2 Chinneroth, the ancient name for the Lake of Galilee, farther down the Jordan River.
11.5 *Waters of Merom*, a stream flowing from the northwest into the Lake of Galilee.
11.8 *Great Sidon*, a major city of the Phoenicians, a Semitic people whose great wealth developed through extensive trade and shipping over the Mediterranean Sea. *Misrephoth-maim* near Sidon, noted for its warm springs. Both cities were adjacent to the territory of the Israelite tribe, Asher. *Mizpeh*, meaning "watchtower," was used for many cities. This one was near Mt. Hermon, which rises to more than 9,000 feet, and is the highest mountain in Syria-Palestine and the source of the Jordan as well as of the Litani river of Syria. Mt. Hermon marked the northern limits of these conquests.
11.12-14 Although the inhabitants of these cities were *utterly* destroyed, the livestock and other captured spoils were kept by the Israelites. *The towns that stood on mounds* probably refers to the stronger, better fortified Canaanite cities built on natural or artificial mounds located on the lowlands between the hill country to the east and the Mediterranean Sea.
11.15 What Joshua has the people do is in accord with what *the LORD had commanded Moses* (Deut 12.3) and passed on to Joshua (Deut 31.1-8), all of which he has now carried out.
11.16-23 Summary of the Geographical Extent of Joshua's Conquests.
11.16-17 The territorial boundaries begin with those in the south. *The Negeb* is the wilderness area south of Palestine toward the Egyptian border. *Goshen* is probably the central and southern hill country in the territory of Judah, with the adjoining *lowland* to the west. *The Arabah* is the great valley which includes the lower end of the Jordan, the Dead Sea and the dry valley to the south.
11.17 *Mount Halak* means "bald mountain," which is nearly identical with the modern Arabic designation for a mountain in the southern Negeb. East of this mountain across the Arabah is Mount *Seir*. The northern limits of the land of Israel are given as Baal-gad, which may be Baal-Bek in what is now eastern Lebanon.
11.18-20 The almost universal hostility that Israel encountered resulted in a long struggle to control the land, but the LORD's having *hardened their hearts* justified Israel's extermination of the native peoples, in accord with the Lord's command. Only the *Hivites...of Gibeon...made peace with Israel*. The Hivites were non-Semitic people, probably originating from what is now Armenia. *Gibeon* was a city a few miles north of Jerusalem in the territory assigned to Benjamin (see Josh 9.3-27).

11.21-22 *The Anakim*, a people mentioned in ancient Egyptian texts but of unknown origin, were expelled under Joshua from the southern city of Hebron, and from Debir and Anab (some twelve miles from Hebron). They were slaughtered or escaped to the Philistine cities along the Mediterranean coast: *Gaza, Gath and Ashdod*. Possibly the Anakim, like the Philistines, were originally from Greece or Asia Minor.
11.23 The conquest of the land under Joshua is summarized, and the division of this *inheritance to Israel* is described in detail in Josh 12-22, preceded by lists of the territories seized and their kings.
12.1-12 The regions east of the Jordan are described as having been divided by Moses among two and one-half Israelite tribes: the half-tribe of Manasseh (descended from Joseph) in the north, Gad in the central district, and Reuben in the south.
12.7-24 The districts west of the Jordan are described as given *to the tribes of Israel*, including the lands formerly belonging to several regional peoples, *the Hittites, Amorites, Canaanites, Perizites, Hivites and Jebusites* (who occupied what was later to be called Jerusalem). The list of *thirty-one* defeated kings of various cities is also included, with some indications of the locations of their territories: *Bethel*, north of Jerusalem; *Carmel*, the mountain to the north of Israel that projects into the Mediterranean Sea; *Golim* in Galilee.
13.1-7 Parts of the land remaining in the hands of local tribes, including the territories of the *Sidonians, Canaanites*, and *Philistines*. It is the responsibility of Yahweh to drive out the inhabitants of these districts. The remainder of the land is to be assigned to the nine tribes and the other half-tribe of Manasseh.

and might receive no mercy, but be exterminated, just as the LORD had commanded
Moses.
21 At that time Joshua came and wiped
out the Anakim from the hill country, from
Hebron, from Debir, from Anab, and from
all the hill country of Judah, and from all
the hill country of Israel; Joshua utterly
destroyed them with their towns. 22None of
the Anakim was left in the land of the
Israelites; some remained only in Gaza, in
Gath, and in Ashdod. 23So Joshua took the
whole land, according to all that the LORD
had spoken to Moses; and Joshua gave it for
an inheritance to Israel according to their
tribal allotments. And the land had rest
from war.

The Kings Conquered by Moses

12 Now these are the kings of the
land, whom the Israelites defeated,
whose land they occupied beyond the Jordan toward the east, from the Wadi Arnon
to Mount Hermon, with all the Arabah
eastward: 2King Sihon of the Amorites who
lived at Heshbon, and ruled from Aroer,
which is on the edge of the Wadi Arnon,
and from the middle of the valley as far as
the river Jabbok, the boundary of the
Ammonites, that is, half of Gilead, 3and the
Arabah to the Sea of Chinneroth eastward,
and in the direction of Beth-jeshimoth, to
the sea of the Arabah, the Dead Sea,[r] southward to the foot of the slopes of Pisgah;
4and King Og[s] of Bashan, one of the last of
the Rephaim, who lived at Ashtaroth and
at Edrei 5and ruled over Mount Hermon and
Salecah and all Bashan to the boundary of
the Geshurites and the Maacathites, and
over half of Gilead to the boundary of King
Sihon of Heshbon. 6Moses, the servant of
the LORD, and the Israelites defeated them;
and Moses the servant of the LORD gave
their land for a possession to the Reubenites
and the Gadites and the half-tribe of
Manasseh.

The Kings Conquered by Joshua

7 The following are the kings of the land
whom Joshua and the Israelites defeated on
the west side of the Jordan, from Baal-gad
in the valley of Lebanon to Mount Halak,
that rises toward Seir (and Joshua gave
their land to the tribes of Israel as a possession according to their allotments, 8in
the hill country, in the lowland, in the
Arabah, in the slopes, in the wilderness,
and in the Negeb, the land of the Hittites,
Amorites, Canaanites, Perizzites, Hivites, and
Jebusites):
9 the king of Jericho one
the king of Ai, which is next
to Bethel one
10 the king of Jerusalem one
the king of Hebron one
11 the king of Jarmuth one
the king of Lachish one
12 the king of Eglon one
the king of Gezer one
13 the king of Debir one
the king of Geder one
14 the king of Hormah one
the king of Arad one
15 the king of Libnah one
the king of Adullam one
16 the king of Makkedah one
the king of Bethel one
17 the king of Tappuah one
the king of Hepher one
18 the king of Aphek one
the king of Lasharon one
19 the king of Madon one
the king of Hazor one
20 the king of Shimron-meron one
the king of Achshaph one
21 the king of Taanach one
the king of Megiddo one
22 the king of Kedesh one
the king of Jokneam in Carmel one
23 the king of Dor in Naphath-dor one
the king of Goiim in Galilee,[t] one
24 the king of Tirzah one
thirty-one kings in all.

The Parts of Canaan Still Unconquered

13 Now Joshua was old and advanced
in years; and the LORD said to him,
"You are old and advanced in years, and
very much of the land still remains to be
possessed. 2This is the land that still remains: all the regions of the Philistines, and
all those of the Geshurites 3(from the Shihor,
which is east of Egypt, northward to the
boundary of Ekron, it is reckoned as
Canaanite; there are five rulers of the
Philistines, those of Gaza, Ashdod, Ashkelon,
Gath, and Ekron), and those of the Avvim,
4in the south, all the land of the Canaanites,
and Mearah that belongs to the Sidonians,

11.21 Num 13.33; Deut 9.2
11.23 Num 34.2ff
12.1 Deut 3.8,9
12.2 Deut 2.33,36
12.3 Josh 11.2; 13.20
12.4 Deut 3.11
12.5 Deut 3.8ff
12.6 Num 21.24,33; 32.29,33
12.7 Josh 11.17,23
12.8 Josh 11.16
12.9 Josh 6.2; 8.29
12.12 Josh 10.33
12.13 Josh 10.38
12.24 Deut 7.24
13.1 Josh 14.10
13.3 Judg 3.3; Deut 2.23

[r] Heb *Salt Sea* [s] Gk: Heb *the boundary of King Og* [t] Gk: Heb *Gilgal*

to Aphek, to the boundary of the Amorites,
[5]and the land of the Gebalites, and all Lebanon, toward the east, from Baal-gad below
Mount Hermon to Lebo-hamath, [6]all the
inhabitants of the hill country from Lebanon to Misrephoth-maim, even all the
Sidonians. I will myself drive them out from
before the Israelites; only allot the land to
Israel for an inheritance, as I have commanded you. [7]Now therefore divide this
land for an inheritance to the nine tribes
and the half-tribe of Manasseh."

The Territory East of the Jordan

8 With the other half-tribe of Manasseh[u]
the Reubenites and the Gadites received
their inheritance, which Moses gave them,
beyond the Jordan eastward, as Moses the
servant of the LORD gave them: [9]from Aroer,
which is on the edge of the Wadi Arnon,
and the town that is in the middle of the
valley, and all the tableland from[v] Medeba
as far as Dibon; [10]and all the cities of King
Sihon of the Amorites, who reigned in
Heshbon, as far as the boundary of the
Ammonites; [11]and Gilead, and the region of
the Geshurites and Maacathites, and all
Mount Hermon, and all Bashan to Salecah;
[12]all the kingdom of Og in Bashan, who
reigned in Ashtaroth and in Edrei (he alone
was left of the survivors of the Rephaim);
these Moses had defeated and driven out.
[13]Yet the Israelites did not drive out the
Geshurites or the Maacathites; but Geshur
and Maacath live within Israel to this day.
14 To the tribe of Levi alone Moses gave
no inheritance; the offerings by fire to the
LORD God of Israel are their inheritance, as
he said to them.

The Territory of Reuben

15 Moses gave an inheritance to the tribe
of the Reubenites according to their clans.
[16]Their territory was from Aroer, which is
on the edge of the Wadi Arnon, and the
town that is in the middle of the valley, and
all the tableland by Medeba; [17]with Heshbon,
and all its towns that are in the tableland;
Dibon, and Bamoth-baal, and Beth-baal-
meon, [18]and Jahaz, and Kedemoth, and
Mephaath, [19]and Kiriathaim, and Sibmah,
and Zereth-shahar on the hill of the valley,
[20]and Beth-peor, and the slopes of Pisgah,
and Beth-jeshimoth, [21]that is, all the towns
of the tableland, and all the kingdom of
King Sihon of the Amorites, who reigned in
Heshbon, whom Moses defeated with the
leaders of Midian, Evi and Rekem and Zur
and Hur and Reba, as princes of Sihon, who
lived in the land. [22]Along with the rest of
those they put to death, the Israelites also
put to the sword Balaam son of Beor, who
practiced divination. [23]And the border of the
Reubenites was the Jordan and its banks.
This was the inheritance of the Reubenites,
according to their families with their towns
and villages.

The Territory of Gad

24 Moses gave an inheritance also to the
tribe of the Gadites, according to their families. [25]Their territory was Jazer, and all the
towns of Gilead, and half the land of the
Ammonites, to Aroer, which is east of
Rabbah, [26]and from Heshbon to Ramath-
mizpeh and Betonim, and from Mahanaim
to the territory of Debir,[w] [27]and in the valley
Beth-haram, Beth-nimrah, Succoth, and
Zaphon, the rest of the kingdom of King
Sihon of Heshbon, the Jordan and its banks,
as far as the lower end of the Sea of
Chinnereth, eastward beyond the Jordan.
[28]This is the inheritance of the Gadites
according to their clans, with their towns
and villages.

The Territory of the Half-Tribe of Manasseh (East)

29 Moses gave an inheritance to the half-
tribe of Manasseh; it was allotted to the
half-tribe of the Manassites according to
their families. [30]Their territory extended from
Mahanaim, through all Bashan, the whole
kingdom of King Og of Bashan, and all the
settlements of Jair, which are in Bashan,
sixty towns, [31]and half of Gilead, and
Ashtaroth, and Edrei, the towns of the kingdom of Og in Bashan; these were allotted to
the people of Machir son of Manasseh according to their clans—for half the
Machirites.
32 These are the inheritances that Moses
distributed in the plains of Moab, beyond
the Jordan east of Jericho. [33]But to the tribe
of Levi Moses gave no inheritance; the LORD
God of Israel is their inheritance, as he said
to them.

[u] Cn: Heb *With it* [v] Compare Gk: Heb lacks *from* [w] Gk Syr Vg: Heb *Lidebir*

13.6 Josh 11.8
13.8 Josh 12.1-6
13.9 ver 16
13.10 Num 21.24,25
13.12 Deut 3.11; Num 21.24,35
13.14 Deut 8.1,2
13.16 Josh 12.2
13.21 Num 31.8
13.22 Num 31.8
13.25 Num 21.32
13.27 Num 34.11
13.30 Num 32.41
13.33 ver 14; Num 18.20; Deut 10.9; 18.1,2

13.8-13 Details of the lands assigned to the half-tribe of Manasseh differ from those already offered in 12.1-6, including the note that not all the land was cleared of its earlier occupants.
13.14 Levi receives no territory, but the tribe is to benefit from the offerings brought to the central sanctuary by the other tribes.
13.15-23 Details of *the Reubenites'* occupancy of their territory east of the Jordan.
13.24-32 Details of the occupancy of their east Jordan territories by the tribe of Gad and the eastern half of the tribe of Manasseh.

14.1-5 The lands west of the Jordan are distributed by a combination of leaders: *the priest Eleazar, and Joshua, and the heads of the families* of the Israelite tribes. The actual assignment of lands is *by lot.* A different detail is the arrangement for the Levites to obtain their own cities and adjacent pasture lands (*cf.* 13.14).
14.6-15 The special allotment of land to Caleb and his descendants was the reward for his having encouraged Israel to invade the land of Canaan (Num 13.30-33). As a result, he and Joshua alone of the original refugees from Egypt were permitted to enter the land (Num 14.30). Hebron was earlier associated with Abraham's initial move into the land of Canaan (Gen 13.18).
15.1-12 The Territory of Judah. This type of assignment of territory proceeds by designation of the boundaries allotted to each tribe.

The Distribution of Territory West of the Jordan

14 These are the inheritances that
the Israelites received in the land
of Canaan, which the priest Eleazar, and
Joshua son of Nun, and the heads of the
families of the tribes of the Israelites distributed to them. [2]Their inheritance was by lot,
as the LORD had commanded Moses for the
nine and one-half tribes. [3]For Moses had
given an inheritance to the two and one-
half tribes beyond the Jordan; but to the
Levites he gave no inheritance among them.
[4]For the people of Joseph were two tribes,
Manasseh and Ephraim; and no portion
was given to the Levites in the land, but
only towns to live in, with their pasture
lands for their flocks and herds. [5]The Israelites did as the LORD commanded Moses;
they allotted the land.

Hebron Allotted to Caleb

6 Then the people of Judah came to Joshua
at Gilgal; and Caleb son of Jephunneh the
Kenizzite said to him, "You know what the
LORD said to Moses the man of God in
Kadesh-barnea concerning you and me. [7]I
was forty years old when Moses the servant
of the LORD sent me from Kadesh-barnea to
spy out the land; and I brought him an
honest report. [8]But my companions who
went up with me made the heart of the
people melt; yet I wholeheartedly followed
the LORD my God. [9]And Moses swore on that
day, saying, 'Surely the land on which your
foot has trodden shall be an inheritance for
you and your children forever, because you
have wholeheartedly followed the LORD my
God.' [10]And now, as you see, the LORD has
kept me alive, as he said, these forty-five
years since the time that the LORD spoke this
word to Moses, while Israel was journeying
through the wilderness; and here I am today,
eighty-five years old. [11]I am still as strong
today as I was on the day that Moses sent
me; my strength now is as my strength was
then, for war, and for going and coming.
[12]So now give me this hill country of which
the LORD spoke on that day; for you heard
on that day how the Anakim were there,
with great fortified cities; it may be that the
LORD will be with me, and I shall drive them
out, as the LORD said."
13 Then Joshua blessed him, and gave
Hebron to Caleb son of Jephunneh for an
inheritance. [14]So Hebron became the inheritance of Caleb son of Jephunneh the Kenizzite
to this day, because he wholeheartedly followed the LORD, the God of Israel. [15]Now the
name of Hebron formerly was Kiriath-arba;[x]
this Arba was[y] the greatest man among the
Anakim. And the land had rest from war.

The Territory of Judah

15 The lot for the tribe of the people
of Judah according to their families reached southward to the boundary of
Edom, to the wilderness of Zin at the farthest south. [2]And their south boundary ran
from the end of the Dead Sea,[z] from the bay
that faces southward; [3]it goes out southward of the ascent of Akrabbim, passes
along to Zin, and goes up south of Kadesh-
barnea, along by Hezron, up to Addar, makes
a turn to Karka, [4]passes along to Azmon,
goes out by the Wadi of Egypt, and comes
to its end at the sea. This shall be your
south boundary. [5]And the east boundary is
the Dead Sea,[z] to the mouth of the Jordan.
And the boundary on the north side runs
from the bay of the sea at the mouth of the
Jordan; [6]and the boundary goes up to
Beth-hoglah, and passes along north of
Beth-arabah; and the boundary goes up to
the Stone of Bohan, Reuben's son; [7]and the
boundary goes up to Debir from the Valley
of Achor, and so northward, turning toward Gilgal, which is opposite the ascent of
Adummim, which is on the south side of
the valley; and the boundary passes along
to the waters of En-shemesh, and ends at
En-rogel; [8]then the boundary goes up by the
valley of the son of Hinnom at the southern
slope of the Jebusites (that is, Jerusalem);
and the boundary goes up to the top of the
mountain that lies over against the valley
of Hinnom, on the west, at the northern
end of the valley of Rephaim; [9]then the
boundary extends from the top of the
mountain to the spring of the Waters of
Nephtoah, and from there to the towns of
Mount Ephron; then the boundary bends
around to Baalah (that is, Kiriath-jearim);
[10]and the boundary circles west of Baalah
to Mount Seir, passes along to the northern
slope of Mount Jearim (that is, Chesalon),
and goes down to Beth-shemesh, and passes
along by Timnah; [11]the boundary goes out
to the slope of the hill north of Ekron, then
the boundary bends around to Shikkeron,

14.1 Num 34.17,18
14.2 Num 26.55
14.3 Num 32.33; Josh 13.14
14.4 Gen 48.5
14.6 Num 13.6,26,30; 14.6,24,30
14.7 Num 13.6; 14.6
14.8 Num 13.31,32; 14.24
14.9 Deut 1.36
14.10 Num 14.30
14.12 Num 13.22
14.13 Josh 22.6; ver 8,9
14.15 Josh 11.23
15.1 Num 34.3,4; 33.36
15.3 Num 34.4
15.4 Num 34.5
15.6 Josh 18.17,19
15.7 Josh 7.24
15.8 ver 63
15.9 Josh 18.15
15.10 Judg 14.1

[x] That is *the city of Arba* [y] Heb lacks *this Arba was* [z] Heb *Salt Sea*

15.12 ver 47
15.13 Jn 14.13-15
15.14 Josh 11.21,22; Num 13.22
15.15 Josh 10.38
15.16 Judg 1.12,13; 3.9
15.18 Judg 1.14
15.28 Gen 21.31
15.31 1 Sam 27.6
15.33 Judg 13.25; 16.31
15.35 1 Sam 22.1
15.38 2 Kings 14.7
15.39 Josh 10.3; 2 Kings 14.19
15.47 ver 4; Num 34.6
15.51 Josh 10.41; 11.16
15.60 Josh 18.14
15.63 Judg 1.21; 2 Sam 5.6
16.1 Josh 18.12
16.2 Josh 18.13
16.3 Josh 18.13; 2 Chr 8.5
16.5 Josh 18.13
16.6 Josh 17.7

and passes along to Mount Baalah, and goes out to Jabneel; then the boundary comes to an end at the sea. [12]And the west boundary was the Mediterranean with its coast. This is the boundary surrounding the people of Judah according to their families.

Caleb Occupies His Portion

13 According to the commandment of the LORD to Joshua, he gave to Caleb son of Jephunneh a portion among the people of Judah, Kiriath-arba,[a] that is, Hebron (Arba was the father of Anak). [14]And Caleb drove out from there the three sons of Anak: Sheshai, Ahiman, and Talmai, the descendants of Anak. [15]From there he went up against the inhabitants of Debir; now the name of Debir formerly was Kiriath-sepher. [16]And Caleb said, "Whoever attacks Kiriath-sepher and takes it, to him I will give my daughter Achsah as wife." [17]Othniel son of Kenaz, the brother of Caleb, took it; and he gave him his daughter Achsah as wife. [18]When she came to him, she urged him to ask her father for a field. As she dismounted from her donkey, Caleb said to her, "What do you wish?" [19]She said to him, "Give me a present; since you have set me in the land of the Negeb, give me springs of water as well." So Caleb gave her the upper springs and the lower springs.

The Towns of Judah

20 This is the inheritance of the tribe of the people of Judah according to their families. [21]The towns belonging to the tribe of the people of Judah in the extreme South, toward the boundary of Edom, were Kabzeel, Eder, Jagur, [22]Kinah, Dimonah, Adadah, [23]Kedesh, Hazor, Ithnan, [24]Ziph, Telem, Bealoth, [25]Hazor-hadattah, Kerioth-hezron (that is, Hazor), [26]Amam, Shema, Moladah, [27]Hazar-gaddah, Heshmon, Beth-pelet, [28]Hazar-shual, Beer-sheba, Biziothiah, [29]Baalah, Iim, Ezem, [30]Eltolad, Chesil, Hormah, [31]Ziklag, Madmannah, Sansannah, [32]Lebaoth, Shilhim, Ain, and Rimmon: in all, twenty-nine towns, with their villages.

33 And in the Lowland, Eshtaol, Zorah, Ashnah, [34]Zanoah, En-gannim, Tappuah, Enam, [35]Jarmuth, Adullam, Socoh, Azekah, [36]Shaaraim, Adithaim, Gederah, Gederothaim: fourteen towns with their villages.

37 Zenan, Hadashah, Migdal-gad, [38]Dilan, Mizpeh, Jokthe-el, [39]Lachish, Bozkath, Eglon, [40]Cabbon, Lahmam, Chitlish, [41]Gederoth, Beth-dagon, Naamah, and Makkedah: sixteen towns with their villages.

42 Libnah, Ether, Ashan, [43]Iphtah, Ashnah, Nezib, [44]Keilah, Achzib, and Mareshah: nine towns with their villages.

45 Ekron, with its dependencies and its villages; [46]from Ekron to the sea, all that were near Ashdod, with their villages.

47 Ashdod, its towns and its villages; Gaza, its towns and its villages; to the Wadi of Egypt, and the Great Sea with its coast.

48 And in the hill country, Shamir, Jattir, Socoh, [49]Dannah, Kiriath-sannah (that is, Debir), [50]Anab, Eshtemoh, Anim, [51]Goshen, Holon, and Giloh: eleven towns with their villages.

52 Arab, Dumah, Eshan, [53]Janim, Beth-tappuah, Aphekah, [54]Humtah, Kiriath-arba (that is, Hebron), and Zior: nine towns with their villages.

55 Maon, Carmel, Ziph, Juttah, [56]Jezreel, Jokdeam, Zanoah, [57]Kain, Gibeah, and Timnah: ten towns with their villages.

58 Halhul, Beth-zur, Gedor, [59]Maarath, Beth-anoth, and Eltekon: six towns with their villages.

60 Kiriath-baal (that is, Kiriath-jearim), and Rabbah: two towns with their villages.

61 In the wilderness, Beth-arabah, Middin, Secacah, [62]Nibshan, the City of Salt, and En-gedi: six towns with their villages.

63 But the people of Judah could not drive out the Jebusites, the inhabitants of Jerusalem; so the Jebusites live with the people of Judah in Jerusalem to this day.

The Territory of Ephraim

16 The allotment of the Josephites went from the Jordan by Jericho, east of the waters of Jericho, into the wilderness, going up from Jericho into the hill country to Bethel; [2]then going from Bethel to Luz, it passes along to Ataroth, the territory of the Archites; [3]then it goes down westward to the territory of the Japhletites, as far as the territory of Lower Beth-horon, then to Gezer, and it ends at the sea.

4 The Josephites—Manasseh and Ephraim—received their inheritance.

5 The territory of the Ephraimites by their families was as follows: the boundary of their inheritance on the east was Ataroth-addar as far as Upper Beth-horon, [6]and the bound-

[a] That is *the city of Arba*

15.13-19 The occupation of the land assigned to Caleb. Caleb's nephew, *Othniel*, captures one of the cities of the region, *Kiriath-sepher*, and as a reward receives a wife and *springs of water* in the arid southern region, *the Negeb*.
15.20-63 The list of cities given to Judah. This is the second type of assignment document. The continuing occupation of the vicinity of Jerusalem by *the Jebusites* is noted.
16.1-10 The assignment of extensive lands to the two half-tribes descended from Joseph, *Ephraim and Manasseh*, is sketched (concluded in 17.1-13), with the note that the Canaanites continued to live in the district around Gezer, a city on the ridge west of Jerusalem which was occupied almost continually for 3500 years until the first century BCE.

17.1-18 The Portion of the Tribes of Joseph. The heritage to the half-tribe of Manasseh is made not only through the male line, but through the *daughters of Zelophad* as well. As a result, the territory assigned is large and dominates central Palestine. Certain towns remain in the control of the *Canaanites.* Even so, the Joseph heirs protest that they need more space, and are encouraged to drive out the Canaanites, in spite of the latter people's superior military equipment, which included *chariots of iron.*
18.1-19.48 Very small sections of the land are apportioned to the remaining seven tribes: Benjamin in the vicinity of Jericho and Jerusalem (18.11-22); Simeon, south of the territory of Judah (19.1-9); Zebulun, west of the Sea of Galilee (19.10-16); Issachar, southeast of the Sea of Galilee (19.17-23); Asher, northwest along the Mediterranean coast (19.24-31); Naphtali, west of the northernmost stretch of the Jordan River (19.23-39); Dan, west of Jerusalem along the coastal plain (19.40-48).

ary goes from there to the sea; on the north is Michmethath; then on the east the boundary makes a turn toward Taanath-shiloh, and passes along beyond it on the east to Janoah, [7]then it goes down from Janoah to Ataroth and to Naarah, and touches Jericho, ending at the Jordan. [8]From Tappuah the boundary goes westward to the Wadi Kanah, and ends at the sea. Such is the inheritance of the tribe of the Ephraimites by their families, [9]together with the towns that were set apart for the Ephraimites within the inheritance of the Manassites, all those towns with their villages. [10]They did not, however, drive out the Canaanites who lived in Gezer: so the Canaanites have lived within Ephraim to this day but have been made to do forced labor.

The Other Half-Tribe of Manasseh (West)

17 Then allotment was made to the tribe of Manasseh, for he was the firstborn of Joseph. To Machir the firstborn of Manasseh, the father of Gilead, were allotted Gilead and Bashan, because he was a warrior. [2]And allotments were made to the rest of the tribe of Manasseh, by their families, Abiezer, Helek, Asriel, Shechem, Hepher, and Shemida; these were the male descendants of Manasseh son of Joseph, by their families.

3 Now Zelophehad son of Hepher son of Gilead son of Machir son of Manasseh had no sons, but only daughters; and these are the names of his daughters: Mahlah, Noah, Hoglah, Milcah, and Tirzah. [4]They came before the priest Eleazar and Joshua son of Nun and the leaders, and said, "The LORD commanded Moses to give us an inheritance along with our male kin." So according to the commandment of the LORD he gave them an inheritance among the kinsmen of their father. [5]Thus there fell to Manasseh ten portions, besides the land of Gilead and Bashan, which is on the other side of the Jordan, [6]because the daughters of Manasseh received an inheritance along with his sons. The land of Gilead was allotted to the rest of the Manassites.

7 The territory of Manasseh reached from Asher to Michmethath, which is east of Shechem; then the boundary goes along southward to the inhabitants of En-tappuah. [8]The land of Tappuah belonged to Manasseh, but the town of Tappuah on the boundary of Manasseh belonged to the Ephraimites. [9]Then the boundary went down to the Wadi Kanah. The towns here, to the south of the wadi, among the towns of Manasseh, belong to Ephraim. Then the boundary of Manasseh goes along the north side of the wadi and ends at the sea. [10]The land to the south is Ephraim's and that to the north is Manasseh's, with the sea forming its boundary; on the north Asher is reached, and on the east Issachar. [11]Within Issachar and Asher, Manasseh had Beth-shean and its villages, Ibleam and its villages, the inhabitants of Dor and its villages, the inhabitants of En-dor and its villages, the inhabitants of Taanach and its villages, and the inhabitants of Megiddo and its villages (the third is Naphath).[b] [12]Yet the Manassites could not take possession of those towns; but the Canaanites continued to live in that land. [13]But when the Israelites grew strong, they put the Canaanites to forced labor, but did not utterly drive them out.

The Tribe of Joseph Protests

14 The tribe of Joseph spoke to Joshua, saying, "Why have you given me but one lot and one portion as an inheritance, since we are a numerous people, whom all along the LORD has blessed?" [15]And Joshua said to them, "If you are a numerous people, go up to the forest, and clear ground there for yourselves in the land of the Perizzites and the Rephaim, since the hill country of Ephraim is too narrow for you." [16]The tribe of Joseph said, "The hill country is not enough for us; yet all the Canaanites who live in the plain have chariots of iron, both those in Beth-shean and its villages and those in the Valley of Jezreel." [17]Then Joshua said to the house of Joseph, to Ephraim and Manasseh, "You are indeed a numerous people, and have great power; you shall not have one lot only, [18]but the hill country shall be yours, for though it is a forest, you shall clear it and possess it to its farthest borders; for you shall drive out the Canaanites, though they have chariots of iron, and though they are strong."

The Territories of the Remaining Tribes

18 Then the whole congregation of the Israelites assembled at Shiloh, and set up the tent of meeting there. The land lay subdued before them.

16.7 1 Chr 7.28
16.8 Josh 17.8,9
16.10 Judg 1.29; 1 Kings 9.16; Josh 17.12
17.1 Gen 41.41; 50.23; Deut 3.15
17.2 Num 26.29-32
17.3 Num 26.33; 27.1-7
17.4 Num 27.5-7
17.6 Josh 13.30,31
17.7 Josh 16.6
17.8 Josh 16.8
17.9 Josh 16.8,9
17.11 1 Chr 7.29
17.12 Judg 1.27,28
17.13 Josh 16.10
17.14 Num 26.34,37
17.16 Judg 1.19; 4.3
18.1 Josh 19.51; Jer 7.12; Judg 18.31

[b] Meaning of Heb uncertain

18.3 Judg 18.9
18.5 Josh 15.1; 16.1,4
18.7 Josh 13.33; 13.8
18.8 ver 1; Judg 18.31
18.10 Josh 19.51
18.13 Gen 28.19; Josh 16.3
18.14 Josh 15.9
18.15 Josh 15.5-9
18.16 2 Kings 23.10
18.20 Josh 21.4,17
18.28 Josh 15.8
19.1 ver 9
19.5 1 Sam 30.1

2 There remained among the Israelites seven tribes whose inheritance had not yet been apportioned. [3]So Joshua said to the Israelites, "How long will you be slack about going in and taking possession of the land that the LORD, the God of your ancestors, has given you? [4]Provide three men from each tribe, and I will send them out that they may begin to go throughout the land, writing a description of it with a view to their inheritances. Then come back to me. [5]They shall divide it into seven portions, Judah continuing in its territory on the south, and the house of Joseph in their territory on the north. [6]You shall describe the land in seven divisions and bring the description here to me; and I will cast lots for you here before the LORD our God. [7]The Levites have no portion among you, for the priesthood of the LORD is their heritage; and Gad and Reuben and the half-tribe of Manasseh have received their inheritance beyond the Jordan eastward, which Moses the servant of the LORD gave them."

8 So the men started on their way; and Joshua charged those who went to write the description of the land, saying, "Go throughout the land and write a description of it, and come back to me; and I will cast lots for you here before the LORD in Shiloh." [9]So the men went and traversed the land and set down in a book a description of it by towns in seven divisions; then they came back to Joshua in the camp at Shiloh, [10]and Joshua cast lots for them in Shiloh before the LORD; and there Joshua apportioned the land to the Israelites, to each a portion.

The Territory of Benjamin

11 The lot of the tribe of Benjamin according to its families came up, and the territory allotted to it fell between the tribe of Judah and the tribe of Joseph. [12]On the north side their boundary began at the Jordan; then the boundary goes up to the slope of Jericho on the north, then up through the hill country westward; and it ends at the wilderness of Beth-aven. [13]From there the boundary passes along southward in the direction of Luz, to the slope of Luz (that is, Bethel), then the boundary goes down to Ataroth-addar, on the mountain that lies south of Lower Beth-horon. [14]Then the boundary goes in another direction, turning on the western side southward from the mountain that lies to the south, opposite Beth-horon, and it ends at Kiriath-baal (that is, Kiriath-jearim), a town belonging to the tribe of Judah. This forms the western side. [15]The southern side begins at the outskirts of Kiriath-jearim; and the boundary goes from there to Ephron,[c] to the spring of the Waters of Nephtoah; [16]then the boundary goes down to the border of the mountain that overlooks the valley of the son of Hinnom, which is at the north end of the valley of Rephaim; and it then goes down the valley of Hinnom, south of the slope of the Jebusites, and downward to En-rogel; [17]then it bends in a northerly direction going on to En-shemesh, and from there goes to Geliloth, which is opposite the ascent of Adummim; then it goes down to the Stone of Bohan, Reuben's son; [18]and passing on to the north of the slope of Beth-arabah[d] it goes down to the Arabah; [19]then the boundary passes on to the north of the slope of Beth-hoglah; and the boundary ends at the northern bay of the Dead Sea,[e] at the south end of the Jordan: this is the southern border. [20]The Jordan forms its boundary on the eastern side. This is the inheritance of the tribe of Benjamin, according to its families, boundary by boundary all around.

21 Now the towns of the tribe of Benjamin according to their families were Jericho, Beth-hoglah, Emek-keziz, [22]Beth-arabah, Zemaraim, Bethel, [23]Avvim, Parah, Ophrah, [24]Chephar-ammoni, Ophni, and Geba—twelve towns with their villages: [25]Gibeon, Ramah, Beeroth, [26]Mizpeh, Chephirah, Mozah, [27]Rekem, Irpeel, Taralah, [28]Zela, Haeleph, Jebus[f] (that is, Jerusalem), Gibeah[g] and Kiriath-jearim[h]—fourteen towns with their villages. This is the inheritance of the tribe of Benjamin according to its families.

The Territory of Simeon

19 The second lot came out for Simeon, for the tribe of Simeon, according to its families; its inheritance lay within the inheritance of the tribe of Judah. [2]It had for its inheritance Beer-sheba, Sheba, Moladah, [3]Hazar-shual, Balah, Ezem, [4]Eltolad, Bethul, Hormah, [5]Ziklag, Beth-marcaboth, Hazar-susah, [6]Beth-lebaoth, and Sharuhen—thirteen towns with their villages; [7]Ain,

[c] Cn See 15.9. Heb *westward* [d] Gk: Heb *to the slope over against the Arabah* [e] Heb *Salt Sea* [f] Gk Syr Vg: Heb *the Jebusite* [g] Heb *Gibeath* [h] Gk: Heb *Kiriath*

Rimmon, Ether, and Ashan—four towns with their villages; [8]together with all the villages all around these towns as far as Baalath-beer, Ramah of the Negeb. This was the inheritance of the tribe of Simeon according to its families. [9]The inheritance of the tribe of Simeon formed part of the territory of Judah; because the portion of the tribe of Judah was too large for them, the tribe of Simeon obtained an inheritance within their inheritance.

The Territory of Zebulun

10 The third lot came up for the tribe of Zebulun, according to its families. The boundary of its inheritance reached as far as Sarid; [11]then its boundary goes up westward, and on to Maralah, and touches Dabbesheth, then the wadi that is east of Jokneam; [12]from Sarid it goes in the other direction eastward toward the sunrise to the boundary of Chisloth-tabor; from there it goes to Daberath, then up to Japhia; [13]from there it passes along on the east toward the sunrise to Gath-hepher, to Eth-kazin, and going on to Rimmon it bends toward Neah; [14]then on the north the boundary makes a turn to Hannathon, and it ends at the valley of Iphtah-el; [15]and Kattath, Nahalal, Shimron, Idalah, and Bethlehem—twelve towns with their villages. [16]This is the inheritance of the tribe of Zebulun, according to its families—these towns with their villages.

The Territory of Issachar

17 The fourth lot came out for Issachar, for the tribe of Issachar, according to its families. [18]Its territory included Jezreel, Chesulloth, Shunem, [19]Hapharaim, Shion, Anaharath, [20]Rabbith, Kishion, Ebez, [21]Remeth, En-gannim, En-haddah, Beth-pazzez; [22]the boundary also touches Tabor, Shahazumah, and Beth-shemesh, and its boundary ends at the Jordan—sixteen towns with their villages. [23]This is the inheritance of the tribe of Issachar, according to its families—the towns with their villages.

The Territory of Asher

24 The fifth lot came out for the tribe of Asher according to its families. [25]Its boundary included Helkath, Hali, Beten, Achshaph, [26]Allammelech, Amad, and Mishal; on the west it touches Carmel and Shihor-libnath, [27]then it turns eastward, goes to Beth-dagon, and touches Zebulun and the valley of Iphtah-el northward to Beth-emek and Neiel; then it continues in the north to Cabul, [28]Ebron, Rehob, Hammon, Kanah, as far as Great Sidon; [29]then the boundary turns to Ramah, reaching to the fortified city of Tyre; then the boundary turns to Hosah, and it ends at the sea; Mahalab,[i] Achzib, [30]Ummah, Aphek, and Rehob—twenty-two towns with their villages. [31]This is the inheritance of the tribe of Asher according to its families—these towns with their villages.

The Territory of Naphtali

32 The sixth lot came out for the tribe of Naphtali, for the tribe of Naphtali, according to its families. [33]And its boundary ran from Heleph, from the oak in Zaanannim, and Adami-nekeb, and Jabneel, as far as Lakkum; and it ended at the Jordan; [34]then the boundary turns westward to Aznoth-tabor, and goes from there to Hukkok, touching Zebulun at the south, and Asher on the west, and Judah on the east at the Jordan. [35]The fortified towns are Ziddim, Zer, Hammath, Rakkath, Chinnereth, [36]Adamah, Ramah, Hazor, [37]Kedesh, Edrei, En-hazor, [38]Iron, Migdal-el, Horem, Beth-anath, and Beth-shemesh—nineteen towns with their villages. [39]This is the inheritance of the tribe of Naphtali according to its families—the towns with their villages.

The Territory of Dan

40 The seventh lot came out for the tribe of Dan, according to its families. [41]The territory of its inheritance included Zorah, Eshtaol, Ir-shemesh, [42]Shaalabbin, Aijalon, Ithlah, [43]Elon, Timnah, Ekron, [44]Eltekeh, Gibbethon, Baalath, [45]Jehud, Bene-berak, Gath-rimmon, [46]Me-jarkon, and Rakkon at the border opposite Joppa. [47]When the territory of the Danites was lost to them, the Danites went up and fought against Leshem, and after capturing it and putting it to the sword, they took possession of it and settled in it, calling Leshem, Dan, after their ancestor Dan. [48]This is the inheritance of the tribe of Dan, according to their families—these towns with their villages.

19.9 ver 1
19.11 Josh 21.34
19.15 Mic 5.2
19.17 2 Sam 2.9
19.28 Josh 11.8
19.30 Josh 21.31
19.34 Deut 33.23
19.42 Judg 1.35
19.47 Judg 18.27-31

[i] Cn Compare Gk: Heb *Mehebel*

19.50 Josh 24.30
19.51 Josh 14.1; 18.1,10
20.2 Num 35.6-34; Deut 4.41; 19.2
20.4 Ruth 4.1,2
20.5 Num 35.12
20.6 Num 35.25
20.7 Josh 21.32; 1 Chr 6.76; Josh 21.11; Lk 1.39
20.8 Josh 21.27,36,38
20.9 Num 35.15; ver 6
21.1 Num 35.1-8
21.2 Num 35.2
21.4 ver 8,19
21.5 ver 20ff
21.6 ver 27ff
21.7 ver 34ff
21.8 ver 3
21.11 Josh 15.13,14; 1 Chr 6.55
21.13 Josh 15.42,54; 20.7; 1 Chr 6.57
21.15 Josh 15.49,51; 1 Chr 6.58
21.16 Josh 15.10,15; 1 Chr 6.59

Joshua's Inheritance

49 When they had finished distributing the several territories of the land as inheritances, the Israelites gave an inheritance among them to Joshua son of Nun. [50]By command of the LORD they gave him the town that he asked for, Timnath-serah in the hill country of Ephraim; he rebuilt the town, and settled in it.

51 These are the inheritances that the priest Eleazar and Joshua son of Nun and the heads of the families of the tribes of the Israelites distributed by lot at Shiloh before the LORD, at the entrance of the tent of meeting. So they finished dividing the land.

The Cities of Refuge

20 Then the LORD spoke to Joshua, saying, [2]"Say to the Israelites, 'Appoint the cities of refuge, of which I spoke to you through Moses, [3]so that anyone who kills a person without intent or by mistake may flee there; they shall be for you a refuge from the avenger of blood. [4]The slayer shall flee to one of these cities and shall stand at the entrance of the gate of the city, and explain the case to the elders of that city; then the fugitive shall be taken into the city, and given a place, and shall remain with them. [5]And if the avenger of blood is in pursuit, they shall not give up the slayer, because the neighbor was killed by mistake, there having been no enmity between them before. [6]The slayer shall remain in that city until there is a trial before the congregation, until the death of the one who is high priest at the time: then the slayer may return home, to the town in which the deed was done.' "

7 So they set apart Kedesh in Galilee in the hill country of Naphtali, and Shechem in the hill country of Ephraim, and Kiriath-arba (that is, Hebron) in the hill country of Judah. [8]And beyond the Jordan east of Jericho, they appointed Bezer in the wilderness on the tableland, from the tribe of Reuben, and Ramoth in Gilead, from the tribe of Gad, and Golan in Bashan, from the tribe of Manasseh. [9]These were the cities designated for all the Israelites, and for the aliens residing among them, that anyone who killed a person without intent could flee there, so as not to die by the hand of the avenger of blood, until there was a trial before the congregation.

Cities Allotted to the Levites

21 Then the heads of the families of the Levites came to the priest Eleazar and to Joshua son of Nun and to the heads of the families of the tribes of the Israelites; [2]they said to them at Shiloh in the land of Canaan, "The LORD commanded through Moses that we be given towns to live in, along with their pasture lands for our livestock." [3]So by command of the LORD the Israelites gave to the Levites the following towns and pasture lands out of their inheritance.

4 The lot came out for the families of the Kohathites. So those Levites who were descendants of Aaron the priest received by lot thirteen towns from the tribes of Judah, Simeon, and Benjamin.

5 The rest of the Kohathites received by lot ten towns from the families of the tribe of Ephraim, from the tribe of Dan, and the half-tribe of Manasseh.

6 The Gershonites received by lot thirteen towns from the families of the tribe of Issachar, from the tribe of Asher, from the tribe of Naphtali, and from the half-tribe of Manasseh in Bashan.

7 The Merarites according to their families received twelve towns from the tribe of Reuben, the tribe of Gad, and the tribe of Zebulun.

8 These towns and their pasture lands the Israelites gave by lot to the Levites, as the LORD had commanded through Moses.

9 Out of the tribe of Judah and the tribe of Simeon they gave the following towns mentioned by name, [10]which went to the descendants of Aaron, one of the families of the Kohathites who belonged to the Levites, since the lot fell to them first. [11]They gave them Kiriath-arba (Arba being the father of Anak), that is Hebron, in the hill country of Judah, along with the pasture lands around it. [12]But the fields of the town and its villages had been given to Caleb son of Jephunneh as his holding.

13 To the descendants of Aaron the priest they gave Hebron, the city of refuge for the slayer, with its pasture lands, Libnah with its pasture lands, [14]Jattir with its pasture lands, Eshtemoa with its pasture lands, [15]Holon with its pasture lands, Debir with its pasture lands, [16]Ain with its pasture lands, Juttah with its pasture lands, and Beth-shemesh with its pasture lands—nine towns out of these two tribes. [17]Out of the

19.49-51 Joshua is granted a city, Timnath-serah, in the territory of Ephraim, northwest of Jerusalem. Joshua and the priestly representative oversee the process of assignment of land to the tribes and others.
20.1-9 Joshua is the one through whom *the cities of refuge* which were earlier promised (Num 35.9-15) are now actually designated. It is in these places – three west of the Jordan and three east of the Jordan – that those who kill others inadvertently may be safe from an *avenger of blood.*
21.1-42 In fulfillment of the instructions given in Num 35.1-8, cities are set aside for the Levites, together with surrounding *pasture lands.* Specific assignments are given to the various families descended from Aaron: the Kohathites (vv. 4-5; 20-26); the Gershonites (vv. 6; 27-33); the Merarites (vv. 7; 34-40). Designated for *the descendants of Aaron* is also *Hebron,* which is elsewhere assigned to Caleb (Josh 14.13-15).

21.43-45 The allotment of territories to the tribes west of the Jordan concludes with an idealized description of the results, according to which *all the land* was from then on subject to the tribes of Israel, and *not one of their enemies withstood them.* Judges, however, gives details of the continuing struggles of Israel to gain and retain these lands.
22.1-9 The eastern tribes had crossed the Jordan in order to assist the other tribes in taking the land (Josh 1.12-15), and are now instructed to return to their assigned territories.

tribe of Benjamin: Gibeon with its pasture lands, Geba with its pasture lands, [18]Anathoth with its pasture lands, and Almon with its pasture lands—four towns. [19]The towns of the descendants of Aaron—the priests—were thirteen in all, with their pasture lands.

20 As to the rest of the Kohathites belonging to the Kohathite families of the Levites, the towns allotted to them were out of the tribe of Ephraim. [21]To them were given Shechem, the city of refuge for the slayer, with its pasture lands in the hill country of Ephraim, Gezer with its pasture lands, [22]Kibzaim with its pasture lands, and Beth-horon with its pasture lands—four towns. [23]Out of the tribe of Dan: Elteke with its pasture lands, Gibbethon with its pasture lands, [24]Aijalon with its pasture lands, Gath-rimmon with its pasture lands—four towns. [25]Out of the half-tribe of Manasseh: Taanach with its pasture lands, and Gath-rimmon with its pasture lands—two towns. [26]The towns of the families of the rest of the Kohathites were ten in all, with their pasture lands.

27 To the Gershonites, one of the families of the Levites, were given out of the half-tribe of Manasseh, Golan in Bashan with its pasture lands, the city of refuge for the slayer, and Beeshterah with its pasture lands—two towns. [28]Out of the tribe of Issachar: Kishion with its pasture lands, Daberath with its pasture lands, [29]Jarmuth with its pasture lands, En-gannim with its pasture lands—four towns; [30]Out of the tribe of Asher: Mishal with its pasture lands, Abdon with its pasture lands, [31]Helkath with its pasture lands, and Rehob with its pasture lands—four towns. [32]Out of the tribe of Naphtali: Kedesh in Galilee with its pasture lands, the city of refuge for the slayer, Hammoth-dor with its pasture lands, and Kartan with its pasture lands—three towns. [33]The towns of the several families of the Gershonites were in all thirteen, with their pasture lands.

34 To the rest of the Levites—the Merarite families—were given out of the tribe of Zebulun: Jokneam with its pasture lands, Kartah with its pasture lands, [35]Dimnah with its pasture lands, Nahalal with its pasture lands—four towns. [36]Out of the tribe of Reuben: Bezer with its pasture lands, Jahzah with its pasture lands, [37]Kedemoth with its pasture lands, and Mephaath with its pasture lands—four towns. [38]Out of the tribe of Gad: Ramoth in Gilead with its pasture lands, the city of refuge for the slayer, Mahanaim with its pasture lands, [39]Heshbon with its pasture lands, Jazer with its pasture lands—four towns in all. [40]As for the towns of the several Merarite families, that is, the remainder of the families of the Levites, those allotted to them were twelve in all.

41 The towns of the Levites within the holdings of the Israelites were in all forty-eight towns with their pasture lands. [42]Each of these towns had its pasture lands around it; so it was with all these towns.

43 Thus the LORD gave to Israel all the land that he swore to their ancestors that he would give them; and having taken possession of it, they settled there. [44]And the LORD gave them rest on every side just as he had sworn to their ancestors; not one of all their enemies had withstood them, for the LORD had given all their enemies into their hands. [45]Not one of all the good promises that the LORD had made to the house of Israel had failed; all came to pass.

The Eastern Tribes Return to Their Territory

22 Then Joshua summoned the Reubenites, the Gadites, and the half-tribe of Manasseh, [2]and said to them, "You have observed all that Moses the servant of the LORD commanded you, and have obeyed me in all that I have commanded you; [3]you have not forsaken your kindred these many days, down to this day, but have been careful to keep the charge of the LORD your God. [4]And now the LORD your God has given rest to your kindred, as he promised them; therefore turn and go to your tents in the land where your possession lies, which Moses the servant of the LORD gave you on the other side of the Jordan. [5]Take good care to observe the commandment and instruction that Moses the servant of the LORD commanded you, to love the LORD your God, to walk in all his ways, to keep his commandments, and to hold fast to him, and to serve him with all your heart and with all your soul." [6]So Joshua blessed them and sent them away, and they went to their tents.

7 Now to the one half of the tribe of Manasseh Moses had given a possession in Bashan; but to the other half Joshua had given a possession beside their fellow Israelites in the land west of the Jordan. And

21.18 1 Chr 6.60
21.21 Josh 20.7
21.27 ver 6
21.32 Josh 20.7
21.34 ver 7
21.36 Josh 20.8
21.41 Num 35.7
21.43 Gen 13.15; Deut 11.31
21.44 Josh 1.13; 11.23; Deut 7.24
21.45 Josh 23.14
22.2 Num 32.20
22.4 Num 32.18; Deut 3.20
22.5 Deut 6.6,17; 10.12
22.7 Num 32.33; Josh 17.5

22.9 Num 32.1,26.29
22.11 ver 19
22.12 Josh 18.1
22.13 Deut 13.14; Num 25.7
22.16 ver 11; Deut 12.13,14
22.17 Num 25.1-9
22.19 ver 11
22.20 Josh 7.1-26
22.22 Deut 10.17; 1 Kings 8.39
22.23 Deut 18.19; 1 Sam 20.16
22.27 Josh 24.27
22.29 Deut 12.13,14
22.31 Lev 26.11,12; 2 Chr 15.2

when Joshua sent them away to their tents and blessed them, [8]he said to them, "Go back to your tents with much wealth, and with very much livestock, with silver, gold, bronze, and iron, and with a great quantity of clothing; divide the spoil of your enemies with your kindred." [9]So the Reubenites and the Gadites and the half-tribe of Manasseh returned home, parting from the Israelites at Shiloh, which is in the land of Canaan, to go to the land of Gilead, their own land of which they had taken possession by command of the LORD through Moses.

A Memorial Altar East of the Jordan

10 When they came to the region[j] near the Jordan that lies in the land of Canaan, the Reubenites and the Gadites and the half-tribe of Manasseh built there an altar by the Jordan, an altar of great size. [11]The Israelites heard that the Reubenites and the Gadites and the half-tribe of Manasseh had built an altar at the frontier of the land of Canaan, in the region[k] near the Jordan, on the side that belongs to the Israelites. [12]And when the people of Israel heard of it, the whole assembly of the Israelites gathered at Shiloh, to make war against them.

13 Then the Israelites sent the priest Phinehas son of Eleazar to the Reubenites and the Gadites and the half-tribe of Manasseh, in the land of Gilead, [14]and with him ten chiefs, one from each of the tribal families of Israel, every one of them the head of a family among the clans of Israel. [15]They came to the Reubenites, the Gadites, and the half-tribe of Manasseh, in the land of Gilead, and they said to them, [16]"Thus says the whole congregation of the LORD, 'What is this treachery that you have committed against the God of Israel in turning away today from following the LORD, by building yourselves an altar today in rebellion against the LORD? [17]Have we not had enough of the sin at Peor from which even yet we have not cleansed ourselves, and for which a plague came upon the congregation of the LORD, [18]that you must turn away today from following the LORD! If you rebel against the LORD today, he will be angry with the whole congregation of Israel tomorrow. [19]But now, if your land is unclean, cross over into the LORD's land where the LORD's tabernacle now stands, and take for yourselves a possession among us; only do not rebel against the LORD, or rebel against us[l] by building yourselves an altar other than the altar of the LORD our God. [20]Did not Achan son of Zerah break faith in the matter of the devoted things, and wrath fell upon all the congregation of Israel? And he did not perish alone for his iniquity!' "

21 Then the Reubenites, the Gadites, and the half-tribe of Manasseh said in answer to the heads of the families of Israel, [22]"The LORD, God of gods! The LORD, God of gods! He knows; and let Israel itself know! If it was in rebellion or in breach of faith toward the LORD, do not spare us today [23]for building an altar to turn away from following the LORD; or if we did so to offer burnt offerings or grain offerings or offerings of well-being on it, may the LORD himself take vengeance. [24]No! We did it from fear that in time to come your children might say to our children, 'What have you to do with the LORD, the God of Israel? [25]For the LORD has made the Jordan a boundary between us and you, you Reubenites and Gadites; you have no portion in the LORD.' So your children might make our children cease to worship the LORD. [26]Therefore we said, 'Let us now build an altar, not for burnt offering, nor for sacrifice, [27]but to be a witness between us and you, and between the generations after us, that we do perform the service of the LORD in his presence with our burnt offerings and sacrifices and offerings of well-being; so that your children may never say to our children in time to come, "You have no portion in the LORD." ' [28]And we thought, If this should be said to us or to our descendants in time to come, we could say, 'Look at this copy of the altar of the LORD, which our ancestors made, not for burnt offerings, nor for sacrifice, but to be a witness between us and you.' [29]Far be it from us that we should rebel against the LORD, and turn away this day from following the LORD by building an altar for burnt offering, grain offering, or sacrifice, other than the altar of the LORD our God that stands before his tabernacle!"

30 When the priest Phinehas and the chiefs of the congregation, the heads of the families of Israel who were with him, heard the words that the Reubenites and the Gadites and the Manassites spoke, they were satisfied. [31]The priest Phinehas son of Eleazar said to the Reubenites and the Gadites and the Manassites, "Today we know that the

22.10-34 The eastern tribes built *an altar of great size* near the Jordan. Although it was at first interpreted by the other tribes as competitive with the central shrine of Yahweh *at Shiloh,* the explanation is given that it was an enduring memorial of the unity of all the tribes on both sides of the Jordan rather than a place for *sacrifice.* It is a shared *witness between us* that the LORD is God.

[j] Or *to Geliloth* [k] Or *at Geliloth* [l] Or *make rebels of us*

23.1-16 Joshua's departing advice to the people of Israel. Having completed the domination of the lands and their distribution to the tribes and Levites, Joshua calls them (23.6) *to observe and do all that is written in the book of the law of Moses*, and to avoid mixing with the other nations, either through worshipping their gods or by intermarriage. They may be assured of God's continuing favor if they remain faithful to the covenant, but are warned of the punishment – including expulsion from the land – that will come if they fail to meet their covenantal obligations.
24.1-28 Renewal of the Covenant at Shechem. The ceremony takes place at the central sacred site whose links go back to the days of Abraham (Gen 12.6) and Jacob (Gen 33.18-20). Joshua rehearses the history of God's people from the time of Abraham through the experience of delivery from slavery in Egypt through Moses and the settlement in the land. It is the acts of God rather than the laws of God which are central here. The people are called to choose between allegiance to Yahweh and serving other gods, whose existence and power is acknowledged. The people commit themselves to Yahweh, the God of Israel, and Joshua responds by giving them a set of statutes and ordinances and establishing a basic copy of these laws and a great rock as a reminder of their commitment at the central sanctuary in Shechem.

LORD is among us, because you have not committed this treachery against the LORD; now you have saved the Israelites from the hand of the LORD."

32 Then the priest Phinehas son of Eleazar and the chiefs returned from the Reubenites and the Gadites in the land of Gilead to the land of Canaan, to the Israelites, and brought back word to them. [33]The report pleased the Israelites; and the Israelites blessed God and spoke no more of making war against them, to destroy the land where the Reubenites and the Gadites were settled. [34]The Reubenites and the Gadites called the altar Witness;[m] "For," said they, "it is a witness between us that the LORD is God."

Joshua Exhorts the People

23 A long time afterward, when the LORD had given rest to Israel from all their enemies all around, and Joshua was old and well advanced in years, [2]Joshua summoned all Israel, their elders and heads, their judges and officers, and said to them, "I am now old and well advanced in years; [3]and you have seen all that the LORD your God has done to all these nations for your sake, for it is the LORD your God who has fought for you. [4]I have allotted to you as an inheritance for your tribes those nations that remain, along with all the nations that I have already cut off, from the Jordan to the Great Sea in the west. [5]The LORD your God will push them back before you, and drive them out of your sight; and you shall possess their land, as the LORD your God promised you. [6]Therefore be very steadfast to observe and do all that is written in the book of the law of Moses, turning aside from it neither to the right nor to the left, [7]so that you may not be mixed with these nations left here among you, or make mention of the names of their gods, or swear by them, or serve them, or bow yourselves down to them, [8]but hold fast to the LORD your God, as you have done to this day. [9]For the LORD has driven out before you great and strong nations; and as for you, no one has been able to withstand you to this day. [10]One of you puts to flight a thousand, since it is the LORD your God who fights for you, as he promised you. [11]Be very careful, therefore, to love the LORD your God. [12]For if you turn back, and join the survivors of these nations left here among you, and intermarry with them, so that you marry their women and they yours, [13]know assuredly that the LORD your God will not continue to drive out these nations before you; but they shall be a snare and a trap for you, a scourge on your sides, and thorns in your eyes, until you perish from this good land that the LORD your God has given you.

14 "And now I am about to go the way of all the earth, and you know in your hearts and souls, all of you, that not one thing has failed of all the good things that the LORD your God promised concerning you; all have come to pass for you, not one of them has failed. [15]But just as all the good things that the LORD your God promised concerning you have been fulfilled for you, so the LORD will bring upon you all the bad things, until he has destroyed you from this good land that the LORD your God has given you. [16]If you transgress the covenant of the LORD your God, which he enjoined on you, and go and serve other gods and bow down to them, then the anger of the LORD will be kindled against you, and you shall perish quickly from the good land that he has given to you."

The Tribes Renew the Covenant

24 Then Joshua gathered all the tribes of Israel to Shechem, and summoned the elders, the heads, the judges, and the officers of Israel; and they presented themselves before God. [2]And Joshua said to all the people, "Thus says the LORD, the God of Israel: Long ago your ancestors—Terah and his sons Abraham and Nahor—lived beyond the Euphrates and served other gods. [3]Then I took your father Abraham from beyond the River and led him through all the land of Canaan and made his offspring many. I gave him Isaac; [4]and to Isaac I gave Jacob and Esau. I gave Esau the hill country of Seir to possess, but Jacob and his children went down to Egypt. [5]Then I sent Moses and Aaron, and I plagued Egypt with what I did in its midst; and afterwards I brought you out. [6]When I brought your ancestors out of Egypt, you came to the sea; and the Egyptians pursued your ancestors with chariots and horsemen to the Red Sea.[n] [7]When they cried out to the LORD, he put darkness between you and the Egyptians, and made the sea come upon them and cover them; and your eyes saw what

[m] Cn Compare Syr: Heb lacks *Witness* [n] Or *Sea of Reeds*

22.33 1 Chr 29.20
22.34 Josh 24.27
23.1 Josh 21.44; 13.1
23.2 Josh 24.1
23.3 Josh 10.14,42
23.5 Num 33.53
23.6 Deut 5.32; Josh 1.7
23.7 Ex 23.33; Deut 7.2,3; Ex 23.13; Ps 16.4
23.8 Deut 10.20
23.9 Deut 11.23; Josh 1.5
23.10 Lev 26.8; ver 3; Deut 3.22
23.12 Ex 34.15,16; Deut 7.3
23.13 Judg 2.3; Ex 23.33; Num 33.55
23.14 1 Kings 2.2; Josh 21.45
23.15 Lev 26.16; Deut 28.15
24.1 Josh 23.2
24.2 Gen 11.27-32
24.3 Gen 12.1; 15.5; 21.3
24.4 Gen 25.25,26; Deut 2.5; Gen 46.6,7
24.5 Ex 3.10
24.6 Ex 12.51; 14.2-31

I did to Egypt. Afterwards you lived in the wilderness a long time. [8]Then I brought you to the land of the Amorites, who lived on the other side of the Jordan; they fought with you, and I handed them over to you, and you took possession of their land, and I destroyed them before you. [9]Then King Balak son of Zippor of Moab, set out to fight against Israel. He sent and invited Balaam son of Beor to curse you, [10]but I would not listen to Balaam; therefore he blessed you; so I rescued you out of his hand. [11]When you went over the Jordan and came to Jericho, the citizens of Jericho fought against you, and also the Amorites, the Perizzites, the Canaanites, the Hittites, the Girgashites, the Hivites, and the Jebusites; and I handed them over to you. [12]I sent the hornet[o] ahead of you, which drove out before you the two kings of the Amorites; it was not by your sword or by your bow. [13]I gave you a land on which you had not labored, and towns that you had not built, and you live in them; you eat the fruit of vineyards and oliveyards that you did not plant.

14 "Now therefore revere the LORD, and serve him in sincerity and in faithfulness; put away the gods that your ancestors served beyond the River and in Egypt, and serve the LORD. [15]Now if you are unwilling to serve the LORD, choose this day whom you will serve, whether the gods your ancestors served in the region beyond the River or the gods of the Amorites in whose land you are living; but as for me and my household, we will serve the LORD."

16 Then the people answered, "Far be it from us that we should forsake the LORD to serve other gods; [17]for it is the LORD our God who brought us and our ancestors up from the land of Egypt, out of the house of slavery, and who did those great signs in our sight. He protected us along all the way that we went, and among all the peoples through whom we passed; [18]and the LORD drove out before us all the peoples, the Amorites who lived in the land. Therefore we also will serve the LORD, for he is our God."

19 But Joshua said to the people, "You cannot serve the LORD, for he is a holy God. He is a jealous God; he will not forgive your transgressions or your sins. [20]If you forsake the LORD and serve foreign gods, then he will turn and do you harm, and consume you, after having done you good." [21]And the people said to Joshua, "No, we will serve the LORD!" [22]Then Joshua said to the people, "You are witnesses against yourselves that you have chosen the LORD, to serve him." And they said, "We are witnesses." [23]He said, "Then put away the foreign gods that are among you, and incline your hearts to the LORD, the God of Israel." [24]The people said to Joshua, "The LORD our God we will serve, and him we will obey." [25]So Joshua made a covenant with the people that day, and made statutes and ordinances for them at Shechem. [26]Joshua wrote these words in the book of the law of God; and he took a large stone, and set it up there under the oak in the sanctuary of the LORD. [27]Joshua said to all the people, "See, this stone shall be a witness against us; for it has heard all the words of the LORD that he spoke to us; therefore it shall be a witness against you, if you deal falsely with your God." [28]So Joshua sent the people away to their inheritances.

Death of Joshua and Eleazar

29 After these things Joshua son of Nun, the servant of the LORD, died, being one hundred ten years old. [30]They buried him in his own inheritance at Timnath-serah, which is in the hill country of Ephraim, north of Mount Gaash.

31 Israel served the LORD all the days of Joshua, and all the days of the elders who outlived Joshua and had known all the work that the LORD did for Israel.

32 The bones of Joseph, which the Israelites had brought up from Egypt, were buried at Shechem, in the portion of ground that Jacob had bought from the children of Hamor, the father of Shechem, for one hundred pieces of money;[p] it became an inheritance of the descendants of Joseph.

33 Eleazar son of Aaron died; and they buried him at Gibeah, the town of his son Phinehas, which had been given him in the hill country of Ephraim.

24.29-33 The Death of Joshua and Eleazar, the priest. Together with burial of the bones of Joseph at Shechem (Gen 50.22-26) which Moses brought out of Egypt (Ex 13.19), the death and burial of these two leaders serve as reminders of continuity with the past as well as indicators of the new stage in the life of God's people that is to begin in the land. The priest's burial place at *Gibeah* is only eight miles from Jerusalem, which was later to become the central shrine of Yahweh.

24.8 Num 21.21-35
24.9 Num 22.2,5
24.11 Josh 3.16,17; 6.1
24.12 Ex 23.28; Deut 7.20; Ps 44.3,6
24.13 Deut 6.10,11
24.14 Deut 10.12; 18.13; 2 Cor 1.12
24.15 Ruth 1.15; 1 Kings 18.21; Ezek 20.39
24.19 Lev 19.2; Ex 20.5; 23.21
24.20 1 Chr 28.9; Josh 23.15
24.23 Judg 10.16
24.24 Ex 19.8; 24.3,7; Deut 5.27
24.25 Ex 24.8
24.27 Josh 22.27
24.29 Judg 2.8
24.30 Josh 19.50
24.31 Judg 2.7
24.32 Gen 50.24,25; Ex 13.19; Gen 33.19
24.33 Josh 22.13

[o] Meaning of Heb uncertain [p] Heb *one hundred qesitah*

JUDGES

See the Introductions, pp. 3, 38, and 41 above.

Israel's Failure to Complete the Conquest of Canaan

1 After the death of Joshua, the Israelites inquired of the LORD, "Who shall go up first for us against the Canaanites, to fight against them?" 2The LORD said, "Judah shall go up. I hereby give the land into his hand." 3Judah said to his brother Simeon, "Come up with me into the territory allotted to me, that we may fight against the Canaanites; then I too will go with you into the territory allotted to you." So Simeon went with him. 4Then Judah went up and the LORD gave the Canaanites and the Perizzites into their hand; and they defeated ten thousand of them at Bezek. 5They came upon Adoni-bezek at Bezek, and fought against him, and defeated the Canaanites and the Perizzites. 6Adoni-bezek fled; but they pursued him, and caught him, and cut off his thumbs and big toes. 7Adoni-bezek said, "Seventy kings with their thumbs and big toes cut off used to pick up scraps under my table; as I have done, so God has paid me back." They brought him to Jerusalem, and he died there.

8 Then the people of Judah fought against Jerusalem and took it. They put it to the sword and set the city on fire. 9Afterward the people of Judah went down to fight against the Canaanites who lived in the hill country, in the Negeb, and in the lowland. 10Judah went against the Canaanites who lived in Hebron (the name of Hebron was formerly Kiriath-arba); and they defeated Sheshai and Ahiman and Talmai.

11 From there they went against the inhabitants of Debir (the name of Debir was formerly Kiriath-sepher). 12Then Caleb said, "Whoever attacks Kiriath-sepher and takes it, I will give him my daughter Achsah as wife." 13And Othniel son of Kenaz, Caleb's younger brother, took it; and he gave him his daughter Achsah as wife. 14When she came to him, she urged him to ask her father for a field. As she dismounted from her donkey, Caleb said to her, "What do you wish?" 15She said to him, "Give me a present; since you have set me in the land of the Negeb, give me also Gulloth-mayim."[a] So Caleb gave her Upper Gulloth and Lower Gulloth.

16 The descendants of Hobab[b] the Kenite, Moses' father-in-law, went up with the people of Judah from the city of palms into the wilderness of Judah, which lies in the Negeb near Arad. Then they went and settled with the Amalekites.[c] 17Judah went with his brother Simeon, and they defeated the Canaanites who inhabited Zephath, and devoted it to destruction. So the city was called Hormah. 18Judah took Gaza with its territory, Ashkelon with its territory, and Ekron with its territory. 19The LORD was with Judah, and he took possession of the hill country, but could not drive out the inhabitants of the plain, because they had chariots of iron. 20Hebron was given to Caleb, as Moses had said; and he drove out from it the three sons of Anak. 21But the Benjaminites did not drive out the Jebusites who lived in Jerusalem; so the Jebusites have lived in Jerusalem among the Benjaminites to this day.

22 The house of Joseph also went up against Bethel; and the LORD was with them. 23The house of Joseph sent out spies to Bethel (the name of the city was formerly Luz). 24When the spies saw a man coming out of the city, they said to him, "Show us the way into the city, and we will deal kindly with you." 25So he showed them the way into the city; and they put the city to the sword, but they let the man and all his family go. 26So the man went to the land of the Hittites and built a city, and named it Luz; that is its name to this day.

27 Manasseh did not drive out the inhabitants of Beth-shean and its villages, or Taanach and its villages, or the inhabitants of Dor and its villages, or the inhabitants of Ibleam and its villages, or the inhabitants of Megiddo and its villages; but the Canaanites continued to live in that land. 28When Israel grew strong, they put the Canaanites to forced labor, but did not in fact drive them out.

29 And Ephraim did not drive out the Canaanites who lived in Gezer; but the Canaanites lived among them in Gezer.

30 Zebulun did not drive out the inhabitants of Kitron, or the inhabitants of Nahalol; but the Canaanites lived among them, and became subject to forced labor.

[a] That is *Basins of Water* [b] Gk: Heb lacks *Hobab* [c] See 1 Sam 15.6: Heb *people*

1.1 Num 27.21
1.3 ver 17
1.4 Gen 13.7
1.8 ver 21; Josh 15.63
1.10 Josh 15.13-19
1.13 Judg 3.9
1.14 Josh 15.18,19
1.16 Judg 4.11,17; Deut 34.3; Judg 3.13
1.17 ver 3; Num 21.3
1.19 ver 2; Josh 17.16,18
1.20 Josh 14.9; 15.13,14; ver 10
1.21 Josh 15.63
1.23 Gen 28.19
1.25 Josh 6.25
1.27 Josh 17.11-13
1.29 Josh 16.10

1.1-20 Judah's Successful Conquest of the Allotted Land. The book begins with a reference to the death of the former leader, *Joshua*, just as the book of Joshua mentioned the death of Moses (Josh 1.1). How *the Israelites inquired of the LORD* is not indicated: it could have been by the sacred oracles, Urim and Thummim (Num 27.21; Ex 28.30) or by a prophet. Unlike the account in Joshua, a major place is given in Judges to the role of one particular tribe: *Judah*. The Canaanites and the Perizzites are some of the Semitic tribes that still occupied the land claimed by Israel and promised to it by Yahweh. **1.4** *Bezek* is a city of unknown location in the southern territory of Judah. *Adoni-bezek* recalls Adoni-zedek, who is named in Josh 10 as king of Jerusalem. The cutting off of the *thumbs and big toes* is typical punishment for a military prisoner in this period. **1.8-10** In addition to the major city, *Jerusalem*, Judah captured three sections of the land: the higher ridge of hills to the east, the more arid plain to the south (*the Negeb*), and the lower hills to the west toward the Mediterranean Sea. The capture of Hebron resulted in its being given to Caleb (1.20; *cf.* Num 14.24; Josh 15.13-19). **1.11-15** The importance of access to water in the semi-arid district known as the *Negeb* is evident in Achsah's request for the additional grant of springs: *Gulloth-mayim*. **1.16-36** *The city of palms* is used elsewhere with reference to Jericho (Deut 34.3; 2 Chr 28.15), but here may refer to a city in the Negeb, the southernmost territory of Israel. The cities along the Mediterranean coast are said to have been captured from the Philistines by Judah (Gaza, Ashkelon, Ekron), but there is no supporting evidence elsewhere for Israel's takeover of these cities. The Benjaminites failed to expel the Jebusites from Jerusalem, just as the other Israelite tribes were unable to gain from the local tribes complete control of the districts that had been assigned to them. Asher, for example, was unable to take over the Mediterranean coastal cities north from Acco to Sidon. Dan had to shift from its original settlement by the Mediterranean Sea up into the *hill country*: that is, the high region near Mt. Hermon, bordering Syria.

31 Asher did not drive out the inhabitants of Acco, or the inhabitants of Sidon, or
of Ahlab, or of Achzib, or of Helbah, or of
Aphik, or of Rehob; 32 but the Asherites lived
among the Canaanites, the inhabitants of
the land; for they did not drive them out.
33 Naphtali did not drive out the inhabitants of Beth-shemesh, or the inhabitants
of Beth-anath, but lived among the
Canaanites, the inhabitants of the land;
nevertheless the inhabitants of Beth-shemesh
and of Beth-anath became subject to forced
labor for them.
34 The Amorites pressed the Danites back
into the hill country; they did not allow
them to come down to the plain. 35 The
Amorites continued to live in Har-heres, in
Aijalon, and in Shaalbim, but the hand of
the house of Joseph rested heavily on them,
and they became subject to forced labor.
36 The border of the Amorites ran from the
ascent of Akrabbim, from Sela and upward.

Israel's Disobedience

2 Now the angel of the LORD went up
from Gilgal to Bochim, and said, "I
brought you up from Egypt, and brought
you into the land that I had promised to
your ancestors. I said, 'I will never break
my covenant with you. 2 For your part, do
not make a covenant with the inhabitants
of this land; tear down their altars.' But you
have not obeyed my command. See what
you have done! 3 So now I say, I will not
drive them out before you; but they shall
become adversaries[d] to you, and their gods
shall be a snare to you." 4 When the angel
of the LORD spoke these words to all the
Israelites, the people lifted up their voices
and wept. 5 So they named that place
Bochim,[e] and there they sacrificed to the
LORD.

Death of Joshua

6 When Joshua dismissed the people, the
Israelites all went to their own inheritances
to take possession of the land. 7 The people
worshiped the LORD all the days of Joshua,
and all the days of the elders who outlived
Joshua, who had seen all the great work
that the LORD had done for Israel. 8 Joshua
son of Nun, the servant of the LORD, died at
the age of one hundred ten years. 9 So they
buried him within the bounds of his inheritance in Timnath-heres, in the hill country
of Ephraim, north of Mount Gaash. 10 Moreover, that whole generation was gathered
to their ancestors, and another generation
grew up after them, who did not know the
LORD or the work that he had done for Israel.

Israel's Unfaithfulness

11 Then the Israelites did what was evil
in the sight of the LORD and worshiped the
Baals; 12 and they abandoned the LORD, the
God of their ancestors, who had brought
them out of the land of Egypt; they followed
other gods, from among the gods of the
peoples who were all around them, and
bowed down to them; and they provoked
the LORD to anger. 13 They abandoned the
LORD, and worshiped Baal and the Astartes.
14 So the anger of the LORD was kindled
against Israel, and he gave them over to
plunderers who plundered them, and he
sold them into the power of their enemies
all around, so that they could no longer
withstand their enemies. 15 Whenever they
marched out, the hand of the LORD was
against them to bring misfortune, as the
LORD had warned them and sworn to them;
and they were in great distress.
16 Then the LORD raised up judges, who
delivered them out of the power of those
who plundered them. 17 Yet they did not
listen even to their judges; for they lusted
after other gods and bowed down to them.
They soon turned aside from the way in
which their ancestors had walked, who had
obeyed the commandments of the LORD;
they did not follow their example. 18 Whenever the LORD raised up judges for them, the
LORD was with the judge, and he delivered
them from the hand of their enemies all the
days of the judge; for the LORD would be
moved to pity by their groaning because of
those who persecuted and oppressed them.
19 But whenever the judge died, they would
relapse and behave worse than their ancestors, following other gods, worshiping them
and bowing down to them. They would not
drop any of their practices or their stubborn
ways. 20 So the anger of the LORD was kindled against Israel; and he said, "Because
this people have transgressed my covenant
that I commanded their ancestors, and have
not obeyed my voice, 21 I will no longer drive
out before them any of the nations that
Joshua left when he died." 22 In order to test

[d] OL Vg Compare Gk: Heb *sides* [e] That is *Weepers*

1.31 Judg 10.6
1.34 Ex 3.17
1.36 Josh 15.3
2.1 ver 5; Judg 6.11; Ex 20.2; Gen 17.7; Deut 7.9
2.2 Ex 23.32; 34.12,13
2.3 Josh 23.13; Judg 3.6; Deut 7.16; Ps 106.36
2.6 Josh 24.28-31
2.10 1 Sam 2.12; 1 Chr 28.9; Gal 4.8
2.11 Judg 3.7,12; 4.1; 6.1,25; 8.33; 10.6
2.12 Deut 31.6
2.13 Judg 10.6
2.14 Judg 3.8; Ps 106.40-42; Deut 28.25
2.16 Ps 106.43-45; Acts 13.20
2.17 ver 7
2.19 Judg 3.12; 4.1; 8.33
2.20 ver 14; Josh 23.16
2.21 Josh 23.13
2.22 Judg 3.1,4

2.1-5 The reason for Israel's failure to gain complete control of the land is said to be that they did not bring to an end the worship of other gods that was carried on at altars in the conquered lands.
2.6-23 Following the death of Joshua, the new generation within Israel knew neither *the LORD* nor what he had done for Israel in bringing his people out of slavery in Egypt and enabling them to enter the new land. Israel's continuing disobedience to God is a theme that is recurrent in Judges: 2.11; 3.7; 3.12; 4.1; 6.1; 10.6; 13.1.

Israel, whether or not they would take care to walk in the way of the LORD as their ancestors did, 23the LORD had left those nations, not driving them out at once, and had not handed them over to Joshua.

Nations Remaining in the Land

3 Now these are the nations that the LORD left to test all those in Israel who had no experience of any war in Canaan 2(it was only that successive generations of Israelites might know war, to teach those who had no experience of it before): 3the five lords of the Philistines, and all the Canaanites, and the Sidonians, and the Hivites who lived on Mount Lebanon, from Mount Baal-hermon as far as Lebo-hamath. 4They were for the testing of Israel, to know whether Israel would obey the commandments of the LORD, which he commanded their ancestors by Moses. 5So the Israelites lived among the Canaanites, the Hittites, the Amorites, the Perizzites, the Hivites, and the Jebusites; 6and they took their daughters as wives for themselves, and their own daughters they gave to their sons; and they worshiped their gods.

Othniel

7 The Israelites did what was evil in the sight of the LORD, forgetting the LORD their God, and worshiping the Baals and the Asherahs. 8Therefore the anger of the LORD was kindled against Israel, and he sold them into the hand of King Cushan-rishathaim of Aram-naharaim; and the Israelites served Cushan-rishathaim eight years. 9But when the Israelites cried out to the LORD, the LORD raised up a deliverer for the Israelites, who delivered them, Othniel son of Kenaz, Caleb's younger brother. 10The spirit of the LORD came upon him, and he judged Israel; he went out to war, and the LORD gave King Cushan-rishathaim of Aram into his hand; and his hand prevailed over Cushan-rishathaim. 11So the land had rest forty years. Then Othniel son of Kenaz died.

Ehud

12 The Israelites again did what was evil in the sight of the LORD; and the LORD strengthened King Eglon of Moab against Israel, because they had done what was evil in the sight of the LORD. 13In alliance with the Ammonites and the Amalekites, he went and defeated Israel; and they took possession of the city of palms. 14So the Israelites served King Eglon of Moab eighteen years.

15 But when the Israelites cried out to the LORD, the LORD raised up for them a deliverer, Ehud son of Gera, the Benjaminite, a left-handed man. The Israelites sent tribute by him to King Eglon of Moab. 16Ehud made for himself a sword with two edges, a cubit in length; and he fastened it on his right thigh under his clothes. 17Then he presented the tribute to King Eglon of Moab. Now Eglon was a very fat man. 18When Ehud had finished presenting the tribute, he sent the people who carried the tribute on their way. 19But he himself turned back at the sculptured stones near Gilgal, and said, "I have a secret message for you, O king." So the king said,[f] "Silence!" and all his attendants went out from his presence. 20Ehud came to him, while he was sitting alone in his cool roof chamber, and said, "I have a message from God for you." So he rose from his seat. 21Then Ehud reached with his left hand, took the sword from his right thigh, and thrust it into Eglon's[g] belly; 22the hilt also went in after the blade, and the fat closed over the blade, for he did not draw the sword out of his belly; and the dirt came out.[h] 23Then Ehud went out into the vestibule,[i] and closed the doors of the roof chamber on him, and locked them.

24 After he had gone, the servants came. When they saw that the doors of the roof chamber were locked, they thought, "He must be relieving himself[j] in the cool chamber." 25So they waited until they were embarrassed. When he still did not open the doors of the roof chamber, they took the key and opened them. There was their lord lying dead on the floor.

26 Ehud escaped while they delayed, and passed beyond the sculptured stones, and escaped to Seirah. 27When he arrived, he sounded the trumpet in the hill country of Ephraim; and the Israelites went down with him from the hill country, having him at their head. 28He said to them, "Follow after me; for the LORD has given your enemies the Moabites into your hand." So they went down after him, and seized the fords of the Jordan against the Moabites, and allowed

[f] Heb *he said* [g] Heb *his* [h] With Tg Vg: Meaning of Heb uncertain [i] Meaning of Heb uncertain [j] Heb *covering his feet*

3.1-6 The non-Israelite tribes are named that continued to live in the land that God had designated for his people on both sides of the Jordan, and continued to worship their own gods: the Canaanites, the Hittites, the Amorites, the Perizzites, the Hivites, and the Jebusites. In addition, the Israelites intermarried with these idolatrous people. As a result, God does not expel these tribes from the land he had assigned to Israel.
3.7-31 Brief Accounts of Three Judges of Israel.
3.7-11 The coming to power of Othniel followed on Israel's idolatrous worship of the male and female fertility gods of the Canaanites: *the Baals and the Asherahs.* This failure on the part of Israel brought divine judgment in the form of domination for *eight years* by an invader from a Mesopotamian region: *Aram Naharaim.* Othniel is described here as *a deliverer for the Israelites,* a term which can also mean "liberator" or "savior." God's intervention in behalf of his people is through *Othniel,* who is also described as one of the first of those who *judged Israel.* Descended from Caleb, he had succeeded in capturing the city of Debir from the Canaanites (Judg 1.13). Empowered by *the Spirit of the LORD,* he then defeated *Cushan-rishathaim* (which may be an altered form of a royal name originating in Elam, now part of Iran). The *forty years* over which his rule is said to have extended is a general term for a long period of time.
3.12-30 *Ehud* freed Israel from domination by *Eglon,* king of the Moabites, and their allies from east of the Jordan, for a period of *eighteen years.* Gaining access to the king by pretending to bring *tribute* from Israel, Ehud assassinated Eglon and *escaped.* The Moabites were slaughtered in huge numbers as they tried to flee eastward across the Jordan to their own land.

3.1 Judg 2.21,22
3.3 Josh 13.3
3.4 Deut 8.2; Judg 2.22
3.6 Ex 34.16; Deut 7.3,4
3.7 Judg 2.11,13; Deut 4.9
3.9 ver 15; Judg 1.13
3.10 Num 11.25,29; 24.2; Judg 6.34
3.12 Judg 2.11,14
3.13 Judg 1.16
3.15 Ps 107.13
3.17 ver 12
3.24 1 Sam 24.3
3.25 2 Kings 2.17; 8.11
3.28 Judg 7.9,15,24; 12.5

no one to cross over. [29]At that time they killed about ten thousand of the Moabites, all strong, able-bodied men; no one escaped. [30]So Moab was subdued that day under the hand of Israel. And the land had rest eighty years.

Shamgar

31 After him came Shamgar son of Anath, who killed six hundred of the Philistines with an oxgoad. He too delivered Israel.

Deborah and Barak

4 The Israelites again did what was evil in the sight of the LORD, after Ehud died. [2]So the LORD sold them into the hand of King Jabin of Canaan, who reigned in Hazor; the commander of his army was Sisera, who lived in Harosheth-ha-goiim. [3]Then the Israelites cried out to the LORD for help; for he had nine hundred chariots of iron, and had oppressed the Israelites cruelly twenty years.

4 At that time Deborah, a prophetess, wife of Lappidoth, was judging Israel. [5]She used to sit under the palm of Deborah between Ramah and Bethel in the hill country of Ephraim; and the Israelites came up to her for judgment. [6]She sent and summoned Barak son of Abinoam from Kedesh in Naphtali, and said to him, "The LORD, the God of Israel, commands you, 'Go, take position at Mount Tabor, bringing ten thousand from the tribe of Naphtali and the tribe of Zebulun. [7]I will draw out Sisera, the general of Jabin's army, to meet you by the Wadi Kishon with his chariots and his troops; and I will give him into your hand.' " [8]Barak said to her, "If you will go with me, I will go; but if you will not go with me, I will not go." [9]And she said, "I will surely go with you; nevertheless, the road on which you are going will not lead to your glory, for the LORD will sell Sisera into the hand of a woman." Then Deborah got up and went with Barak to Kedesh. [10]Barak summoned Zebulun and Naphtali to Kedesh; and ten thousand warriors went up behind him; and Deborah went up with him.

11 Now Heber the Kenite had separated from the other Kenites,[k] that is, the descendants of Hobab the father-in-law of Moses, and had encamped as far away as Elon-bezaanannim, which is near Kedesh.

12 When Sisera was told that Barak son of Abinoam had gone up to Mount Tabor, [13]Sisera called out all his chariots, nine hundred chariots of iron, and all the troops who were with him, from Harosheth-ha-goiim to the Wadi Kishon. [14]Then Deborah said to Barak, "Up! For this is the day on which the LORD has given Sisera into your hand. The LORD is indeed going out before you." So Barak went down from Mount Tabor with ten thousand warriors following him. [15]And the LORD threw Sisera and all his chariots and all his army into a panic[l] before Barak; Sisera got down from his chariot and fled away on foot, [16]while Barak pursued the chariots and the army to Harosheth-ha-goiim. All the army of Sisera fell by the sword; no one was left.

17 Now Sisera had fled away on foot to the tent of Jael wife of Heber the Kenite; for there was peace between King Jabin of Hazor and the clan of Heber the Kenite. [18]Jael came out to meet Sisera, and said to him, "Turn aside, my lord, turn aside to me; have no fear." So he turned aside to her into the tent, and she covered him with a rug. [19]Then he said to her, "Please give me a little water to drink; for I am thirsty." So she opened a skin of milk and gave him a drink and covered him. [20]He said to her, "Stand at the entrance of the tent, and if anybody comes and asks you, 'Is anyone here?' say, 'No.' " [21]But Jael wife of Heber took a tent peg, and took a hammer in her hand, and went softly to him and drove the peg into his temple, until it went down into the ground—he was lying fast asleep from weariness—and he died. [22]Then, as Barak came in pursuit of Sisera, Jael went out to meet him, and said to him, "Come, and I will show you the man whom you are seeking." So he went into her tent; and there was Sisera lying dead, with the tent peg in his temple.

23 So on that day God subdued King Jabin of Canaan before the Israelites. [24]Then the hand of the Israelites bore harder and harder on King Jabin of Canaan, until they destroyed King Jabin of Canaan.

The Song of Deborah

5 Then Deborah and Barak son of Abinoam sang on that day, saying:

2 "When locks are long in Israel,

[k] Heb *from the Kain* [l] Heb adds *to the sword*; compare verse 16

3.30 ver 11
3.31 Judg 5.6
4.1 Judg 2.19
4.2 Josh 11.1,10; ver 13,16; Ps 83.9
4.3 Judg 1.19
4.6 Heb 11.32
4.7 Ps 83.9
4.9 ver 21
4.10 Judg 5.18; ver 14; Judg 5.15
4.11 Judg 1.16; ver 6
4.13 ver 3
4.14 Deut 9.3
4.15 Josh 10.10
4.16 Ps 83.9
4.19 Judg 5.25
4.21 Judg 5.26
5.1 Ex 15.1
5.2 Deut 32.41

3.31 *Shamgar* is said to have *delivered Israel,* in that he killed hundreds of their perennial enemies who inhabited the regions along the Mediterranean coast, *the Philistines.*
4.1-24 Deborah and Barak. The continuing disobedience of Israel leads God to turn them over to Canaanite rule once more, under Jabin, who reigned in Hazor, an important city just west of Lake Huleh in the north of Palestine. The superior cultural and military level of the Canaanites is apparent in their having available *nine hundred chariots of iron* to enforce their cruel control of Israel. Through the encouragement of *Deborah, a prophetess,* Barak assembled *ten thousand* troops from the far northern tribes of *Zebulun and Naphtali,* which pursued and destroyed Jabin's army. Fleeing from this destruction, *Sisera,* their leader, was lured into the tent of *Jael,* wife of Heber the Kenite, who was related to Moses' wife (4.11; 1.16). Jael murdered Sisera while he slept, and the Israelites destroyed King Jabin of Canaan.
5.1-31 The Song of Deborah. Probably the oldest poetical section in the Bible, this song celebrates in poetry the victory of Israel over the Canaanites described in the previous chapter in prose. Keeping the *locks* of hair *long* refers to the custom of allowing one's hair to grow until an objective is achieved or one dies in the attempt. The poetic account of the victory begins by recalling Yahweh's leading his people up from *Sinai* through the region east of the Dead Sea *(Seir...Edom),* and then goes on to celebrate the bravery of the leaders of Israel who risked all to defeat their enemies (5.6-11). The climax came in the victory of *Barak,* even though many of the tribes of Israel did not join the struggle (5.12-18). *Taanach* was strategically important since it guarded access from the south and east to the great fertile plain of Jezreel southwest of the Sea of Galilee. Adapting the imagery of Canaanite religion, *the stars* and the rivers are pictured as joining in the defeat of Israel's enemies (5.19-22). *Meroz* is an unidentified Israelite city whose people failed to help Israel in the battle against the Canaanites (5.23). The heroine is *Jael,* whose shrewd scheme led to the death of the leader of the enemy (5.24-26). The death of Sisera and the reluctance of his mother to acknowledge it are described in vivid poetic language (5.27-30). The song ends with a final contrast between the fate of Yahweh's *enemies* and his *friends* (5.31).

when the people offer themselves
willingly—
bless[m] the LORD!

3 "Hear, O kings; give ear, O princes;
to the LORD I will sing,
I will make melody to the LORD, the
God of Israel.

4 "LORD, when you went out from Seir,
when you marched from the region
of Edom,
the earth trembled,
and the heavens poured,
the clouds indeed poured water.
5 The mountains quaked before the
LORD, the One of Sinai,
before the LORD, the God of Israel.

6 "In the days of Shamgar son of Anath,
in the days of Jael, caravans ceased
and travelers kept to the byways.
7 The peasantry prospered in Israel,
they grew fat on plunder,
because you arose, Deborah,
arose as a mother in Israel.
8 When new gods were chosen,
then war was in the gates.
Was shield or spear to be seen
among forty thousand in Israel?
9 My heart goes out to the commanders
of Israel
who offered themselves willingly
among the people.
Bless the LORD.

10 "Tell of it, you who ride on white
donkeys,
you who sit on rich carpets[n]
and you who walk by the way.
11 To the sound of musicians[n] at the
watering places,
there they repeat the triumphs of
the LORD,
the triumphs of his peasantry in Israel.

"Then down to the gates marched the
people of the LORD.

12 "Awake, awake, Deborah!
Awake, awake, utter a song!
Arise, Barak, lead away your captives,
O son of Abinoam.
13 Then down marched the remnant of
the noble;
the people of the LORD marched down
for him[o] against the mighty.
14 From Ephraim they set out[p] into the
valley,[q]
following you, Benjamin, with your
kin;
from Machir marched down the
commanders,
and from Zebulun those who bear
the marshal's staff;
15 the chiefs of Issachar came with
Deborah,
and Issachar faithful to Barak;
into the valley they rushed out at
his heels.
Among the clans of Reuben
there were great searchings of heart.
16 Why did you tarry among the sheepfolds,
to hear the piping for the flocks?
Among the clans of Reuben
there were great searchings of heart.
17 Gilead stayed beyond the Jordan;
and Dan, why did he abide with
the ships?
Asher sat still at the coast of the sea,
settling down by his landings.
18 Zebulun is a people that scorned death;
Naphtali too, on the heights of the
field.

19 "The kings came, they fought;
then fought the kings of Canaan,
at Taanach, by the waters of Megiddo;
they got no spoils of silver.
20 The stars fought from heaven,
from their courses they fought
against Sisera.
21 The torrent Kishon swept them away,
the onrushing torrent, the torrent
Kishon.
March on, my soul, with might!

22 "Then loud beat the horses' hoofs
with the galloping, galloping of his
steeds.

23 "Curse Meroz, says the angel of the LORD,
curse bitterly its inhabitants,
because they did not come to the help
of the LORD,
to the help of the LORD against the
mighty.

24 "Most blessed of women be Jael,
the wife of Heber the Kenite,

[m] Or *You who offer yourselves willingly among the people, bless* [n] Meaning of Heb uncertain [o] Gk: Heb *me* [p] Cn: Heb *From Ephraim their root* [q] Gk: Heb *in Amalek*

5.3 Ps 27.6
5.4 Deut 33.2; Ps 68.7-9
5.5 Ps 97.5; Isa 64.1,3; Ps 68.8
5.6 Judg 3.31; 4.17
5.8 Deut 32.17
5.11 1 Sam 12.7; Mic 6.5
5.12 Ps 57.8; 68.18
5.14 Judg 3.13,27; Num 32.39
5.15 Judg 4.10
5.16 Num 32.1
5.17 Josh 13.24-28; 19.29,46
5.18 Judg 4.6,10
5.19 Josh 11.1,2; Judg 1.27
5.20 Josh 10.11-14
5.21 Judg 4.7
5.24 Judg 4.17,19-21

5.25 Judg 4.19
5.26 Judg 4.21
5.28 Prov 7.6
5.30 Ex 15.9
5.31 Ps 68.2; 92.9; 19.4,5; Judg 3.11
6.1 Judg 2.11,19; Num 25.15-18; 31.1-3
6.3 Judg 3.13
6.4 Lev 26.16; Deut 28.30,33,51
6.5 Judg 7.12
6.6 Judg 3.15
6.8 Judg 2.1,2
6.9 Ps 44.2,3
6.11 Josh 17.2
6.12 Josh 1.5
6.13 Ps 44.1; 2 Chr 15.2
6.14 Heb 11.32,34; Judg 4.6
6.15 Ex 3.11; 1 Sam 9.21
6.16 Ex 3.12; Josh 1.5
6.17 ver 36,37; Isa 38.7,8
6.19 Gen 18.6-8

of tent-dwelling women most blessed.
25 He asked water and she gave him milk,
she brought him curds in a lordly
bowl.
26 She put her hand to the tent peg
and her right hand to the
workmen's mallet;
she struck Sisera a blow,
she crushed his head,
she shattered and pierced his
temple.
27 He sank, he fell,
he lay still at her feet;
at her feet he sank, he fell;
where he sank, there he fell dead.

28 "Out of the window she peered,
the mother of Sisera gazed[r] through
the lattice:
'Why is his chariot so long in coming?
Why tarry the hoofbeats of his
chariots?'
29 Her wisest ladies make answer,
indeed, she answers the question
herself:
30 'Are they not finding and dividing the
spoil?—
A girl or two for every man;
spoil of dyed stuffs for Sisera,
spoil of dyed stuffs embroidered,
two pieces of dyed work embroidered
for my neck as spoil?'

31 "So perish all your enemies, O
LORD!
But may your friends be like the
sun as it rises in its might."

And the land had rest forty years.

The Midianite Oppression

6 The Israelites did what was evil in the
sight of the LORD, and the LORD gave
them into the hand of Midian seven years.
2The hand of Midian prevailed over Israel;
and because of Midian the Israelites provided for themselves hiding places in the
mountains, caves and strongholds. 3For
whenever the Israelites put in seed, the
Midianites and the Amalekites and the people
of the east would come up against them.
4They would encamp against them and
destroy the produce of the land, as far as
the neighborhood of Gaza, and leave no
sustenance in Israel, and no sheep or ox or
donkey. 5For they and their livestock would
come up, and they would even bring their
tents, as thick as locusts; neither they nor
their camels could be counted; so they wasted
the land as they came in. 6Thus Israel was
greatly impoverished because of Midian; and
the Israelites cried out to the LORD for help.
7 When the Israelites cried to the LORD
on account of the Midianites, 8the LORD sent
a prophet to the Israelites; and he said to
them, "Thus says the LORD, the God of
Israel: I led you up from Egypt, and brought
you out of the house of slavery; 9and I
delivered you from the hand of the Egyptians, and from the hand of all who oppressed you, and drove them out before
you, and gave you their land; 10and I said
to you, 'I am the LORD your God; you shall
not pay reverence to the gods of the Amorites,
in whose land you live.' But you have not
given heed to my voice."

The Call of Gideon

11 Now the angel of the LORD came and
sat under the oak at Ophrah, which belonged to Joash the Abiezrite, as his son
Gideon was beating out wheat in the wine
press, to hide it from the Midianites. 12The
angel of the LORD appeared to him and said
to him, "The LORD is with you, you mighty
warrior." 13Gideon answered him, "But sir,
if the LORD is with us, why then has all this
happened to us? And where are all his
wonderful deeds that our ancestors recounted
to us, saying, 'Did not the LORD bring us up
from Egypt?' But now the LORD has cast us
off, and given us into the hand of Midian."
14Then the LORD turned to him and said, "Go
in this might of yours and deliver Israel
from the hand of Midian; I hereby commission you." 15He responded, "But sir, how
can I deliver Israel? My clan is the weakest
in Manasseh, and I am the least in my
family." 16The LORD said to him, "But I will
be with you, and you shall strike down the
Midianites, every one of them." 17Then he
said to him, "If now I have found favor with
you, then show me a sign that it is you who
speak with me. 18Do not depart from here
until I come to you, and bring out my
present, and set it before you." And he said,
"I will stay until you return."
19 So Gideon went into his house and
prepared a kid, and unleavened cakes from
an ephah of flour; the meat he put in a

[r] Gk Compare Tg: Heb *exclaimed*

6.1-8.35 Gideon's Call, Triumph and Lapse into Idolatry.
6.1-10 Because the Israelites did what was evil in the sight of the LORD, God gave control of them to the *Midianites*, a tribe resident in the area southeast of the Dead Sea and descended from one of Abraham's sons (Gen 25.1-4). A *prophet* sent by the LORD reminds them of his having led them out of slavery in Egypt and warns them against worship of other gods and of their failure to heed God's *voice*.
6.11-24 Gideon, called to his leadership role through *an angel of the LORD*, is addressed as *mighty warrior*, and is instructed to *deliver Israel from the hand of Midian*. His doubts as to whether it is God who is calling him to this role are overcome by the miracle of the *fire* which springs *from the rock* and consumes the meat and cakes he has presented as an offering to God. Gideon's altar to *the LORD is peace* remained standing at Ophrah (location unknown) at the time of the writing of Judges. The *Abiezrites* were part of the tribe of Manasseh (Josh 17.2).

6.25-32 The LORD instructs Gideon to destroy the altar of Baal and the *sacred pole,* which was a symbol of fertility, and to replace them with sacrifices to the LORD. The *townspeople* are ready to kill him, but his father, *Joash,* defines the situation as a test case of the power of Baal. Gideon is given a nickname, *Jerubaal,* as Baal's chief antagonist.
6.33-40 The assembling of the troops for the battle between the followers of Baal and those of Yahweh. Fighters from various northern tribes of Israel join Gideon, who puts God to the test twice with wet and dry fleece in order to be certain of his support.
7.1-25 The Victory over the Midianites. *Gideon's troops... encamped* at the eastern end of the Valley of Jezreel, apparently intending to block the retreat of the Midianites across the Jordan. The orders from the LORD to Gideon to reduce drastically the size of his army are aimed at making it clear that credit for the defeat of the Midianites must go to God and not to the people of Israel. Gideon (7.9-14) overhears the report of a *dream* of one of the Midianites that God is going to deliver *all the army* of Midian into the hands of Gideon. His tactic is one of terrifying the Midianites by having *three hundred men* appear among them in the dark of night with lighted torches suddenly brought out of jars and with blasts of trumpets. In their confusion, the Midianites fought among themselves (7.19-23), and the Israelites pursued them down to *the Jordan,* returning in triumph with *the heads of Oreb and Zeeb,* the two leaders of the Midianite army.

basket, and the broth he put in a pot, and
brought them to him under the oak and
presented them. 20 The angel of God said to
him, "Take the meat and the unleavened
cakes, and put them on this rock, and pour
out the broth." And he did so. 21 Then the
angel of the LORD reached out the tip of the
staff that was in his hand, and touched the
meat and the unleavened cakes; and fire
sprang up from the rock and consumed the
meat and the unleavened cakes; and the
angel of the LORD vanished from his sight.
22 Then Gideon perceived that it was the
angel of the LORD; and Gideon said, "Help
me, Lord GOD! For I have seen the angel of
the LORD face to face." 23 But the LORD said
to him, "Peace be to you; do not fear, you
shall not die." 24 Then Gideon built an altar
there to the LORD, and called it, The LORD is
peace. To this day it still stands at Ophrah,
which belongs to the Abiezrites.
25 That night the LORD said to him, "Take
your father's bull, the second bull seven
years old, and pull down the altar of Baal
that belongs to your father, and cut down
the sacred pole[s] that is beside it; 26 and build
an altar to the LORD your God on the top
of the stronghold here, in proper order; then
take the second bull, and offer it as a burnt
offering with the wood of the sacred pole[s]
that you shall cut down." 27 So Gideon took
ten of his servants, and did as the LORD had
told him; but because he was too afraid of
his family and the townspeople to do it by
day, he did it by night.

Gideon Destroys the Altar of Baal

28 When the townspeople rose early in
the morning, the altar of Baal was broken
down, and the sacred pole[s] beside it was cut
down, and the second bull was offered on
the altar that had been built. 29 So they said
to one another, "Who has done this?" After
searching and inquiring, they were told,
"Gideon son of Joash did it." 30 Then the
townspeople said to Joash, "Bring out your
son, so that he may die, for he has pulled
down the altar of Baal and cut down the
sacred pole[s] beside it." 31 But Joash said to
all who were arrayed against him, "Will
you contend for Baal? Or will you defend his
cause? Whoever contends for him shall be
put to death by morning. If he is a god, let
him contend for himself, because his altar
has been pulled down." 32 Therefore on that
day Gideon[t] was called Jerubbaal, that is
to say, "Let Baal contend against him,"
because he pulled down his altar.
33 Then all the Midianites and the
Amalekites and the people of the east came
together, and crossing the Jordan they
encamped in the Valley of Jezreel. 34 But the
spirit of the LORD took possession of Gideon;
and he sounded the trumpet, and the
Abiezrites were called out to follow him.
35 He sent messengers throughout all
Manasseh, and they too were called out to
follow him. He also sent messengers to
Asher, Zebulun, and Naphtali, and they
went up to meet them.

The Sign of the Fleece

36 Then Gideon said to God, "In order to
see whether you will deliver Israel by my
hand, as you have said, 37 I am going to lay
a fleece of wool on the threshing floor; if
there is dew on the fleece alone, and it is
dry on all the ground, then I shall know
that you will deliver Israel by my hand, as
you have said." 38 And it was so. When he
rose early next morning and squeezed the
fleece, he wrung enough dew from the
fleece to fill a bowl with water. 39 Then
Gideon said to God, "Do not let your anger
burn against me, let me speak one more
time; let me, please, make trial with the
fleece just once more; let it be dry only on
the fleece, and on all the ground let there
be dew." 40 And God did so that night. It was
dry on the fleece only, and on all the
ground there was dew.

Gideon Surprises and Routs the Midianites

7 Then Jerubbaal (that is, Gideon) and
all the troops that were with him rose
early and encamped beside the spring of
Harod; and the camp of Midian was north
of them, below[u] the hill of Moreh, in the
valley.
2 The LORD said to Gideon, "The troops
with you are too many for me to give the
Midianites into their hand. Israel would
only take the credit away from me, saying,
'My own hand has delivered me.' 3 Now
therefore proclaim this in the hearing of the
troops, 'Whoever is fearful and trembling,
let him return home.' " Thus Gideon sifted
them out;[v] twenty-two thousand returned,
and ten thousand remained.

6.20 Judg 13.19
6.21 Lev 9.24
6.22 Judg 13.21
6.25 Ex 34.13; Deut 7.5
6.28 1 Kings 16.32
6.32 Judg 7.1; 1 Sam 12.11
6.33 ver 3; Josh 17.16
6.34 Judg 3.10,27; 1 Chr 12.18; 2 Chr 24.20
6.37 see Ex 4.3-7
6.39 Gen 18.32
7.1 Judg 6.32
7.2 Deut 8.17; Isa 10.13; 2 Cor 4.7
7.3 Deut 20.8

[s] Heb *Asherah* [t] Heb *he* [u] Heb *from* [v] Cn: Heb *home, and depart from Mount Gilead' "*

7.4 1 Sam 14.6
7.7 1 Sam 14.6
7.9 Josh 2.24; 10.8; 11.6
7.11 ver 13-15
7.12 Judg 6.5; 8.10; Josh 11.4
7.14 ver 20
7.15 1 Sam 15.31
7.18 ver 14,20
7.20 ver 14
7.21 2 Kings 7.7
7.22 Josh 6.4,16,20; 1 Sam 14.20
7.23 Judg 6.35
7.24 Judg 3.27,28
7.25 Judg 8.3,4; Ps 83.11; Isa 10.26
8.1 Judg 12.1
8.3 Judg 7.24,25

4 Then the LORD said to Gideon, "The troops are still too many; take them down to the water and I will sift them out for you there. When I say, 'This one shall go with you,' he shall go with you; and when I say, 'This one shall not go with you,' he shall not go." 5So he brought the troops down to the water; and the LORD said to Gideon, "All those who lap the water with their tongues, as a dog laps, you shall put to one side; all those who kneel down to drink, putting their hands to their mouths,[w] you shall put to the other side." 6The number of those that lapped was three hundred; but all the rest of the troops knelt down to drink water. 7Then the LORD said to Gideon, "With the three hundred that lapped I will deliver you, and give the Midianites into your hand. Let all the others go to their homes." 8So he took the jars of the troops from their hands,[x] and their trumpets; and he sent all the rest of Israel back to their own tents, but retained the three hundred. The camp of Midian was below him in the valley.

9 That same night the LORD said to him, "Get up, attack the camp; for I have given it into your hand. 10But if you fear to attack, go down to the camp with your servant Purah; 11and you shall hear what they say, and afterward your hands shall be strengthened to attack the camp." Then he went down with his servant Purah to the outposts of the armed men that were in the camp. 12The Midianites and the Amalekites and all the people of the east lay along the valley as thick as locusts; and their camels were without number, countless as the sand on the seashore. 13When Gideon arrived, there was a man telling a dream to his comrade; and he said, "I had a dream, and in it a cake of barley bread tumbled into the camp of Midian, and came to the tent, and struck it so that it fell; it turned upside down, and the tent collapsed." 14And his comrade answered, "This is no other than the sword of Gideon son of Joash, a man of Israel; into his hand God has given Midian and all the army."

15 When Gideon heard the telling of the dream and its interpretation, he worshiped; and he returned to the camp of Israel, and said, "Get up; for the LORD has given the army of Midian into your hand." 16After he divided the three hundred men into three companies, and put trumpets into the hands of all of them, and empty jars, with torches inside the jars, 17he said to them, "Look at me, and do the same; when I come to the outskirts of the camp, do as I do. 18When I blow the trumpet, I and all who are with me, then you also blow the trumpets around the whole camp, and shout, 'For the LORD and for Gideon!'"

19 So Gideon and the hundred who were with him came to the outskirts of the camp at the beginning of the middle watch, when they had just set the watch; and they blew the trumpets and smashed the jars that were in their hands. 20So the three companies blew the trumpets and broke the jars, holding in their left hands the torches, and in their right hands the trumpets to blow; and they cried, "A sword for the LORD and for Gideon!" 21Every man stood in his place all around the camp, and all the men in camp ran; they cried out and fled. 22When they blew the three hundred trumpets, the LORD set every man's sword against his fellow and against all the army; and the army fled as far as Beth-shittah toward Zererah,[y] as far as the border of Abel-meholah, by Tabbath. 23And the men of Israel were called out from Naphtali and from Asher and from all Manasseh, and they pursued after the Midianites.

24 Then Gideon sent messengers throughout all the hill country of Ephraim, saying, "Come down against the Midianites and seize the waters against them, as far as Beth-barah, and also the Jordan." So all the men of Ephraim were called out, and they seized the waters as far as Beth-barah, and also the Jordan. 25They captured the two captains of Midian, Oreb and Zeeb; they killed Oreb at the rock of Oreb, and Zeeb they killed at the wine press of Zeeb, as they pursued the Midianites. They brought the heads of Oreb and Zeeb to Gideon beyond the Jordan.

Gideon's Triumph and Vengeance

8 Then the Ephraimites said to him, "What have you done to us, not to call us when you went to fight against the Midianites?" And they upbraided him violently. 2So he said to them, "What have I done now in comparison with you? Is not the gleaning of the grapes of Ephraim better than the vintage of Abiezer? 3God has given

8.1-20 Gideon's Defeat of the Midianites and the Resentment of the Israelites. *The Ephraimites* were annoyed because they had not been called to help in the attack on the Midianites (8.1-3), and the inhabitants of several Israelite cities refused to provide food and supplies for Gideon and *the three hundred who were with him.* The Midianite kings, Zebah and Zalmunna, are captured and ask to be executed as compensation for the Israelites they have killed (8.4-21).

[w] Heb places the words *putting their hands to their mouths* after the word *lapped* in verse 6 [x] Cn: Heb *So the people took provisions in their hands* [y] Another reading is *Zeredah*

8.22-28 Gideon's Refusal to Accept the Role of King and his Lapse into Idolatry. After refusing to accept the position of hereditary king of Israel, Gideon requested gold jewelry as compensation for his military successes. From the gold he made an *ephod*, the meaning of which is uncertain, but which was probably an elaborate vestment worn over the shoulders and used as an oracle to determine the divine will. *All Israel* relied upon it instead of on God.

8.29-35 Gideon's Death and the Apostasy of Israel. Gideon's *many wives* bore him *seventy sons*, including *Abimelech*, which means "My father is Melech" (the name of a Canaanite god, sometimes known as Molech; Lev 20.2-5; 2 Kings 23.10; Jer 32.35). Following Gideon's death, Israel abandoned the LORD, turning to the Canaanite god of the covenant, *Baal-berith*.

into your hands the captains of Midian, Oreb and Zeeb; what have I been able to do in comparison with you?" When he said this, their anger against him subsided.

4 Then Gideon came to the Jordan and crossed over, he and the three hundred who were with him, exhausted and famished.[z] 5So he said to the people of Succoth, "Please give some loaves of bread to my followers, for they are exhausted, and I am pursuing Zebah and Zalmunna, the kings of Midian." 6But the officials of Succoth said, "Do you already have in your possession the hands of Zebah and Zalmunna, that we should give bread to your army?" 7Gideon replied, "Well then, when the LORD has given Zebah and Zalmunna into my hand, I will trample your flesh on the thorns of the wilderness and on briers." 8From there he went up to Penuel, and made the same request of them; and the people of Penuel answered him as the people of Succoth had answered. 9So he said to the people of Penuel, "When I come back victorious, I will break down this tower."

10 Now Zebah and Zalmunna were in Karkor with their army, about fifteen thousand men, all who were left of all the army of the people of the east; for one hundred twenty thousand men bearing arms had fallen. 11So Gideon went up by the caravan route east of Nobah and Jogbehah, and attacked the army; for the army was off its guard. 12Zebah and Zalmunna fled; and he pursued them and took the two kings of Midian, Zebah and Zalmunna, and threw all the army into a panic.

13 When Gideon son of Joash returned from the battle by the ascent of Heres, 14he caught a young man, one of the people of Succoth, and questioned him; and he listed for him the officials and elders of Succoth, seventy-seven people. 15Then he came to the people of Succoth, and said, "Here are Zebah and Zalmunna, about whom you taunted me, saying, 'Do you already have in your possession the hands of Zebah and Zalmunna, that we should give bread to your troops who are exhausted?' " 16So he took the elders of the city and he took thorns of the wilderness and briers and with them he trampled[a] the people of Succoth. 17He also broke down the tower of Penuel, and killed the men of the city.

18 Then he said to Zebah and Zalmunna, "What about the men whom you killed at Tabor?" They answered, "As you are, so were they, every one of them; they resembled the sons of a king." 19And he replied, "They were my brothers, the sons of my mother; as the LORD lives, if you had saved them alive, I would not kill you." 20So he said to Jether his firstborn, "Go kill them!" But the boy did not draw his sword, for he was afraid, because he was still a boy. 21Then Zebah and Zalmunna said, "You come and kill us; for as the man is, so is his strength." So Gideon proceeded to kill Zebah and Zalmunna; and he took the crescents that were on the necks of their camels.

Gideon's Idolatry

22 Then the Israelites said to Gideon, "Rule over us, you and your son and your grandson also; for you have delivered us out of the hand of Midian." 23Gideon said to them, "I will not rule over you, and my son will not rule over you; the LORD will rule over you." 24Then Gideon said to them, "Let me make a request of you; each of you give me an earring he has taken as booty." (For the enemy[b] had golden earrings, because they were Ishmaelites.) 25"We will willingly give them," they answered. So they spread a garment, and each threw into it an earring he had taken as booty. 26The weight of the golden earrings that he requested was one thousand seven hundred shekels of gold (apart from the crescents and the pendants and the purple garments worn by the kings of Midian, and the collars that were on the necks of their camels). 27Gideon made an ephod of it and put it in his town, in Ophrah; and all Israel prostituted themselves to it there, and it became a snare to Gideon and to his family. 28So Midian was subdued before the Israelites, and they lifted up their heads no more. So the land had rest forty years in the days of Gideon.

Death of Gideon

29 Jerubbaal son of Joash went to live in his own house. 30Now Gideon had seventy sons, his own offspring, for he had many wives. 31His concubine who was in Shechem also bore him a son, and he named him Abimelech. 32Then Gideon son of Joash died at a good old age, and was buried in the tomb of his father Joash at Ophrah of the Abiezrites.

8.5 Gen 33.17
8.6 ver 15
8.7 Judg 7.15
8.8 Gen 32.30,31
8.9 ver 18
8.12 Ps 83.11
8.15 ver 6
8.16 ver 7
8.17 ver 9
8.18 Judg 4.6
8.21 Ps 83.11; ver 26
8.23 1 Sam 8.7; 10.19; 12.12
8.27 Judg 17.5; Ps 106.39; Deut 7.16
8.28 Judg 5.31
8.29 Judg 7.1
8.30 Judg 9.2,5
8.31 Judg 9.1

[z] Gk: Heb *pursuing* [a] With verse 7, Compare Gk: Heb *he taught* [b] Heb *they*

8.33 Judg 2.17,19; 9.4,46
8.34 Judg 3.7; Deut 4.9
9.1 Judg 8.31
9.2 Judg 8.30; Gen 29.14
9.4 Judg 8.33
9.5 ver 2
9.7 Deut 11.29; 27.12; Jn 4.20
9.15 Isa 30.2; ver 20
9.16 Judg 8.35
9.18 ver 5,6; Judg 8.31
9.19 Judg 8.35
9.23 1 Sam 16.14; 18.9,10
9.24 ver 56,57; Deut 27.25; Num 35.33

33 As soon as Gideon died, the Israelites relapsed and prostituted themselves with the Baals, making Baal-berith their god. 34The Israelites did not remember the LORD their God, who had rescued them from the hand of all their enemies on every side; 35and they did not exhibit loyalty to the house of Jerubbaal (that is, Gideon) in return for all the good that he had done to Israel.

Abimelech Attempts to Establish a Monarchy

9 Now Abimelech son of Jerubbaal went to Shechem to his mother's kinsfolk and said to them and to the whole clan of his mother's family, 2"Say in the hearing of all the lords of Shechem, 'Which is better for you, that all seventy of the sons of Jerubbaal rule over you, or that one rule over you?' Remember also that I am your bone and your flesh." 3So his mother's kinsfolk spoke all these words on his behalf in the hearing of all the lords of Shechem; and their hearts inclined to follow Abimelech, for they said, "He is our brother." 4They gave him seventy pieces of silver out of the temple of Baal-berith with which Abimelech hired worthless and reckless fellows, who followed him. 5He went to his father's house at Ophrah, and killed his brothers the sons of Jerubbaal, seventy men, on one stone; but Jotham, the youngest son of Jerubbaal, survived, for he hid himself. 6Then all the lords of Shechem and all Beth-millo came together, and they went and made Abimelech king, by the oak of the pillar[c] at Shechem.

The Parable of the Trees

7 When it was told to Jotham, he went and stood on the top of Mount Gerizim, and cried aloud and said to them, "Listen to me, you lords of Shechem, so that God may listen to you.

8 The trees once went out
to anoint a king over themselves.
So they said to the olive tree,
'Reign over us.'
9 The olive tree answered them,
'Shall I stop producing my rich oil
by which gods and mortals are honored,
and go to sway over the trees?'
10 Then the trees said to the fig tree,
'You come and reign over us.'
11 But the fig tree answered them,
'Shall I stop producing my sweetness
and my delicious fruit,
and go to sway over the trees?'
12 Then the trees said to the vine,
'You come and reign over us.'
13 But the vine said to them,
'Shall I stop producing my wine
that cheers gods and mortals,
and go to sway over the trees?'
14 So all the trees said to the bramble,
'You come and reign over us.'
15 And the bramble said to the trees,
'If in good faith you are anointing me king over you,
then come and take refuge in my shade;
but if not, let fire come out of the bramble
and devour the cedars of Lebanon.'

16 "Now therefore, if you acted in good faith and honor when you made Abimelech king, and if you have dealt well with Jerubbaal and his house, and have done to him as his actions deserved— 17for my father fought for you, and risked his life, and rescued you from the hand of Midian; 18but you have risen up against my father's house this day, and have killed his sons, seventy men on one stone, and have made Abimelech, the son of his slave woman, king over the lords of Shechem, because he is your kinsman— 19if, I say, you have acted in good faith and honor with Jerubbaal and with his house this day, then rejoice in Abimelech, and let him also rejoice in you; 20but if not, let fire come out from Abimelech, and devour the lords of Shechem, and Beth-millo; and let fire come out from the lords of Shechem, and from Beth-millo, and devour Abimelech." 21Then Jotham ran away and fled, going to Beer, where he remained for fear of his brother Abimelech.

The Downfall of Abimelech

22 Abimelech ruled over Israel three years. 23But God sent an evil spirit between Abimelech and the lords of Shechem; and the lords of Shechem dealt treacherously with Abimelech. 24This happened so that the violence done to the seventy sons of Jerubbaal might be avenged[d] and their blood be laid on their brother Abimelech, who killed them, and on the lords of Shechem,

[c] Cn: Meaning of Heb uncertain [d] Heb *might come*

9.1-6 Abimelech Schemes to Become King of Israel. Basing his operation at Shechem, where the covenant with Jacob had been founded (Gen 33.18-20) and where it was renewed under Joshua (Josh 24), Abimelech used *silver out of the temple of Baal-berith* to buy support for his plan, and proceeded to murder all seventy of his brothers. Only *Jotham, the youngest*, escaped. The leading men in Shechem were joined by those from *Beth-millo*, which may have been a fortified tower adjacent to Shechem.
9.7-57 Jotham's Curse on Abimelech and his Supporters. Delivered from Mount Gerizim, which overlooks the valley where Shechem lies and which became the site of the Samaritan temple, Jotham utters a parable against *the lords of Shechem*, calling into question whether in supporting Abimelech they *acted in good faith*. He reminds them of what his father, Gideon, did for them, and warns that if they did not act in good faith, the fires of divine judgment will consume them and Abimelech. The lords of Shechem turn against Abimelech and renounce him as their king. Forewarned, Abimelech ambushed *Gaal, son of Ebed*, who had come to take over Shechem, then drove him out, and captured the city, killed the people in it, and *razed* it, burning the leaders in *the tower of Shechem*. When Abimelech attacked Thebez (located about twelve miles northeast of Shechem), he was mortally wounded by a woman who dropped a *millstone* on his head from the *tower* of the city. Divine retribution thus fell on the pretender to the throne, Abimelech, as well as on those who sought to destroy him.

who strengthened his hands to kill his brothers. 25 So, out of hostility to him, the lords
of Shechem set ambushes on the mountain
tops. They robbed all who passed by them
along that way; and it was reported to
Abimelech.
26 When Gaal son of Ebed moved into
Shechem with his kinsfolk, the lords of
Shechem put confidence in him. 27 They
went out into the field and gathered the
grapes from their vineyards, trod them, and
celebrated. Then they went into the temple
of their god, ate and drank, and ridiculed
Abimelech. 28 Gaal son of Ebed said, "Who
is Abimelech, and who are we of Shechem,
that we should serve him? Did not the son
of Jerubbaal and Zebul his officer serve the
men of Hamor father of Shechem? Why
then should we serve him? 29 If only this
people were under my command! Then I
would remove Abimelech; I would say[e] to
him, 'Increase your army, and come out.' "
30 When Zebul the ruler of the city heard
the words of Gaal son of Ebed, his anger
was kindled. 31 He sent messengers to
Abimelech at Arumah,[f] saying, "Look, Gaal
son of Ebed and his kinsfolk have come to
Shechem, and they are stirring up[g] the city
against you. 32 Now therefore, go by night,
you and the troops that are with you, and
lie in wait in the fields. 33 Then early in the
morning, as soon as the sun rises, get up
and rush on the city; and when he and the
troops that are with him come out against
you, you may deal with them as best you
can."
34 So Abimelech and all the troops with
him got up by night and lay in wait against
Shechem in four companies. 35 When Gaal
son of Ebed went out and stood in the
entrance of the gate of the city, Abimelech
and the troops with him rose from the
ambush. 36 And when Gaal saw them, he
said to Zebul, "Look, people are coming
down from the mountain tops!" And Zebul
said to him, "The shadows on the mountains look like people to you." 37 Gaal spoke
again and said, "Look, people are coming
down from Tabbur-erez, and one company
is coming from the direction of Elon-
meonenim."[h] 38 Then Zebul said to him,
"Where is your boast[i] now, you who said,
'Who is Abimelech, that we should serve
him?' Are not these the troops you made
light of? Go out now and fight with them."
39 So Gaal went out at the head of the lords
of Shechem, and fought with Abimelech.
40 Abimelech chased him, and he fled before
him. Many fell wounded, up to the entrance
of the gate. 41 So Abimelech resided at
Arumah; and Zebul drove out Gaal and his
kinsfolk, so that they could not live on at
Shechem.
42 On the following day the people went
out into the fields. When Abimelech was
told, 43 he took his troops and divided them
into three companies, and lay in wait in the
fields. When he looked and saw the people
coming out of the city, he rose against them
and killed them. 44 Abimelech and the company that was[j] with him rushed forward
and stood at the entrance of the gate of the
city, while the two companies rushed on all
who were in the fields and killed them.
45 Abimelech fought against the city all that
day; he took the city, and killed the people
that were in it; and he razed the city and
sowed it with salt.
46 When all the lords of the Tower of
Shechem heard of it, they entered the stronghold of the temple of El-berith. 47 Abimelech
was told that all the lords of the Tower of
Shechem were gathered together. 48 So
Abimelech went up to Mount Zalmon, he
and all the troops that were with him.
Abimelech took an ax in his hand, cut
down a bundle of brushwood, and took it
up and laid it on his shoulder. Then he said
to the troops with him, "What you have
seen me do, do quickly, as I have done."
49 So every one of the troops cut down a
bundle and following Abimelech put it
against the stronghold, and they set the
stronghold on fire over them, so that all the
people of the Tower of Shechem also died,
about a thousand men and women.
50 Then Abimelech went to Thebez, and
encamped against Thebez, and took it. 51 But
there was a strong tower within the city,
and all the men and women and all the
lords of the city fled to it and shut themselves in; and they went to the roof of the
tower. 52 Abimelech came to the tower, and
fought against it, and came near to the
entrance of the tower to burn it with fire.
53 But a certain woman threw an upper
millstone on Abimelech's head, and crushed
his skull. 54 Immediately he called to the
young man who carried his armor and said
to him, "Draw your sword and kill me, so

9.27 Judg 8.33
9.28 Gen 34.2,6
9.29 2 Sam 15.4
9.33 1 Sam 10.7
9.37 Ezek 38.12
9.38 ver 28,29
9.39 Gen 35.4
9.45 ver 20; Deut 29.23
9.46 Judg 8.33
9.48 Ps 68.14
9.50 2 Sam 11.21
9.53 ver 50

[e] Gk: Heb *and he said* [f] Cn See 9.41. Heb *Tormah* [g] Cn: Heb *are besieging* [h] That is *Diviners' Oak* [i] Heb *mouth* [j] Vg and some Gk Mss: Heb *companies that were*

people will not say about me, 'A woman
killed him.' " So the young man thrust him
through, and he died. [55]When the Israelites
saw that Abimelech was dead, they all went
home. [56]Thus God repaid Abimelech for the
crime he committed against his father in
killing his seventy brothers; [57]and God also
made all the wickedness of the people of
Shechem fall back on their heads, and on
them came the curse of Jotham son of
Jerubbaal.

Tola and Jair

10 After Abimelech, Tola son of Puah
son of Dodo, a man of Issachar,
who lived at Shamir in the hill country of
Ephraim, rose to deliver Israel. [2]He judged
Israel twenty-three years. Then he died, and
was buried at Shamir.
3 After him came Jair the Gileadite, who
judged Israel twenty-two years. [4]He had
thirty sons who rode on thirty donkeys; and
they had thirty towns, which are in the
land of Gilead, and are called Havvoth-jair
to this day. [5]Jair died, and was buried in
Kamon.

Oppression by the Ammonites

6 The Israelites again did what was evil
in the sight of the LORD, worshiping the
Baals and the Astartes, the gods of Aram,
the gods of Sidon, the gods of Moab, the
gods of the Ammonites, and the gods of the
Philistines. Thus they abandoned the LORD,
and did not worship him. [7]So the anger of
the LORD was kindled against Israel, and he
sold them into the hand of the Philistines
and into the hand of the Ammonites, [8]and
they crushed and oppressed the Israelites
that year. For eighteen years they oppressed
all the Israelites that were beyond the Jordan in the land of the Amorites, which is
in Gilead. [9]The Ammonites also crossed the
Jordan to fight against Judah and against
Benjamin and against the house of Ephraim;
so that Israel was greatly distressed.
10 So the Israelites cried to the LORD,
saying, "We have sinned against you, because we have abandoned our God and
have worshiped the Baals." [11]And the LORD
said to the Israelites, "Did I not deliver you[k]
from the Egyptians and from the Amorites,
from the Ammonites and from the
Philistines? [12]The Sidonians also, and the
Amalekites, and the Maonites, oppressed
you; and you cried to me, and I delivered
you out of their hand. [13]Yet you have
abandoned me and worshiped other gods;
therefore I will deliver you no more. [14]Go
and cry to the gods whom you have chosen; let them deliver you in the time of your
distress." [15]And the Israelites said to the
LORD, "We have sinned; do to us whatever
seems good to you; but deliver us this day!"
[16]So they put away the foreign gods from
among them and worshiped the LORD; and
he could no longer bear to see Israel suffer.
17 Then the Ammonites were called to
arms, and they encamped in Gilead; and the
Israelites came together, and they encamped
at Mizpah. [18]The commanders of the people
of Gilead said to one another, "Who will
begin the fight against the Ammonites? He
shall be head over all the inhabitants of
Gilead."

Jephthah

11 Now Jephthah the Gileadite, the
son of a prostitute, was a mighty
warrior. Gilead was the father of Jephthah.
[2]Gilead's wife also bore him sons; and when
his wife's sons grew up, they drove Jephthah
away, saying to him, "You shall not inherit
anything in our father's house; for you are
the son of another woman." [3]Then Jephthah
fled from his brothers and lived in the land
of Tob. Outlaws collected around Jephthah
and went raiding with him.
4 After a time the Ammonites made war
against Israel. [5]And when the Ammonites
made war against Israel, the elders of Gilead
went to bring Jephthah from the land of
Tob. [6]They said to Jephthah, "Come and be
our commander, so that we may fight with
the Ammonites." [7]But Jephthah said to the
elders of Gilead, "Are you not the very ones
who rejected me and drove me out of my
father's house? So why do you come to me
now when you are in trouble?" [8]The elders
of Gilead said to Jephthah, "Nevertheless,
we have now turned back to you, so that
you may go with us and fight with the
Ammonites, and become head over us, over
all the inhabitants of Gilead." [9]Jephthah
said to the elders of Gilead, "If you bring me
home again to fight with the Ammonites,
and the LORD gives them over to me, I will
be your head." [10]And the elders of Gilead
said to Jephthah, "The LORD will be witness

[k] Heb lacks *Did I not deliver you*

9.56 ver 24; Ps 94.23
9.57 ver 20
10.1 Judg 2.16
10.4 Num 32.41
10.6 Judg 2.11,13; Deut 31.16,17; 32.15
10.7 Judg 2.14
10.10 1 Sam 12.10
10.11 Ex 14.30; Num 21.21,24,25; Judg 13.31
10.12 Judg 5.19; Ps 106.42,43
10.14 Deut 32.37
10.15 1 Sam 3.18
10.16 Josh 24.23; Jer 18.7,8; Deut 32.36; Ps 106.44,45
10.17 Judg 11.29
10.18 Judg 11.8,11
11.1 Heb 11.32
11.3 2 Sam 10.6,8
11.4 Judg 10.9,17
11.8 Judg 10.18
11.10 Jer 42.5

10.1-5 Tola's role as judge is not described, but his base of operations was south of Shechem in the district of *Ephraim*, where the shrines of Yahweh at Shiloh and Bethel were located. The location of *Shamir* is not known. *Jair...judged Israel* in the district of Gilead, east of the Jordan.
10.6-18 Israel's lapse into worship of the Canaanite gods, and the consequent attacks by the Philistines on the west and the Ammonites on the east, led to a call for a new leader to be *head over all the inhabitants of Gilead*.
11.1-40 Jephthah Subdues the Ammonites. Although Jephthah had been driven out by his family because he was the son of a *prostitute*, his effectiveness as the leader of a troop of bandits led them to invite him to become leader of the forces to oppose the Ammonites, who were asserting claims to their ancestral lands, now occupied by the eastern tribes of Israel. Jephthah's recalling of the events *three hundred years* earlier, when the Ammonites refused to let Israel pass through from Egypt on the way to Canaan, does not impress the Ammonites. He vows to offer to the LORD whatever emerges from his house as he returns, and accordingly he is able to *inflict a massive defeat* on the Ammonites. But it is his only child, a daughter, who greets him on his return, and who must be offered to the LORD in fulfillment of his *vow*.

between us; we will surely do as you say." 11 So Jephthah went with the elders of Gilead, and the people made him head and commander over them; and Jephthah spoke all his words before the LORD at Mizpah.

12 Then Jephthah sent messengers to the king of the Ammonites and said, "What is there between you and me, that you have come to me to fight against my land?" 13 The king of the Ammonites answered the messengers of Jephthah, "Because Israel, on coming from Egypt, took away my land from the Arnon to the Jabbok and to the Jordan; now therefore restore it peaceably." 14 Once again Jephthah sent messengers to the king of the Ammonites 15 and said to him: "Thus says Jephthah: Israel did not take away the land of Moab or the land of the Ammonites, 16 but when they came up from Egypt, Israel went through the wilderness to the Red Sea[l] and came to Kadesh. 17 Israel then sent messengers to the king of Edom, saying, 'Let us pass through your land'; but the king of Edom would not listen. They also sent to the king of Moab, but he would not consent. So Israel remained at Kadesh. 18 Then they journeyed through the wilderness, went around the land of Edom and the land of Moab, arrived on the east side of the land of Moab, and camped on the other side of the Arnon. They did not enter the territory of Moab, for the Arnon was the boundary of Moab. 19 Israel then sent messengers to King Sihon of the Amorites, king of Heshbon; and Israel said to him, 'Let us pass through your land to our country.' 20 But Sihon did not trust Israel to pass through his territory; so Sihon gathered all his people together, and encamped at Jahaz, and fought with Israel. 21 Then the LORD, the God of Israel, gave Sihon and all his people into the hand of Israel, and they defeated them; so Israel occupied all the land of the Amorites, who inhabited that country. 22 They occupied all the territory of the Amorites from the Arnon to the Jabbok and from the wilderness to the Jordan. 23 So now the LORD, the God of Israel, has conquered the Amorites for the benefit of his people Israel. Do you intend to take their place? 24 Should you not possess what your god Chemosh gives you to possess? And should we not be the ones to possess everything that the LORD our God has conquered for our benefit? 25 Now are you any better than King Balak son of Zippor of Moab? Did he ever enter into conflict with Israel, or did he ever go to war with them? 26 While Israel lived in Heshbon and its villages, and in Aroer and its villages, and in all the towns that are along the Arnon, three hundred years, why did you not recover them within that time? 27 It is not I who have sinned against you, but you are the one who does me wrong by making war on me. Let the LORD, who is judge, decide today for the Israelites or for the Ammonites." 28 But the king of the Ammonites did not heed the message that Jephthah sent him.

Jephthah's Vow

29 Then the spirit of the LORD came upon Jephthah, and he passed through Gilead and Manasseh. He passed on to Mizpah of Gilead, and from Mizpah of Gilead he passed on to the Ammonites. 30 And Jephthah made a vow to the LORD, and said, "If you will give the Ammonites into my hand, 31 then whoever comes out of the doors of my house to meet me, when I return victorious from the Ammonites, shall be the LORD's, to be offered up by me as a burnt offering." 32 So Jephthah crossed over to the Ammonites to fight against them; and the LORD gave them into his hand. 33 He inflicted a massive defeat on them from Aroer to the neighborhood of Minnith, twenty towns, and as far as Abel-keramim. So the Ammonites were subdued before the people of Israel.

Jephthah's Daughter

34 Then Jephthah came to his home at Mizpah; and there was his daughter coming out to meet him with timbrels and with dancing. She was his only child; he had no son or daughter except her. 35 When he saw her, he tore his clothes, and said, "Alas, my daughter! You have brought me very low; you have become the cause of great trouble to me. For I have opened my mouth to the LORD, and I cannot take back my vow." 36 She said to him, "My father, if you have opened your mouth to the LORD, do to me according to what has gone out of your mouth, now that the LORD has given you vengeance against your enemies, the Ammonites." 37 And she said to her father, "Let this thing be done for me: Grant me two months, so that I may go and wander[m] on

[l] Or *Sea of Reeds* [m] Cn: Heb *go down*

11.11 ver 8; Judg 10.17
11.13 Num 21.24-26
11.15 Deut 2.9,19
11.16 Num 14.25; 20.1,14-21
11.18 Num 21.4; Deut 2.1-9
11.19 Num 21.21,22; Deut 2.26,27
11.20 Num 21.23; Deut 2.32
11.21 Num 21.24,25; Deut 2.33,34
11.22 Deut 2.36
11.24 Num 21.29; 1 Kings 11.7; Josh 3.10
11.25 Num 22.2; Josh 24.9
11.26 Num 21.25; Deut 2.36
11.27 Gen 16.5; 18.25; 31.53; 1 Sam 24.12,15
11.29 Judg 3.10
11.33 Ezek 27.17
11.34 Judg 10.17; Ex 15.20; 1 Sam 18.6; Jer 31.4
11.35 Num 30.2; Eccl 5.2,4,5
11.36 Num 30.2; 2 Sam 18.19,31; Lk 1.38

12.1 Judg 8.1
12.3 1 Sam 19.5; 28.21; Job 13.14
12.4 Judg 3.28; 7.24
12.5 Judg 3.28; 7.24; Josh 22.11
12.7 Heb 11.32
12.14 Judg 5.10; 10.4
13.1 Judg 2.11; 1 Sam 12.9
13.2 Josh 19.41
13.3 ver 6,8,10; Judg 6.12
13.4 ver 14; Num 6.2,3
13.5 Lk 1.15; Num 6.2,5
13.6 1 Sam 2.27; Mt 28.3; ver 17,18
13.8 ver 3,7

the mountains, and bewail my virginity, my
companions and I." [38]"Go," he said and sent
her away for two months. So she departed,
she and her companions, and bewailed her
virginity on the mountains. [39]At the end of
two months, she returned to her father,
who did with her according to the vow he
had made. She had never slept with a man.
So there arose an Israelite custom that [40]for
four days every year the daughters of Israel
would go out to lament the daughter of
Jephthah the Gileadite.

Intertribal Dissension

12 The men of Ephraim were called to
arms, and they crossed to Zaphon
and said to Jephthah, "Why did you cross
over to fight against the Ammonites, and
did not call us to go with you? We will burn
your house down over you!" [2]Jephthah said
to them, "My people and I were engaged in
conflict with the Ammonites who oppressed
us[n] severely. But when I called you, you did
not deliver me from their hand. [3]When I
saw that you would not deliver me, I took
my life in my hand, and crossed over against
the Ammonites, and the LORD gave them
into my hand. Why then have you come up
to me this day, to fight against me?" [4]Then
Jephthah gathered all the men of Gilead and
fought with Ephraim; and the men of Gilead
defeated Ephraim, because they said, "You
are fugitives from Ephraim, you Gileadites—
in the heart of Ephraim and Manasseh."[o]
[5]Then the Gileadites took the fords of the
Jordan against the Ephraimites. Whenever
one of the fugitives of Ephraim said, "Let me
go over," the men of Gilead would say to
him, "Are you an Ephraimite?" When he
said, "No," [6]they said to him, "Then say
Shibboleth," and he said, "Sibboleth," for he
could not pronounce it right. Then they
seized him and killed him at the fords of the
Jordan. Forty-two thousand of the Ephraimites fell at that time.
7 Jephthah judged Israel six years. Then
Jephthah the Gileadite died, and was buried
in his town in Gilead.[p]

Ibzan, Elon, and Abdon

8 After him Ibzan of Bethlehem judged
Israel. [9]He had thirty sons. He gave his
thirty daughters in marriage outside his
clan and brought in thirty young women
from outside for his sons. He judged Israel
seven years. [10]Then Ibzan died, and was
buried at Bethlehem.
11 After him Elon the Zebulunite judged
Israel; and he judged Israel ten years. [12]Then
Elon the Zebulunite died, and was buried at
Aijalon in the land of Zebulun.
13 After him Abdon son of Hillel the
Pirathonite judged Israel. [14]He had forty
sons and thirty grandsons, who rode on
seventy donkeys; he judged Israel eight years.
[15]Then Abdon son of Hillel the Pirathonite
died, and was buried at Pirathon in the land
of Ephraim, in the hill country of the
Amalekites.

The Birth of Samson

13 The Israelites again did what was
evil in the sight of the LORD, and
the LORD gave them into the hand of the
Philistines forty years.
2 There was a certain man of Zorah, of
the tribe of the Danites, whose name was
Manoah. His wife was barren, having borne
no children. [3]And the angel of the LORD
appeared to the woman and said to her,
"Although you are barren, having borne no
children, you shall conceive and bear a son.
[4]Now be careful not to drink wine or strong
drink, or to eat anything unclean, [5]for you
shall conceive and bear a son. No razor is
to come on his head, for the boy shall be
a nazirite[q] to God from birth. It is he who
shall begin to deliver Israel from the hand
of the Philistines." [6]Then the woman came
and told her husband, "A man of God came
to me, and his appearance was like that of
an angel[r] of God, most awe-inspiring; I did
not ask him where he came from, and he
did not tell me his name; [7]but he said to me,
'You shall conceive and bear a son. So then
drink no wine or strong drink, and eat
nothing unclean, for the boy shall be a
nazirite[q] to God from birth to the day of his
death.' "
8 Then Manoah entreated the LORD, and
said, "O, LORD, I pray, let the man of God
whom you sent come to us again and teach
us what we are to do concerning the boy
who will be born." [9]God listened to Manoah,
and the angel of God came again to the
woman as she sat in the field; but her
husband Manoah was not with her. [10]So

12.1-7 Inter-tribal conflict. The Ephraimites resent their not having been asked to join the fight against the Ammonites. This leads to conflict between Ephraim and tribes east of the Jordan (the Gileadites). Differences in pronunciation of Hebrew serve as an indicator of different tribal origin and result in the killing of Ephraimites.

12.8-15 Three Minor Judges of Israel: Ibzan, Elon and Abdon. *Ibzan* comes from the region of Judah, but arranged for his children to intermarry with other tribes. *Elon* was from the district of *Zebulun*, on the plain west of the Sea of Galilee. *Abdon*, a man with many children and considerable wealth, was from the tribe of *Ephraim*, and was buried at *Pirathon*, a few miles southwest of Shechem.

13.1-16.31 Samson. Although the stories of Samson are grouped in this book with the accounts of the judges who delivered the tribes of Israel from their enemies and served as their leaders, more attention is paid to the extraordinary events of his life than to his influence on the life of Israel. With *the Philistines* (Indo-European people who controlled the Mediterranean coast south from Mt. Carmel to the border of Egypt beginning in the twelfth century BCE) dominating Israel, Samson was chosen by God before his birth *to deliver Israel from...the Philistines*. *Zorah*, where his parents lived, was in the southern territory of *Dan:* that is, in the coastal hills west of Jerusalem. His birth to a woman who was *barren* recalls the birth of Samuel (1 Sam 1.5) and those of John the Baptist (Lk 1.7) and Jesus (Lk 1.34). The messenger of God is variously described as *a man of God* (13.6) and an angel of God (13.6,9,16,18-21). The child's special role in the purpose of God is indicated by his being designated a *nazirite*, which means he is to be forever ritually pure and must never cut his hair (13.7,14), unlike the later Nazirite vow of Num 6 which lasted for a briefer, fixed period. The vision of God given to Manoah and his wife convinces them that God has a special purpose for their child, and the coming of God's Spirit upon him confirms this expectation (13.19-25).

[n] Gk OL, Syr H: Heb lacks *who oppressed us* [o] Meaning of Heb uncertain: Gk omits *because . . . Manasseh* [p] Gk: Heb *in the towns of Gilead* [q] That is *one separated* or *one consecrated* [r] Or *the angel*

14.1-20 Samson marries a Philistine woman. Samson's violation of the tradition against marrying outside the tribes of Israel is seen as *a pretext to act against the Philistines*. Empowered by God's *spirit*, he tears apart a lion, returning later to find that bees are producing honey in its carcass. This would make the honey ritually impure, so Samson invents a *riddle* about the source of the honey and his wife lures him into revealing the answer. In anger he *killed thirty men* of the Philistines and temporarily abandoned his new wife.

the woman ran quickly and told her husband, "The man who came to me the other day has appeared to me." 11Manoah got up and followed his wife, and came to the man and said to him, "Are you the man who spoke to this woman?" And he said, "I am." 12Then Manoah said, "Now when your words come true, what is to be the boy's rule of life; what is he to do?" 13The angel of the LORD said to Manoah, "Let the woman give heed to all that I said to her. 14She may not eat of anything that comes from the vine. She is not to drink wine or strong drink, or eat any unclean thing. She is to observe everything that I commanded her."

15 Manoah said to the angel of the LORD, "Allow us to detain you, and prepare a kid for you." 16The angel of the LORD said to Manoah, "If you detain me, I will not eat your food; but if you want to prepare a burnt offering, then offer it to the LORD." (For Manoah did not know that he was the angel of the LORD.) 17Then Manoah said to the angel of the LORD, "What is your name, so that we may honor you when your words come true?" 18But the angel of the LORD said to him, "Why do you ask my name? It is too wonderful."

19 So Manoah took the kid with the grain offering, and offered it on the rock to the LORD, to him who works[s] wonders.[t] 20When the flame went up toward heaven from the altar, the angel of the LORD ascended in the flame of the altar while Manoah and his wife looked on; and they fell on their faces to the ground. 21The angel of the LORD did not appear again to Manoah and his wife. Then Manoah realized that it was the angel of the LORD. 22And Manoah said to his wife, "We shall surely die, for we have seen God." 23But his wife said to him, "If the LORD had meant to kill us, he would not have accepted a burnt offering and a grain offering at our hands, or shown us all these things, or now announced to us such things as these."

24 The woman bore a son, and named him Samson. The boy grew, and the LORD blessed him. 25The spirit of the LORD began to stir him in Mahaneh-dan, between Zorah and Eshtaol.

Samson's Marriage

14 Once Samson went down to Timnah, and at Timnah he saw a Philistine woman. 2Then he came up, and told his father and mother, "I saw a Philistine woman at Timnah; now get her for me as my wife." 3But his father and mother said to him, "Is there not a woman among your kin, or among all our[u] people, that you must go to take a wife from the uncircumcised Philistines?" But Samson said to his father, "Get her for me, because she pleases me." 4His father and mother did not know that this was from the LORD; for he was seeking a pretext to act against the Philistines. At that time the Philistines had dominion over Israel.

5 Then Samson went down with his father and mother to Timnah. When he came to the vineyards of Timnah, suddenly a young lion roared at him. 6The spirit of the LORD rushed on him, and he tore the lion apart barehanded as one might tear apart a kid. But he did not tell his father or his mother what he had done. 7Then he went down and talked with the woman, and she pleased Samson. 8After a while he returned to marry her, and he turned aside to see the carcass of the lion, and there was a swarm of bees in the body of the lion, and honey. 9He scraped it out into his hands, and went on, eating as he went. When he came to his father and mother, he gave some to them, and they ate it. But he did not tell them that he had taken the honey from the carcass of the lion.

10 His father went down to the woman, and Samson made a feast there as the young men were accustomed to do. 11When the people saw him, they brought thirty companions to be with him. 12Samson said to them, "Let me now put a riddle to you. If you can explain it to me within the seven days of the feast, and find it out, then I will give you thirty linen garments and thirty festal garments. 13But if you cannot explain it to me, then you shall give me thirty linen garments and thirty festal garments." So they said to him, "Ask your riddle; let us hear it." 14He said to them,

"Out of the eater came something to
eat.
Out of the strong came something sweet."

But for three days they could not explain the riddle.

15 On the fourth[v] day they said to Samson's wife, "Coax your husband to explain the riddle to us, or we will burn you and your father's house with fire. Have you

[s] Gk Vg: Heb *and working* [t] Heb *wonders, while Manoah and his wife looked on* [u] Cn: Heb *my* [v] Gk Syr: Heb *seventh*

13.13 ver 4,11
13.14 Num 6.4
13.15 ver 3
13.16 Judg 6.20
13.17 Gen 32.29
13.18 Isa 9.6
13.19 Judg 6.20,21
13.20 Lev 9.24
13.21 ver 16
13.22 Judg 6.22; Deut 5.26
13.24 Heb 11.32; 1 Sam 3.19
13.25 Judg 3.10; 18.11
14.2 Gen 21.21; 34.4
14.4 Josh 11.20; Judg 13.1
14.6 Judg 3.10; 13.25
14.7 ver 3
14.12 1 Kings 10.2; Ezek 17.2; Gen 29.27
14.15 Judg 16.5; 15.6

14.18 ver 14
14.19 Judg 3.10
14.20 Judg 15.2; Jn 3.29
15.2 Judg 14.20
15.6 Judg 14.15
15.9 ver 19
15.11 Judg 13.1; 14.4
15.14 Judg 14.19; 1 Sam 11.6
15.15 Lev 26.8; Josh 23.10; Judg 3.31
15.18 Judg 16.28
15.19 Gen 45.27; Isa 40.29
15.20 Heb 11.32; Judg 13.1; 16.31

invited us here to impoverish us?" 16So
Samson's wife wept before him, saying, "You
hate me; you do not really love me. You
have asked a riddle of my people, but you
have not explained it to me." He said to her,
"Look, I have not told my father or my
mother. Why should I tell you?" 17She wept
before him the seven days that their feast
lasted; and because she nagged him, on the
seventh day he told her. Then she explained
the riddle to her people. 18The men of the
town said to him on the seventh day before
the sun went down,

"What is sweeter than honey?
What is stronger than a lion?"

And he said to them,

"If you had not plowed with my heifer,
you would not have found out my
riddle."

19Then the spirit of the LORD rushed on him,
and he went down to Ashkelon. He killed
thirty men of the town, took their spoil, and
gave the festal garments to those who had
explained the riddle. In hot anger he went
back to his father's house. 20And Samson's
wife was given to his companion, who had
been his best man.

Samson Defeats the Philistines

15 After a while, at the time of the
wheat harvest, Samson went to
visit his wife, bringing along a kid. He said,
"I want to go into my wife's room." But her
father would not allow him to go in. 2Her
father said, "I was sure that you had rejected her; so I gave her to your companion.
Is not her younger sister prettier than she?
Why not take her instead?" 3Samson said to
them, "This time, when I do mischief to the
Philistines, I will be without blame." 4So
Samson went and caught three hundred
foxes, and took some torches; and he turned
the foxes[w] tail to tail, and put a torch
between each pair of tails. 5When he had
set fire to the torches, he let the foxes go
into the standing grain of the Philistines,
and burned up the shocks and the standing
grain, as well as the vineyards and[x] olive
groves. 6Then the Philistines asked, "Who
has done this?" And they said, "Samson,
the son-in-law of the Timnite, because he
has taken Samson's wife and given her to
his companion." So the Philistines came up,
and burned her and her father. 7Samson
said to them, "If this is what you do, I swear
I will not stop until I have taken revenge
on you." 8He struck them down hip and
thigh with great slaughter; and he went
down and stayed in the cleft of the rock of
Etam.

9 Then the Philistines came up and encamped in Judah, and made a raid on Lehi.
10The men of Judah said, "Why have you
come up against us?" They said, "We have
come up to bind Samson, to do to him as
he did to us." 11Then three thousand men
of Judah went down to the cleft of the rock
of Etam, and they said to Samson, "Do you
not know that the Philistines are rulers over
us? What then have you done to us?" He
replied, "As they did to me, so I have done
to them." 12They said to him, "We have
come down to bind you, so that we may
give you into the hands of the Philistines."
Samson answered them, "Swear to me that
you yourselves will not attack me." 13They
said to him, "No, we will only bind you and
give you into their hands; we will not kill
you." So they bound him with two new
ropes, and brought him up from the rock.

14 When he came to Lehi, the Philistines
came shouting to meet him; and the spirit
of the LORD rushed on him, and the ropes
that were on his arms became like flax that
has caught fire, and his bonds melted off his
hands. 15Then he found a fresh jawbone of
a donkey, reached down and took it, and
with it he killed a thousand men. 16And
Samson said,

"With the jawbone of a donkey,
heaps upon heaps,
with the jawbone of a donkey
I have slain a thousand men."

17When he had finished speaking, he threw
away the jawbone; and that place was
called Ramath-lehi.[y]

18 By then he was very thirsty, and he
called on the LORD, saying, "You have granted
this great victory by the hand of your servant. Am I now to die of thirst, and fall into
the hands of the uncircumcised?" 19So God
split open the hollow place that is at Lehi,
and water came from it. When he drank,
his spirit returned, and he revived. Therefore it was named En-hakkore,[z] which is at
Lehi to this day. 20And he judged Israel in
the days of the Philistines twenty years.

15.1-20 Samson Defeats the Philistines. Finding that his Philistine wife has been given to another man, Samson *caught three hundred foxes,* and then tying them in pairs with torches between them, he set fire to the fields, *vineyards and olive groves of the Philistines.* On request from the Philistines, and with Samson's acquiescence, *the men of Judah* bound him and turned him over to the Philistines. Breaking his bonds, he attacked them with *a fresh jawbone of a donkey,* killing a thousand of them. When he was thirsty, God provided him with water. Although the nature of his leadership is unclear, he is said to have *judged Israel ...twenty years.*

[w] Heb *them*(15.5) [x] Gk Tg Vg: Heb lacks *and* [y] That is *The Hill of the Jawbone* [z] That is *The Spring of the One who Called*

16.1-22 Samson and Delilah. Escaping from an attempt by the Philistines to kill him while he was with a prostitute in one of their cities, *Gaza*, Samson carried the city gate forty miles to the hill city of Hebron in the territory of Judah. Another attempt to capture him through another woman he loved, *Delilah*, failed until he revealed to her that the secret of his astounding strength was his uncut hair as *a nazirite from [his] mother's womb.* Having cut his hair while he slept, *the Philistines seized him and gouged out his eyes.* But when his hair grew back, his strength returned, and he was able to pull the pillars and roof of the great temple of their god, *Dagon*, down on the rulers of the Philistines and the thousands of people gathered there.

Samson and Delilah

16 Once Samson went to Gaza, where he saw a prostitute and went in to her. 2 The Gazites were told,[a] "Samson has come here." So they circled around and lay in wait for him all night at the city gate. They kept quiet all night, thinking, "Let us wait until the light of the morning; then we will kill him." 3 But Samson lay only until midnight. Then at midnight he rose up, took hold of the doors of the city gate and the two posts, pulled them up, bar and all, put them on his shoulders, and carried them to the top of the hill that is in front of Hebron.

4 After this he fell in love with a woman in the valley of Sorek, whose name was Delilah. 5 The lords of the Philistines came to her and said to her, "Coax him, and find out what makes his strength so great, and how we may overpower him, so that we may bind him in order to subdue him; and we will each give you eleven hundred pieces of silver." 6 So Delilah said to Samson, "Please tell me what makes your strength so great, and how you could be bound, so that one could subdue you." 7 Samson said to her, "If they bind me with seven fresh bowstrings that are not dried out, then I shall become weak, and be like anyone else." 8 Then the lords of the Philistines brought her seven fresh bowstrings that had not dried out, and she bound him with them. 9 While men were lying in wait in an inner chamber, she said to him, "The Philistines are upon you, Samson!" But he snapped the bowstrings, as a strand of fiber snaps when it touches the fire. So the secret of his strength was not known.

10 Then Delilah said to Samson, "You have mocked me and told me lies; please tell me how you could be bound." 11 He said to her, "If they bind me with new ropes that have not been used, then I shall become weak, and be like anyone else." 12 So Delilah took new ropes and bound him with them, and said to him, "The Philistines are upon you, Samson!" (The men lying in wait were in an inner chamber.) But he snapped the ropes off his arms like a thread.

13 Then Delilah said to Samson, "Until now you have mocked me and told me lies; tell me how you could be bound." He said to her, "If you weave the seven locks of my head with the web and make it tight with the pin, then I shall become weak, and be like anyone else." 14 So while he slept, Delilah took the seven locks of his head and wove them into the web,[b] and made them tight with the pin. Then she said to him, "The Philistines are upon you, Samson!" But he awoke from his sleep, and pulled away the pin, the loom, and the web.

15 Then she said to him, "How can you say, 'I love you,' when your heart is not with me? You have mocked me three times now and have not told me what makes your strength so great." 16 Finally, after she had nagged him with her words day after day, and pestered him, he was tired to death. 17 So he told her his whole secret, and said to her, "A razor has never come upon my head; for I have been a nazirite[c] to God from my mother's womb. If my head were shaved, then my strength would leave me; I would become weak, and be like anyone else."

18 When Delilah realized that he had told her his whole secret, she sent and called the lords of the Philistines, saying, "This time come up, for he has told his whole secret to me." Then the lords of the Philistines came up to her, and brought the money in their hands. 19 She let him fall asleep on her lap; and she called a man, and had him shave off the seven locks of his head. He began to weaken,[d] and his strength left him. 20 Then she said, "The Philistines are upon you, Samson!" When he awoke from his sleep, he thought, "I will go out as at other times, and shake myself free." But he did not know that the LORD had left him. 21 So the Philistines seized him and gouged out his eyes. They brought him down to Gaza and bound him with bronze shackles; and he ground at the mill in the prison. 22 But the hair of his head began to grow again after it had been shaved.

Samson's Death

23 Now the lords of the Philistines gathered to offer a great sacrifice to their god Dagon, and to rejoice; for they said, "Our god has given Samson our enemy into our hand." 24 When the people saw him, they praised their god; for they said, "Our god has given our enemy into our hand, the ravager of our country, who has killed many of us." 25 And when their hearts were

16.2 Ps 118.10-12
16.5 Judg 14.15
16.10 ver 13,15
16.13 ver 10,15
16.15 Judg 14.16
16.17 Mic 7.5; Num 6.5; Judg 13.5
16.19 Prov 7.26,27
16.20 Josh 7.12; 1 Sam 16.14; 18.12
16.23 1 Sam 5.2
16.24 Dan 5.4
16.25 Judg 9.27

[a] Gk: Heb lacks *were told* [b] Compare Gk: in verses 13–14, Heb lacks *and make it tight . . . into the web* [c] That is *one separated* or *one consecrated* [d] Gk: Heb *She began to torment him*

16.27 Deut 22.8
16.28 Judg 15.18; Jer 15.15
16.31 Judg 15.20
17.3 Ex 20.4,23; Lev 19.4
17.5 Judg 18.24; 8.27; 18.14; Gen 31.19
17.6 Judg 18.1; 19.1; Deut 12.8
17.7 Judg 19.1; Ruth 1.1,2; Mic 5.2; Mt 2.1
17.10 Judg 18.19
17.12 ver 5; Judg 13.25
18.1 Judg 17.6; 19.1; Josh 19.47
18.2 Judg 13.25; Josh 2.1; Judg 17.1
18.4 Judg 17.10,12
18.5 1 Kings 22.5
18.6 1 Kings 22.6

merry, they said, "Call Samson, and let him
entertain us." So they called Samson out of
the prison, and he performed for them.
They made him stand between the pillars;
26 and Samson said to the attendant who
held him by the hand, "Let me feel the
pillars on which the house rests, so that I
may lean against them." 27 Now the house
was full of men and women; all the lords
of the Philistines were there, and on the
roof there were about three thousand men
and women, who looked on while Samson
performed.
28 Then Samson called to the LORD and
said, "Lord GOD, remember me and strengthen
me only this once, O God, so that with this
one act of revenge I may pay back the
Philistines for my two eyes."[e] 29 And Samson
grasped the two middle pillars on which the
house rested, and he leaned his weight
against them, his right hand on the one and
his left hand on the other. 30 Then Samson
said, "Let me die with the Philistines." He
strained with all his might; and the house
fell on the lords and all the people who were
in it. So those he killed at his death were
more than those he had killed during his
life. 31 Then his brothers and all his family
came down and took him and brought him
up and buried him between Zorah and
Eshtaol in the tomb of his father Manoah.
He had judged Israel twenty years.

Micah and the Levite

17 There was a man in the hill country of Ephraim whose name was
Micah. 2 He said to his mother, "The eleven
hundred pieces of silver that were taken
from you, about which you uttered a curse,
and even spoke it in my hearing,—that
silver is in my possession; I took it; but now
I will return it to you."[f] And his mother
said, "May my son be blessed by the LORD!"
3 Then he returned the eleven hundred pieces
of silver to his mother; and his mother said,
"I consecrate the silver to the LORD from my
hand for my son, to make an idol of cast
metal." 4 So when he returned the money to
his mother, his mother took two hundred
pieces of silver, and gave it to the silversmith, who made it into an idol of cast
metal; and it was in the house of Micah.
5 This man Micah had a shrine, and he
made an ephod and teraphim, and installed
one of his sons, who became his priest. 6 In
those days there was no king in Israel; all
the people did what was right in their own
eyes.
7 Now there was a young man of Bethlehem in Judah, of the clan of Judah. He
was a Levite residing there. 8 This man left
the town of Bethlehem in Judah, to live
wherever he could find a place. He came to
the house of Micah in the hill country of
Ephraim to carry on his work.[g] 9 Micah said
to him, "From where do you come?" He
replied, "I am a Levite of Bethlehem in
Judah, and I am going to live wherever I
can find a place." 10 Then Micah said to him,
"Stay with me, and be to me a father and
a priest, and I will give you ten pieces of
silver a year, a set of clothes, and your
living."[h] 11 The Levite agreed to stay with
the man; and the young man became to
him like one of his sons. 12 So Micah installed the Levite, and the young man became his priest, and was in the house of
Micah. 13 Then Micah said, "Now I know
that the LORD will prosper me, because the
Levite has become my priest."

The Migration of Dan

18 In those days there was no king in
Israel. And in those days the tribe
of the Danites was seeking for itself a territory to live in; for until then no territory
among the tribes of Israel had been allotted
to them. 2 So the Danites sent five valiant
men from the whole number of their clan,
from Zorah and from Eshtaol, to spy out the
land and to explore it; and they said to
them, "Go, explore the land." When they
came to the hill country of Ephraim, to the
house of Micah, they stayed there. 3 While
they were at Micah's house, they recognized the voice of the young Levite; so they
went over and asked him, "Who brought
you here? What are you doing in this place?
What is your business here?" 4 He said to
them, "Micah did such and such for me,
and he hired me, and I have become his
priest." 5 Then they said to him, "Inquire of
God that we may know whether the mission we are undertaking will succeed." 6 The
priest replied, "Go in peace. The mission
you are on is under the eye of the LORD."

[e] Or *so that I may be avenged upon the Philistines for one of my two eyes* [f] The words *but now I will return it to you* are transposed from the end of verse 3 in Heb [g] Or *Ephraim, continuing his journey* [h] Heb *living, and the Levite went*

17.1-21.25 Disorder in Israel Prior to the Establishment of the Monarchy. The concluding chapters of Judges serve as a transition to the Books of Samuel and Kings, where God's rule over his people is no longer through judges, but is mediated through a king (1 Sam 8). This is emphasized in the recurrent note, *There was no king in Israel; all the people did what was right in their own eyes* (17.5; *cf.* 18.1; 19.1; 21.25).

17.1-13 A domestic shrine with a Levite as priest. *Micah,* from the district of *Ephraim,* acknowledged his theft of silver from his mother, who, on his returning *the eleven hundred pieces of silver,* ordered that an idol be made from part of it. Micah installed it in his house, and added to the shrine *an ephod* (a sacred shoulder piece used in consulting the deities) and *teraphim* (objects used to obtain messages from the gods, perhaps linked with ancestor-worship). After first installing *one of his sons* as priest in this domestic shrine, Micah appointed a *Levite of Bethlehem in Judah* to this post. Micah's expectation that this development of shrines and sacred instruments would bring him prosperity (17.13), in spite of its inclusion of idolatrous practices, shows the lack of clarity for guidelines in these matters as contrasted with the later centralization of worship under the kings (David and Solomon) in one sanctuary (the Jerusalem temple).

18.1-31 The Migration of the Tribe of Dan to the Far North. Although Dan was initially assigned territory west of Jerusalem, near the Mediterranean coast (Josh 19.40-48), pressure (probably from the Philistines on the coast) forced them to move far north to an area near the sources of the Jordan River (Josh 19.47; Judg 18). The spies they sent to explore this territory were convinced that there they would be free of interference from the *Sidonians* on the coast and from *the Arameans* in Syria proper to the north and east (18.7). Led by *six hundred men of the Danite clan,* the expedition set out for the north through *Judah,* where they seized the sacred objects from the household shrine of *Micah,* and forced *the Levite* to accompany them. Micah's attempt to regain his *gods* and his *priest* were unsuccessful, and the Danites proceeded with their migration to the northern territory. The *unsuspecting* and unprotected people of *Laish* (north of Lake Huleh) were slaughtered, and the Danites set up the idol for themselves, maintaining a separate sanctuary and priesthood until the time of Israel's *captivity:* that is, in the sixth century BCE.

19.1-30 The Gross Mistreatment of the Levite's Concubine. A Levite living in *the remote parts of the hill country of Ephraim*, northwest of Jerusalem, went to *Bethlehem in Judah* to recover his concubine, who had returned in anger to her parents' home. After several days of cordial hospitality, the Levite and his concubine started the journey back to his residence in the north, passing near Jebus (still in Canaanite hands and not yet known as Jerusalem) on the way. Unwilling to spend the night in territory which would be ethnically and ritually unclean, the Levite sought hospitality in Gibeah, a city of the tribe of Benjamin located a short distance to the north on the main route from Jerusalem. When overnight accommodation was provided (19.20), the *men of the city* demanded that the host turn the Levite over to them for their homosexual indulgence. When he released the concubine to them, they abused her sexually and *wantonly raped her*. The Levite found her lifeless (19.25-28). As a vivid symbol of the moral breakdown in the tribes of Israel, the Levite carved her body into *twelve pieces* and sent one piece to each of the twelve tribes (19.29).

7 The five men went on, and when they came to Laish, they observed the people who were there living securely, after the manner of the Sidonians, quiet and unsuspecting, lacking[i] nothing on earth, and possessing wealth.[j] Furthermore, they were far from the Sidonians and had no dealings with Aram.[k] 8 When they came to their kinsfolk at Zorah and Eshtaol, they said to them, "What do you report?" 9 They said, "Come, let us go up against them; for we have seen the land, and it is very good. Will you do nothing? Do not be slow to go, but enter in and possess the land. 10 When you go, you will come to an unsuspecting people. The land is broad—God has indeed given it into your hands—a place where there is no lack of anything on earth."

11 Six hundred men of the Danite clan, armed with weapons of war, set out from Zorah and Eshtaol, 12 and went up and encamped at Kiriath-jearim in Judah. On this account that place is called Mahaneh-dan[l] to this day; it is west of Kiriath-jearim. 13 From there they passed on to the hill country of Ephraim, and came to the house of Micah.

14 Then the five men who had gone to spy out the land (that is, Laish) said to their comrades, "Do you know that in these buildings there are an ephod, teraphim, and an idol of cast metal? Now therefore consider what you will do." 15 So they turned in that direction and came to the house of the young Levite, at the home of Micah, and greeted him. 16 While the six hundred men of the Danites, armed with their weapons of war, stood by the entrance of the gate, 17 the five men who had gone to spy out the land proceeded to enter and take the idol of cast metal, the ephod, and the teraphim.[m] The priest was standing by the entrance of the gate with the six hundred men armed with weapons of war. 18 When the men went into Micah's house and took the idol of cast metal, the ephod, and the teraphim, the priest said to them, "What are you doing?" 19 They said to him, "Keep quiet! Put your hand over your mouth, and come with us, and be to us a father and a priest. Is it better for you to be priest to the house of one person, or to be priest to a tribe and clan in Israel?" 20 Then the priest accepted the offer. He took the ephod, the teraphim, and the idol, and went along with the people.

21 So they resumed their journey, putting the little ones, the livestock, and the goods in front of them. 22 When they were some distance from the home of Micah, the men who were in the houses near Micah's house were called out, and they overtook the Danites. 23 They shouted to the Danites, who turned around and said to Micah, "What is the matter that you come with such a company?" 24 He replied, "You take my gods that I made, and the priest, and go away, and what have I left? How then can you ask me, 'What is the matter?' " 25 And the Danites said to him, "You had better not let your voice be heard among us or else hot-tempered fellows will attack you, and you will lose your life and the lives of your household." 26 Then the Danites went their way. When Micah saw that they were too strong for him, he turned and went back to his home.

The Danites Settle in Laish

27 The Danites, having taken what Micah had made, and the priest who belonged to him, came to Laish, to a people quiet and unsuspecting, put them to the sword, and burned down the city. 28 There was no deliverer, because it was far from Sidon and they had no dealings with Aram.[n] It was in the valley that belongs to Beth-rehob. They rebuilt the city, and lived in it. 29 They named the city Dan, after their ancestor Dan, who was born to Israel; but the name of the city was formerly Laish. 30 Then the Danites set up the idol for themselves. Jonathan son of Gershom, son of Moses,[o] and his sons were priests to the tribe of the Danites until the time the land went into captivity. 31 So they maintained as their own Micah's idol that he had made, as long as the house of God was at Shiloh.

The Levite's Concubine

19 In those days, when there was no king in Israel, a certain Levite, residing in the remote parts of the hill country of Ephraim, took to himself a concubine from Bethlehem in Judah. 2 But his concubine became angry with[p] him, and

18.7 ver 27,28; Josh 19.47
18.8 ver 2
18.9 Num 13.30; 1 Kings 22.3
18.10 ver 7,27; Deut 8.9
18.12 Judg 13.25
18.13 ver 2
18.14 Judg 17.5
18.16 ver 11
18.17 ver 2,14
18.19 Job 21.5; Judg 17.10
18.24 Judg 17.5
18.27 ver 7,10; Josh 19.47
18.28 ver 7; 2 Sam 10.6
18.29 Josh 19.47
18.30 Judg 17.3,5; Ex 2.22
18.31 Josh 18.1
19.1 Judg 18.1

[i] Cn Compare 18.10: Meaning of Heb uncertain [j] Meaning of Heb uncertain [k] Symmachus: Heb *with anyone* [l] That is *Camp of Dan* [m] Compare 17.4, 5; 18.14: Heb *teraphim and the cast metal* [n] Cn Compare verse 7: Heb *with anyone* [o] Another reading is *son of Manasseh* [p] Gk OL: Heb *prostituted herself against*

she went away from him to her father's
house at Bethlehem in Judah, and was
there some four months. 3 Then her husband set out after her, to speak tenderly to
her and bring her back. He had with him
his servant and a couple of donkeys. When
he reached[q] her father's house, the girl's
father saw him and came with joy to meet
him. 4 His father-in-law, the girl's father,
made him stay, and he remained with him
three days; so they ate and drank, and he[r]
stayed there. 5 On the fourth day they got up
early in the morning, and he prepared to
go; but the girl's father said to his son-in-
law, "Fortify yourself with a bit of food, and
after that you may go." 6 So the two men
sat and ate and drank together; and the
girl's father said to the man, "Why not
spend the night and enjoy yourself?" 7 When
the man got up to go, his father-in-law kept
urging him until he spent the night there
again. 8 On the fifth day he got up early in
the morning to leave; and the girl's father
said, "Fortify yourself." So they lingered[s]
until the day declined, and the two of them
ate and drank.[t] 9 When the man with his
concubine and his servant got up to leave,
his father-in-law, the girl's father, said to
him, "Look, the day has worn on until it is
almost evening. Spend the night. See, the
day has drawn to a close. Spend the night
here and enjoy yourself. Tomorrow you can
get up early in the morning for your journey, and go home."

10 But the man would not spend the
night; he got up and departed, and arrived
opposite Jebus (that is, Jerusalem). He had
with him a couple of saddled donkeys, and
his concubine was with him. 11 When they
were near Jebus, the day was far spent, and
the servant said to his master, "Come now,
let us turn aside to this city of the Jebusites,
and spend the night in it." 12 But his master
said to him, "We will not turn aside into a
city of foreigners, who do not belong to the
people of Israel; but we will continue on to
Gibeah." 13 Then he said to his servant,
"Come, let us try to reach one of these
places, and spend the night at Gibeah or at
Ramah." 14 So they passed on and went
their way; and the sun went down on them
near Gibeah, which belongs to Benjamin.
15 They turned aside there, to go in and
spend the night at Gibeah. He went in and
sat down in the open square of the city, but
no one took them in to spend the night.

16 Then at evening there was an old
man coming from his work in the field. The
man was from the hill country of Ephraim,
and he was residing in Gibeah. (The people
of the place were Benjaminites.) 17 When the
old man looked up and saw the wayfarer
in the open square of the city, he said,
"Where are you going and where do you
come from?" 18 He answered him, "We are
passing from Bethlehem in Judah to the
remote parts of the hill country of Ephraim,
from which I come. I went to Bethlehem in
Judah; and I am going to my home.[u] Nobody has offered to take me in. 19 We your
servants have straw and fodder for our
donkeys, with bread and wine for me and
the woman and the young man along with
us. We need nothing more." 20 The old man
said, "Peace be to you. I will care for all
your wants; only do not spend the night in
the square." 21 So he brought him into his
house, and fed the donkeys; they washed
their feet, and ate and drank.

Gibeah's Crime

22 While they were enjoying themselves,
the men of the city, a perverse lot, surrounded the house, and started pounding
on the door. They said to the old man, the
master of the house, "Bring out the man
who came into your house, so that we may
have intercourse with him." 23 And the man,
the master of the house, went out to them
and said to them, "No, my brothers, do not
act so wickedly. Since this man is my guest,
do not do this vile thing. 24 Here are my
virgin daughter and his concubine; let me
bring them out now. Ravish them and do
whatever you want to them; but against
this man do not do such a vile thing." 25 But
the men would not listen to him. So the
man seized his concubine, and put her out
to them. They wantonly raped her, and
abused her all through the night until the
morning. And as the dawn began to break,
they let her go. 26 As morning appeared, the
woman came and fell down at the door of
the man's house where her master was,
until it was light.

27 In the morning her master got up,
opened the doors of the house, and when
he went out to go on his way, there was
his concubine lying at the door of the house,

19.3 Gen 34.3; 50.21
19.5 ver 8; Gen 18.5
19.6 ver 9,22
19.10 1 Chr 11.4,5
19.11 Judg 1.21
19.12 Heb 11.13
19.15 Heb 13.2
19.16 Ps 104.23; ver 14
19.18 Judg 18.31; 20.18
19.21 Gen 24.32,33
19.22 Gen 19.4; Deut 13.13; Rom 1.26,27
19.23 Gen 34.7; Deut 22.21; 2 Sam 13.12
19.24 Gen 19.8; Deut 21.14

[q] Gk: Heb *she brought him* [r] Compare verse 7 and Gk: Heb *they* [s] Cn: Heb *Linger* [t] Gk: Heb lacks *and drank* [u] Gk Compare 19.29. Heb *to the house of the* LORD

20.1-48 The Tribes of Israel Unite to Punish the Benjaminites. All the Israelites rallied to administer punishment to the tribe of Benjamin, from *Dan* in the far north to *Beersheba* in the southern desert. The huge number of troops assembled is said to have been *four hundred thousand foot soldiers*. They gathered at *Mizpah*, a high hill of nearly 3,000 feet five miles northwest of Jerusalem with a panoramic view of the territories of Benjamin and Judah. After hearing what happened in *Gibeah* to the Levite and the woman who was murdered, the tribes joined in a plan to punish the people of *Gibeah*. The remarkable effectiveness of the Benjaminites in their counterattack on the other tribes (20.19-28) led to the development of an *ambush* which resulted in the death of 25,100 of the tribe of Benjamin. This was seen as an act of the LORD (20.29-35). Yet even as the punishment of Benjamin was being carried out, the leaders of the other tribes inquired of the LORD, whose *ark of the covenant* was located at Bethel just north of Jerusalem (20.27-28). Efforts by Benjamin to escape into *the wilderness* led to further slaughter of members of this tribe and the destruction of their towns and their livestock (20.48).

with her hands on the threshold. 28“Get up,”
he said to her, “we are going.” But there was
no answer. Then he put her on the donkey;
and the man set out for his home. 29When
he had entered his house, he took a knife,
and grasping his concubine he cut her into
twelve pieces, limb by limb, and sent her
throughout all the territory of Israel. 30Then
he commanded the men whom he sent,
saying, “Thus shall you say to all the Israelites, ‘Has such a thing ever happened[v] since
the day that the Israelites came up from the
land of Egypt until this day? Consider it, take
counsel, and speak out.’ ”

The Other Tribes Attack Benjamin

20 Then all the Israelites came out,
from Dan to Beer-sheba, including
the land of Gilead, and the congregation
assembled in one body before the LORD at
Mizpah. 2The chiefs of all the people, of all
the tribes of Israel, presented themselves in
the assembly of the people of God, four
hundred thousand foot-soldiers bearing arms.
3(Now the Benjaminites heard that the people
of Israel had gone up to Mizpah.) And the
Israelites said, “Tell us, how did this criminal act come about?” 4The Levite, the husband of the woman who was murdered,
answered, “I came to Gibeah that belongs
to Benjamin, I and my concubine, to spend
the night. 5The lords of Gibeah rose up
against me, and surrounded the house at
night. They intended to kill me, and they
raped my concubine until she died. 6Then
I took my concubine and cut her into pieces,
and sent her throughout the whole extent
of Israel’s territory; for they have committed
a vile outrage in Israel. 7So now, you Israelites, all of you, give your advice and
counsel here.”
8 All the people got up as one, saying,
“We will not any of us go to our tents, nor
will any of us return to our houses. 9But
now this is what we will do to Gibeah: we
will go up[w] against it by lot. 10We will take
ten men of a hundred throughout all the
tribes of Israel, and a hundred of a thousand, and a thousand of ten thousand, to
bring provisions for the troops, who are
going to repay[x] Gibeah of Benjamin for all
the disgrace that they have done in Israel.”
11So all the men of Israel gathered against
the city, united as one.

12 The tribes of Israel sent men through
all the tribe of Benjamin, saying, “What
crime is this that has been committed among
you? 13Now then, hand over those scoundrels in Gibeah, so that we may put them
to death, and purge the evil from Israel.”
But the Benjaminites would not listen to
their kinsfolk, the Israelites. 14The
Benjaminites came together out of the towns
to Gibeah, to go out to battle against the
Israelites. 15On that day the Benjaminites
mustered twenty-six thousand armed men
from their towns, besides the inhabitants of
Gibeah. 16Of all this force, there were seven
hundred picked men who were left-handed;
every one could sling a stone at a hair, and
not miss. 17And the Israelites, apart from
Benjamin, mustered four hundred thousand
armed men, all of them warriors.
18 The Israelites proceeded to go up to
Bethel, where they inquired of God, “Which
of us shall go up first to battle against the
Benjaminites?” And the LORD answered,
“Judah shall go up first.”
19 Then the Israelites got up in the
morning, and encamped against Gibeah.
20The Israelites went out to battle against
Benjamin; and the Israelites drew up the
battle line against them at Gibeah. 21The
Benjaminites came out of Gibeah, and struck
down on that day twenty-two thousand of
the Israelites. 23[y]The Israelites went up and
wept before the LORD until the evening; and
they inquired of the LORD, “Shall we again
draw near to battle against our kinsfolk the
Benjaminites?” And the LORD said, “Go up
against them.” 22The Israelites took courage, and again formed the battle line in the
same place where they had formed it on the
first day.
24 So the Israelites advanced against the
Benjaminites the second day. 25Benjamin
moved out against them from Gibeah the
second day, and struck down eighteen thousand of the Israelites, all of them armed
men. 26Then all the Israelites, the whole
army, went back to Bethel and wept, sitting
there before the LORD; they fasted that day
until evening. Then they offered burnt offerings and sacrifices of well-being before the
LORD. 27And the Israelites inquired of the
LORD (for the ark of the covenant of God was
there in those days, 28and Phinehas son of
Eleazar, son of Aaron, ministered before it
in those days), saying, “Shall we go out

[v] Compare Gk: Heb 30*And all who saw it said, “Such a thing has not happened or been seen* [w] Gk: Heb lacks *we will go up* [x] Compare Gk: Meaning of Heb uncertain [y] Verses 22 and 23 are transposed

19.28 Judg 20.5
19.29 1 Sam 11.7
19.30 Judg 20.7
20.1 Judg 21.5; 1 Sam 7.5
20.4 Judg 19.15
20.5 Judg 19.22,25,26
20.6 Judg 19.29; Josh 7.15
20.7 Judg 19.30
20.12 Deut 13.14,15
20.13 Judg 19.22
20.18 ver 23,26,27; Num 27.21
20.21 ver 25
20.23 ver 18
20.25 ver 21
20.26 ver 23; Judg 21.2
20.27 Josh 18.1
20.28 Josh 24.33; Deut 18.5; Judg 7.9

20.29 Josh 8.4
20.31 Josh 8.16
20.33 Josh 8.19
20.34 Josh 8.14
20.36 Josh 8.15
20.37 Josh 8.19
20.38 Josh 8.20
20.39 ver 32
20.40 Josh 8.20
20.45 Judg 21.13
20.47 Judg 21.13
21.1 ver 7.18
21.2 Judg 20.18,26
21.4 2 Sam 24.25
21.7 ver 1

once more to battle against our kinsfolk the Benjaminites, or shall we desist?" The Lord answered, "Go up, for tomorrow I will give them into your hand."

29 So Israel stationed men in ambush around Gibeah. [30]Then the Israelites went up against the Benjaminites on the third day, and set themselves in array against Gibeah, as before. [31]When the Benjaminites went out against the army, they were drawn away from the city. As before they began to inflict casualties on the troops, along the main roads, one of which goes up to Bethel and the other to Gibeah, as well as in the open country, killing about thirty men of Israel. [32]The Benjaminites thought, "They are being routed before us, as previously." But the Israelites said, "Let us retreat and draw them away from the city toward the roads." [33]The main body of the Israelites drew back its battle line to Baal-tamar, while those Israelites who were in ambush rushed out of their place west[z] of Geba. [34]There came against Gibeah ten thousand picked men out of all Israel, and the battle was fierce. But the Benjaminites did not realize that disaster was close upon them.

35 The Lord defeated Benjamin before Israel; and the Israelites destroyed twenty-five thousand one hundred men of Benjamin that day, all of them armed.

36 Then the Benjaminites saw that they were defeated.[a]

The Israelites gave ground to Benjamin, because they trusted to the troops in ambush that they had stationed against Gibeah. [37]The troops in ambush rushed quickly upon Gibeah. Then they put the whole city to the sword. [38]Now the agreement between the main body of Israel and the men in ambush was that when they sent up a cloud of smoke out of the city [39]the main body of Israel should turn in battle. But Benjamin had begun to inflict casualties on the Israelites, killing about thirty of them; so they thought, "Surely they are defeated before us, as in the first battle." [40]But when the cloud, a column of smoke, began to rise out of the city, the Benjaminites looked behind them—and there was the whole city going up in smoke toward the sky! [41]Then the main body of Israel turned, and the Benjaminites were dismayed, for they saw that disaster was close upon them. [42]Therefore they turned away from the Israelites in the direction of the wilderness; but the battle overtook them, and those who came out of the city[b] were slaughtering them in between.[c] [43]Cutting down[d] the Benjaminites, they pursued them from Nohah[e] and trod them down as far as a place east of Gibeah. [44]Eighteen thousand Benjaminites fell, all of them courageous fighters. [45]When they turned and fled toward the wilderness to the rock of Rimmon, five thousand of them were cut down on the main roads, and they were pursued as far as Gidom, and two thousand of them were slain. [46]So all who fell that day of Benjamin were twenty-five thousand arms-bearing men, all of them courageous fighters. [47]But six hundred turned and fled toward the wilderness to the rock of Rimmon, and remained at the rock of Rimmon for four months. [48]Meanwhile, the Israelites turned back against the Benjaminites, and put them to the sword—the city, the people, the animals, and all that remained. Also the remaining towns they set on fire.

The Benjaminites Saved from Extinction

21 Now the Israelites had sworn at Mizpah, "No one of us shall give his daughter in marriage to Benjamin." [2]And the people came to Bethel, and sat there until evening before God, and they lifted up their voices and wept bitterly. [3]They said, "O Lord, the God of Israel, why has it come to pass that today there should be one tribe lacking in Israel?" [4]On the next day, the people got up early, and built an altar there, and offered burnt offerings and sacrifices of well-being. [5]Then the Israelites said, "Which of all the tribes of Israel did not come up in the assembly to the Lord?" For a solemn oath had been taken concerning whoever did not come up to the Lord to Mizpah, saying, "That one shall be put to death." [6]But the Israelites had compassion for Benjamin their kin, and said, "One tribe is cut off from Israel this day. [7]What shall we do for wives for those who are left, since we have sworn by the Lord that we will not give them any of our daughters as wives?"

8 Then they said, "Is there anyone from the tribes of Israel who did not come up to

[z] Gk Vg: Heb *in the plain* [a] This sentence is continued by verse 45. [b] Compare Vg and some Gk Mss: Heb *cities* [c] Compare Syr: Meaning of Heb uncertain [d] Gk: Heb *Surrounding* [e] Gk: Heb *pursued them at their resting place*

21.1-15 The Scheme for Saving the Benjaminites from Extinction. In order for Benjamin to survive, there had to be women who could bear children for the Benjaminite males who remained alive. Yet the other tribes had sworn to withold their daughters from *marriage to Benjamin.* It was recalled that the people of *Jabesh Gilead* (in the territory of Gad, or Gilead, east of the Jordan) had not sent troops for the punishment of Benjamin. After killing the populace of this city, except for the *four hundred young virgins* who were found there, the latter were brought to become wives bearing children to the Benjaminites (21.8-14). Another plan to provide wives for Benjamin was the proposal to steal women at Shiloh (north of Bethel) while the throngs were involved in the *yearly festival of the Lord* which was taking place there (21.15-22). The plan was carried out, and the renewal and repopulation of the land of Benjamin began, while the other tribes returned to their own districts (21.23-24). The final note in Judges (21.25) is the disorder that characterized Israel when there was no king as God's agent to implement law and order.

the LORD to Mizpah?" It turned out that no
one from Jabesh-gilead had come to the
camp, to the assembly. 9 For when the roll
was called among the people, not one of the
inhabitants of Jabesh-gilead was there. 10 So
the congregation sent twelve thousand soldiers there and commanded them, "Go, put
the inhabitants of Jabesh-gilead to the sword,
including the women and the little ones.
11 This is what you shall do; every male and
every woman that has lain with a male you
shall devote to destruction." 12 And they
found among the inhabitants of Jabesh-
gilead four hundred young virgins who had
never slept with a man and brought them
to the camp at Shiloh, which is in the land
of Canaan.

13 Then the whole congregation sent
word to the Benjaminites who were at the
rock of Rimmon, and proclaimed peace to
them. 14 Benjamin returned at that time;
and they gave them the women whom they
had saved alive of the women of Jabesh-
gilead; but they did not suffice for them.

15 The people had compassion on
Benjamin because the LORD had made a
breach in the tribes of Israel. 16 So the elders
of the congregation said, "What shall we do
for wives for those who are left, since there
are no women left in Benjamin?" 17 And
they said, "There must be heirs for the
survivors of Benjamin, in order that a tribe
may not be blotted out from Israel. 18 Yet we
cannot give any of our daughters to them
as wives." For the Israelites had sworn,
"Cursed be anyone who gives a wife to
Benjamin." 19 So they said, "Look, the yearly
festival of the LORD is taking place at Shiloh,
which is north of Bethel, on the east of the
highway that goes up from Bethel to
Shechem, and south of Lebonah." 20 And
they instructed the Benjaminites, saying,
"Go and lie in wait in the vineyards, 21 and
watch; when the young women of Shiloh
come out to dance in the dances, then come
out of the vineyards and each of you carry
off a wife for himself from the young women
of Shiloh, and go to the land of Benjamin.
22 Then if their fathers or their brothers
come to complain to us, we will say to
them, 'Be generous and allow us to have
them; because we did not capture in battle
a wife for each man. But neither did you
incur guilt by giving your daughters to
them.' " 23 The Benjaminites did so; they
took wives for each of them from the dancers whom they abducted. Then they went
and returned to their territory, and rebuilt
the towns, and lived in them. 24 So the
Israelites departed from there at that time
by tribes and families, and they went out
from there to their own territories.

25 In those days there was no king in
Israel; all the people did what was right in
their own eyes.

21.11 Num 31.17

21.13 Judg 20.47; Deut 20.10

21.15 ver 6

21.18 ver 18

21.19 Judg 18.31; 1 Sam 1.3

21.21 Ex 15.20; Judg 11.34

21.22 ver 1,18

21.23 Judg 20.48

21.25 Judg 17.6; 18.1; 19.1

RUTH

Elimelech's Family Goes to Moab
1.1 Judg 2.16 1 In the days when the judges ruled,
1.2 there was a famine in the land, and
Gen 35.19; a certain man of Bethlehem in Judah went
Judg 3.30 to live in the country of Moab, he and his
wife and two sons. [2]The name of the man
1.6 Ex 4.31 was Elimelech and the name of his wife
Naomi, and the names of his two sons were
1.8 Mahlon and Chilion; they were Ephrathites
ver 5; Ruth from Bethlehem in Judah. They went into
2.20 the country of Moab and remained there.
1.9 [3]But Elimelech, the husband of Naomi, died,
Ruth 3.1 and she was left with her two sons. [4]These
1.11 took Moabite wives; the name of the one
Deut 25.5 was Orpah and the name of the other Ruth.
When they had lived there about ten years,
1.13 [5]both Mahlon and Chilion also died, so that
Judg 2.15; Ps 32.4 the woman was left without her two sons
and her husband.

1.16 2 Kings 2.2,4,6; Ruth 2.11,12

Naomi and Her Moabite Daughters-in-Law
6 Then she started to return with her
1.18 daughters-in-law from the country of Moab,
Acts 21.14 for she had heard in the country of Moab
that the LORD had considered his people and
1.20 Ex 6.3; given them food. [7]So she set out from the
Job 6.4 place where she had been living, she and
her two daughters-in-law, and they went
1.21 on their way to go back to the land of
Job 1.21 Judah. [8]But Naomi said to her two daugh-
1.22 ters-in-law, "Go back each of you to your
Ex 9.31,32; mother's house. May the LORD deal kindly
Ruth 2.23 with you, as you have dealt with the dead
and with me. [9]The LORD grant that you may
2.1 find security, each of you in the house of
Ruth 1.2; your husband." Then she kissed them, and
3.2,12; 4.21 they wept aloud. [10]They said to her, "No,
2.2 we will return with you to your people."
ver 7; Lev [11]But Naomi said, "Turn back, my daugh-
19.9; Deut ters, why will you go with me? Do I still
24.19 have sons in my womb that they may
become your husbands? [12]Turn back, my
daughters, go your way, for I am too old
to have a husband. Even if I thought there
was hope for me, even if I should have a
husband tonight and bear sons, [13]would
you then wait until they were grown? Would
you then refrain from marrying? No, my
daughters, it has been far more bitter for me
than for you, because the hand of the LORD
has turned against me." [14]Then they wept
aloud again. Orpah kissed her mother-in-
law, but Ruth clung to her.
15 So she said, "See, your sister-in-law
has gone back to her people and to her
gods; return after your sister-in-law." [16]But
Ruth said,

"Do not press me to leave you
or to turn back from following you!
Where you go, I will go;
where you lodge, I will lodge;
your people shall be my people,
and your God my God.
17 Where you die, I will die—
there will I be buried.
May the LORD do thus and so to me,
and more as well,
if even death parts me from you!"

[18]When Naomi saw that she was determined to go with her, she said no more to
her.
19 So the two of them went on until
they came to Bethlehem. When they came
to Bethlehem, the whole town was stirred
because of them; and the women said, "Is
this Naomi?" [20]She said to them,

"Call me no longer Naomi,[a]
call me Mara,[b]
for the Almighty[c] has dealt bitterly
with me.
21 I went away full,
but the LORD has brought me back
empty;
why call me Naomi
when the LORD has dealt harshly
with[d] me,
and the Almighty[c] has brought
calamity upon me?"

22 So Naomi returned together with Ruth
the Moabite, her daughter-in-law, who came
back with her from the country of Moab.
They came to Bethlehem at the beginning
of the barley harvest.

Ruth Meets Boaz
2 Now Naomi had a kinsman on her
husband's side, a prominent rich man,
of the family of Elimelech, whose name was
Boaz. [2]And Ruth the Moabite said to Naomi,
"Let me go to the field and glean among the
ears of grain, behind someone in whose
sight I may find favor." She said to her, "Go,

[a] That is *Pleasant* [b] That is *Bitter* [c] Traditional rendering of Heb *Shaddai* [d] Or *has testified against*

See the Introductions, pp. 4, 39, and 41-42 above.

1.1-5 Introduction: The Wives of Israelites in an Alien Land.
1.1-2 *The days when judges ruled* is a general reference to the time of Israel before the monarchy was established (about 1000 BCE). *Bethlehem* was the town traditionally linked with David in the biblical tradition, both historical (1 Sam 16.4; 17.12-15; 20.6,28; 2 Sam 23.14-17) and prophetic (Mic 5.2). As a result of a *famine*, probably caused by a drought, Elimelech (whose name means, *My God is king*) with his wife, Naomi (*Delight*) and their two sons, migrated across the Jordan Valley to the well-watered plateau of *Moab*. The district from which they came is identified as Ephratha, which may refer to a tribal rather than a strictly geographical area. Traditional hostility of the Israelites toward the Moabites is attested in Deut 23.3-4; Num 25.1-4, and resulted from the latter's having refused to give aid to Israel on its journey from Egypt to Canaan in the time of Joshua.
1.3-5 After the death of their father, the sons of Elimelech married local Moabite women – *Ruth* and *Orpah* – but both men died in their youth (the Hebrew word for *sons* here means *lads*) without offspring.
1.6-22 The Women Return to the Land of Judah.
1.6-14 On learning that the famine is over in Judah, Naomi prepares to return and bids farewell to her daughters-in-law, assuming that they will remain in their native land of Moab and find *security* there through marrying and having children by Moabite husbands. Orpah *kisses* Naomi farewell, but *Ruth* refuses to leave her.
1.15-18 In spite of her mother-in-law's urging her to remain with her *people* and *her gods*, Ruth insists on accompanying Naomi. Her motivation is not only the personal relationship of devotion to her mother-in-law, but also determination to establish for herself a new identity with *your people* and new devotion to *your God*. This is to be a life-long commitment: *There will I be buried*. Archaeological finds from this period show that successive generations of a family were buried in a single tomb through the device of gathering the decomposed bones of a corpse and placing them in a jar (ossuary), thus leaving room for the burial of others. *May the LORD do thus* is part of a solemn formula of an oath, inviting God's intervention if the oath-taker's commitment is not fulfilled even though the contracting parties are parted by death. With this commitment from Ruth, Naomi agrees to have her daughter-in-law accompany her in returning to Judah.
1.19-22 The excitement of the people of Bethlehem over Naomi's return evokes from her a complaint about what *the Almighty* has done to cause her such tragedy and a proposal to change her name from *Delight* (Naomi) to *Bitter* (Mara). *Almighty* here translates El-Shaddai, which appears in ancient Near Eastern texts and inscriptions as a god of the mountains, who had already become identified with the God of Israel in the time of the patriarchs of ancient Israel (Gen 17.1; 28.3; 35.11; 48.3), and continued to be used by the authors of Job and Psalms, as well as the prophets (Isa 13.6; Joel 1.15; Ezek 1.24). The return of the women is said to have taken place at *the beginning of the barley harvest*, which indicates that fertility had returned to the land.
2.1-13 Ruth Receives Favored Treatment from Boaz.
2.1 *Kinsman* translates a term which defines one who stood in close covenant relationship with another. Thus Boaz is obligated to see that someone marries Ruth, the widow of his dead kinsman, so that there will be a son to continue the family line. This is specified as a responsibility for brothers in Deut 25.5-10, but is here seen as extending to other relatives as well.
2.2-7 Ruth carefully chooses to work as a gleaner (collecting grain left behind by the reapers) in a field that belongs to Boaz, a *rich* relative of her late husband.

my daughter." 3So she went. She came and gleaned in the field behind the reapers. As it happened, she came to the part of the field belonging to Boaz, who was of the family of Elimelech. 4Just then Boaz came from Bethlehem. He said to the reapers, "The LORD be with you." They answered, "The LORD bless you." 5Then Boaz said to his servant who was in charge of the reapers, "To whom does this young woman belong?" 6The servant who was in charge of the reapers answered, "She is the Moabite who came back with Naomi from the country of Moab. 7She said, 'Please, let me glean and gather among the sheaves behind the reapers.' So she came, and she has been on her feet from early this morning until now, without resting even for a moment."[e]

8 Then Boaz said to Ruth, "Now listen, my daughter, do not go to glean in another field or leave this one, but keep close to my young women. 9Keep your eyes on the field that is being reaped, and follow behind them. I have ordered the young men not to bother you. If you get thirsty, go to the vessels and drink from what the young men have drawn." 10Then she fell prostrate, with her face to the ground, and said to him, "Why have I found favor in your sight, that you should take notice of me, when I am a foreigner?" 11But Boaz answered her, "All that you have done for your mother-in-law since the death of your husband has been fully told me, and how you left your father and mother and your native land and came to a people that you did not know before. 12May the LORD reward you for your deeds, and may you have a full reward from the LORD, the God of Israel, under whose wings you have come for refuge!" 13Then she said, "May I continue to find favor in your sight, my lord, for you have comforted me and spoken kindly to your servant, even though I am not one of your servants."

14 At mealtime Boaz said to her, "Come here, and eat some of this bread, and dip your morsel in the sour wine." So she sat beside the reapers, and he heaped up for her some parched grain. She ate until she was satisfied, and she had some left over. 15When she got up to glean, Boaz instructed his young men, "Let her glean even among the standing sheaves, and do not reproach her. 16You must also pull out some handfuls for her from the bundles, and leave them for her to glean, and do not rebuke her."

17 So she gleaned in the field until evening. Then she beat out what she had gleaned, and it was about an ephah of barley. 18She picked it up and came into the town, and her mother-in-law saw how much she had gleaned. Then she took out and gave her what was left over after she herself had been satisfied. 19Her mother-in-law said to her, "Where did you glean today? And where have you worked? Blessed be the man who took notice of you." So she told her mother-in-law with whom she had worked, and said, "The name of the man with whom I worked today is Boaz." 20Then Naomi said to her daughter-in-law, "Blessed be he by the LORD, whose kindness has not forsaken the living or the dead!" Naomi also said to her, "The man is a relative of ours, one of our nearest kin."[f] 21Then Ruth the Moabite said, "He even said to me, 'Stay close by my servants, until they have finished all my harvest.' " 22Naomi said to Ruth, her daughter-in-law, "It is better, my daughter, that you go out with his young women, otherwise you might be bothered in another field." 23So she stayed close to the young women of Boaz, gleaning until the end of the barley and wheat harvests; and she lived with her mother-in-law.

Ruth and Boaz at the Threshing Floor

3 Naomi her mother-in-law said to her, "My daughter, I need to seek some security for you, so that it may be well with you. 2Now here is our kinsman Boaz, with whose young women you have been working. See, he is winnowing barley tonight at the threshing floor. 3Now wash and anoint yourself, and put on your best clothes and go down to the threshing floor; but do not make yourself known to the man until he has finished eating and drinking. 4When he lies down, observe the place where he lies; then, go and uncover his feet and lie down; and he will tell you what to do." 5She said to her, "All that you tell me I will do."

6 So she went down to the threshing floor and did just as her mother-in-law had instructed her. 7When Boaz had eaten and drunk, and he was in a contented mood, he went to lie down at the end of the heap of grain. Then she came stealthily and uncovered his feet, and lay down. 8At midnight the man was startled, and turned over, and there, lying at his feet, was a woman! 9He

[e] Compare Gk Vg: Meaning of Heb uncertain [f] Or *one with the right to redeem*

2.8-16 After Ruth has established a reputation for working long and hard, Boaz offers her special favors. She responds by identifying herself as a *foreigner*, and learns that her fidelity to Naomi is already known to Boaz, who asks *the LORD* to reward and protect her.
2.14-17 Boaz gives orders that Ruth is to be given special opportunities to receive food and wine, that she is not to be molested (*reproached*), and that extra grain is to be made available for her to gather. As a result, after beating out the grain at the end of the day, Ruth takes home *an ephah of barley*, which would weigh about forty pounds.
2.18-23 On sharing this grain with her *mother-in-law*, Ruth reports that it was Boaz who gave her such favored treatment as she worked. Encouraged to continue this relationship, Ruth remains in Boaz' fields until the end of both the *barley and the wheat harvests*, a period of about seven weeks (Deut 16.9-12).
3.1-18 Ruth Offers Herself to Boaz.
3.1-5 Naomi counsels Ruth to find the *security* of a marital union and a home with Boaz, who stands in covenant relationship with her dead husband's family and therefore with her. Ruth is to approach him as he sleeps and make herself available sexually (*uncover his feet*). To this Ruth agrees.
3.6-13 Startled to waken and find Ruth lying beside him, he asks what she wants. Her reply is to remind him of his *next-of-kin* obligation (Lev 25.25-49) to his dead relative, including begetting a child through her (Deut 25.5-10). Insisting that he wants to do the right thing, he promises to invite someone even *more closely related* than he to fulfill this covenant obligation. She is recognized to be *worthy* by *all the assembly of my people*, which means the responsible authorities in the community.

2.4 Ps 129.7,8; Lk 1.28
2.6 Ruth 1.22
2.10 1 Sam 25.23
2.11 Ruth 1.14,16,17
2.12 1 Sam 24.19; Ps 17.8; Ruth 1.16
2.14 ver 18
2.18 ver 14
2.19 ver 10
2.20 Ruth 3.10; Prov 17.17; Ruth 3.9; 4.6
2.23 Deut 16.9
3.1 Ruth 1.9
3.2 Deut 25.5-10; Ruth 2.8
3.3 2 Sam 14.2
3.7 Judg 19.6,9,22; 2 Sam 13.28
3.9 ver 12; Ruth 2.20

3.11 Prov 12.4
3.12 ver 9; Ruth 4.1
3.13 Ruth 4.5
3.18 Ps 37.3-5
4.1 Ruth 3.12
4.3 Lev 25.25
4.4 Jer 32.7,8; Lev 25.25
4.5 Deut 25.5,6
4.6 Ruth 3.12,13
4.7 Deut 25.7,9
4.10 Deut 25.6
4.11 Ps 127.3
4.12 ver 18; Gen 38.29
4.13 Ruth 3.11; Gen 29.31; 33.5
4.14 Lk 1.58
4.15 Ruth 1.16,17; 2.11,12

said, "Who are you?" And she answered, "I
am Ruth, your servant; spread your cloak
over your servant, for you are next-of-kin."[g]
10 He said, "May you be blessed by the LORD,
my daughter; this last instance of your
loyalty is better than the first; you have not
gone after young men, whether poor or
rich. 11 And now, my daughter, do not be
afraid, I will do for you all that you ask, for
all the assembly of my people know that
you are a worthy woman. 12 But now, though
it is true that I am a near kinsman, there
is another kinsman more closely related
than I. 13 Remain this night, and in the
morning, if he will act as next-of-kin[g] for
you, good; let him do it. If he is not willing
to act as next-of-kin[g] for you, then, as the
LORD lives, I will act as next-of-kin[g] for you.
Lie down until the morning."
14 So she lay at his feet until morning,
but got up before one person could recognize another; for he said, "It must not be
known that the woman came to the threshing floor." 15 Then he said, "Bring the cloak
you are wearing and hold it out." So she
held it, and he measured out six measures
of barley, and put it on her back; then he
went into the city. 16 She came to her mother-
in-law, who said, "How did things go with
you,[h] my daughter?" Then she told her all
that the man had done for her, 17 saying,
"He gave me these six measures of barley,
for he said, 'Do not go back to your mother-
in-law empty-handed.' " 18 She replied, "Wait,
my daughter, until you learn how the matter
turns out, for the man will not rest, but will
settle the matter today."

The Marriage of Boaz and Ruth

4 No sooner had Boaz gone up to the
gate and sat down there than the
next-of-kin,[g] of whom Boaz had spoken,
came passing by. So Boaz said, "Come over,
friend; sit down here." And he went over
and sat down. 2 Then Boaz took ten men of
the elders of the city, and said, "Sit down
here"; so they sat down. 3 He then said to
the next-of-kin,[g] "Naomi, who has come
back from the country of Moab, is selling
the parcel of land that belonged to our
kinsman Elimelech. 4 So I thought I would
tell you of it, and say: Buy it in the presence
of those sitting here, and in the presence of
the elders of my people. If you will redeem
it, redeem it; but if you will not, tell me, so
that I may know; for there is no one prior
to you to redeem it, and I come after you."
So he said, "I will redeem it." 5 Then Boaz
said, "The day you acquire the field from
the hand of Naomi, you are also acquiring
Ruth[i] the Moabite, the widow of the dead
man, to maintain the dead man's name on
his inheritance." 6 At this, the next-of-kin[g]
said, "I cannot redeem it for myself without
damaging my own inheritance. Take my
right of redemption yourself, for I cannot
redeem it."
7 Now this was the custom in former
times in Israel concerning redeeming and
exchanging: to confirm a transaction, the
one took off a sandal and gave it to the
other; this was the manner of attesting in
Israel. 8 So when the next-of-kin[g] said to
Boaz, "Acquire it for yourself," he took off
his sandal. 9 Then Boaz said to the elders
and all the people, "Today you are witnesses that I have acquired from the hand
of Naomi all that belonged to Elimelech and
all that belonged to Chilion and Mahlon. 10 I
have also acquired Ruth the Moabite, the
wife of Mahlon, to be my wife, to maintain
the dead man's name on his inheritance, in
order that the name of the dead may not
be cut off from his kindred and from the
gate of his native place; today you are
witnesses." 11 Then all the people who were
at the gate, along with the elders, said, "We
are witnesses. May the LORD make the woman
who is coming into your house like Rachel
and Leah, who together built up the house
of Israel. May you produce children in
Ephrathah and bestow a name in Bethlehem; 12 and, through the children that the
LORD will give you by this young woman,
may your house be like the house of Perez,
whom Tamar bore to Judah."

The Genealogy of David

13 So Boaz took Ruth and she became
his wife. When they came together, the
LORD made her conceive, and she bore a
son. 14 Then the women said to Naomi,
"Blessed be the LORD, who has not left you
this day without next-of-kin;[g] and may his
name be renowned in Israel! 15 He shall be
to you a restorer of life and a nourisher of
your old age; for your daughter-in-law who
loves you, who is more to you than seven
sons, has borne him." 16 Then Naomi took
the child and laid him in her bosom, and

[g] Or *one with the right to redeem* [h] Or "*Who are you,* [i] OL Vg: Heb *from the hand of Naomi and from Ruth*

3.14-18 Concerned to keep secret that they have spent the night together, Boaz instructs Ruth to leave before daylight. As a token of his intention to fulfill his next-of-kin obligation to the LORD and to the deceased, he gives her a huge supply of grain to take back to her mother-in-law. This act seems to be done in keeping with the law which requires that those who take on obligations to persons or property must provide an offering of money or goods as evidence before the LORD that the responsibility will be fulfilled completely in the future (Lev 27.1-33).

4.1-12 Boaz Marries Ruth.
4.1-6 *The gate* to which Boaz goes is a typical feature of towns in ancient Israel: a central open space, adjacent to the main city gate, where public discussion and official decisions by the leaders of the community (*elders*) took place. After accosting *the next-of-kin* and assembling a sufficient number of the elders (*ten*) to assure the legality and public nature of the transaction, Boaz invites the closer relative of Ruth's late husband to buy the land from Naomi. In addition to assuring the retaining of property within the tribal group, this procedure required the purchaser to marry the *widow* and thereby guarantee continuity of the family line. The proposal is declined, on the ground that such a purchase would jeopardize his present *inheritance* – for reasons which are not stated. Then Boaz is urged to complete the transaction himself.
4.7-12 Although details are not certain, it is probable that the act by which this close relative gives his *sandal* to Boaz is a public sign of the transfer of responsibility for lands and offspring to someone else. That meaning is implied in Boaz' call to the *witnesses*, which makes official his acquisition of the land and of Ruth. Justification for these acts is provided by his promise to have a son by her in order to *maintain the dead man's name* and his place of honor within the community (*the gate of his native place*). The prayer is that, as happened through the wives of Jacob, *Rachel and Leah* (Gen 29-30), this marriage will help to *build up the house of Israel*, and bring honor to Ephratha and Bethlehem. A second comparison with this impending marriage is that of the fruitful union of Perez, from the tribe of Judah, who was the ancestor of David (Gen 38.29; 46.10-12; 1 Chr 2.4-5).
4.13-21 Ruth Bears a Son, the Grandfather of David. It is through fulfillment of the obligations of Israelite law to assure continuity of property and offspring within the tribe that this union is consummated. Thus what was to be the royal line of Judah is assured when Ruth gives birth to a son, *Obed* (*worshiper*), whose son, Jesse, was to be the father of David. It is the *LORD's* action which *made* Ruth *conceive*, thereby demonstrating that even a non-Israelite who was faithful to God and his law for his people could be the instrument through whom God's purpose is fulfilled.

became his nurse. [17]The women of the
neighborhood gave him a name, saying, "A
son has been born to Naomi." They named
him Obed; he became the father of Jesse, the
father of David.
18 Now these are the descendants of
Perez: Perez became the father of Hezron,
[19]Hezron of Ram, Ram of Amminadab,
[20]Amminadab of Nahshon, Nahshon of
Salmon, [21]Salmon of Boaz, Boaz of Obed,
[22]Obed of Jesse, and Jesse of David.

4.18 Mt 1.3-6

1 SAMUEL

See the Introductions, pp. 3, 38, and 42-43 above.

Samuel's Birth and Dedication

1 There was a certain man of Ramathaim, a Zuphite[a] from the hill country of Ephraim, whose name was Elkanah
son of Jeroham son of Elihu son of Tohu son
of Zuph, an Ephraimite. [2]He had two wives;
the name of the one was Hannah, and the
name of the other Peninnah. Peninnah had
children, but Hannah had no children.
3 Now this man used to go up year by
year from his town to worship and to sacrifice to the LORD of hosts at Shiloh, where
the two sons of Eli, Hophni and Phinehas,
were priests of the LORD. [4]On the day when
Elkanah sacrificed, he would give portions
to his wife Peninnah and to all her sons and
daughters; [5]but to Hannah he gave a double
portion,[b] because he loved her, though the
LORD had closed her womb. [6]Her rival used
to provoke her severely, to irritate her,
because the LORD had closed her womb. [7]So
it went on year by year; as often as she
went up to the house of the LORD, she used
to provoke her. Therefore Hannah wept and
would not eat. [8]Her husband Elkanah said
to her, "Hannah, why do you weep? Why
do you not eat? Why is your heart sad? Am
I not more to you than ten sons?"
9 After they had eaten and drunk at
Shiloh, Hannah rose and presented herself
before the LORD.[c] Now Eli the priest was
sitting on the seat beside the doorpost of the
temple of the LORD. [10]She was deeply distressed and prayed to the LORD, and wept
bitterly. [11]She made this vow: "O LORD of
hosts, if only you will look on the misery
of your servant, and remember me, and not
forget your servant, but will give to your
servant a male child, then I will set him
before you as a nazirite[d] until the day of his
death. He shall drink neither wine nor
intoxicants,[e] and no razor shall touch his
head."
12 As she continued praying before the
LORD, Eli observed her mouth. [13]Hannah
was praying silently; only her lips moved,
but her voice was not heard; therefore Eli
thought she was drunk. [14]So Eli said to her,
"How long will you make a drunken spectacle of yourself? Put away your wine."
[15]But Hannah answered, "No, my lord, I am
a woman deeply troubled; I have drunk
neither wine nor strong drink, but I have
been pouring out my soul before the LORD.
[16]Do not regard your servant as a worthless
woman, for I have been speaking out of my
great anxiety and vexation all this time."
[17]Then Eli answered, "Go in peace; the God
of Israel grant the petition you have made
to him." [18]And she said, "Let your servant
find favor in your sight." Then the woman
went to her quarters,[f] ate and drank with
her husband,[g] and her countenance was
sad no longer.[h]
19 They rose early in the morning and
worshiped before the LORD; then they went
back to their house at Ramah. Elkanah
knew his wife Hannah, and the LORD
remembered her. [20]In due time Hannah
conceived and bore a son. She named him
Samuel, for she said, "I have asked him of
the LORD."

[a] Compare Gk and 1 Chr 6.35–36: Heb *Ramathaim-zophim* [b] Syr: Meaning of Heb uncertain [c] Gk: Heb lacks *and presented herself before the LORD* [d] That is *one separated* or *one consecrated* [e] Cn Compare Gk Q Ms 1.22: MT *then I will give him to the LORD all the days of his life* [f] Gk: Heb *went her way* [g] Gk: Heb lacks *and drank with her husband* [h] Gk: Meaning of Heb uncertain

1.1-7.17 The Early Years of Samuel.
1.1 *Ramathaim* is on the western edge of *the hill country of Ephraim, northwest of Jerusalem.* Elkanah, who lived there, had two sons, but none by his favorite wife, *Hannah.* The term *Zuphite* at times refers to a family group, but later it designates a district in the territory of Ephraim (see 9.5).
1.3 In addition to shrines for the tribes of Israel at Shechem, Bethel and Mizpah, the one at *Shiloh,* about 25 miles north of Jerusalem in the tribal territory of Ephraim, was the place where the sacred box, the ark of God, was kept (3.3). There God was honored as *the LORD of Hosts,* or "armies," which could refer to God's control of the armies of Israel or to the angelic armies which, though unseen, were thought to achieve God's purposes in the world. *Eli* was a priest at Shiloh, along with his two sons, *Hophni and Phineas.*
1.4-8 Even the *double portion* of Elkanah's sacrifice that he gave to *Hannah* and his special words about their relationship could not compensate her for the lack of a child.
1.9-17 Hannah's Plea and Yahweh's Promise.
1.9 Hannah approached the LORD through *Eli the priest.* His location *beside the doorpost of the temple of the LORD* at Shiloh is additional evidence that there were several sanctuaries for the tribes of Israel before the temple of the LORD was built in Jerusalem by Solomon (1 Kings 6.1).
1.11 The complete dedication to the LORD of the longed-for *male child* was to be made publicly evident by his lifelong identity as a *nazirite* (Num 6).
1.12-18 Hannah's earnest struggle in silent prayer led Eli initially to think she was drunk. But her evident devotion to God led Eli to promise her that her *petition* would be answered by the LORD, and she returned to her husband *sad no longer.*
1.19-20 The son conceived and borne by Hannah is named *Samuel,* which means literally "Name of God," or "His name is God," but it is here interpreted as *"I have asked him of the LORD."*

1.1 Josh 17.7,18; 1 Chr 6.27
1.2 Deut 21.15-17; Lk 2.36
1.3 Ex 34.23; Deut 12.5; Josh 18.1
1.4 Deut 12.17
1.5 Gen 16.1; 30.2
1.6 Job 24.21
1.8 Ruth 4.15
1.9 1 Sam 3.3
1.11 Gen 28.20; 29.32; Num 6.5; Judg 13.5
1.13 Gen 24.42-45
1.14 Acts 2.4,13
1.15 Ps 62.8
1.17 Judg 18.6; 1 Sam 25.35; Mk 5.34
1.18 Ruth 2.13; Eccl 9.7
1.19 Gen 4.1; 30.22
1.20 Gen 41.51,52; Ex 2.10,22

21 The man Elkanah and all his household went up to offer to the LORD the yearly
sacrifice, and to pay his vow. 22 But Hannah
did not go up, for she said to her husband,
"As soon as the child is weaned, I will bring
him, that he may appear in the presence of
the LORD, and remain there forever; I will
offer him as a nazirite[i] for all time."[j] 23 Her
husband Elkanah said to her, "Do what
seems best to you, wait until you have
weaned him; only—may the LORD establish
his word."[k] So the woman remained and
nursed her son, until she weaned him.
24 When she had weaned him, she took him
up with her, along with a three-year-old
bull,[l] an ephah of flour, and a skin of wine.
She brought him to the house of the LORD
at Shiloh; and the child was young. 25 Then
they slaughtered the bull, and they brought
the child to Eli. 26 And she said, "Oh, my
lord! As you live, my lord, I am the woman
who was standing here in your presence,
praying to the LORD. 27 For this child I prayed;
and the LORD has granted me the petition
that I made to him. 28 Therefore I have lent
him to the LORD; as long as he lives, he is
given to the LORD."

She left him there for[m] the LORD.

Hannah's Prayer

2 Hannah prayed and said,
"My heart exults in the LORD;
my strength is exalted in my God.[n]
My mouth derides my enemies,
because I rejoice in my[o] victory.

2 "There is no Holy One like the LORD,
no one besides you;
there is no Rock like our God.
3 Talk no more so very proudly,
let not arrogance come from your mouth;
for the LORD is a God of knowledge,
and by him actions are weighed.
4 The bows of the mighty are broken,
but the feeble gird on strength.
5 Those who were full have hired themselves out for bread,
but those who were hungry are fat with spoil.
The barren has borne seven,
but she who has many children is forlorn.
6 The LORD kills and brings to life;
he brings down to Sheol and raises up.
7 The LORD makes poor and makes rich;
he brings low, he also exalts.
8 He raises up the poor from the dust;
he lifts the needy from the ash heap,
to make them sit with princes
and inherit a seat of honor.[p]
For the pillars of the earth are the LORD's,
and on them he has set the world.

9 "He will guard the feet of his faithful ones,
but the wicked shall be cut off in darkness;
for not by might does one prevail.
10 The LORD! His adversaries shall be shattered;
the Most High[q] will thunder in heaven.
The LORD will judge the ends of the earth;
he will give strength to his king,
and exalt the power of his anointed."

Eli's Wicked Sons

11 Then Elkanah went home to Ramah,
while the boy remained to minister to the
LORD, in the presence of the priest Eli.

12 Now the sons of Eli were scoundrels;
they had no regard for the LORD 13 or for the
duties of the priests to the people. When
anyone offered sacrifice, the priest's servant
would come, while the meat was boiling,
with a three-pronged fork in his hand, 14 and
he would thrust it into the pan, or kettle,
or caldron, or pot; all that the fork brought
up the priest would take for himself.[r] This
is what they did at Shiloh to all the Israelites who came there. 15 Moreover, before
the fat was burned, the priest's servant
would come and say to the one who was
sacrificing, "Give meat for the priest to roast;
for he will not accept boiled meat from you,
but only raw." 16 And if the man said to
him, "Let them burn the fat first, and then
take whatever you wish," he would say,
"No, you must give it now; if not, I will take
it by force." 17 Thus the sin of the young

[i] That is *one separated* or *one consecrated* [j] Cn Compare Q Ms: MT lacks *I will offer him as a nazirite for all time* [k] MT: Q Ms Gk Compare Syr *that which goes out of your mouth* [l] Q Ms Gk Syr: MT *three bulls* [m] Gk (Compare Q Ms) and Gk at 2.11: MT *And he* (that is, Elkanah) *worshiped there before* [n] Gk: Heb *the LORD* [o] Q Ms: MT *your* [p] Gk (Compare Q Ms) adds *He grants the vow of the one who vows, and blesses the years of the just* [q] Cn Heb *against him he* [r] Gk Syr Vg: Heb *with it*

1.21 ver 3
1.22 Lk 2.22; 1 Sam 2.11,18
1.23 Num 30.7; ver 17
1.24 Deut 12.5; Josh 18.1
1.25 Lev 1.5; Lk 2.22
1.26 2 Kings 2.2
1.27 ver 11-13
1.28 ver 11,22
2.1 Lk 1.46-55; Ps 89.17; Isa 12.2,3
2.2 Lev 19.2; 2 Sam 22.32; Deut 32.30,31
2.3 Prov 8.13; 1 Sam 16.7; 1 Kings 8.39; Prov 16.2; 24.12
2.4 Ps 76.3
2.5 Ps 113.9; Jer 15.9
2.6 Deut 32.39; Isa 26.19
2.7 Deut 8.17,18; Job 5.11; Ps 75.6,7
2.8 Ps 113.7,8; Job 36.7; 38.4,5
2.9 Ps 91.11,12; Mt 8.12; Ps 33.16,17
2.10 Ps 2.9; 18.13; 96.13; 21.1,7; 89.24
2.11 1 Sam 3.1
2.12 Jer 2.8; 9.3,6
2.13 Lev 7.29-34
2.15 Lev 3.3,4
2.17 Mal 2.7-9

1.21-28 Samuel was presented, or *lent to the LORD,* and was thus dedicated to the LORD for the whole of his life. The Hebrew word for *ask* [sa'al] and a variant form meaning *lend* [sa'ul] are both close to the name of Israel's first king, *Saul,* whom Samuel anointed for his role (10.1).

2.1-10 Hannah's Hymn of Praise to the LORD. This hymn celebrates God's triumph over his enemies and the reversal of fortune for the barren, the poor and the oppressed. There is assurance of God's care for the faithful, for the defeat of his enemies and for the triumph of his justice throughout the earth, as well as for his grant of power to the ruler of his people. This poem served as a model for the hymn of Mary prior to the birth of John the Baptist and Jesus (Lk 1.46-55). The designation of God's agent as *the anointed* was used of both priests and kings (9.16; 10.1; 24.6; 2 Sam 1.14; 19.21).

2.11-17 The wickedness of *the sons of Eli* lies in their appropriating for themselves portions of the priestly offerings in defiance of the detailed regulations about proper priestly procedure and the designating of the beneficiaries of these sacrifices in Lev 7.11-18 and Deut 18.

2.18-21 Samuel's juvenile role in the sanctuary included blessing his parents on the occasion of their annual visit to offer *the yearly sacrifice*, which may be the Day of Atonement described in Lev 16. Elsewhere in the law, three visits each year were required of all males, as in Ex 23.14; 34.23. Samuel's childhood took place, not in the context of home and family, but *in the presence of the LORD*.
2.22-34 Eli is warned of the judgment of God that is to fall on his sons. The sons' sexual exploitation of the women attendants at the sanctuary and their demand for the best of the meat offered in sacrifice contrasts with Samuel's continued growth in stature and in favor with the LORD and the people. These qualities are assigned to Jesus in Lk 2.52. The message from *a man of God* is that these sons' betrayal of their trust as priests will bring down on them the judgment of the God who brought Israel out of Egypt.
2.35-36 But there will remain *a faithful priest* – Samuel – who will serve God *forever*. His role will be carried out in a permanent sanctuary, *a sure house*, and in the presence of the king of God's people: *my anointed one*. Surviving members of the families of Eli's sons will turn to Samuel for bits of money and food.
3.1-4.1 Samuel Called and Commissioned by God as a Prophet.
3.1-9 Samuel's *ministering to the LORD* involved some unspecified forms of service in the sanctuary, which also served as his residence. Neither oracles (*word of the LORD*) nor visions were common in this period, so that both Samuel and Eli had difficulty realizing that it was God who was seeking to communicate with Samuel.

men was very great in the sight of the LORD; for they treated the offerings of the LORD with contempt.

The Child Samuel at Shiloh

18 Samuel was ministering before the LORD, a boy wearing a linen ephod. [19]His mother used to make for him a little robe and take it to him each year, when she went up with her husband to offer the yearly sacrifice. [20]Then Eli would bless Elkanah and his wife, and say, "May the LORD repay[s] you with children by this woman for the gift that she made to[t] the LORD"; and then they would return to their home.

21 And[u] the LORD took note of Hannah; she conceived and bore three sons and two daughters. And the boy Samuel grew up in the presence of the LORD.

Prophecy against Eli's Household

22 Now Eli was very old. He heard all that his sons were doing to all Israel, and how they lay with the women who served at the entrance to the tent of meeting. [23]He said to them, "Why do you do such things? For I hear of your evil dealings from all these people. [24]No, my sons; it is not a good report that I hear the people of the LORD spreading abroad. [25]If one person sins against another, someone can intercede for the sinner with the LORD;[v] but if someone sins against the LORD, who can make intercession?" But they would not listen to the voice of their father; for it was the will of the LORD to kill them.

26 Now the boy Samuel continued to grow both in stature and in favor with the LORD and with the people.

27 A man of God came to Eli and said to him, "Thus the LORD has said, 'I revealed[w] myself to the family of your ancestor in Egypt when they were slaves[x] to the house of Pharaoh. [28]I chose him out of all the tribes of Israel to be my priest, to go up to my altar, to offer incense, to wear an ephod before me; and I gave to the family of your ancestor all my offerings by fire from the people of Israel. [29]Why then look with greedy eye[y] at my sacrifices and my offerings that I commanded, and honor your sons more than me by fattening yourselves on the choicest parts of every offering of my people Israel?' [30]Therefore the LORD the God of Israel declares: 'I promised that your family and the family of your ancestor should go in and out before me forever'; but now the LORD declares: 'Far be it from me; for those who honor me I will honor, and those who despise me shall be treated with contempt. [31]See, a time is coming when I will cut off your strength and the strength of your ancestor's family, so that no one in your family will live to old age. [32]Then in distress you will look with greedy eye[z] on all the prosperity that shall be bestowed upon Israel; and no one in your family shall ever live to old age. [33]The only one of you whom I shall not cut off from my altar shall be spared to weep out his[a] eyes and grieve his[b] heart; all the members of your household shall die by the sword.[c] [34]The fate of your two sons, Hophni and Phinehas, shall be the sign to you—both of them shall die on the same day. [35]I will raise up for myself a faithful priest, who shall do according to what is in my heart and in my mind. I will build him a sure house, and he shall go in and out before my anointed one forever. [36]Everyone who is left in your family shall come to implore him for a piece of silver or a loaf of bread, and shall say, Please put me in one of the priest's places, that I may eat a morsel of bread.' "

Samuel's Calling and Prophetic Activity

3 Now the boy Samuel was ministering to the LORD under Eli. The word of the LORD was rare in those days; visions were not widespread.

2 At that time Eli, whose eyesight had begun to grow dim so that he could not see, was lying down in his room; [3]the lamp of God had not yet gone out, and Samuel was lying down in the temple of the LORD, where the ark of God was. [4]Then the LORD called, "Samuel! Samuel!"[d] and he said, "Here I am!" [5]and ran to Eli, and said, "Here I am, for you called me." But he said, "I did not call; lie down again." So he went and lay down. [6]The LORD called again, "Samuel!" Samuel got up and went to Eli, and said, "Here I am, for you called me." But he said,

[s] Q Ms Gk: MT *give* [t] Q Ms Gk: MT *for the petition that she asked of* [u] Q Ms Gk: MT *When* [v] Gk Compare Q Ms: MT *another, God will mediate for him* [w] Gk Tg Syr: Heb *Did I reveal* [x] Q Ms Gk: MT lacks *slaves* [y] Q Ms Gk: MT *then kick* [z] Q Ms Gk: MT *will kick* [a] Q Ms Gk: MT *your* [b] Q Ms Gk: Heb *your* [c] Q Ms See Gk: MT *die like mortals* [d] Q Ms Gk See 3.10: MT *the LORD called Samuel*

2.18 ver 11.28; 1 Sam 3.1
2.19 1 Sam 1.3
2.20 Lk 2.34; 1 Sam 1.11,27,28
2.21 Gen 21.1; ver 26; 1 Sam 3.19; Lk 2.40
2.22 Ex 38.8
2.24 1 Kings 15.26
2.25 Deut 1.17; Num 15.30; Josh 11.20
2.26 ver 21; Lk 2.52
2.27 1 Kings 13.1; Ex 4.14-16
2.28 Ex 28.1-4; Lev 8.7,8
2.29 ver 13-17; Deut 12.5; Mt 10.37
2.30 Ex 29.9; Ps 91.14; Mal 2.9
2.31 1 Sam 4.11-18; 22.17-20
2.32 1 Kings 2.26,27; Zech 8.4
2.34 1 Kings 13.3; 1 Sam 4.11
2.35 1 Kings 2.35; 2 Sam 7.11,27; 1 Kings 11.38; 1 Sam 12.3; 16.13
2.36 1 Kings 2.27
3.1 1 Sam 2.11,18; Am 8.11
3.2 1 Sam 4.15
3.3 Lev 24.2-4
3.4 Isa 6.8

"I did not call, my son; lie down again." 7 Now Samuel did not yet know the LORD, and the word of the LORD had not yet been revealed to him. 8 The LORD called Samuel again, a third time. And he got up and went to Eli, and said, "Here I am, for you called me." Then Eli perceived that the LORD was calling the boy. 9 Therefore Eli said to Samuel, "Go, lie down; and if he calls you, you shall say, 'Speak, LORD, for your servant is listening.' " So Samuel went and lay down in his place.

10 Now the LORD came and stood there, calling as before, "Samuel! Samuel!" And Samuel said, "Speak, for your servant is listening." 11 Then the LORD said to Samuel, "See, I am about to do something in Israel that will make both ears of anyone who hears of it tingle. 12 On that day I will fulfill against Eli all that I have spoken concerning his house, from beginning to end. 13 For I have told him that I am about to punish his house forever, for the iniquity that he knew, because his sons were blaspheming God,[e] and he did not restrain them. 14 Therefore I swear to the house of Eli that the iniquity of Eli's house shall not be expiated by sacrifice or offering forever."

15 Samuel lay there until morning; then he opened the doors of the house of the LORD. Samuel was afraid to tell the vision to Eli. 16 But Eli called Samuel and said, "Samuel, my son." He said, "Here I am." 17 Eli said, "What was it that he told you? Do not hide it from me. May God do so to you and more also, if you hide anything from me of all that he told you." 18 So Samuel told him everything and hid nothing from him. Then he said, "It is the LORD; let him do what seems good to him."

19 As Samuel grew up, the LORD was with him and let none of his words fall to the ground. 20 And all Israel from Dan to Beer-sheba knew that Samuel was a trustworthy prophet of the LORD. 21 The LORD continued to appear at Shiloh, for the LORD revealed himself to Samuel at Shiloh by the word of the LORD.

4 1 And the word of Samuel came to all Israel.

The Ark of God Captured

In those days the Philistines mustered for war against Israel,[f] and Israel went out to battle against them;[g] they encamped at Ebenezer, and the Philistines encamped at Aphek. 2 The Philistines drew up in line against Israel, and when the battle was joined,[h] Israel was defeated by the Philistines, who killed about four thousand men on the field of battle. 3 When the troops came to the camp, the elders of Israel said, "Why has the LORD put us to rout today before the Philistines? Let us bring the ark of the covenant of the LORD here from Shiloh, so that he may come among us and save us from the power of our enemies." 4 So the people sent to Shiloh, and brought from there the ark of the covenant of the LORD of hosts, who is enthroned on the cherubim. The two sons of Eli, Hophni and Phinehas, were there with the ark of the covenant of God.

5 When the ark of the covenant of the LORD came into the camp, all Israel gave a mighty shout, so that the earth resounded. 6 When the Philistines heard the noise of the shouting, they said, "What does this great shouting in the camp of the Hebrews mean?" When they learned that the ark of the LORD had come to the camp, 7 the Philistines were afraid; for they said, "Gods have[i] come into the camp." They also said, "Woe to us! For nothing like this has happened before. 8 Woe to us! Who can deliver us from the power of these mighty gods? These are the gods who struck the Egyptians with every sort of plague in the wilderness. 9 Take courage, and be men, O Philistines, in order not to become slaves to the Hebrews as they have been to you; be men and fight."

10 So the Philistines fought; Israel was defeated, and they fled, everyone to his home. There was a very great slaughter, for there fell of Israel thirty thousand foot soldiers. 11 The ark of God was captured; and the two sons of Eli, Hophni and Phinehas, died.

Death of Eli

12 A man of Benjamin ran from the battle line, and came to Shiloh the same day, with his clothes torn and with earth upon his head. 13 When he arrived, Eli was sitting upon his seat by the road watching, for his heart trembled for the ark of God. When the man came into the city and told the news, all the city cried out. 14 When Eli

[e] Another reading is *for themselves* [f] Gk: Heb lacks *In those days the Philistines mustered for war against Israel* [g] Gk: Heb *against the Philistines* [h] Meaning of Heb uncertain [i] Or *A god has*

3.7 Acts 19.2
3.11 2 Kings 21.12; Jer 19.3
3.12 1 Sam 2.30-36
3.13 1 Sam 2.12,17,22, 29-31
3.14 Lev 15.30,31; Isa 22.14
3.17 Ruth 1.17; 2 Sam 3.35
3.18 Job 2.10; Isa 39.8
3.19 1 Sam 2.21; Gen 21.22; 39.2; 1 Sam 9.6
3.20 Judg 20.1
3.21 ver 10
4.1 1 Sam 7.12
4.3 Josh 7.7,8; Num 10.35
4.4 2 Sam 6.2; Ex 25.18,22
4.5 Josh 6.5,20
4.6 Ex 15.14
4.9 1 Cor 16.13; Judg 13.1
4.10 ver 2; Deut 28.25; 2 Sam 18.17; 2 Kings 14.12
4.11 1 Sam 2.34; Ps 78.56-64
4.12 Josh 7.6; 2 Sam 1.2; Neh 9.1
4.13 ver 18; 1 Sam 1.9

3.10-18 Because of Eli's sons' wickedness and his failure to *restrain them*, they are all to fall under divine judgment *forever*. Samuel's first task in his prophetic role was to convey this information to the aged Eli, who accepted it as from the LORD.
3.19-4.1 Samuel's prophetic indictments and predictions were all supported by *the LORD*, with the result that he was recognized throughout *all Israel* as God's messenger and agent.
4.2-6.12 The Ark of God and the Philistines.
4.2-3 The Philistines, whose cultural links were with Indo-European peoples living in what is now Greece or Turkey, were repulsed on attempting to invade Egypt, but in the twelfth century BCE they settled on the southern coast of the land that Israel was seeking to occupy. Philistine technical and military equipment was superior to that of Israel, with the result that the army of Israel was defeated.
4.4-11 *The elders of Israel* decided to get God's direct help by bringing into the battle area *the ark of the covenant of the LORD*, in which Moses had been instructed to place the tablets on which the law was inscribed (Ex 25.16,21; 40.20; Deut 10.5). On top of the sacred box were *the cherubim*, which were images of winged animals with human faces (found widely in ancient Near Eastern art) that were set up to guard the presence of the gods and kings. This box had accompanied the Israelites on their long, conflict-filled journey from Egypt through the land east of Jordan into the promised land (Josh 3). Although *the Philistines were afraid* when they heard that the *gods have come into the camp*, they defeated the Israelites and captured *the ark of God*.
4.12-22 Reports of the defeat of Israel and the capture of the ark of God brought death by shock to Eli and his *pregnant* daughter-in-law, who before her death named her son *Ichabod*, which means that, with the disappearance of the sacred box, *the glory [of the God of Israel] has departed* from Israel's midst.

5.1-12 The Ark in the Land of the Philistines. Captured east of Jaffa at *Ebenezer*, the ark was taken to a major commercial city of the Philistines near the coast, *Ashdod*, where it was placed in the temple of their god of the grain, *Dagon*. After the image of the Philistines' god was knocked down and broken, and *tumors* came on the people, the authorities moved the ark to cities farther east in the coastal hills nearer the territory of Israel: first to *Gath*, and then to *Ekron*. Many of the local inhabitants were stricken with tumors, and pleaded with the leaders to send the ark back to the Israelites.

6.1-7.2 The Ark Returned to Israel. By sending along *five gold tumors and five gold mice* when the ark was returned to Israel, the Philistines believed God's wrath would be appeased. The combining of mice and tumors may indicate that the disease that struck the Philistines was bubonic plague. *Milch cows* drew the cart on which the ark rested as it made its way up into the Israelite hills to the east, to *Beth Shemesh*, where many Levites lived. They removed the gold objects from the ark, and the people offered the *sacrifices...to the LORD* which were deemed appropriate for bringing the ark back into the worship life of Israel. Five, the number of the *gold tumors*, matched the number of cities that constituted the Philistine confederacy and its five *lords*.

heard the sound of the outcry, he said, "What is this uproar?" Then the man came quickly and told Eli. [15]Now Eli was ninety-eight years old and his eyes were set, so that he could not see. [16]The man said to Eli, "I have just come from the battle; I fled from the battle today." He said, "How did it go, my son?" [17]The messenger replied, "Israel has fled before the Philistines, and there has also been a great slaughter among the troops; your two sons also, Hophni and Phinehas, are dead, and the ark of God has been captured." [18]When he mentioned the ark of God, Eli[j] fell over backward from his seat by the side of the gate; and his neck was broken and he died, for he was an old man, and heavy. He had judged Israel forty years.

19 Now his daughter-in-law, the wife of Phinehas, was pregnant, about to give birth. When she heard the news that the ark of God was captured, and that her father-in-law and her husband were dead, she bowed and gave birth; for her labor pains overwhelmed her. [20]As she was about to die, the women attending her said to her, "Do not be afraid, for you have borne a son." But she did not answer or give heed. [21]She named the child Ichabod, meaning, "The glory has departed from Israel," because the ark of God had been captured and because of her father-in-law and her husband. [22]She said, "The glory has departed from Israel, for the ark of God has been captured."

The Philistines and the Ark

5 When the Philistines captured the ark of God, they brought it from Ebenezer to Ashdod; [2]then the Philistines took the ark of God and brought it into the house of Dagon and placed it beside Dagon. [3]When the people of Ashdod rose early the next day, there was Dagon, fallen on his face to the ground before the ark of the LORD. So they took Dagon and put him back in his place. [4]But when they rose early on the next morning, Dagon had fallen on his face to the ground before the ark of the LORD, and the head of Dagon and both his hands were lying cut off upon the threshold; only the trunk of[k] Dagon was left to him. [5]This is why the priests of Dagon and all who enter the house of Dagon do not step on the threshold of Dagon in Ashdod to this day.

6 The hand of the LORD was heavy upon the people of Ashdod, and he terrified and struck them with tumors, both in Ashdod and in its territory. [7]And when the inhabitants of Ashdod saw how things were, they said, "The ark of the God of Israel must not remain with us; for his hand is heavy on us and on our god Dagon." [8]So they sent and gathered together all the lords of the Philistines, and said, "What shall we do with the ark of the God of Israel?" The inhabitants of Gath replied, "Let the ark of God be moved on to us."[l] So they moved the ark of the God of Israel to Gath.[m] [9]But after they had brought it to Gath,[n] the hand of the LORD was against the city, causing a very great panic; he struck the inhabitants of the city, both young and old, so that tumors broke out on them. [10]So they sent the ark of the God of Israel[o] to Ekron. But when the ark of God came to Ekron, the people of Ekron cried out, "Why[p] have they brought around to us[q] the ark of the God of Israel to kill us[q] and our[r] people?" [11]They sent therefore and gathered together all the lords of the Philistines, and said, "Send away the ark of the God of Israel, and let it return to its own place, that it may not kill us and our people." For there was a deathly panic[s] throughout the whole city. The hand of God was very heavy there; [12]those who did not die were stricken with tumors, and the cry of the city went up to heaven.

The Ark Returned to Israel

6 The ark of the LORD was in the country of the Philistines seven months. [2]Then the Philistines called for the priests and the diviners and said, "What shall we do with the ark of the LORD? Tell us what we should send with it to its place." [3]They said, "If you send away the ark of the God of Israel, do not send it empty, but by all means return him a guilt offering. Then you will be healed and will be ransomed;[t] will not his hand then turn from you?" [4]And they said, "What is the guilt offering that we shall return to him?" They answered, "Five gold tumors and five gold mice, according to the number of the lords of the

[j] Heb *he* [k] Heb lacks *the trunk of* [l] Gk Compare Q Ms: MT *They answered, "Let the ark of the God of Israel be brought around to Gath."* [m] Gk: Heb lacks *to Gath* [n] Q Ms: MT lacks *to Gath* [o] Q Ms Gk: MT lacks *of Israel* [p] Q Ms Gk: MT lacks *Why* [q] Heb *me* [r] Heb *my* [s] Q Ms reads *a panic from the LORD* [t] Q Ms Gk: MT *and it will be known to you*

4.15 1 Sam 3.2
4.16 2 Sam 1.4
4.18 ver 13
4.20 Gen 35.16-19
4.22 Jer 2.11; ver 11
5.1 1 Sam 4.1; 7.12
5.2 Judg 16.23
5.3 Isa 19.1; 46.1,2,7
5.4 Ezek 6.4,6
5.6 ver 7,11; Ex 9.3; 1 Sam 6.5; Deut 28.27; Ps 78.66
5.8 ver 11
5.9 ver 6,11; 1 Sam 7.13; Ps 78.66
5.11 ver 6,8,9
6.2 Gen 41.8; Ex 7.11; Isa 2.6
6.3 Ex 23.15; Deut 16.16; Lev 5.15,16
6.4 ver 7,18; Josh 13.3; Judg 3.3

Philistines; for the same plague was upon
all of you and upon your lords. [5]So you
must make images of your tumors and
images of your mice that ravage the land,
and give glory to the God of Israel; perhaps
he will lighten his hand on you and your
gods and your land. [6]Why should you harden
your hearts as the Egyptians and Pharaoh
hardened their hearts? After he had made
fools of them, did they not let the people go,
and they departed? [7]Now then, get ready a
new cart and two milch cows that have
never borne a yoke, and yoke the cows to
the cart, but take their calves home, away
from them. [8]Take the ark of the LORD and
place it on the cart, and put in a box at its
side the figures of gold, which you are
returning to him as a guilt offering. Then
send it off, and let it go its way. [9]And watch;
if it goes up on the way to its own land,
to Beth-shemesh, then it is he who has done
us this great harm; but if not, then we shall
know that it is not his hand that struck us;
it happened to us by chance."
10 The men did so; they took two milch
cows and yoked them to the cart, and shut
up their calves at home. [11]They put the ark
of the LORD on the cart, and the box with
the gold mice and the images of their tumors.
[12]The cows went straight in the direction of
Beth-shemesh along one highway, lowing
as they went; they turned neither to the
right nor to the left, and the lords of the
Philistines went after them as far as the
border of Beth-shemesh.
13 Now the people of Beth-shemesh were
reaping their wheat harvest in the valley.
When they looked up and saw the ark, they
went with rejoicing to meet it.[u] [14]The cart
came into the field of Joshua of Beth-shemesh,
and stopped there. A large stone was there;
so they split up the wood of the cart and
offered the cows as a burnt offering to the
LORD. [15]The Levites took down the ark of the
LORD and the box that was beside it, in
which were the gold objects, and set them
upon the large stone. Then the people of
Beth-shemesh offered burnt offerings and
presented sacrifices on that day to the LORD.
[16]When the five lords of the Philistines saw
it, they returned that day to Ekron.
17 These are the gold tumors, which the
Philistines returned as a guilt offering to the
LORD: one for Ashdod, one for Gaza, one for
Ashkelon, one for Gath, one for Ekron;
[18]also the gold mice, according to the number
of all the cities of the Philistines belonging
to the five lords, both fortified cities and
unwalled villages. The great stone, beside
which they set down the ark of the LORD,
is a witness to this day in the field of Joshua
of Beth-shemesh.

The Ark at Kiriath-jearim

19 The descendants of Jeconiah did not
rejoice with the people of Beth-shemesh
when they greeted[v] the ark of the LORD; and
he killed seventy men of them.[wx] The people
mourned because the LORD had made a
great slaughter among the people. [20]Then
the people of Beth-shemesh said, "Who is
able to stand before the LORD, this holy God?
To whom shall he go so that we may be
rid of him?" [21]So they sent messengers to
the inhabitants of Kiriath-jearim, saying,
"The Philistines have returned the ark of
the LORD. Come down and take it up to
you."

7 [1]And the people of Kiriath-jearim came
and took up the ark of the LORD, and
brought it to the house of Abinadab on the
hill. They consecrated his son, Eleazar, to
have charge of the ark of the LORD.
2 From the day that the ark was lodged
at Kiriath-jearim, a long time passed, some
twenty years, and all the house of Israel
lamented[x] after the LORD.

Samuel as Judge

3 Then Samuel said to all the house of
Israel, "If you are returning to the LORD with
all your heart, then put away the foreign
gods and the Astartes from among you.
Direct your heart to the LORD, and serve him
only, and he will deliver you out of the
hand of the Philistines." [4]So Israel put away
the Baals and the Astartes, and they served
the LORD only.
5 Then Samuel said, "Gather all Israel at
Mizpah, and I will pray to the LORD for you."
[6]So they gathered at Mizpah, and drew
water and poured it out before the LORD.
They fasted that day, and said, "We have
sinned against the LORD." And Samuel judged
the people of Israel at Mizpah.
7 When the Philistines heard that the
people of Israel had gathered at Mizpah, the
lords of the Philistines went up against

[u] Gk: Heb *rejoiced to see it* [v] Gk: Heb *And he killed some of the people of Beth-shemesh, because they looked into* [w] Heb *killed seventy men, fifty thousand men* [x] Meaning of Heb uncertain

6.5 1 Sam 5.3-11; Josh 7.19; Isa 42.12
6.6 Ex 8.15; 9.34; 12.31
6.7 2 Sam 6.3; Num 19.2
6.8 ver 3,5
6.9 Josh 15.10; ver 3
6.12 ver 9; Num 20.19
6.14 2 Sam 24.22; 1 Kings 19.21
6.16 Josh 13.3
6.17 ver 4
6.18 ver 14,15
6.19 Num 4.5,15,20; 2 Sam 6.7
6.20 Lev 11.44,45; 2 Sam 6.9
6.21 Josh 9.17; 15.9,60
7.1 2 Sam 6.3,4
7.3 Joel 2.2; Josh 24.14; Judg 2.13; Deut 6.13; Mt 4.10
7.5 Judg 20.1; 1 Sam 8.6
7.6 Ps 62.8; Neh 9.1; Judg 10.10
7.7 1 Sam 17.11

6.19-7.2 The holy power of the ark was further attested when death struck the family of *Jeconiah*, which had failed to take part in the celebration of its return. The decision was made to keep the ark at *Kiriath-jearim*, a town just six miles west of Jerusalem, where under David it was to be permanently located.
Another way to translate *lamented* is "sought to follow" the LORD. Part of Israel's difficulty is seen here to be the lack of adequate leadership.
7.3-15 Samuel's Role in the Transition of Leadership from Judge to King.
7.3-6 Samuel called *all the house of Israel* to turn from the worship of the *foreign* fertility *gods and Astartes*, the goddess who by various names (Ashtoreth, or Anath) was believed to be the giver of life. Devotion to *the LORD* would bring them deliverance from *the Philistines*. Gathered at *Mizpah* (about ten miles north of Jerusalem), Israel engaged in fasting and confession, with Samuel exercising his role as judge.
7.7-14 The attack on Israel by *the Philistines* was repulsed when, after prayer and sacrifice *to the LORD*, he *thundered with a mighty voice*, and so terrified the enemy that they fled in disarray and defeat. Erecting *a stone* was a way of commemorating events which were seen as direct divine actions, and was widely practiced by groups throughout the Middle East in this period. *Ebenezer* attested the help of the LORD in Israel's gaining control of the coastal cities. *Peace* also obtained between Israel and her formerly threatening enemies to the east of the Jordan, *the Amorites*.

7.15-17 Samuel's annual circuit as judge included only cities in the eastern part of the tribal lands of Ephraim and Benjamin, not far from Jerusalem. The altar to the LORD at *Ramah* added one more site to the list of locations of shrines of Israel's God prior to the centralization of worship in Jerusalem under David.
8.1-15.35 Samuel's Role in the Enthronement of Israel's First King: Saul.
8.1-22 The Debate and Decision about a King for Israel. The corrupt, self-serving acts of Samuel's *sons* led the people to demand *a king to govern us like other nations.* God explained that this demand was a rejection of him as their ruler and not merely of his agent, Samuel. This was in keeping with their continuing desire to worship *other gods.* They were forewarned about the demands kings would make on them, in terms of military and other forms of royal service, as well as produce and livestock that would be taken to support the royal establishment. The people, however, saw the king as the agent and symbol of status and power for Israel among the other nations. Samuel is instructed by *the LORD* to *set a king over them,* and the delegates from the various tribes of Israel are instructed to *return home.*

Israel. And when the people of Israel heard
of it they were afraid of the Philistines. [8]The
people of Israel said to Samuel, "Do not
cease to cry out to the LORD our God for us,
and pray that he may save us from the
hand of the Philistines." [9]So Samuel took a
sucking lamb and offered it as a whole
burnt offering to the LORD; Samuel cried out
to the LORD for Israel, and the LORD answered him. [10]As Samuel was offering up
the burnt offering, the Philistines drew near
to attack Israel; but the LORD thundered
with a mighty voice that day against the
Philistines and threw them into confusion;
and they were routed before Israel. [11]And
the men of Israel went out of Mizpah and
pursued the Philistines, and struck them
down as far as beyond Beth-car.
12 Then Samuel took a stone and set it
up between Mizpah and Jeshanah,[y] and
named it Ebenezer;[z] for he said, "Thus far
the LORD has helped us." [13]So the Philistines
were subdued and did not again enter the
territory of Israel; the hand of the LORD was
against the Philistines all the days of Samuel.
[14]The towns that the Philistines had taken
from Israel were restored to Israel, from
Ekron to Gath; and Israel recovered their
territory from the hand of the Philistines.
There was peace also between Israel and
the Amorites.
15 Samuel judged Israel all the days of
his life. [16]He went on a circuit year by year
to Bethel, Gilgal, and Mizpah; and he judged
Israel in all these places. [17]Then he would
come back to Ramah, for his home was
there; he administered justice there to Israel, and built there an altar to the LORD.

Israel Demands a King

8 When Samuel became old, he made
his sons judges over Israel. [2]The name
of his firstborn son was Joel, and the name
of his second, Abijah; they were judges in
Beer-sheba. [3]Yet his sons did not follow in
his ways, but turned aside after gain; they
took bribes and perverted justice.
4 Then all the elders of Israel gathered
together and came to Samuel at Ramah,
[5]and said to him, "You are old and your
sons do not follow in your ways; appoint for
us, then, a king to govern us, like other
nations." [6]But the thing displeased Samuel
when they said, "Give us a king to govern
us." Samuel prayed to the LORD, [7]and the
LORD said to Samuel, "Listen to the voice of
the people in all that they say to you; for
they have not rejected you, but they have
rejected me from being king over them.
[8]Just as they have done to me,[a] from the day
I brought them up out of Egypt to this day,
forsaking me and serving other gods, so also
they are doing to you. [9]Now then, listen to
their voice; only—you shall solemnly warn
them, and show them the ways of the king
who shall reign over them."
10 So Samuel reported all the words of
the LORD to the people who were asking him
for a king. [11]He said, "These will be the
ways of the king who will reign over you:
he will take your sons and appoint them to
his chariots and to be his horsemen, and to
run before his chariots; [12]and he will appoint for himself commanders of thousands
and commanders of fifties, and some to
plow his ground and to reap his harvest,
and to make his implements of war and the
equipment of his chariots. [13]He will take
your daughters to be perfumers and cooks
and bakers. [14]He will take the best of your
fields and vineyards and olive orchards and
give them to his courtiers. [15]He will take
one-tenth of your grain and of your vineyards and give it to his officers and his
courtiers. [16]He will take your male and
female slaves, and the best of your cattle[b]
and donkeys, and put them to his work.
[17]He will take one-tenth of your flocks, and
you shall be his slaves. [18]And in that day
you will cry out because of your king,
whom you have chosen for yourselves; but
the LORD will not answer you in that day."

Israel's Request for a King Granted

19 But the people refused to listen to the
voice of Samuel; they said, "No! but we are
determined to have a king over us, [20]so that
we also may be like other nations, and that
our king may govern us and go out before
us and fight our battles." [21]When Samuel
had heard all the words of the people, he
repeated them in the ears of the LORD. [22]The
LORD said to Samuel, "Listen to their voice
and set a king over them." Samuel then
said to the people of Israel, "Each of you
return home."

[y] Gk Syr: Heb *Shen* [z] That is *Stone of Help* [a] Gk: Heb lacks *to me* [b] Gk: Heb *young men*

7.8 Isa 37.4
7.9 Ps 99.6; Jer 15.1
7.10 Josh 10.10; 1 Sam 2.10; 2 Sam 22.14,15
7.12 Gen 35.14; Josh 4.9
7.13 Judg 13.1; 1 Sam 13.5
7.15 ver 6; 1 Sam 12.11
7.17 1 Sam 1.19
8.1 Deut 16.18,19
8.3 Ex 23.6,8; Deut 16.19; Ps 15.5
8.4 1 Sam 7.17
8.5 Deut 17.14,15
8.6 1 Sam 15.11
8.7 1 Sam 10.19; Ex 16.8
8.9 ver 11
8.11 1 Sam 14.52; 2 Sam 15.1
8.12 1 Sam 22.7
8.14 1 Kings 21.7; Ezek 46.18
8.18 Prov 1.25-28; Mic 3.4
8.20 ver 5
8.22 ver 7

9.1 1 Sam 14.51; 1 Chr 9.36-39
9.2 1 Sam 10.23,24
9.4 Josh 24.33; 2 Kings 4.42; Josh 19.42
9.5 1 Sam 10.2
9.6 Deut 33.1; 1 Sam 3.19
9.7 1 Kings 14.3; 2 Kings 8.8
9.9 2 Sam 24.11; 1 Chr 26.28; Isa 30.10
9.11 Gen 24.15
9.12 Num 28.11-15; 1 Sam 7.17; 10.5
9.16 1 Sam 10.1; Ex 3.7,9
9.17 1 Sam 16.12
9.20 ver 3; 1 Sam 8.5; 12.13
9.21 1 Sam 15.17; Judg 20.46,48
9.24 Lev 7.32,33; Num 18.18
9.25 Deut 22.8; Acts 10.9

Saul Chosen to Be King

9 There was a man of Benjamin whose
name was Kish son of Abiel son of
Zeror son of Becorath son of Aphiah, a
Benjaminite, a man of wealth. 2 He had a
son whose name was Saul, a handsome
young man. There was not a man among
the people of Israel more handsome than
he; he stood head and shoulders above
everyone else.
3 Now the donkeys of Kish, Saul's father,
had strayed. So Kish said to his son Saul,
"Take one of the boys with you; go and look
for the donkeys." 4 He passed through the
hill country of Ephraim and passed through
the land of Shalishah, but they did not find
them. And they passed through the land of
Shaalim, but they were not there. Then he
passed through the land of Benjamin, but
they did not find them.
5 When they came to the land of Zuph,
Saul said to the boy who was with him,
"Let us turn back, or my father will stop
worrying about the donkeys and worry about
us." 6 But he said to him, "There is a man
of God in this town; he is a man held in
honor. Whatever he says always comes
true. Let us go there now; perhaps he will
tell us about the journey on which we have
set out." 7 Then Saul replied to the boy, "But
if we go, what can we bring the man? For
the bread in our sacks is gone, and there
is no present to bring to the man of God.
What have we?" 8 The boy answered Saul
again, "Here, I have with me a quarter
shekel of silver; I will give it to the man of
God, to tell us our way." 9 (Formerly in
Israel, anyone who went to inquire of God
would say, "Come, let us go to the seer"; for
the one who is now called a prophet was
formerly called a seer.) 10 Saul said to the
boy, "Good; come, let us go." So they went
to the town where the man of God was.
11 As they went up the hill to the town,
they met some girls coming out to draw
water, and said to them, "Is the seer here?"
12 They answered, "Yes, there he is just
ahead of you. Hurry; he has come just now
to the town, because the people have a
sacrifice today at the shrine. 13 As soon as
you enter the town, you will find him,
before he goes up to the shrine to eat. For
the people will not eat until he comes, since
he must bless the sacrifice; afterward those
eat who are invited. Now go up, for you will
meet him immediately." 14 So they went up
to the town. As they were entering the
town, they saw Samuel coming out toward
them on his way up to the shrine.
15 Now the day before Saul came, the
LORD had revealed to Samuel: 16 "Tomorrow
about this time I will send to you a man
from the land of Benjamin, and you shall
anoint him to be ruler over my people
Israel. He shall save my people from the
hand of the Philistines; for I have seen the
suffering of[c] my people, because their outcry has come to me." 17 When Samuel saw
Saul, the LORD told him, "Here is the man
of whom I spoke to you. He it is who shall
rule over my people." 18 Then Saul approached Samuel inside the gate, and said,
"Tell me, please, where is the house of the
seer?" 19 Samuel answered Saul, "I am the
seer; go up before me to the shrine, for
today you shall eat with me, and in the
morning I will let you go and will tell you
all that is on your mind. 20 As for your
donkeys that were lost three days ago, give
no further thought to them, for they have
been found. And on whom is all Israel's
desire fixed, if not on you and on all your
ancestral house?" 21 Saul answered, "I am
only a Benjaminite, from the least of the
tribes of Israel, and my family is the hum-
blest of all the families of the tribe of
Benjamin. Why then have you spoken to
me in this way?"
22 Then Samuel took Saul and his serv-
ant-boy and brought them into the hall,
and gave them a place at the head of those
who had been invited, of whom there were
about thirty. 23 And Samuel said to the cook,
"Bring the portion I gave you, the one I
asked you to put aside." 24 The cook took up
the thigh and what went with it[d] and set
them before Saul. Samuel said, "See, what
was kept is set before you. Eat; for it is set[e]
before you at the appointed time, so that
you might eat with the guests."[f]
So Saul ate with Samuel that day. 25 When
they came down from the shrine into the
town, a bed was spread for Saul[g] on the
roof, and he lay down to sleep.[h] 26 Then at
the break of dawn[i] Samuel called to Saul
upon the roof, "Get up, so that I may send
you on your way." Saul got up, and both
he and Samuel went out into the street.

[c] Gk: Heb lacks *the suffering of* [d] Meaning of Heb uncertain [e] Q Ms Gk: MT *it was kept* [f] Cn: Heb *it was kept for you, saying, I have invited the people* [g] Gk: Heb *and he spoke with Saul* [h] Gk: Heb lacks *and he lay down to sleep* [i] Gk: Heb *and they arose early and at break of dawn*

9.1-26 Saul is Chosen to be King of Israel.
9.1-2 The qualifications of Saul to become king of Israel included his genealogical links to the tribe of *Benjamin*, his *handsome* appearance, and his commanding height.
9.3-14 The fruitless search for his father's lost *asses* led Saul to ask the advice of *the man of God*, who was earlier known as a *seer* (one who sees the future and the unknown) and later is designated a *prophet (one who speaks for God)*. The town where the man of God [Samuel] was, was apparently his regular place of residence, Ramah (7.17). There Saul and his companions awaited the appearance of Samuel when he was ready to offer and bless the sacrifice *at the shrine*, or "high place."
9.15-26 Informed by *the LORD* whom he was to meet and what he was to do, Samuel learned that someone from the tribe of Benjamin was to be anointed *ruler over my people Israel*. (The title "king" is not yet bestowed on Saul.) Samuel would also tell him where to find the *lost donkeys*. In a show of humility, Saul noted that he came from *the least of the tribes of Israel*, as well as from a humble family, but Samuel assigned him the largest and choicest part of the sacrificial animal, *the thigh* (see Gen 43.34), in the presence of all the other *guests*. Assigning Saul a sleeping space on the flat *roof* of his house was another sign of special favor.

9.27-10.8 Saul Anointed King. **9.27** The youthfulness of Saul is clear when he is described as a *boy*. **10.1** The details of Saul's rule over Israel and his delivering them from their enemies are found in ancient Greek and Latin versions, but not in the Hebrew text. **10.2-8** The details of what *Saul* will experience on returning to his own native district are foretold by Samuel to persuade the young ruler that God is indeed behind this ceremony and this assignment of responsibility. The *band of prophets* filled with *prophetic frenzy* are typical of the ecstatic manifestations connected with the prophets in this period. The instruction to go to *Gilgal* (Josh 4) indicates yet another historic sacred site where sacrifices continue to be offered to the God of Israel. **10.9-16** Saul's Response to his New Role. For Saul to receive *another heart* indicates the new sense of direction and power that he gained from God, as *the Spirit of God possessed him*. It manifested itself in the *prophetic frenzy* that seized him, but on returning home Saul reported only the recovery of the donkeys and nothing about *the matter of the kingship*. **10.17-26** The Public Proclamation of Saul's Kingship. The designation of Saul as king of Israel is seen here as a concession to the people's demands rather than as God's preference. The process of selection of a ruler is *by lot*, which leads to Saul, who is reluctantly presented to the people and acclaimed as *king*. After Samuel had explained to the people *the rights and duties of the kingship*, the people were dismissed and Saul returned to his hometown, with a group of loyal followers.

Samuel Anoints Saul

27 As they were going down to the outskirts of the town, Samuel said to Saul, "Tell the boy to go on before us, and when he has passed on, stop here yourself for a while, that I may make known to you the word of God."

10 [1]Samuel took a vial of oil and poured it on his head, and kissed him; he said, "The LORD has anointed you ruler over his people Israel. You shall reign over the people of the LORD and you will save them from the hand of their enemies all around. Now this shall be the sign to you that the LORD has anointed you ruler[j] over his heritage: [2]When you depart from me today you will meet two men by Rachel's tomb in the territory of Benjamin at Zelzah; they will say to you, 'The donkeys that you went to seek are found, and now your father has stopped worrying about them and is worrying about you, saying: What shall I do about my son?' [3]Then you shall go on from there further and come to the oak of Tabor; three men going up to God at Bethel will meet you there, one carrying three kids, another carrying three loaves of bread, and another carrying a skin of wine. [4]They will greet you and give you two loaves of bread, which you shall accept from them. [5]After that you shall come to Gibeath-elohim,[k] at the place where the Philistine garrison is; there, as you come to the town, you will meet a band of prophets coming down from the shrine with harp, tambourine, flute, and lyre playing in front of them; they will be in a prophetic frenzy. [6]Then the spirit of the LORD will possess you, and you will be in a prophetic frenzy along with them and be turned into a different person. [7]Now when these signs meet you, do whatever you see fit to do, for God is with you. [8]And you shall go down to Gilgal ahead of me; then I will come down to you to present burnt offerings and offer sacrifices of well-being. Seven days you shall wait, until I come to you and show you what you shall do."

Saul Prophesies

9 As he turned away to leave Samuel, God gave him another heart; and all these signs were fulfilled that day. [10]When they were going from there[l] to Gibeah,[m] a band of prophets met him; and the spirit of God possessed him, and he fell into a prophetic frenzy along with them. [11]When all who knew him before saw how he prophesied with the prophets, the people said to one another, "What has come over the son of Kish? Is Saul also among the prophets?" [12]A man of the place answered, "And who is their father?" Therefore it became a proverb, "Is Saul also among the prophets?" [13]When his prophetic frenzy had ended, he went home.[n]

14 Saul's uncle said to him and to the boy, "Where did you go?" And he replied, "To seek the donkeys; and when we saw they were not to be found, we went to Samuel." [15]Saul's uncle said, "Tell me what Samuel said to you." [16]Saul said to his uncle, "He told us that the donkeys had been found." But about the matter of the kingship, of which Samuel had spoken, he did not tell him anything.

Saul Proclaimed King

17 Samuel summoned the people to the LORD at Mizpah [18]and said to them,[o] "Thus says the LORD, the God of Israel, 'I brought up Israel out of Egypt, and I rescued you from the hand of the Egyptians and from the hand of all the kingdoms that were oppressing you.' [19]But today you have rejected your God, who saves you from all your calamities and your distresses; and you have said, 'No! but set a king over us.' Now therefore present yourselves before the LORD by your tribes and by your clans."

20 Then Samuel brought all the tribes of Israel near, and the tribe of Benjamin was taken by lot. [21]He brought the tribe of Benjamin near by its families, and the family of the Matrites was taken by lot. Finally he brought the family of the Matrites near man by man,[p] and Saul the son of Kish was taken by lot. But when they sought him, he could not be found. [22]So they inquired again of the LORD, "Did the man come here?"[q] and the LORD said, "See, he has hidden himself among the baggage." [23]Then they ran and brought him from there. When he took his stand among the people, he was head and shoulders taller than any of them. [24]Samuel said to all the people, "Do you see the one

[j] Gk: Heb lacks *over his people Israel. You shall . . . anointed you ruler* [k] Or *the Hill of God* [l] Gk: Heb *they came there* [m] Or *the hill* [n] Cn: Heb *he came to the shrine* [o] Heb *to the people of Israel* [p] Gk: Heb lacks *Finally . . . man by man* [q] Gk: Heb *Is there yet a man to come here?*

10.1 1 Sam 16.13; Ps 2.12; Deut 32.9; Ps 78.71
10.2 Gen 35.19,20; 1 Sam 9.3-5
10.3 Gen 28.22; 35.1,3,7,8
10.5 1 Sam 13.3; 9.12; 19.20; 2 Kings 3.15
10.6 Num 11.25,29; ver 10; 1 Sam 19.23,24
10.7 Josh 1.5; Judg 6.12
10.8 1 Sam 11.15; 13.8
10.9 ver 6
10.10 ver 5,6; 1 Sam 19.20
10.11 1 Sam 19.24; Mt 13.54,55; Jn 7.15
10.16 1 Sam 9.20
10.17 1 Sam 7.5,6
10.18 Judg 6.8,9
10.19 1 Sam 8.6,7; Josh 24.1
10.20 Josh 7.14,16,17
10.22 1 Sam 23.2,4,9-11
10.23 1 Sam 9.2
10.24 2 Sam 21.6; 1 Kings 1.25,39

whom the LORD has chosen? There is no one like him among all the people." And all the people shouted, "Long live the king!"

25 Samuel told the people the rights and duties of the kingship; and he wrote them in a book and laid it up before the LORD. Then Samuel sent all the people back to their homes. 26Saul also went to his home at Gibeah, and with him went warriors whose hearts God had touched. 27But some worthless fellows said, "How can this man save us?" They despised him and brought him no present. But he held his peace.

Now Nahash, king of the Ammonites, had been grievously oppressing the Gadites and the Reubenites. He would gouge out the right eye of each of them and would not grant Israel a deliverer. No one was left of the Israelites across the Jordan whose right eye Nahash, king of the Ammonites, had not gouged out. But there were seven thousand men who had escaped from the Ammonites and had entered Jabesh-gilead.[r]

Saul Defeats the Ammonites

11 About a month later,[s] Nahash the Ammonite went up and besieged Jabesh-gilead; and all the men of Jabesh said to Nahash, "Make a treaty with us, and we will serve you." 2But Nahash the Ammonite said to them, "On this condition I will make a treaty with you, namely that I gouge out everyone's right eye, and thus put disgrace upon all Israel." 3The elders of Jabesh said to him, "Give us seven days' respite that we may send messengers through all the territory of Israel. Then, if there is no one to save us, we will give ourselves up to you." 4When the messengers came to Gibeah of Saul, they reported the matter in the hearing of the people; and all the people wept aloud.

5 Now Saul was coming from the field behind the oxen; and Saul said, "What is the matter with the people, that they are weeping?" So they told him the message from the inhabitants of Jabesh. 6And the spirit of God came upon Saul in power when he heard these words, and his anger was greatly kindled. 7He took a yoke of oxen, and cut them in pieces and sent them throughout all the territory of Israel by messengers, saying, "Whoever does not come out after Saul and Samuel, so shall it be done to his oxen!" Then the dread of the LORD fell upon the people, and they came out as one. 8When he mustered them at Bezek, those from Israel were three hundred thousand, and those from Judah seventy[t] thousand. 9They said to the messengers who had come, "Thus shall you say to the inhabitants of Jabesh-gilead: 'Tomorrow, by the time the sun is hot, you shall have deliverance.' " When the messengers came and told the inhabitants of Jabesh, they rejoiced. 10So the inhabitants of Jabesh said, "Tomorrow we will give ourselves up to you, and you may do to us whatever seems good to you." 11The next day Saul put the people in three companies. At the morning watch they came into the camp and cut down the Ammonites until the heat of the day; and those who survived were scattered, so that no two of them were left together.

12 The people said to Samuel, "Who is it that said, 'Shall Saul reign over us?' Give them to us so that we may put them to death." 13But Saul said, "No one shall be put to death this day, for today the LORD has brought deliverance to Israel."

14 Samuel said to the people, "Come, let us go to Gilgal and there renew the kingship." 15So all the people went to Gilgal, and there they made Saul king before the LORD in Gilgal. There they sacrificed offerings of well-being before the LORD, and there Saul and all the Israelites rejoiced greatly.

Samuel's Farewell Address

12 Samuel said to all Israel, "I have listened to you in all that you have said to me, and have set a king over you. 2See, it is the king who leads you now; I am old and gray, but my sons are with you. I have led you from my youth until this day. 3Here I am; testify against me before the LORD and before his anointed. Whose ox have I taken? Or whose donkey have I taken? Or whom have I defrauded? Whom have I oppressed? Or from whose hand have I taken a bribe to blind my eyes with it? Testify against me[u] and I will restore it to you." 4They said, "You have not defrauded us or oppressed us or taken anything from the hand of anyone." 5He said to them, "The LORD is witness against you, and his anointed is witness this day, that you have

[r] Q Ms Compare Josephus, *Antiquities* VI.v.1 (68–71): MT lacks *Now Nahash . . . entered Jabesh-gilead.*
[s] Q Ms Gk: MT lacks *About a month later* [t] Q Ms Gk: MT *thirty* [u] Gk: Heb lacks *Testify against me*

10.25 1 Sam 8.11-18; Deut 17.14-20
10.26 1 Sam 11.4
10.27 1 Kings 10.25; 2 Chr 17.5
11.1 1 Sam 12.12; Judg 21.8; 1 Kings 20.34; Ezek 17.13
11.2 Num 16.14; 1 Sam 17.26
11.4 1 Sam 10.26; 15.34; 30.4; Judg 2.4
11.6 Judg 3.10; 6.34; 13.25; 14.6; 1 Sam 10.10; 16.13
11.7 Judg 19.29; 21.5,8,10
11.8 Judg 1.5; 20.2
11.10 ver 3
11.11 Judg 7.16
11.12 1 Sam 10.27; Lk 19.27
11.13 2 Sam 19.22; Ex 14.13; 1 Sam 19.5
11.14 1 Sam 10.8,25
11.15 1 Sam 10.8
12.1 1 Sam 8.7,9,22; 10.24; 11.14,15
12.2 1 Sam 8.1,5,20
12.3 1 Sam 10.1; 24.6; 2 Sam 1.14; Num 16.15; Acts 20.33; Deut 16.19
12.5 Acts 33.9; 24.20; Ex 22.4

10.27-11.15 Saul Defeats his Opponents and is Acclaimed as King.
10.27 Saul's opponents included some from his own town, *Gibeah.*
11.1-15 The Ammonites from east of the Jordan attacked Israel, besieging the inhabitants of *Jabesh-Gilead,* southeast of the Lake of Galilee, and threatening to disfigure them. Rallying forces from the tribes of both Israel and Judah in large numbers by sending out parts of a dismembered *yoke of oxen* as a symbol of the crisis and the need for common effort to solve it, Saul defeated the Ammonites and scattered them. His victory was taken as a sign of divine support, and after he refused to take action against his earlier opposition, *all the people went to Gilgal* where he was *made king before the LORD,* and appropriate sacrifices were offered.
12.1-5 As Samuel takes leave of his leadership role, he calls to witness concerning his complete integrity in that role the following: the people; *the LORD; and his anointed* (that is, the king). The people agree with Samuel's claim.

not found anything in my hand." And they
said, "He is witness."
6 Samuel said to the people, "The LORD
is witness, who[v] appointed Moses and Aaron
and brought your ancestors up out of the
land of Egypt. [7]Now therefore take your
stand, so that I may enter into judgment
with you before the LORD, and I will declare
to you[w] all the saving deeds of the LORD that
he performed for you and for your ancestors. [8]When Jacob went into Egypt and the
Egyptians oppressed them,[x] then your ancestors cried to the LORD and the LORD sent
Moses and Aaron, who brought forth your
ancestors out of Egypt, and settled them in
this place. [9]But they forgot the LORD their
God; and he sold them into the hand of
Sisera, commander of the army of King
Jabin of[y] Hazor, and into the hand of the
Philistines, and into the hand of the king of
Moab; and they fought against them. [10]Then
they cried to the LORD, and said, 'We have
sinned, because we have forsaken the LORD,
and have served the Baals and the Astartes;
but now rescue us out of the hand of our
enemies, and we will serve you.' [11]And the
LORD sent Jerubbaal and Barak,[z] and
Jephthah, and Samson,[a] and rescued you
out of the hand of your enemies on every
side; and you lived in safety. [12]But when
you saw that King Nahash of the Ammonites came against you, you said to me, 'No,
but a king shall reign over us,' though the
LORD your God was your king. [13]See, here
is the king whom you have chosen, for
whom you have asked; see, the LORD has set
a king over you. [14]If you will fear the LORD
and serve him and heed his voice and not
rebel against the commandment of the LORD,
and if both you and the king who reigns
over you will follow the LORD your God, it
will be well; [15]but if you will not heed the
voice of the LORD, but rebel against the
commandment of the LORD, then the hand
of the LORD will be against you and your
king.[b] [16]Now therefore take your stand and
see this great thing that the LORD will do
before your eyes. [17]Is it not the wheat harvest
today? I will call upon the LORD, that he
may send thunder and rain; and you shall
know and see that the wickedness that you
have done in the sight of the LORD is great
in demanding a king for yourselves." [18]So
Samuel called upon the LORD, and the LORD
sent thunder and rain that day; and all the
people greatly feared the LORD and Samuel.
19 All the people said to Samuel, "Pray
to the LORD your God for your servants, so
that we may not die; for we have added to
all our sins the evil of demanding a king for
ourselves." [20]And Samuel said to the people,
"Do not be afraid; you have done all this
evil, yet do not turn aside from following
the LORD, but serve the LORD with all your
heart; [21]and do not turn aside after useless
things that cannot profit or save, for they
are useless. [22]For the LORD will not cast
away his people, for his great name's sake,
because it has pleased the LORD to make you
a people for himself. [23]Moreover as for me,
far be it from me that I should sin against
the LORD by ceasing to pray for you; and I
will instruct you in the good and the right
way. [24]Only fear the LORD, and serve him
faithfully with all your heart; for consider
what great things he has done for you.
[25]But if you still do wickedly, you shall be
swept away, both you and your king."

Saul's Unlawful Sacrifice

13 Saul was . . .[c] years old when he
began to reign; and he reigned ...
and two[d] years over Israel.
2 Saul chose three thousand out of Israel; two thousand were with Saul in
Michmash and the hill country of Bethel,
and a thousand were with Jonathan in
Gibeah of Benjamin; the rest of the people
he sent home to their tents. [3]Jonathan
defeated the garrison of the Philistines that
was at Geba; and the Philistines heard of it.
And Saul blew the trumpet throughout all
the land, saying, "Let the Hebrews hear!"
[4]When all Israel heard that Saul had defeated the garrison of the Philistines, and
also that Israel had become odious to the
Philistines, the people were called out to
join Saul at Gilgal.
5 The Philistines mustered to fight with
Israel, thirty thousand chariots, and six
thousand horsemen, and troops like the
sand on the seashore in multitude; they
came up and encamped at Michmash, to
the east of Beth-aven. [6]When the Israelites
saw that they were in distress (for the

[v] Gk: Heb lacks *is witness, who* [w] Gk: Heb lacks *and I will declare to you* [x] Gk: Heb lacks *and the Egyptians oppressed them* [y] Gk: Heb lacks *King Jabin of* [z] Gk Syr: Heb *Bedan* [a] Gk: Heb *Samuel* [b] Gk: Heb *and your ancestors* [c] The number is lacking in the Heb text (the verse is lacking in the Septuagint). [d] *Two* is not the entire number; something has dropped out.

12.6-25 Attributed to Samuel, this address embodies the point of view of the deuteronomic historian: that the God who brought Israel out of Egypt and defeated her enemies as she entered the land has – in spite of the people's having worshiped the fertility gods (*the Baals and Astartes*) – now given the nation *a king*. The effectiveness of his rule and the prosperity of the nation depend on whether or not they *rebel against the commandment of the LORD*. Samuel's plea to the people is to be fully obedient, else they will be *swept away, both you and your king*.

13.1-15 Saul's Misguided Preparations for the Battle with the Philistines.

13.1 The Hebrew text omits the numbers for Saul's age and length of reign. Some of the ancient Greek texts say he became king at thirty.

13.2-15 Jonathan, who is later (14.1) identified as the *son of Saul*, accomplishes the first defeat of the Philistines, and the tribes of Israel are called to send troops to Saul at *Gilgal*, located in the Jordan Valley, where Israel under Joshua first began the invasion of the promised land (Josh 4-5). The massing of the *Philistine chariots and troops at Michmash* (on the edge of the eastern hills overlooking the Jordan Valley northeast of Jerusalem) so intimidated the Israelites that they hid in *caves and tombs*. While waiting for the troops to assemble, Saul *offered the burnt offering* at the altar in Gilgal. Samuel tells him that his failure to have a priest make the offering has disqualified him from his position as king. Someone who is *after [the LORD's] own heart* has already been chosen and appointed by God. Yet preparations for the battle with the Philistines continue.

12.6 Ex 6.26
12.7 Isa 1.18; Mic 6.1-5
12.8 Ex 2.23; 3.10; 4.16
12.9 Judg 3.7; 4.2; 10.7; 13.1; 3.12
12.10 Judg 10.10; 2.13; 10.15
12.11 Judg 6.14,32; 4.6; 11.1
12.12 1 Sam 11.1; 8.6,19; Judg 8.23
12.13 1 Sam 10.24; 8.5; Hos 13.11
12.14 Josh 24.14
12.15 Josh 24.20
12.16 Ex 14.13,31
12.17 Prov 26.1; 1 Sam 7.9,10; 8.7
12.18 Ex 14.31
12.19 ver 23; Ex 9.28; Jas 5.15
12.21 Deut 11.16; Jer 16.19; Hab 2.18
12.22 1 Kings 6.13; Josh 7.9; Deut 7.7,8
12.23 Rom 1.9; Col 1.9; 2 Tim 1.3; 1 Kings 8.36
12.24 Eccl 12.13; Deut 10.21
12.25 Josh 24.20; 1 Sam 31.1-5
13.2 1 Sam 10.26
13.3 1 Sam 10.5
13.5 Josh 11.4
13.6 Judg 6.2

13.8 1 Sam 10.8
13.9 2 Sam 24.25
13.10 1 Sam 15.13
13.11 ver 2,5,16,23
13.13 2 Chr 16.9; 1 Sam 15.11,22
13.14 1 Sam 15.28; Acts 13.22
13.15 1 Sam 14.2
13.17 1 Sam 14.15
13.18 Josh 18.13,14; Neh 11.34
13.19 2 Kings 24.14
13.22 Judg 5.8
14.2 1 Sam 13.15
14.3 1 Sam 22.9-12,20; 4.21; 2.28
14.4 1 Sam 13.23
14.6 Judg 7.4,7; 1 Sam 17.46,47
14.10 Gen 24.14; Judg 6.36,37

troops were hard pressed), the people hid themselves in caves and in holes and in rocks and in tombs and in cisterns. [7]Some Hebrews crossed the Jordan to the land of Gad and Gilead. Saul was still at Gilgal, and all the people followed him trembling.

8 He waited seven days, the time appointed by Samuel; but Samuel did not come to Gilgal, and the people began to slip away from Saul.[e] [9]So Saul said, "Bring the burnt offering here to me, and the offerings of well-being." And he offered the burnt offering. [10]As soon as he had finished offering the burnt offering, Samuel arrived; and Saul went out to meet him and salute him. [11]Samuel said, "What have you done?" Saul replied, "When I saw that the people were slipping away from me, and that you did not come within the days appointed, and that the Philistines were mustering at Michmash, [12]I said, 'Now the Philistines will come down upon me at Gilgal, and I have not entreated the favor of the LORD'; so I forced myself, and offered the burnt offering." [13]Samuel said to Saul, "You have done foolishly; you have not kept the commandment of the LORD your God, which he commanded you. The LORD would have established your kingdom over Israel forever, [14]but now your kingdom will not continue; the LORD has sought out a man after his own heart; and the LORD has appointed him to be ruler over his people, because you have not kept what the LORD commanded you." [15]And Samuel left and went on his way from Gilgal.[f] The rest of the people followed Saul to join the army; they went up from Gilgal toward Gibeah of Benjamin.[g]

Preparations for Battle

Saul counted the people who were present with him, about six hundred men. [16]Saul, his son Jonathan, and the people who were present with them stayed in Geba of Benjamin; but the Philistines encamped at Michmash. [17]And raiders came out of the camp of the Philistines in three companies; one company turned toward Ophrah, to the land of Shual, [18]another company turned toward Beth-horon, and another company turned toward the mountain[h] that looks down upon the valley of Zeboim toward the wilderness.

19 Now there was no smith to be found throughout all the land of Israel; for the Philistines said, "The Hebrews must not make swords or spears for themselves"; [20]so all the Israelites went down to the Philistines to sharpen their plowshare, mattocks, axes, or sickles;[i] [21]The charge was two-thirds of a shekel[j] for the plowshares and for the mattocks, and one-third of a shekel for sharpening the axes and for setting the goads.[k] [22]So on the day of the battle neither sword nor spear was to be found in the possession of any of the people with Saul and Jonathan; but Saul and his son Jonathan had them.

Jonathan Surprises and Routs the Philistines

23 Now a garrison of the Philistines had gone out to the pass of Michmash.

14 [1]One day Jonathan son of Saul said to the young man who carried his armor, "Come, let us go over to the Philistine garrison on the other side." But he did not tell his father. [2]Saul was staying in the outskirts of Gibeah under the pomegranate tree that is at Migron; the troops that were with him were about six hundred men, [3]along with Ahijah son of Ahitub, Ichabod's brother, son of Phinehas son of Eli, the priest of the LORD in Shiloh, carrying an ephod. Now the people did not know that Jonathan had gone. [4]In the pass,[l] by which Jonathan tried to go over to the Philistine garrison, there was a rocky crag on one side and a rocky crag on the other; the name of the one was Bozez, and the name of the other Seneh. [5]One crag rose on the north in front of Michmash, and the other on the south in front of Geba.

6 Jonathan said to the young man who carried his armor, "Come, let us go over to the garrison of these uncircumcised; it may be that the LORD will act for us; for nothing can hinder the LORD from saving by many or by few." [7]His armor-bearer said to him, "Do all that your mind inclines to.[m] I am with you; as your mind is, so is mine."[n] [8]Then Jonathan said, "Now we will cross over to those men and will show ourselves to them. [9]If they say to us, 'Wait until we come to you,' then we will stand still in our place, and we will not go up to them. [10]But

13.16-14.23 Jonathan's Success in Battle against the Philistines.
13.19 The great advantage of the Philistines lay in their having chariots and in their metal-working skill with iron, which gave them technical, agricultural, military and financial advantages over the Israelites.
13.23-14.5 While Jonathan was preparing secretly to approach *the Philistine garrison*, which was on a rocky crag across the valley from the Israelites, Saul waited with a priest descended from *Eli, the priest of the LORD in Shiloh*, who was carrying an *ephod*, the sacred shoulder garment which was thought to transmit oracles from God to the people.
14.6-23 The invitation to Jonathan and his armor-bearer from the Philistines to *"Come up to us"* was taken as a sign that God was behind the move into the camp of the enemy. The resultant *panic* among the Philistines led Saul to send in his troops, and the Israelite tribes who had first sided with the Philistines now joined Saul's forces to complete the defeat of the enemy.

[e] Heb *him* [f] Gk: Heb *went up from Gilgal to Gibeah of Benjamin* [g] Gk: Heb lacks *The rest . . . of Benjamin* [h] Cn Compare Gk: Heb *toward the border* [i] Gk: Heb *plowshare* [j] Heb *was a pim* [k] Cn: Meaning of Heb uncertain [l] Heb *Between the passes* [m] Gk: Heb *Do all that is in your mind. Turn* [n] Gk: Heb lacks *so is mine*

if they say, 'Come up to us,' then we will go up; for the LORD has given them into our hand. That will be the sign for us." 11So both of them showed themselves to the garrison of the Philistines; and the Philistines said, "Look, Hebrews are coming out of the holes where they have hidden themselves." 12The men of the garrison hailed Jonathan and his armor-bearer, saying, "Come up to us, and we will show you something." Jonathan said to his armor-bearer, "Come up after me; for the LORD has given them into the hand of Israel." 13Then Jonathan climbed up on his hands and feet, with his armor-bearer following after him. The Philistines[o] fell before Jonathan, and his armor-bearer, coming after him, killed them. 14In that first slaughter Jonathan and his armor-bearer killed about twenty men within an area about half a furrow long in an acre[p] of land. 15There was a panic in the camp, in the field, and among all the people; the garrison and even the raiders trembled; the earth quaked; and it became a very great panic.

16 Saul's lookouts in Gibeah of Benjamin were watching as the multitude was surging back and forth.[q] 17Then Saul said to the troops that were with him, "Call the roll and see who has gone from us." When they had called the roll, Jonathan and his armor-bearer were not there. 18Saul said to Ahijah, "Bring the ark[r] of God here." For at that time the ark[r] of God went with the Israelites. 19While Saul was talking to the priest, the tumult in the camp of the Philistines increased more and more; and Saul said to the priest, "Withdraw your hand." 20Then Saul and all the people who were with him rallied and went into the battle; and every sword was against the other, so that there was very great confusion. 21Now the Hebrews who previously had been with the Philistines and had gone up with them into the camp turned and joined the Israelites who were with Saul and Jonathan. 22Likewise, when all the Israelites who had gone into hiding in the hill country of Ephraim heard that the Philistines were fleeing, they too followed closely after them in the battle. 23So the LORD gave Israel the victory that day.

The battle passed beyond Beth-aven, and the troops with Saul numbered altogether about ten thousand men. The battle spread out over the hill country of Ephraim.

Saul's Rash Oath

24 Now Saul committed a very rash act on that day.[s] He had laid an oath on the troops, saying, "Cursed be anyone who eats food before it is evening and I have been avenged on my enemies." So none of the troops tasted food. 25All the troops[t] came upon a honeycomb; and there was honey on the ground. 26When the troops came upon the honeycomb, the honey was dripping out; but they did not put their hands to their mouths, for they feared the oath. 27But Jonathan had not heard his father charge the troops with the oath; so he extended the staff that was in his hand, and dipped the tip of it in the honeycomb, and put his hand to his mouth; and his eyes brightened. 28Then one of the soldiers said, "Your father strictly charged the troops with an oath, saying, 'Cursed be anyone who eats food this day.' And so the troops are faint." 29Then Jonathan said, "My father has troubled the land; see how my eyes have brightened because I tasted a little of this honey. 30How much better if today the troops had eaten freely of the spoil taken from their enemies; for now the slaughter among the Philistines has not been great."

31 After they had struck down the Philistines that day from Michmash to Aijalon, the troops were very faint; 32so the troops flew upon the spoil, and took sheep and oxen and calves, and slaughtered them on the ground; and the troops ate them with the blood. 33Then it was reported to Saul, "Look, the troops are sinning against the LORD by eating with the blood." And he said, "You have dealt treacherously; roll a large stone before me here."[u] 34Saul said, "Disperse yourselves among the troops, and say to them, 'Let all bring their oxen or their sheep, and slaughter them here, and eat; and do not sin against the LORD by eating with the blood.' " So all of the troops brought their oxen with them that night, and slaughtered them there. 35And Saul built an altar to the LORD; it was the first altar that he built to the LORD.

Jonathan in Danger of Death

36 Then Saul said, "Let us go down after the Philistines by night and despoil them until the morning light; let us not leave one of them." They said, "Do whatever seems

[o] Heb *They* [p] Heb *yoke* [q] Gk: Heb *they went and there* [r] Gk *the ephod* [s] Gk: Heb *The Israelites were distressed that day* [t] Heb *land* [u] Gk: Heb *me this day*

14.24-46 Saul's Foolish Oath and its Consequences.
14.24-35 As though to guarantee military success, Saul pronounced a curse on anyone who ate before nightfall, implying that this abstinence would result in the rout of his *enemies.* The troops heard this decree and abstained, but Jonathan was attracted by the abundant honey and ate some, *and his eyes brightened.* Late in the day, the troops had routed the Philistines and began to indulge in food *taken from their enemies.* Having conquered the Philistines in a large territory stretching from the eastern hills (at *Michmash*) to the edge of the coastal plain (at *Aijalon*), Saul tried to appease the wrath of the LORD with a huge sacrifice of *oxen and sheep.* The *stone* where this was done is said to be Saul's *first altar to the LORD.*
14.36-46 Saul's inability to receive instructions from God about pursuing the Philistines led him to conclude that Jonathan's violation of the oath must be punished by his death. The sacred lot, *Urim and Thummim,* was appealed to and identified Jonathan as guilty, but the people rallied to his support as victor over the Philistines and he was freed from the curse (*"ransomed"*) by some means which is not indicated here.

14.11 1 Sam 13.6
14.12 1 Sam 17.43,44; 2 Sam 5.24
14.15 2 Kings 7.6,7; 1 Sam 13.17
14.16 2 Sam 18.24
14.19 Num 27.21
14.20 Judg 7.22; 2 Chr 20.23
14.22 1 Sam 13.6
14.23 Ex 14.20; Ps 44.6,7; 1 Sam 13.5
14.24 Josh 6.26
14.27 1 Sam 30.12
14.29 1 Kings 18.18
14.32 1 Sam 15.19; Lev 17.10-14
14.35 1 Sam 7.17

good to you." But the priest said, "Let us
draw near to God here." 37So Saul inquired
of God, "Shall I go down after the Philistines?
Will you give them into the hand of Israel?"
But he did not answer him that day. 38Saul
said, "Come here, all you leaders of the
people; and let us find out how this sin has
arisen today. 39For as the LORD lives who
saves Israel, even if it is in my son Jonathan,
he shall surely die!" But there was no one
among all the people who answered him.
40He said to all Israel, "You shall be on one
side, and I and my son Jonathan will be on
the other side." The people said to Saul, "Do
what seems good to you." 41Then Saul said,
"O LORD God of Israel, why have you not
answered your servant today? If this guilt
is in me or in my son Jonathan, O LORD God
of Israel, give Urim; but if this guilt is in
your people Israel,[v] give Thummim." And
Jonathan and Saul were indicated by the
lot, but the people were cleared. 42Then Saul
said, "Cast the lot between me and my son
Jonathan." And Jonathan was taken.
43 Then Saul said to Jonathan, "Tell me
what you have done." Jonathan told him,
"I tasted a little honey with the tip of the
staff that was in my hand; here I am, I will
die." 44Saul said, "God do so to me and more
also; you shall surely die, Jonathan!" 45Then
the people said to Saul, "Shall Jonathan die,
who has accomplished this great victory in
Israel? Far from it! As the LORD lives, not one
hair of his head shall fall to the ground; for
he has worked with God today." So the
people ransomed Jonathan, and he did not
die. 46Then Saul withdrew from pursuing
the Philistines; and the Philistines went to
their own place.

Saul's Continuing Wars

47 When Saul had taken the kingship
over Israel, he fought against all his enemies on every side—against Moab, against
the Ammonites, against Edom, against the
kings of Zobah, and against the Philistines;
wherever he turned he routed them. 48He
did valiantly, and struck down the
Amalekites, and rescued Israel out of the
hands of those who plundered them.
49 Now the sons of Saul were Jonathan,
Ishvi, and Malchishua; and the names of his
two daughters were these: the name of the
firstborn was Merab, and the name of the
younger, Michal. 50The name of Saul's wife
was Ahinoam daughter of Ahimaaz. And
the name of the commander of his army
was Abner son of Ner, Saul's uncle; 51Kish
was the father of Saul, and Ner the father
of Abner was the son of Abiel.
52 There was hard fighting against the
Philistines all the days of Saul; and when
Saul saw any strong or valiant warrior, he
took him into his service.

Saul Defeats the Amalekites but Spares Their King

15 Samuel said to Saul, "The LORD
sent me to anoint you king over
his people Israel; now therefore listen to the
words of the LORD. 2Thus says the LORD of
hosts, 'I will punish the Amalekites for what
they did in opposing the Israelites when
they came up out of Egypt. 3Now go and
attack Amalek, and utterly destroy all that
they have; do not spare them, but kill both
man and woman, child and infant, ox and
sheep, camel and donkey.' "
4 So Saul summoned the people, and
numbered them in Telaim, two hundred
thousand foot soldiers, and ten thousand
soldiers of Judah. 5Saul came to the city of
the Amalekites and lay in wait in the valley.
6Saul said to the Kenites, "Go! Leave! Withdraw from among the Amalekites, or I will
destroy you with them; for you showed
kindness to all the people of Israel when
they came up out of Egypt." So the Kenites
withdrew from the Amalekites. 7Saul defeated the Amalekites, from Havilah as far
as Shur, which is east of Egypt. 8He took
King Agag of the Amalekites alive, but
utterly destroyed all the people with the
edge of the sword. 9Saul and the people
spared Agag, and the best of the sheep and
of the cattle and of the fatlings, and the
lambs, and all that was valuable, and would
not utterly destroy them; all that was despised and worthless they utterly destroyed.

Saul Rejected as King

10 The word of the LORD came to Samuel:
11"I regret that I made Saul king, for he has
turned back from following me, and has not
carried out my commands." Samuel was
angry; and he cried out to the LORD all
night. 12Samuel rose early in the morning
to meet Saul, and Samuel was told, "Saul
went to Carmel, where he set up a monu-

[v] Vg Compare Gk: Heb *41Saul said to the* LORD, *the God of Israel*

14.37 1 Sam 10.22; 28.6
14.38 Josh 7.14; 1 Sam 10.19
14.39 2 Sam 12.5
14.41 Prov 16.33; Acts 1.24
14.43 Josh 7.19; ver 23
14.44 Ruth 1.17; ver 39
14.45 2 Sam 14.11; 1 Kings 1.52; Acts 27.34
14.47 1 Sam 11.1-13; 2 Sam 10.6; ver 52
14.48 1 Sam 15.3,7
14.49 1 Sam 31.2; 1 Chr 8.33; 1 Sam 18.17-20
14.50 2 Sam 2.8
14.51 1 Sam 9.1
14.52 1 Sam 8.11
15.1 1 Sam 9.16
15.2 Ex 17.8-14; Num 24.20; Deut 25.17-19
15.3 Num 24.20; Deut 20.16-18; 1 Sam 22.19
15.6 Judg 1.16; 4.11; Ex 18.10,19; Num 10.29-32
15.7 1 Sam 14.48; Gen 16.7; 25.17,18; Ex 15.22
15.8 1 Kings 20.34ff; 1 Sam 30.1
15.9 ver 3,15
15.11 Gen 6.6,7; 2 Sam 24.16; 1 Kings 9.6,7; 1 Sam 16.1
15.12 Josh 15.55

14.47-52 Saul's Success in Defeating the Hostile Neighbors of Israel.
14.47-48 *All the enemies on every side* whom Saul defeated are named, followed (14.49-51) by a list of all his ancestors and offspring.
15.1-35 Saul's Final, Fatal Mistake. Saul's defeat of the Amalekites was an essential part of his having been anointed as *king over [God's] people Israel.* But his sparing their king, *Agag,* together with all the best of the livestock and other valuables, was in defiance of his commission to *destroy all* their possessions and *kill* all the people. His effort at self-defense by noting that the loot taken from the Amalekites had been sacrificed *to the LORD in Gilgal* evoked from Samuel a poetic response which shows God's priority for obedience over sacrifice. Saul's failure on this point had disqualified him to serve as Israel's king. Saul's penitence cannot overcome God's rejection of him as king for having rejected God's word to him. In his haste to flee, Saul's robe is torn, which Samuel sees as a sign that *the LORD has torn the kingdom* from Saul (15.28). His belated effort to obey by hacking *in pieces* Agag is of no avail, and Saul leaves the scene and forfeits the role of king.

16.1-13 God Chooses David as King.
16.1-5 In order to avoid violent reaction by Saul, Samuel describes his visit to Jesse in Bethlehem as merely an act of *sacrifice to the LORD*. But after seeing Jesse's sons one by one, he recognizes that God's choice among them is *the youngest*, David, and he is *anointed in the presence of his brothers*. The choice is confirmed by the outpouring on David of *the spirit of the LORD*.

ment for himself, and on returning he passed
on down to Gilgal." [13]When Samuel came
to Saul, Saul said to him, "May you be
blessed by the LORD; I have carried out the
command of the LORD." [14]But Samuel said,
"What then is this bleating of sheep in my
ears, and the lowing of cattle that I hear?"
[15]Saul said, "They have brought them from
the Amalekites; for the people spared the
best of the sheep and the cattle, to sacrifice
to the LORD your God; but the rest we have
utterly destroyed." [16]Then Samuel said to
Saul, "Stop! I will tell you what the LORD
said to me last night." He replied, "Speak."
17 Samuel said, "Though you are little
in your own eyes, are you not the head of
the tribes of Israel? The LORD anointed you
king over Israel. [18]And the LORD sent you on
a mission, and said, 'Go, utterly destroy the
sinners, the Amalekites, and fight against
them until they are consumed.' [19]Why then
did you not obey the voice of the LORD? Why
did you swoop down on the spoil, and do
what was evil in the sight of the LORD?"
[20]Saul said to Samuel, "I have obeyed the
voice of the LORD, I have gone on the mission on which the LORD sent me, I have
brought Agag the king of Amalek, and I
have utterly destroyed the Amalekites. [21]But
from the spoil the people took sheep and
cattle, the best of the things devoted to
destruction, to sacrifice to the LORD your
God in Gilgal." [22]And Samuel said,
"Has the LORD as great delight in
burnt offerings and sacrifices,
as in obeying the voice of the LORD?
Surely, to obey is better than sacrifice,
and to heed than the fat of rams.
23 For rebellion is no less a sin than
divination,
and stubbornness is like iniquity and
idolatry.
Because you have rejected the word of
the LORD,
he has also rejected you from being
king."
24 Saul said to Samuel, "I have sinned;
for I have transgressed the commandment
of the LORD and your words, because I
feared the people and obeyed their voice.
[25]Now therefore, I pray, pardon my sin, and
return with me, so that I may worship the
LORD." [26]Samuel said to Saul, "I will not
return with you; for you have rejected the
word of the LORD, and the LORD has rejected
you from being king over Israel." [27]As Samuel
turned to go away, Saul caught hold of the
hem of his robe, and it tore. [28]And Samuel
said to him, "The LORD has torn the kingdom of Israel from you this very day, and
has given it to a neighbor of yours, who is
better than you. [29]Moreover the Glory of
Israel will not recant[w] or change his mind;
for he is not a mortal, that he should
change his mind." [30]Then Saul[x] said, "I
have sinned; yet honor me now before the
elders of my people and before Israel, and
return with me, so that I may worship the
LORD your God." [31]So Samuel turned back
after Saul; and Saul worshiped the LORD.
32 Then Samuel said, "Bring Agag king
of the Amalekites here to me." And Agag
came to him haltingly.[y] Agag said, "Surely
this is the bitterness of death."[z] [33]But Samuel
said,
"As your sword has made women
childless,
so your mother shall be childless
among women."
And Samuel hewed Agag in pieces before
the LORD in Gilgal.
34 Then Samuel went to Ramah; and
Saul went up to his house in Gibeah of Saul.
[35]Samuel did not see Saul again until the
day of his death, but Samuel grieved over
Saul. And the LORD was sorry that he had
made Saul king over Israel.

David Anointed as King

16 The LORD said to Samuel, "How
long will you grieve over Saul? I
have rejected him from being king over
Israel. Fill your horn with oil and set out;
I will send you to Jesse the Bethlehemite, for
I have provided for myself a king among his
sons." [2]Samuel said, "How can I go? If Saul
hears of it, he will kill me." And the LORD
said, "Take a heifer with you, and say, 'I
have come to sacrifice to the LORD.' [3]Invite
Jesse to the sacrifice, and I will show you
what you shall do; and you shall anoint for
me the one whom I name to you." [4]Samuel
did what the LORD commanded, and came
to Bethlehem. The elders of the city came
to meet him trembling, and said, "Do you
come peaceably?" [5]He said, "Peaceably; I
have come to sacrifice to the LORD; sanctify
yourselves and come with me to the sacrifice." And he sanctified Jesse and his sons

[w] Q Ms Gk: MT *deceive* [x] Heb *he* [y] Cn Compare Gk: Meaning of Heb uncertain [z] Q Ms Gk: MT *Surely the bitterness of death is past*

15.13 Gen 14.19; Judg 17.2
15.15 ver 9,21; Gen 3.12
15.17 1 Sam 9.21
15.18 ver 3
15.19 1 Sam 14.32
15.20 ver 13
15.21 ver 15
15.22 Isa 1.11-13; Mic 6.6-8; Heb 10.6-9; Hos 6.6; Mk 12.22
15.23 1 Sam 13.14
15.24 2 Sam 12.13; Prov 29.25; Isa 51.12,13
15.26 1 Sam 13.14
15.27 1 Kings 11.30,31
15.28 1 Sam 28.17
15.29 1 Chr 29.11; Num 23.19; Ezek 24.14
15.30 Jn 12.43; Isa 29.13
15.33 Gen 9.6; Judg 1.7
15.34 1 Sam 7.17; 11.4
15.35 1 Sam 19.24; 16.1
16.1 1 Sam 15.23,35; 9.16; 2 Kings 9.1; Ps 78.70; Acts 13.22
16.2 1 Sam 20.29
16.3 Ex 4.15; 1 Sam 9.16
16.4 Lk 2.4; 1 Kings 2.13; 2 Kings 9.22
16.5 Ex 19.10

and invited them to the sacrifice.
6 When they came, he looked on Eliab
and thought, "Surely the LORD's anointed is
now before the LORD."[a] 7But the LORD said to
Samuel, "Do not look on his appearance or
on the height of his stature, because I have
rejected him; for the LORD does not see as
mortals see; they look on the outward
appearance, but the LORD looks on the heart."
8Then Jesse called Abinadab, and made him
pass before Samuel. He said, "Neither has
the LORD chosen this one." 9Then Jesse made
Shammah pass by. And he said, "Neither
has the LORD chosen this one." 10Jesse made
seven of his sons pass before Samuel, and
Samuel said to Jesse, "The LORD has not
chosen any of these." 11Samuel said to Jesse,
"Are all your sons here?" And he said,
"There remains yet the youngest, but he is
keeping the sheep." And Samuel said to
Jesse, "Send and bring him; for we will not
sit down until he comes here." 12He sent
and brought him in. Now he was ruddy,
and had beautiful eyes, and was handsome.
The LORD said, "Rise and anoint him; for this
is the one." 13Then Samuel took the horn
of oil, and anointed him in the presence of
his brothers; and the spirit of the LORD came
mightily upon David from that day forward.
Samuel then set out and went to Ramah.

David Plays the Lyre for Saul

14 Now the spirit of the LORD departed
from Saul, and an evil spirit from the LORD
tormented him. 15And Saul's servants said
to him, "See now, an evil spirit from God
is tormenting you. 16Let our lord now command the servants who attend you to look
for someone who is skillful in playing the
lyre; and when the evil spirit from God is
upon you, he will play it, and you will feel
better." 17So Saul said to his servants, "Provide for me someone who can play well,
and bring him to me." 18One of the young
men answered, "I have seen a son of Jesse
the Bethlehemite who is skillful in playing,
a man of valor, a warrior, prudent in speech,
and a man of good presence; and the LORD
is with him." 19So Saul sent messengers to
Jesse, and said, "Send me your son David
who is with the sheep." 20Jesse took a donkey loaded with bread, a skin of wine, and
a kid, and sent them by his son David to
Saul. 21And David came to Saul, and entered his service. Saul loved him greatly,
and he became his armor-bearer. 22Saul
sent to Jesse, saying, "Let David remain in
my service, for he has found favor in my
sight." 23And whenever the evil spirit from
God came upon Saul, David took the lyre
and played it with his hand, and Saul would
be relieved and feel better, and the evil spirit
would depart from him.

David and Goliath

17 Now the Philistines gathered their
armies for battle; they were gathered at Socoh, which belongs to Judah, and
encamped between Socoh and Azekah, in
Ephes-dammim. 2Saul and the Israelites
gathered and encamped in the valley of
Elah, and formed ranks against the
Philistines. 3The Philistines stood on the
mountain on the one side, and Israel stood
on the mountain on the other side, with a
valley between them. 4And there came out
from the camp of the Philistines a champion
named Goliath, of Gath, whose height was
six[b] cubits and a span. 5He had a helmet of
bronze on his head, and he was armed with
a coat of mail; the weight of the coat was
five thousand shekels of bronze. 6He had
greaves of bronze on his legs and a javelin
of bronze slung between his shoulders. 7The
shaft of his spear was like a weaver's beam,
and his spear's head weighed six hundred
shekels of iron; and his shield-bearer went
before him. 8He stood and shouted to the
ranks of Israel, "Why have you come out
to draw up for battle? Am I not a Philistine,
and are you not servants of Saul? Choose
a man for yourselves, and let him come
down to me. 9If he is able to fight with me
and kill me, then we will be your servants;
but if I prevail against him and kill him,
then you shall be our servants and serve
us." 10And the Philistine said, "Today I defy
the ranks of Israel! Give me a man, that we
may fight together." 11When Saul and all
Israel heard these words of the Philistine,
they were dismayed and greatly afraid.
12 Now David was the son of an
Ephrathite of Bethlehem in Judah, named
Jesse, who had eight sons. In the days of
Saul the man was already old and advanced
in years.[c] 13The three eldest sons of Jesse
had followed Saul to the battle; the names
of his three sons who went to the battle
were Eliab the firstborn, and next to him
Abinadab, and the third Shammah. 14David

[a] Heb *him* [b] MT: Q Ms Gk *four* [c] Gk Syr: Heb *among men*

16.14-23 David's Special Relationship with Saul.
16.14-15 The coming of the spirit on David is concurrent with its departure from Saul and his becoming possessed by an evil spirit.
16.16-20 David is recommended as one whose music can calm Saul's evil spirit, and David is sent off to Saul.
16.21-23 In addition to his musical therapy, David is *loved greatly* by Saul, and becomes his *armor-bearer*.
17.1-58 David Kills Goliath.
17.1-3 The confrontation of the Philistines and the tribes of Israel took place *between Socoh and Azekah*, west of Bethlehem in the hills that slope down to the Mediterranean coast. The Israelites gathered in *the Valley of Elah*, which is east of the Philistine city of Ashdod.
17.5-7 The weight of the *bronze coat of mail* was about 125 pounds; the weight of the *spear's head*, about 15 pounds.

16.6 1 Sam 7.13
16.7 Isa 55.8; 1 Kings 8.39; 1 Chr 28.9
16.8 1 Sam 17.13
16.9 1 Sam 17.13
16.11 1 Sam 17.12
16.12 1 Sam 17.42; 9.17
16.13 1 Sam 10.1,6,9,10
16.14 Judg 16.20; 1 Sam 18.10
16.16 ver 23; 1 Sam 18.10; 19.9; 2 Kings 3.15
16.18 1 Sam 17.32-36; 3.19
16.20 1 Sam 10.27; Prov 18.16
16.21 Gen 41.46; Prov 22.29
16.23 ver 14-16
17.1 1 Sam 13.5; 2 Chr 28.18
17.2 1 Sam 21.9
17.4 2 Sam 21.19; Josh 11.21
17.6 ver 45
17.7 2 Sam 21.19; ver 41
17.8 1 Sam 8.17
17.10 ver 26,36,45
17.12 Ruth 4.22; 1 Sam 16.18; Gen 35.19; 1 Sam 16.10, 11; 1 Chr 2.13-15
17.13 1 Sam 16.6,8,9

17.17-18 The amount of *parched grain* that David is to take to his brothers in the army is *an ephah*, which is about a half-bushel.
17.26 David articulates the basic issue: Goliath is defying *the armies of the living God*.

was the youngest; the three eldest followed
Saul, 15but David went back and forth from
Saul to feed his father's sheep at Bethlehem.
16For forty days the Philistine came forward
and took his stand, morning and evening.
17 Jesse said to his son David, "Take for
your brothers an ephah of this parched
grain and these ten loaves, and carry them
quickly to the camp to your brothers; 18also
take these ten cheeses to the commander of
their thousand. See how your brothers fare,
and bring some token from them."
19 Now Saul, and they, and all the men
of Israel, were in the valley of Elah, fighting
with the Philistines. 20David rose early in
the morning, left the sheep with a keeper,
took the provisions, and went as Jesse had
commanded him. He came to the encampment as the army was going forth to the
battle line, shouting the war cry. 21Israel
and the Philistines drew up for battle, army
against army. 22David left the things in
charge of the keeper of the baggage, ran to
the ranks, and went and greeted his brothers. 23As he talked with them, the champion, the Philistine of Gath, Goliath by name,
came up out of the ranks of the Philistines,
and spoke the same words as before. And
David heard him.
24 All the Israelites, when they saw the
man, fled from him and were very much
afraid. 25The Israelites said, "Have you seen
this man who has come up? Surely he has
come up to defy Israel. The king will greatly
enrich the man who kills him, and will give
him his daughter and make his family free
in Israel." 26David said to the men who
stood by him, "What shall be done for the
man who kills this Philistine, and takes
away the reproach from Israel? For who is
this uncircumcised Philistine that he should
defy the armies of the living God?" 27The
people answered him in the same way, "So
shall it be done for the man who kills him."
28 His eldest brother Eliab heard him
talking to the men; and Eliab's anger was
kindled against David. He said, "Why have
you come down? With whom have you left
those few sheep in the wilderness? I know
your presumption and the evil of your heart;
for you have come down just to see the
battle." 29David said, "What have I done
now? It was only a question." 30He turned
away from him toward another and spoke
in the same way; and the people answered
him again as before.
31 When the words that David spoke
were heard, they repeated them before Saul;
and he sent for him. 32David said to Saul,
"Let no one's heart fail because of him; your
servant will go and fight with this Philistine." 33Saul said to David, "You are not
able to go against this Philistine to fight
with him; for you are just a boy, and he has
been a warrior from his youth." 34But David
said to Saul, "Your servant used to keep
sheep for his father; and whenever a lion or
a bear came, and took a lamb from the
flock, 35I went after it and struck it down,
rescuing the lamb from its mouth; and if it
turned against me, I would catch it by the
jaw, strike it down, and kill it. 36Your servant has killed both lions and bears; and this
uncircumcised Philistine shall be like one of
them, since he has defied the armies of the
living God." 37David said, "The LORD, who
saved me from the paw of the lion and from
the paw of the bear, will save me from the
hand of this Philistine." So Saul said to
David, "Go, and may the LORD be with you!"
38 Saul clothed David with his armor; he
put a bronze helmet on his head and clothed
him with a coat of mail. 39David strapped
Saul's sword over the armor, and he tried
in vain to walk, for he was not used to
them. Then David said to Saul, "I cannot
walk with these; for I am not used to them."
So David removed them. 40Then he took his
staff in his hand, and chose five smooth
stones from the wadi, and put them in his
shepherd's bag, in the pouch; his sling was
in his hand, and he drew near to the
Philistine.
41 The Philistine came on and drew near
to David, with his shield-bearer in front of
him. 42When the Philistine looked and saw
David, he disdained him, for he was only a
youth, ruddy and handsome in appearance.
43The Philistine said to David, "Am I a dog,
that you come to me with sticks?" And the
Philistine cursed David by his gods. 44The
Philistine said to David, "Come to me, and
I will give your flesh to the birds of the air
and to the wild animals of the field." 45But
David said to the Philistine, "You come to
me with sword and spear and javelin; but
I come to you in the name of the LORD of
hosts, the God of the armies of Israel, whom
you have defied. 46This very day the LORD
will deliver you into my hand, and I will
strike you down and cut off your head; and
I will give the dead bodies of the Philistine
army this very day to the birds of the air
and to the wild animals of the earth, so that

17.15 1 Sam 16.19
17.18 Gen 37.14
17.23 ver 8-11
17.25 Josh 15.16
17.26 1 Sam 11.2; 14.6; ver 10; Deut 5.6
17.27 ver 25
17.28 Gen 37.4ff
17.29 ver 17
17.30 ver 26,27
17.32 Deut 20.1-4; 1 Sam 16.18
17.37 2 Tim 4.17; 1 Sam 20.13; 1 Chr 22.11,16
17.42 Prov 16.18; Ps 123.3,4; 1 Sam 16.12
17.43 1 Sam 24.14; 2 Sam 3.8
17.44 1 Kings 20.10
17.45 2 Chr 32.8; Ps 124.8; Heb 11.34
17.46 1 Kings 18.36; 2 Kings 19.19; Isa 52.10

all the earth may know that there is a God
in Israel, [47]and that all this assembly may
know that the LORD does not save by sword
and spear; for the battle is the LORD's and
he will give you into our hand."

48 When the Philistine drew nearer to
meet David, David ran quickly toward the
battle line to meet the Philistine. [49]David
put his hand in his bag, took out a stone,
slung it, and struck the Philistine on his
forehead; the stone sank into his forehead,
and he fell face down on the ground.

50 So David prevailed over the Philistine
with a sling and a stone, striking down the
Philistine and killing him; there was no
sword in David's hand. [51]Then David ran
and stood over the Philistine; he grasped his
sword, drew it out of its sheath, and killed
him; then he cut off his head with it.

When the Philistines saw that their champion was dead, they fled. [52]The troops of
Israel and Judah rose up with a shout and
pursued the Philistines as far as Gath[d] and
the gates of Ekron, so that the wounded
Philistines fell on the way from Shaaraim as
far as Gath and Ekron. [53]The Israelites came
back from chasing the Philistines, and they
plundered their camp. [54]David took the head
of the Philistine and brought it to Jerusalem; but he put his armor in his tent.

55 When Saul saw David go out against
the Philistine, he said to Abner, the commander of the army, "Abner, whose son is
this young man?" Abner said, "As your soul
lives, O king, I do not know." [56]The king
said, "Inquire whose son the stripling is."
[57]On David's return from killing the Philistine, Abner took him and brought him
before Saul, with the head of the Philistine
in his hand. [58]Saul said to him, "Whose son
are you, young man?" And David answered,
"I am the son of your servant Jesse the
Bethlehemite."

Jonathan's Covenant with David

18 When David[e] had finished speaking to Saul, the soul of Jonathan
was bound to the soul of David, and Jonathan
loved him as his own soul. [2]Saul took him
that day and would not let him return to
his father's house. [3]Then Jonathan made a
covenant with David, because he loved him
as his own soul. [4]Jonathan stripped himself
of the robe that he was wearing, and gave
it to David, and his armor, and even his
sword and his bow and his belt. [5]David
went out and was successful wherever Saul
sent him; as a result, Saul set him over the
army. And all the people, even the servants
of Saul, approved.

6 As they were coming home, when David
returned from killing the Philistine, the
women came out of all the towns of Israel,
singing and dancing, to meet King Saul,
with tambourines, with songs of joy, and
with musical instruments.[f] [7]And the women
sang to one another as they made merry,

"Saul has killed his thousands,
and David his ten thousands."

[8]Saul was very angry, for this saying displeased him. He said, "They have ascribed
to David ten thousands, and to me they
have ascribed thousands; what more can he
have but the kingdom?" [9]So Saul eyed David
from that day on.

Saul Tries to Kill David

10 The next day an evil spirit from God
rushed upon Saul, and he raved within his
house, while David was playing the lyre, as
he did day by day. Saul had his spear in his
hand; [11]and Saul threw the spear, for he
thought, "I will pin David to the wall." But
David eluded him twice.

12 Saul was afraid of David, because the
LORD was with him but had departed from
Saul. [13]So Saul removed him from his presence, and made him a commander of a
thousand; and David marched out and came
in, leading the army. [14]David had success in
all his undertakings; for the LORD was with
him. [15]When Saul saw that he had great
success, he stood in awe of him. [16]But all
Israel and Judah loved David; for it was he
who marched out and came in leading them.

David Marries Michal

17 Then Saul said to David, "Here is my
elder daughter Merab; I will give her to you
as a wife; only be valiant for me and fight
the LORD's battles." For Saul thought, "I will
not raise a hand against him; let the
Philistines deal with him." [18]David said to
Saul, "Who am I and who are my kinsfolk,
my father's family in Israel, that I should be
son-in-law to the king?" [19]But at the time
when Saul's daughter Merab should have
been given to David, she was given to
Adriel the Meholathite as a wife.

17.50-54 David's killing of Goliath is first said to be by the sling stone and then by the *sword.* For David to have taken Goliath's head *to Jerusalem* is strange, since only after David became king was that city occupied by the tribes of Israel.
17.55-58 That these stories of David came from various sources is indicated by the report of Saul's having to ask about David's identity and family origin when, according to 1 Sam 16, David had been Saul's close companion.
18.1-4 Jonathan's Covenant with David. Saul's son's brotherly love for David leads him to give him gifts which unwittingly serve as symbols of the transfer of royal power from himself to David: *robe, armor, sword.*
18.5-16 Saul admires and envies David's successes. Put in charge of Saul's armies, David is acclaimed by the people as ten times superior to the king in his accomplishments, as their song implies: *Saul has killed his thousands, but David his ten thousands.* After his failed attempts to kill David, Saul *stood in awe of him,* but both *Israel and Judah loved David.*
18.17-30 Saul's Ambivalence toward David. He tries simultaneously (1) to link David with his family by giving him one of his daughters in marriage and (2) to get rid of him by sending him to fight the Philistines, who he hopes will kill David. But David is *loved* by Saul's daughter, and has preeminent military success against *the Philistines.*

17.47 1 Sam 14.6; 2 Chr 14.11; Ps 44.6,7
17.51 1 Sam 21.9; Heb 11.34
17.52 Josh 15.36
17.55 1 Sam 16.21,22
17.57 ver 54
17.58 ver 12
18.1 Gen 44.30; Deut 13.6; 1 Sam 20.17; 2 Sam 1.26
18.2 1 Sam 17.15
18.6 Ex 15.20; Judg 11.34; Ps 68.25
18.7 Ex 15.21; 1 Sam 21.11
18.8 1 Sam 15.8
18.10 1 Sam 16.14,23; 19.9,23,24
18.11 1 Sam 19.10; 20.33
18.12 ver 15,29; 1 Sam 16.13; 14.18
18.13 ver 16; 2 Sam 5.2
18.14 1 Sam 16.18; Gen 39.2,3,23
18.16 ver 5
18.17 1 Sam 17.25; 25.28; ver 21,25
18.18 ver 23; 1 Sam 9.21; 2 Sam 7.18
18.19 2 Sam 21.8; Judg 7.22

[d] Gk Syr: Heb *Gai* [e] Heb *he* [f] Or *triangles,* or *three-stringed instruments*

19.1-18 Saul's continuing efforts to kill David. At first Saul is dissuaded from killing David through the intervention of Jonathan. His repeated attempts to kill David or have him killed are frustrated by Saul's daughter (now David's wife), *Michal.* David finally seeks refuge in the tribal territory of Ephraim to the north of Judah, where he finds *Samuel at Ramah.* The prophetic frenzy seizes both *the messengers* sent by Saul to capture David and finally Saul himself.

20 Now Saul's daughter Michal loved
David. Saul was told, and the thing pleased
him. 21Saul thought, "Let me give her to
him that she may be a snare for him and
that the hand of the Philistines may be
against him." Therefore Saul said to David
a second time,[g] "You shall now be my son-
in-law." 22Saul commanded his servants,
"Speak to David in private and say, 'See, the
king is delighted with you, and all his servants love you; now then, become the king's
son-in-law.' " 23So Saul's servants reported
these words to David in private. And David
said, "Does it seem to you a little thing to
become the king's son-in-law, seeing that I
am a poor man and of no repute?" 24The
servants of Saul told him, "This is what
David said." 25Then Saul said, "Thus shall
you say to David, 'The king desires no
marriage present except a hundred foreskins of the Philistines, that he may be
avenged on the king's enemies.' " Now Saul
planned to make David fall by the hand of
the Philistines. 26When his servants told
David these words, David was well pleased
to be the king's son-in-law. Before the
time had expired, 27David rose and went,
along with his men, and killed one hundred[h]
of the Philistines; and David brought their
foreskins, which were given in full number
to the king, that he might become the
king's son-in-law. Saul gave him his daughter Michal as a wife. 28But when Saul
realized that the LORD was with David, and
that Saul's daughter Michal loved him, 29Saul
was still more afraid of David. So Saul was
David's enemy from that time forward.

30 Then the commanders of the Philistines came out to battle; and as often as
they came out, David had more success
than all the servants of Saul, so that his
fame became very great.

Jonathan Intercedes for David

19 Saul spoke with his son Jonathan
and with all his servants about
killing David. But Saul's son Jonathan took
great delight in David. 2Jonathan told David,
"My father Saul is trying to kill you; therefore be on guard tomorrow morning; stay
in a secret place and hide yourself. 3I will
go out and stand beside my father in the field
where you are, and I will speak to my father
about you; if I learn anything I will tell you."
4Jonathan spoke well of David to his father
Saul, saying to him, "The king should not
sin against his servant David, because he has
not sinned against you, and because his
deeds have been of good service to you; 5for
he took his life in his hand when he attacked
the Philistine, and the LORD brought about
a great victory for all Israel. You saw it, and
rejoiced; why then will you sin against an
innocent person by killing David without
cause?" 6Saul heeded the voice of Jonathan;
Saul swore, "As the LORD lives, he shall not
be put to death." 7So Jonathan called David
and related all these things to him. Jonathan
then brought David to Saul, and he was in
his presence as before.

Michal Helps David Escape from Saul

8 Again there was war, and David went
out to fight the Philistines. He launched a
heavy attack on them, so that they fled
before him. 9Then an evil spirit from the
LORD came upon Saul, as he sat in his house
with his spear in his hand, while David was
playing music. 10Saul sought to pin David
to the wall with the spear; but he eluded
Saul, so that he struck the spear into the
wall. David fled and escaped that night.

11 Saul sent messengers to David's house
to keep watch over him, planning to kill
him in the morning. David's wife Michal
told him, "If you do not save your life
tonight, tomorrow you will be killed." 12So
Michal let David down through the window; he fled away and escaped. 13Michal
took an idol[i] and laid it on the bed; she put
a net[j] of goats' hair on its head, and covered
it with the clothes. 14When Saul sent messengers to take David, she said, "He is sick."
15Then Saul sent the messengers to see
David for themselves. He said, "Bring him
up to me in the bed, that I may kill him."
16When the messengers came in, the idol[k]
was in the bed, with the covering[l] of goats'
hair on its head. 17Saul said to Michal,
"Why have you deceived me like this, and
let my enemy go, so that he has escaped?"
Michal answered Saul, "He said to me, 'Let
me go; why should I kill you?' "

David Joins Samuel in Ramah

18 Now David fled and escaped; he came
to Samuel at Ramah, and told him all that

18.20 ver 28
18.21 ver 17.26
18.25 Ex 22.17; 1 Sam 14.24; ver 17
18.26 ver 21
18.27 ver 13; 2 Sam 3.14
18.30 ver 5
19.1 1 Sam 18.1-3,8,9
19.3 1 Sam 20.9,13
19.4 1 Sam 20.32; Gen 42.22
19.5 1 Sam 17.49,50; 11.13; 20.32
19.7 1 Sam 16.21; 18.2,13
19.9 1 Sam 16.14; 18.10,11
19.10 1 Sam 18.11
19.12 Josh 2.15; Acts 9.24,25
19.14 Josh 2.5
19.18 1 Sam 7.17

[g] Heb *by two* [h] Gk Compare 2 Sam 3.14: Heb *two hundred* [i] Heb *took the teraphim* [j] Meaning of Heb uncertain [k] Heb *the teraphim*

19.20 ver 11,14; 1 Sam 10.5,6; Num 11.25
19.23 Isa 20.2; 1 Sam 10.10-12
20.1 1 Sam 24.9
20.5 Num 10.10; 28.11; 1 Sam 19.2
20.6 1 Sam 17.58; Deut 12.5
20.8 1 Sam 18.3; 23.18; 2 Sam 14.32
20.13 1 Sam 3.17; Ruth 1.17; 1 Sam 17.37
20.15 2 Sam 9.1
20.17 1 Sam 18.1
20.18 ver 5,25
20.19 1 Sam 19.2
20.22 ver 37
20.23 ver 14,15; Gen 31.49,53
20.25 ver 18

Saul had done to him. He and Samuel went and settled at Naioth. 19 Saul was told, "David is at Naioth in Ramah." 20 Then Saul sent messengers to take David. When they saw the company of the prophets in a frenzy, with Samuel standing in charge of[l] them, the spirit of God came upon the messengers of Saul, and they also fell into a prophetic frenzy. 21 When Saul was told, he sent other messengers, and they also fell into a frenzy. Saul sent messengers again the third time, and they also fell into a frenzy. 22 Then he himself went to Ramah. He came to the great well that is in Secu;[m] he asked, "Where are Samuel and David?" And someone said, "They are at Naioth in Ramah." 23 He went there, toward Naioth in Ramah; and the spirit of God came upon him. As he was going, he fell into a prophetic frenzy, until he came to Naioth in Ramah. 24 He too stripped off his clothes, and he too fell into a frenzy before Samuel. He lay naked all that day and all that night. Therefore it is said, "Is Saul also among the prophets?"

The Friendship of David and Jonathan

20 David fled from Naioth in Ramah. He came before Jonathan and said, "What have I done? What is my guilt? And what is my sin against your father that he is trying to take my life?" 2 He said to him, "Far from it! You shall not die. My father does nothing either great or small without disclosing it to me; and why should my father hide this from me? Never!" 3 But David also swore, "Your father knows well that you like me; and he thinks, 'Do not let Jonathan know this, or he will be grieved.' But truly, as the LORD lives and as you yourself live, there is but a step between me and death." 4 Then Jonathan said to David, "Whatever you say, I will do for you." 5 David said to Jonathan, "Tomorrow is the new moon, and I should not fail to sit with the king at the meal; but let me go, so that I may hide in the field until the third evening. 6 If your father misses me at all, then say, 'David earnestly asked leave of me to run to Bethlehem his city; for there is a yearly sacrifice there for all the family.' 7 If he says, 'Good!' it will be well with your servant; but if he is angry, then know that evil has been determined by him. 8 Therefore deal kindly with your servant, for you have brought your servant into a sacred covenant[n] with you. But if there is guilt in me, kill me yourself; why should you bring me to your father?" 9 Jonathan said, "Far be it from you! If I knew that it was decided by my father that evil should come upon you, would I not tell you?" 10 Then David said to Jonathan, "Who will tell me if your father answers you harshly?" 11 Jonathan replied to David, "Come, let us go out into the field." So they both went out into the field.

12 Jonathan said to David, "By the LORD, the God of Israel! When I have sounded out my father, about this time tomorrow, or on the third day, if he is well disposed toward David, shall I not then send and disclose it to you? 13 But if my father intends to do you harm, the LORD do so to Jonathan, and more also, if I do not disclose it to you, and send you away, so that you may go in safety. May the LORD be with you, as he has been with my father. 14 If I am still alive, show me the faithful love of the LORD; but if I die,[l] 15 never cut off your faithful love from my house, even if the LORD were to cut off every one of the enemies of David from the face of the earth." 16 Thus Jonathan made a covenant with the house of David, saying, "May the LORD seek out the enemies of David." 17 Jonathan made David swear again by his love for him; for he loved him as he loved his own life.

18 Jonathan said to him, "Tomorrow is the new moon; you will be missed, because your place will be empty. 19 On the day after tomorrow, you shall go a long way down; go to the place where you hid yourself earlier, and remain beside the stone there.[l] 20 I will shoot three arrows to the side of it, as though I shot at a mark. 21 Then I will send the boy, saying, 'Go, find the arrows.' If I say to the boy, 'Look, the arrows are on this side of you, collect them,' then you are to come, for, as the LORD lives, it is safe for you and there is no danger. 22 But if I say to the young man, 'Look, the arrows are beyond you,' then go; for the LORD has sent you away. 23 As for the matter about which you and I have spoken, the LORD is witness[o] between you and me forever."

24 So David hid himself in the field. When the new moon came, the king sat at the feast to eat. 25 The king sat upon his seat, as at other times, upon the seat by the wall. Jonathan stood, while Abner sat by Saul's

20.1-42 David and Jonathan's *sacred covenant* leads them to develop a scheme to determine whether Saul is going to kill David.

[l] Meaning of Heb uncertain [m] Gk reads *to the well of the threshing floor on the bare height* [n] Heb *a covenant of the LORD* [o] Gk: Heb lacks *witness*

20.26. Saul supposes that David's initial absence from the *feast of the new moon* is the result of some temporary ritual uncleanness. **20.31-34** Saul, in his fury, tells Jonathan that David will deprive him of his right to succeed his father as king. But Jonathan refuses to turn against David. **21.1-15** David is Given the Holy Bread. After fleeing to Nob (referred to in 23.19 as *the city of priests*) near Jerusalem, David pretended he was on a secret mission for Saul and persuaded the priest Ahimelech to give him some of the only bread he had. It was *holy bread*, also known as *the bread of the Presence*, which was reserved for the priests (Lev 24.5-9) and specially exhibited in the sanctuary according to the priestly rules (Ex 25.23-30). Above all, no one who was ritually unclean or who had recently had sexual intercourse could touch any sacred item in the sanctuary (Ex 19.9-15). Observing what David said, did and received from the priest was *Doeg the Edomite*, who later reported the incident to Saul (22.9-10). David fled to *Gath*, on the edge of the plain controlled by the Philistines, taking with him *the sword* with which he had killed Goliath. There he escaped the wrath of the local king by pretending *to be mad*.

side; but David's place was empty.

26 Saul did not say anything that day; for he thought, "Something has befallen him; he is not clean, surely he is not clean." 27But on the second day, the day after the new moon, David's place was empty. And Saul said to his son Jonathan, "Why has the son of Jesse not come to the feast, either yesterday or today?" 28Jonathan answered Saul, "David earnestly asked leave of me to go to Bethlehem; 29he said, 'Let me go; for our family is holding a sacrifice in the city, and my brother has commanded me to be there. So now, if I have found favor in your sight, let me get away, and see my brothers.' For this reason he has not come to the king's table."

30 Then Saul's anger was kindled against Jonathan. He said to him, "You son of a perverse, rebellious woman! Do I not know that you have chosen the son of Jesse to your own shame, and to the shame of your mother's nakedness? 31For as long as the son of Jesse lives upon the earth, neither you nor your kingdom shall be established. Now send and bring him to me, for he shall surely die." 32Then Jonathan answered his father Saul, "Why should he be put to death? What has he done?" 33But Saul threw his spear at him to strike him; so Jonathan knew that it was the decision of his father to put David to death. 34Jonathan rose from the table in fierce anger and ate no food on the second day of the month, for he was grieved for David, and because his father had disgraced him.

35 In the morning Jonathan went out into the field to the appointment with David, and with him was a little boy. 36He said to the boy, "Run and find the arrows that I shoot." As the boy ran, he shot an arrow beyond him. 37When the boy came to the place where Jonathan's arrow had fallen, Jonathan called after the boy and said, "Is the arrow not beyond you?" 38Jonathan called after the boy, "Hurry, be quick, do not linger." So Jonathan's boy gathered up the arrows and came to his master. 39But the boy knew nothing; only Jonathan and David knew the arrangement. 40Jonathan gave his weapons to the boy and said to him, "Go and carry them to the city." 41As soon as the boy had gone, David rose from beside the stone heap[p] and prostrated himself with his face to the ground. He bowed three times, and they kissed each other, and wept with each other; David wept the more.[q] 42Then Jonathan said to David, "Go in peace, since both of us have sworn in the name of the LORD, saying, 'The LORD shall be between me and you, and between my descendants and your descendants, forever.' " He got up and left; and Jonathan went into the city.[r]

David and the Holy Bread

21[s] David came to Nob to the priest Ahimelech. Ahimelech came trembling to meet David, and said to him, "Why are you alone, and no one with you?" 2David said to the priest Ahimelech, "The king has charged me with a matter, and said to me, 'No one must know anything of the matter about which I send you, and with which I have charged you.' I have made an appointment[t] with the young men for such and such a place. 3Now then, what have you at hand? Give me five loaves of bread, or whatever is here." 4The priest answered David, "I have no ordinary bread at hand, only holy bread—provided that the young men have kept themselves from women." 5David answered the priest, "Indeed women have been kept from us as always when I go on an expedition; the vessels of the young men are holy even when it is a common journey; how much more today will their vessels be holy?" 6So the priest gave him the holy bread; for there was no bread there except the bread of the Presence, which is removed from before the LORD, to be replaced by hot bread on the day it is taken away.

7 Now a certain man of the servants of Saul was there that day, detained before the LORD; his name was Doeg the Edomite, the chief of Saul's shepherds.

8 David said to Ahimelech, "Is there no spear or sword here with you? I did not bring my sword or my weapons with me, because the king's business required haste." 9The priest said, "The sword of Goliath the Philistine, whom you killed in the valley of Elah, is here wrapped in a cloth behind the ephod; if you will take that, take it, for there is none here except that one." David said, "There is none like it; give it to me."

[p] Gk: Heb *from beside the south* [q] Vg: Meaning of Heb uncertain [r] This sentence is 21.1 in Heb [s] Ch 21.2 in Heb [t] Q Ms Vg Compare Gk: Meaning of MT uncertain

20.26 1 Sam 16.5; Lev 7.20,21
20.28 ver 6
20.30 Deut 21.20
20.32 1 Sam 19.5; Mt 27.23; Lk 23.22
20.33 ver 7
20.36 ver 20,21
20.37 ver 22
20.42 1 Sam 1.17; ver 22
21.1 1 Sam 22.19; 14.3; 16.4
21.4 Lev 24.5-9; Mt 12.4
21.5 Ex 19.14,15
21.6 Mt 12.3,4; Mk 2.25,26; Lev 24.8,9
21.7 1 Sam 22.9
21.9 1 Sam 17.2,51

21.11 1 Sam 18.7; 29.5
21.12 1 Sam 2.19
22.1 2 Sam 23.13
22.2 1 Sam 23.13; 25.13
22.5 2 Sam 24.11; 1 Chr 29.29; 2 Chr 29.25
22.7 1 Sam 8.14
22.8 1 Sam 18.3; 20.16
22.9 1 Sam 21.1; 14.3
22.10 1 Sam 10.22; 21.6,9
22.14 1 Sam 19.4,5
22.17 Ex 1.17
22.18 1 Sam 2.18,31
22.20 1 Sam 23.6,9; 2.33
22.22 1 Sam 21.7

David Flees to Gath

10 David rose and fled that day from Saul; he went to King Achish of Gath. [11]The servants of Achish said to him, "Is this not David the king of the land? Did they not sing to one another of him in dances,

'Saul has killed his thousands,
and David his ten thousands'?"

[12]David took these words to heart and was very much afraid of King Achish of Gath. [13]So he changed his behavior before them; he pretended to be mad when in their presence.[u] He scratched marks on the doors of the gate, and let his spittle run down his beard. [14]Achish said to his servants, "Look, you see the man is mad; why then have you brought him to me? [15]Do I lack madmen, that you have brought this fellow to play the madman in my presence? Shall this fellow come into my house?"

David and His Followers at Adullam

22 David left there and escaped to the cave of Adullam; when his brothers and all his father's house heard of it, they went down there to him. [2]Everyone who was in distress, and everyone who was in debt, and everyone who was discontented gathered to him; and he became captain over them. Those who were with him numbered about four hundred.

3 David went from there to Mizpeh of Moab. He said to the king of Moab, "Please let my father and mother come[v] to you, until I know what God will do for me." [4]He left them with the king of Moab, and they stayed with him all the time that David was in the stronghold. [5]Then the prophet Gad said to David, "Do not remain in the stronghold; leave, and go into the land of Judah." So David left, and went into the forest of Hereth.

Saul Slaughters the Priests at Nob

6 Saul heard that David and those who were with him had been located. Saul was sitting at Gibeah, under the tamarisk tree on the height, with his spear in his hand, and all his servants were standing around him. [7]Saul said to his servants who stood around him, "Hear now, you Benjaminites; will the son of Jesse give every one of you fields and vineyards, will he make you all commanders of thousands and commanders of hundreds? [8]Is that why all of you have conspired against me? No one discloses to me when my son makes a league with the son of Jesse, none of you is sorry for me or discloses to me that my son has stirred up my servant against me, to lie in wait, as he is doing today." [9]Doeg the Edomite, who was in charge of Saul's servants, answered, "I saw the son of Jesse coming to Nob, to Ahimelech son of Ahitub; [10]he inquired of the LORD for him, gave him provisions, and gave him the sword of Goliath the Philistine."

11 The king sent for the priest Ahimelech son of Ahitub and for all his father's house, the priests who were at Nob; and all of them came to the king. [12]Saul said, "Listen now, son of Ahitub." He answered, "Here I am, my lord." [13]Saul said to him, "Why have you conspired against me, you and the son of Jesse, by giving him bread and a sword, and by inquiring of God for him, so that he has risen against me, to lie in wait, as he is doing today?"

14 Then Ahimelech answered the king, "Who among all your servants is so faithful as David? He is the king's son-in-law, and is quick[w] to do your bidding, and is honored in your house. [15]Is today the first time that I have inquired of God for him? By no means! Do not let the king impute anything to his servant or to any member of my father's house; for your servant has known nothing of all this, much or little." [16]The king said, "You shall surely die, Ahimelech, you and all your father's house." [17]The king said to the guard who stood around him, "Turn and kill the priests of the LORD, because their hand also is with David; they knew that he fled, and did not disclose it to me." But the servants of the king would not raise their hand to attack the priests of the LORD. [18]Then the king said to Doeg, "You, Doeg, turn and attack the priests." Doeg the Edomite turned and attacked the priests; on that day he killed eighty-five who wore the linen ephod. [19]Nob, the city of the priests, he put to the sword; men and women, children and infants, oxen, donkeys, and sheep, he put to the sword.

20 But one of the sons of Ahimelech son of Ahitub, named Abiathar, escaped and fled after David. [21]Abiathar told David that Saul had killed the priests of the LORD. [22]David said to Abiathar, "I knew on that day, when Doeg the Edomite was there, that he

22.1-5 David's Family and Followers Join Him in Flight. David becomes a *captain* or chieftain for those with special needs who flock to him. His parents are put under the protection of the non-Israelite *king of Moab*, east of the Dead Sea.
22.6-23 Identified to Saul by Doeg the Edomite as having aided David (21.1-6), *the priests at Nob* are slaughtered by Doeg on Saul's orders, except for one son, *Abiathar*, who escapes and reports the tragedy to David.

[u] Heb *in their hands* [v] Syr Vg: Heb *come out* [w] Heb *and turns aside*

23.1-29 David Pursued by Saul. David's support of the city of *Keilah* (west of Hebron in the coastal hills) attacked by the *Philistines* leads Saul to a futile attempt to capture him there. *David and his men* find safety in *the Wilderness of Ziph*, south of Hebron on the border of the Judean desert, but are pursued by Saul farther south to the *Wilderness of Maon*. They escape capture by Saul only when word comes of another major Philistine attack. David goes farther east to a spring by the Dead Sea: *En-gedi*.

would surely tell Saul. I am responsible[x] for
the lives of all your father's house. 23Stay
with me, and do not be afraid; for the one
who seeks my life seeks your life; you will
be safe with me."

David Saves the City of Keilah

23 Now they told David, "The
Philistines are fighting against
Keilah, and are robbing the threshing floors."
2David inquired of the LORD, "Shall I go and
attack these Philistines?" The LORD said to
David, "Go and attack the Philistines and
save Keilah." 3But David's men said to him,
"Look, we are afraid here in Judah; how
much more then if we go to Keilah against
the armies of the Philistines?" 4Then David
inquired of the LORD again. The LORD answered him, "Yes, go down to Keilah; for I
will give the Philistines into your hand." 5So
David and his men went to Keilah, fought
with the Philistines, brought away their
livestock, and dealt them a heavy defeat.
Thus David rescued the inhabitants of Keilah.
6 When Abiathar son of Ahimelech fled
to David at Keilah, he came down with an
ephod in his hand. 7Now it was told Saul
that David had come to Keilah. And Saul
said, "God has given[y] him into my hand; for
he has shut himself in by entering a town
that has gates and bars." 8Saul summoned
all the people to war, to go down to Keilah,
to besiege David and his men. 9When David
learned that Saul was plotting evil against
him, he said to the priest Abiathar, "Bring
the ephod here." 10David said, "O LORD, the
God of Israel, your servant has heard that
Saul seeks to come to Keilah, to destroy the
city on my account. 11And now, will[z] Saul
come down as your servant has heard? O
LORD, the God of Israel, I beseech you, tell
your servant." The LORD said, "He will come
down." 12Then David said, "Will the men of
Keilah surrender me and my men into the
hand of Saul?" The LORD said, "They will
surrender you." 13Then David and his men,
who were about six hundred, set out and
left Keilah; they wandered wherever they
could go. When Saul was told that David
had escaped from Keilah, he gave up the
expedition. 14David remained in the strongholds in the wilderness, in the hill country
of the Wilderness of Ziph. Saul sought him
every day, but the LORD[a] did not give him
into his hand.

David Eludes Saul in the Wilderness

15 David was in the Wilderness of Ziph
at Horesh when he learned that[b] Saul had
come out to seek his life. 16Saul's son
Jonathan set out and came to David at
Horesh; there he strengthened his hand
through the LORD.[c] 17He said to him, "Do not
be afraid; for the hand of my father Saul
shall not find you; you shall be king over
Israel, and I shall be second to you; my
father Saul also knows that this is so."
18Then the two of them made a covenant
before the LORD; David remained at Horesh,
and Jonathan went home.
19 Then some Ziphites went up to Saul
at Gibeah and said, "David is hiding among
us in the strongholds of Horesh, on the hill
of Hachilah, which is south of Jeshimon.
20Now, O king, whenever you wish to come
down, do so; and our part will be to surrender him into the king's hand." 21Saul
said, "May you be blessed by the LORD for
showing me compassion! 22Go and make
sure once more; find out exactly where he
is, and who has seen him there; for I am
told that he is very cunning. 23Look around
and learn all the hiding places where he
lurks, and come back to me with sure
information. Then I will go with you; and
if he is in the land, I will search him out
among all the thousands of Judah." 24So
they set out and went to Ziph ahead of Saul.
David and his men were in the wilderness
of Maon, in the Arabah to the south of
Jeshimon. 25Saul and his men went to search
for him. When David was told, he went
down to the rock and stayed in the wilderness of Maon. When Saul heard that, he
pursued David into the wilderness of Maon.
26Saul went on one side of the mountain,
and David and his men on the other side
of the mountain. David was hurrying to get
away from Saul, while Saul and his men
were closing in on David and his men to
capture them. 27Then a messenger came to
Saul, saying, "Hurry and come; for the
Philistines have made a raid on the land."
28So Saul stopped pursuing David, and went
against the Philistines; therefore that place
was called the Rock of Escape.[d] 29[e]David

22.23 1 Kings 2.26
23.1 Josh 15.44
23.2 ver 4,6,9; 2 Sam 5.19,23
23.4 Josh 8.7; Judg 7.7
23.6 1 Sam 22.20
23.9 ver 6; 1 Sam 30.7
23.12 ver 20
23.13 1 Sam 22.2; 25.13
23.14 Josh 15.15; Ps 54.3,4
23.16 1 Sam 30.6
23.17 1 Sam 20.31; 24.20
23.18 1 Sam 18.3; 20.16,42; 2 Sam 9.1; 21.7
23.19 1 Sam 26.1
23.20 ver 12
23.21 1 Sam 22.8
23.24 Josh 15.55; 1 Sam 25.2
23.26 Ps 17.9
23.29 2 Chr 20.2

[x] Gk Vg: Meaning of Heb uncertain [y] Gk Tg: Heb *made a stranger of* [z] Q Ms Compare Gk: MT *Will the men of Keilah surrender me into his hand? Will* [a] Q Ms Gk: MT *God* [b] Or *saw that* [c] Compare Q Ms Gk: MT *God* [d] Or *Rock of Division*; Meaning of Heb uncertain [e] Ch 24.1 in Heb

then went up from there, and lived in the strongholds of En-gedi.

David Spares Saul's Life

24 When Saul returned from following the Philistines, he was told, "David is in the wilderness of En-gedi." 2 Then Saul took three thousand chosen men out of all Israel, and went to look for David and his men in the direction of the Rocks of the Wild Goats. 3 He came to the sheepfolds beside the road, where there was a cave; and Saul went in to relieve himself.[f] Now David and his men were sitting in the innermost parts of the cave. 4 The men of David said to him, "Here is the day of which the LORD said to you, 'I will give your enemy into your hand, and you shall do to him as it seems good to you.' " Then David went and stealthily cut off a corner of Saul's cloak. 5 Afterward David was stricken to the heart because he had cut off a corner of Saul's cloak. 6 He said to his men, "The LORD forbid that I should do this thing to my lord, the LORD's anointed, to raise my hand against him; for he is the LORD's anointed." 7 So David scolded his men severely and did not permit them to attack Saul. Then Saul got up and left the cave, and went on his way.

8 Afterwards David also rose up and went out of the cave and called after Saul, "My lord the king!" When Saul looked behind him, David bowed with his face to the ground, and did obeisance. 9 David said to Saul, "Why do you listen to the words of those who say, 'David seeks to do you harm'? 10 This very day your eyes have seen how the LORD gave you into my hand in the cave; and some urged me to kill you, but I spared[g] you. I said, 'I will not raise my hand against my lord; for he is the LORD's anointed.' 11 See, my father, see the corner of your cloak in my hand; for by the fact that I cut off the corner of your cloak, and did not kill you, you may know for certain that there is no wrong or treason in my hands. I have not sinned against you, though you are hunting me to take my life. 12 May the LORD judge between me and you! May the LORD avenge me on you; but my hand shall not be against you. 13 As the ancient proverb says, 'Out of the wicked comes forth wickedness'; but my hand shall not be against you. 14 Against whom has the king of Israel come out? Whom do you pursue? A dead dog? A single flea? 15 May the LORD therefore be judge, and give sentence between me and you. May he see to it, and plead my cause, and vindicate me against you."

16 When David had finished speaking these words to Saul, Saul said, "Is this your voice, my son David?" Saul lifted up his voice and wept. 17 He said to David, "You are more righteous than I; for you have repaid me good, whereas I have repaid you evil. 18 Today you have explained how you have dealt well with me, in that you did not kill me when the LORD put me into your hands. 19 For who has ever found an enemy, and sent the enemy safely away? So may the LORD reward you with good for what you have done to me this day. 20 Now I know that you shall surely be king, and that the kingdom of Israel shall be established in your hand. 21 Swear to me therefore by the LORD that you will not cut off my descendants after me, and that you will not wipe out my name from my father's house." 22 So David swore this to Saul. Then Saul went home; but David and his men went up to the stronghold.

Death of Samuel

25 Now Samuel died; and all Israel assembled and mourned for him. They buried him at his home in Ramah.

Then David got up and went down to the wilderness of Paran.

David and the Wife of Nabal

2 There was a man in Maon, whose property was in Carmel. The man was very rich; he had three thousand sheep and a thousand goats. He was shearing his sheep in Carmel. 3 Now the name of the man was Nabal, and the name of his wife Abigail. The woman was clever and beautiful, but the man was surly and mean; he was a Calebite. 4 David heard in the wilderness that Nabal was shearing his sheep. 5 So David sent ten young men; and David said to the young men, "Go up to Carmel, and go to Nabal, and greet him in my name. 6 Thus you shall salute him: 'Peace be to you, and peace be to your house, and peace be to all that you have. 7 I hear that you have shearers; now your shepherds have been with us, and we did them no harm,

[f] Heb *to cover his feet* [g] Gk Syr Tg Vg: Heb *it* (my eye) *spared*

24.1 1 Sam 23.28,29
24.2 1 Sam 26.2
24.3 Judg 3.24
24.4 1 Sam 23.17; 25.28-30
24.5 2 Sam 24.10
24.6 1 Sam 26.11
24.8 1 Sam 25.23,24
24.11 Ps 7.3; 35.7; 1 Sam 23.14,23; 26.20
24.12 Gen 31.53; Judg 11.27; 1 Sam 26.10; Job 5.8
24.13 Mt 7.16-20
24.14 1 Sam 17.43; 26.20
24.15 ver 12; Ps 35.1; Mic 7.9
24.16 1 Sam 26.17
24.17 1 Sam 26.21; Mt 5.44
24.18 1 Sam 26.23
24.20 1 Sam 23.17
24.21 Gen 21.23; 2 Sam 21.6-8
24.22 1 Sam 23.29
25.1 1 Sam 28.3; Deut 34.8; 2 Chr 33.20; Gen 21.21
25.2 1 Sam 23.24; Josh 15.55
25.6 1 Chr 12.18
25.7 2 Sam 13.23,24; ver 15,21

24.1-22 David's refusal to kill Saul when he had the opportunity to do so moved Saul to forgive David and to acknowledge that he would *surely be king.*
25.1-42 After moving far to the south in the Wilderness of Paran, north of the Gulf of Aqabah, David's request to a wealthy owner of flocks, *Nabal* (meaning "fool") for supplies for his supporters was rejected. *Carmel* was on the edge of the Judean desert west of En-gedi. Nabal's wife, *Abigail,* interceded to keep David from killing her husband and his men, but he died, and she became David's *wife.* His other wives were Ahinoam and Saul's daughter, *Michal.*

and they missed nothing, all the time they
were in Carmel. 8Ask your young men, and
they will tell you. Therefore let my young
men find favor in your sight; for we have
come on a feast day. Please give whatever
you have at hand to your servants and to
your son David.' "
9 When David's young men came, they
said all this to Nabal in the name of David;
and then they waited. 10But Nabal answered
David's servants, "Who is David? Who is
the son of Jesse? There are many servants
today who are breaking away from their
masters. 11Shall I take my bread and my
water and the meat that I have butchered
for my shearers, and give it to men who
come from I do not know where?" 12So
David's young men turned away, and came
back and told him all this. 13David said to
his men, "Every man strap on his sword!"
And every one of them strapped on his
sword; David also strapped on his sword;
and about four hundred men went up after
David, while two hundred remained with
the baggage.
14 But one of the young men told Abigail,
Nabal's wife, "David sent messengers out of
the wilderness to salute our master; and he
shouted insults at them. 15Yet the men were
very good to us, and we suffered no harm,
and we never missed anything when we
were in the fields, as long as we were with
them; 16they were a wall to us both by
night and by day, all the while we were
with them keeping the sheep. 17Now therefore know this and consider what you should
do; for evil has been decided against our
master and against all his house; he is so
ill-natured that no one can speak to him."
18 Then Abigail hurried and took two
hundred loaves, two skins of wine, five
sheep ready dressed, five measures of parched
grain, one hundred clusters of raisins, and
two hundred cakes of figs. She loaded them
on donkeys 19and said to her young men,
"Go on ahead of me; I am coming after
you." But she did not tell her husband
Nabal. 20As she rode on the donkey and
came down under cover of the mountain,
David and his men came down toward her;
and she met them. 21Now David had said,
"Surely it was in vain that I protected all
that this fellow has in the wilderness, so
that nothing was missed of all that belonged to him; but he has returned me evil
for good. 22God do so to David[h] and more
also, if by morning I leave so much as one
male of all who belong to him."
23 When Abigail saw David, she hurried
and alighted from the donkey, fell before
David on her face, bowing to the ground.
24She fell at his feet and said, "Upon me
alone, my lord, be the guilt; please let your
servant speak in your ears, and hear the
words of your servant. 25My lord, do not
take seriously this ill-natured fellow, Nabal;
for as his name is, so is he; Nabal[i] is his
name, and folly is with him; but I, your
servant, did not see the young men of my
lord, whom you sent.
26 Now then, my lord, as the LORD lives,
and as you yourself live, since the LORD has
restrained you from bloodguilt and from
taking vengeance with your own hand,
now let your enemies and those who seek
to do evil to my lord be like Nabal. 27And
now let this present that your servant has
brought to my lord be given to the young
men who follow my lord. 28Please forgive
the trespass of your servant; for the LORD
will certainly make my lord a sure house,
because my lord is fighting the battles of the
LORD; and evil shall not be found in you so
long as you live. 29If anyone should rise up
to pursue you and to seek your life, the life
of my lord shall be bound in the bundle of
the living under the care of the LORD your
God; but the lives of your enemies he shall
sling out as from the hollow of a sling.
30When the LORD has done to my lord according to all the good that he has spoken
concerning you, and has appointed you
prince over Israel, 31my lord shall have no
cause of grief, or pangs of conscience, for
having shed blood without cause or for
having saved himself. And when the LORD
has dealt well with my lord, then remember
your servant."
32 David said to Abigail, "Blessed be the
LORD, the God of Israel, who sent you to
meet me today! 33Blessed be your good sense,
and blessed be you, who have kept me
today from bloodguilt and from avenging
myself by my own hand! 34For as surely as
the LORD the God of Israel lives, who has
restrained me from hurting you, unless you
had hurried and come to meet me, truly by
morning there would not have been left to
Nabal so much as one male." 35Then David
received from her hand what she had
brought him; he said to her, "Go up to your
house in peace; see, I have heeded your

25.8 Neh 8.10-12
25.10 Judg 9.28
25.13 1 Sam 23.13; 30.24
25.15 ver 7
25.16 Ex 14.22
25.18 2 Sam 16.1; 1 Chr 12.40
25.19 Gen 32.16,20
25.21 Ps 109.5
25.22 1 Sam 3.17; 20.13; 1 Kings 14.10
25.23 Josh 15.18
25.24 2 Sam 14.9
25.25 Deut 13.13
25.26 1 Sam 20.3
25.28 1 Sam 2.35; 18.27
25.32 ver 39; Gen 24.27
25.35 1 Sam 20.42; 2 Kings 5.19; Gen 19.21

[h] Gk Compare Syr: Heb *the enemies of David* [i] That is *Fool*

25.36 2 Sam 13.23
25.39 1 Sam 24.15; ver 26.34; 1 Kings 2.44
25.41 Ruth 2.10,13; Mk 1.7
25.42 Gen 24.61-67
25.43 Josh 15.56; 1 Sam 27.3
25.44 2 Sam 3.14; Isa 10.30
26.1 1 Sam 23.19
26.2 1 Sam 13.2; 24.2
26.5 1 Sam 14.50; 17.55
26.6 1 Chr 2.16; Judg 7.10,11
26.9 1 Sam 24.6,7; 2 Sam 1.16
26.10 1 Sam 25.38; Deut 31.14; 1 Sam 31.6
26.11 1 Sam 24.6,12
26.12 Gen 2.21; 16.12
26.17 1 Sam 24.16
26.18 1 Sam 24.9,11-14
26.19 2 Sam 16.11
26.20 1 Sam 24.14

voice, and I have granted your petition."
36 Abigail came to Nabal; he was holding a feast in his house, like the feast of a
king. Nabal's heart was merry within him,
for he was very drunk; so she told him
nothing at all until the morning light. 37In
the morning, when the wine had gone out
of Nabal, his wife told him these things, and
his heart died within him; he became like
a stone. 38About ten days later the LORD
struck Nabal, and he died.
39 When David heard that Nabal was
dead, he said, "Blessed be the LORD who has
judged the case of Nabal's insult to me, and
has kept back his servant from evil; the LORD
has returned the evildoing of Nabal upon
his own head." Then David sent and wooed
Abigail, to make her his wife. 40When David's
servants came to Abigail at Carmel, they
said to her, "David has sent us to you to
take you to him as his wife." 41She rose and
bowed down, with her face to the ground,
and said, "Your servant is a slave to wash
the feet of the servants of my lord." 42Abigail
got up hurriedly and rode away on a donkey; her five maids attended her. She went
after the messengers of David and became
his wife.
43 David also married Ahinoam of Jezreel;
both of them became his wives. 44Saul had
given his daughter Michal, David's wife, to
Palti son of Laish, who was from Gallim.

David Spares Saul's Life a Second Time

26 Then the Ziphites came to Saul at
Gibeah, saying, "David is in hiding
on the hill of Hachilah, which is opposite
Jeshimon."[j] 2So Saul rose and went down to
the Wilderness of Ziph, with three thousand
chosen men of Israel, to seek David in the
Wilderness of Ziph. 3Saul encamped on the
hill of Hachilah, which is opposite Jeshimon[j]
beside the road. But David remained in the
wilderness. When he learned that Saul came
after him into the wilderness, 4David sent
out spies, and learned that Saul had indeed
arrived. 5Then David set out and came to
the place where Saul had encamped; and
David saw the place where Saul lay, with
Abner son of Ner, the commander of his
army. Saul was lying within the encampment, while the army was encamped around
him.
6 Then David said to Ahimelech the
Hittite, and to Joab's brother Abishai son of
Zeruiah, "Who will go down with me into
the camp to Saul?" Abishai said, "I will go
down with you." 7So David and Abishai
went to the army by night; there Saul lay
sleeping within the encampment, with his
spear stuck in the ground at his head; and
Abner and the army lay around him.
8Abishai said to David, "God has given your
enemy into your hand today; now therefore
let me pin him to the ground with one
stroke of the spear; I will not strike him
twice." 9But David said to Abishai, "Do not
destroy him; for who can raise his hand
against the LORD's anointed, and be guiltless?" 10David said, "As the LORD lives, the
LORD will strike him down; or his day will
come to die; or he will go down into battle
and perish. 11The LORD forbid that I should
raise my hand against the LORD's anointed;
but now take the spear that is at his head,
and the water jar, and let us go." 12So David
took the spear that was at Saul's head and
the water jar, and they went away. No one
saw it, or knew it, nor did anyone awake;
for they were all asleep, because a deep
sleep from the LORD had fallen upon them.
13 Then David went over to the other
side, and stood on top of a hill far away,
with a great distance between them. 14David
called to the army and to Abner son of Ner,
saying, "Abner! Will you not answer?" Then
Abner replied, "Who are you that calls to
the king?" 15David said to Abner, "Are you
not a man? Who is like you in Israel? Why
then have you not kept watch over your
lord the king? For one of the people came
in to destroy your lord the king. 16This
thing that you have done is not good. As
the LORD lives, you deserve to die, because
you have not kept watch over your lord,
the LORD's anointed. See now, where is the
king's spear, or the water jar that was at
his head?"
17 Saul recognized David's voice, and
said, "Is this your voice, my son David?"
David said, "It is my voice, my lord, O king."
18And he added, "Why does my lord pursue
his servant? For what have I done? What
guilt is on my hands? 19Now therefore let
my lord the king hear the words of his
servant. If it is the LORD who has stirred you
up against me, may he accept an offering;
but if it is mortals, may they be cursed
before the LORD, for they have driven me out
today from my share in the heritage of the
LORD, saying, 'Go, serve other gods.' 20Now

26.1-25 Saul's repeated pursuit of David into the Wilderness of Ziph led to David's finding him unguarded and refusing to kill him. David shouts across a valley to inform Saul of the failure of his general, *Abner*, to give Saul adequate protection, and questions why Saul wants to kill him. Saul confesses once more, and promises not to raise his hand *against the LORD's anointed:* that is, David.

[j] Or *opposite the wasteland*

27.1-28.2 David Serves a Philistine King. David, his troops of *six hundred*, and his wives take up residence in the southern Philistine city of Gath, from which they conduct raids on non-Israelite tribes (*Amalekites, Geshurites, Girzites*) in the arid area to the southeast toward the border of Egypt for the benefit of the local king, *Achish*. David reported, however, that he had raided the tribe of Judah, with the result that Achish engaged David to fight with him against Israel and to be his *bodyguard for life*. David was rewarded by the king with the gift of the city of *Ziklag*, which was to remain in the hands of the tribe of Judah.

28.3-25 Saul Consults a Medium. Faced with massed Philistine troops at Shunem (on the north of the great Valley of Jezreel in central Palestine), Saul at Gilboa on the hills to the south is unable to get an answer from *the* LORD about the outcome of the impending battle, and consults *a medium at Endor*. When she calls up the recently-dead *Samuel*, he tells Saul that the *kingdom* will be given to *David*, and that Saul's armies will be defeated by *the Philistines*.

therefore, do not let my blood fall to the ground, away from the presence of the LORD; for the king of Israel has come out to seek a single flea, like one who hunts a partridge in the mountains."

21 Then Saul said, "I have done wrong; come back, my son David, for I will never harm you again, because my life was precious in your sight today; I have been a fool, and have made a great mistake." [22]David replied, "Here is the spear, O king! Let one of the young men come over and get it. [23]The LORD rewards everyone for his righteousness and his faithfulness; for the LORD gave you into my hand today, but I would not raise my hand against the LORD's anointed. [24]As your life was precious today in my sight, so may my life be precious in the sight of the LORD, and may he rescue me from all tribulation." [25]Then Saul said to David, "Blessed be you, my son David! You will do many things and will succeed in them." So David went his way, and Saul returned to his place.

David Serves King Achish of Gath

27 David said in his heart, "I shall now perish one day by the hand of Saul; there is nothing better for me than to escape to the land of the Philistines; then Saul will despair of seeking me any longer within the borders of Israel, and I shall escape out of his hand." [2]So David set out and went over, he and the six hundred men who were with him, to King Achish son of Maoch of Gath. [3]David stayed with Achish at Gath, he and his troops, every man with his household, and David with his two wives, Ahinoam of Jezreel, and Abigail of Carmel, Nabal's widow. [4]When Saul was told that David had fled to Gath, he no longer sought for him.

5 Then David said to Achish, "If I have found favor in your sight, let a place be given me in one of the country towns, so that I may live there; for why should your servant live in the royal city with you?" [6]So that day Achish gave him Ziklag; therefore Ziklag has belonged to the kings of Judah to this day. [7]The length of time that David lived in the country of the Philistines was one year and four months.

8 Now David and his men went up and made raids on the Geshurites, the Girzites, and the Amalekites; for these were the landed settlements from Telam[k] on the way to Shur and on to the land of Egypt. [9]David struck the land, leaving neither man nor woman alive, but took away the sheep, the oxen, the donkeys, the camels, and the clothing, and came back to Achish. [10]When Achish asked, "Against whom[l] have you made a raid today?" David would say, "Against the Negeb of Judah," or "Against the Negeb of the Jerahmeelites," or, "Against the Negeb of the Kenites." [11]David left neither man nor woman alive to be brought back to Gath, thinking, "They might tell about us, and say, 'David has done so and so.' " Such was his practice all the time he lived in the country of the Philistines. [12]Achish trusted David, thinking, "He has made himself utterly abhorrent to his people Israel; therefore he shall always be my servant."

28 In those days the Philistines gathered their forces for war, to fight against Israel. Achish said to David, "You know, of course, that you and your men are to go out with me in the army." [2]David said to Achish, "Very well, then you shall know what your servant can do." Achish said to David, "Very well, I will make you my bodyguard for life."

Saul Consults a Medium

3 Now Samuel had died, and all Israel had mourned for him and buried him in Ramah, his own city. Saul had expelled the mediums and the wizards from the land. [4]The Philistines assembled, and came and encamped at Shunem. Saul gathered all Israel, and they encamped at Gilboa. [5]When Saul saw the army of the Philistines, he was afraid, and his heart trembled greatly. [6]When Saul inquired of the LORD, the LORD did not answer him, not by dreams, or by Urim, or by prophets. [7]Then Saul said to his servants, "Seek out for me a woman who is a medium, so that I may go to her and inquire of her." His servants said to him, "There is a medium at Endor."

8 So Saul disguised himself and put on other clothes and went there, he and two men with him. They came to the woman by night. And he said, "Consult a spirit for me, and bring up for me the one whom I name to you." [9]The woman said to him, "Surely you know what Saul has done, how he has cut off the mediums and the wizards from the land. Why then are you laying a

[k] Compare Gk 15.4: Heb *from of old* [l] Q Ms Gk Vg: MT lacks *whom*

26.21 1 Sam 15.24; 24.17
26.22 1 Sam 24.12,19
26.24 Ps 54.7
27.2 1 Sam 25.13; 21.10
27.3 1 Sam 30.3; 25.42,43
27.6 Josh 15.31; 19.5
27.7 1 Sam 29.3
27.8 Josh 13.2,13; Ex 17.8; Ex 15.22
27.9 1 Sam 15.3
27.10 1 Chr 2.9,25; Judg 1.16
28.1 1 Sam 29.1
28.3 1 Sam 25.1; 7.17; 15.23; Lev 19.31; Deut 18.10,11
28.4 2 Kings 4.8; 1 Sam 31.1
28.6 1 Chr 10.13,14; Prov 1.28; Ex 28.30
28.7 Acts 16.16; Josh 17.11
28.8 Isa 8.19; Deut 18.10,11
28.9 ver 3

28.14 1 Sam 15.27; 24.8
28.15 1 Sam 18.12; ver 6
28.17 1 Sam 15.28
28.18 1 Sam 15.9,20.26
28.19 1 Sam 31.2
28.21 1 Sam 19.5
28.23 2 Kings 5.13
29.1 1 Sam 28.1; 4.1; Josh 12.18
29.2 1 Sam 28.1,2
29.3 1 Sam 27.7; Dan 6.5
29.4 1 Chr 12.19; 1 Sam 14.21
29.5 1 Sam 18.7; 21.11
29.6 ver 3
29.9 2 Sam 14.17,20; 19.27; ver 4
29.10 1 Chr 12.19,22

snare for my life to bring about my death?" [10]But Saul swore to her by the LORD, "As the LORD lives, no punishment shall come upon you for this thing." [11]Then the woman said, "Whom shall I bring up for you?" He answered, "Bring up Samuel for me." [12]When the woman saw Samuel, she cried out with a loud voice; and the woman said to Saul, "Why have you deceived me? You are Saul!" [13]The king said to her, "Have no fear; what do you see?" The woman said to Saul, "I see a divine being[m] coming up out of the ground." [14]He said to her, "What is his appearance?" She said, "An old man is coming up; he is wrapped in a robe." So Saul knew that it was Samuel, and he bowed with his face to the ground, and did obeisance.

15 Then Samuel said to Saul, "Why have you disturbed me by bringing me up?" Saul answered, "I am in great distress, for the Philistines are warring against me, and God has turned away from me and answers me no more, either by prophets or by dreams; so I have summoned you to tell me what I should do." [16]Samuel said, "Why then do you ask me, since the LORD has turned from you and become your enemy? [17]The LORD has done to you just as he spoke by me; for the LORD has torn the kingdom out of your hand, and given it to your neighbor, David. [18]Because you did not obey the voice of the LORD, and did not carry out his fierce wrath against Amalek, therefore the LORD has done this thing to you today. [19]Moreover the LORD will give Israel along with you into the hands of the Philistines; and tomorrow you and your sons shall be with me; the LORD will also give the army of Israel into the hands of the Philistines."

20 Immediately Saul fell full length on the ground, filled with fear because of the words of Samuel; and there was no strength in him, for he had eaten nothing all day and all night. [21]The woman came to Saul, and when she saw that he was terrified, she said to him, "Your servant has listened to you; I have taken my life in my hand, and have listened to what you have said to me. [22]Now therefore, you also listen to your servant; let me set a morsel of bread before you. Eat, that you may have strength when you go on your way." [23]He refused, and said, "I will not eat." But his servants, together with the woman, urged him; and he listened to their words. So he got up from the ground and sat on the bed. [24]Now the woman had a fatted calf in the house. She quickly slaughtered it, and she took flour, kneaded it, and baked unleavened cakes. [25]She put them before Saul and his servants, and they ate. Then they rose and went away that night.

The Philistines Reject David

29 Now the Philistines gathered all their forces at Aphek, while the Israelites were encamped by the fountain that is in Jezreel. [2]As the lords of the Philistines were passing on by hundreds and by thousands, and David and his men were passing on in the rear with Achish, [3]the commanders of the Philistines said, "What are these Hebrews doing here?" Achish said to the commanders of the Philistines, "Is this not David, the servant of King Saul of Israel, who has been with me now for days and years? Since he deserted to me I have found no fault in him to this day." [4]But the commanders of the Philistines were angry with him; and the commanders of the Philistines said to him, "Send the man back, so that he may return to the place that you have assigned to him; he shall not go down with us to battle, or else he may become an adversary to us in the battle. For how could this fellow reconcile himself to his lord? Would it not be with the heads of the men here? [5]Is this not David, of whom they sing to one another in dances,

'Saul has killed his thousands,
and David his ten thousands'?"

6 Then Achish called David and said to him, "As the LORD lives, you have been honest, and to me it seems right that you should march out and in with me in the campaign; for I have found nothing wrong in you from the day of your coming to me until today. Nevertheless the lords do not approve of you. [7]So go back now; and go peaceably; do nothing to displease the lords of the Philistines." [8]David said to Achish, "But what have I done? What have you found in your servant from the day I entered your service until now, that I should not go and fight against the enemies of my lord the king?" [9]Achish replied to David, "I know that you are as blameless in my sight as an angel of God; nevertheless, the commanders of the Philistines have said, 'He shall not go up with us to the battle.' [10]Now

29.1-11 David's proposal that he fight with the Philistines against his own people is rejected by the Philistine leaders, and he returns to their territory as they prepare to invade Israel in the Valley of Jezreel.

[m] Or *a god*; or *gods*

30.1-30 David Avenges the Amalekites' Destruction of Ziklag. Returning to find their city (27.6) plundered and their wives and people taken captive by the Amalekites, David is encouraged by the divine instruction through the *ephod* (a garment which was supposed to enable the wearer to receive messages from God) of the priest to attack the Amalekites, whom he is taken to by an Egyptian slave the attackers had left behind for dead. He comes on them in the midst of wild celebration, and all the loot as well as the wives and children is recovered. Even *the two hundred* who were too weary to take part in the pursuit of the Amalekites are permitted by David to share in the *spoil that [was] recovered.* Some of it was also sent to the people of Judah, Benjamin and Ephraim among whom *David and his men had roamed.*

then rise early in the morning, you and the
servants of your lord who came with you,
and go to the place that I appointed for you.
As for the evil report, do not take it to heart,
for you have done well before me.[n] Start
early in the morning, and leave as soon as
you have light." [11]So David set out with his
men early in the morning, to return to the
land of the Philistines. But the Philistines
went up to Jezreel.

David Avenges the Destruction of Ziklag

30 Now when David and his men
came to Ziklag on the third day,
the Amalekites had made a raid on the
Negeb and on Ziklag. They had attacked
Ziklag, burned it down, [2]and taken captive
the women and all[o] who were in it, both
small and great; they killed none of them,
but carried them off, and went their way.
[3]When David and his men came to the city,
they found it burned down, and their wives
and sons and daughters taken captive. [4]Then
David and the people who were with him
raised their voices and wept, until they had
no more strength to weep. [5]David's two
wives also had been taken captive, Ahinoam
of Jezreel, and Abigail the widow of Nabal
of Carmel. [6]David was in great danger; for
the people spoke of stoning him, because all
the people were bitter in spirit for their sons
and daughters. But David strengthened
himself in the LORD his God.
7 David said to the priest Abiathar son of
Ahimelech, "Bring me the ephod." So
Abiathar brought the ephod to David. [8]David
inquired of the LORD, "Shall I pursue this
band? Shall I overtake them?" He answered
him, "Pursue; for you shall surely overtake
and shall surely rescue." [9]So David set out,
he and the six hundred men who were with
him. They came to the Wadi Besor, where
those stayed who were left behind. [10]But
David went on with the pursuit, he and four
hundred men; two hundred stayed behind,
too exhausted to cross the Wadi Besor.
11 In the open country they found an
Egyptian, and brought him to David. They
gave him bread and he ate, they gave him
water to drink; [12]they also gave him a piece
of fig cake and two clusters of raisins. When
he had eaten, his spirit revived; for he had
not eaten bread or drunk water for three
days and three nights. [13]Then David said to
him, "To whom do you belong? Where are
you from?" He said, "I am a young man of
Egypt, servant to an Amalekite. My master
left me behind because I fell sick three days
ago. [14]We had made a raid on the Negeb
of the Cherethites and on that which belongs to Judah and on the Negeb of Caleb;
and we burned Ziklag down." [15]David said
to him, "Will you take me down to this
raiding party?" He said, "Swear to me by
God that you will not kill me, or hand me
over to my master, and I will take you
down to them."
16 When he had taken him down, they
were spread out all over the ground, eating
and drinking and dancing, because of the
great amount of spoil they had taken from
the land of the Philistines and from the land
of Judah. [17]David attacked them from twilight until the evening of the next day. Not
one of them escaped, except four hundred
young men, who mounted camels and fled.
[18]David recovered all that the Amalekites
had taken; and David rescued his two wives.
[19]Nothing was missing, whether small or
great, sons or daughters, spoil or anything
that had been taken; David brought back
everything. [20]David also captured all the
flocks and herds, which were driven ahead
of the other cattle; people said, "This is
David's spoil."
21 Then David came to the two hundred
men who had been too exhausted to follow
David, and who had been left at the Wadi
Besor. They went out to meet David and to
meet the people who were with him. When
David drew near to the people he saluted
them. [22]Then all the corrupt and worthless
fellows among the men who had gone with
David said, "Because they did not go with
us, we will not give them any of the spoil
that we have recovered, except that each
man may take his wife and children, and
leave." [23]But David said, "You shall not do
so, my brothers, with what the LORD has
given us; he has preserved us and handed
over to us the raiding party that attacked
us. [24]Who would listen to you in this matter?
For the share of the one who goes down
into the battle shall be the same as the
share of the one who stays by the baggage;
they shall share alike." [25]From that day
forward he made it a statute and an ordinance for Israel; it continues to the present
day.
26 When David came to Ziklag, he sent
part of the spoil to his friends, the elders of

30.1 1 Sam 29.4,11; 15.7; 27.8
30.5 1 Sam 25.42,43
30.6 Ex 17.4; Ps 27.14; 56.3,4,11
30.7 1 Sam 23.9
30.8 1 Sam 23.2,4; ver 18
30.9 1 Sam 27.2
30.10 ver 9,21
30.12 Judg 15.19
30.14 ver 1,16; 2 Sam 8.18; Ezek 25.16; Josh 14.13
30.16 ver 14
30.17 1 Sam 15.3
30.19 ver 8
30.20 ver 26-31
30.21 ver 10
30.24 Num 31.27; Josh 22.8

[n] Gk: Heb lacks *and go to the place . . . done well before me* [o] Gk: Heb lacks *and all*

Judah, saying, "Here is a present for you from the spoil of the enemies of the LORD"; [27]it was for those in Bethel, in Ramoth of the Negeb, in Jattir, [28]in Aroer, in Siphmoth, in Eshtemoa, [29]in Racal, in the towns of the Jerahmeelites, in the towns of the Kenites, [30]in Hormah, in Bor-ashan, in Athach, [31]in Hebron, all the places where David and his men had roamed.

The Death of Saul and His Sons

31 Now the Philistines fought against Israel; and the men of Israel fled before the Philistines, and many fell[p] on Mount Gilboa. [2]The Philistines overtook Saul and his sons; and the Philistines killed Jonathan and Abinadab and Malchishua, the sons of Saul. [3]The battle pressed hard upon Saul; the archers found him, and he was badly wounded by them. [4]Then Saul said to his armor-bearer, "Draw your sword and thrust me through with it, so that these uncircumcised may not come and thrust me through, and make sport of me." But his armor-bearer was unwilling; for he was terrified. So Saul took his own sword and fell upon it. [5]When his armor-bearer saw that Saul was dead, he also fell upon his sword and died with him. [6]So Saul and his three sons and his armor-bearer and all his men died together on the same day. [7]When the men of Israel who were on the other side of the valley and those beyond the Jordan saw that the men of Israel had fled and that Saul and his sons were dead, they forsook their towns and fled; and the Philistines came and occupied them.

8 The next day, when the Philistines came to strip the dead, they found Saul and his three sons fallen on Mount Gilboa. [9]They cut off his head, stripped off his armor, and sent messengers throughout the land of the Philistines to carry the good news to the houses of their idols and to the people. [10]They put his armor in the temple of Astarte;[q] and they fastened his body to the wall of Beth-shan. [11]But when the inhabitants of Jabesh-gilead heard what the Philistines had done to Saul, [12]all the valiant men set out, traveled all night long, and took the body of Saul and the bodies of his sons from the wall of Beth-shan. They came to Jabesh and burned them there. [13]Then they took their bones and buried them under the tamarisk tree in Jabesh, and fasted seven days.

[p] Heb *and they fell slain* [q] Heb plural

31.1-13 The Death of Saul and His Sons. The utter defeat of *Israel* by *the Philistines* resulted in the death of Saul's sons and in his being fatally wounded, which led him to commit suicide by falling on *his own sword...on Mount Gilboa*, which overlooks the Valley of Jezreel. The news of his death was sent throughout the land of the Philistines, and the body of Saul was affixed to *the wall of Beth-shan*, a major city overlooking the Jordan Valley south of the Lake of Galilee. Israelites from *Jabesh-gilead* on the east side of the Jordan retrieved the bodies of Saul and his sons, and gave them a proper burial.

30.27 Josh 15.30; 19.8; 15.48
30.28 Josh 13.16; 15.50
30.29 1 Sam 27.10; 15.16
30.30 Judg 1.17
30.31 Josh 14.13
31.1 1 Chr 10.1-12; 1 Sam 28.4
31.3 2 Sam 1.6
31.4 Judg 9.54; 2 Sam 1.6,10
31.9 2 Sam 1.20
31.10 1 Sam 7.3; Judg 2.13; 2 Sam 21.12; Josh 17.11
31.11 1 Sam 11.3,9,11
31.12 2 Sam 2.4-7; 2 Chr 16.14
31.13 2 Sam 21.12-14; 1 Sam 22.6; 2 Sam 1.12

2 SAMUEL

See the Introductions, pp. 3, 38, and 42-43 above.

David Mourns for Saul and Jonathan

1 After the death of Saul, when David had returned from defeating the Amalekites, David remained two days in Ziklag. [2]On the third day, a man came from Saul's camp, with his clothes torn and dirt on his head. When he came to David, he fell to the ground and did obeisance. [3]David said to him, "Where have you come from?" He said to him, "I have escaped from the camp of Israel." [4]David said to him, "How did things go? Tell me!" He answered, "The army fled from the battle, but also many of the army fell and died; and Saul and his son Jonathan also died." [5]Then David asked the young man who was reporting to him, "How do you know that Saul and his son Jonathan died?" [6]The young man reporting to him said, "I happened to be on Mount Gilboa; and there was Saul leaning on his spear, while the chariots and the horsemen drew close to him. [7]When he looked behind him, he saw me, and called to me. I answered, 'Here sir.' [8]And he said to me, 'Who are you?' I answered him, 'I am an Amalekite.' [9]He said to me, 'Come, stand over me and kill me; for convulsions have seized me, and yet my life still lingers.' [10]So I stood over him, and killed him, for I knew that he could not live after he had fallen. I took the crown that was on his head and the armlet that was on his arm, and I have brought them here to my lord."

11 Then David took hold of his clothes

1.1-27 David Learns of the Deaths of Saul and Jonathan. **1.1-16** The young *Amalekite* who reports to David that *Saul and Jonathan died* claims that he killed Saul at David's request. This conflicts with the report of Saul's suicide in 1 Sam 31.4. Instead of being rewarded by David, he is executed for having destroyed *the LORD's anointed*.

1.1 1 Sam 31.6; 20.17,26
1.2 1 Sam 4.10,12
1.6 1 Sam 31.2-4
1.8 1 Sam 15.3
1.10 Judg 9.54
1.11 2 Sam 3.31; 13.31

1.17-27 The moving lament of David over the death of Saul and Jonathan is called *the Song of the Bow*, which may be a reference to the warfare carried on by these two (1.22). The lament begins with an instruction to keep the news from the cities of the Philistines – *Gath...Ashkelon – lest the enemies of Israel gloat over the death of Israel's king and his son.* Many scholars attribute this poem to David himself.

2.1-4 David Anointed King in Hebron. Settling with his military supporters in the towns of Hebron, David was in the tribal territory of Judah and in the city where Abraham first settled in the land and built an altar to the LORD (Gen 13.18). It is there that the *people of Judah* come to *anoint David king over them.*

2.8-11 Saul's Son Made King of Israel. *Abner*, commander of Saul's army, installed as king one of Saul's sons, named *Ishbaal*, for the pagan god, Baal. The pious Hebrew tradition would not pronounce that heathen name, but changed it to "Ish-bosheth," meaning "man of shame." All the tribes of Israel except Judah recognized him as king. His military base was at *Mahanaim* in the hills east of the Jordan near the River Jabbok in the territory of Gad.

and tore them; and all the men who were
with him did the same. 12They mourned
and wept, and fasted until evening for Saul
and for his son Jonathan, and for the army
of the LORD and for the house of Israel,
because they had fallen by the sword. 13David
said to the young man who had reported
to him, "Where do you come from?" He
answered, "I am the son of a resident alien,
an Amalekite." 14David said to him, "Were
you not afraid to lift your hand to destroy
the LORD's anointed?" 15Then David called
one of the young men and said, "Come here
and strike him down." So he struck him
down and he died. 16David said to him,
"Your blood be on your head; for your own
mouth has testified against you, saying, 'I
have killed the LORD's anointed.' "

17 David intoned this lamentation over
Saul and his son Jonathan. 18(He ordered
that The Song of the Bow[a] be taught to the
people of Judah; it is written in the Book of
Jashar.) He said:

19 Your glory, O Israel, lies slain upon your high places!
How the mighty have fallen!
20 Tell it not in Gath,
proclaim it not in the streets of Ashkelon;
or the daughters of the Philistines will rejoice,
the daughters of the uncircumcised will exult.

21 You mountains of Gilboa,
let there be no dew or rain upon you,
nor bounteous fields![b]
For there the shield of the mighty was defiled,
the shield of Saul, anointed with oil no more.

22 From the blood of the slain,
from the fat of the mighty,
the bow of Jonathan did not turn back,
nor the sword of Saul return empty.

23 Saul and Jonathan, beloved and lovely!
In life and in death they were not divided;
they were swifter than eagles,
they were stronger than lions.

24 daughters of Israel, weep over Saul,
who clothed you with crimson, in luxury,
who put ornaments of gold on your apparel.

25 How the mighty have fallen
in the midst of the battle!

Jonathan lies slain upon your high places.
26 I am distressed for you, my brother Jonathan;
greatly beloved were you to me;
your love to me was wonderful,
passing the love of women.

27 How the mighty have fallen,
and the weapons of war perished!

David Anointed King of Judah

2 After this David inquired of the LORD,
"Shall I go up into any of the cities
of Judah?" The LORD said to him, "Go up."
David said, "To which shall I go up?" He
said, "To Hebron." 2So David went up there,
along with his two wives, Ahinoam of Jezreel,
and Abigail the widow of Nabal of Carmel.
3David brought up the men who were with
him, every one with his household; and
they settled in the towns of Hebron. 4Then
the people of Judah came, and there they
anointed David king over the house of Judah.
When they told David, "It was the people
of Jabesh-gilead who buried Saul," 5David
sent messengers to the people of Jabesh-
gilead, and said to them, "May you be
blessed by the LORD, because you showed
this loyalty to Saul your lord, and buried
him! 6Now may the LORD show steadfast
love and faithfulness to you! And I too will
reward you because you have done this
thing. 7Therefore let your hands be strong,
and be valiant; for Saul your lord is dead,
and the house of Judah has anointed me
king over them."

Ishbaal King of Israel

8 But Abner son of Ner, commander of
Saul's army, had taken Ishbaal[c] son of Saul,
and brought him over to Mahanaim. 9He
made him king over Gilead, the Ashurites,
Jezreel, Ephraim, Benjamin, and over all
Israel. 10Ishbaal,[c] Saul's son, was forty years

[a] Heb *that The Bow* [b] Meaning of Heb uncertain [c] Gk Compare 1 Chr 8.33; 9.39: Heb *Ish-bosheth*, "man of shame"

1.12 2 Sam 3.35
1.13 ver 8
1.14 1 Sam 24.6; 26.9
1.15 2 Sam 4.10,12
1.16 2 Sam 3.28,29; ver 10
1.17 2 Chr 35.25
1.18 1 Sam 31.3; Josh 10.13
1.19 ver 27
1.20 1 Sam 31.9; Mic 1.10; Ex 15.20; 1 Sam 18.6; 31.4
1.21 1 Sam 31.1; Job 3.3,4; Isa 21.5
1.22 Isa 34.6; 1 Sam 18.4
1.23 Jer 4.13; Judg 14.18
1.25 ver 19,27
1.26 1 Sam 18.1-4
1.27 ver 19,25; 1 Sam 2.4
2.1 1 Sam 23.2,4,9-12; 30.31
2.2 1 Sam 30.5
2.3 1 Sam 30.9; 1 Chr 12.1
2.4 2 Sam 5.3,5; 1 Sam 31.11-13
2.5 1 Sam 23.21
2.8 2 Sam 14.50
2.9 Judg 1.32; 1 Sam 29.1

old when he began to reign over Israel, and
he reigned two years. But the house of
Judah followed David. 11The time that David
was king in Hebron over the house of Judah
was seven years and six months.

The Battle of Gibeon

12 Abner son of Ner, and the servants of
Ishbaal[d] son of Saul, went out from Mahanaim to Gibeon. 13Joab son of Zeruiah, and
the servants of David, went out and met
them at the pool of Gibeon. One group sat
on one side of the pool, while the other sat
on the other side of the pool. 14Abner said
to Joab, "Let the young men come forward
and have a contest before us." Joab said,
"Let them come forward." 15So they came
forward and were counted as they passed
by, twelve for Benjamin and Ishbaal[d] son of
Saul, and twelve of the servants of David.
16Each grasped his opponent by the head,
and thrust his sword in his opponent's side;
so they fell down together. Therefore that
place was called Helkath-hazzurim,[e] which
is at Gibeon. 17The battle was very fierce
that day; and Abner and the men of Israel
were beaten by the servants of David.

18 The three sons of Zeruiah were there,
Joab, Abishai, and Asahel. Now Asahel was
as swift of foot as a wild gazelle. 19Asahel
pursued Abner, turning neither to the right
nor to the left as he followed him. 20Then
Abner looked back and said, "Is it you,
Asahel?" He answered, "Yes, it is." 21Abner
said to him, "Turn to your right or to your
left, and seize one of the young men, and
take his spoil." But Asahel would not turn
away from following him. 22Abner said again
to Asahel, "Turn away from following me;
why should I strike you to the ground? How
then could I show my face to your brother
Joab?" 23But he refused to turn away. So
Abner struck him in the stomach with the
butt of his spear, so that the spear came out
at his back. He fell there, and died where
he lay. And all those who came to the place
where Asahel had fallen and died, stood
still.

24 But Joab and Abishai pursued Abner.
As the sun was going down they came to
the hill of Ammah, which lies before Giah
on the way to the wilderness of Gibeon.
25The Benjaminites rallied around Abner
and formed a single band; they took their
stand on the top of a hill. 26Then Abner
called to Joab, "Is the sword to keep devouring forever? Do you not know that the end
will be bitter? How long will it be before you
order your people to turn from the pursuit
of their kinsmen?" 27Joab said, "As God
lives, if you had not spoken, the people
would have continued to pursue their kinsmen, not stopping until morning." 28Joab
sounded the trumpet and all the people
stopped; they no longer pursued Israel or
engaged in battle any further.

29 Abner and his men traveled all that
night through the Arabah; they crossed the
Jordan, and, marching the whole forenoon,[f]
they came to Mahanaim. 30Joab returned
from the pursuit of Abner; and when he
had gathered all the people together, there
were missing of David's servants nineteen
men besides Asahel. 31But the servants of
David had killed of Benjamin three hundred
sixty of Abner's men. 32They took up Asahel
and buried him in the tomb of his father,
which was at Bethlehem. Joab and his men
marched all night, and the day broke upon
them at Hebron.

Abner Defects to David

3 There was a long war between the
house of Saul and the house of David;
David grew stronger and stronger, while
the house of Saul became weaker and
weaker.

2 Sons were born to David at Hebron: his
firstborn was Amnon, of Ahinoam of Jezreel;
3his second, Chileab, of Abigail the widow
of Nabal of Carmel; the third, Absalom son
of Maacah, daughter of King Talmai of
Geshur; 4the fourth, Adonijah son of Haggith;
the fifth, Shephatiah son of Abital; 5and the
sixth, Ithream, of David's wife Eglah. These
were born to David in Hebron.

6 While there was war between the house
of Saul and the house of David, Abner was
making himself strong in the house of Saul.
7Now Saul had a concubine whose name
was Rizpah daughter of Aiah. And Ishbaal[g]
said to Abner, "Why have you gone in to
my father's concubine?" 8The words of
Ishbaal[d] made Abner very angry; he said,
"Am I a dog's head for Judah? Today I keep
showing loyalty to the house of your father
Saul, to his brothers, and to his friends, and
have not given you into the hand of David;

[d] Gk Compare 1 Chr 8.33; 9.39: Heb *Ish-bosheth*, "man of shame" [e] That is *Field of Sword-edges* [f] Meaning of Heb uncertain [g] Heb *And he*

2.11 2 Sam 5.5
2.12 Josh 18.25
2.13 1 Chr 2.16
2.17 2 Sam 3.1
2.18 1 Chr 2.16; 12.8
2.22 2 Sam 3.27
2.23 2 Sam 3.27; 4.6; 20.10
2.24 Josh 10.41
2.27 ver 14
2.29 ver 8
3.2 1 Chr 3.1-3; 1 Sam 25.42,43
3.3 1 Sam 27.8; 2 Sam 13.37
3.4 1 Kings 1.5
3.7 2 Sam 21.8-11; 16.21
3.8 1 Sam 24.14; 2 Sam 9.8

2.12-32 Contending for Control in Israel. *Joab...and the servants of David* engage in personal combat, rather than mass warfare, in the struggle for control of the tribes of Israel. *Abner and the servants of Ishbaal* invaded the territory of Ephraim, and met the supporters of David at *Gibeon*, northeast of Jerusalem, where the fighting went on until *Abner called to Joab*, and they decided to stop the intertribal killing.
3.1-21 Abner Supports David's Claim to the Throne of Israel.
3.1-5 As the war continued between *the house of Saul* and the supporters of David, his wives bore him six sons *in Hebron*.
3.6-21 Abner Shifts Allegiance to David. Abner's efforts to strengthen his position within the house of Saul were frustrated by the accusation of Ishbaal that he had had sexual relations with a *concubine of Saul*. Abner's response was to announce his intention to help *set up the throne of David over Israel and Judah from Dan* [the northernmost part of the land] *to Beersheba* [the southernmost city]. David agreed to *make a covenant* with Abner, but insisted that he bring with him *Michal, Saul's daughter*, in payment for whom he had given Saul *one hundred foreskins of the Philistines*. Abner then proceeded to gain support for David's kingship from *the whole house of Benjamin* and *all Israel*. Learning of these plans, David *dismissed Abner...in peace*.

3.22-39 Joab, former head of David's troops, was enraged by David's peaceful acceptance of *Abner*, and murdered him. David publicly pronounced a curse on those who killed Abner, then mourned his death and arranged for him to be buried at a hallowed site in *Hebron*, thereby demonstrating to his people that he had no responsibility in Abner's death. He denounced the violence of *the sons of Zeruiah*, including Joab (2.13).

and yet you charge me now with a crime concerning this woman. 9 So may God do to Abner and so may he add to it! For just what the LORD has sworn to David, that will I accomplish for him, 10 to transfer the kingdom from the house of Saul, and set up the throne of David over Israel and over Judah, from Dan to Beer-sheba." 11 And Ishbaal[h] could not answer Abner another word, because he feared him.

12 Abner sent messengers to David at Hebron,[i] saying, "To whom does the land belong? Make your covenant with me, and I will give you my support to bring all Israel over to you." 13 He said, "Good; I will make a covenant with you. But one thing I require of you: you shall never appear in my presence unless you bring Saul's daughter Michal when you come to see me." 14 Then David sent messengers to Saul's son Ishbaal,[j] saying, "Give me my wife Michal, to whom I became engaged at the price of one hundred foreskins of the Philistines." 15 Ishbaal[j] sent and took her from her husband Paltiel the son of Laish. 16 But her husband went with her, weeping as he walked behind her all the way to Bahurim. Then Abner said to him, "Go back home!" So he went back.

17 Abner sent word to the elders of Israel, saying, "For some time past you have been seeking David as king over you. 18 Now then bring it about; for the LORD has promised David: Through my servant David I will save my people Israel from the hand of the Philistines, and from all their enemies." 19 Abner also spoke directly to the Benjaminites; then Abner went to tell David at Hebron all that Israel and the whole house of Benjamin were ready to do.

20 When Abner came with twenty men to David at Hebron, David made a feast for Abner and the men who were with him. 21 Abner said to David, "Let me go and rally all Israel to my lord the king, in order that they may make a covenant with you, and that you may reign over all that your heart desires." So David dismissed Abner, and he went away in peace.

Abner Is Killed by Joab

22 Just then the servants of David arrived with Joab from a raid, bringing much spoil with them. But Abner was not with David at Hebron, for David[k] had dismissed him, and he had gone away in peace. 23 When Joab and all the army that was with him came, it was told Joab, "Abner son of Ner came to the king, and he has dismissed him, and he has gone away in peace." 24 Then Joab went to the king and said, "What have you done? Abner came to you; why did you dismiss him, so that he got away? 25 You know that Abner son of Ner came to deceive you, and to learn your comings and goings and to learn all that you are doing."

26 When Joab came out from David's presence, he sent messengers after Abner, and they brought him back from the cistern of Sirah; but David did not know about it. 27 When Abner returned to Hebron, Joab took him aside in the gateway to speak with him privately, and there he stabbed him in the stomach. So he died for shedding[l] the blood of Asahel, Joab's[m] brother. 28 Afterward, when David heard of it, he said, "I and my kingdom are forever guiltless before the LORD for the blood of Abner son of Ner. 29 May the guilt[n] fall on the head of Joab, and on all his father's house; and may the house of Joab never be without one who has a discharge, or who is leprous,[o] or who holds a spindle, or who falls by the sword, or who lacks food!" 30 So Joab and his brother Abishai murdered Abner because he had killed their brother Asahel in the battle at Gibeon.

31 Then David said to Joab and to all the people who were with him, "Tear your clothes, and put on sackcloth, and mourn over Abner." And King David followed the bier. 32 They buried Abner at Hebron. The king lifted up his voice and wept at the grave of Abner, and all the people wept. 33 The king lamented for Abner, saying,

"Should Abner die as a fool dies?
34 Your hands were not bound,
your feet were not fettered;
as one falls before the wicked
you have fallen."

And all the people wept over him again. 35 Then all the people came to persuade David to eat something while it was still day; but David swore, saying, "So may God do to me, and more, if I taste bread or anything else before the sun goes down!" 36 All the people took notice of it, and it pleased them; just as everything the king did pleased all the people. 37 So all the people and all Israel understood that day that the

[h] Heb *And he* [i] Gk: Heb *where he was* [j] Heb *Ish-bosheth* [k] Heb *he* [l] Heb lacks *shedding* [m] Heb *his* [n] Heb *May it* [o] A term for several skin diseases; precise meaning uncertain

3.9 1 Kings 19.2; 1 Sam 15.8
3.10 Judg 20.1; 1 Sam 3.20
3.13 Gen 43.3; 1 Sam 18.20
3.14 1 Sam 18.25,26
3.15 see 1 Sam 25.44
3.16 2 Sam 16.5
3.18 1 Sam 9.16; 15.28
3.19 1 Sam 10.20,21
3.21 ver 10,12; 1 Kings 11.37
3.22 1 Sam 27.8
3.25 1 Sam 29.6; Isa 37.28
3.27 2 Sam 2.23; 4.6; 20.9,10; 1 Kings 2.5
3.29 1 Kings 2.32
3.30 2 Sam 2.23
3.31 Gen 37.34; 2 Sam 1.2,11
3.33 2 Sam 1.17
3.35 2 Sam 12.17; 1 Sam 3.17; 2 Sam 1.12

3.39 2 Sam 19.5-7; 1 Kings 2.5,6,33,34
4.1 2 Sam 3.27; Ezra 4.4
4.2 Josh 18.25
4.3 Neh 11.33
4.4 2 Sam 9.3,6; 1 Sam 31.1-4
4.5 2 Sam 2.8
4.6 2 Sam 2.23
4.8 1 Sam 23.15; 25.29
4.9 1 Kings 1.29
4.10 2 Sam 1.2,4,15
4.11 Gen 9.5,6
4.12 2 Sam 1.15; 3.32
5.1 1 Chr 11.1; 2 Sam 19.13
5.2 1 Sam 18.13; 16.1,12; 25.30
5.3 1 Chr 11.3; 2 Sam 3.21; 2.4
5.4 Num 4.3; Lk 3.23; 1 Chr 26.31
5.5 2 Sam 2.11
5.6 Josh 15.63; Judg 1.8,21
5.8 ver 9; 2 Sam 6.12,16; 1 Kings 2.10
5.9 ver 7
5.10 2 Sam 3.1
5.11 1 Chr 14.1

king had no part in the killing of Abner son of Ner. [38]And the king said to his servants, "Do you not know that a prince and a great man has fallen this day in Israel? [39]Today I am powerless, even though anointed king; these men, the sons of Zeruiah, are too violent for me. The LORD pay back the one who does wickedly in accordance with his wickedness!"

Ishbaal Assassinated

4 When Saul's son Ishbaal[p] heard that Abner had died at Hebron, his courage failed, and all Israel was dismayed. [2]Saul's son had two captains of raiding bands; the name of the one was Baanah, and the name of the other Rechab. They were sons of Rimmon a Benjaminite from Beeroth—for Beeroth is considered to belong to Benjamin. [3](Now the people of Beeroth had fled to Gittaim and are there as resident aliens to this day).

4 Saul's son Jonathan had a son who was crippled in his feet. He was five years old when the news about Saul and Jonathan came from Jezreel. His nurse picked him up and fled; and, in her haste to flee, it happened that he fell and became lame. His name was Mephibosheth.[q]

5 Now the sons of Rimmon the Beerothite, Rechab and Baanah, set out, and about the heat of the day they came to the house of Ishbaal,[r] while he was taking his noonday rest. [6]They came inside the house as though to take wheat, and they struck him in the stomach; then Rechab and his brother Baanah escaped.[s] [7]Now they had come into the house while he was lying on his couch in his bedchamber; they attacked him, killed him, and beheaded him. Then they took his head and traveled by way of the Arabah all night long. [8]They brought the head of Ishbaal[r] to David at Hebron and said to the king, "Here is the head of Ishbaal,[r] son of Saul, your enemy, who sought your life; the LORD has avenged my lord the king this day on Saul and on his offspring."

9 David answered Rechab and his brother Baanah, the sons of Rimmon the Beerothite, "As the LORD lives, who has redeemed my life out of every adversity, [10]when the one who told me, 'See, Saul is dead,' thought he was bringing good news, I seized him and killed him at Ziklag—this was the reward I gave him for his news. [11]How much more then, when wicked men have killed a righteous man on his bed in his own house! And now shall I not require his blood at your hand, and destroy you from the earth?" [12]So David commanded the young men, and they killed them; they cut off their hands and feet, and hung their bodies beside the pool at Hebron. But the head of Ishbaal[r] they took and buried in the tomb of Abner at Hebron.

David Anointed King of All Israel

5 Then all the tribes of Israel came to David at Hebron, and said, "Look, we are your bone and flesh. [2]For some time, while Saul was king over us, it was you who led out Israel and brought it in. The LORD said to you: It is you who shall be shepherd of my people Israel, you who shall be ruler over Israel." [3]So all the elders of Israel came to the king at Hebron; and King David made a covenant with them at Hebron before the LORD, and they anointed David king over Israel. [4]David was thirty years old when he began to reign, and he reigned forty years. [5]At Hebron he reigned over Judah seven years and six months; and at Jerusalem he reigned over all Israel and Judah thirty-three years.

Jerusalem Made Capital of the United Kingdom

6 The king and his men marched to Jerusalem against the Jebusites, the inhabitants of the land, who said to David, "You will not come in here, even the blind and the lame will turn you back"—thinking, "David cannot come in here." [7]Nevertheless David took the stronghold of Zion, which is now the city of David. [8]David had said on that day, "Whoever would strike down the Jebusites, let him get up the water shaft to attack the lame and the blind, those whom David hates."[t] Therefore it is said, "The blind and the lame shall not come into the house." [9]David occupied the stronghold, and named it the city of David. David built the city all around from the Millo inward. [10]And David became greater and greater, for the LORD, the God of hosts, was with him.

11 King Hiram of Tyre sent messengers to David, along with cedar trees, and car-

[p] Heb lacks *Ishbaal* [q] In 1 Chr 8.34 and 9.40, *Merib-baal* [r] Heb *Ish-bosheth* [s] Meaning of Heb of verse 6 uncertain [t] Another reading is *those who hate David*

4.1-12 The Murder of Ishbaal.
4.1-3 *Rechab and Baanah,* who had been conducting raids for Ishbaal, were disheartened by his loss of *courage* in the contest with David for the throne. The passage reflects the fluidity and mobility of boundaries and populace in the central sections of Israel, with *Benjaminites* living in *Gittaim* on the borders of Philistine territory.
4.4 The parenthetic note about Saul's grandson, *Mephibosheth* (originally, Meri-baal ["hero of Baal"] or Merib-baal ["opponent of Baal"]), prepares the reader for the touching story in 9.1-13 when this cripple becomes a welcome regular guest at *the king's table.*
4.5-12 Rechab and Baanah killed Ishbaal in his sleep, beheaded him and *brought the head to David at Hebron.* Expecting approval, they are executed by David's order, while *the head of Ishbaal* is buried *in the tomb of Abner at Hebron.*
5.1-5 David Anointed as King of All Israel.
5.1-2 David's right to be king was confirmed by his ethnic descent, and by his having led Israel militarily even while Saul was king. He is now to be *shepherd of Israel [and] ruler [or prince] over Israel,* as Saul was (1 Sam 10.1).
5.3 When *the elders of Israel* arrive, however, David is identified as *king over Israel.*
5.4-5 Mention of *Jerusalem* as the seat of his reign anticipates the story to be told of David's capture of this city to serve as his capital.
5.6-16 David Establishes Jerusalem as Capital of Israel.
5.6-10 In spite of scornful opposition from the *Jebusites,* the Canaanite residents of Jerusalem, David was able to take the city, including the central *stronghold,* which became known as *the City of David.* Access to the city was gained through the shaft cut through bedrock to give access from within the city to the spring which lay below and east of the city wall. *The blind and the lame* may have been David's scornful designation of the Jebusites, though later those with such handicaps were excluded from approaching God's altar (Lev 21.17-23) in *the house,* meaning God's temple.
5.11-16 With assistance from *Hiram, king of Tyre,* an economically and culturally advanced Phoenician city-state north of Palestine on the Mediterranean coast, workmen built a royal house for David in his new capital. He greatly enlarged his harem through the acquisition of *concubines and wives,* with the result that the number of his sons and daughters greatly increased.

5.17-25 Philistine Attacks on David are Repulsed. Both the attempted attacks by the Philistines on David began with a massing of their troops in *the valley of Rephaim*, down the slopes which lead from Jerusalem to the Mediterranean and the plain of the Philistines. For David and his army to *go up* against the enemy means to attack them. The first time, the attack is authorized by *the LORD* and is successful. The second time David is to come at them from *their rear*, with the assurance of the support of the invisible heavenly armies which can be heard as *the sound of marching in the tops of the balsam trees*. The Philistines were defeated along a line reaching from Geba (or Gibeah) north of Jerusalem to Gezer on the edge of the Philistine plain.
6.1-23 David Brings the Ark to Jerusalem.
6.1-11 *Baale-judah* is another name for Kirjath-jearim, where the ark had remained since it was brought back from the Philistines (1 Sam 6.19-7.2). Carried on a *new cart*, songs and dancing accompany its transit. When one of the onlookers, *Uzzah*, reached out and touched the ark, he was struck dead. So consternated was David by this that he left the ark in the house of *Obed-edom the Gittite*, from the Philistine city of Gath.
6.12-23 On learning that the ark had brought blessing to the household where it was stored, David decided to bring it into the inner part of Jerusalem, *the city of David*. David's ecstatic dancing in the presence of the ark, which was followed by the appropriate offerings to *the LORD of Hosts* and distribution of food to the people, was interpreted by David's wife *Michal* as vulgar exhibitionism. As a result of her criticism of David, Michal remained childless.

penters and masons who built David a house. 12 David then perceived that the LORD had established him king over Israel, and that he had exalted his kingdom for the sake of his people Israel.

13 In Jerusalem, after he came from Hebron, David took more concubines and wives; and more sons and daughters were born to David. 14 These are the names of those who were born to him in Jerusalem: Shammua, Shobab, Nathan, Solomon, 15 Ibhar, Elishua, Nepheg, Japhia, 16 Elishama, Eliada, and Eliphelet.

Philistine Attack Repulsed

17 When the Philistines heard that David had been anointed king over Israel, all the Philistines went up in search of David; but David heard about it and went down to the stronghold. 18 Now the Philistines had come and spread out in the valley of Rephaim. 19 David inquired of the LORD, "Shall I go up against the Philistines? Will you give them into my hand?" The LORD said to David, "Go up; for I will certainly give the Philistines into your hand." 20 So David came to Baal-perazim, and David defeated them there. He said, "The LORD has burst forth against[u] my enemies before me, like a bursting flood." Therefore that place is called Baal-perazim.[v] 21 The Philistines abandoned their idols there, and David and his men carried them away.

22 Once again the Philistines came up, and were spread out in the valley of Rephaim. 23 When David inquired of the LORD, he said, "You shall not go up; go around to their rear, and come upon them opposite the balsam trees. 24 When you hear the sound of marching in the tops of the balsam trees, then be on the alert; for then the LORD has gone out before you to strike down the army of the Philistines." 25 David did just as the LORD had commanded him; and he struck down the Philistines from Geba all the way to Gezer.

David Brings the Ark to Jerusalem

6 David again gathered all the chosen men of Israel, thirty thousand. 2 David and all the people with him set out and went from Baale-judah, to bring up from there the ark of God, which is called by the name of the LORD of hosts who is enthroned on the cherubim. 3 They carried the ark of God on a new cart, and brought it out of the house of Abinadab, which was on the hill. Uzzah and Ahio,[w] the sons of Abinadab, were driving the new cart 4 with the ark of God;[x] and Ahio[w] went in front of the ark. 5 David and all the house of Israel were dancing before the LORD with all their might, with songs[y] and lyres and harps and tambourines and castanets and cymbals.

6 When they came to the threshing floor of Nacon, Uzzah reached out his hand to the ark of God and took hold of it, for the oxen shook it. 7 The anger of the LORD was kindled against Uzzah; and God struck him there because he reached out his hand to the ark;[z] and he died there beside the ark of God. 8 David was angry because the LORD had burst forth with an outburst upon Uzzah; so that place is called Perez-uzzah,[a] to this day. 9 David was afraid of the LORD that day; he said, "How can the ark of the LORD come into my care?" 10 So David was unwilling to take the ark of the LORD into his care in the city of David; instead David took it to the house of Obed-edom the Gittite. 11 The ark of the LORD remained in the house of Obed-edom the Gittite three months; and the LORD blessed Obed-edom and all his household.

12 It was told King David, "The LORD has blessed the household of Obed-edom and all that belongs to him, because of the ark of God." So David went and brought up the ark of God from the house of Obed-edom to the city of David with rejoicing; 13 and when those who bore the ark of the LORD had gone six paces, he sacrificed an ox and a fatling. 14 David danced before the LORD with all his might; David was girded with a linen ephod. 15 So David and all the house of Israel brought up the ark of the LORD with shouting, and with the sound of the trumpet.

16 As the ark of the LORD came into the city of David, Michal daughter of Saul looked out of the window, and saw King David leaping and dancing before the LORD; and she despised him in her heart.

17 They brought in the ark of the LORD, and set it in its place, inside the tent that David had pitched for it; and David offered burnt offerings and offerings of well-being before the LORD. 18 When David had finished offering the burnt offerings and the offerings

[u] Heb *paraz* [v] That is *Lord of Bursting Forth* [w] Or *and his brother* [x] Compare Gk: Heb *and brought it out of the house of Abinadab, which was on the hill with the ark of God* [y] Q Ms Gk 1 Chr 13.8: Heb *fir-trees* [z] 1 Chr 13.10 Compare Q Ms: Meaning of Heb uncertain [a] That is *Bursting Out Against Uzzah*

5.13 Deut 17.17; 1 Chr 3.9
5.14 1 Chr 3.5-8
5.17 2 Sam 23.14
5.18 Josh 15.18; 17.15; 18.16
5.19 1 Sam 23.2; 2 Sam 2.1
5.20 Isa 28.21
5.21 1 Chr 14.12
5.22 ver 18
5.23 ver 19
5.24 2 Kings 7.6; Judg 4.14
5.25 Josh 12.12; see 1 Chr 14.16
6.2 1 Chr 13.5,6; Lev 24.16; 1 Sam 4.4
6.3 1 Sam 6.7
6.4 1 Sam 7.1
6.5 1 Sam 18.6,7; 1 Chr 13.8
6.6 1 Chr 13.9; Num 4.15,19,20
6.7 1 Sam 6.19
6.10 1 Chr 13.13
6.11 1 Chr 13.14
6.12 1 Chr 15.25; 1 Kings 8.1
6.14 Ex 15.20; 1 Sam 2.18
6.15 1 Chr 15.28
6.16 1 Chr 15.29
6.17 1 Chr 15.1; 16.1; 1 Kings 8.62-65
6.18 1 Kings 8.14,15

of well-being, he blessed the people in the name of the LORD of hosts, 19and distributed food among all the people, the whole multitude of Israel, both men and women, to each a cake of bread, a portion of meat,[b] and a cake of raisins. Then all the people went back to their homes.

20 David returned to bless his household. But Michal the daughter of Saul came out to meet David, and said, "How the king of Israel honored himself today, uncovering himself today before the eyes of his servants' maids, as any vulgar fellow might shamelessly uncover himself!" 21David said to Michal, "It was before the LORD, who chose me in place of your father and all his household, to appoint me as prince over Israel, the people of the LORD, that I have danced before the LORD. 22I will make myself yet more contemptible than this, and I will be abased in my own eyes; but by the maids of whom you have spoken, by them I shall be held in honor." 23And Michal the daughter of Saul had no child to the day of her death.

God's Covenant with David

7 Now when the king was settled in his house, and the LORD had given him rest from all his enemies around him, 2the king said to the prophet Nathan, "See now, I am living in a house of cedar, but the ark of God stays in a tent." 3Nathan said to the king, "Go, do all that you have in mind; for the LORD is with you."

4 But that same night the word of the LORD came to Nathan: 5Go and tell my servant David: Thus says the LORD: Are you the one to build me a house to live in? 6I have not lived in a house since the day I brought up the people of Israel from Egypt to this day, but I have been moving about in a tent and a tabernacle. 7Wherever I have moved about among all the people of Israel, did I ever speak a word with any of the tribal leaders[c] of Israel, whom I commanded to shepherd my people Israel, saying, "Why have you not built me a house of cedar?" 8Now therefore thus you shall say to my servant David: Thus says the LORD of hosts: I took you from the pasture, from following the sheep to be prince over my people Israel; 9and I have been with you wherever you went, and have cut off all your enemies from before you; and I will make for you a great name, like the name of the great ones of the earth. 10And I will appoint a place for my people Israel and will plant them, so that they may live in their own place, and be disturbed no more; and evildoers shall afflict them no more, as formerly, 11from the time that I appointed judges over my people Israel; and I will give you rest from all your enemies. Moreover the LORD declares to you that the LORD will make you a house. 12When your days are fulfilled and you lie down with your ancestors, I will raise up your offspring after you, who shall come forth from your body, and I will establish his kingdom. 13He shall build a house for my name, and I will establish the throne of his kingdom forever. 14I will be a father to him, and he shall be a son to me. When he commits iniquity, I will punish him with a rod such as mortals use, with blows inflicted by human beings. 15But I will not take[d] my steadfast love from him, as I took it from Saul, whom I put away from before you. 16Your house and your kingdom shall be made sure forever before me;[e] your throne shall be established forever. 17In accordance with all these words and with all this vision, Nathan spoke to David.

David's Prayer

18 Then King David went in and sat before the LORD, and said, "Who am I, O Lord GOD, and what is my house, that you have brought me thus far? 19And yet this was a small thing in your eyes, Lord GOD; you have spoken also of your servant's house for a great while to come. May this be instruction for the people,[f] Lord GOD! 20And what more can David say to you? For you know your servant, Lord GOD! 21Because of your promise, and according to your own heart, you have wrought all this greatness, so that your servant may know it. 22Therefore you are great, LORD God; for there is no one like you, and there is no God besides you, according to all that we have heard with our ears. 23Who is like your people, like Israel? Is there another[g] nation on earth whose God went to redeem it as a people, and to make a name for himself,

[b] Vg: Meaning of Heb uncertain [c] Or *any of the tribes* [d] Gk Syr Vg 1 Chr 17.13: Heb *shall not depart* [e] Gk Heb Mss: MT *before you*; Compare 2 Sam 7.26, 29 [f] Meaning of Heb uncertain [g] Gk: Heb *one*

6.20 ver 14.16; 1 Sam 19.24
6.21 1 Sam 13.14; 15.28
7.1 1 Chr 17.1ff
7.2 2 Sam 5.11; Acts 7.46; Ex 26.1
7.3 1 Kings 8.17,18
7.7 Lev 26.11,12; Deut 23.14; 2 Sam 5.2
7.8 1 Sam 16.11,12; Ps 78.70; 2 Sam 6.21
7.9 1 Sam 18.14; 2 Sam 5.10; Ps 18.37-42
7.10 Ex 15.17; Isa 5.2,7; Ps 89.22; Isa 60.18
7.11 Judg 2.16; 1 Sam 12.9-11; ver 1,27; 1 Sam 25.28
7.12 1 Kings 2.1
7.13 1 Kings 5.5; Ps 89.4,29, 36,37; Isa 9.7
7.14 Ps 89.26,27; Heb 1.5; Ps 89.30-33
7.15 1 Sam 15.23,28
7.16 Ps 89.36,37
7.18 Ex 3.11; 1 Sam 18.18
7.20 1 Sam 16.7; Jn 21.17
7.22 Ps 48.1; 86.10; Ex 15.11; Deut 3.24; Ps 44.1
7.23 Deut 4.7,32-38; 10.21; 15.15; 9.26

7.1-17 God's Promise to David. **7.1-3** David, secure in his own new house, proposes to build a permanent structure for *the ark of God,* which had been kept in a mobile tent from the days of the Exodus from Egypt (Ex 27.34) and accompanied Israel as the tribes entered the land of promise (Josh 4.1-13) and began to settle there (Josh 8.30-35; Judg 20.27). *The prophet Nathan,* first mentioned here, had an important role throughout the reign of David. **7.4-17** The message from *the LORD* delivered through *Nathan* is a play on the word *house,* which here refers to a "permanent dwelling place," but also to a "dynasty" or "royal house." God blessed David during his years as shepherd and itinerant military leader; now God will create for him an enduring line of royal successors. But it is one of David's sons, not David himself, who will build *a house for [God's] name.* **7.18-29** David's gratitude to God is not only for the promise of an ongoing dynasty, but even more for the *great and awesome things* God has done for his people, preparing the land for them and overcoming their enemies.

8.1-18 David's Military Successes and Royal Organization. David's armies defeated *the Philistines* on the Mediterranean coast, *the Moabites* southeast of the Dead Sea, *King Hadadezer...of Zobah* north of Damascus, *the Aramaeans of Damascus* (who brought *tribute* to David), and *the Edomites*, on the east side of the Jordan. Tribute was also sent to David from as far away as *Hamath* on the Orontes River in northern Syria. In the list of administrators that David appointed to carry out his rule (8.15-18), those designated *priests* include Zadok and David's sons. Zadok is here linked with Ahitub, as is Ahijah (1 Sam 14.3), but Zadok is not included with the Levites in 1 Chr 16.11, and was probably a priest in the local sanctuary of the Jebusites, where David had him continue to preside when it was dedicated to the LORD. Since David's sons were not descended from Levi or Aaron they would not have been regarded as legitimate priests.
9.1-13 David's Kindness to Mephibosheth. The lame son of Jonathan, Mephibosheth, whose original name was Meribaal (2 Sam 4.4; 1 Chr 8.34), was granted ongoing hospitality in the royal household out of respect for his father, whom David loved (1.26).

doing great and awesome things for them,[h]
by driving out[i] before his people nations
and their gods?[j] 24And you established your
people Israel for yourself to be your people
forever; and you, LORD, became their God.
25And now, LORD God, as for the word that
you have spoken concerning your servant
and concerning his house, confirm it forever; do as you have promised. 26Thus your
name will be magnified forever in the saying, 'The LORD of hosts is God over Israel';
and the house of your servant David will be
established before you. 27For you, LORD of
hosts, the God of Israel, have made this
revelation to your servant, saying, 'I will
build you a house'; therefore your servant
has found courage to pray this prayer to
you. 28And now, Lord GOD, you are God,
and your words are true, and you have
promised this good thing to your servant;
29now therefore may it please you to bless
the house of your servant, so that it may
continue forever before you; for you, Lord
GOD, have spoken, and with your blessing
shall the house of your servant be blessed
forever."

David's Wars

8 Some time afterward, David attacked
the Philistines and subdued them;
David took Metheg-ammah out of the hand
of the Philistines.
2 He also defeated the Moabites and,
making them lie down on the ground,
measured them off with a cord; he measured two lengths of cord for those who were
to be put to death, and one length[k] for those
who were to be spared. And the Moabites
became servants to David and brought
tribute.
3 David also struck down King Hadadezer
son of Rehob of Zobah, as he went to
restore his monument[l] at the river Euphrates. 4David took from him one thousand
seven hundred horsemen, and twenty thousand foot soldiers. David hamstrung all the
chariot horses, but left enough for a hundred chariots. 5When the Arameans of
Damascus came to help King Hadadezer of
Zobah, David killed twenty-two thousand
men of the Arameans. 6Then David put
garrisons among the Arameans of Damascus; and the Arameans became servants to
David and brought tribute. The LORD gave
victory to David wherever he went. 7David
took the gold shields that were carried by
the servants of Hadadezer, and brought them
to Jerusalem. 8From Betah and from Berothai,
towns of Hadadezer, King David took a
great amount of bronze.
9 When King Toi of Hamath heard that
David had defeated the whole army of
Hadadezer, 10Toi sent his son Joram to King
David, to greet him and to congratulate him
because he had fought against Hadadezer
and defeated him. Now Hadadezer had often been at war with Toi. Joram brought
with him articles of silver, gold, and bronze;
11these also King David dedicated to the
LORD, together with the silver and gold that
he dedicated from all the nations he subdued, 12from Edom, Moab, the Ammonites,
the Philistines, Amalek, and from the spoil
of King Hadadezer son of Rehob of Zobah.
13 David won a name for himself. When
he returned, he killed eighteen thousand
Edomites[m] in the Valley of Salt. 14He put
garrisons in Edom; throughout all Edom he
put garrisons, and all the Edomites became
David's servants. And the LORD gave victory
to David wherever he went.

David's Officers

15 So David reigned over all Israel; and
David administered justice and equity to all
his people. 16Joab son of Zeruiah was over
the army; Jehoshaphat son of Ahilud was
recorder; 17Zadok son of Ahitub and
Ahimelech son of Abiathar were priests;
Seraiah was secretary; 18Benaiah son of
Jehoiada was over[n] the Cherethites and the
Pelethites; and David's sons were priests.

David's Kindness to Mephibosheth

9 David asked, "Is there still anyone left
of the house of Saul to whom I may
show kindness for Jonathan's sake?" 2Now
there was a servant of the house of Saul
whose name was Ziba, and he was summoned to David. The king said to him, "Are
you Ziba?" And he said, "At your service!"
3The king said, "Is there anyone remaining
of the house of Saul to whom I may show

[h] Heb *you* [i] Gk 1 Chr 17.21: Heb *for your land* [j] Cn: Heb *before your people, whom you redeemed for yourself from Egypt, nations and its gods* [k] Heb *one full length* [l] Compare 1 Sam 15.12 and 2 Sam 18.18 [m] Gk: Heb *returned from striking down eighteen thousand Arameans* [n] Syr Tg Vg 20.23; 1 Chr 18.17: Heb lacks *was over*

7.24 Deut 26.18; Ps 48.14
7.26 Ps 72.18,19
7.27 ver 13
7.28 Jn 17.17
7.29 Num 6.24-26
8.2 Num 24.17
8.3 2 Sam 10.15-19
8.4 Josh 11.6,9
8.5 1 Kings 11.23-25
8.6 ver 13; 2 Sam 7.9
8.7 1 Kings 10.16
8.10 1 Chr 18.10
8.11 1 Kings 7.51; 1 Chr 18.11; 26.25
8.13 2 Kings 14.7
8.14 Gen 27.29,37,40; Num 24.17,18; ver 6
8.16 2 Sam 19.13; 1 Kings 4.3; 2 Kings 18.18,37
8.17 1 Chr 24.3
8.18 1 Sam 30.14
9.1 1 Sam 20.14-17,42
9.2 2 Sam 16.1-4; 19.17,29
9.3 1 Sam 20.14; 2 Sam 4.4

9.4 2 Sam 17.27
9.6 2 Sam 16.4; 19.24-30
9.7 ver 1,3; 2 Sam 12.8; 19.28
9.8 2 Sam 16.9
9.9 2 Sam 16.4; 19.29
9.10 ver 7,11,13; 2 Sam 19.28
9.12 1 Chr 8.34
9.13 ver 3,7,10
10.1 1 Chr 19.1ff
10.4 Isa 15.2; 20.4
10.6 Gen 34.30; 2 Sam 8.3,5; Judg 18.28
10.8 1 Chr 19.9; Judg 11.3,5
10.12 Deut 31.6; 1 Cor 16.13; 1 Sam 3.18
10.13 1 Kings 20.13-21
10.16 2 Sam 8.3; 1 Chr 19.16
10.18 1 Chr 19.18; 2 Sam 8.6

the kindness of God?" Ziba said to the king, "There remains a son of Jonathan; he is crippled in his feet." [4]The king said to him, "Where is he?" Ziba said to the king, "He is in the house of Machir son of Ammiel, at Lo-debar." [5]Then King David sent and brought him from the house of Machir son of Ammiel, at Lo-debar. [6]Mephibosheth[o] son of Jonathan son of Saul came to David, and fell on his face and did obeisance. David said, "Mephibosheth!"[o] He answered, "I am your servant." [7]David said to him, "Do not be afraid, for I will show you kindness for the sake of your father Jonathan; I will restore to you all the land of your grandfather Saul, and you yourself shall eat at my table always." [8]He did obeisance and said, "What is your servant, that you should look upon a dead dog such as I?"

9 Then the king summoned Saul's servant Ziba, and said to him, "All that belonged to Saul and to all his house I have given to your master's grandson. [10]You and your sons and your servants shall till the land for him, and shall bring in the produce, so that your master's grandson may have food to eat; but your master's grandson Mephibosheth[o] shall always eat at my table." Now Ziba had fifteen sons and twenty servants. [11]Then Ziba said to the king, "According to all that my lord the king commands his servant, so your servant will do." Mephibosheth[o] ate at David's[p] table, like one of the king's sons. [12]Mephibosheth[o] had a young son whose name was Mica. And all who lived in Ziba's house became Mephibosheth's[q] servants. [13]Mephibosheth[o] lived in Jerusalem, for he always ate at the king's table. Now he was lame in both his feet.

The Ammonites and Arameans Are Defeated

10 Some time afterward, the king of the Ammonites died, and his son Hanun succeeded him. [2]David said, "I will deal loyally with Hanun son of Nahash, just as his father dealt loyally with me." So David sent envoys to console him concerning his father. When David's envoys came into the land of the Ammonites, [3]the princes of the Ammonites said to their lord Hanun, "Do you really think that David is honoring your father just because he has sent messengers with condolences to you? Has not David sent his envoys to you to search the city, to spy it out, and to overthrow it?" [4]So Hanun seized David's envoys, shaved off half the beard of each, cut off their garments in the middle at their hips, and sent them away. [5]When David was told, he sent to meet them, for the men were greatly ashamed. The king said, "Remain at Jericho until your beards have grown, and then return."

6 When the Ammonites saw that they had become odious to David, the Ammonites sent and hired the Arameans of Beth-rehob and the Arameans of Zobah, twenty thousand foot soldiers, as well as the king of Maacah, one thousand men, and the men of Tob, twelve thousand men. [7]When David heard of it, he sent Joab and all the army with the warriors. [8]The Ammonites came out and drew up in battle array at the entrance of the gate; but the Arameans of Zobah and of Rehob, and the men of Tob and Maacah, were by themselves in the open country.

9 When Joab saw that the battle was set against him both in front and in the rear, he chose some of the picked men of Israel, and arrayed them against the Arameans; [10]the rest of his men he put in the charge of his brother Abishai, and he arrayed them against the Ammonites. [11]He said, "If the Arameans are too strong for me, then you shall help me; but if the Ammonites are too strong for you, then I will come and help you. [12]Be strong, and let us be courageous for the sake of our people, and for the cities of our God; and may the LORD do what seems good to him." [13]So Joab and the people who were with him moved forward into battle against the Arameans; and they fled before him. [14]When the Ammonites saw that the Arameans fled, they likewise fled before Abishai, and entered the city. Then Joab returned from fighting against the Ammonites, and came to Jerusalem.

15 But when the Arameans saw that they had been defeated by Israel, they gathered themselves together. [16]Hadadezer sent and brought out the Arameans who were beyond the Euphrates; and they came to Helam, with Shobach the commander of the army of Hadadezer at their head. [17]When it was told David, he gathered all Israel together, and crossed the Jordan, and came to Helam. The Arameans arrayed themselves against David and fought with him. [18]The Arameans fled before Israel; and David

10.1-19 Further Military Successes of David's Armies. David's attempt to befriend the *Ammonites* (tribes in the mountains east of the Jordan) evoked shameful treatment of his *envoys*. His troops attacked and defeated them and the *Aramean* mercenaries from Lebanon and Syria who joined them.
The most powerful ruler of this coalition, *Hadadezer*, whose vast domain included Syria and the northern part of the Euphrates valley, *made peace with Israel.*

[o] Or *Merib-baal* : See 4.4 note [p] Gk: Heb *my* [q] Or *Merib-baal's* : See 4.4 note

11.1-5 David's Adultery with Bathsheba, wife of Uriah. David's army, under *Joab*, was engaged in an attack on *Rabbah* (modern Amman), the capital of the *Ammonites. Remaining at home*, David was attracted to *Bathsheba*, and summoned her to the royal house where she became *pregnant*.
11.6-27a David's Schemes to Get Rid of Uriah. The name *Uriah* is pure Hebrew, so his designation as *Hittite* recalls the ethnic origin of his ancestors. The Hittite empire controlled what are now Syria and Turkey, but broke up about 1200 BCE, with its subjects scattering across the Middle East. *Uriah* means "Yahweh is a light." David's calling Uriah back from the army, entertaining him and sending him home was an attempt to make him have sex with his wife (*wash your feet* means to expose your genitals) and thereby to make him think that the child to be born was his son. The successful scheme to get rid of him was to have Joab, the commander of the army, put him in an especially vulnerable place on the battle line. At his death, his wife became David's and *bore him a son*.
11.27b-15 God's Displeasure with David.

killed of the Arameans seven hundred chariot teams, and forty thousand horsemen,[r] and wounded Shobach the commander of their army, so that he died there. [19]When all the kings who were servants of Hadadezer saw that they had been defeated by Israel, they made peace with Israel, and became subject to them. So the Arameans were afraid to help the Ammonites any more.

David Commits Adultery with Bathsheba

11 In the spring of the year, the time when kings go out to battle, David sent Joab with his officers and all Israel with him; they ravaged the Ammonites, and besieged Rabbah. But David remained at Jerusalem.

2 It happened, late one afternoon, when David rose from his couch and was walking about on the roof of the king's house, that he saw from the roof a woman bathing; the woman was very beautiful. [3]David sent someone to inquire about the woman. It was reported, "This is Bathsheba daughter of Eliam, the wife of Uriah the Hittite." [4]So David sent messengers to get her, and she came to him, and he lay with her. (Now she was purifying herself after her period.) Then she returned to her house. [5]The woman conceived; and she sent and told David, "I am pregnant."

6 So David sent word to Joab, "Send me Uriah the Hittite." And Joab sent Uriah to David. [7]When Uriah came to him, David asked how Joab and the people fared, and how the war was going. [8]Then David said to Uriah, "Go down to your house, and wash your feet." Uriah went out of the king's house, and there followed him a present from the king. [9]But Uriah slept at the entrance of the king's house with all the servants of his lord, and did not go down to his house. [10]When they told David, "Uriah did not go down to his house," David said to Uriah, "You have just come from a journey. Why did you not go down to your house?" [11]Uriah said to David, "The ark and Israel and Judah remain in booths;[s] and my lord Joab and the servants of my lord are camping in the open field; shall I then go to my house, to eat and to drink, and to lie with my wife? As you live, and as your soul lives, I will not do such a thing." [12]Then David said to Uriah, "Remain here today also, and tomorrow I will send you back." So Uriah remained in Jerusalem that day. On the next day, [13]David invited him to eat and drink in his presence and made him drunk; and in the evening he went out to lie on his couch with the servants of his lord, but he did not go down to his house.

David Has Uriah Killed

14 In the morning David wrote a letter to Joab, and sent it by the hand of Uriah. [15]In the letter he wrote, "Set Uriah in the forefront of the hardest fighting, and then draw back from him, so that he may be struck down and die." [16]As Joab was besieging the city, he assigned Uriah to the place where he knew there were valiant warriors. [17]The men of the city came out and fought with Joab; and some of the servants of David among the people fell. Uriah the Hittite was killed as well. [18]Then Joab sent and told David all the news about the fighting; [19]and he instructed the messenger, "When you have finished telling the king all the news about the fighting, [20]then, if the king's anger rises, and if he says to you, 'Why did you go so near the city to fight? Did you not know that they would shoot from the wall? [21]Who killed Abimelech son of Jerubbaal?[t] Did not a woman throw an upper millstone on him from the wall, so that he died at Thebez? Why did you go so near the wall?' then you shall say, 'Your servant Uriah the Hittite is dead too.' "

22 So the messenger went, and came and told David all that Joab had sent him to tell. [23]The messenger said to David, "The men gained an advantage over us, and came out against us in the field; but we drove them back to the entrance of the gate. [24]Then the archers shot at your servants from the wall; some of the king's servants are dead; and your servant Uriah the Hittite is dead also." [25]David said to the messenger, "Thus you shall say to Joab, 'Do not let this matter trouble you, for the sword devours now one and now another; press your attack on the city, and overthrow it.' And encourage him."

26 When the wife of Uriah heard that her husband was dead, she made lamentation for him. [27]When the mourning was over, David sent and brought her to his house, and she became his wife, and bore him a son.

11.1 1 Chr 20.1; 1 Kings 20.22,26; 2 Sam 12.26-28
11.2 Deut 22.8; Mt 5.28
11.3 2 Sam 23.39
11.4 Lev 15.19,28; 18.19
11.5 Lev 20.10
11.8 Gen 43.24; Lk 7.44
11.10 2 Sam 7.2,6; 20.6
11.13 ver 9
11.14 1 Kings 21.8-10
11.15 2 Sam 12.9
11.17 ver 21
11.21 Judg 9.50-54
11.26 Deut 34.8; 1 Sam 31.13
11.27 2 Sam 12.9; Ps 51.4,5

[r] 1 Chr 19.18 and some Gk Mss read *foot soldiers* [s] Or *at Succoth* [t] Gk Syr Judg 7.1: Heb *Jerubbesheth*

12.1 2 Sam 14.4-7; 1 Kings 20.35-41
12.5 1 Kings 20.39,40
12.6 Ex 22.1; Lk 19.8
12.7 1 Kings 20.42; 1 Sam 16.13
12.9 1 Sam 15.19; 2 Sam 11.15-17,27
12.10 2 Sam 13.28; 18.14; 1 Kings 2.25
12.11 Deut 28.30; 2 Sam 16.22
12.12 2 Sam 11.4-15; 16.22
12.13 1 Sam 15.24; 2 Sam 24.10; Prov 28.13; Mic 7.18
12.14 Isa 52.5; Rom 2.24
12.15 1 Sam 25.38
12.16 2 Sam 13.31
12.20 Job 1.20
12.22 Isa 38.1,5; Jon 3.9
12.23 Gen 37.35; Job 7.8-10
12.24 Mt 1.6; 1 Chr 22.9
12.26 1 Chr 20.1-3

Nathan Condemns David

But the thing that David had done displeased the LORD,

12 [1]and the LORD sent Nathan to David. He came to him, and said to him, "There were two men in a certain city, the one rich and the other poor. [2]The rich man had very many flocks and herds; [3]but the poor man had nothing but one little ewe lamb, which he had bought. He brought it up, and it grew up with him and with his children; it used to eat of his meager fare, and drink from his cup, and lie in his bosom, and it was like a daughter to him. [4]Now there came a traveler to the rich man, and he was loath to take one of his own flock or herd to prepare for the wayfarer who had come to him, but he took the poor man's lamb, and prepared that for the guest who had come to him." [5]Then David's anger was greatly kindled against the man. He said to Nathan, "As the LORD lives, the man who has done this deserves to die; [6]he shall restore the lamb fourfold, because he did this thing, and because he had no pity."

7 Nathan said to David, "You are the man! Thus says the LORD, the God of Israel: I anointed you king over Israel, and I rescued you from the hand of Saul; [8]I gave you your master's house, and your master's wives into your bosom, and gave you the house of Israel and of Judah; and if that had been too little, I would have added as much more. [9]Why have you despised the word of the LORD, to do what is evil in his sight? You have struck down Uriah the Hittite with the sword, and have taken his wife to be your wife, and have killed him with the sword of the Ammonites. [10]Now therefore the sword shall never depart from your house, for you have despised me, and have taken the wife of Uriah the Hittite to be your wife. [11]Thus says the LORD: I will raise up trouble against you from within your own house; and I will take your wives before your eyes, and give them to your neighbor, and he shall lie with your wives in the sight of this very sun. [12]For you did it secretly; but I will do this thing before all Israel, and before the sun." [13]David said to Nathan, "I have sinned against the LORD." Nathan said to David, "Now the LORD has put away your sin; you shall not die. [14]Nevertheless, because by this deed you have utterly scorned the LORD,[u] the child that is born to you shall die." [15]Then Nathan went to his house.

Bathsheba's Child Dies

The LORD struck the child that Uriah's wife bore to David, and it became very ill. [16]David therefore pleaded with God for the child; David fasted, and went in and lay all night on the ground. [17]The elders of his house stood beside him, urging him to rise from the ground; but he would not, nor did he eat food with them. [18]On the seventh day the child died. And the servants of David were afraid to tell him that the child was dead; for they said, "While the child was still alive, we spoke to him, and he did not listen to us; how then can we tell him the child is dead? He may do himself some harm." [19]But when David saw that his servants were whispering together, he perceived that the child was dead; and David said to his servants, "Is the child dead?" They said, "He is dead."

20 Then David rose from the ground, washed, anointed himself, and changed his clothes. He went into the house of the LORD, and worshiped; he then went to his own house; and when he asked, they set food before him and he ate. [21]Then his servants said to him, "What is this thing that you have done? You fasted and wept for the child while it was alive; but when the child died, you rose and ate food." [22]He said, "While the child was still alive, I fasted and wept; for I said, 'Who knows? The LORD may be gracious to me, and the child may live.' [23]But now he is dead; why should I fast? Can I bring him back again? I shall go to him, but he will not return to me."

Solomon Is Born

24 Then David consoled his wife Bathsheba, and went to her, and lay with her; and she bore a son, and he named him Solomon. The LORD loved him, [25]and sent a message by the prophet Nathan; so he named him Jedidiah,[v] because of the LORD.

The Ammonites Crushed

26 Now Joab fought against Rabbah of the Ammonites, and took the royal city. [27]Joab sent messengers to David, and said, "I have fought against Rabbah; moreover, I have taken the water city. [28]Now, then, gather the rest of the people together, and encamp against the city, and take it; or I

12.1-6 Nathan's Parable of the Theft of the Poor Man's Lamb. The prophet's story evoked David's judgment on the thieving rich man, only to find that he was himself the guilty one in the eyes of the LORD.
12.7-23 God announced his punishment of David, who had been the beneficiary of special divine favor. In spite of his penitence and his period of fasting, he was told that the expected child would die, and *on the seventh day the child died.* David declared that he would one day *go to him* in death, but could not bring him back to life.
12.24-25 The Birth of Solomon. David's name for his son was *Solomon,* based on *shalom,* "peace." Nathan's name for the child was *Jedidiah, "Beloved of the LORD."*
12.26-31 The Capture of the Ammonite Capital. *The royal city* probably refers to the citadel, or heights of the city, where the ruler dwelt. The remainder of *the water city* may have been the fertile section of the city along the river on whose banks it was built. *Joab* urged David to bring the rest of the army with him to complete the capture of the city. David, after taking the city, took as booty the *crown of Milcom* (their god) or the royal crown of gold, which weighed *a talent,* probably 75 pounds or 35 kilograms. The subject *people* were set to work with various tools to build and restore the capital and the other *cities of the Ammonites.*

[u] Ancient scribal tradition: Compare 1 Sam 25.22 note: Heb *scorned the enemies of the LORD* [v] That is *Beloved of the LORD*

13.1-36 Amnon Rapes his Half-sister, Tamar. Tormented by sexual desire for the sister of his half-brother, *Absalom*, David's firstborn *son Amnon* (2 Sam 3.2) feigned illness and schemed to have her come to feed him. After sexually assaulting her, in violation of Mosaic law (Lev 18.9-11; Deut 27.22), he became filled with *great loathing for her*, and sent her away. She *tore* her robe (that of a *virgin* princess) and mourned her condition. David's love for Amnon kept him from punishing the offender, but *Absalom* arranged a feast for all *the king's sons*, at which he had Amnon killed by *the servants*. It was first reported to David that all his sons had been killed, and he was overcome with grief even after they returned.

myself will take the city, and it will be called by my name." 29So David gathered all the people together and went to Rabbah, and fought against it and took it. 30He took the crown of Milcom[w] from his head; the weight of it was a talent of gold, and in it was a precious stone; and it was placed on David's head. He also brought forth the spoil of the city, a very great amount. 31He brought out the people who were in it, and set them to work with saws and iron picks and iron axes, or sent them to the brickworks. Thus he did to all the cities of the Ammonites. Then David and all the people returned to Jerusalem.

Amnon and Tamar

13 Some time passed. David's son Absalom had a beautiful sister whose name was Tamar; and David's son Amnon fell in love with her. 2Amnon was so tormented that he made himself ill because of his sister Tamar, for she was a virgin and it seemed impossible to Amnon to do anything to her. 3But Amnon had a friend whose name was Jonadab, the son of David's brother Shimeah; and Jonadab was a very crafty man. 4He said to him, " son of the king, why are you so haggard morning after morning? Will you not tell me?" Amnon said to him, "I love Tamar, my brother Absalom's sister." 5Jonadab said to him, "Lie down on your bed, and pretend to be ill; and when your father comes to see you, say to him, 'Let my sister Tamar come and give me something to eat, and prepare the food in my sight, so that I may see it and eat it from her hand.' " 6So Amnon lay down, and pretended to be ill; and when the king came to see him, Amnon said to the king, "Please let my sister Tamar come and make a couple of cakes in my sight, so that I may eat from her hand."

7 Then David sent home to Tamar, saying, "Go to your brother Amnon's house, and prepare food for him." 8So Tamar went to her brother Amnon's house, where he was lying down. She took dough, kneaded it, made cakes in his sight, and baked the cakes. 9Then she took the pan and set them[x] out before him, but he refused to eat. Amnon said, "Send out everyone from me." So everyone went out from him. 10Then Amnon said to Tamar, "Bring the food into the chamber, so that I may eat from your hand." So Tamar took the cakes she had made, and brought them into the chamber to Amnon her brother. 11But when she brought them near him to eat, he took hold of her, and said to her, "Come, lie with me, my sister." 12She answered him, "No, my brother, do not force me; for such a thing is not done in Israel; do not do anything so vile! 13As for me, where could I carry my shame? And as for you, you would be as one of the scoundrels in Israel. Now therefore, I beg you, speak to the king; for he will not withhold me from you." 14But he would not listen to her; and being stronger than she, he forced her and lay with her.

15 Then Amnon was seized with a very great loathing for her; indeed, his loathing was even greater than the lust he had felt for her. Amnon said to her, "Get out!" 16But she said to him, "No, my brother;[y] for this wrong in sending me away is greater than the other that you did to me." But he would not listen to her. 17He called the young man who served him and said, "Put this woman out of my presence, and bolt the door after her." 18(Now she was wearing a long robe with sleeves; for this is how the virgin daughters of the king were clothed in earlier times.[z]) So his servant put her out, and bolted the door after her. 19But Tamar put ashes on her head, and tore the long robe that she was wearing; she put her hand on her head, and went away, crying aloud as she went.

20 Her brother Absalom said to her, "Has Amnon your brother been with you? Be quiet for now, my sister; he is your brother; do not take this to heart." So Tamar remained, a desolate woman, in her brother Absalom's house. 21When King David heard of all these things, he became very angry, but he would not punish his son Amnon, because he loved him, for he was his firstborn.[a] 22But Absalom spoke to Amnon neither good nor bad; for Absalom hated Amnon, because he had raped his sister Tamar.

Absalom Avenges the Violation of His Sister

23 After two full years Absalom had sheepshearers at Baal-hazor, which is near Ephraim, and Absalom invited all the king's sons. 24Absalom came to the king, and said,

12.30 1 Chr 20.2
13.1 2 Sam 3.2,3; 1 Chr 3.9
13.3 1 Sam 16.9
13.6 Gen 18.6
13.9 Gen 45.1
13.11 Gen 39.12
13.12 Lev 20.17; Judg 19.23; 20.6
13.13 Gen 20.12; Lev 18.9,11
13.14 Deut 22.25
13.18 Gen 37.3; Judg 5.30
13.19 1 Sam 4.12; 2 Sam 1.2; Jer 2.37
13.20 2 Sam 14.24
13.22 Gen 31.24; Lev 19.17,18

[w] Gk See 1 Kings 11.5, 33: Heb *their kings* [x] Heb *and poured* [y] Cn Compare Gk Vg: Meaning of Heb uncertain [z] Cn: Heb *were clothed in robes* [a] Q Ms Gk: MT lacks *but he would not punish . . . firstborn*

"Your servant has sheepshearers; will the king and his servants please go with your servant?" [25]But the king said to Absalom, "No, my son, let us not all go, or else we will be burdensome to you." He pressed him, but he would not go but gave him his blessing. [26]Then Absalom said, "If not, please let my brother Amnon go with us." The king said to him, "Why should he go with you?" [27]But Absalom pressed him until he let Amnon and all the king's sons go with him. Absalom made a feast like a king's feast.[b] [28]Then Absalom commanded his servants, "Watch when Amnon's heart is merry with wine, and when I say to you, 'Strike Amnon,' then kill him. Do not be afraid; have I not myself commanded you? Be courageous and valiant." [29]So the servants of Absalom did to Amnon as Absalom had commanded. Then all the king's sons rose, and each mounted his mule and fled.

30 While they were on the way, the report came to David that Absalom had killed all the king's sons, and not one of them was left. [31]The king rose, tore his garments, and lay on the ground; and all his servants who were standing by tore their garments. [32]But Jonadab, the son of David's brother Shimeah, said, "Let not my lord suppose that they have killed all the young men the king's sons; Amnon alone is dead. This has been determined by Absalom from the day Amnon[c] raped his sister Tamar. [33]Now therefore, do not let my lord the king take it to heart, as if all the king's sons were dead; for Amnon alone is dead."

34 But Absalom fled. When the young man who kept watch looked up, he saw many people coming from the Horonaim road[d] by the side of the mountain. [35]Jonadab said to the king, "See, the king's sons have come; as your servant said, so it has come about." [36]As soon as he had finished speaking, the king's sons arrived, and raised their voices and wept; and the king and all his servants also wept very bitterly.

37 But Absalom fled, and went to Talmai son of Ammihud, king of Geshur. David mourned for his son day after day. [38]Absalom, having fled to Geshur, stayed there three years. [39]And the heart of[e] the king went out, yearning for Absalom; for he was now consoled over the death of Amnon.

Absalom Returns to Jerusalem

14 Now Joab son of Zeruiah perceived that the king's mind was on Absalom. [2]Joab sent to Tekoa and brought from there a wise woman. He said to her, "Pretend to be a mourner; put on mourning garments, do not anoint yourself with oil, but behave like a woman who has been mourning many days for the dead. [3]Go to the king and speak to him as follows." And Joab put the words into her mouth.

4 When the woman of Tekoa came to the king, she fell on her face to the ground and did obeisance, and said, "Help, king!" [5]The king asked her, "What is your trouble?" She answered, "Alas, I am a widow; my husband is dead. [6]Your servant had two sons, and they fought with one another in the field; there was no one to part them, and one struck the other and killed him. [7]Now the whole family has risen against your servant. They say, 'Give up the man who struck his brother, so that we may kill him for the life of his brother whom he murdered, even if we destroy the heir as well.' Thus they would quench my one remaining ember, and leave to my husband neither name nor remnant on the face of the earth."

8 Then the king said to the woman, "Go to your house, and I will give orders concerning you." [9]The woman of Tekoa said to the king, "On me be the guilt, my lord the king, and on my father's house; let the king and his throne be guiltless." [10]The king said, "If anyone says anything to you, bring him to me, and he shall never touch you again." [11]Then she said, "Please, may the king keep the LORD your God in mind, so that the avenger of blood may kill no more, and my son not be destroyed." He said, "As the LORD lives, not one hair of your son shall fall to the ground."

12 Then the woman said, "Please let your servant speak a word to my lord the king." He said, "Speak." [13]The woman said, "Why then have you planned such a thing against the people of God? For in giving this decision the king convicts himself, inasmuch as the king does not bring his banished one home again. [14]We must all die; we are like water spilled on the ground, which cannot be gathered up. But God will not take away a life; he will devise plans so

[b] Gk Compare Q Ms: MT lacks *Absalom made a feast like a king's feast* [c] Heb *he* [d] Cn Compare Gk: Heb *the road behind him* [e] Q Ms Gk: MT *And David*

13.37-14.33 Absalom's Flight and Return. After *three years* of refuge in *Geshur*, an area east of the Lake of Galilee, Joab, David's military chief, developed a scheme to restore *Absalom* to David's household. *A woman of Tekoa*, south of Bethlehem on the edge of the Judean desert, came to David with a story of fratricide and a plan for revenge which moved the king to invoke the name of *the LORD* as a guarantee that the guilty man would not be put to death. The woman then showed that this principle applied to David himself: he must restore his guilty son. David agreed and brought Absalom to Jerusalem, where *two full years* later, and after setting fire to his brother's field, Joab agreed to take Absalom to David, who *kissed* him as a sign of forgiveness.

13.28 Judg 19.6,9,22; 1 Sam 25.36
13.29 2 Sam 18.9; 1 Kings 1.33,38
13.31 2 Sam 1.11; 12.16
13.32 ver 3
13.33 2 Sam 19.19
13.34 ver 37,38; 2 Sam 18.24
13.37 ver 34; 2 Sam 3.3; 14.23,32
13.39 2 Sam 12.19-23
14.1 2 Sam 13.39
14.2 2 Chr 11.5; 1 Kings 20.35-43; 2 Sam 12.20
14.3 ver 19
14.4 2 Sam 1.12; 2 Kings 6.26-28
14.5 2 Sam 12.1-7
14.7 Num 35.19; Deut 19.12; Mt 21.38
14.9 1 Sam 25.24; Mt 27.25; 1 Kings 2.33
14.11 Num 35.19; 1 Sam 14.45
14.13 2 Sam 12.7; 1 Kings 20.40-42; 2 Sam 13.37,38
14.14 Job 35.15; Heb 9.27; Num 35.15,25,28

15.1-16.14 Absalom's Attempt to Take the Throne and the Flight of David.
15.1-12 By acquiring the equipment of a man of authority – *chariot, horses, fifty men* – and by ingratiating himself with petitioners to the king, Absalom built up popular support and *stole the hearts of the people of Israel.* Pretending to go to Hebron in order to *worship the* L*ORD* there, he sent messages to *all the tribes of Israel* that he had *become king at Hebron.* Ahithophel, formerly *David's counselor,* joined the revolutionary plot with Absalom.

as not to keep an outcast banished forever from his presence.[f] 15 Now I have come to say this to my lord the king because the people have made me afraid; your servant thought, 'I will speak to the king; it may be that the king will perform the request of his servant. 16 For the king will hear, and deliver his servant from the hand of the man who would cut both me and my son off from the heritage of God.' 17 Your servant thought, 'The word of my lord the king will set me at rest'; for my lord the king is like the angel of God, discerning good and evil. The LORD your God be with you!"

18 Then the king answered the woman, "Do not withhold from me anything I ask you." The woman said, "Let my lord the king speak." 19 The king said, "Is the hand of Joab with you in all this?" The woman answered and said, "As surely as you live, my lord the king, one cannot turn right or left from anything that my lord the king has said. For it was your servant Joab who commanded me; it was he who put all these words into the mouth of your servant. 20 In order to change the course of affairs your servant Joab did this. But my lord has wisdom like the wisdom of the angel of God to know all things that are on the earth."

21 Then the king said to Joab, "Very well, I grant this; go, bring back the young man Absalom." 22 Joab prostrated himself with his face to the ground and did obeisance, and blessed the king; and Joab said, "Today your servant knows that I have found favor in your sight, my lord the king, in that the king has granted the request of his servant." 23 So Joab set off, went to Geshur, and brought Absalom to Jerusalem. 24 The king said, "Let him go to his own house; he is not to come into my presence." So Absalom went to his own house, and did not come into the king's presence.

David Forgives Absalom

25 Now in all Israel there was no one to be praised so much for his beauty as Absalom; from the sole of his foot to the crown of his head there was no blemish in him. 26 When he cut the hair of his head (for at the end of every year he used to cut it; when it was heavy on him, he cut it), he weighed the hair of his head, two hundred shekels by the king's weight. 27 There were born to Absalom three sons, and one daughter whose name was Tamar; she was a beautiful woman.

28 So Absalom lived two full years in Jerusalem, without coming into the king's presence. 29 Then Absalom sent for Joab to send him to the king; but Joab would not come to him. He sent a second time, but Joab would not come. 30 Then he said to his servants, "Look, Joab's field is next to mine, and he has barley there; go and set it on fire." So Absalom's servants set the field on fire. 31 Then Joab rose and went to Absalom at his house, and said to him, "Why have your servants set my field on fire?" 32 Absalom answered Joab, "Look, I sent word to you: Come here, that I may send you to the king with the question, 'Why have I come from Geshur? It would be better for me to be there still.' Now let me go into the king's presence; if there is guilt in me, let him kill me!" 33 Then Joab went to the king and told him; and he summoned Absalom. So he came to the king and prostrated himself with his face to the ground before the king; and the king kissed Absalom.

Absalom Usurps the Throne

15 After this Absalom got himself a chariot and horses, and fifty men to run ahead of him. 2 Absalom used to rise early and stand beside the road into the gate; and when anyone brought a suit before the king for judgment, Absalom would call out and say, "From what city are you?" When the person said, "Your servant is of such and such a tribe in Israel," 3 Absalom would say, "See, your claims are good and right; but there is no one deputed by the king to hear you." 4 Absalom said moreover, "If only I were judge in the land! Then all who had a suit or cause might come to me, and I would give them justice." 5 Whenever people came near to do obeisance to him, he would put out his hand and take hold of them, and kiss them. 6 Thus Absalom did to every Israelite who came to the king for judgment; so Absalom stole the hearts of the people of Israel.

7 At the end of four[g] years Absalom said to the king, "Please let me go to Hebron and pay the vow that I have made to the LORD. 8 For your servant made a vow while I lived at Geshur in Aram: If the LORD will indeed bring me back to Jerusalem, then I will worship the LORD in Hebron."[h] 9 The king

14.17 ver 20; 2 Sam 19.27
14.19 ver 3
14.20 ver 17; 2 Sam 19.27
14.23 2 Sam 13.37,38
14.24 2 Sam 3.13
14.25 Isa 1.6
14.26 Ezek 44.20
14.27 2 Sam 18.18
14.28 ver 24
14.32 1 Sam 20.8
14.33 Gen 33.4; Lk 15.20
15.1 2 Sam 12.11; 1 Kings 1.5
15.2 2 Sam 19.8
15.4 Judg 9.29
15.6 Rom 16.18
15.7 2 Sam 3.2,3
15.8 2 Sam 13.37,38; Gen 28.20,21

[f] Meaning of Heb uncertain [g] Gk Syr: Heb *forty* [h] Gk Mss: Heb lacks *in Hebron*

said to him, "Go in peace." So he got up, and went to Hebron. 10But Absalom sent secret messengers throughout all the tribes of Israel, saying, "As soon as you hear the sound of the trumpet, then shout: Absalom has become king at Hebron!" 11Two hundred men from Jerusalem went with Absalom; they were invited guests, and they went in their innocence, knowing nothing of the matter. 12While Absalom was offering the sacrifices, he sent for[i] Ahithophel the Gilonite, David's counselor, from his city Giloh. The conspiracy grew in strength, and the people with Absalom kept increasing.

David Flees from Jerusalem

13 A messenger came to David, saying, "The hearts of the Israelites have gone after Absalom." 14Then David said to all his officials who were with him at Jerusalem, "Get up! Let us flee, or there will be no escape for us from Absalom. Hurry, or he will soon overtake us, and bring disaster down upon us, and attack the city with the edge of the sword." 15The king's officials said to the king, "Your servants are ready to do whatever our lord the king decides." 16So the king left, followed by all his household, except ten concubines whom he left behind to look after the house. 17The king left, followed by all the people; and they stopped at the last house. 18All his officials passed by him; and all the Cherethites, and all the Pelethites, and all the six hundred Gittites who had followed him from Gath, passed on before the king.

19 Then the king said to Ittai the Gittite, "Why are you also coming with us? Go back, and stay with the king; for you are a foreigner, and also an exile from your home. 20You came only yesterday, and shall I today make you wander about with us, while I go wherever I can? Go back, and take your kinsfolk with you; and may the LORD show[j] steadfast love and faithfulness to you." 21But Ittai answered the king, "As the LORD lives, and as my lord the king lives, wherever my lord the king may be, whether for death or for life, there also your servant will be." 22David said to Ittai, "Go then, march on." So Ittai the Gittite marched on, with all his men and all the little ones who were with him. 23The whole country wept aloud as all the people passed by; the king crossed the Wadi Kidron, and all the people moved on toward the wilderness.

24 Abiathar came up, and Zadok also, with all the Levites, carrying the ark of the covenant of God. They set down the ark of God, until the people had all passed out of the city. 25Then the king said to Zadok, "Carry the ark of God back into the city. If I find favor in the eyes of the LORD, he will bring me back and let me see both it and the place where it stays. 26But if he says, 'I take no pleasure in you,' here I am, let him do to me what seems good to him." 27The king also said to the priest Zadok, "Look,[k] go back to the city in peace, you and Abiathar,[l] with your two sons, Ahimaaz your son, and Jonathan son of Abiathar. 28See, I will wait at the fords of the wilderness until word comes from you to inform me." 29So Zadok and Abiathar carried the ark of God back to Jerusalem, and they remained there.

30 But David went up the ascent of the Mount of Olives, weeping as he went, with his head covered and walking barefoot; and all the people who were with him covered their heads and went up, weeping as they went. 31David was told that Ahithophel was among the conspirators with Absalom. And David said, " LORD, I pray you, turn the counsel of Ahithophel into foolishness."

Hushai Becomes David's Spy

32 When David came to the summit, where God was worshiped, Hushai the Archite came to meet him with his coat torn and earth on his head. 33David said to him, "If you go on with me, you will be a burden to me. 34But if you return to the city and say to Absalom, 'I will be your servant, king; as I have been your father's servant in time past, so now I will be your servant,' then you will defeat for me the counsel of Ahithophel. 35The priests Zadok and Abiathar will be with you there. So whatever you hear from the king's house, tell it to the priests Zadok and Abiathar. 36Their two sons are with them there, Zadok's son Ahimaaz and Abiathar's son Jonathan; and by them you shall report to me everything you hear." 37So Hushai, David's friend, came into the city, just as Absalom was entering Jerusalem.

[i] Or *he sent* [j] Gk Compare 2.6: Heb lacks *may the LORD show* [k] Gk: Heb *Are you a seer* or *Do you see?* [l] Cn: Heb lacks *and Abiathar*

15.11 1 Sam 9.13; 22.15
15.12 ver 31; Josh 15.51; Ps 3.1
15.13 ver 6; Judg 9.3
15.14 2 Sam 12.11; 19.9
15.16 2 Sam 16.21,22
15.18 2 Sam 8.18
15.19 2 Sam 18.2
15.20 1 Sam 23.13
15.21 Ruth 1.16,17
15.24 2 Sam 8.17; Num 4.15; 1 Sam 22.20
15.25 Ps 43.3; Jer 25.30
15.26 2 Sam 22.20; 1 Kings 10.9; 1 Sam 3.18
15.27 1 Sam 9.6-9; 2 Sam 7.17
15.28 2 Sam 17.16
15.30 Esth 6.12; 2 Sam 19.4; Isa 20.2-4; Ps 126.6
15.31 ver 12; 2 Sam 16.23; 17.14,23
15.32 Josh 16.2; 2 Sam 1.2
15.33 2 Sam 19.35
15.34 2 Sam 16.19
15.35 2 Sam 17.15,16
15.36 ver 27; 2 Sam 17.17
15.37 2 Sam 16.16,17; 1 Chr 27.33

15.13-31 *David [and] all his officials* fled from Jerusalem, including the non-Israelite mercenaries who supported David's claim to royal power, and stood by him in this crisis: *the Cherethites*, from Crete; *the Pelethites* (probably Philistines); *the Gittites*, from the Philistine city of Gath. The refugees crossed *the Wadi Kidron*, which separates Jerusalem from *the Mount of Olives* on the east of the city, as they proceeded over the Mount toward *the wilderness* of Judea. David dissuaded the priestly leaders, *Abiathar [and] Zadok...with all the Levites*, from taking the *ark of the covenant of God* away from the sanctuary in Jerusalem. The conspiracy against David was called *the counsel of Ahithophel*. Hushai, formerly David's *servant*, was encouraged by David to offer his services to Absalom, so that the plans of the usurper could be reported to David through sons of the priests, *Ahimaaz and Jonathan*. The donkeys and abundant food brought by *Ziba, the servant of Mephibosheth* (4.4; 9.1-13) were supplied for the journey through the wilderness which is visible to the east from *the summit* of the Mount of Olives. At *Bahurim*, a village on the eastern side of the mountain ridge, *Shimei*, a member of the family of Saul, cursed David and pelted the procession with stones. David refused to respond with force, and the refugees proceeded to *the Jordan*.

16.15-18.18 The Failure of Absalom's Plot against David. Ahithophel's challenge of Hushai's *loyalty* to Absalom led to the clever response affirming commitment to the one chosen by God and his people. Ahithophel advised Absalom to demonstrate publicly his repudiation of his father by cohabiting with his concubines, and to launch a large military force to pursue and execute David. Hushai's advice was that Absalom himself should lead the attack, and that tactic was adopted. Through *Ahimaaz and Jonathan*, sons of Zadok the priest, word was sent to David to escape from Absalom and his army by crossing over east of the Jordan, although the recognition of the messengers by *a boy* nearly destroyed the scheme. David's troops were at *Mahanaim* (2.8-29), where supplies were brought by rulers of east Jordan cities subject to David. *The Israelites* supportive of *Absalom* were camped nearby in the region of *Gilead*. In spite of an order from David to *deal gently with...Absalom*, when he was accidentally caught in a tree, Joab sent his men to kill him. After he was buried, *all the Israelites fled to their homes*.

David's Adversaries

16 When David had passed a little
beyond the summit, Ziba the servant of Mephibosheth[m] met him, with a
couple of donkeys saddled, carrying two
hundred loaves of bread, one hundred
bunches of raisins, one hundred of summer
fruits, and one skin of wine. 2 The king said
to Ziba, "Why have you brought these?"
Ziba answered, "The donkeys are for the
king's household to ride, the bread and
summer fruit for the young men to eat, and
the wine is for those to drink who faint in
the wilderness." 3 The king said, "And where
is your master's son?" Ziba said to the king,
"He remains in Jerusalem; for he said, 'Today the house of Israel will give me back
my grandfather's kingdom.' " 4 Then the king
said to Ziba, "All that belonged to Mephibosheth[m] is now yours." Ziba said, "I do
obeisance; let me find favor in your sight,
my lord the king."

Shimei Curses David

5 When King David came to Bahurim, a
man of the family of the house of Saul came
out whose name was Shimei son of Gera;
he came out cursing. 6 He threw stones at
David and at all the servants of King David;
now all the people and all the warriors were
on his right and on his left. 7 Shimei shouted
while he cursed, "Out! Out! Murderer! Scoundrel! 8 The LORD has avenged on all of you
the blood of the house of Saul, in whose
place you have reigned; and the LORD has
given the kingdom into the hand of your
son Absalom. See, disaster has overtaken
you; for you are a man of blood."
9 Then Abishai son of Zeruiah said to the
king, "Why should this dead dog curse my
lord the king? Let me go over and take off
his head." 10 But the king said, "What have
I to do with you, you sons of Zeruiah? If he
is cursing because the LORD has said to him,
'Curse David,' who then shall say, 'Why
have you done so?' " 11 David said to Abishai
and to all his servants, "My own son seeks
my life; how much more now may this
Benjaminite! Let him alone, and let him
curse; for the LORD has bidden him. 12 It may
be that the LORD will look on my distress,[n]
and the LORD will repay me with good for
this cursing of me today." 13 So David and
his men went on the road, while Shimei
went along on the hillside opposite him and
cursed as he went, throwing stones and
flinging dust at him. 14 The king and all the
people who were with him arrived weary at
the Jordan;[o] and there he refreshed himself.

The Counsel of Ahithophel

15 Now Absalom and all the Israelites[p]
came to Jerusalem; Ahithophel was with
him. 16 When Hushai the Archite, David's
friend, came to Absalom, Hushai said to
Absalom, "Long live the king! Long live the
king!" 17 Absalom said to Hushai, "Is this
your loyalty to your friend? Why did you
not go with your friend?" 18 Hushai said to
Absalom, "No; but the one whom the LORD
and this people and all the Israelites have
chosen, his I will be, and with him I will
remain. 19 Moreover, whom should I serve?
Should it not be his son? Just as I have
served your father, so I will serve you."
20 Then Absalom said to Ahithophel,
"Give us your counsel; what shall we do?"
21 Ahithophel said to Absalom, "Go in to
your father's concubines, the ones he has
left to look after the house; and all Israel
will hear that you have made yourself odious
to your father, and the hands of all who are
with you will be strengthened." 22 So they
pitched a tent for Absalom upon the roof;
and Absalom went in to his father's concubines in the sight of all Israel. 23 Now in
those days the counsel that Ahithophel gave
was as if one consulted the oracle[q] of God;
so all the counsel of Ahithophel was esteemed, both by David and by Absalom.
17 Moreover Ahithophel said to
Absalom, "Let me choose twelve
thousand men, and I will set out and pursue David tonight. 2 I will come upon him
while he is weary and discouraged, and
throw him into a panic; and all the people
who are with him will flee. I will strike
down only the king, 3 and I will bring all the
people back to you as a bride comes home
to her husband. You seek the life of only
one man,[r] and all the people will be at
peace." 4 The advice pleased Absalom and all
the elders of Israel.

The Counsel of Hushai

5 Then Absalom said, "Call Hushai the
Archite also, and let us hear too what he

[m] Or *Merib-baal*: See 4.4 note [n] Gk Vg: Heb *iniquity* [o] Gk: Heb lacks *at the Jordan* [p] Gk: Heb *all the people, the men of Israel* [q] Heb *word* [r] Gk: Heb *like the return of the whole (is) the man whom you seek*

16.1 2 Sam 15.32; 9.2-13
16.2 2 Sam 17.29
16.3 2 Sam 9.9,10; 19.26,27
16.5 2 Sam 3.16-18; 19.16-23; 1 Kings 2.8
16.7 2 Sam 12.9
16.8 2 Sam 21.1-9
16.9 2 Sam 19.21; 9.8
16.10 2 Sam 19.22; 1 Pet 2.23; 2 Kings 18.25; Rom 9.20
16.11 2 Sam 12.11; Gen 45.5
16.12 Rom 8.28
16.15 2 Sam 15.37
16.16 2 Sam 15.37
16.17 2 Sam 19.25
16.19 2 Sam 15.34
16.21 2 Sam 15.16; 1 Sam 13.4; 2 Sam 2.7
16.22 2 Sam 12.11,12
16.23 2 Sam 15.12
17.2 2 Sam 16.14; 1 Kings 22.31
17.5 2 Sam 15.31-34

17.8 Hos 13.8; 1 Sam 16.18
17.10 Josh 2.11
17.14 2 Sam 15.31,34
17.15 2 Sam 15.35
17.16 2 Sam 15.28
17.17 2 Sam 15.27,36; Josh 15.7; 18.16
17.18 2 Sam 16.5
17.19 Josh 2.4-6
17.20 Josh 2.3-5; 1 Sam 19.12-17
17.21 ver 15.16
17.23 2 Sam 15.12; 2 Kings 20.1; Mt 27.5
17.24 Gen 32.2; 2 Sam 2.8
17.25 2 Sam 19.13; 20.9-12
17.27 2 Sam 10.1,2; 12.26,29; 19.31,32; 1 Kings 2.7
17.29 2 Sam 16.2
18.1 Ex 18.25; 1 Sam 22.7

has to say." 6 When Hushai came to Absalom,
Absalom said to him, "This is what
Ahithophel has said; shall we do as he
advises? If not, you tell us." 7 Then Hushai
said to Absalom, "This time the counsel
that Ahithophel has given is not good."
8 Hushai continued, "You know that your
father and his men are warriors, and that
they are enraged, like a bear robbed of her
cubs in the field. Besides, your father is
expert in war; he will not spend the night
with the troops. 9 Even now he has hidden
himself in one of the pits, or in some other
place. And when some of our troops[s] fall at
the first attack, whoever hears it will say,
'There has been a slaughter among the
troops who follow Absalom.' 10 Then even
the valiant warrior, whose heart is like the
heart of a lion, will utterly melt with fear;
for all Israel knows that your father is a
warrior, and that those who are with him
are valiant warriors. 11 But my counsel is
that all Israel be gathered to you, from Dan
to Beer-sheba, like the sand by the sea for
multitude, and that you go to battle in
person. 12 So we shall come upon him in
whatever place he may be found, and we
shall light on him as the dew falls on the
ground; and he will not survive, nor will
any of those with him. 13 If he withdraws
into a city, then all Israel will bring ropes
to that city, and we shall drag it into the
valley, until not even a pebble is to be found
there." 14 Absalom and all the men of Israel
said, "The counsel of Hushai the Archite is
better than the counsel of Ahithophel." For
the LORD had ordained to defeat the good
counsel of Ahithophel, so that the LORD
might bring ruin on Absalom.

Hushai Warns David to Escape

15 Then Hushai said to the priests Zadok
and Abiathar, "Thus and so did Ahithophel
counsel Absalom and the elders of Israel;
and thus and so I have counseled. 16 Therefore send quickly and tell David, 'Do not
lodge tonight at the fords of the wilderness,
but by all means cross over; otherwise the
king and all the people who are with him
will be swallowed up.' " 17 Jonathan and
Ahimaaz were waiting at En-rogel; a servant-girl used to go and tell them, and they
would go and tell King David; for they could
not risk being seen entering the city. 18 But
a boy saw them, and told Absalom; so both
of them went away quickly, and came to
the house of a man at Bahurim, who had
a well in his courtyard; and they went
down into it. 19 The man's wife took a covering, stretched it over the well's mouth,
and spread out grain on it; and nothing was
known of it. 20 When Absalom's servants
came to the woman at the house, they said,
"Where are Ahimaaz and Jonathan?" The
woman said to them, "They have crossed
over the brook[t] of water." And when they
had searched and could not find them, they
returned to Jerusalem.

21 After they had gone, the men came
up out of the well, and went and told King
David. They said to David, "Go and cross
the water quickly; for thus and so has
Ahithophel counseled against you." 22 So
David and all the people who were with
him set out and crossed the Jordan; by
daybreak not one was left who had not
crossed the Jordan.

23 When Ahithophel saw that his counsel was not followed, he saddled his donkey
and went off home to his own city. He set
his house in order, and hanged himself; he
died and was buried in the tomb of his
father.

24 Then David came to Mahanaim, while
Absalom crossed the Jordan with all the
men of Israel. 25 Now Absalom had set Amasa
over the army in the place of Joab. Amasa
was the son of a man named Ithra the
Ishmaelite,[u] who had married Abigal daughter of Nahash, sister of Zeruiah, Joab's
mother. 26 The Israelites and Absalom encamped in the land of Gilead.

27 When David came to Mahanaim,
Shobi son of Nahash from Rabbah of the
Ammonites, and Machir son of Ammiel
from Lo-debar, and Barzillai the Gileadite
from Rogelim, 28 brought beds, basins, and
earthen vessels, wheat, barley, meal, parched
grain, beans and lentils,[v] 29 honey and curds,
sheep, and cheese from the herd, for David
and the people with him to eat; for they
said, "The troops are hungry and weary
and thirsty in the wilderness."

The Defeat and Death of Absalom

18 Then David mustered the men who
were with him, and set over them
commanders of thousands and commanders

[s] Gk Mss: Heb *some of them* [t] Meaning of Heb uncertain [u] 1 Chr 2.17: Heb *Israelite* [v] Heb *and lentils and parched grain*

18.19-19.43 David Mourns for Absalom and Returns to Jerusalem.
18.19-33 *Ahimaaz,* one of the messengers of the priestly spy ring (15.36), sought to be the first to inform David of Absalom's death, but then professed ignorance of the outcome of the conflict. *The Cushite,* from what is now Ethiopia or Sudan, first informed David implicitly of the death of his son, whom David then solemnly mourned.

of hundreds. 2 And David divided the army into three groups:[w] one third under the command of Joab, one third under the command of Abishai son of Zeruiah, Joab's brother, and one third under the command of Ittai the Gittite. The king said to the men, "I myself will also go out with you." 3 But the men said, "You shall not go out. For if we flee, they will not care about us. If half of us die, they will not care about us. But you are worth ten thousand of us;[x] therefore it is better that you send us help from the city." 4 The king said to them, "Whatever seems best to you I will do." So the king stood at the side of the gate, while all the army marched out by hundreds and by thousands. 5 The king ordered Joab and Abishai and Ittai, saying, "Deal gently for my sake with the young man Absalom." And all the people heard when the king gave orders to all the commanders concerning Absalom.

6 So the army went out into the field against Israel; and the battle was fought in the forest of Ephraim. 7 The men of Israel were defeated there by the servants of David, and the slaughter there was great on that day, twenty thousand men. 8 The battle spread over the face of all the country; and the forest claimed more victims that day than the sword.

9 Absalom happened to meet the servants of David. Absalom was riding on his mule, and the mule went under the thick branches of a great oak. His head caught fast in the oak, and he was left hanging[y] between heaven and earth, while the mule that was under him went on. 10 A man saw it, and told Joab, "I saw Absalom hanging in an oak." 11 Joab said to the man who told him, "What, you saw him! Why then did you not strike him there to the ground? I would have been glad to give you ten pieces of silver and a belt." 12 But the man said to Joab, "Even if I felt in my hand the weight of a thousand pieces of silver, I would not raise my hand against the king's son; for in our hearing the king commanded you and Abishai and Ittai, saying: For my sake protect the young man Absalom! 13 On the other hand, if I had dealt treacherously against his life[z] (and there is nothing hidden from the king), then you yourself would have stood aloof." 14 Joab said, "I will not waste time like this with you." He took three spears in his hand, and thrust them into the heart of Absalom, while he was still alive in the oak. 15 And ten young men, Joab's armor-bearers, surrounded Absalom and struck him, and killed him.

16 Then Joab sounded the trumpet, and the troops came back from pursuing Israel, for Joab restrained the troops. 17 They took Absalom, threw him into a great pit in the forest, and raised over him a very great heap of stones. Meanwhile all the Israelites fled to their homes. 18 Now Absalom in his lifetime had taken and set up for himself a pillar that is in the King's Valley, for he said, "I have no son to keep my name in remembrance"; he called the pillar by his own name. It is called Absalom's Monument to this day.

David Hears of Absalom's Death

19 Then Ahimaaz son of Zadok said, "Let me run, and carry tidings to the king that the LORD has delivered him from the power of his enemies." 20 Joab said to him, "You are not to carry tidings today; you may carry tidings another day, but today you shall not do so, because the king's son is dead." 21 Then Joab said to a Cushite, "Go, tell the king what you have seen." The Cushite bowed before Joab, and ran. 22 Then Ahimaaz son of Zadok said again to Joab, "Come what may, let me also run after the Cushite." And Joab said, "Why will you run, my son, seeing that you have no reward[a] for the tidings?" 23 "Come what may," he said, "I will run." So he said to him, "Run." Then Ahimaaz ran by the way of the Plain, and outran the Cushite.

24 Now David was sitting between the two gates. The sentinel went up to the roof of the gate by the wall, and when he looked up, he saw a man running alone. 25 The sentinel shouted and told the king. The king said, "If he is alone, there are tidings in his mouth." He kept coming, and drew near. 26 Then the sentinel saw another man running; and the sentinel called to the gatekeeper and said, "See, another man running alone!" The king said, "He also is bringing tidings." 27 The sentinel said, "I think the running of the first one is like the running of Ahimaaz son of Zadok." The king said, "He is a good man, and comes with good tidings."

[w] Gk: Heb *sent forth the army* [x] Gk Vg Symmachus: Heb *for now there are ten thousand such as we* [y] Gk Syr Tg: Heb *was put* [z] Another reading is *at the risk of my life* [a] Meaning of Heb uncertain

18.2 1 Sam 11.11; 2 Sam 15.19
18.3 2 Sam 21.17
18.4 ver 24
18.5 ver 12
18.6 Josh 17.15,18
18.9 2 Sam 14.26
18.12 ver 5
18.14 2 Sam 14.30
18.16 2 Sam 2.28; 20.22
18.17 Josh 7.26; 8.29
18.18 1 Sam 15.12; Gen 14.17; 2 Sam 14.27
18.19 2 Sam 15.36; ver 31
18.24 2 Sam 19.8; 13.34; 2 Kings 9.17

18.28 2 Sam 14.4; 1 Sam 25.23; 17.46
18.29 ver 22
18.31 ver 19; Judg 5.31
18.32 1 Sam 25.26
18.33 2 Sam 19.4; Ex 32.32; Rom 9.3
19.1 2 Sam 18.33
19.4 2 Sam 15.30; 18.33
19.6 Mt 4.46
19.8 2 Sam 15.2; 18.4
19.9 2 Sam 8.1-14; 5.20; 15.14
19.12 2 Sam 5.1
19.13 2 Sam 17.25; 1 Kings 19.2; 8.16; ver 5-7
19.14 Judg 20.1
19.15 Josh 5.9
19.16 2 Sam 16.5; 1 Kings 2.8
19.17 2 Sam 16.1,2
19.19 1 Sam 22.15; 2 Sam 16.6-8; 13.33

28 Then Ahimaaz cried out to the king,
"All is well!" He prostrated himself before
the king with his face to the ground, and
said, "Blessed be the LORD your God, who
has delivered up the men who raised their
hand against my lord the king." 29The king
said, "Is it well with the young man
Absalom?" Ahimaaz answered, "When Joab
sent your servant,[b] I saw a great tumult,
but I do not know what it was." 30The king
said, "Turn aside, and stand here." So he
turned aside, and stood still.
31 Then the Cushite came; and the
Cushite said, "Good tidings for my lord the
king! For the LORD has vindicated you this
day, delivering you from the power of all
who rose up against you." 32The king said
to the Cushite, "Is it well with the young
man Absalom?" The Cushite answered, "May
the enemies of my lord the king, and all
who rise up to do you harm, be like that
young man."

David Mourns for Absalom

33[c] The king was deeply moved, and went
up to the chamber over the gate, and wept;
and as he went, he said, " my son Absalom,
my son, my son Absalom! Would I had died
instead of you, Absalom, my son, my son!"
19 It was told Joab, "The king is weeping and mourning for Absalom."
2So the victory that day was turned into
mourning for all the troops; for the troops
heard that day, "The king is grieving for his
son." 3The troops stole into the city that day
as soldiers steal in who are ashamed when
they flee in battle. 4The king covered his
face, and the king cried with a loud voice,
"O my son Absalom, Absalom, my son, my
son!" 5Then Joab came into the house to the
king, and said, "Today you have covered
with shame the faces of all your officers
who have saved your life today, and the
lives of your sons and your daughters, and
the lives of your wives and your concubines, 6for love of those who hate you and
for hatred of those who love you. You have
made it clear today that commanders and
officers are nothing to you; for I perceive
that if Absalom were alive and all of us
were dead today, then you would be pleased.
7So go out at once and speak kindly to your
servants; for I swear by the LORD, if you do
not go, not a man will stay with you this
night; and this will be worse for you than
any disaster that has come upon you from
your youth until now." 8Then the king got
up and took his seat in the gate. The troops
were all told, "See, the king is sitting in the
gate"; and all the troops came before the
king.

David Recalled to Jerusalem

Meanwhile, all the Israelites had fled to
their homes. 9All the people were disputing
throughout all the tribes of Israel, saying,
"The king delivered us from the hand of our
enemies, and saved us from the hand of the
Philistines; and now he has fled out of the
land because of Absalom. 10But Absalom,
whom we anointed over us, is dead in
battle. Now therefore why do you say nothing about bringing the king back?"
11 King David sent this message to the
priests Zadok and Abiathar, "Say to the
elders of Judah, 'Why should you be the last
to bring the king back to his house? The
talk of all Israel has come to the king.[d]
12You are my kin, you are my bone and my
flesh; why then should you be the last to
bring back the king?' 13And say to Amasa,
'Are you not my bone and my flesh? So
may God do to me, and more, if you are not
the commander of my army from now on,
in place of Joab.' " 14Amasa[e] swayed the
hearts of all the people of Judah as one, and
they sent word to the king, "Return, both
you and all your servants." 15So the king
came back to the Jordan; and Judah came
to Gilgal to meet the king and to bring him
over the Jordan.
16 Shimei son of Gera, the Benjaminite,
from Bahurim, hurried to come down with
the people of Judah to meet King David;
17with him were a thousand people from
Benjamin. And Ziba, the servant of the
house of Saul, with his fifteen sons and his
twenty servants, rushed down to the Jordan
ahead of the king, 18while the crossing was
taking place,[f] to bring over the king's household, and to do his pleasure.

David's Mercy to Shimei

Shimei son of Gera fell down before the
king, as he was about to cross the Jordan,
19and said to the king, "May my lord not
hold me guilty or remember how your

19.1-8a Joab urged David to express gratitude to the *officers* and troops who had risked their lives to protect his.
19.8b-23 David's response to the dispute *throughout all the tribes of Israel* about his failure to return to Jerusalem was to ask *the elders* there to invite him to return. Joab was replaced as head of the army by *Amasa*, whom Absalom had put in that position with his forces. Joab was disqualified for having killed the king's son, Absalom. Benjaminites and *people of Judah* rallied in support of David, welcoming him as he crossed the Jordan at *Gilgal*, where the Israelites first entered the land (Josh 4-5). Saul's relative, *Shimei*, who earlier had cursed David (16.5-8) sought and obtained forgiveness from David.

[b] Heb *the king's servant, your servant* [c] Ch 19.1 in Heb [d] Gk: Heb *to the king, to his house* [e] Heb *He* [f] Cn: Heb *the ford crossed*

servant did wrong on the day my lord the
king left Jerusalem; may the king not bear
it in mind. [20]For your servant knows that
I have sinned; therefore, see, I have come
this day, the first of all the house of Joseph
to come down to meet my lord the king."
[21]Abishai son of Zeruiah answered, "Shall
not Shimei be put to death for this, because
he cursed the LORD's anointed?" [22]But David
said, "What have I to do with you, you sons
of Zeruiah, that you should today become
an adversary to me? Shall anyone be put to
death in Israel this day? For do I not know
that I am this day king over Israel?" [23]The
king said to Shimei, "You shall not die."
And the king gave him his oath.

David and Mephibosheth Meet

24 Mephibosheth[g] grandson of Saul came
down to meet the king; he had not taken
care of his feet, or trimmed his beard, or
washed his clothes, from the day the king
left until the day he came back in safety.
[25]When he came from Jerusalem to meet
the king, the king said to him, "Why did
you not go with me, Mephibosheth?"[g] [26]He
answered, "My lord, king, my servant deceived me; for your servant said to him,
'Saddle a donkey for me,[h] so that I may ride
on it and go with the king.' For your
servant is lame. [27]He has slandered your
servant to my lord the king. But my lord the
king is like the angel of God; do therefore
what seems good to you. [28]For all my father's house were doomed to death before
my lord the king; but you set your servant
among those who eat at your table. What
further right have I, then, to appeal to the
king?" [29]The king said to him, "Why speak
any more of your affairs? I have decided:
you and Ziba shall divide the land."
[30]Mephibosheth[g] said to the king, "Let him
take it all, since my lord the king has
arrived home safely."

David's Kindness to Barzillai

31 Now Barzillai the Gileadite had come
down from Rogelim; he went on with the
king to the Jordan, to escort him over the
Jordan. [32]Barzillai was a very aged man,
eighty years old. He had provided the king
with food while he stayed at Mahanaim, for
he was a very wealthy man. [33]The king said
to Barzillai, "Come over with me, and I will
provide for you in Jerusalem at my side."
[34]But Barzillai said to the king, "How many
years have I still to live, that I should go
up with the king to Jerusalem? [35]Today I
am eighty years old; can I discern what is
pleasant and what is not? Can your servant
taste what he eats or what he drinks? Can
I still listen to the voice of singing men and
singing women? Why then should your
servant be an added burden to my lord the
king? [36]Your servant will go a little way
over the Jordan with the king. Why should
the king recompense me with such a reward? [37]Please let your servant return, so
that I may die in my own town, near the
graves of my father and my mother. But
here is your servant Chimham; let him go
over with my lord the king; and do for him
whatever seems good to you." [38]The king
answered, "Chimham shall go over with
me, and I will do for him whatever seems
good to you; and all that you desire of me
I will do for you." [39]Then all the people
crossed over the Jordan, and the king crossed
over; the king kissed Barzillai and blessed
him, and he returned to his own home.
[40]The king went on to Gilgal, and Chimham
went on with him; all the people of Judah,
and also half the people of Israel, brought
the king on his way.

41 Then all the people of Israel came to
the king, and said to him, "Why have our
kindred the people of Judah stolen you away,
and brought the king and his household
over the Jordan, and all David's men with
him?" [42]All the people of Judah answered
the people of Israel, "Because the king is
near of kin to us. Why then are you angry
over this matter? Have we eaten at all at
the king's expense? Or has he given us any
gift?" [43]But the people of Israel answered the
people of Judah, "We have ten shares in the
king, and in David also we have more than
you. Why then did you despise us? Were we
not the first to speak of bringing back our
king?" But the words of the people of Judah
were fiercer than the words of the people of
Israel.

The Rebellion of Sheba

20 Now a scoundrel named Sheba
son of Bichri, a Benjaminite, happened to be there. He sounded the trumpet
and cried out,

"We have no portion in David,

19.24-30 David offered to restore to the penitent *Mephibosheth* (who had failed to accompany David when he fled from Jerusalem) his property, which David had assigned to his servant, *Ziba* (16.1-5).
19.31-40 David's offer to care for the aged *Barzillai*, who had *provided the king* with necessities while he was in the east Jordan territory of *Gilead*, was declined, but the beneficiary was Barzillai's servant, *Chimham*.
19.41-43 The controversy over special relationships with David on the part of the tribes of Judah and those of Israel anticipated the break that was to come between them (1 Kings 12). A specific example of this tension is given in 20.1-22.
20.1-26 Sheba Leads a Rebellion against David.
20.1-3 *Sheba son of Bichri*, who is from the tribe of Benjamin, sought to unite the northern tribes of Israel against *David*, who was of the southern tribe: *Judah*. *The ten concubines*, whom David had left in charge of the royal house in Jerusalem while he was in the Jordan Valley, were virtually put in prison when he returned to *Jerusalem*.

19.20 2 Sam 16.5
19.21 2 Sam 16.7,8; Ex 22.28
19.22 2 Sam 16.10; 1 Sam 11.13
19.23 1 Kings 2.8
19.24 2 Sam 9.6-10
19.25 2 Sam 16.17
19.26 2 Sam 9.3
19.27 2 Sam 16.3; 14.17,20
19.28 2 Sam 21.6-9; 9.7,10,13
19.31 1 Kings 2.7
19.32 2 Sam 17.27
19.35 Ps 90.10; Isa 5.11,12
19.37 ver 40; 1 Kings 2.7; Jer 41.17
19.39 Gen 31.55
19.41 ver 15
19.42 ver 12
19.43 1 Kings 11.30,31
20.1 2 Sam 19.43; 1 Kings 12.16; 2 Chr 10.16

[g] Or *Merib-baal* : See 4.4 note [h] Gk Syr Vg: Heb *said, I will saddle a donkey for myself*

20.3 2 Sam 15.16; 16.21,22
20.4 2 Sam 19.13
20.6 2 Sam 11.11; 1 Kings 1.33
20.7 2 Sam 8.18; 1 Kings 1.38; 2 Sam 15.18
20.9 Mt 26.49
20.10 2 Sam 2.23; 3.27; 1 Kings 2.5
20.15 1 Kings 15.20; 2 Kings 19.32
20.16 2 Sam 14.2
20.19 1 Sam 26.19; 2 Sam 21.3
20.21 ver 2
20.22 Eccl 9.13-16; ver 1
20.23 2 Sam 8.16-18
20.25 2 Sam 8.17
20.26 2 Sam 23.38
21.2 Josh 9.3,15-17

no share in the son of Jesse!
Everyone to your tents, Israel!"
2 So all the people of Israel withdrew from
David and followed Sheba son of Bichri; but
the people of Judah followed their king
steadfastly from the Jordan to Jerusalem.
3 David came to his house at Jerusalem;
and the king took the ten concubines whom
he had left to look after the house, and put
them in a house under guard, and provided
for them, but did not go in to them. So they
were shut up until the day of their death,
living as if in widowhood.
4 Then the king said to Amasa, "Call the
men of Judah together to me within three
days, and be here yourself." 5 So Amasa
went to summon Judah; but he delayed
beyond the set time that had been appointed him. 6 David said to Abishai, "Now
Sheba son of Bichri will do us more harm
than Absalom; take your lord's servants
and pursue him, or he will find fortified
cities for himself, and escape from us." 7 Joab's
men went out after him, along with the
Cherethites, the Pelethites, and all the
warriors; they went out from Jerusalem to
pursue Sheba son of Bichri. 8 When they
were at the large stone that is in Gibeon,
Amasa came to meet them. Now Joab was
wearing a soldier's garment and over it was
a belt with a sword in its sheath fastened
at his waist; as he went forward it fell out.
9 Joab said to Amasa, "Is it well with you,
my brother?" And Joab took Amasa by the
beard with his right hand to kiss him. 10 But
Amasa did not notice the sword in Joab's
hand; Joab struck him in the belly so that
his entrails poured out on the ground, and
he died. He did not strike a second blow.
Then Joab and his brother Abishai pursued Sheba son of Bichri. 11 And one of
Joab's men took his stand by Amasa, and
said, "Whoever favors Joab, and whoever is
for David, let him follow Joab." 12 Amasa lay
wallowing in his blood on the highway, and
the man saw that all the people were stopping. Since he saw that all who came by
him were stopping, he carried Amasa from
the highway into a field, and threw a garment over him. 13 Once he was removed
from the highway, all the people went on
after Joab to pursue Sheba son of Bichri.
14 Sheba[i] passed through all the tribes of
Israel to Abel of Beth-maacah;[j] and all the
Bichrites[k] assembled, and followed him inside. 15 Joab's forces[l] came and besieged him
in Abel of Beth-maacah; they threw up a
siege ramp against the city, and it stood
against the rampart. Joab's forces were
battering the wall to break it down. 16 Then
a wise woman called from the city, "Listen!
Listen! Tell Joab, 'Come here, I want to
speak to you.' " 17 He came near her; and
the woman said, "Are you Joab?" He answered, "I am." Then she said to him,
"Listen to the words of your servant." He
answered, "I am listening." 18 Then she said,
"They used to say in the old days, 'Let them
inquire at Abel'; and so they would settle
a matter. 19 I am one of those who are
peaceable and faithful in Israel; you seek to
destroy a city that is a mother in Israel;
why will you swallow up the heritage of the
LORD?" 20 Joab answered, "Far be it from me,
far be it, that I should swallow up or destroy! 21 That is not the case! But a man of
the hill country of Ephraim, called Sheba
son of Bichri, has lifted up his hand against
King David; give him up alone, and I will
withdraw from the city." The woman said
to Joab, "His head shall be thrown over the
wall to you." 22 Then the woman went to all
the people with her wise plan. And they cut
off the head of Sheba son of Bichri, and
threw it out to Joab. So he blew the trumpet, and they dispersed from the city, and
all went to their homes, while Joab returned
to Jerusalem to the king.
23 Now Joab was in command of all the
army of Israel;[m] Benaiah son of Jehoiada
was in command of the Cherethites and the
Pelethites; 24 Adoram was in charge of the
forced labor; Jehoshaphat son of Ahilud was
the recorder; 25 Sheva was secretary; Zadok
and Abiathar were priests; 26 and Ira the
Jairite was also David's priest.

David Avenges the Gibeonites

21 Now there was a famine in the
days of David for three years, year
after year; and David inquired of the LORD.
The LORD said, "There is bloodguilt on Saul
and on his house, because he put the
Gibeonites to death." 2 So the king called the
Gibeonites and spoke to them. (Now the
Gibeonites were not of the people of Israel,
but of the remnant of the Amorites; although the people of Israel had sworn to
spare them, Saul had tried to wipe them out

[i] Heb *He* [j] Compare 20.15: Heb *and Beth-maacah* [k] Compare Gk Vg: Heb *Berites* [l] Heb *They* [m] Cn: Heb *Joab to all the army, Israel*

20.4-13 Amasa, whom David had given command of his army, replacing Joab (19.13), delayed rallying the troops against Sheba, and was murdered by Joab at Gibeon, where a major victory over the local Canaanite tribes had been won by the tribes of Israel under Joshua (Josh 10.1-15). After Amasa's bloody corpse was removed from the *highway*, the troops moved quickly to *pursue Bichri*.

20.14-22 When Sheba sought refuge in *Abel of Beth-maacah* (a city in the territory of Dan, north of Lake Huleh), a *wise woman* in the city agreed to have Sheba's head cut off and thrown over the wall to the supporters of David. The rebel troops were dispersed, and Joab and his forces returned *to Jerusalem*.

20.23-26 The various responsibilities in David's government were specified, with Joab commanding the army of Israel, Benaiah in charge of the non-Israelite forces that supported David (*the Cherethites and the Pelethites;* 8.18; 15.18), Adoram supervising the conscripted laborers, and others in recording and priestly functions. *Ira the Jairite* was descended from Jair, who captured territory southeast of the Lake of Galilee for the tribe of Manasseh in the time of Moses (Num 32.41). *Ira* replaced *David's sons* as priests (8.18).

21.1-24.25 Six Appendixes to the Books of Samuel. These materials include both prose and poetry. Some describe incidents which must have occurred much earlier than the end of David's life, especially Saul's bloody treatment of the *Gibeonites*.

(1) 21.1-14 The famine in Israel was seen to be God's punishment for the cruelty of Saul to *the Gibeonites*, a non-Israelite people who lived just north of Jerusalem. *Expiation* for Saul's sin was to be made by the sacrifice of *seven of his sons*. The sparing of *Mephibosheth* has already been described in 9.1-13, but another of Saul's sons by the same name (from a different mother) was put to death. Proper burial for the bones of *Saul and Jonathan* was also arranged in their native territory. Their death was reported in 2 Sam 1.

(2) 21.15-22 A series of battles of the Philistines against David, with various warriors defeating the king's enemies. Concern is expressed about David's taking part in the fighting, since if he were to be killed *the lamp of Israel* would be extinguished.
(3) 22.1-51 David's expression of gratitude to God for victory over his enemies duplicates Ps 18, with a few variations. The first part describes God's sustaining David as he faced the prospect of death, the shaking of the created order, the threatening waters, and how God vindicated him for his obedience to *the ways of the* LORD and the *ordinances* of God. The second part tells how God strengthened him and taught him effective warfare so that he could defeat his *enemies*. The dynasty of David is established *forever*.

in his zeal for the people of Israel and
Judah.) [3]David said to the Gibeonites, "What
shall I do for you? How shall I make expiation, that you may bless the heritage of the
LORD?" [4]The Gibeonites said to him, "It is not
a matter of silver or gold between us and
Saul or his house; neither is it for us to put
anyone to death in Israel." He said, "What
do you say that I should do for you?" [5]They
said to the king, "The man who consumed
us and planned to destroy us, so that we
should have no place in all the territory of
Israel— [6]let seven of his sons be handed
over to us, and we will impale them before
the LORD at Gibeon on the mountain of the
LORD."[n] The king said, "I will hand them
over."

7 But the king spared Mephibosheth,[o] the
son of Saul's son Jonathan, because of the
oath of the LORD that was between them,
between David and Jonathan son of Saul.
[8]The king took the two sons of Rizpah
daughter of Aiah, whom she bore to Saul,
Armoni and Mephibosheth;[o] and the five
sons of Merab[p] daughter of Saul, whom she
bore to Adriel son of Barzillai the Meholathite;
[9]he gave them into the hands of the
Gibeonites, and they impaled them on the
mountain before the LORD. The seven of
them perished together. They were put to
death in the first days of harvest, at the
beginning of barley harvest.

10 Then Rizpah the daughter of Aiah
took sackcloth, and spread it on a rock for
herself, from the beginning of harvest until
rain fell on them from the heavens; she did
not allow the birds of the air to come on
the bodies[q] by day, or the wild animals by
night. [11]When David was told what Rizpah
daughter of Aiah, the concubine of Saul,
had done, [12]David went and took the bones
of Saul and the bones of his son Jonathan
from the people of Jabesh-gilead, who had
stolen them from the public square of Beth-
shan, where the Philistines had hung them
up, on the day the Philistines killed Saul on
Gilboa. [13]He brought up from there the
bones of Saul and the bones of his son
Jonathan; and they gathered the bones of
those who had been impaled. [14]They buried
the bones of Saul and of his son Jonathan
in the land of Benjamin in Zela, in the tomb
of his father Kish; they did all that the king
commanded. After that, God heeded supplications for the land.

Exploits of David's Men

15 The Philistines went to war again
with Israel, and David went down together
with his servants. They fought against the
Philistines, and David grew weary. [16]Ishbi-
benob, one of the descendants of the giants,
whose spear weighed three hundred shekels
of bronze, and who was fitted out with new
weapons,[r] said he would kill David. [17]But
Abishai son of Zeruiah came to his aid, and
attacked the Philistine and killed him. Then
David's men swore to him, "You shall not
go out with us to battle any longer, so that
you do not quench the lamp of Israel."

18 After this a battle took place with the
Philistines, at Gob; then Sibbecai the
Hushathite killed Saph, who was one of the
descendants of the giants. [19]Then there was
another battle with the Philistines at Gob;
and Elhanan son of Jaare-oregim, the
Bethlehemite, killed Goliath the Gittite, the
shaft of whose spear was like a weaver's
beam. [20]There was again war at Gath, where
there was a man of great size, who had six
fingers on each hand, and six toes on each
foot, twenty-four in number; he too was
descended from the giants. [21]When he
taunted Israel, Jonathan son of David's
brother Shimei, killed him. [22]These four were
descended from the giants in Gath; they fell
by the hands of David and his servants.

David's Song of Thanksgiving

22 David spoke to the LORD the words
of this song on the day when the
LORD delivered him from the hand of all his
enemies, and from the hand of Saul. [2]He
said:

The LORD is my rock, my fortress, and
my deliverer,
3 my God, my rock, in whom I take
refuge,
my shield and the horn of my salvation,
my stronghold and my refuge,
my savior; you save me from violence.
4 I call upon the LORD, who is worthy to
be praised,
and I am saved from my enemies.

5 For the waves of death encompassed me,
the torrents of perdition assailed me;
6 the cords of Sheol entangled me,
the snares of death confronted me.

[n] Cn Compare Gk and 21.9: Heb *at Gibeah of Saul, the chosen of the* LORD [o] Or *Merib-baal*: See 4.4 note [p] Two Heb Mss Syr Compare Gk: MT *Michal* [q] Heb *the* [r] Heb *was belted anew*

21.3 2 Sam 20.19
21.4 Num 35.31,32
21.5 1 Sam 10.24,26
21.7 2 Sam 4.4; 9.10; 1 Sam 18.3; 20.8,15; 23.18
21.8 2 Sam 3.7
21.10 ver 8; Deut 21.23; 1 Sam 17.44,46
21.12 1 Sam 31.10-13
21.14 Josh 18.28; 7.26; 2 Sam 24.25
21.17 2 Sam 18.3; 6.17
21.18 1 Chr 20.4; 11.29
21.19 1 Chr 20.5
21.20 1 Chr 20.6
21.21 see 1 Sam 16.9
21.22 1 Chr 20.8
22.1 Ex 15.1; Jude 5.1; Ps 18.2-50
22.2 Deut 32.4; Ps 31.3; 71.3; 91.2; 144.2
22.3 Heb 2.13; Gen 15.1; Lk 1.69; Ps 9.9; 14.6; Jer 16.19
22.4 Ps 48.1
22.5 Ps 93.4; Jon 2.3; Ps 69.14,15
22.6 Ps 116.3

7 In my distress I called upon the LORD;
to my God I called.
From his temple he heard my voice,
and my cry came to his ears.

8 Then the earth reeled and rocked;
the foundations of the heavens trembled
and quaked, because he was angry.
9 Smoke went up from his nostrils,
and devouring fire from his mouth;
glowing coals flamed forth from him.
10 He bowed the heavens, and came down;
thick darkness was under his feet.
11 He rode on a cherub, and flew;
he was seen upon the wings of the wind.
12 He made darkness around him a canopy,
thick clouds, a gathering of water.
13 Out of the brightness before him
coals of fire flamed forth.
14 The LORD thundered from heaven;
the Most High uttered his voice.
15 He sent out arrows, and scattered them
—lightning, and routed them.
16 Then the channels of the sea were seen,
the foundations of the world were laid bare
at the rebuke of the LORD,
at the blast of the breath of his nostrils.

17 He reached from on high, he took me,
he drew me out of mighty waters.
18 He delivered me from my strong enemy,
from those who hated me;
for they were too mighty for me.
19 They came upon me in the day of my calamity,
but the LORD was my stay.
20 He brought me out into a broad place;
he delivered me, because he delighted in me.

21 The LORD rewarded me according to my righteousness;
according to the cleanness of my hands he recompensed me.
22 For I have kept the ways of the LORD,
and have not wickedly departed from my God.
23 For all his ordinances were before me,
and from his statutes I did not turn aside.
24 I was blameless before him,
and I kept myself from guilt.
25 Therefore the LORD has recompensed me according to my righteousness,
according to my cleanness in his sight.

26 With the loyal you show yourself loyal;
with the blameless you show yourself blameless;
27 with the pure you show yourself pure,
and with the crooked you show yourself perverse.
28 You deliver a humble people,
but your eyes are upon the haughty to bring them down.
29 Indeed, you are my lamp, LORD,
the LORD lightens my darkness.
30 By you I can crush a troop,
and by my God I can leap over a wall.
31 This God—his way is perfect;
the promise of the LORD proves true;
he is a shield for all who take refuge in him.

32 For who is God, but the LORD?
And who is a rock, except our God?
33 The God who has girded me with strength[s]
has opened wide my path.[t]
34 He made my[u] feet like the feet of deer,
and set me secure on the heights.
35 He trains my hands for war,
so that my arms can bend a bow of bronze.
36 You have given me the shield of your salvation,
and your help[v] has made me great.
37 You have made me stride freely,
and my feet do not slip;
38 I pursued my enemies and destroyed them,
and did not turn back until they were consumed.
39 I consumed them; I struck them down, so that they did not rise;
they fell under my feet.
40 For you girded me with strength for the battle;

[s] Q Ms Gk Syr Vg Compare Ps 18.32: MT *God is my strong refuge* [t] Meaning of Heb uncertain [u] Another reading is *his* [v] Q Ms: MT *your answering*

22.7 Ps 116.4; 120.1; 34.6,15
22.8 Judg 5.4; Ps 77.18; Job 26.11
22.9 Ps 96.3; Heb 12.29
22.10 Ex 19.16; 1 Kings 8.12; Ps 97.2
22.11 Ps 104.3
22.12 Ps 97.2
22.13 ver 9
22.14 1 Sam 2.10
22.16 Hab 3.11
22.17 Ps 144.7; 32.6
22.19 Ps 23.4
22.20 Ps 31.8; 22.8
22.21 1 Kings 8.32; Ps 24.4
22.22 Gen 18.19; Ps 128.1
22.23 Deut 6.6-9
22.24 Gen 7.1; 17.1; Eph 1.4
22.25 ver 21
22.26 Mt 5.7
22.27 Lev 26.23
22.28 Ps 72.12; Isa 2.11,12,17
22.29 Ps 27.1
22.31 Deut 32.4; Mt 5.48; Ps 12.6; ver 3
22.32 1 Sam 2.2; ver 2
22.33 Ps 27.1; Ps 101.2,6
22.34 Hab 3.19; Deut 32.13
22.35 Ps 144.1
22.37 Prov 4.12
22.39 Mal 4.3
22.40 Ps 44.5

you made my assailants sink under
me.
41 You made my enemies turn their
backs to me,
those who hated me, and I
destroyed them.
42 They looked, but there was no one to
save them;
they cried to the LORD, but he did
not answer them.
43 I beat them fine like the dust of the
earth,
I crushed them and stamped them down
like the mire of the streets.

44 You delivered me from strife with the
peoples;[w]
you kept me as the head of the
nations;
people whom I had not known
served me.
45 Foreigners came cringing to me;
as soon as they heard of me, they
obeyed me.
46 Foreigners lost heart,
and came trembling out of their
strongholds.

47 The LORD lives! Blessed be my rock,
and exalted be my God, the rock of
my salvation,
48 the God who gave me vengeance
and brought down peoples under me,
49 who brought me out from my enemies;
you exalted me above my adversaries,
you delivered me from the violent.

50 For this I will extol you, LORD, among
the nations,
and sing praises to your name.
51 He is a tower of salvation for his king,
and shows steadfast love to his
anointed,
to David and his descendants forever.

The Last Words of David

23 Now these are the last words of
David:
The oracle of David, son of Jesse,
the oracle of the man whom God
exalted,[x]
the anointed of the God of Jacob,
the favorite of the Strong One of Israel:
2 The spirit of the LORD speaks through
me,
his word is upon my tongue.
3 The God of Israel has spoken,
the Rock of Israel has said to me:
One who rules over people justly,
ruling in the fear of God,
4 is like the light of morning,
like the sun rising on a cloudless
morning,
gleaming from the rain on the
grassy land.

5 Is not my house like this with God?
For he has made with me an
everlasting covenant,
ordered in all things and secure.
Will he not cause to prosper
all my help and my desire?
6 But the godless are[y] all like thorns
that are thrown away;
for they cannot be picked up with
the hand;
7 to touch them one uses an iron bar
or the shaft of a spear.
And they are entirely consumed in
fire on the spot.[z]

David's Mighty Men

8 These are the names of the warriors
whom David had: Josheb-basshebeth a
Tahchemonite; he was chief of the Three;[a]
he wielded his spear[b] against eight hundred
whom he killed at one time.
9 Next to him among the three warriors
was Eleazar son of Dodo son of Ahohi. He
was with David when they defied the
Philistines who were gathered there for battle.
The Israelites withdrew, 10but he stood his
ground. He struck down the Philistines until
his arm grew weary, though his hand clung
to the sword. The LORD brought about a
great victory that day. Then the people
came back to him—but only to strip the
dead.
11 Next to him was Shammah son of
Agee, the Hararite. The Philistines gathered
together at Lehi, where there was a plot of
ground full of lentils; and the army fled
from the Philistines. 12But he took his stand
in the middle of the plot, defended it, and
killed the Philistines; and the LORD brought
about a great victory.

[w] Gk: Heb *from strife with my people* [x] Q Ms: MT *who was raised on high* [y] Heb *But worthlessness* [z] Heb *in sitting* [a] Gk Vg Compare 1 Chr 11.11: Meaning of Heb uncertain [b] 1 Chr 11.11: Meaning of Heb uncertain

(4) 23.1-7 The Last Words of David. After identifying himself in terms of his family origin (*son of Jesse*) and as *anointed* and favored of Israel's God, he describes how God speaks through him to his people, and declares that God has made with him *an everlasting covenant.* The godless are to be disposed of like thorns or useless vegetation.

(5) 23.8-38 The great ones who helped David gain and maintain control in his kingdom are here grouped as *the Three* (vv. 8-12) and *the Thirty* (vv. 13-38), although their number comes to *thirty-seven* (vs. 38). They fought for him, risked their lives for him, and defeated humans and wild animals. The *Thirty* appear to be listed in the chronological order of their service to David. Ironically, *Uriah the Hittite* is included, whom David ordered sent into battle to be killed so that he could obtain Uriah's wife (11.1-27).

(6) David's Sin in Taking a Census and the Consequences. Out of pride, David sought to determine how many people were subject to him. This impulse is pictured here as *incited* by the LORD in *anger* against David and Israel, but in the parallel account in 1 Chr 21.1, it is Satan who moves David to launch this project. The reported number of soldiers in *Israel and Judah* – 1,300,000 – is probably greater than the total population of the land actually was. The divine punishment took the form of a *pestilence* which killed a huge segment of the population. The *threshing floor* where David had his encounter with *the angel of the LORD* was purchased by him and became the location for *an altar to the LORD,* and later for the building of the temple in the reign of Solomon.

22.41 Ex 23.27; Josh 10.24
22.42 Ps 50.22; 1 Sam 28.6
22.43 Ps 18.42; Isa 10.6
22.44 2 Sam 3.1; Deut 28.13; Isa 55.5
22.45 Ps 66.3
22.46 Mic 7.17
22.47 Ps 89.26
22.48 Ps 94.1; 144.2
22.49 Ps 44.5; 140.1
22.50 Rom 15.9
22.51 Ps 144.10; 89.20,29; 2 Sam 7.12-16
23.1 2 Sam 7.8,9; Ps 78.70; 89.27; 1 Sam 16.12,13; Ps 89.20
23.2 2 Pet 1.21
23.3 Deut 32.4; 2 Sam 22.2,32; Ex 18.21; 2 Chr 19.7,9
23.4 Judg 5.31; Ps 89.36
23.5 Ps 89.29; Isa 55.3
23.6 Mt 13.42
23.9 1 Chr 27.4
23.10 1 Chr 11.12-14
23.11 1 Chr 11.27

23.13 1 Sam 22.1; 2 Sam 5.18
23.14 1 Sam 22.4,5
23.17 Lev 17.10
23.18 2 Sam 10.10,14; 1 Chr 11.20
23.20 2 Sam 8.18; 20.33; Josh 15.21
23.23 2 Sam 8.18; 20.23
23.24 2 Sam 2.18
23.25 1 Chr 11.27
23.38 2 Sam 20.26
23.39 2 Sam 11.3,6
24.1 2 Sam 20.1,2; 1 Chr 27.23,24
24.2 2 Sam 3.10; Judg 20.1
24.5 Deut 2.36; Josh 13.9,16; Num 32.1,3
24.6 Josh 19.28
24.7 Josh 11.3; Gen 21.22-33
24.9 1 Chr 21.5

13 Towards the beginning of harvest three of the thirty[c] chiefs went down to join David at the cave of Adullam, while a band of Philistines was encamped in the valley of Rephaim. 14 David was then in the stronghold; and the garrison of the Philistines was then at Bethlehem. 15 David said longingly, "that someone would give me water to drink from the well of Bethlehem that is by the gate!" 16 Then the three warriors broke through the camp of the Philistines, drew water from the well of Bethlehem that was by the gate, and brought it to David. But he would not drink of it; he poured it out to the LORD, 17 for he said, "The LORD forbid that I should do this. Can I drink the blood of the men who went at the risk of their lives?" Therefore he would not drink it. The three warriors did these things.

18 Now Abishai son of Zeruiah, the brother of Joab, was chief of the Thirty.[d] With his spear he fought against three hundred men and killed them, and won a name beside the Three. 19 He was the most renowned of the Thirty,[e] and became their commander; but he did not attain to the Three.

20 Benaiah son of Jehoiada was a valiant warrior[f] from Kabzeel, a doer of great deeds; he struck down two sons of Ariel[g] of Moab. He also went down and killed a lion in a pit on a day when snow had fallen. 21 And he killed an Egyptian, a handsome man. The Egyptian had a spear in his hand; but Benaiah went against him with a staff, snatched the spear out of the Egyptian's hand, and killed him with his own spear. 22 Such were the things Benaiah son of Jehoiada did, and won a name beside the three warriors. 23 He was renowned among the Thirty, but he did not attain to the Three. And David put him in charge of his bodyguard.

24 Among the Thirty were Asahel brother of Joab; Elhanan son of Dodo of Bethlehem; 25 Shammah of Harod; Elika of Harod; 26 Helez the Paltite; Ira son of Ikkesh of Tekoa; 27 Abiezer of Anathoth; Mebunnai the Hushathite; 28 Zalmon the Ahohite; Maharai of Netophah; 29 Heleb son of Baanah of Netophah; Ittai son of Ribai of Gibeah of the Benjaminites; 30 Benaiah of Pirathon; Hiddai of the torrents of Gaash; 31 Abi-albon the Arbathite; Azmaveth of Bahurim; 32 Eliahba of Shaalbon; the sons of Jashen: Jonathan 33 son of[h] Shammah the Hararite; Ahiam son of Sharar the Hararite; 34 Eliphelet son of Ahasbai of Maacah; Eliam son of Ahithophel the Gilonite; 35 Hezro[i] of Carmel; Paarai the Arbite; 36 Igal son of Nathan of Zobah; Bani the Gadite; 37 Zelek the Ammonite; Naharai of Beeroth, the armor-bearer of Joab son of Zeruiah; 38 Ira the Ithrite; Gareb the Ithrite; 39 Uriah the Hittite—thirty-seven in all.

David's Census of Israel and Judah

24 Again the anger of the LORD was kindled against Israel, and he incited David against them, saying, "Go, count the people of Israel and Judah." 2 So the king said to Joab and the commanders of the army,[j] who were with him, "Go through all the tribes of Israel, from Dan to Beer-sheba, and take a census of the people, so that I may know how many there are." 3 But Joab said to the king, "May the LORD your God increase the number of the people a hundredfold, while the eyes of my lord the king can still see it! But why does my lord the king want to do this?" 4 But the king's word prevailed against Joab and the commanders of the army. So Joab and the commanders of the army went out from the presence of the king to take a census of the people of Israel. 5 They crossed the Jordan, and began from[k] Aroer and from the city that is in the middle of the valley, toward Gad and on to Jazer. 6 Then they came to Gilead, and to Kadesh in the land of the Hittites;[l] and they came to Dan, and from Dan[m] they went around to Sidon, 7 and came to the fortress of Tyre and to all the cities of the Hivites and Canaanites; and they went out to the Negeb of Judah at Beer-sheba. 8 So when they had gone through all the land, they came back to Jerusalem at the end of nine months and twenty days. 9 Joab reported to the king the number of those who had been recorded: in Israel there were eight hundred thousand soldiers able to draw the sword, and those of Judah were five hundred thousand.

[c] Heb adds *head* [d] Two Heb Mss Syr: MT *Three* [e] Syr Compare 1 Chr 11.25: Heb *Was he the most renowned of the Three?* [f] Another reading is *the son of Ish-hai* [g] Gk: Heb lacks *sons of* [h] Gk: Heb lacks *son of* [i] Another reading is *Hezrai* [j] 1 Chr 21.2 Gk: Heb *to Joab the commander of the army* [k] Gk Mss: Heb *encamped in Aroer south of* [l] Gk: Heb *to the land of Tahtim-hodshi* [m] Cn Compare Gk: Heb *they came to Dan-jaan and*

Judgment on David's Sin

10 But afterward, David was stricken to
the heart because he had numbered the
people. David said to the LORD, "I have
sinned greatly in what I have done. But
now, LORD, I pray you, take away the guilt
of your servant; for I have done very foolishly." 11When David rose in the morning,
the word of the LORD came to the prophet
Gad, David's seer, saying, 12"Go and say to
David: Thus says the LORD: Three things I
offer[n] you; choose one of them, and I will
do it to you." 13So Gad came to David and
told him; he asked him, "Shall three[o] years
of famine come to you on your land? Or will
you flee three months before your foes while
they pursue you? Or shall there be three
days' pestilence in your land? Now consider,
and decide what answer I shall return to
the one who sent me." 14Then David said
to Gad, "I am in great distress; let us fall
into the hand of the LORD, for his mercy is
great; but let me not fall into human hands."

15 So the LORD sent a pestilence on Israel
from that morning until the appointed time;
and seventy thousand of the people died,
from Dan to Beer-sheba. 16But when the
angel stretched out his hand toward Jerusalem to destroy it, the LORD relented concerning the evil, and said to the angel who
was bringing destruction among the people,
"It is enough; now stay your hand." The
angel of the LORD was then by the threshing
floor of Araunah the Jebusite. 17When David
saw the angel who was destroying the people,
he said to the LORD, "I alone have sinned,
and I alone have done wickedly; but these
sheep, what have they done? Let your hand,
I pray, be against me and against my
father's house."

David's Altar on the Threshing Floor

18 That day Gad came to David and said
to him, "Go up and erect an altar to the
LORD on the threshing floor of Araunah the
Jebusite." 19Following Gad's instructions,
David went up, as the LORD had commanded.
20When Araunah looked down, he saw the
king and his servants coming toward him;
and Araunah went out and prostrated himself before the king with his face to the
ground. 21Araunah said, "Why has my lord
the king come to his servant?" David said,
"To buy the threshing floor from you in
order to build an altar to the LORD, so that
the plague may be averted from the people."
22Then Araunah said to David, "Let my lord
the king take and offer up what seems good
to him; here are the oxen for the burnt
offering, and the threshing sledges and the
yokes of the oxen for the wood. 23All this,
king, Araunah gives to the king." And
Araunah said to the king, "May the LORD
your God respond favorably to you."

24 But the king said to Araunah, "No,
but I will buy them from you for a price;
I will not offer burnt offerings to the LORD
my God that cost me nothing." So David
bought the threshing floor and the oxen for
fifty shekels of silver. 25David built there an
altar to the LORD, and offered burnt offerings
and offerings of well-being. So the LORD
answered his supplication for the land, and
the plague was averted from Israel.

24.10 1 Sam 24.5; 2 Sam 12.13; 1 Sam 13.13
24.11 1 Sam 24.5; 9.9; 1Chr 29.29
24.12 1 Chr 21.12
24.14 Ps 103.8,13.14
24.15 1 Chr 21.14; 27.24
24.16 Ex 12.23; Gen 6.6; 1 Sam 15.11
24.17 ver 10; 1 Chr 21.17
24.18 1 Chr 21.18ff
24.21 Num 16.48,50
24.22 1 Kings 19.21
24.23 Ezek 20.40,41
24.24 1 Chr 21.24,25
24.25 2 Sam 21.14; ver 21

[n] Or *hold over* [o] 1 Chr 21.12 Gk: Heb *seven*

1 KINGS

See the Introductions, pp. 3, 38, and 43-44 above.

The Struggle for the Succession

1 King David was old and advanced in years; and although they covered him with clothes, he could not get warm. [2]So his servants said to him, "Let a young virgin be sought for my lord the king, and let her wait on the king, and be his attendant; let her lie in your bosom, so that my lord the king may be warm." [3]So they searched for a beautiful girl throughout all the territory of Israel, and found Abishag the Shunammite, and brought her to the king. [4]The girl was very beautiful. She became the king's attendant and served him, but the king did not know her sexually.

5 Now Adonijah son of Haggith exalted himself, saying, "I will be king"; he prepared for himself chariots and horsemen, and fifty men to run before him. [6]His father had never at any time displeased him by asking, "Why have you done thus and so?" He was also a very handsome man, and he was born next after Absalom. [7]He conferred with Joab son of Zeruiah and with the priest Abiathar, and they supported Adonijah. [8]But the priest Zadok, and Benaiah son of Jehoiada, and the prophet Nathan, and Shimei, and Rei, and David's own warriors did not side with Adonijah.

9 Adonijah sacrificed sheep, oxen, and fatted cattle by the stone Zoheleth, which is beside En-rogel, and he invited all his brothers, the king's sons, and all the royal officials of Judah, [10]but he did not invite the prophet Nathan or Benaiah or the warriors or his brother Solomon.

11 Then Nathan said to Bathsheba, Solomon's mother, "Have you not heard that Adonijah son of Haggith has become king and our lord David does not know it? [12]Now therefore come, let me give you advice, so that you may save your own life and the life of your son Solomon. [13]Go in at once to King David, and say to him, 'Did you not, my lord the king, swear to your servant, saying: Your son Solomon shall succeed me as king, and he shall sit on my throne? Why then is Adonijah king?' [14]Then while you are still there speaking with the king, I will come in after you and confirm your words."

15 So Bathsheba went to the king in his room. The king was very old; Abishag the Shunammite was attending the king. [16]Bathsheba bowed and did obeisance to the king, and the king said, "What do you wish?" [17]She said to him, "My lord, you swore to your servant by the LORD your God, saying: Your son Solomon shall succeed me as king, and he shall sit on my throne. [18]But now suddenly Adonijah has become king, though you, my lord the king, do not know it. [19]He has sacrificed oxen, fatted cattle, and sheep in abundance, and has invited all the children of the king, the priest Abiathar, and Joab the commander of the army; but your servant Solomon he has not invited. [20]But you, my lord the king—the eyes of all Israel are on you to tell them who shall sit on the throne of my lord the king after him. [21]Otherwise it will come to pass, when my lord the king sleeps with his ancestors, that my son Solomon and I will be counted offenders."

22 While she was still speaking with the king, the prophet Nathan came in. [23]The king was told, "Here is the prophet Nathan." When he came in before the king, he did obeisance to the king, with his face to the ground. [24]Nathan said, "My lord the king, have you said, 'Adonijah shall succeed me as king, and he shall sit on my throne'? [25]For today he has gone down and has sacrificed oxen, fatted cattle, and sheep in abundance, and has invited all the king's children, Joab the commander[a] of the army, and the priest Abiathar, who are now eating and drinking before him, and saying, 'Long live King Adonijah!' [26]But he did not invite me, your servant, and the priest Zadok, and Benaiah son of Jehoiada, and your servant Solomon. [27]Has this thing been brought about by my lord the king and you have not let your servants know who should sit on the throne of my lord the king after him?"

The Accession of Solomon

28 King David answered, "Summon Bathsheba to me." So she came into the king's presence, and stood before the king. [29]The king swore, saying, "As the LORD lives, who has saved my life from every adversity, [30]as I swore to you by the LORD, the God of

[a] Gk: Heb *the commanders*

1.3 Josh 19.18
1.5 2 Sam 3.4; 15.1
1.6 2 Sam 3.3,4
1.7 1 Chr 11.6; 2 Sam 20.25; 1 Kings 2.22,28
1.8 2 Sam 20.25; 8.18; 12.1; 23.8
1.9 2 Sam 17.17
1.10 2 Sam 12.24
1.11 2 Sam 3.4
1.13 ver 30; 1 Chr 22.9-13
1.15 ver 1
1.17 ver 13,30
1.19 ver 9
1.21 Deut 31.16; 1 Kings 2.10
1.25 ver 9; 1 Sam 10.24
1.26 ver 8,10
1.29 2 Sam 4.9
1.30 ver 13,17

1.1-2.46 The Death of David and Solomon's Accession to the Throne of Israel.
1.1-4 *A young virgin, Abishag,* was brought from Shunem (southwest of the Lake of Galilee) to care for David in his old age.
1.5-10 The Plot of David's Son and Would-be Successor, Adonijah. *Adonijah,* whose name means "Yahweh is my LORD," David's fourth son born of *Haggith* at Hebron (2 Sam 3.2-5), announced that he was *the king* and successor to David. Support for his claim came from David's military leader, *Joab* (2 Sam 20.23), and one of his priestly leaders, *Abiathar* (2 Sam 20.25). The leaders who opposed Adonijah's claim included *the priest Zadok* (2 Sam 20.25), *Benaiah* the leader of the Philistine troops serving under David (2 Sam 20.23), and *the prophet Nathan* who had conveyed to David God's covenantal promise of the kingdom (2 Sam 7). Adonijah sought to give religious sanction to his seizure of the kingship by offering sacrifices by *the stone Zoheleth,* This may have been a statue of a serpent, which for the pre-Israelite religion was a symbol of life. *En-rogel* was just outside Jerusalem.
1.11-27 First through Bathsheba, wife of David and mother of Solomon, and then personally, *Nathan* informed David of Adonijah's plot to seize the throne and of the mixture of sacrifices and revelry in which he and his followers were engaged.
1.28-48 David Announces that his Successor is Solomon. Nathan and Bathsheba both remind David that he has taken an oath *by the LORD, the God of Israel,* that *Solomon* will succeed him as king. After confirming this to Bathsheba once again (1.30), the prophet and priest are ordered to have Solomon ride David's mule as public evidence of his role as successor. At *Gihon,* the sacred spring just outside Jerusalem, Nathan and Zadok are *to anoint him king,* and he is to mount the throne as *ruler over Israel and Judah.* All the people acclaim him as *King Solomon.* When reports of these developments reached Adonijah and his supporters in the midst of their celebration, they were terrified, but Solomon declined to punish the plotters. After doing *obeisance to King Solomon,* Adonijah was allowed to *go home.*

2.1-4 David's basic instructions to Solomon embody the principles and even the distinctive terms of Deuteronomy (as in Deut 11; 26.16-19): conformity to *the law of Moses* will ensure *prosperity* of the nation and continuity of Israel's royal line.
2.5-9 Although David was bound by oaths not to harm leaders who had turned against him – *Joab and Shimei* (2 Sam 18-20) – Solomon is urged to see that they are killed. The gray head of each of them will not *go down to Sheol*, the abode of the dead, *in peace.*

Israel, 'Your son Solomon shall succeed me as king, and he shall sit on my throne in my place,' so will I do this day." [31]Then Bathsheba bowed with her face to the ground, and did obeisance to the king, and said, "May my lord King David live forever!"

32 King David said, "Summon to me the priest Zadok, the prophet Nathan, and Benaiah son of Jehoiada." When they came before the king, [33]the king said to them, "Take with you the servants of your lord, and have my son Solomon ride on my own mule, and bring him down to Gihon. [34]There let the priest Zadok and the prophet Nathan anoint him king over Israel; then blow the trumpet, and say, 'Long live King Solomon!' [35]You shall go up following him. Let him enter and sit on my throne; he shall be king in my place; for I have appointed him to be ruler over Israel and over Judah." [36]Benaiah son of Jehoiada answered the king, "Amen! May the LORD, the God of my lord the king, so ordain. [37]As the LORD has been with my lord the king, so may he be with Solomon, and make his throne greater than the throne of my lord King David."

38 So the priest Zadok, the prophet Nathan, and Benaiah son of Jehoiada, and the Cherethites and the Pelethites, went down and had Solomon ride on King David's mule, and led him to Gihon. [39]There the priest Zadok took the horn of oil from the tent and anointed Solomon. Then they blew the trumpet, and all the people said, "Long live King Solomon!" [40]And all the people went up following him, playing on pipes and rejoicing with great joy, so that the earth quaked at their noise.

41 Adonijah and all the guests who were with him heard it as they finished feasting. When Joab heard the sound of the trumpet, he said, "Why is the city in an uproar?" [42]While he was still speaking, Jonathan son of the priest Abiathar arrived. Adonijah said, "Come in, for you are a worthy man and surely you bring good news." [43]Jonathan answered Adonijah, "No, for our lord King David has made Solomon king; [44]the king has sent with him the priest Zadok, the prophet Nathan, and Benaiah son of Jehoiada, and the Cherethites and the Pelethites; and they had him ride on the king's mule; [45]the priest Zadok and the prophet Nathan have anointed him king at Gihon; and they have gone up from there rejoicing, so that the city is in an uproar. This is the noise that you heard. [46]Solomon now sits on the royal throne. [47]Moreover the king's servants came to congratulate our lord King David, saying, 'May God make the name of Solomon more famous than yours, and make his throne greater than your throne.' The king bowed in worship on the bed [48]and went on to pray thus, 'Blessed be the LORD, the God of Israel, who today has granted one of my offspring[b] to sit on my throne and permitted me to witness it.' "

49 Then all the guests of Adonijah got up trembling and went their own ways. [50]Adonijah, fearing Solomon, got up and went to grasp the horns of the altar. [51]Solomon was informed, "Adonijah is afraid of King Solomon; see, he has laid hold of the horns of the altar, saying, 'Let King Solomon swear to me first that he will not kill his servant with the sword.' " [52]So Solomon responded, "If he proves to be a worthy man, not one of his hairs shall fall to the ground; but if wickedness is found in him, he shall die." [53]Then King Solomon sent to have him brought down from the altar. He came to do obeisance to King Solomon; and Solomon said to him, "Go home."

David's Instruction to Solomon

2 When David's time to die drew near, he charged his son Solomon, saying: [2]"I am about to go the way of all the earth. Be strong, be courageous, [3]and keep the charge of the LORD your God, walking in his ways and keeping his statutes, his commandments, his ordinances, and his testimonies, as it is written in the law of Moses, so that you may prosper in all that you do and wherever you turn. [4]Then the LORD will establish his word that he spoke concerning me: 'If your heirs take heed to their way, to walk before me in faithfulness with all their heart and with all their soul, there shall not fail you a successor on the throne of Israel.'

5 "Moreover you know also what Joab son of Zeruiah did to me, how he dealt with the two commanders of the armies of Israel, Abner son of Ner, and Amasa son of Jether, whom he murdered, retaliating in time of peace for blood that had been shed in war, and putting the blood of war on the belt around his waist, and on the sandals on his feet. [6]Act therefore according to your

[b] Gk: Heb *one*

1.31 Neh 2.3; Dan 2.4
1.33 2 Sam 20.6,7
1.34 1 Sam 10.1; 16.3,12; 2 Sam 15.10; ver 25
1.37 Josh 1.5,17; 1 Sam 20.13; ver 47
1.38 ver 8,33; 2 Sam 8.18
1.39 Ex 30.23-32; Ps 89.20; 1 Chr 29.22
1.42 2 Sam 15.27,36; 18.27
1.45 ver 40
1.46 1 Chr 29.23
1.47 ver 37; Gen 47.31
1.48 1 Kings 3.6; 2 Sam 7.12
1.50 1 Kings 2.28
1.52 1 Sam 14.45; 2 Sam 14.11
2.1 Gen 47.29; Deut 31.14
2.2 Josh 23.14; Deut 31.7,23; Josh 1.6,7
2.3 Josh 1.7; 1 Chr 22.12,13
2.4 2 Sam 7.25; Ps 132.12; 2 Kings 20.3; 2 Sam 7.12,13
2.5 2 Sam 18.5,12,14; 3.27; 20.10
2.6 ver 9

wisdom, but do not let his gray head go down to Sheol in peace. [7]Deal loyally, however, with the sons of Barzillai the Gileadite, and let them be among those who eat at your table; for with such loyalty they met me when I fled from your brother Absalom. [8]There is also with you Shimei son of Gera, the Benjaminite from Bahurim, who cursed me with a terrible curse on the day when I went to Mahanaim; but when he came down to meet me at the Jordan, I swore to him by the LORD, 'I will not put you to death with the sword.' [9]Therefore do not hold him guiltless, for you are a wise man; you will know what you ought to do to him, and you must bring his gray head down with blood to Sheol."

Death of David

10 Then David slept with his ancestors, and was buried in the city of David. [11]The time that David reigned over Israel was forty years; he reigned seven years in Hebron, and thirty-three years in Jerusalem. [12]So Solomon sat on the throne of his father David; and his kingdom was firmly established.

Solomon Consolidates His Reign

13 Then Adonijah son of Haggith came to Bathsheba, Solomon's mother. She asked, "Do you come peaceably?" He said, "Peaceably." [14]Then he said, "May I have a word with you?" She said, "Go on." [15]He said, "You know that the kingdom was mine, and that all Israel expected me to reign; however, the kingdom has turned about and become my brother's, for it was his from the LORD. [16]And now I have one request to make of you; do not refuse me." She said to him, "Go on." [17]He said, "Please ask King Solomon—he will not refuse you—to give me Abishag the Shunammite as my wife." [18]Bathsheba said, "Very well; I will speak to the king on your behalf."

19 So Bathsheba went to King Solomon, to speak to him on behalf of Adonijah. The king rose to meet her, and bowed down to her; then he sat on his throne, and had a throne brought for the king's mother, and she sat on his right. [20]Then she said, "I have one small request to make of you; do not refuse me." And the king said to her, "Make your request, my mother; for I will not refuse you." [21]She said, "Let Abishag the Shunammite be given to your brother Adonijah as his wife." [22]King Solomon answered his mother, "And why do you ask Abishag the Shunammite for Adonijah? Ask for him the kingdom as well! For he is my elder brother; ask not only for him but also for the priest Abiathar and for Joab son of Zeruiah!" [23]Then King Solomon swore by the LORD, "So may God do to me, and more also, for Adonijah has devised this scheme at the risk of his life! [24]Now therefore as the LORD lives, who has established me and placed me on the throne of my father David, and who has made me a house as he promised, today Adonijah shall be put to death." [25]So King Solomon sent Benaiah son of Jehoiada; he struck him down, and he died.

26 The king said to the priest Abiathar, "Go to Anathoth, to your estate; for you deserve death. But I will not at this time put you to death, because you carried the ark of the Lord GOD before my father David, and because you shared in all the hardships my father endured." [27]So Solomon banished Abiathar from being priest to the LORD, thus fulfilling the word of the LORD that he had spoken concerning the house of Eli in Shiloh.

28 When the news came to Joab—for Joab had supported Adonijah though he had not supported Absalom—Joab fled to the tent of the LORD and grasped the horns of the altar. [29]When it was told King Solomon, "Joab has fled to the tent of the LORD and now is beside the altar," Solomon sent Benaiah son of Jehoiada, saying, "Go, strike him down." [30]So Benaiah came to the tent of the LORD and said to him, "The king commands, 'Come out.' " But he said, "No, I will die here." Then Benaiah brought the king word again, saying, "Thus said Joab, and thus he answered me." [31]The king replied to him, "Do as he has said, strike him down and bury him; and thus take away from me and from my father's house the guilt for the blood that Joab shed without cause. [32]The LORD will bring back his bloody deeds on his own head, because, without the knowledge of my father David, he attacked and killed with the sword two men more righteous and better than himself, Abner son of Ner, commander of the army of Israel, and Amasa son of Jether, commander of the army of Judah. [33]So shall their blood come back on the head of Joab and on the head of his descendants forever; but to David, and to his descendants, and

2.10-12 David's reign of *forty years* lasted for what ancient Israel regarded as a generation, and began about the year 1000. See the chronological chart of the kings of Israel and Judah.
2.13-46 Solomon consolidated his claim to the throne by executing or banishing all who had threatened him or his father, David, in their royal role: *Adonijah* (who was known to have plotted to gain the throne); *the priest, Abiathar; Joab and Shimei* (who violated his promise never to leave his house in Jerusalem). The executioner in each case was *Benaiah son of Jehoida*, whom Solomon put in charge of his army (2.35).

2.7 2 Sam 19.31,38; 9.7,10; 17.27
2.8 2 Sam 16.5-8; 19.18-23
2.9 ver 6
2.10 Acts 2.29; 2 Sam 5.7
2.11 2 Sam 5.4; 1 Chr 29.26,27
2.12 1 Chr 29.23; 2 Chr 1.1
2.13 1 Sam 16.4
2.15 1 Kings 1.5; 1 Chr 22.9,10; 28.5-7
2.17 1 Kings 1.3,4
2.19 Ps 45.9
2.20 ver 6
2.21 1 Kings 1.3,4
2.22 2 Sam 12.8; 1 Kings 1.6,7
2.23 Ruth 1.17
2.24 2 Sam 7.11,13
2.26 Josh 21.18; 1 Sam 23.6; 2 Sam 15.24-29; 1 Sam 22.20-23
2.27 1 Sam 2.31-35
2.28 1 Kings 1.7,50
2.29 ver 25
2.31 Ex 21.14; Num 35.33; Deut 19.13
2.32 Judg 9.24,57; Ps 7.16; 2 Chr 21.13; 2 Sam 3.27; 20.10
2.33 2 Sam 3.29; Prov 25.5

3.1-11.42 The Reign of Solomon. **3.1** Solomon's marriage to *Pharaoh's daughter* was arranged as a form of diplomatic alliance. David's expansion of territory and his military successes made it important for Egypt's ruler to enter into such a relationship. She was housed in what had been David's central residence, while Solomon proceeded with building his house and the temple. **3.2-15** Both *the people* and their king continued to offer sacrifices to *the LORD* at other sacred sites than Jerusalem, and God appeared to Solomon at one of these: *Gibeon* (eight miles north of Jerusalem). Relying upon the *steadfast love* that God showed toward David in establishing the monarchy and placing him as successor, Solomon asked for wisdom in governing God's people. God promised to grant him this wisdom, but to grant him as well what he had not asked for: *riches and honor*. His description of himself as *only a little child* is a form of self-effacement, since his son, Rehoboam, was forty-one when, after Solomon's forty-year reign, he succeeded him as king of Judah (1 Kings 11.41-42; 14.21). **3.16-28** The practical aspects of Solomon's wisdom are evident in his clever scheme to reveal the true mother of *the living boy*.

to his house, and to his throne, there shall be peace from the LORD forevermore." 34 Then Benaiah son of Jehoiada went up and struck him down and killed him; and he was buried at his own house near the wilderness. 35 The king put Benaiah son of Jehoiada over the army in his place, and the king put the priest Zadok in the place of Abiathar.

36 Then the king sent and summoned Shimei, and said to him, "Build yourself a house in Jerusalem, and live there, and do not go out from there to any place whatever. 37 For on the day you go out, and cross the Wadi Kidron, know for certain that you shall die; your blood shall be on your own head." 38 And Shimei said to the king, "The sentence is fair; as my lord the king has said, so will your servant do." So Shimei lived in Jerusalem many days.

39 But it happened at the end of three years that two of Shimei's slaves ran away to King Achish son of Maacah of Gath. When it was told Shimei, "Your slaves are in Gath," 40 Shimei arose and saddled a donkey, and went to Achish in Gath, to search for his slaves; Shimei went and brought his slaves from Gath. 41 When Solomon was told that Shimei had gone from Jerusalem to Gath and returned, 42 the king sent and summoned Shimei, and said to him, "Did I not make you swear by the LORD, and solemnly adjure you, saying, 'Know for certain that on the day you go out and go to any place whatever, you shall die'? And you said to me, 'The sentence is fair; I accept.' 43 Why then have you not kept your oath to the LORD and the commandment with which I charged you?" 44 The king also said to Shimei, "You know in your own heart all the evil that you did to my father David; so the LORD will bring back your evil on your own head. 45 But King Solomon shall be blessed, and the throne of David shall be established before the LORD forever." 46 Then the king commanded Benaiah son of Jehoiada; and he went out and struck him down, and he died.

So the kingdom was established in the hand of Solomon.

Solomon's Prayer for Wisdom

3 Solomon made a marriage alliance with Pharaoh king of Egypt; he took Pharaoh's daughter and brought her into the city of David, until he had finished building his own house and the house of the LORD and the wall around Jerusalem. 2 The people were sacrificing at the high places, however, because no house had yet been built for the name of the LORD.

3 Solomon loved the LORD, walking in the statutes of his father David; only, he sacrificed and offered incense at the high places. 4 The king went to Gibeon to sacrifice there, for that was the principal high place; Solomon used to offer a thousand burnt offerings on that altar. 5 At Gibeon the LORD appeared to Solomon in a dream by night; and God said, "Ask what I should give you." 6 And Solomon said, "You have shown great and steadfast love to your servant my father David, because he walked before you in faithfulness, in righteousness, and in uprightness of heart toward you; and you have kept for him this great and steadfast love, and have given him a son to sit on his throne today. 7 And now, O LORD my God, you have made your servant king in place of my father David, although I am only a little child; I do not know how to go out or come in. 8 And your servant is in the midst of the people whom you have chosen, a great people, so numerous they cannot be numbered or counted. 9 Give your servant therefore an understanding mind to govern your people, able to discern between good and evil; for who can govern this your great people?"

10 It pleased the Lord that Solomon had asked this. 11 God said to him, "Because you have asked this, and have not asked for yourself long life or riches, or for the life of your enemies, but have asked for yourself understanding to discern what is right, 12 I now do according to your word. Indeed I give you a wise and discerning mind; no one like you has been before you and no one like you shall arise after you. 13 I give you also what you have not asked, both riches and honor all your life; no other king shall compare with you. 14 If you will walk in my ways, keeping my statutes and my commandments, as your father David walked, then I will lengthen your life."

15 Then Solomon awoke; it had been a dream. He came to Jerusalem where he stood before the ark of the covenant of the LORD. He offered up burnt offerings and offerings of well-being, and provided a feast for all his servants.

Solomon's Wisdom in Judgment

16 Later, two women who were prosti-

2.35 1 Kings 4.4; 1 Chr 29.22; ver 27
2.36 ver 8
2.37 2 Sam 15.23; Lev 20.9; 2 Sam 1.16
2.39 1 Sam 27.2
2.40 2 Sam 19.16-23
2.44 2 Sam 16.5-13; 1 Sam 25.39; Ezek 17.19
2.45 2 Sam 7.13
2.46 ver 12,25,34; 2 Chr 1.1
3.1 1 Kings 7.8; 9.24; 2 Sam 5.7; 1 Kings 7.1; ch 6; 9.15,19
3.2 Lev 17.3-5; Deut 12.2,4,5
3.3 Deut 6.5; Ps 31.23; 1 Kings 2.3; 9.4; 11.4,6,38
3.4 2 Chr 1.3; 1 Chr 16.39
3.5 1 Kings 9.2; 2 Chr 1.7; Num 12.6; Mt 1.20
3.6 2 Chr 1.8ff; 1 Kings 2.4; 9.4; 1.48
3.7 1 Chr 22.9-13; 29.1; Num 27.17
3.8 Deut 7.6; Gen 13.16; 15.5
3.9 2 Chr 1.10; Prov 2.3-9; Jas 1.5; Ps 72.1,2
3.11 Jas 4.3
3.12 1 Jn 5.14,15; 1 Kings 4.29-31
3.13 Mt 6.33; 1 Kings 4.21-24
3.14 ver 6
3.15 Gen 41.7; 1 Kings 8.65; Esth 1.3; Dan 5.1; Mk 6.21

tutes came to the king and stood before
him. [17]The one woman said, "Please, my
lord, this woman and I live in the same
house; and I gave birth while she was in the
house. [18]Then on the third day after I gave
birth, this woman also gave birth. We were
together; there was no one else with us in
the house, only the two of us were in the
house. [19]Then this woman's son died in the
night, because she lay on him. [20]She got up
in the middle of the night and took my son
from beside me while your servant slept.
She laid him at her breast, and laid her
dead son at my breast. [21]When I rose in the
morning to nurse my son, I saw that he
was dead; but when I looked at him closely
in the morning, clearly it was not the son
I had borne." [22]But the other woman said,
"No, the living son is mine, and the dead
son is yours." The first said, "No, the dead
son is yours, and the living son is mine."
So they argued before the king.
23 Then the king said, "The one says,
'This is my son that is alive, and your son
is dead'; while the other says, 'Not so! Your
son is dead, and my son is the living one.' "
[24]So the king said, "Bring me a sword," and
they brought a sword before the king. [25]The
king said, "Divide the living boy in two;
then give half to the one, and half to the
other." [26]But the woman whose son was
alive said to the king—because compassion
for her son burned within her—"Please, my
lord, give her the living boy; certainly do
not kill him!" The other said, "It shall be
neither mine nor yours; divide it." [27]Then
the king responded: "Give the first woman
the living boy; do not kill him. She is his
mother." [28]All Israel heard of the judgment
that the king had rendered; and they stood
in awe of the king, because they perceived
that the wisdom of God was in him, to
execute justice.

Solomon's Administrative Officers

4 King Solomon was king over all Israel, [2]and these were his high officials:
Azariah son of Zadok was the priest;
[3]Elihoreph and Ahijah sons of Shisha were
secretaries; Jehoshaphat son of Ahilud was
recorder; [4]Benaiah son of Jehoiada was in
command of the army; Zadok and Abiathar
were priests; [5]Azariah son of Nathan was
over the officials; Zabud son of Nathan was
priest and king's friend; [6]Ahishar was in
charge of the palace; and Adoniram son of
Abda was in charge of the forced labor.
7 Solomon had twelve officials over all
Israel, who provided food for the king and
his household; each one had to make provision for one month in the year. [8]These
were their names: Ben-hur, in the hill country of Ephraim; [9]Ben-deker, in Makaz,
Shaalbim, Beth-shemesh, and Elon-beth-
hanan; [10]Ben-hesed, in Arubboth (to him
belonged Socoh and all the land of Hepher);
[11]Ben-abinadab, in all Naphath-dor (he had
Taphath, Solomon's daughter, as his wife);
[12]Baana son of Ahilud, in Taanach, Megiddo,
and all Beth-shean, which is beside Zarethan
below Jezreel, and from Beth-shean to Abel-
meholah, as far as the other side of Jokmeam;
[13]Ben-geber, in Ramoth-gilead (he had the
villages of Jair son of Manasseh, which are
in Gilead, and he had the region of Argob,
which is in Bashan, sixty great cities with
walls and bronze bars); [14]Ahinadab son of
Iddo, in Mahanaim; [15]Ahimaaz, in Naphtali
(he had taken Basemath, Solomon's daughter, as his wife); [16]Baana son of Hushai, in
Asher and Bealoth; [17]Jehoshaphat son of
Paruah, in Issachar; [18]Shimei son of Ela, in
Benjamin; [19]Geber son of Uri, in the land of
Gilead, the country of King Sihon of the
Amorites and of King Og of Bashan. And
there was one official in the land of Judah.

Magnificence of Solomon's Rule

20 Judah and Israel were as numerous
as the sand by the sea; they ate and drank
and were happy. [21c]Solomon was sovereign
over all the kingdoms from the Euphrates
to the land of the Philistines, even to the
border of Egypt; they brought tribute and
served Solomon all the days of his life.
22 Solomon's provision for one day was
thirty cors of choice flour, and sixty cors of
meal, [23]ten fat oxen, and twenty pasture-fed
cattle, one hundred sheep, besides deer,
gazelles, roebucks, and fatted fowl. [24]For he
had dominion over all the region west of
the Euphrates from Tiphsah to Gaza, over
all the kings west of the Euphrates; and he
had peace on all sides. [25]During Solomon's
lifetime Judah and Israel lived in safety,
from Dan even to Beer-sheba, all of them
under their vines and fig trees. [26]Solomon
also had forty thousand stalls of horses for
his chariots, and twelve thousand horsemen. [27]Those officials supplied provisions for

[c] Ch 5.1 in Heb

3.17 Num 27.2
3.20 Ruth 4.16
3.26 Gen 43.30; Isa 49.15; Jer 31.20
3.28 ver 9.11.12
4.5 ver 7
4.8 Josh 24.33
4.9 Josh 1.35; 21.16
4.10 Josh 15.35; 12.17
4.11 Josh 11.1,2
4.12 Josh 5.19; 17.11; 3.16; 1 Kings 19.16; 1 Chr 6.68
4.13 Num 32.41; Deut 3.4
4.14 Josh 13.26
4.15 2 Sam 15.27
4.16 2 Sam 15.32
4.18 1 Kings 1.8
4.19 Deut 3.8-10
4.20 Gen 32.12; 1 Kings 3.8
4.21 2 Chr 9.26; Gen 15.18; Ps 68.29; 72.10,11
4.24 Ps 72.11; 1 Chr 22.9
4.25 Jer 23.6; Mic 4.4; Zech 3.10; Judg 20.1
4.26 1 Kings 10.26; 2 Chr 1.14
4.27 ver 7

4.1-19 Those chosen for leadership roles in Solomon's reign had connections with the reign of David. *Azariah son of Zadok the priest* (2 Sam 20.25; 1 Kings 1.44-45) The designation of *Zabud son of Nathan* as *priest and king's friend* recalls the special relationship of Hushai to David (2 Sam 15.37). The *twelve officials* chosen to provide food for the royal household (4.7) also probably functioned as district administrators throughout the king's realm, which included lands from north to south on both sides of the Jordan, hills and plains, excluding only the strip along the Mediterranean coast.
4.20-28 The prosperity and power of Solomon's reign are evident in the number of subjects in his kingdom (*as the sand by the sea*), the array of neighboring monarchies which he dominated and which paid him *tribute* (from the Euphrates Valley in eastern Syria to the Philistines on the border of Egypt), and from the peace and *safety* (4.25) enjoyed by Israel and Judah. The huge amounts of food needed to feed and maintain the royal establishment included *thirty cors of flour and sixty cors of meal* (a cor was equivalent to more than five bushels). The technological advances of Israel are evident in that Solomon now possessed vast numbers of *chariots*, formerly owned and used in warfare only by the Philistines.

King Solomon and for all who came to King
Solomon's table, each one in his month;
they let nothing be lacking. 28They also
brought to the required place barley and
straw for the horses and swift steeds, each
according to his charge.

Fame of Solomon's Wisdom

29 God gave Solomon very great wisdom, discernment, and breadth of understanding as vast as the sand on the seashore, 30so that Solomon's wisdom surpassed
the wisdom of all the people of the east, and
all the wisdom of Egypt. 31He was wiser
than anyone else, wiser than Ethan the
Ezrahite, and Heman, Calcol, and Darda,
children of Mahol; his fame spread throughout all the surrounding nations. 32He composed three thousand proverbs, and his songs
numbered a thousand and five. 33He would
speak of trees, from the cedar that is in the
Lebanon to the hyssop that grows in the
wall; he would speak of animals, and birds,
and reptiles, and fish. 34People came from
all the nations to hear the wisdom of Solomon; they came from all the kings of the
earth who had heard of his wisdom.

Preparations and Materials for the Temple

5[d] Now King Hiram of Tyre sent his
servants to Solomon, when he heard
that they had anointed him king in place
of his father; for Hiram had always been a
friend to David. 2Solomon sent word to
Hiram, saying, 3"You know that my father
David could not build a house for the name
of the LORD his God because of the warfare
with which his enemies surrounded him,
until the LORD put them under the soles of
his feet.[e] 4But now the LORD my God has
given me rest on every side; there is neither
adversary nor misfortune. 5So I intend to
build a house for the name of the LORD my
God, as the LORD said to my father David,
'Your son, whom I will set on your throne
in your place, shall build the house for my
name.' 6Therefore command that cedars from
the Lebanon be cut for me. My servants will
join your servants, and I will give you
whatever wages you set for your servants;
for you know that there is no one among
us who knows how to cut timber like the
Sidonians."
7 When Hiram heard the words of Solomon, he rejoiced greatly, and said, "Blessed
be the LORD today, who has given to David
a wise son to be over this great people."
8Hiram sent word to Solomon, "I have heard
the message that you have sent to me; I will
fulfill all your needs in the matter of cedar
and cypress timber. 9My servants shall bring
it down to the sea from the Lebanon; I will
make it into rafts to go by sea to the place
you indicate. I will have them broken up
there for you to take away. And you shall
meet my needs by providing food for my
household." 10So Hiram supplied Solomon's
every need for timber of cedar and cypress.
11Solomon in turn gave Hiram twenty thousand cors of wheat as food for his household, and twenty cors of fine oil. Solomon
gave this to Hiram year by year. 12So the
LORD gave Solomon wisdom, as he promised
him. There was peace between Hiram and
Solomon; and the two of them made a
treaty.
13 King Solomon conscripted forced labor
out of all Israel; the levy numbered thirty
thousand men. 14He sent them to the Lebanon, ten thousand a month in shifts; they
would be a month in the Lebanon and two
months at home; Adoniram was in charge
of the forced labor. 15Solomon also had
seventy thousand laborers and eighty
thousand stonecutters in the hill country,
16besides Solomon's three thousand three
hundred supervisors who were over the
work, having charge of the people who did
the work. 17At the king's command, they
quarried out great, costly stones in order to
lay the foundation of the house with dressed
stones. 18So Solomon's builders and Hiram's
builders and the Gebalites did the stonecut-
ting and prepared the timber and the stone
to build the house.

Solomon Builds the Temple

6 In the four hundred eightieth year
after the Israelites came out of the
land of Egypt, in the fourth year of Solomon's reign over Israel, in the month of Ziv,
which is the second month, he began to
build the house of the LORD. 2The house that
King Solomon built for the LORD was sixty
cubits long, twenty cubits wide, and thirty
cubits high. 3The vestibule in front of the
nave of the house was twenty cubits wide,
across the width of the house. Its depth was
ten cubits in front of the house. 4For the

[d] Ch 5.15 in Heb [e] Gk Tg Vg: Heb *my feet* or *his feet*

4.29-34 The Superior Wisdom of Solomon. Not only did his wisdom exceed that of all his contemporaries (including *the Ezrahites*, a group of the legendary wise, and others described as *children of Mahol*, famed for song and dance), but his intellectual gifts involved poetry, music, botany, and zoology. The best known of those who came from other lands to hear Solomon's wisdom was the Queen of Sheba (1 Kings 10; also in the New Testament: Mt 12.42).
5.1-9.14 Solomon Builds the Temple and the Royal House.
5.1-12 *King Hiram of Tyre*, whose realm included most of what is now Lebanon, for both diplomatic and economic reasons, offered to assist Solomon in building the temple. Solomon is said to be able to undertake this project because he *has rest on every side*, and is free from any *adversary* (the Hebrew term for which is *satan*, which later is used for God's cosmic adversary, Satan). Explaining that preoccupation with warfare had prevented David from erecting the temple (although 2 Sam 7.12-13 reports that it was God's intention to have David's son build it), Solomon arranged to have the workers assembled and paid both by *wages* and by supplying *food for his household*. (For definition of *cor*, see note at 4.20-28). The treaty between Hiram and Solomon is described in the Hebrew text as "cutting (or entering) a covenant," which is a mutual agreement.
5.13-18 The materials are prepared and the construction of the temple is begun through *forced labor* conscripted out of all Israel. The stonecutters from Israel prepared the huge foundation, and collaborated with *Hiram's builders* to erect the *house*. The dimensions of the temple, 100 by 20 cubits, were less than those of the multiple buildings which comprised Solomon's house, the basic unit of which was 100 by 50 cubits (7.2).
6.1-22 The details of dimensions and decoration of the temple are given. A *cubit* is about $1\frac{1}{2}$ feet.

4.29 1 Kings 3.12
4.30 Gen 25.6; Acts 7.22
4.31 1 Kings 3.12; 1 Chr 15.19; 2.6; 6.33
4.32 Prov 1.1; Eccl 12.9; Song 1.1
4.34 1 Kings 10.1; 2 Chr 9.23
5.1 ver 10,18; 2 Chr 2.3; 2 Sam 5.11; 1 Chr 14.1
5.3 1 Chr 22.8; 28.3
5.4 1 Kings 4.24; 1 Chr 22.9
5.5 2 Sam 7.12,13; 1 Chr 17.12; 22.10
5.9 2 Chr 2.16; Ezra 3.7; Ezek 27.17; Acts 12.20
5.11 *cf.* 2 Chr 2.10
5.12 1 Kings 3.12
5.14 1 Kings 4.6
5.15 1 Kings 9.20-22; 2 Chr 2.17
5.17 1 Chr 22.2
6.1 2 Chr 3.1,2; Acts 7.47
6.2 *cf.* Ezek 41.1ff
6.4 Ezek 40.16; 41.16

6.5 Ezek 41.6; ver 16.19-21.31
6.7 Deut 27.5.6
6.9 ver 14.38
6.12 1 Kings 2.4; 9.4
6.13 Ex 25.8; Deut 31.6
6.14 ver 9.38
6.16 Ex 26.33; Lev 16.2; 1 Kings 8.6; 2 Chr 3.8
6.18 1 Kings 7.24
6.22 Ex 30.1.3.6
6.23 2 Chr 3.10-12
6.27 Ex 25.20; 37.9; 1 Kings 8.7; 2 Chr 5.8
6.34 Ezek 41.23-25
6.36 1 Kings 7.12
6.37 ver 1

house he made windows with recessed frames.[f] [5]He also built a structure against the wall of the house, running around the walls of the house, both the nave and the inner sanctuary; and he made side chambers all around. [6]The lowest story[g] was five cubits wide, the middle one was six cubits wide, and the third was seven cubits wide; for around the outside of the house he made offsets on the wall in order that the supporting beams should not be inserted into the walls of the house.

7 The house was built with stone finished at the quarry, so that neither hammer nor ax nor any tool of iron was heard in the temple while it was being built.

8 The entrance for the middle story was on the south side of the house: one went up by winding stairs to the middle story, and from the middle story to the third. [9]So he built the house, and finished it; he roofed the house with beams and planks of cedar. [10]He built the structure against the whole house, each story[h] five cubits high, and it was joined to the house with timbers of cedar.

11 Now the word of the LORD came to Solomon, [12]"Concerning this house that you are building, if you will walk in my statutes, obey my ordinances, and keep all my commandments by walking in them, then I will establish my promise with you, which I made to your father David. [13]I will dwell among the children of Israel, and will not forsake my people Israel."

14 So Solomon built the house, and finished it. [15]He lined the walls of the house on the inside with boards of cedar; from the floor of the house to the rafters of the ceiling, he covered them on the inside with wood; and he covered the floor of the house with boards of cypress. [16]He built twenty cubits of the rear of the house with boards of cedar from the floor to the rafters, and he built this within as an inner sanctuary, as the most holy place. [17]The house, that is, the nave in front of the inner sanctuary, was forty cubits long. [18]The cedar within the house had carvings of gourds and open flowers; all was cedar, no stone was seen. [19]The inner sanctuary he prepared in the innermost part of the house, to set there the ark of the covenant of the LORD. [20]The interior of the inner sanctuary was twenty cubits long, twenty cubits wide, and twenty cubits high; he overlaid it with pure gold. He also overlaid the altar with cedar.[i] [21]Solomon overlaid the inside of the house with pure gold, then he drew chains of gold across, in front of the inner sanctuary, and overlaid it with gold. [22]Next he overlaid the whole house with gold, in order that the whole house might be perfect; even the whole altar that belonged to the inner sanctuary he overlaid with gold.

The Furnishings of the Temple

23 In the inner sanctuary he made two cherubim of olivewood, each ten cubits high. [24]Five cubits was the length of one wing of the cherub, and five cubits the length of the other wing of the cherub; it was ten cubits from the tip of one wing to the tip of the other. [25]The other cherub also measured ten cubits; both cherubim had the same measure and the same form. [26]The height of one cherub was ten cubits, and so was that of the other cherub. [27]He put the cherubim in the innermost part of the house; the wings of the cherubim were spread out so that a wing of one was touching the one wall, and a wing of the other cherub was touching the other wall; their other wings toward the center of the house were touching wing to wing. [28]He also overlaid the cherubim with gold.

29 He carved the walls of the house all around about with carved engravings of cherubim, palm trees, and open flowers, in the inner and outer rooms. [30]The floor of the house he overlaid with gold, in the inner and outer rooms.

31 For the entrance to the inner sanctuary he made doors of olivewood; the lintel and the doorposts were five-sided.[i] [32]He covered the two doors of olivewood with carvings of cherubim, palm trees, and open flowers; he overlaid them with gold, and spread gold on the cherubim and on the palm trees.

33 So also he made for the entrance to the nave doorposts of olivewood, four-sided each, [34]and two doors of cypress wood; the two leaves of the one door were folding, and the two leaves of the other door were folding. [35]He carved cherubim, palm trees, and open flowers, overlaying them with gold evenly applied upon the carved work. [36]He built the inner court with three courses of dressed stone to one course of cedar beams.

37 In the fourth year the foundation of

[f] Gk: Meaning of Heb uncertain [g] Gk: Heb *structure* [h] Heb lacks *each story* [i] Meaning of Heb uncertain

6.11-13 express in the language of the Deuteronomist the promise and conditions of God's continuing presence among his people. That the *interior* was *overlaid with pure gold* may mean that it was gilded with liquid gold rather than overlaid with gold plates.

6.23-36 The Furnishings of the Temple. The *cherubim* were probably winged sphinxes which guarded the presence of God in the midst of his people, as they did on the cover of the sacred box or *ark of the covenant* in Ex 25.17-22, which was the place where God would meet his people. Details are given for the doors through which one had to pass to move through successive chambers into the innermost sanctuary where the ark was located.

6.37-38 The process of completion of the temple extended from the fourth to the eleventh year of Solomon's reign.

7.1-51 The group of structures that served as the center for Solomon's monarchy included the House of the Forest (7.2-5), the Hall of Pillars (7.6), the Hall of the Throne (7.7), and his actual residence (7.8). The stones from which these buildings and their foundations were constructed were *costly* and *huge*, up to 12 and 15 feet across a single stone block.

7.13-51 *Hiram*, a bronzeworker from Tyre, was engaged to provide bronze decoration for capitals, as well as containers, wheeled stands, sacred objects and other equipment needed for the ritual carried out in the temple. These were cast in bronze in clay molds set up in *the plain of the Jordan*. The basic furniture – altar, table for the bread of the Presence, lampstands, and other equipment used at the altar – were of gold or covered with gold, and were brought by Solomon into *the treasuries of the house of the LORD*.

the house of the LORD was laid, in the month of Ziv. 38 In the eleventh year, in the month of Bul, which is the eighth month, the house was finished in all its parts, and according to all its specifications. He was seven years in building it.

Solomon's Palace and Other Buildings

7 Solomon was building his own house thirteen years, and he finished his entire house.

2 He built the House of the Forest of the Lebanon one hundred cubits long, fifty cubits wide, and thirty cubits high, built on four rows of cedar pillars, with cedar beams on the pillars. 3 It was roofed with cedar on the forty-five rafters, fifteen in each row, which were on the pillars. 4 There were window frames in the three rows, facing each other in the three rows. 5 All the doorways and doorposts had four-sided frames, opposite, facing each other in the three rows.

6 He made the Hall of Pillars fifty cubits long and thirty cubits wide. There was a porch in front with pillars, and a canopy in front of them.

7 He made the Hall of the Throne where he was to pronounce judgment, the Hall of Justice, covered with cedar from floor to floor.

8 His own house where he would reside, in the other court back of the hall, was of the same construction. Solomon also made a house like this hall for Pharaoh's daughter, whom he had taken in marriage.

9 All these were made of costly stones, cut according to measure, sawed with saws, back and front, from the foundation to the coping, and from outside to the great court. 10 The foundation was of costly stones, huge stones, stones of eight and ten cubits. 11 There were costly stones above, cut to measure, and cedarwood. 12 The great court had three courses of dressed stone to one layer of cedar beams all around; so had the inner court of the house of the LORD, and the vestibule of the house.

Products of Hiram the Bronzeworker

13 Now King Solomon invited and received Hiram from Tyre. 14 He was the son of a widow of the tribe of Naphtali, whose father, a man of Tyre, had been an artisan in bronze; he was full of skill, intelligence, and knowledge in working bronze. He came to King Solomon, and did all his work.

15 He cast two pillars of bronze. Eighteen cubits was the height of the one, and a cord of twelve cubits would encircle it; the second pillar was the same.[j] 16 He also made two capitals of molten bronze, to set on the tops of the pillars; the height of the one capital was five cubits, and the height of the other capital was five cubits. 17 There were nets of checker work with wreaths of chain work for the capitals on the tops of the pillars; seven[k] for the one capital, and seven[l] for the other capital. 18 He made the columns with two rows around each latticework to cover the capitals that were above the pomegranates; he did the same with the other capital. 19 Now the capitals that were on the tops of the pillars in the vestibule were of lily-work, four cubits high. 20 The capitals were on the two pillars and also above the rounded projection that was beside the latticework; there were two hundred pomegranates in rows all around; and so with the other capital. 21 He set up the pillars at the vestibule of the temple; he set up the pillar on the south and called it Jachin; and he set up the pillar on the north and called it Boaz. 22 On the tops of the pillars was lily-work. Thus the work of the pillars was finished.

23 Then he made the molten sea; it was round, ten cubits from brim to brim, and five cubits high. A line of thirty cubits would encircle it completely. 24 Under its brim were panels all around it, each of ten cubits, surrounding the sea; there were two rows of panels, cast when it was cast. 25 It stood on twelve oxen, three facing north, three facing west, three facing south, and three facing east; the sea was set on them. The hindquarters of each were toward the inside. 26 Its thickness was a handbreadth; its brim was made like the brim of a cup, like the flower of a lily; it held two thousand baths.[l]

27 He also made the ten stands of bronze; each stand was four cubits long, four cubits wide, and three cubits high. 28 This was the construction of the stands: they had borders; the borders were within the frames; 29 on the borders that were set in the frames were lions, oxen, and cherubim. On the frames, both above and below the lions and

7.1 1 Kings 9.10; 2 Chr 8.1
7.2 1 Kings 10.17,21
7.7 1 Kings 6.15,16
7.8 1 Kings 3.1; 2 Chr 8.11
7.12 1 Kings 6.36; ver 6
7.13 2 Chr 4.11
7.14 2 Chr 2.14; 4.16
7.15 2 Kings 25.17; 2 Chr 3.15
7.20 2 Chr 3.16; 4.13; Jer 52.23
7.21 2 Chr 3.17; 1 Kings 6.3
7.23 2 Kings 25.13; 2 Chr 4.2; Jer 52.17
7.24 1 Kings 6.18; 2 Chr 4.3
7.25 2 Chr 4.4,5; Jer 52.20
7.27 ver 38; 2 Chr 4.14

[j] Cn: Heb *and a cord of twelve cubits encircled the second pillar* ; Compare Jer 52.21 [k] Heb: Gk *a net* [l] A Heb measure of volume

oxen, there were wreaths of beveled work. [30]Each stand had four bronze wheels and axles of bronze; at the four corners were supports for a basin. The supports were cast with wreaths at the side of each. [31]Its opening was within the crown whose height was one cubit; its opening was round, as a pedestal is made; it was a cubit and a half wide. At its opening there were carvings; its borders were four-sided, not round. [32]The four wheels were underneath the borders; the axles of the wheels were in the stands; and the height of a wheel was a cubit and a half. [33]The wheels were made like a chariot wheel; their axles, their rims, their spokes, and their hubs were all cast. [34]There were four supports at the four corners of each stand; the supports were of one piece with the stands. [35]On the top of the stand there was a round band half a cubit high; on the top of the stand, its stays and its borders were of one piece with it. [36]On the surfaces of its stays and on its borders he carved cherubim, lions, and palm trees, where each had space, with wreaths all around. [37]In this way he made the ten stands; all of them were cast alike, with the same size and the same form.

38 He made ten basins of bronze; each basin held forty baths,[m] each basin measured four cubits; there was a basin for each of the ten stands. [39]He set five of the stands on the south side of the house, and five on the north side of the house; he set the sea on the southeast corner of the house.

40 Hiram also made the pots, the shovels, and the basins. So Hiram finished all the work that he did for King Solomon on the house of the LORD: [41]the two pillars, the two bowls of the capitals that were on the tops of the pillars, the two latticeworks to cover the two bowls of the capitals that were on the tops of the pillars; [42]the four hundred pomegranates for the two latticeworks, two rows of pomegranates for each latticework, to cover the two bowls of the capitals that were on the pillars; [43]the ten stands, the ten basins on the stands; [44]the one sea, and the twelve oxen underneath the sea.

45 The pots, the shovels, and the basins, all these vessels that Hiram made for King Solomon for the house of the LORD were of burnished bronze. [46]In the plain of the Jordan the king cast them, in the clay ground between Succoth and Zarethan. [47]Solomon left all the vessels unweighed, because there were so many of them; the weight of the bronze was not determined.

48 So Solomon made all the vessels that were in the house of the LORD: the golden altar, the golden table for the bread of the Presence, [49]the lampstands of pure gold, five on the south side and five on the north, in front of the inner sanctuary; the flowers, the lamps, and the tongs, of gold; [50]the cups, snuffers, basins, dishes for incense, and firepans, of pure gold; the sockets for the doors of the innermost part of the house, the most holy place, and for the doors of the nave of the temple, of gold.

51 Thus all the work that King Solomon did on the house of the LORD was finished. Solomon brought in the things that his father David had dedicated, the silver, the gold, and the vessels, and stored them in the treasuries of the house of the LORD.

Dedication of the Temple

8 Then Solomon assembled the elders of Israel and all the heads of the tribes, the leaders of the ancestral houses of the Israelites, before King Solomon in Jerusalem, to bring up the ark of the covenant of the LORD out of the city of David, which is Zion. [2]All the people of Israel assembled to King Solomon at the festival in the month Ethanim, which is the seventh month. [3]And all the elders of Israel came, and the priests carried the ark. [4]So they brought up the ark of the LORD, the tent of meeting, and all the holy vessels that were in the tent; the priests and the Levites brought them up. [5]King Solomon and all the congregation of Israel, who had assembled before him, were with him before the ark, sacrificing so many sheep and oxen that they could not be counted or numbered. [6]Then the priests brought the ark of the covenant of the LORD to its place, in the inner sanctuary of the house, in the most holy place, underneath the wings of the cherubim. [7]For the cherubim spread out their wings over the place of the ark, so that the cherubim made a covering above the ark and its poles. [8]The poles were so long that the ends of the poles were seen from the holy place in front of the inner sanctuary; but they could not be seen from outside; they are there to this day. [9]There was nothing in the ark except the two tablets of stone that Moses had placed there at Horeb, where the LORD made a

[m] A Heb measure of volume

7.30 2 Kings 16.17; 25.13,16
7.37 2 Chr 4.14
7.38 2 Chr 4.6
7.41 ver 17,18
7.42 ver 20
7.44 ver 23,25
7.45 2 Chr 4.16
7.46 2 Chr 4.17; Josh 13.27; 3.16
7.48 Ex 37.10ff
7.49 Ex 31-38
7.51 2 Sam 8.11; 2 Chr 5.1
8.1 2 Chr 5.2; 2 Sam 6.17; 2 Sam 5.7,9
8.2 Lev 23.34; 2 Chr 7.8
8.3 Num 7.9
8.4 1 Kings 3.4; 2 Chr 1.3
8.5 2 Sam 6.13
8.6 2 Sam 6.17; 1 Kings 6.19,27
8.8 Ex 25.14
8.9 Ex 25.21; Deut 10.2-5; Heb 9.4; Ex 24.7,8

8.1-66 Dedication of the Temple. **8.1-13** *The elders...heads of the tribes... the leaders of the ancestral houses of the Israelites* joined with Solomon to bring the *ark of the covenant* from its resting place in the *city of David* (located toward the southern end of the ridge called Ophel, on the higher, northern end of which the temple was built) into the newly-built sanctuary. *The priests* carried the ark, and *the holy vessels* were brought up by *the priests and Levites*. The Levites were earlier regarded as authorized priests, but later during the Exile they came to be demoted to a role as servants in the temple cult (Num 18.2-6; Ezek 44.10-14). The cherubim overshadowed the ark in the inner sanctuary, but the poles by which the ark was carried protruded through the curtain. All was invisible from outside. Within, the presence of God was awesomely visible through the cloud – *the glory of the LORD* – which filled the inner room of the sanctuary, the *exalted house* which Solomon built.

8.14-21 Solomon declared the continuity between God's covenant with Israel at Sinai (contained in the ark), his promise to David, and what now stood as God's dwelling place among his people.

8.22-53 Solomon's prayer of dedication recalls the covenantal promise to David, which included continuity of the Davidic royal line. The temple was to serve as the focal point for the prayers of God's people, where petitions would be heard (vv. 27-30), where judgments on the wicked and vindication of the faithful would be confirmed (vv. 31-32), where the disobedience of the covenant people could find forgiveness and restoration (vv. 33-34), where droughts or famine or blight that occurred as God's punishment for his people's failures would find alleviation and renewal (vv. 35-40); where seeking foreigners might find the God of Israel (vv. 41-43), where God's people in battle or captivity in foreign lands could turn for forgiveness and restoration as those privileged to have a special relationship with God (vv. 44-53).

covenant with the Israelites, when they
came out of the land of Egypt. [10]And when
the priests came out of the holy place, a
cloud filled the house of the LORD, [11]so that
the priests could not stand to minister because of the cloud; for the glory of the LORD
filled the house of the LORD.
12 Then Solomon said,
"The LORD has said that he would
dwell in thick darkness.
13 I have built you an exalted house,
a place for you to dwell in forever."

Solomon's Speech

14 Then the king turned around and
blessed all the assembly of Israel, while all
the assembly of Israel stood. [15]He said,
"Blessed be the LORD, the God of Israel, who
with his hand has fulfilled what he promised with his mouth to my father David,
saying, [16]'Since the day that I brought my
people Israel out of Egypt, I have not chosen
a city from any of the tribes of Israel in
which to build a house, that my name
might be there; but I chose David to be over
my people Israel.' [17]My father David had it
in mind to build a house for the name of
the LORD, the God of Israel. [18]But the LORD
said to my father David, 'You did well to
consider building a house for my name;
[19]nevertheless you shall not build the house,
but your son who shall be born to you shall
build the house for my name.' [20]Now the
LORD has upheld the promise that he made;
for I have risen in the place of my father
David; I sit on the throne of Israel, as the
LORD promised, and have built the house for
the name of the LORD, the God of Israel.
[21]There I have provided a place for the ark,
in which is the covenant of the LORD that
he made with our ancestors when he brought
them out of the land of Egypt."

Solomon's Prayer of Dedication

22 Then Solomon stood before the altar
of the LORD in the presence of all the assembly of Israel, and spread out his hands to
heaven. [23]He said, "O LORD, God of Israel,
there is no God like you in heaven above
or on earth beneath, keeping covenant and
steadfast love for your servants who walk
before you with all their heart, [24]the covenant that you kept for your servant my
father David as you declared to him; you
promised with your mouth and have this
day fulfilled with your hand. [25]Therefore, O
LORD, God of Israel, keep for your servant
my father David that which you promised
him, saying, 'There shall never fail you a
successor before me to sit on the throne of
Israel, if only your children look to their
way, to walk before me as you have walked
before me.' [26]Therefore, O God of Israel, let
your word be confirmed, which you promised to your servant my father David.
27 "But will God indeed dwell on the
earth? Even heaven and the highest heaven
cannot contain you, much less this house
that I have built! [28]Regard your servant's
prayer and his plea, O LORD my God, heeding the cry and the prayer that your servant prays to you today; [29]that your eyes
may be open night and day toward this
house, the place of which you said, 'My
name shall be there,' that you may heed the
prayer that your servant prays toward this
place. [30]Hear the plea of your servant and
of your people Israel when they pray toward this place; O hear in heaven your
dwelling place; heed and forgive.
31 "If someone sins against a neighbor
and is given an oath to swear, and comes
and swears before your altar in this house,
[32]then hear in heaven, and act, and judge
your servants, condemning the guilty by
bringing their conduct on their own head,
and vindicating the righteous by rewarding
them according to their righteousness.
33 "When your people Israel, having
sinned against you, are defeated before an
enemy but turn again to you, confess your
name, pray and plead with you in this
house, [34]then hear in heaven, forgive the
sin of your people Israel, and bring them
again to the land that you gave to their
ancestors.
35 "When heaven is shut up and there
is no rain because they have sinned against
you, and then they pray toward this place,
confess your name, and turn from their sin,
because you punish[n] them, [36]then hear in
heaven, and forgive the sin of your servants, your people Israel, when you teach
them the good way in which they should
walk; and grant rain on your land, which
you have given to your people as an inheritance.
37 "If there is famine in the land, if there
is plague, blight, mildew, locust, or caterpillar; if their enemy besieges them in any[o] of

[n] Or *when you answer* [o] Gk Syr: Heb *in the land*

8.10 Ex 40.34,35; 2 Chr 7.1,2
8.12 2 Chr 6.1; Ps 97.2
8.13 2 Sam 7.13; Ps 132.14
8.14 2 Sam 6.18
8.15 1 Chr 29.10,20; Neh 9.5; 2 Sam 7.12,13
8.16 2 Sam 7.4-6; Deut 12.11; 1 Sam 16.1; 2 Sam 7.8
8.17 2 Sam 7.2; 1 Chr 17.1
8.19 2 Sam 7.5,12,13; 1 Kings 5.3,5
8.20 1 Chr 28.5,6
8.21 ver 9
8.22 2 Chr 6.12ff; Ex 9.33; Ezra 9.5
8.23 1 Sam 2.2; 2 Sam 7.22; Deut 7.9; Neh 1.5,9,32
8.25 2 Sam 17.12,16; 1 Kings 2.4
8.26 2 Sam 7.25
8.27 2 Chr 2.6; Isa 66.1; Jer 23.24; Acts 7.49
8.29 Deut 12.11; Dan 6.10
8.30 Neh 1.6
8.31 Ex 22.11
8.32 Deut 25.1
8.33 Lev 26.17; Deut 28.25; Lev 26.39
8.35 Lev 26.19; Deut 28.23
8.36 1 Sam 12.23; Ps 27.11; 94.12
8.37 Lev 26.16,25,26; Deut 28.21-23,38-42

8.39 1 Sam 16.7; 1 Chr 28.9; Ps 11.4; Jer 17.10
8.40 Ps 130.4
8.42 Deut 3.24
8.43 1 Sam 17.46; 2 Kings 19.19; Ps 102.15
8.46 2 Chr 6.36; Prov 20.9; 1 Jn 1.8-10; Lev 26.34-39; Deut 28.36,64
8.47 Lev 26.40; Neh 1.6; Ps 106.6; Dan 9.5
8.48 Jer 29.12-14; Dan 6.10
8.50 2 Chr 30.9; Ps 106.46
8.51 Deut 9.29; Neh 1.10; Deut 4.20; Jer 11.4
8.53 Ex 19.5; Deut 9.26-29
8.55 ver 14
8.56 Josh 21.45; 23.14
8.57 Josh 1.5; Rom 8.28; Heb 13.5
8.58 Ps 119.36
8.60 1 Kings 18.39; Jer 10.10-12
8.61 1 Kings 11.4; 15.3,14; 2 Kings 20.3
8.62 2 Chr 7.4ff
8.64 2 Chr 7.7; 4.1

their cities; whatever plague, whatever sickness there is; [38]whatever prayer, whatever plea there is from any individual or from all your people Israel, all knowing the afflictions of their own hearts so that they stretch out their hands toward this house; [39]then hear in heaven your dwelling place, forgive, act, and render to all whose hearts you know—according to all their ways, for only you know what is in every human heart—[40]so that they may fear you all the days that they live in the land that you gave to our ancestors.

41 "Likewise when a foreigner, who is not of your people Israel, comes from a distant land because of your name [42]—for they shall hear of your great name, your mighty hand, and your outstretched arm—when a foreigner comes and prays toward this house, [43]then hear in heaven your dwelling place, and do according to all that the foreigner calls to you, so that all the peoples of the earth may know your name and fear you, as do your people Israel, and so that they may know that your name has been invoked on this house that I have built.

44 "If your people go out to battle against their enemy, by whatever way you shall send them, and they pray to the LORD toward the city that you have chosen and the house that I have built for your name, [45]then hear in heaven their prayer and their plea, and maintain their cause.

46 "If they sin against you—for there is no one who does not sin—and you are angry with them and give them to an enemy, so that they are carried away captive to the land of the enemy, far off or near; [47]yet if they come to their senses in the land to which they have been taken captive, and repent, and plead with you in the land of their captors, saying, 'We have sinned, and have done wrong; we have acted wickedly'; [48]if they repent with all their heart and soul in the land of their enemies, who took them captive, and pray to you toward their land, which you gave to their ancestors, the city that you have chosen, and the house that I have built for your name; [49]then hear in heaven your dwelling place their prayer and their plea, maintain their cause [50]and forgive your people who have sinned against you, and all their transgressions that they have committed against you; and grant them compassion in the sight of their captors, so that they may have compassion on them [51](for they are your people and heritage, which you brought out of Egypt, from the midst of the iron-smelter). [52]Let your eyes be open to the plea of your servant, and to the plea of your people Israel, listening to them whenever they call to you. [53]For you have separated them from among all the peoples of the earth, to be your heritage, just as you promised through Moses, your servant, when you brought our ancestors out of Egypt, O Lord GOD."

Solomon Blesses the Assembly

54 Now when Solomon finished offering all this prayer and this plea to the LORD, he arose from facing the altar of the LORD, where he had knelt with hands outstretched toward heaven; [55]he stood and blessed all the assembly of Israel with a loud voice:

56 "Blessed be the LORD, who has given rest to his people Israel according to all that he promised; not one word has failed of all his good promise, which he spoke through his servant Moses. [57]The LORD our God be with us, as he was with our ancestors; may he not leave us or abandon us, [58]but incline our hearts to him, to walk in all his ways, and to keep his commandments, his statutes, and his ordinances, which he commanded our ancestors. [59]Let these words of mine, with which I pleaded before the LORD, be near to the LORD our God day and night, and may he maintain the cause of his servant and the cause of his people Israel, as each day requires; [60]so that all the peoples of the earth may know that the LORD is God; there is no other. [61]Therefore devote yourselves completely to the LORD our God, walking in his statutes and keeping his commandments, as at this day."

Solomon Offers Sacrifices

62 Then the king, and all Israel with him, offered sacrifice before the LORD. [63]Solomon offered as sacrifices of well-being to the LORD twenty-two thousand oxen and one hundred twenty thousand sheep. So the king and all the people of Israel dedicated the house of the LORD. [64]The same day the king consecrated the middle of the court that was in front of the house of the LORD; for there he offered the burnt offerings and the grain offerings and the fat pieces of the sacrifices of well-being, because the bronze altar that was before the LORD was too small

8.54-61 The language and emphases of the Deuteronomic historian are set out as the precondition for the words of blessing which Solomon is here reported as pronouncing on the people: to keep *the commandments...statutes...ordinances* which God gave to Israel at Sinai.
8.62-66 Since *all Israel* gathered to participate in the dedicatory sacrifices, the enormous numbers of animals offered may not be exaggerated, since sharing in the meat of the sacrifices was essential for those who belonged to the covenant people. In addition to the offerings in the sanctuary proper, the courtyard in front of it was also dedicated, and there *burnt offerings and grain offerings* were presented, again in large numbers. The ceremonies lasted a full week: *eight days* spent confirming the joy of the participants in the covenant with David and his people.

to receive the burnt offerings and the grain offerings and the fat pieces of the sacrifices of well-being.

65 So Solomon held the festival at that time, and all Israel with him—a great assembly, people from Lebo-hamath to the Wadi of Egypt—before the LORD our God, seven days.[p] 66 On the eighth day he sent the people away; and they blessed the king, and went to their tents, joyful and in good spirits because of all the goodness that the LORD had shown to his servant David and to his people Israel.

God Appears Again to Solomon

9 When Solomon had finished building the house of the LORD and the king's house and all that Solomon desired to build, 2 the LORD appeared to Solomon a second time, as he had appeared to him at Gibeon. 3 The LORD said to him, "I have heard your prayer and your plea, which you made before me; I have consecrated this house that you have built, and put my name there forever; my eyes and my heart will be there for all time. 4 As for you, if you will walk before me, as David your father walked, with integrity of heart and uprightness, doing according to all that I have commanded you, and keeping my statutes and my ordinances, 5 then I will establish your royal throne over Israel forever, as I promised your father David, saying, 'There shall not fail you a successor on the throne of Israel.'

6 "If you turn aside from following me, you or your children, and do not keep my commandments and my statutes that I have set before you, but go and serve other gods and worship them, 7 then I will cut Israel off from the land that I have given them; and the house that I have consecrated for my name I will cast out of my sight; and Israel will become a proverb and a taunt among all peoples. 8 This house will become a heap of ruins;[q] everyone passing by it will be astonished, and will hiss; and they will say, 'Why has the LORD done such a thing to this land and to this house?' 9 Then they will say, 'Because they have forsaken the LORD their God, who brought their ancestors out of the land of Egypt, and embraced other gods, worshiping them and serving them; therefore the LORD has brought this disaster upon them.' "

10 At the end of twenty years, in which Solomon had built the two houses, the house of the LORD and the king's house, 11 King Hiram of Tyre having supplied Solomon with cedar and cypress timber and gold, as much as he desired, King Solomon gave to Hiram twenty cities in the land of Galilee. 12 But when Hiram came from Tyre to see the cities that Solomon had given him, they did not please him. 13 Therefore he said, "What kind of cities are these that you have given me, my brother?" So they are called the land of Cabul[r] to this day. 14 But Hiram had sent to the king one hundred twenty talents of gold.

Other Acts of Solomon

15 This is the account of the forced labor that King Solomon conscripted to build the house of the LORD and his own house, the Millo and the wall of Jerusalem, Hazor, Megiddo, Gezer 16 (Pharaoh king of Egypt had gone up and captured Gezer and burned it down, had killed the Canaanites who lived in the city, and had given it as dowry to his daughter, Solomon's wife; 17 so Solomon rebuilt Gezer), Lower Beth-horon, 18 Baalath, Tamar in the wilderness, within the land, 19 as well as all of Solomon's storage cities, the cities for his chariots, the cities for his cavalry, and whatever Solomon desired to build, in Jerusalem, in Lebanon, and in all the land of his dominion. 20 All the people who were left of the Amorites, the Hittites, the Perizzites, the Hivites, and the Jebusites, who were not of the people of Israel— 21 their descendants who were still left in the land, whom the Israelites were unable to destroy completely—these Solomon conscripted for slave labor, and so they are to this day. 22 But of the Israelites Solomon made no slaves; they were the soldiers, they were his officials, his commanders, his captains, and the commanders of his chariotry and cavalry.

23 These were the chief officers who were over Solomon's work: five hundred fifty, who had charge of the people who carried on the work.

24 But Pharaoh's daughter went up from the city of David to her own house that Solomon had built for her; then he built the Millo.

25 Three times a year Solomon used to

[p] Compare Gk: Heb *seven days and seven days, fourteen days* [q] Syr Old Latin: Heb *will become high* [r] Perhaps meaning *a land good for nothing*

9.1-9 The LORD Appears Again to Solomon. This account of God's coming to Solomon once more to confirm the covenantal promises and give assurance of his continuing presence in *this house* (the newly-completed temple) embodies the perspectives of the Deuteronomist. There is a balance of promises of blessings and warnings of punishment if the commandments are not obeyed or if there is any worship of *other gods*.
9.10-14 Hiram, king of Tyre, was deeply dissatisfied with the *twenty cities* in the land of Galilee which Solomon gave him as additional compensation for the materials and especially for the gold he had provided for the building of the temple. Hiram called the district given him *the land of Cabul*, which means "like nothing."
9.15-28 Solomon's Building, Administrative and Commercial Activities.
9.15-21 The native peoples remaining in the land that Israel occupied were *conscripted* by Solomon to rebuild Jerusalem and other strategic cities throughout his kingdom. *The Millo* was an artifical platform of stone and beaten earth erected on the top of the Ophel ridge above the spring of Gihon to strengthen the fortifications of the city. *Hazor* was an important city for trade and international relations located in Upper Galilee. *Megiddo* was a major center for military and commercial purposes, located at the intersection of major routes from Egypt and Judea in the south to Damascus, Lebanon and Assyria to the north and east. It is mentioned often in Assyrian, Egyptian and biblical literature. *Gezer* guards the intersection where the major road leading west from Jerusalem meets the main coastal road, and is one of the largest excavated ancient sites from the Bronze and Iron Ages. *Lower Beth-horon* defended a major road from Jerusalem to the sea near where it entered the hill country west of the capital. *Baalath* was on the coastal plain south of Joppa (modern Jaffa-Tel-Aviv). *Tamar* was probably located on the edge of the Judean desert in the deep cleft south of the Dead Sea.
9.22-23 *The Israelites* were assigned to military and administrative duties in Solomon's extended realm.
9.24-25 *Pharaoh's daughter* moved into *her own house* in the newer part of Jerusalem on the ridges overlooking *the city of David*. The *three times a year* on which Solomon offered sacrifices may have been the Feast of Unleavened Bread, the Feast of Weeks (at the end of the wheat harvest), and the Feast of Booths, which opened the New Year. *The house* which Solomon completed could be his own, or the temple.

8.65 ver 2; Lev 23.34; Num 34.8; Josh 13.5; Gen 15.18; 2 Chr 7.8
9.1 2 Chr 7.11ff; 1 Kings 7.1; 2 Chr 8.6
9.2 1 Kings 3.5
9.3 2 Kings 20.5; 1 Kings 8.29; Deut 11.12
9.4 Gen 17.1; 1 Kings 15.5
9.5 2 Sam 7.12,16; 1 Kings 2.4; 1 Chr 22.10
9.6 2 Sam 7.14; 2 Chr 7.19,20
9.7 2 Kings 17.23; 25.21; Jer 7.14; Deut 28.37; Ps 44.14
9.8 2 Chr 7.21; Deut 29.24-26; Jer 22.8,9
9.10 1 Kings 6.37,38; 7.1; 2 Chr 8.1
9.11 2 Chr 8.2
9.13 Josh 19.27
9.15 1 Kings 5.13; ver 24; 2 Sam 5.9; Josh 19.36; 17.11; 16.10
9.16 Josh 16.10
9.17 Josh 16.3; 2 Chr 8.5
9.19 1 Kings 4.26; ver 1
9.20 2 Chr 8.7
9.21 Judg 1.21,27,29; Josh 15.63; 17.12; Judg 1.21; Gen 9.25,26; Ezra 2.55,58
9.22 Lev 25.39
9.23 2 Chr 8.10
9.24 1 Kings 3.1; 7.8; 11.27; 2 Chr 32.5
9.25 2 Chr 8.12,13,16

offer up burnt offerings and sacrifices of well-being on the altar that he built for the LORD, offering incense[s] before the LORD. So he completed the house.

Solomon's Commercial Activity

26 King Solomon built a fleet of ships at Ezion-geber, which is near Eloth on the shore of the Red Sea,[t] in the land of Edom. 27Hiram sent his servants with the fleet, sailors who were familiar with the sea, together with the servants of Solomon. 28They went to Ophir, and imported from there four hundred twenty talents of gold, which they delivered to King Solomon.

Visit of the Queen of Sheba

10 When the queen of Sheba heard of the fame of Solomon, (fame due to[u] the name of the LORD), she came to test him with hard questions. 2She came to Jerusalem with a very great retinue, with camels bearing spices, and very much gold, and precious stones; and when she came to Solomon, she told him all that was on her mind. 3Solomon answered all her questions; there was nothing hidden from the king that he could not explain to her. 4When the queen of Sheba had observed all the wisdom of Solomon, the house that he had built, 5the food of his table, the seating of his officials, and the attendance of his servants, their clothing, his valets, and his burnt offerings that he offered at the house of the LORD, there was no more spirit in her.

6 So she said to the king, "The report was true that I heard in my own land of your accomplishments and of your wisdom, 7but I did not believe the reports until I came and my own eyes had seen it. Not even half had been told me; your wisdom and prosperity far surpass the report that I had heard. 8Happy are your wives![v] Happy are these your servants, who continually attend you and hear your wisdom! 9Blessed be the LORD your God, who has delighted in you and set you on the throne of Israel! Because the LORD loved Israel forever, he has made you king to execute justice and righteousness." 10Then she gave the king one hundred twenty talents of gold, a great quantity of spices, and precious stones; never again did spices come in such quantity as that which the queen of Sheba gave to King Solomon.

11 Moreover, the fleet of Hiram, which carried gold from Ophir, brought from Ophir a great quantity of almug wood and precious stones. 12From the almug wood the king made supports for the house of the LORD, and for the king's house, lyres also and harps for the singers; no such almug wood has come or been seen to this day.

13 Meanwhile King Solomon gave to the queen of Sheba every desire that she expressed, as well as what he gave her out of Solomon's royal bounty. Then she returned to her own land, with her servants.

14 The weight of gold that came to Solomon in one year was six hundred sixty-six talents of gold, 15besides that which came from the traders and from the business of the merchants, and from all the kings of Arabia and the governors of the land. 16King Solomon made two hundred large shields of beaten gold; six hundred shekels of gold went into each large shield. 17He made three hundred shields of beaten gold; three minas of gold went into each shield; and the king put them in the House of the Forest of Lebanon. 18The king also made a great ivory throne, and overlaid it with the finest gold. 19The throne had six steps. The top of the throne was rounded in the back, and on each side of the seat were arm rests and two lions standing beside the arm rests, 20while twelve lions were standing, one on each end of a step on the six steps. Nothing like it was ever made in any kingdom. 21All King Solomon's drinking vessels were of gold, and all the vessels of the House of the Forest of Lebanon were of pure gold; none were of silver—it was not considered as anything in the days of Solomon. 22For the king had a fleet of ships of Tarshish at sea with the fleet of Hiram. Once every three years the fleet of ships of Tarshish used to come bringing gold, silver, ivory, apes, and peacocks.[w]

23 Thus King Solomon excelled all the kings of the earth in riches and in wisdom. 24The whole earth sought the presence of Solomon to hear his wisdom, which God had put into his mind. 25Every one of them brought a present, objects of silver and gold, garments, weaponry, spices, horses, and mules, so much year by year.

26 Solomon gathered together chariots

9.26 2 Chr 8.17,18; Num 33.35; Deut 2.8; 1 Kings 22.48
9.27 1 Kings 10.11
9.28 1 Chr 29.4
10.1 2 Chr 9.1ff; Mt 12.42; Judg 14.12
10.5 1 Chr 26.16
10.9 1 Kings 5.7; 2 Sam 8.15
10.11 1 Kings 9.27,28
10.12 2 Chr 9.10,11
10.14 2 Chr 9.13-28
10.16 1 Kings 14.26-28
10.17 1 Kings 7.2
10.18 2 Chr 9.17ff
10.22 1 Kings 9.26-28; 22.48; 2 Chr 20.36
10.23 1 Kings 3.12,13; 4.30
10.24 1 Kings 3.9,12,28
10.26 1 Kings 4.26; 2 Chr 1.14; 9.25; 1 Kings 9.19

9.26-28 Here is resumed the account of Solomon's commercial ventures, based at *Ezion-geber*, on the Gulf of Aqaba. The location of *Ophir* is not known; it could have been in India or Africa, but was accessible through the Red Sea. A *talent* weighed the equivalent of 60 kilograms (132 lbs) in the heavier standard system, or half that by the lighter standard.
10.1-10 Solomon is Visited by the Queen of Sheba. In addition to Solomon's *fame*, his economic and military initiatives in the Red Sea and the Indian Ocean must have caused concern in such an enterprising country as *Sheba* (Saba, in what is now Yemen at the southwest corner of the Arabian peninsula). In addition to producing incense and aromatics, Saba was a major prosperous commercial center for goods from Africa and India. Israel's control of major land and sea routes was a challenge and a threat. That Solomon's *fame [was] due to the name of the LORD* is probably a later pious addition to the original account. It was more likely his *wisdom*, wealth, administrative efficiency and piety that led the Queen of Sheba to visit him. She left behind costly gifts of *gold* and *spices*, as well as congratulations for the special favor God was bestowing on Solomon.
10.11-13 Further exchange of royal gifts and services. Hiram, king of Tyre, brought from *Ophir* not only gold but also a precious wood, *almug*, which was probably a fine-grained red sandalwood. Solomon gave generous gifts to the *Queen of Sheba*, as well.
10.14-29 The enormous wealth of Solomon is detailed, including the costly imports of such exotic items as *ivory, apes and peacocks*. Solomon's fame for his wisdom and the stream of gift-bearing visitors is noted, as well as the extent and costs of some of the imports.

[s] Gk: Heb *offering incense with it that was* [t] Or *Sea of Reeds* [u] Meaning of Heb uncertain [v] Gk Syr: Heb *men* [w] Or *baboons*

and horses; he had fourteen hundred chariots and twelve thousand horses, which he stationed in the chariot cities and with the king in Jerusalem. [27]The king made silver as common in Jerusalem as stones, and he made cedars as numerous as the sycamores of the Shephelah. [28]Solomon's import of horses was from Egypt and Kue, and the king's traders received them from Kue at a price. [29]A chariot could be imported from Egypt for six hundred shekels of silver, and a horse for one hundred fifty; so through the king's traders they were exported to all the kings of the Hittites and the kings of Aram.

Solomon's Errors

11 King Solomon loved many foreign women along with the daughter of Pharaoh: Moabite, Ammonite, Edomite, Sidonian, and Hittite women, [2]from the nations concerning which the LORD had said to the Israelites, "You shall not enter into marriage with them, neither shall they with you; for they will surely incline your heart to follow their gods"; Solomon clung to these in love. [3]Among his wives were seven hundred princesses and three hundred concubines; and his wives turned away his heart. [4]For when Solomon was old, his wives turned away his heart after other gods; and his heart was not true to the LORD his God, as was the heart of his father David. [5]For Solomon followed Astarte the goddess of the Sidonians, and Milcom the abomination of the Ammonites. [6]So Solomon did what was evil in the sight of the LORD, and did not completely follow the LORD, as his father David had done. [7]Then Solomon built a high place for Chemosh the abomination of Moab, and for Molech the abomination of the Ammonites, on the mountain east of Jerusalem. [8]He did the same for all his foreign wives, who offered incense and sacrificed to their gods.

9 Then the LORD was angry with Solomon, because his heart had turned away from the LORD, the God of Israel, who had appeared to him twice, [10]and had commanded him concerning this matter, that he should not follow other gods; but he did not observe what the LORD commanded. [11]Therefore the LORD said to Solomon, "Since this has been your mind and you have not kept my covenant and my statutes that I have commanded you, I will surely tear the kingdom from you and give it to your servant. [12]Yet for the sake of your father David I will not do it in your lifetime; I will tear it out of the hand of your son. [13]I will not, however, tear away the entire kingdom; I will give one tribe to your son, for the sake of my servant David and for the sake of Jerusalem, which I have chosen."

Adversaries of Solomon

14 Then the LORD raised up an adversary against Solomon, Hadad the Edomite; he was of the royal house in Edom. [15]For when David was in Edom, and Joab the commander of the army went up to bury the dead, he killed every male in Edom [16](for Joab and all Israel remained there six months, until he had eliminated every male in Edom); [17]but Hadad fled to Egypt with some Edomites who were servants of his father. He was a young boy at that time. [18]They set out from Midian and came to Paran; they took people with them from Paran and came to Egypt, to Pharaoh king of Egypt, who gave him a house, assigned him an allowance of food, and gave him land. [19]Hadad found great favor in the sight of Pharaoh, so that he gave him his sister-in-law for a wife, the sister of Queen Tahpenes. [20]The sister of Tahpenes gave birth by him to his son Genubath, whom Tahpenes weaned in Pharaoh's house; Genubath was in Pharaoh's house among the children of Pharaoh. [21]When Hadad heard in Egypt that David slept with his ancestors and that Joab the commander of the army was dead, Hadad said to Pharaoh, "Let me depart, that I may go to my own country." [22]But Pharaoh said to him, "What do you lack with me that you now seek to go to your own country?" And he said, "No, do let me go."

23 God raised up another adversary against Solomon,[x] Rezon son of Eliada, who had fled from his master, King Hadadezer of Zobah. [24]He gathered followers around him and became leader of a marauding band, after the slaughter by David; they went to Damascus, settled there, and made him king in Damascus. [25]He was an adversary of Israel all the days of Solomon, making trouble as Hadad did; he despised Israel and reigned over Aram.

[x] Heb *him*

11.1-13 Solomon's acquisition of huge numbers of foreign wives and concubines led him to foster the worship of other deities: *Astarte,* the fertility goddess and consort of Baal, whose worship probably centered in Tyre and Sidon; *Milcom, Chemosh,* and *Molech,* the last two worshipped by Semitic peoples east of the Jordan; to all three of these human sacrifices were offered (2 Kings 3.27). The judgment pronounced on Solomon expresses the Deuteronomic conviction that continuation of God's *covenant* depends on the king's conformity to the *statutes.* Solomon's failure to conform will result in the reduction of the territory to be controlled by his son and successor to that of *one tribe* = Judah.
11.14-22 *Hadad,* of the royal family of *Edom,* had escaped the slaughter of males carried out by *David.* He had fled to Egypt by way of *Midian* (east of the Gulf of Aqabah) and *Paran* (in the Sinai peninsula) and had married Pharaoh's *sister-in-law,* to whom was born a son, *Genubath.* On learning of David's death, Hadad planned to return to his native land, located southeast of the Dead Sea.
11.23-25 *Rezon,* a refugee from *Zobah,* a territory north of Damascus, first organized *a marauding band* and then was made *king of Damascus.* Solomon thus had major threats to his kingdom from north and south of Israel.

10.28 2 Chr 1.16; 9.28
10.29 2 Kings 7.6,7
11.1 Neh 13.26; Deut 17.17
11.2 Ex 34.16; Deut 7.3,4
11.4 1 Kings 8.61; 9.4
11.5 ver 33; Judg 2.13; 2 Kings 23.13
11.7 Num 21.29; Judg 11.24; 2 Kings 23.13
11.9 ver 2,3; 1 Kings 3.5; 9.2
11.10 1 Kings 6.12; 9.6,7
11.11 ver 31; 1 Kings 12.15,16
11.13 2 Sam 7.15; 1 Kings 12.20; Deut 12.11
11.15 2 Sam 8.14; 1 Chr 18.12,13
11.21 1 Kings 2.10
11.23 ver 14; 2 Sam 8.3
11.24 2 Sam 8.3; 10.8,18

11.26 1 Kings 12.2; 2 Chr 13.6; 2 Sam 20.21
11.27 1 Kings 9.24
11.29 1 Kings 14.2
11.30 1 Sam 15.27,28
11.31 ver 11-13
11.33 ver 5-7
11.35 1 Kings 12.16,17
11.36 ver 13; 1 Kings 15.4; 2 Kings 8.19
11.38 Josh 1.5; 2 Sam 7.11,27
11.41 2 Chr 9.29
11.42 2 Chr 9.30
11.43 2 Chr 9.31; 1 Kings 14.21
12.1 2 Chr 10.1ff
12.2 1 Kings 11.26,40
12.4 1 Sam 8.11-18; 1 Kings 4.7
12.5 ver 12
12.7 2 Chr 10.7
12.8 Lev 19.32

Jeroboam's Rebellion

26 Jeroboam son of Nebat, an Ephraimite of Zeredah, a servant of Solomon, whose mother's name was Zeruah, a widow, rebelled against the king. 27 The following was the reason he rebelled against the king. Solomon built the Millo, and closed up the gap in the wall[y] of the city of his father David. 28 The man Jeroboam was very able, and when Solomon saw that the young man was industrious he gave him charge over all the forced labor of the house of Joseph. 29 About that time, when Jeroboam was leaving Jerusalem, the prophet Ahijah the Shilonite found him on the road. Ahijah had clothed himself with a new garment. The two of them were alone in the open country 30 when Ahijah laid hold of the new garment he was wearing and tore it into twelve pieces. 31 He then said to Jeroboam: Take for yourself ten pieces; for thus says the LORD, the God of Israel, "See, I am about to tear the kingdom from the hand of Solomon, and will give you ten tribes. 32 One tribe will remain his, for the sake of my servant David and for the sake of Jerusalem, the city that I have chosen out of all the tribes of Israel. 33 This is because he has[z] forsaken me, worshiped Astarte the goddess of the Sidonians, Chemosh the god of Moab, and Milcom the god of the Ammonites, and has[z] not walked in my ways, doing what is right in my sight and keeping my statutes and my ordinances, as his father David did. 34 Nevertheless I will not take the whole kingdom away from him but will make him ruler all the days of his life, for the sake of my servant David whom I chose and who did keep my commandments and my statutes; 35 but I will take the kingdom away from his son and give it to you—that is, the ten tribes. 36 Yet to his son I will give one tribe, so that my servant David may always have a lamp before me in Jerusalem, the city where I have chosen to put my name. 37 I will take you, and you shall reign over all that your soul desires; you shall be king over Israel. 38 If you will listen to all that I command you, walk in my ways, and do what is right in my sight by keeping my statutes and my commandments, as David my servant did, I will be with you, and will build you an enduring house, as I built for David, and I will give Israel to you. 39 For this reason I will punish the descendants of David, but not forever." 40 Solomon sought therefore to kill Jeroboam; but Jeroboam promptly fled to Egypt, to King Shishak of Egypt, and remained in Egypt until the death of Solomon.

Death of Solomon

41 Now the rest of the acts of Solomon, all that he did as well as his wisdom, are they not written in the Book of the Acts of Solomon? 42 The time that Solomon reigned in Jerusalem over all Israel was forty years. 43 Solomon slept with his ancestors and was buried in the city of his father David; and his son Rehoboam succeeded him.

The Northern Tribes Secede

12 Rehoboam went to Shechem, for all Israel had come to Shechem to make him king. 2 When Jeroboam son of Nebat heard of it (for he was still in Egypt, where he had fled from King Solomon), then Jeroboam returned from[a] Egypt. 3 And they sent and called him; and Jeroboam and all the assembly of Israel came and said to Rehoboam, 4 "Your father made our yoke heavy. Now therefore lighten the hard service of your father and his heavy yoke that he placed on us, and we will serve you." 5 He said to them, "Go away for three days, then come again to me." So the people went away.

6 Then King Rehoboam took counsel with the older men who had attended his father Solomon while he was still alive, saying, "How do you advise me to answer this people?" 7 They answered him, "If you will be a servant to this people today and serve them, and speak good words to them when you answer them, then they will be your servants forever." 8 But he disregarded the advice that the older men gave him, and consulted with the young men who had grown up with him and now attended him. 9 He said to them, "What do you advise that we answer this people who have said to me, 'Lighten the yoke that your father put on us'?" 10 The young men who had grown up with him said to him, "Thus you should say to this people who spoke to you, 'Your father made our yoke heavy, but you must lighten it for us'; thus you should say to them, 'My little finger is thicker than my father's loins. 11 Now, whereas my father laid on you a heavy yoke, I will add to your

11.26-40 Jeroboam, once a trusted labor supervisor for Solomon, was informed by the prophet *Ahijah's* words and symbolic action (tearing his new robe in twelve pieces) that God was about to fulfill his threat to divide the kingdom of Solomon between Judah and Israel (the union of the other ten tribes). The threat repeats the Deuteronomic terms about keeping the *statutes and commandments.* Solomon's attempt to kill Jeroboam led him to flee for safety to *Egypt until the death of Solomon.*
11.41-43 The source reportedly used here, *Book of the Acts of Solomon,* is regrettably lost, but was drawn on by the writer of 1 Kings. Solomon's term of reign may be given in round numbers: *forty years* would be from 962 to 922 BCE.
12.1-19 Israel is Divided into Northern and Southern Kingdoms.
12.1-15 *Rehoboam* went to Shechem to be crowned as king of all Israel, and was advised to lighten the load of forced labor and taxes that his father, Solomon, had imposed on the people. *Jeroboam* returned from Egypt to seek the throne for himself. In vivid images, Rehoboam promised to intensify the burdens on his subjects, thus leading to fulfillment of the prediction about the division of Solomon's kingdom.

[y] Heb lacks *in the wall* [z] Gk Syr Vg: Heb *they have* [a] Gk Vg Compare 2 Chr 10.2: Heb *lived in*

12.16-19 The northern tribes seceded from Judah, and *stoned to death* the agent of Rehoboam who was sent among them. The split between the tribes is noted by the editor as continuing *to this day*, which suggests that the original time of writing the Books of Kings was prior to the dissolution of the northern kingdom, based in Samaria, which did occur in 721 BCE.
12.20-14.20 The Reign of Jeroboam over Israel.
12.20-24 When Jeroboam was established as king *over all Israel*, except Judah, Rehoboam rallied troops from Judah and the small neighboring tribe to the north, Benjamin, to take over the new kingdom of Israel. Forewarned by the prophetic figure, *Shemaiah, the man of God*, the attack was not launched.
12.25-33 *Jeroboam* rebuilt the city of *Shechem*, where the early Israelites had worshipped the LORD since the time of Abraham (Gen 12.6-7) and Jacob (Gen 33.18-20) and the gathering of *all the tribes of Israel* there under Joshua (Josh 24.1). But he also *made two calves of gold*, and established centers for worship of them at the traditional sacred sites of *Bethel*, where the LORD met Abraham and Jacob (Gen 12.8; 28.10-19) and *Dan*, which archaeological remains suggest was a center of the worship of Baal. The *high places* that he built were local centers for worshipping the fertility gods and goddesses. He also changed the process of appointing *priests*, and adapted the calendar of sacred feasts in effect in Jerusalem to conform to the worship of these pagan deities.
13.1-34 Warnings to Jeroboam of the Consequences of his Development of these Pagan Practices. The prediction of *the man of God...out of Judah* about the descendant of David, *Josiah*, who would destroy *the altar at Bethel* is confirmed by the withering of Jeroboam's arm and the collapse of the altar. The disobedience of this man in accepting food from *the prophet* in the vicinity of Bethel was brought under judgment through his tragic death. Even so, *Jeroboam* continued to appoint priests to serve at his pagan *high places*, thereby inviting divine judgment.

yoke. My father disciplined you with whips,
but I will discipline you with scorpions.' "
12 So Jeroboam and all the people came
to Rehoboam the third day, as the king had
said, "Come to me again the third day."
13The king answered the people harshly. He
disregarded the advice that the older men
had given him 14and spoke to them according to the advice of the young men, "My
father made your yoke heavy, but I will add
to your yoke; my father disciplined you with
whips, but I will discipline you with scorpions." 15So the king did not listen to the
people, because it was a turn of affairs
brought about by the LORD that he might
fulfill his word, which the LORD had spoken
by Ahijah the Shilonite to Jeroboam son of
Nebat.
16 When all Israel saw that the king
would not listen to them, the people answered the king,

"What share do we have in David?
We have no inheritance in the son
of Jesse.
To your tents, O Israel!
Look now to your own house, O
David."

So Israel went away to their tents. 17But
Rehoboam reigned over the Israelites who
were living in the towns of Judah. 18When
King Rehoboam sent Adoram, who was
taskmaster over the forced labor, all Israel
stoned him to death. King Rehoboam then
hurriedly mounted his chariot to flee to
Jerusalem. 19So Israel has been in rebellion
against the house of David to this day.

First Dynasty: Jeroboam Reigns over Israel

20 When all Israel heard that Jeroboam
had returned, they sent and called him to
the assembly and made him king over all
Israel. There was no one who followed the
house of David, except the tribe of Judah
alone.
21 When Rehoboam came to Jerusalem,
he assembled all the house of Judah and the
tribe of Benjamin, one hundred eighty thousand chosen troops to fight against the
house of Israel, to restore the kingdom to
Rehoboam son of Solomon. 22But the word
of God came to Shemaiah the man of God:
23Say to King Rehoboam of Judah, son of
Solomon, and to all the house of Judah and
Benjamin, and to the rest of the people,
24"Thus says the LORD, You shall not go up
or fight against your kindred the people of
Israel. Let everyone go home, for this thing
is from me." So they heeded the word of the
LORD and went home again, according to
the word of the LORD.

Jeroboam's Golden Calves

25 Then Jeroboam built Shechem in the
hill country of Ephraim, and resided there;
he went out from there and built Penuel.
26Then Jeroboam said to himself, "Now the
kingdom may well revert to the house of
David. 27If this people continues to go up to
offer sacrifices in the house of the LORD at
Jerusalem, the heart of this people will turn
again to their master, King Rehoboam of
Judah; they will kill me and return to King
Rehoboam of Judah." 28So the king took
counsel, and made two calves of gold. He
said to the people,[b] "You have gone up to
Jerusalem long enough. Here are your gods,
O Israel, who brought you up out of the
land of Egypt." 29He set one in Bethel, and
the other he put in Dan. 30And this thing
became a sin, for the people went to worship before the one at Bethel and before the
other as far as Dan.[c] 31He also made houses[d]
on high places, and appointed priests from
among all the people, who were not Levites.
32Jeroboam appointed a festival on the
fifteenth day of the eighth month like the
festival that was in Judah, and he offered
sacrifices on the altar; so he did in Bethel,
sacrificing to the calves that he had made.
And he placed in Bethel the priests of the
high places that he had made. 33He went up
to the altar that he had made in Bethel on
the fifteenth day in the eighth month, in the
month that he alone had devised; he appointed a festival for the people of Israel,
and he went up to the altar to offer incense.

A Man of God from Judah

13 While Jeroboam was standing by
the altar to offer incense, a man of
God came out of Judah by the word of the
LORD to Bethel 2and proclaimed against the
altar by the word of the LORD, and said, "O
altar, altar, thus says the LORD: 'A son shall
be born to the house of David, Josiah by
name; and he shall sacrifice on you the
priests of the high places who offer incense
on you, and human bones shall be burned
on you.' " 3He gave a sign the same day,

[b] Gk: Heb *to them* [c] Compare Gk: Heb *went to the one as far as Dan* [d] Gk Vg Compare 13.32: Heb *a house*

12.12 ver 5
12.14 Ex 1.13,14; 5.5-9,16-18
12.15 ver 24; Judg 14.4; 2 Chr 10.15; 22.7; 25.20; 1 Kings 11.11,31
12.16 2 Sam 20.1
12.17 1 Kings 11.13,26
12.18 1 Kings 4.6; 5.14
12.19 2 Kings 17.21
12.20 1 Kings 11.13,32
12.21 2 Chr 11.1ff
12.24 ver 15
12.25 Judg 9.45; 8.17
12.27 Deut 12.5,6
12.28 2 Kings 10.29; 17.16; Ex 32.4,8
12.29 Gen 28.19; Judg 18.29
12.30 1 Kings 13.34; 2 Kings 17.21
12.31 1 Kings 13.32,33; Num 3.10; 2 Kings 17.32
12.32 Lev 23.33,34; Num 29.12; Am 7.13
12.33 1 Kings 13.1
13.1 2 Kings 23.17; 1 Kings 12.32,33
13.2 2 Kings 23.15,16
13.3 Isa 7.14; Judg 6.17

13.6 Ex 8.8; 9.28; Acts 8.24; Lk 6.27,28
13.7 1 Sam 9.7,8; 2 Kings 5.15
13.8 ver 16,17; Num 22.18; 24.13
13.11 ver 25
13.16 ver 8,9
13.17 1 Kings 20.35
13.21 1 Sam 15.26
13.24 1 Kings 20.36
13.25 ver 11
13.26 ver 21
13.30 Jer 22.18
13.31 2 Kings 23.17,18
13.32 ver 2; 2 Kings 23.16,17,19; see 1 Kings 16.24
13.33 1 Kings 12.31,32; 2 Chr 11.15; 13.9

saying, "This is the sign that the LORD has spoken: 'The altar shall be torn down, and the ashes that are on it shall be poured out.' " 4 When the king heard what the man of God cried out against the altar at Bethel, Jeroboam stretched out his hand from the altar, saying, "Seize him!" But the hand that he stretched out against him withered so that he could not draw it back to himself. 5 The altar also was torn down, and the ashes poured out from the altar, according to the sign that the man of God had given by the word of the LORD. 6 The king said to the man of God, "Entreat now the favor of the LORD your God, and pray for me, so that my hand may be restored to me." So the man of God entreated the LORD; and the king's hand was restored to him, and became as it was before. 7 Then the king said to the man of God, "Come home with me and dine, and I will give you a gift." 8 But the man of God said to the king, "If you give me half your kingdom, I will not go in with you; nor will I eat food or drink water in this place. 9 For thus I was commanded by the word of the LORD: You shall not eat food, or drink water, or return by the way that you came." 10 So he went another way, and did not return by the way that he had come to Bethel.

11 Now there lived an old prophet in Bethel. One of his sons came and told him all that the man of God had done that day in Bethel; the words also that he had spoken to the king, they told to their father. 12 Their father said to them, "Which way did he go?" And his sons showed him the way that the man of God who came from Judah had gone. 13 Then he said to his sons, "Saddle a donkey for me." So they saddled a donkey for him, and he mounted it. 14 He went after the man of God, and found him sitting under an oak tree. He said to him, "Are you the man of God who came from Judah?" He answered, "I am." 15 Then he said to him, "Come home with me and eat some food." 16 But he said, "I cannot return with you, or go in with you; nor will I eat food or drink water with you in this place; 17 for it was said to me by the word of the LORD: You shall not eat food or drink water there, or return by the way that you came." 18 Then the other[e] said to him, "I also am a prophet as you are, and an angel spoke to me by the word of the LORD: Bring him back with you into your house so that he may eat food and drink water." But he was deceiving him. 19 Then the man of God[e] went back with him, and ate food and drank water in his house.

20 As they were sitting at the table, the word of the LORD came to the prophet who had brought him back; 21 and he proclaimed to the man of God who came from Judah, "Thus says the LORD: Because you have disobeyed the word of the LORD, and have not kept the commandment that the LORD your God commanded you, 22 but have come back and have eaten food and drunk water in the place of which he said to you, 'Eat no food, and drink no water,' your body shall not come to your ancestral tomb." 23 After the man of God[e] had eaten food and had drunk, they saddled for him a donkey belonging to the prophet who had brought him back. 24 Then as he went away, a lion met him on the road and killed him. His body was thrown in the road, and the donkey stood beside it; the lion also stood beside the body. 25 People passed by and saw the body thrown in the road, with the lion standing by the body. And they came and told it in the town where the old prophet lived.

26 When the prophet who had brought him back from the way heard of it, he said, "It is the man of God who disobeyed the word of the LORD; therefore the LORD has given him to the lion, which has torn him and killed him according to the word that the LORD spoke to him." 27 Then he said to his sons, "Saddle a donkey for me." So they saddled one, 28 and he went and found the body thrown in the road, with the donkey and the lion standing beside the body. The lion had not eaten the body or attacked the donkey. 29 The prophet took up the body of the man of God, laid it on the donkey, and brought it back to the city,[f] to mourn and to bury him. 30 He laid the body in his own grave; and they mourned over him, saying, "Alas, my brother!" 31 After he had buried him, he said to his sons, "When I die, bury me in the grave in which the man of God is buried; lay my bones beside his bones. 32 For the saying that he proclaimed by the word of the LORD against the altar in Bethel, and against all the houses of the high places that are in the cities of Samaria, shall surely come to pass."

33 Even after this event Jeroboam did not turn from his evil way, but made priests

[e] Heb *he* [f] Gk: Heb *he came to the town of the old prophet*

14.1-20 God's Judgment on Jeroboam. *The prophet Ahijah,* who had predicted the division of Israel and the ascent of Jeroboam to the throne (1 Kings 11.29-38), when consulted by the king's wife in disguise, told her of God's judgment about to fall on Jeroboam and the approaching destruction of all his offspring. This was fulfilled shortly as predicted. Jeroboam reigned over Israel from 922 to 901.
14.21-31 The reign of *Rehoboam* was also marred by a surge of pagan fertility worship in Judah, including the erection of sexual symbols (sacred *pillars* and *poles*) and the emergence of *male prostitutes.* Judgment fell on Judah in the form of an invasion from Egypt and the stripping of gold and treasures from the temple. Reference is made here to another lost source, *the Book of the Annals of the Kings of Judah.* Rehoboam died in 915 after a reign of seven years.

for the high places again from among all
the people; any who wanted to be priests he
consecrated for the high places. [34]This matter
became sin to the house of Jeroboam, so as
to cut it off and to destroy it from the face
of the earth.

Judgment on the House of Jeroboam

14 At that time Abijah son of Jeroboam fell sick. [2]Jeroboam said to
his wife, "Go, disguise yourself, so that it
will not be known that you are the wife of
Jeroboam, and go to Shiloh; for the prophet
Ahijah is there, who said of me that I
should be king over this people. [3]Take with
you ten loaves, some cakes, and a jar of
honey, and go to him; he will tell you what
shall happen to the child."
4 Jeroboam's wife did so; she set out and
went to Shiloh, and came to the house of
Ahijah. Now Ahijah could not see, for his
eyes were dim because of his age. [5]But the
LORD said to Ahijah, "The wife of Jeroboam
is coming to inquire of you concerning her
son; for he is sick. Thus and thus you shall
say to her."
When she came, she pretended to be
another woman. [6]But when Ahijah heard
the sound of her feet, as she came in at the
door, he said, "Come in, wife of Jeroboam;
why do you pretend to be another? For I am
charged with heavy tidings for you. [7]Go, tell
Jeroboam, 'Thus says the LORD, the God of
Israel: Because I exalted you from among
the people, made you leader over my people
Israel, [8]and tore the kingdom away from
the house of David to give it to you; yet you
have not been like my servant David, who
kept my commandments and followed me
with all his heart, doing only that which
was right in my sight, [9]but you have done
evil above all those who were before you
and have gone and made for yourself other
gods, and cast images, provoking me to
anger, and have thrust me behind your
back; [10]therefore, I will bring evil upon the
house of Jeroboam. I will cut off from Jeroboam every male, both bond and free in
Israel, and will consume the house of Jeroboam, just as one burns up dung until it is
all gone. [11]Anyone belonging to Jeroboam
who dies in the city, the dogs shall eat; and
anyone who dies in the open country, the
birds of the air shall eat; for the LORD has
spoken.' [12]Therefore set out, go to your
house. When your feet enter the city, the
child shall die. [13]All Israel shall mourn for
him and bury him; for he alone of Jeroboam's family shall come to the grave, because in him there is found something pleasing to the LORD, the God of Israel, in the
house of Jeroboam. [14]Moreover the LORD will
raise up for himself a king over Israel, who
shall cut off the house of Jeroboam today,
even right now![g]
15 "The LORD will strike Israel, as a reed
is shaken in the water; he will root up Israel
out of this good land that he gave to their
ancestors, and scatter them beyond the
Euphrates, because they have made their
sacred poles,[h] provoking the LORD to anger.
[16]He will give Israel up because of the sins
of Jeroboam, which he sinned and which he
caused Israel to commit."
17 Then Jeroboam's wife got up and went
away, and she came to Tirzah. As she came
to the threshold of the house, the child died.
[18]All Israel buried him and mourned for
him, according to the word of the LORD,
which he spoke by his servant the prophet
Ahijah.

Death of Jeroboam

19 Now the rest of the acts of Jeroboam,
how he warred and how he reigned, are
written in the Book of the Annals of the
Kings of Israel. [20]The time that Jeroboam
reigned was twenty-two years; then he slept
with his ancestors, and his son Nadab succeeded him.

Rehoboam Reigns over Judah

21 Now Rehoboam son of Solomon
reigned in Judah. Rehoboam was forty-one
years old when he began to reign, and he
reigned seventeen years in Jerusalem, the
city that the LORD had chosen out of all the
tribes of Israel, to put his name there. His
mother's name was Naamah the Ammonite. [22]Judah did what was evil in the sight
of the LORD; they provoked him to jealousy
with their sins that they committed, more
than all that their ancestors had done. [23]For
they also built for themselves high places,
pillars, and sacred poles[h] on every high hill
and under every green tree; [24]there were
also male temple prostitutes in the land.
They committed all the abominations of the
nations that the LORD drove out before the
people of Israel.

[g] Meaning of Heb uncertain [h] Heb *Asherim*

13.34 1 Kings 12.30; 14.10
14.2 1 Sam 28.8; 2 Sam 14.2; 1 Kings 11.29-31
14.3 1 Sam 9.7,8
14.4 1 Kings 11.29; 1 Sam 3.2; 4.15
14.5 2 Sam 14.2
14.7 1 Kings 11.28-31; 16.2
14.8 1 Kings 11.31ff
14.9 1 Kings 12.28; 2 Chr 11.15; Ps 50.17; Ex 34.17; Ezek 23.35
14.10 1 Kings 15.29; 21.21; 2 Kings 9.8; Deut 32.36; 2 Kings 14.26
14.11 1 Kings 16.4; 21.24
14.12 ver 17
14.13 2 Chr 12.12
14.14 1 Kings 15.27-29
14.15 2 Kings 17.6; Josh 23.15,16; 2 Kings 15.29; Ex 34.13; Deut 12.3,4
14.16 1 Kings 12.30; 13.34; 15.30,34
14.19 2 Chr 13.2-20
14.21 2 Chr 12.13; 1 Kings 11.32,36; ver 31
14.22 2 Chr 12.1; Deut 32.21
14.23 Deut 12.2; Ezek 16.24,25; 2 Kings 17.9,10; Isa 57.5
14.24 Deut 23.17; 1 Kings 15.12; 2 Kings 23.7

25 In the fifth year of King Rehoboam, King Shishak of Egypt came up against Jerusalem; 26he took away the treasures of the house of the LORD and the treasures of the king's house; he took everything. He also took away all the shields of gold that Solomon had made; 27so King Rehoboam made shields of bronze instead, and committed them to the hands of the officers of the guard, who kept the door of the king's house. 28As often as the king went into the house of the LORD, the guard carried them and brought them back to the guardroom.

29 Now the rest of the acts of Rehoboam, and all that he did, are they not written in the Book of the Annals of the Kings of Judah? 30There was war between Rehoboam and Jeroboam continually. 31Rehoboam slept with his ancestors and was buried with his ancestors in the city of David. His mother's name was Naamah the Ammonite. His son Abijam succeeded him.

Abijam Reigns over Judah: Idolatry and War

15 Now in the eighteenth year of King Jeroboam son of Nebat, Abijam began to reign over Judah. 2He reigned for three years in Jerusalem. His mother's name was Maacah daughter of Abishalom. 3He committed all the sins that his father did before him; his heart was not true to the LORD his God, like the heart of his father David. 4Nevertheless for David's sake the LORD his God gave him a lamp in Jerusalem, setting up his son after him, and establishing Jerusalem; 5because David did what was right in the sight of the LORD, and did not turn aside from anything that he commanded him all the days of his life, except in the matter of Uriah the Hittite. 6The war begun between Rehoboam and Jeroboam continued all the days of his life. 7The rest of the acts of Abijam, and all that he did, are they not written in the Book of the Annals of the Kings of Judah? There was war between Abijam and Jeroboam. 8Abijam slept with his ancestors, and they buried him in the city of David. Then his son Asa succeeded him.

Asa Reigns over Judah

9 In the twentieth year of King Jeroboam of Israel, Asa began to reign over Judah; 10he reigned forty-one years in Jerusalem. His mother's name was Maacah daughter of Abishalom. 11Asa did what was right in the sight of the LORD, as his father David had done. 12He put away the male temple prostitutes out of the land, and removed all the idols that his ancestors had made. 13He also removed his mother Maacah from being queen mother, because she had made an abominable image for Asherah; Asa cut down her image and burned it at the Wadi Kidron. 14But the high places were not taken away. Nevertheless the heart of Asa was true to the LORD all his days. 15He brought into the house of the LORD the votive gifts of his father and his own votive gifts—silver, gold, and utensils.

Alliance with Aram against Israel

16 There was war between Asa and King Baasha of Israel all their days. 17King Baasha of Israel went up against Judah, and built Ramah, to prevent anyone from going out or coming in to King Asa of Judah. 18Then Asa took all the silver and the gold that were left in the treasures of the house of the LORD and the treasures of the king's house, and gave them into the hands of his servants. King Asa sent them to King Ben-hadad son of Tabrimmon son of Hezion of Aram, who resided in Damascus, saying, 19"Let there be an alliance between me and you, like that between my father and your father: I am sending you a present of silver and gold; go, break your alliance with King Baasha of Israel, so that he may withdraw from me." 20Ben-hadad listened to King Asa, and sent the commanders of his armies against the cities of Israel. He conquered Ijon, Dan, Abel-beth-maacah, and all Chinneroth, with all the land of Naphtali. 21When Baasha heard of it, he stopped building Ramah and lived in Tirzah. 22Then King Asa made a proclamation to all Judah, none was exempt: they carried away the stones of Ramah and its timber, with which Baasha had been building; with them King Asa built Geba of Benjamin and Mizpah. 23Now the rest of all the acts of Asa, all his power, all that he did, and the cities that he built, are they not written in the Book of the Annals of the Kings of Judah? But in his old age he was diseased in his feet. 24Then Asa slept with his ancestors, and was buried with his ancestors in the city of his father David; his son Jehoshaphat succeeded him.

15.1-8 The Reign of Abijam over Judah. Abijam's three-year reign (915-913) was characterized by the worst features of his father's, including idolatry and continuing war with Jeroboam.
15.9-24 The Reign of Asa over Judah. Asa purged the pagan practices, although he allowed the *high places* to remain. His fidelity to the LORD and his *votive gifts* to the temple were matched by his military alliance with the Aramean *King Ben-hadad* of Damascus, which resulted in the destruction of cities and the capture of regions in northern Israel.

14.25 1 Kings 11.40; 2 Chr 12.2,9-11
14.26 1 Kings 15.18; 10.17
14.29 2 Chr 12.15
14.30 1 Kings 12.21-24; 15.6
14.31 2 Chr 12.16; ver 21
15.1 2 Chr 13.1,2
15.3 1 Kings 11.4
15.4 1 Kings 11.36; 2 Chr 21.7
15.5 1 Kings 14.8; 2 Sam 11.4,15-17; 12.9
15.6 1 Kings 14.30
15.7 2 Chr 13.2,3,22
15.8 2 Chr 14.1
15.10 ver 2
15.11 2 Chr 14.2
15.12 1 Kings 14.24; 22.46
15.13 2 Chr 15.16-18; Ex 32.20
15.14 1 Kings 22.43; 2 Chr 15.17,18; ver 3
15.15 1 Kings 7.51
15.16 ver 32
15.17 2 Chr 16.1ff; Josh 18.25; 1 Kings 12.27
15.18 ver 15; 2 Chr 16.2; 1 Kings 11.23,24
15.20 2 Kings 15.29; Judg 18.29; 2 Sam 20.14
15.22 2 Chr 16.6; Josh 21.17
15.23 2 Chr 16.11-14
15.24 2 Chr 17.1

15.25-31 The Reign of Nadab over Israel. *Nadab* followed the evil example of his father, Jeroboam, during his brief reign. Baasha, son of Ahijah (not the prophet of 1 Kings 11.29-30), conspired against Nadab, captured him while he was besieging the Philistine city of *Gibbethon* (south of Joppa), and killed him and all his and Jeroboam's offspring.
15.33-16.7 The Reign of Baasha over Israel. The judgment falls after twenty-four years of Baasha's reign (900-877) because he not only destroyed *the house [descendants] of Jeroboam,* but also followed Jeroboam's idolatrous example.
16.8-20 The brief reigns of Elah (877-876) and Zimri (seven days) over Israel ended respectively in murder and suicide, and the slaughter of all the posterity of Baasha. Popular action in Israel established *Omri,* the head of the army of Israel, as king.

Nadab Reigns over Israel

25 Nadab son of Jeroboam began to reign over Israel in the second year of King Asa of Judah; he reigned over Israel two years. 26 He did what was evil in the sight of the LORD, walking in the way of his ancestor and in the sin that he caused Israel to commit.

27 Baasha son of Ahijah, of the house of Issachar, conspired against him; and Baasha struck him down at Gibbethon, which belonged to the Philistines; for Nadab and all Israel were laying siege to Gibbethon. 28 So Baasha killed Nadab[i] in the third year of King Asa of Judah, and succeeded him. 29 As soon as he was king, he killed all the house of Jeroboam; he left to the house of Jeroboam not one that breathed, until he had destroyed it, according to the word of the LORD that he spoke by his servant Ahijah the Shilonite— 30 because of the sins of Jeroboam that he committed and that he caused Israel to commit, and because of the anger to which he provoked the LORD, the God of Israel.

31 Now the rest of the acts of Nadab, and all that he did, are they not written in the Book of the Annals of the Kings of Israel? 32 There was war between Asa and King Baasha of Israel all their days.

Second Dynasty: Baasha Reigns over Israel

33 In the third year of King Asa of Judah, Baasha son of Ahijah began to reign over all Israel at Tirzah; he reigned twenty-four years. 34 He did what was evil in the sight of the LORD, walking in the way of Jeroboam and in the sin that he caused Israel to commit.

16 The word of the LORD came to Jehu son of Hanani against Baasha, saying, 2 "Since I exalted you out of the dust and made you leader over my people Israel, and you have walked in the way of Jeroboam, and have caused my people Israel to sin, provoking me to anger with their sins, 3 therefore, I will consume Baasha and his house, and I will make your house like the house of Jeroboam son of Nebat. 4 Anyone belonging to Baasha who dies in the city the dogs shall eat; and anyone of his who dies in the field the birds of the air shall eat."

5 Now the rest of the acts of Baasha, what he did, and his power, are they not written in the Book of the Annals of the Kings of Israel? 6 Baasha slept with his ancestors, and was buried at Tirzah; and his son Elah succeeded him. 7 Moreover the word of the LORD came by the prophet Jehu son of Hanani against Baasha and his house, both because of all the evil that he did in the sight of the LORD, provoking him to anger with the work of his hands, in being like the house of Jeroboam, and also because he destroyed it.

Elah Reigns over Israel

8 In the twenty-sixth year of King Asa of Judah, Elah son of Baasha began to reign over Israel in Tirzah; he reigned two years. 9 But his servant Zimri, commander of half his chariots, conspired against him. When he was at Tirzah, drinking himself drunk in the house of Arza, who was in charge of the palace at Tirzah, 10 Zimri came in and struck him down and killed him, in the twenty-seventh year of King Asa of Judah, and succeeded him.

11 When he began to reign, as soon as he had seated himself on his throne, he killed all the house of Baasha; he did not leave him a single male of his kindred or his friends. 12 Thus Zimri destroyed all the house of Baasha, according to the word of the LORD, which he spoke against Baasha by the prophet Jehu— 13 because of all the sins of Baasha and the sins of his son Elah that they committed, and that they caused Israel to commit, provoking the LORD God of Israel to anger with their idols. 14 Now the rest of the acts of Elah, and all that he did, are they not written in the Book of the Annals of the Kings of Israel?

Third Dynasty: Zimri Reigns over Israel

15 In the twenty-seventh year of King Asa of Judah, Zimri reigned seven days in Tirzah. Now the troops were encamped against Gibbethon, which belonged to the Philistines, 16 and the troops who were encamped heard it said, "Zimri has conspired, and he has killed the king"; therefore all Israel made Omri, the commander of the army, king over Israel that day in the camp. 17 So Omri went up from Gibbethon, and all Israel with him, and they besieged Tirzah. 18 When Zimri saw that the city was taken, he went into the citadel of the king's house;

[i] Heb *him*

15.25 1 Kings 14.20
15.26 1 Kings 12.30; 14.16
15.27 1 Kings 14.14; Josh 19.44; 21.23
15.29 1 Kings 14.10,14
15.30 1 Kings 14.9,16
15.31 ver 16
15.34 1 Kings 12.28,29; 13.33; 14.16
16.1 ver 7; 2 Chr 19.2; 20.34
16.2 1 Kings 14.7; 15.34
16.3 ver 11; 1 Kings 14.10; 15.29
16.4 1 Kings 14.11
16.5 1 Kings 14.19; 15.31
16.6 1 Kings 14.17; 15.21
16.7 ver 1; 1 Kings 15.27,29
16.9 2 Kings 9.30-33
16.12 ver 3; 2 Chr 19.2; 20.34
16.13 Deut 32.21; 1 Sam 12.21; Isa 41.29
16.14 ver 5
16.15 1 Kings 15.27
16.18 1 Sam 31.4,5; 2 Sam 17.23

16.19 1 Kings 12.28; 15.26,34
16.20 ver 5,14,27
16.23 1 Kings 15.21
16.24 1 Kings 13.32; Jn 4.4
16.26 Mic 6.16; ver 19
16.30 ver 25; 1 Kings 14.9
16.31 Deut 7.3; 2 Kings 10.18; 17.16
16.32 2 Kings 10.21,26,27
16.33 2 Kings 13.6; ver 29,30
16.34 Josh 6.26
17.1 2 Kings 3.14; Deut 10.8; 1 Kings 18.1; Jas 5.17; Lk 4.25
17.9 Ob 20; Lk 4.26
17.12 ver 1; 2 Kings 4.2-7

he burned down the king's house over himself with fire, and died— [19]because of the sins that he committed, doing evil in the sight of the LORD, walking in the way of Jeroboam, and for the sin that he committed, causing Israel to sin. [20]Now the rest of the acts of Zimri, and the conspiracy that he made, are they not written in the Book of the Annals of the Kings of Israel?

Fourth Dynasty: Omri Reigns over Israel

21 Then the people of Israel were divided into two parts; half of the people followed Tibni son of Ginath, to make him king, and half followed Omri. [22]But the people who followed Omri overcame the people who followed Tibni son of Ginath; so Tibni died, and Omri became king. [23]In the thirty-first year of King Asa of Judah, Omri began to reign over Israel; he reigned for twelve years, six of them in Tirzah.

Samaria the New Capital

24 He bought the hill of Samaria from Shemer for two talents of silver; he fortified the hill, and called the city that he built, Samaria, after the name of Shemer, the owner of the hill.

25 Omri did what was evil in the sight of the LORD; he did more evil than all who were before him. [26]For he walked in all the way of Jeroboam son of Nebat, and in the sins that he caused Israel to commit, provoking the LORD, the God of Israel, to anger by their idols. [27]Now the rest of the acts of Omri that he did, and the power that he showed, are they not written in the Book of the Annals of the Kings of Israel? [28]Omri slept with his ancestors, and was buried in Samaria; his son Ahab succeeded him.

Ahab Reigns over Israel

29 In the thirty-eighth year of King Asa of Judah, Ahab son of Omri began to reign over Israel; Ahab son of Omri reigned over Israel in Samaria twenty-two years. [30]Ahab son of Omri did evil in the sight of the LORD more than all who were before him.

Ahab Marries Jezebel and Worships Baal

31 And as if it had been a light thing for him to walk in the sins of Jeroboam son of Nebat, he took as his wife Jezebel daughter of King Ethbaal of the Sidonians, and went and served Baal, and worshiped him. [32]He erected an altar for Baal in the house of Baal, which he built in Samaria. [33]Ahab also made a sacred pole.[j] Ahab did more to provoke the anger of the LORD, the God of Israel, than had all the kings of Israel who were before him. [34]In his days Hiel of Bethel built Jericho; he laid its foundation at the cost of Abiram his firstborn, and set up its gates at the cost of his youngest son Segub, according to the word of the LORD, which he spoke by Joshua son of Nun.

Elijah Predicts a Drought

17 Now Elijah the Tishbite, of Tishbe[k] in Gilead, said to Ahab, "As the LORD the God of Israel lives, before whom I stand, there shall be neither dew nor rain these years, except by my word." [2]The word of the LORD came to him, saying, [3]"Go from here and turn eastward, and hide yourself by the Wadi Cherith, which is east of the Jordan. [4]You shall drink from the wadi, and I have commanded the ravens to feed you there." [5]So he went and did according to the word of the LORD; he went and lived by the Wadi Cherith, which is east of the Jordan. [6]The ravens brought him bread and meat in the morning, and bread and meat in the evening; and he drank from the wadi. [7]But after a while the wadi dried up, because there was no rain in the land.

The Widow of Zarephath

8 Then the word of the LORD came to him, saying, [9]"Go now to Zarephath, which belongs to Sidon, and live there; for I have commanded a widow there to feed you." [10]So he set out and went to Zarephath. When he came to the gate of the town, a widow was there gathering sticks; he called to her and said, "Bring me a little water in a vessel, so that I may drink." [11]As she was going to bring it, he called to her and said, "Bring me a morsel of bread in your hand." [12]But she said, "As the LORD your God lives, I have nothing baked, only a handful of meal in a jar, and a little oil in a jug; I am now gathering a couple of sticks, so that I may go home and prepare it for myself and my son, that we may eat it, and die." [13]Elijah said to her, "Do not be afraid; go

[j] Heb *Asherah* [k] Gk: Heb *of the settlers*

16.21-28 After an initial split among the tribes of Israel, *Omri* was fully established as king. During his reign (876-869) he *bought the hill of Samaria,* west of Shechem, fortified it and built a new capital there. Though denounced in the Deuteronomic terms, the Assyrians referred to Israel from this time until its fall to the Babylonians as "the house of Omri." After a reign of twelve years (876-869), he was succeeded by his son, *Ahab.*
16.29-22.40 The Reign of Ahab and the Prophets' Challenge.
16.29-34 Ahab's long reign (twenty-two years) is denounced as *evil in the sight of the LORD...more than all* the kings of Israel before him. His actions included promoting the worship of Baal, through his marriage to a Baal-worshiper from Sidon *(Jezebel, daughter of King Ethbaal)* and by the erection of an altar and a fertility symbol: *a sacred pole.* The rebuilding of Jericho was preceded by the sacrifice of two sons of the chief builder, *Hiel,* which was seen as fulfillment of the curse pronounced by Joshua at its destruction (Josh 6.26).
17.1-24 Elijah's Challenge to Ahab and God's Care of the Prophet. *Elijah* (meaning "My God is Yahweh"), who came from *Gilead* (east of the Jordan), warned Ahab of a drought that God would send as judgment for the king's wickedness. At *the Wadi Cherith,* a seasonal stream that flowed into the Jordan from the east, birds of prey – *ravens* – provided the prophet with abundant food until the drought dried up the stream. The widow in *Zarephath* (on the sea-coast between Tyre and Sidon) agreed to feed Elijah, in spite of the seeming loss of meal and oil that she and her son faced. The continual replenishment of the food supply, as *the LORD* promised, and the restoration to life of her son persuaded the widow that Elijah was in truth *a man of God.*

18.1-19 Elijah Confronts Ahab and the Prophets of Baal. The administrator of Ahab's palace, Obadiah (whose name means, "servant of Yahweh"), who had earlier hidden the *prophets* of the LORD when Jezebel sought to kill them, now became the intermediary for *Elijah* to address his would-be killer, *Ahab*. Before all Israel there was to be a public encounter *at Mount Carmel* (overlooking the Mediterranean west of Galilee) between the power of Yahweh and the alleged powers of *Baal* and *Asherah* (or Astarte the fertility goddess). *Baal's prophets* prepared the sacrifice on their altar and implored their god to send fire and consume it, but there was no response. *Elijah...repaired the altar of the LORD* on Carmel, arranged the sacrifice and the wood, and then soaked it all repeatedly with water. Yet *the fire of the LORD fell*, and even the stone altar, the dust and the water were consumed. On Elijah's order, the priests of Baal were seized and killed by the *Wadi Kishon*, the major stream that empties from the Plain of Esdraelon past Mt. Carmel into the sea.

and do as you have said; but first make me a little cake of it and bring it to me, and afterwards make something for yourself and your son. 14 For thus says the LORD the God of Israel: The jar of meal will not be emptied and the jug of oil will not fail until the day that the LORD sends rain on the earth." 15 She went and did as Elijah said, so that she as well as he and her household ate for many days. 16 The jar of meal was not emptied, neither did the jug of oil fail, according to the word of the LORD that he spoke by Elijah.

Elijah Revives the Widow's Son

17 After this the son of the woman, the mistress of the house, became ill; his illness was so severe that there was no breath left in him. 18 She then said to Elijah, "What have you against me, O man of God? You have come to me to bring my sin to remembrance, and to cause the death of my son!" 19 But he said to her, "Give me your son." He took him from her bosom, carried him up into the upper chamber where he was lodging, and laid him on his own bed. 20 He cried out to the LORD, "O LORD my God, have you brought calamity even upon the widow with whom I am staying, by killing her son?" 21 Then he stretched himself upon the child three times, and cried out to the LORD, "O LORD my God, let this child's life come into him again." 22 The LORD listened to the voice of Elijah; the life of the child came into him again, and he revived. 23 Elijah took the child, brought him down from the upper chamber into the house, and gave him to his mother; then Elijah said, "See, your son is alive." 24 So the woman said to Elijah, "Now I know that you are a man of God, and that the word of the LORD in your mouth is truth."

Elijah's Message to Ahab

18 After many days the word of the LORD came to Elijah, in the third year of the drought,[l] saying, "Go, present yourself to Ahab; I will send rain on the earth." 2 So Elijah went to present himself to Ahab. The famine was severe in Samaria. 3 Ahab summoned Obadiah, who was in charge of the palace. (Now Obadiah revered the LORD greatly; 4 when Jezebel was killing off the prophets of the LORD, Obadiah took a hundred prophets, hid them fifty to a cave, and provided them with bread and water.) 5 Then Ahab said to Obadiah, "Go through the land to all the springs of water and to all the wadis; perhaps we may find grass to keep the horses and mules alive, and not lose some of the animals." 6 So they divided the land between them to pass through it; Ahab went in one direction by himself, and Obadiah went in another direction by himself.

7 As Obadiah was on the way, Elijah met him; Obadiah recognized him, fell on his face, and said, "Is it you, my lord Elijah?" 8 He answered him, "It is I. Go, tell your lord that Elijah is here." 9 And he said, "How have I sinned, that you would hand your servant over to Ahab, to kill me? 10 As the LORD your God lives, there is no nation or kingdom to which my lord has not sent to seek you; and when they would say, 'He is not here,' he would require an oath of the kingdom or nation, that they had not found you. 11 But now you say, 'Go, tell your lord that Elijah is here.' 12 As soon as I have gone from you, the spirit of the LORD will carry you I know not where; so, when I come and tell Ahab and he cannot find you, he will kill me, although I your servant have revered the LORD from my youth. 13 Has it not been told my lord what I did when Jezebel killed the prophets of the LORD, how I hid a hundred of the LORD's prophets fifty to a cave, and provided them with bread and water? 14 Yet now you say, 'Go, tell your lord that Elijah is here'; he will surely kill me." 15 Elijah said, "As the LORD of hosts lives, before whom I stand, I will surely show myself to him today." 16 So Obadiah went to meet Ahab, and told him; and Ahab went to meet Elijah.

17 When Ahab saw Elijah, Ahab said to him, "Is it you, you troubler of Israel?" 18 He answered, "I have not troubled Israel; but you have, and your father's house, because you have forsaken the commandments of the LORD and followed the Baals. 19 Now therefore have all Israel assemble for me at Mount Carmel, with the four hundred fifty prophets of Baal and the four hundred prophets of Asherah, who eat at Jezebel's table."

Elijah's Triumph over the Priests of Baal

20 So Ahab sent to all the Israelites, and assembled the prophets at Mount Carmel.

17.14 Lk 4.25,26
17.18 2 Kings 3.13
17.21 2 Kings 4.34,35; see Acts 20.10
17.22 Heb 11.25
17.24 Jn 3.2; 16.30
18.1 1 Kings 17.1; Lk 4.25; Jas 5.17
18.4 ver 13
18.7 2 Kings 1.6-8
18.10 1 Kings 17.1
18.12 2 Kings 2.16; Ezek 3.12,14; Acts 8.39
18.13 ver 4
18.15 1 Kings 17.1
18.17 1 Kings 21.20; Josh 7.25; see Acts 16.20
18.18 2 Chr 15.2; 1 Kings 16.31; 21.25,26
18.19 Josh 19.26; 1 Kings 16.33

[l] Heb lacks *of the drought*

[21]Elijah then came near to all the people,
and said, "How long will you go limping
with two different opinions? If the LORD is
God, follow him; but if Baal, then follow
him." The people did not answer him a
word. [22]Then Elijah said to the people, "I,
even I only, am left a prophet of the LORD;
but Baal's prophets number four hundred
fifty. [23]Let two bulls be given to us; let them
choose one bull for themselves, cut it in
pieces, and lay it on the wood, but put no
fire to it; I will prepare the other bull and
lay it on the wood, but put no fire to it.
[24]Then you call on the name of your god
and I will call on the name of the LORD; the
god who answers by fire is indeed God." All
the people answered, "Well spoken!" [25]Then
Elijah said to the prophets of Baal, "Choose
for yourselves one bull and prepare it first,
for you are many; then call on the name
of your god, but put no fire to it." [26]So they
took the bull that was given them, prepared
it, and called on the name of Baal from
morning until noon, crying, "O
Baal, answer us!" But there was no voice,
and no answer. They limped about the altar
that they had made. [27]At noon Elijah mocked
them, saying, "Cry aloud! Surely he is a
god; either he is meditating, or he has
wandered away, or he is on a journey, or
perhaps he is asleep and must be awakened." [28]Then they cried aloud and, as was
their custom, they cut themselves with
swords and lances until the blood gushed
out over them. [29]As midday passed, they
raved on until the time of the offering of the
oblation, but there was no voice, no answer, and no response.

30 Then Elijah said to all the people,
"Come closer to me"; and all the people
came closer to him. First he repaired the
altar of the LORD that had been thrown
down; [31]Elijah took twelve stones, according
to the number of the tribes of the sons of
Jacob, to whom the word of the LORD came,
saying, "Israel shall be your name"; [32]with
the stones he built an altar in the name of
the LORD. Then he made a trench around
the altar, large enough to contain two
measures of seed. [33]Next he put the wood
in order, cut the bull in pieces, and laid it
on the wood. He said, "Fill four jars with
water and pour it on the burnt offering and
on the wood." [34]Then he said, "Do it a
second time"; and they did it a second time.
Again he said, "Do it a third time"; and they
did it a third time, [35]so that the water ran
all around the altar, and filled the trench
also with water.

36 At the time of the offering of the
oblation, the prophet Elijah came near and
said, "O LORD, God of Abraham, Isaac, and
Israel, let it be known this day that you are
God in Israel, that I am your servant, and
that I have done all these things at your
bidding. [37]Answer me, O LORD, answer me,
so that this people may know that you, O
LORD, are God, and that you have turned
their hearts back." [38]Then the fire of the
LORD fell and consumed the burnt offering,
the wood, the stones, and the dust, and
even licked up the water that was in the
trench. [39]When all the people saw it, they
fell on their faces and said, "The LORD indeed
is God; the LORD indeed is God." [40]Elijah said
to them, "Seize the prophets of Baal; do not
let one of them escape." Then they seized
them; and Elijah brought them down to the
Wadi Kishon, and killed them there.

The Drought Ends

41 Elijah said to Ahab, "Go up, eat and
drink; for there is a sound of rushing rain."
[42]So Ahab went up to eat and to drink.
Elijah went up to the top of Carmel; there
he bowed himself down upon the earth and
put his face between his knees. [43]He said to
his servant, "Go up now, look toward the
sea." He went up and looked, and said,
"There is nothing." Then he said, "Go again
seven times." [44]At the seventh time he said,
"Look, a little cloud no bigger than a person's hand is rising out of the sea." Then
he said, "Go say to Ahab, 'Harness your
chariot and go down before the rain stops
you.' " [45]In a little while the heavens grew
black with clouds and wind; there was a
heavy rain. Ahab rode off and went to
Jezreel. [46]But the hand of the LORD was on
Elijah; he girded up his loins and ran in
front of Ahab to the entrance of Jezreel.

Elijah Flees from Jezebel

19 Ahab told Jezebel all that Elijah
had done, and how he had killed
all the prophets with the sword. [2]Then Jezebel
sent a messenger to Elijah, saying, "So may
the gods do to me, and more also, if I do
not make your life like the life of one of
them by this time tomorrow." [3]Then he was
afraid; he got up and fled for his life, and
came to Beer-sheba, which belongs to Judah;

18.21 2 Kings 17.41; Mt 6.24; Josh 24.15
18.22 1 Kings 19.10,14; ver 19
18.24 ver 38; see 1 Chr 21.26
18.26 Ps 115.5; Jer 10.5; 1 Cor 8.4; 12.2
18.28 Lev 19.28; Deut 14.1
18.29 ver 26
18.30 1 Kings 19.10,14
18.31 Gen 32.28; 35.10; 2 Kings 17.34
18.32 Col 3.17
18.33 Gen 22.9; Lev 1.6-8
18.36 Ex 3.6; 1 Kings 8.43; 2 Kings 19.19; Num 16.28
18.38 Lev 9.24; 1 Chr 21.26; 2 Chr 7.1
18.39 ver 21,24
18.40 Deut 13.5; 18.20; 2 Kings 10.24,25
18.42 ver 19,20; Jas 5.17,18
18.46 2 Kings 3.15; 4.29
19.1 1 Kings 18.40
19.2 1 Kings 20.10; 2 Kings 6.31

18.41-46 Clouds visible from the top of Mt. Carmel coming in off the Mediterranean signaled an end to the drought. *Ahab* hurried inland to the hills at *Jezreel*, but Elijah reached there first.
19.1-21 Elijah Flees and is Met by God at Horeb. Threatened by Jezebel with execution, Elijah fled south. Sustained by divinely provided food, he reached *Horeb* (another name for Sinai), where *the LORD* appeared to him, commissioning him to go to the arid area east of *Damascus*, where he was to anoint three individuals: *Hazael as king over Aram* (the Semitic people living in southern Syria); *Jehu...as king of Israel;* and *Elisha* as successor to him in the role of *prophet* who was to speak and act in God's behalf among his people. They were to slay the idolaters of Israel. The transfer of the *mantle* to Elisha symbolized his assumption of the new role, and the preparation of the feast symbolized his break with his family past.

20.1-34 Ahab Defeats the Invading Arameans. *Ben-hadad* and *the thirty-two kings* allied with him in the siege of *Samaria* became drunk and failed to respond to the attack led by *the young men who served [Israel's] district governors*, and the result was a great slaughter of the Arameans. Another attack by Ben-hadad on *Aphek* (which lay in the coastal hills between Joppa and Shechem) was repulsed, and *Ahab* agreed to let Ben-hadad live in exchange for the return of territory taken earlier from Israel. A prophet, pretending to be a soldier who failed to do his duty, warned *Ahab* of the consequences of his failure to have Ben-hadad killed.

he left his servant there.

4 But he himself went a day's journey into the wilderness, and came and sat down under a solitary broom tree. He asked that he might die: "It is enough; now, O LORD, take away my life, for I am no better than my ancestors." [5]Then he lay down under the broom tree and fell asleep. Suddenly an angel touched him and said to him, "Get up and eat." [6]He looked, and there at his head was a cake baked on hot stones, and a jar of water. He ate and drank, and lay down again. [7]The angel of the LORD came a second time, touched him, and said, "Get up and eat, otherwise the journey will be too much for you." [8]He got up, and ate and drank; then he went in the strength of that food forty days and forty nights to Horeb the mount of God. [9]At that place he came to a cave, and spent the night there.

Then the word of the LORD came to him, saying, "What are you doing here, Elijah?" [10]He answered, "I have been very zealous for the LORD, the God of hosts; for the Israelites have forsaken your covenant, thrown down your altars, and killed your prophets with the sword. I alone am left, and they are seeking my life, to take it away."

Elijah Meets God at Horeb

11 He said, "Go out and stand on the mountain before the LORD, for the LORD is about to pass by." Now there was a great wind, so strong that it was splitting mountains and breaking rocks in pieces before the LORD, but the LORD was not in the wind; and after the wind an earthquake, but the LORD was not in the earthquake; [12]and after the earthquake a fire, but the LORD was not in the fire; and after the fire a sound of sheer silence. [13]When Elijah heard it, he wrapped his face in his mantle and went out and stood at the entrance of the cave. Then there came a voice to him that said, "What are you doing here, Elijah?" [14]He answered, "I have been very zealous for the LORD, the God of hosts; for the Israelites have forsaken your covenant, thrown down your altars, and killed your prophets with the sword. I alone am left, and they are seeking my life, to take it away." [15]Then the LORD said to him, "Go, return on your way to the wilderness of Damascus; when you arrive, you shall anoint Hazael as king over Aram. [16]Also you shall anoint Jehu son of Nimshi as king over Israel; and you shall anoint Elisha son of Shaphat of Abel-meholah as prophet in your place. [17]Whoever escapes from the sword of Hazael, Jehu shall kill; and whoever escapes from the sword of Jehu, Elisha shall kill. [18]Yet I will leave seven thousand in Israel, all the knees that have not bowed to Baal, and every mouth that has not kissed him."

Elisha Becomes Elijah's Disciple

19 So he set out from there, and found Elisha son of Shaphat, who was plowing. There were twelve yoke of oxen ahead of him, and he was with the twelfth. Elijah passed by him and threw his mantle over him. [20]He left the oxen, ran after Elijah, and said, "Let me kiss my father and my mother, and then I will follow you." Then Elijah[m] said to him, "Go back again; for what have I done to you?" [21]He returned from following him, took the yoke of oxen, and slaughtered them; using the equipment from the oxen, he boiled their flesh, and gave it to the people, and they ate. Then he set out and followed Elijah, and became his servant.

Ahab's Wars with the Arameans

20 King Ben-hadad of Aram gathered all his army together; thirty-two kings were with him, along with horses and chariots. He marched against Samaria, laid siege to it, and attacked it. [2]Then he sent messengers into the city to King Ahab of Israel, and said to him: "Thus says Ben-hadad: [3]Your silver and gold are mine; your fairest wives and children also are mine." [4]The king of Israel answered, "As you say, my lord, O king, I am yours, and all that I have." [5]The messengers came again and said: "Thus says Ben-hadad: I sent to you, saying, 'Deliver to me your silver and gold, your wives and children'; [6]nevertheless I will send my servants to you tomorrow about this time, and they shall search your house and the houses of your servants, and lay hands on whatever pleases them,[n] and take it away."

7 Then the king of Israel called all the elders of the land, and said, "Look now! See how this man is seeking trouble; for he sent to me for my wives, my children, my silver, and my gold; and I did not refuse him."

19.4 Num 11.15; Jon 4.3,8
19.8 Ex 34.28; Deut 9.9-11,18; Mt 4.2; Ex 3.1
19.10 Rom 11.3; 1 Kings 18.4,22
19.11 Ex 24.12; Ezek 1.4; 37.7
19.13 Ex 3.6; ver 9
19.14 ver 10
19.15 2 Kings 8.12,13
19.16 2 Kings 9.1-3; ver 19-21; 2 Kings 2.9,15
19.17 2 Kings 8.12; 9.14ff; 13.3,22
19.18 Rom 11.4; Hos 13.2
19.19 2 Kings 2.8,13
19.20 Mt 8.21,22; Lk 9.61,62
19.21 2 Sam 24.22
20.1 1 Kings 15.18,20; 2 Kings 6.24; 1 Kings 22.31; 2 Kings 6.24-29
20.7 2 Kings 5.7

[m] Heb *he* [n] Gk Syr Vg: Heb *you*

20.10 1 Kings 19.2
20.11 Prov 27.1
20.12 ver 16
20.13 ver 28
20.16 ver 12
20.18 2 Kings 14.8-12
20.22 ver 13,26; 2 Sam 11.1
20.23 1 Kings 14.23
20.26 ver 22; 2 Kings 13.7
20.28 ver 13
20.30 ver 26; 1 Kings 22.25; 2 Chr 18.24
20.31 Gen 37.34
20.32 ver 3-6
20.34 1 Kings 15.20

8 Then all the elders and all the people said to him, "Do not listen or consent." 9 So he said to the messengers of Ben-hadad, "Tell my lord the king: All that you first demanded of your servant I will do; but this thing I cannot do." The messengers left and brought him word again. 10 Ben-hadad sent to him and said, "The gods do so to me, and more also, if the dust of Samaria will provide a handful for each of the people who follow me." 11 The king of Israel answered, "Tell him: One who puts on armor should not brag like one who takes it off." 12 When Ben-hadad heard this message—now he had been drinking with the kings in the booths—he said to his men, "Take your positions!" And they took their positions against the city.

Prophetic Opposition to Ahab

13 Then a certain prophet came up to King Ahab of Israel and said, "Thus says the LORD, Have you seen all this great multitude? Look, I will give it into your hand today; and you shall know that I am the LORD." 14 Ahab said, "By whom?" He said, "Thus says the LORD, By the young men who serve the district governors." Then he said, "Who shall begin the battle?" He answered, "You." 15 Then he mustered the young men who serve the district governors, two hundred thirty-two; after them he mustered all the people of Israel, seven thousand.

16 They went out at noon, while Ben-hadad was drinking himself drunk in the booths, he and the thirty-two kings allied with him. 17 The young men who serve the district governors went out first. Ben-hadad had sent out scouts,[o] and they reported to him, "Men have come out from Samaria." 18 He said, "If they have come out for peace, take them alive; if they have come out for war, take them alive."

19 But these had already come out of the city: the young men who serve the district governors, and the army that followed them. 20 Each killed his man; the Arameans fled and Israel pursued them, but King Ben-hadad of Aram escaped on a horse with the cavalry. 21 The king of Israel went out, attacked the horses and chariots, and defeated the Arameans with a great slaughter.

22 Then the prophet approached the king of Israel and said to him, "Come, strengthen yourself, and consider well what you have to do; for in the spring the king of Aram will come up against you."

The Arameans Are Defeated

23 The servants of the king of Aram said to him, "Their gods are gods of the hills, and so they were stronger than we; but let us fight against them in the plain, and surely we shall be stronger than they. 24 Also do this: remove the kings, each from his post, and put commanders in place of them; 25 and muster an army like the army that you have lost, horse for horse, and chariot for chariot; then we will fight against them in the plain, and surely we shall be stronger than they." He heeded their voice, and did so.

26 In the spring Ben-hadad mustered the Arameans and went up to Aphek to fight against Israel. 27 After the Israelites had been mustered and provisioned, they went out to engage them; the people of Israel encamped opposite them like two little flocks of goats, while the Arameans filled the country. 28 A man of God approached and said to the king of Israel, "Thus says the LORD: Because the Arameans have said, 'The LORD is a god of the hills but he is not a god of the valleys,' therefore I will give all this great multitude into your hand, and you shall know that I am the LORD." 29 They encamped opposite one another seven days. Then on the seventh day the battle began; the Israelites killed one hundred thousand Aramean foot soldiers in one day. 30 The rest fled into the city of Aphek; and the wall fell on twenty-seven thousand men that were left.

Ben-hadad also fled, and entered the city to hide. 31 His servants said to him, "Look, we have heard that the kings of the house of Israel are merciful kings; let us put sackcloth around our waists and ropes on our heads, and go out to the king of Israel; perhaps he will spare your life." 32 So they tied sackcloth around their waists, put ropes on their heads, went to the king of Israel, and said, "Your servant Ben-hadad says, 'Please let me live.' " And he said, "Is he still alive? He is my brother." 33 Now the men were watching for an omen; they quickly took it up from him and said, "Yes, Ben-hadad is your brother." Then he said, "Go and bring him." So Ben-hadad came out to him; and he had him come up into the chariot. 34 Ben-hadad[p] said to him, "I will

[o] Heb lacks *scouts* [p] Heb *He*

21.1-28 The Consequences of Ahab's Coveting the Vineyard of Naboth.
21.1-16 Naboth's refusal to exchange his ancestral vineyard for another, as requested by Ahab, led Jezebel to plan a false accusation against him which resulted in his execution.
21.17-28 Elijah charged Ahab with this crime, warning him of the judgment of God that would result in his own death and the termination of his family dynasty, as well as the violent death of Jezebel. Ahab's penitence postponed the tragedy. 21.25 is a Deuteronomic parenthesis showing why Ahab was brought under judgment.

restore the towns that my father took from your father; and you may establish bazaars for yourself in Damascus, as my father did in Samaria." The king of Israel responded,[q] "I will let you go on those terms." So he made a treaty with him and let him go.

A Prophet Condemns Ahab

35 At the command of the LORD a certain member of a company of prophets[r] said to another, "Strike me!" But the man refused to strike him. [36]Then he said to him, "Because you have not obeyed the voice of the LORD, as soon as you have left me, a lion will kill you." And when he had left him, a lion met him and killed him. [37]Then he found another man and said, "Strike me!" So the man hit him, striking and wounding him. [38]Then the prophet departed, and waited for the king along the road, disguising himself with a bandage over his eyes. [39]As the king passed by, he cried to the king and said, "Your servant went out into the thick of the battle; then a soldier turned and brought a man to me, and said, 'Guard this man; if he is missing, your life shall be given for his life, or else you shall pay a talent of silver.' [40]While your servant was busy here and there, he was gone." The king of Israel said to him, "So shall your judgment be; you yourself have decided it." [41]Then he quickly took the bandage away from his eyes. The king of Israel recognized him as one of the prophets. [42]Then he said to him, "Thus says the LORD, 'Because you have let the man go whom I had devoted to destruction, therefore your life shall be for his life, and your people for his people.' " [43]The king of Israel set out toward home, resentful and sullen, and came to Samaria.

Naboth's Vineyard

21 Later the following events took place: Naboth the Jezreelite had a vineyard in Jezreel, beside the palace of King Ahab of Samaria. [2]And Ahab said to Naboth, "Give me your vineyard, so that I may have it for a vegetable garden, because it is near my house; I will give you a better vineyard for it; or, if it seems good to you, I will give you its value in money." [3]But Naboth said to Ahab, "The LORD forbid that I should give you my ancestral inheritance." [4]Ahab went home resentful and sullen because of what Naboth the Jezreelite had said to him; for he had said, "I will not give you my ancestral inheritance." He lay down on his bed, turned away his face, and would not eat.

5 His wife Jezebel came to him and said, "Why are you so depressed that you will not eat?" [6]He said to her, "Because I spoke to Naboth the Jezreelite and said to him, 'Give me your vineyard for money; or else, if you prefer, I will give you another vineyard for it'; but he answered, 'I will not give you my vineyard.' " [7]His wife Jezebel said to him, "Do you now govern Israel? Get up, eat some food, and be cheerful; I will give you the vineyard of Naboth the Jezreelite."

8 So she wrote letters in Ahab's name and sealed them with his seal; she sent the letters to the elders and the nobles who lived with Naboth in his city. [9]She wrote in the letters, "Proclaim a fast, and seat Naboth at the head of the assembly; [10]seat two scoundrels opposite him, and have them bring a charge against him, saying, 'You have cursed God and the king.' Then take him out, and stone him to death." [11]The men of his city, the elders and the nobles who lived in his city, did as Jezebel had sent word to them. Just as it was written in the letters that she had sent to them, [12]they proclaimed a fast and seated Naboth at the head of the assembly. [13]The two scoundrels came in and sat opposite him; and the scoundrels brought a charge against Naboth, in the presence of the people, saying, "Naboth cursed God and the king." So they took him outside the city, and stoned him to death. [14]Then they sent to Jezebel, saying, "Naboth has been stoned; he is dead."

15 As soon as Jezebel heard that Naboth had been stoned and was dead, Jezebel said to Ahab, "Go, take possession of the vineyard of Naboth the Jezreelite, which he refused to give you for money; for Naboth is not alive, but dead." [16]As soon as Ahab heard that Naboth was dead, Ahab set out to go down to the vineyard of Naboth the Jezreelite, to take possession of it.

Elijah Pronounces God's Sentence

17 Then the word of the LORD came to Elijah the Tishbite, saying: [18]Go down to meet King Ahab of Israel, who rules[s] in Samaria; he is now in the vineyard of Naboth, where he has gone to take possession. [19]You shall say to him, "Thus says the

20.35 2 Kings 2.3-7; 1 Kings 13.17,18
20.36 1 Kings 13.24
20.39 2 Kings 10.24
20.42 ver 39; 1 Kings 22.31-37
20.43 1 Kings 21.4
21.1 1 Kings 18.45,46
21.2 1 Sam 8.14
21.3 Lev 25.23; Num 36.7; Ezek 46.18
21.4 1 Kings 20.43
21.7 1 Sam 8.14
21.8 Esth 3.12; 8.8,10
21.10 Ex 22.28; Lev 24.15,16; Acts 6.11
21.13 2 Kings 9.26
21.17 Ps 9.12
21.18 1 Kings 16.29
21.19 1 Kings 22.38; 2 Kings 9.8

[q] Heb lacks *The king of Israel responded* [r] Heb *of the sons of the prophets* [s] Heb *who is*

21.20 1 Kings 18.17; ver 25
21.21 1 Kings 14.10; 2 Kings 9.8
21.22 1 Kings 15.29
21.23 2 Kings 9.10,30-37
21.24 1 Kings 14.11; 16.4
21.25 ver 20; 1 Kings 16.30-33
21.26 Gen 15.16; Lev 18.25-30
21.27 2 Sam 3.31; 2 Kings 6.30
21.29 2 Kings 9.25
22.2 2 Chr 18.2ff; 1 Kings 15.24
22.3 Deut 4.43; Josh 21.38
22.4 2 Kings 3.7
22.6 1 Kings 18.19
22.7 2 Kings 3.11
22.10 ver 6
22.11 Zech 1.18-21; Deut 33.17
22.14 1 Kings 18.10,15; Num 22.18; 24.13
22.15 ver 12
22.17 ver 34-36
22.18 ver 8

LORD: Have you killed, and also taken possession?" You shall say to him, "Thus says
the LORD: In the place where dogs licked up
the blood of Naboth, dogs will also lick up
your blood."
20 Ahab said to Elijah, "Have you found
me, O my enemy?" He answered, "I have
found you. Because you have sold yourself
to do what is evil in the sight of the LORD,
21I will bring disaster on you; I will consume you, and will cut off from Ahab every
male, bond or free, in Israel; 22and I will
make your house like the house of Jeroboam son of Nebat, and like the house of
Baasha son of Ahijah, because you have
provoked me to anger and have caused
Israel to sin. 23Also concerning Jezebel the
LORD said, 'The dogs shall eat Jezebel within
the bounds of Jezreel.' 24Anyone belonging
to Ahab who dies in the city the dogs shall
eat; and anyone of his who dies in the open
country the birds of the air shall eat."
25 (Indeed, there was no one like Ahab,
who sold himself to do what was evil in the
sight of the LORD, urged on by his wife
Jezebel. 26He acted most abominably in going
after idols, as the Amorites had done, whom
the LORD drove out before the Israelites.)
27 When Ahab heard those words, he
tore his clothes and put sackcloth over his
bare flesh; he fasted, lay in the sackcloth,
and went about dejectedly. 28Then the word
of the LORD came to Elijah the Tishbite:
29"Have you seen how Ahab has humbled
himself before me? Because he has humbled
himself before me, I will not bring the disaster in his days; but in his son's days I will
bring the disaster on his house."

Joint Campaign with Judah against Aram

22 For three years Aram and Israel
continued without war. 2But in
the third year King Jehoshaphat of Judah
came down to the king of Israel. 3The king
of Israel said to his servants, "Do you know
that Ramoth-gilead belongs to us, yet we
are doing nothing to take it out of the hand
of the king of Aram?" 4He said to
Jehoshaphat, "Will you go with me to battle
at Ramoth-gilead?" Jehoshaphat replied to
the king of Israel, "I am as you are; my
people are your people, my horses are your
horses."
5 But Jehoshaphat also said to the king
of Israel, "Inquire first for the word of the
LORD." 6Then the king of Israel gathered the
prophets together, about four hundred of
them, and said to them, "Shall I go to battle
against Ramoth-gilead, or shall I refrain?"
They said, "Go up; for the LORD will give it
into the hand of the king." 7But Jehoshaphat
said, "Is there no other prophet of the LORD
here of whom we may inquire?" 8The king
of Israel said to Jehoshaphat, "There is still
one other by whom we may inquire of the
LORD, Micaiah son of Imlah; but I hate him,
for he never prophesies anything favorable
about me, but only disaster." Jehoshaphat
said, "Let the king not say such a thing."
9Then the king of Israel summoned an officer and said, "Bring quickly Micaiah son
of Imlah." 10Now the king of Israel and King
Jehoshaphat of Judah were sitting on their
thrones, arrayed in their robes, at the threshing floor at the entrance of the gate of
Samaria; and all the prophets were prophesying before them. 11Zedekiah son of
Chenaanah made for himself horns of iron,
and he said, "Thus says the LORD: With
these you shall gore the Arameans until
they are destroyed." 12All the prophets were
prophesying the same and saying, "Go up
to Ramoth-gilead and triumph; the LORD
will give it into the hand of the king."

Micaiah Predicts Failure

13 The messenger who had gone to
summon Micaiah said to him, "Look, the
words of the prophets with one accord are
favorable to the king; let your word be like
the word of one of them, and speak
favorably." 14But Micaiah said, "As the LORD
lives, whatever the LORD says to me, that I
will speak."
15 When he had come to the king, the
king said to him, "Micaiah, shall we go to
Ramoth-gilead to battle, or shall we refrain?" He answered him, "Go up and triumph; the LORD will give it into the hand
of the king." 16But the king said to him,
"How many times must I make you swear
to tell me nothing but the truth in the name
of the LORD?" 17Then Micaiah[t] said, "I saw
all Israel scattered on the mountains, like
sheep that have no shepherd; and the LORD
said, 'These have no master; let each one
go home in peace.' " 18The king of Israel
said to Jehoshaphat, "Did I not tell you that
he would not prophesy anything favorable
about me, but only disaster?"

22.1-40 The Disastrous Joint Campaign of Israel and Judah against the Arameans.
22.1-40 King Jehoshaphat of Judah plotted with *Ahab* of Israel to regain from the Arameans control of *Ramoth-gilead* (probably located east of Shechem and across the Jordan Valley). The court prophets encouraged the attempt, but the prophet *Micaiah,* as expected and only reluctantly, foretold the death of Ahab in the attack, and hence was insulted and imprisoned. The focus of the Aramean defenders was *Ahab,* who was fatally wounded and buried in his capital, Samaria. The scene of the dogs licking up Ahab's blood is seen as a fulfillment of Elijah's prophecy (21.24).

[t] Heb *he*

22.41-50 The reign of *Jehoshaphat* (which means, "Yahweh establishes justice" or "sets matters right") was from 873 to 849. The lucrative trade in gold from *Ophir* came to a halt in his reign. Jehoram succeeded him as king of Judah.

19 Then Micaiah[u] said, "Therefore hear the word of the LORD: I saw the LORD sitting on his throne, with all the host of heaven standing beside him to the right and to the left of him. [20]And the LORD said, 'Who will entice Ahab, so that he may go up and fall at Ramoth-gilead?' Then one said one thing, and another said another, [21]until a spirit came forward and stood before the LORD, saying, 'I will entice him.' [22]'How?' the LORD asked him. He replied, 'I will go out and be a lying spirit in the mouth of all his prophets.' Then the LORD[u] said, 'You are to entice him, and you shall succeed; go out and do it.' [23]So you see, the LORD has put a lying spirit in the mouth of all these your prophets; the LORD has decreed disaster for you."

24 Then Zedekiah son of Chenaanah came up to Micaiah, slapped him on the cheek, and said, "Which way did the spirit of the LORD pass from me to speak to you?" [25]Micaiah replied, "You will find out on that day when you go in to hide in an inner chamber." [26]The king of Israel then ordered, "Take Micaiah, and return him to Amon the governor of the city and to Joash the king's son, [27]and say, 'Thus says the king: Put this fellow in prison, and feed him on reduced rations of bread and water until I come in peace.' " [28]Micaiah said, "If you return in peace, the LORD has not spoken by me." And he said, "Hear, you peoples, all of you!"

Defeat and Death of Ahab

29 So the king of Israel and King Jehoshaphat of Judah went up to Ramoth-gilead. [30]The king of Israel said to Jehoshaphat, "I will disguise myself and go into battle, but you wear your robes." So the king of Israel disguised himself and went into battle. [31]Now the king of Aram had commanded the thirty-two captains of his chariots, "Fight with no one small or great, but only with the king of Israel." [32]When the captains of the chariots saw Jehoshaphat, they said, "It is surely the king of Israel." So they turned to fight against him; and Jehoshaphat cried out. [33]When the captains of the chariots saw that it was not the king of Israel, they turned back from pursuing him. [34]But a certain man drew his bow and unknowingly struck the king of Israel between the scale armor and the breastplate; so he said to the driver of his chariot, "Turn around, and carry me out of the battle, for I am wounded." [35]The battle grew hot that day, and the king was propped up in his chariot facing the Arameans, until at evening he died; the blood from the wound had flowed into the bottom of the chariot. [36]Then about sunset a shout went through the army, "Every man to his city, and every man to his country!"

37 So the king died, and was brought to Samaria; they buried the king in Samaria. [38]They washed the chariot by the pool of Samaria; the dogs licked up his blood, and the prostitutes washed themselves in it,[v] according to the word of the LORD that he had spoken. [39]Now the rest of the acts of Ahab, and all that he did, and the ivory house that he built, and all the cities that he built, are they not written in the Book of the Annals of the Kings of Israel? [40]So Ahab slept with his ancestors; and his son Ahaziah succeeded him.

Jehoshaphat Reigns over Judah

41 Jehoshaphat son of Asa began to reign over Judah in the fourth year of King Ahab of Israel. [42]Jehoshaphat was thirty-five years old when he began to reign, and he reigned twenty-five years in Jerusalem. His mother's name was Azubah daughter of Shilhi. [43]He walked in all the way of his father Asa; he did not turn aside from it, doing what was right in the sight of the LORD; yet the high places were not taken away, and the people still sacrificed and offered incense on the high places. [44]Jehoshaphat also made peace with the king of Israel.

45 Now the rest of the acts of Jehoshaphat, and his power that he showed, and how he waged war, are they not written in the Book of the Annals of the Kings of Judah? [46]The remnant of the male temple prostitutes who were still in the land in the days of his father Asa, he exterminated.

47 There was no king in Edom; a deputy was king. [48]Jehoshaphat made ships of the Tarshish type to go to Ophir for gold; but they did not go, for the ships were wrecked at Ezion-geber. [49]Then Ahaziah son of Ahab said to Jehoshaphat, "Let my servants go with your servants in the ships," but Jehoshaphat was not willing. [50]Jehoshaphat slept with his ancestors and was buried with his ancestors in the city of his father David; his son Jehoram succeeded him.

[u] Heb *he* [v] Heb lacks *in it*

22.19 Isa 6.1; Dan 7.9,10

22.22 Judg 9.23; 1 Sam 16.14; 18.10; 19.9; 2 Thess 2.11

22.23 Ezek 14.9

22.24 2 Chr 18.23

22.25 1 Kings 20.30

22.27 2 Chr 18.25-27

22.28 Deut 18.22

22.29 ver 3,4

22.30 2 Chr 25.32

22.31 2 Chr 18.30

22.32 2 Chr 18.31

22.38 1 Kings 21.19

22.39 Am 3.15

22.41 2 Chr 20.31

22.43 2 Chr 17.3; 1 Kings 15.14; 2 Kings 12.3

22.44 2 Chr 19.2

22.45 2 Chr 20.34

22.46 1 Kings 14.24; 15.12

22.47 2 Sam 8.14; 2 Kings 3.9

22.48 2 Chr 20.35ff; 1 Kings 10.22

22.50 2 Chr 21.1

22.51 ver 40
22.52 1 Kings 15.26; 21.25
22.53 1 Kings 16.30-32

Ahaziah Reigns over Israel

51 Ahaziah son of Ahab began to reign over Israel in Samaria in the seventeenth year of King Jehoshaphat of Judah; he reigned two years over Israel. 52 He did what was evil in the sight of the LORD, and walked in the way of his father and mother, and in the way of Jeroboam son of Nebat, who caused Israel to sin. 53 He served Baal and worshiped him; he provoked the LORD, the God of Israel, to anger, just as his father had done.

22.51-53 Ahaziah succeeded Ahab as king of Israel, his brief reign beginning in 850 and ending in 849, and characterized by reversion to the worship of Baal.

2 KINGS

See the Introductions, pp. 3, 38, and 43-44 above.

1.1 2 Sam 8.2; 2 Kings 3.5
1.2 ver 3,6; Mt 10.25; see 2 Kings 8.7-10
1.4 ver 6,16
1.8 Zech 13.4; Mt 3.4
1.10 1 Kings 18.36-38; Lk 9.54
1.13 1 Sam 26.21; Ps 72.14
1.15 ver 3
1.16 ver 3
1.17 2 Kings 3.1; 8.16

Elijah Denounces Ahaziah

1 After the death of Ahab, Moab rebelled against Israel.

2 Ahaziah had fallen through the lattice in his upper chamber in Samaria, and lay injured; so he sent messengers, telling them, "Go, inquire of Baal-zebub, the god of Ekron, whether I shall recover from this injury." 3 But the angel of the LORD said to Elijah the Tishbite, "Get up, go to meet the messengers of the king of Samaria, and say to them, 'Is it because there is no God in Israel that you are going to inquire of Baal-zebub, the god of Ekron?' 4 Now therefore thus says the LORD, 'You shall not leave the bed to which you have gone, but you shall surely die.' " So Elijah went.

5 The messengers returned to the king, who said to them, "Why have you returned?" 6 They answered him, "There came a man to meet us, who said to us, 'Go back to the king who sent you, and say to him: Thus says the LORD: Is it because there is no God in Israel that you are sending to inquire of Baal-zebub, the god of Ekron? Therefore you shall not leave the bed to which you have gone, but shall surely die.' " 7 He said to them, "What sort of man was he who came to meet you and told you these things?" 8 They answered him, "A hairy man, with a leather belt around his waist." He said, "It is Elijah the Tishbite."

9 Then the king sent to him a captain of fifty with his fifty men. He went up to Elijah, who was sitting on the top of a hill, and said to him, "O man of God, the king says, 'Come down.' " 10 But Elijah answered the captain of fifty, "If I am a man of God, let fire come down from heaven and consume you and your fifty." Then fire came down from heaven, and consumed him and his fifty.

11 Again the king sent to him another captain of fifty with his fifty. He went up[a] and said to him, "O man of God, this is the king's order: Come down quickly!" 12 But Elijah answered them, "If I am a man of God, let fire come down from heaven and consume you and your fifty." Then the fire of God came down from heaven and consumed him and his fifty.

13 Again the king sent the captain of a third fifty with his fifty. So the third captain of fifty went up, and came and fell on his knees before Elijah, and entreated him, "O man of God, please let my life, and the life of these fifty servants of yours, be precious in your sight. 14 Look, fire came down from heaven and consumed the two former captains of fifty men with their fifties; but now let my life be precious in your sight." 15 Then the angel of the LORD said to Elijah, "Go down with him; do not be afraid of him." So he set out and went down with him to the king, 16 and said to him, "Thus says the LORD: Because you have sent messengers to inquire of Baal-zebub, the god of Ekron,—is it because there is no God in Israel to inquire of his word?—therefore you shall not leave the bed to which you have gone, but you shall surely die."

Death of Ahaziah

17 So he died according to the word of the LORD that Elijah had spoken. His brother,[b] Jehoram succeeded him as king in the second year of King Jehoram son of Jehoshaphat

1.1-18 Elijah Predicts the Death of Ahaziah. Ahaziah, king of Israel, sent messengers to inquire of *Baal-zebub, the god of Ekron* (on the coastal plain of Philistia) whether he would recover from a severe injury. They are told by *Elijah* that they should have consulted *the God in Israel,* and that Ahaziah will not recover. Other military groups are sent to Elijah, presumably to capture him, but are struck dead. The message from Elijah to the third such group is that the king will die, and he does, to be succeeded by his brother, Jehoram.

[a] Gk Compare verses 9, 13: Heb *He answered* [b] Gk Syr: Heb lacks *His brother*

2.1-18 Elijah Ascends to Heaven and is Succeeded by Elisha. The earlier association of Elijah with Elisha is noted in 1 Kings 19-21, in which the enabling power of Elijah's *mantle* is described. After traveling with Elijah from the sacred sites in the hill country of Benjamin (*Gilgal* and *Bethel*), Elisha descends with him to the Jordan Valley, where the mantle parts the waters as the ark did at the time of Israel's initial entry into the land (Josh 3.14-17). Elijah is taken up to God in a *chariot of fire*, while Elisha picks up the powerful *mantle of Elijah*, which also conveys *the Spirit*. The search to find the body of Elijah is in vain.
2.19-25 The miraculous powers of Elisha are both beneficent (purifying the water source in Jericho) and harmful (causing the death of the children who teased him). His destination was the capital of the northern kingdom: Samaria.

of Judah, because Ahaziah had no son.
[18]Now the rest of the acts of Ahaziah that
he did, are they not written in the Book of
the Annals of the Kings of Israel?

Elijah Ascends to Heaven

2 Now when the LORD was about to
take Elijah up to heaven by a whirlwind, Elijah and Elisha were on their way
from Gilgal. [2]Elijah said to Elisha, "Stay
here; for the LORD has sent me as far as
Bethel." But Elisha said, "As the LORD lives,
and as you yourself live, I will not leave
you." So they went down to Bethel. [3]The
company of prophets[c] who were in Bethel
came out to Elisha, and said to him, "Do
you know that today the LORD will take
your master away from you?" And he said,
"Yes, I know; keep silent."
4 Elijah said to him, "Elisha, stay here;
for the LORD has sent me to Jericho." But he
said, "As the LORD lives, and as you yourself
live, I will not leave you." So they came to
Jericho. [5]The company of prophets[c] who
were at Jericho drew near to Elisha, and
said to him, "Do you know that today the
LORD will take your master away from you?"
And he answered, "Yes, I know; be silent."
6 Then Elijah said to him, "Stay here; for
the LORD has sent me to the Jordan." But he
said, "As the LORD lives, and as you yourself
live, I will not leave you." So the two of
them went on. [7]Fifty men of the company
of prophets[c] also went, and stood at some
distance from them, as they both were standing by the Jordan. [8]Then Elijah took his
mantle and rolled it up, and struck the
water; the water was parted to the one side
and to the other, until the two of them
crossed on dry ground.
9 When they had crossed, Elijah said to
Elisha, "Tell me what I may do for you,
before I am taken from you." Elisha said,
"Please let me inherit a double share of
your spirit." [10]He responded, "You have
asked a hard thing; yet, if you see me as I
am being taken from you, it will be granted
you; if not, it will not." [11]As they continued
walking and talking, a chariot of fire and
horses of fire separated the two of them, and
Elijah ascended in a whirlwind into heaven.
[12]Elisha kept watching and crying out, "Father, father! The chariots of Israel and its
horsemen!" But when he could no longer
see him, he grasped his own clothes and
tore them in two pieces.

Elisha Succeeds Elijah

13 He picked up the mantle of Elijah that
had fallen from him, and went back and
stood on the bank of the Jordan. [14]He took
the mantle of Elijah that had fallen from
him, and struck the water, saying, "Where
is the LORD, the God of Elijah?" When he
had struck the water, the water was parted
to the one side and to the other, and Elisha
went over.
15 When the company of prophets[c] who
were at Jericho saw him at a distance, they
declared, "The spirit of Elijah rests on Elisha."
They came to meet him and bowed to the
ground before him. [16]They said to him, "See
now, we have fifty strong men among your
servants; please let them go and seek your
master; it may be that the spirit of the LORD
has caught him up and thrown him down
on some mountain or into some valley." He
responded, "No, do not send them." [17]But
when they urged him until he was ashamed,
he said, "Send them." So they sent fifty men
who searched for three days but did not find
him. [18]When they came back to him (he
had remained at Jericho), he said to them,
"Did I not say to you, Do not go?"

Elisha Performs Miracles

19 Now the people of the city said to
Elisha, "The location of this city is good, as
my lord sees; but the water is bad, and the
land is unfruitful." [20]He said, "Bring me a
new bowl, and put salt in it." So they
brought it to him. [21]Then he went to the
spring of water and threw the salt into it,
and said, "Thus says the LORD, I have made
this water wholesome; from now on neither
death nor miscarriage shall come from it."
[22]So the water has been wholesome to this
day, according to the word that Elisha spoke.
23 He went up from there to Bethel; and
while he was going up on the way, some
small boys came out of the city and jeered
at him, saying, "Go away, baldhead! Go
away, baldhead!" [24]When he turned around
and saw them, he cursed them in the name
of the LORD. Then two she-bears came out
of the woods and mauled forty-two of the
boys. [25]From there he went on to Mount
Carmel, and then returned to Samaria.

[c] Heb *sons of the prophets*

2.1 Gen 5.24; Heb 11.5; 1 Kings 19.21
2.2 Ruth 1.15,16; ver 4,6; 1 Sam 1.26; 2 Kings 4.30
2.3 ver 5,7,15; 2 Kings 4.1,38
2.4 ver 2; Josh 6.26
2.5 ver 3
2.6 ver 3; Josh 3.8,15-17
2.7 ver 15,16
2.8 1 Kings 19.13,19; ver 14; Ex 14.21,22
2.11 2 Kings 6.17; Ps 104.4
2.12 2 Kings 13.14
2.14 ver 8
2.15 ver 7
2.16 1 Kings 18.12; Acts 8.39
2.17 2 Kings 8.11
2.21 Ex 15.25; 2 Kings 4.41; 6.6
2.24 see Neh 13.25-27
2.25 2 Kings 4.25; 1 Kings 18.19,20

3.1 2 Kings 1.17
3.2 2 Kings 10.18,26-28; 1 Kings 16.31,32
3.3 1 Kings 12.28-32; 14.9,16
3.4 2 Sam 8.2; Isa 16.1
3.5 2 Kings 1.1
3.7 1 Kings 22.4
3.9 ver 1,7; 1 Kings 22.47
3.11 1 Kings 22.7; 19.21
13.13 Ezek 14.3-5; 1 Kings 18.19
3.14 1 Kings 17.1; 2 Kings 5.16
3.15 1 Sam 16.23; Ezek 1.3
3.19 ver 25
3.20 Ex 29.39,40
3.21 Gen 19.37
3.25 ver 19; Isa 16.7,11; Jer 48.31,36
3.27 Am 2.1; Mic 6.7

Jehoram Reigns over Israel

3 In the eighteenth year of King
Jehoshaphat of Judah, Jehoram son of
Ahab became king over Israel in Samaria;
he reigned twelve years. [2]He did what was
evil in the sight of the LORD, though not like
his father and mother, for he removed the
pillar of Baal that his father had made.
[3]Nevertheless he clung to the sin of Jeroboam son of Nebat, which he caused Israel
to commit; he did not depart from it.

War with Moab

4 Now King Mesha of Moab was a sheep
breeder, who used to deliver to the king of
Israel one hundred thousand lambs, and
the wool of one hundred thousand rams.
[5]But when Ahab died, the king of Moab
rebelled against the king of Israel. [6]So King
Jehoram marched out of Samaria at that
time and mustered all Israel. [7]As he went
he sent word to King Jehoshaphat of Judah,
"The king of Moab has rebelled against me;
will you go with me to battle against Moab?"
He answered, "I will; I am with you, my
people are your people, my horses are your
horses." [8]Then he asked, "By which way
shall we march?" Jehoram answered, "By
the way of the wilderness of Edom."

9 So the king of Israel, the king of Judah,
and the king of Edom set out; and when
they had made a roundabout march of
seven days, there was no water for the
army or for the animals that were with
them. [10]Then the king of Israel said, "Alas!
The LORD has summoned us, three kings,
only to be handed over to Moab." [11]But
Jehoshaphat said, "Is there no prophet of
the LORD here, through whom we may
inquire of the LORD?" Then one of the servants of the king of Israel answered, "Elisha
son of Shaphat, who used to pour water on
the hands of Elijah, is here." [12]Jehoshaphat
said, "The word of the LORD is with him."
So the king of Israel and Jehoshaphat and
the king of Edom went down to him.

13 Elisha said to the king of Israel, "What
have I to do with you? Go to your father's
prophets or to your mother's." But the king
of Israel said to him, "No; it is the LORD who
has summoned us, three kings, only to be
handed over to Moab." [14]Elisha said, "As
the LORD of hosts lives, whom I serve, were
it not that I have regard for King Jehoshaphat
of Judah, I would give you neither a look
nor a glance. [15]But get me a musician."
And then, while the musician was playing,
the power of the LORD came on him. [16]And
he said, "Thus says the LORD, 'I will make
this wadi full of pools.' [17]For thus says the
LORD, 'You shall see neither wind nor rain,
but the wadi shall be filled with water, so
that you shall drink, you, your cattle, and
your animals.' [18]This is only a trifle in the
sight of the LORD, for he will also hand Moab
over to you. [19]You shall conquer every
fortified city and every choice city; every
good tree you shall fell, all springs of water
you shall stop up, and every good piece of
land you shall ruin with stones." [20]The next
day, about the time of the morning offering,
suddenly water began to flow from the
direction of Edom, until the country was
filled with water.

21 When all the Moabites heard that the
kings had come up to fight against them,
all who were able to put on armor, from the
youngest to the oldest, were called out and
were drawn up at the frontier. [22]When they
rose early in the morning, and the sun
shone upon the water, the Moabites saw
the water opposite them as red as blood.
[23]They said, "This is blood; the kings must
have fought together, and killed one another. Now then, Moab, to the spoil!" [24]But
when they came to the camp of Israel, the
Israelites rose up and attacked the Moabites,
who fled before them; as they entered Moab
they continued the attack.[d] [25]The cities they
overturned, and on every good piece of land
everyone threw a stone, until it was covered; every spring of water they stopped up,
and every good tree they felled. Only at Kir-
hareseth did the stone walls remain, until
the slingers surrounded and attacked it.
[26]When the king of Moab saw that the
battle was going against him, he took with
him seven hundred swordsmen to break
through, opposite the king of Edom; but
they could not. [27]Then he took his firstborn
son who was to succeed him, and offered
him as a burnt offering on the wall. And
great wrath came upon Israel, so they
withdrew from him and returned to their
own land.

3.1-3 The evaluation of the reign of Jehoram by the Deuteronomic historian is mixed: a sacred symbol of *Baal* was removed, but the basic pattern of disobedience was unchanged.
3.4-27 War between Israel and Moab. *King Mesha of Moab* (a major sheep-producing district east of the lower end of the Dead Sea), who revolted against economic subservience to Israel, is also known from an ancient inscription which mentions his impressive building activity. The coalition of three kings (of Israel, Judah and Edom, Moab's neighbor to the south) joins to attack Mesha, and seek the approval of *the LORD. A musician* helps induce the Spirit, through which Elisha declares that the troops attacking Mesha will receive water, though it is not the rainy season, and that Moab will be destroyed. Mesha's effort to turn the tide of battle by sacrificing his *firstborn son* was futile.

[d] Compare Gk Syr: Meaning of Heb uncertain

4.1-6.7 Elisha's Miracles of Mercy and Retribution.
4.1-7 The widow of a *prophet* was about to lose her children to slavery, but *Elisha* enabled her to produce a great supply of oil which she sold to repay her debts.
4.8-37 At *Shunem* (west of the Lake of Galilee, overlooking the Valley of Jezreel) Elisha was a frequent guest of a wealthy but childless woman. The prophet promised her a son, who was born in due time, but died at an early age. She sent for Elisha, whose servant, *Gehazi*, came first and was unsuccessful in restoring the child to life, but the prophet finally brought him back to life by the ancient equivalent of mouth-to-mouth resuscitation.

Elisha and the Widow's Oil

4 Now the wife of a member of the company of prophets[e] cried to Elisha, "Your servant my husband is dead; and you know that your servant feared the LORD, but a creditor has come to take my two children as slaves." 2 Elisha said to her, "What shall I do for you? Tell me, what do you have in the house?" She answered, "Your servant has nothing in the house, except a jar of oil." 3 He said, "Go outside, borrow vessels from all your neighbors, empty vessels and not just a few. 4 Then go in, and shut the door behind you and your children, and start pouring into all these vessels; when each is full, set it aside." 5 So she left him and shut the door behind her and her children; they kept bringing vessels to her, and she kept pouring. 6 When the vessels were full, she said to her son, "Bring me another vessel." But he said to her, "There are no more." Then the oil stopped flowing. 7 She came and told the man of God, and he said, "Go sell the oil and pay your debts, and you and your children can live on the rest."

Elisha Raises the Shunammite's Son

8 One day Elisha was passing through Shunem, where a wealthy woman lived, who urged him to have a meal. So whenever he passed that way, he would stop there for a meal. 9 She said to her husband, "Look, I am sure that this man who regularly passes our way is a holy man of God. 10 Let us make a small roof chamber with walls, and put there for him a bed, a table, a chair, and a lamp, so that he can stay there whenever he comes to us."

11 One day when he came there, he went up to the chamber and lay down there. 12 He said to his servant Gehazi, "Call the Shunammite woman." When he had called her, she stood before him. 13 He said to him, "Say to her, Since you have taken all this trouble for us, what may be done for you? Would you have a word spoken on your behalf to the king or to the commander of the army?" She answered, "I live among my own people." 14 He said, "What then may be done for her?" Gehazi answered, "Well, she has no son, and her husband is old." 15 He said, "Call her." When he had called her, she stood at the door. 16 He said, "At this season, in due time, you shall embrace a son." She replied, "No, my lord, O man of God; do not deceive your servant."

17 The woman conceived and bore a son at that season, in due time, as Elisha had declared to her.

18 When the child was older, he went out one day to his father among the reapers. 19 He complained to his father, "Oh, my head, my head!" The father said to his servant, "Carry him to his mother." 20 He carried him and brought him to his mother; the child sat on her lap until noon, and he died. 21 She went up and laid him on the bed of the man of God, closed the door on him, and left. 22 Then she called to her husband, and said, "Send me one of the servants and one of the donkeys, so that I may quickly go to the man of God and come back again." 23 He said, "Why go to him today? It is neither new moon nor sabbath." She said, "It will be all right." 24 Then she saddled the donkey and said to her servant, "Urge the animal on; do not hold back for me unless I tell you." 25 So she set out, and came to the man of God at Mount Carmel.

When the man of God saw her coming, he said to Gehazi his servant, "Look, there is the Shunammite woman; 26 run at once to meet her, and say to her, Are you all right? Is your husband all right? Is the child all right?" She answered, "It is all right." 27 When she came to the man of God at the mountain, she caught hold of his feet. Gehazi approached to push her away. But the man of God said, "Let her alone, for she is in bitter distress; the LORD has hidden it from me and has not told me." 28 Then she said, "Did I ask my lord for a son? Did I not say, Do not mislead me?" 29 He said to Gehazi, "Gird up your loins, and take my staff in your hand, and go. If you meet anyone, give no greeting, and if anyone greets you, do not answer; and lay my staff on the face of the child." 30 Then the mother of the child said, "As the LORD lives, and as you yourself live, I will not leave without you." So he rose up and followed her. 31 Gehazi went on ahead and laid the staff on the face of the child, but there was no sound or sign of life. He came back to meet him and told him, "The child has not awakened."

32 When Elisha came into the house, he saw the child lying dead on his bed. 33 So he went in and closed the door on the two of them, and prayed to the LORD. 34 Then he got

[e] Heb *the sons of the prophets*

4.1 2 Kings 2.3; Lev 25.39; Mt 18.25
4.7 1 Kings 12.22
4.8 Josh 19.18
4.9 ver 7
4.12 ver 29-31; 2 Kings 5.20-27; 8.4,5
4.16 Gen 18.10,14; ver 28
4.21 ver 7,32
4.23 Num 10.10; 28.11; 1 Chr 23.31
4.25 2 Kings 2.25
4.28 ver 16
4.29 1 Kings 18.46; 2 Kings 9.1; Lk 10.4; Ex 7.19; 14.16; 2 Kings 2.8,14
4.30 2 Kings 2.2
4.33 ver 4; Mt 6.6; 1 Kings 17.20
4.34 1 Kings 17.21; Acts 20.10

4.35 1 Kings 17.21; 2 Kings 8.1,5
4.37 1 Kings 17.23; Heb 11.35
4.38 2 Kings 2.1,3; 8.1; Lk 10.39; Acts 22.3
4.41 Ex 15.25; 2 Kings 2.21
4.42 1 Sam 9.4,7
4.44 Mt 14.16-21; 15.32-38
5.1 Lk 4.27
5.5 1 Sam 9.8; 2 Kings 8.8,9
5.7 Gen 37.29; 30.2; Deut 32.39; 1 Sam 2.6; 1 Kings 20.7
5.8 1 Kings 12.22
5.10 Jn 9.7
5.13 2 Kings 6.21; 8.9; 1 Sam 28.23
5.14 ver 10; Job 33.25; Lk 4.27
5.15 1 Sam 15.46,47; Dan 2.47; 3.29; 1 Sam 25.27

up on the bed[f] and lay upon the child,
putting his mouth upon his mouth, his eyes
upon his eyes, and his hands upon his
hands; and while he lay bent over him, the
flesh of the child became warm. [35]He got
down, walked once to and fro in the room,
then got up again and bent over him; the
child sneezed seven times, and the child
opened his eyes. [36]Elisha[g] summoned Gehazi
and said, "Call the Shunammite woman."
So he called her. When she came to him,
he said, "Take your son." [37]She came and
fell at his feet, bowing to the ground; then
she took her son and left.

Elisha Purifies the Pot of Stew

38 When Elisha returned to Gilgal, there
was a famine in the land. As the company
of prophets was[h] sitting before him, he said
to his servant, "Put the large pot on, and
make some stew for the company of
prophets."[i] [39]One of them went out into the
field to gather herbs; he found a wild vine
and gathered from it a lapful of wild gourds,
and came and cut them up into the pot of
stew, not knowing what they were. [40]They
served some for the men to eat. But while
they were eating the stew, they cried out,
"O man of God, there is death in the pot!"
They could not eat it. [41]He said, "Then bring
some flour." He threw it into the pot, and
said, "Serve the people and let them eat."
And there was nothing harmful in the pot.

Elisha Feeds One Hundred Men

42 A man came from Baal-shalishah,
bringing food from the first fruits to the
man of God: twenty loaves of barley and
fresh ears of grain in his sack. Elisha said,
"Give it to the people and let them eat."
[43]But his servant said, "How can I set this
before a hundred people?" So he repeated,
"Give it to the people and let them eat, for
thus says the LORD, 'They shall eat and have
some left.' " [44]He set it before them, they
ate, and had some left, according to the
word of the LORD.

The Healing of Naaman

5 Naaman, commander of the army of
the king of Aram, was a great man
and in high favor with his master, because
by him the LORD had given victory to Aram.
The man, though a mighty warrior, suffered from leprosy.[j] [2]Now the Arameans on
one of their raids had taken a young girl
captive from the land of Israel, and she
served Naaman's wife. [3]She said to her
mistress, "If only my lord were with the
prophet who is in Samaria! He would cure
him of his leprosy."[j] [4]So Naaman[g] went in
and told his lord just what the girl from the
land of Israel had said. [5]And the king of
Aram said, "Go then, and I will send along
a letter to the king of Israel."
He went, taking with him ten talents of
silver, six thousand shekels of gold, and ten
sets of garments. [6]He brought the letter to
the king of Israel, which read, "When this
letter reaches you, know that I have sent
to you my servant Naaman, that you may
cure him of his leprosy."[j] [7]When the king
of Israel read the letter, he tore his clothes
and said, "Am I God, to give death or life,
that this man sends word to me to cure a
man of his leprosy?[j] Just look and see how
he is trying to pick a quarrel with me."
8 But when Elisha the man of God heard
that the king of Israel had torn his clothes,
he sent a message to the king, "Why have
you torn your clothes? Let him come to me,
that he may learn that there is a prophet
in Israel." [9]So Naaman came with his horses
and chariots, and halted at the entrance of
Elisha's house. [10]Elisha sent a messenger to
him, saying, "Go, wash in the Jordan seven
times, and your flesh shall be restored and
you shall be clean." [11]But Naaman became
angry and went away, saying, "I thought
that for me he would surely come out, and
stand and call on the name of the LORD his
God, and would wave his hand over the
spot, and cure the leprosy![j] [12]Are not Abana[k]
and Pharpar, the rivers of Damascus, better
than all the waters of Israel? Could I not
wash in them, and be clean?" He turned
and went away in a rage. [13]But his servants
approached and said to him, "Father, if the
prophet had commanded you to do something difficult, would you not have done it?
How much more, when all he said to you
was, 'Wash, and be clean'?" [14]So he went
down and immersed himself seven times in
the Jordan, according to the word of the
man of God; his flesh was restored like the
flesh of a young boy, and he was clean.
15 Then he returned to the man of God,
he and all his company; he came and stood

4.38-44 Elisha countered the effect of poison in a pot of stew, and made it possible for a modest supply of food to feed *a hundred people.*
5.1-15 *Naaman,* commander of the army of the Arameans, afflicted with *leprosy* (or some similar dread skin disease), was sent by *the king* to *the prophet* who was in Samaria, at the suggestion of a captive Israelite slave girl. Messengers were sent to *the king of Israel,* who despaired of curing him, but *Elisha* instructed Naaman to *wash in the Jordan seven times,* which effected the cure. Elisha instructed Naaman to worship only *the LORD,* who responded that he was officially obligated to honor *Rimmon* ("the thunderer," the storm god of the Arameans). The *earth* he took back to Damascus was intended to sanctify the site of an altar of Yahweh.

[f] Heb lacks *on the bed* [g] Heb *he* [h] Heb *sons of the prophets were* [i] Heb *sons of the prophets* [j] A term for several skin diseases; precise meaning uncertain [k] Another reading is *Amana*

5.20-27 The greed of *Gehazi* in asking Naaman for some of the rich gifts that Elisha had refused to accept was met by his being cursed with Naaman's *leprosy.*
6.1-6 The project of the company of prophets to build housing for themselves in the Jordan Valley was hindered temporarily when one worker's iron *ax head* fell into the water. Elisha caused it to float, and it was recovered.
6.8-8.15 Elisha's Miracles in Warfare and Politics.
6.8-23 The military plans of *the king of Aram* are said to be immediately known to Elisha, *the man of God,* who informed the *king of Israel.* The attempt by the king to seize Elisha was frustrated when the leaders of the enemy, which had surrounded with *horses and chariots of fire* the city of Dothan (south of Mt. Carmel and the Plain of Jezreel), were struck blind in response to Elisha's prayer. Led by him to *Samaria,* their sight was restored and the king of Israel, on the advice of the prophet, *prepared for them a great feast* and sent them back to their land.

before him and said, "Now I know that there is no God in all the earth except in Israel; please accept a present from your servant." [16]But he said, "As the LORD lives, whom I serve, I will accept nothing!" He urged him to accept, but he refused. [17]Then Naaman said, "If not, please let two mule-loads of earth be given to your servant; for your servant will no longer offer burnt offering or sacrifice to any god except the LORD. [18]But may the LORD pardon your servant on one count: when my master goes into the house of Rimmon to worship there, leaning on my arm, and I bow down in the house of Rimmon, when I do bow down in the house of Rimmon, may the LORD pardon your servant on this one count." [19]He said to him, "Go in peace."

Gehazi's Greed

But when Naaman had gone from him a short distance, [20]Gehazi, the servant of Elisha the man of God, thought, "My master has let that Aramean Naaman off too lightly by not accepting from him what he offered. As the LORD lives, I will run after him and get something out of him." [21]So Gehazi went after Naaman. When Naaman saw someone running after him, he jumped down from the chariot to meet him and said, "Is everything all right?" [22]He replied, "Yes, but my master has sent me to say, 'Two members of a company of prophets[l] have just come to me from the hill country of Ephraim; please give them a talent of silver and two changes of clothing.' " [23]Naaman said, "Please accept two talents." He urged him, and tied up two talents of silver in two bags, with two changes of clothing, and gave them to two of his servants, who carried them in front of Gehazi.[m] [24]When he came to the citadel, he took the bags[n] from them, and stored them inside; he dismissed the men, and they left.

25 He went in and stood before his master; and Elisha said to him, "Where have you been, Gehazi?" He answered, "Your servant has not gone anywhere at all." [26]But he said to him, "Did I not go with you in spirit when someone left his chariot to meet you? Is this a time to accept money and to accept clothing, olive orchards and vineyards, sheep and oxen, and male and female slaves? [27]Therefore the leprosy[o] of Naaman shall cling to you, and to your descendants forever." So he left his presence leprous,[o] as white as snow.

The Miracle of the Ax Head

6 Now the company of prophets[l] said to Elisha, "As you see, the place where we live under your charge is too small for us. [2]Let us go to the Jordan, and let us collect logs there, one for each of us, and build a place there for us to live." He answered, "Do so." [3]Then one of them said, "Please come with your servants." And he answered, "I will." [4]So he went with them. When they came to the Jordan, they cut down trees. [5]But as one was felling a log, his ax head fell into the water; he cried out, "Alas, master! It was borrowed." [6]Then the man of God said, "Where did it fall?" When he showed him the place, he cut off a stick, and threw it in there, and made the iron float. [7]He said, "Pick it up." So he reached out his hand and took it.

The Aramean Attack Is Thwarted

8 Once when the king of Aram was at war with Israel, he took counsel with his officers. He said, "At such and such a place shall be my camp." [9]But the man of God sent word to the king of Israel, "Take care not to pass this place, because the Arameans are going down there." [10]The king of Israel sent word to the place of which the man of God spoke. More than once or twice he warned such a place[p] so that it was on the alert.

11 The mind of the king of Aram was greatly perturbed because of this; he called his officers and said to them, "Now tell me who among us sides with the king of Israel?" [12]Then one of his officers said, "No one, my lord king. It is Elisha, the prophet in Israel, who tells the king of Israel the words that you speak in your bedchamber." [13]He said, "Go and find where he is; I will send and seize him." He was told, "He is in Dothan." [14]So he sent horses and chariots there and a great army; they came by night, and surrounded the city.

15 When an attendant of the man of God rose early in the morning and went out, an army with horses and chariots was all around the city. His servant said, "Alas, master! What shall we do?" [16]He replied,

[l] Heb *sons of the prophets* [m] Heb *him* [n] Heb lacks *the bags* [o] A term for several skin diseases; precise meaning uncertain [p] Heb *warned it*

5.16 2 Kings 3.14; ver 20,26; Gen 14.22,23
5.18 2 Kings 7.2,17
5.20 2 Kings 4.12,31,36
5.22 2 Kings 4.26; Josh 24.33
5.25 ver 22
5.26 ver 16
5.27 Ex 4.6; Num 12.10; 2 Kings 15.5
6.1 2 Kings 4.38
6.6 2 Kings 2.21
6.9 ver 12
6.13 Gen 37.17
6.16 2 Chr 32.7,8; Ps 55.18; Rom 8.31

6.17 2 Kings 2.11; Ps 68.17; Zech 6.1-7
6.18 Gen 19.11
6.20 ver 17
6.21 2 Kings 2.12; 5.13; 8.9
6.22 Deut 20.11-16; Rom 12.20
6.23 ver 8,9; 2 Kings 5.2
6.24 1 Kings 20.1
6.29 Lev 26.27-29; Deut 28.52,53,57
6.30 1 Kings 21.27
6.31 Ruth 1.17; 1 Kings 19.2
6.32 Ezek 8.1; 20.1; 1 Kings 18.4,13,14
6.33 Job 2.9
7.1 ver 18
7.2 ver 17,19,20; Mal 3.10
7.3 Lev 13.46
7.4 2 Kings 6.24
7.6 2 Sam 5.24; 19.7; 1 Kings 10.29
7.7 Ps 48.4-6

"Do not be afraid, for there are more with
us than there are with them." 17Then Elisha
prayed: "O LORD, please open his eyes that
he may see." So the LORD opened the eyes
of the servant, and he saw; the mountain
was full of horses and chariots of fire all
around Elisha. 18When the Arameans[q] came
down against him, Elisha prayed to the
LORD, and said, "Strike this people, please,
with blindness." So he struck them with
blindness as Elisha had asked. 19Elisha said
to them, "This is not the way, and this is
not the city; follow me, and I will bring you
to the man whom you seek." And he led
them to Samaria.
20 As soon as they entered Samaria,
Elisha said, "O LORD, open the eyes of these
men so that they may see." The LORD opened
their eyes, and they saw that they were
inside Samaria. 21When the king of Israel
saw them he said to Elisha, "Father, shall
I kill them? Shall I kill them?" 22He answered, "No! Did you capture with your
sword and your bow those whom you want
to kill? Set food and water before them so
that they may eat and drink; and let them
go to their master." 23So he prepared for
them a great feast; after they ate and drank,
he sent them on their way, and they went
to their master. And the Arameans no longer
came raiding into the land of Israel.

Ben-hadad's Siege of Samaria

24 Some time later King Ben-hadad of
Aram mustered his entire army; he marched
against Samaria and laid siege to it. 25As the
siege continued, famine in Samaria became
so great that a donkey's head was sold for
eighty shekels of silver, and one-fourth of a
kab of dove's dung for five shekels of silver.
26Now as the king of Israel was walking on
the city wall, a woman cried out to him,
"Help, my lord king!" 27He said, "No! Let the
LORD help you. How can I help you? From
the threshing floor or from the wine press?"
28But then the king asked her, "What is
your complaint?" She answered, "This
woman said to me, 'Give up your son; we
will eat him today, and we will eat my son
tomorrow.' 29So we cooked my son and ate
him. The next day I said to her, 'Give up
your son and we will eat him.' But she has
hidden her son." 30When the king heard the
words of the woman he tore his clothes—
now since he was walking on the city wall,
the people could see that he had sackcloth
on his body underneath— 31and he said,
"So may God do to me, and more, if the
head of Elisha son of Shaphat stays on his
shoulders today." 32So he dispatched a man
from his presence.
Now Elisha was sitting in his house, and
the elders were sitting with him. Before the
messenger arrived, Elisha said to the elders,
"Are you aware that this murderer has sent
someone to take off my head? When the
messenger comes, see that you shut the
door and hold it closed against him. Is not
the sound of his master's feet behind him?"
33While he was still speaking with them, the
king[r] came down to him and said, "This
trouble is from the LORD! Why should I hope
in the LORD any longer?"

7 1But Elisha said, "Hear the word of
the LORD: thus says the LORD, Tomorrow about this time a measure of choice
meal shall be sold for a shekel, and two
measures of barley for a shekel, at the gate
of Samaria." 2Then the captain on whose
hand the king leaned said to the man of
God, "Even if the LORD were to make windows in the sky, could such a thing happen?" But he said, "You shall see it with
your own eyes, but you shall not eat from
it."

The Arameans Flee

3 Now there were four leprous[s] men
outside the city gate, who said to one another, "Why should we sit here until we
die? 4If we say, 'Let us enter the city,' the
famine is in the city, and we shall die there;
but if we sit here, we shall also die. Therefore, let us desert to the Aramean camp; if
they spare our lives, we shall live; and if
they kill us, we shall but die." 5So they
arose at twilight to go to the Aramean
camp; but when they came to the edge of
the Aramean camp, there was no one there
at all. 6For the Lord had caused the Aramean
army to hear the sound of chariots, and of
horses, the sound of a great army, so that
they said to one another, "The king of Israel
has hired the kings of the Hittites and the
kings of Egypt to fight against us." 7So they
fled away in the twilight and abandoned
their tents, their horses, and their donkeys
leaving the camp just as it was, and fled for
their lives. 8When these leprous[s] men had
come to the edge of the camp, they went

6.24-7.20 The (unnamed) king of Israel, during a siege of Samaria which had left the people starving, learned that his subjects were killing and eating their own children. The king put the blame on *Elisha* and *the LORD* whom he represented, but was told that the crisis would pass by the next day. When *four leprous men* approached the camp of the Arameans, they found it deserted, because the besiegers of the city had heard the sound *of a great army*, and, assuming it to have been the Hittite and Egyptian allies come to aid Israel, had fled. First the lepers and then the populace of Samaria *plundered the camp of the Arameans. The captain* who had scoffed at the prediction of an abundance of food was *trampled to death* by the people.

[q] Heb *they* [r] See 7.2: Heb *messenger* [s] A term for several skin diseases; precise meaning uncertain

8.1-6 The restoration of property to *the Shunammite woman* whose son Elisha had brought back to life may have taken place after his death, which is implied by the reference to his work in the past tense and by the role of *Gehazi* as spokesman (8.4).
8.7-15 The seriously ill *Ben-hadad*, king of Damascus, sent *Hazael* (whom Elijah had been told to anoint as king of Aram; 1 Kings 19.15) to Elisha, together with an abundance of gifts and an inquiry about the possibility of his recovery. He was to be told that he would recover, but the prophet foresaw and announced his death. In a kind of vision, he also foresaw both the ascension of *Hazael* to the throne of Aram in his place, and the disaster that he would then bring on Israel. Hazael hastened his becoming king by smothering the ailing incumbent king with wet cloths.

into a tent, ate and drank, carried off silver, gold, and clothing, and went and hid them. Then they came back, entered another tent, carried off things from it, and went and hid them.

9 Then they said to one another, "What we are doing is wrong. This is a day of good news; if we are silent and wait until the morning light, we will be found guilty; therefore let us go and tell the king's household." [10]So they came and called to the gatekeepers of the city, and told them, "We went to the Aramean camp, but there was no one to be seen or heard there, nothing but the horses tied, the donkeys tied, and the tents as they were." [11]Then the gatekeepers called out and proclaimed it to the king's household. [12]The king got up in the night, and said to his servants, "I will tell you what the Arameans have prepared against us. They know that we are starving; so they have left the camp to hide themselves in the open country, thinking, 'When they come out of the city, we shall take them alive and get into the city.' " [13]One of his servants said, "Let some men take five of the remaining horses, since those left here will suffer the fate of the whole multitude of Israel that have perished already;[t] let us send and find out." [14]So they took two mounted men, and the king sent them after the Aramean army, saying, "Go and find out." [15]So they went after them as far as the Jordan; the whole way was littered with garments and equipment that the Arameans had thrown away in their haste. So the messengers returned, and told the king.

16 Then the people went out, and plundered the camp of the Arameans. So a measure of choice meal was sold for a shekel, and two measures of barley for a shekel, according to the word of the LORD. [17]Now the king had appointed the captain on whose hand he leaned to have charge of the gate; the people trampled him to death in the gate, just as the man of God had said when the king came down to him. [18]For when the man of God had said to the king, "Two measures of barley shall be sold for a shekel, and a measure of choice meal for a shekel, about this time tomorrow in the gate of Samaria," [19]the captain had answered the man of God, "Even if the LORD were to make windows in the sky, could such a thing happen?" And he had answered, "You shall see it with your own eyes, but you shall not eat from it." [20]It did indeed happen to him; the people trampled him to death in the gate.

The Shunammite Woman's Land Restored

8 Now Elisha had said to the woman whose son he had restored to life, "Get up and go with your household, and settle wherever you can; for the LORD has called for a famine, and it will come on the land for seven years." [2]So the woman got up and did according to the word of the man of God; she went with her household and settled in the land of the Philistines seven years. [3]At the end of the seven years, when the woman returned from the land of the Philistines, she set out to appeal to the king for her house and her land. [4]Now the king was talking with Gehazi the servant of the man of God, saying, "Tell me all the great things that Elisha has done." [5]While he was telling the king how Elisha had restored a dead person to life, the woman whose son he had restored to life appealed to the king for her house and her land. Gehazi said, "My lord king, here is the woman, and here is her son whom Elisha restored to life." [6]When the king questioned the woman, she told him. So the king appointed an official for her, saying, "Restore all that was hers, together with all the revenue of the fields from the day that she left the land until now."

Death of Ben-hadad

7 Elisha went to Damascus while King Ben-hadad of Aram was ill. When it was told him, "The man of God has come here," [8]the king said to Hazael, "Take a present with you and go to meet the man of God. Inquire of the LORD through him, whether I shall recover from this illness." [9]So Hazael went to meet him, taking a present with him, all kinds of goods of Damascus, forty camel loads. When he entered and stood before him, he said, "Your son King Ben-hadad of Aram has sent me to you, saying, 'Shall I recover from this illness?' " [10]Elisha said to him, "Go, say to him, 'You shall certainly recover'; but the LORD has shown me that he shall certainly die." [11]He fixed his gaze and stared at him, until he was ashamed. Then the man of God wept. [12]Hazael asked, "Why does my lord weep?"

7.9 2 Sam 18.27
7.12 2 Kings 6.25-29
7.16 ver 1
7.18 ver 1
7.19 ver 2
8.1 2 Kings 4.35; Ps 105.16; Hag 1.11
8.4 2 Kings 4.12; 5.20-27
8.5 2 Kings 4.35
8.7 1 Kings 11.24; 2 Kings 6.24
8.8 1 Kings 19.15; 14.3; 2 Kings 1.2
8.10 ver 14,15
8.12 2 Kings 10.32; 12.17; 13.3,7; 15.16; Hos 13.16; Am 1.13

[t] Compare Gk Syr Vg: Meaning of Heb uncertain

He answered, "Because I know the evil that you will do to the people of Israel; you will set their fortresses on fire, you will kill their young men with the sword, dash in pieces their little ones, and rip up their pregnant women." 13 Hazael said, "What is your servant, who is a mere dog, that he should do this great thing?" Elisha answered, "The LORD has shown me that you are to be king over Aram." 14 Then he left Elisha, and went to his master Ben-hadad,[u] who said to him, "What did Elisha say to you?" And he answered, "He told me that you would certainly recover." 15 But the next day he took the bed-cover and dipped it in water and spread it over the king's face, until he died. And Hazael succeeded him.

Jehoram Reigns over Judah

16 In the fifth year of King Joram son of Ahab of Israel,[v] Jehoram son of King Jehoshaphat of Judah began to reign. 17 He was thirty-two years old when he became king, and he reigned eight years in Jerusalem. 18 He walked in the way of the kings of Israel, as the house of Ahab had done, for the daughter of Ahab was his wife. He did what was evil in the sight of the LORD. 19 Yet the LORD would not destroy Judah, for the sake of his servant David, since he had promised to give a lamp to him and to his descendants forever.

20 In his days Edom revolted against the rule of Judah, and set up a king of their own. 21 Then Joram crossed over to Zair with all his chariots. He set out by night and attacked the Edomites and their chariot commanders who had surrounded him;[w] but his army fled home. 22 So Edom has been in revolt against the rule of Judah to this day. Libnah also revolted at the same time. 23 Now the rest of the acts of Joram, and all that he did, are they not written in the Book of the Annals of the Kings of Judah? 24 So Joram slept with his ancestors, and was buried with them in the city of David; his son Ahaziah succeeded him.

Ahaziah Reigns over Judah

25 In the twelfth year of King Joram son of Ahab of Israel, Ahaziah son of King Jehoram of Judah began to reign. 26 Ahaziah was twenty-two years old when he began to reign; he reigned one year in Jerusalem. His mother's name was Athaliah, a granddaughter of King Omri of Israel. 27 He also walked in the way of the house of Ahab, doing what was evil in the sight of the LORD, as the house of Ahab had done, for he was son-in-law to the house of Ahab.

28 He went with Joram son of Ahab to wage war against King Hazael of Aram at Ramoth-gilead, where the Arameans wounded Joram. 29 King Joram returned to be healed in Jezreel of the wounds that the Arameans had inflicted on him at Ramah, when he fought against King Hazael of Aram. King Ahaziah son of Jehoram of Judah went down to see Joram son of Ahab in Jezreel, because he was wounded.

Anointing of Jehu

9 Then the prophet Elisha called a member of the company of prophets[x] and said to him, "Gird up your loins; take this flask of oil in your hand, and go to Ramoth-gilead. 2 When you arrive, look there for Jehu son of Jehoshaphat, son of Nimshi; go in and get him to leave his companions, and take him into an inner chamber. 3 Then take the flask of oil, pour it on his head, and say, 'Thus says the LORD: I anoint you king over Israel.' Then open the door and flee; do not linger."

4 So the young man, the young prophet, went to Ramoth-gilead. 5 He arrived while the commanders of the army were in council, and he announced, "I have a message for you, commander." "For which one of us?" asked Jehu. "For you, commander." 6 So Jehu[y] got up and went inside; the young man poured the oil on his head, saying to him, "Thus says the LORD the God of Israel: I anoint you king over the people of the LORD, over Israel. 7 You shall strike down the house of your master Ahab, so that I may avenge on Jezebel the blood of my servants the prophets, and the blood of all the servants of the LORD. 8 For the whole house of Ahab shall perish; I will cut off from Ahab every male, bond or free, in Israel. 9 I will make the house of Ahab like the house of Jeroboam son of Nebat, and like the house of Baasha son of Ahijah. 10 The dogs shall eat Jezebel in the territory of Jezreel, and no one shall bury her." Then he opened the door and fled.

[u] Heb lacks *Ben-hadad* [v] Gk Syr: Heb adds *Jehoshaphat being king of Judah,* [w] Meaning of Heb uncertain [x] Heb *sons of the prophets* [y] Heb *he*

8.13 1 Sam 17.43; 1 Kings 19.15
8.15 ver 10
8.16 2 Kings 1.17; 3.1; 2 Chr 21.3,4
8.17 2 Chr 21.5-10
8.18 ver 27
8.19 2 Sam 7.13; 1 Kings 11.36; 2 Chr 21.7
8.20 1 Kings 22.4; 2 Kings 3.27; 2 Chr 21.8-10
8.21 2 Sam 18.17; 19.8
8.22 2 Chr 21.10
8.24 2 Chr 21.20; 22.1
8.25 2 Chr 22.1-6
8.28 ver 15; 1 Kings 22.3,29
8.29 2 Kings 9.15; 2 Chr 22.6,7
9.1 2 Kings 2.3; 4.29; 8.28,29
9.2 ver 5,11
9.3 2 Chr 22.7
9.6 ver 3; 1 Kings 19.16; 2 Chr 22.7
9.7 Deut 32.35; 1 Kings 18.4; 21.15; ver 32
9.8 2 Kings 10.17; 1 Kings 21.21; 1 Sam 25.22; Deut 32.36; 2 Kings 14.26
9.9 1 Kings 14.10; 15.29; 16.3-5,11,12
9.10 ver 35,36; 1 Kings 21.23

8.16-13.21 Ongoing Struggle for Power in Israel and Judah down to the Death of Elisha.
8.16-24 *Joram, son of Ahab* and king of Israel (849-842), had probably been co-regent with Jehoshaphat for *five years* earlier, before his sole reign and that of *Jehoram* king of Judah began (also 849-842). The Deuteronomist's criticisms of Ahab, his father-in-law, are applied to him, and during his reign the east Jordan territory of Edom broke away from control by Judah. The reference *to this day* shows that the document has been edited at a later period.
8.25-29 On the death of Jehoram, *Ahaziah,* his son, began his one-year rule over Judah. Having collaborated with *Joram,* king of Israel, in a fight against Ben-hadad of Syria which left Joram seriously wounded, Ahaziah visited him as he recuperated at *Jezreel,* where Ahab had established a royal residence (1 Kings 18.45-46).
9.1-10.36 The violent reign over Israel of *Jehu son of Jehoshaphat,* king of Judah, was launched by *Elisha,* whose young prophetic agent anointed him with *oil,* instructing him to *strike down* all of Ahab's offspring and announcing the gory death of Elijah's royal enemy, *Jezebel* (1 Kings 16.31-33; 19.1-3). The prophecy of Elijah about the dogs licking up Ahab's blood (1 Kings 21.17-19) was now to be fulfilled in the death of Jezebel. *Jehu,* acclaimed by his followers as *king,* decided to kill *Joram* the king of Israel, and thus left his military forces east of the Jordan at *Ramoth-gilead* and crossed to *Jezreel,* where Joram was recuperating. Intimidating the messengers sent to inquire about his purpose, Jehu attacked and killed Joram, linking him with the wickedness of his *mother Jezebel,* and then fatally wounded *King Ahaziah of Judah.*

9.30-37 Jezebel's Death. Adorning herself as a prostitute in Jezreel, Jezebel called Jehu by the name of a man, *Zimri*, who had killed King Elah of Israel and seven days later committed suicide (1 Kings 16.15-20). The *eunuchs* who were with her threw her down to her death on Jehu's order. The prophecy of Elijah about the dogs licking up Ahab's blood (1 Kings 21.17-19) was seen as fulfilled by the dogs who devoured nearly her entire body.

11 When Jehu came back to his master's officers, they said to him, "Is everything all right? Why did that madman come to you?" He answered them, "You know the sort and how they babble." 12 They said, "Liar! Come on, tell us!" So he said, "This is just what he said to me: 'Thus says the LORD, I anoint you king over Israel.' " 13 Then hurriedly they all took their cloaks and spread them for him on the bare[z] steps; and they blew the trumpet, and proclaimed, "Jehu is king."

Joram of Israel Killed

14 Thus Jehu son of Jehoshaphat son of Nimshi conspired against Joram. Joram with all Israel had been on guard at Ramoth-gilead against King Hazael of Aram; 15 but King Joram had returned to be healed in Jezreel of the wounds that the Arameans had inflicted on him, when he fought against King Hazael of Aram. So Jehu said, "If this is your wish, then let no one slip out of the city to go and tell the news in Jezreel." 16 Then Jehu mounted his chariot and went to Jezreel, where Joram was lying ill. King Ahaziah of Judah had come down to visit Joram.

17 In Jezreel, the sentinel standing on the tower spied the company of Jehu arriving, and said, "I see a company." Joram said, "Take a horseman; send him to meet them, and let him say, 'Is it peace?' " 18 So the horseman went to meet him; he said, "Thus says the king, 'Is it peace?' " Jehu responded, "What have you to do with peace? Fall in behind me." The sentinel reported, saying, "The messenger reached them, but he is not coming back." 19 Then he sent out a second horseman, who came to them and said, "Thus says the king, 'Is it peace?' " Jehu answered, "What have you to do with peace? Fall in behind me." 20 Again the sentinel reported, "He reached them, but he is not coming back. It looks like the driving of Jehu son of Nimshi; for he drives like a maniac."

21 Joram said, "Get ready." And they got his chariot ready. Then King Joram of Israel and King Ahaziah of Judah set out, each in his chariot, and went to meet Jehu; they met him at the property of Naboth the Jezreelite. 22 When Joram saw Jehu, he said, "Is it peace, Jehu?" He answered, "What peace can there be, so long as the many whoredoms and sorceries of your mother Jezebel continue?" 23 Then Joram reined about and fled, saying to Ahaziah, "Treason, Ahaziah!" 24 Jehu drew his bow with all his strength, and shot Joram between the shoulders, so that the arrow pierced his heart; and he sank in his chariot. 25 Jehu said to his aide Bidkar, "Lift him out, and throw him on the plot of ground belonging to Naboth the Jezreelite; for remember, when you and I rode side by side behind his father Ahab how the LORD uttered this oracle against him: 26 'For the blood of Naboth and for the blood of his children that I saw yesterday, says the LORD, I swear I will repay you on this very plot of ground.' Now therefore lift him out and throw him on the plot of ground, in accordance with the word of the LORD."

Ahaziah of Judah Killed

27 When King Ahaziah of Judah saw this, he fled in the direction of Beth-haggan. Jehu pursued him, saying, "Shoot him also!" And they shot him[a] in the chariot at the ascent to Gur, which is by Ibleam. Then he fled to Megiddo, and died there. 28 His officers carried him in a chariot to Jerusalem, and buried him in his tomb with his ancestors in the city of David.

29 In the eleventh year of Joram son of Ahab, Ahaziah began to reign over Judah.

Jezebel's Violent Death

30 When Jehu came to Jezreel, Jezebel heard of it; she painted her eyes, and adorned her head, and looked out of the window. 31 As Jehu entered the gate, she said, "Is it peace, Zimri, murderer of your master?" 32 He looked up to the window and said, "Who is on my side? Who?" Two or three eunuchs looked out at him. 33 He said, "Throw her down." So they threw her down; some of her blood spattered on the wall and on the horses, which trampled on her. 34 Then he went in and ate and drank; he said, "See to that cursed woman and bury her; for she is a king's daughter." 35 But when they went to bury her, they found no more of her than the skull and the feet and the palms of her hands. 36 When they came back and told him, he said, "This is the word of the LORD, which he spoke by his servant Elijah the Tishbite, 'In the territory of Jezreel the dogs shall eat the flesh of Jezebel; 37 the corpse of

[z] Meaning of Heb uncertain [a] Syr Vg Compare Gk: Heb lacks *and they shot him*

9.13 Mt 21.7; 2 Sam 15.10; 1 Kings 1.34,39

9.14 2 Kings 8.28

9.15 2 Kings 8.29

9.16 2 Kings 8.29

9.18 ver 19,22

9.20 2 Sam 18.27; 1 Kings 19.17

9.21 2 Chr 22.7, ver 26; 1 Kings 21.1-7,15-19

9.22 1 Kings 16.30-33; 18.19; 2 Chr 21.13

9.23 2 Kings 11.24

9.24 1 Kings 22.34

9.25 1 Kings 21.1,19,24-29

9.26 1 Kings 21.19

9.27 2 Chr 22.9

9.28 2 Kings 23.30

9.30 Jer 4.30; Ezek 23.40

9.31 1 Kings 16.9-20

9.34 1 Kings 21.25; 16.31

9.36 1 Kings 21.23

9.37 Jer 8.1-3

Jezebel shall be like dung on the field in the territory of Jezreel, so that no one can say, This is Jezebel.' "

Massacre of Ahab's Descendants

10 Now Ahab had seventy sons in Samaria. So Jehu wrote letters and sent them to Samaria, to the rulers of Jezreel,[b] to the elders, and to the guardians of the sons of[c] Ahab, saying, 2"Since your master's sons are with you and you have at your disposal chariots and horses, a fortified city, and weapons, 3select the son of your master who is the best qualified, set him on his father's throne, and fight for your master's house." 4But they were utterly terrified and said, "Look, two kings could not withstand him; how then can we stand?" 5So the steward of the palace, and the governor of the city, along with the elders and the guardians, sent word to Jehu: "We are your servants; we will do anything you say. We will not make anyone king; do whatever you think right." 6Then he wrote them a second letter, saying, "If you are on my side, and if you are ready to obey me, take the heads of your master's sons and come to me at Jezreel tomorrow at this time." Now the king's sons, seventy persons, were with the leaders of the city, who were charged with their upbringing. 7When the letter reached them, they took the king's sons and killed them, seventy persons; they put their heads in baskets and sent them to him at Jezreel. 8When the messenger came and told him, "They have brought the heads of the king's sons," he said, "Lay them in two heaps at the entrance of the gate until the morning." 9Then in the morning when he went out, he stood and said to all the people, "You are innocent. It was I who conspired against my master and killed him; but who struck down all these? 10Know then that there shall fall to the earth nothing of the word of the LORD, which the LORD spoke concerning the house of Ahab; for the LORD has done what he said through his servant Elijah." 11So Jehu killed all who were left of the house of Ahab in Jezreel, all his leaders, close friends, and priests, until he left him no survivor.

12 Then he set out and went to Samaria. On the way, when he was at Beth-eked of the Shepherds, 13Jehu met relatives of King Ahaziah of Judah and said, "Who are you?" They answered, "We are kin of Ahaziah; we have come down to visit the royal princes and the sons of the queen mother." 14He said, "Take them alive." They took them alive, and slaughtered them at the pit of Beth-eked, forty-two in all; he spared none of them.

15 When he left there, he met Jehonadab son of Rechab coming to meet him; he greeted him, and said to him, "Is your heart as true to mine as mine is to yours?"[d] Jehonadab answered, "It is." Jehu said,[e] "If it is, give me your hand." So he gave him his hand. Jehu took him up with him into the chariot. 16He said, "Come with me, and see my zeal for the LORD." So he[f] had him ride in his chariot. 17When he came to Samaria, he killed all who were left to Ahab in Samaria, until he had wiped them out, according to the word of the LORD that he spoke to Elijah.

Slaughter of Worshipers of Baal

18 Then Jehu assembled all the people and said to them, "Ahab offered Baal small service; but Jehu will offer much more. 19Now therefore summon to me all the prophets of Baal, all his worshipers, and all his priests; let none be missing, for I have a great sacrifice to offer to Baal; whoever is missing shall not live." But Jehu was acting with cunning in order to destroy the worshipers of Baal. 20Jehu decreed, "Sanctify a solemn assembly for Baal." So they proclaimed it. 21Jehu sent word throughout all Israel; all the worshipers of Baal came, so that there was no one left who did not come. They entered the temple of Baal, until the temple of Baal was filled from wall to wall. 22He said to the keeper of the wardrobe, "Bring out the vestments for all the worshipers of Baal." So he brought out the vestments for them. 23Then Jehu entered the temple of Baal with Jehonadab son of Rechab; he said to the worshipers of Baal, "Search and see that there is no worshiper of the LORD here among you, but only worshipers of Baal." 24Then they proceeded to offer sacrifices and burnt offerings.

Now Jehu had stationed eighty men outside, saying, "Whoever allows any of those to escape whom I deliver into your hands shall forfeit his life." 25As soon as he

[b] Or *of the city*; Vg Compare Gk [c] Gk: Heb lacks *of the sons of* [d] Gk: Heb *Is it right with your heart, as my heart is with your heart?* [e] Gk: Heb lacks *Jehu said* [f] Gk Syr Tg: Heb *they*

10.1 1 Kings 16.24-29
10.5 see 1 Kings 20.4,32
10.7 1 Kings 21.21
10.9 2 Kings 9.14-24; ver 6
10.10 2 Kings 9.7-10; 1 Kings 21.19-29
10.13 2 Kings 8.24,29; 2 Chr 22.8
10.15 Jer 35.6ff; 1 Chr 2.55; Ezra 10.19
10.16 1 Kings 19.10
10.17 2 Kings 9.8; 2 Chr 22.8; ver 10
10.18 1 Kings 16.31,32
10.19 1 Kings 22.6
10.20 Joel 1.14; Ex 32.4-6
10.21 1 Kings 16.32; 2 Kings 11.18
10.24 1 Kings 20.39
10.25 1 Kings 18.40

10.1-17 The Slaughter of Ahab's Descendants and of the Relatives of Ahaziah, King of Judah.
10.1-11 *Seventy* is a round number for the surviving *sons of Ahab* (*cf.* Jacob's sons in Gen 46.27, and Gideon's sons in Judg 8.30; 9.2). Jehu's instructions to the leading figures – *rulers, elders, guardians of the sons – in Samaria* (ancient versions omit "Jezreel" here) were to install as king one of Jehu's sons to replace Joram (9.14-26). Instead of doing so, the leaders turned to Jehu, who ordered them to behead all *the king's sons.* They did so, in addition to killing all the members of his household, *his close friends, and priests.* This was seen as fulfillment of the prophecy of Elijah that judgmental doom would fall on the household of Ahab (1 Kings 21.17-29).
10.12-14 The relatives of King Ahaziah of Judah were on a visit to the rest of the royal family when Jehu met them at Beth-eked (south of Megiddo in the coastal hills) and ordered them to be killed as well.
10.15-17 En route to Samaria, Jehu met *Jehonadab, son of Rechab,* who joined him in a common effort to *wipe out* the worshipers of Baal. The Rechabites, a group of Israelites whose commitment to Yahweh led them to abstain from wine and from planting vineyards or sowing crops, and to live only in tents, were commended by Jeremiah for their ascetic way of life (Jer 35.1-19).
10.18-27 The Slaughter of the Worshipers of Baal. After announcing that he was to offer *a great sacrifice to Baal,* Jehu brought into Baal's temple all his worshipers, made *sacrifices and burnt offerings,* and then ordered all the devotees of Baal to be killed by the sword. Entering *the citadel* or inmost shrine of Baal, the fertility *pillar* and the temple itself were destroyed, and then turned into a symbol of gross uncleanness: *a latrine.*

10.32-36 The summary statement about the reign of Jehu (842-815) is ambivalent: while declaring that he *wiped out Baal from Israel,* and commending him for carrying out God's purpose, it also notes that he shared in the sins of *Jeroboam* and that he failed to rid the Israelite shrines at Bethel and Dan of the golden calves. The typical Deuteronomic conclusion (10.34-36) is prefaced by a promise to Jehu that four generations of his offspring would sit on the throne of Israel, which was fulfilled (2 Kings 13-14). Yet extensive sections of the kingdom were lost to the Syrians under their king, *Hazael:* all the land east of the Jordan *(Gilead)* from where the river empties into the Dead Sea north to the Syrian border *(Bashan).*
11.1-3 Conflict over the Succession to the Throne of Judah. Athaliah, mother of *Ahaziah,* the king of Judah who was murdered by order of Jehu (2 Kings 9.27), was a daughter of Jezebel and Ahab, and a granddaughter of King Omri of Israel (2 Kings 8.26). Determined to preserve the dynasty of her grandfather, she set out to kill all the royal family of her son and to reign herself as queen. *Ahaziah's sister,* however, who was the daughter of King *Joram* (or Jehoram) of Judah, who reigned 849-842, hid one of Ahaziah's children, *Joash,* for six years while Athaliah had seized the throne.
11.4-21 Restoration of the Royal Line of Ahaziah in Judah.
11.4-12 *Jehoiada,* the chief priest, convened the royal bodyguard (*Carites*) and the temple guards to show them Joash, *the king's son.* All the guards were brought together, rather than rotating on and off duty, and equipped with the *spears and shields* kept in the *house of the LORD* since the time of David. The king-designate was given the crown and other tokens of his role and the people's commitment to him (*the covenant*), whereupon he was publicly acclaimed as *king.*
11.13-16 Athaliah, on learning of the coup to replace her with a son of the late king, complained of *treason,* but was executed in the royal *house.*

had finished presenting the burnt offering,
Jehu said to the guards and to the officers,
"Come in and kill them; let no one escape."
So they put them to the sword. The guards
and the officers threw them out, and then
went into the citadel of the temple of Baal.
26 They brought out the pillar[g] that was in
the temple of Baal, and burned it. 27 Then
they demolished the pillar of Baal, and
destroyed the temple of Baal, and made it
a latrine to this day.
28 Thus Jehu wiped out Baal from Israel.
29 But Jehu did not turn aside from the sins
of Jeroboam son of Nebat, which he caused
Israel to commit—the golden calves that
were in Bethel and in Dan. 30 The LORD said
to Jehu, "Because you have done well in
carrying out what I consider right, and in
accordance with all that was in my heart
have dealt with the house of Ahab, your
sons of the fourth generation shall sit on the
throne of Israel." 31 But Jehu was not careful
to follow the law of the LORD the God of
Israel with all his heart; he did not turn
from the sins of Jeroboam, which he caused
Israel to commit.

Death of Jehu

32 In those days the LORD began to trim
off parts of Israel. Hazael defeated them
throughout the territory of Israel: 33 from the
Jordan eastward, all the land of Gilead, the
Gadites, the Reubenites, and the Manassites,
from Aroer, which is by the Wadi Arnon,
that is, Gilead and Bashan. 34 Now the rest
of the acts of Jehu, all that he did, and all
his power, are they not written in the Book
of the Annals of the Kings of Israel? 35 So
Jehu slept with his ancestors, and they
buried him in Samaria. His son Jehoahaz
succeeded him. 36 The time that Jehu reigned
over Israel in Samaria was twenty-eight
years.

Athaliah Reigns over Judah

11 Now when Athaliah, Ahaziah's
mother, saw that her son was dead,
she set about to destroy all the royal family.
2 But Jehosheba, King Joram's daughter,
Ahaziah's sister, took Joash son of Ahaziah,
and stole him away from among the king's
children who were about to be killed; she
put[h] him and his nurse in a bedroom. Thus
she[i] hid him from Athaliah, so that he was
not killed; 3 he remained with her six years,
hidden in the house of the LORD, while
Athaliah reigned over the land.

Jehoiada Anoints the Child Joash

4 But in the seventh year Jehoiada summoned the captains of the Carites and of the
guards and had them come to him in the
house of the LORD. He made a covenant with
them and put them under oath in the house
of the LORD; then he showed them the king's
son. 5 He commanded them, "This is what
you are to do: one-third of you, those who
go off duty on the sabbath and guard the
king's house 6 (another third being at the
gate Sur and a third at the gate behind the
guards), shall guard the palace; 7 and your
two divisions that come on duty in force on
the sabbath and guard the house of the
LORD[j] 8 shall surround the king, each with
weapons in hand; and whoever approaches
the ranks is to be killed. Be with the king
in his comings and goings."
9 The captains did according to all that
the priest Jehoiada commanded; each
brought his men who were to go off duty
on the sabbath, with those who were to
come on duty on the sabbath, and came to
the priest Jehoiada. 10 The priest delivered to
the captains the spears and shields that had
been King David's, which were in the house
of the LORD; 11 the guards stood, every man
with his weapons in his hand, from the
south side of the house to the north side of
the house, around the altar and the house,
to guard the king on every side. 12 Then he
brought out the king's son, put the crown
on him, and gave him the covenant;[k] they
proclaimed him king, and anointed him;
they clapped their hands and shouted, "Long
live the king!"

Death of Athaliah

13 When Athaliah heard the noise of the
guard and of the people, she went into the
house of the LORD to the people; 14 when she
looked, there was the king standing by the
pillar, according to custom, with the captains and the trumpeters beside the king,
and all the people of the land rejoicing and
blowing trumpets. Athaliah tore her clothes
and cried, "Treason! Treason!" 15 Then the

[g] Gk Vg Syr Tg: Heb *pillars* [h] With 2 Chr 22.11: Heb lacks *she put* [i] Gk Syr Vg Compare 2 Chr 22.11: Heb *they* [j] Heb *the LORD to the king* [k] Or *treaty* or *testimony*; Heb *eduth*

10.26 1 Kings 14.23
10.27 Ezra 6.11; Dan 2.5; 3.29
10.29 1 Kings 12.28,29
10.30 ver 35; 2 Kings 15.8,12
10.31 ver 29
10.32 2 Kings 8.12
10.34 Am 1.3-5
11.1 2 Chr 22.10-12
11.2 ver 21; 2 Kings 12.1
11.4 2 Chr 23.1ff; ver 19
11.5 1 Chr 9.25
11.9 2 Chr 23.8
11.10 2 Sam 8.7; 1 Chr 18.7
11.12 1 Sam 10.24
11.13 2 Chr 23.12ff
11.14 2 Kings 23.3; 2 Chr 34.31; 1 Kings 1.39,40; 2 Kings 9.23

priest Jehoiada commanded the captains who were set over the army, "Bring her out between the ranks, and kill with the sword anyone who follows her." For the priest said, "Let her not be killed in the house of the LORD." 16 So they laid hands on her; she went through the horses' entrance to the king's house, and there she was put to death.

17 Jehoiada made a covenant between the LORD and the king and people, that they should be the LORD's people; also between the king and the people. 18 Then all the people of the land went to the house of Baal, and tore it down; his altars and his images they broke in pieces, and they killed Mattan, the priest of Baal, before the altars. The priest posted guards over the house of the LORD. 19 He took the captains, the Carites, the guards, and all the people of the land; then they brought the king down from the house of the LORD, marching through the gate of the guards to the king's house. He took his seat on the throne of the kings. 20 So all the people of the land rejoiced; and the city was quiet after Athaliah had been killed with the sword at the king's house.

21[l] Jehoash[m] was seven years old when he began to reign.

The Temple Repaired

12 In the seventh year of Jehu, Jehoash began to reign; he reigned forty years in Jerusalem. His mother's name was Zibiah of Beer-sheba. 2 Jehoash did what was right in the sight of the LORD all his days, because the priest Jehoiada instructed him. 3 Nevertheless the high places were not taken away; the people continued to sacrifice and make offerings on the high places.

4 Jehoash said to the priests, "All the money offered as sacred donations that is brought into the house of the LORD, the money for which each person is assessed—the money from the assessment of persons—and the money from the voluntary offerings brought into the house of the LORD, 5 let the priests receive from each of the donors; and let them repair the house wherever any need of repairs is discovered." 6 But by the twenty-third year of King Jehoash the priests had made no repairs on the house. 7 Therefore King Jehoash summoned the priest Jehoiada with the other priests and said to them, "Why are you not repairing the house? Now therefore do not accept any more money from your donors but hand it over for the repair of the house." 8 So the priests agreed that they would neither accept more money from the people nor repair the house.

9 Then the priest Jehoiada took a chest, made a hole in its lid, and set it beside the altar on the right side as one entered the house of the LORD; the priests who guarded the threshold put in it all the money that was brought into the house of the LORD. 10 Whenever they saw that there was a great deal of money in the chest, the king's secretary and the high priest went up, counted the money that was found in the house of the LORD, and tied it up in bags. 11 They would give the money that was weighed out into the hands of the workers who had the oversight of the house of the LORD; then they paid it out to the carpenters and the builders who worked on the house of the LORD, 12 to the masons and the stonecutters, as well as to buy timber and quarried stone for making repairs on the house of the LORD, as well as for any outlay for repairs of the house. 13 But for the house of the LORD no basins of silver, snuffers, bowls, trumpets, or any vessels of gold, or of silver, were made from the money that was brought into the house of the LORD, 14 for that was given to the workers who were repairing the house of the LORD with it. 15 They did not ask an accounting from those into whose hand they delivered the money to pay out to the workers, for they dealt honestly. 16 The money from the guilt offerings and the money from the sin offerings was not brought into the house of the LORD; it belonged to the priests.

Hazael Threatens Jerusalem

17 At that time King Hazael of Aram went up, fought against Gath, and took it. But when Hazael set his face to go up against Jerusalem, 18 King Jehoash of Judah took all the votive gifts that Jehoshaphat, Jehoram, and Ahaziah, his ancestors, the kings of Judah, had dedicated, as well as his own votive gifts, all the gold that was found in the treasuries of the house of the LORD and of the king's house, and sent these to King Hazael of Aram. Then Hazael withdrew from Jerusalem.

11.17 2 Chr 23.16; 15.12-14; 2 Sam 5.3
11.18 2 Kings 10.26; Deut 12.3; 2 Chr 23.17ff
11.19 ver 4,6
11.21 2 Chr 24.1
12.3 2 Kings 14.4; 15.35
12.4 2 Kings 22.4; Ex 35.5; 1 Chr 29.3-9
12.6 2 Chr 24.5
12.7 2 Chr 24.6
12.9 2 Chr 24.8; Mk 12.41; Lk 21.1
12.10 2 Kings 19.2
12.12 2 Kings 22.5,6
12.13 2 Chr 24.14; 1 Kings 7.48,50
12.15 2 Kings 22.7
12.16 Lev 5.15-18; 4.24.29; Num 18.9,19
12.17 2 Kings 8.12; 2 Chr 24.23
12.18 1 Kings 15.18; 2 Kings 18.15,16

[l] Ch 12.1 in Heb [m] Another spelling is *Joash*; see verse 19

12.19-21 The reader is referred to the fuller account of *the acts of Joash* in the lost *Book of the Annals of the Kings of Judah.* Murdered by his own servants in *the house of Millo* (the structure built by David with retaining walls to enlarge the level space on the top of the narrow eastern ridge of the ancient city), Joash was buried in the adjacent cemetery, somewhere in the then narrow limits of *the city of David.*
13.1-9 Jehoahaz Reigns over Israel. The description of the reign of *Jehoahaz son of Jehu* is Deuteronomistic, with specification of the length of his kingship (815-801) calculated with beginning and ending years as seventeen, and an indictment of his sharing in the evil deeds of *Jeroboam,* including his permission for Baal-worship to continue even in Samaria. Though Israelites were oppressed by the Syrians (Aram), they remained relatively free. An indication of God's disfavor toward Israel was the reduction of the army horses and chariots to a fraction of the number that had actually belonged to Ahab (2,000) according to an ancient Assyrian inscription of Shalmaneser III (858-824).
13.10-13 Jehoash Reigns over Israel. No more than a Deuteronomistic negatively critical summary account is given of *Jehoash son of Jehoahaz,* the next king of Israel (801-786), including his potent fight with *King Amaziah of Judah.*
13.14-21 The Death of Elisha.
13.14-19 Stricken with a fatal illness, Elisha was visited by King Joash of Israel, who expressed both affection and respect by greeting him as *"My father."* This form of address, as well as mention of *horses and chariots,* recalls the circumstances of Elijah's being taken up to heaven (2 Kings 2.1-12). The instructions of Elisha to King Joash of Israel resemble the symbolic acts of prophets: shooting the arrows and striking the ground with them are to symbolize the defeat of the enemy. Joash's caution in striking the ground only *three times* indicates only a limited victory over *Aram,* the Syrian kingdom.
13.20-21 Continuing evidence of God's power through Elisha comes when the body of a *Moabite... marauder* from east of the Jordan comes back to life on contact with the *bones of Elisha.*
13.22-25 Joash Recovers the Towns Taken by Aram.
13.22-23 In spite of aggression by King Hazael of Aram throughout the reign of Israel's king, Jehoahaz (815-801), the nation was preserved through God's fidelity to the *covenant with Abraham, Isaac and Jacob.*

Death of Joash

19 Now the rest of the acts of Joash, and
all that he did, are they not written in the
Book of the Annals of the Kings of Judah?
[20]His servants arose, devised a conspiracy,
and killed Joash in the house of Millo, on
the way that goes down to Silla. [21]It was
Jozacar son of Shimeath and Jehozabad son
of Shomer, his servants, who struck him
down, so that he died. He was buried with
his ancestors in the city of David; then his
son Amaziah succeeded him.

Jehoahaz Reigns over Israel

13 In the twenty-third year of King
Joash son of Ahaziah of Judah,
Jehoahaz son of Jehu began to reign over
Israel in Samaria; he reigned seventeen years.
[2]He did what was evil in the sight of the
LORD, and followed the sins of Jeroboam son
of Nebat, which he caused Israel to sin; he
did not depart from them. [3]The anger of the
LORD was kindled against Israel, so that he
gave them repeatedly into the hand of King
Hazael of Aram, then into the hand of Ben-
hadad son of Hazael. [4]But Jehoahaz entreated the LORD, and the LORD heeded him;
for he saw the oppression of Israel, how the
king of Aram oppressed them. [5]Therefore
the LORD gave Israel a savior, so that they
escaped from the hand of the Arameans;
and the people of Israel lived in their homes
as formerly. [6]Nevertheless they did not depart
from the sins of the house of Jeroboam,
which he caused Israel to sin, but walked[n]
in them; the sacred pole[o] also remained in
Samaria. [7]So Jehoahaz was left with an
army of not more than fifty horsemen, ten
chariots and ten thousand footmen; for the
king of Aram had destroyed them and made
them like the dust at threshing. [8]Now the
rest of the acts of Jehoahaz and all that he
did, including his might, are they not written in the Book of the Annals of the Kings
of Israel? [9]So Jehoahaz slept with his ancestors, and they buried him in Samaria; then
his son Joash succeeded him.

Jehoash Reigns over Israel

10 In the thirty-seventh year of King
Joash of Judah, Jehoash son of Jehoahaz
began to reign over Israel in Samaria; he
reigned sixteen years. [11]He also did what
was evil in the sight of the LORD; he did not
depart from all the sins of Jeroboam son of
Nebat, which he caused Israel to sin, but he
walked in them. [12]Now the rest of the acts
of Joash, and all that he did, as well as the
might with which he fought against King
Amaziah of Judah, are they not written in
the Book of the Annals of the Kings of Israel?
[13]So Joash slept with his ancestors, and
Jeroboam sat upon his throne; Joash was
buried in Samaria with the kings of Israel.

Death of Elisha

14 Now when Elisha had fallen sick with
the illness of which he was to die, King
Joash of Israel went down to him, and wept
before him, crying, "My father, my father!
The chariots of Israel and its horsemen!"
[15]Elisha said to him, "Take a bow and
arrows"; so he took a bow and arrows.
[16]Then he said to the king of Israel, "Draw
the bow"; and he drew it. Elisha laid his
hands on the king's hands. [17]Then he said,
"Open the window eastward"; and he opened
it. Elisha said, "Shoot"; and he shot. Then
he said, "The LORD's arrow of victory, the
arrow of victory over Aram! For you shall
fight the Arameans in Aphek until you
have made an end of them." [18]He continued, "Take the arrows"; and he took them.
He said to the king of Israel, "Strike the
ground with them"; he struck three times,
and stopped. [19]Then the man of God was
angry with him, and said, "You should
have struck five or six times; then you
would have struck down Aram until you
had made an end of it, but now you will
strike down Aram only three times."
20 So Elisha died, and they buried him.
Now bands of Moabites used to invade the
land in the spring of the year. [21]As a man
was being buried, a marauding band was
seen and the man was thrown into the
grave of Elisha; as soon as the man touched
the bones of Elisha, he came to life and
stood on his feet.

Israel Recaptures Cities from Aram

22 Now King Hazael of Aram oppressed
Israel all the days of Jehoahaz. [23]But the
LORD was gracious to them and had compassion on them; he turned toward them,
because of his covenant with Abraham,
Isaac, and Jacob, and would not destroy
them; nor has he banished them from his
presence until now.

[n] Gk Syr Tg Vg: Heb *he walked* [o] Heb *Asherah*

12.20 2 Kings 14.5; 2 Chr 24.25; 1 Kings 11.27
12.21 2 Chr 24.26,27; 2 Kings 14.1
13.2 1 Kings 12.26-33
13.3 Judg 2.14; 2 Kings 8.12; 12.17
13.4 Num 21.7-9; Ps 78.34; Ex 3.7; 2 Kings 14.26
13.5 ver 25; 2 Kings 14.25,27
13.6 ver 2; 1 Kings 16.33
13.7 Am 1.3
13.9 2 Kings 10.35
13.12 ver 14-19; 2 Kings 14.8-15; 2 Chr 25.17ff
13.14 2 Kings 2.12
13.17 1 Kings 20.26
13.19 ver 25
13.20 see 2 Kings 3.7; 24.2
13.22 2 Kings 8.12
13.23 2 Kings 14.27; Ex 2.24,25; Gen 13.16,17

13.25 2 Kings 10.32,33; 14.25; ver 18,19
14.1 2 Kings 13.10; 2 Chr 25.1
14.4 2 Kings 12.3; 16.4
14.5 2 Kings 12.20
14.6 Deut 24.16; Ezek 18.4,20
14.7 2 Chr 25.11; 2 Sam 8.13; Josh 15.38
14.8 2 Chr 25.17-24
14.9 Judg 9.8-15
14.10 ver 7; Deut 8.14; 2 Chr 26.16; 32.25
14.11 Josh 19.38
14.12 2 Sam 18.17
14.13 Neh 8.16; 12.39; 2 Chr 25.23
14.14 2 Kings 12.18
14.15 2 Kings 13.12
14.17 2 Chr 25.25-28
14.19 Josh 10.31; 2 Kings 18.14,17
14.22 2 Kings 16.6; 2 Chr 26.2
14.25 2 Kings 10.32; 1 Kings 8.65; Deut 3.17; Jon 1.1; Mt 12.39,40; Josh 19.13
14.26 2 Kings 13.4; Deut 32.36
14.27 2 Kings 13.5,23

24 When King Hazael of Aram died, his
son Ben-hadad succeeded him. 25Then
Jehoash son of Jehoahaz took again from
Ben-hadad son of Hazael the towns that he
had taken from his father Jehoahaz in war.
Three times Joash defeated him and recovered the towns of Israel.

Amaziah Reigns over Judah

14 In the second year of King Joash
son of Joahaz of Israel, King
Amaziah son of Joash of Judah, began to
reign. 2He was twenty-five years old when
he began to reign, and he reigned twenty-
nine years in Jerusalem. His mother's name
was Jehoaddin of Jerusalem. 3He did what
was right in the sight of the LORD, yet not
like his ancestor David; in all things he did
as his father Joash had done. 4But the high
places were not removed; the people still
sacrificed and made offerings on the high
places. 5As soon as the royal power was
firmly in his hand he killed his servants
who had murdered his father the king. 6But
he did not put to death the children of the
murderers; according to what is written in
the book of the law of Moses, where the
LORD commanded, "The parents shall not be
put to death for the children, or the children
be put to death for the parents; but all shall
be put to death for their own sins."
7 He killed ten thousand Edomites in the
Valley of Salt and took Sela by storm; he
called it Jokthe-el, which is its name to this
day.
8 Then Amaziah sent messengers to King
Jehoash son of Jehoahaz, son of Jehu, of
Israel, saying, "Come, let us look one another in the face." 9King Jehoash of Israel
sent word to King Amaziah of Judah, "A
thornbush on Lebanon sent to a cedar on
Lebanon, saying, 'Give your daughter to my
son for a wife'; but a wild animal of Lebanon passed by and trampled down the
thornbush. 10You have indeed defeated Edom,
and your heart has lifted you up. Be content
with your glory, and stay at home; for why
should you provoke trouble so that you fall,
you and Judah with you?"
11 But Amaziah would not listen. So
King Jehoash of Israel went up; he and King
Amaziah of Judah faced one another in
battle at Beth-shemesh, which belongs to
Judah. 12Judah was defeated by Israel; everyone fled home. 13King Jehoash of Israel
captured King Amaziah of Judah son of
Jehoash, son of Ahaziah, at Beth-shemesh;
he came to Jerusalem, and broke down the
wall of Jerusalem from the Ephraim Gate to
the Corner Gate, a distance of four hundred
cubits. 14He seized all the gold and silver,
and all the vessels that were found in the
house of the LORD and in the treasuries of
the king's house, as well as hostages; then
he returned to Samaria.
15 Now the rest of the acts that Jehoash
did, his might, and how he fought with
King Amaziah of Judah, are they not written in the Book of the Annals of the Kings
of Israel? 16Jehoash slept with his ancestors,
and was buried in Samaria with the kings
of Israel; then his son Jeroboam succeeded
him.
17 King Amaziah son of Joash of Judah
lived fifteen years after the death of King
Jehoash son of Jehoahaz of Israel. 18Now the
rest of the deeds of Amaziah, are they not
written in the Book of the Annals of the
Kings of Judah? 19They made a conspiracy
against him in Jerusalem, and he fled to
Lachish. But they sent after him to Lachish,
and killed him there. 20They brought him
on horses; he was buried in Jerusalem with
his ancestors in the city of David. 21All the
people of Judah took Azariah, who was
sixteen years old, and made him king to
succeed his father Amaziah. 22He rebuilt
Elath and restored it to Judah, after King
Amaziah[p] slept with his ancestors.

Jeroboam II Reigns over Israel

23 In the fifteenth year of King Amaziah
son of Joash of Judah, King Jeroboam son
of Joash of Israel began to reign in Samaria;
he reigned forty-one years. 24He did what
was evil in the sight of the LORD; he did not
depart from all the sins of Jeroboam son of
Nebat, which he caused Israel to sin. 25He
restored the border of Israel from Lebo-
hamath as far as the Sea of the Arabah,
according to the word of the LORD, the God
of Israel, which he spoke by his servant
Jonah son of Amittai, the prophet, who was
from Gath-hepher. 26For the LORD saw that
the distress of Israel was very bitter; there
was no one left, bond or free, and no one
to help Israel. 27But the LORD had not said
that he would blot out the name of Israel
from under heaven, so he saved them by
the hand of Jeroboam son of Joash.

[p] Heb *the king*

13.24-25 Jehoahaz' son and successor, Jehoash (Joash) was able to regain from Hazael's son and successor, *Ben-hadad,* control over villages of Israel that Hazael had occupied. The threefold victory recalls the symbolic act of striking the ground with the arrows *three times* (13.18).

14.1-22 The Reign of Amaziah in Judah.

14.1-6 Amaziah's reign (800-783) receives a mixed evaluation in the Deuteronomic summary: his actions were right in the sight of the LORD, but he allowed the idolatrous practices to continue in the *high places;* he killed the *servants who had murdered his father* (12.19-21), but allowed their children to live. This concession is said to be in accord with *the Law of Moses* (Deut 24.16), which indicates that the account was written either (1) after the humane features of the Deuteronomic law had begun to develop in Israel, or (2) after Deuteronomy had achieved its present form during the exile of the Jews in Babylon (sixth century BCE) along with the subsequent re-writing of Israel's history.

14.7 Remarkable military successes are reported in attacks on the *Edomites,* whose territory was east and south of the Dead Sea.

14.8-14 The attempts to make peaceful arrangements with *King Jehoash of Israel* are treated as an empty show of strength based on the defeat of the Edomites. Instead of peace, Jehoash defeated and scattered the army of Judah, broke into Jerusalem, stripped the temple of its treasures, and carried them off as well as *hostages* to his capital at *Samaria.*

14.15-16 Summary of the reign and death of Jehoash of Israel.

14.17-22 The summary of the reign of Amaziah is followed by an account of his flight to Lachish (in the coastal hills west of Hebron) from conspirators in Jerusalem, his murder there, and his burial in Jerusalem in *the city of David,* the traditional site of David's residence and entombment. His youthful successor, *Azariah* (also known as Uzziah), whose reign is to be described more fully (15.1-7), is noted here for having *rebuilt Elath,* an important port at the northeastern end of the Gulf of Aqabah, which is probably not to be identified with nearby Ezion-geber, a major commercial center in the time of Solomon (1 Kings 9-10).

14.23-29 The Reign of Jeroboam II over Israel.

14.23-24 The reign of Jeroboam II (786-746) is condemned in this account as repeating the *sins of Jeroboam I* – presumably his fostering of worship of the fertility gods and goddesses (1 Kings 12-14).

14.25 This brief statement contains two important features: (1) the territorial expansion of Israel under Jeroboam II from the *Arabah* (the valley which reaches from the Dead Sea to the Red Sea) to *Lebo-hamath* (a major city in north-central Syria); and (2) the critique of the king offered by the prophet, Jonah. The expansion of the Assyrian empire into Syria at this time created there the power vacuum into which Jeroboam II moved in an unprecedented expansion of the territory controlled by Israel. The prophetic judgment on the king is articulated by the prophet Amos. The prophet mentioned in this account, *Jonah,* is identified as the writer of the Book of Jonah, although the book that bears his name comes from at least a century later.

14.15-29 As hopeless as the fate of Israel seem to be, the writer of this account declares that God is not going to *blot out the name of Israel.*

28 Now the rest of the acts of Jeroboam,
and all that he did, and his might, how he
fought, and how he recovered for Israel
Damascus and Hamath, which had belonged
to Judah, are they not written in the Book
of the Annals of the Kings of Israel? 29Jero-
boam slept with his ancestors, the kings of
Israel; his son Zechariah succeeded him.

Azariah Reigns over Judah

15 In the twenty-seventh year of King
Jeroboam of Israel King Azariah
son of Amaziah of Judah began to reign.
2He was sixteen years old when he began
to reign, and he reigned fifty-two years in
Jerusalem. His mother's name was Jecoliah
of Jerusalem. 3He did what was right in the
sight of the LORD, just as his father Amaziah
had done. 4Nevertheless the high places
were not taken away; the people still sacrificed and made offerings on the high places.
5The LORD struck the king, so that he was
leprous[q] to the day of his death, and lived
in a separate house. Jotham the king's son
was in charge of the palace, governing the
people of the land. 6Now the rest of the acts
of Azariah, and all that he did, are they not
written in the Book of the Annals of the
Kings of Judah? 7Azariah slept with his
ancestors; they buried him with his ancestors in the city of David; his son Jotham
succeeded him.

Zechariah Reigns over Israel

8 In the thirty-eighth year of King Azariah
of Judah, Zechariah son of Jeroboam reigned
over Israel in Samaria six months. 9He did
what was evil in the sight of the LORD, as
his ancestors had done. He did not depart
from the sins of Jeroboam son of Nebat,
which he caused Israel to sin. 10Shallum
son of Jabesh conspired against him, and
struck him down in public and killed him,
and reigned in place of him. 11Now the rest
of the deeds of Zechariah are written in the
Book of the Annals of the Kings of Israel.
12This was the promise of the LORD that he
gave to Jehu, "Your sons shall sit on the
throne of Israel to the fourth generation."
And so it happened.

Shallum Reigns over Israel

13 Shallum son of Jabesh began to reign
in the thirty-ninth year of King Uzziah of
Judah; he reigned one month in Samaria.
14Then Menahem son of Gadi came up from
Tirzah and came to Samaria; he struck
down Shallum son of Jabesh in Samaria
and killed him; he reigned in place of him.
15Now the rest of the deeds of Shallum,
including the conspiracy that he made, are
written in the Book of the Annals of the
Kings of Israel. 16At that time Menahem
sacked Tiphsah, all who were in it and its
territory from Tirzah on; because they did
not open it to him, he sacked it. He ripped
open all the pregnant women in it.

Menahem Reigns over Israel

17 In the thirty-ninth year of King
Azariah of Judah, Menahem son of Gadi
began to reign over Israel; he reigned ten
years in Samaria. 18He did what was evil in
the sight of the LORD; he did not depart all
his days from any of the sins of Jeroboam
son of Nebat, which he caused Israel to sin.
19King Pul of Assyria came against the land;
Menahem gave Pul a thousand talents of
silver, so that he might help him confirm
his hold on the royal power. 20Menahem
exacted the money from Israel, that is, from
all the wealthy, fifty shekels of silver from
each one, to give to the king of Assyria. So
the king of Assyria turned back, and did not
stay there in the land. 21Now the rest of the
deeds of Menahem, and all that he did, are
they not written in the Book of the Annals
of the Kings of Israel? 22Menahem slept with
his ancestors, and his son Pekahiah succeeded him.

Pekahiah Reigns over Israel

23 In the fiftieth year of King Azariah of
Judah, Pekahiah son of Menahem began to
reign over Israel in Samaria; he reigned two
years. 24He did what was evil in the sight
of the LORD; he did not turn away from the
sins of Jeroboam son of Nebat, which he
caused Israel to sin. 25Pekah son of Remaliah,
his captain, conspired against him with fifty
of the Gileadites, and attacked him in
Samaria, in the citadel of the palace along
with Argob and Arieh; he killed him, and
reigned in place of him. 26Now the rest of
the deeds of Pekahiah, and all that he did,
are written in the Book of the Annals of the
Kings of Israel.

[q] A term for several skin diseases; precise meaning uncertain

15.1-7 The Reign of Azariah/Uzziah over Judah. This king's reign, which began at age sixteen, and extended for *fifty-two years* (783-741), is depicted in the summary as mostly good (except for the failure to remove the idolatrous *high places)*. But it was marred by the king's contracting a dread skin disease, which required him to live in a *separate house* (or section of the royal palace) and to have his son, *Jotham*, preside over the government until his father's death. Under the name Uzziah he is mentioned by the prophets (Isa 6.1; 7.1; Hos 1.1; Am 1.1).
15.1-38 Summary Accounts of the Kings of Israel and Judah. Each account is given in the stylized pattern of the deuteronomistic historian, with the age of the rulers and typical denunciations of their reigns, except for that of Jotham, king of Judah. One vivid narrative detail is included in each case.
15.1-8 Zechariah's Reign over Israel. This brief reign of six months (in 746) ended in the murder of the king by *Shallum son of Jabesh*, thereby terminating the dynasty of Jehu (2 Kings 9-10).
15.13-16 Shallum's Reign over Israel. Even briefer than the reign of Zechariah was that of Shallum: *one month* (in 745). It also ended in assassination by his successor, *Menahem* from Tirzah (in the mountain ridges east of Samaria). The plundering and slaughtering by him probably took place at Tappuah (south of Samaria) rather than at *Tiphsah*, which was on the Euphrates River in northeastern Syria.
15.17-22 Menahem's Reign over Israel. His *ten year* reign, which is a round figure (745-738), is here characterized as conforming to the model of wicked Jeroboam I. The territorial aggression of *Assyria* had begun, and Menachem tried to maintain some degree of autonomy for his kingdom by paying huge sums (*a thousand talents of silver)* to the Assyrian king, having extracted the money from *the wealthy* of his own realm.
15.23-26 Pekahiah's Reign over Israel. A similar negative summary of this two-year reign (738-737) is given, with a note of his being expelled from the throne and killed by a group of conspirators, led by one of his military officers, *Pekah*.

14.28 2 Sam 8.6; 1 Kings 11.24; 2 Chr 8.3
14.29 2 Kings 15.8
15.1 2 Kings 14.21; 2 Chr 26.1,3,4
15.2 2 Chr 26.3,4
15.4 2 Kings 12.3; 14.4
15.5 2 Chr 26.19-21
15.7 2 Chr 26.23
15.10 Am 7.9
15.12 2 Kings 10.30
15.13 ver 1,8
15.14 1 Kings 14.17
15.16 1 Kings 4.24; 2 Kings 8.12
15.17 ver 1,8,13
15.19 1 Chr 5.26
15.23 ver 1,8,13,17
15.25 1 Kings 16.18

Pekah Reigns over Israel

27 In the fifty-second year of King Azariah of Judah, Pekah son of Remaliah began to reign over Israel in Samaria; he reigned twenty years. [28]He did what was evil in the sight of the LORD; he did not depart from the sins of Jeroboam son of Nebat, which he caused Israel to sin.

29 In the days of King Pekah of Israel, King Tiglath-pileser of Assyria came and captured Ijon, Abel-beth-maacah, Janoah, Kedesh, Hazor, Gilead, and Galilee, all the land of Naphtali; and he carried the people captive to Assyria. [30]Then Hoshea son of Elah made a conspiracy against Pekah son of Remaliah, attacked him, and killed him; he reigned in place of him, in the twentieth year of Jotham son of Uzziah. [31]Now the rest of the acts of Pekah, and all that he did, are written in the Book of the Annals of the Kings of Israel.

Jotham Reigns over Judah

32 In the second year of King Pekah son of Remaliah of Israel, King Jotham son of Uzziah of Judah began to reign. [33]He was twenty-five years old when he began to reign and reigned sixteen years in Jerusalem. His mother's name was Jerusha daughter of Zadok. [34]He did what was right in the sight of the LORD, just as his father Uzziah had done. [35]Nevertheless the high places were not removed; the people still sacrificed and made offerings on the high places. He built the upper gate of the house of the LORD. [36]Now the rest of the acts of Jotham, and all that he did, are they not written in the Book of the Annals of the Kings of Judah? [37]In those days the LORD began to send King Rezin of Aram and Pekah son of Remaliah against Judah. [38]Jotham slept with his ancestors, and was buried with his ancestors in the city of David, his ancestor; his son Ahaz succeeded him.

Ahaz Reigns over Judah

16 In the seventeenth year of Pekah son of Remaliah, King Ahaz son of Jotham of Judah began to reign. [2]Ahaz was twenty years old when he began to reign; he reigned sixteen years in Jerusalem. He did not do what was right in the sight of the LORD his God, as his ancestor David had done, [3]but he walked in the way of the kings of Israel. He even made his son pass through fire, according to the abominable practices of the nations whom the LORD drove out before the people of Israel. [4]He sacrificed and made offerings on the high places, on the hills, and under every green tree.

5 Then King Rezin of Aram and King Pekah son of Remaliah of Israel came up to wage war on Jerusalem; they besieged Ahaz but could not conquer him. [6]At that time the king of Edom[r] recovered Elath for Edom,[s] and drove the Judeans from Elath; and the Edomites came to Elath, where they live to this day. [7]Ahaz sent messengers to King Tiglath-pileser of Assyria, saying, "I am your servant and your son. Come up, and rescue me from the hand of the king of Aram and from the hand of the king of Israel, who are attacking me." [8]Ahaz also took the silver and gold found in the house of the LORD and in the treasures of the king's house, and sent a present to the king of Assyria. [9]The king of Assyria listened to him; the king of Assyria marched up against Damascus, and took it, carrying its people captive to Kir; then he killed Rezin.

10 When King Ahaz went to Damascus to meet King Tiglath-pileser of Assyria, he saw the altar that was at Damascus. King Ahaz sent to the priest Uriah a model of the altar, and its pattern, exact in all its details. [11]The priest Uriah built the altar; in accordance with all that King Ahaz had sent from Damascus, just so did the priest Uriah build it, before King Ahaz arrived from Damascus. [12]When the king came from Damascus, the king viewed the altar. Then the king drew near to the altar, went up on it, [13]and offered his burnt offering and his grain offering, poured his drink offering, and dashed the blood of his offerings of well-being against the altar. [14]The bronze altar that was before the LORD he removed from the front of the house, from the place between his altar and the house of the LORD, and put it on the north side of his altar. [15]King Ahaz commanded the priest Uriah, saying, "Upon the great altar offer the morning burnt offering, and the evening grain offering, and the king's burnt offering, and his grain offering, with the burnt offering of all the people of the land, their grain offering, and their drink offering; then dash against it all the blood of the burnt offering, and all the blood of the sacrifice; but the bronze altar shall be

[r] Cn: Heb *King Rezin of Aram* [s] Cn: Heb *Aram*

15.27 ver 23; Isa 7.1
15.29 ver 19; 2 Kings 17.6; 1 Chr 5.26
15.32 2 Chr 27.1ff
15.34 ver 3; 2 Chr 26.4,5
15.35 ver 4; 2 Chr 27.3
15.37 2 Kings 16.5; Isa 7.1; ver 27
16.1 2 Chr 28.1ff
16.3 Lev 18.2; 2 Kings 17.17; 21.6; Deut 12.31; 2 Kings 21.2,11
16.4 Deut 12.2; 2 Kings 14.4
16.5 2 Kings 15.37; Isa 7.1; 2 Chr 28.5,6
16.6 2 Kings 14.22; 2 Chr 26.2
16.7 2 Chr 28.16ff; 2 Kings 15.29
16.8 2 Kings 12.17,18
16.9 2 Chr 28.21; Am 1.3-5
16.10 2 Kings 15.29; Isa 8.2
16.14 2 Chr 4.1
16.15 Ex 29.39-41

15.27-31 Pekah's Reign over Israel. This reign, which began in 737, is said to have lasted *twenty years*, but that is difficult to reconcile with the certain date for the fall of Samaria to the Assyrians in 721. The invasion by *Tiglath-pileser* III, who rebuilt and extended the earlier empire of Assyria (in 734-732), resulted in his seizure of territories east, west and north of *Galilee* and the taking of the Israelite inhabitants into captivity in Assyria. These developments are mentioned in the contemporary annals of this ruler, which archaeologists have discovered and deciphered.
15.32-38 Jotham's Reign over Judah. Son of *Uzziah*, this king's rule from 742 to 735 is summarized like those of his predecessors: he *did what was right* but failed to destroy the idolatrous sanctuaries. The pressure on Judah from Syria (*Aram*) and Israel (*Pekah*) is reported as having been sent by *the LORD*.
16.1-20 King Ahaz Allies Judah with Assyria.
16.1-4 During Ahaz' reign (735-715) he adopted idolatrous practices, including having his own son *pass through the fire*, which was offering him as a burnt sacrifice to Baal (Jer 19.5).
16.5-9 Military attacks came from Syria and Israel (*Rezin* and *Pekah*), and the Edomites freed their land from control by Judah. Accordingly, *Ahaz* presented treasures to *the king of Assyria* and cooperated with him militarily, killing *Rezin* (king of Syria), with the result that Judah became a vassal to Assyria.
16.10-20 To ingratiate himself with *Tiglath-pileser*, Ahaz ordered the altar in the Jerusalem temple to be patterned after the pagan sanctuary in Damascus and had the plan of the temple rearranged to serve the Assyrian pattern of sacrifice. *The bronze altar* was no longer used for sacrifice but became a place for the king to obtain divine messages (*inquire by*) through the examination of entrails. The special entrance to the temple reserved for Judah's king was also removed by Ahaz' order, apparently to ingratiate himself with the Assyrian king.

17.1-41 The Exile of Israel to Assyria and the Resettling of Samaria.
17.1-4 *Hoshea*, having murdered and replaced Pekah as Israel's king (15.30), became a *vassal* of the new Assyrian ruler, *Shalmaneser* V, son of Tiglath-pileser, and paid him heavy *tribute*. On learning of Hoshea's having contacted *King So of Egypt* (possibly Osorkon IV, ruled from 727-720), the king of Assyria *imprisoned him*.
17.5-23 After a three-year siege led by Sargon II (whose own official accounts have been found by archaeologists), Samaria was taken by the Assyrians and *the Israelites* were taken into captivity in various cities in the central section of the Tigris-Euphrates Valley and also in Media (now Iran). The explanation of why God let this happen is offered, detailing the failings of the people and the leaders to obey the law and to fulfill their *covenant* obligations to the God of Israel. A parenthetic note (17.19-20) observes that Judah followed the same disobedient pattern and was likewise to be *banished from [God's] presence*. These calamities for Israel are said to have been foretold by God's true *servants the prophets*.

for me to inquire by." [16]The priest Uriah did everything that King Ahaz commanded.

17 Then King Ahaz cut off the frames of the stands, and removed the laver from them; he removed the sea from the bronze oxen that were under it, and put it on a pediment of stone. [18]The covered portal for use on the sabbath that had been built inside the palace, and the outer entrance for the king he removed from[t] the house of the LORD. He did this because of the king of Assyria. [19]Now the rest of the acts of Ahaz that he did, are they not written in the Book of the Annals of the Kings of Judah? [20]Ahaz slept with his ancestors, and was buried with his ancestors in the city of David; his son Hezekiah succeeded him.

Hoshea Reigns over Israel

17 In the twelfth year of King Ahaz of Judah, Hoshea son of Elah began to reign in Samaria over Israel; he reigned nine years. [2]He did what was evil in the sight of the LORD, yet not like the kings of Israel who were before him. [3]King Shalmaneser of Assyria came up against him; Hoshea became his vassal, and paid him tribute. [4]But the king of Assyria found treachery in Hoshea; for he had sent messengers to King So of Egypt, and offered no tribute to the king of Assyria, as he had done year by year; therefore the king of Assyria confined him and imprisoned him.

Israel Carried Captive to Assyria

5 Then the king of Assyria invaded all the land and came to Samaria; for three years he besieged it. [6]In the ninth year of Hoshea the king of Assyria captured Samaria; he carried the Israelites away to Assyria. He placed them in Halah, on the Habor, the river of Gozan, and in the cities of the Medes.

7 This occurred because the people of Israel had sinned against the LORD their God, who had brought them up out of the land of Egypt from under the hand of Pharaoh king of Egypt. They had worshiped other gods [8]and walked in the customs of the nations whom the LORD drove out before the people of Israel, and in the customs that the kings of Israel had introduced.[u] [9]The people of Israel secretly did things that were not right against the LORD their God. They built for themselves high places at all their towns, from watchtower to fortified city; [10]they set up for themselves pillars and sacred poles[v] on every high hill and under every green tree; [11]there they made offerings on all the high places, as the nations did whom the LORD carried away before them. They did wicked things, provoking the LORD to anger; [12]they served idols, of which the LORD had said to them, "You shall not do this." [13]Yet the LORD warned Israel and Judah by every prophet and every seer, saying, "Turn from your evil ways and keep my commandments and my statutes, in accordance with all the law that I commanded your ancestors and that I sent to you by my servants the prophets." [14]They would not listen but were stubborn, as their ancestors had been, who did not believe in the LORD their God. [15]They despised his statutes, and his covenant that he made with their ancestors, and the warnings that he gave them. They went after false idols and became false; they followed the nations that were around them, concerning whom the LORD had commanded them that they should not do as they did. [16]They rejected all the commandments of the LORD their God and made for themselves cast images of two calves; they made a sacred pole,[v] worshiped all the host of heaven, and served Baal. [17]They made their sons and their daughters pass through fire; they used divination and augury; and they sold themselves to do evil in the sight of the LORD, provoking him to anger. [18]Therefore the LORD was very angry with Israel and removed them out of his sight; none was left but the tribe of Judah alone.

19 Judah also did not keep the commandments of the LORD their God but walked in the customs that Israel had introduced. [20]The LORD rejected all the descendants of Israel; he punished them and gave them into the hand of plunderers, until he had banished them from his presence.

21 When he had torn Israel from the house of David, they made Jeroboam son of Nebat king. Jeroboam drove Israel from following the LORD and made them commit great sin. [22]The people of Israel continued in all the sins that Jeroboam committed; they did not depart from them [23]until the LORD removed Israel out of his sight, as he had foretold through all his servants the prophets. So Israel was exiled from their own land to Assyria until this day.

[t] Cn: Heb lacks *from* [u] Meaning of Heb uncertain [v] Heb *Asherim*

16.17 1 Kings 7.23-28
16.20 2 Chr 28.27
17.1 2 Kings 15.30
17.3 2 Kings 18.9-12
17.6 Hos 13.16; Deut 28.64; 29.27,28; 1 Chr 5.26; 2 Kings 18.10,11
17.7 Josh 23.16; Ex 14.15-30; Judg 6.10
17.8 Lev 18.3; Deut 18.9; 2 Kings 16.3
17.9 2 Kings 18.8
17.10 Ex 34.12-14; 1 Kings 14.23; Mic 5.14
17.12 Ex 20.3,4
17.13 1 Sam 9.9; Jer 18.11; 25.5; 35.15
17.14 Ex 32.9; Deut 31.27; Acts 7.51
17.15 Jer 8.9; Deut 29.25; 32.21; Deut 12.30,31
17.16 1 Kings 12.28; 14.15,23; 2 Kings 21.3; 1 Kings 16.31
17.17 Lev 19.26; 2 Kings 16.3; Deut 18.10-12; 1 Kings 21.20
17.18 ver 6; 1 Kings 11.13,32,36
17.20 2 Kings 15.29
17.21 1 Kings 11.11,31; 12.20,28-33

Assyria Resettles Samaria

24 The king of Assyria brought people from Babylon, Cuthah, Avva, Hamath, and Sepharvaim, and placed them in the cities of Samaria in place of the people of Israel; they took possession of Samaria, and settled in its cities. 25When they first settled there, they did not worship the LORD; therefore the LORD sent lions among them, which killed some of them. 26So the king of Assyria was told, "The nations that you have carried away and placed in the cities of Samaria do not know the law of the god of the land; therefore he has sent lions among them; they are killing them, because they do not know the law of the god of the land." 27Then the king of Assyria commanded, "Send there one of the priests whom you carried away from there; let him[w] go and live there, and teach them the law of the god of the land." 28So one of the priests whom they had carried away from Samaria came and lived in Bethel; he taught them how they should worship the LORD.

29 But every nation still made gods of its own and put them in the shrines of the high places that the people of Samaria had made, every nation in the cities in which they lived; 30the people of Babylon made Succoth-benoth, the people of Cuth made Nergal, the people of Hamath made Ashima; 31the Avvites made Nibhaz and Tartak; the Sepharvites burned their children in the fire to Adrammelech and Anammelech, the gods of Sepharvaim. 32They also worshiped the LORD and appointed from among themselves all sorts of people as priests of the high places, who sacrificed for them in the shrines of the high places. 33So they worshiped the LORD but also served their own gods, after the manner of the nations from among whom they had been carried away. 34To this day they continue to practice their former customs.

They do not worship the LORD and they do not follow the statutes or the ordinances or the law or the commandment that the LORD commanded the children of Jacob, whom he named Israel. 35The LORD had made a covenant with them and commanded them, "You shall not worship other gods or bow yourselves to them or serve them or sacrifice to them, 36but you shall worship the LORD, who brought you out of the land of Egypt with great power and with an outstretched arm; you shall bow yourselves to him, and to him you shall sacrifice. 37The statutes and the ordinances and the law and the commandment that he wrote for you, you shall always be careful to observe. You shall not worship other gods; 38you shall not forget the covenant that I have made with you. You shall not worship other gods, 39but you shall worship the LORD your God; he will deliver you out of the hand of all your enemies." 40They would not listen, however, but they continued to practice their former custom.

41 So these nations worshiped the LORD, but also served their carved images; to this day their children and their children's children continue to do as their ancestors did.

Hezekiah's Reign over Judah

18 In the third year of King Hoshea son of Elah of Israel, Hezekiah son of King Ahaz of Judah began to reign. 2He was twenty-five years old when he began to reign; he reigned twenty-nine years in Jerusalem. His mother's name was Abi daughter of Zechariah. 3He did what was right in the sight of the LORD just as his ancestor David had done. 4He removed the high places, broke down the pillars, and cut down the sacred pole.[x] He broke in pieces the bronze serpent that Moses had made, for until those days the people of Israel had made offerings to it; it was called Nehushtan. 5He trusted in the LORD the God of Israel; so that there was no one like him among all the kings of Judah after him, or among those who were before him. 6For he held fast to the LORD; he did not depart from following him but kept the commandments that the LORD commanded Moses. 7The LORD was with him; wherever he went, he prospered. He rebelled against the king of Assyria and would not serve him. 8He attacked the Philistines as far as Gaza and its territory, from watchtower to fortified city.

9 In the fourth year of King Hezekiah, which was the seventh year of King Hoshea son of Elah of Israel, King Shalmaneser of Assyria came up against Samaria, besieged it, 10and at the end of three years, took it. In the sixth year of Hezekiah, which was the ninth year of King Hoshea of Israel, Samaria was taken. 11The king of Assyria carried the Israelites away to Assyria, settled them in Halah, on the Habor, the river of Gozan, and in the cities of the Medes,

[w] Syr Vg: Heb *them* [x] Heb *Asherah*

17.24 Ezra 4.2,10; 2 Kings 18.34
17.27 Mic 3.11
17.30 ver 24
17.31 ver 17,24
17.32 1 Kings 12.31
17.33 Zeph 1.5
17.34 Gen 32.28; 35.10
17.35 Judg 6.10; Ex 20.5
17.36 Ex 6.6; Deut 10.20
17.37 Deut 5.32
17.38 Deut 4.23
17.41 ver 32,33
18.1 2 Kings 17.1; 2 Chr 28.27
18.2 2 Chr 29.1,2
18.4 2 Chr 31.1; Num 21.8,9
18.5 2 Kings 19.10; 23.25
18.6 Deut 10.20
18.7 Gen 39.2,3; 1 Sam 18.14; 2 Kings 16.7
18.8 1 Chr 4.41; Isa 14.29; 2 Kings 17.9
18.9 2 Kings 17.3
18.10 2 Kings 17.6
18.11 2 Kings 17.6

17.24-41 The Assyrians brought peoples from their own territories to settle in the cities of Samaria, but attacks on the new settlers by lions were understood to be the consequence of neglect of the local Israelite deities. Accordingly, a priest was brought back to reinstitute the proper worship of Yahweh, the God of Israel. Idolatrous shrines continued to be built in addition, however, and the Deuteronomic historian adds an explanation of the fate of Israel as a consequence of neglect of proper worship and obedience to the covenant.
18.1-19.37 The Response of Hezekiah and Isaiah to the Invasion of Judah by Sennacherib.
18.1-8 Hezekiah is pictured as a reforming king, who recalled Judah to the commandments and proper worship, and who was therefore successful in maintaining the independence of his people. His reign was from 715 to 687.
18.9-12 A brief summary of the fall of Israel to the Assyrians.

18.13-37 Sennacherib's Invasion of Judah. These events are described not only here (18.13-20.19) and in a slightly different version in Isa 36-39, but also in a very different official Assyrian account preserved on stone tablets found by archaeologists. In the biblical account, the invader's demands for tribute are said to have resulted in Hezekiah's taking more of the royal treasury and even stripping *the gold from the doors of the temple.* From his military base at *Lachish* (west of Hebron in the coastal hills), Sennacherib sent *a great army...to Hezekiah in Jerusalem* led by *the Rabshakeh* (his commander-in-chief) to warn the king of Judah against any alliance with *Egypt* and to remind him of his military impotence in the presence of the Assyrian army. After first addressing his challenge to representatives of the king, the commander then spoke to the people *in the language of Judah,* warning them against military resistance and promising them peace and prosperity if they submitted to the Assyrians. He notes the powerlessness of the gods of the Syrian cities (*Hamath and Arpad*) and of the gods of the Israelite cities. The people respond with silence and sorrow, symbolized by their *torn clothes.* The conduit by which the Rabshakeh stood consisted of a channel cut through the bed rock of the eastern hill of Jerusalem for 1,100 feet to bring water from the only spring in the area into the city, and was probably built to guarantee water in time of siege.

12 because they did not obey the voice of the
LORD their God but transgressed his covenant—all that Moses the servant of the
LORD had commanded; they neither listened
nor obeyed.

Sennacherib Invades Judah

13 In the fourteenth year of King
Hezekiah, King Sennacherib of Assyria came
up against all the fortified cities of Judah
and captured them. 14 King Hezekiah of Judah
sent to the king of Assyria at Lachish,
saying, "I have done wrong; withdraw from
me; whatever you impose on me I will
bear." The king of Assyria demanded of
King Hezekiah of Judah three hundred talents of silver and thirty talents of gold.
15 Hezekiah gave him all the silver that was
found in the house of the LORD and in the
treasuries of the king's house. 16 At that time
Hezekiah stripped the gold from the doors
of the temple of the LORD, and from the
doorposts that King Hezekiah of Judah had
overlaid and gave it to the king of Assyria.
17 The king of Assyria sent the Tartan, the
Rabsaris, and the Rabshakeh with a great
army from Lachish to King Hezekiah at
Jerusalem. They went up and came to Jerusalem. When they arrived, they came and
stood by the conduit of the upper pool,
which is on the highway to the Fuller's
Field. 18 When they called for the king, there
came out to them Eliakim son of Hilkiah,
who was in charge of the palace, and
Shebnah the secretary, and Joah son of
Asaph, the recorder.
19 The Rabshakeh said to them, "Say to
Hezekiah: Thus says the great king, the
king of Assyria: On what do you base this
confidence of yours? 20 Do you think that
mere words are strategy and power for war?
On whom do you now rely, that you have
rebelled against me? 21 See, you are relying
now on Egypt, that broken reed of a staff,
which will pierce the hand of anyone who
leans on it. Such is Pharaoh king of Egypt
to all who rely on him. 22 But if you say to
me, 'We rely on the LORD our God,' is it not
he whose high places and altars Hezekiah
has removed, saying to Judah and to Jerusalem, 'You shall worship before this altar
in Jerusalem'? 23 Come now, make a wager
with my master the king of Assyria: I will
give you two thousand horses, if you are
able on your part to set riders on them.
24 How then can you repulse a single captain among the least of my master's servants, when you rely on Egypt for chariots
and for horsemen? 25 Moreover, is it without
the LORD that I have come up against this
place to destroy it? The LORD said to me, Go
up against this land, and destroy it."
26 Then Eliakim son of Hilkiah, and
Shebnah, and Joah said to the Rabshakeh,
"Please speak to your servants in the Aramaic language, for we understand it; do not
speak to us in the language of Judah within
the hearing of the people who are on the
wall." 27 But the Rabshakeh said to them,
"Has my master sent me to speak these
words to your master and to you, and not
to the people sitting on the wall, who are
doomed with you to eat their own dung
and to drink their own urine?"
28 Then the Rabshakeh stood and called
out in a loud voice in the language of
Judah, "Hear the word of the great king, the
king of Assyria! 29 Thus says the king: 'Do
not let Hezekiah deceive you, for he will not
be able to deliver you out of my hand. 30 Do
not let Hezekiah make you rely on the LORD
by saying, The LORD will surely deliver us,
and this city will not be given into the hand
of the king of Assyria.' 31 Do not listen to
Hezekiah; for thus says the king of Assyria:
'Make your peace with me and come out to
me; then every one of you will eat from
your own vine and your own fig tree, and
drink water from your own cistern, 32 until
I come and take you away to a land like
your own land, a land of grain and wine,
a land of bread and vineyards, a land of
olive oil and honey, that you may live and
not die. Do not listen to Hezekiah when he
misleads you by saying, The LORD will deliver us. 33 Has any of the gods of the nations
ever delivered its land out of the hand of the
king of Assyria? 34 Where are the gods of
Hamath and Arpad? Where are the gods of
Sepharvaim, Hena, and Ivvah? Have they
delivered Samaria out of my hand? 35 Who
among all the gods of the countries have
delivered their countries out of my hand,
that the LORD should deliver Jerusalem out
of my hand?' "
36 But the people were silent and answered him not a word, for the king's command was, "Do not answer him." 37 Then
Eliakim son of Hilkiah, who was in charge
of the palace, and Shebna the secretary, and
Joah son of Asaph, the recorder, came to
Hezekiah with their clothes torn and told
him the words of the Rabshakeh.

18.13 2 Chr 32.1ff; Isa 36.1ff
18.15 2 Kings 16.8
18.17 Isa 20.1; 7.3
18.18 2 Kings 19.2; Isa 22.15,20
18.19 2 Chr 32.10ff
18.21 Ezek 29.6,7
18.22 ver 4; 2 Chr 31.1; 32.12
18.24 Isa 31.1
18.26 Ezra 4.7
18.29 2 Chr 32.15
18.31 1 Kings 4.20, 25
18.32 Deut 8.7-9
18.33 2 Kings 19.12; 2 Chr 32.14; Isa 10.10,11
18.34 2 Kings 19.13; 17.24
18.37 ver 18,26; 2 Kings 6.30

Hezekiah Consults Isaiah

19 When King Hezekiah heard it, he
tore his clothes, covered himself
with sackcloth, and went into the house of
the LORD. [2]And he sent Eliakim, who was in
charge of the palace, and Shebna the secretary, and the senior priests, covered with
sackcloth, to the prophet Isaiah son of Amoz.
[3]They said to him, "Thus says Hezekiah,
This day is a day of distress, of rebuke, and
of disgrace; children have come to the birth,
and there is no strength to bring them
forth. [4]It may be that the LORD your God
heard all the words of the Rabshakeh, whom
his master the king of Assyria has sent to
mock the living God, and will rebuke the
words that the LORD your God has heard;
therefore lift up your prayer for the remnant that is left." [5]When the servants of
King Hezekiah came to Isaiah, [6]Isaiah said
to them, "Say to your master, 'Thus says
the LORD: Do not be afraid because of the
words that you have heard, with which the
servants of the king of Assyria have reviled
me. [7]I myself will put a spirit in him, so that
he shall hear a rumor and return to his
own land; I will cause him to fall by the
sword in his own land.' "

Sennacherib's Threat

8 The Rabshakeh returned, and found
the king of Assyria fighting against Libnah;
for he had heard that the king had left
Lachish. [9]When the king[y] heard concerning
King Tirhakah of Ethiopia,[z] "See, he has set
out to fight against you," he sent messengers again to Hezekiah, saying, [10]"Thus shall
you speak to King Hezekiah of Judah: Do
not let your God on whom you rely deceive
you by promising that Jerusalem will not be
given into the hand of the king of Assyria.
[11]See, you have heard what the kings of
Assyria have done to all lands, destroying
them utterly. Shall you be delivered? [12]Have
the gods of the nations delivered them, the
nations that my predecessors destroyed,
Gozan, Haran, Rezeph, and the people of
Eden who were in Telassar? [13]Where is the
king of Hamath, the king of Arpad, the king
of the city of Sepharvaim, the king of Hena,
or the king of Ivvah?"

Hezekiah's Prayer

14 Hezekiah received the letter from the
hand of the messengers and read it; then
Hezekiah went up to the house of the LORD
and spread it before the LORD. [15]And Hezekiah
prayed before the LORD, and said: "O LORD
the God of Israel, who are enthroned above
the cherubim, you are God, you alone, of
all the kingdoms of the earth; you have
made heaven and earth. [16]Incline your ear,
O LORD, and hear; open your eyes, O LORD,
and see; hear the words of Sennacherib,
which he has sent to mock the living God.
[17]Truly, O LORD, the kings of Assyria have
laid waste the nations and their lands, [18]and
have hurled their gods into the fire, though
they were no gods but the work of human
hands—wood and stone—and so they were
destroyed. [19]So now, O LORD our God, save
us, I pray you, from his hand, so that all
the kingdoms of the earth may know that
you, O LORD, are God alone."

20 Then Isaiah son of Amoz sent to
Hezekiah, saying, "Thus says the LORD, the
God of Israel: I have heard your prayer to
me about King Sennacherib of Assyria. [21]This
is the word that the LORD has spoken concerning him:

She despises you, she scorns you—
  virgin daughter Zion;
she tosses her head—behind your back,
  daughter Jerusalem.

22 Whom have you mocked and reviled?
  Against whom have you raised your
    voice
and haughtily lifted your eyes?
  Against the Holy One of Israel!
23 By your messengers you have mocked
    the Lord,
  and you have said, 'With my many
    chariots
I have gone up the heights of the
    mountains,
  to the far recesses of Lebanon;
I felled its tallest cedars,
  its choicest cypresses;
I entered its farthest retreat,
  its densest forest.
24 I dug wells
  and drank foreign waters,
I dried up with the sole of my foot
  all the streams of Egypt.'

25 Have you not heard
  that I determined it long ago?
I planned from days of old
  what now I bring to pass,
that you should make fortified cities

[y] Heb *he* [z] Or *Nubia;* Heb *Cush*

19.1 2 Chr 32.20-22; Isa 37.1-38; 2 Kings 18.37; 1 Kings 21.27
19.2 Isa 1.1; 2.1
19.4 2 Sam 16.12; 2 Kings 18.35; 1.9
19.6 Isa 37.6ff; 2 Kings 18.17ff
19.7 ver 35-37
19.8 Josh 10.29; 2 Kings 18.14
19.10 2 Kings 18.5,30
19.12 2 Kings 18.33
19.13 2 Kings 18.34
19.14 Isa 37.14
19.15 1 Sam 4.4; 1 Kings 18.39
19.16 Ps 31.2; 2 Chr 6.40; ver 4
19.18 Ps 115.4; Jer 10.3
19.19 Ps 83.18; ver 15
19.20 2 Kings 20.5; Isa 37.21
19.21 Lam 2.13; Job 16.4; Ps 22.7,8
19.22 ver 4,6; Ps 71.22; Isa 5.24
19.23 2 Kings 18.17; Ps 20.7; Isa 10.18
19.24 Isa 19.6
19.25 Isa 45.7; 10.5

19.1-7 Isaiah's Advice to Hezekiah. Hezekiah's message to *the prophet Isaiah* concerned not only the future of the kingdom of Judah, but the credibility of Israel's God in response to his having been mocked by *the king of Assyria.* Isaiah announced that this king will *return to his own land,* where he will be killed.
19.8-13 The scorn of Hezekiah and the God of Judah and the other captive nations is repeated by *Sennacherib,* who also mentions *Tirhakah,* ruler of Egypt (though of Ethiopic origin), the dates of whose reign can be determined from Egyptian sources as 686-664. Since this would be later than the other incidents described above, there may have been a second revolt by Hezekiah against Sennacherib.
19.14-32 Hezekiah's Prayer and Isaiah's Reply. Asserting the complete sovereignty of *the LORD* over the creation, Hezekiah calls on God to deliver his people from the hand of this Assyrian king, as a testimony to *all the kingdoms of the earth* of God's power. Isaiah's vivid message to Sennacherib warns him that God will send him back home from all his conquests, and informs him that *a remnant* from Judah will flourish once more, while this alien invader will never even launch an attack against Jerusalem.

19.35-37 The destruction of his army by *the angel of the* LORD and the murder of Sennacherib by his own sons in *Nineveh* (capital of Assyria, located on the Tigris River) are described.
20.1-21.25 Signs of the End of the Kingdom of Judah.
20.1-11 Hezekiah's Illness. Stricken with what seemed a fatal illness, Hezekiah consulted the prophet Isaiah, who told him that God would deliver Jerusalem from the Assyrians and would extend the life of the king. Confirmation for this promise was given when the *shadow* cast by the sun is said to have moved backward.
20.12-19 Envoys from Babylon as Signs of the Captivity of Judah. *Merodach-baladan,* whose name derives from the Babylonian god, Marduk, had several times seized control of Babylon (city and district in the lower Tigris-Euphrates valley) during the height of the Assyrian empire. *Envoys* from him to Hezekiah were scheming to form an anti-Assyrian coalition against that weakened empire. After Hezekiah showed the Babylonians all his treasures, he was warned by *Isaiah* that all this wealth and all the people would soon be taken off to Babylon as captives, though it would not take place during Hezekiah's lifetime.

crash into heaps of ruins,
26 while their inhabitants, shorn of strength,
are dismayed and confounded;
they have become like plants of the field
and like tender grass,
like grass on the housetops,
blighted before it is grown.

27 "But I know your rising[a] and your sitting,
your going out and coming in,
and your raging against me.
28 Because you have raged against me
and your arrogance has come to my ears,
I will put my hook in your nose
and my bit in your mouth;
I will turn you back on the way
by which you came.

29 "And this shall be the sign for you:
This year you shall eat what grows of itself,
and in the second year what springs from
that; then in the third year sow, reap, plant
vineyards, and eat their fruit. [30]The surviving remnant of the house of Judah shall
again take root downward, and bear fruit
upward; [31]for from Jerusalem a remnant
shall go out, and from Mount Zion a band
of survivors. The zeal of the LORD of hosts
will do this.
32 "Therefore thus says the LORD concerning the king of Assyria: He shall not
come into this city, shoot an arrow there,
come before it with a shield, or cast up a
siege ramp against it. [33]By the way that he
came, by the same he shall return; he shall
not come into this city, says the LORD. [34]For
I will defend this city to save it, for my own
sake and for the sake of my servant David."

Sennacherib's Defeat and Death

35 That very night the angel of the LORD
set out and struck down one hundred eighty-
five thousand in the camp of the Assyrians;
when morning dawned, they were all dead
bodies. [36]Then King Sennacherib of Assyria
left, went home, and lived at Nineveh. [37]As
he was worshiping in the house of his god
Nisroch, his sons Adrammelech and Sharezer
killed him with the sword, and they escaped
into the land of Ararat. His son Esar-haddon
succeeded him.

Hezekiah's Illness

20 In those days Hezekiah became
sick and was at the point of death.
The prophet Isaiah son of Amoz came to
him, and said to him, "Thus says the LORD:
Set your house in order, for you shall die;
you shall not recover." [2]Then Hezekiah
turned his face to the wall and prayed to
the LORD: [3]"Remember now, O LORD, I implore you, how I have walked before you in
faithfulness with a whole heart, and have
done what is good in your sight." Hezekiah
wept bitterly. [4]Before Isaiah had gone out
of the middle court, the word of the LORD
came to him: [5]"Turn back, and say to
Hezekiah prince of my people, Thus says the
LORD, the God of your ancestor David: I have
heard your prayer, I have seen your tears;
indeed, I will heal you; on the third day you
shall go up to the house of the LORD. [6]I will
add fifteen years to your life. I will deliver
you and this city out of the hand of the king
of Assyria; I will defend this city for my own
sake and for my servant David's sake."
[7]Then Isaiah said, "Bring a lump of figs. Let
them take it and apply it to the boil, so that
he may recover."
8 Hezekiah said to Isaiah, "What shall be
the sign that the LORD will heal me, and that
I shall go up to the house of the LORD on
the third day?" [9]Isaiah said, "This is the sign
to you from the LORD, that the LORD will do
the thing that he has promised: the shadow
has now advanced ten intervals; shall it
retreat ten intervals?" [10]Hezekiah answered,
"It is normal for the shadow to lengthen ten
intervals; rather let the shadow retreat ten
intervals." [11]The prophet Isaiah cried to the
LORD; and he brought the shadow back the
ten intervals, by which the sun[b] had declined on the dial of Ahaz.

Envoys from Babylon

12 At that time King Merodach-baladan
son of Baladan of Babylon sent envoys with
letters and a present to Hezekiah, for he had
heard that Hezekiah had been sick.
[13]Hezekiah welcomed them;[c] he showed them
all his treasure house, the silver, the gold,
the spices, the precious oil, his armory, all
that was found in his storehouses; there
was nothing in his house or in all his realm
that Hezekiah did not show them. [14]Then
the prophet Isaiah came to King Hezekiah,

[a] Gk Compare Isa 37.27 Q Ms: MT lacks *rising* [b] Syr See Isa 38.8 and Tg: Heb *it* [c] Gk Vg Syr: Heb *When Hezekiah heard about them*

19.26 Ps 129.6
19.28 Job 41.2; Ezek 29.4; ver 33,36
19.29 1 Sam 2.34; 2 Kings 20.8,9; Lk 2.12
19.30 2 Chr 32.22,23
19.31 Isa 9.7
19.33 ver 28
19.34 2 Kings 20.6; 1 Kings 11.12,13
19.35 2 Chr 32.21; Isa 37.36
19.36 ver 7,28,33; Jon 1.2
19.37 2 Chr 32.21; ver 7; Ezra 4.2
20.1 2 Chr 32.24; Isa 38.1; see 2 Sam 17.23
20.3 Neh 13.22; 2 Kings 18.3-6
20.5 1 Sam 9.16; 10.1; 2 Kings 19.20; Ps 39.12
20.6 2 Kings 19.34
20.7 Isa 38.21
20.11 Josh 10.12-14
20.12 Isa 39.1ff
20.13 2 Chr 32.27

and said to him, "What did these men say? From where did they come to you?" Hezekiah answered, "They have come from a far country, from Babylon." [15]He said, "What have they seen in your house?" Hezekiah answered, "They have seen all that is in my house; there is nothing in my storehouses that I did not show them."

16 Then Isaiah said to Hezekiah, "Hear the word of the LORD: [17]Days are coming when all that is in your house, and that which your ancestors have stored up until this day, shall be carried to Babylon; nothing shall be left, says the LORD. [18]Some of your own sons who are born to you shall be taken away; they shall be eunuchs in the palace of the king of Babylon." [19]Then Hezekiah said to Isaiah, "The word of the LORD that you have spoken is good." For he thought, "Why not, if there will be peace and security in my days?"

Death of Hezekiah

20 The rest of the deeds of Hezekiah, all his power, how he made the pool and the conduit and brought water into the city, are they not written in the Book of the Annals of the Kings of Judah? [21]Hezekiah slept with his ancestors; and his son Manasseh succeeded him.

Manasseh Reigns over Judah

21 Manasseh was twelve years old when he began to reign; he reigned fifty-five years in Jerusalem. His mother's name was Hephzibah. [2]He did what was evil in the sight of the LORD, following the abominable practices of the nations that the LORD drove out before the people of Israel. [3]For he rebuilt the high places that his father Hezekiah had destroyed; he erected altars for Baal, made a sacred pole,[d] as King Ahab of Israel had done, worshiped all the host of heaven, and served them. [4]He built altars in the house of the LORD, of which the LORD had said, "In Jerusalem I will put my name." [5]He built altars for all the host of heaven in the two courts of the house of the LORD. [6]He made his son pass through fire; he practiced soothsaying and augury, and dealt with mediums and with wizards. He did much evil in the sight of the LORD, provoking him to anger. [7]The carved image of Asherah that he had made he set in the house of which the LORD said to David and to his son Solomon, "In this house, and in Jerusalem, which I have chosen out of all the tribes of Israel, I will put my name forever; [8]I will not cause the feet of Israel to wander any more out of the land that I gave to their ancestors, if only they will be careful to do according to all that I have commanded them, and according to all the law that my servant Moses commanded them." [9]But they did not listen; Manasseh misled them to do more evil than the nations had done that the LORD destroyed before the people of Israel.

10 The LORD said by his servants the prophets, [11]"Because King Manasseh of Judah has committed these abominations, has done things more wicked than all that the Amorites did, who were before him, and has caused Judah also to sin with his idols; [12]therefore thus says the LORD, the God of Israel, I am bringing upon Jerusalem and Judah such evil that the ears of everyone who hears of it will tingle. [13]I will stretch over Jerusalem the measuring line for Samaria, and the plummet for the house of Ahab; I will wipe Jerusalem as one wipes a dish, wiping it and turning it upside down. [14]I will cast off the remnant of my heritage, and give them into the hand of their enemies; they shall become a prey and a spoil to all their enemies, [15]because they have done what is evil in my sight and have provoked me to anger, since the day their ancestors came out of Egypt, even to this day."

16 Moreover Manasseh shed very much innocent blood, until he had filled Jerusalem from one end to another, besides the sin that he caused Judah to sin so that they did what was evil in the sight of the LORD.

17 Now the rest of the acts of Manasseh, all that he did, and the sin that he committed, are they not written in the Book of the Annals of the Kings of Judah? [18]Manasseh slept with his ancestors, and was buried in the garden of his house, in the garden of Uzza. His son Amon succeeded him.

Amon Reigns over Judah

19 Amon was twenty-two years old when he began to reign; he reigned two years in Jerusalem. His mother's name was Meshullemeth daughter of Haruz of Jotbah. [20]He did what was evil in the sight of the LORD,

[d] Heb *Asherah*

20.15 ver 13
20.17 2 Kings 24.13; 25.13; Jer 52.17
20.18 2 Kings 24.12; 2 Chr 33.11; Dan 1.3-7
20.19 1 Sam 3.18
20.20 2 Chr 32.32; Neh 3.16
20.21 2 Chr 32.33
21.1 2 Chr 33.1ff
21.2 2 Kings 16.3
21.3 2 Kings 18.4; 1 Kings 16.32,33; 2 Kings 17.16; Deut 17.3
21.4 Jer 32.34; 2 Sam 7.13; 1 Kings 8.29
21.6 Lev 18.21; 2 Kings 16.3; 17.17; Lev 19.26,31; Deut 18.10,11
21.7 1 Kings 8.29; 9.3; 2 Kings 23.27; Jer 32.34
21.8 2 Sam 7.10
21.9 Prov 29.12
21.11 2 Kings 24.3,4; 1 Kings 21.26; ver 16
21.12 1 Sam 3.11; Jer 19.3
21.13 Isa 34.11; Am 7.7,8
21.16 2 Kings 24.4
21.17 2 Chr 33.11-19
21.18 2 Chr 33.20
21.19 2 Chr 33.21-23
21.20 ver 2-6,11,16

20.20-21.18 The Death of Hezekiah and the Reign of Manasseh. Succeeding his father while still a child, Manasseh's reign lasted from 687-642. His importation of the features of the worship of Baal and Asherah are seen in the Deuteronomic assessment of his rule as the reason that God set aside the promises to David of an enduring covenant people.

21.19-26 The Reign of Amon. After following the basic pattern of his father, *Amon* was killed by his servants (probably including court attendants and royal agents), but *the people of the land* (free land-owning citizens) installed the youthful *Josiah* as king in his place.

22.1-23.30 Josiah and the Attempted Reform of Judah.
22.1-2 The reign of Josiah, from 640-609, contrasts sharply with most of his predecessors, in that he sought to obey *the* LORD by following *in the way of his father David.*
22.3-20 In the process of restoration of *the house of the* LORD in Jerusalem, *the book of the law* was found by *the priest Hilkiah.* This was probably the prototype of the Deuteronomic version of the law of Israel. The contrition of the king on hearing the law led to the promise that he would live *in peace until death,* when the judgment of God would fall on his disobedient people.

as his father Manasseh had done. 21He
walked in all the way in which his father
walked, served the idols that his father served,
and worshiped them; 22he abandoned the
LORD, the God of his ancestors, and did not
walk in the way of the LORD. 23The servants
of Amon conspired against him, and killed
the king in his house. 24But the people of
the land killed all those who had conspired
against King Amon, and the people of the
land made his son Josiah king in place of
him. 25Now the rest of the acts of Amon
that he did, are they not written in the Book
of the Annals of the Kings of Judah? 26He
was buried in his tomb in the garden of
Uzza; then his son Josiah succeeded him.

Josiah Reigns over Judah

22 Josiah was eight years old when
he began to reign; he reigned thirty-
one years in Jerusalem. His mother's name
was Jedidah daughter of Adaiah of Bozkath.
2He did what was right in the sight of the
LORD, and walked in all the way of his father
David; he did not turn aside to the right or
to the left.

Hilkiah Finds the Book of the Law

3 In the eighteenth year of King Josiah,
the king sent Shaphan son of Azaliah, son
of Meshullam, the secretary, to the house of
the LORD, saying, 4"Go up to the high priest
Hilkiah, and have him count the entire sum
of the money that has been brought into
the house of the LORD, which the keepers of
the threshold have collected from the people; 5let it be given into the hand of the
workers who have the oversight of the
house of the LORD; let them give it to the
workers who are at the house of the LORD,
repairing the house, 6that is, to the carpenters, to the builders, to the masons; and let
them use it to buy timber and quarried
stone to repair the house. 7But no accounting shall be asked from them for the money
that is delivered into their hand, for they
deal honestly."
8 The high priest Hilkiah said to Shaphan
the secretary, "I have found the book of the
law in the house of the LORD." When Hilkiah
gave the book to Shaphan, he read it. 9Then
Shaphan the secretary came to the king,
and reported to the king, "Your servants
have emptied out the money that was found
in the house, and have delivered it into the
hand of the workers who have oversight of
the house of the LORD." 10Shaphan the secretary informed the king, "The priest Hilkiah
has given me a book." Shaphan then read
it aloud to the king.
11 When the king heard the words of
the book of the law, he tore his clothes.
12Then the king commanded the priest
Hilkiah, Ahikam son of Shaphan, Achbor
son of Micaiah, Shaphan the secretary, and
the king's servant Asaiah, saying, 13"Go,
inquire of the LORD for me, for the people,
and for all Judah, concerning the words of
this book that has been found; for great is
the wrath of the LORD that is kindled against
us, because our ancestors did not obey the
words of this book, to do according to all
that is written concerning us."
14 So the priest Hilkiah, Ahikam, Achbor,
Shaphan, and Asaiah went to the prophetess Huldah the wife of Shallum son of
Tikvah, son of Harhas, keeper of the wardrobe; she resided in Jerusalem in the Second
Quarter, where they consulted her. 15She
declared to them, "Thus says the LORD, the
God of Israel: Tell the man who sent you
to me, 16Thus says the LORD, I will indeed
bring disaster on this place and on its inhabitants—all the words of the book that
the king of Judah has read. 17Because they
have abandoned me and have made offerings to other gods, so that they have provoked me to anger with all the work of their
hands, therefore my wrath will be kindled
against this place, and it will not be
quenched. 18But as to the king of Judah,
who sent you to inquire of the LORD, thus
shall you say to him, Thus says the LORD,
the God of Israel: Regarding the words that
you have heard, 19because your heart was
penitent, and you humbled yourself before
the LORD, when you heard how I spoke
against this place, and against its inhabitants, that they should become a desolation
and a curse, and because you have torn
your clothes and wept before me, I also
have heard you, says the LORD. 20Therefore,
I will gather you to your ancestors, and you
shall be gathered to your grave in peace;
your eyes shall not see all the disaster that
I will bring on this place." They took the
message back to the king.

21.22 1 Kings 11.33
21.23 2 Chr 33.24,25
21.26 ver 18
22.1 2 Chr 34.1; Josh 15.39
22.2 Deut 5.32
22.3 2 Chr 34.8ff
22.4 2 Kings 12.4,9,10
22.5 2 Kings 12.11-14
22.7 2 Kings 12.15
22.8 Deut 31.24-26; 2 Chr 34.14,15
22.12 2 Kings 25.22; 2 Chr 34.20
22.13 Deut 29.27
22.14 2 Chr 34.22
22.17 Deut 29.25-27
22.19 Ps 51.17; Isa 57.15; 1 Kings 21.29; Lev 26.31; Jer 26.6

23.1 2 Chr 34.29-32
23.2 Deut 31.10-13; 2 Kings 22.8
23.3 2 Kings 11.14,17; Deut 13.4
23.4 2 Kings 21.3,7
23.6 ver 15; 2 Chr 34.4
23.7 1 Kings 14.24; 15.12; Ezek 16.16
23.8 1 Kings 15.22
23.9 Ezek 44.10-14
23.10 Isa 30.33; Jer 7.31; Lev 18.21; Deut 18.10
23.12 Jer 19.13; Zeph 1.5; 2 Kings 21.5; ver 4,6
23.13 1 Kings 11.7
23.14 Ex 23.24; Deut 7.5,25
23.15 1 Kings 12.28-33
23.16 1 Kings 13.2
23.17 1 Kings 13.1,30
23.18 1 Kings 13.31
23.19 2 Chr 34.6,7
23.20 2 Kings 10.25; 11.18; 2 Chr 34.5
23.21 2 Chr 35.1; Ex 12.3; Num 9.2; Deut 16.2

Josiah's Reformation

23 Then the king directed that all the elders of Judah and Jerusalem should be gathered to him. [2]The king went up to the house of the LORD, and with him went all the people of Judah, all the inhabitants of Jerusalem, the priests, the prophets, and all the people, both small and great; he read in their hearing all the words of the book of the covenant that had been found in the house of the LORD. [3]The king stood by the pillar and made a covenant before the LORD, to follow the LORD, keeping his commandments, his decrees, and his statutes, with all his heart and all his soul, to perform the words of this covenant that were written in this book. All the people joined in the covenant.

4 The king commanded the high priest Hilkiah, the priests of the second order, and the guardians of the threshold, to bring out of the temple of the LORD all the vessels made for Baal, for Asherah, and for all the host of heaven; he burned them outside Jerusalem in the fields of the Kidron, and carried their ashes to Bethel. [5]He deposed the idolatrous priests whom the kings of Judah had ordained to make offerings in the high places at the cities of Judah and around Jerusalem; those also who made offerings to Baal, to the sun, the moon, the constellations, and all the host of the heavens. [6]He brought out the image of[e] Asherah from the house of the LORD, outside Jerusalem, to the Wadi Kidron, burned it at the Wadi Kidron, beat it to dust and threw the dust of it upon the graves of the common people. [7]He broke down the houses of the male temple prostitutes that were in the house of the LORD, where the women did weaving for Asherah. [8]He brought all the priests out of the towns of Judah, and defiled the high places where the priests had made offerings, from Geba to Beer-sheba; he broke down the high places of the gates that were at the entrance of the gate of Joshua the governor of the city, which were on the left at the gate of the city. [9]The priests of the high places, however, did not come up to the altar of the LORD in Jerusalem, but ate unleavened bread among their kindred. [10]He defiled Topheth, which is in the valley of Ben-hinnom, so that no one would make a son or a daughter pass through fire as an offering to Molech. [11]He removed the horses that the kings of Judah had dedicated to the sun, at the entrance to the house of the LORD, by the chamber of the eunuch Nathan-melech, which was in the precincts;[f] then he burned the chariots of the sun with fire. [12]The altars on the roof of the upper chamber of Ahaz, which the kings of Judah had made, and the altars that Manasseh had made in the two courts of the house of the LORD, he pulled down from there and broke in pieces, and threw the rubble into the Wadi Kidron. [13]The king defiled the high places that were east of Jerusalem, to the south of the Mount of Destruction, which King Solomon of Israel had built for Astarte the abomination of the Sidonians, for Chemosh the abomination of Moab, and for Milcom the abomination of the Ammonites. [14]He broke the pillars in pieces, cut down the sacred poles,[g] and covered the sites with human bones.

15 Moreover, the altar at Bethel, the high place erected by Jeroboam son of Nebat, who caused Israel to sin—he pulled down that altar along with the high place. He burned the high place, crushing it to dust; he also burned the sacred pole.[h] [16]As Josiah turned, he saw the tombs there on the mount; and he sent and took the bones out of the tombs, and burned them on the altar, and defiled it, according to the word of the LORD that the man of God proclaimed,[i] when Jeroboam stood by the altar at the festival; he turned and looked up at the tomb of the man of God who had predicted these things. [17]Then he said, "What is that monument that I see?" The people of the city told him, "It is the tomb of the man of God who came from Judah and predicted these things that you have done against the altar at Bethel." [18]He said, "Let him rest; let no one move his bones." So they let his bones alone, with the bones of the prophet who came out of Samaria. [19]Moreover, Josiah removed all the shrines of the high places that were in the towns of Samaria, which kings of Israel had made, provoking the LORD to anger; he did to them just as he had done at Bethel. [20]He slaughtered on the altars all the priests of the high places who were there, and burned human bones on them. Then he returned to Jerusalem.

The Passover Celebrated

21 The king commanded all the people, "Keep the passover to the LORD your God as

[e] Heb lacks *image of* [f] Meaning of Heb uncertain [g] Heb *Asherim* [h] Heb *Asherah* [i] Gk: Heb *proclaimed, who had predicted these things*

23.1-20 The proper procedures were reinstated in the temple, while *the idolatrous priests* and the prostitutes linked with the shrines were driven out. The pagan altars and *high places, the sacred poles* and tombs treated as sacred, were destroyed. Exception is made for the tomb of *the man of God* who had predicted this divine judgment and consequent renewal.
23.21-25 The Passover was celebrated properly under King Josiah, who halted all the pagan practices of the time *in the land of Judah.* Yet the judgment of God on the disobedient people, the city of Jerusalem, and the temple there was merely postponed.

23.28-30 The attempt by Josiah at Megiddo to stop the attack by Pharaoh Neco of Egypt (ruled 610-595) on the king of Assyria resulted in Josiah's death, with burial in Jerusalem.
23.31-25.30 The Decline and Fall of Judah.
23.31-37 Josiah's immediate successors were (1) Jehoahaz, who was a tool and finally a prisoner of the Egyptians during his brief reign (609); (2) Eliakim, whose name was changed to *Jehoiakim,* and who was installed as a puppet by the Egyptians. Both are said to have done what is *evil in the sight of the LORD.*
24.1-7 With the Babylonians in control of the land *from the Wadi of Egypt* (the present location of the Suez Canal) *to the River Euphrates,* Jehoiakim's futile attempt at a revolt led to an invasion by a multinational force and his death, which is pictured as punishment for his misdeeds.
24.8-16 Jehoiachin, after a brief reign (three months in 598), surrendered to *Nebuchadnezzar of Babylon,* who had successfully besieged Jerusalem, and then took to Babylon the royal family and the treasures of the *king's house* as well as those of the temple. He also forced into exile *ten thousand captives,* including the elite, the military and the productive of the land, leaving behind only *the poorest people.*

prescribed in this book of the covenant." [22]No such passover had been kept since the days of the judges who judged Israel, or during all the days of the kings of Israel or of the kings of Judah; [23]but in the eighteenth year of King Josiah this passover was kept to the LORD in Jerusalem.

24 Moreover Josiah put away the mediums, wizards, teraphim,[j] idols, and all the abominations that were seen in the land of Judah and in Jerusalem, so that he established the words of the law that were written in the book that the priest Hilkiah had found in the house of the LORD. [25]Before him there was no king like him, who turned to the LORD with all his heart, with all his soul, and with all his might, according to all the law of Moses; nor did any like him arise after him.

26 Still the LORD did not turn from the fierceness of his great wrath, by which his anger was kindled against Judah, because of all the provocations with which Manasseh had provoked him. [27]The LORD said, "I will remove Judah also out of my sight, as I have removed Israel; and I will reject this city that I have chosen, Jerusalem, and the house of which I said, My name shall be there."

Josiah Dies in Battle

28 Now the rest of the acts of Josiah, and all that he did, are they not written in the Book of the Annals of the Kings of Judah? [29]In his days Pharaoh Neco king of Egypt went up to the king of Assyria to the river Euphrates. King Josiah went to meet him; but when Pharaoh Neco met him at Megiddo, he killed him. [30]His servants carried him dead in a chariot from Megiddo, brought him to Jerusalem, and buried him in his own tomb. The people of the land took Jehoahaz son of Josiah, anointed him, and made him king in place of his father.

Reign and Captivity of Jehoahaz

31 Jehoahaz was twenty-three years old when he began to reign; he reigned three months in Jerusalem. His mother's name was Hamutal daughter of Jeremiah of Libnah. [32]He did what was evil in the sight of the LORD, just as his ancestors had done. [33]Pharaoh Neco confined him at Riblah in the land of Hamath, so that he might not reign in Jerusalem, and imposed tribute on the land of one hundred talents of silver and a talent of gold. [34]Pharaoh Neco made Eliakim son of Josiah king in place of his father Josiah, and changed his name to Jehoiakim. But he took Jehoahaz away; he came to Egypt, and died there. [35]Jehoiakim gave the silver and the gold to Pharaoh, but he taxed the land in order to meet Pharaoh's demand for money. He exacted the silver and the gold from the people of the land, from all according to their assessment, to give it to Pharaoh Neco.

Jehoiakim Reigns over Judah

36 Jehoiakim was twenty-five years old when he began to reign; he reigned eleven years in Jerusalem. His mother's name was Zebidah daughter of Pedaiah of Rumah. [37]He did what was evil in the sight of the LORD, just as all his ancestors had done.

Judah Overrun by Enemies

24 In his days King Nebuchadnezzar of Babylon came up; Jehoiakim became his servant for three years; then he turned and rebelled against him. [2]The LORD sent against him bands of the Chaldeans, bands of the Arameans, bands of the Moabites, and bands of the Ammonites; he sent them against Judah to destroy it, according to the word of the LORD that he spoke by his servants the prophets. [3]Surely this came upon Judah at the command of the LORD, to remove them out of his sight, for the sins of Manasseh, for all that he had committed, [4]and also for the innocent blood that he had shed; for he filled Jerusalem with innocent blood, and the LORD was not willing to pardon. [5]Now the rest of the deeds of Jehoiakim, and all that he did, are they not written in the Book of the Annals of the Kings of Judah? [6]So Jehoiakim slept with his ancestors; then his son Jehoiachin succeeded him. [7]The king of Egypt did not come again out of his land, for the king of Babylon had taken over all that belonged to the king of Egypt from the Wadi of Egypt to the River Euphrates.

Reign and Captivity of Jehoiachin

8 Jehoiachin was eighteen years old when he began to reign; he reigned three months

[j] Or *household gods*

23.22 2 Chr 35.18,19
23.24 2 Kings 21.6,11,21; Deut 18.10-12
23.25 2 Kings 18.5
23.26 2 Kings 21.11,12; Jer 15.4
23.27 2 Kings 18.11; 21.13,14
23.29 2 Chr 35.20; Zech 12.11
23.30 2 Chr 35.24; 36.1
23.31 1 Chr 3.15; Jer 22.11; 2 Kings 24.18
23.33 2 Kings 25.6; Jer 52.27; 2 Chr 36.3
23.34 2 Chr 36.4; 2 Kings 24.17; Ezek 19.3,4
23.35 ver 33
23.36 2 Chr 36.5
24.1 2 Chr 36.6; Jer 25.1
24.2 Jer 25.9; 35.11; 2 Kings 23.27
24.3 2 Kings 18.25; 23.26
24.4 2 Kings 21.16
24.6 Jer 22.18,19
24.7 Jer 37.5-7; 46.2
24.8 1 Chr 3.16; 2 Chr 36.9

in Jerusalem. His mother's name was Nehushta daughter of Elnathan of Jerusalem. [9]He did what was evil in the sight of the LORD, just as his father had done.

10 At that time the servants of King Nebuchadnezzar of Babylon came up to Jerusalem, and the city was besieged. [11]King Nebuchadnezzar of Babylon came to the city, while his servants were besieging it; [12]King Jehoiachin of Judah gave himself up to the king of Babylon, himself, his mother, his servants, his officers, and his palace officials. The king of Babylon took him prisoner in the eighth year of his reign.

Capture of Jerusalem

13 He carried off all the treasures of the house of the LORD, and the treasures of the king's house; he cut in pieces all the vessels of gold in the temple of the LORD, which King Solomon of Israel had made, all this as the LORD had foretold. [14]He carried away all Jerusalem, all the officials, all the warriors, ten thousand captives, all the artisans and the smiths; no one remained, except the poorest people of the land. [15]He carried away Jehoiachin to Babylon; the king's mother, the king's wives, his officials, and the elite of the land, he took into captivity from Jerusalem to Babylon. [16]The king of Babylon brought captive to Babylon all the men of valor, seven thousand, the artisans and the smiths, one thousand, all of them strong and fit for war. [17]The king of Babylon made Mattaniah, Jehoiachin's uncle, king in his place, and changed his name to Zedekiah.

Zedekiah Reigns over Judah

18 Zedekiah was twenty-one years old when he began to reign; he reigned eleven years in Jerusalem. His mother's name was Hamutal daughter of Jeremiah of Libnah. [19]He did what was evil in the sight of the LORD, just as Jehoiakim had done. [20]Indeed, Jerusalem and Judah so angered the LORD that he expelled them from his presence.

The Fall and Captivity of Judah

Zedekiah rebelled against the king of Babylon.

25 [1]And in the ninth year of his reign, in the tenth month, on the tenth day of the month, King Nebuchadnezzar of Babylon came with all his army against Jerusalem, and laid siege to it; they built siegeworks against it all around. [2]So the city was besieged until the eleventh year of King Zedekiah. [3]On the ninth day of the fourth month the famine became so severe in the city that there was no food for the people of the land. [4]Then a breach was made in the city wall;[k] the king with all the soldiers fled[l] by night by the way of the gate between the two walls, by the king's garden, though the Chaldeans were all around the city. They went in the direction of the Arabah. [5]But the army of the Chaldeans pursued the king, and overtook him in the plains of Jericho; all his army was scattered, deserting him. [6]Then they captured the king and brought him up to the king of Babylon at Riblah, who passed sentence on him. [7]They slaughtered the sons of Zedekiah before his eyes, then put out the eyes of Zedekiah; they bound him in fetters and took him to Babylon.

8 In the fifth month, on the seventh day of the month—which was the nineteenth year of King Nebuchadnezzar, king of Babylon—Nebuzaradan, the captain of the bodyguard, a servant of the king of Babylon, came to Jerusalem. [9]He burned the house of the LORD, the king's house, and all the houses of Jerusalem; every great house he burned down. [10]All the army of the Chaldeans who were with the captain of the guard broke down the walls around Jerusalem. [11]Nebuzaradan the captain of the guard carried into exile the rest of the people who were left in the city and the deserters who had defected to the king of Babylon—all the rest of the population. [12]But the captain of the guard left some of the poorest people of the land to be vinedressers and tillers of the soil.

13 The bronze pillars that were in the house of the LORD, as well as the stands and the bronze sea that were in the house of the LORD, the Chaldeans broke in pieces, and carried the bronze to Babylon. [14]They took away the pots, the shovels, the snuffers, the dishes for incense, and all the bronze vessels used in the temple service, [15]as well as the firepans and the basins. What was made of gold the captain of the guard took away for the gold, and what was made of silver, for the silver. [16]As for the two pillars, the one sea, and the stands, which Solomon had made for the house of the LORD, the bronze

[k] Heb lacks *wall* [l] Gk Compare Jer 39.4; 52.7: Heb lacks *the king* and lacks *fled*

24.10 Dan 1.1
24.12 Jer 24.1; 29.1,2; 25.1; 2 Kings 25.27; Jer 52.28
24.13 2 Kings 20.17; Isa 39.6; 2 Kings 25.13-15; Jer 20.5
24.14 Jer 24.1; 52.28; 2 Kings 25.12; Jer 40.7
24.15 2 Chr 36.10; Jer 22.24-28
24.16 Jer 52.28
24.17 Jer 37.1; 1 Chr 3.15; 2 Chr 36.4,10
24.18 2 Chr 36.11; Jer 52.1ff; 2 Kings 23.31
24.19 2 Chr 36.12
24.20 2 Chr 36.13
25.1 2 Chr 36.3,17-20; Jer 39.1-7; Ezek 24.1,2
25.3 Jer 39.1,2
25.4 Jer 39.4-7
25.6 Jer 34.21,22; 2 Kings 23.33
25.7 Jer 39.6,7; Ezek 12.13
25.8 Jer 52.12-14; 39.9
25.9 2 Chr 36.19; Ps 74.3-7; Am 2.5
25.10 Neh 1.3; Jer 52.14
25.11 2 Chr 36.20; Jer 39.9; 52.15
25.12 2 Kings 24.14; Jer 40.7
25.13 2 Chr 36.18
25.14 1 Kings 7.47-50
25.16 1 Kings 7.47

24.17-20 Another puppet, *Mattaniah,* who was renamed *Zedekiah,* was the last king of Judah (597-586). His disobedience to the law of God resulted in the LORD's expulsion of Jerusalem and Judah *from his presence.*
25.1-21 When Zedekiah rebelled against the Babylonians, a long siege led to capture of the city, the execution of the king's sons, and his being taken as a blind captive to Babylon. In 586 the temple and the king's house, as well as all the fine houses in the city, were destroyed and the city walls broken down. The populace was taken to Babylon, but the priestly and military leaders were executed in the presence of *the king of Babylon* in *Riblah* (northwest of Damascus). The original historical account probably ended here: what follow are two appendixes.

25.22-26 *Gedaliah* served as a puppet king based in *Mizpah* (a few miles north of Jerusalem, earlier visited regularly by Samuel; 1 Sam 7.16-17) which was now the Babylonian provincial capital. He was killed in a revolt by *the royal family* of Judah, and many of his opponents fled to Egypt for safety from *the Chaldeans* (a general term for the Semitic peoples living at the head of the Persian Gulf, who joined to defeat the Assyrians).
25.27-30 The partial freedom of *Jehoiachin* probably took place about the year 560. This account prepares for the end of the Babylonian captivity and the return to the land of Judah described in Ezra and Nehemiah.

of all these vessels was beyond weighing.
17 The height of the one pillar was eighteen
cubits, and on it was a bronze capital; the
height of the capital was three cubits; latticework and pomegranates, all of bronze,
were on the capital all around. The second
pillar had the same, with the latticework.
18 The captain of the guard took the
chief priest Seraiah, the second priest
Zephaniah, and the three guardians of the
threshold; 19 from the city he took an officer
who had been in command of the soldiers,
and five men of the king's council who were
found in the city; the secretary who was the
commander of the army who mustered the
people of the land; and sixty men of the
people of the land who were found in the
city. 20 Nebuzaradan the captain of the guard
took them, and brought them to the king
of Babylon at Riblah. 21 The king of Babylon
struck them down and put them to death
at Riblah in the land of Hamath. So Judah
went into exile out of its land.

Gedaliah Made Governor of Judah

22 He appointed Gedaliah son of Ahikam
son of Shaphan as governor over the people
who remained in the land of Judah, whom
King Nebuchadnezzar of Babylon had left.
23 Now when all the captains of the forces
and their men heard that the king of Babylon
had appointed Gedaliah as governor, they
came with their men to Gedaliah at Mizpah,
namely, Ishmael son of Nethaniah, Johanan
son of Kareah, Seraiah son of Tanhumeth
the Netophathite, and Jaazaniah son of the
Maacathite. 24 Gedaliah swore to them and
their men, saying, "Do not be afraid because
of the Chaldean officials; live in the land,
serve the king of Babylon, and it shall be
well with you." 25 But in the seventh month,
Ishmael son of Nethaniah son of Elishama,
of the royal family, came with ten men;
they struck down Gedaliah so that he died,
along with the Judeans and Chaldeans who
were with him at Mizpah. 26 Then all the
people, high and low[m] and the captains of
the forces set out and went to Egypt; for
they were afraid of the Chaldeans.

Jehoiachin Released from Prison

27 In the thirty-seventh year of the exile
of King Jehoiachin of Judah, in the twelfth
month, on the twenty-seventh day of the
month, King Evil-merodach of Babylon, in
the year that he began to reign, released
King Jehoiachin of Judah from prison; 28 he
spoke kindly to him, and gave him a seat
above the other seats of the kings who were
with him in Babylon. 29 So Jehoiachin put
aside his prison clothes. Every day of his life
he dined regularly in the king's presence.
30 For his allowance, a regular allowance
was given him by the king, a portion every
day, as long as he lived.

[m] Or *young and old*

25.17 1 Kings 7.15-22

25.18 1 Chr 6.14; Ezra 7.1; Jer 21.1; 29.25

25.21 Deut 28.64; 2 Kings 23.27

25.22 Jer 40.5

25.23 Jer 40.7-9

25.25 Jer 41.1,2

25.26 Jer 43.4-7

25.27 Jer 52.31-34; Gen 40.13,20

25.29 2 Sam 9.7

1 CHRONICLES

See the Introductions, pp. 3, 38, and 44-45 above.

From Adam to Abraham
1.1 Gen 4.25-5.32 **1** Adam, Seth, Enosh; [2]Kenan, Mahalalel,
Jared; [3]Enoch, Methuselah, Lamech;
[4]Noah, Shem, Ham, and Japheth.
1.5 Gen 10.2-4 5 The descendants of Japheth: Gomer,
Magog, Madai, Javan, Tubal, Meshech, and
1.8 Gen 10.6ff Tiras. [6]The descendants of Gomer: Ashkenaz,
Diphath,[a] and Togarmah. [7]The descendants
1.10 Gen 10.8,13ff of Javan: Elishah, Tarshish, Kittim, and
Rodanim.[b]
8 The descendants of Ham: Cush, Egypt,
1.17 Gen 10.22ff Put, and Canaan. [9]The descendants of Cush:
Seba, Havilah, Sabta, Raama, and Sabteca.
1.24 Gen 11.10ff The descendants of Raamah: Sheba and
Dedan. [10]Cush became the father of Nimrod;
1.29 Gen 25.13-16 he was the first to be a mighty one on the
earth.
11 Egypt became the father of Ludim,
Anamim, Lehabim, Naphtuhim, [12]Pathrusim,
Casluhim, and Caphtorim, from whom the
1.32 Gen 25.1-4 Philistines come.[c]
1.34 Gen 21.2,3; 25.25,26 13 Canaan became the father of Sidon
his firstborn, and Heth, [14]and the Jebusites,
the Amorites, the Girgashites, [15]the Hivites,
1.35 Gen 36.9,10 the Arkites, the Sinites, [16]the Arvadites, the
Zemarites, and the Hamathites.
17 The descendants of Shem: Elam,
1.38 Gen 36.20-28 Asshur, Arpachshad, Lud, Aram, Uz, Hul,
Gether, and Meshech.[d] [18]Arpachshad be-
came the father of Shelah; and Shelah
1.43 Gen 36.31-43 became the father of Eber. [19]To Eber were
born two sons: the name of the one was
Peleg (for in his days the earth was divided),
and the name of his brother Joktan. [20]Joktan
became the father of Almodad, Sheleph,
Hazarmaveth, Jerah, [21]Hadoram, Uzal,
Diklah, [22]Ebal, Abimael, Sheba, [23]Ophir,
Havilah, and Jobab; all these were the descendants of Joktan.
24 Shem, Arpachshad, Shelah; [25]Eber,
Peleg, Reu; [26]Serug, Nahor, Terah; [27]Abram,
that is, Abraham.

From Abraham to Jacob
28 The sons of Abraham: Isaac and Ish-
mael. [29]These are their genealogies: the
firstborn of Ishmael, Nebaioth; and Kedar,
Adbeel, Mibsam, [30]Mishma, Dumah, Massa,
Hadad, Tema, [31]Jetur, Naphish, and
Kedemah. These are the sons of Ishmael.
[32]The sons of Keturah, Abraham's concu-
bine: she bore Zimran, Jokshan, Medan,
Midian, Ishbak, and Shuah. The sons of
Jokshan: Sheba and Dedan. [33]The sons of
Midian: Ephah, Epher, Hanoch, Abida, and
Eldaah. All these were the descendants of
Keturah.
34 Abraham became the father of Isaac.
The sons of Isaac: Esau and Israel. [35]The
sons of Esau: Eliphaz, Reuel, Jeush, Jalam,
and Korah. [36]The sons of Eliphaz: Teman,
Omar, Zephi, Gatam, Kenaz, Timna, and
Amalek. [37]The sons of Reuel: Nahath, Zerah,
Shammah, and Mizzah.
38 The sons of Seir: Lotan, Shobal, Zibeon,
Anah, Dishon, Ezer, and Dishan. [39]The sons
of Lotan: Hori and Homam; and Lotan's
sister was Timna. [40]The sons of Shobal:
Alian, Manahath, Ebal, Shephi, and Onam.
The sons of Zibeon: Aiah and Anah. [41]The
sons of Anah: Dishon. The sons of Dishon:
Hamran, Eshban, Ithran, and Cheran. [42]The
sons of Ezer: Bilhan, Zaavan, and Jaakan.[e]
The sons of Dishan:[f] Uz and Aran.
43 These are the kings who reigned in
the land of Edom before any king reigned
over the Israelites: Bela son of Beor, whose
city was called Dinhabah. [44]When Bela died,
Jobab son of Zerah of Bozrah succeeded
him. [45]When Jobab died, Husham of the
land of the Temanites succeeded him. [46]When
Husham died, Hadad son of Bedad, who
defeated Midian in the country of Moab,
succeeded him; and the name of his city
was Avith. [47]When Hadad died, Samlah of
Masrekah succeeded him. [48]When Samlah
died, Shaul[g] of Rehoboth on the Euphrates
succeeded him. [49]When Shaul[g] died, Baal-
hanan son of Achbor succeeded him. [50]When
Baal-hanan died, Hadad succeeded him; the
name of his city was Pai, and his wife's
name Mehetabel daughter of Matred, daughter of Me-zahab. [51]And Hadad died.
The clans[h] of Edom were: clans[h] Timna,
Aliah,[i] Jetheth, [52]Oholibamah, Elah, Pinon,
[53]Kenaz, Teman, Mibzar, [54]Magdiel, and Iram;
these are the clans[h] of Edom.

1.1-10.14 The Genealogy of the People of God. The names listed include not only persons mentioned in the biblical narratives, but also some names assigned to individuals that are used elsewhere for places and nations (for example, *Cush, Egypt, Canaan;* 1 Chr 1.8; *cf.* Gen 10.6). Special attention is given to the royal line of Judah descended from *David and Solomon,* to priests, Levites, and temple attendants (such as *musicians;* 1 Chr 6.31-48). The central interests in the genealogy are the royal and priestly lines, with the list of the family of Saul and his unworthy rule serving as preparation for the account of David's model reign over *my people Israel.*
1.19 The earth having been divided in the time of *Peleg* refers to the assignment of territories to the sons of Noah and their descendants, described in Gen 10-11, after the flood and the LORD's scattering these tribes *abroad over the face of all the earth* after the destruction of the Tower of Babel.
1.24-3.24 The major line of genealogical interest is the one traced through Abram (Abraham; 1.24), Isaac and Jacob (Israel; 1.28,34) and the latter's twelve sons (2.1-2), but especially the descendants of Judah (2.3), culminating in *David* (2.13) *and his royal line* (3.1-24).

[a] Gen 10.3 *Ripath;* See Gk Vg [b] Gen 10.4 *Dodanim;* See Syr Vg [c] Heb *Casluhim, from which the Philistines come, Caphtorim;* See Am 9.7, Jer 47.4 [d] *Mash* in Gen 10.23 [e] Or *and Akan;* See Gen 36.27 [f] See 1.38: Heb *Dishon* [g] Or *Saul* [h] Or *chiefs* [i] Or *Alvah;* See Gen 36.40

The Sons of Israel and the Descendants of Judah

2 These are the sons of Israel: Reuben,
Simeon, Levi, Judah, Issachar, Zebulun,
[2]Dan, Joseph, Benjamin, Naphtali, Gad, and
Asher. [3]The sons of Judah: Er, Onan, and
Shelah; these three the Canaanite woman
Bath-shua bore to him. Now Er, Judah's
firstborn, was wicked in the sight of the
LORD, and he put him to death. [4]His daugh-
ter-in-law Tamar also bore him Perez and
Zerah. Judah had five sons in all.

5 The sons of Perez: Hezron and Hamul.
[6]The sons of Zerah: Zimri, Ethan, Heman,
Calcol, and Dara,[j] five in all. [7]The sons of
Carmi: Achar, the troubler of Israel, who
transgressed in the matter of the devoted
thing; [8]and Ethan's son was Azariah.

9 The sons of Hezron, who were born to
him: Jerahmeel, Ram, and Chelubai. [10]Ram
became the father of Amminadab, and
Amminadab became the father of Nahshon,
prince of the sons of Judah. [11]Nahshon
became the father of Salma, Salma of Boaz,
[12]Boaz of Obed, Obed of Jesse. [13]Jesse became
the father of Eliab his firstborn, Abinadab
the second, Shimea the third, [14]Nethanel
the fourth, Raddai the fifth, [15]Ozem the
sixth, David the seventh; [16]and their sisters
were Zeruiah and Abigail. The sons of
Zeruiah: Abishai, Joab, and Asahel, three.
[17]Abigail bore Amasa, and the father of
Amasa was Jether the Ishmaelite.

18 Caleb son of Hezron had children by
his wife Azubah, and by Jerioth; these were
her sons: Jesher, Shobab, and Ardon. [19]When
Azubah died, Caleb married Ephrath, who
bore him Hur. [20]Hur became the father of
Uri, and Uri became the father of Bezalel.

21 Afterward Hezron went in to the
daughter of Machir father of Gilead, whom
he married when he was sixty years old;
and she bore him Segub; [22]and Segub became the father of Jair, who had twenty-
three towns in the land of Gilead. [23]But
Geshur and Aram took from them Havvoth-
jair, Kenath and its villages, sixty towns. All
these were descendants of Machir, father of
Gilead. [24]After the death of Hezron, in Caleb-
ephrathah, Abijah wife of Hezron bore him
Ashhur, father of Tekoa.

25 The sons of Jerahmeel, the firstborn of
Hezron: Ram his firstborn, Bunah, Oren,
Ozem, and Ahijah. [26]Jerahmeel also had
another wife, whose name was Atarah; she
was the mother of Onam. [27]The sons of
Ram, the firstborn of Jerahmeel: Maaz, Jamin,
and Eker. [28]The sons of Onam: Shammai
and Jada. The sons of Shammai: Nadab and
Abishur. [29]The name of Abishur's wife was
Abihail, and she bore him Ahban and Molid.
[30]The sons of Nadab: Seled and Appaim;
and Seled died childless. [31]The son[k] of
Appaim: Ishi. The son[k] of Ishi: Sheshan. The
son[k] of Sheshan: Ahlai. [32]The sons of Jada,
Shammai's brother: Jether and Jonathan;
and Jether died childless. [33]The sons of
Jonathan: Peleth and Zaza. These were the
descendants of Jerahmeel. [34]Now Sheshan
had no sons, only daughters; but Sheshan
had an Egyptian slave, whose name was
Jarha. [35]So Sheshan gave his daughter in
marriage to his slave Jarha; and she bore
him Attai. [36]Attai became the father of
Nathan, and Nathan of Zabad. [37]Zabad
became the father of Ephlal, and Ephlal of
Obed. [38]Obed became the father of Jehu, and
Jehu of Azariah. [39]Azariah became the father of Helez, and Helez of Eleasah. [40]Eleasah
became the father of Sismai, and Sismai of
Shallum. [41]Shallum became the father of
Jekamiah, and Jekamiah of Elishama.

42 The sons of Caleb brother of Jerahmeel:
Mesha[l] his firstborn, who was father of
Ziph. The sons of Mareshah father of Hebron.
[43]The sons of Hebron: Korah, Tappuah,
Rekem, and Shema. [44]Shema became father
of Raham, father of Jorkeam; and Rekem
became the father of Shammai. [45]The son
of Shammai: Maon; and Maon was the
father of Beth-zur. [46]Ephah also, Caleb's
concubine, bore Haran, Moza, and Gazez;
and Haran became the father of Gazez.
[47]The sons of Jahdai: Regem, Jotham, Geshan,
Pelet, Ephah, and Shaaph. [48]Maacah, Caleb's
concubine, bore Sheber and Tirhanah. [49]She
also bore Shaaph father of Madmannah,
Sheva father of Machbenah and father of
Gibea; and the daughter of Caleb was
Achsah. [50]These were the descendants of
Caleb.

The sons[m] of Hur the firstborn of Ephrathah: Shobal father of Kiriath-jearim, [51]Salma
father of Bethlehem, and Hareph father of
Beth-gader. [52]Shobal father of Kiriath-jearim
had other sons: Haroeh, half of the
Menuhoth. [53]And the families of Kiriath-
jearim: the Ithrites, the Puthites, the
Shumathites, and the Mishraites; from these
came the Zorathites and the Eshtaolites.

[j] Or *Darda*; Compare Syr Tg some Gk Mss; See 1 Kings 4.31 [k] Heb *sons* [l] Gk reads *Mareshah* [m] Gk Vg: Heb *son*

2.1 Gen 35.23-26; 46.8-25
2.2 Gen 38.2-10
2.4 Gen 38.29,30
2.5 Gen 46.12
2.6 Josh 7.1; 1 Kings 4.31
2.7 Josh 6.18
2.10 Ruth 4.19,20; Mt 1.4
2.13 1 Sam 16.6,9
2.16 2 Sam 2.18
2.17 2 Sam 17.25
2.19 ver 50
2.20 Ex 31.2
2.21 Num 27.1
2.23 Num 32.41; Deut 3.14; Josh 13.30
2.24 1 Chr 4.5
2.31 ver 34,35
2.36 1 Chr 11.41
2.42 see 1 Chr 2.18,19
2.50 1 Chr 4.4

2.55 Judg 1.16; Jer 35.2
3.1 2 Sam 3.2,3; Josh 15.56
3.3 2 Sam 3.5
3.4 2 Sam 2.11; 5.5
3.5 2 Sam 5.14-16; 2 Sam 12.24; 11.3
3.9 2 Sam 13.1
3.10 1 Kings 11.43
3.16 Mt 1.11
3.22 Ezek 8.2
4.1 Gen 46.12
4.4 1 Chr 2.50
4.5 1 Chr 2.24
4.9 Gen 34.19
4.13 Josh 15.17
4.14 Neh 11.35

54 The sons of Salma: Bethlehem, the Netophathites, Atroth-beth-joab, and half of the Manahathites, the Zorites. 55 The families also of the scribes that lived at Jabez: the Tirathites, the Shimeathites, and the Sucathites. These are the Kenites who came from Hammath, father of the house of Rechab.

Descendants of David and Solomon

3 These are the sons of David who were born to him in Hebron: the firstborn Amnon, by Ahinoam the Jezreelite; the second Daniel, by Abigail the Carmelite; 2 the third Absalom, son of Maacah, daughter of King Talmai of Geshur; the fourth Adonijah, son of Haggith; 3 the fifth Shephatiah, by Abital; the sixth Ithream, by his wife Eglah; 4 six were born to him in Hebron, where he reigned for seven years and six months. And he reigned thirty-three years in Jerusalem. 5 These were born to him in Jerusalem: Shimea, Shobab, Nathan, and Solomon, four by Bath-shua, daughter of Ammiel; 6 then Ibhar, Elishama, Eliphelet, 7 Nogah, Nepheg, Japhia, 8 Elishama, Eliada, and Eliphelet, nine. 9 All these were David's sons, besides the sons of the concubines; and Tamar was their sister.

10 The descendants of Solomon: Rehoboam, Abijah his son, Asa his son, Jehoshaphat his son, 11 Joram his son, Ahaziah his son, Joash his son, 12 Amaziah his son, Azariah his son, Jotham his son, 13 Ahaz his son, Hezekiah his son, Manasseh his son, 14 Amon his son, Josiah his son. 15 The sons of Josiah: Johanan the firstborn, the second Jehoiakim, the third Zedekiah, the fourth Shallum. 16 The descendants of Jehoiakim: Jeconiah his son, Zedekiah his son; 17 and the sons of Jeconiah, the captive: Shealtiel his son, 18 Malchiram, Pedaiah, Shenazzar, Jekamiah, Hoshama, and Nedabiah; 19 The sons of Pedaiah: Zerubbabel and Shimei; and the sons of Zerubbabel: Meshullam and Hananiah, and Shelomith was their sister; 20 and Hashubah, Ohel, Berechiah, Hasadiah, and Jushab-hesed, five. 21 The sons of Hananiah: Pelatiah and Jeshaiah, his son[n] Rephaiah, his son[n] Arnan, his son[n] Obadiah, his son[n] Shecaniah. 22 The son[o] of Shecaniah: Shemaiah. And the sons of Shemaiah: Hattush, Igal, Bariah, Neariah, and Shaphat, six. 23 The sons of Neariah: Elioenai, Hizkiah, and Azrikam, three. 24 The sons of Elioenai: Hodaviah, Eliashib, Pelaiah, Akkub, Johanan, Delaiah, and Anani, seven.

Descendants of Judah

4 The sons of Judah: Perez, Hezron, Carmi, Hur, and Shobal. 2 Reaiah son of Shobal became the father of Jahath, and Jahath became the father of Ahumai and Lahad. These were the families of the Zorathites. 3 These were the sons[p] of Etam: Jezreel, Ishma, and Idbash; and the name of their sister was Hazzelelponi, 4 and Penuel was the father of Gedor, and Ezer the father of Hushah. These were the sons of Hur, the firstborn of Ephrathah, the father of Bethlehem. 5 Ashhur father of Tekoa had two wives, Helah and Naarah; 6 Naarah bore him Ahuzzam, Hepher, Temeni, and Haahashtari.[q] These were the sons of Naarah. 7 The sons of Helah: Zereth, Izhar,[r] and Ethnan. 8 Koz became the father of Anub, Zobebah, and the families of Aharhel son of Harum. 9 Jabez was honored more than his brothers; and his mother named him Jabez, saying, "Because I bore him in pain." 10 Jabez called on the God of Israel, saying, "Oh that you would bless me and enlarge my border, and that your hand might be with me, and that you would keep me from hurt and harm!" And God granted what he asked. 11 Chelub the brother of Shuhah became the father of Mehir, who was the father of Eshton. 12 Eshton became the father of Beth-rapha, Paseah, and Tehinnah the father of Ir-nahash. These are the men of Recah. 13 The sons of Kenaz: Othniel and Seraiah; and the sons of Othniel: Hathath and Meonothai.[s] 14 Meonothai became the father of Ophrah; and Seraiah became the father of Joab father of Ge-harashim,[t] so-called because they were artisans. 15 The sons of Caleb son of Jephunneh: Iru, Elah, and Naam; and the son[o] of Elah: Kenaz. 16 The sons of Jehallelel: Ziph, Ziphah, Tiria, and Asarel. 17 The sons of Ezrah: Jether, Mered, Epher, and Jalon. These are the sons of Bithiah, daughter of Pharaoh, whom Mered married;[u] and she conceived and bore[v] Miriam, Shammai, and Ishbah father of Eshtemoa. 18 And his Judean wife bore Jered father of Gedor, Heber father of Soco, and

[n] Gk Compare Syr Vg: Heb *sons of* [o] Heb *sons* [p] Gk Compare Vg: Heb *the father* [q] Or *Ahashtari* [r] Another reading is *Zohar* [s] Gk Vg: Heb lacks *and Meonothai* [t] That is *Valley of artisans* [u] The clause: *These are . . . married* is transposed from verse 18 [v] Heb lacks *and bore*

4.1-5.26 Of the twelve sons of Jacob, genealogies are offered initially of Judah (4.1-23), Simeon (4.24-43), Reuben (5.1-10), Gad (5.11-22), and the half-tribe of Manasseh (5.23-26). Simeon settled in prosperity and peace at *Gedor*, south of the territory of Judah, while *the Reubenites, the Gadites, and the half-tribe of Manasseh* were reportedly taken off into captivity by the Assyrians (5.26). Assyrian documents attest the collaboration of Manasseh with their king, Esarhaddon, in the seventh century BCE.

Jekuthiel father of Zanoah. [19]The sons of the wife of Hodiah, the sister of Naham, were the fathers of Keilah the Garmite and Eshtemoa the Maacathite. [20]The sons of Shimon: Amnon, Rinnah, Ben-hanan, and Tilon. The sons of Ishi: Zoheth and Benzoheth. [21]The sons of Shelah son of Judah: Er father of Lecah, Laadah father of Mareshah, and the families of the guild of linen workers at Beth-ashbea; [22]and Jokim, and the men of Cozeba, and Joash, and Saraph, who married into Moab but returned to Lehem[w] (now the records[x] are ancient). [23]These were the potters and inhabitants of Netaim and Gederah; they lived there with the king in his service.

Descendants of Simeon

24 The sons of Simeon: Nemuel, Jamin, Jarib, Zerah, Shaul;[y] [25]Shallum was his son, Mibsam his son, Mishma his son. [26]The sons of Mishma: Hammuel his son, Zaccur his son, Shimei his son. [27]Shimei had sixteen sons and six daughters; but his brothers did not have many children, nor did all their family multiply like the Judeans. [28]They lived in Beer-sheba, Moladah, Hazar-shual, [29]Bilhah, Ezem, Tolad, [30]Bethuel, Hormah, Ziklag, [31]Beth-marcaboth, Hazar-susim, Beth-biri, and Shaaraim. These were their towns until David became king. [32]And their villages were Etam, Ain, Rimmon, Tochen, and Ashan, five towns, [33]along with all their villages that were around these towns as far as Baal. These were their settlements. And they kept a genealogical record.

34 Meshobab, Jamlech, Joshah son of Amaziah, [35]Joel, Jehu son of Joshibiah son of Seraiah son of Asiel, [36]Elioenai, Jaakobah, Jeshohaiah, Asaiah, Adiel, Jesimiel, Benaiah, [37]Ziza son of Shiphi son of Allon son of Jedaiah son of Shimri son of Shemaiah— [38]these mentioned by name were leaders in their families, and their clans increased greatly. [39]They journeyed to the entrance of Gedor, to the east side of the valley, to seek pasture for their flocks, [40]where they found rich, good pasture, and the land was very broad, quiet, and peaceful; for the former inhabitants there belonged to Ham. [41]These, registered by name, came in the days of King Hezekiah of Judah, and attacked their tents and the Meunim who were found there, and exterminated them to this day, and settled in their place, because there was pasture there for their flocks. [42]And some of them, five hundred men of the Simeonites, went to Mount Seir, having as their leaders Pelatiah, Neariah, Rephaiah, and Uzziel, sons of Ishi; [43]they destroyed the remnant of the Amalekites that had escaped, and they have lived there to this day.

Descendants of Reuben

5 The sons of Reuben the firstborn of Israel. (He was the firstborn, but because he defiled his father's bed his birthright was given to the sons of Joseph son of Israel, so that he is not enrolled in the genealogy according to the birthright; [2]though Judah became prominent among his brothers and a ruler came from him, yet the birthright belonged to Joseph.) [3]The sons of Reuben, the firstborn of Israel: Hanoch, Pallu, Hezron, and Carmi. [4]The sons of Joel: Shemaiah his son, Gog his son, Shimei his son, [5]Micah his son, Reaiah his son, Baal his son, [6]Beerah his son, whom King Tilgath-pilneser of Assyria carried away into exile; he was a chieftain of the Reubenites. [7]And his kindred by their families, when the genealogy of their generations was reckoned: the chief, Jeiel, and Zechariah, [8]and Bela son of Azaz, son of Shema, son of Joel, who lived in Aroer, as far as Nebo and Baal-meon. [9]He also lived to the east as far as the beginning of the desert this side of the Euphrates, because their cattle had multiplied in the land of Gilead. [10]And in the days of Saul they made war on the Hagrites, who fell by their hand; and they lived in their tents throughout all the region east of Gilead.

Descendants of Gad

11 The sons of Gad lived beside them in the land of Bashan as far as Salecah: [12]Joel the chief, Shapham the second, Janai, and Shaphat in Bashan. [13]And their kindred according to their clans: Michael, Meshullam, Sheba, Jorai, Jacan, Zia, and Eber, seven. [14]These were the sons of Abihail son of Huri, son of Jaroah, son of Gilead, son of Michael, son of Jeshishai, son of Jahdo, son of Buz; [15]Ahi son of Abdiel, son of Guni, was chief in their clan; [16]and they lived in Gilead, in Bashan and in its towns, and in all the pasture lands of Sharon to their limits. [17]All of these were enrolled by genealogies in the

4.21 Gen 38.1,5
4.24 Gen 29.33
4.28 Josh 19.2
4.30 1 Chr 12.1
4.40 Judg 18.7-10
4.41 2 Kings 18.8
4.43 1 Sam 15.8; 30.17; 2 Sam 8.12
5.1 Gen 29.32; 35.22; 49.4; 48.15,22
5.2 Gen 49.8,10; Mic 5.2; Mt 2.6
5.3 Gen 46.9; Num 26.5
5.7 ver 17
5.8 Josh 13.15,16
5.9 Josh 22.9
5.10 ver 18-21
5.11 Josh 13.11,24
5.16 1 Chr 27.29
5.17 2 Kings 15.5,32; 14.16,28

[w] Vg Compare Gk: Heb *and Jashubi-lahem* [x] Or *matters* [y] Or *Saul*

5.19 ver 10; 1 Chr 1.31
5.20 2 Chr 4.11-13; Ps 22.4,5
5.22 2 Kings 15.29; 17.6
5.25 2 Kings 17.7
5.26 2 Kings 15.19,29; 17.6; 18.11
6.1 Ex 6.16; Num 26.57; 1 Chr 23.6
6.3 Lev 10.1
6.8 2 Sam 8.17; 15.27
6.14 Neh 11.11
6.15 2 Kings 25.18
6.16 Ex 6.16
6.20 ver 42
6.25 ver 35,36
6.26 ver 34
6.31 1 Chr 15.16-16.6
6.37 Ex 6.24

days of King Jotham of Judah, and in the days of King Jeroboam of Israel.

18 The Reubenites, the Gadites, and the half-tribe of Manasseh had valiant warriors, who carried shield and sword, and drew the bow, expert in war, forty-four thousand seven hundred sixty, ready for service. [19]They made war on the Hagrites, Jetur, Naphish, and Nodab; [20]and when they received help against them, the Hagrites and all who were with them were given into their hands, for they cried to God in the battle, and he granted their entreaty because they trusted in him. [21]They captured their livestock: fifty thousand of their camels, two hundred fifty thousand sheep, two thousand donkeys, and one hundred thousand captives. [22]Many fell slain, because the war was of God. And they lived in their territory until the exile.

The Half-Tribe of Manasseh

23 The members of the half-tribe of Manasseh lived in the land; they were very numerous from Bashan to Baal-hermon, Senir, and Mount Hermon. [24]These were the heads of their clans: Epher,[z] Ishi, Eliel, Azriel, Jeremiah, Hodaviah, and Jahdiel, mighty warriors, famous men, heads of their clans. [25]But they transgressed against the God of their ancestors, and prostituted themselves to the gods of the peoples of the land, whom God had destroyed before them. [26]So the God of Israel stirred up the spirit of King Pul of Assyria, the spirit of King Tilgath-pilneser of Assyria, and he carried them away, namely, the Reubenites, the Gadites, and the half-tribe of Manasseh, and brought them to Halah, Habor, Hara, and the river Gozan, to this day.

Descendants of Levi

6[a] The sons of Levi: Gershom,[b] Kohath, and Merari. [2]The sons of Kohath: Amram, Izhar, Hebron, and Uzziel. [3]The children of Amram: Aaron, Moses, and Miriam. The sons of Aaron: Nadab, Abihu, Eleazar, and Ithamar. [4]Eleazar became the father of Phinehas, Phinehas of Abishua, [5]Abishua of Bukki, Bukki of Uzzi, [6]Uzzi of Zerahiah, Zerahiah of Meraioth, [7]Meraioth of Amariah, Amariah of Ahitub, [8]Ahitub of Zadok, Zadok of Ahimaaz, [9]Ahimaaz of Azariah, Azariah of Johanan, [10]and Johanan of Azariah (it was he who served as priest in the house that Solomon built in Jerusalem). [11]Azariah became the father of Amariah, Amariah of Ahitub, [12]Ahitub of Zadok, Zadok of Shallum, [13]Shallum of Hilkiah, Hilkiah of Azariah, [14]Azariah of Seraiah, Seraiah of Jehozadak; [15]and Jehozadak went into exile when the LORD sent Judah and Jerusalem into exile by the hand of Nebuchadnezzar.

16[c] The sons of Levi: Gershom, Kohath, and Merari. [17]These are the names of the sons of Gershom: Libni and Shimei. [18]The sons of Kohath: Amram, Izhar, Hebron, and Uzziel. [19]The sons of Merari: Mahli and Mushi. These are the clans of the Levites according to their ancestry. [20]Of Gershom: Libni his son, Jahath his son, Zimmah his son, [21]Joah his son, Iddo his son, Zerah his son, Jeatherai his son. [22]The sons of Kohath: Amminadab his son, Korah his son, Assir his son, [23]Elkanah his son, Ebiasaph his son, Assir his son, [24]Tahath his son, Uriel his son, Uzziah his son, and Shaul his son. [25]The sons of Elkanah: Amasai and Ahimoth, [26]Elkanah his son, Zophai his son, Nahath his son, [27]Eliab his son, Jeroham his son, Elkanah his son. [28]The sons of Samuel: Joel[d] his firstborn, the second Abijah.[e] [29]The sons of Merari: Mahli, Libni his son, Shimei his son, Uzzah his son, [30]Shimea his son, Haggiah his son, and Asaiah his son.

Musicians Appointed by David

31 These are the men whom David put in charge of the service of song in the house of the LORD, after the ark came to rest there. [32]They ministered with song before the tabernacle of the tent of meeting, until Solomon had built the house of the LORD in Jerusalem; and they performed their service in due order. [33]These are the men who served; and their sons were: Of the Kohathites: Heman, the singer, son of Joel, son of Samuel, [34]son of Elkanah, son of Jeroham, son of Eliel, son of Toah, [35]son of Zuph, son of Elkanah, son of Mahath, son of Amasai, [36]son of Elkanah, son of Joel, son of Azariah, son of Zephaniah, [37]son of Tahath, son of Assir, son of Ebiasaph, son of Korah, [38]son of Izhar, son of Kohath, son of Levi, son of Israel; [39]and his brother Asaph, who stood on his right, namely, Asaph son of Berechiah, son of Shimea, [40]son of Michael, son of Baaseiah, son of Malchijah,

[z] Gk Vg: Heb *and Epher* [a] Ch 5.27 in Heb [b] Heb *Gershon*, variant of *Gershom*; See 6.16 [c] Ch 6.1 in Heb [d] Gk Syr Compare verse 33 and 1 Sam 8.2: Heb lacks *Joel* [e] Heb reads *Vashni, and Abijah* for *the second Abijah*, taking *the second* as a proper name

6.1-30 *The sons of Levi* are first described here in terms of their role in the temple rather than by territorial assignment.

6.31-81 Details are given of those who *ministered with song* in the *tent of meeting* before the temple was built. The priestly functions of *Aaron and his sons* are mentioned briefly, followed by a resumption of the genealogies of *the sons of Aaron* (grouped according to the sons of Levi: *Gershom* and *Kohath*) and the towns assigned to them are named. In 6.39 is mentioned *Asaph*, who has a prominent role in the musical aspects of worship in the temple (1 Chr 25).

7.1-8.40 Brief lists of the descendants of the other sons of Jacob are given: Issachar (7.1-5); Naphtali (7.13); Ephraim, Asher (7.30-40). But there is an additional list for the descendants of Manasseh (7.14-19; *cf.* 5.23-26) and a lengthy one for the tribe of Benjamin (8.1-40).
9.1-9 These genealogies are said to have been selected from a source, the *Book of the Kings of Israel*, although the central focus is on the tribe of Judah and those tribes closely linked with it: Benjamin, Ephraim and Manasseh.

[41]son of Ethni, son of Zerah, son of Adaiah,
[42]son of Ethan, son of Zimmah, son of Shimei,
[43]son of Jahath, son of Gershom, son of Levi.
[44]On the left were their kindred the sons of
Merari: Ethan son of Kishi, son of Abdi, son
of Malluch, [45]son of Hashabiah, son of
Amaziah, son of Hilkiah, [46]son of Amzi, son
of Bani, son of Shemer, [47]son of Mahli, son
of Mushi, son of Merari, son of Levi; [48]and
their kindred the Levites were appointed for
all the service of the tabernacle of the house
of God.
49 But Aaron and his sons made offerings on the altar of burnt offering and on
the altar of incense, doing all the work of
the most holy place, to make atonement for
Israel, according to all that Moses the servant of God had commanded. [50]These are the
sons of Aaron: Eleazar his son, Phinehas his
son, Abishua his son, [51]Bukki his son, Uzzi
his son, Zerahiah his son, [52]Meraioth his
son, Amariah his son, Ahitub his son,
[53]Zadok his son, Ahimaaz his son.

Settlements of the Levites

54 These are their dwelling places according to their settlements within their
borders: to the sons of Aaron of the families
of Kohathites—for the lot fell to them first—
[55]to them they gave Hebron in the land of
Judah and its surrounding pasture lands,
[56]but the fields of the city and its villages
they gave to Caleb son of Jephunneh. [57]To
the sons of Aaron they gave the cities of
refuge: Hebron, Libnah with its pasture lands,
Jattir, Eshtemoa with its pasture lands,
[58]Hilen[f] with its pasture lands, Debir with its
pasture lands, [59]Ashan with its pasture lands,
and Beth-shemesh with its pasture lands.
[60]From the tribe of Benjamin, Geba with its
pasture lands, Alemeth with its pasture lands,
and Anathoth with its pasture lands. All
their towns throughout their families were
thirteen.
61 To the rest of the Kohathites were
given by lot out of the family of the tribe,
out of the half-tribe, the half of Manasseh,
ten towns. [62]To the Gershomites according
to their families were allotted thirteen towns
out of the tribes of Issachar, Asher, Naphtali,
and Manasseh in Bashan. [63]To the Merarites
according to their families were allotted
twelve towns out of the tribes of Reuben,
Gad, and Zebulun. [64]So the people of Israel
gave the Levites the towns with their pasture lands. [65]They also gave them by lot out
of the tribes of Judah, Simeon, and Benjamin
these towns that are mentioned by name.
66 And some of the families of the sons
of Kohath had towns of their territory out
of the tribe of Ephraim. [67]They were given
the cities of refuge: Shechem with its pasture lands in the hill country of Ephraim,
Gezer with its pasture lands, [68]Jokmeam
with its pasture lands, Beth-horon with its
pasture lands, [69]Aijalon with its pasture
lands, Gath-rimmon with its pasture lands;
[70]and out of the half-tribe of Manasseh,
Aner with its pasture lands, and Bileam
with its pasture lands, for the rest of the
families of the Kohathites.
71 To the Gershomites: out of the half-
tribe of Manasseh: Golan in Bashan with its
pasture lands and Ashtaroth with its pasture lands; [72]and out of the tribe of Issachar:
Kedesh with its pasture lands, Daberath[g]
with its pasture lands, [73]Ramoth with its
pasture lands, and Anem with its pasture
lands; [74]out of the tribe of Asher: Mashal
with its pasture lands, Abdon with its pasture lands, [75]Hukok with its pasture lands,
and Rehob with its pasture lands; [76]and out
of the tribe of Naphtali: Kedesh in Galilee
with its pasture lands, Hammon with its
pasture lands, and Kiriathaim with its pasture lands. [77]To the rest of the Merarites out
of the tribe of Zebulun: Rimmono with its
pasture lands, Tabor with its pasture lands,
[78]and across the Jordan from Jericho, on the
east side of the Jordan, out of the tribe of
Reuben: Bezer in the steppe with its pasture
lands, Jahzah with its pasture lands,
[79]Kedemoth with its pasture lands, and
Mephaath with its pasture lands; [80]and out
of the tribe of Gad: Ramoth in Gilead with
its pasture lands, Mahanaim with its pasture lands, [81]Heshbon with its pasture lands,
and Jazer with its pasture lands.

Descendants of Issachar

7 The sons[h] of Issachar: Tola, Puah,
Jashub, and Shimron, four. [2]The sons
of Tola: Uzzi, Rephaiah, Jeriel, Jahmai, Ibsam,
and Shemuel, heads of their ancestral houses,
namely of Tola, mighty warriors of their
generations, their number in the days of
David being twenty-two thousand six hundred. [3]The son[i] of Uzzi: Izrahiah. And the

6.41 ver 21
6.49 Ex 27.1-8; 30.1-7,10
6.50 ver 4-8
6.54 Josh 21.4,10
6.55 Josh 21.11,12
6.56 Josh 14.13; 15.13
6.57 Josh 21.13
6.61 ver 66-70; Josh 21.5
6.63 Josh 21.7,34
6.64 Josh 21.3,41,42
6.65 ver 57-60
6.66 ver 61
6.67 Josh 21.21
6.68 see Josh 21.22-35 where some names are differently given
6.73 see Josh 21.29; 19.21
6.76 ver 62
6.77 ver 63
7.1 Gen 46.13; Num 26.23
7.2 2 Sam 24.1,2

[f] Other readings *Hilez, Holon*; See Josh 21.15 [g] Or *Dobrath* [h] Syr Compare Vg: Heb *And to the sons* [i] Heb *sons*

7.5 1 Chr 6.62,72
7.6 Gen 46.21; Num 26.38; 1 Chr 8.1-40
7.12 Num 26.39
7.13 Gen 46.24
7.17 1 Sam 12.11
7.20 Num 26.35
7.24 Josh 16.3,5
7.27 Ex 17.9-14; 24.13
7.28 Josh 16.7
7.30 Gen 46.17; Num 26.44
7.40 ver 30

sons of Izrahiah: Michael, Obadiah, Joel, and
Isshiah, five, all of them chiefs; 4and along
with them, by their generations, according
to their ancestral houses, were units of the
fighting force, thirty-six thousand, for they
had many wives and sons. 5Their kindred
belonging to all the families of Issachar were
in all eighty-seven thousand mighty warriors, enrolled by genealogy.

Descendants of Benjamin

6 The sons of Benjamin: Bela, Becher,
and Jediael, three. 7The sons of Bela: Ezbon,
Uzzi, Uzziel, Jerimoth, and Iri, five, heads of
ancestral houses, mighty warriors; and their
enrollment by genealogies was twenty-two
thousand thirty-four. 8The sons of Becher:
Zemirah, Joash, Eliezer, Elioenai, Omri,
Jeremoth, Abijah, Anathoth, and Alemeth.
All these were the sons of Becher; 9and their
enrollment by genealogies, according to their
generations, as heads of their ancestral
houses, mighty warriors, was twenty thousand two hundred. 10The sons of Jediael:
Bilhan. And the sons of Bilhan: Jeush,
Benjamin, Ehud, Chenaanah, Zethan,
Tarshish, and Ahishahar. 11All these were
the sons of Jediael according to the heads
of their ancestral houses, mighty warriors,
seventeen thousand two hundred, ready for
service in war. 12And Shuppim and Huppim
were the sons of Ir, Hushim the son[j] of
Aher.

Descendants of Naphtali

13 The descendants of Naphtali: Jahziel,
Guni, Jezer, and Shallum, the descendants
of Bilhah.

Descendants of Manasseh

14 The sons of Manasseh: Asriel, whom
his Aramean concubine bore; she bore
Machir the father of Gilead. 15And Machir
took a wife for Huppim and for Shuppim.
The name of his sister was Maacah. And
the name of the second was Zelophehad;
and Zelophehad had daughters. 16Maacah
the wife of Machir bore a son, and she
named him Peresh; the name of his brother
was Sheresh; and his sons were Ulam and
Rekem. 17The son[j] of Ulam: Bedan. These
were the sons of Gilead son of Machir, son
of Manasseh. 18And his sister Hammolecheth
bore Ishhod, Abiezer, and Mahlah. 19The
sons of Shemida were Ahian, Shechem,
Likhi, and Aniam.

Descendants of Ephraim

20 The sons of Ephraim: Shuthelah, and
Bered his son, Tahath his son, Eleadah his
son, Tahath his son, 21Zabad his son,
Shuthelah his son, and Ezer and Elead. Now
the people of Gath, who were born in the
land, killed them, because they came down
to raid their cattle. 22And their father Ephraim
mourned many days, and his brothers came
to comfort him. 23Ephraim[k] went in to his
wife, and she conceived and bore a son; and
he named him Beriah, because disaster[l] had
befallen his house. 24His daughter was
Sheerah, who built both Lower and Upper
Beth-horon, and Uzzen-sheerah. 25Rephah
was his son, Resheph his son, Telah his son,
Tahan his son, 26Ladan his son, Ammihud
his son, Elishama his son, 27Nun[m] his son,
Joshua his son. 28Their possessions and
settlements were Bethel and its towns, and
eastward Naaran, and westward Gezer and
its towns, Shechem and its towns, as far as
Ayyah and its towns; 29also along the borders of the Manassites, Beth-shean and its
towns, Taanach and its towns, Megiddo
and its towns, Dor and its towns. In these
lived the sons of Joseph son of Israel.

Descendants of Asher

30 The sons of Asher: Imnah, Ishvah,
Ishvi, Beriah, and their sister Serah. 31The
sons of Beriah: Heber and Malchiel, who
was the father of Birzaith. 32Heber became
the father of Japhlet, Shomer, Hotham, and
their sister Shua. 33The sons of Japhlet:
Pasach, Bimhal, and Ashvath. These are
the sons of Japhlet. 34The sons of Shemer:
Ahi, Rohgah, Hubbah, and Aram. 35The
sons of Helem[n] his brother: Zophah, Imna,
Shelesh, and Amal. 36The sons of Zophah:
Suah, Harnepher, Shual, Beri, Imrah, 37Bezer,
Hod, Shamma, Shilshah, Ithran, and Beera.
38The sons of Jether: Jephunneh, Pispa, and
Ara. 39The sons of Ulla: Arah, Hanniel, and
Rizia. 40All of these were men of Asher,
heads of ancestral houses, select mighty
warriors, chief of the princes. Their number
enrolled by genealogies, for service in war,
was twenty-six thousand men.

[j] Heb *sons* [k] Heb *He* [l] Heb *beraah* [m] Here spelled *Non*; see Ex 33.11 [n] Or *Hotham*; see 7.32

9.10-34 Following Judah's *exile in Babylon* (from 597 to 582) and return to the Jerusalem area (end of sixth century), the names are given of the heads of households in the city (vv. 3-9), of the priestly families (vv. 10-13), and of the Levites, including the specifics of their responsibilities in the temple (vv. 14-34).

Descendants of Benjamin

8 Benjamin became the father of Bela his
firstborn, Ashbel the second, Aharah
the third, 2 Nohah the fourth, and Rapha the
fifth. 3 And Bela had sons: Addar, Gera,
Abihud,[o] 4 Abishua, Naaman, Ahoah, 5 Gera,
Shephuphan, and Huram. 6 These are the
sons of Ehud (they were heads of ancestral
houses of the inhabitants of Geba, and they
were carried into exile to Manahath):
7 Naaman,[p] Ahijah, and Gera, that is, Heglam,[q]
who became the father of Uzza and Ahihud.
8 And Shaharaim had sons in the country of
Moab after he had sent away his wives
Hushim and Baara. 9 He had sons by his wife
Hodesh: Jobab, Zibia, Mesha, Malcam, 10 Jeuz,
Sachia, and Mirmah. These were his sons,
heads of ancestral houses. 11 He also had sons
by Hushim: Abitub and Elpaal. 12 The sons
of Elpaal: Eber, Misham, and Shemed, who
built Ono and Lod with its towns, 13 and
Beriah and Shema (they were heads of
ancestral houses of the inhabitants of Aijalon,
who put to flight the inhabitants of Gath);
14 and Ahio, Shashak, and Jeremoth.
15 Zebadiah, Arad, Eder, 16 Michael, Ishpah,
and Joha were sons of Beriah. 17 Zebadiah,
Meshullam, Hizki, Heber, 18 Ishmerai, Izliah,
and Jobab were the sons of Elpaal. 19 Jakim,
Zichri, Zabdi, 20 Elienai, Zillethai, Eliel, 21 Adaiah,
Beraiah, and Shimrath were the sons of
Shimei. 22 Ishpan, Eber, Eliel, 23 Abdon, Zichri,
Hanan, 24 Hananiah, Elam, Anthothijah,
25 Iphdeiah, and Penuel were the sons of
Shashak. 26 Shamsherai, Shehariah, Athaliah,
27 Jaareshiah, Elijah, and Zichri were the sons
of Jeroham. 28 These were the heads of ancestral
houses, according to their generations, chiefs.
These lived in Jerusalem.

29 Jeiel[r] the father of Gibeon lived in
Gibeon, and the name of his wife was
Maacah. 30 His firstborn son: Abdon, then
Zur, Kish, Baal,[s] Nadab, 31 Gedor, Ahio,
Zecher, 32 and Mikloth, who became the father
of Shimeah. Now these also lived opposite
their kindred in Jerusalem, with their kin-
dred. 33 Ner became the father of Kish, Kish
of Saul,[t] Saul[t] of Jonathan, Malchishua,
Abinadab, and Esh-baal; 34 and the son of
Jonathan was Merib-baal; and Merib-baal
became the father of Micah. 35 The sons of
Micah: Pithon, Melech, Tarea, and Ahaz.
36 Ahaz became the father of Jehoaddah; and
Jehoaddah became the father of Alemeth,
Azmaveth, and Zimri; Zimri became the
father of Moza. 37 Moza became the father of
Binea; Raphah was his son, Eleasah his son,
Azel his son. 38 Azel had six sons, and these
are their names: Azrikam, Bocheru, Ishmael,
Sheariah, Obadiah, and Hanan; all these
were the sons of Azel. 39 The sons of his
brother Eshek: Ulam his firstborn, Jeush the
second, and Eliphelet the third. 40 The sons
of Ulam were mighty warriors, archers, having many children and grandchildren, one
hundred fifty. All these were Benjaminites.

9 So all Israel was enrolled by genealogies; and these are written in the
Book of the Kings of Israel. And Judah was
taken into exile in Babylon because of their
unfaithfulness. 2 Now the first to live again
in their possessions in their towns were
Israelites, priests, Levites, and temple servants.

Inhabitants of Jerusalem after the Exile

3 And some of the people of Judah,
Benjamin, Ephraim, and Manasseh lived in
Jerusalem: 4 Uthai son of Ammihud, son of
Omri, son of Imri, son of Bani, from the sons
of Perez son of Judah. 5 And of the Shilonites:
Asaiah the firstborn, and his sons. 6 Of the
sons of Zerah: Jeuel and their kin, six hundred ninety. 7 Of the Benjaminites: Sallu son
of Meshullam, son of Hodaviah, son of
Hassenuah, 8 Ibneiah son of Jeroham, Elah
son of Uzzi, son of Michri, and Meshullam
son of Shephatiah, son of Reuel, son of
Ibnijah; 9 and their kindred according to
their generations, nine hundred fifty-six. All
these were heads of families according to
their ancestral houses.

Priestly Families

10 Of the priests: Jedaiah, Jehoiarib,
Jachin, 11 and Azariah son of Hilkiah, son of
Meshullam, son of Zadok, son of Meraioth,
son of Ahitub, the chief officer of the house
of God; 12 and Adaiah son of Jeroham, son
of Pashhur, son of Malchijah, and Maasai
son of Adiel, son of Jahzerah, son of
Meshullam, son of Meshillemith, son of
Immer; 13 besides their kindred, heads of
their ancestral houses, one thousand seven
hundred sixty, qualified for the work of the
service of the house of God.

8.1 Gen 46.21; 1 Chr 7.6
8.6 1 Chr 2.52
8.13 ver 21
8.21 ver 13
8.29 1 Chr 9.35
8.33 1 Chr 9.35-38
8.34 2 Sam 9.12
9.1 1 Chr 5.25,26
9.2 Neh 11.3-22; Ezra 2.43; 8.20
9.3 Neh 11.1
9.10 Neh 11.10-14

[o] Or *father of Ehud*; see 8.6 [p] Heb *and Naaman* [q] Or *he carried them into exile* [r] Compare 9.35: Heb lacks *Jeiel* [s] Gk Ms adds *Ner* ; Compare 8.33 and 9.36 [t] Or *Shaul*

9.14 Neh 11.15-19
9.18 Ezek 46.1,2
9.20 Num 25.7-13
9.21 1 Chr 26.2,14
9.22 1 Chr 26.1,2; 2 Chr 31.15,18
9.25 ver 16; 2 Kings 11.5,7; 2 Chr 23.8
9.27 1 Chr 23.30-32
9.29 1 Chr 23.9
9.30 Ex 30.23-25
9.32 Lev 24.8
9.33 1 Chr 6.31; 25.1; Ps 134.1
9.35 1 Chr 8.29
9.39 1 Chr 8.33
9.41 1 Chr 8.35
10.1 1 Sam 31.1,2
10.4 *cf.* 1 Sam 31.4-7

Levitical Families

14 Of the Levites: Shemaiah son of Hasshub, son of Azrikam, son of Hashabiah, of the sons of Merari; 15and Bakbakkar, Heresh, Galal, and Mattaniah son of Mica, son of Zichri, son of Asaph; 16and Obadiah son of Shemaiah, son of Galal, son of Jeduthun, and Berechiah son of Asa, son of Elkanah, who lived in the villages of the Netophathites.

17 The gatekeepers were: Shallum, Akkub, Talmon, Ahiman; and their kindred Shallum was the chief, 18stationed previously in the king's gate on the east side. These were the gatekeepers of the camp of the Levites. 19Shallum son of Kore, son of Ebiasaph, son of Korah, and his kindred of his ancestral house, the Korahites, were in charge of the work of the service, guardians of the thresholds of the tent, as their ancestors had been in charge of the camp of the LORD, guardians of the entrance. 20And Phinehas son of Eleazar was chief over them in former times; the LORD was with him. 21Zechariah son of Meshelemiah was gatekeeper at the entrance of the tent of meeting. 22All these, who were chosen as gatekeepers at the thresholds, were two hundred twelve. They were enrolled by genealogies in their villages. David and the seer Samuel established them in their office of trust. 23So they and their descendants were in charge of the gates of the house of the LORD, that is, the house of the tent, as guards. 24The gatekeepers were on the four sides, east, west, north, and south; 25and their kindred who were in their villages were obliged to come in every seven days, in turn, to be with them; 26for the four chief gatekeepers, who were Levites, were in charge of the chambers and the treasures of the house of God. 27And they would spend the night near the house of God; for on them lay the duty of watching, and they had charge of opening it every morning.

28 Some of them had charge of the utensils of service, for they were required to count them when they were brought in and taken out. 29Others of them were appointed over the furniture, and over all the holy utensils, also over the choice flour, the wine, the oil, the incense, and the spices. 30Others, of the sons of the priests, prepared the mixing of the spices, 31and Mattithiah, one of the Levites, the firstborn of Shallum the Korahite, was in charge of making the flat cakes. 32Also some of their kindred of the Kohathites had charge of the rows of bread, to prepare them for each sabbath.

33 Now these are the singers, the heads of ancestral houses of the Levites, living in the chambers of the temple free from other service, for they were on duty day and night. 34These were heads of ancestral houses of the Levites, according to their generations; these leaders lived in Jerusalem.

The Family of King Saul

35 In Gibeon lived the father of Gibeon, Jeiel, and the name of his wife was Maacah. 36His firstborn son was Abdon, then Zur, Kish, Baal, Ner, Nadab, 37Gedor, Ahio, Zechariah, and Mikloth; 38and Mikloth became the father of Shimeam; and these also lived opposite their kindred in Jerusalem, with their kindred. 39Ner became the father of Kish, Kish of Saul, Saul of Jonathan, Malchishua, Abinadab, and Esh-baal; 40and the son of Jonathan was Merib-baal; and Merib-baal became the father of Micah. 41The sons of Micah: Pithon, Melech, Tahrea, and Ahaz;[u] 42and Ahaz became the father of Jarah, and Jarah of Alemeth, Azmaveth, and Zimri; and Zimri became the father of Moza. 43Moza became the father of Binea; and Rephaiah was his son, Eleasah his son, Azel his son. 44Azel had six sons, and these are their names: Azrikam, Bocheru, Ishmael, Sheariah, Obadiah, and Hanan; these were the sons of Azel.

Death of Saul and His Sons

10 Now the Philistines fought against Israel; and the men of Israel fled before the Philistines, and fell slain on Mount Gilboa. 2The Philistines overtook Saul and his sons; and the Philistines killed Jonathan and Abinadab and Malchishua, sons of Saul. 3The battle pressed hard on Saul; and the archers found him, and he was wounded by the archers. 4Then Saul said to his armor-bearer, "Draw your sword, and thrust me through with it, so that these uncircumcised may not come and make sport of me." But his armor-bearer was unwilling, for he was terrified. So Saul took his own sword and fell on it. 5When his armor-bearer saw that Saul was dead, he also fell on his sword and died. 6Thus Saul died; he and his three sons and all his house died together. 7When all

[u] Compare 8.35: Heb lacks *and Ahaz*

9.35-44 The genealogy of *Saul*, Israel's first king, is given in association with *Gibeon*, about five miles north of Jerusalem, where there was a *high place*, and where the LORD appeared to Solomon (1 Kings 3.4-15). This genealogy of Saul and the account of his death (10.1-14) serve as a transition to the story of the reign of David.
10.1-14 Omitting any reference to the earlier anointing of Saul by Samuel (1 Sam 10-11), the narrative here notes only Saul's defeat by *the Philistines*, his death and burial, and those of his sons, ending with details of his disobedience to *the LORD*, which led to his death at the LORD's hand.

11.1-29.30 The Reign of David. The Chronicler has omitted (1) the stories of the rivalry between Saul and David that are found in 1 Sam 16-29, as well as the stories (2) of David's struggle for power with Saul's sons (2 Sam 2-4), (3) of his adultery with Bathsheba (2 Sam 11), and (4) of the attempted usurpation of the throne by his son Absalom (2 Sam 13-19). Dominant in this account is the order which David established in his kingdom, but especially in the worship of God in Jerusalem.
11.1-9 David is anointed as *king over Israel* during the reign of Saul in this abbreviated account (*cf.* 1 Sam 16.1-13).
11.4-9 The capture of *Jerusalem* is described briefly (*cf.* 2 Sam 5-6).
11.10-47 This account of David's *mighty warriors*, which shows how they helped him consolidate his rule, builds on 2 Sam 23.8-39.

the men of Israel who were in the valley saw that the army[v] had fled and that Saul and his sons were dead, they abandoned their towns and fled; and the Philistines came and occupied them.

8 The next day when the Philistines came to strip the dead, they found Saul and his sons fallen on Mount Gilboa. [9]They stripped him and took his head and his armor, and sent messengers throughout the land of the Philistines to carry the good news to their idols and to the people. [10]They put his armor in the temple of their gods, and fastened his head in the temple of Dagon. [11]But when all Jabesh-gilead heard everything that the Philistines had done to Saul, [12]all the valiant warriors got up and took away the body of Saul and the bodies of his sons, and brought them to Jabesh. Then they buried their bones under the oak in Jabesh, and fasted seven days.

13 So Saul died for his unfaithfulness; he was unfaithful to the LORD in that he did not keep the command of the LORD; moreover, he had consulted a medium, seeking guidance, [14]and did not seek guidance from the LORD. Therefore the LORD[w] put him to death and turned the kingdom over to David son of Jesse.

David Anointed King of All Israel

11 Then all Israel gathered together to David at Hebron and said, "See, we are your bone and flesh. [2]For some time now, even while Saul was king, it was you who commanded the army of Israel. The LORD your God said to you: It is you who shall be shepherd of my people Israel, you who shall be ruler over my people Israel." [3]So all the elders of Israel came to the king at Hebron, and David made a covenant with them at Hebron before the LORD. And they anointed David king over Israel, according to the word of the LORD by Samuel.

Jerusalem Captured

4 David and all Israel marched to Jerusalem, that is Jebus, where the Jebusites were, the inhabitants of the land. [5]The inhabitants of Jebus said to David, "You will not come in here." Nevertheless David took the stronghold of Zion, now the city of David. [6]David had said, "Whoever attacks the Jebusites first shall be chief and commander." And Joab son of Zeruiah went up first, so he became chief. [7]David resided in the stronghold; therefore it was called the city of David. [8]He built the city all around, from the Millo in complete circuit; and Joab repaired the rest of the city. [9]And David became greater and greater, for the LORD of hosts was with him.

David's Mighty Men and Their Exploits

10 Now these are the chiefs of David's warriors, who gave him strong support in his kingdom, together with all Israel, to make him king, according to the word of the LORD concerning Israel. [11]This is an account of David's mighty warriors: Jashobeam, son of Hachmoni,[x] was chief of the Three;[y] he wielded his spear against three hundred whom he killed at one time.

12 And next to him among the three warriors was Eleazar son of Dodo, the Ahohite. [13]He was with David at Pas-dammim when the Philistines were gathered there for battle. There was a plot of ground full of barley. Now the people had fled from the Philistines, [14]but he and David took their stand in the middle of the plot, defended it, and killed the Philistines; and the LORD saved them by a great victory.

15 Three of the thirty chiefs went down to the rock to David at the cave of Adullam, while the army of Philistines was encamped in the valley of Rephaim. [16]David was then in the stronghold; and the garrison of the Philistines was then at Bethlehem. [17]David said longingly, "O that someone would give me water to drink from the well of Bethlehem that is by the gate!" [18]Then the Three broke through the camp of the Philistines, and drew water from the well of Bethlehem that was by the gate, and they brought it to David. But David would not drink of it; he poured it out to the LORD, [19]and said, "My God forbid that I should do this. Can I drink the blood of these men? For at the risk of their lives they brought it." Therefore he would not drink it. The three warriors did these things.

20 Now Abishai,[z] the brother of Joab, was chief of the Thirty.[a] With his spear he fought against three hundred and killed

10.10 1 Sam 31.10
10.13 1 Sam 13.13; 15.23; 28.7
10.14 1 Sam 15.28; 1 Chr 12.23
11.1 2 Sam 5.1
11.2 2 Sam 5.2; Ps 78.71
11.3 2 Sam 5.3; 1 Sam 16.1,12,13
11.4 Judg 1.21; 19.10
11.6 2 Sam 8.16
11.9 2 Sam 3.1
11.10 2 Sam 23.8-39; ver 3
11.11 2 Sam 23.8
11.13 2 Sam 23.11,12
11.15 2 Sam 23.13; 1 Chr 14.9
11.20 2 Sam 23.18

[v] Heb *they* [w] Heb *he* [x] Or *a Hachmonite* [y] Compare 2 Sam 23.8: Heb *Thirty* or *captains* [z] Gk Vg Tg Compare 2 Sam 23.18: Heb *Abshai* [a] Syr: Heb *Three*

11.21 2 Sam 23.19
11.22 2 Sam 23.20
11.23 1 Sam 17.7
11.26 2 Sam 23.24
11.39 1 Chr 18.15
12.1 1 Sam 27.2-6
12.2 Judg 20.16
12.8 2 Sam 2.18
12.15 Josh 3.15
12.18 Judg 6.34; 2 Sam 17.25
12.19 1 Sam 29.2,4

them, and won a name beside the Three. 21He was the most renowned[b] of the Thirty,[c] and became their commander; but he did not attain to the Three.

22 Benaiah son of Jehoiada was a valiant man[d] of Kabzeel, a doer of great deeds; he struck down two sons of[e] Ariel of Moab. He also went down and killed a lion in a pit on a day when snow had fallen. 23And he killed an Egyptian, a man of great stature, five cubits tall. The Egyptian had in his hand a spear like a weaver's beam; but Benaiah went against him with a staff, snatched the spear out of the Egyptian's hand, and killed him with his own spear. 24Such were the things Benaiah son of Jehoiada did, and he won a name beside the three warriors. 25He was renowned among the Thirty, but he did not attain to the Three. And David put him in charge of his bodyguard.

26 The warriors of the armies were Asahel brother of Joab, Elhanan son of Dodo of Bethlehem, 27Shammoth of Harod,[f] Helez the Pelonite, 28Ira son of Ikkesh of Tekoa, Abiezer of Anathoth, 29Sibbecai the Hushathite, Ilai the Ahohite, 30Maharai of Netophah, Heled son of Baanah of Netophah, 31Ithai son of Ribai of Gibeah of the Benjaminites, Benaiah of Pirathon, 32Hurai of the wadis of Gaash, Abiel the Arbathite, 33Azmaveth of Baharum, Eliahba of Shaalbon, 34Hashem[g] the Gizonite, Jonathan son of Shagee the Hararite, 35Ahiam son of Sachar the Hararite, Eliphal son of Ur, 36Hepher the Mecherathite, Ahijah the Pelonite, 37Hezro of Carmel, Naarai son of Ezbai, 38Joel the brother of Nathan, Mibhar son of Hagri, 39Zelek the Ammonite, Naharai of Beeroth, the armor-bearer of Joab son of Zeruiah, 40Ira the Ithrite, Gareb the Ithrite, 41Uriah the Hittite, Zabad son of Ahlai, 42Adina son of Shiza the Reubenite, a leader of the Reubenites, and thirty with him, 43Hanan son of Maacah, and Joshaphat the Mithnite, 44Uzzia the Ashterathite, Shama and Jeiel sons of Hotham the Aroerite, 45Jediael son of Shimri, and his brother Joha the Tizite, 46Eliel the Mahavite, and Jeribai and Joshaviah sons of Elnaam, and Ithmah the Moabite, 47Eliel, and Obed, and Jaasiel the Mezobaite.

David's Followers in the Wilderness

12 The following are those who came to David at Ziklag, while he could not move about freely because of Saul son of Kish; they were among the mighty warriors who helped him in war. 2They were archers, and could shoot arrows and sling stones with either the right hand or the left; they were Benjaminites, Saul's kindred. 3The chief was Ahiezer, then Joash, both sons of Shemaah of Gibeah; also Jeziel and Pelet sons of Azmaveth; Beracah, Jehu of Anathoth, 4Ishmaiah of Gibeon, a warrior among the Thirty and a leader over the Thirty; Jeremiah,[h] Jahaziel, Johanan, Jozabad of Gederah, 5Eluzai,[i] Jerimoth, Bealiah, Shemariah, Shephatiah the Haruphite; 6Elkanah, Isshiah, Azarel, Joezer, and Jashobeam, the Korahites; 7and Joelah and Zebadiah, sons of Jeroham of Gedor.

8 From the Gadites there went over to David at the stronghold in the wilderness mighty and experienced warriors, expert with shield and spear, whose faces were like the faces of lions, and who were swift as gazelles on the mountains: 9Ezer the chief, Obadiah second, Eliab third, 10Mishmannah fourth, Jeremiah fifth, 11Attai sixth, Eliel seventh, 12Johanan eighth, Elzabad ninth, 13Jeremiah tenth, Machbannai eleventh. 14These Gadites were officers of the army, the least equal to a hundred and the greatest to a thousand. 15These are the men who crossed the Jordan in the first month, when it was overflowing all its banks, and put to flight all those in the valleys, to the east and to the west.

16 Some Benjaminites and Judahites came to the stronghold to David. 17David went out to meet them and said to them, "If you have come to me in friendship, to help me, then my heart will be knit to you; but if you have come to betray me to my adversaries, though my hands have done no wrong, then may the God of our ancestors see and give judgment." 18Then the spirit came upon Amasai, chief of the Thirty, and he said,

"We are yours, O David;
and with you, O son of Jesse!
Peace, peace to you,
and peace to the one who helps you!
For your God is the one who helps
you."

Then David received them, and made them officers of his troops.

19 Some of the Manassites deserted to

12.1-22 Steadily growing support was gained by David from those mentioned here while he was at *Ziklag,* the city given him by the Philistines (1 Sam 27.5-7), which he used as a base of operations *(stronghold in the wilderness)* against *Saul,* who was still on the throne.

[b] Compare 2 Sam 23.19: Heb *more renowned among the two* [c] Syr: Heb *Three* [d] Syr: Heb *the son of a valiant man* [e] See 2 Sam 23.20: Heb lacks *sons of* [f] Compare 2 Sam 23.25: Heb *the Harorite* [g] Compare Gk and 2 Sam 23.32: Heb *the sons of Hashem* [h] Heb verse 5 [i] Heb verse 6

12.23-40 The numbers and capabilities of the military support for David and details of the provision of food are given here in connection with his being anointed as king at *Hebron* (11.1-3). The numbers of the *divisions of the armed troops* are much higher than what would be expected in the historical situation of David.
13.1-14 The story of bringing *the ark of God* from *Kiriath-jearim* (where it had remained since it was recovered from the Philistines; 1 Sam 6.19-7.11) is told here prior to the account of the construction of David's royal house and the assistance of Hiram, king of Tyre (2 Sam 5.11-12; *cf.* 1 Chr 14.1-2). The aim is to show the priority David gave to the worship of God, although the temple had not yet been built as the resting place for the ark (13.14; *cf.* 2 Sam 6.6-10).

David when he came with the Philistines for the battle against Saul. (Yet he did not help them, for the rulers of the Philistines took counsel and sent him away, saying, "He will desert to his master Saul at the cost of our heads.") [20]As he went to Ziklag these Manassites deserted to him: Adnah, Jozabad, Jediael, Michael, Jozabad, Elihu, and Zillethai, chiefs of the thousands in Manasseh. [21]They helped David against the band of raiders,[j] for they were all warriors and commanders in the army. [22]Indeed from day to day people kept coming to David to help him, until there was a great army, like an army of God.

David's Army at Hebron

23 These are the numbers of the divisions of the armed troops who came to David in Hebron to turn the kingdom of Saul over to him, according to the word of the LORD. [24]The people of Judah bearing shield and spear numbered six thousand eight hundred armed troops. [25]Of the Simeonites, mighty warriors, seven thousand one hundred. [26]Of the Levites four thousand six hundred. [27]Jehoiada, leader of the house of Aaron, and with him three thousand seven hundred. [28]Zadok, a young warrior, and twenty-two commanders from his own ancestral house. [29]Of the Benjaminites, the kindred of Saul, three thousand, of whom the majority had continued to keep their allegiance to the house of Saul. [30]Of the Ephraimites, twenty thousand eight hundred, mighty warriors, notables in their ancestral houses. [31]Of the half-tribe of Manasseh, eighteen thousand, who were expressly named to come and make David king. [32]Of Issachar, those who had understanding of the times, to know what Israel ought to do, two hundred chiefs, and all their kindred under their command. [33]Of Zebulun, fifty thousand seasoned troops, equipped for battle with all the weapons of war, to help David[k] with singleness of purpose. [34]Of Naphtali, a thousand commanders, with whom there were thirty-seven thousand armed with shield and spear. [35]Of the Danites, twenty-eight thousand six hundred equipped for battle. [36]Of Asher, forty thousand seasoned troops ready for battle. [37]Of the Reubenites and Gadites and the half-tribe of Manasseh from beyond the Jordan, one hundred twenty thousand armed with all the weapons of war.

38 All these, warriors arrayed in battle order, came to Hebron with full intent to make David king over all Israel; likewise all the rest of Israel were of a single mind to make David king. [39]They were there with David for three days, eating and drinking, for their kindred had provided for them. [40]And also their neighbors, from as far away as Issachar and Zebulun and Naphtali, came bringing food on donkeys, camels, mules, and oxen—abundant provisions of meal, cakes of figs, clusters of raisins, wine, oil, oxen, and sheep, for there was joy in Israel.

The Ark Brought from Kiriath-jearim

13 David consulted with the commanders of the thousands and of the hundreds, with every leader. [2]David said to the whole assembly of Israel, "If it seems good to you, and if it is the will of the LORD our God, let us send abroad to our kindred who remain in all the land of Israel, including the priests and Levites in the cities that have pasture lands, that they may come together to us. [3]Then let us bring again the ark of our God to us; for we did not turn to it in the days of Saul." [4]The whole assembly agreed to do so, for the thing pleased all the people.

5 So David assembled all Israel from the Shihor of Egypt to Lebo-hamath, to bring the ark of God from Kiriath-jearim. [6]And David and all Israel went up to Baalah, that is, to Kiriath-jearim, which belongs to Judah, to bring up from there the ark of God, the LORD, who is enthroned on the cherubim, which is called by his[l] name. [7]They carried the ark of God on a new cart, from the house of Abinadab, and Uzzah and Ahio[m] were driving the cart. [8]David and all Israel were dancing before God with all their might, with song and lyres and harps and tambourines and cymbals and trumpets.

9 When they came to the threshing floor of Chidon, Uzzah put out his hand to hold the ark, for the oxen shook it. [10]The anger of the LORD was kindled against Uzzah; he struck him down because he put out his hand to the ark; and he died there before God. [11]David was angry because the LORD had burst out against Uzzah; so that place is called Perez-uzzah[n] to this day. [12]David

12.21 1 Sam 30.1,9,10
12.23 2 Sam 2.3,4; 1 Chr 11.1; 10.14; 1 Sam 16.1,3
12.28 2 Sam 8.17
12.29 2 Sam 2.8,9
12.32 Esth 1.13
12.33 Ps 12.2
12.38 2 Sam 5.1-3
12.40 1 Sam 25.18
13.2 1 Sam 31.1; Isa 37.4
13.3 1 Sam 7.1,2
13.5 2 Sam 6.1; 1 Chr 15.3; 1 Sam 6.21; 7.1
13.6 Josh 15.9; 2 Kings 19.15
13.7 1 Sam 7.1
13.8 2 Sam 6.5
13.9 2 Sam 6.6
13.10 1 Chr 15.13,15

[j] Or *as officers of his troops* [k] Gk: Heb lacks *David* [l] Heb lacks *his* [m] Or *and his brother* [n] That is *Bursting Out Against Uzzah*

was afraid of God that day; he said, "How
can I bring the ark of God into my care?"
[13]So David did not take the ark into his care
into the city of David; he took it instead to
the house of Obed-edom the Gittite. [14]The
ark of God remained with the household of
Obed-edom in his house three months, and
the LORD blessed the household of Obed-
edom and all that he had.

David Established at Jerusalem

14 King Hiram of Tyre sent messengers to David, along with cedar
logs, and masons and carpenters to build a
house for him. [2]David then perceived that
the LORD had established him as king over
Israel, and that his kingdom was highly
exalted for the sake of his people Israel.
3 David took more wives in Jerusalem,
and David became the father of more sons
and daughters. [4]These are the names of the
children whom he had in Jerusalem:
Shammua, Shobab, and Nathan; Solomon,
[5]Ibhar, Elishua, and Elpelet; [6]Nogah, Nepheg,
and Japhia; [7]Elishama, Beeliada, and
Eliphelet.

Defeat of the Philistines

8 When the Philistines heard that David
had been anointed king over all Israel, all
the Philistines went up in search of David;
and David heard of it and went out against
them. [9]Now the Philistines had come and
made a raid in the valley of Rephaim. [10]David
inquired of God, "Shall I go up against the
Philistines? Will you give them into my
hand?" The LORD said to him, "Go up, and
I will give them into your hand." [11]So he
went up to Baal-perazim, and David defeated them there. David said, "God has
burst out[o] against my enemies by my hand,
like a bursting flood." Therefore that place
is called Baal-perazim.[p] [12]They abandoned
their gods there, and at David's command
they were burned.
13 Once again the Philistines made a
raid in the valley. [14]When David again
inquired of God, God said to him, "You shall
not go up after them; go around and come
on them opposite the balsam trees. [15]When
you hear the sound of marching in the tops
of the balsam trees, then go out to battle;
for God has gone out before you to strike
down the army of the Philistines." [16]David
did as God had commanded him, and they
struck down the Philistine army from Gibeon
to Gezer. [17]The fame of David went out into
all lands, and the LORD brought the fear of
him on all nations.

The Ark Brought to Jerusalem

15 David[q] built houses for himself in
the city of David, and he prepared
a place for the ark of God and pitched a tent
for it. [2]Then David commanded that no one
but the Levites were to carry the ark of God,
for the LORD had chosen them to carry the
ark of the LORD and to minister to him
forever. [3]David assembled all Israel in Jerusalem to bring up the ark of the LORD to its
place, which he had prepared for it. [4]Then
David gathered together the descendants of
Aaron and the Levites: [5]of the sons of Kohath,
Uriel the chief, with one hundred twenty of
his kindred; [6]of the sons of Merari, Asaiah
the chief, with two hundred twenty of his
kindred; [7]of the sons of Gershom, Joel the
chief, with one hundred thirty of his kindred; [8]of the sons of Elizaphan, Shemaiah
the chief, with two hundred of his kindred;
[9]of the sons of Hebron, Eliel the chief, with
eighty of his kindred; [10]of the sons of Uzziel,
Amminadab the chief, with one hundred
twelve of his kindred.
11 David summoned the priests Zadok
and Abiathar, and the Levites Uriel, Asaiah,
Joel, Shemaiah, Eliel, and Amminadab. [12]He
said to them, "You are the heads of families
of the Levites; sanctify yourselves, you and
your kindred, so that you may bring up the
ark of the LORD, the God of Israel, to the
place that I have prepared for it. [13]Because
you did not carry it the first time,[r] the LORD
our God burst out against us, because we
did not give it proper care." [14]So the priests
and the Levites sanctified themselves to bring
up the ark of the LORD, the God of Israel.
[15]And the Levites carried the ark of God on
their shoulders with the poles, as Moses had
commanded according to the word of the
LORD.
16 David also commanded the chiefs of
the Levites to appoint their kindred as the
singers to play on musical instruments, on
harps and lyres and cymbals, to raise loud
sounds of joy. [17]So the Levites appointed
Heman son of Joel; and of his kindred Asaph
son of Berechiah; and of the sons of Merari,
their kindred, Ethan son of Kushaiah; [18]and

14.1-7 David takes up residence in Jerusalem and becomes *the father of more sons and daughters* (*cf.* 1 Sam 5.11-15).
14.8-17 *cf.* 1 Sam 5.17-25. A new feature is the report of an international reputation for David's military and royal prowess (14.17).
15.1-16.6 The account of bringing the ark into the central sanctuary seems based on 2 Sam 6.1-23, but it differs in two respects. (1) There are details of the roles and assignments of the various Levites who were to serve in the temple, although they are not mentioned in 2 Sam 6. This reflects the developments in Israel's worship following their return from the exile in Babylon. (2) David's dancing before the ark is noted here with no mention of his nudity, as in 2 Sam 6.14-23. Initially, *the ark of God* was placed *inside the tent,* with Levites appointed to carry out the worship, including the sacred music to be performed *before the ark of the covenant of God.*

[o] Heb *paraz* [p] That is *Lord of Bursting Out* [q] Heb *He* [r] Meaning of Heb uncertain

13.14 1 Chr 26.4,5
14.1 2 Sam 5.11
14.4 1 Chr 3.5
14.8 2 Sam 5.17
14.9 1 Chr 11.15
14.13 ver 9; 2 Sam 5.22
14.14 2 Sam 5.23
14.16 2 Sam 5.25
14.17 Josh 6.27; 2 Chr 26.8; Deut 2.25
15.1 1 Chr 16.1
15.2 Num 4.15; Deut 10.8; 31.9
15.3 1 Kings 8.1; 1 Chr 13.5
15.8 Ex 6.22
15.9 Ex 6.18
15.11 1 Chr 12.28; 1 Sam 22.20-23
15.12 Ex 19.14,15; 2 Chr 35.6
15.13 2 Sam 6.3; 1 Chr 13.7,10,11
15.14 ver 12
15.15 Ex 25.14; Num 4.5
15.16 1 Chr 25.1
15.17 1 Chr 6.33,39,44

16.7-36 Singing the praise to the LORD is the role assigned to *Asaph and his kindred* (*cf.* 15.17,19). Songs of praise are attributed to David in 2 Sam 1.17-27 and 22.1-23.7, but there is no attribution here. The song includes quotations or paraphrases based on Ps 105.1-15; 96.1-13; 106.47-48.

with them their kindred of the second order, Zechariah, Jaaziel, Shemiramoth, Jehiel, Unni, Eliab, Benaiah, Maaseiah, Mattithiah, Eliphelehu, and Mikneiah, and the gatekeepers Obed-edom and Jeiel. 19 The singers Heman, Asaph, and Ethan were to sound bronze cymbals; 20 Zechariah, Aziel, Shemiramoth, Jehiel, Unni, Eliab, Maaseiah, and Benaiah were to play harps according to Alamoth; 21 but Mattithiah, Eliphelehu, Mikneiah, Obed-edom, Jeiel, and Azaziah were to lead with lyres according to the Sheminith. 22 Chenaniah, leader of the Levites in music, was to direct the music, for he understood it. 23 Berechiah and Elkanah were to be gatekeepers for the ark. 24 Shebaniah, Joshaphat, Nethanel, Amasai, Zechariah, Benaiah, and Eliezer, the priests, were to blow the trumpets before the ark of God. Obed-edom and Jehiah also were to be gatekeepers for the ark.

25 So David and the elders of Israel, and the commanders of the thousands, went to bring up the ark of the covenant of the LORD from the house of Obed-edom with rejoicing. 26 And because God helped the Levites who were carrying the ark of the covenant of the LORD, they sacrificed seven bulls and seven rams. 27 David was clothed with a robe of fine linen, as also were all the Levites who were carrying the ark, and the singers, and Chenaniah the leader of the music of the singers; and David wore a linen ephod. 28 So all Israel brought up the ark of the covenant of the LORD with shouting, to the sound of the horn, trumpets, and cymbals, and made loud music on harps and lyres.

29 As the ark of the covenant of the LORD came to the city of David, Michal daughter of Saul looked out of the window, and saw King David leaping and dancing; and she despised him in her heart.

The Ark Placed in the Tent

16 They brought in the ark of God, and set it inside the tent that David had pitched for it; and they offered burnt offerings and offerings of well-being before God. 2 When David had finished offering the burnt offerings and the offerings of well-being, he blessed the people in the name of the LORD; 3 and he distributed to every person in Israel—man and woman alike—to each a loaf of bread, a portion of meat,[s] and a cake of raisins.

4 He appointed certain of the Levites as ministers before the ark of the LORD, to invoke, to thank, and to praise the LORD, the God of Israel. 5 Asaph was the chief, and second to him Zechariah, Jeiel, Shemiramoth, Jehiel, Mattithiah, Eliab, Benaiah, Obed-edom, and Jeiel, with harps and lyres; Asaph was to sound the cymbals, 6 and the priests Benaiah and Jahaziel were to blow trumpets regularly, before the ark of the covenant of God.

David's Psalm of Thanksgiving

7 Then on that day David first appointed the singing of praises to the LORD by Asaph and his kindred.

8 O give thanks to the LORD, call on his name,
make known his deeds among the peoples.
9 Sing to him, sing praises to him,
tell of all his wonderful works.
10 Glory in his holy name;
let the hearts of those who seek the LORD rejoice.
11 Seek the LORD and his strength,
seek his presence continually.
12 Remember the wonderful works he has done,
his miracles, and the judgments he uttered,
13 O offspring of his servant Israel,[t]
children of Jacob, his chosen ones.

14 He is the LORD our God;
his judgments are in all the earth.
15 Remember his covenant forever,
the word that he commanded, for a thousand generations,
16 the covenant that he made with Abraham,
his sworn promise to Isaac,
17 which he confirmed to Jacob as a statute,
to Israel as an everlasting covenant,
18 saying, "To you I will give the land of Canaan
as your portion for an inheritance."

19 When they were few in number,
of little account, and strangers in the land,[u]

[s] Compare Gk Syr Vg: Meaning of Heb uncertain
[u] Heb *in it*
[t] Another reading is *Abraham* (compare Ps 105.6)

15.24 ver 28; 1 Chr 16.6
15.25 2 Sam 6.12,15; 1 Chr 13.13
15.28 1 Chr 13.8
15.29 2 Sam 6.16
16.1 2 Sam 6.17-19
16.5 Ps 50,73
16.7 2 Sam 23.1
16.8 Ps 105.1-15
16.11 Ps 24.6
16.12 Ps 77.11; 78.43-68
16.14 Isa 26.9
16.16 Gen 17.2; 26.3; 28.13; 35.11
16.17 Gen 35.11,12
16.19 Gen 34.30

16.21 Gen 12.17; 20.3; Ex 7.15-18
16.23 Ps 96.1-13
16.25 Ps 48.1; 89.7
16.26 Ps 96.5
16.28 Ps 29.1,2
16.31 Isa 49.13; Ps 93.1
16.32 Ps 98.7
16.34 Ps 106.1
16.35 Ps 106.47,48
16.36 1 Kings 8.15; Deut 27.15
16.37 ver 4,5; 2 Chr 8.14
16.38 1 Chr 13.14; 26.10
16.39 1 Chr 15.11; 1 Kings 3.4
16.40 Ex 29.38; Num 28.3
16.41 1 Chr 6.33; 25.1-6; 2 Chr 5.13
17.1 2 Sam 7.1-29
17.4 1 Chr 28.2.3
17.5 2 Sam 7.6
17.6 2 Sam 7.7

20 wandering from nation to nation,
from one kingdom to another people,
21 he allowed no one to oppress them;
he rebuked kings on their account,
22 saying, "Do not touch my anointed ones;
do my prophets no harm."

23 Sing to the LORD, all the earth.
Tell of his salvation from day to day.
24 Declare his glory among the nations,
his marvelous works among all the peoples.
25 For great is the LORD, and greatly to be praised;
he is to be revered above all gods.
26 For all the gods of the peoples are idols,
but the LORD made the heavens.
27 Honor and majesty are before him;
strength and joy are in his place.

28 Ascribe to the LORD, O families of the peoples,
ascribe to the LORD glory and strength.
29 Ascribe to the LORD the glory due his name;
bring an offering, and come before him.
Worship the LORD in holy splendor;
30 tremble before him, all the earth.
The world is firmly established; it shall never be moved.
31 Let the heavens be glad, and let the earth rejoice,
and let them say among the nations, "The LORD is king!"
32 Let the sea roar, and all that fills it;
let the field exult, and everything in it.
33 Then shall the trees of the forest sing for joy
before the LORD, for he comes to judge the earth.
34 O give thanks to the LORD, for he is good;
for his steadfast love endures forever.

35 Say also:
"Save us, O God of our salvation,
and gather and rescue us from among the nations,
that we may give thanks to your holy name,
and glory in your praise.
36 Blessed be the LORD, the God of Israel,
from everlasting to everlasting."
Then all the people said "Amen!" and praised the LORD.

Regular Worship Maintained

37 David left Asaph and his kinsfolk there
before the ark of the covenant of the LORD
to minister regularly before the ark as each
day required, 38 and also Obed-edom and
his[v] sixty-eight kinsfolk; while Obed-edom
son of Jeduthun and Hosah were to be
gatekeepers. 39 And he left the priest Zadok
and his kindred the priests before the tabernacle of the LORD in the high place that
was at Gibeon, 40 to offer burnt offerings to
the LORD on the altar of burnt offering regularly, morning and evening, according to all
that is written in the law of the LORD that
he commanded Israel. 41 With them were
Heman and Jeduthun, and the rest of those
chosen and expressly named to render thanks
to the LORD, for his steadfast love endures
forever. 42 Heman and Jeduthun had with
them trumpets and cymbals for the music,
and instruments for sacred song. The sons
of Jeduthun were appointed to the gate.
43 Then all the people departed to their
homes, and David went home to bless his
household.

God's Covenant with David

17 Now when David settled in his
house, David said to the prophet
Nathan, "I am living in a house of cedar,
but the ark of the covenant of the LORD is
under a tent." 2 Nathan said to David, "Do
all that you have in mind, for God is with
you."
3 But that same night the word of the
LORD came to Nathan, saying: 4 Go and tell
my servant David: Thus says the LORD: You
shall not build me a house to live in. 5 For
I have not lived in a house since the day
I brought out Israel to this very day, but I
have lived in a tent and a tabernacle.[w]
6 Wherever I have moved about among all
Israel, did I ever speak a word with any of
the judges of Israel, whom I commanded to
shepherd my people, saying, Why have you
not built me a house of cedar? 7 Now therefore thus you shall say to my servant David:
Thus says the LORD of hosts: I took you from
the pasture, from following the sheep, to be
ruler over my people Israel; 8 and I have
been with you wherever you went, and
have cut off all your enemies before you;
and I will make for you a name, like the
name of the great ones of the earth. 9 I will
appoint a place for my people Israel, and

16.37-43 Here are resumed the assignments of responsibilities to the sanctuary officials, but instead of the Levites it is *Zadok and his kindred* the priests who are mentioned, as in 2 Sam 15.24-37 and 1 Kings 1.8-48. This detail may be drawn from a pre-exilic source, but Ezek 40.46; 43.19; 48.11 and the Dead Sea Scrolls see as legitimate only these priests from the line of Zadok.

17.1-15 Building God's House and the Covenant with David. David's proposal to build a *house* for the LORD to replace the *tent* where the ark of the covenant rested, and the LORD's promise to *build a house* for David, whose son will build *a house for me [the LORD]*, reproduce 2 Sam 7.1-17. Here is evident the same play on words: *house* means both temple and dynasty. In both passages, *the prophet Nathan* is God's messenger to David.

[v] Gk Syr Vg: Heb *their* [w] Gk 2 Sam 7.6: Heb *but I have been from tent to tent and from tabernacle*

17.16-27 David's response to the LORD follows closely 2 Sam 7.18-29, with the expectation that the Davidic *house* will continue forever.
18.1-12 The list of David's victories and his alliances with neighboring nations follows closely 2 Sam 8.1-14.

will plant them, so that they may live in their own place, and be disturbed no more; and evildoers shall wear them down no more, as they did formerly, [10]from the time that I appointed judges over my people Israel; and I will subdue all your enemies.

Moreover I declare to you that the LORD will build you a house. [11]When your days are fulfilled to go to be with your ancestors, I will raise up your offspring after you, one of your own sons, and I will establish his kingdom. [12]He shall build a house for me, and I will establish his throne forever. [13]I will be a father to him, and he shall be a son to me. I will not take my steadfast love from him, as I took it from him who was before you, [14]but I will confirm him in my house and in my kingdom forever, and his throne shall be established forever. [15]In accordance with all these words and all this vision, Nathan spoke to David.

David's Prayer

16 Then King David went in and sat before the LORD, and said, "Who am I, O LORD God, and what is my house, that you have brought me thus far? [17]And even this was a small thing in your sight, O God; you have also spoken of your servant's house for a great while to come. You regard me as someone of high rank,[x] O LORD God! [18]And what more can David say to you for honoring your servant? You know your servant. [19]For your servant's sake, O LORD, and according to your own heart, you have done all these great deeds, making known all these great things. [20]There is no one like you, O LORD, and there is no God besides you, according to all that we have heard with our ears. [21]Who is like your people Israel, one nation on the earth whom God went to redeem to be his people, making for yourself a name for great and terrible things, in driving out nations before your people whom you redeemed from Egypt? [22]And you made your people Israel to be your people forever; and you, O LORD, became their God.

23 "And now, O LORD, as for the word that you have spoken concerning your servant and concerning his house, let it be established forever, and do as you have promised. [24]Thus your name will be established and magnified forever in the saying, 'The LORD of hosts, the God of Israel, is Israel's God'; and the house of your servant David will be established in your presence. [25]For you, my God, have revealed to your servant that you will build a house for him; therefore your servant has found it possible to pray before you. [26]And now, O LORD, you are God, and you have promised this good thing to your servant; [27]therefore may it please you to bless the house of your servant, that it may continue forever before you. For you, O LORD, have blessed and are blessed[y] forever."

David's Kingdom Established and Extended

18 Some time afterward, David attacked the Philistines and subdued them; he took Gath and its villages from the Philistines.

2 He defeated Moab, and the Moabites became subject to David and brought tribute.

3 David also struck down King Hadadezer of Zobah, toward Hamath,[x] as he went to set up a monument at the river Euphrates. [4]David took from him one thousand chariots, seven thousand cavalry, and twenty thousand foot soldiers. David hamstrung all the chariot horses, but left one hundred of them. [5]When the Arameans of Damascus came to help King Hadadezer of Zobah, David killed twenty-two thousand Arameans. [6]Then David put garrisons[z] in Aram of Damascus; and the Arameans became subject to David, and brought tribute. The LORD gave victory to David wherever he went. [7]David took the gold shields that were carried by the servants of Hadadezer, and brought them to Jerusalem. [8]From Tibhath and from Cun, cities of Hadadezer, David took a vast quantity of bronze; with it Solomon made the bronze sea and the pillars and the vessels of bronze.

9 When King Tou of Hamath heard that David had defeated the whole army of King Hadadezer of Zobah, [10]he sent his son Hadoram to King David, to greet him and to congratulate him, because he had fought against Hadadezer and defeated him. Now Hadadezer had often been at war with Tou. He sent all sorts of articles of gold, of silver, and of bronze; [11]these also King David dedicated to the LORD, together with the silver and gold that he had carried off from all the nations, from Edom, Moab, the Ammonites, the Philistines, and Amalek.

12 Abishai son of Zeruiah killed eighteen

17.10 Judg 2.16
17.13 2 Sam 7.14,15; Heb 1.5
17.14 Lk 1.33
17.16 2 Sam 7.18
17.19 Isa 37.35
17.22 Ex 19.5,6
17.24 Ps 46.7,11
18.1 2 Sam 8.1-18
18.5 1 Chr 19.6
18.8 1 Kings 7.15,23; 2 Chr 4.12,15,16
18.10 2 Sam 10.16
18.12 2 Sam 8.13

[x] Meaning of Heb uncertain [y] Or *and it is blessed* [z] Gk Vg 2 Sam 8.6 Compare Syr: Heb lacks *garrisons*

18.15 1 Chr 11.6
18.17 2 Sam 8.18
19.1 2 Sam 10.1
19.3 2 Sam 10.3
19.4 2 Sam 10.4
19.6 1 Chr 18.5,9
19.7 Num 21.30; Josh 13.9,16
19.8 2 Sam 10.7
19.11 2 Sam 10.10
19.12 2 Sam 10.11
19.14 2 Sam 10.13
19.16 2 Sam 10.15
19.17 2 Sam 10.17
19.18 2 Sam 10.18
19.19 2 Sam 10.19
20.1 2 Sam 11.1; 12.26
20.2 2 Sam 12.30,31

thousand Edomites in the Valley of Salt. [13]He put garrisons in Edom; and all the Edomites became subject to David. And the LORD gave victory to David wherever he went.

David's Administration

14 So David reigned over all Israel; and he administered justice and equity to all his people. [15]Joab son of Zeruiah was over the army; Jehoshaphat son of Ahilud was recorder; [16]Zadok son of Ahitub and Ahimelech son of Abiathar were priests; Shavsha was secretary; [17]Benaiah son of Jehoiada was over the Cherethites and the Pelethites; and David's sons were the chief officials in the service of the king.

Defeat of the Ammonites and Arameans

19 Some time afterward, King Nahash of the Ammonites died, and his son succeeded him. [2]David said, "I will deal loyally with Hanun son of Nahash, for his father dealt loyally with me." So David sent messengers to console him concerning his father. When David's servants came to Hanun in the land of the Ammonites, to console him, [3]the officials of the Ammonites said to Hanun, "Do you think, because David has sent consolers to you, that he is honoring your father? Have not his servants come to you to search and to overthrow and to spy out the land?" [4]So Hanun seized David's servants, shaved them, cut off their garments in the middle at their hips, and sent them away; [5]and they departed. When David was told about the men, he sent messengers to them, for they felt greatly humiliated. The king said, "Remain at Jericho until your beards have grown, and then return."

6 When the Ammonites saw that they had made themselves odious to David, Hanun and the Ammonites sent a thousand talents of silver to hire chariots and cavalry from Mesopotamia, from Aram-maacah and from Zobah. [7]They hired thirty-two thousand chariots and the king of Maacah with his army, who came and camped before Medeba. And the Ammonites were mustered from their cities and came to battle. [8]When David heard of it, he sent Joab and all the army of the warriors. [9]The Ammonites came out and drew up in battle array at the entrance of the city, and the kings who had come were by themselves in the open country.

10 When Joab saw that the line of battle was set against him both in front and in the rear, he chose some of the picked men of Israel and arrayed them against the Arameans; [11]the rest of his troops he put in the charge of his brother Abishai, and they were arrayed against the Ammonites. [12]He said, "If the Arameans are too strong for me, then you shall help me; but if the Ammonites are too strong for you, then I will help you. [13]Be strong, and let us be courageous for our people and for the cities of our God; and may the LORD do what seems good to him." [14]So Joab and the troops who were with him advanced toward the Arameans for battle; and they fled before him. [15]When the Ammonites saw that the Arameans fled, they likewise fled before Abishai, Joab's brother, and entered the city. Then Joab came to Jerusalem.

16 But when the Arameans saw that they had been defeated by Israel, they sent messengers and brought out the Arameans who were beyond the Euphrates, with Shophach the commander of the army of Hadadezer at their head. [17]When David was informed, he gathered all Israel together, crossed the Jordan, came to them, and drew up his forces against them. When David set the battle in array against the Arameans, they fought with him. [18]The Arameans fled before Israel; and David killed seven thousand Aramean charioteers and forty thousand foot soldiers, and also killed Shophach the commander of their army. [19]When the servants of Hadadezer saw that they had been defeated by Israel, they made peace with David, and became subject to him. So the Arameans were not willing to help the Ammonites any more.

Siege and Capture of Rabbah

20 In the spring of the year, the time when kings go out to battle, Joab led out the army, ravaged the country of the Ammonites, and came and besieged Rabbah. But David remained at Jerusalem. Joab attacked Rabbah, and overthrew it. [2]David took the crown of Milcom[a] from his head; he found that it weighed a talent of gold, and in it was a precious stone; and it was placed on David's head. He also brought out the booty of the city, a very great

[a] Gk Vg See 1 Kings 11.5, 33: MT *of their king*

18.14-17 The report of David's administrative, military and priestly assignments echoes 2 Sam 8.15-18.
19.1-19 Omitting the material in 2 Sam 9, with its account of David's kindness to the survivors of the family of Saul, this narrative follows 2 Sam 10 in its description of David's defeat of two of Israel's neighbors from east of the Jordan: *the Ammonites* and *the Arameans*, both of which groups were supported by other Semitic peoples from Syria and *Mesopotamia*.
20.1-3 After beginning his account of David's military exploits with material borrowed from 2 Sam 11.1-2, the Chronicler omits the stories in 2 Samuel 11-12 which portray vividly the fallibility of David and Nathan's condemnation of him. The narrative resumes with material from 2 Sam 12.26 concerning the capture of *Rabbah*, chief city of the Ammonites (modern Amman in Jordan).

20.4-8 Passing over the colorful stories of David's conflicts, schemes, and mixture of gracious and despicable actions (2 Sam 13-20), the Chronicler continues his account of David's triumph over the Philistines, based on 2 Sam 21.18-22.
21.1-17 Although this section is based on 2 Sam 24, blame for David's prideful action in conducting a census (the number of God's people was considered to be a divine secret) is placed on *Satan*, rather than on *the anger of the LORD*, as in 2 Sam 24.1. The belief that evil in the world was caused by a being who worked in opposition to God (Satan means "adversary") entered the thinking of Israel during the exile in Babylon, when the Persians dominated the Middle East militarily and culturally. In Persian religion, there were two major deities: the beneficent power of Light, and the evil power of Darkness. The result of David's subjection to Satan was that divine punishment was to fall on Israel.
21.18-22.1 David, faced with a choice as to the form of God's judgment on Israel, accepts responsibility for this sinful act and, when *the LORD sent a pestilence on Israel*, intercedes in behalf of Jerusalem and God's people. To appease the divine wrath, David purchases a *threshing floor*, and on it erects an altar where offerings are presented. Divine approval and reconciliation are evident in the descent of *fire from heaven* upon the offerings on the altar. The Chronicler adds to his sources that it is this location which will replace the altar and tent at *Gibeon* as the only proper place for the worship of the LORD. According to 1 Kings 3.3-15, however, Solomon went to Gibeon to present an offering to God and was granted a vision and promises from the LORD.

amount. 3He brought out the people who were in it, and set them to work[b] with saws and iron picks and axes.[c] Thus David did to all the cities of the Ammonites. Then David and all the people returned to Jerusalem.

Exploits against the Philistines

4 After this, war broke out with the Philistines at Gezer; then Sibbecai the Hushathite killed Sippai, who was one of the descendants of the giants; and the Philistines were subdued. 5Again there was war with the Philistines; and Elhanan son of Jair killed Lahmi the brother of Goliath the Gittite, the shaft of whose spear was like a weaver's beam. 6Again there was war at Gath, where there was a man of great size, who had six fingers on each hand, and six toes on each foot, twenty-four in number; he also was descended from the giants. 7When he taunted Israel, Jonathan son of Shimea, David's brother, killed him. 8These were descended from the giants in Gath; they fell by the hand of David and his servants.

The Census and Plague

21 Satan stood up against Israel, and incited David to count the people of Israel. 2So David said to Joab and the commanders of the army, "Go, number Israel, from Beer-sheba to Dan, and bring me a report, so that I may know their number." 3But Joab said, "May the LORD increase the number of his people a hundredfold! Are they not, my lord the king, all of them my lord's servants? Why then should my lord require this? Why should he bring guilt on Israel?" 4But the king's word prevailed against Joab. So Joab departed and went throughout all Israel, and came back to Jerusalem. 5Joab gave the total count of the people to David. In all Israel there were one million one hundred thousand men who drew the sword, and in Judah four hundred seventy thousand who drew the sword. 6But he did not include Levi and Benjamin in the numbering, for the king's command was abhorrent to Joab.

7 But God was displeased with this thing, and he struck Israel. 8David said to God, "I have sinned greatly in that I have done this thing. But now, I pray you, take away the guilt of your servant; for I have done very foolishly." 9The LORD spoke to Gad, David's seer, saying, 10"Go and say to David, 'Thus says the LORD: Three things I offer you; choose one of them, so that I may do it to you.' " 11So Gad came to David and said to him, "Thus says the LORD, 'Take your choice: 12either three years of famine; or three months of devastation by your foes, while the sword of your enemies overtakes you; or three days of the sword of the LORD, pestilence on the land, and the angel of the LORD destroying throughout all the territory of Israel.' Now decide what answer I shall return to the one who sent me." 13Then David said to Gad, "I am in great distress; let me fall into the hand of the LORD, for his mercy is very great; but let me not fall into human hands."

14 So the LORD sent a pestilence on Israel; and seventy thousand persons fell in Israel. 15And God sent an angel to Jerusalem to destroy it; but when he was about to destroy it, the LORD took note and relented concerning the calamity; he said to the destroying angel, "Enough! Stay your hand." The angel of the LORD was then standing by the threshing floor of Ornan the Jebusite. 16David looked up and saw the angel of the LORD standing between earth and heaven, and in his hand a drawn sword stretched out over Jerusalem. Then David and the elders, clothed in sackcloth, fell on their faces. 17And David said to God, "Was it not I who gave the command to count the people? It is I who have sinned and done very wickedly. But these sheep, what have they done? Let your hand, I pray, O LORD my God, be against me and against my father's house; but do not let your people be plagued!"

David's Altar and Sacrifice

18 Then the angel of the LORD commanded Gad to tell David that he should go up and erect an altar to the LORD on the threshing floor of Ornan the Jebusite. 19So David went up following Gad's instructions, which he had spoken in the name of the LORD. 20Ornan turned and saw the angel; and while his four sons who were with him hid themselves, Ornan continued to thresh wheat. 21As David came to Ornan, Ornan looked and saw David; he went out from the threshing floor, and did obeisance to David with his face to the ground. 22David said to

20.3 2 Sam 12.31
20.4 2 Sam 21.18
20.5 2 Sam 21.19; 1 Sam 17.7
20.6 2 Sam 21.20
21.1 2 Sam 24.1-25
21.2 1 Chr 27.23
21.3 Deut 1.11
21.5 *cf.* 2 Sam 24.9
21.6 1 Chr 27.24
21.8 2 Sam 24.10; 12.13
21.10 1 Chr 29.29; 1 Sam 9.9
21.12 2 Sam 24.13
21.13 Ps 51.1; 130.4,7
21.14 1 Chr 27.24
21.15 2 Sam 24.16
21.16 2 Chr 3.1
21.17 2 Sam 7.8; Ps 74.1
21.18 2 Chr 3.1
21.21 2 Chr 3.1

[b] Compare 2 Sam 12.31: Heb *and he sawed* [c] Compare 2 Sam 12.31: Heb *saws*

Ornan, "Give me the site of the threshing
floor that I may build on it an altar to the
LORD—give it to me at its full price—so that
the plague may be averted from the people."
[23]Then Ornan said to David, "Take it; and
let my lord the king do what seems good
to him; see, I present the oxen for burnt
offerings, and the threshing sledges for the
wood, and the wheat for a grain offering.
I give it all." [24]But King David said to
Ornan, "No; I will buy them for the full
price. I will not take for the LORD what is
yours, nor offer burnt offerings that cost me
nothing." [25]So David paid Ornan six hundred shekels of gold by weight for the site.
[26]David built there an altar to the LORD and
presented burnt offerings and offerings of
well-being. He called upon the LORD, and he
answered him with fire from heaven on the
altar of burnt offering. [27]Then the LORD
commanded the angel, and he put his sword
back into its sheath.

The Place Chosen for the Temple

28 At that time, when David saw that
the LORD had answered him at the threshing
floor of Ornan the Jebusite, he made his
sacrifices there. [29]For the tabernacle of the
LORD, which Moses had made in the wilderness, and the altar of burnt offering were at
that time in the high place at Gibeon; [30]but
David could not go before it to inquire of
God, for he was afraid of the sword of the
angel of the LORD.

22 [1]Then David said, "Here shall be
the house of the LORD God and
here the altar of burnt offering for Israel."

David Prepares to Build the Temple

2 David gave orders to gather together
the aliens who were residing in the land of
Israel, and he set stonecutters to prepare
dressed stones for building the house of God.
[3]David also provided great stores of iron for
nails for the doors of the gates and for
clamps, as well as bronze in quantities beyond
weighing, [4]and cedar logs without number—
for the Sidonians and Tyrians brought great
quantities of cedar to David. [5]For David said,
"My son Solomon is young and inexperienced, and the house that is to be built for
the LORD must be exceedingly magnificent,
famous and glorified throughout all lands;
I will therefore make preparation for it." So
David provided materials in great quantity
before his death.

David's Charge to Solomon and the Leaders

6 Then he called for his son Solomon
and charged him to build a house for the
LORD, the God of Israel. [7]David said to Solomon, "My son, I had planned to build a
house to the name of the LORD my God. [8]But
the word of the LORD came to me, saying,
'You have shed much blood and have waged
great wars; you shall not build a house to
my name, because you have shed so much
blood in my sight on the earth. [9]See, a son
shall be born to you; he shall be a man of
peace. I will give him peace from all his
enemies on every side; for his name shall be
Solomon,[d] and I will give peace[e] and quiet
to Israel in his days. [10]He shall build a
house for my name. He shall be a son to
me, and I will be a father to him, and I will
establish his royal throne in Israel forever.'
[11]Now, my son, the LORD be with you, so
that you may succeed in building the house
of the LORD your God, as he has spoken
concerning you. [12]Only, may the LORD grant
you discretion and understanding, so that
when he gives you charge over Israel you
may keep the law of the LORD your God.
[13]Then you will prosper if you are careful
to observe the statutes and the ordinances
that the LORD commanded Moses for Israel.
Be strong and of good courage. Do not be
afraid or dismayed. [14]With great pains I
have provided for the house of the LORD one
hundred thousand talents of gold, one million talents of silver, and bronze and iron
beyond weighing, for there is so much of it;
timber and stone too I have provided. To
these you must add more. [15]You have an
abundance of workers: stonecutters, masons, carpenters, and all kinds of artisans
without number, skilled in working [16]gold,
silver, bronze, and iron. Now begin the
work, and the LORD be with you."
17 David also commanded all the leaders
of Israel to help his son Solomon, saying,
[18]"Is not the LORD your God with you? Has
he not given you peace on every side? For
he has delivered the inhabitants of the land
into my hand; and the land is subdued
before the LORD and his people. [19]Now set
your mind and heart to seek the LORD your
God. Go and build the sanctuary of the LORD
God so that the ark of the covenant of the

[d] Heb *Shelomoh* [e] Heb *shalom*

21.25 2 Sam 24.24
21.26 Lev 9.24; Judg 6.21
21.29 1 Chr 16.39; 1 Kings 3.4
22.1 1 Chr 21.18-19; 2 Chr 3.1
22.2 1 Kings 9.21; 5.17,18
22.3 1 Chr 29.2,7; ver 14
22.4 1 Kings 5.6
22.5 1 Chr 29.1
22.7 2 Sam 7.2; 1 Chr 17.1; Deut 12.5,11
22.8 1 Kings 5.3; 1 Chr 28.3
22.9 1 Kings 4.20,25; 2 Sam 12.24,25
22.10 2 Sam 7.13; 1 Chr 17.12,13
22.11 ver 16
22.12 1 Kings 3.9-12; 2 Chr 1.10
22.13 1 Chr 28.7; Josh 1.6-9; 1 Chr 28.20
22.14 ver 3
22.16 ver 11
22.17 1 Chr 28.1-6
22.18 2 Sam 7.1; 1 Chr 23.25
22.19 1 Chr 28.9; 1 Kings 8.6; 2 Chr 5.7; ver 7

22.2-5 David's preparation of materials for the later building of the temple by Solomon are aided by contributions from the *Sidonians* and *Tyrians.* In 1 Kings 5, the assistance of *King Hiram of Tyre* is described in detail. The indication that the work was assigned to *the aliens who were residing in the land of Israel* contrasts with the report in 1 Kings 5.13 that Solomon's labor levy consisted of workers from *out of all Israel.*
22.6-19 David Assigns Responsibility for the Temple to Solomon. In 2 Sam 7.13, David is informed that his son will build a house for God, but the emphasis here falls on the establishment and continuity of the Davidic dynasty to rule God's people. The Chronicler asserts the importance of Solomon's observance of *the statutes and the ordinances* that the LORD commanded Moses for Israel, and on details concerning materials and construction workers for erecting the temple. The amount of *gold* and *silver* that David claims to have provided is enormous – the equivalent of many millions of dollars.

Lord and the holy vessels of God may be
brought into a house built for the name of
the Lord."

Families of the Levites and Their Functions

23 When David was old and full of
days, he made his son Solomon
king over Israel.
2 David assembled all the leaders of Israel and the priests and the Levites. 3 The
Levites, thirty years old and upward, were
counted, and the total was thirty-eight
thousand. 4 "Twenty-four thousand of these,"
David said, "shall have charge of the work
in the house of the Lord, six thousand shall
be officers and judges, 5 four thousand gatekeepers, and four thousand shall offer praises
to the Lord with the instruments that I have
made for praise." 6 And David organized them
in divisions corresponding to the sons of
Levi: Gershon,[f] Kohath, and Merari.
7 The sons of Gershon[g] were Ladan and
Shimei. 8 The sons of Ladan: Jehiel the chief,
Zetham, and Joel, three. 9 The sons of Shimei:
Shelomoth, Haziel, and Haran, three. These
were the heads of families of Ladan. 10 And
the sons of Shimei: Jahath, Zina, Jeush, and
Beriah. These four were the sons of Shimei.
11 Jahath was the chief, and Zizah the second; but Jeush and Beriah did not have
many sons, so they were enrolled as a
single family.
12 The sons of Kohath: Amram, Izhar,
Hebron, and Uzziel, four. 13 The sons of
Amram: Aaron and Moses. Aaron was set
apart to consecrate the most holy things, so
that he and his sons forever should make
offerings before the Lord, and minister to
him and pronounce blessings in his name
forever; 14 but as for Moses the man of God,
his sons were to be reckoned among the
tribe of Levi. 15 The sons of Moses: Gershom
and Eliezer. 16 The sons of Gershom: Shebuel
the chief. 17 The sons of Eliezer: Rehabiah
the chief; Eliezer had no other sons, but the
sons of Rehabiah were very numerous. 18 The
sons of Izhar: Shelomith the chief. 19 The
sons of Hebron: Jeriah the chief, Amariah
the second, Jahaziel the third, and Jekameam
the fourth. 20 The sons of Uzziel: Micah the
chief and Isshiah the second.
21 The sons of Merari: Mahli and Mushi.
The sons of Mahli: Eleazar and Kish. 22 Eleazar
died having no sons, but only daughters;
their kindred, the sons of Kish, married
them. 23 The sons of Mushi: Mahli, Eder, and
Jeremoth, three.
24 These were the sons of Levi by their
ancestral houses, the heads of families as
they were enrolled according to the number
of the names of the individuals from twenty
years old and upward who were to do the
work for the service of the house of the
Lord. 25 For David said, "The Lord, the God
of Israel, has given rest to his people; and
he resides in Jerusalem forever. 26 And so the
Levites no longer need to carry the tabernacle or any of the things for its service"—
27 for according to the last words of David
these were the number of the Levites from
twenty years old and upward— 28 "but their
duty shall be to assist the descendants of
Aaron for the service of the house of the
Lord, having the care of the courts and the
chambers, the cleansing of all that is holy,
and any work for the service of the house
of God; 29 to assist also with the rows of
bread, the choice flour for the grain offering,
the wafers of unleavened bread, the baked
offering, the offering mixed with oil, and all
measures of quantity or size. 30 And they
shall stand every morning, thanking and
praising the Lord, and likewise at evening,
31 and whenever burnt offerings are offered
to the Lord on sabbaths, new moons, and
appointed festivals, according to the number
required of them, regularly before the Lord.
32 Thus they shall keep charge of the tent of
meeting and the sanctuary, and shall attend the descendants of Aaron, their kindred, for the service of the house of the
Lord."

Divisions of the Priests

24 The divisions of the descendants of
Aaron were these. The sons of
Aaron: Nadab, Abihu, Eleazar, and Ithamar.
2 But Nadab and Abihu died before their
father, and had no sons; so Eleazar and
Ithamar became the priests. 3 Along with
Zadok of the sons of Eleazar, and Ahimelech
of the sons of Ithamar, David organized
them according to the appointed duties in
their service. 4 Since more chief men were
found among the sons of Eleazar than among
the sons of Ithamar, they organized them
under sixteen heads of ancestral houses of
the sons of Eleazar, and eight of the sons of
Ithamar. 5 They organized them by lot, all
alike, for there were officers of the sanct-

[f] Or *Gershom*; See 1 Chr 6.1, note, and 23.15 [g] Vg Compare Gk Syr: Heb *to the Gershonite*

23.1-32 The responsibilities to be carried out for the assistance of the priests in the temple are divided among the descendants of *the sons of Levi*: Gershon, Kohath, and Merari. On the basis of modern estimates of the population of ancient Israel, the huge numbers of these attendants must be seen as based on extended multiples of 12, representing stylized projections rather than an actual count. The Levites are *to assist the descendants of Aaron*, who in the post-exilic period were regarded as the authentic priests. Here the Levites serve in secondary roles, including culinary and janitorial chores, which are sketched in some detail (23.28-32).
24.1-19 The organization of the priests was *by lot*, and was recorded by a *scribe* (the official record-keeper). Mentioned as witness is *Zadok the priest*, which is in keeping with the special honor given to the Zadokite line of priests by the Chronicler (1 Chr 15.11; 16.39; 29.22).

23.1 1 Kings 1.33-39; 1 Chr 29.28; 28.5
23.3 Num 4.3-49; ver 24
23.4 2 Chr 19.8
23.5 1 Chr 15.16
23.6 2 Chr 8.14; 29.25
23.12 Ex 6.18
23.13 Ex 6.20; 28.1; 30.6-10; Deut 21.5
23.16 1 Chr 26.24ff
23.21 1 Chr 24.26ff
23.24 Num 10.17,21; ver 3
23.25 1 Chr 22.18
23.26 Num 4.5
23.29 Lev 23.5-9; Ex 25.30; Lev 6.20; 2.4-7; 19.35
23.31 Isa 1.13,14; Lev 23.2-4
23.32 Num 1.53; 1 Chr 9.27; Num 3.6
24.1 Ex 6.23
24.2 Lev 10.2; Num 3.4
24.5 ver 31

24.10 Neh 12.4,17; Lk 1.5
24.19 1 Chr 9.25
24.21 1 Chr 23.17
24.23 1 Chr 23.19
24.26 1 Chr 23.21
24.31 ver 5,6
25.1 1 Chr 6.33,39; 15.16
25.3 1 Chr 16.41,42
25.4 1 Chr 6.33; ver 25
25.6 1 Chr 15.16,19
25.8 1 Chr 26.13
25.9 1 Chr 6.39
25.16 ver 4

uary and officers of God among both the sons
of Eleazar and the sons of Ithamar. [6]The
scribe Shemaiah son of Nethanel, a Levite,
recorded them in the presence of the king,
and the officers, and Zadok the priest, and
Ahimelech son of Abiathar, and the heads
of ancestral houses of the priests and of the
Levites; one ancestral house being chosen
for Eleazar and one chosen for Ithamar.
7 The first lot fell to Jehoiarib, the second
to Jedaiah, [8]the third to Harim, the fourth
to Seorim, [9]the fifth to Malchijah, the sixth
to Mijamin, [10]the seventh to Hakkoz, the
eighth to Abijah, [11]the ninth to Jeshua, the
tenth to Shecaniah, [12]the eleventh to Eliashib,
the twelfth to Jakim, [13]the thirteenth to
Huppah, the fourteenth to Jeshebeab, [14]the
fifteenth to Bilgah, the sixteenth to Immer,
[15]the seventeenth to Hezir, the eighteenth to
Happizzez, [16]the nineteenth to Pethahiah,
the twentieth to Jehezkel, [17]the twenty-first
to Jachin, the twenty-second to Gamul, [18]the
twenty-third to Delaiah, the twenty-fourth
to Maaziah. [19]These had as their appointed
duty in their service to enter the house of
the LORD according to the procedure established for them by their ancestor Aaron, as
the LORD God of Israel had commanded him.

Other Levites

20 And of the rest of the sons of Levi: of
the sons of Amram, Shubael; of the sons of
Shubael, Jehdeiah. [21]Of Rehabiah: of the
sons of Rehabiah, Isshiah the chief. [22]Of the
Izharites, Shelomoth; of the sons of
Shelomoth, Jahath. [23]The sons of Hebron:[h]
Jeriah the chief,[i] Amariah the second, Jahaziel
the third, Jekameam the fourth. [24]The sons
of Uzziel, Micah; of the sons of Micah, Shamir.
[25]The brother of Micah, Isshiah; of the sons
of Isshiah, Zechariah. [26]The sons of Merari:
Mahli and Mushi. The sons of Jaaziah: Beno.[j]
[27]The sons of Merari: of Jaaziah, Beno,[j]
Shoham, Zaccur, and Ibri. [28]Of Mahli: Eleazar,
who had no sons. [29]Of Kish, the sons of
Kish: Jerahmeel. [30]The sons of Mushi: Mahli,
Eder, and Jerimoth. These were the sons of
the Levites according to their ancestral
houses. [31]These also cast lots corresponding
to their kindred, the descendants of Aaron,
in the presence of King David, Zadok,
Ahimelech, and the heads of ancestral houses
of the priests and of the Levites, the chief
as well as the youngest brother.

The Temple Musicians

25 David and the officers of the army
also set apart for the service the
sons of Asaph, and of Heman, and of
Jeduthun, who should prophesy with lyres,
harps, and cymbals. The list of those who
did the work and of their duties was: [2]Of the
sons of Asaph: Zaccur, Joseph, Nethaniah,
and Asarelah, sons of Asaph, under the
direction of Asaph, who prophesied under
the direction of the king. [3]Of Jeduthun, the
sons of Jeduthun: Gedaliah, Zeri, Jeshaiah,
Shimei,[k] Hashabiah, and Mattithiah, six,
under the direction of their father Jeduthun,
who prophesied with the lyre in thanksgiving and praise to the LORD. [4]Of Heman, the
sons of Heman: Bukkiah, Mattaniah, Uzziel,
Shebuel, and Jerimoth, Hananiah, Hanani,
Eliathah, Giddalti, and Romamti-ezer, Joshbekashah, Mallothi, Hothir, Mahazioth. [5]All
these were the sons of Heman the king's
seer, according to the promise of God to
exalt him; for God had given Heman fourteen sons and three daughters. [6]They were
all under the direction of their father for the
music in the house of the LORD with cymbals, harps, and lyres for the service of the
house of God. Asaph, Jeduthun, and Heman
were under the order of the king. [7]They and
their kindred, who were trained in singing
to the LORD, all of whom were skillful,
numbered two hundred eighty-eight. [8]And
they cast lots for their duties, small and
great, teacher and pupil alike.
9 The first lot fell for Asaph to Joseph; the
second to Gedaliah, to him and his brothers
and his sons, twelve; [10]the third to Zaccur,
his sons and his brothers, twelve; [11]the
fourth to Izri, his sons and his brothers,
twelve; [12]the fifth to Nethaniah, his sons
and his brothers, twelve; [13]the sixth to
Bukkiah, his sons and his brothers, twelve;
[14]the seventh to Jesarelah,[l] his sons and his
brothers, twelve; [15]the eighth to Jeshaiah,
his sons and his brothers, twelve; [16]the
ninth to Mattaniah, his sons and his brothers, twelve; [17]the tenth to Shimei, his sons
and his brothers, twelve; [18]the eleventh to
Azarel, his sons and his brothers, twelve;
[19]the twelfth to Hashabiah, his sons and his
brothers, twelve; [20]to the thirteenth, Shubael,
his sons and his brothers, twelve; [21]to the
fourteenth, Mattithiah, his sons and his
brothers, twelve; [22]to the fifteenth, to
Jeremoth, his sons and his brothers, twelve;

[h] See 23.19: Heb lacks *Hebron* [i] See 23.19: Heb lacks *the chief* [j] Or *his son*: Meaning of Heb uncertain [k] One Ms: Gk: MT lacks *Shimei* [l] Or *Asarelah*; see 25.2

24.20-31 Other assignments of responsibilities to *the Levites* are indicated here, with the choices made in each case *by lot*.
25.1-31 The sons of Asaph (6.39; 15.19; 16.5-36) are assigned various musical roles, including those who *prophesied with music*, which was a form of ecstatic experience and divine communication. The descendants of Asaph are mentioned in connection with the worship of God after the return from the exile in Ezra (2.41; 3.10) and Nehemiah (7.44; 11.17-22) and in the titles to many of the Psalms (50; 73-83).

26.1-19 The gatekeepers of the temple are from the same genealogical lines – Kore and Asaph – as the musicians (6.37, 39). Even which gate on which side of the city of Jerusalem they are to serve is determined by lot.
26.20-32 Other assignments include supervision of the temple treasuries, as well as *officers and judges* whose duties were to supervise the affairs of the tribes of Israel east and west of the Jordan, both priestly and royal in nature.

23to the sixteenth, to Hananiah, his sons
and his brothers, twelve; 24to the seventeenth, to Joshbekashah, his sons and his
brothers, twelve; 25to the eighteenth, to
Hanani, his sons and his brothers, twelve;
26to the nineteenth, to Mallothi, his sons
and his brothers, twelve; 27to the twentieth,
to Eliathah, his sons and his brothers, twelve;
28to the twenty-first, to Hothir, his sons and
his brothers, twelve; 29to the twenty-second,
to Giddalti, his sons and his brothers, twelve;
30to the twenty-third, to Mahazioth, his sons
and his brothers, twelve; 31to the twenty-
fourth, to Romamti-ezer, his sons and his
brothers, twelve.

The Gatekeepers

26 As for the divisions of the gatekeepers: of the Korahites, Meshelemiah son of Kore, of the sons of Asaph.
2Meshelemiah had sons: Zechariah the
firstborn, Jediael the second, Zebadiah the
third, Jathniel the fourth, 3Elam the fifth,
Jehohanan the sixth, Eliehoenai the seventh. 4Obed-edom had sons: Shemaiah the
firstborn, Jehozabad the second, Joah the
third, Sachar the fourth, Nethanel the fifth,
5Ammiel the sixth, Issachar the seventh,
Peullethai the eighth; for God blessed him.
6Also to his son Shemaiah sons were born
who exercised authority in their ancestral
houses, for they were men of great ability.
7The sons of Shemaiah: Othni, Rephael,
Obed, and Elzabad, whose brothers were
able men, Elihu and Semachiah. 8All these,
sons of Obed-edom with their sons and
brothers, were able men qualified for the
service; sixty-two of Obed-edom. 9Meshelem-
iah had sons and brothers, able men, eighteen. 10Hosah, of the sons of Merari, had
sons: Shimri the chief (for though he was
not the firstborn, his father made him chief),
11Hilkiah the second, Tebaliah the third,
Zechariah the fourth: all the sons and brothers of Hosah totaled thirteen.

12 These divisions of the gatekeepers,
corresponding to their leaders, had duties,
just as their kindred did, ministering in the
house of the LORD; 13and they cast lots by
ancestral houses, small and great alike, for
their gates. 14The lot for the east fell to
Shelemiah. They cast lots also for his son
Zechariah, a prudent counselor, and his lot
came out for the north. 15Obed-edom's came
out for the south, and to his sons was
allotted the storehouse. 16For Shuppim and
Hosah it came out for the west, at the gate
of Shallecheth on the ascending road. Guard
corresponded to guard. 17On the east there
were six Levites each day,[m] on the north
four each day, on the south four each day,
as well as two and two at the storehouse;
18and for the colonnade[n] on the west there
were four at the road and two at the
colonnade.[n] 19These were the divisions of
the gatekeepers among the Korahites and
the sons of Merari.

The Treasurers, Officers, and Judges

20 And of the Levites, Ahijah had charge
of the treasuries of the house of God and the
treasuries of the dedicated gifts. 21The sons
of Ladan, the sons of the Gershonites belonging to Ladan, the heads of families
belonging to Ladan the Gershonite: Jehieli.[o]

22 The sons of Jehieli, Zetham and his
brother Joel, were in charge of the treasuries of the house of the LORD. 23Of the
Amramites, the Izharites, the Hebronites,
and the Uzzielites: 24Shebuel son of Gershom,
son of Moses, was chief officer in charge of
the treasuries. 25His brothers: from Eliezer
were his son Rehabiah, his son Jeshaiah, his
son Joram, his son Zichri, and his son
Shelomoth. 26This Shelomoth and his brothers were in charge of all the treasuries of
the dedicated gifts that King David, and the
heads of families, and the officers of the
thousands and the hundreds, and the commanders of the army, had dedicated. 27From
booty won in battles they dedicated gifts for
the maintenance of the house of the LORD.
28Also all that Samuel the seer, and Saul
son of Kish, and Abner son of Ner, and Joab
son of Zeruiah had dedicated—all dedicated
gifts were in the care of Shelomoth[p] and his
brothers.

29 Of the Izharites, Chenaniah and his
sons were appointed to outside duties for
Israel, as officers and judges. 30Of the
Hebronites, Hashabiah and his brothers, one
thousand seven hundred men of ability, had
the oversight of Israel west of the Jordan for
all the work of the LORD and for the service
of the king. 31Of the Hebronites, Jerijah was
chief of the Hebronites. (In the fortieth year
of David's reign search was made, of whatever genealogy or family, and men of great

[m] Gk: Heb lacks *each day* [n] Heb *parbar*: meaning uncertain [o] The Hebrew text of verse 21 is confused [p] Gk Compare 26.28: Heb *Shelomith*

25.23 ver 4
25.25 ver 4
26.1 ver 19
26.4 1 Chr 15.18
26.10 1 Chr 16.38
26.12 ver 1
26.13 1 Chr 24.5,31; 25.8
26.20 1 Chr 28.12
26.24 1 Chr 23.16
26.25 1 Chr 23.18
26.26 2 Sam 8.11
26.28 1 Sam 9.9
26.29 Neh 11.16; 1 Chr 23.4
26.30 1 Chr 27.17
26.31 1 Chr 23.19

ability among them were found at Jazer in
Gilead.) [32]King David appointed him and his
brothers, two thousand seven hundred men
of ability, heads of families, to have the
oversight of the Reubenites, the Gadites,
and the half-tribe of the Manassites for
everything pertaining to God and for the
affairs of the king.

The Military Divisions

27 This is the list of the people of
Israel, the heads of families, the
commanders of the thousands and the
hundreds, and their officers who served the
king in all matters concerning the divisions
that came and went, month after month
throughout the year, each division numbering twenty-four thousand:
2 Jashobeam son of Zabdiel was in charge
of the first division in the first month; in his
division were twenty-four thousand. [3]He
was a descendant of Perez, and was chief
of all the commanders of the army for the
first month. [4]Dodai the Ahohite was in
charge of the division of the second month;
Mikloth was the chief officer of his division.
In his division were twenty-four thousand.
[5]The third commander, for the third month,
was Benaiah son of the priest Jehoiada, as
chief; in his division were twenty-four thousand. [6]This is the Benaiah who was a mighty
man of the Thirty and in command of the
Thirty; his son Ammizabad was in charge
of his division.[q] [7]Asahel brother of Joab was
fourth, for the fourth month, and his son
Zebadiah after him; in his division were
twenty-four thousand. [8]The fifth commander,
for the fifth month, was Shamhuth, the
Izrahite; in his division were twenty-four
thousand. [9]Sixth, for the sixth month, was
Ira son of Ikkesh the Tekoite; in his division
were twenty-four thousand. [10]Seventh, for
the seventh month, was Helez the Pelonite,
of the Ephraimites; in his division were
twenty-four thousand. [11]Eighth, for the
eighth month, was Sibbecai the Hushathite,
of the Zerahites; in his division were twenty-
four thousand. [12]Ninth, for the ninth month,
was Abiezer of Anathoth, a Benjaminite; in
his division were twenty-four thousand.
[13]Tenth, for the tenth month, was Maharai
of Netophah, of the Zerahites; in his division
were twenty-four thousand. [14]Eleventh, for
the eleventh month, was Benaiah of
Pirathon, of the Ephraimites; in his division
were twenty-four thousand. [15]Twelfth, for
the twelfth month, was Heldai the
Netophathite, of Othniel; in his division were
twenty-four thousand.

Leaders of Tribes

16 Over the tribes of Israel, for the
Reubenites, Eliezer son of Zichri was chief
officer; for the Simeonites, Shephatiah son
of Maacah; [17]for Levi, Hashabiah son of
Kemuel; for Aaron, Zadok; [18]for Judah, Elihu,
one of David's brothers; for Issachar, Omri
son of Michael; [19]for Zebulun, Ishmaiah son
of Obadiah; for Naphtali, Jerimoth son of
Azriel; [20]for the Ephraimites, Hoshea son of
Azaziah; for the half-tribe of Manasseh, Joel
son of Pedaiah; [21]for the half-tribe of
Manasseh in Gilead, Iddo son of Zechariah;
for Benjamin, Jaasiel son of Abner; [22]for
Dan, Azarel son of Jeroham. These were the
leaders of the tribes of Israel. [23]David did not
count those below twenty years of age, for
the LORD had promised to make Israel as
numerous as the stars of heaven. [24]Joab son
of Zeruiah began to count them, but did not
finish; yet wrath came upon Israel for this,
and the number was not entered into the
account of the Annals of King David.

Other Civic Officials

25 Over the king's treasuries was
Azmaveth son of Adiel. Over the treasuries
in the country, in the cities, in the villages
and in the towers, was Jonathan son of
Uzziah. [26]Over those who did the work of
the field, tilling the soil, was Ezri son of
Chelub. [27]Over the vineyards was Shimei
the Ramathite. Over the produce of the
vineyards for the wine cellars was Zabdi the
Shiphmite. [28]Over the olive and sycamore
trees in the Shephelah was Baal-hanan the
Gederite. Over the stores of oil was Joash.
[29]Over the herds that pastured in Sharon
was Shitrai the Sharonite. Over the herds in
the valleys was Shaphat son of Adlai. [30]Over
the camels was Obil the Ishmaelite. Over
the donkeys was Jehdeiah the Meronothite.
Over the flocks was Jaziz the Hagrite. [31]All
these were stewards of King David's property.
32 Jonathan, David's uncle, was a
counselor, being a man of understanding
and a scribe; Jehiel son of Hachmoni attended the king's sons. [33]Ahithophel was

[q] Gk Vg: Heb *Ammizabad was his division*

26.32 2 Chr 19.11
27.2 2 Sam 23.8-30; 1 Chr 11.11-31
27.6 1 Chr 11.22ff
27.7 1 Chr 11.26
27.9 1 Chr 11.28
27.10 1 Chr 11.27
27.11 1 Chr 11.29
27.12 1 Chr 11.28
27.13 1 Chr 11.30
27.14 1 Chr 11.31
27.22 1 Chr 28.1
27.23 Gen 15.5
27.24 2 Sam 24.15; 1 Chr 21.7
27.28 1 Kings 10.27; 2 Chr 1.15
27.33 2 Sam 15.12; 32.37

27.1-15 As with the numbers of the priests and Levites (23.1-4), so the numbers of the military leaders are given in stylized figures combining thousands and multiples of twelve. Taken literally, the army of David as here described would have numbered more than 288,000, which is historically unlikely.
27.16-24 A *chief officer* was set over each of the twelve tribes. Blame for conducting a census of the tribes – which were to be innumerable like the stars – is shifted from *David* to *Joab.*
27.25-31 Supervision of the treasuries (both those of the king and those of the towns and cities), of fields and vineyards, groves and herds, camels and donkeys is assigned to individuals.
27.32-34 The core of aides to David consisted of (1) *Jonathan* (counselor, a man of understanding and a scribe), (2) a second counselor, *Ahithophel;* (3) *Hushai,* who is simply called *the king's friend;* (4) *Jehoiada,* and (5) *Abiathar* (apparently other counselors), and (6) *Joab,* who is in charge of the royal army.

28.1-21 The centrality of David in the establishment of the temple and the institution of the worship of God there is affirmed again; *cf.* Ps 132.8-18; 2 Sam 7; 1 Chr 17.1-14; 22.2-19. Phrased in the language of Deuteronomy (as epitomized in Deut 4.40), God tells David that essential to the continuity of the kingdom in the land is fidelity in *keeping my commandments and ordinances.* The alternative is that disobedience to the law will lead God to *abandon you forever.* The detailed plans that David transmits to Solomon for the structure and furnishing of the temple are in writing and constitute *the plan of all the works.* Solomon is to supervise the entire devoted corps of officers, workers and volunteers. A feature of the sanctuary not mentioned in the other accounts of the shrine and its furnishings is *the golden chariot of the cherubim.* This detail suggests a link with the chariot of God as the symbol of the divine presence and power mentioned in the stories of Elijah and Elisha (2 Kings 2.11-12; 6.17; 7.6), in Ps 68.17 and in Isa 66.15; 29.1-9. In addition to the materials David is said in 21.18-27 and 22.2-5 to have provided for building the temple, he now is reported as making additional offerings in huge amounts of gold, silver and other metals, and as encouraging the heads of Israel's *ancestral houses* to make contributions as well, which they did generously. A Persian coin, *daric of gold,* weighed a little over 8 grams.

the king's counselor, and Hushai the Archite was the king's friend. 34After Ahithophel came Jehoiada son of Benaiah, and Abiathar. Joab was commander of the king's army.

Solomon Instructed to Build the Temple

28 David assembled at Jerusalem all the officials of Israel, the officials of the tribes, the officers of the divisions that served the king, the commanders of the thousands, the commanders of the hundreds, the stewards of all the property and cattle of the king and his sons, together with the palace officials, the mighty warriors, and all the warriors. 2Then King David rose to his feet and said: "Hear me, my brothers and my people. I had planned to build a house of rest for the ark of the covenant of the LORD, for the footstool of our God; and I made preparations for building. 3But God said to me, 'You shall not build a house for my name, for you are a warrior and have shed blood.' 4Yet the LORD God of Israel chose me from all my ancestral house to be king over Israel forever; for he chose Judah as leader, and in the house of Judah my father's house, and among my father's sons he took delight in making me king over all Israel. 5And of all my sons, for the LORD has given me many, he has chosen my son Solomon to sit upon the throne of the kingdom of the LORD over Israel. 6He said to me, 'It is your son Solomon who shall build my house and my courts, for I have chosen him to be a son to me, and I will be a father to him. 7I will establish his kingdom forever if he continues resolute in keeping my commandments and my ordinances, as he is today.' 8Now therefore in the sight of all Israel, the assembly of the LORD, and in the hearing of our God, observe and search out all the commandments of the LORD your God; that you may possess this good land, and leave it for an inheritance to your children after you forever.

9 "And you, my son Solomon, know the God of your father, and serve him with single mind and willing heart; for the LORD searches every mind, and understands every plan and thought. If you seek him, he will be found by you; but if you forsake him, he will abandon you forever. 10Take heed now, for the LORD has chosen you to build a house as the sanctuary; be strong, and act."

11 Then David gave his son Solomon the plan of the vestibule of the temple, and of its houses, its treasuries, its upper rooms, and its inner chambers, and of the room for the mercy seat;[r] 12and the plan of all that he had in mind: for the courts of the house of the LORD, all the surrounding chambers, the treasuries of the house of God, and the treasuries for dedicated gifts; 13for the divisions of the priests and of the Levites, and all the work of the service in the house of the LORD; for all the vessels for the service in the house of the LORD, 14the weight of gold for all golden vessels for each service, the weight of silver vessels for each service, 15the weight of the golden lampstands and their lamps, the weight of gold for each lampstand and its lamps, the weight of silver for a lampstand and its lamps, according to the use of each in the service, 16the weight of gold for each table for the rows of bread, the silver for the silver tables, 17and pure gold for the forks, the basins, and the cups; for the golden bowls and the weight of each; for the silver bowls and the weight of each; 18for the altar of incense made of refined gold, and its weight; also his plan for the golden chariot of the cherubim that spread their wings and covered the ark of the covenant of the LORD.

19 "All this, in writing at the LORD's direction, he made clear to me—the plan of all the works."

20 David said further to his son Solomon, "Be strong and of good courage, and act. Do not be afraid or dismayed; for the LORD God, my God, is with you. He will not fail you or forsake you, until all the work for the service of the house of the LORD is finished. 21Here are the divisions of the priests and the Levites for all the service of the house of God; and with you in all the work will be every volunteer who has skill for any kind of service; also the officers and all the people will be wholly at your command."

Offerings for Building the Temple

29 King David said to the whole assembly, "My son Solomon, whom alone God has chosen, is young and inexperienced, and the work is great; for the temple[s] will not be for mortals but for the LORD God. 2So I have provided for the house of my God, so far as I was able, the gold for the things of gold, the silver for the

[r] Or *the cover* [s] Heb *fortress*

27.34 1 Kings 1.7; 1 Chr 11.6

28.1 1 Chr 27.1-31; 11.10-47

28.2 2 Sam 7.2; 1 Chr 17.1,2; Ps 132.7

28.3 2 Sam 7.5,13; 1 Chr 22.8

28.4 1 Sam 16.6-13; 1 Chr 17.23,27; 5.2; Gen 49.8-10

28.5 1 Chr 3.1-9; 22.9,10

28.6 2 Sam 7.13,14; 1 Chr 22.9,10

28.7 1 Chr 22.13

28.9 Jer 9.24; 1 Chr 29.17-19; 1 Sam 16.7; 2 Chr 15.2; Jer 29.13

28.10 1 Chr 22.13

28.11 ver 12,19; Ex 25.40

28.12 1 Chr 26.20

28.13 1 Chr 24.1; 23.6

28.15 Ex 25.31-39

28.18 Ex 30.1-10; 25.18-22

28.19 ver 11,12

28.20 Josh 1.6,7,9; 1 Chr 22.13; Josh 1.5

28.21 ver 13; Ex 35.25-35; 36.1,2

29.1 1 Chr 22.5; ver 19

29.2 1 Chr 22.3-5

things of silver, and the bronze for the
things of bronze, the iron for the things of
iron, and wood for the things of wood,
besides great quantities of onyx and stones
for setting, antimony, colored stones, all
sorts of precious stones, and marble in
abundance. [3]Moreover, in addition to all
that I have provided for the holy house, I
have a treasure of my own of gold and
silver, and because of my devotion to the
house of my God I give it to the house of
my God: [4]three thousand talents of gold, of
the gold of Ophir, and seven thousand talents of refined silver, for overlaying the
walls of the house, [5]and for all the work to
be done by artisans, gold for the things of
gold and silver for the things of silver. Who
then will offer willingly, consecrating themselves today to the LORD?"
6 Then the leaders of ancestral houses
made their freewill offerings, as did also the
leaders of the tribes, the commanders of the
thousands and of the hundreds, and the
officers over the king's work. [7]They gave for
the service of the house of God five thousand talents and ten thousand darics of
gold, ten thousand talents of silver, eighteen
thousand talents of bronze, and one hundred thousand talents of iron. [8]Whoever
had precious stones gave them to the treasury of the house of the LORD, into the care
of Jehiel the Gershonite. [9]Then the people
rejoiced because these had given willingly,
for with single mind they had offered freely
to the LORD; King David also rejoiced greatly.

David's Praise to God

10 Then David blessed the LORD in the
presence of all the assembly; David said:
"Blessed are you, O LORD, the God of our
ancestor Israel, forever and ever. [11]Yours, O
LORD, are the greatness, the power, the glory,
the victory, and the majesty; for all that is
in the heavens and on the earth is yours;
yours is the kingdom, O LORD, and you are
exalted as head above all. [12]Riches and honor
come from you, and you rule over all. In
your hand are power and might; and it is
in your hand to make great and to give
strength to all. [13]And now, our God, we give
thanks to you and praise your glorious name.
14 "But who am I, and what is my
people, that we should be able to make this
freewill offering? For all things come from
you, and of your own have we given you.
[15]For we are aliens and transients before
you, as were all our ancestors; our days on
the earth are like a shadow, and there is no
hope. [16]O LORD our God, all this abundance
that we have provided for building you a
house for your holy name comes from your
hand and is all your own. [17]I know, my
God, that you search the heart, and take
pleasure in uprightness; in the uprightness
of my heart I have freely offered all these
things, and now I have seen your people,
who are present here, offering freely and
joyously to you. [18]O LORD, the God of
Abraham, Isaac, and Israel, our ancestors,
keep forever such purposes and thoughts in
the hearts of your people, and direct their
hearts toward you. [19]Grant to my son Solomon that with single mind he may keep
your commandments, your decrees, and your
statutes, performing all of them, and that he
may build the temple[t] for which I have
made provision."
20 Then David said to the whole assembly, "Bless the LORD your God." And all the
assembly blessed the LORD, the God of their
ancestors, and bowed their heads and prostrated themselves before the LORD and the
king. [21]On the next day they offered sacrifices and burnt offerings to the LORD, a
thousand bulls, a thousand rams, and a
thousand lambs, with their libations, and
sacrifices in abundance for all Israel; [22]and
they ate and drank before the LORD on that
day with great joy.

Solomon Anointed King

They made David's son Solomon king a
second time; they anointed him as the LORD's
prince, and Zadok as priest. [23]Then Solomon
sat on the throne of the LORD, succeeding his
father David as king; he prospered, and all
Israel obeyed him. [24]All the leaders and the
mighty warriors, and also all the sons of
King David, pledged their allegiance to King
Solomon. [25]The LORD highly exalted Solomon in the sight of all Israel, and bestowed
upon him such royal majesty as had not
been on any king before him in Israel.

Summary of David's Reign

26 Thus David son of Jesse reigned over
all Israel. [27]The period that he reigned over
Israel was forty years; he reigned seven
years in Hebron, and thirty-three years in

[t] Heb *fortress*

29.4 1 Chr 22.14; 1 Kings 9.28
29.6 1 Chr 27.1; 28.1; 27.25ff
29.7 Ezra 2.69; Neh 7.70
29.8 1 Chr 26.21
29.9 1 Kings 8.61; 2 Cor 9.7
29.11 Mt 6.13; 1 Tim 1.17; Rev 5.13
29.12 2 Chr 1.12; Rom 11.36
29.15 Lev 25.23; Ps 39.12; Heb 11.13; 1 Pet 2.11; Job 14.2
29.17 1 Chr 28.9; Prov 11.20
29.19 1 Chr 28.9; Ps 72.1; ver 2; 1 Chr 22.14
29.21 1 Kings 8.62,63
29.22 1 Chr 23.1; 1 Kings 1.33-39
29.25 2 Chr 1.1,12; 1 Kings 3.13
29.26 1 Chr 18.14
29.27 2 Sam 5.4,5; 1 Kings 2.11

29.10-22a David leads *all the assembly* of Israel in praise to God, celebrating God's power over the whole of creation and his care for his people, while appealing to them to be devoted to God and obedient to his commandments. The people then join in the offering of sacrifice and *joy* in the Lord's presence.
29.22b-25 Solomon is confirmed as king (*cf.* 23.1; 1 Kings 1.38-40), and *all Israel*, as well as the leaders and the royal household, acclaim him as such.
29.26-30 David's reign is here depicted affirmatively, without reference to his failures and misdeeds which are recorded in the Books of Samuel and Kings. The Chronicler wants to imply the reliability of this account by claiming that it is based on the *records* allegedly kept by the prophets and seers who advised David during his rule, which is here depicted as a glorious model.

Jerusalem. 28 He died in a good old age, full of days, riches, and honor; and his son Solomon succeeded him. 29 Now the acts of King David, from first to last, are written in the records of the seer Samuel, and in the records of the prophet Nathan, and in the records of the seer Gad, 30 with accounts of all his rule and his might and of the events that befell him and Israel and all the kingdoms of the earth.

29.28 Gen 15.15; 25.8; 1 Chr 23.1

29.30 Dan 2.21; 4.23,25

2 CHRONICLES

See the Introductions, pp. 3, 38, and 44-45 above.

Solomon Requests Wisdom

1 Solomon son of David established himself in his kingdom; the LORD his God was with him and made him exceedingly great.

2 Solomon summoned all Israel, the commanders of the thousands and of the hundreds, the judges, and all the leaders of all Israel, the heads of families. 3 Then Solomon, and the whole assembly with him, went to the high place that was at Gibeon; for God's tent of meeting, which Moses the servant of the LORD had made in the wilderness, was there. 4 (But David had brought the ark of God up from Kiriath-jearim to the place that David had prepared for it; for he had pitched a tent for it in Jerusalem.) 5 Moreover the bronze altar that Bezalel son of Uri, son of Hur, had made, was there in front of the tabernacle of the LORD. And Solomon and the assembly inquired at it. 6 Solomon went up there to the bronze altar before the LORD, which was at the tent of meeting, and offered a thousand burnt offerings on it.

7 That night God appeared to Solomon, and said to him, "Ask what I should give you." 8 Solomon said to God, "You have shown great and steadfast love to my father David, and have made me succeed him as king. 9 O LORD God, let your promise to my father David now be fulfilled, for you have made me king over a people as numerous as the dust of the earth. 10 Give me now wisdom and knowledge to go out and come in before this people, for who can rule this great people of yours?" 11 God answered Solomon, "Because this was in your heart, and you have not asked for possessions, wealth, honor, or the life of those who hate you, and have not even asked for long life, but have asked for wisdom and knowledge for yourself that you may rule my people over whom I have made you king, 12 wisdom and knowledge are granted to you. I will also give you riches, possessions, and honor, such as none of the kings had who were before you, and none after you shall have the like." 13 So Solomon came from[a] the high place at Gibeon, from the tent of meeting, to Jerusalem. And he reigned over Israel.

Solomon's Military and Commercial Activity

14 Solomon gathered together chariots and horses; he had fourteen hundred chariots and twelve thousand horses, which he stationed in the chariot cities and with the king in Jerusalem. 15 The king made silver and gold as common in Jerusalem as stone, and he made cedar as plentiful as the sycamore of the Shephelah. 16 Solomon's horses were imported from Egypt and Kue; the king's traders received them from Kue at the prevailing price. 17 They imported from Egypt, and then exported, a chariot for six hundred shekels of silver, and a horse for one hundred fifty; so through them these were exported to all the kings of the Hittites and the kings of Aram.

Preparations for Building the Temple

2[b] Solomon decided to build a temple for the name of the LORD, and a royal palace for himself. 2[c] Solomon conscripted seventy thousand laborers and eighty thousand stonecutters in the hill country, with three thousand six hundred to oversee them.

[a] Gk Vg: Heb *to* [b] Ch 1.18 in Heb [c] Ch 2.1 in Heb

1.1-9.31 The Glorious Reign of Solomon.

1.1-6 Omitting the accounts of the struggle for the throne in 1 Kings 1-2, and Solomon's strategic marriage with an Egyptian princess (1 Kings 3.1), the Chronicler describes Solomon's first great public act as the assembling at *Gibeon* of all the elaborate leadership that he had developed for Israel: *commanders, judges, leaders, heads of families.* Instead of acknowledging Solomon's error in worshipping at a *high place* (1 Kings 3.3-4), the people are assembled at *Gibeon* as a symbol of continuity with Israel's past, and especially with *Moses* and *the tent of meeting,* which he had made (Ex 26; 39.32), and which is here and in 1 Chr 21.29 reported to be in Gibeon. The difficulty with this claim is apparent in the parenthetical note (1.4) that David had taken *the ark of God* from Kiriath-jearim to Jerusalem. Possibly there were separate traditions in ancient Israel about the tent and the ark. *The bronze altar,* described in Ex 27.1-8, is here attributed to the head of the artisans engaged to build the tent and its sacred equipment, *Bezalel son of Uri* (Ex 31.1-11). The altar, rather than the ark, is pictured as the place where Solomon approached God to *inquire* about his will and purpose.

1.7-17 *God appeared to Solomon,* and in response to Solomon's request for *wisdom* in guiding the kingdom, promises not only *wisdom and knowledge,* but also wealth and honor without equal. The abundance of wealth, military equipment and international trade is enumerated. *Kue* is probably the same as Cilicia: a district including what is now northeastern Syria and southwestern Turkey. *The Hittites* controlled this same general area. *Aram* is western Syria.

2.1-18 Preparations for building the temple included the conscription of huge numbers of workers and supervisors, as well as the acquisition from *Huram of Tyre* (in 1 Kings 5 his name is *Hiram*) of the materials and skilled workers to complete the construction of this complex. *Huram* agreed to fulfill these requests in exchange for food, including grain, wine and oil. His acknowledgment of *the LORD* expands on the source (1 Kings 5.7) to include a declaration of God's having made *heaven and earth,* and an indication that the materials are to build a temple for God and also a *royal palace* for Solomon. In 1 Kings 5.13 the workforce for building and adorning the temple is *conscripted out of all Israel,* but in 2 Chr 2.17-18 the workers are said to have been taken from *all the aliens who were residing in the land.*

1.1 1 Kings 2.12,46; Gen 39.2; 1 Chr 29.25

1.2 1 Chr 28.1

1.3 1 Kings 3.4; Ex 36.8

1.4 2 Sam 6.2,17; 1 Chr 15.1

1.5 Ex 38.1,2

1.6 1 Kings 3.4

1.7 1 Kings 3.5,6

1.8 1 Chr 28.5

1.9 1 Kings 3.7,8

1.10 1 Kings 3.9

1.11 1 Kings 3.11-13

1.12 1 Chr 29.25; 2 Chr 9.22

1.14 1 Kings 4.26; 10.26-29; 2 Chr 9.25

1.15 1 Kings 10.27; 2 Chr 9.27

1.16 1 Kings 10.28,29; 2 Chr 9.28

2.1 1 Kings 5.5

2.2 ver 18; 1 Kings 5.15,16

Alliance with Huram of Tyre

3 Solomon sent word to King Huram of Tyre: "Once you dealt with my father David and sent him cedar to build himself a house to live in. [4]I am now about to build a house for the name of the LORD my God and dedicate it to him for offering fragrant incense before him, and for the regular offering of the rows of bread, and for burnt offerings morning and evening, on the sabbaths and the new moons and the appointed festivals of the LORD our God, as ordained forever for Israel. [5]The house that I am about to build will be great, for our God is greater than other gods. [6]But who is able to build him a house, since heaven, even highest heaven, cannot contain him? Who am I to build a house for him, except as a place to make offerings before him? [7]So now send me an artisan skilled to work in gold, silver, bronze, and iron, and in purple, crimson, and blue fabrics, trained also in engraving, to join the skilled workers who are with me in Judah and Jerusalem, whom my father David provided. [8]Send me also cedar, cypress, and algum timber from Lebanon, for I know that your servants are skilled in cutting Lebanon timber. My servants will work with your servants [9]to prepare timber for me in abundance, for the house I am about to build will be great and wonderful. [10]I will provide for your servants, those who cut the timber, twenty thousand cors of crushed wheat, twenty thousand cors of barley, twenty thousand baths[d] of wine, and twenty thousand baths of oil."

11 Then King Huram of Tyre answered in a letter that he sent to Solomon, "Because the LORD loves his people he has made you king over them." [12]Huram also said, "Blessed be the LORD God of Israel, who made heaven and earth, who has given King David a wise son, endowed with discretion and understanding, who will build a temple for the LORD, and a royal palace for himself.

13 "I have dispatched Huram-abi, a skilled artisan, endowed with understanding, [14]the son of one of the Danite women, his father a Tyrian. He is trained to work in gold, silver, bronze, iron, stone, and wood, and in purple, blue, and crimson fabrics and fine linen, and to do all sorts of engraving and execute any design that may be assigned him, with your artisans, the artisans of my lord, your father David. [15]Now, as for the wheat, barley, oil, and wine, of which my lord has spoken, let him send them to his servants. [16]We will cut whatever timber you need from Lebanon, and bring it to you as rafts by sea to Joppa; you will take it up to Jerusalem."

17 Then Solomon took a census of all the aliens who were residing in the land of Israel, after the census that his father David had taken; and there were found to be one hundred fifty-three thousand six hundred. [18]Seventy thousand of them he assigned as laborers, eighty thousand as stonecutters in the hill country, and three thousand six hundred as overseers to make the people work.

Solomon Builds the Temple

3 Solomon began to build the house of the LORD in Jerusalem on Mount Moriah, where the LORD had appeared to his father David, at the place that David had designated, on the threshing floor of Ornan the Jebusite. [2]He began to build on the second day of the second month of the fourth year of his reign. [3]These are Solomon's measurements[e] for building the house of God: the length, in cubits of the old standard, was sixty cubits, and the width twenty cubits. [4]The vestibule in front of the nave of the house was twenty cubits long, across the width of the house;[f] and its height was one hundred twenty cubits. He overlaid it on the inside with pure gold. [5]The nave he lined with cypress, covered it with fine gold, and made palms and chains on it. [6]He adorned the house with settings of precious stones. The gold was gold from Parvaim. [7]So he lined the house with gold—its beams, its thresholds, its walls, and its doors; and he carved cherubim on the walls.

8 He made the most holy place; its length, corresponding to the width of the house, was twenty cubits, and its width was twenty cubits; he overlaid it with six hundred talents of fine gold. [9]The weight of the nails was fifty shekels of gold. He overlaid the upper chambers with gold.

10 In the most holy place he made two carved cherubim and overlaid[g] them with gold. [11]The wings of the cherubim together extended twenty cubits: one wing of the

[d] A Hebrew measure of volume [e] Syr: Heb *foundations* [f] Compare 1 Kings 6.3: Meaning of Heb uncertain [g] Heb *they overlaid*

2.3 1 Kings 5.2-11; 1 Chr 14.1
2.4 ver 1; Ex 30.7; 25.30; Num 28.9,10
2.5 1 Chr 16.25; Ps 135.5
2.6 1 Kings 8.27; 2 Chr 6.18
2.7 ver 13,14; 1 Chr 22.15
2.8 2 Chr 9.10,11
2.10 1 Kings 5.11
2.11 1 Kings 10.9; 2 Chr 9.8
2.12 1 Kings 5.7; Ps 33.6; 102.25
2.14 1 Kings 7.13,14
2.15 ver 10
2.16 1 Kings 5.8,9
2.17 1 Chr 22.2
2.18 ver 2
3.1 1 Kings 6.1ff; 1 Chr 21.18
3.5 1 Kings 6.17
3.7 1 Kings 6.20-22,29-35
3.8 1 Kings 6.16
3.10 1 Kings 6.23-28

3.1-17 The Construction of the Temple. *The site,* the threshing floor of Ornan the Jebusite, had been selected earlier by David, who bought the place and erected an altar there (2 Sam 24.18-25; 1 Chr 21.18-22.1). *Ornan* is a variant of Araunah, the former owner of the site (2 Sam 24.18). The dimensions and features of the temple are given in idealized numbers, with the *vestibule* reaching a height of *one hundred twenty cubits* (between 180 and 200 feet) and the *gold* overlay of *the holy place* said to have weighed more than 50,000 pounds. *The most holy place,* which is the equivalent of *the inner sanctuary* in 1 Kings 6.17-28, is a term found in Ex 26.31-35 for the inmost section of the sacred tent, where the LORD was believed to be present in the form of a cloud of glory (Ex 40.34-38). *The pillars in front of the house* are described more fully in 1 Kings 7.15-22.

4.1-6 *The molten sea,* about fifteen feet across and 7.5 feet deep, was a huge, elaborate basin in which the priests were to purify themselves. The smaller basins were for washing the offerings and the equipment used in the sacrifices.
4.7-21 Other equipment for the temple was made of bronze (*pots, shovels, basins*) and gold (*lampstands; the golden altar*). The casting of the bronze objects was done in the Jordan Valley, between Succoth and Zeredah, two cities on the far side of the Jordan Valley east of Shechem. A special table was made for *the bread of the Presence,* the sacred bread which was placed before the LORD in the inner sanctuary (1 Sam 21.6; Ex 25.23-30). On the whole, the description here follows the account in 1 Kings 7.13-51.
5.2-14 The account of the bringing of *the ark of the covenant* into the temple is drawn from 1 Kings 8.1-9. The sole contents of the ark (5.10) are *the two tablets that Moses put there at Horeb,* another name for Mount Sinai, where Moses received the law *written with the finger of God* (Ex 31.18). In this account the *Levites* are mentioned, and there is a more extensive list of the priestly officials who were present at the ceremony, with details of their attire and equipment. The brief hymn fragment affirming that the LORD's *steadfast love endures forever* is a recurrent theme in the Psalms (100.5; 106.1; 107.1; 118.1; throughout Ps 136) and in the prophet Jeremiah (33.11).

one, five cubits long, touched the wall of the house, and its other wing, five cubits long, touched the wing of the other cherub; [12]and of this cherub, one wing, five cubits long, touched the wall of the house, and the other wing, also five cubits long, was joined to the wing of the first cherub. [13]The wings of these cherubim extended twenty cubits; the cherubim[h] stood on their feet, facing the nave. [14]And Solomon[i] made the curtain of blue and purple and crimson fabrics and fine linen, and worked cherubim into it.

15 In front of the house he made two pillars thirty-five cubits high, with a capital of five cubits on the top of each. [16]He made encircling[j] chains and put them on the tops of the pillars; and he made one hundred pomegranates, and put them on the chains. [17]He set up the pillars in front of the temple, one on the right, the other on the left; the one on the right he called Jachin, and the one on the left, Boaz.

Furnishings of the Temple

4 He made an altar of bronze, twenty cubits long, twenty cubits wide, and ten cubits high. [2]Then he made the molten sea; it was round, ten cubits from rim to rim, and five cubits high. A line of thirty cubits would encircle it completely. [3]Under it were panels all around, each of ten cubits, surrounding the sea; there were two rows of panels, cast when it was cast. [4]It stood on twelve oxen, three facing north, three facing west, three facing south, and three facing east; the sea was set on them. The hindquarters of each were toward the inside. [5]Its thickness was a handbreadth; its rim was made like the rim of a cup, like the flower of a lily; it held three thousand baths.[k] [6]He also made ten basins in which to wash, and set five on the right side, and five on the left. In these they were to rinse what was used for the burnt offering. The sea was for the priests to wash in.

7 He made ten golden lampstands as prescribed, and set them in the temple, five on the south side and five on the north. [8]He also made ten tables and placed them in the temple, five on the right side and five on the left. And he made one hundred basins of gold. [9]He made the court of the priests, and the great court, and doors for the court; he overlaid their doors with bronze. [10]He set the sea at the southeast corner of the house.

11 And Huram made the pots, the shovels, and the basins. Thus Huram finished the work that he did for King Solomon on the house of God: [12]the two pillars, the bowls, and the two capitals on the top of the pillars; and the two latticeworks to cover the two bowls of the capitals that were on the top of the pillars; [13]the four hundred pomegranates for the two latticeworks, two rows of pomegranates for each latticework, to cover the two bowls of the capitals that were on the pillars. [14]He made the stands, the basins on the stands, [15]the one sea, and the twelve oxen underneath it. [16]The pots, the shovels, the forks, and all the equipment for these Huram-abi made of burnished bronze for King Solomon for the house of the LORD. [17]In the plain of the Jordan the king cast them, in the clay ground between Succoth and Zeredah. [18]Solomon made all these things in great quantities, so that the weight of the bronze was not determined.

19 So Solomon made all the things that were in the house of God: the golden altar, the tables for the bread of the Presence, [20]the lampstands and their lamps of pure gold to burn before the inner sanctuary, as prescribed; [21]the flowers, the lamps, and the tongs, of purest gold; [22]the snuffers, basins, ladles, and firepans, of pure gold. As for the entrance to the temple: the inner doors to the most holy place and the doors of the nave of the temple were of gold.

5 Thus all the work that Solomon did for the house of the LORD was finished. Solomon brought in the things that his father David had dedicated, and stored the silver, the gold, and all the vessels in the treasuries of the house of God.

The Ark Brought into the Temple

2 Then Solomon assembled the elders of Israel and all the heads of the tribes, the leaders of the ancestral houses of the people of Israel, in Jerusalem, to bring up the ark of the covenant of the LORD out of the city of David, which is Zion. [3]And all the Israelites assembled before the king at the festival that is in the seventh month. [4]And all the elders of Israel came, and the Levites carried the ark. [5]So they brought up the ark, the tent of meeting, and all the holy vessels that were in the tent; the priests and the Levites brought them up. [6]King Solomon and all the congregation of Israel, who

[h] Heb *they* [i] Heb *he* [j] Cn: Heb *in the inner sanctuary* [k] A Hebrew measure of volume

3.14 Ex 26.31; Heb 9.3
3.15 1 Kings 7.15-20
3.17 1 Kings 7.21
4.1 Ex 27.1,2; 2 Kings 16.14
4.2 1 Kings 7.23
4.3 1 Kings 7.24-26
4.5 1 Kings 7.26
4.6 1 Kings 7.38
4.7 1 Kings 7.49; Ex 25.31,40
4.8 1 Kings 7.48
4.9 1 Kings 6.36; 2 Kings 21.5
4.10 1 Kings 7.39
4.11 1 Kings 7.40
4.12 1 Kings 7.41
4.13 1 Kings 7.20
4.14 1 Kings 7.27
4.16 1 Kings 7.14
4.17 1 Kings 7.46
4.18 1 Kings 7.47
4.19 1 Kings 7.48-50; Ex 25.30
4.20 Ex 25.31-37
5.1 1 Kings 7.51
5.2 1 Kings 8.1-9; 2 Sam 6.12
5.4 ver 7

had assembled before him, were before the ark, sacrificing so many sheep and oxen that they could not be numbered or counted. [7]Then the priests brought the ark of the covenant of the LORD to its place, in the inner sanctuary of the house, in the most holy place, underneath the wings of the cherubim. [8]For the cherubim spread out their wings over the place of the ark, so that the cherubim made a covering above the ark and its poles. [9]The poles were so long that the ends of the poles were seen from the holy place in front of the inner sanctuary; but they could not be seen from outside; they are there to this day. [10]There was nothing in the ark except the two tablets that Moses put there at Horeb, where the LORD made a covenant[l] with the people of Israel after they came out of Egypt.

11 Now when the priests came out of the holy place (for all the priests who were present had sanctified themselves, without regard to their divisions, [12]and all the levitical singers, Asaph, Heman, and Jeduthun, their sons and kindred, arrayed in fine linen, with cymbals, harps, and lyres, stood east of the altar with one hundred twenty priests who were trumpeters). [13]It was the duty of the trumpeters and singers to make themselves heard in unison in praise and thanksgiving to the LORD, and when the song was raised, with trumpets and cymbals and other musical instruments, in praise to the LORD,

"For he is good,
for his steadfast love endures forever,"

the house, the house of the LORD, was filled with a cloud, [14]so that the priests could not stand to minister because of the cloud; for the glory of the LORD filled the house of God.

Dedication of the Temple

6 Then Solomon said, "The LORD has said that he would reside in thick darkness. [2]I have built you an exalted house, a place for you to reside in forever."

3 Then the king turned around and blessed all the assembly of Israel, while all the assembly of Israel stood. [4]And he said, "Blessed be the LORD, the God of Israel, who with his hand has fulfilled what he promised with his mouth to my father David, saying, [5]'Since the day that I brought my people out of the land of Egypt, I have not chosen a city from any of the tribes of Israel in which to build a house, so that my name might be there, and I chose no one as ruler over my people Israel; [6]but I have chosen Jerusalem in order that my name may be there, and I have chosen David to be over my people Israel.' [7]My father David had it in mind to build a house for the name of the LORD, the God of Israel. [8]But the LORD said to my father David, 'You did well to consider building a house for my name; [9]nevertheless you shall not build the house, but your son who shall be born to you shall build the house for my name.' [10]Now the LORD has fulfilled his promise that he made; for I have succeeded my father David, and sit on the throne of Israel, as the LORD promised, and have built the house for the name of the LORD, the God of Israel. [11]There I have set the ark, in which is the covenant of the LORD that he made with the people of Israel."

Solomon's Prayer of Dedication

12 Then Solomon[m] stood before the altar of the LORD in the presence of the whole assembly of Israel, and spread out his hands. [13]Solomon had made a bronze platform five cubits long, five cubits wide, and three cubits high, and had set it in the court; and he stood on it. Then he knelt on his knees in the presence of the whole assembly of Israel, and spread out his hands toward heaven. [14]He said, "O LORD, God of Israel, there is no God like you, in heaven or on earth, keeping covenant in steadfast love with your servants who walk before you with all their heart— [15]you who have kept for your servant, my father David, what you promised to him. Indeed, you promised with your mouth and this day have fulfilled with your hand. [16]Therefore, O LORD, God of Israel, keep for your servant, my father David, that which you promised him, saying, 'There shall never fail you a successor before me to sit on the throne of Israel, if only your children keep to their way, to walk in my law as you have walked before me.' [17]Therefore, O LORD, God of Israel, let your word be confirmed, which you promised to your servant David.

18 "But will God indeed reside with mortals on earth? Even heaven and the highest heaven cannot contain you, how much less this house that I have built! [19]Regard your servant's prayer and his plea, O LORD my God, heeding the cry and the prayer that your servant prays to you. [20]May

[l] Heb lacks *a covenant* [m] Heb *he*

5.9 1 Kings 8.8,9
5.10 Deut 10.2-5; Heb 9.4
5.11 1 Chr 24.1-5
5.12 1 Chr 25.1-4; 15.24
5.13 2 Chr 7.3; 1 Chr 16.34,42
5.14 1 Kings 8.11; 2 Chr 7.2
6.1 1 Kings 8.12-50
6.6 2 Chr 12.13; 1 Chr 28.4
6.7 1 Chr 28.2
6.11 2 Chr 5.10
6.12 1 Kings 8.22
6.13 1 Kings 8.54
6.14 Ex 15.11; Deut 7.9
6.15 1 Chr 22.9,10
6.16 2 Sam 7.12,16; 1 Kings 2.4; 2 Chr 7.18
6.18 2 Chr 2.6

6.1-11 The Dedication of the Temple by Solomon. Beginning with Solomon's assertion of his role in having built a house where the LORD will *reside forever*, the subsequent narrative follows closely 1 Kings 8.12-21. More specific than in the 1 Kings 8 source are the claims of the uniqueness of the house of David as God's designated rulers over this people, and of a city which did not belong to *any of the tribes of Israel* – that is, Jerusalem – as the location for God's house. Omitting the reference to the covenant having been made with the ancestors of Israel whom God brought out of Egypt (1 Kings 8.21), it is here said to have been made simply *with the people of Israel*.
6.12-42 Solomon's Prayer of Dedication. Since prayer *before the altar of the LORD* was the special prerogative of the priests, a *bronze platform* is described as positioned for Solomon to address God *in the presence of the whole assembly of Israel*. This feature is not found in the account in 1 Kings. In 6.16-17 it is specified that for God's people to *walk in my law* is essential if the Davidic dynasty is to continue. Notable among the themes repeated from the 1 Kings 8 source is the promise that *foreigners* from other nations and lands will come to know God's name and *fear* him. The prayer of repentance with its recollection of the exodus from Egypt in 1 Kings 8.46-53 is abbreviated here (6.36-39), and the petition ends with a paraphrase of Ps 132.8-10, invoking God's support for the priests and the king *(anointed one)*.

7.1-3. The Sign of Divine Approval. The *fire from heaven* not only signifies God's acceptance of the offerings but also results in the filling of the temple with the radiant cloud which was seen as embodying the presence of God there.

your eyes be open day and night toward
this house, the place where you promised
to set your name, and may you heed the
prayer that your servant prays toward this
place. [21]And hear the plea of your servant
and of your people Israel, when they pray
toward this place; may you hear from heaven
your dwelling place; hear and forgive.
22 "If someone sins against another and
is required to take an oath and comes and
swears before your altar in this house, [23]may
you hear from heaven, and act, and judge
your servants, repaying the guilty by bringing their conduct on their own head, and
vindicating those who are in the right by
rewarding them in accordance with their
righteousness.
24 "When your people Israel, having
sinned against you, are defeated before an
enemy but turn again to you, confess your
name, pray and plead with you in this
house, [25]may you hear from heaven, and
forgive the sin of your people Israel, and
bring them again to the land that you gave
to them and to their ancestors.
26 "When heaven is shut up and there
is no rain because they have sinned against
you, and then they pray toward this place,
confess your name, and turn from their sin,
because you punish them, [27]may you hear
in heaven, forgive the sin of your servants,
your people Israel, when you teach them
the good way in which they should walk;
and send down rain upon your land, which
you have given to your people as an inheritance.
28 "If there is famine in the land, if there
is plague, blight, mildew, locust, or caterpillar; if their enemies besiege them in any of
the settlements of the lands; whatever suffering, whatever sickness there is; [29]what-
ever prayer, whatever plea from any individual or from all your people Israel, all
knowing their own suffering and their own
sorrows so that they stretch out their hands
toward this house; [30]may you hear from
heaven, your dwelling place, forgive, and
render to all whose heart you know, according to all their ways, for only you know
the human heart. [31]Thus may they fear you
and walk in your ways all the days that
they live in the land that you gave to our
ancestors.
32 "Likewise when foreigners, who are
not of your people Israel, come from a
distant land because of your great name,
and your mighty hand, and your outstretched arm, when they come and pray
toward this house, [33]may you hear from
heaven your dwelling place, and do whatever the foreigners ask of you, in order that
all the peoples of the earth may know your
name and fear you, as do your people Israel,
and that they may know that your name
has been invoked on this house that I have
built.
34 "If your people go out to battle against
their enemies, by whatever way you shall
send them, and they pray to you toward
this city that you have chosen and the
house that I have built for your name,
[35]then hear from heaven their prayer and
their plea, and maintain their cause.
36 "If they sin against you—for there is
no one who does not sin—and you are
angry with them and give them to an
enemy, so that they are carried away captive to a land far or near; [37]then if they
come to their senses in the land to which
they have been taken captive, and repent,
and plead with you in the land of their
captivity, saying, 'We have sinned, and have
done wrong; we have acted wickedly'; [38]if
they repent with all their heart and soul in
the land of their captivity, to which they
were taken captive, and pray toward their
land, which you gave to their ancestors, the
city that you have chosen, and the house
that I have built for your name, [39]then hear
from heaven your dwelling place their prayer
and their pleas, maintain their cause and
forgive your people who have sinned against
you. [40]Now, O my God, let your eyes be
open and your ears attentive to prayer from
this place.

41 "Now rise up, O LORD God, and go to
your resting place,
you and the ark of your might.
Let your priests, O LORD God, be
clothed with salvation,
and let your faithful rejoice in your
goodness.
42 O LORD God, do not reject your
anointed one.
Remember your steadfast love for
your servant David."

Solomon Dedicates the Temple

7 When Solomon had ended his prayer,
fire came down from heaven and
consumed the burnt offering and the sacrifices; and the glory of the LORD filled the
temple. [2]The priests could not enter the

6.21 Mic 7.18

6.22 Mt 5.33

6.24 2 Chr 7.14

6.26 1 Kings 17.1

6.28 2 Chr 20.9

6.30 1 Sam 16.7; 1 Chr 28.9

6.32 Josh 12.20; Acts 8.27

6.33 2 Chr 7.14

6.36 Job 15.14-16; Jas 3.2; 1 Jn 1.8-10

6.37 2 Chr 7.14

6.40 2 Chr 7.15; Ps 17.1

6.41 Ps 132.8-10; 1 Chr 28.2

7.1 1 Kings 8.54; 18.24,38; 2 Chr 5.13,14

house of the LORD, because the glory of the LORD filled the LORD's house. 3When all the people of Israel saw the fire come down and the glory of the LORD on the temple, they bowed down on the pavement with their faces to the ground, and worshiped and gave thanks to the LORD, saying,

"For he is good,
for his steadfast love endures forever."

4 Then the king and all the people offered sacrifice before the LORD. 5King Solomon offered as a sacrifice twenty-two thousand oxen and one hundred twenty thousand sheep. So the king and all the people dedicated the house of God. 6The priests stood at their posts; the Levites also, with the instruments for music to the LORD that King David had made for giving thanks to the LORD—for his steadfast love endures forever—whenever David offered praises by their ministry. Opposite them the priests sounded trumpets; and all Israel stood.

7 Solomon consecrated the middle of the court that was in front of the house of the LORD; for there he offered the burnt offerings and the fat of the offerings of well-being because the bronze altar Solomon had made could not hold the burnt offering and the grain offering and the fat parts.

8 At that time Solomon held the festival for seven days, and all Israel with him, a very great congregation, from Lebo-hamath to the Wadi of Egypt. 9On the eighth day they held a solemn assembly; for they had observed the dedication of the altar seven days and the festival seven days. 10On the twenty-third day of the seventh month he sent the people away to their homes, joyful and in good spirits because of the goodness that the LORD had shown to David and to Solomon and to his people Israel.

11 Thus Solomon finished the house of the LORD and the king's house; all that Solomon had planned to do in the house of the LORD and in his own house he successfully accomplished.

God's Second Appearance to Solomon

12 Then the LORD appeared to Solomon in the night and said to him: "I have heard your prayer, and have chosen this place for myself as a house of sacrifice. 13When I shut up the heavens so that there is no rain, or command the locust to devour the land, or send pestilence among my people, 14if my people who are called by my name humble themselves, pray, seek my face, and turn from their wicked ways, then I will hear from heaven, and will forgive their sin and heal their land. 15Now my eyes will be open and my ears attentive to the prayer that is made in this place. 16For now I have chosen and consecrated this house so that my name may be there forever; my eyes and my heart will be there for all time. 17As for you, if you walk before me, as your father David walked, doing according to all that I have commanded you and keeping my statutes and my ordinances, 18then I will establish your royal throne, as I made covenant with your father David saying, 'You shall never lack a successor to rule over Israel.'

19 "But if you[n] turn aside and forsake my statutes and my commandments that I have set before you, and go and serve other gods and worship them, 20then I will pluck you[o] up from the land that I have given you;[o] and this house, which I have consecrated for my name, I will cast out of my sight, and will make it a proverb and a byword among all peoples. 21And regarding this house, now exalted, everyone passing by will be astonished, and say, 'Why has the LORD done such a thing to this land and to this house?' 22Then they will say, 'Because they abandoned the LORD the God of their ancestors who brought them out of the land of Egypt, and they adopted other gods, and worshiped them and served them; therefore he has brought all this calamity upon them.' "

Various Activities of Solomon

8 At the end of twenty years, during which Solomon had built the house of the LORD and his own house, 2Solomon rebuilt the cities that Huram had given to him, and settled the people of Israel in them.

3 Solomon went to Hamath-zobah, and captured it. 4He built Tadmor in the wilderness and all the storage towns that he built in Hamath. 5He also built Upper Beth-horon and Lower Beth-horon, fortified cities, with walls, gates, and bars, 6and Baalath, as well as all Solomon's storage towns, and all the towns for his chariots, the towns for his cavalry, and whatever Solomon desired to build, in Jerusalem, in Lebanon, and in all the land of his dominion. 7All the people who were left of the Hittites, the Amorites, the Perizzites, the Hivites, and the Jebusites,

[n] The word *you* in this verse is plural [o] Heb *them*

7.4-22 Solomon Inaugurates the Worship of God in the Temple. Although this section follows closely 1 Kings 8.62-9.9, there are important changes and additions. Emphasis falls on the roles of the priests, musicians and Levites (vv. 4-6), on the special dedicatory service at the altar with the extended participation of the people (vv. 8-10), and on the claim of success for what Solomon did (vs. 11). The description of the LORD's second appearance to Solomon (2 Chr 7.12-22) follows in general 1 Kings 9.2-9, but omits reference to Gibeon as the place where God appeared (since no sacred site is to compete with Jerusalem), while expanding on the manifestations of divine judgment (pestilence, drought, plague) which are to be seen as calls to repentance on the part of God's people. Underscored in 7.19-22 is the apparent prediction of an event that had already occurred by the time the Chronicler was writing: the exile of Israel in Babylon as a form of divine judgment on the disobedient people.

8.1-18 Solomon's Activities: Building, Marital, Sacred and Commercial. In dependence on 1 Kings 9.10-28, the Chronicler gives a fuller list of the building activities of Solomon through the forced labor of subject peoples, and an indication that his Egyptian wife had to be housed separately lest her presence defile the sacred places associated with David and the ark. Also more detail is given for the role of priests and Levites in connection with the annual calendar of sacred feasts. Although there is no mention of Solomon's building a fleet for the purpose, his commerce in importing gold is mentioned. *Ezion-geber* was a port at the upper end of the Gulf of Aqaba, giving access through the Red Sea to ports in South Arabia, India, and Africa.

7.3 2 Chr 5.13; Ps 136.1; 1 Chr 16.41
7.4 1 Kings 8.62.63
7.6 1 Chr 15.16-21; 2 Chr 5.12
7.7 1 Kings 8.64-66
7.8 1 Kings 8.65
7.9 Lev 23.36
7.10 1 Kings 8.66
7.11 1 Kings 9.1-9
7.12 Deut 12.5,11
7.13 2 Chr 6.26-28
7.14 2 Chr 6.27,30,37-39
7.15 2 Chr 6.40
7.16 1 Kings 9.3; 2 Chr 6.6; ver 12
7.17 1 Kings 9.4ff
7.18 2 Chr 6.16
7.19 Lev 26.14,33; Deut 28.15
7.20 Deut 29.28
7.21 Deut 29.24
8.1 1 Kings 9.1-28
8.5 1 Chr 7.24; 2 Chr 14.7

9.1-12 The Visit of the Queen of Sheba. *Sheba* is a variant spelling for Seba or Sabea, which was a commercially prosperous Semitic-speaking realm in the southwest part of the Arabian peninsula, where modern Yemen is. The account here is close to 1 Kings 10.1-13. In both records, Solomon's *wisdom* includes not only proverbial and theoretical insights, but also skill in governance in accordance with *justice and righteousness*. The *algum wood*, which in 1 Kings 10.11 is more accurately spelled *almug*, was prized for making musical instruments.
9.13-25 The Description of Solomon's Wealth. This report of the enormous wealth and trade activity of Solomon is based on 1 Kings 10.14-28, but mentions only Solomon's import of horses, not his trade in them as in 1 Kings 10.29. Only in 1 Chr 9.26 is the claim made that Solomon's kingdom extended over such a vast area: *from the Euphrates* [which is in central Syria] *to the land of the Philistines* [the Mediterranean coast of Palestine], *and to the border of Egypt*. Omitted by the Chronicler is the material from 1 Kings 11.1-40 which reports the huge numbers of Solomon's wives and concubines, his involvement in the worship of alien gods and goddesses, and God's bringing adversaries against him as punishment, culminating in the rebellion of the son of one of his servants, *Jeroboam*.

who were not of Israel, [8]from their descendants who were still left in the land, whom the people of Israel had not destroyed—these Solomon conscripted for forced labor, as is still the case today. [9]But of the people of Israel Solomon made no slaves for his work; they were soldiers, and his officers, the commanders of his chariotry and cavalry. [10]These were the chief officers of King Solomon, two hundred fifty of them, who exercised authority over the people.

11 Solomon brought Pharaoh's daughter from the city of David to the house that he had built for her, for he said, "My wife shall not live in the house of King David of Israel, for the places to which the ark of the LORD has come are holy."

12 Then Solomon offered up burnt offerings to the LORD on the altar of the LORD that he had built in front of the vestibule, [13]as the duty of each day required, offering according to the commandment of Moses for the sabbaths, the new moons, and the three annual festivals—the festival of unleavened bread, the festival of weeks, and the festival of booths. [14]According to the ordinance of his father David, he appointed the divisions of the priests for their service, and the Levites for their offices of praise and ministry alongside the priests as the duty of each day required, and the gatekeepers in their divisions for the several gates; for so David the man of God had commanded. [15]They did not turn away from what the king had commanded the priests and Levites regarding anything at all, or regarding the treasuries.

16 Thus all the work of Solomon was accomplished from[p] the day the foundation of the house of the LORD was laid until the house of the LORD was finished completely.

17 Then Solomon went to Ezion-geber and Eloth on the shore of the sea, in the land of Edom. [18]Huram sent him, in the care of his servants, ships and servants familiar with the sea. They went to Ophir, together with the servants of Solomon, and imported from there four hundred fifty talents of gold and brought it to King Solomon.

Visit of the Queen of Sheba

9 When the queen of Sheba heard of the fame of Solomon, she came to Jerusalem to test him with hard questions, having a very great retinue and camels bearing spices and very much gold and precious stones. When she came to Solomon, she discussed with him all that was on her mind. [2]Solomon answered all her questions; there was nothing hidden from Solomon that he could not explain to her. [3]When the queen of Sheba had observed the wisdom of Solomon, the house that he had built, [4]the food of his table, the seating of his officials, and the attendance of his servants, and their clothing, his valets, and their clothing, and his burnt offerings[q] that he offered at the house of the LORD, there was no more spirit left in her.

5 So she said to the king, "The report was true that I heard in my own land of your accomplishments and of your wisdom, [6]but I did not believe the[r] reports until I came and my own eyes saw it. Not even half of the greatness of your wisdom had been told to me; you far surpass the report that I had heard. [7]Happy are your people! Happy are these your servants, who continually attend you and hear your wisdom! [8]Blessed be the LORD your God, who has delighted in you and set you on his throne as king for the LORD your God. Because your God loved Israel and would establish them forever, he has made you king over them, that you may execute justice and righteousness." [9]Then she gave the king one hundred twenty talents of gold, a very great quantity of spices, and precious stones: there were no spices such as those that the queen of Sheba gave to King Solomon.

10 Moreover the servants of Huram and the servants of Solomon who brought gold from Ophir brought algum wood and precious stones. [11]From the algum wood, the king made steps[s] for the house of the LORD and for the king's house, lyres also and harps for the singers; there never was seen the like of them before in the land of Judah.

12 Meanwhile King Solomon granted the queen of Sheba every desire that she expressed, well beyond what she had brought to the king. Then she returned to her own land, with her servants.

Solomon's Great Wealth

13 The weight of gold that came to Solomon in one year was six hundred sixty-six talents of gold, [14]besides that which the traders and merchants brought; and all the kings of Arabia and the governors of the

[p] Gk Syr Vg: Heb *to* [q] Gk Syr Vg 1 Kings 10.5: Heb *ascent* [r] Heb *their* [s] Gk Vg: Meaning of Heb uncertain

8.8 1 Kings 4.6; 9.21
8.11 1 Kings 3.1; 7.8
8.12 2 Chr 4.1
8.13 Ex 29.38; Num 28.3; Ex 23.14-17
8.14 1 Chr 24.1; 25.1; 26.1; Neh 12.24,36
8.17 1 Kings 9.26
8.18 1 Kings 9.27; 2 Chr 9.10,13
9.1 1 Kings 10.1-13; Mt 12.42; Lk 11.31
9.3 1 Kings 5.12
9.5 1 Kings 10.6
9.8 1 Chr 28.5; 29.23; 2 Chr 2.11
9.9 1 Kings 10.10
9.10 2 Chr 8.18
9.13 1 Kings 10.14-28

9.18 1 Kings 10.18 · **9.19** 1 Kings 10.20 · **9.21** 2 Chr 20.36,37 · **9.22** 2 Chr 1.12; 1 Kings 3.13 · **9.25** 1 Kings 4.26; 10.26; 2 Chr 1.14 · **9.26** 1 Kings 4.21; Ps 72.8 · **9.27** 1 Kings 10.27; 2 Chr 1.15 · **9.28** 1 Kings 10.28; 2 Chr 1.16 · **9.29** 1 Kings 11.41; 1 Chr 29.29 · **9.30** 1 Kings 11.42,43 · **9.31** 1 Kings 2.10 · **10.1** 1 Kings 12.1-20 · **10.2** 1 Kings 11.40 · **10.6** 1 Kings 12.6 · **10.9** 1 Kings 12.9 · **10.12** ver 5 · **10.15** 1 Kings 12.15.24; 2 Chr 25.16-20; 1 Kings 11.29

land brought gold and silver to Solomon.
15 King Solomon made two hundred large
shields of beaten gold; six hundred shekels
of beaten gold went into each large shield.
16 He made three hundred shields of beaten
gold; three hundred shekels of gold went
into each shield; and the king put them in
the House of the Forest of Lebanon. 17 The
king also made a great ivory throne, and
overlaid it with pure gold. 18 The throne had
six steps and a footstool of gold, which were
attached to the throne, and on each side of
the seat were arm rests and two lions standing beside the arm rests, 19 while twelve
lions were standing, one on each end of a
step on the six steps. The like of it was never
made in any kingdom. 20 All King Solomon's
drinking vessels were of gold, and all the
vessels of the House of the Forest of Lebanon were of pure gold; silver was not considered as anything in the days of Solomon.
21 For the king's ships went to Tarshish with
the servants of Huram; once every three
years the ships of Tarshish used to come
bringing gold, silver, ivory, apes, and
peacocks.[t]
22 Thus King Solomon excelled all the
kings of the earth in riches and in wisdom.
23 All the kings of the earth sought the
presence of Solomon to hear his wisdom,
which God had put into his mind. 24 Every
one of them brought a present, objects of
silver and gold, garments, weaponry, spices,
horses, and mules, so much year by year.
25 Solomon had four thousand stalls for horses
and chariots, and twelve thousand horses,
which he stationed in the chariot cities and
with the king in Jerusalem. 26 He ruled over
all the kings from the Euphrates to the land
of the Philistines, and to the border of Egypt.
27 The king made silver as common in Jerusalem as stone, and cedar as plentiful as the
sycamore of the Shephelah. 28 Horses were
imported for Solomon from Egypt and from
all lands.

Death of Solomon

29 Now the rest of the acts of Solomon,
from first to last, are they not written in the
history of the prophet Nathan, and in the
prophecy of Ahijah the Shilonite, and in the
visions of the seer Iddo concerning Jeroboam son of Nebat? 30 Solomon reigned in
Jerusalem over all Israel forty years. 31 Solomon slept with his ancestors and was
buried in the city of his father David; and
his son Rehoboam succeeded him.

The Revolt against Rehoboam

10 Rehoboam went to Shechem, for
all Israel had come to Shechem to
make him king. 2 When Jeroboam son of
Nebat heard of it (for he was in Egypt,
where he had fled from King Solomon),
then Jeroboam returned from Egypt. 3 They
sent and called him; and Jeroboam and all
Israel came and said to Rehoboam, 4 "Your
father made our yoke heavy. Now therefore
lighten the hard service of your father and
his heavy yoke that he placed on us, and
we will serve you." 5 He said to them, "Come
to me again in three days." So the people
went away.
6 Then King Rehoboam took counsel with
the older men who had attended his father
Solomon while he was still alive, saying,
"How do you advise me to answer this
people?" 7 They answered him, "If you will
be kind to this people and please them, and
speak good words to them, then they will
be your servants forever." 8 But he rejected
the advice that the older men gave him,
and consulted the young men who had
grown up with him and now attended him.
9 He said to them, "What do you advise that
we answer this people who have said to me,
'Lighten the yoke that your father put on
us'?" 10 The young men who had grown up
with him said to him, "Thus should you
speak to the people who said to you, 'Your
father made our yoke heavy, but you must
lighten it for us'; tell them, 'My little finger
is thicker than my father's loins. 11 Now,
whereas my father laid on you a heavy
yoke, I will add to your yoke. My father
disciplined you with whips, but I will discipline you with scorpions.' "
12 So Jeroboam and all the people came
to Rehoboam the third day, as the king had
said, "Come to me again the third day."
13 The king answered them harshly. King
Rehoboam rejected the advice of the older
men; 14 he spoke to them in accordance with
the advice of the young men, "My father
made your yoke heavy, but I will add to it;
my father disciplined you with whips, but
I will discipline you with scorpions." 15 So
the king did not listen to the people, because
it was a turn of affairs brought about by
God so that the LORD might fulfill his word,

[t] Or *baboons*

9.29-31 The Death of Solomon. The reported sources for the life of Solomon do not include the *Book of the Acts of Solomon*, as in 1 Kings 11.41, but are rather records said to have been kept by prophets and seers: (1) *Nathan*, who in 2 Sam 7 predicts David's ascent to the throne and Solomon's building the temple of the LORD, (2) *Ahijah*, whose symbolic act of tearing his garment in twelve pieces predicted the partition of Israel under Jeroboam; 1 Kings 11.29-39, and (3) *Iddo the seer*, otherwise unknown, but one of those whose visions were considered by the rulers to be indicative of the intentions of Israel's God (2 Sam 24.11; 1 Chr 21.9; 29.29). Solomon's successor on the throne was his son, *Rehoboam*, born of Naamah, an Ammonite princess (1 Kings 14.31).
10.1-25.28 The Revolt against Rehoboam and the Division between Israel and Judah. From this point on the Chronicler is interested in the destiny of Judah, with only occasional pejorative references to the developments in Israel, the federated northern tribes based at Shechem.
10.1-19 Rehoboam and Jeroboam compete for the throne of Israel, with the resultant partition of the nation. The account here is based on 1 Kings 12.1-19. In spite of the centrality of Jerusalem for David and Solomon as the seat of royal power and of God's presence in the temple, Rehoboam went to Shechem, the traditional center of Israel's covenant with Israel (Gen 33.18-20; Josh 24) to make public his claim to the throne of Israel. Rallying behind the renegade *Jeroboam*, newly returned from exile in Egypt to escape from Solomon (1 Kings 11.26-40), *all Israel* accepted him as leader, joining in his challenge to the rule of the Davidic house, now taken by Rehoboam, who promised a sterner rule than that of his father, Solomon (10.6-11). Reference is made to Ahijah's prediction of the division of Israel (10.15) even though the report of that incident (1 Kings 11.29-39) was omitted by the Chronicler. Also missing is 1 Kings 12.20, which notes that only one tribe of Israel – Judah – sided with Rehoboam.

11.1-17 The struggle to redefine Israel is evident in the account of the fortification and militarization of the cities of Judah, as shown by the phrase, *all Israel in Judah and Benjamin*, which contrasts with 1 Kings 12.21-24, where Israel is equated with the northern tribes. There is no parallel in 1 Kings to 11.5-12, where the resourcefulness and security of *Judah and Benjamin* are sketched. Similarly without parallel is the report in 11.13-17 of the support of the priests and Levites for Judah, to which they had fled after *Jeroboam* began to force them into practices contrary to the Law of Moses. They find *Jerusalem* to be the place where they can obey the LORD, and their coming there helps to solidify the support for Rehoboam. **11.18-22** Curiously there is no parallel in 1 Kings for the account of Rehoboam's gathering many wives. The Chronicler omitted the similar story of Solomon's many wives and concubines, and is perhaps trying to shift this tradition to a less worthy ruler of Israel, Rehoboam, who is credited with wise and effective administration of his realm, however. **12.1-16** Egypt's Attack on Judah. Because of Rehoboam's abandonment of *the law of the LORD*, a huge Egyptian army invaded Judah, but in response to the penitence of the king and his officers, *King Shishak* did not dominate the people, but was content to carry off treasures from the temple and the royal house. This account builds on and modifies 1 Kings 14.21-31. The assertion that it was only *in Jerusalem* that God chose to *put his name* is a direct refutation of Israel's claim to his presence in their northern shrines. The final judgment on Rehoboam is that he was *evil*. Reference to the records of *the prophets* in 12.15 recalls 9.29, but there is no parallel mention of them in Kings.

which he had spoken by Ahijah the Shilonite to Jeroboam son of Nebat.

16 When all Israel saw that the king would not listen to them, the people answered the king,

"What share do we have in David?
We have no inheritance in the son of Jesse.
Each of you to your tents, O Israel!
Look now to your own house, O David."

So all Israel departed to their tents. [17]But Rehoboam reigned over the people of Israel who were living in the cities of Judah. [18]When King Rehoboam sent Hadoram, who was taskmaster over the forced labor, the people of Israel stoned him to death. King Rehoboam hurriedly mounted his chariot to flee to Jerusalem. [19]So Israel has been in rebellion against the house of David to this day.

Judah and Benjamin Fortified

11 When Rehoboam came to Jerusalem, he assembled one hundred eighty thousand chosen troops of the house of Judah and Benjamin to fight against Israel, to restore the kingdom to Rehoboam. [2]But the word of the LORD came to Shemaiah the man of God: [3]Say to King Rehoboam of Judah, son of Solomon, and to all Israel in Judah and Benjamin, [4]"Thus says the LORD: You shall not go up or fight against your kindred. Let everyone return home, for this thing is from me." So they heeded the word of the LORD and turned back from the expedition against Jeroboam.

5 Rehoboam resided in Jerusalem, and he built cities for defense in Judah. [6]He built up Bethlehem, Etam, Tekoa, [7]Beth-zur, Soco, Adullam, [8]Gath, Mareshah, Ziph, [9]Adoraim, Lachish, Azekah, [10]Zorah, Aijalon, and Hebron, fortified cities that are in Judah and in Benjamin. [11]He made the fortresses strong, and put commanders in them, and stores of food, oil, and wine. [12]He also put large shields and spears in all the cities, and made them very strong. So he held Judah and Benjamin.

Priests and Levites Support Rehoboam

13 The priests and the Levites who were in all Israel presented themselves to him from all their territories. [14]The Levites had left their common lands and their holdings and had come to Judah and Jerusalem, because Jeroboam and his sons had prevented them from serving as priests of the LORD, [15]and had appointed his own priests for the high places, and for the goat-demons, and for the calves that he had made. [16]Those who had set their hearts to seek the LORD God of Israel came after them from all the tribes of Israel to Jerusalem to sacrifice to the LORD, the God of their ancestors. [17]They strengthened the kingdom of Judah, and for three years they made Rehoboam son of Solomon secure, for they walked for three years in the way of David and Solomon.

Rehoboam's Marriages

18 Rehoboam took as his wife Mahalath daughter of Jerimoth son of David, and of Abihail daughter of Eliab son of Jesse. [19]She bore him sons: Jeush, Shemariah, and Zaham. [20]After her he took Maacah daughter of Absalom, who bore him Abijah, Attai, Ziza, and Shelomith. [21]Rehoboam loved Maacah daughter of Absalom more than all his other wives and concubines (he took eighteen wives and sixty concubines, and became the father of twenty-eight sons and sixty daughters). [22]Rehoboam appointed Abijah son of Maacah as chief prince among his brothers, for he intended to make him king. [23]He dealt wisely, and distributed some of his sons through all the districts of Judah and Benjamin, in all the fortified cities; he gave them abundant provisions, and found many wives for them.

Egypt Attacks Judah

12 When the rule of Rehoboam was established and he grew strong, he abandoned the law of the LORD, he and all Israel with him. [2]In the fifth year of King Rehoboam, because they had been unfaithful to the LORD, King Shishak of Egypt came up against Jerusalem [3]with twelve hundred chariots and sixty thousand cavalry. A countless army came with him from Egypt—Libyans, Sukkiim, and Ethiopians.[u] [4]He took the fortified cities of Judah and came as far as Jerusalem. [5]Then the prophet Shemaiah came to Rehoboam and to the officers of Judah, who had gathered at Jerusalem because of Shishak, and said to them, "Thus says the LORD: You abandoned me, so I have

[u] Or *Nubians*; Heb *Cushites*

10.16 2 Sam 20.1; ver 19
10.19 1 Kings 12.19
11.1 1 Kings 12.21-24
11.2 2 Chr 12.15
11.4 2 Chr 10.15
11.14 Num 35.2-5; 2 Chr 13.9
11.15 2 Chr 10.15
11.16 2 Chr 15.9
11.17 2 Chr 12.1
11.18 1 Sam 16.6
11.21 Deut 17.17
11.22 Deut 21.15-17
12.1 2 Chr 11.17; 1 Kings 14.22-24
12.2 1 Kings 14.24,25; 11.40
12.3 2 Chr 16.8
12.5 2 Chr 11.2; 15.2; Deut 28.15

12.6 Ex 9.27; Dan 9.14
12.7 1 Kings 21.29
12.8 Deut 28.47,48
12.9 1 Kings 14.25,26; 2 Chr 9.15,16
12.12 2 Chr 19.3
12.13 1 Kings 14.21
12.14 2 Chr 19.3
12.15 1 Kings 14.29,30; 2 Chr 9.29
12.16 1 Kings 14.31; 2 Chr 11.20
13.1 1 Kings 15.1,2
13.2 2 Chr 11.20; 1 Kings 15.7
13.4 Josh 18.22
13.5 2 Sam 7.12,13,16; Num 18.19
13.6 1 Kings 11.26
13.8 1 Kings 12.28; 2 Chr 11.15
13.9 2 Chr 11.14; Ex 29.35; Jer 2.11; 5.7
13.11 2 Chr 2.4; Lev 24.5-9
13.12 Num 10.8,9; Acts 5.39
13.14 2 Chr 14.11
13.15 2 Chr 14.12

abandoned you to the hand of Shishak." 6 Then the officers of Israel and the king humbled themselves and said, "The LORD is in the right." 7 When the LORD saw that they humbled themselves, the word of the LORD came to Shemaiah, saying: "They have humbled themselves; I will not destroy them, but I will grant them some deliverance, and my wrath shall not be poured out on Jerusalem by the hand of Shishak. 8 Nevertheless they shall be his servants, so that they may know the difference between serving me and serving the kingdoms of other lands."

9 So King Shishak of Egypt came up against Jerusalem; he took away the treasures of the house of the LORD and the treasures of the king's house; he took everything. He also took away the shields of gold that Solomon had made; 10 but King Rehoboam made in place of them shields of bronze, and committed them to the hands of the officers of the guard, who kept the door of the king's house. 11 Whenever the king went into the house of the LORD, the guard would come along bearing them, and would then bring them back to the guardroom. 12 Because he humbled himself the wrath of the LORD turned from him, so as not to destroy them completely; moreover, conditions were good in Judah.

Death of Rehoboam

13 So King Rehoboam established himself in Jerusalem and reigned. Rehoboam was forty-one years old when he began to reign; he reigned seventeen years in Jerusalem, the city that the LORD had chosen out of all the tribes of Israel to put his name there. His mother's name was Naamah the Ammonite. 14 He did evil, for he did not set his heart to seek the LORD.

15 Now the acts of Rehoboam, from first to last, are they not written in the records of the prophet Shemaiah and of the seer Iddo, recorded by genealogy? There were continual wars between Rehoboam and Jeroboam. 16 Rehoboam slept with his ancestors and was buried in the city of David; and his son Abijah succeeded him.

Abijah Reigns over Judah

13 In the eighteenth year of King Jeroboam, Abijah began to reign over Judah. 2 He reigned for three years in Jerusalem. His mother's name was Micaiah daughter of Uriel of Gibeah.

Now there was war between Abijah and Jeroboam. 3 Abijah engaged in battle, having an army of valiant warriors, four hundred thousand picked men; and Jeroboam drew up his line of battle against him with eight hundred thousand picked mighty warriors. 4 Then Abijah stood on the slope of Mount Zemaraim that is in the hill country of Ephraim, and said, "Listen to me, Jeroboam and all Israel! 5 Do you not know that the LORD God of Israel gave the kingship over Israel forever to David and his sons by a covenant of salt? 6 Yet Jeroboam son of Nebat, a servant of Solomon son of David, rose up and rebelled against his lord; 7 and certain worthless scoundrels gathered around him and defied Rehoboam son of Solomon, when Rehoboam was young and irresolute and could not withstand them.

8 "And now you think that you can withstand the kingdom of the LORD in the hand of the sons of David, because you are a great multitude and have with you the golden calves that Jeroboam made as gods for you. 9 Have you not driven out the priests of the LORD, the descendants of Aaron, and the Levites, and made priests for yourselves like the peoples of other lands? Whoever comes to be consecrated with a young bull or seven rams becomes a priest of what are no gods. 10 But as for us, the LORD is our God, and we have not abandoned him. We have priests ministering to the LORD who are descendants of Aaron, and Levites for their service. 11 They offer to the LORD every morning and every evening burnt offerings and fragrant incense, set out the rows of bread on the table of pure gold, and care for the golden lampstand so that its lamps may burn every evening; for we keep the charge of the LORD our God, but you have abandoned him. 12 See, God is with us at our head, and his priests have their battle trumpets to sound the call to battle against you. O Israelites, do not fight against the LORD, the God of your ancestors; for you cannot succeed."

13 Jeroboam had sent an ambush around to come on them from behind; thus his troops[v] were in front of Judah, and the ambush was behind them. 14 When Judah turned, the battle was in front of them and behind them. They cried out to the LORD, and the priests blew the trumpets. 15 Then

[v] Heb *they*

13.1-22 The Reign of Abijah over Judah. *Gibeah*, the place of origin of his mother, *Micaiah*, was within the boundaries of Judah. When war broke out between Judah and the northern tribes of Israel under *Jeroboam*, *Abijah* positioned his troops in *the hill country of Ephraim*, which was a buffer zone between the northern and southern tribes. He articulated the claim of exclusive and perpetual title to the kingship of God's people for the Davidic line. Israel's expulsion of the true *priests of the LORD...and the Levites*, as well as the adopting of worship of fertility gods by the northern tribes, has disqualified them from their claim to be God's people. This charge is seen to be confirmed when, in spite of encirclement by Israel's armies, the forces of Judah triumph over Israel, *with great slaughter*. Captured and occupied by Judah are important cities north of Jerusalem: *Bethel, Jeshanah, and Ephron*, with their surrounding territory. As a result, *Jeroboam* did not recover his physical or royal power, *and died*. Again, the records of *the prophet Iddo* are indicated as the source for these accounts.

14.1-16.14 The Reign of Asa over Judah. This account is greatly expanded from its source in 1 Kings 15.9-24. *Asa* is portrayed as an effective reformer, who restored the purity of the worship of Yahweh throughout his realm, while strengthening the defenses of the cities. The contrast between the size of Asa's army and that of the invading horde of *Zerah the Ethiopian* – 300,000 against 1,000,000 – is more symbolic than numerically precise, in that it makes more vivid the LORD's action in behalf of his people. *Mareshah*, where the armies met in battle, is southwest of Jerusalem in the coastal hills, east of Ashkelon. None of the enemy survived against *the LORD and his army*.

15.1-19 Azariah, later identified as a prophet (15.8), advised Asa to give heed to the *teaching priest* and to the *Law*, so that God would continue to preserve and enrich the lives of his people during the time of threat and conflict through which they were passing. Asa heeded the advice, purging the land of idol-worship, rallying to his support people from several tribes (Judah and Benjamin, Ephraim, Manasseh, Simeon), threatening them with death if they did not return to the pure worship of the LORD, and even expelling his own mother from her royal status because of her devotion to the fertility goddess, *Asherah*. Even so, the *high places* where the idolatrous practices were carried out survived.

the people of Judah raised the battle shout. And when the people of Judah shouted, God defeated Jeroboam and all Israel before Abijah and Judah. 16 The Israelites fled before Judah, and God gave them into their hands. 17 Abijah and his army defeated them with great slaughter; five hundred thousand picked men of Israel fell slain. 18 Thus the Israelites were subdued at that time, and the people of Judah prevailed, because they relied on the LORD, the God of their ancestors. 19 Abijah pursued Jeroboam, and took cities from him: Bethel with its villages and Jeshanah with its villages and Ephron[w] with its villages. 20 Jeroboam did not recover his power in the days of Abijah; the LORD struck him down, and he died. 21 But Abijah grew strong. He took fourteen wives, and became the father of twenty-two sons and sixteen daughters. 22 The rest of the acts of Abijah, his behavior and his deeds, are written in the story of the prophet Iddo.

Asa Reigns

14[x] So Abijah slept with his ancestors, and they buried him in the city of David. His son Asa succeeded him. In his days the land had rest for ten years. 2[y] Asa did what was good and right in the sight of the LORD his God. 3 He took away the foreign altars and the high places, broke down the pillars, hewed down the sacred poles,[z] 4 and commanded Judah to seek the LORD, the God of their ancestors, and to keep the law and the commandment. 5 He also removed from all the cities of Judah the high places and the incense altars. And the kingdom had rest under him. 6 He built fortified cities in Judah while the land had rest. He had no war in those years, for the LORD gave him peace. 7 He said to Judah, "Let us build these cities, and surround them with walls and towers, gates and bars; the land is still ours because we have sought the LORD our God; we have sought him, and he has given us peace on every side." So they built and prospered. 8 Asa had an army of three hundred thousand from Judah, armed with large shields and spears, and two hundred eighty thousand troops from Benjamin who carried shields and drew bows; all these were mighty warriors.

Ethiopian Invasion Repulsed

9 Zerah the Ethiopian[a] came out against them with an army of a million men and three hundred chariots, and came as far as Mareshah. 10 Asa went out to meet him, and they drew up their lines of battle in the valley of Zephathah at Mareshah. 11 Asa cried to the LORD his God, "O LORD, there is no difference for you between helping the mighty and the weak. Help us, O LORD our God, for we rely on you, and in your name we have come against this multitude. O LORD, you are our God; let no mortal prevail against you." 12 So the LORD defeated the Ethiopians[b] before Asa and before Judah, and the Ethiopians[b] fled. 13 Asa and the army with him pursued them as far as Gerar, and the Ethiopians[b] fell until no one remained alive; for they were broken before the LORD and his army. The people of Judah[c] carried away a great quantity of booty. 14 They defeated all the cities around Gerar, for the fear of the LORD was on them. They plundered all the cities; for there was much plunder in them. 15 They also attacked the tents of those who had livestock,[d] and carried away sheep and goats in abundance, and camels. Then they returned to Jerusalem.

15 The spirit of God came upon Azariah son of Oded. 2 He went out to meet Asa and said to him, "Hear me, Asa, and all Judah and Benjamin: The LORD is with you, while you are with him. If you seek him, he will be found by you, but if you abandon him, he will abandon you. 3 For a long time Israel was without the true God, and without a teaching priest, and without law; 4 but when in their distress they turned to the LORD, the God of Israel, and sought him, he was found by them. 5 In those times it was not safe for anyone to go or come, for great disturbances afflicted all the inhabitants of the lands. 6 They were broken in pieces, nation against nation and city against city, for God troubled them with every sort of distress. 7 But you, take courage! Do not let your hands be weak, for your work shall be rewarded."

8 When Asa heard these words, the prophecy of Azariah son of Oded,[e] he took courage, and put away the abominable idols from all the land of Judah and Benjamin and from the towns that he had taken in the hill country of Ephraim. He repaired the

[w] Another reading is *Ephrain* [x] Ch 13.23 in Heb [y] Ch 14.1 in Heb [z] Heb *Asherim* [a] Or *Nubian*; Heb *Cushite* [b] Or *Nubians*; Heb *Cushites* [c] Heb *They* [d] Meaning of Heb uncertain [e] Compare Syr Vg: Heb *the prophecy, the prophet Obed*

13.16 2 Chr 16.8
13.18 1 Chr 5.20; 2 Chr 14.11; Ps 22.5
13.20 1 Sam 25.38; 1 Kings 14.20
13.22 2 Chr 12.15
14.1 1 Kings 15.8
14.3 Deut 7.5; 1 Kings 15.12-14; Ex 34.13
14.5 2 Chr 34.4,7
14.6 2 Chr 15.15
14.9 2 Chr 16.8; 11.8
14.11 2 Chr 13.14,18; 1 Sam 14.6; 17.45
14.12 2 Chr 13.15
14.13 Gen 10.19
14.14 Gen 35.5; 2 Chr 17.10
15.1 Num 24.2; 2 Chr 20.14; 24.20
15.2 Jas 4.8; ver 4,15; 2 Chr 24.20
15.3 Hos 3.4; Lev 10.11; 2 Chr 17.9
15.4 Deut 4.29
15.5 Judg 5.6
15.6 Mt 24.7
15.7 Josh 1.7,9
15.8 2 Chr 13.19

altar of the LORD that was in front of the
vestibule of the house of the LORD.[f] [9]He
gathered all Judah and Benjamin, and those
from Ephraim, Manasseh, and Simeon who
were residing as aliens with them, for great
numbers had deserted to him from Israel
when they saw that the LORD his God was
with him. [10]They were gathered at Jerusalem in the third month of the fifteenth year
of the reign of Asa. [11]They sacrificed to the
LORD on that day, from the booty that they
had brought, seven hundred oxen and seven
thousand sheep. [12]They entered into a covenant to seek the LORD, the God of their
ancestors, with all their heart and with all
their soul. [13]Whoever would not seek the
LORD, the God of Israel, should be put to
death, whether young or old, man or woman.
[14]They took an oath to the LORD with a loud
voice, and with shouting, and with trumpets, and with horns. [15]All Judah rejoiced
over the oath; for they had sworn with all
their heart, and had sought him with their
whole desire, and he was found by them,
and the LORD gave them rest all around.
16 King Asa even removed his mother
Maacah from being queen mother because
she had made an abominable image for
Asherah. Asa cut down her image, crushed
it, and burned it at the Wadi Kidron. [17]But
the high places were not taken out of Israel.
Nevertheless the heart of Asa was true all
his days. [18]He brought into the house of
God the votive gifts of his father and his
own votive gifts—silver, gold, and utensils.
[19]And there was no more war until the
thirty-fifth year of the reign of Asa.

Alliance with Aram Condemned

16 In the thirty-sixth year of the reign
of Asa, King Baasha of Israel went
up against Judah, and built Ramah, to
prevent anyone from going out or coming
into the territory of[g] King Asa of Judah.
[2]Then Asa took silver and gold from the
treasures of the house of the LORD and the
king's house, and sent them to King Ben-
hadad of Aram, who resided in Damascus,
saying, [3]"Let there be an alliance between
me and you, like that between my father
and your father; I am sending to you silver
and gold; go, break your alliance with King
Baasha of Israel, so that he may withdraw
from me." [4]Ben-hadad listened to King Asa,
and sent the commanders of his armies
against the cities of Israel. They conquered
Ijon, Dan, Abel-maim, and all the store-
cities of Naphtali. [5]When Baasha heard of
it, he stopped building Ramah, and let his
work cease. [6]Then King Asa brought all
Judah, and they carried away the stones of
Ramah and its timber, with which Baasha
had been building, and with them he built
up Geba and Mizpah.
7 At that time the seer Hanani came to
King Asa of Judah, and said to him, "Because
you relied on the king of Aram, and did not
rely on the LORD your God, the army of the
king of Aram has escaped you. [8]Were not
the Ethiopians[h] and the Libyans a huge army
with exceedingly many chariots and cavalry?
Yet because you relied on the LORD, he gave
them into your hand. [9]For the eyes of the
LORD range throughout the entire earth, to
strengthen those whose heart is true to him.
You have done foolishly in this; for from now
on you will have wars." [10]Then Asa was
angry with the seer, and put him in the
stocks, in prison, for he was in a rage with
him because of this. And Asa inflicted cru-
elties on some of the people at the same time.

Asa's Disease and Death

11 The acts of Asa, from first to last, are
written in the Book of the Kings of Judah
and Israel. [12]In the thirty-ninth year of his
reign Asa was diseased in his feet, and his
disease became severe; yet even in his disease he did not seek the LORD, but sought
help from physicians. [13]Then Asa slept with
his ancestors, dying in the forty-first year of
his reign. [14]They buried him in the tomb
that he had hewn out for himself in the city
of David. They laid him on a bier that had
been filled with various kinds of spices prepared by the perfumer's art; and they made
a very great fire in his honor.

Jehoshaphat's Reign

17 His son Jehoshaphat succeeded him,
and strengthened himself against
Israel. [2]He placed forces in all the fortified
cities of Judah, and set garrisons in the land
of Judah, and in the cities of Ephraim that
his father Asa had taken. [3]The LORD was
with Jehoshaphat, because he walked in the
earlier ways of his father;[i] he did not seek
the Baals, [4]but sought the God of his father

[f] Heb *the vestibule of the LORD* [g] Heb lacks *the territory of* [h] Or *Nubians*; Heb *Cushites* [i] Another reading is *his father David*

15.9 2 Chr 11.16
15.11 2 Chr 14.13-15
15.12 2 Chr 23.16; 34.31
15.13 Ex 22.20; Deut 13.5,9,15
15.15 ver 2; 2 Chr 14.7
15.16 1 Kings 15.13-15; Ex 34.13; 2 Chr 14.2-5
16.1 1 Kings 15.17-22
16.4 1 Kings 15.18,20
16.7 2 Chr 19.2; 14.11; 32.7,8
16.8 2 Chr 14.9; 12.3
16.9 Prov 15.3; Zech 4.10; 1 Sam 13.13
16.11 1 Kings 15.23
16.12 Jer 17.5
16.13 1 Kings 15.24
16.14 Gen 50.2; Jn 19.39,40; 2 Chr 21.19; Jer 34.5
17.1 1 Kings 15.24
17.2 2 Chr 15.8
17.4 1 Kings 12.28

16.1-14 Asa's Final, Fatal Error: Alliance with Syria. Adapting the account in 1 Kings 15.17-22 (including the changing of the date of the incident; *cf.* 1 Kings 16.15 with 2 Chr 16.1), the Chonicler sought to counter the threat to Judah's territory represented by Israel's *King Baasha* building a fortress city only eight miles north of Jerusalem at *Ramah*. Offering Ben-hadad of Aram (Syria) a huge bribe to break his treaty with Israel, Asa persuaded Syria to attack Israel, which it did. Learning of the loss of cities in his northern regions, the *Ramah* project was abandoned. But *the seer Hanani* warned Asa of God's judgment on him and his people for having relied on a human ally rather than *on the LORD*. Divine judgment on Asa took the form of ailing feet, which had fatal consequences for him – a detail expanded from the account in 1 Kings 15.23-24. At this point the Chronicler leaves the Books of Kings, with their accounts of the reigns of the kings of Israel and the roles of Elijah and Elisha, returning at 1 Kings 22.4 = 1 Chr 18.3.

17.1-20.37 The Reign of Jehoshaphat. *Jehoshaphat*, whose name means "Jehovah [Yahweh] sets things right," established military control and *walked in the commandments* of the LORD, as his father had done, avoiding the idolatrous and disobedient *ways of Israel*, the tribes to the north. Further, Jehoshaphat sent *officials* and *Levites* throughout Judah to teach the people, anticipating the later role of Ezra and Nehemiah in instructing the populace in Israel after their return from the Babylonian exile in the sixth century. The favor of the king was courted by non-Israelite neighbors: *the Philistines and the Arabs*, who brought money and flocks. Again, the figures for the army are idealized, since they are given as more than 1,000,000.

18.1-3 The marital and military alliances of Jehoshaphat, king of Israel (869-850), result in a joint attack of Israel and Judah on *Ramoth-gilead*, in the hills east of the Jordan on the fluid border between Israel and Syria.
18.4-34 The Quest for Divine Approval of the Military Expedition. The *four hundred prophets of Israel* claim God is supporting the attack on *Ramoth-Gilead*, but *Micaiah*, one of Ahab's court prophets, at first agrees and then declares that the armies will be scattered, *like sheep without a shepherd*, and that *a lying spirit* is enticing Ahab through the prophets to take on this disastrous attack. Although he was imprisoned, *Micaiah* remained certain that defeat awaited the military enterprise. This passage is unique in 2 Chr, since it reports in detail activities in the northern kingdom of Israel (based on 1 Kings 22.5-35a), but its aim is to show that Israel rejected the true messengers of God and thereby came under disastrous judgment. Though in disguise, King Ahab is fatally wounded by a Syrian bowman and dies.

and walked in his commandments, and not
according to the ways of Israel. 5Therefore
the LORD established the kingdom in his
hand. All Judah brought tribute to
Jehoshaphat, and he had great riches and
honor. 6His heart was courageous in the
ways of the LORD; and furthermore he removed the high places and the sacred poles[j]
from Judah.
7 In the third year of his reign he sent
his officials, Ben-hail, Obadiah, Zechariah,
Nethanel, and Micaiah, to teach in the cities
of Judah. 8With them were the Levites,
Shemaiah, Nethaniah, Zebadiah, Asahel,
Shemiramoth, Jehonathan, Adonijah,
Tobijah, and Tob-adonijah; and with these
Levites, the priests Elishama and Jehoram.
9They taught in Judah, having the book of
the law of the LORD with them; they went
around through all the cities of Judah and
taught among the people.
10 The fear of the LORD fell on all the
kingdoms of the lands around Judah, and
they did not make war against Jehoshaphat.
11Some of the Philistines brought Jehoshaphat
presents, and silver for tribute; and the
Arabs also brought him seven thousand
seven hundred rams and seven thousand
seven hundred male goats. 12Jehoshaphat
grew steadily greater. He built fortresses and
storage cities in Judah. 13He carried out
great works in the cities of Judah. He had
soldiers, mighty warriors, in Jerusalem. 14This
was the muster of them by ancestral houses:
Of Judah, the commanders of the thousands:
Adnah the commander, with three hundred
thousand mighty warriors, 15and next to
him Jehohanan the commander, with two
hundred eighty thousand, 16and next to him
Amasiah son of Zichri, a volunteer for the
service of the LORD, with two hundred thousand mighty warriors. 17Of Benjamin: Eliada,
a mighty warrior, with two hundred thousand armed with bow and shield, 18and next
to him Jehozabad with one hundred eighty
thousand armed for war. 19These were in
the service of the king, besides those whom
the king had placed in the fortified cities
throughout all Judah.

Micaiah Predicts Failure

18 Now Jehoshaphat had great riches
and honor; and he made a mar-
riage alliance with Ahab. 2After some years
he went down to Ahab in Samaria. Ahab
slaughtered an abundance of sheep and
oxen for him and for the people who were
with him, and induced him to go up against
Ramoth-gilead. 3King Ahab of Israel said to
King Jehoshaphat of Judah, "Will you go
with me to Ramoth-gilead?" He answered
him, "I am with you, my people are your
people. We will be with you in the war."
4 But Jehoshaphat also said to the king
of Israel, "Inquire first for the word of the
LORD." 5Then the king of Israel gathered the
prophets together, four hundred of them,
and said to them, "Shall we go to battle
against Ramoth-gilead, or shall I refrain?"
They said, "Go up; for God will give it into
the hand of the king." 6But Jehoshaphat
said, "Is there no other prophet of the LORD
here of whom we may inquire?" 7The king
of Israel said to Jehoshaphat, "There is still
one other by whom we may inquire of the
LORD, Micaiah son of Imlah; but I hate him,
for he never prophesies anything favorable
about me, but only disaster." Jehoshaphat
said, "Let the king not say such a thing."
8Then the king of Israel summoned an officer and said, "Bring quickly Micaiah son
of Imlah." 9Now the king of Israel and King
Jehoshaphat of Judah were sitting on their
thrones, arrayed in their robes; and they
were sitting at the threshing floor at the
entrance of the gate of Samaria; and all the
prophets were prophesying before them.
10Zedekiah son of Chenaanah made for
himself horns of iron, and he said, "Thus
says the LORD: With these you shall gore the
Arameans until they are destroyed." 11All
the prophets were prophesying the same
and saying, "Go up to Ramoth-gilead and
triumph; the LORD will give it into the hand
of the king."
12 The messenger who had gone to
summon Micaiah said to him, "Look, the
words of the prophets with one accord are
favorable to the king; let your word be like
the word of one of them, and speak
favorably." 13But Micaiah said, "As the LORD
lives, whatever my God says, that I will
speak."
14 When he had come to the king, the
king said to him, "Micaiah, shall we go to
Ramoth-gilead to battle, or shall I refrain?"
He answered, "Go up and triumph; they
will be given into your hand." 15But the
king said to him, "How many times must
I make you swear to tell me nothing but the
truth in the name of the LORD?" 16Then

17.5 2 Chr 18.1
17.6 2 Chr 15.17
17.7 2 Chr 15.3
17.8 2 Chr 19.8
17.9 Deut 6.4-9
17.10 2 Chr 14.14
17.11 2 Chr 9.14
17.16 Judg 5.2,9; 1 Chr 29.9
18.1 2 Chr 17.5
18.2 1 Kings 22.2-35
18.4 1 Sam 23.2,4,9; 2 Sam 2.1
18.7 1 Kings 22.8
18.9 Ruth 4.1
18.11 2 Chr 22.5
18.13 Num 22.18-20,35
18.16 Num 27.17; Ezek 34.5-8

[j] Heb *Asherim*

18.20 Job 1.6
18.22 Job 12.16; Ezek 14.9
18.23 Jer 20.2; Mk 14.65; Acts 23.2
18.25 ver 8
18.26 2 Chr 16.10
18.27 Mic 1.9
18.31 2 Chr 13.14,15
18.33 1 Kings 22.34
19.2 1 Kings 16.1; Ps 139.21; 2 Chr 32.25
19.3 2 Chr 12.12,14; 17.6; Ezra 7.10
19.4 2 Chr 15.8-13
19.6 Deut 1.17
19.7 Gen 18.25; Deut 32.4; 10.17,18; Rom 2.11; Col 3.25
19.8 2 Chr 17.8,9
19.9 2 Sam 23.3
19.10 Deut 17.8; ver 2

Micaiah[k] said, "I saw all Israel scattered on
the mountains, like sheep without a shepherd; and the LORD said, 'These have no
master; let each one go home in peace.' "
17The king of Israel said to Jehoshaphat,
"Did I not tell you that he would not prophesy anything favorable about me, but only
disaster?"
18 Then Micaiah[k] said, "Therefore hear
the word of the LORD: I saw the LORD sitting
on his throne, with all the host of heaven
standing to the right and to the left of him.
19And the LORD said, 'Who will entice King
Ahab of Israel, so that he may go up and
fall at Ramoth-gilead?' Then one said one
thing, and another said another, 20until a
spirit came forward and stood before the
LORD, saying, 'I will entice him.' The LORD
asked him, 'How?' 21He replied, 'I will go
out and be a lying spirit in the mouth of
all his prophets.' Then the LORD[k] said, 'You
are to entice him, and you shall succeed; go
out and do it.' 22So you see, the LORD has
put a lying spirit in the mouth of these your
prophets; the LORD has decreed disaster for
you."
23 Then Zedekiah son of Chenaanah
came up to Micaiah, slapped him on the
cheek, and said, "Which way did the spirit
of the LORD pass from me to speak to you?"
24Micaiah replied, "You will find out on that
day when you go in to hide in an inner
chamber." 25The king of Israel then ordered,
"Take Micaiah, and return him to Amon
the governor of the city and to Joash the
king's son; 26and say, 'Thus says the king:
Put this fellow in prison, and feed him on
reduced rations of bread and water until I
return in peace.' " 27Micaiah said, "If you
return in peace, the LORD has not spoken by
me." And he said, "Hear, you peoples, all
of you!"

Defeat and Death of Ahab

28 So the king of Israel and King
Jehoshaphat of Judah went up to Ramoth-
gilead. 29The king of Israel said to Jehoshaphat,
"I will disguise myself and go into battle, but
you wear your robes." So the king of Israel
disguised himself, and they went into battle.
30Now the king of Aram had commanded
the captains of his chariots, "Fight with no
one small or great, but only with the king
of Israel." 31When the captains of the chariots saw Jehoshaphat, they said, "It is the
king of Israel." So they turned to fight
against him; and Jehoshaphat cried out, and
the LORD helped him. God drew them away
from him, 32for when the captains of the
chariots saw that it was not the king of
Israel, they turned back from pursuing him.
33But a certain man drew his bow and
unknowingly struck the king of Israel between the scale armor and the breastplate;
so he said to the driver of his chariot, "Turn
around, and carry me out of the battle, for
I am wounded." 34The battle grew hot that
day, and the king of Israel propped himself
up in his chariot facing the Arameans until
evening; then at sunset he died.
19 King Jehoshaphat of Judah returned
in safety to his house in Jerusalem.
2Jehu son of Hanani the seer went out to
meet him and said to King Jehoshaphat,
"Should you help the wicked and love those
who hate the LORD? Because of this, wrath
has gone out against you from the LORD.
3Nevertheless, some good is found in you,
for you destroyed the sacred poles[l] out of the
land, and have set your heart to seek God."

The Reforms of Jehoshaphat

4 Jehoshaphat resided at Jerusalem; then
he went out again among the people, from
Beer-sheba to the hill country of Ephraim,
and brought them back to the LORD, the God
of their ancestors. 5He appointed judges in
the land in all the fortified cities of Judah,
city by city, 6and said to the judges, "Consider what you are doing, for you judge not
on behalf of human beings but on the
LORD's behalf; he is with you in giving
judgment. 7Now, let the fear of the LORD be
upon you; take care what you do, for there
is no perversion of justice with the LORD our
God, or partiality, or taking of bribes."
8 Moreover in Jerusalem Jehoshaphat
appointed certain Levites and priests and
heads of families of Israel, to give judgment
for the LORD and to decide disputed cases.
They had their seat at Jerusalem. 9He charged
them: "This is how you shall act: in the fear
of the LORD, in faithfulness, and with your
whole heart; 10whenever a case comes to
you from your kindred who live in their
cities, concerning bloodshed, law or commandment, statutes or ordinances, then you
shall instruct them, so that they may not
incur guilt before the LORD and wrath may
not come on you and your kindred. Do so,

19.1-3 The reign of *Jehoshaphat* receives a mixed evaluation: in spite of his collaboration with wicked Israel, his organization of his people in terms of the law and under the guidance of *Levites, priests and heads of families* is commended.

[k] Heb *he* [l] Heb *Asheroth*

20.1-30 The Defeat of the Invaders of Judah from the East. The report of the invasion by tribes from east and south of the Dead Sea, *Moabites and Ammonites*, already taking shape at *En-gedi* (midway down on the western shore of the Dead Sea), led Judah to *seek help from the* LORD. In response to the prayer of *Jehoshaphat, Jahaziel, a Levite*, assures them of victory which God will accomplish without their direct action. *Ziz and Jeruel* were towns on the barren eastern side of the Judean hills as they slope down to the Dead Sea, while *Tekoa* overlooked the area from the crest of the ridge not far from Bethlehem. *The Kohathites* were the branch of the Levites responsible for handling the setting up and dismantling of the inner sanctuary of the LORD, the Holy of Holies (Num 4), when it was portable. *The Korahites* led the music in the temple, as well as serving as gatekeepers (1 Chr 9.19). *Mount Seir* was probably in the Arabah, the barren valley south of the Dead Sea extending down to the Gulf of Aqabah. As a result of the Lord's *ambush*, the invaders were destroyed, Judah claimed the booty, and the troops assembled with joy in *the Valley of Beracah* [blessing] in the wilderness area east of Hebron, before returning to Jerusalem.

and you will not incur guilt. 11See, Amariah the chief priest is over you in all matters of the LORD; and Zebadiah son of Ishmael, the governor of the house of Judah, in all the king's matters; and the Levites will serve you as officers. Deal courageously, and may the LORD be with the good!"

Invasion from the East

20 After this the Moabites and Ammonites, and with them some of the Meunites,[m] came against Jehoshaphat for battle. 2Messengers[n] came and told Jehoshaphat, "A great multitude is coming against you from Edom,[o] from beyond the sea; already they are at Hazazon-tamar" (that is, En-gedi). 3Jehoshaphat was afraid; he set himself to seek the LORD, and proclaimed a fast throughout all Judah. 4Judah assembled to seek help from the LORD; from all the towns of Judah they came to seek the LORD.

Jehoshaphat's Prayer and Victory

5 Jehoshaphat stood in the assembly of Judah and Jerusalem, in the house of the LORD, before the new court, 6and said, "O LORD, God of our ancestors, are you not God in heaven? Do you not rule over all the kingdoms of the nations? In your hand are power and might, so that no one is able to withstand you. 7Did you not, O our God, drive out the inhabitants of this land before your people Israel, and give it forever to the descendants of your friend Abraham? 8They have lived in it, and in it have built you a sanctuary for your name, saying, 9'If disaster comes upon us, the sword, judgment,[p] or pestilence, or famine, we will stand before this house, and before you, for your name is in this house, and cry to you in our distress, and you will hear and save.' 10See now, the people of Ammon, Moab, and Mount Seir, whom you would not let Israel invade when they came from the land of Egypt, and whom they avoided and did not destroy— 11they reward us by coming to drive us out of your possession that you have given us to inherit. 12O our God, will you not execute judgment upon them? For we are powerless against this great multitude that is coming against us. We do not know what to do, but our eyes are on you."

13 Meanwhile all Judah stood before the LORD, with their little ones, their wives, and their children. 14Then the spirit of the LORD came upon Jahaziel son of Zechariah, son of Benaiah, son of Jeiel, son of Mattaniah, a Levite of the sons of Asaph, in the middle of the assembly. 15He said, "Listen, all Judah and inhabitants of Jerusalem, and King Jehoshaphat: Thus says the LORD to you: 'Do not fear or be dismayed at this great multitude; for the battle is not yours but God's. 16Tomorrow go down against them; they will come up by the ascent of Ziz; you will find them at the end of the valley, before the wilderness of Jeruel. 17This battle is not for you to fight; take your position, stand still, and see the victory of the LORD on your behalf, O Judah and Jerusalem.' Do not fear or be dismayed; tomorrow go out against them, and the LORD will be with you."

18 Then Jehoshaphat bowed down with his face to the ground, and all Judah and the inhabitants of Jerusalem fell down before the LORD, worshiping the LORD. 19And the Levites, of the Kohathites and the Korahites, stood up to praise the LORD, the God of Israel, with a very loud voice.

20 They rose early in the morning and went out into the wilderness of Tekoa; and as they went out, Jehoshaphat stood and said, "Listen to me, O Judah and inhabitants of Jerusalem! Believe in the LORD your God and you will be established; believe his prophets." 21When he had taken counsel with the people, he appointed those who were to sing to the LORD and praise him in holy splendor, as they went before the army, saying,

"Give thanks to the LORD,
for his steadfast love endures forever."

22As they began to sing and praise, the LORD set an ambush against the Ammonites, Moab, and Mount Seir, who had come against Judah, so that they were routed. 23For the Ammonites and Moab attacked the inhabitants of Mount Seir, destroying them utterly; and when they had made an end of the inhabitants of Seir, they all helped to destroy one another.

24 When Judah came to the watchtower of the wilderness, they looked toward the multitude; they were corpses lying on the ground; no one had escaped. 25When Jehoshaphat and his people came to take the booty from them, they found livestock[q]

[m] Compare 26.7: Heb *Ammonites* [n] Heb *They* [o] One Ms: MT *Aram* [p] Or *the sword of judgment* [q] Gk: Heb *among them*

19.11 ver 8; 1 Chr 28.20
20.2 Gen 14.7
20.3 2 Chr 19.3
20.6 Deut 4.39; Mt 6.9; 1 Chr 29.11,12; Mt 6.13
20.7 Isa 41.8
20.9 1 Kings 8.33,37; 2 Chr 6.20,28-30
20.10 ver 1,22; Deut 2.4,9,19; Num 20.21
20.11 Ps 83.12
20.12 Judg 11.27; Ps 25.15; 121.1,2
20.14 2 Chr 15.1; 24.20
20.15 Ex 14.13,14; 2 Chr 32.7,8; 1 Sam 17.47
20.17 Ex 14.13,14; 2 Chr 15.2
20.18 Ex 4.31; 2 Chr 7.3
20.20 Isa 7.9
20.21 1 Chr 16.29,34,41; Ps 29.2
20.22 Judg 7.22; 1 Chr 13.13
20.23 1 Sam 14.20

in great numbers, goods, clothing, and precious things, which they took for themselves until they could carry no more. They spent three days taking the booty, because of its abundance. [26]On the fourth day they assembled in the Valley of Beracah, for there they blessed the LORD; therefore that place has been called the Valley of Beracah[r] to this day. [27]Then all the people of Judah and Jerusalem, with Jehoshaphat at their head, returned to Jerusalem with joy, for the LORD had enabled them to rejoice over their enemies. [28]They came to Jerusalem, with harps and lyres and trumpets, to the house of the LORD. [29]The fear of God came on all the kingdoms of the countries when they heard that the LORD had fought against the enemies of Israel. [30]And the realm of Jehoshaphat was quiet, for his God gave him rest all around.

The End of Jehoshaphat's Reign

31 So Jehoshaphat reigned over Judah. He was thirty-five years old when he began to reign; he reigned twenty-five years in Jerusalem. His mother's name was Azubah daughter of Shilhi. [32]He walked in the way of his father Asa and did not turn aside from it, doing what was right in the sight of the LORD. [33]Yet the high places were not removed; the people had not yet set their hearts upon the God of their ancestors.

34 Now the rest of the acts of Jehoshaphat, from first to last, are written in the Annals of Jehu son of Hanani, which are recorded in the Book of the Kings of Israel.

35 After this King Jehoshaphat of Judah joined with King Ahaziah of Israel, who did wickedly. [36]He joined him in building ships to go to Tarshish; they built the ships in Ezion-geber. [37]Then Eliezer son of Dodavahu of Mareshah prophesied against Jehoshaphat, saying, "Because you have joined with Ahaziah, the LORD will destroy what you have made." And the ships were wrecked and were not able to go to Tarshish.

Jehoram's Reign

21 Jehoshaphat slept with his ancestors and was buried with his ancestors in the city of David; his son Jehoram succeeded him. [2]He had brothers, the sons of Jehoshaphat: Azariah, Jehiel, Zechariah, Azariah, Michael, and Shephatiah; all these were the sons of King Jehoshaphat of Judah.[s] [3]Their father gave them many gifts, of silver, gold, and valuable possessions, together with fortified cities in Judah; but he gave the kingdom to Jehoram, because he was the firstborn. [4]When Jehoram had ascended the throne of his father and was established, he put all his brothers to the sword, and also some of the officials of Israel. [5]Jehoram was thirty-two years old when he began to reign; he reigned eight years in Jerusalem. [6]He walked in the way of the kings of Israel, as the house of Ahab had done; for the daughter of Ahab was his wife. He did what was evil in the sight of the LORD. [7]Yet the LORD would not destroy the house of David because of the covenant that he had made with David, and since he had promised to give a lamp to him and to his descendants forever.

Revolt of Edom

8 In his days Edom revolted against the rule of Judah and set up a king of their own. [9]Then Jehoram crossed over with his commanders and all his chariots. He set out by night and attacked the Edomites, who had surrounded him and his chariot commanders. [10]So Edom has been in revolt against the rule of Judah to this day. At that time Libnah also revolted against his rule, because he had forsaken the LORD, the God of his ancestors.

Elijah's Letter

11 Moreover he made high places in the hill country of Judah, and led the inhabitants of Jerusalem into unfaithfulness, and made Judah go astray. [12]A letter came to him from the prophet Elijah, saying: "Thus says the LORD, the God of your father David: Because you have not walked in the ways of your father Jehoshaphat or in the ways of King Asa of Judah, [13]but have walked in the way of the kings of Israel, and have led Judah and the inhabitants of Jerusalem into unfaithfulness, as the house of Ahab led Israel into unfaithfulness, and because you also have killed your brothers, members of your father's house, who were better than yourself, [14]see, the LORD will bring a great plague on your people, your children, your wives, and all your possessions, [15]and you yourself will have a severe sickness with a

[r] That is *Blessing* [s] Gk Syr: Heb *Israel*

20.27 Neh 12.43
20.29 2 Chr 14.14; 17.10
20.30 2 Chr 14.6,7; 15.15
20.31 1 Kings 22.41-43
20.33 2 Chr 17.6; 19.3
20.34 1 Kings 16.1,7
20.35 1 Kings 22.48,49
20.37 2 Chr 9.21
21.1 1 Kings 22.50
21.3 2 Chr 11.5
21.5 2 Kings 8.17-22
21.7 2 Sam 7.12,13; 1 Kings 11.36
21.8 2 Kings 8.20-24
21.11 Lev 20.5
21.12 2 Chr 17.3,4; 14.2-5
21.13 ver 6.11; 1 Kings 16.31-33; ver 4
21.15 ver 18,19

20.31-37 The End of the Reign of Jehoshaphat. The mixed evaluation of the reign of *Jehoshaphat* ends with a critical version of his disastrous collaboration with Israel's king, *Ahaziah*, different from that in 1 Kings 22.45-50.
21.1-20 The Reign of Jehoram. Jehoram (849-842), son and heir to the throne of Jehoshaphat, is portrayed in a completely negative way, from killing his brothers as potential claimants to the kingship, to following the wicked ways of Ahab, whose daughter he married. *Edom*, an east Jordan territory subject to Judah, launched an ongoing revolt, and was joined by *Libnah*, a city on the western borders of Judah in the coastal hills that was earlier designated as assigned to the Levites (Josh 21.13; 1 Chr 6.57). *A letter came to [Jehoram] from the prophet Elijah*, condemning his sanctioning of idolatry and warning him of his protracted and painful death. Since the date of Elijah's life is set in the first half of the ninth century, the author of this message may have been Elisha, whose dates overlap those of the reign of Jehoram, at whose death there was neither *honor* nor *regret*.

22.1-9 The Reign of Ahaziah. The account is based on 2 Kings 8.25-29, but here the king's guilt is intensified. Descended through his mother from Omri, king of Israel (876-869), who founded the new capital at Samaria, the role-model of Ahaziah was Omri's son, *Ahab* (869-850), who permitted Baal-worship and is harshly condemned by the Deuteronomic historian (1 Kings 16-22). Ahaziah's alliance with Ahab resulted in his death at the hands of *Jehu*, who was in process of destroying the descendants of *Ahab*.
22.10-23.21 Athaliah's Attempt to Usurp the Throne of Judah. The account builds on 2 Kings 11.1-20, describing the plot of Athaliah, Ahaziah's mother, to destroy the heirs to the throne of Judah. Through *the priest Jehoiada* and his wife, *Joash son of Ahaziah* is saved and presented to the leaders of the people (*commanders of the hundreds, Levites, heads of the families of Israel*) as the true heir, and then crowned and acclaimed by the people. In spite of her protests, Athaliah is rejected as queen, captured and executed. Through Jehoiada, the covenant is renewed between the people and the LORD, and the land is purged of practices and facilities for idolatrous worship. Those assigned responsibility for *the house of the* LORD are *the levitical priests.*

disease of your bowels, until your bowels come out, day after day, because of the disease."

16 The LORD aroused against Jehoram the anger of the Philistines and of the Arabs who are near the Ethiopians.[t] 17They came up against Judah, invaded it, and carried away all the possessions they found that belonged to the king's house, along with his sons and his wives, so that no son was left to him except Jehoahaz, his youngest son.

Disease and Death of Jehoram

18 After all this the LORD struck him in his bowels with an incurable disease. 19In course of time, at the end of two years, his bowels came out because of the disease, and he died in great agony. His people made no fire in his honor, like the fires made for his ancestors. 20He was thirty-two years old when he began to reign; he reigned eight years in Jerusalem. He departed with no one's regret. They buried him in the city of David, but not in the tombs of the kings.

Ahaziah's Reign

22 The inhabitants of Jerusalem made his youngest son Ahaziah king as his successor; for the troops who came with the Arabs to the camp had killed all the older sons. So Ahaziah son of Jehoram reigned as king of Judah. 2Ahaziah was forty-two years old when he began to reign; he reigned one year in Jerusalem. His mother's name was Athaliah, a granddaughter of Omri. 3He also walked in the ways of the house of Ahab, for his mother was his counselor in doing wickedly. 4He did what was evil in the sight of the LORD, as the house of Ahab had done; for after the death of his father they were his counselors, to his ruin. 5He even followed their advice, and went with Jehoram son of King Ahab of Israel to make war against King Hazael of Aram at Ramoth-gilead. The Arameans wounded Joram, 6and he returned to be healed in Jezreel of the wounds that he had received at Ramah, when he fought King Hazael of Aram. And Ahaziah son of King Jehoram of Judah went down to see Joram son of Ahab in Jezreel, because he was sick.

7 But it was ordained by God that the downfall of Ahaziah should come about through his going to visit Joram. For when he came there he went out with Jehoram to meet Jehu son of Nimshi, whom the LORD had anointed to destroy the house of Ahab. 8When Jehu was executing judgment on the house of Ahab, he met the officials of Judah and the sons of Ahaziah's brothers, who attended Ahaziah, and he killed them. 9He searched for Ahaziah, who was captured while hiding in Samaria and was brought to Jehu, and put to death. They buried him, for they said, "He is the grandson of Jehoshaphat, who sought the LORD with all his heart." And the house of Ahaziah had no one able to rule the kingdom.

Athaliah Seizes the Throne

10 Now when Athaliah, Ahaziah's mother, saw that her son was dead, she set about to destroy all the royal family of the house of Judah. 11But Jehoshabeath, the king's daughter, took Joash son of Ahaziah, and stole him away from among the king's children who were about to be killed; she put him and his nurse in a bedroom. Thus Jehoshabeath, daughter of King Jehoram and wife of the priest Jehoiada—because she was a sister of Ahaziah—hid him from Athaliah, so that she did not kill him; 12he remained with them six years, hidden in the house of God, while Athaliah reigned over the land.

23 But in the seventh year Jehoiada took courage, and entered into a compact with the commanders of the hundreds, Azariah son of Jeroham, Ishmael son of Jehohanan, Azariah son of Obed, Maaseiah son of Adaiah, and Elishaphat son of Zichri. 2They went around through Judah and gathered the Levites from all the towns of Judah, and the heads of families of Israel, and they came to Jerusalem. 3Then the whole assembly made a covenant with the king in the house of God. Jehoiada[u] said to them, "Here is the king's son! Let him reign, as the LORD promised concerning the sons of David. 4This is what you are to do: one third of you, priests and Levites, who come on duty on the sabbath, shall be gatekeepers, 5one third shall be at the king's house, and one third at the Gate of the Foundation; and all the people shall be in the courts of the house of the LORD. 6Do not let anyone enter the house of the LORD except the priests and ministering Levites; they may enter, for they are holy, but all the other[v]

21.16 2 Chr 33.11
21.17 2 Chr 25.23
21.18 ver 15
21.19 2 Chr 16.14
21.20 Jer 22.18,28; 2 Chr 24.25; 28.27
22.1 2 Kings 8.24-29; 2 Chr 21.16,17
22.2 2 Chr 21.6
22.5 2 Kings 8.28ff
22.6 2 Kings 9.15
22.7 2 Chr 10.15; 2 Kings 9.6,7,21
22.8 2 Kings 10.10-14
22.9 2 Kings 9.27,28; 2 Chr 17.4
22.10 2 Kings 11.1-3
23.1 2 Kings 11.4-20
23.3 2 Sam 7.12; 1 Kings 2.4; 2 Chr 6.16; 7.18; 21.7
23.4 1 Chr 9.25

[t] Or *Nubians*; Heb *Cushites* [u] Heb *He* [v] Heb lacks *other*

23.7 1 Chr 23.28-32
23.8 1 Chr 24.1
23.9 ver 1
23.11 Ex 25.16; 1 Sam 10.24
23.12 2 Kings 11.13
23.15 Neh 3.28; Jer 31.40
23.17 Deut 13.9
23.18 2 Chr 5.5; 1 Chr 23.6,30,31; 25.1,2,6
23.19 1 Chr 9.22
23.20 2 Kings 11.19
24.1 2 Kings 11.21; 12.1-15
24.2 2 Chr 26.5
24.4 ver 7
24.6 Ex 30.12-16
24.7 2 Chr 21.17
24.9 ver 6

people shall observe the instructions of the LORD. [7]The Levites shall surround the king, each with his weapons in his hand; and whoever enters the house shall be killed. Stay with the king in his comings and goings."

Joash Crowned King

8 The Levites and all Judah did according to all that the priest Jehoiada commanded; each brought his men, who were to come on duty on the sabbath, with those who were to go off duty on the sabbath; for the priest Jehoiada did not dismiss the divisions. [9]The priest Jehoiada delivered to the captains the spears and the large and small shields that had been King David's, which were in the house of God; [10]and he set all the people as a guard for the king, everyone with weapon in hand, from the south side of the house to the north side of the house, around the altar and the house. [11]Then he brought out the king's son, put the crown on him, and gave him the covenant;[w] they proclaimed him king, and Jehoiada and his sons anointed him; and they shouted, "Long live the king!"

Athaliah Murdered

12 When Athaliah heard the noise of the people running and praising the king, she went into the house of the LORD to the people; [13]and when she looked, there was the king standing by his pillar at the entrance, and the captains and the trumpeters beside the king, and all the people of the land rejoicing and blowing trumpets, and the singers with their musical instruments leading in the celebration. Athaliah tore her clothes, and cried, "Treason! Treason!" [14]Then the priest Jehoiada brought out the captains who were set over the army, saying to them, "Bring her out between the ranks; anyone who follows her is to be put to the sword." For the priest said, "Do not put her to death in the house of the LORD." [15]So they laid hands on her; she went into the entrance of the Horse Gate of the king's house, and there they put her to death.

16 Jehoiada made a covenant between himself and all the people and the king that they should be the LORD's people. [17]Then all the people went to the house of Baal, and tore it down; his altars and his images they broke in pieces, and they killed Mattan, the priest of Baal, in front of the altars. [18]Jehoiada assigned the care of the house of the LORD to the levitical priests whom David had organized to be in charge of the house of the LORD, to offer burnt offerings to the LORD, as it is written in the law of Moses, with rejoicing and with singing, according to the order of David. [19]He stationed the gatekeepers at the gates of the house of the LORD so that no one should enter who was in any way unclean. [20]And he took the captains, the nobles, the governors of the people, and all the people of the land, and they brought the king down from the house of the LORD, marching through the upper gate to the king's house. They set the king on the royal throne. [21]So all the people of the land rejoiced, and the city was quiet after Athaliah had been killed with the sword.

Joash Repairs the Temple

24 Joash was seven years old when he began to reign; he reigned forty years in Jerusalem; his mother's name was Zibiah of Beer-sheba. [2]Joash did what was right in the sight of the LORD all the days of the priest Jehoiada. [3]Jehoiada got two wives for him, and he became the father of sons and daughters.

4 Some time afterward Joash decided to restore the house of the LORD. [5]He assembled the priests and the Levites and said to them, "Go out to the cities of Judah and gather money from all Israel to repair the house of your God, year by year; and see that you act quickly." But the Levites did not act quickly. [6]So the king summoned Jehoiada the chief, and said to him, "Why have you not required the Levites to bring in from Judah and Jerusalem the tax levied by Moses, the servant of the LORD, on[x] the congregation of Israel for the tent of the covenant?"[w] [7]For the children of Athaliah, that wicked woman, had broken into the house of God, and had even used all the dedicated things of the house of the LORD for the Baals.

8 So the king gave command, and they made a chest, and set it outside the gate of the house of the LORD. [9]A proclamation was made throughout Judah and Jerusalem to bring in for the LORD the tax that Moses the servant of God laid on Israel in the wilderness. [10]All the leaders and all the people rejoiced and brought their tax and dropped

24.1-27 The Mixed Record in the Reign of Joash. Expanding and modifying the account in 1 Kings 12, the Chronicler first pictures Joash as diligent in repairing and replacing the equipment of the temple, as well as in requiring his people to contribute to its upkeep in accord with the law of Moses (Ex 30.11-16; 38.26). Then after the death of his priestly counselor, *Jehoiada,* Joash is portrayed as subject to wicked priestly counselors, as a consequence of which *Judah and Jerusalem* are attacked by *Aram* (Syria). Seriously wounded, Joash was put to death by proponents of *Zechariah, son of Jehoiada,* whose message of warning to the king had been rejected by him and his advisors.

[w] Or *treaty,* or *testimony;* Heb *eduth* [x] Compare Vg: Heb *and*

25.1-28 The Reign of Amaziah. Building on 1 Kings 14, the Chronicler again presents a mixed picture of *Amaziah* (800-783). Obedient to the Deuteronomic form of the law of Moses in abstaining from the execution of the children of his father's murderer (Deut 24.16, in contrast to Ex 20.5; 34.7), Amaziah erred in hiring troops from Israel to assist his own army. After achieving victory over *the Edomites* in *the Valley of Salt* (the Arabah, south of the Dead Sea), he imported the worship of their gods into Judah and was then warned by *a prophet* that disaster for Judah would result. This was fulfilled through the destruction of Jerusalem by Israel and Amaziah's subsequent murder at *Lachish* (in the coastal hills southwest of Jerusalem) by conspirators from Judah. Though identified here as *cities of Judah*, *Samaria* was in Israel and *Beth-horon* was in Israel near the border with Judah. Also known as Azariah, Uzziah's reign (783-742) is described in an expanded version of 2 Kings 14.21-22; 15.2-3,5-7. In what is seen as reward for his doing *what was right in the sight of the* LORD, Uzziah was successful militarily to the west (against the Philistines), the east (Arabs and Ammonites), and the south (Egypt). His extensive building activities in Jerusalem are also commended, as are his reorganization and equipping of the army. Yet he is judged for his pride and his usurpation of the priestly role in presenting offerings to the LORD. The judgment falls on him when he is stricken with *leprosy*, which may have been one of several skin diseases. Important in the stylized conclusion of this section is the mention of *the prophet Isaiah the son of Amoz*, whose vision of the LORD enthroned took place *in the year that King Uzziah died* (Isa 6.1).

it into the chest until it was full. [11]Whenever the chest was brought to the king's officers by the Levites, when they saw that there was a large amount of money in it, the king's secretary and the officer of the chief priest would come and empty the chest and take it and return it to its place. So they did day after day, and collected money in abundance. [12]The king and Jehoiada gave it to those who had charge of the work of the house of the LORD, and they hired masons and carpenters to restore the house of the LORD, and also workers in iron and bronze to repair the house of the LORD. [13]So those who were engaged in the work labored, and the repairing went forward at their hands, and they restored the house of God to its proper condition and strengthened it. [14]When they had finished, they brought the rest of the money to the king and Jehoiada, and with it were made utensils for the house of the LORD, utensils for the service and for the burnt offerings, and ladles, and vessels of gold and silver. They offered burnt offerings in the house of the LORD regularly all the days of Jehoiada.

Apostasy of Joash

15 But Jehoiada grew old and full of days, and died; he was one hundred thirty years old at his death. [16]And they buried him in the city of David among the kings, because he had done good in Israel, and for God and his house.

17 Now after the death of Jehoiada the officials of Judah came and did obeisance to the king; then the king listened to them. [18]They abandoned the house of the LORD, the God of their ancestors, and served the sacred poles[y] and the idols. And wrath came upon Judah and Jerusalem for this guilt of theirs. [19]Yet he sent prophets among them to bring them back to the LORD; they testified against them, but they would not listen.

20 Then the spirit of God took possession of[z] Zechariah son of the priest Jehoiada; he stood above the people and said to them, "Thus says God: Why do you transgress the commandments of the LORD, so that you cannot prosper? Because you have forsaken the LORD, he has also forsaken you." [21]But they conspired against him, and by command of the king they stoned him to death in the court of the house of the LORD. [22]King Joash did not remember the kindness that Jehoiada, Zechariah's father, had shown him, but killed his son. As he was dying, he said, "May the LORD see and avenge!"

Death of Joash

23 At the end of the year the army of Aram came up against Joash. They came to Judah and Jerusalem, and destroyed all the officials of the people from among them, and sent all the booty they took to the king of Damascus. [24]Although the army of Aram had come with few men, the LORD delivered into their hand a very great army, because they had abandoned the LORD, the God of their ancestors. Thus they executed judgment on Joash.

25 When they had withdrawn, leaving him severely wounded, his servants conspired against him because of the blood of the son[a] of the priest Jehoiada, and they killed him on his bed. So he died; and they buried him in the city of David, but they did not bury him in the tombs of the kings. [26]Those who conspired against him were Zabad son of Shimeath the Ammonite, and Jehozabad son of Shimrith the Moabite. [27]Accounts of his sons, and of the many oracles against him, and of the rebuilding[b] of the house of God are written in the Commentary on the Book of the Kings. And his son Amaziah succeeded him.

Reign of Amaziah

25 Amaziah was twenty-five years old when he began to reign, and he reigned twenty-nine years in Jerusalem. His mother's name was Jehoaddan of Jerusalem. [2]He did what was right in the sight of the LORD, yet not with a true heart. [3]As soon as the royal power was firmly in his hand he killed his servants who had murdered his father the king. [4]But he did not put their children to death, according to what is written in the law, in the book of Moses, where the LORD commanded, "The parents shall not be put to death for the children, or the children be put to death for the parents; but all shall be put to death for their own sins."

Slaughter of the Edomites

5 Amaziah assembled the people of Judah, and set them by ancestral houses under commanders of the thousands and of the

24.11 2 Kings 12.10

24.13 Neh 10.39

24.16 2 Chr 21.2,20

24.18 ver 4; Ex 34.12-14; 1 Kings 14.23; Josh 22.20; 2 Chr 19.2

24.19 Jer 7.25

24.20 2 Chr 20.14; Num 14.41; 2 Chr 15.2

24.21 Neh 9.26; Mt 23.35; Acts 7.58,59

24.22 Gen 9.5

24.23 2 Kings 12.17

24.24 Lev 26.25; Deut 28.25; 2 Chr 22.8; Isa 10.5

24.25 2 Kings 12.20; ver 21

24.27 2 Kings 12.18,21

25.1 2 Kings 14.1-6

25.2 ver 14

25.4 Deut 24.16; 2 Kings 14.6

25.5 Num 1.3

[y] Heb *Asherim* [z] Heb *clothed itself with* [a] Gk Vg: Heb *sons* [b] Heb *founding*

25.8 2 Chr 14.11; 20.6
25.11 2 Kings 14.7
25.14 2 Chr 28.23; Ex 20.3,5
25.15 Ps 96.5; ver 11,12
25.17 2 Kings 14.8-14
25.18 Judg 9.8-15
25.19 2 Chr 26.16; 32.25
25.20 1 Kings 12.15; 2 Chr 22.7
25.23 2 Chr 21.17; 22.1
25.25 2 Kings 14.17-22
26.1 2 Kings 14.21,22; 15.2,3

hundreds for all Judah and Benjamin. He mustered those twenty years old and upward, and found that they were three hundred thousand picked troops fit for war, able to handle spear and shield. [6]He also hired one hundred thousand mighty warriors from Israel for one hundred talents of silver. [7]But a man of God came to him and said, "O king, do not let the army of Israel go with you, for the LORD is not with Israel—all these Ephraimites. [8]Rather, go by yourself and act; be strong in battle, or God will fling you down before the enemy; for God has power to help or to overthrow." [9]Amaziah said to the man of God, "But what shall we do about the hundred talents that I have given to the army of Israel?" The man of God answered, "The LORD is able to give you much more than this." [10]Then Amaziah discharged the army that had come to him from Ephraim, letting them go home again. But they became very angry with Judah, and returned home in fierce anger.

11 Amaziah took courage, and led out his people; he went to the Valley of Salt, and struck down ten thousand men of Seir. [12]The people of Judah captured another ten thousand alive, took them to the top of Sela, and threw them down from the top of Sela, so that all of them were dashed to pieces. [13]But the men of the army whom Amaziah sent back, not letting them go with him to battle, fell on the cities of Judah from Samaria to Beth-horon; they killed three thousand people in them, and took much booty.

14 Now after Amaziah came from the slaughter of the Edomites, he brought the gods of the people of Seir, set them up as his gods, and worshiped them, making offerings to them. [15]The LORD was angry with Amaziah and sent to him a prophet, who said to him, "Why have you resorted to a people's gods who could not deliver their own people from your hand?" [16]But as he was speaking the king[c] said to him, "Have we made you a royal counselor? Stop! Why should you be put to death?" So the prophet stopped, but said, "I know that God has determined to destroy you, because you have done this and have not listened to my advice."

Israel Defeats Judah

17 Then King Amaziah of Judah took counsel and sent to King Joash son of Jehoahaz son of Jehu of Israel, saying, "Come, let us look one another in the face." [18]King Joash of Israel sent word to King Amaziah of Judah, "A thornbush on Lebanon sent to a cedar on Lebanon, saying, 'Give your daughter to my son for a wife'; but a wild animal of Lebanon passed by and trampled down the thornbush. [19]You say, 'See, I have defeated Edom,' and your heart has lifted you up in boastfulness. Now stay at home; why should you provoke trouble so that you fall, you and Judah with you?"

20 But Amaziah would not listen—it was God's doing, in order to hand them over, because they had sought the gods of Edom. [21]So King Joash of Israel went up; he and King Amaziah of Judah faced one another in battle at Beth-shemesh, which belongs to Judah. [22]Judah was defeated by Israel; everyone fled home. [23]King Joash of Israel captured King Amaziah of Judah, son of Joash, son of Ahaziah, at Beth-shemesh; he brought him to Jerusalem, and broke down the wall of Jerusalem from the Ephraim Gate to the Corner Gate, a distance of four hundred cubits. [24]He seized all the gold and silver, and all the vessels that were found in the house of God, and Obed-edom with them; he seized also the treasuries of the king's house, also hostages; then he returned to Samaria.

Death of Amaziah

25 King Amaziah son of Joash of Judah, lived fifteen years after the death of King Joash son of Jehoahaz of Israel. [26]Now the rest of the deeds of Amaziah, from first to last, are they not written in the Book of the Kings of Judah and Israel? [27]From the time that Amaziah turned away from the LORD they made a conspiracy against him in Jerusalem, and he fled to Lachish. But they sent after him to Lachish, and killed him there. [28]They brought him back on horses; he was buried with his ancestors in the city of David.

Reign of Uzziah

26 Then all the people of Judah took Uzziah, who was sixteen years old, and made him king to succeed his father Amaziah. [2]He rebuilt Eloth and restored it to Judah, after the king slept with his ancestors. [3]Uzziah was sixteen years old when

[c] Heb *he*

27.1-9 The Reign of Jotham (742-735). Based on 2 Kings 15.32-38, the same pattern is evident as in the report of his father's reign: improvements to Jerusalem and Judah, with successful, profitable military endeavors against the Ammonites.

he began to reign, and he reigned fifty-two years in Jerusalem. His mother's name was Jecoliah of Jerusalem. 4 He did what was right in the sight of the LORD, just as his father Amaziah had done. 5 He set himself to seek God in the days of Zechariah, who instructed him in the fear of God; and as long as he sought the LORD, God made him prosper.

6 He went out and made war against the Philistines, and broke down the wall of Gath and the wall of Jabneh and the wall of Ashdod; he built cities in the territory of Ashdod and elsewhere among the Philistines. 7 God helped him against the Philistines, against the Arabs who lived in Gur-baal, and against the Meunites. 8 The Ammonites paid tribute to Uzziah, and his fame spread even to the border of Egypt, for he became very strong. 9 Moreover Uzziah built towers in Jerusalem at the Corner Gate, at the Valley Gate, and at the Angle, and fortified them. 10 He built towers in the wilderness and hewed out many cisterns, for he had large herds, both in the Shephelah and in the plain, and he had farmers and vinedressers in the hills and in the fertile lands, for he loved the soil. 11 Moreover Uzziah had an army of soldiers, fit for war, in divisions according to the numbers in the muster made by the secretary Jeiel and the officer Maaseiah, under the direction of Hananiah, one of the king's commanders. 12 The whole number of the heads of ancestral houses of mighty warriors was two thousand six hundred. 13 Under their command was an army of three hundred seven thousand five hundred, who could make war with mighty power, to help the king against the enemy. 14 Uzziah provided for all the army the shields, spears, helmets, coats of mail, bows, and stones for slinging. 15 In Jerusalem he set up machines, invented by skilled workers, on the towers and the corners for shooting arrows and large stones. And his fame spread far, for he was marvelously helped until he became strong.

Pride and Apostasy

16 But when he had become strong he grew proud, to his destruction. For he was false to the LORD his God, and entered the temple of the LORD to make offering on the altar of incense. 17 But the priest Azariah went in after him, with eighty priests of the LORD who were men of valor; 18 they withstood King Uzziah, and said to him, "It is not for you, Uzziah, to make offering to the LORD, but for the priests the descendants of Aaron, who are consecrated to make offering. Go out of the sanctuary; for you have done wrong, and it will bring you no honor from the LORD God." 19 Then Uzziah was angry. Now he had a censer in his hand to make offering, and when he became angry with the priests a leprous[d] disease broke out on his forehead, in the presence of the priests in the house of the LORD, by the altar of incense. 20 When the chief priest Azariah, and all the priests, looked at him, he was leprous[d] in his forehead. They hurried him out, and he himself hurried to get out, because the LORD had struck him. 21 King Uzziah was leprous[d] to the day of his death, and being leprous[d] lived in a separate house, for he was excluded from the house of the LORD. His son Jotham was in charge of the palace of the king, governing the people of the land.

22 Now the rest of the acts of Uzziah, from first to last, the prophet Isaiah son of Amoz wrote. 23 Uzziah slept with his ancestors; they buried him near his ancestors in the burial field that belonged to the kings, for they said, "He is leprous."[d] His son Jotham succeeded him.

Reign of Jotham

27 Jotham was twenty-five years old when he began to reign; he reigned sixteen years in Jerusalem. His mother's name was Jerushah daughter of Zadok. 2 He did what was right in the sight of the LORD just as his father Uzziah had done—only he did not invade the temple of the LORD. But the people still followed corrupt practices. 3 He built the upper gate of the house of the LORD, and did extensive building on the wall of Ophel. 4 Moreover he built cities in the hill country of Judah, and forts and towers on the wooded hills. 5 He fought with the king of the Ammonites and prevailed against them. The Ammonites gave him that year one hundred talents of silver, ten thousand cors of wheat and ten thousand of barley. The Ammonites paid him the same amount in the second and the third years. 6 So Jotham became strong because he ordered his ways before the LORD his God. 7 Now the rest of the acts of Jotham, and all his wars and his

26.5 2 Chr 24.2; Dan 1.17; 2.19; 2 Chr 15.2
26.6 Isa 14.29
26.7 2 Chr 21.16
26.8 2 Chr 17.11
26.9 2 Chr 25.23; Neh 3.13
26.13 2 Chr 25.5
26.16 Deut 32.15; 2 Chr 25.19; 2 Kings 16.12,13
26.17 1 Chr 6.10
26.18 Num 16.39,40; Ex 30.7,8
26.19 2 Kings 5.25-27
26.21 2 Kings 15.5-7; Lev 13.46; Num 5.2
26.22 Isa 1.1
26.23 2 Kings 15.7; Isa 6.1
27.1 2 Kings 15.33-35
27.2 2 Chr 26.16
27.3 2 Chr 33.14; Neh 3.26
27.6 2 Chr 26.5
27.7 2 Kings 15.36

[d] A term for several skin diseases; precise meaning uncertain

27.8 ver 1
28.1 2 Kings 16.2-4
28.2 2 Chr 22.3; Ex 34.17
28.3 2 Kings 23.10; Lev 18.21; 2 Kings 16.3; 2 Chr 33.6
28.4 ver 25
28.5 Isa 7.1; 2 Kings 16.5,6
28.6 2 Kings 15.27
28.8 2 Chr 11.4
28.9 2 Chr 25.15; Isa 10.5; 47.6; Ezra 9.6; Rev 18.5
28.10 Lev 25.39,42,43, 46
28.11 ver 8
28.15 ver 12; 2 Kings 6.22; Prov 25.21,22; Deut 34.3; Judg 1.16
28.16 2 Kings 16.7
28.18 Ezek 16.57
28.19 2 Chr 21.2
28.20 1 Chr 5.26; 2 Kings 16.8,9
28.23 2 Chr 25.14; Jer 44.17,18

ways, are written in the Book of the Kings of Israel and Judah. 8 He was twenty-five years old when he began to reign; he reigned sixteen years in Jerusalem. 9 Jotham slept with his ancestors, and they buried him in the city of David; and his son Ahaz succeeded him.

Reign of Ahaz

28 Ahaz was twenty years old when he began to reign; he reigned sixteen years in Jerusalem. He did not do what was right in the sight of the LORD, as his ancestor David had done, 2 but he walked in the ways of the kings of Israel. He even made cast images for the Baals; 3 and he made offerings in the valley of the son of Hinnom, and made his sons pass through fire, according to the abominable practices of the nations whom the LORD drove out before the people of Israel. 4 He sacrificed and made offerings on the high places, on the hills, and under every green tree.

Aram and Israel Defeat Judah

5 Therefore the LORD his God gave him into the hand of the king of Aram, who defeated him and took captive a great number of his people and brought them to Damascus. He was also given into the hand of the king of Israel, who defeated him with great slaughter. 6 Pekah son of Remaliah killed one hundred twenty thousand in Judah in one day, all of them valiant warriors, because they had abandoned the LORD, the God of their ancestors. 7 And Zichri, a mighty warrior of Ephraim, killed the king's son Maaseiah, Azrikam the commander of the palace, and Elkanah the next in authority to the king.

Intervention of Oded

8 The people of Israel took captive two hundred thousand of their kin, women, sons, and daughters; they also took much booty from them and brought the booty to Samaria. 9 But a prophet of the LORD was there, whose name was Oded; he went out to meet the army that came to Samaria, and said to them, "Because the LORD, the God of your ancestors, was angry with Judah, he gave them into your hand, but you have killed them in a rage that has reached up to heaven. 10 Now you intend to subjugate the people of Judah and Jerusalem, male and female, as your slaves. But what have you except sins against the LORD your God? 11 Now hear me, and send back the captives whom you have taken from your kindred, for the fierce wrath of the LORD is upon you." 12 Moreover, certain chiefs of the Ephraimites, Azariah son of Johanan, Berechiah son of Meshillemoth, Jehizkiah son of Shallum, and Amasa son of Hadlai, stood up against those who were coming from the war, 13 and said to them, "You shall not bring the captives in here, for you propose to bring on us guilt against the LORD in addition to our present sins and guilt. For our guilt is already great, and there is fierce wrath against Israel." 14 So the warriors left the captives and the booty before the officials and all the assembly. 15 Then those who were mentioned by name got up and took the captives, and with the booty they clothed all that were naked among them; they clothed them, gave them sandals, provided them with food and drink, and anointed them; and carrying all the feeble among them on donkeys, they brought them to their kindred at Jericho, the city of palm trees. Then they returned to Samaria.

Assyria Refuses to Help Judah

16 At that time King Ahaz sent to the king[e] of Assyria for help. 17 For the Edomites had again invaded and defeated Judah, and carried away captives. 18 And the Philistines had made raids on the cities in the Shephelah and the Negeb of Judah, and had taken Beth-shemesh, Aijalon, Gederoth, Soco with its villages, Timnah with its villages, and Gimzo with its villages; and they settled there. 19 For the LORD brought Judah low because of King Ahaz of Israel, for he had behaved without restraint in Judah and had been faithless to the LORD. 20 So King Tilgath-pilneser of Assyria came against him, and oppressed him instead of strengthening him. 21 For Ahaz plundered the house of the LORD and the houses of the king and of the officials, and gave tribute to the king of Assyria; but it did not help him.

Apostasy and Death of Ahaz

22 In the time of his distress he became yet more faithless to the LORD—this same King Ahaz. 23 For he sacrificed to the gods

[e] Gk Syr Vg Compare 2 Kings 16.7: Heb *kings*

28.1-27 The Reign of Ahaz (735-715). Major changes are made from the source in 2 Kings 16 in order to heighten the criticism of Ahaz, including the sacrifices in *the Valley of Hinnom* (just west of the city of Jerusalem and the setting for idolatrous practices); his sacrificial offering of his own sons (*passing through the fire*); and the establishment of *high places* (where offerings were made to the fertility gods and goddesses). The divine punishment for these royal acts is seen in the slaughter of Israelites and in the capturing of huge numbers of the troops of Judah, including the king's sons. *Obed, the prophet,* warns of the coming enslavement of Judah, which is foreshadowed by *Assyria's* invasion and seizure of neighboring lands.

28.16-27 After the failure of Ahaz' plan to gain Assyrian help against his marauding neighbors, *the Edomites and the Philistines*, the king of Assyria, *Tilgath-pilneser* (usually spelled Tiglath-pileser) invaded Judah, accepting tribute for which *Ahaz plundered the house of the LORD.* With the revolts against Assyria crushed in Tyre, Syria and Israel (1 Chr 5.26), Ahaz became a vassal and is so listed in Assyrian documents from this period. In his final years Ahaz turned to worship of the Syrian gods and closed down the worship of Yahweh.

29.1-32.33 The Reign of Hezekiah and the Renewal of the Worship of Yahweh (715-687). After the temple was cleansed by the Levites (29.3-19), and the worship of the LORD was restored under the proper priestly and levitical officials (29.20-36), a special Passover was celebrated (30.1-27). Instead of the traditional first month of Abib (corresponding to March or April as the beginning of spring, and in recollection of the exodus from Egypt; Deut 16), it took place in the *second month*, to be sure that all the celebrants and materials were ritually clean. Even so, special provisions were made for participation by unclean but devout members of neighboring Israelite tribes: *Ephraim, Manasseh, Issachar and Zebulun*, as well as by *resident aliens* (non-Israelites living in the lands of Judah and Israel). The effects of the feast so restored and invigorated the people that it was repeated, and is depicted as a time of great joy.

of Damascus, which had defeated him, and said, "Because the gods of the kings of Aram helped them, I will sacrifice to them so that they may help me." But they were the ruin of him, and of all Israel. 24 Ahaz gathered together the utensils of the house of God, and cut in pieces the utensils of the house of God. He shut up the doors of the house of the LORD and made himself altars in every corner of Jerusalem. 25 In every city of Judah he made high places to make offerings to other gods, provoking to anger the LORD, the God of his ancestors. 26 Now the rest of his acts and all his ways, from first to last, are written in the Book of the Kings of Judah and Israel. 27 Ahaz slept with his ancestors, and they buried him in the city, in Jerusalem; but they did not bring him into the tombs of the kings of Israel. His son Hezekiah succeeded him.

Reign of Hezekiah

29 Hezekiah began to reign when he was twenty-five years old; he reigned twenty-nine years in Jerusalem. His mother's name was Abijah daughter of Zechariah. 2 He did what was right in the sight of the LORD, just as his ancestor David had done.

The Temple Cleansed

3 In the first year of his reign, in the first month, he opened the doors of the house of the LORD and repaired them. 4 He brought in the priests and the Levites and assembled them in the square on the east. 5 He said to them, "Listen to me, Levites! Sanctify yourselves, and sanctify the house of the LORD, the God of your ancestors, and carry out the filth from the holy place. 6 For our ancestors have been unfaithful and have done what was evil in the sight of the LORD our God; they have forsaken him, and have turned away their faces from the dwelling of the LORD, and turned their backs. 7 They also shut the doors of the vestibule and put out the lamps, and have not offered incense or made burnt offerings in the holy place to the God of Israel. 8 Therefore the wrath of the LORD came upon Judah and Jerusalem, and he has made them an object of horror, of astonishment, and of hissing, as you see with your own eyes. 9 Our fathers have fallen by the sword and our sons and our daughters and our wives are in captivity for this. 10 Now it is in my heart to make a covenant with the LORD, the God of Israel, so that his fierce anger may turn away from us. 11 My sons, do not now be negligent, for the LORD has chosen you to stand in his presence to minister to him, and to be his ministers and make offerings to him."

12 Then the Levites arose, Mahath son of Amasai, and Joel son of Azariah, of the sons of the Kohathites; and of the sons of Merari, Kish son of Abdi, and Azariah son of Jehallelel; and of the Gershonites, Joah son of Zimmah, and Eden son of Joah; 13 and of the sons of Elizaphan, Shimri and Jeuel; and of the sons of Asaph, Zechariah and Mattaniah; 14 and of the sons of Heman, Jehuel and Shimei; and of the sons of Jeduthun, Shemaiah and Uzziel. 15 They gathered their brothers, sanctified themselves, and went in as the king had commanded, by the words of the LORD, to cleanse the house of the LORD. 16 The priests went into the inner part of the house of the LORD to cleanse it, and they brought out all the unclean things that they found in the temple of the LORD into the court of the house of the LORD; and the Levites took them and carried them out to the Wadi Kidron. 17 They began to sanctify on the first day of the first month, and on the eighth day of the month they came to the vestibule of the LORD; then for eight days they sanctified the house of the LORD, and on the sixteenth day of the first month they finished. 18 Then they went inside to King Hezekiah and said, "We have cleansed all the house of the LORD, the altar of burnt offering and all its utensils, and the table for the rows of bread and all its utensils. 19 All the utensils that King Ahaz repudiated during his reign when he was faithless, we have made ready and sanctified; see, they are in front of the altar of the LORD."

Temple Worship Restored

20 Then King Hezekiah rose early, assembled the officials of the city, and went up to the house of the LORD. 21 They brought seven bulls, seven rams, seven lambs, and seven male goats for a sin offering for the kingdom and for the sanctuary and for Judah. He commanded the priests the descendants of Aaron to offer them on the altar of the LORD. 22 So they slaughtered the bulls, and the priests received the blood and dashed it against the altar; they slaughtered

28.24 2 Kings 16.17; 2 Chr 29.7; 30.14; 33.3-5

28.26 2 Kings 16.19,20

28.27 2 Chr 24.25

29.1 2 Kings 18.1-3

29.2 2 Chr 28.1

29.3 ver 7; 2 Chr 28.24

29.5 ver 15,34; 2 Chr 35.6

29.6 Jer 2.27; Ezek 8.16

29.8 2 Chr 24.18; 28.5; Deut 28.25; Jer 25.9,18

29.9 2 Chr 28.5-8,17

29.10 2 Chr 15.12; 23.16

29.11 Num 3.6; 8.14

29.12 2 Chr 31.13; Num 3.19,20

29.15 ver 5; 2 Chr 30.12; 1 Chr 23.28

29.17 ver 3

29.19 2 Chr 28.24

29.21 Lev 4.3-14

29.22 Lev 4.18; 8.14

29.23 Lev 4.15 the rams and their blood was dashed against
the altar; they also slaughtered the lambs
29.24 Lev 4.26 and their blood was dashed against the
altar. 23Then the male goats for the sin
offering were brought to the king and the
29.25 1 Chr 25.6; 2 Chr 8.14; 2 Sam 24.11; 7.2 assembly; they laid their hands on them,
24and the priests slaughtered them and made
a sin offering with their blood at the altar,
to make atonement for all Israel. For the
king commanded that the burnt offering
29.26 1 Chr 23.5; 2 Chr 5.12 and the sin offering should be made for all
Israel.
25 He stationed the Levites in the house
29.27 2 Chr 23.18 of the LORD with cymbals, harps, and lyres,
according to the commandment of David
29.29 2 Chr 20.18 and of Gad the king's seer and of the prophet
Nathan, for the commandment was from
the LORD through his prophets. 26The Levites
29.31 2 Chr 13.9; Ex 35.5,22 stood with the instruments of David, and
the priests with the trumpets. 27Then
Hezekiah commanded that the burnt offer-
29.34 2 Chr 35.11; 30.3 ing be offered on the altar. When the burnt
offering began, the song to the LORD began
also, and the trumpets, accompanied by the
29.35 ver 32; Lev 3.16; Num 15.5-10 instruments of King David of Israel. 28The
whole assembly worshiped, the singers sang,
and the trumpeters sounded; all this continued until the burnt offering was finished.
29When the offering was finished, the king
30.2 ver 13,15; Num 9.10,11 and all who were present with him bowed
down and worshiped. 30King Hezekiah and
the officials commanded the Levites to sing
30.3 Ex 12.6,18; 2 Chr 29.34 praises to the LORD with the words of David
and of the seer Asaph. They sang praises
with gladness, and they bowed down and
worshiped.
30.5 Judg 20.1 31 Then Hezekiah said, "You have now
consecrated yourselves to the LORD; come
30.6 Esth 8.14; Job 9.25; Jer 51.31; 2 Chr 20.8 near, bring sacrifices and thank offerings to
the house of the LORD." The assembly brought
sacrifices and thank offerings; and all who
were of a willing heart brought burnt offerings. 32The number of the burnt offerings
30.7 Ezek 20.18; 2 Chr 29.8 that the assembly brought was seventy bulls,
one hundred rams, and two hundred lambs;
all these were for a burnt offering to the
30.8 Ex 32.9; 2 Chr 29.10 LORD. 33The consecrated offerings were six
hundred bulls and three thousand sheep.
34But the priests were too few and could not
30.9 Deut 30.2; Ex 34.6,7; Mic 7.18; Isa 55.7 skin all the burnt offerings, so, until other
priests had sanctified themselves, their kin-
dred, the Levites, helped them until the
work was finished—for the Levites were
more conscientious[f] than the priests in
30.10 2 Chr 36.16 sanctifying themselves. 35Besides the great
number of burnt offerings there was the fat
of the offerings of well-being, and there
were the drink offerings for the burnt offerings. Thus the service of the house of the
LORD was restored. 36And Hezekiah and all
the people rejoiced because of what God had
done for the people; for the thing had come
about suddenly.

30.11 ver 18,21,25

The Great Passover

30 Hezekiah sent word to all Israel
and Judah, and wrote letters also
to Ephraim and Manasseh, that they should
come to the house of the LORD at Jerusalem,
to keep the passover to the LORD the God of
Israel. 2For the king and his officials and all
the assembly in Jerusalem had taken counsel to keep the passover in the second month
3(for they could not keep it at its proper time
because the priests had not sanctified themselves in sufficient number, nor had the
people assembled in Jerusalem). 4The plan
seemed right to the king and all the assembly. 5So they decreed to make a proclamation throughout all Israel, from Beer-sheba
to Dan, that the people should come and
keep the passover to the LORD the God of
Israel, at Jerusalem; for they had not kept
it in great numbers as prescribed. 6So couriers went throughout all Israel and Judah
with letters from the king and his officials,
as the king had commanded, saying, "O
people of Israel, return to the LORD, the God
of Abraham, Isaac, and Israel, so that he
may turn again to the remnant of you who
have escaped from the hand of the kings of
Assyria. 7Do not be like your ancestors and
your kindred, who were faithless to the LORD
God of their ancestors, so that he made
them a desolation, as you see. 8Do not now
be stiff-necked as your ancestors were, but
yield yourselves to the LORD and come to his
sanctuary, which he has sanctified forever,
and serve the LORD your God, so that his
fierce anger may turn away from you. 9For
as you return to the LORD, your kindred and
your children will find compassion with
their captors, and return to this land. For
the LORD your God is gracious and merciful,
and will not turn away his face from you,
if you return to him."
10 So the couriers went from city to city
through the country of Ephraim and
Manasseh, and as far as Zebulun; but they
laughed them to scorn, and mocked them.
11Only a few from Asher, Manasseh, and

[f] Heb *upright in heart*

31.1-21 The purging of the land of idolatrous altars and worship equipment was matched by the arrangement in detail of priests and Levites and the assignment of their responsibilities, for which *Hezekiah* is commended.

Zebulun humbled themselves and came to Jerusalem. [12]The hand of God was also on Judah to give them one heart to do what the king and the officials commanded by the word of the LORD.

13 Many people came together in Jerusalem to keep the festival of unleavened bread in the second month, a very large assembly. [14]They set to work and removed the altars that were in Jerusalem, and all the altars for offering incense they took away and threw into the Wadi Kidron. [15]They slaughtered the passover lamb on the fourteenth day of the second month. The priests and the Levites were ashamed, and they sanctified themselves and brought burnt offerings into the house of the LORD. [16]They took their accustomed posts according to the law of Moses the man of God; the priests dashed the blood that they received[g] from the hands of the Levites. [17]For there were many in the assembly who had not sanctified themselves; therefore the Levites had to slaughter the passover lamb for everyone who was not clean, to make it holy to the LORD. [18]For a multitude of the people, many of them from Ephraim, Manasseh, Issachar, and Zebulun, had not cleansed themselves, yet they ate the passover otherwise than as prescribed. But Hezekiah prayed for them, saying, "The good LORD pardon all [19]who set their hearts to seek God, the LORD the God of their ancestors, even though not in accordance with the sanctuary's rules of cleanness." [20]The LORD heard Hezekiah, and healed the people. [21]The people of Israel who were present at Jerusalem kept the festival of unleavened bread seven days with great gladness; and the Levites and the priests praised the LORD day by day, accompanied by loud instruments for the LORD. [22]Hezekiah spoke encouragingly to all the Levites who showed good skill in the service of the LORD. So the people ate the food of the festival for seven days, sacrificing offerings of well-being and giving thanks to the LORD the God of their ancestors.

23 Then the whole assembly agreed together to keep the festival for another seven days; so they kept it for another seven days with gladness. [24]For King Hezekiah of Judah gave the assembly a thousand bulls and seven thousand sheep for offerings, and the officials gave the assembly a thousand bulls and ten thousand sheep. The priests sanctified themselves in great numbers. [25]The whole assembly of Judah, the priests and the Levites, and the whole assembly that came out of Israel, and the resident aliens who came out of the land of Israel, and the resident aliens who lived in Judah, rejoiced. [26]There was great joy in Jerusalem, for since the time of Solomon son of King David of Israel there had been nothing like this in Jerusalem. [27]Then the priests and the Levites stood up and blessed the people, and their voice was heard; their prayer came to his holy dwelling in heaven.

Pagan Shrines Destroyed

31 Now when all this was finished, all Israel who were present went out to the cities of Judah and broke down the pillars, hewed down the sacred poles,[h] and pulled down the high places and the altars throughout all Judah and Benjamin, and in Ephraim and Manasseh, until they had destroyed them all. Then all the people of Israel returned to their cities, all to their individual properties.

2 Hezekiah appointed the divisions of the priests and of the Levites, division by division, everyone according to his service, the priests and the Levites, for burnt offerings and offerings of well-being, to minister in the gates of the camp of the LORD and to give thanks and praise. [3]The contribution of the king from his own possessions was for the burnt offerings: the burnt offerings of morning and evening, and the burnt offerings for the sabbaths, the new moons, and the appointed festivals, as it is written in the law of the LORD. [4]He commanded the people who lived in Jerusalem to give the portion due to the priests and the Levites, so that they might devote themselves to the law of the LORD. [5]As soon as the word spread, the people of Israel gave in abundance the first fruits of grain, wine, oil, honey, and of all the produce of the field; and they brought in abundantly the tithe of everything. [6]The people of Israel and Judah who lived in the cities of Judah also brought in the tithe of cattle and sheep, and the tithe of the dedicated things that had been consecrated to the LORD their God, and laid them in heaps. [7]In the third month they began to pile up the heaps, and finished them in the seventh month. [8]When Hezekiah and the officials came and saw the heaps, they blessed the

[g] Heb lacks *that they received* [h] Heb *Asherim*

30.13 ver 2

30.14 2 Chr 28.24

30.15 ver 2,3; 2 Chr 29.34

30.16 2 Chr 35.10,15

30.17 2 Chr 29.34

30.18 ver 11,25; Ex 12.43-49

30.19 2 Chr 19.3

30.21 Ex 12.15; 13.6

30.22 2 Chr 32.6; Ezra 10.11

30.23 1 Kings 8.65

30.24 2 Chr 35.7,8; 29.34

30.27 2 Chr 23.18; Num 6.23; Deut 26.15; Ps 68.5

31.1 2 Kings 18.4

31.2 1 Chr 24.1; 23.28-31

31.3 Num 28.29

31.4 Num 18.8; Neh 13.10

31.5 Neh 13.12

31.6 Lev 27.30; Deut 14.28

31.10 Mal 3.10 LORD and his people Israel. [9]Hezekiah questioned the priests and the Levites about the
31.13 2 Chr 35.9 heaps. [10]The chief priest Azariah, who was
of the house of Zadok, answered him, "Since
they began to bring the contributions into
31.15 2 Chr 29.12; Josh 21.9-19 the house of the LORD, we have had enough
to eat and have plenty to spare; for the LORD
has blessed his people, so that we have this
31.16 Ezra 3.4 great supply left over."

31.17 1 Chr 23.24

Reorganization of Priests and Levites

11 Then Hezekiah commanded them to
31.19 Lev 25.34; Num 35.2; ver 12-15 prepare store-chambers in the house of the
LORD; and they prepared them. [12]Faithfully
they brought in the contributions, the tithes
and the dedicated things. The chief officer
31.20 2 Kings 20.3; 22.2 in charge of them was Conaniah the Levite,
with his brother Shimei as second; [13]while
Jehiel, Azaziah, Nahath, Asahel, Jerimoth,
Jozabad, Eliel, Ismachiah, Mahath, and
32.1 2 Kings 18.13-19; Isa 36.1ff Benaiah were overseers assisting Conaniah
and his brother Shimei, by the appointment
of King Hezekiah and of Azariah the chief
officer of the house of God. [14]Kore son of
32.4 2 Kings 20.20; ver 30 Imnah the Levite, keeper of the east gate,
was in charge of the freewill offerings to
God, to apportion the contribution reserved
for the LORD and the most holy offerings.
32.5 2 Chr 25.23; 1 Kings 9.24 [15]Eden, Miniamin, Jeshua, Shemaiah,
Amariah, and Shecaniah were faithfully
assisting him in the cities of the priests, to
32.6 2 Chr 30.22 distribute the portions to their kindred, old
and young alike, by divisions, [16]except those
enrolled by genealogy, males from three
32.7 1 Chr 22.13; 2 Kings 6.16 years old and upwards, all who entered the
house of the LORD as the duty of each day
required, for their service according to their
32.8 Jer 17.5; 2 Chr 13.12; 20.17 offices, by their divisions. [17]The enrollment
of the priests was according to their ances-
tral houses; that of the Levites from twenty
years old and upwards was according to
32.11 2 Kings 18.30 their offices, by their divisions. [18]The priests
were enrolled with all their little children,
their wives, their sons, and their daughters,
32.12 2 Kings 18.22; 2 Chr 31.1 the whole multitude; for they were faithful
in keeping themselves holy. [19]And for the
descendants of Aaron, the priests, who were
in the fields of common land belonging to
their towns, town by town, the people
designated by name were to distribute portions to every male among the priests and
to everyone among the Levites who was
enrolled.

20 Hezekiah did this throughout all Judah;
he did what was good and right and faithful
before the LORD his God. [21]And every work
that he undertook in the service of the
house of God, and in accordance with the
law and the commandments, to seek his
God, he did with all his heart; and he
prospered.

Sennacherib's Invasion

32 After these things and these acts of
faithfulness, King Sennacherib of
Assyria came and invaded Judah and encamped against the fortified cities, thinking
to win them for himself. [2]When Hezekiah
saw that Sennacherib had come and intended to fight against Jerusalem, [3]he planned
with his officers and his warriors to stop the
flow of the springs that were outside the
city; and they helped him. [4]A great many
people were gathered, and they stopped all
the springs and the wadi that flowed through
the land, saying, "Why should the Assyrian
kings come and find water in abundance?"
[5]Hezekiah[i] set to work resolutely and built
up the entire wall that was broken down,
and raised towers on it,[j] and outside it he
built another wall; he also strengthened the
Millo in the city of David, and made weapons and shields in abundance. [6]He appointed
combat commanders over the people, and
gathered them together to him in the square
at the gate of the city and spoke encouragingly to them, saying, [7]"Be strong and of
good courage. Do not be afraid or dismayed
before the king of Assyria and all the horde
that is with him; for there is one greater
with us than with him. [8]With him is an
arm of flesh; but with us is the LORD our
God, to help us and to fight our battles."
The people were encouraged by the words
of King Hezekiah of Judah.

9 After this, while King Sennacherib of
Assyria was at Lachish with all his forces,
he sent his servants to Jerusalem to King
Hezekiah of Judah and to all the people of
Judah that were in Jerusalem, saying, [10]"Thus
says King Sennacherib of Assyria: On what
are you relying, that you undergo the siege
of Jerusalem? [11]Is not Hezekiah misleading
you, handing you over to die by famine and
by thirst, when he tells you, 'The LORD our
God will save us from the hand of the king
of Assyria'? [12]Was it not this same Hezekiah
who took away his high places and his
altars and commanded Judah and Jerusalem, saying, 'Before one altar you shall

32.1-23 This is a condensed version of 2 Kings 18-20. Judah was invaded by *King Sennacherib of Assyria* (705-681) after he had subdued the Babylonians in southern Mesopotamia and then turned to put down the coalition that had formed in the west led by Hezekiah: Judah, southern Syria, and the Philistine cities. In preparation for the defense of Jerusalem, Hezekiah had a tunnel cut more than 1700 feet through the bed rock beneath Jerusalem to provide water during the siege: the Siloam tunnel, for which the ancient inscription was found in the later nineteenth century. **32.9-23** Hezekiah's call to rely on *the LORD our God* rather than on human armies encouraged the people to hold out in spite of Sennacherib's scoffing and the scornful shouts of the enemy to the besieged Jerusalemites. *The prophet Isaiah* encouraged king and people to resist (*cf.* 2 Kings 19.5-7). When the Assyrian king's troops were struck down by *an angel*, he returned in frustration to his own lands and was assassinated by his *own sons* (Isa 36-37 = 2 Kings 18.13-20.11). Hezekiah and his people showed their gratitude by bringing *gifts to the LORD* in Jerusalem.

[i] Heb *He* [j] Vg: Heb *and raised on the towers*

32.24-32 Following a description of *Hezekiah's* great personal wealth and a note about God's letting him make his own decisions about diplomatic dealings with the Babylonians, the section closes with a typical Deuteronomic summary of his reign.
33.1-25 The Reigns of Manasseh and Amon. Manasseh as king (687-642) reinstituted idolatrous practices, thereby foreclosing the covenant promise that God had made to *Solomon*, which presupposed the people's keeping the law. The account is based on 2 Kings 21.1-18.

worship, and upon it you shall make your
offerings'? [13]Do you not know what I and
my ancestors have done to all the peoples
of other lands? Were the gods of the nations
of those lands at all able to save their lands
out of my hand? [14]Who among all the gods
of those nations that my ancestors utterly
destroyed was able to save his people from
my hand, that your God should be able to
save you from my hand? [15]Now therefore do
not let Hezekiah deceive you or mislead you
in this fashion, and do not believe him, for
no god of any nation or kingdom has been
able to save his people from my hand or
from the hand of my ancestors. How much
less will your God save you out of my
hand!"
16 His servants said still more against
the Lord God and against his servant
Hezekiah. [17]He also wrote letters to throw
contempt on the LORD the God of Israel and
to speak against him, saying, "Just as the
gods of the nations in other lands did not
rescue their people from my hands, so the
God of Hezekiah will not rescue his people
from my hand." [18]They shouted it with a
loud voice in the language of Judah to the
people of Jerusalem who were on the wall,
to frighten and terrify them, in order that
they might take the city. [19]They spoke of the
God of Jerusalem as if he were like the gods
of the peoples of the earth, which are the
work of human hands.

Sennacherib's Defeat and Death

20 Then King Hezekiah and the prophet
Isaiah son of Amoz prayed because of this
and cried to heaven. [21]And the LORD sent an
angel who cut off all the mighty warriors
and commanders and officers in the camp
of the king of Assyria. So he returned in
disgrace to his own land. When he came
into the house of his god, some of his own
sons struck him down there with the sword.
[22]So the LORD saved Hezekiah and the inhabitants of Jerusalem from the hand of
King Sennacherib of Assyria and from the
hand of all his enemies; he gave them rest[k]
on every side. [23]Many brought gifts to the
LORD in Jerusalem and precious things to
King Hezekiah of Judah, so that he was
exalted in the sight of all nations from that
time onward.

Hezekiah's Sickness

24 In those days Hezekiah became sick
and was at the point of death. He prayed
to the LORD, and he answered him and gave
him a sign. [25]But Hezekiah did not respond
according to the benefit done to him, for his
heart was proud. Therefore wrath came
upon him and upon Judah and Jerusalem.
[26]Then Hezekiah humbled himself for the
pride of his heart, both he and the inhabitants of Jerusalem, so that the wrath of the
LORD did not come upon them in the days
of Hezekiah.

Hezekiah's Prosperity and Achievements

27 Hezekiah had very great riches and
honor; and he made for himself treasuries
for silver, for gold, for precious stones, for
spices, for shields, and for all kinds of costly
objects; [28]storehouses also for the yield of
grain, wine, and oil; and stalls for all kinds
of cattle, and sheepfolds.[l] [29]He likewise provided cities for himself, and flocks and herds
in abundance; for God had given him very
great possessions. [30]This same Hezekiah
closed the upper outlet of the waters of
Gihon and directed them down to the west
side of the city of David. Hezekiah prospered
in all his works. [31]So also in the matter of
the envoys of the officials of Babylon, who
had been sent to him to inquire about the
sign that had been done in the land, God
left him to himself, in order to test him and
to know all that was in his heart.
32 Now the rest of the acts of Hezekiah,
and his good deeds, are written in the vision
of the prophet Isaiah son of Amoz in the
Book of the Kings of Judah and Israel.
[33]Hezekiah slept with his ancestors, and
they buried him on the ascent to the tombs
of the descendants of David; and all Judah
and the inhabitants of Jerusalem did him
honor at his death. His son Manasseh succeeded him.

Reign of Manasseh

33 Manasseh was twelve years old
when he began to reign; he reigned
fifty-five years in Jerusalem. [2]He did what
was evil in the sight of the LORD, according
to the abominable practices of the nations
whom the LORD drove out before the people

[k] Gk Vg: Heb *guided them* [l] Gk Vg: Heb *flocks for folds*

32.13 2 Kings 18.33-35
32.14 Isa 10.9-11
32.15 2 Kings 18.29
32.17 2 Kings 19.9,12
32.18 2 Kings 18.26-28
32.19 2 Kings 19.18
32.20 2 Kings 19.2,4,15
32.21 2 Kings 19.3ff
32.23 2 Chr 17.5
32.24 2 Kings 20.1-11; Isa 38.1-8
32.25 Ps 116.12; 2 Chr 26.16; 24.18
32.26 Jer 26.18,19
32.29 1 Chr 29.12
32.30 2 Kings 20.20; 1 Kings 1.33
32.31 2 Kings 20.12; Isa 39.1; Deut 8.2,16
32.33 2 Kings 20.21; Prov 10.7
33.1 2 Kings 21.1-9
33.2 Deut 18.9; 2 Chr 28.3

of Israel. 3For he rebuilt the high places that his father Hezekiah had pulled down, and erected altars to the Baals, made sacred poles,[m] worshiped all the host of heaven, and served them. 4He built altars in the house of the LORD, of which the LORD had said, "In Jerusalem shall my name be forever." 5He built altars for all the host of heaven in the two courts of the house of the LORD. 6He made his son pass through fire in the valley of the son of Hinnom, practiced soothsaying and augury and sorcery, and dealt with mediums and with wizards. He did much evil in the sight of the LORD, provoking him to anger. 7The carved image of the idol that he had made he set in the house of God, of which God said to David and to his son Solomon, "In this house, and in Jerusalem, which I have chosen out of all the tribes of Israel, I will put my name forever; 8I will never again remove the feet of Israel from the land that I appointed for your ancestors, if only they will be careful to do all that I have commanded them, all the law, the statutes, and the ordinances given through Moses." 9Manasseh misled Judah and the inhabitants of Jerusalem, so that they did more evil than the nations whom the LORD had destroyed before the people of Israel.

Manasseh Restored after Repentance

10 The LORD spoke to Manasseh and to his people, but they gave no heed. 11Therefore the LORD brought against them the commanders of the army of the king of Assyria, who took Manasseh captive in manacles, bound him with fetters, and brought him to Babylon. 12While he was in distress he entreated the favor of the LORD his God and humbled himself greatly before the God of his ancestors. 13He prayed to him, and God received his entreaty, heard his plea, and restored him again to Jerusalem and to his kingdom. Then Manasseh knew that the LORD indeed was God.

14 Afterward he built an outer wall for the city of David west of Gihon, in the valley, reaching the entrance at the Fish Gate; he carried it around Ophel, and raised it to a very great height. He also put commanders of the army in all the fortified cities in Judah. 15He took away the foreign gods and the idol from the house of the LORD, and all the altars that he had built on the mountain of the house of the LORD and in Jerusalem, and he threw them out of the city. 16He also restored the altar of the LORD and offered on it sacrifices of well-being and of thanksgiving; and he commanded Judah to serve the LORD the God of Israel. 17The people, however, still sacrificed at the high places, but only to the LORD their God.

Death of Manasseh

18 Now the rest of the acts of Manasseh, his prayer to his God, and the words of the seers who spoke to him in the name of the LORD God of Israel, these are in the Annals of the Kings of Israel. 19His prayer, and how God received his entreaty, all his sin and his faithlessness, the sites on which he built high places and set up the sacred poles[n] and the images, before he humbled himself, these are written in the records of the seers.[o] 20So Manasseh slept with his ancestors, and they buried him in his house. His son Amon succeeded him.

Amon's Reign and Death

21 Amon was twenty-two years old when he began to reign; he reigned two years in Jerusalem. 22He did what was evil in the sight of the LORD, as his father Manasseh had done. Amon sacrificed to all the images that his father Manasseh had made, and served them. 23He did not humble himself before the LORD, as his father Manasseh had humbled himself, but this Amon incurred more and more guilt. 24His servants conspired against him and killed him in his house. 25But the people of the land killed all those who had conspired against King Amon; and the people of the land made his son Josiah king to succeed him.

Reign of Josiah

34 Josiah was eight years old when he began to reign; he reigned thirty-one years in Jerusalem. 2He did what was right in the sight of the LORD, and walked in the ways of his ancestor David; he did not turn aside to the right or to the left. 3For in the eighth year of his reign, while he was still a boy, he began to seek the God of his ancestor David, and in the twelfth year he began to purge Judah and Jerusalem of the high places, the sacred poles,[n] and the carved

[m] Heb *Asheroth* [n] Heb *Asherim* [o] One Ms Gk: MT *of Hozai*

33.3 2 Chr 31.1; Deut 16.21; 2 Kings 23.5,6; Deut 17.3
33.4 2 Chr 28.24; 7.16
33.5 2 Chr 4.9
33.6 Lev 18.21; 2 Chr 28.3; Deut 18.10,11; 2 Kings 21.6
33.7 2 Kings 21.7; ver 4,15
33.8 2 Sam 7.10
33.11 Deut 28.36; Ps 107.10,11
33.12 2 Chr 32.26; 1 Pet 5.6
33.13 1 Chr 5.20; Ezra 8.23; Dan 4.25,32
33.14 1 Kings 1.33; Neh 3.3; 2 Chr 27.3
33.15 ver 3-7
33.17 2 Chr 32.12
33.18 ver 10,12,18
33.19 ver 3,13
33.20 2 Kings 21.18
33.21 2 Kings 21.19-24
33.22 ver 2-7
33.23 ver 12
33.24 see 2 Chr 25.27
34.1 2 Kings 22.1,2
34.3 2 Chr 15.2; 1 Kings 13.2; 2 Chr 33.17,22

33.10-20 Captured and taken to *Babylon,* Manasseh repented of his misguided leadership of his people and was enabled to return to Jerusalem, which he endeavored to enlarge and strengthen. A summary reports his death and the succession of his son *Amon* to the throne of Judah.
33.21-25 *Amon* followed the example of the earlier idolatrous practices of his father, and was murdered by his own *servants.* The people installed as king his young son, *Josiah,* at the age of eight.
34.1-35.27 The Reign and Reforms of Josiah.
34.1-33 Josiah's long reign (640-609) is described in terms of a renewal movement. In the earlier account of Josiah (2 Kings 22.1-23.30), the finding of the book of the Law launched his reform of Judah, while here the reform had already begun and was strengthened when the law book was recovered. Rebuilding the temple and reconstituting the priestly leadership enabled the reform to become operative. *Huldah the prophet* warns that *the curses that are written in the book* of the law will indeed fall on the disobedient people when God brings them under judgment, although Josiah will live out his life in peace because of his penitence and humility. Accordingly, Josiah led the people in the renewal of *the covenant,* and sought to remove all idolatrous features from his land.

and the cast images. [4]In his presence they
pulled down the altars of the Baals; he
demolished the incense altars that stood
above them. He broke down the sacred
poles[p] and the carved and the cast images;
he made dust of them and scattered it over
the graves of those who had sacrificed to
them. [5]He also burned the bones of the
priests on their altars, and purged Judah
and Jerusalem. [6]In the towns of Manasseh,
Ephraim, and Simeon, and as far as Naphtali,
in their ruins[q] all around, [7]he broke down
the altars, beat the sacred poles[p] and the
images into powder, and demolished all the
incense altars throughout all the land of
Israel. Then he returned to Jerusalem.

Discovery of the Book of the Law

8 In the eighteenth year of his reign,
when he had purged the land and the
house, he sent Shaphan son of Azaliah,
Maaseiah the governor of the city, and Joah
son of Joahaz, the recorder, to repair the
house of the LORD his God. [9]They came to
the high priest Hilkiah and delivered the
money that had been brought into the house
of God, which the Levites, the keepers of the
threshold, had collected from Manasseh and
Ephraim and from all the remnant of Israel
and from all Judah and Benjamin and from
the inhabitants of Jerusalem. [10]They delivered it to the workers who had the oversight of the house of the LORD, and the
workers who were working in the house of
the LORD gave it for repairing and restoring
the house. [11]They gave it to the carpenters
and the builders to buy quarried stone, and
timber for binders, and beams for the buildings that the kings of Judah had let go to
ruin. [12]The people did the work faithfully.
Over them were appointed the Levites Jahath
and Obadiah, of the sons of Merari, along
with Zechariah and Meshullam, of the sons
of the Kohathites, to have oversight. Other
Levites, all skillful with instruments of music,
[13]were over the burden bearers and directed
all who did work in every kind of service;
and some of the Levites were scribes, and
officials, and gatekeepers.

14 While they were bringing out the
money that had been brought into the house
of the LORD, the priest Hilkiah found the
book of the law of the LORD given through
Moses. [15]Hilkiah said to the secretary
Shaphan, "I have found the book of the law
in the house of the LORD"; and Hilkiah gave
the book to Shaphan. [16]Shaphan brought
the book to the king, and further reported
to the king, "All that was committed to
your servants they are doing. [17]They have
emptied out the money that was found in
the house of the LORD and have delivered it
into the hand of the overseers and the
workers." [18]The secretary Shaphan informed
the king, "The priest Hilkiah has given me
a book." Shaphan then read it aloud to the
king.

19 When the king heard the words of
the law he tore his clothes. [20]Then the king
commanded Hilkiah, Ahikam son of
Shaphan, Abdon son of Micah, the secretary Shaphan, and the king's servant Asaiah:
[21]"Go, inquire of the LORD for me and for
those who are left in Israel and in Judah,
concerning the words of the book that has
been found; for the wrath of the LORD that
is poured out on us is great, because our
ancestors did not keep the word of the LORD,
to act in accordance with all that is written
in this book."

The Prophet Huldah Consulted

22 So Hilkiah and those whom the king
had sent went to the prophet Huldah, the
wife of Shallum son of Tokhath son of
Hasrah, keeper of the wardrobe (who lived
in Jerusalem in the Second Quarter) and
spoke to her to that effect. [23]She declared to
them, "Thus says the LORD, the God of
Israel: Tell the man who sent you to me,
[24]Thus says the LORD: I will indeed bring
disaster upon this place and upon its inhabitants, all the curses that are written in the
book that was read before the king of Judah.
[25]Because they have forsaken me and have
made offerings to other gods, so that they
have provoked me to anger with all the
works of their hands, my wrath will be
poured out on this place and will not be
quenched. [26]But as to the king of Judah,
who sent you to inquire of the LORD, thus
shall you say to him: Thus says the LORD,
the God of Israel: Regarding the words that
you have heard, [27]because your heart was
penitent and you humbled yourself before
God when you heard his words against this
place and its inhabitants, and you have
humbled yourself before me, and have torn
your clothes and wept before me, I also
have heard you, says the LORD. [28]I will

34.4 Lev 26.30; 2 Kings 23.4; Ex 32.20

34.5 1 Kings 13.2; 2 Kings 23.20

34.6 2 Kings 23.15,19

34.7 2 Chr 31.1

34.8 2 Kings 22.3-20

34.9 2 Chr 35.8

34.11 2 Chr 33.4-7

34.12 1 Chr 25.1

34.13 1 Chr 23.4,5

34.14 ver 9

34.16 ver 8

34.19 Josh 7.6

34.21 2 Chr 29.8

34.22 2 Kings 22.14

34.24 2 Chr 36.14-20; Deut 28.15-68

34.25 2 Chr 33.3

34.27 2 Chr 12.7; 32.26

[p] Heb *Asherim* [q] Meaning of Heb uncertain

34.29 2 Kings 23.1-3
34.30 Neh 8.1-3
34.31 2 Kings 11.14; 23.3; 2 Chr 23.3,16; 29.10
34.33 ver 3-7; 2 Chr 33.2-7
35.1 2 Kings 23.21,22; Ex 12.6; Num 9.3
35.2 2 Chr 23.18; 29.11
35.3 Deut 33.10; 2 Chr 5.7; 1 Chr 23.26
35.4 1 Chr 9.10-13; 2 Chr 8.14
35.5 Ps 134.1
35.6 ver 1; 2 Chr 29.5,15; Ezra 6.20
35.7 2 Chr 30.24
35.9 2 Chr 31.12
35.10 ver 5; Ezra 6.18
35.11 ver 1,6; 2 Chr 29.22,34
35.13 Ex 12.8,9; Lev 6.25; 1 Sam 2.13-15
35.15 1 Chr 25.1; 26.12-19
35.17 Ex 12.15; 2 Chr 30.21

gather you to your ancestors and you shall
be gathered to your grave in peace; your
eyes shall not see all the disaster that I will
bring on this place and its inhabitants."
They took the message back to the king.

The Covenant Renewed

29 Then the king sent word and gathered together all the elders of Judah and
Jerusalem. [30]The king went up to the house
of the LORD, with all the people of Judah, the
inhabitants of Jerusalem, the priests and the
Levites, all the people both great and small;
he read in their hearing all the words of the
book of the covenant that had been found
in the house of the LORD. [31]The king stood
in his place and made a covenant before the
LORD, to follow the LORD, keeping his commandments, his decrees, and his statutes,
with all his heart and all his soul, to perform the words of the covenant that were
written in this book. [32]Then he made all
who were present in Jerusalem and in
Benjamin pledge themselves to it. And the
inhabitants of Jerusalem acted according to
the covenant of God, the God of their ancestors. [33]Josiah took away all the abominations from all the territory that belonged to
the people of Israel, and made all who were
in Israel worship the LORD their God. All his
days they did not turn away from following
the LORD the God of their ancestors.

Celebration of the Passover

35 Josiah kept a passover to the
LORD in Jerusalem; they slaughtered the passover lamb on the fourteenth
day of the first month. [2]He appointed the
priests to their offices and encouraged them
in the service of the house of the LORD. [3]He
said to the Levites who taught all Israel and
who were holy to the LORD, "Put the holy
ark in the house that Solomon son of David,
king of Israel, built; you need no longer
carry it on your shoulders. Now serve the
LORD your God and his people Israel. [4]Make
preparations by your ancestral houses by
your divisions, following the written directions of King David of Israel and the written
directions of his son Solomon. [5]Take position in the holy place according to the
groupings of the ancestral houses of your
kindred the people, and let there be Levites
for each division of an ancestral house.[r]
[6]Slaughter the passover lamb, sanctify yourselves, and on behalf of your kindred make
preparations, acting according to the word
of the LORD by Moses."

7 Then Josiah contributed to the people,
as passover offerings for all that were present,
lambs and kids from the flock to the number
of thirty thousand, and three thousand bulls;
these were from the king's possessions. [8]His
officials contributed willingly to the people,
to the priests, and to the Levites. Hilkiah,
Zechariah, and Jehiel, the chief officers of
the house of God, gave to the priests for the
passover offerings two thousand six hundred lambs and kids and three hundred
bulls. [9]Conaniah also, and his brothers
Shemaiah and Nethanel, and Hashabiah
and Jeiel and Jozabad, the chiefs of the
Levites, gave to the Levites for the passover
offerings five thousand lambs and kids and
five hundred bulls.

10 When the service had been prepared
for, the priests stood in their place, and the
Levites in their divisions according to the
king's command. [11]They slaughtered the
passover lamb, and the priests dashed the
blood that they received[s] from them, while
the Levites did the skinning. [12]They set aside
the burnt offerings so that they might distribute them according to the groupings of
the ancestral houses of the people, to offer
to the LORD, as it is written in the book of
Moses. And they did the same with the
bulls. [13]They roasted the passover lamb with
fire according to the ordinance; and they
boiled the holy offerings in pots, in caldrons,
and in pans, and carried them quickly to all
the people. [14]Afterward they made preparations for themselves and for the priests,
because the priests the descendants of Aaron
were occupied in offering the burnt offerings and the fat parts until night; so the
Levites made preparations for themselves
and for the priests, the descendants of Aaron.
[15]The singers, the descendants of Asaph,
were in their place according to the command of David, and Asaph, and Heman,
and the king's seer Jeduthun. The gatekeepers were at each gate; they did not need to
interrupt their service, for their kindred the
Levites made preparations for them.

16 So all the service of the LORD was
prepared that day, to keep the passover and
to offer burnt offerings on the altar of the
LORD, according to the command of King
Josiah. [17]The people of Israel who were

[r] Meaning of Heb uncertain [s] Heb lacks *that they received*

35.1-19 The great celebration of the *Passover,* as in the days of Hezekiah, is to show the repentance and renewal of the covenant people.

35.20-27 King Neco II of Egypt (610-595) sent an expedition to Syria to help the Assyrian king resist the efforts of the Babylonians to take over the empire. *Josiah* offered military resistance to Neco, and was fatally wounded. His death evoked sorrow from *all Judah and Jerusalem*, as well as a *lament* from the prophet Jeremiah (Jer 22.11-17).
36.1-21 The Last Kings of Judah and the Fall of Jerusalem. See 2 Kings 23.30-25.21.
36.1-8 *Jehoahaz'* reign of three months (in 609) was terminated by intervention of *Neco of Egypt*, who exacted tribute from Judah and then installed his own candidate: *Eliakim*, meaning "God raises up." His name was changed to *Jehoiakim* ("the LORD raises up"); he reigned from 609-598. Jerusalem was invaded by Nebuchadnezzar II (605-562), who had led the Babylonians to victory over the Assyrians and now claimed their entire empire. Details of the military exploits are preserved in Babylonian documents and inscriptions recovered over the years by modern archaeologists. The king of Judah and treasures from its temple were taken off to Babylon, which was a foretaste of the full exile of Judah in 586.
36.9-14 The child king, *Jehoiachin*, reigned only *three months and ten days* (in 598) before being taken captive to Babylon, along with more treasures from the temple. His older brother, *Zedekiah* (597-586), who was put on the throne by the Babylonians, rebelled against the God of Israel and ignored the warnings of *the prophet Jeremiah* (see Jer 37-39; 52).

present kept the passover at that time, and
the festival of unleavened bread seven days.
18No passover like it had been kept in Israel
since the days of the prophet Samuel; none
of the kings of Israel had kept such a passover
as was kept by Josiah, by the priests and the
Levites, by all Judah and Israel who were
present, and by the inhabitants of Jerusalem. 19In the eighteenth year of the reign of
Josiah this passover was kept.

Defeat by Pharaoh Neco and Death of Josiah

20 After all this, when Josiah had set the
temple in order, King Neco of Egypt went
up to fight at Carchemish on the Euphrates,
and Josiah went out against him. 21But
Neco[t] sent envoys to him, saying, "What
have I to do with you, king of Judah? I am
not coming against you today, but against
the house with which I am at war; and God
has commanded me to hurry. Cease opposing God, who is with me, so that he will not
destroy you." 22But Josiah would not turn
away from him, but disguised himself in
order to fight with him. He did not listen to
the words of Neco from the mouth of God,
but joined battle in the plain of Megiddo.
23The archers shot King Josiah; and the
king said to his servants, "Take me away,
for I am badly wounded." 24So his servants
took him out of the chariot and carried him
in his second chariot[u] and brought him to
Jerusalem. There he died, and was buried in
the tombs of his ancestors. All Judah and
Jerusalem mourned for Josiah. 25Jeremiah
also uttered a lament for Josiah, and all the
singing men and singing women have spoken of Josiah in their laments to this day.
They made these a custom in Israel; they
are recorded in the Laments. 26Now the rest
of the acts of Josiah and his faithful deeds
in accordance with what is written in the
law of the LORD, 27and his acts, first and last,
are written in the Book of the Kings of Israel
and Judah.

Reign of Jehoahaz

36 The people of the land took
Jehoahaz son of Josiah and made
him king to succeed his father in Jerusalem.
2Jehoahaz was twenty-three years old when
he began to reign; he reigned three months
in Jerusalem. 3Then the king of Egypt
deposed him in Jerusalem and laid on the
land a tribute of one hundred talents of
silver and one talent of gold. 4The king of
Egypt made his brother Eliakim king over
Judah and Jerusalem, and changed his name
to Jehoiakim; but Neco took his brother
Jehoahaz and carried him to Egypt.

Reign and Captivity of Jehoiakim

5 Jehoiakim was twenty-five years old
when he began to reign; he reigned eleven
years in Jerusalem. He did what was evil in
the sight of the LORD his God. 6Against him
King Nebuchadnezzar of Babylon came up,
and bound him with fetters to take him to
Babylon. 7Nebuchadnezzar also carried some
of the vessels of the house of the LORD to
Babylon and put them in his palace in
Babylon. 8Now the rest of the acts of
Jehoiakim, and the abominations that he
did, and what was found against him, are
written in the Book of the Kings of Israel
and Judah; and his son Jehoiachin succeeded him.

Reign and Captivity of Jehoiachin

9 Jehoiachin was eight years old when
he began to reign; he reigned three months
and ten days in Jerusalem. He did what was
evil in the sight of the LORD. 10In the spring
of the year King Nebuchadnezzar sent and
brought him to Babylon, along with the
precious vessels of the house of the LORD,
and made his brother Zedekiah king over
Judah and Jerusalem.

Reign of Zedekiah

11 Zedekiah was twenty-one years old
when he began to reign; he reigned eleven
years in Jerusalem. 12He did what was evil
in the sight of the LORD his God. He did not
humble himself before the prophet Jeremiah
who spoke from the mouth of the LORD. 13He
also rebelled against King Nebuchadnezzar,
who had made him swear by God; he stiffened his neck and hardened his heart against
turning to the LORD, the God of Israel. 14All
the leading priests and the people also were
exceedingly unfaithful, following all the
abominations of the nations; and they polluted the house of the LORD that he had
consecrated in Jerusalem.

35.18 2 Kings 23.21-23
35.20 2 Kings 23.29,30; Isa 10.9; Jer 46.2
35.22 2 Chr 18.29; Judg 5.19
35.24 2 Kings 23.30; Zech 12.11
35.25 Lam 4.20; Jer 22.20
36.1 2 Kings 23.30-34; Jer 22.11
36.5 2 Kings 23.36,37
36.6 2 Kings 24.1; 2 Chr 33.11
36.7 2 Kings 24.13
36.8 2 Kings 24.5; see 1 Chr 3.16
36.9 2 Kings 24.8-17
36.10 2 Sam 11.1; Jer 37.1
36.11 2 Kings 24.18-20; Jer 52.1
36.12 2 Chr 33.23; Jer 21.3-7
36.13 Jer 52.3; 2 Kings 17.14; 2 Chr 30.8

[t] Heb *he* [u] Or *the chariot of his deputy*

36.15 Jer 25.3,4; 35.15; 44.4
36.16 2 Chr 30.10; Jer 5.12,13; Prov 1.25; Ezra 5.12
36.17 2 Kings 25.1-7
36.18 2 Kings 25.13ff
36.19 2 Kings 25.9; Jer 52.13
36.20 2 Kings 25.11; Jer 27.7
36.21 Jer 29.10; Lev 26.34; 25.4
36.22 Ezra 1.1; Jer 25.12; Isa 44.28
36.23 Ezra 1.2,3

The Fall of Jerusalem

15 The LORD, the God of their ancestors,
sent persistently to them by his messengers,
because he had compassion on his people
and on his dwelling place; [16]but they kept
mocking the messengers of God, despising
his words, and scoffing at his prophets, until
the wrath of the LORD against his people
became so great that there was no remedy.
17 Therefore he brought up against them
the king of the Chaldeans, who killed their
youths with the sword in the house of their
sanctuary, and had no compassion on young
man or young woman, the aged or the
feeble; he gave them all into his hand. [18]All
the vessels of the house of God, large and
small, and the treasures of the house of the
LORD, and the treasures of the king and of
his officials, all these he brought to Babylon.
[19]They burned the house of God, broke
down the wall of Jerusalem, burned all its
palaces with fire, and destroyed all its precious vessels. [20]He took into exile in Babylon
those who had escaped from the sword, and
they became servants to him and to his
sons until the establishment of the kingdom
of Persia, [21]to fulfill the word of the LORD by
the mouth of Jeremiah, until the land had
made up for its sabbaths. All the days that
it lay desolate it kept sabbath, to fulfill
seventy years.

Cyrus Proclaims Liberty for the Exiles

22 In the first year of King Cyrus of
Persia, in fulfillment of the word of the LORD
spoken by Jeremiah, the LORD stirred up the
spirit of King Cyrus of Persia so that he sent
a herald throughout all his kingdom and
also declared in a written edict: [23]"Thus
says King Cyrus of Persia: The LORD, the God
of heaven, has given me all the kingdoms
of the earth, and he has charged me to
build him a house at Jerusalem, which is in
Judah. Whoever is among you of all his
people, may the LORD his God be with him!
Let him go up."

36.15-21 *Jerusalem*, the LORD's *dwelling place*, was now seized by the Babylonians. Their actions are here pictured as God's punishment of his disobedient people: the youth were killed, the sanctuary was stripped of its treasures and burned, and the inhabitants were exiled to Babylon, where they became slaves. Only with *the establishment of the kingdom of Persia* would there be any hope of renewal for God's people. The prophecies of *Jeremiah* about judgment and renewal after 70 years appear in Jer 25.1-14; 29.10-14.
36.22-23 Epilogue: The Decree of Cyrus about Judah's Return. In what may be a later addition to 2 Chr, there is mention of the decree of Cyrus II, who ruled Babylon as part of his Persian realm from 539-530, allowing the people of Judah to return to their land and to rebuild God's *house at Jerusalem*.

EZRA

See the Introductions, pp. 3, 38, and 45-46 above.

1.1 2 Chr 36.22,23; Jer 25.12; 29.10; Ezra 5.13,14
1.2 Isa 44.28; 45.1,12,13
1.3 Dan 6.26
1.5 Phil 2.13
1.7 Ezra 5.14; 6.5; 2 Kings 24.13; 2 Chr 36.7
1.8 Ezra 5.14

End of the Babylonian Captivity

1 In the first year of King Cyrus of
Persia, in order that the word of the
LORD by the mouth of Jeremiah might be
accomplished, the LORD stirred up the spirit
of King Cyrus of Persia so that he sent a
herald throughout all his kingdom, and also
in a written edict declared:
2 "Thus says King Cyrus of Persia: The
LORD, the God of heaven, has given me all
the kingdoms of the earth, and he has
charged me to build him a house at Jerusalem
in Judah. [3]Any of those among you who are
of his people—may their God be with them!—
are now permitted to go up to Jerusalem in
Judah, and rebuild the house of the LORD, the
God of Israel—he is the God who is in
Jerusalem; [4]and let all survivors, in whatever
place they reside, be assisted by the people
of their place with silver and gold, with goods
and with animals, besides freewill offerings
for the house of God in Jerusalem."
5 The heads of the families of Judah and
Benjamin, and the priests and the Levites—
everyone whose spirit God had stirred—got
ready to go up and rebuild the house of the
LORD in Jerusalem. [6]All their neighbors aided
them with silver vessels, with gold, with
goods, with animals, and with valuable gifts,
besides all that was freely offered. [7]King
Cyrus himself brought out the vessels of the
house of the LORD that Nebuchadnezzar had
carried away from Jerusalem and placed in
the house of his gods. [8]King Cyrus of Persia
had them released into the charge of
Mithredath the treasurer, who counted them
out to Sheshbazzar the prince of Judah.
[9]And this was the inventory: gold basins,
thirty; silver basins, one thousand; knives,[a]
twenty-nine; [10]gold bowls, thirty; other silver bowls, four hundred ten; other vessels,
one thousand; [11]the total of the gold and
silver vessels was five thousand four hundred. All these Sheshbazzar brought up,
when the exiles were brought up from
Babylonia to Jerusalem.

[a] Vg: Meaning of Heb uncertain

1.1-2.70 The Decree of King Cyrus of Persia Permitting the Jewish Exiles to Return to their Land.
1.1-4 Cyrus II, emperor of Persia, ruled Babylonia from 539-530. His decree was seen by the prophet Jeremiah as fulfillment of his prediction about the people's return (Jer 29.10; 2 Chr 36.21) and he was acclaimed by the prophet Isaiah as the LORD's *anointed*. His decree, which allowed the Jews to return and to rebuild the house of the LORD there, is said to be the result of the LORD stirring up Cyrus' *spirit*.
1.5-11 Preparations for the Return of the Exiles to Jerusalem. In addition to the arrangements for the return made by heads of the families of Judah, the priests and the Levites, Cyrus ordered the release of the sacred vessels that had been brought to Babylon from the Jerusalem temple under *Nebuchadnezzar* and entrusted them to *Sheshbazzar*, someone presumably of Jewish origin but with a Babylonian name. He led the returnees back to Jerusalem.

2.1-70 The list of Babylonian exiles who returned to Jerusalem includes ordinary heads of families, priests (2.36-39), Levites (2.40-42) and temple servants (2.43-58). Also in the number headed for Jerusalem were some who wanted to be included among the priests, but who were not found in the genealogical records and were therefore excluded from the priesthood as *unclean* (2.59-63). Decision as to their ultimate inclusion would be made by appeal to the sacred lot: *Urim and Thummim* (Num 27.21). The total number of those returning is given as 42,360, not counting servants and other attendants. The plan was to rebuild the temple on the traditional site.

List of the Returned Exiles

2 Now these were the people of the province who came from those captive exiles whom King Nebuchadnezzar of Babylon had carried captive to Babylonia; they returned to Jerusalem and Judah, all to their own towns. 2They came with Zerubbabel, Jeshua, Nehemiah, Seraiah, Reelaiah, Mordecai, Bilshan, Mispar, Bigvai, Rehum, and Baanah.

The number of the Israelite people: 3the descendants of Parosh, two thousand one hundred seventy-two. 4Of Shephatiah, three hundred seventy-two. 5Of Arah, seven hundred seventy-five. 6Of Pahath-moab, namely the descendants of Jeshua and Joab, two thousand eight hundred twelve. 7Of Elam, one thousand two hundred fifty-four. 8Of Zattu, nine hundred forty-five. 9Of Zaccai, seven hundred sixty. 10Of Bani, six hundred forty-two. 11Of Bebai, six hundred twenty-three. 12Of Azgad, one thousand two hundred twenty-two. 13Of Adonikam, six hundred sixty-six. 14Of Bigvai, two thousand fifty-six. 15Of Adin, four hundred fifty-four. 16Of Ater, namely of Hezekiah, ninety-eight. 17Of Bezai, three hundred twenty-three. 18Of Jorah, one hundred twelve. 19Of Hashum, two hundred twenty-three. 20Of Gibbar, ninety-five. 21Of Bethlehem, one hundred twenty-three. 22The people of Netophah, fifty-six. 23Of Anathoth, one hundred twenty-eight. 24The descendants of Azmaveth, forty-two. 25Of Kiriatharim, Chephirah, and Beeroth, seven hundred forty-three. 26Of Ramah and Geba, six hundred twenty-one. 27The people of Michmas, one hundred twenty-two. 28Of Bethel and Ai, two hundred twenty-three. 29The descendants of Nebo, fifty-two. 30Of Magbish, one hundred fifty-six. 31Of the other Elam, one thousand two hundred fifty-four. 32Of Harim, three hundred twenty. 33Of Lod, Hadid, and Ono, seven hundred twenty-five. 34Of Jericho, three hundred forty-five. 35Of Senaah, three thousand six hundred thirty.

36 The priests: the descendants of Jedaiah, of the house of Jeshua, nine hundred seventy-three. 37Of Immer, one thousand fifty-two. 38Of Pashhur, one thousand two hundred forty-seven. 39Of Harim, one thousand seventeen.

40 The Levites: the descendants of Jeshua and Kadmiel, of the descendants of Hodaviah, seventy-four. 41The singers: the descendants of Asaph, one hundred twenty-eight. 42The descendants of the gatekeepers: of Shallum, of Ater, of Talmon, of Akkub, of Hatita, and of Shobai, in all one hundred thirty-nine.

43 The temple servants: the descendants of Ziha, Hasupha, Tabbaoth, 44Keros, Siaha, Padon, 45Lebanah, Hagabah, Akkub, 46Hagab, Shamlai, Hanan, 47Giddel, Gahar, Reaiah, 48Rezin, Nekoda, Gazzam, 49Uzza, Paseah, Besai, 50Asnah, Meunim, Nephisim, 51Bakbuk, Hakupha, Harhur, 52Bazluth, Mehida, Harsha, 53Barkos, Sisera, Temah, 54Neziah, and Hatipha.

55 The descendants of Solomon's servants: Sotai, Hassophereth, Peruda, 56Jaalah, Darkon, Giddel, 57Shephatiah, Hattil, Pochereth-hazzebaim, and Ami.

58 All the temple servants and the descendants of Solomon's servants were three hundred ninety-two.

59 The following were those who came up from Tel-melah, Tel-harsha, Cherub, Addan, and Immer, though they could not prove their families or their descent, whether they belonged to Israel: 60the descendants of Delaiah, Tobiah, and Nekoda, six hundred fifty-two. 61Also, of the descendants of the priests: the descendants of Habaiah, Hakkoz, and Barzillai (who had married one of the daughters of Barzillai the Gileadite, and was called by their name). 62These looked for their entries in the genealogical records, but they were not found there, and so they were excluded from the priesthood as unclean; 63the governor told them that they were not to partake of the most holy food, until there should be a priest to consult Urim and Thummim.

64 The whole assembly together was forty-two thousand three hundred sixty, 65besides their male and female servants, of whom there were seven thousand three hundred thirty-seven; and they had two hundred male and female singers. 66They had seven hundred thirty-six horses, two hundred forty-five mules, 67four hundred thirty-five camels, and six thousand seven hundred twenty donkeys.

68 As soon as they came to the house of the LORD in Jerusalem, some of the heads of families made freewill offerings for the house of God, to erect it on its site. 69According to their resources they gave to the building fund sixty-one thousand darics of gold, five thousand minas of silver, and one hundred priestly robes.

70 The priests, the Levites, and some of the people lived in Jerusalem and its vicinity;[b] and the singers, the gatekeepers, and the

2.1 Neh 7.6-73; 2 Kings 24.14-16; 25.11; 2 Chr 36.20
2.5 Neh 7.10
2.6 Neh 7.11
2.16 Neh 7.21
2.21 Neh 7.26
2.31 see ver 7
2.36 1 Chr 24.7-18
2.38 1 Chr 9.12
2.39 1 Chr 24.8
2.43 1 Chr 9.2
2.48 Neh 7.50
2.55 Neh 7.57,60; 11.3
2.58 ver 55
2.61 2 Sam 17.27
2.62 Num 3.10; 16.39,40
2.63 Lev 2.3,19; Ex 28.30
2.64 Neh 7.66ff
2.69 Ezra 8.25-34

[b] 1 Esdras 5.46: Heb lacks *lived in Jerusalem and its vicinity*

temple servants lived in their towns, and all Israel in their towns.

Worship Restored at Jerusalem

3 When the seventh month came, and the Israelites were in the towns, the people gathered together in Jerusalem. [2]Then Jeshua son of Jozadak, with his fellow priests, and Zerubbabel son of Shealtiel with his kin set out to build the altar of the God of Israel, to offer burnt offerings on it, as prescribed in the law of Moses the man of God. [3]They set up the altar on its foundation, because they were in dread of the neighboring peoples, and they offered burnt offerings upon it to the LORD, morning and evening. [4]And they kept the festival of booths,[c] as prescribed, and offered the daily burnt offerings by number according to the ordinance, as required for each day, [5]and after that the regular burnt offerings, the offerings at the new moon and at all the sacred festivals of the LORD, and the offerings of everyone who made a freewill offering to the LORD. [6]From the first day of the seventh month they began to offer burnt offerings to the LORD. But the foundation of the temple of the LORD was not yet laid. [7]So they gave money to the masons and the carpenters, and food, drink, and oil to the Sidonians and the Tyrians to bring cedar trees from Lebanon to the sea, to Joppa, according to the grant that they had from King Cyrus of Persia.

Foundation Laid for the Temple

8 In the second year after their arrival at the house of God at Jerusalem, in the second month, Zerubbabel son of Shealtiel and Jeshua son of Jozadak made a beginning, together with the rest of their people, the priests and the Levites and all who had come to Jerusalem from the captivity. They appointed the Levites, from twenty years old and upward, to have the oversight of the work on the house of the LORD. [9]And Jeshua with his sons and his kin, and Kadmiel and his sons, Binnui and Hodaviah[d] along with the sons of Henadad, the Levites, their sons and kin, together took charge of the workers in the house of God.

10 When the builders laid the foundation of the temple of the LORD, the priests in their vestments were stationed to praise the LORD with trumpets, and the Levites, the sons of Asaph, with cymbals, according to the directions of King David of Israel; [11]and they sang responsively, praising and giving thanks to the LORD,

"For he is good,
for his steadfast love endures forever
toward Israel."

And all the people responded with a great shout when they praised the LORD, because the foundation of the house of the LORD was laid. [12]But many of the priests and Levites and heads of families, old people who had seen the first house on its foundations, wept with a loud voice when they saw this house, though many shouted aloud for joy, [13]so that the people could not distinguish the sound of the joyful shout from the sound of the people's weeping, for the people shouted so loudly that the sound was heard far away.

Resistance to Rebuilding the Temple

4 When the adversaries of Judah and Benjamin heard that the returned exiles were building a temple to the LORD, the God of Israel, [2]they approached Zerubbabel and the heads of families and said to them, "Let us build with you, for we worship your God as you do, and we have been sacrificing to him ever since the days of King Esar-haddon of Assyria who brought us here." [3]But Zerubbabel, Jeshua, and the rest of the heads of families in Israel said to them, "You shall have no part with us in building a house to our God; but we alone will build to the LORD, the God of Israel, as King Cyrus of Persia has commanded us."

4 Then the people of the land discouraged the people of Judah, and made them afraid to build, [5]and they bribed officials to frustrate their plan throughout the reign of King Cyrus of Persia and until the reign of King Darius of Persia.

Rebuilding of Jerusalem Opposed

6 In the reign of Ahasuerus, in his accession year, they wrote an accusation against the inhabitants of Judah and Jerusalem.

7 And in the days of Artaxerxes, Bishlam and Mithredath and Tabeel and the rest of their associates wrote to King Artaxerxes of Persia; the letter was written in Aramaic

[c] Or *tabernacles*; Heb *succoth* [d] Compare 2.40; Neh 7.43; 1 Esdras 5.58: Heb *sons of Judah*

3.1 Neh 7.73; 8.1
3.2 Neh 12.1,8; Ezra 2.2; 1 Chr 3.17; Deut 12.5,6
3.3 Ezra 4.4; Num 28.2-4
3.4 Neh 8.14; Ex 23.16; Num 29.12
3.7 2 Chr 2.10,16; Ezra 1.2; 6.3
3.8 ver 2; Ezra 4.3; 1 Chr 23.24,27
3.9 Ezra 2.40
3.10 1 Chr 16.5,6,42; 6.31; 25.1
3.11 Ex 15.21; 2 Chr 7.3; Neh 12.24; 1 Chr 16.34,41
4.1 ver 7-10
4.2 2 Kings 17.24,32,33; 19.37
4.3 Neh 2.20; Ezra 1.1-3
4.4 Ezra 3.3
4.6 Esth 1.1; Dan 9.1
4.7 2 Kings 18.26; Dan 2.4

3.1-12 Worship Resumed at Jerusalem.
3.1-7 The altar was erected on the earlier site, and the cycle of burnt offerings began. The foundation of the temple itself was not yet laid, but materials were brought from Tyre and Sidon.
3.8-11 With the laying of the foundation of the temple, and the re-establishment of the priestly offices, there were mixed reactions from the people: praise from many, but sorrow among those who remembered the temple of Solomon, which had been far more grand than the modest structure now in process.
4.1-24 Opposition to the Rebuilding of Jerusalem and the Temple.
4.1-3 A subversive scheme of the local residents led them to pose as supporters of the rebuilding project and worshippers of the LORD since the days of *King Esar-haddon* (king of Assyria 681-669) while actually opposing the project. Their attempt was thwarted by *Zerubbabel*, who in spite of his name (*shoot of Babylon*) was of Davidic descent and apparently had been designated as governor of Judah by the Persian ruler, Darius I (522-486). He reaffirmed the decree of *Cyrus* (539-530) for restoring the city and the temple.
4.4-16 The residents of the region frustrated the rebuilding enterprise by threat and bribery from the time of Cyrus until *the reign of Darius* (522-486). The opposition wrote to the Persian ruler, *Ahasuerus* (probably Xerxes, who reigned from 485-464), and then again to *Artaxerxes I* (465-424), to his official staff and to the *rest of the nations* who had been settled in the regions of the tribes of Israel by *Osnappar* (probably Assurbanipal, the Assyrian ruler in 668-630, who had settled other peoples in the former land of Israel and adjacent territories). The letter charged the people now settling in Judah with a scheme of rebellion against Persian rulers.

4.17-24 The initial reaction of the king was to give credence to the charges of a Jewish independence scheme, as expressed in his letter to those in *Samaria and the rest of the province Beyond the River* (meaning, the Persian-controlled territory west and south of the Euphrates). In reaction to this imperial letter, rebuilding ceased in Jerusalem until *the second year of Darius* (which was 521).
5.1-6.22 Resumption of the Building of the Temple.
5.1-17 The prophets Haggai and Zechariah encouraged the rebuilding project, now resumed with imperial permission. In response to a hostile letter from the governor of the province, Tattenai, the Jews wrote to Darius, explaining how and why the earlier city and temple were destroyed – as a divine judgment on the disobedience of his people – and how *Cyrus* (539-530) had granted them permission and provided the materials to rebuild the temple.

and translated.[e] [8]Rehum the royal deputy and Shimshai the scribe wrote a letter against Jerusalem to King Artaxerxes as follows [9](then Rehum the royal deputy, Shimshai the scribe, and the rest of their associates, the judges, the envoys, the officials, the Persians, the people of Erech, the Babylonians, the people of Susa, that is, the Elamites, [10]and the rest of the nations whom the great and noble Osnappar deported and settled in the cities of Samaria and in the rest of the province Beyond the River wrote—and now [11]this is a copy of the letter that they sent):

"To King Artaxerxes: Your servants, the people of the province Beyond the River, send greeting. And now [12]may it be known to the king that the Jews who came up from you to us have gone to Jerusalem. They are rebuilding that rebellious and wicked city; they are finishing the walls and repairing the foundations. [13]Now may it be known to the king that, if this city is rebuilt and the walls finished, they will not pay tribute, custom, or toll, and the royal revenue will be reduced. [14]Now because we share the salt of the palace and it is not fitting for us to witness the king's dishonor, therefore we send and inform the king, [15]so that a search may be made in the annals of your ancestors. You will discover in the annals that this is a rebellious city, hurtful to kings and provinces, and that sedition was stirred up in it from long ago. On that account this city was laid waste. [16]We make known to the king that, if this city is rebuilt and its walls finished, you will then have no possession in the province Beyond the River."

17 The king sent an answer: "To Rehum the royal deputy and Shimshai the scribe and the rest of their associates who live in Samaria and in the rest of the province Beyond the River, greeting. And now [18]the letter that you sent to us has been read in translation before me. [19]So I made a decree, and someone searched and discovered that this city has risen against kings from long ago, and that rebellion and sedition have been made in it. [20]Jerusalem has had mighty kings who ruled over the whole province Beyond the River, to whom tribute, custom, and toll were paid. [21]Therefore issue an order that these people be made to cease, and that this city not be rebuilt, until I make a decree. [22]Moreover, take care not to be slack in this matter; why should damage grow to the hurt of the king?"

23 Then when the copy of King Artaxerxes' letter was read before Rehum and the scribe Shimshai and their associates, they hurried to the Jews in Jerusalem and by force and power made them cease. [24]At that time the work on the house of God in Jerusalem stopped and was discontinued until the second year of the reign of King Darius of Persia.

Restoration of the Temple Resumed

5 Now the prophets, Haggai[f] and Zechariah son of Iddo, prophesied to the Jews who were in Judah and Jerusalem, in the name of the God of Israel who was over them. [2]Then Zerubbabel son of Shealtiel and Jeshua son of Jozadak set out to rebuild the house of God in Jerusalem; and with them were the prophets of God, helping them.

3 At the same time Tattenai the governor of the province Beyond the River and Shethar-bozenai and their associates came to them and spoke to them thus, "Who gave you a decree to build this house and to finish this structure?" [4]They[g] also asked them this, "What are the names of the men who are building this building?" [5]But the eye of their God was upon the elders of the Jews, and they did not stop them until a report reached Darius and then answer was returned by letter in reply to it.

6 The copy of the letter that Tattenai the governor of the province Beyond the River and Shethar-bozenai and his associates the envoys who were in the province Beyond the River sent to King Darius; [7]they sent him a report, in which was written as follows: "To Darius the king, all peace! [8]May it be known to the king that we went to the province of Judah, to the house of the great God. It is being built of hewn stone, and timber is laid in the walls; this work is being done diligently and prospers in their hands. [9]Then we spoke to those elders and asked them, 'Who gave you a decree to build this house and to finish this structure?' [10]We also asked them their names, for your information, so that we might write down the names of the men at their head. [11]This was their reply to us: 'We are the servants of the God of heaven and earth, and we are rebuilding the house that was built many years ago,

4.10 ver 1
4.12 Ezra 5.3,9
4.13 ver 20; Ezra 7.24
4.18 Neh 8.8
4.20 1 Kings 4.21; Ps 72.8
5.1 Hag 1.1; Zech 1.1
5.2 Ezra 3.2
5.3 Ezra 6.6; ver 9; Ezra 1.3
5.4 ver 10
5.5 Ezra 7.6,28; Ps 33.18
5.6 Ezra 4.9
5.9 ver 3,4
5.11 1 Kings 6.1

[e] Heb adds *in Aramaic,* indicating that 4.8–6.18 is in Aramaic. Another interpretation is *The letter was written in the Aramaic script and set forth in the Aramaic language* [f] Aram adds *the prophet* [g] Gk Syr: Aram *We*

which a great king of Israel built and finished.
[12]But because our ancestors had angered the
God of heaven, he gave them into the hand
of King Nebuchadnezzar of Babylon, the
Chaldean, who destroyed this house and
carried away the people to Babylonia. [13]How-
ever, King Cyrus of Babylon, in the first year
of his reign, made a decree that this house
of God should be rebuilt. [14]Moreover, the
gold and silver vessels of the house of God,
which Nebuchadnezzar had taken out of the
temple in Jerusalem and had brought into
the temple of Babylon, these King Cyrus took
out of the temple of Babylon, and they were
delivered to a man named Sheshbazzar,
whom he had made governor. [15]He said to
him, "Take these vessels; go and put them
in the temple in Jerusalem, and let the house
of God be rebuilt on its site." [16]Then this
Sheshbazzar came and laid the foundations
of the house of God in Jerusalem; and from
that time until now it has been under
construction, and it is not yet finished.'
[17]And now, if it seems good to the king, have
a search made in the royal archives there
in Babylon, to see whether a decree was
issued by King Cyrus for the rebuilding of
this house of God in Jerusalem. Let the king
send us his pleasure in this matter."

The Decree of Darius

6 Then King Darius made a decree, and
they searched the archives where the
documents were stored in Babylon. [2]But it
was in Ecbatana, the capital in the province
of Media, that a scroll was found on which
this was written: "A record. [3]In the first
year of his reign, King Cyrus issued a decree: Concerning the house of God at Jerusalem, let the house be rebuilt, the place
where sacrifices are offered and burnt offerings are brought;[h] its height shall be sixty
cubits and its width sixty cubits, [4]with three
courses of hewn stones and one course of
timber; let the cost be paid from the royal
treasury. [5]Moreover, let the gold and silver
vessels of the house of God, which
Nebuchadnezzar took out of the temple in
Jerusalem and brought to Babylon, be restored and brought back to the temple in
Jerusalem, each to its place; you shall put
them in the house of God."
6 "Now you, Tattenai, governor of the
province Beyond the River, Shethar-bozenai,
and you, their associates, the envoys in the
province Beyond the River, keep away; [7]let
the work on this house of God alone; let the
governor of the Jews and the elders of the
Jews rebuild this house of God on its site.
[8]Moreover I make a decree regarding what
you shall do for these elders of the Jews for
the rebuilding of this house of God: the cost
is to be paid to these people, in full and
without delay, from the royal revenue, the
tribute of the province Beyond the River.
[9]Whatever is needed—young bulls, rams, or
sheep for burnt offerings to the God of
heaven, wheat, salt, wine, or oil, as the
priests in Jerusalem require—let that be
given to them day by day without fail, [10]so
that they may offer pleasing sacrifices to the
God of heaven, and pray for the life of the
king and his children. [11]Furthermore I decree
that if anyone alters this edict, a beam shall
be pulled out of the house of the perpetrator,
who then shall be impaled on it. The house
shall be made a dunghill. [12]May the God who
has established his name there overthrow
any king or people that shall put forth a hand
to alter this, or to destroy this house of God
in Jerusalem. I, Darius, make a decree; let
it be done with all diligence."

Completion and Dedication of the Temple

13 Then, according to the word sent by
King Darius, Tattenai, the governor of the
province Beyond the River, Shethar-bozenai,
and their associates did with all diligence
what King Darius had ordered. [14]So the
elders of the Jews built and prospered,
through the prophesying of the prophet
Haggai and Zechariah son of Iddo. They
finished their building by command of the
God of Israel and by decree of Cyrus, Darius,
and King Artaxerxes of Persia; [15]and this
house was finished on the third day of the
month of Adar, in the sixth year of the
reign of King Darius.
16 The people of Israel, the priests and
the Levites, and the rest of the returned
exiles, celebrated the dedication of this house
of God with joy. [17]They offered at the dedication of this house of God one hundred
bulls, two hundred rams, four hundred
lambs, and as a sin offering for all Israel,
twelve male goats, according to the number
of the tribes of Israel. [18]Then they set the
priests in their divisions and the Levites in
their courses for the service of God at Jerusalem, as it is written in the book of Moses.

5.12 2 Chr 36.16.17; 2 Kings 24.2; 25.8,9,11
5.13 Ezra 1.1
5.14 Ezra 1.7; 6.5; Dan 5.2; ver 16; Ezra 1.8
5.16 Ezra 3.8,10; 6.15
5.17 Ezra 6.1,2
6.1 Ezra 5.17
6.3 Ezra 1.1
6.4 1 Kings 6.36
6.5 Ezra 1.7,8; 5.14
6.6 ver 13; Ezra 5.3
6.10 Ezra 7.23
6.11 Ezra 7.26; Dan 2.5; 3.29
6.12 Deut 12.5,11
6.13 ver 6
6.14 Ezra 5.1,2; 1.1; ver 12; Ezra 7.1
6.16 1 Kings 8.63; 2 Chr 7.5
6.17 Ezra 8.35
6.18 2 Chr 35.5; 1 Chr 23.6; Num 3.6; 8.9

6.1-12 Discovery of the decree in *the archives* in *Ecbatana* (the summer imperial residence, located in the mountains south of the Caspian Sea) led to a reaffirmation of the earlier commitment of the Persian rulers to encourage and aid in the rebuilding project.
6.13-22 With the completion of the temple and its dedication, priestly procedures there were resumed in accordance with the Law of Moses (which had been basically revised and edited during the period of Jewish exile in Babylon). *The Passover* was celebrated not only by pious Jewish returnees, but also by non-Israelites who had joined them, separating themselves *from the pollutions of the nations of the land.*

[h] Meaning of Aram uncertain

7.1-10.44 Ezra's Work of Renewal of the People of Judah. **7.1-28** Although Ezra was a descendant of Aaron, and therefore in the priestly line, he was commissioned by *Artaxerxes* (465-424) to go to Jerusalem in order to devote himself to the work of a scribe, which was *to study the law of the LORD...and to teach the statutes and ordinances in Israel.* In the authorizing letter, which was accompanied by generous contributions to the project, the king instructed Ezra to proceed with the preparation of the temple for worship, and ordered the Persian officials to provide financial assistance for the project, while exempting the priests and temple servants from taxes. Administration of justice in the land of the Jews was to be established and maintained by Ezra in accordance with *the laws of your God.* The pattern for Judaism was set by these guidelines, with scribal instruction and interpretation as well as judicial processes carried out by those whose leadership was apart from, though not in opposition to, the priestly system.

The Passover Celebrated

19 On the fourteenth day of the first month the returned exiles kept the passover. [20]For both the priests and the Levites had purified themselves; all of them were clean. So they killed the passover lamb for all the returned exiles, for their fellow priests, and for themselves. [21]It was eaten by the people of Israel who had returned from exile, and also by all who had joined them and separated themselves from the pollutions of the nations of the land to worship the LORD, the God of Israel. [22]With joy they celebrated the festival of unleavened bread seven days; for the LORD had made them joyful, and had turned the heart of the king of Assyria to them, so that he aided them in the work on the house of God, the God of Israel.

The Coming and Work of Ezra

7 After this, in the reign of King Artaxerxes of Persia, Ezra son of Seraiah, son of Azariah, son of Hilkiah, [2]son of Shallum, son of Zadok, son of Ahitub, [3]son of Amariah, son of Azariah, son of Meraioth, [4]son of Zerahiah, son of Uzzi, son of Bukki, [5]son of Abishua, son of Phinehas, son of Eleazar, son of the chief priest Aaron— [6]this Ezra went up from Babylonia. He was a scribe skilled in the law of Moses that the LORD the God of Israel had given; and the king granted him all that he asked, for the hand of the LORD his God was upon him.

7 Some of the people of Israel, and some of the priests and Levites, the singers and gatekeepers, and the temple servants also went up to Jerusalem, in the seventh year of King Artaxerxes. [8]They came to Jerusalem in the fifth month, which was in the seventh year of the king. [9]On the first day of the first month the journey up from Babylon was begun, and on the first day of the fifth month he came to Jerusalem, for the gracious hand of his God was upon him. [10]For Ezra had set his heart to study the law of the LORD, and to do it, and to teach the statutes and ordinances in Israel.

The Letter of Artaxerxes to Ezra

11 This is a copy of the letter that King Artaxerxes gave to the priest Ezra, the scribe, a scholar of the text of the commandments of the LORD and his statutes for Israel: [12]"Artaxerxes, king of kings, to the priest Ezra, the scribe of the law of the God of heaven: Peace.[i] And now [13]I decree that any of the people of Israel or their priests or Levites in my kingdom who freely offers to go to Jerusalem may go with you. [14]For you are sent by the king and his seven counselors to make inquiries about Judah and Jerusalem according to the law of your God, which is in your hand, [15]and also to convey the silver and gold that the king and his counselors have freely offered to the God of Israel, whose dwelling is in Jerusalem, [16]with all the silver and gold that you shall find in the whole province of Babylonia, and with the freewill offerings of the people and the priests, given willingly for the house of their God in Jerusalem. [17]With this money, then, you shall with all diligence buy bulls, rams, and lambs, and their grain offerings and their drink offerings, and you shall offer them on the altar of the house of your God in Jerusalem. [18]Whatever seems good to you and your colleagues to do with the rest of the silver and gold, you may do, according to the will of your God. [19]The vessels that have been given you for the service of the house of your God, you shall deliver before the God of Jerusalem. [20]And whatever else is required for the house of your God, which you are responsible for providing, you may provide out of the king's treasury.

21 "I, King Artaxerxes, decree to all the treasurers in the province Beyond the River: Whatever the priest Ezra, the scribe of the law of the God of heaven, requires of you, let it be done with all diligence, [22]up to one hundred talents of silver, one hundred cors of wheat, one hundred baths[j] of wine, one hundred baths[j] of oil, and unlimited salt. [23]Whatever is commanded by the God of heaven, let it be done with zeal for the house of the God of heaven, or wrath will come upon the realm of the king and his heirs. [24]We also notify you that it shall not be lawful to impose tribute, custom, or toll on any of the priests, the Levites, the singers, the doorkeepers, the temple servants, or other servants of this house of God.

25 "And you, Ezra, according to the God-given wisdom you possess, appoint magistrates and judges who may judge all the people in the province Beyond the River who know the laws of your God; and you shall teach those who do not know them. [26]All who will not obey the law of your God and the law of the king, let judgment be

[i] Syr Vg 1 Esdras 8.9: Aram *Perfect* [j] A Heb measure of volume

6.19 Ezra 1.11; Ex 12.6
6.20 2 Chr 29.34; 30.15; 35.11
6.21 Neh 9.2; 10.28; Ezra 9.11
6.22 Ex 12.15; Ezra 7.27; 1.1; 6.2
7.1 1 Chr 6.4-14; ver 12,21; Neh 2.1
7.6 ver 9,11,12,21, 28
7.7 Ezra 8.1-20
7.9 ver 6
7.10 Ps 119.45; ver 25; Neh 8.1-8
7.12 Ezek 26.7; Dan 2.37
7.14 Esth 1.14
7.15 2 Chr 6.2; Ezra 6.12
7.16 Ezra 8.25; 1 Chr 29.6,9; Ezra 1.4,6
7.17 Num 15.4-13; Deut 12.5-11
7.20 Ezra 6.4
7.21 ver 6
7.23 Ezra 6.10
7.25 Ex 18.21; Deut 16.18; ver 10

strictly executed on them, whether for death or for banishment or for confiscation of their goods or for imprisonment."

27 Blessed be the LORD, the God of our ancestors, who put such a thing as this into the heart of the king to glorify the house of the LORD in Jerusalem, 28 and who extended to me steadfast love before the king and his counselors, and before all the king's mighty officers. I took courage, for the hand of the LORD my God was upon me, and I gathered leaders from Israel to go up with me.

Heads of Families Who Returned with Ezra

8 These are their family heads, and this is the genealogy of those who went up with me from Babylonia, in the reign of King Artaxerxes: 2 Of the descendants of Phinehas, Gershom. Of Ithamar, Daniel. Of David, Hattush, 3 of the descendants of Shecaniah. Of Parosh, Zechariah, with whom were registered one hundred fifty males. 4 Of the descendants of Pahath-moab, Eliehoenai son of Zerahiah, and with him two hundred males. 5 Of the descendants of Zattu,[k] Shecaniah son of Jahaziel, and with him three hundred males. 6 Of the descendants of Adin, Ebed son of Jonathan, and with him fifty males. 7 Of the descendants of Elam, Jeshaiah son of Athaliah, and with him seventy males. 8 Of the descendants of Shephatiah, Zebadiah son of Michael, and with him eighty males. 9 Of the descendants of Joab, Obadiah son of Jehiel, and with him two hundred eighteen males. 10 Of the descendants of Bani,[l] Shelomith son of Josiphiah, and with him one hundred sixty males. 11 Of the descendants of Bebai, Zechariah son of Bebai, and with him twenty-eight males. 12 Of the descendants of Azgad, Johanan son of Hakkatan, and with him one hundred ten males. 13 Of the descendants of Adonikam, those who came later, their names being Eliphelet, Jeuel, and Shemaiah, and with them sixty males. 14 Of the descendants of Bigvai, Uthai and Zaccur, and with them seventy males.

Servants for the Temple

15 I gathered them by the river that runs to Ahava, and there we camped three days. As I reviewed the people and the priests, I found there none of the descendants of Levi. 16 Then I sent for Eliezer, Ariel, Shemaiah, Elnathan, Jarib, Elnathan, Nathan, Zechariah, and Meshullam, who were leaders, and for Joiarib and Elnathan, who were wise, 17 and sent them to Iddo, the leader at the place called Casiphia, telling them what to say to Iddo and his colleagues the temple servants at Casiphia, namely, to send us ministers for the house of our God. 18 Since the gracious hand of our God was upon us, they brought us a man of discretion, of the descendants of Mahli son of Levi son of Israel, namely Sherebiah, with his sons and kin, eighteen; 19 also Hashabiah and with him Jeshaiah of the descendants of Merari, with his kin and their sons, twenty; 20 besides two hundred twenty of the temple servants, whom David and his officials had set apart to attend the Levites. These were all mentioned by name.

Fasting and Prayer for Protection

21 Then I proclaimed a fast there, at the river Ahava, that we might deny ourselves[m] before our God, to seek from him a safe journey for ourselves, our children, and all our possessions. 22 For I was ashamed to ask the king for a band of soldiers and cavalry to protect us against the enemy on our way, since we had told the king that the hand of our God is gracious to all who seek him, but his power and his wrath are against all who forsake him. 23 So we fasted and petitioned our God for this, and he listened to our entreaty.

Gifts for the Temple

24 Then I set apart twelve of the leading priests: Sherebiah, Hashabiah, and ten of their kin with them. 25 And I weighed out to them the silver and the gold and the vessels, the offering for the house of our God that the king, his counselors, his lords, and all Israel there present had offered; 26 I weighed out into their hand six hundred fifty talents of silver, and one hundred silver vessels worth . . . talents,[n] and one hundred talents of gold, 27 twenty gold bowls worth a thousand darics, and two vessels of fine polished bronze as precious as gold. 28 And I said to them, "You are holy to the LORD, and the vessels are holy; and the silver and the gold are a freewill offering to the LORD, the God of your ancestors. 29 Guard them

[k] Gk 1 Esdras 8.32: Heb lacks *of Zattu* [l] Gk 1 Esdras 8.36: Heb lacks *Bani* [m] Or *might fast* [n] The number of talents is lacking

7.27 1 Chr 29.10; Ezra 6.22
7.28 Ezra 9.9; ver 6,9
8.2 1 Chr 3.22
8.3 Ezra 2.3
8.15 ver 21,31; Ezra 7.7
8.17 Ezra 2.43
8.18 Ezra 7.6
8.20 Ezra 2.43
8.21 2 Chr 20.3; Isa 58.3,5
8.22 Ezra 7.6,9,28; Ps 33.18,19; 34.16; 2 Chr 15.2
8.23 2 Chr 33.13
8.25 Ezra 7.15,16
8.26 Ezra 1.9-11
8.28 Lev 21.6-8; 22.2,3
8.29 ver 33,34

7.27-28 The response to the letter expresses gratitude to God for these forms of support for and organization of God's people.
8.1-36 Ezra Accompanied by Jewish Exiles and Temple Servants on his Return to Jerusalem.
8.1-14 Listed are the names and numbers of the families who returned with Ezra.
8.15-20 Special listing is given of the Levites and temple servants who accompanied the returnees.
8.21-23 Preparation for the journey included fasting and prayer.
8.24-30 Gifts and costly materials were assembled for transport to Jerusalem in preparation for rebuilding the temple.

8.31-36 The location of *Ahava* in Babylon is unknown. With the offerings and sacred vessels brought by the *returned exiles* there were messages to the royal Persian officers as to how they were to *support the people and the house of God.*
9.1-4 A major problem to be addressed by Ezra was Judah's involvement by marriage and worship with the non-Jewish people and religions of the land.
9.5-10.5 Ezra's Prayer of Confession. His acknowledgement of the guilt of Israel reached back to their beginnings in the time of Moses. His plea was for marital and cultic separation from non-Jews in order to preserve the ethnic and ritual purity of God's people. To these guidelines the people, as well as the *priests and Levites, agreed under oath.*

and keep them until you weigh them before the chief priests and the Levites and the heads of families in Israel at Jerusalem, within the chambers of the house of the LORD." [30]So the priests and the Levites took over the silver, the gold, and the vessels as they were weighed out, to bring them to Jerusalem, to the house of our God.

The Return to Jerusalem

31 Then we left the river Ahava on the twelfth day of the first month, to go to Jerusalem; the hand of our God was upon us, and he delivered us from the hand of the enemy and from ambushes along the way. [32]We came to Jerusalem and remained there three days. [33]On the fourth day, within the house of our God, the silver, the gold, and the vessels were weighed into the hands of the priest Meremoth son of Uriah, and with him was Eleazar son of Phinehas, and with them were the Levites, Jozabad son of Jeshua and Noadiah son of Binnui. [34]The total was counted and weighed, and the weight of everything was recorded.

35 At that time those who had come from captivity, the returned exiles, offered burnt offerings to the God of Israel, twelve bulls for all Israel, ninety-six rams, seventy-seven lambs, and as a sin offering twelve male goats; all this was a burnt offering to the LORD. [36]They also delivered the king's commissions to the king's satraps and to the governors of the province Beyond the River; and they supported the people and the house of God.

Denunciation of Mixed Marriages

9 After these things had been done, the officials approached me and said, "The people of Israel, the priests, and the Levites have not separated themselves from the peoples of the lands with their abominations, from the Canaanites, the Hittites, the Perizzites, the Jebusites, the Ammonites, the Moabites, the Egyptians, and the Amorites. [2]For they have taken some of their daughters as wives for themselves and for their sons. Thus the holy seed has mixed itself with the peoples of the lands, and in this faithlessness the officials and leaders have led the way." [3]When I heard this, I tore my garment and my mantle, and pulled hair from my head and beard, and sat appalled. [4]Then all who trembled at the words of the God of Israel, because of the faithlessness of the returned exiles, gathered around me while I sat appalled until the evening sacrifice.

Ezra's Prayer

5 At the evening sacrifice I got up from my fasting, with my garments and my mantle torn, and fell on my knees, spread out my hands to the LORD my God, [6]and said,

"O my God, I am too ashamed and embarrassed to lift my face to you, my God, for our iniquities have risen higher than our heads, and our guilt has mounted up to the heavens. [7]From the days of our ancestors to this day we have been deep in guilt, and for our iniquities we, our kings, and our priests have been handed over to the kings of the lands, to the sword, to captivity, to plundering, and to utter shame, as is now the case. [8]But now for a brief moment favor has been shown by the LORD our God, who has left us a remnant, and given us a stake in his holy place, in order that he[o] may brighten our eyes and grant us a little sustenance in our slavery. [9]For we are slaves; yet our God has not forsaken us in our slavery, but has extended to us his steadfast love before the kings of Persia, to give us new life to set up the house of our God, to repair its ruins, and to give us a wall in Judea and Jerusalem.

10 "And now, our God, what shall we say after this? For we have forsaken your commandments, [11]which you commanded by your servants the prophets, saying, 'The land that you are entering to possess is a land unclean with the pollutions of the peoples of the lands, with their abominations. They have filled it from end to end with their uncleanness. [12]Therefore do not give your daughters to their sons, neither take their daughters for your sons, and never seek their peace or prosperity, so that you may be strong and eat the good of the land and leave it for an inheritance to your children forever.' [13]After all that has come upon us for our evil deeds and for our great guilt, seeing that you, our God, have punished us less than our iniquities deserved and have given us such a remnant as this, [14]shall we break your commandments again and intermarry with the peoples who practice these abominations? Would you not be angry with us until you destroy us without

[o] Heb *our God*

8.31 Ezra 7.6,9,28
8.32 Neh 2.11
8.33 ver 26,30
8.35 Ezra 2.1; 6.17
8.36 Ezra 7.21
9.1 Ezra 6.21; Neh 9.2; Lev 18.24-30
9.2 Ezra 10.2,18; Ex 22.31; Neh 13.3
9.3 Job 1.20; Neh 1.4
9.4 Ezra 10.3; Ex 29.39
9.5 Ex 9.29,33
9.6 Dan 9.7,8; 2 Chr 28.9; Rev 18.5
9.7 Dan 9.5,6; Deut 28.36,64; Dan 9.7,8
9.8 Isa 22.23; Ps 13.3; 34.5
9.9 Neh 9.36; Ezra 7.28
9.11 Ezra 6.21
9.12 Deut 7.3; 23.6; Prov 13.22
9.13 ver 6-8
9.14 ver 2; Neh 13.23,27; Deut 9.8,14

remnant or survivor? [15]O LORD, God of Israel, you are just, but we have escaped as a remnant, as is now the case. Here we are before you in our guilt, though no one can face you because of this."

The People's Response

10 While Ezra prayed and made confession, weeping and throwing himself down before the house of God, a very great assembly of men, women, and children gathered to him out of Israel; the people also wept bitterly. [2]Shecaniah son of Jehiel, of the descendants of Elam, addressed Ezra, saying, "We have broken faith with our God and have married foreign women from the peoples of the land, but even now there is hope for Israel in spite of this. [3]So now let us make a covenant with our God to send away all these wives and their children, according to the counsel of my lord and of those who tremble at the commandment of our God; and let it be done according to the law. [4]Take action, for it is your duty, and we are with you; be strong, and do it." [5]Then Ezra stood up and made the leading priests, the Levites, and all Israel swear that they would do as had been said. So they swore.

Foreign Wives and Their Children Rejected

6 Then Ezra withdrew from before the house of God, and went to the chamber of Jehohanan son of Eliashib, where he spent the night.[p] He did not eat bread or drink water, for he was mourning over the faithlessness of the exiles. [7]They made a proclamation throughout Judah and Jerusalem to all the returned exiles that they should assemble at Jerusalem, [8]and that if any did not come within three days, by order of the officials and the elders all their property should be forfeited, and they themselves banned from the congregation of the exiles.

9 Then all the people of Judah and Benjamin assembled at Jerusalem within the three days; it was the ninth month, on the twentieth day of the month. All the people sat in the open square before the house of God, trembling because of this matter and because of the heavy rain. [10]Then Ezra the priest stood up and said to them, "You have trespassed and married foreign women, and so increased the guilt of Israel. [11]Now make confession to the LORD the God of your ancestors, and do his will; separate yourselves from the peoples of the land and from the foreign wives." [12]Then all the assembly answered with a loud voice, "It is so; we must do as you have said. [13]But the people are many, and it is a time of heavy rain; we cannot stand in the open. Nor is this a task for one day or for two, for many of us have transgressed in this matter. [14]Let our officials represent the whole assembly, and let all in our towns who have taken foreign wives come at appointed times, and with them the elders and judges of every town, until the fierce wrath of our God on this account is averted from us." [15]Only Jonathan son of Asahel and Jahzeiah son of Tikvah opposed this, and Meshullam and Shabbethai the Levites supported them.

16 Then the returned exiles did so. Ezra the priest selected men,[q] heads of families, according to their families, each of them designated by name. On the first day of the tenth month they sat down to examine the matter. [17]By the first day of the first month they had come to the end of all the men who had married foreign women.

18 There were found of the descendants of the priests who had married foreign women, of the descendants of Jeshua son of Jozadak and his brothers: Maaseiah, Eliezer, Jarib, and Gedaliah. [19]They pledged themselves to send away their wives, and their guilt offering was a ram of the flock for their guilt. [20]Of the descendants of Immer: Hanani and Zebadiah. [21]Of the descendants of Harim: Maaseiah, Elijah, Shemaiah, Jehiel, and Uzziah. [22]Of the descendants of Pashhur: Elioenai, Maaseiah, Ishmael, Nethanel, Jozabad, and Elasah.

23 Of the Levites: Jozabad, Shimei, Kelaiah (that is, Kelita), Pethahiah, Judah, and Eliezer. [24]Of the singers: Eliashib. Of the gatekeepers: Shallum, Telem, and Uri.

25 And of Israel: of the descendants of Parosh: Ramiah, Izziah, Malchijah, Mijamin, Eleazar, Hashabiah,[r] and Benaiah. [26]Of the descendants of Elam: Mattaniah, Zechariah, Jehiel, Abdi, Jeremoth, and Elijah. [27]Of the descendants of Zattu: Elioenai, Eliashib, Mattaniah, Jeremoth, Zabad, and Aziza. [28]Of the descendants of Bebai: Jehohanan, Hananiah, Zabbai, and Athlai. [29]Of the descendants of Bani: Meshullam, Malluch,

10.6-44 All the returned exiles gathered in Jerusalem to hear Ezra's rebuke and prescription for the problem of mixed marriage of Jew to non-Jew. The men are to separate themselves from *the people of the land* (which in later centuries became a Jewish technical term for non-Israelite residents in the land) and from *foreign wives*. Thus the pattern was set for strict ethnic purity to be observed by those who see themselves as God's covenant people. The rule was applied to Jewish officials, priests, Levites, and the people of Israel in general.

9.15 Neh 9.33; Dan 9.14; ver 6; Ps 130.3
10.1 Dan 9.4,20; 2 Chr 20.9
10.2 Ezra 9.2; Neh 13.27
10.3 2 Chr 34.31; ver 44; Ezra 9.4; Deut 7.2,3
10.4 1 Chr 28.10
10.5 Neh 5.12
10.6 Deut 9.18
10.9 ver 3; Ezra 9.4
10.11 Lev 26.40; ver 3
10.14 2 Chr 29.10; 30.8
10.16 Ezra 4.1
10.19 2 Kings 10.15; 2 Chr 30.8; Lev 5.15; 6.6
10.23 Ex 6.25
10.25 ver 1

[p] 1 Esdras 9.2: Heb *where he went* [q] 1 Esdras 9.16: Syr: Heb *And there were selected Ezra,* [r] 1 Esdras 9.26 Gk: Heb *Malchijah*

10.44 Accordingly, the wives and children of the returning Jews who had intermarried were to be sent away.

Adaiah, Jashub, Sheal, and Jeremoth. [30]Of
the descendants of Pahath-moab: Adna,
Chelal, Benaiah, Maaseiah, Mattaniah,
Bezalel, Binnui, and Manasseh. [31]Of the
descendants of Harim: Eliezer, Isshijah,
Malchijah, Shemaiah, Shimeon, [32]Benjamin,
Malluch, and Shemariah. [33]Of the descend-
ants of Hashum: Mattenai, Mattattah, Zabad,
Eliphelet, Jeremai, Manasseh, and Shimei.
[34]Of the descendants of Bani: Maadai,
Amram, Uel, [35]Benaiah, Bedeiah, Cheluhi,
[36]Vaniah, Meremoth, Eliashib, [37]Mattaniah,
Mattenai, and Jaasu. [38]Of the descendants of
Binnui:[s] Shimei, [39]Shelemiah, Nathan,
Adaiah, [40]Machnadebai, Shashai, Sharai,
[41]Azarel, Shelemiah, Shemariah, [42]Shallum,
Amariah, and Joseph. [43]Of the descendants
of Nebo: Jeiel, Mattithiah, Zabad, Zebina,
Jaddai, Joel, and Benaiah. [44]All these had
married foreign women, and they sent them
away with their children.[t]

[s] Gk: Heb *Bani, Binnui* [t] 1 Esdras 9.36; Meaning of Heb uncertain

10.44
ver 3

See the Introductions, pp. 3, 38, and 45-46 above.

NEHEMIAH

1.1-11 Nehemiah's Response to the Reports from Jerusalem. *Chislev* is the ninth month of the year, approximately November-December. *Susa* was the winter capital of the Persian empire, located north of the upper end of the Persian Gulf. Nehemiah's prayer appeals to God's *covenant*, and acknowledges that Israel's infidelity to its obligations has led to scattering of the people, while fidelity has brought restoration. It is on the basis of these guidelines that he seeks to go to Judah.
2.1-10 Nehemiah Authorized by Artaxerxes to go to Jerusalem. *Nisan*, the first month of the year, is in the spring. *Artaxerxes* may be the first (464-423) or the second (405-359) Persian ruler of that name; probably the former. Unlike Ezra, whose task was to oversee the rebuilding of the temple, Nehemiah was to rebuild the city of Jerusalem, which suggests that his work likely preceded that of Ezra. Letters authorizing his return and rebuilding activities were sent to the governors of the province Beyond the River (Persian-controlled territory south and west of the Euphrates River in Syria) and to *Asaph, the keeper of the king's forest* (probably in Lebanon, where material was provided for rebuilding city and temple). Two local officials were displeased by this proposal. *Sanballat the Horonite* (a native of Beth-horon in what was Israel, but his name is Babylonian) was now governor of *Samaria*, the former capital of the northern tribes of Israel. *Tobiah the Ammonite official* was based south and east of the Dead Sea. Both see a threat of insurrection against the Persians in Nehemiah's restoration project.

Nehemiah Prays for His People

1 The words of Nehemiah son of
Hacaliah. In the month of Chislev, in
the twentieth year, while I was in Susa the
capital, [2]one of my brothers, Hanani, came
with certain men from Judah; and I asked
them about the Jews that survived, those
who had escaped the captivity, and about
Jerusalem. [3]They replied, "The survivors there
in the province who escaped captivity are
in great trouble and shame; the wall of
Jerusalem is broken down, and its gates
have been destroyed by fire."
4 When I heard these words I sat down
and wept, and mourned for days, fasting
and praying before the God of heaven. [5]I
said, "O LORD God of heaven, the great and
awesome God who keeps covenant and
steadfast love with those who love him and
keep his commandments; [6]let your ear be
attentive and your eyes open to hear the
prayer of your servant that I now pray
before you day and night for your servants,
the people of Israel, confessing the sins of
the people of Israel, which we have sinned
against you. Both I and my family have
sinned. [7]We have offended you deeply, failing
to keep the commandments, the statutes,
and the ordinances that you commanded
your servant Moses. [8]Remember the word
that you commanded your servant Moses,
'If you are unfaithful, I will scatter you
among the peoples; [9]but if you return to me
and keep my commandments and do them,
though your outcasts are under the farthest
skies, I will gather them from there and
bring them to the place at which I have
chosen to establish my name.' [10]They are
your servants and your people, whom you
redeemed by your great power and your
strong hand. [11]O Lord, let your ear be attentive to the prayer of your servant, and
to the prayer of your servants who delight
in revering your name. Give success to your
servant today, and grant him mercy in the
sight of this man!"
At the time, I was cupbearer to the king.

Nehemiah Sent to Judah

2 In the month of Nisan, in the twentieth year of King Artaxerxes, when
wine was served him, I carried the wine
and gave it to the king. Now, I had never
been sad in his presence before. [2]So the king
said to me, "Why is your face sad, since you
are not sick? This can only be sadness of the
heart." Then I was very much afraid. [3]I said
to the king, "May the king live forever! Why
should my face not be sad, when the city,
the place of my ancestors' graves, lies waste,
and its gates have been destroyed by fire?"
[4]Then the king said to me, "What do you
request?" So I prayed to the God of heaven.
[5]Then I said to the king, "If it pleases the
king, and if your servant has found favor

1.1 Neh 10.1; 2.1; Esth 1.2; Dan 8.2
1.3 Ne 7.6; 2.17; 2.3
1.4 Ezra 9.3; 10.1; Neh 2.4
1.5 Neh 4.14; 9.32; Ex 20.6
1.6 Dan 9.17; Ezra 10.1; Dan 9.20; 2 Chr 29.6
1.7 Dan 9.5; Deut 28.14,15
1.8 Lev 26.33
1.9 Deut 20.2-4; 12.5
1.10 Deut 9.29; Dan 9.15
1.11 ver 6
2.1 Neh 1.1; Ezra 7.1; Neh 1.11
2.2 Prov 15.13
2.3 Dan 2.4; Neh 1.3
2.4 Neh 1.4

2.6 Neh 5.14; 13.6
2.7 Ezra 7.21; 8.36
2.8 Neh 7.2; ver 18; Ezra 7.6
2.9 ver 7; Ezra 8.22
2.10 ver 19; Neh 4.1
2.13 Neh 3.13; ver 3,17; Neh 1.3
2.14 Neh 3.15; 2 Kings 20.20
2.17 Neh 1.3
2.18 ver 8; 2 Sam 2.7
2.19 Ps 44.13; Neh 6.6
2.20 ver 4
3.1 ver 20,32; Neh 6.1; 7.1; 12.39; Jer 31.38
3.2 Neh 7.36
3.3 Neh 12.39
3.6 Neh 12.39
3.7 Neh 2.7
3.8 ver 31,32; Neh 12.38
3.9 ver 12.17
3.11 Neh 12.38

with you, I ask that you send me to Judah, to the city of my ancestors' graves, so that I may rebuild it." [6]The king said to me (the queen also was sitting beside him), "How long will you be gone, and when will you return?" So it pleased the king to send me, and I set him a date. [7]Then I said to the king, "If it pleases the king, let letters be given me to the governors of the province Beyond the River, that they may grant me passage until I arrive in Judah; [8]and a letter to Asaph, the keeper of the king's forest, directing him to give me timber to make beams for the gates of the temple fortress, and for the wall of the city, and for the house that I shall occupy." And the king granted me what I asked, for the gracious hand of my God was upon me.

9 Then I came to the governors of the province Beyond the River, and gave them the king's letters. Now the king had sent officers of the army and cavalry with me. [10]When Sanballat the Horonite and Tobiah the Ammonite official heard this, it displeased them greatly that someone had come to seek the welfare of the people of Israel.

Nehemiah's Inspection of the Walls

11 So I came to Jerusalem and was there for three days. [12]Then I got up during the night, I and a few men with me; I told no one what my God had put into my heart to do for Jerusalem. The only animal I took was the animal I rode. [13]I went out by night by the Valley Gate past the Dragon's Spring and to the Dung Gate, and I inspected the walls of Jerusalem that had been broken down and its gates that had been destroyed by fire. [14]Then I went on to the Fountain Gate and to the King's Pool; but there was no place for the animal I was riding to continue. [15]So I went up by way of the valley by night and inspected the wall. Then I turned back and entered by the Valley Gate, and so returned. [16]The officials did not know where I had gone or what I was doing; I had not yet told the Jews, the priests, the nobles, the officials, and the rest that were to do the work.

Decision to Restore the Walls

17 Then I said to them, "You see the trouble we are in, how Jerusalem lies in ruins with its gates burned. Come, let us rebuild the wall of Jerusalem, so that we may no longer suffer disgrace." [18]I told them that the hand of my God had been gracious upon me, and also the words that the king had spoken to me. Then they said, "Let us start building!" So they committed themselves to the common good. [19]But when Sanballat the Horonite and Tobiah the Ammonite official, and Geshem the Arab heard of it, they mocked and ridiculed us, saying, "What is this that you are doing? Are you rebelling against the king?" [20]Then I replied to them, "The God of heaven is the one who will give us success, and we his servants are going to start building; but you have no share or claim or historic right in Jerusalem."

Organization of the Work

3 Then the high priest Eliashib set to work with his fellow priests and rebuilt the Sheep Gate. They consecrated it and set up its doors; they consecrated it as far as the Tower of the Hundred and as far as the Tower of Hananel. [2]And the men of Jericho built next to him. And next to them[a] Zaccur son of Imri built.

3 The sons of Hassenaah built the Fish Gate; they laid its beams and set up its doors, its bolts, and its bars. [4]Next to them Meremoth son of Uriah son of Hakkoz made repairs. Next to them Meshullam son of Berechiah son of Meshezabel made repairs. Next to them Zadok son of Baana made repairs. [5]Next to them the Tekoites made repairs; but their nobles would not put their shoulders to the work of their Lord.[b]

6 Joiada son of Paseah and Meshullam son of Besodeiah repaired the Old Gate; they laid its beams and set up its doors, its bolts, and its bars. [7]Next to them repairs were made by Melatiah the Gibeonite and Jadon the Meronothite—the men of Gibeon and of Mizpah—who were under the jurisdiction of[c] the governor of the province Beyond the River. [8]Next to them Uzziel son of Harhaiah, one of the goldsmiths, made repairs. Next to him Hananiah, one of the perfumers, made repairs; and they restored Jerusalem as far as the Broad Wall. [9]Next to them Rephaiah son of Hur, ruler of half the district of[d] Jerusalem, made repairs. [10]Next to them Jedaiah son of Harumaph made repairs opposite his house; and next to him Hattush son of Hashabneiah made repairs. [11]Malch-

[a] Heb *him* [b] Or *lords* [c] Meaning of Heb uncertain [d] Or *supervisor of half the portion assigned to*

2.11-20 The gates and other places mentioned by name here cannot be located certainly. Probably the *Valley Gate* gave access to the city from the Tyropeon Valley, which originally divided Jerusalem on the eastern hill (where the temple was) from the western hill, which was much later incorporated into the city. At the time of Nehemiah's arrival, the local Jewish leaders were unaware of the rebuilding plan.
3.1-31 Assignment of Rebuilding Responsibilities. The locations of the various gates, pools and towers cannot be determined because of the extensive rebuilding of Jerusalem down to medieval times. Some of the districts of Judah mentioned here appear in earlier lists: Mizpeh (Josh 15.37); Keilah (Josh 15.44; 1 Sam 23).

4.1-23 Opposition Mounts as Building the City Progresses. The earlier opponents of the project mock the construction, but plot to capture the city if the fortification is completed. In response, the workers share responsibilities for building and for protecting the city against possible attackers.

ijah son of Harim and Hasshub son of
Pahath-moab repaired another section and
the Tower of the Ovens. 12 Next to him
Shallum son of Hallohesh, ruler of half the
district of[e] Jerusalem, made repairs, he and
his daughters.
13 Hanun and the inhabitants of Zanoah
repaired the Valley Gate; they rebuilt it and
set up its doors, its bolts, and its bars, and
repaired a thousand cubits of the wall, as
far as the Dung Gate.
14 Malchijah son of Rechab, ruler of the
district of[f] Beth-haccherem, repaired the
Dung Gate; he rebuilt it and set up its doors,
its bolts, and its bars.
15 And Shallum son of Col-hozeh, ruler
of the district of[f] Mizpah, repaired the Fountain Gate; he rebuilt it and covered it and
set up its doors, its bolts, and its bars; and
he built the wall of the Pool of Shelah of
the king's garden, as far as the stairs that
go down from the City of David. 16 After him
Nehemiah son of Azbuk, ruler of half the
district of[e] Beth-zur, repaired from a point
opposite the graves of David, as far as the
artificial pool and the house of the warriors.
17 After him the Levites made repairs: Rehum
son of Bani; next to him Hashabiah, ruler
of half the district of[e] Keilah, made repairs
for his district. 18 After him their kin made
repairs: Binnui,[g] son of Henadad, ruler of
half the district of[e] Keilah; 19 next to him
Ezer son of Jeshua, ruler[h] of Mizpah, repaired another section opposite the ascent
to the armory at the Angle. 20 After him
Baruch son of Zabbai repaired another section from the Angle to the door of the house
of the high priest Eliashib. 21 After him
Meremoth son of Uriah son of Hakkoz repaired another section from the door of the
house of Eliashib to the end of the house of
Eliashib. 22 After him the priests, the men of
the surrounding area, made repairs. 23 After
them Benjamin and Hasshub made repairs
opposite their house. After them Azariah
son of Maaseiah son of Ananiah made repairs beside his own house. 24 After him
Binnui son of Henadad repaired another
section, from the house of Azariah to the
Angle and to the corner. 25 Palal son of Uzai
repaired opposite the Angle and the tower
projecting from the upper house of the king
at the court of the guard. After him Pedaiah
son of Parosh 26 and the temple servants
living[i] on Ophel made repairs up to a point
opposite the Water Gate on the east and the
projecting tower. 27 After him the Tekoites
repaired another section opposite the great
projecting tower as far as the wall of Ophel.
28 Above the Horse Gate the priests made
repairs, each one opposite his own house.
29 After them Zadok son of Immer made
repairs opposite his own house. After him
Shemaiah son of Shecaniah, the keeper of
the East Gate, made repairs. 30 After him
Hananiah son of Shelemiah and Hanun sixth
son of Zalaph repaired another section. After
him Meshullam son of Berechiah made repairs
opposite his living quarters. 31 After him
Malchijah, one of the goldsmiths, made repairs
as far as the house of the temple servants
and of the merchants, opposite the Muster
Gate,[j] and to the upper room of the corner.
32 And between the upper room of the corner
and the Sheep Gate the goldsmiths and the
merchants made repairs.

Hostile Plots Thwarted

4[k] Now when Sanballat heard that we
were building the wall, he was angry
and greatly enraged, and he mocked the
Jews. 2 He said in the presence of his associates and of the army of Samaria, "What
are these feeble Jews doing? Will they restore things? Will they sacrifice? Will they
finish it in a day? Will they revive the stones
out of the heaps of rubbish—and burned
ones at that?" 3 Tobiah the Ammonite was
beside him, and he said, "That stone wall
they are building—any fox going up on it
would break it down!" 4 Hear, O our God, for
we are despised; turn their taunt back on
their own heads, and give them over as
plunder in a land of captivity. 5 Do not cover
their guilt, and do not let their sin be blotted
out from your sight; for they have hurled
insults in the face of the builders.
6 So we rebuilt the wall, and all the wall
was joined together to half its height; for
the people had a mind to work.
7[l] But when Sanballat and Tobiah and
the Arabs and the Ammonites and the
Ashdodites heard that the repairing of the
walls of Jerusalem was going forward and
the gaps were beginning to be closed, they
were very angry, 8 and all plotted together
to come and fight against Jerusalem and to

[e] Or *supervisor of half the portion assigned to* [f] Or *supervisor of the portion assigned to* [g] Gk Syr Compare verse 24, 10.9: Heb *Bavvai* [h] Or *supervisor* [i] Cn: Heb *were living* [j] Or *Hammiphkad Gate* [k] Ch 3.33 in Heb [l] Ch 4.1 in Heb

3.12 ver 9
3.13 Neh 2.13
3.15 Neh 2.14; 2 Kings 25.4; Neh 12.37
3.16 ver 9,12,17; 2 Kings 20.20
3.19 ver 15; 2 Chr 26.9
3.20 ver 1; Neh 13.7
3.22 Neh 12.28
3.24 ver 19
3.25 Jer 32.2
3.26 Neh 7.46; 11.21; 8.1
3.28 2 Kings 11.16; 2 Chr 23.15; Jer 31.40
3.31 ver 8,32
3.32 ver 1
4.1 Neh 2.10,19
4.2 ver 10
4.3 Neh 2.10,19
4.4 Ps 123.3; 3.4; 79.12
4.5 Ps 69.27,28; Jer 18.23
4.7 ver 1

4.9 Ps 50.15
4.13 ver 17.18
4.14 Num 14.9; Deut 1.29; 2 Sam 10.12
4.15 2 Sam 17.14; Job 5.12
4.20 Ex 14.14; Deut 1.30; Josh 23.10
5.1 Lev 25.35; Deut 15.7
5.4 Ezra 4.13; 7.24
5.5 Gen 37.27; Lev 25.39
5.7 Ex 22.25; Lev 25.36
5.8 Lev 25.48
5.9 2 Sam 12.14; Neh 4.4; Rom 2.24
5.12 Ezra 10.5
5.13 Acts 18.6; Neh 8.6

cause confusion in it. [9]So we prayed to our God, and set a guard as a protection against them day and night.

10 But Judah said, "The strength of the burden bearers is failing, and there is too much rubbish so that we are unable to work on the wall." [11]And our enemies said, "They will not know or see anything before we come upon them and kill them and stop the work." [12]When the Jews who lived near them came, they said to us ten times, "From all the places where they live[m] they will come up against us."[n] [13]So in the lowest parts of the space behind the wall, in open places, I stationed the people according to their families,[o] with their swords, their spears, and their bows. [14]After I looked these things over, I stood up and said to the nobles and the officials and the rest of the people, "Do not be afraid of them. Remember the LORD, who is great and awesome, and fight for your kin, your sons, your daughters, your wives, and your homes."

15 When our enemies heard that their plot was known to us, and that God had frustrated it, we all returned to the wall, each to his work. [16]From that day on, half of my servants worked on construction, and half held the spears, shields, bows, and body-armor; and the leaders posted themselves behind the whole house of Judah, [17]who were building the wall. The burden bearers carried their loads in such a way that each labored on the work with one hand and with the other held a weapon. [18]And each of the builders had his sword strapped at his side while he built. The man who sounded the trumpet was beside me. [19]And I said to the nobles, the officials, and the rest of the people, "The work is great and widely spread out, and we are separated far from one another on the wall. [20]Rally to us wherever you hear the sound of the trumpet. Our God will fight for us."

21 So we labored at the work, and half of them held the spears from break of dawn until the stars came out. [22]I also said to the people at that time, "Let every man and his servant pass the night inside Jerusalem, so that they may be a guard for us by night and may labor by day." [23]So neither I nor my brothers nor my servants nor the men of the guard who followed me ever took off our clothes; each kept his weapon in his right hand.[p]

Nehemiah Deals with Oppression

5 Now there was a great outcry of the people and of their wives against their Jewish kin. [2]For there were those who said, "With our sons and our daughters, we are many; we must get grain, so that we may eat and stay alive." [3]There were also those who said, "We are having to pledge our fields, our vineyards, and our houses in order to get grain during the famine." [4]And there were those who said, "We are having to borrow money on our fields and vineyards to pay the king's tax. [5]Now our flesh is the same as that of our kindred; our children are the same as their children; and yet we are forcing our sons and daughters to be slaves, and some of our daughters have been ravished; we are powerless, and our fields and vineyards now belong to others."

6 I was very angry when I heard their outcry and these complaints. [7]After thinking it over, I brought charges against the nobles and the officials; I said to them, "You are all taking interest from your own people." And I called a great assembly to deal with them, [8]and said to them, "As far as we were able, we have bought back our Jewish kindred who had been sold to other nations; but now you are selling your own kin, who must then be bought back by us!" They were silent, and could not find a word to say. [9]So I said, "The thing that you are doing is not good. Should you not walk in the fear of our God, to prevent the taunts of the nations our enemies? [10]Moreover I and my brothers and my servants are lending them money and grain. Let us stop this taking of interest. [11]Restore to them, this very day, their fields, their vineyards, their olive orchards, and their houses, and the interest on money, grain, wine, and oil that you have been exacting from them." [12]Then they said, "We will restore everything and demand nothing more from them. We will do as you say." And I called the priests, and made them take an oath to do as they had promised. [13]I also shook out the fold of my garment and said, "So may God shake out everyone from house and from property who does not perform this promise. Thus may they be shaken out and emptied." And all the assembly said, "Amen," and praised the LORD. And the people did as they had promised.

5.1-13 Gross Economic and Personal Injustices among the People. The difficult financial conditions among the returnees led some to foreclose on land for which they had made loans to fellow Jews, and others to sell their impoverished debtors into slavery. Complicating the economic situation was *the king's tax*, which all subjects of the empire were obligated to pay. To ease these difficulties, Nehemiah tells *the great assembly* of the people to restore property and persons to their earlier condition.

[m] Cn: Heb *you return* [n] Compare Gk Syr: Meaning of Heb uncertain [o] Meaning of Heb uncertain [p] Cn: Heb *each his weapon the water*

5.14-19 Nehemiah's Exemplary Generosity. Nehemiah *was appointed governor of Judah* by Artaxerxes for the period of twelve years (probably from 445-433), and in addition to feeding large numbers of people, refused to exercise his claim on local people to supply him with food.
6.1-14 The opposition of Sanballat and Tobiah continued, aided by *Geshem the Arab*, with repeated reports of the Jews' plan to rebel against the Persian ruler, and attempts to intimidate Nehemiah by rumors of plots and false prophetic warnings.
6.15-7.4 The Completion of the City Wall and Control of Access to Jerusalem. In spite of the plots of *Tobiah*, the city wall was finished, but the population and the number of houses inside it were *few*. This confirms the theory that Nehemiah's work preceded Ezra's construction of the temple. Control of the city and arrangements for its security were established.

The Generosity of Nehemiah

14 Moreover from the time that I was
appointed to be their governor in the land
of Judah, from the twentieth year to the
thirty-second year of King Artaxerxes, twelve
years, neither I nor my brothers ate the food
allowance of the governor. 15The former
governors who were before me laid heavy
burdens on the people, and took food and
wine from them, besides forty shekels of
silver. Even their servants lorded it over the
people. But I did not do so, because of the
fear of God. 16Indeed, I devoted myself to the
work on this wall, and acquired no land;
and all my servants were gathered there for
the work. 17Moreover there were at my
table one hundred fifty people, Jews and
officials, besides those who came to us from
the nations around us. 18Now that which
was prepared for one day was one ox and
six choice sheep; also fowls were prepared
for me, and every ten days skins of wine in
abundance; yet with all this I did not demand the food allowance of the governor,
because of the heavy burden of labor on the
people. 19Remember for my good, O my
God, all that I have done for this people.

Intrigues of Enemies Foiled

6 Now when it was reported to Sanballat
and Tobiah and to Geshem the Arab
and to the rest of our enemies that I had
built the wall and that there was no gap left
in it (though up to that time I had not set
up the doors in the gates), 2Sanballat and
Geshem sent to me, saying, "Come and let
us meet together in one of the villages in
the plain of Ono." But they intended to do
me harm. 3So I sent messengers to them,
saying, "I am doing a great work and I
cannot come down. Why should the work
stop while I leave it to come down to you?"
4They sent to me four times in this way,
and I answered them in the same manner.
5In the same way Sanballat for the fifth time
sent his servant to me with an open letter
in his hand. 6In it was written, "It is reported among the nations—and Geshem[q]
also says it—that you and the Jews intend
to rebel; that is why you are building the
wall; and according to this report you wish
to become their king. 7You have also set up
prophets to proclaim in Jerusalem concerning you, 'There is a king in Judah!' And
now it will be reported to the king according
to these words. So come, therefore, and let
us confer together." 8Then I sent to him,
saying, "No such things as you say have
been done; you are inventing them out of
your own mind" 9—for they all wanted to
frighten us, thinking, "Their hands will drop
from the work, and it will not be done." But
now, O God, strengthen my hands.

10 One day when I went into the house
of Shemaiah son of Delaiah son of Mehetabel,
who was confined to his house, he said,
"Let us meet together in the house of God,
within the temple, and let us close the doors
of the temple, for they are coming to kill
you; indeed, tonight they are coming to kill
you." 11But I said, "Should a man like me
run away? Would a man like me go into
the temple to save his life? I will not go in!"
12Then I perceived and saw that God had
not sent him at all, but he had pronounced
the prophecy against me because Tobiah
and Sanballat had hired him. 13He was
hired for this purpose, to intimidate me and
make me sin by acting in this way, and so
they could give me a bad name, in order to
taunt me. 14Remember Tobiah and Sanballat,
O my God, according to these things that
they did, and also the prophetess Noadiah
and the rest of the prophets who wanted to
make me afraid.

The Wall Completed

15 So the wall was finished on the twenty-
fifth day of the month Elul, in fifty-two days.
16And when all our enemies heard of it,
all the nations around us were afraid[r]
and fell greatly in their own esteem; for
they perceived that this work had been
accomplished with the help of our God.
17Moreover in those days the nobles of Judah
sent many letters to Tobiah, and Tobiah's
letters came to them. 18For many in Judah
were bound by oath to him, because he was
the son-in-law of Shecaniah son of Arah:
and his son Jehohanan had married the
daughter of Meshullam son of Berechiah.
19Also they spoke of his good deeds in my
presence, and reported my words to him.
And Tobiah sent letters to intimidate me.

7 Now when the wall had been built
and I had set up the doors, and the
gatekeepers, the singers, and the Levites
had been appointed, 2I gave my brother
Hanani charge over Jerusalem, along with
Hananiah the commander of the citadel—

5.14 Neh 13.6; Ezra 4.13,14
5.15 ver 9
5.17 1 Kings 18.19
5.18 1 Kings 4.22,23; 2 Thess 3.8
5.19 Neh 13.14,22,31
6.1 Neh 2.10,19; 4.1,7; 3.1,3
6.2 1 Chr 8.12
6.6 Neh 2.19
6.10 Jer 36.5
6.12 Ezek 13.22
6.13 ver 6
6.14 Neh 13.29; Ezek 13.17
6.16 Neh 2.10; 4.1,7; Ex 14.25; Ps 126.2
7.1 Neh 6.1,15
7.2 Neh 2.8

[q] Heb *Gashmu* [r] Another reading is *saw*

7.6 Ezra 2.1-70
7.7 Ezra 2.2
7.12 Ezra 2.7
7.17 see Ezra 2.12
7.23 Ezra 2.17
7.27 Ezra 2.23
7.34 Ezra 2.31
7.39 Ezra 2.36
7.43 Ezra 2.40
7.46 Ezra 2.43
7.57 Ezra 2.55
7.60 ver 46
7.63 Ezra 2.61
7.65 Neh 8.9; 10.1

for he was a faithful man and feared God
more than many. 3 And I said to them, "The
gates of Jerusalem are not to be opened
until the sun is hot; while the gatekeepers[s]
are still standing guard, let them shut and
bar the doors. Appoint guards from among
the inhabitants of Jerusalem, some at their
watch posts, and others before their own
houses." 4 The city was wide and large, but
the people within it were few and no houses
had been built.

Lists of the Returned Exiles

5 Then my God put it into my mind to
assemble the nobles and the officials and
the people to be enrolled by genealogy. And
I found the book of the genealogy of those
who were the first to come back, and I
found the following written in it:

6 These are the people of the province
who came up out of the captivity of those
exiles whom King Nebuchadnezzar of
Babylon had carried into exile; they returned to Jerusalem and Judah, each to his
town. 7 They came with Zerubbabel, Jeshua,
Nehemiah, Azariah, Raamiah, Nahamani,
Mordecai, Bilshan, Mispereth, Bigvai, Nehum,
Baanah.

The number of the Israelite people: 8 the
descendants of Parosh, two thousand one
hundred seventy-two. 9 Of Shephatiah, three
hundred seventy-two. 10 Of Arah, six hundred fifty-two. 11 Of Pahath-moab, namely
the descendants of Jeshua and Joab, two
thousand eight hundred eighteen. 12 Of Elam,
one thousand two hundred fifty-four. 13 Of
Zattu, eight hundred forty-five. 14 Of Zaccai,
seven hundred sixty. 15 Of Binnui, six hundred forty-eight. 16 Of Bebai, six hundred
twenty-eight. 17 Of Azgad, two thousand three
hundred twenty-two. 18 Of Adonikam, six
hundred sixty-seven. 19 Of Bigvai, two thousand sixty-seven. 20 Of Adin, six hundred
fifty-five. 21 Of Ater, namely of Hezekiah,
ninety-eight. 22 Of Hashum, three hundred
twenty-eight. 23 Of Bezai, three hundred
twenty-four. 24 Of Hariph, one hundred
twelve. 25 Of Gibeon, ninety-five. 26 The people of Bethlehem and Netophah, one hundred eighty-eight. 27 Of Anathoth, one hundred twenty-eight. 28 Of Beth-azmaveth, forty-
two. 29 Of Kiriath-jearim, Chephirah, and
Beeroth, seven hundred forty-three. 30 Of
Ramah and Geba, six hundred twenty-one.
31 Of Michmas, one hundred twenty-two. 32 Of
Bethel and Ai, one hundred twenty-three.
33 Of the other Nebo, fifty-two. 34 The descendants of the other Elam, one thousand
two hundred fifty-four. 35 Of Harim, three
hundred twenty. 36 Of Jericho, three hundred forty-five. 37 Of Lod, Hadid, and Ono,
seven hundred twenty-one. 38 Of Senaah,
three thousand nine hundred thirty.

39 The priests: the descendants of Jedaiah,
namely the house of Jeshua, nine hundred
seventy-three. 40 Of Immer, one thousand
fifty-two. 41 Of Pashhur, one thousand two
hundred forty-seven. 42 Of Harim, one thousand seventeen.

43 The Levites: the descendants of Jeshua,
namely of Kadmiel of the descendants of
Hodevah, seventy-four. 44 The singers: the
descendants of Asaph, one hundred forty-
eight. 45 The gatekeepers: the descendants of
Shallum, of Ater, of Talmon, of Akkub, of
Hatita, of Shobai, one hundred thirty-eight.

46 The temple servants: the descendants
of Ziha, of Hasupha, of Tabbaoth, 47 of Keros,
of Sia, of Padon, 48 of Lebana, of Hagaba, of
Shalmai, 49 of Hanan, of Giddel, of Gahar,
50 of Reaiah, of Rezin, of Nekoda, 51 of Gazzam,
of Uzza, of Paseah, 52 of Besai, of Meunim,
of Nephushesim, 53 of Bakbuk, of Hakupha,
of Harhur, 54 of Bazlith, of Mehida, of Harsha,
55 of Barkos, of Sisera, of Temah, 56 of Neziah,
of Hatipha.

57 The descendants of Solomon's servants: of Sotai, of Sophereth, of Perida, 58 of
Jaala, of Darkon, of Giddel, 59 of Shephatiah,
of Hattil, of Pochereth-hazzebaim, of Amon.

60 All the temple servants and the descendants of Solomon's servants were three
hundred ninety-two.

61 The following were those who came
up from Tel-melah, Tel-harsha, Cherub,
Addon, and Immer, but they could not
prove their ancestral houses or their descent, whether they belonged to Israel: 62 the
descendants of Delaiah, of Tobiah, of Nekoda,
six hundred forty-two. 63 Also, of the priests:
the descendants of Hobaiah, of Hakkoz, of
Barzillai (who had married one of the daughters of Barzillai the Gileadite and was called
by their name). 64 These sought their registration among those enrolled in the
genealogies, but it was not found there, so
they were excluded from the priesthood as
unclean; 65 the governor told them that they
were not to partake of the most holy food,
until a priest with Urim and Thummim
should come.

7.5-73 Lists of the Families of the Returned Exiles. Names and numbers are given for the returnee families, together with amounts of money involved. The Persian golden *daric* weighed about 8.5 grams, or $\frac{1}{3}$ of an ounce. The priests are settled in the towns that are reported to have been assigned to them, as in Josh 21 and 1 Chr 6.54-81.

[s] Heb *while they*

8.1-10.39 Ezra Reads from the Law and the Covenant is Renewed.
8.1-8 Ezra is said to have read *the book of the law of Moses*, but the version then in use would have been the modified expanded edition, which must have been developed during the decades of Israel's exile in Babylon, and which led to the emergence of *the scribe* as a recognized interpreter of the Law.
8.9-11 Here is depicted the division of labor between the agent of royal power, *Nehemiah the governor*, and the official interpreter of God's will for his people, *Ezra the scribe*. Support for the latter's interpretation of the law was given by *the Levites*.
8.13-18 Celebration of the renewal of life as God's people took the form of the Festival of Booths, which was originally a harvest feast, but which served to recall the experience of Israel in the wilderness of Sinai en route to the land of promise (Ex 23.16; 34.22; Lev 23.33-36; Num 29.12-39; Deut 16.13-17).

66 The whole assembly together was
forty-two thousand three hundred sixty,
[67]besides their male and female slaves, of
whom there were seven thousand three
hundred thirty-seven; and they had two
hundred forty-five singers, male and female.
[68]They had seven hundred thirty-six horses,
two hundred forty-five mules,[t] [69]four hundred thirty-five camels, and six thousand
seven hundred twenty donkeys.
70 Now some of the heads of ancestral
houses contributed to the work. The governor gave to the treasury one thousand
darics of gold, fifty basins, and five hundred
thirty priestly robes. [71]And some of the
heads of ancestral houses gave into the
building fund twenty thousand darics of
gold and two thousand two hundred minas
of silver. [72]And what the rest of the people
gave was twenty thousand darics of gold,
two thousand minas of silver, and sixty-
seven priestly robes.
73 So the priests, the Levites, the gatekeepers, the singers, some of the people, the
temple servants, and all Israel settled in
their towns.

Ezra Summons the People to Obey the Law

When the seventh month came—the people
of Israel being settled in their towns—
8 [1]all the people gathered together into
the square before the Water Gate.
They told the scribe Ezra to bring the book
of the law of Moses, which the LORD had
given to Israel. [2]Accordingly, the priest Ezra
brought the law before the assembly, both
men and women and all who could hear
with understanding. This was on the first
day of the seventh month. [3]He read from it
facing the square before the Water Gate
from early morning until midday, in the
presence of the men and the women and
those who could understand; and the ears
of all the people were attentive to the book
of the law. [4]The scribe Ezra stood on a
wooden platform that had been made for
the purpose; and beside him stood Mattithiah,
Shema, Anaiah, Uriah, Hilkiah, and
Maaseiah on his right hand; and Pedaiah,
Mishael, Malchijah, Hashum, Hash-
baddanah, Zechariah, and Meshullam on
his left hand. [5]And Ezra opened the book in
the sight of all the people, for he was standing above all the people; and when he
opened it, all the people stood up. [6]Then
Ezra blessed the LORD, the great God, and all
the people answered, "Amen, Amen," lifting
up their hands. Then they bowed their
heads and worshiped the LORD with their
faces to the ground. [7]Also Jeshua, Bani,
Sherebiah, Jamin, Akkub, Shabbethai,
Hodiah, Maaseiah, Kelita, Azariah, Jozabad,
Hanan, Pelaiah, the Levites,[u] helped the
people to understand the law, while the
people remained in their places. [8]So they
read from the book, from the law of God,
with interpretation. They gave the sense, so
that the people understood the reading.
9 And Nehemiah, who was the governor, and Ezra the priest and scribe, and the
Levites who taught the people said to all the
people, "This day is holy to the LORD your
God; do not mourn or weep." For all the
people wept when they heard the words of
the law. [10]Then he said to them, "Go your
way, eat the fat and drink sweet wine and
send portions of them to those for whom
nothing is prepared, for this day is holy to
our LORD; and do not be grieved, for the joy
of the LORD is your strength." [11]So the Levites
stilled all the people, saying, "Be quiet, for
this day is holy; do not be grieved." [12]And
all the people went their way to eat and
drink and to send portions and to make
great rejoicing, because they had understood the words that were declared to them.

The Festival of Booths Celebrated

13 On the second day the heads of ancestral houses of all the people, with the
priests and the Levites, came together to the
scribe Ezra in order to study the words of
the law. [14]And they found it written in the
law, which the LORD had commanded by
Moses, that the people of Israel should live
in booths[v] during the festival of the seventh
month, [15]and that they should publish and
proclaim in all their towns and in Jerusalem
as follows, "Go out to the hills and bring
branches of olive, wild olive, myrtle, palm,
and other leafy trees to make booths,[v] as it
is written." [16]So the people went out and
brought them, and made booths[v] for themselves, each on the roofs of their houses,
and in their courts and in the courts of the
house of God, and in the square at the
Water Gate and in the square at the Gate
of Ephraim. [17]And all the assembly of those

7.70 Neh 8.9
7.71 Ezra 2.69
7.73 Ezra 3.1
8.1 Ezra 3.1; Neh 3.26; Ezra 7.6
8.2 Deut 31.11,12; Lev 23.24
8.6 Neh 5.13; Gen 14.22; Ex 4.31
8.7 2 Chr 17.7-9
8.9 Neh 7.65,70; 12.26; Num 29.1; Deut 16.14,15
8.10 Deut 26.11,13
8.12 ver 7,8
8.13 Lev 23.34,42
8.15 Lev 23.4; Deut 16.16; Lev 23.40
8.16 Jer 32.29; Neh 12.39; 2 Kings 14.13
8.17 2 Chr 30.21

[t] Ezra 2.66 and the margins of some Hebrew Mss: MT lacks *They had ... forty-five mules* [u] 1 Esdras 9.48 Vg: Heb *and the Levites* [v] Or *tabernacles*; Heb *succoth*

who had returned from the captivity made booths[w] and lived in them; for from the days of Jeshua son of Nun to that day the people of Israel had not done so. And there was very great rejoicing. [18]And day by day, from the first day to the last day, he read from the book of the law of God. They kept the festival seven days; and on the eighth day there was a solemn assembly, according to the ordinance.

National Confession

9 Now on the twenty-fourth day of this month the people of Israel were assembled with fasting and in sackcloth, and with earth on their heads.[x] [2]Then those of Israelite descent separated themselves from all foreigners, and stood and confessed their sins and the iniquities of their ancestors. [3]They stood up in their place and read from the book of the law of the LORD their God for a fourth part of the day, and for another fourth they made confession and worshiped the LORD their God. [4]Then Jeshua, Bani, Kadmiel, Shebaniah, Bunni, Sherebiah, Bani, and Chenani stood on the stairs of the Levites and cried out with a loud voice to the LORD their God. [5]Then the Levites, Jeshua, Kadmiel, Bani, Hashabneiah, Sherebiah, Hodiah, Shebaniah, and Pethahiah, said, "Stand up and bless the LORD your God from everlasting to everlasting. Blessed be your glorious name, which is exalted above all blessing and praise."

6 And Ezra said:[y] "You are the LORD, you alone; you have made heaven, the heaven of heavens, with all their host, the earth and all that is on it, the seas and all that is in them. To all of them you give life, and the host of heaven worships you. [7]You are the LORD, the God who chose Abram and brought him out of Ur of the Chaldeans and gave him the name Abraham; [8]and you found his heart faithful before you, and made with him a covenant to give to his descendants the land of the Canaanite, the Hittite, the Amorite, the Perizzite, the Jebusite, and the Girgashite; and you have fulfilled your promise, for you are righteous.

9 "And you saw the distress of our ancestors in Egypt and heard their cry at the Red Sea.[z] [10]You performed signs and wonders against Pharaoh and all his servants and all the people of his land, for you knew that they acted insolently against our ancestors. You made a name for yourself, which remains to this day. [11]And you divided the sea before them, so that they passed through the sea on dry land, but you threw their pursuers into the depths, like a stone into mighty waters. [12]Moreover, you led them by day with a pillar of cloud, and by night with a pillar of fire, to give them light on the way in which they should go. [13]You came down also upon Mount Sinai, and spoke with them from heaven, and gave them right ordinances and true laws, good statutes and commandments, [14]and you made known your holy sabbath to them and gave them commandments and statutes and a law through your servant Moses. [15]For their hunger you gave them bread from heaven, and for their thirst you brought water for them out of the rock, and you told them to go in to possess the land that you swore to give them.

16 "But they and our ancestors acted presumptuously and stiffened their necks and did not obey your commandments; [17]they refused to obey, and were not mindful of the wonders that you performed among them; but they stiffened their necks and determined to return to their slavery in Egypt. But you are a God ready to forgive, gracious and merciful, slow to anger and abounding in steadfast love, and you did not forsake them. [18]Even when they had cast an image of a calf for themselves and said, 'This is your God who brought you up out of Egypt,' and had committed great blasphemies, [19]you in your great mercies did not forsake them in the wilderness; the pillar of cloud that led them in the way did not leave them by day, nor the pillar of fire by night that gave them light on the way by which they should go. [20]You gave your good spirit to instruct them, and did not withhold your manna from their mouths, and gave them water for their thirst. [21]Forty years you sustained them in the wilderness so that they lacked nothing; their clothes did not wear out and their feet did not swell. [22]And you gave them kingdoms and peoples, and allotted to them every corner,[a] so they took possession of the land of King Sihon of Heshbon and the land of King Og of Bashan. [23]You multiplied their descendants like the stars of heaven, and brought them into the land that you had told their

[w] Or *tabernacles*; Heb *succoth* [x] Heb *on them* [y] Gk: Heb lacks *And Ezra said* [z] Or *Sea of Reeds* [a] Meaning of Heb uncertain

8.18 Deut 31.11; Lev 23.36; Num 29.35
9.1 Neh 8.2; Ezra 8.23; 1 Sam 4.12
9.2 Ezra 10.11; Neh 13.3,30
9.3 Neh 8.4
9.4 Neh 8.7
9.5 1 Chr 29.13
9.6 2 Kings 19.15; Gen 1.1; Ps 36.6; Col 1.17
9.7 Gen 11.31; 12.1; 17.5
9.8 Gen 15.6,18-21; Josh 21.43-45
9.9 Ex 3.7; 14.10-12
9.10 Ex 5.2; 9.16
9.11 Ex 14.21; 15.5,10
9.12 Ex 13.21,22
9.13 Ex 19.20; 20.1; Ps 19.7-9
9.14 Gen 2.3; Ex 20.8,11
9.15 Ex 16.14; 17.6; Num 20.7-13; Deut 1.8
9.16 Ps 106.6; Deut 31.27
9.17 Ps 78.11; Num 14.4; Ex 34.6,7
9.18 Ex 32.4
9.19 ver 27,31,12
9.20 Num 11.17; Isa 63.11-14; Ex 16.15; 17.6
9.21 Deut 2.7; 8.4; 29.5
9.22 Num 21.21-35
9.23 Gen 15.5

9.1-37 Ezra led the people in a confession of disobedience and a renewed commitment to the covenant relationship with the LORD.

9.38-10.27 The names of those who subscribed to this act of renewal are given.
9.28-39 The summary of the covenantal obligations includes the laws regarding treatment of children, obeying the sabbath requirements, payment of tax to the temple, the cycle of offerings, and support for the priests, Levites and temple attendants.

ancestors to enter and possess. [24]So the descendants went in and possessed the land, and you subdued before them the inhabitants of the land, the Canaanites, and gave them into their hands, with their kings and the peoples of the land, to do with them as they pleased. [25]And they captured fortress cities and a rich land, and took possession of houses filled with all sorts of goods, hewn cisterns, vineyards, olive orchards, and fruit trees in abundance; so they ate, and were filled and became fat, and delighted themselves in your great goodness.

26 "Nevertheless they were disobedient and rebelled against you and cast your law behind their backs and killed your prophets, who had warned them in order to turn them back to you, and they committed great blasphemies. [27]Therefore you gave them into the hands of their enemies, who made them suffer. Then in the time of their suffering they cried out to you and you heard them from heaven, and according to your great mercies you gave them saviors who saved them from the hands of their enemies. [28]But after they had rest, they again did evil before you, and you abandoned them to the hands of their enemies, so that they had dominion over them; yet when they turned and cried to you, you heard from heaven, and many times you rescued them according to your mercies. [29]And you warned them in order to turn them back to your law. Yet they acted presumptuously and did not obey your commandments, but sinned against your ordinances, by the observance of which a person shall live. They turned a stubborn shoulder and stiffened their neck and would not obey. [30]Many years you were patient with them, and warned them by your spirit through your prophets; yet they would not listen. Therefore you handed them over to the peoples of the lands. [31]Nevertheless, in your great mercies you did not make an end of them or forsake them, for you are a gracious and merciful God.

32 "Now therefore, our God—the great and mighty and awesome God, keeping covenant and steadfast love—do not treat lightly all the hardship that has come upon us, upon our kings, our officials, our priests, our prophets, our ancestors, and all your people, since the time of the kings of Assyria until today. [33]You have been just in all that has come upon us, for you have dealt faithfully and we have acted wickedly; [34]our kings, our officials, our priests, and our ancestors have not kept your law or heeded the commandments and the warnings that you gave them. [35]Even in their own kingdom, and in the great goodness you bestowed on them, and in the large and rich land that you set before them, they did not serve you and did not turn from their wicked works. [36]Here we are, slaves to this day—slaves in the land that you gave to our ancestors to enjoy its fruit and its good gifts. [37]Its rich yield goes to the kings whom you have set over us because of our sins; they have power also over our bodies and over our livestock at their pleasure, and we are in great distress."

Those Who Signed the Covenant

38[b] Because of all this we make a firm agreement in writing, and on that sealed document are inscribed the names of our officials, our Levites, and our priests.

10[c] Upon the sealed document are the names of Nehemiah the governor, son of Hacaliah, and Zedekiah; [2]Seraiah, Azariah, Jeremiah, [3]Pashhur, Amariah, Malchijah, [4]Hattush, Shebaniah, Malluch, [5]Harim, Meremoth, Obadiah, [6]Daniel, Ginnethon, Baruch, [7]Meshullam, Abijah, Mijamin, [8]Maaziah, Bilgai, Shemaiah; these are the priests. [9]And the Levites: Jeshua son of Azaniah, Binnui of the sons of Henadad, Kadmiel; [10]and their associates, Shebaniah, Hodiah, Kelita, Pelaiah, Hanan, [11]Mica, Rehob, Hashabiah, [12]Zaccur, Sherebiah, Shebaniah, [13]Hodiah, Bani, Beninu. [14]The leaders of the people: Parosh, Pahath-moab, Elam, Zattu, Bani, [15]Bunni, Azgad, Bebai, [16]Adonijah, Bigvai, Adin, [17]Ater, Hezekiah, Azzur, [18]Hodiah, Hashum, Bezai, [19]Hariph, Anathoth, Nebai, [20]Magpiash, Meshullam, Hezir, [21]Meshezabel, Zadok, Jaddua, [22]Pelatiah, Hanan, Anaiah, [23]Hoshea, Hananiah, Hasshub, [24]Hallohesh, Pilha, Shobek, [25]Rehum, Hashabnah, Maaseiah, [26]Ahiah, Hanan, Anan, [27]Malluch, Harim, and Baanah.

Summary of the Covenant

28 The rest of the people, the priests, the Levites, the gatekeepers, the singers, the temple servants, and all who have separated themselves from the peoples of the

[b] Ch 10.1 in Heb [c] Ch 10.2 in Heb

9.24 Josh 21.43; 18.1
9.25 Deut 3.9; Num 13.27; Deut 6.11; 32.15; 1 Kings 8.66
9.26 Judg 2.11; 1 Kings 14.9; 2 Chr 36.16; ver 30
9.36 Deut 28.48
9.37 Deut 28.33
9.38 2 Chr 29.10; 34.31
10.1 Neh 9.38
10.28 Ezra 2.36-58; Neh 9.2

10.29 Neh 5.12; 2 Chr 34.31
10.30 Ex 34.16; Deut 7.3
10.31 Neh 13.15-22; Ex 23.10,11; Deut 15.1,2
10.32 Ex 30.11-16
10.34 Neh 11.1; 13.31
10.35 Ex 23.19; Deut 26.2
10.36 Ex 13.2; Num 18.15,16
10.37 Lev 23.17; Neh 13.5,9; Lev 27.30
10.38 Num 18.26; Neh 13.12,13
10.39 Deut 12.6; Neh 13.10,11
11.1 Neh 10.34; ver 18; Isa 48.2
11.3 1 Chr 9.2,3; ver 20; Ezra 2.43; Neh 7.57
11.4 1 Chr 9.3ff
11.7 ver 4
11.10 1 Chr 9.10
11.16 1 Chr 26.29

lands to adhere to the law of God, their wives, their sons, their daughters, all who have knowledge and understanding, [29]join with their kin, their nobles, and enter into a curse and an oath to walk in God's law, which was given by Moses the servant of God, and to observe and do all the commandments of the LORD our Lord and his ordinances and his statutes. [30]We will not give our daughters to the peoples of the land or take their daughters for our sons; [31]and if the peoples of the land bring in merchandise or any grain on the sabbath day to sell, we will not buy it from them on the sabbath or on a holy day; and we will forego the crops of the seventh year and the exaction of every debt.

32 We also lay on ourselves the obligation to charge ourselves yearly one-third of a shekel for the service of the house of our God: [33]for the rows of bread, the regular grain offering, the regular burnt offering, the sabbaths, the new moons, the appointed festivals, the sacred donations, and the sin offerings to make atonement for Israel, and for all the work of the house of our God. [34]We have also cast lots among the priests, the Levites, and the people, for the wood offering, to bring it into the house of our God, by ancestral houses, at appointed times, year by year, to burn on the altar of the LORD our God, as it is written in the law. [35]We obligate ourselves to bring the first fruits of our soil and the first fruits of all fruit of every tree, year by year, to the house of the LORD; [36]also to bring to the house of our God, to the priests who minister in the house of our God, the firstborn of our sons and of our livestock, as it is written in the law, and the firstlings of our herds and of our flocks; [37]and to bring the first of our dough, and our contributions, the fruit of every tree, the wine and the oil, to the priests, to the chambers of the house of our God; and to bring to the Levites the tithes from our soil, for it is the Levites who collect the tithes in all our rural towns. [38]And the priest, the descendant of Aaron, shall be with the Levites when the Levites receive the tithes; and the Levites shall bring up a tithe of the tithes to the house of our God, to the chambers of the storehouse. [39]For the people of Israel and the sons of Levi shall bring the contribution of grain, wine, and oil to the storerooms where the vessels of the sanctuary are, and where the priests that minister, and the gatekeepers and the singers are. We will not neglect the house of our God.

Population of the City Increased

11 Now the leaders of the people lived in Jerusalem; and the rest of the people cast lots to bring one out of ten to live in the holy city Jerusalem, while nine-tenths remained in the other towns. [2]And the people blessed all those who willingly offered to live in Jerusalem.

3 These are the leaders of the province who lived in Jerusalem; but in the towns of Judah all lived on their property in their towns: Israel, the priests, the Levites, the temple servants, and the descendants of Solomon's servants. [4]And in Jerusalem lived some of the Judahites and of the Benjaminites. Of the Judahites: Athaiah son of Uzziah son of Zechariah son of Amariah son of Shephatiah son of Mahalalel, of the descendants of Perez; [5]and Maaseiah son of Baruch son of Col-hozeh son of Hazaiah son of Adaiah son of Joiarib son of Zechariah son of the Shilonite. [6]All the descendants of Perez who lived in Jerusalem were four hundred sixty-eight valiant warriors.

7 And these are the Benjaminites: Sallu son of Meshullam son of Joed son of Pedaiah son of Kolaiah son of Maaseiah son of Ithiel son of Jeshaiah. [8]And his brothers[d] Gabbai, Sallai: nine hundred twenty-eight. [9]Joel son of Zichri was their overseer; and Judah son of Hassenuah was second in charge of the city.

10 Of the priests: Jedaiah son of Joiarib, Jachin, [11]Seraiah son of Hilkiah son of Meshullam son of Zadok son of Meraioth son of Ahitub, officer of the house of God, [12]and their associates who did the work of the house, eight hundred twenty-two; and Adaiah son of Jeroham son of Pelaliah son of Amzi son of Zechariah son of Pashhur son of Malchijah, [13]and his associates, heads of ancestral houses, two hundred forty-two; and Amashsai son of Azarel son of Ahzai son of Meshillemoth son of Immer, [14]and their associates, valiant warriors, one hundred twenty-eight; their overseer was Zabdiel son of Haggedolim.

15 And of the Levites: Shemaiah son of Hasshub son of Azrikam son of Hashabiah son of Bunni; [16]and Shabbethai and Jozabad, of the leaders of the Levites, who were over

11.1-12.47 Survey of the Population of Jerusalem and Surrounding Villages, with Assignment of Civic and Cultic Responsibilities.
11.1-33 Those assigned various responsibilities for the life of the city and temple are named and their roles defined. The villages where the people may dwell in the surrounding area are also named.

[d] Gk Mss: Heb *And after him*

12.1-26 The names of the priests and Levites are given, together with indications of the assignments of each group.
12.27-43 The leaders in the ceremonies associated with the dedication of the city wall are named, and a brief description of their roles is included.

the outside work of the house of God; [17]and
Mattaniah son of Mica son of Zabdi son of
Asaph, who was the leader to begin the
thanksgiving in prayer, and Bakbukiah, the
second among his associates; and Abda son
of Shammua son of Galal son of Jeduthun.
[18]All the Levites in the holy city were two
hundred eighty-four.
19 The gatekeepers, Akkub, Talmon and
their associates, who kept watch at the
gates, were one hundred seventy-two. [20]And
the rest of Israel, and of the priests and the
Levites, were in all the towns of Judah, all
of them in their inheritance. [21]But the temple servants lived on Ophel; and Ziha and
Gishpa were over the temple servants.
22 The overseer of the Levites in Jerusalem was Uzzi son of Bani son of Hashabiah
son of Mattaniah son of Mica, of the descendants of Asaph, the singers, in charge
of the work of the house of God. [23]For there
was a command from the king concerning
them, and a settled provision for the singers,
as was required every day. [24]And Pethahiah
son of Meshezabel, of the descendants of
Zerah son of Judah, was at the king's hand
in all matters concerning the people.

Villages outside Jerusalem

25 And as for the villages, with their
fields, some of the people of Judah lived in
Kiriath-arba and its villages, and in Dibon
and its villages, and in Jekabzeel and its
villages, [26]and in Jeshua and in Moladah
and Beth-pelet, [27]in Hazar-shual, in Beer-
sheba and its villages, [28]in Ziklag, in Meconah
and its villages, [29]in En-rimmon, in Zorah,
in Jarmuth, [30]Zanoah, Adullam, and their
villages, Lachish and its fields, and Azekah
and its villages. So they camped from Beer-
sheba to the valley of Hinnom. [31]The people
of Benjamin also lived from Geba onward,
at Michmash, Aija, Bethel and its villages,
[32]Anathoth, Nob, Ananiah, [33]Hazor, Ramah,
Gittaim, [34]Hadid, Zeboim, Neballat, [35]Lod,
and Ono, the valley of artisans. [36]And certain divisions of the Levites in Judah were
joined to Benjamin.

A List of Priests and Levites

12 These are the priests and the Levites
who came up with Zerubbabel son
of Shealtiel, and Jeshua: Seraiah, Jeremiah,
Ezra, [2]Amariah, Malluch, Hattush, [3]Shecan-
iah, Rehum, Meremoth, [4]Iddo, Ginnethoi,
Abijah, [5]Mijamin, Maadiah, Bilgah,
[6]Shemaiah, Joiarib, Jedaiah, [7]Sallu, Amok,
Hilkiah, Jedaiah. These were the leaders of
the priests and of their associates in the
days of Jeshua.
8 And the Levites: Jeshua, Binnui,
Kadmiel, Sherebiah, Judah, and Mattaniah,
who with his associates was in charge of
the songs of thanksgiving. [9]And Bakbukiah
and Unno their associates stood opposite
them in the service. [10]Jeshua was the father
of Joiakim, Joiakim the father of Eliashib,
Eliashib the father of Joiada, [11]Joiada the
father of Jonathan, and Jonathan the father
of Jaddua.
12 In the days of Joiakim the priests,
heads of ancestral houses, were: of Seraiah,
Meraiah; of Jeremiah, Hananiah; [13]of Ezra,
Meshullam; of Amariah, Jehohanan; [14]of
Malluchi, Jonathan; of Shebaniah, Joseph;
[15]of Harim, Adna; of Meraioth, Helkai; [16]of
Iddo, Zechariah; of Ginnethon, Meshullam;
[17]of Abijah, Zichri; of Miniamin, of Moadiah,
Piltai; [18]of Bilgah, Shammua; of Shemaiah,
Jehonathan; [19]of Joiarib, Mattenai; of Jedaiah,
Uzzi; [20]of Sallai, Kallai; of Amok, Eber; [21]of
Hilkiah, Hashabiah; of Jedaiah, Nethanel.
22 As for the Levites, in the days of
Eliashib, Joiada, Johanan, and Jaddua, there
were recorded the heads of ancestral houses;
also the priests until the reign of Darius the
Persian. [23]The Levites, heads of ancestral
houses, were recorded in the Book of the
Annals until the days of Johanan son of
Eliashib. [24]And the leaders of the Levites:
Hashabiah, Sherebiah, and Jeshua son of
Kadmiel, with their associates over against
them, to praise and to give thanks, according to the commandment of David the man
of God, section opposite to section. [25]Mattan-
iah, Bakbukiah, Obadiah, Meshullam,
Talmon, and Akkub were gatekeepers standing guard at the storehouses of the gates.
[26]These were in the days of Joiakim son of
Jeshua son of Jozadak, and in the days of
the governor Nehemiah and of the priest
Ezra, the scribe.

Dedication of the City Wall

27 Now at the dedication of the wall of
Jerusalem they sought out the Levites in all
their places, to bring them to Jerusalem to
celebrate the dedication with rejoicing, with
thanksgivings and with singing, with cymbals, harps, and lyres. [28]The companies of
the singers gathered together from the cir-

11.18 ver 1
11.21 Neh 3.26
11.22 ver 9.14
11.23 Ezra 6.8; 7.20; Neh 12.47
11.25 Josh 14.15; 13.9,17
12.1 Ezra 2.1,2; see Neh 10.2-8
12.7 Ezra 3.2
12.8 Neh 11.17
12.23 1 Chr 9.14ff
12.24 Neh 11.17
12.25 1 Chr 26.15
12.26 Neh 8.8; Ezra 7.6,11
12.27 1 Chr 25.6
12.28 1 Chr 9.16

cuit around Jerusalem and from the villages of the Netophathites; [29]also from Beth-gilgal and from the region of Geba and Azmaveth; for the singers had built for themselves villages around Jerusalem. [30]And the priests and the Levites purified themselves; and they purified the people and the gates and the wall.

31 Then I brought the leaders of Judah up onto the wall, and appointed two great companies that gave thanks and went in procession. One went to the right on the wall to the Dung Gate; [32]and after them went Hoshaiah and half the officials of Judah, [33]and Azariah, Ezra, Meshullam, [34]Judah, Benjamin, Shemaiah, and Jeremiah, [35]and some of the young priests with trumpets: Zechariah son of Jonathan son of Shemaiah son of Mattaniah son of Micaiah son of Zaccur son of Asaph; [36]and his kindred, Shemaiah, Azarel, Milalai, Gilalai, Maai, Nethanel, Judah, and Hanani, with the musical instruments of David the man of God; and the scribe Ezra went in front of them. [37]At the Fountain Gate, in front of them, they went straight up by the stairs of the city of David, at the ascent of the wall, above the house of David, to the Water Gate on the east.

38 The other company of those who gave thanks went to the left,[e] and I followed them with half of the people on the wall, above the Tower of the Ovens, to the Broad Wall, [39]and above the Gate of Ephraim, and by the Old Gate, and by the Fish Gate and the Tower of Hananel and the Tower of the Hundred, to the Sheep Gate; and they came to a halt at the Gate of the Guard. [40]So both companies of those who gave thanks stood in the house of God, and I and half of the officials with me; [41]and the priests Eliakim, Maaseiah, Miniamin, Micaiah, Elioenai, Zechariah, and Hananiah, with trumpets; [42]and Maaseiah, Shemaiah, Eleazar, Uzzi, Jehohanan, Malchijah, Elam, and Ezer. And the singers sang with Jezrahiah as their leader. [43]They offered great sacrifices that day and rejoiced, for God had made them rejoice with great joy; the women and children also rejoiced. The joy of Jerusalem was heard far away.

Temple Responsibilities

44 On that day men were appointed over the chambers for the stores, the contributions, the first fruits, and the tithes, to gather into them the portions required by the law for the priests and for the Levites from the fields belonging to the towns; for Judah rejoiced over the priests and the Levites who ministered. [45]They performed the service of their God and the service of purification, as did the singers and the gatekeepers, according to the command of David and his son Solomon. [46]For in the days of David and Asaph long ago there was a leader of the singers, and there were songs of praise and thanksgiving to God. [47]In the days of Zerubbabel and in the days of Nehemiah all Israel gave the daily portions for the singers and the gatekeepers. They set apart that which was for the Levites; and the Levites set apart that which was for the descendants of Aaron.

Foreigners Separated from Israel

13 On that day they read from the book of Moses in the hearing of the people; and in it was found written that no Ammonite or Moabite should ever enter the assembly of God, [2]because they did not meet the Israelites with bread and water, but hired Balaam against them to curse them—yet our God turned the curse into a blessing. [3]When the people heard the law, they separated from Israel all those of foreign descent.

The Reforms of Nehemiah

4 Now before this, the priest Eliashib, who was appointed over the chambers of the house of our God, and who was related to Tobiah, [5]prepared for Tobiah a large room where they had previously put the grain offering, the frankincense, the vessels, and the tithes of grain, wine, and oil, which were given by commandment to the Levites, singers, and gatekeepers, and the contributions for the priests. [6]While this was taking place I was not in Jerusalem, for in the thirty-second year of King Artaxerxes of Babylon I went to the king. After some time I asked leave of the king [7]and returned to Jerusalem. I then discovered the wrong that Eliashib had done on behalf of Tobiah, preparing a room for him in the courts of the house of God. [8]And I was very angry, and I threw all the household furniture of Tobiah out of the room. [9]Then I gave orders

[e] Cn: Heb *opposite*

12.30 Neh 13.22,30
12.31 ver 38; Neh 2.13; 3.13
12.35 Num 10.2,8
12.36 1 Chr 23.5
12.37 Neh 2.14; 3.15; 3.26
12.38 ver 31; Neh 3.11; 3.8
12.39 Neh 8.16; 3.6; 3.3; 3.1; 3.25
12.44 Neh 13.5,12,13
12.45 1 Chr 25.1; 26.1
12.46 2 Chr 29.30
12.47 Neh 11.23; Num 18.21
13.1 Neh 9.3; Deut 23.3-5
13.2 Num 22.3-11; 23.11
13.3 Neh 9.2; Ex 12.38
13.4 Neh 12.44; 2.10; 6.1,17,18
13.5 Num 18.21
13.6 Neh 5.14; Ezra 6.22
13.7 ver 5
13.9 2 Chr 29.5,15,16

12.44-47 The tasks to be performed by the staff of the temple are mentioned, with special emphasis on the music tradition, which is traced back to *David, Solomon and Asaph* (as reflected in the titles to the Psalms).
13.1-31 Reforms in Defining Israel and in the Practices of its People.
13.1-3 Moabites and Ammonites, perhaps as representatives of Israel's Semitic neighbors, are to be excluded from participation in the life of God's people.
13.4-14 On discovering that *Tobiah*, an Ammonite, had been given space in the temple complex by *Eliashib, the priest*, who was related to Sanballat (13.28), Nehemiah had him expelled. Injustices in supplying the needs of Levites and others were remedied.

13.15-22 Violations of the sabbath law against work were discovered and denounced, with appropriate prayers to God for recognition of Nehemiah's meritorious diligence in seeing that the law was obeyed.
13.23-27 Marriages of Jews to women of adjacent non-Jewish cities are exposed and condemned by Nehemiah.
13.28-31 Nehemiah can boast of his complete purging of the priesthood and the Levites of unworthy members and impure practices. The book ends with an appeal to God to recognize his good deeds.

and they cleansed the chambers, and I
brought back the vessels of the house of
God, with the grain offering and the frankincense.
10 I also found out that the portions of
the Levites had not been given to them; so
that the Levites and the singers, who had
conducted the service, had gone back to
their fields. [11]So I remonstrated with the
officials and said, "Why is the house of God
forsaken?" And I gathered them together
and set them in their stations. [12]Then all
Judah brought the tithe of the grain, wine,
and oil into the storehouses. [13]And I appointed as treasurers over the storehouses
the priest Shelemiah, the scribe Zadok, and
Pedaiah of the Levites, and as their assistant
Hanan son of Zaccur son of Mattaniah, for
they were considered faithful; and their duty
was to distribute to their associates. [14]Re-
member me, O my God, concerning this,
and do not wipe out my good deeds that I
have done for the house of my God and for
his service.

Sabbath Reforms Begun

15 In those days I saw in Judah people
treading wine presses on the sabbath, and
bringing in heaps of grain and loading them
on donkeys; and also wine, grapes, figs, and
all kinds of burdens, which they brought
into Jerusalem on the sabbath day; and I
warned them at that time against selling
food. [16]Tyrians also, who lived in the city,
brought in fish and all kinds of merchandise
and sold them on the sabbath to the people
of Judah, and in Jerusalem. [17]Then I remonstrated with the nobles of Judah and said to
them, "What is this evil thing that you are
doing, profaning the sabbath day? [18]Did not
your ancestors act in this way, and did not
our God bring all this disaster on us and on
this city? Yet you bring more wrath on
Israel by profaning the sabbath."
19 When it began to be dark at the gates
of Jerusalem before the sabbath, I commanded that the doors should be shut and
gave orders that they should not be opened
until after the sabbath. And I set some of
my servants over the gates, to prevent any
burden from being brought in on the sabbath
day. [20]Then the merchants and sellers of all
kinds of merchandise spent the night outside Jerusalem once or twice. [21]But I warned
them and said to them, "Why do you spend
the night in front of the wall? If you do so
again, I will lay hands on you." From that
time on they did not come on the sabbath.
[22]And I commanded the Levites that they
should purify themselves and come and
guard the gates, to keep the sabbath day
holy. Remember this also in my favor, O my
God, and spare me according to the greatness of your steadfast love.

Mixed Marriages Condemned

23 In those days also I saw Jews who
had married women of Ashdod, Ammon,
and Moab; [24]and half of their children spoke
the language of Ashdod, and they could not
speak the language of Judah, but spoke the
language of various peoples. [25]And I contended with them and cursed them and
beat some of them and pulled out their hair;
and I made them take an oath in the name
of God, saying, "You shall not give your
daughters to their sons, or take their daughters for your sons or for yourselves. [26]Did
not King Solomon of Israel sin on account
of such women? Among the many nations
there was no king like him, and he was
beloved by his God, and God made him king
over all Israel; nevertheless, foreign women
made even him to sin. [27]Shall we then listen
to you and do all this great evil and act
treacherously against our God by marrying
foreign women?"
28 And one of the sons of Jehoiada, son
of the high priest Eliashib, was the son-in-
law of Sanballat the Horonite; I chased him
away from me. [29]Remember them, O my
God, because they have defiled the priesthood, the covenant of the priests and the
Levites.
30 Thus I cleansed them from everything foreign, and I established the duties of
the priests and Levites, each in his work;
[31]and I provided for the wood offering, at
appointed times, and for the first fruits.
Remember me, O my God, for good.

13.10 Neh 10.37; 12.28,29
13.11 ver 17,25; Neh 10.39
13.12 Neh 10.37-39; 12.44
13.13 Neh 12.44; 7.2
13.14 ver 22,31; Neh 5.19
13.15 Ex 20.8,10; Neh 10.31
13.17 ver 11,25
13.18 Jer 17.21-23
13.19 Lev 23.32; Jer 17.21
13.21 ver 15
13.22 Neh 12.30; ver 14,31
13.23 Ezra 9.2
13.25 ver 11,17; Deut 25.2; Ezra 10.29,30
13.26 1 Kings 11.1; 3.13; 2 Chr 1.12; 1 Kings 11.4ff
13.27 ver 23; Ezra 10.2
13.28 Neh 12.10; 2.10,19
13.29 Neh 6.14; Num 25.13
13.30 Neh 10.30
13.31 Neh 10.34; ver 14,22

ESTHER

See the Introductions, pp. 4, 39, and 46-47 above.

King Ahasuerus Deposes Queen Vashti

1 This happened in the days of Ahasuerus, the same Ahasuerus who ruled over one hundred twenty-seven provinces from India to Ethiopia.[a] 2In those days when King Ahasuerus sat on his royal throne in the citadel of Susa, 3in the third year of his reign, he gave a banquet for all his officials and ministers. The army of Persia and Media and the nobles and governors of the provinces were present, 4while he displayed the great wealth of his kingdom and the splendor and pomp of his majesty for many days, one hundred eighty days in all.

5 When these days were completed, the king gave for all the people present in the citadel of Susa, both great and small, a banquet lasting for seven days, in the court of the garden of the king's palace. 6There were white cotton curtains and blue hangings tied with cords of fine linen and purple to silver rings[b] and marble pillars. There were couches of gold and silver on a mosaic pavement of porphyry, marble, mother-of-pearl, and colored stones. 7Drinks were served in golden goblets, goblets of different kinds, and the royal wine was lavished according to the bounty of the king. 8Drinking was by flagons, without restraint; for the king had given orders to all the officials of his palace to do as each one desired. 9Furthermore, Queen Vashti gave a banquet for the women in the palace of King Ahasuerus.

10 On the seventh day, when the king was merry with wine, he commanded Mehuman, Biztha, Harbona, Bigtha and Abagtha, Zethar and Carkas, the seven eunuchs who attended him, 11to bring Queen Vashti before the king, wearing the royal crown, in order to show the peoples and the officials her beauty; for she was fair to behold. 12But Queen Vashti refused to come at the king's command conveyed by the eunuchs. At this the king was enraged, and his anger burned within him.

13 Then the king consulted the sages who knew the laws[c] (for this was the king's procedure toward all who were versed in law and custom, 14and those next to him were Carshena, Shethar, Admatha, Tarshish, Meres, Marsena, and Memucan, the seven officials of Persia and Media, who had access to the king, and sat first in the kingdom): 15"According to the law, what is to be done to Queen Vashti because she has not performed the command of King Ahasuerus conveyed by the eunuchs?" 16Then Memucan said in the presence of the king and the officials, "Not only has Queen Vashti done wrong to the king, but also to all the officials and all the peoples who are in all the provinces of King Ahasuerus. 17For this deed of the queen will be made known to all women, causing them to look with contempt on their husbands, since they will say, 'King Ahasuerus commanded Queen Vashti to be brought before him, and she did not come.' 18This very day the noble ladies of Persia and Media who have heard of the queen's behavior will rebel against[d] the king's officials, and there will be no end of contempt and wrath! 19If it pleases the king, let a royal order go out from him, and let it be written among the laws of the Persians and the Medes so that it may not be altered, that Vashti is never again to come before King Ahasuerus; and let the king give her royal position to another who is better than she. 20So when the decree made by the king is proclaimed throughout all his kingdom, vast as it is, all women will give honor to their husbands, high and low alike."

21 This advice pleased the king and the officials, and the king did as Memucan proposed; 22he sent letters to all the royal provinces, to every province in its own script and to every people in its own language, declaring that every man should be master in his own house.[e]

Esther Becomes Queen

2 After these things, when the anger of King Ahasuerus had abated, he remembered Vashti and what she had done and what had been decreed against her. 2Then the king's servants who attended him said, "Let beautiful young virgins be sought out for the king. 3And let the king appoint commissioners in all the provinces of his kingdom to gather all the beautiful young

1.1 Ezra 4.6; Dan 9.1; Esth 8.9; 9.30
1.2 Neh 1.1
1.3 Esth 2.18
1.5 Esth 7.7,8
1.6 Ezek 23.41; Am 6.4
1.7 Esth 2.18
1.10 Judg 16.25; Esth 7.9
1.13 Jer 10.7; Dan 2.12; 1 Chr 12.32
1.14 2 Kings 25.19
1.17 Eph 5.33
1.19 Esth 8.8; Dan 6.8
1.20 Eph 5.22; Col 3.18
1.22 Esth 8.9; Eph 5.22-24; 1 Tim 2.12
2.1 Esth 7.10; 1.19,20
2.3 ver 8.15

1.1-22 King Ahasuerus Deposes his Queen.
1.1 *Ahasuerus* is the equivalent of the Greek Xerxes, who ruled the Persian empire in the fifth century BCE (485-464), following the takeover of the Babylonian empire by his father Darius I (522-486). The Persian dynasty dominated the eastern world from Eastern North Africa to India.
1.2-4 The royal residence was in *Susa*, while the capital of the empire was farther east in Persepolis. *Media* was a region controlled by the Persians in the central part of what is now Iran. Ahasuerus in his citadel showed off his wealth and power to the military and governmental officials.
1.5-9 A sumptuous feast lasting *seven days* displayed the king's wealth and power to the official guests. The practice of having *eunuchs* as court officials was common in the ancient world, perhaps because they offered no competition in the royal harem.
1.10-22 Queen Vashti, ordered by the king to appear before the royal guests, refused and was banished forever from the presence of the king as an example of women's failure to obey their husbands and masters.
2.1-23 Esther, a Jewish Woman, Becomes Queen.
2.1-4 The decision is made to seek for a new queen among virgins in the realm.

[a] Or *Nubia*; Heb *Cush* [b] Or *rods* [c] Cn: Heb *times* [d] Cn: Heb *will tell* [e] Heb adds *and speak according to the language of his people*

2.5-18 The name *Mordecai* derives from Marduk, the king of the Babylonian gods, although he is a leader of the Jewish community. His candidate for queen is *Esther*, whose name comes from Ishtar, the Babylonian goddess whose name means *star*. Her other name is *Hadassah*, which in Hebrew means *myrtle* (Isa 41.19). Mordecai does not reveal to the king the Jewish origins of Esther. Many candidates are taken into the king's presence, and so, after twelve months of cosmetic treatment, is Esther, who spends the night with the king. He chooses her to be queen, and celebrates the event with a great banquet.
2.19-23 After Mordecai discovered a plot by two of the king's *eunuchs* to assassinate him and reported it to Esther, the plotters were executed.
3.1-7.10 Haman's Plot to Destroy Mordecai and its Reversal.
3.1-6 *Haman* is identified as an *Agagite*, a descendant of Agag, who tried to keep Saul from the throne of Judah (1 Sam 15). Mordecai, who is descended from *Kish*, the father of Saul (1 Sam 9.1), refuses to bow down to the Persian king. Haman schemes to destroy Mordecai, as well as *his people*, the Jews.

virgins to the harem in the citadel of Susa
under custody of Hegai, the king's eunuch,
who is in charge of the women; let their
cosmetic treatments be given them. 4And let
the girl who pleases the king be queen
instead of Vashti." This pleased the king,
and he did so.
5 Now there was a Jew in the citadel of
Susa whose name was Mordecai son of Jair
son of Shimei son of Kish, a Benjaminite.
6Kish[f] had been carried away from Jerusalem among the captives carried away with
King Jeconiah of Judah, whom King
Nebuchadnezzar of Babylon had carried
away. 7Mordecai[g] had brought up Hadassah,
that is Esther, his cousin, for she had neither father nor mother; the girl was fair and
beautiful, and when her father and her
mother died, Mordecai adopted her as his
own daughter. 8So when the king's order
and his edict were proclaimed, and when
many young women were gathered in the
citadel of Susa in custody of Hegai, Esther
also was taken into the king's palace and
put in custody of Hegai, who had charge of
the women. 9The girl pleased him and won
his favor, and he quickly provided her with
her cosmetic treatments and her portion of
food, and with seven chosen maids from the
king's palace, and advanced her and her
maids to the best place in the harem. 10Esther
did not reveal her people or kindred, for
Mordecai had charged her not to tell. 11Every
day Mordecai would walk around in front
of the court of the harem, to learn how
Esther was and how she fared.
12 The turn came for each girl to go in
to King Ahasuerus, after being twelve months
under the regulations for the women, since
this was the regular period of their cosmetic
treatment, six months with oil of myrrh and
six months with perfumes and cosmetics for
women. 13When the girl went in to the king
she was given whatever she asked for to
take with her from the harem to the king's
palace. 14In the evening she went in; then
in the morning she came back to the second
harem in custody of Shaashgaz, the king's
eunuch, who was in charge of the concubines; she did not go in to the king again,
unless the king delighted in her and she
was summoned by name.
15 When the turn came for Esther daughter of Abihail the uncle of Mordecai, who
had adopted her as his own daughter, to go
in to the king, she asked for nothing except
what Hegai the king's eunuch, who had
charge of the women, advised. Now Esther
was admired by all who saw her. 16When
Esther was taken to King Ahasuerus in his
royal palace in the tenth month, which is
the month of Tebeth, in the seventh year of
his reign, 17the king loved Esther more than
all the other women; of all the virgins she
won his favor and devotion, so that he set
the royal crown on her head and made her
queen instead of Vashti. 18Then the king
gave a great banquet to all his officials and
ministers—"Esther's banquet." He also
granted a holiday[h] to the provinces, and
gave gifts with royal liberality.

Mordecai Discovers a Plot

19 When the virgins were being gathered together,[i] Mordecai was sitting at the
king's gate. 20Now Esther had not revealed
her kindred or her people, as Mordecai had
charged her; for Esther obeyed Mordecai
just as when she was brought up by him.
21In those days, while Mordecai was sitting
at the king's gate, Bigthan and Teresh, two
of the king's eunuchs, who guarded the
threshold, became angry and conspired to
assassinate[j] King Ahasuerus. 22But the matter came to the knowledge of Mordecai, and
he told it to Queen Esther, and Esther told
the king in the name of Mordecai. 23When
the affair was investigated and found to be
so, both the men were hanged on the gallows. It was recorded in the book of the
annals in the presence of the king.

Haman Undertakes to Destroy the Jews

3 After these things King Ahasuerus
promoted Haman son of Hammedatha
the Agagite, and advanced him and set his
seat above all the officials who were with
him. 2And all the king's servants who were
at the king's gate bowed down and did
obeisance to Haman; for the king had so
commanded concerning him. But Mordecai
did not bow down or do obeisance. 3Then
the king's servants who were at the king's
gate said to Mordecai, "Why do you disobey
the king's command?" 4When they spoke to
him day after day and he would not listen
to them, they told Haman, in order to see
whether Mordecai's words would avail; for
he had told them that he was a Jew. 5When
Haman saw that Mordecai did not bow

2.5 Esth 3.2
2.6 2 Kings 24.14,15; 24.6
2.7 ver 15
2.8 ver 3.15
2.9 ver 3,12
2.10 ver 20
2.15 ver 6; Esth 9.29
2.17 Esth 1.11
2.18 Esth 1.3; 1.7
2.20 ver 10
2.21 Esth 6.2
2.22 Esth 6.1,2
2.23 Esth 10.2
3.2 Esth 2.19; ver 5
3.3 ver 2
3.5 ver 2; Esth 5.9

[f] Heb *a Benjamite* [6]*who* [g] Heb *He* [h] Or *an amnesty* [i] Heb adds *a second time* [j] Heb *to lay hands on*

down or do obeisance to him, Haman was infuriated. [6]But he thought it beneath him to lay hands on Mordecai alone. So, having been told who Mordecai's people were, Haman plotted to destroy all the Jews, the people of Mordecai, throughout the whole kingdom of Ahasuerus.

7 In the first month, which is the month of Nisan, in the twelfth year of King Ahasuerus, they cast Pur—which means "the lot"—before Haman for the day and for the month, and the lot fell on the thirteenth day[k] of the twelfth month, which is the month of Adar. [8]Then Haman said to King Ahasuerus, "There is a certain people scattered and separated among the peoples in all the provinces of your kingdom; their laws are different from those of every other people, and they do not keep the king's laws, so that it is not appropriate for the king to tolerate them. [9]If it pleases the king, let a decree be issued for their destruction, and I will pay ten thousand talents of silver into the hands of those who have charge of the king's business, so that they may put it into the king's treasuries." [10]So the king took his signet ring from his hand and gave it to Haman son of Hammedatha the Agagite, the enemy of the Jews. [11]The king said to Haman, "The money is given to you, and the people as well, to do with them as it seems good to you."

12 Then the king's secretaries were summoned on the thirteenth day of the first month, and an edict, according to all that Haman commanded, was written to the king's satraps and to the governors over all the provinces and to the officials of all the peoples, to every province in its own script and every people in its own language; it was written in the name of King Ahasuerus and sealed with the king's ring. [13]Letters were sent by couriers to all the king's provinces, giving orders to destroy, to kill, and to annihilate all Jews, young and old, women and children, in one day, the thirteenth day of the twelfth month, which is the month of Adar, and to plunder their goods. [14]A copy of the document was to be issued as a decree in every province by proclamation, calling on all the peoples to be ready for that day. [15]The couriers went quickly by order of the king, and the decree was issued in the citadel of Susa. The king and Haman sat down to drink; but the city of Susa was thrown into confusion.

Esther Agrees to Help the Jews

4 When Mordecai learned all that had been done, Mordecai tore his clothes and put on sackcloth and ashes, and went through the city, wailing with a loud and bitter cry; [2]he went up to the entrance of the king's gate, for no one might enter the king's gate clothed with sackcloth. [3]In every province, wherever the king's command and his decree came, there was great mourning among the Jews, with fasting and weeping and lamenting, and most of them lay in sackcloth and ashes.

4 When Esther's maids and her eunuchs came and told her, the queen was deeply distressed; she sent garments to clothe Mordecai, so that he might take off his sackcloth; but he would not accept them. [5]Then Esther called for Hathach, one of the king's eunuchs, who had been appointed to attend her, and ordered him to go to Mordecai to learn what was happening and why. [6]Hathach went out to Mordecai in the open square of the city in front of the king's gate, [7]and Mordecai told him all that had happened to him, and the exact sum of money that Haman had promised to pay into the king's treasuries for the destruction of the Jews. [8]Mordecai also gave him a copy of the written decree issued in Susa for their destruction, that he might show it to Esther, explain it to her, and charge her to go to the king to make supplication to him and entreat him for her people.

9 Hathach went and told Esther what Mordecai had said. [10]Then Esther spoke to Hathach and gave him a message for Mordecai, saying, [11]"All the king's servants and the people of the king's provinces know that if any man or woman goes to the king inside the inner court without being called, there is but one law—all alike are to be put to death. Only if the king holds out the golden scepter to someone, may that person live. I myself have not been called to come in to the king for thirty days." [12]When they told Mordecai what Esther had said, [13]Mordecai told them to reply to Esther, "Do not think that in the king's palace you will escape any more than all the other Jews. [14]For if you keep silence at such a time as this, relief and deliverance will rise for the Jews from another quarter, but you and your father's family will perish. Who knows? Perhaps you have come to royal dignity for just such a time as this." [15]Then Esther said

3.7-15 After casting a *lot* (Pur) to determine the most auspicious day on which to destroy the Jews, Haman told *Ahasuerus* about the disobedience of the Jews to the royal decrees and offered to have them killed throughout the imperial provinces. The king sends out a decree for their death in every province.
4.1-3 As a sign of lamentation in the ancient Near East, people tore their clothing, wrapped themselves in rough fabric made of goat or camel hair (*sackcloth*), and smeared themselves with *ashes*.
4.4-8 Through one of the eunuchs appointed to attend her, Esther learns of Haman's plot against the Jews.
4.9-17 At the urging of Mordecai, Esther agrees to risk her life by going uninvited into the presence of the king in behalf of her people. The hope for *relief for the Jews from another quarter* probably means that God will come to help, although God is never mentioned directly in this book. The fast by the Jews on behalf of Esther is their way of asking God's help in this crisis.

3.6 Ps 83.4
3.7 Esth 9.24; Ezra 6.15
3.8 Ezra 4.12-15; Acts 16.20
3.10 Esth 8.2; Gen 41.42; Esth 7.6
3.12 Esth 8.8-10; 1 Kings 21.8
3.13 Esth 8.10-14
3.14 Esth 8.13,14
3.15 Esth 8.15
4.1 Esth 3.8-10; Jon 3.5,6; Ezek 27.30
4.3 Isa 58.5
4.7 Esth 3.9
4.8 Esth 3.14,15
4.11 Esth 5.1; 6.4; Dan 2.9; Esth 5.2; 8.4
4.15 Esth 5.1

[k] Cn Compare Gk and verse 13 below: Heb *the twelfth month*

5.1-8 The king sees Esther, extends his scepter toward her and invites her to make a request of him. She agrees to state it at a banquet to which the king and Haman are invited.
5.9-14 Haman, furious at Mordecai's failure to be sorrowful or to bow to him, has a huge gallows prepared for his hanging. *Fifty cubits* would equal more than seventy-five feet.
6.1-11 When the king recalls that Mordecai has not been honored for saving the king's life by uncovering the assassination plot (2.19-23) and plans to honor someone who has served him, Haman thinks he is to be honored and suggests elaborate public celebration. Then, ironically, he must lead the honors for *Mordecai the Jew*.

in reply to Mordecai, [16]"Go, gather all the Jews to be found in Susa, and hold a fast on my behalf, and neither eat nor drink for three days, night or day. I and my maids will also fast as you do. After that I will go to the king, though it is against the law; and if I perish, I perish." [17]Mordecai then went away and did everything as Esther had ordered him.

Esther's Banquet

5 On the third day Esther put on her royal robes and stood in the inner court of the king's palace, opposite the king's hall. The king was sitting on his royal throne inside the palace opposite the entrance to the palace. [2]As soon as the king saw Queen Esther standing in the court, she won his favor and he held out to her the golden scepter that was in his hand. Then Esther approached and touched the top of the scepter. [3]The king said to her, "What is it, Queen Esther? What is your request? It shall be given you, even to the half of my kingdom." [4]Then Esther said, "If it pleases the king, let the king and Haman come today to a banquet that I have prepared for the king." [5]Then the king said, "Bring Haman quickly, so that we may do as Esther desires." So the king and Haman came to the banquet that Esther had prepared. [6]While they were drinking wine, the king said to Esther, "What is your petition? It shall be granted you. And what is your request? Even to the half of my kingdom, it shall be fulfilled." [7]Then Esther said, "This is my petition and request: [8]If I have won the king's favor, and if it pleases the king to grant my petition and fulfill my request, let the king and Haman come tomorrow to the banquet that I will prepare for them, and then I will do as the king has said."

Haman Plans to Have Mordecai Hanged

9 Haman went out that day happy and in good spirits. But when Haman saw Mordecai in the king's gate, and observed that he neither rose nor trembled before him, he was infuriated with Mordecai; [10]nevertheless Haman restrained himself and went home. Then he sent and called for his friends and his wife Zeresh, [11]and Haman recounted to them the splendor of his riches, the number of his sons, all the promotions with which the king had honored him, and how he had advanced him above the officials and the ministers of the king. [12]Haman added, "Even Queen Esther let no one but myself come with the king to the banquet that she prepared. Tomorrow also I am invited by her, together with the king. [13]Yet all this does me no good so long as I see the Jew Mordecai sitting at the king's gate." [14]Then his wife Zeresh and all his friends said to him, "Let a gallows fifty cubits high be made, and in the morning tell the king to have Mordecai hanged on it; then go with the king to the banquet in good spirits." This advice pleased Haman, and he had the gallows made.

The King Honors Mordecai

6 On that night the king could not sleep, and he gave orders to bring the book of records, the annals, and they were read to the king. [2]It was found written how Mordecai had told about Bigthana and Teresh, two of the king's eunuchs, who guarded the threshold, and who had conspired to assassinate[l] King Ahasuerus. [3]Then the king said, "What honor or distinction has been bestowed on Mordecai for this?" The king's servants who attended him said, "Nothing has been done for him." [4]The king said, "Who is in the court?" Now Haman had just entered the outer court of the king's palace to speak to the king about having Mordecai hanged on the gallows that he had prepared for him. [5]So the king's servants told him, "Haman is there, standing in the court." The king said, "Let him come in." [6]So Haman came in, and the king said to him, "What shall be done for the man whom the king wishes to honor?" Haman said to himself, "Whom would the king wish to honor more than me?" [7]So Haman said to the king, "For the man whom the king wishes to honor, [8]let royal robes be brought, which the king has worn, and a horse that the king has ridden, with a royal crown on its head. [9]Let the robes and the horse be handed over to one of the king's most noble officials; let him[m] robe the man whom the king wishes to honor, and let him[m] conduct the man on horseback through the open square of the city, proclaiming before him: 'Thus shall it be done for the man whom the king wishes to honor.' " [10]Then the king said to Haman,

5.1 Esth 4.16; 4.11; 6.4
5.2 Prov 21.1; Esth 4.11; 8.4
5.3 Esth 7.2; Mk 6.23
5.5 Esth 6.14
5.6 Esth 7.2; ver 3
5.8 Esth 7.3; 8.5; 6.14
5.9 Esth 2.19; 3.5
5.10 Esth 6.13
5.11 Esth 9.7-10; 3.1
5.12 ver 8
5.13 ver 9
5.14 Esth 6.4; 7.9,10
6.1 Dan 6.18; Esth 2.23; 10.2
6.2 Esth 2.21,22
6.4 Esth 4.11; 5.1; 5.14
6.6 ver 7,9,11
6.8 1 Kings 1.33
6.9 Gen 41.43

[l] Heb *to lay hands on* [m] Heb *them*

"Quickly, take the robes and the horse, as you have said, and do so to the Jew Mordecai who sits at the king's gate. Leave out nothing that you have mentioned." [11]So Haman took the robes and the horse and robed Mordecai and led him riding through the open square of the city, proclaiming, "Thus shall it be done for the man whom the king wishes to honor."

12 Then Mordecai returned to the king's gate, but Haman hurried to his house, mourning and with his head covered. [13]When Haman told his wife Zeresh and all his friends everything that had happened to him, his advisers and his wife Zeresh said to him, "If Mordecai, before whom your downfall has begun, is of the Jewish people, you will not prevail against him, but will surely fall before him."

Haman's Downfall and Mordecai's Advancement

14 While they were still talking with him, the king's eunuchs arrived and hurried Haman off to the banquet that Esther had prepared.

7 [1]So the king and Haman went in to feast with Queen Esther. [2]On the second day, as they were drinking wine, the king again said to Esther, "What is your petition, Queen Esther? It shall be granted you. And what is your request? Even to the half of my kingdom, it shall be fulfilled." [3]Then Queen Esther answered, "If I have won your favor, O king, and if it pleases the king, let my life be given me—that is my petition—and the lives of my people—that is my request. [4]For we have been sold, I and my people, to be destroyed, to be killed, and to be annihilated. If we had been sold merely as slaves, men and women, I would have held my peace; but no enemy can compensate for this damage to the king."[n] [5]Then King Ahasuerus said to Queen Esther, "Who is he, and where is he, who has presumed to do this?" [6]Esther said, "A foe and enemy, this wicked Haman!" Then Haman was terrified before the king and the queen. [7]The king rose from the feast in wrath and went into the palace garden, but Haman stayed to beg his life from Queen Esther, for he saw that the king had determined to destroy him. [8]When the king returned from the palace garden to the banquet hall, Haman had thrown himself on the couch where Esther was reclining; and the king said, "Will he even assault the queen in my presence, in my own house?" As the words left the mouth of the king, they covered Haman's face. [9]Then Harbona, one of the eunuchs in attendance on the king, said, "Look, the very gallows that Haman has prepared for Mordecai, whose word saved the king, stands at Haman's house, fifty cubits high." And the king said, "Hang him on that." [10]So they hanged Haman on the gallows that he had prepared for Mordecai. Then the anger of the king abated.

Esther Saves the Jews

8 On that day King Ahasuerus gave to Queen Esther the house of Haman, the enemy of the Jews; and Mordecai came before the king, for Esther had told what he was to her. [2]Then the king took off his signet ring, which he had taken from Haman, and gave it to Mordecai. So Esther set Mordecai over the house of Haman.

3 Then Esther spoke again to the king; she fell at his feet, weeping and pleading with him to avert the evil design of Haman the Agagite and the plot that he had devised against the Jews. [4]The king held out the golden scepter to Esther, [5]and Esther rose and stood before the king. She said, "If it pleases the king, and if I have won his favor, and if the thing seems right before the king, and I have his approval, let an order be written to revoke the letters devised by Haman son of Hammedatha the Agagite, which he wrote giving orders to destroy the Jews who are in all the provinces of the king. [6]For how can I bear to see the calamity that is coming on my people? Or how can I bear to see the destruction of my kindred?" [7]Then King Ahasuerus said to Queen Esther and to the Jew Mordecai, "See, I have given Esther the house of Haman, and they have hanged him on the gallows, because he plotted to lay hands on the Jews. [8]You may write as you please with regard to the Jews, in the name of the king, and seal it with the king's ring; for an edict written in the name of the king and sealed with the king's ring cannot be revoked."

9 The king's secretaries were summoned at that time, in the third month, which is the month of Sivan, on the twenty-third day; and an edict was written, according to

6.12 2 Sam 15.30
6.13 Esth 5.10
6.14 Esth 5.8
7.2 Esth 5.6; 5.3
7.3 Esth 5.8; 8.5
7.4 Esth 3.9,13
7.6 Esth 3.10
7.8 Esth 1.6
7.9 Esth 1.10; 5.14; Ps 7.16; Prov 11.5,6
8.1 Esth 7.6; 2.7
8.2 Esth 3.10
8.4 Esth 4.11; 5.2
8.5 Esth 5.8; 7.3; 3.13
8.6 Esth 7.4; 9.1
8.7 ver 1
8.8 ver 10; Esth 3.12; 1.19
8.9 Esth 3.12; 1.1; 1.22

6.12-7.10 In spite of warning by his *advisors* that Mordecai will have a role in his downfall, Haman attends Esther's banquet and there is publicly accused by her of plotting the destruction of *her people*. His appeal to Esther is seen by the king as a sexual advance, and his hanging is carried out by the royal decree.
8.1-9.32 The Divine Rescue of the Jews.
8.1-2 Haman's house and authority (symbolized by the *signet ring*) are transferred to Mordecai.
8.3-14 Through Esther's appeal, the king sends a message to all the provinces that the Jews may defend themselves against the attack orders by Haman, and may *take revenge on their enemies*.

[n] Meaning of Heb uncertain

8.15-17 What had been expected by the Jews as a day of destruction and sorrow becomes a festival of rejoicing for their deliverance.
9.1-17 The Jews are attacked by other subject people throughout the Persian empire, rather than by the king's own forces. Huge numbers of their attackers are killed (*seventy-five thousand*), but *no plunder* is taken by the Jews.
9.18-32 All Jews are instructed by a letter from Mordecai, with authorization from Queen Esther, to observe annually the feast of Purim as a remembrance and thanksgiving for the defeat of their enemy, Haman, and the divine preservation of *the Jews*.

all that Mordecai commanded, to the Jews
and to the satraps and the governors and
the officials of the provinces from India to
Ethiopia,[o] one hundred twenty-seven provinces, to every province in its own script
and to every people in its own language,
and also to the Jews in their script and their
language. 10He wrote letters in the name of
King Ahasuerus, sealed them with the king's
ring, and sent them by mounted couriers
riding on fast steeds bred from the royal
herd.[p] 11By these letters the king allowed the
Jews who were in every city to assemble
and defend their lives, to destroy, to kill, and
to annihilate any armed force of any people
or province that might attack them, with
their children and women, and to plunder
their goods 12on a single day throughout all
the provinces of King Ahasuerus, on the
thirteenth day of the twelfth month, which
is the month of Adar. 13A copy of the writ
was to be issued as a decree in every province and published to all peoples, and the
Jews were to be ready on that day to take
revenge on their enemies. 14So the couriers,
mounted on their swift royal steeds, hurried
out, urged by the king's command. The
decree was issued in the citadel of Susa.
15 Then Mordecai went out from the
presence of the king, wearing royal robes of
blue and white, with a great golden crown
and a mantle of fine linen and purple, while
the city of Susa shouted and rejoiced. 16For
the Jews there was light and gladness, joy
and honor. 17In every province and in every
city, wherever the king's command and his
edict came, there was gladness and joy
among the Jews, a festival and a holiday.
Furthermore, many of the peoples of the
country professed to be Jews, because the
fear of the Jews had fallen upon them.

Destruction of the Enemies of the Jews

9 Now in the twelfth month, which is
the month of Adar, on the thirteenth
day, when the king's command and edict
were about to be executed, on the very day
when the enemies of the Jews hoped to gain
power over them, but which had been
changed to a day when the Jews would
gain power over their foes, 2the Jews gathered in their cities throughout all the provinces of King Ahasuerus to lay hands on
those who had sought their ruin; and no
one could withstand them, because the fear
of them had fallen upon all peoples. 3All the
officials of the provinces, the satraps and the
governors, and the royal officials were supporting the Jews, because the fear of Mordecai
had fallen upon them. 4For Mordecai was
powerful in the king's house, and his fame
spread throughout all the provinces as the
man Mordecai grew more and more powerful. 5So the Jews struck down all their
enemies with the sword, slaughtering, and
destroying them, and did as they pleased to
those who hated them. 6In the citadel of
Susa the Jews killed and destroyed five
hundred people. 7They killed Parshandatha,
Dalphon, Aspatha, 8Poratha, Adalia,
Aridatha, 9Parmashta, Arisai, Aridai,
Vaizatha, 10the ten sons of Haman son of
Hammedatha, the enemy of the Jews; but
they did not touch the plunder.
11 That very day the number of those
killed in the citadel of Susa was reported to
the king. 12The king said to Queen Esther,
"In the citadel of Susa the Jews have killed
five hundred people and also the ten sons
of Haman. What have they done in the rest
of the king's provinces? Now what is your
petition? It shall be granted you. And what
further is your request? It shall be fulfilled."
13Esther said, "If it pleases the king, let the
Jews who are in Susa be allowed tomorrow
also to do according to this day's edict, and
let the ten sons of Haman be hanged on the
gallows." 14So the king commanded this to
be done; a decree was issued in Susa, and
the ten sons of Haman were hanged. 15The
Jews who were in Susa gathered also on the
fourteenth day of the month of Adar and
they killed three hundred persons in Susa;
but they did not touch the plunder.
16 Now the other Jews who were in the
king's provinces also gathered to defend
their lives, and gained relief from their
enemies, and killed seventy-five thousand of
those who hated them; but they laid no
hands on the plunder. 17This was on the
thirteenth day of the month of Adar, and
on the fourteenth day they rested and made
that a day of feasting and gladness.

The Feast of Purim Inaugurated

18 But the Jews who were in Susa gathered on the thirteenth day and on the
fourteenth, and rested on the fifteenth day,
making that a day of feasting and gladness.
19Therefore the Jews of the villages, who live

8.10 2 Kings 21.8; Esth 3.12,13
8.11 Esth 9.2,10,15,16; 3.13
8.13 Esth 3.14
8.15 Esth 3.15
8.17 Esth 9.2,19,27
9.1 Esth 8.12; ver 17; Esth 3.13
9.2 ver 15-18; Esth 8.11; Ps 71.13,24; Esth 8.17
9.3 Ezra 8.36
9.5 2 Sam 3.1; Prov 4.18
9.10 Esth 5.11; 8.11
9.12 Esth 7.2
9.13 Esth 8.11
9.15 ver 10
9.16 ver 2,10,15
9.17 ver 1,21
9.18 ver 2,21
9.19 Deut 16.11,14; ver 22; Neh 8.10

[o] Or *Nubia;* Heb *Cush* [p] Meaning of Heb uncertain

in the open towns, hold the fourteenth day
of the month of Adar as a day for gladness
and feasting, a holiday on which they send
gifts of food to one another.
20 Mordecai recorded these things, and
sent letters to all the Jews who were in all
the provinces of King Ahasuerus, both near
and far, [21]enjoining them that they should
keep the fourteenth day of the month Adar
and also the fifteenth day of the same month,
year by year, [22]as the days on which the
Jews gained relief from their enemies, and
as the month that had been turned for them
from sorrow into gladness and from mourning into a holiday; that they should make
them days of feasting and gladness, days for
sending gifts of food to one another and
presents to the poor. [23]So the Jews adopted
as a custom what they had begun to do, as
Mordecai had written to them.
24 Haman son of Hammedatha the
Agagite, the enemy of all the Jews, had
plotted against the Jews to destroy them,
and had cast Pur—that is "the lot"—to
crush and destroy them; [25]but when Esther
came before the king, he gave orders in
writing that the wicked plot that he had
devised against the Jews should come upon
his own head, and that he and his sons
should be hanged on the gallows. [26]There-
fore these days are called Purim, from the
word Pur. Thus because of all that was
written in this letter, and of what they had
faced in this matter, and of what had happened to them, [27]the Jews established and
accepted as a custom for themselves and
their descendants and all who joined them,
that without fail they would continue to
observe these two days every year, as it was
written and at the time appointed. [28]These
days should be remembered and kept
throughout every generation, in every family, province, and city; and these days of
Purim should never fall into disuse among
the Jews, nor should the commemoration of
these days cease among their descendants.
29 Queen Esther daughter of Abihail,
along with the Jew Mordecai, gave full
written authority, confirming this second
letter about Purim. [30]Letters were sent wishing peace and security to all the Jews, to the
one hundred twenty-seven provinces of the
kingdom of Ahasuerus, [31]and giving orders
that these days of Purim should be observed
at their appointed seasons, as the Jew
Mordecai and Queen Esther enjoined on the
Jews, just as they had laid down for themselves and for their descendants regulations
concerning their fasts and their lamentations. [32]The command of Queen Esther fixed
these practices of Purim, and it was recorded in writing.

10 King Ahasuerus laid tribute on the
land and on the islands of the sea.
[2]All the acts of his power and might, and
the full account of the high honor of
Mordecai, to which the king advanced him,
are they not written in the annals of the
kings of Media and Persia? [3]For Mordecai
the Jew was next in rank to King Ahasuerus,
and he was powerful among the Jews and
popular with his many kindred, for he sought
the good of his people and interceded for the
welfare of all his descendants.

9.22 ver 19
9.24 Esth 3.6,7
9.25 Esth 7.4-10; 3.6-15; Ps 7.16
9.26 ver 20
9.27 Esth 8.17; ver 20,21
9.29 Esth 2.15; ver 20,21
9.30 Esth 1.1
9.31 Esth 4.3
9.32 ver 26
10.1 Isa 24.15
10.2 Esth 8.15; 9.4; 2.23
10.3 Gen 41.40; Neh 2.10

10.1-3 Confirmation of this report is said to be available in the official *annals* of the Persian rulers, just as is claimed frequently in the historical books of Israel (1 Kings 14.19; 22.39; 2 Kings 1.18; 23.28; 24.5). This feature intends to lend credibility to this story. The climax of the divine irony is given in the report that the once-threatened Jew *Mordecai* is second in authority only to the King of Persia.

JOB

See the Introductions, pp. 4-5, 48, and 49-50 above.

Job and His Family

1 There was once a man in the land of Uz whose name was Job. That man was blameless and upright, one who feared God and turned away from evil. [2]There were born to him seven sons and three daughters. [3]He had seven thousand sheep, three thousand camels, five hundred yoke of oxen, five hundred donkeys, and very many servants; so that this man was the greatest of all the people of the east. [4]His sons used to go and hold feasts in one another's houses in turn; and they would send and invite their three sisters to eat and drink with them. [5]And when the feast days had run their course, Job would send and sanctify them, and he would rise early in the morning and offer burnt offerings according to the number of them all; for Job said, "It may be that my children have sinned, and cursed God in their hearts." This is what Job always did.

Attack on Job's Character

6 One day the heavenly beings[a] came to present themselves before the LORD, and Satan[b] also came among them. [7]The LORD said to Satan,[b] "Where have you come from?" Satan[b] answered the LORD, "From going to and fro on the earth, and from walking up and down on it." [8]The LORD said to Satan,[b] "Have you considered my servant Job? There is no one like him on the earth, a blameless and upright man who fears God and turns away from evil." [9]Then Satan[b] answered the LORD, "Does Job fear God for nothing? [10]Have you not put a fence around him and his house and all that he has, on every side? You have blessed the work of his hands, and his possessions have increased in the land. [11]But stretch out your hand now, and touch all that he has, and he will curse you to your face." [12]The LORD said to Satan,[b] "Very well, all that he has is in your power; only do not stretch out your hand against him!" So Satan[b] went out from the presence of the LORD.

Job Loses Property and Children

13 One day when his sons and daughters were eating and drinking wine in the eldest brother's house, [14]a messenger came to Job and said, "The oxen were plowing and the donkeys were feeding beside them, [15]and the Sabeans fell on them and carried them off, and killed the servants with the edge of the sword; I alone have escaped to tell you." [16]While he was still speaking, another came and said, "The fire of God fell from heaven and burned up the sheep and the servants, and consumed them; I alone have escaped to tell you." [17]While he was still speaking, another came and said, "The Chaldeans formed three columns, made a raid on the camels and carried them off, and killed the servants with the edge of the sword; I alone have escaped to tell you." [18]While he was still speaking, another came and said, "Your sons and daughters were eating and drinking wine in their eldest brother's house, [19]and suddenly a great wind came across the desert, struck the four corners of the house, and it fell on the young people, and they are dead; I alone have escaped to tell you."

20 Then Job arose, tore his robe, shaved his head, and fell on the ground and worshiped. [21]He said, "Naked I came from my mother's womb, and naked shall I return there; the LORD gave, and the LORD has taken away; blessed be the name of the LORD."

22 In all this Job did not sin or charge God with wrongdoing.

Attack on Job's Health

2 One day the heavenly beings[a] came to present themselves before the LORD, and Satan[b] also came among them to present himself before the LORD. [2]The LORD said to Satan,[b] "Where have you come from?" Satan[b] answered the LORD, "From going to and fro on the earth, and from walking up and down on it." [3]The LORD said to Satan,[b] "Have you considered my servant Job? There is no one like him on the earth, a blameless and upright man who fears God and turns away from evil. He still persists in his integrity, although you incited me against him, to destroy him for no reason." [4]Then Satan[b] answered the LORD, "Skin for skin! All that people have they will give to save their

[a] Heb *sons of God* [b] Or *the Accuser*; Heb *ha-satan*

1.1-5 Prologue: Job's Relationship to God and his Family. The name Job, which appears in the genealogy of Issachar, the son of Jacob in Gen 46.13 and in the prophecy of Ezek 14, could mean *hated* or *penitent*. The land of *Uz* was in northern Arabia or east of the Jordan Valley. To *fear God* means to hold him in awe, and therefore to seek to honor him. Job's enormous wealth is evident in the huge numbers of livestock and servants that he possesses. Job sought *always* to compensate for the indulgent, profligate lives of his children by offering sacrifices in their behalf to *sanctify them*.
1.6-22; 2.1-9 The Charges Raised with God about Job's Character and the Doleful Consequences.
1.6-7 The LORD is pictured as a celestial monarch, with the heavenly beings (*sons of God*) as members of his court. Satan (who is not identical with the Devil as the embodiment of evil, depicted in later Jewish and early Christian writings) is here a kind of prosecuting attorney, whose duty is to discover and prosecute misdeeds in the territories divinely controlled.
1.8-12 The LORD's boast in Job's unique integrity leads Satan to propose that, favored as Job is, he be put to a test: if he experiences difficulties and loses his great possessions, he will show his true character by cursing God. The LORD agrees to put Job to this kind of test.
1.13-22 On learning of the loss of flocks and servants, as well as of sons and daughters, Job performs the appropriate acts of grief (tearing his clothes and shaving his head), but continues to bless the LORD. Those who attacked his herds are Chaldeans (from Babylonia, in what is now southern Iraq) and Sabeans (from south Arabia, also spelled Sheba; Gen 10.7; 1 Kings 10.1-13; Ps 72.10). The *fire of God* is an evidence of God's direct action in human affairs, as in the time of Moses (Ex 19.16-19) and Elijah (1 Kings 18.38; 2 Kings 1.10-12).
2.1-11 Another Test of Job's Faith and Integrity. In a second meeting of the heavenly court, Satan proposes to ruin Job's health in order to test his fidelity to God, and is granted permission to do so. Job, however, accepts this calamity and refuses to rebel against *the hand of God* and thus to renounce his relationship with the LORD.

1.1 Jer 25.20; Ezek 14.14; Jas 5.11; Gen 6.9; 17.1; Ex 18.21
1.2 Job 42.13
1.3 Job 42.12
1.5 Ex 19.10; Gen 8.20; 1 Kings 21.10,13
1.6 Job 38.7; 1 Chr 21.1
1.7 1 Pet 5.8
1.8 Job 42.7,8; ver 1
1.9 1 Tim 6.5
1.10 Job 29.2-6; Ps 128.1,2; Job 31.25
1.11 Job 2.5; 19.21
1.15 Job 6.19
1.16 Gen 19.24; Lev 10.2; Num 11.1-3; 2 Kings 1.10
1.17 Gen 11.28,31
1.18 ver 4,13
1.19 Jer 4.11; 13.24
1.20 Gen 37.29; 1 Pet 5.6
1.21 Eccl 5.15; 1 Tim 6.7; Job 2.10; Eph 5.20; 1 Thess 5.18
1.22 Job 2.10
2.1 Job 1.6
2.2 Job 1.7
2.3 Job 1.1,8; 27.5,6; 9.17

lives.[c] 5But stretch out your hand now and
touch his bone and his flesh, and he will
curse you to your face." 6The LORD said to
Satan,[d] "Very well, he is in your power;
only spare his life."

7 So Satan[d] went out from the presence
of the LORD, and inflicted loathsome sores on
Job from the sole of his foot to the crown
of his head. 8Job[e] took a potsherd with
which to scrape himself, and sat among the
ashes.

9 Then his wife said to him, "Do you still
persist in your integrity? Curse[f] God, and
die." 10But he said to her, "You speak as any
foolish woman would speak. Shall we receive the good at the hand of God, and not
receive the bad?" In all this Job did not sin
with his lips.

Job's Three Friends

11 Now when Job's three friends heard
of all these troubles that had come upon
him, each of them set out from his home—
Eliphaz the Temanite, Bildad the Shuhite,
and Zophar the Naamathite. They met together to go and console and comfort him.
12When they saw him from a distance, they
did not recognize him, and they raised their
voices and wept aloud; they tore their robes
and threw dust in the air upon their heads.
13They sat with him on the ground seven
days and seven nights, and no one spoke a
word to him, for they saw that his suffering
was very great.

Job Curses the Day He Was Born

3 After this Job opened his mouth and
cursed the day of his birth. 2Job said:

3 "Let the day perish in which I was born,
and the night that said,
'A man-child is conceived.'
4 Let that day be darkness!
May God above not seek it,
or light shine on it.
5 Let gloom and deep darkness claim it.
Let clouds settle upon it;
let the blackness of the day terrify it.
6 That night—let thick darkness seize it!
let it not rejoice among the days of the year;
let it not come into the number of the months.
7 Yes, let that night be barren;
let no joyful cry be heard[g] in it.
8 Let those curse it who curse the Sea,[h]
those who are skilled to rouse up Leviathan.
9 Let the stars of its dawn be dark;
let it hope for light, but have none;
may it not see the eyelids of the morning—
10 because it did not shut the doors of my mother's womb,
and hide trouble from my eyes.

11 "Why did I not die at birth,
come forth from the womb and expire?
12 Why were there knees to receive me,
or breasts for me to suck?
13 Now I would be lying down and quiet;
I would be asleep; then I would be at rest
14 with kings and counselors of the earth
who rebuild ruins for themselves,
15 or with princes who have gold,
who fill their houses with silver.
16 Or why was I not buried like a stillborn child,
like an infant that never sees the light?
17 There the wicked cease from troubling,
and there the weary are at rest.
18 There the prisoners are at ease together;
they do not hear the voice of the taskmaster.
19 The small and the great are there,
and the slaves are free from their masters.

20 "Why is light given to one in misery,
and life to the bitter in soul,
21 who long for death, but it does not come,
and dig for it more than for hidden treasures;
22 who rejoice exceedingly,
and are glad when they find the grave?
23 Why is light given to one who cannot see the way,
whom God has fenced in?
24 For my sighing comes like[i] my bread,
and my groanings are poured out like water.
25 Truly the thing that I fear comes upon me,

2.5 Job 1.11
2.6 Job 1.12
2.7 Job 7.5
2.8 Job 42.6; Ezek 27.30; Mt 11.21
2.10 Job 1.21,22; Ps 39.1
2.11 1 Chr 1.45; Gen 25.2; Job 42.11
2.12 Josh 7.6; Lam 2.10; Ezek 27.30
2.13 Gen 50.10; Ezek 3.15
3.3 Job 10.18; Jer 20.14
3.5 Job 10.21; Ps 23.4; Jer 2.6
3.6 Job 23.17
3.8 Job 41.10
3.9 Job 41.18
3.11 Job 10.18
3.12 Gen 30.3; Isa 66.12
3.14 Job 12.17,18; 15.28
3.16 Eccl 6.3
3.17 Job 17.16
3.20 1 Sam 1.10; Prov 31.6; Isa 38.15; Ezek 27.31
3.21 Rev 9.6
3.23 Job 19.6,8,12; Lam 3.7
3.24 Ps 42.3,4

2.11-13 Job's friends' names and places of origin appear in the genealogies of Genesis: *Eliphaz* and *Teman* in Gen 36.4,15; *Shuhite*, as a son of Abraham, in Gen 25.2. As *friends* they come to affirm their loyalty to Job, and to identify with him in his suffering by their spending seven silent *days and nights*.
3.1-26 Job's Lament.
3.1-10 Job's *curse* is followed by a lament (3.11-26). The sequence of items in his lament matches closely those in the creation story of Gen 1.5-19: day, darkness, night, days and years, the struggle with the waters (*Leviathan*, a sea monster), light. Here, however, Job describes not the creation of the world but his own birth as filled with conflict between light and darkness, and as manifesting the power of God against that of Leviathan, who appears in documents from the ancient Near East as the sea monster embodying hostility toward the divine order.
3.11-26 Job's lament consists of a series of questions *why* God has allowed him to continue to live, given the sad, tragic life that he is experiencing. Job pictures the dead as *at rest*, looking back contentedly on their lifetime achievements or relieved from earthly woes, and he asks why those who want to escape from life cannot do so (3.20-26).

[c] Or *the Accuser*; Heb *ha-satan* [d] Or *All that the man has he will give for his life* [e] Heb *He* [f] Heb *Bless* [g] Heb *come* [h] Cn: Heb *day* [i] Heb *before*

4.1-5.27 Eliphaz' Analysis of Job's Situation and his Advice.
4.2-11 Job, who has offered counsel to so many, seems to have forgotten that disaster befalls wrongdoers, just as ferocious animals ultimately meet their doom.
4.12-5.7 Eliphaz' insight was that mortals must accept their fallibility and the transitory quality of their existence, since they are those who inhabit *houses of clay*. There is no point in Job's calling for help from heaven (*the holy ones*), since limitations and suffering are inevitable features of human existence.
5.8-16 It is to God in his *unsearchable* wisdom to whom Job should appeal, since God is the one who exposes human schemes, and who comes to the aid of the *needy* and the *poor*.

and what I dread befalls me.
26 I am not at ease, nor am I quiet;
I have no rest; but trouble comes."

Eliphaz Speaks: Job Has Sinned

4 Then Eliphaz the Temanite answered:
2 "If one ventures a word with
you, will you be offended?
But who can keep from speaking?
3 See, you have instructed many;
you have strengthened the weak
hands.
4 Your words have supported those who
were stumbling,
and you have made firm the feeble
knees.
5 But now it has come to you, and you
are impatient;
it touches you, and you are
dismayed.
6 Is not your fear of God your
confidence,
and the integrity of your ways your
hope?

7 "Think now, who that was innocent
ever perished?
Or where were the upright cut off?
8 As I have seen, those who plow
iniquity
and sow trouble reap the same.
9 By the breath of God they perish,
and by the blast of his anger they
are consumed.
10 The roar of the lion, the voice of the
fierce lion,
and the teeth of the young lions are
broken.
11 The strong lion perishes for lack of
prey,
and the whelps of the lioness are
scattered.

12 "Now a word came stealing to me,
my ear received the whisper of it.
13 Amid thoughts from visions of the
night,
when deep sleep falls on mortals,
14 dread came upon me, and trembling,
which made all my bones shake.
15 A spirit glided past my face;
the hair of my flesh bristled.
16 It stood still,
but I could not discern its
appearance.
A form was before my eyes;
there was silence, then I heard a
voice:
17 'Can mortals be righteous before[j] God?
Can human beings be pure before[j]
their Maker?
18 Even in his servants he puts no trust,
and his angels he charges with error;
19 how much more those who live in
houses of clay,
whose foundation is in the dust,
who are crushed like a moth.
20 Between morning and evening they are
destroyed;
they perish forever without any
regarding it.
21 Their tent-cord is plucked up within
them,
and they die devoid of wisdom.'

Job Is Corrected by God

5 "Call now; is there anyone who will
answer you?
To which of the holy ones will you
turn?
2 Surely vexation kills the fool,
and jealousy slays the simple.
3 I have seen fools taking root,
but suddenly I cursed their dwelling.
4 Their children are far from safety,
they are crushed in the gate,
and there is no one to deliver them.
5 The hungry eat their harvest,
and they take it even out of the
thorns;[k]
and the thirsty[l] pant after their
wealth.
6 For misery does not come from the
earth,
nor does trouble sprout from the
ground;
7 but human beings are born to trouble
just as sparks[m] fly upward.

8 "As for me, I would seek God,
and to God I would commit my cause.
9 He does great things and unsearchable,
marvelous things without number.
10 He gives rain on the earth
and sends waters on the fields;
11 he sets on high those who are lowly,

[j] Or *more than* [k] Meaning of Heb uncertain [l] Aquila Symmachus Syr Vg: Heb *snare* [m] Or *birds*; Heb *sons of Resheph*

4.2 Job 32.18-20
4.3 Isa 35.3; Heb 12.12
4.4 Isa 35.3; Heb 12.12
4.5 Job 6.14; 19.21
4.6 Job 1.1
4.7 Ps 37.25
4.8 Prov 22.8; Hos 10.13; Gal 6.7,8
4.9 Job 15.30; Isa 30.33; Ps 59.13
4.10 Ps 58.6
4.11 Ps 34.10
4.12 Job 26.14
4.14 Jer 23.9
4.17 Job 9.2; 35.10
4.18 Job 15.15
4.19 Job 10.9; 22.16
4.20 Ps 90.5,6; Job 20.7
4.21 Job 36.12
5.1 Job 15.15
5.2 Prov 12.16
5.3 Ps 37.35
5.4 Am 5.12
5.5 Job 18.8-10
5.7 Job 14.1
5.8 Ps 35.23
5.9 Ps 40.5; 72.18
5.10 Ps 65.9
5.11 1 Sam 2.7; Ps 113.7

and those who mourn are lifted to safety.
12 He frustrates the devices of the crafty,
so that their hands achieve no success.
13 He takes the wise in their own craftiness;
and the schemes of the wily are brought to a quick end.
14 They meet with darkness in the daytime,
and grope at noonday as in the night.
15 But he saves the needy from the sword of their mouth,
from the hand of the mighty.
16 So the poor have hope,
and injustice shuts its mouth.

17 "How happy is the one whom God reproves;
therefore do not despise the discipline of the Almighty.[n]
18 For he wounds, but he binds up;
he strikes, but his hands heal.
19 He will deliver you from six troubles;
in seven no harm shall touch you.
20 In famine he will redeem you from death,
and in war from the power of the sword.
21 You shall be hidden from the scourge of the tongue,
and shall not fear destruction when it comes.
22 At destruction and famine you shall laugh,
and shall not fear the wild animals of the earth.
23 For you shall be in league with the stones of the field,
and the wild animals shall be at peace with you.
24 You shall know that your tent is safe,
you shall inspect your fold and miss nothing.
25 You shall know that your descendants will be many,
and your offspring like the grass of the earth.
26 You shall come to your grave in ripe old age,
as a shock of grain comes up to the threshing floor in its season.
27 See, we have searched this out; it is true.
Hear, and know it for yourself."

Job Replies: My Complaint Is Just

6 Then Job answered:
2 "O that my vexation were weighed,
and all my calamity laid in the balances!
3 For then it would be heavier than the sand of the sea;
therefore my words have been rash.
4 For the arrows of the Almighty[n] are in me;
my spirit drinks their poison;
the terrors of God are arrayed against me.
5 Does the wild ass bray over its grass,
or the ox low over its fodder?
6 Can that which is tasteless be eaten without salt,
or is there any flavor in the juice of mallows?[o]
7 My appetite refuses to touch them;
they are like food that is loathsome to me.[o]

8 "O that I might have my request,
and that God would grant my desire;
9 that it would please God to crush me,
that he would let loose his hand and cut me off!
10 This would be my consolation;
I would even exult[o] in unrelenting pain;
for I have not denied the words of the Holy One.
11 What is my strength, that I should wait?
And what is my end, that I should be patient?
12 Is my strength the strength of stones,
or is my flesh bronze?
13 In truth I have no help in me,
and any resource is driven from me.

14 "Those who withhold[p] kindness from a friend
forsake the fear of the Almighty.[n]
15 My companions are treacherous like a torrent-bed,
like freshets that pass away,
16 that run dark with ice,
turbid with melting snow.
17 In time of heat they disappear;
when it is hot, they vanish from their place.

[n] Traditional rendering of Heb *Shaddai* [o] Meaning of Heb uncertain [p] Syr Vg Compare Tg: Meaning of Heb uncertain

5.12 Neh 4.15; Ps 33.10; Isa 8.10
5.14 Job 12.25; Deut 28.29
5.15 Ps 35.10
5.16 Ps 107.42
5.17 Ps 94.12; Jas 1.12; Heb 12.5-11
5.18 Isa 30.26
5.19 Ps 34.19; 91.10
5.20 Ps 33.19; 144.10
5.21 Ps 31.20; 91.5,6
5.22 Ps 91.13; Ezek 34.25
5.23 Ps 91.12; Isa 11.6-9
5.24 Job 8.6; 21.9
5.25 Ps 72.16; 112.2
5.26 Gen 15.15; Prov 9.11
6.2 Job 31.6
6.3 Prov 27.3
6.4 Ps 38.2; Job 21.20; Ps 88.15
6.8 Job 14.13
6.9 1 Kings 19.4
6.10 Job 23.11,12; Lev 19.2; Isa 57.15; Hos 11.9
6.11 Job 21.4
6.13 Job 26.2,3
6.15 Ps 38.11; Jer 15.18
6.17 Job 24.19

5.17-27 God is here called *Shaddai*, a word used in ancient Near Eastern documents with a range of meanings, but it is probably related to a word for mountain, emphasizing immutable strength. His *reproof* and *discipline* are intended to lead humans toward remedy of ills and deliverance from death, toward a life of *peace*, abundance of *offspring*, and length of life. Eliphaz declares that this is *true* and that Job should *know it*.
6.1-7.23 Job is Overcome with Despair, but Not with Guilt.
6.1-7 So massive are the calamities that have befallen Job as a result of *the arrows of the Almighty* (*Shaddai*) that nothing can meet his need for understanding his plight. What his friends offer him as an explanation or comfort he finds *tasteless* and *loathsome*.
6.8-13 Free of any sense of guilt, Job would prefer death to this never-ending agony and perplexity. His resources for dealing with his situation are at an end.
6.14-23 Job is deeply disappointed by his friends for their failure to offer understanding and support. It is not as though he had asked them for money or to risk their lives for him.

6.24-30 Job repeats his petition to them to show him how he may have *gone wrong* toward God. Instead of supporting him, they quibble over words or play mental games over his fate.
6.24-30 In response, he pleads that they will see him as one whose problems with divine justice must be resolved. They cannot charge him with misdeeds, nor is there *any wrong in his tongue*.
7.1-21 Job complains to God about the misery of human life.
7.1-8 All human existence is like slave-labor: relentless demands, bodily discomfort, with no *hope* of escape. Job will never *see good*, and God – here called the All-seeing Eye (Ps 11.4; 33.18) – does not even look at Job in his wretched condition.
7.9-16 Before he goes to the place of death, *Sheol*, from which there is no returning to life on earth, Job will voice his complaint to God, who treats him as though he were the embodiment of evil (here symbolized by the widely-used ancient Near Eastern images of the *Sea* and the *Dragon*). It was these forces which first threatened the order of God's creation (Ps 89.9-10; Gen 1.21; Ps 74.13). Job would prefer sudden death to these endless days of misery and the night of terrifying visions.
7.17-21 Mocking Ps 4.4-8, where God is praised for elevating humans to a status of privilege and to gratifying responsibilities, Job portrays God as relentless in scrutinizing every human action, even to swallowing one's own *spittle*. The intent of this constant divine surveillance by the *Watcher of humanity* (*cf.* the All-seeing Eye of vs. 8) is to expose human sin, which God does not pardon. The grave is surely preferable to such an endless divine examination.
8.1-22 Bildad Invokes the Traditional Arguments that the Wicked are Punished and the Good Rewarded in Life.
8.1-10 Denouncing Job's complaints as *a great wind*, Bildad asserts the justice of God and suggests that the fate of Job's children is the divine recompense for *their transgressions*. He assures Job that, if he is truly upright, he has only to ask God and he will be restored and rewarded. *The wisdom of his ancestors* can teach him this.

18 The caravans turn aside from their course;
they go up into the waste, and perish.
19 The caravans of Tema look,
the travelers of Sheba hope.
20 They are disappointed because they
were confident;
they come there and are confounded.
21 Such you have now become to me;[q]
you see my calamity, and are afraid.
22 Have I said, 'Make me a gift'?
Or, 'From your wealth offer a bribe
for me'?
23 Or, 'Save me from an opponent's hand'?
Or, 'Ransom me from the hand of
oppressors'?

24 "Teach me, and I will be silent;
make me understand how I have
gone wrong.
25 How forceful are honest words!
But your reproof, what does it
reprove?
26 Do you think that you can reprove
words,
as if the speech of the desperate were
wind?
27 You would even cast lots over the
orphan,
and bargain over your friend.

28 "But now, be pleased to look at me;
for I will not lie to your face.
29 Turn, I pray, let no wrong be done.
Turn now, my vindication is at stake.
30 Is there any wrong on my tongue?
Cannot my taste discern calamity?

Job: My Suffering Is without End

7 "Do not human beings have a hard
service on earth,
and are not their days like the days
of a laborer?
2 Like a slave who longs for the shadow,
and like laborers who look for their
wages,
3 so I am allotted months of emptiness,
and nights of misery are apportioned
to me.
4 When I lie down I say, 'When shall I
rise?'
But the night is long,
and I am full of tossing until dawn.
5 My flesh is clothed with worms and dirt;
my skin hardens, then breaks out
again.
6 My days are swifter than a weaver's
shuttle,
and come to their end without hope.[r]

7 "Remember that my life is a breath;
my eye will never again see good.
8 The eye that beholds me will see me
no more;
while your eyes are upon me, I shall
be gone.
9 As the cloud fades and vanishes,
so those who go down to Sheol do
not come up;
10 they return no more to their houses,
nor do their places know them any
more.

11 "Therefore I will not restrain my mouth;
I will speak in the anguish of my spirit;
I will complain in the bitterness of
my soul.
12 Am I the Sea, or the Dragon,
that you set a guard over me?
13 When I say, 'My bed will comfort me,
my couch will ease my complaint,'
14 then you scare me with dreams
and terrify me with visions,
15 so that I would choose strangling
and death rather than this body.
16 I loathe my life; I would not live forever.
Let me alone, for my days are a breath.
17 What are human beings, that you
make so much of them,
that you set your mind on them,
18 visit them every morning,
test them every moment?
19 Will you not look away from me for a
while,
let me alone until I swallow my spittle?
20 If I sin, what do I do to you, you
watcher of humanity?
Why have you made me your target?
Why have I become a burden to you?
21 Why do you not pardon my transgression
and take away my iniquity?
For now I shall lie in the earth;
you will seek me, but I shall not be."

Bildad Speaks: Job Should Repent

8 Then Bildad the Shuhite answered:
2 "How long will you say these
things,
and the words of your mouth be a
great wind?
3 Does God pervert justice?

[q] Cn Compare Gk Syr: Meaning of Heb uncertain　[r] Or *as the thread runs out*

6.19 Gen 25.15; Isa 21.14; 1 Kings 10.1
6.20 Jer 14.3
6.25 Eccl 12.10,11
6.26 Job 8.2
6.27 Joel 3.3; 2 Pet 3.3
6.28 Job 27.4
6.30 Job 27.4; 12.11
7.1 Job 10.17; 14.14; Isa 40.2; Job 14.6
7.2 Lev 19.13
7.3 Lam 1.7; Ps 6.6
7.4 Deut 28.67
7.6 Job 9.25; 13.15; 17.15,16
7.7 Ps 78.39; Job 9.25
7.8 Job 20.9; ver 21
7.9 Job 30.15; 11.8; 2 Sam 12.23
7.10 Job 10.21; Ps 103.16
7.11 Ps 40.9; 1 Sam 1.10
7.12 Ezek 32.2,3
7.14 Job 9.34
7.16 Job 10.1; Eccl 7.15
7.17 Ps 8.4; 144.3; Heb 2.6
7.20 Job 35.3,6; ver 12; Job 16.12
7.21 Job 10.14; Ps 104.29; ver 8
8.3 Gen 18.25; Deut 32.4; 2 Chr 19.7; Dan 9.14; Rom 3.5

8.4 Job 1.5,18,19
8.5 Job 5.8; 11.13; 9.15
8.6 Ps 7.6
8.7 Job 42.12
8.8 Deut 4.32; 32.7; Job 15.18
8.9 Gen 47.9; 1 Chr 29.15; Job 7.6
8.12 Ps 129.6; Jer 17.6
8.13 Ps 9.17; Job 11.20; Prov 10.28
8.15 Job 27.18
8.16 Ps 37.35; 80.11
8.18 Job 7.10; Ps 37.36
8.20 Job 4.7; 21.30
8.21 Ps 126.2; 132.16
8.22 Ps 35.26; 109.29; ver 15
9.2 Ps 143.2; Rom 3.20
9.4 Job 36.5; 2 Chr 13.12
9.6 Isa 2.19,21; Hag 2.6; Heb 12.26; Job 26.11
9.8 Gen 1.6; Ps 104.2,3
9.9 Gen 1.16; Job 38.31; Am 5.8
9.10 Ps 71.15
9.11 Job 23.8,9; 35.14
9.12 Isa 45.9; Rom 9.20; Job 11.10
9.13 Job 26.12; Isa 30.7
9.14 ver 3,32

Or does the Almighty[s] pervert the right?
4 If your children sinned against him,
he delivered them into the power of their transgression.
5 If you will seek God
and make supplication to the Almighty,[s]
6 if you are pure and upright,
surely then he will rouse himself for you
and restore to you your rightful place.
7 Though your beginning was small,
your latter days will be very great.

8 "For inquire now of bygone generations,
and consider what their ancestors have found;
9 for we are but of yesterday, and we know nothing,
for our days on earth are but a shadow.
10 Will they not teach you and tell you
and utter words out of their understanding?

11 "Can papyrus grow where there is no marsh?
Can reeds flourish where there is no water?
12 While yet in flower and not cut down,
they wither before any other plant.
13 Such are the paths of all who forget God;
the hope of the godless shall perish.
14 Their confidence is gossamer,
a spider's house their trust.
15 If one leans against its house, it will not stand;
if one lays hold of it, it will not endure.
16 The wicked thrive[t] before the sun,
and their shoots spread over the garden.
17 Their roots twine around the stoneheap;
they live among the rocks.[u]
18 If they are destroyed from their place,
then it will deny them, saying, 'I have never seen you.'
19 See, these are their happy ways,[v]
and out of the earth still others will spring.

20 "See, God will not reject a blameless person,
nor take the hand of evildoers.
21 He will yet fill your mouth with laughter,
and your lips with shouts of joy.
22 Those who hate you will be clothed with shame,
and the tent of the wicked will be no more."

Job Replies: There Is No Mediator

9 Then Job answered:
2 "Indeed I know that this is so;
but how can a mortal be just before God?
3 If one wished to contend with him,
one could not answer him once in a thousand.
4 He is wise in heart, and mighty in strength
—who has resisted him, and succeeded?—
5 he who removes mountains, and they do not know it,
when he overturns them in his anger;
6 who shakes the earth out of its place,
and its pillars tremble;
7 who commands the sun, and it does not rise;
who seals up the stars;
8 who alone stretched out the heavens
and trampled the waves of the Sea;[w]
9 who made the Bear and Orion,
the Pleiades and the chambers of the south;
10 who does great things beyond understanding,
and marvelous things without number.
11 Look, he passes by me, and I do not see him;
he moves on, but I do not perceive him.
12 He snatches away; who can stop him?
Who will say to him, 'What are you doing?'

13 "God will not turn back his anger;
the helpers of Rahab bowed beneath him.
14 How then can I answer him,
choosing my words with him?

[s] Traditional rendering of Heb *Shaddai* [t] Heb *He thrives* [u] Gk Vg: Meaning of Heb uncertain [v] Meaning of Heb uncertain [w] Or *trampled the back of the sea dragon*

8.11-19 Two kinds of human are compared with two kinds of plant: (1) those plants that lack water are like those persons who *forget God* and thus have nothing to lean upon; (2) others are like plants (omitting *wicked*, which is not in the Hebrew original text) that put down roots and thereby endure. If frustrated in one place, they can *spring* to life in another. Humans can choose to live out their lives in structures as flimsy as *spider* webs or as firm as *rocks*.
8.20-22 Bildad answers and mimics Job's complaints of divine injustice or lack of support by affirming that the *blameless* will be filled with joy, but those hostile toward God are the ones whose dwelling place *will be no more* (8.22; 7.21).
9.1-10.22 Job's Perceptions of God's Power and Inaccessibility.
9.1-3 Another possible translation is *He [God] would not answer him [the human who complains] once in a thousand*. That is, God is not going to respond to human questionings of his justice.
9.6-8 The *pillars of the earth* are the foundations of the platform on which the surface of the earth was perceived to rest, with waters below and around, and with sky, sun, moon, stars and clouds of rain above. God's initial act of creation (Gen 1.1-13) was putting the waters (symbols of chaos) in their place.

9.19 The configurations of stars were identified with various mythical animals and persons in the mythology of the ancient Near East. These star groups are variants of the signs of the zodiac widely used in the hellenistic period, and found on the mosaic floors of ancient (third/fourth century CE) synagogue buildings excavated in Syria and Palestine. The signs were regarded as indicators of the ordering by the divine power(s) which established and maintained the universe. *The chambers of the south* were probably the caves in which the south winds were thought to be kept, as God controlled the winds in the account of the Exodus (Ps 78.26) and in the Song of Solomon (4.16).
9.11-24 Even though God performs marvelous deeds to benefit humanity, he also acts at times in seemingly harsh and harmful ways. Yet there is no way to debate with him about the sad results of his actions. *The helpers of Rahab* are those forces which assist the evil powers that stir up the sea (the waters of chaos) in their opposition to God (Ps 89.10-11). Yet in the past God has overcome these powers for the benefit of his people (Isa 51.9-11). The *accuser* is now bringing charges against Job, but there is no point in appealing to God for support, since he brings catastrophes in his own inscrutable ways and allows *the wicked* to seize control of other human lives.
9.25-35 If in his despair Job were to cease his complaint against God, his accuser would infer from this that Job was admitting his guilt. There is no *umpire* (another translation is, How I wish there were an umpire!) to intercede with God in Job's behalf.
10.1-22 In his deep dismay Job unleashes a series of questions addressed to God, challenging God's compassion and the consistency of his purpose toward his human creatures, his failure to *acquit* Job of the charges of *iniquity*, and his permitting enemies to bring unfounded charges against Job. Why was he born? He prays that he may be granted *a little comfort* before he descends into *the gloom and chaos* of the abode of the dead.

15 Though I am innocent, I cannot
answer him;
I must appeal for mercy to my
accuser.[x]
16 If I summoned him and he answered me,
I do not believe that he would listen
to my voice.
17 For he crushes me with a tempest,
and multiplies my wounds without
cause;
18 he will not let me get my breath,
but fills me with bitterness.
19 If it is a contest of strength, he is the
strong one!
If it is a matter of justice, who can
summon him?[y]
20 Though I am innocent, my own mouth
would condemn me;
though I am blameless, he would
prove me perverse.
21 I am blameless; I do not know myself;
I loathe my life.
22 It is all one; therefore I say,
he destroys both the blameless and
the wicked.
23 When disaster brings sudden death,
he mocks at the calamity[z] of the
innocent.
24 The earth is given into the hand of the
wicked;
he covers the eyes of its judges—
if it is not he, who then is it?

25 "My days are swifter than a runner;
they flee away, they see no good.
26 They go by like skiffs of reed,
like an eagle swooping on the prey.
27 If I say, 'I will forget my complaint;
I will put off my sad countenance
and be of good cheer,'
28 I become afraid of all my suffering,
for I know you will not hold me
innocent.
29 I shall be condemned;
why then do I labor in vain?
30 If I wash myself with soap
and cleanse my hands with lye,
31 yet you will plunge me into filth,
and my own clothes will abhor me.
32 For he is not a mortal, as I am, that I
might answer him,
that we should come to trial together.
33 There is no umpire[a] between us,
who might lay his hand on us both.
34 If he would take his rod away from me,
and not let dread of him terrify me,
35 then I would speak without fear of him,
for I know I am not what I am
thought to be.[b]

Job: I Loathe My Life

10 "I loathe my life;
I will give free utterance to
my complaint;
I will speak in the bitterness of my soul.
2 I will say to God, Do not condemn me;
let me know why you contend
against me.
3 Does it seem good to you to oppress,
to despise the work of your hands
and favor the schemes of the wicked?
4 Do you have eyes of flesh?
Do you see as humans see?
5 Are your days like the days of mortals,
or your years like human years,
6 that you seek out my iniquity
and search for my sin,
7 although you know that I am not guilty,
and there is no one to deliver out of
your hand?
8 Your hands fashioned and made me;
and now you turn and destroy me.[c]
9 Remember that you fashioned me like
clay;
and will you turn me to dust again?
10 Did you not pour me out like milk
and curdle me like cheese?
11 You clothed me with skin and flesh,
and knit me together with bones and
sinews.
12 You have granted me life and steadfast
love,
and your care has preserved my spirit.
13 Yet these things you hid in your heart;
I know that this was your purpose.
14 If I sin, you watch me,
and do not acquit me of my iniquity.
15 If I am wicked, woe to me!
If I am righteous, I cannot lift up my
head,
for I am filled with disgrace
and look upon my affliction.
16 Bold as a lion you hunt me;
you repeat your exploits against me.
17 You renew your witnesses against me,
and increase your vexation toward me;
you bring fresh troops against me.[d]

[x] Or *for my right* [y] Compare Gk: Heb *me* [z] Meaning of Heb uncertain [a] Another reading is *Would that there were an umpire* [b] Cn: Heb *for I am not so in myself* [c] Cn Compare Gk Syr: Heb *made me together all around, and you destroy me* [d] Cn Compare Gk: Heb *toward me; changes and a troop are with me*

9.15 Job 10.15; 8.5
9.17 Job 16.12,14; 2.3
9.18 Job 27.2
9.20 ver 15,29
9.21 Job 1.1; 7.16
9.22 Eccl 9.2,3; Ezek 21.3
9.23 Ps 64.4; Heb 11.36; 1 Pet 1.7
9.24 Job 10.3; 12.6; 12.17
9.26 Hab 1.8
9.29 ver 20
9.30 Jer 2.22
9.32 Eccl 6.10; Rom 9.20; ver 3; Ps 143.2
9.33 1 Sam 2.25
9.34 Job 13.21; Ps 39.10
10.1 1 Kings 19.4; Job 7.16; 7.11
10.2 Job 9.29; Hos 4.1
10.3 ver 8; Job 21.16; 22.18
10.4 1 Sam 16.7
10.5 Ps 90.4; 2 Pet 3.8
10.7 Job 9.21; 9.12
10.8 Ps 119.73
10.9 Gen 2.7; 3.19; Isa 64.8
10.10 Ps 139.14-16
10.12 Job 33.4
10.14 Job 13.27; 9.28
10.15 Isa 3.11; Job 9.12,15; Ps 25.8
10.16 Isa 38.13; Lam 3.10; Job 5.9
10.17 Job 16.8; 7.1

18 "Why did you bring me forth from the womb?
Would that I had died before any eye had seen me,
19 and were as though I had not been,
carried from the womb to the grave.
20 Are not the days of my life few?[e]
Let me alone, that I may find a little comfort[f]
21 before I go, never to return,
to the land of gloom and deep darkness,
22 the land of gloom[g] and chaos,
where light is like darkness."

Zophar Speaks: Job's Guilt Deserves Punishment

11 Then Zophar the Naamathite answered:
2 "Should a multitude of words go unanswered,
and should one full of talk be vindicated?
3 Should your babble put others to silence,
and when you mock, shall no one shame you?
4 For you say, 'My conduct[h] is pure,
and I am clean in God's[i] sight.'
5 But oh, that God would speak,
and open his lips to you,
6 and that he would tell you the secrets of wisdom!
For wisdom is many-sided.[j]
Know then that God exacts of you less than your guilt deserves.

7 "Can you find out the deep things of God?
Can you find out the limit of the Almighty?[k]
8 It is higher than heaven[l]—what can you do?
Deeper than Sheol—what can you know?
9 Its measure is longer than the earth,
and broader than the sea.
10 If he passes through, and imprisons,
and assembles for judgment, who can hinder him?
11 For he knows those who are worthless;
when he sees iniquity, will he not consider it?
12 But a stupid person will get understanding,
when a wild ass is born human.[j]

13 "If you direct your heart rightly,
you will stretch out your hands toward him.
14 If iniquity is in your hand, put it far away,
and do not let wickedness reside in your tents.
15 Surely then you will lift up your face without blemish;
you will be secure, and will not fear.
16 You will forget your misery;
you will remember it as waters that have passed away.
17 And your life will be brighter than the noonday;
its darkness will be like the morning.
18 And you will have confidence, because there is hope;
you will be protected[m] and take your rest in safety.
19 You will lie down, and no one will make you afraid;
many will entreat your favor.
20 But the eyes of the wicked will fail;
all way of escape will be lost to them,
and their hope is to breathe their last."

Job Replies: I Am a Laughingstock

12 Then Job answered:
2 "No doubt you are the people,
and wisdom will die with you.
3 But I have understanding as well as you;
I am not inferior to you.
Who does not know such things as these?
4 I am a laughingstock to my friends;
I, who called upon God and he answered me,
a just and blameless man, I am a laughingstock.
5 Those at ease have contempt for misfortune,[j]
but it is ready for those whose feet are unstable.
6 The tents of robbers are at peace,
and those who provoke God are secure,

[e] Cn Compare Gk Syr: Heb *Are not my days few? Let him cease!* [f] Heb *that I may brighten up a little* [g] Heb *gloom as darkness, deep darkness* [h] Gk: Heb *teaching* [i] Heb *your* [j] Meaning of Heb uncertain [k] Traditional rendering of Heb *Shaddai* [l] Heb *The heights of heaven* [m] Or *you will look around*

11.1-20 Zophar's Response to Job.
11.1-12 Rebuking Job for presumptuous questioning of God's justice, Zophar tells him that God's judgment on him is more lenient than his misdeeds deserve. It is no more likely that *a stupid person* (such as Job is showing himself to be) should become wise than it would be for a wild ass to give birth to a human.
11.13-20 If Job were to reach out to God, and to drive *wickedness* from his life, then light, joy, and *hope* would return to his existence. It is the wicked who never gain this insight, and who, like Job, want only to die.
12.1-14.22 Job's Satirical Challenge to his Counselors' Understanding of God's Wisdom.
12.1-25 Job reviews the popular image of God as a ruthless sovereign who overturns or ignores human aspirations and achievements.

10.18 Job 3.11
10.20 Job 14.1; 7.16,19; 9.27
11.2 Job 8.2
11.3 Jas 3.5; Job 17.2; 21.3
11.4 Job 6.14; 10.7
11.6 Job 28.21; Ezra 9.13
11.7 Eccl 3.11; Rom 11.33
11.8 Job 22.12; 17.16
11.10 Job 9.12; Rev 3.7
11.11 Job 34.21-25; Ps 10.14
11.13 Ps 78.8; 88.9
11.14 Job 22.23; Ps 101.3
11.15 1 Jn 3.21; Ps 27.3
11.16 Isa 65.16; Job 22.11
11.17 Ps 37.6; 112.4; Isa 58.8,10
11.18 Ps 3.5; Prov 3.24
11.19 ver 18
11.20 Deut 28.65; Jer 15.9
12.3 Job 13.2
12.4 Job 6.10,20; 21.3; Ps 91.15; Job 6.29
12.5 Ps 123.4
12.6 Job 9.24; 21.9; 22.18

13.1-19 After denouncing his critics for their foolish claims to wisdom about God and to having the ability to speak for God, Job insists that he must confront God to challenge his justice, and that he will do so in confidence that he will be *vindicated* with regard to the accusations that have been brought against him by his critics. **13.20-28** Addressing his case to God, Job asks to be spared the terrifying divine punishment even before he presents his challenge to God. He wants to know what he has done wrong, why God has hidden his *face* from him, and what the reason is for these destructive punishments he has received from God.

who bring their god in their hands.[n]
7 "But ask the animals, and they will teach you;
the birds of the air, and they will tell you;
8 ask the plants of the earth,[o] and they will teach you;
and the fish of the sea will declare to you.
9 Who among all these does not know
that the hand of the LORD has done this?
10 In his hand is the life of every living thing
and the breath of every human being.
11 Does not the ear test words
as the palate tastes food?
12 Is wisdom with the aged,
and understanding in length of days?

13 "With God[p] are wisdom and strength;
he has counsel and understanding.
14 If he tears down, no one can rebuild;
if he shuts someone in, no one can open up.
15 If he withholds the waters, they dry up;
if he sends them out, they overwhelm the land.
16 With him are strength and wisdom;
the deceived and the deceiver are his.
17 He leads counselors away stripped,
and makes fools of judges.
18 He looses the sash of kings,
and binds a waistcloth on their loins.
19 He leads priests away stripped,
and overthrows the mighty.
20 He deprives of speech those who are trusted,
and takes away the discernment of the elders.
21 He pours contempt on princes,
and looses the belt of the strong.
22 He uncovers the deeps out of darkness,
and brings deep darkness to light.
23 He makes nations great, then destroys them;
he enlarges nations, then leads them away.
24 He strips understanding from the leaders[q] of the earth,
and makes them wander in a pathless waste.
25 They grope in the dark without light;
he makes them stagger like a drunkard.

13 "Look, my eye has seen all this,
my ear has heard and understood it.
2 What you know, I also know;
I am not inferior to you.
3 But I would speak to the Almighty,[r]
and I desire to argue my case with God.
4 As for you, you whitewash with lies;
all of you are worthless physicians.
5 If you would only keep silent,
that would be your wisdom!
6 Hear now my reasoning,
and listen to the pleadings of my lips.
7 Will you speak falsely for God,
and speak deceitfully for him?
8 Will you show partiality toward him,
will you plead the case for God?
9 Will it be well with you when he searches you out?
Or can you deceive him, as one person deceives another?
10 He will surely rebuke you
if in secret you show partiality.
11 Will not his majesty terrify you,
and the dread of him fall upon you?
12 Your maxims are proverbs of ashes,
your defenses are defenses of clay.

13 "Let me have silence, and I will speak,
and let come on me what may.
14 I will take my flesh in my teeth,
and put my life in my hand.[s]
15 See, he will kill me; I have no hope;[t]
but I will defend my ways to his face.
16 This will be my salvation,
that the godless shall not come before him.
17 Listen carefully to my words,
and let my declaration be in your ears.
18 I have indeed prepared my case;
I know that I shall be vindicated.
19 Who is there that will contend with me?
For then I would be silent and die.

Job's Despondent Prayer

20 Only grant two things to me,
then I will not hide myself from your face:
21 withdraw your hand far from me,
and do not let dread of you terrify me.
22 Then call, and I will answer;
or let me speak, and you reply to me.

[n] Or *whom God brought forth by his hand*; Meaning of Heb uncertain [o] Or *speak to the earth* [p] Heb *him* [q] Heb adds *of the people* [r] Traditional rendering of Heb *Shaddai* [s] Gk: Heb *Why should I take . . . in my hand?* [t] Or *Though he kill me, yet I will trust in him*

12.9 Isa 41.20
12.10 Acts 17.28; Job 27.3; 33.4
12.11 Job 34.3
12.12 Job 32.7
12.13 Job 9.4; 11.6
12.14 Job 19.10; 37.7
12.15 1 Kings 8.35; Gen 7.11
12.16 ver 13; Job 13.7,9
12.17 Job 3.14; 19.9; 9.24
12.18 Ps 116.16
12.20 Job 32.9
12.21 Ps 107.40; ver 18
12.22 Dan 2.22; 1 Cor 4.5; Job 3.5
12.23 Ps 107.38; Isa 9.3; Jer 25.9; Deut 12.20; Ps 78.61
12.24 ver 20; Ps 107.40
12.25 Job 5.14; Ps 107.27
13.3 Job 23.3,4; ver 15
13.4 Ps 119.69; Jer 23.32
13.5 Prov 17.28
13.9 Ps 44.21; Gal 6.7
13.12 Job 15.3
13.14 1 Sam 19.5
13.15 Ps 23.4; Prov 14.32; Job 27.5
13.16 Ps 5.5
13.17 Job 21.2
13.19 Isa 50.8; Job 40.4
13.21 Ps 39.10
13.22 Job 14.15

23 How many are my iniquities and my sins?
Make me know my transgression and my sin.
24 Why do you hide your face,
and count me as your enemy?
25 Will you frighten a windblown leaf
and pursue dry chaff?
26 For you write bitter things against me,
and make me reap[u] the iniquities of my youth.
27 You put my feet in the stocks,
and watch all my paths;
you set a bound to the soles of my feet.
28 One wastes away like a rotten thing,
like a garment that is moth-eaten.

14 "A mortal, born of woman, few of days and full of trouble,
2 comes up like a flower and withers,
flees like a shadow and does not last.
3 Do you fix your eyes on such a one?
Do you bring me into judgment with you?
4 Who can bring a clean thing out of an unclean?
No one can.
5 Since their days are determined,
and the number of their months is known to you,
and you have appointed the bounds that they cannot pass,
6 look away from them, and desist,[v]
that they may enjoy, like laborers, their days.

7 "For there is hope for a tree,
if it is cut down, that it will sprout again,
and that its shoots will not cease.
8 Though its root grows old in the earth,
and its stump dies in the ground,
9 yet at the scent of water it will bud
and put forth branches like a young plant.
10 But mortals die, and are laid low;
humans expire, and where are they?
11 As waters fail from a lake,
and a river wastes away and dries up,
12 so mortals lie down and do not rise again;
until the heavens are no more, they will not awake
or be roused out of their sleep.
13 Oh that you would hide me in Sheol,
that you would conceal me until your wrath is past,
that you would appoint me a set time, and remember me!
14 If mortals die, will they live again?
All the days of my service I would wait
until my release should come.
15 You would call, and I would answer you;
you would long for the work of your hands.
16 For then you would not[w] number my steps,
you would not keep watch over my sin;
17 my transgression would be sealed up in a bag,
and you would cover over my iniquity.

18 "But the mountain falls and crumbles away,
and the rock is removed from its place;
19 the waters wear away the stones;
the torrents wash away the soil of the earth;
so you destroy the hope of mortals.
20 You prevail forever against them, and they pass away;
you change their countenance, and send them away.
21 Their children come to honor, and they do not know it;
they are brought low, and it goes unnoticed.
22 They feel only the pain of their own bodies,
and mourn only for themselves."

Eliphaz Speaks: Job Undermines Religion

15 Then Eliphaz the Temanite answered:
2 "Should the wise answer with windy knowledge,
and fill themselves with the east wind?
3 Should they argue in unprofitable talk,
or in words with which they can do no good?
4 But you are doing away with the fear of God,
and hindering meditation before God.
5 For your iniquity teaches your mouth,
and you choose the tongue of the crafty.
6 Your own mouth condemns you, and not I;

[u] Heb *inherit* [v] Cn: Heb *that they may desist* [w] Syr: Heb lacks *not*

13.23 1 Sam 26.18
13.24 Deut 32.20; Ps 13.1; Job 19.11
13.25 Isa 42.3
13.26 Ps 25.7
13.28 Isa 50.9; Jas 5.2
14.1 Job 5.7; Eccl 2.23
14.2 Ps 90.5,6; Jas 1.10; 1 Pet 1.24
14.3 Ps 144.3; 143.2
14.4 Ps 51.2,10; Jn 3.6; Rom 5.12; Eph 2.3
14.5 Ps 139.16; Job 21.21; Acts 17.2
14.6 Job 7.19; 7.1
14.9 Isa 55.10
14.10 Job 13.19
14.11 Isa 19.5
14.12 Ps 102.26; Acts 3.21; Rev 20.11; 21.1
14.13 Isa 26.20
14.14 Job 7.1
14.15 Job 13.22
14.16 Job 10.6; 31.4; 34.21; Prov 5.21; Jer 32.19
14.17 Deut 32.34; Hos 13.12
14.18 Job 18.4
14.20 Job 34.20; Jas 1.10
14.21 Eccl 9.5; Isa 55.10
15.2 Job 6.26
15.5 Ps 36.3; Prov 16.23; Job 5.12,13
15.6 Job 9.20; Lk 19.22

14.1-12 Job affirms that the transiency of human life is ordained by God, but asks that humans might at least enjoy their days while they last. Unlike trees or dried-up streams of water, humans have no hope of renewal.
14.13-17 If death took over human existence for only a limited period and was followed by renewal of life, then God's wrath could be avoided and his loving care might once more be evident to his creatures.
14.18-22 But in fact human beings die and disappear just as rocks and mountains crumble and fall. God's relentless power leads to changes in one's children, to separation from family and friends, and finally to pain and death.
15.1-35 Eliphaz' Severe Rebuke of Job and his Warning of God's Judgment.
15.2-16 In a series of bitterly critical questions to Job, Eliphaz portrays him as full of *wind*, as destroying the *fear of God*, and as articulating wicked thoughts. His arrogance is evident in his pretentious challenge to God and to traditional wisdom; by these statements, he shows himself to be *abominable and corrupt*.

15.17-35 Here Eliphaz appeals to traditional wisdom to claim that it is the wicked who suffer. God will deprive them of security, of prosperity, and of decent homes. They will face disappointment in all their undertakings.
16.1-17.16 Job's Indictment of God.
16.1-22 After an initial rebuke of his *miserable comforters*, who have done nothing to ease his pain, Job details the blame that he places on God for the suffering he has experienced, which is vividly depicted as breaking his bones and goring his body. Filled with a sense of God's injustice, Job calls out for a heavenly arbiter to champion his cause before God, defending *the right of a mortal with God*.

your own lips testify against you.

7 "Are you the firstborn of the human race?
Were you brought forth before the hills?
8 Have you listened in the council of God?
And do you limit wisdom to yourself?
9 What do you know that we do not know?
What do you understand that is not clear to us?
10 The gray-haired and the aged are on our side,
those older than your father.
11 Are the consolations of God too small for you,
or the word that deals gently with you?
12 Why does your heart carry you away,
and why do your eyes flash,[x]
13 so that you turn your spirit against God,
and let such words go out of your mouth?
14 What are mortals, that they can be clean?
Or those born of woman, that they can be righteous?
15 God puts no trust even in his holy ones,
and the heavens are not clean in his sight;
16 how much less one who is abominable and corrupt,
one who drinks iniquity like water!

17 "I will show you; listen to me;
what I have seen I will declare—
18 what sages have told,
and their ancestors have not hidden,
19 to whom alone the land was given,
and no stranger passed among them.
20 The wicked writhe in pain all their days,
through all the years that are laid up for the ruthless.
21 Terrifying sounds are in their ears;
in prosperity the destroyer will come upon them.
22 They despair of returning from darkness,
and they are destined for the sword.
23 They wander abroad for bread, saying, 'Where is it?'
They know that a day of darkness is ready at hand;
24 distress and anguish terrify them;
they prevail against them, like a king prepared for battle.
25 Because they stretched out their hands against God,
and bid defiance to the Almighty,[y]
26 running stubbornly against him
with a thick-bossed shield;
27 because they have covered their faces with their fat,
and gathered fat upon their loins,
28 they will live in desolate cities,
in houses that no one should inhabit,
houses destined to become heaps of ruins;
29 they will not be rich, and their wealth will not endure,
nor will they strike root in the earth;[z]
30 they will not escape from darkness;
the flame will dry up their shoots,
and their blossom[a] will be swept away[b] by the wind.
31 Let them not trust in emptiness, deceiving themselves;
for emptiness will be their recompense.
32 It will be paid in full before their time,
and their branch will not be green.
33 They will shake off their unripe grape, like the vine,
and cast off their blossoms, like the olive tree.
34 For the company of the godless is barren,
and fire consumes the tents of bribery.
35 They conceive mischief and bring forth evil
and their heart prepares deceit."

Job Reaffirms His Innocence

16 Then Job answered:
2 "I have heard many such things;
miserable comforters are you all.
3 Have windy words no limit?
Or what provokes you that you keep on talking?
4 I also could talk as you do,
if you were in my place;
I could join words together against you,
and shake my head at you.
5 I could encourage you with my mouth,
and the solace of my lips would assuage your pain.
6 "If I speak, my pain is not assuaged,
and if I forbear, how much of it leaves me?

7 Surely now God has worn me out;
he has[c] made desolate all my company.

[x] Meaning of Heb uncertain [y] Traditional rendering of Heb *Shaddai* [z] Vg: Meaning of Heb uncertain [a] Gk: Heb *mouth* [b] Cn: Heb *will depart* [c] Heb *you have*

15.7 Job 38.4,21; Ps 90.2; Prov 8.25
15.8 Rom 11.34; Job 12.2
15.9 Job 13.2
15.10 Job 32.6,7
15.11 Job 36.15,16; 2 Cor 1.3,4; Zech 1.13
15.13 Job 33.13
15.14 Job 14.4; Prov 20.9; Eccl 7.20; Job 25.4
15.15 Job 4.18; 25.5
15.16 Ps 14.1,3; Job 34.7
15.18 Job 8.8
15.20 Job 27.13
15.21 Job 18.11; 20.25; 1 Thess 5.3
15.22 ver 30; Job 27.14
15.23 Ps 59.15; 109.10; Job 18.12
15.25 Job 36.9
15.27 Ps 17.10
15.29 Job 27.16,17
15.30 Job 5.14; 22.20; 4.9
15.31 Isa 59.4
15.32 Job 22.16; Ps 55.23; Job 18.16
15.33 Hab 3.17
15.34 Job 16.7; 8.22
15.35 Ps 7.14; Isa 59.4; Hos 10.13
16.2 Job 13.4
16.3 Job 6.26
16.4 Ps 22.7; 109.25; Lam 2.15; Mt 27.39
16.7 Job 7.3; ver 20

8 And he has[d] shriveled me up,
which is a witness against me;
my leanness has risen up against me,
and it testifies to my face.
9 He has torn me in his wrath, and
hated me;
he has gnashed his teeth at me;
my adversary sharpens his eyes
against me.
10 They have gaped at me with their mouths;
they have struck me insolently on
the cheek;
they mass themselves together
against me.
11 God gives me up to the ungodly,
and casts me into the hands of the
wicked.
12 I was at ease, and he broke me in two;
he seized me by the neck and dashed
me to pieces;
he set me up as his target;
13 his archers surround me.
He slashes open my kidneys, and shows
no mercy;
he pours out my gall on the ground.
14 He bursts upon me again and again;
he rushes at me like a warrior.
15 I have sewed sackcloth upon my skin,
and have laid my strength in the dust.
16 My face is red with weeping,
and deep darkness is on my eyelids,
17 though there is no violence in my hands,
and my prayer is pure.

18 "O earth, do not cover my blood;
let my outcry find no resting place.
19 Even now, in fact, my witness is in
heaven,
and he that vouches for me is on high.
20 My friends scorn me;
my eye pours out tears to God,
21 that he would maintain the right of a
mortal with God,
as[e] one does for a neighbor.
22 For when a few years have come,
I shall go the way from which I
shall not return.

Job Prays for Relief

17 My spirit is broken, my days are
extinct,
the grave is ready for me.
2 Surely there are mockers around me,
and my eye dwells on their
provocation.
3 "Lay down a pledge for me with yourself;
who is there that will give surety for
me?
4 Since you have closed their minds to
understanding,
therefore you will not let them triumph.
5 Those who denounce friends for
reward—
the eyes of their children will fail.

6 "He has made me a byword of the
peoples,
and I am one before whom people spit.
7 My eye has grown dim from grief,
and all my members are like a shadow.
8 The upright are appalled at this,
and the innocent stir themselves up
against the godless.
9 Yet the righteous hold to their way,
and they that have clean hands
grow stronger and stronger.
10 But you, come back now, all of you,
and I shall not find a sensible person
among you.
11 My days are past, my plans are broken off,
the desires of my heart.
12 They make night into day;
'The light,' they say, 'is near to the
darkness.'[f]
13 If I look for Sheol as my house,
if I spread my couch in darkness,
14 if I say to the Pit, 'You are my father,'
and to the worm, 'My mother,' or
'My sister,'
15 where then is my hope?
Who will see my hope?
16 Will it go down to the bars of Sheol?
Shall we descend together into the
dust?"

Bildad Speaks: God Punishes the Wicked

18 Then Bildad the Shuhite answered:
2 "How long will you hunt for
words?
Consider, and then we shall speak.
3 Why are we counted as cattle?
Why are we stupid in your sight?
4 You who tear yourself in your anger—
shall the earth be forsaken because
of you,
or the rock be removed out of its place?

5 "Surely the light of the wicked is put out,
and the flame of their fire does not
shine.

16.8 Job 10.17; 19.20
16.9 Ps 35.16; Job 13.24
16.10 Ps 22.13; Lam 3.30; Mic 5.1; Ps 35.15
16.11 Job 1.15,17
16.12 Job 9.17
16.13 Job 19.12; 27.22; 20.25
16.14 Job 9.17; Joel 2.7
16.15 Gen 37.34; Job 30.19
16.16 ver 20
16.17 Job 27.4
16.18 Isa 26.21; Ps 66.18,19
16.19 Rom 1.9
16.21 1 Kings 8.45; Ps 9.4
16.22 Eccl 12.5
17.1 Ps 88.3,4
17.2 ver 6; 1 Sam 1.6,7
17.3 Ps 119.122; Prov 6.1
17.4 Job 12.20
17.5 Lev 19.16; Job 11.20
17.6 Job 30.9,10
17.7 Job 16.16; 16.8
17.9 Prov 4.18; Job 22.30
17.11 Job 7.6
17.13 Job 3.13
17.14 Ps 16.10; Job 21.26; 24.20
17.15 Job 7.6
17.16 Jon 2.6; Job 3.17-19
18.3 Ps 73.22; Job 36.14
18.4 Job 13.14; 14.18
18.5 Prov 13.9; 20.20; 24.20

17.1-16 Faced with despair and death, Job takes an oath (*pledge*), affirming his own integrity and fidelity, in spite of what God and other humans – both traitorous friends and those who regard themselves as *righteous* – have done to him. They have failed to listen to his complaint. Void of *hope*, he looks for death, decay, and the gloom of *the Pit* where the dead remain.
18.1-21 Bildad Details How God Punishes the Wicked. Instead of groping for an explanation and questioning God's justice, Job should recognize that his fate is that of the wicked on whom disaster falls, depriving them of food (vs. 12), health (vs. 13), a dwelling-place (vs. 15), of an enduring reputation (vs. 17) or offspring (vs. 19).

[d] Heb *you have* [e] Syr Vg Tg: Heb *and* [f] Meaning of Heb uncertain

19.1-29 Job Expresses Confidence that He Will Be Vindicated.
19.1-5 Job complains of the abuse he has received from his proud detractors.
19.6-20 He voices his resentment of what God has done to him, leaving him frustrated, humiliated, and despairing. God treats him as an *adversary* and has thwarted him, depriving him of family and friends, who have turned against him. Physically, he is little more than a skeleton.
19.21-29 Crying out for pity from friends and for relief from God's punishment of him, Job hopes there might be a written record of his situation and is confident that someone will come in the future who will support his case before God and vindicate him (a *redeemer*). With this intervention, he is confident that he will see God. Scholarly opinion is divided as to whether the original Hebrew text means that this will occur after his physical body has fallen into decay or in a restored bodily state. In biblical usage, the role of the *redeemer* or *vindicator* was performed by a dead person's next of kin, whose roles included executing vengeance (Num 35.16-28; Deut 19.4-12) and assuring the continuity and freedom of the surviving family (Lev 25.25-28, 47-49; Jer 32.6-11; Deut 25.5-6). In Prov 23.11 and Jer 50.34, it is the LORD who performs the function of redeemer, but here in Job, God is the adversary, and the defender or arbiter (9.33; 16.19) will make his case in Job's behalf before the divine court after Job has died (16.18-22; 17.15-16). Meanwhile, he deplores and denies the charges his friends have brought against him, and warns them of the certainty of the ultimate judgment of God.

6 The light is dark in their tent,
and the lamp above them is put out.
7 Their strong steps are shortened,
and their own schemes throw them down.
8 For they are thrust into a net by their own feet,
and they walk into a pitfall.
9 A trap seizes them by the heel;
a snare lays hold of them.
10 A rope is hid for them in the ground,
a trap for them in the path.
11 Terrors frighten them on every side,
and chase them at their heels.
12 Their strength is consumed by hunger,[g]
and calamity is ready for their stumbling.
13 By disease their skin is consumed,[h]
the firstborn of Death consumes their limbs.
14 They are torn from the tent in which they trusted,
and are brought to the king of terrors.
15 In their tents nothing remains;
sulfur is scattered upon their habitations.
16 Their roots dry up beneath,
and their branches wither above.
17 Their memory perishes from the earth,
and they have no name in the street.
18 They are thrust from light into darkness,
and driven out of the world.
19 They have no offspring or descendant among their people,
and no survivor where they used to live.
20 They of the west are appalled at their fate,
and horror seizes those of the east.
21 Surely such are the dwellings of the ungodly,
such is the place of those who do not know God."

Job Replies: I Know That My Redeemer Lives

19 Then Job answered:
2 "How long will you torment me,
and break me in pieces with words?
3 These ten times you have cast reproach upon me;
are you not ashamed to wrong me?
4 And even if it is true that I have erred,
my error remains with me.
5 If indeed you magnify yourselves against me,
and make my humiliation an argument against me,
6 know then that God has put me in the wrong,
and closed his net around me.
7 Even when I cry out, 'Violence!' I am not answered;
I call aloud, but there is no justice.
8 He has walled up my way so that I cannot pass,
and he has set darkness upon my paths.
9 He has stripped my glory from me,
and taken the crown from my head.
10 He breaks me down on every side, and I am gone,
he has uprooted my hope like a tree.
11 He has kindled his wrath against me,
and counts me as his adversary.
12 His troops come on together;
they have thrown up siegeworks[i] against me,
and encamp around my tent.

13 "He has put my family far from me,
and my acquaintances are wholly estranged from me.
14 My relatives and my close friends have failed me;
15 the guests in my house have forgotten me;
my serving girls count me as a stranger;
I have become an alien in their eyes.
16 I call to my servant, but he gives me no answer;
I must myself plead with him.
17 My breath is repulsive to my wife;
I am loathsome to my own family.
18 Even young children despise me;
when I rise, they talk against me.
19 All my intimate friends abhor me,
and those whom I loved have turned against me.
20 My bones cling to my skin and to my flesh,
and I have escaped by the skin of my teeth.
21 Have pity on me, have pity on me, O you my friends,
for the hand of God has touched me!
22 Why do you, like God, pursue me,
never satisfied with my flesh?

23 "O that my words were written down!
O that they were inscribed in a book!

[g] Or *Disaster is hungry for them* [h] Cn: Heb *It consumes the limbs of his skin* [i] Cn: Heb *their way*

18.7 Prov 4.12; Job 5.13
18.8 Job 22.10; Ps 9.15; 35.8
18.9 Ps 140.5; Job 5.5
18.10 Ps 69.22
18.11 Job 15.21; Jer 6.25; 20.3
18.12 Isa 8.21
18.14 Job 8.22; 15.21
18.15 Ps 11.6
18.16 Isa 5.24; Hos 9.1-16; Am 2.9; Mal 4.1; Job 15.30,32
18.17 Ps 34.16; Prov 2.22; 10.7
18.19 Isa 14.22; Jer 22.30
18.21 Jer 9.3; 1 Thess 4.5
19.4 Job 6.24
19.5 Ps 35.26; 38.16
19.6 Job 27.2; 18.8-10
19.7 Job 30.20
19.8 Job 3.23; 30.26
19.9 Ps 89.44; 89.39
19.10 Job 12.14; 7.6; 24.20
19.11 Job 16.9; 13.24
19.12 Job 30.12
19.14 ver 19
19.15 Gen 14.14; Eccl 2.7
19.18 2 Kings 2.23
19.19 Ps 38.11; 55.13
19.20 Job 33.21; Ps 102.5
19.21 Job 6.14; Ps 38.2
19.22 Job 16.11
19.23 Isa 30.8

24 O that with an iron pen and with lead
they were engraved on a rock forever!
25 For I know that my Redeemer[j] lives,
and that at the last he[k] will stand
upon the earth;[l]
26 and after my skin has been thus
destroyed,
then in[m] my flesh I shall see God,[n]
27 whom I shall see on my side,[o]
and my eyes shall behold, and not
another.
My heart faints within me!
28 If you say, 'How we will persecute him!'
and, 'The root of the matter is found
in him';
29 be afraid of the sword,
for wrath brings the punishment of
the sword,
so that you may know there is a
judgment."

Zophar Speaks: Wickedness Receives Just Retribution

20 Then Zophar the Naamathite
answered:
2 "Pay attention! My thoughts urge me
to answer,
because of the agitation within me.
3 I hear censure that insults me,
and a spirit beyond my
understanding answers me.
4 Do you not know this from of old,
ever since mortals were placed on
earth,
5 that the exulting of the wicked is short,
and the joy of the godless is but for
a moment?
6 Even though they mount up high as
the heavens,
and their head reaches to the clouds,
7 they will perish forever like their own
dung;
those who have seen them will say,
'Where are they?'
8 They will fly away like a dream, and
not be found;
they will be chased away like a
vision of the night.
9 The eye that saw them will see them
no more,
nor will their place behold them any
longer.
10 Their children will seek the favor of the
poor,
and their hands will give back their
wealth.
11 Their bodies, once full of youth,
will lie down in the dust with them.

12 "Though wickedness is sweet in their
mouth,
though they hide it under their
tongues,
13 though they are loath to let it go,
and hold it in their mouths,
14 yet their food is turned in their
stomachs;
it is the venom of asps within them.
15 They swallow down riches and vomit
them up again;
God casts them out of their bellies.
16 They will suck the poison of asps;
the tongue of a viper will kill them.
17 They will not look on the rivers,
the streams flowing with honey and
curds.
18 They will give back the fruit of their
toil,
and will not swallow it down;
from the profit of their trading
they will get no enjoyment.
19 For they have crushed and abandoned
the poor,
they have seized a house that they
did not build.

20 "They knew no quiet in their bellies;
in their greed they let nothing escape.
21 There was nothing left after they had
eaten;
therefore their prosperity will not
endure.
22 In full sufficiency they will be in distress;
all the force of misery will come
upon them.
23 To fill their belly to the full
God[p] will send his fierce anger into
them,
and rain it upon them as their food.[q]
24 They will flee from an iron weapon;
a bronze arrow will strike them
through.
25 It is drawn forth and comes out of
their body,
and the glittering point comes out of
their gall;
terrors come upon them.
26 Utter darkness is laid up for their
treasures;

[j] Or *Vindicator* [k] Or *that he the Last* [l] Heb *dust* [m] Or *without* [n] Meaning of Heb of this verse uncertain [o] Or *for myself* [p] Heb *he* [q] Cn: Meaning of Heb uncertain

19.24 Jer 17.1
19.25 Job 16.19; Ps 78.35; Isa 43.14; Jer 50.34
19.26 Mt 5.8; 1 Cor 13.12; 1 Jn 3.2
19.27 Ps 73.26
19.28 Ps 69.26
19.29 Job 22.4
20.3 Job 19.3
20.4 Deut 4.32
20.5 Ps 37.35; 73.19
20.6 Isa 14.13,14; Ob 3,4
20.7 Job 4.20; 7.10; 8.18
20.8 Ps 73.20; 90.5; Job 18.18; 27.21-23
20.9 Job 7.8,10
20.10 Job 5.4; 27.16,17
20.11 Job 13.26; 21.26
20.12 Prov 20.17; Ps 10.7
20.16 Deut 32.24,33
20.17 Job 29.6; Deut 32.13,14
20.18 ver 10,15
20.19 Job 24.2-4; 35.9
20.20 Eccl 5.13,14
20.21 Job 15.29
20.23 Ps 78.30,31
20.24 Isa 24.18; Jer 48.43; Am 5.19
20.25 Job 16.13; 18.11
20.26 Job 18.18; Ps 21.9

20.1-29 Zophar Repeats the Theme: Job and the Other Wicked People Get What They Deserve. Zophar states the ancient moral principle (*from of old*) that the wicked will ultimately *perish* and disappear in death as a result of their wicked words and acts. None of their efforts in commerce will have enduring results, and after a period of seeming *prosperity* they will fall under the avenging weapons of God, and their apparent achievements will be *dragged off in the day of God's wrath*.

21.1-34 Job Reminds his Critics that the Wicked Often Escape Punishment.
21.1-15 In contrast to Zophar's argument (20.1-29), Job notes that the *wicked* live to a great age, that their *children* prosper and that their houses and flocks flourish, so that they gain *prosperity* in spite of their having told God, *Leave us alone*.
21.16-26 Job abhors these *plans of the wicked*, but even if his critics' teaching that God *stores up* and unleashes his punishment on the children of the wicked were true, it would not deal justly with the wicked themselves.
21.27-34 The wicked die *at ease and secure*, while those who have never experienced the *good* life understandably depart this life in *bitterness of soul*. The rich and powerful are honored even in death, so that Job finds no *comfort* in his critics' false *answers* to his questionings of divine justice.

a fire fanned by no one will devour them;
what is left in their tent will be consumed.
27 The heavens will reveal their iniquity,
and the earth will rise up against them.
28 The possessions of their house will be carried away,
dragged off in the day of God's[r] wrath.
29 This is the portion of the wicked from God,
the heritage decreed for them by God."

Job Replies: The Wicked Often Go Unpunished

21 Then Job answered:
2 "Listen carefully to my words,
and let this be your consolation.
3 Bear with me, and I will speak;
then after I have spoken, mock on.
4 As for me, is my complaint addressed to mortals?
Why should I not be impatient?
5 Look at me, and be appalled,
and lay your hand upon your mouth.
6 When I think of it I am dismayed,
and shuddering seizes my flesh.
7 Why do the wicked live on,
reach old age, and grow mighty in power?
8 Their children are established in their presence,
and their offspring before their eyes.
9 Their houses are safe from fear,
and no rod of God is upon them.
10 Their bull breeds without fail;
their cow calves and never miscarries.
11 They send out their little ones like a flock,
and their children dance around.
12 They sing to the tambourine and the lyre,
and rejoice to the sound of the pipe.
13 They spend their days in prosperity,
and in peace they go down to Sheol.
14 They say to God, 'Leave us alone!
We do not desire to know your ways.
15 What is the Almighty,[s] that we should serve him?
And what profit do we get if we pray to him?'
16 Is not their prosperity indeed their own achievement?[t]
The plans of the wicked are repugnant to me.

17 "How often is the lamp of the wicked put out?
How often does calamity come upon them?
How often does God[u] distribute pains in his anger?
18 How often are they like straw before the wind,
and like chaff that the storm carries away?
19 You say, 'God stores up their iniquity for their children.'
Let it be paid back to them, so that they may know it.
20 Let their own eyes see their destruction,
and let them drink of the wrath of the Almighty.[s]
21 For what do they care for their household after them,
when the number of their months is cut off?
22 Will any teach God knowledge,
seeing that he judges those that are on high?
23 One dies in full prosperity,
being wholly at ease and secure,
24 his loins full of milk
and the marrow of his bones moist.
25 Another dies in bitterness of soul,
never having tasted of good.
26 They lie down alike in the dust,
and the worms cover them.

27 "Oh, I know your thoughts,
and your schemes to wrong me.
28 For you say, 'Where is the house of the prince?
Where is the tent in which the wicked lived?'
29 Have you not asked those who travel the roads,
and do you not accept their testimony,
30 that the wicked are spared in the day of calamity,
and are rescued in the day of wrath?
31 Who declares their way to their face,
and who repays them for what they have done?
32 When they are carried to the grave,
a watch is kept over their tomb.
33 The clods of the valley are sweet to them;
everyone will follow after,

[r] Heb *his* [s] Traditional rendering of Heb *Shaddai* [t] Heb *in their hand* [u] Heb *he*

20.27 Deut 31.28
20.28 Deut 28.31; Job 21.30
20.29 Job 27.13
21.3 Job 16.10
21.4 Job 6.11
21.5 Judg 18.19; Job 29.9; 40.4
21.7 Job 12.6; Ps 73.3,12; Jer 12.1
21.8 Ps 17.14
21.9 Ps 73.5
21.10 Ex 23.26
21.12 Ps 81.2; Job 30.31
21.13 Job 36.11
21.14 Job 22.17; Prov 1.29
21.15 Ex 5.2; Job 34.9; Mal 3.14
21.16 Job 22.18
21.17 Job 18.5,6,12
21.18 Ps 1.4
21.19 Ex 20.5
21.20 Ps 75.8; Isa 51.17; Jer 25.15; Rev 14.10
21.22 Isa 40.13,14
21.26 Eccl 9.2; Job 24.20
21.28 Job 12.21; 8.22
21.30 Prov 16.4; 2 Pet 2.9; Job 20.28; Rom 2.5
21.33 Job 3.22; 17.16; 3.19; 24.24

and those who went before are
innumerable.
34 How then will you comfort me with
empty nothings?
There is nothing left of your answers
but falsehood."

Eliphaz Speaks: Job's Wickedness Is Great

22 Then Eliphaz the Temanite answered:
2 "Can a mortal be of use to God?
Can even the wisest be of service to
him?
3 Is it any pleasure to the Almighty[v] if
you are righteous,
or is it gain to him if you make your
ways blameless?
4 Is it for your piety that he reproves you,
and enters into judgment with you?
5 Is not your wickedness great?
There is no end to your iniquities.
6 For you have exacted pledges from
your family for no reason,
and stripped the naked of their clothing.
7 You have given no water to the weary
to drink,
and you have withheld bread from
the hungry.
8 The powerful possess the land,
and the favored live in it.
9 You have sent widows away empty-handed,
and the arms of the orphans you
have crushed.[w]
10 Therefore snares are around you,
and sudden terror overwhelms you,
11 or darkness so that you cannot see;
a flood of water covers you.

12 "Is not God high in the heavens?
See the highest stars, how lofty they
are!
13 Therefore you say, 'What does God
know?
Can he judge through the deep
darkness?
14 Thick clouds enwrap him, so that he
does not see,
and he walks on the dome of
heaven.'
15 Will you keep to the old way
that the wicked have trod?
16 They were snatched away before their
time;
their foundation was washed away
by a flood.
17 They said to God, 'Leave us alone,'
and 'What can the Almighty[v] do to us?'[x]
18 Yet he filled their houses with good things—
but the plans of the wicked are
repugnant to me.
19 The righteous see it and are glad;
the innocent laugh them to scorn,
20 saying, 'Surely our adversaries are cut off,
and what they left, the fire has
consumed.'

21 "Agree with God,[y] and be at peace;
in this way good will come to you.
22 Receive instruction from his mouth,
and lay up his words in your heart.
23 If you return to the Almighty,[v] you will
be restored,
if you remove unrighteousness from
your tents,
24 if you treat gold like dust,
and gold of Ophir like the stones of
the torrent-bed,
25 and if the Almighty[v] is your gold
and your precious silver,
26 then you will delight yourself in the
Almighty,[v]
and lift up your face to God.
27 You will pray to him, and he will hear
you,
and you will pay your vows.
28 You will decide on a matter, and it will
be established for you,
and light will shine on your ways.
29 When others are humiliated, you say it
is pride;
for he saves the humble.
30 He will deliver even those who are guilty;
they will escape because of the
cleanness of your hands."[z]

Job Replies: My Complaint Is Bitter

23 Then Job answered:
2 "Today also my complaint is
bitter;[a]
his[b] hand is heavy despite my
groaning.
3 Oh, that I knew where I might find him,
that I might come even to his
dwelling!
4 I would lay my case before him,
and fill my mouth with arguments.

[v] Traditional rendering of Heb *Shaddai* [w] Gk Syr Tg Vg: Heb *were crushed* [x] Gk Syr: Heb *them* [y] Heb *him* [z] Meaning of Heb uncertain [a] Syr Vg Tg: Heb *rebellious* [b] Gk Syr: Heb *my*

22.2 Lk 17.10
22.4 Job 14.3; Ps 143.2
22.5 Job 11.6; 15.5
22.6 Ex 22.26; Deut 24.6,17; Ezek 18.12,16
22.7 Mt 10.42; Job 31.31
22.9 Job 24.3; Isa 10.2
22.11 Job 5.14; Ps 69.2
22.13 Ps 10.11
22.16 Job 15.32; 14.19; Mt 7.26,27
22.18 Job 12.6; 21.16
22.19 Ps 58.10; 107.42
22.20 Ps 18.39; Job 15.30
22.21 Jer 9.24; Gal 4.9
22.22 Ps 138.4
22.23 Job 8.5; Isa 19.22; Acts 20.32; Job 11.14
22.24 Ps 19.10
22.25 Isa 33.6; Mt 6.20
22.26 Job 27.10; Isa 58.14
22.27 Job 33.26; Isa 58.9; Job 34.28; Ps 22.25
22.28 Ps 145.19
22.29 Prov 29.23; Mt 23.12; 1 Pet 5.5
22.30 Job 42.7,8; 2 Sam 22.21
23.2 Job 7.11; 6.2,3
23.3 Deut 4.29; Ps 9.4
23.4 Job 13.18

22.1-30 Eliphaz Asserts Job's Wickedness.
22.1-11 By a series of questions, Eliphaz seeks to show that Job's plight is the result of his great *wickedness*, which is evident in his having failed to meet the needs of those around him. He should not be surprised by the *flood* of judgment that now overwhelms him.
22.12-30 Job has asserted that God is remote from the human realm, and thus has taken his position with the wicked who want God to leave them alone. He has declared inconsistently that God allows the wicked to have good things and that he (Job) finds the plans of the wicked to be *repugnant*. It is only the truly righteous who can see clearly and rejoice in God's destruction of the wicked and their possessions.
22.21-30 If Job were to repent of his sins and *return to the Almighty*, he would find joy, his prayers would be answered, and he would be forgiven.
23.1-24.25 Job's Complaint of God's Inaccessibility and of the Unchallenged Wickedness of the Human Race.
23.1-17 Even though he has been faithful in following God's *commandments*, Job does not know where to find him in order to present his case in the divine court. He expresses his terror at the inaccessibility of God and the fearful arbitrariness of his actions.

24.1 No-one is able to see God's daily schedule of activities.
24.2-17 Meanwhile, evil flourishes: property lines are violated, flocks are stolen, the poor are oppressed and left homeless and hungry, in countryside and cities. Yet God *pays no attention*. Murderers and adulterers thrive in the darkness.

5 I would learn what he would answer me,
and understand what he would say
to me.
6 Would he contend with me in the
greatness of his power?
No; but he would give heed to me.
7 There an upright person could reason
with him,
and I should be acquitted forever by
my judge.

8 "If I go forward, he is not there;
or backward, I cannot perceive him;
9 on the left he hides, and I cannot
behold him;
I turn[c] to the right, but I cannot see
him.
10 But he knows the way that I take;
when he has tested me, I shall come
out like gold.
11 My foot has held fast to his steps;
I have kept his way and have not
turned aside.
12 I have not departed from the
commandment of his lips;
I have treasured in[d] my bosom the
words of his mouth.
13 But he stands alone and who can
dissuade him?
What he desires, that he does.
14 For he will complete what he appoints
for me;
and many such things are in his
mind.
15 Therefore I am terrified at his presence;
when I consider, I am in dread of
him.
16 God has made my heart faint;
the Almighty[e] has terrified me;
17 If only I could vanish in darkness,
and thick darkness would cover my
face![f]

Job Complains of Violence on the Earth

24 "Why are times not kept by the
Almighty,[e]
and why do those who know him
never see his days?
2 The wicked[g] remove landmarks;
they seize flocks and pasture them.
3 They drive away the donkey of the
orphan;
they take the widow's ox for a pledge.
4 They thrust the needy off the road;
the poor of the earth all hide
themselves.
5 Like wild asses in the desert
they go out to their toil,
scavenging in the wasteland
food for their young.
6 They reap in a field not their own
and they glean in the vineyard of
the wicked.
7 They lie all night naked, without
clothing,
and have no covering in the cold.
8 They are wet with the rain of the
mountains,
and cling to the rock for want of
shelter.

9 "There are those who snatch the
orphan child from the breast,
and take as a pledge the infant of
the poor.
10 They go about naked, without clothing;
though hungry, they carry the
sheaves;
11 between their terraces[h] they press out oil;
they tread the wine presses, but
suffer thirst.
12 From the city the dying groan,
and the throat of the wounded cries
for help;
yet God pays no attention to their
prayer.

13 "There are those who rebel against the
light,
who are not acquainted with its
ways,
and do not stay in its paths.
14 The murderer rises at dusk
to kill the poor and needy,
and in the night is like a thief.
15 The eye of the adulterer also waits for
the twilight,
saying, 'No eye will see me';
and he disguises his face.
16 In the dark they dig through houses;
by day they shut themselves up;
they do not know the light.
17 For deep darkness is morning to all of
them;
for they are friends with the terrors
of deep darkness.

[c] Syr Vg: Heb *he turns* [d] Gk Vg: Heb *from* [e] Traditional rendering of Heb *Shaddai* [f] Or *But I am not destroyed by the darkness; he has concealed the thick darkness from me* [g] Gk: Heb *they* [h] Meaning of Heb uncertain

23.7 Job 13.3,16
23.8 Job 9.11
23.10 Ps 139.1-3
23.11 Ps 44.18
23.12 Jn 4.32,34
23.13 Job 9.12; 12.14; Ps 115.3
23.14 1 Thess 3.3
23.16 Ps 22.14; Jer 51.46
23.17 Job 10.18,19; 19.8
24.1 Ps 31.15; Jer 46.10
24.2 Deut 19.14; 27.17; 28.31
24.3 Ex 22.26; Deut 24.6,10,12, 17; Job 22.6
24.4 Deut 24.14; Prov 28.28
24.5 Job 39.5-8; Ps 104.23
24.7 Ex 22.26; Job 22.6
24.8 Lam 4.5
24.9 Deut 24.17
24.12 Jer 51.52; Ezek 26.15; Job 9.23,24
24.13 Isa 5.20; Jn 3.19
24.14 Mic 2.1; Ps 10.8
24.15 Prov 7.9; Ps 10.11
24.16 Ex 22.2
24.17 Ps 91.5

18 "Swift are they on the face of the waters;
their portion in the land is cursed;
no treader turns toward their
vineyards.
19 Drought and heat snatch away the
snow waters;
so does Sheol those who have sinned.
20 The womb forgets them;
the worm finds them sweet;
they are no longer remembered;
so wickedness is broken like a tree.

21 "They harm[i] the childless woman,
and do no good to the widow.
22 Yet God[j] prolongs the life of the mighty
by his power;
they rise up when they despair of life.
23 He gives them security, and they are
supported;
his eyes are upon their ways.
24 They are exalted a little while, and
then are gone;
they wither and fade like the
mallow;[k]
they are cut off like the heads of grain.
25 If it is not so, who will prove me a liar,
and show that there is nothing in
what I say?"

Bildad Speaks: How Can a Mortal Be Righteous Before God?

25 Then Bildad the Shuhite answered:
2 "Dominion and fear are with
God;[l]
he makes peace in his high heaven.
3 Is there any number to his armies?
Upon whom does his light not arise?
4 How then can a mortal be righteous
before God?
How can one born of woman be pure?
5 If even the moon is not bright
and the stars are not pure in his sight,
6 how much less a mortal, who is a
maggot,
and a human being, who is a worm!"

Job Replies: God's Majesty Is Unsearchable

26 Then Job answered:
2 "How you have helped one
who has no power!
How you have assisted the arm that
has no strength!
3 How you have counseled one who has
no wisdom,
and given much good advice!
4 With whose help have you uttered words,
and whose spirit has come forth
from you?
5 The shades below tremble,
the waters and their inhabitants.
6 Sheol is naked before God,
and Abaddon has no covering.
7 He stretches out Zaphon[m] over the void,
and hangs the earth upon nothing.
8 He binds up the waters in his thick
clouds,
and the cloud is not torn open by
them.
9 He covers the face of the full moon,
and spreads over it his cloud.
10 He has described a circle on the face of
the waters,
at the boundary between light and
darkness.
11 The pillars of heaven tremble,
and are astounded at his rebuke.
12 By his power he stilled the Sea;
by his understanding he struck down
Rahab.
13 By his wind the heavens were made fair;
his hand pierced the fleeing serpent.
14 These are indeed but the outskirts of
his ways;
and how small a whisper do we hear
of him!
But the thunder of his power who
can understand?"

Job Maintains His Integrity

27 Job again took up his discourse
and said:
2 "As God lives, who has taken away my
right,
and the Almighty,[n] who has made
my soul bitter,
3 as long as my breath is in me
and the spirit of God is in my nostrils,
4 my lips will not speak falsehood,
and my tongue will not utter deceit.
5 Far be it from me to say that you are
right;
until I die I will not put away my
integrity from me.
6 I hold fast my righteousness, and will
not let it go;
my heart does not reproach me for
any of my days.

[i] Gk Tg: Heb *feed on* or *associate with* [j] Heb *he* [k] Gk: Heb *like all others* [l] Heb *him* [m] Or *the North* [n] Traditional rendering of Heb *Shaddai*

24.18 Job 9.26; Ps 90.5
24.19 Job 6.16,17; 21.13
24.20 Ps 31.12; Prov 10.7
24.21 Job 22.9
24.22 Deut 28.66
24.23 Job 12.6; 11.11
24.24 Ps 37.10; Job 14.21; Isa 17.5
25.2 Job 9.4; Rev 1.6; Job 22.12
25.3 Jas 1.17
25.4 Job 4.17; Ps 143.2; Job 14.4
25.5 Job 31.26; 15.15
25.6 Job 7.17; Ps 22.6
26.2 Ps 71.9
26.6 Ps 139.8,11; Heb 4.13
26.7 Job 9.8
26.8 Prov 30.4
26.9 Ps 97.2
26.10 Job 38.8-11; Prov 8.29; Job 38.19; 20.24
26.12 Ex 14.21; Isa 51.15; Jer 31.35
26.13 Job 9.8; Isa 27.1
26.14 Job 36.29
27.1 Job 13.12; 29.1
27.2 Job 34.5; 9.18
27.4 Job 6.28
27.5 Job 2.9; 13.15
27.6 Job 2.3; 13.18; Acts 23.1

24.18-25 The wicked are doomed to disaster and will vanish in death, but meanwhile their evil deeds continue and God allows them length of *life* and *security*. No-one can refute Job's charge.
25.1-6 Bildad Declares that Humans are Unable to Be Righteous Before God. The greatness of the God who rules in heaven and on earth precludes humans' ever gaining status as *righteous* before him.
26.1-27.23 Job on God's Sovereignty and his Own Integrity.
26.1-4 With apparent irony, Job describes the sham *help* that his friends have offered him.
26.5-14 The majesty and omnipotence of God in his control of the universe are evident, even though he does not convey *understanding* to his creatures.
27.1-7 Job declares that, in spite of the *bitter* experience into which God has brought him, he is convinced of his own *integrity, righteousness*, and freedom from guilt, and he calls for judgment on those who criticize him.

27.8-23 Zophar's Final Indictment of Job. Repeating the themes and ideas of his earlier speech in Job 20, there is here insistence that the wicked and their children do suffer from divine punishment. Their wealth and property disappear when *terrors* and *whirlwinds* of divine wrath hit them.
28.1-28 Where Can Wisdom Be Found? The sequence of (1) laments by Job, (2) charges against him by his friends, and (3) responses by him is halted by this poem about wisdom. The pattern of challenges and defenses resumes at 29.1. A description of the various types of search for precious minerals hidden beneath the surface of the earth (vv. 1-11) serves as a metaphor for the human search for priceless wisdom. It cannot be found in the sky above or in the subterranean chambers beneath the earth. God alone in his wisdom *established* and sustains the universe. Essential for humans who seek wisdom is to commit themselves to God and his purpose (*fear the* LORD), and to avoid *evil* acts.

7 "May my enemy be like the wicked,
and may my opponent be like the unrighteous.
8 For what is the hope of the godless when God cuts them off,
when God takes away their lives?
9 Will God hear their cry
when trouble comes upon them?
10 Will they take delight in the Almighty?[o]
Will they call upon God at all times?
11 I will teach you concerning the hand of God;
that which is with the Almighty[o] I will not conceal.
12 All of you have seen it yourselves;
why then have you become altogether vain?

13 "This is the portion of the wicked with God,
and the heritage that oppressors receive from the Almighty:[o]
14 If their children are multiplied, it is for the sword;
and their offspring have not enough to eat.
15 Those who survive them the pestilence buries,
and their widows make no lamentation.
16 Though they heap up silver like dust,
and pile up clothing like clay—
17 they may pile it up, but the just will wear it,
and the innocent will divide the silver.
18 They build their houses like nests,
like booths made by sentinels of the vineyard.
19 They go to bed with wealth, but will do so no more;
they open their eyes, and it is gone.
20 Terrors overtake them like a flood;
in the night a whirlwind carries them off.
21 The east wind lifts them up and they are gone;
it sweeps them out of their place.
22 It[p] hurls at them without pity;
they flee from its[q] power in headlong flight.
23 It[p] claps its[q] hands at them,
and hisses at them from its[q] place.

Interlude: Where Wisdom Is Found

28 "Surely there is a mine for silver,
and a place for gold to be refined.
2 Iron is taken out of the earth,
and copper is smelted from ore.
3 Miners put[r] an end to darkness,
and search out to the farthest bound
the ore in gloom and deep darkness.
4 They open shafts in a valley away from human habitation;
they are forgotten by travelers,
they sway suspended, remote from people.
5 As for the earth, out of it comes bread;
but underneath it is turned up as by fire.
6 Its stones are the place of sapphires,[s]
and its dust contains gold.

7 "That path no bird of prey knows,
and the falcon's eye has not seen it.
8 The proud wild animals have not trodden it;
the lion has not passed over it.

9 "They put their hand to the flinty rock,
and overturn mountains by the roots.
10 They cut out channels in the rocks,
and their eyes see every precious thing.
11 The sources of the rivers they probe;[t]
hidden things they bring to light.

12 "But where shall wisdom be found?
And where is the place of understanding?
13 Mortals do not know the way to it,[u]
and it is not found in the land of the living.
14 The deep says, 'It is not in me,'
and the sea says, 'It is not with me.'
15 It cannot be gotten for gold,
and silver cannot be weighed out as its price.
16 It cannot be valued in the gold of Ophir,
in precious onyx or sapphire.[t]
17 Gold and glass cannot equal it,
nor can it be exchanged for jewels of fine gold.
18 No mention shall be made of coral or of crystal;
the price of wisdom is above pearls.

27.8 Job 8.13; 11.20
27.9 Job 35.12; Prov 1.28; Isa 1.15; Jer 14.12; Mic 3.4
27.10 Job 22.26,27
27.13 Job 20.29; 15.20
27.14 Deut 28.41; Hos 9.13; Job 20.10
27.15 Ps 78.64
27.16 Zech 9.3
27.17 Prov 28.8; Eccl 2.26
27.19 Ezek 29.5; Job 7.8,21
27.20 Job 15.21; 20.8
27.21 Job 21.18; 7.10
27.22 Jer 13.14; Ezek 5.11; Job 11.20
27.23 Lam 2.15; Job 18.18
28.2 Deut 8.9
28.5 Ps 104.14
28.9 Deut 8.15; 32.13
28.12 ver 23.28
28.13 Prov 3.15
28.17 Prov 8.10; 16.16
28.18 Prov 3.15; 8.11

[o] Traditional rendering of Heb *Shaddai* [p] Or *He* (that is God) [q] Or *his* [r] Heb *He puts* [s] Or *lapis lazuli* [t] Gk Vg: Heb *bind* [u] Gk: Heb *its price*

19 The chrysolite of Ethiopia[v] cannot
compare with it,
nor can it be valued in pure gold.

20 "Where then does wisdom come from?
And where is the place of
understanding?
21 It is hidden from the eyes of all living,
and concealed from the birds of the air.
22 Abaddon and Death say,
'We have heard a rumor of it with
our ears.'

23 "God understands the way to it,
and he knows its place.
24 For he looks to the ends of the earth,
and sees everything under the
heavens.
25 When he gave to the wind its weight,
and apportioned out the waters by
measure;
26 when he made a decree for the rain,
and a way for the thunderbolt;
27 then he saw it and declared it;
he established it, and searched it out.
28 And he said to humankind,
'Truly, the fear of the Lord, that is
wisdom;
and to depart from evil is
understanding.' "

Job Finishes His Defense

29 Job again took up his discourse
and said:
2 "Oh, that I were as in the months of
old,
as in the days when God watched
over me;
3 when his lamp shone over my head,
and by his light I walked through
darkness;
4 when I was in my prime,
when the friendship of God was
upon my tent;
5 when the Almighty[w] was still with me,
when my children were around me;
6 when my steps were washed with milk,
and the rock poured out for me
streams of oil!
7 When I went out to the gate of the
city,
when I took my seat in the square,
8 the young men saw me and withdrew,
and the aged rose up and stood;
9 the nobles refrained from talking,
and laid their hands on their mouths;
10 the voices of princes were hushed,
and their tongues stuck to the roof
of their mouths.
11 When the ear heard, it commended me,
and when the eye saw, it approved;
12 because I delivered the poor who cried,
and the orphan who had no helper.
13 The blessing of the wretched came
upon me,
and I caused the widow's heart to
sing for joy.
14 I put on righteousness, and it clothed me;
my justice was like a robe and a
turban.
15 I was eyes to the blind,
and feet to the lame.
16 I was a father to the needy,
and I championed the cause of the
stranger.
17 I broke the fangs of the unrighteous,
and made them drop their prey from
their teeth.
18 Then I thought, 'I shall die in my nest,
and I shall multiply my days like the
phoenix;[x]
19 my roots spread out to the waters,
with the dew all night on my branches;
20 my glory was fresh with me,
and my bow ever new in my hand.'

21 "They listened to me, and waited,
and kept silence for my counsel.
22 After I spoke they did not speak again,
and my word dropped upon them
like dew.[y]
23 They waited for me as for the rain;
they opened their mouths as for the
spring rain.
24 I smiled on them when they had no
confidence;
and the light of my countenance
they did not extinguish.[z]
25 I chose their way, and sat as chief,
and I lived like a king among his
troops,
like one who comforts mourners.

30 "But now they make sport of me,
those who are younger than I,
whose fathers I would have disdained
to set with the dogs of my flock.
2 What could I gain from the strength of
their hands?

[v] Or *Nubia*; Heb *Cush* [w] Traditional rendering of Heb *Shaddai* [x] Or *like sand* [y] Heb lacks *like dew* [z] Meaning of Heb uncertain

29.1-31.40 Job Concludes His Defense of Himself.
29.1-25 Job sadly recalls the days when with the *friendship* of God, he also enjoyed prosperity and respect from his community and its leaders, as well as gratitude for his generosity to those in need and for his ability to triumph over *the unrighteous.* Expecting to have had those experiences and such esteem continue throughout his life, he had encouraged others and was treated virtually as a divine leader by the community, which perceived in *the light of [his] countenance* the counterpart of the glory of God.
30.1-15 Now, however, his *prosperity* has vanished, and he is mocked even by young people from among the poor and the outcasts of society who live by scavenging and in filth.

28.19 Prov 8.19
28.20 ver 23,28
28.22 Job 26.6
28.23 ver 23-28
28.24 Ps 33.13; Prov 15.3
28.25 Ps 135.7; Job 12.15
28.26 Job 37.6,11,12; 37.3; 38.25
28.28 Deut 4.6; Ps 111.10; Prov 1.7; 9.10
29.1 Job 13.12; 27.1
29.2 Jer 31.28
29.3 Job 11.17
29.4 Ps 25.14
29.6 Job 20.17; Deut 32.13,14
29.9 ver 21; Job 21.5
29.10 ver 22
29.12 Job 31.16,17,21
29.13 Job 31.19,20
29.14 Ps 132.9; Isa 59.17; 61.10; Eph 6.14
29.16 Prov 29.7
29.17 Ps 3.7
29.18 Ps 30.6
29.19 Job 18.16; Jer 17.8
29.20 Gen 49.24; Ps 18.34
29.21 ver 9
29.22 ver 10; Job 32.2
29.25 Job 1.3; 31.37; 4.4
30.1 Job 12.4

30.16-31 Though Job's antagonist is not named, the shift of the complaint from *he* to *you* shows that it is God whose attack on Job is being described. Job himself has been kinder to the poor than God now is to him.
31.1-6 Job has made a *covenant* with God to obey his moral principles in all his dealings, and pleads for a fair trial before God. He acknowledges that if he could be proved guilty of adultery or other acts of iniquity, the punishment he has received would be warranted.

All their vigor is gone.
3 Through want and hard hunger
they gnaw the dry and desolate ground,
4 they pick mallow and the leaves of bushes,
and to warm themselves the roots of broom.
5 They are driven out from society;
people shout after them as after a thief.
6 In the gullies of wadis they must live,
in holes in the ground, and in the rocks.
7 Among the bushes they bray;
under the nettles they huddle together.
8 A senseless, disreputable brood,
they have been whipped out of the land.

9 "And now they mock me in song;
I am a byword to them.
10 They abhor me, they keep aloof from me;
they do not hesitate to spit at the sight of me.
11 Because God has loosed my bowstring and humbled me,
they have cast off restraint in my presence.
12 On my right hand the rabble rise up;
they send me sprawling,
and build roads for my ruin.
13 They break up my path,
they promote my calamity;
no one restrains[a] them.
14 As through a wide breach they come;
amid the crash they roll on.
15 Terrors are turned upon me;
my honor is pursued as by the wind,
and my prosperity has passed away like a cloud.

16 "And now my soul is poured out within me;
days of affliction have taken hold of me.
17 The night racks my bones,
and the pain that gnaws me takes no rest.
18 With violence he seizes my garment;[b]
he grasps me by[c] the collar of my tunic.
19 He has cast me into the mire,
and I have become like dust and ashes.
20 I cry to you and you do not answer me;
I stand, and you merely look at me.
21 You have turned cruel to me;
with the might of your hand you persecute me.
22 You lift me up on the wind, you make me ride on it,
and you toss me about in the roar of the storm.
23 I know that you will bring me to death,
and to the house appointed for all living.

24 "Surely one does not turn against the needy,[d]
when in disaster they cry for help.[e]
25 Did I not weep for those whose day was hard?
Was not my soul grieved for the poor?
26 But when I looked for good, evil came;
and when I waited for light, darkness came.
27 My inward parts are in turmoil, and are never still;
days of affliction come to meet me.
28 I go about in sunless gloom;
I stand up in the assembly and cry for help.
29 I am a brother of jackals,
and a companion of ostriches.
30 My skin turns black and falls from me,
and my bones burn with heat.
31 My lyre is turned to mourning,
and my pipe to the voice of those who weep.

31 "I have made a covenant with my eyes;
how then could I look upon a virgin?
2 What would be my portion from God above,
and my heritage from the Almighty[f] on high?
3 Does not calamity befall the unrighteous,
and disaster the workers of iniquity?
4 Does he not see my ways,
and number all my steps?

5 "If I have walked with falsehood,
and my foot has hurried to deceit—
6 let me be weighed in a just balance,
and let God know my integrity!—

[a] Cn: Heb *helps* [b] Gk: Heb *my garment is disfigured* [c] Heb *like* [d] Heb *ruin* [e] Cn: Meaning of Heb uncertain [f] Traditional rendering of Heb *Shaddai*

30.9 Job 12.4; 17.6
30.10 Num 12.14; Deut 25.9; Isa 50.6; Mt 26.67
30.11 Ruth 1.21; Ps 88.7
30.12 Ps 140.4,5; Job 19.12
30.15 Job 3.25; 31.23; Hos 13.3
30.16 Ps 22.14; 42.4
30.17 ver 30
30.19 Ps 69.2,14
30.20 Ps 19.7
30.21 Job 10.3; 16.9,14; 19.6,22
30.22 Job 9.17; 27.21
30.23 Job 9.22; 10.8; 3.19; 17.13
30.24 Job 19.7
30.25 Ps 35.13,14; Rom 12.15
30.26 Job 3.25,26; Jer 8.15; Job 19.8
30.28 Ps 38.6; 42.9; 43.2; Job 19.7
30.29 Mic 1.8
30.30 Ps 119.83; Lam 4.8; Ps 102.3
30.31 Ps 107.1,2
31.1 Mt 5.28
31.4 2 Chr 16.9; Prov 5.21
31.5 Mic 2.11
31.6 Job 6.2,3; 27.5,6

7 if my step has turned aside from the way,
and my heart has followed my eyes,
and if any spot has clung to my hands;
8 then let me sow, and another eat;
and let what grows for me be rooted out.

9 "If my heart has been enticed by a woman,
and I have lain in wait at my neighbor's door;
10 then let my wife grind for another,
and let other men kneel over her.
11 For that would be a heinous crime;
that would be a criminal offense;
12 for that would be a fire consuming down to Abaddon,
and it would burn to the root all my harvest.

13 "If I have rejected the cause of my male or female slaves,
when they brought a complaint against me;
14 what then shall I do when God rises up?
When he makes inquiry, what shall I answer him?
15 Did not he who made me in the womb make them?
And did not one fashion us in the womb?

16 "If I have withheld anything that the poor desired,
or have caused the eyes of the widow to fail,
17 or have eaten my morsel alone,
and the orphan has not eaten from it—
18 for from my youth I reared the orphan[g] like a father,
and from my mother's womb I guided the widow[h]—
19 if I have seen anyone perish for lack of clothing,
or a poor person without covering,
20 whose loins have not blessed me,
and who was not warmed with the fleece of my sheep;
21 if I have raised my hand against the orphan,
because I saw I had supporters at the gate;
22 then let my shoulder blade fall from my shoulder,
and let my arm be broken from its socket.
23 For I was in terror of calamity from God,
and I could not have faced his majesty.

24 "If I have made gold my trust,
or called fine gold my confidence;
25 if I have rejoiced because my wealth was great,
or because my hand had gotten much;
26 if I have looked at the sun[i] when it shone,
or the moon moving in splendor,
27 and my heart has been secretly enticed,
and my mouth has kissed my hand;
28 this also would be an iniquity to be punished by the judges,
for I should have been false to God above.

29 "If I have rejoiced at the ruin of those who hated me,
or exulted when evil overtook them—
30 I have not let my mouth sin
by asking for their lives with a curse—
31 if those of my tent ever said,
'O that we might be sated with his flesh!'[j]—
32 the stranger has not lodged in the street;
I have opened my doors to the traveler—
33 if I have concealed my transgressions as others do,[k]
by hiding my iniquity in my bosom,
34 because I stood in great fear of the multitude,
and the contempt of families terrified me,
so that I kept silence, and did not go out of doors—
35 Oh, that I had one to hear me!
(Here is my signature! let the Almighty[l] answer me!)
Oh, that I had the indictment written by my adversary!
36 Surely I would carry it on my shoulder;
I would bind it on me like a crown;
37 I would give him an account of all my steps;
like a prince I would approach him.

[g] Heb *him* [h] Heb *her* [i] Heb *the light* [j] Meaning of Heb uncertain [k] Or *as Adam did* [l] Traditional rendering of Heb *Shaddai*

31.7 Job 23.11; 9.30
31.8 Lev 26.16; Job 20.18
31.9 Job 24.15
31.10 Jer 8.10
31.11 Gen 38.24; Deut 22.22-24
31.12 Job 15.30; 26.6; 20.28
31.13 Deut 24.14,15
31.15 Mal 2.10
31.16 Job 20.19; 22.7,9
31.17 Job 22.7; 29.12
31.20 Deut 31.20
31.21 Job 22.9
31.22 Job 38.15
31.23 ver 3; Job 13.11
31.24 Mk 10.24
31.25 Ps 62.10
31.26 Deut 4.19; Ezek 8.16
31.28 ver 11
31.29 Prov 17.5
31.30 Mt 5.44
31.31 Job 22.7
31.32 Gen 19.2,3; Rom 12.13
31.33 Gen 3.8; Prov 28.13
31.34 Ex 23.2
31.35 Job 19.7; 30.20,24,28; 35.14
31.37 ver 4; Job 1.3; 29.25

31.7-34 Job then cites the acts for which divine chastisement would have been appropriate, though he insists that he did not perform them. In some cases he specifies what the penalty would be: (vv. 5-8) deceit or theft in any form, to be punished by loss of food and crops; (vv. 9-12) adultery, punished by someone else taking his wife, and by loss of property; (vv. 13-15) injustice or indifference to slaves; (vv. 16-23) failure to come to the aid of the poor or deprived; (vv. 24-28) placing his ultimate trust in his possessions, or the worship of *sun or moon*; (vv. 29-32) allowing himself and his household to rejoice at the *ruin* of his foes, or (vv. 33-34) concealing his own misdeeds.
31.35-40 Job yearns for someone to plead his cause before God, and for a copy of the charges that God (*my adversary*) has against him. He would be happy to make such a list public (*on my shoulder*) and to offer respectfully a complete *account* of misdeeds that he could be shown to have done. He is ready to accept the disasters of judgment if he is indeed proved to be guilty of having violated the covenant with God.

32.1-22 Elihu's Challenge to Job's Friends.
32.1-5 The prose introduction pictures Elihu as angry with Job's friends for their failure to find answers to Job's questions, and with Job for his indictment of God.
32.6-22 Elihu is vividly portrayed as an angry *young* man, who denies that wisdom comes with age, as the failure of Job's friends to *confute* him shows. Now that they have finished their pointless speeches, he is ready to burst in his eagerness to give his own assessment of Job's problem, free of *flattery* or *partiality*.
33.1-36.23 Elihu Challenges Job.
33.1-33 Understanding of God is conveyed, not by human skill, but by *the spirit* or *breath of the Almighty*. Job should not interpret his difficulties as evidence of God's injustice, but see rather that in the midst of terrifying and threatening experiences, sensitive individuals can gain insight and renewal, and will come to acknowledge that they have *sinned* and thereby be *redeemed*. Job must stop complaining and open himself to such divinely-given insight.

38 "If my land has cried out against me,
and its furrows have wept together;
39 if I have eaten its yield without
payment,
and caused the death of its owners;
40 let thorns grow instead of wheat,
and foul weeds instead of barley."

The words of Job are ended.

Elihu Rebukes Job's Friends

32 So these three men ceased to answer Job, because he was righteous in his own eyes. [2]Then Elihu son of
Barachel the Buzite, of the family of Ram,
became angry. He was angry at Job because
he justified himself rather than God; [3]he
was angry also at Job's three friends because they had found no answer, though
they had declared Job to be in the wrong.[m]
[4]Now Elihu had waited to speak to Job,
because they were older than he. [5]But when
Elihu saw that there was no answer in the
mouths of these three men, he became
angry.

6 Elihu son of Barachel the Buzite answered:
"I am young in years,
and you are aged;
therefore I was timid and afraid
to declare my opinion to you.
7 I said, 'Let days speak,
and many years teach wisdom.'
8 But truly it is the spirit in a mortal,
the breath of the Almighty,[n] that
makes for understanding.
9 It is not the old[o] that are wise,
nor the aged that understand what
is right.
10 Therefore I say, 'Listen to me;
let me also declare my opinion.'

11 "See, I waited for your words,
I listened for your wise sayings,
while you searched out what to say.
12 I gave you my attention,
but there was in fact no one that
confuted Job,
no one among you that answered
his words.
13 Yet do not say, 'We have found
wisdom;
God may vanquish him, not a
human.'
14 He has not directed his words against
me,
and I will not answer him with your
speeches.

15 "They are dismayed, they answer no
more;
they have not a word to say.
16 And am I to wait, because they do not
speak,
because they stand there, and
answer no more?
17 I also will give my answer;
I also will declare my opinion.
18 For I am full of words;
the spirit within me constrains me.
19 My heart is indeed like wine that has
no vent;
like new wineskins, it is ready to
burst.
20 I must speak, so that I may find relief;
I must open my lips and answer.
21 I will not show partiality to any person
or use flattery toward anyone.
22 For I do not know how to flatter—
or my Maker would soon put an end
to me!

Elihu Rebukes Job

33 "But now, hear my speech, O Job,
and listen to all my words.
2 See, I open my mouth;
the tongue in my mouth speaks.
3 My words declare the uprightness of
my heart,
and what my lips know they speak
sincerely.
4 The spirit of God has made me,
and the breath of the Almighty[n]
gives me life.
5 Answer me, if you can;
set your words in order before me;
take your stand.
6 See, before God I am as you are;
I too was formed from a piece of clay.
7 No fear of me need terrify you;
my pressure will not be heavy on you.

8 "Surely, you have spoken in my
hearing,
and I have heard the sound of your
words.
9 You say, 'I am clean, without
transgression;

[m] Another ancient tradition reads *answer, and had put God in the wrong* [n] Traditional rendering of Heb *Shaddai* [o] Gk Syr Vg: Heb *many*

31.38 Gen 4.10,11
31.39 Lev 19.13; 1 Kings 21.19; Jas 5.4
31.40 Gen 3.18
32.1 Job 33.9
32.2 Gen 22.21; Jer 25.23
32.3 Job 11.6; 15.16; 22.5
32.6 Job 15.10
32.8 Job 27.3; 33.4; 1 Kings 3.12; Prov 2.6
32.9 1 Cor 1.26
32.11 Job 5.27
32.13 Jer 9.23
32.18 Acts 18.5
32.19 Acts 9.17
32.21 Lev 19.15; Mt 22.16
32.22 1 Thess 2.5
33.3 Job 6.28; 27.4; 36.4
33.4 Gen 2.7; Job 27.3
33.5 ver 32; Job 13.18
33.7 Job 9.34; 13.21; 2 Cor 2.5
33.9 Job 10.7; 13.23; 16.17

I am pure, and there is no iniquity
in me.
10 Look, he finds occasions against me,
he counts me as his enemy;
11 he puts my feet in the stocks,
and watches all my paths.'

12 "But in this you are not right. I will
answer you:
God is greater than any mortal.
13 Why do you contend against him,
saying, 'He will answer none of my[p]
words'?
14 For God speaks in one way,
and in two, though people do not
perceive it.
15 In a dream, in a vision of the night,
when deep sleep falls on mortals,
while they slumber on their beds,
16 then he opens their ears,
and terrifies them with warnings,
17 that he may turn them aside from their
deeds,
and keep them from pride,
18 to spare their souls from the Pit,
their lives from traversing the River.
19 They are also chastened with pain
upon their beds,
and with continual strife in their bones,
20 so that their lives loathe bread,
and their appetites dainty food.
21 Their flesh is so wasted away that it
cannot be seen;
and their bones, once invisible, now
stick out.
22 Their souls draw near the Pit,
and their lives to those who bring
death.
23 Then, if there should be for one of
them an angel,
a mediator, one of a thousand,
one who declares a person upright,
24 and he is gracious to that person, and
says,
'Deliver him from going down into
the Pit;
I have found a ransom;
25 let his flesh become fresh with youth;
let him return to the days of his
youthful vigor.'
26 Then he prays to God, and is accepted
by him,
he comes into his presence with joy,
and God[q] repays him for his
righteousness.
27 That person sings to others and says,
'I sinned, and perverted what was right,
and it was not paid back to me.
28 He has redeemed my soul from going
down to the Pit,
and my life shall see the light.'

29 "God indeed does all these things,
twice, three times, with mortals,
30 to bring back their souls from the Pit,
so that they may see the light of life.[r]
31 Pay heed, Job, listen to me;
be silent, and I will speak.
32 If you have anything to say, answer
me;
speak, for I desire to justify you.
33 If not, listen to me;
be silent, and I will teach you
wisdom."

Elihu Proclaims God's Justice

34 Then Elihu continued and said:
2 "Hear my words, you wise
men,
and give ear to me, you who know;
3 for the ear tests words
as the palate tastes food.
4 Let us choose what is right;
let us determine among ourselves
what is good.
5 For Job has said, 'I am innocent,
and God has taken away my right;
6 in spite of being right I am counted a
liar;
my wound is incurable, though I am
without transgression.'
7 Who is there like Job,
who drinks up scoffing like water,
8 who goes in company with evildoers
and walks with the wicked?
9 For he has said, 'It profits one nothing
to take delight in God.'

10 "Therefore, hear me, you who have
sense,
far be it from God that he should do
wickedness,
and from the Almighty[s] that he
should do wrong.
11 For according to their deeds he will
repay them,
and according to their ways he will
make it befall them.
12 Of a truth, God will not do wickedly,

34.1-20 Elihu denounces Job's claim of innocence and his effort to blame God, since the omnipotent ruler of the universe maintains justice, calling the mighty to account for their abuse of power and caring for the needs of the powerless. Nevertheless, all human life ends in death.

33.10 Job 13.24
33.11 Job 13.27; 14.16
33.13 Job 15.25; Isa 45.9
33.14 Ps 62.11
33.15 Num 12.6; Job 4.13
33.16 Job 36.10,15
33.18 ver 24,28,30
33.19 Job 30.17
33.20 Ps 107.18
33.21 Job 16.8; 19.20
33.22 Ps 88.3
33.23 Mic 6.8
33.24 Isa 38.17
33.25 2 Kings 5.14
33.26 Job 22.27; 34.28; 22.26; Ps 51.12
33.27 Lk 15.21; Rom 6.21
33.28 Ps 103.14; Job 22.28
33.29 Eph 1.11; 1 Cor 12.6; Phil 2.13
33.30 Ps 56.13
33.33 Ps 34.11
34.3 Job 12.11
34.4 1 Thess 5.21
34.6 Jer 15.18; 30.12
34.7 Job 15.16
34.8 Ps 50.18
34.9 Job 21.15; 35.3
34.10 Job 8.3
34.11 Ps 62.12; Mt 16.27; Rom 2.6; 2 Cor 5.10; Rev 22.12
34.12 Job 8.3

[p] Compare Gk: Heb *his* [q] Heb *he* [r] Syr: Heb *to be lighted with the light of life* [s] Traditional rendering of Heb *Shaddai*

34.21-37 No-one can hide from God or escape his judgment. *whether...a nation or an individual.* Any who are truly penitent can be restored, but Job's obstinate charges against God show him to be rebellious and devoid of *knowledge*.
35.1-16 In reaction to Job's charge of God's injustice, Elihu declares that God's concerns are with the rulers and the righteous, calling them to account for misdeeds and subjecting them to punishment. It is foolish and dangerous, therefore, for Job and his counselors to be so obsessed with the condition of those worthless characters like Job who are obviously wicked.

and the Almighty[t] will not pervert
justice.
13 Who gave him charge over the earth
and who laid on him[u] the whole
world?
14 If he should take back his spirit[v] to
himself,
and gather to himself his breath,
15 all flesh would perish together,
and all mortals return to dust.

16 "If you have understanding, hear this;
listen to what I say.
17 Shall one who hates justice govern?
Will you condemn one who is
righteous and mighty,
18 who says to a king, 'You scoundrel!'
and to princes, 'You wicked men!';
19 who shows no partiality to nobles,
nor regards the rich more than the
poor,
for they are all the work of his hands?
20 In a moment they die;
at midnight the people are shaken
and pass away,
and the mighty are taken away by
no human hand.

21 "For his eyes are upon the ways of
mortals,
and he sees all their steps.
22 There is no gloom or deep darkness
where evildoers may hide themselves.
23 For he has not appointed a time[w] for
anyone
to go before God in judgment.
24 He shatters the mighty without
investigation,
and sets others in their place.
25 Thus, knowing their works,
he overturns them in the night, and
they are crushed.
26 He strikes them for their wickedness
while others look on,
27 because they turned aside from
following him,
and had no regard for any of his ways,
28 so that they caused the cry of the poor
to come to him,
and he heard the cry of the afflicted—
29 When he is quiet, who can condemn?
When he hides his face, who can
behold him,
whether it be a nation or an
individual?—
30 so that the godless should not reign,
or those who ensnare the people.

31 "For has anyone said to God,
'I have endured punishment; I will
not offend any more;
32 teach me what I do not see;
if I have done iniquity, I will do it
no more'?
33 Will he then pay back to suit you,
because you reject it?
For you must choose, and not I;
therefore declare what you know.[x]
34 Those who have sense will say to me,
and the wise who hear me will say,
35 'Job speaks without knowledge,
his words are without insight.'
36 Would that Job were tried to the limit,
because his answers are those of the
wicked.
37 For he adds rebellion to his sin;
he claps his hands among us,
and multiplies his words against God."

Elihu Condemns Self-Righteousness

35 Elihu continued and said:
2 "Do you think this to be just?
You say, 'I am in the right before God.'
3 If you ask, 'What advantage have I?
How am I better off than if I had
sinned?'
4 I will answer you
and your friends with you.
5 Look at the heavens and see;
observe the clouds, which are higher
than you.
6 If you have sinned, what do you
accomplish against him?
And if your transgressions are multiplied,
what do you do to him?
7 If you are righteous, what do you give
to him;
or what does he receive from your
hand?
8 Your wickedness affects others like you,
and your righteousness, other
human beings.

9 "Because of the multitude of
oppressions people cry out;
they call for help because of the arm
of the mighty.
10 But no one says, 'Where is God my
Maker,

[t] Traditional rendering of Heb *Shaddai* [u] Heb lacks *on him* [v] Heb *his heart his spirit* [w] Cn: Heb *yet* [x] Meaning of Heb of verses 29–33 uncertain

34.13 Job 38.5,6
34.14 Ps 104.29
34.15 Isa 40.6,7; Gen 3.19
34.17 2 Sam 23.3
34.18 Ex 22.28
34.19 Deut 10.17; Gal 2.6; Job 31.15
34.20 Ex 12.29; Job 12.19
34.21 Job 31.4
34.22 Ps 139.12; Am 9.2,3
34.24 Dan 2.21
34.25 ver 11,20
34.26 Job 26.12
34.27 1 Sam 15.11; Ps 28.5; Isa 5.12
34.28 Job 35.9; Jas 5.4; Ex 22.23
34.29 1 Chr 22.9
34.30 ver 17
34.32 Job 35.11; Ps 25.4
34.35 Job 35.16
34.36 Job 23.10; 22.15
35.2 Job 32.2
35.3 Job 34.9; 9.30,31
35.5 Job 22.12
35.6 Prov 8.36; Jer 7.19
35.7 Job 22.2,3; Prov 9.12; Lk 17.10
35.9 Ex 2.23; Job 12.19
35.10 Job 27.10; Ps 42.8; 149.5; Acts 16.25

who gives strength in the night,
11 who teaches us more than the animals of the earth,
and makes us wiser than the birds of the air?'
12 There they cry out, but he does not answer,
because of the pride of evildoers.
13 Surely God does not hear an empty cry,
nor does the Almighty[y] regard it.
14 How much less when you say that you do not see him,
that the case is before him, and you are waiting for him!
15 And now, because his anger does not punish,
and he does not greatly heed transgression,[z]
16 Job opens his mouth in empty talk,
he multiplies words without knowledge."

Elihu Exalts God's Goodness

36 Elihu continued and said:
2 "Bear with me a little, and I will show you,
for I have yet something to say on God's behalf.
3 I will bring my knowledge from far away,
and ascribe righteousness to my Maker.
4 For truly my words are not false;
one who is perfect in knowledge is with you.

5 "Surely God is mighty and does not despise any;
he is mighty in strength of understanding.
6 He does not keep the wicked alive,
but gives the afflicted their right.
7 He does not withdraw his eyes from the righteous,
but with kings on the throne
he sets them forever, and they are exalted.
8 And if they are bound in fetters
and caught in the cords of affliction,
9 then he declares to them their work
and their transgressions, that they are behaving arrogantly.
10 He opens their ears to instruction,
and commands that they return from iniquity.
11 If they listen, and serve him,
they complete their days in prosperity,
and their years in pleasantness.
12 But if they do not listen, they shall perish by the sword,
and die without knowledge.

13 "The godless in heart cherish anger;
they do not cry for help when he binds them.
14 They die in their youth,
and their life ends in shame.[a]
15 He delivers the afflicted by their affliction,
and opens their ear by adversity.
16 He also allured you out of distress
into a broad place where there was no constraint,
and what was set on your table was full of fatness.

17 "But you are obsessed with the case of the wicked;
judgment and justice seize you.
18 Beware that wrath does not entice you into scoffing,
and do not let the greatness of the ransom turn you aside.
19 Will your cry avail to keep you from distress,
or will all the force of your strength?
20 Do not long for the night,
when peoples are cut off in their place.
21 Beware! Do not turn to iniquity;
because of that you have been tried by affliction.
22 See, God is exalted in his power;
who is a teacher like him?
23 Who has prescribed for him his way,
or who can say, 'You have done wrong'?

Elihu Proclaims God's Majesty

24 "Remember to extol his work,
of which mortals have sung.
25 All people have looked on it;
everyone watches it from far away.
26 Surely God is great, and we do not know him;
the number of his years is unsearchable.
27 For he draws up the drops of water;
he distills[b] his mist in rain,

[y] Traditional rendering of Heb *Shaddai* [z] Theodotion Symmachus Compare Vg: Meaning of Heb uncertain [a] Heb *ends among the temple prostitutes* [b] Cn: Heb *they distill*

36.24-37.24 Elihu's Praise of God. Elihu describes how God uses the powers of nature – rain, clouds, storms, winds, snow, lightning – to bring benefits or disasters on the human world. Humans must learn to acknowledge and respect God Almighty (in Hebrew, *Shaddai*).

35.11 Ps 94.12; Lk 12.24
35.12 Prov 1.28
35.13 Job 27.9; Prov 15.29; Isa 1.15; Jer 11.11
35.14 Ps 37.5,6
35.15 Eccl 8.11
35.16 Job 34.37; 34.35
36.3 Job 8.3; 37.23
36.4 Job 33.3; 37.16
36.5 Ps 22.24; Job 12.13
36.6 Job 8.22; 5.15
36.7 Ps 33.18; 113.8
36.9 Job 15.25
36.10 Job 33.16; 2 Kings 17.13
36.11 Isa 1.19,20
36.12 Job 15.22; 4.21
36.13 Rom 2.5
36.14 Job 15.32; 22.16
36.15 Ps 119.67; ver 10
36.16 Hos 2.14; Ps 118.5; 23.5
36.18 Job 34.33; Jon 4.4,9; Job 33.24
36.20 Job 34.20,25
36.21 Ps 66.18; Heb 11.25
36.22 Isa 40.13; 1 Cor 2.16
36.23 Job 34.13; 8.3
36.24 2 Sam 7.26; Ps 35.27; 59.16
36.26 Ps 102.24
36.27 Ps 147.8

38.1-40.2 God's Response to Job's Challenge. The LORD replies to Job's complaint of divine indifference and injustice with a series of rhetorical questions which point to the absolute sovereignty of God as evident in the establishment of the earth (38.4-7), the control of the seas (38.8-11), and the continuing pattern of alternating day and night (38.12), and in his ability to shape the surface of the earth, and to get rid of the wicked (38.13-14), where the image of shaking dust from a cloth is combined with that of a mold which shapes clay. Under God's sovereignty are access to the *gates of death* (38.16-17), control of the seasons and fertility cycles (38.19-20), the movement of the stars and the clouds (38.31-37), and the life of wild animals and warhorses (38.39-39.30). Job is told to voice his response to this challenge from God.

28 which the skies pour down
and drop upon mortals abundantly.
29 Can anyone understand the spreading of the clouds,
the thunderings of his pavilion?
30 See, he scatters his lightning around him
and covers the roots of the sea.
31 For by these he governs peoples;
he gives food in abundance.
32 He covers his hands with the lightning,
and commands it to strike the mark.
33 Its crashing[c] tells about him;
he is jealous[c] with anger against iniquity.

37 "At this also my heart trembles,
and leaps out of its place.
2 Listen, listen to the thunder of his voice
and the rumbling that comes from his mouth.
3 Under the whole heaven he lets it loose,
and his lightning to the corners of the earth.
4 After it his voice roars;
he thunders with his majestic voice
and he does not restrain the lightnings[d] when his voice is heard.
5 God thunders wondrously with his voice;
he does great things that we cannot comprehend.
6 For to the snow he says, 'Fall on the earth';
and the shower of rain, his heavy shower of rain,
7 serves as a sign on everyone's hand,
so that all whom he has made may know it.[e]
8 Then the animals go into their lairs
and remain in their dens.
9 From its chamber comes the whirlwind,
and cold from the scattering winds.
10 By the breath of God ice is given,
and the broad waters are frozen fast.
11 He loads the thick cloud with moisture;
the clouds scatter his lightning.
12 They turn round and round by his guidance,
to accomplish all that he commands them
on the face of the habitable world.
13 Whether for correction, or for his land,
or for love, he causes it to happen.

14 "Hear this, O Job;
stop and consider the wondrous works of God.
15 Do you know how God lays his command upon them,
and causes the lightning of his cloud to shine?
16 Do you know the balancings of the clouds,
the wondrous works of the one whose knowledge is perfect,
17 you whose garments are hot
when the earth is still because of the south wind?
18 Can you, like him, spread out the skies,
hard as a molten mirror?
19 Teach us what we shall say to him;
we cannot draw up our case because of darkness.
20 Should he be told that I want to speak?
Did anyone ever wish to be swallowed up?
21 Now, no one can look on the light
when it is bright in the skies,
when the wind has passed and cleared them.
22 Out of the north comes golden splendor;
around God is awesome majesty.
23 The Almighty[f]—we cannot find him;
he is great in power and justice,
and abundant righteousness he will not violate.
24 Therefore mortals fear him;
he does not regard any who are wise in their own conceit."

The LORD Answers Job

38 Then the LORD answered Job out of the whirlwind:
2 "Who is this that darkens counsel by words without knowledge?
3 Gird up your loins like a man,
I will question you, and you shall declare to me.

4 "Where were you when I laid the foundation of the earth?
Tell me, if you have understanding.
5 Who determined its measurements—
surely you know!

[c] Meaning of Heb uncertain [d] Heb *them* [e] Meaning of Heb of verse 7 uncertain [f] Traditional rendering of Heb *Shaddai*

36.29 Job 37.11,16; 26.14
36.31 Job 37.13; Ps 136.25
36.32 Job 37.15
36.33 Job 37.2
37.2 Job 36.33
37.3 ver 12
37.4 Ps 29.3
37.5 Job 5.9; 36.26
37.6 Job 38.22; 36.27
37.7 Job 12.14
37.8 Ps 104.22
37.9 Job 9.9; Ps 147.17
37.10 Job 38.29; Ps 147.17
37.11 Job 36.27,29; ver 15
37.12 Ps 148.8; Isa 14.21; 27.6; Prov 8.31
37.13 Ex 9.18; 1 Sam 12.18; Job 38.26; 1 Kings 18.45
37.14 Ps 111.2
37.16 ver 5,14,23; Job 36.4
37.18 Job 9.8; Ps 104.2; Isa 44.24
37.23 1 Tim 6.16; Job 9.4; 8.3; Isa 63.9
37.24 Mt 10.28; 11.25; 1 Cor 1.26
38.1 Job 40.6
38.2 Job 42.3; 35.16; 1 Tim 1.7
38.3 Job 40.7
38.4 Ps 104.5; Prov 8.29

38.6 Job 26.7
38.7 Job 1.6
38.8 Gen 1.9
38.9 Prov 30.4
38.10 Job 26.10
38.11 Ps 89.9
38.12 Ps 74.16
38.13 Ps 104.35
38.15 Job 18.5; Ps 10.15
38.16 Ps 77.19
38.17 Ps 9.13
38.18 Job 28.24
38.20 Job 26.10; 24.13
38.21 Job 15.7
38.22 Job 37.6
38.23 Ex 9.18; Josh 10.11; Isa 30.30; Ezek 13.11,13; Rev 16.21
38.24 Job 26.10; 27.21
38.25 Job 28.26
38.26 Job 36.27; Ps 107.35
38.27 Ps 104.13,14
38.28 Ps 147.8; Jer 14.22
38.29 Ps 147.16,17
38.31 Job 9.9; Am 5.8
38.33 Job 31.35
38.34 ver 37; Job 22.11; 36.27,28
38.35 Job 36.32; 37.3
38.36 Job 32.8; Ps 51.6; Eccl 2.26; Job 32.8

Or who stretched the line upon it?
6 On what were its bases sunk,
or who laid its cornerstone
7 when the morning stars sang together
and all the heavenly beings[g] shouted for joy?

8 "Or who shut in the sea with doors
when it burst out from the womb?—
9 when I made the clouds its garment,
and thick darkness its swaddling band,
10 and prescribed bounds for it,
and set bars and doors,
11 and said, 'Thus far shall you come, and no farther,
and here shall your proud waves be stopped'?

12 "Have you commanded the morning since your days began,
and caused the dawn to know its place,
13 so that it might take hold of the skirts of the earth,
and the wicked be shaken out of it?
14 It is changed like clay under the seal,
and it is dyed[h] like a garment.
15 Light is withheld from the wicked,
and their uplifted arm is broken.

16 "Have you entered into the springs of the sea,
or walked in the recesses of the deep?
17 Have the gates of death been revealed to you,
or have you seen the gates of deep darkness?
18 Have you comprehended the expanse of the earth?
Declare, if you know all this.

19 "Where is the way to the dwelling of light,
and where is the place of darkness,
20 that you may take it to its territory
and that you may discern the paths to its home?
21 Surely you know, for you were born then,
and the number of your days is great!

22 "Have you entered the storehouses of the snow,
or have you seen the storehouses of the hail,
23 which I have reserved for the time of trouble,
for the day of battle and war?
24 What is the way to the place where the light is distributed,
or where the east wind is scattered upon the earth?

25 "Who has cut a channel for the torrents of rain,
and a way for the thunderbolt,
26 to bring rain on a land where no one lives,
on the desert, which is empty of human life,
27 to satisfy the waste and desolate land,
and to make the ground put forth grass?

28 "Has the rain a father,
or who has begotten the drops of dew?
29 From whose womb did the ice come forth,
and who has given birth to the hoarfrost of heaven?
30 The waters become hard like stone,
and the face of the deep is frozen.

31 "Can you bind the chains of the Pleiades,
or loose the cords of Orion?
32 Can you lead forth the Mazzaroth in their season,
or can you guide the Bear with its children?
33 Do you know the ordinances of the heavens?
Can you establish their rule on the earth?

34 "Can you lift up your voice to the clouds,
so that a flood of waters may cover you?
35 Can you send forth lightnings, so that they may go
and say to you, 'Here we are'?
36 Who has put wisdom in the inward parts,[i]
or given understanding to the mind?[i]
37 Who has the wisdom to number the clouds?
Or who can tilt the waterskins of the heavens,

[g] Heb *sons of God* [h] Cn: Heb *and they stand forth* [i] Meaning of Heb uncertain

38 when the dust runs into a mass
and the clods cling together?

39 "Can you hunt the prey for the lion,
or satisfy the appetite of the young lions,
40 when they crouch in their dens,
or lie in wait in their covert?
41 Who provides for the raven its prey,
when its young ones cry to God,
and wander about for lack of food?

39 "Do you know when the mountain goats give birth?
Do you observe the calving of the deer?
2 Can you number the months that they fulfill,
and do you know the time when they give birth,
3 when they crouch to give birth to their offspring,
and are delivered of their young?
4 Their young ones become strong, they grow up in the open;
they go forth, and do not return to them.

5 "Who has let the wild ass go free?
Who has loosed the bonds of the swift ass,
6 to which I have given the steppe for its home,
the salt land for its dwelling place?
7 It scorns the tumult of the city;
it does not hear the shouts of the driver.
8 It ranges the mountains as its pasture,
and it searches after every green thing.

9 "Is the wild ox willing to serve you?
Will it spend the night at your crib?
10 Can you tie it in the furrow with ropes,
or will it harrow the valleys after you?
11 Will you depend on it because its strength is great,
and will you hand over your labor to it?
12 Do you have faith in it that it will return,
and bring your grain to your threshing floor?[j]

13 "The ostrich's wings flap wildly,
though its pinions lack plumage.[k]
14 For it leaves its eggs to the earth,
and lets them be warmed on the ground,
15 forgetting that a foot may crush them,
and that a wild animal may trample them.
16 It deals cruelly with its young, as if they were not its own;
though its labor should be in vain, yet it has no fear;
17 because God has made it forget wisdom,
and given it no share in understanding.
18 When it spreads its plumes aloft,[k]
it laughs at the horse and its rider.

19 "Do you give the horse its might?
Do you clothe its neck with mane?
20 Do you make it leap like the locust?
Its majestic snorting is terrible.
21 It paws[l] violently, exults mightily;
it goes out to meet the weapons.
22 It laughs at fear, and is not dismayed;
it does not turn back from the sword.
23 Upon it rattle the quiver,
the flashing spear, and the javelin.
24 With fierceness and rage it swallows the ground;
it cannot stand still at the sound of the trumpet.
25 When the trumpet sounds, it says 'Aha!'
From a distance it smells the battle,
the thunder of the captains, and the shouting.

26 "Is it by your wisdom that the hawk soars,
and spreads its wings toward the south?
27 Is it at your command that the eagle mounts up
and makes its nest on high?
28 It lives on the rock and makes its home
in the fastness of the rocky crag.
29 From there it spies the prey;
its eyes see it from far away.
30 Its young ones suck up blood;
and where the slain are, there it is."

40 And the LORD said to Job:
2 "Shall a faultfinder contend with the Almighty?[m]
Anyone who argues with God must respond."

[j] Heb *your grain and your threshing floor* [k] Meaning of Heb uncertain [l] Gk Syr Vg: Heb *they dig* [m] Traditional rendering of Heb *Shaddai*

38.39 Ps 104.21
38.40 Job 38.8; Ps 17.12
38.41 Ps 147.9; Mt 6.26
39.1 Ps 29.9
39.3 1 Sam 4.19
39.5 Job 6.5; 11.12; 24.5
39.6 Job 24.5; Jer 2.24; Hos 8.9; Ps 107.34
39.9 Num 23.22; Deut 33.17
39.16 Lam 4.3; ver 22
39.17 Job 35.11
39.19 Ps 147.10
39.20 Joel 2.5; Jer 8.16
39.21 Jer 8.6
39.24 Jer 4.19; Ezek 7.14; Am 3.6
39.25 Josh 6.5; Am 1.14; 2.2
39.27 Jer 46.16; Ob 4
39.29 Job 9.26
39.30 Mt 24.28; Lk 17.37
40.1 Job 33.13; 13.3; 23.4; 31.35

40.4 Job 42.6; 29.9
40.5 Job 9.3,15
40.6 Job 38.1
40.7 Job 38.3; 42.4
40.8 Isa 14.27; Rom 3.4
40.9 2 Chr 32.8; Job 37.5
40.10 Ps 93.1; 104.1
40.11 Isa 42.25; 2.12; Dan 4.37
40.12 1 Sam 2.7; Isa 13.11; 63.3; Job 36.20
40.14 Ps 20.6; 60.5; 108.6
40.15 ver 19
40.19 Job 41.33; ver 15
40.20 Ps 104.26
40.22 Isa 44.1
40.24 Prov 1.17
41.1 Ps 104.26; Isa 27.1
41.2 Isa 37.29
41.10 Job 3.8
41.11 Rom 11.35; Ex 19.5; Deut 10.14; Ps 24.1; 50.12; 1 Cor 10.26

Job's Response to God

3 Then Job answered the LORD:
4 "See, I am of small account; what shall
I answer you?
I lay my hand on my mouth.
5 I have spoken once, and I will not answer;
twice, but will proceed no further."

God's Challenge to Job

6 Then the LORD answered Job out of the
whirlwind:
7 "Gird up your loins like a man;
I will question you, and you declare
to me.
8 Will you even put me in the wrong?
Will you condemn me that you may
be justified?
9 Have you an arm like God,
and can you thunder with a voice
like his?

10 "Deck yourself with majesty and
dignity;
clothe yourself with glory and
splendor.
11 Pour out the overflowings of your anger,
and look on all who are proud, and
abase them.
12 Look on all who are proud, and bring
them low;
tread down the wicked where they
stand.
13 Hide them all in the dust together;
bind their faces in the world below.[n]
14 Then I will also acknowledge to you
that your own right hand can give
you victory.

15 "Look at Behemoth,
which I made just as I made you;
it eats grass like an ox.
16 Its strength is in its loins,
and its power in the muscles of its belly.
17 It makes its tail stiff like a cedar;
the sinews of its thighs are knit
together.
18 Its bones are tubes of bronze,
its limbs like bars of iron.

19 "It is the first of the great acts of God—
only its Maker can approach it with
the sword.
20 For the mountains yield food for it
where all the wild animals play.
21 Under the lotus plants it lies,
in the covert of the reeds and in the
marsh.
22 The lotus trees cover it for shade;
the willows of the wadi surround it.
23 Even if the river is turbulent, it is not
frightened;
it is confident though Jordan rushes
against its mouth.
24 Can one take it with hooks[o]
or pierce its nose with a snare?

41[p] "Can you draw out Leviathan[q]
with a fishhook,
or press down its tongue with a cord?
2 Can you put a rope in its nose,
or pierce its jaw with a hook?
3 Will it make many supplications to you?
Will it speak soft words to you?
4 Will it make a covenant with you
to be taken as your servant forever?
5 Will you play with it as with a bird,
or will you put it on leash for your girls?
6 Will traders bargain over it?
Will they divide it up among the
merchants?
7 Can you fill its skin with harpoons,
or its head with fishing spears?
8 Lay hands on it;
think of the battle; you will not do it
again!
9[r] Any hope of capturing it[s] will be
disappointed;
were not even the gods[t]
overwhelmed at the sight of it?
10 No one is so fierce as to dare to stir it up.
Who can stand before it?[u]
11 Who can confront it[u] and be safe?[v]
—under the whole heaven, who?[w]

12 "I will not keep silence concerning its
limbs,
or its mighty strength, or its splendid
frame.
13 Who can strip off its outer garment?
Who can penetrate its double coat of
mail?[x]
14 Who can open the doors of its face?
There is terror all around its teeth.
15 Its back[y] is made of shields in rows,
shut up closely as with a seal.
16 One is so near to another
that no air can come between them.

[n] Heb *the hidden place* [o] Cn: Heb *in his eyes* [p] Ch 40.25 in Heb [q] Or *the crocodile* [r] Ch 41.1 in Heb [s] Heb *of it* [t] Cn Compare Symmachus Syr: Heb *one is* [u] Heb *me* [v] Gk: Heb *that I shall repay* [w] Heb *to me* [x] Gk: Heb *bridle* [y] Cn Compare Gk Vg: Heb *pride*

40.3-5 Job's Response to God. After the extensive complaints and the petitions for a hearing before God, Job declines to follow his earlier attack with an *answer.* **40.6-41.34** God's Final Challenge to Job. Job is challenged to demonstrate his qualifications for reproaching God, whose *majesty* and power are evident in his destruction of the wicked (40.10-14) and in his having created *Behemoth* (40.15-24) and *Leviathan* (41.1-34). Behemoth, the hippopotamus, and Leviathan, the crocodile, not only represent the marvels of God's creative powers, but also symbolize the historic and cosmic enemies of Israel, past and present. Even huge, powerful creatures like these, which live *without fear,* are subject to the creator. How much more must Job acknowledge the futility of his own opposition to God and his foolish attempt at a *covenant* to prove his innocence. He, like these beasts, is subject to the sovereignty of God, as Job must acknowledge.

42.1-17 Epilogue.
42.1-6 Job's response to the challenge is to acknowledge God's sovereignty and to confess his own false claims of understanding divine wisdom. Since God has graciously addressed him directly (*my eye sees you*), he is ready to repent.
42.7-9 Job's critical friends seek reconciliation with him through their prayers and offerings, and Job's own prayer finds acceptance with the LORD.
42.10-17 The LORD grants to Job twice the amount of his previous possessions, includings flocks and *four generations* of beautiful children.

17 They are joined one to another;
they clasp each other and cannot be separated.
18 Its sneezes flash forth light,
and its eyes are like the eyelids of the dawn.
19 From its mouth go flaming torches;
sparks of fire leap out.
20 Out of its nostrils comes smoke,
as from a boiling pot and burning rushes.
21 Its breath kindles coals,
and a flame comes out of its mouth.
22 In its neck abides strength,
and terror dances before it.
23 The folds of its flesh cling together;
it is firmly cast and immovable.
24 Its heart is as hard as stone,
as hard as the lower millstone.
25 When it raises itself up the gods are afraid;
at the crashing they are beside themselves.
26 Though the sword reaches it, it does not avail,
nor does the spear, the dart, or the javelin.
27 It counts iron as straw,
and bronze as rotten wood.
28 The arrow cannot make it flee;
slingstones, for it, are turned to chaff.
29 Clubs are counted as chaff;
it laughs at the rattle of javelins.
30 Its underparts are like sharp potsherds;
it spreads itself like a threshing sledge on the mire.
31 It makes the deep boil like a pot;
it makes the sea like a pot of ointment.
32 It leaves a shining wake behind it;
one would think the deep to be white-haired.
33 On earth it has no equal,
a creature without fear.
34 It surveys everything that is lofty;
it is king over all that are proud."

Job Is Humbled and Satisfied

42 Then Job answered the LORD:
2 "I know that you can do all things,
and that no purpose of yours can be thwarted.
3 'Who is this that hides counsel without knowledge?'
Therefore I have uttered what I did not understand,
things too wonderful for me, which I did not know.
4 'Hear, and I will speak;
I will question you, and you declare to me.'
5 I had heard of you by the hearing of the ear,
but now my eye sees you;
6 therefore I despise myself,
and repent in dust and ashes."

Job's Friends Are Humiliated

7 After the LORD had spoken these words
to Job, the LORD said to Eliphaz the Temanite:
"My wrath is kindled against you and against
your two friends; for you have not spoken
of me what is right, as my servant Job has.
8Now therefore take seven bulls and seven
rams, and go to my servant Job, and offer
up for yourselves a burnt offering; and my
servant Job shall pray for you, for I will
accept his prayer not to deal with you
according to your folly; for you have not
spoken of me what is right, as my servant
Job has done." 9So Eliphaz the Temanite and
Bildad the Shuhite and Zophar the Naamathite
went and did what the LORD had told them;
and the LORD accepted Job's prayer.

Job's Fortunes Are Restored Twofold

10 And the LORD restored the fortunes of
Job when he had prayed for his friends; and
the LORD gave Job twice as much as he had
before. 11Then there came to him all his
brothers and sisters and all who had known
him before, and they ate bread with him in
his house; they showed him sympathy and
comforted him for all the evil that the LORD
had brought upon him; and each of them
gave him a piece of money[z] and a gold ring.
12The LORD blessed the latter days of Job
more than his beginning; and he had fourteen thousand sheep, six thousand camels,
a thousand yoke of oxen, and a thousand
donkeys. 13He also had seven sons and three
daughters. 14He named the first Jemimah,
the second Keziah, and the third Keren-
happuch. 15In all the land there were no
women so beautiful as Job's daughters; and
their father gave them an inheritance along
with their brothers. 16After this Job lived one
hundred and forty years, and saw his children, and his children's children, four generations. 17And Job died, old and full of days.

41.18 Job 3.9
41.33 Job 40.19
42.2 Gen 18.14; Mt 19.26; Mk 10.27; Lk 18.27
42.3 Job 38.2; Ps 40.5; 131.1; 139.6
42.4 Job 38.3; 40.7
42.5 Job 26.14; Judg 13.22; Isa 6.5
42.6 Ezra 9.6; Job 40.4
42.7 Job 32.3; ver 1-6; 40.3-5
42.8 Num 23.1; Job 1.5; Jas 5.15,16
42.10 Ps 14.7; 126.1
42.11 Job 19.13
42.12 Job 1.10; 8.7; 1.3
42.13 Job 1.2
42.16 Job 5.26; Prov 3.16
42.17 Gen 25.8

[z] Heb *a qesitah*

THE PSALMS

See the Introductions, pp. 4, 48, and 50-51 above.

BOOK I

(Psalms 1–41)

Psalm 1

The Two Ways

1 Happy are those
who do not follow the advice of the wicked,
or take the path that sinners tread,
or sit in the seat of scoffers;
2 but their delight is in the law of the Lord,
and on his law they meditate day and night.
3 They are like trees
planted by streams of water,
which yield their fruit in its season,
and their leaves do not wither.
In all that they do, they prosper.

4 The wicked are not so,
but are like chaff that the wind drives away.
5 Therefore the wicked will not stand in the judgment,
nor sinners in the congregation of the righteous;
6 for the Lord watches over the way of the righteous,
but the way of the wicked will perish.

Psalm 2

God's Promise to His Anointed

1 Why do the nations conspire,
and the peoples plot in vain?
2 The kings of the earth set themselves,
and the rulers take counsel together,
against the Lord and his anointed, saying,
3 "Let us burst their bonds asunder,
and cast their cords from us."

4 He who sits in the heavens laughs;
the Lord has them in derision.
5 Then he will speak to them in his wrath,
and terrify them in his fury, saying,
6 "I have set my king on Zion, my holy hill."
7 I will tell of the decree of the Lord:
He said to me, "You are my son;
today I have begotten you.
8 Ask of me, and I will make the nations your heritage,
and the ends of the earth your possession.
9 You shall break them with a rod of iron,
and dash them in pieces like a potter's vessel."

10 Now therefore, O kings, be wise;
be warned, O rulers of the earth.
11 Serve the Lord with fear,
with trembling 12 kiss his feet,[a]
or he will be angry, and you will perish in the way;
for his wrath is quickly kindled.

Happy are all who take refuge in him.

Psalm 3

Trust in God under Adversity

A Psalm of David, when he fled from his son Absalom.

1 O Lord, how many are my foes!
Many are rising against me;
2 many are saying to me,
"There is no help for you[b] in God."
Selah

3 But you, O Lord, are a shield around me,
my glory, and the one who lifts up my head.
4 I cry aloud to the Lord,
and he answers me from his holy hill.
Selah

5 I lie down and sleep;
I wake again, for the Lord sustains me.
6 I am not afraid of ten thousands of people
who have set themselves against me all around.

7 Rise up, O Lord!
Deliver me, O my God!
For you strike all my enemies on the cheek;
you break the teeth of the wicked.

8 Deliverance belongs to the Lord;
may your blessing be on your people!
Selah

[a] Cn: Meaning of Heb of verses 11b and 12a is uncertain [b] Syr: Heb *him*

Ps 1 Written as an introduction to the entire collection of psalms, this psalm sounds basic themes: the happiness of those whose *delight is in the law of the Lord*, which serves as the subject of their continuing meditation (1.1-2), and produces the fruit of proper living and prosperity (1.3). In contrast with those who ignore or disobey that law and suffer divine punishment (1.4-5), *the righteous* will be watched over by God continually.
Ps 2 Celebrating the enthronement of Israel's king, the rulers of other nations of the earth are warned against challenging his power, since it is God who set him (*the Lord's anointed*, chosen and empowered by God) on the throne in Jerusalem, or *Zion* (2.1-6). The king is invited to ask the Lord for the power to dominate and defeat all other nations of the earth, while they are told to subject themselves wholly to him (2.7-12).
Ps 3 The first of a series of psalms of lament and trust (Ps 3-8), this one deplores the numbers of *foes* that have risen up, but expresses confidence in the protection and access the Lord offers on *his holy hill*, in Jerusalem.

1.1 Prov 4.14; Job 21.16; Ps 17.4; 26.5; Jer 15.17
1.2 Ps 119.35; Josh 1.8
1.3 Jer 17.8; Ezek 47.12; Gen 39.3; Ps 128.2
1.4 Job 21.18; Isa 17.13
1.5 Ps 5.5; 9.7,8,16; 111.1; 149.1
1.6 Ps 37.18; 2 Tim 2.19; Ps 9.3-6
2.1 Acts 4.25; Ps 21.11
2.2 Ps 48.4-6; 74.18,23; Jn 1.41
2.4 Ps 59.8
2.5 Ps 21.8,9
2.6 Ps 3.4
2.7 Acts 13.33; Heb 1.5
2.8 Ps 22.27
2.9 Ps 89.23; Rev 2.27
2.11 Heb 12.28; Ps 119.119,120
2.12 Jn 5.23; Ps 34.8
3.3 Ps 28.7; 27.6
3.4 Ps 34.4; 99.9
3.5 Lev 26.6; Ps 139.18
3.8 Isa 43.11; Jer 3.23; Num 6.23-27

Ps 4 Deploring the shame and deceit heaped on him by enemies, the psalmist advises continuing confidence and offering of sacrifices, which will bring light, joy, and peace to the faithful.
Ps 5 This petition to the LORD declares that the evil and their lies and false claims will be destroyed, while God's *steadfast love* will support and sustain his obedient people.
Ps 6 An appeal to the LORD to be gracious to one who is struck with terror, and who fears death, in whose dark realm (*Sheol*) humans will be able neither to recall what God has done nor to praise him for his kindnesses. The lament turns to gratitude in assurance that God has heard the petition and that the enemies will be smitten with *terror*.

Psalm 4

Confident Plea for Deliverance from Enemies

To the leader: with stringed instruments. A Psalm of David.

1 Answer me when I call, O God of my right!
You gave me room when I was in distress.
Be gracious to me, and hear my prayer.

2 How long, you people, shall my honor suffer shame?
How long will you love vain words, and seek after lies?
Selah
3 But know that the LORD has set apart the faithful for himself;
the LORD hears when I call to him.

4 When you are disturbed,[c] do not sin;
ponder it on your beds, and be silent.
Selah
5 Offer right sacrifices,
and put your trust in the LORD.

6 There are many who say, "O that we might see some good!
Let the light of your face shine on us, O LORD!"
7 You have put gladness in my heart
more than when their grain and wine abound.

8 I will both lie down and sleep in peace;
for you alone, O LORD, make me lie down in safety.

Psalm 5

Trust in God for Deliverance from Enemies

To the leader: for the flutes. A Psalm of David.

1 Give ear to my words, O LORD;
give heed to my sighing.
2 Listen to the sound of my cry,
my King and my God,
for to you I pray.
3 O LORD, in the morning you hear my voice;
in the morning I plead my case to you, and watch.

4 For you are not a God who delights in wickedness;
evil will not sojourn with you.
5 The boastful will not stand before your eyes;
you hate all evildoers.
6 You destroy those who speak lies;
the LORD abhors the bloodthirsty and deceitful.

7 But I, through the abundance of your steadfast love,
will enter your house,
I will bow down toward your holy temple
in awe of you.
8 Lead me, O LORD, in your righteousness
because of my enemies;
make your way straight before me.

9 For there is no truth in their mouths;
their hearts are destruction;
their throats are open graves;
they flatter with their tongues.
10 Make them bear their guilt, O God;
let them fall by their own counsels;
because of their many transgressions cast them out,
for they have rebelled against you.

11 But let all who take refuge in you rejoice;
let them ever sing for joy.
Spread your protection over them,
so that those who love your name may exult in you.
12 For you bless the righteous, O LORD;
you cover them with favor as with a shield.

Psalm 6

Prayer for Recovery from Grave Illness

To the leader: with stringed instruments; according to The Sheminith. A Psalm of David.

1 O LORD, do not rebuke me in your anger,
or discipline me in your wrath.
2 Be gracious to me, O LORD, for I am languishing;
O LORD, heal me, for my bones are shaking with terror.
3 My soul also is struck with terror,
while you, O LORD—how long?

4 Turn, O LORD, save my life;
deliver me for the sake of your steadfast love.
5 For in death there is no remembrance of you;
in Sheol who can give you praise?

6 I am weary with my moaning;
every night I flood my bed with tears;

[c] Or *are angry*

4.1 Ps 27.7; 18.6; 24.5; 18.18; 17.6
4.2 Ps 31.6,18
4.3 Ps 31.23; 6.8,9
4.4 Ps 33.8; Eph 4.26; Ps 77.6
4.5 Deut 33.19; Ps 50.14; 37.3
4.6 Num 6.26
4.7 Acts 14.17; Isa 9.3
4.8 Ps 3.5; Lev 25.18
5.1 Ps 54.2; 19.14
5.2 Ps 3.4; 84.3
5.3 Ps 88.13; Hab 2.1
5.4 Ps 11.5; 92.15
5.5 Ps 73.3; 1.5; 11.5
5.6 Rev 21.8; Ps 55.23
5.7 Ps 69.13; 28.2
5.8 Ps 27.11; 31.1
5.9 Deut 32.20; Lk 11.44; Rom 3.13; Ps 12.2
5.10 Ps 9.16; Lam 1.5; Ps 107.10,11
5.11 Ps 2.12; Isa 65.13; Zech 9.15; Ps 69.36
5.12 Ps 112.2; 32.7,10
6.1 Ps 38.1; 2.5
6.2 Ps 51.1; 41.4
6.3 Jn 12.27; Ps 90.13
6.5 Ps 30.9; Isa 38.18

I drench my couch with my weeping.
7 My eyes waste away because of grief;
they grow weak because of all my foes.

8 Depart from me, all you workers of evil,
for the LORD has heard the sound of my weeping.
9 The LORD has heard my supplication;
the LORD accepts my prayer.
10 All my enemies shall be ashamed and struck with terror;
they shall turn back, and in a moment be put to shame.

Psalm 7

Plea for Help against Persecutors

A Shiggaion of David, which he sang to the LORD *concerning Cush, a Benjaminite.*

1 O LORD my God, in you I take refuge;
save me from all my pursuers, and deliver me,
2 or like a lion they will tear me apart;
they will drag me away, with no one to rescue.

3 O LORD my God, if I have done this,
if there is wrong in my hands,
4 if I have repaid my ally with harm
or plundered my foe without cause,
5 then let the enemy pursue and overtake me,
trample my life to the ground,
and lay my soul in the dust.
Selah

6 Rise up, O LORD, in your anger;
lift yourself up against the fury of my enemies;
awake, O my God;[d] you have appointed a judgment.
7 Let the assembly of the peoples be gathered around you,
and over it take your seat[e] on high.
8 The LORD judges the peoples;
judge me, O LORD, according to my righteousness
and according to the integrity that is in me.

9 O let the evil of the wicked come to an end,
but establish the righteous,
you who test the minds and hearts,
O righteous God.
10 God is my shield,
who saves the upright in heart.
11 God is a righteous judge,
and a God who has indignation every day.

12 If one does not repent, God[f] will whet his sword;
he has bent and strung his bow;
13 he has prepared his deadly weapons,
making his arrows fiery shafts.
14 See how they conceive evil,
and are pregnant with mischief,
and bring forth lies.
15 They make a pit, digging it out,
and fall into the hole that they have made.
16 Their mischief returns upon their own heads,
and on their own heads their violence descends.

17 I will give to the LORD the thanks due to his righteousness,
and sing praise to the name of the LORD, the Most High.

Psalm 8

Divine Majesty and Human Dignity

To the leader: according to The Gittith. A Psalm of David.

1 O LORD, our Sovereign,
how majestic is your name in all the earth!

You have set your glory above the heavens.
2 Out of the mouths of babes and infants
you have founded a bulwark because of your foes,
to silence the enemy and the avenger.

3 When I look at your heavens, the work of your fingers,
the moon and the stars that you have established;
4 what are human beings that you are mindful of them,
mortals[g] that you care for them?

5 Yet you have made them a little lower than God,[h]

[d] Or *awake for me* [e] Cn: Heb *return* [f] Heb *he* [g] Heb *ben adam*, lit. *son of man* [h] Or *than the divine beings* or *angels*: Heb *elohim*

6.7 Ps 31.9
6.8 Ps 119.115; Lk 13.27; Ps 5.5; 28.6
6.9 Ps 116.1; 66.19,20
7.1 Ps 11.1; 31.15
7.2 Ps 17.12; 50.22
7.3 2 Sam 16.7; 1 Sam 24.11
7.4 1 Sam 24.7
7.6 Ps 3.7; 94.2; 44.23
7.7 Ps 68.18
7.8 Ps 96.13; 18.20; 35.24
7.9 Ps 34.21; Isa 54.14; 1 Chr 28.9; Jer 11.20; Rev 2.23
7.10 Ps 18.2; 125.4
7.11 Ps 50.6; Isa 34.2
7.12 Ezek 3.19; 33.9; Deut 32.41; Ps 21.12
7.13 Ps 64.7
7.14 Isa 59.4; Jas 1.15
7.15 Job 4.8; Ps 9.15; Eccl 10.8
7.16 Ps 140.9; Esth 9.25
7.17 Ps 71.15,16; 9.2
8.1 Ps 66.2; 148.13; 113.4
8.2 Mt 21.16; Ps 44.16
8.3 Ps 89.11; 102.5; 136.9
8.4 Job 7.17; Ps 144.3; Heb 2.6
8.5 Ps 103.4; 21.5; Heb 2.9

Ps 7 Another plea for deliverance from antagonists, with an expression that the petitioner has been morally responsible in all his dealings and will ultimately be vindicated by God, while the wicked will suffer the fearful consequences of their moral wrongs.

Ps 8 A psalm of praise to the LORD as the glorious fashioner of all creation, and as the one who has given *human beings (*described here as "children of Adam"), whom God has made as *lower* only than himself, and to whom he has given dominion over *every living thing that he created* (Gen 1.28-30).

Ps 9 A psalm of gratitude for God's *wonderful deeds*, who from his eternal throne has defeated the enemies, ruined their cities, and provided a place of security for his people. The destiny of the wicked is death *in the pit* of *Sheol*, while the needy and the poor will be remembered by God.
Ps 10 This lament pictures the oppression of the poor and helpless by the wicked, who assume that there is no God who will hold them accountable for their misdeeds and injustices, and who now seem to prosper (10.1-11). The call is for God to take the initiative in vindicating *the oppressed* and to demonstrate his role as eternal *king* of the universe by putting the wicked to death, while hearing the cry of the needy and mistreated.

and crowned them with glory and honor.
6 You have given them dominion over the works of your hands;
you have put all things under their feet,
7 all sheep and oxen,
and also the beasts of the field,
8 the birds of the air, and the fish of the sea,
whatever passes along the paths of the seas.

9 O LORD, our Sovereign,
how majestic is your name in all the earth!

Psalm 9

God's Power and Justice

To the leader: according to Muth-labben. A Psalm of David.

1 I will give thanks to the LORD with my whole heart;
I will tell of all your wonderful deeds.
2 I will be glad and exult in you;
I will sing praise to your name, O Most High.

3 When my enemies turned back,
they stumbled and perished before you.
4 For you have maintained my just cause;
you have sat on the throne giving righteous judgment.

5 You have rebuked the nations, you have destroyed the wicked;
you have blotted out their name forever and ever.
6 The enemies have vanished in everlasting ruins;
their cities you have rooted out;
the very memory of them has perished.

7 But the LORD sits enthroned forever,
he has established his throne for judgment.
8 He judges the world with righteousness;
he judges the peoples with equity.

9 The LORD is a stronghold for the oppressed,
a stronghold in times of trouble.
10 And those who know your name put their trust in you,
for you, O LORD, have not forsaken those who seek you.

11 Sing praises to the LORD, who dwells in Zion.
Declare his deeds among the peoples.
12 For he who avenges blood is mindful of them;
he does not forget the cry of the afflicted.

13 Be gracious to me, O LORD.
See what I suffer from those who hate me;
you are the one who lifts me up from the gates of death,
14 so that I may recount all your praises,
and, in the gates of daughter Zion,
rejoice in your deliverance.

15 The nations have sunk in the pit that they made;
in the net that they hid has their own foot been caught.
16 The LORD has made himself known, he has executed judgment;
the wicked are snared in the work of their own hands.
Higgaion. Selah

17 The wicked shall depart to Sheol,
all the nations that forget God.

18 For the needy shall not always be forgotten,
nor the hope of the poor perish forever.

19 Rise up, O LORD! Do not let mortals prevail;
let the nations be judged before you.
20 Put them in fear, O LORD;
let the nations know that they are only human. *Selah*

Psalm 10

Prayer for Deliverance from Enemies

1 Why, O LORD, do you stand far off?
Why do you hide yourself in times of trouble?
2 In arrogance the wicked persecute the poor—
let them be caught in the schemes they have devised.

3 For the wicked boast of the desires of their heart,
those greedy for gain curse and renounce the LORD.

8.6 Gen 1.26; Heb 2.8
8.9 ver 1
9.1 Ps 86.12; 26.7
9.2 Ps 5.11; 83.18
9.3 Ps 56.9; 27.2
9.4 Ps 140.12; 47.8; 67.4; 1 Pet 2.23
9.5 Deut 9.14
9.6 Ps 40.15; 34.16
9.7 Ps 29.10; 89.14
9.8 Ps 96.13
9.9 Ps 18.2; 32.7; 37.39
9.10 Ps 91.14; 37.28
9.11 Ps 76.2; 105.1
9.12 Gen 9.5; ver 18
9.13 Ps 30.10; 25.18; 38.19; 30.3
9.14 Ps 106.2; 87.2; 13.5
9.15 Ps 7.15; 35.8
9.16 Isa 64.2; ver 4
9.17 Ps 49.14; 50.22; Job 8.13
9.18 ver 12; Ps 74.19
9.19 Ps 3.7; 2 Chr 14.11; Ps 110.6
9.20 Ps 83.15; Isa 31.3
10.2 Ps 109.16; 7.15; 9.16
10.3 Ps 94.4; Job 1.5,11; ver 13

4 In the pride of their countenance the
wicked say, "God will not seek it
out";
all their thoughts are, "There is no
God."

5 Their ways prosper at all times;
your judgments are on high, out of
their sight;
as for their foes, they scoff at them.
6 They think in their heart, "We shall not
be moved;
throughout all generations we shall
not meet adversity."

7 Their mouths are filled with cursing and
deceit and oppression;
under their tongues are mischief and
iniquity.
8 They sit in ambush in the villages;
in hiding places they murder the
innocent.

Their eyes stealthily watch for the
helpless;
9 they lurk in secret like a lion in its
covert;
they lurk that they may seize the poor;
they seize the poor and drag them off
in their net.

10 They stoop, they crouch,
and the helpless fall by their might.
11 They think in their heart, "God has
forgotten,
he has hidden his face, he will never
see it."

12 Rise up, O LORD; O God, lift up your
hand;
do not forget the oppressed.
13 Why do the wicked renounce God,
and say in their hearts, "You will not
call us to account"?

14 But you do see! Indeed you note trouble
and grief,
that you may take it into your hands;
the helpless commit themselves to you;
you have been the helper of the
orphan.

15 Break the arm of the wicked and
evildoers;
seek out their wickedness until you
find none.
16 The LORD is king forever and ever;
the nations shall perish from his land.

17 O LORD, you will hear the desire of the
meek;
you will strengthen their heart, you
will incline your ear
18 to do justice for the orphan and the
oppressed,
so that those from earth may strike
terror no more.[i]

Psalm 11

Song of Trust in God

To the leader. Of David.

1 In the LORD I take refuge; how can you
say to me,
"Flee like a bird to the mountains;[j]
2 for look, the wicked bend the bow,
they have fitted their arrow to the
string,
to shoot in the dark at the upright in
heart.
3 If the foundations are destroyed,
what can the righteous do?"

4 The LORD is in his holy temple;
the LORD's throne is in heaven.
His eyes behold, his gaze examines
humankind.
5 The LORD tests the righteous and the
wicked,
and his soul hates the lover of
violence.
6 On the wicked he will rain coals of fire
and sulfur;
a scorching wind shall be the portion
of their cup.
7 For the LORD is righteous;
he loves righteous deeds;
the upright shall behold his face.

Psalm 12

Plea for Help in Evil Times

To the leader: according to The Sheminith. A Psalm of David.

1 Help, O LORD, for there is no longer
anyone who is godly;
the faithful have disappeared from
humankind.
2 They utter lies to each other;
with flattering lips and a double heart
they speak.

3 May the LORD cut off all flattering lips,

10.4 ver 13; Ps 14.1
10.6 Ps 30.6; 49.11
10.7 Rom 3.14; Ps 59.12; 73.8; 140.3
10.8 Prov 1.11; Ps 94.6
10.9 Ps 17.12; 59.3; ver 2; 140.5
10.11 ver 4; Job 22.13; Ps 73.11
10.12 Mic 5.9; Ps 9.12
10.14 Job 11.11; Jer 51.56; Ps 37.5; 68.5; Hos 14.3
10.15 Ps 37.17; 9.12
10.16 Ps 29.10; Deut 8.20
10.17 Ps 145.19; 1 Chr 29.18; Ps 34.15
10.18 Ps 82.3; 9.9; Isa 29.20
11.1 Ps 56.11
11.2 Ps 7.12; 64.3,4
11.3 Ps 82.5
11.4 Ps 18.6; 103.19; 34.15,16
11.5 Gen 22.1; Jas 1.12; Ps 5.5
11.6 Ezek 38.22; Jer 4.11,12; Ps 75.8
11.7 Ps 7.9,11; 33.5; 17.15
12.1 Isa 57.1
12.2 Ps 41.6; 55.21; 1 Chr 12.33
12.3 Ps 73.8,9

Ps 11 A statement of confidence in the LORD, who is in control of the world in spite of the efforts of *the wicked.* Enthroned in heaven, he calls all humans to account: *the righteous and the wicked.* He will punish the evildoers and uphold those who live right and are privileged to see *his face.*
Ps 12 A lament for the seeming prosperity of those who are neither faithful nor truthful, and who pride themselves on their apparent success in their endeavors. But the promise is declared that God will take the initiative (*rise up*) to protect his people and to deal with the proud evildoers.

[i] Meaning of Heb uncertain [j] Gk Syr Jerome Tg: Heb *flee to your mountain, O bird*

Ps 13 Disheartened because of God's apparent loss of interest in the faithful oppressed, the psalmist reminds God that for one of his own to die in such a seemingly abandoned condition would bring joy to the *foes* of God's people. The closing lines reaffirm confidence in the reliable love and generosity of God.
Ps 14 Lamenting the widespread corruption of humanity, the seeming lack of those who are *wise* enough to *seek God*, and the grievous mistreatment that his people are receiving, the psalmist asserts confidence in God's support of *the poor* and in the coming restoration of Israel.
Ps 15 A psalm of praise for and specification of the requirements that God has given to those who will live with access to his presence on his *holy hill*, the temple in Jerusalem.

the tongue that makes great boasts,
4 those who say, "With our tongues we will prevail;
our lips are our own—who is our master?"

5 "Because the poor are despoiled, because the needy groan,
I will now rise up," says the LORD;
"I will place them in the safety for which they long."
6 The promises of the LORD are promises that are pure,
silver refined in a furnace on the ground,
purified seven times.

7 You, O LORD, will protect us;
you will guard us from this generation forever.
8 On every side the wicked prowl,
as vileness is exalted among humankind.

Psalm 13

Prayer for Deliverance from Enemies

To the leader. A Psalm of David.

1 How long, O LORD? Will you forget me forever?
How long will you hide your face from me?
2 How long must I bear pain[k] in my soul,
and have sorrow in my heart all day long?
How long shall my enemy be exalted over me?

3 Consider and answer me, O LORD my God!
Give light to my eyes, or I will sleep the sleep of death,
4 and my enemy will say, "I have prevailed";
my foes will rejoice because I am shaken.

5 But I trusted in your steadfast love;
my heart shall rejoice in your salvation.
6 I will sing to the LORD,
because he has dealt bountifully with me.

Psalm 14

Denunciation of Godlessness

To the leader. Of David.

1 Fools say in their hearts, "There is no God."
They are corrupt, they do abominable deeds;
there is no one who does good.

2 The LORD looks down from heaven on humankind
to see if there are any who are wise,
who seek after God.

3 They have all gone astray, they are all alike perverse;
there is no one who does good,
no, not one.

4 Have they no knowledge, all the evildoers
who eat up my people as they eat bread,
and do not call upon the LORD?

5 There they shall be in great terror,
for God is with the company of the righteous.
6 You would confound the plans of the poor,
but the LORD is their refuge.

7 O that deliverance for Israel would come from Zion!
When the LORD restores the fortunes of his people,
Jacob will rejoice; Israel will be glad.

Psalm 15

Who Shall Abide in God's Sanctuary?

A Psalm of David.

1 O LORD, who may abide in your tent?
Who may dwell on your holy hill?

2 Those who walk blamelessly, and do what is right,
and speak the truth from their heart;
3 who do not slander with their tongue,
and do no evil to their friends,
nor take up a reproach against their neighbors;

12.5 Ps 10.18; 3.7; 34.6
12.6 Ps 18.30; Prov 30.5
12.7 Ps 37.28
12.8 Ps 55.10,11
13.1 Job 13.24; Ps 44.24; 88.14
13.2 Ps 42.4,9; 94.3
13.3 Ps 5.1; Ezra 9.8; Jer 51.39
13.4 Jer 20.10; Ps 25.2
13.5 Ps 52.8; 9.14
13.6 Ps 59.16; 116.7
14.1 Ps 10.4; 53.1-6; 73.8; Rom 3.10-12
14.2 Ps 33.13; 92.6; Ezra 6.21
14.3 Ps 58.3; 2 Pet 2.7; Rev 22.11; Ps 143.2
14.4 Ps 82.5; 27.2; 79.6; Isa 64.7
14.5 Ps 73.15
14.6 Ps 9.9; 40.17
14.7 Ps 53.6; Job 42.10
15.1 Ps 24.3-5; 27.5,6; 2.6
15.2 Ps 24.4; 51.6; Eph 4.25
15.3 Lev 19.16; Ex 23.1

[k] Syr: Heb *hold counsels*

4 in whose eyes the wicked are despised,
but who honor those who fear the LORD;
who stand by their oath even to their hurt;
5 who do not lend money at interest,
and do not take a bribe against the innocent.

Those who do these things shall never be moved.

Psalm 16

Song of Trust and Security in God

A Miktam of David.

1 Protect me, O God, for in you I take refuge.
2 I say to the LORD, "You are my Lord;
I have no good apart from you."[l]

3 As for the holy ones in the land, they are the noble,
in whom is all my delight.

4 Those who choose another god multiply their sorrows;[m]
their drink offerings of blood I will not pour out
or take their names upon my lips.

5 The LORD is my chosen portion and my cup;
you hold my lot.
6 The boundary lines have fallen for me in pleasant places;
I have a goodly heritage.

7 I bless the LORD who gives me counsel;
in the night also my heart instructs me.
8 I keep the LORD always before me;
because he is at my right hand, I shall not be moved.

9 Therefore my heart is glad, and my soul rejoices;
my body also rests secure.
10 For you do not give me up to Sheol,
or let your faithful one see the Pit.

11 You show me the path of life.
In your presence there is fullness of joy;
in your right hand are pleasures forevermore.

Psalm 17

Prayer for Deliverance from Persecutors

A Prayer of David.

1 Hear a just cause, O LORD; attend to my cry;
give ear to my prayer from lips free of deceit.
2 From you let my vindication come;
let your eyes see the right.

3 If you try my heart, if you visit me by night,
if you test me, you will find no wickedness in me;
my mouth does not transgress.
4 As for what others do, by the word of your lips
I have avoided the ways of the violent.
5 My steps have held fast to your paths;
my feet have not slipped.

6 I call upon you, for you will answer me, O God;
incline your ear to me, hear my words.
7 Wondrously show your steadfast love,
O savior of those who seek refuge
from their adversaries at your right hand.

8 Guard me as the apple of the eye;
hide me in the shadow of your wings,
9 from the wicked who despoil me,
my deadly enemies who surround me.
10 They close their hearts to pity;
with their mouths they speak arrogantly.
11 They track me down;[n] now they surround me;
they set their eyes to cast me to the ground.
12 They are like a lion eager to tear,
like a young lion lurking in ambush.

13 Rise up, O LORD, confront them, overthrow them!
By your sword deliver my life from the wicked,
14 from mortals—by your hand, O LORD—
from mortals whose portion in life is in this world.
May their bellies be filled with what you have stored up for them;

[l] Jerome Tg: Meaning of Heb uncertain [m] Cn: Meaning of Heb uncertain [n] One Ms Compare Syr: MT *Our steps*

Ps 16 An expression of gratitude for God's care and provision for his people. *The holy ones in the land* (16.3-4) are the members of the faithful community, who serve as a model for the psalmist, in contrast to those devoted to other gods, from whom all contact must be witheld. Both inward understanding (*my heart)* and bodily security are shared, and there is certainty that the future is one of *joy* in God's presence, rather than gloom in the abode of the dead.
Ps 17 A call for God's attention and vindication in face of the bad example provided by *violent* people and the arrogance of enemies. The appeal is for God's protection of the petitioner as *the apple of [God's] eye*, which means the pupil, the most important and precious part (Zech 2.8; Deut 32.10). The *wings* suggest God's heavenly home and ability to encompass all the earth. Those eager to destroy God's people are to be visited by divine retribution, against them and their *children.* The psalmist's confidence is that he will be vindicated and so be able to see God.

15.4 2 Tim 3.8; Acts 28.10; Judg 11.35
15.5 Ex 22.25; 23.8; Deut 16.19; Ps 112.6
16.1 Ps 17.8; 7.1
16.3 Deut 33.3; Ps 101.6
16.4 Ps 32.10; 106.37,38; Ex 23.13
16.5 Ps 73.26; 23.5; 125.3
16.6 Ps 78.55; Jer 3.19
16.7 Ps 73.24; 77.6
16.8 Ps 54.3; 73.23; 62.2
16.9 Ps 4.7; 30.12; 4.8
16.10 Acts 2.27; 13.35; Ps 49.9
16.11 Mt 7.14; Ps 17.15; 36.7,8
17.3 Ps 26.2; 66.10; Job 23.10; Jer 50.20; Ps 39.1
17.4 Prov 1.15
17.5 Ps 44.18; 18.36
17.6 Ps 86.7; 88.2
17.7 Ps 31.21; 20.6
17.8 Deut 32.10; Ps 36.7
17.10 Ps 73.7; 1 Sam 2.3; Ps 31.18
17.12 Ps 7.2; 10.9
17.13 Ps 73.18; 22.20; 7.12
17.14 Lk 16.8; Ps 73.3-7; Isa 2.7; Job 21.11

Ps 18 This psalm of praise acclaims God as both protector and deliverer of the faithful. The forces pulling the psalmist into the realm of death are overcome when the LORD is appealed to for aid. A series of vivid images depicts the cosmic conflict in earth and sky that ensues as God shows forth his power (18.7-15) and then frees him from the hostile forces, here linked with the chaotic waters that God brought under control when creating the world (Gen 1.1-10). The rightness of his living and the purity of his deeds (*hands*) are rewarded by God, who responds appropriately to all human actions, whether evil or good. God provides the resources and the capacities to defeat one's enemies and to deliver one *from strife.* It is this God, who brings victory to his faithful people, who is here extolled (18.46-50).

may their children have more than enough;
may they leave something over to their little ones.

15 As for me, I shall behold your face in righteousness;
when I awake I shall be satisfied, beholding your likeness.

Psalm 18

Royal Thanksgiving for Victory

To the leader. A Psalm of David the servant of the LORD, who addressed the words of this song to the LORD on the day when the LORD delivered him from the hand of all his enemies, and from the hand of Saul. He said:

1 I love you, O LORD, my strength.
2 The LORD is my rock, my fortress, and my deliverer,
my God, my rock in whom I take refuge,
my shield, and the horn of my salvation, my stronghold.
3 I call upon the LORD, who is worthy to be praised,
so I shall be saved from my enemies.

4 The cords of death encompassed me;
the torrents of perdition assailed me;
5 the cords of Sheol entangled me;
the snares of death confronted me.

6 In my distress I called upon the LORD;
to my God I cried for help.
From his temple he heard my voice,
and my cry to him reached his ears.

7 Then the earth reeled and rocked;
the foundations also of the mountains trembled
and quaked, because he was angry.
8 Smoke went up from his nostrils,
and devouring fire from his mouth;
glowing coals flamed forth from him.
9 He bowed the heavens, and came down;
thick darkness was under his feet.
10 He rode on a cherub, and flew;
he came swiftly upon the wings of the wind.
11 He made darkness his covering around him,
his canopy thick clouds dark with water.
12 Out of the brightness before him
there broke through his clouds
hailstones and coals of fire.
13 The LORD also thundered in the heavens,
and the Most High uttered his voice.[o]
14 And he sent out his arrows, and scattered them;
he flashed forth lightnings, and routed them.
15 Then the channels of the sea were seen,
and the foundations of the world were laid bare
at your rebuke, O LORD,
at the blast of the breath of your nostrils.

16 He reached down from on high, he took me;
he drew me out of mighty waters.
17 He delivered me from my strong enemy,
and from those who hated me;
for they were too mighty for me.
18 They confronted me in the day of my calamity;
but the LORD was my support.
19 He brought me out into a broad place;
he delivered me, because he delighted in me.

20 The LORD rewarded me according to my righteousness;
according to the cleanness of my hands he recompensed me.
21 For I have kept the ways of the LORD,
and have not wickedly departed from my God.
22 For all his ordinances were before me,
and his statutes I did not put away from me.
23 I was blameless before him,
and I kept myself from guilt.
24 Therefore the LORD has recompensed me according to my righteousness,
according to the cleanness of my hands in his sight.

25 With the loyal you show yourself loyal;
with the blameless you show yourself blameless;
26 with the pure you show yourself pure;
and with the crooked you show yourself perverse.
27 For you deliver a humble people,
but the haughty eyes you bring down.
28 It is you who light my lamp;
the LORD, my God, lights up my darkness.

[o] Gk See 2 Sam 22.14: Heb adds *hailstones and coals of fire*

17.15 1 Jn 3.2; Ps 4.6,7; 16.11
18.2 Ps 19.14; 91.2; 40.17; 11.1; 59.11; 75.10; 9.9
18.3 Ps 48.1; Num 10.9
18.4 Ps 116.3; 124.3,4
18.5 Ps 116.3; Prov 14.27
18.6 Ps 86.7; 11.4; 34.15
18.7 Ps 68.7,8; 114.4,6
18.9 Ps 144.5; Ex 20.21
18.10 Ps 80.1; 104.3
18.11 Ps 97.2
18.12 Ps 104.2; 140.10
18.13 Ps 29.3; 104.7
18.14 Ps 7.13; 144.6; Ex 14.24; Judg 4.15
18.15 Ps 106.9; 76.6; Ex 15.8
18.16 Ps 144.7
18.17 ver 48; Ps 35.10
18.19 Ps 31.8; 118.5; 37.23
18.20 Ps 7.8; 1 Kings 8.32; Ps 24.4
18.21 Ps 119.33
18.22 Ps 119.30,83
18.24 1 Sam 26.23
18.25 Mt 5.7
18.26 Job 25.5; Prov 3.34
18.27 Ps 72.12; Prov 6.17
18.28 Job 18.6; 29.3

29 By you I can crush a troop,
and by my God I can leap over a wall.
30 This God—his way is perfect;
the promise of the LORD proves true;
he is a shield for all who take refuge in him.

31 For who is God except the LORD?
And who is a rock besides our God?—
32 the God who girded me with strength,
and made my way safe.
33 He made my feet like the feet of a deer,
and set me secure on the heights.
34 He trains my hands for war,
so that my arms can bend a bow of bronze.
35 You have given me the shield of your salvation,
and your right hand has supported me;
your help[p] has made me great.
36 You gave me a wide place for my steps under me,
and my feet did not slip.
37 I pursued my enemies and overtook them;
and did not turn back until they were consumed.
38 I struck them down, so that they were not able to rise;
they fell under my feet.
39 For you girded me with strength for the battle;
you made my assailants sink under me.
40 You made my enemies turn their backs to me,
and those who hated me I destroyed.
41 They cried for help, but there was no one to save them;
they cried to the LORD, but he did not answer them.
42 I beat them fine, like dust before the wind;
I cast them out like the mire of the streets.

43 You delivered me from strife with the peoples;[q]
you made me head of the nations;
people whom I had not known served me.
44 As soon as they heard of me they obeyed me;
foreigners came cringing to me.
45 Foreigners lost heart,
and came trembling out of their strongholds.

46 The LORD lives! Blessed be my rock,
and exalted be the God of my salvation,
47 the God who gave me vengeance
and subdued peoples under me;
48 who delivered me from my enemies;
indeed, you exalted me above my adversaries;
you delivered me from the violent.

49 For this I will extol you, O LORD, among the nations,
and sing praises to your name.
50 Great triumphs he gives to his king,
and shows steadfast love to his anointed,
to David and his descendants forever.

Psalm 19

God's Glory in Creation and the Law

To the leader. A Psalm of David.

1 The heavens are telling the glory of God;
and the firmament[r] proclaims his handiwork.
2 Day to day pours forth speech,
and night to night declares knowledge.
3 There is no speech, nor are there words;
their voice is not heard;
4 yet their voice[s] goes out through all the earth,
and their words to the end of the world.

In the heavens[t] he has set a tent for the sun,
5 which comes out like a bridegroom from his wedding canopy,
and like a strong man runs its course with joy.
6 Its rising is from the end of the heavens,
and its circuit to the end of them;
and nothing is hid from its heat.

7 The law of the LORD is perfect,
reviving the soul;
the decrees of the LORD are sure,
making wise the simple;
8 the precepts of the LORD are right,
rejoicing the heart;
the commandment of the LORD is clear,
enlightening the eyes;

18.29 2 Cor 12.9; Heb 11.34
18.30 Deut 32.4; Ps 12.6; 17.7
18.31 Deut 32.31,39; Ps 86.8-10; Isa 45.5
18.33 Hab 3.19; Deut 32.13
18.34 Ps 144.1; Job 20.24
18.37 Ps 44.5; 37.20
18.38 Ps 110.6; 36.12; 47.3
18.39 ver 32,47
18.40 Ps 21.21; 94.23
18.41 Ps 50.22; Prov 1.28
18.42 Ps 83.13
18.43 Ps 35.1; Isa 55.5
18.45 Ps 37.2; Mic 7.17
18.46 Ps 42.2; 51.14
18.47 Ps 94.1; 47.3
18.48 Ps 143.94; 27.6; 140.1,4
18.49 Rom 15.9; Ps 108.1
18.50 Ps 144.10; 28.8; 89.4,29
19.1 Gen 1.6; Isa 40.22; Rom 1.19,20
19.2 Ps 74.16
19.4 Rom 10.18
19.5 Eccl 1.5
19.6 Ps 113.3; Deut 30.4
19.7 Ps 119.142; 23.3; 93.5; 111.7; 119.98-100
19.8 Ps 119.128; 12.6; 119.30

Ps 19 God's glory is revealed through the splendor and order of the creation, and especially in the daily cycle of the sun. But God is also disclosed in the wisdom of the Law of Moses, and in the obedience which it elicits from his faithful people, who see in that law both benefits to be gained and *errors* to be avoided. The psalmist prays that both human speech and thought may be *acceptable* to the God who made all this possible.

[p] Or *gentleness* [q] Gk Tg: Heb *people* [r] Or *dome* [s] Gk Jerome Compare Syr: Heb *line* [t] Heb *In them*

Ps 20 Addressed to *the leader,* which is the king of Israel, the psalm promises him God's help, in response to the proper *burnt sacrifices* which have been offered in the temple. Fulfillment of goals and victory in battle are assured to the king and to his people who rely on the power and purpose represented by *the name of the LORD our God.*

Ps 21 Praise to the LORD for answering the petitions of the king and for the bestowal of blessing in response to his trust in the LORD. All the king's enemies and all their schemes against him will come to nothing, and he will defeat them, with the *glory* for this victory to be given to God.

9 the fear of the LORD is pure,
enduring forever;
the ordinances of the LORD are true
and righteous altogether.
10 More to be desired are they than gold,
even much fine gold;
sweeter also than honey,
and drippings of the honeycomb.

11 Moreover by them is your servant
warned;
in keeping them there is great reward.
12 But who can detect their errors?
Clear me from hidden faults.
13 Keep back your servant also from the
insolent;[u]
do not let them have dominion over
me.
Then I shall be blameless,
and innocent of great transgression.

14 Let the words of my mouth and the
meditation of my heart
be acceptable to you,
O LORD, my rock and my redeemer.

Psalm 20

Prayer for Victory

To the leader. A Psalm of David.

1 The LORD answer you in the day of
trouble!
The name of the God of Jacob protect
you!
2 May he send you help from the
sanctuary,
and give you support from Zion.
3 May he remember all your offerings,
and regard with favor your burnt
sacrifices. *Selah*

4 May he grant you your heart's desire,
and fulfill all your plans.
5 May we shout for joy over your victory,
and in the name of our God set up
our banners.
May the LORD fulfill all your petitions.

6 Now I know that the LORD will help his
anointed;
he will answer him from his holy
heaven
with mighty victories by his right
hand.
7 Some take pride in chariots, and some
in horses,
but our pride is in the name of the
LORD our God.
8 They will collapse and fall,
but we shall rise and stand upright.

9 Give victory to the king, O LORD;
answer us when we call.[v]

Psalm 21

Thanksgiving for Victory

To the leader. A Psalm of David.

1 In your strength the king rejoices,
O LORD,
and in your help how greatly he
exults!
2 You have given him his heart's desire,
and have not withheld the request of
his lips. *Selah*
3 For you meet him with rich blessings;
you set a crown of fine gold on his
head.
4 He asked you for life; you gave it to
him—
length of days forever and ever.
5 His glory is great through your help;
splendor and majesty you bestow on
him.
6 You bestow on him blessings forever;
you make him glad with the joy of
your presence.
7 For the king trusts in the LORD,
and through the steadfast love of the
Most High he shall not be
moved.

8 Your hand will find out all your
enemies;
your right hand will find out those
who hate you.
9 You will make them like a fiery furnace
when you appear.
The LORD will swallow them up in his
wrath,
and fire will consume them.
10 You will destroy their offspring from the
earth,
and their children from among
humankind.
11 If they plan evil against you,
if they devise mischief, they will not
succeed.
12 For you will put them to flight;
you will aim at their faces with your
bows.

[u] Or *from proud thoughts* [v] Gk: Heb *give victory, O LORD; let the King answer us when we call*

19.9 Ps 119.42
19.10 Prov 8.10; 16.24
19.11 Ps 17.4; Prov 29.18
19.12 Ps 139.6; 51.1,2; 90.8
19.13 Ps 119.33; 32.2; 25.11
19.14 Ps 104.34; 18.2; Isa 41.14; 43.14
20.1 Ps 102.2; 91.14; 36.7,11; 59.1
20.2 Ps 3.4; 119.28
20.3 Ps 51.19
20.4 Ps 21.2; 145.19
20.5 Ps 9.14; 1 Sam 1.17
20.6 Ps 41.11; Isa 58.9; Ps 28.8
20.7 Isa 36.9; 31.1; 2 Chr 32.8
20.8 Ps 37.24
21.1 Ps 59.16,17; 9.14
21.2 Ps 37.4
21.3 Ps 59.10
21.4 Ps 133.3; 91.16
21.5 Ps 18.50; 45.3,4
21.7 2 Kings 18.5; Ps 16.8
21.8 Isa 10.10
21.9 Mal 4.1; Lam 2.2
21.10 Deut 28.18; Ps 37.28
21.11 Ps 2.1-3; 10.2
21.12 Ps 18.40; 7.12,13

13 Be exalted, O LORD, in your strength!
We will sing and praise your power.

Psalm 22

Plea for Deliverance from Suffering and Hostility

To the leader: according to The Deer of the Dawn. A Psalm of David.

1 My God, my God, why have you
forsaken me?
Why are you so far from helping me,
from the words of my groaning?
2 O my God, I cry by day, but you do not
answer;
and by night, but find no rest.

3 Yet you are holy,
enthroned on the praises of Israel.
4 In you our ancestors trusted;
they trusted, and you delivered them.
5 To you they cried, and were saved;
in you they trusted, and were not put
to shame.

6 But I am a worm, and not human;
scorned by others, and despised by
the people.
7 All who see me mock at me;
they make mouths at me, they shake
their heads;
8 "Commit your cause to the LORD; let him
deliver—
let him rescue the one in whom he
delights!"

9 Yet it was you who took me from the
womb;
you kept me safe on my mother's
breast.
10 On you I was cast from my birth,
and since my mother bore me you
have been my God.
11 Do not be far from me,
for trouble is near
and there is no one to help.

12 Many bulls encircle me,
strong bulls of Bashan surround me;
13 they open wide their mouths at me,
like a ravening and roaring lion.

14 I am poured out like water,
and all my bones are out of joint;
my heart is like wax;
it is melted within my breast;
15 my mouth[w] is dried up like a potsherd,
and my tongue sticks to my jaws;
you lay me in the dust of death.

16 For dogs are all around me;
a company of evildoers encircles me.
My hands and feet have shriveled;[x]
17 I can count all my bones.
They stare and gloat over me;
18 they divide my clothes among themselves,
and for my clothing they cast lots.

19 But you, O LORD, do not be far away!
O my help, come quickly to my aid!
20 Deliver my soul from the sword,
my life[y] from the power of the dog!
21 Save me from the mouth of the lion!

From the horns of the wild oxen you
have rescued[z] me.
22 I will tell of your name to my brothers
and sisters;[a]
in the midst of the congregation I will
praise you:
23 You who fear the LORD, praise him!
All you offspring of Jacob, glorify him;
stand in awe of him, all you offspring
of Israel!
24 For he did not despise or abhor
the affliction of the afflicted;
he did not hide his face from me,[b]
but heard when I[c] cried to him.

25 From you comes my praise in the great
congregation;
my vows I will pay before those who
fear him.
26 The poor[d] shall eat and be satisfied;
those who seek him shall praise the
LORD.
May your hearts live forever!

27 All the ends of the earth shall remember
and turn to the LORD;
and all the families of the nations
shall worship before him.[e]
28 For dominion belongs to the LORD,
and he rules over the nations.

29 To him,[f] indeed, shall all who sleep in[g]
the earth bow down;
before him shall bow all who go

[w] Cn: Heb *strength* [x] Meaning of Heb uncertain [y] Heb *my only one* [z] Heb *answered* [a] Or *kindred* [b] Heb *him* [c] Heb *he* [d] Or *afflicted* [e] Gk Syr Jerome: Heb *you* [f] Cn: Heb *They have eaten and* [g] Cn: Heb *all the fat ones*

Ps 22 A personal lament, which ends in an affirmation of God's intention to rescue not only this oppressed individual, but ultimately all nations and those who have died. There is a series of contrasts (22.1-11) between the seemingly hopeless condition of the psalmist and his rejection by his contemporaries for the folly of his dependence on the LORD, and the power of God to fulfill his promises to the *ancestors* of Israel in the past and to the individual, who is nurtured and sustained from infancy. He describes his wretched condition in a series of vivid images (22.12-19): attacked by animals, athirst, surrounded by mocking enemies. The psalm ends (22.20-31) with praise for the help God has provided, and with a promise to bear witness to God's faithfulness so that not only *the offspring of Israel* but also *the nations* and even the dead *who sleep in the earth* will acknowledge the greatness of God.

21.13 Ps 57.5; 81.1
22.1 Mt 27.46; Ps 10.1
22.2 Ps 42.3
22.3 Ps 99.9; 35.8
22.5 Ps 107.6; 25.2,3; Rom 9.33
22.6 Job 26.6; Isa 41.14; Isa 49.7
22.7 Mt 27.39; Mk 15.29
22.8 Mt 27.43; Mk 1.11
22.9 Ps 71.6
22.10 Isa 43.6
22.12 Ps 68.30; Deut 32.14
22.13 Ps 35.21; 17.12
22.14 Job 30.16; Ps 31.10; 107.26
22.15 Ps 38.10; 137.6; 104.29
22.16 Ps 59.6; Mt 27.35
22.18 Mt 27.35
22.20 Ps 35.17
22.21 ver 13; Ps 34.4
22.22 Heb 2.12
22.23 Ps 135.19; 86.12; 33.8
22.24 Ps 102.17; 69.17; Heb 5.7
22.25 Ps 35.18; 66.13
22.26 Ps 107.9; 40.16; 69.32
22.27 Ps 2.8; 86.9
22.28 Ps 47.7,8; Mt 6.13
22.29 Ps 47.7; Isa 27.13; Ps 95.6

Ps 23 God's faithful provision and constant care of members of his flock is vividly portrayed, including his preservation of his sheep in the face of grave danger, and his supplying their needs for a life of peace and justice for one's *whole life long.*
Ps 24 This psalm of praise is in three parts: (1) 24.1-2, which celebrates God's having created the universe, and in so doing divided the waters on, below and above the earth (Gen 1.6-13); (2) 24.3-6, which specifies the requirements for moral purity of those who come to the temple seeking the blessing of God; (3) 24.7-10, the image of the LORD coming into the sanctuary (whether in Jerusalem or in heaven is not clear) where he is acclaimed as *the king of glory.*
Ps 25 God's instruction of his people is the dominant theme in this psalm. After affirming trust in the LORD to fulfill his promises to those who *wait for* him (25.1-3), the psalmist asks for instruction in God's *ways* and his *truth* so that his *steadfast love and faithfulness* may be experienced by *those who keep his covenant* (25.4-15). The loneliness and affliction by his enemies that he experiences may be overcome as he finds *refuge* in God.

down to the dust,
and I shall live for him.[h]
30 Posterity will serve him;
future generations will be told about the Lord,
31 and[i] proclaim his deliverance to a people yet unborn,
saying that he has done it.

Psalm 23

The Divine Shepherd

A Psalm of David.

1 The LORD is my shepherd, I shall not want.
2 He makes me lie down in green pastures;
he leads me beside still waters;[j]
3 he restores my soul.[k]
He leads me in right paths[l]
for his name's sake.

4 Even though I walk through the darkest valley,[m]
I fear no evil;
for you are with me;
your rod and your staff—
they comfort me.

5 You prepare a table before me
in the presence of my enemies;
you anoint my head with oil;
my cup overflows.
6 Surely[n] goodness and mercy[o] shall follow me
all the days of my life,
and I shall dwell in the house of the LORD
my whole life long.[p]

Psalm 24

Entrance into the Temple

Of David. A Psalm.

1 The earth is the LORD's and all that is in it,
the world, and those who live in it;
2 for he has founded it on the seas,
and established it on the rivers.

3 Who shall ascend the hill of the LORD?
And who shall stand in his holy place?
4 Those who have clean hands and pure hearts,
who do not lift up their souls to what is false,
and do not swear deceitfully.
5 They will receive blessing from the LORD,
and vindication from the God of their salvation.
6 Such is the company of those who seek him,
who seek the face of the God of Jacob.[q] *Selah*

7 Lift up your heads, O gates!
and be lifted up, O ancient doors!
that the King of glory may come in.
8 Who is the King of glory?
The LORD, strong and mighty,
the LORD, mighty in battle.
9 Lift up your heads, O gates!
and be lifted up, O ancient doors!
that the King of glory may come in.
10 Who is this King of glory?
The LORD of hosts,
he is the King of glory.
Selah

Psalm 25

Prayer for Guidance and for Deliverance

Of David.

1 To you, O LORD, I lift up my soul.
2 O my God, in you I trust;
do not let me be put to shame;
do not let my enemies exult over me.
3 Do not let those who wait for you be put to shame;
let them be ashamed who are wantonly treacherous.

4 Make me to know your ways, O LORD;
teach me your paths.
5 Lead me in your truth, and teach me,
for you are the God of my salvation;
for you I wait all day long.

6 Be mindful of your mercy, O LORD, and of your steadfast love,
for they have been from of old.
7 Do not remember the sins of my youth
or my transgressions;
according to your steadfast love
remember me,

[h] Compare Gk Syr Vg: Heb *and he who cannot keep himself alive* [i] Compare Gk: Heb *it will be told about the Lord to the generation, [31] they will come and* [j] Heb *waters of rest* [k] Or *life* [l] Or *paths of righteousness* [m] Or *the valley of the shadow of death* [n] Or *Only* [o] Or *kindness* [p] Heb *for length of days* [q] Gk Syr: Heb *your face, O Jacob*

22.30 Ps 102.28; 71.18
22.31 Ps 78.6
23.1 Isa 40.11; Jn 10.11; 1 Pet 2.25
23.2 Ezek 34.14; Rev 7.17
23.3 Ps 19.7; 5.8
23.4 Ps 138.7; Job 3.5; Ps 27.1; Isa 43.2
23.5 Ps 78.19; 31.19; 92.10; 16.5
23.6 Ps 25.7,10; 27.4-6
24.1 Ex 9.29; Job 41.11; 1 Cor 10.26; Ps 89.11
24.3 Ps 15.1; 2.6; 65.4
24.4 Job 17.9; Mt 5.8; Ps 15.4
24.5 Deut 11.26,27; Isa 46.13; Ps 25.5
24.7 Isa 26.2; 1 Cor 2.8
24.8 Ps 89.13; 78.3-6
24.9 Zech 9.9; Mt 21.5
25.1 Ps 86.4
25.2 Ps 31.6; 41.11
25.3 Isa 49.23; 33.1
25.4 Ps 5.8; 86.11
25.5 Jn 16.13; Ps 24.5; 40.1
25.6 Ps 103.17; Isa 63.15
25.7 Job 13.26; Jer 3.25; Ps 51.1

for your goodness' sake, O LORD!

8 Good and upright is the LORD;
therefore he instructs sinners in the way.
9 He leads the humble in what is right,
and teaches the humble his way.
10 All the paths of the LORD are steadfast love and faithfulness,
for those who keep his covenant and his decrees.

11 For your name's sake, O LORD,
pardon my guilt, for it is great.
12 Who are they that fear the LORD?
He will teach them the way that they should choose.

13 They will abide in prosperity,
and their children shall possess the land.
14 The friendship of the LORD is for those who fear him,
and he makes his covenant known to them.
15 My eyes are ever toward the LORD,
for he will pluck my feet out of the net.

16 Turn to me and be gracious to me,
for I am lonely and afflicted.
17 Relieve the troubles of my heart,
and bring me[r] out of my distress.
18 Consider my affliction and my trouble,
and forgive all my sins.

19 Consider how many are my foes,
and with what violent hatred they hate me.
20 O guard my life, and deliver me;
do not let me be put to shame, for I take refuge in you.
21 May integrity and uprightness preserve me,
for I wait for you.

22 Redeem Israel, O God,
out of all its troubles.

Psalm 26

Plea for Justice and Declaration of Righteousness

Of David.

1 Vindicate me, O LORD,
for I have walked in my integrity,
and I have trusted in the LORD without wavering.
2 Prove me, O LORD, and try me;
test my heart and mind.
3 For your steadfast love is before my eyes,
and I walk in faithfulness to you.[s]

4 I do not sit with the worthless,
nor do I consort with hypocrites;
5 I hate the company of evildoers,
and will not sit with the wicked.

6 I wash my hands in innocence,
and go around your altar, O LORD,
7 singing aloud a song of thanksgiving,
and telling all your wondrous deeds.

8 O LORD, I love the house in which you dwell,
and the place where your glory abides.
9 Do not sweep me away with sinners,
nor my life with the bloodthirsty,
10 those in whose hands are evil devices,
and whose right hands are full of bribes.

11 But as for me, I walk in my integrity;
redeem me, and be gracious to me.
12 My foot stands on level ground;
in the great congregation I will bless the LORD.

Psalm 27

Triumphant Song of Confidence

Of David.

1 The LORD is my light and my salvation;
whom shall I fear?
The LORD is the stronghold[t] of my life;
of whom shall I be afraid?

2 When evildoers assail me
to devour my flesh—
my adversaries and foes—
they shall stumble and fall.

3 Though an army encamp against me,
my heart shall not fear;
though war rise up against me,
yet I will be confident.

4 One thing I asked of the LORD,
that will I seek after:
to live in the house of the LORD

[r] Or *The troubles of my heart are enlarged; bring me* [s] Or *in your faithfulness* [t] Or *refuge*

Ps 26 This prayer for vindication by God recites the fidelity of the petitioner to the law of God and to participation in worship.
Ps 27 In response to the psalmist's faithfulness to the LORD and to worship in the sanctuary, he asks God for continuing support and expresses confidence that God will provide it.

25.8 Ps 106.1; 92.15; 32.8
25.9 Ps 23.3; 27.11
25.10 Ps 40.11; 103.18
25.11 Ps 31.1; Rom 5.20
25.13 Prov 19.23; Ps 37.11
25.14 Prov 3.32; Jn 7.17
25.15 Ps 141.8
25.16 Ps 69.16
25.17 Ps 88.3; 107.6
25.18 2 Sam 16.12
25.19 Ps 3.1; 27.12
25.21 Ps 41.12; ver 3
25.22 Ps 130.8
26.1 Ps 7.8; Prov 20.7; Ps 25.2; Heb 10.23
26.2 Ps 7.9; 66.10
26.3 2 Kings 20.3
26.4 Ps 1.1
26.5 Ps 129.21; 1.1
26.6 Ps 73.13
26.7 Ps 35.18; 9.1
26.8 Ps 27.4
26.9 Ps 28.3
26.10 1 Sam 8.3
26.11 ver 1; Ps 69.18
26.12 Ps 40.2; 27.11; 22.22
27.1 Isa 60.19; Ex 15.2; Ps 62.2
27.2 Ps 14.4
27.3 Ps 3.6
27.4 Ps 26.8; 90.17

Ps 28 This petition is that God will hear this faithful, obedient petitioner and will not mistake him for any of the evildoers who are to be dragged off for punishment. Both God's people and their ruler (*his anointed*) are the special objects of God's care. **Ps 29** The complete sovereignty of the LORD over the creation is celebrated, which his people are called to affirm (29.1-2), and from which they shall benefit (29.11).

all the days of my life,
to behold the beauty of the LORD,
and to inquire in his temple.

5 For he will hide me in his shelter
in the day of trouble;
he will conceal me under the cover of his tent;
he will set me high on a rock.

6 Now my head is lifted up
above my enemies all around me,
and I will offer in his tent
sacrifices with shouts of joy;
I will sing and make melody to the LORD.

7 Hear, O LORD, when I cry aloud,
be gracious to me and answer me!
8 "Come," my heart says, "seek his face!"
Your face, LORD, do I seek.
9 Do not hide your face from me.

Do not turn your servant away in anger,
you who have been my help.
Do not cast me off, do not forsake me,
O God of my salvation!
10 If my father and mother forsake me,
the LORD will take me up.

11 Teach me your way, O LORD,
and lead me on a level path
because of my enemies.
12 Do not give me up to the will of my adversaries,
for false witnesses have risen against me,
and they are breathing out violence.

13 I believe that I shall see the goodness of the LORD
in the land of the living.
14 Wait for the LORD;
be strong, and let your heart take courage;
wait for the LORD!

Psalm 28

Prayer for Help and Thanksgiving for It

Of David.

1 To you, O LORD, I call;
my rock, do not refuse to hear me,
for if you are silent to me,
I shall be like those who go down to the Pit.
2 Hear the voice of my supplication,
as I cry to you for help,
as I lift up my hands
toward your most holy sanctuary.[u]

3 Do not drag me away with the wicked,
with those who are workers of evil,
who speak peace with their neighbors,
while mischief is in their hearts.
4 Repay them according to their work,
and according to the evil of their deeds;
repay them according to the work of their hands;
render them their due reward.
5 Because they do not regard the works of the LORD,
or the work of his hands,
he will break them down and build them up no more.

6 Blessed be the LORD,
for he has heard the sound of my pleadings.
7 The LORD is my strength and my shield;
in him my heart trusts;
so I am helped, and my heart exults,
and with my song I give thanks to him.

8 The LORD is the strength of his people;
he is the saving refuge of his anointed.
9 O save your people, and bless your heritage;
be their shepherd, and carry them forever.

Psalm 29

The Voice of God in a Great Storm

A Psalm of David.

1 Ascribe to the LORD, O heavenly beings,[v]
ascribe to the LORD glory and strength.
2 Ascribe to the LORD the glory of his name;
worship the LORD in holy splendor.

3 The voice of the LORD is over the waters;
the God of glory thunders,
the LORD, over mighty waters.
4 The voice of the LORD is powerful;
the voice of the LORD is full of majesty.

5 The voice of the LORD breaks the cedars;
the LORD breaks the cedars of Lebanon.

[u] Heb *your innermost sanctuary* [v] Heb *sons of gods*

27.5 Ps 31.20; 40.2
27.6 Ps 3.3
27.7 Ps 39.12; 13.3
27.8 Ps 24.6
27.9 Ps 69.17
27.10 Isa 49.15; 40.11
27.11 Ps 25.4; 86.11; 5.8
27.12 Ps 41.2; 35.11; Mt 26.60; Acts 9.1
27.13 Ps 31.19; Jer 11.19
27.14 Ps 40.1; Josh 1.6
28.1 Ps 83.1; 88.4
28.2 Ps 140.6; 5.7; 138.2
28.3 Ps 26.9; 12.2; Jer 9.8
28.4 Rev 18.6
28.5 Isa 5.12
28.6 Ps 116.1
28.7 Ps 18.2; 13.5
28.8 Ps 20.6
28.9 Deut 9.29; Ezra 1.4
29.1 1 Chr 16.28,29; Ps 96.7-9
29.2 2 Chr 20.21
29.3 Job 37.4,5
29.4 Ps 68.33
29.5 Isa 2.13

6 He makes Lebanon skip like a calf,
and Sirion like a young wild ox.

7 The voice of the LORD flashes forth
flames of fire.
8 The voice of the LORD shakes the
wilderness;
the LORD shakes the wilderness of
Kadesh.

9 The voice of the LORD causes the oaks to
whirl,[w]
and strips the forest bare;
and in his temple all say, "Glory!"

10 The LORD sits enthroned over the flood;
the LORD sits enthroned as king
forever.
11 May the LORD give strength to his
people!
May the LORD bless his people with
peace!

Psalm 30

Thanksgiving for Recovery from Grave Illness

A Psalm. A Song at the dedication of the temple. Of David.

1 I will extol you, O LORD, for you have
drawn me up,
and did not let my foes rejoice over
me.
2 O LORD my God, I cried to you for help,
and you have healed me.
3 O LORD, you brought up my soul from
Sheol,
restored me to life from among those
gone down to the Pit.[x]

4 Sing praises to the LORD, O you his
faithful ones,
and give thanks to his holy name.
5 For his anger is but for a moment;
his favor is for a lifetime.
Weeping may linger for the night,
but joy comes with the morning.

6 As for me, I said in my prosperity,
"I shall never be moved."
7 By your favor, O LORD,
you had established me as a strong
mountain;
you hid your face;
I was dismayed.

8 To you, O LORD, I cried,
and to the LORD I made supplication:
9 "What profit is there in my death,
if I go down to the Pit?
Will the dust praise you?
Will it tell of your faithfulness?
10 Hear, O LORD, and be gracious to me!
O LORD, be my helper!"

11 You have turned my mourning into
dancing;
you have taken off my sackcloth
and clothed me with joy,
12 so that my soul[y] may praise you and
not be silent.
O LORD my God, I will give thanks to
you forever.

Psalm 31

Prayer and Praise for Deliverance from Enemies

To the leader. A Psalm of David.

1 In you, O LORD, I seek refuge;
do not let me ever be put to shame;
in your righteousness deliver me.
2 Incline your ear to me;
rescue me speedily.
Be a rock of refuge for me,
a strong fortress to save me.

3 You are indeed my rock and my
fortress;
for your name's sake lead me and
guide me,
4 take me out of the net that is hidden for
me,
for you are my refuge.
5 Into your hand I commit my spirit;
you have redeemed me, O LORD,
faithful God.

6 You hate[z] those who pay regard to
worthless idols,
but I trust in the LORD.
7 I will exult and rejoice in your steadfast
love,
because you have seen my affliction;
you have taken heed of my
adversities,
8 and have not delivered me into the
hand of the enemy;
you have set my feet in a broad place.

[w] Or *causes the deer to calve* [x] Or *that I should not go down to the Pit* [y] Heb *that glory* [z] One Heb Ms Gk Syr Jerome: MT *I hate*

Ps 30 Praise to the LORD here is based on the psalmist's having been delivered from death (*Sheol; the Pit)* and restored to the joy of life.

Ps 31 The reliability of God (*my rock and my fortress)* is affirmed in the face of personal grief (31.9-10) and scorn and threats from enemies (31.11-13). Expected are the silencing of the wicked and the praise of the faithful God by the psalmist and his community.

29.6 Ps 114.4; Deut 3.9
29.8 Num 13.26
29.9 Ps 26.8
29.10 Ps 10.16
29.11 Ps 28.8; 37.11
30.1 Ps 29.9; 25.2
30.2 Ps 88.13; 6.2
30.3 Ps 86.13; 28.1
30.4 Ps 149.1; 50.5; 97.12
30.5 Ps 103.9; 63.3
30.7 Ps 104.29
30.9 Ps 6.5
30.11 Ps 6.8; Jer 31.4,13; Ps 4.7
30.12 Ps 16.9; 44.8
31.1 Ps 22.5; Isa 49.23
31.2 Ps 71.2
31.3 Ps 18.2; 23.3
31.4 Ps 25.15; 28.8
31.5 Lk 23.46; Acts 7.59
31.6 Jon 2.8
31.7 Ps 90.14; 10.14; Jn 10.27
31.8 Deut 32.30; Ps 4.1

Ps 32 Those who have benefited from God's forgiveness (32.1-2) are called to renewal through prayers of confession and petition in *time of distress,* and through instruction in God's purpose. This will lead to fulness of *joy* in the faithful community.

9 Be gracious to me, O LORD, for I am in distress;
my eye wastes away from grief,
my soul and body also.
10 For my life is spent with sorrow,
and my years with sighing;
my strength fails because of my misery,[a]
and my bones waste away.

11 I am the scorn of all my adversaries,
a horror[b] to my neighbors,
an object of dread to my acquaintances;
those who see me in the street flee from me.
12 I have passed out of mind like one who is dead;
I have become like a broken vessel.
13 For I hear the whispering of many—
terror all around!—
as they scheme together against me,
as they plot to take my life.

14 But I trust in you, O LORD;
I say, "You are my God."
15 My times are in your hand;
deliver me from the hand of my enemies and persecutors.
16 Let your face shine upon your servant;
save me in your steadfast love.
17 Do not let me be put to shame, O LORD,
for I call on you;
let the wicked be put to shame;
let them go dumbfounded to Sheol.
18 Let the lying lips be stilled
that speak insolently against the righteous
with pride and contempt.

19 O how abundant is your goodness
that you have laid up for those who fear you,
and accomplished for those who take refuge in you,
in the sight of everyone!
20 In the shelter of your presence you hide them
from human plots;
you hold them safe under your shelter
from contentious tongues.

21 Blessed be the LORD,
for he has wondrously shown his steadfast love to me
when I was beset as a city under siege.
22 I had said in my alarm,
"I am driven far[c] from your sight."
But you heard my supplications
when I cried out to you for help.

23 Love the LORD, all you his saints.
The LORD preserves the faithful,
but abundantly repays the one who acts haughtily.
24 Be strong, and let your heart take courage,
all you who wait for the LORD.

Psalm 32

The Joy of Forgiveness

Of David. A Maskil.

1 Happy are those whose transgression is forgiven,
whose sin is covered.
2 Happy are those to whom the LORD imputes no iniquity,
and in whose spirit there is no deceit.

3 While I kept silence, my body wasted away
through my groaning all day long.
4 For day and night your hand was heavy upon me;
my strength was dried up[d] as by the heat of summer. *Selah*

5 Then I acknowledged my sin to you,
and I did not hide my iniquity;
I said, "I will confess my transgressions to the LORD,"
and you forgave the guilt of my sin. *Selah*

6 Therefore let all who are faithful
offer prayer to you;
at a time of distress,[e] the rush of mighty waters
shall not reach them.
7 You are a hiding place for me;
you preserve me from trouble;
you surround me with glad cries of deliverance. *Selah*

8 I will instruct you and teach you the way you should go;
I will counsel you with my eye upon you.
9 Do not be like a horse or a mule, without understanding,

[a] Gk Syr: Heb *my iniquity* [b] Cn: Heb *exceedingly* [c] Another reading is *cut off* [d] Meaning of Heb uncertain [e] Cn: Heb *at a time of finding only*

31.10 Ps 13.2; 39.11; 38.3
31.11 Isa 53.4; Ps 38.11; 64.8
31.12 Ps 88.4,5
31.13 Jer 20.10; Lam 2.20; Mt 27.1
31.14 Ps 140.6
31.15 Job 24.1; Ps 143.9
31.16 Num 6.25; Ps 4.6
31.17 Ps 25.2,3
31.18 Ps 120.2; 94.4
31.19 Isa 64.4; Rom 11.22; Ps 5.11
31.20 Ps 27.5; Job 5.21
31.21 Ps 17.7; 1 Sam 23.7
31.22 Ps 116.11; Lam 3.54
31.23 Ps 34.9; 145.20; 94.2
31.24 Ps 27.14
32.1 Ps 85.2
32.2 2 Cor 5.19; Jn 1.47
32.3 Ps 39.2,3; 31.10; 38.8
32.4 Job 33.7
32.5 Lev 26.40; Ps 103.12
32.6 Ps 69.13; 144.7; Isa 43.2
32.7 Ps 31.20; 121.7; Ex 15.1
32.8 Ps 25.8; 33.18
32.9 Jas 3.3

32.10 Rom 2.9; Prov 16.20
32.11 Ps 64.10
33.1 Ps 32.11; 147.1
33.2 Ps 92.3
33.3 Ps 96.1; 98.4
33.4 Ps 19.8; 119.90
33.5 Ps 11.7; 119.64
33.6 Gen 11.3; Job 23.13
33.8 Ps 67.7; 96.9
33.9 Gen 1.3; Ps 148.5
33.10 Isa 8.10; 19.3
33.11 Job 23.13; Prov 19.21; Ps 40.5
33.12 Ps 144.15; Ex 19.5; Deut 7.6
33.13 Job 28.24; Ps 11.4
33.15 Jer 32.19
33.16 Ps 44.6
33.17 Ps 20.7; Prov 21.31
33.18 Job 36.7; Ps 34.15; 147.11
33.19 Ps 37.19
33.21 Zech 10.7; Jn 16.22
34.2 Jer 9.24; Ps 119.74
34.3 Lk 1.46
34.4 Mt 7.7; ver 6,17,19
34.5 Ps 36.9; 25.3
34.6 ver 4.17,19
34.7 Dan 6.22; 2 Kings 6.17
34.8 1 Pet 2.3; Ps 2.12

whose temper must be curbed with
bit and bridle,
else it will not stay near you.

10 Many are the torments of the wicked,
but steadfast love surrounds those
who trust in the LORD.
11 Be glad in the LORD and rejoice, O
righteous,
and shout for joy, all you upright in
heart.

Psalm 33

The Greatness and Goodness of God
1 Rejoice in the LORD, O you righteous.
Praise befits the upright.
2 Praise the LORD with the lyre;
make melody to him with the harp of
ten strings.
3 Sing to him a new song;
play skillfully on the strings, with
loud shouts.

4 For the word of the LORD is upright,
and all his work is done in
faithfulness.
5 He loves righteousness and justice;
the earth is full of the steadfast love of
the LORD.

6 By the word of the LORD the heavens
were made,
and all their host by the breath of his
mouth.
7 He gathered the waters of the sea as in
a bottle;
he put the deeps in storehouses.

8 Let all the earth fear the LORD;
let all the inhabitants of the world
stand in awe of him.
9 For he spoke, and it came to be;
he commanded, and it stood firm.

10 The LORD brings the counsel of the
nations to nothing;
he frustrates the plans of the peoples.
11 The counsel of the LORD stands forever,
the thoughts of his heart to all
generations.
12 Happy is the nation whose God is the
LORD,
the people whom he has chosen as
his heritage.

13 The LORD looks down from heaven;
he sees all humankind.
14 From where he sits enthroned he
watches
all the inhabitants of the earth—
15 he who fashions the hearts of them all,
and observes all their deeds.
16 A king is not saved by his great army;
a warrior is not delivered by his great
strength.
17 The war horse is a vain hope for
victory,
and by its great might it cannot save.

18 Truly the eye of the LORD is on those
who fear him,
on those who hope in his steadfast
love,
19 to deliver their soul from death,
and to keep them alive in famine.

20 Our soul waits for the LORD;
he is our help and shield.
21 Our heart is glad in him,
because we trust in his holy name.
22 Let your steadfast love, O LORD, be upon
us,
even as we hope in you.

Psalm 34

Praise for Deliverance from Trouble
Of David, when he feigned madness before Abimelech, so that he drove him out, and he went away.
1 I will bless the LORD at all times;
his praise shall continually be in my
mouth.
2 My soul makes its boast in the LORD;
let the humble hear and be glad.
3 O magnify the LORD with me,
and let us exalt his name together.

4 I sought the LORD, and he answered me,
and delivered me from all my fears.
5 Look to him, and be radiant;
so your[f] faces shall never be ashamed.
6 This poor soul cried, and was heard by
the LORD,
and was saved from every trouble.
7 The angel of the LORD encamps
around those who fear him, and
delivers them.
8 O taste and see that the LORD is good;
happy are those who take refuge in
him.

[f] Gk Syr Jerome: Heb *their*

Ps 33 Praise to God is offered for his faithfulness to his obedient people (33.4-5), and for his sovereign control of the natural world (33.6-7) and over all human affairs (33.7-17), but especially those of the community that trusts in him.
Ps 34 The superscription concerning David does not match the details of the story in 2 Sam 11.14-21. The psalm is an acrostic, each verse beginning with the successive letters of the Hebrew alphabet. From a recital of his own experience of God's support in answer to prayer (34.1-6), the psalmist moves to assure the community that God will punish the *evildoers*, while sustaining and liberating his own people.

Ps 35 An extended recital of the injustices and scornful treatment the psalmist has received is mixed with appeals for God's effective judgment upon them, and concludes with a hope for joy among those who desire his *vindication.*

9 O fear the LORD, you his holy ones,
for those who fear him have no want.
10 The young lions suffer want and hunger,
but those who seek the LORD lack no good thing.

11 Come, O children, listen to me;
I will teach you the fear of the LORD.
12 Which of you desires life,
and covets many days to enjoy good?
13 Keep your tongue from evil,
and your lips from speaking deceit.
14 Depart from evil, and do good;
seek peace, and pursue it.

15 The eyes of the LORD are on the righteous,
and his ears are open to their cry.
16 The face of the LORD is against evildoers,
to cut off the remembrance of them from the earth.
17 When the righteous cry for help, the LORD hears,
and rescues them from all their troubles.
18 The LORD is near to the brokenhearted,
and saves the crushed in spirit.

19 Many are the afflictions of the righteous,
but the LORD rescues them from them all.
20 He keeps all their bones;
not one of them will be broken.
21 Evil brings death to the wicked,
and those who hate the righteous will be condemned.
22 The LORD redeems the life of his servants;
none of those who take refuge in him will be condemned.

Psalm 35

Prayer for Deliverance from Enemies

Of David.

1 Contend, O LORD, with those who contend with me;
fight against those who fight against me!
2 Take hold of shield and buckler,
and rise up to help me!
3 Draw the spear and javelin
against my pursuers;
say to my soul,
"I am your salvation."

4 Let them be put to shame and dishonor
who seek after my life.
Let them be turned back and confounded
who devise evil against me.
5 Let them be like chaff before the wind,
with the angel of the LORD driving them on.
6 Let their way be dark and slippery,
with the angel of the LORD pursuing them.

7 For without cause they hid their net[g] for me;
without cause they dug a pit[h] for my life.
8 Let ruin come on them unawares.
And let the net that they hid ensnare them;
let them fall in it—to their ruin.

9 Then my soul shall rejoice in the LORD,
exulting in his deliverance.
10 All my bones shall say,
"O LORD, who is like you?
You deliver the weak
from those too strong for them,
the weak and needy from those who despoil them."

11 Malicious witnesses rise up;
they ask me about things I do not know.
12 They repay me evil for good;
my soul is forlorn.
13 But as for me, when they were sick,
I wore sackcloth;
I afflicted myself with fasting.
I prayed with head bowed[i] on my bosom,
14 as though I grieved for a friend or a brother;
I went about as one who laments for a mother,
bowed down and in mourning.

15 But at my stumbling they gathered in glee,
they gathered together against me;
ruffians whom I did not know
tore at me without ceasing;
16 they impiously mocked more and more,[j]
gnashing at me with their teeth.

17 How long, O LORD, will you look on?
Rescue me from their ravages,
my life from the lions!

[g] Heb *a pit, their net* [h] The word *pit* is transposed from the preceding line [i] Or *My prayer turned back* [j] Cn Compare Gk: Heb *like the profanest of mockers of a cake*

34.9 Ps 23.1
34.10 Ps 84.11
34.11 Ps 111.10
34.12 1 Pet 3.10
34.13 1 Pet 2.22
34.14 Ps 37.27; Heb 12.14
34.15 Job 36.7; Ps 33.18
34.16 Jer 44.11; Prov 10.7
34.17 Ps 145.19; ver 19
34.18 Ps 145.18; Isa 57.15
34.19 Prov 24.16; ver 4,6,17
34.20 Jn 19.36
34.21 Ps 94.23
34.22 1 Kings 1.29; Ps 71.23
35.1 Ps 43.1
35.4 Ps 70.2,3
35.5 Job 21.18; Ps 1.4; Isa 29.5
35.6 Ps 73.18; Jer 23.12
35.7 Ps 9.15
35.8 1 Thess 5.3
35.9 Isa 61.10; Lk 1.47
35.10 Ex 15.11; Ps 18.17; 37.14
35.11 Ps 27.12
35.12 Jn 10.32
35.13 Job 30.25; Ps 69.10
35.15 Job 30.1,8
35.17 Hab 1.13; Ps 22.20

18 Then I will thank you in the great
congregation;
in the mighty throng I will praise
you.

19 Do not let my treacherous enemies
rejoice over me,
or those who hate me without cause
wink the eye.
20 For they do not speak peace,
but they conceive deceitful words
against those who are quiet in the
land.
21 They open wide their mouths against
me;
they say, "Aha, Aha,
our eyes have seen it."

22 You have seen, O LORD; do not be silent!
O Lord, do not be far from me!
23 Wake up! Bestir yourself for my defense,
for my cause, my God and my Lord!
24 Vindicate me, O LORD, my God,
according to your righteousness,
and do not let them rejoice over me.
25 Do not let them say to themselves,
"Aha, we have our heart's desire."
Do not let them say, "We have
swallowed you[k] up."

26 Let all those who rejoice at my calamity
be put to shame and confusion;
let those who exalt themselves against
me
be clothed with shame and dishonor.

27 Let those who desire my vindication
shout for joy and be glad,
and say evermore,
"Great is the LORD,
who delights in the welfare of his
servant."
28 Then my tongue shall tell of your
righteousness
and of your praise all day long.

Psalm 36

Human Wickedness and Divine Goodness

To the leader. Of David, the servant of the LORD.

1 Transgression speaks to the wicked
deep in their hearts;
there is no fear of God
before their eyes.
2 For they flatter themselves in their own
eyes
that their iniquity cannot be found
out and hated.
3 The words of their mouths are mischief
and deceit;
they have ceased to act wisely and do
good.
4 They plot mischief while on their beds;
they are set on a way that is not
good;
they do not reject evil.

5 Your steadfast love, O LORD, extends to
the heavens,
your faithfulness to the clouds.
6 Your righteousness is like the mighty
mountains,
your judgments are like the great deep;
you save humans and animals alike,
O LORD.

7 How precious is your steadfast love, O God!
All people may take refuge in the
shadow of your wings.
8 They feast on the abundance of your
house,
and you give them drink from the
river of your delights.
9 For with you is the fountain of life;
in your light we see light.

10 O continue your steadfast love to those
who know you,
and your salvation to the upright of
heart!
11 Do not let the foot of the arrogant tread
on me,
or the hand of the wicked drive me
away.
12 There the evildoers lie prostrate;
they are thrust down, unable to rise.

Psalm 37

Exhortation to Patience and Trust

Of David.

1 Do not fret because of the wicked;
do not be envious of wrongdoers,
2 for they will soon fade like the grass,
and wither like the green herb.

3 Trust in the LORD, and do good;
so you will live in the land, and enjoy
security.
4 Take delight in the LORD,
and he will give you the desires of
your heart.

Ps 36 The self-deceit of the wicked is contrasted with the assurance of the faithful that God is active in ordering the universe and in caring for the needs of his own people.
Ps 37 A series of proverbial injunctions to the faithful in acrostic form based on the Hebrew alphabet rehearses the themes of God's punishment of the wicked and his reward of the righteous whose way of life manifests the generosity and loving care of God.

35.18 Ps 22.22,25
35.19 Ps 13.4; 38.19; Prov 6.13; Ps 69.4; Jn 15.25
35.21 Ps 22.13; 40.15
35.22 Ex 3.7; Ps 28.1; 10.1
35.23 Ps 44.23
35.24 Ps 9.4; ver 19
35.25 Lam 2.16
35.26 Ps 40.14; 38.16
35.27 Ps 32.11; 9.4; 40.16; 147.11
35.28 Ps 51.14
36.1 Rom 3.18
36.3 Jer 4.22
36.4 Prov 4.16; Mic 2.1; Isa 65.2
36.6 Job 11.8; Ps 77.19; Rom 11.33
36.7 Ruth 2.12
36.8 Ps 65.4; Job 20.17; Rev 22.1
36.9 Jer 2.13; 1 Pet 2.9
36.12 Ps 140.10
37.1 Ps 73.3; Prov 23.17
37.2 Ps 90.5,6
37.3 Ps 62.8; Deut 30.20; Isa 40.11
37.4 Isa 58.14

[k] Heb *him*

5 Commit your way to the LORD;
trust in him, and he will act.
6 He will make your vindication shine like the light,
and the justice of your cause like the noonday.

7 Be still before the LORD, and wait patiently for him;
do not fret over those who prosper in their way,
over those who carry out evil devices.

8 Refrain from anger, and forsake wrath.
Do not fret—it leads only to evil.
9 For the wicked shall be cut off,
but those who wait for the LORD shall inherit the land.

10 Yet a little while, and the wicked will be no more;
though you look diligently for their place, they will not be there.
11 But the meek shall inherit the land,
and delight themselves in abundant prosperity.

12 The wicked plot against the righteous,
and gnash their teeth at them;
13 but the LORD laughs at the wicked,
for he sees that their day is coming.

14 The wicked draw the sword and bend their bows
to bring down the poor and needy,
to kill those who walk uprightly;
15 their sword shall enter their own heart,
and their bows shall be broken.

16 Better is a little that the righteous person has
than the abundance of many wicked.
17 For the arms of the wicked shall be broken,
but the LORD upholds the righteous.

18 The LORD knows the days of the blameless,
and their heritage will abide forever;
19 they are not put to shame in evil times,
in the days of famine they have abundance.

20 But the wicked perish,
and the enemies of the LORD are like the glory of the pastures;
they vanish—like smoke they vanish away.

21 The wicked borrow, and do not pay back,
but the righteous are generous and keep giving;
22 for those blessed by the LORD shall inherit the land,
but those cursed by him shall be cut off.

23 Our steps[l] are made firm by the LORD,
when he delights in our[m] way;
24 though we stumble,[n] we[o] shall not fall headlong,
for the LORD holds us[p] by the hand.

25 I have been young, and now am old,
yet I have not seen the righteous forsaken
or their children begging bread.
26 They are ever giving liberally and lending,
and their children become a blessing.

27 Depart from evil, and do good;
so you shall abide forever.
28 For the LORD loves justice;
he will not forsake his faithful ones.

The righteous shall be kept safe forever,
but the children of the wicked shall be cut off.
29 The righteous shall inherit the land,
and live in it forever.

30 The mouths of the righteous utter wisdom,
and their tongues speak justice.
31 The law of their God is in their hearts;
their steps do not slip.

32 The wicked watch for the righteous,
and seek to kill them.
33 The LORD will not abandon them to their power,
or let them be condemned when they are brought to trial.

34 Wait for the LORD, and keep to his way,
and he will exalt you to inherit the land;
you will look on the destruction of the wicked.

35 I have seen the wicked oppressing,
and towering like a cedar of Lebanon.[q]

[l] Heb *a man's steps* [m] Heb *his* [n] Heb *he stumbles* [o] Heb *he* [p] Heb *him* [q] Gk: Meaning of Heb uncertain

37.5 Ps 55.22; Prov 16.3; 1 Pet 5.7
37.6 Job 11.17; Mic 7.9
37.7 Ps 62.5; 40.1; ver 1,8
37.8 Ps 73.3; Eph 4.26
37.9 Isa 60.21
37.10 Job 24.24; 7.10
37.11 Mt 5.5
37.12 Ps 35.16
37.13 Ps 2.4; 1 Sam 26.10
37.14 Ps 11.2; 35.10
37.15 Ps 9.16
37.16 Prov 15.16
37.17 Job 38.15; Ps 10.15
37.18 Ps 1.6
37.19 Job 5.20; Ps 33.19
37.20 Ps 72.27; 102.3
37.21 Ps 112.5,9
37.22 Prov 3.33; Job 5.3
37.23 1 Sam 2.9; Ps 147.11
37.24 Prov 24.16; Ps 147.6
37.25 Heb 13.5; Job 15.23
37.26 ver 21; Ps 147.13
37.27 Ps 34.14; ver 18
37.28 Ps 11.7; 21.10; Isa 14.20
37.29 ver 9,18
37.30 Mt 12.35
37.31 Ps 40.8; Isa 51.7; ver 23
37.32 Ps 10.8
37.33 2 Pet 2.9; Ps 109.31
37.34 Ps 27.14; 52.5,6
37.35 Job 5

36 Again I[r] passed by, and they were no
more;
though I sought them, they could not
be found.

37 Mark the blameless, and behold the
upright,
for there is posterity for the peaceable.
38 But transgressors shall be altogether
destroyed;
the posterity of the wicked shall be
cut off.

39 The salvation of the righteous is from
the LORD;
he is their refuge in the time of
trouble.
40 The LORD helps them and rescues them;
he rescues them from the wicked, and
saves them,
because they take refuge in him.

Psalm 38

A Penitent Sufferer's Plea for Healing

A Psalm of David, for the memorial offering.

1 O LORD, do not rebuke me in your anger,
or discipline me in your wrath.
2 For your arrows have sunk into me,
and your hand has come down on me.

3 There is no soundness in my flesh
because of your indignation;
there is no health in my bones
because of my sin.
4 For my iniquities have gone over my
head;
they weigh like a burden too heavy
for me.

5 My wounds grow foul and fester
because of my foolishness;
6 I am utterly bowed down and prostrate;
all day long I go around mourning.
7 For my loins are filled with burning,
and there is no soundness in my
flesh.
8 I am utterly spent and crushed;
I groan because of the tumult of my
heart.

9 O Lord, all my longing is known to you;
my sighing is not hidden from you.
10 My heart throbs, my strength fails me;
as for the light of my eyes—it also
has gone from me.

11 My friends and companions stand aloof
from my affliction,
and my neighbors stand far off.

12 Those who seek my life lay their snares;
those who seek to hurt me speak of ruin,
and meditate treachery all day long.

13 But I am like the deaf, I do not hear;
like the mute, who cannot speak.
14 Truly, I am like one who does not hear,
and in whose mouth is no retort.

15 But it is for you, O LORD, that I wait;
it is you, O Lord my God, who will
answer.
16 For I pray, "Only do not let them rejoice
over me,
those who boast against me when my
foot slips."

17 For I am ready to fall,
and my pain is ever with me.
18 I confess my iniquity;
I am sorry for my sin.
19 Those who are my foes without cause[s]
are mighty,
and many are those who hate me
wrongfully.
20 Those who render me evil for good
are my adversaries because I follow
after good.

21 Do not forsake me, O LORD;
O my God, do not be far from me;
22 make haste to help me,
O Lord, my salvation.

Psalm 39

Prayer for Wisdom and Forgiveness

To the leader: to Jeduthun. A Psalm of David.

1 I said, "I will guard my ways
that I may not sin with my tongue;
I will keep a muzzle on my mouth
as long as the wicked are in my
presence."
2 I was silent and still;
I held my peace to no avail;
my distress grew worse,
3 my heart became hot within me.
While I mused, the fire burned;
then I spoke with my tongue:

4 "LORD, let me know my end,
and what is the measure of my days;

[r] Gk Syr Jerome: Heb *he* [s] Q Ms: MT *my living foes*

37.36 Job 20.5
37.37 Isa 57.1,2
37.38 Ps 1.4; ver 9,20,28
37.39 Ps 3.8; 9.9
37.40 Isa 31.5; 1 Chr 5.20
38.1 Ps 6.1
38.2 Job 6.4; Ps 32.4
38.3 Isa 1.6; Ps 6.2
38.4 Ezra 9.6
38.5 Ps 69.5
38.6 Ps 35.14; 42.9
38.7 Ps 102.3; ver 3
38.8 Job 3.24; Ps 22.1
38.9 Ps 10.17; 6.6
38.11 Ps 31.11; Lk 23.49
38.12 Ps 54.3; 140.5; 35.4,20
38.13 Ps 39.2,9
38.15 Ps 39.7; 17.6
38.16 Ps 13.4; 35.26
38.17 Ps 13.2
38.18 Ps 32.5; 2 Cor 7.9
38.19 Ps 18.17; 35.19
38.20 Ps 35.12; 1 Jn 3.12
38.21 Ps 35.22
38.22 Ps 40.13,17; 27.1
39.1 1 Kings 2.4; Job 2.10; Jas 3.2
39.2 Ps 38.13
39.4 Ps 90.12; 103.14

Ps 38 Confession and contrition for moral sickness mingle with (1) a description of inner pain from guilt and distress, and (2) an acknowledgment of the psalmist's inability to hear or communicate (*deaf...mute*) with God concerning his condition. The end is an appeal for God's continuing concern and *help*.
Ps 39 After having decided to be silent in the presence of *the wicked*, the psalmist is driven to cry out to the LORD in lament for the brevity of human life and his chastisement of *mortals*. The only ground of hope is in God and in aversion of his judgmental *gaze* while life lasts.

Ps 40 The psalmist rejoices in God's rescue and in the new joy he has found among those who trust God. That relationship is not dependent on ceremonial offerings, but on hearing (*an open ear)* and doing the will of God. In spite of evils and antagonists, there is joy in what God has already done and confidence that he will help in the future.

let me know how fleeting my life is.
5 You have made my days a few handbreadths,
and my lifetime is as nothing in your sight.
Surely everyone stands as a mere breath. *Selah*
6 Surely everyone goes about like a shadow.
Surely for nothing they are in turmoil;
they heap up, and do not know who will gather.

7 "And now, O Lord, what do I wait for?
My hope is in you.
8 Deliver me from all my transgressions.
Do not make me the scorn of the fool.
9 I am silent; I do not open my mouth,
for it is you who have done it.
10 Remove your stroke from me;
I am worn down by the blows[t] of your hand.

11 "You chastise mortals
in punishment for sin,
consuming like a moth what is dear to them;
surely everyone is a mere breath. *Selah*

12 "Hear my prayer, O LORD,
and give ear to my cry;
do not hold your peace at my tears.
For I am your passing guest,
an alien, like all my forebears.
13 Turn your gaze away from me, that I may smile again,
before I depart and am no more."

Psalm 40

Thanksgiving for Deliverance and Prayer for Help

To the leader. Of David. A Psalm.

1 I waited patiently for the LORD;
he inclined to me and heard my cry.
2 He drew me up from the desolate pit,[u]
out of the miry bog,
and set my feet upon a rock,
making my steps secure.
3 He put a new song in my mouth,
a song of praise to our God.
Many will see and fear,
and put their trust in the LORD.

4 Happy are those who make
the LORD their trust,
who do not turn to the proud,
to those who go astray after false gods.
5 You have multiplied, O LORD my God,
your wondrous deeds and your thoughts toward us;
none can compare with you.
Were I to proclaim and tell of them,
they would be more than can be counted.

6 Sacrifice and offering you do not desire,
but you have given me an open ear.[v]
Burnt offering and sin offering
you have not required.
7 Then I said, "Here I am;
in the scroll of the book it is written of me.[w]
8 I delight to do your will, O my God;
your law is within my heart."

9 I have told the glad news of deliverance
in the great congregation;
see, I have not restrained my lips,
as you know, O LORD.
10 I have not hidden your saving help within my heart,
I have spoken of your faithfulness and your salvation;
I have not concealed your steadfast love and your faithfulness
from the great congregation.

11 Do not, O LORD, withhold
your mercy from me;
let your steadfast love and your faithfulness
keep me safe forever.
12 For evils have encompassed me
without number;
my iniquities have overtaken me,
until I cannot see;
they are more than the hairs of my head,
and my heart fails me.

13 Be pleased, O LORD, to deliver me;
O LORD, make haste to help me.
14 Let all those be put to shame and confusion
who seek to snatch away my life;
let those be turned back and brought to dishonor
who desire my hurt.

[t] Heb *hostility* [u] Cn: Heb *pit of tumult* [v] Heb *ears you have dug for me* [w] Meaning of Heb uncertain

39.5 Ps 89.47; 144.4; 62.9
39.6 1 Pet 1.24; Ps 127.2; Job 27.17; Lk 12.20
39.7 Ps 38.15
39.8 Ps 51.9; 44.13
39.9 ver 2; Job 2.10
39.10 Job 9.34; Ps 32.4
39.11 2 Pet 2.16; Job 13.28; ver 5
39.12 Ps 102.1; 56.8; Heb 11.13; 1 Pet 2.11
39.13 Job 10.20; 14.10
40.1 Ps 27.14; 34.15
40.2 Ps 69.2; 27.5
40.3 Ps 33.3
40.4 Ps 84.12
40.5 Ps 136.4; Isa 55.8; Ps 139.18
40.6 1 Sam 15.22
40.8 Jn 4.34; Rom 7.22; Ps 37.31
40.9 Ps 22.22; 119.13
40.10 Acts 20.20; Ps 89.1
40.11 Ps 43.3
40.12 Ps 116.3; 38.4; 69.4; 73.26
40.13 Ps 70.1
40.14 Ps 35.4; 63.9

15 Let those be appalled because of their
shame
who say to me, "Aha, Aha!"

16 But may all who seek you
rejoice and be glad in you;
may those who love your salvation
say continually, "Great is the LORD!"
17 As for me, I am poor and needy,
but the Lord takes thought for me.
You are my help and my deliverer;
do not delay, O my God.

Psalm 41

Assurance of God's Help and a Plea for Healing

To the leader. A Psalm of David.

1 Happy are those who consider the poor;[x]
the LORD delivers them in the day of
trouble.
2 The LORD protects them and keeps them
alive;
they are called happy in the land.
You do not give them up to the will
of their enemies.
3 The LORD sustains them on their sickbed;
in their illness you heal all their
infirmities.[y]

4 As for me, I said, "O LORD, be gracious to
me;
heal me, for I have sinned against
you."
5 My enemies wonder in malice
when I will die, and my name perish.
6 And when they come to see me, they
utter empty words,
while their hearts gather mischief;
when they go out, they tell it abroad.
7 All who hate me whisper together about
me;
they imagine the worst for me.

8 They think that a deadly thing has
fastened on me,
that I will not rise again from where I
lie.
9 Even my bosom friend in whom I
trusted,
who ate of my bread, has lifted the
heel against me.
10 But you, O LORD, be gracious to me,
and raise me up, that I may repay
them.
11 By this I know that you are pleased
with me;
because my enemy has not triumphed
over me.
12 But you have upheld me because of my
integrity,
and set me in your presence forever.

13 Blessed be the LORD, the God of Israel,
from everlasting to everlasting.
Amen and Amen.

BOOK II

(Psalms 42–72)

Psalm 42

Longing for God and His Help in Distress

To the leader. A Maskil of the Korahites.

1 As a deer longs for flowing streams,
so my soul longs for you, O God.
2 My soul thirsts for God,
for the living God.
When shall I come and behold
the face of God?
3 My tears have been my food
day and night,
while people say to me continually,
"Where is your God?"

4 These things I remember,
as I pour out my soul:
how I went with the throng,[z]
and led them in procession to the
house of God,
with glad shouts and songs of
thanksgiving,
a multitude keeping festival.
5 Why are you cast down, O my soul,
and why are you disquieted within
me?
Hope in God; for I shall again praise
him,
my help 6and my God.

My soul is cast down within me;
therefore I remember you
from the land of Jordan and of Hermon,
from Mount Mizar.
7 Deep calls to deep
at the thunder of your cataracts;
all your waves and your billows
have gone over me.

[x] Or *weak* [y] Heb *you change all his bed* [z] Meaning of Heb uncertain

40.15 Ps 70.3
40.16 Ps 70.4; 35.27
40.17 Ps 70.5
41.1 Ps 82.3,4; Prov 14.21
41.2 Ps 37.22,28; 27.12
41.3 Ps 6.6
41.4 Ps 6.2; 51.4
41.5 Ps 38.12
41.6 Ps 12.2
41.7 Ps 56.5
41.8 Ps 71.10,11
41.9 Job 19.19; Ps 55.12; Jn 13.18
41.10 Ps 3.3
41.11 Ps 147.11; 25.2
41.12 Ps 37.17; Job 36.7
41.13 Ps 106.48
42.1 Ps 119.131
42.2 Ps 63.1; Jer 10.10; Ps 43.4
42.3 Ps 80.5; 79.10
42.4 Ps 62.8; Isa 30.29; Ps 100.4
42.5 Ps 38.6; 77.3; Lam 3.24; Ps 44.3
42.7 Ps 88.7; Jon 2.3

Ps 41 Affirmations of joy that God cares for the poor and the sick (41.1-3,10-13) bracket a confession of sin and a deploring of the traitorous action of a friend (41.4-9).
Ps 42-43 Originally part of a single psalm, as the lack of an introductory note at the beginning of Ps 43 confirms. Having earlier participated joyously in the worshiping *throng* in the temple courts (42.4), the psalmist now feels alone and estranged from God. From some experience in the mountains at the sources of the Jordan (*Hermon, Mizar*), he is torn between senses of God's dependability and of his remoteness (42.9-43.2). The appeal to God is to bring the petitioner back to the central shrine where he can join in the praise of God.
Ps 42 The Korahites named in the superscription were a Levitical group given responsibility for singing in the temple (2 Chr 20.19; see also Ps 44-49; 84-85; 87-88).

Ps 44 Recalling the great acts of God in behalf of his people in the past (44.1-8), the psalmist asks why there is seeming abandonment of his people by God, even though they have not been *false to the covenant.* In a vivid image, there is a call to God to wake up and come to the rescue of his needy people (44.23-26).

8 By day the LORD commands his steadfast love,
and at night his song is with me,
a prayer to the God of my life.

9 I say to God, my rock,
"Why have you forgotten me?
Why must I walk about mournfully
because the enemy oppresses me?"
10 As with a deadly wound in my body,
my adversaries taunt me,
while they say to me continually,
"Where is your God?"

11 Why are you cast down, O my soul,
and why are you disquieted within me?
Hope in God; for I shall again praise him,
my help and my God.

Psalm 43

Prayer to God in Time of Trouble

1 Vindicate me, O God, and defend my cause
against an ungodly people;
from those who are deceitful and unjust
deliver me!
2 For you are the God in whom I take refuge;
why have you cast me off?
Why must I walk about mournfully
because of the oppression of the enemy?

3 O send out your light and your truth;
let them lead me;
let them bring me to your holy hill
and to your dwelling.
4 Then I will go to the altar of God,
to God my exceeding joy;
and I will praise you with the harp,
O God, my God.

5 Why are you cast down, O my soul,
and why are you disquieted within me?
Hope in God; for I shall again praise him,
my help and my God.

Psalm 44

National Lament and Prayer for Help

To the leader. Of the Korahites. A Maskil.

1 We have heard with our ears, O God,
our ancestors have told us,
what deeds you performed in their days,
in the days of old:
2 you with your own hand drove out the nations,
but them you planted;
you afflicted the peoples,
but them you set free;
3 for not by their own sword did they win the land,
nor did their own arm give them victory;
but your right hand, and your arm,
and the light of your countenance,
for you delighted in them.

4 You are my King and my God;
you command[a] victories for Jacob.
5 Through you we push down our foes;
through your name we tread down our assailants.
6 For not in my bow do I trust,
nor can my sword save me.
7 But you have saved us from our foes,
and have put to confusion those who hate us.
8 In God we have boasted continually,
and we will give thanks to your name forever. *Selah*

9 Yet you have rejected us and abased us,
and have not gone out with our armies.
10 You made us turn back from the foe,
and our enemies have gotten spoil.
11 You have made us like sheep for slaughter,
and have scattered us among the nations.
12 You have sold your people for a trifle,
demanding no high price for them.

13 You have made us the taunt of our neighbors,
the derision and scorn of those around us.
14 You have made us a byword among the nations,
a laughingstock[b] among the peoples.
15 All day long my disgrace is before me,
and shame has covered my face
16 at the words of the taunters and revilers,
at the sight of the enemy and the avenger.

17 All this has come upon us,
yet we have not forgotten you,
or been false to your covenant.

[a] Gk Syr: Heb *You are my King, O God; command* [b] Heb *a shaking of the head*

42.8 Ps 57.3; Job 35.10; Ps 63.6; 149.5
42.9 Ps 38.6
42.10 ver 3
42.11 ver 5
43.1 Ps 26.1; 1 Sam 24.15; Ps 5.6
43.2 Ps 18.1; 44.9; 42.9
43.3 Ps 36.9; 42.4; 84.1
43.4 Ps 26.6; 33.2
43.5 Ps 42.5,11
44.1 Ex 12.26; Ps 78.3,12
44.2 Ex 15.17; Ps 78.55; 80.8
44.3 Josh 24.12; Ps 77.15; Deut 4.37; 7.7,8
44.5 Dan 8.4; Ps 108.13
44.7 Ps 136.24; 53.5
44.8 Ps 34.2; 30.12
44.9 Ps 60.1,10; 74.1
44.10 Lev 26.17; Josh 7.8; Ps 89.41
44.11 ver 22; Deut 4.27; 28.64; Ps 106.27
44.12 Isa 52.3,4; Jer 15.13
44.13 Ps 79.4; 80.6
44.14 Jer 24.9; Ps 109.25
44.16 Ps 74.10; 8.2
44.17 Dan 9.13; Ps 78.7,57

44.18 Ps 78.57; Job 23.11
44.19 Ps 51.8; Job 3.5
44.20 Ps 78.11; 68.31; 81.9
44.21 Ps 139.1.2; Jer 17.10
44.22 Rom 8.36; Isa 53.7
44.23 Ps 7.6; 78.65; 77.7
44.24 Job 13.24; Ps 42.9
44.25 Ps 119.25
44.26 Ps 35.2; 25.22
45.1 Ezra 7.6
45.2 Lk 4.22
45.3 Isa 9.6
45.4 Rev 6.2
45.6 Ps 93.2; Heb 1.8,9; Ps 98.9
45.7 Ps 33.5; Isa 61.1; Ps 79.4; 21.6
45.8 Song 1.3
45.9 Song 6.8; 1 Kings 2.19
45.10 Deut 21.13
45.11 Ps 95.6; Isa 54.5
45.12 Ps 22.29
45.13 Isa 61.10
45.14 Song 1.4; ver 9
45.16 1 Pet 2.9; Rev 1.6; 20.6
45.17 Mal 1.11; Ps 138.4
46.1 Ps 14.6; Deut 4.7; Ps 9.9

18 Our heart has not turned back,
nor have our steps departed from your way,
19 yet you have broken us in the haunt of jackals,
and covered us with deep darkness.

20 If we had forgotten the name of our God,
or spread out our hands to a strange god,
21 would not God discover this?
For he knows the secrets of the heart.
22 Because of you we are being killed all day long,
and accounted as sheep for the slaughter.

23 Rouse yourself! Why do you sleep, O Lord?
Awake, do not cast us off forever!
24 Why do you hide your face?
Why do you forget our affliction and oppression?
25 For we sink down to the dust;
our bodies cling to the ground.
26 Rise up, come to our help.
Redeem us for the sake of your steadfast love.

Psalm 45

Ode for a Royal Wedding

To the leader: according to Lilies. Of the Korahites. A Maskil. A love song.

1 My heart overflows with a goodly theme;
I address my verses to the king;
my tongue is like the pen of a ready scribe.

2 You are the most handsome of men;
grace is poured upon your lips;
therefore God has blessed you forever.
3 Gird your sword on your thigh, O mighty one,
in your glory and majesty.

4 In your majesty ride on victoriously
for the cause of truth and to defend[c] the right;
let your right hand teach you dread deeds.
5 Your arrows are sharp
in the heart of the king's enemies;
the peoples fall under you.

6 Your throne, O God,[d] endures forever and ever.
Your royal scepter is a scepter of equity;
7 you love righteousness and hate wickedness.
Therefore God, your God, has anointed you
with the oil of gladness beyond your companions;
8 your robes are all fragrant with myrrh and aloes and cassia.
From ivory palaces stringed instruments make you glad;
9 daughters of kings are among your ladies of honor;
at your right hand stands the queen in gold of Ophir.

10 Hear, O daughter, consider and incline your ear;
forget your people and your father's house,
11 and the king will desire your beauty.
Since he is your lord, bow to him;
12 the people[e] of Tyre will seek your favor with gifts,
the richest of the people 13 with all kinds of wealth.

The princess is decked in her chamber with gold-woven robes;[f]
14 in many-colored robes she is led to the king;
behind her the virgins, her companions, follow.
15 With joy and gladness they are led along
as they enter the palace of the king.

16 In the place of ancestors you, O king,[g] shall have sons;
you will make them princes in all the earth.
17 I will cause your name to be celebrated in all generations;
therefore the peoples will praise you forever and ever.

Psalm 46

God's Defense of His City and People

To the leader. Of the Korahites. According to Alamoth. A Song.

1 God is our refuge and strength,
a very present[h] help in trouble.

Ps 45 A psalm celebrating the unique place of Israel's king in the purpose of God for his people and for the world. In addition to describing the special eloquence, majesty, power over *enemies*, and affluence of the king (45.2-9), his unique relationship to God is proclaimed (45.6, which could mean that he is superior to all ordinary humans, or that God has provided him with his throne). The bride comes to the king from a non-Israelite people with expensive gifts (45.10-15). Their offspring will rule in his stead and his name will continue to be *celebrated*.

Ps 46 This psalm celebrates the unique sovereignty of God in his own city, when he causes wars to cease and becomes *exalted in the earth*. The city of God could be Jerusalem, renewed in the future (as in Jewish apocalypses and Rev 21), or a new city at the end of the age.

[c] Cn: Heb *and the meekness of* [d] Or *Your throne is a throne of God, it* [e] Heb *daughter* [f] Or *people.* 13 *All glorious is the princess within, gold embroidery is her clothing* [g] Heb lacks *O king* [h] Or *well proved*

Ps 47 God's kingship *over all the earth* is celebrated in this psalm. Even the *princes* of the other nations join *the people of the God of Abraham* in exalting him.
Ps 48 God's rulership over the earth is here described as based on *Mount Zion*, where *kings assemble* to honor him. His praise goes forth *to the ends of the earth*. His rule will endure *forever*.

2 Therefore we will not fear, though the earth should change,
though the mountains shake in the heart of the sea;
3 though its waters roar and foam,
though the mountains tremble with its tumult. *Selah*

4 There is a river whose streams make glad the city of God,
the holy habitation of the Most High.
5 God is in the midst of the city;[i] it shall not be moved;
God will help it when the morning dawns.
6 The nations are in an uproar, the kingdoms totter;
he utters his voice, the earth melts.
7 The LORD of hosts is with us;
the God of Jacob is our refuge.[j]
Selah

8 Come, behold the works of the LORD;
see what desolations he has brought on the earth.
9 He makes wars cease to the end of the earth;
he breaks the bow, and shatters the spear;
he burns the shields with fire.
10 "Be still, and know that I am God!
I am exalted among the nations,
I am exalted in the earth."
11 The LORD of hosts is with us;
the God of Jacob is our refuge.[j]
Selah

Psalm 47

God's Rule over the Nations

To the leader. Of the Korahites. A Psalm.

1 Clap your hands, all you peoples;
shout to God with loud songs of joy.
2 For the LORD, the Most High, is awesome,
a great king over all the earth.
3 He subdued peoples under us,
and nations under our feet.
4 He chose our heritage for us,
the pride of Jacob whom he loves.
Selah

5 God has gone up with a shout,
the LORD with the sound of a trumpet.
6 Sing praises to God, sing praises;
sing praises to our King, sing praises.
7 For God is the king of all the earth;
sing praises with a psalm.[k]

8 God is king over the nations;
God sits on his holy throne.
9 The princes of the peoples gather
as the people of the God of Abraham.
For the shields of the earth belong to God;
he is highly exalted.

Psalm 48

The Glory and Strength of Zion

A Song. A Psalm of the Korahites.

1 Great is the LORD and greatly to be praised
in the city of our God.
His holy mountain, 2beautiful in elevation,
is the joy of all the earth,
Mount Zion, in the far north,
the city of the great King.
3 Within its citadels God
has shown himself a sure defense.

4 Then the kings assembled,
they came on together.
5 As soon as they saw it, they were astounded;
they were in panic, they took to flight;
6 trembling took hold of them there,
pains as of a woman in labor,
7 as when an east wind shatters
the ships of Tarshish.
8 As we have heard, so have we seen
in the city of the LORD of hosts,
in the city of our God,
which God establishes forever.
Selah

9 We ponder your steadfast love, O God,
in the midst of your temple.
10 Your name, O God, like your praise,
reaches to the ends of the earth.
Your right hand is filled with victory.
11 Let Mount Zion be glad,
let the towns[l] of Judah rejoice
because of your judgments.

12 Walk about Zion, go all around it,
count its towers,
13 consider well its ramparts;
go through its citadels,
that you may tell the next generation

[i] Heb *of it* [j] Or *fortress* [k] Heb *Maskil* [l] Heb *daughters*

46.2 Ps 23.4; 82.5; 18.7
46.3 Ps 93.3,4
46.4 Isa 8.7; Ps 48.1,8; Isa 60.14
46.5 Isa 12.6; Ps 37.40
46.6 Ps 2.1; 68.33; Mic 1.4
46.7 2 Chr 13.12; Ps 9.9
46.8 Ps 66.5; Isa 61.4
46.9 Isa 2.4; Ps 76.3; Ezek 39.9
46.10 Ps 100.3; Isa 2.11,17
47.1 Ps 98.8; Isa 55.12; Ps 106.47
47.2 Deut 7.21
47.3 Ps 18.47
47.4 1 Pet 1.4
47.5 Ps 68.33; 98.6
47.6 Ps 68.4; 89.18
47.7 1 Cor 14.15
47.8 1 Chr 16.31
47.9 Ps 72.11; Rom 4.11,12; Ps 89.18; 97.9
48.1 Ps 96.4; Zech 8.3
48.2 Ps 50.2; Lam 2.15; Mt 5.35
48.3 Ps 46.7
48.4 2 Sam 10.6-19
48.5 Ex 15.15
48.7 Jer 18.17
48.10 Josh 7.9; Isa 41.10
48.11 Ps 97.8
48.13 Ps 122.7; 78.5-7

14 that this is God,
our God forever and ever.
He will be our guide forever.

Psalm 49

The Folly of Trust in Riches

To the leader. Of the Korahites. A Psalm.

1 Hear this, all you peoples;
give ear, all inhabitants of the world,
2 both low and high,
rich and poor together.
3 My mouth shall speak wisdom;
the meditation of my heart shall be understanding.
4 I will incline my ear to a proverb;
I will solve my riddle to the music of the harp.

5 Why should I fear in times of trouble,
when the iniquity of my persecutors surrounds me,
6 those who trust in their wealth
and boast of the abundance of their riches?
7 Truly, no ransom avails for one's life,[m]
there is no price one can give to God for it.
8 For the ransom of life is costly,
and can never suffice
9 that one should live on forever
and never see the grave.[n]

10 When we look at the wise, they die;
fool and dolt perish together
and leave their wealth to others.
11 Their graves[o] are their homes forever,
their dwelling places to all generations,
though they named lands their own.
12 Mortals cannot abide in their pomp;
they are like the animals that perish.

13 Such is the fate of the foolhardy,
the end of those[p] who are pleased with their lot. *Selah*
14 Like sheep they are appointed for Sheol;
Death shall be their shepherd;
straight to the grave they descend,[q]
and their form shall waste away;
Sheol shall be their home.[r]
15 But God will ransom my soul from the power of Sheol,
for he will receive me. *Selah*

16 Do not be afraid when some become rich,
when the wealth of their houses increases.
17 For when they die they will carry nothing away;
their wealth will not go down after them.
18 Though in their lifetime they count themselves happy
—for you are praised when you do well for yourself—
19 they[s] will go to the company of their ancestors,
who will never again see the light.
20 Mortals cannot abide in their pomp;
they are like the animals that perish.

Psalm 50

The Acceptable Sacrifice

A Psalm of Asaph.

1 The mighty one, God the LORD,
speaks and summons the earth
from the rising of the sun to its setting.
2 Out of Zion, the perfection of beauty,
God shines forth.

3 Our God comes and does not keep silence,
before him is a devouring fire,
and a mighty tempest all around him.
4 He calls to the heavens above
and to the earth, that he may judge his people:
5 "Gather to me my faithful ones,
who made a covenant with me by sacrifice!"
6 The heavens declare his righteousness,
for God himself is judge. *Selah*

7 "Hear, O my people, and I will speak,
O Israel, I will testify against you.
I am God, your God.
8 Not for your sacrifices do I rebuke you;
your burnt offerings are continually before me.
9 I will not accept a bull from your house,
or goats from your folds.
10 For every wild animal of the forest is mine,
the cattle on a thousand hills.
11 I know all the birds of the air,[t]
and all that moves in the field is mine.

[m] Another reading is *no one can ransom a brother* [n] Heb *the pit* [o] Gk Syr Compare Tg: Heb *their inward* (thought) [p] Tg: Heb *after them* [q] Cn: Heb *the upright shall have dominion over them in the morning* [r] Meaning of Heb uncertain [s] Cn: Heb *you* [t] Gk Syr Tg: Heb *mountains*

48.14 Ps 23.4
49.1 Ps 78.1; 33.8
49.3 Ps 37.30; 119.130
49.4 Ps 78.2; Num 12.8
49.5 Ps 23.4
49.6 Job 31.24
49.7 Mt 25.8,9; Job 36.18
49.8 Mt 16.26
49.9 Ps 22.29; 89.48
49.10 Eccl 2.16,18
49.11 Ps 64.6; 10.6; Deut 3.14
49.12 ver 20
49.13 Lk 12.20
49.14 Ps 9.17; Dan 7.18; Mal 4.3; 1 Cor 6.2; Rev 2.26; Job 24.19
49.15 Ps 56.13; 73.24
49.16 Ps 37.7
49.17 Ps 17.14
49.18 Lk 12.19
49.19 Gen 15.15; Job 33.30
49.20 ver 12
50.1 Josh 22.22; Ps 113.3
50.2 Ps 48.2; Deut 33.2
50.3 Ps 96.13; 97.3; Dan 7.10
50.4 Deut 4.26; Isa 1.2
50.5 Ps 30.4; Ex 24.7; ver 8
50.6 Ps 89.5; 75.7
50.7 Ps 81.8; Ex 20.2
50.8 Ps 40.6; Hos 6.6
50.9 Ps 69.31
50.10 Ps 104.24

Ps 49 A wisdom psalm which contrasts the values and destiny of the rich with those of the righteous. The former enjoy seeming prosperity, but their wealth cannot deliver them from the universal human experience of *Sheol* (death). But God will liberate (ransom) the soul of his faithful one from death, presumably by taking the righteous into his eternal presence. Thus there is nothing to envy in the seeming comfort of the rich.
Ps 50 The ancient editor attributed this psalm to *Asaph,* who was among those David appointed to supervise music in the worship of God (1 Chr 6.31-48). Here there is a contrast between (1) those who think they are meeting their obligations in the covenant with God by the mere act of bringing animal sacrifices while mistreating even their own families, and (2) those who offer to God the true *sacrifice of thanksgiving.* The former will meet destruction, and the latter will find *the salvation of God.*

Ps 51 The introductory insert links this psalm with David's confession of having taken Bathsheba (2 Sam 11-12), but mention of rebuilding Zion (51.18) indicates that it was written after the exile of Israel in Babylon. This confession calls for cleansing by God: the psalmist acknowledges that he has had a sinful disposition since before he was born (51.3-5). He calls to God for his inner cleansing and the renewal of his stance toward life (*heart*), in return for which he will teach God's *ways* to others and sing of God's having freed him from the power of sin. His concern goes beyond his own condition to the renewal of *Jerusalem* and the worship of God there.

12 "If I were hungry, I would not tell you,
for the world and all that is in it is mine.
13 Do I eat the flesh of bulls,
or drink the blood of goats?
14 Offer to God a sacrifice of thanksgiving,[u]
and pay your vows to the Most High.
15 Call on me in the day of trouble;
I will deliver you, and you shall glorify me."

16 But to the wicked God says:
"What right have you to recite my statutes,
or take my covenant on your lips?
17 For you hate discipline,
and you cast my words behind you.
18 You make friends with a thief when you see one,
and you keep company with adulterers.

19 "You give your mouth free rein for evil,
and your tongue frames deceit.
20 You sit and speak against your kin;
you slander your own mother's child.
21 These things you have done and I have been silent;
you thought that I was one just like yourself.
But now I rebuke you, and lay the charge before you.

22 "Mark this, then, you who forget God,
or I will tear you apart, and there will be no one to deliver.
23 Those who bring thanksgiving as their sacrifice honor me;
to those who go the right way[v]
I will show the salvation of God."

Psalm 51

Prayer for Cleansing and Pardon

To the leader. A Psalm of David, when the prophet Nathan came to him, after he had gone in to Bathsheba.

1 Have mercy on me, O God,
according to your steadfast love;
according to your abundant mercy
blot out my transgressions.
2 Wash me thoroughly from my iniquity,
and cleanse me from my sin.

3 For I know my transgressions,
and my sin is ever before me.
4 Against you, you alone, have I sinned,
and done what is evil in your sight,
so that you are justified in your sentence
and blameless when you pass judgment.
5 Indeed, I was born guilty,
a sinner when my mother conceived me.

6 You desire truth in the inward being;[w]
therefore teach me wisdom in my secret heart.
7 Purge me with hyssop, and I shall be clean;
wash me, and I shall be whiter than snow.
8 Let me hear joy and gladness;
let the bones that you have crushed rejoice.
9 Hide your face from my sins,
and blot out all my iniquities.

10 Create in me a clean heart, O God,
and put a new and right[x] spirit within me.
11 Do not cast me away from your presence,
and do not take your holy spirit from me.
12 Restore to me the joy of your salvation,
and sustain in me a willing[y] spirit.

13 Then I will teach transgressors your ways,
and sinners will return to you.
14 Deliver me from bloodshed, O God,
O God of my salvation,
and my tongue will sing aloud of your deliverance.

15 O Lord, open my lips,
and my mouth will declare your praise.
16 For you have no delight in sacrifice;
if I were to give a burnt offering, you would not be pleased.
17 The sacrifice acceptable to God[z] is a broken spirit;
a broken and contrite heart, O God,
you will not despise.

18 Do good to Zion in your good pleasure;
rebuild the walls of Jerusalem,
19 then you will delight in right sacrifices,
in burnt offerings and whole burnt offerings;
then bulls will be offered on your altar.

[u] Or *make thanksgiving your sacrifice to God* [v] Heb *who set a way* [w] Meaning of Heb uncertain [x] Or *steadfast* [y] Or *generous* [z] Or *My sacrifice, O God,*

50.12 Ex 19.5
50.14 Heb 13.15; Deut 23.21
50.15 Ps 91.15; 81.7; 22.23
50.16 Isa 29.13
50.17 Rom 2.21,22; Neh 9.26
50.18 Rom 1.32; 1 Tim 5.22
50.20 Mt 10.21
50.21 Eccl 8.11; Isa 42.14; Ps 90.8
50.22 Job 8.13; Ps 9.17; 7.2
51.1 Ps 4.1; 106.45; Isa 43.25; Acts 3.19
51.2 Heb 9.14; 1 Jn 1.7
51.3 Isa 59.12
51.4 Gen 20.6; Lk 15.21; Rom 3.4
51.5 Ps 58.3; Job 14.4
51.6 Ps 15.2; Prov 2.6
51.7 Lev 14.4; Heb 9.19; Isa 1.18
51.8 Ps 35.10
51.9 Jer 16.17
51.10 Acts 15.9; Eph 2.10; Ps 78.37
51.11 2 Kings 13.23; Eph 4.30
51.12 Ps 13.5; 2 Cor 3.17
51.13 Acts 9.21,22; Ps 22.27
51.14 2 Sam 12.9; Ps 25.5; 35.28
51.15 Ps 9.14
51.16 1 Sam 15.22; Ps 40.6
51.17 Ps 34.18
51.18 Isa 51.3; Ps 102.16
51.19 Ps 4.5; 66.13,15

52.1 1 Sam 22.9; Ps 94.4
52.2 Ps 50.19; 57.4; 59.7
52.3 Jer 9.4,5
52.4 Ps 120.3
52.5 Prov 2.22; Ps 27.13
52.6 Job 22.19; Ps 37.34; 40.3
52.7 Ps 49.6
52.8 Jer 11.16; Ps 13.5
52.9 Ps 30.12; 54.6
53.1 Ps 14.1-7; Rom 3.10
53.2 Ps 33.13
53.3 Rom 3.12
53.4 Jer 4.22
53.5 Lev 26.17,36; Ezek 6.5
53.6 Ps 14.7
54.1 Ps 20.1; 2 Chr 20.6
54.2 Ps 55.1; 5.1
54.3 Ps 86.14; 40.14; 36.1
54.4 Ps 118.7; 41.12
54.5 Ps 94.23; 143.12; 89.49
54.6 Ps 50.14; 52.9
54.7 Ps 34.6; 59.10

Psalm 52

Judgment on the Deceitful

To the leader. A Maskil of David, when Doeg the Edomite came to Saul and said to him, "David has come to the house of Ahimelech."

1 Why do you boast, O mighty one,
of mischief done against the godly?[a]
All day long 2you are plotting
destruction.
Your tongue is like a sharp razor,
you worker of treachery.
3 You love evil more than good,
and lying more than speaking the
truth. *Selah*
4 You love all words that devour,
O deceitful tongue.

5 But God will break you down forever;
he will snatch and tear you from
your tent;
he will uproot you from the land of
the living. *Selah*
6 The righteous will see, and fear,
and will laugh at the evildoer,[b] saying,
7 "See the one who would not take
refuge in God,
but trusted in abundant riches,
and sought refuge in wealth!"[c]

8 But I am like a green olive tree
in the house of God.
I trust in the steadfast love of God
forever and ever.
9 I will thank you forever,
because of what you have done.
In the presence of the faithful
I will proclaim[d] your name, for it is
good.

Psalm 53

Denunciation of Godlessness

To the leader: according to Mahalath. A Maskil of David.

1 Fools say in their hearts, "There is no
God."
They are corrupt, they commit
abominable acts;
there is no one who does good.

2 God looks down from heaven on
humankind
to see if there are any who are wise,
who seek after God.

3 They have all fallen away, they are all
alike perverse;
there is no one who does good,
no, not one.

4 Have they no knowledge, those
evildoers,
who eat up my people as they eat
bread,
and do not call upon God?

5 There they shall be in great terror,
in terror such as has not been.
For God will scatter the bones of the
ungodly;[e]
they will be put to shame,[f] for God
has rejected them.

6 O that deliverance for Israel would come
from Zion!
When God restores the fortunes of his
people,
Jacob will rejoice; Israel will be glad.

Psalm 54

Prayer for Vindication

To the leader: with stringed instruments. A Maskil of David, when the Ziphites went and told Saul, "David is in hiding among us."

1 Save me, O God, by your name,
and vindicate me by your might.
2 Hear my prayer, O God;
give ear to the words of my mouth.

3 For the insolent have risen against me,
the ruthless seek my life;
they do not set God before them.
Selah

4 But surely, God is my helper;
the Lord is the upholder of[g] my life.
5 He will repay my enemies for their evil.
In your faithfulness, put an end to
them.

6 With a freewill offering I will sacrifice to
you;
I will give thanks to your name, O
LORD, for it is good.
7 For he has delivered me from every
trouble,
and my eye has looked in triumph on
my enemies.

[a] Cn Compare Syr: Heb *the kindness of God* [b] Heb *him* [c] Syr Tg: Heb *in his destruction* [d] Cn: Heb *wait for* [e] Cn Compare Gk Syr: Heb *him who encamps against you* [f] Gk: Heb *you will put to shame* [g] Gk Syr Jerome: Heb *is of those who uphold* or *is with those who uphold*

Ps 52 The reference in the superscription to Doeg's betrayal of David to Saul (1 Sam 22.6-10) is anachronistic, since the psalm refers to the temple (house of God, 52.8) which had not been built in David's time. The psalm is a vindictive warning to those who mistreat God's people that they will be punished by God, who will remain secure in *the steadfast love of God*.
Ps 53 This psalm reproduces the denunciation of the wicked in Ps 14 with only minor changes: 53.5 heightens the ferocity of God's judgment on the wicked and omits reference to *the righteous* (14.5). It looks forward, as does Ps 14, to the restoration of God's people.
Ps 54 The title refers to the betrayal of David to Saul by the Ziphites (1 Sam 23.19; 26.1), but the details of that story are not evident in the psalm, which is an appeal that God will save him from his enemies, and promises an offering in thanksgiving.

Ps 55 The *fearful* noise of the enemy and the resultant terror of death are so overwhelming that the psalmist prays to be allowed to escape to quiet and safety (vv.1-8). While he calls for doom on his enemies, he pleads also for God's punishment of his *familiar friend* who has betrayed him and whose deceitful words and cruel attack on another friend have resulted in violation of *a covenant.* The psalmist's confidence is in God's sustaining power, but also in God's punishment of the wicked.

Ps 56 The introduction alludes to David's stay among the Philistines in Gath (1 Sam 21.10-15), but there is no logical link between that event and the content of the psalm. Trust in God has sustained the psalmist in spite of his enemies' plots against him. He asks that they be punished for their misdeeds, and promises appropriate offerings to God for his deliverance.

Psalm 55

Complaint about a Friend's Treachery

To the leader: with stringed instruments. A Maskil of David.

1 Give ear to my prayer, O God;
do not hide yourself from my supplication.
2 Attend to me, and answer me;
I am troubled in my complaint.
I am distraught 3by the noise of the enemy,
because of the clamor of the wicked.
For they bring[h] trouble upon me,
and in anger they cherish enmity against me.

4 My heart is in anguish within me,
the terrors of death have fallen upon me.
5 Fear and trembling come upon me,
and horror overwhelms me.
6 And I say, "O that I had wings like a dove!
I would fly away and be at rest;
7 truly, I would flee far away;
I would lodge in the wilderness; *Selah*
8 I would hurry to find a shelter for myself
from the raging wind and tempest."

9 Confuse, O Lord, confound their speech;
for I see violence and strife in the city.
10 Day and night they go around it
on its walls,
and iniquity and trouble are within it;
11 ruin is in its midst;
oppression and fraud
do not depart from its marketplace.

12 It is not enemies who taunt me—
I could bear that;
it is not adversaries who deal insolently with me—
I could hide from them.
13 But it is you, my equal,
my companion, my familiar friend,
14 with whom I kept pleasant company;
we walked in the house of God with the throng.
15 Let death come upon them;
let them go down alive to Sheol;
for evil is in their homes and in their hearts.

16 But I call upon God,
and the LORD will save me.
17 Evening and morning and at noon
I utter my complaint and moan,
and he will hear my voice.
18 He will redeem me unharmed
from the battle that I wage,
for many are arrayed against me.
19 God, who is enthroned from of old,
Selah
will hear, and will humble them—
because they do not change,
and do not fear God.

20 My companion laid hands on a friend
and violated a covenant with me[i]
21 with speech smoother than butter,
but with a heart set on war;
with words that were softer than oil,
but in fact were drawn swords.

22 Cast your burden[j] on the LORD,
and he will sustain you;
he will never permit
the righteous to be moved.

23 But you, O God, will cast them down
into the lowest pit;
the bloodthirsty and treacherous
shall not live out half their days.
But I will trust in you.

Psalm 56

Trust in God under Persecution

To the leader: according to The Dove on Far-off Terebinths. Of David. A Miktam, when the Philistines seized him in Gath.

1 Be gracious to me, O God, for people trample on me;
all day long foes oppress me;
2 my enemies trample on me all day long,
for many fight against me.
O Most High, 3when I am afraid,
I put my trust in you.
4 In God, whose word I praise,
in God I trust; I am not afraid;
what can flesh do to me?

5 All day long they seek to injure my cause;
all their thoughts are against me for evil.
6 They stir up strife, they lurk,
they watch my steps.
As they hoped to have my life,
7 so repay[k] them for their crime;
in wrath cast down the peoples, O God!

[h] Cn Compare Gk: Heb *they cause to totter* [i] Heb lacks *with me* [j] Or *Cast what he has given you* [k] Cn: Heb *rescue*

55.1 Ps 61.1; 27.9
55.2 Ps 66.19; 77.3; Isa 38.14
55.3 Ps 17.9; 2 Sam 16.7,8; Ps 71.11
55.4 Ps 116.3
55.5 Ps 119.120; Job 21.6
55.6 Job 3.13
55.8 Isa 4.6
55.9 Jer 6.7
55.11 Ps 5.9; 10.7
55.12 Ps 41.9
55.13 2 Sam 15.12; Ps 41.9; Jer 9.4
55.14 Ps 42.4
55.15 Ps 64.7; Num 16.30,33
55.16 Ps 57.2,3
55.17 Ps 141.2; Dan 6.10; Ps 5.3
55.18 Ps 103.4; 2 Chr 32.7,8
55.19 Ps 78.59; Deut 33.27
55.20 Ps 7.4; 89.34
55.21 Ps 28.3; Prov 5.3; Ps 59.7
55.22 Ps 37.5; Mt 6.25; 1 Pet 5.7; Ps 37.24
55.23 Ps 73.18; 5.6; Job 15.32; Ps 25.2
56.1 Ps 57.13
56.2 Ps 57.3; 35.1
56.3 Ps 55.4,5; 11.1
56.4 Ps 118.6; Heb 13.6
56.5 Ps 41.7
56.6 Ps 59.3; 140.2; 19.10,11
56.7 Ps 36.12; 55.23

8 You have kept count of my tossings;
put my tears in your bottle.
Are they not in your record?
9 Then my enemies will retreat
in the day when I call.
This I know, that[l] God is for me.
10 In God, whose word I praise,
in the LORD, whose word I praise,
11 in God I trust; I am not afraid.
What can a mere mortal do to me?

12 My vows to you I must perform, O God;
I will render thank offerings to you.
13 For you have delivered my soul from
death,
and my feet from falling,
so that I may walk before God
in the light of life.

Psalm 57

Praise and Assurance under Persecution

To the leader: Do Not Destroy. Of David. A Miktam, when he fled from Saul, in the cave.

1 Be merciful to me, O God, be merciful to
me,
for in you my soul takes refuge;
in the shadow of your wings I will take
refuge,
until the destroying storms pass by.
2 I cry to God Most High,
to God who fulfills his purpose for me.
3 He will send from heaven and save me,
he will put to shame those who
trample on me. *Selah*
God will send forth his steadfast love
and his faithfulness.

4 I lie down among lions
that greedily devour[m] human prey;
their teeth are spears and arrows,
their tongues sharp swords.

5 Be exalted, O God, above the heavens.
Let your glory be over all the earth.

6 They set a net for my steps;
my soul was bowed down.
They dug a pit in my path,
but they have fallen into it
themselves. *Selah*
7 My heart is steadfast, O God,
my heart is steadfast.
I will sing and make melody.
8 Awake, my soul!
Awake, O harp and lyre!
I will awake the dawn.
9 I will give thanks to you, O Lord, among
the peoples;
I will sing praises to you among the
nations.
10 For your steadfast love is as high as the
heavens;
your faithfulness extends to the clouds.

11 Be exalted, O God, above the heavens.
Let your glory be over all the earth.

Psalm 58

Prayer for Vengeance

To the leader: Do Not Destroy. Of David. A Miktam.

1 Do you indeed decree what is right, you
gods?[n]
Do you judge people fairly?
2 No, in your hearts you devise wrongs;
your hands deal out violence on
earth.

3 The wicked go astray from the womb;
they err from their birth, speaking lies.
4 They have venom like the venom of a
serpent,
like the deaf adder that stops its ear,
5 so that it does not hear the voice of
charmers
or of the cunning enchanter.

6 O God, break the teeth in their mouths;
tear out the fangs of the young lions,
O LORD!
7 Let them vanish like water that runs
away;
like grass let them be trodden down[o]
and wither.
8 Let them be like the snail that dissolves
into slime;
like the untimely birth that never sees
the sun.
9 Sooner than your pots can feel the heat
of thorns,
whether green or ablaze, may he
sweep them away!

10 The righteous will rejoice when they see
vengeance done;
they will bathe their feet in the blood
of the wicked.
11 People will say, "Surely there is a
reward for the righteous;
surely there is a God who judges on
earth."

[l] Or *because* [m] Cn: Heb *are aflame for* [n] Or *mighty lords* [o] Cn: Meaning of Heb uncertain

Ps 57 The reference to Saul and the cave is to the incident in 1 Sam 24, where David escaped but left behind concrete evidence that he had spared Saul's life, not merely that he had fled. The psalm expresses confidence that God has the power and the will to protect his own and fulfill his purpose for them in spite of the schemes of their enemies. Accordingly, the psalmist praises God and prays for his exaltation *over all the earth.*
Ps 58 Here there is a call for God's destruction of the evil powers that pass for gods, and for the foolish people who honor them. *The righteous* will live to see the rout of false divinities and their devotees.

56.8 Ps 139.3; 39.12; Mal 3.26
56.9 Ps 9.3; 102.2; Rom 8.31
56.12 Ps 50.14
56.13 Ps 116.8; Job 33.30
57.1 Ps 2.12; 17.8; Isa 26.20
57.2 Ps 138.8
57.3 Ps 18.16; 56.2; 40.11
57.4 Ps 35.17; Prov 30.14; Ps 55.21
57.5 Ps 108.5
57.6 Ps 35.7; 145.14; 7.15; Prov 28.10
57.7 Ps 108.1
57.8 Ps 16.9; 30.12; 150.3
57.9 Ps 108.3
57.10 Ps 36.5
57.11 ver 5
58.1 Ps 82.2
58.2 Mal 3.15; Ps 94.20
58.3 Ps 51.5; Isa 48.8; Ps 53.3
58.4 Ps 140.3; Eccl 10.11
58.5 Ps 81.11
58.6 Job 4.10; Ps 3.7
58.7 Josh 7.5; Ps 112.10; 64.3
58.8 Job 3.16
58.9 Ps 118.12; Prov 10.25
58.10 Ps 64.10; 91.8; 68.23
58.11 Ps 18.20; 9.8

Ps 59 The introduction refers to David's escape from a plot on his life, described in 1 Sam 19.8-17, although the main focus in the psalm is on the proud, wicked nations. What is prayed for is their humiliation and impotence rather than merely their destruction, while the psalmist is confident in the protective and sustaining power of God.
Ps 60 The superscription refers to David's defeat of the Edomites in 2 Sam 8.13-14, but the details are not exact and the psalm expects defeat rather than victory. The cause of God's anger is not specified, but the result is the weakening of the forces of *those whom you love*, including God's rallying the enemy troops *out of bowshot* of Israel's army. God is in control of all the cities and tribal lands in the vicinity: *Shechem*, the original capital of the northern tribes of Israel; *Succoth*, an important city in what was Israelite territory on the east bank of the Jordan; *Gilead*, east of the Jordan; *Manasseh*, which at one time spanned both sides of the Jordan, while Ephraim and Judah were on the west bank; *Moab and Edom*, east of the Dead Sea, and *Philistia*, on the coastal strip between Israel and the Mediterranean. All these regions are seen as being brought under the control of God's people.

Psalm 59

Prayer for Deliverance from Enemies

To the leader: Do Not Destroy. Of David. A Miktam, when Saul ordered his house to be watched in order to kill him.

1 Deliver me from my enemies, O my God;
protect me from those who rise up against me.
2 Deliver me from those who work evil;
from the bloodthirsty save me.

3 Even now they lie in wait for my life;
the mighty stir up strife against me.
For no transgression or sin of mine, O LORD,
4 for no fault of mine, they run and make ready.

Rouse yourself, come to my help and see!
5 You, LORD God of hosts, are God of Israel.
Awake to punish all the nations;
spare none of those who treacherously plot evil. *Selah*

6 Each evening they come back,
howling like dogs
and prowling about the city.
7 There they are, bellowing with their mouths,
with sharp words[p] on their lips—
for "Who," they think,[q] "will hear us?"

8 But you laugh at them, O LORD;
you hold all the nations in derision.
9 O my strength, I will watch for you;
for you, O God, are my fortress.
10 My God in his steadfast love will meet me;
my God will let me look in triumph on my enemies.

11 Do not kill them, or my people may forget;
make them totter by your power, and bring them down,
O Lord, our shield.
12 For the sin of their mouths, the words of their lips,
let them be trapped in their pride.
For the cursing and lies that they utter,
13 consume them in wrath;
consume them until they are no more.
Then it will be known to the ends of the earth
that God rules over Jacob. *Selah*

14 Each evening they come back,
howling like dogs
and prowling about the city.
15 They roam about for food,
and growl if they do not get their fill.

16 But I will sing of your might;
I will sing aloud of your steadfast love in the morning.
For you have been a fortress for me
and a refuge in the day of my distress.
17 O my strength, I will sing praises to you,
for you, O God, are my fortress,
the God who shows me steadfast love.

Psalm 60

Prayer for National Victory after Defeat

To the leader: according to the Lily of the Covenant. A Miktam of David; for instruction; when he struggled with Aram-naharaim and with Aram-zobah, and when Joab on his return killed twelve thousand Edomites in the Valley of Salt.

1 O God, you have rejected us, broken our defenses;
you have been angry; now restore us!
2 You have caused the land to quake; you have torn it open;
repair the cracks in it, for it is tottering.
3 You have made your people suffer hard things;
you have given us wine to drink that made us reel.

4 You have set up a banner for those who fear you,
to rally to it out of bowshot.[r] *Selah*
5 Give victory with your right hand, and answer us,[s]
so that those whom you love may be rescued.

6 God has promised in his sanctuary:[t]
"With exultation I will divide up Shechem,
and portion out the Vale of Succoth.
7 Gilead is mine, and Manasseh is mine;
Ephraim is my helmet;
Judah is my scepter.
8 Moab is my washbasin;
on Edom I hurl my shoe;
over Philistia I shout in triumph."

[p] Heb *with swords* [q] Heb lacks *they think* [r] Gk Syr Jerome: Heb *because of the truth* [s] Another reading is *me* [t] Or *by his holiness*

59.1 Ps 143.9
59.2 Ps 28.3; 139.19
59.3 Ps 56.6
59.4 Ps 35.19,23
59.5 Ps 9.5; Jer 18.23
59.6 ver 14
59.7 Ps 57.4; 10.11
59.8 Ps 37.13; 2.4
59.9 Ps 9.9
59.10 Ps 21.3; 54.7
59.11 Deut 4.9; Ps 106.27; 84.9
59.12 Prov 12.13; Zeph 3.11; Ps 10.7
59.13 Ps 104.35; 83.18
59.14 ver 6
59.16 Ps 21.13; 101.1; 88.13; ver 9; Ps 46.1
59.17 ver 9,10
60.1 Ps 44.9; 2 Sam 5.20; Ps 79.5; 80.3
60.2 Ps 18.7; 2 Chr 7.14
60.3 Ps 71.20; Isa 51.17,22
60.4 Ps 20.5
60.5 Ps 108.6; 127.2; 17.7
60.6 Ps 89.35; Josh 1.6; Gen 12.6
60.7 Josh 13.31; Deut 33.17; Gen 49.10
60.8 2 Sam 8.1

9 Who will bring me to the fortified city?
Who will lead me to Edom?
10 Have you not rejected us, O God?
You do not go out, O God, with our armies.
11 O grant us help against the foe,
for human help is worthless.
12 With God we shall do valiantly;
it is he who will tread down our foes.

Psalm 61

Assurance of God's Protection

To the leader: with stringed instruments. Of David.

1 Hear my cry, O God;
listen to my prayer.
2 From the end of the earth I call to you,
when my heart is faint.

Lead me to the rock
that is higher than I;
3 for you are my refuge,
a strong tower against the enemy.

4 Let me abide in your tent forever,
find refuge under the shelter of your wings. *Selah*
5 For you, O God, have heard my vows;
you have given me the heritage of those who fear your name.

6 Prolong the life of the king;
may his years endure to all generations!
7 May he be enthroned forever before God;
appoint steadfast love and faithfulness to watch over him!

8 So I will always sing praises to your name,
as I pay my vows day after day.

Psalm 62

Song of Trust in God Alone

To the leader: according to Jeduthun. A Psalm of David.

1 For God alone my soul waits in silence;
from him comes my salvation.
2 He alone is my rock and my salvation,
my fortress; I shall never be shaken.

3 How long will you assail a person,
will you batter your victim, all of you,
as you would a leaning wall, a tottering fence?
4 Their only plan is to bring down a person of prominence.
They take pleasure in falsehood;
they bless with their mouths,
but inwardly they curse. *Selah*

5 For God alone my soul waits in silence,
for my hope is from him.
6 He alone is my rock and my salvation,
my fortress; I shall not be shaken.
7 On God rests my deliverance and my honor;
my mighty rock, my refuge is in God.

8 Trust in him at all times, O people;
pour out your heart before him;
God is a refuge for us. *Selah*

9 Those of low estate are but a breath,
those of high estate are a delusion;
in the balances they go up;
they are together lighter than a breath.
10 Put no confidence in extortion,
and set no vain hopes on robbery;
if riches increase, do not set your heart on them.

11 Once God has spoken;
twice have I heard this:
that power belongs to God,
12 and steadfast love belongs to you, O Lord.
For you repay to all
according to their work.

Psalm 63

Comfort and Assurance in God's Presence

A Psalm of David, when he was in the Wilderness of Judah.

1 O God, you are my God, I seek you,
my soul thirsts for you;
my flesh faints for you,
as in a dry and weary land where there is no water.
2 So I have looked upon you in the sanctuary,
beholding your power and glory.
3 Because your steadfast love is better than life,
my lips will praise you.
4 So I will bless you as long as I live;
I will lift up my hands and call on your name.

5 My soul is satisfied as with a rich feast,[u]
and my mouth praises you with joyful lips

[u] Heb *with fat and fatness*

60.10 ver 1; Ps 44.9
60.11 Ps 146.3
60.12 Num 24.18; Ps 44.5
61.1 Ps 64.1; 86.6
61.2 Ps 77.3; 18.2
61.3 Ps 62.7; Prov 18.10
61.4 Ps 23.6; 91.4
61.5 Ps 56.12; 86.11
61.6 Ps 21.4
61.7 Ps 41.12; 40.11
61.8 Ps 71.22; 65.1
62.1 Ps 33.20
62.2 Ps 89.26; ver 6
62.3 Isa 30.13
62.4 Ps 4.2; 28.3
62.6 ver 2
62.7 Ps 85.9; 46.1
62.8 Ps 37.3; 1 Sam 1.15; Ps 42.4; Lam 2.19
62.9 Ps 39.5,11; Isa 40.15,17; Rom 3.4
62.10 Isa 30.12; 61.8; Job 31.25; Ps 52.7; 1 Tim 6.7
62.11 Job 33.14; 1 Chr 29.11
62.12 Job 34.11; Mt 16.27; Col 3.25
63.1 Ps 42.2; 84.2
63.2 Ps 27.4
63.3 Ps 69.16
63.4 Ps 104.33; 28.2
63.5 Ps 36.8; 71.23

Ps 61 Two themes in this psalm are (1) the appeal to God for security (vv.1-5) under various images: a lofty rock, a strong tower and an enduring shelter (*tent*); (2) long life and divine protection for the king (vv.6-7).
Ps 62 *Jeduthun* is a temple musician mentioned in 1 Chr 25.3 who *prophesied with the lyre.* Confidence is warranted in God alone, since human beings attack others by word and action. Only God provides true security; human conditions of wealth and poverty are alike of no enduring significance. *Power belongs to God.*
Ps 63 God, whom the psalmist has seen *in the sanctuary*, is the one enduring, dependable resource in human life. Human enemies shall be destroyed, but for *the king*, God will be the source of joy.

Ps 64 No matter how shrewdly conceived are human plots against others, God will care for his own and destroy those bent on their destruction. Those obedient to God will *rejoice*.
Ps 65 In God all humanity has a resource for forgiveness (vs.3), and for deliverance from enemies (vs.5), for stability and order in nature and the productivity of the earth (vv.6-13).

6 when I think of you on my bed,
and meditate on you in the watches of the night;
7 for you have been my help,
and in the shadow of your wings I sing for joy.
8 My soul clings to you;
your right hand upholds me.

9 But those who seek to destroy my life
shall go down into the depths of the earth;
10 they shall be given over to the power of the sword,
they shall be prey for jackals.
11 But the king shall rejoice in God;
all who swear by him shall exult,
for the mouths of liars will be stopped.

Psalm 64

Prayer for Protection from Enemies

To the leader. A Psalm of David.

1 Hear my voice, O God, in my complaint;
preserve my life from the dread enemy.
2 Hide me from the secret plots of the wicked,
from the scheming of evildoers,
3 who whet their tongues like swords,
who aim bitter words like arrows,
4 shooting from ambush at the blameless;
they shoot suddenly and without fear.
5 They hold fast to their evil purpose;
they talk of laying snares secretly,
thinking, "Who can see us?[v]
6 Who can search out our crimes?[w]
We have thought out a cunningly conceived plot."
For the human heart and mind are deep.

7 But God will shoot his arrow at them;
they will be wounded suddenly.
8 Because of their tongue he will bring them to ruin;[x]
all who see them will shake with horror.
9 Then everyone will fear;
they will tell what God has brought about,
and ponder what he has done.

10 Let the righteous rejoice in the LORD
and take refuge in him.
Let all the upright in heart glory.

Psalm 65

Thanksgiving for Earth's Bounty

To the leader. A Psalm of David. A Song.

1 Praise is due to you,
O God, in Zion;
and to you shall vows be performed,
2 O you who answer prayer!
To you all flesh shall come.
3 When deeds of iniquity overwhelm us,
you forgive our transgressions.
4 Happy are those whom you choose and bring near
to live in your courts.
We shall be satisfied with the goodness of your house,
your holy temple.

5 By awesome deeds you answer us with deliverance,
O God of our salvation;
you are the hope of all the ends of the earth
and of the farthest seas.
6 By your[y] strength you established the mountains;
you are girded with might.
7 You silence the roaring of the seas,
the roaring of their waves,
the tumult of the peoples.
8 Those who live at earth's farthest bounds are awed by your signs;
you make the gateways of the morning and the evening shout for joy.

9 You visit the earth and water it,
you greatly enrich it;
the river of God is full of water;
you provide the people with grain,
for so you have prepared it.
10 You water its furrows abundantly,
settling its ridges,
softening it with showers,
and blessing its growth.
11 You crown the year with your bounty;
your wagon tracks overflow with richness.
12 The pastures of the wilderness overflow,
the hills gird themselves with joy,
13 the meadows clothe themselves with flocks,
the valleys deck themselves with grain,
they shout and sing together for joy.

[v] Syr: Heb *them* [w] Cn: Heb *They search out crimes* [x] Cn: Heb *They will bring him to ruin, their tongue being against them* [y] Gk Jerome: Heb *his*

63.6 Ps 42.8
63.7 Ps 27.9
63.8 Ps 18.35
63.9 Ps 40.14; 55.15
63.11 Ps 21.1; Deut 6.13; Isa 45.23
64.1 Ps 55.2; 140.1
64.2 Ps 56.6; 59.2
64.3 Ps 58.7
64.4 Ps 11.2; 55.19
64.5 Ps 10.11
64.6 Ps 49.11
64.8 Ps 9.3; Prov 18.7; Ps 22.7
64.9 Jer 50.28
64.10 Ps 32.11; 25.20
65.1 Ps 116.18
65.2 Isa 66.23
65.3 Ps 38.4; Heb 9.14
65.4 Ps 33.12; 4.3; 36.8
65.5 Ps 66.3; 85.4; 22.27; 107.23
65.6 Ps 93.1
65.7 Mt 8.26; Isa 17.12
65.9 Ps 68.9,10; 46.4; 104.14
65.12 Job 38.26,27; Ps 98.8
65.13 Ps 144.13; 72.16; 98.8

Psalm 66

Praise for God's Goodness to Israel

To the leader. A Song. A Psalm.

1 Make a joyful noise to God, all the earth;
2 sing the glory of his name;
give to him glorious praise.
3 Say to God, "How awesome are your deeds!
Because of your great power, your enemies cringe before you.
4 All the earth worships you;
they sing praises to you,
sing praises to your name." *Selah*

5 Come and see what God has done:
he is awesome in his deeds among mortals.
6 He turned the sea into dry land;
they passed through the river on foot.
There we rejoiced in him,
7 who rules by his might forever,
whose eyes keep watch on the nations—
let the rebellious not exalt themselves. *Selah*

8 Bless our God, O peoples,
let the sound of his praise be heard,
9 who has kept us among the living,
and has not let our feet slip.
10 For you, O God, have tested us;
you have tried us as silver is tried.
11 You brought us into the net;
you laid burdens on our backs;
12 you let people ride over our heads;
we went through fire and through water;
yet you have brought us out to a spacious place.[z]

13 I will come into your house with burnt offerings;
I will pay you my vows,
14 those that my lips uttered
and my mouth promised when I was in trouble.
15 I will offer to you burnt offerings of fatlings,
with the smoke of the sacrifice of rams;
I will make an offering of bulls and goats. *Selah*

16 Come and hear, all you who fear God,
and I will tell what he has done for me.
17 I cried aloud to him,
and he was extolled with my tongue.
18 If I had cherished iniquity in my heart,
the Lord would not have listened.
19 But truly God has listened;
he has given heed to the words of my prayer.

20 Blessed be God,
because he has not rejected my prayer
or removed his steadfast love from me.

Psalm 67

The Nations Called to Praise God

To the leader: with stringed instruments. A Psalm. A Song.

1 May God be gracious to us and bless us
and make his face to shine upon us, *Selah*
2 that your way may be known upon earth,
your saving power among all nations.
3 Let the peoples praise you, O God;
let all the peoples praise you.

4 Let the nations be glad and sing for joy,
for you judge the peoples with equity
and guide the nations upon earth. *Selah*
5 Let the peoples praise you, O God;
let all the peoples praise you.

6 The earth has yielded its increase;
God, our God, has blessed us.
7 May God continue to bless us;
let all the ends of the earth revere him.

Psalm 68

Praise and Thanksgiving

To the leader. Of David. A Psalm. A Song.

1 Let God rise up, let his enemies be scattered;
let those who hate him flee before him.
2 As smoke is driven away, so drive them away;
as wax melts before the fire,
let the wicked perish before God.
3 But let the righteous be joyful;
let them exult before God;
let them be jubilant with joy.

4 Sing to God, sing praises to his name;
lift up a song to him who rides upon the clouds[a]—

[z] Cn Compare Gk Syr Jerome Tg: Heb *to a saturation*

[a] Or *cast up a highway for him who rides through the deserts*

66.1 Ps 100.1
66.2 Ps 81.1; 79.9
66.3 Ps 65.5; 18.44
66.4 Ps 22.27; 67.3,4
66.5 Ps 46.8; 106.22
66.6 Ex 14.21; Josh 3.6; Ps 105.43
66.7 Ps 145.13; 11.4; 140.8
66.8 Ps 98.4
66.9 Ps 121.3
66.10 Ps 17.3; Isa 48.10; Zech 13.9; 1 Pet 1.6,7
66.11 Lam 1.13
66.12 Isa 51.23; 43.2
66.13 Eccl 5.4
66.14 Ps 18.6
66.15 Ps 51.19; Num 6.14
66.16 Ps 34.11; 71.15,24
66.18 Job 36.21; Isa 1.15; Jas 4.3
66.19 Ps 116.1,2
66.20 Ps 64.35; 22.24
67.1 Num 6.25; Ps 4.6
67.2 Acts 18.25; Titus 2.11
67.4 Ps 96.10; 98.9
67.5 ver 3
67.6 Lev 26.4; Ps 85.12; Ezek 34.27
67.7 Ps 33.8
68.1 Num 10.35; Isa 33.3
68.2 Isa 9.18; Hos 13.3; Ps 97.5; Mic 1.4
68.3 Ps 32.11
68.4 Ps 66.2; Isa 57.14; 40.3; Ps 83.18

Ps 66 *All the earth* is summoned to join in praising God, who created the earth and orders both nature and human history (vv.1-7). He has cared for his people during their times of difficulty (vv.8-12), and is now approached for worship by the psalmist (vv.13-15), who invites all who *fear God* to join him in honoring the LORD.
Ps 67 The prayer for God's blessing on his people is motivated by the desire that through this *all nations* will know him and acknowledge his universal rule.
Ps 68 This psalm was probably used for symbolic celebrations of God's movement of his people from Sinai to his dwelling place in the sanctuary in Jerusalem. Fire and smoke (vs.2) recall the journeys with the ark of the covenant in Num 9.15-23. His sovereignty is over all the universe (vs.4), but his concern is also for the needy (vv.5-6). Summarized in poetic language are the journey through the wilderness, the victories over enemies (especially those east of the Jordan, represented here by *Bashan*), and the final triumphant ascent to the holy mountain in Jerusalem. All the enemies, symbolized here by wild animals (vs.30), are defeated, and all the *kingdoms of the earth* will join in honoring the God of Israel.

his name is the LORD—
be exultant before him.

5 Father of orphans and protector of widows
is God in his holy habitation.
6 God gives the desolate a home to live in;
he leads out the prisoners to prosperity,
but the rebellious live in a parched land.

7 O God, when you went out before your people,
when you marched through the wilderness, *Selah*
8 the earth quaked, the heavens poured down rain
at the presence of God, the God of Sinai,
at the presence of God, the God of Israel.
9 Rain in abundance, O God, you showered abroad;
you restored your heritage when it languished;
10 your flock found a dwelling in it;
in your goodness, O God, you provided for the needy.

11 The Lord gives the command;
great is the company of those[b] who bore the tidings:
12 "The kings of the armies, they flee, they flee!"
The women at home divide the spoil,
13 though they stay among the sheepfolds—
the wings of a dove covered with silver,
its pinions with green gold.
14 When the Almighty[c] scattered kings there,
snow fell on Zalmon.

15 O mighty mountain, mountain of Bashan;
O many-peaked mountain, mountain of Bashan!
16 Why do you look with envy, O many-peaked mountain,
at the mount that God desired for his abode,
where the LORD will reside forever?

17 With mighty chariotry, twice ten thousand,
thousands upon thousands,
the Lord came from Sinai into the holy place.[d]
18 You ascended the high mount,
leading captives in your train
and receiving gifts from people,
even from those who rebel against the LORD God's abiding there.
19 Blessed be the Lord,
who daily bears us up;
God is our salvation. *Selah*
20 Our God is a God of salvation,
and to GOD, the Lord, belongs escape from death.

21 But God will shatter the heads of his enemies,
the hairy crown of those who walk in their guilty ways.
22 The Lord said,
"I will bring them back from Bashan,
I will bring them back from the depths of the sea,
23 so that you may bathe[e] your feet in blood,
so that the tongues of your dogs may have their share from the foe."

24 Your solemn processions are seen,[f] O God,
the processions of my God, my King, into the sanctuary—
25 the singers in front, the musicians last,
between them girls playing tambourines:
26 "Bless God in the great congregation,
the LORD, O you who are of Israel's fountain!"
27 There is Benjamin, the least of them, in the lead,
the princes of Judah in a body,
the princes of Zebulun, the princes of Naphtali.

28 Summon your might, O God;
show your strength, O God, as you have done for us before.
29 Because of your temple at Jerusalem
kings bear gifts to you.
30 Rebuke the wild animals that live among the reeds,
the herd of bulls with the calves of the peoples.
Trample[g] under foot those who lust after tribute;

[b] Or *company of the women* [c] Traditional rendering of Heb *Shaddai* [d] Cn: Heb *The Lord among them Sinai in the holy* (place) [e] Gk Syr Tg: Heb *shatter* [f] Or *have been seen* [g] Cn: Heb *Trampling*

68.5 Ps 146.9; Deut 10.18; 26.15
68.6 Ps 113.9; Acts 12.6; Ps 107.34
68.7 Ex 13.21; Judg 4.14
68.8 Ex 19.16,18; Judg 5.4
68.9 Deut 11.11
68.10 Deut 26.5; Ps 74.19
68.12 Ps 135.11; 1 Sam 30.24
68.13 Gen 49.14
68.14 Josh 10.10
68.16 Deut 12.5; Ps 87.1,2
68.17 Deut 33.2; Dan 7.10
68.18 Acts 1.9; Eph 4.8; Judg 5.12; 1 Tim 1.13
68.19 Ps 55.22; 65.5
68.20 Ps 49.15; 56.13
68.21 Ps 110.6; 55.23
68.22 Num 21.33; Ex 14.22
68.23 Ps 58.10; 1 Kings 21.9
68.24 Ps 77.13; 63.2
68.25 1 Chr 13.8; Judg 11.34
68.26 Ps 26.12; Deut 33.28; Isa 48.1
68.27 1 Sam 9.21
68.29 Ps 72.10
68.30 Ps 22.12; 89.10

scatter the peoples who delight in war.[h]
31 Let bronze be brought from Egypt;
let Ethiopia[i] hasten to stretch out its hands to God.

32 Sing to God, O kingdoms of the earth;
sing praises to the Lord,
Selah
33 O rider in the heavens, the ancient heavens;
listen, he sends out his voice, his mighty voice.
34 Ascribe power to God,
whose majesty is over Israel;
and whose power is in the skies.
35 Awesome is God in his[j] sanctuary,
the God of Israel;
he gives power and strength to his people.

Blessed be God!

Psalm 69

Prayer for Deliverance from Persecution

To the leader: according to Lilies. Of David.

1 Save me, O God,
for the waters have come up to my neck.
2 I sink in deep mire,
where there is no foothold;
I have come into deep waters,
and the flood sweeps over me.
3 I am weary with my crying;
my throat is parched.
My eyes grow dim
with waiting for my God.

4 More in number than the hairs of my head
are those who hate me without cause;
many are those who would destroy me,
my enemies who accuse me falsely.
What I did not steal
must I now restore?
5 O God, you know my folly;
the wrongs I have done are not hidden from you.

6 Do not let those who hope in you be put to shame because of me,
O Lord GOD of hosts;
do not let those who seek you be dishonored because of me,
O God of Israel.
7 It is for your sake that I have borne reproach,
that shame has covered my face.
8 I have become a stranger to my kindred,
an alien to my mother's children.

9 It is zeal for your house that has consumed me;
the insults of those who insult you have fallen on me.
10 When I humbled my soul with fasting,[k]
they insulted me for doing so.
11 When I made sackcloth my clothing,
I became a byword to them.
12 I am the subject of gossip for those who sit in the gate,
and the drunkards make songs about me.

13 But as for me, my prayer is to you, O LORD.
At an acceptable time, O God,
in the abundance of your steadfast love, answer me.
With your faithful help 14 rescue me
from sinking in the mire;
let me be delivered from my enemies
and from the deep waters.
15 Do not let the flood sweep over me,
or the deep swallow me up,
or the Pit close its mouth over me.

16 Answer me, O LORD, for your steadfast love is good;
according to your abundant mercy, turn to me.
17 Do not hide your face from your servant,
for I am in distress—make haste to answer me.
18 Draw near to me, redeem me,
set me free because of my enemies.

19 You know the insults I receive,
and my shame and dishonor;
my foes are all known to you.
20 Insults have broken my heart,
so that I am in despair.
I looked for pity, but there was none;
and for comforters, but I found none.
21 They gave me poison for food,
and for my thirst they gave me vinegar to drink.

68.31 Isa 19.19; 45.14
68.33 Ps 18.10; Deut 10.14; Ps 44.6; 29.4
68.34 Ps 29.1
68.35 Ps 47.2; 29.11; 66.20
69.1 ver 14,15
69.2 Ps 40.2; Jon 2.3
69.3 Ps 6.6; 119.82; Isa 38.14
69.4 Ps 35.19; Jn 15.25; Ps 38.19; 35.11
69.5 Ps 38.5; 44.21
69.7 Jer 15.15
69.8 Ps 31.11; Isa 53.3
69.9 Jn 2.17; Ps 89.50
69.10 Ps 35.13
69.11 Ps 35.13; Jer 24.9
69.12 Job 30.9
69.13 Isa 49.8; 2 Cor 6.2; Ps 51.1
69.14 ver 2; Ps 144.7
69.15 Ps 124.4,5; Num 16.33
69.16 Ps 63.3; 51.1; 25.16
69.17 Ps 27.9; 66.14
69.19 Ps 22.6,7; Isa 53.3
69.20 Jer 23.9; Isa 63.5; Job 16.2
69.21 Mt 27.34; Jn 19.29

Ps 69 The psalm sounds three themes: (1) lament for hostility from enemies and for misunderstanding from contemporaries; (2) appeal to God for help; (3) invoking judgment on the enemies. 69.1-4,9-12,19-21 sound the lament. 69.6-8,13-18, 29 are the cry to God for vindication. 69.22-28 calls for divine punishment of the oppressors. Vs.5 is a confession of guilt, and the conclusion (vv.30-36) calls for praise to God from the psalmist and from *heaven and earth* when God renews *Zion and the cities of Judah.*

[h] Meaning of Heb of verse 30 is uncertain [i] Or *Nubia*; Heb *Cush* [j] Gk: Heb *from your* [k] Gk Syr: Heb *I wept, with fasting my soul,* or *I made my soul mourn with fasting*

Ps 70 A prayer for divine defense against those bringing threat or harm on the psalmist, and an expression of thanks for God's care for *poor and needy.*
Ps 71 A blend of petitions for safety (vv.1-3) and *rescue* from the attacks of the unjust (vv.4,7-13), and of declarations of gratitude for God's continuing care in the past from childhood down to old age (vv.6,14-24).

22 Let their table be a trap for them,
a snare for their allies.
23 Let their eyes be darkened so that they cannot see,
and make their loins tremble continually.
24 Pour out your indignation upon them,
and let your burning anger overtake them.
25 May their camp be a desolation;
let no one live in their tents.
26 For they persecute those whom you have struck down,
and those whom you have wounded, they attack still more.[l]
27 Add guilt to their guilt;
may they have no acquittal from you.
28 Let them be blotted out of the book of the living;
let them not be enrolled among the righteous.
29 But I am lowly and in pain;
let your salvation, O God, protect me.

30 I will praise the name of God with a song;
I will magnify him with thanksgiving.
31 This will please the LORD more than an ox
or a bull with horns and hoofs.
32 Let the oppressed see it and be glad;
you who seek God, let your hearts revive.
33 For the LORD hears the needy,
and does not despise his own that are in bonds.

34 Let heaven and earth praise him,
the seas and everything that moves in them.
35 For God will save Zion
and rebuild the cities of Judah;
and his servants shall live[m] there and possess it;
36 the children of his servants shall inherit it,
and those who love his name shall live in it.

Psalm 70

Prayer for Deliverance from Enemies

To the leader. Of David, for the memorial offering.

1 Be pleased, O God, to deliver me.
O LORD, make haste to help me!
2 Let those be put to shame and confusion
who seek my life.
Let those be turned back and brought to dishonor
who desire to hurt me.
3 Let those who say, "Aha, Aha!"
turn back because of their shame.

4 Let all who seek you
rejoice and be glad in you.
Let those who love your salvation
say evermore, "God is great!"
5 But I am poor and needy;
hasten to me, O God!
You are my help and my deliverer;
O LORD, do not delay!

Psalm 71

Prayer for Lifelong Protection and Help

1 In you, O LORD, I take refuge;
let me never be put to shame.
2 In your righteousness deliver me and rescue me;
incline your ear to me and save me.
3 Be to me a rock of refuge,
a strong fortress,[n] to save me,
for you are my rock and my fortress.

4 Rescue me, O my God, from the hand of the wicked,
from the grasp of the unjust and cruel.
5 For you, O Lord, are my hope,
my trust, O LORD, from my youth.
6 Upon you I have leaned from my birth;
it was you who took me from my mother's womb.
My praise is continually of you.

7 I have been like a portent to many,
but you are my strong refuge.
8 My mouth is filled with your praise,
and with your glory all day long.
9 Do not cast me off in the time of old age;
do not forsake me when my strength is spent.
10 For my enemies speak concerning me,
and those who watch for my life consult together.
11 They say, "Pursue and seize that person
whom God has forsaken,
for there is no one to deliver."

[l] Gk Syr: Heb *recount the pain of* [m] Syr: Heb *and they shall live* [n] Gk Compare 31.3: Heb *to come continually you have commanded*

69.22 Rom 11.9,10
69.23 Isa 6.9,10; Dan 5.6
69.24 Ps 79.6
69.25 Mt 23.38; Acts 1.20
69.26 Isa 53.4
69.28 Ex 32.32; Phil 4.3; 10.20
69.29 Ps 70.5; 59.1
69.30 Ps 28.7; 34.3; 50.14
69.31 Ps 50.13,14
69.32 Ps 34.2; 22.26
69.33 Ps 12.9; 68.6
69.34 Ps 96.11; 148.1; Isa 44.23; 49.13
69.35 Ps 51.18; Isa 44.26
69.36 Ps 102.28; 37.29
70.1 Ps 40.13
70.2 Ps 35.4,26
70.3 Ps 40.15
70.5 Ps 40.17; 141.1
71.1 Ps 25.2,3
71.2 Ps 31.1; 17.6
71.3 Ps 31.2,3; 44.4
71.4 Ps 140.1,4
71.5 Jer 17.7
71.6 Ps 22.9,10; Isa 46.3; Ps 34.1
71.7 1 Cor 4.9; Ps 61.3
71.8 Ps 35.28
71.9 ver 18
71.10 Ps 56.6; Mt 27.1
71.11 Ps 3.2; 7.2

12 O God, do not be far from me;
O my God, make haste to help me!
13 Let my accusers be put to shame and
consumed;
let those who seek to hurt me
be covered with scorn and disgrace.
14 But I will hope continually,
and will praise you yet more and
more.
15 My mouth will tell of your righteous
acts,
of your deeds of salvation all day
long,
though their number is past my
knowledge.
16 I will come praising the mighty deeds of
the Lord God,
I will praise your righteousness, yours
alone.

17 O God, from my youth you have taught
me,
and I still proclaim your wondrous
deeds.
18 So even to old age and gray hairs,
O God, do not forsake me,
until I proclaim your might
to all the generations to come.[o]
Your power 19and your righteousness,
O God,
reach the high heavens.

You who have done great things,
O God, who is like you?
20 You who have made me see many
troubles and calamities
will revive me again;
from the depths of the earth
you will bring me up again.
21 You will increase my honor,
and comfort me once again.

22 I will also praise you with the harp
for your faithfulness, O my God;
I will sing praises to you with the lyre,
O Holy One of Israel.
23 My lips will shout for joy
when I sing praises to you;
my soul also, which you have
rescued.
24 All day long my tongue will talk of your
righteous help,
for those who tried to do me harm
have been put to shame, and
disgraced.

Psalm 72

Prayer for Guidance and Support for the King

Of Solomon.

1 Give the king your justice, O God,
and your righteousness to a king's son.
2 May he judge your people with
righteousness,
and your poor with justice.
3 May the mountains yield prosperity for
the people,
and the hills, in righteousness.
4 May he defend the cause of the poor of
the people,
give deliverance to the needy,
and crush the oppressor.

5 May he live[p] while the sun endures,
and as long as the moon, throughout
all generations.
6 May he be like rain that falls on the
mown grass,
like showers that water the earth.
7 In his days may righteousness flourish
and peace abound, until the moon is
no more.

8 May he have dominion from sea to sea,
and from the River to the ends of the
earth.
9 May his foes[q] bow down before him,
and his enemies lick the dust.
10 May the kings of Tarshish and of the isles
render him tribute,
may the kings of Sheba and Seba
bring gifts.
11 May all kings fall down before him,
all nations give him service.

12 For he delivers the needy when they call,
the poor and those who have no
helper.
13 He has pity on the weak and the needy,
and saves the lives of the needy.
14 From oppression and violence he
redeems their life;
and precious is their blood in his sight.

15 Long may he live!
May gold of Sheba be given to him.
May prayer be made for him
continually,
and blessings invoked for him all day
long.

[o] Gk Compare Syr: Heb *to a generation, to all that come* [p] Gk: Heb *may they fear you* [q] Cn: Heb *those who live in the wilderness*

Ps 72 A hymn for use when the king is enthroned. The qualities of God to determine what is right (*justice*) and to put it into effect (*righteousness*) are invoked for the king of Israel. His reign is to be characterized by *prosperity*, and care for the poor and needy, by the length of the king's life, by the huge realm over which he rules (*from the River [Euphrates] to the ends of the earth*), by abundance of produce, and by honors and gratitude from other rulers. This psalm and Book II of the edited version of the psalms end with an ascription of praise to God, whose glory will *fill the whole earth*.

71.12 Ps 35.22; 70.1
71.13 Ps 35.4; 109.29; ver 24
71.15 Ps 35.28; 40.5
71.16 Ps 106.2; 51.14
71.17 Deut 4.5; 6.7; Ps 26.7
71.18 ver 9
71.19 Ps 57.10; 35.10
71.20 Ps 60.3; Hos 6.1,2
71.22 Ps 33.2; 78.41
71.23 Ps 5.11; 103.4
71.24 Ps 35.28; ver 13
72.1 Ps 24.5
72.2 Isa 9.7; Ps 82.3
72.3 Ps 85.10; Isa 32.17
72.4 Isa 11.4
72.5 Ps 89.36
72.6 2 Sam 23.4; Hos 6.3
72.7 Ps 92.12
72.8 Ex 23.31; Zech 9.10
72.9 Ps 74.14; Isa 49.23; Mic 7.17
72.10 2 Chr 9.21; Ps 68.29
72.11 Ps 49.23
72.12 Job 29.12
72.14 Ps 116.15
72.15 Isa 60.6

Ps 73 Ps 73-83 are attributed to Asaph, royal musician in the time of David and Solomon (1 Chr 6.39; 2 Chr 5.11-14). A confession of the psalmist's foolish envy of the rich and prosperous whose self-reliant arrogance contrasts with his piety and perplexity. The understanding of how God works for his own people came through insights gained in *the sanctuary,* when he realized the continuing presence of God with the faithful, now and in the future.

16 May there be abundance of grain in the land;
may it wave on the tops of the mountains;
may its fruit be like Lebanon;
and may people blossom in the cities like the grass of the field.
17 May his name endure forever,
his fame continue as long as the sun.
May all nations be blessed in him;[r]
may they pronounce him happy.

18 Blessed be the LORD, the God of Israel,
who alone does wondrous things.
19 Blessed be his glorious name forever;
may his glory fill the whole earth.
Amen and Amen.

20 The prayers of David son of Jesse are ended.

BOOK III

(*Psalms 73–89*)

Psalm 73

Plea for Relief from Oppressors

A Psalm of Asaph.

1 Truly God is good to the upright,[s]
to those who are pure in heart.
2 But as for me, my feet had almost stumbled;
my steps had nearly slipped.
3 For I was envious of the arrogant;
I saw the prosperity of the wicked.

4 For they have no pain;
their bodies are sound and sleek.
5 They are not in trouble as others are;
they are not plagued like other people.
6 Therefore pride is their necklace;
violence covers them like a garment.
7 Their eyes swell out with fatness;
their hearts overflow with follies.
8 They scoff and speak with malice;
loftily they threaten oppression.
9 They set their mouths against heaven,
and their tongues range over the earth.
10 Therefore the people turn and praise them,[t]
and find no fault in them.[u]
11 And they say, "How can God know?
Is there knowledge in the Most High?"
12 Such are the wicked;
always at ease, they increase in riches.
13 All in vain I have kept my heart clean
and washed my hands in innocence.
14 For all day long I have been plagued,
and am punished every morning.

15 If I had said, "I will talk on in this way,"
I would have been untrue to the circle of your children.
16 But when I thought how to understand this,
it seemed to me a wearisome task,
17 until I went into the sanctuary of God;
then I perceived their end.
18 Truly you set them in slippery places;
you make them fall to ruin.
19 How they are destroyed in a moment,
swept away utterly by terrors!
20 They are[v] like a dream when one awakes;
on awaking you despise their phantoms.

21 When my soul was embittered,
when I was pricked in heart,
22 I was stupid and ignorant;
I was like a brute beast toward you.
23 Nevertheless I am continually with you;
you hold my right hand.
24 You guide me with your counsel,
and afterward you will receive me with honor.[w]
25 Whom have I in heaven but you?
And there is nothing on earth that I desire other than you.
26 My flesh and my heart may fail,
but God is the strength[x] of my heart
and my portion forever.

27 Indeed, those who are far from you will perish;
you put an end to those who are false to you.
28 But for me it is good to be near God;
I have made the Lord GOD my refuge,
to tell of all your works.

[r] Or *bless themselves by him* [s] Or *good to Israel* [t] Cn: Heb *his people return here* [u] Cn: Heb *abundant waters are drained by them* [v] Cn: Heb *Lord* [w] Or *to glory* [x] Heb *rock*

72.16 Ps 104.16; Job 5.25
72.17 Ps 89.36; Gen 12.3; 22.18; Lk 1.48
72.18 Ps 41.13; 106.48; 77.14
72.19 Neh 9.5; Zech 14.9
73.1 Ps 86.5; 51.10
73.2 Ps 94.18
73.3 Ps 37.1; Jer 12.1
73.5 Job 21.9
73.6 Ps 109.18
73.7 Job 15.27; Ps 17.10
73.8 Ps 53.1; Jude 16
73.11 Job 22.13
73.12 Ps 49.6; Jer 49.31
73.13 Job 21.15; 34.9; 35.3; Ps 26.6
73.14 Ps 38.6; 118.18
73.16 Eccl 8.17
73.17 Ps 77.13; 37.38
73.18 Ps 35.6,8
73.19 Num 26.21; Job 18.11
73.20 Job 20.8; Ps 78.65; 1 Sam 2.30
73.22 Ps 49.10; Job 18.3
73.24 Ps 32.8; 48.14
73.25 Phil 3.8
73.26 Ps 84.2; 16.5
73.27 Ps 37.20; 119.155
73.28 Heb 10.22; Ps 71.7; 40.5

Psalm 74

Plea for Help in Time of National Humiliation

A Maskil of Asaph.

1 O God, why do you cast us off forever?
Why does your anger smoke against the sheep of your pasture?
2 Remember your congregation, which you acquired long ago,
which you redeemed to be the tribe of your heritage.
Remember Mount Zion, where you came to dwell.
3 Direct your steps to the perpetual ruins;
the enemy has destroyed everything in the sanctuary.

4 Your foes have roared within your holy place;
they set up their emblems there.
5 At the upper entrance they hacked
the wooden trellis with axes.[y]
6 And then, with hatchets and hammers,
they smashed all its carved work.
7 They set your sanctuary on fire;
they desecrated the dwelling place of your name,
bringing it to the ground.
8 They said to themselves, "We will utterly subdue them";
they burned all the meeting places of God in the land.

9 We do not see our emblems;
there is no longer any prophet,
and there is no one among us who knows how long.
10 How long, O God, is the foe to scoff?
Is the enemy to revile your name forever?
11 Why do you hold back your hand;
why do you keep your hand in[z] your bosom?

12 Yet God my King is from of old,
working salvation in the earth.
13 You divided the sea by your might;
you broke the heads of the dragons in the waters.
14 You crushed the heads of Leviathan;
you gave him as food[a] for the creatures of the wilderness.
15 You cut openings for springs and torrents;
you dried up ever-flowing streams.
16 Yours is the day, yours also the night;
you established the luminaries[b] and the sun.
17 You have fixed all the bounds of the earth;
you made summer and winter.

18 Remember this, O LORD, how the enemy scoffs,
and an impious people reviles your name.
19 Do not deliver the soul of your dove to the wild animals;
do not forget the life of your poor forever.

20 Have regard for your[c] covenant,
for the dark places of the land are full of the haunts of violence.
21 Do not let the downtrodden be put to shame;
let the poor and needy praise your name.
22 Rise up, O God, plead your cause;
remember how the impious scoff at you all day long.
23 Do not forget the clamor of your foes,
the uproar of your adversaries that goes up continually.

Psalm 75

Thanksgiving for God's Wondrous Deeds

To the leader: Do Not Destroy. A Psalm of Asaph. A Song.

1 We give thanks to you, O God;
we give thanks; your name is near.
People tell of your wondrous deeds.

2 At the set time that I appoint
I will judge with equity.
3 When the earth totters, with all its inhabitants,
it is I who keep its pillars steady. *Selah*
4 I say to the boastful, "Do not boast,"
and to the wicked, "Do not lift up your horn;
5 do not lift up your horn on high,
or speak with insolent neck."

6 For not from the east or from the west
and not from the wilderness comes lifting up;
7 but it is God who executes judgment,

[y] Cn Compare Gk Syr: Meaning of Heb uncertain [z] Cn: Heb *do you consume your right hand from* [a] Heb *food for the people* [b] Or *moon*; Heb *light* [c] Gk Syr: Heb *the*

74.1 Ps 44.9,23; Deut 29.20; Ps 95.7
74.2 Deut 32.6; Ps 77.15; 68.16
74.3 Isa 61.4; Ps 79.1
74.4 Lam 2.7; Num 2.2
74.5 Jer 46.22
74.7 2 Kings 25.9
74.8 Ps 83.4
74.9 Ps 78.43; 1 Sam 3.1; Ps 79.5
74.10 Ps 44.16; Lev 24.16
74.11 Lam 2.3; Ps 59.13
74.12 Ps 44.4
74.13 Ex 14.21; Isa 51.9
74.15 Ex 17.5,6; Num 20.11; Josh 3.13
74.16 Ps 104.19
74.17 Gen 8.22
74.18 ver 10; Ps 39.8
74.19 Song 2.14; Ps 9.18
74.20 Gen 17.7; Ps 106.45; 88.6
74.21 Ps 103.6; 35.10
74.22 Ps 43.1; ver 18
74.23 ver 10; Ps 65.7
75.1 Ps 79.13; 145.18; 44.1
75.4 Zech 1.21
75.5 Ps 94.4
75.6 Ps 3.3
75.7 Ps 50.6; 1 Sam 2.7; Dan 2.21

Ps 74 After lamenting God's seeming abandonment of his people, as evidenced by the ruined sanctuary (vv.3-8), the lack of a prophet (vs.9), and the scoffing of Israel's enemies about the impotence of her God, the psalmist recalls the majestic power of God in the creation of the world and the defeat of the powers of evil (represented by *Leviathan*, the evil figure from Canaanite mythology who battled with Baal, the high god (Job 41.1-34). He rejoices in the order that God maintains in the creation and calls to mind God's promises in the *covenant*.
Ps 75 A psalm of praise for God's equitable administration of the world, punishing the wicked and the evil powers, but sustaining his own people.

Ps 76 A celebration of the sovereign power of the God who dwells in *Salem* (Jerusalem), whose commanding word (*rebuke*) defeats the hostile forces of earthly and cosmic origin.
Ps 77 To overcome the sense of God's seeming abandonment of the psalmist (vv.1-10) he contemplates God's mighty works in creating and subduing the powers of nature and the enemies of his people Israel (vv.11-20).

putting down one and lifting up
another.
8 For in the hand of the LORD there is a cup
with foaming wine, well mixed;
he will pour a draught from it,
and all the wicked of the earth
shall drain it down to the dregs.
9 But I will rejoice[d] forever;
I will sing praises to the God of Jacob.

10 All the horns of the wicked I will cut off,
but the horns of the righteous shall
be exalted.

Psalm 76

Israel's God—Judge of All the Earth

To the leader: with stringed instruments. A Psalm of Asaph. A Song.

1 In Judah God is known,
his name is great in Israel.
2 His abode has been established in Salem,
his dwelling place in Zion.
3 There he broke the flashing arrows,
the shield, the sword, and the
weapons of war. *Selah*

4 Glorious are you, more majestic
than the everlasting mountains.[e]
5 The stouthearted were stripped of their
spoil;
they sank into sleep;
none of the troops
was able to lift a hand.
6 At your rebuke, O God of Jacob,
both rider and horse lay stunned.

7 But you indeed are awesome!
Who can stand before you
when once your anger is roused?
8 From the heavens you uttered
judgment;
the earth feared and was still
9 when God rose up to establish
judgment,
to save all the oppressed of the earth.
Selah

10 Human wrath serves only to praise you,
when you bind the last bit of your[f]
wrath around you.
11 Make vows to the LORD your God, and
perform them;
let all who are around him bring gifts
to the one who is awesome,
12 who cuts off the spirit of princes,
who inspires fear in the kings of the
earth.

Psalm 77

God's Mighty Deeds Recalled

To the leader: according to Jeduthun. Of Asaph. A Psalm.

1 I cry aloud to God,
aloud to God, that he may hear me.
2 In the day of my trouble I seek the Lord;
in the night my hand is stretched out
without wearying;
my soul refuses to be comforted.
3 I think of God, and I moan;
I meditate, and my spirit faints.
Selah

4 You keep my eyelids from closing;
I am so troubled that I cannot speak.
5 I consider the days of old,
and remember the years of long ago.
6 I commune[g] with my heart in the night;
I meditate and search my spirit:[h]
7 "Will the Lord spurn forever,
and never again be favorable?
8 Has his steadfast love ceased forever?
Are his promises at an end for all time?
9 Has God forgotten to be gracious?
Has he in anger shut up his
compassion?" *Selah*
10 And I say, "It is my grief
that the right hand of the Most High
has changed."

11 I will call to mind the deeds of the LORD;
I will remember your wonders of old.
12 I will meditate on all your work,
and muse on your mighty deeds.
13 Your way, O God, is holy.
What god is so great as our God?
14 You are the God who works wonders;
you have displayed your might
among the peoples.
15 With your strong arm you redeemed
your people,
the descendants of Jacob and Joseph.
Selah

16 When the waters saw you, O God,
when the waters saw you, they were
afraid;
the very deep trembled.
17 The clouds poured out water;
the skies thundered;

[d] Gk: Heb *declare* [e] Gk: Heb *the mountains of prey* [f] Heb lacks *your* [g] Gk Syr: Heb *My music* [h] Syr Jerome: Heb *my spirit searches*

75.8 Ps 60.3; Jer 25.15; Prov 23.30
75.9 Ps 40.10
75.10 Ps 89.17; 148.14
76.1 Ps 48.3
76.2 Ps 27.5; 9.11
76.3 Ps 46.9
76.5 Isa 46.12; Ps 13.3
76.7 Ps 96.4; Nah 1.6
76.8 Ezek 38.20; 2 Chr 20.29,30
76.9 Ps 9.7-9; 72.4
76.10 Ex 9.16; Rom 9.17
76.11 Ps 50.14; 68.29
76.12 Ps 68.35
77.1 Ps 3.4
77.2 Ps 50.15; Isa 26.9,16
77.3 Ps 142.3; 143.4
77.5 Deut 32.7; Ps 143.5; Isa 51.9
77.6 Ps 42.8; 4.4
77.7 Ps 74.1; 85.1
77.8 Ps 89.49; 2 Pet 3.9
77.9 Isa 49.15; Ps 25.6
77.10 Ps 31.22; 44.2,3
77.11 Ps 143.5
77.13 Ps 73.17; Ex 15.11
77.15 Ex 6.6; Deut 9.29
77.16 Ex 14.21
77.17 Judg 5.4; Ps 68.33; 2 Sam 22.15

your arrows flashed on every side.
18 The crash of your thunder was in the whirlwind;
your lightnings lit up the world;
the earth trembled and shook.
19 Your way was through the sea,
your path, through the mighty waters;
yet your footprints were unseen.
20 You led your people like a flock
by the hand of Moses and Aaron.

Psalm 78

God's Goodness and Israel's Ingratitude

A Maskil of Asaph.

1 Give ear, O my people, to my teaching;
incline your ears to the words of my mouth.
2 I will open my mouth in a parable;
I will utter dark sayings from of old,
3 things that we have heard and known,
that our ancestors have told us.
4 We will not hide them from their children;
we will tell to the coming generation
the glorious deeds of the LORD, and his might,
and the wonders that he has done.

5 He established a decree in Jacob,
and appointed a law in Israel,
which he commanded our ancestors
to teach to their children;
6 that the next generation might know them,
the children yet unborn,
and rise up and tell them to their children,
7 so that they should set their hope in God,
and not forget the works of God,
but keep his commandments;
8 and that they should not be like their ancestors,
a stubborn and rebellious generation,
a generation whose heart was not steadfast,
whose spirit was not faithful to God.

9 The Ephraimites, armed with[i] the bow,
turned back on the day of battle.
10 They did not keep God's covenant,
but refused to walk according to his law.
11 They forgot what he had done,
and the miracles that he had shown them.
12 In the sight of their ancestors he worked marvels
in the land of Egypt, in the fields of Zoan.
13 He divided the sea and let them pass through it,
and made the waters stand like a heap.
14 In the daytime he led them with a cloud,
and all night long with a fiery light.
15 He split rocks open in the wilderness,
and gave them drink abundantly as from the deep.
16 He made streams come out of the rock,
and caused waters to flow down like rivers.

17 Yet they sinned still more against him,
rebelling against the Most High in the desert.
18 They tested God in their heart
by demanding the food they craved.
19 They spoke against God, saying,
"Can God spread a table in the wilderness?
20 Even though he struck the rock so that water gushed out
and torrents overflowed,
can he also give bread,
or provide meat for his people?"

21 Therefore, when the LORD heard, he was full of rage;
a fire was kindled against Jacob,
his anger mounted against Israel,
22 because they had no faith in God,
and did not trust his saving power.
23 Yet he commanded the skies above,
and opened the doors of heaven;
24 he rained down on them manna to eat,
and gave them the grain of heaven.
25 Mortals ate of the bread of angels;
he sent them food in abundance.
26 He caused the east wind to blow in the heavens,
and by his power he led out the south wind;
27 he rained flesh upon them like dust,
winged birds like the sand of the seas;
28 he let them fall within their camp,
all around their dwellings.
29 And they ate and were well filled,
for he gave them what they craved.

Ps 78 An extended recital in a mixture of historical and symbolic language of God's dealings with his people Israel, of their infidelity, his judgmental rebukes, and his establishment of the Davidic monarchy. The events referred to include the giving of the *law* (vv.5-8), the disobedience of the tribes as they moved through the wilderness toward the land of Canaan (vv.9-55), and the struggle to take over the land (vv.56-66). The themes of God's forgiveness and the renewal of the relationship run through the psalm as well (vv.23-24,38-39, 51-55). The conclusion celebrates the choice of Judah for leadership (vv.67-72).

77.18 2 Sam 22.8
77.19 Hab 3.15; Ex 14.28
77.20 Ex 13.21; Isa 63.11-13; Ex 6.26
78.1 Isa 51.4
78.2 Mt 13.35
78.3 Ps 44.1
78.4 Ex 12.26; Ps 22.30; 71.17
78.5 Ps 149.19; Deut 4.9
78.6 Ps 102.18
78.7 Deut 6.12; 27.1
78.8 Ezek 20.18; Ex 32.9; ver 37
78.9 1 Chr 12.2; Judg 20.39
78.10 2 Kings 18.12; Ps 119.1
78.11 Ps 106.13
78.12 Ex 7-12; Num 13.22; Isa 19.11,13; Ezek 30.14
78.13 Ex 14.21; 15.8
78.14 Ex 13.21
78.15 Num 20.11; 1 Cor 10.4
78.17 Deut 9.22; Heb 3.16
78.18 Ex 16.2; 1 Cor 10.9
78.19 Num 11.4
78.20 Num 20.11
78.21 Num 11.1
78.22 Heb 3.18
78.23 Mal 3.10
78.24 Jn 6.31
78.26 Num 11.31
78.27 Ps 105.40
78.29 Num 11.20

[i] Heb *armed with shooting*

[30] But before they had satisfied their
craving,
while the food was still in their
mouths,
[31] the anger of God rose against them
and he killed the strongest of them,
and laid low the flower of Israel.

[32] In spite of all this they still sinned;
they did not believe in his wonders.
[33] So he made their days vanish like a
breath,
and their years in terror.
[34] When he killed them, they sought for
him;
they repented and sought God
earnestly.
[35] They remembered that God was their
rock,
the Most High God their redeemer.
[36] But they flattered him with their
mouths;
they lied to him with their tongues.
[37] Their heart was not steadfast toward him;
they were not true to his covenant.
[38] Yet he, being compassionate,
forgave their iniquity,
and did not destroy them;
often he restrained his anger,
and did not stir up all his wrath.
[39] He remembered that they were but
flesh,
a wind that passes and does not come
again.
[40] How often they rebelled against him in
the wilderness
and grieved him in the desert!
[41] They tested God again and again,
and provoked the Holy One of Israel.
[42] They did not keep in mind his power,
or the day when he redeemed them
from the foe;
[43] when he displayed his signs in Egypt,
and his miracles in the fields of Zoan.
[44] He turned their rivers to blood,
so that they could not drink of their
streams.
[45] He sent among them swarms of flies,
which devoured them,
and frogs, which destroyed them.
[46] He gave their crops to the caterpillar,
and the fruit of their labor to the
locust.
[47] He destroyed their vines with hail,
and their sycamores with frost.
[48] He gave over their cattle to the hail,
and their flocks to thunderbolts.
[49] He let loose on them his fierce anger,
wrath, indignation, and distress,
a company of destroying angels.
[50] He made a path for his anger;
he did not spare them from death,
but gave their lives over to the
plague.
[51] He struck all the firstborn in Egypt,
the first issue of their strength in the
tents of Ham.
[52] Then he led out his people like sheep,
and guided them in the wilderness
like a flock.
[53] He led them in safety, so that they were
not afraid;
but the sea overwhelmed their
enemies.
[54] And he brought them to his holy hill,
to the mountain that his right hand
had won.
[55] He drove out nations before them;
he apportioned them for a possession
and settled the tribes of Israel in their
tents.

[56] Yet they tested the Most High God,
and rebelled against him.
They did not observe his decrees,
[57] but turned away and were faithless like
their ancestors;
they twisted like a treacherous bow.
[58] For they provoked him to anger with
their high places;
they moved him to jealousy with
their idols.
[59] When God heard, he was full of wrath,
and he utterly rejected Israel.
[60] He abandoned his dwelling at Shiloh,
the tent where he dwelt among
mortals,
[61] and delivered his power to captivity,
his glory to the hand of the foe.
[62] He gave his people to the sword,
and vented his wrath on his heritage.
[63] Fire devoured their young men,
and their girls had no marriage song.
[64] Their priests fell by the sword,
and their widows made no
lamentation.
[65] Then the Lord awoke as from sleep,
like a warrior shouting because of
wine.
[66] He put his adversaries to rout;
he put them to everlasting disgrace.

[67] He rejected the tent of Joseph,
he did not choose the tribe of Ephraim;

78.31 Num 11.33
78.32 Num 14.16,17; ver 22
78.33 Num 14.29,35
78.34 Hos 5.15
78.35 Deut 32.4; Isa 41.14
78.36 Ezek 33.31; Ex 32.7,8
78.38 Num 14.18; Isa 48.9; 1 Kings 21.29
78.39 Ps 103.14; Gen 6.3; Job 7.7,16
78.40 Ps 95.8-10; Heb 3.16
78.41 Num 14.22; Ps 89.18
78.44 Ex 7.20
78.45 Ex 8.24; Ps 105.31; Ex 8.6
78.47 Ex 9.25
78.48 Ex 9.23
78.49 Ex 15.7
78.51 Ex 12.29; Ps 106.22
78.52 Ps 77.20
78.53 Ex 14.19,27
78.54 Ex 15.17; Ps 44.3
78.55 Ps 44.2; 105.11
78.56 ver 18,40
78.57 Ezek 20.27,28; Hos 7.16
78.58 Deut 32.16,21; 12.2; 1 Kings 11.7
78.60 1 Sam 4.11
78.61 Judg 18.30
78.62 1 Sam 4.10
78.63 Jer 7.34
78.64 1 Sam 22.18; Job 27.15
78.65 Isa 42.13
78.66 1 Sam 5.6

78.68 Ps 87.2
78.69 1 Sam 6.1-38
78.70 1 Sam 16.11,12
78.71 2 Sam 7.8; Gen 33.13; 2 Sam 5.2; 1 Chr 11.2
78.72 1 Kings 9.4
79.1 Ex 15.17; Ps 74.2; 2 Kings 25.9; Mic 3.12
79.2 Jer 7.33
79.3 Jer 14.16
79.4 Ps 44.13
79.5 Ps 74.1,9; Zeph 3.8
79.6 Jer 10.25; Rev 16.1; Isa 45.4,5; 2 Thess 1.8
79.8 Isa 64.9
79.9 2 Chr 14.11; Jer 14.7
79.10 Ps 42.10; 94.1,2
79.11 Ps 102.20
79.12 Isa 65.6,7; Jer 32.18; Lk 6.38; Ps 74.18,22
79.13 Ps 74.1; 95.7; Isa 43.21
80.1 Ps 23.1; 77.20; 99.1
80.2 Ps 35.23
80.3 Lam 5.21; Num 6.25
80.4 Ps 85.5
80.5 Ps 42.3; 102.9
80.6 Ps 44.13; 79.4
80.8 Isa 5.1,7; Jer 2.21; Ezek 15.6; Ps 44.2

68 but he chose the tribe of Judah,
Mount Zion, which he loves.
69 He built his sanctuary like the high heavens,
like the earth, which he has founded forever.
70 He chose his servant David,
and took him from the sheepfolds;
71 from tending the nursing ewes he brought him
to be the shepherd of his people Jacob,
of Israel, his inheritance.
72 With upright heart he tended them,
and guided them with skillful hand.

Psalm 79

Plea for Mercy for Jerusalem

A Psalm of Asaph.

1 O God, the nations have come into your inheritance;
they have defiled your holy temple;
they have laid Jerusalem in ruins.
2 They have given the bodies of your servants
to the birds of the air for food,
the flesh of your faithful to the wild animals of the earth.
3 They have poured out their blood like water
all around Jerusalem,
and there was no one to bury them.
4 We have become a taunt to our neighbors,
mocked and derided by those around us.

5 How long, O LORD? Will you be angry forever?
Will your jealous wrath burn like fire?
6 Pour out your anger on the nations
that do not know you,
and on the kingdoms
that do not call on your name.
7 For they have devoured Jacob
and laid waste his habitation.

8 Do not remember against us the iniquities of our ancestors;
let your compassion come speedily to meet us,
for we are brought very low.
9 Help us, O God of our salvation,
for the glory of your name;
deliver us, and forgive our sins,
for your name's sake.
10 Why should the nations say,
"Where is their God?"
Let the avenging of the outpoured blood of your servants
be known among the nations before our eyes.

11 Let the groans of the prisoners come before you;
according to your great power
preserve those doomed to die.
12 Return sevenfold into the bosom of our neighbors
the taunts with which they taunted you, O Lord!
13 Then we your people, the flock of your pasture,
will give thanks to you forever;
from generation to generation we will recount your praise.

Psalm 80

Prayer for Israel's Restoration

To the leader: on Lilies, a Covenant. Of Asaph. A Psalm.

1 Give ear, O Shepherd of Israel,
you who lead Joseph like a flock!
You who are enthroned upon the cherubim, shine forth
2 before Ephraim and Benjamin and Manasseh.
Stir up your might,
and come to save us!

3 Restore us, O God;
let your face shine, that we may be saved.

4 O LORD God of hosts,
how long will you be angry with your people's prayers?
5 You have fed them with the bread of tears,
and given them tears to drink in full measure.
6 You make us the scorn[j] of our neighbors;
our enemies laugh among themselves.

7 Restore us, O God of hosts;
let your face shine, that we may be saved.

8 You brought a vine out of Egypt;
you drove out the nations and planted it.

Ps 79 In the face of the destruction of Jerusalem and the mockery heaped on Israel, the psalmist pleads with God for vengeance on those who mistreated God's people and the preservation of God's *flock*.
Ps 80 This lament employs a combination of metaphors for Israel and for God: flock and shepherd (vs.1), and vine/vineyard and caretaker (vv.8-18). Recalling the origins of Israel through the exodus from Egypt and the settlement in the land, the settlement and growth of the people there, the question is raised why God has allowed the nation to fall to ruin under enemy attack. God is asked to return to his former *regard for the vine*, and the promise is made to God that the people will *never turn back from you*.

[j] Syr: Heb *strife*

Ps 81 On the occasion of the celebration of a feast, God reminds his people of his care and guidance of them in the past, but also of their idolatry and disobedience. If they will now listen and *walk in [God's] ways*, they will be restored.
Ps 82 God is pictured as convening a council of heavenly beings (*gods*), who are rebuked for their failure to deal justly with the *weak and needy* of the earth. Since these celestial beings lack *knowledge*, their exalted position will not save them from death like any *mortal*. It is only *God* who can rightly rule *the earth*.

9 You cleared the ground for it;
it took deep root and filled the land.
10 The mountains were covered with its shade,
the mighty cedars with its branches;
11 it sent out its branches to the sea,
and its shoots to the River.
12 Why then have you broken down its walls,
so that all who pass along the way pluck its fruit?
13 The boar from the forest ravages it,
and all that move in the field feed on it.

14 Turn again, O God of hosts;
look down from heaven, and see;
have regard for this vine,
15 the stock that your right hand planted.[k]
16 They have burned it with fire, they have cut it down;[l]
may they perish at the rebuke of your countenance.
17 But let your hand be upon the one at your right hand,
the one whom you made strong for yourself.
18 Then we will never turn back from you;
give us life, and we will call on your name.

19 Restore us, O LORD God of hosts;
let your face shine, that we may be saved.

Psalm 81

God's Appeal to Stubborn Israel

To the leader: according to The Gittith. Of Asaph.

1 Sing aloud to God our strength;
shout for joy to the God of Jacob.
2 Raise a song, sound the tambourine,
the sweet lyre with the harp.
3 Blow the trumpet at the new moon,
at the full moon, on our festal day.
4 For it is a statute for Israel,
an ordinance of the God of Jacob.
5 He made it a decree in Joseph,
when he went out over[m] the land of Egypt.

I hear a voice I had not known:
6 "I relieved your[n] shoulder of the burden;
your[n] hands were freed from the basket.
7 In distress you called, and I rescued you;
I answered you in the secret place of thunder;
I tested you at the waters of Meribah. *Selah*
8 Hear, O my people, while I admonish you;
O Israel, if you would but listen to me!
9 There shall be no strange god among you;
you shall not bow down to a foreign god.
10 I am the LORD your God,
who brought you up out of the land of Egypt.
Open your mouth wide and I will fill it.

11 "But my people did not listen to my voice;
Israel would not submit to me.
12 So I gave them over to their stubborn hearts,
to follow their own counsels.
13 O that my people would listen to me,
that Israel would walk in my ways!
14 Then I would quickly subdue their enemies,
and turn my hand against their foes.
15 Those who hate the LORD would cringe before him,
and their doom would last forever.
16 I would feed you[o] with the finest of the wheat,
and with honey from the rock I would satisfy you."

Psalm 82

A Plea for Justice

A Psalm of Asaph.

1 God has taken his place in the divine council;
in the midst of the gods he holds judgment:
2 "How long will you judge unjustly
and show partiality to the wicked? *Selah*
3 Give justice to the weak and the orphan;
maintain the right of the lowly and the destitute.
4 Rescue the weak and the needy;
deliver them from the hand of the wicked."

5 They have neither knowledge nor understanding,

[k] Heb adds from verse 17 *and upon the one whom you made strong for yourself* [l] Cn: Heb *it is cut down* [m] Or *against* [n] Heb *his* [o] Cn Compare verse 16b: Heb *he would feed him*

80.9 Hos 14.5
80.12 Ps 89.40; Nah 2.2
80.13 Jer 5.6
80.14 Isa 63.15
80.16 Ps 39.11; 76.6
80.17 Ps 89.21
80.18 Isa 50.5; Ps 71.20
81.1 Ps 59.16; 66.1
81.3 Num 10.10; Lev 23.24
81.5 Ex 11.4
81.6 Isa 9.4; 10.27
81.7 Ex 2.23; Ps 50.15; Ex 19.19; 17.6,7
81.8 Ps 50.7
81.9 Deut 32.12; Isa 43.12
81.10 Ex 20.2; Ps 103.5
81.11 Ex 32.1
81.12 Acts 7.42; Rom 1.24
81.13 Deut 5.29; Isa 48.18; Ps 128.1
81.14 Ps 47.3; Am 1.8
81.16 Deut 32.13; Ps 147.14
82.1 Isa 3.13; Ex 21.6
82.2 Ps 58.1; Deut 1.17; Prov 18.5
82.3 Deut 24.17
82.4 Job 29.12
82.5 Mic 3.1; Ps 11.3

they walk around in darkness;
all the foundations of the earth are shaken.

6 I say, "You are gods,
children of the Most High, all of you;
7 nevertheless, you shall die like mortals,
and fall like any prince."[p]

8 Rise up, O God, judge the earth;
for all the nations belong to you!

Psalm 83

Prayer for Judgment on Israel's Foes

A Song. A Psalm of Asaph.

1 O God, do not keep silence;
do not hold your peace or be still, O God!
2 Even now your enemies are in tumult;
those who hate you have raised their heads.
3 They lay crafty plans against your people;
they consult together against those you protect.
4 They say, "Come, let us wipe them out as a nation;
let the name of Israel be remembered no more."
5 They conspire with one accord;
against you they make a covenant—
6 the tents of Edom and the Ishmaelites,
Moab and the Hagrites,
7 Gebal and Ammon and Amalek,
Philistia with the inhabitants of Tyre;
8 Assyria also has joined them;
they are the strong arm of the children of Lot. *Selah*

9 Do to them as you did to Midian,
as to Sisera and Jabin at the Wadi Kishon,
10 who were destroyed at En-dor,
who became dung for the ground.
11 Make their nobles like Oreb and Zeeb,
all their princes like Zebah and Zalmunna,
12 who said, "Let us take the pastures of God
for our own possession."

13 O my God, make them like whirling dust,[q]
like chaff before the wind.
14 As fire consumes the forest,
as the flame sets the mountains ablaze,
15 so pursue them with your tempest
and terrify them with your hurricane.
16 Fill their faces with shame,
so that they may seek your name, O LORD.
17 Let them be put to shame and dismayed forever;
let them perish in disgrace.
18 Let them know that you alone,
whose name is the LORD,
are the Most High over all the earth.

Psalm 84

The Joy of Worship in the Temple

To the leader: according to The Gittith. Of the Korahites. A Psalm.

1 How lovely is your dwelling place,
O LORD of hosts!
2 My soul longs, indeed it faints
for the courts of the LORD;
my heart and my flesh sing for joy
to the living God.

3 Even the sparrow finds a home,
and the swallow a nest for herself,
where she may lay her young,
at your altars, O LORD of hosts,
my King and my God.
4 Happy are those who live in your house,
ever singing your praise. *Selah*

5 Happy are those whose strength is in you,
in whose heart are the highways to Zion.[r]
6 As they go through the valley of Baca
they make it a place of springs;
the early rain also covers it with pools.
7 They go from strength to strength;
the God of gods will be seen in Zion.

8 O LORD God of hosts, hear my prayer;
give ear, O God of Jacob! *Selah*
9 Behold our shield, O God;
look on the face of your anointed.

10 For a day in your courts is better
than a thousand elsewhere.
I would rather be a doorkeeper in the house of my God
than live in the tents of wickedness.
11 For the LORD God is a sun and shield;
he bestows favor and honor.
No good thing does the LORD withhold

[p] Or *fall as one man, O princes* [q] Or *a tumbleweed* [r] Heb lacks *to Zion*

Ps 83 God is asked to destroy the enemies of his people now as he did in the past. The present confederacy of enemies includes tribes from east of the Jordan (*Edom, Ishmaelites, Moab, Hagrites, cf.* 1 Chr 5.10), those along the sea coast (*Philistines, Tyre*), now joined by *Assyria* in the late eighth century when Sennacherib invaded Judah. The historic instances of God's defeat of Israel's enemies included here are: *Midian* (Judg 6-8); *Sisera and Jabin* (Judg 4-5); *Oreb and Zeeb* (Judg 7.25); *Zebah and Zalmunna* (Judg 8).
Ps 84 For *Korahites* see Ps 42. This psalm describes the beauties of the temple as God's *dwelling place,* the joys of serving him there, and the happiness of those who make pilgrimages to this place (vv.5-7). *Baca,* an unknown desolate valley, becomes verdant as the pilgrims pass through it. A special prayer is uttered for God's *anointed,* the king of Israel. God protects and shows favor to all who trust him.

82.6 Jn 10.34; Ps 89.26
82.7 Ps 49.12; Ezek 31.14
82.8 Ps 12.5; Mic 7.2,7; Ps 2.8; Rev 11.15
83.1 Ps 28.1; 109.1
83.2 Ps 2.1; 81.15
83.3 Ps 27.5
83.4 Esth 3.6
83.5 Ps 2.2
83.6 2 Chr 20.1,10,11
83.9 Judg 4.22,23
83.11 Judg 8.12,21
83.12 2 Chr 20.11; Ps 132.13
83.13 Isa 7.13; Ps 35.5
83.14 Deut 32.22
83.15 Job 9.17
83.17 Ps 70.2
83.18 Ps 59.13; Ex 6.3; Ps 92.8
84.1 Ps 27.4
84.2 Ps 42.1,2
84.3 Ps 43.4; 5.2
84.4 Ps 65.4
84.5 Ps 81.1
84.6 2 Sam 5.23; Ps 107.35
84.7 Prov 4.18; 2 Cor 3.18; Deut 16.16; Ps 132.13
84.9 Gen 15.1; Ps 2.2
84.10 1 Chr 23.5
84.11 Isa 60.19; Rev 21.23; Ps 34.10

Ps 85 An appeal for a renewal of God's favor to his people in their time of desolation ends with an affirmation of the convergence of God's *steadfast love and faithfulness* with the faithful obedient response of his people.
Ps 86 The themes in this psalm are the needy condition of the psalmist, a petition to God for support and aid, the certainty that ultimately all nations will honor God, a request for instruction in God's *way*, and the contrast between the insolence of the enemies and the gracious dependability of God.
Ps 87 A declaration of certainty of the identity of God's people, who, unlike the evil nations that will fall (*Rahab* [Egypt], *Babylon, Philistia, Tyre, Ethiopia*), will have their names recorded forever in the sanctuary on *Zion*.

from those who walk uprightly.
12 O LORD of hosts,
happy is everyone who trusts in you.

Psalm 85

Prayer for the Restoration of God's Favor

To the leader. Of the Korahites. A Psalm.

1 LORD, you were favorable to your land;
you restored the fortunes of Jacob.
2 You forgave the iniquity of your people;
you pardoned all their sin. *Selah*
3 You withdrew all your wrath;
you turned from your hot anger.

4 Restore us again, O God of our salvation,
and put away your indignation toward us.
5 Will you be angry with us forever?
Will you prolong your anger to all generations?
6 Will you not revive us again,
so that your people may rejoice in you?
7 Show us your steadfast love, O LORD,
and grant us your salvation.

8 Let me hear what God the LORD will speak,
for he will speak peace to his people,
to his faithful, to those who turn to him in their hearts.[s]
9 Surely his salvation is at hand for those who fear him,
that his glory may dwell in our land.

10 Steadfast love and faithfulness will meet;
righteousness and peace will kiss each other.
11 Faithfulness will spring up from the ground,
and righteousness will look down from the sky.
12 The LORD will give what is good,
and our land will yield its increase.
13 Righteousness will go before him,
and will make a path for his steps.

Psalm 86

Supplication for Help against Enemies

A Prayer of David.

1 Incline your ear, O LORD, and answer me,
for I am poor and needy.
2 Preserve my life, for I am devoted to you;
save your servant who trusts in you.
You are my God; 3 be gracious to me, O Lord,
for to you do I cry all day long.
4 Gladden the soul of your servant,
for to you, O Lord, I lift up my soul.
5 For you, O Lord, are good and forgiving,
abounding in steadfast love to all who call on you.
6 Give ear, O LORD, to my prayer;
listen to my cry of supplication.
7 In the day of my trouble I call on you,
for you will answer me.

8 There is none like you among the gods, O Lord,
nor are there any works like yours.
9 All the nations you have made shall come
and bow down before you, O Lord,
and shall glorify your name.
10 For you are great and do wondrous things;
you alone are God.
11 Teach me your way, O LORD,
that I may walk in your truth;
give me an undivided heart to revere your name.
12 I give thanks to you, O Lord my God, with my whole heart,
and I will glorify your name forever.
13 For great is your steadfast love toward me;
you have delivered my soul from the depths of Sheol.

14 O God, the insolent rise up against me;
a band of ruffians seeks my life,
and they do not set you before them.
15 But you, O Lord, are a God merciful and gracious,
slow to anger and abounding in steadfast love and faithfulness.
16 Turn to me and be gracious to me;
give your strength to your servant;
save the child of your serving girl.
17 Show me a sign of your favor,
so that those who hate me may see it and be put to shame,
because you, LORD, have helped me and comforted me.

Psalm 87

The Joy of Living in Zion

Of the Korahites. A Psalm. A Song.

1 On the holy mount stands the city he founded;

[s] Gk: Heb *but let them not turn back to folly*

84.12 Ps 2.12
85.1 Ezra 1.11; Jer 30.18; Ezek 39.25
85.2 Ps 103.3; 32.1
85.5 Ps 74.1; 79.5; 80.4
85.6 Hab 3.2
85.8 Hab 2.1; Zech 7.9
85.9 Isa 46.13; Zech 2.5; Jn 1.14
85.10 Ps 72.3; Isa 32.17; Lk 2.14
85.12 Ps 84.11; Jas 1.17
85.13 Ps 89.14
86.1 Ps 17.6; 40.17
86.2 Ps 25.20; 4.3; 31.14
86.3 Ps 57.1; 88.9
86.4 Ps 25.1; 143.8
86.5 Ps 130.7; 145.9; Joel 2.13
86.6 Ps 55.1
86.7 Ps 50.15; 17.6
86.8 Ex 15.11; Ps 89.6; Deut 3.24
86.9 Ps 22.31; Isa 43.7; Rev 15.4
86.10 Ex 15.11; Ps 72.18; Deut 6.4; Mk 12.29
86.11 Ps 25.4
86.13 Ps 30.3
86.14 Ps 54.3
86.15 Ex 34.6; Neh 9.17; Ps 103.8; Joel 2.13
86.16 Ps 25.16; 68.35; 116.16
86.17 Ps 112.10; 118.13

2 the LORD loves the gates of Zion
more than all the dwellings of Jacob.
3 Glorious things are spoken of you,
O city of God. *Selah*

4 Among those who know me I mention
Rahab and Babylon;
Philistia too, and Tyre, with
Ethiopia[t]—
"This one was born there," they say.

5 And of Zion it shall be said,
"This one and that one were born in
it";
for the Most High himself will
establish it.
6 The LORD records, as he registers the
peoples,
"This one was born there." *Selah*

7 Singers and dancers alike say,
"All my springs are in you."

Psalm 88

Prayer for Help in Despondency

A Song. A Psalm of the Korahites. To the leader: according to Mahalath Leannoth. A Maskil of Heman the Ezrahite.

1 O LORD, God of my salvation,
when, at night, I cry out in your
presence,
2 let my prayer come before you;
incline your ear to my cry.

3 For my soul is full of troubles,
and my life draws near to Sheol.
4 I am counted among those who go
down to the Pit;
I am like those who have no help,
5 like those forsaken among the dead,
like the slain that lie in the grave,
like those whom you remember no
more,
for they are cut off from your hand.
6 You have put me in the depths of the
Pit,
in the regions dark and deep.
7 Your wrath lies heavy upon me,
and you overwhelm me with all your
waves. *Selah*

8 You have caused my companions to
shun me;
you have made me a thing of horror
to them.
I am shut in so that I cannot escape;
9 my eye grows dim through sorrow.
Every day I call on you, O LORD;
I spread out my hands to you.
10 Do you work wonders for the dead?
Do the shades rise up to praise you?
Selah
11 Is your steadfast love declared in the
grave,
or your faithfulness in Abaddon?
12 Are your wonders known in the
darkness,
or your saving help in the land of
forgetfulness?

13 But I, O LORD, cry out to you;
in the morning my prayer comes
before you.
14 O LORD, why do you cast me off?
Why do you hide your face from me?
15 Wretched and close to death from my
youth up,
I suffer your terrors; I am desperate.[u]
16 Your wrath has swept over me;
your dread assaults destroy me.
17 They surround me like a flood all day
long;
from all sides they close in on me.
18 You have caused friend and neighbor to
shun me;
my companions are in darkness.

Psalm 89

God's Covenant with David

A Maskil of Ethan the Ezrahite.

1 I will sing of your steadfast love,
O LORD,[v] forever;
with my mouth I will proclaim your
faithfulness to all generations.
2 I declare that your steadfast love is
established forever;
your faithfulness is as firm as the
heavens.

3 You said, "I have made a covenant with
my chosen one,
I have sworn to my servant David:
4 'I will establish your descendants
forever,
and build your throne for all
generations.' " *Selah*

5 Let the heavens praise your wonders,
O LORD,
your faithfulness in the assembly of
the holy ones.

87.2 Ps 78.67
87.3 Isa 60.1
87.5 Ps 48.8
87.6 Ezek 13.9
87.7 Ps 36.9
88.1 Ps 27.9; 51.14
88.2 Ps 18.6; 86.1
88.3 Ps 107.18,26
88.4 Ps 28.1
88.5 Isa 53.8
88.6 Ps 86.13; 143.3; 69.15
88.7 Ps 42.7
88.8 Job 19.13; Ps 31.11; 142.4; Lam 3.7
88.9 Ps 38.10; 86.3; Job 11.13; Ps 143.6
88.10 Ps 6.5; Isa 38.18
88.12 Job 10.21
88.13 Ps 5.3; 119.147
88.14 Job 13.24; Ps 13.1
88.15 Job 6.4
88.17 Ps 22.16
88.18 Job 19.13; Ps 31.11; 38.11
89.1 Ps 101.1
89.2 Ps 103.17; 36.5
89.3 Kings 8.16; Ps 132.11
89.4 2 Sam 7.16; Isa 9.7; Lk 1.33
89.5 Ps 19.1; 149.1

Ps 88 This lament describes one who is terrified by the prospect of death (variously referred to as *the Pit, Sheol, and Abaddon*) and by the absence (vv.13-14) and *wrath* (vs.16) of God, and who feels wholly abandoned, even by friends.

Ps 89 The first section of this psalm celebrates God's *steadfast love,* as evident through his wondrous power in creation and in history, crushing *Rahab* (Egypt), establishing his people in the land, and founding the eternal dynasty of David and the *covenant with him.* The people will be punished if they violate God's law, but the agreement with David will endure. The second section (vv.38-51) sadly describes God's rejection of David, the covenant and his throne, and asks where now is the hidden God and his *steadfast love.* A formal benediction (vs.52) brings to an end this section of the psalms.

[t] Or *Nubia;* Heb *Cush* [u] Meaning of Heb uncertain [v] Gk: Heb *the steadfast love of the* LORD

6 For who in the skies can be compared to the LORD?
Who among the heavenly beings is like the LORD,
7 a God feared in the council of the holy ones,
great and awesome[w] above all that are around him?
8 O LORD God of hosts,
who is as mighty as you, O LORD?
Your faithfulness surrounds you.
9 You rule the raging of the sea;
when its waves rise, you still them.
10 You crushed Rahab like a carcass;
you scattered your enemies with your mighty arm.
11 The heavens are yours, the earth also is yours;
the world and all that is in it—you have founded them.
12 The north and the south[x]—you created them;
Tabor and Hermon joyously praise your name.
13 You have a mighty arm;
strong is your hand, high your right hand.
14 Righteousness and justice are the foundation of your throne;
steadfast love and faithfulness go before you.
15 Happy are the people who know the festal shout,
who walk, O LORD, in the light of your countenance;
16 they exult in your name all day long,
and extol[y] your righteousness.
17 For you are the glory of their strength;
by your favor our horn is exalted.
18 For our shield belongs to the LORD,
our king to the Holy One of Israel.

19 Then you spoke in a vision to your faithful one, and said:
"I have set the crown[z] on one who is mighty,
I have exalted one chosen from the people.
20 I have found my servant David;
with my holy oil I have anointed him;
21 my hand shall always remain with him;
my arm also shall strengthen him.
22 The enemy shall not outwit him,
the wicked shall not humble him.
23 I will crush his foes before him
and strike down those who hate him.
24 My faithfulness and steadfast love shall be with him;
and in my name his horn shall be exalted.
25 I will set his hand on the sea
and his right hand on the rivers.
26 He shall cry to me, 'You are my Father,
my God, and the Rock of my salvation!'
27 I will make him the firstborn,
the highest of the kings of the earth.
28 Forever I will keep my steadfast love for him,
and my covenant with him will stand firm.
29 I will establish his line forever,
and his throne as long as the heavens endure.
30 If his children forsake my law
and do not walk according to my ordinances,
31 if they violate my statutes
and do not keep my commandments,
32 then I will punish their transgression with the rod
and their iniquity with scourges;
33 but I will not remove from him my steadfast love,
or be false to my faithfulness.
34 I will not violate my covenant,
or alter the word that went forth from my lips.
35 Once and for all I have sworn by my holiness;
I will not lie to David.
36 His line shall continue forever,
and his throne endure before me like the sun.
37 It shall be established forever like the moon,
an enduring witness in the skies."
Selah

38 But now you have spurned and rejected him;
you are full of wrath against your anointed.
39 You have renounced the covenant with your servant;
you have defiled his crown in the dust.
40 You have broken through all his walls;
you have laid his strongholds in ruins.
41 All who pass by plunder him;
he has become the scorn of his neighbors.

[w] Gk Syr: Heb *greatly awesome* [x] Or *Zaphon and Yamin* [y] Cn: Heb *are exalted in* [z] Cn: Heb *help*

89.6 Mic 7.18; Ps 29.1
89.7 Ps 47.2; 96.4
89.8 Ps 71.19
89.9 Ps 65.7
89.10 Ps 87.4; Isa 51.9; Ps 68.1
89.11 1 Chr 29.11; Ps 24.1,2
89.12 Josh 19.22; 12.1
89.13 Ps 98.1
89.14 Ps 97.2; 85.13
89.15 Num 10.10
89.17 Ps 28.8; 75.10
89.18 Ps 47.9; 71.22
89.19 1 Kings 11.34
89.20 Acts 13.22; 1 Sam 16.1,12
89.22 2 Sam 7.10
89.23 2 Sam 7.9
89.24 2 Sam 7.15
89.26 2 Sam 7.14; 22.47
89.27 Col 1.15; Num 24.7; Rev 1.5
89.28 Isa 55.3
89.29 Isa 9.7; Jer 33.17; Deut 11.21
89.30 2 Sam 7.14
89.32 2 Sam 7.14
89.33 2 Sam 7.15
89.34 Deut 7.9; Num 23.19
89.35 Am 4.2
89.36 Ps 72.5
89.38 1 Chr 28.9; Deut 32.19
89.39 Lam 5.16
89.40 Ps 80.12; Lam 2.2,5
89.41 Ps 44.13

42 You have exalted the right hand of his foes;
you have made all his enemies rejoice.
43 Moreover, you have turned back the edge of his sword,
and you have not supported him in battle.
44 You have removed the scepter from his hand,[a]
and hurled his throne to the ground.
45 You have cut short the days of his youth;
you have covered him with shame. *Selah*

46 How long, O LORD? Will you hide yourself forever?
How long will your wrath burn like fire?
47 Remember how short my time is—[b]
for what vanity you have created all mortals!
48 Who can live and never see death?
Who can escape the power of Sheol? *Selah*

49 Lord, where is your steadfast love of old,
which by your faithfulness you swore to David?
50 Remember, O Lord, how your servant is taunted;
how I bear in my bosom the insults of the peoples,[c]
51 with which your enemies taunt, O LORD,
with which they taunted the footsteps of your anointed.

52 Blessed be the LORD forever.
Amen and Amen.

BOOK IV

(*Psalms 90–106*)

Psalm 90

God's Eternity and Human Frailty

A Prayer of Moses, the man of God.

1 Lord, you have been our dwelling place[d]
in all generations.
2 Before the mountains were brought forth,
or ever you had formed the earth and the world,
from everlasting to everlasting you are God.

3 You turn us[e] back to dust,
and say, "Turn back, you mortals."
4 For a thousand years in your sight
are like yesterday when it is past,
or like a watch in the night.

5 You sweep them away; they are like a dream,
like grass that is renewed in the morning;
6 in the morning it flourishes and is renewed;
in the evening it fades and withers.

7 For we are consumed by your anger;
by your wrath we are overwhelmed.
8 You have set our iniquities before you,
our secret sins in the light of your countenance.

9 For all our days pass away under your wrath;
our years come to an end[f] like a sigh.
10 The days of our life are seventy years,
or perhaps eighty, if we are strong;
even then their span[g] is only toil and trouble;
they are soon gone, and we fly away.

11 Who considers the power of your anger?
Your wrath is as great as the fear that is due you.
12 So teach us to count our days
that we may gain a wise heart.

13 Turn, O LORD! How long?
Have compassion on your servants!
14 Satisfy us in the morning with your steadfast love,
so that we may rejoice and be glad all our days.
15 Make us glad as many days as you have afflicted us,
and as many years as we have seen evil.
16 Let your work be manifest to your servants,
and your glorious power to their children.
17 Let the favor of the Lord our God be upon us,

Ps 90 This psalm contrasts the enduring nature of God and the transitory existence of humans (vv.1-6), depicts the power of God's wrath and the *toil and trouble* of limited human life, and concludes with appeals to God's *compassion, love* and favor.

89.42 Ps 13.2; 80.6
89.43 Ps 44.10
89.44 Ezek 28.7
89.45 Ps 102.23; 44.15
89.46 Ps 79.5
89.47 Job 7.7; 10.9; 14.1; Ps 39.5
89.48 Ps 49.9; Heb 11.5
89.49 2 Sam 7.15; Ps 54.5
89.50 Ps 69.9,19
89.51 Ps 74.10
89.52 Ps 41.13
90.1 Deut 33.27; Ezek 11.16
90.2 Prov 8.25; Ps 102.25; 93.2
90.3 Gen 3.19
90.4 2 Pet 3.8; Ps 39.5
90.5 Job 27.20; Ps 73.20; 103.15; Isa 40.6
90.6 Job 14.2; Ps 92.7
90.8 Ps 50.21; Jer 16.17; Ps 19.12
90.9 Ps 78.33
90.10 Eccl 12.2-7
90.11 Ps 76.7
90.12 Ps 39.4
90.13 Deut 32.26; Ps 135.14
90.14 Ps 65.4; 85.6
90.16 Hab 3.2; 1 Kings 8.11
90.17 Ps 27.4; Isa 26.12

[a] Cn: Heb *removed his cleanness* [b] Meaning of Heb uncertain [c] Cn: Heb *bosom all of many peoples* [d] Another reading is *our refuge* [e] Heb *humankind* [f] Syr: Heb *we bring our years to an end* [g] Cn Compare Gk Syr Jerome Tg: Heb *pride*

Ps 91 After an affirmation of the security and loving care of God for his people, the LORD addresses them, inviting their love and their petitions, and promising them support *in trouble*.
Ps 92 The occasion for this psalm of gratitude, accompanied by music and song (vv.2-3), is God's faithfulness and love, to which *the stupid, the wicked, and [God's] enemies* have no access. God's people will flourish and live long, showing forth God's justice and dependability (*my rock*).

and prosper for us the work of our hands—
O prosper the work of our hands!

Psalm 91

Assurance of God's Protection

1 You who live in the shelter of the Most High,
who abide in the shadow of the Almighty,[h]
2 will say to the LORD, "My refuge and my fortress;
my God, in whom I trust."
3 For he will deliver you from the snare of the fowler
and from the deadly pestilence;
4 he will cover you with his pinions,
and under his wings you will find refuge;
his faithfulness is a shield and buckler.
5 You will not fear the terror of the night,
or the arrow that flies by day,
6 or the pestilence that stalks in darkness,
or the destruction that wastes at noonday.

7 A thousand may fall at your side,
ten thousand at your right hand,
but it will not come near you.
8 You will only look with your eyes
and see the punishment of the wicked.

9 Because you have made the LORD your refuge,[i]
the Most High your dwelling place,
10 no evil shall befall you,
no scourge come near your tent.

11 For he will command his angels concerning you
to guard you in all your ways.
12 On their hands they will bear you up,
so that you will not dash your foot against a stone.
13 You will tread on the lion and the adder,
the young lion and the serpent you will trample under foot.

14 Those who love me, I will deliver;
I will protect those who know my name.
15 When they call to me, I will answer them;
I will be with them in trouble,
I will rescue them and honor them.
16 With long life I will satisfy them,
and show them my salvation.

Psalm 92

Thanksgiving for Vindication

A Psalm. A Song for the Sabbath Day.

1 It is good to give thanks to the LORD,
to sing praises to your name, O Most High;
2 to declare your steadfast love in the morning,
and your faithfulness by night,
3 to the music of the lute and the harp,
to the melody of the lyre.
4 For you, O LORD, have made me glad by your work;
at the works of your hands I sing for joy.

5 How great are your works, O LORD!
Your thoughts are very deep!
6 The dullard cannot know,
the stupid cannot understand this:
7 though the wicked sprout like grass
and all evildoers flourish,
they are doomed to destruction forever,
8 but you, O LORD, are on high forever.
9 For your enemies, O LORD,
for your enemies shall perish;
all evildoers shall be scattered.

10 But you have exalted my horn like that of the wild ox;
you have poured over me[j] fresh oil.
11 My eyes have seen the downfall of my enemies;
my ears have heard the doom of my evil assailants.

12 The righteous flourish like the palm tree,
and grow like a cedar in Lebanon.
13 They are planted in the house of the LORD;
they flourish in the courts of our God.
14 In old age they still produce fruit;
they are always green and full of sap,
15 showing that the LORD is upright;
he is my rock, and there is no unrighteousness in him.

[h] Traditional rendering of Heb *Shaddai* [i] Cn: Heb *Because you, LORD, are my refuge; you have made* [j] Syr: Meaning of Heb uncertain

91.1 Ps 27.5; 31:20; 17.8
91.2 Ps 142.5
91.3 Ps 124.7
91.4 Isa 51.16; Ps 57.1; 40.11; 35.2
91.5 Ps 23.4; Song 3.8; Ps 64.4
91.6 ver 10; Job 5.22
91.8 Ps 37.34; Mal 1.5
91.10 Prov 12.21
91.11 Ps 34.7; Mt 4.6; Lk 4.10; Heb 1.14
91.13 Lk 10.19
91.14 Ps 145.20; 59.1; 9.10
91.15 Ps 50.15; 1 Sam 2.30; Jn 12.26
91.16 Ps 21.4; 50.23
92.1 Ps 147.1
92.2 Ps 89.1
92.3 1 Chr 23.5; Ps 33.2
92.5 Ps 40.5; Isa 28.29; Rom 11.33
92.7 Ps 90.5; 94.4; 37.38; 93.4
92.8 Ps 83.18
92.9 Ps 68.1; 89.10
92.11 Ps 54.7; 59.10
92.12 Ps 52.8; Isa 65.22; Hos 14.5,6; Ps 104.16
92.14 Isa 37.31
92.15 Ps 25.8; Deut 32.4; Rom 9.14

Psalm 93

The Majesty of God's Rule
1 The LORD is king, he is robed in majesty;
the LORD is robed, he is girded with strength.
He has established the world; it shall never be moved;
2 your throne is established from of old;
you are from everlasting.

3 The floods have lifted up, O LORD,
the floods have lifted up their voice;
the floods lift up their roaring.
4 More majestic than the thunders of mighty waters,
more majestic than the waves[k] of the sea,
majestic on high is the LORD!

5 Your decrees are very sure;
holiness befits your house,
O LORD, forevermore.

Psalm 94

God the Avenger of the Righteous
1 O LORD, you God of vengeance,
you God of vengeance, shine forth!
2 Rise up, O judge of the earth;
give to the proud what they deserve!
3 O LORD, how long shall the wicked,
how long shall the wicked exult?

4 They pour out their arrogant words;
all the evildoers boast.
5 They crush your people, O LORD,
and afflict your heritage.
6 They kill the widow and the stranger,
they murder the orphan,
7 and they say, "The LORD does not see;
the God of Jacob does not perceive."

8 Understand, O dullest of the people;
fools, when will you be wise?
9 He who planted the ear, does he not hear?
He who formed the eye, does he not see?
10 He who disciplines the nations,
he who teaches knowledge to humankind,
does he not chastise?
11 The LORD knows our thoughts,[l]
that they are but an empty breath.

12 Happy are those whom you discipline, O LORD,
and whom you teach out of your law,
13 giving them respite from days of trouble,
until a pit is dug for the wicked.
14 For the LORD will not forsake his people;
he will not abandon his heritage;
15 for justice will return to the righteous,
and all the upright in heart will follow it.

16 Who rises up for me against the wicked?
Who stands up for me against evildoers?
17 If the LORD had not been my help,
my soul would soon have lived in the land of silence.
18 When I thought, "My foot is slipping,"
your steadfast love, O LORD, held me up.
19 When the cares of my heart are many,
your consolations cheer my soul.
20 Can wicked rulers be allied with you,
those who contrive mischief by statute?
21 They band together against the life of the righteous,
and condemn the innocent to death.
22 But the LORD has become my stronghold,
and my God the rock of my refuge.
23 He will repay them for their iniquity
and wipe them out for their wickedness;
the LORD our God will wipe them out.

Psalm 95

A Call to Worship and Obedience
1 O come, let us sing to the LORD;
let us make a joyful noise to the rock of our salvation!
2 Let us come into his presence with thanksgiving;
let us make a joyful noise to him with songs of praise!
3 For the LORD is a great God,
and a great King above all gods.
4 In his hand are the depths of the earth;
the heights of the mountains are his also.
5 The sea is his, for he made it,
and the dry land, which his hands have formed.

6 O come, let us worship and bow down,
let us kneel before the LORD, our Maker!
7 For he is our God,
and we are the people of his pasture,
and the sheep of his hand.

[k] Cn: Heb *majestic are the waves* [l] Heb *the thoughts of humankind*

93.1 Ps 96.10; 97.1; 99.1; 104.1; 65.6
93.2 Ps 45.6; 90.2
93.4 Ps 65.7; 89.9
93.5 Ps 19.7; 1 Cor 3.17
94.1 Deut 32.35; Ps 50.2
94.2 Ps 7.6; Ps 31.23
94.3 Job 20.5
94.4 Ps 31.18; 10.3
94.7 Ps 10.11
94.8 Ps 92.6
94.9 Ex 4.11; Prov 20.12
94.10 Ps 44.2; Job 35.11; Isa 28.26
94.11 1 Cor 3.20
94.12 Job 5.17; Heb 12.5
94.14 1 Sam 12.22; Rom 11.1,2
94.16 Isa 28.21; Ps 59.2
94.17 Ps 124.1
94.18 Ps 38.16
94.19 Isa 66.13
94.20 Am 6.3; Isa 10.1
94.21 Ps 56.6; Mt 27.1; Prov 17.15
94.22 Ps 59.9; 71.7
94.23 Ps 7.16
95.1 Ps 100.1; Deut 32.15; 2 Sam 22.47
95.2 Mic 6.6; Ps 100.4; 81.2
95.3 Ps 96.4; 97.9; 135.5
95.5 Gen 1.9,10
95.6 Ps 99.5,9; 100.3
95.7 Ps 79.13; 100.3; Heb 3.7-11

Ps 93 The eternal rule and majesty of the LORD, his mastery over the hostile powers (*mighty waters*), and the sureness of his *decrees* are celebrated in this psalm.
Ps 94 After an appeal to God to punish *the wicked* for their failure to recognize or obey God, the psalmist declares that it is essential for all people to accept God's discipline through the wisdom which discloses his purpose and through which the obedient will find justice (vv.8-15). The psalmist declares that only through the LORD has he found stability in life and safety against the schemes of enemies (vv.16-23).
Ps 95 After celebrating the greatness of God and his control of the universe, *sea and land* (vv.1-5), the psalmist calls for God's flock to *worship* him and to avoid the self-will which characterized his people in the wilderness journey at *Meribah and Massah* (Ex 17.1-7; Num 20.1-13).

Ps 96 A hymn of praise to the LORD, calling *all the peoples* to join in acknowledging his sovereignty, bringing offerings to the temple *courts*, confident that his rule will be just. All the creation is invited to unite in praise of the God who is already ruling *the world with righteousness*.
Ps 97 The awesome omnipotence of God is again celebrated here as in Ps 96, but important also are his triumph over his adversaries, and over idolators and the gods they worship. He protects, rescues and illumines those who are *upright in heart*.
Ps 98 Another celebration of the just, sovereign rule of God over the world. His victory over the forces of evil is revealed to *the nations*, but to Israel is disclosed his *steadfast love and faithfulness*. All humans are to join in song and music with the forces of the natural world (*the sea, the floods*) in praise for his righteous reign.

O that today you would listen to his
voice!
8 Do not harden your hearts, as at
Meribah,
as on the day at Massah in the
wilderness,
9 when your ancestors tested me,
and put me to the proof, though they
had seen my work.
10 For forty years I loathed that generation
and said, "They are a people whose
hearts go astray,
and they do not regard my ways."
11 Therefore in my anger I swore,
"They shall not enter my rest."

Psalm 96

Praise to God Who Comes in Judgment
1 O sing to the LORD a new song;
sing to the LORD, all the earth.
2 Sing to the LORD, bless his name;
tell of his salvation from day to day.
3 Declare his glory among the nations,
his marvelous works among all the
peoples.
4 For great is the LORD, and greatly to be
praised;
he is to be revered above all gods.
5 For all the gods of the peoples are idols,
but the LORD made the heavens.
6 Honor and majesty are before him;
strength and beauty are in his
sanctuary.

7 Ascribe to the LORD, O families of the
peoples,
ascribe to the LORD glory and
strength.
8 Ascribe to the LORD the glory due his
name;
bring an offering, and come into his
courts.
9 Worship the LORD in holy splendor;
tremble before him, all the earth.

10 Say among the nations, "The LORD is
king!
The world is firmly established; it
shall never be moved.
He will judge the peoples with
equity."
11 Let the heavens be glad, and let the
earth rejoice;
let the sea roar, and all that fills it;
12 let the field exult, and everything in it.
Then shall all the trees of the forest sing
for joy
13 before the LORD; for he is coming,
for he is coming to judge the earth.
He will judge the world with
righteousness,
and the peoples with his truth.

Psalm 97

The Glory of God's Reign
1 The LORD is king! Let the earth rejoice;
let the many coastlands be glad!
2 Clouds and thick darkness are all
around him;
righteousness and justice are the
foundation of his throne.
3 Fire goes before him,
and consumes his adversaries on
every side.
4 His lightnings light up the world;
the earth sees and trembles.
5 The mountains melt like wax before the
LORD,
before the Lord of all the earth.

6 The heavens proclaim his righteousness;
and all the peoples behold his glory.
7 All worshipers of images are put to
shame,
those who make their boast in
worthless idols;
all gods bow down before him.
8 Zion hears and is glad,
and the towns[m] of Judah rejoice,
because of your judgments, O God.
9 For you, O LORD, are most high over all
the earth;
you are exalted far above all gods.

10 The LORD loves those who hate[n] evil;
he guards the lives of his faithful;
he rescues them from the hand of the
wicked.
11 Light dawns[o] for the righteous,
and joy for the upright in heart.
12 Rejoice in the LORD, O you righteous,
and give thanks to his holy name!

Psalm 98

Praise the Judge of the World
A Psalm.
1 O sing to the LORD a new song,
for he has done marvelous things.
His right hand and his holy arm

[m] Heb *daughters* [n] Cn: Heb *You who love the LORD hate* [o] Gk Syr Jerome: Heb *is sown*

95.8 Ex 17.2,7; Deut 6.16
95.9 Ps 78.18; 1 Cor 10.9
95.10 Heb 3.10,17
95.11 Heb 4.3,5
96.1 1 Chr 16.23-33
96.2 Ps 71.15
96.3 Ps 145.12
96.4 Ps 145.3; 18.3; 95.3
96.5 1 Chr 16.26; Ps 115.15
96.6 Ps 104.1
96.7 Ps 29.1,2
96.8 Ps 79.9
96.9 Ps 29.2
96.10 Ps 93.1; 67.4
96.11 Ps 97.1; 98.7
96.13 Ps 67.4; Rev 19.11
97.1 Ps 96.10,11
97.2 1 Kings 8.12; Ps 18.11; 89.14
97.3 Ps 18.8; Dan 7.10; Hab 3.5; Heb 12.29
97.5 Mic 1.4; Josh 3.11
97.7 Ex 20.4; Lev 26.1; Heb 1.6
97.8 Ps 48.11
97.9 Ps 83.18; Ex 18.11; Ps 95.3
97.10 Ps 34.14; Am 5.15; Prov 2.8; Ps 37.39; Dan 3.28
97.11 Job 22.28; Ps 112.4
98.1 Ps 33.3; Ex 15.6; Isa 52.10

have gotten him victory.
2 The LORD has made known his victory;
he has revealed his vindication in the sight of the nations.
3 He has remembered his steadfast love and faithfulness
to the house of Israel.
All the ends of the earth have seen
the victory of our God.

4 Make a joyful noise to the LORD, all the earth;
break forth into joyous song and sing praises.
5 Sing praises to the LORD with the lyre,
with the lyre and the sound of melody.
6 With trumpets and the sound of the horn
make a joyful noise before the King, the LORD.

7 Let the sea roar, and all that fills it;
the world and those who live in it.
8 Let the floods clap their hands;
let the hills sing together for joy
9 at the presence of the LORD, for he is coming
to judge the earth.
He will judge the world with righteousness,
and the peoples with equity.

Psalm 99

Praise to God for His Holiness

1 The LORD is king; let the peoples tremble!
He sits enthroned upon the cherubim; let the earth quake!
2 The LORD is great in Zion;
he is exalted over all the peoples.
3 Let them praise your great and awesome name.
Holy is he!
4 Mighty King,[p] lover of justice,
you have established equity;
you have executed justice
and righteousness in Jacob.
5 Extol the LORD our God;
worship at his footstool.
Holy is he!

6 Moses and Aaron were among his priests,
Samuel also was among those who called on his name.
They cried to the LORD, and he answered them.
7 He spoke to them in the pillar of cloud;
they kept his decrees,
and the statutes that he gave them.

8 O LORD our God, you answered them;
you were a forgiving God to them,
but an avenger of their wrongdoings.
9 Extol the LORD our God,
and worship at his holy mountain;
for the LORD our God is holy.

Psalm 100

All Lands Summoned to Praise God

A Psalm of thanksgiving.

1 Make a joyful noise to the LORD, all the earth.
2 Worship the LORD with gladness;
come into his presence with singing.

3 Know that the LORD is God.
It is he that made us, and we are his;[q]
we are his people, and the sheep of his pasture.

4 Enter his gates with thanksgiving,
and his courts with praise.
Give thanks to him, bless his name.

5 For the LORD is good;
his steadfast love endures forever,
and his faithfulness to all generations.

Psalm 101

A Sovereign's Pledge of Integrity and Justice

Of David. A Psalm.

1 I will sing of loyalty and of justice;
to you, O LORD, I will sing.
2 I will study the way that is blameless.
When shall I attain it?

I will walk with integrity of heart
within my house;
3 I will not set before my eyes
anything that is base.

I hate the work of those who fall away;
it shall not cling to me.
4 Perverseness of heart shall be far from me;
I will know nothing of evil.

5 One who secretly slanders a neighbor
I will destroy.

[p] Cn: Heb *And a king's strength* [q] Another reading is *and not we ourselves*

98.2 Rom 3.25
98.3 Lk 1.54; Isa 49.6
98.4 Ps 100.1
98.6 Num 10.10
98.7 Ps 96.11; 24.1
98.8 Ps 93.3; 65.12
98.9 Ps 96.10,13
99.1 Ex 25.22
99.2 Ps 97.9
99.4 Ps 11.7; 17.2; 103.6
99.5 Ps 132.7; Lev 19.2
99.6 Jer 15.1; Ex 14.15; 1 Sam 7.9
99.7 Ex 33.9
99.8 Ps 106.44; Num 14.20; Deut 9.20
99.9 Ps 34.3
100.1 Ps 98.4
100.3 Ps 46.10; 95.6,7
100.4 Ps 95.2; 96.2
100.5 Ps 25.8; 119.90
101.1 Ps 89.1
101.2 1 Sam 18.14; 1 Kings 9.4
101.3 Deut 15.9; Ps 40.4
101.4 Prov 11.20
101.5 Ps 50.20; Prov 6.17

Ps 99 The LORD's rule is pictured as based in the inner sanctuary of the temple, where he sits *enthroned upon the cherubim.* Although *all peoples* are enjoined to worship him, it is among his special people (*Jacob*) and through his special agents (*Moses, Aaron and Samuel*) that his law is conveyed and that they obtain forgiveness.
Ps 100 As in Ps 99, *all the earth* is called to join in praise of God, while the special relationship of his people (*the sheep of his pasture*) is also affirmed. In the temple courts God's *steadfast love* is to be celebrated throughout *all generations.*
Ps 101 The claim of *loyalty* to the LORD is matched by *study* of his law, so that personal integrity, rejection of the evil ways of others (vv.4-5,7-8), and *favor* toward the obedient will characterize the life of the psalmist.

Ps 102 This psalm opens with a cry of despair about life (vv.1-11), in which the uncertainty of life is compared with several forms of life – withered grass, lonely birds – and with personal pain and deprivation. The sorrowful theme is resumed in vv.23-24. In between and at the end are affirmations of God's renewal of *Zion* from its *dust*, and of his establishment of his people there to worship the LORD in security.

A haughty look and an arrogant heart
I will not tolerate.

6 I will look with favor on the faithful in the land,
so that they may live with me;
whoever walks in the way that is blameless
shall minister to me.

7 No one who practices deceit
shall remain in my house;
no one who utters lies
shall continue in my presence.

8 Morning by morning I will destroy
all the wicked in the land,
cutting off all evildoers
from the city of the LORD.

Psalm 102

Prayer to the Eternal King for Help

A prayer of one afflicted, when faint and pleading before the LORD.

1 Hear my prayer, O LORD;
let my cry come to you.
2 Do not hide your face from me
in the day of my distress.
Incline your ear to me;
answer me speedily in the day when I call.

3 For my days pass away like smoke,
and my bones burn like a furnace.
4 My heart is stricken and withered like grass;
I am too wasted to eat my bread.
5 Because of my loud groaning
my bones cling to my skin.
6 I am like an owl of the wilderness,
like a little owl of the waste places.
7 I lie awake;
I am like a lonely bird on the housetop.
8 All day long my enemies taunt me;
those who deride me use my name for a curse.
9 For I eat ashes like bread,
and mingle tears with my drink,
10 because of your indignation and anger;
for you have lifted me up and thrown me aside.
11 My days are like an evening shadow;
I wither away like grass.

12 But you, O LORD, are enthroned forever;
your name endures to all generations.
13 You will rise up and have compassion on Zion,
for it is time to favor it;
the appointed time has come.
14 For your servants hold its stones dear,
and have pity on its dust.
15 The nations will fear the name of the LORD,
and all the kings of the earth your glory.
16 For the LORD will build up Zion;
he will appear in his glory.
17 He will regard the prayer of the destitute,
and will not despise their prayer.

18 Let this be recorded for a generation to come,
so that a people yet unborn may praise the LORD:
19 that he looked down from his holy height,
from heaven the LORD looked at the earth,
20 to hear the groans of the prisoners,
to set free those who were doomed to die;
21 so that the name of the LORD may be declared in Zion,
and his praise in Jerusalem,
22 when peoples gather together,
and kingdoms, to worship the LORD.

23 He has broken my strength in midcourse;
he has shortened my days.
24 "O my God," I say, "do not take me away
at the mid-point of my life,
you whose years endure
throughout all generations."

25 Long ago you laid the foundation of the earth,
and the heavens are the work of your hands.
26 They will perish, but you endure;
they will all wear out like a garment.
You change them like clothing, and they pass away;
27 but you are the same, and your years have no end.
28 The children of your servants shall live secure;
their offspring shall be established in your presence.

101.6 Ps 119.1
101.8 Ps 75.10; 118.10-12
102.1 1 Sam 9.16
102.2 Ps 69.17; 71.2
102.3 Jas 4.14; Job 30.30; Ps 31.10
102.4 Ps 37.2
102.5 Lam 4.8
102.6 Isa 34.11
102.7 Ps 77.4; 38.11
102.8 Acts 26.11; 23.12
102.9 Ps 42.3
102.11 Job 14.2; ver 4
102.12 Ps 9.7; Lam 5.19; Ps 135.13
102.13 Isa 60.10; Zech 1.12; Ps 75.2
102.15 1 Kings 8.43; Ps 138.4
102.16 Isa 60.1,2
102.17 Neh 1.6
102.18 Rom 15.4; Ps 22.31
102.19 Deut 26.15; Ps 33.13
102.20 Ps 79.11
102.21 Ps 22.22
102.22 Ps 86.9
102.23 Job 21.21
102.24 Isa 38.10; Ps 90.2; Hab 1.12
102.25 Gen 1.1; Heb 1.10; Ps 96.5
102.26 Isa 34.4; Mt 24.35; 2 Pet 3.7,10; Rev 20.11
102.27 Mal 3.6; Heb 13.8; Jas 1.17
102.28 Ps 69.36; 89.4

103.1 Ps 104.1; 33.21
103.3 Ps 130.8; Isa 43.25; Ex 15.26
103.4 Ps 49.15; 5.12
103.8 Ex 34.6; Neh 9.17; Ps 145.8
103.9 Ps 30.5; Isa 57.16; Jer 3.5
103.10 Ezra 9.13
103.11 Ps 36.5
103.12 2 Sam 12.13; Isa 38.17; Heb 9.26
103.13 Mal 3.17
103.14 Isa 29.16; Gen 3.19
103.15 1 Pet 1.24; Job 14.1,2
103.18 Deut 7.9
103.19 Ps 11.4; 47.2
103.20 Ps 148.2; Mt 6.10; Heb 1.14
103.21 Ps 148.2
104.1 Ps 103.1
104.2 Dan 7.9; Isa 40.22
104.3 Am 9.6; Isa 19.1; Ps 18.10
104.4 Heb 1.7
104.5 Job 26.7; Ps 24.2
104.6 Gen 7.19
104.8 Ps 33.7
104.9 Job 38.10,11; Jer 5.22
104.10 Ps 107.35
104.11 Job 39.5
104.12 Mt 8.20

Psalm 103

Thanksgiving for God's Goodness

Of David.

1 Bless the LORD, O my soul,
and all that is within me,
bless his holy name.
2 Bless the LORD, O my soul,
and do not forget all his benefits—
3 who forgives all your iniquity,
who heals all your diseases,
4 who redeems your life from the Pit,
who crowns you with steadfast love
and mercy,
5 who satisfies you with good as long as
you live[r]
so that your youth is renewed like the
eagle's.

6 The LORD works vindication
and justice for all who are oppressed.
7 He made known his ways to Moses,
his acts to the people of Israel.
8 The LORD is merciful and gracious,
slow to anger and abounding in
steadfast love.
9 He will not always accuse,
nor will he keep his anger forever.
10 He does not deal with us according to
our sins,
nor repay us according to our
iniquities.
11 For as the heavens are high above the
earth,
so great is his steadfast love toward
those who fear him;
12 as far as the east is from the west,
so far he removes our transgressions
from us.
13 As a father has compassion for his
children,
so the LORD has compassion for those
who fear him.
14 For he knows how we were made;
he remembers that we are dust.

15 As for mortals, their days are like grass;
they flourish like a flower of the field;
16 for the wind passes over it, and it is
gone,
and its place knows it no more.
17 But the steadfast love of the LORD is from
everlasting to everlasting
on those who fear him,
and his righteousness to children's
children,
18 to those who keep his covenant
and remember to do his
commandments.

19 The LORD has established his throne in
the heavens,
and his kingdom rules over all.
20 Bless the LORD, O you his angels,
you mighty ones who do his bidding,
obedient to his spoken word.
21 Bless the LORD, all his hosts,
his ministers that do his will.
22 Bless the LORD, all his works,
in all places of his dominion.
Bless the LORD, O my soul.

Psalm 104

God the Creator and Provider

1 Bless the LORD, O my soul.
O LORD my God, you are very great.
You are clothed with honor and majesty,
2 wrapped in light as with a garment.
You stretch out the heavens like a tent,
3 you set the beams of your[s] chambers
on the waters,
you make the clouds your[s] chariot,
you ride on the wings of the wind,
4 you make the winds your[s] messengers,
fire and flame your[s] ministers.

5 You set the earth on its foundations,
so that it shall never be shaken.
6 You cover it with the deep as with a
garment;
the waters stood above the
mountains.
7 At your rebuke they flee;
at the sound of your thunder they
take to flight.
8 They rose up to the mountains, ran
down to the valleys
to the place that you appointed for
them.
9 You set a boundary that they may not
pass,
so that they might not again cover
the earth.

10 You make springs gush forth in the
valleys;
they flow between the hills,
11 giving drink to every wild animal;
the wild asses quench their thirst.
12 By the streams[t] the birds of the air have
their habitation;

Ps 103 The psalmist calls for his inner being (*my soul*) to praise the LORD for his forgiveness, his love, his justice for the oppressed, his *compassion for his children*, and for the faithful quality of his love (in spite of human failures) toward those who *keep his covenant*. The angels and the powers used by God are called to join in praising him.
Ps 104 The greatness of the LORD is extolled for his creating and maintaining the universe, and for sustaining plant, animal and human life on the earth. The psalmist calls all to join him in praising God.

[r] Meaning of Heb uncertain [s] Heb *his* [t] Heb *By them*

Ps 105 Here are recalled the historic events by which God demonstrated his fidelity to his covenant with Israel and the *statutes* that they are called upon to obey.

they sing among the branches.
13 From your lofty abode you water the mountains;
the earth is satisfied with the fruit of your work.

14 You cause the grass to grow for the cattle,
and plants for people to use,[u]
to bring forth food from the earth,
15 and wine to gladden the human heart,
oil to make the face shine,
and bread to strengthen the human heart.
16 The trees of the LORD are watered abundantly,
the cedars of Lebanon that he planted.
17 In them the birds build their nests;
the stork has its home in the fir trees.
18 The high mountains are for the wild goats;
the rocks are a refuge for the coneys.
19 You have made the moon to mark the seasons;
the sun knows its time for setting.
20 You make darkness, and it is night,
when all the animals of the forest come creeping out.
21 The young lions roar for their prey,
seeking their food from God.
22 When the sun rises, they withdraw
and lie down in their dens.
23 People go out to their work
and to their labor until the evening.

24 O LORD, how manifold are your works!
In wisdom you have made them all;
the earth is full of your creatures.
25 Yonder is the sea, great and wide,
creeping things innumerable are there,
living things both small and great.
26 There go the ships,
and Leviathan that you formed to sport in it.

27 These all look to you
to give them their food in due season;
28 when you give to them, they gather it up;
when you open your hand, they are filled with good things.
29 When you hide your face, they are dismayed;
when you take away their breath, they die
and return to their dust.
30 When you send forth your spirit,[v] they are created;
and you renew the face of the ground.

31 May the glory of the LORD endure forever;
may the LORD rejoice in his works—
32 who looks on the earth and it trembles,
who touches the mountains and they smoke.
33 I will sing to the LORD as long as I live;
I will sing praise to my God while I have being.
34 May my meditation be pleasing to him,
for I rejoice in the LORD.
35 Let sinners be consumed from the earth,
and let the wicked be no more.
Bless the LORD, O my soul.
Praise the LORD!

Psalm 105

God's Faithfulness to Israel

1 O give thanks to the LORD, call on his name,
make known his deeds among the peoples.
2 Sing to him, sing praises to him;
tell of all his wonderful works.
3 Glory in his holy name;
let the hearts of those who seek the LORD rejoice.
4 Seek the LORD and his strength;
seek his presence continually.
5 Remember the wonderful works he has done,
his miracles, and the judgments he uttered,
6 O offspring of his servant Abraham,[w]
children of Jacob, his chosen ones.

7 He is the LORD our God;
his judgments are in all the earth.
8 He is mindful of his covenant forever,
of the word that he commanded, for a thousand generations,
9 the covenant that he made with Abraham,
his sworn promise to Isaac,
10 which he confirmed to Jacob as a statute,
to Israel as an everlasting covenant,

[u] Or *to cultivate* [v] Or *your breath* [w] Another reading is *Israel* (compare 1 Chr 16.13)

104.13 Ps 65.9; 147.8
104.14 Ps 147.8; Job 38.27; Gen 1.29; Job 28.5
104.15 Judg 9.13; Ps 23.5
104.18 Prov 30.26
104.19 Gen 1.14
104.20 Isa 45.7
104.21 Job 38.39
104.23 Gen 3.19
104.24 Ps 40.5; Prov 3.19; Ps 65.9
104.26 Ps 107.23; Job 41.1
104.27 Ps 136.25; 145.15
104.29 Job 34.14; Ps 146.4; Eccl 12.7
104.30 Isa 32.15; Ezek 37.9
104.31 Gen 1.31
104.32 Ps 97.4,5; 144.5
104.33 Ps 63.4; 146.2
104.35 Ps 59.13; 37.10; ver 1
105.1. 1 Chr 16.8; Ps 145.12
105.2 Ps 77.12
105.3 Ps 33.21
105.4 Ps 27.8
105.5 Ps 77.11
105.7 Isa 26.9
105.9 Gen 17.2
105.10 Gen 28.13-15

11 saying, "To you I will give the land of
Canaan
as your portion for an inheritance."

12 When they were few in number,
of little account, and strangers in it,
13 wandering from nation to nation,
from one kingdom to another people,
14 he allowed no one to oppress them;
he rebuked kings on their account,
15 saying, "Do not touch my anointed
ones;
do my prophets no harm."

16 When he summoned famine against the
land,
and broke every staff of bread,
17 he had sent a man ahead of them,
Joseph, who was sold as a slave.
18 His feet were hurt with fetters,
his neck was put in a collar of iron;
19 until what he had said came to pass,
the word of the LORD kept testing him.
20 The king sent and released him;
the ruler of the peoples set him free.
21 He made him lord of his house,
and ruler of all his possessions,
22 to instruct[x] his officials at his pleasure,
and to teach his elders wisdom.

23 Then Israel came to Egypt;
Jacob lived as an alien in the land of
Ham.
24 And the LORD made his people very
fruitful,
and made them stronger than their
foes,
25 whose hearts he then turned to hate his
people,
to deal craftily with his servants.

26 He sent his servant Moses,
and Aaron whom he had chosen.
27 They performed his signs among them,
and miracles in the land of Ham.
28 He sent darkness, and made the land
dark;
they rebelled[y] against his words.
29 He turned their waters into blood,
and caused their fish to die.
30 Their land swarmed with frogs,
even in the chambers of their kings.
31 He spoke, and there came swarms of
flies,
and gnats throughout their country.
32 He gave them hail for rain,
and lightning that flashed through
their land.
33 He struck their vines and fig trees,
and shattered the trees of their
country.
34 He spoke, and the locusts came,
and young locusts without number;
35 they devoured all the vegetation in their
land,
and ate up the fruit of their ground.
36 He struck down all the firstborn in their
land,
the first issue of all their strength.

37 Then he brought Israel[z] out with silver
and gold,
and there was no one among their
tribes who stumbled.
38 Egypt was glad when they departed,
for dread of them had fallen upon it.
39 He spread a cloud for a covering,
and fire to give light by night.
40 They asked, and he brought quails,
and gave them food from heaven in
abundance.
41 He opened the rock, and water gushed
out;
it flowed through the desert like a
river.
42 For he remembered his holy promise,
and Abraham, his servant.

43 So he brought his people out with joy,
his chosen ones with singing.
44 He gave them the lands of the nations,
and they took possession of the
wealth of the peoples,
45 that they might keep his statutes
and observe his laws.
Praise the LORD!

Psalm 106

A Confession of Israel's Sins

1 Praise the LORD!
O give thanks to the LORD, for he is
good;
for his steadfast love endures forever.
2 Who can utter the mighty doings of the
LORD,
or declare all his praise?
3 Happy are those who observe justice,
who do righteousness at all times.

4 Remember me, O LORD, when you show
favor to your people;

Ps 106 Here is reported the long series of failures on the part of Israel to obey God as they moved from Egypt to the land of promise. Yet God remembered his *covenant*.

105.11 Gen 13.15; 15.18
105.12 Gen 34.30; Heb 11.9
105.14 Gen 35.5; 12.17
105.16 Lev 26.26; Isa 3.1; Ezek 4.16
105.17 Gen 45.5; 37.28,36
105.18 Gen 39.20
105.19 Gen 40.20,21; Ps 66.10
105.20 Gen 41.14
105.21 Gen 41.40
105.23 Gen 46.6; Acts 13.17
105.24 Ex 1.7
105.25 Ex 1.8,10
105.26 Ex 3.10; Num 16.5
105.27 Ex 7-12; Ps 78.43
105.28 Ex 10.22; Ps 99.7
105.29 Ex 7.20
105.30 Ex 8.6
105.31 Ex 8.16,21
105.32 Ex 9.23
105.34 Ex 10.4; Ps 78.46
105.36 Ex 12.29; Ps 78.51
105.37 Ex 12.35
105.38 Ex 12.33
105.39 Ex 13.21; Neh 9.12
105.40 Ex 16.12ff; Ps 78.24ff
105.41 Ex 17.6; 1 Cor 10.4
105.42 ver 8
105.44 Josh 13.7
105.45 Deut 6.21-25
106.1 Ps 105.1; 100.5; 1 Chr 16.34
106.2 Ps 145.4,12
106.3 Ps 15.2
106.4 Ps 119.132

[x] Gk Syr Jerome: Heb *to bind* [y] Cn Compare Gk Syr: Heb *they did not rebel* [z] Heb *them*

help me when you deliver them;
5 that I may see the prosperity of your chosen ones,
that I may rejoice in the gladness of your nation,
that I may glory in your heritage.

6 Both we and our ancestors have sinned;
we have committed iniquity, have done wickedly.
7 Our ancestors, when they were in Egypt,
did not consider your wonderful works;
they did not remember the abundance of your steadfast love,
but rebelled against the Most High[a] at the Red Sea.[b]
8 Yet he saved them for his name's sake,
so that he might make known his mighty power.
9 He rebuked the Red Sea,[b] and it became dry;
he led them through the deep as through a desert.
10 So he saved them from the hand of the foe,
and delivered them from the hand of the enemy.
11 The waters covered their adversaries;
not one of them was left.
12 Then they believed his words;
they sang his praise.

13 But they soon forgot his works;
they did not wait for his counsel.
14 But they had a wanton craving in the wilderness,
and put God to the test in the desert;
15 he gave them what they asked,
but sent a wasting disease among them.

16 They were jealous of Moses in the camp,
and of Aaron, the holy one of the LORD.
17 The earth opened and swallowed up Dathan,
and covered the faction of Abiram.
18 Fire also broke out in their company;
the flame burned up the wicked.

19 They made a calf at Horeb
and worshiped a cast image.
20 They exchanged the glory of God[c]
for the image of an ox that eats grass.
21 They forgot God, their Savior,
who had done great things in Egypt,
22 wondrous works in the land of Ham,
and awesome deeds by the Red Sea.[b]
23 Therefore he said he would destroy them—
had not Moses, his chosen one,
stood in the breach before him,
to turn away his wrath from destroying them.

24 Then they despised the pleasant land,
having no faith in his promise.
25 They grumbled in their tents,
and did not obey the voice of the LORD.
26 Therefore he raised his hand and swore to them
that he would make them fall in the wilderness,
27 and would disperse[d] their descendants among the nations,
scattering them over the lands.

28 Then they attached themselves to the Baal of Peor,
and ate sacrifices offered to the dead;
29 they provoked the LORD to anger with their deeds,
and a plague broke out among them.
30 Then Phinehas stood up and interceded,
and the plague was stopped.
31 And that has been reckoned to him as righteousness
from generation to generation forever.

32 They angered the LORD[e] at the waters of Meribah,
and it went ill with Moses on their account;
33 for they made his spirit bitter,
and he spoke words that were rash.

34 They did not destroy the peoples,
as the LORD commanded them,
35 but they mingled with the nations
and learned to do as they did.
36 They served their idols,
which became a snare to them.
37 They sacrificed their sons
and their daughters to the demons;
38 they poured out innocent blood,
the blood of their sons and daughters,
whom they sacrificed to the idols of Canaan;

[a] Cn Compare 78.17, 56: Heb *rebelled at the sea* [b] Or *Sea of Reeds* [c] Compare Gk Mss: Heb *exchanged their glory* [d] Syr Compare Ezek 20.23: Heb *cause to fall* [e] Heb *him*

106.5 Ps 1.3; 118.15; 105.3
106.6 Dan 9.5
106.7 Ps 78.11.42; Ex 14.11
106.8 Ex 9.16
106.9 Ex 14.21; Ps 18.15; Nah 1.4; Isa 63.11-14
106.10 Ex 14.30; Ps 107.2
106.11 Ex 14.28; 15.5
106.12 Ex 14.31; 15.1-21
106.13 Ex 15.24
106.14 1 Cor 10.6,9
106.15 Num 11.31
106.16 Num 16.1-3
106.17 Deut 11.6
106.18 Num 16.35
106.19 Ex 32.14
106.20 Jer 2.11; Rom 1.23
106.21 Ps 78.11; Deut 10.21
106.22 Ps 105.27
106.23 Ex 32.10; 32.11-14
106.24 Deut 8.7; Heb 3.18,19
106.25 Num 14.2
106.26 Num 14.28-35; Heb 11.3
106.27 Ps 44.11
106.28 Num 25.2,3
106.30 Num 25.7
106.31 Num 25.11-13
106.32 Num 20.3,13; Ps 81.7
106.33 Num 20.10
106.34 Judg 1.21; Deut 7.2,16
106.35 Judg 3.5,6
106.36 Judg 2.12
106.37 2 Kings 17.7
106.38 Ps 94.21; Num 35.33

and the land was polluted with blood.
39 Thus they became unclean by their acts,
and prostituted themselves in their doings.

40 Then the anger of the LORD was kindled against his people,
and he abhorred his heritage;
41 he gave them into the hand of the nations,
so that those who hated them ruled over them.
42 Their enemies oppressed them,
and they were brought into subjection under their power.
43 Many times he delivered them,
but they were rebellious in their purposes,
and were brought low through their iniquity.
44 Nevertheless he regarded their distress
when he heard their cry.
45 For their sake he remembered his covenant,
and showed compassion according to the abundance of his steadfast love.
46 He caused them to be pitied
by all who held them captive.

47 Save us, O LORD our God,
and gather us from among the nations,
that we may give thanks to your holy name
and glory in your praise.

48 Blessed be the LORD, the God of Israel,
from everlasting to everlasting.
And let all the people say, "Amen."
Praise the LORD!

BOOK V

(Psalms 107–150)

Psalm 107

Thanksgiving for Deliverance from Many Troubles

1 O give thanks to the LORD, for he is good;
for his steadfast love endures forever.
2 Let the redeemed of the LORD say so,
those he redeemed from trouble
3 and gathered in from the lands,
from the east and from the west,
from the north and from the south.[f]

4 Some wandered in desert wastes,
finding no way to an inhabited town;
5 hungry and thirsty,
their soul fainted within them.
6 Then they cried to the LORD in their trouble,
and he delivered them from their distress;
7 he led them by a straight way,
until they reached an inhabited town.
8 Let them thank the LORD for his steadfast love,
for his wonderful works to humankind.
9 For he satisfies the thirsty,
and the hungry he fills with good things.

10 Some sat in darkness and in gloom,
prisoners in misery and in irons,
11 for they had rebelled against the words of God,
and spurned the counsel of the Most High.
12 Their hearts were bowed down with hard labor;
they fell down, with no one to help.
13 Then they cried to the LORD in their trouble,
and he saved them from their distress;
14 he brought them out of darkness and gloom,
and broke their bonds asunder.
15 Let them thank the LORD for his steadfast love,
for his wonderful works to humankind.
16 For he shatters the doors of bronze,
and cuts in two the bars of iron.

17 Some were sick[g] through their sinful ways,
and because of their iniquities endured affliction;
18 they loathed any kind of food,
and they drew near to the gates of death.
19 Then they cried to the LORD in their trouble,
and he saved them from their distress;
20 he sent out his word and healed them,
and delivered them from destruction.

Ps 107 A call to the community to be grateful to God for the support and the forgiveness he has offered over the centuries of the life of his people. *The wise* will recall his works of *steadfast love.*

106.39 Ezek 20.18; Num 15.39
106.40 Ps 78.59
106.41 Judg 2.14; Neh 9.27
106.43 Judg 2.16-18
106.44 Judg 3.9
106.45 Ps 105.8; Judg 2.18
106.46 Ezra 9.9; Jer 42.12
106.47 1 Chr 16.35,36; Ps 147.2
106.48 Ps 41.13
107.1 Ps 106.1
107.2 Ps 106.10
107.3 Ps 106.47; Isa 43.5,6
107.4 Num 14.33; 32.13
107.6 Ps 50.15
107.7 Ezra 8.21
107.8 ver 15,21,31
107.9 Ps 22.26; Lk 1.53
107.10 Lk 1.79; Job 36.8
107.11 Ps 106.7; 2 Chr 36.16
107.12 Ps 22.11
107.13 ver 6
107.14 Ps 116.16; Lk 13.16; Acts 12.7
107.15 ver 8,21,31
107.16 Isa 45.2
107.17 Isa 65.6,7
107.18 Job 33.20,22; Ps 9.13; 88.3
107.20 Mt 8.8; Ps 30.2; 103.3

[f] Cn: Heb *sea* [g] Cn: Heb *fools*

Ps 108 A composite psalm which duplicates Ps 57.7-11 and 60.6-12.

21 Let them thank the LORD for his steadfast love,
for his wonderful works to humankind.
22 And let them offer thanksgiving sacrifices,
and tell of his deeds with songs of joy.

23 Some went down to the sea in ships,
doing business on the mighty waters;
24 they saw the deeds of the LORD,
his wondrous works in the deep.
25 For he commanded and raised the stormy wind,
which lifted up the waves of the sea.
26 They mounted up to heaven, they went down to the depths;
their courage melted away in their calamity;
27 they reeled and staggered like drunkards,
and were at their wits' end.
28 Then they cried to the LORD in their trouble,
and he brought them out from their distress;
29 he made the storm be still,
and the waves of the sea were hushed.
30 Then they were glad because they had quiet,
and he brought them to their desired haven.
31 Let them thank the LORD for his steadfast love,
for his wonderful works to humankind.
32 Let them extol him in the congregation of the people,
and praise him in the assembly of the elders.

33 He turns rivers into a desert,
springs of water into thirsty ground,
34 a fruitful land into a salty waste,
because of the wickedness of its inhabitants.
35 He turns a desert into pools of water,
a parched land into springs of water.
36 And there he lets the hungry live,
and they establish a town to live in;
37 they sow fields, and plant vineyards,
and get a fruitful yield.
38 By his blessing they multiply greatly,
and he does not let their cattle decrease.
39 When they are diminished and brought low
through oppression, trouble, and sorrow,
40 he pours contempt on princes
and makes them wander in trackless wastes;
41 but he raises up the needy out of distress,
and makes their families like flocks.
42 The upright see it and are glad;
and all wickedness stops its mouth.
43 Let those who are wise give heed to these things,
and consider the steadfast love of the LORD.

Psalm 108

Praise and Prayer for Victory

A Song. A Psalm of David.

1 My heart is steadfast, O God, my heart is steadfast;[h]
I will sing and make melody.
Awake, my soul![i]
2 Awake, O harp and lyre!
I will awake the dawn.
3 I will give thanks to you, O LORD, among the peoples,
and I will sing praises to you among the nations.
4 For your steadfast love is higher than the heavens,
and your faithfulness reaches to the clouds.

5 Be exalted, O God, above the heavens,
and let your glory be over all the earth.
6 Give victory with your right hand, and answer me,
so that those whom you love may be rescued.

7 God has promised in his sanctuary:[j]
"With exultation I will divide up Shechem,
and portion out the Vale of Succoth.
8 Gilead is mine; Manasseh is mine;
Ephraim is my helmet;
Judah is my scepter.
9 Moab is my washbasin;
on Edom I hurl my shoe;
over Philistia I shout in triumph."

10 Who will bring me to the fortified city?

[h] Heb Mss Gk Syr: MT lacks *my heart is steadfast* [i] Compare 57.8: Heb *also my soul* [j] Or *by his holiness*

107.22 Lev 7.12; Ps 50.14; 9.11; 73.28; 118.17
107.25 Ps 105.31.34; Jon 1.4; Ps 93.3,4
107.26 Ps 22.14; 119.28
107.27 Job 12.25
107.28 ver 6.13,19
107.29 Ps 89.9; Mt 8.26
107.31 ver 8,15,21
107.32 Ps 22.22,25; 35.18
107.33 Ps 74.15
107.34 Gen 13.10; 14.3; 19.25
107.35 Ps 114.8; Isa 41.18
107.37 Isa 65.21
107.38 Gen 12.2; 17.16,20; Ex 1.7
107.39 Ezek 5.11; Ps 57.6
107.40 Job 12.21,24
107.41 1 Sam 2.8; Ps 113.7-9
107.42 Job 22.19; Ps 52.6; Job 5.16; Ps 63.11; Rom 3.19
107.43 Ps 64.9; Jer 9.12; Hos 14.9
108.1 Ps 57.7
108.2 Ps 57.8-11
108.4 Ps 113.4
108.6 Ps 60.5-12
108.8 Ps 60.7

Who will lead me to Edom?
11 Have you not rejected us, O God?
You do not go out, O God, with our armies.
12 O grant us help against the foe,
for human help is worthless.
13 With God we shall do valiantly;
it is he who will tread down our foes.

Psalm 109

Prayer for Vindication and Vengeance

To the leader. Of David. A Psalm.

1 Do not be silent, O God of my praise.
2 For wicked and deceitful mouths are opened against me,
speaking against me with lying tongues.
3 They beset me with words of hate,
and attack me without cause.
4 In return for my love they accuse me,
even while I make prayer for them.[k]
5 So they reward me evil for good,
and hatred for my love.

6 They say,[l] "Appoint a wicked man against him;
let an accuser stand on his right.
7 When he is tried, let him be found guilty;
let his prayer be counted as sin.
8 May his days be few;
may another seize his position.
9 May his children be orphans,
and his wife a widow.
10 May his children wander about and beg;
may they be driven out of[m] the ruins they inhabit.
11 May the creditor seize all that he has;
may strangers plunder the fruits of his toil.
12 May there be no one to do him a kindness,
nor anyone to pity his orphaned children.
13 May his posterity be cut off;
may his name be blotted out in the second generation.
14 May the iniquity of his father[n] be remembered before the LORD,
and do not let the sin of his mother be blotted out.
15 Let them be before the LORD continually,
and may his[o] memory be cut off from the earth.
16 For he did not remember to show kindness,
but pursued the poor and needy
and the brokenhearted to their death.
17 He loved to curse; let curses come on him.
He did not like blessing; may it be far from him.
18 He clothed himself with cursing as his coat,
may it soak into his body like water,
like oil into his bones.
19 May it be like a garment that he wraps around himself,
like a belt that he wears every day."

20 May that be the reward of my accusers from the LORD,
of those who speak evil against my life.
21 But you, O LORD my Lord,
act on my behalf for your name's sake;
because your steadfast love is good,
deliver me.
22 For I am poor and needy,
and my heart is pierced within me.
23 I am gone like a shadow at evening;
I am shaken off like a locust.
24 My knees are weak through fasting;
my body has become gaunt.
25 I am an object of scorn to my accusers;
when they see me, they shake their heads.

26 Help me, O LORD my God!
Save me according to your steadfast love.
27 Let them know that this is your hand;
you, O LORD, have done it.
28 Let them curse, but you will bless.
Let my assailants be put to shame;[p]
may your servant be glad.
29 May my accusers be clothed with dishonor;
may they be wrapped in their own shame as in a mantle.
30 With my mouth I will give great thanks to the LORD;
I will praise him in the midst of the throng.
31 For he stands at the right hand of the needy,
to save them from those who would condemn them to death.

Ps 109 The lament of one who has been falsely accused; the accusations are made specific in vv.6-19. The psalmist calls for the reversion of the charges to the accuser. In spite of his pathetic weakness (vv.22-25), he is ready to praise God for his rescue.

108.11 Ps 44.9
109.1 Ps 83.1
109.3 Ps 69.4
109.4 Ps 38.20; 69.13
109.5 Ps 35.12; 38.20
109.6 Zech 3.1
109.7 Prov 28.9
109.8 Acts 1.20
109.9 Ex 22.24
109.11 Job 5.5; 18.9
109.12 Isa 9.17
109.13 Ps 37.28; Prov 10.7
109.14 Ex 20.5; Neh 4.5; Jer 18.23
109.15 Ps 34.16
109.16 Ps 37.14,32
109.17 Prov 14.14; Ezek 35.6
109.18 Ps 73.6; Num 5.22
109.20 Ps 94.23; 2 Tim 4.14; Ps 71.10
109.21 Ps 79.9; 69.16
109.22 Ps 40.17; 143.4
109.23 Ps 102.11
109.24 Heb 12.12
109.25 Ps 22.6,7; Mt 27.39; Mk 15.29
109.27 Job 37.7
109.28 2 Sam 16.11,12; Isa 65.14
109.29 Ps 35.26; 132.18
109.30 Ps 35.18
109.31 Ps 16.8; 121.5

[k] Syr: Heb *I prayer* [l] Heb lacks *They say* [m] Gk: Heb *and seek* [n] Cn: Heb *fathers* [o] Gk: Heb *their* [p] Gk: Heb *They have risen up and have been put to shame*

Ps 110 The installation of the king (*my lord*) by God (*the LORD*) is celebrated. His people, including the *youth*, will support the king against his *foes*. But he also has a role as *priest*, on the model of *Melchizedek*, who, as king and priest of *God Most High* in [Jeru-] Salem (Gen 14.17-20), blessed Abraham on his return from victory in the Dead Sea valley. The king is promised victory over hostile kings, effective judgment on the nations, and divine sustenance in this role (vs.7).
Ps 111 Praise to *the LORD* for his fidelity to the covenant, and a reminder to his people to *practice* his law.
Ps 112 The well-being of those who obey the law, their generosity and compassion, their steadfastness and their freedom from fear of *evil tidings* are celebrated in this psalm, which ends with a note on the hostile reaction of *the wicked*.

Psalm 110

Assurance of Victory for God's Priest-King

Of David. A Psalm.

1 The LORD says to my lord,
"Sit at my right hand
until I make your enemies your footstool."

2 The LORD sends out from Zion
your mighty scepter.
Rule in the midst of your foes.
3 Your people will offer themselves willingly
on the day you lead your forces
on the holy mountains.[q]
From the womb of the morning,
like dew, your youth[r] will come to you.
4 The LORD has sworn and will not change his mind,
"You are a priest forever according to the order of Melchizedek."[s]

5 The Lord is at your right hand;
he will shatter kings on the day of his wrath.
6 He will execute judgment among the nations,
filling them with corpses;
he will shatter heads
over the wide earth.
7 He will drink from the stream by the path;
therefore he will lift up his head.

Psalm 111

Praise for God's Wonderful Works

1 Praise the LORD!
I will give thanks to the LORD with my whole heart,
in the company of the upright, in the congregation.
2 Great are the works of the LORD,
studied by all who delight in them.
3 Full of honor and majesty is his work,
and his righteousness endures forever.
4 He has gained renown by his wonderful deeds;
the LORD is gracious and merciful.
5 He provides food for those who fear him;
he is ever mindful of his covenant.
6 He has shown his people the power of his works,
in giving them the heritage of the nations.
7 The works of his hands are faithful and just;
all his precepts are trustworthy.
8 They are established forever and ever,
to be performed with faithfulness and uprightness.
9 He sent redemption to his people;
he has commanded his covenant forever.
Holy and awesome is his name.
10 The fear of the LORD is the beginning of wisdom;
all those who practice it[t] have a good understanding.
His praise endures forever.

Psalm 112

Blessings of the Righteous

1 Praise the LORD!
Happy are those who fear the LORD,
who greatly delight in his commandments.
2 Their descendants will be mighty in the land;
the generation of the upright will be blessed.
3 Wealth and riches are in their houses,
and their righteousness endures forever.
4 They rise in the darkness as a light for the upright;
they are gracious, merciful, and righteous.
5 It is well with those who deal generously and lend,
who conduct their affairs with justice.
6 For the righteous will never be moved;
they will be remembered forever.
7 They are not afraid of evil tidings;
their hearts are firm, secure in the LORD.
8 Their hearts are steady, they will not be afraid;
in the end they will look in triumph on their foes.
9 They have distributed freely, they have given to the poor;
their righteousness endures forever;
their horn is exalted in honor.
10 The wicked see it and are angry;
they gnash their teeth and melt away;
the desire of the wicked comes to nothing.

[q] Another reading is *in holy splendor* [r] Cn: Heb *the dew of your youth* [s] Or *forever, a rightful king by my edict* [t] Gk Syr: Heb *them*

110.1 Mt 22.44; Mk 12.36; Lk 20.42; Acts 2.34; 1 Cor 15.25
110.2 Ps 45.6; 2.9
110.3 Judg 5.2; Ps 96.9
110.4 Heb 5.6,10; 6.20; 7.11,15,21
110.5 Ps 16.8; 2.5,12; Rom 2.5; Rev 11.18
110.6 Isa 2.4; 66.24; Ps 68.21
110.7 Ps 27.6
111.1 Ps 138.1; 149.1
111.3 Ps 145.5
111.4 Ps 86.5; 103.8
111.5 Mt 6.26,33
111.7 Rev 15.3; Ps 19.7
111.8 Mt 5.18; Ps 19.9
111.9 Lk 1.68; Ps 99.3
111.10 Prov 9.10; 3.4; Ps 145.2
112.1 Ps 128.1; 119.16
112.2 Ps 25.13
112.4 Job 11.17; Ps 97.11
112.6 Prov 10.7
112.7 Prov 1.33; Ps 57.7
112.8 Ps 59.10; 118.7
112.9 2 Cor 9.9; Deut 24.13; Ps 75.10
112.10 Ps 86.17; 37.12; 58.7,8; Prov 10.28; 11.7

Psalm 113

God the Helper of the Needy

1 Praise the LORD!
Praise, O servants of the LORD;
praise the name of the LORD.

2 Blessed be the name of the LORD
from this time on and forevermore.
3 From the rising of the sun to its setting
the name of the LORD is to be praised.
4 The LORD is high above all nations,
and his glory above the heavens.

5 Who is like the LORD our God,
who is seated on high,
6 who looks far down
on the heavens and the earth?
7 He raises the poor from the dust,
and lifts the needy from the ash heap,
8 to make them sit with princes,
with the princes of his people.
9 He gives the barren woman a home,
making her the joyous mother of children.
Praise the LORD!

Psalm 114

God's Wonders at the Exodus

1 When Israel went out from Egypt,
the house of Jacob from a people of strange language,
2 Judah became God's[u] sanctuary,
Israel his dominion.

3 The sea looked and fled;
Jordan turned back.
4 The mountains skipped like rams,
the hills like lambs.

5 Why is it, O sea, that you flee?
O Jordan, that you turn back?
6 O mountains, that you skip like rams?
O hills, like lambs?

7 Tremble, O earth, at the presence of the LORD,
at the presence of the God of Jacob,
8 who turns the rock into a pool of water,
the flint into a spring of water.

Psalm 115

The Impotence of Idols and the Greatness of God

1 Not to us, O LORD, not to us, but to your name give glory,
for the sake of your steadfast love and your faithfulness.
2 Why should the nations say,
"Where is their God?"

3 Our God is in the heavens;
he does whatever he pleases.
4 Their idols are silver and gold,
the work of human hands.
5 They have mouths, but do not speak;
eyes, but do not see.
6 They have ears, but do not hear;
noses, but do not smell.
7 They have hands, but do not feel;
feet, but do not walk;
they make no sound in their throats.
8 Those who make them are like them;
so are all who trust in them.

9 O Israel, trust in the LORD!
He is their help and their shield.
10 O house of Aaron, trust in the LORD!
He is their help and their shield.
11 You who fear the LORD, trust in the LORD!
He is their help and their shield.

12 The LORD has been mindful of us; he will bless us;
he will bless the house of Israel;
he will bless the house of Aaron;
13 he will bless those who fear the LORD,
both small and great.

14 May the LORD give you increase,
both you and your children.
15 May you be blessed by the LORD,
who made heaven and earth.

16 The heavens are the LORD's heavens,
but the earth he has given to human beings.
17 The dead do not praise the LORD,
nor do any that go down into silence.
18 But we will bless the LORD
from this time on and forevermore.
Praise the LORD!

Psalm 116

Thanksgiving for Recovery from Illness

1 I love the LORD, because he has heard
my voice and my supplications.
2 Because he inclined his ear to me,
therefore I will call on him as long as I live.

113.1 Ps 135.1
113.2 Dan 2.20
113.3 Ps 50.1
113.4 Ps 97.9; 99.2; 8.1
113.5 Ps 89.6; 103.19
113.6 Ps 11.4; 138.6; Isa 57.15
113.9 1 Sam 2.5; Ps 68.6; Isa 54.1
114.1 Ex 13.3
114.2 Ex 19.6
114.3 Ex 14.21; Josh 3.13,16
114.4 Ps 29.6; Hab 3.6
114.7 Ps 96.9
114.8 Ex 17.6; Num 20.11; Ps 107.35; Deut 8.15
115.1 Isa 84.11; Ezek 36.32; Ps 96.8
115.2 Ps 42.3
115.3 Ps 103.19; 135.6; Dan 4.35
115.4 Deut 4.28; Ps 135.15-17; Jer 10.3ff
115.8 Ps 135.18
115.9 Ps 118.2-4; 33.20
115.11 Ps 135.20
115.14 Deut 1.11
115.15 Gen 14.19; 1.1; Ps 96.5
115.16 Ps 89.11; 8.6
115.17 Ps 6.5; 31.17
115.18 Ps 113.2
116.1 Ps 18.1; 66.19
116.2 Ps 40.1

Ps 113 A celebration of the incomparable power and compassion of the LORD, who *lifts the needy*.
Ps 114 A brief poetic rehearsal of Israel's exodus from Egypt and preservation in the desert. The response of Israel's enemies is described here in cosmic terms (*mountains skip*; rivers turn back), and recalls God's provision of water from the rock for his people on their journey from Egypt (Ex 17.1-6; Num 20.8).
Ps 115 God's *steadfast love* is celebrated, in contrast to the impotence of the idols (vv.3-8). A special call for trust in God is addressed not only to Israel as a whole, but also to the priestly tribe (*house of Aaron*). Continual praise is called for, in contrast to the silence among the dead.
Ps 116 The psalmist praises God for deliverance from suffering and anxiety in what seemed certain death, and he vows continuing signs of gratitude through sacrifices and obedience.

[u] Heb *his*

Ps 117 The briefest of the psalms is a call to *all nations* to join in celebrating God's love and fidelity. **Ps 118** This psalm celebrates the enthronement of Israel's king, beginning with an introductory affirmation of God's steadfast love by various groups, including Gentile converts *who fear the* LORD (vv.1-4), which is followed by the king's recital of the trials he has experienced and how God has delivered him in triumph through all these difficulties so that he is now ready to *enter* his royal duties (vv.5-21). The concluding section (vv.22-29) is the people's acclaim of the one who earlier had been *rejected* by the ruling monarch (which was David's experience at the hand of Saul; 1 Sam 19-31), but now is established as God's chosen ruler over his people. To *bind the festal procession* means that the worshippers whose branches actually touch the altar all share symbolically in the power and blessing of the God who is enthroned there.

3 The snares of death encompassed me;
the pangs of Sheol laid hold on me;
I suffered distress and anguish.
4 Then I called on the name of the LORD:
"O LORD, I pray, save my life!"

5 Gracious is the LORD, and righteous;
our God is merciful.
6 The LORD protects the simple;
when I was brought low, he saved me.
7 Return, O my soul, to your rest,
for the LORD has dealt bountifully with you.

8 For you have delivered my soul from death,
my eyes from tears,
my feet from stumbling.
9 I walk before the LORD
in the land of the living.
10 I kept my faith, even when I said,
"I am greatly afflicted";
11 I said in my consternation,
"Everyone is a liar."

12 What shall I return to the LORD
for all his bounty to me?
13 I will lift up the cup of salvation
and call on the name of the LORD,
14 I will pay my vows to the LORD
in the presence of all his people.
15 Precious in the sight of the LORD
is the death of his faithful ones.
16 O LORD, I am your servant;
I am your servant, the child of your serving girl.
You have loosed my bonds.
17 I will offer to you a thanksgiving sacrifice
and call on the name of the LORD.
18 I will pay my vows to the LORD
in the presence of all his people,
19 in the courts of the house of the LORD,
in your midst, O Jerusalem.
Praise the LORD!

Psalm 117

Universal Call to Worship

1 Praise the LORD, all you nations!
Extol him, all you peoples!
2 For great is his steadfast love toward us,
and the faithfulness of the LORD endures forever.
Praise the LORD!

Psalm 118

A Song of Victory

1 O give thanks to the LORD, for he is good;
his steadfast love endures forever!

2 Let Israel say,
"His steadfast love endures forever."
3 Let the house of Aaron say,
"His steadfast love endures forever."
4 Let those who fear the LORD say,
"His steadfast love endures forever."

5 Out of my distress I called on the LORD;
the LORD answered me and set me in a broad place.
6 With the LORD on my side I do not fear.
What can mortals do to me?
7 The LORD is on my side to help me;
I shall look in triumph on those who hate me.
8 It is better to take refuge in the LORD
than to put confidence in mortals.
9 It is better to take refuge in the LORD
than to put confidence in princes.

10 All nations surrounded me;
in the name of the LORD I cut them off!
11 They surrounded me, surrounded me on every side;
in the name of the LORD I cut them off!
12 They surrounded me like bees;
they blazed[v] like a fire of thorns;
in the name of the LORD I cut them off!
13 I was pushed hard,[w] so that I was falling,
but the LORD helped me.
14 The LORD is my strength and my might;
he has become my salvation.

15 There are glad songs of victory in the tents of the righteous:
"The right hand of the LORD does valiantly;
16 the right hand of the LORD is exalted;
the right hand of the LORD does valiantly."
17 I shall not die, but I shall live,
and recount the deeds of the LORD.
18 The LORD has punished me severely,
but he did not give me over to death.

19 Open to me the gates of righteousness,
that I may enter through them
and give thanks to the LORD.

[v] Gk: Heb *were extinguished* [w] Gk Syr Jerome: Heb *You pushed me hard*

116.3 Ps 18.4-6
116.5 Ps 103.8; Ezra 9.15; Neh 9.8; Ps 145.17; Ex 34.6
116.7 Jer 6.16; Mt 11.29; Ps 13.6
116.8 Ps 56.13
116.11 Ps 31.22; Rom 3.4
116.14 Ps 22.25; Jon 2.9
116.15 Ps 72.14
116.16 Ps 119.125; 143.12; 86.16
116.17 Ps 50.14; ver 13
116.19 Ps 96.8; 135.2
117.1 Ps 22.23; Rom 15.11
117.2 Ps 103.11
118.1 Ps 106.1; 136.1
118.2 Ps 115.9
118.5 Ps 120.1; 18.19
118.6 Ps 27.1; Heb 13.6; Ps 56.4,11
118.7 Ps 54.4; 59.10
118.8 Ps 40.4; Jer 17.5
118.9 Ps 146.3
118.10 Ps 3.6; 18.40
118.13 Ps 140.4; 86.17
118.14 Ex 15.2; Isa 12.2
118.15 Ps 68.3; 89.13
118.16 Ex 15.6
118.17 Hab 1.12; Ps 73.28
118.18 2 Cor 6.9
118.19 Isa 26.2

20 This is the gate of the LORD;
the righteous shall enter through it.

21 I thank you that you have answered me
and have become my salvation.
22 The stone that the builders rejected
has become the chief cornerstone.
23 This is the LORD's doing;
it is marvelous in our eyes.
24 This is the day that the LORD has made;
let us rejoice and be glad in it.[x]
25 Save us, we beseech you, O LORD!
O LORD, we beseech you, give us
success!

26 Blessed is the one who comes in the
name of the LORD.[y]
We bless you from the house of the
LORD.
27 The LORD is God,
and he has given us light.
Bind the festal procession with branches,
up to the horns of the altar.[z]

28 You are my God, and I will give thanks
to you;
you are my God, I will extol you.

29 O give thanks to the LORD, for he is good,
for his steadfast love endures forever.

Psalm 119

The Glories of God's Law

1 Happy are those whose way is
blameless,
who walk in the law of the LORD.
2 Happy are those who keep his decrees,
who seek him with their whole heart,
3 who also do no wrong,
but walk in his ways.
4 You have commanded your precepts
to be kept diligently.
5 O that my ways may be steadfast
in keeping your statutes!
6 Then I shall not be put to shame,
having my eyes fixed on all your
commandments.
7 I will praise you with an upright heart,
when I learn your righteous
ordinances.
8 I will observe your statutes;
do not utterly forsake me.

9 How can young people keep their way
pure?
By guarding it according to your
word.
10 With my whole heart I seek you;
do not let me stray from your
commandments.
11 I treasure your word in my heart,
so that I may not sin against you.
12 Blessed are you, O LORD;
teach me your statutes.
13 With my lips I declare
all the ordinances of your mouth.
14 I delight in the way of your decrees
as much as in all riches.
15 I will meditate on your precepts,
and fix my eyes on your ways.
16 I will delight in your statutes;
I will not forget your word.

17 Deal bountifully with your servant,
so that I may live and observe your
word.
18 Open my eyes, so that I may behold
wondrous things out of your law.
19 I live as an alien in the land;
do not hide your commandments
from me.
20 My soul is consumed with longing
for your ordinances at all times.
21 You rebuke the insolent, accursed ones,
who wander from your
commandments;
22 take away from me their scorn and
contempt,
for I have kept your decrees.
23 Even though princes sit plotting against
me,
your servant will meditate on your
statutes.
24 Your decrees are my delight,
they are my counselors.

25 My soul clings to the dust;
revive me according to your word.
26 When I told of my ways, you answered
me;
teach me your statutes.
27 Make me understand the way of your
precepts,
and I will meditate on your wondrous
works.
28 My soul melts away for sorrow;
strengthen me according to your
word.
29 Put false ways far from me;
and graciously teach me your law.
30 I have chosen the way of faithfulness;

[x] Or *in him* [y] Or *Blessed in the name of the LORD is the one who comes* [z] Meaning of Heb uncertain

Ps 119 The longest of the psalms is an acrostic in which each group of eight verses begins with the successive letters of the Hebrew alphabet. Nearly every verse mentions the law of God directly or by a synonym: law, precept, ways, word, commandments, decrees, statutes, precepts, promise, ordinances. The psalm praises God for having given it to his people, and records the sustaining, renewing, hopeful and admonitory roles that the law fulfills in their lives.

118.20 Ps 24.7; Isa 35.8; Rev 22.14
118.21 Ps 116.1; ver 14
118.22 Mt 21.42; Mk 12.10; Lk 20.17; Acts 4.11; Eph 2.20; 1 Pet 2.4,7
118.26 Mt 21.9; Mk 11.9; Lk 13.35; 19.38; Jn 12.13
118.27 1 Kings 18.39; Esth 8.16; 1 Pet 2.9
118.28 Ex 15.2; Isa 25.1
118.29 ver 1
119.1 Ps 101.2,6; 128.1
119.3 1 Jn 3.9; 5.18
119.6 ver 80
119.7 ver 62
119.9 2 Chr 6.16
119.10 2 Chr 15.15; ver 21,118
119.11 Ps 37.31; Lk 2.19,51
119.12 ver 26,64,68, 108,124, 135,171
119.13 Ps 40.9; ver 72
119.15 ver 23,48,78; Ps 1.2
119.16 Ps 1.2
119.17 Ps 13.6
119.19 Gen 47.9; 1 Chr 29.15; Ps 39.12; 2 Cor 5.6; Heb 11.13
119.20 Ps 42.1,2
119.21 ver 10,118
119.22 Ps 39.8
119.23 ver 15
119.24 ver 16
119.25 Ps 44.25; ver 37
119.26 ver 12
119.27 Ps 145.5
119.28 Ps 107.26; 20.2; 1 Pet 5.10

I set your ordinances before me.
31 I cling to your decrees, O LORD;
let me not be put to shame.
32 I run the way of your commandments,
for you enlarge my understanding.

33 Teach me, O LORD, the way of your
statutes,
and I will observe it to the end.
34 Give me understanding, that I may keep
your law
and observe it with my whole heart.
35 Lead me in the path of your
commandments,
for I delight in it.
36 Turn my heart to your decrees,
and not to selfish gain.
37 Turn my eyes from looking at vanities;
give me life in your ways.
38 Confirm to your servant your promise,
which is for those who fear you.
39 Turn away the disgrace that I dread,
for your ordinances are good.
40 See, I have longed for your precepts;
in your righteousness give me life.

41 Let your steadfast love come to me, O
LORD,
your salvation according to your
promise.
42 Then I shall have an answer for those
who taunt me,
for I trust in your word.
43 Do not take the word of truth utterly
out of my mouth,
for my hope is in your ordinances.
44 I will keep your law continually,
forever and ever.
45 I shall walk at liberty,
for I have sought your precepts.
46 I will also speak of your decrees before
kings,
and shall not be put to shame;
47 I find my delight in your
commandments,
because I love them.
48 I revere your commandments, which I
love,
and I will meditate on your statutes.

49 Remember your word to your servant,
in which you have made me hope.
50 This is my comfort in my distress,
that your promise gives me life.
51 The arrogant utterly deride me,
but I do not turn away from your
law.
52 When I think of your ordinances from of
old,
I take comfort, O LORD.
53 Hot indignation seizes me because of the
wicked,
those who forsake your law.
54 Your statutes have been my songs
wherever I make my home.
55 I remember your name in the night,
O LORD,
and keep your law.
56 This blessing has fallen to me,
for I have kept your precepts.

57 The LORD is my portion;
I promise to keep your words.
58 I implore your favor with all my heart;
be gracious to me according to your
promise.
59 When I think of your ways,
I turn my feet to your decrees;
60 I hurry and do not delay
to keep your commandments.
61 Though the cords of the wicked ensnare
me,
I do not forget your law.
62 At midnight I rise to praise you,
because of your righteous ordinances.
63 I am a companion of all who fear you,
of those who keep your precepts.
64 The earth, O LORD, is full of your
steadfast love;
teach me your statutes.

65 You have dealt well with your servant,
O LORD, according to your word.
66 Teach me good judgment and
knowledge,
for I believe in your commandments.
67 Before I was humbled I went astray,
but now I keep your word.
68 You are good and do good;
teach me your statutes.
69 The arrogant smear me with lies,
but with my whole heart I keep your
precepts.
70 Their hearts are fat and gross,
but I delight in your law.
71 It is good for me that I was humbled,
so that I might learn your statutes.
72 The law of your mouth is better to me
than thousands of gold and silver
pieces.

73 Your hands have made and fashioned me;
give me understanding that I may
learn your commandments.

119.31 Deut 11.22
119.32 1 Kings 4.29; Isa 60.5; 2 Cor 6.11
119.33 ver 5,12
119.34 ver 73; Prov 2.6; Jas 1.5
119.36 1 Kings 8.58; Lk 12.15
119.37 Isa 33.15; Ps 71.20
119.38 2 Sam 7.25
119.40 ver 20,25
119.41 ver 77,116
119.42 Prov 27.11
119.46 Mt 10.18; Acts 26.1,2
119.48 ver 15
119.50 Rom 15.4
119.51 Jer 20.7; Job 23.11; Ps 44.18
119.52 Ps 103.18
119.53 Ezra 9.3; Ps 89.30
119.55 Ps 63.6
119.57 Ps 16.5; Deut 33.9
119.58 1 Kings 13.6; ver 41
119.59 Lk 15.17,18
119.61 Ps 140.5; ver 83
119.62 Acts 16.25
119.63 Ps 101.6
119.64 Ps 33.5; ver 12
119.67 ver 71; Jer 31.18,19; Heb 12.11
119.68 Ps 106.1; Deut 8.16; ver 12
119.69 Job 13.4; ver 56
119.70 Ps 17.10; Isa 6.10; ver 16
119.72 ver 127; Ps 19.10; Prov 8.10,11,19
119.73 Job 10.8; Ps 138.8; ver 34

74 Those who fear you shall see me and rejoice,
because I have hoped in your word.
75 I know, O LORD, that your judgments are right,
and that in faithfulness you have humbled me.
76 Let your steadfast love become my comfort
according to your promise to your servant.
77 Let your mercy come to me, that I may live;
for your law is my delight.
78 Let the arrogant be put to shame,
because they have subverted me with guile;
as for me, I will meditate on your precepts.
79 Let those who fear you turn to me,
so that they may know your decrees.
80 May my heart be blameless in your statutes,
so that I may not be put to shame.

81 My soul languishes for your salvation;
I hope in your word.
82 My eyes fail with watching for your promise;
I ask, "When will you comfort me?"
83 For I have become like a wineskin in the smoke,
yet I have not forgotten your statutes.
84 How long must your servant endure?
When will you judge those who persecute me?
85 The arrogant have dug pitfalls for me;
they flout your law.
86 All your commandments are enduring;
I am persecuted without cause; help me!
87 They have almost made an end of me on earth;
but I have not forsaken your precepts.
88 In your steadfast love spare my life,
so that I may keep the decrees of your mouth.

89 The LORD exists forever;
your word is firmly fixed in heaven.
90 Your faithfulness endures to all generations;
you have established the earth, and it stands fast.
91 By your appointment they stand today,
for all things are your servants.
92 If your law had not been my delight,
I would have perished in my misery.
93 I will never forget your precepts,
for by them you have given me life.
94 I am yours; save me,
for I have sought your precepts.
95 The wicked lie in wait to destroy me,
but I consider your decrees.
96 I have seen a limit to all perfection,
but your commandment is exceedingly broad.

97 Oh, how I love your law!
It is my meditation all day long.
98 Your commandment makes me wiser than my enemies,
for it is always with me.
99 I have more understanding than all my teachers,
for your decrees are my meditation.
100 I understand more than the aged,
for I keep your precepts.
101 I hold back my feet from every evil way,
in order to keep your word.
102 I do not turn away from your ordinances,
for you have taught me.
103 How sweet are your words to my taste,
sweeter than honey to my mouth!
104 Through your precepts I get understanding;
therefore I hate every false way.

105 Your word is a lamp to my feet
and a light to my path.
106 I have sworn an oath and confirmed it,
to observe your righteous ordinances.
107 I am severely afflicted;
give me life, O LORD, according to your word.
108 Accept my offerings of praise, O LORD,
and teach me your ordinances.
109 I hold my life in my hand continually,
but I do not forget your law.
110 The wicked have laid a snare for me,
but I do not stray from your precepts.
111 Your decrees are my heritage forever;
they are the joy of my heart.
112 I incline my heart to perform your statutes
forever, to the end.

113 I hate the double-minded,
but I love your law.
114 You are my hiding place and my shield;

119.74 Ps 34.2; ver 43
119.75 Heb 12.10
119.78 Jer 50.32; ver 86,15
119.81 Ps 84.2
119.82 Ps 69.3
119.83 Job 30.30
119.84 Ps 39.4; Rev 6.10
119.85 Ps 35.7
119.86 ver 78; Ps 35.19; 109.26
119.89 Mt 24.34,35; 1 Pet 1.25
119.90 Ps 36.5; 148.6; Eccl 1.4
119.91 Jer 33.25
119.93 ver 16,25
119.97 Ps 1.2
119.100 Job 32.7-9
119.101 Prov 1.15
119.103 Ps 19.10
119.104 ver 128,130
119.105 Prov 6.23
119.106 Neh 10.29
119.107 ver 25
119.108 Hos 14.2; Heb 13.15; ver 12
119.109 Job 13.14; ver 16
119.110 Ps 140.5; 141.9; ver 10
119.111 Deut 33.4; ver 14,162
119.112 ver 33
119.113 Jas 1.8; ver 47
119.114 Ps 32.7; 91.1; ver 74

I hope in your word.
115 Go away from me, you evildoers,
that I may keep the commandments of my God.
116 Uphold me according to your promise, that I may live,
and let me not be put to shame in my hope.
117 Hold me up, that I may be safe
and have regard for your statutes continually.
118 You spurn all who go astray from your statutes;
for their cunning is in vain.
119 All the wicked of the earth you count as dross;
therefore I love your decrees.
120 My flesh trembles for fear of you,
and I am afraid of your judgments.

121 I have done what is just and right;
do not leave me to my oppressors.
122 Guarantee your servant's well-being;
do not let the godless oppress me.
123 My eyes fail from watching for your salvation,
and for the fulfillment of your righteous promise.
124 Deal with your servant according to your steadfast love,
and teach me your statutes.
125 I am your servant; give me understanding,
so that I may know your decrees.
126 It is time for the LORD to act,
for your law has been broken.
127 Truly I love your commandments
more than gold, more than fine gold.
128 Truly I direct my steps by all your precepts;[a]
I hate every false way.

129 Your decrees are wonderful;
therefore my soul keeps them.
130 The unfolding of your words gives light;
it imparts understanding to the simple.
131 With open mouth I pant,
because I long for your commandments.
132 Turn to me and be gracious to me,
as is your custom toward those who love your name.
133 Keep my steps steady according to your promise,
and never let iniquity have dominion over me.
134 Redeem me from human oppression,
that I may keep your precepts.
135 Make your face shine upon your servant,
and teach me your statutes.
136 My eyes shed streams of tears
because your law is not kept.

137 You are righteous, O LORD,
and your judgments are right.
138 You have appointed your decrees in righteousness
and in all faithfulness.
139 My zeal consumes me
because my foes forget your words.
140 Your promise is well tried,
and your servant loves it.
141 I am small and despised,
yet I do not forget your precepts.
142 Your righteousness is an everlasting righteousness,
and your law is the truth.
143 Trouble and anguish have come upon me,
but your commandments are my delight.
144 Your decrees are righteous forever;
give me understanding that I may live.

145 With my whole heart I cry; answer me, O LORD.
I will keep your statutes.
146 I cry to you; save me,
that I may observe your decrees.
147 I rise before dawn and cry for help;
I put my hope in your words.
148 My eyes are awake before each watch of the night,
that I may meditate on your promise.
149 In your steadfast love hear my voice;
O LORD, in your justice preserve my life.
150 Those who persecute me with evil purpose draw near;
they are far from your law.
151 Yet you are near, O LORD,
and all your commandments are true.
152 Long ago I learned from your decrees
that you have established them forever.

153 Look on my misery and rescue me,
for I do not forget your law.

[a] Gk Jerome: Meaning of Heb uncertain

119.115 Ps 6.8; 139.19; Mt 7.23
119.116 Ps 54.4; 25.2; Rom 5.5; 9.33
119.118 ver 21
119.119 Ezek 22.18
119.120 Hab 3.16
119.122 Job 17.3
119.123 ver 81,82
119.124 ver 12
119.125 Ps 116.16
119.127 Ps 19.10
119.128 ver 104
119.129 ver 18,22
119.130 Prov 6.23; Ps 19.7
119.131 Ps 42.1; ver 20
119.132 Ps 25.16
119.133 Ps 17.15; 19.13
119.134 Ps 142.6
119.135 Ps 4.6; ver 12
119.136 Jer 9.1; Ezek 9.4
119.137 Ezra 9.15; Neh 9.13; Jer 12.1
119.138 Ps 19.7-9
119.139 Ps 69.9
119.140 Ps 12.6
119.142 Ps 19.9; ver 151,160
119.143 ver 24,77
119.144 Ps 19.9; ver 34,73
119.145 ver 10,22,55
119.148 Ps 5.3
119.149 ver 40,154
119.151 Ps 145.18; ver 142
119.152 Lk 21.33
119.153 ver 50; Prov 3.1

119.154 1 Sam 24.15; ver 134
119.155 Job 5.4
119.156 2 Sam 24.14
119.157 Ps 7.1; ver 51
119.158 Ps 139.21
119.159 ver 47,88
119.160 Ps 139.17; ver 142
119.161 1 Sam 24.11
119.162 1 Sam 30.16
119.164 ver 7,160
119.165 Prov 3.2; Isa 26.3; 32.17
119.166 ver 174; Gen 49.18
119.168 ver 22; Prov 5.21
119.169 Ps 18.6; ver 27,65
119.170 Ps 28.2; 31.2
119.171 Ps 51.15; 94.12
119.173 Ps 37.24
119.174 ver 166,24
119.175 Isa 55.3
119.176 Isa 53.6; ver 16

120.1 Ps 102.2; Jon 2.2
120.4 Ps 45.5; 140.10
120.5 Gen 10.2; Ezek 27.13; Gen 25.13; Jer 49.28
121.2 Ps 124.8; 115.15
121.3 Ps 66.9; 127.1
121.5 Isa 25.4; Ps 16.8
121.6 Ps 91.5; Isa 49.10; Rev 7.16
121.7 Ps 91.10-12
121.8 Deut 28.6

122.1 Isa 2.3; Zech 8.21

154 Plead my cause and redeem me;
give me life according to your promise.
155 Salvation is far from the wicked,
for they do not seek your statutes.
156 Great is your mercy, O LORD;
give me life according to your justice.
157 Many are my persecutors and my adversaries,
yet I do not swerve from your decrees.
158 I look at the faithless with disgust,
because they do not keep your commands.
159 Consider how I love your precepts;
preserve my life according to your steadfast love.
160 The sum of your word is truth;
and every one of your righteous ordinances endures forever.

161 Princes persecute me without cause,
but my heart stands in awe of your words.
162 I rejoice at your word
like one who finds great spoil.
163 I hate and abhor falsehood,
but I love your law.
164 Seven times a day I praise you
for your righteous ordinances.
165 Great peace have those who love your law;
nothing can make them stumble.
166 I hope for your salvation, O LORD,
and I fulfill your commandments.
167 My soul keeps your decrees;
I love them exceedingly.
168 I keep your precepts and decrees,
for all my ways are before you.

169 Let my cry come before you, O LORD;
give me understanding according to your word.
170 Let my supplication come before you;
deliver me according to your promise.
171 My lips will pour forth praise,
because you teach me your statutes.
172 My tongue will sing of your promise,
for all your commandments are right.
173 Let your hand be ready to help me,
for I have chosen your precepts.
174 I long for your salvation, O LORD,
and your law is my delight.
175 Let me live that I may praise you,
and let your ordinances help me.
176 I have gone astray like a lost sheep; seek out your servant,
for I do not forget your commandments.

Psalm 120

Prayer for Deliverance from Slanderers

A Song of Ascents.

1 In my distress I cry to the LORD,
that he may answer me:
2 "Deliver me, O LORD,
from lying lips,
from a deceitful tongue."

3 What shall be given to you?
And what more shall be done to you,
you deceitful tongue?
4 A warrior's sharp arrows,
with glowing coals of the broom tree!

5 Woe is me, that I am an alien in Meshech,
that I must live among the tents of Kedar.
6 Too long have I had my dwelling
among those who hate peace.
7 I am for peace;
but when I speak,
they are for war.

Psalm 121

Assurance of God's Protection

A Song of Ascents.

1 I lift up my eyes to the hills—
from where will my help come?
2 My help comes from the LORD,
who made heaven and earth.

3 He will not let your foot be moved;
he who keeps you will not slumber.
4 He who keeps Israel
will neither slumber nor sleep.

5 The LORD is your keeper;
the LORD is your shade at your right hand.
6 The sun shall not strike you by day,
nor the moon by night.

7 The LORD will keep you from all evil;
he will keep your life.
8 The LORD will keep
your going out and your coming in
from this time on and forevermore.

Psalm 122

Song of Praise and Prayer for Jerusalem

A Song of Ascents. Of David.

1 I was glad when they said to me,
"Let us go to the house of the LORD!"

Ps 120 An appeal to the LORD for deliverance from the *deceitful tongue* of his *alien* neighbors (*Meshech* in Asia Minor and *Kedar* in Arabia). Their punishment from God will be *sharp arrows* and *glowing coals* (*cf.* Ps 7.12-13; 64.2-3).
Ps 121 The psalmist looks *to the hills,* that is to the holy mountain of God in Jerusalem where God dwells, for help, for constant protection, and for preservation of life and activity.
Ps 122 A song of pilgrims entering Jerusalem, who rejoice in the tradition of leadership for God's people (*thrones for judgment* and of the monarchy), and in the peace and prosperity which it embodies.

Ps 123 A petition for God's deliverance of his people from their plight, which has evoked *scorn* from their non-Israelite contemporaries.
Ps 124 An utterance of deep gratitude for God's preservation of Israel from the jaws of defeat by her enemies.
Ps 125 The solidity of *Mount Zion* is the symbol for the certitude that God's people have of his continuing care and protection of his faithful, obedient people. A final warning is given to those *who turn aside*.
Ps 126 Rejoicing at God's restoration of his people in the land, which is compared with the dry creek-beds of Israel's southern arid section (*Negeb*) which rush with water following the seasonal rains.

2 Our feet are standing
within your gates, O Jerusalem.

3 Jerusalem—built as a city
that is bound firmly together.
4 To it the tribes go up,
the tribes of the LORD,
as was decreed for Israel,
to give thanks to the name of the LORD.
5 For there the thrones for judgment were set up,
the thrones of the house of David.

6 Pray for the peace of Jerusalem:
"May they prosper who love you.
7 Peace be within your walls,
and security within your towers."
8 For the sake of my relatives and friends
I will say, "Peace be within you."
9 For the sake of the house of the LORD our God,
I will seek your good.

Psalm 123

Supplication for Mercy

A Song of Ascents.

1 To you I lift up my eyes,
O you who are enthroned in the heavens!
2 As the eyes of servants
look to the hand of their master,
as the eyes of a maid
to the hand of her mistress,
so our eyes look to the LORD our God,
until he has mercy upon us.

3 Have mercy upon us, O LORD, have mercy upon us,
for we have had more than enough of contempt.
4 Our soul has had more than its fill
of the scorn of those who are at ease,
of the contempt of the proud.

Psalm 124

Thanksgiving for Israel's Deliverance

A Song of Ascents. Of David.

1 If it had not been the LORD who was on our side
—let Israel now say—
2 if it had not been the LORD who was on our side,
when our enemies attacked us,
3 then they would have swallowed us up alive,
when their anger was kindled against us;
4 then the flood would have swept us away,
the torrent would have gone over us;
5 then over us would have gone
the raging waters.

6 Blessed be the LORD,
who has not given us
as prey to their teeth.
7 We have escaped like a bird
from the snare of the fowlers;
the snare is broken,
and we have escaped.

8 Our help is in the name of the LORD,
who made heaven and earth.

Psalm 125

The Security of God's People

A Song of Ascents.

1 Those who trust in the LORD are like Mount Zion,
which cannot be moved, but abides forever.
2 As the mountains surround Jerusalem,
so the LORD surrounds his people,
from this time on and forevermore.
3 For the scepter of wickedness shall not rest
on the land allotted to the righteous,
so that the righteous might not stretch out
their hands to do wrong.
4 Do good, O LORD, to those who are good,
and to those who are upright in their hearts.
5 But those who turn aside to their own crooked ways
the LORD will lead away with evildoers.
Peace be upon Israel!

Psalm 126

A Harvest of Joy

A Song of Ascents.

1 When the LORD restored the fortunes of Zion,[b]
we were like those who dream.
2 Then our mouth was filled with laughter,

[b] Or *brought back those who returned to Zion*

122.3 Ps 48.13
122.4 Deut 16.16; Ex 16.34
122.5 Deut 17.8; 2 Chr 19.8
122.6 Ps 51.18
122.9 Neh 2.10
123.1 Ps 121.1; 141.8; 2.4; 11.4
123.2 Prov 27.18; Ps 25.15
123.3 Ps 4.1; 51.1
123.4 Ps 79.4
124.1 Ps 94.17; 129.1
124.3 Ps 56.1; 57.3; Prov 1.12
124.5 Ps 69.2
124.6 Ps 27.2
124.7 Prov 6.5; Ps 91.3
124.8 Ps 121.2; Gen 1.1
125.1 Ps 46.5
125.2 Zech 2.5; Ps 121.8
125.3 Prov 22.8; Isa 14.5; Ps 55.20
125.4 Ps 119.68; 7.10; 94.15
125.5 Prov 2.15; Ps 128.6
126.1 Ps 85.1; Acts 12.9
126.2 Job 8.21; Ps 51.14; 71.19

and our tongue with shouts of joy;
then it was said among the nations,
"The LORD has done great things for them."
3 The LORD has done great things for us,
and we rejoiced.

4 Restore our fortunes, O LORD,
like the watercourses in the Negeb.
5 May those who sow in tears
reap with shouts of joy.
6 Those who go out weeping,
bearing the seed for sowing,
shall come home with shouts of joy,
carrying their sheaves.

Psalm 127

God's Blessings in the Home

A Song of Ascents. Of Solomon.

1 Unless the LORD builds the house,
those who build it labor in vain.
Unless the LORD guards the city,
the guard keeps watch in vain.
2 It is in vain that you rise up early
and go late to rest,
eating the bread of anxious toil;
for he gives sleep to his beloved.[c]

3 Sons are indeed a heritage from the LORD,
the fruit of the womb a reward.
4 Like arrows in the hand of a warrior
are the sons of one's youth.
5 Happy is the man who has
his quiver full of them.
He shall not be put to shame
when he speaks with his enemies in the gate.

Psalm 128

The Happy Home of the Faithful

A Song of Ascents.

1 Happy is everyone who fears the LORD,
who walks in his ways.
2 You shall eat the fruit of the labor of your hands;
you shall be happy, and it shall go well with you.

3 Your wife will be like a fruitful vine
within your house;
your children will be like olive shoots
around your table.
4 Thus shall the man be blessed
who fears the LORD.

5 The LORD bless you from Zion.
May you see the prosperity of Jerusalem
all the days of your life.
6 May you see your children's children.
Peace be upon Israel!

Psalm 129

Prayer for the Downfall of Israel's Enemies

A Song of Ascents.

1 "Often have they attacked me from my youth"
—let Israel now say—
2 "often have they attacked me from my youth,
yet they have not prevailed against me.
3 The plowers plowed on my back;
they made their furrows long."
4 The LORD is righteous;
he has cut the cords of the wicked.
5 May all who hate Zion
be put to shame and turned backward.
6 Let them be like the grass on the housetops
that withers before it grows up,
7 with which reapers do not fill their hands
or binders of sheaves their arms,
8 while those who pass by do not say,
"The blessing of the LORD be upon you!
We bless you in the name of the LORD!"

Psalm 130

Waiting for Divine Redemption

A Song of Ascents.

1 Out of the depths I cry to you, O LORD.
2 Lord, hear my voice!
Let your ears be attentive
to the voice of my supplications!

3 If you, O LORD, should mark iniquities,
Lord, who could stand?
4 But there is forgiveness with you,
so that you may be revered.

5 I wait for the LORD, my soul waits,
and in his word I hope;
6 my soul waits for the Lord
more than those who watch for the morning,
more than those who watch for the morning.

[c] Or *for he provides for his beloved during sleep*

Ps 127 An appeal for freedom from anxiety, which is based on confidence in the God who built their chief *city*, and who has continued to provide them with *sons* to assure the continuity of their historic life.
Ps 128 Joy will fill the lives of those who *walk in [God's] ways*, since they will have the reward of their labors and abundance of offspring in the context of an enduring Jerusalem.
Ps 129 Israel's opponents have not *prevailed* over them, nor have their attacks (they *plowed on my back)* killed them. These enemies will be discarded like worthless grass, and will not hear the reassuring prayer of passers-by for God's blessing.
Ps 130 The psalmist's *cry* is from *the depths* of guilt, seeking *forgiveness* for the iniquities that have been committed. He has *hope* that God's *steadfast love* will free *(redeem)* him from this weight of sin.

126.3 Isa 25.9
126.4 Isa 35.6; 43.19
126.5 Jer 31.16; Isa 35.10
127.1 Ps 78.69; 121.4
127.2 Gen 3.17; Job 11.18,19
127.3 Gen 33.5; Josh 24.3,4; Deut 28.4
127.5 Job 5.4; Prov 27.11
128.1 Ps 112.1; 119.3
128.2 Isa 3.10; Ezek 23.29; Eccl 8.12
128.3 Ezek 19.10; Ps 52.8; 144.12
128.5 Ps 134.3; 20.2; 122.9
128.6 Gen 50.23; Job 42.16; Ps 125.5
129.1 Ps 88.15; Hos 2.15; Ps 124.1
129.2 Mt 16.18
129.4 Ps 119.137
129.5 Mic 4.11; Ps 71.13
129.6 Ps 37.2
129.8 Ps 118.26
130.1 Ps 42.7; 69.2
130.2 Ps 64.1; 2 Chr 6.40; Ps 28.2
130.3 Ps 76.7
130.4 Ex 34.7; 1 Kings 8.40; Jer 33.8
130.5 Ps 33.20; Isa 8.17; Ps 119.81
130.6 Ps 63.6; 119.147

Ps 131 Like a contented child satisfied by its nursing mother, so the psalmist is assured that God will continually supply his basic needs.
Ps 132 A song for the annual celebration of the dedication of the temple, which recalls David's diligence in finding the proper place for God's sanctuary (vv.1-7) when the ark was being moved about: *Ephrathah* (Bethlehem) *and Jaar* (Kirjath-jearim), where it rested for a time (1 Sam 7.1-2; 2 Sam 6.1-5). Then God chose to dwell in his holy house in Jerusalem and to reward David by providing *priests* to lead the worship and an ongoing line of descendants (*a horn*) to rule on the throne of David. Vv.8-10 are quoted at the dedication of the temple in 2 Chr 6.41-42.
Ps 133 Kindred living together in unity assumes the extended family where descendants of one father reside in one place, as the law of levirate marriage assumes (Deut 25.5). The happiness of this social system is compared with *precious oil* and with *dew* that originates on *Hermon* in the north and falls on *Zion* in the south.
Ps 134 This brief psalm invokes God's blessing either on pilgrims who spent the night in the temple courts or on the levitical servants who were on duty *day and night* (1 Chr 23).

7 O Israel, hope in the LORD!
For with the LORD there is steadfast love,
and with him is great power to redeem.
8 It is he who will redeem Israel
from all its iniquities.

Psalm 131

Song of Quiet Trust

A Song of Ascents. Of David.

1 O LORD, my heart is not lifted up,
my eyes are not raised too high;
I do not occupy myself with things
too great and too marvelous for me.
2 But I have calmed and quieted my soul,
like a weaned child with its mother;
my soul is like the weaned child that is with me.[d]

3 O Israel, hope in the LORD
from this time on and forevermore.

Psalm 132

The Eternal Dwelling of God in Zion

A Song of Ascents.

1 O LORD, remember in David's favor
all the hardships he endured;
2 how he swore to the LORD
and vowed to the Mighty One of Jacob,
3 "I will not enter my house
or get into my bed;
4 I will not give sleep to my eyes
or slumber to my eyelids,
5 until I find a place for the LORD,
a dwelling place for the Mighty One of Jacob."

6 We heard of it in Ephrathah;
we found it in the fields of Jaar.
7 "Let us go to his dwelling place;
let us worship at his footstool."

8 Rise up, O LORD, and go to your resting place,
you and the ark of your might.
9 Let your priests be clothed with righteousness,
and let your faithful shout for joy.
10 For your servant David's sake
do not turn away the face of your anointed one.

11 The LORD swore to David a sure oath
from which he will not turn back:
"One of the sons of your body
I will set on your throne.
12 If your sons keep my covenant
and my decrees that I shall teach them,
their sons also, forevermore,
shall sit on your throne."

13 For the LORD has chosen Zion;
he has desired it for his habitation:
14 "This is my resting place forever;
here I will reside, for I have desired it.
15 I will abundantly bless its provisions;
I will satisfy its poor with bread.
16 Its priests I will clothe with salvation,
and its faithful will shout for joy.
17 There I will cause a horn to sprout up for David;
I have prepared a lamp for my anointed one.
18 His enemies I will clothe with disgrace,
but on him, his crown will gleam."

Psalm 133

The Blessedness of Unity

A Song of Ascents.

1 How very good and pleasant it is
when kindred live together in unity!
2 It is like the precious oil on the head,
running down upon the beard,
on the beard of Aaron,
running down over the collar of his robes.
3 It is like the dew of Hermon,
which falls on the mountains of Zion.
For there the LORD ordained his blessing,
life forevermore.

Psalm 134

Praise in the Night

A Song of Ascents.

1 Come, bless the LORD, all you servants of the LORD,
who stand by night in the house of the LORD!
2 Lift up your hands to the holy place,
and bless the LORD.

3 May the LORD, maker of heaven and earth,
bless you from Zion.

[d] Or *my soul within me is like a weaned child*

130.7 Ps 131.3; Isa 55.7
130.8 Lk 1.68
131.1 Ps 101.5; Isa 5.15; Rom 12.16
131.2 Ps 62.1; Mt 18.3; 1 Cor 14.20
131.3 Ps 130.7
132.2 Gen 49.24
132.5 Acts 7.46
132.6 1 Sam 17.12; 7.1; 1 Chr 13.5
132.7 Ps 5.7; 99.5
132.8 Num 10.35; 2 Chr 6.41; Ps 78.61
132.9 Job 29.14; Isa 61.10
132.11 Ps 89.3,4; 2 Sam 7.12; 2 Chr 6.16
132.12 Lk 1.32; Acts 2.30
132.13 Ps 48.1,2; 68.16
132.15 Ps 147.14; 107.9
132.17 Ezek 29.21; Lk 1.69; 1 Kings 11.36; 15.4; 2 Chr 21.7
132.18 Ps 35.26; 109.29
133.1 Gen 13.8; Heb 13.1
133.2 Ex 30.25; 39.24
133.3 Deut 4.48; Lev 25.21; Ps 42.8
134.1 Ps 103.21; 1 Chr 9.33
134.2 Ps 28.2; 1 Tim 2.8

Psalm 135

Praise for God's Goodness and Might

1 Praise the LORD!
Praise the name of the LORD;
give praise, O servants of the LORD,
2 you that stand in the house of the LORD,
in the courts of the house of our God.
3 Praise the LORD, for the LORD is good;
sing to his name, for he is gracious.
4 For the LORD has chosen Jacob for himself,
Israel as his own possession.

5 For I know that the LORD is great;
our Lord is above all gods.
6 Whatever the LORD pleases he does,
in heaven and on earth,
in the seas and all deeps.
7 He it is who makes the clouds rise at the end of the earth;
he makes lightnings for the rain
and brings out the wind from his storehouses.

8 He it was who struck down the firstborn of Egypt,
both human beings and animals;
9 he sent signs and wonders
into your midst, O Egypt,
against Pharaoh and all his servants.
10 He struck down many nations
and killed mighty kings—
11 Sihon, king of the Amorites,
and Og, king of Bashan,
and all the kingdoms of Canaan—
12 and gave their land as a heritage,
a heritage to his people Israel.

13 Your name, O LORD, endures forever,
your renown, O LORD, throughout all ages.
14 For the LORD will vindicate his people,
and have compassion on his servants.

15 The idols of the nations are silver and gold,
the work of human hands.
16 They have mouths, but they do not speak;
they have eyes, but they do not see;
17 they have ears, but they do not hear,
and there is no breath in their mouths.
18 Those who make them
and all who trust them
shall become like them.

19 O house of Israel, bless the LORD!
O house of Aaron, bless the LORD!
20 O house of Levi, bless the LORD!
You that fear the LORD, bless the LORD!
21 Blessed be the LORD from Zion,
he who resides in Jerusalem.
Praise the LORD!

Psalm 136

God's Work in Creation and in History

1 O give thanks to the LORD, for he is good,
for his steadfast love endures forever.
2 O give thanks to the God of gods,
for his steadfast love endures forever.
3 O give thanks to the Lord of lords,
for his steadfast love endures forever;

4 who alone does great wonders,
for his steadfast love endures forever;
5 who by understanding made the heavens,
for his steadfast love endures forever;
6 who spread out the earth on the waters,
for his steadfast love endures forever;
7 who made the great lights,
for his steadfast love endures forever;
8 the sun to rule over the day,
for his steadfast love endures forever;
9 the moon and stars to rule over the night,
for his steadfast love endures forever;

10 who struck Egypt through their firstborn,
for his steadfast love endures forever;
11 and brought Israel out from among them,
for his steadfast love endures forever;
12 with a strong hand and an outstretched arm,
for his steadfast love endures forever;
13 who divided the Red Sea[e] in two,
for his steadfast love endures forever;
14 and made Israel pass through the midst of it,
for his steadfast love endures forever;
15 but overthrew Pharaoh and his army in the Red Sea,[e]
for his steadfast love endures forever;
16 who led his people through the wilderness,
for his steadfast love endures forever;
17 who struck down great kings,
for his steadfast love endures forever;

[e] Or *Sea of Reeds*

Ps 135 This summons to praise God in the temple courts recalls God's power in the creation of the world and in the events that made possible Israel's escape from Egypt and settlement in the land of *Canaan*. The worshippers include the people of Israel as a whole, as well as the priests and Levites who lead the worship (vv.19-21).
Ps 136 The same themes – of God's power in creation and in the deliverance and formation of his people in the land – are recited, with the recurrent refrain, *his steadfast love endures forever.* The incidents concerning *the Amorites* and *Og* are reported in Judg 6.10 and Num 21.33-35.

135.2 Lk 2.37; Ps 92.13
135.3 Ps 119.68; 147.1
135.4 Deut 7.6,7; 10.15; Ex 19.5; 1 Pet 2.9
135.5 Ps 48.1; 97.9
135.6 Ps 115.3
135.7 Jer 10.13; Job 28.25; Zech 10.1; Job 38.22
135.8 Ex 12.12; Ps 78.51
135.9 Ps 78.43; 136.15
135.10 Num 21.24; Ps 136.17
135.11 Num 21.21-26,33-35; Josh 12.7
135.12 Ps 78.55
135.13 Ex 3.15; Ps 102.12
135.14 Deut 32.36; Ps 106.45
135.15 Ps 115.4-8
135.19 Ps 115.9
135.20 Ps 118.4
135.21 Ps 134.3; 132.14
136.1 Ps 106.1; 107.1; 118.1; 1 Chr 16.34; 2 Chr 20.21
136.2 Deut 10.17
136.4 Ps 72.18
136.5 Gen 1.1; Prov 3.19; Jer 51.15
136.6 Gen 1.9; Ps 24.2; Jer 10.12
136.7 Gen 1.14,16
136.8 Gen 1.16
136.10 Ex 12.29; Ps 135.8
136.11 Ex 12.51
136.12 Ex 6.6; Ps 44.3; Deut 4.34
136.13 Ex 14.21; Ps 78.13

Ps 137 A lament of the exiles of Israel living in *Babylon,* with an invoking of destruction on that city comparable to what befell *the Edomites,* who had rejoiced in the destruction of the temple in Jerusalem (*cf.* Ob 1-16; Ezek 25.12-14).
Ps 138 A psalm of gratitude for God's abiding love and care for his faithful followers, for whom he fulfills his *purpose.*
Ps 139 God's complete knowledge of his people is here described: It includes inward thoughts (vv.1-6), is effective at any location in the universe (vv.7-12), precedes gestation and birth (vv.13-16), and cannot be measured (vv.17-18). The psalm ends with a call to God to punish the prideful wicked, and to examine the psalmist's inner thoughts.

18 and killed famous kings,
for his steadfast love endures forever;
19 Sihon, king of the Amorites,
for his steadfast love endures forever;
20 and Og, king of Bashan,
for his steadfast love endures forever;
21 and gave their land as a heritage,
for his steadfast love endures forever;
22 a heritage to his servant Israel,
for his steadfast love endures forever.

23 It is he who remembered us in our low estate,
for his steadfast love endures forever;
24 and rescued us from our foes,
for his steadfast love endures forever;
25 who gives food to all flesh,
for his steadfast love endures forever.

26 O give thanks to the God of heaven,
for his steadfast love endures forever.

Psalm 137

Lament over the Destruction of Jerusalem

1 By the rivers of Babylon—
there we sat down and there we wept
when we remembered Zion.
2 On the willows[f] there
we hung up our harps.
3 For there our captors
asked us for songs,
and our tormentors asked for mirth, saying,
"Sing us one of the songs of Zion!"

4 How could we sing the LORD's song
in a foreign land?
5 If I forget you, O Jerusalem,
let my right hand wither!
6 Let my tongue cling to the roof of my mouth,
if I do not remember you,
if I do not set Jerusalem
above my highest joy.

7 Remember, O LORD, against the Edomites
the day of Jerusalem's fall,
how they said, "Tear it down! Tear it down!
Down to its foundations!"
8 O daughter Babylon, you devastator![g]
Happy shall they be who pay you back
what you have done to us!
9 Happy shall they be who take your little ones
and dash them against the rock!

Psalm 138

Thanksgiving and Praise

Of David.

1 I give you thanks, O LORD, with my whole heart;
before the gods I sing your praise;
2 I bow down toward your holy temple
and give thanks to your name for your steadfast love and your faithfulness;
for you have exalted your name and your word
above everything.[h]
3 On the day I called, you answered me,
you increased my strength of soul.[i]

4 All the kings of the earth shall praise you, O LORD,
for they have heard the words of your mouth.
5 They shall sing of the ways of the LORD,
for great is the glory of the LORD.
6 For though the LORD is high, he regards the lowly;
but the haughty he perceives from far away.

7 Though I walk in the midst of trouble,
you preserve me against the wrath of my enemies;
you stretch out your hand,
and your right hand delivers me.
8 The LORD will fulfill his purpose for me;
your steadfast love, O LORD, endures forever.
Do not forsake the work of your hands.

Psalm 139

The Inescapable God

To the leader. Of David. A Psalm.

1 O LORD, you have searched me and known me.
2 You know when I sit down and when I rise up;
you discern my thoughts from far away.
3 You search out my path and my lying down,

[f] Or *poplars* [g] Or *you who are devastated* [h] Cn: Heb *you have exalted your word above all your name* [i] Syr Compare Gk Tg: Heb *you made me arrogant in my soul with strength*

136.14 Ex 14.22
136.15 Ex 14.27; Ps 135.9
136.16 Ex 13.18; 15.22; Deut 8.15
136.17 Ps 135.10-12
136.21 Josh 12.1
136.23 Ps 113.7
136.24 Ps 107.2
136.25 Ps 104.27; 145.15
137.1 Ezek 1.1,3; Neh 1.4
137.3 Ps 80.6
137.6 Ezek 3.26
137.7 Jer 49.7; Lam 4.22; Ezek 25.12; Ob 10-14
137.8 Isa 13.1,6; Jer 25.12; 50.15; Rev 18.6
137.9 2 Kings 8.12; Isa 13.16
138.1 Ps 111.1; 95.3; 96.4
138.2 Ps 28.2; 1 Kings 8.29,30; Isa 42.21
138.3 Ps 118.5; 28.7; 46.1
138.4 Ps 102.15
138.6 Ps 113.5,6; Isa 57.15; Prov 3.34; Jas 4.6
138.7 Ps 23.3,4; 71.20; Jer 51.25; Ps 20.6
138.8 Ps 57.2; Phil 1.6; Ps 136.1; 27.9; Job 10.3,8; 14.15
139.1 Ps 17.3; Jer 12.3
139.2 2 Kings 19.27; Mt 9.4; Jn 2.24
139.3 Job 31.4

139.4 Heb 4.13
139.5 Ps 34.7; Job 9.33
139.6 Rom 11.33; Job 42.3
139.7 Jer 23.24; Jon 1.3
139.8 Am 9.2-4; Job 26.6; Prov 15.11
139.10 Ps 23.2,3
139.11 Job 22.13
139.12 Job 34.22; Dan 2.22; Heb 4.13
139.13 Ps 119.73; Job 10.11
139.14 Ps 40.5
139.15 Job 10.8-10; Ps 63.9
139.17 Ps 40.5
139.19 Isa 11.4; Ps 119.115
139.20 Jude 15
139.21 Ps 119.158
139.23 Job 31.6; Ps 26.2; Jer 11.20
139.24 Prov 15.9; Ps 5.8; 143.10
140.1 Ps 17.13; 18.48
140.2 Ps 36.4; 56.6
140.3 Ps 57.4; 58.4; Jas 3.8
140.4 Ps 71.4
140.5 Ps 35.7; 31.4; 141.9
140.6 Ps 16.2; 143.1; 116.1
140.7 Ps 28.8; 144.10
140.8 Ps 112.10; 10.2
140.9 Ps 7.16
140.10 Ps 11.6; 21.9; 36.12

and are acquainted with all my ways.
4 Even before a word is on my tongue,
O LORD, you know it completely.
5 You hem me in, behind and before,
and lay your hand upon me.
6 Such knowledge is too wonderful for me;
it is so high that I cannot attain it.

7 Where can I go from your spirit?
Or where can I flee from your presence?
8 If I ascend to heaven, you are there;
if I make my bed in Sheol, you are there.
9 If I take the wings of the morning
and settle at the farthest limits of the sea,
10 even there your hand shall lead me,
and your right hand shall hold me fast.
11 If I say, "Surely the darkness shall cover me,
and the light around me become night,"
12 even the darkness is not dark to you;
the night is as bright as the day,
for darkness is as light to you.

13 For it was you who formed my inward parts;
you knit me together in my mother's womb.
14 I praise you, for I am fearfully and wonderfully made.
Wonderful are your works;
that I know very well.
15 My frame was not hidden from you,
when I was being made in secret,
intricately woven in the depths of the earth.
16 Your eyes beheld my unformed substance.
In your book were written
all the days that were formed for me,
when none of them as yet existed.
17 How weighty to me are your thoughts, O God!
How vast is the sum of them!
18 I try to count them—they are more than the sand;
I come to the end[j]—I am still with you.

19 O that you would kill the wicked, O God,
and that the bloodthirsty would depart from me—
20 those who speak of you maliciously,
and lift themselves up against you for evil![k]
21 Do I not hate those who hate you, O LORD?
And do I not loathe those who rise up against you?
22 I hate them with perfect hatred;
I count them my enemies.
23 Search me, O God, and know my heart;
test me and know my thoughts.
24 See if there is any wicked[l] way in me,
and lead me in the way everlasting.[m]

Psalm 140

Prayer for Deliverance from Enemies

To the leader. A Psalm of David.

1 Deliver me, O LORD, from evildoers;
protect me from those who are violent,
2 who plan evil things in their minds
and stir up wars continually.
3 They make their tongue sharp as a snake's,
and under their lips is the venom of vipers. *Selah*

4 Guard me, O LORD, from the hands of the wicked;
protect me from the violent
who have planned my downfall.
5 The arrogant have hidden a trap for me,
and with cords they have spread a net,[n]
along the road they have set snares for me. *Selah*

6 I say to the LORD, "You are my God;
give ear, O LORD, to the voice of my supplications."
7 O LORD, my Lord, my strong deliverer,
you have covered my head in the day of battle.
8 Do not grant, O LORD, the desires of the wicked;
do not further their evil plot.[o] *Selah*

9 Those who surround me lift up their heads;[p]
let the mischief of their lips overwhelm them!
10 Let burning coals fall on them!
Let them be flung into pits, no more to rise!

Ps 140 A prayer for protection against *evildoers*, and invocation of God's punishment of them. A final note affirms God's special care for the *needy* and the upright.

[j] Or *I awake* [k] Cn: Meaning of Heb uncertain [l] Heb *hurtful* [m] Or *the ancient way*. Compare Jer 6.16 [n] Or *they have spread cords as a net* [o] Heb adds *they are exalted* [p] Cn Compare Gk: Heb *those who surround me are uplifted in head*; Heb divides verses 8 and 9 differently

Ps 141 A plea for God's help to guard the psalmist from evil thoughts or misdeeds, even if it requires harsh corrective treatment from other *righteous* people.
Ps 142 Feeling threatened and abandoned, the psalmist calls to God for help, support and deliverance from his *persecutors.*
Ps 143 A call for God to answer this one who is being overwhelmed by his *enemy*, and who is thirsty for God, who needs to be taught God's way and to be led by God's spirit, and to be preserved from his *adversaries.*

11 Do not let the slanderer be established in the land;
let evil speedily hunt down the violent!

12 I know that the LORD maintains the cause of the needy,
and executes justice for the poor.
13 Surely the righteous shall give thanks to your name;
the upright shall live in your presence.

Psalm 141

Prayer for Preservation from Evil

A Psalm of David.

1 I call upon you, O LORD; come quickly to me;
give ear to my voice when I call to you.
2 Let my prayer be counted as incense before you,
and the lifting up of my hands as an evening sacrifice.

3 Set a guard over my mouth, O LORD;
keep watch over the door of my lips.
4 Do not turn my heart to any evil,
to busy myself with wicked deeds
in company with those who work iniquity;
do not let me eat of their delicacies.

5 Let the righteous strike me;
let the faithful correct me.
Never let the oil of the wicked anoint my head,[q]
for my prayer is continually[r] against their wicked deeds.
6 When they are given over to those who shall condemn them,
then they shall learn that my words were pleasant.
7 Like a rock that one breaks apart and shatters on the land,
so shall their bones be strewn at the mouth of Sheol.[s]

8 But my eyes are turned toward you, O GOD, my Lord;
in you I seek refuge; do not leave me defenseless.
9 Keep me from the trap that they have laid for me,
and from the snares of evildoers.
10 Let the wicked fall into their own nets,
while I alone escape.

Psalm 142

Prayer for Deliverance from Persecutors

A Maskil of David. When he was in the cave. A Prayer.

1 With my voice I cry to the LORD;
with my voice I make supplication to the LORD.
2 I pour out my complaint before him;
I tell my trouble before him.
3 When my spirit is faint,
you know my way.

In the path where I walk
they have hidden a trap for me.
4 Look on my right hand and see—
there is no one who takes notice of me;
no refuge remains to me;
no one cares for me.

5 I cry to you, O LORD;
I say, "You are my refuge,
my portion in the land of the living."
6 Give heed to my cry,
for I am brought very low.

Save me from my persecutors,
for they are too strong for me.
7 Bring me out of prison,
so that I may give thanks to your name.
The righteous will surround me,
for you will deal bountifully with me.

Psalm 143

Prayer for Deliverance from Enemies

A Psalm of David.

1 Hear my prayer, O LORD;
give ear to my supplications in your faithfulness;
answer me in your righteousness.
2 Do not enter into judgment with your servant,
for no one living is righteous before you.

3 For the enemy has pursued me,
crushing my life to the ground,
making me sit in darkness like those long dead.

[q] Gk: Meaning of Heb uncertain [r] Cn: Heb *for continually and my prayer* [s] Meaning of Heb of verses 5–7 is uncertain

140.11 Ps 34.21
140.12 Ps 9.4; 35.10
140.13 Ps 97.12; 11.7
141.1 Ps 22.19; 70.5; 143.1
141.2 Rev 5.8; 8.3; Ps 134.2; Ex 29.39
141.4 Ps 119.36; Prov 23.6
141.5 Prov 9.8; Ps 23.5; 35.14
141.7 Ps 53.5
141.8 Ps 25.15; 2.12; 27.9
141.9 Ps 38.12; 140.5
141.10 Ps 35.8
142.1 Ps 77.1; 30.8
142.2 Isa 26.16
142.3 Ps 143.4; 140.5
142.4 Ps 31.11; Job 11.20; Jer 30.17
142.5 Ps 46.1; 16.5; 27.13
142.6 Ps 17.1; 79.8; 116.6
142.7 Ps 146.7; 13.6
143.1 Ps 140.6; 89.1,2; 71.2
143.2 Job 14.3; 4.17; Ps 130.3; Eccl 7.20; Rom 3.20

4 Therefore my spirit faints within me;
my heart within me is appalled.

5 I remember the days of old,
I think about all your deeds,
I meditate on the works of your hands.
6 I stretch out my hands to you;
my soul thirsts for you like a parched land. *Selah*

7 Answer me quickly, O LORD;
my spirit fails.
Do not hide your face from me,
or I shall be like those who go down to the Pit.
8 Let me hear of your steadfast love in the morning,
for in you I put my trust.
Teach me the way I should go,
for to you I lift up my soul.

9 Save me, O LORD, from my enemies;
I have fled to you for refuge.[t]
10 Teach me to do your will,
for you are my God.
Let your good spirit lead me
on a level path.

11 For your name's sake, O LORD, preserve my life.
In your righteousness bring me out of trouble.
12 In your steadfast love cut off my enemies,
and destroy all my adversaries,
for I am your servant.

Psalm 144

Prayer for National Deliverance and Security

Of David.

1 Blessed be the LORD, my rock,
who trains my hands for war, and my fingers for battle;
2 my rock[u] and my fortress,
my stronghold and my deliverer,
my shield, in whom I take refuge,
who subdues the peoples[v] under me.

3 O LORD, what are human beings that you regard them,
or mortals that you think of them?
4 They are like a breath;
their days are like a passing shadow.

5 Bow your heavens, O LORD, and come down;
touch the mountains so that they smoke.
6 Make the lightning flash and scatter them;
send out your arrows and rout them.
7 Stretch out your hand from on high;
set me free and rescue me from the mighty waters,
from the hand of aliens,
8 whose mouths speak lies,
and whose right hands are false.

9 I will sing a new song to you, O God;
upon a ten-stringed harp I will play to you,
10 the one who gives victory to kings,
who rescues his servant David.
11 Rescue me from the cruel sword,
and deliver me from the hand of aliens,
whose mouths speak lies,
and whose right hands are false.

12 May our sons in their youth
be like plants full grown,
our daughters like corner pillars,
cut for the building of a palace.
13 May our barns be filled,
with produce of every kind;
may our sheep increase by thousands,
by tens of thousands in our fields,
14 and may our cattle be heavy with young.
May there be no breach in the walls,[w] no exile,
and no cry of distress in our streets.

15 Happy are the people to whom such blessings fall;
happy are the people whose God is the LORD.

Psalm 145

The Greatness and the Goodness of God

Praise. Of David.

1 I will extol you, my God and King,
and bless your name forever and ever.
2 Every day I will bless you,
and praise your name forever and ever.
3 Great is the LORD, and greatly to be praised;
his greatness is unsearchable.

[t] One Heb Ms Gk: MT *to you I have hidden* [u] With 18.2 and 2 Sam 22.2: Heb *my steadfast love* [v] Heb Mss Syr Aquila Jerome: MT *my people* [w] Heb lacks *in the walls*

Ps 144 The celebration by the king of God's having strengthened him for his task, in spite of his basic human limitations (vv.1-4). An appeal for God's intervention in his behalf against those who attack him (vv.7-8) shifts to a song praising God for the victory that has been achieved (vv.9-10), and then to petitions for the prosperity and safety of land and people (vv.11-14) and a final expression of gratitude for the welfare of God's people (vs.15).
Ps 145 A hymn praising God for his power and goodness (vv.1-9), the splendor and eternity of his rule, or *kingdom* (vv.10-13), and his gracious way of meeting the needs of his people.

143.4 Ps 142.3; Lam 3.11
143.5 Ps 77.5; 77.12; 105.2
143.6 Ps 88.9; 63.1
143.7 Ps 69.17; 27.9; 28.1
143.8 Ps 90.14; 25.2; 27.11; 25.1
143.9 Ps 31.15
143.10 Ps 25.4,5; Neh 9.20; Ps 23.3
143.11 Ps 119.25; 31.1
143.12 Ps 54.5; 52.5; 116.16
144.1 Ps 18.2,34
144.2 Ps 91.2; 59.9; 84.9; 18.39
144.3 Ps 8.4; Heb 2.6
144.4 Ps 39.11; 102.11
144.5 Ps 18.9; Isa 64.1; Ps 104.32
144.6 Ps 18.13,14; 7.13
144.7 Ps 69.1,14; 18.44
144.8 Ps 12.2; Isa 44.20
144.9 Ps 33.2,3
144.10 Ps 18.50; 140.7
144.11 Ps 12.2; Isa 44.20
144.12 Ps 128.3
144.15 Ps 33.12
145.2 Ps 71.6
145.3 Ps 96.4; Job 5.9; Rom 11.33

Ps 146 A declaration of praise to God, who unlike earthly *princes* made *heaven and earth* and who cares for humans in basic need: the oppressed, the hungry, prisoners, the blind, orphans and widows. His reign will be *forever*.
Ps 147 A celebration of the omnipotence of the LORD, who cares for the needy, controls the world of nature, and safeguards his people. All this he has revealed only to *Israel*.

4 One generation shall laud your works to another,
and shall declare your mighty acts.
5 On the glorious splendor of your majesty,
and on your wondrous works, I will meditate.
6 The might of your awesome deeds shall be proclaimed,
and I will declare your greatness.
7 They shall celebrate the fame of your abundant goodness,
and shall sing aloud of your righteousness.

8 The LORD is gracious and merciful,
slow to anger and abounding in steadfast love.
9 The LORD is good to all,
and his compassion is over all that he has made.

10 All your works shall give thanks to you, O LORD,
and all your faithful shall bless you.
11 They shall speak of the glory of your kingdom,
and tell of your power,
12 to make known to all people your[x] mighty deeds,
and the glorious splendor of your[y] kingdom.
13 Your kingdom is an everlasting kingdom,
and your dominion endures throughout all generations.

The LORD is faithful in all his words,
and gracious in all his deeds.[z]
14 The LORD upholds all who are falling,
and raises up all who are bowed down.
15 The eyes of all look to you,
and you give them their food in due season.
16 You open your hand,
satisfying the desire of every living thing.
17 The LORD is just in all his ways,
and kind in all his doings.
18 The LORD is near to all who call on him,
to all who call on him in truth.
19 He fulfills the desire of all who fear him;
he also hears their cry, and saves them.
20 The LORD watches over all who love him,
but all the wicked he will destroy.

21 My mouth will speak the praise of the LORD,
and all flesh will bless his holy name forever and ever.

Psalm 146

Praise for God's Help

1 Praise the LORD!
Praise the LORD, O my soul!
2 I will praise the LORD as long as I live;
I will sing praises to my God all my life long.

3 Do not put your trust in princes,
in mortals, in whom there is no help.
4 When their breath departs, they return to the earth;
on that very day their plans perish.

5 Happy are those whose help is the God of Jacob,
whose hope is in the LORD their God,
6 who made heaven and earth,
the sea, and all that is in them;
who keeps faith forever;
7 who executes justice for the oppressed;
who gives food to the hungry.

The LORD sets the prisoners free;
8 the LORD opens the eyes of the blind.
The LORD lifts up those who are bowed down;
the LORD loves the righteous.
9 The LORD watches over the strangers;
he upholds the orphan and the widow,
but the way of the wicked he brings to ruin.

10 The LORD will reign forever,
your God, O Zion, for all generations.
Praise the LORD!

Psalm 147

Praise for God's Care for Jerusalem

1 Praise the LORD!
How good it is to sing praises to our God;
for he is gracious, and a song of praise is fitting.
2 The LORD builds up Jerusalem;
he gathers the outcasts of Israel.
3 He heals the brokenhearted,
and binds up their wounds.

[x] Gk Jerome Syr: Heb *his* [y] Heb *his* [z] These two lines supplied by Q Ms Gk Syr

145.4 Isa 38.19
145.5 ver 12; Ps 119.27
145.6 Ps 66.3; Deut 32.3
145.7 Isa 63.7; Ps 51.14
145.8 Ex 34.6; Ps 86.5,15
145.9 Ps 100.5; Nah 1.7
145.10 Ps 19.1; 68.26
145.13 Ps 146.10; 2 Pet 1.11
145.14 Ps 37.24; 146.8
145.15 Ps 104.27
145.16 Ps 124.28
145.18 Deut 4.7; Jn 4.24
145.19 Ps 37.4; Prov 15.29
145.20 Ps 31.23; 97.10; 9.5
146.1 Ps 103.1
146.2 Ps 104.33
146.3 Ps 118.8; Isa 2.22
146.4 Ps 104.29; Eccl 12.7; Ps 33.10
146.5 Ps 144.15; 71.5
146.6 Ps 115.15; Acts 14.15; Ps 117.2
146.7 Ps 103.6; 107.9; 68.6
146.8 Mt 9.30; Jn 9.7; Ps 145.14; 11.7
146.9 Ex 22.21; Deut 10.18; Ps 68.5; 147.6
146.10 Ex 15.18; Ps 10.16; Rev 11.15
147.1 Ps 135.3; 33.1
147.2 Ps 102.16; Deut 30.3
147.3 Isa 61.1; 30.26

4 He determines the number of the stars;
he gives to all of them their names.
5 Great is our Lord, and abundant in
power;
his understanding is beyond measure.
6 The LORD lifts up the downtrodden;
he casts the wicked to the ground.

7 Sing to the LORD with thanksgiving;
make melody to our God on the lyre.
8 He covers the heavens with clouds,
prepares rain for the earth,
makes grass grow on the hills.
9 He gives to the animals their food,
and to the young ravens when they
cry.
10 His delight is not in the strength of the
horse,
nor his pleasure in the speed of a
runner;[a]
11 but the LORD takes pleasure in those who
fear him,
in those who hope in his steadfast
love.

12 Praise the LORD, O Jerusalem!
Praise your God, O Zion!
13 For he strengthens the bars of your
gates;
he blesses your children within you.
14 He grants peace[b] within your borders;
he fills you with the finest of wheat.
15 He sends out his command to the earth;
his word runs swiftly.
16 He gives snow like wool;
he scatters frost like ashes.
17 He hurls down hail like crumbs—
who can stand before his cold?
18 He sends out his word, and melts them;
he makes his wind blow, and the
waters flow.
19 He declares his word to Jacob,
his statutes and ordinances to Israel.
20 He has not dealt thus with any other
nation;
they do not know his ordinances.
Praise the LORD!

Psalm 148

Praise for God's Universal Glory

1 Praise the LORD!
Praise the LORD from the heavens;
praise him in the heights!
2 Praise him, all his angels;
praise him, all his host!
3 Praise him, sun and moon;
praise him, all you shining stars!
4 Praise him, you highest heavens,
and you waters above the heavens!

5 Let them praise the name of the LORD,
for he commanded and they were
created.
6 He established them forever and ever;
he fixed their bounds, which cannot
be passed.[c]

7 Praise the LORD from the earth,
you sea monsters and all deeps,
8 fire and hail, snow and frost,
stormy wind fulfilling his command!

9 Mountains and all hills,
fruit trees and all cedars!
10 Wild animals and all cattle,
creeping things and flying birds!

11 Kings of the earth and all peoples,
princes and all rulers of the earth!
12 Young men and women alike,
old and young together!

13 Let them praise the name of the LORD,
for his name alone is exalted;
his glory is above earth and heaven.
14 He has raised up a horn for his people,
praise for all his faithful,
for the people of Israel who are close
to him.
Praise the LORD!

Psalm 149

Praise for God's Goodness to Israel

1 Praise the LORD!
Sing to the LORD a new song,
his praise in the assembly of the
faithful.
2 Let Israel be glad in its Maker;
let the children of Zion rejoice in their
King.
3 Let them praise his name with dancing,
making melody to him with
tambourine and lyre.
4 For the LORD takes pleasure in his
people;
he adorns the humble with victory.
5 Let the faithful exult in glory;
let them sing for joy on their couches.
6 Let the high praises of God be in their
throats

[a] Heb *legs of a person* [b] Or *prosperity* [c] Or *he set a law that cannot pass away*

147.4 Isa 40.26
147.5 Ps 48.1; Isa 40.28
147.8 Job 38.26; Ps 104.13
147.9 Ps 104.27; Job 38.41
147.10 Ps 33.16,17; 1 Sam 16.7
147.14 Isa 60.17; Ps 132.15
147.15 Job 37.12; Ps 104.4
147.16 Job 37.6; 38.29
147.18 Ps 33.9; 107.25
147.19 Deut 33.2; Mal 4.4
147.20 Deut 4.32
148.2 Ps 103.20,21
148.4 1 Kings 8.27; Gen 1.7
148.5 Gen 1.1; Ps 33.6,9
148.6 Jer 33.25; Job 38.33
148.7 Ps 74.13
148.8 Ps 147.15-18
148.9 Isa 44.23; 49.13; 55.12
148.13 Ps 8.1; Isa 12.4; Ps 113.4
148.14 Ps 75.10; Deut 10.21; Eph 2.17
149.1 Ps 33.3; 35.18
149.2 Ps 95.6; 47.6
149.3 Ps 150.4; 81.2
149.4 Ps 35.27; 132.16
149.5 Ps 132.16; Job 35.10
149.6 Ps 66.17; Heb 4.12; Rev 1.16

Ps 148 All creation is summoned to praise the God who made it and all its inhabitants, including earthly rulers and their subject people. The *horn* is God's special presence and effective purpose for and through his people (Ps 89.17; 132.17).
Ps 149 The community is called to join in the praise of God (vv.1-5a), but also to be ready to battle the nations, executing on them *vengeance* and *judgment* (vv.5b-9).

Ps 150 A summons to all of creation to honor God *in his sanctuary* for his deeds in the creation and in behalf of his people. Every creature is called to join this cosmic song of praise.

and two-edged swords in their hands,
7 to execute vengeance on the nations
and punishment on the peoples,
8 to bind their kings with fetters
and their nobles with chains of iron,
9 to execute on them the judgment decreed.
This is glory for all his faithful ones.
Praise the LORD!

Psalm 150

Praise for God's Surpassing Greatness

1 Praise the LORD!
Praise God in his sanctuary;
praise him in his mighty firmament![d]
2 Praise him for his mighty deeds;
praise him according to his surpassing greatness!

3 Praise him with trumpet sound;
praise him with lute and harp!
4 Praise him with tambourine and dance;
praise him with strings and pipe!
5 Praise him with clanging cymbals;
praise him with loud clashing cymbals!
6 Let everything that breathes praise the LORD!
Praise the LORD!

[d] Or *dome*

149.9 Ezek 28.26; Ps 148.14
150.1 Ps 102.19; 19.1
150.2 Ps 145.5,6; Deut 3.24
150.3 Ps 149.3
150.4 Ex 15.20; Isa 38.20
150.5 1 Chr 13.8; 15.16

See the Introductions, pp. 5, 48, and 52 above.

PROVERBS

1.1 Introduction. The attribution of the Proverbs to Solomon is understandable since in 1 Kings 4.29-34 and 10.1-8 he is depicted as a monarch with an international reputation for his superior wisdom. As noted in the Introduction, parts of Prov 25-29 may go back to the time of Solomon, although the book as a whole achieved its present form in the fourth century BCE.
1.2-19 Prologue. The use here of the poetic form (in which there is an ongoing pattern of pairs of matching or contrasting concepts in nearly every verse) shows that there has been a shift from the earlier simple statements of popular wisdom of the ancient Near East to a more elegant literary style. Here the wise are called to take part in a more formal learning process, through which they can master moral principles, increase in knowledge, and unpack the meaning of proverbs and *figures* of speech. What is strikingly different from other eastern wisdom literature, however, is the claim that basic to gaining wisdom is *fear of the LORD*, which means neither fright nor terror, but trust and full respect for God, who grants wisdom to those who look to him to gain it.
1.8-19 What Results from Ignoring Wisdom. To fail to seek wisdom leads to a life of murder and thievery. Those who seek the *blood* of others (1.11,18) receive the punishment announced in Gen 9.6, where Noah is told that the blood will be shed of those who shed the blood of others. To *swallow alive* others is not cannibalism, but a figure for causing others to disappear, just as they vanish from sight in the unseen abode of the dead, *Sheol* or *the Pit*. Those who drive out others will get the same fate in return.
1.20-33 Wisdom's Invitation. Contrasted sharply here are (1) the consequences of refusing wisdom, so as to have no resources when panic strikes, and the results of the rejection are reaped, and (2) the peace and comfort which come when there is *fear of the LORD* (*cf.* note on 1.7).

1 The proverbs of Solomon son of David, king of Israel:

Prologue

2 For learning about wisdom and instruction,
for understanding words of insight,
3 for gaining instruction in wise dealing,
righteousness, justice, and equity;
4 to teach shrewdness to the simple,
knowledge and prudence to the young—
5 Let the wise also hear and gain in learning,
and the discerning acquire skill,
6 to understand a proverb and a figure,
the words of the wise and their riddles.

7 The fear of the LORD is the beginning of knowledge;
fools despise wisdom and instruction.

Warnings against Evil Companions

8 Hear, my child, your father's instruction,
and do not reject your mother's teaching;
9 for they are a fair garland for your head,
and pendants for your neck.
10 My child, if sinners entice you,
do not consent.
11 If they say, "Come with us, let us lie in wait for blood;
let us wantonly ambush the innocent;
12 like Sheol let us swallow them alive
and whole, like those who go down to the Pit.
13 We shall find all kinds of costly things;
we shall fill our houses with booty.
14 Throw in your lot among us;
we will all have one purse"—
15 my child, do not walk in their way,
keep your foot from their paths;
16 for their feet run to evil,
and they hurry to shed blood.
17 For in vain is the net baited
while the bird is looking on;
18 yet they lie in wait—to kill themselves!
and set an ambush—for their own lives!
19 Such is the end[a] of all who are greedy for gain;
it takes away the life of its possessors.

The Call of Wisdom

20 Wisdom cries out in the street;
in the squares she raises her voice.
21 At the busiest corner she cries out;
at the entrance of the city gates she speaks:

[a] Gk: Heb *ways*

1.1 1 Kings 4.32; Eccl 12.9
1.3 Prov 19.20; 2.9
1.4 Prov 8.5,12; 2.10,11
1.5 Prov 9.9; 14.6
1.7 Job 28.28; Ps 111.10; Eccl 12.13
1.8 Prov 4.1; 6.20
1.9 Prov 4.9; Gen 41.42
1.10 Deut 13.8; Eph 5.11
1.11 Prov 12.6; ver 18
1.12 Ps 124.3; 28.1
1.15 Ps 1.1; 119.101
1.16 Isa 59.7
1.19 Prov 15.27
1.20 Prov 8.1

1.22 ver 4,32; Ps 1.1; ver 29
1.23 Joel 2.28
1.24 Isa 65.12; Zech 7.11; Rom 10.21
1.25 Ps 107.11; Lk 7.30; Prov 15.10
1.26 Ps 2.4; Prov 6.15; 10.24
1.28 Isa 1.15; Ezek 8.18; Mic 3.4; Zech 7.13
1.30 Ps 81.11
1.31 Job 4.8; Prov 14.14; Isa 3.11; Jer 6.19
1.32 Jer 2.19
1.33 Ps 25.12
2.1 Prov 4.10
2.4 Prov 3.14; Mt 13.44
2.5 Prov 1.7
2.6 1 Kings 3.9,12; Jas 1.5
2.7 Ps 84.11
2.8 1 Sam 2.9; Ps 66.9
2.9 Prov 8.20; 4.18
2.13 Jn 3.19
2.14 Prov 10.23; Jer 11.15
2.15 Ps 125.5
2.16 Prov 6.24; 23.27
2.18 Prov 7.27
2.21 Ps 37.29; 28.10
2.22 Ps 37.38; Deut 28.63
3.1 Prov 4.5; Ex 20.6; Deut 30.16
3.2 Prov 4.10; Ps 119.165

22 "How long, O simple ones, will you love
being simple?
How long will scoffers delight in their
scoffing
and fools hate knowledge?
23 Give heed to my reproof;
I will pour out my thoughts to you;
I will make my words known to you.
24 Because I have called and you refused,
have stretched out my hand and no
one heeded,
25 and because you have ignored all my
counsel
and would have none of my reproof,
26 I also will laugh at your calamity;
I will mock when panic strikes you,
27 when panic strikes you like a storm,
and your calamity comes like a
whirlwind,
when distress and anguish come
upon you.
28 Then they will call upon me, but I will
not answer;
they will seek me diligently, but will
not find me.
29 Because they hated knowledge
and did not choose the fear of the
LORD,
30 would have none of my counsel,
and despised all my reproof,
31 therefore they shall eat the fruit of their
way
and be sated with their own devices.
32 For waywardness kills the simple,
and the complacency of fools destroys
them;
33 but those who listen to me will be
secure
and will live at ease, without dread of
disaster."

The Value of Wisdom

2 My child, if you accept my words
and treasure up my
commandments within you,
2 making your ear attentive to wisdom
and inclining your heart to
understanding;
3 if you indeed cry out for insight,
and raise your voice for understanding;
4 if you seek it like silver,
and search for it as for hidden
treasures—
5 then you will understand the fear of the
LORD
and find the knowledge of God.
6 For the LORD gives wisdom;
from his mouth come knowledge and
understanding;
7 he stores up sound wisdom for the
upright;
he is a shield to those who walk
blamelessly,
8 guarding the paths of justice
and preserving the way of his faithful
ones.
9 Then you will understand righteousness
and justice
and equity, every good path;
10 for wisdom will come into your heart,
and knowledge will be pleasant to
your soul;
11 prudence will watch over you;
and understanding will guard you.
12 It will save you from the way of evil,
from those who speak perversely,
13 who forsake the paths of uprightness
to walk in the ways of darkness,
14 who rejoice in doing evil
and delight in the perverseness of evil;
15 those whose paths are crooked,
and who are devious in their ways.

16 You will be saved from the loose[b]
woman,
from the adulteress with her smooth
words,
17 who forsakes the partner of her youth
and forgets her sacred covenant;
18 for her way[c] leads down to death,
and her paths to the shades;
19 those who go to her never come back,
nor do they regain the paths of life.

20 Therefore walk in the way of the good,
and keep to the paths of the just.
21 For the upright will abide in the land,
and the innocent will remain in it;
22 but the wicked will be cut off from the
land,
and the treacherous will be rooted out
of it.

Admonition to Trust and Honor God

3 My child, do not forget my teaching,
but let your heart keep my
commandments;
2 for length of days and years of life
and abundant welfare they will give
you.

2.1-22 The Reward for Seeking Wisdom.
2.1-5 Repeated once again is the importance and value of seeking wisdom as a way of understanding in first-hand experience *the fear of the LORD.*
2.6-15 Here are enumerated the benefits of seeking wisdom: understanding, wisdom, knowledge, prudence, protection from evil.
2.16-19 The wisdom-seeker will be preserved from the enticements of extra-marital sexual intercourse, which violates the *sacred covenant* of marriage (Ex 20. 14; Lev 20).
2.20-22 Wisdom is not only a way of gaining insight and understanding, but it develops an enduring way of life in contrast to the punishment that befalls *the wicked.*
3.1-12 Wisdom in Parental Instruction.
3.1-4 Those who maintain Wisdom's basic standards will gain *good repute* from both God and other humans.

[b] Heb *strange* [c] Cn: Heb *house*

3 Do not let loyalty and faithfulness
forsake you;
bind them around your neck,
write them on the tablet of your
heart.
4 So you will find favor and good repute
in the sight of God and of people.

5 Trust in the LORD with all your heart,
and do not rely on your own insight.
6 In all your ways acknowledge him,
and he will make straight your paths.
7 Do not be wise in your own eyes;
fear the LORD, and turn away from evil.
8 It will be a healing for your flesh
and a refreshment for your body.

9 Honor the LORD with your substance
and with the first fruits of all your
produce;
10 then your barns will be filled with plenty,
and your vats will be bursting with
wine.

11 My child, do not despise the LORD's
discipline
or be weary of his reproof,
12 for the LORD reproves the one he loves,
as a father the son in whom he
delights.

The True Wealth

13 Happy are those who find wisdom,
and those who get understanding,
14 for her income is better than silver,
and her revenue better than gold.
15 She is more precious than jewels,
and nothing you desire can compare
with her.
16 Long life is in her right hand;
in her left hand are riches and honor.
17 Her ways are ways of pleasantness,
and all her paths are peace.
18 She is a tree of life to those who lay
hold of her;
those who hold her fast are called
happy.

God's Wisdom in Creation

19 The LORD by wisdom founded the earth;
by understanding he established the
heavens;
20 by his knowledge the deeps broke open,
and the clouds drop down the dew.

The True Security

21 My child, do not let these escape from
your sight:
keep sound wisdom and prudence,
22 and they will be life for your soul
and adornment for your neck.
23 Then you will walk on your way
securely
and your foot will not stumble.
24 If you sit down,[d] you will not be afraid;
when you lie down, your sleep will be
sweet.
25 Do not be afraid of sudden panic,
or of the storm that strikes the
wicked;
26 for the LORD will be your confidence
and will keep your foot from being
caught.

27 Do not withhold good from those to
whom it is due,[e]
when it is in your power to do it.
28 Do not say to your neighbor, "Go, and
come again,
tomorrow I will give it"—when you
have it with you.
29 Do not plan harm against your neighbor
who lives trustingly beside you.
30 Do not quarrel with anyone without
cause,
when no harm has been done to you.
31 Do not envy the violent
and do not choose any of their ways;
32 for the perverse are an abomination to
the LORD,
but the upright are in his confidence.
33 The LORD's curse is on the house of the
wicked,
but he blesses the abode of the
righteous.
34 Toward the scorners he is scornful,
but to the humble he shows favor.
35 The wise will inherit honor,
but stubborn fools, disgrace.

Parental Advice

4 Listen, children, to a father's
instruction,
and be attentive, that you may gain[f]
insight;
2 for I give you good precepts:
do not forsake my teaching.
3 When I was a son with my father,
tender, and my mother's favorite,
4 he taught me, and said to me,

[d] Gk: Heb *lie down* [e] Heb *from its owners* [f] Heb *know*

3.5-10 Human trust is to be in the LORD, rather than in human resources or wisdom. The result will be a clear direction for life, and renewal of the physical *body*. To share one's wealth in behalf of the LORD's work in the world is to assure one's own prosperity.
3.11-12 What might be perceived as the pains of *discipline* and *reproof* are to be seen as expressions of God's concern for the welfare and responsible behavior of his children.
3.13-18 The Benefits of Wisdom. The rewards of pursuing wisdom include length of life, peace and happiness.
3.19-20 Wisdom as the Agent of God in Creating the Universe. Using imagery that matches the creation story in Gen 1, where God is depicted as controlling the waters to bring order to the cosmos, to separate land from sea and heaven from earth, and to control precipitation for the growth of life on the earth, the instrument that God uses to achieve the creation is said to be *wisdom*. According to John 1.1-4, the role of wisdom in creation is echoed in the function of *the Word*.
3.21-35 Wisdom Brings Freedom from Anxiety.
To gain wisdom produces willingness to be generous to others who are in need, and enables one to live trustingly rather than in hostility or plotting harm for others. Those who live in such anti-human ways will receive from God punishment appropriate to their misdeeds.
4.1-27 Advice from a Parent.
4.1-13 To accept parental wisdom as it is transmitted through successive generations is to assure rewards for those who seek wisdom in this way.

3.3 2 Sam 15.20; Prov 1.9; 7.3
3.4 Prov 8.5; Ps 111.10
3.5 Ps 37.3,5; Jer 9.23
3.6 1 Chr 28.9; Isa 45.13
3.7 Rom 12.16; Prov 16.6
3.8 Job 21.24
3.9 Isa 43.23; Ex 23.19
3.10 Deut 28.8
3.11 Heb 12.5,6
3.12 Deut 8.5
3.14 Job 28.13; Prov 8.10,19
3.15 Job 28.18; Prov 8.11
3.16 Prov 8.18
3.17 Prov 16.7
3.18 Prov 11.30; Gen 2.9
3.19 Ps 104.24
3.20 Gen 7.11; Job 36.28
3.22 Prov 4.22; 1.9
3.23 Prov 4.12
3.25 Ps 91.5; Job 5.21
3.27 Rom 13.7; Gal 6.10
3.28 Lev 19.13
3.29 Prov 14.22
3.30 Rom 12.18
3.31 Ps 37.1; Prov 24.1
3.32 Prov 11.20; Ps 25.14
3.33 Deut 11.28; Mal 2.2; Job 8.6
3.34 Jas 4.6; 1 Pet 3.5

4.1 Prov 1.8; 2.2
4.3 1 Chr 22.5
4.4 1 Chr 28.9; Prov 7.2

"Let your heart hold fast my words;
keep my commandments, and live.
5 Get wisdom; get insight: do not forget, nor turn away
from the words of my mouth.
6 Do not forsake her, and she will keep you;
love her, and she will guard you.
7 The beginning of wisdom is this: Get wisdom,
and whatever else you get, get insight.
8 Prize her highly, and she will exalt you;
she will honor you if you embrace her.
9 She will place on your head a fair garland;
she will bestow on you a beautiful crown."

Admonition to Keep to the Right Path

10 Hear, my child, and accept my words,
that the years of your life may be many.
11 I have taught you the way of wisdom;
I have led you in the paths of uprightness.
12 When you walk, your step will not be hampered;
and if you run, you will not stumble.
13 Keep hold of instruction; do not let go;
guard her, for she is your life.
14 Do not enter the path of the wicked,
and do not walk in the way of evildoers.
15 Avoid it; do not go on it;
turn away from it and pass on.
16 For they cannot sleep unless they have done wrong;
they are robbed of sleep unless they have made someone stumble.
17 For they eat the bread of wickedness
and drink the wine of violence.
18 But the path of the righteous is like the light of dawn,
which shines brighter and brighter until full day.
19 The way of the wicked is like deep darkness;
they do not know what they stumble over.
20 My child, be attentive to my words;
incline your ear to my sayings.
21 Do not let them escape from your sight;
keep them within your heart.
22 For they are life to those who find them,
and healing to all their flesh.
23 Keep your heart with all vigilance,
for from it flow the springs of life.
24 Put away from you crooked speech,
and put devious talk far from you.
25 Let your eyes look directly forward,
and your gaze be straight before you.
26 Keep straight the path of your feet,
and all your ways will be sure.
27 Do not swerve to the right or to the left;
turn your foot away from evil.

Warning against Impurity and Infidelity

5 My child, be attentive to my wisdom;
incline your ear to my understanding,
2 so that you may hold on to prudence,
and your lips may guard knowledge.
3 For the lips of a loose[g] woman drip honey,
and her speech is smoother than oil;
4 but in the end she is bitter as wormwood,
sharp as a two-edged sword.
5 Her feet go down to death;
her steps follow the path to Sheol.
6 She does not keep straight to the path of life;
her ways wander, and she does not know it.

7 And now, my child,[h] listen to me,
and do not depart from the words of my mouth.
8 Keep your way far from her,
and do not go near the door of her house;
9 or you will give your honor to others,
and your years to the merciless,
10 and strangers will take their fill of your wealth,
and your labors will go to the house of an alien;
11 and at the end of your life you will groan,
when your flesh and body are consumed,
12 and you say, "Oh, how I hated discipline,
and my heart despised reproof!
13 I did not listen to the voice of my teachers
or incline my ear to my instructors.
14 Now I am at the point of utter ruin
in the public assembly."

[g] Heb *strange* [h] Gk Vg: Heb *children*

4.5 ver 7; Prov 16.16
4.6 2 Thess 2.10
4.7 Prov 23.23
4.8 1 Sam 2.30
4.9 Prov 1.9
4.11 1 Sam 12.23
4.12 Ps 18.36; Prov 3.23
4.14 Ps 1.1; Prov 1.15
4.16 Ps 36.4; Mic 2.1
4.18 Isa 26.7; 2 Sam 23.4; Dan 12.3
4.19 Job 18.5; Isa 59.9,10; Jer 23.12; Jn 12.35
4.21 Prov 3.21; 7.1,2
4.22 Prov 3.8; 12.18
4.23 Mt 12.34; Mk 7.21; Lk 6.45
4.24 Prov 6.12; 19.1
4.26 Heb 12.13; Ps 119.5
4.27 Deut 5.32; 28.14; Prov 1.15
5.1 Prov 4.20; 22.17
5.3 Prov 2.16; Ps 55.21
5.4 Eccl 7.26; Ps 57.4
5.7 Prov 7.24; Ps 119.102
5.8 Prov 7.25; 9.14
5.12 Prov 1.29; 12.1

4.14-19 The consequence of following the example of those obsessed with wrong-doing is a life of *violence* and *darkness*.
4.20-27 The alternative to *the way of the wicked* is to maintain wisdom steadfastly as the path and goal of life.
5.1-13 The Choice between Marital Fidelity and Infidelity.
5.1-14 The solemn warning about submitting to the enticement of a prostitute proceeds to a description of the waste of life and the loss of resources which follow such an involvement.

5.21-23 The section ends by noting that no-one can escape the scrutiny of the LORD, and how he holds responsible those who lack moral *discipline.*
6.1-35 A Series of Brief Moral Injunctions.
6.1-5 A warning against signing a contract (*pledge*) with a *neighbor* or money-lender. It is wiser to get out of any such financial commitment as soon as possible.
6.6-11 Use self-discipline in fulfilling responsibilities rather than relaxing as a *lazybones.*
6.12-15 A warning of the calamity that will fall on liars and cheats.
6.16-19 A list of seven kinds of behavior that *the LORD hates. The heart* is the seat of the will, not merely of the affections.
6.20-35 A reminder of the illuminating *commandments* transmitted through one's parents against marital infidelity, and a warning of the possible consequences of revenge from a betrayed husband.

15 Drink water from your own cistern,
flowing water from your own well.
16 Should your springs be scattered abroad,
streams of water in the streets?
17 Let them be for yourself alone,
and not for sharing with strangers.
18 Let your fountain be blessed,
and rejoice in the wife of your youth,
19 a lovely deer, a graceful doe.
May her breasts satisfy you at all times;
may you be intoxicated always by her love.
20 Why should you be intoxicated, my son, by another woman
and embrace the bosom of an adulteress?
21 For human ways are under the eyes of the LORD,
and he examines all their paths.
22 The iniquities of the wicked ensnare them,
and they are caught in the toils of their sin.
23 They die for lack of discipline,
and because of their great folly they are lost.

Practical Admonitions

6 My child, if you have given your pledge to your neighbor,
if you have bound yourself to another,[i]
2 you are snared by the utterance of your lips,[j]
caught by the words of your mouth.
3 So do this, my child, and save yourself,
for you have come into your neighbor's power:
go, hurry,[k] and plead with your neighbor.
4 Give your eyes no sleep
and your eyelids no slumber;
5 save yourself like a gazelle from the hunter,[l]
like a bird from the hand of the fowler.

6 Go to the ant, you lazybones;
consider its ways, and be wise.
7 Without having any chief
or officer or ruler,
8 it prepares its food in summer,
and gathers its sustenance in harvest.
9 How long will you lie there, O lazybones?
When will you rise from your sleep?
10 A little sleep, a little slumber,
a little folding of the hands to rest,
11 and poverty will come upon you like a robber,
and want, like an armed warrior.

12 A scoundrel and a villain
goes around with crooked speech,
13 winking the eyes, shuffling the feet,
pointing the fingers,
14 with perverted mind devising evil,
continually sowing discord;
15 on such a one calamity will descend suddenly;
in a moment, damage beyond repair.

16 There are six things that the LORD hates,
seven that are an abomination to him:
17 haughty eyes, a lying tongue,
and hands that shed innocent blood,
18 a heart that devises wicked plans,
feet that hurry to run to evil,
19 a lying witness who testifies falsely,
and one who sows discord in a family.

20 My child, keep your father's commandment,
and do not forsake your mother's teaching.
21 Bind them upon your heart always;
tie them around your neck.
22 When you walk, they[m] will lead you;
when you lie down, they[m] will watch over you;
and when you awake, they[m] will talk with you.
23 For the commandment is a lamp and the teaching a light,
and the reproofs of discipline are the way of life,
24 to preserve you from the wife of another,[n]
from the smooth tongue of the adulteress.
25 Do not desire her beauty in your heart,
and do not let her capture you with her eyelashes;
26 for a prostitute's fee is only a loaf of bread,[o]
but the wife of another stalks a man's very life.

[i] Or *a stranger* [j] Cn Compare Gk Syr: Heb *the words of your mouth* [k] Or *humble yourself* [l] Cn: Heb *from the hand* [m] Heb *it* [n] Gk: MT *the evil woman* [o] Cn Compare Gk Syr Vg Tg: Heb *for because of a harlot to a piece of bread*

5.16 Prov 9.17
5.18 Eccl 9.9; Mal 2.14
5.19 Song 2.9; 4.5; 7.3
5.20 Prov 2.16; 7.5
5.21 Job 31.4; 34.21; Prov 15.3; Jer 16.17; 32.19; Hos 7.2; Heb 4.13
5.22 Ps 9.15
5.23 Job 4.21; 36.12

6.1 Prov 11.15; 17.18; 20.16; 22.26; 27.13
6.4 Ps 132.4
6.5 Ps 91.3
6.6 Prov 30.24,25
6.8 Prov 10.5
6.9 Prov 24.33
6.11 Prov 10.4; 13.4; 20.4
6.12 Prov 16.27; 10.32
6.13 Ps 35.19; Prov 10.10
6.14 Mic 2.1; ver 19
6.15 Prov 24.22; Jer 19.11; 2 Chr 36.16
6.17 Ps 18.27; 120.2; Isa 1.15
6.18 Gen 6.5; Prov 1.16
6.19 Ps 27.12; ver 4
6.20 Prov 7.1; 1.8
6.21 Prov 3.3
6.22 Prov 3.23,24
6.23 Ps 19.8
6.24 Prov 2.16; 5.3
6.25 Mt 5.28
6.26 Prov 29.3; 7.23; Ezek 13.18

27 Can fire be carried in the bosom
without burning one's clothes?
28 Or can one walk on hot coals
without scorching the feet?
29 So is he who sleeps with his neighbor's
wife;
no one who touches her will go
unpunished.
30 Thieves are not despised who steal only
to satisfy their appetite when they are
hungry.
31 Yet if they are caught, they will pay
sevenfold;
they will forfeit all the goods of their
house.
32 But he who commits adultery has no
sense;
he who does it destroys himself.
33 He will get wounds and dishonor,
and his disgrace will not be wiped
away.
34 For jealousy arouses a husband's fury,
and he shows no restraint when he
takes revenge.
35 He will accept no compensation,
and refuses a bribe no matter how
great.

The False Attractions of Adultery

7 My child, keep my words
and store up my
commandments with you;
2 keep my commandments and live,
keep my teachings as the apple of
your eye;
3 bind them on your fingers,
write them on the tablet of your
heart.
4 Say to wisdom, "You are my sister,"
and call insight your intimate friend,
5 that they may keep you from the loose[p]
woman,
from the adulteress with her smooth
words.

6 For at the window of my house
I looked out through my lattice,
7 and I saw among the simple ones,
I observed among the youths,
a young man without sense,
8 passing along the street near her corner,
taking the road to her house
9 in the twilight, in the evening,
at the time of night and darkness.

10 Then a woman comes toward him,
decked out like a prostitute, wily of
heart.[q]
11 She is loud and wayward;
her feet do not stay at home;
12 now in the street, now in the squares,
and at every corner she lies in wait.
13 She seizes him and kisses him,
and with impudent face she says to
him:
14 "I had to offer sacrifices,
and today I have paid my vows;
15 so now I have come out to meet you,
to seek you eagerly, and I have found
you!
16 I have decked my couch with coverings,
colored spreads of Egyptian linen;
17 I have perfumed my bed with myrrh,
aloes, and cinnamon.
18 Come, let us take our fill of love until
morning;
let us delight ourselves with love.
19 For my husband is not at home;
he has gone on a long journey.
20 He took a bag of money with him;
he will not come home until full
moon."

21 With much seductive speech she
persuades him;
with her smooth talk she compels
him.
22 Right away he follows her,
and goes like an ox to the slaughter,
or bounds like a stag toward the trap[r]
23 until an arrow pierces its entrails.
He is like a bird rushing into a snare,
not knowing that it will cost him his
life.

24 And now, my children, listen to me,
and be attentive to the words of my
mouth.
25 Do not let your hearts turn aside to her
ways;
do not stray into her paths.
26 for many are those she has laid low,
and numerous are her victims.
27 Her house is the way to Sheol,
going down to the chambers of death.

7.1-27 Additional Warnings against Adultery.
7.1-5 Wisdom is here personified as a sister or friend who keeps one from violating the commandments against sexual promiscuity.
7.6-23 A vivid picture of the strategy carried out by an adulteress.
7.24-27 A solemn reminder that the consequences of adultery may be *death*.

6.29 Ezek 18.6; 33.26
6.31 Ex 22.1-4
6.32 Prov 7.7
6.34 Prov 27.4; 11.4
7.1 Prov 2.1
7.2 Prov 4.4; Deut 32.10
7.3 Deut 6.8; Prov 3.3
7.5 Prov 2.16; 5.3; 6.24
7.7 Prov 1.22; 6.32
7.8 ver 12,27
7.9 Job 24.15
7.11 Prov 9.13; 1 Tim 5.13
7.12 Prov 23.28
7.14 Prov 7.11,16
7.16 Prov 31.22; Isa 19.9
7.21 Prov 5.3
7.23 Eccl 9.12
7.24 Prov 5.7
7.25 Prov 5.8
7.26 Prov 9.18
7.27 Prov 2.18; 5.5; 9.18

[p] Heb *strange* [q] Meaning of Heb uncertain [r] Cn Compare Gk: Meaning of Heb uncertain

8.1-9.18 The Benefits Offered by Wisdom.
Personified wisdom invites all to partake of the benefits she offers: prudence, intelligence, truth, discretion, hatred of arrogance and evil. Those who give heed to her, she leads to *honor and justice.*
8.22-36 Here is developed further the theme of wisdom's role in the creation of the world, as mentioned briefly in 3.19-20. Detailed are God's having created wisdom as the embodiment of his plan and purpose for the world, and his use of wisdom as the agent to shape the world and the human race that inhabits it. Specified are the benefits of heeding wisdom and the dire consequences of failure to do so.

The Gifts of Wisdom

8 Does not wisdom call,
and does not understanding
raise her voice?
2 On the heights, beside the way,
at the crossroads she takes her stand;
3 beside the gates in front of the town,
at the entrance of the portals she cries
out:
4 "To you, O people, I call,
and my cry is to all that live.
5 O simple ones, learn prudence;
acquire intelligence, you who lack it.
6 Hear, for I will speak noble things,
and from my lips will come what is
right;
7 for my mouth will utter truth;
wickedness is an abomination to my
lips.
8 All the words of my mouth are
righteous;
there is nothing twisted or crooked in
them.
9 They are all straight to one who
understands
and right to those who find
knowledge.
10 Take my instruction instead of silver,
and knowledge rather than choice gold;
11 for wisdom is better than jewels,
and all that you may desire cannot
compare with her.
12 I, wisdom, live with prudence,[s]
and I attain knowledge and
discretion.
13 The fear of the LORD is hatred of evil.
Pride and arrogance and the way of evil
and perverted speech I hate.
14 I have good advice and sound wisdom;
I have insight, I have strength.
15 By me kings reign,
and rulers decree what is just;
16 by me rulers rule,
and nobles, all who govern rightly.
17 I love those who love me,
and those who seek me diligently find
me.
18 Riches and honor are with me,
enduring wealth and prosperity.
19 My fruit is better than gold, even fine
gold,
and my yield than choice silver.
20 I walk in the way of righteousness,
along the paths of justice,
21 endowing with wealth those who love
me,
and filling their treasuries.

Wisdom's Part in Creation

22 The LORD created me at the beginning[t] of
his work,[u]
the first of his acts of long ago.
23 Ages ago I was set up,
at the first, before the beginning of
the earth.
24 When there were no depths I was
brought forth,
when there were no springs
abounding with water.
25 Before the mountains had been shaped,
before the hills, I was brought forth—
26 when he had not yet made earth and
fields,[s]
or the world's first bits of soil.
27 When he established the heavens, I was
there,
when he drew a circle on the face of
the deep,
28 when he made firm the skies above,
when he established the fountains of
the deep,
29 when he assigned to the sea its limit,
so that the waters might not
transgress his command,
when he marked out the foundations of
the earth,
30 then I was beside him, like a master
worker;[v]
and I was daily his[w] delight,
rejoicing before him always,
31 rejoicing in his inhabited world
and delighting in the human race.

32 And now, my children, listen to me:
happy are those who keep my ways.
33 Hear instruction and be wise,
and do not neglect it.
34 Happy is the one who listens to me,
watching daily at my gates,
waiting beside my doors.
35 For whoever finds me finds life
and obtains favor from the LORD;
36 but those who miss me injure
themselves;
all who hate me love death."

[s] Meaning of Heb uncertain [t] Or *me as the beginning* [u] Heb *way* [v] Another reading is *little child* [w] Gk: Heb lacks *his*

8.1 Prov 1.20; 9.3
8.3 Job 29.7
8.5 Prov 1.4,22,32
8.6 Prov 22.20; 23.16
8.7 Ps 37.30
8.9 Prov 14.6; 3.13
8.10 Prov 3.14,15
8.11 Job 28.18; Prov 3.15
8.12 ver 5; Prov 1.4
8.13 Prov 16.6; 16.18; 15.9; 6.12
8.14 Prov 1.25; 2.7; Eccl 7.19
8.15 Dan 2.21; Rom 13.1
8.17 1 Sam 2.30; Ps 91.14; Jn 14.21; Jas 1.5
8.18 Prov 3.16; Mt 6.33
8.19 Prov 3.14; 10.20
8.21 Prov 24.4
8.22 Prov 3.19
8.23 Jn 17.5
8.25 Ps 90.2
8.27 Prov 3.19; Job 26.10
8.29 Job 38.10; Ps 104.9; Job 38.6
8.30 Jn 1.1-3
8.31 Ps 16.3
8.32 Prov 5.7; Ps 119.1,2; Lk 11.28
8.34 Prov 3.13,18
8.35 Prov 4.22; 12.2
8.36 Prov 20.2

Wisdom's Feast

9 Wisdom has built her house,
she has hewn her seven pillars.
2 She has slaughtered her animals, she has mixed her wine,
she has also set her table.
3 She has sent out her servant-girls, she calls
from the highest places in the town,
4 "You that are simple, turn in here!"
To those without sense she says,
5 "Come, eat of my bread
and drink of the wine I have mixed.
6 Lay aside immaturity,[x] and live,
and walk in the way of insight."

General Maxims

7 Whoever corrects a scoffer wins abuse;
whoever rebukes the wicked gets hurt.
8 A scoffer who is rebuked will only hate you;
the wise, when rebuked, will love you.
9 Give instruction[y] to the wise, and they will become wiser still;
teach the righteous and they will gain in learning.
10 The fear of the LORD is the beginning of wisdom,
and the knowledge of the Holy One is insight.
11 For by me your days will be multiplied,
and years will be added to your life.
12 If you are wise, you are wise for yourself;
if you scoff, you alone will bear it.

Folly's Invitation and Promise

13 The foolish woman is loud;
she is ignorant and knows nothing.
14 She sits at the door of her house,
on a seat at the high places of the town,
15 calling to those who pass by,
who are going straight on their way,
16 "You who are simple, turn in here!"
And to those without sense she says,
17 "Stolen water is sweet,
and bread eaten in secret is pleasant."
18 But they do not know that the dead[z] are there,
that her guests are in the depths of Sheol.

Wise Sayings of Solomon

10 The proverbs of Solomon.

A wise child makes a glad father,
but a foolish child is a mother's grief.
2 Treasures gained by wickedness do not profit,
but righteousness delivers from death.
3 The LORD does not let the righteous go hungry,
but he thwarts the craving of the wicked.
4 A slack hand causes poverty,
but the hand of the diligent makes rich.
5 A child who gathers in summer is prudent,
but a child who sleeps in harvest brings shame.
6 Blessings are on the head of the righteous,
but the mouth of the wicked conceals violence.
7 The memory of the righteous is a blessing,
but the name of the wicked will rot.
8 The wise of heart will heed commandments,
but a babbling fool will come to ruin.
9 Whoever walks in integrity walks securely,
but whoever follows perverse ways will be found out.
10 Whoever winks the eye causes trouble,
but the one who rebukes boldly makes peace.[a]
11 The mouth of the righteous is a fountain of life,
but the mouth of the wicked conceals violence.
12 Hatred stirs up strife,
but love covers all offenses.
13 On the lips of one who has understanding wisdom is found,
but a rod is for the back of one who lacks sense.
14 The wise lay up knowledge,
but the babbling of a fool brings ruin near.
15 The wealth of the rich is their fortress;
the poverty of the poor is their ruin.
16 The wage of the righteous leads to life,
the gain of the wicked to sin.
17 Whoever heeds instruction is on the path to life,
but one who rejects a rebuke goes astray.

[x] Or *simpleness* [y] Heb lacks *instruction* [z] Heb *shades* [a] Gk: Heb *but a babbling fool will come to ruin*

9.1 Mt 16.18; Eph 2.20,22; 1 Pet 2.5 **9.2** Mt 22.4; Lk 14.16,17 **9.3** Ps 68.11; Mt 22.3; Prov 8.1,2 **9.4** Prov 8.5; 6.32 **9.5** Song 5.1; Isa 55.1; Jn 6.27 **9.6** Ezek 11.20; 37.24 **9.7** Prov 23.9 **9.8** Mt 7.6; Ps 141.5 **9.9** Prov 1.5 **9.10** Job 28.28; Prov 1.7 **9.11** Prov 3.16; 10.27 **9.12** Prov 19.29 **9.13** Prov 7.11; 5.6 **9.17** Prov 20.17 **9.18** Prov 7.27

10.1 Prov 1.1; 15.20; 29.3,15 **10.3** Ps 34.9,10; Mt 6.33; Ps 112.10 **10.4** Prov 12.24; 13.4 **10.5** Prov 6.8; 17.2 **10.6** Esth 7.8 **10.7** Ps 9.5,6; Eccl 8.10 **10.8** Prov 13.3 **10.9** Ps 23.4; Prov 28.18; Isa 33.15; Prov 26.26 **10.10** Prov 6.13 **10.11** Ps 37.30 **10.12** 1 Pet 4.8 **10.13** Prov 26.3 **10.15** Job 31.24; Ps 52.7; Prov 18.11; 19.7

9.1-6 Described are wisdom's abode and her invitation for humans to share in the sustenance she offers.
9.7-18 This section of Proverbs ends with a series of contrasts between the behavior and destiny of (1) the fools and scoffers, and (2) the wise. The crucial shift from the former mode of life to the latter occurs when one gains *the fear of the LORD*, which is further described here as *the knowledge of the Holy One*. This theme was sounded in Prov 1.7 and 3.7.
10.1-22.16 Proverbial Sayings. This major section of Proverbs consists of sentences of wisdom, phrased as parallel statements in which there are comparisons or contrasts between two aspects of the subject under consideration in each proverb. These may be grouped under three types: (1) advice by which individuals can gain a life of contentment and prosperity; (2) the effects of individual behavior on the life of the community; (3) human behavior as called for in response to God. Some of the material seems to have been grouped on the basis of similar initial letters or words in the original Hebrew, but the meanings of the sentences are largely self-contained. The whole collection is attributed to Solomon (see note on Prov 1.1).
10.10 To *wink the eye* means to make a sign to someone as a device for covering up an evil deed. The translation here, which is based on the Greek version, fits well the adjacent proverbs which contrast the candor of the righteous and the deceitfulness of the wicked.
10.13 Punishment is inescapable for anyone who lacks wisdom.

10.25 *The tempest* means a time of difficulty which tests the basic quality of the individual.
11.16 In contrast to Stoic philosophy and the teaching of Jesus (Mt 23.12) about humility as virtue, this proverb recommends aggressiveness as leading to wealth, in contrast to timidity which leads to poverty.

18 Lying lips conceal hatred,
and whoever utters slander is a fool.
19 When words are many, transgression is not lacking,
but the prudent are restrained in speech.
20 The tongue of the righteous is choice silver;
the mind of the wicked is of little worth.
21 The lips of the righteous feed many,
but fools die for lack of sense.
22 The blessing of the LORD makes rich,
and he adds no sorrow with it.[b]
23 Doing wrong is like sport to a fool,
but wise conduct is pleasure to a person of understanding.
24 What the wicked dread will come upon them,
but the desire of the righteous will be granted.
25 When the tempest passes, the wicked are no more,
but the righteous are established forever.
26 Like vinegar to the teeth, and smoke to the eyes,
so are the lazy to their employers.
27 The fear of the LORD prolongs life,
but the years of the wicked will be short.
28 The hope of the righteous ends in gladness,
but the expectation of the wicked comes to nothing.
29 The way of the LORD is a stronghold for the upright,
but destruction for evildoers.
30 The righteous will never be removed,
but the wicked will not remain in the land.
31 The mouth of the righteous brings forth wisdom,
but the perverse tongue will be cut off.
32 The lips of the righteous know what is acceptable,
but the mouth of the wicked what is perverse.

11 A false balance is an abomination to the LORD,
but an accurate weight is his delight.
2 When pride comes, then comes disgrace;
but wisdom is with the humble.
3 The integrity of the upright guides them,
but the crookedness of the treacherous destroys them.
4 Riches do not profit in the day of wrath,
but righteousness delivers from death.
5 The righteousness of the blameless keeps their ways straight,
but the wicked fall by their own wickedness.
6 The righteousness of the upright saves them,
but the treacherous are taken captive by their schemes.
7 When the wicked die, their hope perishes,
and the expectation of the godless comes to nothing.
8 The righteous are delivered from trouble,
and the wicked get into it instead.
9 With their mouths the godless would destroy their neighbors,
but by knowledge the righteous are delivered.
10 When it goes well with the righteous, the city rejoices;
and when the wicked perish, there is jubilation.
11 By the blessing of the upright a city is exalted,
but it is overthrown by the mouth of the wicked.
12 Whoever belittles another lacks sense,
but an intelligent person remains silent.
13 A gossip goes about telling secrets,
but one who is trustworthy in spirit keeps a confidence.
14 Where there is no guidance, a nation[c] falls,
but in an abundance of counselors there is safety.
15 To guarantee loans for a stranger brings trouble,
but there is safety in refusing to do so.
16 A gracious woman gets honor,
but she who hates virtue is covered with shame.[d]
The timid become destitute,[e]
but the aggressive gain riches.
17 Those who are kind reward themselves,
but the cruel do themselves harm.
18 The wicked earn no real gain,
but those who sow righteousness get a true reward.
19 Whoever is steadfast in righteousness will live,

[b] Or *and toil adds nothing to it* [c] Or *an army* [d] Compare Gk Syr: Heb lacks *but she ... shame* [e] Gk: Heb lacks *The timid ... destitute*

10.19 Prov 18.21; Eccl 5.3; Jas 3.2
10.20 Prov 8.19
10.22 Gen 24.35; Ps 37.22
10.23 Prov 15.21
10.24 Ps 145.19; Mt 5.6; 1 Jn 5.14,15
10.25 Prov 12.7; Ps 15.5; Mt 7.24; 16.18
10.26 Prov 26.6
10.27 Prov 9.11; Ps 55.23
10.29 Ps 28.8; Prov 21.15
10.30 Ps 37.29
10.31 Ps 37.30; Prov 17.20
11.1 Lev 19.35; Deut 25.13-16
11.2 Prov 16.18
11.3 Prov 13.6
11.4 Ezek 7.19; Zeph 1.18; Gen 7.1
11.6 Eccl 10.8
11.7 Prov 10.28
11.8 Prov 21.18
11.10 Prov 28.12
11.11 Prov 29.8
11.12 Prov 14.21; 10.19
11.13 Lev 19.6; Prov 20.19; 1 Tim 5.13; Prov 19.11
11.14 Prov 15.22; 20.18; 24.6
11.16 Prov 31.30
11.18 Hos 10.12; Gal 6.8,9

but whoever pursues evil will die.
20 Crooked minds are an abomination to
the LORD,
but those of blameless ways are his
delight.
21 Be assured, the wicked will not go
unpunished,
but those who are righteous will
escape.
22 Like a gold ring in a pig's snout
is a beautiful woman without good
sense.
23 The desire of the righteous ends only in
good;
the expectation of the wicked in
wrath.
24 Some give freely, yet grow all the richer;
others withhold what is due, and only
suffer want.
25 A generous person will be enriched,
and one who gives water will get
water.
26 The people curse those who hold back
grain,
but a blessing is on the head of those
who sell it.
27 Whoever diligently seeks good seeks
favor,
but evil comes to the one who
searches for it.
28 Those who trust in their riches will
wither,[f]
but the righteous will flourish like
green leaves.
29 Those who trouble their households will
inherit wind,
and the fool will be servant to the
wise.
30 The fruit of the righteous is a tree of life,
but violence[g] takes lives away.
31 If the righteous are repaid on earth,
how much more the wicked and the
sinner!

12 Whoever loves discipline loves
knowledge,
but those who hate to be rebuked are
stupid.
2 The good obtain favor from the LORD,
but those who devise evil he
condemns.
3 No one finds security by wickedness,
but the root of the righteous will
never be moved.
4 A good wife is the crown of her
husband,
but she who brings shame is like
rottenness in his bones.
5 The thoughts of the righteous are just;
the advice of the wicked is
treacherous.
6 The words of the wicked are a deadly
ambush,
but the speech of the upright delivers
them.
7 The wicked are overthrown and are no
more,
but the house of the righteous will
stand.
8 One is commended for good sense,
but a perverse mind is despised.
9 Better to be despised and have a servant,
than to be self-important and lack
food.
10 The righteous know the needs of their
animals,
but the mercy of the wicked is cruel.
11 Those who till their land will have
plenty of food,
but those who follow worthless
pursuits have no sense.
12 The wicked covet the proceeds of
wickedness,[h]
but the root of the righteous bears
fruit.
13 The evil are ensnared by the
transgression of their lips,
but the righteous escape from trouble.
14 From the fruit of the mouth one is filled
with good things,
and manual labor has its reward.
15 Fools think their own way is right,
but the wise listen to advice.
16 Fools show their anger at once,
but the prudent ignore an insult.
17 Whoever speaks the truth gives honest
evidence,
but a false witness speaks deceitfully.
18 Rash words are like sword thrusts,
but the tongue of the wise brings
healing.
19 Truthful lips endure forever,
but a lying tongue lasts only a
moment.
20 Deceit is in the mind of those who plan
evil,
but those who counsel peace have joy.
21 No harm happens to the righteous,
but the wicked are filled with trouble.
22 Lying lips are an abomination to the
LORD,
but those who act faithfully are his
delight.

[f] Cn: Heb *fall* [g] Cn Compare Gk Syr: Heb *a wise man* [h] Or *covet the catch of the wicked*

11.27 The *favor* sought and gained is the welfare of the community, in contrast to the evil outcome of the actions of those who foster anti-social activities.
11.19 Those who exploit or misuse family possessions are going to *inherit wind;* that is, to cause a storm of conflict. The result will be that the guilty member of the family will be subjected like a *servant* to the faithful and wise in the family.
11.31 In contrast with ideas in later Judaism and Christianity about future rewards and punishments, the consequences of good or bad deeds are here said to be experienced in this life.
12.14 The results of helpful, constructive speech include the welfare of the one who utters it, just as constructive hard work brings its own reward.

11.20 Prov 12.22; Ps 119.1
11.21 Prov 16.5; Ps 112.2
11.24 Prov 13.7; 19.17
11.25 2 Cor 9.6-10; Mt 5.7
11.26 Am 8.5,6; Job 29.13
11.27 Esth 7.10; Ps 7.15; 10.2
11.28 Ps 52.7; Mk 10.24; 1 Tim 6.17; Ps 1.3; Jer 17.8
11.30 1 Cor 9.19; Jas 5.20
11.31 Prov 13.21; 2 Sam 22.21,25
12.1 Prov 9.8; 15.10
12.2 Prov 8.35
12.3 Prov 10.25
12.4 Prov 31.23; 1 Cor 11.7; Prov 14.30
12.6 Prov 1.11; 14.3
12.7 Ps 37.36; Mt 7.24
12.10 Deut 25.4
12.11 Prov 28.19; Judg 9.4
12.13 Prov 18.7; 2 Pet 2.9
12.14 Prov 13.2; Job 34.11; Isa 3.10,11
12.15 Prov 14.12; Lk 18.11
12.16 Prov 29.11
12.17 Prov 14.5
12.18 Ps 57.4
12.19 Ps 52.5
12.20 ver 5
12.21 Ps 91.10; 1 Pet 3.13; Prov 14.14
12.22 Prov 6.17; 11.20; Rev 22.15

12.23 The shrewd individual does not publicly disclose his limitations or ignorance, but the *fool* displays his foolishness by his loose talk.
12.27 The lazy set out on a hunt, but never catch their prey and hence have nothing to eat, while the diligent achieve their goals.
13.8 The rich man spends his wealth to pay off a blackmailer, but the poor man, who has nothing to pay, gets no such *threats*.
13.12 A tree of life is a common figure in the literature of the ancient Near East for the enduring source of life in creation and in subsequent existence, as in Gen 2.9.
13.13 The *word* and the *commandment* could be those of the wisdom teacher or those of God.
13.25 A recurring theme is that prosperity is the reward of the righteous.
14.3 What fools say results in their punishment: *a rod for their backs*.
14.4 Work is essential if there is to be productivity, just as plowing with oxen is necessary for producing grain.

23 One who is clever conceals knowledge,
but the mind of a fool[i] broadcasts folly.
24 The hand of the diligent will rule,
while the lazy will be put to forced labor.
25 Anxiety weighs down the human heart,
but a good word cheers it up.
26 The righteous gives good advice to friends,[j]
but the way of the wicked leads astray.
27 The lazy do not roast[k] their game,
but the diligent obtain precious wealth.[k]
28 In the path of righteousness there is life,
in walking its path there is no death.

13 A wise child loves discipline,[l]
but a scoffer does not listen to rebuke.
2 From the fruit of their words good persons eat good things,
but the desire of the treacherous is for wrongdoing.
3 Those who guard their mouths preserve their lives;
those who open wide their lips come to ruin.
4 The appetite of the lazy craves, and gets nothing,
while the appetite of the diligent is richly supplied.
5 The righteous hate falsehood,
but the wicked act shamefully and disgracefully.
6 Righteousness guards one whose way is upright,
but sin overthrows the wicked.
7 Some pretend to be rich, yet have nothing;
others pretend to be poor, yet have great wealth.
8 Wealth is a ransom for a person's life,
but the poor get no threats.
9 The light of the righteous rejoices,
but the lamp of the wicked goes out.
10 By insolence the heedless make strife,
but wisdom is with those who take advice.
11 Wealth hastily gotten[m] will dwindle,
but those who gather little by little will increase it.
12 Hope deferred makes the heart sick,
but a desire fulfilled is a tree of life.
13 Those who despise the word bring destruction on themselves,
but those who respect the commandment will be rewarded.
14 The teaching of the wise is a fountain of life,
so that one may avoid the snares of death.
15 Good sense wins favor,
but the way of the faithless is their ruin.[n]
16 The clever do all things intelligently,
but the fool displays folly.
17 A bad messenger brings trouble,
but a faithful envoy, healing.
18 Poverty and disgrace are for the one who ignores instruction,
but one who heeds reproof is honored.
19 A desire realized is sweet to the soul,
but to turn away from evil is an abomination to fools.
20 Whoever walks with the wise becomes wise,
but the companion of fools suffers harm.
21 Misfortune pursues sinners,
but prosperity rewards the righteous.
22 The good leave an inheritance to their children's children,
but the sinner's wealth is laid up for the righteous.
23 The field of the poor may yield much food,
but it is swept away through injustice.
24 Those who spare the rod hate their children,
but those who love them are diligent to discipline them.
25 The righteous have enough to satisfy their appetite,
but the belly of the wicked is empty.

14 The wise woman[o] builds her house,
but the foolish tears it down with her own hands.
2 Those who walk uprightly fear the LORD,
but one who is devious in conduct despises him.
3 The talk of fools is a rod for their backs,[p]
but the lips of the wise preserve them.
4 Where there are no oxen, there is no grain;

[i] Heb *the heart of fools* [j] Syr: Meaning of Heb uncertain [k] Meaning of Heb uncertain [l] Cn: Heb *A wise child the discipline of his father* [m] Gk Vg: Heb *from vanity* [n] Cn Compare Gk Syr Vg Tg: Heb *is enduring* [o] Heb *Wisdom of women* [p] Cn: Heb *a rod of pride*

12.23 Prov 13.16; 15.2
12.25 Prov 15.13; Isa 50.4
12.28 Prov 11.19
13.1 Prov 10.1; 15.12
13.3 Ps 39.1; Jas 3.2
13.4 Prov 10.4
13.6 Prov 11.3,5
13.7 Prov 11.24; Lk 12.20, 21,33; 2 Cor 6.10
13.9 Job 18.5; Prov 24.20
13.10 Prov 11.14
13.11 Prov 10.2; 14.23
13.13 2 Chr 36.16
13.14 Prov 10.11; Ps 18.5
13.15 Prov 34; 21.8
13.16 Prov 12.23; 15.2
13.17 Prov 25.13
13.18 Prov 15.5,31,32
13.20 Prov 15.31; 28.19
13.21 Ps 32.10
13.22 Job 27.16,17; Prov 28.8; Eccl 2.26
13.23 Prov 12.11
13.24 Prov 19.18; 22.15; 29.15,17
13.25 Ps 34.10; 37.3
14.2 Prov 19.1; Rom 2.4
14.3 Prov 12.6

abundant crops come by the strength
of the ox.
5 A faithful witness does not lie,
but a false witness breathes out lies.
6 A scoffer seeks wisdom in vain,
but knowledge is easy for one who
understands.
7 Leave the presence of a fool,
for there you do not find words of
knowledge.
8 It is the wisdom of the clever to
understand where they go,
but the folly of fools misleads.
9 Fools mock at the guilt offering,[q]
but the upright enjoy God's favor.
10 The heart knows its own bitterness,
and no stranger shares its joy.
11 The house of the wicked is destroyed,
but the tent of the upright flourishes.
12 There is a way that seems right to a
person,
but its end is the way to death.[r]
13 Even in laughter the heart is sad,
and the end of joy is grief.
14 The perverse get what their ways
deserve,
and the good, what their deeds
deserve.[s]
15 The simple believe everything,
but the clever consider their steps.
16 The wise are cautious and turn away
from evil,
but the fool throws off restraint and is
careless.
17 One who is quick-tempered acts
foolishly,
and the schemer is hated.
18 The simple are adorned with[t] folly,
but the clever are crowned with
knowledge.
19 The evil bow down before the good,
the wicked at the gates of the
righteous.
20 The poor are disliked even by their
neighbors,
but the rich have many friends.
21 Those who despise their neighbors are
sinners,
but happy are those who are kind to
the poor.
22 Do they not err that plan evil?
Those who plan good find loyalty and
faithfulness.
23 In all toil there is profit,
but mere talk leads only to poverty.
24 The crown of the wise is their wisdom,[u]
but folly is the garland[v] of fools.
25 A truthful witness saves lives,
but one who utters lies is a betrayer.
26 In the fear of the LORD one has strong
confidence,
and one's children will have a refuge.
27 The fear of the LORD is a fountain of life,
so that one may avoid the snares of
death.
28 The glory of a king is a multitude of
people;
without people a prince is ruined.
29 Whoever is slow to anger has great
understanding,
but one who has a hasty temper
exalts folly.
30 A tranquil mind gives life to the flesh,
but passion makes the bones rot.
31 Those who oppress the poor insult their
Maker,
but those who are kind to the needy
honor him.
32 The wicked are overthrown by their
evildoing,
but the righteous find a refuge in
their integrity.[w]
33 Wisdom is at home in the mind of one
who has understanding,
but it is not[x] known in the heart of
fools.
34 Righteousness exalts a nation,
but sin is a reproach to any people.
35 A servant who deals wisely has the
king's favor,
but his wrath falls on one who acts
shamefully.

15

A soft answer turns away wrath,
but a harsh word stirs up
anger.
2 The tongue of the wise dispenses
knowledge,[y]
but the mouths of fools pour out folly.
3 The eyes of the LORD are in every place,
keeping watch on the evil and the
good.
4 A gentle tongue is a tree of life,
but perverseness in it breaks the
spirit.
5 A fool despises a parent's instruction,
but the one who heeds admonition is
prudent.
6 In the house of the righteous there is

[q] Meaning of Heb uncertain [r] Heb *ways of death* [s] Cn: Heb *from upon him* [t] Or *inherit* [u] Cn Compare Gk: Heb *riches* [v] Cn: Heb *is the folly* [w] Gk Syr: Heb *in their death* [x] Gk Syr: Heb lacks *not* [y] Cn: Heb *makes knowledge good*

14.5 Ex 20.16; Prov 6.19; 12.17
14.8 Prov 15.21; ver 24
14.11 Prov 3.33; 12.7; 15.25
14.12 Prov 16.25; Rom 6.21
14.13 Prov 5.4; Eccl 2.2
14.14 Prov 1.31; 12.14
14.16 Prov 22.3
14.17 ver 29
14.18 Prov 18.15
14.19 Prov 11.29
14.20 Prov 19.7
14.21 Prov 11.12; Ps 41.1
14.25 ver 5
14.26 Prov 19.23; Isa 33.6
14.27 Prov 13.14
14.29 Prov 16.32; Jas 1.19; Prov 29.20
14.30 Prov 12.4
14.31 Prov 17.5; ver 21
14.32 Job 13.15; Ps 23.4; 2 Cor 1.9; 2 Tim 4.18
14.33 Prov 2.10; 12.16
14.34 Prov 11.11
14.35 Mt 24.45
15.1 Judg 8.1-3; 1 Sam 25.10-13
15.2 Prov 12.23; 13.16
15.3 Job 34.21; Heb 4.13
15.5 Prov 13.1,18

14.6-9 *Knowledge* or the lack of it are matters of inherent human qualities rather than the results of human achievement.
14.12-13 Even for the upright, sorrow and frustration are inevitable.
14.21 Love of neighbor is a theme that runs through both the Old and the New Testament: *cf.* Lev 19.18; Mk 12.31; Mt 5.43; Lk 10.27; Rom 13.9. Concern for *the poor* is a theme in the teaching of both Jesus (Lk 6.20; 14.21) and Paul (Gal 2.10).
14.29 Being slow to anger is a quality of God, according to the prophets (Joel 2.13; Nahum 1.3).
14.31 See note on 14.21.
14.34 God honors a righteous *nation*, but judges sternly a sinful *people*.

15.8-10 The moral condition of one who opposes God determines the acceptability or non-acceptability of whatever is brought to God.
15.11 If even such areas as the places of the dead (*Sheol* and *Abaddon*), which are inaccessible to human eyes, are known to God, then surely he can discern human motivations (*hearts*).
15.15-19 Set side by side are (1) the promise of prosperity to those with a sense of rightness with God (*cheerful heart*); and (2) assurance that the relationship achieved through *fear of the* LORD is more to be prized than material abundance.
15.24 The path that leads *upward* means the life of obedience and reward (not the path to heaven), and is contrasted with the route to the grave (*Sheol*).
15.25 The *widow's boundaries* are the limits of her property.
15.30 *Light of the eyes* means the glowing appearance which communicates joy, while *good news* refreshes the total person (*body*).
15.33 Humility refers to acceptance of God's will, which transcends in importance the desire of the individual for *honor*.
16.1-9 How *the fear of the* LORD shapes the lives, attitudes and actions of his faithful people.

much treasure,
but trouble befalls the income of the wicked.
7 The lips of the wise spread knowledge;
not so the minds of fools.
8 The sacrifice of the wicked is an abomination to the LORD,
but the prayer of the upright is his delight.
9 The way of the wicked is an abomination to the LORD,
but he loves the one who pursues righteousness.
10 There is severe discipline for one who forsakes the way,
but one who hates a rebuke will die.
11 Sheol and Abaddon lie open before the LORD,
how much more human hearts!
12 Scoffers do not like to be rebuked;
they will not go to the wise.
13 A glad heart makes a cheerful countenance,
but by sorrow of heart the spirit is broken.
14 The mind of one who has understanding seeks knowledge,
but the mouths of fools feed on folly.
15 All the days of the poor are hard,
but a cheerful heart has a continual feast.
16 Better is a little with the fear of the LORD
than great treasure and trouble with it.
17 Better is a dinner of vegetables where love is
than a fatted ox and hatred with it.
18 Those who are hot-tempered stir up strife,
but those who are slow to anger calm contention.
19 The way of the lazy is overgrown with thorns,
but the path of the upright is a level highway.
20 A wise child makes a glad father,
but the foolish despise their mothers.
21 Folly is a joy to one who has no sense,
but a person of understanding walks straight ahead.
22 Without counsel, plans go wrong,
but with many advisers they succeed.
23 To make an apt answer is a joy to anyone,
and a word in season, how good it is!
24 For the wise the path of life leads upward,
in order to avoid Sheol below.
25 The LORD tears down the house of the proud,
but maintains the widow's boundaries.
26 Evil plans are an abomination to the LORD,
but gracious words are pure.
27 Those who are greedy for unjust gain make trouble for their households,
but those who hate bribes will live.
28 The mind of the righteous ponders how to answer,
but the mouth of the wicked pours out evil.
29 The LORD is far from the wicked,
but he hears the prayer of the righteous.
30 The light of the eyes rejoices the heart,
and good news refreshes the body.
31 The ear that heeds wholesome admonition
will lodge among the wise.
32 Those who ignore instruction despise themselves,
but those who heed admonition gain understanding.
33 The fear of the LORD is instruction in wisdom,
and humility goes before honor.

16 The plans of the mind belong to mortals,
but the answer of the tongue is from the LORD.
2 All one's ways may be pure in one's own eyes,
but the LORD weighs the spirit.
3 Commit your work to the LORD,
and your plans will be established.
4 The LORD has made everything for its purpose,
even the wicked for the day of trouble.
5 All those who are arrogant are an abomination to the LORD;
be assured, they will not go unpunished.
6 By loyalty and faithfulness iniquity is atoned for,
and by the fear of the LORD one avoids evil.
7 When the ways of people please the LORD,
he causes even their enemies to be at peace with them.
8 Better is a little with righteousness

15.8 Isa 1.11; Jer 6.20; Mic 6.7
15.9 Prov 21.21; 1 Tim 6.11
15.10 Prov 1.29-32; 5.12
15.11 Job 26.6; Ps 139.8; 2 Chr 6.30
15.12 Prov 13.1; Am 5.10
15.13 Prov 17.22; 12.25
15.16 Ps 37.16; Prov 16.8; 1 Tim 6.6
15.17 Prov 17.1
15.18 Prov 26.21; 29.22; 14.29
15.19 Prov 22.5
15.20 Prov 10.1; 30.17
15.21 Prov 10.23; Eph 5.15
15.22 Prov 11.14; 20.18
15.23 Prov 25.11
15.24 Prov 4.18
15.25 Prov 12.7; Ps 68.5,6
15.26 Prov 6.16-19; 16.24
15.27 Prov 28.25; 1 Tim 6.10; Isa 33.15
15.28 1 Pet 3.15
15.29 Ps 34.16; 145.18
15.32 Prov 1.7; 8.36; 15.5
15.33 Prov 1.7; 18.12
16.2 Prov 21.2
16.3 Ps 37.5
16.4 Isa 43.7; Job 21.20
16.5 Prov 6.17; 11.21
16.6 Dan 4.27; Prov 14.16
16.7 2 Chr 17.10

than large income with injustice.
9 The human mind plans the way,
but the LORD directs the steps.
10 Inspired decisions are on the lips of a king;
his mouth does not sin in judgment.
11 Honest balances and scales are the LORD'S;
all the weights in the bag are his work.
12 It is an abomination to kings to do evil,
for the throne is established by righteousness.
13 Righteous lips are the delight of a king,
and he loves those who speak what is right.
14 A king's wrath is a messenger of death,
and whoever is wise will appease it.
15 In the light of a king's face there is life,
and his favor is like the clouds that bring the spring rain.
16 How much better to get wisdom than gold!
To get understanding is to be chosen rather than silver.
17 The highway of the upright avoids evil;
those who guard their way preserve their lives.
18 Pride goes before destruction,
and a haughty spirit before a fall.
19 It is better to be of a lowly spirit among the poor
than to divide the spoil with the proud.
20 Those who are attentive to a matter will prosper,
and happy are those who trust in the LORD.
21 The wise of heart is called perceptive,
and pleasant speech increases persuasiveness.
22 Wisdom is a fountain of life to one who has it,
but folly is the punishment of fools.
23 The mind of the wise makes their speech judicious,
and adds persuasiveness to their lips.
24 Pleasant words are like a honeycomb,
sweetness to the soul and health to the body.
25 Sometimes there is a way that seems to be right,
but in the end it is the way to death.
26 The appetite of workers works for them;
their hunger urges them on.
27 Scoundrels concoct evil,
and their speech is like a scorching fire.
28 A perverse person spreads strife,
and a whisperer separates close friends.
29 The violent entice their neighbors,
and lead them in a way that is not good.
30 One who winks the eyes plans[z] perverse things;
one who compresses the lips brings evil to pass.
31 Gray hair is a crown of glory;
it is gained in a righteous life.
32 One who is slow to anger is better than the mighty,
and one whose temper is controlled than one who captures a city.
33 The lot is cast into the lap,
but the decision is the LORD'S alone.

17 Better is a dry morsel with quiet
than a house full of feasting with strife.
2 A slave who deals wisely will rule over a child who acts shamefully,
and will share the inheritance as one of the family.
3 The crucible is for silver, and the furnace is for gold,
but the LORD tests the heart.
4 An evildoer listens to wicked lips;
and a liar gives heed to a mischievous tongue.
5 Those who mock the poor insult their Maker;
those who are glad at calamity will not go unpunished.
6 Grandchildren are the crown of the aged,
and the glory of children is their parents.
7 Fine speech is not becoming to a fool;
still less is false speech to a ruler.[a]
8 A bribe is like a magic stone in the eyes of those who give it;
wherever they turn they prosper.
9 One who forgives an affront fosters friendship,
but one who dwells on disputes will alienate a friend.
10 A rebuke strikes deeper into a discerning person
than a hundred blows into a fool.
11 Evil people seek only rebellion,
but a cruel messenger will be sent against them.
12 Better to meet a she-bear robbed of its cubs
than to confront a fool immersed in folly.

[z] Gk Syr Vg Tg: Heb *to plan* [a] Or *a noble person*

16.10-15 This series of proverbs details the resources and responsibilities of rulers in relationship with their people.
16.16-33 Contrasted is the mode of life of the wise with that of the foolish; the former foster peace and the latter *concoct evil.*
17.1-28 Commendation of peace, love of family, moral sensitivity, discipline and obedient wisdom, in contrast with the cruelty, perversity and defensiveness of those of *the crooked mind.*

16.9 Ps 37.23; Prov 20.24; Jer 10.23
16.11 Prov 11.1
16.12 Prov 25.5
16.13 Prov 14.35
16.14 Prov 19.12
16.15 Job 29.23
16.16 Prov 8.10,19
16.18 Prov 11.2
16.20 Ps 2.12; 34.8; Jer 17.7
16.22 Prov 13.14; 7.22
16.23 Prov 37.30
16.25 Prov 14.12
16.27 Prov 6.12,14,18; Jas 3.6
16.28 Prov 15.18; 17.9
16.29 Prov 1.10
16.31 Prov 20.29
16.32 Prov 19.11
17.1 Prov 15.17
17.2 Prov 10.5
17.3 Prov 27.21; Ps 26.2
17.5 Prov 14.31; Job 31.29
17.6 Prov 13.22
17.8 Prov 21.14; Isa 1.23; Am 5.12
17.9 Prov 10.12; Jas 5.20; 1 Pet 4.8; Prov 16.28
17.12 Hos 13.8

18.1-24 Integrity, candor, fairness in dealings with others, and the value of acquiring knowledge are praised.

13 Evil will not depart from the house
of one who returns evil for good.
14 The beginning of strife is like letting out water;
so stop before the quarrel breaks out.
15 One who justifies the wicked and one who condemns the righteous
are both alike an abomination to the LORD.
16 Why should fools have a price in hand
to buy wisdom, when they have no mind to learn?
17 A friend loves at all times,
and kinsfolk are born to share adversity.
18 It is senseless to give a pledge,
to become surety for a neighbor.
19 One who loves transgression loves strife;
one who builds a high threshold invites broken bones.
20 The crooked of mind do not prosper,
and the perverse of tongue fall into calamity.
21 The one who begets a fool gets trouble;
the parent of a fool has no joy.
22 A cheerful heart is a good medicine,
but a downcast spirit dries up the bones.
23 The wicked accept a concealed bribe
to pervert the ways of justice.
24 The discerning person looks to wisdom,
but the eyes of a fool to the ends of the earth.
25 Foolish children are a grief to their father
and bitterness to her who bore them.
26 To impose a fine on the innocent is not right,
or to flog the noble for their integrity.
27 One who spares words is knowledgeable;
one who is cool in spirit has understanding.
28 Even fools who keep silent are considered wise;
when they close their lips, they are deemed intelligent.

18 The one who lives alone is self-indulgent,
showing contempt for all who have sound judgment.[b]
2 A fool takes no pleasure in understanding,
but only in expressing personal opinion.
3 When wickedness comes, contempt comes also;
and with dishonor comes disgrace.
4 The words of the mouth are deep waters;
the fountain of wisdom is a gushing stream.
5 It is not right to be partial to the guilty,
or to subvert the innocent in judgment.
6 A fool's lips bring strife,
and a fool's mouth invites a flogging.
7 The mouths of fools are their ruin,
and their lips a snare to themselves.
8 The words of a whisperer are like delicious morsels;
they go down into the inner parts of the body.
9 One who is slack in work
is close kin to a vandal.
10 The name of the LORD is a strong tower;
the righteous run into it and are safe.
11 The wealth of the rich is their strong city;
in their imagination it is like a high wall.
12 Before destruction one's heart is haughty,
but humility goes before honor.
13 If one gives answer before hearing,
it is folly and shame.
14 The human spirit will endure sickness;
but a broken spirit—who can bear?
15 An intelligent mind acquires knowledge,
and the ear of the wise seeks knowledge.
16 A gift opens doors;
it gives access to the great.
17 The one who first states a case seems right,
until the other comes and cross-examines.
18 Casting the lot puts an end to disputes
and decides between powerful contenders.
19 An ally offended is stronger than a city;[c]
such quarreling is like the bars of a castle.
20 From the fruit of the mouth one's stomach is satisfied;
the yield of the lips brings satisfaction.
21 Death and life are in the power of the tongue,
and those who love it will eat its fruits.
22 He who finds a wife finds a good thing,
and obtains favor from the LORD.

[b] Meaning of Heb uncertain [c] Gk Syr Vg Tg: Meaning of Heb uncertain

17.13 Ps 109.4,5; Jer 18.20
17.14 Prov 20.3
17.15 Ex 23.7; Isa 5.23
17.17 Ruth 1.16; Prov 18.24
17.18 Prov 6.1
17.19 Prov 29.22; 16.18
17.20 Jas 3.8
17.21 Prov 10.1; 19.13
17.22 Prov 15.13; Ps 22.15
17.23 Ex 23.8
17.24 Eccl 2.14
17.25 Prov 10.1
17.26 Prov 18.5
17.27 Jas 1.19
17.28 Job 13.5
18.2 Prov 12.23
18.4 Prov 20.5; 10.11
18.5 Lev 19.15; Deut 1.17; Prov 24.23
18.7 Prov 10.14; Eccl 10.12
18.8 Prov 26.22
18.9 Prov 28.24
18.10 2 Sam 22.3; Ps 18.2
18.11 Prov 10.15
18.12 Prov 11.2
18.13 Jn 7.51
18.16 Gen 32.20; 1 Sam 25.27
18.18 Prov 16.33
18.20 Prov 12.14
18.21 Mt 12.37
18.22 Prov 19.14; 8.35

18.23 Jas 2.3
18.24 Prov 17.17
19.1 Prov 28.6
19.3 Prov 11.3; Ps 37.7
19.4 Prov 14.20
19.5 Ex 23.1; Prov 6.19
19.6 Prov 19.26; 17.8
19.7 ver 4; Ps 38.11
19.8 Prov 16.20
19.9 ver 5
19.10 Eccl 10.6,7
19.11 Jas 1.19; Prov 16.32
19.12 Prov 16.14; Hos 14.5
19.13 Prov 10.1; 21.9
19.14 2 Cor 12.14; Prov 18.22
19.15 Prov 6.9; 10.4
19.16 Lk 10.28
19.17 Eccl 11.1; Mt 10.42; 2 Cor 9.6-8; Heb 6.10
19.18 Prov 13.24
19.20 Prov 8.33
19.21 Prov 16.1,9; Ps 33.10,11
19.23 1 Tim 4.8; Ps 25.13; Prov 12.21
19.24 Prov 26.15
19.25 Prov 21.11; 9.8
19.28 Job 15.16
19.29 Prov 10.13; 26.3
20.1 Gen 9.21; Isa 5.22
20.2 Prov 19.12; 8.36; 1 Kings 2.23
20.3 Prov 17.14
20.4 Prov 10.4; 19.15,24
20.5 Prov 18.4

23 The poor use entreaties,
but the rich answer roughly.
24 Some[d] friends play at friendship[e]
but a true friend sticks closer than
one's nearest kin.

19 Better the poor walking in
integrity
than one perverse of speech who is a
fool.
2 Desire without knowledge is not good,
and one who moves too hurriedly
misses the way.
3 One's own folly leads to ruin,
yet the heart rages against the LORD.
4 Wealth brings many friends,
but the poor are left friendless.
5 A false witness will not go unpunished,
and a liar will not escape.
6 Many seek the favor of the generous,
and everyone is a friend to a giver of
gifts.
7 If the poor are hated even by their kin,
how much more are they shunned by
their friends!
When they call after them, they are not
there.[f]
8 To get wisdom is to love oneself;
to keep understanding is to prosper.
9 A false witness will not go unpunished,
and the liar will perish.
10 It is not fitting for a fool to live in luxury,
much less for a slave to rule over
princes.
11 Those with good sense are slow to anger,
and it is their glory to overlook an
offense.
12 A king's anger is like the growling of a
lion,
but his favor is like dew on the grass.
13 A stupid child is ruin to a father,
and a wife's quarreling is a continual
dripping of rain.
14 House and wealth are inherited from
parents,
but a prudent wife is from the LORD.
15 Laziness brings on deep sleep;
an idle person will suffer hunger.
16 Those who keep the commandment will
live;
those who are heedless of their ways
will die.
17 Whoever is kind to the poor lends to the
LORD,
and will be repaid in full.
18 Discipline your children while there is
hope;
do not set your heart on their
destruction.
19 A violent tempered person will pay the
penalty;
if you effect a rescue, you will only
have to do it again.[f]
20 Listen to advice and accept instruction,
that you may gain wisdom for the
future.
21 The human mind may devise many plans,
but it is the purpose of the LORD that
will be established.
22 What is desirable in a person is loyalty,
and it is better to be poor than a liar.
23 The fear of the LORD is life indeed;
filled with it one rests secure
and suffers no harm.
24 The lazy person buries a hand in the
dish,
and will not even bring it back to the
mouth.
25 Strike a scoffer, and the simple will learn
prudence;
reprove the intelligent, and they will
gain knowledge.
26 Those who do violence to their father
and chase away their mother
are children who cause shame and
bring reproach.
27 Cease straying, my child, from the
words of knowledge,
in order that you may hear
instruction.
28 A worthless witness mocks at justice,
and the mouth of the wicked devours
iniquity.
29 Condemnation is ready for scoffers,
and flogging for the backs of fools.

20 Wine is a mocker, strong drink a
brawler,
and whoever is led astray by it is not
wise.
2 The dread anger of a king is like the
growling of a lion;
anyone who provokes him to anger
forfeits life itself.
3 It is honorable to refrain from strife,
but every fool is quick to quarrel.
4 The lazy person does not plow in
season;
harvest comes, and there is nothing
to be found.
5 The purposes in the human mind are
like deep water,
but the intelligent will draw them
out.

19.1-23 Among the virtues here extolled are earnest search for knowledge, love of oneself, patience, kindness to the poor, and *loyalty*. These lead those who *fear the LORD* to a life of security. **19.24-29** A series of predictions about what awaits the lazy, scoffers and fools. **20.1-30** This mixture of warnings and encouragements includes such unusual images as (vs.8) the king winnowing evil with his eyes (distinguishing on sight between the valuable and the worthless); (vs.25) saying *rashly, "It is holy"* means to make a vow before God without having considered the cost or the consequences; (vs.26) *the wise king* can – figuratively – drive the wheels of the chariot over the grain (which represents a matter under analysis) and thus separate the valuable from the useless. The chapter closes with a reminder (vs.30) that the trials and sufferings of the faithful have a cleansing effect, and are not to be regarded as punitive or meaningless.

[d] Syr Tg: Heb *A man of* [e] Cn Compare Syr Vg Tg: Meaning of Heb uncertain [f] Meaning of Heb uncertain

21.1-31 The human failings here exposed and contrasted with God's purpose for *the wise* include pride (vs.4), haste (vs.5), lying (vs.6), violence (vs.7), crooked behavior (vs.8), contentiousness on the part of a spouse (vv.9,19), evil desire (vs.10), scoffing (vv.11,24), refusal to heed the needs of the poor (vs.13), love of sensual pleasure (vs.17), laziness (vs.25), false witness (vs.28). Paying off one's accuser or antagonist is here recommended as a way of escaping the anger of one's opponent.

6 Many proclaim themselves loyal,
but who can find one worthy of trust?
7 The righteous walk in integrity—
happy are the children who follow them!
8 A king who sits on the throne of judgment
winnows all evil with his eyes.
9 Who can say, "I have made my heart clean;
I am pure from my sin"?
10 Diverse weights and diverse measures
are both alike an abomination to the LORD.
11 Even children make themselves known by their acts,
by whether what they do is pure and right.
12 The hearing ear and the seeing eye—
the LORD has made them both.
13 Do not love sleep, or else you will come to poverty;
open your eyes, and you will have plenty of bread.
14 "Bad, bad," says the buyer,
then goes away and boasts.
15 There is gold, and abundance of costly stones;
but the lips informed by knowledge are a precious jewel.
16 Take the garment of one who has given surety for a stranger;
seize the pledge given as surety for foreigners.
17 Bread gained by deceit is sweet,
but afterward the mouth will be full of gravel.
18 Plans are established by taking advice;
wage war by following wise guidance.
19 A gossip reveals secrets;
therefore do not associate with a babbler.
20 If you curse father or mother,
your lamp will go out in utter darkness.
21 An estate quickly acquired in the beginning
will not be blessed in the end.
22 Do not say, "I will repay evil";
wait for the LORD, and he will help you.
23 Differing weights are an abomination to the LORD,
and false scales are not good.
24 All our steps are ordered by the LORD;
how then can we understand our own ways?
25 It is a snare for one to say rashly, "It is holy,"
and begin to reflect only after making a vow.
26 A wise king winnows the wicked,
and drives the wheel over them.
27 The human spirit is the lamp of the LORD,
searching every inmost part.
28 Loyalty and faithfulness preserve the king,
and his throne is upheld by righteousness.[g]
29 The glory of youths is their strength,
but the beauty of the aged is their gray hair.
30 Blows that wound cleanse away evil;
beatings make clean the innermost parts.

21 The king's heart is a stream of water in the hand of the LORD;
he turns it wherever he will.
2 All deeds are right in the sight of the doer,
but the LORD weighs the heart.
3 To do righteousness and justice
is more acceptable to the LORD than sacrifice.
4 Haughty eyes and a proud heart—
the lamp of the wicked—are sin.
5 The plans of the diligent lead surely to abundance,
but everyone who is hasty comes only to want.
6 The getting of treasures by a lying tongue
is a fleeting vapor and a snare[h] of death.
7 The violence of the wicked will sweep them away,
because they refuse to do what is just.
8 The way of the guilty is crooked,
but the conduct of the pure is right.
9 It is better to live in a corner of the housetop
than in a house shared with a contentious wife.
10 The souls of the wicked desire evil;
their neighbors find no mercy in their eyes.
11 When a scoffer is punished, the simple become wiser;
when the wise are instructed, they increase in knowledge.
12 The Righteous One observes the house of the wicked;

[g] Gk: Heb *loyalty* [h] Gk: Heb *seekers*

20.6 Prov 25.14; Mt 6.2; Lk 18.11; Ps 12.1; Lk 18.8
20.7 2 Cor 1.12; Ps 37.26
20.8 ver 26
20.9 1 Kings 8.46; 1 Jn 1.8
20.10 Deut 25.13; ver 23
20.11 Mt 7.16
20.12 Ex 4.11
20.13 Prov 6.9,10; Rom 12.11
20.17 Prov 9.17
20.18 Prov 15.22; 24.6; Lk 14.31
20.19 Prov 11.13; Rom 16.18
20.20 Mt 15.4; Job 18.5
20.21 Prov 28.20
20.22 Rom 12.17; 1 Pet 3.9; Ps 27.14
20.24 Ps 37.23; Prov 16.9; Jer 10.23
20.25 Eccl 5.4,5
20.27 1 Cor 2.11
20.28 Prov 29.14
20.29 Prov 16.31
21.2 Prov 16.2; 24.12; Lk 16.15
21.3 1 Sam 15.22; Prov 15.8; Isa 1.11-17; Hos 6.6; Mic 6.7,8
21.4 Prov 6.17
21.5 Prov 10.4; 28.22
21.6 2 Pet 2.3
21.7 Prov 10.25
21.9 Prov 25.24
21.10 Prov 2.14; 14.21
21.11 Prov 19.25
21.12 Prov 14.11

he casts the wicked down to ruin.
[13] If you close your ear to the cry of the poor,
you will cry out and not be heard.
[14] A gift in secret averts anger;
and a concealed bribe in the bosom,
strong wrath.
[15] When justice is done, it is a joy to the
righteous,
but dismay to evildoers.
[16] Whoever wanders from the way of
understanding
will rest in the assembly of the dead.
[17] Whoever loves pleasure will suffer want;
whoever loves wine and oil will not
be rich.
[18] The wicked is a ransom for the righteous,
and the faithless for the upright.
[19] It is better to live in a desert land
than with a contentious and fretful wife.
[20] Precious treasure remains[i] in the house
of the wise,
but the fool devours it.
[21] Whoever pursues righteousness and
kindness
will find life[j] and honor.
[22] One wise person went up against a city
of warriors
and brought down the stronghold in
which they trusted.
[23] To watch over mouth and tongue
is to keep out of trouble.
[24] The proud, haughty person, named
"Scoffer,"
acts with arrogant pride.
[25] The craving of the lazy person is fatal,
for lazy hands refuse to labor.
[26] All day long the wicked covet,[k]
but the righteous give and do not
hold back.
[27] The sacrifice of the wicked is an
abomination;
how much more when brought with
evil intent.
[28] A false witness will perish,
but a good listener will testify
successfully.
[29] The wicked put on a bold face,
but the upright give thought to[l] their
ways.
[30] No wisdom, no understanding, no
counsel,
can avail against the LORD.
[31] The horse is made ready for the day of
battle,
but the victory belongs to the LORD.

22 A good name is to be chosen
rather than great riches,
and favor is better than silver or
gold.
[2] The rich and the poor have this in
common:
the LORD is the maker of them all.
[3] The clever see danger and hide;
but the simple go on, and suffer for it.
[4] The reward for humility and fear of the
LORD
is riches and honor and life.
[5] Thorns and snares are in the way of the
perverse;
the cautious will keep far from them.
[6] Train children in the right way,
and when old, they will not stray.
[7] The rich rules over the poor,
and the borrower is the slave of the
lender.
[8] Whoever sows injustice will reap
calamity,
and the rod of anger will fail.
[9] Those who are generous are blessed,
for they share their bread with the poor.
[10] Drive out a scoffer, and strife goes out;
quarreling and abuse will cease.
[11] Those who love a pure heart and are
gracious in speech
will have the king as a friend.
[12] The eyes of the LORD keep watch over
knowledge,
but he overthrows the words of the
faithless.
[13] The lazy person says, "There is a lion
outside!
I shall be killed in the streets!"
[14] The mouth of a loose[m] woman is a deep pit;
he with whom the LORD is angry falls
into it.
[15] Folly is bound up in the heart of a boy,
but the rod of discipline drives it far
away.
[16] Oppressing the poor in order to enrich
oneself,
and giving to the rich, will lead only
to loss.

Sayings of the Wise

[17] The words of the wise:

Incline your ear and hear my words,[n]
and apply your mind to my teaching;
[18] for it will be pleasant if you keep them

21.13 Mt 18.30-34; 1 Jn 3.17; Jas 2.13
21.14 Prov 18.16; 19.6
21.16 Ps 49.14
21.18 Prov 11.8
21.19 ver 9
21.20 Prov 22.4; Job 20.15,18
21.21 Mt 5.6
21.22 Eccl 9.15,16
21.23 Prov 12.13; Jas 3.2
21.24 Ps 1.1; Prov 1.22; Isa 16.6; Jer 48.29
21.25 Prov 13.4; 20.4
21.26 Ps 37.26; Mt 5.42; Eph 4.28
21.27 Isa 66.3; Jer 6.20; Am 5.22
21.28 Prov 19.5,9
21.29 Eccl 8.1
21.30 Isa 8.9,10; Jer 9.23; Acts 5.39
21.31 Isa 31.1; Ps 3.8; 1 Cor 15.28
22.1 Eccl 7.1
22.5 Prov 15.19
22.6 Eph 6.4
22.7 Prov 18.23; Jas 2.6
22.8 Prov 24.16; Ps 125.3
22.9 2 Cor 9.6
22.10 Prov 18.6; 26.20
22.11 Mt 5.8; Prov 16.13
22.12 Prov 21.12
22.13 Prov 26.13
22.15 Prov 13.24; 23.14

22.1-16 Many of these proverbs deal with social and economic status. Integrity and generosity are esteemed above wealth, but *the reward* for those who fear the LORD is *riches, honor and life.* Diligence and discipline are also praised.
22.17-24.34 Sayings of the Wise. There are parallels between these proverbs and older Egyptian wisdom from about 1500 BCE.
22.17-21 The introduction to this collection of *sayings of admonition and knowledge* calls for *trust in the LORD,* and reminds the hearer of the speaker's repeated declarations of wisdom which an emissary is to convey to the ruler who sent him to investigate.

[i] Gk: Heb *and oil* [j] Gk: Heb *life and righteousness* [k] Gk: Heb *all day long one covets covetously* [l] Another reading is *establish* [m] Heb *strange* [n] Cn Compare Gk: Heb *Incline your ear, and hear the words of the wise*

22.22-24.34 The wide range of subjects covered includes temperance in eating and drinking (23.1-7,19-21,29-35), the transmission of wisdom through parents and families (23.12-15, 22-125), stability and security achieved through wisdom (24.3-7), and generosity toward neighbors (24.28-29).

within you,
if all of them are ready on your lips.
19 So that your trust may be in the LORD,
I have made them known to you
today—yes, to you.
20 Have I not written for you thirty sayings
of admonition and knowledge,
21 to show you what is right and true,
so that you may give a true answer
to those who sent you?

22 Do not rob the poor because they are
poor,
or crush the afflicted at the gate;
23 for the LORD pleads their cause
and despoils of life those who despoil
them.
24 Make no friends with those given to anger,
and do not associate with hotheads,
25 or you may learn their ways
and entangle yourself in a snare.
26 Do not be one of those who give pledges,
who become surety for debts.
27 If you have nothing with which to pay,
why should your bed be taken from
under you?
28 Do not remove the ancient landmark
that your ancestors set up.
29 Do you see those who are skillful in
their work?
they will serve kings;
they will not serve common people.

23

When you sit down to eat with a
ruler,
observe carefully what[o] is before you,
2 and put a knife to your throat
if you have a big appetite.
3 Do not desire the ruler's[p] delicacies,
for they are deceptive food.
4 Do not wear yourself out to get rich;
be wise enough to desist.
5 When your eyes light upon it, it is gone;
for suddenly it takes wings to itself,
flying like an eagle toward heaven.
6 Do not eat the bread of the stingy;
do not desire their delicacies;
7 for like a hair in the throat, so are they.[q]
"Eat and drink!" they say to you;
but they do not mean it.
8 You will vomit up the little you have
eaten,
and you will waste your pleasant words.
9 Do not speak in the hearing of a fool,
who will only despise the wisdom of
your words.
10 Do not remove an ancient landmark
or encroach on the fields of orphans,
11 for their redeemer is strong;
he will plead their cause against you.
12 Apply your mind to instruction
and your ear to words of knowledge.
13 Do not withhold discipline from your
children;
if you beat them with a rod, they will
not die.
14 If you beat them with the rod,
you will save their lives from Sheol.
15 My child, if your heart is wise,
my heart too will be glad.
16 My soul will rejoice
when your lips speak what is right.
17 Do not let your heart envy sinners,
but always continue in the fear of the
LORD.
18 Surely there is a future,
and your hope will not be cut off.

19 Hear, my child, and be wise,
and direct your mind in the way.
20 Do not be among winebibbers,
or among gluttonous eaters of meat;
21 for the drunkard and the glutton will
come to poverty,
and drowsiness will clothe them with
rags.

22 Listen to your father who begot you,
and do not despise your mother when
she is old.
23 Buy truth, and do not sell it;
buy wisdom, instruction, and
understanding.
24 The father of the righteous will greatly
rejoice;
he who begets a wise son will be glad
in him.
25 Let your father and mother be glad;
let her who bore you rejoice.

26 My child, give me your heart,
and let your eyes observe[r] my ways.
27 For a prostitute is a deep pit;
an adulteress[s] is a narrow well.
28 She lies in wait like a robber
and increases the number of the
faithless.

29 Who has woe? Who has sorrow?
Who has strife? Who has
complaining?
Who has wounds without cause?

[o] Or *who* [p] Heb *his* [q] Meaning of Heb uncertain [r] Another reading is *delight in* [s] Heb *an alien woman*

22.19 Prov 3.5
22.20 Prov 8.6,10
22.21 Lk 1.3,4
22.22 Zech 7.10; Mal 3.5
22.23 1 Sam 25.39; Ps 12.5; 35.10; Prov 23.11
22.26 Prov 11.15
22.28 Prov 23.10
22.29 Rom 12.11; 1 Kings 10.8
23.3 ver 6; Ps 141.4
23.4 Prov 28.20; 1 Tim 6.9,10; Rom 12.16
23.6 Ps 141.4
23.7 Prov 26.24,25
23.9 Mt 7.6; Prov 1.7
23.10 Prov 22.28; Jer 22.3; Zech 7.10
23.11 Prov 22.23
23.12 Prov 22.17
23.13 Prov 13.24; 19.18; 22.15
23.17 Ps 37.1; Prov 28.14
23.20 Isa 5.22; Mt 24.49; Lk 21.34; Rom 13.13; Eph 5.18
23.21 Prov 21.17; 6.10,11
23.22 Prov 1.8; 30.17; Eph 6.1
23.23 Prov 4.5,7; Mt 13.44
23.24 Prov 10.1; 15.20
23.26 Prov 3.1; 4.4; Ps 1.2
23.27 Prov 22.14
23.28 Prov 7.12; Eccl 7.26
23.29 Isa 5.11,22

23.30 Eph 5.18; Ps 75.8
23.33 Prov 2.12
23.35 Jer 5.3
24.1 Ps 37.1; 73.3; Prov 3.31
24.2 Jer 22.17; Job 15.35
24.3 Prov 9.1
24.5 Prov 21.22
24.6 Lk 14.31
24.7 Ps 10.5
24.8 Prov 6.14; Rom 1.30
24.10 Jer 51.46; Heb 12.3
24.11 Ps 82.4; Isa 58.6,7
24.12 Prov 21.2; Eccl 5.8; Ps 121.3-8; 94.9-11; Prov 12.14
24.13 Song 5.1
24.14 Prov 2.10
24.15 Ps 10.9,10
24.16 Ps 34.19; Mic 7.8; ver 22
24.17 Job 31.29; Ob 12
24.19 Ps 37.1
24.20 Prov 13.9
24.21 Rom 13.1-7; 1 Pet 2.17
24.23 Prov 1.6; 18.5; Lev 19.15; Deut 1.17
24.24 Prov 17.15
24.25 Prov 28.23

Who has redness of eyes?
30 Those who linger late over wine,
those who keep trying mixed wines.
31 Do not look at wine when it is red,
when it sparkles in the cup
and goes down smoothly.
32 At the last it bites like a serpent,
and stings like an adder.
33 Your eyes will see strange things,
and your mind utter perverse things.
34 You will be like one who lies down in
the midst of the sea,
like one who lies on the top of a
mast.[t]
35 "They struck me," you will say,[u] "but I
was not hurt;
they beat me, but I did not feel it.
When shall I awake?
I will seek another drink."

24 Do not envy the wicked,
nor desire to be with them;
2 for their minds devise violence,
and their lips talk of mischief.

3 By wisdom a house is built,
and by understanding it is established;
4 by knowledge the rooms are filled
with all precious and pleasant riches.
5 Wise warriors are mightier than strong
ones,[v]
and those who have knowledge than
those who have strength;
6 for by wise guidance you can wage your
war,
and in abundance of counselors there
is victory.
7 Wisdom is too high for fools;
in the gate they do not open their
mouths.

8 Whoever plans to do evil
will be called a mischief-maker.
9 The devising of folly is sin,
and the scoffer is an abomination to all.

10 If you faint in the day of adversity,
your strength being small;
11 if you hold back from rescuing those
taken away to death,
those who go staggering to the
slaughter;
12 if you say, "Look, we did not know
this"—
does not he who weighs the heart
perceive it?
Does not he who keeps watch over your
soul know it?
And will he not repay all according to
their deeds?

13 My child, eat honey, for it is good,
and the drippings of the honeycomb
are sweet to your taste.
14 Know that wisdom is such to your soul;
if you find it, you will find a future,
and your hope will not be cut off.

15 Do not lie in wait like an outlaw against
the home of the righteous;
do no violence to the place where the
righteous live;
16 for though they fall seven times, they
will rise again;
but the wicked are overthrown by
calamity.

17 Do not rejoice when your enemies fall,
and do not let your heart be glad
when they stumble,
18 or else the LORD will see it and be
displeased,
and turn away his anger from them.

19 Do not fret because of evildoers.
Do not envy the wicked;
20 for the evil have no future;
the lamp of the wicked will go out.

21 My child, fear the LORD and the king,
and do not disobey either of them;[w]
22 for disaster comes from them suddenly,
and who knows the ruin that both
can bring?

Further Sayings of the Wise

23 These also are sayings of the wise:

Partiality in judging is not good.
24 Whoever says to the wicked, "You are
innocent,"
will be cursed by peoples, abhorred by
nations;
25 but those who rebuke the wicked will
have delight,
and a good blessing will come upon
them.
26 One who gives an honest answer
gives a kiss on the lips.

[t] Meaning of Heb uncertain [u] Gk Syr Vg Tg: Heb lacks *you will say* [v] Gk Compare Syr Tg: Heb *A wise man is strength* [w] Gk: Heb *do not associate with those who change*

25.1-29.27 Wise Sayings Attributed to Solomon. This is probably the oldest segment of the Book of Proverbs, and may include material which goes back to Solomon, as claimed in 25.1. King Hezekiah of Judah (reigned 715-687 BCE) is given credit for having copied these documents, perhaps as part of the restoration projects for the temple and priesthood launched by him according to 2 Chr 29-31. The themes considered in this material include the wisdom and power of kings (25.1-10,15), generosity toward one's enemies (25.21-23), and appropriate compensation for the hostile, the lazy and fools (26.1-27.3). To *heap coals of fire on the heads* of one's enemies is to make them penitent and put them to shame by one's generosity, although the figure of speech may build on an Egyptian custom by which a penitent person literally put hot coals on his head as evidence of his contrition.

27 Prepare your work outside,
get everything ready for you in the field;
and after that build your house.

28 Do not be a witness against your neighbor without cause,
and do not deceive with your lips.
29 Do not say, "I will do to others as they have done to me;
I will pay them back for what they have done."

30 I passed by the field of one who was lazy,
by the vineyard of a stupid person;
31 and see, it was all overgrown with thorns;
the ground was covered with nettles,
and its stone wall was broken down.
32 Then I saw and considered it;
I looked and received instruction.
33 A little sleep, a little slumber,
a little folding of the hands to rest,
34 and poverty will come upon you like a robber,
and want, like an armed warrior.

Further Wise Sayings of Solomon

25 These are other proverbs of Solomon that the officials of King Hezekiah of Judah copied.

2 It is the glory of God to conceal things,
but the glory of kings is to search things out.
3 Like the heavens for height, like the earth for depth,
so the mind of kings is unsearchable.
4 Take away the dross from the silver,
and the smith has material for a vessel;
5 take away the wicked from the presence of the king,
and his throne will be established in righteousness.
6 Do not put yourself forward in the king's presence
or stand in the place of the great;
7 for it is better to be told, "Come up here,"
than to be put lower in the presence of a noble.
What your eyes have seen
8 do not hastily bring into court;
for[x] what will you do in the end,
when your neighbor puts you to shame?
9 Argue your case with your neighbor directly,
and do not disclose another's secret;
10 or else someone who hears you will bring shame upon you,
and your ill repute will have no end.

11 A word fitly spoken
is like apples of gold in a setting of silver.
12 Like a gold ring or an ornament of gold
is a wise rebuke to a listening ear.
13 Like the cold of snow in the time of harvest
are faithful messengers to those who send them;
they refresh the spirit of their masters.
14 Like clouds and wind without rain
is one who boasts of a gift never given.
15 With patience a ruler may be persuaded,
and a soft tongue can break bones.
16 If you have found honey, eat only enough for you,
or else, having too much, you will vomit it.
17 Let your foot be seldom in your neighbor's house,
otherwise the neighbor will become weary of you and hate you.
18 Like a war club, a sword, or a sharp arrow
is one who bears false witness against a neighbor.
19 Like a bad tooth or a lame foot
is trust in a faithless person in time of trouble.
20 Like vinegar on a wound[y]
is one who sings songs to a heavy heart.
Like a moth in clothing or a worm in wood,
sorrow gnaws at the human heart.[z]
21 If your enemies are hungry, give them bread to eat;
and if they are thirsty, give them water to drink;
22 for you will heap coals of fire on their heads,
and the LORD will reward you.

[x] Cn: Heb *or else* [y] Gk: Heb *Like one who takes off a garment on a cold day, like vinegar on lye* [z] Gk Syr Tg: Heb lacks *Like a moth ... human heart*

24.28 Prov 25.18; Eph 4.25
24.29 Prov 20.22; Mt 5.39; Rom 12.17
24.30 Prov 6.6-11
24.33 Prov 6.9; 20.13
25.1 Prov 1.1
25.2 Deut 29.29; Ezra 6.1
25.4 2 Tim 2.21
25.5 Prov 20.8; 16.12
25.7 Lk 14.7-11
25.8 Mt 5.25
25.9 Mt 18.15; Prov 11.13
25.11 Prov 15.23
25.12 Prov 15.31; 20.12
25.13 ver 25; Prov 13.17
25.14 Prov 20.6; Jude 12
25.15 Gen 32.4; 1 Sam 25.24; Prov 15.1; 16.14
25.16 ver 27
25.18 Ps 57.4; Prov 12.18
25.21 Ex 23.4,5; Mt 5.44; Rom 12.20
25.22 2 Sam 16.12

23 The north wind produces rain,
and a backbiting tongue, angry looks.
24 It is better to live in a corner of the housetop
than in a house shared with a contentious wife.
25 Like cold water to a thirsty soul,
so is good news from a far country.
26 Like a muddied spring or a polluted fountain
are the righteous who give way before the wicked.
27 It is not good to eat much honey,
or to seek honor on top of honor.
28 Like a city breached, without walls,
is one who lacks self-control.

26 Like snow in summer or rain in harvest,
so honor is not fitting for a fool.
2 Like a sparrow in its flitting, like a swallow in its flying,
an undeserved curse goes nowhere.
3 A whip for the horse, a bridle for the donkey,
and a rod for the back of fools.
4 Do not answer fools according to their folly,
or you will be a fool yourself.
5 Answer fools according to their folly,
or they will be wise in their own eyes.
6 It is like cutting off one's foot and drinking down violence,
to send a message by a fool.
7 The legs of a disabled person hang limp;
so does a proverb in the mouth of a fool.
8 It is like binding a stone in a sling
to give honor to a fool.
9 Like a thornbush brandished by the hand of a drunkard
is a proverb in the mouth of a fool.
10 Like an archer who wounds everybody
is one who hires a passing fool or drunkard.[a]
11 Like a dog that returns to its vomit
is a fool who reverts to his folly.
12 Do you see persons wise in their own eyes?
There is more hope for fools than for them.
13 The lazy person says, "There is a lion in the road!
There is a lion in the streets!"
14 As a door turns on its hinges,
so does a lazy person in bed.
15 The lazy person buries a hand in the dish,
and is too tired to bring it back to the mouth.
16 The lazy person is wiser in self-esteem
than seven who can answer discreetly.
17 Like somebody who takes a passing dog by the ears
is one who meddles in the quarrel of another.
18 Like a maniac who shoots deadly firebrands and arrows,
19 so is one who deceives a neighbor
and says, "I am only joking!"
20 For lack of wood the fire goes out,
and where there is no whisperer, quarreling ceases.
21 As charcoal is to hot embers and wood to fire,
so is a quarrelsome person for kindling strife.
22 The words of a whisperer are like delicious morsels;
they go down into the inner parts of the body.
23 Like the glaze[b] covering an earthen vessel
are smooth[c] lips with an evil heart.
24 An enemy dissembles in speaking
while harboring deceit within;
25 when an enemy speaks graciously, do not believe it,
for there are seven abominations concealed within;
26 though hatred is covered with guile,
the enemy's wickedness will be exposed in the assembly.
27 Whoever digs a pit will fall into it,
and a stone will come back on the one who starts it rolling.
28 A lying tongue hates its victims,
and a flattering mouth works ruin.

27 Do not boast about tomorrow,
for you do not know what a day may bring.
2 Let another praise you, and not your own mouth—
a stranger, and not your own lips.
3 A stone is heavy, and sand is weighty,
but a fool's provocation is heavier than both.
4 Wrath is cruel, anger is overwhelming,
but who is able to stand before jealousy?
5 Better is open rebuke
than hidden love.
6 Well meant are the wounds a friend inflicts,

[a] Meaning of Heb uncertain [b] Cn: Heb *silver of dross* [c] Gk: Heb *burning*

25.23 Ps 101.5 **25.24** Prov 21.9 **25.25** ver 13; Prov 15.30 **25.26** Ezek 32.2; 34.18,19 **25.27** ver 16; Prov 27.2 **25.28** Prov 16.32 **26.1** 1 Sam 12.17 **26.2** Num 23.8; Deut 23.5 **26.3** Ps 32.9 **26.4** Prov 23.9; 29.9 **26.5** Mt 16.1-4; 21.24-27 **26.7** ver 9 **26.8** ver 1 **26.9** ver 7 **26.11** 2 Pet 2.22; Ex 8.15 **26.12** ver 5; Prov 3.7; 29.20 **26.13** Prov 22.13 **26.15** Prov 19.24 **26.17** Prov 3.30 **26.18** Isa 50.11 **26.19** Prov 24.28 **26.20** Prov 16.28; 22.10 **26.21** Prov 15.18 **26.22** Prov 18.8 **26.24** Prov 10.18; 12.20 **26.25** Ps 28.3; Jer 9.8 **26.26** Mt 23.28; Lk 8.17 **26.27** Ps 7.15; Prov 28.10; Eccl 10.8 **26.28** Prov 29.5 **27.1** Lk 12.19,20; Jas 4.14 **27.2** Prov 25.27; 2 Cor 10.12,18 **27.3** Prov 12.16 **27.5** Prov 28.23

27.4-22 Human relations are depicted here in matters of love, jealousy, insults, fidelity toward one's neighbors and masters, the temptation to become proud when praised, and the impossibility of changing a fool even through disaster.

27.23-29.27 The qualities commended here are integrity (28.19), trust in the LORD (28.25), generosity (28.27), restraint (29.11), humility (29.23), and uprightness (29.27). An important theme is advice to rulers: 28.3,16; 29.2,4,14,16. Wisdom manifests itself through keeping the law (28.4,7,9). This is linked in 29.18 with attention to *prophecy*, which refers to obedience to the word of God through the ones empowered to speak for him, rather than to prophetic predictions alone. The section ends (25.27) with an assertion of the basic incompatibility of the righteous and the wicked.

but profuse are the kisses of an
enemy.
7 The sated appetite spurns honey,
but to a ravenous appetite even the
bitter is sweet.
8 Like a bird that strays from its nest
is one who strays from home.
9 Perfume and incense make the heart
glad,
but the soul is torn by trouble.[d]
10 Do not forsake your friend or the friend
of your parent;
do not go to the house of your
kindred in the day of your
calamity.
Better is a neighbor who is nearby
than kindred who are far away.
11 Be wise, my child, and make my heart
glad,
so that I may answer whoever
reproaches me.
12 The clever see danger and hide;
but the simple go on, and suffer for it.
13 Take the garment of one who has given
surety for a stranger;
seize the pledge given as surety for
foreigners.[e]
14 Whoever blesses a neighbor with a loud
voice,
rising early in the morning,
will be counted as cursing.
15 A continual dripping on a rainy day
and a contentious wife are alike;
16 to restrain her is to restrain the wind
or to grasp oil in the right hand.[f]
17 Iron sharpens iron,
and one person sharpens the wits[g] of
another.
18 Anyone who tends a fig tree will eat its
fruit,
and anyone who takes care of a
master will be honored.
19 Just as water reflects the face,
so one human heart reflects another.
20 Sheol and Abaddon are never satisfied,
and human eyes are never satisfied.
21 The crucible is for silver, and the
furnace is for gold,
so a person is tested[h] by being praised.
22 Crush a fool in a mortar with a pestle
along with crushed grain,
but the folly will not be driven out.

23 Know well the condition of your flocks,
and give attention to your herds;
24 for riches do not last forever,
nor a crown for all generations.
25 When the grass is gone, and new
growth appears,
and the herbage of the mountains is
gathered,
26 the lambs will provide your clothing,
and the goats the price of a field;
27 there will be enough goats' milk for
your food,
for the food of your household
and nourishment for your servant-
girls.

28 The wicked flee when no one
pursues,
but the righteous are as bold as a lion.
2 When a land rebels
it has many rulers;
but with an intelligent ruler
there is lasting order.[f]
3 A ruler[i] who oppresses the poor
is a beating rain that leaves no food.
4 Those who forsake the law praise the
wicked,
but those who keep the law struggle
against them.
5 The evil do not understand justice,
but those who seek the LORD
understand it completely.
6 Better to be poor and walk in integrity
than to be crooked in one's ways
even though rich.
7 Those who keep the law are wise
children,
but companions of gluttons shame
their parents.
8 One who augments wealth by
exorbitant interest
gathers it for another who is kind to
the poor.
9 When one will not listen to the law,
even one's prayers are an
abomination.
10 Those who mislead the upright into evil
ways
will fall into pits of their own making,
but the blameless will have a goodly
inheritance.
11 The rich is wise in self-esteem,
but an intelligent poor person sees
through the pose.
12 When the righteous triumph, there is
great glory,
but when the wicked prevail, people
go into hiding.

[d] Gk: Heb *the sweetness of a friend is better than one's own counsel* [e] Vg and 20.16: Heb *for a foreign woman* [f] Meaning of Heb uncertain [g] Heb *face* [h] Heb lacks *is tested* [i] Cn: Heb *A poor person*

27.7 Prov 25.16
27.10 2 Chr 10.6-8; Prov 17.17; 18.24
27.11 Prov 10.1; 23.15; Ps 119.42
27.12 Prov 22.3
27.13 Prov 20.16
27.15 Prov 19.13
27.18 1 Cor 9.7; Lk 12.42-44; 19.17
27.20 Hab 2.5; Eccl 1.8
27.21 Lk 6.26
27.22 Prov 23.35; Jer 5.3
27.24 Prov 23.5; Job 19.9
27.25 Ps 104.14
28.1 Lev 26.17; Ps 53.5
28.2 Prov 11.11
28.3 Mt 18.28
28.4 Rom 1.32; 1 Kings 18.18
28.5 Ps 92.6; Jn 7.17; 1 Cor 2.15
28.6 Prov 19.1; ver 18
28.7 Prov 23.20
28.8 Lev 26.36; Prov 13.22; 14.31
28.9 Ps 66.18; Prov 15.8
28.10 Prov 26.27; Mt 6.33; Heb 6.12
28.11 Prov 26.5,12; 18.17
28.12 Prov 11.10; Eccl 10.5,6

28.13 Ps 32.3,5
28.14 Ps 16.8; Rom 2.5
28.15 1 Pet 5.8; Mt 2.16
28.17 Gen 9.6; Ex 21.14
28.18 Prov 10.9,25; ver 6
28.19 Prov 12.11
28.20 Prov 10.6; ver 22; 1 Tim 6.9
28.23 Prov 27.5,6
28.24 Prov 19.26; 18.9
28.25 Prov 15.27; 29.25
28.27 Deut 15.7; Prov 19.17; 21.13
29.1 1 Sam 2.25; 2 Chr 36.16; Prov 6.15
29.2 Esth 8.15; Prov 28.15
29.3 Prov 10.1; 5.9,10; Lk 15.13
29.7 Job 29.16; Ps 41.1
29.8 Prov 11.11; 16.14
29.10 1 Jn 3.12
29.11 Prov 12.16; 19.11
29.13 Ps 13.3
29.14 Ps 72.4; Isa 11.4; Prov 16.12; 25.5
29.15 Prov 13.24; 10.1
29.16 Ps 37.36; 58.10; 91.8; 92.11
29.17 ver 15; Prov 10.1
29.18 1 Sam 3.1; Am 8.11,12; Jn 13.17

13 No one who conceals transgressions will prosper,
but one who confesses and forsakes them will obtain mercy.
14 Happy is the one who is never without fear,
but one who is hard-hearted will fall into calamity.
15 Like a roaring lion or a charging bear
is a wicked ruler over a poor people.
16 A ruler who lacks understanding is a cruel oppressor;
but one who hates unjust gain will enjoy a long life.
17 If someone is burdened with the blood of another,
let that killer be a fugitive until death;
let no one offer assistance.
18 One who walks in integrity will be safe,
but whoever follows crooked ways will fall into the Pit.[j]
19 Anyone who tills the land will have plenty of bread,
but one who follows worthless pursuits will have plenty of poverty.
20 The faithful will abound with blessings,
but one who is in a hurry to be rich will not go unpunished.
21 To show partiality is not good—
yet for a piece of bread a person may do wrong.
22 The miser is in a hurry to get rich
and does not know that loss is sure to come.
23 Whoever rebukes a person will afterward find more favor
than one who flatters with the tongue.
24 Anyone who robs father or mother
and says, "That is no crime,"
is partner to a thug.
25 The greedy person stirs up strife,
but whoever trusts in the LORD will be enriched.
26 Those who trust in their own wits are fools;
but those who walk in wisdom come through safely.
27 Whoever gives to the poor will lack nothing,
but one who turns a blind eye will get many a curse.
28 When the wicked prevail, people go into hiding;
but when they perish, the righteous increase.

29

One who is often reproved, yet remains stubborn,
will suddenly be broken beyond healing.
2 When the righteous are in authority, the people rejoice;
but when the wicked rule, the people groan.
3 A child who loves wisdom makes a parent glad,
but to keep company with prostitutes is to squander one's substance.
4 By justice a king gives stability to the land,
but one who makes heavy exactions ruins it.
5 Whoever flatters a neighbor
is spreading a net for the neighbor's feet.
6 In the transgression of the evil there is a snare,
but the righteous sing and rejoice.
7 The righteous know the rights of the poor;
the wicked have no such understanding.
8 Scoffers set a city aflame,
but the wise turn away wrath.
9 If the wise go to law with fools,
there is ranting and ridicule without relief.
10 The bloodthirsty hate the blameless,
and they seek the life of the upright.
11 A fool gives full vent to anger,
but the wise quietly holds it back.
12 If a ruler listens to falsehood,
all his officials will be wicked.
13 The poor and the oppressor have this in common:
the LORD gives light to the eyes of both.
14 If a king judges the poor with equity,
his throne will be established forever.
15 The rod and reproof give wisdom,
but a mother is disgraced by a neglected child.
16 When the wicked are in authority, transgression increases,
but the righteous will look upon their downfall.
17 Discipline your children, and they will give you rest;
they will give delight to your heart.
18 Where there is no prophecy, the people cast off restraint,
but happy are those who keep the law.

[j] Syr: Heb *fall all at once*

30.1-33 The Wise Sayings of Agur.
30.1 *Agur* and *Jakeh* are mentioned only here. The original Hebrew text may have contained a reference to the tribe of Massa in North Arabia, from which *Lemuel* (31.1) also came, as descendants from Abraham's son, Ishmael (Gen 25.2-18). Some ancient translations of Prov 30.1 are obscure in meaning. As translated here, vs.1 begins the cry of despair at the speaker's inability to comprehend the wisdom of God that is embodied in the complexities of the creation.
30.5-6 Here are affirmed the reliability and the immutability of God's word to his people.
30.7-9 The experience of either prosperity or poverty can undercut reliance upon God.
30.10-14 A series of warnings against denouncing others and exalting oneself.
30.15-31 A group of vivid comparisons and contrasts. The first presents the chronic demands of (1) *Sheol* for more dead bodies, of (2) the *barren womb* for children, of (3) *the earth* for water to allow things to grow, and of (4) *the fire* for fuel. Interspersed among these comparisons are warnings about disobedience to parents (vs.17), the complacency of an adulteress (vs.20), and the effects on humans of inflated pride and unrestrained anger (vv.32-33).

19 By mere words servants are not
disciplined,
for though they understand, they will
not give heed.
20 Do you see someone who is hasty in
speech?
There is more hope for a fool than for
anyone like that.
21 A slave pampered from childhood
will come to a bad end.[k]
22 One given to anger stirs up strife,
and the hothead causes much
transgression.
23 A person's pride will bring humiliation,
but one who is lowly in spirit will
obtain honor.
24 To be a partner of a thief is to hate
one's own life;
one hears the victim's curse, but
discloses nothing.[l]
25 The fear of others[m] lays a snare,
but one who trusts in the LORD is
secure.
26 Many seek the favor of a ruler,
but it is from the LORD that one gets
justice.
27 The unjust are an abomination to the
righteous,
but the upright are an abomination
to the wicked.

Sayings of Agur

30 The words of Agur son of Jakeh. An oracle.

Thus says the man: I am weary, O God,
I am weary, O God. How can I
prevail?[n]
2 Surely I am too stupid to be human;
I do not have human understanding.
3 I have not learned wisdom,
nor have I knowledge of the holy ones.[o]
4 Who has ascended to heaven and come
down?
Who has gathered the wind in the
hollow of the hand?
Who has wrapped up the waters in a
garment?
Who has established all the ends of
the earth?
What is the person's name?
And what is the name of the person's
child?
Surely you know!

5 Every word of God proves true;
he is a shield to those who take
refuge in him.
6 Do not add to his words,
or else he will rebuke you, and you
will be found a liar.

7 Two things I ask of you;
do not deny them to me before I die:
8 Remove far from me falsehood and
lying;
give me neither poverty nor riches;
feed me with the food that I need,
9 or I shall be full, and deny you,
and say, "Who is the LORD?"
or I shall be poor, and steal,
and profane the name of my God.

10 Do not slander a servant to a master,
or the servant will curse you, and
you will be held guilty.

11 There are those who curse their fathers
and do not bless their mothers.
12 There are those who are pure in their
own eyes
yet are not cleansed of their filthiness.
13 There are those—how lofty are their
eyes,
how high their eyelids lift!
14 There are those whose teeth are swords,
whose teeth are knives,
to devour the poor from off the earth,
the needy from among mortals.

15 The leech[l] has two daughters;
"Give, give," they cry.
Three things are never satisfied;
four never say, "Enough":
16 Sheol, the barren womb,
the earth ever thirsty for water,
and the fire that never says, "Enough."[l]

17 The eye that mocks a father
and scorns to obey a mother
will be pecked out by the ravens of the
valley
and eaten by the vultures.

18 Three things are too wonderful for me;
four I do not understand:
19 the way of an eagle in the sky,
the way of a snake on a rock,
the way of a ship on the high seas,
and the way of a man with a girl.

[k] Vg: Meaning of Heb uncertain [l] Meaning of Heb uncertain [m] Or *human fear* [n] Or *I am spent.* Meaning of Heb uncertain [o] Or *Holy One*

29.20 Jas 1.19; Prov 26.12
29.22 Prov 15.18; 17.19
29.23 Job 22.29; Isa 66.2; Dan 4.30; Mt 23.12
29.24 Lev 5.1
29.25 Gen 12.12; Ps 91.1-16
29.26 Isa 49.4
30.1 Prov 31.1
30.2 Ps 73.22
30.3 Prov 9.10
30.4 Jn 3.13; Ps 104.3; Isa 40.12; Job 38.8,9; Isa 45.18
30.5 Ps 12.6; 18.30; 84.11
30.6 Deut 4.2; 12.32; Rev 22.18
30.8 Mt 6.11
30.9 Deut 8.12; Neh 9.25; Job 31.24; Hos 13.6
30.10 Eccl 7.21
30.11 Prov 20.20
30.12 Lk 18.11
30.13 Ps 131.1; Prov 6.17
30.14 Job 29.17; Ps 52.2; 14.4; Am 8.4
30.16 Prov 27.20
30.17 Gen 9.22; Prov 23.22; Deut 28.26

20 This is the way of an adulteress:
she eats, and wipes her mouth,
and says, "I have done no wrong."

21 Under three things the earth trembles;
under four it cannot bear up:
22 a slave when he becomes king,
and a fool when glutted with food;
23 an unloved woman when she gets a
husband,
and a maid when she succeeds her
mistress.

24 Four things on earth are small,
yet they are exceedingly wise:
25 the ants are a people without strength,
yet they provide their food in the
summer;
26 the badgers are a people without power,
yet they make their homes in the
rocks;
27 the locusts have no king,
yet all of them march in rank;
28 the lizard[p] can be grasped in the hand,
yet it is found in kings' palaces.

29 Three things are stately in their stride;
four are stately in their gait:
30 the lion, which is mightiest among wild
animals
and does not turn back before any;
31 the strutting rooster,[q] the he-goat,
and a king striding before[r] his people.

32 If you have been foolish, exalting
yourself,
or if you have been devising evil,
put your hand on your mouth.
33 For as pressing milk produces curds,
and pressing the nose produces blood,
so pressing anger produces strife.

The Teaching of King Lemuel's Mother

31 The words of King Lemuel. An
oracle that his mother taught him:

2 No, my son! No, son of my womb!
No, son of my vows!
3 Do not give your strength to women,
your ways to those who destroy
kings.
4 It is not for kings, O Lemuel,
it is not for kings to drink wine,
or for rulers to desire[s] strong drink;
5 or else they will drink and forget what
has been decreed,
and will pervert the rights of all the
afflicted.
6 Give strong drink to one who is
perishing,
and wine to those in bitter distress;
7 let them drink and forget their poverty,
and remember their misery no more.
8 Speak out for those who cannot speak,
for the rights of all the destitute.[t]
9 Speak out, judge righteously,
defend the rights of the poor and
needy.

Ode to a Capable Wife

10 A capable wife who can find?
She is far more precious than jewels.
11 The heart of her husband trusts in her,
and he will have no lack of gain.
12 She does him good, and not harm,
all the days of her life.
13 She seeks wool and flax,
and works with willing hands.
14 She is like the ships of the merchant,
she brings her food from far away.
15 She rises while it is still night
and provides food for her household
and tasks for her servant-girls.
16 She considers a field and buys it;
with the fruit of her hands she plants
a vineyard.
17 She girds herself with strength,
and makes her arms strong.
18 She perceives that her merchandise is
profitable.
Her lamp does not go out at night.
19 She puts her hands to the distaff,
and her hands hold the spindle.
20 She opens her hand to the poor,
and reaches out her hands to the
needy.
21 She is not afraid for her household
when it snows,
for all her household are clothed in
crimson.
22 She makes herself coverings;
her clothing is fine linen and purple.
23 Her husband is known in the city gates,
taking his seat among the elders of
the land.
24 She makes linen garments and sells
them;
she supplies the merchant with sashes.

[p] Or *spider* [q] Gk Syr Tg Compare Vg: Meaning of Heb uncertain [r] Meaning of Heb uncertain [s] Cn: Heb *where* [t] Heb *all children of passing away*

31.1-31 King Lemuel's Instructions from his Mother. Similar patterns for providing instruction for a ruler have been found in several ancient Near Eastern texts from Egypt and Babylonia.
31.1 As in 30.1, there may be reference to Massa, the North Arabian tribe descended from Abraham through Ishmael (Gen 25.14).
31.2-5 The king is to maintain his strength to rule by avoiding excessive sexual activity and too much wine.
31.6-7 *Strong drink* does, however, have uses: for easing the pain of those near death and for those in hopeless misery.
31.8-9 The major positive recommendation is for the king to uphold the rights of the poor.
31.10-31 Here is offered a detailed description of the roles and qualities of *a capable wife*. Her productivity includes providing textiles (*wool and flax*) and food for *the household*, purchasing and planting vineyards, helping *the poor and needy*, and making clothes for herself and for sale to others. Her personal qualities are to be *strength and dignity*, as well as confidence even in face of the uncertain future. She should convey wisdom and kindness, and be diligent in caring for her household. Her husband and children will join in praising her, and her *fear of the LORD* will result in her being praised for her work (*the fruit of her hand*) by the populace at large (*in the city gates*).

30.20 Prov 5.6
30.22 Prov 19.10
30.25 Prov 6.6-8
30.26 Ps 104.18
30.30 Judg 14.18; Mic 5.8
30.32 Job 21.5; 40.4; Mic 7.16
30.33 Prov 10.12; 29.22
31.1 Prov 30.1
31.2 Isa 49.15
31.3 Prov 5.9; Deut 17.17; 1 Kings 11.1; Neh 13.26
31.4 Eccl 10.17; Prov 20.1
31.5 Hos 4.11
31.8 Job 29.12-17
31.9 Lev 19.15; Deut 1.16
31.10 Prov 12.4; 19.14
31.13 ver 21-24
31.15 Rom 12.11; Lk 12.42
31.20 Eph 4.28; Heb 13.16
31.21 1 Sam 1.24
31.23 Ruth 4.1,11; Prov 12.4

25 Strength and dignity are her clothing,
and she laughs at the time to come.
26 She opens her mouth with wisdom,
and the teaching of kindness is on her tongue.
27 She looks well to the ways of her household,
and does not eat the bread of idleness.
28 Her children rise up and call her happy;
her husband too, and he praises her:
29 "Many women have done excellently,
but you surpass them all."
30 Charm is deceitful, and beauty is vain,
but a woman who fears the LORD is to be praised.
31 Give her a share in the fruit of her hands,
and let her works praise her in the city gates.

31.25 ver 17

31.26 Prov 10.31

31.27 Prov 19.15

31.29 Prov 12.4

31.30 Prov 6.25; 22.4

ECCLESIASTES

See the Introductions, pp. 4, 5, 48, and 52-53 above.

1.1 The Hebrew title, *Qoheleth*, means *one who gathers*, which could refer to assembling the people or to collecting proverbial wisdom. The latter seems to be the subject of this Collector's work. The English title derives from the ancient Latin version, which translated this term as *Ecclesiastes*. The king in Jerusalem would be Solomon, to whom was attributed superiority in wisdom (1 Kings 4.29-34), a claim for him which is repeated in Eccl 1.12-18 and 12.9-10.
1.2-11 Human Existence is Completely Vain. Like the cycles of natural forces (sun, wind, rivers) which repeat themselves, so all human life and experience is *wearisome* in its repetition. Nothing new happens, and the people of the past are lost to human memory.
1.12-18 The Emptiness of the Collector's Efforts. Even though he has made superlative achievements in *experience* and *wisdom*, the whole of the search was as vain as *chasing after wind*, and resulted in sorrow rather than the joy of true and full understanding.

Reflections of a Royal Philosopher

1 The words of the Teacher,[a] the son of David, king in Jerusalem.
2 Vanity of vanities, says the Teacher,[a]
vanity of vanities! All is vanity.
3 What do people gain from all the toil
at which they toil under the sun?
4 A generation goes, and a generation comes,
but the earth remains forever.
5 The sun rises and the sun goes down,
and hurries to the place where it rises.
6 The wind blows to the south,
and goes around to the north;
round and round goes the wind,
and on its circuits the wind returns.
7 All streams run to the sea,
but the sea is not full;
to the place where the streams flow,
there they continue to flow.
8 All things[b] are wearisome;
more than one can express;
the eye is not satisfied with seeing,
or the ear filled with hearing.
9 What has been is what will be,
and what has been done is what will be done;
there is nothing new under the sun.
10 Is there a thing of which it is said,
"See, this is new"?
It has already been,
in the ages before us.
11 The people of long ago are not remembered,
nor will there be any remembrance
of people yet to come
by those who come after them.

The Futility of Seeking Wisdom

12 I, the Teacher,[a] when king over Israel
in Jerusalem, 13applied my mind to seek and
to search out by wisdom all that is done
under heaven; it is an unhappy business
that God has given to human beings to be
busy with. 14I saw all the deeds that are
done under the sun; and see, all is vanity
and a chasing after wind.[c]
15 What is crooked cannot be made straight,
and what is lacking cannot be counted.
16 I said to myself, "I have acquired
great wisdom, surpassing all who were over
Jerusalem before me; and my mind has had
great experience of wisdom and knowledge."
17And I applied my mind to know wisdom
and to know madness and folly. I perceived
that this also is but a chasing after wind.[c]
18 For in much wisdom is much vexation,
and those who increase knowledge increase sorrow.

[a] Heb *Qoheleth*, traditionally rendered *Preacher* [b] Or *words* [c] Or *a feeding on wind.* See Hos 12.1

1.1 ver 12; Eccl 7.27; 12.8-10

1.2 Ps 39.5,6; 62.9; 144.4; Eccl 12.8

1.3 Eccl 2.22; 3.9

1.4 Ps 104.5; 119.90

1.5 Ps 19.5,6

1.6 Eccl 11.5; Jn 3.8

1.8 Prov 27.20

1.9 Eccl 2.12; 3.15

1.13 ver 17; Eccl 3.10

1.14 Eccl 2.11,17

1.15 Eccl 7.13

1.16 1 Kings 3.12,13; 4.30; 10.23; Eccl 2.9

1.17 Eccl 2.3,12; 7.23,25

1.18 Eccl 12.12

The Futility of Self-Indulgence

2 I said to myself, "Come now, I will make a test of pleasure; enjoy yourself." But again, this also was vanity. 2 I said of laughter, "It is mad," and of pleasure, "What use is it?" 3 I searched with my mind how to cheer my body with wine—my mind still guiding me with wisdom—and how to lay hold on folly, until I might see what was good for mortals to do under heaven during the few days of their life. 4 I made great works; I built houses and planted vineyards for myself; 5 I made myself gardens and parks, and planted in them all kinds of fruit trees. 6 I made myself pools from which to water the forest of growing trees. 7 I bought male and female slaves, and had slaves who were born in my house; I also had great possessions of herds and flocks, more than any who had been before me in Jerusalem. 8 I also gathered for myself silver and gold and the treasure of kings and of the provinces; I got singers, both men and women, and delights of the flesh, and many concubines.[d]

9 So I became great and surpassed all who were before me in Jerusalem; also my wisdom remained with me. 10 Whatever my eyes desired I did not keep from them; I kept my heart from no pleasure, for my heart found pleasure in all my toil, and this was my reward for all my toil. 11 Then I considered all that my hands had done and the toil I had spent in doing it, and again, all was vanity and a chasing after wind,[e] and there was nothing to be gained under the sun.

Wisdom and Joy Given to One Who Pleases God

12 So I turned to consider wisdom and madness and folly; for what can the one do who comes after the king? Only what has already been done. 13 Then I saw that wisdom excels folly as light excels darkness.

14 The wise have eyes in their head,
but fools walk in darkness.

Yet I perceived that the same fate befalls all of them. 15 Then I said to myself, "What happens to the fool will happen to me also; why then have I been so very wise?" And I said to myself that this also is vanity. 16 For there is no enduring remembrance of the wise or of fools, seeing that in the days to come all will have been long forgotten. How can the wise die just like fools? 17 So I hated life, because what is done under the sun was grievous to me; for all is vanity and a chasing after wind.[e]

18 I hated all my toil in which I had toiled under the sun, seeing that I must leave it to those who come after me 19 —and who knows whether they will be wise or foolish? Yet they will be master of all for which I toiled and used my wisdom under the sun. This also is vanity. 20 So I turned and gave my heart up to despair concerning all the toil of my labors under the sun, 21 because sometimes one who has toiled with wisdom and knowledge and skill must leave all to be enjoyed by another who did not toil for it. This also is vanity and a great evil. 22 What do mortals get from all the toil and strain with which they toil under the sun? 23 For all their days are full of pain, and their work is a vexation; even at night their minds do not rest. This also is vanity.

24 There is nothing better for mortals than to eat and drink, and find enjoyment in their toil. This also, I saw, is from the hand of God; 25 for apart from him[f] who can eat or who can have enjoyment? 26 For to the one who pleases him God gives wisdom and knowledge and joy; but to the sinner he gives the work of gathering and heaping, only to give to one who pleases God. This also is vanity and a chasing after wind.[e]

Everything Has Its Time

3 For everything there is a season, and a time for every matter under heaven:
2 a time to be born, and a time to die;
a time to plant, and a time to pluck up what is planted;
3 a time to kill, and a time to heal;
a time to break down, and a time to build up;
4 a time to weep, and a time to laugh;
a time to mourn, and a time to dance;
5 a time to throw away stones, and a time to gather stones together;
a time to embrace, and a time to refrain from embracing;
6 a time to seek, and a time to lose;
a time to keep, and a time to throw away;
7 a time to tear, and a time to sew;
a time to keep silence, and a time to speak;
8 a time to love, and a time to hate;
a time for war, and a time for peace.

[d] Meaning of Heb uncertain [e] Or *a feeding on wind.* See Hos 12.1 [f] Gk Syr: Heb *apart from me*

2.1-11 The Futility of Pursuing Pleasure. Abundance of fertile lands, gardens, houses, slaves, wives and personal influence produced for the Collector no enduring satisfaction: *all was vanity.*
2.12-16 The Futility of Pursuing Wisdom. Exploring possibilities as successor to *the king* (David), the Collector pursued *wisdom*, only to find that it provided no *enduring* values. For those who please him, God does provide the basic necessities: to *eat* and *drink*, to gain *knowledge and joy*. But these, too, are only transitory and soon vanish.
3.1-4.3 God's Present and Future Ordering of the World and Human Life.
3.1-8 The ceaseless sequence of time-bound human existence is sketched.

2.1 Lk 12.19; Eccl 1.2
2.2 Prov 14.13; Eccl 7.6
2.4 1 Kings 7.1-12; Song 8.10,11
2.5 Song 4.16; 5.1; Neh 2.8
2.8 1 Kings 9.28; 10.10,14,21; 4.21; 20.14; 2 Sam 19.35
2.9 Eccl 1.16
2.10 Eccl 3.22; 5.18; 9.9
2.11 Eccl 1.3,14
2.12 Eccl 1.17; 7.25
2.14 Prov 17.24; Ps 49.10; Eccl 9.2,3,11
2.15 Eccl 6.8,11
2.17 Eccl 4.2; ver 22,23
2.18 ver 11; Ps 39.6; 49.10
2.20 ver 11
2.21 Eccl 4.4; ver 18
2.22 Eccl 1.3; 3.9
2.23 Job 5.7; 14.1; Eccl 1.18; Ps 127.2
2.24 Eccl 3.12,13,22; 5.18; 8.15
2.26 Job 32.8; 27.16,17; Eccl 1.14
3.1 ver 17; Eccl 8.6
3.2 Heb 9.27
3.4 Rom 12.15; Ps 126.2; Ex 15.20
3.5 1 Cor 7.5
3.7 Am 5.13
3.8 Lk 14.26

The God-Given Task

9 What gain have the workers from their toil? [10]I have seen the business that God has given to everyone to be busy with. [11]He has made everything suitable for its time; moreover he has put a sense of past and future into their minds, yet they cannot find out what God has done from the beginning to the end. [12]I know that there is nothing better for them than to be happy and enjoy themselves as long as they live; [13]moreover, it is God's gift that all should eat and drink and take pleasure in all their toil. [14]I know that whatever God does endures forever; nothing can be added to it, nor anything taken from it; God has done this, so that all should stand in awe before him. [15]That which is, already has been; that which is to be, already is; and God seeks out what has gone by.[g]

Judgment and the Future Belong to God

16 Moreover I saw under the sun that in the place of justice, wickedness was there, and in the place of righteousness, wickedness was there as well. [17]I said in my heart, God will judge the righteous and the wicked, for he has appointed a time for every matter, and for every work. [18]I said in my heart with regard to human beings that God is testing them to show that they are but animals. [19]For the fate of humans and the fate of animals is the same; as one dies, so dies the other. They all have the same breath, and humans have no advantage over the animals; for all is vanity. [20]All go to one place; all are from the dust, and all turn to dust again. [21]Who knows whether the human spirit goes upward and the spirit of animals goes downward to the earth? [22]So I saw that there is nothing better than that all should enjoy their work, for that is their lot; who can bring them to see what will be after them?

4 Again I saw all the oppressions that are practiced under the sun. Look, the tears of the oppressed—with no one to comfort them! On the side of their oppressors there was power—with no one to comfort them. [2]And I thought the dead, who have already died, more fortunate than the living, who are still alive; [3]but better than both is the one who has not yet been, and has not seen the evil deeds that are done under the sun.

4 Then I saw that all toil and all skill in work come from one person's envy of another. This also is vanity and a chasing after wind.[h]

5 Fools fold their hands
and consume their own flesh.
6 Better is a handful with quiet
than two handfuls with toil,
and a chasing after wind.[h]

7 Again, I saw vanity under the sun: [8]the case of solitary individuals, without sons or brothers; yet there is no end to all their toil, and their eyes are never satisfied with riches. "For whom am I toiling," they ask, "and depriving myself of pleasure?" This also is vanity and an unhappy business.

The Value of a Friend

9 Two are better than one, because they have a good reward for their toil. [10]For if they fall, one will lift up the other; but woe to one who is alone and falls and does not have another to help. [11]Again, if two lie together, they keep warm; but how can one keep warm alone? [12]And though one might prevail against another, two will withstand one. A threefold cord is not quickly broken.

13 Better is a poor but wise youth than an old but foolish king, who will no longer take advice. [14]One can indeed come out of prison to reign, even though born poor in the kingdom. [15]I saw all the living who, moving about under the sun, follow that[i] youth who replaced the king;[j] [16]there was no end to all those people whom he led. Yet those who come later will not rejoice in him. Surely this also is vanity and a chasing after wind.[h]

Reverence, Humility, and Contentment

5 [k] Guard your steps when you go to the house of God; to draw near to listen is better than the sacrifice offered by fools; for they do not know how to keep from doing evil.[l] [2m]Never be rash with your mouth, nor let your heart be quick to utter a word before God, for God is in heaven, and you upon earth; therefore let your words be few.

3 For dreams come with many cares, and a fool's voice with many words.

4 When you make a vow to God, do not delay fulfilling it; for he has no pleasure in fools. Fulfill what you vow. [5]It is better that you should not vow than that you should

[g] Heb *what is pursued* [h] Or *a feeding on wind.* See Hos 12.1 [i] Heb *the second* [j] Heb *him* [k] Ch 4.17 in Heb [l] Cn: Heb *they do not know how to do evil* [m] Ch 5.1 in Heb

3.9-22 Since God assigns to every creature its time for existence, there is no greater happiness than taking *pleasure* in one's life and work, conscious that all human and animal life will *turn to dust,* with no prospect of future existence.
4.1-3 Never to have lived at all is preferable to the frustrations and oppressiveness of human life.
4.4-6.12 The Frustrations of Human Existence. A series of proverbial statements about the futility of striving for possessions or security.
4.4-8 It is vain for the envious, for fools or for *solitary individuals* to strive for personal gain, since all their efforts will have no enduring results. *Fools* who decide to do nothing (*fold their hands*) will end by destroying themselves (*consuming their own flesh*).
4.9-12 There are modest benefits from mutual support between friends.
4.13-16 Even though *a wise youth* might have the good fortune to replace a king on the throne (a foolish old man) and gain wide support, he will be forgotten by later generations.
5.1-7 Careful listening in the house of God is better than offering a mindless sacrifice, just as thoughtfulness in addressing God is preferable to *rash* prayers or *many words.* Promises made to God are to be *fulfilled* by the petitioner. God will punish those who speak rashly and will *destroy* vain human efforts.

3.9 Eccl 1.3
3.10 Eccl 1.13
3.11 Gen 1.31; Eccl 8.17; Rom 11.33
3.14 Jas 1.17; Eccl 5.7
3.15 Eccl 1.9; 6.10
3.17 Mt 16.27; Rom 2.6-8; 2 Cor 5.10; 2 Thess 1.6,7; ver 1
3.19 Ps 73.22; Eccl 9.12
3.20 Gen 3.19; Eccl 12.7
3.21 Eccl 12.7
3.22 Eccl 2.24; 5.18; 6.12; 8.7; 10.14
4.1 Eccl 3.16; 5.8
4.3 Eccl 6.3
4.4 Eccl 2.21; 1.14
4.5 Prov 6.10; Isa 9.20
4.6 Prov 15.16,17; 16.8
4.8 Prov 27.20; 1 Jn 2.16
4.11 1 Kings 1.1
4.13 Eccl 9.15
4.14 Gen 41.14,41-43
4.16 Eccl 1.14
5.1 Ex 3.5; Isa 1.12; 1 Sam 15.22; Prov 15.8; 21-27; Hos 6.6
5.2 Prov 20.25; 10.19; Mt 6.7
5.4 Deut 23.21-23; Ps 50.14; 76.11; 66.13,14
5.5 Prov 20.25; Acts 5.4

vow and not fulfill it. [6]Do not let your mouth lead you into sin, and do not say before the messenger that it was a mistake; why should God be angry at your words, and destroy the work of your hands?

7 With many dreams come vanities and a multitude of words;[n] but fear God.

8 If you see in a province the oppression of the poor and the violation of justice and right, do not be amazed at the matter; for the high official is watched by a higher, and there are yet higher ones over them. [9]But all things considered, this is an advantage for a land: a king for a plowed field.[n]

10 The lover of money will not be satisfied with money; nor the lover of wealth, with gain. This also is vanity.

11 When goods increase, those who eat them increase; and what gain has their owner but to see them with his eyes?

12 Sweet is the sleep of laborers, whether they eat little or much; but the surfeit of the rich will not let them sleep.

13 There is a grievous ill that I have seen under the sun: riches were kept by their owners to their hurt, [14]and those riches were lost in a bad venture; though they are parents of children, they have nothing in their hands. [15]As they came from their mother's womb, so they shall go again, naked as they came; they shall take nothing for their toil, which they may carry away with their hands. [16]This also is a grievous ill: just as they came, so shall they go; and what gain do they have from toiling for the wind? [17]Besides, all their days they eat in darkness, in much vexation and sickness and resentment.

18 This is what I have seen to be good: it is fitting to eat and drink and find enjoyment in all the toil with which one toils under the sun the few days of the life God gives us; for this is our lot. [19]Likewise all to whom God gives wealth and possessions and whom he enables to enjoy them, and to accept their lot and find enjoyment in their toil—this is the gift of God. [20]For they will scarcely brood over the days of their lives, because God keeps them occupied with the joy of their hearts.

The Frustration of Desires

6 There is an evil that I have seen under the sun, and it lies heavy upon humankind: [2]those to whom God gives wealth, possessions, and honor, so that they lack nothing of all that they desire, yet God does not enable them to enjoy these things, but a stranger enjoys them. This is vanity; it is a grievous ill. [3]A man may beget a hundred children, and live many years; but however many are the days of his years, if he does not enjoy life's good things, or has no burial, I say that a stillborn child is better off than he. [4]For it comes into vanity and goes into darkness, and in darkness its name is covered; [5]moreover it has not seen the sun or known anything; yet it finds rest rather than he. [6]Even though he should live a thousand years twice over, yet enjoy no good—do not all go to one place?

7 All human toil is for the mouth, yet the appetite is not satisfied. [8]For what advantage have the wise over fools? And what do the poor have who know how to conduct themselves before the living? [9]Better is the sight of the eyes than the wandering of desire; this also is vanity and a chasing after wind.[o]

10 Whatever has come to be has already been named, and it is known what human beings are, and that they are not able to dispute with those who are stronger. [11]The more words, the more vanity, so how is one the better? [12]For who knows what is good for mortals while they live the few days of their vain life, which they pass like a shadow? For who can tell them what will be after them under the sun?

A Disillusioned View of Life

7 A good name is better than precious
ointment,
and the day of death, than the day of
birth.
2 It is better to go to the house of
mourning
than to go to the house of feasting;
for this is the end of everyone,
and the living will lay it to heart.
3 Sorrow is better than laughter,
for by sadness of countenance the
heart is made glad.
4 The heart of the wise is in the house of
mourning;
but the heart of fools is in the house
of mirth.
5 It is better to hear the rebuke of the
wise
than to hear the song of fools.

[n] Meaning of Heb uncertain [o] Or *a feeding on wind.* See Hos 12.1

5.7 Eccl 3.14; 12.13
5.8 Eccl 4.1; Ps 12.5; 58.11; 82.1
5.10 Eccl 2.10,11
5.11 Eccl 2.9
5.12 Prov 3.24
5.13 Eccl 6.1,2
5.15 Job 1.21; Ps 49.17; 1 Tim 6.7
5.16 Eccl 1.3; Prov 11.29
5.17 Eccl 2.23
5.18 Eccl 2.10,24; 3.22
5.19 2 Chr 1.12; Eccl 2.24; 3.13; 6.2
6.1 Eccl 5.13
6.2 1 Kings 3.13; Ps 17.14; 73.7
6.3 2 Kings 9.35; Isa 14.19,20; Jer 22.19; Eccl 4.3
6.7 Prov 16.26
6.8 Eccl 2.15
6.9 Eccl 11.9; 1.14
6.10 Eccl 1.9; Job 9.32; Isa 45.9; Jer 49.19
6.12 Jas 4.14; Ps 39.6; Eccl 8.7
7.1 Prov 15.30; 22.1; Eccl 4.2
7.2 Eccl 2.16; Ps 90.12
7.3 2 Cor 7.10
7.5 Ps 141.5; Prov 13.18; 15.31,32

5.8-20 Warning is given concerning those whose yearning for wealth leads them to commit injustice and deceit. God will hold accountable those who *oppress the poor,* and the efforts of those whose chief aim is to gain riches will be in vain. What is truly *good* is to enjoy one's work and God-given *possession* during the brief span (*few days*) of human life.
6.1-12 Abundance of possessions and offspring is vain unless they are simply accepted as from God: given and enjoyed day by day during the *few days* that humans are granted to live.
7.1-9.18 The Futility of Traditional Human Values.
7.1-4 Sorrow and acceptance of death are preferable to such meaningless activities as revelry and empty mirth.
7.5-14 To accept *rebuke* and *oppression* as divine punishment is wiser than to admire the mindless frivolity of fools. Yet *anger* and worrying over present injustices and human mortality are useless, especially when compared with the satisfaction and comfort that wisdom can bring.

7.15-19 To try to sort out and solve all the riddles and conflicts of human existence is useless. Few men and no women undertake such a task. The Collector found, however, that the puzzles of life are the product of humans, not of God.
8.1-9 There are some modest advantages to gaining *wisdom* (it improves one's appearance) and to obeying the king, even though his rule is temporally limited and may be arbitrary.
8.10-17 Although the *wicked* are honored, and *sinners* continue their wicked ways, God will call them to account. Yet the *righteous* suffer and some of the wicked prosper, so that the only certain value for the wise is the *enjoyment* of life while it lasts. No one can comprehend the *work of God*, so it is useless to try.

6 For like the crackling of thorns under a
pot,
so is the laughter of fools;
this also is vanity.
7 Surely oppression makes the wise
foolish,
and a bribe corrupts the heart.
8 Better is the end of a thing than its
beginning;
the patient in spirit are better than
the proud in spirit.
9 Do not be quick to anger,
for anger lodges in the bosom of fools.
10 Do not say, "Why were the former days
better than these?"
For it is not from wisdom that you
ask this.
11 Wisdom is as good as an inheritance,
an advantage to those who see the
sun.
12 For the protection of wisdom is like the
protection of money,
and the advantage of knowledge is
that wisdom gives life to the one
who possesses it.
13 Consider the work of God;
who can make straight what he has
made crooked?

14 In the day of prosperity be joyful, and
in the day of adversity consider; God has
made the one as well as the other, so that
mortals may not find out anything that will
come after them.

The Riddles of Life

15 In my vain life I have seen everything; there are righteous people who perish in their righteousness, and there are
wicked people who prolong their life in their
evildoing. 16 Do not be too righteous, and do
not act too wise; why should you destroy
yourself? 17 Do not be too wicked, and do not
be a fool; why should you die before your
time? 18 It is good that you should take hold
of the one, without letting go of the other;
for the one who fears God shall succeed
with both.
19 Wisdom gives strength to the wise
more than ten rulers that are in a city.
20 Surely there is no one on earth so
righteous as to do good without ever sinning.
21 Do not give heed to everything that
people say, or you may hear your servant
cursing you; 22 your heart knows that many
times you have yourself cursed others.
23 All this I have tested by wisdom; I
said, "I will be wise," but it was far from
me. 24 That which is, is far off, and deep,
very deep; who can find it out? 25 I turned
my mind to know and to search out and to
seek wisdom and the sum of things, and to
know that wickedness is folly and that foolishness is madness. 26 I found more bitter
than death the woman who is a trap, whose
heart is snares and nets, whose hands are
fetters; one who pleases God escapes her,
but the sinner is taken by her. 27 See, this
is what I found, says the Teacher,[p] adding
one thing to another to find the sum, 28 which
my mind has sought repeatedly, but I have
not found. One man among a thousand I
found, but a woman among all these I have
not found. 29 See, this alone I found, that
God made human beings straightforward,
but they have devised many schemes.

Obey the King and Enjoy Yourself

8 Who is like the wise man?
And who knows the
interpretation of a thing?
Wisdom makes one's face shine,
and the hardness of one's
countenance is changed.
2 Keep[q] the king's command because of
your sacred oath. 3 Do not be terrified; go
from his presence, do not delay when the
matter is unpleasant, for he does whatever
he pleases. 4 For the word of the king is
powerful, and who can say to him, "What
are you doing?" 5 Whoever obeys a command will meet no harm, and the wise
mind will know the time and way. 6 For
every matter has its time and way, although the troubles of mortals lie heavy
upon them. 7 Indeed, they do not know
what is to be, for who can tell them how
it will be? 8 No one has power over the wind[r]
to restrain the wind,[r] or power over the day
of death; there is no discharge from the
battle, nor does wickedness deliver those
who practice it. 9 All this I observed, applying my mind to all that is done under the
sun, while one person exercises authority
over another to the other's hurt.

God's Ways Are Inscrutable

10 Then I saw the wicked buried; they
used to go in and out of the holy place, and
were praised in the city where they had

[p] *Qoheleth*, traditionally rendered *Preacher* [q] Heb *I keep* [r] Or *breath*

7.7 Ex 23.8; Deut 16.19
7.8 ver 1; Prov 14.29; Gal 5.22; Eph 4.2
7.9 Prov 14.17; Jas 1.19
7.11 Prov 8.10,11
7.13 Eccl 3.11; 8.17; 1.15; Isa 14.27
7.14 Eccl 3.4; Deut 8.5
7.15 Eccl 6.12; 8.14
7.16 Rom 12.3
7.19 Eccl 9.13-18
7.20 1 Kings 8.46; 2 Chr 6.36; Prov 20.9; Rom 3.23
7.23 Rom 1.22
7.24 Job 28.12; Rom 11.33
7.25 Eccl 1.17; 2.12
7.26 Prov 5.3,4; 22.14
7.27 Eccl 1.1,2
7.29 Gen 1.27; 3.6,7
8.1 Prov 4.8,9; Deut 28.50
8.2 Ezek 17.18
8.4 Job 9.12; Dan 4.35
8.6 Eccl 3.1,17
8.7 Prov 24.22; Eccl 6.12; 9.12; 10.14
8.8 Ps 49.6,7; Deut 20.5-8; ver 13
8.9 Eccl 4.1; 5.8

8.12 Isa 65.20; Ps 37.11; 18.19; Prov 1.32,33; Isa 3.10,11
8.13 ver 8; Isa 3.11; Eccl 6.12
8.14 Ps 73.14; Eccl 7.15; Job 21.7; Mal 3.15
8.15 Eccl 2.24; 3.12,13; 5.18; 9.7
8.17 Job 5.9; Eccl 3.11; Rom 11.33; Eccl 8.7; Ps 73.16
9.2 Job 9.22; Eccl 6.6; 7.2
9.3 ver 2; Eccl 8.11; 1.17
9.5 Job 14.21; Eccl 1.11; 2.16; Ps 88.12; Isa 26.14
9.6 Eccl 3.22
9.7 Eccl 8.15
9.8 Rev 3.4; Ps 23.5
9.9 Eccl 6.12; 7.15
9.10 Rom 12.11;' Col 3.23; Isa 38.10
9.11 Am 2.14,15; Deut 8.17,18; 1 Sam 6.9
9.12 Eccl 8.7; Prov 29.6; Isa 24.18; Lk 21.34,35
9.15 Eccl 4.13; 2.16; 8.10
9.16 Prov 21.22; Eccl 7.19
9.17 Eccl 7.5; 10.12
9.18 ver 16; Josh 7.1,11,12

done such things.[s] This also is vanity. 11Be-
cause sentence against an evil deed is not
executed speedily, the human heart is fully
set to do evil. 12Though sinners do evil a
hundred times and prolong their lives, yet
I know that it will be well with those who
fear God, because they stand in fear before
him, 13but it will not be well with the
wicked, neither will they prolong their days
like a shadow, because they do not stand
in fear before God.
14 There is a vanity that takes place on
earth, that there are righteous people who
are treated according to the conduct of the
wicked, and there are wicked people who
are treated according to the conduct of the
righteous. I said that this also is vanity. 15So
I commend enjoyment, for there is nothing
better for people under the sun than to eat,
and drink, and enjoy themselves, for this
will go with them in their toil through the
days of life that God gives them under the
sun.
16 When I applied my mind to know
wisdom, and to see the business that is done
on earth, how one's eyes see sleep neither
day nor night, 17then I saw all the work of
God, that no one can find out what is
happening under the sun. However much
they may toil in seeking, they will not find
it out; even though those who are wise
claim to know, they cannot find it out.

Take Life as It Comes

9 All this I laid to heart, examining it
all, how the righteous and the wise
and their deeds are in the hand of God;
whether it is love or hate one does not
know. Everything that confronts them 2is
vanity,[t] since the same fate comes to all, to
the righteous and the wicked, to the good
and the evil,[u] to the clean and the unclean,
to those who sacrifice and those who do not
sacrifice. As are the good, so are the sinners;
those who swear are like those who shun
an oath. 3This is an evil in all that happens
under the sun, that the same fate comes to
everyone. Moreover, the hearts of all are full
of evil; madness is in their hearts while they
live, and after that they go to the dead. 4But
whoever is joined with all the living has
hope, for a living dog is better than a dead
lion. 5The living know that they will die, but
the dead know nothing; they have no more
reward, and even the memory of them is
lost. 6Their love and their hate and their
envy have already perished; never again
will they have any share in all that happens
under the sun.
7 Go, eat your bread with enjoyment,
and drink your wine with a merry heart; for
God has long ago approved what you do.
8Let your garments always be white; do not
let oil be lacking on your head. 9Enjoy life
with the wife whom you love, all the days
of your vain life that are given you under
the sun, because that is your portion in life
and in your toil at which you toil under the
sun. 10Whatever your hand finds to do, do
with your might; for there is no work or
thought or knowledge or wisdom in Sheol,
to which you are going.
11 Again I saw that under the sun the
race is not to the swift, nor the battle to the
strong, nor bread to the wise, nor riches to
the intelligent, nor favor to the skillful; but
time and chance happen to them all. 12For
no one can anticipate the time of disaster.
Like fish taken in a cruel net, and like birds
caught in a snare, so mortals are snared at
a time of calamity, when it suddenly falls
upon them.

Wisdom Superior to Folly

13 I have also seen this example of wisdom under the sun, and it seemed great to
me. 14There was a little city with few people
in it. A great king came against it and
besieged it, building great siegeworks against
it. 15Now there was found in it a poor wise
man, and he by his wisdom delivered the
city. Yet no one remembered that poor
man. 16So I said, "Wisdom is better than
might; yet the poor man's wisdom is despised, and his words are not heeded."

17 The quiet words of the wise are more to
be heeded
than the shouting of a ruler among
fools.
18 Wisdom is better than weapons of war,
but one bungler destroys much good.

Miscellaneous Observations

10 Dead flies make the perfumer's
ointment give off a foul odor;
so a little folly outweighs wisdom and
honor.
2 The heart of the wise inclines to the
right,

[s] Meaning of Heb uncertain [t] Syr Compare Gk: Heb *Everything that confronts them 2is everything* [u] Gk Syr Vg: Heb lacks *and the evil*

9.1-12 Although the *wise* are *in the hand of God*, both the *righteous* and the *evil* face the same end: death. In the place of the dead there is neither knowledge nor *reward*, and all human deeds are gone forever. The wise path, therefore, is to enjoy life – food and drink, spouse and daily work – but all these will also disappear in Sheol, the gloomy realm of the dead. There is no escape from *time and chance*, both of which lead to death.
9.13-11.6 Words of Wisdom.
9.13-18 Even though the advice of *a poor wise man* could save a city under siege, his words are *not heeded*, and he is simply forgotten. The effectiveness of the superior *weapons* of wisdom can be counteracted by the act of a single stupid *bungler*.
10.1-15 *Folly* will easily win out over *wisdom*, so that its champions attain to positions of power *in high places*. Yet the one who possesses wisdom must remain calmly in his *post*, fulfilling his responsibilities, in spite of the anger of the *ruler*, confident that the consequences of human misdeeds will lead to appropriate retribution just as there will be harmful results of the activities of workmen dangerously exposed in pits, quarries and forests. Like a snake-charmer who must use his skill to control a deadly snake, the wise must utilize their insights to avoid harm. *The wise* are not to emulate *the fools* who *talk on and on*, even though they do not know the *future*. The fools could not even find their *way to town*.

10.16-19 Two styles of royal rule are contrasted here: (1) the young upstart *king*, who spends his time in drunken revelry, with the result that *the roof* of his kingdom caves in, while he simply assumes that his new-found wealth will *meet every need*. (2) The truly noble king regulates the life of his subjects and rules with *strength*. No matter what the king is like, those who are wise will not in private *curse* the king and his rich supporters, since they realize that reports of such critical thoughts and comments will surely reach those in power.
10.20-11.6 The Need for the Wise to Gain Foresight and Caution. Like a merchant who *sends out* merchandise overseas with no way of knowing for certain what his profits for the trade may be, the wise are advised to take multiple calculated risks as an offset to possible *disaster*, rather than placing all their resources behind a single transaction. No-one can predict when rain will come or in which direction a tree will fall, but it is wise to observe closely winds and clouds before sowing crops. Just as no-one can understand how the human fetus comes alive in the womb, so no-one can fully comprehend *the work of God*. Diligence is required of wise human beings, since they cannot predict which of their efforts will *prosper*.
11.7-12.8 Preparing Oneself for Old Age. Everyone enjoys the bright days of youth, but all must remember that *the days of darkness* in advanced age will come inevitably. Meanwhile, youth should enjoy life – tempered by the reminder of God's future judgment of all humanity – free of *anxiety* and *pain*. Yet there are solemn reminders of the later years of human life when failing eyesight dims *sun, moon and stars*, when *clouds* overshadow life, when hands *tremble*, backs are *bent*, teeth cease *grinding*, eyes and ears become *shut*, and sexual urges diminish (*the sound of the grinding is low* and *desire fails*; see Judg 16.18-22). One awakes early, is fearful of heights and of travel, and in spite of external stimuli (*the almond blossom*), one drags through life like a decrepit insect. The end of all this is the death of the body and the return of the breath to its source in God (Gen 2.7). The whole human story is absurd: a super-vanity.

but the heart of a fool to the left.
3 Even when fools walk on the road, they lack sense,
and show to everyone that they are fools.
4 If the anger of the ruler rises against you, do not leave your post,
for calmness will undo great offenses.

5 There is an evil that I have seen under
the sun, as great an error as if it proceeded
from the ruler: 6folly is set in many high
places, and the rich sit in a low place. 7I
have seen slaves on horseback, and princes
walking on foot like slaves.

8 Whoever digs a pit will fall into it;
and whoever breaks through a wall will be bitten by a snake.
9 Whoever quarries stones will be hurt by them;
and whoever splits logs will be endangered by them.
10 If the iron is blunt, and one does not whet the edge,
then more strength must be exerted;
but wisdom helps one to succeed.
11 If the snake bites before it is charmed,
there is no advantage in a charmer.

12 Words spoken by the wise bring them favor,
but the lips of fools consume them.
13 The words of their mouths begin in foolishness,
and their talk ends in wicked madness;
14 yet fools talk on and on.
No one knows what is to happen,
and who can tell anyone what the future holds?
15 The toil of fools wears them out,
for they do not even know the way to town.

16 Alas for you, O land, when your king is a servant,[v]
and your princes feast in the morning!
17 Happy are you, O land, when your king is a nobleman,
and your princes feast at the proper time—
for strength, and not for drunkenness!
18 Through sloth the roof sinks in,
and through indolence the house leaks.
19 Feasts are made for laughter;
wine gladdens life,
and money meets every need.
20 Do not curse the king, even in your thoughts,
or curse the rich, even in your bedroom;
for a bird of the air may carry your voice,
or some winged creature tell the matter.

The Value of Diligence

11 Send out your bread upon the waters,
for after many days you will get it back.
2 Divide your means seven ways, or even eight,
for you do not know what disaster may happen on earth.
3 When clouds are full,
they empty rain on the earth;
whether a tree falls to the south or to the north,
in the place where the tree falls, there it will lie.
4 Whoever observes the wind will not sow;
and whoever regards the clouds will not reap.

5 Just as you do not know how the
breath comes to the bones in the mother's
womb, so you do not know the work of
God, who makes everything.

6 In the morning sow your seed, and at
evening do not let your hands be idle; for
you do not know which will prosper, this
or that, or whether both alike will be good.

Youth and Old Age

7 Light is sweet, and it is pleasant for the
eyes to see the sun.

8 Even those who live many years should
rejoice in them all; yet let them remember
that the days of darkness will be many. All
that comes is vanity.

9 Rejoice, young man, while you are
young, and let your heart cheer you in the
days of your youth. Follow the inclination
of your heart and the desire of your eyes,
but know that for all these things God will
bring you into judgment.

10 Banish anxiety from your mind, and
put away pain from your body; for youth
and the dawn of life are vanity.

[v] Or *a child*

10.3 Prov 13.16; 18.2
10.4 Eccl 8.3; 1 Sam 25.24-33; Prov 25.15
10.6 Esth 3.1
10.8 Ps 7.15; Prov 26.27
10.11 Ps 58.4,5; Jer 8.17
10.12 Prov 10.32; Lk 4.22; Prov 10.14; 18.7
10.13 Eccl 7.25
10.14 Prov 15.2; Eccl 3.22; 6.12; 8.7
10.16 Isa 3.4,5.12; 5.11
10.17 Prov 31.4; Isa 5.11
10.18 Prov 24.30-34
10.19 Ps 104.15; Eccl 7.12
10.20 Ex 22.28; Acts 23.5; 2 Kings 6.12; Lk 12.3
11.1 Isa 32.20; Deut 15.10; Prov 19.17; Mt 10.42; 2 Cor 9.8; Gal 6.9,10; Heb 6.10
11.2 Ps 112.9; Lk 6.30; 1 Tim 6.18,19; Eccl 12.1
11.5 Jn 3.8; Ps 139.14,15
11.6 Eccl 9.10
11.7 Eccl 7.11
11.8 Eccl 9.7; 12.1
11.9 Eccl 2.10; Num 15.39; Eccl 3.17; 12.14; Rom 14.10
11.10 2 Cor 7.1; 2 Tim 2.22

12.4 Jer 25.10; 2 Sam 19.35
12.5 Job 17.13; Jer 9.17
12.7 Gen 3.19; Job 34.15; Ps 90.3; Job 34.14; Isa 57.16; Zech 12.1
12.9 1 Kings 4.32
12.10 Prov 10.32; 22.20,21
12.11 Eccl 7.5; Acts 2.37; Ezra 9.8; Isa 22.23
12.13 Deut 4.2; Eccl 8.5; Mic 6.8
12.14 Mt 10.26; 12.36; 1 Cor 4.5

12 Remember your creator in the days of your youth, before the days of trouble come, and the years draw near when you will say, "I have no pleasure in them"; 2 before the sun and the light and the moon and the stars are darkened and the clouds return with[w] the rain; 3 in the day when the guards of the house tremble, and the strong men are bent, and the women who grind cease working because they are few, and those who look through the windows see dimly; 4 when the doors on the street are shut, and the sound of the grinding is low, and one rises up at the sound of a bird, and all the daughters of song are brought low; 5 when one is afraid of heights, and terrors are in the road; the almond tree blossoms, the grasshopper drags itself along[x] and desire fails; because all must go to their eternal home, and the mourners will go about the streets; 6 before the silver cord is snapped,[y] and the golden bowl is broken, and the pitcher is broken at the fountain, and the wheel broken at the cistern, 7 and the dust returns to the earth as it was, and the breath[z] returns to God who gave it. 8 Vanity of vanities, says the Teacher;[a] all is vanity.

Epilogue

9 Besides being wise, the Teacher[a] also taught the people knowledge, weighing and studying and arranging many proverbs. 10 The Teacher[a] sought to find pleasing words, and he wrote words of truth plainly.

11 The sayings of the wise are like goads, and like nails firmly fixed are the collected sayings that are given by one shepherd.[b] 12 Of anything beyond these, my child, beware. Of making many books there is no end, and much study is a weariness of the flesh.

13 The end of the matter; all has been heard. Fear God, and keep his commandments; for that is the whole duty of everyone. 14 For God will bring every deed into judgment, including[c] every secret thing, whether good or evil.

[w] Or *after* ; Heb *'ahar* [x] Or *is a burden* [y] Syr Vg Compare Gk: Heb *is removed* [z] Or *the spirit* [a] *Qoheleth,* traditionally rendered *Preacher* [b] Meaning of Heb uncertain [c] Or *into the judgment on*

12.9-14 Epilogue. First there is a sketch (12.9-10) of the role of the Collector, who gathered this wisdom and conveyed it in such a way as to prod (with *goads* and *nails*) his hearers. His aim as *shepherd* is to care for God's people as his flock. Then (12.11-14) a warning is given to the student (*my child*) to avoid other wisdom collections. What is really necessary *has been heard* already. Now what is essential is that the *fear of God* will be evident through obedience to *his commandments,* since God will call everyone to account for *every deed,* public or private, good or evil.

THE SONG OF SOLOMON

See the Introductions, pp. 4, 48, and 53-54 above.

1.1 1 Kings 4.32
1.2 Song 4.10
1.3 Song 4.10; Eccl 7.1
1.4 Ps 45.14,15
1.5 Song 2.14; 4.3; 2.7; 5.8
1.6 Ps 69.8; Song 8.11
1.7 Song 3.1-4; 2.16; 8.13

1 The Song of Songs, which is Solomon's.

Colloquy of Bride and Friends

2 Let him kiss me with the kisses of his mouth!
For your love is better than wine,
3 your anointing oils are fragrant,
your name is perfume poured out;
therefore the maidens love you.
4 Draw me after you, let us make haste.
The king has brought me into his chambers.
We will exult and rejoice in you;
we will extol your love more than wine;
rightly do they love you.

5 I am black and beautiful,
O daughters of Jerusalem,
like the tents of Kedar,
like the curtains of Solomon.
6 Do not gaze at me because I am dark,
because the sun has gazed on me.
My mother's sons were angry with me;
they made me keeper of the vineyards,
but my own vineyard I have not kept!
7 Tell me, you whom my soul loves,
where you pasture your flock,
where you make it lie down at noon;
for why should I be like one who is veiled
beside the flocks of your companions?

1.1 *Song of Songs* could mean "the greatest song" but here indicates a collection of love songs.
1.2-8 The First Song: The Arrival of the Bride.
1.2-4 The bride-to-be arrives at the royal palace eager to be kissed and taken to the *king's chambers,* since she knows his reputation as a lover. Her attendants, *the girls,* are also attracted by him and *rejoice* in his fame.
1.5-7 The new bride is *dark* because she is from *Kedar* in northern Arabia, where a tribe lived that was linked with Abraham's son, Ishmael (Gen 25.13). Although she has been assigned responsibility for the family *vineyards,* she does not protect her *own vineyard,* which is a symbol for her virginity. In search of the king as her sexual companion, she asks where his flock *lies down* – that is, where he keeps his harem. The newcomer does not want to be treated as a widow (*veiled*) and thereby to be excluded from access to the king.

8 If you do not know,
O fairest among women,
follow the tracks of the flock,
and pasture your kids
beside the shepherds' tents.

Colloquy of Bridegroom, Friends, and Bride

9 I compare you, my love,
to a mare among Pharaoh's chariots.
10 Your cheeks are comely with
ornaments,
your neck with strings of jewels.
11 We will make you ornaments of gold,
studded with silver.

12 While the king was on his couch,
my nard gave forth its fragrance.
13 My beloved is to me a bag of myrrh
that lies between my breasts.
14 My beloved is to me a cluster of henna
blossoms
in the vineyards of En-gedi.

15 Ah, you are beautiful, my love;
ah, you are beautiful;
your eyes are doves.
16 Ah, you are beautiful, my beloved,
truly lovely.
Our couch is green;
17 the beams of our house are cedar,
our rafters[a] are pine.

2 I am a rose[b] of Sharon,
a lily of the valleys.

2 As a lily among brambles,
so is my love among maidens.

3 As an apple tree among the trees of the
wood,
so is my beloved among young men.
With great delight I sat in his shadow,
and his fruit was sweet to my taste.
4 He brought me to the banqueting house,
and his intention toward me was love.
5 Sustain me with raisins,
refresh me with apples;
for I am faint with love.
6 O that his left hand were under my head,
and that his right hand embraced me!
7 I adjure you, O daughters of Jerusalem,
by the gazelles or the wild does:
do not stir up or awaken love
until it is ready!

Springtime Rhapsody

8 The voice of my beloved!
Look, he comes,
leaping upon the mountains,
bounding over the hills.
9 My beloved is like a gazelle
or a young stag.
Look, there he stands
behind our wall,
gazing in at the windows,
looking through the lattice.
10 My beloved speaks and says to me:
"Arise, my love, my fair one,
and come away;
11 for now the winter is past,
the rain is over and gone.
12 The flowers appear on the earth;
the time of singing has come,
and the voice of the turtledove
is heard in our land.
13 The fig tree puts forth its figs,
and the vines are in blossom;
they give forth fragrance.
Arise, my love, my fair one,
and come away.
14 O my dove, in the clefts of the rock,
in the covert of the cliff,
let me see your face,
let me hear your voice;
for your voice is sweet,
and your face is lovely.
15 Catch us the foxes,
the little foxes,
that ruin the vineyards—
for our vineyards are in blossom."

16 My beloved is mine and I am his;
he pastures his flock among the lilies.
17 Until the day breathes
and the shadows flee,
turn, my beloved, be like a gazelle
or a young stag on the cleft
mountains.[c]

Love's Dream

3 Upon my bed at night
I sought him whom my soul loves;
I sought him, but found him not;
I called him, but he gave no answer.[d]
2 "I will rise now and go about the city,
in the streets and in the squares;
I will seek him whom my soul loves."
I sought him, but found him not.
3 The sentinels found me,

[a] Meaning of Heb uncertain [b] Heb *crocus* [c] Or *on the mountains of Bether*: meaning of Heb uncertain [d] Gk: Heb lacks this line

1.8 The *daughters* (vs.5) urge the new prospective bride (*fairest among women*) to follow the crowd of prospective sleeping companions of the king to his *tents*, and to take her attendants (*kids*) with her.
1.9-2.7 The Second Song: The King and the Bride Converse.
1.9-11 The king's first reaction to the woman is to note that she is as richly adorned as a horse drawing the chariot of *Pharaoh*.
1.12-14 The bride remarks that she is bathed in aphrodisiac fragrances, including *henna* from *En-gedi*, a site located on the western shore of the Dead Sea, where archaeologists have found traces of an ancient perfume industry.
1.15 The king is attracted by the woman's beauty, especially by her fluttering *eyes*.
1.16-2.2 After commending the king on the beauty of the bridal chamber and furnishings that he has provided, the bride refers to herself as a simple wildflower (*crocus* is to be preferred to *rose*). The calyx, or rod in the bloom of this lily, combined with mention of the *valley*, are allusions to male and female sexual organs. This fits with the bride's description of his previous love relations with other women as *brambles*.
2.3-7 Picturing her attraction to the king and her eager expectation of a love relationship with him, as is his intention, she feels *faint* at the prospect of this experience and calls for *raisins* and *apples*, both of which were erotic symbols. The union is not yet to be completed, so the present relationship is limited to fondling and caressing. The other women of the harem (*daughters of Jerusalem*) are not to stimulate him further until the proper time for her union with him has come.
2.8-17 The Third Song: The King Approaches.
2.8-10a The bride hears and sees the king approaching, bounding like a young *stag* across the terrain until he reaches and peers into the enclosure (*our wall*) where the women of his harem are.
2.10b-15 His invitation to her includes a celebration of the change she has made in him, which is compared with the dramatic shift of seasons from the gloomy *rain* of winter to the outburst of *flowers*, fruit and wildlife (*turtledoves*) in the spring and early summer. The *clefts* and caves (*covert of the cliffs*) are sexual symbols, as are the muzzles of the foxes which penetrate the *vineyards*.
2.16-17 The bride rejoices at his choice of her from among his *flock* (his harem) to spend the night with him until *the shadows flee*. She invites him now to follow his instincts and take the initiative in the sexual relations.
3.1-5 The Fourth Song: Pre-Marital Relations. Abandoned by the king during the night, the bride *sought* him, at first in vain, as she wandered the *streets* (the palace corridors). Then, on finding him, she clutches him and entices him to penetrate her womb (*mother's house*). Understood literally, the house of her mother would have been that of her father, located in far-off Arabia. Until the sexual union is complete, the *daughters* are ordered to refrain from any advances to the king.

1.8 Song 5.9; 6.1
1.9 Song 2.2,10,13; 2 Chr 1.16
1.10 Ezek 16.11–13
1.14 Song 4.13
1.15 Song 4.1; 5.12
1.17 1 Kings 6.9,10; 2 Chr 3.5
2.1 Isa 35.1,2; Song 5.13; 7.2
2.3 Song 8.5; 4.13
2.4 Ps 20.5
2.5 Song 7.8; 5.8
2.6 Song 8.3
2.7 Song 3.5; 8.4
2.8 ver 17
2.9 ver 17
2.10 ver 13
2.12 Ps 74.19
2.13 Mt 24.32; Song 7.12; ver 10
2.14 Song 5.2; Jer 48.28; Song 8.13; 1.5
2.15 Ezek 13.4
2.16 Song 6.3; 7.10
2.17 Song 4.6; ver 8,9
3.1 Isa 26.9; Song 1.7; 5.6
3.2 Jer 5.1
3.3 Song 5.7

3.4 Song 8.2
3.5 Song 2.7; 8.4
3.6 Song 8.5; 1.13; 4.6,14
3.8 Jer 50.9; Ps 45.3; 91.5
3.10 Song 1.5
3.11 Song 3.16,17
4.1 Song 1.15; 5.12; 6.5,7
4.2 Song 6.6
4.3 Song 6.7
4.4 Song 7.4; Neh 3.19
4.5 Song 7.3; 2.16; 6.2,3
4.6 Song 2.17; ver 14
4.7 Song 1.15
4.8 Song 5.1; Deut 3.9
4.9 ver 10,12; Prov 1.9; Ezek 16.11
4.10 Song 1.2-4
4.11 Prov 5.3; 24.13; Gen 27.27; Hos 14.6
4.12 Prov 5.15-18; Gen 29.3
4.13 Eccl 2.5; Song 6.11; 7.12; ver 16; Song 1.14
4.14 Song 1.12; Ex 30.23; ver 6; Song 3.6; Jn 19.39
4.15 Jn 4.10; 7.38

as they went about in the city.
"Have you seen him whom my soul
loves?"
4 Scarcely had I passed them,
when I found him whom my soul
loves.
I held him, and would not let him go
until I brought him into my mother's
house,
and into the chamber of her that
conceived me.
5 I adjure you, O daughters of Jerusalem,
by the gazelles or the wild does:
do not stir up or awaken love
until it is ready!

The Groom and His Party Approach

6 What is that coming up from the
wilderness,
like a column of smoke,
perfumed with myrrh and frankincense,
with all the fragrant powders of the
merchant?
7 Look, it is the litter of Solomon!
Around it are sixty mighty men
of the mighty men of Israel,
8 all equipped with swords
and expert in war,
each with his sword at his thigh
because of alarms by night.
9 King Solomon made himself a palanquin
from the wood of Lebanon.
10 He made its posts of silver,
its back of gold, its seat of purple;
its interior was inlaid with love.[e]
Daughters of Jerusalem,
11 come out.
Look, O daughters of Zion,
at King Solomon,
at the crown with which his mother
crowned him
on the day of his wedding,
on the day of the gladness of his heart.

The Bride's Beauty Extolled

4 How beautiful you are, my love,
how very beautiful!
Your eyes are doves
behind your veil.
Your hair is like a flock of goats,
moving down the slopes of Gilead.
2 Your teeth are like a flock of shorn ewes
that have come up from the washing,
all of which bear twins,
and not one among them is bereaved.
3 Your lips are like a crimson thread,
and your mouth is lovely.
Your cheeks are like halves of a
pomegranate
behind your veil.
4 Your neck is like the tower of David,
built in courses;
on it hang a thousand bucklers,
all of them shields of warriors.
5 Your two breasts are like two fawns,
twins of a gazelle,
that feed among the lilies.
6 Until the day breathes
and the shadows flee,
I will hasten to the mountain of myrrh
and the hill of frankincense.
7 You are altogether beautiful, my love;
there is no flaw in you.
8 Come with me from Lebanon, my bride;
come with me from Lebanon.
Depart[f] from the peak of Amana,
from the peak of Senir and Hermon,
from the dens of lions,
from the mountains of leopards.

9 You have ravished my heart, my sister,
my bride,
you have ravished my heart with a
glance of your eyes,
with one jewel of your necklace.
10 How sweet is your love, my sister, my
bride!
how much better is your love than
wine,
and the fragrance of your oils than
any spice!
11 Your lips distill nectar, my bride;
honey and milk are under your
tongue;
the scent of your garments is like the
scent of Lebanon.
12 A garden locked is my sister, my bride,
a garden locked, a fountain sealed.
13 Your channel[e] is an orchard of
pomegranates
with all choicest fruits,
henna with nard,
14 nard and saffron, calamus and
cinnamon,
with all trees of frankincense,
myrrh and aloes,
with all chief spices—
15 a garden fountain, a well of living
water,
and flowing streams from Lebanon.

[e] Meaning of Heb uncertain [f] Or *Look*

3.6-11 The Fifth Song: The Wedding Procession. The royal wedding procession pictures the bride as coming to Jerusalem from the desert. Surrounded by both exotic odors and military escorts, Solomon's *litter* or *palanquin* is made of costly wood and metals. The king wears a special nuptial *crown,* given him by his mother as a sign of approval of this impending union.
4.1-7 The Sixth Song: The Wedding. The beauty of the bride's detailed features is extolled by the king: her *eyes* are visible through her *veil;* her *hair,* which is curly, moves about like *goats* on a mountain. Her *teeth* are white, even and without gaps; her lips and cheeks are bright with color. Her *neck* is decked with necklaces; her breasts are compared with the graceful heads of deer. The king then approaches her perfume-laden presence.
4.8-5.1 Seventh Song: the Consummation of the Marriage.
4.8-15a Now addressing her as *bride,* the king delights in her breasts, which are compared with glistening, snow-covered mountains. He commends her love-making, calling her *sister,* now that the consummation has made her a member of the covenant people. The former prohibitions to their union (*a garden locked*) are now removed, and all her attractions invite him to complete the sexual act.
4.15b-16 The bride responds by urging him to *enter his garden.*

5.1 After announcing that the consummation is complete, the royal companions encourage the pair to continue the relationship: *Be drunk with love.*
5.2-9 The Eighth Song: The Lover Abandons his Bride. After awakening the bride and asking to be let in, the king tries to enter her chamber, but becomes impatient as she tries to slide the bolt and admit him. After he leaves, she searches for him. The aroused guards beat her and she appeals for help to the other women. Lamenting that she is *faint* because of her unfulfilled *love*, she is told by the women that in spite of her being the *fairest* among them, she has no right to appeal to them for help.
5.10-6.3 The Ninth Song: Longing for the Lost Lover.
5.10-16 Picturing her lost lover, the bride describes his features from his head down to his legs, as he depicted her in 4.1-7. The word translated *body* probably refers to the king's loins. The reference to Lebanon and its cedars suggests the height and majesty of this friend and lover for whom she longs.
6.1-3 The other women now offer to help her find him, but she declares that he has now turned to other loves (*beds of spices*), even though she still considers him to be *mine*.
6.4-12 The Tenth Song: Praise of the Bride. Tirzah, the ancient capital of the northern tribes of Israel (1 Kings 14.17; 16.8-15), and Jerusalem were splendid cities, "awesome" (rather than *terrible*) as the *army* of the stars. The king's description of the bride's ravishing beauty reaches a climax in his declaring her to be incomparably more beautiful than all the other women in his harem (*queens, concubines, and maidens*). And the latter also acknowledge this. The meaning of the present Hebrew text of vs.12 is wholly unclear, but the original may have expressed the king's joy at being united with the bride, or her rejoicing at being joined with him (placed in his *chariot*).

16 Awake, O north wind,
and come, O south wind!
Blow upon my garden
that its fragrance may be wafted abroad.
Let my beloved come to his garden,
and eat its choicest fruits.

5 I come to my garden, my sister, my bride;
I gather my myrrh with my spice,
I eat my honeycomb with my honey,
I drink my wine with my milk.

Eat, friends, drink,
and be drunk with love.

Another Dream

2 I slept, but my heart was awake.
Listen! my beloved is knocking.
"Open to me, my sister, my love,
my dove, my perfect one;
for my head is wet with dew,
my locks with the drops of the night."
3 I had put off my garment;
how could I put it on again?
I had bathed my feet;
how could I soil them?
4 My beloved thrust his hand into the opening,
and my inmost being yearned for him.
5 I arose to open to my beloved,
and my hands dripped with myrrh,
my fingers with liquid myrrh,
upon the handles of the bolt.
6 I opened to my beloved,
but my beloved had turned and was gone.
My soul failed me when he spoke.
I sought him, but did not find him;
I called him, but he gave no answer.
7 Making their rounds in the city
the sentinels found me;
they beat me, they wounded me,
they took away my mantle,
those sentinels of the walls.
8 I adjure you, O daughters of Jerusalem,
if you find my beloved,
tell him this:
I am faint with love.

Colloquy of Friends and Bride

9 What is your beloved more than another beloved,
O fairest among women?
What is your beloved more than another beloved,
that you thus adjure us?

10 My beloved is all radiant and ruddy,
distinguished among ten thousand.
11 His head is the finest gold;
his locks are wavy,
black as a raven.
12 His eyes are like doves
beside springs of water,
bathed in milk,
fitly set.[g]
13 His cheeks are like beds of spices,
yielding fragrance.
His lips are lilies,
distilling liquid myrrh.
14 His arms are rounded gold,
set with jewels.
His body is ivory work,[g]
encrusted with sapphires.[h]
15 His legs are alabaster columns,
set upon bases of gold.
His appearance is like Lebanon,
choice as the cedars.
16 His speech is most sweet,
and he is altogether desirable.
This is my beloved and this is my friend,
O daughters of Jerusalem.

6 Where has your beloved gone,
O fairest among women?
Which way has your beloved turned,
that we may seek him with you?

2 My beloved has gone down to his garden,
to the beds of spices,
to pasture his flock in the gardens,
and to gather lilies.
3 I am my beloved's and my beloved is mine;
he pastures his flock among the lilies.

The Bride's Matchless Beauty

4 You are beautiful as Tirzah, my love,
comely as Jerusalem,
terrible as an army with banners.
5 Turn away your eyes from me,
for they overwhelm me!
Your hair is like a flock of goats,
moving down the slopes of Gilead.
6 Your teeth are like a flock of ewes,
that have come up from the washing;

4.16 Song 5.1; 6.2
5.1 Song 6.2; 4.9,11,14; Lk 15.7,10; Jn 3.29
5.2 Song 4.9; 6.9; ver 11
5.3 Lk 11.7; Gen19.2
5.5 ver 13
5.6 Song 6.1; 3.1; Prov 1.28
5.7 Song 3.3
5.8 Song 2.7; 3.5; 2.5
5.9 Song 1.8; 6.1
5.12 Song 1.15; 4.1
5.13 Song 6.2; 2.1
5.16 Song 7.9; 2 Sam 1.23
6.1 Song 5.6; 1.8
6.2 Song 4.16; 5.1,13; 1.7; 2.1
6.3 Song 2.16; 7.10
6.4 Song 1.15; ver 10
6.5 Song 4.1
6.6 Song 4.2

[g] Meaning of Heb uncertain [h] Heb *lapis lazuli*

6.7 Song 4.3
6.8 1 Kings 11.3; Song 1.3
6.9 Song 2.14; 5.2; Gen 30.13
6.10 ver 4
6.11 Song 7.12
6.13 Judg 21.21; Gen 32.2
7.1 Ps 45.13
7.3 Song 4.5
7.4 Song 4.4
7.5 Isa 35.2
7.6 Song 1.15,16
7.8 Song 2.5
7.10 Song 2.16; 6.3; Ps 45.11
7.12 Song 6.11
7.13 Gen 30.14; Song 2.3; 4.13,16
8.2 Song 3.4
8.3 Song 2.6
8.4 Song 2.7; 3.5

all of them bear twins,
and not one among them is bereaved.
7 Your cheeks are like halves of a pomegranate
behind your veil.
8 There are sixty queens and eighty concubines,
and maidens without number.
9 My dove, my perfect one, is the only one,
the darling of her mother,
flawless to her that bore her.
The maidens saw her and called her happy;
the queens and concubines also, and they praised her.
10 "Who is this that looks forth like the dawn,
fair as the moon, bright as the sun,
terrible as an army with banners?"

11 I went down to the nut orchard,
to look at the blossoms of the valley,
to see whether the vines had budded,
whether the pomegranates were in bloom.
12 Before I was aware, my fancy set me
in a chariot beside my prince.[i]

13[j] Return, return, O Shulammite!
Return, return, that we may look upon you.

Why should you look upon the Shulammite,
as upon a dance before two armies?[k]

Expressions of Praise

7 How graceful are your feet in sandals,
O queenly maiden!
Your rounded thighs are like jewels,
the work of a master hand.
2 Your navel is a rounded bowl
that never lacks mixed wine.
Your belly is a heap of wheat,
encircled with lilies.
3 Your two breasts are like two fawns,
twins of a gazelle.
4 Your neck is like an ivory tower.
Your eyes are pools in Heshbon,
by the gate of Bath-rabbim.
Your nose is like a tower of Lebanon,
overlooking Damascus.
5 Your head crowns you like Carmel,
and your flowing locks are like purple;
a king is held captive in the tresses.[l]

6 How fair and pleasant you are,
O loved one, delectable maiden![m]
7 You are stately[n] as a palm tree,
and your breasts are like its clusters.
8 I say I will climb the palm tree
and lay hold of its branches.
Oh, may your breasts be like clusters of the vine,
and the scent of your breath like apples,
9 and your kisses[o] like the best wine
that goes down[p] smoothly,
gliding over lips and teeth.[q]

10 I am my beloved's,
and his desire is for me.
11 Come, my beloved,
let us go forth into the fields,
and lodge in the villages;
12 let us go out early to the vineyards,
and see whether the vines have budded,
whether the grape blossoms have opened
and the pomegranates are in bloom.
There I will give you my love.
13 The mandrakes give forth fragrance,
and over our doors are all choice fruits,
new as well as old,
which I have laid up for you, O my beloved.

8 O that you were like a brother to me,
who nursed at my mother's breast!
If I met you outside, I would kiss you,
and no one would despise me.
2 I would lead you and bring you
into the house of my mother,
and into the chamber of the one who bore me.[r]
I would give you spiced wine to drink,
the juice of my pomegranates.
3 O that his left hand were under my head,
and that his right hand embraced me!
4 I adjure you, O daughters of Jerusalem,
do not stir up or awaken love
until it is ready!

6.13 Interlude. A call is addressed to the bride, who is identified here by her north Arabian origins as a *Shulammite*, from the city of Shunem (or Sulam), where David's companion and comforter in his last days came from (1 Kings 1.3-4). Her reply to this call is to say that she has not come to fulfill her relationship with the king as a public spectacle (*before armies* or in a choral dance). **7.1-10** The Eleventh Song: Praise of the Bride's Beauty. In this description of the bride's beauty, the details begin with her feet and move upward to her hair, which holds the king *captive*. Comparing her *stately* figure to a *tree*, he indicates his intention to make love to her, to which she responds by declaring her availability. **7.11-8.4** Twelfth Song: The Bride Sings of Love in the Country. Now the king's love for the bride is about to be consummated. She urges that they go out *into the fields* where the beauties of nature will surround them as they are joined sexually, which is symbolized here by her references to opening of *doors* and entering *the house of my mother* (her vagina and womb). There is another plea to the other women not to spoil this prospective experience by arousing the king sexually.

[i] Cn: Meaning of Heb uncertain [j] Ch 7.1 in Heb [k] Or *dance of Mahanaim* [l] Meaning of Heb uncertain [m] Syr: Heb *in delights* [n] Heb *This your stature is* [o] Heb *palate* [p] Heb *down for my lover* [q] Gk Syr Vg: Heb *lips of sleepers* [r] Gk Syr: Heb *my mother; she* (or *you*) *will teach me*

8.5-20 Thirteenth Song: The Bride Again Calls for the King's Love. The poet, speaking like the chorus in classic drama, asks who this is that comes with her *beloved* companion. She has aroused love in him in the gardens of the royal palace (*under the apple tree*), and now asks to share with him a full and enduring love: as indispensable as the royal *seal;* as sure as *death* or the *grave;* as mysterious and unpredictable as *fire.* Love cannot be *quenched,* and it is beyond price in its value. Her family had regarded her as a *little sister,* not physically developed and not ready for pregnancy (*she is a door*). But now she is physically attractive to the king with her breasts *like towers,* and she has brought him full satisfaction (*peace*).
8.11-14 The Fourteenth Song: An Epilogue. Contrasted are the huge remunerations from vineyards owned by Solomon and operated by tenants and the rewards that she and the king have received from their relationship. Her companions are listening to her lovely voice, but he wants to hear it again for himself. She urges him to come to her quickly, and with his characteristic grace.

Homecoming

5 Who is that coming up from the
wilderness,
leaning upon her beloved?

Under the apple tree I awakened you.
There your mother was in labor with you;
there she who bore you was in labor.

6 Set me as a seal upon your heart,
as a seal upon your arm;
for love is strong as death,
passion fierce as the grave.
Its flashes are flashes of fire,
a raging flame.
7 Many waters cannot quench love,
neither can floods drown it.
If one offered for love
all the wealth of his house,
it would be utterly scorned.

8 We have a little sister,
and she has no breasts.
What shall we do for our sister,
on the day when she is spoken for?
9 If she is a wall,
we will build upon her a battlement
of silver;
but if she is a door,
we will enclose her with boards of
cedar.
10 I was a wall,
and my breasts were like towers;
then I was in his eyes
as one who brings[u] peace.
11 Solomon had a vineyard at Baal-hamon;
he entrusted the vineyard to keepers;
each one was to bring for its fruit a
thousand pieces of silver.
12 My vineyard, my very own, is for
myself;
you, O Solomon, may have the
thousand,
and the keepers of the fruit two
hundred!

13 O you who dwell in the gardens,
my companions are listening for your
voice;
let me hear it.

14 Make haste, my beloved,
and be like a gazelle
or a young stag
upon the mountains of spices!

[u] Or *finds*

8.5 Song 3.6; 2.3
8.6 Isa 49.16; Jer 22.24; Hag 2.23; Prov 6.34
8.8 Ezek 16.7
8.11 Eccl 2.4; Mt 21.33; Song 1.6; 2.3; Isa 7.23
8.13 Song 1.7; 2.14
8.14 Song 2.17; 4.6

ISAIAH

See the Introductions, pp. 6, 54-56, and 57-58 above.

1.1 *The vision of Isaiah* is not a dream or a fantasy, but a three-dimensional set of insights: (1) backward into the historical origins of Israel and its covenant relationship with the LORD; (2) into the present situation of Israel's disobedience and impending judgment; (3) into the future, when God's intended relationship with his people may be restored. The kings of Judah mentioned here ruled in sequence from 783 to 687, and their reigns are described in 2 Kings 14-20.
1.2-20 God's Diagnosis and Prescription for Israel's Ailment.
1.2-4 Addressed to the disobedient and corrupt *people* of the LORD in Judah; they are called by the traditional name, *Israel.*
1.5-6 As a result of the divine punishment that has already come, Israel is depicted as a sick and wounded human body.

1 The vision of Isaiah son of Amoz,
which he saw concerning Judah and
Jerusalem in the days of Uzziah, Jotham,
Ahaz, and Hezekiah, kings of Judah.

The Wickedness of Judah

2 Hear, O heavens, and listen, O earth;
for the LORD has spoken:
I reared children and brought them up,
but they have rebelled against me.
3 The ox knows its owner,
and the donkey its master's crib;
but Israel does not know,
my people do not understand.

4 Ah, sinful nation,
people laden with iniquity,
offspring who do evil,
children who deal corruptly,
who have forsaken the LORD,
who have despised the Holy One of
Israel,
who are utterly estranged!

5 Why do you seek further beatings?
Why do you continue to rebel?
The whole head is sick,
and the whole heart faint.
6 From the sole of the foot even to the
head,
there is no soundness in it,
but bruises and sores
and bleeding wounds;
they have not been drained, or bound up,
or softened with oil.

1.1 Num 12.6; Isa 2.1; 2 Kings 15.1,13,32; 16.1; 18.1
1.2 Deut 32.1
1.3 Jer 8.7; 9.3,6
1.4 Isa 14.20; ver 28; Isa 5.24
1.5 Isa 31.6; 33.24
1.6 Job 2.7; Ps 38.3; Isa 30.26; Lk 10.34

1.7 Isa 6.11; Jer 44.6

1.9 Rom 9.29; Isa 10.20-22

1.10 Isa 28.14; 3.9; Ezek 16.46; Rev 11.8

1.11 1 Sam 15.22; Jer 6.20; Mic 6.7

1.12 Ex 23.17

1.13 Isa 66.3; 1 Chr 23.31; Ex 12.16; Jer 7.9,10

1.14 Num 28.11; Lev 23.2; Isa 7.13; 43.24

1.15 1 Kings 8.22; Isa 8.17; 59.2; Mic 3.4; Isa 59.3

1.16 Jer 4.14; Isa 52.11; 55.7; Jer 25.5

1.17 Jer 22.3; Isa 58.6; Ps 82.3

1.18 Isa 43.26; Ps 51.7; Rev 7.14

1.19 Deut 30.15,16

1.20 Isa 3.25; 34.16

1.21 Jer 2.20; Isa 59.7

1.22 Ezek 22.18

1.23 Hos 9.15; Ex 23.8; Mic 7.3; Jer 5.28; Zech 7.10

1.24 Isa 49.26; 35.4

1.25 Mal 3.3

1.26 Jer 33.7; Zech 8.3

1.28 Isa 24.20; Ps 9.5; 2 Thess 1.8,9

1.29 Isa 57.5; 65.3

7 Your country lies desolate,
your cities are burned with fire;
in your very presence
aliens devour your land;
it is desolate, as overthrown by foreigners.
8 And daughter Zion is left
like a booth in a vineyard,
like a shelter in a cucumber field,
like a besieged city.
9 If the LORD of hosts
had not left us a few survivors,
we would have been like Sodom,
and become like Gomorrah.

10 Hear the word of the LORD,
you rulers of Sodom!
Listen to the teaching of our God,
you people of Gomorrah!
11 What to me is the multitude of your sacrifices?
says the LORD;
I have had enough of burnt offerings of rams
and the fat of fed beasts;
I do not delight in the blood of bulls,
or of lambs, or of goats.

12 When you come to appear before me,[a]
who asked this from your hand?
Trample my courts no more;
13 bringing offerings is futile;
incense is an abomination to me.
New moon and sabbath and calling of convocation—
I cannot endure solemn assemblies with iniquity.
14 Your new moons and your appointed festivals
my soul hates;
they have become a burden to me,
I am weary of bearing them.
15 When you stretch out your hands,
I will hide my eyes from you;
even though you make many prayers,
I will not listen;
your hands are full of blood.
16 Wash yourselves; make yourselves clean;
remove the evil of your doings
from before my eyes;
cease to do evil,
17 learn to do good;
seek justice,
rescue the oppressed,
defend the orphan,
plead for the widow.

18 Come now, let us argue it out,
says the LORD:
though your sins are like scarlet,
they shall be like snow;
though they are red like crimson,
they shall become like wool.
19 If you are willing and obedient,
you shall eat the good of the land;
20 but if you refuse and rebel,
you shall be devoured by the sword;
for the mouth of the LORD has spoken.

The Degenerate City

21 How the faithful city
has become a whore!
She that was full of justice,
righteousness lodged in her—
but now murderers!
22 Your silver has become dross,
your wine is mixed with water.
23 Your princes are rebels
and companions of thieves.
Everyone loves a bribe
and runs after gifts.
They do not defend the orphan,
and the widow's cause does not come before them.

24 Therefore says the Sovereign, the LORD of hosts, the Mighty One of Israel:
Ah, I will pour out my wrath on my enemies,
and avenge myself on my foes!
25 I will turn my hand against you;
I will smelt away your dross as with lye
and remove all your alloy.
26 And I will restore your judges as at the first,
and your counselors as at the beginning.
Afterward you shall be called the city of righteousness,
the faithful city.

27 Zion shall be redeemed by justice,
and those in her who repent, by righteousness.
28 But rebels and sinners shall be destroyed together,
and those who forsake the LORD shall be consumed.
29 For you shall be ashamed of the oaks
in which you delighted;
and you shall blush for the gardens
that you have chosen.

[a] Or *see my face*

1.7-9 The destruction of the cities and the seizure of the lands of Judah had already begun, as was evident in the invasion of the country and the taking of 46 cities by Sennacherib, the Assyrian king (705-701). Jerusalem, here called *Zion*, has not yet been seized. Its lonely desolation is compared to *Sodom and Gomorrah*, the cities destroyed by God in judgment for the depravity of their inhabitants (Gen 18.16-19.29).
1.11-15 The sanctuary originally designed for the exclusive honoring of the LORD has now become a royal chapel devoted to enhancing the prestige and wealth of the ruler and his rich supporters, who together exploit the poor and seize their lands.
1.16-17 The leaders of Judah have forgotten the basic intent of the covenant: to create and sustain a people mutually supportive and concerned for the welfare of all as God's people.
1.18-25 The option is open to renew the covenant and rebuild responsibility within the community. Otherwise the prospect is of divine judgment, which will take the form of invasion by the enemy power. Ironically, the faithlessness and corruption of the city has converted those who should be God's people into *my enemies*, on whom his wrath will now fall. The result of this fiery outpouring will be purification, however, not destruction.
1.26-31 The vision is of the replacement of the self-serving monarchs by the earlier forms of leadership: *judges* and *counselors*, who will be concerned for the welfare of all. *The city of righteousness* will be a transformed community, where things are set right, so that God's intended order and mutual support of the people prevail. At the same time there is warning of utter destruction on those who prize personal gain above responsibility for all of God's people.

2.1-4 The Future Dwelling-Place of God.
2.1 *Word* implies not only "message" but also "insight" – in this case, into the purpose of God for his people.
2.2-4 This image of the elevation of *the* LORD*'s house* is not physical, but symbolizes universal acknowledgment of the sovereignty of the God of Israel. This will lead to an end to warfare and the triumph of peace.
2.5-4.1 God's Judgment Falls on Human Arrogance.
2.5-22 Human pride is bolstered by the *soothsayers* who claim to predict a rosy future, by those who accumulate wealth through exploiting the weak, and by humanly-contrived idols. All these sources of human pride will be brought down, as is symbolized by the fall of trees and mountains, of towers and ship masts, and ultimately of the idols.

30 For you shall be like an oak
whose leaf withers,
and like a garden without water.
31 The strong shall become like tinder,
and their work[b] like a spark;
they and their work shall burn together,
with no one to quench them.

The Future House of God

2 The word that Isaiah son of Amoz saw concerning Judah and Jerusalem.

2 In days to come
the mountain of the LORD's house
shall be established as the highest of the mountains,
and shall be raised above the hills;
all the nations shall stream to it.
3 Many peoples shall come and say,
"Come, let us go up to the mountain of the LORD,
to the house of the God of Jacob;
that he may teach us his ways
and that we may walk in his paths."
For out of Zion shall go forth instruction,
and the word of the LORD from Jerusalem.
4 He shall judge between the nations,
and shall arbitrate for many peoples;
they shall beat their swords into plowshares,
and their spears into pruning hooks;
nation shall not lift up sword against nation,
neither shall they learn war any more.

Judgment Pronounced on Arrogance

5 O house of Jacob,
come, let us walk
in the light of the LORD!
6 For you have forsaken the ways of[c] your people,
O house of Jacob.
Indeed they are full of diviners[d] from the east
and of soothsayers like the Philistines,
and they clasp hands with foreigners.
7 Their land is filled with silver and gold,
and there is no end to their treasures;
their land is filled with horses,
and there is no end to their chariots.
8 Their land is filled with idols;
they bow down to the work of their hands,
to what their own fingers have made.
9 And so people are humbled,
and everyone is brought low—
do not forgive them!
10 Enter into the rock,
and hide in the dust
from the terror of the LORD,
and from the glory of his majesty.
11 The haughty eyes of people shall be brought low,
and the pride of everyone shall be humbled;
and the LORD alone will be exalted
in that day.
12 For the LORD of hosts has a day
against all that is proud and lofty,
against all that is lifted up and high;[e]
13 against all the cedars of Lebanon,
lofty and lifted up;
and against all the oaks of Bashan;
14 against all the high mountains,
and against all the lofty hills;
15 against every high tower,
and against every fortified wall;
16 against all the ships of Tarshish,
and against all the beautiful craft.[f]
17 The haughtiness of people shall be humbled,
and the pride of everyone shall be brought low;
and the LORD alone will be exalted on that day.
18 The idols shall utterly pass away.
19 Enter the caves of the rocks
and the holes of the ground,
from the terror of the LORD,
and from the glory of his majesty,
when he rises to terrify the earth.
20 On that day people will throw away
to the moles and to the bats
their idols of silver and their idols of gold,
which they made for themselves to worship,
21 to enter the caverns of the rocks
and the clefts in the crags,
from the terror of the LORD,
and from the glory of his majesty,
when he rises to terrify the earth.
22 Turn away from mortals,
who have only breath in their nostrils,
for of what account are they?

[b] Or *its makers* [c] Heb lacks *the ways of* [d] Cn: Heb lacks *of diviners* [e] Cn Compare Gk: Heb *low* [f] Compare Gk: Meaning of Heb uncertain

1.31 Isa 5.24; 66.24; Mt 3.12
2.1 Isa 1.1
2.2 Mic 4.1-3; Isa 27.13; 66.20; 56.7
2.3 Isa 55.5; 66.18; Zech 8.20-23; Lk 24.47
2.4 Isa 32.17,18; Hos 2.18
2.5 Isa 58.1; 60.1,2,19; 18.14
2.6 Deut 31.17; 2 Kings 16.7,8
2.7 Deut 17.16
2.8 Isa 10.11; 17.8
2.9 Isa 5.15; Neh 4.5
2.10 Rev 6.15; 2 Thess 1.9
2.11 Isa 13.11; Zech 9.16
2.12 Isa 24.4,21
2.13 Isa 10.33,34; Zech 11.2
2.14 Isa 30.25
2.16 1 Kings 10.22
2.17 ver 11
2.18 Isa 21.9
2.19 Hos 10.8; Rev 9.6; 2 Thess 1.9; Heb 12.26
2.20 Isa 30.22
2.21 ver 10,19
2.22 Ps 146.3; Job 27.3; Jas 4.14

3 For now the Sovereign, the LORD of
hosts,
is taking away from Jerusalem and
from Judah
support and staff—
all support of bread,
and all support of water—
2 warrior and soldier,
judge and prophet,
diviner and elder,
3 captain of fifty
and dignitary,
counselor and skillful magician
and expert enchanter.
4 And I will make boys their princes,
and babes shall rule over them.
5 The people will be oppressed,
everyone by another
and everyone by a neighbor;
the youth will be insolent to the elder,
and the base to the honorable.

6 Someone will even seize a relative,
a member of the clan, saying,
"You have a cloak;
you shall be our leader,
and this heap of ruins
shall be under your rule."
7 But the other will cry out on that day,
saying,
"I will not be a healer;
in my house there is neither bread
nor cloak;
you shall not make me
leader of the people."
8 For Jerusalem has stumbled
and Judah has fallen,
because their speech and their deeds are
against the LORD,
defying his glorious presence.

9 The look on their faces bears witness
against them;
they proclaim their sin like Sodom,
they do not hide it.
Woe to them!
For they have brought evil on
themselves.
10 Tell the innocent how fortunate they
are,
for they shall eat the fruit of their
labors.
11 Woe to the guilty! How unfortunate
they are,
for what their hands have done shall
be done to them.
12 My people—children are their
oppressors,
and women rule over them.
O my people, your leaders mislead you,
and confuse the course of your paths.

13 The LORD rises to argue his case;
he stands to judge the peoples.
14 The LORD enters into judgment
with the elders and princes of his
people:
It is you who have devoured the
vineyard;
the spoil of the poor is in your
houses.
15 What do you mean by crushing my
people,
by grinding the face of the poor? says
the Lord GOD of hosts.

16 The LORD said:
Because the daughters of Zion are
haughty
and walk with outstretched necks,
glancing wantonly with their eyes,
mincing along as they go,
tinkling with their feet;
17 the Lord will afflict with scabs
the heads of the daughters of Zion,
and the LORD will lay bare their secret
parts.

18 In that day the Lord will take away
the finery of the anklets, the headbands,
and the crescents; 19 the pendants, the bracelets, and the scarfs; 20 the headdresses, the
armlets, the sashes, the perfume boxes, and
the amulets; 21 the signet rings and nose
rings; 22 the festal robes, the mantles, the
cloaks, and the handbags; 23 the garments of
gauze, the linen garments, the turbans, and
the veils.
24 Instead of perfume there will be a
stench;
and instead of a sash, a rope;
and instead of well-set hair, baldness;
and instead of a rich robe, a binding
of sackcloth;
instead of beauty, shame.[g]
25 Your men shall fall by the sword
and your warriors in battle.
26 And her gates shall lament and mourn;
ravaged, she shall sit upon the
ground.

[g] Q Ms: MT lacks *shame*

3.1 Jer 37.21; Lev 26.26
3.2 2 Kings 24.14
3.4 Eccl 10.16
3.5 Mic 7.3-6; Isa 9.19
3.6 Isa 4.1
3.7 Ezek 34.4
3.8 Isa 1.7; 6.11; 9.17; 65.3,5
3.9 Isa 1.10; Gen 13.13
3.10 Deut 28.1-14
3.11 Isa 65.6,7
3.12 ver 4; Isa 9.16
3.13 Isa 66.16; Mic 6.2
3.14 Ezek 20.35,36; Isa 10.1,2; Jas 2.6
3.15 Ps 94.5
3.16 Isa 4.4
3.17 Isa 47.3
3.18 Judg 8.21
3.20 Ex 39.28
3.21 Ezek 16.12
3.24 Prov 31.24; Isa 22.12; 15.3
3.25 Isa 1.20; 65.12
3.26 Jer 14.2; Lam 2.10

3.1-4.1 The judgment of God on *Jerusalem and Judah* will shatter all the present economic, social and political structures, because the leaders – *elders and princes* – have oppressed and exploited *the poor.* Similarly, the showy dress and manners of the women will be brought under judgment.

4.2-6 The Renewal of Zion: God's Glory in the Midst of his People.
4.2 *The branch of the LORD* is an image widely used by the prophets for the ruler of Israel, chosen and empowered by God, whose reign will be in accord with God's purpose for his people (Jer 23.5-6; 33.15-16; Hag 2.21-23; Zech 3.8; 6.12; also in Ps 132.17).
4.3 *Holy* means purged and renewed, in readiness for right relationship with God and his people.
4.5 *Cloud...glory* recalls the visible, powerful presence of God in and over the tabernacle when the covenant was established through Moses at Sinai (Ex 40.34-38).
5.1-7 The Ruin of the Vineyard as Symbol of God's Judgment.
5.1 The symbolic meanings of *my beloved* and *his vineyard* are given in 5.7, where the owner is identified as the LORD of hosts, and the vineyard is the people of Israel and Judah. The *grapes* represent the expected moral fruits: *justice* and *righteousness*.
5.5 The image of the destruction of the vineyard foreshadows God's judgment in the form of disaster and withdrawal of support from Israel.
5.8-30 Details of Israel's Social Injustice.
5.8-10 Greed, which regards wealth as the highest human value.
5.11-13 Self-indulgence, which is devoted to drink and revelry.
5.14-17 The consequence is inevitably (1) the death of the populace, here pictured as going down to *Sheol*, the traditional subterranean gloomy and hopeless abode of the dead; (2) the ruin of the cities.

4 Seven women shall take hold of one
man in that day, saying,
"We will eat our own bread and wear
our own clothes;
just let us be called by your name;
take away our disgrace."

The Future Glory of the Survivors in Zion

2 On that day the branch of the LORD
shall be beautiful and glorious, and the fruit
of the land shall be the pride and glory of
the survivors of Israel. [3]Whoever is left in
Zion and remains in Jerusalem will be called
holy, everyone who has been recorded for
life in Jerusalem, [4]once the Lord has washed
away the filth of the daughters of Zion and
cleansed the bloodstains of Jerusalem from
its midst by a spirit of judgment and by a
spirit of burning. [5]Then the LORD will create
over the whole site of Mount Zion and over
its places of assembly a cloud by day and
smoke and the shining of a flaming fire by
night. Indeed over all the glory there will
be a canopy. [6]It will serve as a pavilion, a
shade by day from the heat, and a refuge
and a shelter from the storm and rain.

The Song of the Unfruitful Vineyard

5 Let me sing for my beloved
my love-song concerning his
vineyard:
My beloved had a vineyard
on a very fertile hill.
2 He dug it and cleared it of stones,
and planted it with choice vines;
he built a watchtower in the midst of it,
and hewed out a wine vat in it;
he expected it to yield grapes,
but it yielded wild grapes.

3 And now, inhabitants of Jerusalem
and people of Judah,
judge between me
and my vineyard.
4 What more was there to do for my
vineyard
that I have not done in it?
When I expected it to yield grapes,
why did it yield wild grapes?

5 And now I will tell you
what I will do to my vineyard.
I will remove its hedge,
and it shall be devoured;
I will break down its wall,
and it shall be trampled down.
6 I will make it a waste;
it shall not be pruned or hoed,
and it shall be overgrown with briers
and thorns;
I will also command the clouds
that they rain no rain upon it.

7 For the vineyard of the LORD of hosts
is the house of Israel,
and the people of Judah
are his pleasant planting;
he expected justice,
but saw bloodshed;
righteousness,
but heard a cry!

Social Injustice Denounced

8 Ah, you who join house to house,
who add field to field,
until there is room for no one but you,
and you are left to live alone
in the midst of the land!
9 The LORD of hosts has sworn in my
hearing:
Surely many houses shall be desolate,
large and beautiful houses, without
inhabitant.
10 For ten acres of vineyard shall yield but
one bath,
and a homer of seed shall yield a
mere ephah.[h]

11 Ah, you who rise early in the morning
in pursuit of strong drink,
who linger in the evening
to be inflamed by wine,
12 whose feasts consist of lyre and harp,
tambourine and flute and wine,
but who do not regard the deeds of the
LORD,
or see the work of his hands!
13 Therefore my people go into exile
without knowledge;
their nobles are dying of hunger,
and their multitude is parched with
thirst.

14 Therefore Sheol has enlarged its appetite
and opened its mouth beyond
measure;
the nobility of Jerusalem[i] and her
multitude go down,
her throng and all who exult in her.

4.1 Isa 13.12; 2 Thess 3.12; Isa 54.4
4.2 Isa 11.1; Zech 3.8; 6.12; Ps 72.16; Isa 10.20
4.3 Isa 28.5; 60.21; 52.1; Lk 10.20
4.4 Isa 3.16,24; 1.15; 28.6; Mal 3.2,3
4.5 Ex 13.21; Isa 60.1,2
4.6 Isa 25.4
5.1 Ps 80.8; Mt 21.33; Mk 12.1; Lk 20.9
5.2 Jer 2.21; Mt 21.19; Mk 11.13; Lk 13.6
5.3 Mt 21.40
5.4 Mt 23.37
5.5 Ps 89.40; Isa 6.13; Ps 80.12; Isa 10.6; Lk 21.24; Rev 11.2
5.6 Isa 24.1,3; Heb 6.8; 1 Kings 8.35
5.7 Ps 80.8-11; Isa 3.14,15
5.8 Mic 2.2
5.9 Isa 22.14; 6.11,12
5.10 Isa 7.23; Ezek 45.11
5.11 Prov 23.29,30; Eccl 10.16
5.12 Am 6.5,6; Job 34.27; Ps 28.5
5.13 Hos 4.6; Isa 1.3; 3.3; 9.14,15
5.14 Prov 30.16; Num 16.30-34; Ps 141.7

[h] The Heb *bath, homer,* and *ephah* are measures of quantity [i] Heb *her nobility*

15 People are bowed down, everyone is
brought low,
and the eyes of the haughty are
humbled.
16 But the LORD of hosts is exalted by
justice,
and the Holy God shows himself holy
by righteousness.
17 Then the lambs shall graze as in their
pasture,
fatlings and kids[j] shall feed among
the ruins.

18 Ah, you who drag iniquity along with
cords of falsehood,
who drag sin along as with cart
ropes,
19 who say, "Let him make haste,
let him speed his work
that we may see it;
let the plan of the Holy One of Israel
hasten to fulfillment,
that we may know it!"
20 Ah, you who call evil good
and good evil,
who put darkness for light
and light for darkness,
who put bitter for sweet
and sweet for bitter!
21 Ah, you who are wise in your own eyes,
and shrewd in your own sight!
22 Ah, you who are heroes in drinking
wine
and valiant at mixing drink,
23 who acquit the guilty for a bribe,
and deprive the innocent of their
rights!

Foreign Invasion Predicted

24 Therefore, as the tongue of fire devours
the stubble,
and as dry grass sinks down in the
flame,
so their root will become rotten,
and their blossom go up like dust;
for they have rejected the instruction of
the LORD of hosts,
and have despised the word of the
Holy One of Israel.

25 Therefore the anger of the LORD was
kindled against his people,
and he stretched out his hand against
them and struck them;
the mountains quaked,
and their corpses were like refuse
in the streets.
For all this his anger has not turned
away,
and his hand is stretched out still.

26 He will raise a signal for a nation far
away,
and whistle for a people at the ends of
the earth;
Here they come, swiftly, speedily!
27 None of them is weary, none stumbles,
none slumbers or sleeps,
not a loincloth is loose,
not a sandal-thong broken;
28 their arrows are sharp,
all their bows bent,
their horses' hoofs seem like flint,
and their wheels like the whirlwind.
29 Their roaring is like a lion,
like young lions they roar;
they growl and seize their prey,
they carry it off, and no one can
rescue.
30 They will roar over it on that day,
like the roaring of the sea.
And if one look to the land—
only darkness and distress;
and the light grows dark with clouds.

A Vision of God in the Temple

6 In the year that King Uzziah died, I
saw the Lord sitting on a throne, high
and lofty; and the hem of his robe filled the
temple. 2Seraphs were in attendance above
him; each had six wings: with two they
covered their faces, and with two they
covered their feet, and with two they flew.
3And one called to another and said:
"Holy, holy, holy is the LORD of hosts;
the whole earth is full of his glory."
4The pivots[k] on the thresholds shook at the
voices of those who called, and the house
filled with smoke. 5And I said: "Woe is me!
I am lost, for I am a man of unclean lips,
and I live among a people of unclean lips;
yet my eyes have seen the King, the LORD
of hosts!"
6 Then one of the seraphs flew to me,
holding a live coal that had been taken
from the altar with a pair of tongs. 7The
seraph[l] touched my mouth with it and said:
"Now that this has touched your lips, your
guilt has departed and your sin is blotted
out." 8Then I heard the voice of the Lord

[j] Cn Compare Gk: Heb *aliens* [k] Meaning of Heb uncertain [l] Heb *He*

5.15 Isa 2.9,11
5.16 Isa 2.11,17; 8.13; 29.23
5.18 Isa 59.4-8
5.19 Ezek 12.22; 2 Pet 3.3,4
5.20 Prov 17.15; Mt 6.22,23; Lk 11.34,35
5.21 Rom 12.16
5.22 ver 11
5.23 Isa 10.1,2; Ps 94.21
5.24 Isa 9.18,19; Job 18.16; Hos 5.12; Acts 13.41
5.25 2 Kings 22.13; Jer 4.24; Isa 14.19; 9.12,17,21; 23.11
5.26 Isa 13.2,3; 7.18; Deut 28.49; Isa 13.4,5
5.27 Joel 2.7,8; Dan 5.6
5.28 Ps 7.12,13; Jer 4.13
5.29 Jer 51.38; Isa 10.6; 42.22
5.30 Isa 17.12; 8.22
6.1 Isa 1.1; 2 Kings 15.7; 1 Kings 22.9
6.2 Rev 4.8; Ezek 1.11
6.3 Rev 4.8; Ps 72.19
6.5 Ex 33.20; Jer 9.3-8; 51.57
6.7 Jer 1.9; Isa 40.2; 1 Jn 1.7
6.8 Ezek 10.5; Acts 9.4; 26.19

5.18-23 Depicted here are the forms of self-deceit of the wicked.
5.24-30 Inescapable is God's judgment on Israel, effected through an invasion of Judah and Jerusalem by *a nation far away*, which in this historical situation was the Babylonians in 586. The result will be *darkness and distress*.
6.1-13 The Vision of the LORD in the Temple.
6.1 The year that King Uzziah died was 742.
6.2 *Seraphs* were messengers or agents of God, characterized by their flaming appearance and by their three pairs of wings: one pair covered their faces, in the awesome presence of God; one covered their genitals (*feet*) as a sign of commitment to purity; one was for flight, to fulfill the commission from God.
6.4 *Pivots* may refer to the devices on which the temple gates turned, or to the foundations on which they rested.
6.5 Isaiah's vision of God leaves him overcome with a sense of his uncleanness and of that of his associates.
6.8 The purification of the prophet's *lips* renders him fit and qualified to speak God's word to his people.

saying, "Whom shall I send, and who will
go for us?" And I said, "Here am I; send
me!" [9]And he said, "Go and say to this
people:

'Keep listening, but do not comprehend;
keep looking, but do not understand.'
10 Make the mind of this people dull,
and stop their ears,
and shut their eyes,
so that they may not look with their
eyes,
and listen with their ears,
and comprehend with their minds,
and turn and be healed."
11 Then I said, "How long, O Lord?" And
he said:
"Until cities lie waste
without inhabitant,
and houses without people,
and the land is utterly desolate;
12 until the LORD sends everyone far away,
and vast is the emptiness in the midst
of the land.
13 Even if a tenth part remain in it,
it will be burned again,
like a terebinth or an oak
whose stump remains standing
when it is felled."[m]
The holy seed is its stump.

Isaiah Reassures King Ahaz

7 In the days of Ahaz son of Jotham son
of Uzziah, king of Judah, King Rezin
of Aram and King Pekah son of Remaliah
of Israel went up to attack Jerusalem, but
could not mount an attack against it. [2]When
the house of David heard that Aram had
allied itself with Ephraim, the heart of Ahaz[n]
and the heart of his people shook as the
trees of the forest shake before the wind.
3 Then the LORD said to Isaiah, Go out to
meet Ahaz, you and your son Shear-jashub,[o]
at the end of the conduit of the upper pool
on the highway to the Fuller's Field, [4]and
say to him, Take heed, be quiet, do not fear,
and do not let your heart be faint because
of these two smoldering stumps of firebrands,
because of the fierce anger of Rezin and
Aram and the son of Remaliah. [5]Because
Aram—with Ephraim and the son of
Remaliah—has plotted evil against you,
saying, [6]Let us go up against Judah and cut
off Jerusalem[p] and conquer it for ourselves
and make the son of Tabeel king in it;
[7]therefore thus says the Lord GOD:
It shall not stand,
and it shall not come to pass.
8 For the head of Aram is Damascus,
and the head of Damascus is Rezin.
(Within sixty-five years Ephraim will be
shattered, no longer a people.)
9 The head of Ephraim is Samaria,
and the head of Samaria is the son of
Remaliah.
If you do not stand firm in faith,
you shall not stand at all.

Isaiah Gives Ahaz the Sign of Immanuel

10 Again the LORD spoke to Ahaz, saying,
[11]Ask a sign of the LORD your God; let it be
deep as Sheol or high as heaven. [12]But Ahaz
said, I will not ask, and I will not put the
LORD to the test. [13]Then Isaiah[q] said: "Hear
then, O house of David! Is it too little for you
to weary mortals, that you weary my God
also? [14]Therefore the Lord himself will give
you a sign. Look, the young woman[r] is with
child and shall bear a son, and shall name
him Immanuel.[s] [15]He shall eat curds and
honey by the time he knows how to refuse
the evil and choose the good. [16]For before
the child knows how to refuse the evil and
choose the good, the land before whose two
kings you are in dread will be deserted.
[17]The LORD will bring on you and on your
people and on your ancestral house such
days as have not come since the day that
Ephraim departed from Judah—the king of
Assyria."
18 On that day the LORD will whistle for
the fly that is at the sources of the streams
of Egypt, and for the bee that is in the land
of Assyria. [19]And they will all come and
settle in the steep ravines, and in the clefts
of the rocks, and on all the thornbushes,
and on all the pastures.
20 On that day the Lord will shave with
a razor hired beyond the River—with the
king of Assyria—the head and the hair of
the feet, and it will take off the beard as
well.
21 On that day one will keep alive a
young cow and two sheep, [22]and will eat
curds because of the abundance of milk that
they give; for everyone that is left in the
land shall eat curds and honey.
23 On that day every place where there
used to be a thousand vines, worth a thousand shekels of silver, will become briers
and thorns. [24]With bow and arrows one

[m] Meaning of Heb uncertain [n] Heb *his heart* [o] That is *A remnant shall return* [p] Heb *cut it off* [q] Heb *he* [r] Gk *the virgin* [s] That is *God is with us*

6.9-13 God's inescapable judgment on his people will leave them desolate, with only a *stump* remaining, which symbolizes the survival of the royal line through which ultimate restoration of the covenant people will take place.
7.1-25 Isaiah's Promise and Warning to King Ahaz.
7.1-2 *Ahaz,* Judah's king (735-715), was terrified by the coalition between the northern tribes of Israel under *Pekah* (737-732) and *Rezin,* the king of Syria (*Aram*).
7.3-9 The name of Isaiah's son, *Shear-jashub,* which means "a remnant shall return," indicates that God has a future purpose for his people, which will not be thwarted by these feeble kings, here described as *smoldering stumps of firebrands.* The shattering of the northern tribes, here referred to as *Ephraim,* is promised to take place within sixty-five years, although Samaria actually fell to the Assyrians in 721. The specific locations in Jerusalem mentioned here (*upper pool; Fuller's field,* where bleaching and cleaning were done) cannot now be determined. If the attack on Jerusalem by the Syrians and the northern tribes were to succeed, their candidate for king of Judah would be *Tabeel,* which means, *God is good.* Judah must *stand firm* by trusting God against such feeble, transient adversaries as the rulers in *Damascus and Samaria.*
7.10-23 The Sign of God's Fulfillment of his Promise.
7.11-12 Ahaz refuses to ask God for a sign that the prophetic promise will be fulfilled, although he has the choice that it can range from the lowest depths (*Sheol,* the underground abode of the dead) to the greatest heights (*heaven,* the canopy above the earth where God dwells).
7.13-20 A pregnant young woman (the ancient Greek version renders this as *parthenos,* meaning "virgin") is about to have a son who will be called *Immanuel,* which means "God with us." Before he has reached the decision-making stage of development, the land of *the two kings* – Israel and Syria – will be subject to Assyria, which, in alliance with *Egypt,* will take over the region, including eventually Judah as well.
7.21-25 There will be a shortage of cultivated crops because of ruined fields and vineyards, but since there is only a small remaining population, there will be enough of the food of nomads (curds and honey; Gen 18.8; Judg 5.25) for the inhabitants to survive.

6.9 Ezek 3.11; Mt 13.14,15; Mk 4.12; Lk 8.10; Jn 12.40; Rom 11.8
6.10 Ps 119.70; Jer 5.21
6.11 Mic 3.12
6.12 Jer 4.29
6.13 Isa 1.9; Job 14.7; Ezra 9.2
7.1 2 Kings 16.1; 15.37; 15.25
7.2 ver 13; Isa 8.12
7.3 Isa 10.21; 2 Kings 18.17
7.4 Isa 30.15; 10.24; 35.4
7.7 Isa 8.10
7.8 Isa 17.1-3
7.9 2 Chr 20.20
7.11 Isa 37.30; 38.7,8; 2 Kings 19.29
7.14 Mt 1.23; Lk 1.31; Isa 9.6; 8.8
7.15 ver 22
7.16 Isa 8.4
7.17 2 Chr 28.19; 1 Kings 12.16
7.18 Isa 5.26
7.19 Isa 2.19; Jer 16.16
7.20 Isa 24.1; Ezek 5.1-4; Isa 10.5,15; 8.7

8.1 Isa 30.8; Hab 2.2
8.2 2 Kings 16.10
8.4 Isa 7.16; 7.8,9
8.6 Neh 3.15; Jn 9.7; Isa 7.1,2,6
8.8 Isa 10.6; 30.28; 7.14
8.10 Job 5.12; Isa 7.7; Rom 8.31
8.11 Ezek 3.14; 2.8
8.12 Isa 7.2; 1 Pet 3.14,15
8.13 Isa 5.16; 29.23; Num 20.12
8.14 Ezek 11.16; Lk 2.34; Rom 9.33; 1 Pet 2.8
8.15 Isa 28.13; Mt 21.44; Lk 20.18; Rom 9.32
8.16 ver 1,2; Dan 12.4
8.17 Isa 54.8; Hab 2.3
8.18 Heb 2.13; Ps 71.7; Zech 3.8
8.19 1 Sam 28.8; Isa 19.3; 30.2; 45.11
8.20 Lk 16.29; Mic 3.6
8.21 Isa 9.20,21; Rev 16.11
8.22 Isa 5.30; 9.1
9.1 2 Kings 15.29; 2 Chr 16.4
9.2 Mt 4.15,16
9.3 Isa 26.15; 35.10; 1 Sam 30.16
9.4 Isa 10.27; 14.4; 10.26

will go there, for all the land will be briers and thorns; 25and as for all the hills that used to be hoed with a hoe, you will not go there for fear of briers and thorns; but they will become a place where cattle are let loose and where sheep tread.

Isaiah's Son a Sign of the Assyrian Invasion

8 Then the LORD said to me, Take a large tablet and write on it in common characters, "Belonging to Maher-shalal-hash-baz,"[t] 2and have it attested[u] for me by reliable witnesses, the priest Uriah and Zechariah son of Jeberechiah. 3And I went to the prophetess, and she conceived and bore a son. Then the LORD said to me, Name him Maher-shalal-hash-baz; 4for before the child knows how to call "My father" or "My mother," the wealth of Damascus and the spoil of Samaria will be carried away by the king of Assyria.

5 The LORD spoke to me again: 6Because this people has refused the waters of Shiloah that flow gently, and melt in fear before[v] Rezin and the son of Remaliah; 7therefore, the Lord is bringing up against it the mighty flood waters of the River, the king of Assyria and all his glory; it will rise above all its channels and overflow all its banks; 8it will sweep on into Judah as a flood, and, pouring over, it will reach up to the neck; and its outspread wings will fill the breadth of your land, O Immanuel.

9 Band together, you peoples, and be dismayed;
listen, all you far countries;
gird yourselves and be dismayed;
gird yourselves and be dismayed!
10 Take counsel together, but it shall be brought to naught;
speak a word, but it will not stand,
for God is with us.[w]

11 For the LORD spoke thus to me while his hand was strong upon me, and warned me not to walk in the way of this people, saying: 12Do not call conspiracy all that this people calls conspiracy, and do not fear what it fears, or be in dread. 13But the LORD of hosts, him you shall regard as holy; let him be your fear, and let him be your dread. 14He will become a sanctuary, a stone one strikes against; for both houses of Israel he will become a rock one stumbles over—a trap and a snare for the inhabitants of Jerusalem. 15And many among them shall stumble; they shall fall and be broken; they shall be snared and taken.

Disciples of Isaiah

16 Bind up the testimony, seal the teaching among my disciples. 17I will wait for the LORD, who is hiding his face from the house of Jacob, and I will hope in him. 18See, I and the children whom the LORD has given me are signs and portents in Israel from the LORD of hosts, who dwells on Mount Zion. 19Now if people say to you, "Consult the ghosts and the familiar spirits that chirp and mutter; should not a people consult their gods, the dead on behalf of the living, 20for teaching and for instruction?" Surely, those who speak like this will have no dawn! 21They will pass through the land,[x] greatly distressed and hungry; when they are hungry, they will be enraged and will curse[y] their king and their gods. They will turn their faces upward, 22or they will look to the earth, but will see only distress and darkness, the gloom of anguish; and they will be thrust into thick darkness.[z]

The Righteous Reign of the Coming King

9[a] But there will be no gloom for those who were in anguish. In the former time he brought into contempt the land of Zebulun and the land of Naphtali, but in the latter time he will make glorious the way of the sea, the land beyond the Jordan, Galilee of the nations.

2[b] The people who walked in darkness
have seen a great light;
those who lived in a land of deep darkness—
on them light has shined.
3 You have multiplied the nation,
you have increased its joy;
they rejoice before you
as with joy at the harvest,
as people exult when dividing plunder.
4 For the yoke of their burden,
and the bar across their shoulders,
the rod of their oppressor,
you have broken as on the day of Midian.

[t] That is *The spoil speeds, the prey hastens* [u] Q Ms Gk Syr: MT *and I caused to be attested* [v] Cn: Meaning of Heb uncertain [w] Heb *immanu el* [x] Heb *it* [y] Or *curse by* [z] Meaning of Heb uncertain [a] Ch 8.23 in Heb [b] Ch 9.1 in Heb

8.1-22 Isaiah's Son and Disciples as Signs to Israel.
8.1-4 The name given to the prophet's son before he was conceived, *Maher-shalal-hash-baz,* which means "The spoil speeds; the prey hastens," is a warning that Assyria will soon loot the lands of Syria (*Damascus*) and Israel (*Samaria*). Thus it is foolish of Judah to fear these neighboring kings.
8.5-8 Because Judah refused to depend on what the LORD provided (symbolized by the water supply of Jerusalem, which flowed from the spring of Gihon into the city through the channel of Siloam, or *Shiloah*), and relied instead on the petty kings of Damascus and Samaria, there will come on Judah a flood of judgment, symbolized by *the River* (which is the mighty Tigris-Euphrates in Assyria). In this oracle *Immanuel* seems to refer to God's people rather than only to their king.
8.9-15 Human plans and schemes for survival are fruitless, as is the notion that taking refuge in the temple will guarantee safety, since God will be a *rock,* not as the ground of security but as what will cause the nation to stumble and fall.
8.16-22 The *disciples* and *the children* of the prophet are the sources of information about what God is going to do, rather than the foolish oracles (*ghosts and spirits that chirp and mutter*) to which the people may vainly turn for advice. There is no escaping the judgment of God.
9.1-10.4 Ultimate Deliverance for God's People and the Establishment of God's Rule over the Earth.
9.1 These lines reflect the seizure of the regions of Galilee, here called *the land of Zebulon and...Naphtali,* by Tiglath-Pileser III in 738. Ultimate freeing of the entire region from Assyrian domination is promised.
9.2-7 Here the prophet's promise leads to assurance that God will bless Judah, and ultimately all nations of the world, through the establishment on the throne of a descendant of David, whose rule will be one of everlasting *justice and righteousness,* instead of the ruthless greed and exploitation which now prevails in Judah. This will be accomplished by *the zeal* which *the LORD of hosts* (= armies) will manifest. The king will share the timeless, limitless, benign powers of God.

9.8-10.4 The Prospect of Judgment on Israel in the Near Future. What has happened to Israel through its defeat by foreign powers, its loss of control of its lands and its exile to Babylon is all pictured by the prophet as evidence of the effectiveness of God's judgment on his disobedient people.
9.9 *Ephraim and the inhabitants of Samaria* refers to the people of Israel living just north of the territory of Judah and the population of Israel's capital, Samaria. The intertribal conflict that had taken place within Israel is described as *Manasseh devoured Ephraim.* The injustice of the leaders of these tribes toward the weak and poor will be met by God's judgment on those who perpetrate these wrongs.

5 For all the boots of the tramping warriors
and all the garments rolled in blood
shall be burned as fuel for the fire.
6 For a child has been born for us,
a son given to us;
authority rests upon his shoulders;
and he is named
Wonderful Counselor, Mighty God,
Everlasting Father, Prince of Peace.
7 His authority shall grow continually,
and there shall be endless peace
for the throne of David and his kingdom.
He will establish and uphold it
with justice and with righteousness
from this time onward and forevermore.
The zeal of the LORD of hosts will do this.

Judgment on Arrogance and Oppression

8 The Lord sent a word against Jacob,
and it fell on Israel;
9 and all the people knew it—
Ephraim and the inhabitants of Samaria—
but in pride and arrogance of heart they said:
10 "The bricks have fallen,
but we will build with dressed stones;
the sycamores have been cut down,
but we will put cedars in their place."
11 So the LORD raised adversaries[c] against them,
and stirred up their enemies,
12 the Arameans on the east and the Philistines on the west,
and they devoured Israel with open mouth.
For all this his anger has not turned away;
his hand is stretched out still.

13 The people did not turn to him who struck them,
or seek the LORD of hosts.
14 So the LORD cut off from Israel head and tail,
palm branch and reed in one day—
15 elders and dignitaries are the head,
and prophets who teach lies are the tail;
16 for those who led this people led them astray,
and those who were led by them were left in confusion.
17 That is why the Lord did not have pity on[d] their young people,
or compassion on their orphans and widows;
for everyone was godless and an evildoer,
and every mouth spoke folly.
For all this his anger has not turned away,
his hand is stretched out still.

18 For wickedness burned like a fire,
consuming briers and thorns;
it kindled the thickets of the forest,
and they swirled upward in a column of smoke.
19 Through the wrath of the LORD of hosts
the land was burned,
and the people became like fuel for the fire;
no one spared another.
20 They gorged on the right, but still were hungry,
and they devoured on the left, but were not satisfied;
they devoured the flesh of their own kindred;[e]
21 Manasseh devoured Ephraim, and Ephraim Manasseh,
and together they were against Judah.
For all this his anger has not turned away;
his hand is stretched out still.

10 Ah, you who make iniquitous decrees,
who write oppressive statutes,
2 to turn aside the needy from justice
and to rob the poor of my people of their right,
that widows may be your spoil,
and that you may make the orphans your prey!
3 What will you do on the day of punishment,
in the calamity that will come from far away?
To whom will you flee for help,
and where will you leave your wealth,
4 so as not to crouch among the prisoners
or fall among the slain?
For all this his anger has not turned away;
his hand is stretched out still.

[c] Cn: Heb *the adversaries of Rezin* [d] Q Ms: MT *rejoice over* [e] Or *arm*

9.5 Isa 2.4
9.6 Isa 7.14; Lk 2.11; Jn 3.16; Mt 28.18; 1 Cor 15.25; Isa 28.29; 10.21; 63.16; Eph 2.14
9.7 Dan 2.44; Lk 1.32,33; Isa 16.15; 11.4,5; 37.32
9.9 Isa 7.8,9; 46.12
9.11 Isa 7.1,8
9.12 2 Kings 16.6; 2 Chr 28.18; Ps 79.7; Isa 5.25
9.13 Jer 5.3; Hos 7.10; Isa 31.1
9.14 Isa 19.15; Rev 18.8
9.15 Isa 3.2,3; 28.15
9.16 Isa 3.12
9.17 Jer 18.21; Isa 27.11; 10.6; Mic 7.2; Isa 5.25
9.18 Isa 10.17; Mal 4.1
9.19 Isa 10.6; Joel 2.3; Isa 1.31; 24.6; Mic 7.2,6
9.20 Isa 8.21,22; 49.26
9.21 Isa 5.25
10.1 Ps 94.20
10.2 Isa 5.23; 1.23
10.3 Job 31.14; Hos 9.7; Lk 19.44; Isa 5.26; 20.6
10.4 Isa 24.22; 22.2; 5.25

Arrogant Assyria Also Judged

5 Ah, Assyria, the rod of my anger—
the club in their hands is my fury!
6 Against a godless nation I send him,
and against the people of my wrath I command him,
to take spoil and seize plunder,
and to tread them down like the mire of the streets.
7 But this is not what he intends,
nor does he have this in mind;
but it is in his heart to destroy,
and to cut off nations not a few.
8 For he says:
"Are not my commanders all kings?
9 Is not Calno like Carchemish?
Is not Hamath like Arpad?
Is not Samaria like Damascus?
10 As my hand has reached to the kingdoms of the idols
whose images were greater than those of Jerusalem and Samaria,
11 shall I not do to Jerusalem and her idols
what I have done to Samaria and her images?"

12 When the Lord has finished all his
work on Mount Zion and on Jerusalem, he[f]
will punish the arrogant boasting of the
king of Assyria and his haughty pride. 13 For
he says:
"By the strength of my hand I have done it,
and by my wisdom, for I have understanding;
I have removed the boundaries of peoples,
and have plundered their treasures;
like a bull I have brought down those who sat on thrones.
14 My hand has found, like a nest,
the wealth of the peoples;
and as one gathers eggs that have been forsaken,
so I have gathered all the earth;
and there was none that moved a wing,
or opened its mouth, or chirped."

15 Shall the ax vaunt itself over the one who wields it,
or the saw magnify itself against the one who handles it?
As if a rod should raise the one who lifts it up,
or as if a staff should lift the one who is not wood!
16 Therefore the Sovereign, the LORD of hosts,
will send wasting sickness among his stout warriors,
and under his glory a burning will be kindled,
like the burning of fire.
17 The light of Israel will become a fire,
and his Holy One a flame;
and it will burn and devour
his thorns and briers in one day.
18 The glory of his forest and his fruitful land
the LORD will destroy, both soul and body,
and it will be as when an invalid wastes away.
19 The remnant of the trees of his forest will be so few
that a child can write them down.

The Repentant Remnant of Israel

20 On that day the remnant of Israel and
the survivors of the house of Jacob will no
more lean on the one who struck them, but
will lean on the LORD, the Holy One of Israel,
in truth. 21 A remnant will return, the remnant of Jacob, to the mighty God. 22 For
though your people Israel were like the
sand of the sea, only a remnant of them will
return. Destruction is decreed, overflowing
with righteousness. 23 For the Lord GOD of
hosts will make a full end, as decreed, in all
the earth.[g]
24 Therefore thus says the Lord GOD of
hosts: O my people, who live in Zion, do not
be afraid of the Assyrians when they beat
you with a rod and lift up their staff against
you as the Egyptians did. 25 For in a very
little while my indignation will come to an
end, and my anger will be directed to their
destruction. 26 The LORD of hosts will wield
a whip against them, as when he struck
Midian at the rock of Oreb; his staff will be
over the sea, and he will lift it as he did in
Egypt. 27 On that day his burden will be
removed from your shoulder, and his yoke
will be destroyed from your neck.

He has gone up from Rimmon,[h]
28 he has come to Aiath;
he has passed through Migron,
at Michmash he stores his baggage;
29 they have crossed over the pass,
at Geba they lodge for the night;

[f] Heb *I* [g] Or *land* [h] Cn: Heb *and his yoke from your neck, and a yoke will be destroyed because of fatness*

10.5-19 God's Judgment on Assyria.
10.5-11 Initially, the prophet shows that it is God who is using Assyria to punish disobedient Israel. Like the foolishly self-confident cities of Syria which soon fell into the hands of the Assyrians in the later eighth century (*Calno, Carchemish and Arpad* in northern Syria; *Hamath* (on-the-Orontes) in central Syria), the takeover of Damascus and Samaria is foretold. These defeats actually occurred in 732 and 721 respectively. Jerusalem may expect the same fate.
10.12-19 Beyond these disasters will come the doom of Assyria, which in the interim will continue to be the instrument for accomplishing God's purpose in punishing his disobedient people. Assyria has no basis for pride in its victories: it is merely serving as God's *ax*.
10.20-34 The Promise of Renewal of the Faithful Remnant of Israel.
10.20-23 The promise to *the remnant of Israel...and of Jacob* applies to the reconstituted people of God, which will not consist of the present northern or southern groups of tribes, but will include the faithful from whatever tribe, all of whom will be gathered to worship God in Jerusalem (10.32). The promise of the remnant's return recalls the name of Isaiah's son (7.3). The destruction which is soon to be experienced is countered by the act of God in setting things right with and among his people, as the term *righteousness* implies. God is sure to complete his purpose to *a full end*.
10.24-27 As God's earlier judgments on the other nations – Egypt in the time of the exodus; Midian in the time of Joshua (Judg 6-8) – come to an end, so God will remove the *burden of punishment* from Israel, and do so *in a very little while*.
10.27b-34 Following the list of cities near Jerusalem and the threat to the city itself is the assurance that God will *cut down Assyria* like a great cedar of *Lebanon*.

10.5 Jer 51.20
10.6 Isa 9.17,19; Jer 34.22; Isa 5.25,29
10.7 Gen 50.20
10.8 2 Kings 18.24,34; 19.10ff
10.9 Am 6.2; 2 Chr 35.20; 2 Kings 16.9
10.10 2 Kings 19.17,18
10.12 2 Kings 19.31; Jer 50.18; Isa 37.23
10.13 Isa 37.24; Ezek 28.4; Dan 4.30
10.14 Job 31.25
10.15 Jer 51.20; Rom 9.20,21; ver 5
10.16 Isa 17.4; Ps 106.15; ver 18
10.17 Isa 30.33; 37.23; 27.4
10.18 Jer 21.14
10.19 Isa 21.17
10.20 2 Kings 16.7; 2 Chr 28.20; Isa 17.7,8
10.21 Isa 6.13; 9.6
10.22 Rom 9.27,28; Isa 28.22
10.23 Dan 9.27
10.25 Isa 17.14; ver 5
10.26 Isa 37.36-38; Judg 7.25; Ex 14.16,27
10.27 Isa 9.4; 30.23
10.28 1 Sam 14.2; 13.2,5; 17.22
10.29 Josh 21.17; 18.25; 1 Sam 10.26

11.1-9 The Renewal of Humanity and of Creation in the Future Rule of David's Son.
11.1 The *stump of Jesse* is the remainder of the Davidic royal line.
11.2-4 God's purpose, the ability to understand it, and the power to effect it are granted to David's son through the gift of God's *spirit.* Unlike most of the rulers of Israel and Judah, this king will be concerned for the welfare of the poor and the powerless, and he will destroy *the wicked.* His ability to understand God's intention for his people is *righteousness.* His courage and persistence in putting that purpose into operation exhibit his *faithfulness.*
11.6-9 Not only will human relations within the community of God's people be transformed, but also the destructive and hostile peoples of the created world will be transformed and made peaceable as the world comes to understand and live by the LORD's plan for it.
11.10-16 The Ingathering of Israel and Judah. Presupposed here is the return of Judah from Babylon after 586, and the renewal of the people in the land.
11.10 The nations take note of the Davidic ruler and ask about him and the divine glory that accompanies his rule.
11.11-12 Israel and Judah will be brought back *a second time* from the lands where they have been scattered; the implied "first time" refers to Israel's exodus from Egypt to the promised land.
11.13-16 The antipathy that had developed historically between Israel (the northern tribes) and Judah (the southern tribes) will be overcome. All will join in a common effort to defeat their enemies: *the Philistines, Edom, Moab, Egypt. The River* is the Euphrates, which the returning tribes of Israel will be enabled by God to cross as they come back to the land from exile in Babylon. Their return did take place in the late sixth century.

Ramah trembles,
Gibeah of Saul has fled.
30 Cry aloud, O daughter Gallim!
Listen, O Laishah!
Answer her, O Anathoth!
31 Madmenah is in flight,
the inhabitants of Gebim flee for safety.
32 This very day he will halt at Nob,
he will shake his fist
at the mount of daughter Zion,
the hill of Jerusalem.

33 Look, the Sovereign, the LORD of hosts,
will lop the boughs with terrifying power;
the tallest trees will be cut down,
and the lofty will be brought low.
34 He will hack down the thickets of the forest with an ax,
and Lebanon with its majestic trees[i] will fall.

The Peaceful Kingdom

11 A shoot shall come out from the stump of Jesse,
and a branch shall grow out of his roots.
2 The spirit of the LORD shall rest on him,
the spirit of wisdom and understanding,
the spirit of counsel and might,
the spirit of knowledge and the fear of the LORD.
3 His delight shall be in the fear of the LORD.

He shall not judge by what his eyes see,
or decide by what his ears hear;
4 but with righteousness he shall judge the poor,
and decide with equity for the meek of the earth;
he shall strike the earth with the rod of his mouth,
and with the breath of his lips he shall kill the wicked.
5 Righteousness shall be the belt around his waist,
and faithfulness the belt around his loins.

6 The wolf shall live with the lamb,
the leopard shall lie down with the kid,
the calf and the lion and the fatling together,
and a little child shall lead them.
7 The cow and the bear shall graze,
their young shall lie down together;
and the lion shall eat straw like the ox.
8 The nursing child shall play over the hole of the asp,
and the weaned child shall put its hand on the adder's den.
9 They will not hurt or destroy
on all my holy mountain;
for the earth will be full of the knowledge of the LORD
as the waters cover the sea.

Return of the Remnant of Israel and Judah

10 On that day the root of Jesse shall
stand as a signal to the peoples; the nations
shall inquire of him, and his dwelling shall
be glorious.
11 On that day the Lord will extend his
hand yet a second time to recover the
remnant that is left of his people, from
Assyria, from Egypt, from Pathros, from
Ethiopia,[j] from Elam, from Shinar, from
Hamath, and from the coastlands of the sea.
12 He will raise a signal for the nations,
and will assemble the outcasts of Israel,
and gather the dispersed of Judah
from the four corners of the earth.
13 The jealousy of Ephraim shall depart,
the hostility of Judah shall be cut off;
Ephraim shall not be jealous of Judah,
and Judah shall not be hostile towards Ephraim.
14 But they shall swoop down on the backs of the Philistines in the west,
together they shall plunder the people of the east.
They shall put forth their hand against Edom and Moab,
and the Ammonites shall obey them.
15 And the LORD will utterly destroy
the tongue of the sea of Egypt;
and will wave his hand over the River
with his scorching wind;
and will split it into seven channels,
and make a way to cross on foot;
16 so there shall be a highway from Assyria
for the remnant that is left of his people,
as there was for Israel
when they came up from the land of Egypt.

[i] Cn Compare Gk Vg: Heb *with a majestic one* [j] Or *Nubia*; Heb *Cush*

10.30 1 Sam 25.44; Josh 21.18
10.31 Josh 15.31
10.32 1 Sam 21.1; Neh 11.32; Isa 13.2; 37.22
10.33 Am 2.9
11.1 Zech 6.12; Rev 5.5; Acts 13.23; Isa 4.2
11.2 Isa 61.1; Mt 3.16; Jn 1.32
11.3 Jn 2.25; 7.25
11.4 Isa 9.7; 3.14; 29.19; Mal 4.6; Job 4.9; 2 Thess 2.8
11.5 Eph 6.14; Isa 25.1
11.6 Isa 65.26
11.9 Job 5.23; Hab 2.14
11.10 Rom 15.12; Jn 3.14,15; Lk 2.32; Isa 14.3
11.11 Zech 10.10; Mic 7.12; Isa 66.19
11.12 ver 10; Zech 10.6; Isa 24.16
11.13 Jer 3.18; Ezek 37.16,17,22; Hos 1.11
11.14 Dan 11.41; Joel 3.19; Isa 16.14; 25.10
11.15 Isa 43.16; 19.16; 7.20; 8.7
11.16 Isa 19.23; 62.10; Ex 14.26-29; Isa 51.10; 63.12,13

Thanksgiving and Praise

12 You will say in that day:
I will give thanks to you, O LORD,
for though you were angry with me,
your anger turned away,
and you comforted me.

2 Surely God is my salvation;
I will trust, and will not be afraid,
for the LORD GOD[k] is my strength and my
might;
he has become my salvation.

3 With joy you will draw water from the
wells of salvation. 4And you will say in that
day:
Give thanks to the LORD,
call on his name;
make known his deeds among the
nations;
proclaim that his name is exalted.

5 Sing praises to the LORD, for he has done
gloriously;
let this be known[l] in all the earth.
6 Shout aloud and sing for joy, O royal[m]
Zion,
for great in your midst is the Holy
One of Israel.

Proclamation against Babylon

13 The oracle concerning Babylon that Isaiah son of Amoz saw.

2 On a bare hill raise a signal,
cry aloud to them;
wave the hand for them to enter
the gates of the nobles.
3 I myself have commanded my
consecrated ones,
have summoned my warriors, my
proudly exulting ones,
to execute my anger.

4 Listen, a tumult on the mountains
as of a great multitude!
Listen, an uproar of kingdoms,
of nations gathering together!
The LORD of hosts is mustering
an army for battle.
5 They come from a distant land,
from the end of the heavens,
the LORD and the weapons of his
indignation,
to destroy the whole earth.

6 Wail, for the day of the LORD is near;
it will come like destruction from the
Almighty![n]
7 Therefore all hands will be feeble,
and every human heart will melt,
8 and they will be dismayed.
Pangs and agony will seize them;
they will be in anguish like a woman
in labor.
They will look aghast at one another;
their faces will be aflame.
9 See, the day of the LORD comes,
cruel, with wrath and fierce anger,
to make the earth a desolation,
and to destroy its sinners from it.
10 For the stars of the heavens and their
constellations
will not give their light;
the sun will be dark at its rising,
and the moon will not shed its light.
11 I will punish the world for its evil,
and the wicked for their iniquity;
I will put an end to the pride of the
arrogant,
and lay low the insolence of tyrants.
12 I will make mortals more rare than fine
gold,
and humans than the gold of Ophir.
13 Therefore I will make the heavens
tremble,
and the earth will be shaken out of its
place,
at the wrath of the LORD of hosts
in the day of his fierce anger.
14 Like a hunted gazelle,
or like sheep with no one to gather
them,
all will turn to their own people,
and all will flee to their own lands.
15 Whoever is found will be thrust
through,
and whoever is caught will fall by the
sword.
16 Their infants will be dashed to pieces
before their eyes;
their houses will be plundered,
and their wives ravished.
17 See, I am stirring up the Medes against
them,
who have no regard for silver
and do not delight in gold.
18 Their bows will slaughter the young
men;
they will have no mercy on the fruit
of the womb;
their eyes will not pity children.

[k] Heb *for Yah, the* LORD [l] Or *this is made known* [m] Or *O inhabitant of* [n] Traditional rendering of Heb *Shaddai*

12.1-6 Israel's Gratitude toward God. Gratitude is expressed that God's anger, as manifest in defeat and exile, has now been *turned away*. This is now to be evident in the restoration of the people to the land (*salvation*). The people are to be nurtured in the new situation by God through *waters out of the wells of salvation*, and are to proclaim to all *the nations* the good news of what God has done for them and to declare that present in their midst (in the restored temple) is *the Holy One of Israel*. Some scholars date this oracle after the return of Israel from Babylonian captivity, which began in 521.
13.1-22 The Oracle against Babylon.
13.1 This *oracle* concerning Babylon is probably from after the time of Isaiah of Jerusalem, since the nation that took the people of Judah into exile was not Assyria, but Babylon, which under Nebuchadnezzar seized control of the empire from the Assyrians in 605, and took away the first exiles from Judah in 597.
13.9-11 The wrath of God is reflected in the darkening of the universe and its celestial sources of light. Certain are the punishment and destruction of the very pagan powers which God used to effect judgment on his disobedient people.
13.12 *Ophir*, the source of gold, was probably in east Africa near the Gulf of Suez.
13.17 *The Medes* were a people based south of the Caspian Sea who came to control the whole of Persia.

12.1 Isa 26.1; 25.1; 40.1,2
12.2 Isa 33.2; 26.3; Ex 15.2; Ps 118.14
12.3 Jn 4.10; 7.37,38; Isa 41.18
12.5 Isa 24.14; Ex 15.1; Ps 98.1
12.6 Zeph 3.14; Isa 49.26
13.1 Jer 50,51
13.2 Jer 50.2; 51.25; Isa 10.32
13.3 Joel 3.11; Ps 149.2
13.4 Isa 5.30
13.5 Isa 5.26; 42.13; 10.5; 24.1
13.6 Zeph 1.7; Isa 10.25; Joel 1.15
13.7 Ezek 7.17; 21.7
13.8 Isa 21.3; 26.17
13.9 Isa 66.15,16
13.10 Isa 5.30; Joel 2.10; Mt 24.29; Mk 13.24; Lk 21.25
13.11 Isa 26.21; 11.4; 2.11; Jer 48.29
13.13 Isa 34.4; 51.6; Jer 10.10; Am 8.8; Hag 2.6
13.14 1 Kings 22.17; Jer 50.16; 51.9
13.16 Ps 137.9; Nah 3.10; Zech 14.2
13.17 Isa 21.2; Jer 51.11; Dan 5.28
13.18 2 Kings 8.12; Ezek 9.5,10

13.19 *The Chaldeans* were a Semitic-speaking people who lived at the head of the Persian Gulf. This area was the home of Abraham and his ancestors (Gen 11.27-32). The Chaldeans joined with the Medes to overthrow the domination of the region by the Assyrians in the late seventh century. *Sodom and Gomorrah,* the cities whose destruction by God's judgment is depicted in Gen 19, became the recurrent symbols of divine destruction in later epochs. **13.20** *Arabs* is a general term for nomadic people, which probably derives from the Semitic word for desert, "Arabah." **14.1-2** Judah Restored to her Land. This will be accomplished through the LORD's *compassion on Jacob,* but will be aided by help from *the nations,* in a reversal of their previously hostile roles. Israel will be accompanied on her return by *aliens,* who are non-Israelites but choose to attach themselves to God's people. **14.3-23** An Oracle against Babylon. **14.3-21** Other nations join Israel in rejoicing at the fall of prideful, aggressive Babylon. The designation of Babylon as *Day Star, son of Dawn* is drawn from Canaanite mythology, in which one of the stars aspires to the dominant role of the sun and is subsequently thrown down. Having sought to put itself in the place of *the Most High,* Babylon is now to be utterly debased.

19 And Babylon, the glory of kingdoms,
the splendor and pride of the Chaldeans,
will be like Sodom and Gomorrah
when God overthrew them.
20 It will never be inhabited
or lived in for all generations;
Arabs will not pitch their tents there,
shepherds will not make their flocks lie down there.
21 But wild animals will lie down there,
and its houses will be full of howling creatures;
there ostriches will live,
and there goat-demons will dance.
22 Hyenas will cry in its towers,
and jackals in the pleasant palaces;
its time is close at hand,
and its days will not be prolonged.

Restoration of Judah

14 But the LORD will have compassion
on Jacob and will again choose
Israel, and will set them in their own land;
and aliens will join them and attach themselves to the house of Jacob. 2 And the nations
will take them and bring them to their
place, and the house of Israel will possess
the nations[o] as male and female slaves in
the LORD's land; they will take captive those
who were their captors, and rule over those
who oppressed them.

Downfall of the King of Babylon

3 When the LORD has given you rest from
your pain and turmoil and the hard service
with which you were made to serve, 4 you
will take up this taunt against the king of
Babylon:

How the oppressor has ceased!
How his insolence[p] has ceased!
5 The LORD has broken the staff of the wicked,
the scepter of rulers,
6 that struck down the peoples in wrath
with unceasing blows,
that ruled the nations in anger
with unrelenting persecution.
7 The whole earth is at rest and quiet;
they break forth into singing.
8 The cypresses exult over you,
the cedars of Lebanon, saying,
"Since you were laid low,
no one comes to cut us down."
9 Sheol beneath is stirred up
to meet you when you come;
it rouses the shades to greet you,
all who were leaders of the earth;
it raises from their thrones
all who were kings of the nations.
10 All of them will speak
and say to you:
"You too have become as weak as we!
You have become like us!"
11 Your pomp is brought down to Sheol,
and the sound of your harps;
maggots are the bed beneath you,
and worms are your covering.

12 How you are fallen from heaven,
O Day Star, son of Dawn!
How you are cut down to the ground,
you who laid the nations low!
13 You said in your heart,
"I will ascend to heaven;
I will raise my throne
above the stars of God;
I will sit on the mount of assembly
on the heights of Zaphon;[q]
14 I will ascend to the tops of the clouds,
I will make myself like the Most High."
15 But you are brought down to Sheol,
to the depths of the Pit.
16 Those who see you will stare at you,
and ponder over you:
"Is this the man who made the earth tremble,
who shook kingdoms,
17 who made the world like a desert
and overthrew its cities,
who would not let his prisoners go home?"
18 All the kings of the nations lie in glory,
each in his own tomb;
19 but you are cast out, away from your grave,
like loathsome carrion,[r]
clothed with the dead, those pierced by the sword,
who go down to the stones of the Pit,
like a corpse trampled underfoot.
20 You will not be joined with them in burial,
because you have destroyed your land,
you have killed your people.

May the descendants of evildoers
nevermore be named!

[o] Heb *them* [p] Q Ms Compare Gk Syr Vg: Meaning of MT uncertain [q] Or *assembly in the far north* [r] Cn Compare Gk: Heb *like a loathed branch*

13.19 Isa 21.9; Dan 4.30; Gen 19.24; Deut 29.23; Jer 49.18
13.20 Jer 51.37-43
13.21 Isa 34.11-15
13.22 Jer 51.33
14.1 Ps 102.13; Zech 1.17; 2.12; Isa 60.4,5,10; Eph 2.12-19
14.2 Isa 49.22; 60.9,10; 66.20; 60.14
14.3 Isa 40.2
14.4 Isa 13.19; Hab 2.6; Rev 18.6
14.6 Isa 10.14; 47.6
14.8 Isa 55.12
14.9 Ezek 32.21
14.11 Isa 5.14; Ezek 28.13; Isa 51.8
14.12 Isa 34.4; Lk 10.18
14.13 Ezek 28.2; Dan 8.10
14.14 Isa 47.8; 2 Thess 2.4
14.15 Mt 11.23
14.16 Jer 50.23
14.17 Joel 2.3; Isa 45.13
14.19 Isa 22.16-18; Jer 41.7,9; Isa 5.25
14.20 Job 18.19; Ps 21.10; 37.28; Isa 31.2

14.21 Ex 20.5; Isa 13.16; Mt 23.35; Isa 27.6
14.22 Isa 26.14; Prov 10.7; Isa 47.9
14.23 Isa 34.11-15; Zeph 2.14; Isa 13.6
14.24 Isa 45.23; 55.8,9; Acts 4.28
14.25 Isa 10.12,27
14.26 Isa 23.9; Ex 15.12
14.27 2 Chr 20.6; Isa 43.13; Dan 4.31,35
14.28 2 Kings 16.20
14.29 Jer 47.1-7; 2 Chr 26.6
14.30 Isa 3.14,15; 7.21; 8.21; Jer 25.16,20
14.31 Isa 3.26; ver 29; Jer 1.14; Isa 34.16
14.32 Isa 37.9; Ps 87.1,5; Zeph 3.12; Zech 11.11
15.1 Isa 11.14; Jer 48; Ezek 25.8-11; Jer 48.41
15.2 Lev 21.5
15.3 Jon 3.6-8; Jer 48.38; Isa 22.4
15.5 Jer 48.5,31,34; Isa 59.7
15.6 Isa 19.5-7; Joel 1.10-12
15.7 Isa 30.6
15.9 2 Kings 17.25; Jer 50.17

21 Prepare slaughter for his sons
because of the guilt of their father.[s]
Let them never rise to possess the earth
or cover the face of the world with cities.

22 I will rise up against them, says the
LORD of hosts, and will cut off from Babylon
name and remnant, offspring and posterity,
says the LORD. 23And I will make it a possession of the hedgehog, and pools of water,
and I will sweep it with the broom of
destruction, says the LORD of hosts.

An Oracle concerning Assyria

24 The LORD of hosts has sworn:
As I have designed,
so shall it be;
and as I have planned,
so shall it come to pass:
25 I will break the Assyrian in my land,
and on my mountains trample him under foot;
his yoke shall be removed from them,
and his burden from their shoulders.
26 This is the plan that is planned
concerning the whole earth;
and this is the hand that is stretched out
over all the nations.
27 For the LORD of hosts has planned,
and who will annul it?
His hand is stretched out,
and who will turn it back?

An Oracle concerning Philistia

28In the year that King Ahaz died this oracle
came:

29 Do not rejoice, all you Philistines,
that the rod that struck you is broken,
for from the root of the snake will come forth an adder,
and its fruit will be a flying fiery serpent.
30 The firstborn of the poor will graze,
and the needy lie down in safety;
but I will make your root die of famine,
and your remnant I[t] will kill.
31 Wail, O gate; cry, O city;
melt in fear, O Philistia, all of you!
For smoke comes out of the north,
and there is no straggler in its ranks.
32 What will one answer the messengers of the nation?
"The LORD has founded Zion,
and the needy among his people
will find refuge in her."

An Oracle concerning Moab

15 An oracle concerning Moab.

Because Ar is laid waste in a night,
Moab is undone;
because Kir is laid waste in a night,
Moab is undone.
2 Dibon[u] has gone up to the temple,
to the high places to weep;
over Nebo and over Medeba
Moab wails.
On every head is baldness,
every beard is shorn;
3 in the streets they bind on sackcloth;
on the housetops and in the squares
everyone wails and melts in tears.
4 Heshbon and Elealeh cry out,
their voices are heard as far as Jahaz;
therefore the loins of Moab quiver;[v]
his soul trembles.
5 My heart cries out for Moab;
his fugitives flee to Zoar,
to Eglath-shelishiyah.
For at the ascent of Luhith
they go up weeping;
on the road to Horonaim
they raise a cry of destruction;
6 the waters of Nimrim
are a desolation;
the grass is withered, the new growth fails,
the verdure is no more.
7 Therefore the abundance they have gained
and what they have laid up
they carry away
over the Wadi of the Willows.
8 For a cry has gone
around the land of Moab;
the wailing reaches to Eglaim,
the wailing reaches to Beer-elim.
9 For the waters of Dibon[w] are full of blood;
yet I will bring upon Dibon[w] even more—
a lion for those of Moab who escape,
for the remnant of the land.

[s] Syr Compare Gk: Heb *fathers* [t] Q Ms Vg: MT *he* [u] Cn: Heb *the house and Dibon* [v] Cn Compare Gk Syr: Heb *the armed men of Moab cry aloud* [w] Q Ms Vg Compare Syr: MT *Dimon*

14.22-23 The poetic announcement of God's judgment on Babylon is followed by a brief oracle in prose which affirms the ruin of the proud city.
14.24-27 An Oracle against Assyria. Probably dating from the time of Isaiah himself, this prediction of doom was appropriate prior to the rise of Babylon to power. God is sovereign over all the earth, and his purpose will triumph in spite of arrogant human schemes and systems.
14.28-32 An Oracle against Philistia. This longtime power on the Mediterranean coast west of Israel and Judah is not to be pleased by the fall of Assyria, since a fearful fate is in store for the Philistines in the plan of God.
15.1-16.14 An Oracle against Moab.
15.1-9 Mentioned as lamenting their ruin are the cities of Moab, the area east of the Dead Sea through which Israel had passed on the way into the promised land (Num 33; Deut 1): *Kir*, the capital of Moab, located on a promontory overlooking the great valley leading down to the Gulf of Aqabah; *Dibon*, an important city on the main trade route through the area, the King's Highway; *Medeba*, a city and area 25 miles south of Amman (the latter was known in antiquity as Rabbah and Philadelphia), and center of a fertile area; *Heshbon*, a strategic city back to the time of the exodus (Num 21.21-30; Deut 32.49). *The remnant of the land* refers to the small group of Moabites who will survive the impending judgment of God on this nation.

16.1 *Lambs* are to be sent to the ruler of Judah, to be offered to the God of Israel at the temple on Mt. Zion.
16.2 The *Arnon* was the main river flowing through Moab and emptying into the Dead Sea.
16.4-5 Once the wicked have been punished, Moab will become part of the realm of the descendant of *David.*
16.8-13 Cities claimed by Moab, such as *Sibmah* and *Elealeh,* which were assigned to the Israelite tribe of Reuben (Num 32), will fall to ruin when judgment descends on Moab, as will the people's shrines.
17.1-14 Oracles concerning Damascus and Israel.
17.1-3 *Damascus,* the capital of Syria, will be destroyed, as will Samaria, the capital of Israel in *Ephraim.*
17.4-11 God's judgment will fall on Judah in the midst of her seeming prosperity and military successes. *The Valley of Rephaim* led southwest from the hills west of Jerusalem toward the coastal plain. *The Hivites and Amorites* were descendants of the former occupants of Palestine and Transjordan before Israel's exodus from Egypt. Both those now living in the land in apparent prosperity and their enemies from other lands will fall under God's judgment.

16 Send lambs
to the ruler of the land,
from Sela, by way of the desert,
to the mount of daughter Zion.
2 Like fluttering birds,
like scattered nestlings,
so are the daughters of Moab
at the fords of the Arnon.
3 "Give counsel,
grant justice;
make your shade like night
at the height of noon;
hide the outcasts,
do not betray the fugitive;
4 let the outcasts of Moab
settle among you;
be a refuge to them
from the destroyer."

When the oppressor is no more,
and destruction has ceased,
and marauders have vanished from the land,
5 then a throne shall be established in steadfast love
in the tent of David,
and on it shall sit in faithfulness
a ruler who seeks justice
and is swift to do what is right.

6 We have heard of the pride of Moab
—how proud he is!—
of his arrogance, his pride, and his insolence;
his boasts are false.
7 Therefore let Moab wail,
let everyone wail for Moab.
Mourn, utterly stricken,
for the raisin cakes of Kir-hareseth.

8 For the fields of Heshbon languish,
and the vines of Sibmah,
whose clusters once made drunk
the lords of the nations,
reached to Jazer
and strayed to the desert;
their shoots once spread abroad
and crossed over the sea.
9 Therefore I weep with the weeping of Jazer
for the vines of Sibmah;
I drench you with my tears,
O Heshbon and Elealeh;
for the shout over your fruit harvest
and your grain harvest has ceased.
10 Joy and gladness are taken away
from the fruitful field;
and in the vineyards no songs are sung,
no shouts are raised;
no treader treads out wine in the presses;
the vintage-shout is hushed.[x]
11 Therefore my heart throbs like a harp for Moab,
and my very soul for Kir-heres.

12 When Moab presents himself, when
he wearies himself upon the high place,
when he comes to his sanctuary to pray, he
will not prevail.
13 This was the word that the LORD spoke
concerning Moab in the past. 14But now the
LORD says, In three years, like the years of
a hired worker, the glory of Moab will be
brought into contempt, in spite of all its
great multitude; and those who survive will
be very few and feeble.

An Oracle concerning Damascus

17 An oracle concerning Damascus.

See, Damascus will cease to be a city,
and will become a heap of ruins.
2 Her towns will be deserted forever;[y]
they will be places for flocks,
which will lie down, and no one will make them afraid.
3 The fortress will disappear from Ephraim,
and the kingdom from Damascus;
and the remnant of Aram will be
like the glory of the children of Israel,
says the LORD of hosts.

4 On that day
the glory of Jacob will be brought low,
and the fat of his flesh will grow lean.
5 And it shall be as when reapers gather standing grain
and their arms harvest the ears,
and as when one gleans the ears of grain
in the Valley of Rephaim.
6 Gleanings will be left in it,
as when an olive tree is beaten—
two or three berries
in the top of the highest bough,
four or five
on the branches of a fruit tree,
says the LORD God of Israel.

7 On that day people will regard their
Maker, and their eyes will look to the Holy

[x] Gk: Heb *I have hushed* [y] Cn Compare Gk: Heb *the cities of Aroer are deserted*

16.1 2 Kings 3.4; 14.7; Isa 10.32
16.2 Num 21.13,14
16.3 Isa 25.4
16.4 Isa 9.4; 54.14
16.5 Dan 7.14; Mic 4.7; Lk 1.33; Isa 9.7
16.6 Jer 48.29,30; Zeph 2.8,10
16.7 1 Chr 16.3; 2 Kings 3.25; Jer 48.31
16.8 Isa 15.4; Num 32.38; Jer 48.32
16.9 Jer 48.32; Isa 15.4; Jer 40.10,12
16.10 Isa 24.7,8; Jer 48.33; Job 24.11
16.11 Isa 15.5; 63.15; Jer 48.36
16.12 Jer 48.35; 1 Kings 18.29; Isa 15.2; 2 Kings 19.12
16.14 Isa 21.16; 25.10
17.1 2 Kings 16.9; Jer 49.23; Am 1.3; Zech 9.1; Isa 8.4; 10.9
17.2 Jer 7.33
17.3 Isa 7.16; 8.4
17.4 Isa 10.3,16
17.5 Jer 51.33; 2 Sam 5.18,22
17.6 Isa 24.13; 27.12
17.7 Isa 10.20; Mic 7.7

17.8 Isa 27.9; 30.22; 31.7; Ex 34.13; Deut 7.5
17.9 Isa 7.25
17.10 Isa 51.13; Ps 68.19; Isa 26.4; 30.29
17.11 Ps 90.6; Job 4.8
17.12 Jer 6.23; Ezek 43.2; Ps 18.4
17.13 Isa 33.3; Ps 9.5; Isa 13.14; 29.5; 41.15,16
17.14 Isa 41.12; 2 Kings 19.35
18.1 Isa 20.3-5; Ezek 30.4,5,9; Zeph 2.12; 3.10
18.2 Ex 2.3; ver 7; 2 Chr 12.2-4
18.3 Ps 49.1; Isa 5.26; 26.11
18.4 Isa 26.21; 2 Sam 23.4; Isa 26.19
18.5 Ezek 17.6-10; Isa 27.11
18.6 Isa 46.11; 56.9; Jer 7.33
18.7 Ps 68.31; Isa 45.14; Zeph 3.10; Zech 14.16,17
19.1 Isa 13.1; Jer 46.13-26; Ezek 29,30; Ps 18.10; 104.3; Ex 12.12; Jer 43.12
19.2 Judg 7.22; 1 Sam 14.16,20; 2 Chr 20.23; Mt 10.21,36
19.3 ver 11-14; Isa 8.19

One of Israel; 8 they will not have regard for
the altars, the work of their hands, and they
will not look to what their own fingers have
made, either the sacred poles[z] or the altars
of incense.

9 On that day their strong cities will be
like the deserted places of the Hivites and
the Amorites,[a] which they deserted because
of the children of Israel, and there will be
desolation.

10 For you have forgotten the God of your salvation,
  and have not remembered the Rock of your refuge;
therefore, though you plant pleasant plants
  and set out slips of an alien god,
11 though you make them grow on the day that you plant them,
  and make them blossom in the morning that you sow;
yet the harvest will flee away
  in a day of grief and incurable pain.

12 Ah, the thunder of many peoples,
  they thunder like the thundering of the sea!
Ah, the roar of nations,
  they roar like the roaring of mighty waters!
13 The nations roar like the roaring of many waters,
  but he will rebuke them, and they will flee far away,
chased like chaff on the mountains before the wind
  and whirling dust before the storm.
14 At evening time, lo, terror!
  Before morning, they are no more.
This is the fate of those who despoil us,
  and the lot of those who plunder us.

An Oracle concerning Ethiopia

18 Ah, land of whirring wings
  beyond the rivers of Ethiopia,[b]
2 sending ambassadors by the Nile
  in vessels of papyrus on the waters!
Go, you swift messengers,
  to a nation tall and smooth,
to a people feared near and far,
  a nation mighty and conquering,
  whose land the rivers divide.

3 All you inhabitants of the world,
  you who live on the earth,
when a signal is raised on the mountains, look!
  When a trumpet is blown, listen!
4 For thus the LORD said to me:
I will quietly look from my dwelling
  like clear heat in sunshine,
  like a cloud of dew in the heat of harvest.
5 For before the harvest, when the blossom is over
  and the flower becomes a ripening grape,
he will cut off the shoots with pruning hooks,
  and the spreading branches he will hew away.
6 They shall all be left
  to the birds of prey of the mountains
  and to the animals of the earth.
And the birds of prey will summer on them,
  and all the animals of the earth will winter on them.

7 At that time gifts will be brought to the
LORD of hosts from[c] a people tall and smooth,
from a people feared near and far, a nation
mighty and conquering, whose land the
rivers divide, to Mount Zion, the place of the
name of the LORD of hosts.

An Oracle concerning Egypt

19 An oracle concerning Egypt.

See, the LORD is riding on a swift cloud
  and comes to Egypt;
the idols of Egypt will tremble at his presence,
  and the heart of the Egyptians will melt within them.
2 I will stir up Egyptians against Egyptians,
  and they will fight, one against the other,
  neighbor against neighbor,
  city against city, kingdom against kingdom;
3 the spirit of the Egyptians within them will be emptied out,
  and I will confound their plans;
they will consult the idols and the spirits of the dead

[a] Heb *Asherim* [b] Cn Compare Gk: Heb *places of the wood and the highest bough* [c] Or *Nubia*; Heb *Cush* [d] Q Ms Gk Vg: MT *of*

18.1-7 Oracle concerning Ethiopia.
18.2 *Papyrus* is a substance made from reeds which grow in the Nile. When sliced and pressed together in layers, it forms a durable water-resistant material used to write on and as an outer surface for river boats.
18.4-6 *Ethiopia.* In spite of the seeming prosperity of this land up the Nile from Egypt, judgment is about to fall.
18.7 Subsequently, members of this *tall, smooth people* will bring gifts to the sanctuary of Israel's God in Jerusalem.
19.1-25 An Oracle about Egypt.
19.1-17 *The LORD* will bring about major difficulties for the Egyptians, and (probably due to a change in the ruling dynasty) they will have *a fierce king over them.* The physical evidence of this divine judgment will take the form of a decrease in the flow of *the Nile.* The royal residence in the Nile delta at *Zoan,* where miracles and oracles used to take place, will fall into confusion as God's plan for Judah begins to unfold. Tiny *Judah* will strike *terror* in the hearts of the Egyptians as a consequence of the plan of *the LORD of hosts.*

19.18-22 The presence of Hebrew-speaking (*language of Canaan*) cities and the worship of the LORD there will transform Egypt, which will be aided by the God of Israel in its times of difficulty. The commercial links between Egypt and Assyria will then create a triad of nations blessed by *the LORD of hosts:* Israel, Egypt and Assyria. The replacement of Assyrian rule by that of the Babylonians in 538 precluded a literal fulfillment of this prophecy.
20.1-6 The Folly of Trusting in Egypt and Ethiopia.
20.1 The capture of the important Phoenician seaport of *Ashdod* by the Assyrians after 715 under their king, *Sargon*, led some in Judah to turn to an alliance with Egypt and Ethiopia in the hope of preserving their national identity.
20.2 Isaiah stripped himself of clothes and footwear to symbolize the folly of relying on such powers for safety.

and the ghosts and the familiar
spirits;
4 I will deliver the Egyptians
into the hand of a hard master;
a fierce king will rule over them,
says the Sovereign, the LORD of hosts.

5 The waters of the Nile will be dried up,
and the river will be parched and dry;
6 its canals will become foul,
and the branches of Egypt's Nile will
diminish and dry up,
reeds and rushes will rot away.
7 There will be bare places by the Nile,
on the brink of the Nile;
and all that is sown by the Nile will dry
up,
be driven away, and be no more.
8 Those who fish will mourn;
all who cast hooks in the Nile will
lament,
and those who spread nets on the
water will languish.
9 The workers in flax will be in despair,
and the carders and those at the loom
will grow pale.
10 Its weavers will be dismayed,
and all who work for wages will be
grieved.

11 The princes of Zoan are utterly foolish;
the wise counselors of Pharaoh give
stupid counsel.
How can you say to Pharaoh,
"I am one of the sages,
a descendant of ancient kings"?
12 Where now are your sages?
Let them tell you and make known
what the LORD of hosts has planned
against Egypt.
13 The princes of Zoan have become fools,
and the princes of Memphis are
deluded;
those who are the cornerstones of its
tribes
have led Egypt astray.
14 The LORD has poured into them[e]
a spirit of confusion;
and they have made Egypt stagger in all
its doings
as a drunkard staggers around in
vomit.
15 Neither head nor tail, palm branch or
reed,
will be able to do anything for Egypt.

16 On that day the Egyptians will be like
women, and tremble with fear before the
hand that the LORD of hosts raises against
them. 17 And the land of Judah will become
a terror to the Egyptians; everyone to whom
it is mentioned will fear because of the plan
that the LORD of hosts is planning against
them.

Egypt, Assyria, and Israel Blessed

18 On that day there will be five cities in
the land of Egypt that speak the language
of Canaan and swear allegiance to the LORD
of hosts. One of these will be called the City
of the Sun.
19 On that day there will be an altar to
the LORD in the center of the land of Egypt,
and a pillar to the LORD at its border. 20 It will
be a sign and a witness to the LORD of hosts
in the land of Egypt; when they cry to the
LORD because of oppressors, he will send
them a savior, and will defend and deliver
them. 21 The LORD will make himself known
to the Egyptians; and the Egyptians will
know the LORD on that day, and will worship with sacrifice and burnt offering, and
they will make vows to the LORD and perform them. 22 The LORD will strike Egypt,
striking and healing; they will return to the
LORD, and he will listen to their supplications and heal them.
23 On that day there will be a highway
from Egypt to Assyria, and the Assyrian will
come into Egypt, and the Egyptian into
Assyria, and the Egyptians will worship
with the Assyrians.
24 On that day Israel will be the third
with Egypt and Assyria, a blessing in the
midst of the earth, 25 whom the LORD of hosts
has blessed, saying, "Blessed be Egypt my
people, and Assyria the work of my hands,
and Israel my heritage."

Isaiah Dramatizes the Conquest of Egypt and Ethiopia

20 In the year that the commander-
in-chief, who was sent by King
Sargon of Assyria, came to Ashdod and
fought against it and took it— 2 at that time
the LORD had spoken to Isaiah son of Amoz,
saying, "Go, and loose the sackcloth from
your loins and take your sandals off your
feet," and he had done so, walking naked

[d] Gk Compare Tg: Heb *it*

19.4 Isa 20.4; Jer 46.26; Ezek 29.19
19.5 Jer 51.36; Ezek 30.12
19.6 Ex 7.18; Isa 37.25; 15.6
19.10 Ps 11.3
19.11 Num 13.22; 1 Kings 4.30; Acts 7.22
19.12 1 Cor 1.20; Isa 14.24; Rom 9.17
19.13 Jer 2.16; Ezek 30.13; Zech 10.4
19.14 Isa 29.10; Mt 17.17; Isa 3.12; 9.16; 28.7
19.16 Jer 51.30; Isa 2.19; 11.15; 30.32
19.17 Isa 14.24
19.18 Isa 45.23; 65.16
19.19 Isa 56.7; Gen 28.18; Ex 24.4; Josh 22.10,26,27
19.20 Isa 43.3,11; 49.25
19.21 Isa 11.9; Mal 1.11; Isa 44.5
19.22 Isa 30.26; 27.13; 45.14
19.23 Isa 11.16; 27.13
19.25 Isa 45.14; Hos 2.23; Eph 2.10
20.1 2 Kings 18.17; 1 Sam 5.1
20.2 Zech 13.4; Ezek 24.17,23; 1 Sam 19.24; Mic 1.8

and barefoot. [3]Then the LORD said, "Just as
my servant Isaiah has walked naked and
barefoot for three years as a sign and a
portent against Egypt and Ethiopia,[e] [4]so shall
the king of Assyria lead away the Egyptians
as captives and the Ethiopians[f] as exiles,
both the young and the old, naked and
barefoot, with buttocks uncovered, to the
shame of Egypt. [5]And they shall be dismayed and confounded because of Ethiopia[e]
their hope and of Egypt their boast. [6]In that
day the inhabitants of this coastland will
say, 'See, this is what has happened to
those in whom we hoped and to whom we
fled for help and deliverance from the king
of Assyria! And we, how shall we escape?' "

Oracles concerning Babylon, Edom, and Arabia

21 The oracle concerning the wilderness of the sea.

As whirlwinds in the Negeb sweep on,
 it comes from the desert,
 from a terrible land.
2 A stern vision is told to me;
 the betrayer betrays,
 and the destroyer destroys.
Go up, O Elam,
 lay siege, O Media;
all the sighing she has caused
 I bring to an end.
3 Therefore my loins are filled with anguish;
 pangs have seized me,
 like the pangs of a woman in labor;
I am bowed down so that I cannot hear,
 I am dismayed so that I cannot see.
4 My mind reels, horror has appalled me;
 the twilight I longed for
 has been turned for me into trembling.
5 They prepare the table,
 they spread the rugs,
 they eat, they drink.
Rise up, commanders,
 oil the shield!
6 For thus the Lord said to me:
"Go, post a lookout,
 let him announce what he sees.
7 When he sees riders, horsemen in pairs,
 riders on donkeys, riders on camels,
let him listen diligently,
 very diligently."
8 Then the watcher[g] called out:
"Upon a watchtower I stand, O Lord,
 continually by day,
and at my post I am stationed
 throughout the night.
9 Look, there they come, riders,
 horsemen in pairs!"
Then he responded,
 "Fallen, fallen is Babylon;
and all the images of her gods
 lie shattered on the ground."
10 O my threshed and winnowed one,
 what I have heard from the LORD of hosts,
 the God of Israel, I announce to you.

11 The oracle concerning Dumah.

One is calling to me from Seir,
 "Sentinel, what of the night?
 Sentinel, what of the night?"
12 The sentinel says:
"Morning comes, and also the night.
 If you will inquire, inquire;
 come back again."

13 The oracle concerning the desert plain.

In the scrub of the desert plain you will lodge,
 O caravans of Dedanites.
14 Bring water to the thirsty,
 meet the fugitive with bread,
 O inhabitants of the land of Tema.
15 For they have fled from the swords,
 from the drawn sword,
from the bent bow,
 and from the stress of battle.
16 For thus the Lord said to me: Within
a year, according to the years of a hired
worker, all the glory of Kedar will come to
an end; [17]and the remaining bows of Kedar's
warriors will be few; for the LORD, the God
of Israel, has spoken.

A Warning of Destruction of Jerusalem

22 The oracle concerning the valley of vision.

What do you mean that you have gone up,
 all of you, to the housetops,
2 you that are full of shoutings,
 tumultuous city, exultant town?
Your slain are not slain by the sword,
 nor are they dead in battle.

[e] Or *Nubia*; Heb *Cush* [f] Or *Nubians*; Heb *Cushites* [g] Q Ms: MT *a lion*

20.3-6 The prophet's nakedness foreshadows Assyria's stripping of Egypt and Ethiopia of their wealth and populations.
21.1-16 Oracles concerning Babylon, Edom and Arabia.
21.1-10 A series of ecstatic visions portrays the fearful judgment that is to fall (1) on the city of Babylon (21.1-10), which will be taken by *Elam* (territory east of the lower Tigris-Euphrates valley) and by *Media* (located in the mountains northeast of the Tigris and below the Caspian Sea); (2) on Edom (*Dumah*) in the northwestern part of the Arabian desert, astride major commercial routes (21.11-12); and (3) on *Dedan*, the center of the Arabian peoples in the *Kedar*, in the desert east of Damascus, at a strategic position on trade routes from the east to the Mediterranean coast (21.13-16). All these centers are to lose power as a result of the work of *the God of Israel*.
22.1-25 Isaiah's Response to the End of the Siege of Jerusalem.
22.1-14 The prophet sees no cause for rejoicing in the lifting of the siege of Jerusalem (701), since the defenders of the city have fled and much of it has been ruined in an effort to rebuild the walls. The defenders had counted on the weapons stored in the huge armory, *the House of the Forest*, built from cedars of Lebanon by Solomon (1 Kings 7.2; 10.17), but they were useless. The people's lack of contrition about their disobedience, which brought this catastrophe on them as divine judgment, is disheartening to the prophet.

20.3 Isa 8.18; 37.9; 43.3
20.4 Isa 19.4; 3.17; Jer 13.22,26
20.5 2 Kings 18.21; Isa 30.3,5,7; Ezek 29.6,7
20.6 Isa 10.3; 30.7; Mt 23.33; Heb 2.3
21.1 Isa 31.1; Jer 51.42; Zech 9.14
21.2 Isa 33.1; 13.17; Jer 49.34
21.3 Isa 15.5; 16.11; 13.8
21.4 Deut 28.67
21.5 Jer 51.39,57; Dan 5.1-4
21.7 ver 9
21.8 Hab 2.1
21.9 Jer 51.8; Rev 14.8; 18.2; Isa 46.1; Jer 50.2; 51.44
21.10 Jer 51.33
21.11 Gen 25.14; 32.3
21.13 Isa 13.1; Jer 49.28; 1 Chr 1.9,32
21.14 Gen 25.15; Job 6.19
21.15 Isa 13.14,15; 17.13
21.16 Isa 16.14; 17.4; Ps 120.5; Isa 60.7
21.17 Isa 10.19; Num 23.19; Zech 1.6
22.1 Isa 13.1; Joel 3.12,14; Isa 15.3
22.2 Isa 32.13; Jer 14.18; Lam 2.20

22.15-25 Hezekiah is still king of Judah (715-687), but his chief aide, *Shebna*, is interested only in constructing a monumental tomb for himself and his family, rather than in the welfare of the wounded and dispossessed. *Eliakim* will replace him, and he will show courage and responsibility in his role, for which he will be honored. His negotiations with the Assyrian leader, Sennacherib, while Jerusalem was besieged, are reported in Isa 36-39 (2 Kings 18.13-19.7).
23.1-8 The Oracle against Tyre.
23.1-12 The theme of oracles concerning the nations is resumed here from Isa 14-20. *Tarshish* was an important shipping center, perhaps on *Cyprus*, or possibly identical with Tarsus, a major commercial and cultural city since the Stone Age on the southeast coast of what is now Turkey. *Shihor* was probably a port in the Nile delta of Egypt. *Tyre* and *Sidon* were major commercial centers for the Phoenicians in what is now Lebanon. *The* LORD is about to deflate the foolish pride of these economically flourishing centers.

3 Your rulers have all fled together;
they were captured without the use of a bow.[h]
All of you who were found were captured,
though they had fled far away.[i]
4 Therefore I said:
Look away from me,
let me weep bitter tears;
do not try to comfort me
for the destruction of my beloved people.

5 For the Lord GOD of hosts has a day
of tumult and trampling and confusion
in the valley of vision,
a battering down of walls
and a cry for help to the mountains.
6 Elam bore the quiver
with chariots and cavalry,[j]
and Kir uncovered the shield.
7 Your choicest valleys were full of chariots,
and the cavalry took their stand at the gates.
8 He has taken away the covering of Judah.

On that day you looked to the weapons
of the House of the Forest, [9]and you saw
that there were many breaches in the city
of David, and you collected the waters of the
lower pool. [10]You counted the houses of
Jerusalem, and you broke down the houses
to fortify the wall. [11]You made a reservoir
between the two walls for the water of the
old pool. But you did not look to him who
did it, or have regard for him who planned
it long ago.

12 In that day the Lord GOD of hosts
called to weeping and mourning,
to baldness and putting on sackcloth;
13 but instead there was joy and festivity,
killing oxen and slaughtering sheep,
eating meat and drinking wine.
"Let us eat and drink,
for tomorrow we die."
14 The LORD of hosts has revealed himself in my ears:
Surely this iniquity will not be forgiven you until you die,
says the Lord GOD of hosts.

Denunciation of Self-Seeking Officials

15 Thus says the Lord GOD of hosts: Come,
go to this steward, to Shebna, who is master
of the household, and say to him: [16]What
right do you have here? Who are your
relatives here, that you have cut out a tomb
here for yourself, cutting a tomb on the
height, and carving a habitation for yourself
in the rock? [17]The LORD is about to hurl you
away violently, my fellow. He will seize firm
hold on you, [18]whirl you round and round,
and throw you like a ball into a wide land;
there you shall die, and there your splendid
chariots shall lie, O you disgrace to your
master's house! [19]I will thrust you from
your office, and you will be pulled down
from your post.
20 On that day I will call my servant
Eliakim son of Hilkiah, [21]and will clothe him
with your robe and bind your sash on him.
I will commit your authority to his hand,
and he shall be a father to the inhabitants
of Jerusalem and to the house of Judah. [22]I
will place on his shoulder the key of the
house of David; he shall open, and no one
shall shut; he shall shut, and no one shall
open. [23]I will fasten him like a peg in a
secure place, and he will become a throne
of honor to his ancestral house. [24]And they
will hang on him the whole weight of his
ancestral house, the offspring and issue,
every small vessel, from the cups to all the
flagons. [25]On that day, says the LORD of
hosts, the peg that was fastened in a secure
place will give way; it will be cut down and
fall, and the load that was on it will perish,
for the LORD has spoken.

An Oracle concerning Tyre

23

The oracle concerning Tyre.

Wail, O ships of Tarshish,
for your fortress is destroyed.[k]
When they came in from Cyprus
they learned of it.
2 Be still, O inhabitants of the coast,
O merchants of Sidon,
your messengers crossed over the sea[l]
3 and were on the mighty waters;
your revenue was the grain of Shihor,
the harvest of the Nile;
you were the merchant of the nations.

[h] Or *without their bows* [i] Gk Syr Vg: Heb *fled from far away* [j] Meaning of Heb uncertain [k] Cn Compare verse 14: Heb *for it is destroyed, without houses* [l] Q Ms: MT *crossing over the sea, they replenished you*

22.3 Isa 21.15
22.4 Isa 15.3; Jer 4.19; 9.1
22.5 Isa 37.3; 63.3; Lam 1.5; 2.2; ver 1
22.6 Jer 49.35; 2 Kings 16.9
22.7 2 Chr 32.1
22.8 2 Chr 32.3-5,30; 1 Kings 7.2; 10.17
22.9 Neh 3.16
22.11 2 Kings 25.4; 20.20; 2 Chr 32.3,4; Isa 37.26
22.12 Joel 1.13; Isa 15.2; Mic 1.16
22.13 Isa 5.11,22; 56.12; 1 Cor 15.32
22.14 Isa 5.9; 65.7,20
22.15 2 Kings 18.37; Isa 36.3
22.16 2 Sam 18.18; 2 Chr 16.14; Mt 27.60
22.18 Isa 17.13; Job 18.18
22.20 2 Kings 18.18; Isa 36.3
22.22 Rev 3.7; Isa 7.2,13; Job 12.14
22.23 Ezra 9.8; Job 36.7
22.25 ver 23; Isa 46.11; Mic 4.4
23.1 Jer 25.22; 47.4; Ezek 26,27,28; ver 12
23.2 Isa 47.5
23.3 Jer 2.18; Ezek 27.3-23

4 Be ashamed, O Sidon, for the sea has
spoken,
the fortress of the sea, saying:
"I have neither labored nor given birth,
I have neither reared young men
nor brought up young women."
5 When the report comes to Egypt,
they will be in anguish over the
report about Tyre.
6 Cross over to Tarshish—
wail, O inhabitants of the coast!
7 Is this your exultant city
whose origin is from days of old,
whose feet carried her
to settle far away?
8 Who has planned this
against Tyre, the bestower of crowns,
whose merchants were princes,
whose traders were the honored of
the earth?
9 The LORD of hosts has planned it—
to defile the pride of all glory,
to shame all the honored of the earth.
10 Cross over to your own land,
O ships of[m] Tarshish;
this is a harbor[n] no more.
11 He has stretched out his hand over the
sea,
he has shaken the kingdoms;
the LORD has given command
concerning Canaan
to destroy its fortresses.
12 He said:
You will exult no longer,
O oppressed virgin daughter Sidon;
rise, cross over to Cyprus—
even there you will have no rest.

13 Look at the land of the Chaldeans!
This is the people; it was not Assyria. They
destined Tyre for wild animals. They erected
their siege towers, they tore down her
palaces, they made her a ruin.[o]
14 Wail, O ships of Tarshish,
for your fortress is destroyed.
15 From that day Tyre will be forgotten for
seventy years, the lifetime of one king. At
the end of seventy years, it will happen to
Tyre as in the song about the prostitute:
16 Take a harp,
go about the city,
you forgotten prostitute!
Make sweet melody,
sing many songs,
that you may be remembered.
17 At the end of seventy years, the LORD will
visit Tyre, and she will return to her trade,
and will prostitute herself with all the kingdoms of the world on the face of the earth.
18 Her merchandise and her wages will be
dedicated to the LORD; her profits[p] will not
be stored or hoarded, but her merchandise
will supply abundant food and fine clothing
for those who live in the presence of the
LORD.

Impending Judgment on the Earth

24 Now the LORD is about to lay
waste the earth and make it
desolate,
and he will twist its surface and
scatter its inhabitants.
2 And it shall be, as with the people, so
with the priest;
as with the slave, so with his master;
as with the maid, so with her
mistress;
as with the buyer, so with the seller;
as with the lender, so with the
borrower;
as with the creditor, so with the
debtor.
3 The earth shall be utterly laid waste and
utterly despoiled;
for the LORD has spoken this word.

4 The earth dries up and withers,
the world languishes and withers;
the heavens languish together with
the earth.
5 The earth lies polluted
under its inhabitants;
for they have transgressed laws,
violated the statutes,
broken the everlasting covenant.
6 Therefore a curse devours the earth,
and its inhabitants suffer for their
guilt;
therefore the inhabitants of the earth
dwindled,
and few people are left.
7 The wine dries up,
the vine languishes,
all the merry-hearted sigh.
8 The mirth of the timbrels is stilled,
the noise of the jubilant has ceased,
the mirth of the lyre is stilled.
9 No longer do they drink wine with
singing;
strong drink is bitter to those who
drink it.

[m] Cn Compare Gk: Heb *like the Nile, daughter* [n] Cn: Heb *restraint* [o] Meaning of Heb uncertain [p] Heb *it*

23.4 Ezek 28.21,22
23.7 Isa 22.2; 32.13
23.9 Isa 2.11; 13.11; Job 40.11,12; Isa 5.13; 9.15
23.11 Isa 14.26; 50.2; 25.2
23.12 Rev 18.22; Isa 47.1; ver 1
23.13 Isa 10.5,7
23.14 ver 1
23.15 Jer 25.11,22
23.17 Rev 17.2
23.18 Isa 60.5-9; Zech 14.20
24.1 ver 19,20; Isa 13.13,14
24.2 Hos 4.9; Lev 25.36,37; Deut 23.19,20
24.3 Isa 6.11,12
24.5 Gen 3.17; Num 35.33; Isa 59.12
24.6 Isa 34.5; Mal 4.6; Isa 5.24; 9.19
24.7 Isa 16.8-10; Joel 1.10-12
24.8 Jer 7.34; 16.9; 25.10; Ezek 26.13; Hos 2.11; Rev 18.22

23.13 is probably a later insert to shift the original force of the oracle from Assyria (705-701) to Babylon, which conquered Assyria in the period from 612 to 605.
23.13-18 *Tyre* is destined for ruin, in accord with God's judgment on the city. This will be in effect for *seventy years* – which is probably a round figure for a generation. The city which now tries to buy happiness and fulfillment through traffic with prostitutes will in the future find true satisfaction by devoting its wealth and prosperity to the people of *the LORD.*
24.1-23 Universal Judgment to Fall on the Human Race.
24.1-13 Recalling the chaos that preceded the creation of the universe (Gen 1.1-12), the prophet pictures a future situation of cosmic and social disorder, in which all human joy is overwhelmed by God's judgment on the human race for having broken the everlasting covenant that was to have brought all humanity into right relationship with God.

24.14-23 Even though there still are those who *give glory to God*, their influence is not sufficient to call people as a whole from despair and *treacherous* behavior. Warning comes of a day when *the foundations of the earth tremble* and punishment will come down on a cosmic scale from the God who reigns *on Mount Zion and in Jerusalem*.
25.1-12 God's Plan Includes Disaster in Jerusalem and Punishment of Israel's Enemies.
25.1-5 The destruction of Jerusalem is part of God's plan, and this provides an ironic occasion for rejoicing by the prophet.
25.6-10a It is on the mountain of *the LORD of hosts* in Jerusalem that blessing will be poured out by God *over all people*, and death itself will be *swallowed up forever*.

10 The city of chaos is broken down,
every house is shut up so that no one can enter.
11 There is an outcry in the streets for lack of wine;
all joy has reached its eventide;
the gladness of the earth is banished.
12 Desolation is left in the city,
the gates are battered into ruins.
13 For thus it shall be on the earth
and among the nations,
as when an olive tree is beaten,
as at the gleaning when the grape harvest is ended.

14 They lift up their voices, they sing for joy;
they shout from the west over the majesty of the LORD.
15 Therefore in the east give glory to the LORD;
in the coastlands of the sea glorify the name of the LORD, the God of Israel.
16 From the ends of the earth we hear songs of praise,
of glory to the Righteous One.
But I say, I pine away,
I pine away. Woe is me!
For the treacherous deal treacherously,
the treacherous deal very treacherously.

17 Terror, and the pit, and the snare
are upon you, O inhabitant of the earth!
18 Whoever flees at the sound of the terror
shall fall into the pit;
and whoever climbs out of the pit
shall be caught in the snare.
For the windows of heaven are opened,
and the foundations of the earth tremble.
19 The earth is utterly broken,
the earth is torn asunder,
the earth is violently shaken.
20 The earth staggers like a drunkard,
it sways like a hut;
its transgression lies heavy upon it,
and it falls, and will not rise again.

21 On that day the LORD will punish
the host of heaven in heaven,
and on earth the kings of the earth.
22 They will be gathered together
like prisoners in a pit;
they will be shut up in a prison,
and after many days they will be punished.
23 Then the moon will be abashed,
and the sun ashamed;
for the LORD of hosts will reign
on Mount Zion and in Jerusalem,
and before his elders he will manifest his glory.

Praise for Deliverance from Oppression

25 O LORD, you are my God;
I will exalt you, I will praise your name;
for you have done wonderful things,
plans formed of old, faithful and sure.
2 For you have made the city a heap,
the fortified city a ruin;
the palace of aliens is a city no more,
it will never be rebuilt.
3 Therefore strong peoples will glorify you;
cities of ruthless nations will fear you.
4 For you have been a refuge to the poor,
a refuge to the needy in their distress,
a shelter from the rainstorm and a shade from the heat.
When the blast of the ruthless was like a winter rainstorm,
5 the noise of aliens like heat in a dry place,
you subdued the heat with the shade of clouds;
the song of the ruthless was stilled.

6 On this mountain the LORD of hosts will make for all peoples
a feast of rich food, a feast of well-aged wines,
of rich food filled with marrow, of well-aged wines strained clear.
7 And he will destroy on this mountain
the shroud that is cast over all peoples,
the sheet that is spread over all nations;
8 he will swallow up death forever.
Then the Lord GOD will wipe away the tears from all faces,
and the disgrace of his people he will take away from all the earth,
for the LORD has spoken.
9 It will be said on that day,
Lo, this is our God; we have waited for him, so that he might save us.
This is the LORD for whom we have waited;

24.10 Isa 23.1
24.11 Jer 14.2; 46.12; Isa 16.10; 32.13
24.13 Isa 17.5,6
24.14 Isa 12.6; 42.10
24.15 Isa 25.3; Mal 1.11; Isa 66.19
24.16 Isa 11.12; 28.5; Jer 5.11
24.17 1 Kings 19.17
24.18 Jer 48.43,44; Gen 7.11; Ps 18.7
24.19 ver 1; Jer 4.23
24.20 Isa 19.14; 66.24; Dan 11.19; Am 8.14
24.21 Ps 76.12
24.22 Isa 10.4; 42.22; Ezek 38.8; Zech 9.11,12
24.23 Isa 13.10; 60.19; Zech 14.6,7; Mic 4.7; Heb 12.22
25.1 Ps 118.28; 98.1; Num 23.19
25.2 Isa 17.1; 13.22; 32.14
25.4 Isa 14.32; 11.4; 32.2; 49.25
25.5 Jer 51.54-56
25.6 Isa 2.2-4; Prov 9.2; Mt 22.4; Dan 7.14; Mt 8.11
25.8 Hos 13.14; 1 Cor 15.54; Rev 7.17; 21.4; Isa 54.4
25.9 Isa 40.9; 30.18; 33.22; 66.10; Ps 20.5

let us be glad and rejoice in his
salvation.
10 For the hand of the LORD will rest on
this mountain.

The Moabites shall be trodden down in
their place
as straw is trodden down in a dung-pit.
11 Though they spread out their hands in
the midst of it,
as swimmers spread out their hands
to swim,
their pride will be laid low despite the
struggle[q] of their hands.
12 The high fortifications of his walls will
be brought down,
laid low, cast to the ground, even to
the dust.

Judah's Song of Victory

26 On that day this song will be
sung in the land of Judah:
We have a strong city;
he sets up victory
like walls and bulwarks.
2 Open the gates,
so that the righteous nation that
keeps faith
may enter in.
3 Those of steadfast mind you keep in
peace—
in peace because they trust in you.
4 Trust in the LORD forever,
for in the LORD GOD[r]
you have an everlasting rock.
5 For he has brought low
the inhabitants of the height;
the lofty city he lays low.
He lays it low to the ground,
casts it to the dust.
6 The foot tramples it,
the feet of the poor,
the steps of the needy.

7 The way of the righteous is level;
O Just One, you make smooth the
path of the righteous.
8 In the path of your judgments,
O LORD, we wait for you;
your name and your renown
are the soul's desire.
9 My soul yearns for you in the night,
my spirit within me earnestly seeks
you.
For when your judgments are in the
earth,
the inhabitants of the world learn
righteousness.
10 If favor is shown to the wicked,
they do not learn righteousness;
in the land of uprightness they deal
perversely
and do not see the majesty of the
LORD.
11 O LORD, your hand is lifted up,
but they do not see it.
Let them see your zeal for your people,
and be ashamed.
Let the fire for your adversaries
consume them.
12 O LORD, you will ordain peace for us,
for indeed, all that we have done, you
have done for us.
13 O LORD our God,
other lords besides you have ruled
over us,
but we acknowledge your name
alone.
14 The dead do not live;
shades do not rise—
because you have punished and
destroyed them,
and wiped out all memory of them.
15 But you have increased the nation, O
LORD,
you have increased the nation; you
are glorified;
you have enlarged all the borders of
the land.

16 O LORD, in distress they sought you,
they poured out a prayer[q]
when your chastening was on them.
17 Like a woman with child,
who writhes and cries out in her pangs
when she is near her time,
so were we because of you, O LORD;
18 we were with child, we writhed,
but we gave birth only to wind.
We have won no victories on earth,
and no one is born to inhabit the
world.
19 Your dead shall live, their corpses[s] shall
rise.
O dwellers in the dust, awake and
sing for joy!
For your dew is a radiant dew,
and the earth will give birth to those
long dead.[t]

[q] Meaning of Heb uncertain [r] Heb *in Yah, the LORD* [s] Cn Compare Syr Tg: Heb *my corpse* [t] Heb *to the shades*

25.10 Isa 16.14
26.1 Isa 4.2; 12.1; 14.31; 60.18
26.2 Isa 60.11,18; 61.3; 62.1,2
26.4 Isa 12.2; 17.10
26.5 Isa 25.12; Job 40.11-13
26.6 Isa 28.3; 3.14,15
26.7 Isa 57.2; 42.16
26.8 Isa 51.4; 56.1; ver 13; Ex 3.15
26.9 Ps 63.6; Isa 55.6; Hos 5.15
26.10 Rom 2.4; Isa 22.12,13; Hos 11.7; Jn 5.37,38
26.11 Isa 5.12; 9.7; 10.17; 66.15,24
26.12 ver 3; Isa 64.8
26.13 Isa 2.8; 10.11; 63.7
26.14 Isa 8.19; Hab 2.19; Isa 10.3
26.15 Isa 9.3; 33.17
26.16 Hos 5.15
26.17 Isa 13.8; Jn 16.21
26.18 Isa 33.11; Ps 17.14
26.19 Ezek 37.1-14; Dan 12.2

25.10b-12 The enemies of God's people, here represented by the *Moabites*, will be punished and their cities destroyed.
26.1-21 The Vindication of the Faithful and the Defeat of Evil. The courageous, obedient nation will be vindicated by *the LORD God*, and the haughty and ruthless will be brought down in judgment, since they do not perceive or obey God's commands. Even death itself, which seems to conquer all of human existence, will be overcome when God brings life again to his faithful people. This confidence will enable them to endure the time of stress and suffering that is coming on the world.

27.1 The Defeat of the Cosmic Evil Serpent. The *serpent*, here identified as *Leviathan*, recalls the agent of the temptation and disobedience of the first human in Gen 3. Now it meets final and total defeat.
27.2-11 Images of the Renewal of God's People.
27.1-11 Building on the image of Israel as God's unproductive vineyard in Isa 5, where the people's disobedience is portrayed, the prophet here envisions their renewal, while the disobedient fall under divine judgment. *Israel*, the faithful remnant of God's people, manifests the fruit of obedience, and their guilt is *expiated*. The disobedient for their lack of *understanding* face destruction, like a fortified city visited by ruin and death.
27.12-13 God's people will be regathered in Jerusalem, returning from territory reaching from *Egypt* to Babylon (*the Euphrates*). There they will *worship the LORD*.
28.1-19 An Oracle against Israel and its Leaders.
28.1-4 The proud, self-indulgent leaders of Israel in *Ephraim*, just north of Judah's borders, will be *trampled under foot* by God's judgment, which will come on them through the invasion of a foreign army.

20 Come, my people, enter your chambers,
and shut your doors behind you;
hide yourselves for a little while
until the wrath is past.
21 For the LORD comes out from his place
to punish the inhabitants of the earth
for their iniquity;
the earth will disclose the blood shed on it,
and will no longer cover its slain.

Israel's Redemption

27 On that day the LORD with his
cruel and great and strong sword
will punish Leviathan the fleeing serpent,
Leviathan the twisting serpent, and he will
kill the dragon that is in the sea.

2 On that day:
A pleasant vineyard, sing about it!
3 I, the LORD, am its keeper;
every moment I water it.
I guard it night and day
so that no one can harm it;
4 I have no wrath.
If it gives me thorns and briers,
I will march to battle against it.
I will burn it up.
5 Or else let it cling to me for protection,
let it make peace with me,
let it make peace with me.

6 In days to come[u] Jacob shall take root,
Israel shall blossom and put forth shoots,
and fill the whole world with fruit.

7 Has he struck them down as he struck down those who struck them?
Or have they been killed as their killers were killed?
8 By expulsion,[v] by exile you struggled against them;
with his fierce blast he removed them in the day of the east wind.
9 Therefore by this the guilt of Jacob will be expiated,
and this will be the full fruit of the removal of his sin:
when he makes all the stones of the altars
like chalkstones crushed to pieces,
no sacred poles[w] or incense altars will remain standing.
10 For the fortified city is solitary,
a habitation deserted and forsaken,
like the wilderness;
the calves graze there,
there they lie down, and strip its branches.
11 When its boughs are dry, they are broken;
women come and make a fire of them.
For this is a people without understanding;
therefore he that made them will not have compassion on them,
he that formed them will show them no favor.

12 On that day the LORD will thresh from
the channel of the Euphrates to the Wadi
of Egypt, and you will be gathered one by
one, O people of Israel. 13And on that day
a great trumpet will be blown, and those
who were lost in the land of Assyria and
those who were driven out to the land of
Egypt will come and worship the LORD on
the holy mountain at Jerusalem.

Judgment on Corrupt Rulers, Priests, and Prophets

28 Ah, the proud garland of the drunkards of Ephraim,
and the fading flower of its glorious beauty,
which is on the head of those bloated with rich food, of those overcome with wine!
2 See, the Lord has one who is mighty and strong;
like a storm of hail, a destroying tempest,
like a storm of mighty, overflowing waters;
with his hand he will hurl them down to the earth.
3 Trampled under foot will be
the proud garland of the drunkards of Ephraim.
4 And the fading flower of its glorious beauty,
which is on the head of those bloated with rich food,
will be like a first-ripe fig before the summer;
whoever sees it, eats it up
as soon as it comes to hand.

[u] Heb *Those to come* [v] Meaning of Heb uncertain [w] Heb *Asherim*

26.20 Ex 12.22,23; Ps 30.5; Isa 54.7,8; 2 Cor 4.17
26.21 Mic 1.3; Jude 14; Isa 13.11; Job 16.18
27.1 Isa 34.5,6; Job 3.8; Ps 74.14; Isa 51.9
27.2 Ps 5.7; 80.8; Jer 2.21
27.3 Isa 58.11; 31.5; 1 Sam 2.9
27.4 2 Sam 23.6; Isa 33.12
27.5 Isa 25.4; Job 22.21
27.6 Isa 37.31; Hos 14.5,6
27.7 Isa 10.12,17
27.8 Job 23.6; Jer 10.23; Ps 78.38
27.9 Isa 1.25; Rom 11.27; Isa 17.8
27.10 Isa 32.13,14; Jer 26.6,18
27.11 Deut 32.28; Isa 1.3; Jer 8.7; Deut 32.18; Isa 43.1,7; 44.2,21,24
27.12 Isa 11.11; Gen 15.18; Deut 30.3,4
27.13 Lev 25.9; Mt 24.31; Rev 11.15; Isa 19.23-25
28.1 ver 3,4,7
28.2 Isa 40.10; 30.30; Ezek 13.11; Isa 29.6; 30.28
28.3 ver 1,18
28.4 Hos 9.10; Mic 7.1; Nah 3.12

5 In that day the LORD of hosts will be a
garland of glory,
and a diadem of beauty, to the
remnant of his people;
6 and a spirit of justice to the one who sits
in judgment,
and strength to those who turn back
the battle at the gate.

7 These also reel with wine
and stagger with strong drink;
the priest and the prophet reel with
strong drink,
they are confused with wine,
they stagger with strong drink;
they err in vision,
they stumble in giving judgment.
8 All tables are covered with filthy vomit;
no place is clean.

9 "Whom will he teach knowledge,
and to whom will he explain the
message?
Those who are weaned from milk,
those taken from the breast?
10 For it is precept upon precept, precept
upon precept,
line upon line, line upon line,
here a little, there a little."[x]

11 Truly, with stammering lip
and with alien tongue
he will speak to this people,
12 to whom he has said,
"This is rest;
give rest to the weary;
and this is repose";
yet they would not hear.
13 Therefore the word of the LORD will be to
them,
"Precept upon precept, precept upon
precept,
line upon line, line upon line,
here a little, there a little;"[x]
in order that they may go, and fall
backward,
and be broken, and snared, and
taken.

14 Therefore hear the word of the LORD,
you scoffers
who rule this people in Jerusalem.
15 Because you have said, "We have made
a covenant with death,
and with Sheol we have an
agreement;
when the overwhelming scourge passes
through
it will not come to us;
for we have made lies our refuge,
and in falsehood we have taken
shelter";
16 therefore thus says the Lord GOD,
See, I am laying in Zion a foundation
stone,
a tested stone,
a precious cornerstone, a sure
foundation:
"One who trusts will not panic."
17 And I will make justice the line,
and righteousness the plummet;
hail will sweep away the refuge of lies,
and waters will overwhelm the
shelter.
18 Then your covenant with death will be
annulled,
and your agreement with Sheol will
not stand;
when the overwhelming scourge passes
through
you will be beaten down by it.
19 As often as it passes through, it will take
you;
for morning by morning it will pass
through,
by day and by night;
and it will be sheer terror to understand
the message.
20 For the bed is too short to stretch
oneself on it,
and the covering too narrow to wrap
oneself in it.
21 For the LORD will rise up as on Mount
Perazim,
he will rage as in the valley of
Gibeon;
to do his deed—strange is his deed!
and to work his work—alien is his
work!
22 Now therefore do not scoff,
or your bonds will be made stronger;
for I have heard a decree of destruction
from the Lord GOD of hosts upon the
whole land.

23 Listen, and hear my voice;
Pay attention, and hear my speech.
24 Do those who plow for sowing plow
continually?
Do they continually open and harrow
their ground?
25 When they have leveled its surface,

[x] Meaning of Heb of this verse uncertain

28.5-6 Only a *remnant of his people* will survive this catastrophe to witness the disclosure of the LORD's *glory*, which experience will benefit the leaders *who sit in judgment* and who *turn back the battle*.
28.7-13 Those who should be providing guidance and purification – the *prophets* and the *priests* – are gluttonous and drunkards, with the result that God's efforts to instruct his people are perverted or ignored.
28.14-29 The solution to this crisis is not for the leaders to make a *covenant with death* in the vain effort to escape punishment, but for them to rely solely on the *foundation stone*, which is God's promise to purify his people as they experience the imminent exile to Babylon. This purging experience requires time, like a farmer's protracted efforts with growing things.

28.5 Isa 41.16; 62.3; 4.2
28.6 Isa 11.2; 32.15; 25.4
28.7 Prov 20.1; Hos 4.11; Isa 56.10,12
28.8 Jer 48.26
28.9 ver 26; Ps 131.2; Heb 5.12,13
28.10 Neh 9.30
28.11 1 Cor 14.21
28.12 Jer 6.16; Mt 11.28,29
28.13 Mt 21.44
28.14 ver 22; Isa 29.20
28.15 ver 18,2; Isa 49.3,4; 29.15
28.16 Ps 118.22; Mt 21.42; Acts 4.11; Rom 9.33; 10.11; Eph 2.20; 1 Pet 2.4-6
28.17 Isa 5.16; ver 2
28.18 ver 15
28.19 Isa 50.4; Ps 88.15; Jer 15.8
28.21 2 Sam 5.20; 1 Chr 14.11; Josh 10.10,12; 2 Sam 5.25; 1 Chr 14.16; Lam 3.33
28.22 ver 14; Isa 10.22,23

29.1-24 The Capture of Jerusalem in God's Plan for his People.
29.1-10 The LORD is behind the impending siege and capture of Jerusalem, here referred to as *Ariel*, which in the ancient language of Babylon (Akkadian) meant "mountain of God." David once took this city (then known as Jebus) because *the LORD of hosts* was with him (2 Sam 5.6-10). The present inhabitants of the city are to be prepared for its capture in spite of the unduly optimistic predictions of the local *prophets* about successful resistance against the Babylonians.
29.11-16 The inability of the people as a whole to *read* and accept the prophet's message of the God-sent judgment that is about to fall on the city is matched by the empty routine of their worship and their inability to accept the sovereignty of the God who like a *potter* shapes his people's existence.

do they not scatter dill, sow cummin,
and plant wheat in rows
and barley in its proper place,
and spelt as the border?
26 For they are well instructed;
their God teaches them.

27 Dill is not threshed with a threshing sledge,
nor is a cart wheel rolled over cummin;
but dill is beaten out with a stick,
and cummin with a rod.
28 Grain is crushed for bread,
but one does not thresh it forever;
one drives the cart wheel and horses over it,
but does not pulverize it.
29 This also comes from the LORD of hosts;
he is wonderful in counsel,
and excellent in wisdom.

The Siege of Jerusalem

29 Ah, Ariel, Ariel,
the city where David encamped!
Add year to year;
let the festivals run their round.
2 Yet I will distress Ariel,
and there shall be moaning and lamentation,
and Jerusalem[y] shall be to me like an Ariel.[z]
3 And like David[a] I will encamp against you;
I will besiege you with towers
and raise siegeworks against you.
4 Then deep from the earth you shall speak,
from low in the dust your words shall come;
your voice shall come from the ground
like the voice of a ghost,
and your speech shall whisper out of the dust.

5 But the multitude of your foes[b] shall be like small dust,
and the multitude of tyrants like flying chaff.
And in an instant, suddenly,
6 you will be visited by the LORD of hosts
with thunder and earthquake and great noise,
with whirlwind and tempest, and the flame of a devouring fire.
7 And the multitude of all the nations that fight against Ariel,
all that fight against her and her stronghold, and who distress her,
shall be like a dream, a vision of the night.
8 Just as when a hungry person dreams of eating
and wakes up still hungry,
or a thirsty person dreams of drinking
and wakes up faint, still thirsty,
so shall the multitude of all the nations be
that fight against Mount Zion.

9 Stupefy yourselves and be in a stupor,
blind yourselves and be blind!
Be drunk, but not from wine;
stagger, but not from strong drink!
10 For the LORD has poured out upon you
a spirit of deep sleep;
he has closed your eyes, you prophets,
and covered your heads, you seers.
11 The vision of all this has become for
you like the words of a sealed document. If
it is given to those who can read, with the
command, "Read this," they say, "We cannot, for it is sealed." 12And if it is given to
those who cannot read, saying, "Read this,"
they say, "We cannot read."

13 The Lord said:
Because these people draw near with their mouths
and honor me with their lips,
while their hearts are far from me,
and their worship of me is a human commandment learned by rote;
14 so I will again do
amazing things with this people,
shocking and amazing.
The wisdom of their wise shall perish,
and the discernment of the discerning shall be hidden.

15 Ha! You who hide a plan too deep for the LORD,
whose deeds are in the dark,
and who say, "Who sees us? Who knows us?"
16 You turn things upside down!
Shall the potter be regarded as the clay?
Shall the thing made say of its maker,

[y] Heb *she* [z] Probable meaning, *altar hearth*; compare Ezek 43.15 [a] Gk: Meaning of Heb uncertain [b] Cn: Heb *strangers*

28.27 Am 1.3
28.29 Isa 9.6; 31.2; Rom 11.33
29.1 2 Sam 5.9; ver 9,13
29.2 Isa 3.26; Lam 2.5
29.3 Lk 19.43,44
29.4 Isa 8.19; Lev 20.6; Deut 18.10,11; 1 Sam 28.8,15; 2 Chr 33.6
29.5 Isa 17.13,14; 25.3-5; 30.13; 1 Thess 5.3
29.6 Isa 28.2; Mt 24.7; Mk 13.8; Lk 21.11; Rev 11.13,19; 16.18
29.7 Mic 4.11,12; Zech 12.9; Job 20.8; Ps 73.20
29.8 Isa 54.17
29.9 Isa 51.17,21,22
29.10 Rom 11.8; Ps 69.23; Isa 6.9,10; Mic 3.6
29.11 Isa 27.7; 8.16; Dan 12.4,9; Mt 13.11
29.13 Ezek 33.31; Mt 15.8,9; Mk 7.6,7
29.14 Hab 1.5; Jer 8.9; 49.7; 1 Cor 1.19
29.15 Isa 30.1; 57.12; Ps 94.7
29.16 Isa 45.9; Jer 18.1-6; Rom 9.19-21

"He did not make me";
or the thing formed say of the one who formed it,
"He has no understanding"?

Hope for the Future

17 Shall not Lebanon in a very little while
become a fruitful field,
and the fruitful field be regarded as a forest?
18 On that day the deaf shall hear
the words of a scroll,
and out of their gloom and darkness
the eyes of the blind shall see.
19 The meek shall obtain fresh joy in the LORD,
and the neediest people shall exult in the Holy One of Israel.
20 For the tyrant shall be no more,
and the scoffer shall cease to be;
all those alert to do evil shall be cut off—
21 those who cause a person to lose a lawsuit,
who set a trap for the arbiter in the gate,
and without grounds deny justice to the one in the right.

22 Therefore thus says the LORD, who redeemed Abraham, concerning the house of Jacob:
No longer shall Jacob be ashamed,
no longer shall his face grow pale.
23 For when he sees his children,
the work of my hands, in his midst,
they will sanctify my name;
they will sanctify the Holy One of Jacob,
and will stand in awe of the God of Israel.
24 And those who err in spirit will come to understanding,
and those who grumble will accept instruction.

The Futility of Reliance on Egypt

30 Oh, rebellious children, says the LORD,
who carry out a plan, but not mine;
who make an alliance, but against my will,
adding sin to sin;
2 who set out to go down to Egypt
without asking for my counsel,
to take refuge in the protection of Pharaoh,
and to seek shelter in the shadow of Egypt;
3 Therefore the protection of Pharaoh shall become your shame,
and the shelter in the shadow of Egypt your humiliation.
4 For though his officials are at Zoan
and his envoys reach Hanes,
5 everyone comes to shame
through a people that cannot profit them,
that brings neither help nor profit,
but shame and disgrace.

6 An oracle concerning the animals of the Negeb.
Through a land of trouble and distress,
of lioness and roaring[c] lion,
of viper and flying serpent,
they carry their riches on the backs of donkeys,
and their treasures on the humps of camels,
to a people that cannot profit them.
7 For Egypt's help is worthless and empty,
therefore I have called her,
"Rahab who sits still."[d]

A Rebellious People

8 Go now, write it before them on a tablet,
and inscribe it in a book,
so that it may be for the time to come
as a witness forever.
9 For they are a rebellious people,
faithless children,
children who will not hear
the instruction of the LORD;
10 who say to the seers, "Do not see";
and to the prophets, "Do not prophesy to us what is right;
speak to us smooth things,
prophesy illusions,
11 leave the way, turn aside from the path,
let us hear no more about the Holy One of Israel."
12 Therefore thus says the Holy One of Israel:
Because you reject this word,
and put your trust in oppression and deceit,
and rely on them;
13 therefore this iniquity shall become for you

29.17 Isa 32.15
29.18 Isa 35.5; ver 11
29.19 Isa 61.1; Mt 11.5; Jas 2.5
29.20 ver 5; Isa 28.14,22; 59.4
29.21 Am 5.10,12; Prov 28.21
29.22 Isa 41.8; 45.17; 54.4
29.23 Isa 49.20-26; 45.11; 5.16; 8.13
29.24 Isa 28.7
30.1 ver 9; Isa 29.15; 8.11,12
30.2 Isa 31.1; Num 27.21; Josh 9.14; 1 Kings 22.7; Jer 21.2
30.3 Isa 20.5; Jer 37.3,5
30.4 Isa 19.11
30.5 Jer 2.36; ver 7
30.6 Isa 46.1,2; 8.22; 14.29; 15.7
30.7 Jer 37.7; ver 15
30.8 Isa 8.1; Hab 2.2
30.9 ver 1; Isa 28.15; 24.5
30.10 Isa 29.10; 5.20; 1 Kings 22.8,13
30.11 Job 21.14
30.12 Isa 5.24; 59.13
30.13 Isa 26.21; Ps 62.3; Isa 29.5

29.17-24 Beyond the present gloom is the assurance that God will purge his people of the wicked leaders, the *scoffers*, and the cheats. In the future, the people will honor *the God of Israel*, and will come to an *understanding* of his purpose for them.
30.1-7 The Folly of Relying on Egypt. There is no safety in depending on Egypt to protect Judah from seizure by the Babylonians. The seats of Egyptian power at this time were *Zoan*, where the Pharaohs of this period lived, and *Hanes*, near the earlier capital, Memphis. The expectation of help from this *Rahab* (a disdainful term for Egypt; Ps 87.4) is futile, in contrast to the Rahab in Joshua's day, who made possible Israel's seizing Jericho (Josh 2).
30.8-26 Facing Up to the Crisis and Seeing Ultimate Victory.
30.8-18 Even though many of God's people are determined not to face up to the enormous difficulties that confront them, they will indeed experience this ruinous judgment. It is only those who calmly trust God and his purpose for them who will share in the final triumph of God over their enemies.

[c] Cn: Heb *from them* [d] Meaning of Heb uncertain

30.19-26 Beyond the *adversity* and *affliction* that are imminent, they will soon experience renewal through (1) instruction in God's *way* for them; (2) expulsion of the idols from their midst, and (3) transformation of the created order so that light and water, flocks and crops will be available in unprecedented abundance. This section of Isaiah on cosmic renewal is considered by some scholars to be a post-exilic insertion among the authentic oracles.
30.27-33 Israel's Joy at God's Judgment on Assyria.
30.27-28 God's control of human affairs among the nations is complete.
30.29-33 Israel is called to rejoice as the fires and blows of divine judgment fall on Assyria.

like a break in a high wall, bulging
out, and about to collapse,
whose crash comes suddenly, in an
instant;
14 its breaking is like that of a potter's
vessel
that is smashed so ruthlessly
that among its fragments not a sherd is
found
for taking fire from the hearth,
or dipping water out of the cistern.

15 For thus said the Lord GOD, the Holy
One of Israel:
In returning and rest you shall be saved;
in quietness and in trust shall be your
strength.
But you refused 16 and said,
"No! We will flee upon horses"—
therefore you shall flee!
and, "We will ride upon swift steeds"—
therefore your pursuers shall be swift!
17 A thousand shall flee at the threat of
one,
at the threat of five you shall flee,
until you are left
like a flagstaff on the top of a
mountain,
like a signal on a hill.

God's Promise to Zion

18 Therefore the LORD waits to be gracious
to you;
therefore he will rise up to show
mercy to you.
For the LORD is a God of justice;
blessed are all those who wait for him.

19 Truly, O people in Zion, inhabitants of
Jerusalem, you shall weep no more. He will
surely be gracious to you at the sound of
your cry; when he hears it, he will answer
you. 20 Though the Lord may give you the
bread of adversity and the water of affliction, yet your Teacher will not hide himself
any more, but your eyes shall see your
Teacher. 21 And when you turn to the right
or when you turn to the left, your ears shall
hear a word behind you, saying, "This is
the way; walk in it." 22 Then you will defile
your silver-covered idols and your gold-
plated images. You will scatter them like
filthy rags; you will say to them, "Away
with you!"
23 He will give rain for the seed with
which you sow the ground, and grain, the
produce of the ground, which will be rich
and plenteous. On that day your cattle will
graze in broad pastures; 24 and the oxen and
donkeys that till the ground will eat silage,
which has been winnowed with shovel and
fork. 25 On every lofty mountain and every
high hill there will be brooks running with
water—on a day of the great slaughter,
when the towers fall. 26 Moreover the light
of the moon will be like the light of the sun,
and the light of the sun will be sevenfold,
like the light of seven days, on the day
when the LORD binds up the injuries of his
people, and heals the wounds inflicted by
his blow.

Judgment on Assyria

27 See, the name of the LORD comes from
far away,
burning with his anger, and in thick
rising smoke;[e]
his lips are full of indignation,
and his tongue is like a devouring
fire;
28 his breath is like an overflowing stream
that reaches up to the neck—
to sift the nations with the sieve of
destruction,
and to place on the jaws of the
peoples a bridle that leads them
astray.

29 You shall have a song as in the night
when a holy festival is kept; and gladness
of heart, as when one sets out to the sound
of the flute to go to the mountain of the
LORD, to the Rock of Israel. 30 And the LORD
will cause his majestic voice to be heard and
the descending blow of his arm to be seen,
in furious anger and a flame of devouring
fire, with a cloudburst and tempest and
hailstones. 31 The Assyrian will be terror-
stricken at the voice of the LORD, when he
strikes with his rod. 32 And every stroke of
the staff of punishment that the LORD lays
upon him will be to the sound of timbrels
and lyres; battling with brandished arm he
will fight with him. 33 For his burning place[f]
has long been prepared; truly it is made
ready for the king,[g] its pyre made deep and
wide, with fire and wood in abundance; the
breath of the LORD, like a stream of sulfur,
kindles it.

30.14 Ps 2.9; Jer 19.10,11
30.15 Isa 7.4; 28.12; 32.17
30.16 Isa 31.1,3
30.17 Lev 26.8; Deut 28.25; 32.30; Josh 23.10
30.18 Isa 42.14; 33.5; 5.16; 25.19
30.19 Isa 65.9; 60.20; 61.1-3; Mt 7.7-11
30.20 1 Kings 22.27; Ps 80.5; 74.9; Am 8.11
30.21 Isa 35.8,9; Prov 3.6; Isa 29.24
30.22 Isa 2.20; 31.7; 46.6; Mt 4.10
30.23 Ps 65.9-13; Isa 65.21,22; 32.20
30.26 Isa 60.19,20; Rev 21.23; 22.5; Isa 61.1; 1.6; Jer 33.6
30.27 Isa 59.19; 10.5,13,17; 66.15
30.28 Isa 11.4; 2 Thess 2.8; Isa 8.8; 37.29
30.29 Ps 42.4; Isa 2.3; 17.10
30.30 Isa 28.2; 32.19
30.31 Isa 31.8
30.32 Isa 10.24; Jer 31.4; Ezek 32.10
30.33 Jer 7.3; 19.6; ver 27,28; Isa 34.9

[i] Meaning of Heb uncertain [j] Or *Topheth* [k] Or *Molech*

Alliance with Egypt Is Futile

31 Alas for those who go down to Egypt for help
and who rely on horses,
who trust in chariots because they are many
and in horsemen because they are very strong,
but do not look to the Holy One of Israel
or consult the LORD!
2 Yet he too is wise and brings disaster;
he does not call back his words,
but will rise against the house of the evildoers,
and against the helpers of those who work iniquity.
3 The Egyptians are human, and not God;
their horses are flesh, and not spirit.
When the LORD stretches out his hand,
the helper will stumble, and the one helped will fall,
and they will all perish together.

4 For thus the LORD said to me,
As a lion or a young lion growls over its prey,
and—when a band of shepherds is called out against it—
is not terrified by their shouting
or daunted at their noise,
so the LORD of hosts will come down
to fight upon Mount Zion and upon its hill.
5 Like birds hovering overhead, so the LORD of hosts
will protect Jerusalem;
he will protect and deliver it,
he will spare and rescue it.

6 Turn back to him whom you[h] have
deeply betrayed, O people of Israel. 7For on
that day all of you shall throw away your
idols of silver and idols of gold, which your
hands have sinfully made for you.
8 "Then the Assyrian shall fall by a sword, not of mortals;
and a sword, not of humans, shall devour him;
he shall flee from the sword,
and his young men shall be put to forced labor.
9 His rock shall pass away in terror,
and his officers desert the standard in panic,"
says the LORD, whose fire is in Zion,
and whose furnace is in Jerusalem.

Government with Justice Predicted

32 See, a king will reign in righteousness,
and princes will rule with justice.
2 Each will be like a hiding place from the wind,
a covert from the tempest,
like streams of water in a dry place,
like the shade of a great rock in a weary land.
3 Then the eyes of those who have sight will not be closed,
and the ears of those who have hearing will listen.
4 The minds of the rash will have good judgment,
and the tongues of stammerers will speak readily and distinctly.
5 A fool will no longer be called noble,
nor a villain said to be honorable.
6 For fools speak folly,
and their minds plot iniquity:
to practice ungodliness,
to utter error concerning the LORD,
to leave the craving of the hungry unsatisfied,
and to deprive the thirsty of drink.
7 The villainies of villains are evil;
they devise wicked devices
to ruin the poor with lying words,
even when the plea of the needy is right.
8 But those who are noble plan noble things,
and by noble things they stand.

Complacent Women Warned of Disaster

9 Rise up, you women who are at ease, hear my voice;
you complacent daughters, listen to my speech.
10 In little more than a year
you will shudder, you complacent ones;
for the vintage will fail,
the fruit harvest will not come.
11 Tremble, you women who are at ease,
shudder, you complacent ones;
strip, and make yourselves bare,
and put sackcloth on your loins.
12 Beat your breasts for the pleasant fields,
for the fruitful vine,
13 for the soil of my people
growing up in thorns and briers;
yes, for all the joyous houses
in the jubilant city.

[h] Heb *they*

31.1 Isa 30.2; Ezek 17.15; Isa 2.7; Ps 20.7; Dan 9.13; Isa 10.17
31.2 Isa 28.29; Rom 16.27; Isa 45.7; Num 23.19; Isa 14.20; 22.14
31.3 Ezek 28.9; Isa 36.9; 9.17; 30.5.7
31.4 Hos 11.10; Am 3.8; Isa 42.13
31.5 Ps 91.4; Isa 17.13
31.6 Isa 44.22; 1.2,5
31.7 Isa 2.20
31.8 Isa 10.12; 66.16; 21.15; 14.2
31.9 Deut 32.31,37; Isa 5.26; 10.16
32.1 Isa 9.6,7; Jer 23.5; Zech 9.9
32.2 Isa 4.6; 35.6; 41.18; 43.19,20
32.3 Isa 29.18
32.4 Isa 29.24
32.5 1 Sam 25.25
32.6 Isa 59.7,13; 10.6; 9.15,16; 3.15
32.7 Jer 5.26-28; Isa 11.4; 5.23
32.8 2 Cor 9.6-11
32.9 Isa 47.8; 28.23
32.10 Isa 5.5,6
32.11 Isa 22.12; 47.2
32.12 Nah 2.7
32.13 Isa 34.13; 22.2

31.1-9 The Futility of Reliance on Egypt.
31.1-5 The human limitations of Egypt are contrasted with the cosmic power of God to defeat his enemies, to vindicate his faithful people and to protect Jerusalem.
31.6-9 When God's time comes, *idols of gold* are to be discarded, and Assyria *shall fall,* while *Zion* will be delivered from her enemies.
32.1-20 The Rule of the Ideal King.
32.1-8 The coming to power of this new king will bring sight and insight to his subjects, expose the folly of many, and encourage *the noble* to plan wisely.
32.9-15 Women who are complacent about the future are warned of the disaster that will befall Jerusalem, until God's purpose triumphs and the land and people are renewed.

32.16-20 Both the land itself and its inhabitants will be transformed as the agent of God's rule takes over.
33.1-16 God's Triumph over Evil Powers and Sinful People.
33.1 *The destroyer* refers to Babylon, which took Israel into exile and will itself be destroyed.
33.2-6 It is *the LORD* alone who gains victory and honor in the new era that is about to dawn.
33.7-9 The present interim period may be characterized by human despair, as symbolized by the decline into aridity of such splendid places as *Lebanon*, with its great mountains covered with cedar forests, *Sharon* and *Carmel*, the fertile plain in central Israel and the grand peak that overlooks it and the sea, and *Bashan*, a plateau in southern Syria famous for its fine flocks and herds.
33.10-16 *The LORD* will bring judgment on *sinners in Zion*, but prosperity and exaltation to the *righteous*.

14 For the palace will be forsaken,
the populous city deserted;
the hill and the watchtower
will become dens forever,
the joy of wild asses,
a pasture for flocks;
15 until a spirit from on high is poured out on us,
and the wilderness becomes a fruitful field,
and the fruitful field is deemed a forest.

The Peace of God's Reign

16 Then justice will dwell in the wilderness,
and righteousness abide in the fruitful field.
17 The effect of righteousness will be peace,
and the result of righteousness,
quietness and trust forever.
18 My people will abide in a peaceful habitation,
in secure dwellings, and in quiet resting places.
19 The forest will disappear completely,[i]
and the city will be utterly laid low.
20 Happy will you be who sow beside every stream,
who let the ox and the donkey range freely.

A Prophecy of Deliverance from Foes

33 Ah, you destroyer,
who yourself have not been destroyed;
you treacherous one,
with whom no one has dealt treacherously!
When you have ceased to destroy,
you will be destroyed;
and when you have stopped dealing treacherously,
you will be dealt with treacherously.

2 O LORD, be gracious to us; we wait for you.
Be our arm every morning,
our salvation in the time of trouble.
3 At the sound of tumult, peoples fled;
before your majesty, nations scattered.
4 Spoil was gathered as the caterpillar gathers;
as locusts leap, they leaped[j] upon it.
5 The LORD is exalted, he dwells on high;
he filled Zion with justice and righteousness;
6 he will be the stability of your times,
abundance of salvation, wisdom, and knowledge;
the fear of the LORD is Zion's treasure.[k]

7 Listen! the valiant[j] cry in the streets;
the envoys of peace weep bitterly.
8 The highways are deserted,
travelers have quit the road.
The treaty is broken,
its oaths[l] are despised,
its obligation[m] is disregarded.
9 The land mourns and languishes;
Lebanon is confounded and withers away;
Sharon is like a desert;
and Bashan and Carmel shake off their leaves.

10 "Now I will arise," says the LORD,
"now I will lift myself up;
now I will be exalted.
11 You conceive chaff, you bring forth stubble;
your breath is a fire that will consume you.
12 And the peoples will be as if burned to lime,
like thorns cut down, that are burned in the fire."

13 Hear, you who are far away, what I have done;
and you who are near, acknowledge my might.
14 The sinners in Zion are afraid;
trembling has seized the godless:
"Who among us can live with the devouring fire?
Who among us can live with everlasting flames?"
15 Those who walk righteously and speak uprightly,
who despise the gain of oppression,
who wave away a bribe instead of accepting it,
who stop their ears from hearing of bloodshed
and shut their eyes from looking on evil,
16 they will live on the heights;
their refuge will be the fortresses of rocks;
their food will be supplied, their water assured.

32.14 Isa 13.22; 6.11; 13.21
32.15 Isa 11.2; Ezek 39.29; Joel 2.28; Isa 29.17; 35.2
32.16 Isa 33.5
32.17 Rom 14.17; Jas 3.18; Isa 30.15
32.19 Isa 30.30; Zech 11.2
32.20 Isa 30.24
33.1 Isa 21.2; Hab 2.8; Isa 24.16; Jer 25.12-14; Mt 7.2
33.2 Isa 25.9
33.3 Isa 17.13; Jer 25.30,31
33.5 Ps 97.9
33.6 ver 20; Isa 45.17; 11.9; Mt 6.33
33.7 2 Kings 18.18,37

[i] Cn: Heb *And it will hail when the forest comes down* [j] Meaning of Heb uncertain [k] Heb *his treasure*; meaning of Heb uncertain [l] Q Ms: MT *cities* [m] Or *everyone*

33.18 Isa 17.14; 1 Cor 1.20
33.19 2 Kings 19.32; Deut 28.49,50; Jer 5.15
33.20 Ps 48.12; 46.5; 125.1,2; Isa 37.33; 54.2
33.21 Isa 41.18
33.22 Isa 2.4; Jas 4.12; ver 17; Zech 9.9; Isa 35.4
33.23 2 Kings 7.8,16
33.24 Jer 30.17; 50.20
34.1 Ps 49.1; Deut 32.1
34.2 Isa 26.20,21; 13.5; 30.25
34.3 Joel 2.20; Ezek 14.19
34.4 Ezek 32.7,8; Joel 2.31; Mt 24.29; 2 Pet 3.10; Rev 6.13,14
34.5 Jer 46.10; 49.7; Mal 1.4
34.6 Jer 49.13; Isa 63.1
34.7 Ps 22.21; 68.30; Isa 29.9; 49.26
34.8 Isa 63.4
34.9 Deut 29.23
34.10 Isa 66.24; Rev 14.11; 19.3; Mal 1.4; Ezek 29.11
34.11 Isa 14.23; Zeph 2.14; Rev 18.2; 2 Kings 21.13; Lam 2.8
34.13 Isa 13.22; 32.13; Jer 9.11; 10.22
34.14 Isa 13.21

The Land of the Majestic King

17 Your eyes will see the king in his beauty;
they will behold a land that stretches far away.
18 Your mind will muse on the terror:
"Where is the one who counted?
Where is the one who weighed the tribute?
Where is the one who counted the towers?"
19 No longer will you see the insolent people,
the people of an obscure speech that you cannot comprehend,
stammering in a language that you cannot understand.
20 Look on Zion, the city of our appointed festivals!
Your eyes will see Jerusalem,
a quiet habitation, an immovable tent,
whose stakes will never be pulled up,
and none of whose ropes will be broken.
21 But there the LORD in majesty will be for us
a place of broad rivers and streams,
where no galley with oars can go,
nor stately ship can pass.
22 For the LORD is our judge, the LORD is our ruler,
the LORD is our king; he will save us.

23 Your rigging hangs loose;
it cannot hold the mast firm in its place,
or keep the sail spread out.

Then prey and spoil in abundance will be divided;
even the lame will fall to plundering.
24 And no inhabitant will say, "I am sick";
the people who live there will be forgiven their iniquity.

Judgment on the Nations

34 Draw near, O nations, to hear;
O peoples, give heed!
Let the earth hear, and all that fills it;
the world, and all that comes from it.
2 For the LORD is enraged against all the nations,
and furious against all their hoards;
he has doomed them, has given them over for slaughter.
3 Their slain shall be cast out,
and the stench of their corpses shall rise;
the mountains shall flow with their blood.
4 All the host of heaven shall rot away,
and the skies roll up like a scroll.
All their host shall wither
like a leaf withering on a vine,
or fruit withering on a fig tree.

5 When my sword has drunk its fill in the heavens,
lo, it will descend upon Edom,
upon the people I have doomed to judgment.
6 The LORD has a sword; it is sated with blood,
it is gorged with fat,
with the blood of lambs and goats,
with the fat of the kidneys of rams.
For the LORD has a sacrifice in Bozrah,
a great slaughter in the land of Edom.
7 Wild oxen shall fall with them,
and young steers with the mighty bulls.
Their land shall be soaked with blood,
and their soil made rich with fat.

8 For the LORD has a day of vengeance,
a year of vindication by Zion's cause.[n]
9 And the streams of Edom[o] shall be turned into pitch,
and her soil into sulfur;
her land shall become burning pitch.
10 Night and day it shall not be quenched;
its smoke shall go up forever.
From generation to generation it shall lie waste;
no one shall pass through it forever and ever.
11 But the hawk[p] and the hedgehog[p] shall possess it;
the owl[p] and the raven shall live in it.
He shall stretch the line of confusion over it,
and the plummet of chaos over[q] its nobles.
12 They shall name it No Kingdom There,
and all its princes shall be nothing.
13 Thorns shall grow over its strongholds,
nettles and thistles in its fortresses.
It shall be the haunt of jackals,
an abode for ostriches.
14 Wildcats shall meet with hyenas,
goat-demons shall call to each other;

[n] Or *of recompense by Zion's defender* [o] Heb *her streams* [p] Identification uncertain [q] Heb lacks *over*

33.17-24 The New King and the Renewed Jerusalem.
33.17-19 A new *king* will preside over a renewed land which is no longer troubled by those who pay *tribute* to foreign rulers, or by occupying forces *of alien speech.*
33.20-24 The city will enjoy enduring peace, with the LORD himself as king. How God is to be present and active in and through the new ruler is not explained by the prophet. The pirates of the past will be out of business, so that even *the lame* will be able to share in the loot. Forgiveness of the people's *iniquity* is reflected in the healing of *the sick.*
34.1-17 Warning of Defeat to God's Enemies in Earth and Heaven.
34.1-4 All the earth, and *all the nations,* as well as the disobedient *host of heaven* (the fallen angels and the hostile powers), are told of the coming outburst of God's wrath and their consequent doom.
34.5-15 The chief focus of the divine judgment will be *Edom,* which exploited the land of Judah during the exile of its people in Babylon, according to the prophet Obadiah (Ob 10-16).

there too Lilith shall repose,
and find a place to rest.
15 There shall the owl nest
and lay and hatch and brood in its shadow;
there too the buzzards shall gather,
each one with its mate.
16 Seek and read from the book of the LORD:
Not one of these shall be missing;
none shall be without its mate.
For the mouth of the LORD has commanded,
and his spirit has gathered them.
17 He has cast the lot for them,
his hand has portioned it out to them with the line;
they shall possess it forever,
from generation to generation they shall live in it.

The Return of the Redeemed to Zion

35 The wilderness and the dry land shall be glad,
the desert shall rejoice and blossom;
like the crocus 2 it shall blossom abundantly,
and rejoice with joy and singing.
The glory of Lebanon shall be given to it,
the majesty of Carmel and Sharon.
They shall see the glory of the LORD,
the majesty of our God.

3 Strengthen the weak hands,
and make firm the feeble knees.
4 Say to those who are of a fearful heart,
"Be strong, do not fear!
Here is your God.
He will come with vengeance,
with terrible recompense.
He will come and save you."

5 Then the eyes of the blind shall be opened,
and the ears of the deaf unstopped;
6 then the lame shall leap like a deer,
and the tongue of the speechless sing for joy.
For waters shall break forth in the wilderness,
and streams in the desert;
7 the burning sand shall become a pool,
and the thirsty ground springs of water;
the haunt of jackals shall become a swamp,[r]
the grass shall become reeds and rushes.
8 A highway shall be there,
and it shall be called the Holy Way;
the unclean shall not travel on it,[s]
but it shall be for God's people;[t]
no traveler, not even fools, shall go astray.
9 No lion shall be there,
nor shall any ravenous beast come up on it;
they shall not be found there,
but the redeemed shall walk there.
10 And the ransomed of the LORD shall return,
and come to Zion with singing;
everlasting joy shall be upon their heads;
they shall obtain joy and gladness,
and sorrow and sighing shall flee away.

Sennacherib Threatens Jerusalem

36 In the fourteenth year of King
Hezekiah, King Sennacherib of
Assyria came up against all the fortified
cities of Judah and captured them. 2 The
king of Assyria sent the Rabshakeh from
Lachish to King Hezekiah at Jerusalem, with
a great army. He stood by the conduit of the
upper pool on the highway to the Fuller's
Field. 3 And there came out to him Eliakim
son of Hilkiah, who was in charge of the
palace, and Shebna the secretary, and Joah
son of Asaph, the recorder.
4 The Rabshakeh said to them, "Say to
Hezekiah: Thus says the great king, the
king of Assyria: On what do you base this
confidence of yours? 5 Do you think that
mere words are strategy and power for war?
On whom do you now rely, that you have
rebelled against me? 6 See, you are relying
on Egypt, that broken reed of a staff, which
will pierce the hand of anyone who leans
on it. Such is Pharaoh king of Egypt to all
who rely on him. 7 But if you say to me, 'We
rely on the LORD our God,' is it not he whose
high places and altars Hezekiah has removed, saying to Judah and to Jerusalem,
'You shall worship before this altar'? 8 Come
now, make a wager with my master the
king of Assyria: I will give you two thousand horses, if you are able on your part to
set riders on them. 9 How then can you
repulse a single captain among the least of
my master's servants, when you rely on
Egypt for chariots and for horsemen?
10 Moreover, is it without the LORD that I

[r] Cn: Heb *in the haunt of jackals is her resting place* [s] Or *pass it by* [t] Cn: Heb *for them*

34.16-17 By contrast, *the LORD* will restore and renew his people: *Not one of them shall be missing.* They will possess the land *forever.*
35.1-10 God's People Return to a Renewed Land.
35.1 The return of the people will be accompanied by a renewal of the creation itself, so that what has been barren will now *blossom abundantly.*
35.2 The territory to be occupied by this restored people includes not only the land of the northern tribes of Israel, as indicated by mention of *Carmel and Sharon* (reversing the judgment of Isa 33.9), but also lands not previously part of Israel: *Lebanon.*
35.3-7 Vivid images depict God's judgment (*terrible recompense*), but even more his renewal of the world, evident in the overcoming of basic human limitations (*blind, deaf*) and the provision of an abundance of water to increase greatly the fertility of the land.
35.8-10 All these changes prepare for the return of Israel from exile, which is to occur on a transformed highway through the Arabian desert, over which *the ransomed of the LORD* come to enjoy their liberation and restoration to the land.
36.1-22 Sennacherib's Siege of Jerusalem. Beginning at this point, the book of Isaiah follows closely the source also used in 2 Kings 18.13-20.19, which describes the last years of the reign of Hezekiah. A major addition to that source is the psalm of gratitude in Isa 38.9-20. A major omission is the lack of mention of Hezekiah's offer to buy off the Assyrians from their siege of Jerusalem by stripping the temple and its treasury (2 Kings 18.14-16). Hezekiah's reign was from 715 to 687.
36.1-2 In 701 Sennacherib's troops, under *the Rabshakeh* (which was the Assyrian term for "chief steward"), laid siege to Jerusalem *with a great army.*
36.3 Slightly different roles are assigned to *Shebna* and *Eliakim* here than in Isa 22.15-25. Here they are respectively *secretary* and *in charge of the palace.*
36.6 The warning against reliance on Egypt recalls the oracles of Isa 30 and 31.

34.15 Deut 14.13
34.16 Isa 30.8; 40.5
34.17 Jer 13.25; ver 10,11
35.1 Isa 55.12; 51.3
35.2 Isa 32.15; ver 10; Isa 60.13; 25.9
35.3 Job 4.3,4; Heb 12.12
35.4 Isa 1.24; 34.8; Ps 145.19
35.5 Isa 29.18; Mt 11.5; Jn 9.6,7
35.6 Mt 15.20; Jn 5.8,9; Acts 3.8; Mt 9.32; Isa 41.18; 43.19; Jn 7.38
35.7 Isa 49.10; 34.13
35.8 Isa 62.10; Mt 7.13,14; Jer 14.8
35.9 Isa 30.6; 34.14; 62.12
35.10 Isa 51.11; 25.8; 65.19; Rev 7.17; 21.4
36.1 2 Kings 18.13; Isa 1.1
36.2 2 Kings 18.17-20; Isa 7.3
36.3 Isa 22.15,20
36.4 2 Kings 18.19
36.5 2 Kings 18.7
36.6 Ezek 29.6,7; Isa 30.3,5,7
36.7 2 Kings 18.4,5
36.9 Isa 37.29; 20.5

36.11 Ezra 4.7; ver 13
36.13 2 Chr 32.18
36.14 Isa 37.10
36.15 ver 18
36.16 Zech 3.10; Prov 5.15
36.18 ver 15
36.19 Isa 37.11-13; 2 Kings 17.6
36.20 1 Kings 20.23,28; ver 15
36.22 ver 3; Isa 22.15,20
37.1 2 Kings 19.1-37
37.2 Isa 22.15,20
37.3 Isa 26.16-18
37.4 Isa 36.15,18,20
37.6 Isa 7.4; 35.4
37.7 ver 9,37,38
37.9 ver 7; Isa 18.1; 20.5
37.10 Isa 36.15
37.11 Isa 10.9-11; 36.18-20
37.12 2 Kings 17.6; 18.11; Gen 11.31; 12.1-4; Acts 7.2
37.16 Ex 25.22; Deut 10.17; Isa 42.5; 45.12
37.17 Dan 9.18; Ps 74.22; ver 4

have come up against this land to destroy it? The LORD said to me, Go up against this land, and destroy it."

11 Then Eliakim, Shebna, and Joah said to the Rabshakeh, "Please speak to your servants in Aramaic, for we understand it; do not speak to us in the language of Judah within the hearing of the people who are on the wall." 12But the Rabshakeh said, "Has my master sent me to speak these words to your master and to you, and not to the people sitting on the wall, who are doomed with you to eat their own dung and drink their own urine?"

13 Then the Rabshakeh stood and called out in a loud voice in the language of Judah, "Hear the words of the great king, the king of Assyria! 14Thus says the king: 'Do not let Hezekiah deceive you, for he will not be able to deliver you. 15Do not let Hezekiah make you rely on the LORD by saying, The LORD will surely deliver us; this city will not be given into the hand of the king of Assyria.' 16Do not listen to Hezekiah; for thus says the king of Assyria: 'Make your peace with me and come out to me; then everyone of you will eat from your own vine and your own fig tree and drink water from your own cistern, 17until I come and take you away to a land like your own land, a land of grain and wine, a land of bread and vineyards. 18Do not let Hezekiah mislead you by saying, The LORD will save us. Has any of the gods of the nations saved their land out of the hand of the king of Assyria? 19Where are the gods of Hamath and Arpad? Where are the gods of Sepharvaim? Have they delivered Samaria out of my hand? 20Who among all the gods of these countries have saved their countries out of my hand, that the LORD should save Jerusalem out of my hand?' "

21 But they were silent and answered him not a word, for the king's command was, "Do not answer him." 22Then Eliakim son of Hilkiah, who was in charge of the palace, and Shebna the secretary, and Joah son of Asaph, the recorder, came to Hezekiah with their clothes torn, and told him the words of the Rabshakeh.

Hezekiah Consults Isaiah

37 When King Hezekiah heard it, he tore his clothes, covered himself with sackcloth, and went into the house of the LORD. 2And he sent Eliakim, who was in charge of the palace, and Shebna the secretary, and the senior priests, covered with sackcloth, to the prophet Isaiah son of Amoz. 3They said to him, "Thus says Hezekiah, This day is a day of distress, of rebuke, and of disgrace; children have come to the birth, and there is no strength to bring them forth. 4It may be that the LORD your God heard the words of the Rabshakeh, whom his master the king of Assyria has sent to mock the living God, and will rebuke the words that the LORD your God has heard; therefore lift up your prayer for the remnant that is left."

5 When the servants of King Hezekiah came to Isaiah, 6Isaiah said to them, "Say to your master, 'Thus says the LORD: Do not be afraid because of the words that you have heard, with which the servants of the king of Assyria have reviled me. 7I myself will put a spirit in him, so that he shall hear a rumor, and return to his own land; I will cause him to fall by the sword in his own land.' "

8 The Rabshakeh returned, and found the king of Assyria fighting against Libnah; for he had heard that the king had left Lachish. 9Now the king[u] heard concerning King Tirhakah of Ethiopia,[v] "He has set out to fight against you." When he heard it, he sent messengers to Hezekiah, saying, 10"Thus shall you speak to King Hezekiah of Judah: Do not let your God on whom you rely deceive you by promising that Jerusalem will not be given into the hand of the king of Assyria. 11See, you have heard what the kings of Assyria have done to all lands, destroying them utterly. Shall you be delivered? 12Have the gods of the nations delivered them, the nations that my predecessors destroyed, Gozan, Haran, Rezeph, and the people of Eden who were in Telassar? 13Where is the king of Hamath, the king of Arpad, the king of the city of Sepharvaim, the king of Hena, or the king of Ivvah?"

Hezekiah's Prayer

14 Hezekiah received the letter from the hand of the messengers and read it; then Hezekiah went up to the house of the LORD and spread it before the LORD. 15And Hezekiah prayed to the LORD, saying: 16"O LORD of hosts, God of Israel, who are enthroned above the cherubim, you are God, you alone, of all the kingdoms of the earth; you have made heaven and earth. 17Incline your ear, O LORD, and hear; open your eyes, O LORD,

36.11-12 *The Rabshakeh* vividly pictures the food and drink available to the besieged Jerusalemites as *dung* and *urine*. **36.13-22** He then mocks Hezekiah's claim that the LORD can deliver Jerusalem from the Assyrian forces, which have been all-conquering. Hezekiah's aides return to him in despair. **37.1-37** The Confrontation with Sennacherib and his Retreat. This account closely follows 2 Kings 19: Hezekiah's appeal to Isaiah (37.1-4), the counsel of Isaiah to the king (37.5-7), the prayer of Hezekiah (37.14-20), and the prophet's response (37.21-35), which affirms God's sovereignty over all human schemes and the certain subjugation of Sennacherib. This prediction of the defeat of the Assyrians is followed by an account of the king's humiliating retreat to his own city, gods and family (37.36-37).

[u] Heb *he* [v] Or *Nubia*; Heb *Cush*

38.1-39.8 Hezekiah's Illness, Psalm of Praise, and Foolish Final Actions.
38.1-5 With variations in detail, this report parallels 2 Kings 20.1-3 in its report of Hezekiah's serious illness, his appeal to the LORD, the divine promise of recovery and extension of life, and the liberation of Jerusalem from *the King of Assyria.*

and see; hear all the words of Sennacherib,
which he has sent to mock the living God.
[18]Truly, O LORD, the kings of Assyria have
laid waste all the nations and their lands,
[19]and have hurled their gods into the fire,
though they were no gods, but the work of
human hands—wood and stone—and so
they were destroyed. [20]So now, O LORD our
God, save us from his hand, so that all the
kingdoms of the earth may know that you
alone are the LORD."

21 Then Isaiah son of Amoz sent to
Hezekiah, saying: "Thus says the LORD, the
God of Israel: Because you have prayed to
me concerning King Sennacherib of Assyria,
[22]this is the word that the LORD has spoken
concerning him:

She despises you, she scorns you—
virgin daughter Zion;
she tosses her head—behind your back,
daughter Jerusalem.

[23] Whom have you mocked and reviled?
Against whom have you raised your voice
and haughtily lifted your eyes?
Against the Holy One of Israel!
[24] By your servants you have mocked the Lord,
and you have said, 'With my many chariots
I have gone up the heights of the mountains,
to the far recesses of Lebanon;
I felled its tallest cedars,
its choicest cypresses;
I came to its remotest height,
its densest forest.
[25] I dug wells
and drank waters,
I dried up with the sole of my foot
all the streams of Egypt.'

[26] Have you not heard
that I determined it long ago?
I planned from days of old
what now I bring to pass,
that you should make fortified cities
crash into heaps of ruins,
[27] while their inhabitants, shorn of strength,
are dismayed and confounded;
they have become like plants of the field
and like tender grass,
like grass on the housetops,
blighted[w] before it is grown.

[28] I know your rising up[x] and your sitting down,
your going out and coming in,
and your raging against me.
[29] Because you have raged against me
and your arrogance has come to my ears,
I will put my hook in your nose
and my bit in your mouth;
I will turn you back on the way
by which you came.

30 "And this shall be the sign for you:
This year eat what grows of itself, and in
the second year what springs from that;
then in the third year sow, reap, plant
vineyards, and eat their fruit. [31]The surviving remnant of the house of Judah shall
again take root downward, and bear fruit
upward; [32]for from Jerusalem a remnant
shall go out, and from Mount Zion a band
of survivors. The zeal of the LORD of hosts
will do this.

33 "Therefore thus says the LORD concerning the king of Assyria: He shall not
come into this city, shoot an arrow there,
come before it with a shield, or cast up a
siege ramp against it. [34]By the way that he
came, by the same he shall return; he shall
not come into this city, says the LORD. [35]For
I will defend this city to save it, for my own
sake and for the sake of my servant David."

Sennacherib's Defeat and Death

36 Then the angel of the LORD set out
and struck down one hundred eighty-five
thousand in the camp of the Assyrians;
when morning dawned, they were all dead
bodies. [37]Then King Sennacherib of Assyria
left, went home, and lived at Nineveh. [38]As
he was worshiping in the house of his god
Nisroch, his sons Adrammelech and Sharezer
killed him with the sword, and they escaped
into the land of Ararat. His son Esar-haddon
succeeded him.

Hezekiah's Illness

38 In those days Hezekiah became
sick and was at the point of death.
The prophet Isaiah son of Amoz came to
him, and said to him, "Thus says the LORD:
Set your house in order, for you shall die;
you shall not recover." [2]Then Hezekiah
turned his face to the wall, and prayed to

[w] With 2 Kings 19.26: Heb *field* [x] Q Ms Gk: MT lacks *your rising up*

37.18 2 Kings 15.29; 1 Chr 5.26; Nah 2.11,12

37.19 Isa 2.8; 26.14

37.20 Isa 25.9; Ps 46.10; Ezek 36.23

37.21 ver 2

37.22 Jer 14.17; Lam 2.13; Zech 2.10; Job 16.4

37.23 ver 4; Isa 2.11; 5.15,21; Ezek 39.7; Hab 1.12

37.24 Isa 8.7,8; 10.18,33,34; 14.8

37.26 Isa 40.21,28; Acts 2.23; 4.27,28; Isa 46.11; 10.6; 17.1

37.27 Isa 40.7; Ps 129.6

37.28 Ps 139.1

37.29 Isa 10.12; 30.28; Ezek 38.4; ver 34

37.31 ver 4; Isa 4.2; 10.20; 27.6

37.32 ver 4; 2 Kings 19.31; Isa 9.7; Zech 1.14

37.35 2 Kings 20.6; Isa 38.6; 48.9,11

37.36 2 Kings 19.35; Isa 10.12,33,34

37.38 Jer 51.27; Ezra 4.2

38.1 2 Kings 20.1-6,9-11; 2 Chr 32.24; 2 Sam 17.23

38.3 Neh 13.14; 2 Kings 18.5,6; 1 Chr 28.9; 29.19; Deut 6.18
38.5 2 Kings 18.2,13
38.6 Isa 37.35
38.7 Isa 7.11
38.8 2 Kings 20.9-11; Josh 10.12-14
38.10 Ps 102.24; 107.18; Job 17.11,15; 2 Cor 1.9
38.11 Ps 27.13; 116.9
38.12 2 Cor 5.1,4; Heb 1.12; Job 7.6; 6.9; Ps 73.14
38.13 Job 10.16; 16.12; Ps 51.8; 32.4
38.14 Isa 59.11; Ps 119.122,123
38.15 Ps 39.9; 1 Kings 21.27; Job 7.11; 10.1
38.17 Ps 30.3; Isa 43.25; Jer 31.34; Mic 7.19
38.18 Ps 6.5; 88.11; 115.17; Eccl 9.10; Ps 28.1
38.19 Ps 118.17; Deut 6.7; Ps 78.5-7
38.20 Ps 86.5; 33.1-3; 104.33; 116.17-19
38.21 2 Kings 20.7,8
39.1 2 Kings 20.12-19; 2 Chr 32.31
39.2 2 Chr 32.25,31; 2 Kings 18.15,16
39.3 2 Sam 12.1; 2 Chr 16.7; Jer 5.15
39.5 1 Sam 13.13,14; 15.16

the LORD: 3"Remember now, O LORD, I implore you, how I have walked before you in
faithfulness with a whole heart, and have
done what is good in your sight." And
Hezekiah wept bitterly.
4 Then the word of the LORD came to
Isaiah: 5"Go and say to Hezekiah, Thus says
the LORD, the God of your ancestor David:
I have heard your prayer, I have seen your
tears; I will add fifteen years to your life. 6I
will deliver you and this city out of the
hand of the king of Assyria, and defend this
city.
7 "This is the sign to you from the LORD,
that the LORD will do this thing that he has
promised: 8See, I will make the shadow cast
by the declining sun on the dial of Ahaz
turn back ten steps." So the sun turned
back on the dial the ten steps by which it
had declined.[y]

9 A writing of King Hezekiah of Judah,
after he had been sick and had
recovered from his sickness:
10 I said: In the noontide of my days
I must depart;
I am consigned to the gates of Sheol
for the rest of my years.
11 I said, I shall not see the LORD
in the land of the living;
I shall look upon mortals no more
among the inhabitants of the world.
12 My dwelling is plucked up and removed
from me
like a shepherd's tent;
like a weaver I have rolled up my life;
he cuts me off from the loom;
from day to night you bring me to an
end;[y]
13 I cry for help[z] until morning;
like a lion he breaks all my bones;
from day to night you bring me to an
end.[y]

14 Like a swallow or a crane[y] I clamor,
I moan like a dove.
My eyes are weary with looking
upward.
O Lord, I am oppressed; be my
security!
15 But what can I say? For he has spoken
to me,
and he himself has done it.
All my sleep has fled[a]
because of the bitterness of my soul.
16 O Lord, by these things people live,
and in all these is the life of my spirit.[y]
Oh, restore me to health and make
me live!
17 Surely it was for my welfare
that I had great bitterness;
but you have held back[b] my life
from the pit of destruction,
for you have cast all my sins
behind your back.
18 For Sheol cannot thank you,
death cannot praise you;
those who go down to the Pit cannot
hope
for your faithfulness.
19 The living, the living, they thank you,
as I do this day;
fathers make known to children
your faithfulness.

20 The LORD will save me,
and we will sing to stringed
instruments[c]
all the days of our lives,
at the house of the LORD.

21 Now Isaiah had said, "Let them take
a lump of figs, and apply it to the boil, so
that he may recover." 22Hezekiah also had
said, "What is the sign that I shall go up
to the house of the LORD?"

Envoys from Babylon Welcomed

39 At that time King Merodach-
baladan son of Baladan of Babylon
sent envoys with letters and a present to
Hezekiah, for he heard that he had been
sick and had recovered. 2Hezekiah welcomed
them; he showed them his treasure house,
the silver, the gold, the spices, the precious
oil, his whole armory, all that was found in
his storehouses. There was nothing in his
house or in all his realm that Hezekiah did
not show them. 3Then the prophet Isaiah
came to King Hezekiah and said to him,
"What did these men say? From where did
they come to you?" Hezekiah answered,
"They have come to me from a far country,
from Babylon." 4He said, "What have they
seen in your house?" Hezekiah answered,
"They have seen all that is in my house;
there is nothing in my storehouses that I
did not show them."
5 Then Isaiah said to Hezekiah, "Hear

[y] Meaning of Heb uncertain [z] Cn: Meaning of Heb uncertain [a] Cn Compare Syr: Heb *I will walk slowly all my years* [b] Cn Compare Gk Vg: Heb *loved* [c] Heb *my stringed instruments*

38.7-8 A briefer version is given of the supportive sign from God through the reversal of the sun's shadow on the sun-dial than the account in 2 Kings 20.7-11. There it is linked with the report of Hezekiah's being healed, a detail only briefly noted in 38.21.

38.9-20 Hezekiah's psalm-like response to God's promise (not found in 2 Kings) reports his expectation that his life will be short, but following his prayer, he is assured of an extension of his life and offers praise to God for this gift.

39.1-8 closely match 2 Kings 21.12-19, with the story of Hezekiah's ostentatious display of his *treasure*, his *house*, his *weapons* and his *storehouses*. This evokes from the prophet the warning that in the future all this wealth and some of the king's children will be carried off to Babylon. The king is content, however, because these tragedies will not occur during his own lifetime, which will pass in *peace and security*.

40.1-11 Comfort to God's People and the Revelation of God to All Humanity.
40.1-2 God's people have paid their debt to him for their disobedience, and their time of exile in Babylon is soon to end.
40.3-5 All the human race will see God's work of deliverance for his people by the way he will prepare for them to return (*cf.* 35.8-10).
40.6-11 In contrast to the inconsistency of human behavior and the transiency of all earthly life, *the word of our God* is fully reliable and his promise will be fulfilled in his tender care and restoration of his people to their land.
40.13-31 The Omnipotence and Compassion of God. The impossibility of measuring God's power over nature and history, or of offering him advice, is contrasted with his concern for helpless humanity and his special care for those who rely upon him: *who wait for the LORD.*

the word of the LORD of hosts: 6 Days are
coming when all that is in your house, and
that which your ancestors have stored up
until this day, shall be carried to Babylon;
nothing shall be left, says the LORD. 7 Some
of your own sons who are born to you shall
be taken away; they shall be eunuchs in the
palace of the king of Babylon." 8 Then
Hezekiah said to Isaiah, "The word of the
LORD that you have spoken is good." For he
thought, "There will be peace and security
in my days."

God's People Are Comforted

40 Comfort, O comfort my people,
says your God.
2 Speak tenderly to Jerusalem,
and cry to her
that she has served her term,
that her penalty is paid,
that she has received from the LORD's hand
double for all her sins.

3 A voice cries out:
"In the wilderness prepare the way of the LORD,
make straight in the desert a highway for our God.
4 Every valley shall be lifted up,
and every mountain and hill be made low;
the uneven ground shall become level,
and the rough places a plain.
5 Then the glory of the LORD shall be revealed,
and all people shall see it together,
for the mouth of the LORD has spoken."

6 A voice says, "Cry out!"
And I said, "What shall I cry?"
All people are grass,
their constancy is like the flower of the field.
7 The grass withers, the flower fades,
when the breath of the LORD blows upon it;
surely the people are grass.
8 The grass withers, the flower fades;
but the word of our God will stand forever.
9 Get you up to a high mountain,
O Zion, herald of good tidings;[d]
lift up your voice with strength,
O Jerusalem, herald of good tidings,[e]
lift it up, do not fear;
say to the cities of Judah,
"Here is your God!"
10 See, the Lord GOD comes with might,
and his arm rules for him;
his reward is with him,
and his recompense before him.
11 He will feed his flock like a shepherd;
he will gather the lambs in his arms,
and carry them in his bosom,
and gently lead the mother sheep.

12 Who has measured the waters in the hollow of his hand
and marked off the heavens with a span,
enclosed the dust of the earth in a measure,
and weighed the mountains in scales
and the hills in a balance?
13 Who has directed the spirit of the LORD,
or as his counselor has instructed him?
14 Whom did he consult for his enlightenment,
and who taught him the path of justice?
Who taught him knowledge,
and showed him the way of understanding?
15 Even the nations are like a drop from a bucket,
and are accounted as dust on the scales;
see, he takes up the isles like fine dust.
16 Lebanon would not provide fuel enough,
nor are its animals enough for a burnt offering.
17 All the nations are as nothing before him;
they are accounted by him as less than nothing and emptiness.

18 To whom then will you liken God,
or what likeness compare with him?
19 An idol? —A workman casts it,
and a goldsmith overlays it with gold,
and casts for it silver chains.
20 As a gift one chooses mulberry wood[f]
—wood that will not rot—
then seeks out a skilled artisan
to set up an image that will not topple.

21 Have you not known? Have you not heard?
Has it not been told you from the beginning?

[d] Or *O herald of good tidings to Zion* [e] Or *O herald of good tidings to Jerusalem* [f] Meaning of Heb uncertain

39.6 Jer 20.5
39.7 Dan 1.2-7
39.8 2 Chr 32.26; 1 Sam 3.18; 2 Chr 34.28
40.1 Isa 12.1
40.2 Isa 35.4; 41.11-13; 33.24; Jer 16.18
40.3 Mt 3.3; Mk 1.3; Lk 3.4-6; Jn 1.23; Mal 3.1
40.4 Isa 45.2
40.6 Job 14.2; Ps 102.11; 103.15; 1 Pet 1.24,25
40.7 Ps 90.5,6; ver 24
40.8 Isa 55.11; Mt 5.18; 1 Pet 1.24,25
40.9 Isa 60.1; 52.7; Acts 10.36; Rom 10.15
40.10 Isa 59.16,18; 62.11; Rev 22.27,12
40.11 Ezek 34.23; Mic 5.4; Jn 10.11; Heb 13.20
40.12 Isa 48.13; Job 38.8-11; Heb 1.10-12
40.13 Rom 11.34; 1 Cor 2.16
40.15 Jer 10.10; Isa 17.13; 29.5
40.17 Isa 29.7; 30.28
40.18 ver 25; Isa 46.5; Mic 7.18; Acts 17.29
40.19 Isa 41.6,7; 44.12; Jer 10.3
40.20 Isa 41.7; Jer 10.3-5
40.21 Ps 19.1; Acts 14.17; Rom 1.19

40.22 Job 22.14; Num 13.33; Isa 42.5; 44.24; Ps 104.2
40.23 Job 12.21; Ps 107.40; Isa 5.21
40.24 Isa 17.10,11; ver 7; Isa 17.13; 41.16
40.25 ver 18
40.26 Isa 51.6; 42.5; Ps 147.4; 89.11-13; Isa 34.16
40.27 Isa 49.4,14; 54.8; Lk 18.7,8; Isa 25.1
40.28 Ps 90.2; 147.5; Rom 11.33
40.29 Isa 50.4; Jer 31.25; Isa 41.10
40.31 Ps 103.5; 2 Cor 4.8-10,16; Deut 32.11; 2 Cor 4.1; Heb 12.3
41.1 Zech 2.13; Isa 40.31; 34.1; 43.26
41.2 Isa 45.1-3; 46.11; 42.6; 2 Chr 36.23; Isa 29.5; 40.24
41.4 Isa 44.7; 46.10; 43.10; 44.6; Rev 1.17; 22.13
41.5 Ps 67.7
41.6 Isa 40.19
41.7 Isa 40.19,20
41.8 Isa 44.1; 2 Chr 20.7; Jas 2.23
41.9 Isa 11.11; 43.5-7; 42.1; Ps 135.4
41.10 Isa 43.5; Rom 8.31; Isa 44.2
41.11 Isa 45.24; 17.13
41.12 Isa 17.14; 29.20

Have you not understood from the foundations of the earth?
22 It is he who sits above the circle of the earth,
and its inhabitants are like grasshoppers;
who stretches out the heavens like a curtain,
and spreads them like a tent to live in;
23 who brings princes to naught,
and makes the rulers of the earth as nothing.

24 Scarcely are they planted, scarcely sown,
scarcely has their stem taken root in the earth,
when he blows upon them, and they wither,
and the tempest carries them off like stubble.

25 To whom then will you compare me,
or who is my equal? says the Holy One.
26 Lift up your eyes on high and see:
Who created these?
He who brings out their host and numbers them,
calling them all by name;
because he is great in strength,
mighty in power,
not one is missing.

27 Why do you say, O Jacob,
and speak, O Israel,
"My way is hidden from the LORD,
and my right is disregarded by my God"?
28 Have you not known? Have you not heard?
The LORD is the everlasting God,
the Creator of the ends of the earth.
He does not faint or grow weary;
his understanding is unsearchable.
29 He gives power to the faint,
and strengthens the powerless.
30 Even youths will faint and be weary,
and the young will fall exhausted;
31 but those who wait for the LORD shall renew their strength,
they shall mount up with wings like eagles,
they shall run and not be weary,
they shall walk and not faint.

Israel Assured of God's Help

41 Listen to me in silence, O coastlands;
let the peoples renew their strength;
let them approach, then let them speak;
let us together draw near for judgment.

2 Who has roused a victor from the east,
summoned him to his service?
He delivers up nations to him,
and tramples kings under foot;
he makes them like dust with his sword,
like driven stubble with his bow.
3 He pursues them and passes on safely,
scarcely touching the path with his feet.
4 Who has performed and done this,
calling the generations from the beginning?
I, the LORD, am first,
and will be with the last.
5 The coastlands have seen and are afraid,
the ends of the earth tremble;
they have drawn near and come.
6 Each one helps the other,
saying to one another, "Take courage!"
7 The artisan encourages the goldsmith,
and the one who smooths with the hammer encourages the one who strikes the anvil,
saying of the soldering, "It is good";
and they fasten it with nails so that it cannot be moved.
8 But you, Israel, my servant,
Jacob, whom I have chosen,
the offspring of Abraham, my friend;
9 you whom I took from the ends of the earth,
and called from its farthest corners,
saying to you, "You are my servant,
I have chosen you and not cast you off";
10 do not fear, for I am with you,
do not be afraid, for I am your God;
I will strengthen you, I will help you,
I will uphold you with my victorious right hand.

11 Yes, all who are incensed against you
shall be ashamed and disgraced;
those who strive against you
shall be as nothing and shall perish.
12 You shall seek those who contend with you,

41.1-10 Special Care for Israel from the Lord of History.
41.1-7 Nations whose destiny is being shaped by the God of Israel continue to turn for assurance to idols, the products of human invention.
41.8-20 God's special link with his people, which goes back to Abraham, is his role as *Redeemer*, who provides what is required to restore his people to right relationship with him. As *the Holy One of Israel* he purifies them to be worthy of this relationship. His work will be evident in the defeat of their enemies and – in a mixed metaphor – in his use of them as a *threshing sledge* which will level *mountains*, thus symbolizing both the forceful preparation of the lands for their return and the defeat of those people who may stand in their way (Isa 40.4). The theme of meeting the needs of the weak and deprived is also repeated from Isa 40.29-31.

41.21-29 The Folly of Dependence on Idols. Unlike *the LORD,* the idols can neither predict nor bring about changes in human destiny. By contrast, God has *stirred up* his agent *from the north* – that is, Cyrus – to enable the Jews to return to their land (*cf.* 41.2; 45.13). This image is anticipated in Isa 13.4-9 and Jer 50.9; 51.11. The coming action was disclosed by God only to Zion, his people. All other claimants to predicting the future are *empty wind.*

42.1-4 The Servant of the LORD (1). This is the first of four poems about *the servant,* describing him as the special agent of God to fulfill the divine purpose for the faithful community (see 49.1-6; 50.4-9; 52.13-53.12). The image of God's servant is used variously in this section of Isaiah: it may refer to a specially endowed individual through whom God's purpose will be achieved, or to a community through which the divine intention is fulfilled. Christians interpreted these poems as predictions of Jesus Christ. The poems depict the work of the servant, but do not disclose his identity. In this poem God chose the servant and empowered him by his *spirit.* His role of establishing *justice to the nations* will be carried out in a gentle, unobtrusive but persistent way.

but you shall not find them;
those who war against you
shall be as nothing at all.
13 For I, the LORD your God,
hold your right hand;
it is I who say to you, "Do not fear,
I will help you."

14 Do not fear, you worm Jacob,
you insect[g] Israel!
I will help you, says the LORD;
your Redeemer is the Holy One of Israel.
15 Now, I will make of you a threshing sledge,
sharp, new, and having teeth;
you shall thresh the mountains and crush them,
and you shall make the hills like chaff.
16 You shall winnow them and the wind shall carry them away,
and the tempest shall scatter them.
Then you shall rejoice in the LORD;
in the Holy One of Israel you shall glory.

17 When the poor and needy seek water,
and there is none,
and their tongue is parched with thirst,
I the LORD will answer them,
I the God of Israel will not forsake them.
18 I will open rivers on the bare heights,[h]
and fountains in the midst of the valleys;
I will make the wilderness a pool of water,
and the dry land springs of water.
19 I will put in the wilderness the cedar,
the acacia, the myrtle, and the olive;
I will set in the desert the cypress,
the plane and the pine together,
20 so that all may see and know,
all may consider and understand,
that the hand of the LORD has done this,
the Holy One of Israel has created it.

The Futility of Idols

21 Set forth your case, says the LORD;
bring your proofs, says the King of Jacob.
22 Let them bring them, and tell us
what is to happen.
Tell us the former things, what they are,
so that we may consider them,
and that we may know their outcome;
or declare to us the things to come.
23 Tell us what is to come hereafter,
that we may know that you are gods;
do good, or do harm,
that we may be afraid and terrified.
24 You, indeed, are nothing
and your work is nothing at all;
whoever chooses you is an abomination.

25 I stirred up one from the north, and he has come,
from the rising of the sun he was summoned by name.[i]
He shall trample[j] on rulers as on mortar,
as the potter treads clay.
26 Who declared it from the beginning, so that we might know,
and beforehand, so that we might say, "He is right"?
There was no one who declared it, none who proclaimed,
none who heard your words.
27 I first have declared it to Zion,[k]
and I give to Jerusalem a herald of good tidings.
28 But when I look there is no one;
among these there is no counselor
who, when I ask, gives an answer.
29 No, they are all a delusion;
their works are nothing;
their images are empty wind.

The Servant, a Light to the Nations

42 Here is my servant, whom I uphold,
my chosen, in whom my soul delights;
I have put my spirit upon him;
he will bring forth justice to the nations.
2 He will not cry or lift up his voice,
or make it heard in the street;
3 a bruised reed he will not break,
and a dimly burning wick he will not quench;
he will faithfully bring forth justice.
4 He will not grow faint or be crushed
until he has established justice in the earth;

[g] Syr: Heb *men of* [h] Or *trails* [i] Cn Compare Q Ms Gk: MT *and he shall call on my name* [j] Cn: Heb *come* [k] Cn: Heb *First to Zion—Behold, behold them*

41.13 Isa 42.6; ver 10
41.14 Job 25.6; Isa 43.14
41.15 Mic 4.13
41.16 Jer 51.2; Isa 45.25
41.17 Isa 43.20; 30.19; 42.16
41.18 Isa 35.6,7; 43.19
41.20 Isa 40.5; Job 12.9
41.21 ver 1; Isa 43.15
41.22 Isa 45.21; 43.9
41.23 Isa 42.9; 44.7,8; 45.3; Jn 13.19; Jer 10.5
41.24 Ps 115.8; Isa 44.9; 1 Cor 8.4; ver 29
41.25 ver 2; Isa 10.6
41.26 Isa 44.7; 45.21; Hab 2.18,19
41.27 ver 4; Isa 40.9
41.28 Isa 63.5; 40.13,14; 46.7
41.29 ver 24; Isa 44.9; Jer 5.13
42.1 Isa 43.10; 53.11; Mt 12.18-20; 3.16,17; 17.5; Isa 2.4
42.3 Isa 57.15; Ps 72.2
42.4 Isa 40.28; ver 10,12

and the coastlands wait for his
teaching.

5 Thus says God, the LORD,
who created the heavens and
stretched them out,
who spread out the earth and what
comes from it,
who gives breath to the people upon it
and spirit to those who walk in it:
6 I am the LORD, I have called you in
righteousness,
I have taken you by the hand and
kept you;
I have given you as a covenant to the
people,[l]
a light to the nations,
7 to open the eyes that are blind,
to bring out the prisoners from the
dungeon,
from the prison those who sit in
darkness.
8 I am the LORD, that is my name;
my glory I give to no other,
nor my praise to idols.
9 See, the former things have come to pass,
and new things I now declare;
before they spring forth,
I tell you of them.

A Hymn of Praise

10 Sing to the LORD a new song,
his praise from the end of the earth!
Let the sea roar[m] and all that fills it,
the coastlands and their inhabitants.
11 Let the desert and its towns lift up their
voice,
the villages that Kedar inhabits;
let the inhabitants of Sela sing for joy,
let them shout from the tops of the
mountains.
12 Let them give glory to the LORD,
and declare his praise in the
coastlands.
13 The LORD goes forth like a soldier,
like a warrior he stirs up his fury;
he cries out, he shouts aloud,
he shows himself mighty against his
foes.

14 For a long time I have held my peace,
I have kept still and restrained myself;
now I will cry out like a woman in
labor,
I will gasp and pant.
15 I will lay waste mountains and hills,
and dry up all their herbage;
I will turn the rivers into islands,
and dry up the pools.
16 I will lead the blind
by a road they do not know,
by paths they have not known
I will guide them.
I will turn the darkness before them into
light,
the rough places into level ground.
These are the things I will do,
and I will not forsake them.
17 They shall be turned back and utterly
put to shame—
those who trust in carved images,
who say to cast images,
"You are our gods."

18 Listen, you that are deaf;
and you that are blind, look up and
see!
19 Who is blind but my servant,
or deaf like my messenger whom I
send?
Who is blind like my dedicated one,
or blind like the servant of the LORD?
20 He sees many things, but does[n] not
observe them;
his ears are open, but he does not
hear.

Israel's Disobedience

21 The LORD was pleased, for the sake of his
righteousness,
to magnify his teaching and make it
glorious.
22 But this is a people robbed and
plundered,
all of them are trapped in holes
and hidden in prisons;
they have become a prey with no one to
rescue,
a spoil with no one to say, "Restore!"
23 Who among you will give heed to this,
who will attend and listen for the
time to come?
24 Who gave up Jacob to the spoiler,
and Israel to the robbers?
Was it not the LORD, against whom we
have sinned,
in whose ways they would not walk,
and whose law they would not obey?

[l] Meaning of Heb uncertain [m] Cn Compare Ps 96.11; 98.7: Heb *Those who go down to the sea* [n] Heb *You see many things but do*

42.5 Isa 44.24; Zech 12.1; Acts 17.25
42.6 Isa 43.1; 49.6,8; Lk 2.32; Acts 13.47
42.7 Isa 35.5; 61.1; Lk 4.18; 2 Tim 2.26; Heb 2.14
42.8 Isa 48.11
42.9 Isa 48.3,6
42.10 Isa 33.3; 40.3; 98.1; 107.23
42.12 Isa 24.15; ver 4
42.13 Isa 9.7; Ex 15.3; Hos 11.10; Isa 66.14-16
42.14 Isa 57.11
42.15 Isa 2.12-16; 44.27
42.16 Isa 29.18; Lk 1.78,79; 3.5; Isa 41.17
42.17 Ps 97.7; Isa 1.29; 44.11; 45.16
42.19 Isa 43.8; Ezek 12.2
42.20 Jer 6.10
42.21 Isa 58.13
42.22 Isa 24.18,22; 10.6
42.24 Isa 30.15; 48.18

42.5-9 The Role God Intends for his People. The special covenantal relationship and activity of God's people are not for their benefit alone, but are intended to bring knowledge of God *as a light to the nations.*
42.10-20 All Humanity Called to Praise God.
42.10-12 All people from all over the world are called to join in praise of God, even those from such remote places as *Kedar* and *Sela* in the Arabian desert.
42.13 It is through his mighty acts that the LORD declares who he is.
42.14-17 God will no longer restrain himself, but will soon renew the creation in order to *put to shame* those who honor idols instead of the creator.
42.18-20 Even those who claim to be God's servant people are too *blind* and *deaf* to hear and obey his word.
42.21-43.28 Israel Renewed by God in Spite of Disobedience.
42.21-43.28 Although *the LORD* was ready to display his power to set things right in the world (*righteousness*) and to make known his teaching, his people's disobedience led to their being *trapped* and *consumed* by his judgment on them.

43.1-7 Now, however, *the Holy One of Israel* is calling and freeing his people, and changing the status of other nations – *Egypt, Ethiopia, Seba (*modern Yemen) – in order to renew his own nation, which he identifies as *called by my name.*
43.8-13 None of the nations of the world could have predicted this transformation of a seemingly vanishing subject people: Israel. Only the LORD could have achieved this.
43.14-21 This liberation process is already under way through the God who rules nations, wildlife, and even the surface of the earth in order to accomplish his will for his people.
43.22-28 Although his people have been disobedient and negligent in worship, God will forgive their failures. But they are reminded that it was their misdeeds that led to what seemed *utter destruction* for Israel.

25 So he poured upon him the heat of his anger
and the fury of war;
it set him on fire all around, but he did not understand;
it burned him, but he did not take it to heart.

Restoration and Protection Promised

43 But now thus says the LORD,
he who created you, O Jacob,
he who formed you, O Israel:
Do not fear, for I have redeemed you;
I have called you by name, you are mine.
2 When you pass through the waters, I will be with you;
and through the rivers, they shall not overwhelm you;
when you walk through fire you shall not be burned,
and the flame shall not consume you.
3 For I am the LORD your God,
the Holy One of Israel, your Savior.
I give Egypt as your ransom,
Ethiopia[o] and Seba in exchange for you.
4 Because you are precious in my sight,
and honored, and I love you,
I give people in return for you,
nations in exchange for your life.
5 Do not fear, for I am with you;
I will bring your offspring from the east,
and from the west I will gather you;
6 I will say to the north, "Give them up,"
and to the south, "Do not withhold;
bring my sons from far away
and my daughters from the end of the earth—
7 everyone who is called by my name,
whom I created for my glory,
whom I formed and made."

8 Bring forth the people who are blind, yet have eyes,
who are deaf, yet have ears!
9 Let all the nations gather together,
and let the peoples assemble.
Who among them declared this,
and foretold to us the former things?
Let them bring their witnesses to justify them,
and let them hear and say, "It is true."
10 You are my witnesses, says the LORD,
and my servant whom I have chosen,
so that you may know and believe me
and understand that I am he.
Before me no god was formed,
nor shall there be any after me.
11 I, I am the LORD,
and besides me there is no savior.
12 I declared and saved and proclaimed,
when there was no strange god among you;
and you are my witnesses, says the LORD.
13 I am God, and also henceforth I am He;
there is no one who can deliver from my hand;
I work and who can hinder it?

14 Thus says the LORD,
your Redeemer, the Holy One of Israel:
For your sake I will send to Babylon
and break down all the bars,
and the shouting of the Chaldeans
will be turned to lamentation.[p]
15 I am the LORD, your Holy One,
the Creator of Israel, your King.
16 Thus says the LORD,
who makes a way in the sea,
a path in the mighty waters,
17 who brings out chariot and horse,
army and warrior;
they lie down, they cannot rise,
they are extinguished, quenched like a wick:
18 Do not remember the former things,
or consider the things of old.
19 I am about to do a new thing;
now it springs forth, do you not perceive it?
I will make a way in the wilderness
and rivers in the desert.
20 The wild animals will honor me,
the jackals and the ostriches;
for I give water in the wilderness,
rivers in the desert,
to give drink to my chosen people,
21 the people whom I formed for myself
so that they might declare my praise.

22 Yet you did not call upon me, O Jacob;
but you have been weary of me, O Israel!
23 You have not brought me your sheep for burnt offerings,
or honored me with your sacrifices.

[o] Or *Nubia*; Heb *Cush* [p] Meaning of Heb uncertain

42.25 Isa 5.25; 2 Kings 25.9; Hos 7.9
43.1 ver 7.15.21; Isa 44.2.6.21
43.2 Ps 66.12; Deut 31.6.8; Dan 3.25.27
43.3 Ex 20.2; ver 11; Prov 11.8; 21.18
43.4 Isa 63.9
43.5 Isa 41.10.14; 44.2; Jer 30.10.11; 46.27.28
43.6 Ps 107.3; Isa 14.2
43.7 Ps 100.3; Isa 29.23; Eph 2.10; ver 1
43.8 Isa 6.9; 42.19; Ezek 12.2
43.9 Isa 41.21.22.26
43.10 Isa 44.8; 42.1; 41.4; 44.6
43.11 Isa 45.21
43.12 Deut 32.16; Ps 81.9; ver 10; Isa 44.8
43.13 Ps 90.2; Job 9.12; Isa 14.27
43.14 Isa 41.14; 13.14.15
43.16 Ex 14.16; Ps 77.19; Isa 51.10; Josh 3.13
43.17 Ex 14.4-9.25
43.18 Jer 16.14
43.19 2 Cor 5.17; Rev 21.5; Ex 17.6; Num 20.11; Isa 35.6
43.20 Isa 48.21
43.21 ver 1; Ps 102.18; Lk 1.74.75
43.22 Isa 30.9-11; Mal 1.13
43.23 Am 5.25; Mal 1.6-8

I have not burdened you with offerings,
or wearied you with frankincense.
24 You have not bought me sweet cane
with money,
or satisfied me with the fat of your
sacrifices.
But you have burdened me with your
sins;
you have wearied me with your
iniquities.

25 I, I am He
who blots out your transgressions for
my own sake,
and I will not remember your sins.
26 Accuse me, let us go to trial;
set forth your case, so that you may
be proved right.
27 Your first ancestor sinned,
and your interpreters transgressed
against me.
28 Therefore I profaned the princes of the
sanctuary,
I delivered Jacob to utter destruction,
and Israel to reviling.

God's Blessing on Israel

44 But now hear, O Jacob my
servant,
Israel whom I have chosen!
2 Thus says the LORD who made you,
who formed you in the womb and
will help you:
Do not fear, O Jacob my servant,
Jeshurun whom I have chosen.
3 For I will pour water on the thirsty
land,
and streams on the dry ground;
I will pour my spirit upon your
descendants,
and my blessing on your offspring.
4 They shall spring up like a green
tamarisk,
like willows by flowing streams.
5 This one will say, "I am the LORD's,"
another will be called by the name of
Jacob,
yet another will write on the hand, "The
LORD's,"
and adopt the name of Israel.

6 Thus says the LORD, the King of Israel,
and his Redeemer, the LORD of hosts:
I am the first and I am the last;
besides me there is no god.
7 Who is like me? Let them proclaim it,
let them declare and set it forth before
me.
Who has announced from of old the
things to come?[q]
Let them tell us[r] what is yet to be.
8 Do not fear, or be afraid;
have I not told you from of old and
declared it?
You are my witnesses!
Is there any god besides me?
There is no other rock; I know not one.

The Absurdity of Idol Worship

9 All who make idols are nothing, and
the things they delight in do not profit; their
witnesses neither see nor know. And so
they will be put to shame. 10Who would
fashion a god or cast an image that can do
no good? 11Look, all its devotees shall be put
to shame; the artisans too are merely human. Let them all assemble, let them stand
up; they shall be terrified, they shall all be
put to shame.
12 The ironsmith fashions it[s] and works
it over the coals, shaping it with hammers,
and forging it with his strong arm; he
becomes hungry and his strength fails, he
drinks no water and is faint. 13The carpenter stretches a line, marks it out with a
stylus, fashions it with planes, and marks it
with a compass; he makes it in human
form, with human beauty, to be set up in
a shrine. 14He cuts down cedars or chooses
a holm tree or an oak and lets it grow
strong among the trees of the forest. He
plants a cedar and the rain nourishes it.
15Then it can be used as fuel. Part of it he
takes and warms himself; he kindles a fire
and bakes bread. Then he makes a god and
worships it, makes it a carved image and
bows down before it. 16Half of it he burns
in the fire; over this half he roasts meat,
eats it and is satisfied. He also warms himself and says, "Ah, I am warm, I can feel
the fire!" 17The rest of it he makes into a
god, his idol, bows down to it and worships
it; he prays to it and says, "Save me, for you
are my god!"
18 They do not know, nor do they comprehend; for their eyes are shut, so that
they cannot see, and their minds as well, so
that they cannot understand. 19No one
considers, nor is there knowledge or discernment to say, "Half of it I burned in the

[q] Cn: Heb *from my placing an eternal people and things to come* [r] Tg: Heb *them* [s] Cn: Heb *an ax*

44.1-8 One Sovereign God and One People of God.
44.1-5 *Jacob my servant* receives assurance from *the LORD* of the people's renewal. Then many will identify themselves as *Israel*, probably both Jews and Gentiles, who *adopt the name*.
44.6-8 Human history from first to last is foreseen and controlled by *the LORD*. No other deity warrants human trust.
44.9-20 The Folly of Idolatry (1). This is the first in a series of prophetic oracles about human foolishness in honoring humanly-made images of the gods.
44.9-11 Both the *devotees* of the idols and the *artisans* who make them are fools.
44.12-20 Such people foolishly assume that some object made of wood – which can be used for fuel to warm oneself or to prepare food, and then turns to ashes – is the deity they should worship.

43.24 Ex 30.23; Isa 1.14; Mal 2.17
43.25 Isa 44.23; Ezek 36.22; Jer 31.34
43.26 Isa 1.18; ver 9
43.28 Isa 47.6; Lam 2.2,6; Zech 8.13
44.1 Isa 41.8; Jer 30.10; 46.27,28
44.2 Isa 43.1,7; Deut 32.15
44.3 Isa 35.7; Joel 2.28; Jn 7.38; Acts 2.18
44.5 Isa 19.21; Zech 8.20-22
44.6 Isa 43.1,14; 41.4; 48.12; Rev 1.8,17; 22.13
44.7 Isa 41.4,22
44.8 Isa 41.22; 43.10; Deut 4.35; 1 Sam 2.2; Isa 26.4
44.9 Isa 41.24; 66.3; 43.9; 42.17
44.10 Jer 10.5; Hab 2.18
44.11 Isa 1.29; 42.17
44.12 Isa 40.19; 41.6; Jer 10.3-5
44.13 Isa 41.7; Ps 115.5-7
44.15 ver 17,19; 2 Chr 25.14
44.17 ver 15; Isa 45.20; 1 Kings 18.26,28
44.18 Isa 1.3; 6.9,10
44.19 Isa 5.13; 45.20; 27.11; Deut 27.15

44.21-28 God as Reliable and Resourceful.
44.21-22 Israel has not been forgotten by God, but forgiven and set free.
44.23-28 God's control of creation and of all humanity is now evident in the renewal of Jerusalem and in his choice of the Persian king, *Cyrus*, who ruled Babylon 539-530, to be the agent for rebuilding the city and its *temple*.
45.1-19 Cyrus as God's Agent of Renewal.
45.1-8 Designated here as *the LORD's anointed*, Cyrus is told that his military successes in taking over the empire from the Babylonians and his subsequent reconstituting and enriching of the area are the gift of God, and that these achievements were accomplished *for the sake of my servant Jacob*. Even though Cyrus does not recognize God's absolute sovereignty, through what he does divine blessing and renewal will be manifest on the earth, which is God's creation.
45.9-19 In spite of the folly of those who question God's wisdom as evident in his work in the world, *Cyrus* has been used by God to free his *people* and to bestow on them *the wealth of nations*, including Egypt and Ethiopia. This will be their possession solely through the *salvation* which the LORD has been accomplishing from creation through the present renewal of *Jacob*.

fire; I also baked bread on its coals, I roasted
meat and have eaten. Now shall I make the
rest of it an abomination? Shall I fall down
before a block of wood?" 20He feeds on
ashes; a deluded mind has led him astray,
and he cannot save himself or say, "Is not
this thing in my right hand a fraud?"

Israel Is Not Forgotten

21 Remember these things, O Jacob,
and Israel, for you are my servant;
I formed you, you are my servant;
O Israel, you will not be forgotten by me.
22 I have swept away your transgressions like a cloud,
and your sins like mist;
return to me, for I have redeemed you.

23 Sing, O heavens, for the LORD has done it;
shout, O depths of the earth;
break forth into singing, O mountains,
O forest, and every tree in it!
For the LORD has redeemed Jacob,
and will be glorified in Israel.

24 Thus says the LORD, your Redeemer,
who formed you in the womb:
I am the LORD, who made all things,
who alone stretched out the heavens,
who by myself spread out the earth;
25 who frustrates the omens of liars,
and makes fools of diviners;
who turns back the wise,
and makes their knowledge foolish;
26 who confirms the word of his servant,
and fulfills the prediction of his messengers;
who says of Jerusalem, "It shall be inhabited,"
and of the cities of Judah, "They shall be rebuilt,
and I will raise up their ruins";
27 who says to the deep, "Be dry—
I will dry up your rivers";
28 who says of Cyrus, "He is my shepherd,
and he shall carry out all my purpose";
and who says of Jerusalem, "It shall be rebuilt,"
and of the temple, "Your foundation shall be laid."

Cyrus, God's Instrument

45 Thus says the LORD to his anointed, to Cyrus,
whose right hand I have grasped
to subdue nations before him
and strip kings of their robes,
to open doors before him—
and the gates shall not be closed:
2 I will go before you
and level the mountains,[t]
I will break in pieces the doors of bronze
and cut through the bars of iron,
3 I will give you the treasures of darkness
and riches hidden in secret places,
so that you may know that it is I, the LORD,
the God of Israel, who call you by your name.
4 For the sake of my servant Jacob,
and Israel my chosen,
I call you by your name,
I surname you, though you do not know me.
5 I am the LORD, and there is no other;
besides me there is no god.
I arm you, though you do not know me,
6 so that they may know, from the rising of the sun
and from the west, that there is no one besides me;
I am the LORD, and there is no other.
7 I form light and create darkness,
I make weal and create woe;
I the LORD do all these things.

8 Shower, O heavens, from above,
and let the skies rain down righteousness;
let the earth open, that salvation may spring up,[u]
and let it cause righteousness to sprout up also;
I the LORD have created it.

9 Woe to you who strive with your Maker,
earthen vessels with the potter![v]
Does the clay say to the one who fashions it, "What are you making"?
or "Your work has no handles"?
10 Woe to anyone who says to a father,
"What are you begetting?"
or to a woman, "With what are you in labor?"

[t] Q Ms Gk: MT *the swellings* [u] Q Ms: MT *that they may bring forth salvation* [v] Cn: Heb *with the potsherds, or with the potters*

44.20 Ps 102.9; Job 15.31; Isa 57.11
44.21 Isa 46.8; ver 1,2; Isa 49.15
44.22 Isa 43.25; 55.7; 43.1; 1 Pet 1.18,19
44.23 Isa 42.10; 55.12; 43.1; 61.3
44.24 Isa 43.14; ver 2; Isa 40.14,22
44.25 Isa 40.14; 29.14; 1 Cor 1.20,27
44.26 Isa 55.11; 49.7-20; Jer 32.15,44
44.27 Isa 43.16; 42.15
44.28 Isa 45.1; 14.32; 45.13
45.1 Isa 44.28; Jer 50.3,35; ver 5
45.2 Isa 40.4; Ps 107.16; Jer 51.30
45.3 Jer 41.8; Isa 43.1
45.4 Isa 41.8; 43.1; Acts 17.23
45.5 ver 6; Isa 44.6,8; Ps 18.39
45.6 Mal 1.11; Isa 43.5; ver 5
45.7 Isa 42.16; Ps 104.20; Am 3.6
45.8 Ps 72.6; 85.11; Isa 12.3; 60.21
45.9 Isa 29.16; Rom 9.20,21

11 Thus says the LORD,
the Holy One of Israel, and its Maker:
Will you question me[w] about my
children,
or command me concerning the work
of my hands?
12 I made the earth,
and created humankind upon it;
it was my hands that stretched out the
heavens,
and I commanded all their host.
13 I have aroused Cyrus[x] in righteousness,
and I will make all his paths straight;
he shall build my city
and set my exiles free,
not for price or reward,
says the LORD of hosts.
14 Thus says the LORD:
The wealth of Egypt and the
merchandise of Ethiopia,[y]
and the Sabeans, tall of stature,
shall come over to you and be yours,
they shall follow you;
they shall come over in chains and
bow down to you.
They will make supplication to you,
saying,
"God is with you alone, and there is
no other;
there is no god besides him."
15 Truly, you are a God who hides himself,
O God of Israel, the Savior.
16 All of them are put to shame and
confounded,
the makers of idols go in confusion
together.
17 But Israel is saved by the LORD
with everlasting salvation;
you shall not be put to shame or
confounded
to all eternity.

18 For thus says the LORD,
who created the heavens
(he is God!),
who formed the earth and made it
(he established it;
he did not create it a chaos,
he formed it to be inhabited!):
I am the LORD, and there is no other.
19 I did not speak in secret,
in a land of darkness;
I did not say to the offspring of Jacob,
"Seek me in chaos."
I the LORD speak the truth,
I declare what is right.

Idols Cannot Save Babylon

20 Assemble yourselves and come together,
draw near, you survivors of the
nations!
They have no knowledge—
those who carry about their wooden
idols,
and keep on praying to a god
that cannot save.
21 Declare and present your case;
let them take counsel together!
Who told this long ago?
Who declared it of old?
Was it not I, the LORD?
There is no other god besides me,
a righteous God and a Savior;
there is no one besides me.

22 Turn to me and be saved,
all the ends of the earth!
For I am God, and there is no other.
23 By myself I have sworn,
from my mouth has gone forth in
righteousness
a word that shall not return:
"To me every knee shall bow,
every tongue shall swear."

24 Only in the LORD, it shall be said of me,
are righteousness and strength;
all who were incensed against him
shall come to him and be ashamed.
25 In the LORD all the offspring of Israel
shall triumph and glory.

46 Bel bows down, Nebo stoops,
their idols are on beasts and cattle;
these things you carry are loaded
as burdens on weary animals.
2 They stoop, they bow down together;
they cannot save the burden,
but themselves go into captivity.

3 Listen to me, O house of Jacob,
all the remnant of the house of Israel,
who have been borne by me from your
birth,
carried from the womb;
4 even to your old age I am he,
even when you turn gray I will carry
you.
I have made, and I will bear;
I will carry and will save.

[w] Cn: Heb *Ask me of things to come* [x] Heb *him* [y] Or *Nubia*; Heb *Cush*

45.11 Isa 43.15; 54.5; 8.19; Jer 31.9; 60.21
45.12 ver 18; Isa 42.5; Neh 9.6
45.13 Isa 41.2; ver 2; Isa 44.28; 52.3
45.14 Isa 14.1,2; Ps 149.8; Isa 49.23; Jer 16.19; 1 Cor 14.25
45.15 Isa 8.17; 43.3
45.16 Isa 44.9,11
45.17 Isa 26.4; Rom 11.26; Isa 49.23
45.18 Isa 42.5; ver 12; Gen 1.2,26; ver 5
45.19 Isa 48.16; 41.8; Jer 29.13,14; Isa 63.1; 44.8
45.20 Isa 43.9; 44.18,19; Jer 10.5; Isa 46.6,7
45.21 Isa 41.23,26; ver 5; Isa 43.3,11
45.22 Num 21.8,9; Isa 30.15; 49.6,12
45.23 Isa 62.8; Rom 14.11; Isa 55.11; 65.16
45.24 Isa 54.17; 41.11
45.25 Isa 53.11; 60.19
46.1 Jer 50.2-4; Isa 45.20
46.2 Jer 43.12,13
46.3 ver 12; Isa 45.19; 10.21,22; 63.9
46.4 Isa 43.13; Ps 71.18

45.20-46.13 The Folly of Idolatry.
45.20-25 People from all the nations are informed that their worship of other gods is futile, since there is no other god who is able to set things right (*righteous*) and to renew and fulfill his plan for this people (*savior*). Everyone is called to acknowledge this from *the ends of the earth* so that *every knee shall bow* to honor *the LORD.*
46.1-13 *The remnant of the house of Israel* (*cf.* Isa 10.21-22; 11.11) is reminded of the impotence of the regional gods: *Bel* (a name of the king of the Babylonian gods, Marduk) and *Nebo* (his son, whose name is a component in the names of the Babylonian rulers, Nebuchadnezzar and Nabonidus). The powers and purpose of Israel's God are beyond comparison with the costly idols used in the worship of the Babylonian gods, and he alone will fulfil his purpose *in Zion.*

47.1-15 The Foolish Confidence of Babylon.
47.1-4 The silly, sordid and self-indulgent life of the Babylonians is contrasted with the holiness of Israel's liberating and renewing *Redeemer*.
47.5-15 The apparent triumph of the Babylonians over Israel and the other kingdoms occurred because God *gave them into your [the Babylonians'] hand*. Their false, self-congratulatory sense of security in the midst of their present prosperity, supported by their magical and astrological practices, will go up in smoke through the *fire* of God's judgment on them.

5 To whom will you liken me and make me equal,
and compare me, as though we were alike?
6 Those who lavish gold from the purse,
and weigh out silver in the scales—
they hire a goldsmith, who makes it into a god;
then they fall down and worship!
7 They lift it to their shoulders, they carry it,
they set it in its place, and it stands there;
it cannot move from its place.
If one cries out to it, it does not answer
or save anyone from trouble.

8 Remember this and consider,[z]
recall it to mind, you transgressors,
9 remember the former things of old;
for I am God, and there is no other;
I am God, and there is no one like me,
10 declaring the end from the beginning
and from ancient times things not yet done,
saying, "My purpose shall stand,
and I will fulfill my intention,"
11 calling a bird of prey from the east,
the man for my purpose from a far country.
I have spoken, and I will bring it to pass;
I have planned, and I will do it.

12 Listen to me, you stubborn of heart,
you who are far from deliverance:
13 I bring near my deliverance, it is not far off,
and my salvation will not tarry;
I will put salvation in Zion,
for Israel my glory.

The Humiliation of Babylon

47 Come down and sit in the dust,
virgin daughter Babylon!
Sit on the ground without a throne,
daughter Chaldea!
For you shall no more be called
tender and delicate.
2 Take the millstones and grind meal,
remove your veil,
strip off your robe, uncover your legs,
pass through the rivers.
3 Your nakedness shall be uncovered,
and your shame shall be seen.
I will take vengeance,
and I will spare no one.
4 Our Redeemer—the LORD of hosts is his name—
is the Holy One of Israel.

5 Sit in silence, and go into darkness,
daughter Chaldea!
For you shall no more be called
the mistress of kingdoms.
6 I was angry with my people,
I profaned my heritage;
I gave them into your hand,
you showed them no mercy;
on the aged you made your yoke
exceedingly heavy.
7 You said, "I shall be mistress forever,"
so that you did not lay these things to heart
or remember their end.

8 Now therefore hear this, you lover of pleasures,
who sit securely,
who say in your heart,
"I am, and there is no one besides me;
I shall not sit as a widow
or know the loss of children"—
9 both these things shall come upon you
in a moment, in one day:
the loss of children and widowhood
shall come upon you in full measure,
in spite of your many sorceries
and the great power of your enchantments.

10 You felt secure in your wickedness;
you said, "No one sees me."
Your wisdom and your knowledge
led you astray,
and you said in your heart,
"I am, and there is no one besides me."
11 But evil shall come upon you,
which you cannot charm away;
disaster shall fall upon you,
which you will not be able to ward off;
and ruin shall come on you suddenly,
of which you know nothing.

12 Stand fast in your enchantments
and your many sorceries,
with which you have labored from your youth;
perhaps you may be able to succeed,
perhaps you may inspire terror.
13 You are wearied with your many consultations;

[z] Meaning of Heb uncertain

46.5 Isa 40.18,25
46.6 Isa 40.19; 44.15.17
46.7 ver 1; Isa 40.20; 44.17; 41.26,28; 45.20
46.8 Isa 44.19,21; 48.8
46.9 Isa 45.5,21; 41.26,27
46.10 Isa 45.21; 14.24; Acts 5.39
46.11 Isa 18.6; 41.2,25; 37.26
46.12 ver 3; Isa 48.4; Jer 2.5
46.13 Isa 61.11; 43.7; 44.23
47.1 Jer 48.18; 46.11; 51.33
47.3 Ezek 16.37; Isa 34.8; 63.4
47.4 Isa 41.14
47.5 Isa 23.2; 13.10; ver 7; 13.19; Dan 2.37
47.6 Zech 1.15; Isa 43.28; 10.14; Deut 28.50
47.7 ver 5; Isa 42.25; 45.21
47.8 Isa 32.9,11; Zeph 2.15; Rev 18.7
47.9 Isa 13.16,18; 1 Thess 5.3; Nah 3.4
47.10 Ps 52.7; Isa 29.15; 44.20; ver 8
47.11 Isa 57.1; 1 Thess 5.3; ver 9
47.12 ver 9
47.13 Isa 57.10; Dan 2.2

let those who study[a] the heavens
stand up and save you,
those who gaze at the stars,
and at each new moon predict
what[b] shall befall you.

14 See, they are like stubble,
the fire consumes them;
they cannot deliver themselves
from the power of the flame.
No coal for warming oneself is this,
no fire to sit before!
15 Such to you are those with whom you have labored,
who have trafficked with you from your youth;
they all wander about in their own paths;
there is no one to save you.

God the Creator and Redeemer

48 Hear this, O house of Jacob,
who are called by the name of Israel,
and who came forth from the loins[c] of Judah;
who swear by the name of the LORD,
and invoke the God of Israel,
but not in truth or right.
2 For they call themselves after the holy city,
and lean on the God of Israel;
the LORD of hosts is his name.

3 The former things I declared long ago,
they went out from my mouth and I made them known;
then suddenly I did them and they came to pass.
4 Because I know that you are obstinate,
and your neck is an iron sinew
and your forehead brass,
5 I declared them to you from long ago,
before they came to pass I announced them to you,
so that you would not say, "My idol did them,
my carved image and my cast image commanded them."

6 You have heard; now see all this;
and will you not declare it?
From this time forward I make you hear new things,
hidden things that you have not known.
7 They are created now, not long ago;
before today you have never heard of them,
so that you could not say, "I already knew them."
8 You have never heard, you have never known,
from of old your ear has not been opened.
For I knew that you would deal very treacherously,
and that from birth you were called a rebel.

9 For my name's sake I defer my anger,
for the sake of my praise I restrain it for you,
so that I may not cut you off.
10 See, I have refined you, but not like[d] silver;
I have tested you in the furnace of adversity.
11 For my own sake, for my own sake, I do it,
for why should my name[e] be profaned?
My glory I will not give to another.

12 Listen to me, O Jacob,
and Israel, whom I called:
I am He; I am the first,
and I am the last.
13 My hand laid the foundation of the earth,
and my right hand spread out the heavens;
when I summon them,
they stand at attention.

14 Assemble, all of you, and hear!
Who among them has declared these things?
The LORD loves him;
he shall perform his purpose on Babylon,
and his arm shall be against the Chaldeans.
15 I, even I, have spoken and called him,
I have brought him, and he will prosper in his way.
16 Draw near to me, hear this!
From the beginning I have not spoken in secret,

[a] Meaning of Heb uncertain [b] Gk Syr Compare Vg: Heb *from what* [c] Cn: Heb *waters* [d] Cn: Heb *with* [e] Gk Old Latin: Heb *for why should it*

47.14 Nah 1.10; Mal 4.1
47.15 Rev 18.11; Isa 43.13; 46.7
48.1 Isa 46.12; Num 24.7; Ps 68.26; Isa 45.23
48.2 Isa 52.1; Mic 3.11; Rom 2.17
48.3 Isa 41.22; 42.9; 43.9; 44.7,8; 45.21; Josh 21.45
48.4 Ezek 2.4; Ex 32.9; Deut 31.27; Ezek 3.7-9
48.5 Ezek 2.4; 3.7
48.6 Isa 42.9; 43.19
48.8 Isa 42.25; 46.8; Ps 58.3
48.9 ver 11; Ps 78.38; Isa 30.18
48.10 Jer 9.7; Ezek 22.18-22; Jer 11.4
48.11 ver 9; Deut 32.26; Ezek 20.9; Isa 42.8
48.12 Deut 32.39; Isa 41.4; Rev 1.17; 22.13
48.13 Ps 102.25; Isa 40.26
48.14 Isa 43.9; 45.21; 46.10,11; Jer 50.21-29
48.15 Isa 41.2; 45.1,2
48.16 Isa 41.1; 45.19; 43.13; Zech 2.9,11

48.1-22 The Certainty of Israel's Liberation from Babylonia.
48.1-2 Those who call themselves *Israel* or *Judah* are here warned against assuming that an *idol* or *another god* that some human made *not long ago* is the agent that achieved their freedom and renewal. It is solely God who planned to take them into this exile, which *refined* them. He alone will *perform his [judgmental] purpose on Babylon,* as he explained to his people from the beginning.

48.17-22 The people might have escaped this punishment of exile if they *had paid attention to [God's] commandments*, but now they are called to leave Babylon. As God once led and cared for Moses and the Israelites *through the deserts*, so he will lead his people back to the land of Judah.
49.1-7 The Servant of the LORD (2). The prophet here speaks for the faithful component of historic *Israel* to describe the role of that remnant as *my servant*, whose task is to renew God's people: *to bring back Jacob to him*. Not only will the faithful *survivors of Israel* experience freedom and renewal, but they will also become the instruments through whom *light* will reach out to all nations, *to the end of the earth*. Though other nations now despise Israel and her God, the rulers of these hostile peoples will one day *prostrate* themselves before *the Holy One of Israel*.
49.8-26 The Return of God's People to Zion.
49.8-13 The faithful remnant will demonstrate God's inclusive plan for his people by inviting the deprived and oppressed to share in the new era of blessing. God will prepare the way for those coming from all over the world – including *Syene*, which is far up the Nile in Egypt. All of *heaven* and *earth* are called to share in the rejoicing over God's deliverance and renewal of his people.

from the time it came to be I have been there.
And now the Lord GOD has sent me and his spirit.

17 Thus says the LORD,
your Redeemer, the Holy One of Israel:
I am the LORD your God,
who teaches you for your own good,
who leads you in the way you should go.
18 O that you had paid attention to my commandments!
Then your prosperity would have been like a river,
and your success like the waves of the sea;
19 your offspring would have been like the sand,
and your descendants like its grains;
their name would never be cut off
or destroyed from before me.

20 Go out from Babylon, flee from Chaldea,
declare this with a shout of joy,
proclaim it,
send it forth to the end of the earth;
say, "The LORD has redeemed his servant Jacob!"
21 They did not thirst when he led them through the deserts;
he made water flow for them from the rock;
he split open the rock and the water gushed out.

22 "There is no peace," says the LORD, "for the wicked."

The Servant's Mission

49 Listen to me, O coastlands,
pay attention, you peoples from far away!
The LORD called me before I was born,
while I was in my mother's womb he named me.
2 He made my mouth like a sharp sword,
in the shadow of his hand he hid me;
he made me a polished arrow,
in his quiver he hid me away.
3 And he said to me, "You are my servant,
Israel, in whom I will be glorified."
4 But I said, "I have labored in vain,
I have spent my strength for nothing and vanity;
yet surely my cause is with the LORD,
and my reward with my God."

5 And now the LORD says,
who formed me in the womb to be his servant,
to bring Jacob back to him,
and that Israel might be gathered to him,
for I am honored in the sight of the LORD,
and my God has become my strength—
6 he says,
"It is too light a thing that you should be my servant
to raise up the tribes of Jacob
and to restore the survivors of Israel;
I will give you as a light to the nations,
that my salvation may reach to the end of the earth."

7 Thus says the LORD,
the Redeemer of Israel and his Holy One,
to one deeply despised, abhorred by the nations,
the slave of rulers,
"Kings shall see and stand up,
princes, and they shall prostrate themselves,
because of the LORD, who is faithful,
the Holy One of Israel, who has chosen you."

Zion's Children to Be Brought Home

8 Thus says the LORD:
In a time of favor I have answered you,
on a day of salvation I have helped you;
I have kept you and given you
as a covenant to the people,[f]
to establish the land,
to apportion the desolate heritages;
9 saying to the prisoners, "Come out,"
to those who are in darkness, "Show yourselves."
They shall feed along the ways,
on all the bare heights[g] shall be their pasture;
10 they shall not hunger or thirst,
neither scorching wind nor sun shall strike them down,

[f] Meaning of Heb uncertain [g] Or *the trails*

48.17 Isa 43.14; Ps 32.8
48.18 Deut 32.29; Ps 119.165; Isa 61.10,11
48.19 Gen 22.17; Jer 32.22; Isa 56.5; 66.22
48.20 Jer 50.8; Isa 42.10; 62.11; 43.1
48.21 Isa 41.17; Ex 17.6; Ps 105.41
48.22 Isa 57.21
49.1 Isa 42.4; 66.19; 44.2,24; Isa 7.14; 9.6; Mt 1.20; Gal 1.15
49.2 Isa 11.4; Heb 4.12; Isa 51.16; Hab 3.11
49.3 Isa 42.1; 44.23
49.4 Isa 65.23
49.5 Isa 44.2,23; 27.12; 43.4; 12.2
49.6 Isa 42.6; Lk 2.32; Acts 13.47; 26.23
49.7 Isa 48.17; 53.3; Ps 22.6-8; Isa 52.15; 66.23
49.8 Ps 69.13; 2 Cor 6.2; Isa 42.6; 44.26
49.9 Isa 42.7; Lk 4.18; Isa 41.18
49.10 Rev 7.16; Ps 121.6; Isa 14.1; 40.11; 41.17

for he who has pity on them will lead them,
and by springs of water will guide them.
11 And I will turn all my mountains into a road,
and my highways shall be raised up.
12 Lo, these shall come from far away,
and lo, these from the north and from the west,
and these from the land of Syene.[h]

13 Sing for joy, O heavens, and exult, O earth;
break forth, O mountains, into singing!
For the LORD has comforted his people,
and will have compassion on his suffering ones.

14 But Zion said, "The LORD has forsaken me,
my Lord has forgotten me."
15 Can a woman forget her nursing child,
or show no compassion for the child of her womb?
Even these may forget,
yet I will not forget you.
16 See, I have inscribed you on the palms of my hands;
your walls are continually before me.
17 Your builders outdo your destroyers,[i]
and those who laid you waste go away from you.
18 Lift up your eyes all around and see;
they all gather, they come to you.
As I live, says the LORD,
you shall put all of them on like an ornament,
and like a bride you shall bind them on.

19 Surely your waste and your desolate places
and your devastated land—
surely now you will be too crowded for your inhabitants,
and those who swallowed you up will be far away.
20 The children born in the time of your bereavement
will yet say in your hearing:
"The place is too crowded for me;
make room for me to settle."
21 Then you will say in your heart,
"Who has borne me these?
I was bereaved and barren,
exiled and put away—
so who has reared these?
I was left all alone—
where then have these come from?"

22 Thus says the Lord GOD:
I will soon lift up my hand to the nations,
and raise my signal to the peoples;
and they shall bring your sons in their bosom,
and your daughters shall be carried on their shoulders.
23 Kings shall be your foster fathers,
and their queens your nursing mothers.
With their faces to the ground they shall bow down to you,
and lick the dust of your feet.
Then you will know that I am the LORD;
those who wait for me shall not be put to shame.

24 Can the prey be taken from the mighty,
or the captives of a tyrant[j] be rescued?
25 But thus says the LORD:
Even the captives of the mighty shall be taken,
and the prey of the tyrant be rescued;
for I will contend with those who contend with you,
and I will save your children.
26 I will make your oppressors eat their own flesh,
and they shall be drunk with their own blood as with wine.
Then all flesh shall know
that I am the LORD your Savior,
and your Redeemer, the Mighty One of Jacob.

50 Thus says the LORD:
Where is your mother's bill of divorce
with which I put her away?
Or which of my creditors is it
to whom I have sold you?
No, because of your sins you were sold,
and for your transgressions your mother was put away.
2 Why was no one there when I came?
Why did no one answer when I called?
Is my hand shortened, that it cannot redeem?
Or have I no power to deliver?

[h] Q Ms: MT *Sinim* [i] Or *Your children come swiftly; your destroyers* [j] Q Ms Syr Vg: MT *of a righteous person*

49.11 Isa 40.4; 62.10
49.12 Isa 43.5,6
49.13 Isa 44.23; 40.1; 54.7,8,10; Rev 12.12; 18.20
49.14 Isa 40.27
49.15 Isa 44.21
49.16 Song 8.6; Isa 62.6,7
49.17 ver 19
49.18 Isa 60.4; 43.5; 45.23; 52.1
49.19 Isa 51.3; 54.1,2; Zech 10.10; Ps 56.1,2
49.20 Isa 54.1-3
49.21 Isa 54.6,7; 27.10; 5.13; 1.8
49.22 Isa 62.10; 60.4; 66.20
49.23 Isa 60.16; 45.14; Ps 72.9; Mic 7.17; Isa 43.10; 25.9; Ps 25.3
49.25 Isa 14.1,2; 25.9
49.26 Isa 9.4,20; 45.6; 43.3; ver 7
50.1 Deut 24.1,3; Jer 3.8; Isa 54.6,7; Deut 32.30; Isa 52.3; 48.8
50.2 Isa 65.12; 66.4; Num 11.23; Isa 59.1; Ex 14.21; Josh 3.16

49.14-26 *Zion,* the sacred mount where the temple was built and which came to designate Jerusalem as a city, cannot complain that it was abandoned by *the LORD,* since his care continues and the names of his people are ever with him. The rebuilding will continue, the land will be renewed, and will become *crowded* by the returnees, whose coming to Zion will be supported by the rulers of many nations. The LORD will punish their oppressors and thereby demonstrate that he is their *Savior and Redeemer, the Mighty One of Jacob.*
50.1-3 God's Sovereign Control of Human History. Comparing the separation of God's people from their land to the divorce of a wife and a husband, the prophet represents God as first reminding them of their failure to respond to his appeal for restoration of relationship with him, and then affirming his power to free or to punish the entire universe.

50.4-9 A Servant Poem (3). Although the term *servant* is not used in this portrait of God's agent, his role as a faithful *teacher* leads to his being tortured and *insulted*, as is the fate of the servant in the other poems. God rewards and confirms him in the face of his adversaries.
50.10-11 A Warning to the Opponents of God's Servant. No-one seems to heed the message of the *servant*, yet the response of violence toward him is to be more than matched by God's punitive treatment of its perpetrators.
51.1-52.12 God's Promise of Deliverance for His People.
51.1-3 Those who *seek the Lord* are counselled to turn back to the bed-rock of the covenant with *Abraham*, confident that the *desert* of judgment that the world is about to experience will be turned by God into an Eden of blessing.
51.4-11 The people of God are to have no anxiety about the forces that threaten them, since his *salvation has gone out*, and the God who overcame the forces of evil in the past (symbolized by *Rahab...the dragon*; Ps 74.12-14; 89.11) will preserve and restore his people in the near future.

By my rebuke I dry up the sea,
I make the rivers a desert;
their fish stink for lack of water,
and die of thirst.[k]
3 I clothe the heavens with blackness,
and make sackcloth their covering.

The Servant's Humiliation and Vindication

4 The Lord God has given me
the tongue of a teacher,[l]
that I may know how to sustain
the weary with a word.
Morning by morning he wakens—
wakens my ear
to listen as those who are taught.
5 The Lord God has opened my ear,
and I was not rebellious,
I did not turn backward.
6 I gave my back to those who struck me,
and my cheeks to those who pulled
out the beard;
I did not hide my face
from insult and spitting.

7 The Lord God helps me;
therefore I have not been disgraced;
therefore I have set my face like flint,
and I know that I shall not be put to
shame;
8 he who vindicates me is near.
Who will contend with me?
Let us stand up together.
Who are my adversaries?
Let them confront me.
9 It is the Lord God who helps me;
who will declare me guilty?
All of them will wear out like a
garment;
the moth will eat them up.

10 Who among you fears the Lord
and obeys the voice of his servant,
who walks in darkness
and has no light,
yet trusts in the name of the Lord
and relies upon his God?
11 But all of you are kindlers of fire,
lighters of firebrands.[m]
Walk in the flame of your fire,
and among the brands that you have
kindled!
This is what you shall have from my
hand:
you shall lie down in torment.

Blessings in Store for God's People

51 Listen to me, you that pursue
righteousness,
you that seek the Lord.
Look to the rock from which you were
hewn,
and to the quarry from which you
were dug.
2 Look to Abraham your father
and to Sarah who bore you;
for he was but one when I called him,
but I blessed him and made him
many.
3 For the Lord will comfort Zion;
he will comfort all her waste places,
and will make her wilderness like Eden,
her desert like the garden of the Lord;
joy and gladness will be found in her,
thanksgiving and the voice of song.

4 Listen to me, my people,
and give heed to me, my nation;
for a teaching will go out from me,
and my justice for a light to the
peoples.
5 I will bring near my deliverance swiftly,
my salvation has gone out
and my arms will rule the peoples;
the coastlands wait for me,
and for my arm they hope.
6 Lift up your eyes to the heavens,
and look at the earth beneath;
for the heavens will vanish like smoke,
the earth will wear out like a
garment,
and those who live on it will die like
gnats;[n]
but my salvation will be forever,
and my deliverance will never be ended.

7 Listen to me, you who know
righteousness,
you people who have my teaching in
your hearts;
do not fear the reproach of others,
and do not be dismayed when they
revile you.
8 For the moth will eat them up like a
garment,
and the worm will eat them like wool;
but my deliverance will be forever,
and my salvation to all generations.

9 Awake, awake, put on strength,
O arm of the Lord!

[k] Or *die on the thirsty ground* [l] Cn: Heb *of those who are taught* [m] Syr: Heb *you gird yourselves with firebrands* [n] Or *in like manner*

50.3 Isa 13.10; Rev 6.12
50.4 Isa 54.13; Jer 31.25; Ps 143.8
50.5 Ps 40.6; Mt 26.39; Jn 8.29; 14.31; Phil 2.8
50.6 Isa 53.5; Mt 26.67; Lk 22.63
50.7 Isa 49.8; 54.4; Ezek 3.8,9
50.8 Rom 8.32-34
50.9 Isa 41.10; 54.17; 51.8
50.10 Isa 49.2,3; 9.2; Eph 5.8; Isa 12.2
50.11 Ps 35.8; Isa 65.13-15
51.1 ver 7; Ps 94.15
51.2 Rom 4.16; Heb 11.11,12; Gen 12.1; 24.35
51.3 Isa 40.1; 52.9; Joel 2.3; Gen 13.10; Isa 66.10
51.4 Ps 50.7; Isa 2.3; 42.4,6
51.5 Isa 46.13; 40.10; 42.4; 63.5
51.6 Isa 40.26; Ps 102.26; Mt 24.35; 2 Pet 3.10; Isa 45.17
51.7 ver 1; Ps 37.31; Mt 5.11; Acts 5.41
51.8 Isa 50.9; ver 6
51.9 Isa 52.1; Deut 4.34; Ps 89.10; 74.13; Ezek 29.3

Awake, as in days of old,
the generations of long ago!
Was it not you who cut Rahab in pieces,
who pierced the dragon?
10 Was it not you who dried up the sea,
the waters of the great deep;
who made the depths of the sea a way
for the redeemed to cross over?
11 So the ransomed of the LORD shall return,
and come to Zion with singing;
everlasting joy shall be upon their heads;
they shall obtain joy and gladness,
and sorrow and sighing shall flee away.

12 I, I am he who comforts you;
why then are you afraid of a mere mortal who must die,
a human being who fades like grass?
13 You have forgotten the LORD, your Maker,
who stretched out the heavens
and laid the foundations of the earth.
You fear continually all day long
because of the fury of the oppressor,
who is bent on destruction.
But where is the fury of the oppressor?
14 The oppressed shall speedily be released;
they shall not die and go down to the Pit,
nor shall they lack bread.
15 For I am the LORD your God,
who stirs up the sea so that its waves roar—
the LORD of hosts is his name.
16 I have put my words in your mouth,
and hidden you in the shadow of my hand,
stretching out[o] the heavens
and laying the foundations of the earth,
and saying to Zion, "You are my people."

17 Rouse yourself, rouse yourself!
Stand up, O Jerusalem,
you who have drunk at the hand of the LORD
the cup of his wrath,
who have drunk to the dregs
the bowl of staggering.
18 There is no one to guide her
among all the children she has borne;
there is no one to take her by the hand
among all the children she has brought up.
19 These two things have befallen you
—who will grieve with you?—
devastation and destruction, famine and sword—
who will comfort you?[p]
20 Your children have fainted,
they lie at the head of every street
like an antelope in a net;
they are full of the wrath of the LORD,
the rebuke of your God.

21 Therefore hear this, you who are wounded,[q]
who are drunk, but not with wine:
22 Thus says your Sovereign, the LORD,
your God who pleads the cause of his people:
See, I have taken from your hand the cup of staggering;
you shall drink no more
from the bowl of my wrath.
23 And I will put it into the hand of your tormentors,
who have said to you,
"Bow down, that we may walk on you";
and you have made your back like the ground
and like the street for them to walk on.

Let Zion Rejoice

52 Awake, awake,
put on your strength, O Zion!
Put on your beautiful garments,
O Jerusalem, the holy city;
for the uncircumcised and the unclean
shall enter you no more.
2 Shake yourself from the dust, rise up,
O captive[r] Jerusalem;
loose the bonds from your neck,
O captive daughter Zion!

3 For thus says the LORD: You were sold
for nothing, and you shall be redeemed
without money. 4For thus says the Lord GOD:
Long ago, my people went down into Egypt
to reside there as aliens; the Assyrian, too,
has oppressed them without cause. 5Now
therefore what am I doing here, says the
LORD, seeing that my people are taken away
without cause? Their rulers howl, says the
LORD, and continually, all day long, my name

[o] Syr: Heb *planting* [p] Q Ms Gk Syr Vg: MT *how may I comfort you?* [q] Or *humbled* [r] Cn: Heb *rise up, sit*

51.10 Ex 14.21; Isa 43.16; 63.9,16
51.11 Isa 35.10; 60.19; Rev 7.17; 22.3
51.12 ver 3; 2 Cor 1.3; Ps 118.6; Isa 40.6,7; 1 Pet 1.24
51.13 Isa 17.10; Job 9.8; Ps 104.2; Isa 40.22; 7.4; 49.26
51.14 Isa 52.2; 38.18; 49.10
51.15 Jer 31.35
51.16 Deut 18.18; Isa 59.21; 49.2; 65.17
51.17 Isa 52.1; Job 21.20; Jer 25.15
51.18 Isa 59.21
51.19 Isa 9.20
51.20 Isa 5.25; 42.25; 66.15
51.21 Isa 54.11; 29.9
51.22 Jer 50.34; ver 17
51.23 Jer 25.15-17,26,28; Zech 12.2; Josh 10.24
52.1 Isa 51.9,17; Neh 11.1; Mt 4.5; Rev 21.2,27
52.2 sa 29.4; 9.4; 51.14
52.3 's 44.12; Isa 63.4; 45.13
52.4 Gen 46.6
52.5 Ezek 36.20; Rom 2.24

51.12-23 They are to have no fear of a mere mortal enemy. Their future is in the hands of God, who will free *the oppressed* and vindicate his *people.* In spite of the past *devastation and destruction* that Jerusalem has experienced, the people will no longer be subject to God's *wrath,* but will see the humiliation of their oppressors whom God brought against them as a judgment.
52.1-2 They are to arouse themselves in preparation for this coming time of liberation.
52.3-6 Their former oppressors will now become aware of what God is doing for the renewal of his people.

52.7-12 With joy in their response to God's message of deliverance, the people are to leave Babylon in a pure state, confident of their future in God's plan.
52.13-53.12 A Servant Poem (4).
52.13-53.3 The last and longest of the Servant Poems announces the ultimate exaltation of God's *servant*, but it then quickly turns to a depiction of his horrible sufferings and gross disfigurement, and of the scornful rejection he experiences.
53.4-6 The servant's sufferings are not the result of his own misdeeds, but are vicarious, in that he bears the gross punishment of others through his acceptance of the penalty for the iniquity of us all.
53.7-12 His oppression evoked no complaint from him, and his death led to his being buried among the wicked and the wealthy. All this happened to him according to *the will of the LORD* as an *offering for sin*. His self-sacrifice will make *many righteous*, through his *intercessions* in their behalf.

is despised. [6]Therefore my people shall know
my name; therefore in that day they shall
know that it is I who speak; here am I.

7 How beautiful upon the mountains
are the feet of the messenger who
announces peace,
who brings good news,
who announces salvation,
who says to Zion, "Your God reigns."
8 Listen! Your sentinels lift up their voices,
together they sing for joy;
for in plain sight they see
the return of the LORD to Zion.
9 Break forth together into singing,
you ruins of Jerusalem;
for the LORD has comforted his people,
he has redeemed Jerusalem.
10 The LORD has bared his holy arm
before the eyes of all the nations;
and all the ends of the earth shall see
the salvation of our God.

11 Depart, depart, go out from there!
Touch no unclean thing;
go out from the midst of it, purify
yourselves,
you who carry the vessels of the LORD.
12 For you shall not go out in haste,
and you shall not go in flight;
for the LORD will go before you,
and the God of Israel will be your
rear guard.

The Suffering Servant

13 See, my servant shall prosper;
he shall be exalted and lifted up,
and shall be very high.
14 Just as there were many who were
astonished at him[s]
—so marred was his appearance,
beyond human semblance,
and his form beyond that of mortals—
15 so he shall startle[t] many nations;
kings shall shut their mouths because
of him;
for that which had not been told them
they shall see,
and that which they had not heard
they shall contemplate.

53 Who has believed what we have
heard?
And to whom has the arm of the
LORD been revealed?
2 For he grew up before him like a young
plant,
and like a root out of dry ground;
he had no form or majesty that we
should look at him,
nothing in his appearance that we
should desire him.
3 He was despised and rejected by others;
a man of suffering[u] and acquainted
with infirmity;
and as one from whom others hide their
faces[v]
he was despised, and we held him of
no account.

4 Surely he has borne our infirmities
and carried our diseases;
yet we accounted him stricken,
struck down by God, and afflicted.
5 But he was wounded for our
transgressions,
crushed for our iniquities;
upon him was the punishment that
made us whole,
and by his bruises we are healed.
6 All we like sheep have gone astray;
we have all turned to our own way,
and the LORD has laid on him
the iniquity of us all.

7 He was oppressed, and he was afflicted,
yet he did not open his mouth;
like a lamb that is led to the slaughter,
and like a sheep that before its
shearers is silent,
so he did not open his mouth.
8 By a perversion of justice he was taken
away.
Who could have imagined his future?
For he was cut off from the land of the
living,
stricken for the transgression of my
people.
9 They made his grave with the wicked
and his tomb[w] with the rich,[x]
although he had done no violence,
and there was no deceit in his mouth.

10 Yet it was the will of the LORD to crush
him with pain.[y]
When you make his life an offering for sin,[t]
he shall see his offspring, and shall
prolong his days;
through him the will of the LORD shall
prosper.

[s] Syr Tg: Heb *you* [t] Meaning of Heb uncertain [u] Or *a man of sorrows* [v] Or *as one who hides his face from us* [w] Q Ms: MT *and in his death* [x] Cn: Heb *with a rich person* [y] Or *by disease*; meaning of Heb uncertain

52.6 Isa 49.23
52.7 Nah 1.15; Rom 10.15; Ps 93.1
52.8 Isa 62.6
52.9 Isa 44.23,26; 48.20
52.10 Ps 98.2,3; Isa 45.22; 48.20; Lk 3.6
52.11 Jer 50.8; 2 Cor 6.17; 2 Tim 2.19; Isa 1.16
52.12 Ex 12.33; Isa 42.16; 58.8
52.13 Isa 42.1; Phil 2.9
52.14 Ps 22.6,7; Isa 53.2,3
52.15 Ezek 36.25; Rom 15.21
53.1 Jn 12.38; Rom 10.16
53.2 Isa 11.1; 52.14
53.3 Ps 22.6; ver 10; Jn 1.10,11
53.4 Mt 8.17; Heb 9.28; 1 Pet 2.24
53.5 Rom 4.25; 1 Cor 15.3; 1 Pet 2.24
53.6 ver 11
53.7 Mt 26.63; Acts 8.32
53.8 ver 5,12
53.9 Mt 27.57; 1 Pet 2.22
53.10 ver 3-6; Isa 54.3; 46.10

53.11 Jn 10.14-18; Rom 5.18,19; ver 5,6
53.12 Isa 52.13; Mt 26.38,39,42; Lk 22.37; 2 Cor 5.21
54.1 Gal 4.27; 1 Sam 2.5; Isa 62.4
54.2 Isa 49.19,20
54.3 Isa 43.5,6; 49.19,23
54.4 Isa 45.17; Jer 31.19; Isa 4.1; 25.8
54.5 Jer 3.14; Isa 43.14; 48.17; 6.3
54.6 Isa 62.4
54.7 Isa 26.20; 43.5
54.8 Isa 60.10; ver 10; Isa 49.10,13; ver 5
54.9 Gen 9.11; Isa 12.1
54.10 Isa 51.6; Ps 89.33,34; ver 8
54.11 1 Chr 29.2; Rev 21.18
54.13 Jer 31.34; Jn 6.45; Ps 119.165
54.14 Isa 62.1; 9.4; 14.4; ver 4
54.15 Isa 41.11-16
54.17 Isa 29.8; 50.8,9; 45.24

11 Out of his anguish he shall see light;[z]
he shall find satisfaction through his knowledge.
The righteous one,[a] my servant, shall make many righteous,
and he shall bear their iniquities.
12 Therefore I will allot him a portion with the great,
and he shall divide the spoil with the strong;
because he poured out himself to death,
and was numbered with the transgressors;
yet he bore the sin of many,
and made intercession for the transgressors.

The Eternal Covenant of Peace

54 Sing, O barren one who did not bear;
burst into song and shout,
you who have not been in labor!
For the children of the desolate woman will be more
than the children of her that is married, says the LORD.
2 Enlarge the site of your tent,
and let the curtains of your habitations be stretched out;
do not hold back; lengthen your cords
and strengthen your stakes.
3 For you will spread out to the right and to the left,
and your descendants will possess the nations
and will settle the desolate towns.

4 Do not fear, for you will not be ashamed;
do not be discouraged, for you will not suffer disgrace;
for you will forget the shame of your youth,
and the disgrace of your widowhood you will remember no more.
5 For your Maker is your husband,
the LORD of hosts is his name;
the Holy One of Israel is your Redeemer,
the God of the whole earth he is called.
6 For the LORD has called you
like a wife forsaken and grieved in spirit,
like the wife of a man's youth when she is cast off,
says your God.
7 For a brief moment I abandoned you,
but with great compassion I will gather you.
8 In overflowing wrath for a moment
I hid my face from you,
but with everlasting love I will have compassion on you,
says the LORD, your Redeemer.

9 This is like the days of Noah to me:
Just as I swore that the waters of Noah
would never again go over the earth,
so I have sworn that I will not be angry with you
and will not rebuke you.
10 For the mountains may depart
and the hills be removed,
but my steadfast love shall not depart from you,
and my covenant of peace shall not be removed,
says the LORD, who has compassion on you.

11 O afflicted one, storm-tossed, and not comforted,
I am about to set your stones in antimony,
and lay your foundations with sapphires.[b]
12 I will make your pinnacles of rubies,
your gates of jewels,
and all your wall of precious stones.
13 All your children shall be taught by the LORD,
and great shall be the prosperity of your children.
14 In righteousness you shall be established;
you shall be far from oppression, for you shall not fear;
and from terror, for it shall not come near you.
15 If anyone stirs up strife,
it is not from me;
whoever stirs up strife with you
shall fall because of you.
16 See it is I who have created the smith
who blows the fire of coals,
and produces a weapon fit for its purpose;
I have also created the ravager to destroy.
17 No weapon that is fashioned against you shall prosper,

54.1-17 The Eternal Covenant of Peace.
54.1-10 In her restricted situation of exile, Israel is compared with a childless woman, but she is about to become the mother of many in the dawning era of unprecedented growth of God's people. As in the reconciliation of an estranged wife, the LORD will *have compassion* on his people and pour out on them his *everlasting love.*
54.11-17 Changing the imagery, the prophet compares renewed Israel first with a splendid, bejewelled building and then with a victorious people, whose enemies will be utterly defeated.

[z] Q Mss: MT lacks *light* [a] Or *and he shall find satisfaction. Through his knowledge, the righteous one* [b] Or *lapis lazuli*

55.1-13 The Invitation to Share in the Life of God's People.
55.1-5 Human economic status is of no significance as a condition for responding to God's invitation to share in *the everlasting covenant*, nor is ethnic origin, since *nations* unknown to Israel are going to come seeking *the LORD your God*.
55.6-9 God's invitation to take part in the life of this new community is open to all, including the wicked, who will find *pardon*. This divine plan does not match with human schemes or value systems, but far transcends them.
55.10-11 The results are certain, since God always accomplishes his *purpose*.
55.12-13 The renewal of God's people will be matched by the renewal of the creation itself.
Isa 56.1-8. Israel as an Inclusive Community.
56.1-2. God's people must obey the law, including keeping the sabbath, if God's *deliverance* of his people from the hostile powers is to take place.
56.3-8 Non-Israelites and those whose physical condition excludes them from full participation in the community (Deut 23.2), as well as Israelites who have been expelled, if they now observe the sabbath and do what pleases God, will share in the life and worship of the covenant people.

and you shall confute every tongue
that rises against you in judgment.
This is the heritage of the servants of the LORD
and their vindication from me, says the LORD.

An Invitation to Abundant Life

55 Ho, everyone who thirsts,
come to the waters;
and you that have no money,
come, buy and eat!
Come, buy wine and milk
without money and without price.
2 Why do you spend your money for that which is not bread,
and your labor for that which does not satisfy?
Listen carefully to me, and eat what is good,
and delight yourselves in rich food.
3 Incline your ear, and come to me;
listen, so that you may live.
I will make with you an everlasting covenant,
my steadfast, sure love for David.
4 See, I made him a witness to the peoples,
a leader and commander for the peoples.
5 See, you shall call nations that you do not know,
and nations that do not know you shall run to you,
because of the LORD your God, the Holy One of Israel,
for he has glorified you.

6 Seek the LORD while he may be found,
call upon him while he is near;
7 let the wicked forsake their way,
and the unrighteous their thoughts;
let them return to the LORD, that he may have mercy on them,
and to our God, for he will abundantly pardon.
8 For my thoughts are not your thoughts,
nor are your ways my ways, says the LORD.
9 For as the heavens are higher than the earth,
so are my ways higher than your ways
and my thoughts than your thoughts.
10 For as the rain and the snow come down from heaven,
and do not return there until they have watered the earth,
making it bring forth and sprout,
giving seed to the sower and bread to the eater,
11 so shall my word be that goes out from my mouth;
it shall not return to me empty,
but it shall accomplish that which I purpose,
and succeed in the thing for which I sent it.

12 For you shall go out in joy,
and be led back in peace;
the mountains and the hills before you
shall burst into song,
and all the trees of the field shall clap their hands.
13 Instead of the thorn shall come up the cypress;
instead of the brier shall come up the myrtle;
and it shall be to the LORD for a memorial,
for an everlasting sign that shall not be cut off.

The Covenant Extended to All Who Obey

56 Thus says the LORD:
Maintain justice, and do what is right,
for soon my salvation will come,
and my deliverance be revealed.

2 Happy is the mortal who does this,
the one who holds it fast,
who keeps the sabbath, not profaning it,
and refrains from doing any evil.

3 Do not let the foreigner joined to the LORD say,
"The LORD will surely separate me from his people";
and do not let the eunuch say,
"I am just a dry tree."
4 For thus says the LORD:
To the eunuchs who keep my sabbaths,
who choose the things that please me
and hold fast my covenant,
5 I will give, in my house and within my walls,
a monument and a name

55.1 Isa 41.17; Jn 4.14; 7.37; Mt 13.44; Rev 3.18
55.2 Hos 8.7; Isa 62.8,9; 25.6
55.3 Isa 51.4; Rom 10.5; Isa 61.8; Acts 13.34
55.4 Jer 30.9; Ezek 34.23,24; Dan 9.25
55.5 Isa 49.6,12,23; Zech 8.22; Isa 60.9
55.6 Ps 32.6; Isa 49.8; 2 Cor 6.1,2
55.7 Isa 1.16; 59.7; 31.6; 54.8,10; 44.22
55.9 Ps 103.11
55.10 Isa 30.23; 2 Cor 9.10
55.11 Isa 45.23; 59.21; 46.10
55.12 Isa 51.11; 54.10,13; 44.23; 1 Chr 16.33
55.13 Isa 41.19; 32.13; 63.12,14; 19.20
56.1 Isa 61.8; 46.13
56.2 Isa 58.13
56.3 ver 6; Acts 8.27
56.4 ver 2,6
56.5 ver 7; Isa 66.20; 26.1; 62.2; 48.19

56.6 Isa 60.10; 61.5; ver 2,4
56.7 Isa 11.9; 65.25; Rom 12.1; Heb 13.15; Mt 21.13; Mk 11.17; Lk 19.46
56.8 Isa 11.12; 60.3-11; Jn 10.16
56.9 Jer 12.9
56.10 Isa 29.9-14; Nah 3.18
57.1 Ps 12.1; Isa 42.25; 47.7,11
57.2 Isa 26.7
57.3 Mt 16.4; Isa 1.21
57.4 Isa 48.8
57.5 2 Kings 16.4; Lev 18.21; 2 Kings 16.3; Jer 7.31
57.6 Jer 3.9; 7.18; 5.9,29
57.7 Ezek 16.16; 23.14
57.8 Ezek 23.7,18; 16.26,28
57.9 Ezek 23.16,40
57.10 Isa 47.13; Jer 2.25
57.11 Isa 51.12; Jer 2.32; ver 1; Ps 50.21

better than sons and daughters;
I will give them an everlasting name
that shall not be cut off.

6 And the foreigners who join themselves
to the LORD,
to minister to him, to love the name
of the LORD,
and to be his servants,
all who keep the sabbath, and do not
profane it,
and hold fast my covenant—
7 these I will bring to my holy mountain,
and make them joyful in my house of
prayer;
their burnt offerings and their sacrifices
will be accepted on my altar;
for my house shall be called a house of
prayer
for all peoples.
8 Thus says the Lord GOD,
who gathers the outcasts of Israel,
I will gather others to them
besides those already gathered.[c]

The Corruption of Israel's Rulers

9 All you wild animals,
all you wild animals in the forest,
come to devour!
10 Israel's[d] sentinels are blind,
they are all without knowledge;
they are all silent dogs
that cannot bark;
dreaming, lying down,
loving to slumber.
11 The dogs have a mighty appetite;
they never have enough.
The shepherds also have no
understanding;
they have all turned to their own
way,
to their own gain, one and all.
12 "Come," they say, "let us[e] get wine;
let us fill ourselves with strong drink.
And tomorrow will be like today,
great beyond measure."

Israel's Futile Idolatry

57 The righteous perish,
and no one takes it to heart;
the devout are taken away,
while no one understands.
For the righteous are taken away from
calamity,
2 and they enter into peace;
those who walk uprightly
will rest on their couches.
3 But as for you, come here,
you children of a sorceress,
you offspring of an adulterer and a
whore.[f]
4 Whom are you mocking?
Against whom do you open your
mouth wide
and stick out your tongue?
Are you not children of transgression,
the offspring of deceit—
5 you that burn with lust among the
oaks,
under every green tree;
you that slaughter your children in the
valleys,
under the clefts of the rocks?
6 Among the smooth stones of the valley
is your portion;
they, they, are your lot;
to them you have poured out a drink
offering,
you have brought a grain offering.
Shall I be appeased for these things?
7 Upon a high and lofty mountain
you have set your bed,
and there you went up to offer
sacrifice.
8 Behind the door and the doorpost
you have set up your symbol;
for, in deserting me,[g] you have
uncovered your bed,
you have gone up to it,
you have made it wide;
and you have made a bargain for
yourself with them,
you have loved their bed,
you have gazed on their nakedness.[h]
9 You journeyed to Molech[i] with oil,
and multiplied your perfumes;
you sent your envoys far away,
and sent down even to Sheol.
10 You grew weary from your many
wanderings,
but you did not say, "It is useless."
You found your desire rekindled,
and so you did not weaken.

11 Whom did you dread and fear
so that you lied,

56.9-12. The predatory wild animals are summoned to devour the disobedient Israelites, who are preoccupied with their self-indulgent way of life.
57.1-13 Israel's Futile Idolatry.
57.1-2 The death of *the devout* goes unnoticed, even though they will surely enter safely the place of rest.
57.5-13 Those whose origins and way of life are corrupted by devotion to the false gods and who are characterized by *lust* and sacrificing their own *children* are warned that their trust in idols is utterly futile. Only those who rely solely on God will share in the renewed land and temple.

[c] Heb *besides his gathered ones* [d] Heb *His* [e] Q Ms Syr Vg Tg: MT *me* [f] Heb *an adulterer and she plays the whore* [g] Meaning of Heb uncertain [h] Or *their phallus*; Heb *the hand* [i] Or *the king*

57.14-21 A Promise of Help and Healing.
As God enabled the tribes of Israel in the days of Moses and Joshua to overcome every obstacle and to reach the land where the sanctuary of Yahweh was established (Ex 15; Josh 24; Ps 68), so he will now forgive and renew his people. They will live in peace, but the wicked will have only turmoil.
58.1-14 False and True Worship.
58.1-9 The Power of God's Presence among his People.
Although the misguided Israelites claim to be seeking God and his *ways* for them, their selfish lives and false show of humility are in sharp contrast with God's call to them to free the oppressed, to care for the *hungry* and the *homeless* and the *naked*. When they do these acts of mercy, a new day will *dawn* for them: God will set things right, protect and help them by his glorious presence.

and did not remember me
or give me a thought?
Have I not kept silent and closed my eyes,[j]
and so you do not fear me?
12 I will concede your righteousness and your works,
but they will not help you.
13 When you cry out, let your collection of idols deliver you!
The wind will carry them off,
a breath will take them away.
But whoever takes refuge in me shall possess the land
and inherit my holy mountain.

A Promise of Help and Healing
14 It shall be said,
"Build up, build up, prepare the way,
remove every obstruction from my people's way."
15 For thus says the high and lofty one
who inhabits eternity, whose name is Holy:
I dwell in the high and holy place,
and also with those who are contrite and humble in spirit,
to revive the spirit of the humble,
and to revive the heart of the contrite.
16 For I will not continually accuse,
nor will I always be angry;
for then the spirits would grow faint before me,
even the souls that I have made.
17 Because of their wicked covetousness I was angry;
I struck them, I hid and was angry;
but they kept turning back to their own ways.
18 I have seen their ways, but I will heal them;
I will lead them and repay them with comfort,
creating for their mourners the fruit of the lips.[k]
19 Peace, peace, to the far and the near,
says the LORD;
and I will heal them.
20 But the wicked are like the tossing sea
that cannot keep still;
its waters toss up mire and mud.
21 There is no peace, says my God, for the wicked.

False and True Worship
58 Shout out, do not hold back!
Lift up your voice like a trumpet!
Announce to my people their rebellion,
to the house of Jacob their sins.
2 Yet day after day they seek me
and delight to know my ways,
as if they were a nation that practiced righteousness
and did not forsake the ordinance of their God;
they ask of me righteous judgments,
they delight to draw near to God.
3 "Why do we fast, but you do not see?
Why humble ourselves, but you do not notice?"
Look, you serve your own interest on your fast day,
and oppress all your workers.
4 Look, you fast only to quarrel and to fight
and to strike with a wicked fist.
Such fasting as you do today
will not make your voice heard on high.
5 Is such the fast that I choose,
a day to humble oneself?
Is it to bow down the head like a bulrush,
and to lie in sackcloth and ashes?
Will you call this a fast,
a day acceptable to the LORD?

6 Is not this the fast that I choose:
to loose the bonds of injustice,
to undo the thongs of the yoke,
to let the oppressed go free,
and to break every yoke?
7 Is it not to share your bread with the hungry,
and bring the homeless poor into your house;
when you see the naked, to cover them,
and not to hide yourself from your own kin?
8 Then your light shall break forth like the dawn,
and your healing shall spring up quickly;
your vindicator[l] shall go before you,
the glory of the LORD shall be your rear guard.
9 Then you shall call, and the LORD will answer;

57.13 Jer 22.20; Isa 25.4; 60.21; 65.9
57.14 Isa 62.10; Jer 18.15
57.15 Isa 52.13; 40.28; 66.1; Ps 34.18; 51.17; 14.2,3; Isa 61.1
57.16 Gen 6.3; Ps 85.5; 103.9; Mic 7.18; Job 34.14; Isa 42.5
57.17 Jer 6.13; Isa 1.4
57.18 Isa 53.5; 52.12; 61.1-3
57.19 Heb 13.15; Acts 2.39; Eph 2.17
57.20 Job 18.5-14
57.21 Isa 48.22
58.1 Isa 48.8; 50.1; 59.12
58.2 Isa 1.11; 48.1; 59.13; 29.13
58.3 Mal 3.14; Isa 22.12,13
58.4 1 Kings 21.9,12,13; Isa 59.2
58.5 Zech 7.5; Esth 4.3; Job 2.8
58.6 Neh 5.10-12; Jer 34.9
58.7 Ezek 18.7,16; Mt 25.35; Job 31.19; Gen 29.14; Neh 5.5
58.8 ver 10; Isa 30.26; 62.1; Ex 14.19; Isa 52.12
58.9 Isa 55.6; ver 6; Ps 12.2

[j] Gk Vg: Heb *silent even for a long time* [k] Meaning of Heb uncertain [l] Or *vindication*

you shall cry for help, and he will
say, Here I am.

If you remove the yoke from among you,
the pointing of the finger, the
speaking of evil,
10 if you offer your food to the hungry
and satisfy the needs of the afflicted,
then your light shall rise in the darkness
and your gloom be like the noonday.
11 The LORD will guide you continually,
and satisfy your needs in parched
places,
and make your bones strong;
and you shall be like a watered garden,
like a spring of water,
whose waters never fail.
12 Your ancient ruins shall be rebuilt;
you shall raise up the foundations of
many generations;
you shall be called the repairer of the
breach,
the restorer of streets to live in.

13 If you refrain from trampling the
sabbath,
from pursuing your own interests on
my holy day;
if you call the sabbath a delight
and the holy day of the LORD
honorable;
if you honor it, not going your own
ways,
serving your own interests, or
pursuing your own affairs;[m]
14 then you shall take delight in the LORD,
and I will make you ride upon the
heights of the earth;
I will feed you with the heritage of your
ancestor Jacob,
for the mouth of the LORD has spoken.

Injustice and Oppression to Be Punished

59 See, the LORD's hand is not too
short to save,
nor his ear too dull to hear.
2 Rather, your iniquities have been
barriers
between you and your God,
and your sins have hidden his face from
you
so that he does not hear.
3 For your hands are defiled with blood,
and your fingers with iniquity;
your lips have spoken lies,
your tongue mutters wickedness.
4 No one brings suit justly,
no one goes to law honestly;
they rely on empty pleas, they speak lies,
conceiving mischief and begetting
iniquity.
5 They hatch adders' eggs,
and weave the spider's web;
whoever eats their eggs dies,
and the crushed egg hatches out a
viper.
6 Their webs cannot serve as clothing;
they cannot cover themselves with
what they make.
Their works are works of iniquity,
and deeds of violence are in their
hands.
7 Their feet run to evil,
and they rush to shed innocent blood;
their thoughts are thoughts of iniquity,
desolation and destruction are in their
highways.
8 The way of peace they do not know,
and there is no justice in their paths.
Their roads they have made crooked;
no one who walks in them knows
peace.

9 Therefore justice is far from us,
and righteousness does not reach us;
we wait for light, and lo! there is
darkness;
and for brightness, but we walk in
gloom.
10 We grope like the blind along a wall,
groping like those who have no eyes;
we stumble at noon as in the twilight,
among the vigorous[n] as though we
were dead.
11 We all growl like bears;
like doves we moan mournfully.
We wait for justice, but there is none;
for salvation, but it is far from us.
12 For our transgressions before you are
many,
and our sins testify against us.
Our transgressions indeed are with us,
and we know our iniquities:
13 transgressing, and denying the LORD,
and turning away from following our
God,
talking oppression and revolt,
conceiving lying words and uttering
them from the heart.
14 Justice is turned back,
and righteousness stands at a distance;

[m] Heb *or speaking words* [n] Meaning of Heb uncertain

58.10-14 They need to abandon false and futile modes of worship. Instead of accusing others (*pointing the finger*) and making a public display of sabbath piety, they are to assist others in need, and bring *light* to those in darkness. God will restore and refresh them and rebuild their city, and thus they will be honored throughout *the earth* and God's promise to *Jacob* will be fulfilled.
59.1-15a Injustice and Oppression to be Punished.
59.1-8 Israel's predicament is the result, not of God's inability to act, but of the nation's sins: lies, dishonesty, evil plots (*adders' eggs*) and efforts to hide what they are doing (*webs*). Their way of life is devoid of justice and *peace*.
59.9-15a They wander in the dark, overwhelmed by their own misdeeds, devoid of justice or *truth*.

58.10 ver 7; Ps 37.6
58.11 Isa 49.10; 41.17; 66.14; Jn 4.14; 7.38
58.12 Isa 49.8; 44.28; 30.13; Am 9.11
58.13 Isa 56.2; Ps 84.2,10; Isa 55.8; 59.13
58.14 Isa 61.10; Deut 32.13; Isa 1.19,20
59.1 Num 11.23; Isa 50.2; 58.9
59.2 Isa 1.15; 58.4
59.3 Isa 1.15; Jer 2.30; ver 13; Isa 28.15
59.4 ver 14,15; Isa 30.12; Job 15.35; Ps 7.14
59.5 Isa 14.29; Job 8.14
59.6 Isa 28.20; 57.12; 58.4
59.7 Rom 3.15-17; Isa 65.2
59.8 ver 9,11; Ps 125.5; ver 14
59.9 ver 14; Isa 5.30; 8.21,22
59.10 Deut 28.29; Job 5.14; Am 8.9; Isa 8.4,15
59.11 Isa 38.14; Ezek 7.16; ver 9,14
59.12 Isa 58.1; Jer 14.7
59.13 Josh 24.27; Titus 1.16; Isa 30.12; ver 3,4
59.14 Isa 1.21; 46.21; 48.1

59.15b-21 God's Action to Renew his People.
Into Israel's hopeless condition God has come like a powerful, wholly effective military leader. His reputation to achieve his purpose is respected fully by his *enemies* and by Israel's hostile neighbors. His renewed people will fully obey his *words*, generation after generation.
60.1-22 The Ingathering of the Dispersed of Israel.
60.1-7 The radiant glory of God's presence among his people will attract rulers (*kings*) and *nations*. His scattered people will be restored from distant lands. Valuable gifts will be brought to the temple, including *gold and frankincense* (Mt 2.11) and animals for offerings.
60.8-18 All means of travel will be used to bring God's people back, and leaders of other nations will help to restore Jerusalem, which will be open to receive gifts and to welcome even those who formerly oppressed Israel. Food will be abundant, and the dominant forces in the *City of the* LORD will be *peace* and *justice*.

for truth stumbles in the public square,
and uprightness cannot enter.
15 Truth is lacking,
and whoever turns from evil is despoiled.

The LORD saw it, and it displeased him
that there was no justice.
16 He saw that there was no one,
and was appalled that there was no one to intervene;
so his own arm brought him victory,
and his righteousness upheld him.
17 He put on righteousness like a breastplate,
and a helmet of salvation on his head;
he put on garments of vengeance for clothing,
and wrapped himself in fury as in a mantle.
18 According to their deeds, so will he repay;
wrath to his adversaries, requital to his enemies;
to the coastlands he will render requital.
19 So those in the west shall fear the name of the LORD,
and those in the east, his glory;
for he will come like a pent-up stream
that the wind of the LORD drives on.

20 And he will come to Zion as Redeemer,
to those in Jacob who turn from transgression, says the LORD.
21 And as for me, this is my covenant with
them, says the LORD: my spirit that is upon
you, and my words that I have put in your
mouth, shall not depart out of your mouth,
or out of the mouths of your children, or
out of the mouths of your children's children, says the LORD, from now on and
forever.

The Ingathering of the Dispersed

60 Arise, shine; for your light has come,
and the glory of the LORD has risen upon you.
2 For darkness shall cover the earth,
and thick darkness the peoples;
but the LORD will arise upon you,
and his glory will appear over you.
3 Nations shall come to your light,
and kings to the brightness of your dawn.

4 Lift up your eyes and look around;
they all gather together, they come to you;
your sons shall come from far away,
and your daughters shall be carried on their nurses' arms.
5 Then you shall see and be radiant;
your heart shall thrill and rejoice,[o]
because the abundance of the sea shall be brought to you,
the wealth of the nations shall come to you.
6 A multitude of camels shall cover you,
the young camels of Midian and Ephah;
all those from Sheba shall come.
They shall bring gold and frankincense,
and shall proclaim the praise of the LORD.
7 All the flocks of Kedar shall be gathered to you,
the rams of Nebaioth shall minister to you;
they shall be acceptable on my altar,
and I will glorify my glorious house.

8 Who are these that fly like a cloud,
and like doves to their windows?
9 For the coastlands shall wait for me,
the ships of Tarshish first,
to bring your children from far away,
their silver and gold with them,
for the name of the LORD your God,
and for the Holy One of Israel,
because he has glorified you.
10 Foreigners shall build up your walls,
and their kings shall minister to you;
for in my wrath I struck you down,
but in my favor I have had mercy on you.
11 Your gates shall always be open;
day and night they shall not be shut,
so that nations shall bring you their wealth,
with their kings led in procession.
12 For the nation and kingdom
that will not serve you shall perish;
those nations shall be utterly laid waste.
13 The glory of Lebanon shall come to you,
the cypress, the plane, and the pine,
to beautify the place of my sanctuary;
and I will glorify where my feet rest.
14 The descendants of those who oppressed you
shall come bending low to you,

59.15 Isa 5.23; 1.21-23
59.16 Isa 63.5; Ezek 22.30; Ps 98.1
59.17 Eph 6.14; 1 Thess 5.8; Isa 63.2,3
59.18 Isa 65.6,7; 66.6
59.19 Ps 113.3; Isa 66.12
59.20 Rom 11.26,27; Ezek 18.30,31; Acts 2.38,39
59.21 Jer 31.31-34; Isa 44.3,26; 54.10; Jer 32.40
60.1 Eph 5.14; Mal 4.2
60.2 Col 1.13; Isa 4.5
60.3 Isa 49.6,23; ver 11
60.4 Isa 49.18,20-22
60.5 Ps 34.5; Isa 23.18; 24.14; 61.6
60.6 Gen 25.4; Ps 72.10; Isa 43.23; 42.10
60.7 Gen 25.13; Isa 56.7; Hag 2.7,9
60.9 Isa 66.19; 2.16; 49.22; 55.5
60.10 Zech 6.15; Isa 49.23; 54.8
60.11 ver 18.5; Ps 149.8
60.12 Zech 14.17
60.13 Isa 35.2; 41.19; 1 Chr 28.2; Ps 132.7
60.14 Isa 49.23; Heb 12.22; Rev 3.9

[o] Heb *be enlarged*

and all who despised you
shall bow down at your feet;
they shall call you the City of the LORD,
the Zion of the Holy One of Israel.
15 Whereas you have been forsaken and
hated,
with no one passing through,
I will make you majestic forever,
a joy from age to age.
16 You shall suck the milk of nations,
you shall suck the breasts of kings;
and you shall know that I, the LORD, am
your Savior
and your Redeemer, the Mighty One
of Jacob.

17 Instead of bronze I will bring gold,
instead of iron I will bring silver;
instead of wood, bronze,
instead of stones, iron.
I will appoint Peace as your overseer
and Righteousness as your
taskmaster.
18 Violence shall no more be heard in your
land,
devastation or destruction within
your borders;
you shall call your walls Salvation,
and your gates Praise.

God the Glory of Zion

19 The sun shall no longer be
your light by day,
nor for brightness shall the moon
give light to you by night;[p]
but the LORD will be your everlasting
light,
and your God will be your glory.
20 Your sun shall no more go down,
or your moon withdraw itself;
for the LORD will be your everlasting
light,
and your days of mourning shall be
ended.
21 Your people shall all be righteous;
they shall possess the land forever.
They are the shoot that I planted, the
work of my hands,
so that I might be glorified.
22 The least of them shall become a clan,
and the smallest one a mighty nation;
I am the LORD;
in its time I will accomplish it quickly.

The Good News of Deliverance

61 The spirit of the Lord GOD is upon
me,
because the LORD has anointed me;
he has sent me to bring good news to
the oppressed,
to bind up the brokenhearted,
to proclaim liberty to the captives,
and release to the prisoners;
2 to proclaim the year of the LORD's favor,
and the day of vengeance of our God;
to comfort all who mourn;
3 to provide for those who mourn in
Zion—
to give them a garland instead of
ashes,
the oil of gladness instead of mourning,
the mantle of praise instead of a faint
spirit.
They will be called oaks of
righteousness,
the planting of the LORD, to display his
glory.
4 They shall build up the ancient ruins,
they shall raise up the former
devastations;
they shall repair the ruined cities,
the devastations of many generations.

5 Strangers shall stand and feed your
flocks,
foreigners shall till your land and
dress your vines;
6 but you shall be called priests of the LORD,
you shall be named ministers of our
God;
you shall enjoy the wealth of the
nations,
and in their riches you shall glory.
7 Because their[q] shame was double,
and dishonor was proclaimed as their
lot,
therefore they shall possess a double
portion;
everlasting joy shall be theirs.

8 For I the LORD love justice,
I hate robbery and wrongdoing;[r]
I will faithfully give them their
recompense,
and I will make an everlasting
covenant with them.
9 Their descendants shall be known
among the nations,

60.19-22 The promise is repeated of the divine illumination through the LORD's presence, together with a description of the people's renewal and vast increase in number.
61.1-11 The Good News of Deliverance.
61.1-7 As promised to the future king descended from David (Isa 11.1-2), the ruler of God's people will receive power to acocmplish God's purpose in the world. Those who benefit most will be those now deprived and oppressed. He will also punish the wicked, while pouring out benefits on his people, their city and their land. The renewed people will serve as intermediaries (*priests*) between God and the former outsiders (*strangers, foreigners*), who will be doubly blessed by God.
61.8-11 God's faithfulness in fulfilling his covenant promises to Israel will be recognized and valued among other nations. His chosen agent of renewal rejoices in his work of setting right with God the world and its inhabitants.

60.15 Jer 30.17; Isa 66.5; 33.8,9; 65.18
60.16 Isa 49.23; 66.11; 63.8,16
60.18 Isa 54.14; 51.19; 26.1; ver 11
60.19 Rev 21.23; 22.5; Isa 9.2; Zech 2.5
60.20 Isa 30.26; 65.19
60.21 Isa 52.1; Ps 37.11,22; Isa 29.23; 45.11
60.22 Isa 51.2
61.1 Isa 11.2; Lk 4.18; Ps 45.7; Isa 57.15; 42.7
61.2 Isa 49.8; 34.8; 57.18; Mt 5.4
61.3 Isa 60.20; Ps 45.7; Isa 60.21
61.4 Isa 49.8; Ezek 36.33
61.5 Isa 60.10
61.6 Isa 66.21; 60.5,11
61.7 Isa 54.4; 40.2; Zech 9.12; Isa 60.15; Ps 16.11
61.8 Isa 30.18; 55.3
61.9 Isa 54.3; 44.3

[p] Q Ms Gk Old Latin Tg: MT lacks *by night* [q] Heb *your* [r] Or *robbery with a burnt offering*

62.1-12 The Vindication and Salvation of Zion.
The renewal of God's people will be a universal sign of God's power and love. Jerusalem is invited to send constant reminders to the LORD to accomplish what he has promised: to establish and maintain his faithful people. All the earth will acknowledge that this special (*holy*) people have been restored and renewed by God.
63.1-6 Vengeance on the Enemies.
The cruel figure coming from Edom (a region south and east of the Dead Sea) and crushing his opponents represents the fate of the historic and the future enemies of God's people.

and their offspring among the peoples;
all who see them shall acknowledge
that they are a people whom the LORD
has blessed.
10 I will greatly rejoice in the LORD,
my whole being shall exult in my
God;
for he has clothed me with the garments
of salvation,
he has covered me with the robe of
righteousness,
as a bridegroom decks himself with a
garland,
and as a bride adorns herself with her
jewels.
11 For as the earth brings forth its shoots,
and as a garden causes what is sown
in it to spring up,
so the Lord GOD will cause righteousness
and praise
to spring up before all the nations.

The Vindication and Salvation of Zion

62 For Zion's sake I will not keep
silent,
and for Jerusalem's sake I will not
rest,
until her vindication shines out like the
dawn,
and her salvation like a burning
torch.
2 The nations shall see your vindication,
and all the kings your glory;
and you shall be called by a new name
that the mouth of the LORD will give.
3 You shall be a crown of beauty in the
hand of the LORD,
and a royal diadem in the hand of
your God.
4 You shall no more be termed Forsaken,[s]
and your land shall no more be
termed Desolate;[t]
but you shall be called My Delight Is in
Her,[u]
and your land Married;[v]
for the LORD delights in you,
and your land shall be married.
5 For as a young man marries a young
woman,
so shall your builder[w] marry you,
and as the bridegroom rejoices over the
bride,
so shall your God rejoice over you.
6 Upon your walls, O Jerusalem,
I have posted sentinels;
all day and all night
they shall never be silent.
You who remind the LORD,
take no rest,
7 and give him no rest
until he establishes Jerusalem
and makes it renowned throughout
the earth.
8 The LORD has sworn by his right hand
and by his mighty arm:
I will not again give your grain
to be food for your enemies,
and foreigners shall not drink the wine
for which you have labored;
9 but those who garner it shall eat it
and praise the LORD,
and those who gather it shall drink it
in my holy courts.

10 Go through, go through the gates,
prepare the way for the people;
build up, build up the highway,
clear it of stones,
lift up an ensign over the peoples.
11 The LORD has proclaimed
to the end of the earth:
Say to daughter Zion,
"See, your salvation comes;
his reward is with him,
and his recompense before him."
12 They shall be called, "The Holy People,
The Redeemed of the LORD";
and you shall be called, "Sought Out,
A City Not Forsaken."

Vengeance on Edom

63 "Who is this that comes from
Edom,
from Bozrah in garments stained
crimson?
Who is this so splendidly robed,
marching in his great might?"

"It is I, announcing vindication,
mighty to save."

2 "Why are your robes red,
and your garments like theirs who
tread the wine press?"

3 "I have trodden the wine press alone,
and from the peoples no one was
with me;
I trod them in my anger
and trampled them in my wrath;

[s] Heb *Azubah* [t] Heb *Shemamah* [u] Heb *Hephzibah* [v] Heb *Beulah* [w] Cn: Heb *your sons*

61.10 Isa 12.1,2; 49.4,18; Rev 21.2
61.11 Isa 55.10; 45.23,24; Ps 72.3; 85.11; Isa 60.18
62.1 Isa 61.11; 52.10
62.2 Isa 60.3; ver 4,12; Isa 65.15
62.3 Zech 9.16
62.4 Hos 1.10; Isa 54.6,7; Jer 32.41; 3.14
62.5 Isa 65.19
62.6 Isa 52.8; Jer 6.17; Ezek 3.17; Ps 74.2
62.7 Mt 15.21-28; Lk 18.1-8; Jer 33.9
62.8 Isa 45.23; Deut 28.31,33; Jer 5.17
62.9 Isa 65.13,21-23
62.10 Isa 57.14; 49.11; 11.10,12
62.11 Isa 49.6; Zech 9.9; Mt 21.5; Isa 51.5; 40.10
62.12 Isa 4.3; 51.10; ver 4
63.1 Isa 34.5,6; Am 1.12; Zeph 3.17
63.2 Rev 19.13,15
63.3 Isa 22.5; 28.3; Mic 7.10; Rev 19.15

their juice spattered on my garments,
and stained all my robes.
4 For the day of vengeance was in my
heart,
and the year for my redeeming work
had come.
5 I looked, but there was no helper;
I stared, but there was no one to
sustain me;
so my own arm brought me victory,
and my wrath sustained me.
6 I trampled down peoples in my anger,
I crushed them in my wrath,
and I poured out their lifeblood on
the earth."

God's Mercy Remembered

7 I will recount the gracious deeds of the
LORD,
the praiseworthy acts of the LORD,
because of all that the LORD has done for us,
and the great favor to the house of
Israel
that he has shown them according to
his mercy,
according to the abundance of his
steadfast love.
8 For he said, "Surely they are my people,
children who will not deal falsely";
and he became their savior
9 in all their distress.
It was no messenger[x] or angel
but his presence that saved them;[y]
in his love and in his pity he redeemed
them;
he lifted them up and carried them all
the days of old.

10 But they rebelled
and grieved his holy spirit;
therefore he became their enemy;
he himself fought against them.
11 Then they[z] remembered the days of old,
of Moses his servant.[a]
Where is the one who brought them up
out of the sea
with the shepherds of his flock?
Where is the one who put within them
his holy spirit,
12 who caused his glorious arm
to march at the right hand of Moses,
who divided the waters before them
to make for himself an everlasting
name,
13 who led them through the depths?
Like a horse in the desert,
they did not stumble.
14 Like cattle that go down into the valley,
the spirit of the LORD gave them rest.
Thus you led your people,
to make for yourself a glorious name.

A Prayer of Penitence

15 Look down from heaven and see,
from your holy and glorious
habitation.
Where are your zeal and your might?
The yearning of your heart and your
compassion?
They are withheld from me.
16 For you are our father,
though Abraham does not know us
and Israel does not acknowledge us;
you, O LORD, are our father;
our Redeemer from of old is your
name.
17 Why, O LORD, do you make us stray
from your ways
and harden our heart, so that we do
not fear you?
Turn back for the sake of your servants,
for the sake of the tribes that are your
heritage.
18 Your holy people took possession for a
little while;
but now our adversaries have
trampled down your sanctuary.
19 We have long been like those whom
you do not rule,
like those not called by your name.

64 O that you would tear open the
heavens and come down,
so that the mountains would quake
at your presence—
2[b] as when fire kindles brushwood
and the fire causes water to boil—
to make your name known to your
adversaries,
so that the nations might tremble at
your presence!
3 When you did awesome deeds that we
did not expect,
you came down, the mountains
quaked at your presence.
4 From ages past no one has heard,
no ear has perceived,
no eye has seen any God besides you,

63.7-14 God's Mercy Remembered.
Depicted here are are both the *gracious* and enduring love of God for his people, in spite of their failures, and the punishment that he has brought on them in his role as their *enemy*. The same power that chastened them has now freed them and brought them into the land of rest and peace.
63.15-64.12 A Prayer of Penitence.
63.15-19 The prayer begins with rebuking and questioning God's seeming indifference and neglect of his people's needs. He has caused them to wander from his ways and has allowed Israel's *adversaries* to take over the land and the *sanctuary*.
64.1-4 The prophet pleads with God to show his power over creation and the nations of the world, since there is no God like him who can do these mighty acts.

63.4 Isa 34.8; 61.2
63.5 Isa 59.16; Ps 98.1; Isa 52.10
63.6 Isa 65.12; 51.17,21,22; 34.3
63.7 Isa 54.8,10; 1 Kings 8.66; Ps 51.1
63.9 Judg 10.16; Ex 23.20-23; Deut 7.7,8; Ex 19.4; Deut 1.31
63.10 Ps 78.40; Acts 7.51; Eph 4.30; Ps 106.40
63.11 Ps 106.44,45; Ex 14.30; Isa 51.9,10; Num 11.17
63.12 Ex 15.6; 14.21; Isa 50.10,11
63.13 Ps 106.9
63.14 Deut 32.12
63.15 Deut 26.15; Ps 80.14; Jer 31.20; Hos 11.8
63.16 Isa 64.8; 51.2; 44.6; 60.16
63.17 Ezek 14.7-9; Isa 29.13,14; Num 10.36
63.18 Deut 7.6; Ps 74.3-7
63.19 Lam 3.43-45
64.1 Ps 144.5; Judg 5.5
64.2 Jer 5.22
64.3 Ps 65.5; 66.3,5; 106.22
64.4 1 Cor 2.9; Isa 40.31

[x] Gk: Heb *anguish* [y] Or *savior.* 9 *In all their distress he was distressed; the angel of his presence saved them;* [z] Heb *he* [a] Cn: Heb *his people* [b] Ch 64.1 in Heb

64.5-12 God's anger and seeming withdrawal are understandable and appropriate, because his people have neglected and disobeyed him. He shapes human affairs, as is evident in his punishing them by causing the destruction of their cities, the desolation of the land, and the ruin of the temple.
65.1-16 God's Address to the Faithful and Unfaithful in Israel. God's offering of himself to his people has been met by their disobedience and continuing participaiton in fertility rites (*in gardens*) and the cult of the dead (in *tombs*). They are to receive punishment for their defiance of God and their idolatrous practices. Yet God will preserve a faithful line (*my servants*) from Jacob and Judah, in contrast to the destruction (*curse*) that will fall on the disobedient. All this will prove his *faithfulness* to both his promises and his warnings.

who works for those who wait for
him.
5 You meet those who gladly do right,
those who remember you in your
ways.
But you were angry, and we sinned;
because you hid yourself we
transgressed.[c]
6 We have all become like one who is
unclean,
and all our righteous deeds are like a
filthy cloth.
We all fade like a leaf,
and our iniquities, like the wind, take
us away.
7 There is no one who calls on your
name,
or attempts to take hold of you;
for you have hidden your face from us,
and have delivered[d] us into the hand
of our iniquity.
8 Yet, O LORD, you are our Father;
we are the clay, and you are our
potter;
we are all the work of your hand.
9 Do not be exceedingly angry, O LORD,
and do not remember iniquity forever.
Now consider, we are all your people.
10 Your holy cities have become a
wilderness,
Zion has become a wilderness,
Jerusalem a desolation.
11 Our holy and beautiful house,
where our ancestors praised you,
has been burned by fire,
and all our pleasant places have
become ruins.
12 After all this, will you restrain yourself,
O LORD?
Will you keep silent, and punish us so
severely?

The Righteousness of God's Judgment

65 I was ready to be sought out by
those who did not ask,
to be found by those who did not seek
me.
I said, "Here I am, here I am,"
to a nation that did not call on my
name.
2 I held out my hands all day long
to a rebellious people,
who walk in a way that is not good,
following their own devices;
3 a people who provoke me
to my face continually,
sacrificing in gardens
and offering incense on bricks;
4 who sit inside tombs,
and spend the night in secret places;
who eat swine's flesh,
with broth of abominable things in
their vessels;
5 who say, "Keep to yourself,
do not come near me, for I am too
holy for you."
These are a smoke in my nostrils,
a fire that burns all day long.
6 See, it is written before me:
I will not keep silent, but I will repay;
I will indeed repay into their laps
7 their[e] iniquities and their[e] ancestors'
iniquities together,
says the LORD;
because they offered incense on the
mountains
and reviled me on the hills,
I will measure into their laps
full payment for their actions.
8 Thus says the LORD:
As the wine is found in the cluster,
and they say, "Do not destroy it,
for there is a blessing in it,"
so I will do for my servants' sake,
and not destroy them all.
9 I will bring forth descendants[f] from
Jacob,
and from Judah inheritors[g] of my
mountains;
my chosen shall inherit it,
and my servants shall settle there.
10 Sharon shall become a pasture for
flocks,
and the Valley of Achor a place for
herds to lie down,
for my people who have sought me.
11 But you who forsake the LORD,
who forget my holy mountain,
who set a table for Fortune
and fill cups of mixed wine for
Destiny;
12 I will destine you to the sword,
and all of you shall bow down to the
slaughter;
because, when I called, you did not
answer,
when I spoke, you did not listen,
but you did what was evil in my sight,
and chose what I did not delight in.

[c] Meaning of Heb uncertain [d] Gk Syr Old Latin Tg: Heb *melted* [e] Gk Syr: Heb *your* [f] Or *a descendant* [g] Or *an inheritor*

64.5 Ex 20.24; Isa 56.1; 63.7,10
64.6 Isa 6.5; 46.12; Ps 90.5,6; Isa 50.1
64.7 Isa 59.4; 27.5; 54.8; 9.18
64.8 Isa 63.16; 29.16; 60.21
64.9 Isa 60.10; 43.25; 63.8
64.10 Isa 6.11
64.11 Isa 63.18; Ps 74.5-7; Isa 7.23
64.12 Isa 42.14; Ps 83.1
65.1 Rom 10.20; Hos 1.10
65.2 Rom 10.21; Isa 30.1,9; 59.7
65.3 Isa 3.8; 66.3,17
65.4 Lev 11.7; Isa 66.3,17
65.5 Mt 9.11; Lk 18.9-12
65.6 Ps 50.3; 79.12; Jer 16.18
65.7 Isa 30.13,14; 57.7; Ezek 20.27,28; Jer 5.29
65.9 Isa 45.19,25; 49.8; 57.13; 32.18
65.10 Isa 33.9; Josh 7.24; Hos 2.15
65.11 Deut 29.24,25; Isa 56.7
65.12 Isa 34.5,6; 63.6; 2 Chr 36.15,16; Prov 1.24; Jer 7.13

13 Therefore thus says the Lord GOD:
My servants shall eat,
but you shall be hungry;
my servants shall drink,
but you shall be thirsty;
my servants shall rejoice,
but you shall be put to shame;
14 my servants shall sing for gladness of heart,
but you shall cry out for pain of heart,
and shall wail for anguish of spirit.
15 You shall leave your name to my chosen to use as a curse,
and the Lord GOD will put you to death;
but to his servants he will give a different name.
16 Then whoever invokes a blessing in the land
shall bless by the God of faithfulness,
and whoever takes an oath in the land
shall swear by the God of faithfulness;
because the former troubles are forgotten
and are hidden from my sight.

The Glorious New Creation

17 For I am about to create new heavens
and a new earth;
the former things shall not be remembered
or come to mind.
18 But be glad and rejoice forever
in what I am creating;
for I am about to create Jerusalem as a joy,
and its people as a delight.
19 I will rejoice in Jerusalem,
and delight in my people;
no more shall the sound of weeping be heard in it,
or the cry of distress.
20 No more shall there be in it
an infant that lives but a few days,
or an old person who does not live out a lifetime;
for one who dies at a hundred years will be considered a youth,
and one who falls short of a hundred will be considered accursed.
21 They shall build houses and inhabit them;
they shall plant vineyards and eat their fruit.
22 They shall not build and another inhabit;
they shall not plant and another eat;
for like the days of a tree shall the days of my people be,
and my chosen shall long enjoy the work of their hands.
23 They shall not labor in vain,
or bear children for calamity;[h]
for they shall be offspring blessed by the LORD—
and their descendants as well.
24 Before they call I will answer,
while they are yet speaking I will hear.
25 The wolf and the lamb shall feed together,
the lion shall eat straw like the ox;
but the serpent—its food shall be dust!
They shall not hurt or destroy
on all my holy mountain,
says the LORD.

The Worship God Demands

66 Thus says the LORD:
Heaven is my throne
and the earth is my footstool;
what is the house that you would build for me,
and what is my resting place?
2 All these things my hand has made,
and so all these things are mine,[i]
says the LORD.
But this is the one to whom I will look,
to the humble and contrite in spirit,
who trembles at my word.

3 Whoever slaughters an ox is like one who kills a human being;
whoever sacrifices a lamb, like one who breaks a dog's neck;
whoever presents a grain offering, like one who offers swine's blood;[j]
whoever makes a memorial offering of frankincense, like one who blesses an idol.
These have chosen their own ways,
and in their abominations they take delight;
4 I also will choose to mock[k] them,
and bring upon them what they fear;
because, when I called, no one answered,
when I spoke, they did not listen;
but they did what was evil in my sight,
and chose what did not please me.

[h] Or *sudden terror* [i] Gk Syr: Heb *these things came to be* [j] Meaning of Heb uncertain [k] Or *to punish*

65.13 Isa 1.19; 8.21; 41.17,18; 5.13; 66.5,14
65.14 Mt 8.12; Lk 13.28
65.15 Zech 8.13; Isa 62.2
65.16 Ps 72.17; 31.5; Isa 45.23; Jer 31.12
65.17 2 Pet 3.13; Isa 43.18
65.18 Isa 61.10
65.19 Isa 62.5; 35.10; Rev 7.17
65.20 Deut 4.40; Eccl 8.12,13
65.21 Am 9.14; Isa 37.30
65.22 Isa 62.8,9; Ps 92.12-14; Deut 32.46,47
65.23 Isa 55.2; 61.9
65.24 Dan 9.27
65.25 Isa 11.6,7,9; Gen 3.14
66.1 1 Kings 8.27; 2 Chr 6.18; Mt 5.34,35; Jer 7.4; Acts 7.49,50
66.2 Isa 40.26; 57.15; Mt 5.3,4; ver 5
66.3 Isa 1.11,13; 65.2,4
66.4 Prov 1.24; Isa 65.12; Jer 7.13

65.17-25 The Renewal of the Creation.
Not only will the people of God be restored to right relationship with him, but the whole created order will be renewed. There will be unprecedented length of life for the people and fruitfulness of crops. Even conflict between animal species (*wolf* and *lamb*) will cease, and life in the holy city (*mountain*) will be free of conflict.

66.1-6 What God Expects from his Renewed People.
Although God's power is universal and sovereign, he has chosen to associate with his human creatures who are *humble and contrite*. The sacrificial offering system of the Mosaic code and of the temple will end, since they did not evoke the obedience he sought. The false claims of the wicked that they are glorifying God will be met with divine punishment.

66.7-13 The People of Israel as God's Child.
Mingling images linked with childbirth – mother, child, obstetrician, parent – the prophet looks forward with joy to the rebirth of God's people, who will be prosperous and surrounded by love.
66.14-17 The Divine Punishment of the Wicked.
In contrast to the fruitful relation between God and his people is this prophecy of wrath to be poured out on the wicked, especially on those who persist in idolatry.
66.18-24 The Ultimate Vision of God's Glory.
People from all nations, including those who have not heard of the LORD, will be gathered in Jerusalem to see the radiant glory of God that will reside there. The nations' help for the people of Israel to return to the *holy mountain* will be their offering to God. Some from the nations will serve in the temple as *priests and Levites*, and all humanity will join in the worship of God. But they will also see the gruesome fate of rebellious humanity.

The LORD Vindicates Zion

5 Hear the word of the LORD,
you who tremble at his word:
Your own people who hate you
and reject you for my name's sake
have said, "Let the LORD be glorified,
so that we may see your joy";
but it is they who shall be put to shame.

6 Listen, an uproar from the city!
A voice from the temple!
The voice of the LORD,
dealing retribution to his enemies!

7 Before she was in labor
she gave birth;
before her pain came upon her
she delivered a son.
8 Who has heard of such a thing?
Who has seen such things?
Shall a land be born in one day?
Shall a nation be delivered in one moment?
Yet as soon as Zion was in labor
she delivered her children.
9 Shall I open the womb and not deliver?
says the LORD;
shall I, the one who delivers, shut the womb?
says your God.

10 Rejoice with Jerusalem, and be glad for her,
all you who love her;
rejoice with her in joy,
all you who mourn over her—
11 that you may nurse and be satisfied
from her consoling breast;
that you may drink deeply with delight
from her glorious bosom.

12 For thus says the LORD:
I will extend prosperity to her like a river,
and the wealth of the nations like an overflowing stream;
and you shall nurse and be carried on her arm,
and dandled on her knees.
13 As a mother comforts her child,
so I will comfort you;
you shall be comforted in Jerusalem.

The Reign and Indignation of God

14 You shall see, and your heart shall rejoice;
your bodies[l] shall flourish like the grass;
and it shall be known that the hand of the LORD is with his servants,
and his indignation is against his enemies.
15 For the LORD will come in fire,
and his chariots like the whirlwind,
to pay back his anger in fury,
and his rebuke in flames of fire.
16 For by fire will the LORD execute judgment,
and by his sword, on all flesh;
and those slain by the LORD shall be many.

17 Those who sanctify and purify themselves to go into the gardens, following the one in the center, eating the flesh of pigs, vermin, and rodents, shall come to an end together, says the LORD.

18 For I know[m] their works and their
thoughts, and I am[n] coming to gather all
nations and tongues; and they shall come
and shall see my glory, 19 and I will set a
sign among them. From them I will send
survivors to the nations, to Tarshish, Put,[o]
and Lud—which draw the bow—to Tubal
and Javan, to the coastlands far away that
have not heard of my fame or seen my
glory; and they shall declare my glory among
the nations. 20 They shall bring all your
kindred from all the nations as an offering
to the LORD, on horses, and in chariots, and
in litters, and on mules, and on dromedaries, to my holy mountain Jerusalem, says
the LORD, just as the Israelites bring a grain
offering in a clean vessel to the house of the
LORD. 21 And I will also take some of them
as priests and as Levites, says the LORD.

22 For as the new heavens and the new earth,
which I will make,
shall remain before me, says the LORD;
so shall your descendants and your name remain.
23 From new moon to new moon,
and from sabbath to sabbath,
all flesh shall come to worship before me,
says the LORD.

24 And they shall go out and look at the dead bodies of the people who have rebelled against me; for their worm shall not die, their fire shall not be quenched, and they shall be an abhorrence to all flesh.

[l] Heb *bones* [m] Gk Syr: Heb lacks *know* [n] Gk Syr Vg Tg: Heb *it is* [o] Gk: Heb *Pul*

66.5 ver 2; Isa 60.15; Mt 5.10-12; Lk 13.17
66.6 Isa 6.1,8; 65.6
66.7 Isa 37.3
66.8 Isa 64.4
66.10 Isa 65.18; Ps 26.8; 137.6
66.11 Isa 60.16
66.12 Isa 48.18; 60.4,5
66.13 2 Cor 1.3,4
66.14 Isa 33.20; Zech 10.7; Isa 58.11; Ezra 7.9; Isa 34.2
66.15 Isa 31.9; 2 Thess 1.8; Ps 78.16
66.16 Isa 30.30; 65.12; 34.3
66.17 Isa 65.3,4; Ps 37.20
66.18 Isa 59.7; 45.22-25
66.19 Isa 62.10; 42.12
66.20 Isa 60.4; 65.11,25; 52.11
66.21 Isa 61.6; 1 Pet 2.5,9
66.22 Isa 65.17; 2 Pet 3.13; Rev 21.1; Isa 65.22,23; 56.5
66.23 Isa 1.13,14; 49.7
66.24 Isa 5.25; 24.20; Mk 9.48; Isa 1.31; Dan 12.2

JEREMIAH

See the Introductions, pp. 6, 54-57, and 59-60 above.

1 The words of Jeremiah son of Hilkiah,
of the priests who were in Anathoth
in the land of Benjamin, 2to whom the word
of the LORD came in the days of King Josiah
son of Amon of Judah, in the thirteenth
year of his reign. 3It came also in the days
of King Jehoiakim son of Josiah of Judah,
and until the end of the eleventh year of
King Zedekiah son of Josiah of Judah, until
the captivity of Jerusalem in the fifth month.

Jeremiah's Call and Commission

4 Now the word of the LORD came to me
saying,

5 "Before I formed you in the womb I
knew you,
and before you were born I consecrated
you;
I appointed you a prophet to the
nations."

6Then I said, "Ah, Lord GOD! Truly I do not
know how to speak, for I am only a boy."
7But the LORD said to me,

"Do not say, 'I am only a boy';
for you shall go to all to whom I send
you,
and you shall speak whatever I
command you.
8 Do not be afraid of them,
for I am with you to deliver you,
says the LORD."

9Then the LORD put out his hand and touched
my mouth; and the LORD said to me,

"Now I have put my words in your
mouth.
10 See, today I appoint you over nations
and over kingdoms,
to pluck up and to pull down,
to destroy and to overthrow,
to build and to plant."

11 The word of the LORD came to me,
saying, "Jeremiah, what do you see?" And
I said, "I see a branch of an almond tree."[a]
12Then the LORD said to me, "You have seen
well, for I am watching[b] over my word to
perform it." 13The word of the LORD came to
me a second time, saying, "What do you
see?" And I said, "I see a boiling pot, tilted
away from the north."

14 Then the LORD said to me: Out of the
north disaster shall break out on all the
inhabitants of the land. 15For now I am
calling all the tribes of the kingdoms of the
north, says the LORD; and they shall come
and all of them shall set their thrones at the
entrance of the gates of Jerusalem, against
all its surrounding walls and against all the
cities of Judah. 16And I will utter my judgments against them, for all their wickedness
in forsaking me; they have made offerings
to other gods, and worshiped the works of
their own hands. 17But you, gird up your
loins; stand up and tell them everything
that I command you. Do not break down
before them, or I will break you before
them. 18And I for my part have made you
today a fortified city, an iron pillar, and a
bronze wall, against the whole land—against
the kings of Judah, its princes, its priests,
and the people of the land. 19They will fight
against you; but they shall not prevail against
you, for I am with you, says the LORD, to
deliver you.

God Pleads with Israel to Repent

2 The word of the LORD came to me,
saying: 2Go and proclaim in the hearing of Jerusalem, Thus says the LORD:

I remember the devotion of your youth,
your love as a bride,
how you followed me in the wilderness,
in a land not sown.
3 Israel was holy to the LORD,
the first fruits of his harvest.
All who ate of it were held guilty;
disaster came upon them,
says the LORD.

4 Hear the word of the LORD, O house of
Jacob, and all the families of the house of
Israel. 5Thus says the LORD:

What wrong did your ancestors find in
me
that they went far from me,
and went after worthless things, and
became worthless themselves?
6 They did not say, "Where is the LORD
who brought us up from the land of
Egypt,
who led us in the wilderness,
in a land of deserts and pits,
in a land of drought and deep darkness,

[a] Heb *shaqed* [b] Heb *shoqed*

1.1 2 Chr 35.25; 1 Chr 6.60; Isa 32.7-9
1.2 1 Kings 13.2; 2 Kings 21.18,24
1.3 Jer 25.1; 39.2; 52.12
1.5 Ps 139.15,16; Isa 49.1,5
1.6 Ex 4.10; Isa 6.5
1.8 Ezek 2.6; Jer 15.20
1.9 Isa 6.7; Ex 4.11-16
1.10 Jer 18.7; 2 Cor 10.4,5
1.11 Jer 24.3
1.13 Zech 4.2; Ezek 11.3,7; 24.3
1.14 Jer 4.6; 6.1
1.15 Isa 22.7; Jer 9.11
1.16 Deut 28.20; Jer 17.13; 7.9; 10.3-5
1.17 1 Kings 18.46; Ex 3.12; Ezek 2.6
1.18 Isa 50.7; Jer 6.27; 15.20
1.19 Jer 11.19; 15.10,11; ver 8
2.2 Jer 7.2; 11.6; Ezek 16.8; Deut 2.7
2.3 Ex 19.5,6; Jer 30.16; 50.7
2.5 Isa 5.4; Mic 6.3; Jer 8.19; 2 Kings 17.15
2.6 Ex 20.2; Isa 63.11; Hos 13.4; Deut 8.15; 32.10

1.1-3 The Time and Place of Jeremiah's Prophetic Work.
1.1 From a priestly family, Jeremiah was born in *Anathoth,* located a few miles north of Jerusalem, one of the towns assigned to priests and Levites, according to Josh 21.18. The period of his public activity extended from the reign of *Josiah* as king of Judah (640-609) to those of *Jehoiakim* (609-598) and (omitting Jehoicahin, who ruled for only 3 months) *Zedekiah* (597-586). The progressive takeover of Jerusalem by the Babylonians began in 597 and was complete by 586.
1.4-19 Jeremiah Called by God as a Prophet.
1.4-10 Jeremiah's role as *prophet to the nations* is said to have been part of God's plan before his birth. His commissioning took place while he was *only a boy,* yet he was to proclaim fearlessly what God put in his *mouth.* His role was not merely to describe the destruction that was coming but also to bring about the restructuring of the nations.
1.11-19 A pun in Hebrew links the image of the growth of the almond branch (in Hebrew, *shaqed)* with God's continuing concern (*shoqed*) for Judah. The *boiling pot, tilted away from the north,* symbolizes the divine wrath that is about to boil over on Judah, bringing the *kingdoms of the north* to punish disobedient, idolatrous *Jerusalem and all the cities of Judah.* Jeremiah is himself the stronghold which will be protected and preserved by God.
2.1-37 Israel's Faithlessness to God.
2.1-3 The prophet recalls both the initial fidelity of God to Israel in the time of the exodus and the wilderness journeys and the punishment that fell on those who disobeyed such laws as the sanctity of the *first fruits* of the crops.
2.4-32 The people, the priests, and the leaders of Israel have disobeyed God's law, or have ignored its demands upon them. They have turned instead to rely on *Egypt* or *Assyria* for gods to worship and as the base for confidence about the future of their nation.

in a land that no one passes through,
where no one lives?"
7 I brought you into a plentiful land
to eat its fruits and its good things.
But when you entered you defiled my land,
and made my heritage an abomination.
8 The priests did not say, "Where is the LORD?"
Those who handle the law did not know me;
the rulers[c] transgressed against me;
the prophets prophesied by Baal,
and went after things that do not profit.

9 Therefore once more I accuse you,
says the LORD,
and I accuse your children's children.
10 Cross to the coasts of Cyprus and look,
send to Kedar and examine with care;
see if there has ever been such a thing.
11 Has a nation changed its gods,
even though they are no gods?
But my people have changed their glory
for something that does not profit.
12 Be appalled, O heavens, at this,
be shocked, be utterly desolate,
says the LORD,
13 for my people have committed two evils:
they have forsaken me,
the fountain of living water,
and dug out cisterns for themselves,
cracked cisterns
that can hold no water.

14 Is Israel a slave? Is he a homeborn servant?
Why then has he become plunder?
15 The lions have roared against him,
they have roared loudly.
They have made his land a waste;
his cities are in ruins, without inhabitant.
16 Moreover, the people of Memphis and Tahpanhes
have broken the crown of your head.
17 Have you not brought this upon yourself
by forsaking the LORD your God,
while he led you in the way?
18 What then do you gain by going to Egypt,
to drink the waters of the Nile?
Or what do you gain by going to Assyria,
to drink the waters of the Euphrates?
19 Your wickedness will punish you,
and your apostasies will convict you.
Know and see that it is evil and bitter
for you to forsake the LORD your God;
the fear of me is not in you,
says the Lord GOD of hosts.

20 For long ago you broke your yoke
and burst your bonds,
and you said, "I will not serve!"
On every high hill
and under every green tree
you sprawled and played the whore.
21 Yet I planted you as a choice vine,
from the purest stock.
How then did you turn degenerate
and become a wild vine?
22 Though you wash yourself with lye
and use much soap,
the stain of your guilt is still before me,
says the Lord GOD.
23 How can you say, "I am not defiled,
I have not gone after the Baals"?
Look at your way in the valley;
know what you have done—
a restive young camel interlacing her tracks,
24 a wild ass at home in the wilderness,
in her heat sniffing the wind!
Who can restrain her lust?
None who seek her need weary themselves;
in her month they will find her.
25 Keep your feet from going unshod
and your throat from thirst.
But you said, "It is hopeless,
for I have loved strangers,
and after them I will go."

26 As a thief is shamed when caught,
so the house of Israel shall be shamed—
they, their kings, their officials,
their priests, and their prophets,
27 who say to a tree, "You are my father,"
and to a stone, "You gave me birth."
For they have turned their backs to me,
and not their faces.
But in the time of their trouble they say,
"Come and save us!"
28 But where are your gods
that you made for yourself?
Let them come, if they can save you,

[c] Heb *shepherds*

2.7 Num 13.27; Lev 18.25; Ps 78.58
2.8 Jer 10.21; Mal 2.6,7; Rom 2.20; Jer 23.13; 16.19
2.9 Ezek 20.35,36; Mic 6.2
2.11 Mic 4.5; Ps 106.20; Rom 1.23
2.13 Ps 36.9; Jer 17.13; Jn 4.14; Jer 14.3
2.14 Ex 4.22; Jer 5.19
2.15 Jer 50.17; 4.7
2.16 Jer 44.1; 43.7-9; 48.45
2.17 Jer 4.18; Deut 32.10
2.18 Isa 30.1,2; Josh 13.3; Jer 50.17
2.19 Isa 3.9; Hos 5.5; 11.7; Jer 5.24; Ps 36.1
2.20 Lev 26.13; ver 25; Deut 12.2; Isa 57.5,7
2.21 Ex 15.17; Isa 5.4
2.22 Jer 4.14
2.23 Prov 30.12; Jer 9.14; 7.31
2.24 Jer 14.6
2.25 Jer 18.12; 14.10; Deut 32.16
2.26 Jer 48.27
2.27 Jer 3.9; 18.17; 22.23; Isa 26.16
2.28 Deut 32.37; Isa 45.20; Jer 11.13

2.29 Jer 5.1; 6.13
2.30 Isa 1.5; Jer 26.20-24
2.31 Isa 45.19; Deut 32.15
2.32 Isa 17.10; Hos 8.14
2.34 Jer 19.4; Ex 22.2
2.35 ver 23; Jer 25.31; 1 Jn 1.8,10
2.36 ver 23; Hos 12.1; Isa 30.3; 2 Chr 28.16,20,21
2.37 2 Sam 13.19; Jer 37.7-10
3.1 Deut 24.4; Jer 2.20; Ezek 16.26,28,29; Zech 1.3
3.2 Deut 12.2; Jer 2.20; Prov 23.28; Jer 2.7
3.3 Lev 26.19; Jer 6.15; Ezek 3.7
3.4 ver 19; Ps 71.17
3.5 ver 12; Isa 57.16
3.6 Jer 7.24; 17.2
3.7 Ezek 16.46,47
3.8 2 Kings 17.6; Isa 50.1; Ezek 23.11
3.9 Jer 2.7,27
3.10 Hos 7.14
3.11 Ezek 16.51; ver 7
3.12 2 Kings 17.6; Ps 86.15
3.13 Deut 30.1-3; Jer 2.20,25; Deut 12.2

in your time of trouble;
for you have as many gods
as you have towns, O Judah.

29 Why do you complain against me?
You have all rebelled against me,
says the LORD.
30 In vain I have struck down your children;
they accepted no correction.
Your own sword devoured your prophets
like a ravening lion.
31 And you, O generation, behold the word of the LORD![d]
Have I been a wilderness to Israel,
or a land of thick darkness?
Why then do my people say, "We are free,
we will come to you no more"?
32 Can a girl forget her ornaments,
or a bride her attire?
Yet my people have forgotten me,
days without number.

33 How well you direct your course
to seek lovers!
So that even to wicked women
you have taught your ways.
34 Also on your skirts is found
the lifeblood of the innocent poor,
though you did not catch them breaking in.
Yet in spite of all these things[d]
35 you say, "I am innocent;
surely his anger has turned from me."
Now I am bringing you to judgment
for saying, "I have not sinned."
36 How lightly you gad about,
changing your ways!
You shall be put to shame by Egypt
as you were put to shame by Assyria.
37 From there also you will come away
with your hands on your head;
for the LORD has rejected those in whom you trust,
and you will not prosper through them.

Unfaithful Israel

3 If[e] a man divorces his wife
and she goes from him
and becomes another man's wife,
will he return to her?
Would not such a land be greatly polluted?
You have played the whore with many lovers;
and would you return to me?
says the LORD.
2 Look up to the bare heights,[f] and see!
Where have you not been lain with?
By the waysides you have sat waiting for lovers,
like a nomad in the wilderness.
You have polluted the land
with your whoring and wickedness.
3 Therefore the showers have been withheld,
and the spring rain has not come;
yet you have the forehead of a whore,
you refuse to be ashamed.
4 Have you not just now called to me,
"My Father, you are the friend of my youth—
5 will he be angry forever,
will he be indignant to the end?"
This is how you have spoken,
but you have done all the evil that you could.

A Call to Repentance

6 The LORD said to me in the days of King
Josiah: Have you seen what she did, that
faithless one, Israel, how she went up on
every high hill and under every green tree,
and played the whore there? 7 And I thought,
"After she has done all this she will return
to me"; but she did not return, and her false
sister Judah saw it. 8 She[g] saw that for all
the adulteries of that faithless one, Israel, I
had sent her away with a decree of divorce;
yet her false sister Judah did not fear, but
she too went and played the whore. 9 Because she took her whoredom so lightly,
she polluted the land, committing adultery
with stone and tree. 10 Yet for all this her
false sister Judah did not return to me with
her whole heart, but only in pretense, says
the LORD.

11 Then the LORD said to me: Faithless
Israel has shown herself less guilty than
false Judah. 12 Go, and proclaim these words
toward the north, and say:
Return, faithless Israel,
says the LORD.
I will not look on you in anger,
for I am merciful,
says the LORD;
I will not be angry forever.
13 Only acknowledge your guilt,

[d] Meaning of Heb uncertain [e] Q Ms Gk Syr: MT *Saying, If* [f] Or *the trails* [g] Q Ms Gk Mss Syr: MT *I*

2.33-37 The people are warned of the consequences of their adopting these foreign ways, which will lead to withdrawal of God's support.
3.1-10 Judah as an Unfaithful Wife. In spite of her infidelity to *the LORD*, as evident in her whoring after other deities, Judah expects easy and quick forgiveness from her God. She has not learned the price of being unfaithful, even though the northern tribes of Israel have already been taken away in exile.
3.11-4.4 Israel and Judah as Unfaithful Children.
3.11-14 Unlike unrepentant Judah, some in Israel now seem ready to confess their faults and to hope for restoration to *Zion*.

3.15-25 Instructed by *shepherds*, some from both Israel and Judah will regain their heritage if they truly repent their earlier idolatry and disobedience. The essential requirement is repentance.
4.1-4 A mixture of threat and promise tells Israel and Judah of the possibility of the renewal of God's favor if there is a genuine commitment *to the LORD*, which is here symbolized by *circumcision of your hearts*.
4.5-31 The Impending Fall of Jerusalem.
Using a series of images for oncoming destruction, the prophet announces the doom of Judah and Jerusalem through an invasion from *the north*, which means Babylon.
4.5-8 This image is of a marauding *lion*, which is the *destroyer* that is coming on Judah.

that you have rebelled against the
LORD your God,
and scattered your favors among
strangers under every green tree,
and have not obeyed my voice,
says the LORD.
14 Return, O faithless children,
says the LORD,
for I am your master;
I will take you, one from a city and two
from a family,
and I will bring you to Zion.

15 I will give you shepherds after my
own heart, who will feed you with knowledge and understanding. 16And when you
have multiplied and increased in the land,
in those days, says the LORD, they shall no
longer say, "The ark of the covenant of the
LORD." It shall not come to mind, or be
remembered, or missed; nor shall another
one be made. 17At that time Jerusalem shall
be called the throne of the LORD, and all
nations shall gather to it, to the presence of
the LORD in Jerusalem, and they shall no
longer stubbornly follow their own evil will.
18In those days the house of Judah shall join
the house of Israel, and together they shall
come from the land of the north to the land
that I gave your ancestors for a heritage.

19 I thought
how I would set you among my
children,
and give you a pleasant land,
the most beautiful heritage of all the
nations.
And I thought you would call me, My
Father,
and would not turn from following
me.
20 Instead, as a faithless wife leaves her
husband,
so you have been faithless to me,
O house of Israel,
says the LORD.

21 A voice on the bare heights[h] is heard,
the plaintive weeping of Israel's
children,
because they have perverted their way,
they have forgotten the LORD their
God:
22 Return, O faithless children,
I will heal your faithlessness.
"Here we come to you;
for you are the LORD our God.
23 Truly the hills are[i] a delusion,
the orgies on the mountains.
Truly in the LORD our God
is the salvation of Israel.
24 "But from our youth the shameful
thing has devoured all for which our ancestors had labored, their flocks and their herds,
their sons and their daughters. 25Let us lie
down in our shame, and let our dishonor
cover us; for we have sinned against the
LORD our God, we and our ancestors, from
our youth even to this day; and we have
not obeyed the voice of the LORD our God."

4 If you return, O Israel,
says the LORD,
if you return to me,
if you remove your abominations from
my presence,
and do not waver,
2 and if you swear, "As the LORD lives!"
in truth, in justice, and in
uprightness,
then nations shall be blessed[j] by him,
and by him they shall boast.
3 For thus says the LORD to the people of
Judah and to the inhabitants of
Jerusalem:
Break up your fallow ground,
and do not sow among thorns.
4 Circumcise yourselves to the LORD,
remove the foreskin of your hearts,
O people of Judah and inhabitants of
Jerusalem,
or else my wrath will go forth like fire,
and burn with no one to quench it,
because of the evil of your doings.

Invasion and Desolation of Judah Threatened

5 Declare in Judah, and proclaim in
Jerusalem, and say:
Blow the trumpet through the land;
shout aloud[k] and say,
"Gather together, and let us go
into the fortified cities!"
6 Raise a standard toward Zion,
flee for safety, do not delay,
for I am bringing evil from the north,
and a great destruction.
7 A lion has gone up from its thicket,
a destroyer of nations has set out;
he has gone out from his place

[h] Or *the trails* [i] Gk Syr Vg: Heb *Truly from the hills is* [j] Or *shall bless themselves* [k] Or *shout, take your weapons*: Heb *shout, fill* (your hand)

3.14 Hos 2.19; Jer 50.4,5
3.15 Jer 23.4; Acts 20.28
3.16 Isa 65.17
3.17 Jer 17.12; ver 19; Isa 60.9; Jer 11.8
3.18 Isa 11.13; Hos 1.11; Jer 31.8; Am 9.15
3.19 Dan 8.9; Ps 16.6; Isa 63.16
3.20 ver 6,7; Isa 48.8
3.21 Isa 15.2; Jer 2.32
3.22 ver 14; Hos 6.1; 14.4; Jer 31.6
3.23 Ps 121.1,2; 3.8
3.25 Ezra 9.7; Jer 22.21
4.1 Jer 3.1,22; Joel 2.12; Jer 7.3,7
4.2 Deut 10.20; Gen 22.18; Gal 3.8; Isa 45.25; 1 Cor 1.31
4.3 Hos 10.12; Mt 13.7,22
4.4 Deut 10.16; 30.6; Jer 9.26; Rom 2.28,29; Jer 21.12; Mk 9.43,48
4.5 Jer 6.1; 8.14
4.6 Jer 1.13-15; 6.1,22
4.7 2 Kings 24.1; Jer 5.6; Dan 7.4; Jer 25.9; Isa 1.7; Jer 2.15

to make your land a waste;
your cities will be ruins
without inhabitant.
8 Because of this put on sackcloth,
lament and wail:
"The fierce anger of the LORD
has not turned away from us."

9 On that day, says the LORD, courage shall
fail the king and the officials; the priests
shall be appalled and the prophets astounded.
10 Then I said, "Ah, Lord GOD, how utterly
you have deceived this people and Jerusalem, saying, 'It shall be well with you,' even
while the sword is at the throat!"

11 At that time it will be said to this
people and to Jerusalem: A hot wind comes
from me out of the bare heights[l] in the
desert toward my poor people, not to winnow or cleanse— 12 a wind too strong for
that. Now it is I who speak in judgment
against them.
13 Look! He comes up like clouds,
his chariots like the whirlwind;
his horses are swifter than eagles—
woe to us, for we are ruined!
14 O Jerusalem, wash your heart clean of
wickedness
so that you may be saved.
How long shall your evil schemes
lodge within you?
15 For a voice declares from Dan
and proclaims disaster from Mount
Ephraim.
16 Tell the nations, "Here they are!"
Proclaim against Jerusalem,
"Besiegers come from a distant land;
they shout against the cities of Judah.
17 They have closed in around her like
watchers of a field,
because she has rebelled against me,
says the LORD.
18 Your ways and your doings
have brought this upon you.
This is your doom; how bitter it is!
It has reached your very heart."

Sorrow for a Doomed Nation

19 My anguish, my anguish! I writhe in pain!
Oh, the walls of my heart!
My heart is beating wildly;
I cannot keep silent;
for I[m] hear the sound of the trumpet,
the alarm of war.
20 Disaster overtakes disaster,
the whole land is laid waste.
Suddenly my tents are destroyed,
my curtains in a moment.
21 How long must I see the standard,
and hear the sound of the trumpet?
22 "For my people are foolish,
they do not know me;
they are stupid children,
they have no understanding.
They are skilled in doing evil,
but do not know how to do good."

23 I looked on the earth, and lo, it was
waste and void;
and to the heavens, and they had no
light.
24 I looked on the mountains, and lo, they
were quaking,
and all the hills moved to and fro.
25 I looked, and lo, there was no one at all,
and all the birds of the air had fled.
26 I looked, and lo, the fruitful land was a
desert,
and all its cities were laid in ruins
before the LORD, before his fierce
anger.

27 For thus says the LORD: The whole
land shall be a desolation; yet I will not
make a full end.
28 Because of this the earth shall mourn,
and the heavens above grow black;
for I have spoken, I have purposed;
I have not relented nor will I turn
back.

29 At the noise of horseman and archer
every town takes to flight;
they enter thickets; they climb among
rocks;
all the towns are forsaken,
and no one lives in them.
30 And you, O desolate one,
what do you mean that you dress in
crimson,
that you deck yourself with
ornaments of gold,
that you enlarge your eyes with
paint?
In vain you beautify yourself.
Your lovers despise you;
they seek your life.
31 For I heard a cry as of a woman in
labor,
anguish as of one bringing forth her
first child,

[l] Or *the trails* [m] Another reading is *for you, O my soul,*

4.8 Isa 22.12; Jer 6.26; 30.24
4.9 Isa 22.3-5; 29.9,10
4.10 Ezek 14.9; 2 Thess 2.11; Jer 5.12; 14.13
4.11 Jer 51.1; Ezek 17.10; Hos 13.15
4.12 Jer 1.16
4.13 Isa 19.1; 5.28; Deut 28.49; Lam 4.19; Isa 3.8
4.14 Isa 1.16; Jas 4.8; Jer 6.19; 13.27
4.16 Jer 5.6,15; Isa 39.3; Ezek 21.22
4.17 2 Kings 25.1,4; Jer 5.23
4.18 Ps 107.17; Isa 50.1; Jer 2.17,19
4.19 Isa 15.5; 16.11; 21.3; 22.4; Jer 9.1,10
4.20 Ps 42.7; Ezek 7.26; Jer 10.20
4.22 Jer 10.8; 2.8; Rom 16.19
4.23 Gen 1.2; Isa 24.19
4.24 Isa 5.25; Ezek 38.20
4.25 Zeph 1.3
4.26 Jer 9.10
4.27 Jer 12.11,12; 5.10,18; 30.11; 46.28
4.28 Hos 4.3; Isa 5.30; 50.3; Num 23.19; Jer 7.16
4.29 Jer 6.23; 16.16
4.30 Jer 13.21; 2 Kings 9.30; Ezek 23.40; Jer 22.20,22
4.31 Jer 13.21; Isa 42.14; 1.15; Lam 1.17

4.9-10 All the leaders of the people will be astounded when, in spite of false assurances of safety from false prophets, disaster strikes.
4.11-26 Like a *whirlwind,* the disaster is coming in response to Judah's evil *ways* and lack of *understanding.* This will result in the desolation of the land.
4.27-31 Mourning will replace the religious ostentation of the past.

5.1-31 The Reasons for God's Judgment on his People.
5.1-17 Both poor and rich have been obstinate in their disobedient ways, so destruction will come on *the house of Israel and the house of Judah.* In spite of false complacency, judgment will occur through an alien *nation* chosen as God's instrument: Babylon.

the cry of daughter Zion gasping for breath,
stretching out her hands,
"Woe is me! I am fainting before killers!"

The Utter Corruption of God's People

5 Run to and fro through the streets of Jerusalem,
look around and take note!
Search its squares and see
if you can find one person
who acts justly
and seeks truth—
so that I may pardon Jerusalem.[n]
2 Although they say, "As the LORD lives,"
yet they swear falsely.
3 O LORD, do your eyes not look for truth?
You have struck them,
but they felt no anguish;
you have consumed them,
but they refused to take correction.
They have made their faces harder than rock;
they have refused to turn back.

4 Then I said, "These are only the poor,
they have no sense;
for they do not know the way of the LORD,
the law of their God.
5 Let me go to the rich[o]
and speak to them;
surely they know the way of the LORD,
the law of their God."
But they all alike had broken the yoke,
they had burst the bonds.

6 Therefore a lion from the forest shall kill them,
a wolf from the desert shall destroy them.
A leopard is watching against their cities;
everyone who goes out of them shall be torn in pieces—
because their transgressions are many,
their apostasies are great.

7 How can I pardon you?
Your children have forsaken me,
and have sworn by those who are no gods.
When I fed them to the full,
they committed adultery
and trooped to the houses of prostitutes.
8 They were well-fed lusty stallions,
each neighing for his neighbor's wife.
9 Shall I not punish them for these things?
says the LORD;
and shall I not bring retribution
on a nation such as this?

10 Go up through her vine-rows and destroy,
but do not make a full end;
strip away her branches,
for they are not the LORD's.
11 For the house of Israel and the house of Judah
have been utterly faithless to me,
says the LORD.
12 They have spoken falsely of the LORD,
and have said, "He will do nothing.
No evil will come upon us,
and we shall not see sword or famine."
13 The prophets are nothing but wind,
for the word is not in them.
Thus shall it be done to them!

14 Therefore thus says the LORD, the God of hosts:
Because they[p] have spoken this word,
I am now making my words in your mouth a fire,
and this people wood, and the fire shall devour them.
15 I am going to bring upon you
a nation from far away, O house of Israel,
says the LORD.
It is an enduring nation,
it is an ancient nation,
a nation whose language you do not know,
nor can you understand what they say.
16 Their quiver is like an open tomb;
all of them are mighty warriors.
17 They shall eat up your harvest and your food;
they shall eat up your sons and your daughters;
they shall eat up your flocks and your herds;
they shall eat up your vines and your fig trees;
they shall destroy with the sword
your fortified cities in which you trust.

[n] Heb *it* [o] Or *the great* [p] Heb *you*

5.1 2 Chr 16.9; Ezek 22.30; Gen 18.23,26,32
5.2 Titus 1.16; Jer 4.2; 7.9
5.3 Isa 1.5; 9.13; Jer 2.30; Zeph 3.2; Jer 7.26; 19.15
5.4 Jer 4.22; 8.7
5.5 Mic 3.1; Ps 2.3
5.6 Hab 1.8; Zeph 3.3; Hos 13.7; Jer 30.14,15
5.7 Josh 23.7; Zeph 1.5; Deut 32.21; Gal 4.8; Jer 7.9; Num 25.1-3
5.8 Ezek 22.11; Jer 13.27
5.9 Jer 9.9; 44.22
5.10 Jer 39.8; ver 18; Jer 4.27
5.11 Jer 3.20
5.12 2 Chr 36.16; Isa 28.15; Jer 23.17; 14.13
5.13 Jer 14.13,15
5.14 Jer 1.9; 23.29
5.15 Deut 28.49; Isa 5.26; Jer 1.15; 6.22; 4.16; Isa 39.3
5.16 Isa 5.28; 13.18
5.17 Lev 26.16; Deut 28.31,33; Jer 8.13; Hos 8.14

18 But even in those days, says the LORD,
I will not make a full end of you. 19 And
when your people say, "Why has the LORD
our God done all these things to us?" you
shall say to them, "As you have forsaken
me and served foreign gods in your land, so
you shall serve strangers in a land that is
not yours."

20 Declare this in the house of Jacob,
proclaim it in Judah:
21 Hear this, O foolish and senseless people,
who have eyes, but do not see,
who have ears, but do not hear.
22 Do you not fear me? says the LORD;
Do you not tremble before me?
I placed the sand as a boundary for the sea,
a perpetual barrier that it cannot pass;
though the waves toss, they cannot prevail,
though they roar, they cannot pass over it.
23 But this people has a stubborn and rebellious heart;
they have turned aside and gone away.
24 They do not say in their hearts,
"Let us fear the LORD our God,
who gives the rain in its season,
the autumn rain and the spring rain,
and keeps for us
the weeks appointed for the harvest."
25 Your iniquities have turned these away,
and your sins have deprived you of good.
26 For scoundrels are found among my people;
they take over the goods of others.
Like fowlers they set a trap;[q]
they catch human beings.
27 Like a cage full of birds,
their houses are full of treachery;
therefore they have become great and rich,
28 they have grown fat and sleek.
They know no limits in deeds of wickedness;
they do not judge with justice
the cause of the orphan, to make it prosper,
and they do not defend the rights of the needy.
29 Shall I not punish them for these things?
says the LORD,
and shall I not bring retribution
on a nation such as this?

30 An appalling and horrible thing
has happened in the land:
31 the prophets prophesy falsely,
and the priests rule as the prophets direct;[r]
my people love to have it so,
but what will you do when the end comes?

The Imminence and Horror of the Invasion

6 Flee for safety, O children of Benjamin,
from the midst of Jerusalem!
Blow the trumpet in Tekoa,
and raise a signal on Beth-haccherem;
for evil looms out of the north,
and great destruction.
2 I have likened daughter Zion
to the loveliest pasture.[s]
3 Shepherds with their flocks shall come against her.
They shall pitch their tents around her;
they shall pasture, all in their places.
4 "Prepare war against her;
up, and let us attack at noon!"
"Woe to us, for the day declines,
the shadows of evening lengthen!"
5 "Up, and let us attack by night,
and destroy her palaces!"
6 For thus says the LORD of hosts:
Cut down her trees;
cast up a siege ramp against Jerusalem.
This is the city that must be punished;[t]
there is nothing but oppression within her.
7 As a well keeps its water fresh,
so she keeps fresh her wickedness;
violence and destruction are heard within her;
sickness and wounds are ever before me.
8 Take warning, O Jerusalem,
or I shall turn from you in disgust,
and make you a desolation,
an uninhabited land.

9 Thus says the LORD of hosts:
Glean[u] thoroughly as a vine

[q] Meaning of Heb uncertain [r] Or *rule by their own authority* [s] Or *I will destroy daughter Zion, the loveliest pasture* [t] Or *the city of license* [u] Cn: Heb *They shall glean*

5.18-19 The poetic oracle is interrupted by a prose note (perhaps written after the return from exile) that this judgmental experience will not result in *the full end* of God's people.
5.20-31 God has established order in the creation, but this has no equivalent in the moral order of his people, where the rich and powerful exploit the weak, and corrupt officials – *prophets* and *priests* – are welcomed and honored by the people.
6.1-30 The Impending Invasion. *Tekoa* and *Beth-haccherem*, villages on ridges south of Jerusalem from which enemy attacks on the city could be foreseen, are here warned of the imminent invasion. It will take place because of the *oppression* which characterizes the people, whose worship is an *abomination* because they refuse to *walk in God's ways*.

5.18 Jer 4.27
5.19 Deut 29.24-26; 1 Kings 9.8,9; Jer 16.10-13; Deut 28.48
5.21 ver 4; Isa 6.9; Ezek 12.2; Mt 13.14; Jer 6.10
5.22 Jer 2.19; Job 26.10; Ps 104.9
5.23 Jer 4.17; 6.28
5.24 Ps 147.8; Mt 5.45; Joel 2.23; Gen 8.22
5.25 Jer 2.17; 4.18
5.26 Ps 10.9; Prov 1.11; Hab 1.15
5.27 Jer 9.6; 12.1
5.28 Deut 32.15; Isa 1.23; Zech 7.10; Jer 2.34
5.29 Mal 3.5
5.30 Hos 6.10
5.31 Jer 14.14; Ezek 13.6; Mic 2.11
6.1 2 Chr 11.6; Neh 3.14; Jer 1.14; 4.6
6.2 Deut 28.56; Jer 4.31
6.3 Jer 12.10; 2 Kings 25.1; Jer 4.17
6.4 Joel 3.9; Jer 15.8
6.5 Jer 52.13
6.6 Deut 20.19,20; Jer 32.24; 22.17
6.7 Isa 57.20; Ps 55.9-11; Jer 20.8; Ezek 7.11,23
6.8 Jer 7.28; Ezek 23.18; Hos 9.12
6.9 Jer 49.9; 8.3

6.21-30 The enemy will overwhelm the people of Judah, and the suffering they will experience is not aimed at refining them, but is leading to their rejection.

the remnant of Israel;
like a grape-gatherer, pass your hand again
over its branches.

10 To whom shall I speak and give warning,
that they may hear?
See, their ears are closed,[v]
they cannot listen.
The word of the LORD is to them an object of scorn;
they take no pleasure in it.
11 But I am full of the wrath of the LORD;
I am weary of holding it in.

Pour it out on the children in the street,
and on the gatherings of young men as well;
both husband and wife shall be taken,
the old folk and the very aged.
12 Their houses shall be turned over to others,
their fields and wives together;
for I will stretch out my hand
against the inhabitants of the land,
says the LORD.

13 For from the least to the greatest of them,
everyone is greedy for unjust gain;
and from prophet to priest,
everyone deals falsely.
14 They have treated the wound of my people carelessly,
saying, "Peace, peace,"
when there is no peace.
15 They acted shamefully, they committed abomination;
yet they were not ashamed,
they did not know how to blush.
Therefore they shall fall among those who fall;
at the time that I punish them, they shall be overthrown,
says the LORD.
16 Thus says the LORD:
Stand at the crossroads, and look,
and ask for the ancient paths,
where the good way lies; and walk in it,
and find rest for your souls.
But they said, "We will not walk in it."
17 Also I raised up sentinels for you:
"Give heed to the sound of the trumpet!"
But they said, "We will not give heed."
18 Therefore hear, O nations,
and know, O congregation, what will happen to them.
19 Hear, O earth; I am going to bring disaster on this people,
the fruit of their schemes,
because they have not given heed to my words;
and as for my teaching, they have rejected it.
20 Of what use to me is frankincense that comes from Sheba,
or sweet cane from a distant land?
Your burnt offerings are not acceptable,
nor are your sacrifices pleasing to me.
21 Therefore thus says the LORD:
See, I am laying before this people
stumbling blocks against which they shall stumble;
parents and children together,
neighbor and friend shall perish.

22 Thus says the LORD:
See, a people is coming from the land of the north,
a great nation is stirring from the farthest parts of the earth.
23 They grasp the bow and the javelin,
they are cruel and have no mercy,
their sound is like the roaring sea;
they ride on horses,
equipped like a warrior for battle,
against you, O daughter Zion!

24 "We have heard news of them,
our hands fall helpless;
anguish has taken hold of us,
pain as of a woman in labor.
25 Do not go out into the field,
or walk on the road;
for the enemy has a sword,
terror is on every side."

26 O my poor people, put on sackcloth,
and roll in ashes;
make mourning as for an only child,
most bitter lamentation:
for suddenly the destroyer
will come upon us.

27 I have made you a tester and a refiner[w]
among my people
so that you may know and test their ways.
28 They are all stubbornly rebellious,
going about with slanders;

[v] Heb *are uncircumcised* [w] Or *a fortress*

6.10 Jer 7.26; Acts 7.51; Jer 20.8
6.11 Job 32.18,19; Jer 20.9; 9.21
6.12 Deut 28.30; Jer 8.10; 15.6
6.13 Isa 56.11; Jer 8.10; 22.17; Mic 3.5,11
6.14 Jer 8.11; Ezek 13.10; Jer 4.10; 23.17
6.16 Isa 8.20; Jer 18.15; Mal 4.4; Lk 16.29; Mt 11.29
6.17 Isa 21.11; 58.1; Jer 25.4; Ezek 3.17; Hab 2.1
6.19 Isa 1.2; Jer 19.3,15; Prov 1.31; Jer 8.9
6.20 Isa 1.11; Am 5.21; Mic 6.6; Isa 60.6; Jer 7.21
6.21 Isa 8.14; Jer 13.16; 9.21,22
6.22 Jer 1.15; 5.15; 10.22; 50.41-43; Neh 1.9
6.23 Jer 4.29; 50.42; Isa 5.30
6.24 Jer 4.31; 13.21; 49.24; 50.43
6.25 Jer 14.18; 12.12; 20.10
6.26 Jer 4.8; 25.34; Mic 1.10; Zech 12.10
6.28 Jer 5.23; 9.4; Ezek 22.18

they are bronze and iron,
  all of them act corruptly.
29 The bellows blow fiercely,
  the lead is consumed by the fire;
in vain the refining goes on,
  for the wicked are not removed.
30 They are called "rejected silver,"
  for the LORD has rejected them.

Jeremiah Proclaims God's Judgment on the Nation

7 The word that came to Jeremiah from the LORD: 2Stand in the gate of the LORD's house, and proclaim there this word, and say, Hear the word of the LORD, all you people of Judah, you that enter these gates to worship the LORD. 3Thus says the LORD of hosts, the God of Israel: Amend your ways and your doings, and let me dwell with you[x] in this place. 4Do not trust in these deceptive words: "This is[y] the temple of the LORD, the temple of the LORD, the temple of the LORD."

5 For if you truly amend your ways and your doings, if you truly act justly one with another, 6if you do not oppress the alien, the orphan, and the widow, or shed innocent blood in this place, and if you do not go after other gods to your own hurt, 7then I will dwell with you in this place, in the land that I gave of old to your ancestors forever and ever.

8 Here you are, trusting in deceptive words to no avail. 9Will you steal, murder, commit adultery, swear falsely, make offerings to Baal, and go after other gods that you have not known, 10and then come and stand before me in this house, which is called by my name, and say, "We are safe!"—only to go on doing all these abominations? 11Has this house, which is called by my name, become a den of robbers in your sight? You know, I too am watching, says the LORD. 12Go now to my place that was in Shiloh, where I made my name dwell at first, and see what I did to it for the wickedness of my people Israel. 13And now, because you have done all these things, says the LORD, and when I spoke to you persistently, you did not listen, and when I called you, you did not answer, 14therefore I will do to the house that is called by my name, in which you trust, and to the place that I gave to you and to your ancestors, just what I did to Shiloh. 15And I will cast you out of my sight, just as I cast out all your kinsfolk, all the offspring of Ephraim.

The People's Disobedience

16 As for you, do not pray for this people, do not raise a cry or prayer on their behalf, and do not intercede with me, for I will not hear you. 17Do you not see what they are doing in the towns of Judah and in the streets of Jerusalem? 18The children gather wood, the fathers kindle fire, and the women knead dough, to make cakes for the queen of heaven; and they pour out drink offerings to other gods, to provoke me to anger. 19Is it I whom they provoke? says the LORD. Is it not themselves, to their own hurt? 20Therefore thus says the Lord GOD: My anger and my wrath shall be poured out on this place, on human beings and animals, on the trees of the field and the fruit of the ground; it will burn and not be quenched.

21 Thus says the LORD of hosts, the God of Israel: Add your burnt offerings to your sacrifices, and eat the flesh. 22For in the day that I brought your ancestors out of the land of Egypt, I did not speak to them or command them concerning burnt offerings and sacrifices. 23But this command I gave them, "Obey my voice, and I will be your God, and you shall be my people; and walk only in the way that I command you, so that it may be well with you." 24Yet they did not obey or incline their ear, but, in the stubbornness of their evil will, they walked in their own counsels, and looked backward rather than forward. 25From the day that your ancestors came out of the land of Egypt until this day, I have persistently sent all my servants the prophets to them, day after day; 26yet they did not listen to me, or pay attention, but they stiffened their necks. They did worse than their ancestors did.

27 So you shall speak all these words to them, but they will not listen to you. You shall call to them, but they will not answer you. 28You shall say to them: This is the nation that did not obey the voice of the LORD their God, and did not accept discipline; truth has perished; it is cut off from their lips.

29 Cut off your hair and throw it away;
  raise a lamentation on the bare
    heights,[z]
for the LORD has rejected and forsaken

[x] Or *and I will let you dwell* [y] Heb *They are* [z] Or *the trails*

7.5 Jer 4.1,2; 22.3
7.6 Deut 6.14,15; 8.19; Jer 13.10
7.8 Jer 13.25
7.9 Ex 20.3; Jer 11.13,17; 19.4
7.10 Ezek 23.39; Jer 32.34; 2.23,35
7.11 Mt 21.13; Mk 11.17; Lk 19.46
7.12 Jer 26.6; 1 Sam 4.10,11
7.13 2 Chr 36.15; Jer 35.17; Isa 65.12
7.14 1 Kings 9.7; ver 4,12
7.15 Jer 15.1; 2 Kings 17.23; Ps 78.67
7.16 Ex 32.10; Jer 11.14; 15.1
7.18 Jer 44.17; 19.13; 11.17
7.19 Deut 32.16,21
7.21 Isa 1.11; Am 5.21; Hos 8.13
7.22 1 Sam 15.22; Ps 51.16; Hos 6.6
7.23 Ex 15.26; Lev 26.12; Isa 3.10
7.24 Ps 81.11,12; Jer 15.16
7.25 Jer 25.4; Lk 11.49
7.26 Jer 19.15; 16.12
7.27 Ezek 2.7; 3.7; Isa 50.2
7.28 Jer 6.17; 5.3; 9.5
7.29 Job 1.20; Isa 15.2; Jer 16.6; Mic 1.16; Jer 3.21; 14.19

7.1-38 A Challenge to Attitudes toward the Temple.
7.1-4 The prophet is to challenge the assumption that the existence of the temple is a sure guarantee of the welfare of the covenant people.
7.5-7 If basic failures are remedied, God will continue to *dwell* there, as he did with their *ancestors.*
7.8-15 The people's disobedience to the commandments and worship of other gods will result in the destruction of the temple, as happened at Shiloh, the early center of worship of the Israelite tribes and the location of the ark of the covenant (Josh 18; Judg 21.19). As at that time, God's people do not now heed his voice and will be *cast out.*
7.16-34 A recital of the people's gross misdeeds in offering sacrifices to *the queen of heaven,* a mother goddess worshipped in various countries, early and late in the ancient world, and under a variety of names: Artemis, Atargatis, Isis. These practices will evoke God's judgment on his people. God did not tell their *ancestors* as they left Egypt that they should offer *burnt offerings and sacrifices.* (This denial implies that these features of the Mosaic law as found in Exodus to Deuteronomy were later additions.) Even though God has *persistently sent...prophets* to them, they have not heeded and obeyed *the voice of the LORD,* but have offered human sacrifices in Topeth (also known as Hinnom, a valley west of Jerusalem where idol-worship and child sacrifice were practised). Accordingly, they are to be rejected by God, with the result that birds of prey will feast on their corpses there, and the bones of their former leaders will lie exposed as a sign of God's disfavor toward his people. For the faithful remnant, death will be more attractive than life.

8.4-17 The Failure of Leadership and the Doom of the Nation. **8.4-12** Instead of summoning the people to obey *the ordinance of the* LORD, the religious leaders claim wisdom but act shamefully: *the scribes*, whose interpretations of God's law are *false; the wise*, who have in fact *rejected the word of the* LORD*; the prophets and priests*, who are greedy and shameful in their activities in the name of God. **8.13-17** The people do not produce the fruit of righteousness, and so their search for peace will be met by a disastrous invasion through the northern territory of the tribe of *Dan*, which borders Syria.

the generation that provoked his
wrath.

30 For the people of Judah have done
evil in my sight, says the LORD; they have
set their abominations in the house that is
called by my name, defiling it. 31And they
go on building the high place[a] of Topheth,
which is in the valley of the son of Hinnom,
to burn their sons and their daughters in
the fire—which I did not command, nor did
it come into my mind. 32Therefore, the days
are surely coming, says the LORD, when it
will no more be called Topheth, or the
valley of the son of Hinnom, but the valley
of Slaughter: for they will bury in Topheth
until there is no more room. 33The corpses
of this people will be food for the birds of
the air, and for the animals of the earth;
and no one will frighten them away. 34And
I will bring to an end the sound of mirth
and gladness, the voice of the bride and
bridegroom in the cities of Judah and in the
streets of Jerusalem; for the land shall become a waste.

8 At that time, says the LORD, the bones
of the kings of Judah, the bones of its
officials, the bones of the priests, the bones
of the prophets, and the bones of the inhabitants of Jerusalem shall be brought out of
their tombs; 2and they shall be spread before the sun and the moon and all the host
of heaven, which they have loved and served,
which they have followed, and which they
have inquired of and worshiped; and they
shall not be gathered or buried; they shall
be like dung on the surface of the ground.
3Death shall be preferred to life by all the
remnant that remains of this evil family in
all the places where I have driven them,
says the LORD of hosts.

The Blind Perversity of the Whole Nation

4 You shall say to them, Thus says the
LORD:
When people fall, do they not get up
again?
If they go astray, do they not turn
back?
5 Why then has this people[b] turned away
in perpetual backsliding?
They have held fast to deceit,
they have refused to return.
6 I have given heed and listened,
but they do not speak honestly;
no one repents of wickedness,
saying, "What have I done!"
All of them turn to their own course,
like a horse plunging headlong into
battle.
7 Even the stork in the heavens
knows its times;
and the turtledove, swallow, and crane[c]
observe the time of their coming;
but my people do not know
the ordinance of the LORD.

8 How can you say, "We are wise,
and the law of the LORD is with us,"
when, in fact, the false pen of the scribes
has made it into a lie?
9 The wise shall be put to shame,
they shall be dismayed and taken;
since they have rejected the word of the
LORD,
what wisdom is in them?
10 Therefore I will give their wives to
others
and their fields to conquerors,
because from the least to the greatest
everyone is greedy for unjust gain;
from prophet to priest
everyone deals falsely.
11 They have treated the wound of my
people carelessly,
saying, "Peace, peace,"
when there is no peace.
12 They acted shamefully, they committed
abomination;
yet they were not at all ashamed,
they did not know how to blush.
Therefore they shall fall among those
who fall;
at the time when I punish them, they
shall be overthrown,
says the LORD.
13 When I wanted to gather them, says the
LORD,
there are[d] no grapes on the vine,
nor figs on the fig tree;
even the leaves are withered,
and what I gave them has passed
away from them.[c]

14 Why do we sit still?
Gather together, let us go into the
fortified cities
and perish there;
for the LORD our God has doomed us to
perish,

7.30 2 Kings 21.4; 2 Chr 33.4,5,7; Jer 23.11; Ezek 7.20; Dan 9.27
7.31 2 Kings 23.10; Jer 19.5; Ps 106.38; Deut 17.3
7.32 Jer 19.6,7,11; 2 Kings 23.10
7.34 Isa 24.7,8; Ezek 26.13; Hos 2.11; Rev 18.23; Isa 1.7
8.1 Ezek 6.5
8.2 Acts 7.42; Jer 22.19
8.3 Job 3.21; 7.15,16; Rev 9.6; Jer 23.3,8
8.4 Prov 24.16
8.5 Jer 5.6; 7.24; 5.27; 9.6
8.6 Ps 14.2; Ezek 22.30; Rev 9.20; Job 39.21-25
8.7 Isa 1.3; Song 2.12; Jer 5.4,5
8.8 Jer 4.22; Rom 2.17
8.9 Jer 6.15,19
8.10 Deut 28.30; Isa 56.11
8.11 Jer 6.14; Ezek 13.10
8.12 Jer 3.3; 6.21; 10.15
8.13 Jer 14.12; Ezek 22.20,21; Isa 5.2; Joel 1.7; Mt 21.19
8.14 Jer 4.5; 35.11; 9.15; Mt 27.34; Jer 3.25; 14.20

[a] Gk Tg: Heb *high places* [b] One Ms Gk: MT *this people, Jerusalem,* [c] Meaning of Heb uncertain [d] Or *I will make an end of them, says the* LORD*. There are*

and has given us poisoned water to
drink,
because we have sinned against the
LORD.
15 We look for peace, but find no good,
for a time of healing, but there is
terror instead.

16 The snorting of their horses is heard
from Dan;
at the sound of the neighing of their
stallions
the whole land quakes.
They come and devour the land and all
that fills it,
the city and those who live in it.
17 See, I am letting snakes loose among you,
adders that cannot be charmed,
and they shall bite you,
says the LORD.

The Prophet Mourns for the People

18 My joy is gone, grief is upon me,
my heart is sick.
19 Hark, the cry of my poor people
from far and wide in the land:
"Is the LORD not in Zion?
Is her King not in her?"
("Why have they provoked me to anger
with their images,
with their foreign idols?")
20 "The harvest is past, the summer is
ended,
and we are not saved."
21 For the hurt of my poor people I am hurt,
I mourn, and dismay has taken hold
of me.

22 Is there no balm in Gilead?
Is there no physician there?
Why then has the health of my poor
people
not been restored?

9[e] O that my head were a spring of water,
and my eyes a fountain of tears,
so that I might weep day and night
for the slain of my poor people!
2[f] O that I had in the desert
a traveler's lodging place,
that I might leave my people
and go away from them!
For they are all adulterers,
a band of traitors.
3 They bend their tongues like bows;
they have grown strong in the land
for falsehood, and not for truth;
for they proceed from evil to evil,
and they do not know me, says the
LORD.

4 Beware of your neighbors,
and put no trust in any of your kin;[g]
for all your kin[h] are supplanters,
and every neighbor goes around like
a slanderer.
5 They all deceive their neighbors,
and no one speaks the truth;
they have taught their tongues to speak
lies;
they commit iniquity and are too
weary to repent.[i]
6 Oppression upon oppression, deceit[j]
upon deceit!
They refuse to know me, says the LORD.

7 Therefore thus says the LORD of hosts:
I will now refine and test them,
for what else can I do with my sinful
people?[k]
8 Their tongue is a deadly arrow;
it speaks deceit through the mouth.
They all speak friendly words to their
neighbors,
but inwardly are planning to lay an
ambush.
9 Shall I not punish them for these things?
says the LORD;
and shall I not bring retribution
on a nation such as this?

10 Take up[l] weeping and wailing for the
mountains,
and a lamentation for the pastures of
the wilderness,
because they are laid waste so that no
one passes through,
and the lowing of cattle is not heard;
both the birds of the air and the animals
have fled and are gone.
11 I will make Jerusalem a heap of ruins,
a lair of jackals;
and I will make the towns of Judah a
desolation,
without inhabitant.

12 Who is wise enough to understand
this? To whom has the mouth of the LORD

[e] Ch 8.23 in Heb [f] Ch 9.1 in Heb [g] Heb *in a brother* [h] Heb *for every brother* [i] Cn Compare Gk: Heb *they weary themselves with iniquity.* [6]*Your dwelling* [j] Cn: Heb *Your dwelling in the midst of deceit* [k] Or *my poor people* [l] Gk Syr: Heb *I will take up*

8.18-9.11 The Prophet's Lament over the Doomed People.
8.18-22 The prophet's *heart is sick,* because the whole people is sick as a consequence of their provocative idolatry, their refusal to repent, and the seeming lack of a healer or a remedy to restore *the health of my people.*
9.1-2 The prophet's responses range from depth of sorrow to the desire to flee away from them.
9.3-6 Their behavior is characterized by lies, evil acts toward *their neighbors,* and *deceit.*
9.7-11 God will *refine* them by punishing them for such misdeeds through his desolating their land and ruining Jerusalem.
9.12-16 Failure to Obey the Law will Bring Exile. The ruin of the land and the scattering of its people are the direct consequence of their having *forsaken [God's] law.* Here is sounded the Deuteronomic theme (as in Deuteronomy and the Books of Kings) about God's judgment for failure to obey the commandments (*cf.* 1 Kings 11.9-11).

8.15 Jer 14.19
8.16 Jer 4.15; Judg 5.22; Jer 3.24; 10.25
8.17 Num 21.6; Ps 58.4,5
8.19 Jer 4.16; Isa 39.3; Jer 14.9; Deut 32.21; Ps 31.6
8.21 Jer 14.17; Joel 2.6; Nah 2.10
8.22 Gen 37.25; Jer 14.19; 30.13
9.1 Isa 22.4; Lam 2.11; Jer 6.26; 8.21.22
9.2 Isa 55.6,7; Jer 5.7,8,11; 12.1,6
9.3 Ps 64.3; Isa 59.4; Jer 4.22; 1 Sam 2.12; Hos 4.1
9.4 ver 8; Jer 12.6; Gen 27.35; Jer 6.28
9.5 Mic 6.12; Jer 12.13; 51.58,64
9.6 Jer 5.27; 11.10; Jn 3.19,20
9.7 Isa 1.25; Mal 3.3; Hos 11.8
9.8 Ps 12.2; 28.3; Jer 5.26
9.9 Jer 5.9,29
9.10 Jer 4.24-26; Hos 4.3; Ezek 14.15
9.11 Isa 25.2; 13.22; 34.13; Jer 4.27; 26.9
9.12 Ps 107.43; Hos 14.9; Jer 23.10,16

spoken, so that they may declare it? Why
is the land ruined and laid waste like a
wilderness, so that no one passes through?
13 And the LORD says: Because they have
forsaken my law that I set before them, and
have not obeyed my voice, or walked in
accordance with it, 14 but have stubbornly
followed their own hearts and have gone
after the Baals, as their ancestors taught
them. 15 Therefore thus says the LORD of
hosts, the God of Israel: I am feeding this
people with wormwood, and giving them
poisonous water to drink. 16 I will scatter
them among nations that neither they nor
their ancestors have known; and I will send
the sword after them, until I have consumed them.

The People Mourn in Judgment

17 Thus says the LORD of hosts:
Consider, and call for the mourning
women to come;
send for the skilled women to come;
18 let them quickly raise a dirge over us,
so that our eyes may run down with
tears,
and our eyelids flow with water.
19 For a sound of wailing is heard from
Zion:
"How we are ruined!
We are utterly shamed,
because we have left the land,
because they have cast down our
dwellings."

20 Hear, O women, the word of the LORD,
and let your ears receive the word of
his mouth;
teach to your daughters a dirge,
and each to her neighbor a lament.
21 "Death has come up into our windows,
it has entered our palaces,
to cut off the children from the streets
and the young men from the
squares."
22 Speak! Thus says the LORD:
"Human corpses shall fall
like dung upon the open field,
like sheaves behind the reaper,
and no one shall gather them."

23 Thus says the LORD: Do not let the
wise boast in their wisdom, do not let the
mighty boast in their might, do not let the
wealthy boast in their wealth; 24 but let
those who boast boast in this, that they
understand and know me, that I am the
LORD; I act with steadfast love, justice, and
righteousness in the earth, for in these things
I delight, says the LORD.

25 The days are surely coming, says the
LORD, when I will attend to all those who
are circumcised only in the foreskin: 26 Egypt,
Judah, Edom, the Ammonites, Moab, and
all those with shaven temples who live in
the desert. For all these nations are
uncircumcised, and all the house of Israel
is uncircumcised in heart.

Idolatry Has Brought Ruin on Israel

10 Hear the word that the LORD speaks
to you, O house of Israel. 2 Thus
says the LORD:
Do not learn the way of the nations,
or be dismayed at the signs of the
heavens;
for the nations are dismayed at them.
3 For the customs of the peoples are false:
a tree from the forest is cut down,
and worked with an ax by the hands
of an artisan;
4 people deck it with silver and gold;
they fasten it with hammer and nails
so that it cannot move.
5 Their idols[m] are like scarecrows in a
cucumber field,
and they cannot speak;
they have to be carried,
for they cannot walk.
Do not be afraid of them,
for they cannot do evil,
nor is it in them to do good.

6 There is none like you, O LORD;
you are great, and your name is great
in might.
7 Who would not fear you, O King of the
nations?
For that is your due;
among all the wise ones of the nations
and in all their kingdoms
there is no one like you.
8 They are both stupid and foolish;
the instruction given by idols
is no better than wood![n]
9 Beaten silver is brought from Tarshish,
and gold from Uphaz.
They are the work of the artisan and of
the hands of the goldsmith;
their clothing is blue and purple;

[m] Heb *They* [n] Meaning of Heb uncertain

9.17-22 Judgment Brings Death. The professional women mourners are summoned and ordered to teach others to mourn, because the young women will not live long enough to replace them.
9.23-24 True Wisdom: To Know the LORD. The truly wise understand how God acts: in *love, justice and righteousness.*
9.25-26 True Circumcision. Circumcision is an essential rite for God's people, but the physical operation alone is inadequate for gaining membership in God's people, since many non-Israelites practise it as well. It must be matched by purification of the *heart*, which is the seat of the will, and must be renewed.
10.1-16 The Folly of Idolatry.
10.1-9 The impotence of the idols, which are contrived by humans, is described, as is the folly of the *instruction* given by them, even though the materials from which they are made are costly.

9.13 Jer 5.19; Ps 89.30
9.14 Rom 1.21-24; Gal 1.14; 1 Pet 1.18
9.15 Jer 8.14; 23.15
9.16 Lev 26.33; Deut 28.64; Jer 44.27; Ezek 5.2
9.17 2 Chr 35.25; Eccl 12.5; Am 5.16
9.18 Jer 14.17
9.19 Jer 4.13; 7.15; 15.1
9.20 Isa 32.9
9.21 Jer 15.7; 18.21; 6.11
9.22 Jer 8.2; 16.4
9.23 Eccl 9.11; Isa 10.8-12; Ps 49.6-9
9.24 1 Cor 1.31; 2 Cor 10.17; Gal 6.14; Ps 36.5,7; Mic 7.18
9.25 Rom 2.8,9
9.26 Jer 25.23; Lev 26.41; Ezek 44.7; Rom 2.28
10.2 Lev 18.3; Isa 47.12-14
10.3 Isa 40.19; 45.20
10.4 ver 14; Isa 41.7
10.5 Ps 115.5; 1 Cor 12.2; Isa 46.1,7; 41.23
10.6 Deut 33.26; Isa 12.6; Jer 32.18
10.7 Ps 22.28; Dan 2.27,28; 1 Cor 1.19,20
10.8 ver 14; Jer 4.22; 2.27
10.9 Isa 40.19; Ps 72.10; Dan 10.5; Ps 115.4

they are all the product of skilled
workers.
10 But the LORD is the true God;
he is the living God and the
everlasting King.
At his wrath the earth quakes,
and the nations cannot endure his
indignation.

11 Thus shall you say to them: The gods
who did not make the heavens and the
earth shall perish from the earth and from
under the heavens.[o]

12 It is he who made the earth by his
power,
who established the world by his
wisdom,
and by his understanding stretched
out the heavens.
13 When he utters his voice, there is a
tumult of waters in the heavens,
and he makes the mist rise from the
ends of the earth.
He makes lightnings for the rain,
and he brings out the wind from his
storehouses.
14 Everyone is stupid and without
knowledge;
goldsmiths are all put to shame by
their idols;
for their images are false,
and there is no breath in them.
15 They are worthless, a work of delusion;
at the time of their punishment they
shall perish.
16 Not like these is the LORD,[p] the portion of
Jacob,
for he is the one who formed all
things,
and Israel is the tribe of his inheritance;
the LORD of hosts is his name.

The Coming Exile

17 Gather up your bundle from the ground,
O you who live under siege!
18 For thus says the LORD:
I am going to sling out the inhabitants
of the land
at this time,
and I will bring distress on them,
so that they shall feel it.

19 Woe is me because of my hurt!
My wound is severe.
But I said, "Truly this is my
punishment,
and I must bear it."
20 My tent is destroyed,
and all my cords are broken;
my children have gone from me,
and they are no more;
there is no one to spread my tent again,
and to set up my curtains.
21 For the shepherds are stupid,
and do not inquire of the LORD;
therefore they have not prospered,
and all their flock is scattered.

22 Hear, a noise! Listen, it is coming—
a great commotion from the land of
the north
to make the cities of Judah a desolation,
a lair of jackals.

23 I know, O LORD, that the way of human
beings is not in their control,
that mortals as they walk cannot
direct their steps.
24 Correct me, O LORD, but in just measure;
not in your anger, or you will bring
me to nothing.

25 Pour out your wrath on the nations
that do not know you,
and on the peoples that do not call on
your name;
for they have devoured Jacob;
they have devoured him and
consumed him,
and have laid waste his habitation.

Israel and Judah Have Broken the Covenant

11 The word that came to Jeremiah
from the LORD: 2Hear the words of
this covenant, and speak to the people of
Judah and the inhabitants of Jerusalem.
3You shall say to them, Thus says the LORD,
the God of Israel: Cursed be anyone who
does not heed the words of this covenant,
4which I commanded your ancestors when
I brought them out of the land of Egypt,
from the iron-smelter, saying, Listen to my
voice, and do all that I command you. So
shall you be my people, and I will be your
God, 5that I may perform the oath that I
swore to your ancestors, to give them a
land flowing with milk and honey, as at this
day. Then I answered, "So be it, LORD."
6 And the LORD said to me: Proclaim all

[o] This verse is in Aramaic [p] Heb lacks *the LORD*

10.10-16 The omnipotence of God is contrasted with the weakness of the *stupid* idols.
10.17-25 The Siege and Fall of Judah and Jerusalem. The LORD is pictured in this oracle (probably written after the fall of Jerusalem) as using the Babylonian invaders to expel his disobedient people, and yet as being sad at the cessation of worship they offer in God's *tent:* the temple in Jerusalem. The power of Babylon, coming *from the land of the north,* has been used by God to desolate Judah and to *devour Jacob.*
11.1-17 The Violation of the Covenant by Israel and Judah. The failure of this people to fulfill their obligations under the covenant, which their ancestors agreed to when God brought them out of Egypt, has now reached the level of conspiracy. They have reverted to polytheism and idolatry – including offerings to *Baal* – which has *provoked [God] to anger,* and the people shall be destroyed.

10.10 Isa 65.16; Jer 4.2; 50.46; Ps 76.7
10.11 Ps 96.5; Isa 2.18; Zeph 2.11
10.12 Jer 51.15-19; Ps 78.69; Job 9.8; Isa 40.22
10.13 Ps 29.3-9; Job 36.27-29; Ps 135.7
10.14 Jer 51.17; Isa 42.17; Hab 2.18
10.15 Jer 8.19; 51.18
10.16 Ps 73.26; Jer 51.19; Isa 45.7; Deut 32.9; Jer 31.35
10.19 Jer 4.19,31; 14.17; Mic 7.9
10.20 Jer 4.20; 31.15; Isa 51.18
10.21 Jer 2.8; 23.2
10.22 Jer 4.15; 1.14; 9.11
10.23 Prov 20.24; Isa 26.7
10.24 Ps 6.1
10.25 Ps 79.6.7; Job 18.21; Jer 8.16; 50.7,17
11.3 Deut 27.26; Gal 3.10
11.4 Ex 24.3-8; Deut 4.20; 1 Kings 8.51; Jer 7.23; 24.7
11.5 Ex 13.5; Deut 7.12; Jer 32.22; 28.6

11.18-23 Jeremiah's Prayer and the LORD's Response.
11.18-20 The prophet discovers the plot to assassinate him, and commits his future to *the LORD.*
11.21-23 The people trying to kill Jeremiah are those of his hometown, Anathoth. He announces to them God's devastating judgment upon them.
12.1-17 Jeremiah's Complaint and God's Response.
12.1-4 The prophet asks why God allows the wicked to prosper, since they honor God only with *their mouths* and not in their *hearts.* He pleads for the LORD to slaughter them, and thus to disprove the charge that God is *blind* to the ways of these evil ones.
12.5-13 God notifies the prophet of his intention to abandon his people and to make desolate their land, since his former love for them has been replaced by *hate* and *anger* toward them.

these words in the cities of Judah, and in
the streets of Jerusalem: Hear the words of
this covenant and do them. 7 For I solemnly
warned your ancestors when I brought them
up out of the land of Egypt, warning them
persistently, even to this day, saying, Obey
my voice. 8 Yet they did not obey or incline
their ear, but everyone walked in the stubbornness of an evil will. So I brought upon
them all the words of this covenant, which
I commanded them to do, but they did not.
9 And the LORD said to me: Conspiracy
exists among the people of Judah and the
inhabitants of Jerusalem. 10 They have turned
back to the iniquities of their ancestors of
old, who refused to heed my words; they
have gone after other gods to serve them;
the house of Israel and the house of Judah
have broken the covenant that I made with
their ancestors. 11 Therefore, thus says the
LORD, assuredly I am going to bring disaster
upon them that they cannot escape; though
they cry out to me, I will not listen to them.
12 Then the cities of Judah and the inhabitants of Jerusalem will go and cry out to the
gods to whom they make offerings, but they
will never save them in the time of their
trouble. 13 For your gods have become as
many as your towns, O Judah; and as many
as the streets of Jerusalem are the altars you
have set up to shame, altars to make offerings to Baal.
14 As for you, do not pray for this people, or lift up a cry or prayer on their behalf,
for I will not listen when they call to me
in the time of their trouble. 15 What right
has my beloved in my house, when she has
done vile deeds? Can vows[q] and sacrificial
flesh avert your doom? Can you then exult?
16 The LORD once called you, "A green olive
tree, fair with goodly fruit"; but with the
roar of a great tempest he will set fire to it,
and its branches will be consumed. 17 The
LORD of hosts, who planted you, has pronounced evil against you, because of the
evil that the house of Israel and the house
of Judah have done, provoking me to anger
by making offerings to Baal.

Jeremiah's Life Threatened

18 It was the LORD who made it known to me, and I knew;
then you showed me their evil deeds.
19 But I was like a gentle lamb
led to the slaughter.
And I did not know it was against me
that they devised schemes, saying,
"Let us destroy the tree with its fruit,
let us cut him off from the land of the living,
so that his name will no longer be remembered!"
20 But you, O LORD of hosts, who judge righteously,
who try the heart and the mind,
let me see your retribution upon them,
for to you I have committed my cause.

21 Therefore thus says the LORD concerning the people of Anathoth, who seek your
life, and say, "You shall not prophesy in the
name of the LORD, or you will die by our
hand"— 22 therefore thus says the LORD of
hosts: I am going to punish them; the
young men shall die by the sword; their
sons and their daughters shall die by famine; 23 and not even a remnant shall be left
of them. For I will bring disaster upon the
people of Anathoth, the year of their punishment.

Jeremiah Complains to God

12 You will be in the right, O LORD,
when I lay charges against you;
but let me put my case to you.
Why does the way of the guilty prosper?
Why do all who are treacherous thrive?
2 You plant them, and they take root;
they grow and bring forth fruit;
you are near in their mouths
yet far from their hearts.
3 But you, O LORD, know me;
You see me and test me—my heart is with you.
Pull them out like sheep for the slaughter,
and set them apart for the day of slaughter.
4 How long will the land mourn,
and the grass of every field wither?
For the wickedness of those who live in it
the animals and the birds are swept away,
and because people said, "He is blind to our ways."[r]

God Replies to Jeremiah

5 If you have raced with foot-runners and they have wearied you,

[q] Gk: Heb *Can many* [r] Gk: Heb *to our future*

11.7 1 Sam 8.9; Jer 7.13,25
11.8 Jer 7.26; Mic 7.9; Lev 26.14-43
11.9 Ezek 22.25; Hos 6.9
11.10 1 Sam 15.11; Jer 13.10; Judg 2.11-13; Jer 3.6-11
11.11 ver 17; Jer 25.35; ver 14; Jer 14.12
11.12 Deut 32.37; Jer 44.17
11.14 Ex 32.10; ver 11; Ps 66.18
11.15 Jer 12.7; 13.27; 4.22
11.16 Ps 52.8; 83.2; Jer 21.14
11.17 Jer 12.2; 16.10,11; 32.27
11.19 Isa 53.7; Jer 18.18; Ps 83.4; 52.5; 109.13
11.20 Jer 20.12; Ps 7.9
11.21 Jer 12.5,6; Am 2.12; Jer 26.8; 38.4
11.23 Jer 6.9; 23.12; 48.44
12.1 Jer 11.20; Job 13.3; Jer 5.27,28; 20.5,11
12.2 Jer 11.17; Isa 29.13; Ezek 33.31
12.3 Ps 139.1-4; Jer 11.20; 17.18
12.4 Jer 9.10; Joel 1.10-17; Hos 4.3; Jer 4.25
12.5 Jer 26.8; 38.4-6; 49.19; 50.44

how will you compete with horses?
And if in a safe land you fall down,
how will you fare in the thickets of the Jordan?
6 For even your kinsfolk and your own family,
even they have dealt treacherously with you;
they are in full cry after you;
do not believe them,
though they speak friendly words to you.

7 I have forsaken my house,
I have abandoned my heritage;
I have given the beloved of my heart
into the hands of her enemies.
8 My heritage has become to me
like a lion in the forest;
she has lifted up her voice against me—
therefore I hate her.
9 Is the hyena greedy[s] for my heritage at my command?
Are the birds of prey all around her?
Go, assemble all the wild animals;
bring them to devour her.
10 Many shepherds have destroyed my vineyard,
they have trampled down my portion,
they have made my pleasant portion
a desolate wilderness.
11 They have made it a desolation;
desolate, it mourns to me.
The whole land is made desolate,
but no one lays it to heart.
12 Upon all the bare heights[t] in the desert
spoilers have come;
for the sword of the LORD devours
from one end of the land to the other;
no one shall be safe.
13 They have sown wheat and have reaped thorns,
they have tired themselves out but profit nothing.
They shall be ashamed of their[u] harvests
because of the fierce anger of the LORD.

14 Thus says the LORD concerning all my
evil neighbors who touch the heritage that
I have given my people Israel to inherit: I
am about to pluck them up from their land,
and I will pluck up the house of Judah from
among them. 15 And after I have plucked
them up, I will again have compassion on
them, and I will bring them again to their
heritage and to their land, everyone of them.
16 And then, if they will diligently learn the
ways of my people, to swear by my name,
"As the LORD lives," as they taught my
people to swear by Baal, then they shall be
built up in the midst of my people. 17 But if
any nation will not listen, then I will completely uproot it and destroy it, says the
LORD.

The Linen Loincloth

13 Thus said the LORD to me, "Go and
buy yourself a linen loincloth, and
put it on your loins, but do not dip it in
water." 2 So I bought a loincloth according
to the word of the LORD, and put it on my
loins. 3 And the word of the LORD came to
me a second time, saying, 4 "Take the loincloth that you bought and are wearing, and
go now to the Euphrates,[v] and hide it there
in a cleft of the rock." 5 So I went, and hid
it by the Euphrates,[v] as the LORD commanded
me. 6 And after many days the LORD said to
me, "Go now to the Euphrates,[v] and take
from there the loincloth that I commanded
you to hide there." 7 Then I went to the
Euphrates,[v] and dug, and I took the loincloth from the place where I had hidden it.
But now the loincloth was ruined; it was
good for nothing.
8 Then the word of the LORD came to me:
9 Thus says the LORD: Just so I will ruin the
pride of Judah and the great pride of Jerusalem. 10 This evil people, who refuse to hear
my words, who stubbornly follow their own
will and have gone after other gods to serve
them and worship them, shall be like this
loincloth, which is good for nothing. 11 For
as the loincloth clings to one's loins, so I
made the whole house of Israel and the
whole house of Judah cling to me, says the
LORD, in order that they might be for me a
people, a name, a praise, and a glory. But
they would not listen.

Symbol of the Wine-Jars

12 You shall speak to them this word:
Thus says the LORD, the God of Israel: Every
wine-jar should be filled with wine. And
they will say to you, "Do you think we do
not know that every wine-jar should be
filled with wine?" 13 Then you shall say to
them: Thus says the LORD: I am about to fill
all the inhabitants of this land—the kings

[s] Cn: Heb *Is the hyena, the bird of prey* [t] Or *the trails* [u] Heb *your* [v] Or *to Parah*; Heb *perath*

12.6 Jer 9.4; Ps 12.2; Prov 26.25
12.7 Jer 7.29; 11.15; Lam 2.1
12.8 Isa 59.13; Hos 9.15
12.9 2 Kings 24.2; Isa 56.9
12.10 Jer 23.1; Isa 5.1-7; 63.18; Jer 3.19
12.11 Jer 4.20,27; Isa 42.25
12.12 Jer 3.2,21; Isa 34.6; Jer 16.5; 30.5
12.13 Lev 26.16; Deut 28.38; Mic 6.15; Hag 1.6; Jer 9.5; 17.10
12.14 Zech 2.8-10; Deut 30.3; Isa 11.11-16
12.15 Ezek 28.25; Jer 48.47; 49.6,39; Am 9.14
12.16 Isa 42.6; Jer 4.2; 5.7; Eph 2.20,21
12.17 Isa 60.12
13.1 ver 11
13.2 Isa 20.2
13.4 Jer 51.63
13.5 Ex 39.42,43; 40.16
13.9 Lev 26.19; ver 15-17
13.10 Jer 9.14; 11.8; 16.12
13.11 Ex 19.5,6; Jer 7.23; 32.20; 33.9
13.13 Isa 51.17,21; 63.6; Jer 25.27; 51.7

12.14-17 Not only the exile of Judah as punishment is in store for her, but also the possibility of her return if she learns *the ways* God intended for her. Refusal to give heed to these choices, however, will lead to her destruction.
13.1-15.9 Oracles Announcing Judah's Exile.
13.1-11 The prophet is told to act a parable of God's judgment on Judah by placing a *linen loincloth* in a crevice in the rock by the Euphrates River, beyond which the people will soon be exiled. The gross deterioration of the cloth symbolizes the calamitous state of God's people.
13.12-14 Like drunken people who lose complete self-control, the structures for stability and hope are about to be shattered, including the Davidic dynasty and the temple of God's presence.

13.15-27 *The* LORD's *flock* are about to be taken captive, while the royal house and cities across the land as far south as the barren Negeb are all to lie in ruins. The Babylonian power *from the north*, with which Judah at times sought an alliance, will now take over the land because of the people's wickedness and participation in idolatries, here designated as adulteries, in part because of the sexual aspects of the worship of the fertility deities.
14.1-12 A drought that struck the land is seen to symbolize the drying up of God's support for his people, as a consequence of their disobedience. Belated petitions and offerings to God will not stave off the disastrous judgment about to fall.

who sit on David's throne, the priests, the
prophets, and all the inhabitants of Jerusalem—with drunkenness.
14 And I will dash
them one against another, parents and
children together, says the LORD. I will not
pity or spare or have compassion when I
destroy them.

Exile Threatened

15 Hear and give ear; do not be haughty,
for the LORD has spoken.
16 Give glory to the LORD your God
before he brings darkness,
and before your feet stumble
on the mountains at twilight;
while you look for light,
he turns it into gloom
and makes it deep darkness.
17 But if you will not listen,
my soul will weep in secret for your pride;
my eyes will weep bitterly and run down with tears,
because the LORD's flock has been taken captive.

18 Say to the king and the queen mother:
"Take a lowly seat,
for your beautiful crown
has come down from your head."[w]
19 The towns of the Negeb are shut up
with no one to open them;
all Judah is taken into exile,
wholly taken into exile.

20 Lift up your eyes and see
those who come from the north.
Where is the flock that was given you,
your beautiful flock?
21 What will you say when they set as head over you
those whom you have trained
to be your allies?
Will not pangs take hold of you,
like those of a woman in labor?
22 And if you say in your heart,
"Why have these things come upon me?"
it is for the greatness of your iniquity
that your skirts are lifted up,
and you are violated.
23 Can Ethiopians[x] change their skin
or leopards their spots?
Then also you can do good
who are accustomed to do evil.
24 I will scatter you[y] like chaff
driven by the wind from the desert.
25 This is your lot,
the portion I have measured out to you, says the LORD,
because you have forgotten me
and trusted in lies.
26 I myself will lift up your skirts over your face,
and your shame will be seen.
27 I have seen your abominations,
your adulteries and neighings, your shameless prostitutions
on the hills of the countryside.
Woe to you, O Jerusalem!
How long will it be
before you are made clean?

The Great Drought

14 The word of the LORD that came to Jeremiah concerning the drought:
2 Judah mourns
and her gates languish;
they lie in gloom on the ground,
and the cry of Jerusalem goes up.
3 Her nobles send their servants for water;
they come to the cisterns,
they find no water,
they return with their vessels empty.
They are ashamed and dismayed
and cover their heads,
4 because the ground is cracked.
Because there has been no rain on the land
the farmers are dismayed;
they cover their heads.
5 Even the doe in the field forsakes her newborn fawn
because there is no grass.
6 The wild asses stand on the bare heights,[z]
they pant for air like jackals;
their eyes fail
because there is no herbage.

7 Although our iniquities testify against us,
act, O LORD, for your name's sake;
our apostasies indeed are many,
and we have sinned against you.
8 O hope of Israel,
its savior in time of trouble,
why should you be like a stranger in the land,
like a traveler turning aside for the night?
9 Why should you be like someone confused,

[w] Gk Syr Vg: Meaning of Heb uncertain [x] Or *Nubians*; Heb *Cushites* [y] Heb *them* [z] Or *the trails*

13.14 Jer 19.9-11; 6.21; 16.5; Isa 27.11
13.15 Prov 16.5
13.16 Ps 96.8; Isa 59.9; Jer 23.12; 2.6
13.17 Mal 2.2; Jer 9.1; 14.17; 23.1,2
13.18 2 Chr 33.12,19; Isa 3.20; Ezek 24.17,23
13.19 Jer 32.44; 20.4; 52.27-30
13.20 Jer 6.22; ver 17
13.21 Jer 5.31; 2.25; 4.31
13.22 Deut 7.17; Jer 5.19; 16.10
13.23 Prov 27.22; Jer 4.22
13.24 Jer 9.16; 4.11; 18.17
13.25 Ps 11.6; Jer 2.32; 3.21
13.26 Ezek 16.37; Hos 2.10
13.27 Jer 5.7,8; 11.15; 2.20; 4.14; Hos 8.5
14.1 Jer 17.8
14.2 Isa 3.26; Jer 8.21; 11.11; 46.12
14.3 1 Kings 18.5; 2 Kings 18.31; 2 Sam 15.30
14.4 Joel 1.19,20; Jer 3.3; Joel 1.11
14.6 Jer 2.24; Joel 1.18
14.7 Isa 59.12; Jer 5.6; 8.5
14.8 Jer 17.13; Isa 43.3; 63.8; Ps 50.15
14.9 Isa 50.2; Jer 8.19; 15.16; Isa 63.19

like a mighty warrior who cannot
give help?
Yet you, O LORD, are in the midst of us,
and we are called by your name;
do not forsake us!

10 Thus says the LORD concerning this
people:
Truly they have loved to wander,
they have not restrained their feet;
therefore the LORD does not accept them,
now he will remember their iniquity
and punish their sins.

11 The LORD said to me: Do not pray for
the welfare of this people. 12 Although they
fast, I do not hear their cry, and although
they offer burnt offering and grain offering,
I do not accept them; but by the sword, by
famine, and by pestilence I consume them.

Denunciation of Lying Prophets

13 Then I said: "Ah, Lord GOD! Here are
the prophets saying to them, 'You shall not
see the sword, nor shall you have famine,
but I will give you true peace in this place.' "
14 And the LORD said to me: The prophets are
prophesying lies in my name; I did not send
them, nor did I command them or speak to
them. They are prophesying to you a lying
vision, worthless divination, and the deceit
of their own minds. 15 Therefore thus says
the LORD concerning the prophets who prophesy in my name though I did not send
them, and who say, "Sword and famine
shall not come on this land": By sword and
famine those prophets shall be consumed.
16 And the people to whom they prophesy
shall be thrown out into the streets of Jerusalem, victims of famine and sword. There
shall be no one to bury them—themselves,
their wives, their sons, and their daughters.
For I will pour out their wickedness upon
them.

17 You shall say to them this word:
Let my eyes run down with tears night
and day,
and let them not cease,
for the virgin daughter—my people—is
struck down with a crushing
blow,
with a very grievous wound.
18 If I go out into the field,
look—those killed by the sword!
And if I enter the city,
look—those sick with[a] famine!
For both prophet and priest ply their
trade throughout the land,
and have no knowledge.

The People Plead for Mercy

19 Have you completely rejected Judah?
Does your heart loathe Zion?
Why have you struck us down
so that there is no healing for us?
We look for peace, but find no good;
for a time of healing, but there is
terror instead.
20 We acknowledge our wickedness, O
LORD,
the iniquity of our ancestors,
for we have sinned against you.
21 Do not spurn us, for your name's sake;
do not dishonor your glorious throne;
remember and do not break your
covenant with us.
22 Can any idols of the nations bring rain?
Or can the heavens give showers?
Is it not you, O LORD our God?
We set our hope on you,
for it is you who do all this.

Punishment Is Inevitable

15 Then the LORD said to me: Though
Moses and Samuel stood before
me, yet my heart would not turn toward
this people. Send them out of my sight, and
let them go! 2 And when they say to you,
"Where shall we go?" you shall say to
them: Thus says the LORD:
Those destined for pestilence, to
pestilence,
and those destined for the sword, to
the sword;
those destined for famine, to famine,
and those destined for captivity, to
captivity.
3 And I will appoint over them four kinds of
destroyers, says the LORD: the sword to kill,
the dogs to drag away, and the birds of the
air and the wild animals of the earth to
devour and destroy. 4 I will make them a
horror to all the kingdoms of the earth
because of what King Manasseh son of
Hezekiah of Judah did in Jerusalem.

5 Who will have pity on you, O Jerusalem,
or who will bemoan you?

[a] Heb *look—the sicknesses of*

14.10 Jer 2.25; Jer 6.20; Hos 8.13
14.11 Ex 32.10; Jer 7.16
14.12 Isa 1.15; Jer 11.11; 6.20; 7.21; 9.16; 21.9
14.13 Jer 5.12; 23.17; 6.14
14.14 Jer 5.31; 27.15; 23.16,26; Ezek 12.24
14.15 Jer 5.12,13; Ezek 14.10
14.16 Isa 9.16; Jer 7.33; 8.1,2; 13.22-25
14.17 Jer 9.1; Lam 1.15,16; Jer 10.19; 30.14,15
14.18 Jer 6.25; Ezek 7.15; Jer 6.13; 2.8; 5.5
14.19 Jer 6.30; 30.13; 8.15; 1 Thess 5.3
14.20 Jer 3.25; 8.14
14.21 ver 7; Jer 3.17; 17.12
14.22 Isa 41.29; Jer 10.3; 5.24; Isa 41.4; 43.10; Lam 3.26
15.1 Ezek 14.14,20; Ex 32.11,12; 1 Sam 7.9; 12.23; 2 Kings 17.20; Jer 7.15; 10.20
15.2 Jer 43.11; Ezek 5.2,12; Zech 11.9
15.3 Lev 26.16; 1 Kings 21.23,24; Deut 28.26; Jer 7.33
15.4 Deut 28.25; 2 Kings 21.11ff; 23.26

14.13-16 No evidence is offered to the *lying prophets* who in God's name deny that disaster is impending. They and their families will suffer death and the disgrace of lying unburied.
14.17-18 The true prophet rightly predicts doom, contradicting the false prophets and priests.
14.19-22 The prophet's abject confession of *our wickedness* is followed by his declaration that *the LORD* is the only one who can restore his people.
15.1-9 The destruction of the people and the desolation of the land are depicted in vivid images. The chief blame for the decline of Judah is placed on *Manasseh,* the king of Judah (687-642), who revived the high places and altars for the worship of Baal in Judah (2 Kings 21).

15.10-21 Jeremiah's Prayer and the LORD's Response.
15.10-18 The prophet pleads for God's continuing care for him, recalling the *delight* he found when he took within himself God's words of instruction (*ate them*), but he also reflects on the anger he felt because of Israel's disobedience. He asks why God makes this painful sorrow continue.
15.19-21 God's reply reaffirms Jeremiah's role as the one who speaks for God, as well as the promise to him of protection and deliverance.
16.1-23 Jeremiah's Life as Symbol of Judgment. Jeremiah is to have neither wife nor children, since a wretched future in life and death awaits the wicked people of Judah, who have forsaken God and worshipped other gods. God will *hurl* them out of his land and will show them no *favor*. The failure to break bread with the mourners or to offer them a *cup* is a violation of the common practice of kindness to members of a bereaved family.

Who will turn aside
  to ask about your welfare?
6 You have rejected me, says the LORD,
  you are going backward;
so I have stretched out my hand against
      you and destroyed you—
  I am weary of relenting.
7 I have winnowed them with a
      winnowing fork
  in the gates of the land;
I have bereaved them, I have destroyed
      my people;
  they did not turn from their ways.
8 Their widows became more numerous
  than the sand of the seas;
I have brought against the mothers of
      youths
  a destroyer at noonday;
I have made anguish and terror
  fall upon her suddenly.
9 She who bore seven has languished;
  she has swooned away;
her sun went down while it was yet
      day;
  she has been shamed and disgraced.
And the rest of them I will give to the
      sword
  before their enemies,
        says the LORD.

Jeremiah Complains Again and Is Reassured

10 Woe is me, my mother, that you ever
bore me, a man of strife and contention to
the whole land! I have not lent, nor have
I borrowed, yet all of them curse me. 11The
LORD said: Surely I have intervened in your
life[b] for good, surely I have imposed enemies
on you in a time of trouble and in a time
of distress.[c] 12Can iron and bronze break
iron from the north?

13 Your wealth and your treasures I will
give as plunder, without price, for all your
sins, throughout all your territory. 14I will
make you serve your enemies in a land that
you do not know, for in my anger a fire is
kindled that shall burn forever.

15 O LORD, you know;
  remember me and visit me,
  and bring down retribution for me on
      my persecutors.
In your forbearance do not take me
      away;
  know that on your account I suffer
      insult.
16 Your words were found, and I ate them,
  and your words became to me a joy
  and the delight of my heart;
for I am called by your name,
  O LORD, God of hosts.
17 I did not sit in the company of
      merrymakers,
  nor did I rejoice;
under the weight of your hand I sat
      alone,
  for you had filled me with
      indignation.
18 Why is my pain unceasing,
  my wound incurable,
  refusing to be healed?
Truly, you are to me like a deceitful
      brook,
  like waters that fail.

19 Therefore thus says the LORD:
If you turn back, I will take you back,
  and you shall stand before me.
If you utter what is precious, and not
      what is worthless,
  you shall serve as my mouth.
It is they who will turn to you,
  not you who will turn to them.
20 And I will make you to this people
  a fortified wall of bronze;
they will fight against you,
  but they shall not prevail over you,
for I am with you
  to save you and deliver you,
        says the LORD.
21 I will deliver you out of the hand of the
      wicked,
  and redeem you from the grasp of the
      ruthless.

Jeremiah's Celibacy and Message

16 The word of the LORD came to me:
2You shall not take a wife, nor
shall you have sons or daughters in this
place. 3For thus says the LORD concerning
the sons and daughters who are born in
this place, and concerning the mothers who
bear them and the fathers who beget them
in this land: 4They shall die of deadly diseases. They shall not be lamented, nor shall
they be buried; they shall become like dung
on the surface of the ground. They shall
perish by the sword and by famine, and
their dead bodies shall become food for the
birds of the air and for the wild animals of
the earth.

5 For thus says the LORD: Do not enter

[b] Heb *intervened with you* [c] Meaning of Heb uncertain

15.6 Jer 6.19; 7.24; 6.11,12; 7.16
15.7 Jer 51.2; 18.21; 5.3
15.9 1 Sam 2.5; Isa 47.9; Jer 6.4; Am 8.9; Jer 50.12; 21.7
15.10 Job 3.1; Jer 20.14; Deut 23.19
15.11 Isa 41.10; Jer 39.11,12; 40.4,5
15.13 Ps 44.12; Jer 17.3; Isa 52.3,5
15.14 Jer 16.13; 17.4; Deut 32.22
15.15 Jer 12.3; 20.11; Ps 69.7-9
15.16 Ezek 3.1-3; Ps 119.72; Jer 14.9
15.17 Jer 16.8; Ezek 3.24,25
15.18 Jer 30.15; Mic 1.9; Jer 14.3
15.19 Jer 4.1; Ezek 22.26
15.20 Jer 1.18,19; 20.11; Isa 41.10
15.21 Jer 20.13; 31.11
16.1 Jer 1.2,4
16.2 1 Cor 7.26
16.3 Jer 6.11; 15.8; 6.21
16.4 Ps 83.10; Jer 9.22; 15.3; 34.20
16.5 Ezek 24.16-23; Jer 12.12; 13.14

the house of mourning, or go to lament, or bemoan them; for I have taken away my peace from this people, says the LORD, my steadfast love and mercy. 6 Both great and small shall die in this land; they shall not be buried, and no one shall lament for them; there shall be no gashing, no shaving of the head for them. 7 No one shall break bread[d] for the mourner, to offer comfort for the dead; nor shall anyone give them the cup of consolation to drink for their fathers or their mothers. 8 You shall not go into the house of feasting to sit with them, to eat and drink. 9 For thus says the LORD of hosts, the God of Israel: I am going to banish from this place, in your days and before your eyes, the voice of mirth and the voice of gladness, the voice of the bridegroom and the voice of the bride.

10 And when you tell this people all these words, and they say to you, "Why has the LORD pronounced all this great evil against us? What is our iniquity? What is the sin that we have committed against the LORD our God?" 11 then you shall say to them: It is because your ancestors have forsaken me, says the LORD, and have gone after other gods and have served and worshiped them, and have forsaken me and have not kept my law; 12 and because you have behaved worse than your ancestors, for here you are, every one of you, following your stubborn evil will, refusing to listen to me. 13 Therefore I will hurl you out of this land into a land that neither you nor your ancestors have known, and there you shall serve other gods day and night, for I will show you no favor.

God Will Restore Israel

14 Therefore, the days are surely coming, says the LORD, when it shall no longer be said, "As the LORD lives who brought the people of Israel up out of the land of Egypt," 15 but "As the LORD lives who brought the people of Israel up out of the land of the north and out of all the lands where he had driven them." For I will bring them back to their own land that I gave to their ancestors.

16 I am now sending for many fishermen, says the LORD, and they shall catch them; and afterward I will send for many hunters, and they shall hunt them from every mountain and every hill, and out of the clefts of the rocks. 17 For my eyes are on all their ways; they are not hidden from my presence, nor is their iniquity concealed from my sight. 18 And[e] I will doubly repay their iniquity and their sin, because they have polluted my land with the carcasses of their detestable idols, and have filled my inheritance with their abominations.

19 O LORD, my strength and my stronghold,
  my refuge in the day of trouble,
to you shall the nations come
  from the ends of the earth and say:
Our ancestors have inherited nothing
    but lies,
  worthless things in which there is no
    profit.
20 Can mortals make for themselves gods?
  Such are no gods!

21 "Therefore I am surely going to teach them, this time I am going to teach them my power and my might, and they shall know that my name is the LORD."

Judah's Sin and Punishment

17 The sin of Judah is written with an iron pen; with a diamond point it is engraved on the tablet of their hearts, and on the horns of their altars, 2 while their children remember their altars and their sacred poles,[f] beside every green tree, and on the high hills, 3 on the mountains in the open country. Your wealth and all your treasures I will give for spoil as the price of your sin[g] throughout all your territory. 4 By your own act you shall lose the heritage that I gave you, and I will make you serve your enemies in a land that you do not know, for in my anger a fire is kindled[h] that shall burn forever.

5 Thus says the LORD:
Cursed are those who trust in mere
    mortals
  and make mere flesh their strength,
  whose hearts turn away from the
    LORD.
6 They shall be like a shrub in the desert,
  and shall not see when relief comes.
They shall live in the parched places of
    the wilderness,
  in an uninhabited salt land.

[d] Two Mss Gk: MT *break for them* [e] Gk: Heb *And first* [f] Heb *Asherim* [g] Cn: Heb *spoil your high places for sin* [h] Two Mss Theodotion: *you kindled*

16.6 Ezek 9.6; Jer 41.5; 47.5
16.7 Ezek 24.17; Hos 9.4
16.8 Jer 15.17
16.9 Jer 7.34; 25.10; Hos 2.11; Rev 18.23
16.10 Deut 29.24; 1 Kings 9.8,9; Jer 5.19
16.11 Jer 22.9; Ezek 11.21; 1 Pet 4.3
16.12 Jer 7.26; 13.10; Eccl 9.3
16.13 Deut 4.26-28; 28.36; Jer 15.4; 5.19
16.14 Isa 43.18; Jer 23.7,8; Ex 20.2
16.15 Ps 106.47; Isa 11.11-16; Jer 24.6
16.16 Am 4.2; Hab 1.14,15; Mic 7.2; Isa 2.21
16.17 Ps 90.8; 1 Cor 4.5; Heb 4.13; Jer 2.22
16.18 Rev 18.6; Ezek 11.18,21
16.19 Jer 15.11; Ps 14.6; Hab 2.18,19
16.20 Isa 37.19; Jer 2.11; Gal 4.8
16.21 Ps 9.16; Jer 33.2; Am 5.8
17.1 Jer 2.22; Job 19.24; Prov 3.3; 2 Cor 3.3
17.4 Jer 12.7; 15.14; 7.20
17.5 Isa 30.1-3; 2 Chr 32.8
17.6 Jer 48.6; Deut 29.23

16.14-17.13 Oracles of Judgment and Renewal.
16.14-15 This brief promise of restoration of Israel to the land may have been added here later (after the return from the exile) to ease the harshness of the judgment theme (*cf.* Jer 23.7-8).
16.16-18 Returning to the theme of judgment, the LORD is pictured as sending out hunters to gather the wicked from their hiding places so that they can receive the punishment that befits their misdeeds.
16.19-20 A fragmentary oracle promises that other *nations* will come to the LORD, confessing the folly of idolatry. They are to be instructed that the true name of God is *the LORD.*
17.1-4 Judah's participation in idolatry defies the prohibition against it in the covenant code, from which it is *engraved on the tablet of their hearts.* They should know not only the law, but also the inevitable consequences of disobedience to it.
17.5-13 After contrasting the hopeless fate of idolaters with the abundant resources available to those who *trust in the LORD,* the oracle considers the perversity of the human mind, which relies on its own acquisitions and achievements (*wealth*) and turns from God, the only source of *living water.*

17.14-18 A Prayer of Jeremiah. Here the prophet recalls his fidelity to God, and asks for protection in the difficult times ahead, as well as for the humiliation of his *persecutors.*
17.19-18.17 Warnings of the Consequences of Disobedience.
17.19-27 The Major Importance of Sabbath Observance. Avoidance of carrying anything into Jerusalem or of performing work there will assure continuance of the Davidic line of kings, and the life of the city will continue *forever.* Sabbath violation, however, will result in the burning of the city.
18.1-11 Comparing God to a potter, Jeremiah sees God as *shaping evil* in response to the *evil ways* of the people.

7 Blessed are those who trust in the LORD,
whose trust is the LORD.
8 They shall be like a tree planted by water,
sending out its roots by the stream.
It shall not fear when heat comes,
and its leaves shall stay green;
in the year of drought it is not anxious,
and it does not cease to bear fruit.

9 The heart is devious above all else;
it is perverse—
who can understand it?
10 I the LORD test the mind
and search the heart,
to give to all according to their ways,
according to the fruit of their doings.

11 Like the partridge hatching what it did not lay,
so are all who amass wealth unjustly;
in mid-life it will leave them,
and at their end they will prove to be fools.

12 O glorious throne, exalted from the beginning,
shrine of our sanctuary!
13 O hope of Israel! O LORD!
All who forsake you shall be put to shame;
those who turn away from you[i] shall be recorded in the underworld,[j]
for they have forsaken the fountain of living water, the LORD.

Jeremiah Prays for Vindication

14 Heal me, O LORD, and I shall be healed;
save me, and I shall be saved;
for you are my praise.
15 See how they say to me,
"Where is the word of the LORD?
Let it come!"
16 But I have not run away from being a shepherd[k] in your service,
nor have I desired the fatal day.
You know what came from my lips;
it was before your face.
17 Do not become a terror to me;
you are my refuge in the day of disaster;
18 Let my persecutors be shamed,
but do not let me be shamed;
let them be dismayed,
but do not let me be dismayed;
bring on them the day of disaster;
destroy them with double destruction!

Hallow the Sabbath Day

19 Thus said the LORD to me: Go and
stand in the People's Gate, by which the
kings of Judah enter and by which they go
out, and in all the gates of Jerusalem, 20and
say to them: Hear the word of the LORD, you
kings of Judah, and all Judah, and all the
inhabitants of Jerusalem, who enter by these
gates. 21Thus says the LORD: For the sake of
your lives, take care that you do not bear
a burden on the sabbath day or bring it in
by the gates of Jerusalem. 22And do not
carry a burden out of your houses on the
sabbath or do any work, but keep the sabbath
day holy, as I commanded your ancestors.
23Yet they did not listen or incline their ear;
they stiffened their necks and would not
hear or receive instruction.
24 But if you listen to me, says the LORD,
and bring in no burden by the gates of this
city on the sabbath day, but keep the sabbath
day holy and do no work on it, 25then there
shall enter by the gates of this city kings[l]
who sit on the throne of David, riding
in chariots and on horses, they and their
officials, the people of Judah and the inhabitants of Jerusalem; and this city shall be
inhabited forever. 26And people shall come
from the towns of Judah and the places
around Jerusalem, from the land of Benjamin,
from the Shephelah, from the hill country,
and from the Negeb, bringing burnt offerings and sacrifices, grain offerings and frankincense, and bringing thank offerings to the
house of the LORD. 27But if you do not listen
to me, to keep the sabbath day holy, and
to carry in no burden through the gates of
Jerusalem on the sabbath day, then I will
kindle a fire in its gates; it shall devour the
palaces of Jerusalem and shall not be
quenched.

The Potter and the Clay

18 The word that came to Jeremiah
from the LORD: 2"Come, go down to
the potter's house, and there I will let you
hear my words." 3So I went down to the
potter's house, and there he was working
at his wheel. 4The vessel he was making of
clay was spoiled in the potter's hand, and
he reworked it into another vessel, as seemed
good to him.
5 Then the word of the LORD came to me:
6Can I not do with you, O house of Israel,
just as this potter has done? says the LORD.

[i] Heb *me* [j] Or *in the earth* [k] Meaning of Heb uncertain [l] Cn: Heb *kings and officials*

17.7 Ps 34.8; 84.12; 40.4; Prov 16.20
17.8 Ps 1.3; Jer 14.1-6
17.9 Mk 7.21,22; Rom 7.11; Eph 4.22
17.10 1 Sam 16.7; Jer 11.20; 20.12; Rom 8.27; Jer 32.19; Rom 2.6
17.13 Jer 14.8; Ps 73.27; Isa 1.28; Jer 2.13,17
17.14 Jer 30.17; Ps 54.1; Deut 10.21; Ps 109.1
17.15 Isa 5.19; Am 5.18
17.17 Ps 88.15; Jer 16.19
17.18 Ps 35.4,26; Ps 35.8; Jer 16.18
17.20 Jer 19.3; 22.2; Hos 5.1
17.21 Deut 4.9,15,23; Num 15.32-36; Neh 13.15-21
17.22 Ex 20.8; 23.12; 31.13; Ezek 20.12
17.23 Jer 7.24,26; 11.10; 19.15
17.24 Deut 11.13; Ex 20.8-11; Ezek 20.20
17.25 Jer 22.4; Isa 9.7; Lk 1.32; Heb 12.22
17.26 Zech 7.7; Ps 107.22
17.27 Jer 22.5; Isa 9.18,19; Jer 11.16; Am 2.5; 7.20
18.2 Jer 19.1,2; 23.22
18.6 Isa 45.9; Mt 20.15; Rom 9.20,21

Just like the clay in the potter's hand, so are
you in my hand, O house of Israel. 7 At one
moment I may declare concerning a nation
or a kingdom, that I will pluck up and
break down and destroy it, 8 but if that
nation, concerning which I have spoken,
turns from its evil, I will change my mind
about the disaster that I intended to bring
on it. 9 And at another moment I may declare concerning a nation or a kingdom
that I will build and plant it, 10 but if it does
evil in my sight, not listening to my voice,
then I will change my mind about the good
that I had intended to do to it. 11 Now,
therefore, say to the people of Judah and the
inhabitants of Jerusalem: Thus says the LORD:
Look, I am a potter shaping evil against you
and devising a plan against you. Turn now,
all of you from your evil way, and amend
your ways and your doings.

Israel's Stubborn Idolatry

12 But they say, "It is no use! We will follow our own plans, and each of us will act according to the stubbornness of our evil will."

13 Therefore thus says the LORD:
Ask among the nations:
 Who has heard the like of this?
The virgin Israel has done
 a most horrible thing.
14 Does the snow of Lebanon leave
 the crags of Sirion?[m]
Do the mountain[n] waters run dry,[o]
 the cold flowing streams?
15 But my people have forgotten me,
 they burn offerings to a delusion;
they have stumbled[p] in their ways,
 in the ancient roads,
and have gone into bypaths,
 not the highway,
16 making their land a horror,
 a thing to be hissed at forever.
All who pass by it are horrified
 and shake their heads.
17 Like the wind from the east,
 I will scatter them before the enemy.
I will show them my back, not my face,
 in the day of their calamity.

A Plot against Jeremiah

18 Then they said, "Come, let us make plots against Jeremiah—for instruction shall not perish from the priest, nor counsel from the wise, nor the word from the prophet. Come, let us bring charges against him,[q] and let us not heed any of his words."

19 Give heed to me, O LORD,
 and listen to what my adversaries say!
20 Is evil a recompense for good?
 Yet they have dug a pit for my life.
Remember how I stood before you
 to speak good for them,
 to turn away your wrath from them.
21 Therefore give their children over to
 famine;
 hurl them out to the power of the
 sword,
let their wives become childless and
 widowed.
 May their men meet death by
 pestilence,
 their youths be slain by the sword in
 battle.
22 May a cry be heard from their houses,
 when you bring the marauder
 suddenly upon them!
For they have dug a pit to catch me,
 and laid snares for my feet.
23 Yet you, O LORD, know
 all their plotting to kill me.
Do not forgive their iniquity,
 do not blot out their sin from your
 sight.
Let them be tripped up before you;
 deal with them while you are angry.

The Broken Earthenware Jug

19 Thus said the LORD: Go and buy a
potter's earthenware jug. Take with
you[r] some of the elders of the people and
some of the senior priests, 2 and go out to
the valley of the son of Hinnom at the entry
of the Potsherd Gate, and proclaim there
the words that I tell you. 3 You shall say:
Hear the word of the LORD, O kings of Judah
and inhabitants of Jerusalem. Thus says the
LORD of hosts, the God of Israel: I am going
to bring such disaster upon this place that
the ears of everyone who hears of it will
tingle. 4 Because the people have forsaken
me, and have profaned this place by making
offerings in it to other gods whom neither
they nor their ancestors nor the kings of
Judah have known; and because they have
filled this place with the blood of the inno-

[m] Cn: Heb *of the field* [n] Cn: Heb *foreign* [o] Cn: Heb *Are ... plucked up?* [p] Gk Syr Vg: Heb *they made them stumble* [q] Heb *strike him with the tongue* [r] Syr Tg Compare Gk: Heb lacks *take with you*

18.12-17 Determined to follow their *own plans* rather than to seek and fulfill God's will, the people have *forgotten* their source in God's purpose, and have accordingly become a ruin and a disgrace. *Sirion* was a name used by the people of Sidon and vicinity for Mt. Hermon (Deut 3.9; 4.48).
18.18-23 A Prayer of Jeremiah. The *plots against Jeremiah* were instigated by the religious leaders who thought that they alone had a right to speak for God: *priests, the wise, prophets.* Jeremiah's prayer calls for God's retaliation against them in the form of childlessness, *famine, pestilence,* robbery, and death in battle.
19.1-15 Jeremiah's Symbolic Act Portraying Judah's Destruction. After announcing to the leaders of the people (*elders, senior priests*) the doom that is to fall on *Judah and Jerusalem* for the murder, idolatry, and child-sacrifice they have committed, Jeremiah is to tell them as they gather in the valley where idolatrous practices were commonly performed (*Topheth,* or *Hinnom*) that death will overtake the city. The symbolic breaking of the jar announces the impending destruction of the idolatrous city, where roof-tops have been converted into high places to worship *the host of heaven*: the mass of invisible spirits that the local religions believed must be appeased and honored for human safety.

18.8 Ezek 18.21; Jer 26.3; Jon 3.10
18.9 Jer 1.10; 31.28
18.10 Jer 7.24-28; Ezek 33.18
18.11 Jer 4.6; 2 Kings 17.13; Isa 1.16-19; Acts 26.20
18.12 Jer 2.25; 7.24; 16.12
18.13 Jer 2.10,11; 14.17; 5.30; 23.14
18.15 Isa 65.7; Jer 7.9; 6.16; Isa 57.14; 62.10
18.16 Jer 25.9; 50.13; 48.27
18.17 Job 27.21; Jer 13.24; 2.27; 46.21
18.18 Jer 11.19; Mal 2.7; Jer 8.8; 5.13; 20.10; 43.2
18.20 Ps 35.7; 57.6; 106.23
18.21 Ps 109.9,10; Isa 13.18; Jer 15.8; Ezek 22.25; Jer 9.21; 11.22
18.22 Jer 6.26; Ps 140.5
18.23 Ps 109.14; Isa 2.9; Jer 6.15,21; 7.20
19.2 Josh 15.8; Jer 7.31
19.3 Jer 17.20; 1 Sam 3.11; 4.18
19.4 Deut 28.20; Isa 65.11; 2 Kings 21.16; Jer 2.34

20.1-6 A Leading Priest Persecutes Jeremiah. After being struck by Pashhur, the chief priest, Jeremiah was put *in stocks* overnight in one of the temple gates. The name Pashhur probably means "to go about quietly"; the prophet's new name for him sounds somewhat similar, *Magor*, with the added term, *missabib*, which together mean *Terror-all-around*. There follows a recital of sad events: the fall of the city, the plundering of its wealth, and the exile of its populace.
20.7-18 A Prayer of Jeremiah. Describing his role as having been *enticed* by the LORD to announce the doom of his people, the prophet describes his own inner compulsion (*like a burning fire*) to proclaim his message, and how he expects to be vindicated by the calamitous events which will befall Judah. Even so, he laments his birth into a life of *toil and sorrow* in fulfilling his tragic role as prophet of God's judgment.

cent, [5]and gone on building the high places
of Baal to burn their children in the fire as
burnt offerings to Baal, which I did not
command or decree, nor did it enter my
mind. [6]Therefore the days are surely coming, says the LORD, when this place shall no
more be called Topheth, or the valley of the
son of Hinnom, but the valley of Slaughter.
[7]And in this place I will make void the plans
of Judah and Jerusalem, and will make
them fall by the sword before their enemies,
and by the hand of those who seek their life.
I will give their dead bodies for food to the
birds of the air and to the wild animals of
the earth. [8]And I will make this city a
horror, a thing to be hissed at; everyone
who passes by it will be horrified and will
hiss because of all its disasters. [9]And I will
make them eat the flesh of their sons and
the flesh of their daughters, and all shall eat
the flesh of their neighbors in the siege, and
in the distress with which their enemies and
those who seek their life afflict them.

10 Then you shall break the jug in the
sight of those who go with you, [11]and shall
say to them: Thus says the LORD of hosts:
So will I break this people and this city, as
one breaks a potter's vessel, so that it can
never be mended. In Topheth they shall
bury until there is no more room to bury.
[12]Thus will I do to this place, says the LORD,
and to its inhabitants, making this city like
Topheth. [13]And the houses of Jerusalem and
the houses of the kings of Judah shall be
defiled like the place of Topheth—all the
houses upon whose roofs offerings have
been made to the whole host of heaven, and
libations have been poured out to other
gods.

14 When Jeremiah came from Topheth,
where the LORD had sent him to prophesy,
he stood in the court of the LORD's house
and said to all the people: [15]Thus says the
LORD of hosts, the God of Israel: I am now
bringing upon this city and upon all its
towns all the disaster that I have pronounced
against it, because they have stiffened their
necks, refusing to hear my words.

Jeremiah Persecuted by Pashhur

20 Now the priest Pashhur son of
Immer, who was chief officer in
the house of the LORD, heard Jeremiah prophesying these things. [2]Then Pashhur struck
the prophet Jeremiah, and put him in the
stocks that were in the upper Benjamin
Gate of the house of the LORD. [3]The next
morning when Pashhur released Jeremiah
from the stocks, Jeremiah said to him, The
LORD has named you not Pashhur but "Terror-all-around." [4]For thus says the LORD: I
am making you a terror to yourself and to
all your friends; and they shall fall by the
sword of their enemies while you look on.
And I will give all Judah into the hand of
the king of Babylon; he shall carry them
captive to Babylon, and shall kill them with
the sword. [5]I will give all the wealth of this
city, all its gains, all its prized belongings,
and all the treasures of the kings of Judah
into the hand of their enemies, who shall
plunder them, and seize them, and carry
them to Babylon. [6]And you, Pashhur, and
all who live in your house, shall go into
captivity, and to Babylon you shall go; there
you shall die, and there you shall be buried,
you and all your friends, to whom you have
prophesied falsely.

Jeremiah Denounces His Persecutors

7 O LORD, you have enticed me,
and I was enticed;
you have overpowered me,
and you have prevailed.
I have become a laughingstock all day
long;
everyone mocks me.
8 For whenever I speak, I must cry out,
I must shout, "Violence and
destruction!"
For the word of the LORD has become for
me
a reproach and derision all day long.
9 If I say, "I will not mention him,
or speak any more in his name,"
then within me there is something like a
burning fire
shut up in my bones;
I am weary with holding it in,
and I cannot.
10 For I hear many whispering:
"Terror is all around!
Denounce him! Let us denounce him!"
All my close friends
are watching for me to stumble.
"Perhaps he can be enticed,
and we can prevail against him,
and take our revenge on him."
11 But the LORD is with me like a dread
warrior;
therefore my persecutors will stumble,
and they will not prevail.

19.5 Jer 32.35; 2 Kings 17.17; Lev 18.21
19.6 Jer 7.32; Josh 15.8
19.7 Jer 15.2,9; Ps 79.2; Jer 16.4
19.8 Jer 18.16; 49.13; 1 Kings 9.8; 2 Chr 7.21
19.9 Deut 28.53,55; Isa 9.20; Lam 4.10
19.11 Ps 2.9; Isa 30.14; Rev 2.27; Jer 7.32
19.13 Jer 52.13; 7.18; Ezek 20.28; Acts 7.42
19.14 Jer 26.2
19.15 Jer 7.26; 17.23; Ps 58.4
20.1 1 Chr 24.14; 2 Kings 25.18
20.2 Jer 1.19; Job 13.27; Jer 37.13; 38.7
20.4 Job 18.11-21; Jer 29.21; 21.4-10; 52.27
20.5 Jer 15.13; 17.3; 2 Kings 20.17; 2 Chr 36.10; Jer 3.24
20.6 ver 1; Jer 28.15-17; 14.13-15; 29.21
20.7 Jer 1.6-8; Mic 3.8; Jer 38.19
20.8 Jer 6.7,10; 2 Chr 36.16
20.9 1 Kings 19.3,4; Ps 39.3; Job 32.18-20; Acts 4.20
20.10 Ps 31.13; Ps 41.9; Lk 11.53,54
20.11 Jer 1.8,19; 15.20; 17.18; 23.40

20.12 Jer 11.20; 17.10; Ps 54.7; 59.10
20.13 Jer 31.7; Ps 35.9,10; Jer 15.21
20.14 Job 3.3; Jer 15.10
20.15 Gen 21.6,7
20.16 Gen 19.25; Jer 18.22
20.17 Job 3.10,11; 10.18,19
20.18 Job 3.20; Ps 90.9; Jer 3.25
21.1 2 Kings 24.17,18; Jer 38.1; 2 Kings 25.18; Jer 29.25; 37.3
21.2 Jer 37.3,7
21.4 Zech 14.2
21.5 Isa 63.10; Jer 32.37
21.7 Jer 37.17; 39.5; 52.9; 13.14
21.8 Deut 30.15,19
21.9 Jer 38.2,17,18; 14.12; 39.18; 45.5
21.10 Jer 44.11,27; 39.16; 32.28,29; 38.18,23; 52.13
21.11 Jer 13.18; 17.20
21.12 Isa 7.2,13; Jer 22.3; Zech 7.9; Jer 7.20
21.13 Ezek 13.8; Jer 49.4
21.14 Isa 3.10,11; Ezek 20.46,48; 2 Chr 36.19; Jer 52.13

They will be greatly shamed,
for they will not succeed.
Their eternal dishonor
will never be forgotten.
12 O LORD of hosts, you test the righteous,
you see the heart and the mind;
let me see your retribution upon them,
for to you I have committed my cause.

13 Sing to the LORD;
praise the LORD!
For he has delivered the life of the needy
from the hands of evildoers.

14 Cursed be the day
on which I was born!
The day when my mother bore me,
let it not be blessed!
15 Cursed be the man
who brought the news to my father,
saying,
"A child is born to you, a son,"
making him very glad.
16 Let that man be like the cities
that the LORD overthrew without pity;
let him hear a cry in the morning
and an alarm at noon,
17 because he did not kill me in the womb;
so my mother would have been my
grave,
and her womb forever great.
18 Why did I come forth from the womb
to see toil and sorrow,
and spend my days in shame?

Jerusalem Will Fall to Nebuchadrezzar

21 This is the word that came to
Jeremiah from the LORD, when King
Zedekiah sent to him Pashhur son of
Malchiah and the priest Zephaniah son of
Maaseiah, saying, 2"Please inquire of the
LORD on our behalf, for King Nebuchadrezzar
of Babylon is making war against us; perhaps the LORD will perform a wonderful deed
for us, as he has often done, and will make
him withdraw from us."
3 Then Jeremiah said to them: 4Thus you
shall say to Zedekiah: Thus says the LORD,
the God of Israel: I am going to turn back
the weapons of war that are in your hands
and with which you are fighting against the
king of Babylon and against the Chaldeans
who are besieging you outside the walls;
and I will bring them together into the
center of this city. 5I myself will fight against
you with outstretched hand and mighty
arm, in anger, in fury, and in great wrath.
6And I will strike down the inhabitants of
this city, both human beings and animals;
they shall die of a great pestilence. 7After-
ward, says the LORD, I will give King Zedekiah
of Judah, and his servants, and the people
in this city—those who survive the pestilence, sword, and famine—into the hands
of King Nebuchadrezzar of Babylon, into the
hands of their enemies, into the hands of
those who seek their lives. He shall strike
them down with the edge of the sword; he
shall not pity them, or spare them, or have
compassion.
8 And to this people you shall say: Thus
says the LORD: See, I am setting before you
the way of life and the way of death. 9Those
who stay in this city shall die by the sword,
by famine, and by pestilence; but those who
go out and surrender to the Chaldeans who
are besieging you shall live and shall have
their lives as a prize of war. 10For I have set
my face against this city for evil and not for
good, says the LORD: it shall be given into
the hands of the king of Babylon, and he
shall burn it with fire.

Message to the House of David

11 To the house of the king of Judah say:
Hear the word of the LORD, 12O house of
David! Thus says the LORD:
Execute justice in the morning,
and deliver from the hand of the
oppressor
anyone who has been robbed,
or else my wrath will go forth like fire,
and burn, with no one to quench it,
because of your evil doings.

13 See, I am against you, O inhabitant of
the valley,
O rock of the plain,
says the LORD;
you who say, "Who can come down
against us,
or who can enter our places of
refuge?"
14 I will punish you according to the fruit
of your doings,
says the LORD;
I will kindle a fire in its forest,
and it shall devour all that is around it.

21.1-22.30 Messages of Divine Judgment for the House of Judah. **21.1-14** Responding to a request from *King Zedekiah* (597-586) for a favorable word from the LORD about the outcome of the attack on Judah by *Nebuchadrezzar of Babylon* in 597, Jeremiah announces the certain defeat of Judah, since the LORD will *fight against* his people. The king and the majority of the people will be taken into exile. Those remaining will be beset by *pestilence, sword, and famine.* The only positive alternative for the people is to surrender to the Chaldeans. The royal family is to *execute justice,* but the *fire* of God's justice will consume Judah in any case.

22.1-9 This note of hope for survival of the Davidic dynasty may represent an earlier period in Jeremiah's career – perhaps at the time of Josiah's reform of Judah (626-609; 2 Kings 22-23). Yet the solemn warning is sounded of punishment which will follow failure to fulfill *the covenant.*
22.10-12 More lamentable than the death of their king, Josiah, in 609 will be the exile of the people of Judah, including Josiah's son, *Shallum,* also known as Jehoahaz, who reigned for only three months and was a captive of the Egyptians (2 Kings 23.31-34).
22.11-23 Both these oracles are addressed to *Jehoiakim* (609-598), although only before the second is that explicit (22.18). Installed as king by Pharaoh Necho of Egypt (2 Kings 23.34-37), Jehoiakim devoted his time and wealth to erecting a splendid royal palace, ignoring the perilous condition of the nation and the people (*cf.* 2 Kings 24.1-6). There is in 2 Kings 24 no report of the expulsion of his corpse from the city as refuse. The richness of the palace was symbolized by the *cedars from Lebanon* of which he built it, while ignoring the impending *pain* of divine judgment.

Exhortation to Repent

22 Thus says the LORD: Go down to
the house of the king of Judah,
and speak there this word, [2]and say: Hear
the word of the LORD, O King of Judah sitting
on the throne of David—you, and your
servants, and your people who enter these
gates. [3]Thus says the LORD: Act with justice
and righteousness, and deliver from the
hand of the oppressor anyone who has been
robbed. And do no wrong or violence to the
alien, the orphan, and the widow, or shed
innocent blood in this place. [4]For if you will
indeed obey this word, then through the
gates of this house shall enter kings who sit
on the throne of David, riding in chariots
and on horses, they, and their servants, and
their people. [5]But if you will not heed these
words, I swear by myself, says the LORD,
that this house shall become a desolation.
[6]For thus says the LORD concerning the
house of the king of Judah:

You are like Gilead to me,
like the summit of Lebanon;
but I swear that I will make you a desert,
an uninhabited city.[s]

7 I will prepare destroyers against you,
all with their weapons;
they shall cut down your choicest cedars
and cast them into the fire.

8 And many nations will pass by this
city, and all of them will say one to another,
"Why has the LORD dealt in this way with
that great city?" [9]And they will answer,
"Because they abandoned the covenant of
the LORD their God, and worshiped other
gods and served them."

10 Do not weep for him who is dead,
nor bemoan him;
weep rather for him who goes away,
for he shall return no more
to see his native land.

Message to the Sons of Josiah

11 For thus says the LORD concerning
Shallum son of King Josiah of Judah, who
succeeded his father Josiah, and who went
away from this place: He shall return here
no more, [12]but in the place where they have
carried him captive he shall die, and he
shall never see this land again.

13 Woe to him who builds his house by unrighteousness,
and his upper rooms by injustice;
who makes his neighbors work for nothing,
and does not give them their wages;

14 who says, "I will build myself a spacious house
with large upper rooms,"
and who cuts out windows for it,
paneling it with cedar,
and painting it with vermilion.

15 Are you a king
because you compete in cedar?
Did not your father eat and drink
and do justice and righteousness?
Then it was well with him.

16 He judged the cause of the poor and needy;
then it was well.
Is not this to know me?
says the LORD.

17 But your eyes and heart
are only on your dishonest gain,
for shedding innocent blood,
and for practicing oppression and violence.

18 Therefore thus says the LORD concerning King Jehoiakim son of Josiah of Judah:

They shall not lament for him, saying,
"Alas, my brother!" or "Alas, sister!"
They shall not lament for him, saying,
"Alas, lord!" or "Alas, his majesty!"

19 With the burial of a donkey he shall be buried—
dragged off and thrown out beyond
the gates of Jerusalem.

20 Go up to Lebanon, and cry out,
and lift up your voice in Bashan;
cry out from Abarim,
for all your lovers are crushed.

21 I spoke to you in your prosperity,
but you said, "I will not listen."
This has been your way from your youth,
for you have not obeyed my voice.

22 The wind shall shepherd all your shepherds,
and your lovers shall go into captivity;
then you will be ashamed and dismayed
because of all your wickedness.

23 O inhabitant of Lebanon,
nested among the cedars,
how you will groan[t] when pangs come upon you,
pain as of a woman in labor!

[s] Cn: Heb *uninhabited cities* [t] Gk Vg Syr: Heb *will be pitied*

22.1 Jer 21.11; 2 Chr 25.15,16
22.2 Jer 19.3; 29.20
22.3 Jer 21.12; Ps 72.4; Ex 22.21-24
22.5 Jer 17.27; 26.4; Heb 6.13; Jer 7.14; 26.6,9
22.6 Jer 7.34
22.7 Isa 10.3-6; Jer 4.6,7; Isa 10.33,34
22.8 Deut 29.24,25; 1 Kings 9.8,9; Jer 16.10
22.9 2 Kings 22.17; 2 Chr 34.25
22.10 2 Kings 22.20; ver 18; Jer 16.7; 44.14
22.13 Mic 3.10; Hab 2.9; Jas 5.4
22.14 Isa 5.8,9; Sam 7.2
22.15 2 Kings 23.25; Jer 7.5; 42.6
22.16 Ps 72.1-4,12,13; 1 Chr 28.9; Jer 9.24
22.17 Jer 6.13; 8.10; Jer 6.6
22.18 1 Kings 13.30; Jer 34.5
22.19 Jer 36.30
22.20 Deut 32.49; Jer 2.25; 3.1
22.21 Jer 13.10; 19.15; 3.24,25; 32.30
22.22 Jer 5.13; 30.14; Isa 65.13; Jer 20.11

Judgment on Coniah (Jehoiachin)

24 As I live, says the LORD, even if King
Coniah son of Jehoiakim of Judah were the
signet ring on my right hand, even from
there I would tear you off 25 and give you
into the hands of those who seek your life,
into the hands of those of whom you are
afraid, even into the hands of King
Nebuchadrezzar of Babylon and into the
hands of the Chaldeans. 26 I will hurl you
and the mother who bore you into another
country, where you were not born, and
there you shall die. 27 But they shall not
return to the land to which they long to
return.

28 Is this man Coniah a despised broken pot,
  a vessel no one wants?
Why are he and his offspring hurled out
  and cast away in a land that they do not know?
29 O land, land, land,
  hear the word of the LORD!
30 Thus says the LORD:
Record this man as childless,
  a man who shall not succeed in his days;
for none of his offspring shall succeed
  in sitting on the throne of David,
  and ruling again in Judah.

Restoration after Exile

23 Woe to the shepherds who destroy
and scatter the sheep of my pas-
ture! says the LORD. 2 Therefore thus says the
LORD, the God of Israel, concerning the
shepherds who shepherd my people: It is
you who have scattered my flock, and have
driven them away, and you have not attended to them. So I will attend to you for
your evil doings, says the LORD. 3 Then I
myself will gather the remnant of my flock
out of all the lands where I have driven
them, and I will bring them back to their
fold, and they shall be fruitful and multiply.
4 I will raise up shepherds over them who
will shepherd them, and they shall not fear
any longer, or be dismayed, nor shall any
be missing, says the LORD.

The Righteous Branch of David

5 The days are surely coming, says the
LORD, when I will raise up for David a
righteous Branch, and he shall reign as
king and deal wisely, and shall execute
justice and righteousness in the land. 6 In his
days Judah will be saved and Israel will live
in safety. And this is the name by which he
will be called: "The LORD is our righteousness."
7 Therefore, the days are surely coming,
says the LORD, when it shall no longer be
said, "As the LORD lives who brought the
people of Israel up out of the land of Egypt,"
8 but "As the LORD lives who brought out
and led the offspring of the house of Israel
out of the land of the north and out of all
the lands where he[u] had driven them."
Then they shall live in their own land.

False Prophets of Hope Denounced

9 Concerning the prophets:
My heart is crushed within me,
  all my bones shake;
I have become like a drunkard,
  like one overcome by wine,
because of the LORD
  and because of his holy words.
10 For the land is full of adulterers;
  because of the curse the land mourns,
  and the pastures of the wilderness are dried up.
Their course has been evil,
  and their might is not right.
11 Both prophet and priest are ungodly;
  even in my house I have found their wickedness,
    says the LORD.
12 Therefore their way shall be to them
  like slippery paths in the darkness,
  into which they shall be driven and fall;
for I will bring disaster upon them
  in the year of their punishment,
    says the LORD.
13 In the prophets of Samaria
  I saw a disgusting thing:
they prophesied by Baal
  and led my people Israel astray.
14 But in the prophets of Jerusalem
  I have seen a more shocking thing:
they commit adultery and walk in lies;
  they strengthen the hands of evildoers,
  so that no one turns from wickedness;
all of them have become like Sodom to me,
  and its inhabitants like Gomorrah.
15 Therefore thus says the LORD of hosts
  concerning the prophets:

[u] Gk: Heb *I*

22.24 Jer 37.1; Song 8.6; Hag 2.23
22.25 2 Kings 24.15,16; Jer 34.20
22.26 2 Kings 24.15; 2 Chr 36.10; 2 Kings 24.8
22.29 Deut 32.1; Jer 6.19; Mic 1.2
22.30 1 Chr 3.16,17; Mt 1.12
23.1 Ezek 13.3; Jer 10.21; 50.6; Ezek 34.31
23.3 Isa 11.11-16; Jer 32.37; Ezek 34.13-16
23.4 Jer 3.15; Ezek 34.23; Jer 30.10; Jn 6.39; 10.28
23.5 Isa 4.2; 11.1; 53.2; Jer 33.14-16; Zech 3.8; 6.12; Isa 9.7; Lk 1.32,33
23.6 Deut 33.28; Zech 14.11; Isa 7.14; 9.6; Mt 1.21-23; Jer 33.16; Rom 3.22; 1 Cor 1.30
23.7 Isa 43.18,19; Jer 16.14,15
23.9 Hab 3.16; Jer 20.8,9
23.10 Jer 5.7,8; Hos 4.2,3; Jer 9.10; 12.4
23.11 Jer 6.13; 8.10; 7.9,10; 32.34
23.12 Ps 35.6; Jn 12.35; Jer 11.23
23.13 Hos 9.7,8; Jer 2.8
23.14 Jer 5.30; 29.23; Ezek 13.22; Isa 1.9,10; Jer 20.16
23.15 Jer 8.14; 9.15

22.24-30 *Coniah* (or Jehoiachin) also reigned but three months (598) before he was taken to Egypt as a captive. This oracle declares that none of Coniah's descendants through the authentic royal line will sit on *the throne of David.*
23.1-40 True and False Prophets concerning Israel's Future. Some scholars date these oracles late in the career of Jeremiah, while others think they come from a still later time, when Israel returned from exile in Babylon (after 521). Details of Jeremiah's encounters with the official court prophets are given in Jer 27-28.
23.1-4 Indicting the faithless leaders of Israel as those who *scattered [God's] flock* (13.15-17), the prophet foretells the coming of faithful shepherds who will renew and restore God's people.
23.5-8 The re-establishment of the Davidic rulers will result in reigns far different from those of the recent occupants of the throne: these will be characterized by *justice and righteousness.* In a play on the name of the king imposed on Judah by Babylon and renamed Zedekiah [*tzedekiyah*] (2 Kings 24.17-20), the true future king will be *Yahweh tzidkenu,* "the LORD is our righteousness."
23.9-15 Jeremiah is disheartened by the activities of the local prophets, who are worse than those earlier in the northern kingdom (*Samaria*), who relied on Baal for their oracles. The prophets in Judah break the law of God and support *evildoers among the leaders of the nation.* All these false prophets are doomed to destruction for fostering such *ungodliness.*

23.16-17 These false prophets delude the people by their false messages of hope.
23.18-32 The LORD is against these falsely optimistic, lying prophets.
23.33-40 The Hebrew word *massa* can mean *oracle* or *burden*. What should have been an oracle from the LORD calling for repentance and renewal from his true prophet has been perverted into burdens which require God's judgment on his people for their weighty disobedience.
24.1-10 The Parable of the Good and the Bad Figs. This depicts the first phase of the exile of Judah to Babylon in 597, which involved *King Jeconiah, officials, artisans and smiths* – all of them important for the political and economic stability of Judah.

"I am going to make them eat
wormwood,
and give them poisoned water to
drink;
for from the prophets of Jerusalem
ungodliness has spread throughout
the land."

16 Thus says the LORD of hosts: Do not
listen to the words of the prophets who
prophesy to you; they are deluding you.
They speak visions of their own minds, not
from the mouth of the LORD. 17They keep
saying to those who despise the word of the
LORD, "It shall be well with you"; and to all
who stubbornly follow their own stubborn
hearts, they say, "No calamity shall come
upon you."

18 For who has stood in the council of the
LORD
so as to see and to hear his word?
Who has given heed to his word so as
to proclaim it?
19 Look, the storm of the LORD!
Wrath has gone forth,
a whirling tempest;
it will burst upon the head of the
wicked.
20 The anger of the LORD will not turn back
until he has executed and
accomplished
the intents of his mind.
In the latter days you will understand it
clearly.

21 I did not send the prophets,
yet they ran;
I did not speak to them,
yet they prophesied.
22 But if they had stood in my council,
then they would have proclaimed my
words to my people,
and they would have turned them from
their evil way,
and from the evil of their doings.

23 Am I a God near by, says the LORD,
and not a God far off? 24Who can hide in
secret places so that I cannot see them? says
the LORD. Do I not fill heaven and earth?
says the LORD. 25I have heard what the
prophets have said who prophesy lies in my
name, saying, "I have dreamed, I have
dreamed!" 26How long? Will the hearts of
the prophets ever turn back—those who
prophesy lies, and who prophesy the deceit
of their own heart? 27They plan to make my
people forget my name by their dreams that
they tell one another, just as their ancestors
forgot my name for Baal. 28Let the prophet
who has a dream tell the dream, but let the
one who has my word speak my word
faithfully. What has straw in common with
wheat? says the LORD. 29Is not my word like
fire, says the LORD, and like a hammer that
breaks a rock in pieces? 30See, therefore, I
am against the prophets, says the LORD, who
steal my words from one another. 31See, I
am against the prophets, says the LORD, who
use their own tongues and say, "Says the
LORD." 32See, I am against those who prophesy lying dreams, says the LORD, and who
tell them, and who lead my people astray
by their lies and their recklessness, when I
did not send them or appoint them; so they
do not profit this people at all, says the LORD.
33 When this people, or a prophet, or a
priest asks you, "What is the burden of the
LORD?" you shall say to them, "You are the
burden,[v] and I will cast you off, says the
LORD." 34And as for the prophet, priest, or
the people who say, "The burden of the
LORD," I will punish them and their households. 35Thus shall you say to one another,
among yourselves, "What has the LORD
answered?" or "What has the LORD spoken?"
36But "the burden of the Lord" you shall
mention no more, for the burden is everyone's own word, and so you pervert the
words of the living God, the LORD of hosts,
our God. 37Thus you shall ask the prophet,
"What has the LORD answered you?" or
"What has the LORD spoken?" 38But if you
say, "the burden of the LORD," thus says the
LORD: Because you have said these words,
"the burden of the LORD," when I sent to
you, saying, You shall not say, "the burden
of the LORD," 39therefore, I will surely lift you
up[w] and cast you away from my presence,
you and the city that I gave to you and
your ancestors. 40And I will bring upon you
everlasting disgrace and perpetual shame,
which shall not be forgotten.

The Good and the Bad Figs

24 The LORD showed me two baskets
of figs placed before the temple of
the LORD. This was after King Nebuchadrezzar
of Babylon had taken into exile from Jerusalem King Jeconiah son of Jehoiakim of

[v] Gk Vg: Heb *What burden* [w] Heb Mss Gk Vg: MT *forget you*

23.16 Jer 27.9,10,14; Mt 7.15; Jer 14.14; Jer 9.20
23.17 Jer 8.11; 13.10; 18.12; 5.12; Mic 3.11
23.18 Job 15.8; 33.31
23.19 Jer 25.32; 30.23
23.20 Jer 30.24; Gen 49.1
23.21 Jer 14.14; 27.15; 29.9
23.22 Jer 9.12; 35.15; 1 Thess 1.9,10
23.23 Ps 139.1-10; Jer 50.51
23.24 Ps 139.7-12; Isa 29.15; Am 9.2; 1 Kings 8.27
23.25 Jer 8.6; 14.14; 29.8
23.27 Judg 3.7; 8.33,34
23.28 Jer 9.12,20
23.29 Jer 5.14; 20.9; 2 Cor 10.4,5
23.30 Ezek 13.8
23.33 Isa 13.1; Hab 1.1; Mal 1.1; ver 39
23.34 Lam 2.14; Zech 13.3
23.35 Jer 33.3; 42.4
23.36 Jer 10.10
23.39 Jer 7.14,15; Ezek 8.18
23.40 Jer 20.11

24.1 Am 8.1; 2 Kings 24.10-16; 2 Chr 36.10; Jer 22.24; 29.2

Judah, together with the officials of Judah, the artisans, and the smiths, and had brought them to Babylon. 2One basket had very good figs, like first-ripe figs, but the other basket had very bad figs, so bad that they could not be eaten. 3And the LORD said to me, "What do you see, Jeremiah?" I said, "Figs, the good figs very good, and the bad figs very bad, so bad that they cannot be eaten."

4 Then the word of the LORD came to me: 5Thus says the LORD, the God of Israel: Like these good figs, so I will regard as good the exiles from Judah, whom I have sent away from this place to the land of the Chaldeans. 6I will set my eyes upon them for good, and I will bring them back to this land. I will build them up, and not tear them down; I will plant them, and not pluck them up. 7I will give them a heart to know that I am the LORD; and they shall be my people and I will be their God, for they shall return to me with their whole heart.

8 But thus says the LORD: Like the bad figs that are so bad they cannot be eaten, so will I treat King Zedekiah of Judah, his officials, the remnant of Jerusalem who remain in this land, and those who live in the land of Egypt. 9I will make them a horror, an evil thing, to all the kingdoms of the earth—a disgrace, a byword, a taunt, and a curse in all the places where I shall drive them. 10And I will send sword, famine, and pestilence upon them, until they are utterly destroyed from the land that I gave to them and their ancestors.

The Babylonian Captivity Foretold

25 The word that came to Jeremiah concerning all the people of Judah, in the fourth year of King Jehoiakim son of Josiah of Judah (that was the first year of King Nebuchadrezzar of Babylon), 2which the prophet Jeremiah spoke to all the people of Judah and all the inhabitants of Jerusalem: 3For twenty-three years, from the thirteenth year of King Josiah son of Amon of Judah, to this day, the word of the LORD has come to me, and I have spoken persistently to you, but you have not listened. 4And though the LORD persistently sent you all his servants the prophets, you have neither listened nor inclined your ears to hear 5when they said, "Turn now, everyone of you, from your evil way and wicked doings, and you will remain upon the land that the LORD has given to you and your ancestors from of old and forever; 6do not go after other gods to serve and worship them, and do not provoke me to anger with the work of your hands. Then I will do you no harm." 7Yet you did not listen to me, says the LORD, and so you have provoked me to anger with the work of your hands to your own harm.

8 Therefore thus says the LORD of hosts: Because you have not obeyed my words, 9I am going to send for all the tribes of the north, says the LORD, even for King Nebuchadrezzar of Babylon, my servant, and I will bring them against this land and its inhabitants, and against all these nations around; I will utterly destroy them, and make them an object of horror and of hissing, and an everlasting disgrace.[x] 10And I will banish from them the sound of mirth and the sound of gladness, the voice of the bridegroom and the voice of the bride, the sound of the millstones and the light of the lamp. 11This whole land shall become a ruin and a waste, and these nations shall serve the king of Babylon seventy years. 12Then after seventy years are completed, I will punish the king of Babylon and that nation, the land of the Chaldeans, for their iniquity, says the LORD, making the land an everlasting waste. 13I will bring upon that land all the words that I have uttered against it, everything written in this book, which Jeremiah prophesied against all the nations. 14For many nations and great kings shall make slaves of them also; and I will repay them according to their deeds and the work of their hands.

The Cup of God's Wrath

15 For thus the LORD, the God of Israel, said to me: Take from my hand this cup of the wine of wrath, and make all the nations to whom I send you drink it. 16They shall drink and stagger and go out of their minds because of the sword that I am sending among them.

17 So I took the cup from the LORD's hand, and made all the nations to whom the LORD sent me drink it: 18Jerusalem and the towns of Judah, its kings and officials, to make them a desolation and a waste, an object of hissing and of cursing, as they are today; 19Pharaoh king of Egypt, his servants, his officials, and all his people; 20all the

[x] Gk Compare Syr: Heb *and everlasting desolations*

24.2 Nah 3.12; Jer 27.19
24.3 Jer 1.11,13
24.6 Jer 29.10; Ezek 11.17; Jer 33.7; 42.10
24.7 Jer 31.33; 32.40; Zech 8.8; Heb 8.10; Jer 29.13
24.8 Jer 29.17; 39.5,9; 44.26-30
24.9 Jer 15.4; 29.18; 34.17; 1 Kings 9.7; Ps 44.13,14; Isa 65.15
24.10 Isa 51.19; Jer 21.9; 27.8
25.1 Jer 36.1; 2 Kings 24.1,2
25.3 Jer 1.2; 2 Chr 34.1-3,8; Jer 36.2; 7.13; 22.21
25.4 Jer 7.13,25; 26.5
25.5 Isa 55.6,7; Jer 4.1; Jer 7.7
25.7 Deut 32.21; 2 Kings 17.17; 21.15; Jer 7.19
25.9 Jer 1.15; 27.6; 18.16
25.10 Isa 24.7; Ezek 26.13; Eccl 12.4; Isa 47.2
25.12 Ezra 1.1; Jer 29.10; Isa 13.14; 13.19; 14.23
25.14 Jer 50.9; 51.27,28; 50.41; 51.6,24
25.15 Ps 75.8; Isa 51.17
25.16 Jer 51.7; Nah 3.11
25.18 Isa 51.17; Jer 24.9; 44.22
25.20 Job 1.1; Jer 47.1-7; Isa 20.1

25.1-38 Oracles of Judgment on Judah and Jerusalem.
25.1-14 Dated from *the first year of King Nebuchadrezzar of Babylon*, which would be 605, Jeremiah's declaration is that *the word* has been coming to him *for twenty-three years* (since the thirteenth year of Josiah, in 628), but that the people have listened neither to him nor to the other *prophets* who have called them to *turn* from their evil ways. That change was an essential condition for their remaining in the land. So God will *send* for the Babylonians to destroy *the land and its inhabitants*, and the people will serve these invaders for *seventy years*. The deportation actually began in 597.
25.15-38 The disaster about to fall on Judah will also strike the nations adjacent to Judah (Egypt and the coastal cities from Gaza in the south to Tyre and Sidon in the north), as well as the realms of *Arabia* and the countries north and east of the Euphrates River (*Elam, Media*). If disaster is coming on the city called by [God's] name, how much more will it fall on these other nations that God has used to punish his disobedient people. The corpses of those who fall in this encompassing judgment will extend across the whole earth. The leaders (*shepherds)* of these doomed nations will not be able to escape. *Sheshach* is a cryptogram for Babel (= Babylon), as in Jer 51.41. Some scholars want to assign these oracles of doom on other nations to a later writer among Jeremiah's disciples, but the theme is in any case a natural development of this prophet's conviction that God uses evil instruments to achieve his purposes.

26.1-24 Jeremiah's Prophecy in the Temple. Jeremiah's warning that *this house* (the temple) will be destroyed as the sanctuary at Shiloh was (Josh 18.1; Jer 7.12-14) is based on the people's refusal to heed the voice of the prophet. In reaction, a coalition (*priests, prophets, people*) is determined to put him to death, but they reconsider when a council of leaders recalls that when Micah uttered a similar prophecy in the reign of Hezekiah (715-687), the decision was reached not to kill him. Not followed is the precedent of Jehoiakim (609-598) in murdering the prophet Uriah for his pronouncements of doom on city and land.

mixed people;[d] all the kings of the land of Uz; all the kings of the land of the Philistines—Ashkelon, Gaza, Ekron, and the remnant of Ashdod; [21]Edom, Moab, and the Ammonites; [22]all the kings of Tyre, all the kings of Sidon, and the kings of the coastland across the sea; [23]Dedan, Tema, Buz, and all who have shaven temples; [24]all the kings of Arabia and all the kings of the mixed peoples[e] that live in the desert; [25]all the kings of Zimri, all the kings of Elam, and all the kings of Media; [26]all the kings of the north, far and near, one after another, and all the kingdoms of the world that are on the face of the earth. And after them the king of Sheshach[f] shall drink.

27 Then you shall say to them, Thus says the LORD of hosts, the God of Israel: Drink, get drunk and vomit, fall and rise no more, because of the sword that I am sending among you.

28 And if they refuse to accept the cup from your hand to drink, then you shall say to them: Thus says the LORD of hosts: You must drink! [29]See, I am beginning to bring disaster on the city that is called by my name, and how can you possibly avoid punishment? You shall not go unpunished, for I am summoning a sword against all the inhabitants of the earth, says the LORD of hosts.

30 You, therefore, shall prophesy against them all these words, and say to them:

The LORD will roar from on high,
and from his holy habitation utter his voice;
he will roar mightily against his fold,
and shout, like those who tread grapes,
against all the inhabitants of the earth.
31 The clamor will resound to the ends of the earth,
for the LORD has an indictment against the nations;
he is entering into judgment with all flesh,
and the guilty he will put to the sword,
says the LORD.

32 Thus says the LORD of hosts:
See, disaster is spreading
from nation to nation,
and a great tempest is stirring
from the farthest parts of the earth!

33 Those slain by the LORD on that day shall extend from one end of the earth to the other. They shall not be lamented, or gathered, or buried; they shall become dung on the surface of the ground.

34 Wail, you shepherds, and cry out;
roll in ashes, you lords of the flock,
for the days of your slaughter have come—and your dispersions,[g]
and you shall fall like a choice vessel.
35 Flight shall fail the shepherds,
and there shall be no escape for the lords of the flock.
36 Hark! the cry of the shepherds,
and the wail of the lords of the flock!
For the LORD is despoiling their pasture,
37 and the peaceful folds are devastated,
because of the fierce anger of the LORD.
38 Like a lion he has left his covert;
for their land has become a waste
because of the cruel sword,
and because of his fierce anger.

Jeremiah's Prophecies in the Temple

26 At the beginning of the reign of King Jehoiakim son of Josiah of Judah, this word came from the LORD: [2]Thus says the LORD: Stand in the court of the LORD's house, and speak to all the cities of Judah that come to worship in the house of the LORD; speak to them all the words that I command you; do not hold back a word. [3]It may be that they will listen, all of them, and will turn from their evil way, that I may change my mind about the disaster that I intend to bring on them because of their evil doings. [4]You shall say to them: Thus says the LORD: If you will not listen to me, to walk in my law that I have set before you, [5]and to heed the words of my servants the prophets whom I send to you urgently—though you have not heeded— [6]then I will make this house like Shiloh, and I will make this city a curse for all the nations of the earth.

7 The priests and the prophets and all the people heard Jeremiah speaking these words in the house of the LORD. [8]And when Jeremiah had finished speaking all that the LORD had commanded him to speak to all the people, then the priests and the prophets and all the people laid hold of him, saying, "You shall die! [9]Why have you prophesied in the name of the LORD, saying,

[g] Meaning of Heb uncertain [f] *Sheshach* is a cryptogram for *Babel*, Babylon

25.21 Jer 49.1-22; 48.1-47

25.22 Jer 47.4; 49.23

25.23 Jer 49.7,8; Jer 9.26; 49.32

25.24 2 Chr 9.14

25.26 Jer 50.9

25.27 Hab 2.16; Ezek 21.4,5

25.29 Ezek 9.6; 1 Pet 4.17; 1 Kings 8.43; ver 31

25.30 Isa 42.13; Joel 3.16; Am 1.2; Isa 16.9

25.31 Hos 4.1; Mic 6.2; Joel 3.2

25.33 Isa 66.16; Ps 79.3; Jer 16.4; Isa 5.25

25.34 Jer 6.26; Ezek 27.30; Isa 34.7; Jer 50.27

26.1 2 Kings 23.36; 2 Chr 36.4,5; Jer 7.1,2

26.2 Jer 19.14; Lk 19.47,48; Jer 1.17; Acts 20.20,27; Deut 4.2

26.3 Jer 36.3-7; 18.8

26.4 Lev 26.14; Deut 28.15; Jer 17.27; 32.23; 44.10,23

26.5 2 Kings 9.7; Jer 25.3,4

26.6 1 Sam 4.10,11; Isa 65.15; Jer 24.9

26.8 Jer 20.1,2; 11.19; 18.23

26.9 Jer 9.11; 33.10

'This house shall be like Shiloh, and this
city shall be desolate, without inhabitant'?"
And all the people gathered around Jeremiah in the house of the LORD.
10 When the officials of Judah heard
these things, they came up from the king's
house to the house of the LORD and took
their seat in the entry of the New Gate of
the house of the LORD. 11 Then the priests
and the prophets said to the officials and to
all the people, "This man deserves the sentence of death because he has prophesied
against this city, as you have heard with
your own ears."
12 Then Jeremiah spoke to all the officials and all the people, saying, "It is the
LORD who sent me to prophesy against this
house and this city all the words you have
heard. 13 Now therefore amend your ways
and your doings, and obey the voice of the
LORD your God, and the LORD will change his
mind about the disaster that he has pronounced against you. 14 But as for me, here
I am in your hands. Do with me as seems
good and right to you. 15 Only know for
certain that if you put me to death, you will
be bringing innocent blood upon yourselves
and upon this city and its inhabitants, for
in truth the LORD sent me to you to speak
all these words in your ears."
16 Then the officials and all the people
said to the priests and the prophets, "This
man does not deserve the sentence of death,
for he has spoken to us in the name of the
LORD our God." 17 And some of the elders of
the land arose and said to all the assembled
people, 18 "Micah of Moresheth, who prophesied during the days of King Hezekiah of
Judah, said to all the people of Judah: 'Thus
says the LORD of hosts,

Zion shall be plowed as a field;
  Jerusalem shall become a heap of
    ruins,
  and the mountain of the house a
    wooded height.'

19 Did King Hezekiah of Judah and all Judah
actually put him to death? Did he not fear
the LORD and entreat the favor of the LORD,
and did not the LORD change his mind about
the disaster that he had pronounced against
them? But we are about to bring great
disaster on ourselves!"
20 There was another man prophesying
in the name of the LORD, Uriah son of
Shemaiah from Kiriath-jearim. He prophesied against this city and against this land
in words exactly like those of Jeremiah.
21 And when King Jehoiakim, with all his
warriors and all the officials, heard his words,
the king sought to put him to death; but
when Uriah heard of it, he was afraid and
fled and escaped to Egypt. 22 Then King
Jehoiakim sent[a] Elnathan son of Achbor
and men with him to Egypt, 23 and they took
Uriah from Egypt and brought him to King
Jehoiakim, who struck him down with the
sword and threw his dead body into the
burial place of the common people.
24 But the hand of Ahikam son of
Shaphan was with Jeremiah so that he was
not given over into the hands of the people
to be put to death.

The Sign of the Yoke

27 In the beginning of the reign of
King Zedekiah[b] son of Josiah of
Judah, this word came to Jeremiah from the
LORD. 2 Thus the LORD said to me: Make
yourself a yoke of straps and bars, and put
them on your neck. 3 Send word[c] to the king
of Edom, the king of Moab, the king of the
Ammonites, the king of Tyre, and the king
of Sidon by the hand of the envoys who
have come to Jerusalem to King Zedekiah
of Judah. 4 Give them this charge for their
masters: Thus says the LORD of hosts, the
God of Israel: This is what you shall say to
your masters: 5 It is I who by my great
power and my outstretched arm have made
the earth, with the people and animals that
are on the earth, and I give it to whomever
I please. 6 Now I have given all these lands
into the hand of King Nebuchadnezzar of
Babylon, my servant, and I have given him
even the wild animals of the field to serve
him. 7 All the nations shall serve him and
his son and his grandson, until the time of
his own land comes; then many nations
and great kings shall make him their slave.
8 But if any nation or kingdom will not
serve this king, Nebuchadnezzar of Babylon,
and put its neck under the yoke of the king
of Babylon, then I will punish that nation
with the sword, with famine, and with
pestilence, says the LORD, until I have completed its[d] destruction by his hand. 9 You,
therefore, must not listen to your prophets,
your diviners, your dreamers,[e] your soothsayers, or your sorcerers, who are saying to

[a] Heb adds *men to Egypt* [b] Another reading is *Jehoiakim* [c] Cn: Heb *send them* [d] Heb *their* [e] Gk Syr Vg: Heb *dreams*

26.10 Jer 36.10
26.11 Jer 18.23; Deut 18.20; Mt 26.66; Jer 38.4; Acts 6.11-14
26.12 Jer 1.17,18
26.13 Jer 7.3,5; 18.11; Joel 2.14; Jon 3.9; 4.2
26.15 Prov 6.16,17; Jer 7.6
26.18 Mic 1.1; Ps 79.1; Mic 3.12; Zech 8.3
26.19 2 Chr 29.6-11; 32.26; 2 Sam 24.16; Acts 5.39
26.20 Josh 9.17; 1 Sam 6.21; 7.2
26.21 1 Kings 19.2-4; Mt 10.23,28
26.22 Jer 36.12
26.24 2 Kings 22.12-14; Jer 39.14
27.1 Jer 26.1
27.2 Jer 28.10,13
27.3 Jer 25.21,22
27.5 Jer 10.12; 51.15; Ps 115.15,16; Acts 17.26
27.6 Ezek 29.18-20; Jer 25.9; 28.14
27.7 Jer 44.30; 46.13; 25.12; Isa 14.4-6
27.8 Jer 38.17-19; Ezek 17.19-21; Jer 29.17,18; Ezek 14.21
27.9 Ex 22.18; Deut 18.10; Isa 8.19; Mal 3.5

27.1-28.17 Jeremiah's Rejection of the Proposal for an Alliance against Babylon.
27.1-22 When envoys from surrounding nations (*Edom, Moab, Tyre, Sidon*) propose to Zedekiah (597-586) an alliance to free the region from Babylonian control, Jeremiah protests that it is *the LORD of hosts* who has put all these nations under Babylon. The prophet symbolizes the need for submission by placing a yoke on his own neck, asserting that failure to submit – as proposed by *prophets, diviners, soothsayers, sorcerers* – will result in permanent expulsion from the land. If they accept this form of divine judgment, they may remain there. Confirmation of this rejection of resistance to Babylon will come when the remaining *vessels left in the house of the LORD* are carried off to Babylon as the others have been.

28.1-17 One of the prophets, *Hananiah*, announced the end of Judah's subjection to Babylon and the return of the sacred objects to Jerusalem. He broke Jeremiah's yoke as a sign of the release he announced, but Jeremiah declared that, like an *iron* yoke, God's will could not be broken. He then announced the death of *Hananiah*, and it shortly occurred.

you, 'You shall not serve the king of Babylon.'
[10]For they are prophesying a lie to you, with
the result that you will be removed far from
your land; I will drive you out, and you will
perish. [11]But any nation that will bring its
neck under the yoke of the king of Babylon
and serve him, I will leave on its own land,
says the LORD, to till it and live there.

12 I spoke to King Zedekiah of Judah in
the same way: Bring your necks under the
yoke of the king of Babylon, and serve him
and his people, and live. [13]Why should you
and your people die by the sword, by famine, and by pestilence, as the LORD has
spoken concerning any nation that will not
serve the king of Babylon? [14]Do not listen
to the words of the prophets who are telling
you not to serve the king of Babylon, for
they are prophesying a lie to you. [15]I have
not sent them, says the LORD, but they are
prophesying falsely in my name, with the
result that I will drive you out and you will
perish, you and the prophets who are prophesying to you.

16 Then I spoke to the priests and to all
this people, saying, Thus says the LORD: Do
not listen to the words of your prophets
who are prophesying to you, saying, "The
vessels of the LORD's house will soon be
brought back from Babylon," for they are
prophesying a lie to you. [17]Do not listen to
them; serve the king of Babylon and live.
Why should this city become a desolation?
[18]If indeed they are prophets, and if the
word of the LORD is with them, then let
them intercede with the LORD of hosts, that
the vessels left in the house of the LORD, in
the house of the king of Judah, and in
Jerusalem may not go to Babylon. [19]For
thus says the LORD of hosts concerning the
pillars, the sea, the stands, and the rest of
the vessels that are left in this city, [20]which
King Nebuchadnezzar of Babylon did not
take away when he took into exile from
Jerusalem to Babylon King Jeconiah son of
Jehoiakim of Judah, and all the nobles of
Judah and Jerusalem— [21]thus says the LORD
of hosts, the God of Israel, concerning the
vessels left in the house of the LORD, in the
house of the king of Judah, and in Jerusalem: [22]They shall be carried to Babylon, and
there they shall stay, until the day when I
give attention to them, says the LORD. Then
I will bring them up and restore them to
this place.

Hananiah Opposes Jeremiah and Dies

28 In that same year, at the beginning of the reign of King Zedekiah
of Judah, in the fifth month of the fourth
year, the prophet Hananiah son of Azzur,
from Gibeon, spoke to me in the house of
the LORD, in the presence of the priests and
all the people, saying, [2]"Thus says the LORD
of hosts, the God of Israel: I have broken the
yoke of the king of Babylon. [3]Within two
years I will bring back to this place all the
vessels of the LORD's house, which King
Nebuchadnezzar of Babylon took away from
this place and carried to Babylon. [4]I will
also bring back to this place King Jeconiah
son of Jehoiakim of Judah, and all the exiles
from Judah who went to Babylon, says the
LORD, for I will break the yoke of the king
of Babylon."

5 Then the prophet Jeremiah spoke to
the prophet Hananiah in the presence of the
priests and all the people who were standing in the house of the LORD; [6]and the
prophet Jeremiah said, "Amen! May the
LORD do so; may the LORD fulfill the words
that you have prophesied, and bring back
to this place from Babylon the vessels of the
house of the LORD, and all the exiles. [7]But
listen now to this word that I speak in your
hearing and in the hearing of all the people.
[8]The prophets who preceded you and me
from ancient times prophesied war, famine,
and pestilence against many countries and
great kingdoms. [9]As for the prophet who
prophesies peace, when the word of that
prophet comes true, then it will be known
that the LORD has truly sent the prophet."

10 Then the prophet Hananiah took the
yoke from the neck of the prophet Jeremiah,
and broke it. [11]And Hananiah spoke in the
presence of all the people, saying, "Thus
says the LORD: This is how I will break the
yoke of King Nebuchadnezzar of Babylon
from the neck of all the nations within two
years." At this, the prophet Jeremiah went
his way.

12 Sometime after the prophet Hananiah
had broken the yoke from the neck of the
prophet Jeremiah, the word of the LORD
came to Jeremiah: [13]Go, tell Hananiah, Thus
says the LORD: You have broken wooden
bars only to forge iron bars in place of them!
[14]For thus says the LORD of hosts, the God
of Israel: I have put an iron yoke on the
neck of all these nations so that they may

27.10 Jer 23.25; 8.19; 32.31
27.11 Jer 21.9
27.12 Jer 28.1
27.13 Ezek 18.31
27.14 Jer 14.14; Ezek 13.22
27.15 Jer 23.21,25; Jer 6.13-15; 14.15,16
27.16 2 Chr 36.7,10; Jer 28.3; Dan 1.2; ver 10
27.18 1 Sam 7.8; 12.19,23
27.19 2 Kings 25.13,17; Jer 52.17-23
27.20 2 Kings 24.14-16; Jer 24.1
27.22 2 Kings 25.13; 2 Chr 36.18; Jer 29.10; 32.5; Ezra 1.7; 7.19
28.1 Jer 27.1,3,12; Josh 9.3; 10.12
28.3 2 Kings 24.13; 2 Chr 36.10; Jer 27.12
28.4 Jer 22.24,26,27; 27.8
28.6 1 Kings 1.36; Jer 11.5
28.7 1 Kings 22.28
28.8 1 Kings 14.15; Isa 5.5-7; Joel 1.20; Am 1.2; Nah 1.2
28.9 Deut 18.22
28.10 Jer 27.2
28.11 Jer 14.14; 27.10
28.12 Jer 1.2
28.13 Ps 107.16; Isa 45.2
28.14 Deut 28.48; Jer 27.6-8; 25.11

serve King Nebuchadnezzar of Babylon, and they shall indeed serve him; I have even given him the wild animals. [15]And the prophet Jeremiah said to the prophet Hananiah, "Listen, Hananiah, the LORD has not sent you, and you made this people trust in a lie. [16]Therefore thus says the LORD: I am going to send you off the face of the earth. Within this year you will be dead, because you have spoken rebellion against the LORD."

17 In that same year, in the seventh month, the prophet Hananiah died.

Jeremiah's Letter to the Exiles in Babylon

29 These are the words of the letter that the prophet Jeremiah sent from Jerusalem to the remaining elders among the exiles, and to the priests, the prophets, and all the people, whom Nebuchadnezzar had taken into exile from Jerusalem to Babylon. [2]This was after King Jeconiah, and the queen mother, the court officials, the leaders of Judah and Jerusalem, the artisans, and the smiths had departed from Jerusalem. [3]The letter was sent by the hand of Elasah son of Shaphan and Gemariah son of Hilkiah, whom King Zedekiah of Judah sent to Babylon to King Nebuchadnezzar of Babylon. It said: [4]Thus says the LORD of hosts, the God of Israel, to all the exiles whom I have sent into exile from Jerusalem to Babylon: [5]Build houses and live in them; plant gardens and eat what they produce. [6]Take wives and have sons and daughters; take wives for your sons, and give your daughters in marriage, that they may bear sons and daughters; multiply there, and do not decrease. [7]But seek the welfare of the city where I have sent you into exile, and pray to the LORD on its behalf, for in its welfare you will find your welfare. [8]For thus says the LORD of hosts, the God of Israel: Do not let the prophets and the diviners who are among you deceive you, and do not listen to the dreams that they dream,[f] [9]for it is a lie that they are prophesying to you in my name; I did not send them, says the LORD.

10 For thus says the LORD: Only when Babylon's seventy years are completed will I visit you, and I will fulfill to you my promise and bring you back to this place. [11]For surely I know the plans I have for you, says the LORD, plans for your welfare and not for harm, to give you a future with hope. [12]Then when you call upon me and come and pray to me, I will hear you. [13]When you search for me, you will find me; if you seek me with all your heart, [14]I will let you find me, says the LORD, and I will restore your fortunes and gather you from all the nations and all the places where I have driven you, says the LORD, and I will bring you back to the place from which I sent you into exile.

15 Because you have said, "The LORD has raised up prophets for us in Babylon,"— [16]Thus says the LORD concerning the king who sits on the throne of David, and concerning all the people who live in this city, your kinsfolk who did not go out with you into exile: [17]Thus says the LORD of hosts, I am going to let loose on them sword, famine, and pestilence, and I will make them like rotten figs that are so bad they cannot be eaten. [18]I will pursue them with the sword, with famine, and with pestilence, and will make them a horror to all the kingdoms of the earth, to be an object of cursing, and horror, and hissing, and a derision among all the nations where I have driven them, [19]because they did not heed my words, says the LORD, when I persistently sent to you my servants the prophets, but they[g] would not listen, says the LORD. [20]But now, all you exiles whom I sent away from Jerusalem to Babylon, hear the word of the LORD: [21]Thus says the LORD of hosts, the God of Israel, concerning Ahab son of Kolaiah and Zedekiah son of Maaseiah, who are prophesying a lie to you in my name: I am going to deliver them into the hand of King Nebuchadrezzar of Babylon, and he shall kill them before your eyes. [22]And on account of them this curse shall be used by all the exiles from Judah in Babylon: "The LORD make you like Zedekiah and Ahab, whom the king of Babylon roasted in the fire," [23]because they have perpetrated outrage in Israel and have committed adultery with their neighbors' wives, and have spoken in my name lying words that I did not command them; I am the one who knows and bears witness, says the LORD.

The Letter of Shemaiah

24 To Shemaiah of Nehelam you shall say: [25]Thus says the LORD of hosts, the God of Israel: In your own name you sent a

[f] Cn: Heb *your dreams that you cause to dream* [g] Syr: Heb *you*

28.15 Jer 29.31; Ezek 13.22
28.16 Deut 6.15; Deut 13.5; Jer 29.32
29.2 2 Kings 24.12-16; Jer 22.24-28; 24.1; 28.4
29.4 Isa 10.5,6; Jer 24.5
29.6 Jer 16.2-4
29.7 Ezra 6.10; Dan 4.19; 1 Tim 2.2
29.8 Jer 27.9; 14.14; 23.21,25,27
29.9 Jer 27.15; ver 31
29.10 2 Chr 36.21,22; Jer 25.12; 27.22; Dan 9.2
29.11 Isa 40.9-11; Jer 30.18-22; 31.17
29.12 Ps 50.15; Jer 33.3; Ps 145.19
29.13 1 Chr 22.19; 2 Chr 22.9; Jer 24.7
29.14 Deut 30.1-10; Jer 30.3; Isa 43.5,6; Jer 3.14
29.16 Jer 38.2,3,17-23
29.17 Jer 27.8; 32.24; 24.3,8-10
29.18 Isa 65.15; Jer 42.18; 25.9
29.19 Jer 6.19; 25.4; 26.5
29.20 Jer 24.5
29.22 Isa 65.15; Dan 3.6
29.23 2 Sam 13.12; Prov 5.21; Jer 16.17
29.25 ver 1,29; 2 Kings 25.18; Jer 21.1

29.1-32 Jeremiah's Letter to the Exiles In Babylon and a Hostile Response.
29.1-14 Jeremiah's letter to the exiles, sent in the reign of Zedekiah (597-586), urges them to settle there, produce large families, and seek the welfare of that city. They will not be speedily returning to Jerusalem, as the false prophets claim, but only after *seventy years*.
29.15-23 Solemn warning is given as well to those remaining in the land of Judah that failure to obey the LORD's words will bring horrible judgment on them, as it did on two of the false prophets in Babylon, Ahab and Zedekiah, whom the king of Babylon roasted in the fire.
29.24-32 One of the leading prophets in Babylon, Shemaiah, writes to the high priest in Jerusalem to silence this madman, Jeremiah, from his encouraging the exiles to be content in Babylon. In response, Jeremiah declares Shemaiah's divine punishment.

30.1-31.39 Restoration and Renewal of God's Covenant with Israel and Judah.
30.1-24 Restoration is promised for both *Israel and Judah*, thus reuniting the long-divided northern and southern kingdoms (since 922, when Rehoboam and Jeroboam divided the land and the people; 1 Kings 12-14). This unprecedented event of reunion (*none like it*) will bring God's people back from exile, but will also make *an end of all nations.* Meanwhile the experience of the people of God will be painful, but their *health* and *fortunes* will be restored. Jerusalem will be rebuilt, and *one of their own* will rule as *prince.* The result will be the ultimate reunion of God and his people, but first will come a time of suffering. Absent from this series of promises is mention of restoration of the priesthood, the temple, or the specifically Davidic line of kings.

letter to all the people who are in Jerusalem,
and to the priest Zephaniah son of Maaseiah,
and to all the priests, saying, 26The LORD
himself has made you priest instead of the
priest Jehoiada, so that there may be officers
in the house of the LORD to control any
madman who plays the prophet, to put him
in the stocks and the collar. 27So now why
have you not rebuked Jeremiah of Anathoth
who plays the prophet for you? 28For he has
actually sent to us in Babylon, saying, "It
will be a long time; build houses and live
in them, and plant gardens and eat what
they produce."
29 The priest Zephaniah read this letter
in the hearing of the prophet Jeremiah.
30Then the word of the LORD came to Jeremiah: 31Send to all the exiles, saying, Thus
says the LORD concerning Shemaiah of
Nehelam: Because Shemaiah has prophesied
to you, though I did not send him, and has
led you to trust in a lie, 32therefore thus says
the LORD: I am going to punish Shemaiah
of Nehelam and his descendants; he shall
not have anyone living among this people
to see[h] the good that I am going to do to
my people, says the LORD, for he has spoken
rebellion against the LORD.

Restoration Promised for Israel and Judah

30 The word that came to Jeremiah
from the LORD: 2Thus says the LORD,
the God of Israel: Write in a book all the
words that I have spoken to you. 3For the
days are surely coming, says the LORD, when
I will restore the fortunes of my people,
Israel and Judah, says the LORD, and I will
bring them back to the land that I gave to
their ancestors and they shall take possession of it.
4 These are the words that the LORD
spoke concerning Israel and Judah:
5 Thus says the LORD:
We have heard a cry of panic,
of terror, and no peace.
6 Ask now, and see,
can a man bear a child?
Why then do I see every man
with his hands on his loins like a woman in labor?
Why has every face turned pale?
7 Alas! that day is so great
there is none like it;
it is a time of distress for Jacob;
yet he shall be rescued from it.

8 On that day, says the LORD of hosts, I
will break the yoke from off his[i] neck, and
I will burst his[i] bonds, and strangers shall
no more make a servant of him. 9But they
shall serve the LORD their God and David
their king, whom I will raise up for them.

10 But as for you, have no fear, my servant Jacob, says the LORD,
and do not be dismayed, O Israel;
for I am going to save you from far away,
and your offspring from the land of their captivity.
Jacob shall return and have quiet and ease,
and no one shall make him afraid.
11 For I am with you, says the LORD, to save you;
I will make an end of all the nations
among which I scattered you,
but of you I will not make an end.
I will chastise you in just measure,
and I will by no means leave you unpunished.

12 For thus says the LORD:
Your hurt is incurable,
your wound is grievous.
13 There is no one to uphold your cause,
no medicine for your wound,
no healing for you.
14 All your lovers have forgotten you;
they care nothing for you;
for I have dealt you the blow of an enemy,
the punishment of a merciless foe,
because your guilt is great,
because your sins are so numerous.
15 Why do you cry out over your hurt?
Your pain is incurable.
Because your guilt is great,
because your sins are so numerous,
I have done these things to you.
16 Therefore all who devour you shall be devoured,
and all your foes, everyone of them,
shall go into captivity;
those who plunder you shall be plundered,
and all who prey on you I will make a prey.
17 For I will restore health to you,
and your wounds I will heal,
says the LORD,
because they have called you an outcast:
"It is Zion; no one cares for her!"

[h] Gk: Heb *and he shall not see* [i] Cn: Heb *your*

29.26 Jer 20.1; 2 Kings 9.11; Acts 26.24; Jer 20.2

29.31 ver 20,24; Jer 14.14,15; 28.15

29.32 Jer 36.31; 22.30; 17.6; 28.16

30.2 Jer 25.13; Hab 2.2

30.3 Jer 29.10; Ps 53.6; Zeph 3.20; Jer 16.15; Ezek 20.42

30.5 Isa 5.30; Am 5.16-18

30.6 Jer 4.31; 6.24

30.7 Isa 2.12; Joel 2.11; Lam 1.12; Jer 2.27,28; ver 10

30.8 Isa 9.4; Jer 27.2; Ezek 34.27

30.9 Isa 55.3,4; Ezek 34.23; 37.24; Hos 3.5; Lk 1.69; Acts 2.30; 13.23

30.10 Isa 43.5; 44.2; Jer 46.27,28; Isa 60.4; Jer 33.16; Mic 4.4

30.11 Jer 46.28; 4.27; 10.24

30.12 ver 15; Jer 15.18

30.13 Jer 14.19; 46.11

30.14 Lam 1.2; 2.4,5; Jer 5.6; 32.30-35

30.16 Isa 33.1; 41.11; Jer 10.25; Jer 50.10

30.17 Jer 8.22; 22.33; Jer 33.24

18 Thus says the LORD:
I am going to restore the fortunes of the tents of Jacob,
and have compassion on his dwellings;
the city shall be rebuilt upon its mound,
and the citadel set on its rightful site.
19 Out of them shall come thanksgiving,
and the sound of merrymakers.
I will make them many, and they shall not be few;
I will make them honored, and they shall not be disdained.
20 Their children shall be as of old,
their congregation shall be established before me;
and I will punish all who oppress them.
21 Their prince shall be one of their own,
their ruler shall come from their midst;
I will bring him near, and he shall approach me,
for who would otherwise dare to approach me?
says the LORD.
22 And you shall be my people,
and I will be your God.

23 Look, the storm of the LORD!
Wrath has gone forth,
a whirling[j] tempest;
it will burst upon the head of the wicked.
24 The fierce anger of the LORD will not turn back
until he has executed and accomplished
the intents of his mind.
In the latter days you will understand this.

The Joyful Return of the Exiles

31 At that time, says the LORD, I will be the God of all the families of Israel, and they shall be my people.
2 Thus says the LORD:
The people who survived the sword
found grace in the wilderness;
when Israel sought for rest,
3 the LORD appeared to him[k] from far away.[l]
I have loved you with an everlasting love;
therefore I have continued my faithfulness to you.
4 Again I will build you, and you shall be built,
O virgin Israel!
Again you shall take[m] your tambourines,
and go forth in the dance of the merrymakers.
5 Again you shall plant vineyards
on the mountains of Samaria;
the planters shall plant,
and shall enjoy the fruit.
6 For there shall be a day when sentinels will call
in the hill country of Ephraim:
"Come, let us go up to Zion,
to the LORD our God."

7 For thus says the LORD:
Sing aloud with gladness for Jacob,
and raise shouts for the chief of the nations;
proclaim, give praise, and say,
"Save, O LORD, your people,
the remnant of Israel."
8 See, I am going to bring them from the land of the north,
and gather them from the farthest parts of the earth,
among them the blind and the lame,
those with child and those in labor, together;
a great company, they shall return here.
9 With weeping they shall come,
and with consolations[n] I will lead them back,
I will let them walk by brooks of water,
in a straight path in which they shall not stumble;
for I have become a father to Israel,
and Ephraim is my firstborn.

10 Hear the word of the LORD, O nations,
and declare it in the coastlands far away;
say, "He who scattered Israel will gather him,
and will keep him as a shepherd a flock."
11 For the LORD has ransomed Jacob,
and has redeemed him from hands too strong for him.
12 They shall come and sing aloud on the height of Zion,

31.1-26 The ground of the exiles' return is God's *everlasting love,* which will result in the renewal not only *of* Zion in Judah, but of *Samaria* and *Ephraim* as well. In addition, returnees will come from many nations across the earth, including the disabled, as *the LORD* gathers his scattered *flock.* Temple and sacrifices are not mentioned, but *priests* will be there and will flourish. The penitent will recall their earlier disobedience, and the *weary* will be renewed. God is creating a *new thing:* the traditionally adulterous bride, Israel (Hosea 2; Jer 2.23-25) will now eagerly seek renewal of relationship with her husband (=God).

30.18 Jer 31.23; Ps 102.13; Jer 31.4,38-40
30.19 Isa 35.10; Jer 31.4,12,13; 33.10,11,22
30.21 Num 16.5; Jer 50.44
30.22 Jer 32.38; Ezek 11.20; 36.28; Zech 13.9
30.23 Jer 23.19,20; 25.32
30.24 Jer 4.8; 23.20
31.1 Jer 30.22,24; Isa 41.10; Rom 11.26-28
31.2 Num 14.20; Josh 1.13; Isa 63.14
31.3 Deut 7.8; Ps 25.6; Hos 11.4
31.4 Jer 30.19
31.5 Isa 65.21; Jer 50.19
31.6 Isa 2.3; Mic 4.2
31.7 Ps 14.7; Deut 28.13; Isa 61.9; Ps 28.9; Isa 37.31
31.8 Jer 3.18; 23.8; Isa 43.6; Ezek 20.34,41; Isa 42.16; 40.11
31.9 Isa 43.19; 49.10,11; 64.8; Jer 3.4,19
31.10 Isa 66.19; Jer 50.19; Isa 40.11
31.11 Isa 44.23; 48.20; Jer 50.34; Isa 49.24,25
31.12 Ezek 17.23; Hos 3.5; Isa 58.11; 35.10; 65.19; Rev 21.4

[j] One Ms: Meaning of MT uncertain [k] Gk: Heb *me* [l] Or *to him long ago* [m] Or *adorn yourself with* [n] Gk Compare Vg Tg: Heb *supplications*

31.27-30 As God renews his people, instead of later generations suffering for the sins of their ancestors, each generation will accept its own moral responsibility.
31.31-38 The earlier covenant of the LORD with *Israel and Judah* was inscribed on tablets of stone (Ex 31.18; Ex 34). But the *new covenant* will be written *on their hearts,* meaning that its message will be directly accessible to their wills and consciousness. Instruction will not be needed, since everyone will *know the LORD.* The covenant will be as durable as the universe itself. So large will be God's people that the city of Jerusalem must be enlarged to contain them.

and they shall be radiant over the
goodness of the LORD,
over the grain, the wine, and the oil,
and over the young of the flock and
the herd;
their life shall become like a watered
garden,
and they shall never languish again.
13 Then shall the young women rejoice in
the dance,
and the young men and the old shall
be merry.
I will turn their mourning into joy,
I will comfort them, and give them
gladness for sorrow.
14 I will give the priests their fill of fatness,
and my people shall be satisfied with
my bounty,
says the LORD.

15 Thus says the LORD:
A voice is heard in Ramah,
lamentation and bitter weeping.
Rachel is weeping for her children;
she refuses to be comforted for her
children,
because they are no more.
16 Thus says the LORD:
Keep your voice from weeping,
and your eyes from tears;
for there is a reward for your work,
says the LORD:
they shall come back from the land of
the enemy;
17 there is hope for your future,
says the LORD:
your children shall come back to their
own country.

18 Indeed I heard Ephraim pleading:
"You disciplined me, and I took the
discipline;
I was like a calf untrained.
Bring me back, let me come back,
for you are the LORD my God.
19 For after I had turned away I repented;
and after I was discovered, I struck
my thigh;
I was ashamed, and I was dismayed
because I bore the disgrace of my
youth."
20 Is Ephraim my dear son?
Is he the child I delight in?
As often as I speak against him,
I still remember him.
Therefore I am deeply moved for him;
I will surely have mercy on him,
says the LORD.

21 Set up road markers for yourself,
make yourself guideposts;
consider well the highway,
the road by which you went.
Return, O virgin Israel,
return to these your cities.
22 How long will you waver,
O faithless daughter?
For the LORD has created a new thing on
the earth:
a woman encompasses[o] a man.

23 Thus says the LORD of hosts, the God
of Israel: Once more they shall use these
words in the land of Judah and in its towns
when I restore their fortunes:
"The LORD bless you, O abode of
righteousness,
O holy hill!"
24 And Judah and all its towns shall live
there together, and the farmers and those
who wander[p] with their flocks.
25 I will satisfy the weary,
and all who are faint I will replenish.
26 Thereupon I awoke and looked, and
my sleep was pleasant to me.

Individual Retribution

27 The days are surely coming, says the
LORD, when I will sow the house of Israel
and the house of Judah with the seed of
humans and the seed of animals. 28 And just
as I have watched over them to pluck up
and break down, to overthrow, destroy, and
bring evil, so I will watch over them to
build and to plant, says the LORD. 29 In those
days they shall no longer say:
"The parents have eaten sour grapes,
and the children's teeth are set on
edge."
30 But all shall die for their own sins; the
teeth of everyone who eats sour grapes shall
be set on edge.

A New Covenant

31 The days are surely coming, says the
LORD, when I will make a new covenant
with the house of Israel and the house of
Judah. 32 It will not be like the covenant that
I made with their ancestors when I took
them by the hand to bring them out of the

[o] Meaning of Heb uncertain [p] Cn Compare Syr Vg Tg: Heb *and they shall wander*

31.13 Ps 30.11; Zech 8.4,5; Isa 61.3; 51.11
31.14 ver 25; Jer 50.19
31.15 Mt 2.17,18; Gen 37.35; Ps 77.2; Jer 10.20
31.16 Isa 25.8; 30.19; Heb 6.10; ver 4,5; Jer 30.3; Ezek 11.17
31.17 Jer 29.11
31.18 Job 5.17; Ps 94.12; Hos 4.16; Ps 80.3,7,19; Jer 17.14; Acts 3.26
31.19 Ezek 36.31; Zech 12.10; Ezek 21.12; Jer 3.25; Ps 25.7; Jer 22.21
31.20 Hos 11.8; Gen 43.30; Isa 63.15; 55.7; Hos 14.4
31.21 Jer 6.16; 50.5; Isa 48.20; ver 4
31.23 Jer 30.18; 32.44; Isa 1.26; Jer 50.7; Zech 8.3
31.24 Jer 33.12,13
31.25 Mt 5.6
31.27 Ezek 36.9-11; Hos 2.23
31.28 Jer 44.27; 1.10
31.29 Ezek 18.2
31.30 Deut 24.16; Ezek 18.4,20; Gal 6.5,7
31.31 Jer 32.40; Ezek 37.26; Heb 8.8-12
31.32 Ex 19.5; 24.6-8; Deut 1.31; Jer 11.7,8; 3.14

31.33 Jer 32.40; 24.7; 32.38
31.34 1 Thess 4.9; Isa 54.13; Jn 6.45; Mic 7.18; Rom 11.27
31.35 Gen 1.16; Ps 19.1-6; Jer 10.16
31.36 Isa 54.9,10; Jer 33.20; Am 9.8,9
31.37 Jer 33.22-26
31.38 Neh 3.1; Zech 14.10; 2 Kings 14.13
31.40 Jer 7.32; 2 Sam 15.23; 2 Kings 23.6; Joel 3.17
32.2 Neh 3.25; Jer 37.21; 39.14
32.3 2 Kings 6.31,32; Jer 26.8,9; 34.2,3
32.4 Jer 38.18,23; 39.5
32.5 Jer 39.7; Jer 27.22; 34.4,5; 21.4
32.7 Jer 1.1; Lev 25.25; Ruth 4.4
32.9 Gen 23.16; 24.22; Ex 21.32
32.10 Ruth 4.1,9
32.11 Lk 2.27
32.12 Jer 36.4; 51.59
32.15 Jer 33.12,13; Zech 3.10

land of Egypt—a covenant that they broke,
though I was their husband,[q] says the LORD.
[33]But this is the covenant that I will make
with the house of Israel after those days,
says the LORD: I will put my law within
them, and I will write it on their hearts; and
I will be their God, and they shall be my
people. [34]No longer shall they teach one
another, or say to each other, "Know the
LORD," for they shall all know me, from the
least of them to the greatest, says the LORD;
for I will forgive their iniquity, and remember their sin no more.

[35] Thus says the LORD,
who gives the sun for light by day
and the fixed order of the moon and the stars for light by night,
who stirs up the sea so that its waves roar—
the LORD of hosts is his name:
[36] If this fixed order were ever to cease
from my presence, says the LORD,
then also the offspring of Israel would cease
to be a nation before me forever.

[37] Thus says the LORD:
If the heavens above can be measured,
and the foundations of the earth below can be explored,
then I will reject all the offspring of Israel
because of all they have done,
says the LORD.

Jerusalem to Be Enlarged

38 The days are surely coming, says the
LORD, when the city shall be rebuilt for the
LORD from the tower of Hananel to the
Corner Gate. [39]And the measuring line shall
go out farther, straight to the hill Gareb,
and shall then turn to Goah. [40]The whole
valley of the dead bodies and the ashes, and
all the fields as far as the Wadi Kidron, to
the corner of the Horse Gate toward the
east, shall be sacred to the LORD. It shall
never again be uprooted or overthrown.

Jeremiah Buys a Field During the Siege

32 The word that came to Jeremiah
from the LORD in the tenth year of
King Zedekiah of Judah, which was the
eighteenth year of Nebuchadrezzar. [2]At that
time the army of the king of Babylon was
besieging Jerusalem, and the prophet Jeremiah was confined in the court of the
guard that was in the palace of the king of
Judah, [3]where King Zedekiah of Judah had
confined him. Zedekiah had said, "Why do
you prophesy and say: Thus says the LORD:
I am going to give this city into the hand
of the king of Babylon, and he shall take it;
[4]King Zedekiah of Judah shall not escape
out of the hands of the Chaldeans, but shall
surely be given into the hands of the king
of Babylon, and shall speak with him face
to face and see him eye to eye; [5]and he shall
take Zedekiah to Babylon, and there he
shall remain until I attend to him, says the
LORD; though you fight against the Chaldeans,
you shall not succeed?"
6 Jeremiah said, The word of the LORD
came to me: [7]Hanamel son of your uncle
Shallum is going to come to you and say,
"Buy my field that is at Anathoth, for the
right of redemption by purchase is yours."
[8]Then my cousin Hanamel came to me in
the court of the guard, in accordance with
the word of the LORD, and said to me, "Buy
my field that is at Anathoth in the land of
Benjamin, for the right of possession and
redemption is yours; buy it for yourself."
Then I knew that this was the word of the
LORD.
9 And I bought the field at Anathoth
from my cousin Hanamel, and weighed out
the money to him, seventeen shekels of
silver. [10]I signed the deed, sealed it, got
witnesses, and weighed the money on scales.
[11]Then I took the sealed deed of purchase,
containing the terms and conditions, and
the open copy; [12]and I gave the deed of
purchase to Baruch son of Neriah son of
Mahseiah, in the presence of my cousin
Hanamel, in the presence of the witnesses
who signed the deed of purchase, and in the
presence of all the Judeans who were sitting
in the court of the guard. [13]In their presence
I charged Baruch, saying, [14]Thus says the
LORD of hosts, the God of Israel: Take these
deeds, both this sealed deed of purchase and
this open deed, and put them in an earthenware jar, in order that they may last for
a long time. [15]For thus says the LORD of
hosts, the God of Israel: Houses and fields
and vineyards shall again be bought in this
land.

32.1-33.26 Assurance of Renewal.
32.1-15 The decision of Jeremiah, imprisoned in Jerusalem while it was besieged by the Babylonians, to obey the word of the LORD by purchasing a field near his hometown of *Anathoth* (Jer 1.1; 11.21-23) was a public symbolic act of confidence in the future restoration of God's people. The deed for the field was given to *Baruch son of Neriah*, who later appears as Jeremiah's scribe, recording the prophet's words from the LORD.

[q] Or *master* [r] Or *to thousands*

32.16-25 Jeremiah's prayer, with its praise of God for his mighty deeds and the assurance of deliverance for those who obey God's laws, sounds like Deuteronomy and the Deuteronomic history in style and wording (Deut 26; 2 Kings 23). **32.16-44** God offers reassurance to Jeremiah about why Jerusalem is falling to the Babylonians – because of their idolatry and evil deeds – and about the *everlasting covenant*, which will be in effect after the renewal of the people.

Jeremiah Prays for Understanding

16 After I had given the deed of purchase to Baruch son of Neriah, I prayed to the LORD, saying: 17 Ah Lord GOD! It is you who made the heavens and the earth by your great power and by your outstretched arm! Nothing is too hard for you. 18 You show steadfast love to the thousandth generation,[z] but repay the guilt of parents into the laps of their children after them, O great and mighty God whose name is the LORD of hosts, 19 great in counsel and mighty in deed; whose eyes are open to all the ways of mortals, rewarding all according to their ways and according to the fruit of their doings. 20 You showed signs and wonders in the land of Egypt, and to this day in Israel and among all humankind, and have made yourself a name that continues to this very day. 21 You brought your people Israel out of the land of Egypt with signs and wonders, with a strong hand and outstretched arm, and with great terror; 22 and you gave them this land, which you swore to their ancestors to give them, a land flowing with milk and honey; 23 and they entered and took possession of it. But they did not obey your voice or follow your law; of all you commanded them to do, they did nothing. Therefore you have made all these disasters come upon them. 24 See, the siege ramps have been cast up against the city to take it, and the city, faced with sword, famine, and pestilence, has been given into the hands of the Chaldeans who are fighting against it. What you spoke has happened, as you yourself can see. 25 Yet you, O Lord GOD, have said to me, "Buy the field for money and get witnesses"—though the city has been given into the hands of the Chaldeans.

God's Assurance of the People's Return

26 The word of the LORD came to Jeremiah: 27 See, I am the LORD, the God of all flesh; is anything too hard for me? 28 Therefore, thus says the LORD: I am going to give this city into the hands of the Chaldeans and into the hand of King Nebuchadrezzar of Babylon, and he shall take it. 29 The Chaldeans who are fighting against this city shall come, set it on fire, and burn it, with the houses on whose roofs offerings have been made to Baal and libations have been poured out to other gods, to provoke me to anger. 30 For the people of Israel and the people of Judah have done nothing but evil in my sight from their youth; the people of Israel have done nothing but provoke me to anger by the work of their hands, says the LORD. 31 This city has aroused my anger and wrath, from the day it was built until this day, so that I will remove it from my sight 32 because of all the evil of the people of Israel and the people of Judah that they did to provoke me to anger—they, their kings and their officials, their priests and their prophets, the citizens of Judah and the inhabitants of Jerusalem. 33 They have turned their backs to me, not their faces; though I have taught them persistently, they would not listen and accept correction. 34 They set up their abominations in the house that bears my name, and defiled it. 35 They built the high places of Baal in the valley of the son of Hinnom, to offer up their sons and daughters to Molech, though I did not command them, nor did it enter my mind that they should do this abomination, causing Judah to sin.

36 Now therefore thus says the LORD, the God of Israel, concerning this city of which you say, "It is being given into the hand of the king of Babylon by the sword, by famine, and by pestilence": 37 See, I am going to gather them from all the lands to which I drove them in my anger and my wrath and in great indignation; I will bring them back to this place, and I will settle them in safety. 38 They shall be my people, and I will be their God. 39 I will give them one heart and one way, that they may fear me for all time, for their own good and the good of their children after them. 40 I will make an everlasting covenant with them, never to draw back from doing good to them; and I will put the fear of me in their hearts, so that they may not turn from me. 41 I will rejoice in doing good to them, and I will plant them in this land in faithfulness, with all my heart and all my soul.

42 For thus says the LORD: Just as I have brought all this great disaster upon this people, so I will bring upon them all the good fortune that I now promise them. 43 Fields shall be bought in this land of which you are saying, It is a desolation, without human beings or animals; it has been given into the hands of the Chaldeans. 44 Fields shall be bought for money, and deeds shall be signed and sealed and witnessed, in the land of Benjamin, in the places around Jerusalem, and in the cities

32.17 Jer 1.6; 4.10; 2 Kings 19.15; Isa 40.26-28
32.18 Ex 34.7; Jer 20.11; 10.16
32.19 Isa 28.29; Jer 16.17; 17.10
32.20 Ex 9.16; Dan 9.15
32.21 Ex 6.6; 1 Chr 17.21
32.22 Ex 3.8,17; Jer 11.5
32.23 Jer 2.7; 26.4; 44.10; Neh 9.26; Jer 11.8; Dan 9.10-14
32.24 Jer 33.4; Ezek 14.21; Deut 4.26; Zech 1.6
32.27 Num 16.22
32.28 Jer 34.2,3
32.29 Jer 21.10; 37.8,10; 52.13; 19.13
32.30 Jer 2.7; 22.21; 25.7
32.31 2 Kings 23.27; 24.3
32.32 Isa 1.4-6; Dan 9.8
32.33 Jer 2.27; Ezek 8.16; Jer 35.15
32.34 Jer 7.30,31; Ezek 8.5,6
32.35 Jer 7.31; 19.5; Lev 18.21; 1 Kings 11.33
32.37 Deut 30.3; Jer 23.3; 23.6; Zech 14.11
32.39 Jer 24.7; Ezek 11.19,20; 37.25
32.41 Deut 30.9; Zeph 3.17; Am 9.15
32.42 Jer 31.28; Zech 8.14,15; Jer 33.14
32.44 Jer 17.26; 33.7,11,26

33.1 Jer 32.2,3
33.2 Jer 10.16; 51.19; Ex 15.3
33.3 Ps 50.15; Jer 29.12; 32.17,27; Isa 48.6
33.4 Jer 32.13,14,24
33.5 Isa 8.17; Jer 21.10
33.6 Isa 66.12; Gal 5.22,23
33.7 Jer 32.44; Am 9.14,15
33.8 Mic 7.18; Zech 13.1; Heb 9.13,14
33.9 Isa 62.7; Jer 13.11; Isa 60.5
33.11 Isa 35.10; 51.3,11; 1 Chr 16.8, 34; 2 Chr 5.13; Lev 7.12
33.12 Isa 65.10; Ezek 34.12-14
33.13 Jer 17.26; Lev 27.32; Lk 15.4
33.14 Jer 23.5; Ezek 34.23-25
33.15 Isa 4.2; 11.1; Zech 3.8; Ps 72.1-5
33.16 Jer 23.6; Isa 45.24,25; Phil 3.9
33.17 2 Sam 7.16; 1 Kings 2.4; Lk 1.32,33
33.18 Deut 18.1; 24.8; Heb 13.15
33.20 Ps 89.37; Isa 54.9; Jer 31.36
33.21 Ps 89.34
33.22 Gen 15.5; 22.17; Jer 30.19
33.24 Neh 4.2-4; Ezek 36.2
33.25 Ps 74.16,17; Jer 31.35,36
33.26 Jer 31.37; Isa 14.1; Hos 1.7; 2.23

of Judah, of the hill country, of the Shephelah,
and of the Negeb; for I will restore their
fortunes, says the LORD.

Healing after Punishment

33 The word of the LORD came to
Jeremiah a second time, while he
was still confined in the court of the guard:
[2]Thus says the LORD who made the earth,[s]
the LORD who formed it to establish it—the
LORD is his name: [3]Call to me and I will
answer you, and will tell you great and
hidden things that you have not known.
[4]For thus says the LORD, the God of Israel,
concerning the houses of this city and the
houses of the kings of Judah that were torn
down to make a defense against the siege
ramps and before the sword:[t] [5]The Chaldeans
are coming in to fight[u] and to fill them with
the dead bodies of those whom I shall strike
down in my anger and my wrath, for I have
hidden my face from this city because of all
their wickedness. [6]I am going to bring it
recovery and healing; I will heal them and
reveal to them abundance[t] of prosperity and
security. [7]I will restore the fortunes of Judah
and the fortunes of Israel, and rebuild them
as they were at first. [8]I will cleanse them
from all the guilt of their sin against me,
and I will forgive all the guilt of their sin
and rebellion against me. [9]And this city[v]
shall be to me a name of joy, a praise and
a glory before all the nations of the earth
who shall hear of all the good that I do for
them; they shall fear and tremble because
of all the good and all the prosperity I
provide for it.
10 Thus says the LORD: In this place of
which you say, "It is a waste without human
beings or animals," in the towns of Judah
and the streets of Jerusalem that are desolate, without inhabitants, human or animal, there shall once more be heard [11]the
voice of mirth and the voice of gladness, the
voice of the bridegroom and the voice of the
bride, the voices of those who sing, as they
bring thank offerings to the house of the
LORD:

"Give thanks to the LORD of hosts,
  for the LORD is good,
  for his steadfast love endures forever!"

For I will restore the fortunes of the land as
at first, says the LORD.
12 Thus says the LORD of hosts: In this
place that is waste, without human beings
or animals, and in all its towns there shall
again be pasture for shepherds resting their
flocks. [13]In the towns of the hill country, of
the Shephelah, and of the Negeb, in the
land of Benjamin, the places around Jerusalem, and in the towns of Judah, flocks
shall again pass under the hands of the one
who counts them, says the LORD.

The Righteous Branch and the Covenant with David

14 The days are surely coming, says the
LORD, when I will fulfill the promise I made
to the house of Israel and the house of Judah.
[15]In those days and at that time I will cause
a righteous Branch to spring up for David;
and he shall execute justice and righteousness in the land. [16]In those days Judah will
be saved and Jerusalem will live in safety.
And this is the name by which it will be
called: "The LORD is our righteousness."
17 For thus says the LORD: David shall
never lack a man to sit on the throne of the
house of Israel, [18]and the levitical priests
shall never lack a man in my presence to
offer burnt offerings, to make grain offerings, and to make sacrifices for all time.
19 The word of the LORD came to Jeremiah: [20]Thus says the LORD: If any of you
could break my covenant with the day and
my covenant with the night, so that day
and night would not come at their appointed time, [21]only then could my covenant with my servant David be broken, so
that he would not have a son to reign on
his throne, and my covenant with my
ministers the Levites. [22]Just as the host of
heaven cannot be numbered and the sands
of the sea cannot be measured, so I will
increase the offspring of my servant David,
and the Levites who minister to me.
23 The word of the LORD came to Jeremiah: [24]Have you not observed how these
people say, "The two families that the LORD
chose have been rejected by him," and how
they hold my people in such contempt that
they no longer regard them as a nation?
[25]Thus says the LORD: Only if I had not
established my covenant with day and night
and the ordinances of heaven and earth,
[26]would I reject the offspring of Jacob and
of my servant David and not choose any of
his descendants as rulers over the offspring

[s] Gk: Heb *it* [t] Meaning of Heb uncertain [u] Cn: Heb *They are coming in to fight against the Chaldeans* [v] Heb *And it*

33.1-26 The destruction of Jerusalem is detailed, which leads some scholars to say that this oracle was written after the events had occurred. The promise is that the flocks and the land will be renewed, a king of the line of David – *a righteous Branch* – will sit on the throne, and the *levitical priests* will resume their roles in the temple.

of Abraham, Isaac, and Jacob. For I will
restore their fortunes, and will have mercy
upon them.

Death in Captivity Predicted for Zedekiah

34 The word that came to Jeremiah
from the LORD, when King Nebuchadrezzar of Babylon and all his army and
all the kingdoms of the earth and all the
peoples under his dominion were fighting
against Jerusalem and all its cities: [2]"Thus
says the LORD, the God of Israel: Go and
speak to King Zedekiah of Judah and say to
him: Thus says the LORD: I am going to give
this city into the hand of the king of Babylon,
and he shall burn it with fire. [3]And you
yourself shall not escape from his hand, but
shall surely be captured and handed over to
him; you shall see the king of Babylon eye
to eye and speak with him face to face; and
you shall go to Babylon. [4]Yet hear the word
of the LORD, O King Zedekiah of Judah! Thus
says the LORD concerning you: You shall not
die by the sword; [5]you shall die in peace.
And as spices were burned[w] for your ancestors, the earlier kings who preceded you, so
they shall burn spices[x] for you and lament
for you, saying, "Alas, lord!" For I have
spoken the word, says the LORD.
6 Then the prophet Jeremiah spoke all
these words to Zedekiah king of Judah, in
Jerusalem, [7]when the army of the king of
Babylon was fighting against Jerusalem and
against all the cities of Judah that were left,
Lachish and Azekah; for these were the
only fortified cities of Judah that remained.

Treacherous Treatment of Slaves

8 The word that came to Jeremiah from
the LORD, after King Zedekiah had made a
covenant with all the people in Jerusalem
to make a proclamation of liberty to them,
[9]that all should set free their Hebrew slaves,
male and female, so that no one should
hold another Judean in slavery. [10]And they
obeyed, all the officials and all the people
who had entered into the covenant that all
would set free their slaves, male or female,
so that they would not be enslaved again;
they obeyed and set them free. [11]But afterward they turned around and took back the
male and female slaves they had set free,
and brought them again into subjection as
slaves. [12]The word of the LORD came to
Jeremiah from the LORD: [13]Thus says the
LORD, the God of Israel: I myself made a
covenant with your ancestors when I
brought them out of the land of Egypt, out
of the house of slavery, saying, [14]"Every
seventh year each of you must set free any
Hebrews who have been sold to you and
have served you six years; you must set
them free from your service." But your
ancestors did not listen to me or incline
their ears to me. [15]You yourselves recently
repented and did what was right in my
sight by proclaiming liberty to one another,
and you made a covenant before me in the
house that is called by my name; [16]but then
you turned around and profaned my name
when each of you took back your male and
female slaves, whom you had set free according to their desire, and you brought
them again into subjection to be your slaves.
[17]Therefore, thus says the LORD: You have
not obeyed me by granting a release to your
neighbors and friends; I am going to grant
a release to you, says the LORD—a release
to the sword, to pestilence, and to famine.
I will make you a horror to all the kingdoms of the earth. [18]And those who transgressed my covenant and did not keep the
terms of the covenant that they made before me, I will make like[y] the calf when they
cut it in two and passed between its parts:
[19]the officials of Judah, the officials of Jerusalem, the eunuchs, the priests, and all the
people of the land who passed between the
parts of the calf [20]shall be handed over to
their enemies and to those who seek their
lives. Their corpses shall become food for
the birds of the air and the wild animals of
the earth. [21]And as for King Zedekiah of
Judah and his officials, I will hand them
over to their enemies and to those who seek
their lives, to the army of the king of Babylon,
which has withdrawn from you. [22]I am
going to command, says the LORD, and will
bring them back to this city; and they will
fight against it, and take it, and burn it with
fire. The towns of Judah I will make a
desolation without inhabitant.

The Rechabites Commended

35 The word that came to Jeremiah
from the LORD in the days of King
Jehoiakim son of Josiah of Judah: [2]Go to the
house of the Rechabites, and speak with
them, and bring them to the house of the

[w] Heb *as there was burning* [x] Heb *shall burn* [y] Cn: Heb lacks *like*

34.1-26 Warnings of God's Punishment of Judah.
34.1-7 As Judah and Jerusalem are being besieged by Nebuchadrezzar of Babylon, Jeremiah informs *King Zedekiah,* who has been placed on the throne by the Babylonians (2 Kings 24.17-20), that the city will soon fall and that he will be taken off to Babylon. Only the fortified cities of *Lachish and Azekah* in the hills overlooking the coastal plain southwest of Jerusalem are holding out against the invaders.
34.8-22 After Zedekiah has decreed that all enslaved Hebrews in Judah are to be freed, the people at first conform to the royal *covenant,* but then resume ownership of the briefly freed slaves. Jeremiah's *word from the LORD* reminds these slave-owners of the provision in the law of Moses for freeing slaves every seventh year (Ex 21.2; Deut 15.12). He then announces that he will *release* these violators of the law to fearful suffering and to control by the invaders. They are to be hacked in pieces like the sacrificial calves who were cut in two as offerings (Gen 15.7-11, 17-18). Jerusalem and *the towns of Judah* are to become *a desolation.*
35.1-19 The Rechabites as Models of Fidelity.
In the reign of Jehoiakim in Judah (609-598) a group formed whose members abstained from wine and lived only in *tents* like the early nomadic Israelites. They attributed these rules to their ancestor, Jehonadab son of Rechab, who supported the reforms of Jehu (842-815) in Israel (2 Kings 10.15-17), and hence they took the name of *Rechabites.* Jeremiah does not adopt their rules, but commends their fidelity to ancient regulations, contrasting it with the infidelity of the people of Judah in his own time. He promises that God will preserve the Rechabites.

34.1 2 Kings 25.1ff; Jer 39.1; 1.15; Dan 2.37,38

34.2 Jer 22.1,2; 37.1-4; Jer 32.29

34.5 2 Chr 16.14; 21.19; Jer 22.18

34.7 2 Chr 11.9; 2 Kings 18.13; 19.8

34.8 Ex 21.2; Lev 25.10

34.9 Neh 5.11; Lev 25.39-46

34.13 Ex 24.3,7,8; Deut 15.22

34.14 Ex 21.2; 23.10; Deut 15.12; 1 Sam 8.7,8; 2 Kings 17.13,14

34.15 2 Kings 23.3; Neh 10.29; Jer 7.10,11; 32.34

34.16 Ex 20.7; Lev 19.12

34.17 Mt 7.2; Gal 6.7; Deut 28.25,64

34.18 Deut 17.2; Hos 6.7; Gen 15.10,17

34.20 Jer 11.21; Jer 7.33; 19.7

34.21 Jer 37.5,11

34.22 Jer 37.8,10; Jer 4.7; 33.10; 44.22

35.1 2 Kings 24.1; Jer 1.3; 27.20

35.2 2 Kings 10.15; 1 Chr 2.55; 1 Kings 6.5

LORD, into one of the chambers; then offer them wine to drink. 3So I took Jaazaniah son of Jeremiah son of Habazziniah, and his brothers, and all his sons, and the whole house of the Rechabites. 4I brought them to the house of the LORD into the chamber of the sons of Hanan son of Igdaliah, the man of God, which was near the chamber of the officials, above the chamber of Maaseiah son of Shallum, keeper of the threshold. 5Then I set before the Rechabites pitchers full of wine, and cups; and I said to them, "Have some wine." 6But they answered, "We will drink no wine, for our ancestor Jonadab son of Rechab commanded us, 'You shall never drink wine, neither you nor your children; 7nor shall you ever build a house, or sow seed; nor shall you plant a vineyard, or even own one; but you shall live in tents all your days, that you may live many days in the land where you reside.' 8We have obeyed the charge of our ancestor Jonadab son of Rechab in all that he commanded us, to drink no wine all our days, ourselves, our wives, our sons, or our daughters, 9and not to build houses to live in. We have no vineyard or field or seed; 10but we have lived in tents, and have obeyed and done all that our ancestor Jonadab commanded us. 11But when King Nebuchadrezzar of Babylon came up against the land, we said, 'Come, and let us go to Jerusalem for fear of the army of the Chaldeans and the army of the Arameans.' That is why we are living in Jerusalem."

12 Then the word of the LORD came to Jeremiah: 13Thus says the LORD of hosts, the God of Israel: Go and say to the people of Judah and the inhabitants of Jerusalem, Can you not learn a lesson and obey my words? says the LORD. 14The command has been carried out that Jonadab son of Rechab gave to his descendants to drink no wine; and they drink none to this day, for they have obeyed their ancestor's command. But I myself have spoken to you persistently, and you have not obeyed me. 15I have sent to you all my servants the prophets, sending them persistently, saying, 'Turn now everyone of you from your evil way, and amend your doings, and do not go after other gods to serve them, and then you shall live in the land that I gave to you and your ancestors.' But you did not incline your ear or obey me. 16The descendants of Jonadab son of Rechab have carried out the command that their ancestor gave them, but this people has not obeyed me. 17Therefore, thus says the LORD, the God of hosts, the God of Israel: I am going to bring on Judah and on all the inhabitants of Jerusalem every disaster that I have pronounced against them; because I have spoken to them and they have not listened, I have called to them and they have not answered.

18 But to the house of the Rechabites Jeremiah said: Thus says the LORD of hosts, the God of Israel: Because you have obeyed the command of your ancestor Jonadab, and kept all his precepts, and done all that he commanded you, 19therefore thus says the LORD of hosts, the God of Israel: Jonadab son of Rechab shall not lack a descendant to stand before me for all time.

The Scroll Read in the Temple

36 In the fourth year of King Jehoiakim son of Josiah of Judah, this word came to Jeremiah from the LORD: 2Take a scroll and write on it all the words that I have spoken to you against Israel and Judah and all the nations, from the day I spoke to you, from the days of Josiah until today. 3It may be that when the house of Judah hears of all the disasters that I intend to do to them, all of them may turn from their evil ways, so that I may forgive their iniquity and their sin.

4 Then Jeremiah called Baruch son of Neriah, and Baruch wrote on a scroll at Jeremiah's dictation all the words of the LORD that he had spoken to him. 5And Jeremiah ordered Baruch, saying, "I am prevented from entering the house of the LORD; 6so you go yourself, and on a fast day in the hearing of the people in the LORD's house you shall read the words of the LORD from the scroll that you have written at my dictation. You shall read them also in the hearing of all the people of Judah who come up from their towns. 7It may be that their plea will come before the LORD, and that all of them will turn from their evil ways, for great is the anger and wrath that the LORD has pronounced against this people." 8And Baruch son of Neriah did all that the prophet Jeremiah ordered him about reading from the scroll the words of the LORD in the LORD's house.

9 In the fifth year of King Jehoiakim son of Josiah of Judah, in the ninth month, all the people in Jerusalem and all the people who came from the towns of Judah to

35.4 Deut 33.1; 1 Kings 12.22; 2 Kings 12.9; 25.18; 1 Chr 9.18,19
35.5 Am 2.12
35.6 2 Kings 10.15; 1 Chr 2.55; Lev 10.9; Lk 1.15
35.7 Gen 25.27; Heb 11.9; Ex 20.12; Eph 6.2,3
35.8 Prov 1.8,9; Eph 6.1; Col 3.20
35.11 2 Kings 24.1,2; Jer 4.5-7; 8.14
35.13 Isa 28.9-12; Jer 32.33
35.14 2 Chr 36.15; Jer 7.13; 25.3; Isa 30.9; 50.2
35.15 Jer 26.5; 32.33; Isa 1.16,17; Jer 4.1; 18.11; 7.6; 13.10; 22.4; 34.14
35.16 ver 14
35.17 Jer 19.3,15; Mic 3.12; Prov 1.24; Isa 65.12; 66.4; Jer 7.13
35.19 Jer 33.17; 15.19
36.1 2 Kings 24.1; Jer 25.1,3
36.2 ver 6,23,28; Zech 5.1; Jer 1.9,10; 25.9-29; 25.3
36.3 ver 7; Jer 26.3; Isa 55.7; Jer 18.8; Jon 3.8; Mk 4.12; Acts 3.19
36.4 ver 18; Jer 32.12; ver 14; Ezek 2.9
36.5 Jer 32.2; 33.1
36.7 2 Kings 22.13; Jer 4.4; 21.5
36.9 ver 6; Esth 4.16; Jon 3.5

36.1-32 The Recording of the LORD's Words to Jeremiah.
36.1-9 The fourth year of Jehoiakim would be 606 or 605. All the words of the LORD to Jeremiah were dictated by him to *Baruch son of Neriah*, who wrote them on a scroll and read them to the people in the temple courts, calling them to repent and thus to have the weight of God's judgment on them eased. The role of Baruch in relation to Jeremiah is described more fully in Jer 45. This section of Jeremiah (Jer 36-45) depicts vividly the final struggles of the prophet to convey the word of the LORD to the rulers and people of Judah.

36.11-19 When a court official heard Baruch reading these oracles in public, he summoned him to read them in the royal palace.
36.20-26 When the king heard them, he cut up the scroll and burned it. He then ordered the arrest of Baruch and Jeremiah, but *the LORD hid them.*
36.27-32 The LORD thereupon informed Jeremiah that the king would have no descendants to replace him on the throne, and that his body would be exposed rather than buried, which was viewed as a disgraceful end to life. Jeremiah dictated the oracles again, but added *many similar words*. The extent to which our present book of Jeremiah includes further additions is difficult to determine with certainty.
37.1-10 Jeremiah's Warning to Zedekiah. Zedekiah (597-586), installed by the Babylonians as king of Judah, sought a *word* from the LORD through Jeremiah. The message that came was that the Egyptians would withdraw and the *Chaldeans* (Babylonians) would continue the siege of Jerusalem.

Jerusalem proclaimed a fast before the LORD.
10 Then, in the hearing of all the people,
Baruch read the words of Jeremiah from the scroll, in the house of the LORD, in the chamber of Gemariah son of Shaphan the secretary, which was in the upper court, at the entry of the New Gate of the LORD's house.

The Scroll Read in the Palace

11 When Micaiah son of Gemariah son of Shaphan heard all the words of the LORD
from the scroll, 12 he went down to the
king's house, into the secretary's chamber; and all the officials were sitting there: Elishama the secretary, Delaiah son of Shemaiah, Elnathan son of Achbor, Gemariah son of Shaphan, Zedekiah son of
Hananiah, and all the officials. 13 And Micaiah
told them all the words that he had heard, when Baruch read the scroll in the hearing
of the people. 14 Then all the officials sent
Jehudi son of Nethaniah son of Shelemiah son of Cushi to say to Baruch, "Bring the scroll that you read in the hearing of the people, and come." So Baruch son of Neriah took the scroll in his hand and came to
them. 15 And they said to him, "Sit down
and read it to us." So Baruch read it to
them. 16 When they heard all the words,
they turned to one another in alarm, and said to Baruch, "We certainly must report
all these words to the king." 17 Then they
questioned Baruch, "Tell us now, how did you write all these words? Was it at his
dictation?" 18 Baruch answered them, "He
dictated all these words to me, and I wrote
them with ink on the scroll." 19 Then the
officials said to Baruch, "Go and hide, you and Jeremiah, and let no one know where you are."

Jehoiakim Burns the Scroll

20 Leaving the scroll in the chamber of Elishama the secretary, they went to the court of the king; and they reported all the
words to the king. 21 Then the king sent
Jehudi to get the scroll, and he took it from the chamber of Elishama the secretary; and Jehudi read it to the king and all the officials
who stood beside the king. 22 Now the king
was sitting in his winter apartment (it was the ninth month), and there was a fire
burning in the brazier before him. 23 As
Jehudi read three or four columns, the king[z]
would cut them off with a penknife and throw them into the fire in the brazier, until the entire scroll was consumed in the fire
that was in the brazier. 24 Yet neither the
king, nor any of his servants who heard all these words, was alarmed, nor did they tear
their garments. 25 Even when Elnathan and
Delaiah and Gemariah urged the king not to burn the scroll, he would not listen to
them. 26 And the king commanded Jerahmeel
the king's son and Seraiah son of Azriel and Shelemiah son of Abdeel to arrest the secretary Baruch and the prophet Jeremiah. But the LORD hid them.

Jeremiah Dictates Another

27 Now, after the king had burned the scroll with the words that Baruch wrote at Jeremiah's dictation, the word of the LORD
came to Jeremiah: 28 Take another scroll and
write on it all the former words that were in the first scroll, which King Jehoiakim of
Judah has burned. 29 And concerning King
Jehoiakim of Judah you shall say: Thus says the LORD, You have dared to burn this scroll, saying, Why have you written in it that the king of Babylon will certainly come and destroy this land, and will cut off from it
human beings and animals? 30 Therefore thus
says the LORD concerning King Jehoiakim of Judah: He shall have no one to sit upon the throne of David, and his dead body shall be cast out to the heat by day and the frost by
night. 31 And I will punish him and his
offspring and his servants for their iniquity; I will bring on them, and on the inhabitants of Jerusalem, and on the people of Judah, all the disasters with which I have threatened them—but they would not listen.
32 Then Jeremiah took another scroll and gave it to the secretary Baruch son of Neriah, who wrote on it at Jeremiah's dictation all the words of the scroll that King Jehoiakim of Judah had burned in the fire; and many similar words were added to them.

Zedekiah's Vain Hope

37 Zedekiah son of Josiah, whom King Nebuchadrezzar of Babylon made king in the land of Judah, succeeded Coniah
son of Jehoiakim. 2 But neither he nor his
servants nor the people of the land listened to the words of the LORD that he spoke through the prophet Jeremiah.

[z] Heb *he*

36.10 Jer 26.10
36.11 ver 13
36.12 ver 20,25; Jer 26.22
36.13 2 Kings 22.10
36.14 ver 21
36.15 ver 21
36.16 ver 24; Acts 24.25; Jer 13.18; Am 7.10,11
36.19 ver 26; Jer 26.20-24
36.21 ver 14; 2 Chr 34.18
36.22 Am 3.15
36.24 2 Kings 19.1,2; 22.11; Isa 36.22; 37.1
36.25 Acts 5.34-39
36.26 1 Kings 19.1ff; Jer 15.20,21
36.27 ver 23,4,18
36.28 Jer 28.13,14
36.29 Job 15.24,25; Isa 45.9; 30.10; Jer 26.9; 32.3; 25.9-11
36.30 2 Kings 24.12-15; Jer 22.30; 22.19
36.31 Jer 23.34; Deut 28.15; Jer 19.15
37.1 2 Kings 24.17; 2 Chr 36.10; Jer 22.24; Ezek 16.12-21
37.2 2 Chr 36.12,14

3 King Zedekiah sent Jehucal son of Shelemiah and the priest Zephaniah son of Maaseiah to the prophet Jeremiah saying, "Please pray for us to the LORD our God." [4]Now Jeremiah was still going in and out among the people, for he had not yet been put in prison. [5]Meanwhile, the army of Pharaoh had come out of Egypt; and when the Chaldeans who were besieging Jerusalem heard news of them, they withdrew from Jerusalem.

6 Then the word of the LORD came to the prophet Jeremiah: [7]Thus says the LORD, God of Israel: This is what the two of you shall say to the king of Judah, who sent you to me to inquire of me, Pharaoh's army, which set out to help you, is going to return to its own land, to Egypt. [8]And the Chaldeans shall return and fight against this city; they shall take it and burn it with fire. [9]Thus says the LORD: Do not deceive yourselves, saying, "The Chaldeans will surely go away from us," for they will not go away. [10]Even if you defeated the whole army of Chaldeans who are fighting against you, and there remained of them only wounded men in their tents, they would rise up and burn this city with fire.

Jeremiah Is Imprisoned

11 Now when the Chaldean army had withdrawn from Jerusalem at the approach of Pharaoh's army, [12]Jeremiah set out from Jerusalem to go to the land of Benjamin to receive his share of property[a] among the people there. [13]When he reached the Benjamin Gate, a sentinel there named Irijah son of Shelemiah son of Hananiah arrested the prophet Jeremiah saying, "You are deserting to the Chaldeans." [14]And Jeremiah said, "That is a lie; I am not deserting to the Chaldeans." But Irijah would not listen to him, and arrested Jeremiah and brought him to the officials. [15]The officials were enraged at Jeremiah, and they beat him and imprisoned him in the house of the secretary Jonathan, for it had been made a prison. [16]Thus Jeremiah was put in the cistern house, in the cells, and remained there many days.

17 Then King Zedekiah sent for him, and received him. The king questioned him secretly in his house, and said, "Is there any word from the LORD?" Jeremiah said, "There is!" Then he said, "You shall be handed over to the king of Babylon." [18]Jeremiah also said to King Zedekiah, "What wrong have I done to you or your servants or this people, that you have put me in prison? [19]Where are your prophets who prophesied to you, saying, 'The king of Babylon will not come against you and against this land'? [20]Now please hear me, my lord king: be good enough to listen to my plea, and do not send me back to the house of the secretary Jonathan to die there." [21]So King Zedekiah gave orders, and they committed Jeremiah to the court of the guard; and a loaf of bread was given him daily from the bakers' street, until all the bread of the city was gone. So Jeremiah remained in the court of the guard.

Jeremiah in the Cistern

38 Now Shephatiah son of Mattan, Gedaliah son of Pashhur, Jucal son of Shelemiah, and Pashhur son of Malchiah heard the words that Jeremiah was saying to all the people, [2]Thus says the LORD, Those who stay in this city shall die by the sword, by famine, and by pestilence; but those who go out to the Chaldeans shall live; they shall have their lives as a prize of war, and live. [3]Thus says the LORD, This city shall surely be handed over to the army of the king of Babylon and be taken. [4]Then the officials said to the king, "This man ought to be put to death, because he is discouraging the soldiers who are left in this city, and all the people, by speaking such words to them. For this man is not seeking the welfare of this people, but their harm." [5]King Zedekiah said, "Here he is; he is in your hands; for the king is powerless against you." [6]So they took Jeremiah and threw him into the cistern of Malchiah, the king's son, which was in the court of the guard, letting Jeremiah down by ropes. Now there was no water in the cistern, but only mud, and Jeremiah sank in the mud.

Jeremiah Is Rescued by Ebed-melech

7 Ebed-melech the Ethiopian,[b] a eunuch in the king's house, heard that they had put Jeremiah into the cistern. The king happened to be sitting at the Benjamin Gate, [8]So Ebed-melech left the king's house and spoke to the king, [9]"My lord king, these men have acted wickedly in all they did to

[a] Meaning of Heb uncertain [b] Or *Nubian*; Heb *Cushite*

37.11-38.28 Jeremiah in Prison.
37.11-21 Seized, beaten and imprisoned, Jeremiah was consulted secretly by Zedekiah. The message to him repeated the certainty of his exile in Babylon. Jeremiah's plea not to be returned to the officer who had imprisoned him was honored, and the prophet was put under guard in the royal palace.
38.1-13 Some officers who heard Jeremiah's prediction that those who turned themselves over to the Babylonian besiegers would survive threw him into a muddy cistern, on the charge of aiding the enemy. He was rescued by an *Ethiopian*, and placed under guard.

37.3 Jer 21.1,2; 29.25; 52.24; 1 Kings 13.6; Acts 8.24
37.5 2 Kings 24.7; Ezek 17.15; Jer 34.21
37.7 Jer 21.1; Isa 30.1-3; 31.1-3; Ezek 17.17
37.8 Jer 34.22
37.9 Jer 29.8
37.10 Jer 21.4,5; Joel 2.11
37.13 Jer 38.7; Zech 14.10; Jer 18.18; 20.10; Lk 23.2; Acts 24.5-9,13
37.15 Jer 18.23; 2 Chr 16.10; 18.26
37.16 Jer 38.6
37.17 Jer 38.5,14-16,24-27
37.18 Dan 6.22; Jn 10.32; Acts 25.8,11,25
37.19 Jer 2.28; 6.14; 29.31
37.21 Jer 32.2; 38.13,28; Isa 33.16; Jer 38.9; 52.6; 39.14,15
38.1 Jer 37.3; 21.1.8
38.2 Jer 21.9; 42.17; 45.5
38.3 Jer 21.10; 32.3
38.4 Jer 18.23; 26.11; 1 Kings 18.17,18; Am 7.10; Acts 16.20; Jer 29.7
38.5 2 Sam 3.39
38.6 Jer 37.21; Acts 16.24; Zech 9.11
38.7 Jer 39.16; 37.13; Am 5.10
38.9 Jer 37.21; 52.6

38.14-28 In a second *secret* consultation with Zedekiah, Jeremiah repeated the prediction that the king's *wives and children*, as well as the king himself, would be taken by the *Chaldeans*. Efforts by officials to discover the substance of this conversation failed.
39.1-40.16 Jeremiah's Experiences During and After the Fall of Jerusalem.
39.1-10 When the Babylonians took Jerusalem, Zedekiah tried to escape, but was captured at *Jericho* and taken back to Jerusalem, where his *sons* and *all the nobles of Judah* were killed before his eyes, and he was then blinded. Only *some of the poor* were allowed to remain in the area; all others were exiled to Babylon.

the prophet Jeremiah by throwing him into
the cistern to die there of hunger, for there
is no bread left in the city." 10Then the king
commanded Ebed-melech the Ethiopian,[c]
"Take three men with you from here, and
pull the prophet Jeremiah up from the cistern before he dies." 11So Ebed-melech took
the men with him and went to the house
of the king, to a wardrobe of[d] the storehouse, and took from there old rags and
worn-out clothes, which he let down to
Jeremiah in the cistern by ropes. 12Then
Ebed-melech the Ethiopian[c] said to Jeremiah,
"Just put the rags and clothes between your
armpits and the ropes." Jeremiah did so.
13Then they drew Jeremiah up by the ropes
and pulled him out of the cistern. And
Jeremiah remained in the court of the guard.

Zedekiah Consults Jeremiah Again
14 King Zedekiah sent for the prophet
Jeremiah and received him at the third
entrance of the temple of the LORD. The king
said to Jeremiah, "I have something to ask
you; do not hide anything from me." 15Jer-
emiah said to Zedekiah, "If I tell you, you
will put me to death, will you not? And if
I give you advice, you will not listen to me."
16So King Zedekiah swore an oath in secret
to Jeremiah, "As the LORD lives, who gave
us our lives, I will not put you to death or
hand you over to these men who seek your
life."
17 Then Jeremiah said to Zedekiah, "Thus
says the LORD, the God of hosts, the God of
Israel, If you will only surrender to the
officials of the king of Babylon, then your
life shall be spared, and this city shall not
be burned with fire, and you and your
house shall live. 18But if you do not surrender to the officials of the king of Babylon,
then this city shall be handed over to the
Chaldeans, and they shall burn it with fire,
and you yourself shall not escape from their
hand." 19King Zedekiah said to Jeremiah, "I
am afraid of the Judeans who have deserted
to the Chaldeans, for I might be handed
over to them and they would abuse me."
20Jeremiah said, "That will not happen. Just
obey the voice of the LORD in what I say to
you, and it shall go well with you, and your
life shall be spared. 21But if you are determined not to surrender, this is what the
LORD has shown me— 22a vision of all the
women remaining in the house of the king
of Judah being led out to the officials of the
king of Babylon and saying,
'Your trusted friends have seduced you
and have overcome you;
Now that your feet are stuck in the
mud,
they desert you.'
23All your wives and your children shall be
led out to the Chaldeans, and you yourself
shall not escape from their hand, but shall
be seized by the king of Babylon; and this
city shall be burned with fire."
24 Then Zedekiah said to Jeremiah, "Do
not let anyone else know of this conversation, or you will die. 25If the officials should
hear that I have spoken with you, and they
should come and say to you, 'Just tell us
what you said to the king; do not conceal
it from us, or we will put you to death.
What did the king say to you?' 26then you
shall say to them, 'I was presenting my plea
to the king not to send me back to the
house of Jonathan to die there.'<|>" 27All
the officials did come to Jeremiah and questioned him; and he answered them in the
very words the king had commanded. So
they stopped questioning him, for the conversation had not been overheard. 28And
Jeremiah remained in the court of the guard
until the day that Jerusalem was taken.

The Fall of Jerusalem
39 In the ninth year of King Zedekiah
of Judah, in the tenth month, King
Nebuchadrezzar of Babylon and all his army
came against Jerusalem and besieged it; 2in
the eleventh year of Zedekiah, in the fourth
month, on the ninth day of the month, a
breach was made in the city. 3When Jerusalem was taken,[e] all the officials of the king
of Babylon came and sat in the middle gate:
Nergal-sharezer, Samgar-nebo, Sarsechim the
Rabsaris, Nergal-sharezer the Rabmag, with
all the rest of the officials of the king of
Babylon. 4When King Zedekiah of Judah
and all the soldiers saw them, they fled,
going out of the city at night by way of the
king's garden through the gate between the
two walls; and they went toward the Arabah.
5But the army of the Chaldeans pursued
them, and overtook Zedekiah in the plains
of Jericho; and when they had taken him,
they brought him up to King Nebuchadrezzar

[c] Or *Nubian*; Heb *Cushite* [d] Cn: Heb *to under* [e] Or *Nubian*; Heb *Cushite* [f] This clause has been transposed from 38.28

38.13 Jer 37.21; 39.14,15
38.14 Jer 21.1,2; 37.17; 15.11; 42.2-5,20
38.15 Lk 22.67,68
38.16 Jer 37.17; Isa 57.16; Zech 12.1; ver 4-6
38.17 Ps 80.7,14; 1 Chr 17.24; Ezek 8.4; 2 Kings 24.12; 26.27-30
38.18 Jer 27.8; 32.4; 34.3
38.19 Isa 51.12,13; Jn 12.42; 19.12,13; Jer 39.9; 2 Chr 30.10; Neh 4.1
38.20 Jer 11.4.8; 7.23; Isa 55.3
38.22 Jer 6.12; 8.10; 43.6
38.23 Jer 39.6; 41.10
38.25 ver 4-6,27
38.26 Jer 37.15,20
38.27 1 Sam 10.15,16; 16.2-5
38.28 Jer 37.21; 39.14
39.1 2 Kings 25.1-4; Jer 52.4-7; Ezek 24.1,2
39.2 2 Kings 25.4; Jer 52.7
39.3 Jer 38.17
39.4 2 Kings 25.4; Jer 52.7; Am 2.14; 2 Chr 32.5
39.5 Jer 32.4; 38.18,23; Josh 4.13; 2 Kings 23.33

of Babylon, at Riblah, in the land of Hamath; and he passed sentence on him. [6]The king of Babylon slaughtered the sons of Zedekiah at Riblah before his eyes; also the king of Babylon slaughtered all the nobles of Judah. [7]He put out the eyes of Zedekiah, and bound him in fetters to take him to Babylon. [8]The Chaldeans burned the king's house and the houses of the people, and broke down the walls of Jerusalem. [9]Then Nebuzaradan the captain of the guard exiled to Babylon the rest of the people who were left in the city, those who had deserted to him, and the people who remained. [10]Nebuzaradan the captain of the guard left in the land of Judah some of the poor people who owned nothing, and gave them vineyards and fields at the same time.

Jeremiah, Set Free, Remembers Ebed-melech

11 King Nebuchadrezzar of Babylon gave command concerning Jeremiah through Nebuzaradan, the captain of the guard, saying, [12]"Take him, look after him well and do him no harm, but deal with him as he may ask you." [13]So Nebuzaradan the captain of the guard, Nebushazban the Rabsaris, Nergal-sharezer the Rabmag, and all the chief officers of the king of Babylon sent [14]and took Jeremiah from the court of the guard. They entrusted him to Gedaliah son of Ahikam son of Shaphan to be brought home. So he stayed with his own people.

15 The word of the LORD came to Jeremiah while he was confined in the court of the guard: [16]Go and say to Ebed-melech the Ethiopian:[f] Thus says the LORD of hosts, the God of Israel: I am going to fulfill my words against this city for evil and not for good, and they shall be accomplished in your presence on that day. [17]But I will save you on that day, says the LORD, and you shall not be handed over to those whom you dread. [18]For I will surely save you, and you shall not fall by the sword; but you shall have your life as a prize of war, because you have trusted in me, says the LORD.

Jeremiah with Gedaliah the Governor

40 The word that came to Jeremiah from the LORD after Nebuzaradan the captain of the guard had let him go from Ramah, when he took him bound in fetters along with all the captives of Jerusalem and Judah who were being exiled to Babylon. [2]The captain of the guard took Jeremiah and said to him, "The LORD your God threatened this place with this disaster; [3]and now the LORD has brought it about, and has done as he said, because all of you sinned against the LORD and did not obey his voice. Therefore this thing has come upon you. [4]Now look, I have just released you today from the fetters on your hands. If you wish to come with me to Babylon, come, and I will take good care of you; but if you do not wish to come with me to Babylon, you need not come. See, the whole land is before you; go wherever you think it good and right to go. [5]If you remain,[g] then return to Gedaliah son of Ahikam son of Shaphan, whom the king of Babylon appointed governor of the towns of Judah, and stay with him among the people; or go wherever you think it right to go." So the captain of the guard gave him an allowance of food and a present, and let him go. [6]Then Jeremiah went to Gedaliah son of Ahikam at Mizpah, and stayed with him among the people who were left in the land.

7 When all the leaders of the forces in the open country and their troops heard that the king of Babylon had appointed Gedaliah son of Ahikam governor in the land, and had committed to him men, women, and children, those of the poorest of the land who had not been taken into exile to Babylon, [8]they went to Gedaliah at Mizpah—Ishmael son of Nethaniah, Johanan son of Kareah, Seraiah son of Tanhumeth, the sons of Ephai the Netophathite, Jezaniah son of the Maacathite, they and their troops. [9]Gedaliah son of Ahikam son of Shaphan swore to them and their troops, saying, "Do not be afraid to serve the Chaldeans. Stay in the land and serve the king of Babylon, and it shall go well with you. [10]As for me, I am staying at Mizpah to represent you before the Chaldeans who come to us; but as for you, gather wine and summer fruits and oil, and store them in your vessels, and live in the towns that you have taken over." [11]Likewise, when all the Judeans who were in Moab and among the Ammonites and in Edom and in other lands heard that the king of Babylon had left a remnant in Judah and had appointed Gedaliah son of Ahikam son of Shaphan as governor over them, [12]then all the Judeans returned from all the places to which they had been scattered

[f] Or *Nubian*; Heb *Cushite* [g] Syr: Meaning of Heb uncertain

39.6 2 Kings 25.7; Jer 34.19-21
39.7 2 Kings 25.7; Jer 52.11; Ezek 12.13; Jer 32.5
39.8 2 Kings 25.9,10; Jer 38.18; 52.13
39.9 2 Kings 25.11,20; Jer 52.12-16; 24.8; 38.19
39.10 2 Kings 25.12; Jer 52.16
39.11 Jer 1.8; 15.20,21; Acts 24.23
39.14 Jer 38.28; 40.1-6; 2 Kings 22.12,14; 2 Chr 34.20
39.16 Jer 38.7,12; 21.10; Dan 9.12; Zech 1.6
39.17 Ps 41.1,2; 50.15
39.18 Jer 21.9; 45.5; Ps 34.22; Jer 17.7,8
40.1 Jer 39.9,11,14; 31.15; Eph 6.20
40.2 Jer 22.8,9; 50.7
40.3 Deut 29.24,25; Dan 9.11
40.4 Jer 39.11,12; Gen 20.15
40.5 Jer 39.14; 2 Kings 25.23; ver 4; Jer 52.34
40.6 Jer 39.14; Judg 20.1
40.7 2 Kings 25.23,24; Jer 39.10; 52.16
40.8 Jer 41.1
40.10 ver 6; Jer 35.19; 39.10; ver 12; Jer 48.32
40.11 Isa 16.4; 1 Sam 11.1; 12.12; Isa 11.14
40.12 Jer 43.5; ver 10

40.1-16 Jeremiah chose to remain in Judah, under the custody of Gedaliah, whom the Babylonians appointed governor, and who set up his seat of government at *Mizpah* (about eight miles north of Jerusalem) and urged the remaining Judahites to submit to Babylonian rule. Others who had fled across the Jordan returned to live in prosperity in Judah under the new governor.

41.1-44.30 Jeremiah Denounces the Futile Effort to Find Safety in Egypt.
41.1-18 *Ishmael*, a member of *the royal family*, organized a revolt, killed Gedaliah because of his collaboration with the Babylonians, and slaughtered scores of worshippers who had come to *the temple of the LORD* from cities of the northern tribes of Israel: *Shechem, Shiloh*, and *Samaria*. Leading as captives the governor's family and others from Mizpah, Ishmael fled across the Jordan to the Ammonites. The leader of the forces loyal to Gedaliah intercepted Ishmael and freed his captives. Many, however, decided to migrate to Egypt.
42.1-22 When the *commanders of the forces* consulted with Jeremiah about what this *remnant* of the people still in Judah should do, his *word from the LORD* was that they should *remain in this land*. If they were to go to Egypt, fighting (*the sword*) and famine would overtake them.

and came to the land of Judah, to Gedaliah at Mizpah; and they gathered wine and summer fruits in great abundance.

13 Now Johanan son of Kareah and all the leaders of the forces in the open country came to Gedaliah at Mizpah [14]and said to him, "Are you at all aware that Baalis king of the Ammonites has sent Ishmael son of Nethaniah to take your life?" But Gedaliah son of Ahikam would not believe them. [15]Then Johanan son of Kareah spoke secretly to Gedaliah at Mizpah, "Please let me go and kill Ishmael son of Nethaniah, and no one else will know. Why should he take your life, so that all the Judeans who are gathered around you would be scattered, and the remnant of Judah would perish?" [16]But Gedaliah son of Ahikam said to Johanan son of Kareah, "Do not do such a thing, for you are telling a lie about Ishmael."

Insurrection against Gedaliah

41 In the seventh month, Ishmael son of Nethaniah son of Elishama, of the royal family, one of the chief officers of the king, came with ten men to Gedaliah son of Ahikam, at Mizpah. As they ate bread together there at Mizpah, [2]Ishmael son of Nethaniah and the ten men with him got up and struck down Gedaliah son of Ahikam son of Shaphan with the sword and killed him, because the king of Babylon had appointed him governor in the land. [3]Ishmael also killed all the Judeans who were with Gedaliah at Mizpah, and the Chaldean soldiers who happened to be there.

4 On the day after the murder of Gedaliah, before anyone knew of it, [5]eighty men arrived from Shechem and Shiloh and Samaria, with their beards shaved and their clothes torn, and their bodies gashed, bringing grain offerings and incense to present at the temple of the LORD. [6]And Ishmael son of Nethaniah came out from Mizpah to meet them, weeping as he came. As he met them, he said to them, "Come to Gedaliah son of Ahikam." [7]When they reached the middle of the city, Ishmael son of Nethaniah and the men with him slaughtered them, and threw them[h] into a cistern. [8]But there were ten men among them who said to Ishmael, "Do not kill us, for we have stores of wheat, barley, oil, and honey hidden in the fields." So he refrained, and did not kill them along with their companions.

9 Now the cistern into which Ishmael had thrown all the bodies of the men whom he had struck down was the large cistern[i] that King Asa had made for defense against King Baasha of Israel; Ishmael son of Nethaniah filled that cistern with those whom he had killed. [10]Then Ishmael took captive all the rest of the people who were in Mizpah, the king's daughters and all the people who were left at Mizpah, whom Nebuzaradan, the captain of the guard, had committed to Gedaliah son of Ahikam. Ishmael son of Nethaniah took them captive and set out to cross over to the Ammonites.

11 But when Johanan son of Kareah and all the leaders of the forces with him heard of all the crimes that Ishmael son of Nethaniah had done, [12]they took all their men and went to fight against Ishmael son of Nethaniah. They came upon him at the great pool that is in Gibeon. [13]And when all the people who were with Ishmael saw Johanan son of Kareah and all the leaders of the forces with him, they were glad. [14]So all the people whom Ishmael had carried away captive from Mizpah turned around and came back, and went to Johanan son of Kareah. [15]But Ishmael son of Nethaniah escaped from Johanan with eight men, and went to the Ammonites. [16]Then Johanan son of Kareah and all the leaders of the forces with him took all the rest of the people whom Ishmael son of Nethaniah had carried away captive[j] from Mizpah after he had slain Gedaliah son of Ahikam—soldiers, women, children, and eunuchs, whom Johanan brought back from Gibeon.[k] [17]And they set out, and stopped at Geruth Chimham near Bethlehem, intending to go to Egypt [18]because of the Chaldeans; for they were afraid of them, because Ishmael son of Nethaniah had killed Gedaliah son of Ahikam, whom the king of Babylon had made governor over the land.

Jeremiah Advises Survivors Not to Migrate

42 Then all the commanders of the forces, and Johanan son of Kareah and Azariah[l] son of Hoshaiah, and all the people from the least to the greatest, approached [2]the prophet Jeremiah and said, "Be good enough to listen to our plea, and pray to the LORD your God for us—for all

[h] Syr: Heb lacks *and threw them*; compare verse 9 [i] Gk: Heb *whom he had killed by the hand of Gedaliah* [j] Cn: Heb *whom he recovered from Ishmael son of Nethaniah* [k] Meaning of Heb uncertain [l] Gk: Heb *Jezaniah*

40.13 ver 8
40.14 Jer 41.10
40.15 1 Sam 26.8; 2 Sam 21.17; Jer 42.2
40.16 Mt 10.16
41.1 2 Kings 25.25; Jer 40.6,8,14
41.2 2 Kings 25.25; Jer 40.5
41.5 Gen 33.18; Josh 18.1; 1 Kings 16.24,29; Jer 16.6; 2 Kings 25.9
41.6 Jer 50.4
41.7 Isa 59.7; Ezek 22.27
41.9 1 Kings 15.22; 2 Chr 16.6
41.10 Jer 40.11,12; 43.6; 40.7,14
41.11 Jer 40.7,8,13-16
41.12 2 Sam 2.13
41.13 ver 10,14
41.15 ver 2
41.16 Jer 42.8; 43.4-7
41.17 2 Sam 19.37,38; Jer 42.14
41.18 Jer 42.11,16; Lk 12.4,5; Jer 40.5
42.1 Jer 40.8,13; 41.11
42.2 Jer 36.7; 37.20; ver 20; 1 Kings 13.6; Acts 8.24; Deut 28.62; Lam 1.1

42.3 Ps 86.11; Mic 4.2
42.4 1 Sam 12.23; 1 Kings 22.14; Jer 23.28; 1 Sam 3.17,18; Ps 40.10
42.6 Deut 6.3; Jer 7.23
42.10 Jer 24.6; 31.28; Ezek 36.36; Jon 3.10; 4.2
42.11 Jer 41.18; Isa 43.5; Rom 8.31
42.13 Jer 44.16
42.14 Jer 41.17; 4.19,21
42.15 Jer 44.12-14
42.17 Jer 44.13,14,28
42.18 Jer 7.20; 33.5; Isa 65.15; Jer 29.18; 22.10,27
42.19 Deut 17.16; Isa 30.1-7; Neh 9.26,29,30
42.21 Jer 43.1; Ezek 2.7; Jer 43.4
42.22 Jer 43.11; Hos 9.6
43.1 Jer 26.8; 51.63; 42.10-18
43.2 Jer 42.1; 2 Chr 36.13; Jer 42.5
43.3 Jer 38.4
43.4 Jer 42.5,6,10-12
43.6 Jer 41.10; 39.10; 40.7
43.8 Jer 2.16; 44.1; 46.14

this remnant. For there are only a few of us left out of many, as your eyes can see. [3]Let the LORD your God show us where we should go and what we should do." [4]The prophet Jeremiah said to them, "Very well: I am going to pray to the LORD your God as you request, and whatever the LORD answers you I will tell you; I will keep nothing back from you." [5]They in their turn said to Jeremiah, "May the LORD be a true and faithful witness against us if we do not act according to everything that the LORD your God sends us through you. [6]Whether it is good or bad, we will obey the voice of the LORD our God to whom we are sending you, in order that it may go well with us when we obey the voice of the LORD our God."

7 At the end of ten days the word of the LORD came to Jeremiah. [8]Then he summoned Johanan son of Kareah and all the commanders of the forces who were with him, and all the people from the least to the greatest, [9]and said to them, "Thus says the LORD, the God of Israel, to whom you sent me to present your plea before him: [10]If you will only remain in this land, then I will build you up and not pull you down; I will plant you, and not pluck you up; for I am sorry for the disaster that I have brought upon you. [11]Do not be afraid of the king of Babylon, as you have been; do not be afraid of him, says the LORD, for I am with you, to save you and to rescue you from his hand. [12]I will grant you mercy, and he will have mercy on you and restore you to your native soil. [13]But if you continue to say, 'We will not stay in this land,' thus disobeying the voice of the LORD your God [14]and saying, 'No, we will go to the land of Egypt, where we shall not see war, or hear the sound of the trumpet, or be hungry for bread, and there we will stay,' [15]then hear the word of the LORD, O remnant of Judah. Thus says the LORD of hosts, the God of Israel: If you are determined to enter Egypt and go to settle there, [16]then the sword that you fear shall overtake you there, in the land of Egypt; and the famine that you dread shall follow close after you into Egypt; and there you shall die. [17]All the people who have determined to go to Egypt to settle there shall die by the sword, by famine, and by pestilence; they shall have no remnant or survivor from the disaster that I am bringing upon them.

18 "For thus says the LORD of hosts, the God of Israel: Just as my anger and my wrath were poured out on the inhabitants of Jerusalem, so my wrath will be poured out on you when you go to Egypt. You shall become an object of execration and horror, of cursing and ridicule. You shall see this place no more. [19]The LORD has said to you, O remnant of Judah, Do not go to Egypt. Be well aware that I have warned you today [20]that you have made a fatal mistake. For you yourselves sent me to the LORD your God, saying, 'Pray for us to the LORD our God, and whatever the LORD our God says, tell us and we will do it.' [21]So I have told you today, but you have not obeyed the voice of the LORD your God in anything that he sent me to tell you. [22]Be well aware, then, that you shall die by the sword, by famine, and by pestilence in the place where you desire to go and settle."

Taken to Egypt, Jeremiah Warns of Judgment

43 When Jeremiah finished speaking to all the people all these words of the LORD their God, with which the LORD their God had sent him to them, [2]Azariah son of Hoshaiah and Johanan son of Kareah and all the other insolent men said to Jeremiah, "You are telling a lie. The LORD our God did not send you to say, 'Do not go to Egypt to settle there'; [3]but Baruch son of Neriah is inciting you against us, to hand us over to the Chaldeans, in order that they may kill us or take us into exile in Babylon." [4]So Johanan son of Kareah and all the commanders of the forces and all the people did not obey the voice of the LORD, to stay in the land of Judah. [5]But Johanan son of Kareah and all the commanders of the forces took all the remnant of Judah who had returned to settle in the land of Judah from all the nations to which they had been driven— [6]the men, the women, the children, the princesses, and everyone whom Nebuzaradan the captain of the guard had left with Gedaliah son of Ahikam son of Shaphan; also the prophet Jeremiah and Baruch son of Neriah. [7]And they came into the land of Egypt, for they did not obey the voice of the LORD. And they arrived at Tahpanhes.

8 Then the word of the LORD came to Jeremiah in Tahpanhes: [9]Take some large stones in your hands, and bury them in the clay pavement[m] that is at the entrance to

[m] Meaning of Heb uncertain

43.1-7 Accusing Jeremiah of heeding the advice of *Baruch*, his companion and scribe, the leaders forced *all the remnant of the people*, as well as those who had recently returned to Judah, to migrate to Egypt – including Baruch and Jeremiah. They settled in the northeast section of the Nile delta, at *Tahpanhes*.
43.8-13 Jeremiah buried large stones in the pavement before *Pharaoh's palace*, as signs that the Babylonian king would soon take over Egypt as well, destroying the foolish notion of the emigrants from Judah that in Egypt they could escape God's judgment on them.

44.1-14 Jeremiah reminds the refugees in Egypt of the persistent rejection by their leaders of God's message for his people through the prophets, and of the consequent judgment that has fallen on Judah and Jerusalem.
44.15-19 The Jewish people living in *Pathros* (far up the Nile Valley) claim that they are benefiting from their new practice of idolatrous offerings to *the queen of heaven*, the Egyptian fertility goddess.

Pharaoh's palace in Tahpanhes. Let the Judeans see you do it, [10]and say to them, Thus says the LORD of hosts, the God of Israel: I am going to send and take my servant King Nebuchadrezzar of Babylon, and he[n] will set his throne above these stones that I have buried, and he will spread his royal canopy over them. [11]He shall come and ravage the land of Egypt, giving

those who are destined for pestilence, to pestilence,
and those who are destined for captivity, to captivity,
and those who are destined for the sword, to the sword.

[12]He[o] shall kindle a fire in the temples of the gods of Egypt; and he shall burn them and carry them away captive; and he shall pick clean the land of Egypt, as a shepherd picks his cloak clean of vermin; and he shall depart from there safely. [13]He shall break the obelisks of Heliopolis, which is in the land of Egypt; and the temples of the gods of Egypt he shall burn with fire.

Denunciation of Persistent Idolatry

44 The word that came to Jeremiah for all the Judeans living in the land of Egypt, at Migdol, at Tahpanhes, at Memphis, and in the land of Pathros, [2]Thus says the LORD of hosts, the God of Israel: You yourselves have seen all the disaster that I have brought on Jerusalem and on all the towns of Judah. Look at them; today they are a desolation, without an inhabitant in them, [3]because of the wickedness that they committed, provoking me to anger, in that they went to make offerings and serve other gods that they had not known, neither they, nor you, nor your ancestors. [4]Yet I persistently sent to you all my servants the prophets, saying, "I beg you not to do this abominable thing that I hate!" [5]But they did not listen or incline their ear, to turn from their wickedness and make no offerings to other gods. [6]So my wrath and my anger were poured out and kindled in the towns of Judah and in the streets of Jerusalem; and they became a waste and a desolation, as they still are today. [7]And now thus says the LORD God of hosts, the God of Israel: Why are you doing such great harm to yourselves, to cut off man and woman, child and infant, from the midst of Judah, leaving yourselves without a remnant? [8]Why do you provoke me to anger with the works of your hands, making offerings to other gods in the land of Egypt where you have come to settle? Will you be cut off and become an object of cursing and ridicule among all the nations of the earth? [9]Have you forgotten the crimes of your ancestors, of the kings of Judah, of their[p] wives, your own crimes and those of your wives, which they committed in the land of Judah and in the streets of Jerusalem? [10]They have shown no contrition or fear to this day, nor have they walked in my law and my statutes that I set before you and before your ancestors.

11 Therefore thus says the LORD of hosts, the God of Israel: I am determined to bring disaster on you, to bring all Judah to an end. [12]I will take the remnant of Judah who are determined to come to the land of Egypt to settle, and they shall perish, everyone; in the land of Egypt they shall fall; by the sword and by famine they shall perish; from the least to the greatest, they shall die by the sword and by famine; and they shall become an object of execration and horror, of cursing and ridicule. [13]I will punish those who live in the land of Egypt, as I have punished Jerusalem, with the sword, with famine, and with pestilence, [14]so that none of the remnant of Judah who have come to settle in the land of Egypt shall escape or survive or return to the land of Judah. Although they long to go back to live there, they shall not go back, except some fugitives.

15 Then all the men who were aware that their wives had been making offerings to other gods, and all the women who stood by, a great assembly, all the people who lived in Pathros in the land of Egypt, answered Jeremiah: [16]"As for the word that you have spoken to us in the name of the LORD, we are not going to listen to you. [17]Instead, we will do everything that we have vowed, make offerings to the queen of heaven and pour out libations to her, just as we and our ancestors, our kings and our officials, used to do in the towns of Judah and in the streets of Jerusalem. We used to have plenty of food, and prospered, and saw no misfortune. [18]But from the time we stopped making offerings to the queen of heaven and pouring out libations to her, we have lacked everything and have perished by the sword and by famine." [19]And the women said,[q] "Indeed we will go on making

[n] Gk Syr: Heb *I* [o] Gk Syr Vg: Heb *I* [p] Heb *his* [q] Compare Syr: Heb lacks *And the women said*

43.10 Jer 25.9,11; 27.5,6; 31.20
43.11 Isa 19.1-25; Jer 44.13; 46.13; Ezek 29.19,20; Jer 15.2
43.12 Isa 19.1; Jer 46.25; Ezek 30.13
44.1 Jer 46.14; 43.7; Isa 19.13
44.2 Jer 9.11; 34.22; Mic 3.12
44.3 Ezek 8.17,18; Dan 9.5; Isa 3.8; Jer 19.4; Deut 13.6; 32.17
44.4 2 Chr 36.15; Jer 7.25; 25.4; 26.5; Ezek 8.10
44.6 Jer 42.18
44.7 Jer 26.19; Ezek 33.11; Jer 9.21; 51.22
44.8 2 Kings 17.15-17; Jer 25.6,7; Jer 42.18
44.9 Jer 7.9,10,17,18
44.10 Jer 6.15; 8.12; 26.4; 32.23
44.11 Lev 26.17; Jer 21.10; Am 9.4
44.12 Jer 42.15-18,22
44.14 Jer 22.26,27; Isa 4.2; 10.20; ver 28; Rom 9.27
44.15 Jer 5.1-5
44.16 Jer 8.6,12; 13.10
44.17 2 Kings 17.16; Jer 7.18; Hos 2.5-9; Phil 3.19
44.18 Jer 40.12
44.19 Jer 7.18; Num 30.6,7

offerings to the queen of heaven and pouring out libations to her; do you think that we made cakes for her, marked with her image, and poured out libations to her without our husbands' being involved?"

20 Then Jeremiah said to all the people, men and women, all the people who were giving him this answer: 21 "As for the offerings that you made in the towns of Judah and in the streets of Jerusalem, you and your ancestors, your kings and your officials, and the people of the land, did not the LORD remember them? Did it not come into his mind? 22 The LORD could no longer bear the sight of your evil doings, the abominations that you committed; therefore your land became a desolation and a waste and a curse, without inhabitant, as it is to this day. 23 It is because you burned offerings, and because you sinned against the LORD and did not obey the voice of the LORD or walk in his law and in his statutes and in his decrees, that this disaster has befallen you, as is still evident today."

24 Jeremiah said to all the people and all the women, "Hear the word of the LORD, all you Judeans who are in the land of Egypt, 25 Thus says the LORD of hosts, the God of Israel: You and your wives have accomplished in deeds what you declared in words, saying, 'We are determined to perform the vows that we have made, to make offerings to the queen of heaven and to pour out libations to her.' By all means, keep your vows and make your libations! 26 Therefore hear the word of the LORD, all you Judeans who live in the land of Egypt: Lo, I swear by my great name, says the LORD, that my name shall no longer be pronounced on the lips of any of the people of Judah in all the land of Egypt, saying, 'As the Lord GOD lives.' 27 I am going to watch over them for harm and not for good; all the people of Judah who are in the land of Egypt shall perish by the sword and by famine, until not one is left. 28 And those who escape the sword shall return from the land of Egypt to the land of Judah, few in number; and all the remnant of Judah, who have come to the land of Egypt to settle, shall know whose words will stand, mine or theirs! 29 This shall be the sign to you, says the LORD, that I am going to punish you in this place, in order that you may know that my words against you will surely be carried out: 30 Thus says the LORD, I am going to give Pharaoh Hophra, king of Egypt, into the hands of his enemies, those who seek his life, just as I gave King Zedekiah of Judah into the hand of King Nebuchadrezzar of Babylon, his enemy who sought his life."

A Word of Comfort to Baruch

45 The word that the prophet Jeremiah spoke to Baruch son of Neriah, when he wrote these words in a scroll at the dictation of Jeremiah, in the fourth year of King Jehoiakim son of Josiah of Judah: 2 Thus says the LORD, the God of Israel, to you, O Baruch: 3 You said, "Woe is me! The LORD has added sorrow to my pain; I am weary with my groaning, and I find no rest." 4 Thus you shall say to him, "Thus says the LORD: I am going to break down what I have built, and pluck up what I have planted—that is, the whole land. 5 And you, do you seek great things for yourself? Do not seek them; for I am going to bring disaster upon all flesh, says the LORD; but I will give you your life as a prize of war in every place to which you may go."

Judgment on Egypt

46 The word of the LORD that came to the prophet Jeremiah concerning the nations.

2 Concerning Egypt, about the army of Pharaoh Neco, king of Egypt, which was by the river Euphrates at Carchemish and which King Nebuchadrezzar of Babylon defeated in the fourth year of King Jehoiakim son of Josiah of Judah:

3 Prepare buckler and shield,
  and advance for battle!
4 Harness the horses;
  mount the steeds!
Take your stations with your helmets,
  whet your lances,
  put on your coats of mail!
5 Why do I see them terrified?
  They have fallen back;
their warriors are beaten down,
  and have fled in haste.
They do not look back—
  terror is all around!
says the LORD.
6 The swift cannot flee away,
  nor can the warrior escape;
in the north by the river Euphrates
  they have stumbled and fallen.

44.21 Ezek 8.10,11; 16.24; Isa 64.9; Jer 14.10; Hos 7.2
44.22 Isa 7.13; Jer 4.4; 21.12; 25.11,18,38
44.23 Jer 40.3; ver 10,2; Dan 9.11,12
44.24 Jer 42.15; ver 15; Jer 43.7
44.25 Mt 14.9; Acts 23.12
44.26 Gen 22.16; Am 6.8; Heb 6.13,18; Ezek 20.39; Jer 5.2
44.27 Jer 1.10; 31.28; Ezek 7.6
44.28 Isa 27.13; ver 17,25,26
44.29 Isa 7.11,14; 8.18; Prov 19.21; Isa 40.8
44.30 Jer 46.25,26; Ezek 29.3; 2 Kings 25.4-7; Jer 39.5
45.1 Jer 36.1,4,18,32
45.3 Ps 6.6; 2 Cor 4.1,16
45.4 Isa 5.5; Jer 11.17; 18.7-10
45.5 1 Kings 3.9,11; Mt 6.25,32,33; Rom 12.16; Jer 25.31; 21.9; 38.2; 39.18
46.2 2 Kings 23.29; 2 Chr 35.20; Jer 45.1
46.3 Jer 51.11,12; Nah 2.1; 3.14
46.5 Isa 42.17; Ezek 39.18; Jer 6.25; 49.29
46.6 Isa 30.16; Dan 11.19

44.20-30 Jeremiah responds that they have learned nothing from the disasters which have befallen this people because of their idolatry in the land of Judah and their failure to obey the law of God. The result will be the death of nearly all those who sought to escape in Egypt. The death of the reigning *Pharaoh Hophra* will be a sign confirming Jeremiah's prophecy of doom. The Greek historian Herodotus reports that he was murdered in 570.
45.1-5 Jeremiah's Final Word to Baruch. Jeremiah's message to Baruch stands as a fitting conclusion to the prophet's career: service to the LORD has brought him unrelenting pain. Disaster will come *upon all flesh* (humanity), but Baruch's own survival will be a gift from the LORD.
46.1-28 Oracles against Egypt. These oracles against the nations, in Jer 46-51 of the Hebrew text, are found in the Septuagint (ancient Greek) version of the Jewish scriptures following Jer 25, which is a logical location for them.
46.1-12 The Oracle Against Egypt. Egypt's attack on Babylon, in which she was joined by other nations (Ethiopia; *Put*, on the east coast of Africa; and the *Ludim*, or Lydians from Asia Minor) met defeat at *Carchemish* in the *fourth year of King Jehoiakim* (=605). The folly of the attack is vividly pictured, and the defeat is seen as a *sacrifice* offered by the LORD.

46.13-26 The Babylonian invasion of Egypt is here foretold, including the ruin of its major city, *Memphis*. *Tabor* and *Carmel*, prominent mountains in Israel, are symbols of God's initiative in the defeat of Egypt.
46.27-28 A brief interlude offers assurance to Israel that, beyond the present period when she is being *chastised*, she will be restored.

7 Who is this, rising like the Nile,
like rivers whose waters surge?
8 Egypt rises like the Nile,
like rivers whose waters surge.
It said, Let me rise, let me cover the earth,
let me destroy cities and their inhabitants.
9 Advance, O horses,
and dash madly, O chariots!
Let the warriors go forth:
Ethiopia[r] and Put who carry the shield,
the Ludim, who draw[s] the bow.
10 That day is the day of the Lord GOD of hosts,
a day of retribution,
to gain vindication from his foes.
The sword shall devour and be sated,
and drink its fill of their blood.
For the Lord GOD of hosts holds a sacrifice
in the land of the north by the river Euphrates.
11 Go up to Gilead, and take balm,
O virgin daughter Egypt!
In vain you have used many medicines;
there is no healing for you.
12 The nations have heard of your shame,
and the earth is full of your cry;
for warrior has stumbled against warrior;
both have fallen together.

Babylonia Will Strike Egypt

13 The word that the LORD spoke to the
prophet Jeremiah about the coming of King
Nebuchadrezzar of Babylon to attack the
land of Egypt:

14 Declare in Egypt, and proclaim in Migdol;
proclaim in Memphis and Tahpanhes;
Say, "Take your stations and be ready,
for the sword shall devour those around you."
15 Why has Apis fled?[t]
Why did your bull not stand?
—because the LORD thrust him down.
16 Your multitude stumbled[u] and fell,
and one said to another,[v]
"Come, let us go back to our own people
and to the land of our birth,
because of the destroying sword."
17 Give Pharaoh, king of Egypt, the name
"Braggart who missed his chance."
18 As I live, says the King,
whose name is the LORD of hosts,
one is coming
like Tabor among the mountains,
and like Carmel by the sea.
19 Pack your bags for exile,
sheltered daughter Egypt!
For Memphis shall become a waste,
a ruin, without inhabitant.

20 A beautiful heifer is Egypt—
a gadfly from the north lights upon her.
21 Even her mercenaries in her midst
are like fatted calves;
they too have turned and fled together,
they did not stand;
for the day of their calamity has come upon them,
the time of their punishment.

22 She makes a sound like a snake gliding away;
for her enemies march in force,
and come against her with axes,
like those who fell trees.
23 They shall cut down her forest,
says the LORD,
though it is impenetrable,
because they are more numerous than locusts;
they are without number.
24 Daughter Egypt shall be put to shame;
she shall be handed over to a people from the north.

25 The LORD of hosts, the God of Israel,
said: See, I am bringing punishment upon
Amon of Thebes, and Pharaoh, and Egypt
and her gods and her kings, upon Pharaoh
and those who trust in him. 26 I will hand
them over to those who seek their life, to
King Nebuchadrezzar of Babylon and his
officers. Afterward Egypt shall be inhabited
as in the days of old, says the LORD.

God Will Save Israel

27 But as for you, have no fear, my servant Jacob,
and do not be dismayed, O Israel;
for I am going to save you from far away,
and your offspring from the land of their captivity.

[r] Or *Nubia*; Heb *Cush* [s] Cn: Heb *who grasp, who draw* [t] Gk: Heb *Why was it swept away* [u] Gk: Meaning of Heb uncertain [v] Gk: Heb *and fell one to another and they said*

46.7 Jer 47.2
46.8 Isa 37.24; 10.13
46.9 Jer 47.3; Nah 2.4; 3.9; Isa 66.19
46.10 Isa 13.6; Joel 1.15; 2.1; Jer 50.15,28; Isa 34.6; Zeph 1.7
46.11 Jer 8.22; 51.8; Isa 47.1; Jer 31.4,21; 30.13; Ezek 30.21
46.12 Jer 2.36; Nah 3.8-10; Jer 14.2
46.13 Isa 19.1; Jer 43.10,11
46.14 Jer 44.1; 43.8; Nah 2.13
46.16 Lev 26.36,37; Jer 51.9; 50.16
46.17 Isa 19.11-16
46.18 Jer 48.15; Ps 89.12; 1 Kings 18.42
46.19 Jer 48.18; Isa 20.4; ver 4; Ezek 30.13
46.20 Jer 50.11; ver 24
46.21 ver 5; Ps 37.13; Jer 50.27
46.22 Isa 29.4
46.23 Isa 10.34; Jer 21.14; Judg 6.5; Joel 2.25
46.24 ver 19; Jer 1.15
46.25 Jer 43.12; Ezek 30.14-16; Jer 44.30; Ezek 30.13; Isa 20.5
46.26 Jer 44.30; Ezek 32.11; 29.11-14
46.27 Isa 41.13; 43.5; Jer 30.10,11; 23.3,4,6; 50.19

Jacob shall return and have quiet and
ease,
and no one shall make him afraid.
28 As for you, have no fear, my servant
Jacob,
says the LORD,
for I am with you.
I will make an end of all the nations
among which I have banished you,
but I will not make an end of you!
I will chastise you in just measure,
and I will by no means leave you
unpunished.

Judgment on the Philistines

47 The word of the LORD that came to
the prophet Jeremiah concerning
the Philistines, before Pharaoh attacked Gaza:
2 Thus says the LORD:
See, waters are rising out of the north
and shall become an overflowing
torrent;
they shall overflow the land and all that
fills it,
the city and those who live in it.
People shall cry out,
and all the inhabitants of the land
shall wail.
3 At the noise of the stamping of the hoofs
of his stallions,
at the clatter of his chariots, at the
rumbling of their wheels,
parents do not turn back for children,
so feeble are their hands,
4 because of the day that is coming
to destroy all the Philistines,
to cut off from Tyre and Sidon
every helper that remains.
For the LORD is destroying the Philistines,
the remnant of the coastland of
Caphtor.
5 Baldness has come upon Gaza,
Ashkelon is silenced.
O remnant of their power![w]
How long will you gash yourselves?
6 Ah, sword of the LORD!
How long until you are quiet?
Put yourself into your scabbard,
rest and be still!
7 How can it[x] be quiet,
when the LORD has given it an order?
Against Ashkelon and against the
seashore—
there he has appointed it.

Judgment on Moab

48 Concerning Moab.

Thus says the Lord of hosts, the God of
Israel:
Alas for Nebo, it is laid waste!
Kiriathaim is put to shame, it is
taken;
the fortress is put to shame and broken
down;
2 the renown of Moab is no more.
In Heshbon they planned evil against
her:
"Come, let us cut her off from being a
nation!"
You also, O Madmen, shall be brought
to silence;[y]
the sword shall pursue you.

3 Hark! a cry from Horonaim,
"Desolation and great destruction!"
4 "Moab is destroyed!"
her little ones cry out.
5 For at the ascent of Luhith
they go[z] up weeping bitterly;
for at the descent of Horonaim
they have heard the distressing cry of
anguish.
6 Flee! Save yourselves!
Be like a wild ass[a] in the desert!

7 Surely, because you trusted in your
strongholds[b] and your treasures,
you also shall be taken;
Chemosh shall go out into exile,
with his priests and his attendants.
8 The destroyer shall come upon every
town,
and no town shall escape;
the valley shall perish,
and the plain shall be destroyed,
as the LORD has spoken.

9 Set aside salt for Moab,
for she will surely fall;
her towns shall become a desolation,
with no inhabitant in them.

10 Accursed is the one who is slack in
doing the work of the LORD; and accursed
is the one who keeps back the sword from
bloodshed.

11 Moab has been at ease from his youth,
settled like wine[c] on its dregs;

[w] Gk: Heb *their valley* [x] Gk Vg: Heb *you* [y] The place-name *Madmen* sounds like the Hebrew verb *to be silent* [z] Cn: Heb *he goes* [a] Gk Aquila: Heb *like Aroer* [b] Gk: Heb *works* [c] Heb lacks *like wine*

46.28 Isa 8.9,10; Jer 1.19; 4.27; Am 9.8,9; Jer 10.24; 30.11
47.1 Jer 25.17,20; Am 1.6; Zeph 2.4
47.2 Isa 14.31; Jer 46.20,24; Isa 8.7; 15.2-5; Jer 46.12
47.3 Jer 8.16; Nah 3.2
47.4 Isa 14.31; 23.5,6,11; Joel 3.4; Zech 9.2-4; Gen 10.14
47.5 Mic 1.16; Jer 25.20; 16.6; 41.5
47.6 Jer 12.12; 4.21
47.7 Ezek 14.17; Mic 6.9
48.1 Isa 15.2; ver 22,23; Num 32.37
48.2 Isa 16.14; 15.4; Jer 49.3
48.3 Isa 15.5; ver 5,34
48.5 Isa 15.5
48.6 Jer 51.6; 17.6
48.7 Jer 9.23; Num 21.29; 1 Kings 11.33; Jer 49.3
48.8 Jer 6.26
48.9 Isa 16.2; Jer 44.22
48.10 Jer 11.3; 1 Sam 15.3,9; 1 Kings 20.42; Jer 47.6,7
48.11 Jer 22.21; Zech 1.15; Zeph 1.12; Nah 2.2

47.1-7 The Philistines, neighbors to Israel and Judah to the west along the Mediterranean coast, are warned that the Babylonian power *out of the north* will come to destroy their cities, from Gaza in the south to Tyre in the north. **48.1-47** A series of oracles predicts the destruction of Moab, the Semitic people located east of the Dead Sea. Mentioned are specific Moabite cities: *Kiriathaim, Nebo,* and *Horonaim,* in addition to extended lists of cities in 48.21-24 and 34. *Chemosh,* who will *go into exile,* was the national god of the Moabites (Num 21.29; 1 Kings 11.7). Worship of him will cease, and the people will be ashamed of him when they realize his impotence. The specific focus of the lament includes the cities of *Jazer* (west of modern Amman); *Kir-heres* (probably identical with Kir-hareseth, east of the Dead Sea and well situated on a rocky promontory for safety against attack), and *Heshbon* (an important city in northern Moab). The *house of Sihon* was the royal family of the Ammonites, a nation to the north and east of Moab, mentioned in connection with the Israelites' struggles in their move from Sinai to the promised land (Num 21.24). *Nimrim* was a stream flowing into the Dead Sea from the east. The images used in depicting the desolation of Moab include defeat in warfare (48.14-17), drought (48.18), failure of crops (48.28-33), birds of prey (48.40-43), and fire (48.45-46). A final note assures the ultimate restoration of Moab (48.47).

he has not been emptied from vessel to
vessel,
nor has he gone into exile;
therefore his flavor has remained
and his aroma is unspoiled.

12 Therefore, the time is surely coming,
says the LORD, when I shall send to him
decanters to decant him, and empty his
vessels, and break his[d] jars in pieces. 13 Then
Moab shall be ashamed of Chemosh, as the
house of Israel was ashamed of Bethel, their
confidence.

14 How can you say, "We are heroes
and mighty warriors"?
15 The destroyer of Moab and his towns
has come up,
and the choicest of his young men
have gone down to slaughter,
says the King, whose name is the
LORD of hosts.
16 The calamity of Moab is near at hand
and his doom approaches swiftly.
17 Mourn over him, all you his neighbors,
and all who know his name;
say, "How the mighty scepter is broken,
the glorious staff!"

18 Come down from glory,
and sit on the parched ground,
enthroned daughter Dibon!
For the destroyer of Moab has come up
against you;
he has destroyed your strongholds.
19 Stand by the road and watch,
you inhabitant of Aroer!
Ask the man fleeing and the woman
escaping;
say, "What has happened?"
20 Moab is put to shame, for it is broken
down;
wail and cry!
Tell it by the Arnon,
that Moab is laid waste.

21 Judgment has come upon the tableland, upon Holon, and Jahzah, and
Mephaath, 22 and Dibon, and Nebo, and Beth-
diblathaim, 23 and Kiriathaim, and Beth-
gamul, and Beth-meon, 24 and Kerioth, and
Bozrah, and all the towns of the land of
Moab, far and near. 25 The horn of Moab is
cut off, and his arm is broken, says the LORD.
26 Make him drunk, because he magnified himself against the LORD; let Moab wallow
in his vomit; he too shall become a
laughingstock. 27 Israel was a laughingstock
for you, though he was not caught among
thieves; but whenever you spoke of him you
shook your head!

28 Leave the towns, and live on the rock,
O inhabitants of Moab!
Be like the dove that nests
on the sides of the mouth of a gorge.
29 We have heard of the pride of Moab—
he is very proud—
of his loftiness, his pride, and his
arrogance,
and the haughtiness of his heart.
30 I myself know his insolence, says the
LORD;
his boasts are false,
his deeds are false.
31 Therefore I wail for Moab;
I cry out for all Moab;
for the people of Kir-heres I mourn.
32 More than for Jazer I weep for you,
O vine of Sibmah!
Your branches crossed over the sea,
reached as far as Jazer;[e]
upon your summer fruits and your
vintage
the destroyer has fallen.
33 Gladness and joy have been taken away
from the fruitful land of Moab;
I have stopped the wine from the wine
presses;
no one treads them with shouts of
joy;
the shouting is not the shout of joy.

34 Heshbon and Elealeh cry out;[f] as far
as Jahaz they utter their voice, from Zoar
to Horonaim and Eglath-shelishiyah. For
even the waters of Nimrim have become
desolate. 35 And I will bring to an end in
Moab, says the LORD, those who offer sacrifice at a high place and make offerings to
their gods. 36 Therefore my heart moans for
Moab like a flute, and my heart moans like
a flute for the people of Kir-heres; for the
riches they gained have perished.
37 For every head is shaved and every
beard cut off; on all the hands there are
gashes, and on the loins sackcloth. 38 On all
the housetops of Moab and in the squares
there is nothing but lamentation; for I have
broken Moab like a vessel that no one
wants, says the LORD. 39 How it is broken!

[d] Gk Aquila: Heb *their* [e] Two Mss and Isa 16.8: MT *the sea of Jazer* [f] Cn: Heb *From the cry of Heshbon to Elealeh*

48.13 Isa 45.16; ver 39; Hos 10.6; 1 Kings 12.29
48.14 Isa 10.13-16
48.15 Jer 50.27; 46.18
48.16 Isa 13.22
48.17 Jer 9.17-20; Isa 14.5
48.18 Isa 47.1; Jer 46.19; ver 8
48.19 Deut 2.36; 1 Sam 4.13,16
48.20 Isa 16.7; Num 21.13
48.24 Am 2.2
48.25 Ps 75.10; Ezek 30.21
48.26 Jer 25.15,27
48.27 Zeph 2.8; Jer 2.26; 18.16
48.28 Jer 49.16; Ps 55.6,7; Song 2.14
48.29 Isa 16.6; Zeph 2.8; Ps 138.6
48.30 Isa 37.28; 16.6
48.31 Isa 15.5; 16.7,11
48.32 Isa 16.8,9; Num 21.32
48.33 Isa 16.10; Joel 1.12; Isa 5.10; Hag 2.16
48.34 Isa 15.4-6
48.35 Isa 15.2; 16.12; Jer 7.9; 11.13
48.36 Isa 16.11; 15.7
48.37 Isa 15.2,3; Jer 47.5
48.38 Jer 22.28; 25.34
48.39 Ezek 26.16

How they wail! How Moab has turned his back in shame! So Moab has become a derision and a horror to all his neighbors.
40 For thus says the LORD:
Look, he shall swoop down like an eagle,
and spread his wings against Moab;
41 the towns[g] shall be taken
and the strongholds seized.
The hearts of the warriors of Moab, on that day,
shall be like the heart of a woman in labor.
42 Moab shall be destroyed as a people,
because he magnified himself against the LORD.
43 Terror, pit, and trap
are before you, O inhabitants of Moab!
says the LORD.
44 Everyone who flees from the terror
shall fall into the pit,
and everyone who climbs out of the pit
shall be caught in the trap.
For I will bring these things[h] upon Moab
in the year of their punishment,
says the LORD.

45 In the shadow of Heshbon
fugitives stop exhausted;
for a fire has gone out from Heshbon,
a flame from the house of Sihon;
it has destroyed the forehead of Moab,
the scalp of the people of tumult.[i]
46 Woe to you, O Moab!
The people of Chemosh have perished,
for your sons have been taken captive,
and your daughters into captivity.
47 Yet I will restore the fortunes of Moab
in the latter days, says the LORD.
Thus far is the judgment on Moab.

Judgment on the Ammonites

49 Concerning the Ammonites.

Thus says the Lord:
Has Israel no sons?
Has he no heir?
Why then has Milcom dispossessed Gad,
and his people settled in its towns?
2 Therefore, the time is surely coming,
says the LORD,
when I will sound the battle alarm
against Rabbah of the Ammonites;
it shall become a desolate mound,
and its villages shall be burned with fire;
then Israel shall dispossess those who dispossessed him,
says the LORD.

3 Wail, O Heshbon, for Ai is laid waste!
Cry out, O daughters[j] of Rabbah!
Put on sackcloth,
lament, and slash yourselves with whips![k]
For Milcom shall go into exile,
with his priests and his attendants.
4 Why do you boast in your strength?
Your strength is ebbing,
O faithless daughter.
You trusted in your treasures, saying,
"Who will attack me?"
5 I am going to bring terror upon you,
says the Lord GOD of hosts,
from all your neighbors,
and you will be scattered, each headlong,
with no one to gather the fugitives.
6 But afterward I will restore the fortunes of the Ammonites, says the LORD.

Judgment on Edom

7 Concerning Edom.

Thus says the Lord of hosts:
Is there no longer wisdom in Teman?
Has counsel perished from the prudent?
Has their wisdom vanished?
8 Flee, turn back, get down low,
inhabitants of Dedan!
For I will bring the calamity of Esau upon him,
the time when I punish him.
9 If grape-gatherers came to you,
would they not leave gleanings?
If thieves came by night,
even they would pillage only what they wanted.
10 But as for me, I have stripped Esau bare,
I have uncovered his hiding places,
and he is not able to conceal himself.
His offspring are destroyed, his kinsfolk
and his neighbors; and he is no more.
11 Leave your orphans, I will keep them alive;
and let your widows trust in me.
12 For thus says the LORD: If those who
do not deserve to drink the cup still have
to drink it, shall you be the one to go
unpunished? You shall not go unpunished;
you must drink it. 13For by myself I have
sworn, says the LORD, that Bozrah shall

48.40 Jer 49.22; Dan 7.4; Hos 8.1; Isa 8.8
48.41 Isa 21.3; Jer 30.6; 49.22,24; Mic 4.9
48.42 ver 2; Ps 83.4; ver 26; Isa 37.23
48.43 Isa 24.17,18; Lam 3.47
48.44 1 Kings 19.17; Jer 11.23; 46.21
48.45 ver 2; Num 21.21,26,28, 29; 24.17
48.46 Num 21.29; ver 7
48.47 Jer 49.6,39
49.1 Ezek 21.28; 25.2; Am 1.13; Zeph 2.8,9
49.2 Jer 4.19; Ezek 21.20; Isa 14.2
49.3 Jer 48.2; Josh 7.2-5; 8.1-29; Isa 32.11; Jer 4.8; 48.7
49.4 Jer 9.23; 31.22; Ps 62.10; Ezek 28.4,5
49.5 Jer 48.43,44; 16.16; 46.5; Lam 4.15
49.6 ver 39; Jer 48.47
49.7 Isa 34.5,6; Ezek 25.12; Am 1.11,12; Jer 8.9; ver 20
49.8 ver 30; Jer 25.23; 46.21
49.9 Ob 5
49.10 Jer 13.26; Mal 1.3; Isa 17.14
49.11 Ps 68.5
49.12 Jer 25.28,29; 1 Pet 4.17
49.13 Jer 44.26; Isa 34.6; 34.9-15

49.1-6 Announcement of judgment which is to fall on the *Ammonites*, whose god, *Milcom* (another name for Baal), helped them take land east of the Jordan from the Israelite tribe of *Gad*. Now their cities and lands will be laid waste, yet they too will be restored one day.
49.7-22 Edom is at the southernmost part of what is now Jordan, bordering on the Gulf of Aqabah. *Teman* was one of the Edomite cities, while *Dedan* was a city and tribe living on the edge of the Arabian desert. *Bozrah* was the chief city in northern Edom, noted for its strong fortifications and regarded by its inhabitants as impregnable. *Sodom and Gomorrah*, probably located in Edom by the Dead Sea, were prime examples of cities destroyed through divine judgment (Gen 19.1-11; Deut 29.16-18), such as is now to fall on Edom. The people's cry of lament will be audible at the Red Sea, more than 100 miles to the south.

[g] Or *Kerioth* [h] Gk Syr: Heb *bring upon it* [i] Or *of Shaon* [j] Or *villages* [k] Cn: Meaning of Heb uncertain

49.23-27 *Damascus*, capital of Syria, is described as in *panic* because of the destruction of her cities and her troops. *Hamath* is a major city on the Orontes River in central Syria; *Arpad* is in the north. *Ben-hadad* is a recurrent designation for the royal line in Syria (1 Kings 15.18-21; 2 Kings 8.7-15; 13.24-25).
49.28-33 *Kedar* was an Arab tribe that controlled trade routes from Arabia to the major cities of Syria and Palestine. *Hazor* as a city was destroyed under Tiglath-Pileser (745-727) according to 2 Kings 15.29, but was rebuilt. This reference to *Hazor* may be to the territory east of the upper Jordan River, dominated by Hazor. Herds of *camels* will be taken by Nebuchadrezzar. Those with *shaven temples* are the desert Arabs, as in Jer 9.26.

become an object of horror and ridicule, a
waste, and an object of cursing; and all her
towns shall be perpetual wastes.

14 I have heard tidings from the LORD,
and a messenger has been sent
among the nations:
"Gather yourselves together and come
against her,
and rise up for battle!"
15 For I will make you least among the
nations,
despised by humankind.
16 The terror you inspire
and the pride of your heart have
deceived you,
you who live in the clefts of the rock,[l]
who hold the height of the hill.
Although you make your nest as high
as the eagle's,
from there I will bring you down,
says the LORD.

17 Edom shall become an object of horror; everyone who passes by it will be
horrified and will hiss because of all its
disasters. 18As when Sodom and Gomorrah
and their neighbors were overthrown, says
the LORD, no one shall live there, nor shall
anyone settle in it. 19Like a lion coming up
from the thickets of the Jordan against a
perennial pasture, I will suddenly chase
Edom[m] away from it; and I will appoint over
it whomever I choose.[n] For who is like me?
Who can summon me? Who is the shepherd who can stand before me? 20Therefore
hear the plan that the LORD has made against
Edom and the purposes that he has formed
against the inhabitants of Teman: Surely
the little ones of the flock shall be dragged
away; surely their fold shall be appalled at
their fate. 21At the sound of their fall the
earth shall tremble; the sound of their cry
shall be heard at the Red Sea.[o] 22Look, he
shall mount up and swoop down like an
eagle, and spread his wings against Bozrah,
and the heart of the warriors of Edom in
that day shall be like the heart of a woman
in labor.

Judgment on Damascus

23 Concerning Damascus.

Hamath and Arpad are confounded,
for they have heard bad news;
they melt in fear, they are troubled like
the sea[p]
that cannot be quiet.
24 Damascus has become feeble, she turned
to flee,
and panic seized her;
anguish and sorrows have taken hold of
her,
as of a woman in labor.
25 How the famous city is forsaken,[q]
the joyful town![r]
26 Therefore her young men shall fall in
her squares,
and all her soldiers shall be destroyed
in that day,
says the LORD of hosts.
27 And I will kindle a fire at the wall of
Damascus,
and it shall devour the strongholds of
Ben-hadad.

Judgment on Kedar and Hazor

28 Concerning Kedar and the kingdoms
of Hazor that King Nebuchadrezzar of
Babylon defeated.

Thus says the LORD:
Rise up, advance against Kedar!
Destroy the people of the east!
29 Take their tents and their flocks,
their curtains and all their goods;
carry off their camels for yourselves,
and a cry shall go up: "Terror is all
around!"
30 Flee, wander far away, hide in deep
places,
O inhabitants of Hazor!
says the LORD.
For King Nebuchadrezzar of Babylon
has made a plan against you
and formed a purpose against you.

31 Rise up, advance against a nation at ease,
that lives secure,
says the LORD,
that has no gates or bars,
that lives alone.
32 Their camels shall become booty,
their herds of cattle a spoil.
I will scatter to every wind
those who have shaven temples,
and I will bring calamity
against them from every side,
says the LORD.

[l] Or *of Sela* [m] Heb *him* [n] Or *and I will single out the choicest of his rams*: Meaning of Heb uncertain [o] Or *Sea of Reeds* [p] Cn: Heb *there is trouble in the sea* [q] Vg: Heb *is not forsaken* [r] Syr Vg Tg: Heb *the town of my joy*

49.14 Ob 1-4; Isa 18.2; 30.4; Jer 50.14
49.16 Isa 25.5; 14.13-15; Am 9.2
49.17 Jer 50.13; 1 Kings 9.8; Jer 51.37
49.18 Gen 19.25; Deut 29.23; Am 4.11
49.19 Jer 50.44; 12.5; Isa 46.9
49.20 Jer 50.45; Mal 1.3,4
49.21 Jer 50.46; Ezek 26.15,18
49.22 Jer 4.13; 48.40,41
49.23 2 Chr 16.2; Jer 39.5; Isa 10.9; 57.20
49.25 Jer 33.9; 51.41
49.26 Jer 50.30; 51.4; Am 4.10
49.27 Jer 43.12; Am 1.3-5; 1 Kings 15.18-20
49.28 Isa 21.16,17; Jer 2.10; Ezek 27.21; Isa 11.14
49.29 Jer 6.25; 20.3,10; 46.5
49.30 Jer 25.9
49.31 Isa 47.8; Ezek 38.11; Deut 33.28
49.32 Ezek 12.14,15; Jer 9.26; 25.23

33 Hazor shall become a lair of jackals,
an everlasting waste;
no one shall live there,
nor shall anyone settle in it.

Judgment on Elam

34 The word of the LORD that came to the
prophet Jeremiah concerning Elam, at the
beginning of the reign of King Zedekiah of
Judah.
35 Thus says the LORD of hosts: I am
going to break the bow of Elam, the main-
stay of their might; 36 and I will bring upon
Elam the four winds from the four quarters
of heaven; and I will scatter them to all
these winds, and there shall be no nation
to which the exiles from Elam shall not
come. 37 I will terrify Elam before their enemies, and before those who seek their life;
I will bring disaster upon them, my fierce
anger, says the LORD. I will send the sword
after them, until I have consumed them;
38 and I will set my throne in Elam, and
destroy their king and officials, says the
LORD.
39 But in the latter days I will restore the
fortunes of Elam, says the LORD.

Judgment on Babylon

50 The word that the LORD spoke
concerning Babylon, concerning
the land of the Chaldeans, by the prophet
Jeremiah:

2 Declare among the nations and proclaim,
set up a banner and proclaim,
do not conceal it, say:
Babylon is taken,
Bel is put to shame,
Merodach is dismayed.
Her images are put to shame,
her idols are dismayed.

3 For out of the north a nation has come
up against her; it shall make her land a
desolation, and no one shall live in it; both
human beings and animals shall flee away.

4 In those days and in that time, says the
LORD, the people of Israel shall come, they
and the people of Judah together; they shall
come weeping as they seek the LORD their
God. 5 They shall ask the way to Zion, with
faces turned toward it, and they shall come
and join[s] themselves to the LORD by an
everlasting covenant that will never be forgotten.

6 My people have been lost sheep; their
shepherds have led them astray, turning
them away on the mountains; from mountain to hill they have gone, they have forgotten their fold. 7 All who found them have
devoured them, and their enemies have
said, "We are not guilty, because they have
sinned against the LORD, the true pasture,
the LORD, the hope of their ancestors."

8 Flee from Babylon, and go out of the
land of the Chaldeans, and be like male
goats leading the flock. 9 For I am going to
stir up and bring against Babylon a company of great nations from the land of the
north; and they shall array themselves
against her; from there she shall be taken.
Their arrows are like the arrows of a skilled
warrior who does not return empty-handed.
10 Chaldea shall be plundered; all who plunder her shall be sated, says the LORD.

11 Though you rejoice, though you exult,
O plunderers of my heritage,
though you frisk about like a heifer on
the grass,
and neigh like stallions,
12 your mother shall be utterly shamed,
and she who bore you shall be disgraced.
Lo, she shall be the last of the nations,
a wilderness, dry land, and a desert.
13 Because of the wrath of the LORD she
shall not be inhabited,
but shall be an utter desolation;
everyone who passes by Babylon shall
be appalled
and hiss because of all her wounds.
14 Take up your positions around Babylon,
all you that bend the bow;
shoot at her, spare no arrows,
for she has sinned against the LORD.
15 Raise a shout against her from all sides,
"She has surrendered;
her bulwarks have fallen,
her walls are thrown down."
For this is the vengeance of the LORD:
take vengeance on her,
do to her as she has done.
16 Cut off from Babylon the sower,
and the wielder of the sickle in time
of harvest;
because of the destroying sword
all of them shall return to their own
people,
and all of them shall flee to their own
land.

[s] Gk: Heb *toward it. Come! They shall join*

49.34-39 *Elam* was an area east of the lower Tigris Valley. It served as an important source of food and other basic supplies for the region. The skill of its warriors was notable, although its capital, Susa, was destroyed by Ashurbanipal in 646. Another destruction of Susa is predicted by Ezekiel (32.24-25). Jews resident in Elam returned to Israel in the time of Ezra (Ezra 2.7,31). A final note promises restoration of Elam.
50.1-51.58 Oracles against Babylon.
50.1-10 The first group of pronouncements describes the Babylonian god, *Merodach* (Marduk; Bel is his title of honor) as dismayed because the nation honoring him has been taken over by a people *out of the north.* The reference is to Persia, although when Cyrus took over Babylon in 538 he respected and preserved the city, rather than destroying it as here predicted. This prophecy of an invader from the north matches the prediction of Babylon's invasion of Judah (Jer 6.1; 13.20; 16.15 etc). Both *Israel and Judah* will be restored to the land of *Zion,* in spite of the earlier irresponsibility of their leaders (*shepherds*). Babylon will be plundered by *a company of great nations.* Historically, the Medes and Persians were joined to seize Babylon and its empire.
50.11-20 Oracles in poetry (50.11-16) and prose (50.17-20) foretell the destruction of Babylon, while *Israel and Judah* will be pardoned and restored to their lands.

49.33 Jer 10.22; Zeph 2.9,13-15
49.34 Ezek 32.24; 2 Kings 24.17,18; Jer 28.1
49.35 Isa 22.6; Jer 51.56
49.36 Rev 7.1; Ezek 5.10; Am 9.9
49.37 Jer 8.9; 17.18; 6.19; 30.24; 9.16
50.1 Isa 13.1; Rev 14.8
50.2 Jer 51.27; 51.31; Isa 46.1; Jer 51.44,47
50.3 Jer 51.48; Jer 9.10; Zeph 1.3
50.4 Hos 1.11; Ezra 3.12,13; Jer 31.9; Zech 12.10; Hos 3.5
50.6 Isa 53.6; Ezek 34.15,16; Jer 23.11-14; 2.20; 3.6,23; 33.12
50.7 Jer 40.2,3; 31.23; 14.8; 17.13
50.8 Jer 51.6,45; Rev 18.4
50.9 Jer 51.1,2
50.11 Jer 12.14; 46.20
50.12 Jer 22.6; 51.43
50.13 Jer 25.12; 49.17
50.14 Jer 49.35; Hab 2.8,17
50.15 Jer 51.14; 1 Chr 29.24; Ezek 17.18; Jer 51.44,58; 46.10
50.16 Joel 1.11; Jer 51.9

17 Israel is a hunted sheep driven away
by lions. First the king of Assyria devoured
it, and now at the end King Nebuchadrezzar
of Babylon has gnawed its bones. 18 Therefore, thus says the LORD of hosts, the God of
Israel: I am going to punish the king of
Babylon and his land, as I punished the
king of Assyria. 19 I will restore Israel to its
pasture, and it shall feed on Carmel and in
Bashan, and on the hills of Ephraim and in
Gilead its hunger shall be satisfied. 20 In
those days and at that time, says the LORD,
the iniquity of Israel shall be sought, and
there shall be none; and the sins of Judah,
and none shall be found; for I will pardon
the remnant that I have spared.

21 Go up to the land of Merathaim;[t]
go up against her,
and attack the inhabitants of Pekod[u]
and utterly destroy the last of them,[v]
says the LORD;
do all that I have commanded you.
22 The noise of battle is in the land,
and great destruction!
23 How the hammer of the whole earth
is cut down and broken!
How Babylon has become
a horror among the nations!
24 You set a snare for yourself and you
were caught, O Babylon,
but you did not know it;
you were discovered and seized,
because you challenged the LORD.
25 The LORD has opened his armory,
and brought out the weapons of his
wrath,
for the Lord GOD of hosts has a task to
do
in the land of the Chaldeans.
26 Come against her from every quarter;
open her granaries;
pile her up like heaps of grain, and
destroy her utterly;
let nothing be left of her.
27 Kill all her bulls,
let them go down to the slaughter.
Alas for them, their day has come,
the time of their punishment!

28 Listen! Fugitives and refugees from
the land of Babylon are coming to declare
in Zion the vengeance of the LORD our God,
vengeance for his temple.

29 Summon archers against Babylon, all
who bend the bow. Encamp all around her;
let no one escape. Repay her according to
her deeds; just as she has done, do to her—
for she has arrogantly defied the LORD, the
Holy One of Israel. 30 Therefore her young
men shall fall in her squares, and all her
soldiers shall be destroyed on that day, says
the LORD.

31 I am against you, O arrogant one,
says the Lord GOD of hosts;
for your day has come,
the time when I will punish you.
32 The arrogant one shall stumble and fall,
with no one to raise him up,
and I will kindle a fire in his cities,
and it will devour everything around
him.

33 Thus says the LORD of hosts: The people
of Israel are oppressed, and so too are the
people of Judah; all their captors have held
them fast and refuse to let them go. 34 Their
Redeemer is strong; the LORD of hosts is his
name. He will surely plead their cause, that
he may give rest to the earth, but unrest to
the inhabitants of Babylon.

35 A sword against the Chaldeans, says the
LORD,
and against the inhabitants of
Babylon,
and against her officials and her
sages!
36 A sword against the diviners,
so that they may become fools!
A sword against her warriors,
so that they may be destroyed!
37 A sword against her[w] horses and against
her[w] chariots,
and against all the foreign troops in
her midst,
so that they may become women!
A sword against all her treasures,
that they may be plundered!
38 A drought[x] against her waters,
that they may be dried up!
For it is a land of images,
and they go mad over idols.

39 Therefore wild animals shall live with
hyenas in Babylon,[y] and ostriches shall inhabit her; she shall never again be peopled,

[t] Or *of Double Rebellion* [u] Or *of Punishment* [v] Tg: Heb *destroy after them* [w] Cn: Heb *his* [x] Another reading is *A sword* [y] Heb lacks *in Babylon*

50.21-32 Babylon is here referred to under the names of *Merathaim* (a region at the head of the Persian Gulf) and *Pekod* (a district in eastern Babylonia). These names resemble respectively the Semitic roots for "rebellion" and "punishment," which correspond to what Babylon is about to experience when God's *wrath* is vented on her, and her enemies surround her for an attack.
50.33-34 A prose interlude promises God's intervention on behalf of Israel and Judah, but vows *unrest* for Babylon.
50.35-46 God's attack will be on the whole range of Babylonian society: *officials, sages, diviners, warriors, mercenary troops.* Babylon will degenerate into an area inhabited only by wild animals – literally or figuratively. Confronted by the invaders from the north, the king of Babylon will become helpless. The final pronouncement echoes the oracle against Edom in 49.19-21.

50.17 Jer 2.15; 2 Kings 17.6; 24.10,14
50.19 Jer 31.10; 33.12; 31.5
50.20 Jer 31.34; Mic 7.19; Isa 1.9; Jer 33.8
50.21 Ezek 23.23; Isa 10.6; 44.28; 48.14; Jer 34.22
50.22 Jer 51.54-56
50.23 Isa 14.6; Jer 51.20-24
50.24 Jer 48.43,44; 51.8,31,39, 57; Dan 5.30,31
50.25 Isa 13.5; Jer 51.12,25,55
50.26 ver 41; Isa 14.23
50.27 Isa 34.7; Ezek 7.7; Jer 48.44
50.28 Isa 48.20; Jer 51.6; 51.10,11
50.29 Jer 51.56; Rev 18.6; Isa 47.10
50.30 Isa 13.17,18; Jer 49.26; 51.56,67
50.31 Jer 21.13; Nah 2.13
50.32 Isa 10.12-15; Jer 21.14; 49.27
50.33 Isa 14.17; 58.6
50.34 Isa 43.14; Jer 15.21; 31.11; 32.18; 51.19; 51.36; Isa 14.3-7
50.35 Dan 5.1,2,7,8,30
50.36 Isa 44.25; Jer 49.22
50.37 Jer 51.21,22; 25.30; Ezek 30.5; Jer 51.30; Nah 3.13
50.38 Jer 51.32,36,42, 47,52
50.39 Isa 13.21,22; Jer 51.37; Isa 13.20

or inhabited for all generations. 40As when
God overthrew Sodom and Gomorrah and
their neighbors, says the LORD, so no one shall
live there, nor shall anyone settle in her.

41 Look, a people is coming from the north;
a mighty nation and many kings
are stirring from the farthest parts of
the earth.
42 They wield bow and spear,
they are cruel and have no mercy.
The sound of them is like the roaring sea;
they ride upon horses,
set in array as a warrior for battle,
against you, O daughter Babylon!

43 The king of Babylon heard news of them,
and his hands fell helpless;
anguish seized him,
pain like that of a woman in labor.

44 Like a lion coming up from the
thickets of the Jordan against a perennial
pasture, I will suddenly chase them away
from her; and I will appoint over her whomever I choose.[z] For who is like me? Who can
summon me? Who is the shepherd who can
stand before me? 45Therefore hear the plan
that the LORD has made against Babylon,
and the purposes that he has formed against
the land of the Chaldeans: Surely the little
ones of the flock shall be dragged away;
surely their[a] fold shall be appalled at their
fate. 46At the sound of the capture of Babylon
the earth shall tremble, and her cry shall be
heard among the nations.

Israel the Creator's Instrument

51 Thus says the LORD:
I am going to stir up a destructive
wind[b]
against Babylon
and against the inhabitants of Leb-
qamai;[c]
2 and I will send winnowers to Babylon,
and they shall winnow her.
They shall empty her land
when they come against her from
every side
on the day of trouble.
3 Let not the archer bend his bow,
and let him not array himself in his
coat of mail.
Do not spare her young men;
utterly destroy her entire army.
4 They shall fall down slain in the land of
the Chaldeans,
and wounded in her streets.
5 Israel and Judah have not been forsaken
by their God, the LORD of hosts,
though their land is full of guilt
before the Holy One of Israel.

6 Flee from the midst of Babylon,
save your lives, each of you!
Do not perish because of her guilt,
for this is the time of the LORD's
vengeance;
he is repaying her what is due.
7 Babylon was a golden cup in the LORD's
hand,
making all the earth drunken;
the nations drank of her wine,
and so the nations went mad.
8 Suddenly Babylon has fallen and is
shattered;
wail for her!
Bring balm for her wound;
perhaps she may be healed.
9 We tried to heal Babylon,
but she could not be healed.
Forsake her, and let each of us go
to our own country;
for her judgment has reached up to
heaven
and has been lifted up even to the
skies.
10 The LORD has brought forth our
vindication;
come, let us declare in Zion
the work of the LORD our God.

11 Sharpen the arrows!
Fill the quivers!
The LORD has stirred up the spirit of the
kings of the Medes, because his purpose
concerning Babylon is to destroy it, for that
is the vengeance of the LORD, vengeance for
his temple.
12 Raise a standard against the walls of
Babylon;
make the watch strong;
post sentinels;
prepare the ambushes;
for the LORD has both planned and done
what he spoke concerning the
inhabitants of Babylon.
13 You who live by mighty waters,
rich in treasures,

[z] Or *and I will single out the choicest of her rams*: Meaning of Heb uncertain [a] Syr Gk Tg Compare 49.20: Heb lacks *their* [b] Or *stir up the spirit of a destroyer* [c] *Leb-qamai* is a cryptogram for *Kasdim*, Chaldea

51.1-18 *Leb-qamai* is a cryptogram of *Kasdim*, which represents Chaldea (*cf.* 50.45). This *Chaldean* regime will be destroyed, but Israel and Judah will be preserved. Babylon, which was once an instrument in the LORD's hands to effect punishment of disobedient Judah, is now seen as a nation *fallen and shattered*, while God's people will experience *vindication*. It is the Medes who are here predicted to destroy Babylon, and historically they did conquer it in 538. The folly of Babylonian idolatry is vividly described.

50.40 Gen 19.25; Jer 49.18; Lk 17.28-30
50.41 Jer 6.22; Rev 17.16
50.42 Jer 6.23; Isa 13.18; 5.30
50.43 Jer 51.31; 49.24
50.44 Jer 49.19-21; Isa 46.9; Job 41.10; Jer 49.19
50.45 Isa 14.24; Jer 51.11; 49.20
50.46 Rev 18.9; Ezek 27.28
51.1 Jer 4.11; Hos 13.15
51.2 Isa 41.16; Jer 15.7; Mt 3.12
51.3 Jer 50.14; 46.4; 50.21
51.5 Isa 54.7,8; Jer 33.24-26
51.6 Jer 50.8; Rev 18.4; Num 16.26; Jer 50.15; 25.14
51.7 Rev 17.4; Jer 25.15; Rev 14.8; 18.3; Jer 25.16
51.8 Isa 21.9; Rev 14.8; 18.2; Jer 48.20; Rev 18.9,11,19
51.9 Isa 13.14; Jer 50.16; Rev 18.5
51.10 Ps 37.6; Mic 7.9; Isa 40.2; Jer 50.28
51.11 Jer 46.4; Joel 3.9,10; Jer 50.3,9,28
51.12 Isa 13.2; Jer 50.2
51.13 Rev 17.1,15

51.19-23 Contrasted with the end of Babylon is the *LORD's* continuing use of Israel as his instrument of punishment for disobedient humanity.
51.24-58 In addition to *the Medes*, the nations that God will use to destroy Babylon include kingdoms in what is now Armenia: *Ararat, Minni, and Ashkenaz* (possibly the Scythians). *The inhabitants of Zion* will *be avenged* by the punishment Babylon experiences. *Sheshach* is another cryptogram for Babylon, which will become an international symbol for the horrors of human destiny, a place from which to flee, and a vicarious sacrifice for *the slain of Israel*. Ultimate responsibility for this disaster rests with the LORD, who will *lay Babylon waste*.

your end has come,
the thread of your life is cut.
14 The LORD of hosts has sworn by himself:
Surely I will fill you with troops like a swarm of locusts,
and they shall raise a shout of victory over you.

15 It is he who made the earth by his power,
who established the world by his wisdom,
and by his understanding stretched out the heavens.
16 When he utters his voice there is a tumult of waters in the heavens,
and he makes the mist rise from the ends of the earth.
He makes lightnings for the rain,
and he brings out the wind from his storehouses.
17 Everyone is stupid and without knowledge;
goldsmiths are all put to shame by their idols;
for their images are false,
and there is no breath in them.
18 They are worthless, a work of delusion;
at the time of their punishment they shall perish.
19 Not like these is the LORD,[d] the portion of Jacob,
for he is the one who formed all things,
and Israel is the tribe of his inheritance;
the LORD of hosts is his name.

Israel the Creator's Instrument
20 You are my war club, my weapon of battle:
with you I smash nations;
with you I destroy kingdoms;
21 with you I smash the horse and its rider;
with you I smash the chariot and the charioteer;
22 with you I smash man and woman;
with you I smash the old man and the boy;
with you I smash the young man and the girl;
23 with you I smash shepherds and their flocks;
with you I smash farmers and their teams;
with you I smash governors and deputies.

The Doom of Babylon
24 I will repay Babylon and all the inhabitants of Chaldea before your very eyes
for all the wrong that they have done in
Zion, says the LORD.

25 I am against you, O destroying mountain,
says the LORD,
that destroys the whole earth;
I will stretch out my hand against you,
and roll you down from the crags,
and make you a burned-out mountain.
26 No stone shall be taken from you for a corner
and no stone for a foundation,
but you shall be a perpetual waste,
says the LORD.

27 Raise a standard in the land,
blow the trumpet among the nations;
prepare the nations for war against her,
summon against her the kingdoms,
Ararat, Minni, and Ashkenaz;
appoint a marshal against her,
bring up horses like bristling locusts.
28 Prepare the nations for war against her,
the kings of the Medes, with their governors and deputies,
and every land under their dominion.
29 The land trembles and writhes,
for the LORD's purposes against Babylon stand,
to make the land of Babylon a desolation,
without inhabitant.
30 The warriors of Babylon have given up fighting,
they remain in their strongholds;
their strength has failed,
they have become women;
her buildings are set on fire,
her bars are broken.
31 One runner runs to meet another,
and one messenger to meet another,
to tell the king of Babylon
that his city is taken from end to end:
32 the fords have been seized,
the marshes have been burned with fire,
and the soldiers are in panic.
33 For thus says the LORD of hosts, the God of Israel:
Daughter Babylon is like a threshing floor

[d] Heb lacks *the LORD*

51.14 Jer 49.13; Am 6.8; Nah 3.15; Jer 50.15
51.15 Gen 1.1,6; Jer 10.12-16; Acts 14.15; Rom 1.20; Job 9.8; Ps 104.2; Isa 40.22
51.16 Ps 18.13; Jer 10.13; Ps 135.7
51.17 Jer 10.14; 50.2; Hab 2.18,19
51.18 Jer 10.15
51.19 Jer 10.16; 50.34
51.20 Isa 10.5,15; Jer 50.23; Isa 41.15,16; Mic 4.12,13
51.22 2 Chr 36.17
51.24 Jer 50.10,15,29
51.25 Jer 50.31; Zech 4.7; Rev 8.8
51.26 ver 29; Jer 50.13
51.27 Isa 13.2; Jer 50.2; 25.14; 50.41,42
51.29 Jer 8.16; 10.10; 50.46; Am 8.8; Isa 13.19,20; 47.11
51.30 Ps 76.5; Jer 50.36,37; Isa 13.7,8; Lam 2.9; Am 1.5; Nah 3.13
51.31 2 Chr 30.6; 2 Sam 18.19-31; Jer 50.24
51.32 Jer 50.37,38
51.33 Isa 21.10; 41.15; Hab 3.12; Isa 17.5-7; Hos 6.11; Joel 3.13

at the time when it is trodden;
yet a little while
and the time of her harvest will come.

34 "King Nebuchadrezzar of Babylon has
devoured me,
he has crushed me;
he has made me an empty vessel,
he has swallowed me like a monster;
he has filled his belly with my delicacies,
he has spewed me out.
35 May my torn flesh be avenged on
Babylon,"
the inhabitants of Zion shall say.
"May my blood be avenged on the
inhabitants of Chaldea,"
Jerusalem shall say.
36 Therefore thus says the LORD:
I am going to defend your cause
and take vengeance for you.
I will dry up her sea
and make her fountain dry;
37 and Babylon shall become a heap of
ruins,
a den of jackals,
an object of horror and of hissing,
without inhabitant.

38 Like lions they shall roar together;
they shall growl like lions' whelps.
39 When they are inflamed, I will set out
their drink
and make them drunk, until they
become merry
and then sleep a perpetual sleep
and never wake, says the LORD.
40 I will bring them down like lambs to the
slaughter,
like rams and goats.

41 How Sheshach[e] is taken,
the pride of the whole earth seized!
How Babylon has become
an object of horror among the
nations!
42 The sea has risen over Babylon;
she has been covered by its
tumultuous waves.
43 Her cities have become an object of
horror,
a land of drought and a desert,
a land in which no one lives,
and through which no mortal passes.
44 I will punish Bel in Babylon,
and make him disgorge what he has
swallowed.
The nations shall no longer stream to him;
the wall of Babylon has fallen.

45 Come out of her, my people!
Save your lives, each of you,
from the fierce anger of the LORD!
46 Do not be fainthearted or fearful
at the rumors heard in the land—
one year one rumor comes,
the next year another,
rumors of violence in the land
and of ruler against ruler.

47 Assuredly, the days are coming
when I will punish the images of
Babylon;
her whole land shall be put to shame,
and all her slain shall fall in her midst.
48 Then the heavens and the earth,
and all that is in them,
shall shout for joy over Babylon;
for the destroyers shall come against
them out of the north,
says the LORD.
49 Babylon must fall for the slain of Israel,
as the slain of all the earth have
fallen because of Babylon.

50 You survivors of the sword,
go, do not linger!
Remember the LORD in a distant land,
and let Jerusalem come into your mind:
51 We are put to shame, for we have heard
insults;
dishonor has covered our face,
for aliens have come
into the holy places of the LORD's house.

52 Therefore the time is surely coming,
says the LORD,
when I will punish her idols,
and through all her land
the wounded shall groan.
53 Though Babylon should mount up to
heaven,
and though she should fortify her
strong height,
from me destroyers would come upon her,
says the LORD.

54 Listen!—a cry from Babylon!
A great crashing from the land of the
Chaldeans!
55 For the LORD is laying Babylon waste,
and stilling her loud clamor.
Their waves roar like mighty waters,

[e] *Sheshach* is a cryptogram for *Babel*, Babylon

51.34 Jer 50.17; Isa 24.1-3; Am 8.4
51.35 Ps 137.8; ver 24
51.36 Ps 140.12; Jer 50.34; Rom 12.19; Jer 50.38
51.37 Isa 13.22; Jer 50.39; Rev 18.2; Jer 49.33; 50.13
51.39 Jer 25.27
51.40 Jer 50.27
51.41 Jer 25.26; Isa 13.19; Jer 49.25
51.42 Isa 8.7,8; Dan 9.26
51.43 Jer 50.12; Isa 13.20
51.44 Isa 46.1; Jer 50.2; ver 34,58
51.45 ver 6; Jer 50.8; Rev 18.4; Acts 2.40
51.46 Jer 46.27,28; 2 Kings 19.7; Isa 13.3-5; 19.2
51.47 Isa 46.1,2; ver 52; Jer 50.2; 50.12,35-37
51.48 Isa 44.23; 49.13; Rev 12.12; 18.20; ver 11,27
51.49 Jer 50.29
51.50 ver 45; Ps 137.6
51.51 Ps 79.4
51.52 ver 47; Jer 50.38
51.53 Isa 14.12,13; Jer 49.16; Isa 13.3
51.54 Jer 50.46
51.55 ver 42

51.59-64 Jeremiah's Final Word to Babylon. To *Seraiah*, a member of the staff of King Zedekiah who is about to be taken captive to Babylon, Jeremiah gives a copy of the oracles describing *the disasters* slated for Babylon. They are to be read aloud there, and the scroll tied to a stone and thrown into the Euphrates to symbolize the inescapable doom of Babylon. This section marks the end of *the words of Jeremiah.*
52.1-34 Historical Appendix. Drawn from 2 Kings 24.18-25.30, this editorial addition to the oracles of Jeremiah shows in part how they were fulfilled within the historical experience of Israel and Judah. The editor's one major supplement to his source is the list of figures on the numbers of those taken into exile in Babylon. This seems to be overstated. The reign of Jehoiachin began in 598 and is briefly described, including his being taken captive to Babylon in 2 Kings 24.8-17. The supplement therefore ends, like 2 Kings, on a positive note, with the special favor granted to the former king of Judah.

the sound of their clamor resounds;
56 for a destroyer has come against her,
against Babylon;
her warriors are taken,
their bows are broken;
for the LORD is a God of recompense,
he will repay in full.
57 I will make her officials and her sages
drunk,
also her governors, her deputies, and
her warriors;
they shall sleep a perpetual sleep and
never wake,
says the King, whose name is the
LORD of hosts.

58 Thus says the LORD of hosts:
The broad wall of Babylon
shall be leveled to the ground,
and her high gates
shall be burned with fire.
The peoples exhaust themselves for
nothing,
and the nations weary themselves
only for fire.[f]

Jeremiah's Command to Seraiah
59 The word that the prophet Jeremiah
commanded Seraiah son of Neriah son of
Mahseiah, when he went with King Zedekiah
of Judah to Babylon, in the fourth year of
his reign. Seraiah was the quartermaster.
60Jeremiah wrote in a[g] scroll all the disasters
that would come on Babylon, all these words
that are written concerning Babylon. 61And
Jeremiah said to Seraiah: "When you come
to Babylon, see that you read all these
words, 62and say, 'O LORD, you yourself
threatened to destroy this place so that
neither human beings nor animals shall live
in it, and it shall be desolate forever.' 63When
you finish reading this scroll, tie a stone to
it, and throw it into the middle of the
Euphrates, 64and say, 'Thus shall Babylon
sink, to rise no more, because of the disasters that I am bringing on her.' "[h]
Thus far are the words of Jeremiah.

The Destruction of Jerusalem Reviewed
52 Zedekiah was twenty-one years old
when he began to reign; he reigned
eleven years in Jerusalem. His mother's name
was Hamutal daughter of Jeremiah of Libnah.
2He did what was evil in the sight of the
LORD, just as Jehoiakim had done. 3Indeed,
Jerusalem and Judah so angered the LORD
that he expelled them from his presence.
Zedekiah rebelled against the king of
Babylon. 4And in the ninth year of his
reign, in the tenth month, on the tenth day
of the month, King Nebuchadrezzar of
Babylon came with all his army against
Jerusalem, and they laid siege to it; they
built siegeworks against it all around. 5So
the city was besieged until the eleventh
year of King Zedekiah. 6On the ninth day
of the fourth month the famine became so
severe in the city that there was no food for
the people of the land. 7Then a breach was
made in the city wall;[i] and all the soldiers
fled and went out from the city by night by
the way of the gate between the two walls,
by the king's garden, though the Chaldeans
were all around the city. They went in the
direction of the Arabah. 8But the army of
the Chaldeans pursued the king, and overtook Zedekiah in the plains of Jericho; and
all his army was scattered, deserting him.
9Then they captured the king, and brought
him up to the king of Babylon at Riblah in
the land of Hamath, and he passed sentence
on him. 10The king of Babylon killed the
sons of Zedekiah before his eyes, and also
killed all the officers of Judah at Riblah. 11He
put out the eyes of Zedekiah, and bound
him in fetters, and the king of Babylon took
him to Babylon, and put him in prison until
the day of his death.
12 In the fifth month, on the tenth day
of the month—which was the nineteenth
year of King Nebuchadrezzar, king of
Babylon—Nebuzaradan the captain of the
bodyguard who served the king of Babylon,
entered Jerusalem. 13He burned the house of
the LORD, the king's house, and all the
houses of Jerusalem; every great house he
burned down. 14All the army of the
Chaldeans, who were with the captain of
the guard, broke down all the walls around
Jerusalem. 15Nebuzaradan the captain of the
guard carried into exile some of the poorest
of the people and the rest of the people who
were left in the city and the deserters who
had defected to the king of Babylon, together with the rest of the artisans. 16But
Nebuzaradan the captain of the guard left
some of the poorest people of the land to be
vinedressers and tillers of the soil.
17 The pillars of bronze that were in the

[f] Gk Syr Compare Hab 2.13: Heb *and the nations for fire, and they are weary* [g] Or *one* [h] Gk: Heb *on her. And they shall weary themselves* [i] Heb lacks *wall*

51.56 ver 48; Hab 2.8; Ps 94.1,2; ver 6,24
51.57 ver 39; Ps 76.5,6; Jer 46.18; 48.15
51.58 ver 44; Jer 50.15; Hab 2.13; ver 64
51.59 Jer 32.12; 28.1
51.60 Jer 30.2,3; 36.2,4,32
51.62 Jer 25.12; 50.3,39; ver 43; Ezek 35.9
51.63 Rev 18.21
51.64 Nah 1.8,9; ver 58
52.1 2 Kings 24.18; 2 Chr 36.11-13
52.2 Jer 36.30,31
52.3 Isa 3.1,4,5; 2 Chr 36.13
52.4 2 Kings 25.1-7; Jer 39.1; Ezek 24.1,2; Jer 32.24
52.6 Jer 38.9
52.7 Jer 39.2; 39.4-7
52.8 Jer 21.7; 32.4; 34.21; 37.17; 38.23
52.9 Jer 32.4; 2 Kings 25.6; Jer 39.5
52.10 Jer 39.6
52.11 Jer 39.7; Ezek 12.13
52.12 2 Kings 25.8-21; Jer 39.9
52.13 2 Chr 36.19; Lam 2.7; Mic 3.12; Jer 39.8
52.14 2 Kings 25.10
52.15 2 Kings 25.11; Jer 39.9
52.16 2 Kings 25.12; Jer 39.10; 40.2-6
52.17 1 Kings 7.15-36; Jer 27.19-22

house of the LORD, and the stands and the
bronze sea that were in the house of the
LORD, the Chaldeans broke in pieces, and
carried all the bronze to Babylon. [18]They
took away the pots, the shovels, the snuffers, the basins, the ladles, and all the vessels
of bronze used in the temple service. [19]The
captain of the guard took away the small
bowls also, the firepans, the basins, the pots,
the lampstands, the ladles, and the bowls
for libation, both those of gold and those of
silver. [20]As for the two pillars, the one sea,
the twelve bronze bulls that were under the
sea, and the stands,[u] which King Solomon
had made for the house of the LORD, the
bronze of all these vessels was beyond
weighing. [21]As for the pillars, the height of
the one pillar was eighteen cubits, its circumference was twelve cubits; it was hollow and its thickness was four fingers. [22]Upon
it was a capital of bronze; the height of the
one capital was five cubits; latticework and
pomegranates, all of bronze, encircled the
top of the capital. And the second pillar had
the same, with pomegranates. [23]There were
ninety-six pomegranates on the sides; all
the pomegranates encircling the latticework
numbered one hundred.

24 The captain of the guard took the
chief priest Seraiah, the second priest
Zephaniah, and the three guardians of the
threshold; [25]and from the city he took an
officer who had been in command of the
soldiers, and seven men of the king's council who were found in the city; the secretary
of the commander of the army who mustered the people of the land; and sixty men
of the people of the land who were found
inside the city. [26]Then Nebuzaradan the
captain of the guard took them, and brought
them to the king of Babylon at Riblah.
[27]And the king of Babylon struck them
down, and put them to death at Riblah in
the land of Hamath. So Judah went into
exile out of its land.

28 This is the number of the people whom
Nebuchadrezzar took into exile: in the seventh year, three thousand twenty-three
Judeans; [29]in the eighteenth year of
Nebuchadrezzar he took into exile from
Jerusalem eight hundred thirty-two persons;
[30]in the twenty-third year of Nebuchadrezzar,
Nebuzaradan the captain of the guard took
into exile of the Judeans seven hundred
forty-five persons; all the persons were four
thousand six hundred.

Jehoiachin Favored in Captivity

31 In the thirty-seventh year of the exile
of King Jehoiachin of Judah, in the twelfth
month, on the twenty-fifth day of the month,
King Evil-merodach of Babylon, in the year
he began to reign, showed favor to King
Jehoiachin of Judah and brought him out of
prison; [32]he spoke kindly to him, and gave
him a seat above the seats of the other
kings who were with him in Babylon. [33]So
Jehoiachin put aside his prison clothes, and
every day of his life he dined regularly at
the king's table. [34]For his allowance, a regular daily allowance was given him by the
king of Babylon, as long as he lived, up to
the day of his death.

52.18 1 Kings 7.40,45
52.19 1 Kings 7.49,50
52.20 1 Kings 7.47
52.21 1 Kings 7.15
52.22 1 Kings 7.16,20,42
52.24 2 Kings 25.18; Jer 21.1; 29.25; 37.3; 35.4
52.26 ver 12,15,16; 2 Kings 25.20,21; ver 9
52.27 Isa 6.11,12; Jer 13.19; Ezek 33.28; Mic 4.10
52.28 2 Kings 24.2,3,12-16; Neh 7.6; Dan 1.1-3
52.30 2 Kings 25.11; Jer 39.9
52.31 2 Kings 25.27-30; Gen 40.13
52.33 Gen 41.14,42; 2 Sam 9.13; 1 Kings 2.7
52.34 2 Sam 9.10

[j] Cn: Heb *that were under the stands*

LAMENTATIONS

See the Introductions, pp. 4 and 60-61 above.

1.1-22 Judah's Plight as the Result of God's Judgment. The lamentation pictures the loneliness of Jerusalem now that most of its inhabitants have been taken off into captivity by the Babylonians. Judah's former *friends* have become her enemies and her *masters*.
1.4 There are none who come to the holy city to celebrate the festivals, now that the temple is ruined.
1.8-9 The reason for these disasters is that *Jerusalem sinned*, and her disobedience to God has become obvious to all.
1.10 The temple sanctuary, formerly accessible only to the priests, is now *invaded* by people from non-Israelite *nations* who before the disaster could not even have associated with the *congregation* of God's people.
1.11-12 The poverty of the people searching for *bread* and selling off their prized possessions to obtain *food* evokes no sympathy from the neighboring people who see the condition of the city.
1.13-17 Jerusalem is personified by the poet, who laments the present pain and disobedience that caused these troubles and led to God's seeming rejection of his people.

The Deserted City

1 How lonely sits the city
that once was full of people!
How like a widow she has become,
she that was great among the nations!
She that was a princess among the provinces
has become a vassal.

2 She weeps bitterly in the night,
with tears on her cheeks;
among all her lovers
she has no one to comfort her;
all her friends have dealt treacherously with her,
they have become her enemies.

3 Judah has gone into exile with suffering
and hard servitude;
she lives now among the nations,
and finds no resting place;
her pursuers have all overtaken her
in the midst of her distress.

4 The roads to Zion mourn,
for no one comes to the festivals;
all her gates are desolate,
her priests groan;
her young girls grieve,[a]
and her lot is bitter.

5 Her foes have become the masters,
her enemies prosper,
because the LORD has made her suffer
for the multitude of her transgressions;
her children have gone away,
captives before the foe.

6 From daughter Zion has departed
all her majesty.
Her princes have become like stags
that find no pasture;
they fled without strength
before the pursuer.

7 Jerusalem remembers,
in the days of her affliction and wandering,
all the precious things
that were hers in days of old.
When her people fell into the hand of the foe,
and there was no one to help her,
the foe looked on mocking
over her downfall.

8 Jerusalem sinned grievously,
so she has become a mockery;
all who honored her despise her,
for they have seen her nakedness;
she herself groans,
and turns her face away.

9 Her uncleanness was in her skirts;
she took no thought of her future;
her downfall was appalling,
with none to comfort her.
"O LORD, look at my affliction,
for the enemy has triumphed!"

10 Enemies have stretched out their hands
over all her precious things;
she has even seen the nations
invade her sanctuary,
those whom you forbade
to enter your congregation.

11 All her people groan
as they search for bread;
they trade their treasures for food
to revive their strength.
Look, O LORD, and see
how worthless I have become.

12 Is it nothing to you,[a] all you who pass by?
Look and see
if there is any sorrow like my sorrow,
which was brought upon me,
which the LORD inflicted
on the day of his fierce anger.

13 From on high he sent fire;
it went deep into my bones;
he spread a net for my feet;
he turned me back;
he has left me stunned,
faint all day long.

14 My transgressions were bound[a] into a yoke;
by his hand they were fastened together;

[a] Meaning of Heb uncertain

1.1 Isa 3.26; 54.4; Ezra 4.20; Jer 40.9
1.2 Ps 6.6; Jer 2.25; 4.30
1.3 Jer 13.19; Deut 28.64,65; 2 Kings 25.4,5
1.4 Jer 9.11; 10.22; Joel 1.8-13
1.5 Deut 28.43,44; Jer 30.14,15; 39.9; 52.28
1.6 Jer 13.18; 2 Kings 25.4,5
1.7 Ps 42.4; Isa 5.1-4; Jer 37.7; Lam 4.17; Jer 48.27
1.8 1 Kings 8.46; ver 5,20,17; Jer 13.22,26; ver 4,11,21,22
1.9 Ezek 24.13; Deut 32.29; Isa 47.7; Jer 13.17,18; 16.7
1.10 Isa 64.10,11; Jer 51.51; Deut 23.3
1.11 Jer 38.9; 52.6; 1 Sam 30.12
1.12 Jer 18.16; 48.27; ver 18; Jer 30.23,24; 4.8
1.13 Job 30.30; Hab 3.16; Job 19.6; Jer 44.6
1.14 Deut 28.48; Isa 47.6; Jer 28.13,14; 32.3,5; Ezek 25.4,7

they weigh on my neck,
sapping my strength;
the Lord handed me over
to those whom I cannot withstand.

15 The LORD has rejected
all my warriors in the midst of me;
he proclaimed a time against me
to crush my young men;
the Lord has trodden as in a wine press
the virgin daughter Judah.

16 For these things I weep;
my eyes flow with tears;
for a comforter is far from me,
one to revive my courage;
my children are desolate,
for the enemy has prevailed.

17 Zion stretches out her hands,
but there is no one to comfort her;
the LORD has commanded against Jacob
that his neighbors should become his foes;
Jerusalem has become
a filthy thing among them.

18 The LORD is in the right,
for I have rebelled against his word;
but hear, all you peoples,
and behold my suffering;
my young women and young men
have gone into captivity.

19 I called to my lovers
but they deceived me;
my priests and elders
perished in the city
while seeking food
to revive their strength.

20 See, O LORD, how distressed I am;
my stomach churns,
my heart is wrung within me,
because I have been very rebellious.
In the street the sword bereaves;
in the house it is like death.

21 They heard how I was groaning,
with no one to comfort me.
All my enemies heard of my trouble;
they are glad that you have done it.
Bring on the day you have announced,
and let them be as I am.

22 Let all their evil doing come before you;
and deal with them
as you have dealt with me
because of all my transgressions;
for my groans are many
and my heart is faint.

God's Warnings Fulfilled

2 How the Lord in his anger
has humiliated[b] daughter Zion!
He has thrown down from heaven to earth
the splendor of Israel;
he has not remembered his footstool
in the day of his anger.

2 The Lord has destroyed without mercy
all the dwellings of Jacob;
in his wrath he has broken down
the strongholds of daughter Judah;
he has brought down to the ground in dishonor
the kingdom and its rulers.

3 He has cut down in fierce anger
all the might of Israel;
he has withdrawn his right hand from them
in the face of the enemy;
he has burned like a flaming fire in Jacob,
consuming all around.

4 He has bent his bow like an enemy,
with his right hand set like a foe;
he has killed all in whom we took pride
in the tent of daughter Zion;
he has poured out his fury like fire.

5 The Lord has become like an enemy;
he has destroyed Israel;
He has destroyed all its palaces,
laid in ruins its strongholds,
and multiplied in daughter Judah
mourning and lamentation.

6 He has broken down his booth like a garden,
he has destroyed his tabernacle;
the LORD has abolished in Zion
festival and sabbath,
and in his fierce indignation has spurned
king and priest.

[b] Meaning of Heb uncertain

1.15 Isa 41.2; Jer 13.24; 18.21; Isa 28.18; Mic 7.10; Rev 14.19
1.16 Jer 13.17; 14.17; Lam 2.18; ver 2,9
1.17 Jer 4.31; 2 Kings 24.2-4; ver 8
1.18 Jer 12.1; 1 Sam 12.14; ver 12; Deut 28.32,41
1.19 Jer 30.14; 14.15; Lam 2.20
1.20 Isa 16.11; Jer 4.19; Lam 2.11; Deut 32.29; Ezek 7.15
1.21 Lam 2.15; Isa 14.5,6; Jer 30.16
1.22 Neh 4.4,5; Ps 137.7,8
2.1 Lam 3.43,44; Ezek 28.14-16; Isa 64.11; Ps 99.5; 132.7
2.2 Ps 21.9; Lam 3.43; Mic 5.11,14; Isa 25.12; Ps 89.39
2.3 Ps 75.5,10; 74.11; Jer 21.4,5; 21.14
2.4 Lam 3.12,13; Ezek 24.25; Isa 42.25; Jer 7.20
2.5 Jer 30.14; 6.26; 9.17-20
2.6 Jer 7.14; 52.13; Lam 1.4; Zeph 3.18; Lam 4.16,20; 5.12

1.18-20 The poet acknowledges that God is justified in what he has done to punish Judah, even though the inward parts of the people *churn* as they endure these horrors.
1.21-22 The glee of the neighboring peoples (*enemies*) at Judah's plight leads to a call for God to bring comparable judgment on them.
2.1-22 God Brought the Punishment: Judah Must Repent.
2.1-9 God is portrayed here as the active agent in the destruction of Jerusalem and its temple. His *anger* and enmity toward the people are described, including his having *disowned his sanctuary*. All these tragic events were not chance, but the consequence of what God *determined* to do in destroying the city, scattering its leaders, and depriving the people of reliable *prophets* who would bring God's message to them.

2.10-16 Depicted are the silent weeping of the people at their plight, their crying out for food, and the lack of anyone to *heal* or of *prophets* to tell the people the truth. Instead, there is mockery from enemies at the desolation of the once splendid city.
2.17 This disaster came because the Lord *demolished without pity* the great city and its temple.
2.18-22 The lament resumes for the city (*wall*) of Zion, where food is so scarce that *children* are hungry and some are eaten by their starving mothers. Other people have died from sickness or starvation, or *by the sword*. God *invited* Judah's *enemies* to come and see the ghastly sight as though it were a day of *festival*.

7 The Lord has scorned his altar,
disowned his sanctuary;
he has delivered into the hand of the enemy
the walls of her palaces;
a clamor was raised in the house of the LORD
as on a day of festival.

8 The LORD determined to lay in ruins
the wall of daughter Zion;
he stretched the line;
he did not withhold his hand from destroying;
he caused rampart and wall to lament;
they languish together.

9 Her gates have sunk into the ground;
he has ruined and broken her bars;
her king and princes are among the nations;
guidance is no more,
and her prophets obtain
no vision from the LORD.

10 The elders of daughter Zion
sit on the ground in silence;
they have thrown dust on their heads
and put on sackcloth;
the young girls of Jerusalem
have bowed their heads to the ground.

11 My eyes are spent with weeping;
my stomach churns;
my bile is poured out on the ground
because of the destruction of my people,
because infants and babes faint
in the streets of the city.

12 They cry to their mothers,
"Where is bread and wine?"
as they faint like the wounded
in the streets of the city,
as their life is poured out
on their mothers' bosom.

13 What can I say for you, to what compare you,
O daughter Jerusalem?
To what can I liken you, that I may comfort you,
O virgin daughter Zion?
For vast as the sea is your ruin;
who can heal you?

14 Your prophets have seen for you
false and deceptive visions;
they have not exposed your iniquity
to restore your fortunes,
but have seen oracles for you
that are false and misleading.

15 All who pass along the way
clap their hands at you;
they hiss and wag their heads
at daughter Jerusalem;
"Is this the city that was called
the perfection of beauty,
the joy of all the earth?"

16 All your enemies
open their mouths against you;
they hiss, they gnash their teeth,
they cry: "We have devoured her!
Ah, this is the day we longed for;
at last we have seen it!"

17 The LORD has done what he purposed,
he has carried out his threat;
as he ordained long ago,
he has demolished without pity;
he has made the enemy rejoice over you,
and exalted the might of your foes.

18 Cry aloud[c] to the Lord!
O wall of daughter Zion!
Let tears stream down like a torrent
day and night!
Give yourself no rest,
your eyes no respite!

19 Arise, cry out in the night,
at the beginning of the watches!
Pour out your heart like water
before the presence of the Lord!
Lift your hands to him
for the lives of your children,
who faint for hunger
at the head of every street.

20 Look, O LORD, and consider!
To whom have you done this?
Should women eat their offspring,
the children they have borne?
Should priest and prophet be killed
in the sanctuary of the Lord?

21 The young and the old are lying
on the ground in the streets;
my young women and my young men
have fallen by the sword;

[c] Cn: Heb *Their heart cried*

2.7 Isa 64.11; Ezek 7.20-22; Jer 33.4,5; Ps 74.4
2.8 Jer 5.10; 2 Kings 21.13; Isa 34.11; 3.26; Jer 14.2
2.9 Neh 1.3; Jer 51.30; Deut 28.36; 2 Kings 24.15; 2 Chr 15.3; Jer 14.14; 23.16; Ezek 7.26
2.10 Job 2.13; Isa 3.26; Am 8.3; Job 2.12; Ezek 27.30,31; Isa 15.3; Lam 1.4
2.11 Ps 6.7; Lam 3.48; 1.20; Job 16.13; Ps 22.14; Lam 4.4
2.12 Jer 5.17; Lam 4.4; Job 30.16
2.13 Lam 1.12; Isa 37.22; Jer 14.17; 8.22; 30.12-15
2.14 Jer 2.8; 29.8,9; Isa 58.1; Jer 23.36; Ezek 22.25,28
2.15 Jer 19.8; Zeph 2.15; Isa 37.22; Ps 48.2; 50.2
2.16 Ps 22.13; Lam 3.46; Ps 37.12; 56.2; Ob 12-15
2.17 Deut 28.15; Jer 18.11; ver 1,2; Ps 35.24,26; Lam 1.5
2.18 Hos 7.14; Jer 9.1; Lam 1.2,16
2.19 Ps 42.3; Isa 26.9; Ps 62.8; Isa 51.20
2.20 Jer 19.9; 14.15; Lam 4.13,16
2.21 2 Chr 36.17; Jer 6.11; Ps 78.62,63; Jer 13.14; Zech 11.6

in the day of your anger you have killed
them,
slaughtering without mercy.

22 You invited my enemies from all around
as if for a day of festival;
and on the day of the anger of the LORD
no one escaped or survived;
those whom I bore and reared
my enemy has destroyed.

God's Steadfast Love Endures

3 I am one who has seen affliction
under the rod of God's[d] wrath;
2 he has driven and brought me
into darkness without any light;
3 against me alone he turns his hand,
again and again, all day long.

4 He has made my flesh and my skin
waste away,
and broken my bones;
5 he has besieged and enveloped me
with bitterness and tribulation;
6 he has made me sit in darkness
like the dead of long ago.

7 He has walled me about so that I
cannot escape;
he has put heavy chains on me;
8 though I call and cry for help,
he shuts out my prayer;
9 he has blocked my ways with hewn
stones,
he has made my paths crooked.

10 He is a bear lying in wait for me,
a lion in hiding;
11 he led me off my way and tore me to
pieces;
he has made me desolate;
12 he bent his bow and set me
as a mark for his arrow.

13 He shot into my vitals
the arrows of his quiver;
14 I have become the laughingstock of all
my people,
the object of their taunt-songs all day
long.
15 He has filled me with bitterness,
he has sated me with wormwood.

16 He has made my teeth grind on gravel,
and made me cower in ashes;
17 my soul is bereft of peace;
I have forgotten what happiness is;
18 so I say, "Gone is my glory,
and all that I had hoped for from the
LORD."

19 The thought of my affliction and my
homelessness
is wormwood and gall!
20 My soul continually thinks of it
and is bowed down within me.
21 But this I call to mind,
and therefore I have hope:

22 The steadfast love of the LORD never
ceases,[e]
his mercies never come to an end;
23 they are new every morning;
great is your faithfulness.
24 "The LORD is my portion," says my soul,
"therefore I will hope in him."

25 The LORD is good to those who wait for
him,
to the soul that seeks him.
26 It is good that one should wait quietly
for the salvation of the LORD.
27 It is good for one to bear
the yoke in youth,
28 to sit alone in silence
when the Lord has imposed it,
29 to put one's mouth to the dust
(there may yet be hope),
30 to give one's cheek to the smiter,
and be filled with insults.

31 For the Lord will not
reject forever.
32 Although he causes grief, he will have
compassion
according to the abundance of his
steadfast love;
33 for he does not willingly afflict
or grieve anyone.

34 When all the prisoners of the land
are crushed under foot,
35 when human rights are perverted
in the presence of the Most High,
36 when one's case is subverted
—does the Lord not see it?

37 Who can command and have it done,
if the Lord has not ordained it?
38 Is it not from the mouth of the Most High
that good and bad come?

[d] Heb *his* [e] Syr Tg: Heb *LORD, we are not cut off*

2.22 Ps 31.13; Jer 6.25; Hos 9.12,13
3.1 Job 19.21; Jer 15.17,18
3.3 Isa 5.25
3.4 Job 16.8; Ps 51.8; Isa 38.13; Jer 50.17
3.6 Ps 88.5,6
3.7 Job 3.23; Jer 40.4
3.8 Job 30.20; Ps 22.2
3.10 Job 10.16; Isa 38.13
3.12 Ps 7.12,13; Job 7.20
3.14 Jer 20.7; Job 30.9
3.19 Jer 9.15
3.20 Ps 42.5,6,11
3.22 Mal 3.6
3.23 Zeph 3.5
3.24 Ps 16.5; 33.18
3.25 Isa 25.9; 30.18; 26.9
3.26 Ps 37.7; 40.1; Isa 30.15
3.27 Ps 94.12
3.28 Jer 15.17
3.30 Isa 50.6; Mt 5.39
3.31 Ps 94.14
3.32 Ps 78.38; Hos 11.8
3.33 Ezek 33.11; Heb 12.10
3.35 Ps 140.12
3.36 Hab 1.13
3.37 Ps 33.9
3.38 Job 2.10; Isa 45.7; Jer 32.42

3.1-66 The City Confesses its Sin and Calls for Renewal and Retribution.
3.1-20 God's punitive judgment has brought ruin to his people, so that all that they once *hoped for* is gone, and bitterness prevails.
3.21-39 God's love endures and will prevail beyond the present time of punishment of the people for their disobedience. God *sees* and calls to account injustice, as well as sending both *good and bad* on the world.

3.40-42 What is called for is repentance and confession on the part of the people.
3.43-54 Again the details of the plight of Judah are recounted, and the sense of being *lost* through estrangement from God is expressed.
3.55-66 Appeal is made to God to bring judgment on the enemies of his people, so that those who *taunt* Judah will be *destroyed* from the face of the earth.
4.1-22 Jerusalem's Ruin was Punishment by God.
4.1-10 Again the wretched condition of the survivors left behind in Jerusalem is vividly depicted: the sanctuary is robbed of its beauty; children are abandoned by their mothers, like an *ostrich* left behind in the desert sands; infants are not nursed, and some are eaten. Those people once regarded as privileged are now *shriveled* and dry from lack of food and water. Those killed in battle are better off than those who have survived.

39 Why should any who draw breath
complain
about the punishment of their sins?

40 Let us test and examine our ways,
and return to the LORD.
41 Let us lift up our hearts as well as our
hands
to God in heaven.
42 We have transgressed and rebelled,
and you have not forgiven.

43 You have wrapped yourself with anger
and pursued us,
killing without pity;
44 you have wrapped yourself with a cloud
so that no prayer can pass through.
45 You have made us filth and rubbish
among the peoples.

46 All our enemies
have opened their mouths against us;
47 panic and pitfall have come upon us,
devastation and destruction.
48 My eyes flow with rivers of tears
because of the destruction of my
people.

49 My eyes will flow without ceasing,
without respite,
50 until the LORD from heaven
looks down and sees.
51 My eyes cause me grief
at the fate of all the young women in
my city.

52 Those who were my enemies without
cause
have hunted me like a bird;
53 they flung me alive into a pit
and hurled stones on me;
54 water closed over my head;
I said, "I am lost."

55 I called on your name, O LORD,
from the depths of the pit;
56 you heard my plea, "Do not close your ear
to my cry for help, but give me relief!"
57 You came near when I called on you;
you said, "Do not fear!"

58 You have taken up my cause, O Lord,
you have redeemed my life.
59 You have seen the wrong done to me,
O LORD;
judge my cause.

60 You have seen all their malice,
all their plots against me.

61 You have heard their taunts, O LORD,
all their plots against me.
62 The whispers and murmurs of my
assailants
are against me all day long.
63 Whether they sit or rise—see,
I am the object of their taunt-songs.

64 Pay them back for their deeds, O LORD,
according to the work of their hands!
65 Give them anguish of heart;
your curse be on them!
66 Pursue them in anger and destroy them
from under the LORD's heavens.

The Punishment of Zion

4 How the gold has grown dim,
how the pure gold is changed!
The sacred stones lie scattered
at the head of every street.

2 The precious children of Zion,
worth their weight in fine gold—
how they are reckoned as earthen pots,
the work of a potter's hands!

3 Even the jackals offer the breast
and nurse their young,
but my people has become cruel,
like the ostriches in the wilderness.

4 The tongue of the infant sticks
to the roof of its mouth for thirst;
the children beg for food,
but no one gives them anything.

5 Those who feasted on delicacies
perish in the streets;
those who were brought up in purple
cling to ash heaps.

6 For the chastisement[f] of my people has
been greater
than the punishment[g] of Sodom,
which was overthrown in a moment,
though no hand was laid on it.[h]

7 Her princes were purer than snow,
whiter than milk;
their bodies were more ruddy than
coral,
their hair[h] like sapphire.[i]

[f] Or *iniquity* [g] Or *sin* [h] Meaning of Heb uncertain [i] Or *lapis lazuli*

3.39 Mic 7.9; Heb 12.5,6
3.40 Ps 119.59; 2 Cor 13.5
3.41 Ps 25.1; 28.2
3.42 Dan 9.5; Jer 5.7,9
3.43 Lam 2.21; Ps 83.15
3.44 Ps 97.2; ver 8
3.45 1 Cor 4.13
3.46 Lam 2.16
3.47 Isa 24.17; Jer 48.43; Isa 51.19
3.48 Lam 1.16; 2.11,18
3.49 Ps 77.2
3.50 Isa 63.15
3.52 Ps 35.7
3.53 Jer 37.16
3.54 Ps 69.2; Isa 38.10
3.55 Jon 2.2
3.56 Ps 116.1,2
3.57 Ps 145.18; Isa 41.10,14
3.58 Jer 51.36; Ps 71.23
3.60 Jer 11.19,20; 18.18
3.62 Ezek 36.3
3.64 Ps 28.4
3.66 Ps 8.3
4.2 Isa 51.18; 30.14; Jer 19.11
4.3 Isa 34.13; 49.15; Job 39.14,16
4.4 Jer 14.3; Lam 2.12
4.6 Ezek 16.48; Gen 19.23; Jer 20.16
4.7 Ps 51.7

8 Now their visage is blacker than soot;
they are not recognized in the streets.
Their skin has shriveled on their bones;
it has become as dry as wood.

9 Happier were those pierced by the sword
than those pierced by hunger,
whose life drains away, deprived
of the produce of the field.

10 The hands of compassionate women
have boiled their own children;
they became their food
in the destruction of my people.

11 The LORD gave full vent to his wrath;
he poured out his hot anger,
and kindled a fire in Zion
that consumed its foundations.

12 The kings of the earth did not believe,
nor did any of the inhabitants of the world,
that foe or enemy could enter
the gates of Jerusalem.

13 It was for the sins of her prophets
and the iniquities of her priests,
who shed the blood of the righteous
in the midst of her.

14 Blindly they wandered through the streets,
so defiled with blood
that no one was able
to touch their garments.

15 "Away! Unclean!" people shouted at them;
"Away! Away! Do not touch!"
So they became fugitives and wanderers;
it was said among the nations,
"They shall stay here no longer."

16 The LORD himself has scattered them,
he will regard them no more;
no honor was shown to the priests,
no favor to the elders.

17 Our eyes failed, ever watching
vainly for help;
we were watching eagerly
for a nation that could not save.

18 They dogged our steps
so that we could not walk in our streets;
our end drew near; our days were numbered;
for our end had come.

19 Our pursuers were swifter
than the eagles in the heavens;
they chased us on the mountains,
they lay in wait for us in the wilderness.

20 The LORD's anointed, the breath of our life,
was taken in their pits—
the one of whom we said, "Under his shadow
we shall live among the nations."

21 Rejoice and be glad, O daughter Edom,
you that live in the land of Uz;
but to you also the cup shall pass;
you shall become drunk and strip yourself bare.

22 The punishment of your iniquity,
O daughter Zion, is accomplished,
he will keep you in exile no longer;
but your iniquity, O daughter Edom, he will punish,
he will uncover your sins.

A Plea for Mercy

5 Remember, O LORD, what has befallen us;
look, and see our disgrace!
2 Our inheritance has been turned over to strangers,
our homes to aliens.
3 We have become orphans, fatherless;
our mothers are like widows.
4 We must pay for the water we drink;
the wood we get must be bought.
5 With a yoke[j] on our necks we are hard driven;
we are weary, we are given no rest.
6 We have made a pact with[k] Egypt and Assyria,
to get enough bread.
7 Our ancestors sinned; they are no more,
and we bear their iniquities.
8 Slaves rule over us;
there is no one to deliver us from their hand.
9 We get our bread at the peril of our lives,

[j] Symmachus: Heb lacks *With a yoke* [k] Heb *have given the hand to*

4.11-16 All this has happened, unexpected by Judah and her enemies, because of the nation's disobedience. The people are exiled, and the leadership crushed. **4.17-22** The folly of the people and their leaders prior to the Babylonian seizure of Jerusalem led them to look to some other nation to rescue them, such as Egypt (Jer 37.1-10). Their own king, *the Lord's anointed*, Zedekiah, tried to resist the Babylonians but was captured, blinded and *taken* as captive to Babylon (Jer 52.1-11). Although Judah's neighbor to the east of the Jordan, Edom, may feel secure and complacent, it too will fall under God's judgment.
5.1-22 A Review of the Calamity that Befell Judah.
5.1-15 The cruel, oppressive, inhuman conditions of the people are detailed. To obtain sufficient food, they must make *pacts* with their former enemies, Egypt and Assyria. Both women and members of the ruling class (*princes* and *elders*) have been grossly abused.

4.8 Job 30.30; Lam 5.10; Ps 102.5
4.9 Jer 15.2; Ezek 24.23
4.10 Lam 2.20; 2 Kings 6.29; Deut 28.57
4.11 Jer 7.20; ver 22; Deut 32.22; Jer 21.14
4.12 1 Kings 9.8,9; Jer 21.13
4.13 Jer 5.31; 6.13; Ezek 22.26; Mic 3.11,12; Mt 23.31
4.14 Isa 56.10; 59.9,10; Jer 19.4; 2.34
4.15 Lev 13.45; Jer 49.5
4.16 Lam 5.12
4.17 2 Kings 24.7; Isa 20.5; Jer 37.7; Ezek 29.16
4.18 2 Kings 25.4; Ezek 7.2,3; Am 8.2
4.19 Deut 28.49; Jer 4.13; Hab 1.8
4.20 2 Sam 1.14; 19.21; Ezek 12.13; 19.4,8
4.21 Isa 34.7; Am 1.11,12; Ob 1,16
4.22 Isa 40.2; Mal 1.3,4
5.1 Ps 89.50; 44.13-16
5.2 Ps 79.1; Zeph 1.13
5.5 Jer 28.14; Neh 9.36,37
5.6 Jer 2.36; Hos 5.13; 7.11; 9.3
5.7 Jer 14.20; 16.12
5.8 Neh 5.15; Zech 11.6

5.16-18 These disasters and the desolation of the temple area (*Mount Zion*) are the direct consequences of the people's sins.
5.19-22 The final lines of this lamentation alternate between affirmation of God's eternal rule and appeal to the LORD for restoration of his people.

because of the sword in the
wilderness.
10 Our skin is black as an oven
from the scorching heat of famine.
11 Women are raped in Zion,
virgins in the towns of Judah.
12 Princes are hung up by their hands;
no respect is shown to the elders.
13 Young men are compelled to grind,
and boys stagger under loads of
wood.
14 The old men have left the city gate,
the young men their music.
15 The joy of our hearts has ceased;
our dancing has been turned to
mourning.
16 The crown has fallen from our head;
woe to us, for we have sinned!
17 Because of this our hearts are sick,
because of these things our eyes have
grown dim:
18 because of Mount Zion, which lies
desolate;
jackals prowl over it.

19 But you, O LORD, reign forever;
your throne endures to all
generations.
20 Why have you forgotten us completely?
Why have you forsaken us these
many days?
21 Restore us to yourself, O LORD, that we
may be restored;
renew our days as of old—
22 unless you have utterly rejected us,
and are angry with us beyond measure.

5.10 Lam 4.8
5.11 Isa 13.16; Zech 14.2
5.12 Lam 4.16
5.13 Jer 7.18
5.15 Jer 25.10
5.17 Isa 1.5; Ps 6.7
5.19 Ps 9.7; 102.12,25-27; 45.6
5.20 Ps 13.1
5.21 Jer 31.18
5.22 Jer 7.29; Isa 64.9

EZEKIEL

See the Introductions, pp. 6, 54-57, and 61-62 above.

1.1-3 Introduction. *Thirtieth year* may be a reference to Ezekiel's age when he was commissioned as a prophet. *Among the exiles* refers to the Judahites who were taken to Babylon in 597. *The fifth year of the exile of King Jehoiachin* was 592, since his reign began in 597 (2 Kings 24.8-12). Ezekiel's prophetic role probably was from 593-571. His identification as a *priest* shows that there was no sharp division between priests and prophets, as scholars have sometimes suggested. *Chebar* was a canal tributary to the Euphrates River, southeast of Babylon. That *the hand of the LORD was on him there* shows that the activity of the LORD is by no means limited to the land of Israel.
1.4-28 Ezekiel's Vision of the LORD. This vision is depicted, not as a direct, revelatory experience, but as involving features which resemble but are not simply equivalent to ordinary human experience. The frequently-repeated word *like...* emphasizes this. Ezekiel is influenced by and contributes to the belief in Israel that God transcends human dimensions and therefore cannot be reduced to direct physical descriptions.
1.4-14 *Out of the north* pictures God as coming from his dwelling place in Jerusalem, crossing to Syria and then southward down the Tigris-Euphrates valley to Babylon. The four-sided creatures *of human form* with faces and feet of animals symbolize the multiple powers and aspects of God's activity in the world.
1.15-21 *The LORD* is conveyed in a kind of chariot, just as Elijah was taken up into the presence of God by horses and a chariot of fire (2 Kings 2.9-12).

The Vision of the Chariot

1 In the thirtieth year, in the fourth
month, on the fifth day of the month,
as I was among the exiles by the river
Chebar, the heavens were opened, and I
saw visions of God. 2 On the fifth day of the
month (it was the fifth year of the exile of
King Jehoiachin), 3 the word of the LORD
came to the priest Ezekiel son of Buzi, in the
land of the Chaldeans by the river Chebar;
and the hand of the LORD was on him there.
4 As I looked, a stormy wind came out
of the north: a great cloud with brightness
around it and fire flashing forth continually,
and in the middle of the fire, something like
gleaming amber. 5 In the middle of it was
something like four living creatures. This
was their appearance: they were of human
form. 6 Each had four faces, and each of
them had four wings. 7 Their legs were
straight, and the soles of their feet were like
the sole of a calf's foot; and they sparkled
like burnished bronze. 8 Under their wings
on their four sides they had human hands.
And the four had their faces and their
wings thus: 9 their wings touched one another; each of them moved straight ahead,
without turning as they moved. 10 As for the
appearance of their faces: the four had the
face of a human being, the face of a lion on
the right side, the face of an ox on the left
side, and the face of an eagle; 11 such were
their faces. Their wings were spread out
above; each creature had two wings, each
of which touched the wing of another, while
two covered their bodies. 12 Each moved
straight ahead; wherever the spirit would
go, they went, without turning as they
went. 13 In the middle of[a] the living creatures
there was something that looked like burning coals of fire, like torches moving to and
fro among the living creatures; the fire was
bright, and lightning issued from the fire.
14 The living creatures darted to and fro, like
a flash of lightning.
15 As I looked at the living creatures, I
saw a wheel on the earth beside the living
creatures, one for each of the four of them.[b]
16 As for the appearance of the wheels and
their construction: their appearance was
like the gleaming of beryl; and the four had
the same form, their construction being
something like a wheel within a wheel.
17 When they moved, they moved in any of

[a] Gk OL: Heb *And the appearance of* [b] Heb *of their faces*

1.1 Ezek 3.15,23; Mt 3.16; Acts 7.56
1.2 2 Kings 24.12
1.4 Isa 21.1
1.5 Rev 4.6; Ezek 10.8,14
1.6 ver 10,23
1.7 Rev 1.15; 2.18
1.8 Ezek 10.8,21
1.10 Rev 4.7; Ezek 10.14
1.11 Ezek 10.16,19; Isa 6.2
1.13 Ps 104.4; Rev 4.5
1.14 Mt 24.27
1.15 ver 19-21
1.16 Ezek 10.9-11; Dan 10.6
1.17 ver 12

1.18 Ezek 10.12; Rev 4.6,8
1.19 Ezek 10.16,17,19
1.20 ver 12; Ezek 10.17
1.21 Ezek 10.17
1.22 Ezek 10.1
1.24 Ezek 10.5; 43.2; Rev 1.15; 19.6; 2 Kings 7.6
1.26 Ezek 10.1; Ex 24.10; Ezek 43.6,7; Rev 1.13
1.27 ver 4; Ezek 8.2
1.28 Rev 4.3; 10.1; Ezek 3.23; 8.4; Dan 8.17; Rev 1.17
2.1 Dan 10.11
2.2 Dan 8.18; Ezek 3.24
2.3 Jer 3.25; Ezek 20.18,30
2.4 Jer 5.3; Ezek 3.7
2.5 Ezek 3.11,26,27; 33.33
2.6 Jer 1.8,17; Isa 9.18; Mic 7.4; Ezek 3.9
2.7 Jer 1.7,17
2.8 Isa 50.5; Rev 10.9
2.9 Ezek 8.3; 3.1
3.1 Ezek 2.8,9
3.3 Rev 10.9,10; Jer 15.16; Ps 19.10, 119.103
3.6 Mt 11.21,23; Acts 13.46-48
3.7 Jn 15.20; Ezek 2.4
3.9 Isa 50.7; Mic 3.8; Ezek 2.6

the four directions without veering as they
moved. 18Their rims were tall and awesome,
for the rims of all four were full of eyes all
around. 19When the living creatures moved,
the wheels moved beside them; and when
the living creatures rose from the earth, the
wheels rose. 20Wherever the spirit would go,
they went, and the wheels rose along with
them; for the spirit of the living creatures
was in the wheels. 21When they moved, the
others moved; when they stopped, the others stopped; and when they rose from the
earth, the wheels rose along with them; for
the spirit of the living creatures was in the
wheels.

22 Over the heads of the living creatures
there was something like a dome, shining
like crystal,[c] spread out above their heads.
23Under the dome their wings were stretched
out straight, one toward another; and each
of the creatures had two wings covering its
body. 24When they moved, I heard the sound
of their wings like the sound of mighty
waters, like the thunder of the Almighty,[d]
a sound of tumult like the sound of an
army; when they stopped, they let down
their wings. 25And there came a voice from
above the dome over their heads; when
they stopped, they let down their wings.

26 And above the dome over their heads
there was something like a throne, in appearance like sapphire;[e] and seated above
the likeness of a throne was something that
seemed like a human form. 27Upward from
what appeared like the loins I saw something like gleaming amber, something that
looked like fire enclosed all around; and
downward from what looked like the loins
I saw something that looked like fire, and
there was a splendor all around. 28Like the
bow in a cloud on a rainy day, such was
the appearance of the splendor all around.
This was the appearance of the likeness of
the glory of the LORD.

When I saw it, I fell on my face, and I
heard the voice of someone speaking.

The Vision of the Scroll

2 He said to me: O mortal,[f] stand up on
your feet, and I will speak with you.
2And when he spoke to me, a spirit entered
into me and set me on my feet; and I heard
him speaking to me. 3He said to me, Mortal,
I am sending you to the people of Israel, to
a nation[g] of rebels who have rebelled against
me; they and their ancestors have transgressed against me to this very day. 4The
descendants are impudent and stubborn. I
am sending you to them, and you shall say
to them, "Thus says the Lord GOD." 5Whether
they hear or refuse to hear (for they are a
rebellious house), they shall know that there
has been a prophet among them. 6And you,
O mortal, do not be afraid of them, and do
not be afraid of their words, though briers
and thorns surround you and you live among
scorpions; do not be afraid of their words,
and do not be dismayed at their looks, for
they are a rebellious house. 7You shall speak
my words to them, whether they hear or
refuse to hear; for they are a rebellious
house.

8 But you, mortal, hear what I say to
you; do not be rebellious like that rebellious
house; open your mouth and eat what I
give you. 9I looked, and a hand was stretched
out to me, and a written scroll was in it.
10He spread it before me; it had writing on
the front and on the back, and written on
it were words of lamentation and mourning
and woe.

3 He said to me, O mortal, eat what is
offered to you; eat this scroll, and go,
speak to the house of Israel. 2So I opened
my mouth, and he gave me the scroll to eat.
3He said to me, Mortal, eat this scroll that
I give you and fill your stomach with it.
Then I ate it; and in my mouth it was as
sweet as honey.

4 He said to me: Mortal, go to the house
of Israel and speak my very words to them.
5For you are not sent to a people of obscure
speech and difficult language, but to the
house of Israel— 6not to many peoples of
obscure speech and difficult language, whose
words you cannot understand. Surely, if I
sent you to them, they would listen to you.
7But the house of Israel will not listen to
you, for they are not willing to listen to me;
because all the house of Israel have a hard
forehead and a stubborn heart. 8See, I have
made your face hard against their faces,
and your forehead hard against their foreheads. 9Like the hardest stone, harder than
flint, I have made your forehead; do not fear
them or be dismayed at their looks, for they
are a rebellious house. 10He said to me:
Mortal, all my words that I shall speak to
you receive in your heart and hear with

[c] Gk: Heb *like the awesome crystal* [d] Traditional rendering of Heb *Shaddai* [e] Or *lapis lazuli* [f] Or *son of man*; Heb *ben adam* (and so throughout the book when Ezekiel is addressed) [g] Syr: Heb *to nations*

1.22-25 The *dome* which separates earth from heaven in this vision recalls the dome images used in the description of the creation of the world (Gen 1.1-19). The voice of the LORD comes from *above the dome*, while he is only indirectly described as *something that seemed like a human form*, which again recalls the imagery of Gen 1.26, where humans are created in God's image. *The glory of the LORD* was the radiant cloud in which God's presence became visible to humans, as at the giving of the law through Moses (Ex 16.10) and in the sacred tent or tabernacle (Ex 40.34; Num 20.6) and later in the temple (1 Kings 8.9-13; Ps 24.7-10).

2.1-3.27 The LORD's Commissioning of Ezekiel.

2.1-9 The specifics of the prophet's commissioning for his role begin with repeated reminders of his human, mortal nature. He is commissioned to speak for God to the *rebellious* people of Israel. The course of history which God has fixed as a result of the disobedience of the people is contained in, and symbolized by, the *written scroll*, with its message of *mourning and woe*.

3.1-11 For the prophet to *eat* this scroll is to symbolize his complete absorption of and involvement in God's message. Fully warned of the people's lack of understanding and hostility, he is to tell them what *the LORD says*, and yet must be ready to accept that they will *refuse to hear*.

3.12-15 The prophet is being transported to where the exiles are living (at *Tel-abib*, which means "mound formed by the flood," near Nippur, about 10 miles south of Babylon). On his journey he is accompanied by the presence of God: *the glory of the* LORD, and the sounds of angel wings and of chariot wheels.
3.16-27 The prophet's personal involvement in conveying the message to *the house of Israel* includes his exoneration when his hearers do not heed the message, as well as his personal responsibility if he fails to warn them. The temporary binding and silencing of the prophet dramatize this involvement, but show that many in Israel will refuse to hear the word from God through the prophet.
4.1-6.14 Ezekiel's Symbolic Actions Depict God's Judgment.
4.1-3 The prophet's drawing portrays the siege of Jerusalem that historically was soon to take place (586). Lying on his left side for *390 days* symbolizes the 390 years of *punishment* for Israel, which had begun with the fall of Samaria to the Assyrians in 722.
4.4-15 The briefer *forty days* on the right side represent the years of punishment for *Judah*. The supply of food and water during the siege will be meagre: twenty shekels of food would equal about eight ounces; a *hin* is equivalent to about half a quart. The use of *human dung* as fuel to bake the *barley-cake* would make the food ritually impure, and so Ezekiel refuses the suggestion.

your ears; 11then go to the exiles, to your people, and speak to them. Say to them, "Thus says the Lord GOD"; whether they hear or refuse to hear.

Ezekiel at the River Chebar

12 Then the spirit lifted me up, and as the glory of the LORD rose[h] from its place, I heard behind me the sound of loud rumbling; 13it was the sound of the wings of the living creatures brushing against one another, and the sound of the wheels beside them, that sounded like a loud rumbling. 14The spirit lifted me up and bore me away; I went in bitterness in the heat of my spirit, the hand of the LORD being strong upon me. 15I came to the exiles at Tel-abib, who lived by the river Chebar.[i] And I sat there among them, stunned, for seven days.

16 At the end of seven days, the word of the LORD came to me: 17Mortal, I have made you a sentinel for the house of Israel; whenever you hear a word from my mouth, you shall give them warning from me. 18If I say to the wicked, "You shall surely die," and you give them no warning, or speak to warn the wicked from their wicked way, in order to save their life, those wicked persons shall die for their iniquity; but their blood I will require at your hand. 19But if you warn the wicked, and they do not turn from their wickedness, or from their wicked way, they shall die for their iniquity; but you will have saved your life. 20Again, if the righteous turn from their righteousness and commit iniquity, and I lay a stumbling block before them, they shall die; because you have not warned them, they shall die for their sin, and their righteous deeds that they have done shall not be remembered; but their blood I will require at your hand. 21If, however, you warn the righteous not to sin, and they do not sin, they shall surely live, because they took warning; and you will have saved your life.

Ezekiel Isolated and Silenced

22 Then the hand of the LORD was upon me there; and he said to me, Rise up, go out into the valley, and there I will speak with you. 23So I rose up and went out into the valley; and the glory of the LORD stood there, like the glory that I had seen by the river Chebar; and I fell on my face. 24The spirit entered into me, and set me on my feet; and he spoke with me and said to me: Go, shut yourself inside your house. 25As for you, mortal, cords shall be placed on you, and you shall be bound with them, so that you cannot go out among the people; 26and I will make your tongue cling to the roof of your mouth, so that you shall be speechless and unable to reprove them; for they are a rebellious house. 27But when I speak with you, I will open your mouth, and you shall say to them, "Thus says the Lord GOD"; let those who will hear, hear; and let those who refuse to hear, refuse; for they are a rebellious house.

The Siege of Jerusalem Portrayed

4 And you, O mortal, take a brick and set it before you. On it portray a city, Jerusalem; 2and put siegeworks against it, and build a siege wall against it, and cast up a ramp against it; set camps also against it, and plant battering rams against it all around. 3Then take an iron plate and place it as an iron wall between you and the city; set your face toward it, and let it be in a state of siege, and press the siege against it. This is a sign for the house of Israel.

4 Then lie on your left side, and place the punishment of the house of Israel upon it; you shall bear their punishment for the number of the days that you lie there. 5For I assign to you a number of days, three hundred ninety days, equal to the number of the years of their punishment; and so you shall bear the punishment of the house of Israel. 6When you have completed these, you shall lie down a second time, but on your right side, and bear the punishment of the house of Judah; forty days I assign you, one day for each year. 7You shall set your face toward the siege of Jerusalem, and with your arm bared you shall prophesy against it. 8See, I am putting cords on you so that you cannot turn from one side to the other until you have completed the days of your siege.

9 And you, take wheat and barley, beans and lentils, millet and spelt; put them into one vessel, and make bread for yourself. During the number of days that you lie on your side, three hundred ninety days, you shall eat it. 10The food that you eat shall be

[h] Cn: Heb *and blessed be the glory of the* LORD [i] Two Mss Syr: Heb *Chebar, and to where they lived.* Another reading is *Chebar, and I sat where they sat*

3.11 Ezek 2.5,7
3.12 Ezek 8.3; Acts 8.39; 2.2
3.14 Jer 6.11; Ezek 1.3; 8.1
3.15 Ezek 1.1; Job 2.13
3.17 Ezek 33.7-9; Isa 52.8; 56.10; Jer 6.17
3.18 Gen 2.17; Ezek 33.6; Jn 8.21,24
3.19 Ezek 33.3,9; Acts 18.6; 20.26
3.20 Ezek 18.24; 33.12,13; Jer 6.21
3.21 Acts 20.31; ver 19
3.22 ver 14; Ezek 8.4; Acts 9.6
3.23 Ezek 1.28; 1.1
3.24 Ezek 2.2
3.25 Ezek 4.8
3.26 Ezek 24.27; Lk 1.20,22; Ezek 2.5-7
3.27 Ezek 24.27; 33.22; ver 11,9,26
4.1 Isa 20.2; Ezek 5.1
4.2 Ezek 21.22
4.3 Ezek 5.2; 12.6,11; 24.24,27
4.4 Lev 10.17; Num 18.1
4.5 Num 14.34
4.7 ver 3; Ezek 21.1
4.8 Ezek 3.25

twenty shekels a day by weight; at fixed times you shall eat it. [11]And you shall drink water by measure, one-sixth of a hin; at fixed times you shall drink. [12]You shall eat it as a barley-cake, baking it in their sight on human dung. [13]The LORD said, "Thus shall the people of Israel eat their bread, unclean, among the nations to which I will drive them." [14]Then I said, "Ah Lord GOD! I have never defiled myself; from my youth up until now I have never eaten what died of itself or was torn by animals, nor has carrion flesh come into my mouth." [15]Then he said to me, "See, I will let you have cow's dung instead of human dung, on which you may prepare your bread."

16 Then he said to me, Mortal, I am going to break the staff of bread in Jerusalem; they shall eat bread by weight and with fearfulness; and they shall drink water by measure and in dismay. [17]Lacking bread and water, they will look at one another in dismay, and waste away under their punishment.

A Sword against Jerusalem

5 And you, O mortal, take a sharp sword; use it as a barber's razor and run it over your head and your beard; then take balances for weighing, and divide the hair. [2]One third of the hair you shall burn in the fire inside the city, when the days of the siege are completed; one third you shall take and strike with the sword all around the city;[j] and one third you shall scatter to the wind, and I will unsheathe the sword after them. [3]Then you shall take from these a small number, and bind them in the skirts of your robe. [4]From these, again, you shall take some, throw them into the fire and burn them up; from there a fire will come out against all the house of Israel.

5 Thus says the Lord GOD: This is Jerusalem; I have set her in the center of the nations, with countries all around her. [6]But she has rebelled against my ordinances and my statutes, becoming more wicked than the nations and the countries all around her, rejecting my ordinances and not following my statutes. [7]Therefore thus says the Lord GOD: Because you are more turbulent than the nations that are all around you, and have not followed my statutes or kept my ordinances, but have acted according to the ordinances of the nations that are all around you; [8]therefore thus says the Lord GOD: I, I myself, am coming against you; I will execute judgments among you in the sight of the nations. [9]And because of all your abominations, I will do to you what I have never yet done, and the like of which I will never do again. [10]Surely, parents shall eat their children in your midst, and children shall eat their parents; I will execute judgments on you, and any of you who survive I will scatter to every wind. [11]Therefore, as I live, says the Lord GOD, surely, because you have defiled my sanctuary with all your detestable things and with all your abominations—therefore I will cut you down;[k] my eye will not spare, and I will have no pity. [12]One third of you shall die of pestilence or be consumed by famine among you; one third shall fall by the sword around you; and one third I will scatter to every wind and will unsheathe the sword after them.

13 My anger shall spend itself, and I will vent my fury on them and satisfy myself; and they shall know that I, the LORD, have spoken in my jealousy, when I spend my fury on them. [14]Moreover I will make you a desolation and an object of mocking among the nations around you, in the sight of all that pass by. [15]You shall be[l] a mockery and a taunt, a warning and a horror, to the nations around you, when I execute judgments on you in anger and fury, and with furious punishments—I, the LORD, have spoken— [16]when I loose against you[m] my deadly arrows of famine, arrows for destruction, which I will let loose to destroy you, and when I bring more and more famine upon you, and break your staff of bread. [17]I will send famine and wild animals against you, and they will rob you of your children; pestilence and bloodshed shall pass through you; and I will bring the sword upon you. I, the LORD, have spoken.

Judgment on Idolatrous Israel

6 The word of the LORD came to me: [2]O mortal, set your face toward the mountains of Israel, and prophesy against them, [3]and say, You mountains of Israel, hear the word of the Lord GOD! Thus says the Lord GOD to the mountains and the hills, to the ravines and the valleys: I, I myself will bring a sword upon you, and I will destroy your high places. [4]Your altars shall

[j] Heb *it* [k] Another reading is *I will withdraw* [l] Gk Syr Vg Tg: Heb *It shall be* [m] Heb *them*

4.12 Isa 36.12 **4.13** Hos 9.3 **4.14** Ezek 9.8; Acts 10.14; Ex 22.31; Lev 17.15; Deut 14.3; Isa 65.4 **4.16** Lev 26.26; Isa 3.1; Ezek 5.16; 14.13; ver 10,11; Ezek 12.19 **4.17** Lev 26.39; Ezek 24.13 **5.1** Lev 21.5; Isa 7.20; Ezek 44.20 **5.2** ver 12; Ezek 4.2-8; Lev 26.33 **5.3** Jer 39.10 **5.4** Jer 41.1,2; 44.14 **5.5** Ezek 4.1; Lam 1.1 **5.6** Ezek 16.47,48,51; Jer 11.10; Zech 7.11 **5.7** 2 Chr 33.9; Ezek 16.47 **5.8** Ezek 15.7 **5.9** Dan 9.12; Mt 24.21 **5.10** Lev 26.29; Ezek 12.14; Zech 2.6 **5.11** 2 Chr 36.14; Ezek 7.4,9; 8.18 **5.12** Jer 43.10,11; Ezek 12.14 **5.13** Lam 4.11; Ezek 21.17; 36.6 **5.14** Lev 26.31,32; Neh 2.17 **5.15** Deut 28.37; 1 Kings 9.7; Jer 24.9; Ezek 25.17 **5.16** Deut 32.23,24; Ezek 4.16 **5.17** Ezek 14.21; 28.23 **6.3** Ezek 36.4,6 **6.4** Lev 26.30

4.16-17 *The staff of bread* that is to be broken probably refers to the practice of baking bread with a hole in the center, which was then placed high up on a pole as a reserve, out of reach of mice or other varmints. So severe is the effect of the siege that every resource must be used to survive. **5.1-17** The instructions to the prophet to shave his head and beard are symbols of divine judgment. Male hair and beard were supposed to remain uncut, according to the law of Moses (Lev 19.27), and cutting was expressly forbidden as a sign of mourning among God's people (Deut 14.1-2), but especially for priests (Lev 21.5). To cut a beard was to put the victim to shame (2 Sam 10.4-5). Yet the LORD's detailed instructions to Ezekiel are to cut his hair and beard as a sign of impending judgment by God. The shame from this loss of hair will fall, not on the prophet, but on Jerusalem. The gross misuse of the sanctuary of God there will result in its people practising cannibalism (5.9), and being subject to *pestilence*, death in battle, and dispersion *to every wind* (5.12). As a result of these disasters, Israel will be a *mockery to the nations* (5.15). **6.1-14** By the prophet's facing in the direction of *the mountains of Israel*, his pronouncements assure that judgment will fall on the people for their worship of *idols*, and for their having erected altars and *high places* in honor of the other gods. The warnings of death by *pestilence, sword and famine* are repeated. The entire land of Israel will be *desolate* from *the wilderness* (probably the Negeb in the south) to *Riblah*, a city on the Orontes River north of Damascus in Syria.

7.1-12.28 Oracles of Judgment on Israel and Jerusalem.
7.1-27 In each of these oracles is stressed the imminence of the destruction that is to fall because of the *abominations* that have been committed by God's people. Their wealth and the commerce that created it are finished (7.10-13). There is no point in trying to fight off the disaster, since everyone will be powerless when confronted by God's judgment (7.14-19). Jerusalem's *beautiful ornament*, the temple, will be destroyed, as well as the order and structure of society in Judah (7.20-27).

become desolate, and your incense stands
shall be broken; and I will throw down your
slain in front of your idols. 5I will lay the
corpses of the people of Israel in front of
their idols; and I will scatter your bones
around your altars. 6Wherever you live,
your towns shall be waste and your high
places ruined, so that your altars will be
waste and ruined,[n] your idols broken and
destroyed, your incense stands cut down,
and your works wiped out. 7The slain shall
fall in your midst; then you shall know that
I am the LORD.
8 But I will spare some. Some of you
shall escape the sword among the nations
and be scattered through the countries.
9Those of you who escape shall remember
me among the nations where they are carried
captive, how I was crushed by their wanton
heart that turned away from me, and their
wanton eyes that turned after their idols.
Then they will be loathsome in their own
sight for the evils that they have committed,
for all their abominations. 10And they shall
know that I am the LORD; I did not threaten
in vain to bring this disaster upon them.
11 Thus says the Lord GOD: Clap your
hands and stamp your foot, and say, Alas
for all the vile abominations of the house of
Israel! For they shall fall by the sword, by
famine, and by pestilence. 12Those far off
shall die of pestilence; those nearby shall fall
by the sword; and any who are left and are
spared shall die of famine. Thus I will spend
my fury upon them. 13And you shall know
that I am the LORD, when their slain lie
among their idols around their altars, on
every high hill, on all the mountain tops,
under every green tree, and under every
leafy oak, wherever they offered pleasing
odor to all their idols. 14I will stretch out my
hand against them, and make the land
desolate and waste, throughout all their
settlements, from the wilderness to Riblah.[o]
Then they shall know that I am the LORD.

Impending Disaster

7 The word of the LORD came to me:
2You, O mortal, thus says the Lord
GOD to the land of Israel:
An end! The end has come
upon the four corners of the land.
3 Now the end is upon you,
I will let loose my anger upon you;
I will judge you according to your ways,
I will punish you for all your
abominations.
4 My eye will not spare you, I will have
no pity.
I will punish you for your ways,
while your abominations are among
you.
Then you shall know that I am the LORD.
5 Thus says the Lord GOD:
Disaster after disaster! See, it comes.
6 An end has come, the end has come.
It has awakened against you; see, it
comes!
7 Your doom[p] has come to you,
O inhabitant of the land.
The time has come, the day is near—
of tumult, not of reveling on the
mountains.
8 Soon now I will pour out my wrath
upon you;
I will spend my anger against you.
I will judge you according to your ways,
and punish you for all your
abominations.
9 My eye will not spare; I will have no
pity.
I will punish you according to your
ways,
while your abominations are among
you.
Then you shall know that it is I the LORD
who strike.
10 See, the day! See, it comes!
Your doom[p] has gone out.
The rod has blossomed, pride has
budded.
11 Violence has grown into a rod of
wickedness.
None of them shall remain,
not their abundance, not their
wealth;
no pre-eminence among them.[p]
12 The time has come, the day draws near;
let not the buyer rejoice, nor the
seller mourn,
for wrath is upon all their multitude.
13For the sellers shall not return to what
has been sold as long as they remain alive.
For the vision concerns all their multitude;
it shall not be revoked. Because of their
iniquity, they cannot maintain their lives.[p]
14 They have blown the horn and made
everything ready;
but no one goes to battle,
for my wrath is upon all their
multitude.

[n] Syr Vg Tg: Heb *and be made guilty* [o] Another reading is *Diblah* [p] Meaning of Heb uncertain

6.6 Lev 26.31; Zech 13.2
6.7 Ezek 11.10,12
6.8 Jer 44.28; Ezek 5.2,12; 12.16; 14.22
6.9 Jer 51.50; Ps 78.40; Isa 7.13; Ezek 43.24; 20.7,24; 20.43
6.11 Ezek 21.14; 25.6; 5.12; 7.15
6.12 Dan 9.7; Ezek 5.13
6.13 ver 7; Jer 2.20; Hos 4.13; Isa 57.5
6.14 Isa 5.25; Ezek 14.13; Num 33.46
7.2 Am 8.2; Ezek 11.13; Rev 7.1; 20.8
7.4 Ezek 5.11; 8.18; 11.21; 6.7
7.5 2 Kings 21.12,13
7.7 ver 12; Isa 22.5
7.8 Ezek 20.8,21; 6.12; ver 3
7.11 Jer 6.7; 16.5,6; Ezek 24.16,22

[15] The sword is outside, pestilence and
famine are inside;
those in the field die by the sword;
those in the city—famine and
pestilence devour them.
[16] If any survivors escape,
they shall be found on the mountains
like doves of the valleys,
all of them moaning over their iniquity.
[17] All hands shall grow feeble,
all knees turn to water.
[18] They shall put on sackcloth,
horror shall cover them.
Shame shall be on all faces,
baldness on all their heads.
[19] They shall fling their silver into the streets,
their gold shall be treated as unclean.
Their silver and gold cannot save them on
the day of the wrath of the LORD. They shall
not satisfy their hunger or fill their stomachs with it. For it was the stumbling block
of their iniquity. [20]From their[q] beautiful
ornament, in which they took pride, they
made their abominable images, their detestable things; therefore I will make of it an
unclean thing to them.
[21] I will hand it over to strangers as booty,
to the wicked of the earth as plunder;
they shall profane it.
[22] I will avert my face from them,
so that they may profane my
treasured[r] place;
the violent shall enter it,
they shall profane it.
[23] Make a chain![s]
For the land is full of bloody crimes;
the city is full of violence.
[24] I will bring the worst of the nations
to take possession of their houses.
I will put an end to the arrogance of the
strong,
and their holy places shall be
profaned.
[25] When anguish comes, they will seek
peace,
but there shall be none.
[26] Disaster comes upon disaster,
rumor follows rumor;
they shall keep seeking a vision from the
prophet;
instruction shall perish from the
priest,
and counsel from the elders.
[27] The king shall mourn,
the prince shall be wrapped in
despair,
and the hands of the people of the
land shall tremble.
According to their way I will deal with
them;
according to their own judgments I
will judge them.
And they shall know that I am the LORD.

Abominations in the Temple

8 In the sixth year, in the sixth month,
on the fifth day of the month, as I sat
in my house, with the elders of Judah sitting
before me, the hand of the Lord GOD fell
upon me there. [2]I looked, and there was a
figure that looked like a human being;[t]
below what appeared to be its loins it was
fire, and above the loins it was like the
appearance of brightness, like gleaming
amber. [3]It stretched out the form of a hand,
and took me by a lock of my head; and the
spirit lifted me up between earth and heaven,
and brought me in visions of God to Jerusalem, to the entrance of the gateway of the
inner court that faces north, to the seat of
the image of jealousy, which provokes to
jealousy. [4]And the glory of the God of Israel
was there, like the vision that I had seen in
the valley.
5 Then God[u] said to me, "O mortal, lift
up your eyes now in the direction of the
north." So I lifted up my eyes toward the
north, and there, north of the altar gate, in
the entrance, was this image of jealousy.
[6]He said to me, "Mortal, do you see what
they are doing, the great abominations that
the house of Israel are committing here, to
drive me far from my sanctuary? Yet you
will see still greater abominations."
7 And he brought me to the entrance of
the court; I looked, and there was a hole in
the wall. [8]Then he said to me, "Mortal, dig
through the wall"; and when I dug through
the wall, there was an entrance. [9]He said
to me, "Go in, and see the vile abominations
that they are committing here." [10]So I went
in and looked; there, portrayed on the wall
all around, were all kinds of creeping things,
and loathsome animals, and all the idols of
the house of Israel. [11]Before them stood
seventy of the elders of the house of Israel,
with Jaazaniah son of Shaphan standing
among them. Each had his censer in his
hand, and the fragrant cloud of incense was
ascending. [12]Then he said to me, "Mortal,
have you seen what the elders of the house

7.15 Deut 32.25; Ezek 5.12 **7.16** Ezek 6.8; 14.22; Isa 38.14; 59.11 **7.17** Isa 13.7; Ezek 21.7; Heb 12.12 **7.18** Isa 15.2,3; Am 8.10; Ezek 27.31 **7.19** Isa 30.22; Prov 11.4; Zeph 1.18; Ezek 13.5; 14.3,4 **7.20** Jer 7.30 **7.21** Ps 74.2-8 **7.22** Ezek 39.23,24 **7.23** 2 Kings 21.16; Ezek 9.9; 8.17 **7.24** Ezek 21.31; 33.28; 24.21 **7.25** Ezek 13.10,16 **7.26** Deut 32.23; Jer 4.20; Ezek 21.7; Ps 74.9; Ezek 20.1,3 **7.27** Ps 35.26; Ezek 26.16; ver 3,4,8; Ezek 18.20 **8.1** Ezek 14.1; 20.1; 33.31; 1.3; 3.22 **8.2** Ezek 1.4,27 **8.3** Dan 5.5; Ezek 3.12,14; 11.1; Jer 32.34; Ezek 5.11 **8.4** Ezek 1.28 **8.5** Zech 5.5; ver 3 **8.6** ver 9,17; Ezek 5.11; 7.22,24; ver 11,14,16 **8.10** Ex 20.4; Ezek 14.3 **8.11** Jer 19.1; Num 16.17,35; Ezek 16.18; 23.41

8.1-18 With details that recall Ezekiel's vision when commissioned as a prophet (Ezek 1), there is pictured a human-like figure accompanied by *the glory of God* who appears to Ezekiel, directing his attention toward *the north*, which in this context means Jerusalem, which lay beyond and to the east of the northern end of the Tigris-Euphrates Valley. The prophet is then transported by *the spirit* to the temple, where he hears of the *great abominations* practised there, and sees the images of idolatrous worship carried out by the *seventy elders* who are the leaders of Judah, the ceremonial *weeping* performed to honor *Tammuz* (a fertility god worshiped by many peoples over the centuries in Mesopotamia as a way of guaranteeing annual crops), and finally the sun-worship carried out by the people of Judah facing the sun *with their backs to the temple of the LORD*. God's wrath is seen to be fully justified.

[q] Syr Symmachus: Heb *its* [r] Or *secret* [s] Meaning of Heb uncertain [t] Gk: Heb *like fire* [u] Heb *he*

9.1-11 *The executioners of the city* are summoned to kill all who bear on their foreheads *the mark* of their having participated in the idolatries. These include both old and young, male and female. The slaughter of the guilty begins within the *courts* of the temple. The *glory of the God of Israel* has already gone up from *the cherub* (winged creatures comprised of features from several animals; they stood on top of the ark of the covenant; Ex 25-26). Although the people cry out that *the LORD has forsaken the land,* he is seen here as directly at work through *the man clothed in linen* who is carrying out the judgment of God on disobedient Israel.

10.1-22 Again recalling details of the prophet's initial vision (Ezek 1), the radiant cloud which is *the glory of the LORD* rises up out of the temple, accompanied and supported by the cherubim and the multiple-wheeled chariot, as a symbol of the departure of God's presence from the midst of his people.

of Israel are doing in the dark, each in his room of images? For they say, 'The LORD does not see us, the LORD has forsaken the land.' " [13]He said also to me, "You will see still greater abominations that they are committing."

14 Then he brought me to the entrance of the north gate of the house of the LORD; women were sitting there weeping for Tammuz. [15]Then he said to me, "Have you seen this, O mortal? You will see still greater abominations than these."

16 And he brought me into the inner court of the house of the LORD; there, at the entrance of the temple of the LORD, between the porch and the altar, were about twenty-five men, with their backs to the temple of the LORD, and their faces toward the east, prostrating themselves to the sun toward the east. [17]Then he said to me, "Have you seen this, O mortal? Is it not bad enough that the house of Judah commits the abominations done here? Must they fill the land with violence, and provoke my anger still further? See, they are putting the branch to their nose! [18]Therefore I will act in wrath; my eye will not spare, nor will I have pity; and though they cry in my hearing with a loud voice, I will not listen to them."

The Slaughter of the Idolaters

9 Then he cried in my hearing with a loud voice, saying, "Draw near, you executioners of the city, each with his destroying weapon in his hand." [2]And six men came from the direction of the upper gate, which faces north, each with his weapon for slaughter in his hand; among them was a man clothed in linen, with a writing case at his side. They went in and stood beside the bronze altar.

3 Now the glory of the God of Israel had gone up from the cherub on which it rested to the threshold of the house. The LORD called to the man clothed in linen, who had the writing case at his side; [4]and said to him, "Go through the city, through Jerusalem, and put a mark on the foreheads of those who sigh and groan over all the abominations that are committed in it." [5]To the others he said in my hearing, "Pass through the city after him, and kill; your eye shall not spare, and you shall show no pity. [6]Cut down old men, young men and young women, little children and women, but touch no one who has the mark. And begin at my sanctuary." So they began with the elders who were in front of the house. [7]Then he said to them, "Defile the house, and fill the courts with the slain. Go!" So they went out and killed in the city. [8]While they were killing, and I was left alone, I fell prostrate on my face and cried out, "Ah Lord GOD! will you destroy all who remain of Israel as you pour out your wrath upon Jerusalem?" [9]He said to me, "The guilt of the house of Israel and Judah is exceedingly great; the land is full of bloodshed and the city full of perversity; for they say, 'The LORD has forsaken the land, and the LORD does not see.' [10]As for me, my eye will not spare, nor will I have pity, but I will bring down their deeds upon their heads."

11 Then the man clothed in linen, with the writing case at his side, brought back word, saying, "I have done as you commanded me."

God's Glory Leaves Jerusalem

10 Then I looked, and above the dome that was over the heads of the cherubim there appeared above them something like a sapphire,[v] in form resembling a throne. [2]He said to the man clothed in linen, "Go within the wheelwork underneath the cherubim; fill your hands with burning coals from among the cherubim, and scatter them over the city." He went in as I looked on. [3]Now the cherubim were standing on the south side of the house when the man went in; and a cloud filled the inner court. [4]Then the glory of the LORD rose up from the cherub to the threshold of the house; the house was filled with the cloud, and the court was full of the brightness of the glory of the LORD. [5]The sound of the wings of the cherubim was heard as far as the outer court, like the voice of God Almighty[w] when he speaks.

6 When he commanded the man clothed in linen, "Take fire from within the wheelwork, from among the cherubim," he went in and stood beside a wheel. [7]And a cherub stretched out his hand from among the cherubim to the fire that was among the cherubim, took some of it and put it into the hands of the man clothed in linen, who took it and went out. [8]The cherubim appeared to have the form of a human hand under their wings.

[v] Or *lapis lazuli* [w] Traditional rendering of Heb *El Shaddai*

8.13 Ezek 9.3
8.14 Ezek 44.4; 46.9
8.16 Ezek 11.1; Jer 2.27; Deut 4.19; Job 31.26; Jer 44.17
8.17 Ezek 9.9; Mic 2.2; Jer 7.18,19; Ezek 16.26
8.18 Ezek 5.13; 7.4; 9.5,10; Isa 1.15; Jer 11.11; Mic 3.4; Zech 7.13
9.2 Ezek 10.2; Rev 15.6
9.3 Ezek 8.4; 10.4,18; 11.22,23
9.4 Ex 12.7; 1 Pet 4.17; Rev 7.3; 9.4; Ps 119.53, 136; Jer 13.17
9.5 Ezek 5.11; 7.4,9
9.6 2 Chr 36.17; Rev 9.4; Jer 25.29; Am 3.2; Ezek 8.11,12,16
9.7 2 Chr 36.17; Ezek 7.20-22; 6.4
9.8 1 Chr 21.16; Josh 7.6; Ezek 11.13
9.9 Ezek 7.23; 22.29; 8.12
9.10 Isa 65.6; Ezek 8.18; 7.4; 11.21
10.1 Ezek 1.22,26; Rev 4.2
10.2 Ezek 9.2,3; ver 13; Isa 6.6; Rev 8.5
10.3 Ezek 8.3,16
10.4 Ezek 1.28; 9.3; Ex 40.34,35; 1 Kings 8.10,11
10.5 Ezek 1.24
10.8 Ezek 1.8

9 I looked, and there were four wheels beside the cherubim, one beside each cherub; and the appearance of the wheels was like gleaming beryl. 10 And as for their appearance, the four looked alike, something like a wheel within a wheel. 11 When they moved, they moved in any of the four directions without veering as they moved; but in whatever direction the front wheel faced, the others followed without veering as they moved. 12 Their entire body, their rims, their spokes, their wings, and the wheels—the wheels of the four of them—were full of eyes all around. 13 As for the wheels, they were called in my hearing "the wheelwork." 14 Each one had four faces: the first face was that of the cherub, the second face was that of a human being, the third that of a lion, and the fourth that of an eagle.

15 The cherubim rose up. These were the living creatures that I saw by the river Chebar. 16 When the cherubim moved, the wheels moved beside them; and when the cherubim lifted up their wings to rise up from the earth, the wheels at their side did not veer. 17 When they stopped, the others stopped, and when they rose up, the others rose up with them; for the spirit of the living creatures was in them.

18 Then the glory of the LORD went out from the threshold of the house and stopped above the cherubim. 19 The cherubim lifted up their wings and rose up from the earth in my sight as they went out with the wheels beside them. They stopped at the entrance of the east gate of the house of the LORD; and the glory of the God of Israel was above them.

20 These were the living creatures that I saw underneath the God of Israel by the river Chebar; and I knew that they were cherubim. 21 Each had four faces, each four wings, and underneath their wings something like human hands. 22 As for what their faces were like, they were the same faces whose appearance I had seen by the river Chebar. Each one moved straight ahead.

Judgment on Wicked Counselors

11 The spirit lifted me up and brought me to the east gate of the house of the LORD, which faces east. There, at the entrance of the gateway, were twenty-five men; among them I saw Jaazaniah son of Azzur, and Pelatiah son of Benaiah, officials of the people. 2 He said to me, "Mortal, these are the men who devise iniquity and who give wicked counsel in this city; 3 they say, 'The time is not near to build houses; this city is the pot, and we are the meat.' 4 Therefore prophesy against them; prophesy, O mortal."

5 Then the spirit of the LORD fell upon me, and he said to me, "Say, Thus says the LORD: This is what you think, O house of Israel; I know the things that come into your mind. 6 You have killed many in this city, and have filled its streets with the slain. 7 Therefore thus says the Lord GOD: The slain whom you have placed within it are the meat, and this city is the pot; but you shall be taken out of it. 8 You have feared the sword; and I will bring the sword upon you, says the Lord GOD. 9 I will take you out of it and give you over to the hands of foreigners, and execute judgments upon you. 10 You shall fall by the sword; I will judge you at the border of Israel. And you shall know that I am the LORD. 11 This city shall not be your pot, and you shall not be the meat inside it; I will judge you at the border of Israel. 12 Then you shall know that I am the LORD, whose statutes you have not followed, and whose ordinances you have not kept, but you have acted according to the ordinances of the nations that are around you."

13 Now, while I was prophesying, Pelatiah son of Benaiah died. Then I fell down on my face, cried with a loud voice, and said, "Ah Lord GOD! will you make a full end of the remnant of Israel?"

God Will Restore Israel

14 Then the word of the LORD came to me: 15 Mortal, your kinsfolk, your own kin, your fellow exiles,[x] the whole house of Israel, all of them, are those of whom the inhabitants of Jerusalem have said, "They have gone far from the LORD; to us this land is given for a possession." 16 Therefore say: Thus says the Lord GOD: Though I removed them far away among the nations, and though I scattered them among the countries, yet I have been a sanctuary to them for a little while[y] in the countries where they have gone. 17 Therefore say: Thus says the Lord GOD: I will gather you from the peoples, and assemble you out of the countries where you have been scattered, and I

[x] Gk Syr: Heb *people of your kindred* [y] Or *to some extent*

10.9 Ezek 1.15,16
10.11 Ezek 1.17; ver 22
10.12 Rev 4.6,8; Ezek 1.18
10.14 Ezek 1.6,10; Rev 4.7
10.16 Ezek 1.19
10.17 Ezek 1.12,20,21
10.19 Ezek 11.1,22
10.20 ver 15; Ezek 1.22; 1.1
10.21 Ezek 1.6,8
10.22 Ezek 1.10,12
11.1 Ezek 3.12,14; 8.3; 10.19; 8.16
11.2 Isa 30.1; Mic 2.1
11.3 Ezek 12.22,27; 2 Pet 3.4; Jer 1.13; Ezek 24.3,6
11.4 Ezek 3.4,17
11.5 Ezek 2.2; 3.24; Jer 11.20; Ezek 38.10
11.6 Ezek 7.23; 22.3,4
11.7 Ezek 24.3,6,10,11; Mic 3.3; ver 9
11.9 Ps 106.41; Ezek 5.8
11.10 2 Kings 25.19-21; Jer 52.10; 2 Kings 14.25; Ezek 6.7
11.12 ver 10; Ezek 18.8,9; 8.10,14,16
11.13 ver 1; Ezek 9.8
11.15 Ezek 33.24
11.16 Isa 8.14
11.17 Jer 24.5; Ezek 28.25; 34.13

11.1-13 Chief responsibility for the gross condition of Jerusalem lies with its *officials.* They boast that their operation of the city has been so fine that there is no further need to *build houses,* and that they are the ones who control the city (*the pot*) and are hence its most desirable feature (*the meat*). Ezekiel transforms their metaphor to show that instead of building the city they have *killed* many of its inhabitants, so that God will now remove them from their leadership roles in *the pot* (11.7,11) because they have not followed God's *statutes and ordinances* for the life of God's people. On hearing this message of doom from the prophet, one of the leaders of the city, *Pelatiah,* falls dead, to which Ezekiel responds by asking God if he will now destroy completely *the remnant of Israel.* **11.14-21** An interlude (perhaps written after the destruction of Jerusalem had taken place in 586) contains the promise of the restoration of Israel. Those who occupy this land during the dispersion of God's people *among the nations* are to be told that God will one day bring them back and give them *the land of Israel,* from which they will then *remove* the idolatrous features. There God will renew the people in *heart* (will and purpose) and *spirit* (power and commitment), which will result in their obedience to God's *statutes and ordinances* for them. But those who persist in idolatry will suffer punishment for their *deeds.*

11.22-25 The *radiant cloud* of *the glory of the* LORD arises from the temple and pauses briefly on the Mount of Olives *east of the city* as it returns to heaven. Ezekiel is taken back *into Chaldea* with these messages for the exiles there.
12.1-16 The instruction from the LORD to Ezekiel to take up his luggage and dig through the mud-brick wall of his house is to be a *sign* to the exiles that their situation is in accord with God's plan. *The prince* who is among the exiles is Zedekiah, the king of Judah who had tried to escape from Jerusalem during the Babylonian siege through a *breach* in the walls of the city (2 Kings 25.1-7), but was caught and taken captive to Babylon. The people of God have been scattered, but some (*a few*) will survive the *sword, famine, and pestilence* of the dispersion and will bear witness later to their experiences in fulfillment of God's judgment on his disobedient people.
12.17-28 A series of messages (*word of the* LORD) to the prophet is intended to inform those still in the land of Israel that terrifying experiences await them (*quaking, trembling*), and to instruct all God's people that his words are certain of fulfillment, which will not be *delayed any longer*.

will give you the land of Israel. 18 When they
come there, they will remove from it all its
detestable things and all its abominations.
19 I will give them one[z] heart, and put a new
spirit within them; I will remove the heart
of stone from their flesh and give them a
heart of flesh, 20 so that they may follow my
statutes and keep my ordinances and obey
them. Then they shall be my people, and I
will be their God. 21 But as for those whose
heart goes after their detestable things and
their abominations,[a] I will bring their deeds
upon their own heads, says the Lord GOD.
22 Then the cherubim lifted up their
wings, with the wheels beside them; and
the glory of the God of Israel was above
them. 23 And the glory of the LORD ascended
from the middle of the city, and stopped on
the mountain east of the city. 24 The spirit
lifted me up and brought me in a vision by
the spirit of God into Chaldea, to the exiles.
Then the vision that I had seen left me.
25 And I told the exiles all the things that the
LORD had shown me.

Judah's Captivity Portrayed

12 The word of the LORD came to me:
2 Mortal, you are living in the midst
of a rebellious house, who have eyes to see
but do not see, who have ears to hear but
do not hear; 3 for they are a rebellious house.
Therefore, mortal, prepare for yourself an
exile's baggage, and go into exile by day in
their sight; you shall go like an exile from
your place to another place in their sight.
Perhaps they will understand, though they
are a rebellious house. 4 You shall bring out
your baggage by day in their sight, as
baggage for exile; and you shall go out
yourself at evening in their sight, as those
do who go into exile. 5 Dig through the wall
in their sight, and carry the baggage through
it. 6 In their sight you shall lift the baggage
on your shoulder, and carry it out in the
dark; you shall cover your face, so that you
may not see the land; for I have made you
a sign for the house of Israel.
7 I did just as I was commanded. I brought
out my baggage by day, as baggage for
exile, and in the evening I dug through the
wall with my own hands; I brought it out
in the dark, carrying it on my shoulder in
their sight.
8 In the morning the word of the LORD
came to me: 9 Mortal, has not the house of
Israel, the rebellious house, said to you,
"What are you doing?" 10 Say to them, "Thus
says the Lord GOD: This oracle concerns the
prince in Jerusalem and all the house of
Israel in it." 11 Say, "I am a sign for you: as
I have done, so shall it be done to them;
they shall go into exile, into captivity."
12 And the prince who is among them shall
lift his baggage on his shoulder in the dark,
and shall go out; he[b] shall dig through the
wall and carry it through; he shall cover his
face, so that he may not see the land with
his eyes. 13 I will spread my net over him,
and he shall be caught in my snare; and I
will bring him to Babylon, the land of the
Chaldeans, yet he shall not see it; and he
shall die there. 14 I will scatter to every wind
all who are around him, his helpers and all
his troops; and I will unsheathe the sword
behind them. 15 And they shall know that I
am the LORD, when I disperse them among
the nations and scatter them through the
countries. 16 But I will let a few of them
escape from the sword, from famine and
pestilence, so that they may tell of all their
abominations among the nations where they
go; then they shall know that I am the
LORD.

Judgment Not Postponed

17 The word of the LORD came to me:
18 Mortal, eat your bread with quaking, and
drink your water with trembling and with
fearfulness; 19 and say to the people of the
land, Thus says the Lord GOD concerning
the inhabitants of Jerusalem in the land of
Israel: They shall eat their bread with fearfulness, and drink their water in dismay,
because their land shall be stripped of all it
contains, on account of the violence of all
those who live in it. 20 The inhabited cities
shall be laid waste, and the land shall become a desolation; and you shall know that
I am the LORD.
21 The word of the LORD came to me:
22 Mortal, what is this proverb of yours about
the land of Israel, which says, "The days are
prolonged, and every vision comes to nothing"? 23 Tell them therefore, "Thus says the
Lord GOD: I will put an end to this proverb,
and they shall use it no more as a proverb
in Israel." But say to them, The days are
near, and the fulfillment of every vision.

[z] Another reading is *a new* [a] Cn: Heb *And to the heart of their detestable things and their abominations their heart goes* [b] Gk Syr: Heb *they*

11.18 Ezek 37.23; 5.11
11.19 Jer 32.39; Ezek 36.26,27; 18.31; Zech 7.12; 2 Cor 3.3
11.20 Ps 105.45; Ezek 14.11
11.21 Ezek 9.10
11.22 Ezek 1.19; 10.19
11.23 Ezek 8.4; 9.3; Zech 14.4
12.2 Ezek 2.6-8; Jer 5.21; Mt 13.13,14
12.3 Jer 26.3; 36.3,7; 2 Tim 2.25
12.4 Jer 39.4; ver 12
12.6 ver 12,13; Isa 8.18; Ezek 4.3; 24.24
12.9 Ezek 2.5; 17.12; 24.19
12.10 Mal 1.1
12.11 ver 6; 2 Kings 25.4-7
12.12 Jer 39.4
12.13 Isa 24.17,18; Hos 7.12; Jer 52.11; Ezek 17.16
12.14 2 Kings 25.4,5; Ezek 5.2,12
12.15 Ezek 6.7,14
12.16 Ezek 6.8-10; 14.22; Jer 22.8,9
12.19 Ezek 4.16; 23.33; Zech 7.14
12.20 Ezek 5.14; 36.3
12.22 Ezek 16.44; 11.3; ver 27; Am 6.3; 2 Pet 3.4
12.23 Joel 2.1; Zeph 1.14

[24]For there shall no longer be any false vision or flattering divination within the house of Israel. [25]But I the LORD will speak the word that I speak, and it will be fulfilled. It will no longer be delayed; but in your days, O rebellious house, I will speak the word and fulfill it, says the Lord GOD.

26 The word of the LORD came to me: [27]Mortal, the house of Israel is saying, "The vision that he sees is for many years ahead; he prophesies for distant times." [28]Therefore say to them, Thus says the Lord GOD: None of my words will be delayed any longer, but the word that I speak will be fulfilled, says the Lord GOD.

False Prophets Condemned

13 The word of the LORD came to me: [2]Mortal, prophesy against the prophets of Israel who are prophesying; say to those who prophesy out of their own imagination: "Hear the word of the LORD!" [3]Thus says the Lord GOD, Alas for the senseless prophets who follow their own spirit, and have seen nothing! [4]Your prophets have been like jackals among ruins, O Israel. [5]You have not gone up into the breaches, or repaired a wall for the house of Israel, so that it might stand in battle on the day of the LORD. [6]They have envisioned falsehood and lying divination; they say, "Says the LORD," when the LORD has not sent them, and yet they wait for the fulfillment of their word! [7]Have you not seen a false vision or uttered a lying divination, when you have said, "Says the LORD," even though I did not speak?

8 Therefore thus says the Lord GOD: Because you have uttered falsehood and envisioned lies, I am against you, says the Lord GOD. [9]My hand will be against the prophets who see false visions and utter lying divinations; they shall not be in the council of my people, nor be enrolled in the register of the house of Israel, nor shall they enter the land of Israel; and you shall know that I am the Lord GOD. [10]Because, in truth, because they have misled my people, saying, "Peace," when there is no peace; and because, when the people build a wall, these prophets[c] smear whitewash on it. [11]Say to those who smear whitewash on it that it shall fall. There will be a deluge of rain,[d] great hailstones will fall, and a stormy wind will break out. [12]When the wall falls, will it not be said to you, "Where is the whitewash you smeared on it?" [13]Therefore thus says the Lord GOD: In my wrath I will make a stormy wind break out, and in my anger there shall be a deluge of rain, and hailstones in wrath to destroy it. [14]I will break down the wall that you have smeared with whitewash, and bring it to the ground, so that its foundation will be laid bare; when it falls, you shall perish within it; and you shall know that I am the LORD. [15]Thus I will spend my wrath upon the wall, and upon those who have smeared it with whitewash; and I will say to you, The wall is no more, nor those who smeared it— [16]the prophets of Israel who prophesied concerning Jerusalem and saw visions of peace for it, when there was no peace, says the Lord GOD.

17 As for you, mortal, set your face against the daughters of your people, who prophesy out of their own imagination; prophesy against them [18]and say, Thus says the Lord GOD: Woe to the women who sew bands on all wrists, and make veils for the heads of persons of every height, in the hunt for human lives! Will you hunt down lives among my people, and maintain your own lives? [19]You have profaned me among my people for handfuls of barley and for pieces of bread, putting to death persons who should not die and keeping alive persons who should not live, by your lies to my people, who listen to lies.

20 Therefore thus says the Lord GOD: I am against your bands with which you hunt lives;[e] I will tear them from your arms, and let the lives go free, the lives that you hunt down like birds. [21]I will tear off your veils, and save my people from your hands; they shall no longer be prey in your hands; and you shall know that I am the LORD. [22]Because you have disheartened the righteous falsely, although I have not disheartened them, and you have encouraged the wicked not to turn from their wicked way and save their lives; [23]therefore you shall no longer see false visions or practice divination; I will save my people from your hand. Then you will know that I am the LORD.

God's Judgments Justified

14 Certain elders of Israel came to me and sat down before me. [2]And the word of the LORD came to me: [3]Mortal, these men have taken their idols into their hearts,

[c] Heb *they* [d] Heb *rain and you* [e] Gk Syr: Heb *lives for birds*

12.24 Ezek 13.23; Zech 13.2-4
12.25 ver 28; Isa 55.11; Dan 9.12; Hab 1.5; ver 2
12.27 ver 22; Dan 10.14; 2 Pet 3.4
12.28 ver 25; Mt 24.48-50
13.2 Jer 37.19; ver 17; Jer 14.14; 23.16,26; Am 7.16
13.3 Lam 2.14; Jer 23.28-32
13.5 Ps 106.23,30; Ezek 22.30; Isa 58.12; Ezek 7.19
13.6 ver 22; Ezek 22.28; Jer 28.15
13.9 Ezra 2.59,62; Neh 7.5; Ps 69.28; Ezek 11.10,12
13.10 Jer 50.6; 8.11; ver 16; Ezek 22.28
13.11 Ezek 38.22
13.14 Mic 1.6; ver 9; Ezek 14.8
13.16 Ezek 6.14; Isa 57.21
13.17 Ezek 20.46; 21.2; ver 2
13.18 Ezek 22.25; 2 Pet 2.14
13.19 Ezek 20.39; Prov 28.21; Mic 3.5; Jer 23.14,17
13.22 Am 5.12; Jer 23.14; Ezek 33.14-16
13.23 ver 6; Ezek 12.24; Mic 3.6; ver 9; Ezek 14.8
14.1 Ezek 8.1; 20.1; 33.31
14.3 Ezek 20.16; 7.19; Jer 11.11; Ezek 20.3,31

13.1-14.11 Ezekiel and the False Prophets.
13.1-16 Ezekiel is called to expose and denounce the false prophets who have uttered predictions *out of their own imaginations*, but have done nothing concrete to safeguard Israel, such as repair *breaches* in the city walls. The LORD has not spoken through them, and so there is no basis for their prophecies. They will be excluded from the register of the house of Israel. Their tactics are compared with those of a builder who, having constructed a flimsy masonry wall, tries to make it look solid by smearing it with *whitewash*. The Hebrew term for this white plaster also means "nonsense." The waters of God's *wrath* will wash off the deceptive cover of these false prophets and expose the falsity of their claim for the *peace* of Jerusalem.
13.17-23 A special denunciation is uttered against women who, in exchange for food (*barley, bread*), prepare magical objects (*bands, veils*) which their buyers use to bring good or harm on others. Both the dependence on such magical devices and those who use them are condemned, but God promises that they will be ineffective on his own *people*.
14.1-11 Israelite and non-Israelite dwellers in their land (*aliens*) who try to consult the LORD through a prophet will receive no answer except God's denunciation of their idolatry and a warning that they will be *cut off* from among God's people. Prophets who misunderstand God's message and are hence *deceived* will be destroyed, and those who inquire of them will also be *punished*.

14.12-20.44 Lessons to be Learned from Israel's Past.
14.12-23 Even if such great figures of Israel's history as *Noah, Daniel* and *Job* were to be present among his people in later generations, God would deliver only these worthies and not the others from *famine, wild animals, pestilence, and sword* (military attack). Although the books that bear their names come from a much later time (see introductions to Daniel and Job), these two figures were legendary men of wisdom and piety in the wider Middle East, as is shown by Ezek 28.3 and the introductory story in Job 1.1-5. Disaster is about to fall on Jerusalem, but *some survivors...will be brought out* who will bear testimony to the severity of God's punishment of his people when they are disobedient.
15.1-8 *The vine* appears in other biblical texts as a symbol for God's people (Hos 10; Isa 5; Ps 80.8-18). Here the vine is seen to be useless as material for the construction of objects or even as fuel, and hence serves as a fitting image for useless *Jerusalem*, whose people are bound for destruction.

and placed their iniquity as a stumbling
block before them; shall I let myself be
consulted by them? [4]Therefore speak to them,
and say to them, Thus says the Lord GOD:
Any of those of the house of Israel who take
their idols into their hearts and place their
iniquity as a stumbling block before them,
and yet come to the prophet—I the LORD
will answer those who come with the
multitude of their idols, [5]in order that I may
take hold of the hearts of the house of
Israel, all of whom are estranged from me
through their idols.
6 Therefore say to the house of Israel,
Thus says the Lord GOD: Repent and turn
away from your idols; and turn away your
faces from all your abominations. [7]For any
of those of the house of Israel, or of the
aliens who reside in Israel, who separate
themselves from me, taking their idols into
their hearts and placing their iniquity as a
stumbling block before them, and yet come
to a prophet to inquire of me by him, I the
LORD will answer them myself. [8]I will set my
face against them; I will make them a sign
and a byword and cut them off from the
midst of my people; and you shall know
that I am the LORD.
9 If a prophet is deceived and speaks a
word, I, the LORD, have deceived that prophet,
and I will stretch out my hand against him,
and will destroy him from the midst of my
people Israel. [10]And they shall bear their
punishment—the punishment of the inquirer
and the punishment of the prophet shall be
the same— [11]so that the house of Israel
may no longer go astray from me, nor defile
themselves any more with all their transgressions. Then they shall be my people,
and I will be their God, says the Lord GOD.
12 The word of the LORD came to me:
[13]Mortal, when a land sins against me by
acting faithlessly, and I stretch out my hand
against it, and break its staff of bread and
send famine upon it, and cut off from it
human beings and animals, [14]even if Noah,
Daniel,[f] and Job, these three, were in it, they
would save only their own lives by their
righteousness, says the Lord GOD. [15]If I send
wild animals through the land to ravage it,
so that it is made desolate, and no one may
pass through because of the animals; [16]even
if these three men were in it, as I live, says
the Lord GOD, they would save neither sons
nor daughters; they alone would be saved,
but the land would be desolate. [17]Or if I
bring a sword upon that land and say, 'Let
a sword pass through the land,' and I cut
off human beings and animals from it;
[18]though these three men were in it, as I
live, says the Lord GOD, they would save
neither sons nor daughters, but they alone
would be saved. [19]Or if I send a pestilence
into that land, and pour out my wrath
upon it with blood, to cut off humans and
animals from it; [20]even if Noah, Daniel,[f] and
Job were in it, as I live, says the Lord GOD,
they would save neither son nor daughter;
they would save only their own lives by
their righteousness.
21 For thus says the Lord GOD: How
much more when I send upon Jerusalem
my four deadly acts of judgment, sword,
famine, wild animals, and pestilence, to cut
off humans and animals from it! [22]Yet,
survivors shall be left in it, sons and daughters who will be brought out; they will
come out to you. When you see their ways
and their deeds, you will be consoled for the
evil that I have brought upon Jerusalem, for
all that I have brought upon it. [23]They shall
console you, when you see their ways and
their deeds; and you shall know that it was
not without cause that I did all that I have
done in it, says the Lord GOD.

The Useless Vine

15 The word of the LORD came to me:
2 O mortal, how does the wood
of the vine surpass all other
wood—
the vine branch that is among the
trees of the forest?
3 Is wood taken from it to make
anything?
Does one take a peg from it on which
to hang any object?
4 It is put in the fire for fuel;
when the fire has consumed both
ends of it
and the middle of it is charred,
is it useful for anything?
5 When it was whole it was used for
nothing;
how much less—when the fire has
consumed it,
and it is charred—
can it ever be used for anything!
6 Therefore thus says the Lord GOD: Like
the wood of the vine among the trees of the
forest, which I have given to the fire for

[f] Or, as otherwise read, *Danel*

14.5 Isa 1.4; Jer 2.11; Zech 11.8
14.6 Isa 2.20; 30.22; Ezek 18.30; 8.6
14.7 Ex 12.48; 20.10; ver 4
14.8 Jer 44.11; Ezek 15.7; Isa 65.15; Ezek 5.15; 6.7
14.9 1 Kings 22.23; Job 12.16; Jer 4.10; 2 Thess 2.11; Jer 14.15
14.11 Ezek 44.10,15; 11.20; 37.27
14.13 Ezek 15.8; 6.14; 5.16; ver 17,19,21
14.14 Jer 15.1; Gen 6.8; Dan 1.6; Job 1.1,5; ver 16,18,20
14.15 Ezek 5.17
14.17 Ezek 5.12; 21.3,4; 25.13; Zeph 1.3
14.19 ver 21; Ezek 38.22; 7.8
14.21 Ezek 5.17; Jer 15.2,3; Rev 6.8
14.22 Ezek 12.16; 7.16; 20.43; 16.54
14.23 Jer 22.8,9
15.2 Isa 5.1-7; Jer 2.21; Hos 10.1
15.4 ver 6; Ezek 19.14; Jn 15.6
15.6 ver 2; Ezek 17.3-10

fuel, so I will give up the inhabitants of Jerusalem. [7]I will set my face against them; although they escape from the fire, the fire shall still consume them; and you shall know that I am the LORD, when I set my face against them. [8]And I will make the land desolate, because they have acted faithlessly, says the Lord GOD.

God's Faithless Bride

16 The word of the LORD came to me: [2]Mortal, make known to Jerusalem her abominations, [3]and say, Thus says the Lord GOD to Jerusalem: Your origin and your birth were in the land of the Canaanites; your father was an Amorite, and your mother a Hittite. [4]As for your birth, on the day you were born your navel cord was not cut, nor were you washed with water to cleanse you, nor rubbed with salt, nor wrapped in cloths. [5]No eye pitied you, to do any of these things for you out of compassion for you; but you were thrown out in the open field, for you were abhorred on the day you were born.

6 I passed by you, and saw you flailing about in your blood. As you lay in your blood, I said to you, "Live! [7]and grow up[g] like a plant of the field." You grew up and became tall and arrived at full womanhood;[h] your breasts were formed, and your hair had grown; yet you were naked and bare.

8 I passed by you again and looked on you; you were at the age for love. I spread the edge of my cloak over you, and covered your nakedness: I pledged myself to you and entered into a covenant with you, says the Lord GOD, and you became mine. [9]Then I bathed you with water and washed off the blood from you, and anointed you with oil. [10]I clothed you with embroidered cloth and with sandals of fine leather; I bound you in fine linen and covered you with rich fabric.[i] [11]I adorned you with ornaments: I put bracelets on your arms, a chain on your neck, [12]a ring on your nose, earrings in your ears, and a beautiful crown upon your head. [13]You were adorned with gold and silver, while your clothing was of fine linen, rich fabric,[i] and embroidered cloth. You had choice flour and honey and oil for food. You grew exceedingly beautiful, fit to be a queen. [14]Your fame spread among the nations on account of your beauty, for it was perfect because of my splendor that I had bestowed on you, says the Lord GOD.

15 But you trusted in your beauty, and played the whore because of your fame, and lavished your whorings on any passer-by.[j] [16]You took some of your garments, and made for yourself colorful shrines, and on them played the whore; nothing like this has ever been or ever shall be.[i] [17]You also took your beautiful jewels of my gold and my silver that I had given you, and made for yourself male images, and with them played the whore; [18]and you took your embroidered garments to cover them, and set my oil and my incense before them. [19]Also my bread that I gave you—I fed you with choice flour and oil and honey—you set it before them as a pleasing odor; and so it was, says the Lord GOD. [20]You took your sons and your daughters, whom you had borne to me, and these you sacrificed to them to be devoured. As if your whorings were not enough! [21]You slaughtered my children and delivered them up as an offering to them. [22]And in all your abominations and your whorings you did not remember the days of your youth, when you were naked and bare, flailing about in your blood.

23 After all your wickedness (woe, woe to you! says the Lord GOD), [24]you built yourself a platform and made yourself a lofty place in every square; [25]at the head of every street you built your lofty place and prostituted your beauty, offering yourself to every passer-by, and multiplying your whoring. [26]You played the whore with the Egyptians, your lustful neighbors, multiplying your whoring, to provoke me to anger. [27]Therefore I stretched out my hand against you, reduced your rations, and gave you up to the will of your enemies, the daughters of the Philistines, who were ashamed of your lewd behavior. [28]You played the whore with the Assyrians, because you were insatiable; you played the whore with them, and still you were not satisfied. [29]You multiplied your whoring with Chaldea, the land of merchants; and even with this you were not satisfied.

30 How sick is your heart, says the Lord GOD, that you did all these things, the deeds of a brazen whore; [31]building your platform at the head of every street, and making your lofty place in every square! Yet you were not like a whore, because you scorned

16.1-58 Israel as God's Unfaithful Wife. The marital image for the relationship of God to his people occurs in other prophetic traditions (Hosea 1-9; Jer 2.23-25). It was natural to transfer this symbol from the worship of the fertility god, Baal, and his consort, Anath. An elaborate allegory begins by picturing the mixed ethnic origins of Israel with an *Amorite father* (a loose term for the Semitic tribes that lived in the region before the emergence of Israel; Gen 15.16) and *a Hittite mother* (a term used for non-Semitic peoples living in this area; Gen 23.1-16), and the resultant birth of the nation in *the land of Canaan*, which was the dominant tribe in the land where Israel finally settled. Abandoned and in desperate condition (enslaved in *Egypt*), Israel was rescued by God, and then flourished in the land under the judges and the royal line of David. But she made herself available to other gods, erecting high places and altars (*lofty places*) everywhere in honor of *Egyptian, Assyrian and Chaldean* divinities, instead of remaining faithful to her *husband*, the LORD. Now all her *lovers* – the nations whose deities she worshiped – will become her oppressors and destroyers, stripping her *naked and bare*. These traditions of idolatry and disobedience have been passed through successive generations, from *mother* to *daughter. The daughters* are *Samaria* (the northern tribes of Israel) and *Sodom* (Gen 18-19; a people to the south, perhaps Edom). Israel has gone beyond her sisters by acting *more abominably* than they.

15.7 Lev 17.10; Ezek 14.8; Isa 24.18; Ezek 6.7; 7.4; 14.8
15.8 Ezek 14.13
16.2 Ezek 20.4; 22.2; 8.9-17
16.3 Ezek 21.30; ver 45
16.4 Hos 2.3
16.5 Deut 32.10
16.6 ver 22; Ex 19.4
16.7 Ex 1.7; ver 22
16.8 Ruth 3.9; Gen 22.16-18; Ex 24.7,8; 19.5; Jer 2.2
16.11 Ezek 23.40; Gen 24.22,47; Prov 1.9
16.13 Deut 32.13,14; 1 Sam 10.1
16.15 Isa 57.8; Jer 2.20; Ezek 23.3,8,11,12
16.16 ver 10; Ezek 6.3,6; Hos 2.8
16.17 Ezek 7.20
16.20 2 Kings 16.3; Isa 57.5
16.21 2 Kings 17.17; Jer 19.5
16.22 Hos 11.1; ver 4-6
16.24 Isa 57.5,7; Jer 2.20; 3.2
16.25 Prov 9.14; ver 15
16.26 Ezek 8.17; 20.7,8; 23.19-21
16.27 Ezek 14.13; 20.33,34; 2 Chr 28.18,19
16.28 2 Kings 16.7,10; 2 Chr 28.23
16.29 Ezek 23.14-17

[g] Gk Syr: Heb *Live! I made you a myriad* [h] Cn: Heb *ornament of ornaments* [i] Meaning of Heb uncertain [j] Heb adds *let it be his*

16.53-58 Possibly a later addition, the promise of restoration of Israel is initially said to be aimed at drawing the attention of the nations to her lewd behavior. But the theme then shifts to the hope of renewing *the everlasting covenant* with the LORD, which will come about through his granting Israel forgiveness for all that the people have done.

payment. 32 Adulterous wife, who receives
strangers instead of her husband! 33 Gifts are
given to all whores; but you gave your gifts
to all your lovers, bribing them to come to
you from all around for your whorings. 34 So
you were different from other women in
your whorings: no one solicited you to play
the whore; and you gave payment, while
no payment was given to you; you were
different.

35 Therefore, O whore, hear the word of
the LORD: 36 Thus says the Lord GOD, Because
your lust was poured out and your nakedness uncovered in your whoring with your
lovers, and because of all your abominable
idols, and because of the blood of your
children that you gave to them, 37 therefore,
I will gather all your lovers, with whom
you took pleasure, all those you loved and
all those you hated; I will gather them
against you from all around, and will uncover your nakedness to them, so that they
may see all your nakedness. 38 I will judge
you as women who commit adultery and
shed blood are judged, and bring blood
upon you in wrath and jealousy. 39 I will
deliver you into their hands, and they shall
throw down your platform and break down
your lofty places; they shall strip you of
your clothes and take your beautiful objects
and leave you naked and bare. 40 They shall
bring up a mob against you, and they shall
stone you and cut you to pieces with their
swords. 41 They shall burn your houses and
execute judgments on you in the sight of
many women; I will stop you from playing
the whore, and you shall also make no
more payments. 42 So I will satisfy my fury
on you, and my jealousy shall turn away
from you; I will be calm, and will be angry
no longer. 43 Because you have not remembered the days of your youth, but have
enraged me with all these things; therefore,
I have returned your deeds upon your head,
says the Lord GOD.

Have you not committed lewdness beyond all your abominations? 44 See, everyone who uses proverbs will use this proverb
about you, "Like mother, like daughter."
45 You are the daughter of your mother,
who loathed her husband and her children;
and you are the sister of your sisters, who
loathed their husbands and their children.
Your mother was a Hittite and your father
an Amorite. 46 Your elder sister is Samaria,
who lived with her daughters to the north
of you; and your younger sister, who lived
to the south of you, is Sodom with her
daughters. 47 You not only followed their
ways, and acted according to their abominations; within a very little time you were
more corrupt than they in all your ways.
48 As I live, says the Lord GOD, your sister
Sodom and her daughters have not done as
you and your daughters have done. 49 This
was the guilt of your sister Sodom: she and
her daughters had pride, excess of food, and
prosperous ease, but did not aid the poor
and needy. 50 They were haughty, and did
abominable things before me; therefore I
removed them when I saw it. 51 Samaria has
not committed half your sins; you have
committed more abominations than they,
and have made your sisters appear righteous by all the abominations that you have
committed. 52 Bear your disgrace, you also,
for you have brought about for your sisters
a more favorable judgment; because of your
sins in which you acted more abominably
than they, they are more in the right than
you. So be ashamed, you also, and bear
your disgrace, for you have made your
sisters appear righteous.

53 I will restore their fortunes, the fortunes of Sodom and her daughters and the
fortunes of Samaria and her daughters, and
I will restore your own fortunes along with
theirs, 54 in order that you may bear your
disgrace and be ashamed of all that you
have done, becoming a consolation to them.
55 As for your sisters, Sodom and her daughters shall return to their former state, Samaria
and her daughters shall return to their
former state, and you and your daughters
shall return to your former state. 56 Was not
your sister Sodom a byword in your mouth
in the day of your pride, 57 before your
wickedness was uncovered? Now you are a
mockery to the daughters of Aram[k] and all
her neighbors, and to the daughters of the
Philistines, those all around who despise
you. 58 You must bear the penalty of your
lewdness and your abominations, says the
LORD.

An Everlasting Covenant

59 Yes, thus says the Lord GOD: I will
deal with you as you have done, you who
have despised the oath, breaking the covenant; 60 yet I will remember my covenant
with you in the days of your youth, and I

[k] Another reading is *Edom*

16.33 Isa 30.6; Hos 8.9,10
16.36 ver 15; Ezek 23.10,18,29; Jer 19.5
16.37 Jer 13.22,26; Hos 2.10; Nah 3.5; Isa 47.3
16.38 Lev 20.10; Ezek 23.45; Jer 18.21
16.39 Ezek 21.31; ver 24,31; Ezek 23.26
16.40 Ezek 23.46,47; Jn 8.5,7
16.41 Deut 13.16; 2 Kings 25.9; Jer 52.13; Ezek 23.10,27,48
16.43 Ps 78.42; ver 22; Ezek 6.9; 11.21; 22.31
16.44 Ezek 12.22,23
16.46 Gen 13.11-13; Isa 1.10
16.47 2 Kings 21.9; Ezek 5.6,7
16.48 Mt 10.15; 11.24
16.49 Isa 3.9; Gen 13.10; Lk 12.16-20; Ezek 18.7,12,16
16.50 Ezek 7.10
16.51 Ezek 5.6; Jer 3.11; Mt 12.41,42
16.53 ver 60,61; Isa 19.24,25
16.54 Ezek 14.22,23
16.57 2 Kings 16.5; 2 Chr 28.18; Ezek 5.14
16.58 Ezek 23.49
16.59 Ezek 17.13; Deut 29.12
16.60 Jer 2.2; Hos 2.15; Jer 32.40; Ezek 37.26

will establish with you an everlasting covenant. [61]Then you will remember your ways,
and be ashamed when I[l] take your sisters,
both your elder and your younger, and give
them to you as daughters, but not on account of my[m] covenant with you. [62]I will
establish my covenant with you, and you
shall know that I am the LORD, [63]in order
that you may remember and be confounded,
and never open your mouth again because
of your shame, when I forgive you all that
you have done, says the Lord GOD.

The Two Eagles and the Vine

17 The word of the LORD came to me:
[2]O mortal, propound a riddle, and
speak an allegory to the house of Israel.
[3]Say: Thus says the Lord GOD:

A great eagle, with great wings and
long pinions,
rich in plumage of many colors,
came to the Lebanon.
He took the top of the cedar,
4 broke off its topmost shoot;
He carried it to a land of trade,
set it in a city of merchants.
5 Then he took a seed from the land,
placed it in fertile soil;
A plant[n] by abundant waters,
he set it like a willow twig.
6 It sprouted and became a vine
spreading out, but low;
Its branches turned toward him,
its roots remained where it stood.
So it became a vine;
it brought forth branches,
put forth foliage.

7 There was another great eagle,
with great wings and much plumage.
And see! This vine stretched out
its roots toward him;
It shot out its branches toward him,
so that he might water it.
From the bed where it was planted
8 it was transplanted
to good soil by abundant waters,
so that it might produce branches
and bear fruit
and become a noble vine.

[9]Say: Thus says the Lord GOD:
Will it prosper?
Will he not pull up its roots,
cause its fruit to rot[n] and wither,
its fresh sprouting leaves to fade?
No strong arm or mighty army will be
needed
to pull it from its roots.
10 When it is transplanted, will it thrive?
When the east wind strikes it,
will it not utterly wither,
wither on the bed where it grew?

11 Then the word of the LORD came to
me: [12]Say now to the rebellious house: Do
you not know what these things mean? Tell
them: The king of Babylon came to Jerusalem, took its king and its officials, and
brought them back with him to Babylon.
[13]He took one of the royal offspring and
made a covenant with him, putting him
under oath (he had taken away the chief
men of the land), [14]so that the kingdom
might be humble and not lift itself up, and
that by keeping his covenant it might stand.
[15]But he rebelled against him by sending
ambassadors to Egypt, in order that they
might give him horses and a large army.
Will he succeed? Can one escape who does
such things? Can he break the covenant
and yet escape? [16]As I live, says the Lord
GOD, surely in the place where the king
resides who made him king, whose oath he
despised, and whose covenant with him he
broke—in Babylon he shall die. [17]Pharaoh
with his mighty army and great company
will not help him in war, when ramps are
cast up and siege walls built to cut off many
lives. [18]Because he despised the oath and
broke the covenant, because he gave his
hand and yet did all these things, he shall
not escape. [19]Therefore thus says the Lord
GOD: As I live, I will surely return upon his
head my oath that he despised, and my
covenant that he broke. [20]I will spread my
net over him, and he shall be caught in my
snare; I will bring him to Babylon and enter
into judgment with him there for the treason he has committed against me. [21]All the
pick[o] of his troops shall fall by the sword,
and the survivors shall be scattered to every
wind; and you shall know that I, the LORD,
have spoken.

Israel Exalted at Last

22 Thus says the Lord GOD:
I myself will take a sprig
from the lofty top of a cedar;
I will set it out.
I will break off a tender one
from the topmost of its young twigs;

[l] Syr: Heb *you* [m] Heb lacks *my* [n] Meaning of Heb uncertain [o] Another reading is *fugitives*

17.1-21 This allegory of the eagle and the vine draws on Israel's recent past for its lesson concerning the nation's future. The first *great eagle* is the Babylonian empire, which carried Israel off to live in its lands *by abundant waters*, where the exiles did well. The second *eagle* represents the attempt of King Zedekiah of Judah to find safety for his people through an alliance with Egypt – a scheme which Jeremiah also describes as misguided (Jer 37). Babylon has already reduced Judah and Jerusalem to a vassal state by *taking away the chief men of the land*, including the king, who was exiled because of the *treason* he committed by trying to avoid God's judgment: the exile.

17.22-24 It is God's action which will relocate Israel and make the nation fruitful, so that all the other nations of the world (*trees of the field*) will recognize the LORD as the prime instrument of purpose and power in human history.

16.61 Ezek 20.43; Isa 54.1; 60.4; Jer 31.31
16.62 Ezek 20.37; Hos 2.19,20; Ezek 20.43,44
16.63 ver 61; Rom 3.19
17.2 Ezek 20.49; 24.3
17.3 Jer 22.23
17.5 Deut 8.7-9; Isa 44.4
17.7 ver 15
17.10 ver 15; Ezek 19.14; Hos 13.15
17.12 Ezek 2.5; 12.9; ver 3; 2 Kings 24.11-16
17.13 2 Kings 24.15-17; 2 Chr 36.13
17.14 ver 6; Ezek 29.14
17.15 2 Kings 24.20; 2 Chr 36.13
17.16 ver 13,18,19; Jer 52.11; Ezek 12.13
17.17 Jer 37.7; Ezek 29.6,7; 4.2
17.18 Lam 5.6
17.20 Ezek 12.13; 32.3; 20.36
17.21 2 Kings 25.5,11; Ezek 12.14; 6.7,10
17.22 Isa 11.1; Jer 23.5; Zech 3.8; Ezek 36.36; 20.40

18.1-32 Contrary to the traditional notion that God brings judgment on successive generations for the misdeeds of their ancestors, Ezekiel insists that individuals are responsible for their own actions, whether they disobey the laws of God or repent and turn to the way of obedience. What constitutes righteous living is summarized in Ezek 18.5-9, where there is an epitome of the law of Moses. God cannot be called *unfair*, since he holds each person accountable for his or her own actions. Hence, the prophet calls all people to repent and gain *a new heart and a new spirit*, which embody the purpose and power to obey the LORD.

I myself will plant it
on a high and lofty mountain.
23 On the mountain height of Israel
I will plant it,
in order that it may produce boughs
and bear fruit,
and become a noble cedar.
Under it every kind of bird will live;
in the shade of its branches will nest
winged creatures of every kind.
24 All the trees of the field shall know
that I am the LORD.
I bring low the high tree,
I make high the low tree;
I dry up the green tree
and make the dry tree flourish.
I the LORD have spoken;
I will accomplish it.

Individual Retribution

18 The word of the LORD came to me:
2What do you mean by repeating
this proverb concerning the land of Israel,
"The parents have eaten sour grapes, and
the children's teeth are set on edge"? 3As I
live, says the Lord GOD, this proverb shall no
more be used by you in Israel. 4Know that
all lives are mine; the life of the parent as
well as the life of the child is mine: it is only
the person who sins that shall die.
5 If a man is righteous and does what is
lawful and right— 6if he does not eat upon
the mountains or lift up his eyes to the idols
of the house of Israel, does not defile his
neighbor's wife or approach a woman during her menstrual period, 7does not oppress
anyone, but restores to the debtor his pledge,
commits no robbery, gives his bread to the
hungry and covers the naked with a garment, 8does not take advance or accrued
interest, withholds his hand from iniquity,
executes true justice between contending
parties, 9follows my statutes, and is careful
to observe my ordinances, acting faithfully—
such a one is righteous; he shall surely live,
says the Lord GOD.
10 If he has a son who is violent, a
shedder of blood, 11who does any of these
things (though his father[p] does none of
them), who eats upon the mountains, defiles his neighbor's wife, 12oppresses the poor
and needy, commits robbery, does not restore the pledge, lifts up his eyes to the idols,
commits abomination, 13takes advance or
accrued interest; shall he then live? He shall
not. He has done all these abominable things;
he shall surely die; his blood shall be upon
himself.
14 But if this man has a son who sees
all the sins that his father has done, considers, and does not do likewise, 15who does
not eat upon the mountains or lift up his
eyes to the idols of the house of Israel, does
not defile his neighbor's wife, 16does not
wrong anyone, exacts no pledge, commits
no robbery, but gives his bread to the hungry
and covers the naked with a garment, 17with-
holds his hand from iniquity,[q] takes no
advance or accrued interest, observes my
ordinances, and follows my statutes; he shall
not die for his father's iniquity; he shall
surely live. 18As for his father, because he
practiced extortion, robbed his brother, and
did what is not good among his people, he
dies for his iniquity.
19 Yet you say, "Why should not the
son suffer for the iniquity of the father?"
When the son has done what is lawful and
right, and has been careful to observe all
my statutes, he shall surely live. 20The person
who sins shall die. A child shall not suffer
for the iniquity of a parent, nor a parent
suffer for the iniquity of a child; the righteousness of the righteous shall be his own,
and the wickedness of the wicked shall be
his own.
21 But if the wicked turn away from all
their sins that they have committed and
keep all my statutes and do what is lawful
and right, they shall surely live; they shall
not die. 22None of the transgressions that
they have committed shall be remembered
against them; for the righteousness that
they have done they shall live. 23Have I any
pleasure in the death of the wicked, says the
Lord GOD, and not rather that they should
turn from their ways and live? 24But when
the righteous turn away from their righteousness and commit iniquity and do the
same abominable things that the wicked do,
shall they live? None of the righteous deeds
that they have done shall be remembered;
for the treachery of which they are guilty
and the sin they have committed, they shall
die.
25 Yet you say, "The way of the Lord is
unfair." Hear now, O house of Israel: Is my
way unfair? Is it not your ways that are
unfair? 26When the righteous turn away
from their righteousness and commit iniquity, they shall die for it; for the iniquity

[p] Heb *he* [q] Gk: Heb *the poor*

17.23 Isa 2.2,3; Ezek 20.40; Hos 14.5-7; Mt 13.31,32
17.24 Ps 96.12; Ezek 21.26; 19.12; 22.14; 24.14
18.2 Jer 31.29; Lam 5.7
18.4 Isa 42.5; ver 20; Rom 6.23
18.6 Ezek 22.9; ver 12,15; Lev 18.19; 20.18; Ezek 22.10
18.7 Ex 22.21; Lev 19.15; Deut 24.12,13; Lev 19.13
18.8 Ex 22.25; Lev 25.36,37; Deut 23.19; 1.16; Zech 8.16
18.9 Ezek 20.11; Am 5.4
18.10 Ex 21.12; Num 35.31
18.12 Am 4.1; Isa 59.6,7; Ezek 8.6,17
18.13 ver 8,17; Ezek 33.4,5
18.14 Prov 23.24
18.16 Ps 41.1
18.19 Ex 20.5; Deut 5.9; 2 Kings 23.26
18.20 Deut 24.16; Isa 3.10,11; Rom 2.9
18.21 Ezek 33.12,19; Ezek 3.21
18.22 Ezek 33.16; Mic 7.19; Ps 18.20-24
18.23 Ezek 33.11; 1 Tim 2.4; 2 Pet 3.9
18.24 Ezek 3.20; 33.12,13,18; 2 Pet 2.20
18.25 ver 29; Ezek 33.17,20; Zeph 3.5

that they have committed they shall die.
[27]Again, when the wicked turn away from
the wickedness they have committed and
do what is lawful and right, they shall save
their life. [28]Because they considered and
turned away from all the transgressions
that they had committed, they shall surely
live; they shall not die. [29]Yet the house of
Israel says, "The way of the Lord is unfair."
O house of Israel, are my ways unfair? Is
it not your ways that are unfair?

30 Therefore I will judge you, O house of
Israel, all of you according to your ways,
says the Lord GOD. Repent and turn from all
your transgressions; otherwise iniquity will
be your ruin.[r] [31]Cast away from you all the
transgressions that you have committed
against me, and get yourselves a new heart
and a new spirit! Why will you die, O house
of Israel? [32]For I have no pleasure in the
death of anyone, says the Lord GOD. Turn,
then, and live.

Israel Degraded

19 As for you, raise up a lamentation
for the princes of Israel, [2]and say:

What a lioness was your mother
among lions!
She lay down among young lions,
rearing her cubs.
3 She raised up one of her cubs;
he became a young lion,
and he learned to catch prey;
he devoured humans.
4 The nations sounded an alarm against
him;
he was caught in their pit;
and they brought him with hooks
to the land of Egypt.
5 When she saw that she was thwarted,
that her hope was lost,
she took another of her cubs
and made him a young lion.
6 He prowled among the lions;
he became a young lion,
and he learned to catch prey;
he devoured people.
7 And he ravaged their strongholds,[s]
and laid waste their towns;
the land was appalled, and all in it,
at the sound of his roaring.
8 The nations set upon him
from the provinces all around;
they spread their net over him;
he was caught in their pit.
9 With hooks they put him in a cage,
and brought him to the king of
Babylon;
they brought him into custody,
so that his voice should be heard no
more
on the mountains of Israel.
10 Your mother was like a vine in a
vineyard[t]
transplanted by the water,
fruitful and full of branches
from abundant water.
11 Its strongest stem became
a ruler's scepter;[u]
it towered aloft
among the thick boughs;
it stood out in its height
with its mass of branches.
12 But it was plucked up in fury,
cast down to the ground;
the east wind dried it up;
its fruit was stripped off,
its strong stem was withered;
the fire consumed it.
13 Now it is transplanted into the
wilderness,
into a dry and thirsty land.
14 And fire has gone out from its stem,
has consumed its branches and fruit,
so that there remains in it no strong
stem,
no scepter for ruling.

This is a lamentation, and it is used as
a lamentation.

Israel's Continuing Rebellion

20 In the seventh year, in the fifth
month, on the tenth day of the
month, certain elders of Israel came to
consult the LORD, and sat down before me.
[2]And the word of the LORD came to me:
[3]Mortal, speak to the elders of Israel, and
say to them: Thus says the Lord GOD: Why
are you coming? To consult me? As I live,
says the Lord GOD, I will not be consulted
by you. [4]Will you judge them, mortal, will
you judge them? Then let them know the
abominations of their ancestors, [5]and say to
them: Thus says the Lord GOD: On the day
when I chose Israel, I swore to the offspring
of the house of Jacob—making myself known
to them in the land of Egypt—I swore to

[r] Or *so that they shall not be a stumbling block of iniquity to you* [s] Heb *his widows* [t] Cn: Heb *in your blood* [u] Heb *Its strongest stems became rulers' scepters*

18.30 Ezek 7.3; 33.20; Mt 3.2; Rev 2.5
18.31 Isa 1.16,17; 55.7; Ezek 11.19; 36.26
18.32 Ezek 33.11; 2 Pet 3.9
19.1 Ezek 26.17; 27.2
19.2 Nah 2.11,12; Isa 5.29; Zech 11.3
19.3 2 Kings 23.31,32; ver 6
19.4 2 Kings 23.33; 2 Chr 36.4
19.5 2 Kings 23.34
19.6 2 Kings 24.9; ver 3
19.7 Ezek 12.19; 30.12
19.8 2 Kings 24.2; ver 4
19.9 2 Chr 36.6; Jer 22.18; Ezek 6.2
19.10 Ps 80.8-11
19.11 Ezek 31.3; Dan 4.11
19.12 Jer 31.28; Ezek 28.17; 17.10; Hos 13.15
19.13 Hos 2.3
19.14 Ezek 15.4; Lam 4.20
20.1 Ezek 8.1,11,12; 9.6
20.4 Ezek 16.2; 22.2
20.5 Ex 6.7; Deut 7.6; Ex 6.2,3; 20.2

19.1-9 *The princes of Israel* and their disobedience are described here allegorically. One *young lion* was taken to Egypt (that is, Jehoahaz; 2 Kings 23.31-35) and the other young lion was taken to *the king of Babylon* (Jehoiachin; 2 Kings 24.8-12).
19.10-14 The images change to depict the uprooting of Judah, *the vine,* and its transplanting (to Babylon). *Its strongest stem* was Jehoiachin, who in this oracle was expected to suffer a fate similar to that of his father, Jehoiakim (2 Kings 23.36-24.7), but who historically was treated throughout the remainder of his life as a royal guest in Babylon, according to 2 Kings 25.27-30.
20.1-32 *The elders of Israel* came to inquire of the LORD through Ezekiel *in the seventh year* following the exile: 591. These leaders of the community in exile are told that consultation with the LORD is impossible. Instead, they receive a recital of God's acts in behalf of his people and of their perennial disobedience, beginning with their time of slavery in Egypt and continuing during their flight from Egypt, the giving of the law, and their journeys through the wilderness. Not only had they rejected the law, but they went so far as to pervert it by performing as religious acts the very things it prohibited: child sacrifice and offering sacrifices to local gods on high places.

them, saying, I am the LORD your God. 6On that day I swore to them that I would bring them out of the land of Egypt into a land that I had searched out for them, a land flowing with milk and honey, the most glorious of all lands. 7And I said to them, Cast away the detestable things your eyes feast on, every one of you, and do not defile yourselves with the idols of Egypt; I am the LORD your God. 8But they rebelled against me and would not listen to me; not one of them cast away the detestable things their eyes feasted on, nor did they forsake the idols of Egypt.

Then I thought I would pour out my wrath upon them and spend my anger against them in the midst of the land of Egypt. 9But I acted for the sake of my name, that it should not be profaned in the sight of the nations among whom they lived, in whose sight I made myself known to them in bringing them out of the land of Egypt. 10So I led them out of the land of Egypt and brought them into the wilderness. 11I gave them my statutes and showed them my ordinances, by whose observance everyone shall live. 12Moreover I gave them my sabbaths, as a sign between me and them, so that they might know that I the LORD sanctify them. 13But the house of Israel rebelled against me in the wilderness; they did not observe my statutes but rejected my ordinances, by whose observance everyone shall live; and my sabbaths they greatly profaned.

Then I thought I would pour out my wrath upon them in the wilderness, to make an end of them. 14But I acted for the sake of my name, so that it should not be profaned in the sight of the nations, in whose sight I had brought them out. 15Moreover I swore to them in the wilderness that I would not bring them into the land that I had given them, a land flowing with milk and honey, the most glorious of all lands, 16because they rejected my ordinances and did not observe my statutes, and profaned my sabbaths; for their heart went after their idols. 17Nevertheless my eye spared them, and I did not destroy them or make an end of them in the wilderness.

18 I said to their children in the wilderness, Do not follow the statutes of your parents, nor observe their ordinances, nor defile yourselves with their idols. 19I the LORD am your God; follow my statutes, and be careful to observe my ordinances, 20and hallow my sabbaths that they may be a sign between me and you, so that you may know that I the LORD am your God. 21But the children rebelled against me; they did not follow my statutes, and were not careful to observe my ordinances, by whose observance everyone shall live; they profaned my sabbaths.

Then I thought I would pour out my wrath upon them and spend my anger against them in the wilderness. 22But I withheld my hand, and acted for the sake of my name, so that it should not be profaned in the sight of the nations, in whose sight I had brought them out. 23Moreover I swore to them in the wilderness that I would scatter them among the nations and disperse them through the countries, 24because they had not executed my ordinances, but had rejected my statutes and profaned my sabbaths, and their eyes were set on their ancestors' idols. 25Moreover I gave them statutes that were not good and ordinances by which they could not live. 26I defiled them through their very gifts, in their offering up all their firstborn, in order that I might horrify them, so that they might know that I am the LORD.

27 Therefore, mortal, speak to the house of Israel and say to them, Thus says the Lord GOD: In this again your ancestors blasphemed me, by dealing treacherously with me. 28For when I had brought them into the land that I swore to give them, then wherever they saw any high hill or any leafy tree, there they offered their sacrifices and presented the provocation of their offering; there they sent up their pleasing odors, and there they poured out their drink offerings. 29(I said to them, What is the high place to which you go? So it is called Bamah[v] to this day.) 30Therefore say to the house of Israel, Thus says the Lord GOD: Will you defile yourselves after the manner of your ancestors and go astray after their detestable things? 31When you offer your gifts and make your children pass through the fire, you defile yourselves with all your idols to this day. And shall I be consulted by you, O house of Israel? As I live, says the Lord GOD, I will not be consulted by you.

32 What is in your mind shall never happen—the thought, "Let us be like the nations, like the tribes of the countries, and worship wood and stone."

[v] That is *High Place*

20.6 Ex 3.8,17; Deut 8.7-9; Jer 32.22; Ps 48.2; Dan 8.9

20.7 Ezek 18.31; Deut 29.16,18; Ex 20.2

20.8 Isa 63.10; Ezek 7.8

20.9 Ex 32.12; Num 14.13ff; Ezek 36.21; 39.7

20.10 Ex 13.18

20.11 Deut 4.8; Lev 18.5; Rom 10.5; Gal 3.12

20.12 Ex 31.13,17; ver 20

20.13 Num 14.22; Ps 78.40; 95.8-10; Prov 1.25; Num 14.29; Ps 106.23

20.15 Num 14.28; Ps 95.11; ver 6

20.16 Num 15.39; Ps 78.37; Am 5.25

20.19 Ex 6.7; 20.2; Deut 5.32

20.21 Num 25.1; ver 8,13,16

20.22 ver 17; Ps 78.38; ver 9,14

20.23 Lev 26.33; Deut 28.64; Ps 106.27; Jer 15.4

20.25 Ps 81.12; Rom 1.24; 2 Thess 2.11

20.26 ver 30; 2 Kings 17.17; 2 Chr 28.3; Ezek 16.20,21; 6.7

20.27 Ezek 2.7; Rom 2.24; Ezek 18.24; 39.23,26

20.28 Isa 57.5-7; Ezek 6.13; 16.19

20.31 Ps 106.37-39; Jer 7.31; Ezek 16.20

20.33 Jer 21.5
20.35 Ezek 17.20
20.36 ver 13.21; 1 Cor 10.5-10; Deut 32.10
20.37 Lam 27.32; Jer 33.13; Ezek 16.60,62
20.38 Ezek 34.17,20; Am 9.9,10; Jer 44.14; Ezek 6.7
20.39 Jer 44.25,26; Am 4.4; Isa 1.13; Ezek 23.38,39
20.40 Ezek 17.23; Mic 4.1; Ezek 37.22,24; Isa 56.7; 60.7; Mal 3.4
20.41 Eph 5.2; Phil 4.18
20.42 Ezek 34.13; 36.24
20.43 Ezek 16.61; Hos 5.15; Ezek 36.31; Zech 12.10
20.44 Ezek 24.44; 36.22
20.46 Ezek 6.2; 21.2
20.47 Jer 21.14; 17.24; 21.4
20.48 Jer 7.20; 17.27
20.49 Ezek 17.2; Mt 13.13,14
21.2 Ezek 20.46; Am 7.16
21.3 Jer 21.13; Ezek 5.8; ver 9-11,19; Job 9.22
21.6 Isa 22.4
21.9 Deut 32.41
21.12 Jer 31.19

God Will Restore Israel

33 As I live, says the Lord GOD, surely with a mighty hand and an outstretched arm, and with wrath poured out, I will be king over you. [34]I will bring you out from the peoples and gather you out of the countries where you are scattered, with a mighty hand and an outstretched arm, and with wrath poured out; [35]and I will bring you into the wilderness of the peoples, and there I will enter into judgment with you face to face. [36]As I entered into judgment with your ancestors in the wilderness of the land of Egypt, so I will enter into judgment with you, says the Lord GOD. [37]I will make you pass under the staff, and will bring you within the bond of the covenant. [38]I will purge out the rebels among you, and those who transgress against me; I will bring them out of the land where they reside as aliens, but they shall not enter the land of Israel. Then you shall know that I am the LORD.

39 As for you, O house of Israel, thus says the Lord GOD: Go serve your idols, everyone of you now and hereafter, if you will not listen to me; but my holy name you shall no more profane with your gifts and your idols.

40 For on my holy mountain, the mountain height of Israel, says the Lord GOD, there all the house of Israel, all of them, shall serve me in the land; there I will accept them, and there I will require your contributions and the choicest of your gifts, with all your sacred things. [41]As a pleasing odor I will accept you, when I bring you out from the peoples, and gather you out of the countries where you have been scattered; and I will manifest my holiness among you in the sight of the nations. [42]You shall know that I am the LORD, when I bring you into the land of Israel, the country that I swore to give to your ancestors. [43]There you shall remember your ways and all the deeds by which you have polluted yourselves; and you shall loathe yourselves for all the evils that you have committed. [44]And you shall know that I am the LORD, when I deal with you for my name's sake, not according to your evil ways, or corrupt deeds, O house of Israel, says the Lord GOD.

A Prophecy against the Negeb

45[w] The word of the LORD came to me: [46]Mortal, set your face toward the south, preach against the south, and prophesy against the forest land in the Negeb; [47]say to the forest of the Negeb, Hear the word of the LORD: Thus says the Lord GOD, I will kindle a fire in you, and it shall devour every green tree in you and every dry tree; the blazing flame shall not be quenched, and all faces from south to north shall be scorched by it. [48]All flesh shall see that I the LORD have kindled it; it shall not be quenched. [49]Then I said, "Ah Lord GOD! they are saying of me, 'Is he not a maker of allegories?' "

The Drawn Sword of God

21[x] The word of the LORD came to me: [2]Mortal, set your face toward Jerusalem and preach against the sanctuaries; prophesy against the land of Israel [3]and say to the land of Israel, Thus says the LORD: I am coming against you, and will draw my sword out of its sheath, and will cut off from you both righteous and wicked. [4]Because I will cut off from you both righteous and wicked, therefore my sword shall go out of its sheath against all flesh from south to north; [5]and all flesh shall know that I the LORD have drawn my sword out of its sheath; it shall not be sheathed again. [6]Moan therefore, mortal; moan with breaking heart and bitter grief before their eyes. [7]And when they say to you, "Why do you moan?" you shall say, "Because of the news that has come. Every heart will melt and all hands will be feeble, every spirit will faint and all knees will turn to water. See, it comes and it will be fulfilled," says the Lord GOD.

8 And the word of the LORD came to me: [9]Mortal, prophesy and say: Thus says the Lord; Say:

A sword, a sword is sharpened,
  it is also polished;
10 It is sharpened for slaughter,
  honed to flash like lightning!
How can we make merry?
  You have despised the rod,
  and all discipline.[y]
11 The sword[z] is given to be polished,
  to be grasped in the hand;
It is sharpened, the sword is polished,
  to be placed in the slayer's hand.
12 Cry and wail, O mortal,
  for it is against my people;
it is against all Israel's princes;
  they are thrown to the sword,
  together with my people.

[w] Ch 21.1 in Heb [x] Ch 21.6 in Heb [y] Meaning of Heb uncertain [z] Heb *It*

20.33-44 Yet one day God will be the *king* of his people and will bring them into conformity with the covenant, so that they will at last bear testimony to the LORD when they *manifest [God's] holiness in the sight of the nations.* Then they will be restored to the land, and will acknowledge God as *the LORD*, worshiping him *on my holy mountain*, which is his chosen dwelling place in Jerusalem among his people.
20.45-24.27 Oracles against Jerusalem.
20.45-49 In the ancient versions of Ezekiel, Chapter 21 begins at this point. The prediction of judgment *against the south* is shown by 21.2 to be aimed at Jerusalem, rather than literally toward the semi-arid Negeb district south of Jerusalem. Most travellers from Babylon to Jerusalem would go north up the Tigris-Euphrates valley into Syria, and then turn southwest toward Israel and Jerusalem. It is this perspective that is adopted in this oracle. The fire of judgment that is to fall is not fortuitous, but the direct action of God.
21.1-17 The image changes when the fearful effects of God's judgment on his disobedient people are represented by a sharpened *sword*. The results of its use will be great *slaughter*.

21.18-22 It is Nebuchadnezzar, the king of Babylon, who serves as the sword of the LORD. When at a crossroads the king had to decide whether to attack the Ammonite capital, *Rabbah*, or the Israelite capital, Jerusalem, he made his decision by (1) *divination:* shaken *arrows* (specially marked arrows were shaken together and the one that emerged was the indicator for action); (2) *teraphim* (images of the gods, specially marked to indicate alternatives); and (3) *liver* inspection, by which the configuration on the liver of a sacrificial animal was interpreted to determine action. On this basis, the king laid siege to Jerusalem. It was the *guilt* of the Jerusalemites that caused this attack, and only *ruin, slaughter and blood* will remain after the sword of the LORD has struck.
22.1-32 The *city of blood* is so called because of the bloody offerings to idols and the bloody deeds of its leaders (*princes*), who mistreat parents, orphans, widows, and *aliens* (resident non-Israelites) and who perform perverted sexual acts. The dispersion of this people among the nations will make a mockery of their claim to be God's own and will profane the LORD's name.

Ah! Strike the thigh!
13 For consider: What! If you despise the rod,
will it not happen?[a] says the Lord GOD.
14 And you, mortal, prophesy;
Strike hand to hand.
Let the sword fall twice, thrice;
it is a sword for killing.
A sword for great slaughter—
it surrounds them;
15 therefore hearts melt
and many stumble.
At all their gates I have set
the point[a] of the sword.
Ah! It is made for flashing,
it is polished[b] for slaughter.
16 Attack to the right!
Engage to the left!
Wherever your edge is directed.
17 I too will strike hand to hand,
I will satisfy my fury;
I the LORD have spoken.

18 The word of the LORD came to me:
19 Mortal, mark out two roads for the sword
of the king of Babylon to come; both of
them shall issue from the same land. And
make a signpost, make it for a fork in the
road leading to a city; 20 mark out the road
for the sword to come to Rabbah of the
Ammonites or to Judah and to[c] Jerusalem
the fortified. 21 For the king of Babylon stands
at the parting of the way, at the fork in the
two roads, to use divination; he shakes the
arrows, he consults the teraphim,[d] he in-
spects the liver. 22 Into his right hand comes
the lot for Jerusalem, to set battering rams,
to call out for slaughter, for raising the
battle cry, to set battering rams against the
gates, to cast up ramps, to build siege towers. 23 But to them it will seem like a false
divination; they have sworn solemn oaths;
but he brings their guilt to remembrance,
bringing about their capture.

24 Therefore thus says the Lord God:
Because you have brought your guilt to
remembrance, in that your transgressions
are uncovered, so that in all your deeds
your sins appear—because you have come
to remembrance, you shall be taken in
hand.[e]

25 As for you, vile, wicked prince of Israel,
you whose day has come,
the time of final punishment,
26 thus says the Lord GOD:
Remove the turban, take off the crown;
things shall not remain as they are.
Exalt that which is low,
abase that which is high.
27 A ruin, a ruin, a ruin—
I will make it!
(Such has never occurred.)
Until he comes whose right it is;
to him I will give it.

28 As for you, mortal, prophesy, and
say, Thus says the Lord GOD concerning the
Ammonites, and concerning their reproach;
say:
A sword, a sword! Drawn for slaughter
Polished to consume,[f] to flash like
lightning.
29 Offering false visions for you,
divining lies for you,
they place you over the necks
of the vile, wicked ones—
those whose day has come,
the time of final punishment.
30 Return it to its sheath!
In the place where you were created,
in the land of your origin,
I will judge you.
31 I will pour out my indignation upon you,
with the fire of my wrath
I will blow upon you.
I will deliver you into brutish hands,
those skillful to destroy.
32 You shall be fuel for the fire,
your blood shall enter the earth;
You shall be remembered no more,
for I the LORD have spoken.

The Bloody City

22 The word of the LORD came to me:
2 You, mortal, will you judge, will
you judge the bloody city? Then declare to
it all its abominable deeds. 3 You shall say,
Thus says the Lord GOD: A city! Shedding
blood within itself; its time has come; making its idols, defiling itself. 4 You have become guilty by the blood that you have
shed, and defiled by the idols that you have
made; you have brought your day near, the
appointed time of your years has come.
Therefore I have made you a disgrace before
the nations, and a mockery to all the countries. 5 Those who are near and those who
are far from you will mock you, you infa-
mous one, full of tumult.

6 The princes of Israel in you, everyone
according to his power, have been bent on
shedding blood. 7 Father and mother are

[a] Meaning of Heb uncertain [b] Tg: Heb *wrapped up* [c] Gk Syr: Heb *Judah in* [d] Or *the household gods* [e] Or *be taken captive* [f] Cn: Heb *to contain*

21.14 Num 24.10; Ezek 6.11; Lev 26.21,24; Ezek 30.24
21.17 ver 14; Ezek 22.13; 5.13
21.19 Ezek 4.1-3; ver 15
21.20 Jer 49.2; Ezek 25.5; Am 1.14
21.21 Num 23.23; Prov 16.33; Judg 17.5
21.23 Ezek 17.13,15,16, 18; 29.16
21.25 Ezek 7.2,3,7; 35.5
21.26 Jer 13.18; Ezek 16.12; 17.24; Lk 1.52
21.27 Hag 2.21,22; Ps 2.6; Jer 23.5,6; Ezek 34.24; 37.24
21.28 Jer 49.1; Ezek 25.2,3; Zeph 2.8; Isa 31.8; Jer 12.12
21.29 Ezek 13.6-9; 22.28; ver 25; Ezek 35.5
21.30 Jer 47.6,7; Ezek 16.3
21.31 Ezek 7.8; 14.19; 22.20,21; Jer 6.22,23; 51.20,21
21.32 Mal 4.1; Ezek 25.10
22.2 Ezek 20.4; 24.6-9; Nah 3.1; Ezek 16.2; 20.4
22.6 Isa 1.23
22.7 Deut 27.16; Ex 22.21,22

treated with contempt in you; the alien
residing within you suffers extortion; the
orphan and the widow are wronged in you.
8You have despised my holy things, and
profaned my sabbaths. 9In you are those
who slander to shed blood, those in you
who eat upon the mountains, who commit
lewdness in your midst. 10In you they uncover their fathers' nakedness; in you they
violate women in their menstrual periods.
11One commits abomination with his
neighbor's wife; another lewdly defiles his
daughter-in-law; another in you defiles his
sister, his father's daughter. 12In you, they
take bribes to shed blood; you take both
advance interest and accrued interest, and
make gain of your neighbors by extortion;
and you have forgotten me, says the Lord
GOD.
13 See, I strike my hands together at the
dishonest gain you have made, and at the
blood that has been shed within you. 14Can
your courage endure, or can your hands
remain strong in the days when I shall deal
with you? I the LORD have spoken, and I will
do it. 15I will scatter you among the nations
and disperse you through the countries,
and I will purge your filthiness out of you.
16And I[g] shall be profaned through you in
the sight of the nations; and you shall know
that I am the LORD.
17 The word of the LORD came to me:
18Mortal, the house of Israel has become
dross to me; all of them, silver,[h] bronze, tin,
iron, and lead. In the smelter they have
become dross. 19Therefore thus says the
Lord God: Because you have all become
dross, I will gather you into the midst of
Jerusalem. 20As one gathers silver, bronze,
iron, lead, and tin into a smelter, to blow
the fire upon them in order to melt them;
so I will gather you in my anger and in my
wrath, and I will put you in and melt you.
21I will gather you and blow upon you with
the fire of my wrath, and you shall be
melted within it. 22As silver is melted in a
smelter, so you shall be melted in it; and
you shall know that I the LORD have poured
out my wrath upon you.
23 The word of the LORD came to me:
24Mortal, say to it: You are a land that is
not cleansed, not rained upon in the day of
indignation. 25Its princes[i] within it are like
a roaring lion tearing the prey; they have
devoured human lives; they have taken
treasure and precious things; they have
made many widows within it. 26Its priests
have done violence to my teaching and
have profaned my holy things; they have
made no distinction between the holy and
the common, neither have they taught the
difference between the unclean and the clean,
and they have disregarded my sabbaths, so
that I am profaned among them. 27Its officials within it are like wolves tearing the
prey, shedding blood, destroying lives to get
dishonest gain. 28Its prophets have smeared
whitewash on their behalf, seeing false visions and divining lies for them, saying,
"Thus says the Lord GOD," when the LORD
has not spoken. 29The people of the land
have practiced extortion and committed
robbery; they have oppressed the poor and
needy, and have extorted from the alien
without redress. 30And I sought for anyone
among them who would repair the wall
and stand in the breach before me on behalf
of the land, so that I would not destroy it;
but I found no one. 31Therefore I have
poured out my indignation upon them; I
have consumed them with the fire of my
wrath; I have returned their conduct upon
their heads, says the Lord GOD.

Oholah and Oholibah

23 The word of the LORD came to me:
2Mortal, there were two women,
the daughters of one mother; 3they played
the whore in Egypt; they played the whore
in their youth; their breasts were caressed
there, and their virgin bosoms were fondled.
4Oholah was the name of the elder and
Oholibah the name of her sister. They became mine, and they bore sons and daughters. As for their names, Oholah is Samaria,
and Oholibah is Jerusalem.
5 Oholah played the whore while she
was mine; she lusted after her lovers the
Assyrians, warriors[j] 6clothed in blue, governors and commanders, all of them handsome young men, mounted horsemen. 7She
bestowed her favors upon them, the choicest men of Assyria all of them; and she
defiled herself with all the idols of everyone
for whom she lusted. 8She did not give up
her whorings that she had practiced since
Egypt; for in her youth men had lain with
her and fondled her virgin bosom and poured
out their lust upon her. 9Therefore I deliv-

[g] Gk Syr Vg: Heb *you* [h] Transposed from the end of the verse; compare verse 20 [i] Gk: Heb *indignation.* 25*A conspiracy of its prophets* [j] Meaning of Heb uncertain

22.23-31 *Princes, priests and prophets* have all betrayed and corrupted their roles and responsibilities. There is no-one to intercede with God in their behalf to forestall the outpouring of his judgment on the people and these evil leaders.
23.1-49 Israel and Judah are portrayed as *whores* who have violated their special relationship with God for what they foolishly think will be personal gain. First *Oholah* (Israel), through the worship of the gods of Egypt and Assyria, and then *Oholibah* (Judah), through worship of the gods of Babylon, practised whoredom. They went to the extreme of offering their own children to these deities, while violating the sabbath laws and defiling God's proper sanctuary. Ironically, it is the very people to whose gods they have turned who will now come against them to plunder, kill and exile them.

22.8 ver 26; Lev 19.30; Ezek 23.38,39
22.9 Ezek 18.6,11,15
22.10 Lev 18.8,19; Ezek 18.6
22.11 Ezek 18.11; Lev 18.15; 18.9
22.12 Mic 7.2,3; Lev 25.36; 19.13; Jer 3.21
22.14 Ezek 21.7; 24.14
22.15 Deut 4.27; Zech 4.17; Ezek 23.27
22.18 Isa 1.22; Jer 6.28
22.22 Ezek 21.7; 20.8,33
22.25 Hos 6.9; Ps 10.9; Jer 15.8
22.26 Mal 2.8; Lev 10.10; Ezek 44.23; Hag 2.11-14; Ezek 20.12,13; 36.20
22.27 Isa 1.23
22.28 Ezek 13.10-16; 13.6,7
22.29 Isa 5.7; Am 3.10; Ex 22.21; 23.9
22.30 Jer 5.1; Ezek 13.5; Ps 106.23
22.31 Isa 13.5; Ezek 9.10; 11.21; 16.43
23.3 Josh 24.14; Ezek 20.8; 16.22
23.4 Ezek 16.8,20
23.5 1 Kings 12.28-30; Ezek 16.28; Hos 8.9,10
23.7 ver 30; Ezek 16.15; 20.7; Hos 5.3; 6.10
23.8 Ex 32.4; ver 3; Ezek 16.15
23.9 ver 22; Ezek 16.37; 2 Kings 18.9-11; Hos 11.5

ered her into the hands of her lovers, into
the hands of the Assyrians, for whom she
lusted. [10]These uncovered her nakedness;
they seized her sons and her daughters; and
they killed her with the sword. Judgment
was executed upon her, and she became a
byword among women.

11 Her sister Oholibah saw this, yet she
was more corrupt than she in her lusting
and in her whorings, which were worse
than those of her sister. [12]She lusted after
the Assyrians, governors and commanders,
warriors[k] clothed in full armor, mounted
horsemen, all of them handsome young
men. [13]And I saw that she was defiled; they
both took the same way. [14]But she carried
her whorings further; she saw male figures
carved on the wall, images of the Chaldeans
portrayed in vermilion, [15]with belts around
their waists, with flowing turbans on their
heads, all of them looking like officers—a
picture of Babylonians whose native land
was Chaldea. [16]When she saw them she
lusted after them, and sent messengers to
them in Chaldea. [17]And the Babylonians
came to her into the bed of love, and they
defiled her with their lust; and after she
defiled herself with them, she turned from
them in disgust. [18]When she carried on her
whorings so openly and flaunted her nakedness, I turned in disgust from her, as I had
turned from her sister. [19]Yet she increased
her whorings, remembering the days of her
youth, when she played the whore in the
land of Egypt [20]and lusted after her para-
mours there, whose members were like those
of donkeys, and whose emission was like
that of stallions. [21]Thus you longed for the
lewdness of your youth, when the Egyptians[l]
fondled your bosom and caressed[m] your
young breasts.

22 Therefore, O Oholibah, thus says the
Lord GOD: I will rouse against you your
lovers from whom you turned in disgust,
and I will bring them against you from
every side: [23]the Babylonians and all the
Chaldeans, Pekod and Shoa and Koa, and
all the Assyrians with them, handsome
young men, governors and commanders all
of them, officers and warriors,[n] all of them
riding on horses. [24]They shall come against
you from the north[o] with chariots and
wagons and a host of peoples; they shall set
themselves against you on every side with
buckler, shield, and helmet, and I will commit the judgment to them, and they shall
judge you according to their ordinances. [25]I
will direct my indignation against you, in
order that they may deal with you in fury.
They shall cut off your nose and your ears,
and your survivors shall fall by the sword.
They shall seize your sons and your daughters, and your survivors shall be devoured
by fire. [26]They shall also strip you of your
clothes and take away your fine jewels. [27]So
I will put an end to your lewdness and your
whoring brought from the land of Egypt;
you shall not long for them, or remember
Egypt any more. [28]For thus says the Lord
God: I will deliver you into the hands of
those whom you hate, into the hands of
those from whom you turned in disgust;
[29]and they shall deal with you in hatred,
and take away all the fruit of your labor,
and leave you naked and bare, and the
nakedness of your whorings shall be exposed. Your lewdness and your whorings
[30]have brought this upon you, because you
played the whore with the nations, and
polluted yourself with their idols. [31]You have
gone the way of your sister; therefore I will
give her cup into your hand. [32]Thus says
the Lord GOD:

You shall drink your sister's cup,
  deep and wide;
you shall be scorned and derided,
  it holds so much.
33 You shall be filled with drunkenness and
    sorrow.
A cup of horror and desolation
  is the cup of your sister Samaria;
34 you shall drink it and drain it out,
  and gnaw its sherds,
  and tear out your breasts;

for I have spoken, says the Lord GOD. [35]There-
fore thus says the Lord GOD: Because you
have forgotten me and cast me behind your
back, therefore bear the consequences of
your lewdness and whorings.

36 The LORD said to me: Mortal, will you
judge Oholah and Oholibah? Then declare
to them their abominable deeds. [37]For they
have committed adultery, and blood is on
their hands; with their idols they have
committed adultery; and they have even
offered up to them for food the children
whom they had borne to me. [38]Moreover
this they have done to me: they have defiled
my sanctuary on the same day and profaned my sabbaths. [39]For when they had

[k] Meaning of Heb uncertain [l] Two Mss: MT *from Egypt* [m] Cn: Heb *for the sake of* [n] Compare verses 6 and 12: Heb *officers and called ones* [o] Gk: Meaning of Heb uncertain

23.10 Ezek 16.37; Hos 2.10; ver 47; Ezek 16.57

23.11 Jer 3.8-11; Ezek 16.47

23.12 2 Kings 16.7-10; 2 Chr 28.16-23; ver 6,23

23.14 Ezek 8.10; 16.29; Jer 22.14

23.17 ver 28,30

23.18 ver 10; Jer 6.8

23.20 Ezek 16.26

23.21 ver 3

23.22 ver 28; Ezek 16.37

23.23 Ezek 21.19; 2 Kings 24.2; Jer 50.21; ver 6,12

23.24 Ezek 21.15,19; Jer 47.3; Ezek 16.40; Jer 39.5,6

23.26 Ezek 16.39

23.27 Ezek 16.41; 22.15; ver 3,19

23.29 ver 26; Ezek 16.39

23.32 Isa 51.17; Jer 25.15; Ezek 22.4,5

23.34 Ps 75.8; Isa 51.17

23.35 Jer 3.21; Hos 8.14; 1 Kings 14.9; Neh 9.26

23.36 Ezek 20.4; 22.2; Isa 58.1

23.37 ver 3,45; Ezek 16.20,21,36,45

23.39 2 Kings 21.4

slaughtered their children for their idols, on the same day they came into my sanctuary to profane it. This is what they did in my house.

40 They even sent for men to come from far away, to whom a messenger was sent, and they came. For them you bathed yourself, painted your eyes, and decked yourself with ornaments; [41]you sat on a stately couch, with a table spread before it on which you had placed my incense and my oil. [42]The sound of a raucous multitude was around her, with many of the rabble brought in drunken from the wilderness; and they put bracelets on the arms[p] of the women, and beautiful crowns upon their heads.

43 Then I said, Ah, she is worn out with adulteries, but they carry on their sexual acts with her. [44]For they have gone in to her, as one goes in to a whore. Thus they went in to Oholah and to Oholibah, wanton women. [45]But righteous judges shall declare them guilty of adultery and of bloodshed; because they are adulteresses and blood is on their hands.

46 For thus says the Lord GOD: Bring up an assembly against them, and make them an object of terror and of plunder. [47]The assembly shall stone them and with their swords they shall cut them down; they shall kill their sons and their daughters, and burn up their houses. [48]Thus will I put an end to lewdness in the land, so that all women may take warning and not commit lewdness as you have done. [49]They shall repay you for your lewdness, and you shall bear the penalty for your sinful idolatry; and you shall know that I am the Lord GOD.

The Boiling Pot

24 In the ninth year, in the tenth month, on the tenth day of the month, the word of the LORD came to me: [2]Mortal, write down the name of this day, this very day. The king of Babylon has laid siege to Jerusalem this very day. [3]And utter an allegory to the rebellious house and say to them, Thus says the Lord GOD:

Set on the pot, set it on,
pour in water also;
4 put in it the pieces,
all the good pieces, the thigh and the shoulder;
fill it with choice bones.
5 Take the choicest one of the flock,
pile the logs[q] under it;
boil its pieces,[r]
seethe[s] also its bones in it.

6 Therefore thus says the Lord GOD:
Woe to the bloody city,
the pot whose rust is in it,
whose rust has not gone out of it!
Empty it piece by piece,
making no choice at all.[t]
7 For the blood she shed is inside it;
she placed it on a bare rock;
she did not pour it out on the ground,
to cover it with earth.
8 To rouse my wrath, to take vengeance,
I have placed the blood she shed
on a bare rock,
so that it may not be covered.
9Therefore thus says the Lord GOD:
Woe to the bloody city!
I will even make the pile great.
10 Heap up the logs, kindle the fire;
boil the meat well, mix in the spices,
let the bones be burned.
11 Stand it empty upon the coals,
so that it may become hot, its copper glow,
its filth melt in it, its rust be consumed.
12 In vain I have wearied myself;[u]
its thick rust does not depart.
To the fire with its rust![v]
13 Yet, when I cleansed you in your filthy lewdness,
you did not become clean from your filth;
you shall not again be cleansed
until I have satisfied my fury upon you.

[14]I the LORD have spoken; the time is coming, I will act. I will not refrain, I will not spare, I will not relent. According to your ways and your doings I will judge you, says the Lord GOD.

Ezekiel's Bereavement

15 The word of the LORD came to me: [16]Mortal, with one blow I am about to take away from you the delight of your eyes; yet you shall not mourn or weep, nor shall your tears run down. [17]Sigh, but not aloud; make no mourning for the dead. Bind on your turban, and put your sandals on your feet; do not cover your upper lip or eat the

[p] Heb *hands* [q] Compare verse 10: Heb *the bones* [r] Two Mss: Heb *its boilings* [s] Cn: Heb *its bones seethe* [t] Heb *piece, no lot has fallen on it* [u] Cn: Meaning of Heb uncertain [v] Meaning of Heb uncertain

23.40 Isa 57.9; 2 Kings 9.30; Jer 4.30; Ezek 16.13-16
23.41 Esth 1.6; Am 6.4; Prov 7.17; Hos 2.8
23.42 Ezek 16.49; Jer 51.7; Ezek 16.11,12
23.45 Ezek 16.38; Hos 6.5; Lev 20.10
23.47 Ezek 16.40; 2 Chr 36.17,19; Ezek 24.21; Jer 39.8
23.48 ver 27; Ezek 22.15; 2 Pet 2.6
24.1 Ezek 1.2; 8.1; 20.1; 26.1
24.2 Isa 8.1; 2 Kings 25.1; Jer 39.1; 52.4
24.3 Ezek 17.2; Jer 1.13; Ezek 11.3
24.6 ver 9; Ezek 22.3; Mic 7.2; Joel 3.3; Nah 3.10
24.7 Ezek 23.37,45; Lev 17.13; Deut 12.16
24.9 ver 6; Nah 3.1; Hab 2.12
24.13 Jer 6.28-30; Ezek 22.24; 5.13; 8.18; 16.42
24.14 1 Sam 15.29; Isa 55.11; Ezek 9.10; 18.30; 36.19
24.16 Job 23.2; Jer 16.5; 22.10; 13.17
24.17 Jer 16.5-7; 2 Sam 15.30; Mic 3.7

24.1-14 The exact date when the siege of Jerusalem begins is revealed to Ezekiel: the *ninth year* of Jehoiakim was 588. A boiling pot containing pieces of a sheep symbolizes the punishment and dismemberment of God's people (*house*), and the protracted cleansing process which is fired by God's *fury* with them; *cf.* Jer 1.3.
24.15-27 The death of the prophet's *wife* and his refraining from the customary signs of mourning for her symbolize the necessity for the people to accept, sadly and solemnly, God's having deprived them of Jerusalem, *their stronghold, their delight.*

25.1-32.32 Oracles against the Foreign Nations.
25.1-7 The Ammonites, a Semitic tribe based east of the Jordan River across from central Palestine, are to be punished for their glee over the desolation and *exile* of Judah. Their land is to be taken by other *nations*, and they will be destroyed.
25.8-11 *Moab*, south of Ammon and east of the Dead Sea, is to be seized by *people of the east*, meaning tribes located in north central Arabia.
25.12-14 *Edom*, which was located below the southern end of the Dead Sea, figured prominently in Israel's migration from Egypt to the land of Canaan (Num 20). These people also are to become targets of God's *wrath*.
25.15-17 The Philistines in their prosperous cities along the Mediterranean coast competed with and harrassed Israel from the time of the initial settlement in the land and continuing through the period of the monarchy: 1 Chr 14; 2 Chr 26.6-15; 28.18. The *Cherethites* were probably a colony of Cretans who lived south of the Philistines. Some of them served as mercenaries for that nation as well as for Israel (2 Sam 8.18; 20.23).

bread of mourners.[w] 18 So I spoke to the people in the morning, and at evening my wife died. And on the next morning I did as I was commanded.

19 Then the people said to me, "Will you not tell us what these things mean for us, that you are acting this way?" 20 Then I said to them: The word of the LORD came to me: 21 Say to the house of Israel, Thus says the Lord GOD: I will profane my sanctuary, the pride of your power, the delight of your eyes, and your heart's desire; and your sons and your daughters whom you left behind shall fall by the sword. 22 And you shall do as I have done; you shall not cover your upper lip or eat the bread of mourners.[v] 23 Your turbans shall be on your heads and your sandals on your feet; you shall not mourn or weep, but you shall pine away in your iniquities and groan to one another. 24 Thus Ezekiel shall be a sign to you; you shall do just as he has done. When this comes, then you shall know that I am the Lord GOD.

25 And you, mortal, on the day when I take from them their stronghold, their joy and glory, the delight of their eyes and their heart's affection, and also[x] their sons and their daughters, 26 on that day, one who has escaped will come to you to report to you the news. 27 On that day your mouth shall be opened to the one who has escaped, and you shall speak and no longer be silent. So you shall be a sign to them; and they shall know that I am the LORD.

Proclamation against Ammon

25 The word of the LORD came to me: 2 Mortal, set your face toward the Ammonites and prophesy against them. 3 Say to the Ammonites, Hear the word of the Lord GOD: Thus says the Lord GOD, Because you said, "Aha!" over my sanctuary when it was profaned, and over the land of Israel when it was made desolate, and over the house of Judah when it went into exile; 4 therefore I am handing you over to the people of the east for a possession. They shall set their encampments among you and pitch their tents in your midst; they shall eat your fruit, and they shall drink your milk. 5 I will make Rabbah a pasture for camels and Ammon a fold for flocks. Then you shall know that I am the LORD. 6 For thus says the Lord GOD: Because you have clapped your hands and stamped your feet and rejoiced with all the malice within you against the land of Israel, 7 therefore I have stretched out my hand against you, and will hand you over as plunder to the nations. I will cut you off from the peoples and will make you perish out of the countries; I will destroy you. Then you shall know that I am the LORD.

Proclamation against Moab

8 Thus says the Lord GOD: Because Moab[y] said, The house of Judah is like all the other nations, 9 therefore I will lay open the flank of Moab from the towns[z] on its frontier, the glory of the country, Beth-jeshimoth, Baal-meon, and Kiriathaim. 10 I will give it along with Ammon to the people of the east as a possession. Thus Ammon shall be remembered no more among the nations, 11 and I will execute judgments upon Moab. Then they shall know that I am the LORD.

Proclamation against Edom

12 Thus says the Lord GOD: Because Edom acted revengefully against the house of Judah and has grievously offended in taking vengeance upon them, 13 therefore thus says the Lord God, I will stretch out my hand against Edom, and cut off from it humans and animals, and I will make it desolate; from Teman even to Dedan they shall fall by the sword. 14 I will lay my vengeance upon Edom by the hand of my people Israel; and they shall act in Edom according to my anger and according to my wrath; and they shall know my vengeance, says the Lord GOD.

Proclamation against Philistia

15 Thus says the Lord GOD: Because with unending hostilities the Philistines acted in vengeance, and with malice of heart took revenge in destruction; 16 therefore thus says the Lord GOD, I will stretch out my hand against the Philistines, cut off the Cherethites, and destroy the rest of the seacoast. 17 I will execute great vengeance on them with wrathful punishments. Then they shall know that I am the LORD, when I lay my vengeance on them.

24.21 Jer 7.14; Ps 27.4; Jer 6.11; Ezek 23.47
24.23 Job 27.15; Ps 78.64; Ezek 33.10
24.24 Ezek 4.3; 12.6,11; Jer 17.15; Ezek 6.7; 25.5
24.25 Jer 11.22
24.27 Ezek 3.26,27; 33.22; ver 24
25.2 Jer 27.3; Ezek 21.28; Am 1.13; Zeph 2.8,9
25.3 Prov 17.5; Ezek 26.2
25.5 Ezek 21.20; Isa 17.2; Zeph 2.14
25.6 Job 27.23; Lam 2.15; Zeph 2.8,10
25.7 Ezek 26.5; Am 1.14,15; Ezek 6.14
25.12 Lam 4.21,22; Ezek 35.2; Am 1.11; Ob 10-16
25.13 Am 1.12; Jer 25.23
25.14 Isa 11.14; Jer 49.2
25.15 Jer 25.20; Isa 14.29-31; Joel 3.4; 2 Chr 28.18
25.16 Zeph 2.4,5; 1 Sam 30.14; Jer 47.1-7
25.17 Ezek 5.15; Ps 9.16

[w] Vg Tg: Heb *of men* [x] Heb lacks *and also* [y] Gk Old Latin: Heb *Moab and Seir* [z] Heb *towns from its towns*

26.2 Isa 23; Jer 25.22; Ezek 25.3; 36.2
26.3 Mic 4.11; Isa 5.30; Jer 50.42
26.4 Am 1.10
26.5 Ezek 27.32; 29.19
26.6 Ezek 25.5
26.7 Jer 27.3-6; Ezra 7.12; Dan 2.37; Ezek 23.24
26.8 ver 6; Ezek 21.22; Jer 6.6; 32.24
26.9 Ezek 21.22
26.10 Jer 4.13; 39.3; Ezek 27.28
26.11 Hab 1.8; Isa 26.5; Jer 43.13
26.13 Isa 14.11; 25.10; Isa 23.16; Rev 18.22
26.15 ver 18; Ezek 31.16
26.16 Ezek 27.35; Jon 3.6; Job 2.13
26.17 Ezek 27.32; Rev 18.9; Isa 23.4; Ezek 28.2
26.18 ver 15
26.20 Ezek 32.18,24; Am 9.2; Jer 33.9
26.21 Ezek 27.36; 28.19; ver 14
27.2 Ezek 28.12
27.3 Ezek 28.2; ver 33; Ezek 28.12

Proclamation against Tyre

26 In the eleventh year, on the first
day of the month, the word of the
LORD came to me: 2Mortal, because Tyre said
concerning Jerusalem,

"Aha, broken is the gateway of the
peoples;
it has swung open to me;
I shall be replenished,
now that it is wasted."

3Therefore, thus says the Lord GOD:
See, I am against you, O Tyre!
I will hurl many nations against you,
as the sea hurls its waves.
4 They shall destroy the walls of Tyre
and break down its towers.
I will scrape its soil from it
and make it a bare rock.
5 It shall become, in the midst of the sea,
a place for spreading nets.
I have spoken, says the Lord GOD.
It shall become plunder for the nations,
6 and its daughter-towns in the country
shall be killed by the sword.
Then they shall know that I am the LORD.

7 For thus says the Lord GOD: I will bring
against Tyre from the north King Nebuchadrezzar of Babylon, king of kings, together
with horses, chariots, cavalry, and a great
and powerful army.

8 Your daughter-towns in the country
he shall put to the sword.
He shall set up a siege wall against you,
cast up a ramp against you,
and raise a roof of shields against you.
9 He shall direct the shock of his battering
rams against your walls
and break down your towers with his
axes.
10 His horses shall be so many
that their dust shall cover you.
At the noise of cavalry, wheels, and
chariots
your very walls shall shake,
when he enters your gates
like those entering a breached city.
11 With the hoofs of his horses
he shall trample all your streets.
He shall put your people to the sword,
and your strong pillars shall fall to
the ground.
12 They will plunder your riches
and loot your merchandise;
they shall break down your walls
and destroy your fine houses.
Your stones and timber and soil
they shall cast into the water.
13 I will silence the music of your songs;
the sound of your lyres shall be heard
no more.
14 I will make you a bare rock;
you shall be a place for spreading nets.
You shall never again be rebuilt,
for I the LORD have spoken,
says the Lord GOD.

15 Thus says the Lord GOD to Tyre: Shall
not the coastlands shake at the sound of
your fall, when the wounded groan, when
slaughter goes on within you? 16Then all
the princes of the sea shall step down from
their thrones; they shall remove their robes
and strip off their embroidered garments.
They shall clothe themselves with trembling, and shall sit on the ground; they shall
tremble every moment, and be appalled at
you. 17And they shall raise a lamentation
over you, and say to you:

How you have vanished[a] from the seas,
O city renowned,
once mighty on the sea,
you and your inhabitants,[b]
who imposed your[c] terror
on all the mainland![d]
18 Now the coastlands tremble
on the day of your fall;
the coastlands by the sea
are dismayed at your passing.

19 For thus says the Lord GOD: When I
make you a city laid waste, like cities that
are not inhabited, when I bring up the deep
over you, and the great waters cover you,
20then I will thrust you down with those
who descend into the Pit, to the people of
long ago, and I will make you live in the
world below, among primeval ruins, with
those who go down to the Pit, so that you
will not be inhabited or have a place[e] in the
land of the living. 21I will bring you to a
dreadful end, and you shall be no more;
though sought for, you will never be found
again, says the Lord GOD.

Lamentation over Tyre

27 The word of the LORD came to me:
2Now you, mortal, raise a lamentation over Tyre, 3and say to Tyre, which
sits at the entrance to the sea, merchant of
the peoples on many coastlands, Thus says
the Lord God:

[a] Gk OL Aquila: Heb *have vanished, O inhabited one, inhabitants* [b] Heb *it and its inhabitants* [c] Heb *their* [d] Cn: Heb *its* [e] Gk: Heb *I will give beauty*

26.1-21 The first of a series of oracles and lamentations concerning Phoenicia, Israel's prosperous neighbor to the northwest along the sea coast. Its king, Hiram, had provided the material (cedar) and skilled artisans essential for the construction of the Jerusalem temple by Solomon (1 Kings 7.13-46). Earlier Phoenicia's chief city, Tyre, had paid tribute money to Assyria, but Sennacherib (705-681) tried without success to capture the city in its militarily strong location on an island just off the coast of what is now Lebanon. Nebuchadnezzar's forces besieged Tyre from 586 to 573 and could not take it, but the city surrendered nonetheless. It is this latter assault on Tyre which is pictured in this oracle, although the fall of the impregnable city to its attackers is described. Tyre, *once mighty* commercially and militarily, is here seen in ruins and its inhabitants are driven down to *the Pit*, the unseen abode of the dead.
27.1-36 The mercantile wealth and contacts of Tyre are portrayed here through the image of the city as a splendid ship, made from rich woods of the region (*Senir* is Mt. Hermon, and *Bashan* is a region just south of that lofty peak in southern Syria). The ship is served by a crew from other Phoenician cities (*Arvad, Sidon, Zemer,* and *Gebal* [which was later known as Byblos], and by mercenaries from regions of Africa (*Paras, Lud, Put*). The city's walls are guarded by those from the northern cities of *Arvad and Gamad* (*Helech* is probably a reference to the army). Tyre's trading partners are named in a prose insert in the oracle, and they range across the Mediterranean and Middle Eastern worlds: *Javan* is Ionia, land of the Greeks; *Tubal and Meshech* were tribes living in central Asia Minor; *the Rhodians* lived on Rhodes, an island off the southwest coast of Asia Minor; *Minnith* was a town in Ammon, east of the Jordan; *Helbon,* north of Damascus, was famed for its wine; *Vedan* is either an unknown place or a manuscript error for Dan, the district of upper Israel just south of Mt. Hermon; *Dedan and Kedar* are in Arabia; *Sheba and Raamah* are located at the southern end of the Arabian peninsula; *Haran, Canneh* and *Eden* were cities along the Euphrates River, while *Asshur* refers to the nation Assyria. *Chilmad* is an unknown location in Mesopotamia. The oracle concludes (27.25-36) with the vivid picture of all this vast wealth lost at sea, in spite of the efforts of the mariners. The ruin of Tyre *by the sea* symbolizes the destruction of this great commercial nation, Phoenicia.

O Tyre, you have said,
"I am perfect in beauty."
4 Your borders are in the heart of the seas;
your builders made perfect your beauty.
5 They made all your planks
of fir trees from Senir;
they took a cedar from Lebanon
to make a mast for you.
6 From oaks of Bashan
they made your oars;
they made your deck of pines[f]
from the coasts of Cyprus,
inlaid with ivory.
7 Of fine embroidered linen from Egypt
was your sail,
serving as your ensign;
blue and purple from the coasts of Elishah
was your awning.
8 The inhabitants of Sidon and Arvad
were your rowers;
skilled men of Zemer[g] were within you,
they were your pilots.
9 The elders of Gebal and its artisans were within you,
caulking your seams;
all the ships of the sea with their mariners were within you,
to barter for your wares.
10 Paras[h] and Lud and Put
were in your army,
your mighty warriors;
they hung shield and helmet in you;
they gave you splendor.
11 Men of Arvad and Helech[i]
were on your walls all around;
men of Gamad were at your towers.
They hung their quivers all around your walls;
they made perfect your beauty.

12 Tarshish did business with you out of
the abundance of your great wealth; silver,
iron, tin, and lead they exchanged for your
wares. 13 Javan, Tubal, and Meshech traded
with you; they exchanged human beings
and vessels of bronze for your merchandise.
14 Beth-togarmah exchanged for your wares
horses, war horses, and mules. 15 The
Rhodians[j] traded with you; many coastlands
were your own special markets; they brought
you in payment ivory tusks and ebony.
16 Edom[k] did business with you because of
your abundant goods; they exchanged for
your wares turquoise, purple, embroidered
work, fine linen, coral, and rubies. 17 Judah
and the land of Israel traded with you; they
exchanged for your merchandise wheat from
Minnith, millet,[l] honey, oil, and balm. 18 Damascus traded with you for your abundant
goods—because of your great wealth of
every kind—wine of Helbon, and white wool.
19 Vedan and Javan from Uzal[k] entered into
trade for your wares; wrought iron, cassia,
and sweet cane were bartered for your
merchandise. 20 Dedan traded with you in
saddlecloths for riding. 21 Arabia and all the
princes of Kedar were your favored dealers
in lambs, rams, and goats; in these they did
business with you. 22 The merchants of Sheba
and Raamah traded with you; they exchanged for your wares the best of all kinds
of spices, and all precious stones, and gold.
23 Haran, Canneh, Eden, the merchants of
Sheba, Asshur, and Chilmad traded with
you. 24 These traded with you in choice
garments, in clothes of blue and embroidered work, and in carpets of colored material, bound with cords and made secure;
in these they traded with you.[m] 25 The ships
of Tarshish traveled for you in your trade.

So you were filled and heavily laden
in the heart of the seas.
26 Your rowers have brought you
into the high seas.
The east wind has wrecked you
in the heart of the seas.
27 Your riches, your wares, your merchandise,
your mariners and your pilots,
your caulkers, your dealers in merchandise,
and all your warriors within you,
with all the company
that is with you,
sink into the heart of the seas
on the day of your ruin.
28 At the sound of the cry of your pilots
the countryside shakes,
29 and down from their ships
come all that handle the oar.
The mariners and all the pilots of the sea
stand on the shore
30 and wail aloud over you,
and cry bitterly.
They throw dust on their heads
and wallow in ashes;

[f] Or *boxwood* [g] Cn Compare Gen 10.18: Heb *your skilled men, O Tyre* [h] Or *Persia* [i] Or *and your army* [j] Gk: Heb *The Dedanites* [k] Another reading is *Aram* [l] Meaning of Heb uncertain [m] Cn: Heb *in your market*

27.4 ver 25-27
27.5 Deut 3.9
27.6 Zech 11.12; Isa 2.13; Jer 2.10
27.8 1 Kings 9.27
27.9 1 Kings 5.18; ver 27
27.10 Ezek 30.5; 38.5; ver 11
27.11 ver 3,8,10
27.12 2 Chr 20.36; Isa 23.6,10; ver 18,33
27.13 Gen 10.2; Isa 66.19; Ezek 38.2; Joel 3.3; Rev 18.13
27.14 Gen 10.3; Ezek 38.6
27.15 Gen 10.7; Rev 18.12
27.16 Ezek 28.13; 16.13,18
27.17 Judg 11.33; Jer 8.22
27.18 Jer 49.23; Ezek 47.16-18; ver 12,33
27.21 Jer 25.24; 49.28; Isa 60.7
27.22 Gen 10.7; 1 Kings 10.1,2; Isa 60.6
27.23 Gen 11.31; 2 Kings 19.12; Am 1.5
27.25 Isa 2.16; 23.14; ver 4
27.26 Ezek 26.19; Ps 48.7; ver 4,25,27
27.27 Prov 11.4; Rev 18.9-19
27.28 Ezek 26.15
27.29 Rev 18.17-19
27.30 Job 2.12; Rev 18.19; Esth 4.1,3; Jer 6.26

27.31 Jer 16.6; Ezek 29.18; Isa 22.12; 16.9
27.32 ver 2; Ezek 26.17; Rev 18.18
27.33 Rev 18.19
27.34 ver 26,27; Ezek 26.19; Zech 9.3,4
27.35 Ezek 26.15,16; 32.10
27.36 Jer 18.16; Zeph 2.15; Ezek 26.21; Ps 37.10,36
28.2 Ezek 27.25-27; Isa 31.3; ver 6
28.3 Dan 1.20
28.4 Ezek 27.33
28.5 Ps 62.10; Zech 9.3; Hos 13.6
28.6 ver 2
28.7 Ezek 26.7; 30.11; 31.12; 32.12; ver 17
28.8 Ezek 32.30; 27.26,27.34
28.9 ver 2
28.10 Ezek 31.18; 32.19,21,25, 27
28.12 Ezek 27.2; ver 3; Ezek 27.3
28.13 Ezek 31.8,9; 36.35
28.14 Ex 25.20; ver 16; Ezek 20.40; Rev 18.16
28.15 Ezek 27.3,4; Isa 14.12; ver 17,18
28.16 Ezek 27.12ff; 8.17; Gen 3.24; ver 14
28.17 ver 2,5; Ezek 31.10; 27.3,4; 26.16

31 they make themselves bald for you,
  and put on sackcloth,
and they weep over you in bitterness of soul,
  with bitter mourning.
32 In their wailing they raise a lamentation for you,
  and lament over you:
"Who was ever destroyed[n] like Tyre
  in the midst of the sea?
33 When your wares came from the seas,
  you satisfied many peoples;
with your abundant wealth and merchandise
  you enriched the kings of the earth.
34 Now you are wrecked by the seas,
  in the depths of the waters;
your merchandise and all your crew
  have sunk with you.
35 All the inhabitants of the coastlands
  are appalled at you;
and their kings are horribly afraid,
  their faces are convulsed.
36 The merchants among the peoples hiss at you;
  you have come to a dreadful end
  and shall be no more forever."

Proclamation against the King of Tyre

28 The word of the LORD came to me:
2Mortal, say to the prince of Tyre,
Thus says the Lord GOD:
Because your heart is proud
  and you have said, "I am a god;
I sit in the seat of the gods,
  in the heart of the seas,"
yet you are but a mortal, and no god,
  though you compare your mind
  with the mind of a god.
3 You are indeed wiser than Daniel;[o]
  no secret is hidden from you;
4 by your wisdom and your understanding
  you have amassed wealth for yourself,
and have gathered gold and silver
  into your treasuries.
5 By your great wisdom in trade
  you have increased your wealth,
  and your heart has become proud in your wealth.
6 Therefore thus says the Lord GOD:
Because you compare your mind
  with the mind of a god,
7 therefore, I will bring strangers against you,
  the most terrible of the nations;
they shall draw their swords against the beauty of your wisdom
  and defile your splendor.
8 They shall thrust you down to the Pit,
  and you shall die a violent death
  in the heart of the seas.
9 Will you still say, "I am a god,"
  in the presence of those who kill you,
though you are but a mortal, and no god,
  in the hands of those who wound you?
10 You shall die the death of the uncircumcised
  by the hand of foreigners;
  for I have spoken, says the Lord GOD.

Lamentation over the King of Tyre

11 Moreover the word of the LORD came
to me: 12Mortal, raise a lamentation over
the king of Tyre, and say to him, Thus says
the Lord GOD:
You were the signet of perfection,[p] full of wisdom and perfect in beauty.
13 You were in Eden, the garden of God;
  every precious stone was your covering,
carnelian, chrysolite, and moonstone,
  beryl, onyx, and jasper,
sapphire,[q] turquoise, and emerald;
  and worked in gold were your settings
  and your engravings.[p]
On the day that you were created
  they were prepared.
14 With an anointed cherub as guardian I placed you;[p]
  you were on the holy mountain of God;
  you walked among the stones of fire.
15 You were blameless in your ways
  from the day that you were created,
  until iniquity was found in you.
16 In the abundance of your trade
  you were filled with violence, and you sinned;
so I cast you as a profane thing from the mountain of God,
  and the guardian cherub drove you out
  from among the stones of fire.
17 Your heart was proud because of your beauty;
  you corrupted your wisdom for the sake of your splendor.
I cast you to the ground;
  I exposed you before kings,

28.1-10 The oracle addressed to *the prince of Tyre* denounces him for his self-deification (*I am a god*) and for his abuse of his wisdom, which exceeds that of *Daniel* (the wise man in documents dating from about 1500 BCE, from Ugarit on the coast of northern Syria), but which he has used primarily for gaining wealth. His death at the hands of *attackers* is foretold. **28.11-19** In this oracle *the king of Tyre* is linked with a creation myth that resembles at several points the creation story of Gen 2. But it goes on to show that the pride of the king's *heart* has *corrupted* his wisdom, so that from his present place of *splendor* he will fall to *a dreadful end*.

[n] Tg Vg: Heb *like silence* [o] Or, as otherwise read, *Danel* [p] Meaning of Heb uncertain [q] Or *lapis lazuli*

28.20-23 Sidon, the second greatest Phoenician city, is told of the *judgment and bloodshed* that God is about to send upon it, which will lead to its recognition of God as *the* LORD.
28.25-26 Contrasting with the oracles of judgment on the nations is this promise of the return of God's people to *their own land*, where they will *live in safety* while disaster falls on the others.
29.1-21 The date assigned to this series of oracles concerning Egypt, *in the twenty-fifth year*, would be 571. The first of the oracles exposes the *Pharaoh* for his claims to divinity (*cf.* the king of Tyre in 28.9), which include designating himself as the one who made *the Nile*. He will be caught like a *fish*, and his body will be exposed to vultures, in order that Egypt may learn not to rely on him as divine. From *Migdol* (in the northern part of the Nile delta) to *Syene* (modern Aswan, about 750 miles upstream [south] from the mouth of the river) the land of Egypt will become a waste for *forty years*, and its people will be scattered *among the nations*. Then they will be restored, though no longer as a world power, but as *the most lowly of the kingdoms*, since God's chastisement of them will have made them aware of *their iniquity* and the power of the LORD. The instrument of God's judgment will be *King Nebuchadrezzar of Babylon*, who will strip the land of its wealth, in contrast to his unrewarding siege of Tyre. His gaining the *land of Egypt* will serve as payment for the service he is doing God by punishing Egypt. A parenthetic note in 29.21 promises that, as a result of this fall of Egypt, Israel will *know that I am the* LORD.

to feast their eyes on you.
18 By the multitude of your iniquities,
in the unrighteousness of your trade,
you profaned your sanctuaries.
So I brought out fire from within you;
it consumed you,
and I turned you to ashes on the earth
in the sight of all who saw you.
19 All who know you among the peoples
are appalled at you;
you have come to a dreadful end
and shall be no more forever.

Proclamation against Sidon

20 The word of the LORD came to me:
21 Mortal, set your face toward Sidon, and
prophesy against it, 22 and say, Thus says
the Lord GOD:
I am against you, O Sidon,
and I will gain glory in your midst.
They shall know that I am the LORD
when I execute judgments in it,
and manifest my holiness in it;
23 for I will send pestilence into it,
and bloodshed into its streets;
and the dead shall fall in its midst,
by the sword that is against it on
every side.
And they shall know that I am the LORD.
24 The house of Israel shall no longer
find a pricking brier or a piercing thorn
among all their neighbors who have treated
them with contempt. And they shall know
that I am the Lord GOD.

Future Blessing for Israel

25 Thus says the Lord GOD: When I gather
the house of Israel from the peoples among
whom they are scattered, and manifest my
holiness in them in the sight of the nations,
then they shall settle on their own soil that
I gave to my servant Jacob. 26 They shall live
in safety in it, and shall build houses and
plant vineyards. They shall live in safety,
when I execute judgments upon all their
neighbors who have treated them with
contempt. And they shall know that I am
the LORD their God.

Proclamation against Egypt

29 In the tenth year, in the tenth
month, on the twelfth day of the
month, the word of the LORD came to me:
2 Mortal, set your face against Pharaoh king
of Egypt, and prophesy against him and
against all Egypt; 3 speak, and say, Thus says
the Lord GOD:
I am against you,
Pharaoh king of Egypt,
the great dragon sprawling
in the midst of its channels,
saying, "My Nile is my own;
I made it for myself."
4 I will put hooks in your jaws,
and make the fish of your channels
stick to your scales.
I will draw you up from your channels,
with all the fish of your channels
sticking to your scales.
5 I will fling you into the wilderness,
you and all the fish of your channels;
you shall fall in the open field,
and not be gathered and buried.
To the animals of the earth and to the
birds of the air
I have given you as food.
6 Then all the inhabitants of Egypt shall
know
that I am the LORD
because you[r] were a staff of reed
to the house of Israel;
7 when they grasped you with the hand,
you broke,
and tore all their shoulders;
and when they leaned on you, you
broke,
and made all their legs unsteady.[s]
8 Therefore, thus says the Lord GOD: I
will bring a sword upon you, and will cut
off from you human being and animal; 9 and
the land of Egypt shall be a desolation and
a waste. Then they shall know that I am
the LORD.
Because you[t] said, "The Nile is mine, and
I made it," 10 therefore, I am against you,
and against your channels, and I will make
the land of Egypt an utter waste and desolation, from Migdol to Syene, as far as the
border of Ethiopia.[u] 11 No human foot shall
pass through it, and no animal foot shall
pass through it; it shall be uninhabited forty
years. 12 I will make the land of Egypt a
desolation among desolated countries; and
her cities shall be a desolation forty years
among cities that are laid waste. I will
scatter the Egyptians among the nations,
and disperse them among the countries.
13 Further, thus says the Lord GOD: At
the end of forty years I will gather the
Egyptians from the peoples among whom

[r] Gk Syr Vg: Heb *they* [s] Syr: Heb *stand* [t] Gk Syr Vg: Heb *he* [u] Or *Nubia*; Heb *Cush*

28.18 ver 16; Am 1.9,10; Mal 4.3
28.19 Ezek 26.21; 27.36; Jer 51.64
28.21 Ezek 6.2; 25.2; Isa 23.4,12; Ezek 32.30
28.22 Ezek 26.3; 39.13; Ps 9.16; ver 26; Ezek 38.16
28.23 Ezek 38.22; Jer 51.52; ver 24,26
28.24 Num 33.55; Josh 23.13; Isa 55.13; Ezek 25.6; 36.5
28.25 Isa 11.12; Jer 32.37; Ezek 20.41; Jer 23.8; 27.11; Ezek 37.25
28.26 Jer 23.6; Isa 65.21; Am 9.13,14
29.2 Ezek 28.21; Jer 44.30; Isa 19.1; Jer 25.19; 46.2,25
29.3 Jer 44.30; Ezek 28.22; Isa 27.1; 51.9; Ezek 32.2
29.4 2 Kings 19.28; Isa 37.29; Ezek 38.4
29.5 Ezek 32.4-6; Jer 7.33; 34.20; Ezek 39.4
29.6 Isa 36.6
29.7 Jer 37.5-11; Ezek 17.17
29.8 Ezek 14.17; 32.11-13
29.10 Ezek 30.12; 30.6
29.11 Jer 43.11,12; Ezek 32.13
29.12 Ezek 30.7,26
29.13 Isa 19.22,23; Jer 46.26

they were scattered; 14 and I will restore the
fortunes of Egypt, and bring them back to
the land of Pathros, the land of their origin;
and there they shall be a lowly kingdom.
15 It shall be the most lowly of the kingdoms,
and never again exalt itself above the nations; and I will make them so small that
they will never again rule over the nations.
16 The Egyptians[v] shall never again be the
reliance of the house of Israel; they will
recall their iniquity, when they turned to
them for aid. Then they shall know that I
am the Lord GOD.

Babylonia Will Plunder Egypt

17 In the twenty-seventh year, in the
first month, on the first day of the month,
the word of the LORD came to me: 18 Mortal,
King Nebuchadrezzar of Babylon made his
army labor hard against Tyre; every head
was made bald and every shoulder was
rubbed bare; yet neither he nor his army
got anything from Tyre to pay for the labor
that he had expended against it. 19 Therefore
thus says the Lord GOD: I will give the land
of Egypt to King Nebuchadrezzar of Babylon;
and he shall carry off its wealth and despoil
it and plunder it; and it shall be the wages
for his army. 20 I have given him the land
of Egypt as his payment for which he labored,
because they worked for me, says the Lord
GOD.

21 On that day I will cause a horn to
sprout up for the house of Israel, and I will
open your lips among them. Then they
shall know that I am the LORD.

Lamentation for Egypt

30 The word of the LORD came to me:
2 Mortal, prophesy, and say, Thus
says the Lord GOD:

Wail, "Alas for the day!"
3 For a day is near,
the day of the LORD is near;
it will be a day of clouds,
a time of doom[w] for the nations.
4 A sword shall come upon Egypt,
and anguish shall be in Ethiopia,[x]
when the slain fall in Egypt,
and its wealth is carried away,
and its foundations are torn down.
5 Ethiopia,[x] and Put, and Lud, and all Arabia,
and Libya,[y] and the people of the allied land[z]
shall fall with them by the sword.

6 Thus says the LORD:
Those who support Egypt shall fall,
and its proud might shall come down;
from Migdol to Syene
they shall fall within it by the sword,
says the Lord GOD.
7 They shall be desolated among other
desolated countries,
and their cities shall lie among cities
laid waste.
8 Then they shall know that I am the LORD,
when I have set fire to Egypt,
and all who help it are broken.

9 On that day, messengers shall go out
from me in ships to terrify the unsuspecting
Ethiopians;[a] and anguish shall come upon
them on the day of Egypt's doom;[b] for it is
coming!

10 Thus says the Lord GOD:
I will put an end to the hordes of Egypt,
by the hand of King Nebuchadrezzar
of Babylon.
11 He and his people with him, the most
terrible of the nations,
shall be brought in to destroy the land;
and they shall draw their swords
against Egypt,
and fill the land with the slain.
12 I will dry up the channels,
and will sell the land into the hand of
evildoers;
I will bring desolation upon the land
and everything in it
by the hand of foreigners;
I the LORD have spoken.

13 Thus says the Lord GOD:
I will destroy the idols
and put an end to the images in
Memphis;
there shall no longer be a prince in the
land of Egypt;
so I will put fear in the land of Egypt.
14 I will make Pathros a desolation,
and will set fire to Zoan,
and will execute acts of judgment on
Thebes.
15 I will pour my wrath upon Pelusium,
the stronghold of Egypt,
and cut off the hordes of Thebes.
16 I will set fire to Egypt;
Pelusium shall be in great agony;
Thebes shall be breached,
and Memphis face adversaries by day.

[v] Heb *It* [w] Heb lacks *of doom* [x] Or *Nubia;* Heb *Cush* [y] Compare Gk Syr Vg: Heb *Cub* [z] Meaning of Heb uncertain [a] Or *Nubians:* Heb *Cush* [b] Heb *the day of Egypt*

30.1-19 Another oracle against Egypt predicts disaster not only for that land but also for *Ethiopia* or Cush to the south, for *Put and Lud* (also in Africa), for *all Arabia* and for *Libya* in north Africa. Repeated is the prediction that these disasters will come through *Nebuchadrezzar of Babylon.* Accompanying the slaughter will be drought, since God will *dry up the channels* of the Nile. The images of the sacred city of *Memphis* will be destroyed, as will *Pathros and Zoan.* Zoan, more commonly known by its Greek name as Tanis, was a major commercial city, a military stronghold, and for a time the royal residence. Other centers which will fall are *Pelusium* (or Sin, on the eastern frontier) and *Thebes* (in Hebrew, "No"), which was 330 miles south (up the Nile) from modern Cairo, and a major center for the worship of Egyptian deities in the second and first millennia BCE. *Tehaphnehes,* or Tahpanes, was a frontier fortress on the border with Israel, where Jeremiah and others sought to escape from Nebuchadrezzar when he invaded Judah (Jer 43.7; 44.1).

29.16 Isa 30.2,3; 36.4,6; Jer 14.10; Hos 8.13; ver 6,9,21

29.18 Jer 27.6; Ezek 26.7,8; 27.31

29.19 Ezek 30.10; Jer 43.10-13; Ezek 30.4

29.20 Isa 45.1-3; Jer 25.9

29.21 Ps 132.17; Ezek 24.27; 33.22; Lk 21.15; Ezek 6.7; ver 6

30.2 Isa 13.6; Ezek 21.12; Joel 1.5,11,13

30.3 Ezek 7.7,12; Joel 2.1; Ob 15; Zeph 1.7; ver 18

30.4 ver 11,5,9; Ezek 29.19

30.5 Jer 25.20,24

30.6 Isa 20.3-6; Ezek 29.10

30.7 Ezek 29.12

30.8 Ezek 29.6,9,16; ver 14,16,5,6

30.9 Isa 18.1,2; Ezek 38.11; 32.9,10

30.10 Ezek 29.19

30.11 Ezek 28.7; ver 4

30.12 Isa 19.5,6; Ezek 29.3,9

30.13 Isa 19.1; Zech 13.2; ver 16; Zech 10.11; Isa 19.16

30.14 Ezek 29.14; Ps 78.12,43; ver 15,16

30.15 Jer 46.25; ver 16

30.20-26 The *eleventh year* would be 587. An oracle predicts the shattering of the power of *Pharaoh of Egypt*, by the *arms of the king of Babylon*. Mention of Pharaoh's *broken arm* may be an allusion to an earlier unsuccessful effort by Egypt to help Israel (Jer 37.5-7).
31.1-18 A lofty *cedar of Lebanon* (which grew to a great height and might live for 2,000 years, and which might be considered superior to the trees in the garden of Eden) is compared with Egypt, which, as a consequence of *its wickedness*, is about to fall at *the hand of the prince of nations*. This humiliation is to serve as a lesson to other nations not to aspire to such grand splendor. The target of the parable is specified: *This is Pharaoh and all his horde*.

17 The young men of On and of Pi-beseth
shall fall by the sword;
and the cities themselves[c] shall go
into captivity.
18 At Tehaphnehes the day shall be dark,
when I break there the dominion of
Egypt,
and its proud might shall come to an end;
the city[d] shall be covered by a cloud,
and its daughter-towns shall go into
captivity.
19 Thus I will execute acts of judgment on
Egypt.
Then they shall know that I am the LORD.

Proclamation against Pharaoh

20 In the eleventh year, in the first month,
on the seventh day of the month, the word
of the LORD came to me: [21]Mortal, I have
broken the arm of Pharaoh king of Egypt;
it has not been bound up for healing or
wrapped with a bandage, so that it may
become strong to wield the sword. [22]There-
fore thus says the Lord GOD: I am against
Pharaoh king of Egypt, and will break his
arms, both the strong arm and the one that
was broken; and I will make the sword fall
from his hand. [23]I will scatter the Egyptians
among the nations, and disperse them
throughout the lands. [24]I will strengthen
the arms of the king of Babylon, and put my
sword in his hand; but I will break the arms
of Pharaoh, and he will groan before him
with the groans of one mortally wounded.
[25]I will strengthen the arms of the king of
Babylon, but the arms of Pharaoh shall fall.
And they shall know that I am the LORD,
when I put my sword into the hand of the
king of Babylon. He shall stretch it out
against the land of Egypt, [26]and I will scatter the Egyptians among the nations and
disperse them throughout the countries. Then
they shall know that I am the LORD.

The Lofty Cedar

31 In the eleventh year, in the third
month, on the first day of the
month, the word of the LORD came to me:
[2]Mortal, say to Pharaoh king of Egypt and
to his hordes:
Whom are you like in your greatness?
3 Consider Assyria, a cedar of Lebanon,
with fair branches and forest shade,
and of great height,
its top among the clouds.[e]
4 The waters nourished it,
the deep made it grow tall,
making its rivers flow[f]
around the place it was planted,
sending forth its streams
to all the trees of the field.
5 So it towered high
above all the trees of the field;
its boughs grew large
and its branches long,
from abundant water in its shoots.
6 All the birds of the air
made their nests in its boughs;
under its branches all the animals of the
field
gave birth to their young;
and in its shade
all great nations lived.
7 It was beautiful in its greatness,
in the length of its branches;
for its roots went down
to abundant water.
8 The cedars in the garden of God could
not rival it,
nor the fir trees equal its boughs;
the plane trees were as nothing
compared with its branches;
no tree in the garden of God
was like it in beauty.
9 I made it beautiful
with its mass of branches,
the envy of all the trees of Eden
that were in the garden of God.

10 Therefore thus says the Lord GOD:
Because it[g] towered high and set its top
among the clouds,[e] and its heart was proud
of its height, [11]I gave it into the hand of the
prince of the nations; he has dealt with it
as its wickedness deserves. I have cast it
out. [12]Foreigners from the most terrible of
the nations have cut it down and left it. On
the mountains and in all the valleys its
branches have fallen, and its boughs lie
broken in all the watercourses of the land;
and all the peoples of the earth went away
from its shade and left it.
13 On its fallen trunk settle
all the birds of the air,
and among its boughs lodge
all the wild animals.
14All this is in order that no trees by the
waters may grow to lofty height or set their
tops among the clouds,[e] and that no trees
that drink water may reach up to them in
height.

[c] Heb *and they* [d] Heb *she* [e] Gk: Heb *thick boughs* [f] Gk: Heb *rivers going* [g] Syr Vg: Heb *you*

30.18 Jer 43.8-13; Ezek 34.27; ver 3
30.19 ver 14,25,26
30.21 Ps 10.15; Jer 46.11
30.22 Ezek 29.3; Ps 37.17
30.23 Ezek 29.12; ver 26
30.24 ver 10,25; Zech 10.12; Zeph 2.12; Ezek 26.15; 21.14,25
30.25 ver 24,22,11; Isa 5.25
30.26 Ezek 29.12
31.2 Ezek 29.19; 30.10; ver 18
31.3 Nah 3.1ff; Ezek 17.23; ver 5,10
31.4 Ezek 17.5,8; Rev 17.1,15
31.5 Ps 37.35; Ezek 17.5
31.6 Ezek 17.23; Dan 4.12; Mt 13.32; Mk 4.32; Lk 13.19
31.8 Gen 2.8; 13.10; Ezek 28.13; ver 16,18
31.10 Isa 14.13,14; Ezek 28.17; Dan 5.20
31.11 Ezek 30.10,11; Nah 3.18
31.12 Ezek 28.7; Hab 1.6; Ezek 32.5; 35.8; Nah 3.17,18
31.13 Isa 18.6; Ezek 32.4
31.14 ver 16,17; Ps 63.9; ver 18; Ezek 32.24

For all of them are handed over to
death,
to the world below;
along with all mortals,
with those who go down to the Pit.

15 Thus says the Lord GOD: On the day
it went down to Sheol I closed the deep over
it and covered it; I restrained its rivers, and
its mighty waters were checked. I clothed
Lebanon in gloom for it, and all the trees
of the field fainted because of it. 16 I made the
nations quake at the sound of its fall, when
I cast it down to Sheol with those who go
down to the Pit; and all the trees of Eden,
the choice and best of Lebanon, all that
were well watered, were consoled in the
world below. 17 They also went down to
Sheol with it, to those killed by the sword,
along with its allies,[h] those who lived in its
shade among the nations.

18 Which among the trees of Eden was
like you in glory and in greatness? Now you
shall be brought down with the trees of
Eden to the world below; you shall lie among
the uncircumcised, with those who are killed
by the sword. This is Pharaoh and all his
horde, says the Lord GOD.

Lamentation over Pharaoh and Egypt

32 In the twelfth year, in the twelfth month, on the first day of the month, the word of the LORD came to me:
2 Mortal, raise a lamentation over Pharaoh king of Egypt, and say to him:

You consider yourself a lion among the
nations,
but you are like a dragon in the seas;
you thrash about in your streams,
trouble the water with your feet,
and foul your[i] streams.

3 Thus says the Lord GOD:
In an assembly of many peoples
I will throw my net over you;
and I[j] will haul you up in my
dragnet.

4 I will throw you on the ground,
on the open field I will fling you,
and will cause all the birds of the air to
settle on you,
and I will let the wild animals of the
whole earth gorge themselves
with you.

5 I will strew your flesh on the
mountains,
and fill the valleys with your carcass.[k]

6 I will drench the land with your flowing
blood
up to the mountains,
and the watercourses will be filled
with you.

7 When I blot you out, I will cover the
heavens,
and make their stars dark;
I will cover the sun with a cloud,
and the moon shall not give its light.

8 All the shining lights of the heavens
I will darken above you,
and put darkness on your land,
says the Lord GOD.

9 I will trouble the hearts of many
peoples,
as I carry you captive[l] among the
nations,
into countries you have not known.

10 I will make many peoples appalled at you;
their kings shall shudder because of
you.
When I brandish my sword before them,
they shall tremble every moment
for their lives, each one of them,
on the day of your downfall.

11 For thus says the Lord GOD:
The sword of the king of Babylon shall
come against you.

12 I will cause your hordes to fall
by the swords of mighty ones,
all of them most terrible among the
nations.
They shall bring to ruin the pride of
Egypt,
and all its hordes shall perish.

13 I will destroy all its livestock
from beside abundant waters;
and no human foot shall trouble them
any more,
nor shall the hoofs of cattle trouble
them.

14 Then I will make their waters clear,
and cause their streams to run like
oil, says the Lord GOD.

15 When I make the land of Egypt desolate
and when the land is stripped of all
that fills it,
when I strike down all who live in it,
then they shall know that I am the
LORD.

16 This is a lamentation; it shall be
chanted.
The women of the nations shall chant it.

[h] Heb *its arms* [i] Heb *their* [j] Gk Vg: Heb *they* [k] Symmachus Syr Vg: Heb *your height* [l] Gk: Heb *bring your destruction*

31.15 Ezek 32.7; Nah 2.10
31.16 Ezek 26.15; Isa 14.15; Ezek 32.18; Isa 14.8; Ezek 32.31
31.17 Ps 9.17; Ezek 32.18-20
31.18 Ezek 32.19; ver 8,9,14; Ezek 28.10; 32.19,21
32.2 Ezek 27.2; 19.3,6; 38.13; 34.18
32.3 Ezek 12.13; 17.20; Hos 7.12
32.4 Ezek 29.5; 31.13; Isa 18.6
32.6 Ezek 35.6; Rev 14.20
32.7 Prov 13.9; Isa 34.4; 13.10; Joel 2.31; 3.15; Am 8.9; Mt 24.29; Rev 6.12,13
32.9 Ezek 28.19; Rev 18.10-15; Ex 15.14-16
32.10 Ezek 27.35; 26.16; Jer 46.10
32.11 Jer 46.26; Ezek 30.4
32.12 Ezek 28.7; 31.12; 30.18
32.13 Ezek 29.8,11
32.15 Ezek 29.12,19,20; Ps 9.16; Ezek 6.7
32.16 2 Sam 1.17; 2 Chr 35.25; Ezek 26.17

32.1-16 Here the image of Egypt's fall under God's judgment changes to the capture and killing of a wild animal, the corpse of which will feed birds of prey and wild animals. Life-giving water and light are cut off from Egypt when the *king of Babylon* defeats and desolates it. This *lamentation* for Egypt is to be *chanted.*

32.17-32 The dead from Egypt find on arrival in *the Pit* (the abode of the dead; also known as *Sheol*) that other formerly great nations have preceded them: *Assyria, Elam* (an area east of the Tigris on the border of modern Persia), *Meshech* and *Tubal* (names also found in the genealogy of Gen 10, but which here refer to districts in the mountain region of Asia Minor). Other fallen nations in the Pit are closer neighbors of Israel: *Edom* (south of the Dead Sea) and *Sidon* (on the coast of modern Lebanon). The death of *Pharaoh and all his multitude* brings to these other fallen nations a kind of consolation.
33.1-48.35 Ezekiel's Messages for the Future of Israel.
33.1-9 Ezekiel is the sentry promised by God to warn the people of impending disaster. Those who ignore his message will *surely die.*

Over Egypt and all its hordes they shall
 chant it,
says the Lord GOD.

Dirge over Egypt

17 In the twelfth year, in the first month,[m] on the fifteenth day of the month, the word of the LORD came to me:

18 Mortal, wail over the hordes of Egypt,
 and send them down,
with Egypt[n] and the daughters of
 majestic nations,
 to the world below,
 with those who go down to the Pit.
19 "Whom do you surpass in beauty?
 Go down! Be laid to rest with the
 uncircumcised!"

20They shall fall among those who are killed by the sword. Egypt[n] has been handed over to the sword; carry away both it and its hordes. 21The mighty chiefs shall speak of them, with their helpers, out of the midst of Sheol: "They have come down, they lie still, the uncircumcised, killed by the sword."

22 Assyria is there, and all its company, their graves all around it, all of them killed, fallen by the sword. 23Their graves are set in the uttermost parts of the Pit. Its company is all around its grave, all of them killed, fallen by the sword, who spread terror in the land of the living.

24 Elam is there, and all its hordes around its grave; all of them killed, fallen by the sword, who went down uncircumcised into the world below, who spread terror in the land of the living. They bear their shame with those who go down to the Pit. 25They have made Elam[n] a bed among the slain with all its hordes, their graves all around it, all of them uncircumcised, killed by the sword; for terror of them was spread in the land of the living, and they bear their shame with those who go down to the Pit; they are placed among the slain.

26 Meshech and Tubal are there, and all their multitude, their graves all around them, all of them uncircumcised, killed by the sword; for they spread terror in the land of the living. 27And they do not lie with the fallen warriors of long ago[o] who went down to Sheol with their weapons of war, whose swords were laid under their heads, and whose shields[p] are upon their bones; for the terror of the warriors was in the land of the living. 28So you shall be broken and lie among the uncircumcised, with those who are killed by the sword.

29 Edom is there, its kings and all its princes, who for all their might are laid with those who are killed by the sword; they lie with the uncircumcised, with those who go down to the Pit.

30 The princes of the north are there, all of them, and all the Sidonians, who have gone down in shame with the slain, for all the terror that they caused by their might; they lie uncircumcised with those who are killed by the sword, and bear their shame with those who go down to the Pit.

31 When Pharaoh sees them, he will be consoled for all his hordes—Pharaoh and all his army, killed by the sword, says the Lord GOD. 32For he[q] spread terror in the land of the living; therefore he shall be laid to rest among the uncircumcised, with those who are slain by the sword—Pharaoh and all his multitude, says the Lord GOD.

Ezekiel Israel's Sentry

33 The word of the LORD came to me: 2O Mortal, speak to your people and say to them, If I bring the sword upon a land, and the people of the land take one of their number as their sentinel; 3and if the sentinel sees the sword coming upon the land and blows the trumpet and warns the people; 4then if any who hear the sound of the trumpet do not take warning, and the sword comes and takes them away, their blood shall be upon their own heads. 5They heard the sound of the trumpet and did not take warning; their blood shall be upon themselves. But if they had taken warning, they would have saved their lives. 6But if the sentinel sees the sword coming and does not blow the trumpet, so that the people are not warned, and the sword comes and takes any of them, they are taken away in their iniquity, but their blood I will require at the sentinel's hand.

7 So you, mortal, I have made a sentinel for the house of Israel; whenever you hear a word from my mouth, you shall give them warning from me. 8If I say to the wicked, "O wicked ones, you shall surely die," and you do not speak to warn the wicked to turn from their ways, the wicked shall die in their iniquity, but their blood I

[m] Gk: Heb lacks *in the first month* [n] Heb *it* [o] Gk Old Latin: Heb *of the uncircumcised* [p] Cn: Heb *iniquities* [q] Cn: Heb *I*

32.18 ver 2,16; Mic 1.8; Ezek 26.20; 31.14; ver 24
32.19 Ezek 31.2,18; 28.10; ver 21,24,29
32.21 Isa 1.31; 14.9,10; ver 27,31,32
32.22 Ezek 31.3,16
32.23 Isa 14.15; ver 24-27,32
32.24 Jer 49.34-39; Ps 27.13; Isa 38.11; Jer 11.19; ver 25,30
32.25 Ps 139.8; ver 19,23,24
32.26 Gen 10.2; Ezek 27.13; 38.2; ver 19,32
32.27 Isa 14.18,19,21,23
32.29 Isa 34.5-15; Jer 49.7-22; Ezek 25.13
32.30 Ezek 38.6,15; 39.2; 28.21
33.2 Ezek 3.11; Jer 12.12; Zech 13.7; 2 Sam 18.24,25; 2 Kings 9.17
33.3 Hos 8.1; Joel 2.1
33.4 Jer 6.17; Zech 1.4; Ezek 18.13; Acts 18.6
33.5 Heb 11.7
33.6 Isa 56.10,11; ver 8; Ezek 3.18,20
33.7 Ezek 3.17-21; Jer 26.2; Acts 5.20

33.9 Acts 13.40,41,46; Ezek 3.19,21
33.10 Ezek 18.2; 24.23; Ezek 37.11
33.11 2 Sam 14.14; Ezek 18.23,32; 2 Pet 3.9; Ezek 18.30,31
33.12 Ezek 3.20; 2 Chr 7.14
33.13 Ezek 3.20; 18.24; 2 Pet 2.20,21
33.14 Ezek 3.18,19; 18.27
33.15 Lev 6.2,4,5; Num 5.6,7; Lk 19.8; Ezek 20.11
33.16 Ezek 18.22
33.18 Ezek 18.26
33.19 ver 12,14
33.20 Ezek 18.25; ver 17
33.21 Ezek 1.2; 24.26; 2 Kings 25.4
33.22 Ezek 1.3; 24.27; Lk 1.64
33.24 Ezek 36.4; Isa 51.2; Acts 7.5
33.25 Deut 12.16; Ezek 20.24; 22.6,9
33.26 Ezek 18.6; 22.11
33.27 Ezek 39.4; 1 Sam 13.6; Isa 2.19
33.28 Jer 44.2,6,22; Ezek 7.24; 36.34,35
33.29 Ezek 23.33,35
33.31 Ezek 14.1; 20.1; 8.1; Ps 78.36,37; Isa 29.13; Mt 13.22
33.33 1 Sam 3.20; Ezek 2.5

will require at your hand. 9But if you warn the wicked to turn from their ways, and they do not turn from their ways, the wicked shall die in their iniquity, but you will have saved your life.

God's Justice and Mercy

10 Now you, mortal, say to the house of Israel, Thus you have said: "Our transgressions and our sins weigh upon us, and we waste away because of them; how then can we live?" 11Say to them, As I live, says the Lord GOD, I have no pleasure in the death of the wicked, but that the wicked turn from their ways and live; turn back, turn back from your evil ways; for why will you die, O house of Israel? 12And you, mortal, say to your people, The righteousness of the righteous shall not save them when they transgress; and as for the wickedness of the wicked, it shall not make them stumble when they turn from their wickedness; and the righteous shall not be able to live by their righteousness[r] when they sin. 13Though I say to the righteous that they shall surely live, yet if they trust in their righteousness and commit iniquity, none of their righteous deeds shall be remembered; but in the iniquity that they have committed they shall die. 14Again, though I say to the wicked, "You shall surely die," yet if they turn from their sin and do what is lawful and right—15if the wicked restore the pledge, give back what they have taken by robbery, and walk in the statutes of life, committing no iniquity—they shall surely live, they shall not die. 16None of the sins that they have committed shall be remembered against them; they have done what is lawful and right, they shall surely live.

17 Yet your people say, "The way of the Lord is not just," when it is their own way that is not just. 18When the righteous turn from their righteousness, and commit iniquity, they shall die for it.[s] 19And when the wicked turn from their wickedness, and do what is lawful and right, they shall live by it.[s] 20Yet you say, "The way of the Lord is not just." O house of Israel, I will judge all of you according to your ways!

The Fall of Jerusalem

21 In the twelfth year of our exile, in the tenth month, on the fifth day of the month, someone who had escaped from Jerusalem came to me and said, "The city has fallen." 22Now the hand of the LORD had been upon me the evening before the fugitive came; but he had opened my mouth by the time the fugitive came to me in the morning; so my mouth was opened, and I was no longer unable to speak.

The Survivors in Judah

23 The word of the LORD came to me: 24Mortal, the inhabitants of these waste places in the land of Israel keep saying, "Abraham was only one man, yet he got possession of the land; but we are many; the land is surely given us to possess." 25Therefore say to them, Thus says the Lord GOD: You eat flesh with the blood, and lift up your eyes to your idols, and shed blood; shall you then possess the land? 26You depend on your swords, you commit abominations, and each of you defiles his neighbor's wife; shall you then possess the land? 27Say this to them, Thus says the Lord GOD: As I live, surely those who are in the waste places shall fall by the sword; and those who are in the open field I will give to the wild animals to be devoured; and those who are in strongholds and in caves shall die by pestilence. 28I will make the land a desolation and a waste, and its proud might shall come to an end; and the mountains of Israel shall be so desolate that no one will pass through. 29Then they shall know that I am the LORD, when I have made the land a desolation and a waste because of all their abominations that they have committed.

30 As for you, mortal, your people who talk together about you by the walls, and at the doors of the houses, say to one another, each to a neighbor, "Come and hear what the word is that comes from the LORD." 31They come to you as people come, and they sit before you as my people, and they hear your words, but they will not obey them. For flattery is on their lips, but their heart is set on their gain. 32To them you are like a singer of love songs,[t] one who has a beautiful voice and plays well on an instrument; they hear what you say, but they will not do it. 33When this comes—and come it will!—then they shall know that a prophet has been among them.

[r] Heb *by it* [s] Heb *them* [t] Cn: Heb *like a love song*

33.10-20 The charge that God is unjust to punish Israel and destroy many of his people is met by the message that the crucial factor is the response of the individual to God's call to righteousness: those who obey will find life, and those who pursue *wickedness* will die.
33.21-33 Following the rumor of the siege of Jerusalem (24.1-2) comes the direct report of its fall *in the twelfth year*, which is 586. Ezekiel is reminded of the futility of his message to the people of Judah, who have come claiming to seek *the word from the LORD*, but in fact ignoring it in their disobedient manner of life.

34.1-31 The failure to provide for the needs of the people of Israel by its self-serving leaders (*shepherds*) resulted in their present plight and dispersion, and God will hold the former leaders accountable. God promises to be the true and faithful shepherd, seeking out the sheep (*Israel*), feeding them and restoring them. The sheep, however, must behave properly and submit to the *one shepherd*, a descendant of David, whom God will place over them. In this new situation there will be peace and prosperity, as well as *safety* from attack by other nations. Then Israel will truly know their God.

Israel's False Shepherds

34 The word of the LORD came to me:
2Mortal, prophesy against the shepherds of Israel: prophesy, and say to them—
to the shepherds: Thus says the Lord GOD:
Ah, you shepherds of Israel who have been
feeding yourselves! Should not shepherds
feed the sheep? 3You eat the fat, you clothe
yourselves with the wool, you slaughter the
fatlings; but you do not feed the sheep. 4You
have not strengthened the weak, you have
not healed the sick, you have not bound up
the injured, you have not brought back the
strayed, you have not sought the lost, but
with force and harshness you have ruled
them. 5So they were scattered, because there
was no shepherd; and scattered, they became food for all the wild animals. 6My
sheep were scattered, they wandered over
all the mountains and on every high hill;
my sheep were scattered over all the face of
the earth, with no one to search or seek for
them.
7 Therefore, you shepherds, hear the word
of the LORD: 8As I live, says the Lord GOD,
because my sheep have become a prey, and
my sheep have become food for all the wild
animals, since there was no shepherd; and
because my shepherds have not searched
for my sheep, but the shepherds have fed
themselves, and have not fed my sheep;
9therefore, you shepherds, hear the word of
the LORD: 10Thus says the Lord GOD, I am
against the shepherds; and I will demand
my sheep at their hand, and put a stop to
their feeding the sheep; no longer shall the
shepherds feed themselves. I will rescue my
sheep from their mouths, so that they may
not be food for them.

God, the True Shepherd

11 For thus says the Lord GOD: I myself
will search for my sheep, and will seek them
out. 12As shepherds seek out their flocks
when they are among their scattered sheep,
so I will seek out my sheep. I will rescue
them from all the places to which they have
been scattered on a day of clouds and thick
darkness. 13I will bring them out from the
peoples and gather them from the countries, and will bring them into their own
land; and I will feed them on the mountains
of Israel, by the watercourses, and in all the
inhabited parts of the land. 14I will feed
them with good pasture, and the mountain
heights of Israel shall be their pasture; there
they shall lie down in good grazing land,
and they shall feed on rich pasture on the
mountains of Israel. 15I myself will be the
shepherd of my sheep, and I will make them
lie down, says the Lord GOD. 16I will seek the
lost, and I will bring back the strayed, and
I will bind up the injured, and I will
strengthen the weak, but the fat and the
strong I will destroy. I will feed them with
justice.
17 As for you, my flock, thus says the
Lord GOD: I shall judge between sheep and
sheep, between rams and goats: 18Is it not
enough for you to feed on the good pasture,
but you must tread down with your feet the
rest of your pasture? When you drink of
clear water, must you foul the rest with
your feet? 19And must my sheep eat what
you have trodden with your feet, and drink
what you have fouled with your feet?
20 Therefore, thus says the Lord GOD to
them: I myself will judge between the fat
sheep and the lean sheep. 21Because you
pushed with flank and shoulder, and butted
at all the weak animals with your horns
until you scattered them far and wide, 22I
will save my flock, and they shall no longer
be ravaged; and I will judge between sheep
and sheep.
23 I will set up over them one shepherd,
my servant David, and he shall feed them:
he shall feed them and be their shepherd.
24And I, the LORD, will be their God, and my
servant David shall be prince among them;
I, the LORD, have spoken.
25 I will make with them a covenant of
peace and banish wild animals from the
land, so that they may live in the wild and
sleep in the woods securely. 26I will make
them and the region around my hill a
blessing; and I will send down the showers
in their season; they shall be showers of
blessing. 27The trees of the field shall yield
their fruit, and the earth shall yield its
increase. They shall be secure on their soil;
and they shall know that I am the LORD,
when I break the bars of their yoke, and
save them from the hands of those who
enslaved them. 28They shall no more be
plunder for the nations, nor shall the animals of the land devour them; they shall
live in safety, and no one shall make them
afraid. 29I will provide for them a splendid
vegetation so that they shall no more be
consumed with hunger in the land, and no
longer suffer the insults of the nations. 30They
shall know that I, the LORD their God, am

34.2 Jer 10.21; ver 8-10,14,15; Jn 10.11; 21.15-17
34.3 Isa 56.11; Zech 11.16; Ezek 22.25,27
34.4 Zech 11.16; Mt 9.36; Lk 15.4; 1 Pet 5.3
34.5 Jer 10.21; 50.6,7; Jer 23.2; Mt 9.36
34.8 Acts 20.29; ver 5,6,2
34.10 Ezek 3.18; Heb 13.17; ver 2,8
34.11 Ezek 11.17; 20.41
34.12 Jn 10.16; Ezek 30.3; Joel 2.2
34.13 Isa 65.9,10; Jer 23.3; Ezek 37.22; Isa 30.25
34.14 Ps 23.1,2; Ezek 20.40; 28.25,26
34.16 Mt 18.11; Lk 5.32; Isa 49.26
34.17 Ezek 20.37,38; Zech 10.3; Mt 25.32,33
34.23 Isa 40.11; Jer 23.4,5; 30.9; Hos 3.5
34.24 Ezek 36.28; 37.27; 37.24,25; Hos 3.5
34.25 Isa 11.6-9; Hos 2.18; Jer 23.6
34.26 Isa 56.7; Zech 8.13
34.27 Ps 85.12; Isa 4.2; Jer 2.20
34.28 Jer 30.10
34.29 Isa 60.21; Ezek 36.29; 36.3,6

with them, and that they, the house of
Israel, are my people, says the Lord GOD.
31 You are my sheep, the sheep of my pasture[u]
and I am your God, says the Lord GOD.

Judgment on Mount Seir

35 The word of the LORD came to me:
2 Mortal, set your face against
Mount Seir, and prophesy against it, 3 and
say to it, Thus says the Lord GOD:
I am against you, Mount Seir;
I stretch out my hand against you
to make you a desolation and a waste.
4 I lay your towns in ruins;
you shall become a desolation,
and you shall know that I am the LORD.
5 Because you cherished an ancient enmity,
and gave over the people of Israel to the
power of the sword at the time of their
calamity, at the time of their final punishment; 6 therefore, as I live, says the Lord
GOD, I will prepare you for blood, and blood
shall pursue you; since you did not hate
bloodshed, bloodshed shall pursue you. 7 I
will make Mount Seir a waste and a desolation; and I will cut off from it all who
come and go. 8 I will fill its mountains with
the slain; on your hills and in your valleys
and in all your watercourses those killed
with the sword shall fall. 9 I will make you
a perpetual desolation, and your cities shall
never be inhabited. Then you shall know
that I am the LORD.
10 Because you said, "These two nations
and these two countries shall be mine, and
we will take possession of them,"—although
the LORD was there— 11 therefore, as I live,
says the Lord GOD, I will deal with you
according to the anger and envy that you
showed because of your hatred against them;
and I will make myself known among you,[v]
when I judge you. 12 You shall know that I,
the LORD, have heard all the abusive speech
that you uttered against the mountains of
Israel, saying, "They are laid desolate, they
are given us to devour." 13 And you magnified yourselves against me with your mouth,
and multiplied your words against me; I
heard it. 14 Thus says the Lord God: As the
whole earth rejoices, I will make you desolate. 15 As you rejoiced over the inheritance
of the house of Israel, because it was desolate, so I will deal with you; you shall be
desolate, Mount Seir, and all Edom, all of it.
Then they shall know that I am the LORD.

Blessing on Israel

36 And you, mortal, prophesy to the
mountains of Israel, and say: O
mountains of Israel, hear the word of the
LORD. 2 Thus says the Lord GOD: Because the
enemy said of you, "Aha!" and, "The ancient heights have become our possession,"
3 therefore prophesy, and say: Thus says the
Lord GOD: Because they made you desolate
indeed, and crushed you from all sides, so
that you became the possession of the rest
of the nations, and you became an object
of gossip and slander among the people;
4 therefore, O mountains of Israel, hear the
word of the Lord GOD: Thus says the Lord
GOD to the mountains and the hills, the
watercourses and the valleys, the desolate
wastes and the deserted towns, which have
become a source of plunder and an object
of derision to the rest of the nations all
around; 5 therefore thus says the Lord GOD:
I am speaking in my hot jealousy against
the rest of the nations, and against all
Edom, who, with wholehearted joy and
utter contempt, took my land as their possession, because of its pasture, to plunder it.
6 Therefore prophesy concerning the land of
Israel, and say to the mountains and hills,
to the watercourses and valleys, Thus says
the Lord GOD: I am speaking in my jealous
wrath, because you have suffered the insults of the nations; 7 therefore thus says the
Lord GOD: I swear that the nations that are
all around you shall themselves suffer insults.
8 But you, O mountains of Israel, shall
shoot out your branches, and yield your
fruit to my people Israel; for they shall soon
come home. 9 See now, I am for you; I will
turn to you, and you shall be tilled and
sown; 10 and I will multiply your population,
the whole house of Israel, all of it; the towns
shall be inhabited and the waste places
rebuilt; 11 and I will multiply human beings
and animals upon you. They shall increase
and be fruitful; and I will cause you to be
inhabited as in your former times, and will
do more good to you than ever before. Then
you shall know that I am the LORD. 12 I will
lead people upon you—my people Israel—
and they shall possess you, and you shall
be their inheritance. No longer shall you
bereave them of children.
13 Thus says the Lord GOD: Because they
say to you, "You devour people, and you
bereave your nation of children," 14 there-

[u] Gk OL: Heb *pasture, you are people* [v] Gk: Heb *them*

34.31 Ps 100.3; Jn 10.11
35.2 Jer 49.7,8
35.5 Ezek 25.12; Ob 10; Ezek 7.2; 21.25,29
35.7 Ezek 25.13; 29.11
35.8 Isa 34.5,6; Ezek 31.12; 32.4,5
35.9 Jer 49.13; Ezek 6.7; 36.11
35.10 Ezek 36.2,5; Ps 48.1,3; Ezek 48.35
35.11 Am 1.11; Mt 7.2; Ps 9.16
35.13 Ezek 36.3; Jer 7.11; 29.23
35.14 Isa 49.13; Jer 51.48
35.15 Jer 50.11; Ob 4,21; Ezek 6.7
36.2 Ezek 25.3; Hab 3.19; Ezek 35.10
36.3 Jer 2.15; 51.34; 18.16; Ezek 35.13
36.4 Ezek 6.3; 34.28; Ps 79.4; Jer 48.27
36.5 Ezek 38.19; 25.12-14; 35.10,12; Jer 50.11; Mic 7.8
36.6 Ps 123.3,4; Ezek 34.29
36.10 Isa 27.6; Ezek 32.21,22; ver 33
36.11 Jer 30.18; Ezek 16.55; 35.9

35.1-15 The oracle of judgment against *Mount Seir* (a high mountain east of the rift below the Dead Sea and a symbol for the people of Edom) is the result of the Edomites' persistent efforts to exploit the difficulties experienced by Israel and Judah (*two nations*). As a result of this greedy attitude, Edom shall become *desolate*.
36.1-38 The renewal of *the mountains of Israel* (symbolizing the land and its people) will compensate for the desolation and exploitation of its lands by hostile nations and will backfire on them so that they will receive *insults*. Instead of the disaster hoped for by its enemies, Israel will be fruitful in population and produce, and a rewarding place of residence for God's people. The past misdeeds and their consequences are rehearsed here, but the renewal of the people will be a testimony – not only to them, but also to the nations which God used as instruments to discipline Israel. The restored land will resemble *the garden of Eden*, and the ruined towns will be filled with *flocks of people*.

37.1-28 Two vivid images depict the reconstitution of Israel: (1) the reassembling and restoration to life of bare human bones scattered across a valley, and (2) the joining together of two sticks as a symbol of the reuniting of the divided peoples of Israel (called here *Joseph and Ephraim*) and *Judah*. There will be a single Davidic ruler over the united kingdom, and the people will be joined in a *covenant of peace*, worshiping *their God* at a single sanctuary. This passage provides an effective preparation for the description of the rebuilt temple and the reassignment of tribal lands in 40.1-48.35, but an extended apocalyptic passage, Ezek 38-39, has been inserted by a later writer-editor; *cf.* Isa 14-27; Dan 7-11.

fore you shall no longer devour people and no longer bereave your nation of children, says the Lord GOD; 15 and no longer will I let you hear the insults of the nations, no longer shall you bear the disgrace of the peoples; and no longer shall you cause your nation to stumble, says the Lord GOD.

The Renewal of Israel

16 The word of the LORD came to me: 17 Mortal, when the house of Israel lived on their own soil, they defiled it with their ways and their deeds; their conduct in my sight was like the uncleanness of a woman in her menstrual period. 18 So I poured out my wrath upon them for the blood that they had shed upon the land, and for the idols with which they had defiled it. 19 I scattered them among the nations, and they were dispersed through the countries; in accordance with their conduct and their deeds I judged them. 20 But when they came to the nations, wherever they came, they profaned my holy name, in that it was said of them, "These are the people of the LORD, and yet they had to go out of his land." 21 But I had concern for my holy name, which the house of Israel had profaned among the nations to which they came.

22 Therefore say to the house of Israel, Thus says the Lord GOD: It is not for your sake, O house of Israel, that I am about to act, but for the sake of my holy name, which you have profaned among the nations to which you came. 23 I will sanctify my great name, which has been profaned among the nations, and which you have profaned among them; and the nations shall know that I am the LORD, says the Lord GOD, when through you I display my holiness before their eyes. 24 I will take you from the nations, and gather you from all the countries, and bring you into your own land. 25 I will sprinkle clean water upon you, and you shall be clean from all your uncleannesses, and from all your idols I will cleanse you. 26 A new heart I will give you, and a new spirit I will put within you; and I will remove from your body the heart of stone and give you a heart of flesh. 27 I will put my spirit within you, and make you follow my statutes and be careful to observe my ordinances. 28 Then you shall live in the land that I gave to your ancestors; and you shall be my people, and I will be your God. 29 I will save you from all your uncleannesses, and I will summon the grain and make it abundant and lay no famine upon you. 30 I will make the fruit of the tree and the produce of the field abundant, so that you may never again suffer the disgrace of famine among the nations. 31 Then you shall remember your evil ways, and your dealings that were not good; and you shall loathe yourselves for your iniquities and your abominable deeds. 32 It is not for your sake that I will act, says the Lord GOD; let that be known to you. Be ashamed and dismayed for your ways, O house of Israel.

33 Thus says the Lord GOD: On the day that I cleanse you from all your iniquities, I will cause the towns to be inhabited, and the waste places shall be rebuilt. 34 The land that was desolate shall be tilled, instead of being the desolation that it was in the sight of all who passed by. 35 And they will say, "This land that was desolate has become like the garden of Eden; and the waste and desolate and ruined towns are now inhabited and fortified." 36 Then the nations that are left all around you shall know that I, the LORD, have rebuilt the ruined places, and replanted that which was desolate; I, the LORD, have spoken, and I will do it.

37 Thus says the Lord GOD: I will also let the house of Israel ask me to do this for them: to increase their population like a flock. 38 Like the flock for sacrifices,[w] like the flock at Jerusalem during her appointed festivals, so shall the ruined towns be filled with flocks of people. Then they shall know that I am the LORD.

The Valley of Dry Bones

37 The hand of the LORD came upon me, and he brought me out by the spirit of the LORD and set me down in the middle of a valley; it was full of bones. 2 He led me all around them; there were very many lying in the valley, and they were very dry. 3 He said to me, "Mortal, can these bones live?" I answered, "O Lord GOD, you know." 4 Then he said to me, "Prophesy to these bones, and say to them: O dry bones, hear the word of the LORD. 5 Thus says the Lord GOD to these bones: I will cause breath[x] to enter you, and you shall live. 6 I will lay sinews on you, and will cause flesh to come upon you, and cover you with skin, and put breath[x] in you, and you shall live; and you

[w] Heb *flock of holy things* [x] Or *spirit*

36.15 Ezek 34.29; 22.4; Jer 13.16; 18.15
36.17 Lev 18.25,26,28; Jer 2.7
36.18 Ezek 22.20; 16.36-38; 23.37
36.19 Am 9.9; Ezek 39.24; Rom 2.6
36.20 Isa 52.5; Rom 2.24; Jer 33.24
36.21 Ps 74.18; Isa 48.9; Ezek 20.44
36.22 Ps 106.8
36.23 Ezek 20.41; Ps 126.2; Ezek 28.25; 39.27
36.24 Ezek 34.13; 37.21
36.25 Isa 52.15; Heb 10.22; Zech 13.1
36.26 Ps 51.10; Ezek 11.19
36.27 Ezek 11.19; 37.14
36.28 Jer 30.22; Ezek 11.20; 37.27
36.29 Zech 13.1; 36.20; Ezek 34.27,29; Hos 2.21-23
36.31 Ezek 16.61-63; 20.43; 6.9
36.32 Ezek 20.44; ver 22
36.35 Isa 51.3; Ezek 31.9; Joel 2.3
36.36 Ezek 39.27,28; 22.14; 37.14
36.38 1 Kings 8.63; ver 33-35; Zech 11.17
37.1 Ezek 1.3; 8.3; 11.24; Lk 4.1; Acts 8.39
37.3 Isa 26.19; Deut 32.39; 1 Sam 2.6
37.5 Ps 104.29,30; ver 9,10
37.6 ver 8-10; Ezek 6.7; 35.12; Joel 2.27; 3.17

shall know that I am the LORD."

7 So I prophesied as I had been commanded; and as I prophesied, suddenly there was a noise, a rattling, and the bones came together, bone to its bone. [8]I looked, and there were sinews on them, and flesh had come upon them, and skin had covered them; but there was no breath in them. [9]Then he said to me, "Prophesy to the breath, prophesy, mortal, and say to the breath:[x] Thus says the Lord GOD: Come from the four winds, O breath,[y] and breathe upon these slain, that they may live." [10]I prophesied as he commanded me, and the breath came into them, and they lived, and stood on their feet, a vast multitude.

11 Then he said to me, "Mortal, these bones are the whole house of Israel. They say, 'Our bones are dried up, and our hope is lost; we are cut off completely.' [12]Therefore prophesy, and say to them, Thus says the Lord GOD: I am going to open your graves, and bring you up from your graves, O my people; and I will bring you back to the land of Israel. [13]And you shall know that I am the LORD, when I open your graves, and bring you up from your graves, O my people. [14]I will put my spirit within you, and you shall live, and I will place you on your own soil; then you shall know that I, the LORD, have spoken and will act," says the LORD.

The Two Sticks

15 The word of the LORD came to me: [16]Mortal, take a stick and write on it, "For Judah, and the Israelites associated with it"; then take another stick and write on it, "For Joseph (the stick of Ephraim) and all the house of Israel associated with it"; [17]and join them together into one stick, so that they may become one in your hand. [18]And when your people say to you, "Will you not show us what you mean by these?" [19]say to them, Thus says the Lord GOD: I am about to take the stick of Joseph (which is in the hand of Ephraim) and the tribes of Israel associated with it; and I will put the stick of Judah upon it,[z] and make them one stick, in order that they may be one in my hand. [20]When the sticks on which you write are in your hand before their eyes, [21]then say to them, Thus says the Lord GOD: I will take the people of Israel from the nations among which they have gone, and will gather them from every quarter, and bring them to their own land. [22]I will make them one nation in the land, on the mountains of Israel; and one king shall be king over them all. Never again shall they be two nations, and never again shall they be divided into two kingdoms. [23]They shall never again defile themselves with their idols and their detestable things, or with any of their transgressions. I will save them from all the apostasies into which they have fallen,[a] and will cleanse them. Then they shall be my people, and I will be their God.

24 My servant David shall be king over them; and they shall all have one shepherd. They shall follow my ordinances and be careful to observe my statutes. [25]They shall live in the land that I gave to my servant Jacob, in which your ancestors lived; they and their children and their children's children shall live there forever; and my servant David shall be their prince forever. [26]I will make a covenant of peace with them; it shall be an everlasting covenant with them; and I will bless[b] them and multiply them, and will set my sanctuary among them forevermore. [27]My dwelling place shall be with them; and I will be their God, and they shall be my people. [28]Then the nations shall know that I the LORD sanctify Israel, when my sanctuary is among them forevermore.

Invasion by Gog

38 The word of the LORD came to me: [2]Mortal, set your face toward Gog, of the land of Magog, the chief prince of Meshech and Tubal. Prophesy against him [3]and say: Thus says the Lord GOD: I am against you, O Gog, chief prince of Meshech and Tubal; [4]I will turn you around and put hooks into your jaws, and I will lead you out with all your army, horses and horsemen, all of them clothed in full armor, a great company, all of them with shield and buckler, wielding swords. [5]Persia, Ethiopia,[c] and Put are with them, all of them with buckler and helmet; [6]Gomer and all its troops; Beth-togarmah from the remotest parts of the north with all its troops—many peoples are with you.

7 Be ready and keep ready, you and all the companies that are assembled around you, and hold yourselves in reserve for

[y] Or *wind* or *spirit* [z] Heb *I will put them upon it* [a] Another reading is *from all the settlements in which they have sinned* [b] Tg: Heb *give* [c] Or *Nubia*; Heb *Cush*

37.9 Ps 104.30; ver 5; Hos 13.14
37.10 ver 5,6; Rev 11.11
37.11 Ezek 36.10; 39.25; Ps 141.7; Isa 49.14
37.12 Isa 26.19; Hos 13.14; ver 25; Ezek 36.24; Am 9.14,15
37.13 Ezek 6.7; ver 6.12
37.14 Ezek 36.27; 39.29; 36.36
37.16 Num 17.2; 2 Chr 11.11-17; 15.9
37.19 Zech 10.6; ver 16,17
37.21 Ezek 36.24; 39.27
37.22 Isa 11.13; Jer 3.18; Hos 1.11; Ezek 34.23
37.23 Ezek 11.18; 43.7; 36.25; 36.28
37.24 Jer 30.9; Isa 40.11; Hos 3.5; Ezek 36.27
37.25 Ezek 28.25; 36.28; Zech 6.12
37.26 Isa 55.3; Ezek 36.10; 20.40; 43.7
37.27 Lev 26.11; Jn 1.14
37.28 Ezek 36.23; 20.12
38.2 Ezek 39.1; Rev 20.8; Ezek 39.1
38.4 2 Kings 19.28; Ezek 39.2
38.5 Ezek 27.10; 30.4,5
38.6 Gen 10.2; Ezek 27.14

38.1-39.20 The Invasion of Israel by the King from the North. **38.1-16** The reference in 38.17 to *the prophets of Israel* as having lived *in former days* shows that this section of Ezekiel was written at a considerably later time, and may reflect the historical development in the fourth century when Alexander began his conquest of the Middle East. *Gog* is not a known historical figure, but may derive from Gyges, a seventh century king of Lydia in southern Asia Minor, which is in the vicinity of *Meshech and Tubal* (Ezek 32.26). *Magog*, the name of the land, derives from the name of this symbolic king, Gog. Allied with *Persia* (a nation mentioned only in the sixth century and later levels of the biblical historical books), *Ethiopia and Put* (probably Libya in north Africa), *Gomer* (from southern Russia), and *Beth-togarmah* (Armenia) from *the remotest parts of the north*, Gog's army is instructed to invade *the land restored from war* (which is another indication of the post-exilic date of this section). Distant peoples from *Tarshish* (in the western Mediterranean), *Sheba and Dedan* (from central and southern Arabia) will inquire about what Gog intends. The writer sees this mass invasion as the plan of God.

38.17-23 All of the natural order – the earth, fish, land animals, insects – will be thrown into cosmic disorder as an indication of God's wrath toward Gog, the audacious antagonist of God's people. Gog's utter defeat will *display God's greatness to the nations.*

39.1-10 A different version of this apocalyptic vision depicts in detail the destruction of Gog and the land of Magog, so that all *the nations* will see how God has vindicated his people and freed them from the necessity to fight their enemies.

them. 8After many days you shall be mustered; in the latter years you shall go against a land restored from war, a land where people were gathered from many nations on the mountains of Israel, which had long lain waste; its people were brought out from the nations and now are living in safety, all of them. 9You shall advance, coming on like a storm; you shall be like a cloud covering the land, you and all your troops, and many peoples with you.

10 Thus says the Lord GOD: On that day thoughts will come into your mind, and you will devise an evil scheme. 11You will say, "I will go up against the land of unwalled villages; I will fall upon the quiet people who live in safety, all of them living without walls, and having no bars or gates"; 12to seize spoil and carry off plunder; to assail the waste places that are now inhabited, and the people who were gathered from the nations, who are acquiring cattle and goods, who live at the center[d] of the earth. 13Sheba and Dedan and the merchants of Tarshish and all its young warriors[e] will say to you, "Have you come to seize spoil? Have you assembled your horde to carry off plunder, to carry away silver and gold, to take away cattle and goods, to seize a great amount of booty?"

14 Therefore, mortal, prophesy, and say to Gog: Thus says the Lord GOD: On that day when my people Israel are living securely, you will rouse yourself[f] 15and come from your place out of the remotest parts of the north, you and many peoples with you, all of them riding on horses, a great horde, a mighty army; 16you will come up against my people Israel, like a cloud covering the earth. In the latter days I will bring you against my land, so that the nations may know me, when through you, O Gog, I display my holiness before their eyes.

Judgment on Gog

17 Thus says the Lord GOD: Are you he of whom I spoke in former days by my servants the prophets of Israel, who in those days prophesied for years that I would bring you against them? 18On that day, when Gog comes against the land of Israel, says the Lord GOD, my wrath shall be aroused. 19For in my jealousy and in my blazing wrath I declare: On that day there shall be a great shaking in the land of Israel; 20the fish of the sea, and the birds of the air, and the animals of the field, and all creeping things that creep on the ground, and all human beings that are on the face of the earth, shall quake at my presence, and the mountains shall be thrown down, and the cliffs shall fall, and every wall shall tumble to the ground. 21I will summon the sword against Gog[g] in[h] all my mountains, says the Lord GOD; the swords of all will be against their comrades. 22With pestilence and bloodshed I will enter into judgment with him; and I will pour down torrential rains and hailstones, fire and sulfur, upon him and his troops and the many peoples that are with him. 23So I will display my greatness and my holiness and make myself known in the eyes of many nations. Then they shall know that I am the LORD.

Gog's Armies Destroyed

39 And you, mortal, prophesy against Gog, and say: Thus says the Lord GOD: I am against you, O Gog, chief prince of Meshech and Tubal! 2I will turn you around and drive you forward, and bring you up from the remotest parts of the north, and lead you against the mountains of Israel. 3I will strike your bow from your left hand, and will make your arrows drop out of your right hand. 4You shall fall upon the mountains of Israel, you and all your troops and the peoples that are with you; I will give you to birds of prey of every kind and to the wild animals to be devoured. 5You shall fall in the open field; for I have spoken, says the Lord GOD. 6I will send fire on Magog and on those who live securely in the coastlands; and they shall know that I am the LORD.

7 My holy name I will make known among my people Israel; and I will not let my holy name be profaned any more; and the nations shall know that I am the LORD, the Holy One in Israel. 8It has come! It has happened, says the Lord GOD. This is the day of which I have spoken.

9 Then those who live in the towns of Israel will go out and make fires of the weapons and burn them—bucklers and shields, bows and arrows, handpikes and spears—and they will make fires of them for seven years. 10They will not need to take wood out of the field or cut down any trees in the forests, for they will make their fires

[d] Heb *navel* [e] Heb *young lions* [f] Gk: Heb *will you not know?* [g] Heb *him* [h] Heb *to* or *for*

38.8 Isa 24.22; Ezek 36.24
38.9 Isa 28.2; Joel 2.2
38.10 Mic 2.1
38.11 Zech 2.4; Jer 49.31; ver 8
38.12 Isa 10.6; Ezek 29.19; ver 8
38.13 Ezek 27.22; 27.15; Nah 2.11-13
38.14 Jer 23.6; Zech 2.5,8
38.15 ver 6; Ezek 39.2
38.16 Ezek 36.23
38.17 Isa 34.1-6
38.18 ver 2; Ps 18.8,15
38.19 Ezek 36.5,6; Nah 1.2; Hag 2.6,7; Rev 16.18
38.20 Jer 4.24; Hos 4.3; Nah 1.5,6; Zech 14.4
38.21 Ezek 14.17; Judg 7.22; 1 Sam 14.20; 2 Chr 20.23
38.22 Isa 66.16; Jer 25.31; Rev 16.21; Ps 11.6
38.23 Ezek 36.23; Ps 9.16; Ezek 37.28
39.1 Ezek 38.2-4
39.2 Ezek 38.15
39.3 Ezek 30.21-24; Hos 1.5
39.4 Ezek 38.21; 33.27
39.6 Ezek 38.22; Am 1.4; Ps 72.10; Jer 25.22
39.7 Ezek 36.20-22; ver 25; Ezek 20.39; 38.16; Isa 60.9,14
39.9 Ps 46.9
39.10 Isa 14.2; Hab 2.8

of the weapons; they will despoil those who despoiled them, and plunder those who plundered them, says the Lord GOD.

The Burial of Gog

11 On that day I will give to Gog a place for burial in Israel, the Valley of the Travelers[i] east of the sea; it shall block the path of the travelers, for there Gog and all his horde will be buried; it shall be called the Valley of Hamon-gog.[j] 12Seven months the house of Israel shall spend burying them, in order to cleanse the land. 13All the people of the land shall bury them; and it will bring them honor on the day that I show my glory, says the Lord GOD. 14They will set apart men to pass through the land regularly and bury any invaders[k] who remain on the face of the land, so as to cleanse it; for seven months they shall make their search. 15As the searchers[k] pass through the land, anyone who sees a human bone shall set up a sign by it, until the buriers have buried it in the Valley of Hamon-gog.[j] 16(A city Hamonah[l] is there also.) Thus they shall cleanse the land.

17 As for you, mortal, thus says the Lord GOD: Speak to the birds of every kind and to all the wild animals: Assemble and come, gather from all around to the sacrificial feast that I am preparing for you, a great sacrificial feast on the mountains of Israel, and you shall eat flesh and drink blood. 18You shall eat the flesh of the mighty, and drink the blood of the princes of the earth—of rams, of lambs, and of goats, of bulls, all of them fatlings of Bashan. 19You shall eat fat until you are filled, and drink blood until you are drunk, at the sacrificial feast that I am preparing for you. 20And you shall be filled at my table with horses and charioteers,[m] with warriors and all kinds of soldiers, says the Lord GOD.

Israel Restored to the Land

21 I will display my glory among the nations; and all the nations shall see my judgment that I have executed, and my hand that I have laid on them. 22The house of Israel shall know that I am the LORD their God, from that day forward. 23And the nations shall know that the house of Israel went into captivity for their iniquity, because they dealt treacherously with me. So I hid my face from them and gave them into the hand of their adversaries, and they all fell by the sword. 24I dealt with them according to their uncleanness and their transgressions, and hid my face from them.

25 Therefore thus says the Lord GOD: Now I will restore the fortunes of Jacob, and have mercy on the whole house of Israel; and I will be jealous for my holy name. 26They shall forget[n] their shame, and all the treachery they have practiced against me, when they live securely in their land with no one to make them afraid, 27when I have brought them back from the peoples and gathered them from their enemies' lands, and through them have displayed my holiness in the sight of many nations. 28Then they shall know that I am the LORD their God because I sent them into exile among the nations, and then gathered them into their own land. I will leave none of them behind; 29and I will never again hide my face from them, when I pour out my spirit upon the house of Israel, says the Lord GOD.

The Vision of the New Temple

40 In the twenty-fifth year of our exile, at the beginning of the year, on the tenth day of the month, in the fourteenth year after the city was struck down, on that very day, the hand of the LORD was upon me, and he brought me there. 2He brought me, in visions of God, to the land of Israel, and set me down upon a very high mountain, on which was a structure like a city to the south. 3When he brought me there, a man was there, whose appearance shone like bronze, with a linen cord and a measuring reed in his hand; and he was standing in the gateway. 4The man said to me, "Mortal, look closely and listen attentively, and set your mind upon all that I shall show you, for you were brought here in order that I might show it to you; declare all that you see to the house of Israel."

5 Now there was a wall all around the outside of the temple area. The length of the measuring reed in the man's hand was six long cubits, each being a cubit and a handbreadth in length; so he measured the thickness of the wall, one reed; and the height, one reed. 6Then he went into the gateway facing east, going up its steps, and meas-

[i] Or *of the Abarim* [j] That is, *the Horde of Gog* [k] Heb *travelers* [l] That is *The Horde* [m] Heb *chariots* [n] Another reading is *They shall bear*

39.11 Ezek 38.2; ver 1,15
39.13 Jer 33.9; Ezek 28.22
39.14 Jer 14.16; ver 12
39.17 ver 4; Rev 19.17; Isa 34.6,7; Jer 46.10; Zeph 1.7
39.18 Rev 19.18; Deut 32.14; Ps 22.12; Am 4.1
39.20 Ps 76.6; Ezek 38.4; Rev 19.18
39.21 Ezek 38.16,23; ver 13
39.23 Ezek 36.18-20,23; 20.27; ver 26; Isa 59.2; ver 29
39.24 Ezek 36.19; ver 23
39.25 Jer 30.3,18; Ezek 34.13; 36.24; 20.40; Hos 1.11
39.26 Ezek 34.25-28; Isa 17.2; Mic 4.4
39.27 Ezek 28.25,26; 36.23,24; 38.16
39.28 Ezek 34.30; ver 22
39.29 Isa 32.15; Ezek 36.27; 37.14; Joel 2.28; Acts 2.17
40.1 Ezek 33.21; 1.2,3
40.2 Ezek 8.3; Dan 7.1,7; Ezek 17.23; Rev 21.10
40.3 Ezek 1.7; Dan 10.6; Ezek 47.3; Rev 11.1; 21.15
40.4 Ezek 44.5; 43.10; Jer 26.2; Acts 20.27
40.6 ver 20,26

39.11-20 *Gog*, as a symbol of aggression against God's people, will be buried along with his army in the *Valley of Travelers*, which may be the deep valley south of the Dead Sea. All the people of the land of Israel will assist in the burial process of these divinely slaughtered troops. (*Hamonah* may not be an actual place, but a play on the Hebrew word for horde: Hamon; 39.11.) Birds of carrion enjoy an unprecedented feast on the carcasses of the fallen invaders.
39.21-29 Both *the nations* and *the house of Israel* will finally learn who the sovereign of the universe is – the LORD – and that he treats human beings in ways that are appropriate to their behavior. All Israel will be brought back from *exile* among the nations, and God will *pour out his spirit* upon them.
40.1-48.35 The Restored Temple, Cultus and Land of Israel. The actual reconstruction of the temple began, with permission from the Persian rulers, in 520 (Ezra 3.1-13). The resulting building was greeted with mixed emotions, probably since it was a modest structure as compared with the splendor of Solomon's temple (1 Kings 6.2-38). Here in Ezekiel, as in the Temple Scroll (discovered in 1960 among the Qumran, or Dead Sea Scrolls), there is a detailed but idealized description of the structure and the worship activities to be carried out there in the future.
40.1-4 *The twenty-eighth year* since Ezekiel's exile was 573. His vision of being *set down upon a very high mountain* with *a structure like a city* opposite him may refer to the Mount of Olives, which overlooks the temple area from the east, but it more likely implies a major geological transformation of the area by which the temple hill became a lofty mountain, just as the tiny spring of Gihon (1 Kings 1.32-48) is transformed into an abundant, rushing river (Ezek 40). *The man* who measures the temple structure and shows it to the prophet is a heavenly being. Ezekiel is reminded of this contrast with himself when he is addressed as *son of man*, which means a human with all the human limitations (Ps 8.3-4).
40.5-47 As for the measurements, a *reed* is just over ten feet in length, and a *cubit* varied from 17 to 20 inches. Detailed descriptions are given of the four gates of the temple complex, each of which faces one of the points of the compass, and has associated chambers. A decorative feature found in architectural remains throughout the ancient Middle East is the *palm tree*. At each of the gates there are provisions for ceremonial killing of sacrificial animals. Other chambers are assigned to *singers*, to priests in general, and to those priests descended from *Zadok* (2 Sam 20.25; 1 Kings 1.39-45) who alone were permitted to enter the holy place.

ured the threshold of the gate, one reed
deep.[o] There were [7]recesses, and each recess
was one reed wide and one reed deep; and
the space between the recesses, five cubits;
and the threshold of the gate by the vestibule of the gate at the inner end was one
reed deep. [8]Then he measured the inner
vestibule of the gateway, one cubit. [9]Then
he measured the vestibule of the gateway,
eight cubits; and its pilasters, two cubits;
and the vestibule of the gate was at the
inner end. [10]There were three recesses on
either side of the east gate; the three were
of the same size; and the pilasters on either
side were of the same size. [11]Then he
measured the width of the opening of the
gateway, ten cubits; and the width of the
gateway, thirteen cubits. [12]There was a
barrier before the recesses, one cubit on
either side; and the recesses were six cubits
on either side. [13]Then he measured the gate
from the back[p] of the one recess to the back[p]
of the other, a width of twenty-five cubits,
from wall to wall.[q] [14]He measured[r] also the
vestibule, twenty cubits; and the gate next
to the pilaster on every side of the court.[s]
[15]From the front of the gate at the entrance
to the end of the inner vestibule of the gate
was fifty cubits. [16]The recesses and their
pilasters had windows, with shutters[s] on
the inside of the gateway all around, and
the vestibules also had windows on the
inside all around; and on the pilasters were
palm trees.

17 Then he brought me into the outer
court; there were chambers there, and a
pavement, all around the court; thirty
chambers fronted on the pavement. [18]The
pavement ran along the side of the gates,
corresponding to the length of the gates;
this was the lower pavement. [19]Then he
measured the distance from the inner front
of[t] the lower gate to the outer front of the
inner court, one hundred cubits.[u]

20 Then he measured the gate of the
outer court that faced north—its depth and
width. [21]Its recesses, three on either side,
and its pilasters and its vestibule were of the
same size as those of the first gate; its depth
was fifty cubits, and its width twenty-five
cubits. [22]Its windows, its vestibule, and its
palm trees were of the same size as those
of the gate that faced toward the east. Seven
steps led up to it; and its vestibule was on
the inside.[v] [23]Opposite the gate on the north,
as on the east, was a gate to the inner
court; he measured from gate to gate, one
hundred cubits.

24 Then he led me toward the south,
and there was a gate on the south; and he
measured its pilasters and its vestibule; they
had the same dimensions as the others.
[25]There were windows all around in it and
in its vestibule, like the windows of the
others; its depth was fifty cubits, and its
width twenty-five cubits. [26]There were seven
steps leading up to it; its vestibule was on
the inside.[v] It had palm trees on its pilasters,
one on either side. [27]There was a gate on
the south of the inner court; and he measured from gate to gate toward the south,
one hundred cubits.

28 Then he brought me to the inner
court by the south gate, and he measured
the south gate; it was of the same dimensions as the others. [29]Its recesses, its pilasters, and its vestibule were of the same size
as the others; and there were windows all
around in it and in its vestibule; its depth
was fifty cubits, and its width twenty-five
cubits. [30]There were vestibules all around,
twenty-five cubits deep and five cubits wide.
[31]Its vestibule faced the outer court, and
palm trees were on its pilasters, and its
stairway had eight steps.

32 Then he brought me to the inner
court on the east side, and he measured the
gate; it was of the same size as the others.
[33]Its recesses, its pilasters, and its vestibule
were of the same dimensions as the others;
and there were windows all around in it
and in its vestibule; its depth was fifty cubits,
and its width twenty-five cubits. [34]Its vestibule faced the outer court, and it had palm
trees on its pilasters, on either side; and its
stairway had eight steps.

35 Then he brought me to the north
gate, and he measured it; it had the same
dimensions as the others. [36]Its recesses, its
pilasters, and its vestibule were of the same
size as the others;[w] and it had windows all
around. Its depth was fifty cubits, and its
width twenty-five cubits. [37]Its vestibule[x] faced
the outer court, and it had palm trees on
its pilasters, on either side; and its stairway
had eight steps.

[o] Heb *deep, and one threshold, one reed deep* [p] Gk: Heb *roof* [q] Heb *opening facing opening* [r] Heb *made* [s] Meaning of Heb uncertain [t] Compare Gk: Heb *from before* [u] Heb adds *the east and the north* [v] Gk: Heb *before them* [w] One Ms: Compare verses 29 and 33: MT lacks *were of the same size as the others* [x] Gk Vg Compare verses 26, 31, 34: Heb *pilasters*

40.7 ver 10-16,21,29,33,36
40.10 ver 7
40.14 ver 9,16; 1 Chr 28.6; Isa 62.9; Ezek 42.1
40.16 1 Kings 6.4; ver 21,22,26,31,34,37
40.17 Rev 11.2; 1 Chr 9.26; 2 Chr 31.11; Ezek 41.6; 45.5
40.19 ver 23,27
40.21 ver 7,16,30
40.22 ver 16,6,26,31,34,37,49
40.23 ver 19,27
40.24 ver 21
40.25 ver 16,22,21,33
40.26 ver 6,22,16
40.27 ver 23,32,19
40.28 ver 32,35
40.29 ver 7,10,21,16,22,25
40.30 ver 16,21,25
40.31 ver 16,22,26,34,37
40.32 ver 28-31,35
40.33 ver 29,16,21
40.34 ver 16,22,37
40.35 Ezek 44.4; 47.2
40.36 ver 7,29,16
40.37 ver 16,35

40.38 Ezek 41.10; 42.13; 2 Chr 4.6
40.39 Lev 4.2,3; Lev 5.6; 6.6; 7.1
40.41 ver 39.40
40.42 ver 39; Ex 20.25
40.44 ver 23.27.17.38; 1 Chr 6.31; 25.1-7
40.45 ver 17.38; Lev 8.35; 1 Chr 9.23; 2 Chr 13.11
40.46 ver 17.38; Num 18.5; Ezek 44.15; 43.19; 1 Kings 2.35
40.47 ver 19.23.27
40.49 1 Kings 6.3; 2 Kings 7.21; Jer 52.17-23; Rev 3.12
41.1 Ezek 40.2,3,17; ver 21.23; Ezek 40.9
41.2 1 Kings 6.2,17; 2 Chr 3.3
41.3 Ezek 40.16; ver 1
41.4 1 Kings 6.20; 2 Chr 3.8
41.5 ver 6-11
41.6 1 Kings 6.5,6
41.7 1 Kings 6.8
41.8 Ezek 40.5
41.9 ver 11
41.10 Ezek 40.17
41.11 ver 9
41.12 ver 13-15; Ezek 42.1
41.13 Ezek 40.47; ver 13-15
41.14 Ezek 40.47
41.15 Ezek 42.1,10,13; 40.6; ver 25

38 There was a chamber with its door in
the vestibule of the gate,[y] where the burnt
offering was to be washed. [39]And in the
vestibule of the gate were two tables on
either side, on which the burnt offering and
the sin offering and the guilt offering were
to be slaughtered. [40]On the outside of the
vestibule[z] at the entrance of the north gate
were two tables; and on the other side of
the vestibule of the gate were two tables.
[41]Four tables were on the inside, and four
tables on the outside of the side of the gate,
eight tables, on which the sacrifices were to
be slaughtered. [42]There were also four tables of hewn stone for the burnt offering, a
cubit and a half long, and one cubit and a
half wide, and one cubit high, on which the
instruments were to be laid with which the
burnt offerings and the sacrifices were slaughtered. [43]There were pegs, one handbreadth
long, fastened all around the inside. And on
the tables the flesh of the offering was to be
laid.
44 On the outside of the inner gateway
there were chambers for the singers in the
inner court, one[a] at the side of the north
gate facing south, the other at the side of
the east gate facing north. [45]He said to me,
"This chamber that faces south is for the
priests who have charge of the temple,
[46]and the chamber that faces north is for
the priests who have charge of the altar;
these are the descendants of Zadok, who
alone among the descendants of Levi may
come near to the LORD to minister to him."
[47]He measured the court, one hundred cubits
deep, and one hundred cubits wide, a square;
and the altar was in front of the temple.

The Temple

48 Then he brought me to the vestibule
of the temple and measured the pilasters of
the vestibule, five cubits on either side; and
the width of the gate was fourteen cubits;
and the sidewalls of the gate were three
cubits[b] on either side. [49]The depth of the
vestibule was twenty cubits, and the width
twelve[c] cubits; ten steps led up[d] to it; and
there were pillars beside the pilasters on
either side.

41 Then he brought me to the nave,
and measured the pilasters; on each
side six cubits was the width of the pilasters.[e]
[2]The width of the entrance was ten cubits;
and the sidewalls of the entrance were five
cubits on either side. He measured the length
of the nave, forty cubits, and its width,
twenty cubits. [3]Then he went into the inner
room and measured the pilasters of the
entrance, two cubits; and the width of the
entrance, six cubits; and the sidewalls[f] of
the entrance, seven cubits. [4]He measured
the depth of the room, twenty cubits, and
its width, twenty cubits, beyond the nave.
And he said to me, This is the most holy
place.
5 Then he measured the wall of the temple, six cubits thick; and the width of the
side chambers, four cubits, all around the
temple. [6]The side chambers were in three
stories, one over another, thirty in each
story. There were offsets[g] all around the
wall of the temple to serve as supports for
the side chambers, so that they should not
be supported by the wall of the temple. [7]The
passageway[h] of the side chambers widened
from story to story; for the structure was
supplied with a stairway all around the
temple. For this reason the structure became
wider from story to story. One ascended
from the bottom story to the uppermost
story by way of the middle one. [8]I saw
also that the temple had a raised platform
all around; the foundations of the side
chambers measured a full reed of six long
cubits. [9]The thickness of the outer wall of
the side chambers was five cubits; and the
free space between the side chambers of the
temple [10]and the chambers of the court was
a width of twenty cubits all around the
temple on every side. [11]The side chambers
opened onto the area left free, one door
toward the north, and another door toward
the south; and the width of the part that
was left free was five cubits all around.
12 The building that was facing the temple yard on the west side was seventy cubits
wide; and the wall of the building was five
cubits thick all around, and its depth ninety
cubits.
13 Then he measured the temple, one
hundred cubits deep; and the yard and the
building with its walls, one hundred cubits
deep; [14]also the width of the east front of the
temple and the yard, one hundred cubits.
15 Then he measured the depth of the
building facing the yard at the west,

40.48-42.20 The dimensions of the sanctuary itself are detailed, with specific mention of decorative features: faces of humans, lions, cherubim, palm trees – some of which appear on doors, gates, walls and windows. The multiple storeys of the inner courtyard are described, including the *vacant chambers* where only the priests, clothed in proper vestments, may go to eat *the most holy offerings*. Finally the exterior dimensions of the entire structure are measured.

[y] Cn: Heb *at the pilasters of the gates* [z] Cn: Heb *to him who goes up* [a] Heb lacks *one* [b] Gk: Heb *and the width of the gate was three cubits* [c] Gk: Heb *eleven* [d] Gk: Heb *and by steps that went up* [e] Compare Gk: Heb *tent* [f] Gk: Heb *width* [g] Gk Compare 1 Kings 6.6: Heb *they entered* [h] Cn: Heb *it was surrounded*

together with its galleries[i] on either side,
one hundred cubits.
The nave of the temple and the inner
room and the outer[j] vestibule 16 were paneled,[k]
and, all around, all three had windows with
recessed[l] frames. Facing the threshold the
temple was paneled with wood all around,
from the floor up to the windows (now the
windows were covered), 17 to the space above
the door, even to the inner room, and on
the outside. And on all the walls all around
in the inner room and the nave there was
a pattern.[m] 18 It was formed of cherubim and
palm trees, a palm tree between cherub and
cherub. Each cherub had two faces: 19 a
human face turned toward the palm tree on
the one side, and the face of a young lion
turned toward the palm tree on the other
side. They were carved on the whole temple
all around; 20 from the floor to the area
above the door, cherubim and palm trees
were carved on the wall.[n]
21 The doorposts of the nave were square.
In front of the holy place was something
resembling 22 an altar of wood, three cubits
high, two cubits long, and two cubits wide;[o]
its corners, its base,[p] and its walls were of
wood. He said to me, "This is the table that
stands before the LORD." 23 The nave and the
holy place had each a double door. 24 The
doors had two leaves apiece, two swinging
leaves for each door. 25 On the doors of the
nave were carved cherubim and palm trees,
such as were carved on the walls; and there
was a canopy of wood in front of the
vestibule outside. 26 And there were recessed
windows and palm trees on either side, on
the sidewalls of the vestibule.[q]

The Holy Chambers and the Outer Wall

42 Then he led me out into the outer
court, toward the north, and he
brought me to the chambers that were
opposite the temple yard and opposite the
building on the north. 2 The length of the
building that was on the north side[r] was[s]
one hundred cubits, and the width fifty
cubits. 3 Across the twenty cubits that belonged to the inner court, and facing the
pavement that belonged to the outer court,
the chambers rose[t] gallery[u] by gallery[u] in
three stories. 4 In front of the chambers was
a passage on the inner side, ten cubits wide
and one hundred cubits deep,[v] and its[w]
entrances were on the north. 5 Now the
upper chambers were narrower, for the
galleries[u] took more away from them than
from the lower and middle chambers in the
building. 6 For they were in three stories,
and they had no pillars like the pillars of the
outer[x] court; for this reason the upper chambers were set back from the ground more
than the lower and the middle ones. 7 There
was a wall outside parallel to the chambers,
toward the outer court, opposite the chambers, fifty cubits long. 8 For the chambers on
the outer court were fifty cubits long, while
those opposite the temple were one hundred
cubits long. 9 At the foot of these chambers
ran a passage that one entered from the
east in order to enter them from the outer
court. 10 The width of the passage[y] is fixed
by the wall of the court.
On the south[z] also, opposite the vacant
area and opposite the building, there were
chambers 11 with a passage in front of them;
they were similar to the chambers on the
north, of the same length and width, with
the same exits[a] and arrangements and doors.
12 So the entrances of the chambers to the
south were entered through the entrance at
the head of the corresponding passage, from
the east, along the matching wall.[u]
13 Then he said to me, "The north chambers and the south chambers opposite the
vacant area are the holy chambers, where
the priests who approach the LORD shall eat
the most holy offerings; there they shall
deposit the most holy offerings—the grain
offering, the sin offering, and the guilt
offering, for the place is holy. 14 When the
priests enter the holy place, they shall not
go out of it into the outer court without
laying there the vestments in which they
minister, for these are holy; they shall put
on other garments before they go near to
the area open to the people."
15 When he had finished measuring the
interior of the temple area, he led me out
by the gate that faces east, and measured
the temple area all around. 16 He measured

[i] Cn: Meaning of Heb uncertain [j] Gk: Heb *of the court* [k] Gk: Heb *the thresholds* [l] Cn Compare Gk 1 Kings 6.4: Meaning of Heb uncertain [m] Heb *measures* [n] Cn Compare verse 25: Heb *and the wall* [o] Gk: Heb lacks *two cubits wide* [p] Gk: Heb *length* [q] Cn: Heb *vestibule. And the side chambers of the temple and the canopies* [r] Gk: Heb *door* [s] Gk: Heb *before the length* [t] Heb lacks *the chambers rose* [u] Meaning of Heb uncertain [v] Gk Syr: Heb *a way of one cubit* [w] Heb *their* [x] Gk: Heb lacks *outer* [y] Heb lacks *of the passage* [z] Gk: Heb *east* [a] Heb *and all their exits*

41.16 ver 25,26; Ezek 40.16; ver 15; Ezek 42.3; 1 Kings 6.15
41.18 1 Kings 6.29; 7.36; Ezek 40.16; 2 Chr 3.5
41.19 Ezek 1.10; 10.14
41.21 ver 1; 1 Kings 6.33; Ezek 40.9,14,16
41.22 Ex 30.1; Rev 8.3; Ezek 44.16; Mal 1.7,12; Ex 30.8
41.23 1 Kings 6.31-35; ver 1,4
41.26 ver 16; Ezek 40.9,16,48
42.1 Ezek 40.17,28; 41.1,12; ver 10,13
42.3 Ezek 41.10,16
42.4 Ezek 46.19
42.6 Ezek 41.6
42.8 Ezek 41.13,14
42.9 Ezek 44.5; 46.19
42.13 Lev 7.6; 10.13,14,17; Lev 6.25,29; Num 18.9,10
42.14 Ezek 44.19; Ex 29.4-9; Zech 3.4,5
42.15 Ezek 40.6; 43.1

the east side with the measuring reed, five hundred cubits by the measuring reed. [17]Then he turned and measured[b] the north side, five hundred cubits by the measuring reed. [18]Then he turned and measured[b] the south side, five hundred cubits by the measuring reed. [19]Then he turned to the west side and measured, five hundred cubits by the measuring reed. [20]He measured it on the four sides. It had a wall around it, five hundred cubits long and five hundred cubits wide, to make a separation between the holy and the common.

The Divine Glory Returns to the Temple

43 Then he brought me to the gate, the gate facing east. [2]And there, the glory of the God of Israel was coming from the east; the sound was like the sound of mighty waters; and the earth shone with his glory. [3]The[c] vision I saw was like the vision that I had seen when he came to destroy the city, and[d] like the vision that I had seen by the river Chebar; and I fell upon my face. [4]As the glory of the LORD entered the temple by the gate facing east, [5]the spirit lifted me up, and brought me into the inner court; and the glory of the LORD filled the temple.

6 While the man was standing beside me, I heard someone speaking to me out of the temple. [7]He said to me: Mortal, this is the place of my throne and the place for the soles of my feet, where I will reside among the people of Israel forever. The house of Israel shall no more defile my holy name, neither they nor their kings, by their whoring, and by the corpses of their kings at their death.[e] [8]When they placed their threshold by my threshold and their doorposts beside my doorposts, with only a wall between me and them, they were defiling my holy name by their abominations that they committed; therefore I have consumed them in my anger. [9]Now let them put away their idolatry and the corpses of their kings far from me, and I will reside among them forever.

10 As for you, mortal, describe the temple to the house of Israel, and let them measure the pattern; and let them be ashamed of their iniquities. [11]When they are ashamed of all that they have done, make known to them the plan of the temple, its arrangement, its exits and its entrances, and its whole form—all its ordinances and its entire plan and all its laws; and write it down in their sight, so that they may observe and follow the entire plan and all its ordinances. [12]This is the law of the temple: the whole territory on the top of the mountain all around shall be most holy. This is the law of the temple.

The Altar

13 These are the dimensions of the altar by cubits (the cubit being one cubit and a handbreadth): its base shall be one cubit high,[f] and one cubit wide, with a rim of one span around its edge. This shall be the height of the altar: [14]From the base on the ground to the lower ledge, two cubits, with a width of one cubit; and from the smaller ledge to the larger ledge, four cubits, with a width of one cubit; [15]and the altar hearth, four cubits; and from the altar hearth projecting upward, four horns. [16]The altar hearth shall be square, twelve cubits long by twelve wide. [17]The ledge also shall be square, fourteen cubits long by fourteen wide, with a rim around it half a cubit wide, and its surrounding base, one cubit. Its steps shall face east.

18 Then he said to me: Mortal, thus says the Lord GOD: These are the ordinances for the altar: On the day when it is erected for offering burnt offerings upon it and for dashing blood against it, [19]you shall give to the levitical priests of the family of Zadok, who draw near to me to minister to me, says the Lord GOD, a bull for a sin offering. [20]And you shall take some of its blood, and put it on the four horns of the altar, and on the four corners of the ledge, and upon the rim all around; thus you shall purify it and make atonement for it. [21]You shall also take the bull of the sin offering, and it shall be burnt in the appointed place belonging to the temple, outside the sacred area.

22 On the second day you shall offer a male goat without blemish for a sin offering; and the altar shall be purified, as it was purified with the bull. [23]When you have finished purifying it, you shall offer a bull without blemish and a ram from the flock without blemish. [24]You shall present them before the LORD, and the priests shall throw salt on them and offer them up as a burnt

[b] Gk: Heb *measuring reed all around. He measured* [c] Gk: Heb *Like the vision* [d] Syr: Heb *and the visions* [e] Or *on their high places* [f] Gk: Heb lacks *high*

42.20 Ezek 40.5; Zech 2.5; Ezek 45.2
43.1 Ezek 10.19; 44.1; 46.1
43.2 Ezek 11.23; 1.24; Rev 1.15; 18.1; Ezek 10.4
43.3 Ezek 1.4,28; Jer 1.10; Ezek 1.3; 3.23
43.4 Ezek 10.19; 44.2
43.5 Ezek 3.14; 8.3; 1 Kings 8.10,11; Ezek 44.4
43.6 Ezek 1.26; 40.3
43.7 Ps 47.8; Ezek 1.26; 37.26,28; Jer 16.18; Ezek 6.5,13
43.8 Ezek 8.3; 23.39; 44.7
43.9 Ezek 18.30,31
43.10 Ezek 40.4; ver 11
43.11 Ezek 44.5; 12.3; 11.20; 36.27
43.12 Ezek 40.2
43.13 Ezek 40.5; 41.8
43.14 ver 17,20; Ezek 45.19
43.15 Ex 27.2; Lev 9.9; 1 Kings 1.50
43.16 Ex 27.1
43.17 Ex 20.26; Ezek 40.6
43.18 Ezek 2.1; Ex 40.29; Lev 1.5
43.19 Ezek 44.15; Num 16.5,40
43.21 Ex 29.14; Heb 13.11
43.23 Ex 29.1
43.24 Lev 2.13; Mk 9.49,50; Col 4.6

43.1-12 Before resuming the description of his vision of the interior of the temple, the prophet describes the return of the radiant cloud, *the glory of the God of Israel,* which event is accompanied by God's own declaration that it is here he *will reside among the people of Israel forever.* His presence requires them to abstain from any violation of ritual purity as defined by his law.
43.13-27 Instructions are given about the dimensions and the detailed structure of the altar, as well as the essential preparations and procedures for offering sacrifices there, if they are to be acceptable to *the LORD God.*

44.1-3 The gate of the inner sanctuary, where God is present, must remain shut at all times. The *prince of Israel* may, however, enter this chamber through the vestibule to eat a meal in the presence of God.
44.4-31 Admission to the temple as a whole is forbidden to *foreigners uncircumcised in heart and flesh,* which means that even those on whom the physical rite has been performed, but whose life is not in accord with the requirements of the law, are to be excluded. The *Levites* are relegated to servile roles: killing the sacrificial animals and other *chores.* They may not come before God as priests: only levitical priests who are descended from Zadok may *approach [God's] table.* Even they must be clothed properly, and must have avoided certain disqualifying activities (including marrying a divorced woman, or contacting a corpse, for which a purification process is prescribed). Qualified priests are to eat the food offerings brought to the temple and are to be the recipients of other items presented to God there. Unlike the plan which David is reported in 1 Chr 28.11-19 as having given to Solomon as a guide to the construction of the temple, Ezekiel's vision does not provide an architectural plan for future builders of the temple, but a heavenly vision of the ideal holy place where God would dwell and his people come to worship him.

offering to the LORD. 25 For seven days you shall provide daily a goat for a sin offering; also a bull and a ram from the flock, without blemish, shall be provided. 26 Seven days shall they make atonement for the altar and cleanse it, and so consecrate it. 27 When these days are over, then from the eighth day onward the priests shall offer upon the altar your burnt offerings and your offerings of well-being; and I will accept you, says the Lord GOD.

The Closed Gate

44 Then he brought me back to the outer gate of the sanctuary, which faces east; and it was shut. 2 The LORD said to me: This gate shall remain shut; it shall not be opened, and no one shall enter by it; for the LORD, the God of Israel, has entered by it; therefore it shall remain shut. 3 Only the prince, because he is a prince, may sit in it to eat food before the LORD; he shall enter by way of the vestibule of the gate, and shall go out by the same way.

Admission to the Temple

4 Then he brought me by way of the north gate to the front of the temple; and I looked, and lo! the glory of the LORD filled the temple of the LORD; and I fell upon my face. 5 The LORD said to me: Mortal, mark well, look closely, and listen attentively to all that I shall tell you concerning all the ordinances of the temple of the LORD and all its laws; and mark well those who may be admitted to[g] the temple and all those who are to be excluded from the sanctuary. 6 Say to the rebellious house,[h] to the house of Israel, Thus says the Lord GOD: O house of Israel, let there be an end to all your abominations 7 in admitting foreigners, uncircumcised in heart and flesh, to be in my sanctuary, profaning my temple when you offer to me my food, the fat and the blood. You[i] have broken my covenant with all your abominations. 8 And you have not kept charge of my sacred offerings; but you have appointed foreigners[j] to act for you in keeping my charge in my sanctuary.

9 Thus says the Lord GOD: No foreigner, uncircumcised in heart and flesh, of all the foreigners who are among the people of Israel, shall enter my sanctuary. 10 But the Levites who went far from me, going astray from me after their idols when Israel went astray, shall bear their punishment. 11 They shall be ministers in my sanctuary, having oversight at the gates of the temple, and serving in the temple; they shall slaughter the burnt offering and the sacrifice for the people, and they shall attend on them and serve them. 12 Because they ministered to them before their idols and made the house of Israel stumble into iniquity, therefore I have sworn concerning them, says the Lord God, that they shall bear their punishment. 13 They shall not come near to me, to serve me as priest, nor come near any of my sacred offerings, the things that are most sacred; but they shall bear their shame, and the consequences of the abominations that they have committed. 14 Yet I will appoint them to keep charge of the temple, to do all its chores, all that is to be done in it.

The Levitical Priests

15 But the levitical priests, the descendants of Zadok, who kept the charge of my sanctuary when the people of Israel went astray from me, shall come near to me to minister to me; and they shall attend me to offer me the fat and the blood, says the Lord GOD. 16 It is they who shall enter my sanctuary, it is they who shall approach my table, to minister to me, and they shall keep my charge. 17 When they enter the gates of the inner court, they shall wear linen vestments; they shall have nothing of wool on them, while they minister at the gates of the inner court, and within. 18 They shall have linen turbans on their heads, and linen undergarments on their loins; they shall not bind themselves with anything that causes sweat. 19 When they go out into the outer court to the people, they shall remove the vestments in which they have been ministering, and lay them in the holy chambers; and they shall put on other garments, so that they may not communicate holiness to the people with their vestments. 20 They shall not shave their heads or let their locks grow long; they shall only trim the hair of their heads. 21 No priest shall drink wine when he enters the inner court. 22 They shall not marry a widow, or a divorced woman, but only a virgin of the stock of the house of Israel, or a widow who is the widow of a priest. 23 They shall teach my people the difference between the holy and the com-

[g] Cn: Heb *the entrance of* [h] Gk: Heb lacks *house* [i] Gk Syr Vg: Heb *They* [j] Heb lacks *foreigners*

43.25 Ex 29.35,36; Lev 8.33

43.27 Lev 9.1; 3.1; 17.5; Ezek 20.40

44.3 Ezek 37.25; Gen 31.54; 1 Cor 10.18; Ezek 46.2,8

44.4 Ezek 40.20,40; 3.23; 43.5; 1.28; Rev 15.8

44.5 Ezek 40.4; 43.10,11

44.6 Ezek 2.5; 3.9; 45.9; 1 Pet 4.3

44.7 Ex 12.43-49; Lev 26.41; Deut 10.16; Jer 4.4; 9.26; Lev 22.25

44.10 2 Kings 23.8,9; Ezek 22.26; Num 18.23

44.11 1 Chr 26.1; 2 Chr 29.34; Num 16.9

44.12 2 Kings 16.10-16; Ezek 14.3,4; Ps 106.26

44.13 Num 18.3; 2 Kings 23.9; Ezek 32.30; 39.26

44.14 Num 18.4; ver 11

44.15 Ezek 40.46; 48.11; Deut 10.8

44.17 Ex 28.39,40. 43; 39.27,28

44.18 Ex 28.40,42; Isa 3.20

44.19 Ezek 42.14; 46.20

44.21 Lev 10.9

44.22 Lev 21.7,13,14

44.23 Lev 10.10; Mal 2.7

44.24 Deut 17.8,9; Ezek 20.12,20
44.25 Lev 21.1-3
44.26 Num 19.13-19
44.28 Num 18.20; Deut 10.9; Josh 13.14,33
44.29 Num 18.9,14; Lev 27.21,28
44.30 Ex 29.19; Num 3.13; 15.20; Neh 10.37; Mal 3.10
44.31 Ex 22.31; Lev 22.8
45.4 ver 1; Ezek 48.10,11
45.5 Ezek 48.13
45.6 Ezek 48.15
45.7 Ezek 46.16-18; 48.21
45.8 Isa 11.3-5; Jer 23.5; Ezek 22.27; 46.18; Josh 11.23
45.9 Ezek 45.6; Jer 6.7; 22.3; Neh 5.1-5
45.10 Lev 19.35,36; Prov 11.1
45.12 Ex 30.13; Lev 27.25; Num 3.47
45.15 ver 17; Lev 1.4; 6.30
45.17 Ezek 46.4-12; 1 Kings 8.64; 2 Chr 31.3; Lev 23.1-44; Ezek 43.27

mon, and show them how to distinguish between the unclean and the clean. 24 In a controversy they shall act as judges, and they shall decide it according to my judgments. They shall keep my laws and my statutes regarding all my appointed festivals, and they shall keep my sabbaths holy. 25 They shall not defile themselves by going near to a dead person; for father or mother, however, and for son or daughter, and for brother or unmarried sister they may defile themselves. 26 After he has become clean, they shall count seven days for him. 27 On the day that he goes into the holy place, into the inner court, to minister in the holy place, he shall offer his sin offering, says the Lord GOD.

28 This shall be their inheritance: I am their inheritance; and you shall give them no holding in Israel; I am their holding. 29 They shall eat the grain offering, the sin offering, and the guilt offering; and every devoted thing in Israel shall be theirs. 30 The first of all the first fruits of all kinds, and every offering of all kinds from all your offerings, shall belong to the priests; you shall also give to the priests the first of your dough, in order that a blessing may rest on your house. 31 The priests shall not eat of anything, whether bird or animal, that died of itself or was torn by animals.

The Holy District

45 When you allot the land as an inheritance, you shall set aside for the LORD a portion of the land as a holy district, twenty-five thousand cubits long and twenty[k] thousand cubits wide; it shall be holy throughout its entire extent. 2 Of this, a square plot of five hundred by five hundred cubits shall be for the sanctuary, with fifty cubits for an open space around it. 3 In the holy district you shall measure off a section twenty-five thousand cubits long and ten thousand wide, in which shall be the sanctuary, the most holy place. 4 It shall be a holy portion of the land; it shall be for the priests, who minister in the sanctuary and approach the LORD to minister to him; and it shall be both a place for their houses and a holy place for the sanctuary. 5 Another section, twenty-five thousand cubits long and ten thousand cubits wide, shall be for the Levites who minister at the temple, as their holding for cities to live in.[l]

6 Alongside the portion set apart as the holy district you shall assign as a holding for the city an area five thousand cubits wide, and twenty-five thousand cubits long; it shall belong to the whole house of Israel.

7 And to the prince shall belong the land on both sides of the holy district and the holding of the city, alongside the holy district and the holding of the city, on the west and on the east, corresponding in length to one of the tribal portions, and extending from the western to the eastern boundary 8 of the land. It is to be his property in Israel. And my princes shall no longer oppress my people; but they shall let the house of Israel have the land according to their tribes.

9 Thus says the Lord GOD: Enough, O princes of Israel! Put away violence and oppression, and do what is just and right. Cease your evictions of my people, says the Lord GOD.

Weights and Measures

10 You shall have honest balances, an honest ephah, and an honest bath.[m] 11 The ephah and the bath shall be of the same measure, the bath containing one-tenth of a homer, and the ephah one-tenth of a homer; the homer shall be the standard measure. 12 The shekel shall be twenty gerahs. Twenty shekels, twenty-five shekels, and fifteen shekels shall make a mina for you.

Offerings

13 This is the offering that you shall make: one-sixth of an ephah from each homer of wheat, and one-sixth of an ephah from each homer of barley, 14 and as the fixed portion of oil,[n] one-tenth of a bath from each cor (the cor,[o] like the homer, contains ten baths); 15 and one sheep from every flock of two hundred, from the pastures of Israel. This is the offering for grain offerings, burnt offerings, and offerings of well-being, to make atonement for them, says the Lord GOD. 16 All the people of the land shall join with the prince in Israel in making this offering. 17 But this shall be the obligation of the prince regarding the burnt offerings, grain offerings, and drink offerings, at the festivals, the new moons, and the sabbaths, all the appointed festivals of

45.1-9 Three districts – idealized and strictly geometric – are to be set aside in Jerusalem: one for the priests, one for the Levites, and one for the sanctuary itself, with bordering districts for *the prince,* who is to avoid all *violence and oppression* as he rules God's people.
45.10-25 The scales, as well as the weights and measures, are to be uniform and honest: *bath* = 6 gallons; *homer, cor* = 6.5 bushels; *ephah* = 20+ quarts; *shekel* weighs 175 grains; *gerah,* 8+ grains; *mina* = 20 ounces. These precise measures are considered essential to ensure proper amounts in grain and drink offerings. All offerings are to be performed at carefully prescribed times of the year, and serve as an *atonement,* to restore right relationship between God and his wayward people. The dates assigned here for these offerings, as well as for Atonement and Passover, differ from those in Lev 16 and 23.

[k] Gk: Heb *ten* [l] Gk: Heb *as their holding, twenty chambers* [m] A Heb measure of volume [n] Cn: Heb *oil, the bath the oil* [o] Vg: Heb *homer*

46.1-15 Detailed regulations are given for entering or leaving the temple, particularly for the *prince*, who is to offer more elaborate sacrifices than his subjects do.
46.16-18 The prince is to maintain his wealth within his family: gifts to servants must be returned to him when slaves are freed.

the house of Israel: he shall provide the sin offerings, grain offerings, the burnt offerings, and the offerings of well-being, to make atonement for the house of Israel.

Festivals

18 Thus says the Lord GOD: In the first month, on the first day of the month, you shall take a young bull without blemish, and purify the sanctuary. [19]The priest shall take some of the blood of the sin offering and put it on the doorposts of the temple, the four corners of the ledge of the altar, and the posts of the gate of the inner court. [20]You shall do the same on the seventh day of the month for anyone who has sinned through error or ignorance; so you shall make atonement for the temple.

21 In the first month, on the fourteenth day of the month, you shall celebrate the festival of the passover, and for seven days unleavened bread shall be eaten. [22]On that day the prince shall provide for himself and all the people of the land a young bull for a sin offering. [23]And during the seven days of the festival he shall provide as a burnt offering to the LORD seven young bulls and seven rams without blemish, on each of the seven days; and a male goat daily for a sin offering. [24]He shall provide as a grain offering an ephah for each bull, an ephah for each ram, and a hin of oil to each ephah. [25]In the seventh month, on the fifteenth day of the month and for the seven days of the festival, he shall make the same provision for sin offerings, burnt offerings, and grain offerings, and for the oil.

Miscellaneous Regulations

46 Thus says the Lord GOD: The gate of the inner court that faces east shall remain closed on the six working days; but on the sabbath day it shall be opened and on the day of the new moon it shall be opened. [2]The prince shall enter by the vestibule of the gate from outside, and shall take his stand by the post of the gate. The priests shall offer his burnt offering and his offerings of well-being, and he shall bow down at the threshold of the gate. Then he shall go out, but the gate shall not be closed until evening. [3]The people of the land shall bow down at the entrance of that gate before the LORD on the sabbaths and on the new moons. [4]The burnt offering that the prince offers to the LORD on the sabbath day shall be six lambs without blemish and a ram without blemish; [5]and the grain offering with the ram shall be an ephah, and the grain offering with the lambs shall be as much as he wishes to give, together with a hin of oil to each ephah. [6]On the day of the new moon he shall offer a young bull without blemish, and six lambs and a ram, which shall be without blemish; [7]as a grain offering he shall provide an ephah with the bull and an ephah with the ram, and with the lambs as much as he wishes, together with a hin of oil to each ephah. [8]When the prince enters, he shall come in by the vestibule of the gate, and he shall go out by the same way.

9 When the people of the land come before the LORD at the appointed festivals, whoever enters by the north gate to worship shall go out by the south gate; and whoever enters by the south gate shall go out by the north gate: they shall not return by way of the gate by which they entered, but shall go out straight ahead. [10]When they come in, the prince shall come in with them; and when they go out, he shall go out.

11 At the festivals and the appointed seasons the grain offering with a young bull shall be an ephah, and with a ram an ephah, and with the lambs as much as one wishes to give, together with a hin of oil to an ephah. [12]When the prince provides a freewill offering, either a burnt offering or offerings of well-being as a freewill offering to the LORD, the gate facing east shall be opened for him; and he shall offer his burnt offering or his offerings of well-being as he does on the sabbath day. Then he shall go out, and after he has gone out the gate shall be closed.

13 He shall provide a lamb, a yearling, without blemish, for a burnt offering to the LORD daily; morning by morning he shall provide it. [14]And he shall provide a grain offering with it morning by morning regularly, one-sixth of an ephah, and one-third of a hin of oil to moisten the choice flour, as a grain offering to the LORD; this is the ordinance for all time. [15]Thus the lamb and the grain offering and the oil shall be provided, morning by morning, as a regular burnt offering.

16 Thus says the Lord GOD: If the prince makes a gift to any of his sons out of his inheritance,[p] it shall belong to his sons, it

[p] Gk: Heb *it is his inheritance*

45.18 Ezek 46.1,3,6; Lev 16.16
45.19 Ezek 43.20
45.20 Lev 4.27; 16.20; ver 15,18
45.21 Ex 12.18; Lev 23.5,6; Num 9.2,3; 28.16,17
45.22 Lev 4.14
45.23 Lev 23.8; Num 28.16-25; Job 42.8
45.25 Lev 23.34; Num 29.12; Deut 16.13
46.1 Ezek 45.17-19
46.2 ver 8; Ezek 44.3; 45.9; ver 12
46.3 Lk 1.10; ver 1
46.4 Ezek 45.17
46.5 Ezek 45.24; ver 7,11
46.6 ver 1
46.7 ver 5
46.8 Ezek 44.3; ver 2
46.9 Ex 23.14-17; Deut 16.16
46.11 Ezek 45.17; ver 5,7
46.12 2 Chr 29.31; Ezek 44.3; ver 2; Ezek 45.17
46.13 Ex 29.38; Num 28.3; Isa 50.4
46.14 Num 28.5
46.15 Ex 29.42; Num 28.6
46.16 2 Chr 21.3

46.17 Lev 27.10
46.18 Ezek 45.8; Mic 2.1,2; Ezek 34.3-6,21
46.19 Ezek 42.9,13
46.20 2 Chr 35.13; Lev 2.4,5,7; Ezek 44.19
46.24 Ezek 44.11; ver 20
47.1 Jer 2.13; Joel 3.18; Zech 13.1; 14.8
47.2 Ezek 44.1,2,4
47.3 Ezek 40.3
47.6 Ezek 2.1; 8.6; 40.4; 44.5
47.7 ver 12; Rev 22.2
47.8 Deut 3.17; Isa 35.6,7; Josh 3.16
47.10 Gen 14.7; 2 Chr 20.2; Ezek 26.5,15; Num 34.6; Josh 23.4
47.12 ver 7; Job 8.16; Ps 1.3; Jer 17.8; Rev 22.2
47.13 Num 34.2-12; Gen 48.5; 1 Chr 5.1; Ezek 48.4
47.14 Gen 12.7; Deut 1.8; Ezek 20.5,6
47.15 Num 34.8; Ezek 48.1
47.16 ver 17,20; Ezek 48.1; ver 18
47.17 Num 34.9; Ezek 48.1; ver 16
47.18 ver 16; Jer 50.19; Gen 13.10,11

is their holding by inheritance. 17But if he makes a gift out of his inheritance to one of his servants, it shall be his to the year of liberty; then it shall revert to the prince; only his sons may keep a gift from his inheritance. 18The prince shall not take any of the inheritance of the people, thrusting them out of their holding; he shall give his sons their inheritance out of his own holding, so that none of my people shall be dispossessed of their holding.

19 Then he brought me through the entrance, which was at the side of the gate, to the north row of the holy chambers for the priests; and there I saw a place at the extreme western end of them. 20He said to me, "This is the place where the priests shall boil the guilt offering and the sin offering, and where they shall bake the grain offering, in order not to bring them out into the outer court and so communicate holiness to the people."

21 Then he brought me out to the outer court, and led me past the four corners of the court; and in each corner of the court there was a court— 22in the four corners of the court were small[q] courts, forty cubits long and thirty wide; the four were of the same size. 23On the inside, around each of the four courts[r] was a row of masonry, with hearths made at the bottom of the rows all around. 24Then he said to me, "These are the kitchens where those who serve at the temple shall boil the sacrifices of the people."

Water Flowing from the Temple

47 Then he brought me back to the entrance of the temple; there, water was flowing from below the threshold of the temple toward the east (for the temple faced east); and the water was flowing down from below the south end of the threshold of the temple, south of the altar. 2Then he brought me out by way of the north gate, and led me around on the outside to the outer gate that faces toward the east;[s] and the water was coming out on the south side.

3 Going on eastward with a cord in his hand, the man measured one thousand cubits, and then led me through the water; and it was ankle-deep. 4Again he measured one thousand, and led me through the water; and it was knee-deep. Again he measured one thousand, and led me through the water; and it was up to the waist. 5Again he measured one thousand, and it was a river that I could not cross, for the water had risen; it was deep enough to swim in, a river that could not be crossed. 6He said to me, "Mortal, have you seen this?"

Then he led me back along the bank of the river. 7As I came back, I saw on the bank of the river a great many trees on the one side and on the other. 8He said to me, "This water flows toward the eastern region and goes down into the Arabah; and when it enters the sea, the sea of stagnant waters, the water will become fresh. 9Wherever the river goes,[t] every living creature that swarms will live, and there will be very many fish, once these waters reach there. It will become fresh; and everything will live where the river goes. 10People will stand fishing beside the sea[u] from En-gedi to En-eglaim; it will be a place for the spreading of nets; its fish will be of a great many kinds, like the fish of the Great Sea. 11But its swamps and marshes will not become fresh; they are to be left for salt. 12On the banks, on both sides of the river, there will grow all kinds of trees for food. Their leaves will not wither nor their fruit fail, but they will bear fresh fruit every month, because the water for them flows from the sanctuary. Their fruit will be for food, and their leaves for healing."

The New Boundaries of the Land

13 Thus says the Lord God: These are the boundaries by which you shall divide the land for inheritance among the twelve tribes of Israel. Joseph shall have two portions. 14You shall divide it equally; I swore to give it to your ancestors, and this land shall fall to you as your inheritance.

15 This shall be the boundary of the land: On the north side, from the Great Sea by way of Hethlon to Lebo-hamath, and on to Zedad,[v] 16Berothah, Sibraim (which lies between the border of Damascus and the border of Hamath), as far as Hazer-hatticon, which is on the border of Hauran. 17So the boundary shall run from the sea to Hazar-enon, which is north of the border of Damascus, with the border of Hamath to the north.[w] This shall be the north side.

18 On the east side, between Hauran

[q] Gk Syr Vg: Meaning of Heb uncertain [r] Heb *the four of them* [s] Meaning of Heb uncertain [t] Gk Syr Vg Tg: Heb *the two rivers go* [u] Heb *it* [v] Gk: Heb *Lebo-zedad,* [16]*Hamath* [w] Meaning of Heb uncertain

46.19-24 Special kitchen space is to be set aside for preparing the priests' own sacrificial offerings, in order to avoid conveying the sacrifices' special quality of holiness to the common people.
47.1-12 Water flowing in huge quantities from the temple transforms the valley through which it flows, and the salty Dead Sea into which it empties, which (unlike its present and historic highly saline condition) becomes full of fish. Curiously, the *swamps and marshes* on its banks remain salty. This apparently was regarded as desirable because the Dead Sea was historically a major source of salt for inhabitants of the whole region. The trees watered by the river, however, produce crops each month, and their leaves are effective for healing purposes.
47.13-20 The new boundaries of Israel's land far exceed those of its extent historically: (1) the northern boundary goes from Hethlon (between Tyre and Sidon on what is now the Lebanese coast) to Lebo-hamath (on the Orontes River northwest of Damascus), and southeastward above Damascus to the Hauran (a broad plain south and east of Damascus; (2) the eastern border follows the Jordan to the *eastern* (Dead) *sea,* and then to the town of Tamar, south of the Dead Sea; (3) the southern border goes across to the west from Tamar through towns (Meribath-kadesh) and dry valleys (Wadi of Egypt) to the Mediterranean coast; (4) the western boundary follows the Mediterranean coast northward to Hamath in Syria.

47.21-48.35 This land is to be divided up among the twelve tribes, except for the holy districts around Jerusalem and its sanctuary, where there are special plots for the Levites and the *consecrated priests.* Appended to this list are further details of the city of Jerusalem, including the allotment of gates to the various groups of tribes. The circumference of the city will be over 6 miles (*18,000 cubits*), and it will receive a new name, suitable for the unique place of God's presence: *the LORD is there.*

and Damascus; along the Jordan between Gilead and the land of Israel; to the eastern sea and as far as Tamar.[x] This shall be the east side.

19 On the south side, it shall run from Tamar as far as the waters of Meribath-kadesh, from there along the Wadi of Egypt[y] to the Great Sea. This shall be the south side.

20 On the west side, the Great Sea shall be the boundary to a point opposite Lebo-hamath. This shall be the west side.

21 So you shall divide this land among you according to the tribes of Israel. 22You shall allot it as an inheritance for yourselves and for the aliens who reside among you and have begotten children among you. They shall be to you as citizens of Israel; with you they shall be allotted an inheritance among the tribes of Israel. 23In whatever tribe aliens reside, there you shall assign them their inheritance, says the Lord GOD.

The Tribal Portions

48 These are the names of the tribes: Beginning at the northern border, on the Hethlon road,[z] from Lebo-hamath, as far as Hazar-enon (which is on the border of Damascus, with Hamath to the north), and[a] extending from the east side to the west,[b] Dan, one portion. 2Adjoining the territory of Dan, from the east side to the west, Asher, one portion. 3Adjoining the territory of Asher, from the east side to the west, Naphtali, one portion. 4Adjoining the territory of Naphtali, from the east side to the west, Manasseh, one portion. 5Adjoining the territory of Manasseh, from the east side to the west, Ephraim, one portion. 6Adjoining the territory of Ephraim, from the east side to the west, Reuben, one portion. 7Adjoining the territory of Reuben, from the east side to the west, Judah, one portion.

8 Adjoining the territory of Judah, from the east side to the west, shall be the portion that you shall set apart, twenty-five thousand cubits in width, and in length equal to one of the tribal portions, from the east side to the west, with the sanctuary in the middle of it. 9The portion that you shall set apart for the LORD shall be twenty-five thousand cubits in length, and twenty[c] thousand in width. 10These shall be the allotments of the holy portion: the priests shall have an allotment measuring twenty-five thousand cubits on the northern side, ten thousand cubits in width on the western side, ten thousand in width on the eastern side, and twenty-five thousand in length on the southern side, with the sanctuary of the LORD in the middle of it. 11This shall be for the consecrated priests, the descendants[d] of Zadok, who kept my charge, who did not go astray when the people of Israel went astray, as the Levites did. 12It shall belong to them as a special portion from the holy portion of the land, a most holy place, adjoining the territory of the Levites. 13Alongside the territory of the priests, the Levites shall have an allotment twenty-five thousand cubits in length and ten thousand in width. The whole length shall be twenty-five thousand cubits and the width twenty[e] thousand. 14They shall not sell or exchange any of it; they shall not transfer this choice portion of the land, for it is holy to the LORD.

15 The remainder, five thousand cubits in width and twenty-five thousand in length, shall be for ordinary use for the city, for dwellings and for open country. In the middle of it shall be the city; 16and these shall be its dimensions: the north side four thousand five hundred cubits, the south side four thousand five hundred, the east side four thousand five hundred, and the west side four thousand five hundred. 17The city shall have open land: on the north two hundred fifty cubits, on the south two hundred fifty, on the east two hundred fifty, on the west two hundred fifty. 18The remainder of the length alongside the holy portion shall be ten thousand cubits to the east, and ten thousand to the west, and it shall be alongside the holy portion. Its produce shall be food for the workers of the city. 19The workers of the city, from all the tribes of Israel, shall cultivate it. 20The whole portion that you shall set apart shall be twenty-five thousand cubits square, that is, the holy portion together with the property of the city.

21 What remains on both sides of the holy portion and of the property of the city shall belong to the prince. Extending from the twenty-five thousand cubits of the holy portion to the east border, and westward

[x] Compare Syr: Heb *you shall measure* [y] Heb lacks *of Egypt* [z] Compare 47.15: Heb *by the side of the way* [a] Cn: Heb *and they shall be his* [b] Gk Compare verses 2–8: Heb *the east side the west* [c] Compare 45.1: Heb *ten* [d] One Ms Gk: Heb *of the descendants* [e] Gk: Heb *ten*

47.19 Ezek 48.28; Deut 32.51; Isa 27.12

47.20 Num 34.6; ver 10,15; Ezek 48.1; Am 6.14

47.22 Num 26.55,56; Isa 56.6,7; Rom 10.12; Eph 2.12-14; 3.6; Col 3.11

48.1 Ezek 47.15-17,20; Josh 19.40-48

48.2 Josh 19.24-31

48.3 Josh 19.32-39

48.4 Josh 13.29-31; 17.1-11

48.5 Josh 16.5-9; 17.8-10,14-18

48.6 Josh 13.15-21

48.7 Josh 15.1-63

48.8 Ezek 45.1-6

48.10 Ezek 44.28; 45.4; ver 8

48.11 Ezek 44.15; 44.10,12

48.12 Ezek 45.4

48.13 Ezek 45.3

48.14 Lev 25.32-34

48.15 Ezek 42.20; 45.6

48.16 Rev 21.16

48.17 Ezek 45.2

48.18 ver 8

48.19 Ezek 45.6

48.20 ver 16

48.21 Ezek 34.24; 45.7; ver 22,8,10

from the twenty-five thousand cubits to the west border, parallel to the tribal portions, it shall belong to the prince. The holy portion with the sanctuary of the temple in the middle of it, [22]and the property of the Levites and of the city, shall be in the middle of that which belongs to the prince. The portion of the prince shall lie between the territory of Judah and the territory of Benjamin.

23 As for the rest of the tribes: from the east side to the west, Benjamin, one portion. [24]Adjoining the territory of Benjamin, from the east side to the west, Simeon, one portion. [25]Adjoining the territory of Simeon, from the east side to the west, Issachar, one portion. [26]Adjoining the territory of Issachar, from the east side to the west, Zebulun, one portion. [27]Adjoining the territory of Zebulun, from the east side to the west, Gad, one portion. [28]And adjoining the territory of Gad to the south, the boundary shall run from Tamar to the waters of Meribath-kadesh, from there along the Wadi of Egypt[f] to the Great Sea. [29]This is the land that you shall allot as an inheritance among the tribes of Israel, and these are their portions, says the Lord GOD.

30 These shall be the exits of the city: On the north side, which is to be four thousand five hundred cubits by measure, [31]three gates, the gate of Reuben, the gate of Judah, and the gate of Levi, the gates of the city being named after the tribes of Israel. [32]On the east side, which is to be four thousand five hundred cubits, three gates, the gate of Joseph, the gate of Benjamin, and the gate of Dan. [33]On the south side, which is to be four thousand five hundred cubits by measure, three gates, the gate of Simeon, the gate of Issachar, and the gate of Zebulun. [34]On the west side, which is to be four thousand five hundred cubits, three gates,[g] the gate of Gad, the gate of Asher, and the gate of Naphtali. [35]The circumference of the city shall be eighteen thousand cubits. And the name of the city from that time on shall be, The LORD is There.

48.23 ver 1-7; Josh 18.21-28
48.24 Josh 19.1-9
48.25 Josh 19.17-23
48.26 Josh 19.10-16
48.27 Josh 13.24-28
48.28 Ezek 47.19,20
48.29 Ezek 47.13-20
48.30 ver 31-34
48.31 Rev 21.12,13
48.35 Isa 12.6; 24.23; Jer 3.17; 14.9; Joel 3.21; Rev 21.3; 22.3

[f] Heb lacks *of Egypt* [g] One Ms Gk Syr: MT *their gates three*

DANIEL

See the Introductions, pp. 6, 56-57, and 63-65 above.

Four Young Israelites at the Babylonian Court

1 In the third year of the reign of King Jehoiakim of Judah, King Nebuchadnezzar of Babylon came to Jerusalem and besieged it. [2]The Lord let King Jehoiakim of Judah fall into his power, as well as some of the vessels of the house of God. These he brought to the land of Shinar,[a] and placed the vessels in the treasury of his gods.

3 Then the king commanded his palace master Ashpenaz to bring some of the Israelites of the royal family and of the nobility, [4]young men without physical defect and handsome, versed in every branch of wisdom, endowed with knowledge and insight, and competent to serve in the king's palace; they were to be taught the literature and language of the Chaldeans. [5]The king assigned them a daily portion of the royal rations of food and wine. They were to be educated for three years, so that at the end of that time they could be stationed in the king's court. [6]Among them were Daniel, Hananiah, Mishael, and Azariah, from the tribe of Judah. [7]The palace master gave them other names: Daniel he called Belteshazzar, Hananiah he called Shadrach, Mishael he called Meshach, and Azariah he called Abednego.

8 But Daniel resolved that he would not defile himself with the royal rations of food and wine; so he asked the palace master to allow him not to defile himself. [9]Now God allowed Daniel to receive favor and compassion from the palace master. [10]The palace master said to Daniel, "I am afraid of my lord the king; he has appointed your food and your drink. If he should see you in poorer condition than the other young men of your own age, you would endanger my head with the king." [11]Then Daniel asked

[a] Gk Theodotion: Heb adds *to the house of his own gods*

1.1 2 Kings 24.1; 2 Chr 36.6
1.2 Jer 27.19,20; Isa 11.11; Zech 5.11
1.4 2 Sam 14.25; Dan 2.4
1.5 ver 8,18; 1 Kings 10.8; ver 19
1.6 Ezek 14.14,20; 28.3
1.7 Dan 4.8; 5.12; 2.49; 3.12
1.8 Deut 32.38; Ezek 4.13; Hos 9.3
1.9 Job 5.15,16; Ps 106.46; Prov 16.7

1.1-3 Introduction. The *third year of the reign of Jehoiakim* was 606 BCE. *Nebuchadnezzar* (the Hebrew form of the Babylonian name Nabuchadrezzar) seized Jerusalem in 597, and began carrying away to Babylon (*Shinar*) the treasures of the temple, the people and its king. The *god* worshiped in Babylon was Marduk.
1.4-21 Preparation of Daniel for his Role as Interpreter of God's Purpose.
1.4-7 To encourage acceptance of the Babylonian language and culture by the Jewish expatriates, able young Jewish men were given instruction and assigned roles in the royal palace. Babylonian names were even given to them, including *Belteshazzar* (Daniel), which is based on Bel, a Babylonian god.
1.8-15 Refusing to eat the food served to the royal household on account of Jewish dietary restrictions, Daniel and his friends gave evidence of God's favor toward them in that they flourished on a vegetable diet.

1.17-21 When the period of instruction and training was over, Daniel and his friends exceeded in *wisdom and understanding* the traditional consultants to the king concerning the future of the state, identified here as *magicians and enchanters*.
2.1-13 The Inability of the Official Soothsayers to Understand the King's Dream.
2.1-9 The designations of the court advisors, when joined with those in 1.20 (*sorcerers and Chaldeans* [=astrologers]), indicate that they were all of the astrological variety, interpreting dreams and celestial signs in order to predict the future. Here they are all called upon to bring back to the king's memory the content of his dream, under penalty of horrible execution if they fail.
2.10-16 The astrologers insist that the king is making an impossible demand, but Daniel intercedes with the king and offers to recall the dream and give an interpretation of it.
2.17-49 Daniel Recalls and Interprets the King's Dream.
2.17-23 On petition to God from Daniel and his friends, *the mystery* of the king's dream is disclosed to Daniel, and he expresses gratitude to the God who controls time, history and the operation of the natural order for the insight and wisdom which he discloses to his chosen instruments. The mystery is the secret divine plan for the future of humanity. Before the exile of Israel to Babylon, the prophets perceived these as disclosed to them as God's servants (Am 3.7), while those who predicted prosperity for the disobedient nation were denounced by God (Jer 23.18, 22). Later, in the Dead Sea Scrolls, the prophets are perceived as having foretold in detail what the destiny of this faithful remnant community will be. In the Qumran document 4Q 174, for example, the quotations from the prophets are followed by declarations such as *This means...*, or *This is...*, or *Interpreted, this saying concerns...* In 4Q 175, the promise of a prophet like Moses is quoted from Deut 18.8-19 as being fulfilled in the end time.

the guard whom the palace master had appointed over Daniel, Hananiah, Mishael, and Azariah: [12]"Please test your servants for ten days. Let us be given vegetables to eat and water to drink. [13]You can then compare our appearance with the appearance of the young men who eat the royal rations, and deal with your servants according to what you observe." [14]So he agreed to this proposal and tested them for ten days. [15]At the end of ten days it was observed that they appeared better and fatter than all the young men who had been eating the royal rations. [16]So the guard continued to withdraw their royal rations and the wine they were to drink, and gave them vegetables. [17]To these four young men God gave knowledge and skill in every aspect of literature and wisdom; Daniel also had insight into all visions and dreams.

18 At the end of the time that the king had set for them to be brought in, the palace master brought them into the presence of Nebuchadnezzar, [19]and the king spoke with them. And among them all, no one was found to compare with Daniel, Hananiah, Mishael, and Azariah; therefore they were stationed in the king's court. [20]In every matter of wisdom and understanding concerning which the king inquired of them, he found them ten times better than all the magicians and enchanters in his whole kingdom. [21]And Daniel continued there until the first year of King Cyrus.

Nebuchadnezzar's Dream

2 In the second year of Nebuchadnezzar's reign, Nebuchadnezzar dreamed such dreams that his spirit was troubled and his sleep left him. [2]So the king commanded that the magicians, the enchanters, the sorcerers, and the Chaldeans be summoned to tell the king his dreams. When they came in and stood before the king, [3]he said to them, "I have had such a dream that my spirit is troubled by the desire to understand it." [4]The Chaldeans said to the king (in Aramaic),[b] "O king, live forever! Tell your servants the dream, and we will reveal the interpretation." [5]The king answered the Chaldeans, "This is a public decree: if you do not tell me both the dream and its interpretation, you shall be torn limb from limb, and your houses shall be laid in ruins. [6]But if you do tell me the dream and its interpretation, you shall receive from me gifts and rewards and great honor. Therefore tell me the dream and its interpretation." [7]They answered a second time, "Let the king first tell his servants the dream, then we can give its interpretation." [8]The king answered, "I know with certainty that you are trying to gain time, because you see I have firmly decreed: [9]if you do not tell me the dream, there is but one verdict for you. You have agreed to speak lying and misleading words to me until things take a turn. Therefore, tell me the dream, and I shall know that you can give me its interpretation." [10]The Chaldeans answered the king, "There is no one on earth who can reveal what the king demands! In fact no king, however great and powerful, has ever asked such a thing of any magician or enchanter or Chaldean. [11]The thing that the king is asking is too difficult, and no one can reveal it to the king except the gods, whose dwelling is not with mortals."

12 Because of this the king flew into a violent rage and commanded that all the wise men of Babylon be destroyed. [13]The decree was issued, and the wise men were about to be executed; and they looked for Daniel and his companions, to execute them. [14]Then Daniel responded with prudence and discretion to Arioch, the king's chief executioner, who had gone out to execute the wise men of Babylon; [15]he asked Arioch, the royal official, "Why is the decree of the king so urgent?" Arioch then explained the matter to Daniel. [16]So Daniel went in and requested that the king give him time and he would tell the king the interpretation.

God Reveals Nebuchadnezzar's Dream

17 Then Daniel went to his home and informed his companions, Hananiah, Mishael, and Azariah, [18]and told them to seek mercy from the God of heaven concerning this mystery, so that Daniel and his companions with the rest of the wise men of Babylon might not perish. [19]Then the mystery was revealed to Daniel in a vision of the night, and Daniel blessed the God of heaven.

[20] Daniel said:
"Blessed be the name of God from age to age,
for wisdom and power are his.
[21] He changes times and seasons,

[b] The text from this point to the end of chapter 7 is in Aramaic

1.15 Ex 23.25; Prov 10.22
1.16 ver 12
1.17 1 Kings 3.12; Jas 1.5,17; Dan 2.19; 7.1; 8.1
1.18 ver 5,3,7
1.19 Gen 41.46; 1 Kings 10.8; Jer 15.1
1.20 Dan 2.27,28,46, 48; 2.2
1.21 Dan 6.28; 10.1
2.1 Gen 41.8; Dan 4.5; Esth 6.1; Dan 6.18
2.2 Gen 41.8; Ex 7.11; ver 10,27; Dan 5.7
2.3 Gen 40.8; 41.15; Dan 4.5
2.4 Isa 36.11; 1 Kings 1.31; Dan 3.9; 5.10; 6.6,21
2.5 Ezra 6.11; ver 12; Dan 3.29
2.6 Dan 5.7,16,29
2.7 ver 4
2.9 Esth 4.11; Isa 41.23
2.11 Dan 5.11; Isa 57.15
2.14 ver 24; Jer 52.12,14
2.15 Dan 3.22; ver 1-12
2.18 Isa 37.4; Jer 33.3; Dan 9.9
2.19 ver 22,27-29; Num 12.6; Job 33.15,16
2.20 Ps 113.2; Jer 32.19; ver 21-23
2.21 Esth 1.13; Dan 7.25; Job 12.18; Ps 75.6,7; Jas 1.5

deposes kings and sets up kings;
he gives wisdom to the wise
and knowledge to those who have understanding.
22 He reveals deep and hidden things;
he knows what is in the darkness,
and light dwells with him.
23 To you, O God of my ancestors,
I give thanks and praise,
for you have given me wisdom and power,
and have now revealed to me what we asked of you,
for you have revealed to us what the king ordered."

Daniel Interprets the Dream

24 Therefore Daniel went to Arioch, whom the king had appointed to destroy the wise men of Babylon, and said to him, "Do not destroy the wise men of Babylon; bring me in before the king, and I will give the king the interpretation."

25 Then Arioch quickly brought Daniel before the king and said to him: "I have found among the exiles from Judah a man who can tell the king the interpretation." 26 The king said to Daniel, whose name was Belteshazzar, "Are you able to tell me the dream that I have seen and its interpretation?" 27 Daniel answered the king, "No wise men, enchanters, magicians, or diviners can show to the king the mystery that the king is asking, 28 but there is a God in heaven who reveals mysteries, and he has disclosed to King Nebuchadnezzar what will happen at the end of days. Your dream and the visions of your head as you lay in bed were these: 29 To you, O king, as you lay in bed, came thoughts of what would be hereafter, and the revealer of mysteries disclosed to you what is to be. 30 But as for me, this mystery has not been revealed to me because of any wisdom that I have more than any other living being, but in order that the interpretation may be known to the king and that you may understand the thoughts of your mind.

31 "You were looking, O king, and lo! there was a great statue. This statue was huge, its brilliance extraordinary; it was standing before you, and its appearance was frightening. 32 The head of that statue was of fine gold, its chest and arms of silver, its middle and thighs of bronze, 33 its legs of iron, its feet partly of iron and partly of clay. 34 As you looked on, a stone was cut out, not by human hands, and it struck the statue on its feet of iron and clay and broke them in pieces. 35 Then the iron, the clay, the bronze, the silver, and the gold, were all broken in pieces and became like the chaff of the summer threshing floors; and the wind carried them away, so that not a trace of them could be found. But the stone that struck the statue became a great mountain and filled the whole earth.

36 "This was the dream; now we will tell the king its interpretation. 37 You, O king, the king of kings—to whom the God of heaven has given the kingdom, the power, the might, and the glory, 38 into whose hand he has given human beings, wherever they live, the wild animals of the field, and the birds of the air, and whom he has established as ruler over them all—you are the head of gold. 39 After you shall arise another kingdom inferior to yours, and yet a third kingdom of bronze, which shall rule over the whole earth. 40 And there shall be a fourth kingdom, strong as iron; just as iron crushes and smashes everything,[c] it shall crush and shatter all these. 41 As you saw the feet and toes partly of potter's clay and partly of iron, it shall be a divided kingdom; but some of the strength of iron shall be in it, as you saw the iron mixed with the clay. 42 As the toes of the feet were part iron and part clay, so the kingdom shall be partly strong and partly brittle. 43 As you saw the iron mixed with clay, so will they mix with one another in marriage,[d] but they will not hold together, just as iron does not mix with clay. 44 And in the days of those kings the God of heaven will set up a kingdom that shall never be destroyed, nor shall this kingdom be left to another people. It shall crush all these kingdoms and bring them to an end, and it shall stand forever; 45 just as you saw that a stone was cut from the mountain not by hands, and that it crushed the iron, the bronze, the clay, the silver, and the gold. The great God has informed the king what shall be hereafter. The dream is certain, and its interpretation trustworthy."

Daniel and His Friends Promoted

46 Then King Nebuchadnezzar fell on his face, worshiped Daniel, and commanded that a grain offering and incense be offered

[c] Gk Theodotion Syr Vg: Aram adds *and like iron that crushes* [d] Aram *by human seed*

2.22 Job 12.22; Ps 25.14; 139.11,12; Isa 45.7; Jer 23.24
2.25 Gen 41.14; Dan 1.6; 5.13; 6.13
2.28 Gen 40.8; 41.16; 49.1; Isa 2.2; Mic 4.1; Dan 4.5
2.29 ver 22,28
2.30 Gen 41.16; Isa 45.3; Ps 139.2
2.31 Dan 7.7; Hab 1.7
2.34 Dan 8.25; Zech 4.6; Isa 2.9; 60.12
2.35 Ps 1.4; Hos 13.3; Ps 37.10,36; Isa 2.2,3
2.37 Isa 47.5; Jer 27.6,7; Ezek 26.7; Ezra 1.2; Ps 62.11
2.38 Jer 27.6; Dan 4.21,22; ver 32
2.39 ver 32
2.40 Dan 7.7,23
2.41 ver 33
2.44 Ps 2.9; Isa 60.12; 1 Cor 15.24
2.45 Isa 28.16; ver 35; Dan 8.25; ver 29; Mal 1.11; Gen 41.28,32
2.46 Dan 8.17; Acts 10.25; 14.13; 28.6; Rev 19.10

2.24-45 After interceding with the king in behalf of the court advisors who could not discover the king's dream, Daniel offers his own interpretation of it. He gives credit to *the God in heaven who reveals mysteries*. The different parts of the *great statue* seen by the king in his dream included a head of gold, chest and arms of silver, middle and thighs of bronze, legs of iron, and feet of mixed iron and clay. These are the successive ages of human history, which are depicted in other ways in such Greco-Roman writers as Hesiod (*Works and Days*) and Ovid (*Metamorphoses*). The king of Babylon is the golden head; the three other parts of the body are the successive empires: Median, Persian and Greek (Alexander the Great). The latter's empire was divided into Ptolemaic and Seleucid segments, based in Egypt and Syria respectively – each with shifting rulers. All these are to be shattered and then replaced by God's rule, which will dominate the whole earth and endure forever.
2.46-49 The Babylonian king honors Daniel and his friends, calls for acknowledgement of their God, and offers them gifts and positions of power in the kingdom.

to him. [47]The king said to Daniel, "Truly, your God is God of gods and Lord of kings and a revealer of mysteries, for you have been able to reveal this mystery!" [48]Then the king promoted Daniel, gave him many great gifts, and made him ruler over the whole province of Babylon and chief prefect over all the wise men of Babylon. [49]Daniel made a request of the king, and he appointed Shadrach, Meshach, and Abednego over the affairs of the province of Babylon. But Daniel remained at the king's court.

The Golden Image

3 King Nebuchadnezzar made a golden statue whose height was sixty cubits and whose width was six cubits; he set it up on the plain of Dura in the province of Babylon. [2]Then King Nebuchadnezzar sent for the satraps, the prefects, and the governors, the counselors, the treasurers, the justices, the magistrates, and all the officials of the provinces to assemble and come to the dedication of the statue that King Nebuchadnezzar had set up. [3]So the satraps, the prefects, and the governors, the counselors, the treasurers, the justices, the magistrates, and all the officials of the provinces, assembled for the dedication of the statue that King Nebuchadnezzar had set up. When they were standing before the statue that Nebuchadnezzar had set up, [4]the herald proclaimed aloud, "You are commanded, O peoples, nations, and languages, [5]that when you hear the sound of the horn, pipe, lyre, trigon, harp, drum, and entire musical ensemble, you are to fall down and worship the golden statue that King Nebuchadnezzar has set up. [6]Whoever does not fall down and worship shall immediately be thrown into a furnace of blazing fire." [7]Therefore, as soon as all the peoples heard the sound of the horn, pipe, lyre, trigon, harp, drum, and entire musical ensemble, all the peoples, nations, and languages fell down and worshiped the golden statue that King Nebuchadnezzar had set up.

8 Accordingly, at this time certain Chaldeans came forward and denounced the Jews. [9]They said to King Nebuchadnezzar, "O king, live forever! [10]You, O king, have made a decree, that everyone who hears the sound of the horn, pipe, lyre, trigon, harp, drum, and entire musical ensemble, shall fall down and worship the golden statue, [11]and whoever does not fall down and worship shall be thrown into a furnace of blazing fire. [12]There are certain Jews whom you have appointed over the affairs of the province of Babylon: Shadrach, Meshach, and Abednego. These pay no heed to you, O King. They do not serve your gods and they do not worship the golden statue that you have set up."

13 Then Nebuchadnezzar in furious rage commanded that Shadrach, Meshach, and Abednego be brought in; so they brought those men before the king. [14]Nebuchadnezzar said to them, "Is it true, O Shadrach, Meshach, and Abednego, that you do not serve my gods and you do not worship the golden statue that I have set up? [15]Now if you are ready when you hear the sound of the horn, pipe, lyre, trigon, harp, drum, and entire musical ensemble to fall down and worship the statue that I have made, well and good.[e] But if you do not worship, you shall immediately be thrown into a furnace of blazing fire, and who is the god that will deliver you out of my hands?"

16 Shadrach, Meshach, and Abednego answered the king, "O Nebuchadnezzar, we have no need to present a defense to you in this matter. [17]If our God whom we serve is able to deliver us from the furnace of blazing fire and out of your hand, O king, let him deliver us.[f] [18]But if not, be it known to you, O king, that we will not serve your gods and we will not worship the golden statue that you have set up."

The Fiery Furnace

19 Then Nebuchadnezzar was so filled with rage against Shadrach, Meshach, and Abednego that his face was distorted. He ordered the furnace heated up seven times more than was customary, [20]and ordered some of the strongest guards in his army to bind Shadrach, Meshach, and Abednego and to throw them into the furnace of blazing fire. [21]So the men were bound, still wearing their tunics,[g] their trousers,[g] their hats, and their other garments, and they were thrown into the furnace of blazing fire. [22]Because the king's command was urgent and the furnace was so overheated, the raging flames killed the men who lifted

[e] Aram lacks *well and good* [f] Or *If our God whom we serve is able to deliver us, he will deliver us from the furnace of blazing fire and out of your hand, O king.* [g] Meaning of Aram word uncertain

3.1-12 The King's Command to All to Worship the Great Image. The image stands ninety feet tall and is covered with gold. Worship of the image is to be led by all the officers and agents of the empire, and participated in by all the subjects. The titles of those summoned to fall down before it include the Persian term *satrap.* The musical instruments that are to be played in celebration have names that derive from Greek (*gitaras,* lyre; *psalterion,* harp; *symphonias,* pipe). This linguistic evidence shows that Daniel is writing after the Persians have been replaced by Greeks as the dominant cultural force in the east: that is, in the hellenistic period. The *Chaldeans* who denounce Daniel and his associates to the king are astrologers who want to predict a happier future for the king and his realm. The story may antedate the reign of Antiochus IV Epiphanes (175-163 BCE) who had a statue of himself erected in the Jerusalem temple in 168 BCE, but the crisis created in Daniel 3 closely resembles the one which took place under Antiochus. Daniel was written in reaction to that hellenistic ruler.
3.13-30 Nebuchadnezzar orders these three who refuse to obey the royal decree by worshiping *the golden statue* to be thrown into the *furnace.* They are joined in the furnace by a fourth figure who resembles a *god* and they are miraculously delivered. This companion who *has the appearance of a god* is said in 3.28 to be an angel or agent of God. The king's addressing Daniel and his friends as *servants of the Most High God* does not indicate his conversion to Jewish faith, but is the term used by other non-Israelites who acknowledge the power of their God: Balaam (Num 24.16), and the Babylonian king in Isa 14.14. The king decrees punishment for anyone who reproaches the god of this faithful three.

2.47 Dan 11.36; ver 22,28
2.48 ver 6; Dan 4.9; 5.11
2.49 Dan 3.12; Esth 2.19,21; Dan 3.2
3.1 Isa 46.6; Hab 2.19; ver 30; Dan 2.48
3.2 ver 3,27
3.4 Isa 40.9; 58.1; Rev 18.2; Dan 4.1; 6.25
3.5 ver 7,10,15
3.6 ver 11,15,21; Jer 29.22; Rev 14.11
3.7 ver 4,5
3.8 Dan 4.7; 6.12
3.9 Dan 2.4; 5.10
3.10 ver 4-6; Dan 6.2; ver 5,7,15
3.12 Dan 2.49; 1.7; 6.13
3.13 Dan 2.12; ver 19
3.14 Isa 46.1; Jer 50.2; ver 1
3.15 ver 5,6; Ex 5.2; Isa 36.18-20; Dan 2.47

Shadrach, Meshach, and Abednego. 23But
the three men, Shadrach, Meshach, and
Abednego, fell down, bound, into the furnace of blazing fire.
24 Then King Nebuchadnezzar was astonished and rose up quickly. He said to his
counselors, "Was it not three men that we
threw bound into the fire?" They answered
the king, "True, O king." 25He replied, "But
I see four men unbound, walking in the
middle of the fire, and they are not hurt;
and the fourth has the appearance of a
god."[h] 26Nebuchadnezzar then approached
the door of the furnace of blazing fire and
said, "Shadrach, Meshach, and Abednego,
servants of the Most High God, come out!
Come here!" So Shadrach, Meshach, and
Abednego came out from the fire. 27And the
satraps, the prefects, the governors, and the
king's counselors gathered together and saw
that the fire had not had any power over
the bodies of those men; the hair of their
heads was not singed, their tunics[i] were not
harmed, and not even the smell of fire came
from them. 28Nebuchadnezzar said, "Blessed
be the God of Shadrach, Meshach, and
Abednego, who has sent his angel and
delivered his servants who trusted in him.
They disobeyed the king's command and
yielded up their bodies rather than serve
and worship any god except their own God.
29Therefore I make a decree: Any people,
nation, or language that utters blasphemy
against the God of Shadrach, Meshach, and
Abednego shall be torn limb from limb, and
their houses laid in ruins; for there is no
other god who is able to deliver in this
way." 30Then the king promoted Shadrach,
Meshach, and Abednego in the province of
Babylon.

Nebuchadnezzar's Second Dream

4[j] King Nebuchadnezzar to all peoples,
nations, and languages that live
throughout the earth: May you have abundant prosperity! 2The signs and wonders
that the Most High God has worked for me
I am pleased to recount.

3 How great are his signs,
how mighty his wonders!
His kingdom is an everlasting kingdom,
and his sovereignty is from generation
to generation.

4[k] I, Nebuchadnezzar, was living at ease
in my home and prospering in my palace.
5I saw a dream that frightened me; my
fantasies in bed and the visions of my head
terrified me. 6So I made a decree that all the
wise men of Babylon should be brought
before me, in order that they might tell me
the interpretation of the dream. 7Then the
magicians, the enchanters, the Chaldeans,
and the diviners came in, and I told them
the dream, but they could not tell me its
interpretation. 8At last Daniel came in before me—he who was named Belteshazzar
after the name of my god, and who is
endowed with a spirit of the holy gods[l]—
and I told him the dream: 9"O Belteshazzar,
chief of the magicians, I know that you are
endowed with a spirit of the holy gods[l] and
that no mystery is too difficult for you.
Hear[m] the dream that I saw; tell me its
interpretation.

10[n] Upon my bed this is what I saw;
there was a tree at the center of the
earth,
and its height was great.
11 The tree grew great and strong,
its top reached to heaven,
and it was visible to the ends of the
whole earth.
12 Its foliage was beautiful,
its fruit abundant,
and it provided food for all.
The animals of the field found shade
under it,
the birds of the air nested in its
branches,
and from it all living beings were fed.

13I continued looking, in the visions of my
head as I lay in bed, and there was a holy
watcher, coming down from heaven. 14He
cried aloud and said:

'Cut down the tree and chop off its
branches,
strip off its foliage and scatter its fruit.
Let the animals flee from beneath it
and the birds from its branches.
15 But leave its stump and roots in the
ground,
with a band of iron and bronze,
in the tender grass of the field.
Let him be bathed with the dew of heaven,
and let his lot be with the animals of
the field

[h] Aram *a son of the gods* [i] Meaning of Aram word uncertain [j] Ch 3.31 in Aram [k] Ch 4.1 in Aram [l] Or *a holy, divine spirit* [m] Theodotion: Aram *The visions of* [n] Theodotion Syr Compare Gk: Aram adds *The visions of my head*

3.27 ver 2; Isa 43.2; Heb 11.34; ver 21
3.28 ver 15,25; Acts 5.19; 12.7; Ps 34.7,8; Jer 17.7; ver 18
3.29 Dan 6.26; ver 12; Dan 2.5; 2.47; 6.27
3.30 Dan 2.49
4.1 Dan 6.25
4.2 Dan 3.26
4.3 Dan 6.27; ver 34; Dan 2.44; 6.26
4.4 Isa 47.7,8
4.5 Dan 2.28,29; 2.1
4.6 Dan 2.2
4.7 Dan 2.2
4.8 Dan 1.7; 2.26; 5.11,14
4.9 Dan 2.48; 5.11; 2.47,4,5
4.10 ver 5,20; Ezek 31.3-6
4.12 Ezek 31.6,7; Lam 4.20; Mt 13.32; Lk 13.19
4.13 Dan 7.1; ver 17,23; Dan 8.13; Zech 14.5
4.14 Ezek 31.10-14; Mt 3.10; Ezek 31.12,13

4.1-37 Nebuchadnezzar's Second Dream, its Interpretation and Consequences.
4.1-3 Nebuchadnezzar's praise of the Most High is repeated, as in Dan 3.28-29. God's *everlasting rule* is timeless in duration and limitless in power.
4.4-9 The court *Chaldeans* (astrologers) are once again unable to interpret the king's dream. Daniel (*Belteshazzar*) is summoned and the king recounts his dream, unlike 2.25-35 where he could not recall it.
4.10-27 The *tree* which is the subject of the dream symbolizes the mighty rule of Nebuchadnezzar, which is recognized across the world by humans and animals. The world-tree symbol appears in Ezek 31, where the tree is chopped down (31.10-14), just as the *stump* of a monarchy appears in the prophetic oracles of Isaiah (11.1). The coming of the *watcher from heaven* (an angel or sentinel, who perceives God's purpose and is the agent by which it is accomplished) indicates that divine judgment is about to fall on the king of Babylon.

4.28-33 The king's adopting the location and lifestyle of an animal is a kind of insanity, as his subsequent recovery of *reason* (vs. 36) makes clear. Ancient accounts of the kings of Babylon report no such interruption in the reign of Nebuchadnezzar, but a later king, Nabonidus (556-539 BCE), did disappear from the throne for an extended period, and this story in Daniel may reflect that historical recollection. The aim of the humiliation of the king is to enable him to recognize that *the Most High* is sovereign over all human affairs. Nebuchadnezzar's subsequent acts of mercy to his subjects will *atone* for his sins, but in spite of his lament, the divine decree is put into effect and the king begins to live like a wild animal.
4.34-37 Penitent, Nebuchadnezzar at the end of his period of banishment acknowledges the sovereignty of the Most High, and is *restored* to the *glory* of his kingdom.

in the grass of the earth.
16 Let his mind be changed from that of a human,
and let the mind of an animal be given to him.
And let seven times pass over him.
17 The sentence is rendered by decree of the watchers,
the decision is given by order of the holy ones,
in order that all who live may know
that the Most High is sovereign over the kingdom of mortals;
he gives it to whom he will
and sets over it the lowliest of human beings.'

18 This is the dream that I, King Nebuchadnezzar, saw. Now you, Belteshazzar, declare
the interpretation, since all the wise men of
my kingdom are unable to tell me the
interpretation. You are able, however, for
you are endowed with a spirit of the holy
gods."[o]

Daniel Interprets the Second Dream

19 Then Daniel, who was called
Belteshazzar, was severely distressed for a
while. His thoughts terrified him. The king
said, "Belteshazzar, do not let the dream or
the interpretation terrify you." Belteshazzar
answered, "My lord, may the dream be for
those who hate you, and its interpretation
for your enemies! 20 The tree that you saw,
which grew great and strong, so that its top
reached to heaven and was visible to the
end of the whole earth, 21 whose foliage was
beautiful and its fruit abundant, and which
provided food for all, under which animals
of the field lived, and in whose branches the
birds of the air had nests— 22 it is you, O
king! You have grown great and strong.
Your greatness has increased and reaches
to heaven, and your sovereignty to the ends
of the earth. 23 And whereas the king saw
a holy watcher coming down from heaven
and saying, 'Cut down the tree and destroy
it, but leave its stump and roots in the
ground, with a band of iron and bronze, in
the grass of the field; and let him be bathed
with the dew of heaven, and let his lot be
with the animals of the field, until seven
times pass over him'— 24 this is the interpretation, O king, and it is a decree of the Most
High that has come upon my lord the king:
25 You shall be driven away from human
society, and your dwelling shall be with the
wild animals. You shall be made to eat
grass like oxen, you shall be bathed with
the dew of heaven, and seven times shall
pass over you, until you have learned that
the Most High has sovereignty over the
kingdom of mortals, and gives it to whom
he will. 26 As it was commanded to leave the
stump and roots of the tree, your kingdom
shall be re-established for you from the time
that you learn that Heaven is sovereign.
27 Therefore, O king, may my counsel be
acceptable to you: atone for[p] your sins with
righteousness, and your iniquities with mercy
to the oppressed, so that your prosperity
may be prolonged."

Nebuchadnezzar's Humiliation

28 All this came upon King Nebuchadnezzar. 29 At the end of twelve months he
was walking on the roof of the royal palace
of Babylon, 30 and the king said, "Is this not
magnificent Babylon, which I have built as
a royal capital by my mighty power and for
my glorious majesty?" 31 While the words
were still in the king's mouth, a voice came
from heaven: "O King Nebuchadnezzar, to
you it is declared: The kingdom has departed from you! 32 You shall be driven away
from human society, and your dwelling
shall be with the animals of the field. You
shall be made to eat grass like oxen, and
seven times shall pass over you, until you
have learned that the Most High has sovereignty over the kingdom of mortals and
gives it to whom he will." 33 Immediately the
sentence was fulfilled against Nebuchadnezzar. He was driven away from human
society, ate grass like oxen, and his body
was bathed with the dew of heaven, until
his hair grew as long as eagles' feathers and
his nails became like birds' claws.

Nebuchadnezzar Praises God

34 When that period was over, I,
Nebuchadnezzar, lifted my eyes to heaven,
and my reason returned to me.
I blessed the Most High,
and praised and honored the one who lives forever.
For his sovereignty is an everlasting sovereignty,
and his kingdom endures from

[o] Or *a holy, divine spirit* [p] Aram *break off*

4.16 Dan 7.25; 11.13; 12.7
4.17 Ps 9.16; ver 2,25; Dan 5.18,19; 11.21
4.18 Gen 41.8,15; Dan 5.8,15; ver 7-9
4.19 Dan 7.15,28; 2 Sam 18.32; Jer 29.7
4.20 ver 10-12
4.22 2 Sam 12.7; Dan 2.37,38; 5.18,19; Jer 27.6-8
4.23 ver 13-17; Dan 5.21
4.25 Dan 5.21; Ps 83.18; Jer 27.5
4.26 Mt 21.25; Lk 15.18
4.27 Isa 55.6,7; Ezek 18.21,22; Ps 41.1-3; 1 Kings 21.29
4.28 Zech 1.6
4.30 Hab 2.4; ver 25; Dan 5.20,21; Isa 37.24,25
4.31 Dan 5.5; ver 13,14,23
4.33 Dan 5.21
4.34 ver 16,25,32,36, 2; Dan 5.18,21; 12.7; Rev 4.10; Lk 1.33

generation to generation.
35 All the inhabitants of the earth are
accounted as nothing,
and he does what he wills with the
host of heaven
and the inhabitants of the earth.
There is no one who can stay his hand
or say to him, "What are you doing?"

36At that time my reason returned to me; and my majesty and splendor were restored to me for the glory of my kingdom. My counselors and my lords sought me out, I was re-established over my kingdom, and still more greatness was added to me. 37Now I, Nebuchadnezzar, praise and extol and honor the King of heaven,

for all his works are truth,
and his ways are justice;
and he is able to bring low
those who walk in pride.

Belshazzar's Feast

5 King Belshazzar made a great festival for a thousand of his lords, and he was drinking wine in the presence of the thousand.

2 Under the influence of the wine, Belshazzar commanded that they bring in the vessels of gold and silver that his father Nebuchadnezzar had taken out of the temple in Jerusalem, so that the king and his lords, his wives, and his concubines might drink from them. 3So they brought in the vessels of gold and silver[q] that had been taken out of the temple, the house of God in Jerusalem, and the king and his lords, his wives, and his concubines drank from them. 4They drank the wine and praised the gods of gold and silver, bronze, iron, wood, and stone.

The Writing on the Wall

5 Immediately the fingers of a human hand appeared and began writing on the plaster of the wall of the royal palace, next to the lampstand. The king was watching the hand as it wrote. 6Then the king's face turned pale, and his thoughts terrified him. His limbs gave way, and his knees knocked together. 7The king cried aloud to bring in the enchanters, the Chaldeans, and the diviners; and the king said to the wise men of Babylon, "Whoever can read this writing and tell me its interpretation shall be clothed in purple, have a chain of gold around his neck, and rank third in the kingdom." 8Then all the king's wise men came in, but they could not read the writing or tell the king the interpretation. 9Then King Belshazzar became greatly terrified and his face turned pale, and his lords were perplexed.

10 The queen, when she heard the discussion of the king and his lords, came into the banqueting hall. The queen said, "O king, live forever! Do not let your thoughts terrify you or your face grow pale. 11There is a man in your kingdom who is endowed with a spirit of the holy gods.[r] In the days of your father he was found to have enlightenment, understanding, and wisdom like the wisdom of the gods. Your father, King Nebuchadnezzar, made him chief of the magicians, enchanters, Chaldeans, and diviners,[s] 12because an excellent spirit, knowledge, and understanding to interpret dreams, explain riddles, and solve problems were found in this Daniel, whom the king named Belteshazzar. Now let Daniel be called, and he will give the interpretation."

The Writing on the Wall Interpreted

13 Then Daniel was brought in before the king. The king said to Daniel, "So you are Daniel, one of the exiles of Judah, whom my father the king brought from Judah? 14I have heard of you that a spirit of the gods[t] is in you, and that enlightenment, understanding, and excellent wisdom are found in you. 15Now the wise men, the enchanters, have been brought in before me to read this writing and tell me its interpretation, but they were not able to give the interpretation of the matter. 16But I have heard that you can give interpretations and solve problems. Now if you are able to read the writing and tell me its interpretation, you shall be clothed in purple, have a chain of gold around your neck, and rank third in the kingdom."

17 Then Daniel answered in the presence of the king, "Let your gifts be for yourself, or give your rewards to someone else! Nevertheless I will read the writing to the king and let him know the interpretation. 18O king, the Most High God gave your father Nebuchadnezzar kingship, greatness, glory, and majesty. 19And because of the

[q] Theodotion Vg: Aram lacks *and silver* [r] Or *a holy, divine spirit* [s] Aram adds *the king your father* [t] Or *a divine spirit*

4.35 Isa 40.15,17; Ps 135.6; Isa 43.13; 45.9; Rom 9.20
4.36 ver 34,30; Dan 2.31; ver 26
4.37 Ps 33.4,5; Ex 18.11; Dan 5.20
5.1 Esth 1.3
5.2 Dan 1.2; Jer 52.19; ver 23
5.4 ver 23; Rev 9.20
5.5 Dan 4.31; ver 24
5.6 Dan 4.5,19; Nah 2.10; Ezek 7.17; 21.7
5.7 Isa 47.13; Dan 2.6; Ezek 16.11; Dan 6.2,3
5.8 Dan 2.10,27; 4.7
5.9 Isa 21.2-4; Jer 6.24; ver 6
5.10 Dan 2.4; 3.9
5.11 Dan 2.47,48; 4.8,9,18; 1.17
5.12 Dan 6.3; 1.7
5.13 Dan 2.25; 6.13; 1.1,2
5.16 Gen 40.8; ver 7,29
5.17 2 Kings 5.16
5.18 ver 21; Dan 2.37,38; 4.17; Jer 27.5-7
5.19 Dan 3.4; 2.12,13

5.1-30 Belshazzar's Feast and his Death.
5.1-4 This vivid story combines features of historical recollections with creative imagination: Belshazzar was actually the son of Nabonidus, king of Babylon (556-539), not Nebuchadnezzar (605-562), and was co-regent with his father when the city was captured by the Persians under Cyrus in 539. There was a legend that the king of Babylon was in the midst of a drunken feast when his empire was attacked and taken over. The symbolic force of this story in Daniel stands in spite of the mix of fact and fiction that it represents. Added to the tradition here are the details of the defilement at a royal, secular orgy of the sacred *vessels* from the Jerusalem temple, which served as an insult to the God of Israel.
5.5-12 As in the Nebuchadnezzar stories (Dan 2,4), the inability of the royal predicters of the future to understand the message from God contrasts with Daniel's God-given capability.
5.13-28 Recalling God's humiliation of Nebuchadnezzar when he left the splendor of his palace and lived like a wild animal, the message inscribed by the mysterious fingers on the palace wall is read and interpreted by Daniel. The literal meanings of the words refer to units of weight: *Mene*, a mina; *Tekel*, a shekel; *Parsin*, a half-shekel. But as vs. 27 shows, each of these words is a pun: Mene= [God] has numbered; Tekel=you have been weighed; Parsin = you have been divided [by God].

5.29-30 Daniel is honored by the king for his skill in interpreting these messages, but the seizure of the kingdom by the Persians takes place that night. *Darius the Mede* is not found in any historical sources. The Medes, who competed with the Persians for control of what is now Iran and part of Iraq, were defeated by Cyrus of Persia in 550. It was he who captured Babylon in 539. There was a Darius of Persia who ascended the throne after the death of Cyrus' son, Cambyses (530-522). These historical traditions are blended and altered by the author of Daniel.
6.1-28 Daniel Delivered from the Lions.
6.1-9 In the hierarchical administrative structure of Darius, *satraps* (regional governors) reported to three *presidents* (or chief ministers), of whom Daniel stood out for his efficiency and integrity. He was being considered by the king for appointment as a kind of prime minister when the other royal leaders conspired to have him condemned as a violator of the king's decree prohibiting anyone from offering prayers to any divinity except the king.
6.10-28 The decree did not deter Daniel from praying thrice daily to the God who dwelt in Jerusalem. Reported to the king as a violator of the royal prohibition, Daniel was placed in a den of lions, which was sealed with the royal insignia. After a sleepless night, the king found Daniel alive, since God had protected him from the lions because of his fidelity to God and the king. Daniel's enemies are eaten by the lions, and the king sends out a decree through all his realm honoring and acknowledging the power of *the living God* who saved Daniel.

greatness that he gave him, all peoples, nations, and languages trembled and feared before him. He killed those he wanted to kill, kept alive those he wanted to keep alive, honored those he wanted to honor, and degraded those he wanted to degrade. 20 But when his heart was lifted up and his spirit was hardened so that he acted proudly, he was deposed from his kingly throne, and his glory was stripped from him. 21 He was driven from human society, and his mind was made like that of an animal. His dwelling was with the wild asses, he was fed grass like oxen, and his body was bathed with the dew of heaven, until he learned that the Most High God has sovereignty over the kingdom of mortals, and sets over it whomever he will. 22 And you, Belshazzar his son, have not humbled your heart, even though you knew all this! 23 You have exalted yourself against the Lord of heaven! The vessels of his temple have been brought in before you, and you and your lords, your wives and your concubines have been drinking wine from them. You have praised the gods of silver and gold, of bronze, iron, wood, and stone, which do not see or hear or know; but the God in whose power is your very breath, and to whom belong all your ways, you have not honored.

24 "So from his presence the hand was sent and this writing was inscribed. 25 And this is the writing that was inscribed: MENE, MENE, TEKEL, and PARSIN. 26 This is the interpretation of the matter: MENE, God has numbered the days of[u] your kingdom and brought it to an end; 27 TEKEL, you have been weighed on the scales and found wanting; 28 PERES,[v] your kingdom is divided and given to the Medes and Persians."

29 Then Belshazzar gave the command, and Daniel was clothed in purple, a chain of gold was put around his neck, and a proclamation was made concerning him that he should rank third in the kingdom.

30 That very night Belshazzar, the Chaldean king, was killed. 31 [w]And Darius the Mede received the kingdom, being about sixty-two years old.

The Plot against Daniel

6 It pleased Darius to set over the kingdom one hundred twenty satraps, stationed throughout the whole kingdom, 2 and over them three presidents, including Daniel; to these the satraps gave account, so that the king might suffer no loss. 3 Soon Daniel distinguished himself above all the other presidents and satraps because an excellent spirit was in him, and the king planned to appoint him over the whole kingdom. 4 So the presidents and the satraps tried to find grounds for complaint against Daniel in connection with the kingdom. But they could find no grounds for complaint or any corruption, because he was faithful, and no negligence or corruption could be found in him. 5 The men said, "We shall not find any ground for complaint against this Daniel unless we find it in connection with the law of his God."

6 So the presidents and satraps conspired and came to the king and said to him, "O King Darius, live forever! 7 All the presidents of the kingdom, the prefects and the satraps, the counselors and the governors are agreed that the king should establish an ordinance and enforce an interdict, that whoever prays to anyone, divine or human, for thirty days, except to you, O king, shall be thrown into a den of lions. 8 Now, O king, establish the interdict and sign the document, so that it cannot be changed, according to the law of the Medes and the Persians, which cannot be revoked." 9 Therefore King Darius signed the document and interdict.

Daniel in the Lions' Den

10 Although Daniel knew that the document had been signed, he continued to go to his house, which had windows in its upper room open toward Jerusalem, and to get down on his knees three times a day to pray to his God and praise him, just as he had done previously. 11 The conspirators came and found Daniel praying and seeking mercy before his God. 12 Then they approached the king and said concerning the interdict, "O king! Did you not sign an interdict, that anyone who prays to anyone, divine or human, within thirty days except to you, O king, shall be thrown into a den of lions?" The king answered, "The thing stands fast, according to the law of the Medes and Persians, which cannot be revoked." 13 Then they responded to the king, "Daniel, one of the exiles from Judah, pays no attention to you, O king, or to the interdict you have signed, but he is saying his prayers three times a day."

[u] Aram lacks *the days of* [v] The singular of *Parsin* [w] Ch 6.1 in Aram

5.20 Dan 4.30,37; 2 Kings 17.14; 2 Chr 36.13; Jer 13.18
5.21 Dan 4.32-34; 4.16; Ezek 17.24; Dan 4.34,35
5.22 2 Chr 33.23; 36.12
5.23 Jer 50.29; ver 3,4; Ps 115.5,6; Hab 2.18,19; Job 12.10; 31.4; Jer 10.23
5.24 ver 5
5.26 Isa 13.6,17; Jer 27.7; 50.41-43
5.27 Job 31.6; Ps 62.9
5.30 Isa 21.4-9; Jer 51.31,39, 57
5.31 Dan 6.1; 9.1
6.1 Esth 1.1; Dan 5.31
6.2 Dan 2.48,49; Ezra 4.22
6.3 Dan 1.20; 5.12,14; Esth 10.3
6.4 Gen 43.18; ver 22
6.6 ver 21; Neh 2.3; Dan 2.4
6.7 Dan 3.2,27; Ps 59.3; Dan 3.6; ver 16
6.8 ver 12,15; Esth 1.19; 8.8
6.9 Ps 118.9; 146.3
6.10 1 Kings 8.48,49; Ps 95.6; 55.17; 1 Thess 5.17,18
6.12 Dan 3.8; Acts 16.19-21
6.13 Dan 1.6; 5.13; Esth 3.8; Dan 3.12; Acts 5.29

14 When the king heard the charge, he
was very much distressed. He was determined to save Daniel, and until the sun
went down he made every effort to rescue
him. 15 Then the conspirators came to the
king and said to him, "Know, O king, that
it is a law of the Medes and Persians that
no interdict or ordinance that the king
establishes can be changed."
16 Then the king gave the command,
and Daniel was brought and thrown into
the den of lions. The king said to Daniel,
"May your God, whom you faithfully serve,
deliver you!" 17 A stone was brought and
laid on the mouth of the den, and the king
sealed it with his own signet and with the
signet of his lords, so that nothing might be
changed concerning Daniel. 18 Then the king
went to his palace and spent the night
fasting; no food was brought to him, and
sleep fled from him.

Daniel Saved from the Lions

19 Then, at break of day, the king got up
and hurried to the den of lions. 20 When he
came near the den where Daniel was, he
cried out anxiously to Daniel, "O Daniel,
servant of the living God, has your God
whom you faithfully serve been able to
deliver you from the lions?" 21 Daniel then
said to the king, "O king, live forever! 22 My
God sent his angel and shut the lions'
mouths so that they would not hurt me,
because I was found blameless before him;
and also before you, O king, I have done no
wrong." 23 Then the king was exceedingly
glad and commanded that Daniel be taken
up out of the den. So Daniel was taken up
out of the den, and no kind of harm was
found on him, because he had trusted in his
God. 24 The king gave a command, and
those who had accused Daniel were brought
and thrown into the den of lions—they,
their children, and their wives. Before they
reached the bottom of the den the lions
overpowered them and broke all their bones
in pieces.
25 Then King Darius wrote to all peoples
and nations of every language throughout
the whole world: "May you have abundant
prosperity! 26 I make a decree, that in all my
royal dominion people should tremble and
fear before the God of Daniel:

For he is the living God,
  enduring forever.
His kingdom shall never be destroyed,
  and his dominion has no end.
27 He delivers and rescues,
  he works signs and wonders in
    heaven and on earth;
for he has saved Daniel
  from the power of the lions."

28 So this Daniel prospered during the reign
of Darius and the reign of Cyrus the
Persian.

Visions of the Four Beasts

7 In the first year of King Belshazzar of
Babylon, Daniel had a dream and
visions of his head as he lay in bed. Then
he wrote down the dream:[x] 2 I,[y] Daniel, saw
in my vision by night the four winds of
heaven stirring up the great sea, 3 and four
great beasts came up out of the sea, different from one another. 4 The first was like a
lion and had eagles' wings. Then, as I
watched, its wings were plucked off, and it
was lifted up from the ground and made to
stand on two feet like a human being; and
a human mind was given to it. 5 Another
beast appeared, a second one, that looked
like a bear. It was raised up on one side, had
three tusks[z] in its mouth among its teeth
and was told, "Arise, devour many bodies!"
6 After this, as I watched, another appeared,
like a leopard. The beast had four wings of
a bird on its back and four heads; and
dominion was given to it. 7 After this I saw
in the visions by night a fourth beast, terrifying and dreadful and exceedingly strong.
It had great iron teeth and was devouring,
breaking in pieces, and stamping what was
left with its feet. It was different from all the
beasts that preceded it, and it had ten horns.
8 I was considering the horns, when another
horn appeared, a little one coming up among
them; to make room for it, three of the
earlier horns were plucked up by the roots.
There were eyes like human eyes in this
horn, and a mouth speaking arrogantly.

Judgment before the Ancient One

9 As I watched,
thrones were set in place,
  and an Ancient One[a] took his throne,
his clothing was white as snow,

6.14 Mk 6.26
6.15 Esth 8.8; ver 8
6.16 Jer 38.5; ver 7,20; Ps 37,39,40
6.18 2 Sam 12.16,17; Esth 6.1; Dan 2.1
6.20 ver 26,27; Jer 32.17; Dan 3.17
6.22 Acts 12.11; 2 Tim 4.17; Heb 11.33; 1 Sam 24.10
6.23 ver 14,18; Dan 3.25,27; Isa 26.3; Heb 11.33
6.24 2 Kings 14.6; Ps 54.5; Isa 38.13
6.25 Ezra 1.1,2; Esth 3.12; 8.9; Dan 4.1; 1 Pet 1.2
6.26 Dan 3.29; Ps 99.1; Dan 4.34; Ps 93.1,2; Dan 4.3; 7.14,27
6.28 Ezra 1.1,2; Dan 1.21; 10.1
7.1 Dan 5.1,22,30; 1.17; ver 7,13,15; Jer 36.4,32
7.3 ver 17; Rev 13.1
7.4 Jer 48.40; Ezek 17.3; Hab 1.8
7.6 ver 12
7.7 Rev 12.3; 13.1; 17.3
7.8 ver 20,21; Rev 9.7; ver 11,25
7.9 Mk 9.3; Rev 1.14; Ezek 1.13,26; 10.2,6

7.1-28 Daniel's Vision of the Four Beasts.
7.1-8 The weird composite animals that Daniel sees in his dream (which is said to have come to him during the Babylonian period) emerge from a stormy *sea*. This is a common Near Eastern and Biblical symbol for the primeval chaos out of which the ordered creation emerged (Gen 1; Isa 17.12-14; Nah 1.3-5). The beasts are (1) a lion with eagle's wings, (2) a bear with tusks (or ribs) in its mouth, (3) a leopard with four wings and four heads, and (4) an unnamed beast with iron teeth and multiple horns. The last of these rulers is depicted contemptuously as *a little horn*, with eyes like a human, who speaks *arrogantly*.
7.9-10 Contrasted with these aggressive symbols of earthly rule is the serene sovereignty of God, portrayed as an elderly man (*the Ancient One*) whose power and whose agents surround his seat of power: the chariot throne (*cf. wheels*; Ezek 1).

[x] Q Ms Theodotion: MT adds *the beginning of the words; he said* [y] Theodotion: Aram *Daniel answered and said, "I* [z] Or *ribs* [a] Aram *an Ancient of Days*

and the hair of his head like pure wool;
his throne was fiery flames,
and its wheels were burning fire.
10 A stream of fire issued
and flowed out from his presence.
A thousand thousands served him,
and ten thousand times ten thousand
stood attending him.
The court sat in judgment,
and the books were opened.
11 I watched then because of the noise of the
arrogant words that the horn was speaking.
And as I watched, the beast was put to
death, and its body destroyed and given
over to be burned with fire. 12 As for the rest
of the beasts, their dominion was taken
away, but their lives were prolonged for a
season and a time. 13 As I watched in the
night visions,
I saw one like a human being[b]
coming with the clouds of heaven.
And he came to the Ancient One[c]
and was presented before him.
14 To him was given dominion
and glory and kingship,
that all peoples, nations, and languages
should serve him.
His dominion is an everlasting dominion
that shall not pass away,
and his kingship is one
that shall never be destroyed.

Daniel's Visions Interpreted

15 As for me, Daniel, my spirit was troubled within me,[d] and the visions of my head
terrified me. 16 I approached one of the attendants to ask him the truth concerning
all this. So he said that he would disclose
to me the interpretation of the matter: 17 "As
for these four great beasts, four kings shall
arise out of the earth. 18 But the holy ones
of the Most High shall receive the kingdom
and possess the kingdom forever—forever
and ever."
19 Then I desired to know the truth
concerning the fourth beast, which was
different from all the rest, exceedingly terrifying, with its teeth of iron and claws of
bronze, and which devoured and broke in
pieces, and stamped what was left with its
feet; 20 and concerning the ten horns that
were on its head, and concerning the other
horn, which came up and to make room for
which three of them fell out—the horn that
had eyes and a mouth that spoke arrogantly, and that seemed greater than the
others. 21 As I looked, this horn made war
with the holy ones and was prevailing over
them, 22 until the Ancient One[c] came; then
judgment was given for the holy ones of the
Most High, and the time arrived when the
holy ones gained possession of the kingdom.
23 This is what he said: "As for the
fourth beast,
there shall be a fourth kingdom on
earth
that shall be different from all the
other kingdoms;
it shall devour the whole earth,
and trample it down, and break it to
pieces.
24 As for the ten horns,
out of this kingdom ten kings shall arise,
and another shall arise after them.
This one shall be different from the
former ones,
and shall put down three kings.
25 He shall speak words against the Most
High,
shall wear out the holy ones of the
Most High,
and shall attempt to change the
sacred seasons and the law;
and they shall be given into his power
for a time, two times,[e] and half a
time.
26 Then the court shall sit in judgment,
and his dominion shall be taken
away,
to be consumed and totally destroyed.
27 The kingship and dominion
and the greatness of the kingdoms
under the whole heaven
shall be given to the people of the
holy ones of the Most High;
their kingdom shall be an everlasting
kingdom,
and all dominions shall serve and
obey them."
28 Here the account ends. As for me,
Daniel, my thoughts greatly terrified me,
and my face turned pale; but I kept the
matter in my mind.

Vision of a Ram and a Goat

8 In the third year of the reign of King
Belshazzar a vision appeared to me,
Daniel, after the one that had appeared to
me at first. 2 In the vision I was looking and
saw myself in Susa the capital, in the prov-

[b] Aram *one like a son of man* [c] Aram *the Ancient of Days* [d] Aram *troubled in its sheath* [e] Aram *a time, times*

7.11-14 The evil beasts are deprived of their *dominion* and God's rule is administered through *one like a human being.* It is a kingdom universal in scope, everlasting and unconquerable.
7.15-28 Daniel receives the *interpretation* of his dream from *one of the attendants* (an angel or a member of the heavenly council that continues in God's presence). The *four great beasts* represent the successive world empires: Babylonian, Median, Persian and Greek (Alexander and his successors: the Seleucids in Syria and the Ptolemies in Egypt). The *little horn* is again Antiochus IV Epiphanes, in whose reign (175-164 BCE) the effort to force Jews and all subjects to honor him as divine provoked the Jewish revolt led by Mattathias and his sons. They became known as the Maccabees, from the nickname Maccabee (for *hammer*) that was given to Judah, their leader (in 167-164). The revolt ended in the defeat of the Seleucids under Antiochus and the purification of the temple in 164.
7.18-21 *The holy ones*, referred to in vs. 13 as *one like a human being* (which is sometimes translated, *one like a son of man*) are the faithful, courageous Jews who defied the royal decree and supported the Maccabean revolt. To them God gives *the kingdom*, which involves the recovery of an independent Jewish state.
7.23-28 The explanation of the dream about the four beasts expands what is implied in the description of the vision: God rewards the faithful *holy ones* who do not yield to the demands of the pagan idolatrous ruler, and they receive from God an *everlasting kingdom*.
8.1-25 Daniel's Vision of the Ram and the Goat.
8.1-14 Daniel's next vision, which is said to have taken place during the reign of *Belshazzar*, occurs at the eastern *Ulai* gate of the Persian *capital* city of Susa *in the province of Elam.* Daniel sees a *goat* with one *horn* from the west attacking a two-horned *ram*. Subsequently, the goat's horn is broken and replaced by *four horns*. The *little* horn which sprouts from one of these succeeds in dominating the *south* and *east*, including *the beautiful land*, which is Judah. There he prohibits the making of offerings in the *sanctuary*, and then desecrates it. This pollution of the sanctuary will continue for 1150 days (two sacrifices were offered each day, morning and evening) until it is restored.

7.10 Ps 50.3; 97.3; Isa 30.33; Rev 5.11; 20.12

7.11 ver 7,8; Rev 19.20

7.13 Ezek 1.26; Mt 24.30; 26.64; Mk 13.26; Lk 21.27; Rev 1.7,13

7.14 Ps 2.6-8; 1 Cor 15.27; Eph 1.22; Phil 2.9-11; Ps 72.11; 102.22; Dan 2.44; Mic 4.7; Heb 12.28

7.15 ver 1,28

7.16 Rev 5.5; 7.13,14; Dan 8.16,17

7.18 Isa 60.12-14; Rev 2.26; 20.4

7.21 Rev 13.7

7.22 ver 9,13; 1 Cor 6.2,3; ver 18

7.23 ver 7,19

7.24 ver 7,8; Rev 17.12

7.25 Isa 37.23; Dan 8.24,25; Rev 13.5; 17.6; 18.24; Dan 2.21; 12.7; Rev 12.14

7.26 ver 10,22

7.27 ver 14,18,22; Lk 1.33; Jn 12.34; Rev 11.15; Ps 2.6-12; Isa 60.12

7.28 ver 15; Dan 8.27; Lk 2.19

8.1 Dan 7.1,15,28

8.2 Dan 7.2,15; Esth 1.2; Ezek 32.24; ver 16

ince of Elam,[f] and I was by the river Ulai.[g] 3I looked up and saw a ram standing beside the river.[h] It had two horns. Both horns were long, but one was longer than the other, and the longer one came up second. 4I saw the ram charging westward and northward and southward. All beasts were powerless to withstand it, and no one could rescue from its power; it did as it pleased and became strong.

5 As I was watching, a male goat appeared from the west, coming across the face of the whole earth without touching the ground. The goat had a horn[i] between its eyes. 6It came toward the ram with the two horns that I had seen standing beside the river,[j] and it ran at it with savage force. 7I saw it approaching the ram. It was enraged against it and struck the ram, breaking its two horns. The ram did not have power to withstand it; it threw the ram down to the ground and trampled upon it, and there was no one who could rescue the ram from its power. 8Then the male goat grew exceedingly great; but at the height of its power, the great horn was broken, and in its place there came up four prominent horns toward the four winds of heaven.

9 Out of one of them came another[k] horn, a little one, which grew exceedingly great toward the south, toward the east, and toward the beautiful land. 10It grew as high as the host of heaven. It threw down to the earth some of the host and some of the stars, and trampled on them. 11Even against the prince of the host it acted arrogantly; it took the regular burnt offering away from him and overthrew the place of his sanctuary. 12Because of wickedness, the host was given over to it together with the regular burnt offering;[l] it cast truth to the ground, and kept prospering in what it did. 13Then I heard a holy one speaking, and another holy one said to the one that spoke, "For how long is this vision concerning the regular burnt offering, the transgression that makes desolate, and the giving over of the sanctuary and host to be trampled?"[l] 14And he answered him,[m] "For two thousand three hundred evenings and mornings; then the sanctuary shall be restored to its rightful state."

Gabriel Interprets the Vision

15 When I, Daniel, had seen the vision, I tried to understand it. Then someone appeared standing before me, having the appearance of a man, 16and I heard a human voice by the Ulai, calling, "Gabriel, help this man understand the vision." 17So he came near where I stood; and when he came, I became frightened and fell prostrate. But he said to me, "Understand, O mortal,[n] that the vision is for the time of the end."

18 As he was speaking to me, I fell into a trance, face to the ground; then he touched me and set me on my feet. 19He said, "Listen, and I will tell you what will take place later in the period of wrath; for it refers to the appointed time of the end. 20As for the ram that you saw with the two horns, these are the kings of Media and Persia. 21The male goat[o] is the king of Greece, and the great horn between its eyes is the first king. 22As for the horn that was broken, in place of which four others arose, four kingdoms shall arise from his[p] nation, but not with his power.

23 At the end of their rule,
when the transgressions have reached
their full measure,
a king of bold countenance shall arise,
skilled in intrigue.
24 He shall grow strong in power,[q]
shall cause fearful destruction,
and shall succeed in what he does.
He shall destroy the powerful
and the people of the holy ones.
25 By his cunning
he shall make deceit prosper under
his hand,
and in his own mind he shall be great.
Without warning he shall destroy many
and shall even rise up against the
Prince of princes.
But he shall be broken, and not by
human hands.

26The vision of the evenings and the mornings that has been told is true. As for you, seal up the vision, for it refers to many days from now."

27 So I, Daniel, was overcome and lay sick for some days; then I arose and went about the king's business. But I was dismayed by the vision and did not understand it.

[f] Gk Theodotion: MT Q Ms repeat *in the vision I was looking* [g] Or *the Ulai Gate* [h] Or *gate* [i] Theodotion: Gk *one horn*; Heb *a horn of vision* [j] Or *gate* [k] Cn Compare 7.8: Heb *one* [l] Meaning of Heb uncertain [m] Gk Theodotion Syr Vg: Heb *me* [n] Heb *son of man* [o] Or *shaggy male goat* [p] Gk Theodotion Vg: Heb *the* [q] Theodotion and one Gk Ms: Heb repeats (from 8.22) *but not with his power*

8.15-25 *Gabriel* (meaning, God is my mighty one) is a leading angel who serves as God's messenger (Dan 9.21; Lk 1.19,26). He explains the vision of *the time of the end,* which means the end of the present age and the establishment of God's rule through his people and over the world. As in the vision of Daniel 7, the rulers of *Media and Persia* are overcome by *the king of Greece,* Alexander, whose empire is soon divided among his successors into four kingdoms. The *little horn* of vs. 9 is here called *a king of bold countenance,* which refers again to Antiochus Epiphanes and his effort to force faithful Jews (*the people of the holy ones*) to worship him as divine. His arrogance against God, who is *the Prince of princes,* will result in his own destruction, which will take place *not by human hands.* **8.26-27** The reference to these events occurring *many days from now* is part of the logic of apocalyptic writers who date back into the past visions and predictions about recent or impending events to show that what happens is the outworking of the plan of God. The inability of Daniel to comprehend what is happening, apart from the divine disclosure, is also part of the method of apocalyptic writers.

8.3 Dan 10.5; ver 20
8.4 ver 7
8.5 ver 21
8.6 ver 3
8.7 Dan 11.11; 7.7
8.8 2 Chr 26.16; Dan 5.20; ver 22; Dan 7.2; Rev 7.1
8.9 ver 23; Dan 11.16,41
8.10 Rev 12.4
8.11 Dan 11.36,37; Josh 5.14; Dan 11.31; 12.11; Ezek 46.13,14
8.13 Dan 4.13,23; 12.6,8; Rev 11.2
8.15 ver 1; Dan 7.13
8.16 Dan 9.21; Lk 1.19,26
8.17 Ezek 1.28; Rev 1.17
8.18 Dan 10.9; 10.10,16,18; Ezek 2.2
8.19 Hab 2.3
8.21 ver 5; Dan 10.20
8.22 ver 8
8.24 Dan 11.36
8.25 Dan 11.21; ver 11; Dan 2.34,45
8.26 Dan 10.1; 12.4,9; 10.14
8.27 Dan 7.28; Hab 3.16

Daniel's Prayer for the People

9 In the first year of Darius son of
Ahasuerus, by birth a Mede, who
became king over the realm of the
Chaldeans— [2]in the first year of his reign,
I, Daniel, perceived in the books the number
of years that, according to the word of the
LORD to the prophet Jeremiah, must be fulfilled for the devastation of Jerusalem,
namely, seventy years.
3 Then I turned to the Lord God, to seek
an answer by prayer and supplication with
fasting and sackcloth and ashes. [4]I prayed
to the LORD my God and made confession,
saying,
"Ah, Lord, great and awesome God, keeping covenant and steadfast love with those
who love you and keep your commandments, [5]we have sinned and done wrong,
acted wickedly and rebelled, turning aside
from your commandments and ordinances.
[6]We have not listened to your servants the
prophets, who spoke in your name to our
kings, our princes, and our ancestors, and
to all the people of the land.
7 "Righteousness is on your side, O Lord,
but open shame, as at this day, falls on us,
the people of Judah, the inhabitants of Jerusalem, and all Israel, those who are near
and those who are far away, in all the lands
to which you have driven them, because of
the treachery that they have committed
against you. [8]Open shame, O LORD, falls on
us, our kings, our officials, and our ancestors,
because we have sinned against you. [9]To the
Lord our God belong mercy and forgiveness,
for we have rebelled against him, [10]and have
not obeyed the voice of the LORD our God
by following his laws, which he set before
us by his servants the prophets.
11 "All Israel has transgressed your law
and turned aside, refusing to obey your
voice. So the curse and the oath written in
the law of Moses, the servant of God, have
been poured out upon us, because we have
sinned against you. [12]He has confirmed his
words, which he spoke against us and against
our rulers, by bringing upon us a calamity
so great that what has been done against
Jerusalem has never before been done under the whole heaven. [13]Just as it is written
in the law of Moses, all this calamity has
come upon us. We did not entreat the favor
of the LORD our God, turning from our
iniquities and reflecting on his[r] fidelity. [14]So
the LORD kept watch over this calamity until
he brought it upon us. Indeed, the LORD our
God is right in all that he has done; for we
have disobeyed his voice.
15 "And now, O Lord our God, who
brought your people out of the land of Egypt
with a mighty hand and made your name
renowned even to this day—we have sinned,
we have done wickedly. [16]O Lord, in view
of all your righteous acts, let your anger
and wrath, we pray, turn away from your
city Jerusalem, your holy mountain; because of our sins and the iniquities of our
ancestors, Jerusalem and your people have
become a disgrace among all our neighbors.
[17]Now therefore, O our God, listen to the
prayer of your servant and to his supplication, and for your own sake, Lord,[s] let your
face shine upon your desolated sanctuary.
[18]Incline your ear, O my God, and hear.
Open your eyes and look at our desolation
and the city that bears your name. We do
not present our supplication before you on
the ground of our righteousness, but on the
ground of your great mercies. [19]O Lord,
hear; O Lord, forgive; O Lord, listen and act
and do not delay! For your own sake, O my
God, because your city and your people
bear your name!"

The Seventy Weeks

20 While I was speaking, and was praying and confessing my sin and the sin of my
people Israel, and presenting my supplication before the LORD my God on behalf of the
holy mountain of my God— [21]while I was
speaking in prayer, the man Gabriel, whom
I had seen before in a vision, came to me
in swift flight at the time of the evening
sacrifice. [22]He came[t] and said to me, "Daniel, I have now come out to give you wisdom and understanding. [23]At the beginning
of your supplications a word went out, and
I have come to declare it, for you are greatly
beloved. So consider the word and understand the vision:
24 "Seventy weeks are decreed for your
people and your holy city: to finish the
transgression, to put an end to sin, and to
atone for iniquity, to bring in everlasting
righteousness, to seal both vision and prophet,
and to anoint a most holy place.[u] [25]Know
therefore and understand: from the time
that the word went out to restore and

[r] Heb *your* [s] Theodotion Vg Compare Syr: Heb *for the Lord's sake* [t] Gk Syr: Heb *He made to understand* [u] Or *thing* or *one*

9.1-19 Daniel's Prayer for the Forgiveness of God's People. **9.1-2** The date here is anachronistic, since the reign of Darius I (who was a Persian, not a Median) began after the time of Cyrus (550-530) in 522. *Ahasuerus* (Xerxes) was not Darius' father but his son. Daniel's prediction about the future of God's people, which is charted over a period of *seventy weeks* (of years = 490), builds on the prophecy of Jeremiah 25.1-12; 29.10. Jeremiah announced in about 587 BCE that the Jewish exiles in Babylon would return after 70 years of punishment. Having read this *in the books* that were beginning to take on authority as the Jewish scriptures, Daniel recalculates God's time to seventy successive periods of seven years each, after which the divine liberation of God's people and the renewal of the sanctuary in Jerusalem will take place. **9.3-19** Clothed in the garb of mourning and contrition, *sackcloth and ashes* (2 Sam 3.31; Isa 15.3; Jer 4.8; Ezek 27.31), Daniel begins his *confession*. He contrasts God's faithfulness to his *covenant* and the *righteousness* of his dealings with his people with their infidelity and violations of the *law of Moses*. He pleads for forgiveness and for relief from the punishment that God has rightly sent on his irresponsible people. At stake is the reputation of the God whose *city* and *people* are known by his name. **9.20-27** The Seventy Weeks of Years: The Catastrophes that Will Precede the Coming of the End of the Age. Instead of a vision or dream requiring interpretation, Daniel is now given instruction by *the man Gabriel* (see 8.15-16) concerning the future of Jerusalem and its sanctuary on *the holy mountain of God*. The 490 years here sketched begin with the Persian decree to permit restoration of Jerusalem in the time of Ezra and Nehemiah (Neh 2-6) and end with the installation by Antiochus Epiphanes of a statue of himself in the temple as an object of mandatory worship. The *anointed prince* in the first fifty years (*seven weeks*) is probably one of the priests who returned from Babylon in the time of Ezra and restored the worship of God in the temple (Ezra 2.36; Neh 7.39). Or it may be Cyrus, who gave permission for the exiles to return and rebuild the temple, and who is called the *anointed* of the LORD in Isa 45.1.

9.1 Dan 5.31; 11.1
9.2 2 Chr 36.21; Jer 29.10; Zech 7.5
9.3 Neh 1.4; Jer 29.12; Jas 4.8
9.4 Deut 7.21; Neh 9.32; Deut 7.9
9.5 Ps 106.6; Lam 1.18,20; ver 11
9.6 2 Chr 36.15,16; ver 8
9.7 Jer 23.6; 33.16; Am 9.9
9.9 Neh 9.17; Ps 130.4
9.11 Isa 1.4-6; Jer 8.5,10; Deut 27.15
9.12 Isa 44.26; Zech 1.6; Ezek 5.9
9.13 Isa 9.13; Jer 2.30
9.14 Jer 31.28; 44.27; ver 7,10
9.15 Ex 6.1,6; Jer 32.21; Neh 9.10; Jer 32.20
9.16 1 Sam 12.7; Ps 31.1; Zech 8.3
9.17 Num 6.25; Lam 5.18
9.18 Isa 37.17; Jer 25.29; 36.7
9.19 Ps 44.23; 74.10,11
9.20 ver 3; Isa 58.9; 6.5
9.21 Dan 8.16; Isa 6.2; Dan 8.18; 10.10,16,18
9.23 Dan 10.12; Lk 1.28; Mt 24.15
9.24 Isa 53.10; Rom 5.10; Acts 3.14
9.25 Ezra 4.24; Neh 2.1-8; 3.1; Jn 1.41; 4.25; Isa 9.6

rebuild Jerusalem until the time of an
anointed prince, there shall be seven weeks;
and for sixty-two weeks it shall be built
again with streets and moat, but in a troubled time. 26 After the sixty-two weeks, an
anointed one shall be cut off and shall have
nothing, and the troops of the prince who
is to come shall destroy the city and the
sanctuary. Its[v] end shall come with a flood,
and to the end there shall be war. Desolations
are decreed. 27 He shall make a strong covenant with many for one week, and for half
of the week he shall make sacrifice and
offering cease; and in their place[w] shall be
an abomination that desolates, until the
decreed end is poured out upon the desolator."

Conflict of Nations and Heavenly Powers

10 In the third year of King Cyrus of
Persia a word was revealed to
Daniel, who was named Belteshazzar. The
word was true, and it concerned a great
conflict. He understood the word, having
received understanding in the vision.
2 At that time I, Daniel, had been mourning for three weeks. 3 I had eaten no rich
food, no meat or wine had entered my
mouth, and I had not anointed myself at all,
for the full three weeks. 4 On the twenty-
fourth day of the first month, as I was
standing on the bank of the great river (that
is, the Tigris), 5 I looked up and saw a man
clothed in linen, with a belt of gold from
Uphaz around his waist. 6 His body was like
beryl, his face like lightning, his eyes like
flaming torches, his arms and legs like the
gleam of burnished bronze, and the sound
of his words like the roar of a multitude. 7 I,
Daniel, alone saw the vision; the people
who were with me did not see the vision,
though a great trembling fell upon them,
and they fled and hid themselves. 8 So I was
left alone to see this great vision. My strength
left me, and my complexion grew deathly
pale, and I retained no strength. 9 Then I
heard the sound of his words; and when I
heard the sound of his words, I fell into a
trance, face to the ground.
10 But then a hand touched me and
roused me to my hands and knees. 11 He
said to me, "Daniel, greatly beloved, pay
attention to the words that I am going to
speak to you. Stand on your feet, for I have
now been sent to you." So while he was
speaking this word to me, I stood up trembling. 12 He said to me, "Do not fear, Daniel,
for from the first day that you set your mind
to gain understanding and to humble yourself before your God, your words have been
heard, and I have come because of your
words. 13 But the prince of the kingdom of
Persia opposed me twenty-one days. So
Michael, one of the chief princes, came to
help me, and I left him there with the prince
of the kingdom of Persia,[x] 14 and have come
to help you understand what is to happen
to your people at the end of days. For there
is a further vision for those days."
15 While he was speaking these words
to me, I turned my face toward the ground
and was speechless. 16 Then one in human
form touched my lips, and I opened my
mouth to speak, and said to the one who
stood before me, "My lord, because of the
vision such pains have come upon me that
I retain no strength. 17 How can my lord's
servant talk with my lord? For I am shaking,[y]
no strength remains in me, and no breath
is left in me."
18 Again one in human form touched
me and strengthened me. 19 He said, "Do not
fear, greatly beloved, you are safe. Be strong
and courageous!" When he spoke to me, I
was strengthened and said, "Let my lord
speak, for you have strengthened me." 20 Then
he said, "Do you know why I have come
to you? Now I must return to fight against
the prince of Persia, and when I am through
with him, the prince of Greece will come.
21 But I am to tell you what is inscribed in
the book of truth. There is no one with me
who contends against these princes except
Michael, your prince.
11 1 As for me, in the first year of
Darius the Mede, I stood up to
support and strengthen him.
2 "Now I will announce the truth to you.
Three more kings shall arise in Persia. The
fourth shall be far richer than all of them,
and when he has become strong through
his riches, he shall stir up all against the
kingdom of Greece. 3 Then a warrior king
shall arise, who shall rule with great dominion and take action as he pleases. 4 And
while still rising in power, his kingdom shall
be broken and divided toward the four winds
of heaven, but not to his posterity, nor
according to the dominion with which he
ruled; for his kingdom shall be uprooted and

[v] Or *His* [w] Cn: Meaning of Heb uncertain [x] Gk Theodotion: Heb *I was left there with the kings of Persia* [y] Gk: Heb *from now*

9.26 Isa 53.8; Mk 9.12; Lk 19.43,44; Nah 1.8
9.27 Dan 11.31; Mt 24.15; Lk 21.20; Isa 10.23
10.1 Dan 6.28; 1.7; 8.26; 2.21
10.2 Ezra 9.4,5; Neh 1.4
10.4 Dan 8.2; Gen 2.14
10.5 Dan 12.6,7; Rev 1.13; Jer 10.9
10.6 Mt 17.2; Rev 1.16,14,15; 2.18
10.7 2 Kings 6.17; Acts 9.7; Ezek 12.18
10.8 Gen 32.24; Dan 7.28; 8.27
10.9 Dan 8.18
10.10 Jer 1.9; Dan 9.21; Rev 1.17
10.11 Dan 9.23
10.12 Rev 1.17; Dan 9.3; 9.20-23
10.13 ver 20,21; Dan 12.1; Jude 9; Rev 12.7
10.14 Dan 2.28; 8.26; Hab 2.3
10.15 Ezek 24.27; Lk 1.20
10.16 Dan 8.15; ver 10; Jer 1.9; ver 8
10.19 ver 11,12; Judg 6.23
10.21 Dan 11.2; ver 13
11.1 Dan 9.1; 5.31
11.3 Dan 8.4,5,21
11.4 Dan 8.8,22; Ezek 37.9; Zech 2.6; Rev 7.1

9.26-27 *The anointed one* who is cut off at the end of this period may be Onias III, the high priest who was murdered in 171 (2 Macc 4; *cf.* Dan 11.22). *The prince who is to come* is Antiochus IV, who plundered the temple on his return from defeating the Ptolemies in Egypt in 169 (1 Macc 1.20-35). His prohibition of sacrifices in the temple lasted for *one week*, until God's *decreed end* of him took place.
10.1-12.45 Daniel is Given Assurance through Visions of God.
10.1-9 The revelatory experience of Daniel is dated to the third year of Cyrus (reigned 550-530) and consists of a *word*, or revelatory oracle. Prepared for this experience by his fasting and standing on the bank of the *Tigris* in Babylonia, there appears to him *a man* with a dazzling appearance, who is a revelatory messenger from God and before whom he prostrates himself. The detail about the inability of Daniel's companions to see what is happening to him resembles the private experiences of God's revelation granted to Moses and Elijah, to Jesus (Mk 9.1-8) and to Paul (2 Cor 12.1-10).
10.10-11.1 The heavenly messenger's *arrival* was delayed by hostile demonic powers (*the prince of the kingdom of Persia*), but then became possible through angelic intervention by *Michael*. This angel, whose name means *Who is like God?*, was assigned by God to guard and preserve his special people. His title of *prince* recalls Josh 5.13-15, where the commander of the *army of the* L*ORD* is disclosed to Joshua as the attack on Jericho is prepared. The struggle with the powers of evil that Daniel sees will continue, however.
11.2-35 The events and chief characters in this drama that leads to the end of the age took place in the successive reigns of the Persian and Greek kings. *The warrior king* is Alexander, but his realm is soon split among his successors: the Ptolemies (*king of the south*) and the Seleucids (*king of the north*). The details of these struggles for power as portrayed in 11.5-20 match remarkably well what is known of these events from Greek and Jewish historical sources. *The contemptible person* in 11.22 is Antiochus IV. *The prince of the covenant* is the high priest – a post which was so prestigious and financially rewarding that candidates fought each other and offered bribes to obtain it. Those *who forsake the covenant* are people who conformed to the hellenistic culture and obeyed the decrees of Antiochus which forbade sacrifices in the temple (1 Macc 1.45). Even *the wise among the people* will in some cases give in to the paganizing pressures, while others will be put to death (*fall*). This experience will purify them and thus prepare them for entrance into the new age (*the time appointed*).

go to others besides these.
5 "Then the king of the south shall grow
strong, but one of his officers shall grow
stronger than he and shall rule a realm
greater than his own realm. [6]After some
years they shall make an alliance, and the
daughter of the king of the south shall come
to the king of the north to ratify the agreement. But she shall not retain her power,
and his offspring shall not endure. She shall
be given up, she and her attendants and her
child and the one who supported her.
"In those times [7]a branch from her roots
shall rise up in his place. He shall come
against the army and enter the fortress of
the king of the north, and he shall take
action against them and prevail. [8]Even their
gods, with their idols and with their precious vessels of silver and gold, he shall
carry off to Egypt as spoils of war. For some
years he shall refrain from attacking the
king of the north; [9]then the latter shall
invade the realm of the king of the south,
but will return to his own land.
10 "His sons shall wage war and assemble a multitude of great forces, which shall
advance like a flood and pass through, and
again shall carry the war as far as his
fortress. [11]Moved with rage, the king of the
south shall go out and do battle against the
king of the north, who shall muster a great
multitude, which shall, however, be defeated by his enemy. [12]When the multitude
has been carried off, his heart shall be
exalted, and he shall overthrow tens of
thousands, but he shall not prevail. [13]For
the king of the north shall again raise a
multitude, larger than the former, and after
some years[z] he shall advance with a great
army and abundant supplies.
14 "In those times many shall rise against
the king of the south. The lawless among
your own people shall lift themselves up in
order to fulfill the vision, but they shall fail.
[15]Then the king of the north shall come and
throw up siegeworks, and take a well-
fortified city. And the forces of the south
shall not stand, not even his picked troops,
for there shall be no strength to resist. [16]But
he who comes against him shall take the
actions he pleases, and no one shall withstand him. He shall take a position in the
beautiful land, and all of it shall be in his
power. [17]He shall set his mind to come with
the strength of his whole kingdom, and he
shall bring terms of peace[a] and perform
them. In order to destroy the kingdom,[b] he
shall give him a woman in marriage; but
it shall not succeed or be to his advantage.
[18]Afterward he shall turn to the coastlands,
and shall capture many. But a commander
shall put an end to his insolence; indeed,[c]
he shall turn his insolence back upon him.
[19]Then he shall turn back toward the fortresses of his own land, but he shall stumble
and fall, and shall not be found.
20 "Then shall arise in his place one who
shall send an official for the glory of the
kingdom; but within a few days he shall be
broken, though not in anger or in battle.
[21]In his place shall arise a contemptible
person on whom royal majesty had not been
conferred; he shall come in without warning
and obtain the kingdom through intrigue.
[22]Armies shall be utterly swept away and
broken before him, and the prince of the
covenant as well. [23]And after an alliance is
made with him, he shall act deceitfully and
become strong with a small party. [24]Without
warning he shall come into the richest
parts[d] of the province and do what none of
his predecessors had ever done, lavishing
plunder, spoil, and wealth on them. He shall
devise plans against strongholds, but only
for a time. [25]He shall stir up his power and
determination against the king of the south
with a great army, and the king of the south
shall wage war with a much greater and
stronger army. But he shall not succeed, for
plots shall be devised against him [26]by those
who eat of the royal rations. They shall
break him, his army shall be swept away,
and many shall fall slain. [27]The two kings,
their minds bent on evil, shall sit at one table
and exchange lies. But it shall not succeed,
for there remains an end at the time appointed. [28]He shall return to his land with
great wealth, but his heart shall be set
against the holy covenant. He shall work his
will, and return to his own land.
29 "At the time appointed he shall return and come into the south, but this time
it shall not be as it was before. [30]For ships
of Kittim shall come against him, and he
shall lose heart and withdraw. He shall be
enraged and take action against the holy
covenant. He shall turn back and pay heed
to those who forsake the holy covenant.
[31]Forces sent by him shall occupy and profane the temple and fortress. They shall

[z] Heb *and at the end of the times years* [a] Gk: Heb *kingdom, and upright ones with him* [b] Heb *it* [c] Meaning of Heb uncertain [d] Or *among the richest men*

11.6 ver 13,15,40
11.7 ver 19,38,39
11.8 Isa 37.19; 46.1,2; Jer 43.12,13
11.10 Isa 8.8; Jer 46.7,8; Dan 9.26; ver 7
11.11 ver 5; Dan 8.7; ver 13,10
11.13 Dan 4.16; 12.7
11.15 Jer 6.6; Ezek 4.2; 17.17
11.16 Dan 8.4,7; ver 3,36; Josh 1.5; ver 41,45
11.17 2 Kings 12.17; Ezek 4.3,7
11.18 Isa 66.19; Jer 31.10; Hos 12.14
11.19 Ps 27.2; Job 20.8; Ezek 26.21
11.20 Isa 60.17
11.21 ver 24,32,34
11.22 ver 10; Dan 8.10,11
11.23 Dan 8.25
11.24 ver 21; Ezek 34.14
11.26 ver 10,40
11.27 Ps 52.1; 64.6; Jer 9.3-5; ver 35,40; Hab 2.3
11.30 Gen 10.4; Num 24.24; Jer 2.10
11.31 Dan 8.11; 9.27; Mt 24.15; Mk 13.14

abolish the regular burnt offering and set up the abomination that makes desolate. 32 He shall seduce with intrigue those who violate the covenant; but the people who are loyal to their God shall stand firm and take action. 33 The wise among the people shall give understanding to many; for some days, however, they shall fall by sword and flame, and suffer captivity and plunder. 34 When they fall victim, they shall receive a little help, and many shall join them insincerely. 35 Some of the wise shall fall, so that they may be refined, purified, and cleansed,[e] until the time of the end, for there is still an interval until the time appointed.

36 "The king shall act as he pleases. He shall exalt himself and consider himself greater than any god, and shall speak horrendous things against the God of gods. He shall prosper until the period of wrath is completed, for what is determined shall be done. 37 He shall pay no respect to the gods of his ancestors, or to the one beloved by women; he shall pay no respect to any other god, for he shall consider himself greater than all. 38 He shall honor the god of fortresses instead of these; a god whom his ancestors did not know he shall honor with gold and silver, with precious stones and costly gifts. 39 He shall deal with the strongest fortresses by the help of a foreign god. Those who acknowledge him he shall make more wealthy, and shall appoint them as rulers over many, and shall distribute the land for a price.

The Time of the End

40 "At the time of the end the king of the south shall attack him. But the king of the north shall rush upon him like a whirlwind, with chariots and horsemen, and with many ships. He shall advance against countries and pass through like a flood. 41 He shall come into the beautiful land, and tens of thousands shall fall victim, but Edom and Moab and the main part of the Ammonites shall escape from his power. 42 He shall stretch out his hand against the countries, and the land of Egypt shall not escape. 43 He shall become ruler of the treasures of gold and of silver, and all the riches of Egypt; and the Libyans and the Ethiopians[f] shall follow in his train. 44 But reports from the east and the north shall alarm him, and he shall go out with great fury to bring ruin and complete destruction to many. 45 He shall pitch his palatial tents between the sea and the beautiful holy mountain. Yet he shall come to his end, with no one to help him.

The Resurrection of the Dead

12 "At that time Michael, the great prince, the protector of your people, shall arise. There shall be a time of anguish, such as has never occurred since nations first came into existence. But at that time your people shall be delivered, everyone who is found written in the book. 2 Many of those who sleep in the dust of the earth[g] shall awake, some to everlasting life, and some to shame and everlasting contempt. 3 Those who are wise shall shine like the brightness of the sky,[h] and those who lead many to righteousness, like the stars forever and ever. 4 But you, Daniel, keep the words secret and the book sealed until the time of the end. Many shall be running back and forth, and evil[i] shall increase."

5 Then I, Daniel, looked, and two others appeared, one standing on this bank of the stream and one on the other. 6 One of them said to the man clothed in linen, who was upstream, "How long shall it be until the end of these wonders?" 7 The man clothed in linen, who was upstream, raised his right hand and his left hand toward heaven. And I heard him swear by the one who lives forever that it would be for a time, two times, and half a time,[j] and that when the shattering of the power of the holy people comes to an end, all these things would be accomplished. 8 I heard but could not understand; so I said, "My lord, what shall be the outcome of these things?" 9 He said, "Go your way, Daniel, for the words are to remain secret and sealed until the time of the end. 10 Many shall be purified, cleansed, and refined, but the wicked shall continue to act wickedly. None of the wicked shall understand, but those who are wise shall understand. 11 From the time that the regular burnt offering is taken away and the abomination that desolates is set up, there shall be one thousand two hundred ninety days. 12 Happy are those who persevere and attain the thousand three hundred thirty-five days. 13 But you, go your way,[k] and rest; you shall rise for your reward at the end of the days."

[e] Heb *made them white* [f] Or *Nubians*; Heb *Cushites* [g] Or *the land of dust* [h] Or *dome* [i] Cn Compare Gk: Heb *knowledge* [j] Heb *a time, times, and a half* [k] Gk Theodotion: Heb adds *to the end*

11.32 ver 21,34; Mic 5.7-9
11.33 Mt 24.9; Jn 16.2; Heb 11.36-38
11.34 Mt 7.15; Rom 16.18
11.35 Zech 13.9; Jn 15.2; ver 27,40
11.36 2 Thess 2.4; Rev 13.5,6; Dan 2.47; 8.12,19; 9.27
11.40 ver 10.13,15,26; Isa 5.28
11.41 Jer 48.47; 49.6
11.43 2 Chr 12.3; Ezek 30.4,5; Nah 3.9
11.45 ver 16.41; Isa 65.25; 66.20; Dan 9.16,20
12.1 Dan 10.13,21; 9.12; Mt 24.21; Rev 16.18; ver 4
12.2 Isa 26.19; Mt 25.46; Jn 5.28; Acts 24.15
12.3 Mt 13.43; Dan 11.33
12.4 Rev 22.10; Dan 11.33
12.6 Dan 8.13; 10.5
12.7 Rev 10.5,6; Dan 4.34; 7.25; Rev 12.14; Lk 21.24; Rev 10.7
12.8 ver 6
12.9 ver 13,4
12.10 Dan 11.35; Isa 32.6,7
12.11 Dan 8.11-14; 9.27; 11.31; Mt 24.15; Mk 13.14
12.12 Isa 30.18; Rev 11.2; 12.6; 13.5
12.13 ver 9,4; Rev 14.13

11.36-39 Antiochus' final blasphemies against his own ancestral deities as well as against the God of Israel have for him a common motivation: to strengthen his position of power and thus to be able to reward his supporters. **11.40-45** Here are described the final schemes and tactics of Antiochus, including his return to Judah, *the beautiful land.* But he was soon to come to *his end,* when the support system he had built failed him. His death in *the beautiful holy mountain* is predicted to take place in the vicinity of Jerusalem, where prophets expected God's judgment of the evil powers to occur: Ezek 38.14-23; Joel 3.11-15; Zech 14.1-5. He actually died in Persia, after stealing treasures from the temple of the fertility goddess, Artemis (1 Macc 6.1-16).

12.1-10 The Final Revelation of God's Victory and the Vindication of God's People.

12.1-3 The *time of anguish* is typical of apocalyptic writings: the unprecedented conflict and suffering that the people will endure before God's final victory comes. Only those recorded *in the book* as God's chosen and faithful people will survive this crisis. The awakening to life of the dead *who sleep in the dust* will include those blessed with resurrection life as well as those doomed to *everlasting* rejection by God for their wickedness. Those given life in the age to come are *the wise* who heard and trusted God's message and who led others to share in the life of *righteousness.* This passage, the earliest teaching in Jewish scriptures about the resurrection of the faithful, is affirmed also in 2 Macc 7.7-23; 12.38-46; 14.45-46.

12.4-10 This revelation is not to be made public in the present evil age, but is to be preserved secretly in writing (*the book sealed*) until the crisis comes to its final conclusion. Standing on *the bank of the stream* (Tigris) are two witnesses (in this case, angels) as required by the law of Moses to confirm testimony (Deut 19.15). The *man clothed in linen* who reveals to Daniel the divine plan for the future (Dan 10.5-6) is now asked when it will be *accomplished,* to which his answer, *a time, two times, and half a time* means three and one-half years, as already indicated in 7.25 and 9.27. Daniel's request for more specific information about *the outcome* of God's plan is turned aside with the declaration that these are *secret* matters, to be revealed only at *the time of the end.* Until then, some people will continue to be wicked, but only *the wise,* who are God's obedient people, will be able to *understand.*

12.11-13 Revised Time-Schedules for the End of the Age. The interim between (1) the final desecration of the temple, including the erecting of the statue of Antiochus Epiphanes (*the abomination*) and (2) the dawn of the new age is calculated first as 1290 days (instead of 1150, as in Dan 8.14), and then as 13,335 days. A final note promises a reward for those who remain faithful to God.

See the Introductions, pp. 6, 54-57, and 65-66 above.

HOSEA

1 The word of the LORD that came to Hosea son of Beeri, in the days of Kings Uzziah, Jotham, Ahaz, and Hezekiah of Judah, and in the days of King Jeroboam son of Joash of Israel.

The Family of Hosea

2 When the LORD first spoke through Hosea, the LORD said to Hosea, "Go, take for yourself a wife of whoredom and have children of whoredom, for the land commits great whoredom by forsaking the LORD." 3So he went and took Gomer daughter of Diblaim, and she conceived and bore him a son.

4 And the LORD said to him, "Name him Jezreel;[a] for in a little while I will punish the house of Jehu for the blood of Jezreel, and I will put an end to the kingdom of the house of Israel. 5On that day I will break the bow of Israel in the valley of Jezreel."

6 She conceived again and bore a daughter. Then the LORD said to him, "Name her Lo-ruhamah,[b] for I will no longer have pity on the house of Israel or forgive them. 7But I will have pity on the house of Judah, and I will save them by the LORD their God; I will not save them by bow, or by sword, or by war, or by horses, or by horsemen."

8 When she had weaned Lo-ruhamah, she conceived and bore a son. 9Then the LORD said, "Name him Lo-ammi,[c] for you are not my people and I am not your God."[d]

The Restoration of Israel

10[e] Yet the number of the people of Israel shall be like the sand of the sea, which can be neither measured nor numbered; and in the place where it was said to them, "You are not my people," it shall be said to them, "Children of the living God." 11The people of Judah and the people of Israel shall be gathered together, and they shall appoint for themselves one head; and they shall take possession of[f] the land, for great shall be the day of Jezreel.

2[g] Say to your brother,[h] Ammi,[i] and to your sister,[j] Ruhamah.[k]

Israel's Infidelity, Punishment, and Redemption

2 Plead with your mother, plead—
for she is not my wife,
and I am not her husband—
that she put away her whoring from her face,
and her adultery from between her breasts,
3 or I will strip her naked
and expose her as in the day she was born,
and make her like a wilderness,
and turn her into a parched land,
and kill her with thirst.
4 Upon her children also I will have no pity,
because they are children of whoredom.
5 For their mother has played the whore;
she who conceived them has acted shamefully.
For she said, "I will go after my lovers;
they give me my bread and my water,
my wool and my flax, my oil and my drink."
6 Therefore I will hedge up her[l] way with thorns;
and I will build a wall against her,
so that she cannot find her paths.
7 She shall pursue her lovers,
but not overtake them;
and she shall seek them,
but shall not find them.
Then she shall say, "I will go
and return to my first husband,
for it was better with me then than now."
8 She did not know
that it was I who gave her
the grain, the wine, and the oil,
and who lavished upon her silver
and gold that they used for Baal.
9 Therefore I will take back
my grain in its time,
and my wine in its season;
and I will take away my wool and my flax,
which were to cover her nakedness.

[a] That is *God sows* [b] That is *Not pitied* [c] That is *Not my people* [d] Heb *I am not yours* [e] Ch 2.1 in Heb [f] Heb *rise up from* [g] Ch 2.3 in Heb [h] Gk: Heb *brothers* [i] That is *My People* [j] Gk Vg: Heb *sisters* [k] That is *Pitied* [l] Gk Syr: Heb *your*

1.2 Hos 3.1; Jer 3.1,12,14; Hos 2.5; 3.5

1.4 2 Kings 10.1-14; 15.10

1.5 2 Kings 15.29

1.6 ver 3,9; Hos 2.4

1.7 Isa 30.18; Jer 25.5,6; Zech 9.9,10

1.10 Gen 32.12; Jer 33.22; Rom 9.25-27; ver 9; Isa 63.16; 64.8

1.11 Isa 11.12; Jer 23.5,6; Ezek 37.21-24; Hos 3.5

2.2 ver 5; Hos 4.5; Isa 50.1; Hos 1.2

2.3 Ezek 16.7,22,39; Isa 32.13,14; Am 8.11

2.4 Jer 13.14; Ezek 8.18

2.5 Isa 1.21; Jer 3.1,2,6; 44.17,18

2.6 Job 3.23; 19.8; Hos 9.6; 10.8

2.7 Jer 2.2; 3.1; Ezek 16.8; Hos 13.6

2.8 Isa 1.3; Ezek 16.19; Hos 8.4

1.1 Introduction. The only other biblical occurrence of *Beeri*, the name of Hosea's father, is in Gen 26.34, where Esau is reputed to have married the daughter of a Hittite of that name. The Hittites were a people living in the mountains of Canaan, but more numerous in Syria and Asia Minor. Perhaps Beeri's name is of Hittite origin. The reigns of the kings of Judah were: Uzziah (783-742), Jotham (742-735), Ahaz (735-715) and Hezekiah (687). Taken as it stands, this list of rulers would imply as much as a century of prophetic activity by Hosea. In the northern kingdom of Israel, Jeroboam II ruled from 786-746. All that can be inferred is that Hosea was probably active from about 750 down to the fall of Israel to the Assyrians in 722. **1.2-9** Hosea's Unfaithful Wife and their Children as Symbols of Faithless Israel. **1.2-3** Hosea marries *Gomer* in full knowledge of her sexual infidelity, which becomes a major symbol of the disobedient, idolatrous people of God who have *forsaken the LORD*. **1.4-5** Each of the children of this pair is given a name symbolic of Israel's disobedience and violation of the covenant relationship with God. *Jezreel* (God sows) points to the harvest of judgment that God is about to bring on the *kingdom* of Israel, and is also the name of the city which was the residence of the kings of Israel (1 Kings 18.45-46; 21.1), and the place where the wicked Queen Jezebel was put to death by Jehu (2 Kings 9.30-37) when he ruthlessly installed himself as king of Israel (2 Kings 9-10). Now his dynasty (*house*) is about to be destroyed. **1.6-7** The daughter born to Gomer is named *Lo-ruhamah* (meaning, not shown compassion). God's mercy will be withheld from Israel, but will be extended to *the house of Judah* (the group of southern tribes based in Jerusalem), which will be *saved* from defeat or exile by *the LORD their God* through means which are not specified but do not include military resources. **1.8-9** The third child born to Gomer and Hosea is a son named *Lo-ammi* (Not my people), which indicates that God has broken the relationship with the northern tribes of Israel and is no longer their God. **1.10-2.1** God's Renewal of Relationship with both Israel and Judah. A change in vocabulary and imagery in this section may indicate that it was written later, following the exile of Judah to Babylon in 586, but it could originate with Hosea. This prophecy expects the reunion of Israel and Judah under one ruler (*head*) in *the land* (occupied by both northern and southern tribes), and the restoration of relationship between *the living God* and *all his children*. This renewal is symbolized by the change of the children's names to *Ammi* (my people) and *Ruhamah* (shown compassion). **2.2-23** How Israel's Relationship with God was Broken and How it will be Restored. **2.2-6** The infidelity of God's people, which will lead to his abandonment of them, is expressed in terms of *whoring*, as evident in their seeking aid from, and giving credit to, the gods (*Baals*) of neighboring tribes for supplying their basic necessities: food, water, and crops. This misguided search for security will result in God's thwarting Israel, symbolized by his *building a wall* of frustration to enclose them. **2.7-13** Failure to recognize that it was God's hand and not that of the other gods (*lovers*) that was providing Israel with her basic needs (*silver and gold, grain, wine and oil*) will result in God's *taking away* these necessities. This will expose the futility (*nakedness*) of the people's idolatry. Their modes of festival worship will be ended, as will the rewards they thought they were receiving from the worship of the *Baals*. These *lords* were the fertility deities who were honored by ceremonies and sacrifices as a means of assuring agricultural and community prosperity.

10 Now I will uncover her shame
in the sight of her lovers,
and no one shall rescue her out of my hand.
11 I will put an end to all her mirth,
her festivals, her new moons, her sabbaths,
and all her appointed festivals.
12 I will lay waste her vines and her fig trees,
of which she said,
"These are my pay,
which my lovers have given me."
I will make them a forest,
and the wild animals shall devour them.
13 I will punish her for the festival days of the Baals,
when she offered incense to them
and decked herself with her ring and jewelry,
and went after her lovers,
and forgot me, says the LORD.

14 Therefore, I will now allure her,
and bring her into the wilderness,
and speak tenderly to her.
15 From there I will give her her vineyards,
and make the Valley of Achor a door of hope.
There she shall respond as in the days of her youth,
as at the time when she came out of the land of Egypt.

16 On that day, says the LORD, you will call
me, "My husband," and no longer will you
call me, "My Baal."[m] 17 For I will remove the
names of the Baals from her mouth, and
they shall be mentioned by name no more.
18 I will make for you[n] a covenant on that
day with the wild animals, the birds of the
air, and the creeping things of the ground;
and I will abolish[o] the bow, the sword, and
war from the land; and I will make you lie
down in safety. 19 And I will take you for my
wife forever; I will take you for my wife in
righteousness and in justice, in steadfast
love, and in mercy. 20 I will take you for my
wife in faithfulness; and you shall know the
LORD.

21 On that day I will answer, says the LORD,
I will answer the heavens
and they shall answer the earth;
22 and the earth shall answer the grain,
the wine, and the oil,
and they shall answer Jezreel;[p]
23 and I will sow him[q] for myself in the land.
And I will have pity on Lo-ruhamah,[r]
and I will say to Lo-ammi,[s] "You are my people";
and he shall say, "You are my God."

Further Assurances of God's Redeeming Love

3 The LORD said to me again, "Go, love
a woman who has a lover and is an
adulteress, just as the LORD loves the people
of Israel, though they turn to other gods
and love raisin cakes." 2 So I bought her for
fifteen shekels of silver and a homer of
barley and a measure of wine.[t] 3 And I said
to her, "You must remain as mine for many
days; you shall not play the whore, you
shall not have intercourse with a man, nor
I with you." 4 For the Israelites shall remain
many days without king or prince, without
sacrifice or pillar, without ephod or teraphim.
5 Afterward the Israelites shall return and
seek the LORD their God, and David their
king; they shall come in awe to the LORD
and to his goodness in the latter days.

God Accuses Israel

4 Hear the word of the LORD, O people of Israel;
for the LORD has an indictment
against the inhabitants of the land.
There is no faithfulness or loyalty,
and no knowledge of God in the land.
2 Swearing, lying, and murder,
and stealing and adultery break out;
bloodshed follows bloodshed.
3 Therefore the land mourns,
and all who live in it languish;
together with the wild animals
and the birds of the air,
even the fish of the sea are perishing.

4 Yet let no one contend,
and let none accuse,
for with you is my contention, O priest.[u]
5 You shall stumble by day;
the prophet also shall stumble with you by night,
and I will destroy your mother.
6 My people are destroyed for lack of knowledge;

[m] That is, *"My master"* [n] Heb *them* [o] Heb *break* [p] That is *God sows* [q] Cn: Heb *her* [r] That is *Not pitied* [s] That is *Not my people* [t] Gk: Heb *a homer of barley and a lethech of barley* [u] Cn: Meaning of Heb uncertain

2.14-23 God will entice the people to return to honoring him alone, and their time of despair (*Valley of Achor*; Josh 7.24-26) will give way to an era of *hope* like that of the days of deliverance from slavery in Egypt. When this relationship with the LORD is restored, devotion to *Baal* will cease and the *covenant* will be renewed for the benefit of those who will once more be known as God's people.
3.1-5 Beyond Israel's Impending Disasters Lies Renewal of Relationship with God. Recalling the instruction of 1.2 about loving unfaithful Gomer just as God loves disobedient Israel, the people's violation of the covenant is evident in their enjoying *raisin cakes*, which were eaten as part of the worship of the fertility goddess (2 Sam 6.19; Jer 7.18; 44.15-19). Purchasing this woman for *fifteen shekels of silver* is an ironic way of showing that God wants the relationship restored, even if it requires the moral compromise of paying the symbolic equivalent of a huge prostitute's fee. The cost to the unfaithful wife is total sexual abstinence: a complete break with the pagan practices, which include the *pillar* (a male fertility symbol erected to honor Baal), an *ephod* (perhaps a sacred garment, or a device used to determine the will of the god), and *teraphim* (small, portable idols; 1 Sam 19.9-17; Gen 31.19-35). The linking of the call to *seek the LORD* with *David the king* may mean that the prophet expected all twelve of the tribes of Israel to be reunited in a single realm as in the time of David.
4.1-5.15 God's Indictment of Israel.
4.1-11 Responsibility for the gross infidelity and immorality of the people, as well as for the natural disasters that have fallen on *the land* and the *wild animals*, rests with the *priests* and the *prophets* (those involved in the pagan cults). Instead of instructing the people in *the knowledge of God* and for moral renewal, the religious leaders *have forgotten the law of God* and thus have fostered *iniquity* and *whoredom* (idolatry).

2.10 Ezek 16.37
2.11 Jer 7.34; 16.9; Am 8.10; Isa 1.13,14
2.12 ver 5; Isa 5.5; Hos 13.8
2.13 Ezek 16.12,17; Hos 4.6; 8.14; 13.6
2.14 Ezek 20.33-38
2.15 Ezek 28.25,26; Josh 7.26; Jer 2.2; Ex 15.1,2; Hos 11.1
2.17 Ex 23.13; Josh 23.7; Ps 16.4; Zech 13.2; ver 13
2.18 Job 5.23; Isa 11.6-9; Ps 46.9; Ezek 34.25
2.19 Isa 62.4,5; Jer 3.14; Isa 1.27
2.20 Hos 6.6; 13.4
2.22 Jer 31.12; Joel 2.19
2.23 Jer 31.27; Hos 1.6,9,10; Zech 13.9; Rom 9.25,26
3.1 Hos 1.2; 2 Sam 6.19; 1 Chr 16.3
3.2 Ruth 4.10
3.4 Hos 13.10,11; 2.11; Ex 28.6; Judg 17.5; Zech 10.2
3.5 Jer 50.4,5; Ezek 34.23,24; Jer 31.9; Mic 4.1
4.1 Hos 5.1; 12.2; Mic 6.2; Isa 59.4; Jer 7.28; Hos 6.6; 5.4
4.3 Jer 4.28; Zeph 1.3; Jer 4.25
4.4 Ezek 3.26; Deut 17.12

4.12-19 Not only do the people dishonor *their God* by their offerings to the fertility gods (*a piece of wood*), but the men have sex with the *temple prostitutes* in order to assure the fertility of their crops. The people are told to avoid the sacred sites of Israel's earlier history: *Gilgal* (Josh 4.19-24; 1 Sam 7.16; 11.14-15) and Bethel, here called *Beth-aven* (Gen 28.10-22; 1 Sam 7.16; 10.3), which had become a center for idolatrous worship under Jeroboam (1 Kings 12.25-33). The prophet hopes that *Judah* will not participate in these wicked practices, but *Ephraim* (symbolizing the northern tribes) has already *joined* in sexual activities, and in drunkenness. They have been swept along into these *orgies* as by a *wind*, but the result will be their humiliation (*shame*).
5.1-7 The indictment of the faithless *priests* is now joined with a warning to the royal leaders (*house of the king*). Involved in idolatry are other important sites in Israel's past: *Mizpah* (Judg 20-21; 1 Sam 7; 10.17-27); *Tabor* (Judg 4); and *Shittim* (Num 25.1; Josh 2.1; 3.1). Judah is now following the bad example of *Ephraim* by participating in these evil rites, and the divine judgment will fall within a month (*the new moon*).
5.8-15 The foolish attempts of Israel and Judah to work out an accommodation with Assyria, their aggressive neighbor to the northeast, are described in 2 Kings 16.5-9 and Isa 7. Now both the northern tribes (indicated by the names of the cities that rally to fight: *Gibeah, Ramah, Beth-aven*) and Judah will fall victim to God's judgment, which will include Assyria's attack from without (God will *tear* them *like a lion*) and decay from within (*maggots...rottenness*). Until the people acknowledge their guilt, there will be no *rescue*, nor will God pay attention to their pleas, since he will withdraw to his *place*, which could be Sinai or his heavenly abode.

because you have rejected knowledge,
I reject you from being a priest to me.
And since you have forgotten the law of your God,
I also will forget your children.

7 The more they increased,
the more they sinned against me;
they changed[v] their glory into shame.
8 They feed on the sin of my people;
they are greedy for their iniquity.
9 And it shall be like people, like priest;
I will punish them for their ways,
and repay them for their deeds.
10 They shall eat, but not be satisfied;
they shall play the whore, but not multiply;
because they have forsaken the LORD
to devote themselves to 11 whoredom.

The Idolatry of Israel

Wine and new wine
take away the understanding.
12 My people consult a piece of wood,
and their divining rod gives them oracles.
For a spirit of whoredom has led them astray,
and they have played the whore,
forsaking their God.
13 They sacrifice on the tops of the mountains,
and make offerings upon the hills,
under oak, poplar, and terebinth,
because their shade is good.

Therefore your daughters play the whore,
and your daughters-in-law commit adultery.
14 I will not punish your daughters when they play the whore,
nor your daughters-in-law when they commit adultery;
for the men themselves go aside with whores,
and sacrifice with temple prostitutes;
thus a people without understanding
comes to ruin.

15 Though you play the whore, O Israel,
do not let Judah become guilty.
Do not enter into Gilgal,
or go up to Beth-aven,
and do not swear, "As the LORD lives."
16 Like a stubborn heifer,
Israel is stubborn;
can the LORD now feed them
like a lamb in a broad pasture?

17 Ephraim is joined to idols—
let him alone.
18 When their drinking is ended, they indulge in sexual orgies;
they love lewdness more than their glory.[w]
19 A wind has wrapped them[x] in its wings,
and they shall be ashamed because of their altars.[y]

Impending Judgment on Israel and Judah

5 Hear this, O priests!
Give heed, O house of Israel!
Listen, O house of the king!
For the judgment pertains to you;
for you have been a snare at Mizpah,
and a net spread upon Tabor,
2 and a pit dug deep in Shittim;[z]
but I will punish all of them.

3 I know Ephraim,
and Israel is not hidden from me;
for now, O Ephraim, you have played the whore;
Israel is defiled.
4 Their deeds do not permit them
to return to their God.
For the spirit of whoredom is within them,
and they do not know the LORD.

5 Israel's pride testifies against him;
Ephraim[a] stumbles in his guilt;
Judah also stumbles with them.
6 With their flocks and herds they shall go
to seek the LORD,
but they will not find him;
he has withdrawn from them.
7 They have dealt faithlessly with the LORD;
for they have borne illegitimate children.
Now the new moon shall devour
them along with their fields.

8 Blow the horn in Gibeah,
the trumpet in Ramah.
Sound the alarm at Beth-aven;

[v] Ancient Heb tradition: MT *I will change* [w] Cn Compare Gk: Meaning of Heb uncertain [x] Heb *her* [y] Gk Syr: Heb *sacrifices* [z] Cn: Meaning of Heb uncertain [a] Heb *Israel and Ephraim*

4.5 Hos 5.5; Ezek 14.3,7; Hos 2.2,5
4.6 ver 1; Mal 2.7,8; Hos 2.13; 8.1,12
4.7 Hos 10.1; 13.6; Hab 2.16; Mal 2.9
4.9 Isa 24.2; Jer 5.31; Hos 9.9
4.10 Lev 26.26; Mic 6.14; Hos 7.14; 9.17
4.11 Hos 5.4; Isa 28.7
4.12 Jer 2.27; Hab 2.19; Hos 5.4; 9.1
4.13 Jer 3.6; Ezek 6.13; Hos 2.13; 11.2; Am 7.17; Rom 1.28
4.14 ver 18; Deut 23.17; ver 6,11
4.15 Am 4.4; 1 Kings 12.28,29
4.16 Ps 78.8; Isa 5.17; 7.25
4.18 ver 14,7
4.19 Hos 12.1; 13.15; Isa 1.29
5.1 Hos 4.1; 6.9
5.3 Am 3.2; Hos 6.10
5.4 Hos 4.11,12
5.5 Hos 7.10; 4.5; Ezek 23.31-35
5.6 Mic 6.6,7; Isa 1.15; Ezek 8.6
5.7 Isa 48.8; Hos 6.7; 2.4,11,12
5.8 Hos 9.9; 10.9; Isa 10.29,30; Hos 4.15

look behind you, Benjamin!
9 Ephraim shall become a desolation
in the day of punishment;
among the tribes of Israel
I declare what is sure.
10 The princes of Judah have become
like those who remove the landmark;
on them I will pour out
my wrath like water.
11 Ephraim is oppressed, crushed in judgment,
because he was determined to go after vanity.[b]
12 Therefore I am like maggots to Ephraim,
and like rottenness to the house of Judah.
13 When Ephraim saw his sickness,
and Judah his wound,
then Ephraim went to Assyria,
and sent to the great king.[c]
But he is not able to cure you
or heal your wound.
14 For I will be like a lion to Ephraim,
and like a young lion to the house of Judah.
I myself will tear and go away;
I will carry off, and no one shall rescue.
15 I will return again to my place
until they acknowledge their guilt
and seek my face.
In their distress they will beg my favor:

A Call to Repentance

6 "Come, let us return to the LORD;
for it is he who has torn, and he will heal us;
he has struck down, and he will bind us up.
2 After two days he will revive us;
on the third day he will raise us up,
that we may live before him.
3 Let us know, let us press on to know the LORD;
his appearing is as sure as the dawn;
he will come to us like the showers,
like the spring rains that water the earth."

Impenitence of Israel and Judah

4 What shall I do with you, O Ephraim?
What shall I do with you, O Judah?
Your love is like a morning cloud,
like the dew that goes away early.
5 Therefore I have hewn them by the prophets,
I have killed them by the words of my mouth,
and my[d] judgment goes forth as the light.
6 For I desire steadfast love and not sacrifice,
the knowledge of God rather than burnt offerings.

7 But at[e] Adam they transgressed the covenant;
there they dealt faithlessly with me.
8 Gilead is a city of evildoers,
tracked with blood.
9 As robbers lie in wait[f] for someone,
so the priests are banded together;[g]
they murder on the road to Shechem,
they commit a monstrous crime.
10 In the house of Israel I have seen a horrible thing;
Ephraim's whoredom is there, Israel is defiled.

11 For you also, O Judah, a harvest is appointed.

When I would restore the fortunes of my people,
7 [1]when I would heal Israel,
the corruption of Ephraim is revealed,
and the wicked deeds of Samaria;
for they deal falsely,
the thief breaks in,
and the bandits raid outside.
2 But they do not consider
that I remember all their wickedness.
Now their deeds surround them,
they are before my face.
3 By their wickedness they make the king glad,
and the officials by their treachery.
4 They are all adulterers;
they are like a heated oven,
whose baker does not need to stir the fire,
from the kneading of the dough until it is leavened.
5 On the day of our king the officials
became sick with the heat of wine;
he stretched out his hand with mockers.

[b] Gk: Meaning of Heb uncertain [c] Cn: Heb *to a king who will contend* [d] Gk Syr: Heb *your* [e] Cn: Heb *like* [f] Cn: Meaning of Heb uncertain [g] Syr: Heb *are a company*

6.1-11 God's People are Called to Repentance.
6.1-3 The appeal to return to the LORD requires the acknowledgement that it was God's punitive action by which Israel was *torn* and *struck down*. Themes from the nature cults are used to describe this promised renewal: the god who dies and rises after a brief time (*three days*, which the early Christians allude to in connection with the resurrection of Jesus: Lk 24.46; 1 Cor 15.4); the rising sun and the *spring rain* as symbols of restoration of life.
6.4-11a The disloyalty of the people to God and the covenant continue in spite of God's stern rebuke of them through the prophet's imagery as *hewn...killed* and struck by God's *light*. The prophet's contrast of *steadfast love* and knowledge of God with *sacrifice* and *burnt offerings* could mean a repudiation of the sacrificial system (as is claimed in Mt 9.13; 12.7) or it may affirm God's preferring human devotion to animal sacrifices. *Adam* is Admah, a city in the Jordan Valley reported by Hosea (11.8) as destroyed with Gilead (an Israelite tribal region east of the Jordan) for gross violation of the *covenant*. The priests organized groups of bandits to prey on travelers on the main road that led up from the Jordan to *Shechem*, where the historic portable sanctuary of God had been located in the time of Joshua (Josh 24). There and throughout *Ephraim* was being carried out *whoredom* or participation in the worship of the fertility deities. As with Israel, the time for judgment on Judah has already been *appointed* by God.
6.11b-7.16 Details of the Degeneracy of the Covenant People.
6.11b-7.3 The people's unrelenting wickedness and cruelty hinders God from following his inclination to *restore* and *heal* Israel. Even the *officials* of this nation are pleased by the gross misdeeds and *treachery* of the people.
7.4-10 By an extended comparison of Israel with the baking of bread, the prophet describes the *heated* sexual passions of the *adulteress* (= the nation), the king and his officials joining the people in a drunken orgy, the rising and falling (like yeast) of the evil urges of the people, and the resemblance of Ephraim to a half-baked loaf. Unaware of their waning powers, like hair turning *white*, and filled with pride, they refuse to return to the LORD.

5.9 Isa 37.3; 46.10; Zech 1.6
5.10 Deut 19.14; Ezek 7.8; Ps 93.3,4
5.12 Ps 39.11; Prov 12.4
5.13 Jer 30.12; Hos 7.11; 8.9; 10.6; 14.3
5.14 Hos 13.7,8; Ps 50.22; Mic 5.8
5.15 Isa 64.7-9; Jer 2.27; Hos 3.5
6.1 Jer 50.4,5; Hos 5.14; 14.4; Isa 30.26
6.3 Isa 2.3; Mic 4.2; Ps 19.6; Mic 5.2; Joel 2.23
6.4 Hos 7.1; 11.8; 13.3
6.5 Jer 1.10,18; Heb 4.12; ver 3
6.6 Mt 9.13; Ps 50.8,9; Hos 2.20
6.9 Hos 7.1; Jer 7.9,10; Ezek 22.9; 23.27
6.10 Jer 5.30,31; Hos 5.3
6.11 Joel 3.13; Zeph 2.7
7.1 ver 13; Hos 6.4; 11.8; 4.2; 6.9
7.2 Hos 8.13; 9.9; Am 8.7; Jer 2.19; Hos 4.9
7.4 Jer 9.2; 23.10
7.5 Isa 28.1,7,8

7.11-16 Like a pigeon (*dove*) chattering nonsense, Ephraim wants to turn to the pagan, hostile neighboring powers for help: *Egypt* and *Assyria*. God will catch them all in the *net* of his disciplining judgment. As is evident from their lies and plots, the people's alienation has taken place in spite of God's having *trained* and *strengthened* them, and will result in the uselessness of their weapons and the futility of their foreign alliances.
8.1-14 Israel Has Turned from God to Foolish Resources.
8.1-6 Two symbols of impending judgment: *the trumpet* announcing the doom of the nation, and *the vulture* that will feast on the corpses of the fallen, disobedient *covenant* people. Claiming to *know God*, they have ignored *the good*, selected their own *kings* and defiled the sanctuary in Samaria with images of bulls (symbols of fertility), just as Jeroboam did at Bethel and Dan (1 Kings 12.25-33).
8.7-10 Israel's attempt to solve its problems through an alliance with Assyria is compared with a farmer's foolish tactics, a *useless vessel* and a *wild ass* separated from its herd. All such efforts will fall under God's judgment.
8.11-14 Israel will suffer punishment and exile for having set up *altars* to alien divinities while at the same time going through the routines of offering *sacrifices* to the LORD. The grand cities she constructed will come under judgment because she forgot her *Maker*.

6 For they are kindled[h] like an oven, their
heart burns within them;
all night their anger smolders;
in the morning it blazes like a flaming
fire.
7 All of them are hot as an oven,
and they devour their rulers.
All their kings have fallen;
none of them calls upon me.

8 Ephraim mixes himself with the peoples;
Ephraim is a cake not turned.
9 Foreigners devour his strength,
but he does not know it;
gray hairs are sprinkled upon him,
but he does not know it.
10 Israel's pride testifies against[i] him;
yet they do not return to the LORD
their God,
or seek him, for all this.

Futile Reliance on the Nations

11 Ephraim has become like a dove,
silly and without sense;
they call upon Egypt, they go to
Assyria.
12 As they go, I will cast my net over
them;
I will bring them down like birds of
the air;
I will discipline them according to the
report made to their assembly.[j]
13 Woe to them, for they have strayed
from me!
Destruction to them, for they have
rebelled against me!
I would redeem them,
but they speak lies against me.

14 They do not cry to me from the heart,
but they wail upon their beds;
they gash themselves for grain and
wine;
they rebel against me.
15 It was I who trained and strengthened
their arms,
yet they plot evil against me.
16 They turn to that which does not profit;[k]
they have become like a defective
bow;
their officials shall fall by the sword
because of the rage of their tongue.
So much for their babbling in the land
of Egypt.

Israel's Apostasy

8 Set the trumpet to your lips!
One like a vulture[l] is over the
house of the LORD,
because they have broken my covenant,
and transgressed my law.
2 Israel cries to me,
"My God, we—Israel—know you!"
3 Israel has spurned the good;
the enemy shall pursue him.

4 They made kings, but not through me;
they set up princes, but without my
knowledge.
With their silver and gold they made
idols
for their own destruction.
5 Your calf is rejected, O Samaria.
My anger burns against them.
How long will they be incapable of
innocence?
6 For it is from Israel,
an artisan made it;
it is not God.
The calf of Samaria
shall be broken to pieces.[l]

7 For they sow the wind,
and they shall reap the whirlwind.
The standing grain has no heads,
it shall yield no meal;
if it were to yield,
foreigners would devour it.
8 Israel is swallowed up;
now they are among the nations
as a useless vessel.
9 For they have gone up to Assyria,
a wild ass wandering alone;
Ephraim has bargained for lovers.
10 Though they bargain with the nations,
I will now gather them up.
They shall soon writhe
under the burden of kings and
princes.

11 When Ephraim multiplied altars to
expiate sin,
they became to him altars for sinning.
12 Though I write for him the multitude of
my instructions,
they are regarded as a strange thing.
13 Though they offer choice sacrifices,[k]
though they eat flesh,
the LORD does not accept them.
Now he will remember their iniquity,

[h] Gk Syr: Heb *brought near* [i] Or *humbles* [j] Meaning of Heb uncertain [k] Cn: Meaning of Heb uncertain [l] Or *shall go up in flames*

7.7 Ps 21.9; ver 16; Isa 64.7
7.9 Isa 1.7; Hos 4.6
7.10 Hos 5.5; ver 7,14; Hos 5.4
7.11 Hos 11.11; 4.6,11,14; ver 16; Hos 5.13; 8.9; 12.1
7.12 Ezek 12.13
7.13 Hos 9.12,17; Jer 14.10; Ezek 34.6; ver 1; Mt 23.37
7.14 Jer 3.10; Am 2.8; Mic 2.11; Hos 13.16
7.15 Hos 11.13; Nah 1.9
7.16 Ps 78.57; ver 7; Ezek 23.32
8.1 Hos 5.8; Hab 1.8; Hos 6.7; 4.6
8.2 Hos 7.14
8.4 Hos 13.10,11; 2.8
8.5 ver 6; Hos 10.5; 13.2; Jer 13.27
8.6 Hos 13.2
8.7 Hos 10.12,13; Isa 66.15; Nah 1.3
8.8 Jer 51.34; Hos 13.15
8.9 Hos 7.11; Jer 2.24; Ezek 16.33
8.10 Ezek 16.37; 22.20; Jer 42.2
8.12 ver 1; Hos 4.6
8.13 Jer 7.21; Hos 7.2; 1 Cor 4.5; Hos 4.9; 9.7; 9.3,6

and punish their sins;
they shall return to Egypt.
14 Israel has forgotten his Maker,
and built palaces;
and Judah has multiplied fortified cities;
but I will send a fire upon his cities,
and it shall devour his strongholds.

Punishment for Israel's Sin

9 Do not rejoice, O Israel!
Do not exult[m] as other nations do;
for you have played the whore,
departing from your God.
You have loved a prostitute's pay
on all threshing floors.
2 Threshing floor and wine vat shall not
feed them,
and the new wine shall fail them.
3 They shall not remain in the land of the
LORD;
but Ephraim shall return to Egypt,
and in Assyria they shall eat unclean
food.

4 They shall not pour drink offerings of
wine to the LORD,
and their sacrifices shall not please
him.
Such sacrifices shall be like mourners'
bread;
all who eat of it shall be defiled;
for their bread shall be for their hunger
only;
it shall not come to the house of the
LORD.

5 What will you do on the day of
appointed festival,
and on the day of the festival of the
LORD?
6 For even if they escape destruction,
Egypt shall gather them,
Memphis shall bury them.
Nettles shall possess their precious
things of silver;[n]
thorns shall be in their tents.

7 The days of punishment have come,
the days of recompense have come;
Israel cries,[o]
"The prophet is a fool,
the man of the spirit is mad!"
Because of your great iniquity,
your hostility is great.
8 The prophet is a sentinel for my God
over Ephraim,
yet a fowler's snare is on all his ways,
and hostility in the house of his God.
9 They have deeply corrupted themselves
as in the days of Gibeah;
he will remember their iniquity,
he will punish their sins.

10 Like grapes in the wilderness,
I found Israel.
Like the first fruit on the fig tree,
in its first season,
I saw your ancestors.
But they came to Baal-peor,
and consecrated themselves to a thing
of shame,
and became detestable like the thing
they loved.
11 Ephraim's glory shall fly away like a bird—
no birth, no pregnancy, no conception!
12 Even if they bring up children,
I will bereave them until no one is left.
Woe to them indeed
when I depart from them!
13 Once I saw Ephraim as a young palm
planted in a lovely meadow,[n]
but now Ephraim must lead out his
children for slaughter.
14 Give them, O LORD—
what will you give?
Give them a miscarrying womb
and dry breasts.

15 Every evil of theirs began at Gilgal;
there I came to hate them.
Because of the wickedness of their deeds
I will drive them out of my house.
I will love them no more;
all their officials are rebels.

16 Ephraim is stricken,
their root is dried up,
they shall bear no fruit.
Even though they give birth,
I will kill the cherished offspring of
their womb.
17 Because they have not listened to him,
my God will reject them;
they shall become wanderers among
the nations.

Israel's Sin and Captivity

10 Israel is a luxuriant vine
that yields its fruit.
The more his fruit increased
the more altars he built;
as his country improved,

9.1-10.15 God's Judgment on Israel.
9.1-6 The foolish *exultation* of Israel is a sham, since God knows of her having courted the foreign gods like a *prostitute*. Their *festival celebrations* with *wine* and *sacrifices* are empty and hence have no place in *the house of the LORD*. Now the people are to be exiled to Egypt and Assyria (9.3), and *thorns* will take over their former dwelling-places.
9.7-17 The *prophet's* message of *punishment* for Israel leads the people to denounce him as a *fool*, so that he meets *hostility* even in the sanctuary of God. Their corruption is compared with that of the men of Gibeah who grossly mistreated visitors when Israel first came to the land (Judg 19-20). God's original call to Israel *in the wilderness* has now degenerated into a people who devote themselves to pagan deities, as they did to Baal Peor earlier (Num 25.18; Josh 22.17). Accordingly, Ephraim will have no more offspring. God now hates his people, whose monarchy began at *Gilgal* under Saul (1 Sam 11.15); it has now become a center of Baal-worship (Am 4.4; 5.5). They will lose their homes and their children, and will again be *wanderers* among the nations. The sacred calf statue which they have admired will, like them, be taken to *Assyria*.
10.1-8 Foolishly, Israel has celebrated its prosperity by erecting *altars* and *pillars* (fertility symbols), which God will now destroy. The people will be left without a *king*, even as they mourn the loss of their fertility objects (*calves*) and are taken off to exile, bitterly disillusioned (*put to shame*).

8.14 Hos 2.13; 13.6; Jer 17.27
9.1 Isa 22.12,13; Hos 10.5; 4.12; Jer 44.17
9.2 Hos 2.9
9.3 Jer 2.7; Hos 8.13; Ezek 4.13; Hos 7.11
9.4 Jer 6.20; Hos 5.6; 8.13; Hag 2.14
9.5 Isa 10.3; Jer 5.31; Joel 1.13
9.6 ver 3; Jer 2.16; Ezek 30.13,16; Isa 5.6; Hos 10.8
9.7 Jer 10.15; Mic 7.4; Isa 34.8; Jer 16.18; Ezek 14.9,10
9.8 Hos 5.1
9.9 Isa 31.6; Judg 19.12; Hos 5.8; 10.9; 7.2; 8.13
9.10 Mic 7.1; Jer 24.2; Num 25.3; Hos 4.14; Jer 11.13
9.11 Hos 4.7; 10.5; ver 14
9.12 ver 16; Hos 7.13
9.13 Ezek 27.3,4
9.15 Hos 4.9; 7.2; 12.2; Isa 1.23
9.16 Hos 5.11; 8.7; ver 12
9.17 Hos 4.10; Deut 28.65
10.1 Ezek 15.1-5; Hos 8.11; 3.4

[m] Gk: Heb *To exultation* [n] Meaning of Heb uncertain [o] Cn Compare Gk: Heb *shall know*

10.9-15 Both the *king* of Israel and the idolatrous system, identified here as *Aven*, will be destroyed. This was originally the Egyptian shrine of the sun (later known as Heliopolis), but here it probably refers to Bethel (as in 10.5). Instead of preparing the people for growth of *righteousness* and love among those who *seek the LORD*, the leaders are harvesting the results of their reliance on raw power and fortifications rather than on God. They will be destroyed just as *Shalman* (Shalmaneser III, ruler of Assyria) demolished *Beth-arbel* (probably Arbela, a major city east of Nineveh, the Assyrian capital). Now *Bethel* (a city since the days of Abraham, site of the sanctuary of the LORD built to compete with the Jerusalem temple; Gen 28.11-17; 1 Sam 7.16; 1 Kings 12.29-33) will also be destroyed and Israel's king will be *cut off*.
11.1-12.13 Israel's Determination to Shatter the Parent-Child Relationship with God.
11.1-4 Comparing the exodus of Israel from Egypt with a parent nurturing a child with *bands of love*, the people are seen as rebelling against God's compassionate treatment of them.
11.5-7 Now they are to return to exile in Egypt and Assyria, and in spite of pleas to God, they are not to return to their land soon.

he improved his pillars.
2 Their heart is false;
now they must bear their guilt.
The LORD[p] will break down their altars,
and destroy their pillars.

3 For now they will say:
"We have no king,
for we do not fear the LORD,
and a king—what could he do for us?"
4 They utter mere words;
with empty oaths they make
covenants;
so litigation springs up like poisonous
weeds
in the furrows of the field.
5 The inhabitants of Samaria tremble
for the calf[q] of Beth-aven.
Its people shall mourn for it,
and its idolatrous priests shall wail[r]
over it,
over its glory that has departed from it.
6 The thing itself shall be carried to
Assyria
as tribute to the great king.[s]
Ephraim shall be put to shame,
and Israel shall be ashamed of his
idol.[t]

7 Samaria's king shall perish
like a chip on the face of the waters.
8 The high places of Aven, the sin of
Israel,
shall be destroyed.
Thorn and thistle shall grow up
on their altars.
They shall say to the mountains, Cover
us,
and to the hills, Fall on us.

9 Since the days of Gibeah you have
sinned, O Israel;
there they have continued.
Shall not war overtake them in
Gibeah?
10 I will come[u] against the wayward people
to punish them;
and nations shall be gathered against
them
when they are punished[v] for their
double iniquity.

11 Ephraim was a trained heifer
that loved to thresh,
and I spared her fair neck;
but I will make Ephraim break the
ground;
Judah must plow;
Jacob must harrow for himself.
12 Sow for yourselves righteousness;
reap steadfast love;
break up your fallow ground;
for it is time to seek the LORD,
that he may come and rain
righteousness upon you.

13 You have plowed wickedness,
you have reaped injustice,
you have eaten the fruit of lies.
Because you have trusted in your power
and in the multitude of your warriors,
14 therefore the tumult of war shall rise
against your people,
and all your fortresses shall be
destroyed,
as Shalman destroyed Beth-arbel on the
day of battle
when mothers were dashed in pieces
with their children.
15 Thus it shall be done to you, O Bethel,
because of your great wickedness.
At dawn the king of Israel
shall be utterly cut off.

God's Compassion Despite Israel's Ingratitude

11 When Israel was a child, I loved
him,
and out of Egypt I called my son.
2 The more I[w] called them,
the more they went from me;[x]
they kept sacrificing to the Baals,
and offering incense to idols.

3 Yet it was I who taught Ephraim to
walk,
I took them up in my[y] arms;
but they did not know that I healed
them.
4 I led them with cords of human kindness,
with bands of love.
I was to them like those
who lift infants to their cheeks.[z]
I bent down to them and fed them.

5 They shall return to the land of Egypt,
and Assyria shall be their king,

[p] Heb *he* [q] Gk Syr: Heb *calves* [r] Cn: Heb *exult* [s] Cn: Heb *to a king who will contend* [t] Cn: Heb *counsel* [u] Cn Compare Gk: Heb *In my desire* [v] Gk: Heb *bound* [w] Gk: Heb *they* [x] Gk: Heb *them* [y] Gk Syr Vg: Heb *his* [z] Or *who ease the yoke on their jaws*

10.2 1 Kings 18.21; Mt 6.24; Hos 13.16; ver 8
10.4 Ezek 17.13-19; Hos 4.2; Deut 31.16,17
10.5 Hos 8.5,6; 9.11
10.6 Hos 11.5; 5.13; 4.7; Isa 30.3; Jer 7.24
10.7 Hos 13.11
10.8 ver 5; 1 Kings 12.30; ver 2; Hos 9.6; Lk 23.30; Rev 6.16
10.9 Hos 5.8; 9.9
10.10 Ezek 5.13; Hos 4.9
10.11 Jer 50.11; Hos 4.16; Jer 28.14; Ps 66.12
10.12 Prov 11.18; Jer 4.3; Hos 12.6; 6.3; Isa 44.3; 45.8
10.13 Job 4.8; Gal 6.7,8; Hos 4.2; 7.3
10.14 Isa 17.3; Hos 13.16
10.15 ver 7
11.1 Hos 2.15; 12.9,13; 13.4; Mt 2.15
11.2 2 Kings 17.13-15; Hos 2.13; Isa 65.7; Jer 18.15
11.3 Hos 7.15; Deut 1.31; Jer 30.17
11.4 Jer 31.2,3; Lev 26.13; Ex 16.32; Ps 78.25
11.5 Hos 10.6; 7.16

because they have refused to return
to me.
6 The sword rages in their cities,
it consumes their oracle-priests,
and devours because of their schemes.
7 My people are bent on turning away
from me.
To the Most High they call,
but he does not raise them up at all.[a]

8 How can I give you up, Ephraim?
How can I hand you over, O Israel?
How can I make you like Admah?
How can I treat you like Zeboiim?
My heart recoils within me;
my compassion grows warm and
tender.
9 I will not execute my fierce anger;
I will not again destroy Ephraim;
for I am God and no mortal,
the Holy One in your midst,
and I will not come in wrath.[a]

10 They shall go after the LORD,
who roars like a lion;
when he roars,
his children shall come trembling
from the west.
11 They shall come trembling like birds
from Egypt,
and like doves from the land of Assyria;
and I will return them to their homes,
says the LORD.

12[b] Ephraim has surrounded me with lies,
and the house of Israel with deceit;
but Judah still walks[c] with God,
and is faithful to the Holy One.

12 Ephraim herds the wind,
and pursues the east wind all day
long;
they multiply falsehood and violence;
they make a treaty with Assyria,
and oil is carried to Egypt.

The Long History of Rebellion

2 The LORD has an indictment against
Judah,
and will punish Jacob according to
his ways,
and repay him according to his deeds.
3 In the womb he tried to supplant his
brother,
and in his manhood he strove with God.
4 He strove with the angel and prevailed,
he wept and sought his favor;
he met him at Bethel,
and there he spoke with him.[d]
5 The LORD the God of hosts,
the LORD is his name!
6 But as for you, return to your God,
hold fast to love and justice,
and wait continually for your God.

7 A trader, in whose hands are false
balances,
he loves to oppress.
8 Ephraim has said, "Ah, I am rich,
I have gained wealth for myself;
in all of my gain
no offense has been found in me
that would be sin."[d]
9 I am the LORD your God
from the land of Egypt;
I will make you live in tents again,
as in the days of the appointed festival.

10 I spoke to the prophets;
it was I who multiplied visions,
and through the prophets I will bring
destruction.
11 In Gilead[e] there is iniquity,
they shall surely come to nothing.
In Gilgal they sacrifice bulls,
so their altars shall be like stone heaps
on the furrows of the field.
12 Jacob fled to the land of Aram,
there Israel served for a wife,
and for a wife he guarded sheep.[f]
13 By a prophet the LORD brought Israel up
from Egypt,
and by a prophet he was guarded.
14 Ephraim has given bitter offense,
so his Lord will bring his crimes down
on him
and pay him back for his insults.

Relentless Judgment on Israel

13 When Ephraim spoke, there was
trembling;
he was exalted in Israel;
but he incurred guilt through Baal
and died.
2 And now they keep on sinning
and make a cast image for themselves,
idols of silver made according to their
understanding,
all of them the work of artisans.

[a] Meaning of Heb uncertain [b] Ch 12.1 in Heb [c] Heb *roams* or *rules* [d] Gk Syr: Heb *us* [e] Compare Syr: Heb *Gilead* [f] Heb lacks *sheep*

11.6 Hos 13.16; 4.16,17
11.7 Jer 8.5; ver 2
11.8 Hos 6.4; Gen 14.8; Isa 63.15
11.9 Deut 13.17; Jer 26.3; Isa 41.14,16; 55.8,9; Mal 3.6
11.10 Hos 6.1-3; Joel 3.16; Isa 66.2,5
11.11 Isa 11.11; 60.8; Ezek 28.25,26
11.12 Hos 4.2; 7.3
12.1 2 Kings 17.4; Isa 30.6
12.2 Mic 6.2; Hos 4.9
12.3 Gen 25.26; 32.24,28
12.4 Gen 32.26; 28.12-15
12.6 Mic 6.8; Hos 6.6; Mic 7.7
12.7 Am 8.5; Mic 6.11
12.8 Hos 13.6; Rev 3.17; Hos 4.8; 14.1
12.9 Hos 11.1; 13.4; Lev 23.42; Neh 8.17
12.10 2 Kings 17.13; Jer 7.25; Ezek 17.2; 20.49
12.11 Hos 6.8; 4.15; 9.15; 10.1,2
12.12 Gen 28.5; 29.20
12.13 Ex 13.3
12.14 Ezek 18.10-13; Dan 11.18; Mic 6.16
13.1 Judg 8.1; 12.1; Hos 2.8-17
13.2 Isa 46.6; Hos 8.6

11.8-11 But God, whose *wrath* is not like that of humans, will not bring on their cities such utter destruction as fell on *Admah* and *Zeboiim*, which were destroyed with Sodom and Gomorrah (Deut. 29.23). Instead, Israel will be restored to the land, as will Judah (perhaps a later addition, since Judah went into exile in Babylon much later, in 586).
11.12-12.9 Israel's behavior, which is characterized by *deceit, falsehood and violence*, and by reliance on pagan powers, is contrasted with Judah's maintenance of fidelity to the Holy One. Yet Judah, like Jacob (Gen 32.22-32) competes with her *brother* tribes and wrestles with God. The tribes of Israel are rebuked for their pride and false claims of innocence, which will result in their return to a migratory life (*in tents*), which ironically is what they act out annually in the Feast of Booths, recalling their journey through the desert of Sinai to Canaan.
12.10-13 God is still speaking to his people through prophets, who offer instruction as well as predictions of impending punishment for their disobedience, such as has already fallen on Gilead (6.8) and Gilgal (4.15; 10.15), where altars honoring the hill-gods were once as common as heaps of stones in a field. Yet God does achieve his purpose for his people in other lands: Jacob spent time in *Aram* (Syria) in order to get a wife (Gen 28-29); it was out of Egypt that God's prophet Moses led his people (Deut 26.5-9).
12.14-13.16 God's Inescapable Judgment on Israel.
12.14-13.3 God will surely call *Ephraim* to account for the *crimes* done in violation of God's law, especially making images to which the people were encouraged to make *sacrifices*. Therefore these people will disappear like *morning mist* or *chaff* that is blown away.

13.4-11 The God who has controlled the destiny of Israel since the tribes were freed from slavery in *Egypt* and supported through the *wilderness* will attack and *devour* them. The kings, who were granted to them as a concession, are now to be taken away.
13.12-16 Stubborn Israel is like a foetus that refuses to emerge from the womb – that is, to face life and accept responsibility. God shows no *compassion* with respect to their imminent *death*, but instead will visit them with disaster as from a parching *wind* from the desert, from a stripped treasury, or from an attack that leaves behind dead children and mutilated mothers.
14.1-8 A Final Plea for Israel to Repent. Confession of guilt, as well as renunciation of dependence on other nations (*Assyria*) or on their own schemes for national deliverance (*the work of our hands*), will unleash God's forgiveness of his people and restore them to a flourishing, fruitful common life. It is not *the idols* that sustain God's people, but the fidelity and concern which he has for their welfare.

"Sacrifice to these," they say.[g]
People are kissing calves!
3 Therefore they shall be like the morning mist
or like the dew that goes away early,
like chaff that swirls from the threshing floor
or like smoke from a window.

4 Yet I have been the LORD your God
ever since the land of Egypt;
you know no God but me,
and besides me there is no savior.
5 It was I who fed[h] you in the wilderness,
in the land of drought.
6 When I fed[i] them, they were satisfied;
they were satisfied, and their heart was proud;
therefore they forgot me.
7 So I will become like a lion to them,
like a leopard I will lurk beside the way.
8 I will fall upon them like a bear robbed of her cubs,
and will tear open the covering of their heart;
there I will devour them like a lion,
as a wild animal would mangle them.

9 I will destroy you, O Israel;
who can help you?[j]
10 Where now is[k] your king, that he may save you?
Where in all your cities are your rulers,
of whom you said,
"Give me a king and rulers"?
11 I gave you a king in my anger,
and I took him away in my wrath.

12 Ephraim's iniquity is bound up;
his sin is kept in store.
13 The pangs of childbirth come for him,
but he is an unwise son;
for at the proper time he does not present himself
at the mouth of the womb.

14 Shall I ransom them from the power of Sheol?
Shall I redeem them from Death?
O Death, where are[l] your plagues?
O Sheol, where is[l] your destruction?
Compassion is hidden from my eyes.
15 Although he may flourish among rushes,[m]
the east wind shall come, a blast from the LORD,
rising from the wilderness;
and his fountain shall dry up,
his spring shall be parched.
It shall strip his treasury
of every precious thing.
16[n] Samaria shall bear her guilt,
because she has rebelled against her God;
they shall fall by the sword,
their little ones shall be dashed in pieces,
and their pregnant women ripped open.

A Plea for Repentance

14 Return, O Israel, to the LORD your God,
for you have stumbled because of your iniquity.
2 Take words with you
and return to the LORD;
say to him,
"Take away all guilt;
accept that which is good,
and we will offer
the fruit[o] of our lips.
3 Assyria shall not save us;
we will not ride upon horses;
we will say no more, 'Our God,'
to the work of our hands.
In you the orphan finds mercy."

Assurance of Forgiveness

4 I will heal their disloyalty;
I will love them freely,
for my anger has turned from them.
5 I will be like the dew to Israel;
he shall blossom like the lily,
he shall strike root like the forests of Lebanon.[p]
6 His shoots shall spread out;
his beauty shall be like the olive tree,
and his fragrance like that of Lebanon.
7 They shall again live beneath my[q] shadow,
they shall flourish as a garden;[r]

[g] Cn Compare Gk: Heb *To these they say sacrifices of people* [h] Gk Syr: Heb *knew* [i] Cn: Heb *according to their pasture* [j] Gk Syr: Heb *for in me is your help* [k] Gk Syr Vg: Heb *I will be* [l] Gk Syr: Heb *I will be* [m] Or *among brothers* [n] Ch 14.1 in Heb [o] Gk Syr: Heb *bulls* [p] Cn: Heb *like Lebanon* [q] Heb *his* [r] Cn: Heb *they shall grow grain*

13.3 Hos 6.4; Dan 2.35; Ps 68.2
13.4 Hos 12.9; Isa 43.11
13.5 Deut 2.7; 8.15; 32.10
13.6 Deut 8.12,14; 32.15; Hos 2.13; 4.6; 8.14
13.7 Lam 3.10; Jer 5.6
13.10 2 Kings 17.4; Hos 8.4
13.11 1 Sam 8.7; 1 Kings 14.7-10
13.12 Deut 32.34; Rom 2.5
13.13 Mic 4.9,10; Isa 37.3; 66.9
13.14 Ezek 37.12,13; 1 Cor 15.54,55; Rom 11.29
13.15 Hos 10.1; Ezek 17.10; 19.12; Jer 51.36; 20.5
13.16 Hos 10.2; 7.14; Isa 13.16; Hos 10.14; 2 Kings 15.16
14.1 Hos 10.12; 14.6; Joel 2.13
14.2 Mic 7.18,19; Heb 13.15
14.3 Hos 5.13; Isa 31.1; Hos 8.6; 13.2; Ps 10.14
14.4 Zeph 3.17; Isa 12.1
14.5 Job 29.19; Mt 6.28; Isa 35.2
14.6 Ps 52.8; Song 4.11
14.7 Ps 91.4; Ezek 17.23; Hos 2.21,22

they shall blossom like the vine,
  their fragrance shall be like the wine
    of Lebanon.

8 O Ephraim, what have I[s] to do with
    idols?
  It is I who answer and look after
    you.[t]
I am like an evergreen cypress;
  your faithfulness[u] comes from me.
9 Those who are wise understand these
    things;
  those who are discerning know them.
For the ways of the LORD are right,
  and the upright walk in them,
  but transgressors stumble in them.

[s] Or *What more has Ephraim* [t] Heb *him* [u] Heb *your fruit*

14.8 ver 3; Isa 41.19; Ezek 17.23
14.9 Ps 107.43; Acts 13.10; Isa 26.7; 1.28

14.9 Epilogue. A concluding appeal to the hearers or readers to be *wise* by recognizing the righteousness of the LORD's *ways*, which serve as a path for the *upright* but a stumbling block to *transgressors*.

JOEL

See the Introductions, pp. 6, 54-57, and 66-67 above.

1 The word of the LORD that came to
Joel son of Pethuel:

Lament over the Ruin of the Country

2 Hear this, O elders,
  give ear, all inhabitants of the land!
Has such a thing happened in your days,
  or in the days of your ancestors?
3 Tell your children of it,
  and let your children tell their
    children,
  and their children another generation.

4 What the cutting locust left,
  the swarming locust has eaten.
What the swarming locust left,
  the hopping locust has eaten,
and what the hopping locust left,
  the destroying locust has eaten.

5 Wake up, you drunkards, and weep;
  and wail, all you wine-drinkers,
over the sweet wine,
  for it is cut off from your mouth.
6 For a nation has invaded my land,
  powerful and innumerable;
its teeth are lions' teeth,
  and it has the fangs of a lioness.
7 It has laid waste my vines,
  and splintered my fig trees;
it has stripped off their bark and thrown
    it down;
  their branches have turned white.

8 Lament like a virgin dressed in sackcloth
  for the husband of her youth.
9 The grain offering and the drink offering
    are cut off
  from the house of the LORD.
The priests mourn,
  the ministers of the LORD.
10 The fields are devastated,
  the ground mourns;
for the grain is destroyed,
  the wine dries up,
  the oil fails.

11 Be dismayed, you farmers,
  wail, you vinedressers,
over the wheat and the barley;
  for the crops of the field are ruined.
12 The vine withers,
  the fig tree droops.
Pomegranate, palm, and apple—
  all the trees of the field are dried up;
surely, joy withers away
  among the people.

A Call to Repentance and Prayer

13 Put on sackcloth and lament, you
    priests;
  wail, you ministers of the altar.
Come, pass the night in sackcloth,
  you ministers of my God!
Grain offering and drink offering
  are withheld from the house of your
    God.

14 Sanctify a fast,
  call a solemn assembly.
Gather the elders
  and all the inhabitants of the land

1.1 Jer 1.2; Ezek 1.3; Hos 1.1; Acts 2.16
1.2 Hos 4.1; 5.1; ver 14; Joel 2.2
1.3 Ps 78.4
1.4 Deut 28.38; Joel 2.25; Nah 3.15,16; Isa 33.4
1.6 Joel 2.2,11; Rev 9.8
1.7 Isa 5.6; Am 4.9
1.8 ver 13; Am 8.10
1.9 Joel 2.14,17
1.10 Isa 24.4-7; Hos 9.2
1.11 Jer 14.3,4; Isa 17.11; Jer 9.12
1.12 Hab 3.17,18; Isa 16.10; 24.11; Jer 48.33
1.13 ver 8; Jer 4.8; ver 9; Joel 2.17; 1 Kings 21.27
1.14 2 Chr 20.3,4; Joel 2.15,16; ver 2; Jon 3.8

1.1 Introduction. *Joel* means *Yahweh [the LORD] is God.* There is no indication, as in other prophetic writings, of the time or circumstances of his having received the *word of the LORD.* His father's name, *Pethuel*, means *God opens the way.*
1.2-7 The Devastation of the Land by Locusts. This unprecedented disaster is to be recounted to posterity: the successive stages of the invasion of the locusts are – in natural order – the *destroying* (grubs), *hopping* (devouring) and *swarming* (flying) stages of these insects. The people who are eager for the *sweet wine* of the annual harvest festival are in for shock and disappointment: the *nation*, or horde of locusts, has devoured the crops, including those of the *vines* and *fig trees*.
1.8-2.18 How To Respond to the Disaster: Repent!
1.8 The mourning over the calamity is compared with that of a newly-married woman whose husband has died.
1.9-12 The details of the catastrophe are amplified to include the loss of *offerings* for the sanctuary and the resultant sorrow of the *priests*, the drying up of fields and vineyards, the ruin of the grain crops (*wheat and barley*) and that of the produce of the orchards. With the loss of these crops *joy withers away* for the people.
1.13-14 The *priests* are to prepare for lamentations in the temple (*house of God*), and the leaders of the community (*elders*) are to convene the people so that they may call on the LORD for help.

1.15-20 The crisis is more than a rare plague: it is *the day of the LORD* which has come near: that event or moment when God calls his people to account and brings devastating judgment upon them. This *day* is frequently announced by the prophets and is often pictured as God's anger and hostility against his opponents. At times it is seen as a war against Israel's enemies, but it comes to be directed against Israel (Isa 2.5-22; Am 5.18-25; Isa 28.21; Lam 1.12; Jer 46.10; Ezek 39.8). The plague and the resultant deprivation have occurred for the purpose of divine punishment.
2.1-11 Mingling the images of the locusts' invasion with that of the army of God, the prophet calls for *the trumpet* to be sounded, which was the traditional way to notify the people of an impending battle or attack. *Thick darkness* pervades the land, and the army leaves *desolate* what were formerly fertile fields (*Garden of Eden*). The locusts are compared with horses and chariots of battle, moving inexorably on their intended *paths*, invading the *city* and its *houses*. Cosmic disturbances accompany this invasion by the *vast* army of God, and the question is whether anyone can survive.
2.12-17 The Call to Repentance. Even in the face of such seemingly inevitable disaster, the prophet calls the people to perform the acts of penitence (*fasting, weeping, mourning*) and to *return* to the *gracious* LORD, who may yet *relent* from carrying out this destruction. The people are to *assemble* as an expression of their corporate penitence, and the *priests* are to intercede with God in behalf of the people so that other *nations* will not be able to charge that God has abandoned his own people.

to the house of the LORD your God,
and cry out to the LORD.

15 Alas for the day!
For the day of the LORD is near,
and as destruction from the Almighty[a]
it comes.
16 Is not the food cut off
before our eyes,
joy and gladness
from the house of our God?

17 The seed shrivels under the clods,[b]
the storehouses are desolate;
the granaries are ruined
because the grain has failed.
18 How the animals groan!
The herds of cattle wander about
because there is no pasture for them;
even the flocks of sheep are dazed.[c]

19 To you, O LORD, I cry.
For fire has devoured
the pastures of the wilderness,
and flames have burned
all the trees of the field.
20 Even the wild animals cry to you
because the watercourses are dried
up,
and fire has devoured
the pastures of the wilderness.

2 Blow the trumpet in Zion;
sound the alarm on my holy
mountain!
Let all the inhabitants of the land
tremble,
for the day of the LORD is coming, it is
near—
2 a day of darkness and gloom,
a day of clouds and thick darkness!
Like blackness spread upon the
mountains
a great and powerful army comes;
their like has never been from of old,
nor will be again after them
in ages to come.

3 Fire devours in front of them,
and behind them a flame burns.
Before them the land is like the garden
of Eden,
but after them a desolate wilderness,
and nothing escapes them.

4 They have the appearance of horses,
and like war-horses they charge.
5 As with the rumbling of chariots,
they leap on the tops of the
mountains,
like the crackling of a flame of fire
devouring the stubble,
like a powerful army
drawn up for battle.

6 Before them peoples are in anguish,
all faces grow pale.[b]
7 Like warriors they charge,
like soldiers they scale the wall.
Each keeps to its own course,
they do not swerve from[d] their paths.
8 They do not jostle one another,
each keeps to its own track;
they burst through the weapons
and are not halted.
9 They leap upon the city,
they run upon the walls;
they climb up into the houses,
they enter through the windows like
a thief.

10 The earth quakes before them,
the heavens tremble.
The sun and the moon are darkened,
and the stars withdraw their shining.
11 The LORD utters his voice
at the head of his army;
how vast is his host!
Numberless are those who obey his
command.
Truly the day of the LORD is great;
terrible indeed—who can endure it?

12 Yet even now, says the LORD,
return to me with all your heart,
with fasting, with weeping, and with
mourning;
13 rend your hearts and not your
clothing.
Return to the LORD, your God,
for he is gracious and merciful,
slow to anger, and abounding in
steadfast love,
and relents from punishing.
14 Who knows whether he will not turn
and relent,
and leave a blessing behind him,
a grain offering and a drink offering
for the LORD, your God?

[a] Traditional rendering of Heb *Shaddai* [b] Meaning of Heb uncertain [c] Compare Gk Syr Vg: Meaning of Heb uncertain [d] Gk Syr Vg: Heb *they do not take a pledge along*

1.15 Jer 30.7; Isa 13.6,9; Joel 2.1,11,31
1.16 Isa 3.7; Deut 12.6,7; Ps 43.4
1.18 1 Kings 18.5; Jer 14.5,6; Hos 4.3
1.19 Ps 50.15; Jer 9.10; Joel 2.3
1.20 Job 38.41; Ps 104.21; 1 Kings 17.7; 18.5
2.1 Jer 4.5; Num 10.9; Zeph 1.14-16; ver 11,31; Joel 1.15
2.2 Am 5.18; Joel 1.6; Lam 1.12; Joel 1.2
2.3 Joel 1.19,20; Gen 2.8; Isa 51.3; Ps 105.34,35
2.4 Rev 9.7
2.5 Rev 9.9; Isa 5.24; 30.30
2.6 Isa 13.8; Nah 2.10; Jer 30.6
2.9 ver 7; Jer 9.21; Jn 10.1
2.10 Ps 18.7; Isa 13.10; Joel 2.15; Mt 24.29
2.11 Joel 3.16; Am 1.2; ver 2,25; Jer 50.34; Rev 18.8
2.12 Jer 4.1; Hos 12.6
2.13 Ps 34.18; Isa 57.15; 2 Sam 1.11; Jon 4.2; Jer 18.8; 42.10
2.14 Jer 26.3; Hag 2.19; Joel 1.9,13

2.15 Num 10.3; ver 1; Jer 36.9; Joel 1.14
2.16 Ex 19.10,22; Ps 19.5
2.17 Ezek 8.16; Mt 23.35; Joel 1.9; Deut 9.26-29; Isa 37.20
2.18 Zech 1.14; Isa 60.10
2.19 Hos 2.21,22; Ezek 34.29; 36.15
2.20 Jer 1.14,15; Zech 14.8; Deut 11.24; Isa 34.3; Am 4.10
2.22 Ps 65.12,13
2.23 Ps 149.2; Isa 41.16; Deut 11.14; Jer 5.24; Hos 6.3
2.25 Joel 1.4
2.26 Isa 62.9; Ps 67.5-7; Isa 25.1; 45.17
2.27 Joel 3.17,21; Isa 45.5,21; 49.23
2.28 Acts 2.17-21; Zech 39.29; Isa 40.5
2.29 1 Cor 12.13; Gal 3.28
2.30 Mt 24.29; Lk 21.11,25; Acts 2.19
2.31 Isa 13.9,10; Mt 24.29; Mal 4.1,5; Rev 6.12
2.32 Isa 46.13; Mic 4.7; Rom 9.27
3.1 Jer 30.3; Ezek 38.14
3.2 Isa 66.16; Ezek 34.6; 35.10; 36.1-5

15 Blow the trumpet in Zion;
sanctify a fast;
call a solemn assembly;
16 gather the people.
Sanctify the congregation;
assemble the aged;
gather the children,
even infants at the breast.
Let the bridegroom leave his room,
and the bride her canopy.

17 Between the vestibule and the altar
let the priests, the ministers of the LORD, weep.
Let them say, "Spare your people, O LORD,
and do not make your heritage a mockery,
a byword among the nations.
Why should it be said among the peoples,
'Where is their God?' "

God's Response and Promise

18 Then the LORD became jealous for his land,
and had pity on his people.
19 In response to his people the LORD said:
I am sending you
grain, wine, and oil,
and you will be satisfied;
and I will no more make you
a mockery among the nations.

20 I will remove the northern army far from you,
and drive it into a parched and desolate land,
its front into the eastern sea,
and its rear into the western sea;
its stench and foul smell will rise up.
Surely he has done great things!

21 Do not fear, O soil;
be glad and rejoice,
for the LORD has done great things!
22 Do not fear, you animals of the field,
for the pastures of the wilderness are green;
the tree bears its fruit,
the fig tree and vine give their full yield.

23 O children of Zion, be glad
and rejoice in the LORD your God;
for he has given the early rain[e] for your vindication,
he has poured down for you
abundant rain,
the early and the later rain, as before.
24 The threshing floors shall be full of grain,
the vats shall overflow with wine and oil.

25 I will repay you for the years
that the swarming locust has eaten,
the hopper, the destroyer, and the cutter,
my great army, which I sent against you.

26 You shall eat in plenty and be satisfied,
and praise the name of the LORD your God,
who has dealt wondrously with you.
And my people shall never again be put to shame.
27 You shall know that I am in the midst of Israel,
and that I, the LORD, am your God
and there is no other.
And my people shall never again be put to shame.

God's Spirit Poured Out

28[f] Then afterward
I will pour out my spirit on all flesh;
your sons and your daughters shall prophesy,
your old men shall dream dreams,
and your young men shall see visions.
29 Even on the male and female slaves,
in those days, I will pour out my spirit.

30 I will show portents in the heavens
and on the earth, blood and fire and columns of smoke. 31 The sun shall be turned
to darkness, and the moon to blood, before
the great and terrible day of the LORD comes.
32 Then everyone who calls on the name of
the LORD shall be saved; for in Mount Zion
and in Jerusalem there shall be those who
escape, as the LORD has said, and among the
survivors shall be those whom the LORD
calls.

3[g] For then, in those days and at that
time, when I restore the fortunes of
Judah and Jerusalem, 2 I will gather all the
nations and bring them down to the valley
of Jehoshaphat, and I will enter into judgment with them there, on account of my

[e] Meaning of Heb uncertain [f] Ch 3.1 in Heb [g] Ch 4.1 in Heb

2.18-27 The LORD Promises Renewal.
2.18-19 What the people lost through God's judgment on them will now be restored, and thus their reputation and that of their God will rise among the nations.
2.20 *The northern army* could refer to the locust plague, although these came from the east (Ex 10.13), but it more likely symbolizes the enemy armies that invaded Israel from the north (Assyria and Babylon). They will be driven into the desert and the seas, both the Persian Gulf to the east and the Mediterranean to the west.
2.21-22 The *soil* and the plants and animals are encouraged to resume their normal patterns of productivity.
2.23-27 The period of plague and drought will be replaced by an epoch of fertility and plenty, for which the people are to praise God, and be assured that he who alone is God will not punish them again.
2.28-3.21 The Glorious Future of Judah and the Judgment of the Nations.
2.28-32 *Afterward* implies that the oracles which follow concern the more distant future for God's people. The outpouring of *the spirit* of God on all the people (*flesh*) will benefit sons and daughters, old and young, slaves and free, and will give purpose and power for the renewal of the whole community. Unlike Acts 2.17-21, where this passage is quoted to confirm the universal outreach of the gospel, here *everyone who calls on the name of the LORD* means the people of Judah, including the *survivors* of its wars and the exiles who returned (3.2). They are to be *saved* from the gloom and judgment that will fall on the earth, and they are to find refuge in *Zion and Jerusalem*.
3.1-8 While preparations are made to *restore Judah and Jerusalem*, all the *nations* will be gathered in the *Valley of Jehoshaphat* (meaning, Yahweh is Judge). Punishment will be meted out to them for their having scattered God's people, divided up the land of Judah and Israel, exploited the youth, stolen Judah's wealth, and sold the people as slaves for export to Greece. With the restoration of God's people to their land, these procedures will be reversed, so that the children of their former oppressors will be sold as slaves to the *Sabeans*, an Arab people in what is now Yemen in South Arabia.

3.9-16 The nations are to assemble in the Valley of Judgment – also known as the Valley of Decision – where God will do the judging. The instruction to them reverses that given in Isa 2.4 and Mic 4.3 for the nations to change their weapons into farm tools. Arriving for war, they find that the *harvest* that is *ripe* is the outpouring of God's wrath on these wicked nations. With the heavens darkened, the judgment will issue from God's dwelling place in *Zion*, where he will also provide a *stronghold for his people*.
3.17-21 The fertility of the land will exceed that of its earlier times, as symbolized by the stream which will flow out from the temple (*house of the LORD*) through the *Wadi Shittim* (Valley of Acacias). This is one of the seasonally dry valleys which, after the winter rains, drain water from the hills near Jerusalem into the Dead Sea (*cf.* Zech 14.8). Punishment will fall on *Egypt* and *Edom*, the land east of the Dead Sea, because of the harm they did to Judah, which with Jerusalem *shall be inhabited forever*, while judgment will fall on those who harmed God's people.

people and my heritage Israel, because they
have scattered them among the nations.
They have divided my land, 3and cast lots
for my people, and traded boys for prostitutes, and sold girls for wine, and drunk it
down.
4 What are you to me, O Tyre and Sidon,
and all the regions of Philistia? Are you
paying me back for something? If you are
paying me back, I will turn your deeds back
upon your own heads swiftly and speedily.
5For you have taken my silver and my gold,
and have carried my rich treasures into
your temples.[h] 6You have sold the people of
Judah and Jerusalem to the Greeks, removing them far from their own border. 7But
now I will rouse them to leave the places
to which you have sold them, and I will
turn your deeds back upon your own heads.
8I will sell your sons and your daughters
into the hand of the people of Judah, and
they will sell them to the Sabeans, to a
nation far away; for the LORD has spoken.

Judgment in the Valley of Jehoshaphat

9 Proclaim this among the nations:
Prepare war,[i]
stir up the warriors.
Let all the soldiers draw near,
let them come up.
10 Beat your plowshares into swords,
and your pruning hooks into spears;
let the weakling say, "I am a warrior."

11 Come quickly,[j]
all you nations all around,
gather yourselves there.
Bring down your warriors, O LORD.
12 Let the nations rouse themselves,
and come up to the valley of
Jehoshaphat;
for there I will sit to judge
all the neighboring nations.

13 Put in the sickle,
for the harvest is ripe.
Go in, tread,
for the wine press is full.
The vats overflow,
for their wickedness is great.

14 Multitudes, multitudes,
in the valley of decision!
For the day of the LORD is near
in the valley of decision.
15 The sun and the moon are darkened,
and the stars withdraw their shining.

16 The LORD roars from Zion,
and utters his voice from Jerusalem,
and the heavens and the earth shake.
But the LORD is a refuge for his people,
a stronghold for the people of Israel.

The Glorious Future of Judah

17 So you shall know that I, the LORD your
God,
dwell in Zion, my holy mountain.
And Jerusalem shall be holy,
and strangers shall never again pass
through it.

18 In that day
the mountains shall drip sweet wine,
the hills shall flow with milk,
and all the stream beds of Judah
shall flow with water;
a fountain shall come forth from the
house of the LORD
and water the Wadi Shittim.

19 Egypt shall become a desolation
and Edom a desolate wilderness,
because of the violence done to the
people of Judah,
in whose land they have shed
innocent blood.
20 But Judah shall be inhabited forever,
and Jerusalem to all generations.
21 I will avenge their blood, and I will not
clear the guilty,[k]
for the LORD dwells in Zion.

[h] Or *palaces* [i] Heb *sanctify war* [j] Meaning of Heb uncertain [k] Gk Syr: Heb *I will hold innocent their blood that I have not held innocent*

3.3 Ob 11; Nah 3.10
3.4 Am 1.9,10; Ezek 25.12-17
3.7 Isa 43.5,6; Jer 23.8
3.8 Isa 14.2; 60.14; Ezek 23.42; Jer 6.20
3.10 Isa 2.4; Mic 4.3; Zech 12.8
3.11 Ezek 38.15,16; Isa 13.3
3.12 Isa 2.4; 3.13
3.13 Mt 13.39; Rev 14.15; Isa 63.3; Rev 14.19
3.14 Isa 34.2-8; Joel 1.15; 2.1
3.16 Am 1.2; Joel 2.11; Hag 2.6; Jer 17.17
3.17 ver 21; Ezek 20.40; Ob 17; Isa 52.1; Nah 1.15
3.18 Am 9.13; Isa 30.25; 35.6; Ezek 47.1-12; Rev 22.1
3.19 Ob 10
3.20 Ezek 37.25; Am 9.15
3.21 Ezek 36.25; ver 17

AMOS

1 The words of Amos, who was among
the shepherds of Tekoa, which he saw
concerning Israel in the days of King Uzziah
of Judah and in the days of King Jeroboam
son of Joash of Israel, two years[a] before the
earthquake.

Judgment on Israel's Neighbors

[2]And he said:
The LORD roars from Zion,
  and utters his voice from Jerusalem;
the pastures of the shepherds wither,
  and the top of Carmel dries up.

[3] Thus says the LORD:
For three transgressions of Damascus,
  and for four, I will not revoke the
    punishment;[b]
because they have threshed Gilead
  with threshing sledges of iron.
[4] So I will send a fire on the house of
    Hazael,
  and it shall devour the strongholds of
    Ben-hadad.
[5] I will break the gate bars of Damascus,
  and cut off the inhabitants from the
    Valley of Aven,
and the one who holds the scepter from
    Beth-eden;
  and the people of Aram shall go into
    exile to Kir,
        says the LORD.

[6] Thus says the LORD:
For three transgressions of Gaza,
  and for four, I will not revoke the
    punishment;[b]
because they carried into exile entire
    communities,
  to hand them over to Edom.
[7] So I will send a fire on the wall of Gaza,
  fire that shall devour its strongholds.
[8] I will cut off the inhabitants from
    Ashdod,
  and the one who holds the scepter
    from Ashkelon;
I will turn my hand against Ekron,
  and the remnant of the Philistines
    shall perish,
        says the Lord GOD.

[9] Thus says the LORD:
For three transgressions of Tyre,
  and for four, I will not revoke the
    punishment;[b]
because they delivered entire
    communities over to Edom,
  and did not remember the covenant
    of kinship.
[10] So I will send a fire on the wall of Tyre
  fire that shall devour its strongholds.

[11] Thus says the LORD:
For three transgressions of Edom,
  and for four, I will not revoke the
    punishment;[b]
because he pursued his brother with th
    sword
  and cast off all pity;
he maintained his anger perpetually,[c]
  and kept his wrath[d] forever.
[12] So I will send a fire on Teman,
  and it shall devour the strongholds o
    Bozrah.

[13] Thus says the LORD:
For three transgressions of the
    Ammonites,
  and for four, I will not revoke the
    punishment;[b]
because they have ripped open pregnar
    women in Gilead
  in order to enlarge their territory.
[14] So I will kindle a fire against the wall o
    Rabbah,
  fire that shall devour its strongholds,
with shouting on the day of battle,
  with a storm on the day of the
    whirlwind;
[15] then their king shall go into exile,
  he and his officials together,
        says the LOR

2 Thus says the LORD:
For three transgressions of Moab,
  and for four, I will not revoke the
    punishment;[b]
because he burned to lime
  the bones of the king of Edom.
[2] So I will send a fire on Moab,
  and it shall devour the strongholds o
    Kerioth,

[a] Or *during two years* [b] Heb *cause it to return* [c] Syr Vg: Heb *and his anger tore perpetually* [d] Gk Syr V
Heb *and his wrath kept*

1.1 2 Sam 14.2; 2 Kings 14.23-29; Zech 14.5
1.2 Jer 25.30; Joel 3.16; 1.18,19; Am 9.3
1.3 Isa 7.8; 8.4; ver 13
1.4 Jer 49.27; 1 Kings 20.1; 2 Kings 6.24
1.5 Jer 51.30; 2 Kings 16.9; Am 9.7
1.6 1 Sam 6.17; Jer 47.1,5; ver 9; Ob 11
1.8 Zeph 2.4; Zech 9.6; Ps 81.14
1.9 Isa 23.1-18; Ezek 26.2-4; 1 Kings 5.1; 9.11-14
1.10 Zech 9.4
1.11 Isa 34.5,6; 63.1-6; Jer 49.7-22; Ob 10-12; Isa 57.16; Mic 7.18
1.12 Jer 49.7,20; Ob 9.10
1.13 Jer 49.1-6; Ezek 25.2-7; 2 Kings 15.16
1.14 Jer 49.2; Am 2.2; Ezek 21.22; Isa 29.6; 30.30
1.15 Jer 49.3
2.1 Isa 15; 16; Jer 48; Zeph 2.8,9
2.2 Jer 48.41,45

See the Introductions, pp. 6, 54-57, and 67-68 above.

1.1 Introduction. *The words of Amos*, rather than his life or acts, are reported. *Tekoa* is a small town near the Judean desert, south of Jerusalem. His life *among the shepherds*, combined with his major interest in the sanctuaries, may indicate that he procured sacrificial animals. His prophecies are based on first-hand observation: *what he saw*. His activity is said to have been during the reigns of Uzziah in Judah (779-738) and Jeroboam II in Israel (784-744), probably around 750. *The earthquake* is also mentioned in Zech 14.5, but its date cannot be determined.
1.2-2.5 God's Impending Judgment on Israel's Neighbors.
1.2 The introduction to this series of pronouncements of *punishment* implies that the LORD manifests himself in *Jerusalem* only, and not in the other sanctuaries of Israel. From there his voice, which echoes across Israel from *Zion* in the south to *Carmel* in the north, *withers* the land.
1.3-5 *Damascus* refers to the nation of which it is capital: Syria. It is to be called to account for its multiple misdeeds: stealing the wealth of Gilead (Israel's rich territory east of the Jordan). *Hazael* and *Ben-hadad* are familiar as names of the kings of Syria a century before Amos (2 Kings 8.7-15). The devastation of Syria will include the *Valley of Aven* (probably Baalbek, the mountain valley where the temple of the sun was located) and two other unidentified cities, *Beth-eden* and *Kir*. *Aram* is a basic name for Syria, where the language was Aramaic. Damascus was taken over by Assyria in 732.
1.6-8 *Gaza, Ashdod, Ashkelon* and *Ekron* were the prosperous cities of the Philistines on the Mediterranean coast to the west of Israel. They will be destroyed for having sold into slavery *entire communities* (probably from within Judah) to the east Jordan people of Edom.
1.9-10 *Tyre*, the chief port of the Phoenicians (in what is now Lebanon), was a major commercial power in the eastern Mediterranean in the eighth century BCE. Like Gaza, Tyre is charged with selling whole *communities* of Israelites to the Edomites as slaves. This violated the *covenant of kingship* which Solomon made with Hiram, king of Tyre (1 Kings 5.1-12). As a result, *fire* will fall on their fortified city.
1.11-12 The *transgressions of Edom* may reflect the early conflicts between Jacob (Israel) and Esau (Edom) reported in Gen 25.19-28.9. But since Edom was controlled by Judah in the time of Amos (2 Kings 14.7-22), this oracle may come from after the fall of Jerusalem in 586, when Edom conducted raids on the land of Judah (*cf.* Ob 10-12; Isa 34.5-17; Jer 49.7-22). *Teman* and *Bozrah* were Edom's largest cities, north and south respectively.
1.13-14 *The Ammonites* inhabited the territory farther east of the Jordan beyond *Gilead* and north of Moab. Their attack on the Israelites in Gilead had included slaughtering *pregnant women*. The divine judgment on them will include the devastation of their capital, *Rabbah* (or Rabbath-Ammon) in a *storm* of divine wrath (2 Kings 2.1; Job 38.1; Jer 23.19) which will lead to the *exile* of their king.
2.1-3 *Moab*, the region east of the Dead Sea, is to suffer for its cremation of the *bones* of the king of Edom, an act which was regarded in the law of Moses as appropriate only for those found guilty of gross acts (Lev 20.14; 21.9).

2.4-5 Coming closer to Israel. Amos' next oracle is against *Judah* for its failure to observe the law received from the people's ancestors, which is here referred to as *statutes*, a term characteristic of Deuteronomy (4.40; 6.17; 11.32; 17.19; 26.16-17; 27.10). Use of that term here may indicate that this oracle dates from after the return of Israel from exile in Babylon, when the Deuteronomic editing of the law was complete.
2.6-16 The Judgment to Fall on Israel.
2.6-8 *Israel*, where Amos is now living, is the target of the longest and most severe of the judgment oracles. Poor and *righteous* people of Israel are being sold into slavery by the wealthy. In payment they take *money*, but also cheat on real estate transactions, where *sandals* or *garments* were offered as down payments. Father and sons sexually exploit servant *girls*, in direct violation of Ex 21.8. Those who perform such acts take part in the religious festivities in the sanctuary, using funds that they obtained by theft and cheating.
2.9-12 Israel is reminded of God's outstanding acts in the past in behalf of Israel: (1) the destruction of the *Amorites*, who here represent all the Semitic peoples who were living in Canaan at the time of Israel's conquest (Num 21.21-31); (2) the deliverance of Israel from slavery in Egypt. Although God *raised up* individuals to communicate his purpose to his people – such as the *nazirites*, like Samson (Judg 13-16) and Samuel (1 Sam 1.1-28) – Israel has regularly hindered the *prophets* from communicating God's message to them.
2.13-16 There is no escape from the doom that is to fall on Israel.
3.1-4.13 Punishment for Israel is Inevitable. The focus now shifts to Israel alone as recipient of God's judgment.
3.1-8 Amos' carrying out of his assignment to predict judgment for Israel – the beneficiaries of God's special favor – is unavoidable, as this series of inevitable outcomes among animals and humans attests. The prophet cannot avoid *prophesying* what God has told him.

and Moab shall die amid uproar,
amid shouting and the sound of the trumpet;
3 I will cut off the ruler from its midst,
and will kill all its officials with him,
says the LORD.

Judgment on Judah

4 Thus says the LORD:
For three transgressions of Judah,
and for four, I will not revoke the punishment;[e]
because they have rejected the law of the LORD,
and have not kept his statutes,
but they have been led astray by the same lies
after which their ancestors walked.
5 So I will send a fire on Judah,
and it shall devour the strongholds of Jerusalem.

Judgment on Israel

6 Thus says the LORD:
For three transgressions of Israel,
and for four, I will not revoke the punishment;[e]
because they sell the righteous for silver,
and the needy for a pair of sandals—
7 they who trample the head of the poor
into the dust of the earth,
and push the afflicted out of the way;
father and son go in to the same girl,
so that my holy name is profaned;
8 they lay themselves down beside every altar
on garments taken in pledge;
and in the house of their God they drink
wine bought with fines they imposed.

9 Yet I destroyed the Amorite before them,
whose height was like the height of cedars,
and who was as strong as oaks;
I destroyed his fruit above,
and his roots beneath.
10 Also I brought you up out of the land of Egypt,
and led you forty years in the wilderness,
to possess the land of the Amorite.
11 And I raised up some of your children to be prophets
and some of your youths to be nazirites.[f]
Is it not indeed so, O people of Israel?
says the LORD.

12 But you made the nazirites[f] drink wine,
and commanded the prophets,
saying, "You shall not prophesy."

13 So, I will press you down in your place,
just as a cart presses down
when it is full of sheaves.[g]
14 Flight shall perish from the swift,
and the strong shall not retain their strength,
nor shall the mighty save their lives;
15 those who handle the bow shall not stand,
and those who are swift of foot shall not save themselves,
nor shall those who ride horses save their lives;
16 and those who are stout of heart among the mighty
shall flee away naked in that day,
says the LORD.

Israel's Guilt and Punishment

3 Hear this word that the LORD has spoken against you, O people of Israel, against the whole family that I brought up out of the land of Egypt:
2 You only have I known
of all the families of the earth;
therefore I will punish you
for all your iniquities.

3 Do two walk together
unless they have made an appointment?
4 Does a lion roar in the forest,
when it has no prey?
Does a young lion cry out from its den,
if it has caught nothing?
5 Does a bird fall into a snare on the earth,
when there is no trap for it?
Does a snare spring up from the ground,
when it has taken nothing?
6 Is a trumpet blown in a city,
and the people are not afraid?
Does disaster befall a city,
unless the LORD has done it?
7 Surely the Lord GOD does nothing,
without revealing his secret
to his servants the prophets.
8 The lion has roared;
who will not fear?
The Lord GOD has spoken;
who can but prophesy?

[e] Heb *cause it to return* [f] That is, *those separated* or *those consecrated* [g] Meaning of Heb uncertain

2.3 Am 5.7,12; 6.12; Ps 2.10; Isa 40.23; Jer 48.7
2.4 2 Kings 17.19; Joel 3.2; Jer 6.19; Ezek 20.13,16,18
2.5 Jer 17.27; Hos 8.14
2.6 2 Kings 18.12; Joel 3.3; Am 5.11,12; 8.6
2.7 Am 8.4; 5.12; Lev 20.3; Hos 4.14
2.8 1 Cor 8.10; Ex 22.26; Am 4.1; 6.6
2.9 Deut 2.31; Num 13.33; Isa 5.24; Mal 4.1
2.10 Ex 12.51; Deut 2.7; Ex 3.8
2.11 Jer 7.25; Num 6.2,3
2.12 Isa 30.10; Jer 11.21; Am 7.12,13; Mic 2.6
2.13 Joel 3.13
2.14 Isa 30.16,17; Jer 9.23; Ps 33.16
2.15 Jer 51.26; Ezek 39.3; Isa 31.3
2.16 Jer 48.41
3.1 Jer 8.3; 13.11; Am 2.10; 9.7
3.2 Deut 7.6; Jer 14.20; Ezek 20.36; Lk 12.47; Rom 2.9
3.3 Lev 26.23,24
3.4 Hos 11.10
3.6 Jer 6.1; Hos 5.8; Isa 14.24-27; 45.7
3.7 Gen 18.17; Jn 15.15; Rev 10.7

9 Proclaim to the strongholds in Ashdod,
and to the strongholds in the land of Egypt,
and say, "Assemble yourselves on Mount[h] Samaria,
and see what great tumults are within it,
and what oppressions are in its midst."
10 They do not know how to do right, says the LORD,
those who store up violence and robbery in their strongholds.
11 Therefore thus says the Lord GOD:
An adversary shall surround the land,
and strip you of your defense;
and your strongholds shall be plundered.

12 Thus says the LORD: As the shepherd
rescues from the mouth of the lion two legs,
or a piece of an ear, so shall the people of
Israel who live in Samaria be rescued, with
the corner of a couch and part[i] of a bed.

13 Hear, and testify against the house of Jacob,
says the Lord GOD, the God of hosts:
14 On the day I punish Israel for its transgressions,
I will punish the altars of Bethel,
and the horns of the altar shall be cut off
and fall to the ground.
15 I will tear down the winter house as well as the summer house;
and the houses of ivory shall perish,
and the great houses[j] shall come to an end,
says the LORD.

4 Hear this word, you cows of Bashan
who are on Mount Samaria,
who oppress the poor, who crush the needy,
who say to their husbands, "Bring something to drink!"
2 The Lord GOD has sworn by his holiness:
The time is surely coming upon you,
when they shall take you away with hooks,
even the last of you with fishhooks.
3 Through breaches in the wall you shall leave,
each one straight ahead;
and you shall be flung out into Harmon,[i]
says the LORD.

4 Come to Bethel—and transgress;
to Gilgal—and multiply transgression;
bring your sacrifices every morning,
your tithes every three days;
5 bring a thank offering of leavened bread,
and proclaim freewill offerings,
publish them;
for so you love to do, O people of Israel!
says the Lord GOD.

Israel Rejects Correction

6 I gave you cleanness of teeth in all your cities,
and lack of bread in all your places,
yet you did not return to me,
says the LORD.

7 And I also withheld the rain from you
when there were still three months to the harvest;
I would send rain on one city,
and send no rain on another city;
one field would be rained upon,
and the field on which it did not rain withered;
8 so two or three towns wandered to one town
to drink water, and were not satisfied;
yet you did not return to me,
says the LORD.

9 I struck you with blight and mildew;
I laid waste[k] your gardens and your vineyards;
the locust devoured your fig trees and your olive trees;
yet you did not return to me,
says the LORD.

10 I sent among you a pestilence after the manner of Egypt;
I killed your young men with the sword;
I carried away your horses;[l]
and I made the stench of your camp
go up into your nostrils;
yet you did not return to me,
says the LORD.

11 I overthrew some of you,
as when God overthrew Sodom and Gomorrah,
and you were like a brand snatched from the fire;

[h] Gk Syr: Heb *the mountains of* [i] Meaning of Heb uncertain [j] Or *many houses* [k] Cn: Heb *the multitude of* [l] Heb *with the captivity of your horses*

3.8 Am 1.2; Jon 1.1; 3.1; Jer 20.9; Acts 4.20
3.9 Am 1.8; 4.1; 6.1; 8.6
3.10 Jer 4.22; Am 5.7; 6.12; Hab 2.8-11; Zeph 1.9; Zech 5.3,4
3.11 Am 6.14; 2.14; 2.5
3.12 1 Sam 17.34-37; Am 6.4; Ps 132.3
3.13 Ezek 2.7
3.15 Jer 36.22; Judg 3.20; 1 Kings 22.39
4.1 Ps 22.12; Ezek 39.18; Am 3.9; 6.1; 5.11; 8.6; 2.8; 6.6
4.2 Ps 89.25; Am 6.8; 8.7; Isa 37.29; Ezek 38.4; 29.4
4.4 Am 3.14; 5.5; Hos 4.15; Num 28.3,4; Deut 14.28
4.5 Lev 7.13; 22.18,21; Hos 9.1,10
4.6 Isa 3.1; Jer 14.18; 5.3; Hag 2.17
4.8 Jer 14.4; Ezek 4.16; Jer 3.7
4.9 Deut 28.22; Hag 2.17; Joel 1.4; 2.25; Jer 3.10
4.10 Ex 9.3,6; Deut 28.27,60; Jer 11.22; 18.21; 48.15; Joel 2.20
4.11 Isa 13.19; Zech 3.2; Jer 23.14

3.9-15 The traditional enemies of Israel, *Ashdod* and *Egypt*, are encouraged to come and see how God will use a foreign *adversary* to *surround* and defeat Samaria and its people, from which only a few of the people (*the piece of an ear*) and bits of their possessions (*corner of a couch*) will escape. Major targets of the attack will be the corrupted altars (as at Bethel) and the luxurious *houses* of the wealthy Israelites.
4.1-5 The wealthy *cows of Bashan* (an area east of Jordan famous for its fine cattle), who have lived by exploiting *the poor* and by ordering about their servants, are now warned that the day of judgment is at hand. They cannot escape from the *hooks* of God's judgment (Isa 37.29; Ezek 29.4), not even by crawling out through a crevice in the city wall when the attack occurs. Instead, they will be thrown out on the dung heap (probable meaning of *Harmon*). Ironically, these aristocrats are invited to proceed with the presentation of their vain, idolatrous offerings in the corrupted sanctuaries where once the Lord was honored: Bethel and Gilgal.
4.6-13 God's earlier efforts to shock Israel into listening to him have failed: famine (*cleanness of teeth*), drought, blight, pestilence, fiery destruction as in Sodom and Gomorrah (Gen 19.24-25). Now God will confront them directly.

5.1-27 The Prophet Laments Israel's Inability to Respond to God's Message.
5.1-17 Israel is now pictured as *fallen*. Her capital city, *Samaria*, will retain only a fraction of its population (*out of a hundred, ten left*). The nation is called to abandon its idolatrous ways and to be prepared for the *fire* of God's wrath against its perversion of *justice*. The God who created the constellations (*Pleiades and Orion*) will now pour out *destruction*. The security of houses and fortresses and vineyards will be forfeited because of the corruption and insensitivity to the needs of the *poor*. Although the people are still called to *establish justice*, they are warned that disaster will fall on the city streets as well as the farms and vineyards when God's judgment hits them.
5.18-24 For the wealthy, the festive *day of the LORD* was an occasion for indulgent eating and drinking, so that God *despises* their fraudulent religious celebrations, and will visit death and destruction on his disobedient people, no matter how generous their offerings or how resonant their festal songs. What must be poured out is not wine or music, but *justice* according to God's law and a life in right relationship with God (*righteousness*).

yet you did not return to me,
says the LORD.

12 Therefore thus I will do to you, O Israel;
because I will do this to you,
prepare to meet your God, O Israel!

13 For lo, the one who forms the mountains, creates the wind,
reveals his thoughts to mortals,
makes the morning darkness,
and treads on the heights of the earth—
the LORD, the God of hosts, is his name!

A Lament for Israel's Sin

5 Hear this word that I take up over
you in lamentation, O house of Israel:
2 Fallen, no more to rise,
is maiden Israel;
forsaken on her land,
with no one to raise her up.

3 For thus says the Lord God:
The city that marched out a thousand
shall have a hundred left,
and that which marched out a hundred
shall have ten left.[m]

4 For thus says the LORD to the house of Israel:
Seek me and live;
5 but do not seek Bethel,
and do not enter into Gilgal
or cross over to Beer-sheba;
for Gilgal shall surely go into exile,
and Bethel shall come to nothing.

6 Seek the LORD and live,
or he will break out against the house of Joseph like fire,
and it will devour Bethel, with no one to quench it.
7 Ah, you that turn justice to wormwood,
and bring righteousness to the ground!

8 The one who made the Pleiades and Orion,
and turns deep darkness into the morning,
and darkens the day into night,
who calls for the waters of the sea,
and pours them out on the surface of the earth,
the LORD is his name,
9 who makes destruction flash out against the strong,
so that destruction comes upon the fortress.

10 They hate the one who reproves in the gate,
and they abhor the one who speaks the truth.
11 Therefore because you trample on the poor
and take from them levies of grain,
you have built houses of hewn stone,
but you shall not live in them;
you have planted pleasant vineyards,
but you shall not drink their wine.
12 For I know how many are your transgressions,
and how great are your sins—
you who afflict the righteous, who take a bribe,
and push aside the needy in the gate.
13 Therefore the prudent will keep silent in such a time;
for it is an evil time.

14 Seek good and not evil,
that you may live;
and so the LORD, the God of hosts, will be with you,
just as you have said.
15 Hate evil and love good,
and establish justice in the gate;
it may be that the LORD, the God of hosts,
will be gracious to the remnant of Joseph.

16 Therefore thus says the LORD, the God of hosts, the Lord:
In all the squares there shall be wailing;
and in all the streets they shall say,
"Alas! alas!"
They shall call the farmers to mourning,
and those skilled in lamentation, to wailing;
17 in all the vineyards there shall be wailing,
for I will pass through the midst of you,
says the LORD.

The Day of the LORD a Dark Day

18 Alas for you who desire the day of the LORD!
Why do you want the day of the LORD?

[m] Heb adds *to the house of Israel*

4.12 ver 2; Ezek 13.5
4.13 Jer 10.13; Ps 139.2; Dan 2.28; Jer 13.16; Mic 1.3; Am 5.8,27
5.1 Ezek 19.1
5.2 Jer 14.17; Am 8.14; Isa 51.18; Jer 50.32
5.3 Isa 6.13; Am 6.9
5.4 Jer 29.3; Isa 55.3
5.5 Am 4.4; 1 Sam 7.16; 11.14; Am 8.14
5.6 Isa 55.3,6,7; ver 14; Deut 4.24; Am 3.14
5.8 Job 9.9; 12.22; Isa 42.16; Am 8.9; Ps 104.6-9; Am 9.6
5.10 Isa 29.21; 1 Kings 22.8; Isa 59.15
5.11 Am 3.9; 8.6; 3.15; 6.11; Mic 6.15
5.12 Am 6.2,7; Isa 29.21
5.14 ver 6; Mic 3.11
5.15 Ps 97.10; Rom 12.9; Joel 2.14; Mic 5.3,7,8
5.16 Jer 9.17; Joel 1.11; 2 Chr 35.25
5.17 Isa 16.10; Jer 48.33; Nah 1.2
5.18 Isa 5.19; Joel 1.15; 2.1,11,31; 2 Pet 3.4; Jer 30.7

It is darkness, not light;
19 as if someone fled from a lion,
and was met by a bear;
or went into the house and rested a hand against the wall,
and was bitten by a snake.
20 Is not the day of the LORD darkness, not light,
and gloom with no brightness in it?

21 I hate, I despise your festivals,
and I take no delight in your solemn assemblies.
22 Even though you offer me your burnt offerings and grain offerings,
I will not accept them;
and the offerings of well-being of your fatted animals
I will not look upon.
23 Take away from me the noise of your songs;
I will not listen to the melody of your harps.
24 But let justice roll down like waters,
and righteousness like an ever-flowing stream.

25 Did you bring to me sacrifices and
offerings the forty years in the wilderness,
O house of Israel? 26 You shall take up
Sakkuth your king, and Kaiwan your star-
god, your images,[n] which you made for
yourselves; 27 therefore I will take you into
exile beyond Damascus, says the LORD, whose
name is the God of hosts.

Complacent Self-Indulgence Will Be Punished

6 Alas for those who are at ease in Zion,
and for those who feel secure on Mount Samaria,
the notables of the first of the nations,
to whom the house of Israel resorts!
2 Cross over to Calneh, and see;
from there go to Hamath the great;
then go down to Gath of the Philistines.
Are you better[o] than these kingdoms?
Or is your[p] territory greater than their[q] territory,
3 O you that put far away the evil day,
and bring near a reign of violence?

4 Alas for those who lie on beds of ivory,
and lounge on their couches,
and eat lambs from the flock,
and calves from the stall;
5 who sing idle songs to the sound of the harp,
and like David improvise on instruments of music;
6 who drink wine from bowls,
and anoint themselves with the finest oils,
but are not grieved over the ruin of Joseph!
7 Therefore they shall now be the first to go into exile,
and the revelry of the loungers shall pass away.

8 The Lord GOD has sworn by himself
(says the LORD, the God of hosts):
I abhor the pride of Jacob
and hate his strongholds;
and I will deliver up the city and all that is in it.

9 If ten people remain in one house, they
shall die. 10 And if a relative, one who burns
the dead,[r] shall take up the body to bring
it out of the house, and shall say to someone in the innermost parts of the house, "Is
anyone else with you?" the answer will
come, "No." Then the relative[s] shall say,
"Hush! We must not mention the name of
the LORD."

11 See, the LORD commands,
and the great house shall be shattered to bits,
and the little house to pieces.
12 Do horses run on rocks?
Does one plow the sea with oxen?[t]
But you have turned justice into poison
and the fruit of righteousness into wormwood—
13 you who rejoice in Lo-debar,[u]
who say, "Have we not by our own strength
taken Karnaim[v] for ourselves?"
14 Indeed, I am raising up against you a nation,
O house of Israel, says the LORD, the God of hosts,
and they shall oppress you from Lebohamath
to the Wadi Arabah.

[n] Heb *your images, your star-god* [o] Or *Are they better* [p] Heb *their* [q] Heb *your* [r] Or *who makes a burning for him* [s] Heb *he* [t] Or *Does one plow them with oxen* [u] Or *in a thing of nothingness* [v] Or *horns*

5.25-27 The answer here implied to the question whether Israel offered sacrifices to the LORD during the *forty years* of wandering from Egypt to the land of Canaan is negative. Although the books of Exodus through Deuteronomy indicate that they did, for this prophet and others (Hos 6.6; Mic 6.6-8; Jer 6.20) what God wants is obedience and right living, as Am 5.24 states. The alienation of Israel from God will be evident in its adopting Babylonian deities, *Sakkuth* and *Kaiwan*, and even making images of them. God's judgment on his people will take the form of his exiling them *beyond Damascus*, a threat that is repeated in 6.7; 7.11,17, and which was fulfilled when Israel was taken off to Assyria (2 Kings 17).
6.1-14 The Doom of Affluent, Complacent Israel.
6.1-7 The mountains of *Zion* and *Samaria* symbolize the false pride and self-indulgence of the rich leadership groups in Judah and Israel, who compare their situation favorably with those of leading cities in Syria, *Calneh* and *Hamath*, and with that of the Philistine city of *Gath* on the sea coast west of Judah. They now wallow in luxury, but they (*Joseph* represents Israel) face *ruin* and exile.
6.8-9 The fortifications of the city will crumble and its inhabitants will be taken away, with the remaining population crowded into the ruins (*ten in one house*). Corpses of the fallen will be secretly cremated.
6.10-14 With their social and moral structures perverted and shattered, the leadership group remains proud of what they regard as accomplishments, including the Israelite military successes east of the Jordan at Debir and Karnaim. Amos uses these names ironically, changing the former to *Lo-debar* (nothing!) and implying that the supposed horns (*Karnaim*) of power will prove useless in face of the impending invasion by *a nation*, which is Assyria. *Hamath* had once marked the northern limit of land claimed by Israel (2 Kings 14.25), and *Arabah*, at the foot of the Dead Sea, was the southern limit.

5.19 Jer 48.44
5.20 Isa 13.10; Zeph 1.15
5.21 Isa 1.11-16; Lev 26.31
5.22 Isa 66.3; Mic 6.6,7; Am 4.5
5.24 Jer 22.3; Ezek 45.9; Mic 6.8
5.25 Deut 32.17; Ezek 20.8,16,24; Acts 7.42
5.27 2 Kings 17.6; Am 4.13
6.1 Isa 32.9-11; Lk 6.24; Ex 19.5; Am 3.2
6.2 Jer 2.10; Isa 10.9; 2 Kings 18.34; 2 Chr 26.6; Nah 3.8
6.3 Isa 56.12; Am 9.10
6.4 Am 3.15,12; Ezek 34.2,3
6.5 Isa 5.12; Am 5.23; 1 Chr 23.5
6.6 Am 2.8; 4.1; Gen 37.25; Ezek 9.4
6.7 Am 7.11,17; Dan 5.4-6,30; ver 4
6.8 Jer 51.14; Heb 6.13; Deut 32.19; Ps 106.40; Am 3.10,11
6.11 Isa 55.11; Am 3.15
6.12 Isa 59.13,14; Am 5.7
6.14 Jer 5.15; Am 3.11; Num 34.8; 1 Kings 8.65

7.1-8.3 Images of the Coming Judgment on Israel and a Priestly Complaint. A series of images depicts the judgment that God is about to bring on Israel: (1) locusts that arrive at harvest time: 7.1-3; (2) a rain of fire: 7.4-6; (3) a plumb line: 7.7-9; (4) a basket of summer fruit: 8.1-3. Each report includes a conversation between the LORD and Amos. Inserted between (3) and (4) is a report by *Amaziah*, the priest to the king, Jeroboam II, that Amos is conspiring against him and the nation (7.10-17). This is followed by Amos' response.
7.1-3 The locust's devouring the second growth of grass (the first having been donated to the *king*) symbolizes God's cutting down his people. Amos' intercession moves the LORD to *relent*.
7.4-6 The second imminent disaster is pictured as a *rain of fire*, which has already dried up the cosmic sea (*the great deep*) and is now about to consume God's people. Again Amos is effective in turning aside disaster.
7.7-9 *The plumb line* symbolizes God's calling his people to account for their deeds. He will not ignore (*pass by*) their failures again, and therefore destruction will come on all the shrines, whether of the fertility deities or of the LORD, and also on the royal family.
7.10-17 The priest's report to the king, Jeroboam, that Amos has predicted his death and the exile of Israel evokes a royal decree for Amos to leave the country and return to his native Judah, which he refuses to obey. A former shepherd and farmer, Amos is not one of the official court prophets who say what the king wants to hear. He takes orders from the LORD alone. Disaster for the royal family and exile for the people are inevitable.
8.1-3 With a grim pun on the word for *summer fruit* (*qayits*), Amos learns that *the end* (*qayits*) has come for Israel, its temple, and many of its people.
8.4-9.12 The Causes and Consequences of God's Judgment on Israel.
8.4-6 The exploitation of the poor by the wealthy and the merchant class is described.

Locusts, Fire, and a Plumb Line

7 This is what the Lord GOD showed me:
he was forming locusts at the time the
latter growth began to sprout (it was the
latter growth after the king's mowings).
[2]When they had finished eating the grass of
the land, I said,

"O Lord GOD, forgive, I beg you!
How can Jacob stand?
He is so small!"
3 The LORD relented concerning this;
"It shall not be," said the LORD.

4 This is what the Lord GOD showed me:
the Lord GOD was calling for a shower of
fire,[w] and it devoured the great deep and
was eating up the land. [5]Then I said,

"O Lord GOD, cease, I beg you!
How can Jacob stand?
He is so small!"
6 The LORD relented concerning this;
"This also shall not be," said the Lord GOD.

7 This is what he showed me: the Lord
was standing beside a wall built with a
plumb line, with a plumb line in his hand.
[8]And the LORD said to me, "Amos, what do
you see?" And I said, "A plumb line." Then
the Lord said,

"See, I am setting a plumb line
in the midst of my people Israel;
I will never again pass them by;
9 the high places of Isaac shall be made desolate,
and the sanctuaries of Israel shall be laid waste,
and I will rise against the house of Jeroboam with the sword."

Amaziah Complains to the King

10 Then Amaziah, the priest of Bethel,
sent to King Jeroboam of Israel, saying,
"Amos has conspired against you in the
very center of the house of Israel; the land
is not able to bear all his words. [11]For thus
Amos has said,

'Jeroboam shall die by the sword,
and Israel must go into exile
away from his land.' "

[12]And Amaziah said to Amos, "O seer, go,
flee away to the land of Judah, earn your
bread there, and prophesy there; [13]but never
again prophesy at Bethel, for it is the king's
sanctuary, and it is a temple of the kingdom."

14 Then Amos answered Amaziah,
"I am[x] no prophet, nor a prophet's son; but
I am[x] a herdsman, and a dresser of sycamore trees, [15]and the LORD took me from
following the flock, and the LORD said to me,
'Go, prophesy to my people Israel.'
16 "Now therefore hear the word of the LORD.
You say, 'Do not prophesy against Israel,
and do not preach against the house of Isaac.'
17 Therefore thus says the LORD:
'Your wife shall become a prostitute in the city,
and your sons and your daughters shall fall by the sword,
and your land shall be parceled out by line;
you yourself shall die in an unclean land,
and Israel shall surely go into exile away from its land.' "

The Basket of Fruit

8 This is what the Lord GOD showed
me—a basket of summer fruit.[y] [2]He
said, "Amos, what do you see?" And I said,
"A basket of summer fruit."[y] Then the LORD
said to me,

"The end[z] has come upon my people Israel;
I will never again pass them by.
3 The songs of the temple[a] shall become wailings in that day,"
says the Lord GOD;
"the dead bodies shall be many,
cast out in every place. Be silent!"

4 Hear this, you that trample on the needy,
and bring to ruin the poor of the land,
5 saying, "When will the new moon be over
so that we may sell grain;
and the sabbath,
so that we may offer wheat for sale?
We will make the ephah small and the shekel great,
and practice deceit with false balances,
6 buying the poor for silver
and the needy for a pair of sandals,
and selling the sweepings of the wheat."

[w] Or *for a judgment by fire* [x] Or *was* [y] Heb *qayits* [z] Heb *qets* [a] Or *palace*

7.1 ver 4.7; Am 8.1; Joel 1.4; Am 4.9; Nah 3.15
7.2 Ex 10.14,15; Ezek 9.8; 11.13; Isa 37.4; Jer 42.2
7.3 Deut 32.36; Jer 26.19; Jon 3.10
7.5 ver 2
7.6 ver 3
7.8 Am 8.2; Isa 28.17; 34.11; Lam 2.8; Mic 7.18
7.9 Hos 10.8; Mic 1.5; Isa 63.18; 2 Kings 15.10
7.10 1 Kings 12.32; 2 Kings 14.23; Jer 26.8-11
7.11 ver 9.17
7.13 Am 2.12; 1 Kings 12.32; 13.1
7.14 1 Kings 20.35; 2 Kings 2.5; 4.38; 2 Chr 19.2; Am 1.1
7.15 2 Sam 7.8; Am 3.8; Jer 7.1; Ezek 2.3,4
7.16 Am 2.12; Ezek 21.2; Mic 2.6
7.17 Jer 29.21; Hos 4.13,14; Jer 14.16; Ezek 4.13; Hos 9.3
8.2 Am 7.8; Jer 24.3; Ezek 7.2
8.3 Am 5.23; 6.9,10
8.4 Ps 14.4; Am 5.11,12
8.5 2 Kings 4.23; Neh 13.15,16; Mic 6.10-11
8.6 Am 2.6

7 The LORD has sworn by the pride of
Jacob:
Surely I will never forget any of their
deeds.
8 Shall not the land tremble on this
account,
and everyone mourn who lives in it,
and all of it rise like the Nile,
and be tossed about and sink again,
like the Nile of Egypt?

9 On that day, says the Lord GOD,
I will make the sun go down at noon,
and darken the earth in broad daylight.
10 I will turn your feasts into mourning,
and all your songs into lamentation;
I will bring sackcloth on all loins,
and baldness on every head;
I will make it like the mourning for an
only son,
and the end of it like a bitter day.

11 The time is surely coming, says the Lord
GOD,
when I will send a famine on the land;
not a famine of bread, or a thirst for
water,
but of hearing the words of the LORD.
12 They shall wander from sea to sea,
and from north to east;
they shall run to and fro, seeking the
word of the LORD,
but they shall not find it.

13 In that day the beautiful young women
and the young men
shall faint for thirst.
14 Those who swear by Ashimah of
Samaria,
and say, "As your god lives, O Dan,"
and, "As the way of Beer-sheba lives"—
they shall fall, and never rise again.

The Destruction of Israel

9 I saw the LORD standing beside[b] the
altar, and he said:
Strike the capitals until the thresholds
shake,
and shatter them on the heads of all
the people;[c]
and those who are left I will kill with
the sword;
not one of them shall flee away,
not one of them shall escape.

2 Though they dig into Sheol,
from there shall my hand take them;
though they climb up to heaven,
from there I will bring them down.
3 Though they hide themselves on the top
of Carmel,
from there I will search out and take
them;
and though they hide from my sight at
the bottom of the sea,
there I will command the sea-serpent,
and it shall bite them.
4 And though they go into captivity in
front of their enemies,
there I will command the sword, and
it shall kill them;
and I will fix my eyes on them
for harm and not for good.

5 The Lord, GOD of hosts,
he who touches the earth and it melts,
and all who live in it mourn,
and all of it rises like the Nile,
and sinks again, like the Nile of Egypt;
6 who builds his upper chambers in the
heavens,
and founds his vault upon the earth;
who calls for the waters of the sea,
and pours them out upon the surface
of the earth—
the LORD is his name.

7 Are you not like the Ethiopians[d] to me,
O people of Israel? says the LORD.
Did I not bring Israel up from the land
of Egypt,
and the Philistines from Caphtor and
the Arameans from Kir?
8 The eyes of the Lord GOD are upon the
sinful kingdom,
and I will destroy it from the face of
the earth
—except that I will not utterly
destroy the house of Jacob,
says the LORD.

9 For lo, I will command,
and shake the house of Israel among
all the nations
as one shakes with a sieve,
but no pebble shall fall to the ground.
10 All the sinners of my people shall die by
the sword,
who say, "Evil shall not overtake or
meet us."

[b] Or *on* [c] Heb *all of them* [d] Or *Nubians*; Heb *Cushites*

8.7 Am 6.8; Deut 33.26,29; Hos 8.13; 9.9
8.8 Isa 5.25; Hos 4.3; Am 9.5
8.9 Isa 13.10; Jer 15.9; Mic 3.6; Am 4.13; 5.8
8.10 Am 5.21; 6.4,5; Jer 48.37; Ezek 7.18; Jer 6.26; Zech 12.10
8.11 1 Sam 3.1; 2 Chr 15.3; Ezek 7.26; Mic 3.6
8.12 Ezek 20.3,31
8.13 Lam 1.18; Isa 41.17; Hos 2.3
8.14 Hos 4.15; 1 Kings 12.28,29; Am 5.5
9.1 Am 3.14; Zeph 2.14; Hab 3.13; ver 4; Am 2.14
9.2 Ps 139.8; Jer 51.53; Ob 4
9.3 Am 1.2; Jer 16.16,17; Isa 27.1
9.4 Lev 26.33; Ezek 5.12; Jer 44.11
9.5 Mic 1.4; Am 8.8
9.6 Ps 104.3; Am 5.8; 4.13
9.7 Isa 43.3; Am 2.10; 3.1; Jer 47.4; Am 1.5
9.8 Jer 44.27; ver 4,10; Jer 30.11; Joel 2.32
9.9 Isa 30.28
9.10 Am 8.14; 6.3

8.7-8 God's charging Israel with responsibility for its misdeeds will result in a judgment here compared to an earthquake in which the land will rise and fall like the annual flooding and receding of the Nile.
8.9-10 The raucous festivities of Israel will be changed into funereal lamentations.
8.11-14 Even those who seek *the words of the LORD* will not be able to find them, and those who hope to be sustained by visiting the polluted sanctuaries of Israel and Judah – in Samaria, Dan (in the north) and Beersheba (far in the south) – will *fall* without possibility of renewal.
9.1-10 There is no escape from the judgment of God, not on the mountain tops (*Carmel*) or in the *bottom of the sea*, and not even after the people are taken into *captivity*. The God who controls the heavens and the earth, who moves nations from place to place (Israel from *Egypt*, the Philistines from *Caphtor* [Crete], the Arameans from *Kir*) will achieve his purpose in destroying his faithless people, all of whom shall die. The latter part of 9.8, with its promise to preserve a remnant of *Jacob*, is a later addition, as are vv. 11-15.

9.11-15 Promise of Restoration of the Monarchy and of the People of Israel. The promise of the restoration of the Davidic monarchy is anachronistic here, since it was still flourishing and would continue for another century and a half (until 586). Here there is a promise that it will recover its control of the land of *Edom*, east of the Jordan, which was occupied by David (2 Sam 8.13-14) for the sake of its rich mineral deposits and its strategic location on the King's Highway, the main north-south regional trade route. *The nations called by my name* are the trophies of future wars, like those given to David according to Ps 60.6-12. Here the disasters that are to strike the land are reversed, and unprecedented prosperity, fertility and rebuilding are expected to occur.

The Restoration of David's Kingdom

11 On that day I will raise up
the booth of David that is fallen,
and repair its[e] breaches,
and raise up its[f] ruins,
and rebuild it as in the days of old;
12 in order that they may possess the remnant of Edom
and all the nations who are called by my name,
says the LORD who does this.

13 The time is surely coming, says the LORD,
when the one who plows shall overtake the one who reaps,
and the treader of grapes the one who sows the seed;
the mountains shall drip sweet wine,
and all the hills shall flow with it.
14 I will restore the fortunes of my people Israel,
and they shall rebuild the ruined cities and inhabit them;
they shall plant vineyards and drink their wine,
and they shall make gardens and eat their fruit.
15 I will plant them upon their land,
and they shall never again be plucked up
out of the land that I have given them,
says the LORD your God.

[e] Gk: Heb *their* [f] Gk: Heb *his*

9.11 Acts 15.16,17; Ps 80.12; Isa 63.11; Jer 46.26

9.12 Ob 19; Isa 11.14; 43.7

9.13 Lev 26.5; Joel 3.18

9.14 Isa 60.4; Jer 30.18; Isa 61.4; Ezek 36.35; 28.26

9.15 Jer 24.6; 31.28; Isa 60.21; Jer 32.41; Ezek 34.28

OBADIAH

See the Introductions, pp. 6, 54-57, and 68-69 above.

1a The briefest of introductions for the shortest of the Old Testament books. *Obadiah* means *servant of Yahweh*.
1b-4 The vision concerns the destruction of Edom as a nation, when its neighbors will rise up, subdue, and absorb it. This occurred historically, probably through the incursion of Arabian tribes about 450 BCE. The rocky *heights* and narrow inhabited canyons (*clefts of the rock*) of this area east of the Dead Sea were used by later non-Israelite occupants, as is evident from the impressive ruins of the Nabatean capital of Petra built after 100 BCE. This oracle resembles Jer 49.14-16.
5-9 *Edom* is identified with Esau, the son of Isaac who contested with Jacob (Israel) the role of primary heir (Gen 27). The prediction that Edom will be shattered matches prophecies against this nation in Am 1.11-12; Jer 49.7-22; Isa 63.1-6; Ezek 25.12-14; 35.1-15. *Teman*, an Edomite city, serves here as a symbol for Edom, and so do the references to the mountains. This section resembles Jer 49.9-10.

Proud Edom Will Be Brought Low

1 The vision of Obadiah.

Thus says the Lord GOD concerning Edom:
We have heard a report from the LORD,
and a messenger has been sent among the nations:
"Rise up! Let us rise against it for battle!"
2 I will surely make you least among the nations;
you shall be utterly despised.
3 Your proud heart has deceived you,
you that live in the clefts of the rock,[a]
whose dwelling is in the heights.
You say in your heart,
"Who will bring me down to the ground?"
4 Though you soar aloft like the eagle,
though your nest is set among the stars,
from there I will bring you down,
says the LORD.

Pillage and Slaughter Will Repay Edom's Cruelty

5 If thieves came to you,
if plunderers by night
—how you have been destroyed!—
would they not steal only what they wanted?
If grape-gatherers came to you,
would they not leave gleanings?
6 How Esau has been pillaged,
his treasures searched out!
7 All your allies have deceived you,
they have driven you to the border;
your confederates have prevailed against you;
those who ate[b] your bread have set a trap for you—
there is no understanding of it.
8 On that day, says the LORD,
I will destroy the wise out of Edom,
and understanding out of Mount Esau.
9 Your warriors shall be shattered, O Teman,
so that everyone from Mount Esau will be cut off.

[a] Or *clefts of Sela* [b] Cn: Heb lacks *those who ate*

1 Isa 34.5; Ezek 25.12; Joel 3.19; Jer 49.14; Isa 30.4; Jer 6.4,5

3 Isa 16.6; Jer 49.16; 2 Kings 14.7; Isa 14.13-15; Rev 18.7

4 Job 20.6; Hab 2.9; Isa 14.13-15

5 Jer 49.9; ver 9,10; Isa 17.6

7 Jer 30.14; 38.22; Ps 41.9; Jer 49.7

8 Job 5.12; Isa 29.14

9 Jer 49.22; Am 1.12; Hab 3.3; ver 5

Edom Mistreated His Brother

10 For the slaughter and violence done to
your brother Jacob,
shame shall cover you,
and you shall be cut off forever.
11 On the day that you stood aside,
on the day that strangers carried off
his wealth,
and foreigners entered his gates
and cast lots for Jerusalem,
you too were like one of them.
12 But you should not have gloated[c] over[d]
your brother
on the day of his misfortune;
you should not have rejoiced over the
people of Judah
on the day of their ruin;
you should not have boasted
on the day of distress.
13 You should not have entered the gate of
my people
on the day of their calamity;
you should not have joined in the
gloating over Judah's[e] disaster
on the day of his calamity;
you should not have looted his goods
on the day of his calamity.
14 You should not have stood at the
crossings
to cut off his fugitives;
you should not have handed over his
survivors
on the day of distress.

15 For the day of the LORD is near against
all the nations.
As you have done, it shall be done to you;
your deeds shall return on your own
head.
16 For as you have drunk on my holy
mountain,
all the nations around you shall drink;
they shall drink and gulp down,[f]
and shall be as though they had
never been.

Israel's Final Triumph

17 But on Mount Zion there shall be those
that escape,
and it shall be holy;
and the house of Jacob shall take
possession of those who
dispossessed them.
18 The house of Jacob shall be a fire,
the house of Joseph a flame,
and the house of Esau stubble;
they shall burn them and consume
them,
and there shall be no survivor of the
house of Esau;
for the LORD has spoken.
19 Those of the Negeb shall possess Mount
Esau,
and those of the Shephelah the land
of the Philistines;
they shall possess the land of Ephraim
and the land of Samaria,
and Benjamin shall possess Gilead.
20 The exiles of the Israelites who are in
Halah[g]
shall possess[h] Phoenicia as far as
Zarephath;
and the exiles of Jerusalem who are in
Sepharad
shall possess the towns of the Negeb.
21 Those who have been saved[i] shall go up
to Mount Zion
to rule Mount Esau;
and the kingdom shall be the LORD's.

10 Ps 137.7; Joel 3.3; Nah 3.10
11 Ps 137.7; Joel 3.19; Am 1.11
12 Mic 4.11; Ezek 35.15; 36.5; Ps 31.18
13 Ezek 35.5,10; 36.2,3
15 Ezek 30.3; Joel 1.15; Jer 50.29; Hab 2.8; Ezek 35.11
16 Jer 49.12,13; 25.15,16
17 Isa 4.2,3; Am 9.11-15
18 Isa 10.17; Jer 11.23; Am 1.8
19 Am 9.12; Isa 11.14; Zeph 2.7; Jer 31.5; 32.44
20 1 Kings 17.9; Jer 32.44; 33.13
21 Neh 9.27; Ps 22.28; 67.4; Dan 2.44; Zech 14.9

10-16 The reason for this harsh judgment is that Edom participated in the looting of Jerusalem at the time of the city's fall to the Babylonians in 587, as reflected in Ps 137.7. The prediction is that Edom will experience at the hands of surrounding nations what she did to Jerusalem. They will *gulp* her down, so that she will disappear. **17-21** The contrast between the ultimate fate of Edom and that of Judah will be complete when the once-pillaged city of Jerusalem is restored on *Mount Zion*; the house of *Jacob* will be a fiery instrument of God for Edom's destruction without a *survivor*. Judah will take over wider territory, including Edom: those in the south of Judah (*Negeb*) will occupy Edom; those in the lower hills toward the coast (*Shephelah*) will control the former Philistine coastal district; *Benjamin* just north of Jerusalem will take over *Gilead* east of the Jordan; all of the land of the northern tribes (*Samaria*) will be part of the new kingdom. Exiles returning from *Halah* near Nineveh will dominate the Phoenician territory in what is now Lebanon, while those formerly from Jerusalem but more recently exiled in *Sepharad* (possibly north Africa, or Asia Minor) will reoccupy the southern district (*Negeb*). The beneficiaries (*saved*) – or agents of renewal (*saviors*) – in the purpose of God will share the rule from Mt. Zion.

[c] Heb *But do not gloat* (and similarly through verse 14) [d] Heb *on the day of* [e] Heb *his* [f] Meaning of Heb uncertain [g] Cn: Heb *in this army* [h] Cn: Meaning of Heb uncertain [i] Or *Saviors*

JONAH

See the Introductions, pp. 6, 39, and 69-70 above.

1.1-3 Jonah is told to go to *Nineveh*, the great ancient city (Gen 10.11) which was the capital of the Assyrian empire from 705 to 612 BCE, situated in what is now Iraq. Instead, he tries to escape from God by taking a ship from Joppa (on the Mediterranean coast) for Tarshish, which was probably a port in what is now Spain.
1.4-16 By lot, the passenger whose guilt brought on the fierce storm is identified as Jonah. After asking *the LORD* to spare them further punishment and offering sacrifices, the sailors follow Jonah's suggestion and throw him off the ship.
1.17-2.10 While travelling back to the eastern Mediterranean in the divinely-provided *fish*, Jonah recites a psalm-like hymn of thanksgiving, in which the physical danger and deliverance he is experiencing become metaphors for his spiritual distress and renewal.

Jonah Tries to Run Away from God

1 Now the word of the LORD came to
Jonah son of Amittai, saying, 2“Go at
once to Nineveh, that great city, and cry
out against it; for their wickedness has
come up before me.” 3But Jonah set out to
flee to Tarshish from the presence of the
LORD. He went down to Joppa and found a
ship going to Tarshish; so he paid his fare
and went on board, to go with them to
Tarshish, away from the presence of the
LORD.
4 But the LORD hurled a great wind upon
the sea, and such a mighty storm came
upon the sea that the ship threatened to
break up. 5Then the mariners were afraid,
and each cried to his god. They threw the
cargo that was in the ship into the sea, to
lighten it for them. Jonah, meanwhile, had
gone down into the hold of the ship and
had lain down, and was fast asleep. 6The
captain came and said to him, “What are
you doing sound asleep? Get up, call on
your god! Perhaps the god will spare us a
thought so that we do not perish.”
7 The sailors[a] said to one another, “Come,
let us cast lots, so that we may know on
whose account this calamity has come upon
us.” So they cast lots, and the lot fell on
Jonah. 8Then they said to him, “Tell us why
this calamity has come upon us. What is
your occupation? Where do you come from?
What is your country? And of what people
are you?” 9“I am a Hebrew,” he replied. “I
worship the LORD, the God of heaven, who
made the sea and the dry land.” 10Then the
men were even more afraid, and said to
him, “What is this that you have done!” For
the men knew that he was fleeing from the
presence of the LORD, because he had told
them so.
11 Then they said to him, “What shall
we do to you, that the sea may quiet down
for us?” For the sea was growing more and
more tempestuous. 12He said to them, “Pick
me up and throw me into the sea; then the
sea will quiet down for you; for I know it
is because of me that this great storm has
come upon you.” 13Nevertheless the men
rowed hard to bring the ship back to land,
but they could not, for the sea grew more
and more stormy against them. 14Then they
cried out to the LORD, “Please, O LORD, we
pray, do not let us perish on account of this
man's life. Do not make us guilty of innocent blood; for you, O LORD, have done as
it pleased you.” 15So they picked Jonah up
and threw him into the sea; and the sea
ceased from its raging. 16Then the men
feared the LORD even more, and they offered
a sacrifice to the LORD and made vows.
17[b] But the LORD provided a large fish to
swallow up Jonah; and Jonah was in the
belly of the fish three days and three nights.

A Psalm of Thanksgiving

2 Then Jonah prayed to the LORD his
God from the belly of the fish, 2saying,
“I called to the LORD out of my distress,
and he answered me;
out of the belly of Sheol I cried,
and you heard my voice.
3 You cast me into the deep,
into the heart of the seas,
and the flood surrounded me;
all your waves and your billows
passed over me.
4 Then I said, ‘I am driven away
from your sight;
how[c] shall I look again
upon your holy temple?’
5 The waters closed in over me;
the deep surrounded me;
weeds were wrapped around my head
6 at the roots of the mountains.
I went down to the land
whose bars closed upon me forever;
yet you brought up my life from the Pit,
O LORD my God.
7 As my life was ebbing away,
I remembered the LORD;
and my prayer came to you,
into your holy temple.
8 Those who worship vain idols
forsake their true loyalty.
9 But I with the voice of thanksgiving
will sacrifice to you;
what I have vowed I will pay.
Deliverance belongs to the LORD!”
10Then the LORD spoke to the fish, and it
spewed Jonah out upon the dry land.

1.1 2 Kings 14.25; Mt 12.39
1.2 Jon 3.2,3; 4.1; Ezra 9.6
1.3 Ps 139.7,9,10; Acts 9.36
1.4 Ps 107.25
1.5 Acts 27.18; 1 Sam 24.3
1.6 Ps 107.28; Jon 3.9
1.7 Josh 7.14; 1 Sam 10.20; 14.41,42; Acts 1.26
1.8 Josh 7.19; 1 Sam 14.43
1.9 Ps 146.6; Acts 17.24
1.10 Job 27.22
1.12 2 Sam 24.17; Jn 11.50; 1 Chr 21.17
1.14 ver 16; Deut 21.8; Ps 115.3
1.16 1 Sam 6.2-5
1.17 Jon 4.6; Mt 12.40; 16.4; Lk 11.30
2.3 Ps 88.6; 42.7
2.4 Ps 31.22; 1 Kings 8.38
2.5 Ps 69.1; Lam 3.54
2.6 Ps 16.10
2.7 Ps 142.3; 77.10,11; 18.6
2.8 2 Kings 17.15; Ps 31.6; Jer 10.8; 16.19
2.9 Ps 50.14; Hos 14.2; Heb 13.15; Job 22.27; Ps 3.8

[a] Heb *They* [b] Ch 2.1 in Heb [c] Theodotion: Heb *surely*

3.1 Jon 1.1,2
3.5 Dan 9.3; Joel 1.14; Jer 31.34
3.6 Job 2.8; Jer 6.26; Dan 9.3
3.7 ver 5; 2 Chr 20.3
3.8 Ps 130.1; Jon 1.6,14; Isa 55.6,7; Jer 18.11
3.9 2 Sam 12.22; Joel 2.14
3.10 Jer 31.18; Ex 32.14; Jer 18.8; Am 7.3,6
4.1 ver 4,9; Mt 20.15; Lk 15.28
4.2 Jon 1.3; Ex 34.6; Ps 86.5; Joel 2.13
4.3 1 Kings 19.4; ver 8; Job 7.15,16
4.4 ver 9; Mt 20.11,15
4.5 1 Kings 19.9,13
4.11 Jon 1.2; 3.2,3; Deut 1.39; Ps 36.6

Conversion of Nineveh

3 The word of the LORD came to Jonah a second time, saying, 2"Get up, go to Nineveh, that great city, and proclaim to it the message that I tell you." 3So Jonah set out and went to Nineveh, according to the word of the LORD. Now Nineveh was an exceedingly large city, a three days' walk across. 4Jonah began to go into the city, going a day's walk. And he cried out, "Forty days more, and Nineveh shall be overthrown!" 5And the people of Nineveh believed God; they proclaimed a fast, and everyone, great and small, put on sackcloth.

6 When the news reached the king of Nineveh, he rose from his throne, removed his robe, covered himself with sackcloth, and sat in ashes. 7Then he had a proclamation made in Nineveh: "By the decree of the king and his nobles: No human being or animal, no herd or flock, shall taste anything. They shall not feed, nor shall they drink water. 8Human beings and animals shall be covered with sackcloth, and they shall cry mightily to God. All shall turn from their evil ways and from the violence that is in their hands. 9Who knows? God may relent and change his mind; he may turn from his fierce anger, so that we do not perish."

10 When God saw what they did, how they turned from their evil ways, God changed his mind about the calamity that he had said he would bring upon them; and he did not do it.

Jonah's Anger

4 But this was very displeasing to Jonah, and he became angry. 2He prayed to the LORD and said, "O LORD! Is not this what I said while I was still in my own country? That is why I fled to Tarshish at the beginning; for I knew that you are a gracious God and merciful, slow to anger, and abounding in steadfast love, and ready to relent from punishing. 3And now, O LORD, please take my life from me, for it is better for me to die than to live." 4And the LORD said, "Is it right for you to be angry?" 5Then Jonah went out of the city and sat down east of the city, and made a booth for himself there. He sat under it in the shade, waiting to see what would become of the city.

6 The LORD God appointed a bush,[d] and made it come up over Jonah, to give shade over his head, to save him from his discomfort; so Jonah was very happy about the bush. 7But when dawn came up the next day, God appointed a worm that attacked the bush, so that it withered. 8When the sun rose, God prepared a sultry east wind, and the sun beat down on the head of Jonah so that he was faint and asked that he might die. He said, "It is better for me to die than to live."

Jonah Is Reproved

9 But God said to Jonah, "Is it right for you to be angry about the bush?" And he said, "Yes, angry enough to die." 10Then the LORD said, "You are concerned about the bush, for which you did not labor and which you did not grow; it came into being in a night and perished in a night. 11And should I not be concerned about Nineveh, that great city, in which there are more than a hundred and twenty thousand persons who do not know their right hand from their left, and also many animals?"

[d] Heb *qiqayon*, possibly *the castor bean plant*

3.1-10 *The great city* of Nineveh has been shown by excavations to have been very large. That the population was more than 120,000 (4.11) is fully credible. Jonah's announcement of God's impending judgment and his call to the people to repent are heeded by the city.
4.1-11 Jonah's initial anger when the people repent gives way to a mixture of acknowledging God's love and forgiveness with self-pity and a desire for death. His lament over the withering of the bush that shaded him evokes from God a rebuke for his lack of compassion toward the people of this great city to which he has brought God's message.

MICAH

See the Introductions, pp. 6, 54-57, and 70 above.

1 The word of the Lord that came to Micah of Moresheth in the days of Kings Jotham, Ahaz, and Hezekiah of Judah, which he saw concerning Samaria and Jerusalem.

Judgment Pronounced against Samaria

2 Hear, you peoples, all of you;
listen, O earth, and all that is in it;
and let the Lord God be a witness
against you,
the Lord from his holy temple.
3 For lo, the Lord is coming out of his
place,
and will come down and tread upon
the high places of the earth.
4 Then the mountains will melt under
him
and the valleys will burst open,
like wax near the fire,
like waters poured down a steep place.
5 All this is for the transgression of Jacob
and for the sins of the house of Israel.
What is the transgression of Jacob?
Is it not Samaria?
And what is the high place[a] of Judah?
Is it not Jerusalem?
6 Therefore I will make Samaria a heap in
the open country,
a place for planting vineyards.
I will pour down her stones into the
valley,
and uncover her foundations.
7 All her images shall be beaten to pieces,
all her wages shall be burned with fire,
and all her idols I will lay waste;
for as the wages of a prostitute she
gathered them,
and as the wages of a prostitute they
shall again be used.

The Doom of the Cities of Judah

8 For this I will lament and wail;
I will go barefoot and naked;
I will make lamentation like the jackals,
and mourning like the ostriches.
9 For her wound[b] is incurable.
It has come to Judah;
it has reached to the gate of my people,
to Jerusalem.
10 Tell it not in Gath,
weep not at all;
in Beth-leaphrah
roll yourselves in the dust.
11 Pass on your way,
inhabitants of Shaphir,
in nakedness and shame;
the inhabitants of Zaanan
do not come forth;
Beth-ezel is wailing
and shall remove its support from
you.
12 For the inhabitants of Maroth
wait anxiously for good,
yet disaster has come down from the
Lord
to the gate of Jerusalem.
13 Harness the steeds to the chariots,
inhabitants of Lachish;
it was the beginning of sin
to daughter Zion,
for in you were found
the transgressions of Israel.
14 Therefore you shall give parting gifts
to Moresheth-gath;
the houses of Achzib shall be a
deception
to the kings of Israel.
15 I will again bring a conqueror upon
you,
inhabitants of Mareshah;
the glory of Israel
shall come to Adullam.
16 Make yourselves bald and cut off your
hair
for your pampered children;
make yourselves as bald as the eagle,
for they have gone from you into
exile.

Social Evils Denounced

2 Alas for those who devise wickedness
and evil deeds[c] on their beds!
When the morning dawns, they perform
it,
because it is in their power.
2 They covet fields, and seize them;
houses, and take them away;
they oppress householder and house,
people and their inheritance.
3 Therefore thus says the Lord:

[a] Heb *what are the high places* [b] Gk Syr Vg: Heb *wounds* [c] Cn: Heb *work evil*

1.1 Introduction. *Micah* is a shortened form of Michaiah, which means, Who is like God? Micah was active during the reigns of three kings of Judah: Jotham (742-735), Ahaz (735-715) and Hezekiah (715-687). The central event for Micah seems to have been the fall of Samaria to the Assyrians in 721. His oracles are addressed to the capitals of the northern and southern groups of tribes: *Samaria* and *Jerusalem*.
1.2-16 Oracles against Israel and Judah.
1.2-9 The form is that of a lawsuit, calling *all peoples* as witnesses, and announcing the presence of God, the ultimate judge, specifying the accusation and pronouncing the penalty. God appears striding across the earth from his heavenly *dwelling-place*, stepping on the high *mountains* which melt *like wax* at his touch. He comes because of Israel's *transgression*, which is specified as her perversion of the supposed sanctuaries of God in Samaria and Jerusalem into places of idol-worship and cult prostitution. The destruction of Israel's capital, Samaria, will be followed by that of Jerusalem in such a drastic manner that all of Judah will feel threatened as well.
1.10-16 Micah informs the towns in his native area southwest of Jerusalem (*Gath...Lachish*) that their region will be conquered by the Assyrians, even if the king (*glory of Israel*) should hide in the cave of *Adullam* as David did (1 Sam 22.1-2). Signs of the mourning and penitence of the *pampered children* of Israel over the capture of the land include their rolling *in the dust* and cutting their *hair*.
2.1-3.12 The Prophet's Accusation.
2.1-11 The greedy schemers plot to seize the property of others, but the Lord has a plan to take away all their buildings through an invader (*an evil*) who will seize all their land. Then these very thieves will – ironically – complain that God is *altering* the basic pattern of distribution and *inheritance* of property which was supposed to have taken place when Israel first entered the land (Num 34-35). Now there will be no one in the future *assembly of the Lord's people* to take their side in adjudicating the reassignment (*by lot*) of the boundaries of their land. Instead, they continue to exhaust *the Lord's patience* by their refusal to listen to the warnings that are being *preached* to them, calling attention to their unjust acts, their thefts from *the peaceful* and their expulsion of *women and children* from their homes. There will be no place of *rest* or escape from judgment for those who commit such filthy, cruel deeds. The only prophet or preacher they want to hear is one who utters *empty falsehoods*.

1.1 Jer 26.18; 2 Kings 15.5,7,32-38; 16.1-20; 18.1-21
1.2 Jer 6.19; 22.29; Ps 50.7; 11.4
1.3 Isa 26.21; Am 4.13
1.4 Isa 64.1,2; Nah 1.5
1.5 Isa 28.1; Am 8.14; 2 Chr 34.3,4
1.6 Jer 31.5; Am 5.11; Ezek 13.14
1.7 Deut 9.21; 2 Chr 34.7; Isa 23.17
1.8 Isa 22.4; 32.11; 13.21,22
1.9 Jer 30.12,15; 2 Kings 18.13; ver 12
1.10 2 Sam 1.20
1.11 Ezek 23.29
1.12 Isa 59.9-11; Jer 14.19
1.13 2 Kings 14.19; Isa 36.2
1.14 2 Kings 16.8; Josh 15.44; Jer 15.18
1.15 Josh 15.44; Mic 5.2; Josh 12.15; 2 Sam 23.13
1.16 Isa 15.2; 22.12; Lam 4.5; Am 7.11
2.1 Isa 32.7; Nah 1.11; Hos 7.6,7; Prov 3.27
2.2 Am 8.4; Isa 5.8; 1 Kings 21.1-15
2.3 Am 3.1,2; Deut 28.48; Jer 18.11; Isa 2.11,12; Am 5.13

Now, I am devising against this family
an evil
from which you cannot remove your
necks;
and you shall not walk haughtily,
for it will be an evil time.
4 On that day they shall take up a taunt
song against you,
and wail with bitter lamentation,
and say, "We are utterly ruined;
the LORD[d] alters the inheritance of my
people;
how he removes it from me!
Among our captors[e] he parcels out
our fields."
5 Therefore you will have no one to cast
the line by lot
in the assembly of the LORD.

6 "Do not preach"—thus they preach—
"one should not preach of such
things;
disgrace will not overtake us."
7 Should this be said, O house of Jacob?
Is the LORD's patience exhausted?
Are these his doings?
Do not my words do good
to one who walks uprightly?
8 But you rise up against my people[f] as
an enemy;
you strip the robe from the peaceful,[g]
from those who pass by trustingly
with no thought of war.
9 The women of my people you drive out
from their pleasant houses;
from their young children you take
away
my glory forever.
10 Arise and go;
for this is no place to rest,
because of uncleanness that destroys
with a grievous destruction.[h]
11 If someone were to go about uttering
empty falsehoods,
saying, "I will preach to you of wine
and strong drink,"
such a one would be the preacher for
this people!

A Promise for the Remnant of Israel

12 I will surely gather all of you, O Jacob,
I will gather the survivors of Israel;
I will set them together
like sheep in a fold,
like a flock in its pasture;
it will resound with people.
13 The one who breaks out will go up
before them;
they will break through and pass the
gate,
going out by it.
Their king will pass on before them,
the LORD at their head.

Wicked Rulers and Prophets

3 And I said:
Listen, you heads of Jacob
and rulers of the house of Israel!
Should you not know justice?—
2 you who hate the good and love the
evil,
who tear the skin off my people,[i]
and the flesh off their bones;
3 who eat the flesh of my people,
flay their skin off them,
break their bones in pieces,
and chop them up like meat[j] in a kettle,
like flesh in a caldron.

4 Then they will cry to the LORD,
but he will not answer them;
he will hide his face from them at that
time,
because they have acted wickedly.

5 Thus says the LORD concerning the
prophets
who lead my people astray,
who cry "Peace"
when they have something to eat,
but declare war against those
who put nothing into their mouths.
6 Therefore it shall be night to you,
without vision,
and darkness to you, without
revelation.
The sun shall go down upon the
prophets,
and the day shall be black over them;
7 the seers shall be disgraced,
and the diviners put to shame;
they shall all cover their lips,
for there is no answer from God.
8 But as for me, I am filled with power,
with the spirit of the LORD,
and with justice and might,
to declare to Jacob his transgression
and to Israel his sin.

[d] Heb *he* [e] Cn: Heb *the rebellious* [f] Cn: Heb *But yesterday my people rose* [g] Cn: Heb *from before a garment* [h] Meaning of Heb uncertain [i] Heb *from them* [j] Gk: Heb *as*

2.12-13 Probably written after the exile; the *survivors of Israel* are promised that they will be led out of captivity like sheep, when God *breaks* open the way for them to return to the land. *The LORD*, their true *king*, will be leading them.
3.1-7 Returning to the judgment theme, the prophet directs his attack against the leaders of Israel who violate the law of justice, fleecing and flaying and lacerating their own people. God will give no heed to those who are superficially penitent and *cry to the LORD*, or to those who are led *astray* by the false *prophets*, *seers*, and *diviners* who for a fee will convey what they claim is an *answer from God*.
3.8-12 By contrast with these charlatans, Micah – filled with God's *spirit* and concerned for *justice* – is unrelenting in his criticism of Israel's *rulers* and prophets who will do anything *for a price*. The prophet confronts these unscrupulous leaders, as well as the people who go along with them. They all claim to be *leaning on the LORD*, but he knows their deceitful and grasping ways. Accordingly, the city of Jerusalem and its temple mount (*Zion*) will become useless territory.

2.4 Hab 2.6; Mic 1.8; Isa 24.3; Jer 4.13; 6.12; 8.10
2.5 Josh 18.4,10
2.6 Isa 30.10; Am 2.12; 7.16; Mic 3.6; 6.16
2.10 Lev 18.25,28,29; Deut 12.9; Ps 106.38
2.11 Jer 5.13,31; Isa 28.7; 30.10,11
2.12 Mic 4.6,7; 5.7,8; 7.18; Jer 33.22
2.13 Hos 3.5; Isa 52.12
3.1 Jer 5.4,5
3.2 Mic 2.8; 7.2,3; Ezek 22.27
3.3 Ps 14.4; Zeph 3.3; Ezek 34.2,3; 11.3
3.4 Ps 18.41; Prov 1.28; Isa 1.15; Zech 7.13; Isa 59.2; Mic 7.13
3.5 Isa 56.10; Ezek 13.10; Jer 14.14,15; Mic 2.11; Jer 6.14; Ezek 13.18,19
3.6 Isa 8.20,22; Ezek 13.23; Am 8.9
3.7 Zech 13.4; Isa 44.25; Mic 7.16; 1 Sam 28.6; ver 4
3.8 Isa 61.1,2; 58.1

4.1-5.1 Renewal of Jerusalem and the Faithful People of God.
4.1-4 This picture of *many nations* coming to the *LORD's house* for instruction includes the role of God as *judge* of all disputes among his people, the renunciation of war by all the nations, and the peaceful life that all enjoy as they heed the words of *the LORD of hosts*. Symbolic of the unique role of the temple as the focus of God's administration of the world is the transformation of Mt. Zion into *the highest of the mountains*. These words appear also in Isa 2.2-4, and 4.4 closely resembles Zech 3.10. Some scholars would assign this section to the post-exilic period, but it differs from the more likely post-exilic passage in 4.6-13 which claims political sovereignty for Jerusalem.
4.5 This prophecy expects only Israel to follow *the LORD*, while all other nations go the way of their respective *gods*.
4.6-13 This oracle resembles the apocalyptic visions of Daniel and Zechariah. *The remnant* of the nation, having been *afflicted* by God, will become a *strong nation*. After suffering the pains of the Babylonian exile – like a *woman in labor* – they will be vindicated by God, while their proud enemies will become like *sheaves* on God's *threshing floor* and will be trampled and hacked to pieces by the weapons and the horses' hooves of the triumphal new people of God. Only the latter are wholly devoted to him.

9 Hear this, you rulers of the house of
Jacob
and chiefs of the house of Israel,
who abhor justice
and pervert all equity,
10 who build Zion with blood
and Jerusalem with wrong!
11 Its rulers give judgment for a bribe,
its priests teach for a price,
its prophets give oracles for money;
yet they lean upon the LORD and say,
"Surely the LORD is with us!
No harm shall come upon us."
12 Therefore because of you
Zion shall be plowed as a field;
Jerusalem shall become a heap of ruins,
and the mountain of the house a
wooded height.

Peace and Security through Obedience

4 In days to come
the mountain of the LORD's house
shall be established as the highest of the
mountains,
and shall be raised up above the hills.
Peoples shall stream to it,
2 and many nations shall come and
say:
"Come, let us go up to the mountain of
the LORD,
to the house of the God of Jacob;
that he may teach us his ways
and that we may walk in his paths."
For out of Zion shall go forth
instruction,
and the word of the LORD from
Jerusalem.
3 He shall judge between many peoples,
and shall arbitrate between strong
nations far away;
they shall beat their swords into
plowshares,
and their spears into pruning hooks;
nation shall not lift up sword against
nation,
neither shall they learn war any
more;
4 but they shall all sit under their own
vines and under their own fig
trees,
and no one shall make them afraid;
for the mouth of the LORD of hosts has
spoken.
5 For all the peoples walk,
each in the name of its god,
but we will walk in the name of the
LORD our God
forever and ever.

Restoration Promised after Exile

6 In that day, says the LORD,
I will assemble the lame
and gather those who have been driven
away,
and those whom I have afflicted.
7 The lame I will make the remnant,
and those who were cast off, a strong
nation;
and the LORD will reign over them in
Mount Zion
now and forevermore.

8 And you, O tower of the flock,
hill of daughter Zion,
to you it shall come,
the former dominion shall come,
the sovereignty of daughter
Jerusalem.

9 Now why do you cry aloud?
Is there no king in you?
Has your counselor perished,
that pangs have seized you like a
woman in labor?
10 Writhe and groan,[k] O daughter Zion,
like a woman in labor;
for now you shall go forth from the city
and camp in the open country;
you shall go to Babylon.
There you shall be rescued,
there the LORD will redeem you
from the hands of your enemies.

11 Now many nations
are assembled against you,
saying, "Let her be profaned,
and let our eyes gaze upon Zion."
12 But they do not know
the thoughts of the LORD;
they do not understand his plan,
that he has gathered them as sheaves
to the threshing floor.
13 Arise and thresh,
O daughter Zion,
for I will make your horn iron
and your hoofs bronze;

[k] Meaning of Heb uncertain

3.9 ver 1; Isa 1.23
3.10 Jer 22.13; Ezek 22.27; Hab 2.12
3.11 Isa 1.23; Hos 4.18; Jer 6.13; Isa 48.2; Jer 7.4
3.12 Jer 26.18; Mic 4.1,2
4.1 Isa 2.2-4; Ezek 17.22; 43.12; Jer 3.17
4.2 Zech 2.11; 14.16; Jer 31.6; Isa 54.13; 42.1-4; Zech 14.8,9
4.3 Isa 2.4; Joel 3.10; Ps 72.7
4.4 1 Kings 4.25; Zech 3.10; Isa 1.20; 40.5
4.5 2 Kings 17.29; Isa 26.8,13; Zech 10.12
4.6 Ezek 34.16; Zeph 3.19; Ps 147.2; Ezek 34.13
4.7 Mic 2.12; 5.7,8; 7.18; Isa 9.6; Dan 7.14; Lk 1.33; Rev 11.15
4.8 Mic 2.12; Isa 1.26; Zech 9.10
4.9 Jer 8.19; Isa 13.8; Jer 30.6
4.10 Hos 2.14; Isa 45.13; Mic 7.8-12; Isa 48.20; 52.9-12
4.11 Lam 2.16; Ob 12; Mic 7.10
4.12 Isa 55.8; Rom 11.33; Isa 21.10
4.13 Isa 41.15; Dan 2.44; Zech 4.14

you shall beat in pieces many peoples,
and shall[l] devote their gain to the LORD,
their wealth to the Lord of the whole earth.

5 [m] Now you are walled around with a wall;[n]
siege is laid against us;
with a rod they strike the ruler of Israel
upon the cheek.

The Ruler from Bethlehem

2 [o] But you, O Bethlehem of Ephrathah,
who are one of the little clans of Judah,
from you shall come forth for me
one who is to rule in Israel,
whose origin is from of old,
from ancient days.
3 Therefore he shall give them up until the time
when she who is in labor has brought forth;
then the rest of his kindred shall return
to the people of Israel.
4 And he shall stand and feed his flock in the strength of the LORD,
in the majesty of the name of the LORD his God.
And they shall live secure, for now he shall be great
to the ends of the earth;
5 and he shall be the one of peace.

If the Assyrians come into our land
and tread upon our soil,[p]
we will raise against them seven shepherds
and eight installed as rulers.
6 They shall rule the land of Assyria with the sword,
and the land of Nimrod with the drawn sword;[q]
they[r] shall rescue us from the Assyrians
if they come into our land
or tread within our border.

The Future Role of the Remnant

7 Then the remnant of Jacob,
surrounded by many peoples,
shall be like dew from the LORD,
like showers on the grass,
which do not depend upon people
or wait for any mortal.
8 And among the nations the remnant of Jacob,
surrounded by many peoples,
shall be like a lion among the animals of the forest,
like a young lion among the flocks of sheep,
which, when it goes through, treads down
and tears in pieces, with no one to deliver.
9 Your hand shall be lifted up over your adversaries,
and all your enemies shall be cut off.

10 In that day, says the LORD,
I will cut off your horses from among you
and will destroy your chariots;
11 and I will cut off the cities of your land
and throw down all your strongholds;
12 and I will cut off sorceries from your hand,
and you shall have no more soothsayers;
13 and I will cut off your images
and your pillars from among you,
and you shall bow down no more
to the work of your hands;
14 and I will uproot your sacred poles[s]
from among you
and destroy your towns.
15 And in anger and wrath I will execute vengeance
on the nations that did not obey.

God Challenges Israel

6 Hear what the LORD says:
Rise, plead your case before the mountains,
and let the hills hear your voice.
2 Hear, you mountains, the controversy of the LORD,
and you enduring foundations of the earth;
for the LORD has a controversy with his people,
and he will contend with Israel.

3 "O my people, what have I done to you?
In what have I wearied you? Answer me!

5.1-6 Now, however, Israel is surrounded by the enemy and their *ruler* is under attack, but one day from the little city of David in Judah – that is, *Bethlehem* – will appear Israel's new ruler. Meanwhile, Israel has been *given up* to oppression until the royal heir comes. When the new king has been *brought forth*, he shall care for his people (*flock*) through the authority of *the name of the LORD*, providing them with security and extending his realm *to the ends of the earth*. Even though the Assyrians now threaten an invasion of Israel, their territory will one day be ruled by agents (*rulers*) appointed by this king, and all Israelites who are there in exile will be *rescued*.
5.7-9 Another later apocalyptic oracle promises preservation of the *remnant of Jacob*, which will one day turn against its present oppressors and destroy them.
5.10-15 The prophecy turns once more to the theme of the purging from Israel of all its sources of pride (*chariots, cities, strongholds*), and of its participation in pagan practices (*sorcery, images*, and fertility symbols such as *pillars* and *poles*). God's *wrath* will destroy all of these features of Israel's perverted worship.
6.1-8 God's Plea and Promise to Israel.
6.1-5 In the manner of a court process, Israel is called to respond in public (*before the mountains*) to God's charge against his people of ingratitude and infidelity. He reminds them of his care and protection of them in the events of the exodus from Egypt, and of their escape from attacks by rulers east of the Jordan (Balak of Moab: Num 22-24) and from enticement to worship Baal (Num 25), as well as his shaping events for them to enter the promised land (Josh 2-4). These are God's *saving acts* in behalf of his people.

5.1 Jer 5.7; 1 Kings 22.24; Lam 3.30
5.2 Mt 2.6; 1 Sam 17.12; 23.23; Lk 2.4; Isa 9.6
5.3 Mic 4.10; Hos 11.8; Isa 10.20-22
5.4 Isa 40.11; Ezek 34.23; Isa 52.13; Lk 1.32
5.5 Isa 9.6; Rev 11.15; Isa 8.7,8
5.6 Nah 2.11-13; Zeph 2.13; Gen 10.8; Isa 37.36,37
5.7 Mic 2.12; Deut 32.2; Hos 14.5
5.8 Mic 4.13; Zech 10.5; Hos 5.14; Ps 50.22
5.9 Ps 10.12; 21.8; Isa 26.11
5.10 Isa 2.7; Hos 14.3; Zech 9.10
5.11 Isa 1.7; Hos 10.14; Am 5.9
5.12 Deut 18.10-12; Isa 2.6
5.14 Ex 34.13; Isa 17.8; 27.9
5.15 Ps 149.7; Isa 65.12
6.1 Ps 50.1; Ezek 6.2,3
6.2 Deut 32.1; Hos 12.2; Isa 1.8; Hos 4.1
6.3 Ps 50.7; Jer 2.5; Isa 43.22,23

[l] Gk Syr Tg: Heb *and I will* [m] Ch 4.14 in Heb [n] Cn Compare Gk: Meaning of Heb uncertain [o] Ch 5.1 in Heb [p] Gk: Heb *in our palaces* [q] Cn: Heb *in its entrances* [r] Heb *he* [s] Heb *Asherim*

6.6-8 What God expects from his people is not an abundance of sacrifices (*thousands of rams, ten thousand rivers of oil*) but *justice, love, kindness*, which are to characterize the lives of the true covenant community.
6.9-16 How God will Deal with Israel's Gross Disobedience. The LORD, whose sacred name evokes *fear*, addresses the people of Israel (*tribe, assembly*), reminding them that he knows and will punish them for amassing wealth, for their *dishonest* business transactions and their rampant *lies*. All of their false confidence about the security they have built – including money and food reserves – will be of no help in preserving them. Their model for living has been the ruthless, power-oriented style of the outwardly successful earlier kings of Israel, Omri and Ahab (1 Kings 17-22), who were denounced by the prophet Elijah. Similarly, the destiny of this ruthless, power-mad people will be *desolation* and *scorn* by other nations.
7.1-20 The Prophet's Despair, Confidence and Hope.
7.1-7 The prophet feels that his efforts have been in vain: there is no *fruit* to be gathered in the form of repentance. There are no faithful people remaining, only would-be murderers and the corrupt officials who manipulate the community for their own advantage. Relationships between friends, and between parents and children, have become perverted and hostile. With *no one left who is upright*, the prophet looks only *to the LORD* for a remedy.

4 For I brought you up from the land of Egypt,
and redeemed you from the house of slavery;
and I sent before you Moses,
Aaron, and Miriam.
5 O my people, remember now what King Balak of Moab devised,
what Balaam son of Beor answered him,
and what happened from Shittim to Gilgal,
that you may know the saving acts of the LORD."

What God Requires

6 "With what shall I come before the LORD,
and bow myself before God on high?
Shall I come before him with burnt offerings,
with calves a year old?
7 Will the LORD be pleased with thousands of rams,
with ten thousands of rivers of oil?
Shall I give my firstborn for my transgression,
the fruit of my body for the sin of my soul?"
8 He has told you, O mortal, what is good;
and what does the LORD require of you
but to do justice, and to love kindness,
and to walk humbly with your God?

Cheating and Violence to Be Punished

9 The voice of the LORD cries to the city
(it is sound wisdom to fear your name):
Hear, O tribe and assembly of the city![t]
10 Can I forget[u] the treasures of wickedness in the house of the wicked,
and the scant measure that is accursed?
11 Can I tolerate wicked scales
and a bag of dishonest weights?
12 Your[v] wealthy are full of violence;
your[w] inhabitants speak lies,
with tongues of deceit in their mouths.
13 Therefore I have begun[x] to strike you down,
making you desolate because of your sins.
14 You shall eat, but not be satisfied,
and there shall be a gnawing hunger within you;
you shall put away, but not save,
and what you save, I will hand over to the sword.
15 You shall sow, but not reap;
you shall tread olives, but not anoint yourselves with oil;
you shall tread grapes, but not drink wine.
16 For you have kept the statutes of Omri[y]
and all the works of the house of Ahab,
and you have followed their counsels.
Therefore I will make you a desolation,
and your[z] inhabitants an object of hissing;
so you shall bear the scorn of my people.

The Total Corruption of the People

7 Woe is me! For I have become like one who,
after the summer fruit has been gathered,
after the vintage has been gleaned,
finds no cluster to eat;
there is no first-ripe fig for which I hunger.
2 The faithful have disappeared from the land,
and there is no one left who is upright;
they all lie in wait for blood,
and they hunt each other with nets.
3 Their hands are skilled to do evil;
the official and the judge ask for a bribe,
and the powerful dictate what they desire;
thus they pervert justice.[a]
4 The best of them is like a brier,
the most upright of them a thorn hedge.
The day of their[b] sentinels, of their[b] punishment, has come;
now their confusion is at hand.
5 Put no trust in a friend,
have no confidence in a loved one;
guard the doors of your mouth

[t] Cn Compare Gk: Heb *tribe, and who has appointed it yet?* [u] Cn: Meaning of Heb uncertain [v] Heb *Whose* [w] Heb *whose* [x] Gk Syr Vg: Heb *have made sick* [y] Gk Syr Vg Tg: Heb *the statutes of Omri are kept* [z] Heb *its* [a] Cn: Heb *they weave it* [b] Heb *your*

6.4 Ex 12.51; Deut 4.20; 7.8; Ps 77.20; Ex 15.20
6.5 Num 22.5,6; Rev 2.14; Num 25.1; Josh 4.19; 5.9,10; Judg 5.11; 1 Sam 12.7
6.7 2 Kings 16.3; 21.6; Jer 7.31
6.8 Deut 10.12; 1 Sam 15.22; Hos 6.6; 12.6; Isa 56.1; 57.15; 66.2
6.10 Jer 5.26,27; Am 3.10; 8.5
6.11 Hos 12.7
6.13 Mic 1.9; Isa 1.7; 6.11
6.14 Lev 26.26; Isa 9.20; 30.6
6.15 Deut 28.38; Jer 12.13; Am 5.11; Zeph 1.13
6.16 1 Kings 16.25-33; 7.24; 19.8; 29.18; 51.51
7.1 Isa 24.13; 28.4; Hos 9.10
7.2 Ps 12.1; Isa 57.1; 59.7; Jer 5.26; Hos 5.1
7.3 Prov 4.16,17; Am 5.12; Mic 3.11
7.4 Ezek 2.6; 28.24; Nah 1.10; Isa 10.3; Hos 9.7; Isa 22.5

from her who lies in your embrace;
6 for the son treats the father with contempt,
the daughter rises up against her mother,
the daughter-in-law against her mother-in-law;
your enemies are members of your own household.
7 But as for me, I will look to the LORD,
I will wait for the God of my salvation;
my God will hear me.

Penitence and Trust in God

8 Do not rejoice over me, O my enemy;
when I fall, I shall rise;
when I sit in darkness,
the LORD will be a light to me.
9 I must bear the indignation of the LORD,
because I have sinned against him,
until he takes my side
and executes judgment for me.
He will bring me out to the light;
I shall see his vindication.
10 Then my enemy will see,
and shame will cover her who said to me,
"Where is the LORD your God?"
My eyes will see her downfall;[c]
now she will be trodden down
like the mire of the streets.

A Prophecy of Restoration

11 A day for the building of your walls!
In that day the boundary shall be far extended.
12 In that day they will come to you
from Assyria to[d] Egypt,
and from Egypt to the River,
from sea to sea and from mountain to mountain.
13 But the earth will be desolate
because of its inhabitants,
for the fruit of their doings.

14 Shepherd your people with your staff,
the flock that belongs to you,
which lives alone in a forest
in the midst of a garden land;
let them feed in Bashan and Gilead
as in the days of old.
15 As in the days when you came out of the land of Egypt,
show us[e] marvelous things.
16 The nations shall see and be ashamed
of all their might;
they shall lay their hands on their mouths;
their ears shall be deaf;
17 they shall lick dust like a snake,
like the crawling things of the earth;
they shall come trembling out of their fortresses;
they shall turn in dread to the LORD our God,
and they shall stand in fear of you.

God's Compassion and Steadfast Love

18 Who is a God like you, pardoning iniquity
and passing over the transgression
of the remnant of your[f] possession?
He does not retain his anger forever,
because he delights in showing clemency.
19 He will again have compassion upon us;
he will tread our iniquities under foot.
You will cast all our[g] sins
into the depths of the sea.
20 You will show faithfulness to Jacob
and unswerving loyalty to Abraham,
as you have sworn to our ancestors
from the days of old.

7.6 Ezek 22.7; Mt 10.21,35,36; Lk 12.53
7.7 Hab 2.1; Ps 130.5; 4.3
7.8 Prov 24.17; Lam 4.21; Ps 37.24; Isa 9.2
7.9 Lam 3.39,40; Isa 42.7,16; 56.1
7.10 Ps 35.26; Isa 51.23; Zech 10.5
7.11 Isa 54.11; Zeph 2.2
7.12 Isa 11.16; 19.23-25
7.13 Jer 25.11; Mic 6.13; Isa 3.10,11; Mic 3.4
7.15 Ex 3.20; 20.34; Ps 78.12
7.16 Job 21.5; Mic 3.7
7.17 Ps 72.9; Isa 49.23; Deut 32.24; Ps 18.45; Isa 59.19
7.18 Ex 34.7,9; Isa 43.25; Jer 32.41
7.19 Jer 50.20; Isa 38.17; 43.25; Jer 31.34
7.20 Lk 1.55,72; Deut 7.8,12

7.8-17 The scornful *enemy* who denied the power of the LORD will now have to see God's *vindication* of the prophet and will be *trodden down*. But Israel's capital will be rebuilt and its territory of control extended to include that of her historic enemies *Assyria* and *Egypt*. The rest of the earth is here portrayed as *desolate*, while Israel flourishes like the proverbially fertile fields and pastures of *Bashan and Gilead*. Meanwhile, the defeated nations will come grovelling *like snakes*, out of *fear* of Israel's God. This section also appears to have come from the time of the exile or later.
7.18-20 In a liturgical conclusion the prophet offers praise to God for *pardoning* Israel's *iniquity*, and for his favor to *the remnant* of the people. Since their sins have been *cast...into the depths of the sea*, they can be certain that God will be faithful to them and their posterity through the covenant made with Jacob and Abraham.

[c] Heb lacks *downfall* [d] One Ms: MT *Assyria and cities of* [e] Cn: Heb *I will show him* [f] Heb *his* [g] Gk Syr Vg Tg: Heb *their*

NAHUM

See the Introductions, pp. 6, 54-57, and 71 above.

1 An oracle concerning Nineveh. The book of the vision of Nahum of Elkosh.

The Consuming Wrath of God

2 A jealous and avenging God is the LORD,
the LORD is avenging and wrathful;
the LORD takes vengeance on his adversaries
and rages against his enemies.
3 The LORD is slow to anger but great in power,
and the LORD will by no means clear the guilty.

His way is in whirlwind and storm,
and the clouds are the dust of his feet.
4 He rebukes the sea and makes it dry,
and he dries up all the rivers;
Bashan and Carmel wither,
and the bloom of Lebanon fades.
5 The mountains quake before him,
and the hills melt;
the earth heaves before him,
the world and all who live in it.

6 Who can stand before his indignation?
Who can endure the heat of his anger?
His wrath is poured out like fire,
and by him the rocks are broken in pieces.
7 The LORD is good,
a stronghold in a day of trouble;
he protects those who take refuge in him,
8 even in a rushing flood.
He will make a full end of his adversaries,[a]
and will pursue his enemies into darkness.
9 Why do you plot against the LORD?
He will make an end;
no adversary will rise up twice.
10 Like thorns they are entangled,
like drunkards they are drunk;
they are consumed like dry straw.
11 From you one has gone out
who plots evil against the LORD,
who counsels wickedness.

Good News for Judah

12 Thus says the LORD,
"Though they are at full strength and many,[b]
they will be cut off and pass away.
Though I have afflicted you,
I will afflict you no more.
13 And now I will break off his yoke from you
and snap the bonds that bind you."

14 The LORD has commanded concerning you:
"Your name shall be perpetuated no longer;
from the house of your gods I will cut off
the carved image and the cast image.
I will make your grave, for you are worthless."

15[c] Look! On the mountains the feet of one
who brings good tidings,
who proclaims peace!
Celebrate your festivals, O Judah,
fulfill your vows,
for never again shall the wicked invade you;
they are utterly cut off.

The Destruction of the Wicked City

2 A shatterer[d] has come up against you.
Guard the ramparts;
watch the road;
gird your loins;
collect all your strength.

2 (For the LORD is restoring the majesty of Jacob,
as well as the majesty of Israel,
though ravagers have ravaged them
and ruined their branches.)

3 The shields of his warriors are red;
his soldiers are clothed in crimson.
The metal on the chariots flashes
on the day when he musters them;
the chargers[e] prance.
4 The chariots race madly through the streets,

[a] Gk: Heb *of her place* [b] Meaning of Heb uncertain [c] Ch 2.1 in Heb [d] Cn: Heb *scatterer* [e] Cn Compare Gk Syr: Heb *cypresses*

1.1 Introduction. *Nineveh*, the subject of this oracle, was a city founded in about 5000 BCE. As capital of the Assyrian empire, which in the eighth century BCE extended across upper Mesopotamia and Syria to the Mediterranean, it was the symbol for dominance of this vast territory. The northern tribes of Israel were controlled by Assyria after the fall of Samaria in 721 (2 Kings 17), and Judah came under pressure from Assyria for nearly a century. The oracle describes the fall of Nineveh to the Babylonians, probably in anticipation of the event which took place in 612. *Nahum* means *comfort*; he comes from *Elkosh*, the location of which is not now known.
1.2-11 The Wrath of God Falls on Nineveh. The real power behind the expected fall of Nineveh is the wrathful God, whose sovereignty is evident in his control of the *sea and the rivers* and the *mountains*, of which are named those east of the Jordan (*Bashan*), west of Israel (*Carmel*) and to the north (*Lebanon*). For the objects of God's *anger* there is no withstanding him, but for those who look to him for *refuge*, he is *good* and protective. All human plots against him will come to nought.
1.12-15 The Promised Liberation of God's People. No matter how powerful have been the attacks of enemies on the people, they will now end and Israel will be liberated. The reputation (*name*) of the enemy will pass into oblivion, and the messenger with *good tidings* will appear with his announcement of *peace* and joyous *festivals*. The threat of the *wicked* will be ended forever.
2.1-3.19 The Doom of Nineveh and Assyria.
2.1 The city is to brace itself for the impending attack.
2.2 A parenthetic note repeats the assurance that God will restore Israel.
2.3-12 The destruction of Nineveh is foretold. Its agents of war – *soldiers, chariots* – are prepared for battle. Troops ascend the fortified *walls* and erect shelters (*mantelets*) for protection against arrows and hurled stones. But with the opening of the sluice *gates* on the Tigris River, the city is flooded and its walls are undermined. The people – including slave women, who may be fertility cult prostitutes – flee the city and looters take over. Nineveh, which often pictured itself as a lion (with its patron goddess, Ishtar, as a *lioness*) is now destroyed along with its people (*whelps*).

1.1 Isa 13.1; Hab 1.1; Nah 2.8; 3.7; Zeph 2.13
1.2 Ex 20.5; Deut 4.24; 32.35,41; Ps 94.1
1.3 Ex 34.6,7; Ps 103.8; Isa 29.6; Ps 104.3
1.5 Ex 19.18; Mic 1.4; Isa 24.1,20
1.6 Jer 10.10; Mal 3.2; Isa 66.15; 1 Kings 19.11
1.8 Isa 28.2,18; 13.9,10
1.9 Ps 2.1; Isa 28.22
1.10 2 Sam 23.6; Mal 4.1
1.11 ver 9; Ezek 11.2
1.12 Isa 10.16-19,33,34; 54.7,8
1.13 Isa 9.4; Jer 2.20
1.14 Isa 46.1,2; Mic 5.13,14; Ezek 32.22,23
1.15 Isa 40.9; Ps 52.7; Rom 10.15; Lev 23.2,4; Isa 52.1; Joel 3.17; Isa 29.7,8
2.1 Jer 51.20-23; Nah 3.12,14
2.2 Isa 60.15; Ezek 37.21-23
2.3 Ezek 23.14,15; Job 39.23
2.4 Ezek 26.10; Jer 4.13

they rush to and fro through the
squares;
their appearance is like torches,
they dart like lightning.
5 He calls his officers;
they stumble as they come forward;
they hasten to the wall,
and the mantelet[f] is set up.
6 The river gates are opened,
the palace trembles.
7 It is decreed[f] that the city[g] be exiled,
its slave women led away,
moaning like doves
and beating their breasts.
8 Nineveh is like a pool
whose waters[h] run away.
"Halt! Halt!"—
but no one turns back.
9 "Plunder the silver,
plunder the gold!
There is no end of treasure!
An abundance of every precious
thing!"

10 Devastation, desolation, and destruction!
Hearts faint and knees tremble,
all loins quake,
all faces grow pale!
11 What became of the lions' den,
the cave[i] of the young lions,
where the lion goes,
and the lion's cubs, with no one to
disturb them?
12 The lion has torn enough for his whelps
and strangled prey for his lionesses;
he has filled his caves with prey
and his dens with torn flesh.

13 See, I am against you, says the LORD
of hosts, and I will burn your[j] chariots in
smoke, and the sword shall devour your
young lions; I will cut off your prey from
the earth, and the voice of your messengers
shall be heard no more.

Ruin Imminent and Inevitable

3 Ah! City of bloodshed,
utterly deceitful, full of booty—
no end to the plunder!
2 The crack of whip and rumble of wheel,
galloping horse and bounding chariot!
3 Horsemen charging,
flashing sword and glittering spear,
piles of dead,
heaps of corpses,
dead bodies without end—
they stumble over the bodies!
4 Because of the countless debaucheries of
the prostitute,
gracefully alluring, mistress of sorcery,
who enslaves[k] nations through her
debaucheries,
and peoples through her sorcery,
5 I am against you,
says the LORD of hosts,
and will lift up your skirts over your
face;
and I will let nations look on your
nakedness
and kingdoms on your shame.
6 I will throw filth at you
and treat you with contempt,
and make you a spectacle.
7 Then all who see you will shrink from
you and say,
"Nineveh is devastated; who will
bemoan her?"
Where shall I seek comforters for you?

8 Are you better than Thebes[l]
that sat by the Nile,
with water around her,
her rampart a sea,
water her wall?
9 Ethiopia[m] was her strength,
Egypt too, and that without limit;
Put and the Libyans were her[n] helpers.

10 Yet she became an exile,
she went into captivity;
even her infants were dashed in pieces
at the head of every street;
lots were cast for her nobles,
all her dignitaries were bound in
fetters.
11 You also will be drunken,
you will go into hiding;[f]
you will seek
a refuge from the enemy.
12 All your fortresses are like fig trees
with first-ripe figs—
if shaken they fall
into the mouth of the eater.
13 Look at your troops:
they are women in your midst.
The gates of your land
are wide open to your foes;
fire has devoured the bars of your
gates.

[f] Meaning of Heb uncertain [g] Heb *it* [h] Cn Compare Gk: Heb *a pool, from the days that she has become, and they* [i] Cn: Heb *pasture* [j] Heb *her* [k] Heb *sells* [l] Heb *No-amon* [m] Or *Nubia*; Heb *Cush* [n] Gk: Heb *your*

2.7 Isa 59.11; 32.12
2.8 Nah 3.7; Jer 46.5; 47.3
2.10 Ps 22.14; Isa 13.7,8; Joel 2.6
2.11 Isa 5.29; Jer 4.7; Nah 3.1
2.12 Isa 10.6-14; Jer 51.34
2.13 Nah 3.5; Ps 46.9; Isa 49.24,25
3.1 Ezek 24.6,9
3.2 Nah 2.3,4; Jer 47.3
3.3 Hab 3.11; Isa 34.3; 66.16; 2 Kings 19.35
3.4 Isa 23.17; Rev 17.1,2; Isa 47.9; Rev 18.3
3.5 Nah 2.13; Isa 47.2,3; Jer 13.22; Ezek 16.37
3.6 Job 9.31; Mal 2.9; Isa 14.16; Jer 51.37
3.7 Jer 51.9; Nah 2.8; Zeph 2.13; Isa 51.19; Jer 15.5
3.8 Jer 46.25; Ezek 30.14-16; Isa 19.6-8
3.9 Isa 20.5; Ezek 27.10; 30.5; 38.5; 2 Chr 12.3; 16.8
3.10 Isa 20.4; 13.16; Hos 13.16; Lam 2.19; Joel 3.3; Ob 11
3.11 Jer 25.27; Isa 2.10,19
3.12 Isa 28.4; Rev 6.13
3.13 Jer 50.37; 51.30; Ps 147.13

2.13 The threat is repeated in prose, using the same imagery of the *young lions*.
3.1-7 After further details about the ruins of the city and the *piles of the dead*, the oracle describes the gross excesses of the sexual rites and exploitation that were part of the worship of Ishtar, the fertility goddess. He then pictures her as laid bare and shamed, with her *skirts lifted up over her face* for all the *nations* to see. Pelted with *filth*, the once proud city will be the focus of shame.
3.8-19 Foolishly confident of what she assumes is an impregnable position beside the river, Nineveh is like *Thebes*, the capital of Egypt on the *Nile*, which relied for support on adjoining African nations: *Ethiopia, Put* (Somalia), *and Libya*. Instead, the populace of Nineveh will experience *exile* and enslavement. The fortifications will fall, the resources will be depleted, and the armies will fly away like *locusts*. The leaders are now *asleep*, and when the disaster comes, there will be no way to heal the city's fatal wound. Those of other nations who hear of her fate will *clap their hands* in vindictive joy.

14 Draw water for the siege,
strengthen your forts;
trample the clay,
tread the mortar,
take hold of the brick mold!
15 There the fire will devour you,
the sword will cut you off.
It will devour you like the locust.

Multiply yourselves like the locust,
multiply like the grasshopper!
16 You increased your merchants
more than the stars of the heavens.
The locust sheds its skin and flies
away.
17 Your guards are like grasshoppers,
your scribes like swarms[a] of locusts
settling on the fences
on a cold day—
when the sun rises, they fly away;
no one knows where they have gone.

18 Your shepherds are asleep,
O king of Assyria;
your nobles slumber.
Your people are scattered on the
mountains
with no one to gather them.
19 There is no assuaging your hurt,
your wound is mortal.
All who hear the news about you
clap their hands over you.
For who has ever escaped
your endless cruelty?

[a] Meaning of Heb uncertain

3.15 ver 13; Joel 1.4
3.18 Ps 76.5,6; Isa 56.10; Jer 51.57; Nah 2.5; 1 Kings 22.17
3.19 Mic 1.9; Lam 2.15; Zeph 2.15

HABAKKUK

See the Introductions, pp. 6, 54-57, and 71-72 above.

1.1 Introduction. *Oracle*, sometimes translated as *burden*, is a message of doom, often pronounced against other nations, as in Nahum 1.1, but this oracle concerns God's people and their impending punishment.
1.2-17 The Prophet Complains to God about the Invasion.
1.1-4 The prophet's prayers to the LORD have gone unheeded, while *wrongdoing* and *destruction* are everywhere, and *justice* seems to have no place in the life of the people.
1.5-11 Unprecedented destruction is appearing with the invasion of the land by the *Chaldeans* (Babylonians), with their swift cavalry, their disdain for all regional rulers, and their overmastering everything by their proud power.
1.12-14 Resuming his complaint against God, the prophet reminds God of the certainty of his ultimate punishment of the evil powers, but asks why God now allows this misery to happen to his people.

1 The oracle that the prophet Habakkuk saw.

The Prophet's Complaint

2 O LORD, how long shall I cry for help,
and you will not listen?
Or cry to you "Violence!"
and you will not save?
3 Why do you make me see wrongdoing
and look at trouble?
Destruction and violence are before me;
strife and contention arise.
4 So the law becomes slack
and justice never prevails.
The wicked surround the righteous—
therefore judgment comes forth perverted.

5 Look at the nations, and see!
Be astonished! Be astounded!
For a work is being done in your days
that you would not believe if you
were told.
6 For I am rousing the Chaldeans,
that fierce and impetuous nation,
who march through the breadth of the
earth
to seize dwellings not their own.
7 Dread and fearsome are they;
their justice and dignity proceed from
themselves.
8 Their horses are swifter than leopards,
more menacing than wolves at dusk;
their horses charge.
Their horsemen come from far away;
they fly like an eagle swift to devour.
9 They all come for violence,
with faces pressing[a] forward;
they gather captives like sand.
10 At kings they scoff,
and of rulers they make sport.
They laugh at every fortress,
and heap up earth to take it.
11 Then they sweep by like the wind;
they transgress and become guilty;
their own might is their god!

12 Are you not from of old,
O LORD my God, my Holy One?
You[b] shall not die.
O LORD, you have marked them for
judgment;
and you, O Rock, have established
them for punishment.

[a] Meaning of Heb uncertain [b] Ancient Heb tradition: MT *We*

1.2 Ps 13.1,2; 22.1,2
1.3 ver 13; Jer 20.8
1.4 Ps 119.126; 22.12; Isa 5.20
1.5 Acts 13.41; Isa 29.9,14
1.6 2 Kings 24.2; Jer 4.11-13; 5.15; 8.10
1.7 Isa 18.2,7; Jer 39.5-9
1.8 Jer 4.13; 5.6; Ezek 17.3; Hos 8.1
1.9 Hab 2.5
1.10 2 Chr 36.6,10; Isa 10.9; 14.16; Jer 32.24; Ezek 26.8
1.11 Jer 4.11,12; Jer 2.3; Dan 4.30
1.12 Deut 33.27; Ps 90.2; Isa 10.5-7; Deut 32.4

13 Your eyes are too pure to behold evil,
and you cannot look on wrongdoing;
why do you look on the treacherous,
and are silent when the wicked swallow
those more righteous than they?
14 You have made people like the fish of the sea,
like crawling things that have no ruler.

15 The enemy[c] brings all of them up with a hook;
he drags them out with his net,
he gathers them in his seine;
so he rejoices and exults.
16 Therefore he sacrifices to his net
and makes offerings to his seine;
for by them his portion is lavish,
and his food is rich.
17 Is he then to keep on emptying his net,
and destroying nations without mercy?

God's Reply to the Prophet's Complaint

2 I will stand at my watchpost,
and station myself on the rampart;
I will keep watch to see what he will say to me,
and what he[d] will answer concerning my complaint.
2 Then the LORD answered me and said:
Write the vision;
make it plain on tablets,
so that a runner may read it.
3 For there is still a vision for the appointed time;
it speaks of the end, and does not lie.
If it seems to tarry, wait for it;
it will surely come, it will not delay.
4 Look at the proud!
Their spirit is not right in them,
but the righteous live by their faith.[e]
5 Moreover, wealth[f] is treacherous;
the arrogant do not endure.
They open their throats wide as Sheol;
like Death they never have enough.
They gather all nations for themselves,
and collect all peoples as their own.

The Woes of the Wicked

6 Shall not everyone taunt such people
and, with mocking riddles, say about them,
"Alas for you who heap up what is not your own!"
How long will you load yourselves
with goods taken in pledge?
7 Will not your own creditors suddenly rise,
and those who make you tremble wake up?
Then you will be booty for them.
8 Because you have plundered many nations,
all that survive of the peoples shall plunder you—
because of human bloodshed, and violence to the earth,
to cities and all who live in them.

9 "Alas for you who get evil gain for your houses,
setting your nest on high
to be safe from the reach of harm!"
10 You have devised shame for your house
by cutting off many peoples;
you have forfeited your life.
11 The very stones will cry out from the wall,
and the plaster[g] will respond from the woodwork.

12 "Alas for you who build a town by bloodshed,
and found a city on iniquity!"
13 Is it not from the LORD of hosts
that peoples labor only to feed the flames,
and nations weary themselves for nothing?
14 But the earth will be filled
with the knowledge of the glory of the LORD,
as the waters cover the sea.

15 "Alas for you who make your neighbors drink,
pouring out your wrath[h] until they are drunk,
in order to gaze on their nakedness!"
16 You will be sated with contempt instead of glory.
Drink, you yourself, and stagger![i]
The cup in the LORD's right hand
will come around to you,
and shame will come upon your glory!
17 For the violence done to Lebanon will overwhelm you;

[c] Heb *He* [d] Syr: Heb *I* [e] Or *faithfulness* [f] Other Heb Mss read *wine* [g] Or *beam* [h] Or *poison* [i] Q Ms Gk: MT *be uncircumcised*

1.15-17 The enemy is as merciless and self-serving toward God's people as a fisherman is who hooks, cooks and eats the fish he catches.
2.1-20 God's Reply: The Support of the Righteous and the Woes of the Wicked.
2.1 Like a watchman, the prophet awaits God's response to his complaint.
2.2-5 God has a plan for the future which will reward the faithful and punish the wicked. The prophet is to prepare for sending out this message to the people in *plain* and readable words, and is assured that it will surely happen at God's *appointed time*. *The proud* will not heed it, but the *righteous* will trust it and live by it. This verse (2.4) in the Greek translation is quoted in the New Testament (Rom 1.17; Gal 3.11; Heb 10.38) with the implied meaning that trust in God is the sole ground of right relationship with him.
2.6-8 A series of woes, introduced by *alas*, notes in detail who will fall under God's judgment and why. The first are those whose greed at both the personal and the international level leads them to steal, to plunder other nations, and to cause *bloodshed*.
2.9-11 The second woe describes those who falsely assume that a strongly-built house will protect them from the consequences of their misdeeds. *House* can also mean *dynasty*, and the warning applies to nations that exploit their neighbors and have a false sense of security.
2.12-14 The third woe is a warning of the futility of the effort to build cities and nations by exploiting other people (*by bloodshed*) as a way of trying to guarantee survival and power. What will fill *the earth* and make it secure will not be these vain efforts, but *the knowledge of the LORD*.
2.15-19 The fourth woe is against those who get others drunk in order to exploit them sexually, perhaps in connection with fertility rites in service of other deities. The *violence* these evil ones do will come back on them. The *idols* they worship – although covered by precious metals – are shown to be lifeless, useless products of wood.

1.13 Jer 12.1,2; Isa 24.16; Ps 50.21; 56.1,2
1.14 Eccl 9.12
1.15 Jer 16.16; Am 4.2; Ps 10.9
1.17 Isa 19.8; 14.5,6
2.1 Isa 21.8,11; Ps 5.3; 85.8
2.2 Deut 27.8; Isa 8.1; Rev 1.19
2.3 Dan 8.17,19; 10.14; Ezek 12.25; Heb 10.37,38
2.4 Rom 1.17; Gal 3.11; Heb 10.38,39
2.5 Prov 20.1; 21.24; 2 Kings 14.10; Jer 25.9
2.6 Jer 50.13; ver 12; Ezek 18.12; Am 2.8
2.8 Isa 33.1; Zech 2.8; ver 17
2.9 Jer 22.13; Ezek 22.27; Jer 49.16
2.10 2 Kings 9.26; ver 16; Prov 1.18; Jer 26.19
2.12 Mic 3.10; Nah 3.1
2.14 Isa 11.9; Zech 14.8,9
2.15 Isa 28.7,8; Hos 7.5
2.16 ver 10; Lam 4.21; Jer 25.15,27; Nah 3.6
2.17 Zech 11.1; ver 8; Jer 51.35

2.20 In contrast to these foolish activities and the false deities, *the* LORD continues to dwell in his *holy* place. Before him all the earth must stand in awe.
3.1-19 The Prophet's Prayer.
3.1 Instructions are given for singing this hymn in the assembly, with additional instructions at the end of 3.19.
3.2-12 The awesome activity (*work*) of the LORD is here recounted, reviewing for *our own time* what God did in the past: creating the world and bringing the *nations* under control. God's coming on the scene is from *Teman* and *Paran*, regions southeast of the Dead Sea through which he led Israel from Egypt into the promised land. Gleaming *like the sun* and acclaimed by *the earth*, his presence is avoided by the fleeing evil forces (*pestilence* and *plague*), but before him the earth's surface changes shape. The dwellings of nomads (*tents*) east and west of the Red Sea (*Cushan* in Africa; *Midian* in Arabia) flutter at his passing. As in the time of creation, God brings the *sea* and *rivers* under control and fixes *the sun* and *moon* in their courses. On the earth, all the *nations* are brought into submission (*trampled*) by his presence.
3.13-16 God's purpose in coming was to free his chosen (*anointed*) people and to *crush* their opponents, symbolized by the chaotic *sea* which is subdued by God's power. Now the prophet is filled with awe and trembling as he awaits the *day of calamity* that is in store for the enemies of God's people.
3.17-19 In spite of the present scene of ruin of crops, groves and flocks, the prophet *exults* in confidence that God will bring about the deliverance and renewal (*salvation*) of his people.

the destruction of the animals will
terrify you—[j]
because of human bloodshed and
violence to the earth,
to cities and all who live in them.

18 What use is an idol
once its maker has shaped it—
a cast image, a teacher of lies?
For its maker trusts in what has been made,
though the product is only an idol
that cannot speak!
19 Alas for you who say to the wood,
"Wake up!"
to silent stone, "Rouse yourself!"
Can it teach?
See, it is gold and silver plated,
and there is no breath in it at all.

20 But the LORD is in his holy temple;
let all the earth keep silence before him!

3 A prayer of the prophet Habakkuk according to Shigionoth.

The Prophet's Prayer

2 O LORD, I have heard of your renown,
and I stand in awe, O LORD, of your
work.
In our own time revive it;
in our own time make it known;
in wrath may you remember mercy.
3 God came from Teman,
the Holy One from Mount Paran.
Selah
His glory covered the heavens,
and the earth was full of his praise.
4 The brightness was like the sun;
rays came forth from his hand,
where his power lay hidden.
5 Before him went pestilence,
and plague followed close behind.
6 He stopped and shook the earth;
he looked and made the nations
tremble.
The eternal mountains were shattered;
along his ancient pathways
the everlasting hills sank low.
7 I saw the tents of Cushan under affliction;
the tent-curtains of the land of Midian
trembled.
8 Was your wrath against the rivers,[k] O LORD?
Or your anger against the rivers,[k]
or your rage against the sea,[l]
when you drove your horses,
your chariots to victory?
9 You brandished your naked bow,
sated[m] were the arrows at your
command.[n] *Selah*
You split the earth with rivers.
10 The mountains saw you, and writhed;
a torrent of water swept by;
the deep gave forth its voice.
The sun[o] raised high its hands;
11 the moon[p] stood still in its exalted place,
at the light of your arrows speeding by,
at the gleam of your flashing spear.
12 In fury you trod the earth,
in anger you trampled nations.
13 You came forth to save your people,
to save your anointed.
You crushed the head of the wicked
house,
laying it bare from foundation to
roof.[n] *Selah*
14 You pierced with his own arrows the
head[q] of his warriors,[r]
who came like a whirlwind to scatter us,[s]
gloating as if ready to devour the
poor who were in hiding.
15 You trampled the sea with your horses,
churning the mighty waters.

16 I hear, and I tremble within;
my lips quiver at the sound.
Rottenness enters into my bones,
and my steps tremble[t] beneath me.
I wait quietly for the day of calamity
to come upon the people who attack us.

Trust and Joy in the Midst of Trouble

17 Though the fig tree does not blossom,
and no fruit is on the vines;
though the produce of the olive fails
and the fields yield no food;
though the flock is cut off from the fold
and there is no herd in the stalls,
18 yet I will rejoice in the LORD;
I will exult in the God of my salvation.
19 GOD, the Lord, is my strength;
he makes my feet like the feet of a
deer,
and makes me tread upon the
heights.[u]

To the leader: with stringed[v]
instruments.

[j] Gk Syr: Meaning of Heb uncertain [k] Or *against River* [l] Or *against Sea* [m] Cn: Heb *oaths* [n] Meaning of Heb uncertain [o] Heb *It* [p] Heb *sun, moon* [q] Or *leader* [r] Vg Compare Gk Syr: Meaning of Heb uncertain [s] Heb *me* [t] Cn Compare Gk: Meaning of Heb uncertain [u] Heb *my heights* [v] Heb *my stringed*

2.18 Isa 42.17; Jer 2.27,28; 10.8,14; Zech 10.2; Ps 115.4,8
2.19 Jer 2.27,28; 1 Kings 18.26-29; Jer 10.9,14; Ps 135.17
2.20 Mic 1.2; Zeph 1.7; Zech 2.13
3.2 Job 42.5,6; Ps 119.120; Jer 10.7; Ps 85.6; Isa 54.8
3.3 Am 1.12; Deut 33.2; Ps 113.4; 48.10
3.4 Ps 18.12; Job 26.14
3.5 Ex 12.29,30; Num 16.46-49
3.6 Ps 35.5; 114.1-6; Mic 5.2
3.8 Ex 7.19,20; 14.16,21; Deut 33.26; Ps 68.17
3.9 Gen 26.3; Deut 7.8; Ps 78.16; 105.41
3.10 Ps 114.1-6; 98.7,8; Ex 14.22
3.11 Josh 10.12-14; Ps 18.9,11,14
3.12 Ps 68.7; Isa 41.15; Jer 51.33
3.13 Ex 15.2; Ps 68.19,20; 110.6; Ezek 13.14
3.15 Ps 77.19; Ex 15.8
3.16 Jer 23.9; Jer 5.15
3.17 Joel 1.18; Jer 5.17
3.18 Isa 61.10; Ps 46.1-5; Isa 12.2
3.19 2 Sam 22.34; Ps 18.33; Deut 33.29

ZEPHANIAH

1 The word of the LORD that came to Zephaniah son of Cushi son of Gedaliah son of Amariah son of Hezekiah, in the days of King Josiah son of Amon of Judah.

The Coming Judgment on Judah

2 I will utterly sweep away everything
from the face of the earth, says the LORD.
3 I will sweep away humans and animals;
I will sweep away the birds of the air
and the fish of the sea.
I will make the wicked stumble.[a]
I will cut off humanity
from the face of the earth, says the LORD.
4 I will stretch out my hand against Judah,
and against all the inhabitants of Jerusalem;
and I will cut off from this place every remnant of Baal
and the name of the idolatrous priests;[b]
5 those who bow down on the roofs
to the host of the heavens;
those who bow down and swear to the LORD,
but also swear by Milcom;[c]
6 those who have turned back from following the LORD,
who have not sought the LORD or inquired of him.

7 Be silent before the Lord GOD!
For the day of the LORD is at hand;
the LORD has prepared a sacrifice,
he has consecrated his guests.
8 And on the day of the LORD's sacrifice
I will punish the officials and the king's sons
and all who dress themselves in foreign attire.
9 On that day I will punish
all who leap over the threshold,
who fill their master's house
with violence and fraud.

10 On that day, says the LORD,
a cry will be heard from the Fish Gate,
a wail from the Second Quarter,
a loud crash from the hills.
11 The inhabitants of the Mortar wail,
for all the traders have perished;
all who weigh out silver are cut off.
12 At that time I will search Jerusalem with lamps,
and I will punish the people
who rest complacently[d] on their dregs,
those who say in their hearts,
"The LORD will not do good,
nor will he do harm."
13 Their wealth shall be plundered,
and their houses laid waste.
Though they build houses,
they shall not inhabit them;
though they plant vineyards,
they shall not drink wine from them.

The Great Day of the LORD

14 The great day of the LORD is near,
near and hastening fast;
the sound of the day of the LORD is bitter,
the warrior cries aloud there.
15 That day will be a day of wrath,
a day of distress and anguish,
a day of ruin and devastation,
a day of darkness and gloom,
a day of clouds and thick darkness,
16 a day of trumpet blast and battle cry
against the fortified cities
and against the lofty battlements.

17 I will bring such distress upon people
that they shall walk like the blind;
because they have sinned against the LORD,
their blood shall be poured out like dust,
and their flesh like dung.
18 Neither their silver nor their gold
will be able to save them
on the day of the LORD's wrath;
in the fire of his passion
the whole earth shall be consumed;
for a full, a terrible end
he will make of all the inhabitants of the earth.

Judgment on Israel's Enemies

2 Gather together, gather,
O shameless nation,
2 before you are driven away
like the drifting chaff,[e]
before there comes upon you

[a] Cn: Heb *sea, and those who cause the wicked to stumble* [b] Compare Gk: Heb *the idolatrous priests with the priests* [c] Gk Mss Syr Vg: Heb *Malcam* (or, *their king*) [d] Heb *who thicken* [e] Cn Compare Gk Syr: Heb *before a decree is born; like chaff a day has passed away*

1.1 2 Kings 22.1-23,34; 21.18-26 **1.2** Ezek 33.27 **1.3** Isa 6.11,12; Jer 9.10; Ezek 7.19 **1.4** Ezek 6.14; Mic 5.13; Hos 10.5 **1.5** Jer 19.13; 5.2,7; 49.1 **1.6** Isa 1.4; Jer 2.13; Isa 9.13; Hos 7.7 **1.7** Hab 2.20; Zech 2.13; Isa 13.6; ver 14; Isa 34.6; Jer 46.10 **1.8** Isa 24.21; Jer 39.6; Isa 2.6 **1.9** Jer 5.27; Am 3.10 **1.10** Am 8.3; 2 Chr 33.14; 34.22; Ezek 6.13 **1.12** Jer 16.16,17; 48.11; Am 6.1; Ezek 8.12; 9.9 **1.13** Deut 28.30,39; Am 5.11; Mic 6.15 **1.14** Joel 2.1,11 **1.15** Isa 22.5; Jer 30.7; Am 5.18-20 **1.17** Jer 10.18; Isa 59.10; Ps 79.3; Jer 9.22 **1.18** Prov 11.4; Zeph 3.8; ver 2.3 **2.1** Joel 1.14; Jer 3.3; 6.15 **2.2** Isa 17.13; Hos 13.3; Nah 1.6; Zeph 1.18

See the Introductions, pp. 6, 54-57, and 72 above.

1.1 Introduction. *Zephaniah* means *the Lord protects,* but may derive from the name of a Canaanite god, Zephan, who was identified with Yahweh: Zephan is Yah[weh]. The claim to be the bearer of God's message (*the word of the LORD*) is typical of the claims of prophets, but the number of ancestral names mentioned is unusual, as well as the probable reference to a king, *Hezekiah,* the reforming king of Judah (715-687), whose efforts to make alliances with the Assyrians and Egyptians (2 Kings 18) were criticized by Isaiah (Isa 37). *Josiah's* reign (640-609) also involved reform efforts, which were stimulated by the discovery of a copy of the Law (2 Kings 22.3-20). **1.2-13** God's Coming Purge of Judah. **1.2-3** The cleansing activity of God will affect animals, birds, fish and humans, recalling the stories of the fall and the flood (Gen 6-8). **1.4-6** The major focus of the purge will be Judah, because of its having participated in the cult of *Baal.* Going up on house-tops, they worshiped the stars, which they regarded as deities, and *Milcom* (their king), which was the name of the chief god among the Ammonites east of the Jordan. **1.7-13** *The day of the LORD* is the coming time when God will punish his disobedient people. The victims of that judgment are here pictured symbolically as offerings being prepared for *sacrifice.* Those punished will include the royal establishment, whose members mimic the *dress* of their pagan neighbors, as well as those who perform sacred dances (*leap*) like the idolators, but are ruthless and deceitful in their dealings with others. God will seek out *with lamps* and punish those who have profited from *trade* in items of *silver* made for idol worship, as well as those in a drunken state (*on their dregs*). Their houses and vineyards, which are signs of their seeming prosperity, will be destroyed. **1.14-18** The Coming Day of the LORD. The troops and the cities will alike be destroyed, and the sinful people will lose all sense of direction (*walk like the blind*). All the inhabitants of the earth and their possessions will fall victim to the LORD's *wrath.* **2.1-15** The Ruin of Israel's Enemies. As a further warning to Judah to avoid God's *wrath* by returning to obedience and *righteousness* as a way of life, there follows a series of pronouncements of judgment on Israel's hostile neighbors: (1) vv.1-7: on the Philistine coastal cities (*Gaza, Ashkelon, Ekron*), including *the Cherethites* (Cretans, who first settled the Palestinian coast and became known as the *Philistines*); (2) vv. 8-11: on the nations east of the Jordan (*Moab, the Ammonites*), whose fate will be burning, like that of Sodom and Gomorrah (Gen 19.24-25; Am 4.11); (3) vs. 12: on *the Ethiopians*; (4) vv.13-15: on *Assyria,* as symbolized by its capital, *Nineveh,* which claimed for itself unique power and importance (*I am, and there is no one else*), but which will become a den of wild birds and animals, and an object of scorn; *cf.* the fate of Babylon as depicted in Isa 47.8-10.

3.1-7 The Destruction of Jerusalem. The failure of the city to *trust in the Lord* is matched by that of its leaders: *officials, judges, prophets, priests.* Their behavior is the opposite of what the Lord does daily in prescribing justice for the city. Instead of learning a lesson from being cut off from outside contact and experiencing ruin, the people are only *the more eager* to pursue their corrupt objectives.
3.8-13 Beyond Punishment, Renewal. God's sovereignty over the affairs of all *nations* will be evident not only through the *fire* of divine judgment, but also in the subsequent renewal which will restore the common language of humanity, which was lost at the tower of Babel (Gen 11.1-9) and will aid in the return of God's scattered people from the lands to which they have wandered. Their leadership will be purged of *the proud,* and the *remnant of Israel* will live in peace, humility and truth.

the fierce anger of the Lord,
before there comes upon you
the day of the Lord's wrath.
3 Seek the Lord, all you humble of the land,
who do his commands;
seek righteousness, seek humility;
perhaps you may be hidden
on the day of the Lord's wrath.
4 For Gaza shall be deserted,
and Ashkelon shall become a desolation;
Ashdod's people shall be driven out at noon,
and Ekron shall be uprooted.

5 Ah, inhabitants of the seacoast,
you nation of the Cherethites!
The word of the Lord is against you,
O Canaan, land of the Philistines;
and I will destroy you until no inhabitant is left.
6 And you, O seacoast, shall be pastures,
meadows for shepherds
and folds for flocks.
7 The seacoast shall become the possession
of the remnant of the house of Judah,
on which they shall pasture,
and in the houses of Ashkelon
they shall lie down at evening.
For the Lord their God will be mindful of them
and restore their fortunes.

8 I have heard the taunts of Moab
and the revilings of the Ammonites,
how they have taunted my people
and made boasts against their territory.
9 Therefore, as I live, says the Lord of hosts,
the God of Israel,
Moab shall become like Sodom
and the Ammonites like Gomorrah,
a land possessed by nettles and salt pits,
and a waste forever.
The remnant of my people shall plunder them,
and the survivors of my nation shall possess them.
10 This shall be their lot in return for their pride,
because they scoffed and boasted
against the people of the Lord of hosts.
11 The Lord will be terrible against them;
he will shrivel all the gods of the earth,
and to him shall bow down,
each in its place,
all the coasts and islands of the nations.

12 You also, O Ethiopians,[f]
shall be killed by my sword.

13 And he will stretch out his hand against the north,
and destroy Assyria;
and he will make Nineveh a desolation,
a dry waste like the desert.
14 Herds shall lie down in it,
every wild animal;[g]
the desert owl[h] and the screech owl[h]
shall lodge on its capitals;
the owl[i] shall hoot at the window,
the raven[j] croak on the threshold;
for its cedar work will be laid bare.
15 Is this the exultant city
that lived secure,
that said to itself,
"I am, and there is no one else"?
What a desolation it has become,
a lair for wild animals!
Everyone who passes by it
hisses and shakes the fist.

The Wickedness of Jerusalem

3 Ah, soiled, defiled,
oppressing city!
2 It has listened to no voice;
it has accepted no correction.
It has not trusted in the Lord;
it has not drawn near to its God.

3 The officials within it
are roaring lions;
its judges are evening wolves
that leave nothing until the morning.
4 Its prophets are reckless,
faithless persons;
its priests have profaned what is sacred,
they have done violence to the law.
5 The Lord within it is righteous;
he does no wrong.
Every morning he renders his judgment,
each dawn without fail;
but the unjust knows no shame.

[f] Or *Nubians;* Heb *Cushites* [g] Tg Compare Gk: Heb *nation* [h] Meaning of Heb uncertain [i] Cn: Heb *a voice* [j] Gk Vg: Heb *desolation*

2.3 Am 5.6; Ps 76.9; Am 5.14,15; Ps 57.1
2.4 Am 1.7,8; Zech 9.5-7
2.5 Ezek 25.16; Am 3.1; Isa 14.29-31; Zeph 3.6
2.6 Isa 17.2
2.7 Mic 4.7; Isa 32.14; Ps 80.14; Lk 1.68; Ps 126.1,4
2.8 Ezek 25.3,6,8; Jer 49.1
2.9 Isa 15.1-16; 14; Am 1.13; Deut 29.23; Isa 11.14
2.10 Isa 16.6; Jer 48.29; ver 8
2.11 Joel 2.11; Zeph 1.4; 3.9; Mal 1.11; Isa 24.15
2.12 Isa 18.1
2.13 Isa 14.26; 10.12; Nah 3.7
2.14 ver 6; Isa 13.21; 34.11,14; Jer 22.14
2.15 Isa 22.2; 47.8; 32.14; Jer 18.16; 19.8
3.1 Jer 5.23; Ezek 23.30; Jer 6.6
3.2 Jer 22.21; 5.3; Ps 78.22; 73.28
3.3 Ezek 22.27; Hab 1.8
3.4 Hos 9.7; Ezek 22.26
3.5 ver 15,17; Deut 32.4; Jer 3.3

6 I have cut off nations;
their battlements are in ruins;
I have laid waste their streets
so that no one walks in them;
their cities have been made desolate,
without people, without inhabitants.
7 I said, "Surely the city[k] will fear me,
it will accept correction;
it will not lose sight[l]
of all that I have brought upon it."
But they were the more eager
to make all their deeds corrupt.

Punishment and Conversion of the Nations

8 Therefore wait for me, says the LORD,
for the day when I arise as a witness.
For my decision is to gather nations,
to assemble kingdoms,
to pour out upon them my indignation,
all the heat of my anger;
for in the fire of my passion
all the earth shall be consumed.

9 At that time I will change the speech of the peoples
to a pure speech,
that all of them may call on the name of the LORD
and serve him with one accord.
10 From beyond the rivers of Ethiopia[m]
my suppliants, my scattered ones,
shall bring my offering.

11 On that day you shall not be put to shame
because of all the deeds by which you have rebelled against me;
for then I will remove from your midst
your proudly exultant ones,
and you shall no longer be haughty
in my holy mountain.
12 For I will leave in the midst of you
a people humble and lowly.
They shall seek refuge in the name of the LORD—
13 the remnant of Israel;
they shall do no wrong
and utter no lies,
nor shall a deceitful tongue
be found in their mouths.
Then they will pasture and lie down,
and no one shall make them afraid.

A Song of Joy

14 Sing aloud, O daughter Zion;
shout, O Israel!
Rejoice and exult with all your heart,
O daughter Jerusalem!
15 The LORD has taken away the judgments against you,
he has turned away your enemies.
The king of Israel, the LORD, is in your midst;
you shall fear disaster no more.
16 On that day it shall be said to Jerusalem:
Do not fear, O Zion;
do not let your hands grow weak.
17 The LORD, your God, is in your midst,
a warrior who gives victory;
he will rejoice over you with gladness,
he will renew you[n] in his love;
he will exult over you with loud singing
18 as on a day of festival.[o]
I will remove disaster from you,[p]
so that you will not bear reproach for it.
19 I will deal with all your oppressors
at that time.
And I will save the lame
and gather the outcast,
and I will change their shame into praise
and renown in all the earth.
20 At that time I will bring you home,
at the time when I gather you;
for I will make you renowned and praised
among all the peoples of the earth,
when I restore your fortunes
before your eyes, says the LORD.

3.14-20 Zion's Song of Rejoicing. Israel's *enemies* will be defeated and the nation will no more be threatened with *disaster*. God will be present as *king* in their midst, her *oppressors* will be overcome, and the renewed people – including the *lame* and the *outcast* – will share in the joy and honor of God's people *among the nations of the earth*.

3.6 Zeph 1.16; Isa 6.11; Zeph 2.5
3.7 ver 2; Jer 7.7; Hos 9.9
3.8 Ps 27.14; Zeph 2.2; Joel 3.2; Zeph 1.18
3.9 Isa 19.18; Ps 22.27; Zeph 2.11
3.10 Ps 68.31; Isa 18.1,7; 60.6,7
3.11 Isa 45.17; Joel 2.26,27; Isa 2.12; 5.15; Ezek 20.40
3.12 Isa 14.32; Nah 1.7
3.13 Mic 4.7; Isa 60.21; Zech 8.3,16; Rev 14.5; Ezek 34.28; Mic 4.4
3.14 Isa 12.6; Zech 2.10
3.15 Ezek 37.26-28; ver 5; Isa 54.14
3.16 Isa 35.3,4; Heb 12.12
3.17 ver 5,15; Isa 63.1; 62.5
3.19 Isa 60.14; Ezek 34.16; Mic 4.6,7
3.20 Ezek 37.12,21; Isa 56.5; 66.22; Zeph 2.7

[k] Heb *it* [l] Gk Syr: Heb *its dwelling will not be cut off* [m] Or *Nubia*; Heb *Cush* [n] Gk Syr: Heb *he will be silent* [o] Gk Syr: Meaning of Heb uncertain [p] Cn: Heb *I will remove from you; they were*

HAGGAI

See the Introductions, pp. 6, 54-57, and 73 above.

1.1-2 Introduction. *The second year of King Darius*, following his taking power in the Persian empire, was 520. *Zerubbabel*, in spite of his Babylonian name, is pictured as a Jew who returned to Judah from exile as Persian-appointed *governor* (Ezra 2.2) and was descended from David (1 Chr 3.1-19). *Joshua* is in the line of descent of the high priests (1 Chr 6.14-15).
1.3-11 The Plight of Judah. The reason that the people of Judah are living at the subsistence level is that they have been interested chiefly in building their own houses, while neglecting to *build the house* of the LORD, which has lain *in ruins* since its destruction by the Babylonians in 587. Their situation will become worse, including drought and famine.
1.12-15 Construction of the Temple Begun. There are to be three modes of leadership for Judah: the governor, Zerubbabel; the high priest, Joshua; and the prophet, Haggai. The faithful remnant of the people rally to support the project, and the work is begun.
2.1-9 Encouragement about the Future Splendor of the Temple. As construction began, those who had seen the glory of the earlier temple were disappointed with the modest new beginnings, but were reassured that the gifts that would come from all over creation and from *all the nations* (Isa 60.6) would result in a temple that would surpass in beauty that of Solomon.
2.10-19 The parallel is drawn between the ritual impurity that results from physical contact with an unclean object (*meat, food*) and the people's association with other deities. Unless the altar and worship in the temple are pure, there will be no recovery of prosperity. Yet the possibility of full renewal has existed since the first *stone was placed* to rebuild the temple

The Command to Rebuild the Temple

1 In the second year of King Darius, in the sixth month, on the first day of the month, the word of the LORD came by the prophet Haggai to Zerubbabel son of Shealtiel, governor of Judah, and to Joshua son of Jehozadak, the high priest: [2]Thus says the LORD of hosts: These people say the time has not yet come to rebuild the LORD's house. [3]Then the word of the LORD came by the prophet Haggai, saying: [4]Is it a time for you yourselves to live in your paneled houses, while this house lies in ruins? [5]Now therefore thus says the LORD of hosts: Consider how you have fared. [6]You have sown much, and harvested little; you eat, but you never have enough; you drink, but you never have your fill; you clothe yourselves, but no one is warm; and you that earn wages earn wages to put them into a bag with holes.

7 Thus says the LORD of hosts: Consider how you have fared. [8]Go up to the hills and bring wood and build the house, so that I may take pleasure in it and be honored, says the LORD. [9]You have looked for much, and, lo, it came to little; and when you brought it home, I blew it away. Why? says the LORD of hosts. Because my house lies in ruins, while all of you hurry off to your own houses. [10]Therefore the heavens above you have withheld the dew, and the earth has withheld its produce. [11]And I have called for a drought on the land and the hills, on the grain, the new wine, the oil, on what the soil produces, on human beings and animals, and on all their labors.

12 Then Zerubbabel son of Shealtiel, and Joshua son of Jehozadak, the high priest, with all the remnant of the people, obeyed the voice of the LORD their God, and the words of the prophet Haggai, as the LORD their God had sent him; and the people feared the LORD. [13]Then Haggai, the messenger of the LORD, spoke to the people with the LORD's message, saying, I am with you, says the LORD. [14]And the LORD stirred up the spirit of Zerubbabel son of Shealtiel, governor of Judah, and the spirit of Joshua son of Jehozadak, the high priest, and the spirit of all the remnant of the people; and they came and worked on the house of the LORD of hosts, their God, [15]on the twenty-fourth day of the month, in the sixth month.

The Future Glory of the Temple

2 In the second year of King Darius, [1]in the seventh month, on the twenty-first day of the month, the word of the LORD came by the prophet Haggai, saying: [2]Speak now to Zerubbabel son of Shealtiel, governor of Judah, and to Joshua son of Jehozadak, the high priest, and to the remnant of the people, and say, [3]Who is left among you that saw this house in its former glory? How does it look to you now? Is it not in your sight as nothing? [4]Yet now take courage, O Zerubbabel, says the LORD; take courage, O Joshua, son of Jehozadak, the high priest; take courage, all you people of the land, says the LORD; work, for I am with you, says the LORD of hosts, [5]according to the promise that I made you when you came out of Egypt. My spirit abides among you; do not fear. [6]For thus says the LORD of hosts: Once again, in a little while, I will shake the heavens and the earth and the sea and the dry land; [7]and I will shake all the nations, so that the treasure of all nations shall come, and I will fill this house with splendor, says the LORD of hosts. [8]The silver is mine, and the gold is mine, says the LORD of hosts. [9]The latter splendor of this house shall be greater than the former, says the LORD of hosts; and in this place I will give prosperity, says the LORD of hosts.

A Rebuke and a Promise

10 On the twenty-fourth day of the ninth month, in the second year of Darius, the word of the LORD came by the prophet Haggai, saying: [11]Thus says the LORD of hosts: Ask the priests for a ruling: [12]If one carries consecrated meat in the fold of one's garment, and with the fold touches bread, or stew, or wine, or oil, or any kind of food, does it become holy? The priests answered, "No." [13]Then Haggai said, "If one who is unclean by contact with a dead body touches any of these, does it become unclean?" The priests answered, "Yes, it becomes unclean." [14]Haggai then said, So is it with this people, and with this nation before me, says the LORD; and so with every work of their hands; and what they offer there is unclean. [15]But now, consider what will come to pass from

1.1 Zech 1.1; 1 Chr 3.17; Ezra 3.2; Zech 6.11
1.4 2 Sam 7.2; ver 9
1.5 Lam 3.40
1.6 Deut 28.38; Mic 6.14; Zech 8.10
1.8 Ezra 3.7; Ps 132.13,14; Hag 2.7,9
1.9 ver 6; Isa 40.7
1.10 Lev 26.19; Deut 28.23; 1 Kings 8.35
1.11 Mal 3.9-11; Deut 28.22; Hag 2.17
1.12 Hag 2.2; Isa 1.19; 50.10
1.13 Mal 2.7; 3.1; Mt 28.30; Rom 8.31
1.14 2 Chr 36.22; Ezra 1.1; 5.2,8
2.3 Ezra 3.12; Zech 4.10
2.4 Zech 8.9; Acts 7.9
2.5 Ex 29.45,46; Neh 9.20; Isa 63.11,14
2.6 Heb 12.26; Isa 10.25; 29.17; ver 21
2.7 Dan 2.44; Isa 60.4-9
2.9 Isa 66.12; Zech 2.5
2.11 Lev 10.10; Deut 33.10; Mal 2.7
2.12 Ezek 44.19; Mt 23.19
2.13 Num 19.11,22
2.14 Prov 15.8; Isa 1.11-15
2.15 Hag 1.5; Ezra 3.10; 4.24

2.16 Hag 1.6,9; Zech 8.10
2.17 1 Kings 8.37; Am 4.9; Isa 9.13
2.18 Zech 8.9
2.21 Hag 1.14; Zech 4.6-10; Heb 12.26
2.22 Dan 2.44; Mic 5.10; Zech 4.6; 2 Chr 20.23
2.23 Song 8.6; Jer 22.24; Isa 42.1; 43.10

this day on. Before a stone was placed upon a stone in the LORD's temple, [16]how did you fare?[a] When one came to a heap of twenty measures, there were but ten; when one came to the wine vat to draw fifty measures, there were but twenty. [17]I struck you and all the products of your toil with blight and mildew and hail; yet you did not return to me, says the LORD. [18]Consider from this day on, from the twenty-fourth day of the ninth month. Since the day that the foundation of the LORD's temple was laid, consider: [19]Is there any seed left in the barn? Do the vine, the fig tree, the pomegranate, and the olive tree still yield nothing? From this day on I will bless you.

God's Promise to Zerubbabel

20 The word of the LORD came a second time to Haggai on the twenty-fourth day of the month: [21]Speak to Zerubbabel, governor of Judah, saying, I am about to shake the heavens and the earth, [22]and to overthrow the throne of kingdoms; I am about to destroy the strength of the kingdoms of the nations, and overthrow the chariots and their riders; and the horses and their riders shall fall, every one by the sword of a comrade. [23]On that day, says the LORD of hosts, I will take you, O Zerubbabel my servant, son of Shealtiel, says the LORD, and make you like a signet ring; for I have chosen you, says the LORD of hosts.

[a] Gk: Heb *since they were*

2.20-23 *Zerubbabel,* the governor, is promised that God will overthrow the power of the surrounding nations and that members of their armies will kill each other. He will become the symbol and agent (*signet ring*) of God's authority over this renewed people, because God has *chosen* him for this role.

ZECHARIAH

1.1 Ezra 4.24; Hag 1.1; Neh 12.4,16
1.3 Isa 31.6; Mal 3.7; Jas 4.8
1.4 2 Chr 36.15; Hos 14.1; Jer 6.17; 11.7,8
1.6 Jer 12.16,17; Lam 2.17
1.8 Josh 5.13; Rev 6.4; Zech 6.2-7
1.9 Zech 2.3; 4.5
1.10 Heb 1.14
1.11 Isa 14.7
1.12 Hab 1.2; Dan 9.2
1.13 Zech 4.1; Isa 40.1,2
1.14 Zech 8.2
1.15 Ps 123.4; Am 1.11

Israel Urged to Repent

1 In the eighth month, in the second year of Darius, the word of the LORD came to the prophet Zechariah son of Berechiah son of Iddo, saying: [2]The LORD was very angry with your ancestors. [3]Therefore say to them, Thus says the LORD of hosts: Return to me, says the LORD of hosts, and I will return to you, says the LORD of hosts. [4]Do not be like your ancestors, to whom the former prophets proclaimed, "Thus says the LORD of hosts, Return from your evil ways and from your evil deeds." But they did not hear or heed me, says the LORD. [5]Your ancestors, where are they? And the prophets, do they live forever? [6]But my words and my statutes, which I commanded my servants the prophets, did they not overtake your ancestors? So they repented and said, "The LORD of hosts has dealt with us according to our ways and deeds, just as he planned to do."

First Vision: The Horsemen

7 On the twenty-fourth day of the eleventh month, the month of Shebat, in the second year of Darius, the word of the LORD came to the prophet Zechariah son of Berechiah son of Iddo; and Zechariah[a] said, [8]In the night I saw a man riding on a red horse! He was standing among the myrtle trees in the glen; and behind him were red, sorrel, and white horses. [9]Then I said, "What are these, my lord?" The angel who talked with me said to me, "I will show you what they are." [10]So the man who was standing among the myrtle trees answered, "They are those whom the LORD has sent to patrol the earth." [11]Then they spoke to the angel of the LORD who was standing among the myrtle trees, "We have patrolled the earth, and lo, the whole earth remains at peace." [12]Then the angel of the LORD said, "O LORD of hosts, how long will you withhold mercy from Jerusalem and the cities of Judah, with which you have been angry these seventy years?" [13]Then the LORD replied with gracious and comforting words to the angel who talked with me. [14]So the angel who talked with me said to me, Proclaim this message: Thus says the LORD of hosts; I am very jealous for Jerusalem and for Zion. [15]And I am extremely angry with the nations that are at ease; for while I was only a little angry, they made the disaster worse.

[a] Heb *and he*

See the Introductions, pp. 6, 54-57, and 73-75 above.

1.1-6 Prologue. The date of the beginning of Zechariah's prophetic activity corresponds to the year 521 and follows by two months that of Haggai (Hag 1.1). The prophet's ancestry, *son of Berechiah son of Iddo,* differs from that in Ezra 5.1; 6.14, where he is *son of Iddo.* He may have been among the people of Judah exiled to Babylon, or among those who remained in the land. God's *anger* was aimed at the disobedient *ancestors* whom he sent into exile. Now they are called to *return* to their land in an obedient relationship to *the LORD of Hosts,* but the exiles died in the interim between the exile in 586 and the permission for the Judahites to return granted in 521 by Darius of Persia, ruler of what was Babylonia. The *ancestors* in Babylonia had come to realize that it was their violations of *the words and statutes* of God that had led him to *plan* their expulsion from their land.

1.7-17 The First Vision: The Horsemen.

1.7 The date – in the second year of Darius' reign – matches the year given in Haggai 1.1, but is two months later than Haggai's visions (2.18,20-23) of God shattering the cosmic and political order of the Persian empire – which did not occur.

1.8-11 The horses and riders in the grove of trees are interpreted by the unidentified *man* among them as having completed their *patrol* and found all the *earth at peace.* This reflects Darius' successful suppression of many revolts at the outset of his reign.

1.12-17 *The angel of the LORD* explains that the cities of Judah have been subjected to God's wrath for *seventy years,* as predicted in Jer 25.11-13; 29.10. The punishment of *Babylon* had already taken place when the Persians seized the empire. The new promise is of *prosperity* for *Zion* and *Jerusalem.*

16 Therefore, thus says the LORD, I have returned to Jerusalem with compassion; my
house shall be built in it, says the LORD of
hosts, and the measuring line shall be
stretched out over Jerusalem. 17 Proclaim
further: Thus says the LORD of hosts: My
cities shall again overflow with prosperity;
the LORD will again comfort Zion and again
choose Jerusalem.

Second Vision: The Horns and the Smiths

18[b] And I looked up and saw four horns.
19 I asked the angel who talked with me,
"What are these?" And he answered me,
"These are the horns that have scattered
Judah, Israel, and Jerusalem." 20 Then the
LORD showed me four blacksmiths. 21 And I
asked, "What are they coming to do?" He
answered, "These are the horns that scattered Judah, so that no head could be raised;
but these have come to terrify them, to
strike down the horns of the nations that
lifted up their horns against the land of
Judah to scatter its people."[c]

Third Vision: The Man with a Measuring Line

2[d] I looked up and saw a man with a
measuring line in his hand. 2 Then I
asked, "Where are you going?" He answered
me, "To measure Jerusalem, to see what is
its width and what is its length." 3 Then the
angel who talked with me came forward,
and another angel came forward to meet
him, 4 and said to him, "Run, say to that
young man: Jerusalem shall be inhabited
like villages without walls, because of the
multitude of people and animals in it. 5 For
I will be a wall of fire all around it, says the
LORD, and I will be the glory within it."

Interlude: An Appeal to the Exiles

6 Up, up! Flee from the land of the north,
says the LORD; for I have spread you abroad
like the four winds of heaven, says the LORD.
7 Up! Escape to Zion, you that live with
daughter Babylon. 8 For thus said the LORD
of hosts (after his glory[e] sent me) regarding
the nations that plundered you: Truly, one
who touches you touches the apple of my
eye.[f] 9 See now, I am going to raise[g] my
hand against them, and they shall become
plunder for their own slaves. Then you will
know that the LORD of hosts has sent me.
10 Sing and rejoice, O daughter Zion! For lo,
I will come and dwell in your midst, says
the LORD. 11 Many nations shall join themselves to the LORD on that day, and shall be
my people; and I will dwell in your midst.
And you shall know that the LORD of hosts
has sent me to you. 12 The LORD will inherit
Judah as his portion in the holy land, and
will again choose Jerusalem.

13 Be silent, all people, before the LORD;
for he has roused himself from his holy
dwelling.

Fourth Vision: Joshua and Satan

3 Then he showed me the high priest
Joshua standing before the angel of
the LORD, and Satan[h] standing at his right
hand to accuse him. 2 And the LORD said to
Satan,[h] "The LORD rebuke you, O Satan![h]
The LORD who has chosen Jerusalem rebuke
you! Is not this man a brand plucked from
the fire?" 3 Now Joshua was dressed with
filthy clothes as he stood before the angel.
4 The angel said to those who were standing
before him, "Take off his filthy clothes."
And to him he said, "See, I have taken your
guilt away from you, and I will clothe you
with festal apparel." 5 And I said, "Let them
put a clean turban on his head." So they
put a clean turban on his head and clothed
him with the apparel; and the angel of the
LORD was standing by.

6 Then the angel of the LORD assured
Joshua, saying 7 "Thus says the LORD of hosts:
If you will walk in my ways and keep my
requirements, then you shall rule my house
and have charge of my courts, and I will
give you the right of access among those
who are standing here. 8 Now listen, Joshua,
high priest, you and your colleagues who
sit before you! For they are an omen of
things to come: I am going to bring my
servant the Branch. 9 For on the stone that
I have set before Joshua, on a single stone
with seven facets, I will engrave its inscription, says the LORD of hosts, and I will
remove the guilt of this land in a single day.
10 On that day, says the LORD of hosts, you
shall invite each other to come under your
vine and fig tree."

[b] Ch 2.1 in Heb [c] Heb *it* [d] Ch 2.5 in Heb [e] Cn: Heb *after glory he* [f] Heb *his eye* [g] Or *wave* [h] Or *the Accuser*; Heb *the Adversary*

1.18-21 The Second Vision: The Horns and the Blacksmiths. The *horns* are frequently used symbols of the power of hostile nations, as in Deut 33.17 (Moab). *Judah and Jerusalem*, as well as *Israel*, have been *scattered* into the wider world by these Gentile powers, but God has his own strong weapons, symbolized by the *blacksmiths*, which will *strike down* the hostile nations.
2.1-5 The Third Vision: The Man with the Measuring Line. The man who is about to measure the dimensions of Jerusalem in preparation for its rebuilding is told that it will have no walls because (1) the number of people and animals in it will exceed any limits set by walls, and (2) God himself will protect the city like *a wall of fire around it*. As in the temple of old, God's *glory* will reside in Jerusalem, which indicates that the temple will be rebuilt.
2.6-13 Appeals and Promises Concerning the Exiles' Return to Zion.
2.6-9 God's people are now scattered to *the four winds*, but they are to *flee* from Babylonia (*the land of the north*; Jer 6.22; 16.15; 31.8). The nations that *plundered* God's favorite people (*the apple of my eye*) are now to be plundered by those whom they oppressed, which will show God's support for his own.
2.10-13 The restoration of Judah and Jerusalem will include the dwelling of God *in their midst*, and the conversion of *many nations* who will become members of God's *people*, as in Isa 56.6-7. From that *holy dwelling* comes a solemn warning that God is setting things right for his people and punishing the hostile nations, as in Hab 2.20 and Zeph 2.1-15.
3.1-10 The Fourth Vision: Vindication and Purification of the High Priest and the Promise of the Branch. Like Job 1, this scene takes place in the presence of the (*angel of the*) LORD, with *Satan* in his role as accuser.
3.1-2 The LORD *rebukes* Satan, speaking the commanding word which brings him under control (as in the Jesus tradition; Mk 3.11-27; Lk 11.14-23), and thereby saves the attacked priest from the judgment *fire*.
3.3-5 The target of Satan's accusation is *Joshua*, whose father (Jehozadak) and grandfather (Seraiah) preceded him in this post, with the former exiled to Babylon in 587 (1 Chr 6.14-15) and the latter executed by the Babylonians (2 Kings 25.18-21). Joshua's *filthy clothes* symbolize the corrupting of God's people that took place during the exile in Babylon. His *festal apparel* and his *turban* (not the ordinary term for the priestly headdress, but one implying royal status, as in Ezek 21.25-26) indicate that the cultic establishment in Jerusalem will be purified, and suggest the special role of the priest when Israel has no king.
3.6-10 If Joshua and the people obey God's *ways* and *requirements*, this high priest will *rule* and have *access* to God's presence in the temple as well as to the heavenly court, represented by *those standing here*. In addition, the establishment of a royal leader is indicated by *the Branch* (Isa 11.1; Jer 23.5) who is God's *servant*, a title often linked with David as king in the Psalms (78.70; 89.3; 132.10; 144.10) and the prophets (Ezek 34.27; 37.24-26). The priest's role is indicated by the precious *stone with seven facets*, which recalls the engraving fastened on the priest's turban in Ex 28.36-38. The inscription, Holiness to the Lord, served to purify God's covenant people.

1.16 Isa 54.8; Zech 2.1,2.10
1.17 Isa 44.26; 51.3; Zech 2.12; 3.2
1.21 Ps 75.10
2.1 Zech 1.18; Ezek 40.3
2.2 Ezek 40.3; Rev 21.15-17
2.4 Ezek 38.11; Jer 30.19
2.5 Isa 26.1; Zech 9.8; Rev 21.23
2.6 Isa 48.20; Jer 1.14; Ezek 17.21
2.8 Isa 60.7-9; Deut 30.10
2.9 Isa 11.15; Zech 4.9
2.10 Isa 12.6; Zeph 3.14; Lev 26.12; Ezek 37.27
2.12 Deut 32.9; Zech 1.17
2.13 Hab 2.20; Ps 78.65; Isa 51.9
3.1 Hag 1.1; Ps 109.6
3.2 Jude 9.23; Am 4.11
3.4 Isa 43.25; Rev 19.8
3.5 Ex 29.6
3.7 1 Kings 3.14; Ezek 44.16; Deut 17.9; Zech 4.14
3.8 Isa 20.3; Ezek 12.11; Isa 4.2; 53.2; Jer 33.15
3.9 Isa 28.16; Zech 4.10; Jer 31.34; Mic 7.18
3.10 1 Kings 4.25; Isa 36.16

Fifth Vision: The Lampstand and Olive Trees

4 The angel who talked with me came again, and wakened me, as one is wakened from sleep. 2 He said to me, "What do you see?" And I said, "I see a lampstand all of gold, with a bowl on the top of it; there are seven lamps on it, with seven lips on each of the lamps that are on the top of it. 3 And by it there are two olive trees, one on the right of the bowl and the other on its left." 4 I said to the angel who talked with me, "What are these, my lord?" 5 Then the angel who talked with me answered me, "Do you not know what these are?" I said, "No, my lord." 6 He said to me, "This is the word of the LORD to Zerubbabel: Not by might, nor by power, but by my spirit, says the LORD of hosts. 7 What are you, O great mountain? Before Zerubbabel you shall become a plain; and he shall bring out the top stone amid shouts of 'Grace, grace to it!' "

8 Moreover the word of the LORD came to me, saying, 9 "The hands of Zerubbabel have laid the foundation of this house; his hands shall also complete it. Then you will know that the LORD of hosts has sent me to you. 10 For whoever has despised the day of small things shall rejoice, and shall see the plummet in the hand of Zerubbabel.

"These seven are the eyes of the LORD, which range through the whole earth." 11 Then I said to him, "What are these two olive trees on the right and the left of the lampstand?" 12 And a second time I said to him, "What are these two branches of the olive trees, which pour out the oil[i] through the two golden pipes?" 13 He said to me, "Do you not know what these are?" I said, "No, my lord." 14 Then he said, "These are the two anointed ones who stand by the Lord of the whole earth."

Sixth Vision: The Flying Scroll

5 Again I looked up and saw a flying scroll. 2 And he said to me, "What do you see?" I answered, "I see a flying scroll; its length is twenty cubits, and its width ten cubits." 3 Then he said to me, "This is the curse that goes out over the face of the whole land; for everyone who steals shall be cut off according to the writing on one side, and everyone who swears falsely[j] shall be cut off according to the writing on the other side. 4 I have sent it out, says the LORD of hosts, and it shall enter the house of the thief, and the house of anyone who swears falsely by my name; and it shall abide in that house and consume it, both timber and stones."

Seventh Vision: The Woman in a Basket

5 Then the angel who talked with me came forward and said to me, "Look up and see what this is that is coming out." 6 I said, "What is it?" He said, "This is a basket[k] coming out." And he said, "This is their iniquity[l] in all the land." 7 Then a leaden cover was lifted, and there was a woman sitting in the basket![k] 8 And he said, "This is Wickedness." So he thrust her back into the basket,[k] and pressed the leaden weight down on its mouth. 9 Then I looked up and saw two women coming forward. The wind was in their wings; they had wings like the wings of a stork, and they lifted up the basket[k] between earth and sky. 10 Then I said to the angel who talked with me, "Where are they taking the basket?"[k] 11 He said to me, "To the land of Shinar, to build a house for it; and when this is prepared, they will set the basket[k] down there on its base."

Eighth Vision: Four Chariots

6 And again I looked up and saw four chariots coming out from between two mountains—mountains of bronze. 2 The first chariot had red horses, the second chariot black horses, 3 the third chariot white horses, and the fourth chariot dappled gray[m] horses. 4 Then I said to the angel who talked with me, "What are these, my lord?" 5 The angel answered me, "These are the four winds[n] of heaven going out, after presenting themselves before the LORD of all the earth. 6 The chariot with the black horses goes toward the north country, the white ones go toward the west country,[o] and the dappled ones go toward the south country." 7 When the steeds came out, they were impatient to get off and patrol the earth. And he said, "Go, patrol the earth." So they patrolled the earth. 8 Then he cried out to me, "Lo, those who go toward the north country have set my spirit at rest in the north country."

[i] Cn: Heb *gold* [j] The word *falsely* added from verse 4 [k] Heb *ephah* [l] Gk Compare Syr: Heb *their eye* [m] Compare Gk: Meaning of Heb uncertain [n] Or *spirits* [o] Cn: Heb *go after them*

4.1-14 The Fifth Vision: The Lampstand and the Two Olive Trees.

4.1-3 This elaborate version of the seven-branched lampstand, known as the *menorah*, has a reservoir (*bowl*) at the top, and *seven lips* on each lamp where the flame burns. In the restored temple this would replace the space above the ark of the covenant (destroyed in 586) where the radiant cloud of glory showed the presence of God. Here the multiple manifestations of light symbolize God's surveillance of the whole earth (4.10b). The meaning of the *two olive trees* is supplied in vv. 11-14.

4.4-10 The prophet is puzzled by what he sees, but the intended recipient of this vision is *Zerubbabel*, who has a Babylonian name, but who is a descendant of David (1 Chr 3.17-19) and who returned from Babylon to Judah as *governor* (Ezra 2.2; 3.2). This arrangement increased the esteem of the people of Judah for the Persian rulers, just as Cyrus was called *God's anointed* (Isa 45.1). The new ruler's sole resource will be God's *spirit*, through which obstacles will be overcome and the divine purpose will be accomplished in the laying of the foundation of the temple (*this house*). The term translated *plummet* could be either a builder's tool or a memorial tablet to be embedded in the newly-laid foundation.

4.11-14 The answer to the repeated question about the two trees and the olive oil which flows from them does not concern the source of light for the lamps, but the supply of oil by which the omnipotent God anointed these two, priest and king, to rule and guide his people.

5.1-4 The Sixth Vision: The Flying Scroll. Measuring about fifteen by forty-five feet, the rolled-up document is a record of God's decree of judgment on all who violate his covenant (Deut 29.20-21) and on their property, including even *houses* of *stone*.

5.5-11.The Woman in a Basket. The container (in Hebrew, *ephah*) recalls other warnings of God's judgment recorded in the law (Lev 19.37; Deut 25.16) and the prophets (Am 8.5; Ezek 45.10; Mic 6.11), but here container and contents (*Wickedness*) are to be taken back to *Shinar*, where human pride first perverted society by the attempt to build a tower that would reach up to God (Gen 11.1-9). A new structure will house Wickedness there.

6.1-8 The Eighth Vision: The Four Chariots. As in Jer 4.12-13, Ps 68.17 and Deut 33.26-27, the LORD is pictured as flying in a chariot, leading his armies in triumph over Israel's enemies. The scope of the control these chariots achieve extends to the four corners of the earth. As a result, the LORD is *at rest* concerning the accomplishment of his purpose *in the north country*, which is Babylon.

4.1 Zech 1.9; 2.3; Dan 8.18
4.2 Ex 25.31; Rev 1.12; Ex 25.37; Rev 4.5
4.3 Rev 11.4
4.6 Hag 2.4,5; Hos 1.7; Eph 6.17
4.7 Jer 52.25; Ps 118.22; Ezra 3.10,11
4.9 Ezra 3.10; 6.15; Zech 2.9,11; 6.15; Isa 48.16; Zech 2.8
4.10 Hag 2.3; Zech 3.9; Rev 8.2; Zech 1.10
4.14 Rev 11.4; Zech 3.1-7; Mic 4.13
5.1 Ezek 2.9
5.3 Jer 26.6; Ex 20.15; Mal 3.8,9; ver 4
5.4 Mal 3.5; Hos 4.2,3; Lev 14.45; Hab 2.9-11
5.8 Hos 12.7; Am 8.5; Mic 6.11
5.11 Jer 29.5,28; Gen 10.10
6.2 Rev 6.4,5
6.3 Rev 6.2
6.5 Jer 49.36; Ezek 37.9; Mt 24.31; Rev 7.1
6.6 Jer 1.14; Ezek 1.4; Dan 11.5
6.8 Ezek 5.13

6.9-15 The Branch is to be Crowned. Precious metal is to be collected from four former exiles (otherwise unknown), and from it is to be made a *crown* to be placed *on the head of the high priest Joshua*. The Hebrew reads, *crowns*, which may indicate one for the priest and one for the future king, who is identified as *the Branch* (*cf.* 3.8), and whose rule will be coordinated with that of the priest in *peaceful understanding*. Both crowns are to remain in the temple until the great day of coronation arrives. The builders of the temple will come from *far off* to aid the construction, which will confirm that the prophet's message was from the LORD – so long as the people are obedient to his will.
7.1-14 The People's Hypocrisy and Disobedience Exposed.
7.1 Two years after the initial visions of the prophet (1.1), another message from *the LORD* comes to him.
7.2-7 *People of Bethel* could refer to the site of an important sanctuary in Israel from the time of Abraham (Gen 12.8) to Jeroboam (1 Kings 12.29-33), or it could be part of a proper name, *Bethel-sharezer*. The messengers ask whether the people should continue to observe the fast *in the fifth month* commemorating the fall of Jerusalem to the Babylonians in 586. The other fast, in the *seventh* month, recalled the murder of Gedaliah, the governor of Judah appointed by the Babylonians (Jer 41.1-3). The response is that Judah had fasted *seventy years* (Jer 29.10) to gratify the people's own religious impulses but had taken no steps toward renewal of commitment to the covenant, even though the *words* of the LORD have been continually warning them through the prophets of the consequences of their characteristic disobedience.
7.8-14 What is required of Judah is renewal of moral responsibility and gracious concern for the members of the community. What led to God's not heeding their call as the disasters fell and to their being scattered was their own moral failure.
8.1-23 God Renews his Promises to his People.
8.1-8 God's *jealous* (or zealous) purpose for *Jerusalem* is to restore its holiness and its inhabitants, who will include the very old and little children, brought from *east and west* to live in the holy city in fidelity and obedience.
8.9-23 The discouraging prospects in the impoverished city as rebuilding the temple begins will be replaced by peace and prosperity. Judah and Israel – here addressed as one – and their God will be sought after by the other nations rather than scorned. People from all language groups will follow the Jews returning to Jerusalem and there will seek *favor with the LORD*.

The Coronation of the Branch

9 The word of the LORD came to me:
[10]Collect silver and gold[p] from the exiles—
from Heldai, Tobijah, and Jedaiah—who
have arrived from Babylon; and go the
same day to the house of Josiah son of
Zephaniah. [11]Take the silver and gold and
make a crown,[q] and set it on the head of
the high priest Joshua son of Jehozadak;
[12]say to him: Thus says the LORD of hosts:
Here is a man whose name is Branch: for
he shall branch out in his place, and he
shall build the temple of the LORD. [13]It is he
that shall build the temple of the LORD; he
shall bear royal honor, and shall sit and
rule on his throne. There shall be a priest
by his throne, with peaceful understanding
between the two of them. [14]And the crown[r]
shall be in the care of Heldai,[s] Tobijah,
Jedaiah, and Josiah[t] son of Zephaniah, as a
memorial in the temple of the LORD.
15 Those who are far off shall come and
help to build the temple of the LORD; and
you shall know that the LORD of hosts has
sent me to you. This will happen if you
diligently obey the voice of the LORD your
God.

Hypocritical Fasting Condemned

7 In the fourth year of King Darius, the
word of the LORD came to Zechariah
on the fourth day of the ninth month,
which is Chislev. [2]Now the people of Bethel
had sent Sharezer and Regem-melech and
their men, to entreat the favor of the LORD,
[3]and to ask the priests of the house of the
LORD of hosts and the prophets, "Should I
mourn and practice abstinence in the fifth
month, as I have done for so many years?"
[4]Then the word of the LORD of hosts came
to me: [5]Say to all the people of the land and
the priests: When you fasted and lamented
in the fifth month and in the seventh, for
these seventy years, was it for me that you
fasted? [6]And when you eat and when you
drink, do you not eat and drink only for
yourselves? [7]Were not these the words that
the LORD proclaimed by the former prophets,
when Jerusalem was inhabited and in prosperity, along with the towns around it, and
when the Negeb and the Shephelah were
inhabited?

Punishment for Rejecting God's Demands

8 The word of the LORD came to Zechariah,
saying: [9]Thus says the LORD of hosts: Render
true judgments, show kindness and mercy
to one another; [10]do not oppress the widow,
the orphan, the alien, or the poor; and do
not devise evil in your hearts against one
another. [11]But they refused to listen, and
turned a stubborn shoulder, and stopped
their ears in order not to hear. [12]They made
their hearts adamant in order not to hear
the law and the words that the LORD of hosts
had sent by his spirit through the former
prophets. Therefore great wrath came from
the LORD of hosts. [13]Just as, when I[u] called,
they would not hear, so, when they called,
I would not hear, says the LORD of hosts,
[14]and I scattered them with a whirlwind
among all the nations that they had not
known. Thus the land they left was desolate, so that no one went to and fro, and
a pleasant land was made desolate.

God's Promises to Zion

8 The word of the LORD of hosts came
to me, saying: [2]Thus says the LORD of
hosts: I am jealous for Zion with great
jealousy, and I am jealous for her with
great wrath. [3]Thus says the LORD: I will
return to Zion, and will dwell in the midst
of Jerusalem; Jerusalem shall be called the
faithful city, and the mountain of the LORD
of hosts shall be called the holy mountain.
[4]Thus says the LORD of hosts: Old men and
old women shall again sit in the streets of
Jerusalem, each with staff in hand because
of their great age. [5]And the streets of the
city shall be full of boys and girls playing
in its streets. [6]Thus says the LORD of hosts:
Even though it seems impossible to the
remnant of this people in these days, should
it also seem impossible to me, says the LORD
of hosts? [7]Thus says the LORD of hosts: I will
save my people from the east country and
from the west country; [8]and I will bring
them to live in Jerusalem. They shall be my
people and I will be their God, in faithfulness and in righteousness.
9 Thus says the LORD of hosts: Let your
hands be strong—you that have recently
been hearing these words from the mouths
of the prophets who were present when the

[p] Cn Compare verse 11: Heb lacks *silver and gold* [q] Gk Mss Syr Tg: Heb *crowns* [r] Gk Syr: Heb *crowns* [s] Syr Compare verse 10: Heb *Helem* [t] Syr Compare verse 10: Heb *Hen* [u] Heb *he*

6.10 Jer 28.6
6.11 Ezra 3.2; Hag 1.1
6.12 Isa 11.1; Zech 3.8; Isa 53.2
6.13 Isa 9.6; 22.24; 9.7; Ps 110.14
6.15 Isa 57.19; 60.10; Zech 4.9; 3.7
7.1 Zech 1.1,7; Neh 1.1
7.2 Jer 26.19; Zech 8.21
7.3 Jer 52.12; Zech 8.19; 12.12-14
7.5 Isa 58.5; Zech 8.19; Jer 41.1; Rom 14.6
7.9 Ezek 18.8; Zech 8.16; Mic 6.8
7.10 Deut 24.17; Jer 7.6; Mic 2.1
7.11 Jer 11.10; 17.23; 5.21; Acts 7.57
7.12 Ezek 11.19; 36.26; Neh 9.29,30; Dan 9.11
7.13 Prov 1.24; Isa 1.15
7.14 Deut 4.27; Jer 23.19; 44.6; Isa 60.15
8.2 Zech 1.14
8.3 Zech 1.16; 2.10,11; Jer 31.23
8.4 Isa 65.20
8.5 Jer 30.19,20
8.6 Ps 118.23; Jer 32.17,27
8.7 Isa 11.11; 43.5,6; Am 9.14
8.8 Zech 10.10; Ezek 37.25; Zech 2.11
8.9 Hag 2.4; Ezra 5.1

8.10 Hag 1.6
8.12 Joel 2.22; Hag 1.10; Isa 61.7
8.13 Jer 42.18; Gen 12.2; Ruth 4.11
8.14 Jer 31.28; Ezek 24.14
8.16 Zech 7.9; Eph 4.25
8.17 Prov 3.29; Zech 7.10; 5.4; Hab 1.13
8.19 Zech 7.3,5; Jer 39.2; 52.4; Isa 12.1; ver 16
8.21 Mic 4.1,2
8.22 Isa 60.3; 66.23; ver 21
8.23 Isa 45.14,24; 60.14; 1 Cor 14.25; 2 Chr 15.5; Isa 19.2
9.2 Jer 49.23; Ezek 28.3-5,12,21
9.3 2 Sam 24.7; Ezek 27.33; 1 Kings 10.21,27
9.4 Isa 23.1; Ezek 28.18
9.5 Am 1.6-8
9.6 Am 1.6-8
9.7 Ezek 25.15-17
9.8 Zech 2.5; Isa 52.1; 54.14; 60.18
9.9 Zeph 3.14,15; Isa 9.6,7; Mt 21.5; Isa 43.3,11; 57.15

foundation was laid for the rebuilding of the temple, the house of the LORD of hosts. [10]For before those days there were no wages for people or for animals, nor was there any safety from the foe for those who went out or came in, and I set them all against one other. [11]But now I will not deal with the remnant of this people as in the former days, says the LORD of hosts. [12]For there shall be a sowing of peace; the vine shall yield its fruit, the ground shall give its produce, and the skies shall give their dew; and I will cause the remnant of this people to possess all these things. [13]Just as you have been a cursing among the nations, O house of Judah and house of Israel, so I will save you and you shall be a blessing. Do not be afraid, but let your hands be strong.

14 For thus says the LORD of hosts: Just as I purposed to bring disaster upon you, when your ancestors provoked me to wrath, and I did not relent, says the LORD of hosts, [15]so again I have purposed in these days to do good to Jerusalem and to the house of Judah; do not be afraid. [16]These are the things that you shall do: Speak the truth to one another, render in your gates judgments that are true and make for peace, [17]do not devise evil in your hearts against one another, and love no false oath; for all these are things that I hate, says the LORD.

Joyful Fasting

18 The word of the LORD of hosts came to me, saying: [19]Thus says the LORD of hosts: The fast of the fourth month, and the fast of the fifth, and the fast of the seventh, and the fast of the tenth, shall be seasons of joy and gladness, and cheerful festivals for the house of Judah: therefore love truth and peace.

Many Peoples Drawn to Jerusalem

20 Thus says the LORD of hosts: Peoples shall yet come, the inhabitants of many cities; [21]the inhabitants of one city shall go to another, saying, "Come, let us go to entreat the favor of the LORD, and to seek the LORD of hosts; I myself am going." [22]Many peoples and strong nations shall come to seek the LORD of hosts in Jerusalem, and to entreat the favor of the LORD. [23]Thus says the LORD of hosts: In those days ten men from nations of every language shall take hold of a Jew, grasping his garment and saying, "Let us go with you, for we have heard that God is with you."

Judgment on Israel's Enemies

9 An Oracle.

The word of the LORD is against the land of Hadrach
and will rest upon Damascus.
For to the LORD belongs the capital[v] of Aram,[w]
as do all the tribes of Israel;
2 Hamath also, which borders on it,
Tyre and Sidon, though they are very wise.
3 Tyre has built itself a rampart,
and heaped up silver like dust,
and gold like the dirt of the streets.
4 But now, the Lord will strip it of its possessions
and hurl its wealth into the sea,
and it shall be devoured by fire.

5 Ashkelon shall see it and be afraid;
Gaza too, and shall writhe in anguish;
Ekron also, because its hopes are withered.
The king shall perish from Gaza;
Ashkelon shall be uninhabited;
6 a mongrel people shall settle in Ashdod,
and I will make an end of the pride of Philistia.
7 I will take away its blood from its mouth,
and its abominations from between its teeth;
it too shall be a remnant for our God;
it shall be like a clan in Judah,
and Ekron shall be like the Jebusites.
8 Then I will encamp at my house as a guard,
so that no one shall march to and fro;
no oppressor shall again overrun them,
for now I have seen with my own eyes.

The Coming Ruler of God's People

9 Rejoice greatly, O daughter Zion!
Shout aloud, O daughter Jerusalem!
Lo, your king comes to you;
triumphant and victorious is he,
humble and riding on a donkey,
on a colt, the foal of a donkey.

[v] Heb *eye* [w] Cn: Heb *of Adam* (or *of humankind*)

9.1-8 The Word of the LORD Crushes Israel's Hostile Neighbors. Picturing *the word* as an instrument of power and purpose, the cities and districts of Syria and the Philistine coastal cities are seen here as the targets of God's destruction. He will protect his own people (*house*) and will give them continuing attention (*with my own eyes*).
9.9-11.3 The New Ruler and the Renewal of God's People.
9.9-10 The people are called to *rejoice* now that a king is coming who has *triumphed* over injustice and disobedience, but is so humble that he rides on a lowly donkey instead of a grand war-horse. He will bring *peace* to the nations, and his domain will be universal.

9.11-17 Now that the people's covenant relationship with God has been confirmed by their obedient suffering (*blood*), they will be set free to return to the land and their oppressors will be defeated. These include *Greece*, which conquered Syria-Palestine in the later fourth century BCE, suggesting a late date for this oracle. The LORD's appearance in a storm recalls Ex 19.16-20. He will enable his people to defeat their enemies, as in the holy wars when Israel invaded Canaan (Num 21.21-30; Judg 5.1-31). Understood literally, to *drink blood* would violate ritual law (Lev 7.26-27), but it here serves as a symbol of victory for those who are God's *flock* and who will glow like *jewels* in their regained prosperity.

10.1-12 Restoration of Judah and Israel will be achieved by the LORD, whose purpose will come down like *rain*. To be avoided are messages from the household gods (*teraphim*) and the *diviners* who claim to foretell the future, but who have in fact led astray God's people. God will find among the people all the necessary equipment and skills (*tent peg, bow, commander*) for overcoming his enemies and theirs. Both Judah and Israel (*Joseph, Ephraim*) will share in this renewal, which will return them to the land from the nations where they have been scattered – from *Egypt to Assyria* – and God will strengthen them to *walk in his name*.

10 He[x] will cut off the chariot from Ephraim
and the war horse from Jerusalem;
and the battle bow shall be cut off,
and he shall command peace to the nations;
his dominion shall be from sea to sea,
and from the River to the ends of the earth.

11 As for you also, because of the blood of my covenant with you,
I will set your prisoners free from the waterless pit.
12 Return to your stronghold, O prisoners of hope;
today I declare that I will restore to you double.
13 For I have bent Judah as my bow;
I have made Ephraim its arrow.
I will arouse your sons, O Zion,
against your sons, O Greece,
and wield you like a warrior's sword.

14 Then the LORD will appear over them,
and his arrow go forth like lightning;
the Lord GOD will sound the trumpet
and march forth in the whirlwinds of the south.
15 The LORD of hosts will protect them,
and they shall devour and tread down the slingers;[y]
they shall drink their blood[z] like wine,
and be full like a bowl,
drenched like the corners of the altar.

16 On that day the LORD their God will save them
for they are the flock of his people;
for like the jewels of a crown
they shall shine on his land.
17 For what goodness and beauty are his!
Grain shall make the young men flourish,
and new wine the young women.

Restoration of Judah and Israel

10 Ask rain from the LORD
in the season of the spring rain,
from the LORD who makes the storm clouds,
who gives showers of rain to you,[a]
the vegetation in the field to everyone.
2 For the teraphim[b] utter nonsense,
and the diviners see lies;
the dreamers tell false dreams,
and give empty consolation.
Therefore the people wander like sheep;
they suffer for lack of a shepherd.

3 My anger is hot against the shepherds,
and I will punish the leaders;[c]
for the LORD of hosts cares for his flock,
the house of Judah,
and will make them like his proud war horse.
4 Out of them shall come the cornerstone,
out of them the tent peg,
out of them the battle bow,
out of them every commander.
5 Together they shall be like warriors in battle,
trampling the foe in the mud of the streets;
they shall fight, for the LORD is with them,
and they shall put to shame the riders on horses.

6 I will strengthen the house of Judah,
and I will save the house of Joseph.
I will bring them back because I have compassion on them,
and they shall be as though I had not rejected them;
for I am the LORD their God and I will answer them.
7 Then the people of Ephraim shall become like warriors,
and their hearts shall be glad as with wine.
Their children shall see it and rejoice,
their hearts shall exult in the LORD.

8 I will signal for them and gather them in,
for I have redeemed them,
and they shall be as numerous as they were before.
9 Though I scattered them among the nations,
yet in far countries they shall remember me,
and they shall rear their children and return.
10 I will bring them home from the land of Egypt,
and gather them from Assyria;
I will bring them to the land of Gilead and to Lebanon,
until there is no room for them.
11 They[d] shall pass through the sea of distress,

[x] Gk: Heb *I* [y] Cn: Heb *the slingstones* [z] Gk: Heb *shall drink* [a] Heb *them* [b] Or *household gods* [c] Or *male goats* [d] Gk: Heb *He*

9.10 Hos 1.7; 2.18; Hag 2.22; Isa 57.19; Ps 72.8; Isa 60.12
9.11 Ex 24.8; Heb 10.29; Isa 51.14
9.12 Jer 16.19; 17.13; Isa 61.7
9.13 Jer 51.20; Joel 3.6; Ps 45.3; Isa 49.2
9.14 Isa 31.5; Ps 18.14; Isa 27.13; 21.1; 66.15
9.15 Isa 37.35; Zech 12.6; Job 41.28; Ps 78.65; Ex 27.2
9.16 Jer 31.10,11; Isa 62.3
9.17 Jer 31.12,14
10.1 Jer 14.22; 10.13; Isa 30.23
10.2 Ezek 21.21; Hos 3.4; Jer 27.9; Job 13.4; Ezek 34.5
10.3 Jer 25.34-36; Ezek 34.12,17
10.4 Zech 9.10
10.5 2 Sam 22.43; Hag 2.22
10.6 ver 12; Zech 9.16; 8.8; 1.16; 13.9
10.7 Zech 9.13,15; Isa 54.13
10.8 Isa 5.26; Jer 33.22; Ezek 36.11
10.9 Ezek 6.9
10.10 Isa 11.11; Jer 50.19; Isa 49.19,20
10.11 Isa 51.9,10; 19.5-7; Zeph 2.13; Ezek 30.13

and the waves of the sea shall be
struck down,
and all the depths of the Nile dried up.
The pride of Assyria shall be laid low,
and the scepter of Egypt shall depart.
12 I will make them strong in the LORD,
and they shall walk in his name,
says the LORD.

11 Open your doors, O Lebanon,
so that fire may devour your
cedars!
2 Wail, O cypress, for the cedar has fallen,
for the glorious trees are ruined!
Wail, oaks of Bashan,
for the thick forest has been felled!
3 Listen, the wail of the shepherds,
for their glory is despoiled!
Listen, the roar of the lions,
for the thickets of the Jordan are
destroyed!

Two Kinds of Shepherds

4 Thus said the LORD my God: Be a shepherd of the flock doomed to slaughter. 5 Those who buy them kill them and go unpunished; and those who sell them say, "Blessed be the LORD, for I have become rich"; and their own shepherds have no pity on them. 6 For I will no longer have pity on the inhabitants of the earth, says the LORD. I will cause them, every one, to fall each into the hand of a neighbor, and each into the hand of the king; and they shall devastate the earth, and I will deliver no one from their hand.

7 So, on behalf of the sheep merchants, I became the shepherd of the flock doomed to slaughter. I took two staffs; one I named Favor, the other I named Unity, and I tended the sheep. 8 In one month I disposed of the three shepherds, for I had become impatient with them, and they also detested me. 9 So I said, "I will not be your shepherd. What is to die, let it die; what is to be destroyed, let it be destroyed; and let those that are left devour the flesh of one another!" 10 I took my staff Favor and broke it, annulling the covenant that I had made with all the peoples. 11 So it was annulled on that day, and the sheep merchants, who were watching me, knew that it was the word of the LORD. 12 I then said to them, "If it seems right to you, give me my wages; but if not, keep them." So they weighed out as my wages thirty shekels of silver. 13 Then the LORD said to me, "Throw it into the treasury"[e]—this lordly price at which I was valued by them. So I took the thirty shekels of silver and threw them into the treasury[e] in the house of the LORD. 14 Then I broke my second staff Unity, annulling the family ties between Judah and Israel.

15 Then the LORD said to me: Take once more the implements of a worthless shepherd. 16 For I am now raising up in the land a shepherd who does not care for the perishing, or seek the wandering,[f] or heal the maimed, or nourish the healthy,[g] but devours the flesh of the fat ones, tearing off even their hoofs.

17 Oh, my worthless shepherd,
who deserts the flock!
May the sword strike his arm
and his right eye!
Let his arm be completely withered,
his right eye utterly blinded!

Jerusalem's Victory

12 An Oracle.

The word of the LORD concerning Israel: Thus says the LORD, who stretched out the heavens and founded the earth and formed the human spirit within: 2 See, I am about to make Jerusalem a cup of reeling for all the surrounding peoples; it will be against Judah also in the siege against Jerusalem. 3 On that day I will make Jerusalem a heavy stone for all the peoples; all who lift it shall grievously hurt themselves. And all the nations of the earth shall come together against it. 4 On that day, says the LORD, I will strike every horse with panic, and its rider with madness. But on the house of Judah I will keep a watchful eye, when I strike every horse of the peoples with blindness. 5 Then the clans of Judah shall say to themselves, "The inhabitants of Jerusalem have strength through the LORD of hosts, their God."

6 On that day I will make the clans of Judah like a blazing pot on a pile of wood, like a flaming torch among sheaves; and they shall devour to the right and to the left all the surrounding peoples, while Jerusalem shall again be inhabited in its place, in Jerusalem.

7 And the LORD will give victory to the tents of Judah first, that the glory of the

[e] Syr: Heb *it to the potter* [f] Syr Compare Gk Vg: Heb *the youth* [g] Meaning of Heb uncertain

10.12 Mic 4.5
11.1 Jer 22.6,7; Ezek 31.3
11.2 Isa 32.19
11.3 Jer 25.34-36; 50.44
11.4 ver 7
11.5 Jer 50.7; Hos 12.8
11.6 Jer 13.14; Zech 14.13; Mic 5.8
11.7 Zeph 3.12; Ezek 37.16; ver 10,14
11.8 Hos 5.7
11.10 ver 7; Jer 14.21
11.11 Zeph 3.12
11.12 1 Kings 5.6; Gen 37.28; Ex 21.32; Mt 26.15; 27.9,10
11.13 Mt 27.9
11.15 Ezek 34.2-4
11.17 Jer 23.1; Jn 10.12; Ezek 30.21,22; Mic 3.6,7
12.1 Isa 42.5; 57.16; Heb 12.9
12.2 Isa 51.22,23; Zech 14.14
12.3 Dan 2.34,35,44, 45; Mt 21.44; Zech 14.2
12.4 Ps 76.6; Ezek 38.4; Zech 9.10
12.5 Zech 10.5,12
12.6 Isa 10.17,18; Ob 18; Zech 2.4; 8.3-5
12.7 Jer 30.18; Am 9.11

11.1-3 The neighboring lands of *Lebanon* to the north and *Bashan* to the east of Galilee are warned of the destruction that will strike them.
11.4-17 The Slaughter of God's Flock.
11.4-14 The complex imagery of this oracle is pessimistic in its import. The prophet is assigned to *shepherd* God's *flock*, here seen as doomed to slaughter, as in 12.3. The *rich* who pitilessly exploit the poor take pride in their wealth, while all the *inhabitants of the earth* are being destroyed by each other and by *the king*, and *the earth* is laid waste. Accepting the task as *shepherd of the doomed flock*, the prophet takes *two staffs* to deal with the sheep: *Favor* (or *presence of God*, as in the temple; Ps 18.6; 27.4) and *Unity* (of God's people, Israel and Judah). Vv. 8-9 interrupt the flow of the oracle: there is no indication of the identity or role of the *three shepherds*, and in what follows (vv. 10-17) the prophet has not renounced his role as shepherd. The breaking of the *staff Favor* symbolizes the shattering of the covenant relationship between God and his people, and the ensuing slaughter is profitable for *the merchants* who make money from the loot and throw it into the temple *treasury* (or into the smelter for making temple coins). The staff of *Unity* of the northern and southern tribes is also broken.
11.15-17 With the prophet-shepherd gone, leadership of the people now passes to *a worthless shepherd* who has no concern for the sheep, but only for feeding himself. He will be smitten by God for his irresponsibility.
12.1-9 Judah's Victory. All the nations will join in an attack on Jerusalem, but will be crushed *(grievously hurt)* and driven mad as a result, while the people of the city will be strengthened through the LORD. Like a blazing fire, the *clans of Judah* will consume their opponents. The simple (*tents*) and the *feeblest* of Judah will triumph, after which the king and the glorious inhabitants will assume power *like God*, and the opposing nations will be defeated.

12.10-13.1 Mourning for the Pierced One. Reading *me* instead of *the one*, the prophet foresees the time when, having experienced severe suffering or death (*pierced*), the people are filled with *compassion* and mourning for what they have done to God's messenger. Ironically, their laments will resemble and match those of the devotees of the fertility god, *Hadad*, whose annual ritual death and passage to the underworld many Israelites took part in. The mourners as seen by the prophet will include various groups: royal (*house of David*), prophetic (*Nathan*; 2 Sam 7), priestly (*Levi*) and other temple functionaries (*Shimei*; 1 Chr 25.17). The new *fountain* will purify the penitent people of Jerusalem.
13.2-6 The Purging of Idols and False Prophets. Even *the names of the idols* will be removed, and the false prophets will be killed (*pierced*) by their own parents unless they renounce their prophetic claims. The *wounds* are the masochistic acts of ecstatic prophets (1 Kings 18.28).
13.7-9 The Slaughter of the Flock and the Survival of the Remnant. Resuming the imagery of 11.4-17, God's judgment is pronounced against the irresponsible leaders, and the doom of two-thirds of God's people (*the sheep*) is announced. The faithful remnant will be purged and *refined*, and God and his people will identify with each other.
14.1-21 God's Universal Rule and the Renewal of Jerusalem.
14.1-15 The final assault of *all nations* against Jerusalem will be encountered by *the* LORD and his *holy ones*, whose coming will result in the splitting of the Mount of Olives, which lies east of the temple mount. While the faithful flee for refuge, cosmic and seismic disturbances (like those said to have taken place in the time of Uzziah, according to the Jewish historian, Josephus, in his *Antiquities* 9.10.4) will change the face of the earth and the movements of the heavenly bodies. Alternating seasons and the sequence of day/night will disappear. Water will flow year-round east and west from Jerusalem, and the LORD will be sovereign over all the earth. Those who attack Jerusalem will be stricken with ghastly ailments, as will their beasts of burden.

house of David and the glory of the inhabitants of Jerusalem may not be exalted over
that of Judah. 8On that day the LORD will
shield the inhabitants of Jerusalem so that
the feeblest among them on that day shall
be like David, and the house of David shall
be like God, like the angel of the LORD, at
their head. 9And on that day I will seek to
destroy all the nations that come against
Jerusalem.

Mourning for the Pierced One

10 And I will pour out a spirit of compassion and supplication on the house of
David and the inhabitants of Jerusalem, so
that, when they look on the one[h] whom
they have pierced, they shall mourn for
him, as one mourns for an only child, and
weep bitterly over him, as one weeps over
a firstborn. 11On that day the mourning in
Jerusalem will be as great as the mourning
for Hadad-rimmon in the plain of Megiddo.
12The land shall mourn, each family by
itself; the family of the house of David by
itself, and their wives by themselves; the
family of the house of Nathan by itself, and
their wives by themselves; 13the family of
the house of Levi by itself, and their wives
by themselves; the family of the Shimeites
by itself, and their wives by themselves;
14and all the families that are left, each by
itself, and their wives by themselves.

13 On that day a fountain shall be
opened for the house of David and
the inhabitants of Jerusalem, to cleanse them
from sin and impurity.

Idolatry Cut Off

2 On that day, says the LORD of hosts, I
will cut off the names of the idols from the
land, so that they shall be remembered no
more; and also I will remove from the land
the prophets and the unclean spirit. 3And if
any prophets appear again, their fathers
and mothers who bore them will say to
them, "You shall not live, for you speak lies
in the name of the LORD"; and their fathers
and their mothers who bore them shall
pierce them through when they prophesy.
4On that day the prophets will be ashamed,
every one, of their visions when they prophesy; they will not put on a hairy mantle in
order to deceive, 5but each of them will say,
"I am no prophet, I am a tiller of the soil;
for the land has been my possession[i] since
my youth." 6And if anyone asks them, "What
are these wounds on your chest?"[j] the
answer will be "The wounds I received in
the house of my friends."

The Shepherd Struck, the Flock Scattered

7 "Awake, O sword, against my shepherd,
against the man who is my
associate,"
says the LORD of hosts.
Strike the shepherd, that the sheep may
be scattered;
I will turn my hand against the little
ones.
8 In the whole land, says the LORD,
two-thirds shall be cut off and perish,
and one-third shall be left alive.
9 And I will put this third into the fire,
refine them as one refines silver,
and test them as gold is tested.
They will call on my name,
and I will answer them.
I will say, "They are my people";
and they will say, "The LORD is our God."

Future Warfare and Final Victory

14 See, a day is coming for the LORD,
when the plunder taken from you
will be divided in your midst. 2For I will
gather all the nations against Jerusalem to
battle, and the city shall be taken and the
houses looted and the women raped; half
the city shall go into exile, but the rest of
the people shall not be cut off from the city.
3Then the LORD will go forth and fight against
those nations as when he fights on a day
of battle. 4On that day his feet shall stand
on the Mount of Olives, which lies before
Jerusalem on the east; and the Mount of
Olives shall be split in two from east to west
by a very wide valley; so that one half of
the Mount shall withdraw northward, and
the other half southward. 5And you shall
flee by the valley of the LORD's mountain,[k]
for the valley between the mountains shall
reach to Azal;[l] and you shall flee as you fled
from the earthquake in the days of King
Uzziah of Judah. Then the LORD my God will
come, and all the holy ones with him.

[h] Heb *on me* [i] Cn: Heb *for humankind has caused me to possess* [j] Heb *wounds between your hands* [k] Heb *my mountains* [l] Meaning of Heb uncertain

12.8 Zech 9.14,15; Mic 7.8; Ps 8.5; 82.6
12.9 ver 3; Zech 14.2,3
12.10 Isa 44.3; Ezek 39.29; Joel 2.28; Jn 19.34; Rev 1.7; Jer 6.26
12.11 2 Kings 23.29
13.1 Jer 2.13; Heb 9.14; Ps 51.2,7; Ezek 36.25
13.2 Ex 23.13; Hos 2.17; Jer 23.14,15; Ezek 36.25,29
13.3 Jer 23.34; Deut 18.20; 13.6-11
13.4 Mic 3.6,7; 2 Kings 1.8; Mt 3.4
13.7 Jer 47.6; Mic 5.2,4; Jer 23.5,6; Isa 53.4,5,10; Mt 26.31
13.8 Isa 6.13
13.9 Isa 48.10; 1 Pet 1.6; Zech 10.6; Jer 30.22; Hos 2.23
14.1 Isa 13.9; Joel 2.1; Mal 4.1; ver 14
14.2 Zech 12.2,3; Isa 13.6; Zech 13.8
14.3 Zech 9.14,15
14.4 Ezek 11.23; Mic 1.3,4; Hab 3.6
14.5 Am 1.1; Isa 66.15,16 Mt 25.31; Jude 14

6 On that day there shall not be[m] either
cold or frost.[n] [7]And there shall be continuous day (it is known to the LORD), not day
and not night, for at evening time there
shall be light.
8 On that day living waters shall flow
out from Jerusalem, half of them to the
eastern sea and half of them to the western
sea; it shall continue in summer as in winter.
9 And the LORD will become king over all
the earth; on that day the LORD will be one
and his name one.
10 The whole land shall be turned into
a plain from Geba to Rimmon south of
Jerusalem. But Jerusalem shall remain aloft
on its site from the Gate of Benjamin to the
place of the former gate, to the Corner Gate,
and from the Tower of Hananel to the king's
wine presses. [11]And it shall be inhabited, for
never again shall it be doomed to destruction; Jerusalem shall abide in security.
12 This shall be the plague with which
the LORD will strike all the peoples that wage
war against Jerusalem: their flesh shall rot
while they are still on their feet; their eyes
shall rot in their sockets, and their tongues
shall rot in their mouths. [13]On that day a
great panic from the LORD shall fall on them,
so that each will seize the hand of a neighbor,
and the hand of the one will be raised
against the hand of the other; [14]even Judah
will fight at Jerusalem. And the wealth of
all the surrounding nations shall be collected—gold, silver, and garments in great
abundance. [15]And a plague like this plague
shall fall on the horses, the mules, the
camels, the donkeys, and whatever animals
may be in those camps.
16 Then all who survive of the nations
that have come against Jerusalem shall go
up year after year to worship the King, the
LORD of hosts, and to keep the festival of
booths.[o] [17]If any of the families of the earth
do not go up to Jerusalem to worship the
King, the LORD of hosts, there will be no rain
upon them. [18]And if the family of Egypt do
not go up and present themselves, then on
them shall[p] come the plague that the LORD
inflicts on the nations that do not go up to
keep the festival of booths.[o] [19]Such shall be
the punishment of Egypt and the punishment of all the nations that do not go up
to keep the festival of booths.[o]
20 On that day there shall be inscribed
on the bells of the horses, "Holy to the
LORD." And the cooking pots in the house
of the LORD shall be as holy as[q] the bowls
in front of the altar; [21]and every cooking pot
in Jerusalem and Judah shall be sacred to
the LORD of hosts, so that all who sacrifice
may come and use them to boil the flesh of
the sacrifice. And there shall no longer be
traders[r] in the house of the LORD of hosts on
that day.

14.7 Isa 30.26; Rev 21.23
14.8 Ezek 47.1; Joel 3.18; Rev 22.1
14.9 Rev 11.15; Isa 45.21-24; Eph 4.5,6
14.10 Am 9.11; Zech 12.6; Jer 37.13; 38.7; 31.38
14.11 Zech 2.4; Rev 22.3; Jer 23.5,6
14.12 Deut 28.21,22
14.13 1 Sam 14.15,20; Zech 11.6; Ezek 38.21
14.14 Zech 12.2,5; Isa 23.18
14.15 ver 12
14.16 Isa 60.6,7,9; ver 9
14.17 ver 9,16; Am 4.7
14.18 ver 12
14.19 ver 12
14.20 Ex 28.36-38; Zech 9.15
14.21 Neh 8.10; 1 Cor 10.31; Ezek 44.9; Zech 9.8

14.16-21 All nations will come to Jerusalem annually to worship *the LORD of Hosts*, with famine as a penalty for any who fail to do so. In a reversal of history, *Egypt* will take part in the *feast of booths* which celebrates Israel's liberation from Egypt under Moses. Insignia and dishes earlier used only by the priest will now be used by all the holy people, and commerce in the temple will cease.

[m] Cn: Heb *there shall not be light* [n] Compare Gk Syr Vg Tg: Meaning of Heb uncertain [o] Or *tabernacles*; Heb *succoth* [p] Gk Syr: Heb *shall not* [q] Heb *shall be like* [r] Or *Canaanites*

See the Introductions, pp. 6, 54-57, and 75-76 above.

MALACHI

1 An oracle. The word of the LORD to Israel by Malachi.[a]

Israel Preferred to Edom

2 I have loved you, says the LORD. But you say, "How have you loved us?" Is not Esau Jacob's brother? says the LORD. Yet I have loved Jacob 3but I have hated Esau; I have made his hill country a desolation and his heritage a desert for jackals. 4If Edom says, "We are shattered but we will rebuild the ruins," the LORD of hosts says: They may build, but I will tear down, until they are called the wicked country, the people with whom the LORD is angry forever. 5Your own eyes shall see this, and you shall say, "Great is the LORD beyond the borders of Israel!"

Corruption of the Priesthood

6 A son honors his father, and servants their master. If then I am a father, where is the honor due me? And if I am a master, where is the respect due me? says the LORD of hosts to you, O priests, who despise my name. You say, "How have we despised your name?" 7By offering polluted food on my altar. And you say, "How have we polluted it?"[b] By thinking that the LORD's table may be despised. 8When you offer blind animals in sacrifice, is that not wrong? And when you offer those that are lame or sick, is that not wrong? Try presenting that to your governor; will he be pleased with you or show you favor? says the LORD of hosts. 9And now implore the favor of God, that he may be gracious to us. The fault is yours. Will he show favor to any of you? says the LORD of hosts. 10Oh, that someone among you would shut the temple[c] doors, so that you would not kindle fire on my altar in vain! I have no pleasure in you, says the LORD of hosts, and I will not accept an offering from your hands. 11For from the rising of the sun to its setting my name is great among the nations, and in every place incense is offered to my name, and a pure offering; for my name is great among the nations, says the LORD of hosts. 12But you profane it when you say that the Lord's table is polluted, and the food for it[d] may be despised. 13"What a weariness this is," you say, and you sniff at me,[e] says the LORD of hosts. You bring what has been taken by violence or is lame or sick, and this you bring as your offering! Shall I accept that from your hand? says the LORD. 14Cursed be the cheat who has a male in the flock and vows to give it, and yet sacrifices to the Lord what is blemished; for I am a great King, says the LORD of hosts, and my name is reverenced among the nations.

2 And now, O priests, this command is for you. 2If you will not listen, if you will not lay it to heart to give glory to my name, says the LORD of hosts, then I will send the curse on you and I will curse your blessings; indeed I have already cursed them,[f] because you do not lay it to heart. 3I will rebuke your offspring, and spread dung on your faces, the dung of your offerings, and I will put you out of my presence.[g]

4 Know, then, that I have sent this command to you, that my covenant with Levi may hold, says the LORD of hosts. 5My covenant with him was a covenant of life and well-being, which I gave him; this called for reverence, and he revered me and stood in awe of my name. 6True instruction was in his mouth, and no wrong was found on his lips. He walked with me in integrity and uprightness, and he turned many from iniquity. 7For the lips of a priest should guard knowledge, and people should seek instruction from his mouth, for he is the messenger of the LORD of hosts. 8But you have turned aside from the way; you have caused many to stumble by your instruction; you have corrupted the covenant of Levi, says the LORD of hosts, 9and so I make you despised and abased before all the people, inasmuch as you have not kept my ways but have shown partiality in your instruction.

The Covenant Profaned by Judah

10 Have we not all one father? Has not one God created us? Why then are we faithless to one another, profaning the covenant of our ancestors? 11Judah has been

[a] Or *by my messenger* [b] Gk: Heb *you* [c] Heb lacks *temple* [d] Compare Syr Tg: Heb *its fruit, its food* [e] Another reading is *at it* [f] Heb *it* [g] Cn Compare Gk Syr: Heb *and he shall bear you to it*

1.1 Introduction. Both the term *oracle* and the criticisms of the priest and temple also appear in Zech 9-14, together with the promise of vindication of the faithful community. *Edom* here stands for the descendants of Esau who lived in the area east of the Dead Sea.
1.2-5 God's Judgment on Edom. Pointing to the precedent of God's radical distinction between Isaac's two sons, Jacob and Esau (Gen 27.30-4), the oracle implies that being born into the covenant family of Abraham and his God-given son, Isaac, does not guarantee participation in the benefits of the covenant. God's greatness is able to achieve his purposes *beyond the borders of Israel.*
1.6-2.3 The Priests' Failure to Maintain Purity. The corruption of the priesthood is evident in that they allow *polluted, lame, and sick* animals to be offered as sacrifices in violation of the requirement of the law that they be *without blemish* (Lev 1-4). *The LORD* would prefer having the *temple doors* shut with no sacrifices offered to having these impure offerings brought. Although the reputation (*name*) of God is *great among the nations,* and suitable offerings are being made across the world (perhaps by Jews scattered throughout the nations), the priests in Jerusalem debase the worship of God by their lax procedures in direct violation of the Law of Moses. If they persist in this disgrace to the name *of the great king* (God), he will bring a curse on them, denounce (*rebuke*) their offspring, smear them with filth, and expel them from his *presence.*
2.4-9 The Betrayal of the Covenant with Levi. Although in Num 25.10-13 it is the descendants of Aaron and not of Levi who are the priests, here the latter serve as priests and are designated as having a *covenant* form of obligation to God to do so. Unlike that of the priests in Leviticus, their task now includes as a major role the *instruction* of the people. This reflects the kind of priestly assignment to teaching the law which is described in the post-exilic strand of Numbers (3.5-10) and is undertaken by Ezra and Nehemiah (Ezra 7.10; Neh 8.1-12). These Levites are not giving proper instruction but are leading the people astray, including *showing partiality* – making exceptions in applying the law.
2.10-17 The Infidelity of Judah. Building on the image of Israel and Judah as the wife of the LORD (Hos 2), Judah is here seen as having corrupted her relationship with God by marrying non-Israelite wives and participating in the worship of alien gods and goddesses. The people of Judah shed tears at the altar of God because of his failure to accept their offerings, which is shown by his lack of favor toward them. They fail to realize that this disfavor is the direct consequence of their having betrayed their special relationship with God. Their *evil* mode of life exemplifies the violation of their obligation to *the God of justice.*

1.2 Isa 41.8,9; Jer 31.3; Rom 9.13
1.3 Jer 49.18; Ezek 35.3-9
1.5 Ps 35.27; Job 42.8
1.6 Ex 20.12; Mal 2.10; Lk 6.46; Mal 3.5; 2.1-9
1.7 Lev 21.6,8; ver 12
1.8 Lev 22.22
1.9 Am 5.22; Lev 23.34-44
1.10 Isa 1.13; Jer 14.10-12; Hos 5.6
1.11 Isa 45.6; 60.3,5,6; Rev 8.3; Jer 10.6,7
1.13 Isa 43.22; 61.8; Lev 22.20
1.14 Lev 22.18-20; Zech 14.9; Zeph 2.11
2.2 Lev 26.14; Deut 28.15-20
2.4 Num 3.45; 18.21
2.5 Num 25.12; Ezek 34.25; Deut 33.9
2.6 Deut 33.8-10; Jer 23.22; Jas 5.20
2.7 Lev 10.11; Jer 18.18; Num 27.21
2.8 Mal 3.7; Jer 18.15; Ezek 44.10
2.9 1 Sam 2.30; Deut 1.17; Mic 3.11
2.10 Isa 63.16; 1 Cor 8.6; Jer 9.4,5; Ex 19.4-6
2.11 Jer 3.7-9; Ezra 9.1; Neh 13.23

faithless, and abomination has been committed in Israel and in Jerusalem; for Judah has profaned the sanctuary of the LORD, which he loves, and has married the daughter of a foreign god. 12May the LORD cut off from the tents of Jacob anyone who does this—any to witness[h] or answer, or to bring an offering to the LORD of hosts.

13 And this you do as well: You cover the LORD's altar with tears, with weeping and groaning because he no longer regards the offering or accepts it with favor at your hand. 14You ask, "Why does he not?" Because the LORD was a witness between you and the wife of your youth, to whom you have been faithless, though she is your companion and your wife by covenant. 15Did not one God make her?[i] Both flesh and spirit are his.[j] And what does the one God[k] desire? Godly offspring. So look to yourselves, and do not let anyone be faithless to the wife of his youth. 16For I hate[l] divorce, says the LORD, the God of Israel, and covering one's garment with violence, says the LORD of hosts. So take heed to yourselves and do not be faithless.

17 You have wearied the LORD with your words. Yet you say, "How have we wearied him?" By saying, "All who do evil are good in the sight of the LORD, and he delights in them." Or by asking, "Where is the God of justice?"

The Coming Messenger

3 See, I am sending my messenger to prepare the way before me, and the Lord whom you seek will suddenly come to his temple. The messenger of the covenant in whom you delight—indeed, he is coming, says the LORD of hosts. 2But who can endure the day of his coming, and who can stand when he appears?

For he is like a refiner's fire and like fullers' soap; 3he will sit as a refiner and purifier of silver, and he will purify the descendants of Levi and refine them like gold and silver, until they present offerings to the LORD in righteousness.[m] 4Then the offering of Judah and Jerusalem will be pleasing to the LORD as in the days of old and as in former years.

5 Then I will draw near to you for judgment; I will be swift to bear witness against the sorcerers, against the adulterers, against those who swear falsely, against those who oppress the hired workers in their wages, the widow and the orphan, against those who thrust aside the alien, and do not fear me, says the LORD of hosts.

6 For I the LORD do not change; therefore you, O children of Jacob, have not perished. 7Ever since the days of your ancestors you have turned aside from my statutes and have not kept them. Return to me, and I will return to you, says the LORD of hosts. But you say, "How shall we return?"

Do Not Rob God

8 Will anyone rob God? Yet you are robbing me! But you say, "How are we robbing you?" In your tithes and offerings! 9You are cursed with a curse, for you are robbing me—the whole nation of you! 10Bring the full tithe into the storehouse, so that there may be food in my house, and thus put me to the test, says the LORD of hosts; see if I will not open the windows of heaven for you and pour down for you an overflowing blessing. 11I will rebuke the locust[n] for you, so that it will not destroy the produce of your soil; and your vine in the field shall not be barren, says the LORD of hosts. 12Then all nations will count you happy, for you will be a land of delight, says the LORD of hosts.

13 You have spoken harsh words against me, says the LORD. Yet you say, "How have we spoken against you?" 14You have said, "It is vain to serve God. What do we profit by keeping his command or by going about as mourners before the LORD of hosts? 15Now we count the arrogant happy; evildoers not only prosper, but when they put God to the test they escape."

The Reward of the Faithful

16 Then those who revered the LORD spoke with one another. The LORD took note and listened, and a book of remembrance was written before him of those who revered the LORD and thought on his name. 17They shall be mine, says the LORD of hosts, my special possession on the day when I act, and I will spare them as parents spare their children who serve them. 18Then once more you shall see the difference between the righteous and the wicked, between one who serves God and one who does not serve him.

[h] Cn Compare Gk: Heb *arouse* [i] Or *Has he not made one?* [j] Cn: Heb *and a remnant of spirit was his* [k] Heb *he* [l] Cn: Heb *he hates* [m] Or *right offerings to the LORD* [n] Heb *devourer*

2.12 Hos 9.12; Mal 1.10,13
2.14 Prov 5.18; 2.17
2.15 Gen 2.24; Mt 19.4; Ex 20.14; Lev 20.10
2.17 Isa 43.24; 5.19,20
3.1 Mt 11.10; Mk 1.2; Lk 1.76; 7.27
3.2 Ezek 22.14; Zech 13.9; Mt 3.10-12; 1 Cor 3.13-15
3.3 Isa 1.25; Zech 13.9
3.5 Deut 18.10; Ezek 22.9-11; Zech 5.4; Lev 19.13
3.6 Num 23.19; Jas 1.17
3.7 Acts 7.51; Zech 1.3
3.8 Neh 13.10-12
3.10 Prov 3.9,10; Ps 78.23-29; 2 Chr 31.10
3.13 Mal 2.17
3.14 Ps 73.13; Jer 2.25; 18.12; Isa 58.3
3.15 Mal 4.1; Jer 7.10
3.16 Ps 34.15; 56.8; Rev 20.12
3.17 1 Pet 2.9; Isa 26.20
3.18 Gen 18.25; Am 5.15

3.1-5 God's Messenger and the Coming Judgment. In Hebrew *my messenger* is Malachi, which is the name of the prophet. The call to *prepare the way* of the LORD is also found in Isa 40.3. The basic point of this passage is clear: God's *messenger* is *coming* to prepare for God's judgment on Israel, with its *sorcerers, adulterers* and those who *oppress* workers and the deprived (*aliens, widows, orphans*). But *the LORD* in this passage is not the distinctive Hebrew name of God, Yahweh. Yet he is coming to *his temple.* The *messenger* could be the prophet or some powerful agent of God, or, less likely, it could refer to God himself. Although his identity is not clear, the role of the *messenger of the covenant* is to purify the priests so that once again they will offer acceptable sacrifices.
3.6-15 The Call to Return to God. The pattern of Israel's disobedience is clear in the people's having turned from the *statutes* of the law. Yet God remains willing to accept them if they *return* to full obedience. A clear evidence of their disobedience is their persistent failure to bring to the temple of the LORD the *full tithes* (ten per cent of their earnings and produce; Num 18; Lev 27). If they meet that obligation in the future, God will offer abundant blessing and protection from disasters such as a plague of *locusts.* All nations will recognize this special favor which they enjoy with God. Currently, however, the *arrogant* and the *evil-doers* seem to be prospering.
3.16-4.4 The Contrast between the Fate of the Faithful and of the Disobedient.
3.16-18 The faithful within Israel will join together in mutual support (*spoke with one another*) in distinction from the disobedient majority. God has the names of the obedient recorded in a sacred book, as in Ps 69.28; Ex 32.30-34, so that the sharp distinction between *the righteous and the wicked* within Israel is clear.

The Great Day of the LORD

4 [o]See, the day is coming, burning like
an oven, when all the arrogant and
all evildoers will be stubble; the day that
comes shall burn them up, says the LORD of
hosts, so that it will leave them neither root
nor branch. 2 But for you who revere my
name the sun of righteousness shall rise,
with healing in its wings. You shall go out
leaping like calves from the stall. 3 And you
shall tread down the wicked, for they will
be ashes under the soles of your feet, on the
day when I act, says the LORD of hosts.
4 Remember the teaching of my servant
Moses, the statutes and ordinances that I
commanded him at Horeb for all Israel.
5 Lo, I will send you the prophet Elijah
before the great and terrible day of the LORD
comes. 6 He will turn the hearts of parents
to their children and the hearts of children
to their parents, so that I will not come and
strike the land with a curse.[p]

[o] Ch 4.1–6 are Ch 3.19–24 in Heb [p] Or *a ban of utter destruction*

4.1-3 Here are contrasted the fiery punishment of the *arrogant* in the day of judgment, and the healing of the faithful. The agent of healing is the *sun of righteousness*, whose role of bringing life and light is assigned to God himself in Ps 84.11 and Isa 60.19-20, and to the people of God in Isa 60.1-3. The righteous will *leap* for joy, while treading under foot the *ashes* of the wicked.
4.4-5 Conclusion.
(1) In the language of Deuteronomy 4-5, there is a reminder to the people to obey the Law of Moses, which became available in its edited form through Ezra after the return of Israel from exile in Babylon. (2) There is a solemn warning that Elijah – who was God's agent of judgment in the reign of wicked King Ahab (1 Kings 17-21) – will return on *the day of the* LORD. Since Elijah was taken up to heaven, according to 2 Kings 2.1-12, it was believed that God would send him back to fulfill his task of renewal of God's people (Sir 48.1-12; Mk 6.15; 9.2-13; 15.35; Lk 9.7-8,19). His future coming and call to repentance will ward off further divine judgment.

4.1
Joel 2.31; Ob 18; Am 2.9

4.2
Mal 3.16; Lk 1.78; Eph 5.14

4.3
Mic 7.10; Zech 10.5

4.4
Ex 20.3

4.5
Mt 11.14; Mk 9.11; Lk 1.17

THE NEW COVENANT COMMONLY CALLED THE NEW TESTAMENT OF OUR LORD AND SAVIOR JESUS CHRIST

New Revised Standard Version

ALPHABETICAL LIST OF BOOKS OF THE NEW TESTAMENT

The Gospel According to

MATTHEW

The Genealogy of Jesus the Messiah

1 An account of the genealogy[a] of Jesus
the Messiah,[b] the son of David, the
son of Abraham.
2 Abraham was the father of Isaac, and
Isaac the father of Jacob, and Jacob the
father of Judah and his brothers, [3]and Judah
the father of Perez and Zerah by Tamar,
and Perez the father of Hezron, and Hezron
the father of Aram, [4]and Aram the father
of Aminadab, and Aminadab the father of
Nahshon, and Nahshon the father of Salmon,
[5]and Salmon the father of Boaz by Rahab,
and Boaz the father of Obed by Ruth, and
Obed the father of Jesse, [6]and Jesse the
father of King David.
And David was the father of Solomon by
the wife of Uriah, [7]and Solomon the father
of Rehoboam, and Rehoboam the father of
Abijah, and Abijah the father of Asaph,[c]
[8]and Asaph[c] the father of Jehoshaphat, and
Jehoshaphat the father of Joram, and Joram
the father of Uzziah, [9]and Uzziah the father
of Jotham, and Jotham the father of Ahaz,
and Ahaz the father of Hezekiah, [10]and
Hezekiah the father of Manasseh, and
Manasseh the father of Amos,[d] and Amos[d]
the father of Josiah, [11]and Josiah the father
of Jechoniah and his brothers, at the time
of the deportation to Babylon.
12 And after the deportation to Babylon:
Jechoniah was the father of Salathiel, and
Salathiel the father of Zerubbabel, [13]and
Zerubbabel the father of Abiud, and Abiud
the father of Eliakim, and Eliakim the father
of Azor, [14]and Azor the father of Zadok, and
Zadok the father of Achim, and Achim the
father of Eliud, [15]and Eliud the father of
Eleazar, and Eleazar the father of Matthan,
and Matthan the father of Jacob, [16]and
Jacob the father of Joseph the husband of
Mary, of whom Jesus was born, who is
called the Messiah.[e]
17 So all the generations from Abraham
to David are fourteen generations; and from
David to the deportation to Babylon, fourteen generations; and from the deportation
to Babylon to the Messiah,[e] fourteen generations.

The Birth of Jesus the Messiah

18 Now the birth of Jesus the Messiah[b]
took place in this way. When his mother
Mary had been engaged to Joseph, but before
they lived together, she was found to be
with child from the Holy Spirit. [19]Her husband Joseph, being a righteous man and
unwilling to expose her to public disgrace,
planned to dismiss her quietly. [20]But just
when he had resolved to do this, an angel
of the Lord appeared to him in a dream and
said, "Joseph, son of David, do not be afraid
to take Mary as your wife, for the child
conceived in her is from the Holy Spirit.
[21]She will bear a son, and you are to name
him Jesus, for he will save his people from
their sins." [22]All this took place to fulfill
what had been spoken by the Lord through
the prophet:
23 "Look, the virgin shall conceive and bear
a son,
and they shall name him Emmanuel,"
which means, "God is with us." [24]When
Joseph awoke from sleep, he did as the
angel of the Lord commanded him; he took
her as his wife, [25]but had no marital relations with her until she had borne a son;[f]
and he named him Jesus.

The Visit of the Wise Men

2 In the time of King Herod, after Jesus
was born in Bethlehem of Judea, wise
men[g] from the East came to Jerusalem,
[2]asking, "Where is the child who has been
born king of the Jews? For we observed his
star at its rising,[h] and have come to pay him
homage." [3]When King Herod heard this, he
was frightened, and all Jerusalem with him;
[4]and calling together all the chief priests
and scribes of the people, he inquired of
them where the Messiah[e] was to be born.
[5]They told him, "In Bethlehem of Judea; for
so it has been written by the prophet:
6 'And you, Bethlehem, in the land of Judah,
are by no means least among the rulers
of Judah;
for from you shall come a ruler
who is to shepherd[i] my people Israel.'"

1.1 Ps 132.11; Isa 11.1; Lk 1.32; Jn 7.42; Acts 2.30; 13.23; Rom 1.3; Gen 12.3; 22.18; Gal 3.16
1.2 Gen 21.1,3; 25.26; 29.35
1.3 Gen 38.27ff; Ruth 4.18ff; 1 Chr 2.5,9ff
1.6 1 Sam 16.1; 17.12; 2 Sam 17.24
1.7 1 Chr 3.10
1.10 2 Kings 20.21; 1 Chr 3.13
1.11 2 Kings 24.14-16; Jer 27.20; 39.9
1.12 1 Chr 3.17,19
1.16 Lk 1.27
1.18 Lk 1.27; 1.35
1.19 Deut 22.13-21
1.21 Lk 2.21; Jn 1.29; Acts 4.12; 13.23,38
1.23 Isa 7.14
1.25 Ex 13.2; Lk 2.21
2.1 Lk 2.4-7; 1.5
2.2 Jer 23.5; Zech 9.9; Mk 15.2; Jn 1.49
2.5 Jn 7.42
2.6 Mic 5.2; Jn 21.16

[a]Or *birth* [b]Or *Jesus Christ* [c]Other ancient authorities read *Asa* [d]Other ancient authorities read *Amon* [e]Or *the Christ* [f]Other ancient authorities read *her firstborn son* [g]Or *astrologers*; Gk *magi* [h]Or *in the East* [i]Or *rule*

See the Introductions, pp. 7–8 and 77–78 above.

1.1 *Messiah.* From the Hebrew word meaning "anointed one." It was applied to anyone chosen or sent by God, especially a political or priestly agent commissioned by God to set the people in a right relationship with their Creator. *Son of David* and *son of Abraham* link Jesus to the covenants of promise between God and his people (Gen 12.1-3; 2 Sam 7.8-16).
1.1-16 This genealogy of Jesus differs from the one in Lk 3.23-28: Matthew's version places Jesus in the history of Israel, beginning with Abraham; Luke's version links Jesus with the whole human race, beginning with Adam.
1.17 *Fourteen generations.* These multiples of seven recall the sacredness of that number, and may point to the Davidic descent of Jesus, since the numerical equivalent of the Hebrew consonants in David is fourteen.
1.18-25 The first of Matthew's five opening stories based on Old Testament themes or quotations: (1) the birth of Jesus (cf. Isa 7.14); (2) the visit of the wise men (2.13-15); (3) the escape to Egypt (2.13-15); (4) the massacre of the infants (2.16-18); (5) the return from Egypt (2.19-23). Old Testament themes recalled here include Israel's exodus from Egypt; Joseph's dream; the ruler who killed children; the escape of the child; the return to the land of promise. The ministry and significance of Jesus are pictured by Matthew as God's renewal of the true covenant people.
1.18 *Engaged.* Engagement involved the formal exchange of consent before witnesses and the transfer of legal rights over the bride, and thus was virtually as binding as marriage. *From the Holy Spirit.* The Spirit is the unseen agent at work in all these events, as in Gen 1.2; Ps 104.30; Mt 3.16; 27.50; Lk 1.35.
1.19 *Public disgrace...dismiss her quietly.* Termination of engagement or marriage usually included a public act before witnesses, but Joseph seems to have tried to ease the situation by avoiding this.
1.20 *Angel of the Lord.* Like the Hebrew word, *angel* means "messenger"; here an agent of God with message or action (1.24; 2.13,19; 28.2; Gen 31.11; 37.5,9). *In a dream.* Dreams were a common means of divine communication in the biblical tradition (Gen 31.11; 1 Kings 3.5; Dan 2.3).
1.21 *Jesus.* In Hebrew, "Yeshua," meaning "Yahweh [the distinctive name of the God of Israel] is my salvation."
1.23 The quotation is from Isa 7.14 (see note there). *The virgin shall conceive* is from the Greek translation (*parthenos*), but the Hebrew original (*almah*) means "young woman."
2.1-12 The second story, the visit of the wise men, shows the influence of Mic 5.2 (*Bethlehem*) and 2 Sam 5.2,9 (*shepherd*).
2.1-4 *Herod.* Called Herod the Great, he ruled as a puppet of the Romans from 37 to 4 BCE. *Wise men* is in Greek *magoi*, a term for magicians and for astrologers, who claim to read the future by the movement of the stars. *From the East* refers to Babylonia or Persia. Herod and his supporters were *frightened* because they feared some supernatural threat to his rule. The *chief priests* and *scribes* who were consulted about the birthplace of the Messiah later become Jesus' bitterest enemies (23.1 ff; 26.57-68). *Scribes* were consulted to give interpretations of scripture and applications of the law.
2.6 The quotation is from Mic 5.2, but the new *ruler* will serve as a *shepherd* of his people (2 Sam 5.2).

7 Then Herod secretly called for the wise
men[j] and learned from them the exact time
when the star had appeared. [8]Then he sent
them to Bethlehem, saying, "Go and search
diligently for the child; and when you have
found him, bring me word so that I may
also go and pay him homage." [9]When they
had heard the king, they set out; and there,
ahead of them, went the star that they had
seen at its rising,[k] until it stopped over the
place where the child was. [10]When they
saw that the star had stopped,[l] they were
overwhelmed with joy. [11]On entering the
house, they saw the child with Mary his
mother; and they knelt down and paid him
homage. Then, opening their treasure chests,
they offered him gifts of gold, frankincense,
and myrrh. [12]And having been warned in
a dream not to return to Herod, they left for
their own country by another road.

The Escape to Egypt

13 Now after they had left, an angel of
the Lord appeared to Joseph in a dream and
said, "Get up, take the child and his mother,
and flee to Egypt, and remain there until I
tell you; for Herod is about to search for the
child, to destroy him." [14]Then Joseph[m] got
up, took the child and his mother by night,
and went to Egypt, [15]and remained there
until the death of Herod. This was to fulfill
what had been spoken by the Lord through
the prophet, "Out of Egypt I have called my
son."

The Massacre of the Infants

16 When Herod saw that he had been
tricked by the wise men,[n] he was infuriated,
and he sent and killed all the children in
and around Bethlehem who were two years
old or under, according to the time that he
had learned from the wise men.[n] [17]Then
was fulfilled what had been spoken through
the prophet Jeremiah:

[18] "A voice was heard in Ramah,
wailing and loud lamentation,
Rachel weeping for her children;
she refused to be consoled, because
they are no more."

The Return from Egypt

19 When Herod died, an angel of the
Lord suddenly appeared in a dream to Joseph
in Egypt and said, [20]"Get up, take the child
and his mother, and go to the land of Israel,
for those who were seeking the child's life
are dead." [21]Then Joseph[o] got up, took the
child and his mother, and went to the land
of Israel. [22]But when he heard that Archelaus
was ruling over Judea in place of his father
Herod, he was afraid to go there. And after
being warned in a dream, he went away to
the district of Galilee. [23]There he made his
home in a town called Nazareth, so that
what had been spoken through the prophets might be fulfilled, "He will be called a
Nazorean."

The Proclamation of John the Baptist

3 In those days John the Baptist appeared in the wilderness of Judea,
proclaiming, [2]"Repent, for the kingdom of
heaven has come near."[p] [3]This is the one
of whom the prophet Isaiah spoke when he
said,

"The voice of one crying out in the wilderness:
'Prepare the way of the Lord,
make his paths straight.'"

[4]Now John wore clothing of camel's hair
with a leather belt around his waist, and his
food was locusts and wild honey. [5]Then the
people of Jerusalem and all Judea were going
out to him, and all the region along the
Jordan, [6]and they were baptized by him in
the river Jordan, confessing their sins.

7 But when he saw many Pharisees and
Sadducees coming for baptism, he said to
them, "You brood of vipers! Who warned
you to flee from the wrath to come? [8]Bear
fruit worthy of repentance. [9]Do not presume
to say to yourselves, 'We have Abraham as
our ancestor'; for I tell you, God is able from
these stones to raise up children to Abraham.
[10]Even now the ax is lying at the root of the
trees; every tree therefore that does not bear
good fruit is cut down and thrown into the
fire.

11 "I baptize you with[q] water for repentance, but one who is more powerful than
I is coming after me; I am not worthy
to carry his sandals. He will baptize you

[j] Or *astrologers*; Gk *magi* [k] Or *in the East* [l] Gk *saw the star* [m] Gk *he* [n] Or *astrologers*; Gk *magi* [o] Gk *he* [p] Or *is at hand* [q] Or *in*

2.11 Mt 1.18; Ps 72.10; Isa 60.6
2.12 Mt 2.22
2.13 ver 19,20
2.14 Hos 11.1
2.18 Jer 31.15
2.22 Mt 3.13; Lk 2.39
2.23 Lk 1.26; Mk 1.24
3.2 Dan 2.44; Mt 4.17; 10.7
3.3 Isa 40.3; Mk 1.3; Lk 3.4; Jn 1.23; Lk 1.76
3.4 2 Kings 1.8; Lev 11.22
3.6 Acts 19.4,18
3.7 Mt 12.34; 23.33; Rom 5.9; 1 Thess 1.10
3.8 Acts 26.20
3.9 Jn 8.33,39; Acts 13.26; Rom 4.1,11,16
3.10 Mt 7.19
3.11 Acts 1.5; 11.16; 19.4; Isa 4.4; Acts 2.3,4

2.11 Mention of their *house* in Bethlehem indicates that Mary and Joseph lived there, and after returning from Egypt, moved to Nazareth (2.22-23), in contrast to Lk 2.1-7, where their original home is there.
2.13-15 The third story: the flight to Egypt.
2.15 Quoted from Hos 11.1, the original reference is to Israel as God's *son.* Matthew shows the new exodus of the new Israel, formed through Jesus.
2.16-18 The fourth story recalls Pharaoh's decision to kill all the new-born males in Israel (Ex 1.22).
2.18 The quotation is from Jer 31.15. *Ramah* is an Ephraimite town between Bethel and Jerusalem, where the women of Israel, symbolized by *Rachel,* bemoan the loss of their offspring, as occurred during Israel's exile in Babylon (*cf.* Jer 40.1). Rachel herself died near Bethlehem as she gave birth to Benjamin (Gen 30.22-24; 35.16-20; 41.52).
2.19-23 The fifth story describes the return of Mary and Joseph from Egypt after Herod's death, and their subsequent move to Nazareth.
2.22 *Archelaus.* Son of Herod, ruler of Judea from 4 BCE to 6 CE, when the Romans deposed him for incompetence.
2.23 *Nazareth.* An obscure village near Sepphoris, the capital of Galilee during the Roman period. *He shall be called a Nazarene* is not a direct Old Testament quotation, but may link this town with either the messianic "branch" (Heb. *netzer*) or the strict-living Nazirites (such as Samson, Judg 13.5); see Acts 24.5.
3.1-7.29 Narrative-Discourse Section One (see Introductions, pp. 77–8 above): Preparation for Ministry. The clue at the end of each major section of Matthew is a form of the statement, "When Jesus had finished...": 7.28; 11.1; 13.53; 19.1; 26.1.
3.1-17 *cf.* Mk 1.1-11; Lk 3.1-22. Jesus and John the Baptist. Matthew's account of Jesus and John emphasizes John's role as in accord with the Jewish scriptures, while Luke's stresses the potential inclusion in the new community of those excluded by Jewish standards.
3.1-3 John is the one whose coming was prophesied in Isa 40.3, calling out *in the wilderness* for the renewal of God's people. (The original call was to prepare the way in the wilderness for Israel to return from exile in Babylon.) Later John will be acclaimed as the greatest of the prophets (11.11) and as the new Elijah (11.14). His call to Israel to *repent* (meaning "turn around," in the sense of change one's mind and direction) is echoed by Jesus (4.17). *The kingdom of heaven* (literally, "of the heavens") refers to the coming new era when the God who is sovereign ruler in the heavens will rule over the earth and its inhabitants.
3.4-6 John's clothing recalls that of the prophet Elijah (2 Kings 1.8), who is later identified with John (11.14). Baptism by John is purification for a new beginning in the life of God's people, accompanied by God's grant of forgiveness of sins, rather than a periodic ritual washing (Ex 40.12-15; Lev 16.4,24).
3.7-10 *cf.* Lk 3.7-9. John's challenge to the Jewish leadership.
3.7 *Pharisees and Sadducees.* The Pharisees were laypeople who met in homes for study of the Law and the prophets, for worship and for table fellowship. They wanted to understand the relevance of the Law for their daily lives and how to maintain purity as God's people. The Sadducees were a group of supporters for the priests and the temple who cooperated with the Romans and were thus given power through the local council established by the Romans for regional control. They recognized only the Law of Moses as authoritative for God's people.
3.9 John's radical theme is that descent from Abraham is no guarantee of sharing in God's people. See Jn 8.39; Gal 3.9; 4.21; Rom 4.13-25.
3.11-12 The One who is *Coming.* John's preparatory role through his call to repentance and baptism resembles the purification rites of the Dead Sea community. But the one who is *coming* will purify God's new people with *Holy Spirit and fire.* Spirit (Greek, *pneuma,* which can mean "wind" or "breath") is the power of God to shape or reshape the world, as "fire" is the power to judge and purge (*burn*) it.

3.12 Mal 3.3; Mt 13.30
3.13 Jn 1.31-34
3.16 Isa 11.2; 42.1; Jn 1.32
3.17 Ps 2.7; Mt 12.18; 17.5; Mk 9.7; Lk 9.35
4.2 Ex 34.28; 1 Kings 19.8
4.3 1 Thess 3.5
4.4 Deut 8.3
4.5 Neh 11.1; Dan 9.24; Mt 27.53; Rev 21.10
4.6 Ps 91.11,12
4.7 Deut 6.16
4.10 1 Chr 21.1; Deut 6.13
4.11 Mt 26.53; Lk 22.43; Heb 1.14
4.15 Isa 9.1,2
4.16 Isa 42.7; Lk 2.32
4.17 Mt 3.2; 10.7
4.18 Jn 1.35-42
4.20 Lk 18.28
4.23 Mk 1.39; Lk 4.15,44; Mt 9.35; 13.54; Mk 1.21; 1.34
4.24 Lk 2.2; Mt 8.16,28,33; Mk 1.32; Lk 8.36; Mt 17.15; 8.6; 9.2,6
4.25 Mk 3.7,8; Lk 6.17

with[r] the Holy Spirit and fire. 12 His winnowing fork is in his hand, and he will clear his threshing floor and will gather his wheat into the granary; but the chaff he will burn with unquenchable fire."

The Baptism of Jesus

13 Then Jesus came from Galilee to John at the Jordan, to be baptized by him. 14 John would have prevented him, saying, "I need to be baptized by you, and do you come to me?" 15 But Jesus answered him, "Let it be so now; for it is proper for us in this way to fulfill all righteousness." Then he consented. 16 And when Jesus had been baptized, just as he came up from the water, suddenly the heavens were opened to him and he saw the Spirit of God descending like a dove and alighting on him. 17 And a voice from heaven said, "This is my Son, the Beloved,[s] with whom I am well pleased."

The Temptation of Jesus

4 Then Jesus was led up by the Spirit into the wilderness to be tempted by the devil. 2 He fasted forty days and forty nights, and afterwards he was famished. 3 The tempter came and said to him, "If you are the Son of God, command these stones to become loaves of bread." 4 But he answered, "It is written,

'One does not live by bread alone,
but by every word that comes from the mouth of God.'"

5 Then the devil took him to the holy city and placed him on the pinnacle of the temple, 6 saying to him, "If you are the Son of God, throw yourself down; for it is written,

'He will command his angels concerning you,'
and 'On their hands they will bear you up,
so that you will not dash your foot against a stone.'"

7 Jesus said to him, "Again it is written, 'Do not put the Lord your God to the test.'"

8 Again, the devil took him to a very high mountain and showed him all the kingdoms of the world and their splendor; 9 and he said to him, "All these I will give you, if you will fall down and worship me." 10 Jesus said to him, "Away with you, Satan! for it is written,

'Worship the Lord your God,
and serve only him.'"

11 Then the devil left him, and suddenly angels came and waited on him.

Jesus Begins His Ministry in Galilee

12 Now when Jesus[t] heard that John had been arrested, he withdrew to Galilee. 13 He left Nazareth and made his home in Capernaum by the sea, in the territory of Zebulun and Naphtali, 14 so that what had been spoken through the prophet Isaiah might be fulfilled:

15 "Land of Zebulun, land of Naphtali,
on the road by the sea, across the Jordan, Galilee of the Gentiles—
16 the people who sat in darkness
have seen a great light,
and for those who sat in the region and shadow of death
light has dawned."

17 From that time Jesus began to proclaim, "Repent, for the kingdom of heaven has come near."[u]

Jesus Calls the First Disciples

18 As he walked by the Sea of Galilee, he saw two brothers, Simon, who is called Peter, and Andrew his brother, casting a net into the sea—for they were fishermen. 19 And he said to them, "Follow me, and I will make you fish for people." 20 Immediately they left their nets and followed him. 21 As he went from there, he saw two other brothers, James son of Zebedee and his brother John, in the boat with their father Zebedee, mending their nets, and he called them. 22 Immediately they left the boat and their father, and followed him.

Jesus Ministers to Crowds of People

23 Jesus[v] went throughout Galilee, teaching in their synagogues and proclaiming the good news[w] of the kingdom and curing every disease and every sickness among the people. 24 So his fame spread throughout all Syria, and they brought to him all the sick, those who were afflicted with various diseases and pains, demoniacs, epileptics, and paralytics, and he cured them. 25 And great crowds followed him from Galilee, the Decapolis, Jerusalem, Judea, and from beyond the Jordan.

[r] Or *in* [s] Or *my beloved Son* [t] Gk *he* [u] Or *is at hand* [v] Gk *He* [w] Gk *gospel*

3.13-17 The Baptism of Jesus. See Mk 1.9-11; Lk 3.21-22. **3.13** *At the Jordan.* John chose to perform the rite of baptism as preparation for the new era of God's rule at the same place that Israel entered the land of promise under Joshua (Josh 3). **3.16-17** Jesus is confirmed by God as the agent of renewal of his people by the coming of the *Spirit,* which will provide him with God's wisdom, knowledge and power (Isa 11.1-2), and by the voice from God, acclaiming him as *Son* and agent of God's rule (Ps 2.7), in whom God is *well-pleased* (Isa 42.1). The *dove* symbolizes the coming of a new covenant relationship, as it did in the days of Noah (Gen 8.1-5). **4.1-11** Jesus' temptation is a series of testings to see if he will use his extraordinary powers in self-gratifying ways, with the *devil* (meaning "accuser" or *tempter*) quoting scripture. To each of them he responds with a verse from scripture pointing to dedication solely to the will and purpose of God. His time of testing lasts *forty days,* as did those of Moses (Ex 24.18) and Elijah (1 Kings 19.8). All three of them were preparing for their roles as agents of renewal for the covenant people. **4.3-4** The need for food: Deut 8.3. **4.5-7** The proposal (Ps 91.11-12) to test God's power in public: Deut 6.16. **4.8-10** The promise of universal rule if Jesus *worships* the devil: Deut 6.13. Identified as *Satan,* the tempter is not so much an "accuser" (Job 1.6-12) as an adversary, seeking to thwart God's purposes for his people (1 Chr 12.1). **4.12-17** Jesus' Ministry is launched in Galilee. John's arrest marks the beginning of Jesus' bringing the light of the good news, as in Mk 1.14-15, and calling his hearers to make an about face (*repent*) in preparation for the new era. The wide scope of Jesus' activity in both Jewish and Gentile regions is indicated in the quotation from Isa 9.1-2. The *road by the sea* runs through *Capernaum,* a commercial fishing town on the shore of the lake of *Galilee,* where Jesus moves his residence from Nazareth. Galilee was dominated by *Gentiles* and hellenistic culture from the time of Seleucid control of Syria-Palestine (second century BCE). **4.18-22** *cf.* Mk 1.16-20. Four of the local fishermen are called by Jesus and join him to spread the good news: *Peter* (Simon, whose nickname, Rock, in Greek is Petros, and in Hebrew, Cephas; 1 Cor 1.12); *Andrew* (Peter's brother, and originally a follower of John the Baptist, Jn 1.35-41); the sons of Zebedee, *James,* and *John,* who are prominent in the lists of the twelve followers (Mt 10.2-4; Mk 3.16-19; Lk 6.14-16; Acts 1.13). **4.23-25** The range of Jesus' activities and the geographical spread of the movement. *Cf.* Mk 1.39; 3.7-10; Lk 4.44; 6.17-19. In addition to announcing the coming of God's kingdom, Jesus' healing and control of the demons (evil powers which were thought to warp human lives) attract hearers and those seeking cures from not only Jewish territory north and south and on both sides of the Jordan, but also from the *Decapolis,* a group of ten cities of developed hellenistic culture, with temples, baths, and Greek-style marketplaces.

The Beatitudes

5 When Jesus[x] saw the crowds, he went
up the mountain; and after he sat
down, his disciples came to him. 2 Then he
began to speak, and taught them, saying:
3 "Blessed are the poor in spirit, for theirs
is the kingdom of heaven.
4 "Blessed are those who mourn, for they
will be comforted.
5 "Blessed are the meek, for they will
inherit the earth.
6 "Blessed are those who hunger and
thirst for righteousness, for they will be
filled.
7 "Blessed are the merciful, for they will
receive mercy.
8 "Blessed are the pure in heart, for they
will see God.
9 "Blessed are the peacemakers, for they
will be called children of God.
10 "Blessed are those who are persecuted
for righteousness' sake, for theirs is the
kingdom of heaven.
11 "Blessed are you when people revile
you and persecute you and utter all kinds
of evil against you falsely[y] on my account.
12 Rejoice and be glad, for your reward is
great in heaven, for in the same way they
persecuted the prophets who were before
you.

Salt and Light

13 "You are the salt of the earth; but if
salt has lost its taste, how can its saltiness
be restored? It is no longer good for anything, but is thrown out and trampled under
foot.
14 "You are the light of the world. A city
built on a hill cannot be hid. 15 No one after
lighting a lamp puts it under the bushel
basket, but on the lampstand, and it gives
light to all in the house. 16 In the same way,
let your light shine before others, so that
they may see your good works and give
glory to your Father in heaven.

The Law and the Prophets

17 "Do not think that I have come to
abolish the law or the prophets; I have
come not to abolish but to fulfill. 18 For truly
I tell you, until heaven and earth pass
away, not one letter,[z] not one stroke of a
letter, will pass from the law until all is
accomplished. 19 Therefore, whoever breaks[a]
one of the least of these commandments,
and teaches others to do the same, will be
called least in the kingdom of heaven; but
whoever does them and teaches them will
be called great in the kingdom of heaven.
20 For I tell you, unless your righteousness
exceeds that of the scribes and Pharisees,
you will never enter the kingdom of heaven.

Concerning Anger

21 "You have heard that it was said to
those of ancient times, 'You shall not
murder'; and 'Whoever murders shall be
liable to judgment.' 22 But I say to you that
if you are angry with a brother or sister,[b]
you will be liable to judgment; and if you
insult[c] a brother or sister,[d] you will be liable
to the council; and if you say, 'You fool,'
you will be liable to the hell[e] of fire. 23 So
when you are offering your gift at the altar,
if you remember that your brother or sister[f]
has something against you, 24 leave your gift
there before the altar and go; first be reconciled to your brother or sister,[f] and then
come and offer your gift. 25 Come to terms
quickly with your accuser while you are on
the way to court[g] with him, or your accuser
may hand you over to the judge, and the
judge to the guard, and you will be thrown
into prison. 26 Truly I tell you, you will never
get out until you have paid the last penny.

Concerning Adultery

27 "You have heard that it was said,
'You shall not commit adultery.' 28 But I say
to you that everyone who looks at a woman
with lust has already committed adultery
with her in his heart. 29 If your right eye
causes you to sin, tear it out and throw it
away; it is better for you to lose one of your
members than for your whole body to be
thrown into hell.[e] 30 And if your right hand
causes you to sin, cut it off and throw it
away; it is better for you to lose one of your
members than for your whole body to go
into hell.[e]

[x] Gk *he* [y] Other ancient authorities lack *falsely* [z] Gk *one iota* [a] Or *annuls* [b] Gk *a brother*; other ancient authorities add *without cause* [c] Gk *say Raca to* (an obscure term of abuse) [d] Gk *a brother* [e] Gk *Gehenna* [f] Gk *your brother* [g] Gk lacks *to court*

5.1-7.29 First Major Discourse: Sermon on the Mount. Jesus' role as teacher is central in Matthew (23.8) and his followers' primary task is to instruct others (28.20). But first he leaves the *crowds* and teaches his *disciples*, which means "learners." As Moses first instructed Israel from the *mountain* in Sinai (Ex 19), so Jesus teaches his followers from a mountain (5.1). The teachings recorded here are in large part from the sayings source also used by Luke, but many are unique to Matthew.
5.2-10 Each of these pronouncements (traditionally called "beatitudes") by Jesus begins with "blessed," which means that God honors and rewards his people as they obey him and do his work. Luke's version of these blessings is addressed to the hearers (*you poor*; Lk 6.20), but Matthew's speak in more general terms (*the poor in spirit* [5.3], who live in dependence upon God alone). *Cf.* Rom 15.26; Gal 2.10; Acts 2.24.
5.4 *cf. those who weep* in Lk 6.21, whose sorrow will be turned into joy as God's rule is established in the world.
5.5 *Meek* means "humble," those who do not press for personal advantages. They will share in God's rule over the whole *earth*.
5.6 Those whose chief desire is for them and the world to be in right relationship (*righteousness*) with God will find fulfillment.
5.8 Purity of *heart* concerns clarity of insight about God's will and purpose for his people, as stated in Prov 3.3-6.
5.9-12 The faithful community will work to reconcile others to God (*peacemakers*), but will be involved in persecution as a result of their efforts to prepare others for God's rule. God's *reward* for their courage and fidelity is already stored up for them *in heaven*.
5.13 Just as salt improves the taste of food, so they are to fulfill their role as bringers of peace and justice in *the earth*, or else be thrown out as useless.
5.14-16 Just as lights are lighted to provide illumination, so the followers through their good deeds are to bring light to others and thus bring *glory* to God.
5.17-20 Jesus speaks first of the role of the law in the life of the new community: its aims for God's people are to be *fulfilled*, including both the five books of Moses (*law*) and the *prophets*, which for Jews includes the Former Prophets (Joshua through Kings) and the Latter Prophets (Isaiah, Jeremiah, Ezekiel and the Twelve Minor Prophets). The Writings are the other historical and poetic books. Together they comprise the Jewish scriptures. Not even the tiniest letter (*iota*) or the smallest bit of writing will disappear. The teachers in the Jesus movement are to demand strict obedience, with standards and integrity exceeding those of the official teachers of the first century (*scribes and Pharisees*), if the members are to share in the new rule of God.
5.21-48 The contrasts between Jesus' understanding of the law (which is quoted on each issue) and those of the Jewish teachers. In each case, Jesus speaks on his own authority: *I say to you*.
5.21-26 Concerning Murder (Ex 20.13; Deut 5.17). More basic than prevention of murder or punishing culprits are (1) avoidance of anger or insults toward others and (2) efforts to effect reconciliation. The *court* was the regional council empowered by the Romans and composed of priests and their wealthy supporters with permission to adjudicate intra-Jewish disputes. The *hell of fire* was named for and symbolized by the ever-burning trash dump in the valley of Hinnom just south of Jerusalem (2 Kings 23.10).
5.27-30 Concerning Adultery (Ex 20.14; Deut 5.18). As serious a violation of a woman as adultery is a lustful look. Eyes and other bodily members are to be kept under strict self-control.

5.1 Mk 3.13; Jn 6.3
5.3 Mk 10.14; Lk 22.29
5.4 Isa 61.2,3
5.6 Isa 55.1,2
5.8 Heb 12.14; 1 Jn 3.2
5.9 Rom 8.14
5.10 1 Pet 3.14
5.11 1 Pet 4.14
5.12 Acts 7.52; 1 Thess 2.15; Jas 5.10
5.13 Mk 9.50; Lk 14.34,35
5.14 Phil 2.15
5.15 Mk 4.21; Lk 8.16
5.16 1 Pet 2.12
5.17 Rom 3.31; Gal 3.24
5.18 Lk 16.17
5.19 Jas 2.10
5.21 Ex 20.13; Deut 5.17
5.22 1 Jn 3.15; Jas 2.20
5.23 Mt 8.4; 23.19
5.25 Prov 25.8; Lk 12.57-59
5.27 Ex 20.14; Deut 5.18
5.28 Job 31.1; Prov 6.25
5.29 Mt 18.9; Mk 9.43-47

Concerning Divorce

31 "It was also said, 'Whoever divorces his wife, let him give her a certificate of divorce.' 32But I say to you that anyone who divorces his wife, except on the ground of unchastity, causes her to commit adultery; and whoever marries a divorced woman commits adultery.

Concerning Oaths

33 "Again, you have heard that it was said to those of ancient times, 'You shall not swear falsely, but carry out the vows you have made to the Lord.' 34But I say to you, Do not swear at all, either by heaven, for it is the throne of God, 35or by the earth, for it is his footstool, or by Jerusalem, for it is the city of the great King. 36And do not swear by your head, for you cannot make one hair white or black. 37Let your word be 'Yes, yes' or 'No, no'; anything more than this comes from the evil one.[h]

Concerning Retaliation

38 "You have heard that it was said, 'An eye for an eye and a tooth for a tooth.' 39But I say to you, Do not resist an evildoer. But if anyone strikes you on the right cheek, turn the other also; 40and if anyone wants to sue you and take your coat, give your cloak as well; 41and if anyone forces you to go one mile, go also the second mile. 42Give to everyone who begs from you, and do not refuse anyone who wants to borrow from you.

Love for Enemies

43 "You have heard that it was said, 'You shall love your neighbor and hate your enemy.' 44But I say to you, Love your enemies and pray for those who persecute you, 45so that you may be children of your Father in heaven; for he makes his sun rise on the evil and on the good, and sends rain on the righteous and on the unrighteous. 46For if you love those who love you, what reward do you have? Do not even the tax collectors do the same? 47And if you greet only your brothers and sisters,[i] what more are you doing than others? Do not even the Gentiles do the same? 48Be perfect, therefore, as your heavenly Father is perfect.

Concerning Almsgiving

6 "Beware of practicing your piety before others in order to be seen by them; for then you have no reward from your Father in heaven.

2 "So whenever you give alms, do not sound a trumpet before you, as the hypocrites do in the synagogues and in the streets, so that they may be praised by others. Truly I tell you, they have received their reward. 3But when you give alms, do not let your left hand know what your right hand is doing, 4so that your alms may be done in secret; and your Father who sees in secret will reward you.[j]

Concerning Prayer

5 "And whenever you pray, do not be like the hypocrites; for they love to stand and pray in the synagogues and at the street corners, so that they may be seen by others. Truly I tell you, they have received their reward. 6But whenever you pray, go into your room and shut the door and pray to your Father who is in secret; and your Father who sees in secret will reward you.[j]

7 "When you are praying, do not heap up empty phrases as the Gentiles do; for they think that they will be heard because of their many words. 8Do not be like them, for your Father knows what you need before you ask him.

9 "Pray then in this way:
Our Father in heaven,
hallowed be your name.
10 Your kingdom come.
Your will be done,
on earth as it is in heaven.
11 Give us this day our daily bread.[k]
12 And forgive us our debts,
as we also have forgiven our debtors.
13 And do not bring us to the time of trial,[l]
but rescue us from the evil one.[m]

14For if you forgive others their trespasses, your heavenly Father will also forgive you; 15but if you do not forgive others, neither will your Father forgive your trespasses.

[h] Or *evil* [i] Gk *your brothers* [j] Other ancient authorities add *openly* [k] Or *our bread for tomorrow* [l] Or *us into temptation* [m] Or *from evil.* Other ancient authorities add, in some form, *For the kingdom and the power and the glory are yours forever. Amen.*

5.31 Deut 24.1-4; Mk 10.11,12; Lk 16.18
5.33 Lev 19.12; Num 30.2; Deut 23.21; Mt 23.16
5.34 Jas 5.12; Isa 66.1
5.38 Ex 21.24; Lev 24.20; Deut 19.21
5.39 Prov 24.29; Lk 6.29; Rom 12.17,19; 1 Cor 6.7; 1 Pet 3.9
5.42 Deut 15.8; Lk 6.30
5.43 Lev 19.18; Deut 23.6; Ps 41.10
5.44 Rom 12.14; Acts 7.60; 1 Cor 4.12; 1 Pet 2.23
5.45 Job 25.3
5.48 Lev 19.2; Col 1.28; Jas 1.4
6.1 Mt 23.5
6.2 Rom 12.8
6.4 Col 3.23,24
6.5 Mk 11.25; Lk 18.10-14
6.6 2 Kings 4.33
6.7 Eccl 5.2; 1 Kings 18.26,29
6.10 Mt 26.39,42
6.11 Prov 30.8
6.12 Mt 18.21
6.13 Jn 17.15; 2 Thess 3.3; Jas 1.13
6.14 Mk 11.15,26; Eph 4.32; Col 3.13
6.15 Mt 18.35

5.31-32 Concerning Divorce (Deut 24.1-4). Jesus' strict rules on adultery are explained more fully in Mt 19.1-12. See also Mk 10.1-12. As was not the case in Jewish law, males are said by Jesus to be equally responsible for the breakdown of marriage.
5.33-37 Concerning Oaths (Lev 19.12; Num 30.2; Ex 20.7; Deut 5.11). Rather than determine one's responsibility to meet an obligation by deciding the sincerity and authority of one's oath, it is essential that all one's statements are reliable and unequivocal.
5.38-42 Concerning Retaliation (Ex 21.24; Deut 19.21). Rather than demand equal compensation for what others have taken, God's people are to overcome greed by generosity toward the wrongdoer.
5.43-48 Concerning Love for Enemies (Lev 19.18). There was debate as to who was one's neighbor and a widespread assumption that outsiders were enemies and thus targets of hatred, although no scripture directly states this. Ps 58.6-11; 68.21-31; 83.13-15 call for punishment of one's enemies, and the Dead Sea Scrolls call for hatred of them (Manual of Discipline 1.3-4). Jesus calls for responding to enemies with love, which can transform them.
5.46 *Tax collectors* were those who collected taxes for the Romans. They contracted for an annual amount, but could keep what they collected beyond the agreed-upon figure. Their work involved assessing goods in transit through Palestine, which put them in contact with ritually unclean items. Accordingly, they were classed by pious Jews as sinners.
5.48 *Perfect* means "mature," that which achieves its intended objectives.
6.1-18 Jesus' View of the Three Major Features of Jewish Piety: Alms, Prayer and Fasting.
6.1-8 Gifts to others in need are to be private rather than ostentatious public acts in the presence of the pious (*synagogues*) or on the *streets.* Prayers are addressed to God, not to impress the public with pompous language. God rewards genuine acts of charity and heeds the requests of his faithful people.
6.9-15 The model of prayer is given in a simpler form in Lk 11.2-4, where God is addressed intimately and affectionately as Father (given in Mk 14.36 in the Semitic form as "Abba," equivalent to "Pappa" or "Daddy").
6.11 *Daily bread* may mean "bread for the following day," enough for one to survive on from day to day in total dependence on God, as Israel survived by God's daily supply of manna in the wilderness (Ex 16).

6.16-18 Fasting is to be a means of self-discipline, not a mode of showing off one's piety. Only in Matthew.
6.19-7.27 General Instructions for the Faithful Community.
6.19-21 As in Lk 12.33-34, *treasures in heaven* are God's rewards for obedience and fidelity, in contrast with tangible possessions.
6.22-23 *cf.* Lk 11.33-34. The *eye* was perceived as the mode of illumination for the body. When the eye is not attuned to the light of God, the whole inner being is overcome with darkness.
6.24-34 *Wealth* translates Mammon, the Aramaic word for tangible possessions, which can take control of human life. God's faithful people are to be free from anxiety and the need to rely on physical possessions to guarantee the future. The primary concern is to be for the coming of God's rule and for his scheme of setting things right in the world (*righteousness*).
7.1-5 Self-evaluation is essential, and rules out judging others. *Cf.* fuller tradition in Lk 6.37-38,41,42; also Rom 14.1-13.
7.6 Valuable insights and resources are to be retained for the faithful community, not distributed indiscriminately. Only in Matthew.
7.7-11 Returning to the theme of prayer. God is pictured as the one who answers the requests and meets the needs of his people. *Cf.* Lk 11.9-13. Even *evil* humans care for their loved ones. God the *Father* meets the needs of all earnest petitioners.

Concerning Fasting

16 "And whenever you fast, do not look dismal, like the hypocrites, for they disfigure their faces so as to show others that they are fasting. Truly I tell you, they have received their reward. [17]But when you fast, put oil on your head and wash your face, [18]so that your fasting may be seen not by others but by your Father who is in secret; and your Father who sees in secret will reward you.[n]

Concerning Treasures

19 "Do not store up for yourselves treasures on earth, where moth and rust[o] consume and where thieves break in and steal; [20]but store up for yourselves treasures in heaven, where neither moth nor rust[o] consumes and where thieves do not break in and steal. [21]For where your treasure is, there your heart will be also.

The Sound Eye

22 "The eye is the lamp of the body. So, if your eye is healthy, your whole body will be full of light; [23]but if your eye is unhealthy, your whole body will be full of darkness. If then the light in you is darkness, how great is the darkness!

Serving Two Masters

24 "No one can serve two masters; for a slave will either hate the one and love the other, or be devoted to the one and despise the other. You cannot serve God and wealth.[p]

Do Not Worry

25 "Therefore I tell you, do not worry about your life, what you will eat or what you will drink,[q] or about your body, what you will wear. Is not life more than food, and the body more than clothing? [26]Look at the birds of the air; they neither sow nor reap nor gather into barns, and yet your heavenly Father feeds them. Are you not of more value than they? [27]And can any of you by worrying add a single hour to your span of life?[r] [28]And why do you worry about clothing? Consider the lilies of the field, how they grow; they neither toil nor spin, [29]yet I tell you, even Solomon in all his glory was not clothed like one of these. [30]But if God so clothes the grass of the field, which is alive today and tomorrow is thrown into the oven, will he not much more clothe you—you of little faith? [31]Therefore do not worry, saying, 'What will we eat?' or 'What will we drink?' or 'What will we wear?' [32]For it is the Gentiles who strive for all these things; and indeed your heavenly Father knows that you need all these things. [33]But strive first for the kingdom of God[s] and his[t] righteousness, and all these things will be given to you as well.

34 "So do not worry about tomorrow, for tomorrow will bring worries of its own. Today's trouble is enough for today.

Judging Others

7 "Do not judge, so that you may not be judged. [2]For with the judgment you make you will be judged, and the measure you give will be the measure you get. [3]Why do you see the speck in your neighbor's[u] eye, but do not notice the log in your own eye? [4]Or how can you say to your neighbor,[v] 'Let me take the speck out of your eye,' while the log is in your own eye? [5]You hypocrite, first take the log out of your own eye, and then you will see clearly to take the speck out of your neighbor's[u] eye.

Profaning the Holy

6 "Do not give what is holy to dogs; and do not throw your pearls before swine, or they will trample them under foot and turn and maul you.

Ask, Search, Knock

7 "Ask, and it will be given you; search, and you will find; knock, and the door will be opened for you. [8]For everyone who asks receives, and everyone who searches finds, and for everyone who knocks, the door will be opened. [9]Is there anyone among you who, if your child asks for bread, will give a stone? [10]Or if the child asks for a fish, will give a snake? [11]If you then, who are evil,

6.19 Prov 23.4; 1 Tim 6.17; Heb 13.5; Jas 5.1
6.20 Lk 12.33,34; 18.22; 1 Tim 6.19; 1 Pet 1.4
6.22 Mt 20.15; Mk 7.22; Lk 11.34-36
6.24 Lk 16.13
6.25 Ps 55.22; Phil 4.6; 1 Pet 5.7
6.26 Job 38.41; Ps 147.9; Lk 12.24
6.33 Mt 19.28; Mk 10.29,30; Lk 18.29,30
7.1 Mk 4.24; Rom 2.1; 14.10; 1 Cor 4.3
7.6 Prov 9.7,8; Acts 13.45
7.7 Mk 11.24; Jn 15.7; 16.23,24; Jas 4.3; 1 Jn 3.22; 5.14,15
7.8 Jer 29.12,13

[n] Other ancient authorities add *openly* [o] Gk *eating* [p] Gk *mammon* [q] Other ancient authorities lack *or what you will drink* [r] Or *add one cubit to your height* [s] Other ancient authorities lack *of God* [t] Or *its* [u] Gk *brother's* [v] Gk *brother*

7.12 Lk 6.31; Rom 13.8-10; Gal 5.14
7.13 Lk 13.24
7.15 Jer 23.16; Mt 24.11,24; Mk 13.22; 2 Pet 2.1; 1 Jn 4.1; Rev 16.13; 19.20; Acts 20.29
7.16 Mt 12.33; Mk 3.10; Jas 3.12
7.19 Mt 3.10; Lk 3.9; Jn 15.2,6
7.21 Hos 8.2; Mt 25.11,12; Acts 19.13; Rom 2.13; Jas 1.22
7.22 Mt 25.12; Lk 13.25-27
7.23 Ps 6.8; Mt 25.12; Lk 13.25,27
7.24 Lk 6.47-49; Jas 1.22-25
7.28 Mt 11.1; 13.53; 19.1; 26.1; 13.54; Mk 1.22; 6.2; Lk 4.32; Jn 7.46
8.2 Mt 9.18; 15.25; 18.26; 20.20; Jn 9.38
8.4 Lev 14.3,4,10; Mk 3.12; 5.43; 7.36; 8.30; 9.9
8.8 Ps 107.20
8.11 Isa 49.12; 59.19; Mal 1.11; Lk 13.29; Acts 10.45
8.12 Mt 13.42,50; 22.13; 25.30; Lk 13.28

know how to give good gifts to your children, how much more will your Father in
heaven give good things to those who ask
him!

The Golden Rule

12 "In everything do to others as you
would have them do to you; for this is the
law and the prophets.

The Narrow Gate

13 "Enter through the narrow gate; for
the gate is wide and the road is easy[w] that
leads to destruction, and there are many
who take it. 14For the gate is narrow and
the road is hard that leads to life, and there
are few who find it.

A Tree and Its Fruit

15 "Beware of false prophets, who come
to you in sheep's clothing but inwardly are
ravenous wolves. 16You will know them by
their fruits. Are grapes gathered from thorns,
or figs from thistles? 17In the same way,
every good tree bears good fruit, but the bad
tree bears bad fruit. 18A good tree cannot
bear bad fruit, nor can a bad tree bear good
fruit. 19Every tree that does not bear good
fruit is cut down and thrown into the fire.
20Thus you will know them by their fruits.

Concerning Self-Deception

21 "Not everyone who says to me, 'Lord,
Lord,' will enter the kingdom of heaven, but
only the one who does the will of my Father
in heaven. 22On that day many will say to
me, 'Lord, Lord, did we not prophesy in
your name, and cast out demons in your
name, and do many deeds of power in your
name?' 23Then I will declare to them, 'I
never knew you; go away from me, you
evildoers.'

Hearers and Doers

24 "Everyone then who hears these words
of mine and acts on them will be like a wise
man who built his house on rock. 25The
rain fell, the floods came, and the winds
blew and beat on that house, but it did not
fall, because it had been founded on rock.
26And everyone who hears these words of
mine and does not act on them will be like
a foolish man who built his house on sand.
27The rain fell, and the floods came, and the
winds blew and beat against that house,
and it fell—and great was its fall!"
28 Now when Jesus had finished saying
these things, the crowds were astounded at
his teaching, 29for he taught them as one
having authority, and not as their scribes.

Jesus Cleanses a Leper

8 When Jesus[x] had come down from
the mountain, great crowds followed
him; 2and there was a leper[y] who came to
him and knelt before him, saying, "Lord, if
you choose, you can make me clean." 3He
stretched out his hand and touched him,
saying, "I do choose. Be made clean!" Immediately his leprosy[y] was cleansed. 4Then
Jesus said to him, "See that you say nothing
to anyone; but go, show yourself to the
priest, and offer the gift that Moses commanded, as a testimony to them."

Jesus Heals a Centurion's Servant

5 When he entered Capernaum, a
centurion came to him, appealing to him
6and saying, "Lord, my servant is lying at
home paralyzed, in terrible distress." 7And
he said to him, "I will come and cure him."
8The centurion answered, "Lord, I am not
worthy to have you come under my roof;
but only speak the word, and my servant
will be healed. 9For I also am a man under
authority, with soldiers under me; and I say
to one, 'Go,' and he goes, and to another,
'Come,' and he comes, and to my slave, 'Do
this,' and the slave does it." 10When Jesus
heard him, he was amazed and said to
those who followed him, "Truly I tell you,
in no one[z] in Israel have I found such faith.
11I tell you, many will come from east and
west and will eat with Abraham and Isaac
and Jacob in the kingdom of heaven, 12while
the heirs of the kingdom will be thrown into
the outer darkness, where there will be
weeping and gnashing of teeth." 13And to
the centurion Jesus said, "Go; let it be done
for you according to your faith." And the
servant was healed in that hour.

[w] Other ancient authorities read *for the road is wide and easy* [x] Gk *he* [y] The terms *leper* and *leprosy* can refer to several diseases [z] Other ancient authorities read *Truly I tell you, not even*

7.12 The instruction to act toward others as you would like them to treat you is expressed in negative mode ("do not do to anyone what you hate") in the apocryphal writings Tobit (4.15) and the Wisdom of Sirach (31.15). It is only implicit in the scriptural tradition (*"law and the prophets"*). *Cf.* Lk 6.31.

7.13-14 The majority are going to take the *easy road* which ends in destruction, rather than the demanding way that leads to *life*. *Cf.* Lk 13.23-24.

7.15-20 The true quality of those who claim to speak (*prophesy*) and act in the *name* of God or to belong to his people will be evident by what they produce (*fruit*). *Cf.* Lk 6.43-46. God will dismiss the frauds as *evildoers*. *Cf.* Lk 13.26-27.

7.24-28 The first discourse ends with a parable contrasting the sound structure (*on rock*) of the *wise* who hear and obey God with the *ruin* of the lives of the disobedient. "When Jesus had finished" marks the end of the first narrative-discourse section (4.1-7.28).

8.1-11.1 Narrative-Discourse Section Two: Jesus' Authority and the Sending of the Twelve Disciples. Jesus' authority as agent of God and founder of the new people of God is evident in the healings and exorcisms which he performs, and in his invitation to participate in the new community extended to those excluded by Jewish legal standards.

8.1-4 In healing the leper (of a serious skin disorder which today cannot be precisely identified), Jesus *touched him*, which would have resulted in his own ritual defilement (Lev 13; 14.2-7). Also in a longer version in Mk 1.40-45 and Lk 5.12-16.

8.5-13 *cf.* Lk 7.1-10. The *centurion* (commander of one hundred men in a Roman military legion) asks Jesus to heal his ailing *servant*, while recognizing that Jesus would be defiled if he visited or touched him. Jesus uses the invitation to announce that joining *Abraham, Isaac and Jacob* in God's new rule will be faithful participants from all over the world, while traditional *heirs* will be expelled into the realm of *darkness*. There the pain and sorrow of the excluded will be evident in *weeping and gnashing of teeth*, a favorite term of Matthew (13.42,50; 24.51; 25.30). Also in Lk 13.28.

Jesus Heals Many at Peter's House

14 When Jesus entered Peter's house, he saw his mother-in-law lying in bed with a fever; 15he touched her hand, and the fever left her, and she got up and began to serve him. 16That evening they brought to him many who were possessed with demons; and he cast out the spirits with a word, and cured all who were sick. 17This was to fulfill what had been spoken through the prophet Isaiah, "He took our infirmities and bore our diseases."

Would-Be Followers of Jesus

18 Now when Jesus saw great crowds around him, he gave orders to go over to the other side. 19A scribe then approached and said, "Teacher, I will follow you wherever you go." 20And Jesus said to him, "Foxes have holes, and birds of the air have nests; but the Son of Man has nowhere to lay his head." 21Another of his disciples said to him, "Lord, first let me go and bury my father." 22But Jesus said to him, "Follow me, and let the dead bury their own dead."

Jesus Stills the Storm

23 And when he got into the boat, his disciples followed him. 24A windstorm arose on the sea, so great that the boat was being swamped by the waves; but he was asleep. 25And they went and woke him up, saying, "Lord, save us! We are perishing!" 26And he said to them, "Why are you afraid, you of little faith?" Then he got up and rebuked the winds and the sea; and there was a dead calm. 27They were amazed, saying, "What sort of man is this, that even the winds and the sea obey him?"

Jesus Heals the Gadarene Demoniacs

28 When he came to the other side, to the country of the Gadarenes,[a] two demoniacs coming out of the tombs met him. They were so fierce that no one could pass that way. 29Suddenly they shouted, "What have you to do with us, Son of God? Have you come here to torment us before the time?" 30Now a large herd of swine was feeding at some distance from them. 31The demons begged him, "If you cast us out, send us into the herd of swine." 32And he said to them, "Go!" So they came out and entered the swine; and suddenly, the whole herd rushed down the steep bank into the sea and perished in the water. 33The swineherds ran off, and on going into the town, they told the whole story about what had happened to the demoniacs. 34Then the whole town came out to meet Jesus; and when they saw him, they begged him to leave their neighborhood.

9 1And after getting into a boat he crossed the sea and came to his own town.

Jesus Heals a Paralytic

2 And just then some people were carrying a paralyzed man lying on a bed. When Jesus saw their faith, he said to the paralytic, "Take heart, son; your sins are forgiven." 3Then some of the scribes said to themselves, "This man is blaspheming." 4But Jesus, perceiving their thoughts, said, "Why do you think evil in your hearts? 5For which is easier, to say, 'Your sins are forgiven,' or to say, 'Stand up and walk'? 6But so that you may know that the Son of Man has authority on earth to forgive sins"—he then said to the paralytic—"Stand up, take your bed and go to your home." 7And he stood up and went to his home. 8When the crowds saw it, they were filled with awe, and they glorified God, who had given such authority to human beings.

The Call of Matthew

9 As Jesus was walking along, he saw a man called Matthew sitting at the tax booth; and he said to him, "Follow me." And he got up and followed him.

10 And as he sat at dinner[b] in the house, many tax collectors and sinners came and were sitting[c] with him and his disciples. 11When the Pharisees saw this, they said to his disciples, "Why does your teacher eat with tax collectors and sinners?" 12But when he heard this, he said, "Those who are well have no need of a physician, but those who are sick. 13Go and learn what this means, 'I desire mercy, not sacrifice.' For I have come to call not the righteous but sinners."

The Question about Fasting

14 Then the disciples of John came to

[a] Other ancient authorities read *Gergesenes*; others, *Gerasenes* [b] Gk *reclined* [c] Gk *were reclining*

8.14-17 Reference to *Peter's mother-in-law* indicates that he was married (Mk 1.19-31; Lk 4.38-39). Sickness and being possessed by demons are regarded as evidence of the powers of evil; overcoming them is a sign of Jesus as fulfillment of God's purpose for the renewal of his people (8.17=Isa 53.4). *Cf.* Mk 1.29-34; Lk 4.38-40.
8.18-22 Those who want to follow Jesus are warned that they must be willing to abandon all ordinary physical and family securities and obligations. *Cf.* Lk 9.57-60. Jesus' reference to himself as *Son of Man* not only links him with humanity in general (Ps 8.4; Ezek 2.1) but also identifies him as God's agent of renewal at the end of the present age (Dan 7.14).
8.23-27 The power granted by God to Jesus extends even to the calming of a storm (*cf.* Gen 1.1-10; Ex 14.16-29; Ps 29.10; Isa 63.12). *Cf.* Mk 4.35-41; Lk 8.22-25.
8.28-9.1 Jesus' healing activity now reaches east of the Jordan to Gadara, one of the hellenistic cities of the Decapolis. The demons acknowledge Jesus as God's agent for transforming the world and its people (*Son of God*; Ps 2.7; Dead Sea Scrolls 4QFl 4-10). Although the abundance of *swine* there shows that it is not a predominantly Jewish city (Lev 11.7-8), the *whole town* comes out to meet Jesus, and then asks him to leave since he threatens their possessions. He returns to Capernaum, *his own town*.
9.2-8 To pronounce forgiveness of sins is solely God's role (Isa 43.25), so for Jesus to do so is seen by pious Jews as *blasphemy*. But since sickness was seen as the result of sin, Jesus' ability to heal the man convinces the *crowds* that God has granted him the *authority* to effect forgiveness (16.19; 18.18; Jn 20.23).
9.9-13 Jesus not only befriends and associates with *tax collectors and sinners*, but invites one of them, *Matthew* (called Levi in Mk 2.14; Lk 5.27), to be one of his inner circle of followers. This act is a symbol of the extension of grace and healing to those in deepest need: *sinners* (9.13; *cf.* Hos 6.6).
9.14-17 Three images are offered by Jesus to show why he and his followers do not engage in fasting as a sign of penitence: (1) his presence with them – *as the bridegroom* – brings joy, not regrets; (2) to lament in the presence of God's agent of renewal is as inappropriate as to put a patch on an *old cloak*; (3) the old models cannot contain the new power that Jesus brings any more than a stiff old wineskin could hold newly fermenting wine.

8.14 1 Cor 9.5
8.17 Isa 53.4
8.18 Mk 4.35; Lk 8.22
8.22 Mt 9.9; Jn 1.43; 2.19
8.26 Mt 6.30; 4.31; 16.8; Ps 65.7; 89.9; 107.29
8.29 Judg 11.12; 2 Sam 16.10; Mk 1.24; Jn 2.4
9.1 Mt 4.13
9.2 Mt 9.22; Mk 6.50; 10.49; Acts 23.11
9.4 Mt 12.25; Lk 6.8; 9.47; 11.17
9.8 Mt 5.16; 15.31; Lk 7.16; 13.13; 17.15; 23.47; Jn 15.8; Acts 4.21; 11.18; 21.20
9.11 Mt 11.19; Gal 2.15
9.13 Hos 6.6; Mic 6.6-8; Mt 12.7; 1 Tim 1.15
9.14 Lk 18.12

9.15 Jn 3.29; Acts 13.2,3; 14.23
9.18 Mt 8.2; Jn 9.38
9.20 Mt 14.36; Mk 3.10
9.21 see Lk 6.19
9.22 Mk 10.52; Lk 7.50; 17.19; 18.42; Mt 9.9; 15.28
9.23 see 2 Chr 35.25; Jer 9.17; 16.6; Ezek 24.17
9.24 see Jn 11.13; Acts 20.10
9.27 Mt 15.22; Mk 10.47,48; Lk 18.38,39
9.30 Mt 8.4; 17.9
9.31 Mk 7.36
9.32 Mt 12.22-24; Lk 11.14
9.34 Mt 12.24; Mk 3.22; Lk 11.15
9.35 Mk 6.6; Lk 13.22
9.36 Mk 6.34; Ezek 34.5; Zech 10.2
9.37 Lk 10.2; Jn 4.35
10.1 Mk 3.13-15; Lk 6.14-16; Acts 1.13
10.4 Lk 6.16; Acts 1.13; Jn 13.26
10.5 Lk 9.52; Acts 8.5,25
10.6 Mt 15.24; Ezek 34.5
10.7 Mt 3.2; Lk 10.9

him, saying, "Why do we and the Pharisees fast often,[d] but your disciples do not fast?" 15 And Jesus said to them, "The wedding guests cannot mourn as long as the bridegroom is with them, can they? The days will come when the bridegroom is taken away from them, and then they will fast. 16 No one sews a piece of unshrunk cloth on an old cloak, for the patch pulls away from the cloak, and a worse tear is made. 17 Neither is new wine put into old wineskins; otherwise, the skins burst, and the wine is spilled, and the skins are destroyed; but new wine is put into fresh wineskins, and so both are preserved."

A Girl Restored to Life and a Woman Healed

18 While he was saying these things to them, suddenly a leader of the synagogue[e] came in and knelt before him, saying, "My daughter has just died; but come and lay your hand on her, and she will live." 19 And Jesus got up and followed him, with his disciples. 20 Then suddenly a woman who had been suffering from hemorrhages for twelve years came up behind him and touched the fringe of his cloak, 21 for she said to herself, "If I only touch his cloak, I will be made well." 22 Jesus turned, and seeing her he said, "Take heart, daughter; your faith has made you well." And instantly the woman was made well. 23 When Jesus came to the leader's house and saw the flute players and the crowd making a commotion, 24 he said, "Go away; for the girl is not dead but sleeping." And they laughed at him. 25 But when the crowd had been put outside, he went in and took her by the hand, and the girl got up. 26 And the report of this spread throughout that district.

Jesus Heals Two Blind Men

27 As Jesus went on from there, two blind men followed him, crying loudly, "Have mercy on us, Son of David!" 28 When he entered the house, the blind men came to him; and Jesus said to them, "Do you believe that I am able to do this?" They said to him, "Yes, Lord." 29 Then he touched their eyes and said, "According to your faith let it be done to you." 30 And their eyes were opened. Then Jesus sternly ordered them, "See that no one knows of this." 31 But they went away and spread the news about him throughout that district.

Jesus Heals One Who Was Mute

32 After they had gone away, a demoniac who was mute was brought to him. 33 And when the demon had been cast out, the one who had been mute spoke; and the crowds were amazed and said, "Never has anything like this been seen in Israel." 34 But the Pharisees said, "By the ruler of the demons he casts out the demons."[f]

The Harvest Is Great, the Laborers Few

35 Then Jesus went about all the cities and villages, teaching in their synagogues, and proclaiming the good news of the kingdom, and curing every disease and every sickness. 36 When he saw the crowds, he had compassion for them, because they were harassed and helpless, like sheep without a shepherd. 37 Then he said to his disciples, "The harvest is plentiful, but the laborers are few; 38 therefore ask the Lord of the harvest to send out laborers into his harvest."

The Twelve Apostles

10 Then Jesus[g] summoned his twelve disciples and gave them authority over unclean spirits, to cast them out, and to cure every disease and every sickness. 2 These are the names of the twelve apostles: first, Simon, also known as Peter, and his brother Andrew; James son of Zebedee, and his brother John; 3 Philip and Bartholomew; Thomas, and Matthew the tax collector; James son of Alphaeus, and Thaddaeus;[h] 4 Simon the Cananaean, and Judas Iscariot, the one who betrayed him.

The Mission of the Twelve

5 These twelve Jesus sent out with the following instructions: "Go nowhere among the Gentiles, and enter no town of the Samaritans, 6 but go rather to the lost sheep of the house of Israel. 7 As you go, proclaim the good news, 'The kingdom of heaven has come near.'[i] 8 Cure the sick, raise the dead,

[d] Other ancient authorities lack *often* [e] Gk lacks *of the synagogue* [f] Other ancient authorities lack this verse [g] Gk *he* [h] Other ancient authorities read *Lebbaeus*, or *Lebbaeus called Thaddaeus* [i] Or *is at hand*

9.18 Jesus' touching the corpse of the dead child and the body of the woman with *hemorrhages* would be seen as polluting him, but instead it heals the sick and restores the dead to life. *Cf.* Mk 5.21-43; Lk 8.40-56.
9.27-34 The healing of the *two blind men* and the *mute demoniac* are evidence of Jesus' power for human renewal, but they also symbolize the transformation of those who cannot see or speak about what God is doing through Jesus, hailed as *Son of David*, God's Messiah (1.1), to establish his kingdom. But since Jesus does not observe ritual purity, his opponents see him as in league with the *prince of demons*.
9.35-38 The transition to the discourse section (10.1-11.1) is a summary of Jesus' activity, an indication that God's people lack a leader (*without a shepherd*), and the observation that the fulfillment of God's purpose (*harvest*) is about to begin.
10.1-11.1 Discourse on Sending the Twelve.
10.1-4 The twelve *disciples* who are commissioned to carry out the ministry of healing and exorcisms that signal the coming of God's kingdom in their midst (12.28) are for the first time in the gospels called *apostles*, meaning "those sent" or "commissioned." The names listed here are the same as in the basic core of other lists (Mk 7.16-19; Lk 6.14-16; Acts 1.13), but there are differences in some of the less well-known figures. *Cananaean* refers to Simon's character as an enthusiast, which is rendered in Luke 6.16 as *zealot*, a term which was used for the Jewish nationalists only after the outbreak against the Romans around 66 CE. *Iscariot* may refer to Judas' origin in Kerioth, a town west of the Dead Sea.
10.3-15 The twelve are commissioned to concentrate their preaching and healing efforts on Jews: *lost sheep of the house of Israel*. After Jesus' resurrection, they will be charged to go to *all nations* (28.19). They are now to go out with all speed, making no provisions for long term needs, confident that those who reject their message will fall under divine *judgment*.

10.16-25 Conflict and persecution are to be expected by these apostolic messengers. Matthew places emphasis on the opposition that the gospel messengers will experience from the Jewish leadership, both civil (in the regional *councils*) and religious (*in their synagogues*). The charges against them will give opportunity for testimony before the Roman authorities as well. They are to persevere in their witness for Christ to *the end* of the present age and the coming of the *Son of Man*, which will take place before they have completed their witness to the *towns of Israel*. This emphasis in picturing the role of the new community is unique to Matthew.
10.25 See 12.24 on the accusation that Jesus works with Beelzebul, the prince of the demons.
10.26-33 Assurance that God will reveal his purpose to his people, and that he will preserve them in spite of the persecution and martyrdom they will experience at the hands of their opponents. Their faithfulness in their witness to Christ on earth will be confirmed (*acknowledged*) by God, as will the infidelity of those who deny Jesus. *Cf.* Lk 12.2-9.
10.34-39 The lives of the faithful will be characterized by conflict, even within families, so that their ultimate devotion must be to Christ and his way of life which may lead to martyrdom (*take up the cross*). *Cf.* Lk 12.51-53; 14.26-27; 17.3.
10.40-42 Those who receive and help the messengers of Jesus will be rewarded by God.
11.1 Concludes the period of special instruction to the *disciples.*

cleanse the lepers,[j] cast out demons. You
received without payment; give without
payment. 9Take no gold, or silver, or copper
in your belts, 10no bag for your journey, or
two tunics, or sandals, or a staff; for laborers
deserve their food. 11Whatever town or village you enter, find out who in it is worthy,
and stay there until you leave. 12As you
enter the house, greet it. 13If the house is
worthy, let your peace come upon it; but if
it is not worthy, let your peace return to
you. 14If anyone will not welcome you or
listen to your words, shake off the dust from
your feet as you leave that house or town.
15Truly I tell you, it will be more tolerable
for the land of Sodom and Gomorrah on the
day of judgment than for that town.

Coming Persecutions

16 "See, I am sending you out like sheep
into the midst of wolves; so be wise as
serpents and innocent as doves. 17Beware of
them, for they will hand you over to councils and flog you in their synagogues; 18and
you will be dragged before governors and
kings because of me, as a testimony to them
and the Gentiles. 19When they hand you
over, do not worry about how you are to
speak or what you are to say; for what you
are to say will be given to you at that time;
20for it is not you who speak, but the Spirit
of your Father speaking through you.
21Brother will betray brother to death, and
a father his child, and children will rise
against parents and have them put to death;
22and you will be hated by all because of my
name. But the one who endures to the end
will be saved. 23When they persecute you in
one town, flee to the next; for truly I tell
you, you will not have gone through all the
towns of Israel before the Son of Man comes.
24 "A disciple is not above the teacher,
nor a slave above the master; 25it is enough
for the disciple to be like the teacher, and
the slave like the master. If they have called
the master of the house Beelzebul, how
much more will they malign those of his
household!

Whom to Fear

26 "So have no fear of them; for nothing
is covered up that will not be uncovered,
and nothing secret that will not become
known. 27What I say to you in the dark, tell
in the light; and what you hear whispered,
proclaim from the housetops. 28Do not fear
those who kill the body but cannot kill the
soul; rather fear him who can destroy both
soul and body in hell.[k] 29Are not two sparrows sold for a penny? Yet not one of them
will fall to the ground apart from your
Father. 30And even the hairs of your head
are all counted. 31So do not be afraid; you
are of more value than many sparrows.
32 "Everyone therefore who acknowledges me before others, I also will acknowledge before my Father in heaven; 33but
whoever denies me before others, I also will
deny before my Father in heaven.

Not Peace, but a Sword

34 "Do not think that I have come to
bring peace to the earth; I have not come
to bring peace, but a sword.
35 For I have come to set a man against his
father,
and a daughter against her mother,
and a daughter-in-law against her mother-
in-law;
36 and one's foes will be members of one's
own household.
37Whoever loves father or mother more than
me is not worthy of me; and whoever loves
son or daughter more than me is not worthy
of me; 38and whoever does not take up the
cross and follow me is not worthy of me.
39Those who find their life will lose it, and
those who lose their life for my sake will
find it.

Rewards

40 "Whoever welcomes you welcomes
me, and whoever welcomes me welcomes
the one who sent me. 41Whoever welcomes
a prophet in the name of a prophet will
receive a prophet's reward; and whoever
welcomes a righteous person in the name
of a righteous person will receive the reward of the righteous; 42and whoever gives
even a cup of cold water to one of these
little ones in the name of a disciple—truly
I tell you, none of these will lose their
reward."

11 Now when Jesus had finished instructing his twelve disciples, he
went on from there to teach and proclaim
his message in their cities.

[j] The terms *leper* and *leprosy* can refer to several diseases [k] Gk *Gehenna*

10.10 1 Cor 9.7; 1 Tim 5.18
10.14 Lk 10.10,11; Acts 13.51; 18.6
10.15 Mt 11.22
10.16 Lk 10.3; Rom 16.19
10.18 Acts 25.24-26
10.20 2 Sam 23.2; Jn 16.7-11; Acts 4.8
10.22 Lk 21.17; Dan 12.12; Mt 24.13; Mk 13.13
10.24 Lk 6.40; Jn 13.16; 15.20
10.25 Mt 12.24; Mk 3.22; Lk 11.15
10.26 Mk 4.22; Lk 8.17; 12.2,3; Isa 8.12,13; Heb 10.31
10.30 Lk 21.18; Acts 27.34
10.32 Rom 10.9; 2 Tim 2.12; Rev 3.5
10.34 Lk 12.51-53; Mk 13.12
10.35 Mic 7.6
10.36 Mic 7.6
10.37 Lk 14.26
10.38 Mt 16.24
10.39 Mt 16.25; Lk 17.33; Jn 12.25
10.40 Lk 9.48; Jn 12.44; Gal 4.14
10.42 Mt 25.40; Heb 6.10

Messengers from John the Baptist

2 When John heard in prison what the Messiah[l] was doing, he sent word by his[m] disciples 3 and said to him, "Are you the one who is to come, or are we to wait for another?" 4 Jesus answered them, "Go and tell John what you hear and see: 5 the blind receive their sight, the lame walk, the lepers[n] are cleansed, the deaf hear, the dead are raised, and the poor have good news brought to them. 6 And blessed is anyone who takes no offense at me."

Jesus Praises John the Baptist

7 As they went away, Jesus began to speak to the crowds about John: "What did you go out into the wilderness to look at? A reed shaken by the wind? 8 What then did you go out to see? Someone[o] dressed in soft robes? Look, those who wear soft robes are in royal palaces. 9 What then did you go out to see? A prophet?[p] Yes, I tell you, and more than a prophet. 10 This is the one about whom it is written,

'See, I am sending my messenger ahead of you,
who will prepare your way before you.'

11 Truly I tell you, among those born of women no one has arisen greater than John the Baptist; yet the least in the kingdom of heaven is greater than he. 12 From the days of John the Baptist until now the kingdom of heaven has suffered violence,[q] and the violent take it by force. 13 For all the prophets and the law prophesied until John came; 14 and if you are willing to accept it, he is Elijah who is to come. 15 Let anyone with ears[r] listen!

16 "But to what will I compare this generation? It is like children sitting in the marketplaces and calling to one another,

17 'We played the flute for you, and you did not dance;
we wailed, and you did not mourn.'

18 For John came neither eating nor drinking, and they say, 'He has a demon'; 19 the Son of Man came eating and drinking, and they say, 'Look, a glutton and a drunkard, a friend of tax collectors and sinners!' Yet wisdom is vindicated by her deeds."[s]

Woes to Unrepentant Cities

20 Then he began to reproach the cities in which most of his deeds of power had been done, because they did not repent. 21 "Woe to you, Chorazin! Woe to you, Bethsaida! For if the deeds of power done in you had been done in Tyre and Sidon, they would have repented long ago in sackcloth and ashes. 22 But I tell you, on the day of judgment it will be more tolerable for Tyre and Sidon than for you. 23 And you, Capernaum,

will you be exalted to heaven?
No, you will be brought down to Hades.

For if the deeds of power done in you had been done in Sodom, it would have remained until this day. 24 But I tell you that on the day of judgment it will be more tolerable for the land of Sodom than for you."

Jesus Thanks His Father

25 At that time Jesus said, "I thank[t] you, Father, Lord of heaven and earth, because you have hidden these things from the wise and the intelligent and have revealed them to infants; 26 yes, Father, for such was your gracious will.[u] 27 All things have been handed over to me by my Father; and no one knows the Son except the Father, and no one knows the Father except the Son and anyone to whom the Son chooses to reveal him.

28 "Come to me, all you that are weary and are carrying heavy burdens, and I will give you rest. 29 Take my yoke upon you, and learn from me; for I am gentle and humble in heart, and you will find rest for your souls. 30 For my yoke is easy, and my burden is light."

Plucking Grain on the Sabbath

12 At that time Jesus went through the grainfields on the sabbath; his disciples were hungry, and they began to pluck heads of grain and to eat. 2 When the Pharisees saw it, they said to him, "Look, your disciples are doing what is not lawful to do on the sabbath." 3 He said to them,

[l] Or *the Christ* [m] Other ancient authorities read *two of his* [n] The terms *leper* and *leprosy* can refer to several diseases [o] Or *Why then did you go out? To see someone* [p] Other ancient authorities read *Why then did you go out? To see a prophet?* [q] Or *has been coming violently* [r] Other ancient authorities add *to hear* [s] Other ancient authorities read *children* [t] Or *praise* [u] Or *for so it was well-pleasing in your sight*

11.2 Mt 14.3; Mk 6.17; Lk 9.7ff
11.3 Jn 11.27
11.5 Isa 35.4-6; 61.1; Lk 4.18,19
11.6 Isa 8.14,15; Rom 9.32; 1 Pet 2.8
11.7 Mt 3.1
11.9 Lk 1.76
11.10 Mal 3.1; Mk 1.2
11.12 Lk 16.16
11.14 Mal 4.5; Mt 17.12; Lk 1.17
11.15 Mt 13.9,43; Mk 4.23; Rev 13.9
11.19 Mt 9.11; Lk 15.2
11.21 Jon 3.7,8
11.22 ver 24; Mt 10.15
11.23 Isa 14.13; Lam 2.1
11.24 Mt 10.15
11.25 1 Cor 1.26-29
11.27 Mt 28.18; Jn 3.35; 13.3; 17.2
11.28 see Jer 31.25; Jn 7.37
11.29 Jn 13.15; Phil 2.5; 1 Pet 2.21; 1 Jn 2.6; Jer 6.16
12.1 Deut 23.25
12.2 Ex 20.10
12.3 1 Sam 21.6

11.2-13.58 Narrative-Discourse Section Three: The Kingdom and its Coming.
11.2-12.50 Words and Actions in Preparation for the Kingdom.
11.2-19 John, *in prison* because he denounced Herod Antipas for marrying his brother's wife (14.3-4), sends to ask Jesus if he is God's agent for renewal (*the one who is to come*). Jesus' response is to point to his healing activities which match the prophetic promises to the outsiders in Isa 29.18-19; 35.5-6; 61.1-2. This may be an *offense* to the strict, law-abiding John (neither *eating nor drinking*), in contrast to Jesus' friendship with those whose way of life puts them outside the covenant people (*tax collectors and sinners*). John is the greatest of humans, but his role is to prepare God's people for the coming of God's rule (*Elijah; cf.* Mal 4.5-6), to which all the scriptures (*prophets and the law*) point. With the coming of Jesus, conflict has intensified, as Jesus and his followers work to defeat the powers of Satan. His contemporaries will denounce him (*Son of Man*) as a violator of the traditional covenant with Israel: *a glutton and a drunkard* (Deut 21.18-21). God's *wisdom* at work through Jesus will be *vindicated* by the results. *Cf.* Lk 7.18-35; 16.16.
11.20-24 The hostility of the people in the cities around the Sea of Galilee (*Capernaum* and *Chorazin* on the west bank, and *Bethsaida* on the east side) is contrasted with the readiness to hear and repent at Jesus' message in the great pagan cities, *Tyre and Sidon*, symbolized by their putting on coarse garments (*sackcloth*) as a sign of penitence (Gen 37.34; 1 Kings 21.27; Jon 3.5-8). As a result of the hostility of the Galilean cities, doom will fall on them as it did on ancient *Sodom* (Gen 19), and they will be sent to *Hades* (the unseen realm of the dead below the surface of the earth), just as Babylon was warned (Isa 14.3-21). *Cf.* Lk 10.13-15.
11.25-27 Jesus' gratitude to the *Father* is for what God has *revealed* to and through Jesus for the renewal of his simple people (*infants*), in contrast to the religious leaders who think themselves to be *wise and intelligent*. *Cf.* Lk 10.21-22.
11.28-30 Only in Matthew is this invitation to the diligent seekers who are willing to accept the heavy responsibility (*burden*) of discipleship, which he makes *light*.
12.1-50 Jesus' Controversy with the Pharisees over the Basis for Participation in God's People. The issues include sabbath observance, the inclusion of Gentiles, and the source of his power over the evil spirits.
12.1-8 Jesus cites examples from scripture when human need took precedence over the Mosaic law, as when David and his friends ate the holy Bread of the Presence reserved for the priests (1 Sam 21.1-6; Lev 24.5-9), and as when the priests must perform their duties even on the sabbath (Num 28.9-10). Quoting the prophet Hosea (6.6) on the priority of *mercy* over legal obligations, Jesus identifies himself (*Son of Man*) as *Lord of the sabbath*. *Cf.* Mk 2.23-28

12.9-14 The same point is made with regard to Jesus' healing activity: human need is more important than sabbath law. *Cf.* Mk 3.1-6; Lk 6.6-11.
12.15-21 Quoting Isa 41.1-4, Jesus implies that he is God's *servant*, and that his role is to bring *justice* and *hope* to the Gentiles. *Cf.* Mk 3.7-12; Lk 6.17-19.
12.22-32 Jesus' effectiveness in healing and expelling demons leads his critics to assert that his ability derives from *Beelzebul*, originally the name of a Philistine god which was changed by Jews to mean "lord of dung" and whose role was chief of the demonic powers. Jesus asserts that for Satan to enable him to overcome the demons would be self-defeating and that his true source of power is the Spirit of God. This claim is heard as *blasphemy*. *Cf.* Mk 3.19-30; Lk 11.14-23.
12.33-37 A series of proverbial sayings describes how what one says discloses what one is inwardly. God will call everyone to account for whatever is uttered. *Cf.* Lk 6.43-45.
12.38-42 *cf.* Lk 11.29-32, where the *sign of Jonah* is his calling to repentance the pagan city of *Nineveh*. Here it is the *three days and nights* in the *sea monster* which are seen as pointing to Jesus' burial and resurrection. But the final point is that this Gentile city repented, just as the *queen* of a Gentile land (Sheba, in southern Arabia; 1 Kings 10.1-10) sought the wisdom of God through Solomon, whose name is linked in Jewish tradition with Proverbs, Ecclesiastes and the Wisdom of Solomon.

"Have you not read what David did when
he and his companions were hungry? 4He
entered the house of God and ate the bread
of the Presence, which it was not lawful for
him or his companions to eat, but only for
the priests. 5Or have you not read in the law
that on the sabbath the priests in the temple
break the sabbath and yet are guiltless? 6I
tell you, something greater than the temple
is here. 7But if you had known what this
means, 'I desire mercy and not sacrifice,'
you would not have condemned the guiltless. 8For the Son of Man is lord of the
sabbath."

The Man with a Withered Hand

9 He left that place and entered their
synagogue; 10a man was there with a withered hand, and they asked him, "Is it lawful
to cure on the sabbath?" so that they might
accuse him. 11He said to them, "Suppose
one of you has only one sheep and it falls
into a pit on the sabbath; will you not lay
hold of it and lift it out? 12How much more
valuable is a human being than a sheep! So
it is lawful to do good on the sabbath."
13Then he said to the man, "Stretch out
your hand." He stretched it out, and it was
restored, as sound as the other. 14But the
Pharisees went out and conspired against
him, how to destroy him.

God's Chosen Servant

15 When Jesus became aware of this, he
departed. Many crowds[v] followed him, and
he cured all of them, 16and he ordered them
not to make him known. 17This was to fulfill
what had been spoken through the prophet
Isaiah:

18 "Here is my servant, whom I have chosen,
my beloved, with whom my soul is well pleased.
I will put my Spirit upon him,
and he will proclaim justice to the Gentiles.
19 He will not wrangle or cry aloud,
nor will anyone hear his voice in the streets.
20 He will not break a bruised reed
or quench a smoldering wick
until he brings justice to victory.
21 And in his name the Gentiles will hope."

Jesus and Beelzebul

22 Then they brought to him a demoniac who was blind and mute; and he cured
him, so that the one who had been mute
could speak and see. 23All the crowds were
amazed and said, "Can this be the Son of
David?" 24But when the Pharisees heard it,
they said, "It is only by Beelzebul, the ruler
of the demons, that this fellow casts out the
demons." 25He knew what they were thinking and said to them, "Every kingdom divided against itself is laid waste, and no city
or house divided against itself will stand. 26If
Satan casts out Satan, he is divided against
himself; how then will his kingdom stand?
27If I cast out demons by Beelzebul, by
whom do your own exorcists[w] cast them
out? Therefore they will be your judges.
28But if it is by the Spirit of God that I cast
out demons, then the kingdom of God has
come to you. 29Or how can one enter a
strong man's house and plunder his property, without first tying up the strong man?
Then indeed the house can be plundered.
30Whoever is not with me is against me,
and whoever does not gather with me scatters. 31Therefore I tell you, people will be
forgiven for every sin and blasphemy, but
blasphemy against the Spirit will not be
forgiven. 32Whoever speaks a word against
the Son of Man will be forgiven, but whoever speaks against the Holy Spirit will not
be forgiven, either in this age or in the age
to come.

A Tree and Its Fruit

33 "Either make the tree good, and its
fruit good; or make the tree bad, and its
fruit bad; for the tree is known by its fruit.
34You brood of vipers! How can you speak
good things, when you are evil? For out of
the abundance of the heart the mouth speaks.
35The good person brings good things out of
a good treasure, and the evil person brings
evil things out of an evil treasure. 36I tell
you, on the day of judgment you will have
to give an account for every careless word
you utter; 37for by your words you will be
justified, and by your words you will be
condemned."

The Sign of Jonah

38 Then some of the scribes and Pharisees said to him, "Teacher, we wish to see

12.4 Ex 25.30; Lev 24.5,9
12.5 Num 28.9,10
12.6 ver 41,42
12.7 Hos 6.6; Mt 9.13
12.10 Lk 13.14; 14.3; Jn 9.16
12.11 Lk 14.5
12.12 Mt 10.31
12.14 Mt 27.1; Mk 3.6; Lk 6.11; Jn 5.18; 11.53
12.15 Mt 10.23; 19.2
12.16 Mt 9.30
12.18 Isa 42.1-6; 49.6
12.22 Mt 9.32,33
12.23 Mt 9.27
12.24 Mt 9.34; 10.25; Jn 7.20; 8.52; 10.20
12.25 Mt 9.4
12.27 Mt 9.34; 10.25; Acts 19.13
12.28 Dan 2.44; 7.14; Lk 1.33; 17.20, 21
12.30 Mk 9.40; Lk 9.50
12.31 Lk 12.10
12.32 Mt 11.19; 13.55; Jn 7.12,52
12.33 Mt 7.17; Lk 6.43,44
12.34 Mt 3.7; 23.33; Lk 6.45
12.38 Mt 16.1; Mk 8,12; Jn 2.18; 6.30; 1 Cor 1.22

[v] Other ancient authorities lack *crowds* [w] Gk *sons*

12.39 Mt 16.4
12.40 Jon 1.17
12.41 Jon 1.2; 3.5
12.42 1 Kings 10.2; 2 Chr 9.1
12.45 2 Pet 2.20
12.46 Mt 13.55; Mk 6.3; Jn 2.12; 7.3,5; Acts 1.4; 1 Cor 9.5; Gal 1.9
12.50 Jn 15.14
13.2 Lk 5.3
13.8 Gen 26.12
13.9 Mt 11.15
13.11 Mt 11.25; 19.11; Jn 6.65; 1 Cor 2.10; 1 Jn 2.27
13.12 Mt 29.29; Lk 19.26
13.13 Jer 5.21; Ezek 12.2
13.14 Isa 6.9,10; Ezek 12.2; Jn 12.40; Acts 28.26,27; Rom 11.8
13.15 Heb 5.11
13.16 Mt 16.17; Lk 10.23,24; Jn 20.29
13.17 Heb 11.13; 1 Pet 1.10,11
13.19 Mt 4.23

a sign from you." [39]But he answered them, "An evil and adulterous generation asks for a sign, but no sign will be given to it except the sign of the prophet Jonah. [40]For just as Jonah was three days and three nights in the belly of the sea monster, so for three days and three nights the Son of Man will be in the heart of the earth. [41]The people of Nineveh will rise up at the judgment with this generation and condemn it, because they repented at the proclamation of Jonah, and see, something greater than Jonah is here! [42]The queen of the South will rise up at the judgment with this generation and condemn it, because she came from the ends of the earth to listen to the wisdom of Solomon, and see, something greater than Solomon is here!

The Return of the Unclean Spirit

43 "When the unclean spirit has gone out of a person, it wanders through waterless regions looking for a resting place, but it finds none. [44]Then it says, 'I will return to my house from which I came.' When it comes, it finds it empty, swept, and put in order. [45]Then it goes and brings along seven other spirits more evil than itself, and they enter and live there; and the last state of that person is worse than the first. So will it be also with this evil generation."

The True Kindred of Jesus

46 While he was still speaking to the crowds, his mother and his brothers were standing outside, wanting to speak to him. [47]Someone told him, "Look, your mother and your brothers are standing outside, wanting to speak to you."[x] [48]But to the one who had told him this, Jesus[y] replied, "Who is my mother, and who are my brothers?" [49]And pointing to his disciples, he said, "Here are my mother and my brothers! [50]For whoever does the will of my Father in heaven is my brother and sister and mother."

The Parable of the Sower

13 That same day Jesus went out of the house and sat beside the sea. [2]Such great crowds gathered around him that he got into a boat and sat there, while the whole crowd stood on the beach. [3]And he told them many things in parables, saying: "Listen! A sower went out to sow. [4]And as he sowed, some seeds fell on the path, and the birds came and ate them up. [5]Other seeds fell on rocky ground, where they did not have much soil, and they sprang up quickly, since they had no depth of soil. [6]But when the sun rose, they were scorched; and since they had no root, they withered away. [7]Other seeds fell among thorns, and the thorns grew up and choked them. [8]Other seeds fell on good soil and brought forth grain, some a hundredfold, some sixty, some thirty. [9]Let anyone with ears[z] listen!"

The Purpose of the Parables

10 Then the disciples came and asked him, "Why do you speak to them in parables?" [11]He answered, "To you it has been given to know the secrets[a] of the kingdom of heaven, but to them it has not been given. [12]For to those who have, more will be given, and they will have an abundance; but from those who have nothing, even what they have will be taken away. [13]The reason I speak to them in parables is that 'seeing they do not perceive, and hearing they do not listen, nor do they understand.' [14]With them indeed is fulfilled the prophecy of Isaiah that says:

'You will indeed listen, but never understand,
and you will indeed look, but never perceive.
[15] For this people's heart has grown dull,
and their ears are hard of hearing,
and they have shut their eyes;
so that they might not look with their eyes,
and listen with their ears,
and understand with their heart and turn—
and I would heal them.'

[16]But blessed are your eyes, for they see, and your ears, for they hear. [17]Truly I tell you, many prophets and righteous people longed to see what you see, but did not see it, and to hear what you hear, but did not hear it.

The Parable of the Sower Explained

18 "Hear then the parable of the sower. [19]When anyone hears the word of the kingdom and does not understand it, the evil

[x] Other ancient authorities lack verse 47 [y] Gk *he* [z] Other ancient authorities add *to hear* [a] Or *mysteries*

12.43-45 The transformation that Jesus brings to a human life (*swept, put in order*) can be lost by the return of evil spirits. *Cf.* Lk 11.24-26.
12.46-50 The most basic form of personal identity – the family – is here redefined by Jesus in terms of the community obedient to God's *will*. *Cf.* Mk 3.31-35; Lk 8.19-21.
13.1-52 The Third Major Discourse: The Parables concerning the Spread of the Good News and the Results. The parables are presented to the *crowds*, but their meaning is explained only to the inner circle of the disciples (13.10-17,34-36).
13.1-9 The Parable of the Sower. Contrasted are (1) the mixed conditions in which the seed is sown and (2) the astonishingly rich results (*one hundredfold, sixty, thirty*). *Cf.* Mk 4.1-9; Lk 8.4-8.
13.10-15 The explanation, which builds on Isa 6.9-10, makes the point that the meaning and power of what Jesus says and does are available only for those to whom God has *given* the insights concerning his purpose. Others can discern nothing. *Cf.* Mk 4.10-12; Lk 8.9-10.
13.16-17 The insights given to Jesus' followers have not previously been available, not even to seeking *prophets and righteous people*. *Cf.* Lk 10.23-24.
13.18-23 The private explanation of the parable of the sower differentiates the various kinds of response to Jesus' message of the coming of God's rule, ranging from those who lack comprehension or perseverance to those whose lives and works are fruitful. *Cf.* Mk 4.12-20; Lk 8.11-15.

13.24-30 The Parable of the Weeds among the Wheat. Unique to Matthew; the private explanation is given in Mt 13.36-43.
13.31-32 The Parable of the Mustard Seed contrasts the small beginnings of the proclamation of the coming kingdom and the astonishing results. *Cf.* Mk 4.30-32; Lk 13.18-19.
13.33 The Parable of the Leaven points to the hidden but effective power of the gospel.
13.34-35 Reaffirms the contrast between Jesus' public proclamation of the good news and the hidden meanings which are disclosed to the community (Ps 78.2). *Cf.* Mk 4.33-34, where the privacy of the explanation is even more emphatic.
13.36-43 The Parable of the Weeds has become an allegory of the events at the end of the age, when the forces and agents of evil will be removed from the *kingdom* of the *Son of Man* (in the present age), and the *kingdom of the Father* will be established for *the righteous*. Only in Matthew.
13.44-52 Four Unique Matthean Parables: (1) the giving up of all one's possessions in order to gain (*buy*) a share in the kingdom; (2) the surrender of all in order to possess the kingdom (a single costly *pearl*); (3) the end-time sorting out of those who have found their way into the present community, and the punishment of the excluded; (4) the interpreter (*scribe*) who can disclose both new and traditional insights.

one comes and snatches away what is sown
in the heart; this is what was sown on the
path. 20As for what was sown on rocky
ground, this is the one who hears the word
and immediately receives it with joy; 21yet
such a person has no root, but endures only
for a while, and when trouble or persecution arises on account of the word, that
person immediately falls away.[b] 22As for
what was sown among thorns, this is the
one who hears the word, but the cares of
the world and the lure of wealth choke the
word, and it yields nothing. 23But as for
what was sown on good soil, this is the one
who hears the word and understands it,
who indeed bears fruit and yields, in one
case a hundredfold, in another sixty, and in
another thirty."

The Parable of Weeds among the Wheat

24 He put before them another parable:
"The kingdom of heaven may be compared
to someone who sowed good seed in his
field; 25but while everybody was asleep, an
enemy came and sowed weeds among the
wheat, and then went away. 26So when the
plants came up and bore grain, then the
weeds appeared as well. 27And the slaves of
the householder came and said to him,
'Master, did you not sow good seed in your
field? Where, then, did these weeds come
from?' 28He answered, 'An enemy has done
this.' The slaves said to him, 'Then do you
want us to go and gather them?' 29But he
replied, 'No; for in gathering the weeds you
would uproot the wheat along with them.
30Let both of them grow together until the
harvest; and at harvest time I will tell the
reapers, Collect the weeds first and bind
them in bundles to be burned, but gather
the wheat into my barn.' "

The Parable of the Mustard Seed

31 He put before them another parable:
"The kingdom of heaven is like a mustard
seed that someone took and sowed in his
field; 32it is the smallest of all the seeds, but
when it has grown it is the greatest of
shrubs and becomes a tree, so that the birds
of the air come and make nests in its
branches."

The Parable of the Yeast

33 He told them another parable: "The
kingdom of heaven is like yeast that a
woman took and mixed in with[c] three
measures of flour until all of it was leavened."

The Use of Parables

34 Jesus told the crowds all these things
in parables; without a parable he told them
nothing. 35This was to fulfill what had been
spoken through the prophet:[d]

"I will open my mouth to speak in parables;
I will proclaim what has been hidden from the foundation of the world."[e]

Jesus Explains the Parable of the Weeds

36 Then he left the crowds and went
into the house. And his disciples approached
him, saying, "Explain to us the parable of
the weeds of the field." 37He answered, "The
one who sows the good seed is the Son of
Man; 38the field is the world, and the good
seed are the children of the kingdom; the
weeds are the children of the evil one, 39and
the enemy who sowed them is the devil; the
harvest is the end of the age, and the
reapers are angels. 40Just as the weeds are
collected and burned up with fire, so will it
be at the end of the age. 41The Son of Man
will send his angels, and they will collect
out of his kingdom all causes of sin and all
evildoers, 42and they will throw them into
the furnace of fire, where there will be
weeping and gnashing of teeth. 43Then the
righteous will shine like the sun in the
kingdom of their Father. Let anyone with
ears[f] listen!

Three Parables

44 "The kingdom of heaven is like treasure hidden in a field, which someone found
and hid; then in his joy he goes and sells
all that he has and buys that field.

45 "Again, the kingdom of heaven is like
a merchant in search of fine pearls; 46on
finding one pearl of great value, he went
and sold all that he had and bought it.

47 "Again, the kingdom of heaven is like

[b] Gk *stumbles* [c] Gk *hid in* [d] Other ancient authorities read *the prophet Isaiah* [e] Other ancient authorities lack *of the world* [f] Other ancient authorities add *to hear*

13.21 Mt 11.6
13.22 Rom 12.2; 1 Cor 1.20; 2 Cor 4.4; Gal 1.4; Eph 2.2; Mt 19.23
13.23 ver 8
13.24 Lk 13.19,20
13.30 Mt 3.12
13.31 see Isa 2.2,3; Mic 4.1
13.32 Ps 104.12; Ezek 17.23; 31.6; Dan 4.12
13.33 Gen 18.6; Gal 5.9
13.34 Mk 4.33,34
13.35 Ps 78.2; Rom 16.25,26; 1 Cor 2.7; Eph 3.9; Col 1.26
13.38 Mt 24.14; 28.19; Lk 24.47; Jn 8.44; 1 Jn 8.44; 1 Jn 3.10
13.39 Joel 3.13; Mt 24.3; 28.20; Rev 14.15
13.40 1 Cor 10.11; Heb 9.26
13.41 Mt 24.31
13.42 Mt 24.51; 25.30; Lk 13.28
13.43 Dan 12.3; Mt 11.15
13.44 see Phil 3.7,8; Isa 55.1
13.47 Mt 22.10

13.49 Mt 25.32
13.50 ver 42
13.53 Mt 7.28; 11.1; 19.1; 26.1
13.54 Mt 4.23; 7.28
13.55 Lk 3.23; Jn 6.42
13.57 Jn 4.44
14.1 Mk 8.15; Lk 3.1,19; 8.3; 13.31; 23.7,8; Acts 4.27; 12.1
14.3 Lk 3.19,20
14.4 Lev 18.16; 20.21
14.5 Mt 21.26; Lk 20.6
14.14 Mt 9.36
14.17 Mt 16.9
14.19 1 Sam 9.13; Mt 15.36; Mk 14.22; Lk 24.30
14.23 Lk 6.12; 9.28

a net that was thrown into the sea and
caught fish of every kind; [48]when it was full,
they drew it ashore, sat down, and put the
good into baskets but threw out the bad.
[49]So it will be at the end of the age. The
angels will come out and separate the evil
from the righteous [50]and throw them into
the furnace of fire, where there will be
weeping and gnashing of teeth.

Treasures New and Old

51 "Have you understood all this?" They
answered, "Yes." [52]And he said to them,
"Therefore every scribe who has been trained
for the kingdom of heaven is like the master
of a household who brings out of his treasure what is new and what is old." [53]When
Jesus had finished these parables, he left
that place.

The Rejection of Jesus at Nazareth

54 He came to his hometown and began
to teach the people[g] in their synagogue, so
that they were astounded and said, "Where
did this man get this wisdom and these
deeds of power? [55]Is not this the carpenter's
son? Is not his mother called Mary? And are
not his brothers James and Joseph and Simon
and Judas? [56]And are not all his sisters with
us? Where then did this man get all this?"
[57]And they took offense at him. But Jesus
said to them, "Prophets are not without
honor except in their own country and in
their own house." [58]And he did not do
many deeds of power there, because of their
unbelief.

The Death of John the Baptist

14 At that time Herod the ruler[h] heard
reports about Jesus; [2]and he said
to his servants, "This is John the Baptist; he
has been raised from the dead, and for this
reason these powers are at work in him."
[3]For Herod had arrested John, bound him,
and put him in prison on account of
Herodias, his brother Philip's wife,[i] [4]because
John had been telling him, "It is not lawful
for you to have her." [5]Though Herod[j] wanted
to put him to death, he feared the crowd,
because they regarded him as a prophet.
[6]But when Herod's birthday came, the
daughter of Herodias danced before the
company, and she pleased Herod [7]so much
that he promised on oath to grant her
whatever she might ask. [8]Prompted by her
mother, she said, "Give me the head of John
the Baptist here on a platter." [9]The king
was grieved, yet out of regard for his oaths
and for the guests, he commanded it to be
given; [10]he sent and had John beheaded in
the prison. [11]The head was brought on a
platter and given to the girl, who brought
it to her mother. [12]His disciples came and
took the body and buried it; then they went
and told Jesus.

Feeding the Five Thousand

13 Now when Jesus heard this, he withdrew from there in a boat to a deserted
place by himself. But when the crowds
heard it, they followed him on foot from the
towns. [14]When he went ashore, he saw a
great crowd; and he had compassion for
them and cured their sick. [15]When it was
evening, the disciples came to him and said,
"This is a deserted place, and the hour is
now late; send the crowds away so that
they may go into the villages and buy food
for themselves." [16]Jesus said to them, "They
need not go away; you give them something to eat." [17]They replied, "We have
nothing here but five loaves and two fish."
[18]And he said, "Bring them here to me."
[19]Then he ordered the crowds to sit down
on the grass. Taking the five loaves and the
two fish, he looked up to heaven, and blessed
and broke the loaves, and gave them to the
disciples, and the disciples gave them to the
crowds. [20]And all ate and were filled; and
they took up what was left over of the
broken pieces, twelve baskets full. [21]And
those who ate were about five thousand
men, besides women and children.

Jesus Walks on the Water

22 Immediately he made the disciples get
into the boat and go on ahead to the other
side, while he dismissed the crowds. [23]And
after he had dismissed the crowds, he went
up the mountain by himself to pray. When
evening came, he was there alone, [24]but by
this time the boat, battered by the waves,
was far from the land,[k] for the wind was
against them. [25]And early in the morning
he came walking toward them on the sea.

[g] Gk *them* [h] Gk *tetrarch* [i] Other ancient authorities read *his brother's wife* [j] Gk *he* [k] Other ancient authorities read *was out on the sea*

13.53-58 Conclusion of Narrative-Discourse Section Three. Note of Jesus having *finished these parables* concludes the section, followed by the report of the rejection of Jesus in *his own hometown* after his *teaching* there. Mention of *their* synagogue (as in 4.23; 10.27; 12.9; 23.34) indicates that Matthew makes a sharp distinction between the gatherings of the Jews and those of the members of the new community. The villagers know his parents and his family, but they take offense at his claims to speak for God (*prophet*).
14.1-18.35 Narrative-Discourse Section Four: The Life and Work of the New Community.
14.1-12 The Death of John the Baptist. Herod Antipas, tetrarch (ruler of the fourth part of the realm of his father, Herod the Great), assumes Jesus is the resurrected John the Baptist (*cf.* Mk 6.14-29). Herod had executed John on the request of the daughter of his new wife, Herodias, who divorced her husband, Herod's brother (Deut 24.1-4), in violation of the Jewish law (Lev 18.16; 20.21), and thus was denounced by John. The daughter was named Salome, according to the Jewish historian, Josephus.
14.13-21 The Feeding of the Five Thousand. The event occurs when Jesus, having withdrawn *to a deserted place*, re-enacts the miracle of God's supply of food for his people during the Exodus of Israel, when the people were fed in the desert through Moses. A second miraculous feeding is described in Mt 15.32-39; Mk 8.1-10; Jn 6.1-13. In both sets of stories, the action words – *took, blessed, broke, gave* – in the distribution of the bread mirror the language of the Christian eucharist (Mt 26.26; Acts 2.46). Even *women and children* participate. *Cf.* Mk 6.30-44; Lk 9.10-17.
14.22-33 Jesus Walks on the Water. Further divine confirmation of Jesus as God's agent of renewal is given by his coming over the lake during a storm and rescuing the doubting Peter, thereby demonstrating God's control of the waters (as in Gen 1.6-7; Ps 89.9-10). The phrase by which Jesus identifies himself is in Greek, "I Am," recalling Yahweh's self-disclosure in Ex 3.14. *Cf.* Mk 6.45-52.

14.34-36 Growing trust in Jesus is evident at *Gennesaret* on the northwestern shore of Galilee, near Capernaum, where the sick are brought to him and seek healing by merely touching his *cloak*. *Cf.* Mk 6.53-56.
15.1-20 Conflict between Jesus and the religious leaders is intensified here in the light of the sharp disagreements between the late first century community behind this gospel and emergent rabbinic Judaism: the issue is which aspects of the Mosaic legal traditions are binding on the covenant people. The major points of contention are (1) the later ritual features added by the Pharisees, such as washing hands before eating, and (2) using humanly-contrived rules to evade direct moral responsibility, such as providing for one's parents. Isa 29.13 is quoted. The basic principle of dietary purity is called into question by the affirmation that defilement comes from within humans, not from without (15.10-12).The Pharisees cannot perceive this truth. *Cf.* Mk 7.1-13.
15.21-31 Jesus enacts the extension of his healing powers to non-Israelites (*dogs*), in this case from *Tyre and Sidon*, and to those excluded by physical ailments from contact with the pious, thereby reflecting the prophecies of Isa 35.1-10 about the renewal of God's people. These outsiders now praise *the God of Israel*. *Cf.* Mk 7.24-37.

[26]But when the disciples saw him walking
on the sea, they were terrified, saying, "It
is a ghost!" And they cried out in fear. [27]But
immediately Jesus spoke to them and said,
"Take heart, it is I; do not be afraid."
28 Peter answered him, "Lord, if it is
you, command me to come to you on the
water." [29]He said, "Come." So Peter got out
of the boat, started walking on the water,
and came toward Jesus. [30]But when he
noticed the strong wind,[l] he became frightened, and beginning to sink, he cried out,
"Lord, save me!" [31]Jesus immediately reached
out his hand and caught him, saying to
him, "You of little faith, why did you doubt?"
[32]When they got into the boat, the wind
ceased. [33]And those in the boat worshiped
him, saying, "Truly you are the Son of
God."

Jesus Heals the Sick in Gennesaret

34 When they had crossed over, they
came to land at Gennesaret. [35]After the
people of that place recognized him, they
sent word throughout the region and
brought all who were sick to him, [36]and
begged him that they might touch even the
fringe of his cloak; and all who touched it
were healed.

The Tradition of the Elders

15 Then Pharisees and scribes came
to Jesus from Jerusalem and said,
[2]"Why do your disciples break the tradition
of the elders? For they do not wash their
hands before they eat." [3]He answered them,
"And why do you break the commandment
of God for the sake of your tradition? [4]For
God said,[m] 'Honor your father and your
mother,' and, 'Whoever speaks evil of father
or mother must surely die.' [5]But you say
that whoever tells father or mother, 'Whatever support you might have had from me
is given to God,'[n] then that person need not
honor the father.[o] [6]So, for the sake of your
tradition, you make void the word[p] of God.
[7]You hypocrites! Isaiah prophesied rightly
about you when he said:
[8] 'This people honors me with their lips,
but their hearts are far from me;
[9] in vain do they worship me,
teaching human precepts as doctrines.'"

Things That Defile

10 Then he called the crowd to him and
said to them, "Listen and understand: [11]it is
not what goes into the mouth that defiles
a person, but it is what comes out of the
mouth that defiles." [12]Then the disciples
approached and said to him, "Do you know
that the Pharisees took offense when they
heard what you said?" [13]He answered, "Every
plant that my heavenly Father has not
planted will be uprooted. [14]Let them alone;
they are blind guides of the blind.[q] And if
one blind person guides another, both will
fall into a pit." [15]But Peter said to him,
"Explain this parable to us." [16]Then he said,
"Are you also still without understanding?
[17]Do you not see that whatever goes into
the mouth enters the stomach, and goes out
into the sewer? [18]But what comes out of the
mouth proceeds from the heart, and this is
what defiles. [19]For out of the heart come evil
intentions, murder, adultery, fornication,
theft, false witness, slander. [20]These are what
defile a person, but to eat with unwashed
hands does not defile."

The Canaanite Woman's Faith

21 Jesus left that place and went away
to the district of Tyre and Sidon. [22]Just then
a Canaanite woman from that region came
out and started shouting, "Have mercy on
me, Lord, Son of David; my daughter is
tormented by a demon." [23]But he did not
answer her at all. And his disciples came
and urged him, saying, "Send her away, for
she keeps shouting after us." [24]He answered,
"I was sent only to the lost sheep of the
house of Israel." [25]But she came and knelt
before him, saying, "Lord, help me." [26]He
answered, "It is not fair to take the children's food and throw it to the dogs." [27]She
said, "Yes, Lord, yet even the dogs eat the
crumbs that fall from their masters' table."
[28]Then Jesus answered her, "Woman, great
is your faith! Let it be done for you as you
wish." And her daughter was healed instantly.

Jesus Cures Many People

29 After Jesus had left that place, he

[l] Other ancient authorities read *the wind* [m] Other ancient authorities read *commanded, saying* [n] Or *is an offering* [o] Other ancient authorities add *or the mother* [p] Other ancient authorities read *law*; others, *commandment* [q] Other ancient authorities lack *of the blind*

14.26 see Lk 24.37

14.27 Mt 9.2; 17.7; 28.10; Rev 1.17

14.31 Mt 6.30; 8.26; 16.8

14.33 Ps 2.7; Mt 16.16; 26.63; Lk 4.41; Jn 11.27; Acts 8.37; Rom 1.4

14.36 Mt 9.20; Mk 3.10

15.2 Lk 11.38

15.4 Ex 20.12; Deut 5.16; Eph 6.2

15.5 Ex 21.17; Lev 20.9; Deut 27.16

15.8 Isa 29.13

15.9 Col 2.18-22

15.11 Acts 10.14,15; 1 Tim 4.3

15.13 Isa 60.21; Jn 15.2; 1 Cor 3.9ff

15.14 Mt 23.16; Lk 6.39; Rom 2.19

15.15 Mt 13.36

15.16 Mt 16.9

15.18 Mt 12.34; Jas 3.6

15.19 Gal 5.19-21; 1 Cor 6.9,10; Rom 14.14

15.22 Mt 9.27; 4.24

15.24 Mt 10.6,23

15.25 Mt 8.2; 18.26; 20.20; Jn 9.38

15.28 Mt 9.22,28; Mk 10.52; Lk 7.50; 17.19

15.30 Lk 7.22 passed along the Sea of Galilee, and he went
up the mountain, where he sat down. [30]Great
15.31 Mt 9.8 crowds came to him, bringing with them
the lame, the maimed, the blind, the mute,
and many others. They put them at his feet,
15.32 Mt 9.36 and he cured them, [31]so that the crowd was
amazed when they saw the mute speaking,
15.36 Mt 14.19; 1 Sam 9.13 the maimed whole, the lame walking, and
the blind seeing. And they praised the God
of Israel.

16.1 Mt 12.38; Lk 11.16,29; 12.54-56

Feeding the Four Thousand

32 Then Jesus called his disciples to him
and said, "I have compassion for the crowd,
16.4 Jon 3.4,5; Mt 12.39 because they have been with me now for
three days and have nothing to eat; and I
do not want to send them away hungry, for
16.6 Lk 12.1 they might faint on the way." [33]The disciples said to him, "Where are we to get
enough bread in the desert to feed so great
16.8 Mt 6.30; 8.26; 14.31 a crowd?" [34]Jesus asked them, "How many
loaves have you?" They said, "Seven, and
a few small fish." [35]Then ordering the crowd
16.9 Mt 14.17-21 to sit down on the ground, [36]he took the
seven loaves and the fish; and after giving
16.10 Mt 15.34-38 thanks he broke them and gave them to the
disciples, and the disciples gave them to the
crowds. [37]And all of them ate and were
16.14 Mt 14.2; Jn 1.21 filled; and they took up the broken pieces
left over, seven baskets full. [38]Those who
had eaten were four thousand men, besides
16.16 Mt 14.33; Jn 6.69; 11.27 women and children. [39]After sending away
the crowds, he got into the boat and went
to the region of Magadan.[r]

16.17 1 Cor 15.50; Gal 1.16; Eph 6.12

The Demand for a Sign

16 The Pharisees and Sadducees came,
16.18 Jn 1.42 and to test Jesus[s] they asked him
to show them a sign from heaven. [2]He
answered them, "When it is evening, you
16.19 Mt 18.18; Jn 20.23 say, 'It will be fair weather, for the sky is
red.' [3]And in the morning, 'It will be stormy
today, for the sky is red and threatening.'
16.20 Mk 3.12; 5.43; 7.36; 9.9 You know how to interpret the appearance
of the sky, but you cannot interpret the
signs of the times.[t] [4]An evil and adulterous
generation asks for a sign, but no sign will
16.21 Mt 17.22,23; 20.17-19; Lk 17.25 be given to it except the sign of Jonah."
Then he left them and went away.

The Yeast of the Pharisees and Sadducees

5 When the disciples reached the other
side, they had forgotten to bring any bread.
[6]Jesus said to them, "Watch out, and beware of the yeast of the Pharisees and
Sadducees." [7]They said to one another, "It
is because we have brought no bread."
[8]And becoming aware of it, Jesus said, "You
of little faith, why are you talking about
having no bread? [9]Do you still not perceive?
Do you not remember the five loaves for the
five thousand, and how many baskets you
gathered? [10]Or the seven loaves for the four
thousand, and how many baskets you gathered? [11]How could you fail to perceive that
I was not speaking about bread? Beware of
the yeast of the Pharisees and Sadducees!"
[12]Then they understood that he had not
told them to beware of the yeast of bread,
but of the teaching of the Pharisees and
Sadducees.

Peter's Declaration about Jesus

13 Now when Jesus came into the district of Caesarea Philippi, he asked his disciples, "Who do people say that the Son of
Man is?" [14]And they said, "Some say John
the Baptist, but others Elijah, and still others Jeremiah or one of the prophets." [15]He
said to them, "But who do you say that I
am?" [16]Simon Peter answered, "You are the
Messiah,[u] the Son of the living God." [17]And
Jesus answered him, "Blessed are you, Simon
son of Jonah! For flesh and blood has not
revealed this to you, but my Father in
heaven. [18]And I tell you, you are Peter,[v] and
on this rock[w] I will build my church, and
the gates of Hades will not prevail against
it. [19]I will give you the keys of the kingdom
of heaven, and whatever you bind on earth
will be bound in heaven, and whatever you
loose on earth will be loosed in heaven."
[20]Then he sternly ordered the disciples not
to tell anyone that he was[x] the Messiah.[u]

Jesus Foretells His Death and Resurrection

21 From that time on, Jesus began to
show his disciples that he must go to Jerusalem and undergo great suffering at the
hands of the elders and chief priests and
scribes, and be killed, and on the third day
be raised. [22]And Peter took him aside and
began to rebuke him, saying, "God forbid it,
Lord! This must never happen to you."

[r] Other ancient authorities read *Magdala* or *Magdalan* [s] Gk *him* [t] Other ancient authorities lack [2]*When it is . . . of the times* [u] Or *the Christ* [v] Gk *Petros* [w] Gk *petra* [x] Other ancient authorities add *Jesus*

5.32-39 It is these outsiders who now share in the fellowship meal of the new people of God – linked in the Greek with eucharist (giving thanks, *broke, gave*) – as did the Jewish followers (*cf.* Mt 14.13-21; Mk 8.1-10).

16.1-4 The request for a divine confirmation (*sign*) is here advanced by a combination of *Pharisees and Sadducees* – groups which normally would not cooperate. The request is rejected and their ability to discern signs of what God is doing in the changing *times* is denied. The *sign of Jonah* is recalled (*cf.* 12.39). *Cf.* Mk 8.11-13; Lk 11.19; 12.54-56.

16.5-12 The question about *yeast of bread* (Lev 23.5-8,15-21; Deut 16.9-12) becomes here a double metaphor: (1) for the sustenance which Jesus has provided for his people (*loaves*) and (2) for the unacceptability of *the teaching of the Pharisees and Sadducees*. *Cf.* Mk 8.14-21.

16.13-28 The Faith, Authority and Conflicts of the New Community. *Caesarea Philippi* was a Gentile city and district in northern Galilee at one of the sources of the Jordan. Peter's response to Jesus' question about who the disciples think he is (*Son of Man*, see note Mk 8.31). Peter's response, that Jesus is the *Messiah, the Son of the living God*, recalls Ps 2.4-11 where God acclaims the king of his people as his *Son* and as sovereign over the earth. Only here in the gospels is direct mention made of the *church* and of the decision-making role of *Peter* and the other apostles. The basic meaning of *church*, like synagogue, is a gathering or assembly. Both of Simon's nicknames, *Peter* and Cephas (Jn 1.42), mean *rock*, the foundation on which the new community will be built. Using terminology found in the rabbinic traditions (*bind, loose*), Peter and the apostles will make decisions about regulations to guide the life of the community, which will be confirmed by God *in heaven*. *Cf.* Mt 18.18. Until Jesus' death and resurrection, his identity as *Messiah* is not to be told to *anyone*. *Cf.* Mk 8.27-9.1; Lk 9.18-27.

16.21-28 Jesus' linking of these promises of power to the announcement of his *suffering, death* and resurrection is rejected by Peter, whose viewpoint is linked with *Satan*, since these are essential to God's method of renewal of his people. They must be ready to share in suffering and death (*forfeit their life*), although some will survive until Jesus enters his *kingdom* in triumph.

17.1-13 Like the transforming experiences of *Moses* and *Elijah* (Ex 34.29-35; 2 Kings 2.1-12), Jesus receives heavenly confirmation of his special role in God's purpose for his people (*This is my Son*). The coming of *Elijah*, predicted in Mal 4.5, has already occurred through the person and ministry of *John the Baptist*.
17.14-21 Jesus' expulsion of the demon from the *epileptic* boy contrasts with the inability of the disciples through their *little faith*. Moving a *mountain* as a metaphor for great faith recalls Isa 40.4 and 49.11. *Cf.* the longer version in Mk 9.14-29.
17.22-23 The disciples are still unable to understand the suffering and death predicted by Jesus. *Cf.* Mk 9.30-33.
17.24-27 Only in Matthew is the issue of the *temple tax* discussed. After the temple was destroyed (66-70 CE), Jews had to pay this tax (which amounted to about two days' wages) directly to Rome. The question was, should God's people resist the demand for support of a pagan power? Jesus' answer is that it should be paid to avoid conflict (*offense*), and that God will provide it.

23 But he turned and said to Peter, "Get
behind me, Satan! You are a stumbling
block to me; for you are setting your mind
not on divine things but on human things."

The Cross and Self-Denial

24 Then Jesus told his disciples, "If any
want to become my followers, let them
deny themselves and take up their cross and
follow me. 25 For those who want to save
their life will lose it, and those who lose
their life for my sake will find it. 26 For what
will it profit them if they gain the whole
world but forfeit their life? Or what will they
give in return for their life?
27 "For the Son of Man is to come with
his angels in the glory of his Father, and
then he will repay everyone for what has
been done. 28 Truly I tell you, there are some
standing here who will not taste death
before they see the Son of Man coming in
his kingdom."

The Transfiguration

17 Six days later, Jesus took with him
Peter and James and his brother
John and led them up a high mountain, by
themselves. 2 And he was transfigured before them, and his face shone like the sun,
and his clothes became dazzling white. 3 Suddenly there appeared to them Moses and
Elijah, talking with him. 4 Then Peter said to
Jesus, "Lord, it is good for us to be here; if
you wish, I[y] will make three dwellings[z]
here, one for you, one for Moses, and one
for Elijah." 5 While he was still speaking,
suddenly a bright cloud overshadowed them,
and from the cloud a voice said, "This is my
Son, the Beloved;[a] with him I am well
pleased; listen to him!" 6 When the disciples
heard this, they fell to the ground and were
overcome by fear. 7 But Jesus came and
touched them, saying, "Get up and do not
be afraid." 8 And when they looked up, they
saw no one except Jesus himself alone.
9 As they were coming down the mountain, Jesus ordered them, "Tell no one about
the vision until after the Son of Man has
been raised from the dead." 10 And the disciples asked him, "Why, then, do the scribes
say that Elijah must come first?" 11 He
replied, "Elijah is indeed coming and will
restore all things; 12 but I tell you that Elijah
has already come, and they did not recognize him, but they did to him whatever they
pleased. So also the Son of Man is about to
suffer at their hands." 13 Then the disciples
understood that he was speaking to them
about John the Baptist.

Jesus Cures a Boy with a Demon

14 When they came to the crowd, a man
came to him, knelt before him, 15 and said,
"Lord, have mercy on my son, for he is an
epileptic and he suffers terribly; he often
falls into the fire and often into the water.
16 And I brought him to your disciples, but
they could not cure him." 17 Jesus answered,
"You faithless and perverse generation, how
much longer must I be with you? How
much longer must I put up with you? Bring
him here to me." 18 And Jesus rebuked the
demon,[b] and it[c] came out of him, and the
boy was cured instantly. 19 Then the disciples
came to Jesus privately and said, "Why
could we not cast it out?" 20 He said to them,
"Because of your little faith. For truly I tell
you, if you have faith the size of a[d] mustard
seed, you will say to this mountain, 'Move
from here to there,' and it will move; and
nothing will be impossible for you."[e]

Jesus Again Foretells His Death and Resurrection

22 As they were gathering[f] in Galilee,
Jesus said to them, "The Son of Man is
going to be betrayed into human hands,
23 and they will kill him, and on the third
day he will be raised." And they were greatly
distressed.

Jesus and the Temple Tax

24 When they reached Capernaum, the
collectors of the temple tax[g] came to Peter
and said, "Does your teacher not pay the
temple tax?"[g] 25 He said, "Yes, he does." And
when he came home, Jesus spoke of it
first, asking, "What do you think, Simon?
From whom do kings of the earth take toll
or tribute? From their children or from
others?" 26 When Peter[h] said, "From others,"

[y] Other ancient authorities read *we* [z] Or *tents* [a] Or *my beloved Son* [b] Gk *it* or *him* [c] Gk *the demon* [d] Gk *faith as a grain of* [e] Other ancient authorities add verse 21, *But this kind does not come out except by prayer and fasting* [f] Other ancient authorities read *living* [g] Gk *didrachma* [h] Gk *he*

16.24 Mt 10.38,39; Lk 14.27; 17.33; Jn 12.25
16.27 Mt 10.33; Lk 12.9; Jn 2.28; Rom 2.6; Rev 22.12
16.28 Mt 10.23; 1 Cor 16.22; 1 Thess 4.15-18; Rev 1.7; Jas 5.7
17.1 Mt 26.37; Mk 5.37; 13.3
17.5 2 Pet 1.17; Mt 3.17; Isa 42.1; Acts 3.22,23
17.7 Mt 14.27
17.9 Mt 8.4; 16.20; Mk 3.12; 5.43; 7.36
17.10 Mal 4.5; Mt 11.14
17.11 Mal 4.6; Lk 1.16,17
17.12 Mt 11.14; 14.3,10; 16.21
17.20 Mt 21.21; Mk 11.23; Lk 17.6; 1 Cor 12.9
17.22 Mt 16.21; 20.17; Lk 18.31; 24.6,7
17.24 Ex 30.13; 38.26
17.25 Rom 13.7; Mt 22.17,19

Jesus said to him, "Then the children are free. 27However, so that we do not give offense to them, go to the sea and cast a hook; take the first fish that comes up; and when you open its mouth, you will find a coin;[i] take that and give it to them for you and me."

True Greatness

18 At that time the disciples came to Jesus and asked, "Who is the greatest in the kingdom of heaven?" 2He called a child, whom he put among them, 3and said, "Truly I tell you, unless you change and become like children, you will never enter the kingdom of heaven. 4Whoever becomes humble like this child is the greatest in the kingdom of heaven. 5Whoever welcomes one such child in my name welcomes me.

Temptations to Sin

6 "If any of you put a stumbling block before one of these little ones who believe in me, it would be better for you if a great millstone were fastened around your neck and you were drowned in the depth of the sea. 7Woe to the world because of stumbling blocks! Occasions for stumbling are bound to come, but woe to the one by whom the stumbling block comes!

8 "If your hand or your foot causes you to stumble, cut it off and throw it away; it is better for you to enter life maimed or lame than to have two hands or two feet and to be thrown into the eternal fire. 9And if your eye causes you to stumble, tear it out and throw it away; it is better for you to enter life with one eye than to have two eyes and to be thrown into the hell[j] of fire.

The Parable of the Lost Sheep

10 "Take care that you do not despise one of these little ones; for, I tell you, in heaven their angels continually see the face of my Father in heaven.[k] 12What do you think? If a shepherd has a hundred sheep, and one of them has gone astray, does he not leave the ninety-nine on the mountains and go in search of the one that went astray? 13And if he finds it, truly I tell you, he rejoices over it more than over the ninety-nine that never went astray. 14So it is not the will of your[l] Father in heaven that one of these little ones should be lost.

Reproving Another Who Sins

15 "If another member of the church[m] sins against you,[n] go and point out the fault when the two of you are alone. If the member listens to you, you have regained that one.[o] 16But if you are not listened to, take one or two others along with you, so that every word may be confirmed by the evidence of two or three witnesses. 17If the member refuses to listen to them, tell it to the church; and if the offender refuses to listen even to the church, let such a one be to you as a Gentile and a tax collector. 18Truly I tell you, whatever you bind on earth will be bound in heaven, and whatever you loose on earth will be loosed in heaven. 19Again, truly I tell you, if two of you agree on earth about anything you ask, it will be done for you by my Father in heaven. 20For where two or three are gathered in my name, I am there among them."

Forgiveness

21 Then Peter came and said to him, "Lord, if another member of the church[p] sins against me, how often should I forgive? As many as seven times?" 22Jesus said to him, "Not seven times, but, I tell you, seventy-seven[q] times.

The Parable of the Unforgiving Servant

23 "For this reason the kingdom of heaven may be compared to a king who wished to settle accounts with his slaves. 24When he began the reckoning, one who owed him ten thousand talents[r] was brought to him; 25and, as he could not pay, his lord ordered him to be sold, together with his wife and children and all his possessions, and payment to be made. 26So the slave fell on his knees before him, saying, 'Have patience with me, and I will pay you everything.' 27And out of pity for him, the lord of that slave released him and forgave him

17.27 Mt 5.29,30; 18.6,8; Lk 17.2; Jn 6.61; 1 Cor 8.13
18.3 Mt 19.14; Mk 10.15; Lk 18.17; 1 Pet 2.2
18.5 Mt 10.40; Lk 18.17
18.6 Lk 17.1,2
18.7 Lk 17.1; 1 Cor 11.19
18.8 Mt 5.29,30; Mk 9.43,45
18.9 Mt 5.29; Mk 9.47; Mt 17.27
18.10 Ps 34.7; Acts 12.11; Heb 1.14
18.15 Lev 19.17; Lk 17.3; Gal 6.1; Jas 5.19,20
18.16 Deut 19.15; Jn 8.17; 2 Cor 13.1; Heb 10.28
18.17 1 Cor 6.1-6; 2 Thess 3.6, 14
18.18 Mt 16.19; Jn 20.23
18.19 Mt 5.24; 1 Jn 5.14

18.1-5 Instead of striving for power and prestige in the community, they are to accept the lowly role assigned by the culture of the time to a *child*. *Cf.* Mk 9.33-37; Lk 9.46-48.
18.6-9 *Stumbling blocks* are temptations and tests through which God's people pass which are intended by their opponents, or by inner urges, to divert them from obedience and fidelity to God. *Cf.* Mk 9.42-48; Lk 17.1-2; Mt 5.29-30.
18.10-14 God provides *angels* to guard his people, and, like a *shepherd*, is concerned for any who may go astray. *Cf.* Lk 15.3-7.
18.15-20 Members of the community are to take responsibility for reproving erring brothers and sisters, with referral of the case to the whole community (*church*) if the counsel is rejected. The group decisions will be confirmed by God, who is present (*there among them*) when they gather.
18.21-22 The times that members are to be forgiven are not to be counted (*seventy times seven*). *Cf.* Lk 17.4.
18.23-35 The person who was forgiven a huge debt (the equivalent of millions of dollars) by the *king* refuses to forgive a minor obligation and so is subjected to *torture* by his *lord*. So God will punish those who refuse to forgive other members of the community.

[i] Gk *stater*; the stater was worth two didrachma [j] Gk *Gehenna* [k] Other ancient authorities add verse 11, *For the Son of Man came to save the lost* [l] Other ancient authorities read *my* [m] Gk *If your brother* [n] Other ancient authorities lack *against you* [o] Gk *the brother* [p] Gk *if my brother* [q] Or *seventy times seven* [r] A talent was worth more than fifteen years' wages of a laborer

19.1-2 *When Jesus had finished* marks the transition to the next major section of Matthew, with a note of Jesus' transfer of activity from Galilee to Judea, the center of Jewish life and tradition.
19.3-26.2 Narrative-Discourse Section Five: Preparation for the Coming Judgment on Israel and on God's New People.
19.3-12 The issue is, When is divorce permitted by the law of God? Since male and female sexual identity were present from the beginning of creation (Gen 1.27), marriage is the primary pattern for human relationships (Gen 2.24). Divorce is a concession to human stubbornness (*hardhearted*), and is to be permitted only when one of the partners is guilty of unchastity. No conditions for divorce are granted in Mk 10.12.
19.13-15 The share of children in the blessings of the new community is challenged by the *disciples*, but encouraged by Jesus, who formally accepts them by laying on them his *hands*. *Cf.* Mt 18.3; Mk 10.13-16; Lk 18.15-17.
19.16-30 Jesus tells the story of a rich *young man* who (1) asks about *deeds* to be performed in order to participate in the *life* of the age to come, (2) is reminded of the *commandments*, and (3) when told to get rid of all his *possessions* and to give all to the *poor*, retreats *grieving* because of the great sacrifice required of him. *Camel through the eye of a needle* is an image of the impossible, here compared with the *rich* entering God's kingdom. To be *saved* is to become what God intended humans to be when they were created, including their relationship to God and to each other, and is impossible of achievement by mortals. Jesus as future judge (*Son of Man*) will share the role with the faithful disciples who replace the *twelve tribes* and who reward those who have left all to follow Jesus. *Cf.* Mk 10.17-31; Lk 18.18-30.

the debt. 28But that same slave, as he went
out, came upon one of his fellow slaves who
owed him a hundred denarii;[s] and seizing
him by the throat, he said, 'Pay what you
owe.' 29Then his fellow slave fell down and
pleaded with him, 'Have patience with me,
and I will pay you.' 30But he refused; then
he went and threw him into prison until he
would pay the debt. 31When his fellow slaves
saw what had happened, they were greatly
distressed, and they went and reported to
their lord all that had taken place. 32Then
his lord summoned him and said to him,
'You wicked slave! I forgave you all that
debt because you pleaded with me. 33Should
you not have had mercy on your fellow
slave, as I had mercy on you?' 34And in
anger his lord handed him over to be tortured until he would pay his entire debt.
35So my heavenly Father will also do to
every one of you, if you do not forgive your
brother or sister[t] from your heart."

Teaching about Divorce

19 When Jesus had finished saying
these things, he left Galilee and
went to the region of Judea beyond the
Jordan. 2Large crowds followed him, and he
cured them there.
3 Some Pharisees came to him, and to
test him they asked, "Is it lawful for a man
to divorce his wife for any cause?" 4He
answered, "Have you not read that the one
who made them at the beginning 'made
them male and female,' 5and said, 'For this
reason a man shall leave his father and
mother and be joined to his wife, and the
two shall become one flesh'? 6So they are
no longer two, but one flesh. Therefore
what God has joined together, let no one
separate." 7They said to him, "Why then did
Moses command us to give a certificate of
dismissal and to divorce her?" 8He said to
them, "It was because you were so hard-
hearted that Moses allowed you to divorce
your wives, but from the beginning it was
not so. 9And I say to you, whoever divorces
his wife, except for unchastity, and marries
another commits adultery."[u]
10 His disciples said to him, "If such is
the case of a man with his wife, it is better
not to marry." 11But he said to them, "Not
everyone can accept this teaching, but only
those to whom it is given. 12For there are
eunuchs who have been so from birth, and
there are eunuchs who have been made
eunuchs by others, and there are eunuchs
who have made themselves eunuchs for the
sake of the kingdom of heaven. Let anyone
accept this who can."

Jesus Blesses Little Children

13 Then little children were being brought
to him in order that he might lay his hands
on them and pray. The disciples spoke sternly
to those who brought them; 14but Jesus
said, "Let the little children come to me, and
do not stop them; for it is to such as these
that the kingdom of heaven belongs." 15And
he laid his hands on them and went on his
way.

The Rich Young Man

16 Then someone came to him and said,
"Teacher, what good deed must I do to
have eternal life?" 17And he said to him,
"Why do you ask me about what is good?
There is only one who is good. If you wish
to enter into life, keep the commandments."
18He said to him, "Which ones?" And Jesus
said, "You shall not murder; You shall not
commit adultery; You shall not steal; You
shall not bear false witness; 19Honor your
father and mother; also, You shall love your
neighbor as yourself." 20The young man
said to him, "I have kept all these;[v] what
do I still lack?" 21Jesus said to him, "If you
wish to be perfect, go, sell your possessions,
and give the money[w] to the poor, and you
will have treasure in heaven; then come,
follow me." 22When the young man heard
this word, he went away grieving, for he
had many possessions.
23 Then Jesus said to his disciples, "Truly
I tell you, it will be hard for a rich person
to enter the kingdom of heaven. 24Again I
tell you, it is easier for a camel to go
through the eye of a needle than for someone who is rich to enter the kingdom of
God." 25When the disciples heard this, they
were greatly astounded and said, "Then
who can be saved?" 26But Jesus looked at

19.1 Mk 10.1; Jn 10.40
19.2 Mt 4.23
19.3 Mt 5.31
19.4 Gen 1.27; 5.2
19.5 Gen 2.24; 1 Cor 6.16; Eph 5.31
19.7 Deut 24.1-4; Mt 5.31
19.9 Mk 5.32; Lk 16.18; 1 Cor 7.10-13
19.11 1 Cor 7.7-9
19.14 Mt 18.3; 1 Cor 14.20; 1 Pet 2.2
19.16 Lev 18.5; Lk 10.25
19.18 Ex 20.13; Deut 5.17; Rom 13.9; Jas 2.11
19.19 Lev 19.18; Mt 22.39; Rom 13.9; Gal 5.14
19.21 Mt 6.20; Lk 12.33; 16.9; Acts 2.45; 4.34,35
19.23 Mt 13.22; 1 Cor 1.26; 1 Tim 6.9,10
19.26 Gen 18.14; Job 42.2; Jer 32.17; Zech 8.6

[s] The denarius was the usual day's wage for a laborer [t] Gk *brother* [u] Other ancient authorities read *except on the ground of unchastity, causes her to commit adultery*; others add at the end of the verse *and he who marries a divorced woman commits adultery* [v] Other ancient authorities add *from my youth* [w] Gk lacks *the money*

them and said, "For mortals it is impossible, but for God all things are possible."

27 Then Peter said in reply, "Look, we have left everything and followed you. What then will we have?" [28]Jesus said to them, "Truly I tell you, at the renewal of all things, when the Son of Man is seated on the throne of his glory, you who have followed me will also sit on twelve thrones, judging the twelve tribes of Israel. [29]And everyone who has left houses or brothers or sisters or father or mother or children or fields, for my name's sake, will receive a hundredfold,[x] and will inherit eternal life. [30]But many who are first will be last, and the last will be first.

The Laborers in the Vineyard

20 "For the kingdom of heaven is like a landowner who went out early in the morning to hire laborers for his vineyard. [2]After agreeing with the laborers for the usual daily wage,[y] he sent them into his vineyard. [3]When he went out about nine o'clock, he saw others standing idle in the marketplace; [4]and he said to them, 'You also go into the vineyard, and I will pay you whatever is right.' So they went. [5]When he went out again about noon and about three o'clock, he did the same. [6]And about five o'clock he went out and found others standing around; and he said to them, 'Why are you standing here idle all day?' [7]They said to him, 'Because no one has hired us.' He said to them, 'You also go into the vineyard.' [8]When evening came, the owner of the vineyard said to his manager, 'Call the laborers and give them their pay, beginning with the last and then going to the first.' [9]When those hired about five o'clock came, each of them received the usual daily wage.[y] [10]Now when the first came, they thought they would receive more; but each of them also received the usual daily wage.[y] [11]And when they received it, they grumbled against the landowner, [12]saying, 'These last worked only one hour, and you have made them equal to us who have borne the burden of the day and the scorching heat.' [13]But he replied to one of them, 'Friend, I am doing you no wrong; did you not agree with me for the usual daily wage?[y] [14]Take what belongs to you and go; I choose to give to this last the same as I give to you. [15]Am I not allowed to do what I choose with what belongs to me? Or are you envious because I am generous?'[z] [16]So the last will be first, and the first will be last."[a]

A Third Time Jesus Foretells His Death and Resurrection

17 While Jesus was going up to Jerusalem, he took the twelve disciples aside by themselves, and said to them on the way, [18]"See, we are going up to Jerusalem, and the Son of Man will be handed over to the chief priests and scribes, and they will condemn him to death; [19]then they will hand him over to the Gentiles to be mocked and flogged and crucified; and on the third day he will be raised."

The Request of the Mother of James and John

20 Then the mother of the sons of Zebedee came to him with her sons, and kneeling before him, she asked a favor of him. [21]And he said to her, "What do you want?" She said to him, "Declare that these two sons of mine will sit, one at your right hand and one at your left, in your kingdom." [22]But Jesus answered, "You do not know what you are asking. Are you able to drink the cup that I am about to drink?"[b] They said to him, "We are able." [23]He said to them, "You will indeed drink my cup, but to sit at my right hand and at my left, this is not mine to grant, but it is for those for whom it has been prepared by my Father."

24 When the ten heard it, they were angry with the two brothers. [25]But Jesus called them to him and said, "You know that the rulers of the Gentiles lord it over them, and their great ones are tyrants over them. [26]It will not be so among you; but whoever wishes to be great among you must be your servant, [27]and whoever wishes to be first among you must be your slave; [28]just as the Son of Man came not to be served but to serve, and to give his life a ransom for many."

Jesus Heals Two Blind Men

29 As they were leaving Jericho, a large crowd followed him. [30]There were two blind

[x] Other ancient authorities read *manifold* [y] Gk *a denarius* [z] Gk *is your eye evil because I am good?* [a] Other ancient authorities add *for many are called but few are chosen* [b] Other ancient authorities add *or to be baptized with the baptism that I am baptized with?*

19.27 Mt 4.20; Lk 5.11
19.28 Mt 20.21; Lk 22.28-30; Rev 3.21
19.30 Mt 20.16; Lk 13.30
20.1 Mt 13.24; 21.28,33
20.8 Lev 19.3; Deut 24.15
20.12 Jon 4.8; Lk 12.55; Jas 1.11
20.13 Mt 22.12; 26.50
20.15 Deut 15.9; Mt 6.23; Mk 7.22
20.16 Mt 19.30
20.18 Mt 16.21
20.19 Mt 16.21; 27.2; Acts 2.23; 3.13
20.20 Mt 4.21; 8.2; 9.18; Jn 9.38
20.21 Mt 19.28
20.22 Mt 26.39,42; Lk 22.42; Jn 18.11
20.23 Acts 12.2; Rev 1.9; Mt 25.34
20.24 Lk 22.24,25
20.25 Lk 22.25-27
20.26 Mt 23.11; Mk 9.35; Lk 9.48
20.28 Jn 13.4; Phil 2.7; Jn 13.14; Isa 53.10; 1 Tim 2.6; Titus 2.14; 1 Pet 1.19; Mt 26.28; Heb 9.28
20.30 Mt 9.27

20.1-16 The vineyard is an important prophetic symbol for the people of God in their need (Isa 5; Jer 12). Here the point is the varying degrees of fidelity that the *laborers* there have demonstrated and of reward that they receive. God's sovereign will is determinative, and will reverse human estimates (*the first will be last*). Only in Matthew.
20.17-19 The third prediction of Jesus' death and resurrection: see 16.21; 17.22. *Cf.* Mk 10.32-34; Lk 18.31-34.
20.20-28 The request of the *mother of the sons of Zebedee* (James and John) for granting them special status in the age to come is countered by Jesus' declaration that that is the prerogative of the *Father*, and that her sons' role is to share in Christ's suffering (*drink my cup*), to accept the role of a *servant*, which is to be willing to give one's life for the relief (*ransom*) of others from death. *Cf.* Mk 10.35-45; Lk 22.24-27.
20.29-34 One blind man named Bartimaeus is healed by Jesus in the parallel story in Mk 10.46-52 (*cf.* Lk 18.35-43). The symbolism includes Jesus' *compassion* for those in need, and the gift of *sight* for those who cannot clearly see what God is doing through him.

21.1-11 The approach to *Jerusalem* seems to be up through the wilderness of Judea by way of *Bethphage*, a village on the slope of the *Mount of Olives*, probably near Bethany. Matthew makes explicit the reference to Isa 62.11 and Zech 9.9 in Jesus' riding into Jerusalem on a *donkey*. Since, in the poetic form of Zech 9, two animals are mentioned, Matthew reports Jesus as acquiring a *donkey* as well as a *colt*. The crowd that welcomes him on the way quotes Ps 118.25-26, acclaiming him as heir to the throne of *David*. *Hosanna* means in Hebrew, "Save us now." In the city he is recognized instead as a Galilean *prophet*. *Cf.* Mk 11.1-10; Lk 19.28-38.
21.12-17 Jesus' disruptive actions are in the outer area of the temple, the Court of the Gentiles, where the latter were permitted to come and where Jewish visitors could buy sacrificial animals and exchange money for special temple coinage, actions essential to the functioning of the temple cult. Jesus contrasts these greedy entrepreneurs (*den of robbers*) with the intention that the place be a *house of prayer* (Isa 56.7; Jer 7.11). In response to the challenge from the priestly and scribal leaders to the crowd's acclaim of him, Jesus quotes Ps 8.2 concerning the praise for him.
21.18-22 Jesus' cursing of the *fig tree* recalls Jer 8.13, where Yahweh compares disobedient Israel with unfruitful vines and trees. The ability to accomplish such curses is promised to his followers. *Cf.* Mk 11.12-24, where instruction to forgive others is included.
21.23-32.Jesus refuses to identify the source of his *authority* when his interrogators will not even acknowledge that John's was from God (*from heaven*). Cf. Mk 11.27-33. Matthew adds the parable of the penitent and impenitent sons, the first of whom finally obeyed the father and worked, thus symbolizing those excluded from the community (*tax collectors and harlots*) who repented at the message of John.

men sitting by the roadside. When they heard that Jesus was passing by, they shouted, "Lord,[c] have mercy on us, Son of David!" 31The crowd sternly ordered them to be quiet; but they shouted even more loudly, "Have mercy on us, Lord, Son of David!" 32Jesus stood still and called them, saying, "What do you want me to do for you?" 33They said to him, "Lord, let our eyes be opened." 34Moved with compassion, Jesus touched their eyes. Immediately they regained their sight and followed him.

Jesus' Triumphal Entry into Jerusalem

21 When they had come near Jerusalem and had reached Bethphage, at the Mount of Olives, Jesus sent two disciples, 2saying to them, "Go into the village ahead of you, and immediately you will find a donkey tied, and a colt with her; untie them and bring them to me. 3If anyone says anything to you, just say this, 'The Lord needs them.' And he will send them immediately.[d]" 4This took place to fulfill what had been spoken through the prophet, saying,

5 "Tell the daughter of Zion,
Look, your king is coming to you,
humble, and mounted on a donkey,
and on a colt, the foal of a donkey."

6The disciples went and did as Jesus had directed them; 7they brought the donkey and the colt, and put their cloaks on them, and he sat on them. 8A very large crowd[e] spread their cloaks on the road, and others cut branches from the trees and spread them on the road. 9The crowds that went ahead of him and that followed were shouting,

"Hosanna to the Son of David!
Blessed is the one who comes in the name of the Lord!
Hosanna in the highest heaven!"

10When he entered Jerusalem, the whole city was in turmoil, asking, "Who is this?" 11The crowds were saying, "This is the prophet Jesus from Nazareth in Galilee."

Jesus Cleanses the Temple

12 Then Jesus entered the temple[f] and drove out all who were selling and buying in the temple, and he overturned the tables of the money changers and the seats of those who sold doves. 13He said to them, "It is written,

'My house shall be called a house of prayer';
but you are making it a den of robbers."

14 The blind and the lame came to him in the temple, and he cured them. 15But when the chief priests and the scribes saw the amazing things that he did, and heard[g] the children crying out in the temple, "Hosanna to the Son of David," they became angry 16and said to him, "Do you hear what these are saying?" Jesus said to them, "Yes; have you never read,

'Out of the mouths of infants and nursing babies
you have prepared praise for yourself'?"

17He left them, went out of the city to Bethany, and spent the night there.

Jesus Curses the Fig Tree

18 In the morning, when he returned to the city, he was hungry. 19And seeing a fig tree by the side of the road, he went to it and found nothing at all on it but leaves. Then he said to it, "May no fruit ever come from you again!" And the fig tree withered at once. 20When the disciples saw it, they were amazed, saying, "How did the fig tree wither at once?" 21Jesus answered them, "Truly I tell you, if you have faith and do not doubt, not only will you do what has been done to the fig tree, but even if you say to this mountain, 'Be lifted up and thrown into the sea,' it will be done. 22Whatever you ask for in prayer with faith, you will receive."

The Authority of Jesus Questioned

23 When he entered the temple, the chief priests and the elders of the people came to him as he was teaching, and said, "By what authority are you doing these things, and who gave you this authority?" 24Jesus said to them, "I will also ask you one question; if you tell me the answer, then I will also tell you by what authority I do these things. 25Did the baptism of John come from heaven, or was it of human origin?" And they argued with one another, "If we say, 'From heaven,' he will say to us, 'Why then did

[c] Other ancient authorities lack *Lord* [d] Or *'The Lord needs them and will send them back immediately.'* [e] Or *Most of the crowd* [f] Other ancient authorities add *of God* [g] Gk lacks *heard*

21.5 Isa 62.11; Zech 9.9
21.8 2 Kings 9.13
21.9 Ps 118.26; ver 15; Mt 23.39
21.11 Jn 6.14; 7.40; Acts 3.22; Mk 6.15; Lk 13.33
21.12 Ex 30.13; Deut 14.25
21.13 Isa 56.7; Jer 7.11
21.15 ver 9; Lk 19.39
21.16 Ps 8.2
21.21 Mt 17.20; Lk 17.6; Jas 1.6
21.22 Mt 7.7; Jn 14.13,14; 16.23; Jas 5.16
21.23 Acts 4.7; 7.27

you not believe him?' 26But if we say, 'Of human origin,' we are afraid of the crowd; for all regard John as a prophet." 27So they answered Jesus, "We do not know." And he said to them, "Neither will I tell you by what authority I am doing these things.

The Parable of the Two Sons

28 "What do you think? A man had two sons; he went to the first and said, 'Son, go and work in the vineyard today.' 29He answered, 'I will not'; but later he changed his mind and went. 30The father[h] went to the second and said the same; and he answered, 'I go, sir'; but he did not go. 31Which of the two did the will of his father?" They said, "The first." Jesus said to them, "Truly I tell you, the tax collectors and the prostitutes are going into the kingdom of God ahead of you. 32For John came to you in the way of righteousness and you did not believe him, but the tax collectors and the prostitutes believed him; and even after you saw it, you did not change your minds and believe him.

The Parable of the Wicked Tenants

33 "Listen to another parable. There was a landowner who planted a vineyard, put a fence around it, dug a wine press in it, and built a watchtower. Then he leased it to tenants and went to another country. 34When the harvest time had come, he sent his slaves to the tenants to collect his produce. 35But the tenants seized his slaves and beat one, killed another, and stoned another. 36Again he sent other slaves, more than the first; and they treated them in the same way. 37Finally he sent his son to them, saying, 'They will respect my son.' 38But when the tenants saw the son, they said to themselves, 'This is the heir; come, let us kill him and get his inheritance.' 39So they seized him, threw him out of the vineyard, and killed him. 40Now when the owner of the vineyard comes, what will he do to those tenants?" 41They said to him, "He will put those wretches to a miserable death, and lease the vineyard to other tenants who will give him the produce at the harvest time."

42 Jesus said to them, "Have you never read in the scriptures:

'The stone that the builders rejected
has become the cornerstone;[i]
this was the Lord's doing,
and it is amazing in our eyes'?

43Therefore I tell you, the kingdom of God will be taken away from you and given to a people that produces the fruits of the kingdom.[j] 44The one who falls on this stone will be broken to pieces; and it will crush anyone on whom it falls."[k]

45 When the chief priests and the Pharisees heard his parables, they realized that he was speaking about them. 46They wanted to arrest him, but they feared the crowds, because they regarded him as a prophet.

The Parable of the Wedding Banquet

22 Once more Jesus spoke to them in parables, saying: 2"The kingdom of heaven may be compared to a king who gave a wedding banquet for his son. 3He sent his slaves to call those who had been invited to the wedding banquet, but they would not come. 4Again he sent other slaves, saying, 'Tell those who have been invited: Look, I have prepared my dinner, my oxen and my fat calves have been slaughtered, and everything is ready; come to the wedding banquet.' 5But they made light of it and went away, one to his farm, another to his business, 6while the rest seized his slaves, mistreated them, and killed them. 7The king was enraged. He sent his troops, destroyed those murderers, and burned their city. 8Then he said to his slaves, 'The wedding is ready, but those invited were not worthy. 9Go therefore into the main streets, and invite everyone you find to the wedding banquet.' 10Those slaves went out into the streets and gathered all whom they found, both good and bad; so the wedding hall was filled with guests.

11 "But when the king came in to see the guests, he noticed a man there who was not wearing a wedding robe, 12and he said to him, 'Friend, how did you get in here without a wedding robe?' And he was speechless. 13Then the king said to the attendants, 'Bind him hand and foot, and throw him into the outer darkness, where there will be weeping and gnashing of teeth.' 14For many are called, but few are chosen."

The Question about Paying Taxes

15 Then the Pharisees went and plotted to entrap him in what he said. 16So they sent their disciples to him, along with the

[h] Gk *He* [i] Or *keystone* [j] Gk *the fruits of it* [k] Other ancient authorities lack verse 44

21.26 Mt 14.5; Mk 6.20
21.28 ver 33; Mt 20.21
21.31 Lk 7.29,50
21.32 Mt 3.1ff; Lk 7.29,30; 3.12,13
21.33 Ps 80.8; Isa 5.1-7; Mt 25.14,15
21.34 Mt 22.3
21.35 2 Chr 24.21; Mt 23.34,37; Heb 11.36,37
21.38 Ps 2.8; Heb 1.2; Mt 26.3; 27.1
21.41 Mt 8.11; Acts 13.46; 18.6; 28.28
21.42 Ps 118.22, 23; Acts 4.11; 1 Pet 2.7
21.43 Mt 8.12
21.46 ver 26,11
22.2 Mt 13.24
22.3 Mt 21.34
22.4 Mt 21.36
22.7 Lk 19.27
22.8 Mt 10.11,13
22.10 Mt 13.47
22.11 2 Cor 5.3; Eph 4.24; Col 3.10,12; Rev 3.4; 16.15; 19.8
22.12 Mt 20.13; 26.50
22.13 Mt 8.12; Lk 13.28
22.16 Mk 3.6; 8.15

21.33-46 Developing allegorically the prophetic image of disobedient Israel as an unfruitful vineyard (Isa 5), Jesus pictures the various responses of the people to God's messengers and to him: beaten and killed, including the owner's *son* (=Jesus). The result will be the punishment and death of these irresponsible *tenants* (the Jewish leaders) and the assignment of the role to others – i.e., the new community. Changing the image, the rejected *stone* (Jesus) is the cornerstone of the new *nation* of God's people.
22.1-14 The parable of the marriage feast builds on the symbolic husband–wife relationship of Yahweh to Israel (Hos 2). Those invited to participate in the feast for the king's *son* mistreat and kill the messengers who invited them, and are in turn punished by the *king* and their city is destroyed (thus pointing to the destruction of Jerusalem in 66-70 CE). Now the invitation goes to those on the margin of society (the outsiders by Jewish standards), and those who are unfit (*not wearing a wedding robe*) are condemned. Different version in Lk 14.16-24.
22.15-22 Questions debated among Jews: (1) Paying Taxes to Caesar. *Herodians* were supporters of Herod and his successors as puppet kings, appointed by Rome. With the *Pharisees*, they try to trick Jesus into a public statement that would be subversive of Roman law. *Cf.* Mk 12.13-17; Lk 20.20-26.

22.23-33 (2) The question concerning resurrection. The Sadducees denied the resurrection because there is no explicit support for it in the Law of Moses, which was their sole scriptural authority. They pose a hypothetical problem of the situation in the resurrection life of a woman married successively by seven brothers, six of them to fulfill the levirate law requiring brothers to beget sons by a childless widow (Deut 25.5-6). Jesus responds by noting that God *is* – in the present tense – the God of each succeeding generation of the founders of Israel, so that these seemingly dead are to be among the *living. Cf.* Mk 12.18-27; Lk 20.27-40.
22.34-40 (3) The question of which of the commandments of the law was the *greatest* was raised often in Judaism of the post-biblical period, as it is here by the *lawyer* (someone who specializes in interpreting the Law of Moses). Love of God and neighbor are the essence of both the *law and the prophets. Cf.* Mk 12.28-34, which gives a fuller account.
22.41-46 Quoting Ps 110.1, Jesus raises the question (4) how David's *son* (heir to the throne of David) is also his *Lord*, which early became the central title for Jesus (Phil 2.11; Rom 10.9). *Cf.* Mk 12.35-37; Lk 20.41-44.
23.1-36 Matthew has uniquely brought together sayings of Jesus critical of the *scribes* (those devoted to interpretation of the law) and the Pharisees (Jews concerned for the direct relevance of the law) who *sit on Moses' seat*, claiming divinely confirmed interpretation of the Law. The critique here is that they prescribe (teach) for others but do not conform their lives to their own principles. *Phylacteries* (leather cases containing texts from the Law; Ex 13.1-6; Deut 6.4-9; 11.13-21) and *fringes* (tassels on prayer shawls) were worn to impress others rather than as personal reminders of legal obligations. Similarly, they prefer *seats* and a title of honor (*rabbi*, which only later became the designation for a synagogue leader). Seven deprecations against these pious show-offs begin with the word *Woe*, the Greek term for which conveys sorrow rather than vengeance: (1) their restrictions *lock out* prospective participants in the kingdom of God; (2) they put forth great effort to *convert* one Gentile, who becomes twice as unfit as they are; (3) their rules about *oaths* evade the basic obligation to God; (4) their preoccupation with such details as *tithing* spices and with such external factors as (5) ritual cleansing and outward appearance (6) distract them from the purity of inner condition; (7) they honor the dead prophets, but copy the behavior of those who murdered God's messengers. They will persecute and kill the *prophets, sages and scribes* of the new community in *their synagogues*, just as the Bible reports the killing of God's messengers from the first book (death of Abel in Gen 4.8) to the last in the Hebrew canon (Zechariah in 2 Chr 24.20-22).

Herodians, saying, "Teacher, we know that you are sincere, and teach the way of God in accordance with truth, and show deference to no one; for you do not regard people with partiality. 17 Tell us, then, what you think. Is it lawful to pay taxes to the emperor, or not?" 18 But Jesus, aware of their malice, said, "Why are you putting me to the test, you hypocrites? 19 Show me the coin used for the tax." And they brought him a denarius. 20 Then he said to them, "Whose head is this, and whose title?" 21 They answered, "The emperor's." Then he said to them, "Give therefore to the emperor the things that are the emperor's, and to God the things that are God's." 22 When they heard this, they were amazed; and they left him and went away.

The Question about the Resurrection

23 The same day some Sadducees came to him, saying there is no resurrection;[l] and they asked him a question, saying, 24 "Teacher, Moses said, 'If a man dies childless, his brother shall marry the widow, and raise up children for his brother.' 25 Now there were seven brothers among us; the first married, and died childless, leaving the widow to his brother. 26 The second did the same, so also the third, down to the seventh. 27 Last of all, the woman herself died. 28 In the resurrection, then, whose wife of the seven will she be? For all of them had married her."

29 Jesus answered them, "You are wrong, because you know neither the scriptures nor the power of God. 30 For in the resurrection they neither marry nor are given in marriage, but are like angels[m] in heaven. 31 And as for the resurrection of the dead, have you not read what was said to you by God, 32 'I am the God of Abraham, the God of Isaac, and the God of Jacob'? He is God not of the dead, but of the living." 33 And when the crowd heard it, they were astounded at his teaching.

The Greatest Commandment

34 When the Pharisees heard that he had silenced the Sadducees, they gathered together, 35 and one of them, a lawyer, asked him a question to test him. 36 "Teacher, which commandment in the law is the greatest?" 37 He said to him, " 'You shall love the Lord your God with all your heart, and with all your soul, and with all your mind.' 38 This is the greatest and first commandment. 39 And a second is like it: 'You shall love your neighbor as yourself.' 40 On these two commandments hang all the law and the prophets."

The Question about David's Son

41 Now while the Pharisees were gathered together, Jesus asked them this question: 42 "What do you think of the Messiah?[n] Whose son is he?" They said to him, "The son of David." 43 He said to them, "How is it then that David by the Spirit[o] calls him Lord, saying,

44 'The Lord said to my Lord,
"Sit at my right hand,
until I put your enemies under your feet" '?

45 If David thus calls him Lord, how can he be his son?" 46 No one was able to give him an answer, nor from that day did anyone dare to ask him any more questions.

Jesus Denounces Scribes and Pharisees

23 Then Jesus said to the crowds and to his disciples, 2 "The scribes and the Pharisees sit on Moses' seat; 3 therefore, do whatever they teach you and follow it; but do not do as they do, for they do not practice what they teach. 4 They tie up heavy burdens, hard to bear,[p] and lay them on the shoulders of others; but they themselves are unwilling to lift a finger to move them. 5 They do all their deeds to be seen by others; for they make their phylacteries broad and their fringes long. 6 They love to have the place of honor at banquets and the best seats in the synagogues, 7 and to be greeted with respect in the marketplaces, and to have people call them rabbi. 8 But you are not to be called rabbi, for you have one teacher, and you are all students.[q] 9 And call no one your father on earth, for you have one Father—the one in heaven. 10 Nor are you to be called instructors, for you have one instructor, the Messiah.[r] 11 The greatest among you will be your servant. 12 All who exalt themselves will be humbled, and all who humble themselves will be exalted.

13 "But woe to you, scribes and Phari-

[l] Other ancient authorities read *who say that there is no resurrection* [m] Other ancient authorities add *of God* [n] Or *Christ* [o] Gk *in spirit* [p] Other ancient authorities lack *hard to bear* [q] Gk *brothers* [r] Or *the Christ*

22.17 Mt 17.25
22.21 Rom 13.7
22.23 Acts 23.8
22.24 Deut 25.5
22.29 Jn 20.9
22.32 Ex 3.6,16; Acts 7.32; Heb 11.16
22.33 Mt 7.28
22.35 Lk 7.30; 10.25; 11.45; 14.3
22.37 Deut 6.5
22.39 Lev 19.18; Mt 19.19; Rom 13.9; Gal 5.14; Jas 2.8
22.40 Mt 7.12
22.42 Mt 9.27
22.44 Ps 110.1; Acts 2.34; Heb 1.13; 10.13
22.46 Mk 12.34; Lk 20.40
23.2 Ezra 7.6,25; Neh 8.4
23.4 Lk 11.46; Acts 15.10; Gal 6.13
23.5 Mt 6.1,2,5,16; Deut 6.8
23.6 Lk 11.43; 14.7; 20.46
23.8 Jas 3.1
23.9 Mal 1.6
23.11 Mt 20.26
23.12 Lk 14.11; 18.14; Jas 4.6; 1 Pet 5.5
23.13 Lk 11.52

23.16 ver 24; Mt 15.14; 5.33-35
23.17 Ex 30.29
23.19 Ex 29.37
23.22 Ps 11.4; Mt 5.34
23.23 Mt 11.42; Lev 27.30; Mic 6.8
23.39 Ps 118.26; Mt 21.9
24.1 Mk 13.1
24.2 Mt 26.61; 27.39,40; Lk 19.44; Jn 2.19
24.4 Jer 29.8; 2 Thess 2.3

sees, hypocrites! For you lock people out of the kingdom of heaven. For you do not go in yourselves, and when others are going in, you stop them.[s] [15]Woe to you, scribes and Pharisees, hypocrites! For you cross sea and land to make a single convert, and you make the new convert twice as much a child of hell[t] as yourselves.

16 "Woe to you, blind guides, who say, 'Whoever swears by the sanctuary is bound by nothing, but whoever swears by the gold of the sanctuary is bound by the oath.' [17]You blind fools! For which is greater, the gold or the sanctuary that has made the gold sacred? [18]And you say, 'Whoever swears by the altar is bound by nothing, but whoever swears by the gift that is on the altar is bound by the oath.' [19]How blind you are! For which is greater, the gift or the altar that makes the gift sacred? [20]So whoever swears by the altar, swears by it and by everything on it; [21]and whoever swears by the sanctuary, swears by it and by the one who dwells in it; [22]and whoever swears by heaven, swears by the throne of God and by the one who is seated upon it.

23 "Woe to you, scribes and Pharisees, hypocrites! For you tithe mint, dill, and cummin, and have neglected the weightier matters of the law: justice and mercy and faith. It is these you ought to have practiced without neglecting the others. [24]You blind guides! You strain out a gnat but swallow a camel!

25 "Woe to you, scribes and Pharisees, hypocrites! For you clean the outside of the cup and of the plate, but inside they are full of greed and self-indulgence. [26]You blind Pharisee! First clean the inside of the cup,[u] so that the outside also may become clean.

27 "Woe to you, scribes and Pharisees, hypocrites! For you are like whitewashed tombs, which on the outside look beautiful, but inside they are full of the bones of the dead and of all kinds of filth. [28]So you also on the outside look righteous to others, but inside you are full of hypocrisy and lawlessness.

29 "Woe to you, scribes and Pharisees, hypocrites! For you build the tombs of the prophets and decorate the graves of the righteous, [30]and you say, 'If we had lived in the days of our ancestors, we would not have taken part with them in shedding the blood of the prophets.' [31]Thus you testify against yourselves that you are descendants of those who murdered the prophets. [32]Fill up, then, the measure of your ancestors. [33]You snakes, you brood of vipers! How can you escape being sentenced to hell?[t] [34]Therefore I send you prophets, sages, and scribes, some of whom you will kill and crucify, and some you will flog in your synagogues and pursue from town to town, [35]so that upon you may come all the righteous blood shed on earth, from the blood of righteous Abel to the blood of Zechariah son of Barachiah, whom you murdered between the sanctuary and the altar. [36]Truly I tell you, all this will come upon this generation.

The Lament over Jerusalem

37 "Jerusalem, Jerusalem, the city that kills the prophets and stones those who are sent to it! How often have I desired to gather your children together as a hen gathers her brood under her wings, and you were not willing! [38]See, your house is left to you, desolate.[v] [39]For I tell you, you will not see me again until you say, 'Blessed is the one who comes in the name of the Lord.' "

The Destruction of the Temple Foretold

24 As Jesus came out of the temple and was going away, his disciples came to point out to him the buildings of the temple. [2]Then he asked them, "You see all these, do you not? Truly I tell you, not one stone will be left here upon another; all will be thrown down."

Signs of the End of the Age

3 When he was sitting on the Mount of Olives, the disciples came to him privately, saying, "Tell us, when will this be, and what will be the sign of your coming and of the end of the age?" [4]Jesus answered them, "Beware that no one leads you astray. [5]For many will come in my name, saying, 'I am the Messiah!'[w] and they will lead many astray. [6]And you will hear of wars and rumors of wars; see that you are not

[s] Other authorities add here (or after verse 12) verse 14, *Woe to you, scribes and Pharisees, hypocrites! For you devour widows' houses and for the sake of appearance you make long prayers; therefore you will receive the greater condemnation* [t] Gk *Gehenna* [u] Other ancient authorities add *and of the plate* [v] Other ancient authorities lack *desolate* [w] Or *the Christ*

23.37-39 Jesus' lament for *Jerusalem* concerns the rejection of him and his message concerning the re-defined *children* of God. *Cf.* Lk 13.34-35.
24.1-25.46 The Fifth Discourse: The Destruction of the Temple and the Judgment of the Nations. Since it appears in Mark (13.1-37) and Luke (21.5-36), though in shorter forms, scholars have called it the Synoptic Apocalypse (a type of literature which depicts the conflicts and deliverance that God's people will experience at the end of the present age).
24.1-2 *The buildings of the temple* were the magnificent structures built by Herod the Great, beginning in 20 BCE and still unfinished at the time of Jesus. The destruction did occur when the Romans besieged and destroyed the city at the end of the Jewish revolt (66-70 CE).
24.3-8 This catastrophe will be the prelude to the *coming* of Jesus in triumph. The *sign* for this event will be a series of difficulties (false claimants to the role of *Messiah*; international conflicts and cosmic disturbances) which are only the first of the pains leading to the *birth* of the new age.

24.9-14 The community will experience persecution and martyrdom, the rise of *false prophets*, and the apostasy of some members. Only the faithful will *endure to the end* and spread the good news across the *world*.
24.15-31 The final sign of the end will be the *desolating sacrilege*, a term from Dan 9.27 and 11.1 referring to the decree of the Syrian ruler, Antiochus IV Epiphanes, in 168 BCE to have a statue of himself as divine erected in the Jerusalem temple. The Roman emperor Caligula (37-41 CE) gave a similar order for a statue of himself as Jupiter to be placed in the temple. When the pagan ruler takes a similar action, God's people are to flee, no matter what their condition may be. Unprecedented *suffering* is to occur, and unparalleled pressure on the faithful to deny their trust in Jesus. Jesus, the *Son of Man*, will come in triumph and *glory*, the corpses of those killed in the cosmic conflict will feed the vultures, but the faithful (*elect*) will be gathered from everywhere.
24.32-36 On the analogy of the steady growth and development of a *fig tree*, the community is to discern the signs of these divine acts of renewal of the creation and of God's people, which are certain to take place within *this generation*, although God alone knows exactly when it will occur.
24.37-44 As the time of the *coming of the Son of Man* nears, most people will be preoccupied with routine affairs, as in the time of *Noah* (Gen 7.7). The faithful are to be watchful, like the responsible *owner* of a home on guard against a *thief*, who might come at any *hour*. *Cf.* Lk 17.26-27,34-35; 12.39-40.

alarmed; for this must take place, but the end is not yet. 7 For nation will rise against nation, and kingdom against kingdom, and there will be famines[x] and earthquakes in various places: 8 all this is but the beginning of the birth pangs.

Persecutions Foretold

9 "Then they will hand you over to be tortured and will put you to death, and you will be hated by all nations because of my name. 10 Then many will fall away,[y] and they will betray one another and hate one another. 11 And many false prophets will arise and lead many astray. 12 And because of the increase of lawlessness, the love of many will grow cold. 13 But the one who endures to the end will be saved. 14 And this good news[z] of the kingdom will be proclaimed throughout the world, as a testimony to all the nations; and then the end will come.

The Desolating Sacrilege

15 "So when you see the desolating sacrilege standing in the holy place, as was spoken of by the prophet Daniel (let the reader understand), 16 then those in Judea must flee to the mountains; 17 the one on the housetop must not go down to take what is in the house; 18 the one in the field must not turn back to get a coat. 19 Woe to those who are pregnant and to those who are nursing infants in those days! 20 Pray that your flight may not be in winter or on a sabbath. 21 For at that time there will be great suffering, such as has not been from the beginning of the world until now, no, and never will be. 22 And if those days had not been cut short, no one would be saved; but for the sake of the elect those days will be cut short. 23 Then if anyone says to you, 'Look! Here is the Messiah!'[a] or 'There he is!'—do not believe it. 24 For false messiahs[b] and false prophets will appear and produce great signs and omens, to lead astray, if possible, even the elect. 25 Take note, I have told you beforehand. 26 So, if they say to you, 'Look! He is in the wilderness,' do not go out. If they say, 'Look! He is in the inner rooms,' do not believe it. 27 For as the lightning comes from the east and flashes as far as the west, so will be the coming of the Son of Man. 28 Wherever the corpse is, there the vultures will gather.

The Coming of the Son of Man

29 "Immediately after the suffering of those days

the sun will be darkened,
and the moon will not give its light;
the stars will fall from heaven,
and the powers of heaven will be shaken.

30 Then the sign of the Son of Man will appear in heaven, and then all the tribes of the earth will mourn, and they will see 'the Son of Man coming on the clouds of heaven' with power and great glory. 31 And he will send out his angels with a loud trumpet call, and they will gather his elect from the four winds, from one end of heaven to the other.

The Lesson of the Fig Tree

32 "From the fig tree learn its lesson: as soon as its branch becomes tender and puts forth its leaves, you know that summer is near. 33 So also, when you see all these things, you know that he[c] is near, at the very gates. 34 Truly I tell you, this generation will not pass away until all these things have taken place. 35 Heaven and earth will pass away, but my words will not pass away.

The Necessity for Watchfulness

36 "But about that day and hour no one knows, neither the angels of heaven, nor the Son,[d] but only the Father. 37 For as the days of Noah were, so will be the coming of the Son of Man. 38 For as in those days before the flood they were eating and drinking, marrying and giving in marriage, until the day Noah entered the ark, 39 and they knew nothing until the flood came and swept them all away, so too will be the coming of the Son of Man. 40 Then two will be in the field; one will be taken and one will be left. 41 Two women will be grinding meal together; one will be taken and one will be left. 42 Keep awake therefore, for you do not know on what day[e] your Lord is coming. 43 But understand this: if the owner of the house had known in what part of the

[x] Other ancient authorities add *and pestilences* [y] Or *stumble* [z] Or *gospel* [a] Or *the Christ* [b] Or *christs* [c] Or *it* [d] Other ancient authorities lack *nor the Son* [e] Other ancient authorities read *at what hour*

24.7 Isa 19.2; Hag 2.22; Zech 14.13
24.9 Mt 10.17,22; Jn 15.18; 16.2
24.10 Mt 11.6
24.11 Mt 7.15; Acts 20.29; 1 Tim 4.1
24.13 Mt 10.22; Rev 2.7
24.14 Rom 10.18; Col 1.6,23
24.15 Dan 9.27; 11.31; 12.11; Acts 21.28
24.21 Dan 12.1; Joel 2.2
24.22 Isa 65.8,9
24.23 Lk 17.23; 21.8
24.24 2 Thess 2.9-11; Rev 13.13
24.27 Lk 17.24
24.29 Isa 13.10; Ezek 32.7; Joel 2.10; Rev 8.12
24.30 Dan 7.13; Mt 16.27; Rev 1.7
24.31 Isa 27.13; Zech 9.14; 1 Cor 15.52; 1 Thess 4.16
24.34 Mt 16.28; 23.36
24.35 Mt 5.18
24.37 Gen 6.5; 7.6-23; Lk 17.26,27
24.40 Lk 17.34,35
24.42 Mt 25.13; Lk 12.40
24.43 1 Thess 5.2; 2 Pet 3.10; Rev 3.3; 16.15

night the thief was coming, he would have stayed awake and would not have let his house be broken into. 44Therefore you also must be ready, for the Son of Man is coming at an unexpected hour.

The Faithful or the Unfaithful Slave

45 "Who then is the faithful and wise slave, whom his master has put in charge of his household, to give the other slaves[f] their allowance of food at the proper time? 46Blessed is that slave whom his master will find at work when he arrives. 47Truly I tell you, he will put that one in charge of all his possessions. 48But if that wicked slave says to himself, 'My master is delayed,' 49and he begins to beat his fellow slaves, and eats and drinks with drunkards, 50the master of that slave will come on a day when he does not expect him and at an hour that he does not know. 51He will cut him in pieces[g] and put him with the hypocrites, where there will be weeping and gnashing of teeth.

The Parable of the Ten Bridesmaids

25 "Then the kingdom of heaven will be like this. Ten bridesmaids[h] took their lamps and went to meet the bridegroom.[i] 2Five of them were foolish, and five were wise. 3When the foolish took their lamps, they took no oil with them; 4but the wise took flasks of oil with their lamps. 5As the bridegroom was delayed, all of them became drowsy and slept. 6But at midnight there was a shout, 'Look! Here is the bridegroom! Come out to meet him.' 7Then all those bridesmaids[h] got up and trimmed their lamps. 8The foolish said to the wise, 'Give us some of your oil, for our lamps are going out.' 9But the wise replied, 'No! there will not be enough for you and for us; you had better go to the dealers and buy some for yourselves.' 10And while they went to buy it, the bridegroom came, and those who were ready went with him into the wedding banquet; and the door was shut. 11Later the other bridesmaids[h] came also, saying, 'Lord, lord, open to us.' 12But he replied, 'Truly I tell you, I do not know you.' 13Keep awake therefore, for you know neither the day nor the hour.[j]

The Parable of the Talents

14 "For it is as if a man, going on a journey, summoned his slaves and entrusted his property to them; 15to one he gave five talents,[k] to another two, to another one, to each according to his ability. Then he went away. 16The one who had received the five talents went off at once and traded with them, and made five more talents. 17In the same way, the one who had the two talents made two more talents. 18But the one who had received the one talent went off and dug a hole in the ground and hid his master's money. 19After a long time the master of those slaves came and settled accounts with them. 20Then the one who had received the five talents came forward, bringing five more talents, saying, 'Master, you handed over to me five talents; see, I have made five more talents.' 21His master said to him, 'Well done, good and trustworthy slave; you have been trustworthy in a few things, I will put you in charge of many things; enter into the joy of your master.' 22And the one with the two talents also came forward, saying, 'Master, you handed over to me two talents; see, I have made two more talents.' 23His master said to him, 'Well done, good and trustworthy slave; you have been trustworthy in a few things, I will put you in charge of many things; enter into the joy of your master.' 24Then the one who had received the one talent also came forward, saying, 'Master, I knew that you were a harsh man, reaping where you did not sow, and gathering where you did not scatter seed; 25so I was afraid, and I went and hid your talent in the ground. Here you have what is yours.' 26But his master replied, 'You wicked and lazy slave! You knew, did you, that I reap where I did not sow, and gather where I did not scatter? 27Then you ought to have invested my money with the bankers, and on my return I would have received what was my own with interest. 28So take the talent from him, and give it to the one with the ten talents. 29For to all those who have, more will be given, and they will have an abundance; but from those who have nothing, even what they have will be taken away. 30As for this worthless slave, throw him into the outer darkness, where there will be weeping and gnashing of teeth.'

[f] Gk *to give them* [g] Or *cut him off* [h] Gk *virgins* [i] Other ancient authorities add *and the bride* [j] Other ancient authorities add *in which the Son of Man is coming* [k] A talent was worth more than fifteen years' wages of a laborer

24.44 1 Thess 5.6
24.45 Mt 25.21,23
24.46 Rev 16.15
24.47 Mt 25.21,23
24.51 Mt 8.12; 13.42,50; 25.30
25.1 Mt 24.42,44; Mk 13.35; Lk 12.40; 1 Thess 5.6
25.2 Mt 7.24; 10.16; 24.45
25.5 1 Thess 5.6
25.7 Lk 12.35
25.10 Lk 13.25; Rev 19.9
25.11 Mt 7.21-23
25.13 Mt 24.42,44; Mk 13.35; Lk 12.40; 1 Thess 5.6
25.14 Lk 19.12; Mt 21.33
25.15 Mt 18.23,24; Lk 19.13
25.19 Mt 18.23
25.21 Mt 24.45,47; Lk 16.10
25.24 Jn 10.28,29; 2 Thess 2.9-11; 2 Tim 2.19; Rev 13.13
25.27 Lk 17.24
25.29 Mt 13.12; Mk 4.25; Lk 8.18
25.30 Mt 8.12; 3.42,50; 22.13; Lk 13.28

24.45-51 The figure changes to the way a *slave* spends his time and energies while his *master* is absent; the slave who abuses others and is self-indulgent is depicted as *cut in pieces* along with the *hypocrites* (meaning "play actor," a favorite term of Matthew for those who merely make a show of obedience to God) when the *master* (Christ) returns. *Cf.* Lk 12.42-46.
25.1-13 The Parable of the Ten Bridesmaids (only in Matthew) pictures those who are, and those who are not, ready for the climactic event: the temporally unpredictable but certain return of the bridegroom (Jesus) to consummate the union.
25.14-30 The Parable of the Talents depicts the range of ways in which slaves handle their responsibilities (symbolized by *talents*, coins of very high value) during the absence of their master. The venturesome are rewarded, but the timid are denounced as *wicked* and *lazy*, and are doomed to be cast into outer *darkness*. *Cf.* Lk 19.12-27, which is an allegory of the crowning of Christ as king.

25.31-46 The Final Judgment (only in Matthew) is not a parable but a description of the *Son of Man* commending the *nations* which ministered to the needs of the *members of his family* (the new covenant people) as they went about carrying his message, and condemning those *nations* which failed to meet the needs of his people when they were hungry, sick, or in prison. Only the nations which responded with compassion can share in *eternal life*.
26.1-28.20 The Death and Resurrection of Jesus.
26.1-2 Matthew's characteristic transitional phrase (*when Jesus had finished...*) leads to the account of Jesus' last days among his followers. The *Passover* (see Ex 12 for its origins) was linked with phases of the moon and could thus fall on any day of the week. The synoptic gospels report this Passover as falling on Friday (sundown Thursday to sundown Friday). *Two days* before the Passover would be sundown Tuesday to sundown Wednesday. *Cf.* Jn 19.14.
26.3-5 The priestly and lay leaders are convened by *Caiaphas* (high priest 18-36 CE) to get rid of Jesus, but to avoid a popular uprising in his support *during the festival*.
26.6-13 Symbolic anointing of Jesus (which he describes as preparation for his burial) is performed by a *woman* of means in a ritually impure setting: the home of a *leper*.
26.14-16 *Judas Iscariot* (see note at 10.4) offered to *betray* Jesus to the Jewish authorities, by making certain for them his location and identity. Matthew specifies the amount of compensation he receives: *thirty pieces of silver* (see Zech 11.12, where the prophet annuls the covenant and is paid this amount).
26.17-25 *Unleavened Bread* refers to an originally agricultural festival (Ex 34.18-20) which was later combined with Passover (Ex 12.1-20; Ezek 45.21-24) and began on the fifteenth of the Jewish month Nisan. That morning all leaven was removed from Jewish households and the Passover lamb was sacrificed. The Passover meal took place after sunset. Contrast Jn 19.4, where Jesus' last meal was eaten on the evening of the Day of Preparation and Jesus died on the following afternoon, before Passover began at sunset on Friday. Here (as in Mark and Luke) Jesus shares the actual Passover meal, which was eaten in homes. Bread was *dipped* by participants into a common bowl containing sauce. Betrayal by an intimate friend is pictured in Ps 41.9, and the death of an "anointed one" is predicted by Daniel (9.26), who foretells the coming of God's *kingdom* through "one like a *son of man*" (Dan 7.13-14). *Cf.* Mt 8.20; 19.28.

The Judgment of the Nations

31 "When the Son of Man comes in his
glory, and all the angels with him, then he
will sit on the throne of his glory. 32All the
nations will be gathered before him, and he
will separate people one from another as a
shepherd separates the sheep from the goats,
33and he will put the sheep at his right hand
and the goats at the left. 34Then the king
will say to those at his right hand, 'Come,
you that are blessed by my Father, inherit
the kingdom prepared for you from the
foundation of the world; 35for I was hungry
and you gave me food, I was thirsty and
you gave me something to drink, I was a
stranger and you welcomed me, 36I was
naked and you gave me clothing, I was sick
and you took care of me, I was in prison
and you visited me.' 37Then the righteous
will answer him, 'Lord, when was it that we
saw you hungry and gave you food, or
thirsty and gave you something to drink?
38And when was it that we saw you a
stranger and welcomed you, or naked and
gave you clothing? 39And when was it that
we saw you sick or in prison and visited
you?' 40And the king will answer them,
'Truly I tell you, just as you did it to one
of the least of these who are members of my
family,[l] you did it to me.' 41Then he will say
to those at his left hand, 'You that are
accursed, depart from me into the eternal
fire prepared for the devil and his angels;
42for I was hungry and you gave me no
food, I was thirsty and you gave me nothing to drink, 43I was a stranger and you did
not welcome me, naked and you did not
give me clothing, sick and in prison and
you did not visit me.' 44Then they also will
answer, 'Lord, when was it that we saw
you hungry or thirsty or a stranger or
naked or sick or in prison, and did not take
care of you?' 45Then he will answer them,
'Truly I tell you, just as you did not do it
to one of the least of these, you did not do
it to me.' 46And these will go away into
eternal punishment, but the righteous into
eternal life."

The Plot to Kill Jesus

26 When Jesus had finished saying all
these things, he said to his disciples, 2"You know that after two days the
Passover is coming, and the Son of Man will
be handed over to be crucified."
3 Then the chief priests and the elders of
the people gathered in the palace of the
high priest, who was called Caiaphas, 4and
they conspired to arrest Jesus by stealth and
kill him. 5But they said, "Not during the
festival, or there may be a riot among the
people."

The Anointing at Bethany

6 Now while Jesus was at Bethany in the
house of Simon the leper,[m] 7a woman came
to him with an alabaster jar of very costly
ointment, and she poured it on his head as
he sat at the table. 8But when the disciples
saw it, they were angry and said, "Why this
waste? 9For this ointment could have been
sold for a large sum, and the money given
to the poor." 10But Jesus, aware of this, said
to them, "Why do you trouble the woman?
She has performed a good service for me.
11For you always have the poor with you,
but you will not always have me. 12By
pouring this ointment on my body she has
prepared me for burial. 13Truly I tell you,
wherever this good news[n] is proclaimed in
the whole world, what she has done will be
told in remembrance of her."

Judas Agrees to Betray Jesus

14 Then one of the twelve, who was
called Judas Iscariot, went to the chief priests
15and said, "What will you give me if I
betray him to you?" They paid him thirty
pieces of silver. 16And from that moment he
began to look for an opportunity to betray
him.

The Passover with the Disciples

17 On the first day of Unleavened Bread
the disciples came to Jesus, saying, "Where
do you want us to make the preparations
for you to eat the Passover?" 18He said, "Go
into the city to a certain man, and say to
him, 'The Teacher says, My time is near; I
will keep the Passover at your house with
my disciples.' " 19So the disciples did as Jesus
had directed them, and they prepared the
Passover meal.
20 When it was evening, he took his
place with the twelve;[o] 21and while they
were eating, he said, "Truly I tell you, one

[l] Gk *these my brothers* [m] The terms *leper* and *leprosy* can refer to several diseases [n] Or *gospel* [o] Other ancient authorities add *disciples*

25.31 Mt 16.27; 19.28
25.32 Ezek 34.17,20
25.34 Lk 12.32; 1 Cor 6.9; 15.50; Gal 5.21; Rev 13.8; 17.8
25.35 Isa 58.7; Ezek 18.7; Jas 1.27; Heb 13.2
25.36 Jas 2.15,16; 2 Tim 1.16
25.40 Prov 14.31; 19.17; Mt 10.42; Heb 6.10
25.41 Mt 7.23; Mk 9.48; Lk 16.24; Jude 7; 2 Pet 2.4
25.45 Prov 14.31; 17.5
25.46 Dan 12.2; Jn 5.29; Rom 2.7; Gal 6.8
26.1 Mt 7.28; 11.1; 13.53; 19.1
26.2 Jn 13.1
26.3 Ps 2.2; Jn 11.47-53
26.4 Mt 12.14
26.5 Mt 27.24
26.6 Mt 21.17
26.11 Deut 15.11
26.12 Jn 19.40
26.15 Ex 21.32; Zech 11.12
26.18 Jn 7.6,8; 12.23; 13.1; 17.1
26.19 Deut 16.5-8

of you will betray me." 22And they became greatly distressed and began to say to him one after another, "Surely not I, Lord?" 23He answered, "The one who has dipped his hand into the bowl with me will betray me. 24The Son of Man goes as it is written of him, but woe to that one by whom the Son of Man is betrayed! It would have been better for that one not to have been born." 25Judas, who betrayed him, said, "Surely not I, Rabbi?" He replied, "You have said so."

The Institution of the Lord's Supper

26 While they were eating, Jesus took a loaf of bread, and after blessing it he broke it, gave it to the disciples, and said, "Take, eat; this is my body." 27Then he took a cup, and after giving thanks he gave it to them, saying, "Drink from it, all of you; 28for this is my blood of the[p] covenant, which is poured out for many for the forgiveness of sins. 29I tell you, I will never again drink of this fruit of the vine until that day when I drink it new with you in my Father's kingdom."

30 When they had sung the hymn, they went out to the Mount of Olives.

Peter's Denial Foretold

31 Then Jesus said to them, "You will all become deserters because of me this night; for it is written,

'I will strike the shepherd,
and the sheep of the flock will be scattered.'

32But after I am raised up, I will go ahead of you to Galilee." 33Peter said to him, "Though all become deserters because of you, I will never desert you." 34Jesus said to him, "Truly I tell you, this very night, before the cock crows, you will deny me three times." 35Peter said to him, "Even though I must die with you, I will not deny you." And so said all the disciples.

Jesus Prays in Gethsemane

36 Then Jesus went with them to a place called Gethsemane; and he said to his disciples, "Sit here while I go over there and pray." 37He took with him Peter and the two sons of Zebedee, and began to be grieved and agitated. 38Then he said to them, "I am deeply grieved, even to death; remain here, and stay awake with me." 39And going a little farther, he threw himself on the ground and prayed, "My Father, if it is possible, let this cup pass from me; yet not what I want but what you want." 40Then he came to the disciples and found them sleeping; and he said to Peter, "So, could you not stay awake with me one hour? 41Stay awake and pray that you may not come into the time of trial;[q] the spirit indeed is willing, but the flesh is weak." 42Again he went away for the second time and prayed, "My Father, if this cannot pass unless I drink it, your will be done." 43Again he came and found them sleeping, for their eyes were heavy. 44So leaving them again, he went away and prayed for the third time, saying the same words. 45Then he came to the disciples and said to them, "Are you still sleeping and taking your rest? See, the hour is at hand, and the Son of Man is betrayed into the hands of sinners. 46Get up, let us be going. See, my betrayer is at hand."

The Betrayal and Arrest of Jesus

47 While he was still speaking, Judas, one of the twelve, arrived; with him was a large crowd with swords and clubs, from the chief priests and the elders of the people. 48Now the betrayer had given them a sign, saying, "The one I will kiss is the man; arrest him." 49At once he came up to Jesus and said, "Greetings, Rabbi!" and kissed him. 50Jesus said to him, "Friend, do what you are here to do." Then they came and laid hands on Jesus and arrested him. 51Suddenly, one of those with Jesus put his hand on his sword, drew it, and struck the slave of the high priest, cutting off his ear. 52Then Jesus said to him, "Put your sword back into its place; for all who take the sword will perish by the sword. 53Do you think that I cannot appeal to my Father, and he will at once send me more than twelve legions of angels? 54But how then would the scriptures be fulfilled, which say it must happen in this way?" 55At that hour Jesus said to the crowds, "Have you come out with swords and clubs to arrest me as though I were a bandit? Day after day I sat in the temple teaching, and you did not arrest me. 56But all this has taken place, so that the scriptures of the prophets may be fulfilled." Then all the disciples deserted him and fled.

[p] Other ancient authorities add *new* [q] Or *into temptation*

26.23 Ps 41.9; Lk 22.21; Jn 13.18; Isa 53; Dan 9.26; Acts 17.2,3; 1 Cor 15.3
26.26 1 Cor 10.16; 11.23-25
26.28 Ex 24.6-8; Mt 20.28; Mk 1.4; Heb 9.20
26.29 Acts 10.41
26.30 Mk 14.26
26.31 Jn 16.32; Mt 11.6; Zech 13.7
26.32 Mt 28.7,10,16
26.34 Jn 13.37
26.35 Jn 13.37
26.37 Mt 4.21
26.38 Jn 12.27
26.39 Jn 12.27; Mt 20.22; Jn 6.38; Phil 2.8
26.40 ver 38
26.41 Mt 6.13; Lk 11.4
26.42 Jn 4.34; 5.30; 6.38
26.45 ver 18; Jn 12.23,27; 13.1; 17.1
26.49 ver 25
26.50 Mt 20.13; 22.12
26.52 Gen 9.6; Rev 13.10
26.53 2 Kings 6.17; Dan 7.10
26.54 ver 24; Lk 24.25,44,46
26.56 ver 54

26.26-30 The shared *loaf* and *cup*, for which thanks are given (in Greek, *eucharistesas*), comprise the sign of the *covenant*, in which God's new people are forgiven and united, now and in preparation for the coming of *the Father's kingdom*.
26.31-35 Jesus predicts that after he has been struck, his followers will be *scattered* (Zech 13.9), but he will rejoin them in *Galilee*. *Cf.* Mt 28.7,16-20; Mk 16.7. Peter's predicted denial occurs that evening: 26.69-79.
26.36-46 Jesus' prayerful struggle is in *Gethsemane* (probably on the western slopes of the Mount of Olives, but the exact site is unknown) while the disciples were *sleeping*. He employs the image of the *cup* of suffering which God is calling him to undergo.
26.47-56 The *crowd* that comes to seize Jesus, led by *Judas*, is from the Jewish leaders. Judas addresses Jesus as *Rabbi* (Hebrew for "My master"; only later used for honored teachers of the law). Rejecting efforts by his followers at physical retaliation, he reminds them of the potential of angelic support (*legion* was a Roman infantry unit of five to six thousand), and tells the mob (*crowds*) that he is not a *bandit* (threat to law and order), and that his arrest and pending death are in accord with scriptural prophecy. Mention of the many occasions when he was teaching in the temple suggests that Jesus was in Jerusalem more often than is mentioned in Matthew's account (Jn 2.23). *Cf.* Mk 14.43-52.

Jesus before the High Priest

57 Those who had arrested Jesus took him to Caiaphas the high priest, in whose house the scribes and the elders had gathered. 58But Peter was following him at a distance, as far as the courtyard of the high priest; and going inside, he sat with the guards in order to see how this would end. 59Now the chief priests and the whole council were looking for false testimony against Jesus so that they might put him to death, 60but they found none, though many false witnesses came forward. At last two came forward 61and said, "This fellow said, 'I am able to destroy the temple of God and to build it in three days.' " 62The high priest stood up and said, "Have you no answer? What is it that they testify against you?" 63But Jesus was silent. Then the high priest said to him, "I put you under oath before the living God, tell us if you are the Messiah,[r] the Son of God." 64Jesus said to him, "You have said so. But I tell you,

From now on you will see the Son of Man
seated at the right hand of Power
and coming on the clouds of heaven."

65Then the high priest tore his clothes and said, "He has blasphemed! Why do we still need witnesses? You have now heard his blasphemy. 66What is your verdict?" They answered, "He deserves death." 67Then they spat in his face and struck him; and some slapped him, 68saying, "Prophesy to us, you Messiah![r] Who is it that struck you?"

Peter's Denial of Jesus

69 Now Peter was sitting outside in the courtyard. A servant-girl came to him and said, "You also were with Jesus the Galilean." 70But he denied it before all of them, saying, "I do not know what you are talking about." 71When he went out to the porch, another servant-girl saw him, and she said to the bystanders, "This man was with Jesus of Nazareth."[s] 72Again he denied it with an oath, "I do not know the man." 73After a little while the bystanders came up and said to Peter, "Certainly you are also one of them, for your accent betrays you." 74Then he began to curse, and he swore an oath, "I do not know the man!" At that moment the cock crowed. 75Then Peter remembered what Jesus had said: "Before the cock crows, you will deny me three times." And he went out and wept bitterly.

Jesus Brought before Pilate

27 When morning came, all the chief priests and the elders of the people conferred together against Jesus in order to bring about his death. 2They bound him, led him away, and handed him over to Pilate the governor.

The Suicide of Judas

3 When Judas, his betrayer, saw that Jesus[t] was condemned, he repented and brought back the thirty pieces of silver to the chief priests and the elders. 4He said, "I have sinned by betraying innocent[u] blood." But they said, "What is that to us? See to it yourself." 5Throwing down the pieces of silver in the temple, he departed; and he went and hanged himself. 6But the chief priests, taking the pieces of silver, said, "It is not lawful to put them into the treasury, since they are blood money." 7After conferring together, they used them to buy the potter's field as a place to bury foreigners. 8For this reason that field has been called the Field of Blood to this day. 9Then was fulfilled what had been spoken through the prophet Jeremiah,[v] "And they took[w] the thirty pieces of silver, the price of the one on whom a price had been set,[x] on whom some of the people of Israel had set a price, 10and they gave[y] them for the potter's field, as the Lord commanded me."

Pilate Questions Jesus

11 Now Jesus stood before the governor; and the governor asked him, "Are you the King of the Jews?" Jesus said, "You say so." 12But when he was accused by the chief priests and elders, he did not answer. 13Then Pilate said to him, "Do you not hear how many accusations they make against you?" 14But he gave him no answer, not even to a single charge, so that the governor was greatly amazed.

[r] Or *Christ* [s] Gk *the Nazorean* [t] Gk *he* [u] Other ancient authorities read *righteous* [v] Other ancient authorities read *Zechariah* or *Isaiah* [w] Or *I took* [x] Or *the price of the precious One* [y] Other ancient authorities read *I gave*

26.57-68 The leaders who examine Jesus are the local regional council (Greek, *synedrion*) of the kind set up by the Romans throughout the empire to give a degree of local autonomy to the indigenous power group. By the later second century CE, that title was adopted for the rabbinical council (Sanhedrin) which presided over Jewish religious affairs. The *false testimony* against Jesus includes the alteration of his prediction that the temple would be destroyed (24.2) to the charge that he was going to destroy it and rebuild it. In answer to the *high priest's* question if Jesus is the *Messiah*, Jesus replies, *You have said so*, meaning, "The words are yours," following this with the implicit claim of his vindication and return as triumphant *Son of Man*. See note on 26.17-25; Dan 7.13-14. Although Jesus is said to *deserve death*, and the Jewish council could execute violators of its laws, the leaders' decision is to turn him over to the jurisdiction of the Romans (27.1-2). *Cf.* Mk 14.53-65; Lk 22.54-70.
26.69-75 In response to young women and other *bystanders*, Peter fulfills Jesus' prediction of three denials of his association with Jesus (26.34), and is deeply contrite. *Cf.* Mk 14.66-72; Lk 22.56-72.
27.1-2 After conferring next morning, the leaders turn Jesus over to the Roman governor's jurisdiction.
27.3-10 Matthew alone of the gospels reports the death of Judas, which is by suicide; in Acts 1.18-19, his abdomen burst open in the *potter's field* he had purchased with the bribe (see Zech 11.13; Jer 32.6-15).
27.11-26 The Hearing before Pilate. *Pilate* was procurator (emperor's agent) governing Judea from 26 to 36 CE under Tiberius, and was recalled for his ruthlessness and cynical methods of making decisions, as is evident from other ancient historical sources. In response to the question whether he aspires to be *King of the Jews*, Jesus again responds (26.64) with *You say so*. Pilate offers to release Jesus, in fulfillment of the agreement to liberate annually one political prisoner (27.15), but the leaders choose instead the *notorious Barabbas*, and call for Jesus' *crucifixion*. Capital crimes were punished among the Jews by stoning (Ex 21; Lev 24; Num 14; Deut 17), but the Romans nailed the hands of major offenders to a cross-piece of wood, which was then suspended at the top of a pole until the condemned had died. Only in Matthew is Jesus' innocence declared by the Romans (27.19,24), and only in Matthew is responsibility for his death explicitly accepted by the Jewish leaders (Mt 27.25).

26.58 Jn 18.15
26.60 Ps 27.12; 35.11; Acts 6.13; Deut 19.15
26.61 Mt 27.40
26.63 Isa 53.7; Mt 27.12,14; Lev 5.1; Jn 18.33
26.64 Ps 110.1; Dan 7.13; Mt 16.27,28
26.65 Num 14.6; Acts 14.14; Lev 24.16
26.66 Jn 19.7
26.67 Isa 53.3; Mt 27.30; Jn 19.3
26.75 ver 34; Jn 13.38
27.2 Mt 20.19; Acts 3.13
27.3 Mt 26.14,15
27.4 ver 24
27.5 Acts 1.18
27.8 Acts 1.19
27.9 Zech 11.12,13
27.12 Mt 26.63; Jn 19.9
27.13 Mt 26.62; Jn 19.10
27.14 1 Tim 6.13

Barabbas or Jesus?

15 Now at the festival the governor was
accustomed to release a prisoner for the
crowd, anyone whom they wanted. 16At
that time they had a notorious prisoner,
called Jesus[z] Barabbas. 17So after they had
gathered, Pilate said to them, "Whom do
you want me to release for you, Jesus[z]
Barabbas or Jesus who is called the
Messiah?"[a] 18For he realized that it was out
of jealousy that they had handed him over.
19While he was sitting on the judgment
seat, his wife sent word to him, "Have
nothing to do with that innocent man, for
today I have suffered a great deal because
of a dream about him." 20Now the chief
priests and the elders persuaded the crowds
to ask for Barabbas and to have Jesus killed.
21The governor again said to them, "Which
of the two do you want me to release for
you?" And they said, "Barabbas." 22Pilate
said to them, "Then what should I do with
Jesus who is called the Messiah?"[a] All of
them said, "Let him be crucified!" 23Then he
asked, "Why, what evil has he done?" But
they shouted all the more, "Let him be
crucified!"

Pilate Hands Jesus over to Be Crucified

24 So when Pilate saw that he could do
nothing, but rather that a riot was beginning, he took some water and washed his
hands before the crowd, saying, "I am innocent of this man's blood;[b] see to it yourselves." 25Then the people as a whole answered, "His blood be on us and on our
children!" 26So he released Barabbas for
them; and after flogging Jesus, he handed
him over to be crucified.

The Soldiers Mock Jesus

27 Then the soldiers of the governor took
Jesus into the governor's headquarters,[c] and
they gathered the whole cohort around him.
28They stripped him and put a scarlet robe
on him, 29and after twisting some thorns
into a crown, they put it on his head. They
put a reed in his right hand and knelt before
him and mocked him, saying, "Hail, King
of the Jews!" 30They spat on him, and took
the reed and struck him on the head. 31Af-
ter mocking him, they stripped him of the
robe and put his own clothes on him. Then
they led him away to crucify him.

The Crucifixion of Jesus

32 As they went out, they came upon a
man from Cyrene named Simon; they compelled this man to carry his cross. 33And
when they came to a place called Golgotha
(which means Place of a Skull), 34they offered him wine to drink, mixed with gall;
but when he tasted it, he would not drink
it. 35And when they had crucified him, they
divided his clothes among themselves by
casting lots;[d] 36then they sat down there
and kept watch over him. 37Over his head
they put the charge against him, which
read, "This is Jesus, the King of the Jews."
38 Then two bandits were crucified with
him, one on his right and one on his left.
39Those who passed by derided[e] him, shaking their heads 40and saying, "You who
would destroy the temple and build it in
three days, save yourself! If you are the Son
of God, come down from the cross." 41In the
same way the chief priests also, along with
the scribes and elders, were mocking him,
saying, 42"He saved others; he cannot save
himself.[f] He is the King of Israel; let him
come down from the cross now, and we will
believe in him. 43He trusts in God; let God
deliver him now, if he wants to; for he said,
'I am God's Son.' " 44The bandits who were
crucified with him also taunted him in the
same way.

The Death of Jesus

45 From noon on, darkness came over
the whole land[g] until three in the afternoon. 46And about three o'clock Jesus cried
with a loud voice, "Eli, Eli, lema sabachthani?" that is, "My God, my God, why
have you forsaken me?" 47When some of
the bystanders heard it, they said, "This
man is calling for Elijah." 48At once one of
them ran and got a sponge, filled it with
sour wine, put it on a stick, and gave it to
him to drink. 49But the others said, "Wait,
let us see whether Elijah will come to save

[z] Other ancient authorities lack *Jesus* [a] Or *the Christ* [b] Other ancient authorities read *this righteous blood*, or *this righteous man's blood* [c] Gk *the praetorium* [d] Other ancient authorities add *in order that what had been spoken through the prophet might be fulfilled, "They divided my clothes among themselves, and for my clothing they cast lots."* [e] Or *blasphemed* [f] Or *is he unable to save himself?* [g] Or *earth*

27.19 Acts 12.21; ver 24
27.20 Acts 3.14
27.24 Mt 26.5; Deut 21.6-8; Ps 26.6; ver 19
27.25 Josh 2.19; Acts 5.28
27.26 Isa 53.5
27.27 Jn 18.28,33; Acts 10.1
27.29 Ps 69.19; Isa 53.3
27.30 Mt 26.67; Mk 10.34; 14.65
27.31 Isa 53.7
27.32 Heb 13.12
27.33 Ps 69.21
27.35 Ps 22.18
27.36 ver 54
27.38 Isa 53.12
27.39 Ps 22.7; 109.25
27.40 Mt 26.61; Acts 6.14; Jn 2.19
27.42 Jn 1.49; 12.13
27.43 Ps 22.8
27.45 Am 8.9
27.46 Ps 22.1
27.48 Ps 69.21

27.27-44 The Crucifixion. The soldiers' mocking of Jesus begins in the Roman government *headquarters* (praetorium), when, before they crucify him, they give him mock royal equipment – *scarlet robe*, crown (*of thorns*), and scepter (*reed*) – and hail him as *king of the Jews*. The man compelled to carry the cross-bar for Jesus is *Simon* from *Cyrene* (a Greek city on the coast of North Africa). The *wine* and *gall* offered to him are a narcotic; *cf.* Ps 69.21. The accusation of claiming to be *king* is placed above him, and false charges of threats to destroy the temple are repeated by the people, the priests and the *bandits* crucified beside him.
27.45-56 The Death of Jesus. His cry of agony (27.46) is a quotation from Ps 22 in Aramaic, the remainder of which is a declaration of divine deliverance. *Eli* is confused by his hearers with *Elijah*, whose coming at the end of the age is promised in Mal 4.5-6. That the *curtain of the temple* (before the Holy of Holies, which could be entered only by the high priest) is torn from the top at the moment of Jesus' death implies that it was an act of God, opening access to his presence. The divine affirmation of Jesus and the hope of life beyond the grave are given in the earthquake and the resurrection of *the saints* (true people of God), reported only in Matthew. This leads the Roman officer to acknowledge Jesus as God's *Son*. Only the faithful *women* are on hand to witness these events.

27.57-66 The Entombment of Jesus. Burial of a violator of the covenant on the same day as his execution was decreed by the Law of Moses (Deut 21.22-23). Joseph from *Arimathea* (probably a city north of Jerusalem), identified by Matthew *as a disciple* of Jesus, is permitted by Pilate to bury Jesus in his own *new tomb*. After partial preparation of the body, a *great stone* seals the tomb shut. All this is observed by the two Marys. Only Matthew reports the precaution taken at the urging of the Jewish leaders that a Roman military guard be placed to prevent the removal of Jesus' body by his *disciples*.
28.1-10 No indication is given of the women's intention to prepare Jesus' body for burial, as in Mk 16.1-2. Only Matthew reports the earthquake and descent of the *angel of the Lord* to instruct the women who went *to see the tomb* that Jesus has risen and will meet the *disciples* in *Galilee*, and that Jesus himself met them and confirmed the angel's instruction.
28.11-15 Unique to Matthew is the account of the *guard's* report to the *chief priests* of what happened at the tomb, and the bribe given them to tell that the *disciples* had stolen the body *while we were asleep*. How they would have known what happened while they were asleep is not considered.
28.16-20 Matthew's account of the appearance of Jesus to the disciples takes place in *Galilee*, rather than in Jerusalem and vicinity, as in Lk 24.13-49. As in 5.1; 15.29; 17.1, it is on a *mountain* that Jesus reveals his purpose to his followers. The *authority* given to him by God is the basis for commissioning the disciples: *Go therefore*. Their task is to *make disciples* or "give instruction" to *all the nations*, not simply to Israel, as in 10.5-6. Baptism is to be performed with the trinitarian formula (unique in the gospel tradition), and instruction is to stress what Jesus *commanded*. His presence is promised throughout the present *age*.

him."[h] 50 Then Jesus cried again with a loud voice and breathed his last.[i] 51 At that moment the curtain of the temple was torn in two, from top to bottom. The earth shook, and the rocks were split. 52 The tombs also were opened, and many bodies of the saints who had fallen asleep were raised. 53 After his resurrection they came out of the tombs and entered the holy city and appeared to many. 54 Now when the centurion and those with him, who were keeping watch over Jesus, saw the earthquake and what took place, they were terrified and said, "Truly this man was God's Son!"[j]

55 Many women were also there, looking on from a distance; they had followed Jesus from Galilee and had provided for him. 56 Among them were Mary Magdalene, and Mary the mother of James and Joseph, and the mother of the sons of Zebedee.

The Burial of Jesus

57 When it was evening, there came a rich man from Arimathea, named Joseph, who was also a disciple of Jesus. 58 He went to Pilate and asked for the body of Jesus; then Pilate ordered it to be given to him. 59 So Joseph took the body and wrapped it in a clean linen cloth 60 and laid it in his own new tomb, which he had hewn in the rock. He then rolled a great stone to the door of the tomb and went away. 61 Mary Magdalene and the other Mary were there, sitting opposite the tomb.

The Guard at the Tomb

62 The next day, that is, after the day of Preparation, the chief priests and the Pharisees gathered before Pilate 63 and said, "Sir, we remember what that impostor said while he was still alive, 'After three days I will rise again.' 64 Therefore command the tomb to be made secure until the third day; otherwise his disciples may go and steal him away, and tell the people, 'He has been raised from the dead,' and the last deception would be worse than the first." 65 Pilate said to them, "You have a guard[k] of soldiers; go, make it as secure as you can."[l] 66 So they went with the guard and made the tomb secure by sealing the stone.

The Resurrection of Jesus

28 After the sabbath, as the first day of the week was dawning, Mary Magdalene and the other Mary went to see the tomb. 2 And suddenly there was a great earthquake; for an angel of the Lord, descending from heaven, came and rolled back the stone and sat on it. 3 His appearance was like lightning, and his clothing white as snow. 4 For fear of him the guards shook and became like dead men. 5 But the angel said to the women, "Do not be afraid; I know that you are looking for Jesus who was crucified. 6 He is not here; for he has been raised, as he said. Come, see the place where he[m] lay. 7 Then go quickly and tell his disciples, 'He has been raised from the dead,[n] and indeed he is going ahead of you to Galilee; there you will see him.' This is my message for you." 8 So they left the tomb quickly with fear and great joy, and ran to tell his disciples. 9 Suddenly Jesus met them and said, "Greetings!" And they came to him, took hold of his feet, and worshiped him. 10 Then Jesus said to them, "Do not be afraid; go and tell my brothers to go to Galilee; there they will see me."

The Report of the Guard

11 While they were going, some of the guard went into the city and told the chief priests everything that had happened. 12 After the priests[o] had assembled with the elders, they devised a plan to give a large sum of money to the soldiers, 13 telling them, "You must say, 'His disciples came by night and stole him away while we were asleep.' 14 If this comes to the governor's ears, we will satisfy him and keep you out of trouble." 15 So they took the money and did as they were directed. And this story is still told among the Jews to this day.

The Commissioning of the Disciples

16 Now the eleven disciples went to Galilee, to the mountain to which Jesus had directed them. 17 When they saw him, they worshiped him; but some doubted. 18 And Jesus came and said to them, "All authority in heaven and on earth has been given to me. 19 Go therefore and make disciples of all

[h] Other ancient authorities add *And another took a spear and pierced his side, and out came water and blood* [i] Or *gave up his spirit* [j] Or *a son of God* [k] Or *Take a guard* [l] Gk *you know how* [m] Other ancient authorities read *the Lord* [n] Other ancient authorities lack *from the dead* [o] Gk *they*

27.51 Ex 26.31; Heb 9.3; ver 54
27.54 Mt 3.17; 17.5
27.55 Lk 8.2,3
27.56 Mk 15.40,47; Lk 24.10
27.57 Acts 13.29
27.60 Mt 28.2; Mk 16.4
27.63 Mt 16.21; 17.23; 20.19; Mk 8.31; 10.34; Lk 9.22; 18.33; 24.6,7; Jn 2.19
27.65 Mt 28.11
27.66 ver 60; Mt 28.11-15
28.1 Lk 8.2; Mt 27.56
28.2 Mt 27.51,60
28.5 ver 10; Mt 14.27
28.6 Mt 12.40; 16.21; 17.23; 20.19
28.7 Mt 26.32; ver 16
28.9 Jn 20.14-18
28.10 Rom 8.29; Heb 2.11
28.11 Mt 27.65,66
28.14 Mt 27.2
28.16 ver 7; Mt 26.32
28.18 Dan 7.13,14; Lk 10.22; Phil 2.9,10; 1 Pet 3.22
28.19 Lk 24.47; Acts 1.8

nations, baptizing them in the name of the Father and of the Son and of the Holy Spirit, [20]and teaching them to obey everything that I have commanded you. And remember, I am with you always, to the end of the age."[p]

[p] Other ancient authorities add *Amen*

The Gospel According to

MARK

See the Introductions, pp. 7–8 and 78–79 above.

The Proclamation of John the Baptist

1 The beginning of the good news[a] of Jesus Christ, the Son of God.[b]

2 As it is written in the prophet Isaiah,[c]

"See, I am sending my messenger ahead of you,[d]
who will prepare your way;
3 the voice of one crying out in the wilderness:
'Prepare the way of the Lord,
make his paths straight,'"

[4]John the baptizer appeared[e] in the wilderness, proclaiming a baptism of repentance for the forgiveness of sins. [5]And people from the whole Judean countryside and all the people of Jerusalem were going out to him, and were baptized by him in the river Jordan, confessing their sins. [6]Now John was clothed with camel's hair, with a leather belt around his waist, and he ate locusts and wild honey. [7]He proclaimed, "The one who is more powerful than I is coming after me; I am not worthy to stoop down and untie the thong of his sandals. [8]I have baptized you with[f] water; but he will baptize you with[f] the Holy Spirit."

The Baptism of Jesus

9 In those days Jesus came from Nazareth of Galilee and was baptized by John in the Jordan. [10]And just as he was coming up out of the water, he saw the heavens torn apart and the Spirit descending like a dove on him. [11]And a voice came from heaven, "You are my Son, the Beloved;[g] with you I am well pleased."

The Temptation of Jesus

12 And the Spirit immediately drove him out into the wilderness. [13]He was in the wilderness forty days, tempted by Satan; and he was with the wild beasts; and the angels waited on him.

The Beginning of the Galilean Ministry

14 Now after John was arrested, Jesus came to Galilee, proclaiming the good news[a] of God,[h] [15]and saying, "The time is fulfilled, and the kingdom of God has come near;[i] repent, and believe in the good news."[a]

Jesus Calls the First Disciples

16 As Jesus passed along the Sea of Galilee, he saw Simon and his brother Andrew casting a net into the sea—for they were fishermen. [17]And Jesus said to them, "Follow me and I will make you fish for people." [18]And immediately they left their nets and followed him. [19]As he went a little farther, he saw James son of Zebedee and his brother John, who were in their boat mending the nets. [20]Immediately he called them; and they left their father Zebedee in the boat with the hired men, and followed him.

[a] Or *gospel* [b] Other ancient authorities lack *the Son of God* [c] Other ancient authorities read *in the prophets* [d] Gk *before your face* [e] Other ancient authorities read *John was baptizing* [f] Or *in* [g] Or *my beloved Son* [h] Other ancient authorities read *of the kingdom* [i] Or *is at hand*

1.1 Mt 4.3
1.2 Mal 3.1; Mt 11.10; Lk 7.27
1.3 Isa 40.3
1.4 Acts 13.24; Lk 1.77
1.6 Lev 11.22
1.7 Acts 13.25
1.8 Acts 1.5; Isa 44.3; Joel 2.28
1.9 Mt 2.23
1.10 Jn 1.32
1.11 Ps 2.7; Isa 42.1
1.14 Mt 4.23
1.15 Gal 4.4; Eph 1.10; Acts 20.21
1.18 Mt 19.27

1.1 Introduction. *Beginning:* John the Baptist marks the transition from the epoch of the old covenant to that of the new, which Jesus brings. The term *good news*, or gospel, functions as the title for this book, and became the accepted designation for this type of writing. *The Son of God.* See 1.11 (see note); 3.11; 5.7; 14.61; 15.39.
1.2-6 The scriptures quoted are from Mal 3.1, preparing for God's *messenger*, and Isa 40.3, preparing for the *Lord* (Yahweh in Isaiah; Jesus in Mark). *Cf.* Mt 1.1-3; Lk 3.4-6. *John the baptizer* (later called the Baptist) was imprisoned (1.14) and executed (6.17-29) by Herod Antipas. Details about John's birth in Lk 1.5-25,57-80; and his preaching in Lk 3.10-18. *Baptism of repentance* (which means "change the mind") is a public act by which a new beginning in life is sought. On John's clothing, see note on Mt 3.4-6. John is in Israel's prophetic tradition.
1.7-8 *cf.* notes on Mt 3.11-12.
1.9-11 *cf.* Mt 3.13-17; Lk 3.21-22. *Nazareth* was a small village near Sepphoris, the capital of the province of *Galilee*. In Mark, only Jesus sees the heavens opened and the Spirit descending, and the voice is addressed to him: *You are my Son.*
1.12-13 Jesus' testing by *Satan* (the adversary [1 Chr 21.1] and accuser [Zech 3.1-3]) takes place in the *wilderness*, which recalls the experiences of Moses (Ex 24.18) and Elijah (1 Kings 19.8), and is told in greater detail in Matthew (4.1-11) and Luke (4.1-13).
1.14-15 Returning from the Jordan Valley, Jesus launches his ministry in *Galilee*. His message is that the *time* for fulfillment of God's purpose in the world (*kingdom*) has now fully come. That is the *good news* to which his hearers are to turn (*repent*) and in which they are to trust (*believe*).
1.16-20 The First Followers. *cf.* Mt 4.18-22. The relative wealth of the second pair of brothers is indicated by the fact that their father carries on his fishing business with *hired servants*.

The Man with an Unclean Spirit

21 They went to Capernaum; and when
the sabbath came, he entered the synagogue and taught. [22]They were astounded
at his teaching, for he taught them as one
having authority, and not as the scribes.
[23]Just then there was in their synagogue a
man with an unclean spirit, [24]and he cried
out, "What have you to do with us, Jesus
of Nazareth? Have you come to destroy us?
I know who you are, the Holy One of God."
[25]But Jesus rebuked him, saying, "Be silent,
and come out of him!" [26]And the unclean
spirit, convulsing him and crying with a
loud voice, came out of him. [27]They were
all amazed, and they kept on asking one
another, "What is this? A new teaching—
with authority! He[j] commands even the
unclean spirits, and they obey him." [28]At
once his fame began to spread throughout
the surrounding region of Galilee.

Jesus Heals Many at Simon's House

29 As soon as they[k] left the synagogue,
they entered the house of Simon and
Andrew, with James and John. [30]Now
Simon's mother-in-law was in bed with a
fever, and they told him about her at once.
[31]He came and took her by the hand and
lifted her up. Then the fever left her, and
she began to serve them.

32 That evening, at sundown, they
brought to him all who were sick or possessed with demons. [33]And the whole city
was gathered around the door. [34]And he
cured many who were sick with various
diseases, and cast out many demons; and
he would not permit the demons to speak,
because they knew him.

A Preaching Tour in Galilee

35 In the morning, while it was still very
dark, he got up and went out to a deserted
place, and there he prayed. [36]And Simon
and his companions hunted for him. [37]When
they found him, they said to him, "Everyone is searching for you." [38]He answered,
"Let us go on to the neighboring towns, so
that I may proclaim the message there also;
for that is what I came out to do." [39]And
he went throughout Galilee, proclaiming
the message in their synagogues and casting out demons.

Jesus Cleanses a Leper

40 A leper[l] came to him begging him,
and kneeling[m] he said to him, "If you choose,
you can make me clean." [41]Moved with
pity,[n] Jesus[o] stretched out his hand and
touched him, and said to him, "I do choose.
Be made clean!" [42]Immediately the leprosy[p]
left him, and he was made clean. [43]After
sternly warning him he sent him away at
once, [44]saying to him, "See that you say
nothing to anyone; but go, show yourself to
the priest, and offer for your cleansing what
Moses commanded, as a testimony to them."
[45]But he went out and began to proclaim
it freely, and to spread the word, so that
Jesus[o] could no longer go into a town openly,
but stayed out in the country; and people
came to him from every quarter.

Jesus Heals a Paralytic

2 When he returned to Capernaum after some days, it was reported that he
was at home. [2]So many gathered around
that there was no longer room for them,
not even in front of the door; and he was
speaking the word to them. [3]Then some
people[q] came, bringing to him a paralyzed
man, carried by four of them. [4]And when
they could not bring him to Jesus because
of the crowd, they removed the roof above
him; and after having dug through it, they
let down the mat on which the paralytic
lay. [5]When Jesus saw their faith, he said to
the paralytic, "Son, your sins are forgiven."
[6]Now some of the scribes were sitting there,
questioning in their hearts, [7]"Why does this
fellow speak in this way? It is blasphemy!
Who can forgive sins but God alone?" [8]At
once Jesus perceived in his spirit that they
were discussing these questions among
themselves; and he said to them, "Why do
you raise such questions in your hearts?
[9]Which is easier, to say to the paralytic,
'Your sins are forgiven,' or to say, 'Stand up
and take your mat and walk'? [10]But so that
you may know that the Son of Man has
authority on earth to forgive sins"—he said
to the paralytic— [11]"I say to you, stand up,
take your mat and go to your home." [12]And
he stood up, and immediately took the mat
and went out before all of them; so that
they were all amazed and glorified God,
saying, "We have never seen anything like
this!"

[j] Or *A new teaching! With authority he* [k] Other ancient authorities read *he* [l] The terms *leper* and *leprosy* can refer to several diseases [m] Other ancient authorities lack *kneeling* [n] Other ancient authorities read *anger* [o] Gk *he* [p] The terms *leper* and *leprosy* can refer to several diseases [q] Gk *they*

1.21-28 *Capernaum* was a prosperous town on a main trade route from eastern Syria to Palestine and its port cities. *Synagogue* in the first century was the term for the meeting of Jews seeking fuller understanding of their tradition through study and worship, gathering in homes or public halls. *Scribes* were those who specialized in the interpretation and application of the Mosaic law to daily life. Jesus' expulsion of the demon (*unclean spirit*) shows his *holy* calling, which is acknowledged by the evil powers which become subject to his control (*rebuke*). *Cf.* Lk 4.31-37.
1.29-34 The core of Jesus' followers consists of the four brothers whom he called from their daily work (1.16-20). The mention of Peter's *mother-in-law* assumes his married status, as in 1 Cor 9.5. The wide response to Jesus' healings attracts large numbers of the ailing and the demon-possessed. His order to the demons to be silent indicates that he wants to disclose his identity as God's agent on his own terms. *Cf.* Mt 8.14-17; Lk 4.38-41.
1.35-39 Jesus' withdrawal to a *deserted place* recalls his initial preparation by the Spirit for ministry in the *wilderness* (1.12). The proclamation of the good news moves *throughout Galilee*, beginning in each town with the assembly of faithful Jews (*their synagogues*). *Cf.* Lk 4.42-44.
1.40-45 Physical contact with a *leper* (with an unidentified skin ailment, probably a type of mold; not Hansen's disease, commonly called leprosy) made persons and houses unclean (Lev 14). Those cured had to be ritually cleansed by the *priest*, as Jesus here instructs the man. *Stern warning*, which effects the cure, may be a variant of Jesus' commanding word to the demons (*rebuke*; 1.25).
2.1-12 Jesus Heals a Paralytic. The next section of Mark (2.1-3.6) treats of important features of Jewish piety and group identity which Jesus challenges. The first scene is in a typical one-room house with a roof of hardened mud laid over sticks. To reach Jesus in the crowded space, the friends of the *paralytic dug through* the roof in order to lower the man to where Jesus was. The forgiveness of sins implies a link between sickness and sin, but is to be granted by God alone. Jesus' healing the man is a sign of his authority *on earth* as *Son of Man*, which he claims includes the right to pronounce forgiveness. See note on Mt 8.20. *Cf.* Mt 9.1-8; Lk 5.17-26.

1.21 Mt 4.23
1.22 Mt 7.28
1.24 Mt 8.29; Mk 10.47; 14.67; Jn 6.69; Acts 3.14
1.25 ver 34
1.27 Mk 10.24,32
1.29 ver 21,23
1.32 Mk 4.24
1.34 Mt 4.23; Mk 3.12; Acts 16.17,18
1.35 Mt 14.23; Lk 5.16
1.38 Isa 61.1
1.39 Mt 4.23-25
1.40 Mk 10.17
1.44 Lev 13.49; 14.2-32
1.45 Lk 5.15; Mt 28.15; Mk 2.13; Lk 5.17; Jn 6.2
2.2 ver 13
2.3 Mt 4.24
2.7 Isa 43.25
2.12 Mt 9.33

2.13 Mk 1.45
2.14 Mt 8.22
2.16 Acts 23.9
2.17 Lk 19.10; 1 Tim 1.15
2.20 Lk 17.22
2.23 Deut 23.25
2.26 1 Sam 21.1-6; 2 Sam 8.17; Ex 29.32,33; Lev 24.9
2.27 Ex 23.12; Deut 5.14
3.1 Mk 1.21,39
3.2 Lk 14.1; 20.20; Mt 12.10
3.6 Mt 12.14; 22.16; Mk 12.13
3.7 Mt 4.25
3.8 Mt 11.21
3.10 Mt 4.23; Mk 5.29,34; 6.56; 8.22
3.11 Mk 1.23,24; Lk 4.41; Mt 14.33
3.12 Mk 1.25,34
3.13 Mt 5.1; Lk 9.1

Jesus Calls Levi

13 Jesus[r] went out again beside the sea; the whole crowd gathered around him, and he taught them. 14 As he was walking along, he saw Levi son of Alphaeus sitting at the tax booth, and he said to him, "Follow me." And he got up and followed him.

15 And as he sat at dinner[s] in Levi's[t] house, many tax collectors and sinners were also sitting[u] with Jesus and his disciples—for there were many who followed him. 16 When the scribes of[v] the Pharisees saw that he was eating with sinners and tax collectors, they said to his disciples, "Why does he eat[w] with tax collectors and sinners?" 17 When Jesus heard this, he said to them, "Those who are well have no need of a physician, but those who are sick; I have come to call not the righteous but sinners."

The Question about Fasting

18 Now John's disciples and the Pharisees were fasting; and people[x] came and said to him, "Why do John's disciples and the disciples of the Pharisees fast, but your disciples do not fast?" 19 Jesus said to them, "The wedding guests cannot fast while the bridegroom is with them, can they? As long as they have the bridegroom with them, they cannot fast. 20 The days will come when the bridegroom is taken away from them, and then they will fast on that day.

21 "No one sews a piece of unshrunk cloth on an old cloak; otherwise, the patch pulls away from it, the new from the old, and a worse tear is made. 22 And no one puts new wine into old wineskins; otherwise, the wine will burst the skins, and the wine is lost, and so are the skins; but one puts new wine into fresh wineskins."[y]

Pronouncement about the Sabbath

23 One sabbath he was going through the grainfields; and as they made their way his disciples began to pluck heads of grain. 24 The Pharisees said to him, "Look, why are they doing what is not lawful on the sabbath?" 25 And he said to them, "Have you never read what David did when he and his companions were hungry and in need of food? 26 He entered the house of God, when Abiathar was high priest, and ate the bread of the Presence, which it is not lawful for any but the priests to eat, and he gave some to his companions." 27 Then he said to them, "The sabbath was made for humankind, and not humankind for the sabbath; 28 so the Son of Man is lord even of the sabbath."

The Man with a Withered Hand

3 Again he entered the synagogue, and a man was there who had a withered hand. 2 They watched him to see whether he would cure him on the sabbath, so that they might accuse him. 3 And he said to the man who had the withered hand, "Come forward." 4 Then he said to them, "Is it lawful to do good or to do harm on the sabbath, to save life or to kill?" But they were silent. 5 He looked around at them with anger; he was grieved at their hardness of heart and said to the man, "Stretch out your hand." He stretched it out, and his hand was restored. 6 The Pharisees went out and immediately conspired with the Herodians against him, how to destroy him.

A Multitude at the Seaside

7 Jesus departed with his disciples to the sea, and a great multitude from Galilee followed him; 8 hearing all that he was doing, they came to him in great numbers from Judea, Jerusalem, Idumea, beyond the Jordan, and the region around Tyre and Sidon. 9 He told his disciples to have a boat ready for him because of the crowd, so that they would not crush him; 10 for he had cured many, so that all who had diseases pressed upon him to touch him. 11 Whenever the unclean spirits saw him, they fell down before him and shouted, "You are the Son of God!" 12 But he sternly ordered them not to make him known.

Jesus Appoints the Twelve

13 He went up the mountain and called to him those whom he wanted, and they came to him. 14 And he appointed twelve, whom he also named apostles,[z] to be with him, and to be sent out to proclaim the

[r] Gk *He* [s] Gk *reclined* [t] Gk *his* [u] Gk *reclining* [v] Other ancient authorities read *and* [w] Other ancient authorities add *and drink* [x] Gk *they* [y] Other ancient authorities lack *but one puts new wine into fresh wineskins* [z] Other ancient authorities lack *whom he also named apostles*

2.13-17 The Call of Levi. Identified in Mt 9.9 as *Matthew*, Jesus calls a *tax collector* (under contract to the Romans to collect sales and transit taxes) to become one of his followers. On the grounds of their inescapable and constant violation of both Jewish ritual purity and nationalist loyalty, tax collectors were despised by pious Jews. Jesus defends his action on the ground that his mission is to call to the life of the new community those denounced on ritual, moral and other grounds as *sinners*. *Cf.* Mt 9.9-13; Lk 5.27-32.
2.18-22 Fasting. Abstinence from food on certain occasions was seen by many Jews as a sign of pious personal discipline. Jesus dismisses the practice as inappropriate in view of his presence (*the bridegroom*) among the people. Old patterns (*cloaks; wineskins*) will be shattered by the new reality which he brings. *Cf.* Mt 9.14-17; Lk 5.33-39.
2.23-28 Sabbath. For Jesus' appeal to precedents for setting aside the law against work on the sabbath, see notes on Matthew's fuller account in 12.1-8. Jesus has the sovereign power (*lord*) of even such a basic Jewish principle as the sabbath law. *Cf.* Lk 6.1-5.
3.1-6 Healing on the Sabbath. Healing the man on the sabbath, Jesus poses the issue of the legality of doing *good or harm* on the sabbath. Now a plot *to destroy* him is hatched by a strange Jewish coalition: the *Pharisees*, who stress personal purity and separateness from the corrupt culture, and *Herodians*, who support the puppet rulers empowered by the Roman empire. *Cf.* Mt 12.9-14; Lk 6.6-11.
3.7-12 A summary picture of the huge response to Jesus' healing activity, with people coming from the south (*Judea*), east of the Jordan (*Idumea*) and from the major Gentile cities north of Palestine (*Tyre and Sidon*). The *unclean spirits* acknowledge Jesus as *Son of God* (*cf.* Mt 3.13), though he orders them to stop. See note on 1.34. *Cf.* Mt 12.15-21, where Jesus' activity is linked with the prophecy of "justice to the Gentiles."
3.13-19a Jesus Appoints the Twelve. This matches the number of the tribes of Israel, the covenant people. Their roles are *to be with him*, as witnesses of his words and works; to *proclaim* the good news; to overcome the powers of evil (*demons*). There are slight variations among the lists of Jesus' followers found in the gospel accounts and Acts (Mt 10.14; Lk 6.12-16; Acts 1.13). Some ancient manuscripts of Mark do not identify them here as *apostles* (those sent or commissioned).

message, 15 and to have authority to cast out
demons. 16 So he appointed the twelve:[a]
Simon (to whom he gave the name Peter);
17 James son of Zebedee and John the brother
of James (to whom he gave the name
Boanerges, that is, Sons of Thunder); 18 and
Andrew, and Philip, and Bartholomew, and
Matthew, and Thomas, and James son of
Alphaeus, and Thaddaeus, and Simon the
Cananaean, 19 and Judas Iscariot, who be-
trayed him.

Jesus and Beelzebul

Then he went home; 20 and the crowd came
together again, so that they could not even
eat. 21 When his family heard it, they went
out to restrain him, for people were saying,
"He has gone out of his mind." 22 And the
scribes who came down from Jerusalem
said, "He has Beelzebul, and by the ruler of
the demons he casts out demons." 23 And he
called them to him, and spoke to them in
parables, "How can Satan cast out Satan?
24 If a kingdom is divided against itself, that
kingdom cannot stand. 25 And if a house is
divided against itself, that house will not be
able to stand. 26 And if Satan has risen up
against himself and is divided, he cannot
stand, but his end has come. 27 But no one
can enter a strong man's house and plunder his property without first tying up the
strong man; then indeed the house can be
plundered.
28 "Truly I tell you, people will be forgiven for their sins and whatever blasphemies they utter; 29 but whoever blasphemes
against the Holy Spirit can never have forgiveness, but is guilty of an eternal sin"—
30 for they had said, "He has an unclean
spirit."

The True Kindred of Jesus

31 Then his mother and his brothers
came; and standing outside, they sent to
him and called him. 32 A crowd was sitting
around him; and they said to him, "Your
mother and your brothers and sisters[b] are
outside, asking for you." 33 And he replied,
"Who are my mother and my brothers?"
34 And looking at those who sat around him,
he said, "Here are my mother and my
brothers! 35 Whoever does the will of God is
my brother and sister and mother."

The Parable of the Sower

4 Again he began to teach beside the
sea. Such a very large crowd gathered
around him that he got into a boat on the
sea and sat there, while the whole crowd
was beside the sea on the land. 2 He began
to teach them many things in parables, and
in his teaching he said to them: 3 "Listen! A
sower went out to sow. 4 And as he sowed,
some seed fell on the path, and the birds
came and ate it up. 5 Other seed fell on rocky
ground, where it did not have much soil,
and it sprang up quickly, since it had no
depth of soil. 6 And when the sun rose, it
was scorched; and since it had no root, it
withered away. 7 Other seed fell among
thorns, and the thorns grew up and choked
it, and it yielded no grain. 8 Other seed fell
into good soil and brought forth grain,
growing up and increasing and yielding
thirty and sixty and a hundredfold." 9 And
he said, "Let anyone with ears to hear
listen!"

The Purpose of the Parables

10 When he was alone, those who were
around him along with the twelve asked
him about the parables. 11 And he said to
them, "To you has been given the secret[c]
of the kingdom of God, but for those outside, everything comes in parables; 12 in order
that

'they may indeed look, but not perceive,
and may indeed listen, but not understand;
so that they may not turn again and be
forgiven.'"

13 And he said to them, "Do you not
understand this parable? Then how will you
understand all the parables? 14 The sower
sows the word. 15 These are the ones on the
path where the word is sown: when they
hear, Satan immediately comes and takes
away the word that is sown in them. 16 And
these are the ones sown on rocky ground:
when they hear the word, they immediately
receive it with joy. 17 But they have no root,
and endure only for a while; then, when
trouble or persecution arises on account of
the word, immediately they fall away.[d] 18 And
others are those sown among the thorns:
these are the ones who hear the word, 19 but
the cares of the world, and the lure of
wealth, and the desire for other things come

[a] Other ancient authorities lack *So he appointed the twelve* [b] Other ancient authorities lack *and sisters* [c] Or *mystery* [d] Or *stumble*

3.19b-30 On his returning to Capernaum *(home)*, Jesus' *family* (mother and brothers; 3.31; 6.3) arrive to put him in custody, thinking that he has lost his *mind* (noted only by Mark). The professional interpreters of the law (*scribes*) think he is in league with the *prince of demons, Beelzebul*. (See note on Mt 12.22-24.) He claims instead to be *plundering* Satan's sphere of power, and charges with *blasphemy* those who attribute to Satan the powers granted him by God's Spirit.
3.31-35 Jesus' true family is comprised of those who *do the will of God*. Notable is the inclusion of women in the new community: *sister and mother*.
4.1-34 The Parables of Jesus. Expanded by Matthew (13.1-52), this group of sayings includes not only the basic symbolic stories (*parables*) to illustrate what God and his coming kingdom are like, but also interpretations (4.13-20) and reasons why Jesus speaks in parables (4.21-25,33-34).
4.1-2 So great is the *crowd* that comes to hear Jesus that he must address them from a boat on the *sea* of Galilee.
4.3-9 The range of results from sowing seed is compared with the different responses to the good news, including astonishingly rich increase in those who accept it (*a hundredfold*). *Cf.* Mt 13.1-9; Lk 8.4-8.
4.10-12 Jesus uses *parables* in order to convey truth to those granted a share in God's *kingdom*, but the impossibility for outsiders to grasp the message is confirmed by quoting Isa 6.9. *Cf.* Mt 13.10-15, where the quotation from Isa 6 is extended; Lk 8.9-10.
4.13-20 The interpretation of the Parable of the Sower focuses on the range of responses of the hearers of the good news (including superficial acceptance, discouragement by subsequent persecution, worldly preoccupation, and fruitful reaction) and the activity of *Satan* to prevent it from taking root. *Cf.* Mt 13.18-23; Lk 8.11-15.

3.16 Jn 1.42
3.20 Mk 6.31
3.21 Jn 10.20; Acts 26.24
3.22 Mt 9.34; 10.25; Jn 7.20; 8.48,52
3.23 Mk 4.2ff
3.27 Isa 49.24,25
3.28 Lk 12.10
3.31 Mt 12.46; Lk 8.19
4.1 Mk 2.13; 3.7
4.2 Mk 3.23
4.8 Jn 15.5; Col 1.6
4.9 Mt 11.15
4.11 1 Cor 5.12; Col 4.5; 1 Thess 4.12; 1 Tim 3.7
4.12 Isa 6.9; Jn 12.40; Acts 28.26; Rom 11.8
4.15 Mk 3.23,26

4.22 Mt 10.26; Lk 8.17; 12.2
4.23 Mt 11.15
4.24 Mt 7.2; Lk 6.38
4.25 Mt 13.12; 25.29; Lk 8.18; 19.26
4.26 Mt 13.24
4.29 Rev 14.15
4.30 Mt 13.24
4.33 Jn 16.12
4.34 Mt 13.34; Jn 16.25
4.36 Mk 5.2.21
4.40 Mt 14.31,32; Mk 16.14
5.2 Mt 4.1; 1.23
5.6 Mt 4.9; 18.26
5.7 Mt 8.29; 4.3; Lk 8.28; Acts 16.17; Heb 7.1

in and choke the word, and it yields nothing. 20And these are the ones sown on the
good soil: they hear the word and accept it
and bear fruit, thirty and sixty and a hundredfold."

A Lamp under a Bushel Basket

21 He said to them, "Is a lamp brought
in to be put under the bushel basket, or
under the bed, and not on the lampstand?
22For there is nothing hidden, except to be
disclosed; nor is anything secret, except to
come to light. 23Let anyone with ears to
hear listen!" 24And he said to them, "Pay
attention to what you hear; the measure
you give will be the measure you get, and
still more will be given you. 25For to those
who have, more will be given; and from
those who have nothing, even what they
have will be taken away."

The Parable of the Growing Seed

26 He also said, "The kingdom of God is
as if someone would scatter seed on the
ground, 27and would sleep and rise night
and day, and the seed would sprout and
grow, he does not know how. 28The earth
produces of itself, first the stalk, then the
head, then the full grain in the head. 29But
when the grain is ripe, at once he goes in
with his sickle, because the harvest has
come."

The Parable of the Mustard Seed

30 He also said, "With what can we
compare the kingdom of God, or what
parable will we use for it? 31It is like a
mustard seed, which, when sown upon the
ground, is the smallest of all the seeds on
earth; 32yet when it is sown it grows up and
becomes the greatest of all shrubs, and puts
forth large branches, so that the birds of the
air can make nests in its shade."

The Use of Parables

33 With many such parables he spoke
the word to them, as they were able to hear
it; 34he did not speak to them except in
parables, but he explained everything in
private to his disciples.

Jesus Stills a Storm

35 On that day, when evening had come,
he said to them, "Let us go across to the
other side." 36And leaving the crowd behind, they took him with them in the boat,
just as he was. Other boats were with him.
37A great windstorm arose, and the waves
beat into the boat, so that the boat was
already being swamped. 38But he was in the
stern, asleep on the cushion; and they woke
him up and said to him, "Teacher, do you
not care that we are perishing?" 39He woke
up and rebuked the wind, and said to the
sea, "Peace! Be still!" Then the wind ceased,
and there was a dead calm. 40He said to
them, "Why are you afraid? Have you still
no faith?" 41And they were filled with great
awe and said to one another, "Who then is
this, that even the wind and the sea obey
him?"

Jesus Heals the Gerasene Demoniac

5 They came to the other side of the
sea, to the country of the Gerasenes.[e]
2And when he had stepped out of the boat,
immediately a man out of the tombs with
an unclean spirit met him. 3He lived among
the tombs; and no one could restrain him
any more, even with a chain; 4for he had
often been restrained with shackles and
chains, but the chains he wrenched apart,
and the shackles he broke in pieces; and no
one had the strength to subdue him. 5Night
and day among the tombs and on the
mountains he was always howling and
bruising himself with stones. 6When he saw
Jesus from a distance, he ran and bowed
down before him; 7and he shouted at the
top of his voice, "What have you to do with
me, Jesus, Son of the Most High God? I
adjure you by God, do not torment me."
8For he had said to him, "Come out of the
man, you unclean spirit!" 9Then Jesus[f] asked
him, "What is your name?" He replied, "My
name is Legion; for we are many." 10He
begged him earnestly not to send them out
of the country. 11Now there on the hillside
a great herd of swine was feeding; 12and the
unclean spirits[g] begged him, "Send us into
the swine; let us enter them." 13So he gave
them permission. And the unclean spirits
came out and entered the swine; and the
herd, numbering about two thousand, rushed
down the steep bank into the sea, and were
drowned in the sea.

4.21-25. As an explanation for Jesus' use of parables, the extended analogy is offered of what one does with a lamp: it is not concealed but used to bring light to those in darkness. The point is to heed the light, to listen and understand the message. *Cf.* Mt 13.12; Lk 8.16-18. Similar declarations by Jesus in Mt 10.26; Lk 12.2.
4.26-29 Like seed that has been sown, the good news contains the power to assure growth and results by the time of harvest (= the coming day of divine judgment). Only in Mark.
4.30-32 The analogy here is between the small beginning and the astonishing results of the proclamation of the gospel. *Cf.* Mt 13.31-32; Lk 13.18-19.
4.33-34 Jesus is said to have used consistently the symbolic story method (*parables*) to convey truth to the chosen followers who alone can grasp its meaning.
4.35-41 The symbolic stories are followed by a series of symbolic actions. The first is Jesus' stilling the storm, which not only saves the lives of his disciples, but demonstrates the cosmic power granted to him by God. See note on Mt 8.23-27. Also in Lk 8.22-25.
5.1-20 *Country of the Gerasenes* in other manuscripts reads Gergesenes and Gadarenes; all three cities lie east of the Jordan, but Gerasa, a model of Greco-Roman culture, is farthest from the Lake of Galilee where the pigs drown. The demon-possessed man who comes to Jesus had become ritually impure by living *among the tombs* (Lev 22.4; Num 5.2; 6.6; 9.6) and in a Gentile area with large herds of *swine* (Lev 11.7-8). Even the demons who possess the man identify themselves by a Roman military term: *legion*, a unit of 5,400 to 6,000 soldiers. Jesus' action elicits fear from the local people, but arouses a desire to be a follower of Jesus in the cured man, who is instructed to tell his *friends* what God has done for him, and he does so in the *Decapolis*, the federation of ten Greco-Roman cities, most of them east of the Jordan, but including Damascus to the north. *Cf.* the briefer versions of the story in Mt 8.28-34; Lk 8.26-39.

[e] Other ancient authorities read *Gergesenes*; others, *Gadarenes* [f] Gk *he* [g] Gk *they*

5.21-43 A Girl Restored to Life and a Woman Healed. Returning to the west bank of the Lake of Galilee, Jesus is asked by a *leader of the synagogue* (at this stage a lay movement with lay leaders) to heal his dying daughter. Delayed by a woman seeking a cure for her menstrual *hemorrhages* who touches him (which would defile him ritually; Lev 12.2-8; 15.19-30) and is healed by his word on the basis of her *faith* (or trust in him), news comes of the child's death. Again, Jesus calls for *faith* (trust) on the part of the synagogue leader. On reaching the home where the child has died, Jesus enters and touches her (*took her by the hand*) in defiance of ritual restrictions about contact with corpses (Num 19.11-13), and she is restored to life. *Cf.* Mt 9.18-26; Lk 8.40-56.

6.1-6a The Rejection of Jesus at Nazareth. Jesus, who in Mk 14-15 is going to experience rejection by the Jewish leadership in Jerusalem, already experiences hostility from the residents of his home town, *Nazareth* (see note on 1.9). His astonishing teaching and the reports of his amazing *deeds* (healings and exorcisms) do not match with his humble occupation as a *carpenter* (wood-worker, or builder). The *brothers* mentioned are apparently older sons born to Mary and Joseph. *James* became the leader of the Jerusalem church (1 Cor 15.37; Acts 12.17; Gal 1.19; 2.9). The other brothers and sisters are otherwise unknown. Jesus implies his place in the tradition of the *prophets* whose message from God is rejected by their own people. *Cf.* Mt 13.53-58.

14 The swineherds ran off and told it in
the city and in the country. Then people
came to see what it was that had happened.
15 They came to Jesus and saw the demoniac
sitting there, clothed and in his right mind,
the very man who had had the legion; and
they were afraid. 16 Those who had seen
what had happened to the demoniac and to
the swine reported it. 17 Then they began to
beg Jesus[h] to leave their neighborhood. 18 As
he was getting into the boat, the man who
had been possessed by demons begged him
that he might be with him. 19 But Jesus[i]
refused, and said to him, "Go home to your
friends, and tell them how much the Lord
has done for you, and what mercy he has
shown you." 20 And he went away and
began to proclaim in the Decapolis how
much Jesus had done for him; and everyone
was amazed.

A Girl Restored to Life and a Woman Healed

21 When Jesus had crossed again in the
boat[j] to the other side, a great crowd gathered around him; and he was by the sea.
22 Then one of the leaders of the synagogue
named Jairus came and, when he saw him,
fell at his feet 23 and begged him repeatedly,
"My little daughter is at the point of death.
Come and lay your hands on her, so that
she may be made well, and live." 24 So he
went with him.
And a large crowd followed him and
pressed in on him. 25 Now there was a woman
who had been suffering from hemorrhages
for twelve years. 26 She had endured much
under many physicians, and had spent all
that she had; and she was no better, but
rather grew worse. 27 She had heard about
Jesus, and came up behind him in the
crowd and touched his cloak, 28 for she said,
"If I but touch his clothes, I will be made
well." 29 Immediately her hemorrhage stopped;
and she felt in her body that she was healed
of her disease. 30 Immediately aware that
power had gone forth from him, Jesus turned
about in the crowd and said, "Who touched
my clothes?" 31 And his disciples said to him,
"You see the crowd pressing in on you; how
can you say, 'Who touched me?'" 32 He
looked all around to see who had done it.
33 But the woman, knowing what had happened to her, came in fear and trembling,
fell down before him, and told him the
whole truth. 34 He said to her, "Daughter,
your faith has made you well; go in peace,
and be healed of your disease."
35 While he was still speaking, some
people came from the leader's house to say,
"Your daughter is dead. Why trouble the
teacher any further?" 36 But overhearing[k]
what they said, Jesus said to the leader of
the synagogue, "Do not fear, only believe."
37 He allowed no one to follow him except
Peter, James, and John, the brother of James.
38 When they came to the house of the
leader of the synagogue, he saw a commotion, people weeping and wailing loudly.
39 When he had entered, he said to them,
"Why do you make a commotion and weep?
The child is not dead but sleeping." 40 And
they laughed at him. Then he put them all
outside, and took the child's father and
mother and those who were with him, and
went in where the child was. 41 He took her
by the hand and said to her, "Talitha cum,"
which means, "Little girl, get up!" 42 And
immediately the girl got up and began to
walk about (she was twelve years of age).
At this they were overcome with amazement. 43 He strictly ordered them that no
one should know this, and told them to give
her something to eat.

The Rejection of Jesus at Nazareth

6 He left that place and came to his
hometown, and his disciples followed
him. 2 On the sabbath he began to teach in
the synagogue, and many who heard him
were astounded. They said, "Where did this
man get all this? What is this wisdom that
has been given to him? What deeds of
power are being done by his hands! 3 Is not
this the carpenter, the son of Mary[l] and
brother of James and Joses and Judas and
Simon, and are not his sisters here with
us?" And they took offense[m] at him. 4 Then
Jesus said to them, "Prophets are not without honor, except in their hometown, and
among their own kin, and in their own
house." 5 And he could do no deed of power
there, except that he laid his hands on a few
sick people and cured them. 6 And he was
amazed at their unbelief.

5.15 ver 16.18; Mt 4.24; ver 9
5.18 Acts 16.39
5.20 Mk 7.31; Mt 4.25
5.21 Mt 9.1
5.22 Lk 8.49; 13.14; Acts 13.15; 18.8,17
5.23 Mk 6.5; 7.32; 8.23; Acts 9.17; 28.8
5.25 Lev 15.25
6.2 Mt 4.23; 7.28; Mk 1.21
6.3 Mt 12.46; 11.6
6.4 Jn 4.44
6.5 Mt 5.23; 7.32; 8.23
6.6 Mt 9.35; Lk 13.22

[h] Gk *him* [i] Gk *he* [j] Other ancient authorities lack *in the boat* [k] Or *ignoring*; other ancient authorities read *hearing* [l] Other ancient authorities read *son of the carpenter and of Mary* [m] Or *stumbled*

6.7 Mk 3.13; Lk 10.1
6.12 Mt 11.1; Lk 9.6
6.13 Jas 5.14
6.15 Mt 16.14; Mk 8.28; Mt 21.11
6.16 Lk 3.19
6.18 Lev 18.16; 20.21
6.20 Mt 21.26
6.21 Esth 1.3; 2.18
6.23 Esth 5.3,6; 7.2
6.31 Mk 3.20
6.32 ver 45
6.34 Mt 9.36
6.37 2 Kings 4.42-44
6.38 Mt 15.34; Mk 8.5
6.41 Mt 26.26; Mk 14.22; Lk 24.30,31

The Mission of the Twelve

Then he went about among the villages
teaching. 7He called the twelve and began
to send them out two by two, and gave
them authority over the unclean spirits. 8He
ordered them to take nothing for their journey except a staff; no bread, no bag, no
money in their belts; 9but to wear sandals
and not to put on two tunics. 10He said to
them, "Wherever you enter a house, stay
there until you leave the place. 11If any
place will not welcome you and they refuse
to hear you, as you leave, shake off the dust
that is on your feet as a testimony against
them." 12So they went out and proclaimed
that all should repent. 13They cast out many
demons, and anointed with oil many who
were sick and cured them.

The Death of John the Baptist

14 King Herod heard of it, for Jesus'[n]
name had become known. Some were[o] saying, "John the baptizer has been raised from
the dead; and for this reason these powers
are at work in him." 15But others said, "It
is Elijah." And others said, "It is a prophet,
like one of the prophets of old." 16But when
Herod heard of it, he said, "John, whom I
beheaded, has been raised."

17 For Herod himself had sent men who
arrested John, bound him, and put him in
prison on account of Herodias, his brother
Philip's wife, because Herod[p] had married
her. 18For John had been telling Herod, "It
is not lawful for you to have your brother's
wife." 19And Herodias had a grudge against
him, and wanted to kill him. But she could
not, 20for Herod feared John, knowing that
he was a righteous and holy man, and he
protected him. When he heard him, he was
greatly perplexed;[q] and yet he liked to listen
to him. 21But an opportunity came when
Herod on his birthday gave a banquet for
his courtiers and officers and for the leaders
of Galilee. 22When his daughter Herodias[r]
came in and danced, she pleased Herod and
his guests; and the king said to the girl,
"Ask me for whatever you wish, and I will
give it." 23And he solemnly swore to her,
"Whatever you ask me, I will give you,
even half of my kingdom." 24She went out
and said to her mother, "What should I ask
for?" She replied, "The head of John the
baptizer." 25Immediately she rushed back to
the king and requested, "I want you to give
me at once the head of John the Baptist on
a platter." 26The king was deeply grieved;
yet out of regard for his oaths and for the
guests, he did not want to refuse her. 27Im-
mediately the king sent a soldier of the
guard with orders to bring John's[n] head. He
went and beheaded him in the prison,
28brought his head on a platter, and gave
it to the girl. Then the girl gave it to her
mother. 29When his disciples heard about it,
they came and took his body, and laid it in
a tomb.

Feeding the Five Thousand

30 The apostles gathered around Jesus,
and told him all that they had done and
taught. 31He said to them, "Come away to
a deserted place all by yourselves and rest
a while." For many were coming and going,
and they had no leisure even to eat. 32And
they went away in the boat to a deserted
place by themselves. 33Now many saw them
going and recognized them, and they hurried there on foot from all the towns and
arrived ahead of them. 34As he went ashore,
he saw a great crowd; and he had compassion for them, because they were like sheep
without a shepherd; and he began to teach
them many things. 35When it grew late, his
disciples came to him and said, "This is a
deserted place, and the hour is now very
late; 36send them away so that they may go
into the surrounding country and villages
and buy something for themselves to eat."
37But he answered them, "You give them
something to eat." They said to him, "Are
we to go and buy two hundred denarii[s]
worth of bread, and give it to them to eat?"
38And he said to them, "How many loaves
have you? Go and see." When they had
found out, they said, "Five, and two fish."
39Then he ordered them to get all the people
to sit down in groups on the green grass.
40So they sat down in groups of hundreds
and of fifties. 41Taking the five loaves and
the two fish, he looked up to heaven, and
blessed and broke the loaves, and gave
them to his disciples to set before the people;
and he divided the two fish among them all.
42And all ate and were filled; 43and they
took up twelve baskets full of broken pieces

6.6b-13 The *twelve* are sent out to extend the healing and preaching activity of Jesus. The urgency of their message and activities is underscored by the instruction to take only minimal equipment and to accept whatever hospitality is offered them as they journey from town to town. *Cf.* Mt 9.35; 10.1,9-11; Lk 9.1-6.
6.14-29 *Herod* Antipas, see note on Mt 14.1-12; Mark's account is fuller. Jesus' extraordinary powers are explained by the assumption that he is *John the baptizer* (or the John who baptizes), risen from the dead. Only later is he given the title, the Baptist (Mt 3.1; 14.2). Expected in scripture to return to life on earth were *Elijah* (Mal 4.5) and *a prophet* like Moses (Deut 18.15). Unlike Jesus, John had a faithful group of *disciples* who prepared his body for burial.
6.30-44 Feeding the Five Thousand. The fullest account is in Mark (*cf.* Mt 14.13-21; Lk 9.10-17; also in Jn 6.1-14). The emphasis on the *deserted place* as a retreat and the need to feed the multitude gathered there heightens the parallel with the miraculous feeding of Israel through Moses in the Sinai desert (Ex 16; Num 11). The procedure and language correspond with those of the Christian communal meal of the New Covenant evident in Paul's letters and Acts: *Took the loaves; blessed* God, the provider for his people; *broke the loaves; gave them to the people. Cf.* 1 Cor 11.23-26; Acts 2.46; 20.11; 27.35.

[n] Gk *his* [o] Other ancient authorities read *He was* [p] Gk *he* [q] Other ancient authorities read *he did many things* [r] Other ancient authorities read *the daughter of Herodias herself* [s] The denarius was the usual day's wage for a laborer

6.45-52 See note on Mt 14.22-33 for Jesus' power over the waters. *Bethsaida* was on the mostly Gentile populated northeastern shore of the lake, opposite Capernaum on the northwest shore. *Gennesaret* was a coastal plain south of Capernaum. The response of the powers of *wind* and *sea*, manifesting divine authority, *astounds* the disciples, who are unable to comprehend the significance of the miraculous feeding.
6.53-56. Jesus' reputation as a healer attracts throngs. Touching him brings healing to the sick, but ritual pollution to him, which is the theme of the next section of Mark (7.1-23). *Cf.* Mt 14.34-36.
7.1-23 Defilement and Purity. The stress is on the central importance of purity of food and food containers for *all the Jews*, but especially for the *Pharisees* (the name for whose group means "pure ones") and the *scribes*, who are those responsible for showing the relevance and specific requirements of the Law of Moses. Jesus appeals here to the prophet *Isaiah* (29.13) to show that of primary importance is personal dedication to God and his will, rather than formal – often evasive – conformity to legal precepts. The real source of evil is not ritual pollution from without but corruption within the human *heart* (seat of the will, and not merely of emotions).
7.24-30 This woman – Gentile by origin (*Syrophoenician*), culture (*Greek*) and place of residence (*the region of Tyre and Sidon*) – beseeches Jesus to expel the demon from her daughter. She persists in spite of Jesus' question whether such benefits (*children's bread*) ought to be made available to non-Israelites (*dogs*), and the demon is expelled. *Cf.* Mt 15.21-28.

and of the fish. [44]Those who had eaten the
loaves numbered five thousand men.

Jesus Walks on the Water

45 Immediately he made his disciples get
into the boat and go on ahead to the other
side, to Bethsaida, while he dismissed the
crowd. [46]After saying farewell to them, he
went up on the mountain to pray.
47 When evening came, the boat was
out on the sea, and he was alone on the
land. [48]When he saw that they were straining at the oars against an adverse wind, he
came towards them early in the morning,
walking on the sea. He intended to pass
them by. [49]But when they saw him walking
on the sea, they thought it was a ghost and
cried out; [50]for they all saw him and were
terrified. But immediately he spoke to them
and said, "Take heart, it is I; do not be
afraid." [51]Then he got into the boat with
them and the wind ceased. And they were
utterly astounded, [52]for they did not understand about the loaves, but their hearts
were hardened.

Healing the Sick in Gennesaret

53 When they had crossed over, they
came to land at Gennesaret and moored the
boat. [54]When they got out of the boat,
people at once recognized him, [55]and rushed
about that whole region and began to bring
the sick on mats to wherever they heard he
was. [56]And wherever he went, into villages
or cities or farms, they laid the sick in the
marketplaces, and begged him that they
might touch even the fringe of his cloak;
and all who touched it were healed.

The Tradition of the Elders

7 Now when the Pharisees and some of
the scribes who had come from Jerusalem gathered around him, [2]they noticed
that some of his disciples were eating with
defiled hands, that is, without washing them.
[3](For the Pharisees, and all the Jews, do not
eat unless they thoroughly wash their hands,[t]
thus observing the tradition of the elders;
[4]and they do not eat anything from the
market unless they wash it;[u] and there are
also many other traditions that they observe, the washing of cups, pots, and bronze
kettles.[v]) [5]So the Pharisees and the scribes
asked him, "Why do your disciples not live[w]
according to the tradition of the elders, but
eat with defiled hands?" [6]He said to them,
"Isaiah prophesied rightly about you hypocrites, as it is written,
'This people honors me with their lips,
but their hearts are far from me;
7 in vain do they worship me,
teaching human precepts as doctrines.'
[8]You abandon the commandment of God
and hold to human tradition."
9 Then he said to them, "You have a fine
way of rejecting the commandment of God
in order to keep your tradition! [10]For Moses
said, 'Honor your father and your mother';
and, 'Whoever speaks evil of father or mother
must surely die.' [11]But you say that if anyone tells father or mother, 'Whatever support you might have had from me is Corban'
(that is, an offering to God[x])— [12]then you
no longer permit doing anything for a father
or mother, [13]thus making void the word of
God through your tradition that you have
handed on. And you do many things like
this."
14 Then he called the crowd again and
said to them, "Listen to me, all of you, and
understand: [15]there is nothing outside a
person that by going in can defile, but the
things that come out are what defile."[y]
17 When he had left the crowd and
entered the house, his disciples asked him
about the parable. [18]He said to them, "Then
do you also fail to understand? Do you not
see that whatever goes into a person from
outside cannot defile, [19]since it enters, not
the heart but the stomach, and goes out
into the sewer?" (Thus he declared all foods
clean.) [20]And he said, "It is what comes out
of a person that defiles. [21]For it is from
within, from the human heart, that evil
intentions come: fornication, theft, murder,
[22]adultery, avarice, wickedness, deceit, licentiousness, envy, slander, pride, folly. [23]All
these evil things come from within, and
they defile a person."

The Syrophoenician Woman's Faith

24 From there he set out and went away
to the region of Tyre.[z] He entered a house

[t] Meaning of Gk uncertain [u] Other ancient authorities read *and when they come from the marketplace, they do not eat unless they purify themselves* [v] Other ancient authorities add *and beds* [w] Gk *walk* [x] Gk lacks *to God* [y] Other ancient authorities add verse 16, *"Let anyone with ears to hear listen"* [z] Other ancient authorities add *and Sidon*

6.45 ver 32; Mt 11.21; Mk 8.22
6.48 Mt 13.35; 24.43
6.50 Mt 9.2
6.51 ver 32
6.52 Mk 8.17,18; 3.5
6.53 Jn 6.24,25
6.56 Mk 3.10; Mt 9.20
7.3 ver 5; Acts 10.14,28; 11.8
7.4 Mt 2.25; Lk 11.39
7.5 ver 3,8,9,13; Gal 1.14
7.6 Isa 29.13
7.8 ver 5,9,13
7.9 ver 5,8,13
7.10 Ex 20.12; Deut 5.6; Ex 21.17; Lev 20.9
7.11 Mt 23.18

7.32 Mk 5.23; Mt 9.32; Lk 11.14
7.33 Mk 8.23
7.34 Mk 6.41; 8.12
7.35 Isa 35.5,6
7.36 Mk 1.44; 5.43
8.2 Mt 9.36
8.5 Mk 6.38
8.7 Mt 14.19; Mk 6.41
8.11 Mt 12.38,39; Lk 11.29; Jn 6.30
8.12 Mk 7.34
8.15 Lk 12.1; Mk 16.4; 12.13
8.17 Mk 6.52; Isa 6.9,10
8.19 Mt 14.20; Mk 6.43; Lk 9.17; Jn 6.13
8.20 ver 6-9; Mt 15.37
8.21 Mk 6.52
8.22 Mt 11.21; Mk 6.45; Lk 9.10
8.23 Mk 7.33; 5.23

and did not want anyone to know he was there. Yet he could not escape notice, 25but a woman whose little daughter had an unclean spirit immediately heard about him, and she came and bowed down at his feet. 26Now the woman was a Gentile, of Syrophoenician origin. She begged him to cast the demon out of her daughter. 27He said to her, "Let the children be fed first, for it is not fair to take the children's food and throw it to the dogs." 28But she answered him, "Sir,[a] even the dogs under the table eat the children's crumbs." 29Then he said to her, "For saying that, you may go—the demon has left your daughter." 30So she went home, found the child lying on the bed, and the demon gone.

Jesus Cures a Deaf Man

31 Then he returned from the region of Tyre, and went by way of Sidon towards the Sea of Galilee, in the region of the Decapolis. 32They brought to him a deaf man who had an impediment in his speech; and they begged him to lay his hand on him. 33He took him aside in private, away from the crowd, and put his fingers into his ears, and he spat and touched his tongue. 34Then looking up to heaven, he sighed and said to him, "Ephphatha," that is, "Be opened." 35And immediately his ears were opened, his tongue was released, and he spoke plainly. 36Then Jesus[b] ordered them to tell no one; but the more he ordered them, the more zealously they proclaimed it. 37They were astounded beyond measure, saying, "He has done everything well; he even makes the deaf to hear and the mute to speak."

Feeding the Four Thousand

8 In those days when there was again a great crowd without anything to eat, he called his disciples and said to them, 2"I have compassion for the crowd, because they have been with me now for three days and have nothing to eat. 3If I send them away hungry to their homes, they will faint on the way—and some of them have come from a great distance." 4His disciples replied, "How can one feed these people with bread here in the desert?" 5He asked them, "How many loaves do you have?" They said, "Seven." 6Then he ordered the crowd to sit down on the ground; and he took the seven loaves, and after giving thanks he broke them and gave them to his disciples to distribute; and they distributed them to the crowd. 7They had also a few small fish; and after blessing them, he ordered that these too should be distributed. 8They ate and were filled; and they took up the broken pieces left over, seven baskets full. 9Now there were about four thousand people. And he sent them away. 10And immediately he got into the boat with his disciples and went to the district of Dalmanutha.[c]

The Demand for a Sign

11 The Pharisees came and began to argue with him, asking him for a sign from heaven, to test him. 12And he sighed deeply in his spirit and said, "Why does this generation ask for a sign? Truly I tell you, no sign will be given to this generation." 13And he left them, and getting into the boat again, he went across to the other side.

The Yeast of the Pharisees and of Herod

14 Now the disciples[d] had forgotten to bring any bread; and they had only one loaf with them in the boat. 15And he cautioned them, saying, "Watch out—beware of the yeast of the Pharisees and the yeast of Herod."[e] 16They said to one another, "It is because we have no bread." 17And becoming aware of it, Jesus said to them, "Why are you talking about having no bread? Do you still not perceive or understand? Are your hearts hardened? 18Do you have eyes, and fail to see? Do you have ears, and fail to hear? And do you not remember? 19When I broke the five loaves for the five thousand, how many baskets full of broken pieces did you collect?" They said to him, "Twelve." 20"And the seven for the four thousand, how many baskets full of broken pieces did you collect?" And they said to him, "Seven." 21Then he said to them, "Do you not yet understand?"

Jesus Cures a Blind Man at Bethsaida

22 They came to Bethsaida. Some people[f] brought a blind man to him and begged him to touch him. 23He took the blind man

[a] Or *Lord*; other ancient authorities prefix *Yes* [b] Gk *he* [c] Other ancient authorities read *Mageda* or *Magdala* [d] Gk *they* [e] Other ancient authorities read *the Herodians* [f] Gk *They*

7.31-37 Jesus' activity continues in Gentile territory (*Sidon; region of the Decapolis*, see note on 5.1-20), and includes a deaf-mute. Jesus' use of spittle and his touching the ailing man's ears would violate ritual purity laws (Num 12.14-15; Deut 25.9; Job 17.6). Jesus' effort to halt the spread of news about him (apparently until the full disclosure of God's purpose through him is given in Jerusalem) does not stop the testimony. The prediction in Isa 35.5 about God's renewal of the creation is already taking place (Mt 11.5; Lk 7.22). *Cf.* Mt 15.29-31.

8.1-10 The Feeding of the Four Thousand apparently occurs while Jesus is still in Gentile territory. The basic outline of the story is the same as in Mk 6.30-44, and the language used corresponds to the Christian eucharist: *giving thanks* (in Greek, *eucharistesas*), *broke, gave*. The different number of loaves and baskets (*seven*) matches the distinction made in Acts 6.3 between the number of leaders chosen for the Gentile (hellenistic) wing of the church – seven – and the number of apostles chosen for the Jewish Christian community (*twelve*); see 8.19-21. The Gentile Christian community is launched here symbolically. *Cf.* Mt 15.32-39.

8.11-13 In contrast to the response of Jesus to a request for a *sign from heaven* (a miracle to confirm that God is with him) in other gospel tradition (the sign of Jonah; *cf.* Mt 12.39; 16.4; Lk 11.29), here *no sign* is given.

8.14-21 See note on Mt 16.9-12. Here are mentioned the *yeast of the Pharisees* (conformity to legal regulations) and the *yeast of Herod* (slavish cooperation with the Roman empire). Jesus rejects both in favor of a new community that transcends Jew–Gentile distinctions. *Cf.* Mt 16.5-12; Lk 12.1.

8.22-26 The cure of the blind man in Bethsaida (see note on 6.45), reported only in Mark, is another act of healing in predominantly Gentile territory, with a prohibition against spreading news of Jesus' healing powers.

8.27-33 Outside Jewish territory near the foot of Mt. Hermon, originally a shrine for the nature god, Pan (or Paneas), *Caesarea Philippi* was refounded and rebuilt by Herod's son, Philip, in honor of the emperor and himself. It is in this center of Gentile tradition and power that Jesus requests and receives from his followers reports as to who they and others judge him to be. Again, they are not yet to divulge this insight. *Cf.* Mt 16.13-23 (see notes there on expanded version); Lk 9.18-22.
8.34-9.1 Jesus predicts in detail his suffering, rejection and death, denouncing Peter's pious but purely human response, and advising the disciples of the self-denial and death they will undergo, on the model of his *cross*. Beyond that is the promise of God's vindication and disclosure of Jesus in *glory*, which will occur during the lifetime of some of his followers.
9.2-8 *After six days* means here "within one week." See note on the presence of *Moses and Elijah* at Mt 17.1-13. Jesus' radical change of appearance as a sign of God's presence (*cf.* Dan 10) is a foretaste of his ultimate glorification as God's *Son*.
9.9-13 The predicted coming of *Elijah* in preparation for a new age (Mal 4.5) is now said to have already occurred (John the Baptist), but Jesus must experience *sufferings* as an essential stage in his disclosure as triumphant *Son of Man*. In a Jewish apocalypse, Moses was also pictured as being taken up to heaven without having died. *Cf.* Lk 9.28-36.
9.14-29 Jesus' expulsion of the demon (*unclean spirit*) which was understood to have caused the epilepsy-like ailment of the young boy succeeds where the disciples failed. Their failure was the result of a lack of *prayer*, to which some ancient manuscripts add."and fasting." *Cf.* Mt 17.14-21; Lk 9.37-43.

by the hand and led him out of the village;
and when he had put saliva on his eyes and
laid his hands on him, he asked him, "Can
you see anything?" [24]And the man[g] looked
up and said, "I can see people, but they look
like trees, walking." [25]Then Jesus[g] laid his
hands on his eyes again; and he looked
intently and his sight was restored, and he
saw everything clearly. [26]Then he sent him
away to his home, saying, "Do not even go
into the village."[h]

Peter's Declaration about Jesus

27 Jesus went on with his disciples to the
villages of Caesarea Philippi; and on the
way he asked his disciples, "Who do people
say that I am?" [28]And they answered him,
"John the Baptist; and others, Elijah; and
still others, one of the prophets." [29]He asked
them, "But who do you say that I am?"
Peter answered him, "You are the Messiah."[i]
[30]And he sternly ordered them not to tell
anyone about him.

Jesus Foretells His Death and Resurrection

31 Then he began to teach them that the
Son of Man must undergo great suffering,
and be rejected by the elders, the chief
priests, and the scribes, and be killed, and
after three days rise again. [32]He said all this
quite openly. And Peter took him aside and
began to rebuke him. [33]But turning and
looking at his disciples, he rebuked Peter
and said, "Get behind me, Satan! For you
are setting your mind not on divine things
but on human things."

34 He called the crowd with his disciples,
and said to them, "If any want to become
my followers, let them deny themselves and
take up their cross and follow me. [35]For
those who want to save their life will lose
it, and those who lose their life for my sake,
and for the sake of the gospel,[j] will save it.
[36]For what will it profit them to gain the
whole world and forfeit their life? [37]Indeed,
what can they give in return for their life?
[38]Those who are ashamed of me and of my
words[k] in this adulterous and sinful generation, of them the Son of Man will also be
ashamed when he comes in the glory of his

9 Father with the holy angels." [1]And he
said to them, "Truly I tell you, there
are some standing here who will not taste
death until they see that the kingdom of
God has come with[l] power."

The Transfiguration

2 Six days later, Jesus took with him
Peter and James and John, and led them up
a high mountain apart, by themselves. And
he was transfigured before them, [3]and his
clothes became dazzling white, such as no
one[m] on earth could bleach them. [4]And
there appeared to them Elijah with Moses,
who were talking with Jesus. [5]Then Peter
said to Jesus, "Rabbi, it is good for us to be
here; let us make three dwellings,[n] one for
you, one for Moses, and one for Elijah." [6]He
did not know what to say, for they were
terrified. [7]Then a cloud overshadowed them,
and from the cloud there came a voice,
"This is my Son, the Beloved;[o] listen to
him!" [8]Suddenly when they looked around,
they saw no one with them any more, but
only Jesus.

The Coming of Elijah

9 As they were coming down the mountain, he ordered them to tell no one about
what they had seen, until after the Son of
Man had risen from the dead. [10]So they kept
the matter to themselves, questioning what
this rising from the dead could mean. [11]Then
they asked him, "Why do the scribes say
that Elijah must come first?" [12]He said to
them, "Elijah is indeed coming first to restore all things. How then is it written
about the Son of Man, that he is to go
through many sufferings and be treated
with contempt? [13]But I tell you that Elijah
has come, and they did to him whatever
they pleased, as it is written about him."

The Healing of a Boy with a Spirit

14 When they came to the disciples, they
saw a great crowd around them, and some
scribes arguing with them. [15]When the whole
crowd saw him, they were immediately
overcome with awe, and they ran forward
to greet him. [16]He asked them, "What are

8.26 Mt 8.4
8.27 Jn 6.66-69
8.28 Mk 6.14
8.29 Jn 6.69; 11.27
8.30 Mk 9.9
8.32 Jn 18.20
8.33 Mt 4.10
8.34 Mt 10.38; Lk 14.27
8.35 Mt 10.39; Lk 17.33; Jn 12.25
8.38 Mt 10.33; Lk 12.9; Mt 8.20; Mk 13.26
9.1 Mt 24.30; 25.31; Mk 13.30; Lk 22.18
9.2 Mk 5.37; 13.3
9.3 Mt 28.3
9.5 Mt 23.7
9.7 2 Pet 1.17,18; Mk 1.11

[g] Gk *he* [h] Other ancient authorities add *or tell anyone in the village* [i] Or *the Christ* [j] Other ancient authorities read *lose their life for the sake of the gospel* [k] Other ancient authorities read *and of mine* [l] Or *in* [m] Gk *no fuller* [n] Or *tents* [o] Or *my beloved Son*

9.28 Mk 7.17
9.31 Mt 16.21; Mk 8.31
9.32 Jn 12.16
9.34 Lk 22.24
9.35 Mt 20.26,27; Mk 10.43; Lk 22.26
9.36 Mk 10.16
9.37 Mt 10.40; Jn 12.44; 13.20
9.38 Num 11.27-29
9.40 Mt 12.30
9.41 Mt 10.42
9.42 Lk 17.1,2; 1 Cor 8.12
9.43 Mt 5.29,30; 5.22; 25.41
9.45 Mt 5.22
9.47 Mt 5.29
9.48 Isa 66.24
9.49 Lev 2.13
9.50 Mt 5.13; Lk 14.34,35; Col 4.6; Rom 12.18; 2 Cor 13.11; 1 Thess 5.13

you arguing about with them?" [17]Someone
from the crowd answered him, "Teacher, I
brought you my son; he has a spirit that
makes him unable to speak; [18]and whenever it seizes him, it dashes him down; and
he foams and grinds his teeth and becomes
rigid; and I asked your disciples to cast it
out, but they could not do so." [19]He answered them, "You faithless generation, how
much longer must I be among you? How
much longer must I put up with you? Bring
him to me." [20]And they brought the boy[p]
to him. When the spirit saw him, immediately it convulsed the boy,[p] and he fell on
the ground and rolled about, foaming at the
mouth. [21]Jesus[q] asked the father, "How long
has this been happening to him?" And he
said, "From childhood. [22]It has often cast
him into the fire and into the water, to
destroy him; but if you are able to do
anything, have pity on us and help us."
[23]Jesus said to him, "If you are able!—All
things can be done for the one who believes." [24]Immediately the father of the child
cried out,[r] "I believe; help my unbelief!"
[25]When Jesus saw that a crowd came running together, he rebuked the unclean spirit,
saying to it, "You spirit that keeps this boy
from speaking and hearing, I command
you, come out of him, and never enter him
again!" [26]After crying out and convulsing
him terribly, it came out, and the boy was
like a corpse, so that most of them said, "He
is dead." [27]But Jesus took him by the hand
and lifted him up, and he was able to stand.
[28]When he had entered the house, his disciples asked him privately, "Why could we
not cast it out?" [29]He said to them, "This
kind can come out only through prayer."[s]

Jesus Again Foretells His Death and Resurrection

30 They went on from there and passed
through Galilee. He did not want anyone to
know it; [31]for he was teaching his disciples,
saying to them, "The Son of Man is to be
betrayed into human hands, and they will
kill him, and three days after being killed,
he will rise again." [32]But they did not
understand what he was saying and were
afraid to ask him.

Who Is the Greatest?

33 Then they came to Capernaum; and
when he was in the house he asked them,
"What were you arguing about on the
way?" [34]But they were silent, for on the
way they had argued with one another
who was the greatest. [35]He sat down, called
the twelve, and said to them, "Whoever
wants to be first must be last of all and
servant of all." [36]Then he took a little child
and put it among them; and taking it in his
arms, he said to them, [37]"Whoever welcomes one such child in my name welcomes me, and whoever welcomes me
welcomes not me but the one who sent
me."

Another Exorcist

38 John said to him, "Teacher, we saw
someone[t] casting out demons in your name,
and we tried to stop him, because he was
not following us." [39]But Jesus said, "Do not
stop him; for no one who does a deed of
power in my name will be able soon afterward to speak evil of me. [40]Whoever is not
against us is for us. [41]For truly I tell you,
whoever gives you a cup of water to drink
because you bear the name of Christ will by
no means lose the reward.

Temptations to Sin

42 "If any of you put a stumbling block
before one of these little ones who believe
in me,[u] it would be better for you if a great
millstone were hung around your neck and
you were thrown into the sea. [43]If your
hand causes you to stumble, cut it off; it is
better for you to enter life maimed than to
have two hands and to go to hell,[v] to the
unquenchable fire.[w] [45]And if your foot causes
you to stumble, cut it off; it is better for you
to enter life lame than to have two feet and
to be thrown into hell.[v,w] [47]And if your eye
causes you to stumble, tear it out; it is better
for you to enter the kingdom of God with
one eye than to have two eyes and to be
thrown into hell,[v] [48]where their worm never
dies, and the fire is never quenched.
49 "For everyone will be salted with fire.[x]
[50]Salt is good; but if salt has lost its saltiness,

9.30-32 The second of Jesus' detailed predictions of his suffering, death and resurrection, which the disciples still do not *understand*. *Cf.* note on 8.31-33; Mt 17.22-23; Lk 9.43-45.
9.33-37 The dispute among the disciples as to which is the *greatest* evokes from Jesus an instruction to abandon seeking a position of power or prestige. His model is that of a *child*, who is simply to be *welcomed*, as God *welcomes* those who come to him in simple trust. *Cf.* Mt 18.1-5; Mk 10.15; Lk 9.46-48.
9.38-41 Jesus commends acceptance of those who perform acts of healing or kindness (*a cup of water*) in his name, even by those who are not members of the community. *Cf.* Lk 9.49-50.
9.42-48 God's people are to avoid causing difficulties for others (*stumbling blocks*) and failing to control their own actions and the impulses of various parts of the body. God will bring severe punishment on such undisciplined behavior: they will be *thrown into hell* (in Greek, *Gehenna*, the valley of Hinnom outside Jerusalem, where rubbish was gathered and burned). *Cf.* Mt 18.6-9; Lk 17.1-2.
9.49-50 Two sayings about *salt* with different meanings: the first is the image of purification (*with fire*); the second is the essential function of making life palatable (*at peace*).

[p] Gk *him* [q] Gk *He* [r] Other ancient authorities add *with tears* [s] Other ancient authorities add *and fasting* [t] Other ancient authorities add *who does not follow us* [u] Other ancient authorities lack *in me* [v] Gk *Gehenna* [w] Verses 44 and 46 (which are identical with verse 48) are lacking in the best ancient authorities [x] Other ancient authorities either add or substitute *and every sacrifice will be salted with salt*

10.1-52 Guidelines for the life of the new community, with warnings about inescapable sufferings.
10.1-12 Divorce is inadmissible for God's people, in contrast to Jewish rules of the first century and the tradition in Mt 19.1-12, where adultery is sufficient ground for terminating marriage.
10.13-16 The theme of *children* in God's *kingdom* is treated more fully than in 9.36-37. Here the point is that children will accept as a gift what is offered to them, and that is how everyone should accept a place among God's new people. *Laying his hands* on the children became a formal sign of their acceptance in the covenant community. *Cf.* Mt 19.13-15; Lk 18.15-17.
10.17-31 The issue of wealth as an obstacle to admission to the new life of God's people is discussed here, as in Mt 19.16-30 and Lk 18.18-30, with an additional feature: not only will the faithful be assured of new life in *the age to come*, but in the present community the shared life will involve new family-like relationships with others, new possessions, as well as *persecutions*.
10.32-34 The poignancy of this prediction of Jesus' suffering, death and resurrection is heightened by the detail that it is uttered as he is on his final journey *up to Jerusalem*. *Cf.* Mt 20.17-19; Lk 18.31-34.

how can you season it?[y] Have salt in yourselves, and be at peace with one another."

Teaching about Divorce

10 He left that place and went to the
region of Judea and[z] beyond the
Jordan. And crowds again gathered around
him; and, as was his custom, he again
taught them.
2 Some Pharisees came, and to test him
they asked, "Is it lawful for a man to divorce
his wife?" 3 He answered them, "What did
Moses command you?" 4 They said, "Moses
allowed a man to write a certificate of
dismissal and to divorce her." 5 But Jesus
said to them, "Because of your hardness of
heart he wrote this commandment for you.
6 But from the beginning of creation, 'God
made them male and female.' 7 'For this
reason a man shall leave his father and
mother and be joined to his wife,[a] 8 and the
two shall become one flesh.' So they are no
longer two, but one flesh. 9 Therefore what
God has joined together, let no one separate."
10 Then in the house the disciples asked
him again about this matter. 11 He said to
them, "Whoever divorces his wife and
marries another commits adultery against
her; 12 and if she divorces her husband and
marries another, she commits adultery."

Jesus Blesses Little Children

13 People were bringing little children to
him in order that he might touch them; and
the disciples spoke sternly to them. 14 But
when Jesus saw this, he was indignant and
said to them, "Let the little children come
to me; do not stop them; for it is to such
as these that the kingdom of God belongs.
15 Truly I tell you, whoever does not receive
the kingdom of God as a little child will
never enter it." 16 And he took them up in
his arms, laid his hands on them, and
blessed them.

The Rich Man

17 As he was setting out on a journey,
a man ran up and knelt before him, and
asked him, "Good Teacher, what must I do
to inherit eternal life?" 18 Jesus said to him,
"Why do you call me good? No one is good
but God alone. 19 You know the commandments: 'You shall not murder; You shall not
commit adultery; You shall not steal; You
shall not bear false witness; You shall not
defraud; Honor your father and mother.' "
20 He said to him, "Teacher, I have kept all
these since my youth." 21 Jesus, looking at
him, loved him and said, "You lack one
thing; go, sell what you own, and give the
money[b] to the poor, and you will have
treasure in heaven; then come, follow me."
22 When he heard this, he was shocked and
went away grieving, for he had many possessions.
23 Then Jesus looked around and said to
his disciples, "How hard it will be for those
who have wealth to enter the kingdom of
God!" 24 And the disciples were perplexed at
these words. But Jesus said to them again,
"Children, how hard it is[c] to enter the
kingdom of God! 25 It is easier for a camel to
go through the eye of a needle than for
someone who is rich to enter the kingdom
of God." 26 They were greatly astounded and
said to one another,[d] "Then who can be
saved?" 27 Jesus looked at them and said,
"For mortals it is impossible, but not for
God; for God all things are possible."
28 Peter began to say to him, "Look, we
have left everything and followed you."
29 Jesus said, "Truly I tell you, there is no
one who has left house or brothers or sisters
or mother or father or children or fields, for
my sake and for the sake of the good news,[e]
30 who will not receive a hundredfold now
in this age—houses, brothers and sisters,
mothers and children, and fields with
persecutions—and in the age to come eternal life. 31 But many who are first will be
last, and the last will be first."

A Third Time Jesus Foretells His Death and Resurrection

32 They were on the road, going up to
Jerusalem, and Jesus was walking ahead of
them; they were amazed, and those who
followed were afraid. He took the twelve
aside again and began to tell them what
was to happen to him, 33 saying, "See, we
are going up to Jerusalem, and the Son of
Man will be handed over to the chief priests
and the scribes, and they will condemn him

[y] Or *how can you restore its saltiness?* [z] Other ancient authorities lack *and* [a] Other ancient authorities lack *and be joined to his wife* [b] Gk lacks *the money* [c] Other ancient authorities add *for those who trust in riches* [d] Other ancient authorities read *to him* [e] Or *gospel*

10.1 Mt 19.1; Jn 10.40; 11.7
10.4 Deut 24.1-4; Mt 5.31; 19.7
10.6 Gen 1.27; 5.2
10.7 Gen 2.24; 1 Cor 6.16
10.11 Mt 5.32; Lk 16.18; Rom 7.3; 1 Cor 7.10,11
10.15 Mt 18.3; 1 Cor 14.20; 1 Pet 2.2
10.16 Mk 9.36
10.17 Mk 1.40; Lk 10.25; Eph 1.18
10.19 Ex 20.12-16; Deut 5.16-20
10.21 Mt 6.20; Lk 12.33; Acts 2.35; 4.34,35
10.23 Mt 19.23; Lk 18.24
10.24 Ps 52.7; 62.10; 1 Tim 6.17
10.27 Jer 32.17
10.28 Mt 4.20-22
10.29 Mt 6.33
10.31 Mt 20.16; Lk 13.30
10.32 Mk 8.31; 9.31; Lk 9.22

10.34 Mt 26.67; 27.30; Mk 14.65
10.37 Mt 19.28; Lk 22.30
10.38 Lk 12.50; Jn 18.11
10.39 Acts 12.2; Rev 1.9; 10.41; Lk 22.25-27
10.43 Mt 9.35
10.45 Jn 13.14; 1 Tim 2.5,6
10.47 Mt 9.27
10.51 Jn 20.16; Mt 23.7
10.52 Mt 9.22; Mk 5.34; Lk 7.50; 8.48; 17.19
11.1 Mt 21.17
11.4 Mk 14.16
11.9 Ps 118.26; Mt 23.39
11.11 Mt 21.10,11,17
11.12 Lk 13.6-9

to death; then they will hand him over to
the Gentiles; [34]they will mock him, and spit
upon him, and flog him, and kill him; and
after three days he will rise again."

The Request of James and John

35 James and John, the sons of Zebedee,
came forward to him and said to him,
"Teacher, we want you to do for us whatever we ask of you." [36]And he said to them,
"What is it you want me to do for you?"
[37]And they said to him, "Grant us to sit, one
at your right hand and one at your left, in
your glory." [38]But Jesus said to them, "You
do not know what you are asking. Are you
able to drink the cup that I drink, or be
baptized with the baptism that I am baptized with?" [39]They replied, "We are able."
Then Jesus said to them, "The cup that I
drink you will drink; and with the baptism
with which I am baptized, you will be
baptized; [40]but to sit at my right hand or at
my left is not mine to grant, but it is for
those for whom it has been prepared."
41 When the ten heard this, they began
to be angry with James and John. [42]So Jesus
called them and said to them, "You know
that among the Gentiles those whom they
recognize as their rulers lord it over them,
and their great ones are tyrants over them.
[43]But it is not so among you; but whoever
wishes to become great among you must be
your servant, [44]and whoever wishes to be
first among you must be slave of all. [45]For
the Son of Man came not to be served but
to serve, and to give his life a ransom for
many."

The Healing of Blind Bartimaeus

46 They came to Jericho. As he and his
disciples and a large crowd were leaving
Jericho, Bartimaeus son of Timaeus, a blind
beggar, was sitting by the roadside. [47]When
he heard that it was Jesus of Nazareth, he
began to shout out and say, "Jesus, Son of
David, have mercy on me!" [48]Many sternly
ordered him to be quiet, but he cried out
even more loudly, "Son of David, have mercy
on me!" [49]Jesus stood still and said, "Call
him here." And they called the blind man,
saying to him, "Take heart; get up, he is
calling you." [50]So throwing off his cloak, he
sprang up and came to Jesus. [51]Then Jesus
said to him, "What do you want me to do
for you?" The blind man said to him, "My
teacher,[f] let me see again." [52]Jesus said to
him, "Go; your faith has made you well."
Immediately he regained his sight and followed him on the way.

Jesus' Triumphal Entry into Jerusalem

11 When they were approaching
Jerusalem, at Bethphage and Bethany, near the Mount of Olives, he sent two
of his disciples [2]and said to them, "Go into
the village ahead of you, and immediately
as you enter it, you will find tied there a colt
that has never been ridden; untie it and
bring it. [3]If anyone says to you, 'Why are
you doing this?' just say this, 'The Lord
needs it and will send it back here immediately.'" [4]They went away and found a
colt tied near a door, outside in the street.
As they were untying it, [5]some of the bystanders said to them, "What are you doing, untying the colt?" [6]They told them
what Jesus had said; and they allowed them
to take it. [7]Then they brought the colt to
Jesus and threw their cloaks on it; and he
sat on it. [8]Many people spread their cloaks
on the road, and others spread leafy branches
that they had cut in the fields. [9]Then those
who went ahead and those who followed
were shouting,
"Hosanna!
Blessed is the one who comes in the
name of the Lord!
10 Blessed is the coming kingdom of our
ancestor David!
Hosanna in the highest heaven!"
11 Then he entered Jerusalem and went
into the temple; and when he had looked
around at everything, as it was already late,
he went out to Bethany with the twelve.

Jesus Curses the Fig Tree

12 On the following day, when they came
from Bethany, he was hungry. [13]Seeing in
the distance a fig tree in leaf, he went to see
whether perhaps he would find anything on
it. When he came to it, he found nothing
but leaves, for it was not the season for figs.
[14]He said to it, "May no one ever eat fruit
from you again." And his disciples heard it.

10.35-45 Ironically this prediction of suffering (see 8.31; 9.31) is followed by the disciples' vying for superior roles in Jesus' day of glorification. Here the brothers (rather than their mother, as in Mt 20.20) ask Jesus for the seats of honor *in your glory*. The *cup* and the *baptism* are symbols of the suffering and death which Jesus must undergo. God alone has *prepared* the places of honor for the faithful in the new age. The other disciples are resentful, but all are called to the role of *slave of all*. Jesus' own role is death as a *ransom*, liberating others from punishment and death for their sins. *Cf.* Mt 20.20-28; Lk 22.24-27.
10.46-52 *cf.* Mt 20.29-34. Here there is a single blind man, who is a *beggar*. Jesus, addressed by the Aramaic term of respect, Rabbouni (*master*), announces that it is the man's faith that has made him well. *Cf.* Lk 18.35-43.
11.1-13.37 Jesus' Final Public Ministry in Jerusalem.
11.1-11 Entry into Jerusalem. Mention of *Bethphage* and *Bethany* (home of Mary, Martha and Lazarus; Jn 11.1) indicates that Jesus' route to Jerusalem from Galilee was through the Jordan Valley and up through the wilderness of Judea on the Jericho – Jerusalem road past the south end of the Mount of Olives, which is across the Kidron Valley from the Jerusalem temple hill. His entry to the city on a *colt* recalls Isa 62.11 but especially Zech 9.9, which predicts the coming of Israel's king on this lowly beast. His acclaim by the throng includes an appeal to God to free his people, *Hosanna* ("Save us now") and an announcement of the coming rule of God in the tradition of David, quoting Ps 118.25-26, and expecting a nationalist restoration. There is no popular response in the *temple*.
11.12-14,20-25 On the cursing of the fig tree, see note on Mt 21.18-22. Included in Mark are appeals to trust God to do the humanly impossible (*a mountain thrown into the sea*), and a call to reflect in dealings with others God's forgiveness of his people.

[f] Aramaic *Rabbouni*

11.15-19 See note on Mt 21.12-17. Mark alone notes Jesus' hindering the commercial traffic *through the temple*, and includes the words from Isa 56.7 that the temple is to be a place of prayer *for all the nations*, not merely for Israel. His bold act provokes hostility from a coalition of Jewish leaders: *chief priests* and *scribes* (the self-appointed interpreters of the Jewish law).
11.27-33 See notes on Mt 21.23-27; Lk 20.1-8. Jesus implies that the purpose of God at work through John, and rejected by the religious leaders, is being carried forward through him.
12.1-12 The Parable of the Wicked Tenants. See note on Mt 21.33-46. The mention in v.5 of *another slave* whom the tenants of the vineyard (the Jewish leaders) *killed* may be a reference to the death of John the Baptist. The *others* who are given responsibility for God's work (*the vineyard*) are the leaders of the new people of God. The final quotation is from Ps 118.22-23, which pictures God's new people as a building. The Jewish leaders are fearful of the popular support for Jesus, and so are eager to remove him from the public scene.
12.13-17 Mark turns again to a series of basic issues among Jews of the early first century. The first is a combined attempt by the ritual purists (*Pharisees*) and those collaborating with the Romans (*Herodians*) to elicit from Jesus a subversive statement against Jews paying taxes to the Romans, which would lead to his condemnation by the Roman authorities. See note on Mt 22.15-22.

Jesus Cleanses the Temple

15 Then they came to Jerusalem. And he entered the temple and began to drive out those who were selling and those who were buying in the temple, and he overturned the tables of the money changers and the seats of those who sold doves; [16]and he would not allow anyone to carry anything through the temple. [17]He was teaching and saying, "Is it not written,

'My house shall be called a house of prayer for all the nations'?
But you have made it a den of robbers."

[18]And when the chief priests and the scribes heard it, they kept looking for a way to kill him; for they were afraid of him, because the whole crowd was spellbound by his teaching. [19]And when evening came, Jesus and his disciples[g] went out of the city.

The Lesson from the Withered Fig Tree

20 In the morning as they passed by, they saw the fig tree withered away to its roots. [21]Then Peter remembered and said to him, "Rabbi, look! The fig tree that you cursed has withered." [22]Jesus answered them, "Have[h] faith in God. [23]Truly I tell you, if you say to this mountain, 'Be taken up and thrown into the sea,' and if you do not doubt in your heart, but believe that what you say will come to pass, it will be done for you. [24]So I tell you, whatever you ask for in prayer, believe that you have received[i] it, and it will be yours.

25 "Whenever you stand praying, forgive, if you have anything against anyone; so that your Father in heaven may also forgive you your trespasses."[j]

Jesus' Authority Is Questioned

27 Again they came to Jerusalem. As he was walking in the temple, the chief priests, the scribes, and the elders came to him [28]and said, "By what authority are you doing these things? Who gave you this authority to do them?" [29]Jesus said to them, "I will ask you one question; answer me, and I will tell you by what authority I do these things. [30]Did the baptism of John come from heaven, or was it of human origin? Answer me." [31]They argued with one another, "If we say, 'From heaven,' he will say, 'Why then did you not believe him?' [32]But shall we say, 'Of human origin'?"—they were afraid of the crowd, for all regarded John as truly a prophet. [33]So they answered Jesus, "We do not know." And Jesus said to them, "Neither will I tell you by what authority I am doing these things."

The Parable of the Wicked Tenants

12 Then he began to speak to them in parables. "A man planted a vineyard, put a fence around it, dug a pit for the wine press, and built a watchtower; then he leased it to tenants and went to another country. [2]When the season came, he sent a slave to the tenants to collect from them his share of the produce of the vineyard. [3]But they seized him, and beat him, and sent him away empty-handed. [4]And again he sent another slave to them; this one they beat over the head and insulted. [5]Then he sent another, and that one they killed. And so it was with many others; some they beat, and others they killed. [6]He had still one other, a beloved son. Finally he sent him to them, saying, 'They will respect my son.' [7]But those tenants said to one another, 'This is the heir; come, let us kill him, and the inheritance will be ours.' [8]So they seized him, killed him, and threw him out of the vineyard. [9]What then will the owner of the vineyard do? He will come and destroy the tenants and give the vineyard to others. [10]Have you not read this scripture:

'The stone that the builders rejected
has become the cornerstone;[k]
[11] this was the Lord's doing,
and it is amazing in our eyes'?"

12 When they realized that he had told this parable against them, they wanted to arrest him, but they feared the crowd. So they left him and went away.

The Question about Paying Taxes

13 Then they sent to him some Pharisees and some Herodians to trap him in what he said. [14]And they came and said to him, "Teacher, we know that you are sincere, and show deference to no one; for you do not regard people with partiality, but teach

[g] Gk *they*: other ancient authorities read *he* [h] Other ancient authorities read *"If you have* [i] Other ancient authorities read *are receiving* [j] Other ancient authorities add verse 26, *"But if you do not forgive, neither will your Father in heaven forgive your trespasses."* [k] Or *keystone*

11.17 Isa 56.7; Jer 7.11
11.18 Mt 21.46; 7.28
11.20 Mt 21.19
11.21 Mt 23.7
11.22 Mt 17.20
11.23 Mt 21.21; Lk 17.6
11.24 Mt 7.7; Jn 14.13,14; 15.7; 16.23,24; Jas 1.5,6
11.25 Mt 6.14,15; Col 3.13
11.32 Mt 14.5
12.1 Isa 5.1-7; *cf.* Heb 1.1-3
12.10 Ps 118.22,23; Acts 4.11; 1 Pet 2.7
12.12 Mt 21.45,46; Mk 11.18; Mt 22.22
12.13 Mk 3.6; Lk 11.54

12.17 Rom 13.7
12.19 Deut 25.5
12.25 1 Cor 15.42,49,52
12.26 Ex 3.6
12.28 Lk 10.25-28; 20.39
12.29 Deut 6.4
12.31 Lev 19.18; Rom 13.9; Gal 5.14; Jas 2.8
12.32 Deut 4.39; Isa 45.6,14; 46.9
12.33 1 Sam 15.22; Hos 6.6; Mic 6.6-8
12.34 Mt 22.46
12.35 Mt 26.55; 9.27
12.36 Ps 110.1; Acts 2.34,35; Heb 1.13
12.37 Jn 12.9
12.38 Lk 11.43
12.41 Jn 8.20; 2 Kings 12.9
12.43 2 Cor 8.12

the way of God in accordance with truth. Is it lawful to pay taxes to the emperor, or not? [15]Should we pay them, or should we not?" But knowing their hypocrisy, he said to them, "Why are you putting me to the test? Bring me a denarius and let me see it." [16]And they brought one. Then he said to them, "Whose head is this, and whose title?" They answered, "The emperor's." [17]Jesus said to them, "Give to the emperor the things that are the emperor's, and to God the things that are God's." And they were utterly amazed at him.

The Question about the Resurrection

18 Some Sadducees, who say there is no resurrection, came to him and asked him a question, saying, [19]"Teacher, Moses wrote for us that if a man's brother dies, leaving a wife but no child, the man[l] shall marry the widow and raise up children for his brother. [20]There were seven brothers; the first married and, when he died, left no children; [21]and the second married her and died, leaving no children; and the third likewise; [22]none of the seven left children. Last of all the woman herself died. [23]In the resurrection[m] whose wife will she be? For the seven had married her."

24 Jesus said to them, "Is not this the reason you are wrong, that you know neither the scriptures nor the power of God? [25]For when they rise from the dead, they neither marry nor are given in marriage, but are like angels in heaven. [26]And as for the dead being raised, have you not read in the book of Moses, in the story about the bush, how God said to him, 'I am the God of Abraham, the God of Isaac, and the God of Jacob'? [27]He is God not of the dead, but of the living; you are quite wrong."

The First Commandment

28 One of the scribes came near and heard them disputing with one another, and seeing that he answered them well, he asked him, "Which commandment is the first of all?" [29]Jesus answered, "The first is, 'Hear, O Israel: the Lord our God, the Lord is one; [30]you shall love the Lord your God with all your heart, and with all your soul, and with all your mind, and with all your strength.' [31]The second is this, 'You shall love your neighbor as yourself.' There is no other commandment greater than these." [32]Then the scribe said to him, "You are right, Teacher; you have truly said that 'he is one, and besides him there is no other'; [33]and 'to love him with all the heart, and with all the understanding, and with all the strength,' and 'to love one's neighbor as oneself,'—this is much more important than all whole burnt offerings and sacrifices." [34]When Jesus saw that he answered wisely, he said to him, "You are not far from the kingdom of God." After that no one dared to ask him any question.

The Question about David's Son

35 While Jesus was teaching in the temple, he said, "How can the scribes say that the Messiah[n] is the son of David? [36]David himself, by the Holy Spirit, declared,

'The Lord said to my Lord,
"Sit at my right hand,
until I put your enemies under your feet." '

[37]David himself calls him Lord; so how can he be his son?" And the large crowd was listening to him with delight.

Jesus Denounces the Scribes

38 As he taught, he said, "Beware of the scribes, who like to walk around in long robes, and to be greeted with respect in the marketplaces, [39]and to have the best seats in the synagogues and places of honor at banquets! [40]They devour widows' houses and for the sake of appearance say long prayers. They will receive the greater condemnation."

The Widow's Offering

41 He sat down opposite the treasury, and watched the crowd putting money into the treasury. Many rich people put in large sums. [42]A poor widow came and put in two small copper coins, which are worth a penny. [43]Then he called his disciples and said to them, "Truly I tell you, this poor widow has put in more than all those who are contributing to the treasury. [44]For all of them have contributed out of their abundance; but she out of her poverty has put in everything she had, all she had to live on."

12.18-27 The second issue to divide Jews, since Pharisees affirmed the resurrection of the faithful dead, and Sadducees denied it. See note on Mt 22.23-33; also Lk 20.27-40.
12.28-34 An issue long debated among Jewish interpreters of the law was, Which commandment should have priority over the others? Jesus' solution is to point to two: Love of God (Deut 6.4-5), and love of your neighbor as yourself (Lev 19.18). In Mark the *scribe*, a professional interpreter of the Jewish law, expounds this theme, emphasizing acts of love as more important than *sacrifices*. The threat to the temple-based religion is implicit but clear.
12.35-37 Based on Ps 110.1, Jesus answers the question about the relation of David and Messiah by declaring that the *Messiah* is to be not merely a descendant (*son*) of David, but also his *Lord*, who will be exalted by God and triumph over all his *enemies*. His words delight the *crowd* of hearers.
12.38-40 Jesus' controversy with the professional interpreters of the law: *scribes*. *Cf.* the much longer version in Mt 23.1-36. Here Jesus denounces the scribes' ostentation in dress and piety, as well as their financial exploitation of those who seek their advice.
12.41-44 Contrasted with the scribes' exploiting religion for financial gain is the simple piety of the *widow* who contributes to the temple *treasury* all that she has.

[l] Gk *his brother* [m] Other ancient authorities add *when they rise* [n] Or *the Christ*

13.1-37 The End of the Temple and the Consummation of the Age. *Cf.* notes on Mt 24.1-25.46; Lk 21.5-36.
13.1-4 After predicting the destruction of the great temple complex built in Jerusalem by Herod, Jesus explains to only four of the disciples when this will take place and what its implications are for God's people. *Cf.* Mt 24.1-3; Lk 21.5-7.
13.5-8 A warning against false claimants to be God's agent of renewal (I am he) and predictions of cosmic and political disturbances which will precede the *birth pangs* of the new age.
13.9-13 The community members will undergo trials before religious and civil authorities, but are to rely on the *Holy Spirit* as to how they shall testify. Families will be split and the community will be universally *hated*, but they are to remain faithful until the *end* of the age. *Cf.* Mt 24.9-14; Lk 21.12-19.
13.14-23 See note on Mt 24.15-31 on the *desolating sacrilege*, which will be the ultimate effort to divinize the Roman emperor and to desecrate the temple. The faithful community is to flee the scene, but their suffering will be great, as will be their need to reject *false messiahs*.
13.24-27 The cosmic disturbances will precede God's sending from heaven his agent of renewal and triumph: the *Son of Man* (Dan 7.9-14), who will assemble God's elect people of the new covenant from all over the world, in accord with Old Testament expectations: Deut 30.4; Isa 27.12-13. *Cf.* Mt 24.29-31; Lk 21.25-28.
13.28-32 The appearance in spring of leaves on the fig tree assures the nearness of summer; just so, the signs sketched above assure that the consummation of the age will take place within *this generation*. The promise is sure; the exact time is the secret of the *Father*.
13.33-37 Mark's (original) version of the apocalypse ends with a series of sayings about the need for watchfulness which have parallels scattered in Mt (25.14-15; 24.42; 25.13) and Luke (12.38,40; 19.12-13). Mark's emphasis is on the need for diligence on the part of the *servants* whom the master has left in charge.

The Destruction of the Temple Foretold

13 As he came out of the temple, one
of his disciples said to him, "Look,
Teacher, what large stones and what large
buildings!" 2Then Jesus asked him, "Do you
see these great buildings? Not one stone will
be left here upon another; all will be thrown
down."
3 When he was sitting on the Mount of
Olives opposite the temple, Peter, James,
John, and Andrew asked him privately, 4"Tell
us, when will this be, and what will be the
sign that all these things are about to be
accomplished?" 5Then Jesus began to say to
them, "Beware that no one leads you astray.
6Many will come in my name and say, 'I
am he!'[o] and they will lead many astray.
7When you hear of wars and rumors of
wars, do not be alarmed; this must take
place, but the end is still to come. 8For
nation will rise against nation, and kingdom against kingdom; there will be earthquakes in various places; there will be famines. This is but the beginning of the birth
pangs.

Persecution Foretold

9 "As for yourselves, beware; for they
will hand you over to councils; and you will
be beaten in synagogues; and you will stand
before governors and kings because of me,
as a testimony to them. 10And the good
news[p] must first be proclaimed to all nations. 11When they bring you to trial and
hand you over, do not worry beforehand
about what you are to say; but say whatever is given you at that time, for it is not
you who speak, but the Holy Spirit. 12Brother
will betray brother to death, and a father
his child, and children will rise against
parents and have them put to death; 13and
you will be hated by all because of my
name. But the one who endures to the end
will be saved.

The Desolating Sacrilege

14 "But when you see the desolating
sacrilege set up where it ought not to be (let
the reader understand), then those in Judea
must flee to the mountains; 15the one on the
housetop must not go down or enter the
house to take anything away; 16the one in
the field must not turn back to get a coat.
17Woe to those who are pregnant and to
those who are nursing infants in those
days! 18Pray that it may not be in winter.
19For in those days there will be suffering,
such as has not been from the beginning of
the creation that God created until now, no,
and never will be. 20And if the Lord had not
cut short those days, no one would be
saved; but for the sake of the elect, whom
he chose, he has cut short those days.
21And if anyone says to you at that time,
'Look! Here is the Messiah!'[q] or 'Look! There
he is!'—do not believe it. 22False messiahs[r]
and false prophets will appear and produce
signs and omens, to lead astray, if possible,
the elect. 23But be alert; I have already told
you everything.

The Coming of the Son of Man

24 "But in those days, after that suffering,
the sun will be darkened,
and the moon will not give its light,
25 and the stars will be falling from heaven,
and the powers in the heavens will be
shaken.
26Then they will see 'the Son of Man coming in clouds' with great power and glory.
27Then he will send out the angels, and
gather his elect from the four winds, from
the ends of the earth to the ends of heaven.

The Lesson of the Fig Tree

28 "From the fig tree learn its lesson: as
soon as its branch becomes tender and puts
forth its leaves, you know that summer is
near. 29So also, when you see these things
taking place, you know that he[s] is near, at
the very gates. 30Truly I tell you, this generation will not pass away until all these
things have taken place. 31Heaven and earth
will pass away, but my words will not pass
away.

The Necessity for Watchfulness

32 "But about that day or hour no one
knows, neither the angels in heaven, nor
the Son, but only the Father. 33Beware, keep
alert;[t] for you do not know when the time
will come. 34It is like a man going on a
journey, when he leaves home and puts his
slaves in charge, each with his work, and
commands the doorkeeper to be on the
watch. 35Therefore, keep awake—for you do

[o] Gk *I am* [p] Gk *gospel* [q] Or *the Christ* [r] Or *christs* [s] Or *it* [t] Other ancient authorities add *and pray*

13.2 Lk 19.44; Mk 14.58; 15.29; Acts 6.14
13.3 Mk 5.37; 9.2
13.5 Eph 5.6; 1 Thess 2.3
13.6 Jn 8.24
13.9 Mt 10.17
13.11 Mt 10.17
13.12 Mic 7.6; Mt 10.21
13.13 Jn 15.21; Mt 10.22; Rev 2.10
13.14 Dan 9.27; 11.31; 12.11
13.17 Lk 23.29
13.19 Dan 9.26; 12.1; Joel 2.2
13.21 Lk 17.23; 21.8
13.22 Mt 7.15; Jn 4.48
13.23 2 Pet 3.17
13.24 Zeph 1.15
13.26 Dan 7.13; Mt 16.27; Mk 14.62; 1 Thess 4.16; 2 Thess 1.7,10
13.30 Mk 9.1
13.31 Mt 5.18; Lk 16.17
13.32 Acts 1.7
13.33 Eph 6.18; Col 4.2; 1 Thess 5.6
13.34 Mt 25.14
13.35 Lk 12.35-40

14.1 Jn 11.55; 13.1; Mt 12.14
14.3 Lk 7.37-39; Mt 21.17
14.7 Deut 15.11
14.8 Jn 19.20
14.10 Lk 22.3,4; Jn 6.71
14.12 Ex 12.11
14.18 ver 44,45
14.22 Mk 6.41; 8.6; Lk 24.30; 1 Cor 11.23-25
14.23 1 Cor 10.16
14.24 Ex 24.8; Heb 9.20
14.26 Mt 21.1
14.27 Zech 13.7
14.28 Mk 16.7
14.29 Jn 13.37,38

not know when the master of the house will come, in the evening, or at midnight, or at cockcrow, or at dawn, [36]or else he may find you asleep when he comes suddenly. [37]And what I say to you I say to all: Keep awake."

The Plot to Kill Jesus

14 It was two days before the Passover and the festival of Unleavened Bread. The chief priests and the scribes were looking for a way to arrest Jesus[u] by stealth and kill him; [2]for they said, "Not during the festival, or there may be a riot among the people."

The Anointing at Bethany

3 While he was at Bethany in the house of Simon the leper,[v] as he sat at the table, a woman came with an alabaster jar of very costly ointment of nard, and she broke open the jar and poured the ointment on his head. [4]But some were there who said to one another in anger, "Why was the ointment wasted in this way? [5]For this ointment could have been sold for more than three hundred denarii,[w] and the money given to the poor." And they scolded her. [6]But Jesus said, "Let her alone; why do you trouble her? She has performed a good service for me. [7]For you always have the poor with you, and you can show kindness to them whenever you wish; but you will not always have me. [8]She has done what she could; she has anointed my body beforehand for its burial. [9]Truly I tell you, wherever the good news[x] is proclaimed in the whole world, what she has done will be told in remembrance of her."

Judas Agrees to Betray Jesus

10 Then Judas Iscariot, who was one of the twelve, went to the chief priests in order to betray him to them. [11]When they heard it, they were greatly pleased, and promised to give him money. So he began to look for an opportunity to betray him.

The Passover with the Disciples

12 On the first day of Unleavened Bread, when the Passover lamb is sacrificed, his disciples said to him, "Where do you want us to go and make the preparations for you to eat the Passover?" [13]So he sent two of his disciples, saying to them, "Go into the city, and a man carrying a jar of water will meet you; follow him, [14]and wherever he enters, say to the owner of the house, 'The Teacher asks, Where is my guest room where I may eat the Passover with my disciples?' [15]He will show you a large room upstairs, furnished and ready. Make preparations for us there." [16]So the disciples set out and went to the city, and found everything as he had told them; and they prepared the Passover meal.

17 When it was evening, he came with the twelve. [18]And when they had taken their places and were eating, Jesus said, "Truly I tell you, one of you will betray me, one who is eating with me." [19]They began to be distressed and to say to him one after another, "Surely, not I?" [20]He said to them, "It is one of the twelve, one who is dipping bread[y] into the bowl[z] with me. [21]For the Son of Man goes as it is written of him, but woe to that one by whom the Son of Man is betrayed! It would have been better for that one not to have been born."

The Institution of the Lord's Supper

22 While they were eating, he took a loaf of bread, and after blessing it he broke it, gave it to them, and said, "Take; this is my body." [23]Then he took a cup, and after giving thanks he gave it to them, and all of them drank from it. [24]He said to them, "This is my blood of the[a] covenant, which is poured out for many. [25]Truly I tell you, I will never again drink of the fruit of the vine until that day when I drink it new in the kingdom of God."

Peter's Denial Foretold

26 When they had sung the hymn, they went out to the Mount of Olives. [27]And Jesus said to them, "You will all become deserters; for it is written,

'I will strike the shepherd,
and the sheep will be scattered.'

[28]But after I am raised up, I will go before you to Galilee." [29]Peter said to him, "Even though all become deserters, I will not."

[u] Gk *him* [v] The terms *leper* and *leprosy* can refer to several diseases [w] The denarius was the usual day's wage for a laborer [x] Or *gospel* [y] Gk lacks *bread* [z] Other ancient authorities read *same bowl* [a] Other ancient authorities add *new*

14.1-2 In Mark's chronology, *the Passover* here falls on the day extending from sundown Thursday to sundown Friday, which is the fourteenth of the Jewish month Nisan. *Two days before the Passover* would be from sundown Tuesday to sundown Wednesday. It is on that day that the coalition of *priests* and *scribes* conspires to *kill* Jesus prior to the *festival*, in order to avoid a popular uprising (riot) in support of him. For further details, see notes on Mt 26.1-5.
14.3-9 On the anointing of Jesus' body in preparation for his burial, see notes on Mt 26.6-13. Far more important than a gift to the *poor* is this perceptive act for which an unnamed *woman* will be renowned throughout *the whole world*.
14.10-11 *cf.* Mt 26.14-16. The money is merely *promised* to Judas, who, outside the city and at night, will show the priestly group where and who Jesus is.
14.12-21 Preparation for the Passover with the Disciples. On *the first day of Unleavened Bread*, see Ex 12.15-20 and notes on Mt 26.17-25. The institution of the Passover is detailed in Ex 12.1-13; in Judaism it was celebrated in homes, just as the early gatherings of Christians were. The common *bowl* was both symbol and instrument of shared life within the community, so Jesus' announcement that one of their number *will betray* him heightens the tragedy and irony.
14.22-25 *cf.* Mt 26.26-29; Lk 22.15-20. One of the few features of the gospels to be found also in the New Testament letters (1 Cor 11.23-25). The re-enactment of this meal in the subsequent life of the church recalls the past event, celebrates the present communion of God's people, and looks forward to their liberation and reunion with Jesus in the *kingdom of God*.
14.26-31 Peter's denial of his association with Jesus is foretold, as is the abandonment of Jesus by all the disciples after his arrest and crucifixion. Both events are in accord with scripture (14.27; cf. Zech 13.7). Also predicted by Jesus are his resurrection and appearance to his followers *in Galilee*. *Cf.* Mt 26.31-35; Lk 22.31-34,39.

14.32-42 *Cf.* notes on Mt 26.36-46; Lk 22.40-46. Only Mark reports Jesus' prayer that he might escape the period (*hour*) of agony through which he is soon to pass, and his addressing God as *Abba*, an intensely personal Aramaic term for one's father. Here the disciples are unable to explain why they are *sleeping* at this time of Jesus' most severe testing.
14.43-52 *cf.* notes on Mt 26.47-56 for details of Judas' betrayal, and Jesus' challenge to the armed crowd who have come to seize him. Only Mark mentions the unidentified *young man* who leaves his clothing behind as he flees.
14.53-65 See notes on Mt 26.57-68 for the nature of the Jewish *council* led by the *chief priests* which interrogates Jesus concerning his reported threat to destroy the temple. Mark notes the disagreements in the *testimony* brought against Jesus. His answer to the direct question about his being *Messiah* is a simple affirmation, *I am*, followed by a prediction of his heavenly exaltation as *Son of Man. Cf.* note on Mt 26.17-25. This claim to divine power is heard as *blasphemy*, and thus he deserves death by stoning as a violator of Jewish law (Num 24.16). The crowd and the guards join in shameful treatment of him.
14.65-72 In response to the declarations of various bystanders that *Peter* is associated with Jesus, he not only denies his participation in the movement, but confirms by a *curse* his lack of links with Jesus.

30 Jesus said to him, "Truly I tell you, this day, this very night, before the cock crows twice, you will deny me three times." 31 But he said vehemently, "Even though I must die with you, I will not deny you." And all of them said the same.

Jesus Prays in Gethsemane

32 They went to a place called Gethsemane; and he said to his disciples, "Sit here while I pray." 33 He took with him Peter and James and John, and began to be distressed and agitated. 34 And he said to them, "I am deeply grieved, even to death; remain here, and keep awake." 35 And going a little farther, he threw himself on the ground and prayed that, if it were possible, the hour might pass from him. 36 He said, "Abba,[b] Father, for you all things are possible; remove this cup from me; yet, not what I want, but what you want." 37 He came and found them sleeping; and he said to Peter, "Simon, are you asleep? Could you not keep awake one hour? 38 Keep awake and pray that you may not come into the time of trial;[c] the spirit indeed is willing, but the flesh is weak." 39 And again he went away and prayed, saying the same words. 40 And once more he came and found them sleeping, for their eyes were very heavy; and they did not know what to say to him. 41 He came a third time and said to them, "Are you still sleeping and taking your rest? Enough! The hour has come; the Son of Man is betrayed into the hands of sinners. 42 Get up, let us be going. See, my betrayer is at hand."

The Betrayal and Arrest of Jesus

43 Immediately, while he was still speaking, Judas, one of the twelve, arrived; and with him there was a crowd with swords and clubs, from the chief priests, the scribes, and the elders. 44 Now the betrayer had given them a sign, saying, "The one I will kiss is the man; arrest him and lead him away under guard." 45 So when he came, he went up to him at once and said, "Rabbi!" and kissed him. 46 Then they laid hands on him and arrested him. 47 But one of those who stood near drew his sword and struck the slave of the high priest, cutting off his ear. 48 Then Jesus said to them, "Have you come out with swords and clubs to arrest me as though I were a bandit? 49 Day after day I was with you in the temple teaching, and you did not arrest me. But let the scriptures be fulfilled." 50 All of them deserted him and fled.

51 A certain young man was following him, wearing nothing but a linen cloth. They caught hold of him, 52 but he left the linen cloth and ran off naked.

Jesus before the Council

53 They took Jesus to the high priest; and all the chief priests, the elders, and the scribes were assembled. 54 Peter had followed him at a distance, right into the courtyard of the high priest; and he was sitting with the guards, warming himself at the fire. 55 Now the chief priests and the whole council were looking for testimony against Jesus to put him to death; but they found none. 56 For many gave false testimony against him, and their testimony did not agree. 57 Some stood up and gave false testimony against him, saying, 58 "We heard him say, 'I will destroy this temple that is made with hands, and in three days I will build another, not made with hands.'" 59 But even on this point their testimony did not agree. 60 Then the high priest stood up before them and asked Jesus, "Have you no answer? What is it that they testify against you?" 61 But he was silent and did not answer. Again the high priest asked him, "Are you the Messiah,[d] the Son of the Blessed One?" 62 Jesus said, "I am; and
'you will see the Son of Man
seated at the right hand of the Power,'
and 'coming with the clouds of heaven.'"

63 Then the high priest tore his clothes and said, "Why do we still need witnesses? 64 You have heard his blasphemy! What is your decision?" All of them condemned him as deserving death. 65 Some began to spit on him, to blindfold him, and to strike him, saying to him, "Prophesy!" The guards also took him over and beat him.

Peter Denies Jesus

66 While Peter was below in the courtyard, one of the servant-girls of the high priest came by. 67 When she saw Peter warming himself, she stared at him and said, "You also were with Jesus, the man from Nazareth." 68 But he denied it, saying,

14.30 ver 66-72; Jn 13.38
14.34 Jn 12.27
14.35 ver 41
14.36 Rom 8.15; Gal 4.6; Jn 5.30; 6.38
14.38 Mt 6.13; Lk 11.4; Rom 7.23; Gal 5.17
14.41 ver 35; Jn 13.1
14.45 Mt 23.7
14.49 Mk 12.35; Isa 53.7ff; Lk 19.47; Jn 18.19-21
14.50 Ps 88.8; ver 27
14.54 ver 68; Mt 26.3; Jn 18.18
14.58 Mk 15.29; Jn 2.19; Acts 6.14
14.61 Isa 53.7
14.62 Dan 7.13; Mt 24.30; Mk 13.26
14.63 Num 14.6; Acts 14.14
14.64 Lev 24.16
14.65 Mk 10.34; Esth 7.8; Lk 22.64
14.66 ver 30,54
14.67 ver 54; Mk 1.24
14.68 ver 54

[b] Aramaic for *Father* [c] Or *into temptation* [d] Or *the Christ*

"I do not know or understand what you are talking about." And he went out into the forecourt.[e] Then the cock crowed.[f] 69 And the servant-girl, on seeing him, began again to say to the bystanders, "This man is one of them." 70 But again he denied it. Then after a little while the bystanders again said to Peter, "Certainly you are one of them; for you are a Galilean." 71 But he began to curse, and he swore an oath, "I do not know this man you are talking about." 72 At that moment the cock crowed for the second time. Then Peter remembered that Jesus had said to him, "Before the cock crows twice, you will deny me three times." And he broke down and wept.

Jesus before Pilate

15 As soon as it was morning, the chief priests held a consultation with the elders and scribes and the whole council. They bound Jesus, led him away, and handed him over to Pilate. 2 Pilate asked him, "Are you the King of the Jews?" He answered him, "You say so." 3 Then the chief priests accused him of many things. 4 Pilate asked him again, "Have you no answer? See how many charges they bring against you." 5 But Jesus made no further reply, so that Pilate was amazed.

Pilate Hands Jesus over to Be Crucified

6 Now at the festival he used to release a prisoner for them, anyone for whom they asked. 7 Now a man called Barabbas was in prison with the rebels who had committed murder during the insurrection. 8 So the crowd came and began to ask Pilate to do for them according to his custom. 9 Then he answered them, "Do you want me to release for you the King of the Jews?" 10 For he realized that it was out of jealousy that the chief priests had handed him over. 11 But the chief priests stirred up the crowd to have him release Barabbas for them instead. 12 Pilate spoke to them again, "Then what do you wish me to do[g] with the man you call[h] the King of the Jews?" 13 They shouted back, "Crucify him!" 14 Pilate asked them, "Why, what evil has he done?" But they shouted all the more, "Crucify him!" 15 So Pilate, wishing to satisfy the crowd, released Barabbas for them; and after flogging Jesus, he handed him over to be crucified.

The Soldiers Mock Jesus

16 Then the soldiers led him into the courtyard of the palace (that is, the governor's headquarters[i]); and they called together the whole cohort. 17 And they clothed him in a purple cloak; and after twisting some thorns into a crown, they put it on him. 18 And they began saluting him, "Hail, King of the Jews!" 19 They struck his head with a reed, spat upon him, and knelt down in homage to him. 20 After mocking him, they stripped him of the purple cloak and put his own clothes on him. Then they led him out to crucify him.

The Crucifixion of Jesus

21 They compelled a passer-by, who was coming in from the country, to carry his cross; it was Simon of Cyrene, the father of Alexander and Rufus. 22 Then they brought Jesus[j] to the place called Golgotha (which means the place of a skull). 23 And they offered him wine mixed with myrrh; but he did not take it. 24 And they crucified him, and divided his clothes among them, casting lots to decide what each should take.

25 It was nine o'clock in the morning when they crucified him. 26 The inscription of the charge against him read, "The King of the Jews." 27 And with him they crucified two bandits, one on his right and one on his left.[k] 29 Those who passed by derided[l] him, shaking their heads and saying, "Aha! You who would destroy the temple and build it in three days, 30 save yourself, and come down from the cross!" 31 In the same way the chief priests, along with the scribes, were also mocking him among themselves and saying, "He saved others; he cannot save himself. 32 Let the Messiah,[m] the King of Israel, come down from the cross now, so that we may see and believe." Those who were crucified with him also taunted him.

The Death of Jesus

33 When it was noon, darkness came over the whole land[n] until three in the afternoon. 34 At three o'clock Jesus cried out

14.70 ver 68; Acts 2.7
14.72 ver 30
15.1 Mt 5.22; Lk 22.66; 23.1; Jn 18.28
15.5 Isa 53.7
15.6 Mt 27.15; Lk 23.17; Jn 18.39
15.11 Acts 3.14
15.15 Jn 19.1,16
15.16 Acts 10.1
15.21 Lk 23.26; Rom 16.13
15.24 Ps 22.18
15.29 Ps 22.7; Mk 13.2; 14.58; Jn 2.19
15.31 Ps 22.8
15.32 ver 26,27
15.34 Ps 22.1

15.1-5 The priestly and scribal leaders meet with the regional *council*, and decide to turn Jesus over to the Roman authority, *Pilate*, to decide his fate on the political charge that he claimed to be *King of the Jews*. Jesus neither agrees nor disputes that he made such a claim: *You say so*.
15.6-15 Since the charge is not clear, *Pilate* seeks an escape by offering to free Jesus as a political prisoner, as the governors are said to have done annually at the time of the great Jewish festival. The Jerusalem crowd asks instead for the release of a known revolutionary, *Barabbas*, and calls for the *crucifixion* of Jesus, a Roman mode of execution reserved for the worst offenders. Pilate accedes to the crowd's demand to order Jesus to be crucified. *Cf.* Mt 27.11-26; Lk 23.2-5,17-25.
15.16-20 *cf.* notes on Mt 27.27-44 for the soldiers' cruel treatment of Jesus as an aspirant to Jewish kingship.
15.21-32 The names are given for the *passer-by* who is forced to carry the heavy cross-piece (*Simon of Cyrene*) and his sons, *Alexander and Rufus*, who may have been known to Mark's original readers but are otherwise unknown, unless Rufus is the one greeted by Paul in Rom 16.13. The claim that Jesus promised to rebuild the temple in three days distorts Jesus' prediction that he will rise from the dead after three days. The accusers confuse his destiny with the fate of the temple.
15.33-41 See notes on Mt 27.45-56, where the text closely matches Mark. After a *loud cry*, Jesus expelled his breath, which implies that his acceptance of death was a voluntary action. The family connections of the women who remain faithfully at the crucifixion are with *James the younger*, who may be James the son of Alphaeus (Mk 3.18; Acts 1.13), and *Joses*, one of Jesus' brothers (Mk 6.3; *Joseph* in Mt 13.55). The name of *Salome*, not found in Matthew's account, may be that of the wife of one of the disciples. These women had been followers and supporters of Jesus in Galilee, as were the *many other women* who accompanied them.

[e] Or *gateway* [f] Other ancient authorities lack *Then the cock crowed* [g] Other ancient authorities read *what should I do* [h] Other ancient authorities lack *the man you call* [i] Gk *the praetorium* [j] Gk *him* [k] Other ancient authorities add verse 28, *And the scripture was fulfilled that says, "And he was counted among the lawless."* [l] Or *blasphemed* [m] Or *the Christ* [n] Or *earth*

15.42-47 Since it was late on Friday afternoon before the sabbath began at sundown, it was an urgent matter to bury Jesus. See notes on Mt 27.57-66. *Joseph* is here identified as a *respected member of the council* (see note on 14.32-42), indicating the importance of his place in the regional Jewish ruling body set up by the Romans. Death of the crucified often came only after many hours or even days, so *Pilate* needs confirmation of Jesus' death within a period of only three hours (15.33). Burial and closure of the *rock-hewn* tomb are completed hastily. Two of the women see the place of burial (15.47).
16.1-8 Three of the women come *very early* on the morning after the sabbath, having *bought spices* to *anoint* the body of Jesus and thus prepare him properly for burial. The sanctity of spices and oil in the worship of Israel is at the highest level (Ex 30.34-36). Only Mark mentions the *young man* seated beside the empty tomb who explains why Jesus is not there (*he has been raised*) and where his followers will next see him: in *Galilee*, as he promised (14.28). The *terror and amazement* which seize the *disciples and Peter* at this disclosure recall the reaction of Daniel when he is told of the cosmic conflict and destruction of the traditional sanctuary of God that will precede the coming of the new age of God's rule (Dan 10.8-12). The Greek text ends awkwardly and abruptly with a conjunction.

The Shorter Ending. An early and widely-adopted ending attempts to bring Mark to a smoother conclusion, conveying the message to Peter and the inner circle of the disciples, and attesting to the power of Jesus in the spread of the good news *from east to west.*

The Longer Ending. Found in many manuscripts, but not in those most widely regarded as accurate, the stories of Jesus' appearances to his followers here given reflect traditions preserved in the other canonical and non-canonical gospels, including Lk 24.13-15,50-51 and Jn 20.11-23.

with a loud voice, "Eloi, Eloi, lema sabachthani?" which means, "My God, my God, why have you forsaken me?"[o] 35When some of the bystanders heard it, they said, "Listen, he is calling for Elijah." 36And someone ran, filled a sponge with sour wine, put it on a stick, and gave it to him to drink, saying, "Wait, let us see whether Elijah will come to take him down." 37Then Jesus gave a loud cry and breathed his last. 38And the curtain of the temple was torn in two, from top to bottom. 39Now when the centurion, who stood facing him, saw that in this way he[p] breathed his last, he said, "Truly this man was God's Son!"[q]

40 There were also women looking on from a distance; among them were Mary Magdalene, and Mary the mother of James the younger and of Joses, and Salome. 41These used to follow him and provided for him when he was in Galilee; and there were many other women who had come up with him to Jerusalem.

The Burial of Jesus

42 When evening had come, and since it was the day of Preparation, that is, the day before the sabbath, 43Joseph of Arimathea, a respected member of the council, who was also himself waiting expectantly for the kingdom of God, went boldly to Pilate and asked for the body of Jesus. 44Then Pilate wondered if he were already dead; and summoning the centurion, he asked him whether he had been dead for some time. 45When he learned from the centurion that he was dead, he granted the body to Joseph. 46Then Joseph[r] bought a linen cloth, and taking down the body,[s] wrapped it in the linen cloth, and laid it in a tomb that had been hewn out of the rock. He then rolled a stone against the door of the tomb. 47Mary Magdalene and Mary the mother of Joses saw where the body[s] was laid.

The Resurrection of Jesus

16 When the sabbath was over, Mary Magdalene, and Mary the mother of James, and Salome bought spices, so that they might go and anoint him. 2And very early on the first day of the week, when the sun had risen, they went to the tomb. 3They had been saying to one another, "Who will roll away the stone for us from the entrance to the tomb?" 4When they looked up, they saw that the stone, which was very large, had already been rolled back. 5As they entered the tomb, they saw a young man, dressed in a white robe, sitting on the right side; and they were alarmed. 6But he said to them, "Do not be alarmed; you are looking for Jesus of Nazareth, who was crucified. He has been raised; he is not here. Look, there is the place they laid him. 7But go, tell his disciples and Peter that he is going ahead of you to Galilee; there you will see him, just as he told you." 8So they went out and fled from the tomb, for terror and amazement had seized them; and they said nothing to anyone, for they were afraid.[t]

The Shorter Ending of Mark

[And all that had been commanded them they told briefly to those around Peter. And afterward Jesus himself sent out through them, from east to west, the sacred and imperishable proclamation of eternal salvation.[u]]

The Longer Ending of Mark

Jesus Appears to Mary Magdalene

9 [Now after he rose early on the first day of the week, he appeared first to Mary Magdalene, from whom he had cast out seven demons. 10She went out and told those who had been with him, while they were mourning and weeping. 11But when they heard that he was alive and had been seen by her, they would not believe it.

[o] Other ancient authorities read *made me a reproach* [p] Other ancient authorities add *cried out and* [q] Or *a son of God* [r] Gk *he* [s] Gk *it* [t] Some of the most ancient authorities bring the book to a close at the end of verse 8. One authority concludes the book with the shorter ending; others include the shorter ending and then continue with verses 9–20. In most authorities verses 9–20 follow immediately after verse 8, though in some of these authorities the passage is marked as being doubtful. [u] Other ancient authorities add *Amen*

15.36 Ps 69.21
15.38 Heb 10.19,20
15.39 Mk 1.11; 9.7
15.40 Ps 38.11; Jn 19.25; Mk 16.1
15.41 Lk 8.1-3
15.42 Deut 21.22,23; Mt 27.62
15.43 Acts 13.50; 17.12; Lk 2.25,38
15.45 ver 39
16.1 Lk 23.56; Jn 19.39
16.3 Mk 15.46
16.5 Mk 9.15
16.6 ver 5; Mk 1.24
16.7 Mk 14.28; Jn 21.1-23

Jesus Appears to Two Disciples
12 After this he appeared in another form
to two of them, as they were walking into
the country. 13And they went back and told
the rest, but they did not believe them.

Jesus Commissions the Disciples
14 Later he appeared to the eleven themselves as they were sitting at the table; and
he upbraided them for their lack of faith
and stubbornness, because they had not
believed those who saw him after he had
risen.[v] 15And he said to them, "Go into all
the world and proclaim the good news[w] to
the whole creation. 16The one who believes
and is baptized will be saved; but the one
who does not believe will be condemned.
17And these signs will accompany those
who believe: by using my name they will
cast out demons; they will speak in new
tongues; 18they will pick up snakes in their
hands,[x] and if they drink any deadly thing,
it will not hurt them; they will lay their
hands on the sick, and they will recover."

The Ascension of Jesus
19 So then the Lord Jesus, after he had
spoken to them, was taken up into heaven
and sat down at the right hand of God.
20And they went out and proclaimed the
good news everywhere, while the Lord
worked with them and confirmed the message by the signs that accompanied it.[y]]

[v] Other ancient authorities add, in whole or in part, *And they excused themselves, saying, "This age of lawlessness and unbelief is under Satan, who does not allow the truth and power of God to prevail over the unclean things of the spirits. Therefore reveal your righteousness now"—thus they spoke to Christ. And Christ replied to them, "The term of years of Satan's power has been fulfilled, but other terrible things draw near. And for those who have sinned I was handed over to death, that they may return to the truth and sin no more, that they may inherit the spiritual and imperishable glory of righteousness that is in heaven."* [w] Or *gospel* [x] Other ancient authorities lack *in their hands* [y] Other ancient authorities add *Amen*

The Gospel According to

LUKE

See the Introductions, pp. 7–8 and 79–80 above.

Dedication to Theophilus
1 Since many have undertaken to set
down an orderly account of the events
that have been fulfilled among us, 2just as
they were handed on to us by those who
from the beginning were eyewitnesses and
servants of the word, 3I too decided, after
investigating everything carefully from the
very first,[a] to write an orderly account for
you, most excellent Theophilus, 4so that
you may know the truth concerning the
things about which you have been instructed.

The Birth of John the Baptist Foretold
5 In the days of King Herod of Judea,
there was a priest named Zechariah, who
belonged to the priestly order of Abijah. His
wife was a descendant of Aaron, and her
name was Elizabeth. 6Both of them were
righteous before God, living blamelessly
according to all the commandments and
regulations of the Lord. 7But they had no
children, because Elizabeth was barren, and
both were getting on in years.
8 Once when he was serving as priest
before God and his section was on duty, 9he
was chosen by lot, according to the custom
of the priesthood, to enter the sanctuary of
the Lord and offer incense. 10Now at the
time of the incense offering, the whole assembly of the people was praying outside.
11Then there appeared to him an angel of
the Lord, standing at the right side of the
altar of incense. 12When Zechariah saw him,
he was terrified; and fear overwhelmed him.

[a] Or *for a long time*

1.2 Heb 2.3; 1 Pet 5.1; 2 Pet 1.16; 1 Jn 1.1; Mk 1.1; Jn 15.27
1.3 Acts 11.4; 18.23; 1.1
1.5 Mt 2.1; 1 Chr 24.10
1.6 Gen 7.1; 1 Kings 9.4; 2 Kings 20.3
1.8 1 Chr 24.19; 2 Chr 8.14
1.9 Ex 30.7,8; 1 Chr 23.13; 2 Chr 29.11
1.10 Lev 16.17

1.1-4 Introduction.
In a literary style used by Greco-Roman authors, the writer (who is here given the traditional name of Luke) affirms that his narrative *account* is one among *many*, that it will be *orderly*, that it depends on the testimony of *eyewitnesses*, and that his aim is to impart the *truth* to his patron, *Theophilus* (whose name means *friend of God*).
1.5-4.13 The Preparations for Jesus' Birth and Ministry.
1.5-25 Dated to the reign of Herod of Judea (37-4 BCE), the story of the birth of John the Baptist recalls the account in 1 Sam 1, of an elderly couple who were unable to have a child but were given a son who was dedicated to the LORD (Samuel) and whose major role was to prepare for a new leader of God's people: Saul and then David (1 Sam 8-10, 15-16). The *angel's* instruction to *Zechariah*, John's priestly father, resembles Hannah's hymnic prayer in 1 Sam 2. John's role is compared with that of *Elijah*, who called God's people to account in a time of a wicked ruler (1 Kings 21-2 Kings 2). The climactic feature of John's work is to prepare *a people* for *the Lord*.

1.26-38 While Elizabeth is still pregnant with John (*in the sixth month*) Mary has an angelic visitor who promises her a son, who will take the place of his ancestor David as the ruler of God's people, but his rule will last *forever*. God's *power*, through the *Holy Spirit*, will come upon her, and without sexual union she will bear a son. Mary accepts this promise as in accord with God's *word*.

1.39-56 The convergence of these angelic messages comes when Mary visits Elizabeth and the child leaps in her womb, at which she acclaims the unborn child of Mary as *my Lord* and commends Mary's confidence in the divine promise of a son. Mary's praise of the Lord resembles closely Hannah's as reported in 1 Sam 2.1-10, including God's exaltation of the poor, and anticipates the inclusion of a wide segment of humanity in the people of *Abraham*.

13 But the angel said to him, "Do not be afraid, Zechariah, for your prayer has been heard. Your wife Elizabeth will bear you a son, and you will name him John. 14 You will have joy and gladness, and many will rejoice at his birth, 15 for he will be great in the sight of the Lord. He must never drink wine or strong drink; even before his birth he will be filled with the Holy Spirit. 16 He will turn many of the people of Israel to the Lord their God. 17 With the spirit and power of Elijah he will go before him, to turn the hearts of parents to their children, and the disobedient to the wisdom of the righteous, to make ready a people prepared for the Lord." 18 Zechariah said to the angel, "How will I know that this is so? For I am an old man, and my wife is getting on in years." 19 The angel replied, "I am Gabriel. I stand in the presence of God, and I have been sent to speak to you and to bring you this good news. 20 But now, because you did not believe my words, which will be fulfilled in their time, you will become mute, unable to speak, until the day these things occur."

21 Meanwhile the people were waiting for Zechariah, and wondered at his delay in the sanctuary. 22 When he did come out, he could not speak to them, and they realized that he had seen a vision in the sanctuary. He kept motioning to them and remained unable to speak. 23 When his time of service was ended, he went to his home.

24 After those days his wife Elizabeth conceived, and for five months she remained in seclusion. She said, 25 "This is what the Lord has done for me when he looked favorably on me and took away the disgrace I have endured among my people."

The Birth of Jesus Foretold

26 In the sixth month the angel Gabriel was sent by God to a town in Galilee called Nazareth, 27 to a virgin engaged to a man whose name was Joseph, of the house of David. The virgin's name was Mary. 28 And he came to her and said, "Greetings, favored one! The Lord is with you."[b] 29 But she was much perplexed by his words and pondered what sort of greeting this might be. 30 The angel said to her, "Do not be afraid, Mary, for you have found favor with God. 31 And now, you will conceive in your womb and bear a son, and you will name him Jesus. 32 He will be great, and will be called the Son of the Most High, and the Lord God will give to him the throne of his ancestor David. 33 He will reign over the house of Jacob forever, and of his kingdom there will be no end." 34 Mary said to the angel, "How can this be, since I am a virgin?"[c] 35 The angel said to her, "The Holy Spirit will come upon you, and the power of the Most High will overshadow you; therefore the child to be born[d] will be holy; he will be called Son of God. 36 And now, your relative Elizabeth in her old age has also conceived a son; and this is the sixth month for her who was said to be barren. 37 For nothing will be impossible with God." 38 Then Mary said, "Here am I, the servant of the Lord; let it be with me according to your word." Then the angel departed from her.

Mary Visits Elizabeth

39 In those days Mary set out and went with haste to a Judean town in the hill country, 40 where she entered the house of Zechariah and greeted Elizabeth. 41 When Elizabeth heard Mary's greeting, the child leaped in her womb. And Elizabeth was filled with the Holy Spirit 42 and exclaimed with a loud cry, "Blessed are you among women, and blessed is the fruit of your womb. 43 And why has this happened to me, that the mother of my Lord comes to me? 44 For as soon as I heard the sound of your greeting, the child in my womb leaped for joy. 45 And blessed is she who believed that there would be[e] a fulfillment of what was spoken to her by the Lord."

Mary's Song of Praise

46 And Mary[f] said,
"My soul magnifies the Lord,
47 and my spirit rejoices in God my Savior,
48 for he has looked with favor on the lowliness of his servant.
Surely, from now on all generations will call me blessed;
49 for the Mighty One has done great things for me,
and holy is his name.
50 His mercy is for those who fear him
from generation to generation.
51 He has shown strength with his arm;
he has scattered the proud in the

[b] Other ancient authorities add *Blessed are you among women* [c] Gk *I do not know a man* [d] Other ancient authorities add *of you* [e] Or *believed, for there will be* [f] Other ancient authorities read *Elizabeth*

1.13 ver 30,60,63
1.14 ver 58
1.15 Num 6.3; Judg 13.4; Lk 7.33; Jer 1.5; Gal 1.15
1.16 Mal 4.5,6
1.17 Mt 11.14; 17.13
1.18 Gen 17.17; ver 34
1.19 Dan 21-23; Mt 18.10
1.20 Ezek 3.26; 24.27
1.25 Gen 30.23; Isa 4.1
1.26 Mt 2.23
1.27 Mt 1.16; ver 19
1.28 Dan 9.23; 10.19
1.31 Isa 7.14; Lk 2.21
1.32 Mk 5.7; Isa 9.6,7; Jer 23.5; Rev 3.7
1.33 Dan 2.44; 7.14,27; Mt 28.18; Heb 1.8
1.35 ver 32; Mk 1.24; Mt 4.3
1.37 Gen 18.14; Jer 32.17; Mt 19.26; Mk 10.27; Lk 18.27; Rom 4.21
1.42 Judg 5.24; Lk 11.27,28
1.43 Lk 2.11
1.46 1 Sam 2.1-10; Ps 34.2,3
1.47 Ps 35.9; 1 Tim 1.1; 2.3; Titus 2.10; Jude 25
1.48 Ps 138.6; Lk 11.27
1.49 Ps 71.19; 111.9
1.50 Ps 103.17
1.51 Ps 98.1; Isa 40.10; Ps 33.10; 1 Pet 5.5

1.52 Job 5.11
1.53 Ps 34.10
1.54 Ps 98.3
1.55 Gen 17.19; Ps 132.11; Gal 3.16
1.58 Gen 19.19
1.59 Gen 17.12; Lev 12.3
1.66 Lk 2.19,51; Gen 39.2; Acts 11.21
1.67 ver 41; Joel 2.28
1.68 Ps 72.18; 111.9; Lk 7.16
1.69 Ps 18.2; 89.17; 132.17; Ezek 29.21
1.70 Jer 23.5; Dan 9.24; Acts 3.21; Rom 1.2
1.72 Mic 7.20; Ps 105.8,9; 106.45; Ezek 16.60
1.74 Rom 6.18; Heb 9.14
1.75 Eph 4.24; Titus 2.12
1.76 Mal 3.1; 4.5; Mt 11.9,10
1.77 Mk 1.4
1.79 Mt 9.2; Mk 4.16; Acts 26.18
1.80 Lk 2.40,52
2.4 Lk 1.27

thoughts of their hearts.
52 He has brought down the powerful from their thrones,
and lifted up the lowly;
53 he has filled the hungry with good things,
and sent the rich away empty.
54 He has helped his servant Israel,
in remembrance of his mercy,
55 according to the promise he made to our ancestors,
to Abraham and to his descendants forever."

56 And Mary remained with her about three months and then returned to her home.

The Birth of John the Baptist

57 Now the time came for Elizabeth to give birth, and she bore a son. 58 Her neighbors and relatives heard that the Lord had shown his great mercy to her, and they rejoiced with her.

59 On the eighth day they came to circumcise the child, and they were going to name him Zechariah after his father. 60 But his mother said, "No; he is to be called John." 61 They said to her, "None of your relatives has this name." 62 Then they began motioning to his father to find out what name he wanted to give him. 63 He asked for a writing tablet and wrote, "His name is John." And all of them were amazed. 64 Immediately his mouth was opened and his tongue freed, and he began to speak, praising God. 65 Fear came over all their neighbors, and all these things were talked about throughout the entire hill country of Judea. 66 All who heard them pondered them and said, "What then will this child become?" For, indeed, the hand of the Lord was with him.

Zechariah's Prophecy

67 Then his father Zechariah was filled with the Holy Spirit and spoke this prophecy:
68 "Blessed be the Lord God of Israel,
for he has looked favorably on his people and redeemed them.
69 He has raised up a mighty savior[g] for us
in the house of his servant David,
70 as he spoke through the mouth of his holy prophets from of old,
71 that we would be saved from our enemies and from the hand of all who hate us.
72 Thus he has shown the mercy promised to our ancestors,
and has remembered his holy covenant,
73 the oath that he swore to our ancestor Abraham,
to grant us 74 that we, being rescued from the hands of our enemies,
might serve him without fear, 75 in holiness and righteousness
before him all our days.
76 And you, child, will be called the prophet of the Most High;
for you will go before the Lord to prepare his ways,
77 to give knowledge of salvation to his people
by the forgiveness of their sins.
78 By the tender mercy of our God,
the dawn from on high will break upon[h] us,
79 to give light to those who sit in darkness
and in the shadow of death,
to guide our feet into the way of peace."

80 The child grew and became strong in spirit, and he was in the wilderness until the day he appeared publicly to Israel.

The Birth of Jesus

2 In those days a decree went out from Emperor Augustus that all the world should be registered. 2 This was the first registration and was taken while Quirinius was governor of Syria. 3 All went to their own towns to be registered. 4 Joseph also went from the town of Nazareth in Galilee to Judea, to the city of David called Bethlehem, because he was descended from the house and family of David. 5 He went to be registered with Mary, to whom he was engaged and who was expecting a child. 6 While they were there, the time came for her to deliver her child. 7 And she gave birth to her firstborn son and wrapped him in bands of cloth, and laid him in a manger, because there was no place for them in the inn.

The Shepherds and the Angels

8 In that region there were shepherds living in the fields, keeping watch over their

1.57-66. At the birth of John, his father writes down the child's name and recovers his power of speech, to the astonishment of the whole *hill country of Judea.* His prophecy concerns, not his new-born son, but the royal figure and the renewal of the covenant with God's people that he will achieve, bringing *light to those in darkness.* John lives the ascetic life in the *wilderness,* like Elijah (1 Kings 19), but is also to prepare there *the way of the Lord* (3.4; Isa 40.3-5).

2.1-20 Here and throughout his gospel and Acts, Luke mentions the secular authorities (*Emperor Augustus...Quirinius, governor of Syria*) in order to emphasize the public nature of the events he reports and how God works through human agents to achieve his purposes. Joseph and Mary live in *Nazareth in Galilee* but travel south to *Bethlehem* in Judea, which was the ancestral town of Joseph where they had to register for the imperial census. The details of the new-born child in the *manger* and the visit of the shepherds emphasize the simple human aspects of Jesus, while the angelic song shows the divine purpose to be achieved through him.

[g] Gk *a horn of salvation* [h] Other ancient authorities read *has broken upon*

2.21-38 The continuity between the traditions of Israel and what God was to do through Jesus is exemplified (1) by the presentation of him in the temple and the sacrifices offered (Lev 12.1-8; Ex 13.11-16), (2) by *Simeon's* recognition and affirmation of Jesus as *Messiah* and bringer of *revelation to the Gentiles* (Isa 49.6) as well as a cause of controversy within *Israel* (Isa 8.14), and (3) by the prophetess *Anna's* acclaim of Jesus as the one who will redeem *Jerusalem*, the symbol of God's people (Isa 52.7-10).
2.39-52 The piety of Jesus' family is evident in their annual participation in the *festival of the Passover*, which is here seen as linking the annual celebration of Israel's deliverance from Egypt (Deut 16) with that of unleavened bread (Lev 23), which symbolized the beginning of the new year. Jesus' growth in *wisdom* is exemplified by his interrogating the offical *teachers* in the temple and by his involvement in matters which concern *my Father*.

flock by night. 9 Then an angel of the Lord
stood before them, and the glory of the Lord
shone around them, and they were terrified.
10 But the angel said to them, "Do not be
afraid; for see—I am bringing you good
news of great joy for all the people: 11 to you
is born this day in the city of David a Savior,
who is the Messiah,[i] the Lord. 12 This will be
a sign for you: you will find a child wrapped
in bands of cloth and lying in a manger."
13 And suddenly there was with the angel a
multitude of the heavenly host,[j] praising
God and saying,
14 "Glory to God in the highest heaven,
and on earth peace among those whom
he favors!"[k]
15 When the angels had left them and
gone into heaven, the shepherds said to one
another, "Let us go now to Bethlehem and
see this thing that has taken place, which
the Lord has made known to us." 16 So they
went with haste and found Mary and Joseph,
and the child lying in the manger. 17 When
they saw this, they made known what had
been told them about this child; 18 and all
who heard it were amazed at what the
shepherds told them. 19 But Mary treasured
all these words and pondered them in her
heart. 20 The shepherds returned, glorifying
and praising God for all they had heard and
seen, as it had been told them.

Jesus Is Named

21 After eight days had passed, it was
time to circumcise the child; and he was
called Jesus, the name given by the angel
before he was conceived in the womb.

Jesus Is Presented in the Temple

22 When the time came for their purification according to the law of Moses, they
brought him up to Jerusalem to present him
to the Lord 23 (as it is written in the law of
the Lord, "Every firstborn male shall be
designated as holy to the Lord"), 24 and they
offered a sacrifice according to what is stated
in the law of the Lord, "a pair of turtledoves
or two young pigeons."
25 Now there was a man in Jerusalem
whose name was Simeon;[l] this man was
righteous and devout, looking forward to
the consolation of Israel, and the Holy Spirit
rested on him. 26 It had been revealed to him
by the Holy Spirit that he would not see
death before he had seen the Lord's Messiah.[m]
27 Guided by the Spirit, Simeon[n] came into
the temple; and when the parents brought
in the child Jesus, to do for him what was
customary under the law, 28 Simeon[o] took
him in his arms and praised God, saying,
29 "Master, now you are dismissing your
servant[p] in peace,
according to your word;
30 for my eyes have seen your salvation,
31 which you have prepared in the presence of all peoples,
32 a light for revelation to the Gentiles
and for glory to your people Israel."
33 And the child's father and mother
were amazed at what was being said about
him. 34 Then Simeon[l] blessed them and said
to his mother Mary, "This child is destined
for the falling and the rising of many in
Israel, and to be a sign that will be opposed
35 so that the inner thoughts of many will
be revealed—and a sword will pierce your
own soul too."
36 There was also a prophet, Anna[q] the
daughter of Phanuel, of the tribe of Asher.
She was of a great age, having lived with
her husband seven years after her marriage,
37 then as a widow to the age of eighty-four.
She never left the temple but worshiped
there with fasting and prayer night and
day. 38 At that moment she came, and began to praise God and to speak about the
child[r] to all who were looking for the redemption of Jerusalem.

The Return to Nazareth

39 When they had finished everything
required by the law of the Lord, they returned to Galilee, to their own town of
Nazareth. 40 The child grew and became
strong, filled with wisdom; and the favor of
God was upon him.

The Boy Jesus in the Temple

41 Now every year his parents went to
Jerusalem for the festival of the Passover.
42 And when he was twelve years old, they
went up as usual for the festival. 43 When
the festival was ended and they started to
return, the boy Jesus stayed behind in Jerusalem, but his parents did not know it.
44 Assuming that he was in the group of

[i] Or *the Christ* [j] Gk *army* [k] Other ancient authorities read *peace, goodwill among people* [l] Gk *Symeon* [m] Or *the Lord's Christ* [n] Gk *In the Spirit, he* [o] Gk *he* [p] Gk *slave* [q] Gk *Hanna* [r] Gk *him*

2.10 Mt 14.27
2.11 Jn 4.42; Mt 1.16; 16.16; Lk 1.43; Acts 2.36
2.12 1 Sam 2.34; 2 Kings 19.29; Isa 7.14
2.13 Dan 7.10; Rev 5.11
2.14 Isa 57.19; Lk 1.79; Rom 5.1; Eph 1.9; Phil 2.13
2.19 ver 51
2.20 Mt 9.8
2.21 Lk 1.59; 1.31
2.22 Lev 12.2-6
2.23 Ex 13.2,12; Num 3.13
2.25 ver 38; Lk 23.51
2.26 Ps 89.48; Heb 11.5
2.27 ver 22
2.29 ver 26
2.30 Isa 52.10; Lk 3.6
2.32 Isa 42.6; 49.6; Acts 13.47; 26.23
2.34 Mt 21.44; 1 Cor 1.23,24; 2 Cor 2.16; 1 Pet 2.7,8
2.36 Acts 21.9; Josh 19.24; 1 Tim 5.9
2.37 Acts 13.3; 1 Tim 5.5
2.38 ver 25; Lk 24.21
2.39 ver 51
2.40 ver 52; Lk 1.80
2.41 Ex 23.15; Deut 16.1-6

2.47 Mt 7.28; Mk 4.22,32; Jn 7.15,46
2.48 Mk 3.31-35
2.49 Jn 2.16
2.50 Mk 9.32; Lk 9.45
2.51 ver 19.39
2.52 ver 40; 1 Sam 2.26
3.1 Mt 27.2; 14.1
3.2 Jn 11.49; 18.13; Acts 4.6; Mt 26.3
3.4 Isa 40.3-5
3.6 Ps 98.2; Isa 52.10; Lk 2.30
3.7 Mt 12.34; 23.33
3.8 Jn 8.33,39
3.9 Mt 7.19; Heb 6.7,8
3.10 Acts 2.37
3.11 Jas 2.15,16
3.12 Lk 7.29
3.13 Lk 19.8
3.14 Ex 23.1; Lev 19.11
3.15 Acts 13.25
3.16 Acts 1.5; 11.16; 19.4
3.17 Isa 30.24; Mic 4.12; Mt 13.30
3.19 Mt 14.3,4; Mk 6.17,18
3.21 Lk 5.15; 6.12; 9.18,28; 11.1
3.22 Ps 2.7; Isa 42.1; Lk 9.35; Acts 10.38; 2 Pet 1.17
3.23 Mt 4.17; Acts 1.1; Jn 8.57; Lk 1.27

travelers, they went a day's journey. Then
they started to look for him among their
relatives and friends. 45When they did not
find him, they returned to Jerusalem to
search for him. 46After three days they found
him in the temple, sitting among the teachers, listening to them and asking them
questions. 47And all who heard him were
amazed at his understanding and his answers. 48When his parents[s] saw him they
were astonished; and his mother said to
him, "Child, why have you treated us like
this? Look, your father and I have been
searching for you in great anxiety." 49He
said to them, "Why were you searching for
me? Did you not know that I must be in my
Father's house?"[t] 50But they did not understand what he said to them. 51Then he went
down with them and came to Nazareth,
and was obedient to them. His mother treasured all these things in her heart.
52 And Jesus increased in wisdom and in
years,[u] and in divine and human favor.

The Proclamation of John the Baptist

3 In the fifteenth year of the reign of
Emperor Tiberius, when Pontius Pilate
was governor of Judea, and Herod was
ruler[v] of Galilee, and his brother Philip ruler[v]
of the region of Ituraea and Trachonitis,
and Lysanias ruler[v] of Abilene, 2during the
high priesthood of Annas and Caiaphas, the
word of God came to John son of Zechariah
in the wilderness. 3He went into all the
region around the Jordan, proclaiming a
baptism of repentance for the forgiveness of
sins, 4as it is written in the book of the
words of the prophet Isaiah,

"The voice of one crying out in the wilderness:
'Prepare the way of the Lord,
make his paths straight.
5 Every valley shall be filled,
and every mountain and hill shall be made low,
and the crooked shall be made straight,
and the rough ways made smooth;
6 and all flesh shall see the salvation of God.' "

7 John said to the crowds that came out
to be baptized by him, "You brood of vipers!
Who warned you to flee from the wrath to
come? 8Bear fruits worthy of repentance. Do
not begin to say to yourselves, 'We have
Abraham as our ancestor'; for I tell you,
God is able from these stones to raise up
children to Abraham. 9Even now the ax is
lying at the root of the trees; every tree
therefore that does not bear good fruit is cut
down and thrown into the fire."
10 And the crowds asked him, "What
then should we do?" 11In reply he said to
them, "Whoever has two coats must share
with anyone who has none; and whoever
has food must do likewise." 12Even tax
collectors came to be baptized, and they
asked him, "Teacher, what should we do?"
13He said to them, "Collect no more than
the amount prescribed for you." 14Soldiers
also asked him, "And we, what should we
do?" He said to them, "Do not extort money
from anyone by threats or false accusation,
and be satisfied with your wages."
15 As the people were filled with expectation, and all were questioning in their
hearts concerning John, whether he might
be the Messiah,[w] 16John answered all of
them by saying, "I baptize you with water;
but one who is more powerful than I is
coming; I am not worthy to untie the thong
of his sandals. He will baptize you with[x] the
Holy Spirit and fire. 17His winnowing fork
is in his hand, to clear his threshing floor
and to gather the wheat into his granary;
but the chaff he will burn with unquenchable
fire."
18 So, with many other exhortations, he
proclaimed the good news to the people.
19But Herod the ruler,[v] who had been rebuked by him because of Herodias, his
brother's wife, and because of all the evil
things that Herod had done, 20added to
them all by shutting up John in prison.

The Baptism of Jesus

21 Now when all the people were baptized, and when Jesus also had been baptized and was praying, the heaven was
opened, 22and the Holy Spirit descended
upon him in bodily form like a dove. And
a voice came from heaven, "You are my
Son, the Beloved;[y] with you I am well
pleased."[z]

The Ancestors of Jesus

23 Jesus was about thirty years old when
he began his work. He was the son (as was

[s] Gk *they* [t] Or *be about my Father's interests?* [u] Or *in stature* [v] Gk *tetrarch* [w] Or *the Christ* [x] Or *in* [y] Or *my beloved Son* [z] Other ancient authorities read *You are my Son, today I have begotten you*

3.1-20 John the Baptist's launching of his public prophetic activity is, like Jesus' birth, placed by Luke in the historical context of earthly rulers apparently in charge of these districts east (*Judea, Galilee*) and west (*Iturea, Trachonitis*) of the Jordan, and in Syria (*Abilene*, northwest of Damascus), while the real mover of history is God. John defines his role *in the wilderness* in terms of Isa 40.3-5, where the coming of *the Lord* leads to all humanity (*all flesh*) seeing God's salvation. Ethnic origin is irrelevant for membership in God's people (*children of Abraham*), as are such occupations as *tax-collector* or even Roman *soldier*. The commitment to a new life found public expression in the rite of *baptism*, but yet to come is the *more powerful* agent of God who will accomplish this renewal and purge God's people. The official hostility to John's message comes to a climax in the imprisonment of John by *Herod* (Antipas; ruled 4 BCE-39 CE).
3.21-22 The baptism of Jesus is described without mention of John, but with the public event of the Spirit's descent *bodily*, and with the private disclosure to Jesus that he is God's *Son*.
3.23-38 The genealogy of Jesus is here traced backward to *Adam*, the father of the human race, unlike Matthew's version (which moves from Abraham to Jesus; Mt 1.2-16).

4.1-13 Emphasizing the power of the *Spirit* upon Jesus, Luke parallels Matthew (Mt 4.1-11) in the account of the devil's effort – reinforced by a quotation from Scripture (4.10-11 = Ps 91.11-12) – to have Jesus exploit his special relationship to God (*Son*) for personal benefit or public show. The scriptures quoted by Jesus in rejecting the devil's proposals are Deut 8.3; 6.13,16.
4.14-9.50 Jesus' Public Ministry.
4.14-30 Emphasis on *the Spirit* is evident in the account of Jesus launching his ministry of proclamation and healing in Galilee. His strategy alternates between more formal presentations in the *synagogues* and public, spontaneous actions and statements. In his address to the gathering in Nazareth (4.18-19), he quotes from the prophet Isaiah (Isa 61.1-2; 58.6) and claims it is now being *fulfilled* in their midst. Anticipating rejection by his own people, Jesus recalls that it was among non-Israelites that *Elijah* and *Elisha* were able to cure human ills (1 Kings 17.1,8-9; 18.1-2; 2 Kings 5.14); this enrages his hearers, who try to execute him.

thought) of Joseph son of Heli, 24son of
Matthat, son of Levi, son of Melchi, son of
Jannai, son of Joseph, 25son of Mattathias,
son of Amos, son of Nahum, son of Esli, son
of Naggai, 26son of Maath, son of Mattathias,
son of Semein, son of Josech, son of Joda,
27son of Joanan, son of Rhesa, son of
Zerubbabel, son of Shealtiel,[a] son of Neri,
28son of Melchi, son of Addi, son of Cosam,
son of Elmadam, son of Er, 29son of Joshua,
son of Eliezer, son of Jorim, son of Matthat,
son of Levi, 30son of Simeon, son of Judah,
son of Joseph, son of Jonam, son of Eliakim,
31son of Melea, son of Menna, son of
Mattatha, son of Nathan, son of David,
32son of Jesse, son of Obed, son of Boaz, son
of Sala,[b] son of Nahshon, 33son of
Amminadab, son of Admin, son of Arni,[c]
son of Hezron, son of Perez, son of Judah,
34son of Jacob, son of Isaac, son of Abraham,
son of Terah, son of Nahor, 35son of Serug,
son of Reu, son of Peleg, son of Eber, son
of Shelah, 36son of Cainan, son of Arphaxad,
son of Shem, son of Noah, son of Lamech,
37son of Methuselah, son of Enoch, son of
Jared, son of Mahalaleel, son of Cainan,
38son of Enos, son of Seth, son of Adam, son
of God.

The Temptation of Jesus

4 Jesus, full of the Holy Spirit, returned
from the Jordan and was led by the
Spirit in the wilderness, 2where for forty
days he was tempted by the devil. He ate
nothing at all during those days, and when
they were over, he was famished. 3The devil
said to him, "If you are the Son of God,
command this stone to become a loaf of
bread." 4Jesus answered him, "It is written,
'One does not live by bread alone.'"
5 Then the devil[d] led him up and showed
him in an instant all the kingdoms of the
world. 6And the devil[d] said to him, "To you
I will give their glory and all this authority;
for it has been given over to me, and I give
it to anyone I please. 7If you, then, will
worship me, it will all be yours." 8Jesus
answered him, "It is written,
'Worship the Lord your God,
and serve only him.'"
9 Then the devil[d] took him to Jerusalem,
and placed him on the pinnacle of the
temple, saying to him, "If you are the Son
of God, throw yourself down from here,
10for it is written,
'He will command his angels concerning
you,
to protect you,'
11and
'On their hands they will bear you up,
so that you will not dash your foot
against a stone.'"
12Jesus answered him, "It is said, 'Do not
put the Lord your God to the test.'" 13When
the devil had finished every test, he departed from him until an opportune time.

The Beginning of the Galilean Ministry

14 Then Jesus, filled with the power of
the Spirit, returned to Galilee, and a report
about him spread through all the surrounding country. 15He began to teach in their
synagogues and was praised by everyone.

The Rejection of Jesus at Nazareth

16 When he came to Nazareth, where he
had been brought up, he went to the synagogue on the sabbath day, as was his custom. He stood up to read, 17and the scroll
of the prophet Isaiah was given to him. He
unrolled the scroll and found the place
where it was written:
18 "The Spirit of the Lord is upon me,
because he has anointed me
to bring good news to the poor.
He has sent me to proclaim release to the
captives
and recovery of sight to the blind,
to let the oppressed go free,
19 to proclaim the year of the Lord's favor."
20And he rolled up the scroll, gave it back
to the attendant, and sat down. The eyes of
all in the synagogue were fixed on him.
21Then he began to say to them, "Today
this scripture has been fulfilled in your
hearing." 22All spoke well of him and were
amazed at the gracious words that came
from his mouth. They said, "Is not this
Joseph's son?" 23He said to them, "Doubtless
you will quote to me this proverb, 'Doctor,
cure yourself!' And you will say, 'Do here
also in your hometown the things that we
have heard you did at Capernaum.'" 24And
he said, "Truly I tell you, no prophet is
accepted in the prophet's hometown. 25But
the truth is, there were many widows in
Israel in the time of Elijah, when the heaven

[a] Gk *Salathiel* [b] Other ancient authorities read *Salmon* [c] Other ancient authorities read *Amminadab, son of Aram*; others vary widely [d] Gk *he*

3.27 Mt 1.12
3.31 2 Sam 5.14; 1 Chr 3.5
3.32 Ruth 4.88ff; 1 Chr 2.10ff
3.34 Gen 11.24,26
3.36 Gen 11.12; 5.6ff
3.38 Gen 5.2,2
4.1 ver 14; Lk 2.27
4.2 Ex 34.28; 1 Kings 19.8
4.4 Deut 8.3
4.6 Jn 12.31; 14.30; 1 Jn 5.19
4.8 Deut 6.13
4.10 Ps 91.11,12
4.12 Deut 6.16
4.13 Jn 14.30; Heb 4.15
4.14 Mt 9.26
4.15 Mt 9.35; 11.1
4.16 Mt 13.54; Mk 6.1; Acts 13.14-16
4.18 Isa 61.1,2; Mt 12.18
4.19 Lev 25.10
4.20 ver 17
4.22 Ps 45.2; Mt 13.54,55 Mk 6.2,3; Jn 6.42; 7.15
4.23 Mk 1.2ff; 2.1ff; ver 16
4.24 Mt 13.57; Mk 6.4; Jn 4.44
4.25 1 Kings 17.9 8-16; 18.1; Jas 5.17,18

4.27 2 Kings 5.1-14
4.29 Num 15.35; Acts 7.58; Heb 13.12
4.30 Jn 8.59; 10.39
4.31 Mt 4.13
4.32 Mt 7.28; Mk 11.18; Jn 7.46
4.34 ver 41; Ps 16.10; Dan 9.24
4.35 ver 39,41; Mt 8.26; Mk 4.39; Lk 8.24
4.36 ver 32
4.37 ver 14
4.39 ver 35,41
4.40 Mk 5.23; Mt 4.23
4.41 Mt 4.3; 8.4
4.42 Mk 1.35-38
4.44 Mt 4.18-22; Mk 1.16-20; Jn 1.40-42
5.3 Mt 13.1,2; Mk 4.1
5.4 Jn 21.6
5.5 Lk 8.24,45; 9.33,49; 17.13
5.10 Mt 14.27
5.11 ver 28; Mt 19.29
5.12 Lk 17.11-19

was shut up three years and six months,
and there was a severe famine over all the
land; 26yet Elijah was sent to none of them
except to a widow at Zarephath in Sidon.
27There were also many lepers[e] in Israel in
the time of the prophet Elisha, and none of
them was cleansed except Naaman the
Syrian." 28When they heard this, all in the
synagogue were filled with rage. 29They got
up, drove him out of the town, and led him
to the brow of the hill on which their town
was built, so that they might hurl him off
the cliff. 30But he passed through the midst
of them and went on his way.

The Man with an Unclean Spirit

31 He went down to Capernaum, a city
in Galilee, and was teaching them on the
sabbath. 32They were astounded at his teaching, because he spoke with authority. 33In
the synagogue there was a man who had
the spirit of an unclean demon, and he cried
out with a loud voice, 34"Let us alone! What
have you to do with us, Jesus of Nazareth?
Have you come to destroy us? I know who
you are, the Holy One of God." 35But Jesus
rebuked him, saying, "Be silent, and come
out of him!" When the demon had thrown
him down before them, he came out of him
without having done him any harm. 36They
were all amazed and kept saying to one
another, "What kind of utterance is this?
For with authority and power he commands the unclean spirits, and out they
come!" 37And a report about him began to
reach every place in the region.

Healings at Simon's House

38 After leaving the synagogue he entered Simon's house. Now Simon's mother-
in-law was suffering from a high fever, and
they asked him about her. 39Then he stood
over her and rebuked the fever, and it left
her. Immediately she got up and began to
serve them.
40 As the sun was setting, all those who
had any who were sick with various kinds
of diseases brought them to him; and he
laid his hands on each of them and cured
them. 41Demons also came out of many,
shouting, "You are the Son of God!" But he
rebuked them and would not allow them to
speak, because they knew that he was the
Messiah.[f]

Jesus Preaches in the Synagogues

42 At daybreak he departed and went
into a deserted place. And the crowds were
looking for him; and when they reached
him, they wanted to prevent him from leaving them. 43But he said to them, "I must
proclaim the good news of the kingdom of
God to the other cities also; for I was sent
for this purpose." 44So he continued proclaiming the message in the synagogues of
Judea.[g]

Jesus Calls the First Disciples

5 Once while Jesus[h] was standing beside
the lake of Gennesaret, and the crowd
was pressing in on him to hear the word
of God, 2he saw two boats there at the shore
of the lake; the fishermen had gone out of
them and were washing their nets. 3He got
into one of the boats, the one belonging to
Simon, and asked him to put out a little
way from the shore. Then he sat down and
taught the crowds from the boat. 4When he
had finished speaking, he said to Simon,
"Put out into the deep water and let down
your nets for a catch." 5Simon answered,
"Master, we have worked all night long but
have caught nothing. Yet if you say so, I
will let down the nets." 6When they had
done this, they caught so many fish that
their nets were beginning to break. 7So they
signaled their partners in the other boat to
come and help them. And they came and
filled both boats, so that they began to sink.
8But when Simon Peter saw it, he fell down
at Jesus' knees, saying, "Go away from me,
Lord, for I am a sinful man!" 9For he and
all who were with him were amazed at the
catch of fish that they had taken; 10and so
also were James and John, sons of Zebedee,
who were partners with Simon. Then Jesus
said to Simon, "Do not be afraid; from now
on you will be catching people." 11When
they had brought their boats to shore, they
left everything and followed him.

Jesus Cleanses a Leper

12 Once, when he was in one of the
cities, there was a man covered with leprosy.[e]
When he saw Jesus, he bowed with his face
to the ground and begged him, "Lord, if you
choose, you can make me clean." 13Then
Jesus[h] stretched out his hand, touched him,

[e] The terms *leper* and *leprosy* can refer to several diseases [f] Or *the Christ* [g] Other ancient authorities read *Galilee* [h] Gk *he*

4.31-41 *Capernaum,* a small city on the shore of Galilee, is the setting for Jesus' early activity according to Mark (1.16-21) and now his home, as well as the home of his first disciples (Mk 2.1). The *demon* recognizes in Jesus the power of destruction of the powers of evil, and is overcome by Jesus' word of *authority.* Simon's [Peter's] marriage is mentioned in 1 Cor 9.5. The *fever* of his *mother-in-law* is controlled by Jesus' commanding word (*rebuked*), as are the demons, who recognize in Jesus their conqueror as *Son of God.* He orders them to be silent, since it is not their kind of testimony that he seeks as *Messiah.*
4.42-44 Luke's survey of the launching of Jesus' ministry shows him alternating between public proclamation (*in the synagogues*) and retreat to remote private (*deserted*) places. Although there is mention of his activity *in Judea,* the story which follows has him in Galilee, according to some ancient manuscripts.
5.1-11 The *Lake of Genessaret,* another name for the Sea of Galilee, derives from a district on the southwest shore of the lake. Although the story initially resembles that of Jesus' call of the fishermen in Mk 1.16-20 (Mt 4.18-22), the details of the miraculous catch of fish correspond with John 21.1-11. Central in the narrative are the disbelief and subsequent confession of Simon Peter and the comparison between this catch and the disciples' call to *catch people.*
5.12-16 The story of the cleansing of the leper by Jesus follows the account in Mk 1.40-45, including the instruction to make the offering before the priest, as commanded in Lev 13.49; 14.2-32.

5.17-26 Again the story of the healing of the paralytic follows Mk 2.1-12, but the roof is made with *tiles* instead of mud, and the man is lowered on a *bed* instead of a pallet. The grant of healing is linked, as in Mark, with the forgiveness of sins which Jesus pronounces.
5.27-31 As in Mk 2.13-17, Jesus invites a tax collector – one of a group despised for violation of both ritual and national Jewish standards – to become a member of his inner circle of followers.
5.33-39 Jesus' refusal to demand ascetic behavior of his *disciples* is defended by him on the ground that the newness of the way of life that he brings is incompatible with the old standards. 5.39, which is omitted in some ancient manuscripts, notes that those fond of the old ways will not accept the new.
6.1-5 The climax of this incident, in which Jesus' followers help themselves to grain (as allowed in the Jewish law; Deut 23.25) but do so on the sabbath (Ex 20.10), comes with an appeal to the precedent of David's having eaten out of necessity bread forbidden to non-priests (1 Sam 21.1-7) and with the affirmation of Jesus' (*the Son of Man's*) lordship over *the sabbath*.

and said, "I do choose. Be made clean."
Immediately the leprosy[i] left him. 14 And he
ordered him to tell no one. "Go," he said,
"and show yourself to the priest, and, as
Moses commanded, make an offering for
your cleansing, for a testimony to them."
15 But now more than ever the word about
Jesus[j] spread abroad; many crowds would
gather to hear him and to be cured of their
diseases. 16 But he would withdraw to deserted places and pray.

Jesus Heals a Paralytic

17 One day, while he was teaching,
Pharisees and teachers of the law were
sitting near by (they had come from every
village of Galilee and Judea and from Jerusalem); and the power of the Lord was with
him to heal.[k] 18 Just then some men came,
carrying a paralyzed man on a bed. They
were trying to bring him in and lay him
before Jesus;[j] 19 but finding no way to bring
him in because of the crowd, they went up
on the roof and let him down with his bed
through the tiles into the middle of the
crowd[l] in front of Jesus. 20 When he saw
their faith, he said, "Friend,[m] your sins are
forgiven you." 21 Then the scribes and the
Pharisees began to question, "Who is this
who is speaking blasphemies? Who can
forgive sins but God alone?" 22 When Jesus
perceived their questionings, he answered
them, "Why do you raise such questions in
your hearts? 23 Which is easier, to say, 'Your
sins are forgiven you,' or to say, 'Stand up
and walk'? 24 But so that you may know
that the Son of Man has authority on earth
to forgive sins"—he said to the one who
was paralyzed—"I say to you, stand up and
take your bed and go to your home." 25 Immediately he stood up before them, took
what he had been lying on, and went to his
home, glorifying God. 26 Amazement seized
all of them, and they glorified God and were
filled with awe, saying, "We have seen
strange things today."

Jesus Calls Levi

27 After this he went out and saw a tax
collector named Levi, sitting at the tax booth;
and he said to him, "Follow me." 28 And he
got up, left everything, and followed him.
29 Then Levi gave a great banquet for
him in his house; and there was a large
crowd of tax collectors and others sitting at
the table[n] with them. 30 The Pharisees and
their scribes were complaining to his disciples, saying, "Why do you eat and drink
with tax collectors and sinners?" 31 Jesus
answered, "Those who are well have no
need of a physician, but those who are sick;
32 I have come to call not the righteous but
sinners to repentance."

The Question about Fasting

33 Then they said to him, "John's disciples, like the disciples of the Pharisees, frequently fast and pray, but your disciples eat
and drink. 34 Jesus said to them, "You cannot make wedding guests fast while the
bridegroom is with them, can you? 35 The
days will come when the bridegroom will be
taken away from them, and then they will
fast in those days." 36 He also told them a
parable: "No one tears a piece from a new
garment and sews it on an old garment;
otherwise the new will be torn, and the
piece from the new will not match the old.
37 And no one puts new wine into old wineskins; otherwise the new wine will burst the
skins and will be spilled, and the skins will
be destroyed. 38 But new wine must be put
into fresh wineskins. 39 And no one after
drinking old wine desires new wine, but
says, 'The old is good.'"[o]

The Question about the Sabbath

6 One sabbath[p] while Jesus[q] was going
through the grainfields, his disciples
plucked some heads of grain, rubbed them
in their hands, and ate them. 2 But some of
the Pharisees said, "Why are you doing
what is not lawful[r] on the sabbath?" 3 Jesus
answered, "Have you not read what David
did when he and his companions were
hungry? 4 He entered the house of God and
took and ate the bread of the Presence,
which it is not lawful for any but the priests
to eat, and gave some to his companions?"
5 Then he said to them, "The Son of Man is
lord of the sabbath."

[i] The terms *leper* and *leprosy* can refer to several diseases [j] Gk *him* [k] Other ancient authorities read *was present to heal them* [l] Gk *into the midst* [m] Gk *Man* [n] Gk *reclining* [o] Other ancient authorities read *better*; others lack verse 39 [p] Other ancient authorities read *On the second first sabbath* [q] Gk *he* [r] Other ancient authorities add *to do*

5.14 Lev 13.49; 14.2-32
5.15 Mt 9.26; Lk 4.14,37
5.16 Mt 14.13; Mk 6.46; Lk 3.21; 6.12; 9.18,28; 11.1
5.17 Mt 15.1; Mk 5.30; Lk 6.19
5.19 Mt 24.17
5.20 Lk 7.48,49
5.21 Isa 43.25
5.26 Lk 7.16
5.28 ver 11
5.29 Lk 15.1
5.30 Acts 23.9
5.32 1 Tim 1.15
5.33 Lk 7.18; Jn 3.25,26
5.35 Lk 9.22; 17.22
6.1 Deut 23.25
6.2 Ex 20.10; 23.12; Deut 5.14
6.3 1 Sam 21.6
6.4 Lev 24.9

The Man with a Withered Hand

6 On another sabbath he entered the
synagogue and taught, and there was a
man there whose right hand was withered.
[7]The scribes and the Pharisees watched him
to see whether he would cure on the sabbath,
so that they might find an accusation against
him. [8]Even though he knew what they
were thinking, he said to the man who had
the withered hand, "Come and stand here."
He got up and stood there. [9]Then Jesus said
to them, "I ask you, is it lawful to do good
or to do harm on the sabbath, to save life
or to destroy it?" [10]After looking around at
all of them, he said to him, "Stretch out
your hand." He did so, and his hand was
restored. [11]But they were filled with fury
and discussed with one another what they
might do to Jesus.

Jesus Chooses the Twelve Apostles

12 Now during those days he went out
to the mountain to pray; and he spent the
night in prayer to God. [13]And when day
came, he called his disciples and chose twelve
of them, whom he also named apostles:
[14]Simon, whom he named Peter, and his
brother Andrew, and James, and John, and
Philip, and Bartholomew, [15]and Matthew,
and Thomas, and James son of Alphaeus,
and Simon, who was called the Zealot,
[16]and Judas son of James, and Judas Iscariot,
who became a traitor.

Jesus Teaches and Heals

17 He came down with them and stood
on a level place, with a great crowd of his
disciples and a great multitude of people
from all Judea, Jerusalem, and the coast of
Tyre and Sidon. [18]They had come to hear
him and to be healed of their diseases; and
those who were troubled with unclean spirits
were cured. [19]And all in the crowd were
trying to touch him, for power came out
from him and healed all of them.

Blessings and Woes

20 Then he looked up at his disciples and
said:
"Blessed are you who are poor,
for yours is the kingdom of God.
21 "Blessed are you who are hungry now,
for you will be filled.
"Blessed are you who weep now,
for you will laugh.

22 "Blessed are you when people hate
you, and when they exclude you, revile
you, and defame you[s] on account of the
Son of Man. [23]Rejoice in that day and leap
for joy, for surely your reward is great in
heaven; for that is what their ancestors did
to the prophets.
24 "But woe to you who are rich,
for you have received your consolation.
25 "Woe to you who are full now,
for you will be hungry.
"Woe to you who are laughing now,
for you will mourn and weep.

26 "Woe to you when all speak well of
you, for that is what their ancestors did to
the false prophets.

Love for Enemies

27 "But I say to you that listen, Love
your enemies, do good to those who hate
you, [28]bless those who curse you, pray for
those who abuse you. [29]If anyone strikes
you on the cheek, offer the other also; and
from anyone who takes away your coat do
not withhold even your shirt. [30]Give to
everyone who begs from you; and if anyone
takes away your goods, do not ask for them
again. [31]Do to others as you would have
them do to you.

32 "If you love those who love you,
what credit is that to you? For even sinners
love those who love them. [33]If you do good
to those who do good to you, what credit
is that to you? For even sinners do the
same. [34]If you lend to those from whom you
hope to receive, what credit is that to you?
Even sinners lend to sinners, to receive as
much again. [35]But love your enemies, do
good, and lend, expecting nothing in return.[t]
Your reward will be great, and you will be
children of the Most High; for he is kind to
the ungrateful and the wicked. [36]Be merciful,
just as your Father is merciful.

Judging Others

37 "Do not judge, and you will not be
judged; do not condemn, and you will not
be condemned. Forgive, and you will be
forgiven; [38]give, and it will be given to you.
A good measure, pressed down, shaken
together, running over, will be put into

[s] Gk *cast out your name as evil* [t] Other ancient authorities read *despairing of no one*

6.6-11 The critics in this version of the story of the healing of the man with the withered hand (Mk 3.1-6) are specified to be *scribes* (the professional interpreters of the law) and *Pharisees*.
6.12-16 Luke's account of Jesus' call of the twelve followers (see Mk 3.13-19) notes the special time of preparation through extended prayer all night long. They are here designated as *apostles*, rather than disciples (also in Mk 6.30; Mt 10.2). The list of the twelve varies from that of Mark in sequence and in its inclusion of a second Judas, and in its calling Simon *the Zealot* (which before the Jewish revolt of 66-70 CE indicated a strong commitment rather than Jewish nationalism).
6.17-4 The Sermon on the Plain.
6.17-19 Unlike Matthew's version of Jesus' instruction to his disciples, which (like Moses' giving the Law to Israel) occurs on a mountain (Mt 5.1), he here speaks to a crowd gathered from all over the region *on a level place*. They have come not only to hear but also to be healed.
6.20-26 Luke's version of Jesus' pronouncements of blessing (often called the Beatitudes) differs from Matthew's (5.3-12) in that (1) they are in the second person (*you who are poor*); (2) they are promises for God's future reversal of the plight of his people (*you who weep now will laugh*); and (3) they are matched by warnings of the deprivations that are coming for those now enjoying power and plenty.
6.27-36 The commandment to *love your enemies* involves not merely attitude but action, and the model for this transforming mode of human dealings is God, whose children are called to match his compassion and generosity (*cf.* Mt 5.39-42,44-48).
6.37-42 To abstain from critical attitudes toward others and to be generous instead will result in forgiveness and generosity from God (*will be given* by God). Essential is self-examination, of one's own modest position (a *disciple* means a learner) and failures (*the log* in one's eye).

6.6 Lk 13.14; 14.3; Jn 9.16
6.8 Mt 9.4
6.12 Mt 14.23; Lk 9.28
6.13 Mk 6.30
6.16 Jude 1
6.17 Mt 4.25; Mk 3.7,8
6.19 Mt 9.21; 14.36; Mk 3.10; Lk 5.17
6.21 Isa 61.3
6.22 1 Pet 4.14; Jn 9.22; 16.2
6.23 Acts 5.41; Col 1.24; Mal 4.2; Acts 7.51
6.24 Jas 5.1; Lk 16.25
6.25 Isa 65.13; Prov 14.13
6.26 Jn 15.19
6.27 ver 35; Rom 12.20
6.28 Lk 23.34; Acts 7.60
6.30 Deut 15.7,8,10; Prov 21.26
6.31 Mt 7.12
6.35 ver 27,30
6.37 Rom 2.1
6.38 Mk 4.24; Jas 2.13

6.43-49 The surest evidence of the inner condition of anyone is the outward manner of life, *good* or *evil*. Similarly, Jesus' true follower will not merely address him as *Lord*, but will obey his words. Those who do obey are compared with a well-founded building that can withstand the powerful destructive currents of life.
7.1-10 Luke's version of this story (see Mt 8.5-13) reports the Roman military officer (*centurion*, in charge of one hundred soldiers) sending his request for the healing of his *slave* through *some Jewish elders*, who report that he has built a *synagogue* for them (one of two New Testament references to a synagogue as a building rather than a meeting; see Acts 18.7). His unique confidence (*faith*) in Jesus' power to heal results in a cure of the slave and a commendation from Jesus.
7.11-17 Found only in Luke, this story, which extends Jesus' healing power to restoring life to the dead, recalls Elijah's raising a widow's son (1 Kings 17.8-24) and leads to his acclaim as *a great prophet*. *Nain* is in southern Galilee.
7.18-35 Jesus in Contrast with John the Baptist. The question sent to Jesus by the imprisoned John is whether Jesus is the agent for the renewal of God's people (*the one who is to come*). Instead of a simple verbal answer, Jesus points to what he has been doing in his ministry of healing and proclamation of good news to the ailing, the dead and *the poor*, using phrases from Isaiah (29.18-19; 35.5-6; 61.1) which describe the transformation that will take place when the rule of God is established in the new order of creation. Some will find his claims *an offense*. Describing John in terms of Elijah, the prophet in the wilderness (1 Kings 17.3-7; 19.4), Jesus declares that John is the God-sent messenger (Ex.23.20; Mal 3.1) to prepare the way for him, a role which also prepared many people, including even *tax collectors*, through *baptism* for a place in *the kingdom of God*. Many pious Jews and their leaders were offended by John's asceticism (*no bread...no wine*), and also by Jesus' free and open ways, which they considered to be rebellious (*glutton and drunkard*; Deut 21.18-21) and in violation of the limits for God's people (*friend of tax collectors and sinners*). God's *wisdom* will provide its own vindication in future events (*children*).

your lap; for the measure you give will be the measure you get back."

39 He also told them a parable: "Can a blind person guide a blind person? Will not both fall into a pit? 40A disciple is not above the teacher, but everyone who is fully qualified will be like the teacher. 41Why do you see the speck in your neighbor's[u] eye, but do not notice the log in your own eye? 42Or how can you say to your neighbor,[v] 'Friend,[v] let me take out the speck in your eye,' when you yourself do not see the log in your own eye? You hypocrite, first take the log out of your own eye, and then you will see clearly to take the speck out of your neighbor's[u] eye.

A Tree and Its Fruit

43 "No good tree bears bad fruit, nor again does a bad tree bear good fruit; 44for each tree is known by its own fruit. Figs are not gathered from thorns, nor are grapes picked from a bramble bush. 45The good person out of the good treasure of the heart produces good, and the evil person out of evil treasure produces evil; for it is out of the abundance of the heart that the mouth speaks.

The Two Foundations

46 "Why do you call me 'Lord, Lord,' and do not do what I tell you? 47I will show you what someone is like who comes to me, hears my words, and acts on them. 48That one is like a man building a house, who dug deeply and laid the foundation on rock; when a flood arose, the river burst against that house but could not shake it, because it had been well built.[w] 49But the one who hears and does not act is like a man who built a house on the ground without a foundation. When the river burst against it, immediately it fell, and great was the ruin of that house."

Jesus Heals a Centurion's Servant

7 After Jesus[x] had finished all his sayings in the hearing of the people, he entered Capernaum. 2A centurion there had a slave whom he valued highly, and who was ill and close to death. 3When he heard about Jesus, he sent some Jewish elders to him, asking him to come and heal his slave. 4When they came to Jesus, they appealed to him earnestly, saying, "He is worthy of having you do this for him, 5for he loves our people, and it is he who built our synagogue for us." 6And Jesus went with them, but when he was not far from the house, the centurion sent friends to say to him, "Lord, do not trouble yourself, for I am not worthy to have you come under my roof; 7therefore I did not presume to come to you. But only speak the word, and let my servant be healed. 8For I also am a man set under authority, with soldiers under me; and I say to one, 'Go,' and he goes, and to another, 'Come,' and he comes, and to my slave, 'Do this,' and the slave does it." 9When Jesus heard this he was amazed at him, and turning to the crowd that followed him, he said, "I tell you, not even in Israel have I found such faith." 10When those who had been sent returned to the house, they found the slave in good health.

Jesus Raises the Widow's Son at Nain

11 Soon afterwards[y] he went to a town called Nain, and his disciples and a large crowd went with him. 12As he approached the gate of the town, a man who had died was being carried out. He was his mother's only son, and she was a widow; and with her was a large crowd from the town. 13When the Lord saw her, he had compassion for her and said to her, "Do not weep." 14Then he came forward and touched the bier, and the bearers stood still. And he said, "Young man, I say to you, rise!" 15The dead man sat up and began to speak, and Jesus[x] gave him to his mother. 16Fear seized all of them; and they glorified God, saying, "A great prophet has risen among us!" and "God has looked favorably on his people!" 17This word about him spread throughout Judea and all the surrounding country.

Messengers from John the Baptist

18 The disciples of John reported all these things to him. So John summoned two of his disciples 19and sent them to the Lord to ask, "Are you the one who is to come, or are we to wait for another?" 20When the men had come to him, they said, "John the Baptist has sent us to you to ask, 'Are you

[u] Gk *brother's* [v] Gk *brother* [w] Other ancient authorities read *founded upon the rock* [x] Gk *he* [y] Other ancient authorities read *Next day*

6.39 Mt 15.4
6.40 Mt 10.24; Jn 13.16; 15.20
6.43 Mt 7.15,16,20
6.44 Mt 12.33
6.45 Mt 12.34,35; Mk 7.20
6.46 Mt 7.21
6.47 Jas 1.22-25
7.1 Mt 7.28
7.9 ver 50
7.11 1 Kings 17.17-24; 2 Kings 4.32-37; Mk 5.21-24,35-43; Jn 11.1-44
7.13 ver 19; Lk 10.1; 11.1,39; 12.42; 13.15; 17.5,6; 18.6; 19.8; 22.61; 24.34
7.14 Lk 8.54; Jn 11.43; Acts 9.40
7.16 Lk 1.65; Jn 6.14; Lk 1.68

7.21 Mt 4.23; Mk 3.10
7.22 Isa 29.18,19; 35.5,6; Lk 4.18
7.29 Mt 21.32; Lk 3.12
7.30 Mt 22.35; Acts 20.27
7.33 Lk 1.15
7.34 Lk 5.29; 15.1,2
7.36 Mt 26.6-13; 4.3-9; Jn 12.1-8
7.39 ver 16; Lk 24.19; Jn 6.14
7.41 Mt 18.28
7.44 Gen 18.4; 19.2; 43.24; Judg 19.21; 1 Tim 5.10
7.46 Ps 23.5
7.48 Mt 9.2; Mk 2.5; Lk 5.20
7.50 Mt 9.22; Mk 5.34; Lk 8.48
8.1 Mt 4.23
8.2 Mt 27.55,56

the one who is to come, or are we to wait
for another?'" 21 Jesus[z] had just then cured
many people of diseases, plagues, and evil
spirits, and had given sight to many who
were blind. 22 And he answered them, "Go
and tell John what you have seen and
heard: the blind receive their sight, the lame
walk, the lepers[a] are cleansed, the deaf
hear, the dead are raised, the poor have
good news brought to them. 23 And blessed
is anyone who takes no offense at me."

24 When John's messengers had gone,
Jesus[b] began to speak to the crowds about
John:[c] "What did you go out into the wilderness to look at? A reed shaken by the
wind? 25 What then did you go out to see?
Someone[d] dressed in soft robes? Look, those
who put on fine clothing and live in luxury
are in royal palaces. 26 What then did you
go out to see? A prophet? Yes, I tell you,
and more than a prophet. 27 This is the one
about whom it is written,

'See, I am sending my messenger ahead
of you,
who will prepare your way before you.'

28 I tell you, among those born of women no
one is greater than John; yet the least in the
kingdom of God is greater than he." 29 (And
all the people who heard this, including the
tax collectors, acknowledged the justice of
God,[e] because they had been baptized with
John's baptism. 30 But by refusing to be
baptized by him, the Pharisees and the
lawyers rejected God's purpose for themselves.)

31 "To what then will I compare the
people of this generation, and what are they
like? 32 They are like children sitting in the
marketplace and calling to one another,

'We played the flute for you, and you did
not dance;
we wailed, and you did not weep.'

33 For John the Baptist has come eating no
bread and drinking no wine, and you say,
'He has a demon'; 34 the Son of Man has
come eating and drinking, and you say,
'Look, a glutton and a drunkard, a friend
of tax collectors and sinners!' 35 Nevertheless, wisdom is vindicated by all her children."

A Sinful Woman Forgiven

36 One of the Pharisees asked Jesus[c] to
eat with him, and he went into the Pharisee's house and took his place at the table.
37 And a woman in the city, who was a
sinner, having learned that he was eating
in the Pharisee's house, brought an alabaster jar of ointment. 38 She stood behind him
at his feet, weeping, and began to bathe his
feet with her tears and to dry them with her
hair. Then she continued kissing his feet
and anointing them with the ointment.
39 Now when the Pharisee who had invited
him saw it, he said to himself, "If this man
were a prophet, he would have known who
and what kind of woman this is who is
touching him—that she is a sinner." 40 Jesus
spoke up and said to him, "Simon, I have
something to say to you." "Teacher," he
replied, "Speak." 41 "A certain creditor had
two debtors; one owed five hundred denarii,[f]
and the other fifty. 42 When they could not
pay, he canceled the debts for both of them.
Now which of them will love him more?"
43 Simon answered, "I suppose the one for
whom he canceled the greater debt." And
Jesus[b] said to him, "You have judged rightly."
44 Then turning toward the woman, he said
to Simon, "Do you see this woman? I entered your house; you gave me no water for
my feet, but she has bathed my feet with
her tears and dried them with her hair.
45 You gave me no kiss, but from the time
I came in she has not stopped kissing my
feet. 46 You did not anoint my head with oil,
but she has anointed my feet with ointment. 47 Therefore, I tell you, her sins, which
were many, have been forgiven; hence she
has shown great love. But the one to whom
little is forgiven, loves little." 48 Then he said
to her, "Your sins are forgiven." 49 But those
who were at the table with him began to
say among themselves, "Who is this who
even forgives sins?" 50 And he said to the
woman, "Your faith has saved you; go in
peace."

Some Women Accompany Jesus

8 Soon afterwards he went on through
cities and villages, proclaiming and
bringing the good news of the kingdom of
God. The twelve were with him, 2 as well as
some women who had been cured of evil
spirits and infirmities: Mary, called
Magdalene, from whom seven demons had
gone out, 3 and Joanna, the wife of Herod's
steward Chuza, and Susanna, and many

[z] Gk *He* [a] The terms *leper* and *leprosy* can refer to several diseases [b] Gk *he* [c] Gk *him* [d] Or *Why then did you go out? To see someone* [e] Or *praised God* [f] The denarius was the usual day's wage for a laborer

7.36-50 The festive occasion to which the *Pharisee* (later identified as Simon; 7.40, 44) invited Jesus is indicated by the guests reclining at the meal (the literal meaning of *took his place*). The nature of the sin of the notorious *woman* is not disclosed, but Jesus permits her to touch him even though contact with her would be ritually defiling. Jesus is aware of her moral condition, and illustrates both it and his forgiveness of her by the parable of the debtor, adding commendation for her loving concern for him. A *denarius* was the equivalent of a day's labor.

8.1-3 Of the *many* women who provide financial support for Jesus and *the twelve* is a core of those who have been *cured* by him, including *Mary Magdalene* (who becomes a witness of the empty tomb – (23.49; 24.10) and *Joanna*, wife of the manager (*steward*) of Herod Antipas' affairs.

8.4-15 The Parable of the Sower and the explanation of it are given in a shorter version than in Mark (4.1-9). Here those who *fall away* from the faith are contrasted with those who *hold it fast...with patient endurance.*
8.16-18 The parable-like words about putting the lamp on the stand point to the disclosure of God's purpose in the future, as in Mk 4.21-25, but warn about *how* one listens and the self-deceit of those who only *seem to have* accepted the message.
8.19-21 This shortened version of Mk 3.31-35 defines his true family as those who hear and do God's word, rather than those who *do the will of God.*
8.22-25 In Luke's account of Jesus' stilling the storm on Galilee, he is addressed by his disciples, not as *Teacher* (Mk 4.38), but as *Master* (in Greek literature the word means "master-teacher").
8.26-39 Luke's report of the exorcism of the man at Gerasa follows closely Mark's (5.1-20), but here the former demoniac *proclaims what Jesus had done for him* only in that city rather than throughout the *Decapolis*, the confederation of Hellenistic cities (Mk 5.20).

others, who provided for them[g] out of their resources.

The Parable of the Sower

4 When a great crowd gathered and people from town after town came to him, he said in a parable: 5"A sower went out to sow his seed; and as he sowed, some fell on the path and was trampled on, and the birds of the air ate it up. 6Some fell on the rock; and as it grew up, it withered for lack of moisture. 7Some fell among thorns, and the thorns grew with it and choked it. 8Some fell into good soil, and when it grew, it produced a hundredfold." As he said this, he called out, "Let anyone with ears to hear listen!"

The Purpose of the Parables

9 Then his disciples asked him what this parable meant. 10He said, "To you it has been given to know the secrets[h] of the kingdom of God; but to others I speak[i] in parables, so that

'looking they may not perceive,
and listening they may not understand.'

The Parable of the Sower Explained

11 "Now the parable is this: The seed is the word of God. 12The ones on the path are those who have heard; then the devil comes and takes away the word from their hearts, so that they may not believe and be saved. 13The ones on the rock are those who, when they hear the word, receive it with joy. But these have no root; they believe only for a while and in a time of testing fall away. 14As for what fell among the thorns, these are the ones who hear; but as they go on their way, they are choked by the cares and riches and pleasures of life, and their fruit does not mature. 15But as for that in the good soil, these are the ones who, when they hear the word, hold it fast in an honest and good heart, and bear fruit with patient endurance.

A Lamp under a Jar

16 "No one after lighting a lamp hides it under a jar, or puts it under a bed, but puts it on a lampstand, so that those who enter may see the light. 17For nothing is hidden that will not be disclosed, nor is anything secret that will not become known and come to light. 18Then pay attention to how you listen; for to those who have, more will be given; and from those who do not have, even what they seem to have will be taken away."

The True Kindred of Jesus

19 Then his mother and his brothers came to him, but they could not reach him because of the crowd. 20And he was told, "Your mother and your brothers are standing outside, wanting to see you." 21But he said to them, "My mother and my brothers are those who hear the word of God and do it."

Jesus Calms a Storm

22 One day he got into a boat with his disciples, and he said to them, "Let us go across to the other side of the lake." So they put out, 23and while they were sailing he fell asleep. A windstorm swept down on the lake, and the boat was filling with water, and they were in danger. 24They went to him and woke him up, shouting, "Master, Master, we are perishing!" And he woke up and rebuked the wind and the raging waves; they ceased, and there was a calm. 25He said to them, "Where is your faith?" They were afraid and amazed, and said to one another, "Who then is this, that he commands even the winds and the water, and they obey him?"

Jesus Heals the Gerasene Demoniac

26 Then they arrived at the country of the Gerasenes,[j] which is opposite Galilee. 27As he stepped out on land, a man of the city who had demons met him. For a long time he had worn[k] no clothes, and he did not live in a house but in the tombs. 28When he saw Jesus, he fell down before him and shouted at the top of his voice, "What have you to do with me, Jesus, Son of the Most High God? I beg you, do not torment me"— 29for Jesus[l] had commanded the unclean spirit to come out of the man. (For many

[g] Other ancient authorities read *him* [h] Or *mysteries* [i] Gk lacks *I speak* [j] Other ancient authorities read *Gadarenes*; others, *Gergesenes* [k] Other ancient authorities read *a man of the city who had had demons for a long time met him. He wore* [l] Gk *he*

8.8 Mt 11.15
8.9 Isa 6.9,10; Jer 5.21; Ezek 12.2
8.11 1 Thess 2.13; 1 Pet 1.23
8.16 Mt 5.15; Mk 4.21; Lk 11.33
8.17 Mt 10.26; Mk 4.22; Lk 12.2
8.18 Mt 13.12; 25.29; Lk 19.26
8.21 Lk 11.28; Jn 15.14
8.22 Mk 6.47-52; Jn 6.16-21
8.24 Lk 5.5; 4.39
8.28 Mk 1.24

8.31 Rom 10.7; Rev 20.1,3
8.33 ver 22,23
8.35 Lk 10.39
8.36 Mt 4.24
8.37 Acts 16.39
8.45 Lk 5.5
8.46 Lk 5.17; 6.19
8.48 Lk 7.50; 17.19; 18.42
8.49 ver 41
8.52 Lk 23.27; Jn 11.11,13
8.54 Lk 7.14; Jn 11.43
8.56 Mt 8.4; Mk 3.12; 7.36; Lk 9.21
9.1 Mk 3.13,14
9.2 Lk 10.1,9
9.3 Lk 10.4; 22.35
9.5 Acts 13.51
9.7 ver 19

times it had seized him; he was kept under guard and bound with chains and shackles, but he would break the bonds and be driven by the demon into the wilds.) 30 Jesus then asked him, "What is your name?" He said, "Legion"; for many demons had entered him. 31 They begged him not to order them to go back into the abyss.

32 Now there on the hillside a large herd of swine was feeding; and the demons[m] begged Jesus[n] to let them enter these. So he gave them permission. 33 Then the demons came out of the man and entered the swine, and the herd rushed down the steep bank into the lake and was drowned.

34 When the swineherds saw what had happened, they ran off and told it in the city and in the country. 35 Then people came out to see what had happened, and when they came to Jesus, they found the man from whom the demons had gone sitting at the feet of Jesus, clothed and in his right mind. And they were afraid. 36 Those who had seen it told them how the one who had been possessed by demons had been healed. 37 Then all the people of the surrounding country of the Gerasenes[o] asked Jesus[n] to leave them; for they were seized with great fear. So he got into the boat and returned. 38 The man from whom the demons had gone begged that he might be with him; but Jesus[p] sent him away, saying, 39 "Return to your home, and declare how much God has done for you." So he went away, proclaiming throughout the city how much Jesus had done for him.

A Girl Restored to Life and a Woman Healed

40 Now when Jesus returned, the crowd welcomed him, for they were all waiting for him. 41 Just then there came a man named Jairus, a leader of the synagogue. He fell at Jesus' feet and begged him to come to his house, 42 for he had an only daughter, about twelve years old, who was dying.

As he went, the crowds pressed in on him. 43 Now there was a woman who had been suffering from hemorrhages for twelve years; and though she had spent all she had on physicians,[q] no one could cure her. 44 She came up behind him and touched the fringe of his clothes, and immediately her hemorrhage stopped. 45 Then Jesus asked, "Who touched me?" When all denied it, Peter[r] said, "Master, the crowds surround you and press in on you." 46 But Jesus said, "Someone touched me; for I noticed that power had gone out from me." 47 When the woman saw that she could not remain hidden, she came trembling; and falling down before him, she declared in the presence of all the people why she had touched him, and how she had been immediately healed. 48 He said to her, "Daughter, your faith has made you well; go in peace."

49 While he was still speaking, someone came from the leader's house to say, "Your daughter is dead; do not trouble the teacher any longer." 50 When Jesus heard this, he replied, "Do not fear. Only believe, and she will be saved." 51 When he came to the house, he did not allow anyone to enter with him, except Peter, John, and James, and the child's father and mother. 52 They were all weeping and wailing for her; but he said, "Do not weep; for she is not dead but sleeping." 53 And they laughed at him, knowing that she was dead. 54 But he took her by the hand and called out, "Child, get up!" 55 Her spirit returned, and she got up at once. Then he directed them to give her something to eat. 56 Her parents were astounded; but he ordered them to tell no one what had happened.

The Mission of the Twelve

9 Then Jesus[p] called the twelve together and gave them power and authority over all demons and to cure diseases, 2 and he sent them out to proclaim the kingdom of God and to heal. 3 He said to them, "Take nothing for your journey, no staff, nor bag, nor bread, nor money—not even an extra tunic. 4 Whatever house you enter, stay there, and leave from there. 5 Wherever they do not welcome you, as you are leaving that town shake the dust off your feet as a testimony against them." 6 They departed and went through the villages, bringing the good news and curing diseases everywhere.

Herod's Perplexity

7 Now Herod the ruler[s] heard about all that had taken place, and he was perplexed,

8.40-56 The linked stories of the restoration to life of the daughter of *the leader of the synagogue* and of the woman with a bloody flow are somewhat abbreviated here (*cf.* Mk 5.21-43), but there are detailed differences: Peter, as spokesman for the disciples, addresses Jesus as *Master;* Jesus says that *power* has gone out of him at her touch; the woman's identification of herself as the one who touched him is not privately to him but *in the presence of all the people;* the result of trusting Jesus is that the child will *be saved* (meaning, made well); at Jesus' word, her *spirit* [or *breath*] *returned.*
9.1-6 Having shifted the story of Jesus' preaching in the Nazareth synagogue (Mk 6.1-6) to an earlier point in his narrative (Lk 4.16-30), Luke here describes his sending the *twelve.* Their assignment includes preaching *the kingdom of God* and healing.
9.7-9 The account of Herod Antipas' puzzlement over whether Jesus was John raised from the dead includes the detail that Herod *tried to see him.* Mark's detailed account of the death of John (6.17-29) is replaced by Luke with a brief mention of Herod's having imprisoned John when he rebuked the ruler (3.19-20). Luke avoids putting secular rulers in an unfavorable light.

[m] Gk *they* [n] Gk *him* [o] Other ancient authorities read *Gadarenes;* others, *Gergesenes* [p] Gk *he* [q] Other ancient authorities lack *and had spent all she had on physicians* [r] Other ancient authorities add *and those who were with him* [s] Gk *tetrarch*

9.10-17 Luke's report of Jesus feeding the five thousand is briefer than Mark's (6.30-44) and differs in details: its location in *a city called Bethsaida*, northeast from the Lake of Galilee, although it is also described as *a deserted place*; his message to the crowd concerns *the kingdom of God*; the *bread* and *fish* are distributed in a single act.
9.18-27 Jesus' disclosure of his identity to the disciples takes place in a situation of prayer (rather than while on a preaching tour, as in Mk 8.27), and Peter acclaims him simply as *the Messiah of God*. His prediction of his own suffering, death and resurrection is followed by (1) his call to them to *take up the cross*, (2) the warning of rejection by the *Son of Man* for those who fail to trust (*are ashamed of*) his word, and (3) the promise of a vision of *the kingdom of God*.
9.28-36 As in the feeding story (9.18), this vision takes place when Jesus has withdrawn with his followers to pray. Jesus' impending death (*departure*; in Greek, *exodos*) is the subject of conversation with *Moses and Elijah*, both of whom were reported in Jewish tradition as having been taken up to God without dying. The LORD's secret burial of Moses (Deut 34.6) led to the tradition that he had not died but ascended; Elijah's being taken up is described in 2 Kings 2.1-12. Peter's proposal to make the situation permanent by erecting *dwellings* is a sign of his lack of knowledge. The heavenly voice acclaims Jesus as *my Chosen*, which is probably referring to the conception of Israel in Isa 42.1 as God's *child* and *chosen one* – terms here seen as embodied in Jesus, the agent of the new covenant people.
9.37-43a Luke's short version of the story of the curing of the *child* with demonic seizures (Mk 9.14-29) highlights the perversity of Jesus' contemporaries and *the greatness of God* that is manifest in this healing act of Jesus.

because it was said by some that John had been raised from the dead, [8]by some that Elijah had appeared, and by others that one of the ancient prophets had arisen. [9]Herod said, "John I beheaded; but who is this about whom I hear such things?" And he tried to see him.

Feeding the Five Thousand

10 On their return the apostles told Jesus[t] all they had done. He took them with him and withdrew privately to a city called Bethsaida. [11]When the crowds found out about it, they followed him; and he welcomed them, and spoke to them about the kingdom of God, and healed those who needed to be cured.

12 The day was drawing to a close, and the twelve came to him and said, "Send the crowd away, so that they may go into the surrounding villages and countryside, to lodge and get provisions; for we are here in a deserted place." [13]But he said to them, "You give them something to eat." They said, "We have no more than five loaves and two fish—unless we are to go and buy food for all these people." [14]For there were about five thousand men. And he said to his disciples, "Make them sit down in groups of about fifty each." [15]They did so and made them all sit down. [16]And taking the five loaves and the two fish, he looked up to heaven, and blessed and broke them, and gave them to the disciples to set before the crowd. [17]And all ate and were filled. What was left over was gathered up, twelve baskets of broken pieces.

Peter's Declaration about Jesus

18 Once when Jesus[u] was praying alone, with only the disciples near him, he asked them, "Who do the crowds say that I am?" [19]They answered, "John the Baptist; but others, Elijah; and still others, that one of the ancient prophets has arisen." [20]He said to them, "But who do you say that I am?" Peter answered, "The Messiah[v] of God."

Jesus Foretells His Death and Resurrection

21 He sternly ordered and commanded them not to tell anyone, [22]saying, "The Son of Man must undergo great suffering, and be rejected by the elders, chief priests, and scribes, and be killed, and on the third day be raised."

23 Then he said to them all, "If any want to become my followers, let them deny themselves and take up their cross daily and follow me. [24]For those who want to save their life will lose it, and those who lose their life for my sake will save it. [25]What does it profit them if they gain the whole world, but lose or forfeit themselves? [26]Those who are ashamed of me and of my words, of them the Son of Man will be ashamed when he comes in his glory and the glory of the Father and of the holy angels. [27]But truly I tell you, there are some standing here who will not taste death before they see the kingdom of God."

The Transfiguration

28 Now about eight days after these sayings Jesus[u] took with him Peter and John and James, and went up on the mountain to pray. [29]And while he was praying, the appearance of his face changed, and his clothes became dazzling white. [30]Suddenly they saw two men, Moses and Elijah, talking to him. [31]They appeared in glory and were speaking of his departure, which he was about to accomplish at Jerusalem. [32]Now Peter and his companions were weighed down with sleep; but since they had stayed awake,[w] they saw his glory and the two men who stood with him. [33]Just as they were leaving him, Peter said to Jesus, "Master, it is good for us to be here; let us make three dwellings,[x] one for you, one for Moses, and one for Elijah"—not knowing what he said. [34]While he was saying this, a cloud came and overshadowed them; and they were terrified as they entered the cloud. [35]Then from the cloud came a voice that said, "This is my Son, my Chosen;[y] listen to him!" [36]When the voice had spoken, Jesus was found alone. And they kept silent and in those days told no one any of the things they had seen.

Jesus Heals a Boy with a Demon

37 On the next day, when they had come down from the mountain, a great crowd met him. [38]Just then a man from the crowd shouted, "Teacher, I beg you to look

[t] Gk *him* [u] Gk *he* [v] Or *The Christ* [w] Or *but when they were fully awake* [x] Or *tents* [y] Other ancient authorities read *my Beloved*

9.8 Mt 16.14
9.9 Lk 23.8
9.10 ver 17
9.13 2 Kings 4.42-44
9.16 Lk 22.19; 24.30,31; Acts 2.42; 20.11; 27.35
9.18 Jn 1.49; 6.66-69; 11.27
9.19 ver 7.8; Mk 9.11-13
9.20 Jn 6.69
9.21 Mt 16.20
9.22 ver 43-45; Lk 18.31-34
9.23 Mt 10.38; Lk 14.27
9.24 Mt 10.39
9.25 Jn 12.25
9.26 Mt 10.33; Lk 12.9; 2 Tim 2.12; 1 Jn 2.28
9.27 Lk 22.18; Jn 21.22
9.28 Lk 3.21; 5.16; 6.12
9.31 2 Pet 1.15
9.32 Mt 26.43; Mk 14.40
9.33 Lk 5.8; 8.24,45; 17.13
9.35 2 Pet 1.17,18; Mt 3.17
9.36 Mt 17.9

at my son; he is my only child. 39Suddenly a spirit seizes him, and all at once he[z] shrieks. It convulses him until he foams at the mouth; it mauls him and will scarcely leave him. 40I begged your disciples to cast it out, but they could not." 41Jesus answered, "You faithless and perverse generation, how much longer must I be with you and bear with you? Bring your son here." 42While he was coming, the demon dashed him to the ground in convulsions. But Jesus rebuked the unclean spirit, healed the boy, and gave him back to his father. 43And all were astounded at the greatness of God.

Jesus Again Foretells His Death

While everyone was amazed at all that he was doing, he said to his disciples, 44"Let these words sink into your ears: The Son of Man is going to be betrayed into human hands." 45But they did not understand this saying; its meaning was concealed from them, so that they could not perceive it. And they were afraid to ask him about this saying.

True Greatness

46 An argument arose among them as to which one of them was the greatest. 47But Jesus, aware of their inner thoughts, took a little child and put it by his side, 48and said to them, "Whoever welcomes this child in my name welcomes me, and whoever welcomes me welcomes the one who sent me; for the least among all of you is the greatest."

Another Exorcist

49 John answered, "Master, we saw someone casting out demons in your name, and we tried to stop him, because he does not follow with us." 50But Jesus said to him, "Do not stop him; for whoever is not against you is for you."

A Samaritan Village Refuses to Receive Jesus

51 When the days drew near for him to be taken up, he set his face to go to Jerusalem. 52And he sent messengers ahead of him. On their way they entered a village of the Samaritans to make ready for him; 53but they did not receive him, because his face was set toward Jerusalem. 54When his disciples James and John saw it, they said, "Lord, do you want us to command fire to come down from heaven and consume them?"[a] 55But he turned and rebuked them. 56Then[b] they went on to another village.

Would-Be Followers of Jesus

57 As they were going along the road, someone said to him, "I will follow you wherever you go." 58And Jesus said to him, "Foxes have holes, and birds of the air have nests; but the Son of Man has nowhere to lay his head." 59To another he said, "Follow me." But he said, "Lord, first let me go and bury my father." 60But Jesus[c] said to him, "Let the dead bury their own dead; but as for you, go and proclaim the kingdom of God." 61Another said, "I will follow you, Lord; but let me first say farewell to those at my home." 62Jesus said to him, "No one who puts a hand to the plow and looks back is fit for the kingdom of God."

The Mission of the Seventy

10 After this the Lord appointed seventy[d] others and sent them on ahead of him in pairs to every town and place where he himself intended to go. 2He said to them, "The harvest is plentiful, but the laborers are few; therefore ask the Lord of the harvest to send out laborers into his harvest. 3Go on your way. See, I am sending you out like lambs into the midst of wolves. 4Carry no purse, no bag, no sandals; and greet no one on the road. 5Whatever house you enter, first say, 'Peace to this house!' 6And if anyone is there who shares in peace, your peace will rest on that person; but if not, it will return to you. 7Remain in the same house, eating and drinking whatever they provide, for the laborer deserves to be paid. Do not move about from house to house. 8Whenever you enter a town and its people welcome you, eat what is set before you; 9cure the sick who are there, and say to them, 'The kingdom of God has come near to you.'[e] 10But

[z] Or *it* [a] Other ancient authorities add *as Elijah did* [b] Other ancient authorities read *rebuked them, and said, "You do not know what spirit you are of, 56for the Son of Man has not come to destroy the lives of human beings but to save them." Then* [c] Gk *he* [d] Other ancient authorities read *seventy-two* [e] Or *is at hand for you*

9.43 2 Pet 1.16
9.44 ver 22
9.45 Lk 2.50; 18.34
9.48 Mt 10.40; Jn 12.44; 13.20; Mt 23.11,12
9.49 Mk 9.38
9.50 Mt 12.30
9.51 Lk 13.22; 17.11; 18.31; 19.11,28
9.52 Mt 10.5; Jn 4.4
9.54 Mk 3.17; 1 Kings 1.10,12
9.59 Mt 8.21,22
10.1 Mt 10.1; Mk 6.7; Lk 9.1,2,51,52
10.2 Mt 9.37,38; Jn 4.35
10.3 Mt 10.16
10.4 Mt 10.9,10; Mk 6.8; Lk 9.3
10.5 Mk 10.12
10.7 Mt 10.10; 1 Cor 9.14; 1 Tim 5.18
10.9 Mt 3.2; 10.7

9.43b-48 The disciples' inability to understand this second prediction of his arrest and death (*delivered into human hands*) is the result of its *meaning* having been *concealed* from them. Their vying for places of honor as his followers leads Jesus to contrast their lust for power with the *child*, who is seemingly *the least* among them, but by simplicity and trust symbolizes *the greatest*.
9.49-50 Dependence on the power of Jesus' name is more important than public membership in the community of his followers.
9.51-19.27 Preparing for the Confrontation in Jerusalem.
9.51-55 That Jesus' face is *set to go to Jerusalem* prepares the reader for a series of his challenges to the assumptions about God's people and the criteria for participation that prevailed in Judaism in the first century. That this process is part of God's plan is evident in the refusal of the *Samaritans* to *receive him*.
9.57-62 In an expanded form of the so-called Q source that Luke shared with Matthew, would-be followers of Jesus are told that acceptance of this role will obligate them to abandon the security of a home (*to lay one's head*) and the traditional family responsibilities, even to the burial of parents. Once the commitment has been made, there is to be no turning back.
10.1-16 Providing a symbolic model for the gospel mission to non-Israelites, Luke pictures Jesus sending out *seventy* (the traditional Jewish number for the nations of the world) *laborers* on a mission similar to that of the twelve (9.1-6), but now they are to reach out to those beyond the limits of the community of Israel. By their words and acts, they show that *the kingdom of God has come near*. Judgment will fall on the Jewish cities (*Chorazin, Bethsaida, Capernaum*) for their failure to receive the message, while Gentile cities (*Tyre, Sidon*) will respond to such works done in them.

10.17-24 The joy of the *seventy* over the success of their mission leads to Jesus' declaration that these events are the prelude to the defeat of *Satan*, and to his warning against pride in their accomplishments. Instead, he rejoices that God's purpose has been revealed to him, and through him to his followers. **10.25-37** Linked with the question of a *lawyer* (devoted to interpretation of the Jewish law), Luke adapts Mark's version of this incident to highlight the twin laws of love of God and neighbor (Mk 12.28-31), but then adds Jesus' definition of what a neighbor does in his story of the *Samaritan* (despised by the Israelites) who risks his ritual purity, his life and his resources to come to the aid of another human being in need. **10.38-42** These sisters represent two possible priorities for Jesus' followers: service or listening to his teaching. The latter is the *better part.*

whenever you enter a town and they do not
welcome you, go out into its streets and say,
11‘Even the dust of your town that clings to
our feet, we wipe off in protest against you.
Yet know this: the kingdom of God has
come near.’[f] 12I tell you, on that day it will
be more tolerable for Sodom than for that
town.

Woes to Unrepentant Cities

13 “Woe to you, Chorazin! Woe to you,
Bethsaida! For if the deeds of power done in
you had been done in Tyre and Sidon, they
would have repented long ago, sitting in
sackcloth and ashes. 14But at the judgment
it will be more tolerable for Tyre and Sidon
than for you. 15And you, Capernaum,
will you be exalted to heaven?
No, you will be brought down to Hades.
16 “Whoever listens to you listens to me,
and whoever rejects you rejects me, and
whoever rejects me rejects the one who sent
me.”

The Return of the Seventy

17 The seventy[g] returned with joy, saying, “Lord, in your name even the demons
submit to us!” 18He said to them, “I watched
Satan fall from heaven like a flash of lightning. 19See, I have given you authority to
tread on snakes and scorpions, and over all
the power of the enemy; and nothing will
hurt you. 20Nevertheless, do not rejoice at
this, that the spirits submit to you, but
rejoice that your names are written in
heaven.”

Jesus Rejoices

21 At that same hour Jesus[h] rejoiced in
the Holy Spirit[i] and said, “I thank[j] you,
Father, Lord of heaven and earth, because
you have hidden these things from the wise
and the intelligent and have revealed them
to infants; yes, Father, for such was your
gracious will.[k] 22All things have been handed
over to me by my Father; and no one
knows who the Son is except the Father, or
who the Father is except the Son and anyone to whom the Son chooses to reveal
him.”
23 Then turning to the disciples, Jesus[h]
said to them privately, “Blessed are the eyes
that see what you see! 24For I tell you that
many prophets and kings desired to see
what you see, but did not see it, and to hear
what you hear, but did not hear it.”

The Parable of the Good Samaritan

25 Just then a lawyer stood up to test
Jesus.[l] “Teacher,” he said, “what must I do
to inherit eternal life?” 26He said to him,
“What is written in the law? What do you
read there?” 27He answered, “You shall love
the Lord your God with all your heart, and
with all your soul, and with all your strength,
and with all your mind; and your neighbor
as yourself.” 28And he said to him, “You
have given the right answer; do this, and
you will live.”
29 But wanting to justify himself, he
asked Jesus, “And who is my neighbor?”
30Jesus replied, “A man was going down
from Jerusalem to Jericho, and fell into the
hands of robbers, who stripped him, beat
him, and went away, leaving him half dead.
31Now by chance a priest was going down
that road; and when he saw him, he passed
by on the other side. 32So likewise a Levite,
when he came to the place and saw him,
passed by on the other side. 33But a Samaritan while traveling came near him; and
when he saw him, he was moved with pity.
34He went to him and bandaged his wounds,
having poured oil and wine on them. Then
he put him on his own animal, brought
him to an inn, and took care of him. 35The
next day he took out two denarii,[m] gave
them to the innkeeper, and said, ‘Take care
of him; and when I come back, I will repay
you whatever more you spend.’ 36Which of
these three, do you think, was a neighbor
to the man who fell into the hands of the
robbers?” 37He said, “The one who showed
him mercy.” Jesus said to him, “Go and do
likewise.”

Jesus Visits Martha and Mary

38 Now as they went on their way, he
entered a certain village, where a woman
named Martha welcomed him into her home.
39She had a sister named Mary, who sat at
the Lord's feet and listened to what he was
saying. 40But Martha was distracted by her

[f] Or *is at hand* [g] Other ancient authorities read *seventy-two* [h] Gk *he* [i] Other authorities read *in the spirit* [j] Or *praise* [k] Or *for so it was well-pleasing in your sight* [l] Gk *him* [m] The denarius was the usual day's wage for a laborer

10.11 Mt 10.14; Mk 6.11; Lk 9.5
10.12 Mt 10.15; 11.24
10.13 Mt 11.21; Lk 6.24-26
10.15 Mt 11.23
10.16 Mt 10.40; Mk 9.37; Lk 9.48; Jn 13.20
10.17 ver 1
10.18 Jn 12.31; Rev 9.1; 12.8,9
10.19 Acts 28.5
10.20 Ex 32.32; Ps 69.28; Dan 12.1; Phil 4.3; Heb 12.23; Rev 13.8; 21.27
10.21 Mt 11.25; 1 Cor 1.26-29
10.22 Mt 28.18; Jn 3.35; 17.2
10.23 Mt 13.16
10.24 1 Pet 1.10
10.25 Mt 19.16; Mk 10.17; Lk 18.18
10.27 Deut 6.5; Lev 19.18; Rom 13.9; Gal 5.14; Jas 2.8
10.28 Lev 18.5; Mk 11.25
10.29 Lk 16.15
10.33 Lk 9.52; Jn 4.9
10.38 Jn 11.1; 12.2,3
10.39 Lk 8.35; Acts 22.3

10.42 Ps 27.4

11.1 Mk 1.35; Lk 3.21

11.4 Mt 18.35; Mk 11.25

11.8 Lk 18.1-6

11.9 Mt 7.7-11; 18.19; 21.22; Mk 11.14; Jas 1.5-8; 1 Jn 5.14,15

11.14 Mt 9.32-34

11.16 Mt 16.1; Mk 8.11

11.17 Jn 2.25

11.20 Ex 8.19

11.23 Lk 9.50

11.26 Heb 10.26; 2 Pet 2.20

11.27 Lk 23.29

many tasks; so she came to him and asked,
"Lord, do you not care that my sister has
left me to do all the work by myself? Tell
her then to help me." 41But the Lord answered her, "Martha, Martha, you are
worried and distracted by many things;
42there is need of only one thing.[n] Mary has
chosen the better part, which will not be
taken away from her."

The Lord's Prayer

11 He was praying in a certain place,
and after he had finished, one of
his disciples said to him, "Lord, teach us to
pray, as John taught his disciples." 2He said
to them, "When you pray, say:

Father,[o] hallowed be your name.
Your kingdom come.[p]
3 Give us each day our daily bread.[q]
4 And forgive us our sins,
for we ourselves forgive everyone
indebted to us.
And do not bring us to the time of
trial."[r]

Perseverance in Prayer

5 And he said to them, "Suppose one of
you has a friend, and you go to him at
midnight and say to him, 'Friend, lend me
three loaves of bread; 6for a friend of mine
has arrived, and I have nothing to set before
him.' 7And he answers from within, 'Do not
bother me; the door has already been locked,
and my children are with me in bed; I
cannot get up and give you anything.' 8I tell
you, even though he will not get up and
give him anything because he is his friend,
at least because of his persistence he will get
up and give him whatever he needs.
9 "So I say to you, Ask, and it will be
given you; search, and you will find; knock,
and the door will be opened for you. 10For
everyone who asks receives, and everyone
who searches finds, and for everyone who
knocks, the door will be opened. 11Is there
anyone among you who, if your child asks
for[s] a fish, will give a snake instead of a fish?
12Or if the child asks for an egg, will give
a scorpion? 13If you then, who are evil,
know how to give good gifts to your children, how much more will the heavenly
Father give the Holy Spirit[t] to those who
ask him!"

Jesus and Beelzebul

14 Now he was casting out a demon
that was mute; when the demon had gone
out, the one who had been mute spoke, and
the crowds were amazed. 15But some of
them said, "He casts out demons by
Beelzebul, the ruler of the demons." 16Oth-
ers, to test him, kept demanding from him
a sign from heaven. 17But he knew what
they were thinking and said to them, "Every
kingdom divided against itself becomes a
desert, and house falls on house. 18If Satan
also is divided against himself, how will his
kingdom stand?—for you say that I cast out
the demons by Beelzebul. 19Now if I cast out
the demons by Beelzebul, by whom do your
exorcists[u] cast them out? Therefore they will
be your judges. 20But if it is by the finger
of God that I cast out the demons, then the
kingdom of God has come to you. 21When
a strong man, fully armed, guards his castle, his property is safe. 22But when one
stronger than he attacks him and overpow-
ers him, he takes away his armor in which
he trusted and divides his plunder. 23Who-
ever is not with me is against me, and
whoever does not gather with me scatters.

The Return of the Unclean Spirit

24 "When the unclean spirit has gone
out of a person, it wanders through waterless regions looking for a resting place, but
not finding any, it says, 'I will return to my
house from which I came.' 25When it comes,
it finds it swept and put in order. 26Then it
goes and brings seven other spirits more evil
than itself, and they enter and live there;
and the last state of that person is worse
than the first."

True Blessedness

27 While he was saying this, a woman
in the crowd raised her voice and said to

11.1-13 A simpler, more likely original form of the prayer that Jesus *taught his disciples.* While awaiting the universal honoring (*hallowing*) of God's authority (*name*), Jesus tells his followers to ask for daily physical and moral renewal, to be forgiving as well, and to pray for deliverance from *the time of trial* that will precede the coming of God's kingdom. God's readiness to answer the prayers of his people is compared with someone asleep with his whole family when a needy neighbor comes to borrow some bread. God's people are to expect God to meet their requests, including his grant of the Holy Spirit (which will be a major factor in Luke's second volume, especially in Acts 2.)
11.14-26 As in Mk 3.22-27, the significance of Jesus' exorcisms is not his alliance with *Beelzebul, the prince of demons*, but the added feature here is that this activity of Jesus is a sign of the ultimate defeat of the demons and the coming of God's rule. *The finger of God* recalls God's deliverance of Israel from slavery in Egypt (Ex 8.19). Jesus is the *stronger* one who is defeating Satan (*the strong man*), and his hearers must decide on which side of this struggle they will align themselves. Even when the evil power has been expelled from a person, there remains the possibility of possession by other evil *spirits*.
11.27-28 More blessed even than Jesus' mother is the one who hears and obeys God's word.

[n] Other ancient authorities read *few things are necessary, or only one* [o] Other ancient authorities read *Our Father in heaven* [p] A few ancient authorities read *Your Holy Spirit come upon us and cleanse us.* Other ancient authorities add *Your will be done, on earth as in heaven* [q] Or *our bread for tomorrow* [r] Or *us into temptation.* Other ancient authorities add *but rescue us from the evil one* (or *from evil*) [s] Other ancient authorities add *bread, will give a stone; or if your child asks for* [t] Other ancient authorities read *the Father give the Holy Spirit from heaven* [u] Gk *sons*

11.29-32 While *this generation* says it seeks for a *sign* from God, it ignores his message, unlike the Gentile *people of Nineveh* (Jon 3.5-10) and *the queen of the south* (1 Kings 10.1-14), who respectively repented on hearing the prophet and sought the wisdom of God through Solomon.
11.33-36 The purpose of Jesus' coming is to bring light to his people. How one responds to that light discloses one's inner condition.
11.37-54 Jesus' controversy with the *Pharisees* – much expanded in Mt 23 – concerns several themes: external vs. inner cleansing; giving priority to such important issues as *justice and love* vs. tithing; seeking acclaim for one's piety or placing heavy burdens on others as a requirement for religious devotion; honoring the memory of the prophets while rejecting them and their message. God will call to account those whose tradition of rejection of his messengers reaches from the first murder in the Jewish scriptures (Abel in Gen 4.8) to the last (Zechariah, in 2 Chr 24.20-21). These severe criticisms crystallize the determination of the Pharisees to be rid of him.
12.1-34 A series of brief sayings and a parable indicate major themes in Jesus' teaching: the *hypocrisy* of the Pharisees leads them to cover up their misdeeds and misstatements (1-3); most to be feared are not those who may kill but those who will cause disqualification from the life of God's people (4-5); God cares for all his creation, but especially for his own people (5-6); those with courage to *acknowledge* Jesus will be confirmed by God and given courage to bear their testimony before hostile authorities (8-12); avoid the fate of the *fool* whose reliance was on his possessions rather than on his relationship (*treasures*) with God (13-21); God's providential care of his people makes unnecessary anxiety about appearance or daily needs, since a share in the life of God's *kingdom* is not gained by human merit but by the *Father's* gift.

him, "Blessed is the womb that bore you and the breasts that nursed you!" [28]But he said, "Blessed rather are those who hear the word of God and obey it!"

The Sign of Jonah

29 When the crowds were increasing, he began to say, "This generation is an evil generation; it asks for a sign, but no sign will be given to it except the sign of Jonah. [30]For just as Jonah became a sign to the people of Nineveh, so the Son of Man will be to this generation. [31]The queen of the South will rise at the judgment with the people of this generation and condemn them, because she came from the ends of the earth to listen to the wisdom of Solomon, and see, something greater than Solomon is here! [32]The people of Nineveh will rise up at the judgment with this generation and condemn it, because they repented at the proclamation of Jonah, and see, something greater than Jonah is here!

The Light of the Body

33 "No one after lighting a lamp puts it in a cellar,[v] but on the lampstand so that those who enter may see the light. [34]Your eye is the lamp of your body. If your eye is healthy, your whole body is full of light; but if it is not healthy, your body is full of darkness. [35]Therefore consider whether the light in you is not darkness. [36]If then your whole body is full of light, with no part of it in darkness, it will be as full of light as when a lamp gives you light with its rays."

Jesus Denounces Pharisees and Lawyers

37 While he was speaking, a Pharisee invited him to dine with him; so he went in and took his place at the table. [38]The Pharisee was amazed to see that he did not first wash before dinner. [39]Then the Lord said to him, "Now you Pharisees clean the outside of the cup and of the dish, but inside you are full of greed and wickedness. [40]You fools! Did not the one who made the outside make the inside also? [41]So give for alms those things that are within; and see, everything will be clean for you.

42 "But woe to you Pharisees! For you tithe mint and rue and herbs of all kinds, and neglect justice and the love of God; it is these you ought to have practiced, without neglecting the others. [43]Woe to you Pharisees! For you love to have the seat of honor in the synagogues and to be greeted with respect in the marketplaces. [44]Woe to you! For you are like unmarked graves, and people walk over them without realizing it."

45 One of the lawyers answered him, "Teacher, when you say these things, you insult us too." [46]And he said, "Woe also to you lawyers! For you load people with burdens hard to bear, and you yourselves do not lift a finger to ease them. [47]Woe to you! For you build the tombs of the prophets whom your ancestors killed. [48]So you are witnesses and approve of the deeds of your ancestors; for they killed them, and you build their tombs. [49]Therefore also the Wisdom of God said, 'I will send them prophets and apostles, some of whom they will kill and persecute,' [50]so that this generation may be charged with the blood of all the prophets shed since the foundation of the world, [51]from the blood of Abel to the blood of Zechariah, who perished between the altar and the sanctuary. Yes, I tell you, it will be charged against this generation. [52]Woe to you lawyers! For you have taken away the key of knowledge; you did not enter yourselves, and you hindered those who were entering."

53 When he went outside, the scribes and the Pharisees began to be very hostile toward him and to cross-examine him about many things, [54]lying in wait for him, to catch him in something he might say.

A Warning against Hypocrisy

12 Meanwhile, when the crowd gathered by the thousands, so that they trampled on one another, he began to speak first to his disciples, "Beware of the yeast of the Pharisees, that is, their hypocrisy. [2]Nothing is covered up that will not be uncovered, and nothing secret that will not become known. [3]Therefore whatever you have said in the dark will be heard in the light, and what you have whispered behind closed doors will be proclaimed from the housetops.

Exhortation to Fearless Confession

4 "I tell you, my friends, do not fear those who kill the body, and after that can

[v] Other ancient authorities add *or under the bushel basket*

11.28 Lk 8.21; Jn 15.14
11.29 Mt 16.4; Mk 8.12; ver 16
11.31 1 Kings 10.1; 2 Chr 9.1
11.32 Jon 3.5
11.33 Mt 5.15; Mk 4.21; Lk 8.16
11.34 Mt 6.22,23
11.37 Lk 7.36; 14.1
11.38 Mk 7.3,4
11.39 Mt 23.25,26
11.41 Lk 12.33; Mk 7.19; Titus 1.15
11.42 Mt 23.23; Lk 18.12
11.43 Mt 23.6,7; Mk 12.38,39; Lk 20.46
11.44 Mt 23.27
11.46 Mt 23.4
11.47 Mt 23.29-32; Acts 7.51-53
11.49 Mt 23.24-36; 1 Cor 1.24; Col 2.3
11.51 Gen 4.8; 2 Chr 24.20,21
11.52 Mt 23.13
11.54 Mk 12.13
12.1 Mt 16.6; Mk 8.15; Mt 16.12
12.2 Mt 10.26,27; Mk 4.22; Lk 8.17; Eph 5.13
12.4 Mt 10.28-33; Jn 15.14,15

12.5 Heb 10.31
12.7 Mt 12.12; Lk 21.18; Acts 27.34
12.8 Mk 8.38; 2 Tim 2.12; 1 Jn 2.23
12.10 Mt 12.31,32; Mk 3.28,29
12.11 Mt 10.19; Mk 13.11; Lk 21.14
12.14 Mic 6.8; Rom 2.1,3
12.15 1 Tim 6.6-10
12.19 Eccl 11.9; Jas 5.5
12.20 Jer 17.11; Job 27.8; Ps 39.6
12.21 ver 33
12.24 Job 38.41
12.25 Ps 39.5
12.27 1 Kings 10.4-7
12.30 Mt 6.8
12.32 Jn 21.15-17
12.33 Mt 19.21; Mk 6.20
12.34 Mt 6.21
12.35 Mt 25.1-13; Mk 13.33-37; Eph 6.14
12.37 Mt 24.42,46; Lk 17.8; Jn 13.4
12.39 Mt 24.43; 1 Thess 5.2; 2 Pet 3.10; Rev 3.3; 16.15
12.40 Mt 24.44; Mk 13.33; Lk 21.36

do nothing more. [5]But I will warn you
whom to fear: fear him who, after he has
killed, has authority[w] to cast into hell.[x] Yes,
I tell you, fear him! [6]Are not five sparrows
sold for two pennies? Yet not one of them
is forgotten in God's sight. [7]But even the
hairs of your head are all counted. Do not
be afraid; you are of more value than many
sparrows.
8 "And I tell you, everyone who acknowledges me before others, the Son of
Man also will acknowledge before the angels of God; [9]but whoever denies me before
others will be denied before the angels of
God. [10]And everyone who speaks a word
against the Son of Man will be forgiven; but
whoever blasphemes against the Holy Spirit
will not be forgiven. [11]When they bring you
before the synagogues, the rulers, and the
authorities, do not worry about how[y] you
are to defend yourselves or what you are to
say; [12]for the Holy Spirit will teach you at
that very hour what you ought to say."

The Parable of the Rich Fool

13 Someone in the crowd said to him,
"Teacher, tell my brother to divide the family inheritance with me." [14]But he said to
him, "Friend, who set me to be a judge or
arbitrator over you?" [15]And he said to them,
"Take care! Be on your guard against all
kinds of greed; for one's life does not consist
in the abundance of possessions." [16]Then he
told them a parable: "The land of a rich
man produced abundantly. [17]And he thought
to himself, 'What should I do, for I have no
place to store my crops?' [18]Then he said, 'I
will do this: I will pull down my barns and
build larger ones, and there I will store all
my grain and my goods. [19]And I will say
to my soul, 'Soul, you have ample goods
laid up for many years; relax, eat, drink, be
merry.' [20]But God said to him, 'You fool!
This very night your life is being demanded
of you. And the things you have prepared,
whose will they be?' [21]So it is with those
who store up treasures for themselves but
are not rich toward God."

Do Not Worry

22 He said to his disciples, "Therefore I
tell you, do not worry about your life, what
you will eat, or about your body, what you
will wear. [23]For life is more than food, and
the body more than clothing. [24]Consider the
ravens: they neither sow nor reap, they
have neither storehouse nor barn, and yet
God feeds them. Of how much more value
are you than the birds! [25]And can any of
you by worrying add a single hour to your
span of life?[z] [26]If then you are not able to
do so small a thing as that, why do you
worry about the rest? [27]Consider the lilies,
how they grow: they neither toil nor spin;[a]
yet I tell you, even Solomon in all his glory
was not clothed like one of these. [28]But if
God so clothes the grass of the field, which
is alive today and tomorrow is thrown into
the oven, how much more will he clothe
you—you of little faith! [29]And do not keep
striving for what you are to eat and what
you are to drink, and do not keep worrying.
[30]For it is the nations of the world that
strive after all these things, and your Father
knows that you need them. [31]Instead, strive
for his[b] kingdom, and these things will be
given to you as well.
32 "Do not be afraid, little flock, for it is
your Father's good pleasure to give you the
kingdom. [33]Sell your possessions, and give
alms. Make purses for yourselves that do
not wear out, an unfailing treasure in
heaven, where no thief comes near and no
moth destroys. [34]For where your treasure is,
there your heart will be also.

Watchful Slaves

35 "Be dressed for action and have your
lamps lit; [36]be like those who are waiting for
their master to return from the wedding
banquet, so that they may open the door for
him as soon as he comes and knocks.
[37]Blessed are those slaves whom the master
finds alert when he comes; truly I tell you,
he will fasten his belt and have them sit
down to eat, and he will come and serve
them. [38]If he comes during the middle of the
night, or near dawn, and finds them so,
blessed are those slaves.
39 "But know this: if the owner of the
house had known at what hour the thief
was coming, he[c] would not have let his
house be broken into. [40]You also must be
ready, for the Son of Man is coming at an
unexpected hour."

[w] Or *power* [x] Gk *Gehenna* [y] Other ancient authorities add *or what* [z] Or *add a cubit to your stature* [a] Other ancient authorities read *Consider the lilies; they neither spin nor weave* [b] Other ancient authorities read *God's* [c] Other ancient authorities add *would have watched and*

12.35-13.9 Another series of images depicts the accountability of God's people. Pictures of slaves (12.35-48) present two themes: (1) the importance of fidelity to God and his work until the unpredictable coming of the master, *the Son of Man;* (2) the rewards and punishments that depend on the faithfulness of service prior to his return. The domestic conflicts that will result from commitments made to Jesus are depicted (12.49-53). Those concerned with various kinds of portents cannot see the significance of God's work through Jesus in the *present time* (12.54-56). It is essential to come to terms with one's situation now, lest severe punishment await one in the future (12.57-59). Harsh military actions and natural catastrophes are not to be compared with the judgment that God is to bring on the unrepentant human race (13.1-5). Yet God does allow more time for people to repent, just as a thoughtful owner of a seemingly sluggish *vineyard* or *fig tree* gives it time to produce (13.6-9).

13.10-17 Jesus justifies his having healed a woman on the Sabbath on the ground that human need must take precedence even over such an ancient law as abstaining from work on the seventh day.

The Faithful or the Unfaithful Slave

41 Peter said, "Lord, are you telling this parable for us or for everyone?" 42And the Lord said, "Who then is the faithful and prudent manager whom his master will put in charge of his slaves, to give them their allowance of food at the proper time? 43Blessed is that slave whom his master will find at work when he arrives. 44Truly I tell you, he will put that one in charge of all his possessions. 45But if that slave says to himself, 'My master is delayed in coming,' and if he begins to beat the other slaves, men and women, and to eat and drink and get drunk, 46the master of that slave will come on a day when he does not expect him and at an hour that he does not know, and will cut him in pieces,[d] and put him with the unfaithful. 47That slave who knew what his master wanted, but did not prepare himself or do what was wanted, will receive a severe beating. 48But the one who did not know and did what deserved a beating will receive a light beating. From everyone to whom much has been given, much will be required; and from the one to whom much has been entrusted, even more will be demanded.

Jesus the Cause of Division

49 "I came to bring fire to the earth, and how I wish it were already kindled! 50I have a baptism with which to be baptized, and what stress I am under until it is completed! 51Do you think that I have come to bring peace to the earth? No, I tell you, but rather division! 52From now on five in one household will be divided, three against two and two against three; 53they will be divided:

father against son
  and son against father,
mother against daughter
  and daughter against mother,
mother-in-law against her daughter-in-law
  and daughter-in-law against mother-in-law."

Interpreting the Time

54 He also said to the crowds, "When you see a cloud rising in the west, you immediately say, 'It is going to rain'; and so it happens. 55And when you see the south wind blowing, you say, 'There will be scorching heat'; and it happens. 56You hypocrites! You know how to interpret the appearance of earth and sky, but why do you not know how to interpret the present time?

Settling with Your Opponent

57 "And why do you not judge for yourselves what is right? 58Thus, when you go with your accuser before a magistrate, on the way make an effort to settle the case,[e] or you may be dragged before the judge, and the judge hand you over to the officer, and the officer throw you in prison. 59I tell you, you will never get out until you have paid the very last penny."

Repent or Perish

13 At that very time there were some present who told him about the Galileans whose blood Pilate had mingled with their sacrifices. 2He asked them, "Do you think that because these Galileans suffered in this way they were worse sinners than all other Galileans? 3No, I tell you; but unless you repent, you will all perish as they did. 4Or those eighteen who were killed when the tower of Siloam fell on them—do you think that they were worse offenders than all the others living in Jerusalem? 5No, I tell you; but unless you repent, you will all perish just as they did."

The Parable of the Barren Fig Tree

6 Then he told this parable: "A man had a fig tree planted in his vineyard; and he came looking for fruit on it and found none. 7So he said to the gardener, 'See here! For three years I have come looking for fruit on this fig tree, and still I find none. Cut it down! Why should it be wasting the soil?' 8He replied, 'Sir, let it alone for one more year, until I dig around it and put manure on it. 9If it bears fruit next year, well and good; but if not, you can cut it down.' "

Jesus Heals a Crippled Woman

10 Now he was teaching in one of the synagogues on the sabbath. 11And just then there appeared a woman with a spirit that had crippled her for eighteen years. She was bent over and was quite unable to stand up straight. 12When Jesus saw her, he called her over and said, "Woman, you are set free

[d] Or *cut him off* [e] Gk *settle with him*

12.42 Lk 7.13
12.47 Num 15.30; Deut 25.2
12.48 Lev 5.17
12.50 Mk 10.38; Jn 12.27
12.51 Mt 10.34-36; ver 49
12.53 Mic 7.6; Mt 10.21
12.54 Mt 16.2
12.55 Mt 20.12
12.56 Mt 16.3
12.58 Mt 5.25,26
12.59 Mk 12.42
13.1 Mt 27.2
13.2 Jn 9.2,3
13.4 Lk 11.4
13.6 Mt 21.19
13.7 Mt 3.10; 7.19; Lk 3.9

13.13 Mk 5.23
13.14 Ex 20.9; Lk 6.7; 14.3
13.15 Lk 7.13; 14.5
13.16 Lk 19.9
13.22 Lk 9.51
13.34 Mt 7.13
13.25 Mt 25.10-12; 7.23
13.27 Mt 7.23; 25.41
13.28 Mt 8.11,12
13.30 Mt 19.30; Mk 10.31
13.32 Heb 2.10; 7.28
13.34 Mt 23.37-39; Lk 19.41
13.35 Ps 118.26; Mt 21.9; Lk 19.38
14.1 Mk 3.2
14.3 Mt 12.10; Mk 3.4; Lk 6.9
14.5 Ex 23.5; Lk 13.15
14.7 Mt 23.6
14.8 Prov 25.6,7

from your ailment." 13 When he laid his
hands on her, immediately she stood up
straight and began praising God. 14 But the
leader of the synagogue, indignant because
Jesus had cured on the sabbath, kept saying
to the crowd, "There are six days on which
work ought to be done; come on those days
and be cured, and not on the sabbath day."
15 But the Lord answered him and said,
"You hypocrites! Does not each of you on
the sabbath untie his ox or his donkey from
the manger, and lead it away to give it
water? 16 And ought not this woman, a
daughter of Abraham whom Satan bound
for eighteen long years, be set free from this
bondage on the sabbath day?" 17 When he
said this, all his opponents were put to
shame; and the entire crowd was rejoicing
at all the wonderful things that he was
doing.

The Parable of the Mustard Seed

18 He said therefore, "What is the kingdom of God like? And to what should I
compare it? 19 It is like a mustard seed that
someone took and sowed in the garden; it
grew and became a tree, and the birds of
the air made nests in its branches."

The Parable of the Yeast

20 And again he said, "To what should
I compare the kingdom of God? 21 It is like
yeast that a woman took and mixed in
with[f] three measures of flour until all of it
was leavened."

The Narrow Door

22 Jesus[g] went through one town and
village after another, teaching as he made
his way to Jerusalem. 23 Someone asked him,
"Lord, will only a few be saved?" He said
to them, 24 "Strive to enter through the
narrow door; for many, I tell you, will try
to enter and will not be able. 25 When once
the owner of the house has got up and shut
the door, and you begin to stand outside
and to knock at the door, saying, 'Lord,
open to us,' then in reply he will say to you,
'I do not know where you come from.'
26 Then you will begin to say, 'We ate and
drank with you, and you taught in our
streets.' 27 But he will say, 'I do not know
where you come from; go away from me,
all you evildoers!' 28 There will be weeping
and gnashing of teeth when you see
Abraham and Isaac and Jacob and all the
prophets in the kingdom of God, and you
yourselves thrown out. 29 Then people will
come from east and west, from north and
south, and will eat in the kingdom of God.
30 Indeed, some are last who will be first, and
some are first who will be last."

The Lament over Jerusalem

31 At that very hour some Pharisees
came and said to him, "Get away from here,
for Herod wants to kill you." 32 He said to
them, "Go and tell that fox for me,[h] 'Listen,
I am casting out demons and performing
cures today and tomorrow, and on the third
day I finish my work. 33 Yet today, tomorrow, and the next day I must be on my
way, because it is impossible for a prophet
to be killed outside of Jerusalem.' 34 Jerusalem, Jerusalem, the city that kills the prophets and stones those who are sent to it! How
often have I desired to gather your children
together as a hen gathers her brood under
her wings, and you were not willing! 35 See,
your house is left to you. And I tell you, you
will not see me until the time comes when[i]
you say, 'Blessed is the one who comes in
the name of the Lord.' "

Jesus Heals the Man with Dropsy

14 On one occasion when Jesus[j] was
going to the house of a leader of the
Pharisees to eat a meal on the sabbath, they
were watching him closely. 2 Just then, in
front of him, there was a man who had
dropsy. 3 And Jesus asked the lawyers and
Pharisees, "Is it lawful to cure people on the
sabbath, or not?" 4 But they were silent. So
Jesus[j] took him and healed him, and sent
him away. 5 Then he said to them, "If one
of you has a child[k] or an ox that has fallen
into a well, will you not immediately pull
it out on a sabbath day?" 6 And they could
not reply to this.

Humility and Hospitality

7 When he noticed how the guests chose
the places of honor, he told them a parable.
8 "When you are invited by someone to a

[f] Gk *hid in* [g] Gk *He* [h] Gk lacks *for me* [i] Other ancient authorities lack *the time comes when* [j] Gk *he* [k] Other ancient authorities read *a donkey*

13.18-14.35 A series of sayings and parables depicts the coming of God's kingdom and the qualifications for participation in it. The parables of *the mustard seed* and the *yeast* contrast the tiny beginnings and the remarkable results (13.18-21). *The narrow door* symbolizes Jesus' radical redefinition of admission to the kingdom, from which many of the traditionally pious will be excluded, while others from across the world will find entrance. In announcing his impending death in Jerusalem (13.31-35), Jesus laments his rejection by so many there and warns that in the future they will see him vindicated *in the name of the Lord.* Another healing on the Sabbath (14.1-6) is justified as an act of mercy that transcends the traditional law. The image of a banquet as a symbol of the time of blessing in the new age is set forth in successive passages: (1) allowing the host to assign the seats of honor instead of striving to occupy them (14.7-11); (2) the advice to invite those who would normally be excluded (*poor, crippled, blind, lame; cf.* 7.22) to share in the time of rejoicing (14.12-14); (3) the parable of the great banquet, to which those originally invited do not come because of preoccupation with daily affairs, but which is shared by the incapacitated (as in 14.13) and by complete outsiders (14.15-24). To be a follower of Jesus demands a break with the security of one's family, the willingness to live under the threat of martyrdom (*take up the cross*), the necessity of long-range planning like that of a builder or a military leader, and the abandonment of one's *possessions* (14.25-33). If they are not true to their original call and identity with him, they are to be *thrown away* as useless.

15.1-32 Jesus defends his welcoming *sinners* into his community through three parables which depict God's joy at recovery of the lost. Recovery of the single lost sheep brings more joy than the docile ninety-nine (15.3-7). The joyful housewife is elated on recovering her lost coin (15.8-10). The rejoicing of the father at his reconciliation with the errant son has to be explained to the son who followed tradition and stayed at home.

wedding banquet, do not sit down at the place of honor, in case someone more distinguished than you has been invited by your host; 9and the host who invited both of you may come and say to you, 'Give this person your place,' and then in disgrace you would start to take the lowest place. 10But when you are invited, go and sit down at the lowest place, so that when your host comes, he may say to you, 'Friend, move up higher'; then you will be honored in the presence of all who sit at the table with you. 11For all who exalt themselves will be humbled, and those who humble themselves will be exalted."

12 He said also to the one who had invited him, "When you give a luncheon or a dinner, do not invite your friends or your brothers or your relatives or rich neighbors, in case they may invite you in return, and you would be repaid. 13But when you give a banquet, invite the poor, the crippled, the lame, and the blind. 14And you will be blessed, because they cannot repay you, for you will be repaid at the resurrection of the righteous."

The Parable of the Great Dinner

15 One of the dinner guests, on hearing this, said to him, "Blessed is anyone who will eat bread in the kingdom of God!" 16Then Jesus[l] said to him, "Someone gave a great dinner and invited many. 17At the time for the dinner he sent his slave to say to those who had been invited, 'Come; for everything is ready now.' 18But they all alike began to make excuses. The first said to him, 'I have bought a piece of land, and I must go out and see it; please accept my regrets.' 19Another said, 'I have bought five yoke of oxen, and I am going to try them out; please accept my regrets.' 20Another said, 'I have just been married, and therefore I cannot come.' 21So the slave returned and reported this to his master. Then the owner of the house became angry and said to his slave, 'Go out at once into the streets and lanes of the town and bring in the poor, the crippled, the blind, and the lame.' 22And the slave said, 'Sir, what you ordered has been done, and there is still room.' 23Then the master said to the slave, 'Go out into the roads and lanes, and compel people to come in, so that my house may be filled. 24For I tell you,[m] none of those who were invited will taste my dinner.'"

The Cost of Discipleship

25 Now large crowds were traveling with him; and he turned and said to them, 26"Whoever comes to me and does not hate father and mother, wife and children, brothers and sisters, yes, and even life itself, cannot be my disciple. 27Whoever does not carry the cross and follow me cannot be my disciple. 28For which of you, intending to build a tower, does not first sit down and estimate the cost, to see whether he has enough to complete it? 29Otherwise, when he has laid a foundation and is not able to finish, all who see it will begin to ridicule him, 30saying, 'This fellow began to build and was not able to finish.' 31Or what king, going out to wage war against another king, will not sit down first and consider whether he is able with ten thousand to oppose the one who comes against him with twenty thousand? 32If he cannot, then, while the other is still far away, he sends a delegation and asks for the terms of peace. 33So therefore, none of you can become my disciple if you do not give up all your possessions.

About Salt

34 "Salt is good; but if salt has lost its taste, how can its saltiness be restored?[n] 35It is fit neither for the soil nor for the manure pile; they throw it away. Let anyone with ears to hear listen!"

The Parable of the Lost Sheep

15 Now all the tax collectors and sinners were coming near to listen to him. 2And the Pharisees and the scribes were grumbling and saying, "This fellow welcomes sinners and eats with them."

3 So he told them this parable: 4"Which one of you, having a hundred sheep and losing one of them, does not leave the ninety-nine in the wilderness and go after the one that is lost until he finds it? 5When he has found it, he lays it on his shoulders and rejoices. 6And when he comes home, he calls together his friends and neighbors, saying to them, 'Rejoice with me, for I have

14.10 Prov 25.6,7

14.11 Mt 23.12; Lk 18.14; Jas 4.6; 1 Pet 5.5,6

14.13 ver 21

14.15 Rev 19.9

14.17 Prov 9.2,5

14.20 Deut 24.5; 1 Cor 7.33

14.21 ver 13

14.24 Mt 21.43; Acts 13.46

14.25 Mt 10.37,38

14.27 Mt 16.24; Mk 8.34; Lk 9.23

14.33 Lk 18.29,30; Phil 3.7; Heb 11.26

14.34 Mt 5.13; Mk 9.50

14.35 Mt 11.15

15.1 Lk 5.29

15.2 Mt 9.11

[l] Gk *he* [m] The Greek word for *you* here is plural [n] Or *how can it be used for seasoning?*

15.7 ver 10; Lk 19.10; Jas 5.20
15.10 ver 7
15.11 Mt 21.28
15.12 Deut 21.17
15.20 Gen 45.14; 46.29; Acts 20.37
15.21 Ps 51.4
15.22 Zech 3.4; Gen 41.42
15.24 ver 32; 1 Tim 5.6; Eph 2.1; 5.14
15.30 ver 12
15.32 ver 24
16.1 Lk 15.13

found my sheep that was lost.' [7]Just so, I
tell you, there will be more joy in heaven
over one sinner who repents than over
ninety-nine righteous persons who need no
repentance.

The Parable of the Lost Coin

8 "Or what woman having ten silver
coins,[o] if she loses one of them, does not
light a lamp, sweep the house, and search
carefully until she finds it? [9]When she has
found it, she calls together her friends and
neighbors, saying, 'Rejoice with me, for I
have found the coin that I had lost.' [10]Just
so, I tell you, there is joy in the presence
of the angels of God over one sinner who
repents."

The Parable of the Prodigal and His Brother

11 Then Jesus[p] said, "There was a man
who had two sons. [12]The younger of them
said to his father, 'Father, give me the share
of the property that will belong to me.' So
he divided his property between them. [13]A
few days later the younger son gathered all
he had and traveled to a distant country,
and there he squandered his property in
dissolute living. [14]When he had spent everything, a severe famine took place throughout that country, and he began to be in
need. [15]So he went and hired himself out to
one of the citizens of that country, who sent
him to his fields to feed the pigs. [16]He would
gladly have filled himself with[q] the pods
that the pigs were eating; and no one gave
him anything. [17]But when he came to himself he said, 'How many of my father's hired
hands have bread enough and to spare, but
here I am dying of hunger! [18]I will get up
and go to my father, and I will say to him,
"Father, I have sinned against heaven and
before you; [19]I am no longer worthy to be
called your son; treat me like one of your
hired hands."' [20]So he set off and went to
his father. But while he was still far off, his
father saw him and was filled with compassion; he ran and put his arms around him
and kissed him. [21]Then the son said to him,
'Father, I have sinned against heaven and
before you; I am no longer worthy to be
called your son.'[r] [22]But the father said to his
slaves, 'Quickly, bring out a robe—the best
one—and put it on him; put a ring on his
finger and sandals on his feet. [23]And get the
fatted calf and kill it, and let us eat and
celebrate; [24]for this son of mine was dead
and is alive again; he was lost and is found!'
And they began to celebrate.

25 "Now his elder son was in the field;
and when he came and approached the
house, he heard music and dancing. [26]He
called one of the slaves and asked what was
going on. [27]He replied, 'Your brother has
come, and your father has killed the fatted
calf, because he has got him back safe and
sound.' [28]Then he became angry and refused to go in. His father came out and
began to plead with him. [29]But he answered
his father, 'Listen! For all these years I have
been working like a slave for you, and I
have never disobeyed your command; yet
you have never given me even a young
goat so that I might celebrate with my
friends. [30]But when this son of yours came
back, who has devoured your property with
prostitutes, you killed the fatted calf for
him!' [31]Then the father[p] said to him, 'Son,
you are always with me, and all that is
mine is yours. [32]But we had to celebrate
and rejoice, because this brother of yours
was dead and has come to life; he was lost
and has been found.'"

The Parable of the Dishonest Manager

16 Then Jesus[p] said to the disciples,
"There was a rich man who had
a manager, and charges were brought to
him that this man was squandering his
property. [2]So he summoned him and said to
him, 'What is this that I hear about you?
Give me an accounting of your manage-
ment, because you cannot be my manager
any longer.' [3]Then the manager said to
himself, 'What will I do, now that my
master is taking the position away from me?
I am not strong enough to dig, and I am
ashamed to beg. [4]I have decided what to do
so that, when I am dismissed as manager,
people may welcome me into their homes.'
[5]So, summoning his master's debtors one by
one, he asked the first, 'How much do you
owe my master?' [6]He answered, 'A hundred
jugs of olive oil.' He said to him, 'Take your
bill, sit down quickly, and make it fifty.'
[7]Then he asked another, 'And how much
do you owe?' He replied, 'A hundred containers of wheat.' He said to him, 'Take

16.1-9 The parable of the clever manager, in which he is commended for having *acted shrewdly* by granting favors to those in debt to his master, makes the point that one can learn even from the dishonest. One should plan ahead for a future day of reckoning.

[o] Gk *drachmas*, each worth about a day's wage for a laborer [p] Gk *he* [q] Other ancient authorities read *filled his stomach with* [r] Other ancient authorities add *treat me as one of your hired servants*

16.10-15 A series of sayings calls for careful acceptance of one's responsibilities in the service of God, and for avoiding reliance on material possessions.
16.16-18 Observations on the Jewish law include the claim that the epoch of the law (*until John*) has been replaced by the inbreaking kingdom of God, into which *everyone* (Jew and Gentile, pious or sinner) is now *urged to enter.* Through Jesus' fullfillment of the scriptures (4.21; 24.26-27, 32), every *stroke of a letter* is preserved. The saying prohibiting divorce and remarriage here is stricter than the Mosaic law itself (Deut 24.1).
16.19-31 The story of the rich man and Lazarus depicts the reversal of human conditions in the life to come: the *rich man* dies and suffers *torment* in *Hades* (the underworld abode of the dead), while *Lazarus* (a shortened form of Eleazar, son of Aaron the priest; Ex 6.23), the beggar at the door of the rich man, is far across a great gulf and at the place of honor next to the founder of the covenant people, *Abraham.* The rich man's suggestion of sending someone from the dead to warn the complacent is declared to be futile, since *Moses and the prophets* have been ignored by many, and from Luke's viewpoint, *someone* (Jesus) has indeed returned from the dead and his message is being rejected by many.
17.1-10 Another series of sayings points up the themes of responsibility of members of the new community toward each other on such issues as causing others to *sin,* forgiving those who sin against oneself, increasing one's faith, and accepting even a menial role (cooking and serving meals) within the new community.

your bill and make it eighty.' 8 And his master commended the dishonest manager because he had acted shrewdly; for the children of this age are more shrewd in dealing with their own generation than are the children of light. 9 And I tell you, make friends for yourselves by means of dishonest wealth[s] so that when it is gone, they may welcome you into the eternal homes.[t]

10 "Whoever is faithful in a very little is faithful also in much; and whoever is dishonest in a very little is dishonest also in much. 11 If then you have not been faithful with the dishonest wealth,[s] who will entrust to you the true riches? 12 And if you have not been faithful with what belongs to another, who will give you what is your own? 13 No slave can serve two masters; for a slave will either hate the one and love the other, or be devoted to the one and despise the other. You cannot serve God and wealth."[s]

The Law and the Kingdom of God

14 The Pharisees, who were lovers of money, heard all this, and they ridiculed him. 15 So he said to them, "You are those who justify yourselves in the sight of others; but God knows your hearts; for what is prized by human beings is an abomination in the sight of God.

16 "The law and the prophets were in effect until John came; since then the good news of the kingdom of God is proclaimed, and everyone tries to enter it by force.[u] 17 But it is easier for heaven and earth to pass away, than for one stroke of a letter in the law to be dropped.

18 "Anyone who divorces his wife and marries another commits adultery, and whoever marries a woman divorced from her husband commits adultery.

The Rich Man and Lazarus

19 "There was a rich man who was dressed in purple and fine linen and who feasted sumptuously every day. 20 And at his gate lay a poor man named Lazarus, covered with sores, 21 who longed to satisfy his hunger with what fell from the rich man's table; even the dogs would come and lick his sores. 22 The poor man died and was carried away by the angels to be with Abraham.[v] The rich man also died and was buried. 23 In Hades, where he was being tormented, he looked up and saw Abraham far away with Lazarus by his side.[w] 24 He called out, 'Father Abraham, have mercy on me, and send Lazarus to dip the tip of his finger in water and cool my tongue; for I am in agony in these flames.' 25 But Abraham said, 'Child, remember that during your lifetime you received your good things, and Lazarus in like manner evil things; but now he is comforted here, and you are in agony. 26 Besides all this, between you and us a great chasm has been fixed, so that those who might want to pass from here to you cannot do so, and no one can cross from there to us.' 27 He said, 'Then, father, I beg you to send him to my father's house— 28 for I have five brothers—that he may warn them, so that they will not also come into this place of torment.' 29 Abraham replied, 'They have Moses and the prophets; they should listen to them.' 30 He said, 'No, father Abraham; but if someone goes to them from the dead, they will repent.' 31 He said to him, 'If they do not listen to Moses and the prophets, neither will they be convinced even if someone rises from the dead.' "

Some Sayings of Jesus

17 Jesus[x] said to his disciples, "Occasions for stumbling are bound to come, but woe to anyone by whom they come! 2 It would be better for you if a millstone were hung around your neck and you were thrown into the sea than for you to cause one of these little ones to stumble. 3 Be on your guard! If another disciple[y] sins, you must rebuke the offender, and if there is repentance, you must forgive. 4 And if the same person sins against you seven times a day, and turns back to you seven times and says, 'I repent,' you must forgive."

5 The apostles said to the Lord, "Increase our faith!" 6 The Lord replied, "If you had faith the size of a[z] mustard seed, you could say to this mulberry tree, 'Be uprooted and planted in the sea,' and it would obey you.

7 "Who among you would say to your slave who has just come in from plowing or tending sheep in the field, 'Come here at once and take your place at the table'? 8 Would you not rather say to him, 'Prepare supper for me, put on your apron and serve

[s] Gk *mammon* [t] Gk *tents* [u] Or *everyone is strongly urged to enter it* [v] Gk *to Abraham's bosom* [w] Gk *in his bosom* [x] Gk *He* [y] Gk *your brother* [z] Gk *faith as a grain of*

16.8 Jn 12.36; Eph 5.8; 1 Thess 5.5
16.9 Mt 6.19,24; 19.21; Lk 11.41; 12.33
16.10 Mt 25.21; Lk 19.17
16.11 ver 9
16.13 Mt 6.24
16.14 2 Tim 3.2; Lk 23.35
16.15 Lk 10.29; 1 Sam 16.7; Prov 21.2; Acts 1.24
16.16 Mt 11.12,13; 4.23
16.17 Isa 40.8; Mt 5.17,18; Lk 21.33
16.18 Mt 5.31,32; 19.19; Mk 10.11; 1 Cor 7.10,11
16.20 Acts 3.2
16.22 Jn 13.23
16.23 Mt 11.23
16.24 ver 30; Mt 25.41
16.25 Lk 6.24
16.29 Lk 4.17; Jn 5.45-47; Acts 15.21
16.30 Lk 3.8; 19.9
17.1 Mt 18.6,7; Mk 9.42; 1 Cor 11.19
17.2 1 Cor 8.12
17.3 Mt 18.15
17.4 Mt 18.21,22
17.5 Mk 6.30
17.6 Mt 17.20; 21.21; Mk 9.23; Lk 9.22
17.8 Lk 12.37

17.11 Lk 9.51,52; Jn 4.3,4
17.12 Lev 13.46
17.14 Lev 13.2; 14.2; Mt 8.4
17.15 Mt 9.8
17.16 Mt 10.5
17.19 Mt 9.22; Mk 5.34; Lk 7.50; 8.48; 18.42
17.21 ver 23
17.22 Mt 9.15; Mk 2.20; Lk 5.35
17.23 Mt 24.23; Mk 13.21; Lk 21.8
17.24 Mt 24.27
17.25 Mt 16.21; Lk 9.22
17.26 Mt 24.37-39; Gen 7
17.28 Gen 18.20-33; 19.24,25

me while I eat and drink; later you may eat and drink'? 9Do you thank the slave for doing what was commanded? 10So you also, when you have done all that you were ordered to do, say, 'We are worthless slaves; we have done only what we ought to have done!' "

Jesus Cleanses Ten Lepers

11 On the way to Jerusalem Jesus[a] was going through the region between Samaria and Galilee. 12As he entered a village, ten lepers[b] approached him. Keeping their distance, 13they called out, saying, "Jesus, Master, have mercy on us!" 14When he saw them, he said to them, "Go and show yourselves to the priests." And as they went, they were made clean. 15Then one of them, when he saw that he was healed, turned back, praising God with a loud voice. 16He prostrated himself at Jesus'[c] feet and thanked him. And he was a Samaritan. 17Then Jesus asked, "Were not ten made clean? But the other nine, where are they? 18Was none of them found to return and give praise to God except this foreigner?" 19Then he said to him, "Get up and go on your way; your faith has made you well."

The Coming of the Kingdom

20 Once Jesus[a] was asked by the Pharisees when the kingdom of God was coming, and he answered, "The kingdom of God is not coming with things that can be observed; 21nor will they say, 'Look, here it is!' or 'There it is!' For, in fact, the kingdom of God is among[d] you."

22 Then he said to the disciples, "The days are coming when you will long to see one of the days of the Son of Man, and you will not see it. 23They will say to you, 'Look there!' or 'Look here!' Do not go, do not set off in pursuit. 24For as the lightning flashes and lights up the sky from one side to the other, so will the Son of Man be in his day.[e] 25But first he must endure much suffering and be rejected by this generation. 26Just as it was in the days of Noah, so too it will be in the days of the Son of Man. 27They were eating and drinking, and marrying and being given in marriage, until the day Noah entered the ark, and the flood came and destroyed all of them. 28Likewise, just as it was in the days of Lot: they were eating and drinking, buying and selling, planting and building, 29but on the day that Lot left Sodom, it rained fire and sulfur from heaven and destroyed all of them 30—it will be like that on the day that the Son of Man is revealed. 31On that day, anyone on the housetop who has belongings in the house must not come down to take them away; and likewise anyone in the field must not turn back. 32Remember Lot's wife. 33Those who try to make their life secure will lose it, but those who lose their life will keep it. 34I tell you, on that night there will be two in one bed; one will be taken and the other left. 35There will be two women grinding meal together; one will be taken and the other left."[f] 37Then they asked him, "Where, Lord?" He said to them, "Where the corpse is, there the vultures will gather."

The Parable of the Widow and the Unjust Judge

18 Then Jesus[a] told them a parable about their need to pray always and not to lose heart. 2He said, "In a certain city there was a judge who neither feared God nor had respect for people. 3In that city there was a widow who kept coming to him and saying, 'Grant me justice against my opponent.' 4For a while he refused; but later he said to himself, 'Though I have no fear of God and no respect for anyone, 5yet because this widow keeps bothering me, I will grant her justice, so that she may not wear me out by continually coming.' "[g] 6And the Lord said, "Listen to what the unjust judge says. 7And will not God grant justice to his chosen ones who cry to him day and night? Will he delay long in helping them? 8I tell you, he will quickly grant justice to them. And yet, when the Son of Man comes, will he find faith on earth?"

The Parable of the Pharisee and the Tax Collector

9 He also told this parable to some who trusted in themselves that they were righteous and regarded others with contempt: 10"Two men went up to the temple to pray, one a Pharisee and the other a tax collector.

[a] Gk *he* [b] The terms *leper* and *leprosy* can refer to several diseases [c] Gk *his* [d] Or *within* [e] Other ancient authorities lack *in his day* [f] Other ancient authorities add verse 36, *"Two will be in the field; one will be taken and the other left."* [g] Or *so that she may not finally come and slap me in the face*

17.11-19 Mention of *the way to Jerusalem* reminds the reader of this stage in Luke's account of Jesus' career (9.51; 19.28). The only leper of the ten healed by Jesus who returned to express his gratitude was a *Samaritan*, who is referred to as a *foreigner* since he was not a member of the Jewish community.
17.20-37 In answer to the question about when God's kingdom would come, Jesus replies that it is already *among* them through his words and actions of renewal, but that its full coming will be so sudden and unexpected, and most people will be so preoccupied with their daily routines (*eating and drinking...*), that they will be unprepared for the grim judgment that will fall on the world. The remains of those that are struck down in the judgment of God will be food for the *vultures*.
18.1-8 The insistent but effective appeals of the *widow* to the judge are compared with the readiness of God to heed the prayers of his people and set matters right. But the question remains whether there will still be people of *faith* when the *Son of Man* returns.
18.9-14 This story contrasts the *Pharisee's* proud recitation of his moral superiority with the *tax collector's* confession of sin and plea for mercy.

18.15-30 A series of teachings about qualifications for participation in the *kingdom of God*: (1) Children are welcome, since the kingdom is to be received just as a child would accept a gift: freely and with gratitude (*cf.* 9.46-48); (2) the rich *ruler* story (18.18-30) closely parallels Mk 10.17-31 with the demand to strip off one's possessions, as symbolized by the impossibility of a huge, awkward camel passing through the tiny opening in a needle; (3) present self-denial for the sake of the *kingdom*, such as Peter claims, will lead to divine reward in the age to come.

18.31-43 Two brief stories present in dramatic contrast (1) the inability of the disciples to understand Jesus' prophecy of his suffering and death in *Jerusalem* with (2) the ability of the *blind* beggar in *Jericho* to recognize Jesus as *son of David* and *Lord*, which results in his receiving sight and in the people's praise of God.

19.1-10 A third story describes Jesus' call to Zacchaeus, *the chief tax collector*, whose great wealth, gained by collaboration with the Roman occupying power, would have made him an object of envy and hatred. Luke reports his generosity and honesty, and Jesus acclaims him as *a son of Abraham* – a true member of the covenant people in spite of his *lost* condition by Jewish standards.

11The Pharisee, standing by himself, was praying thus, 'God, I thank you that I am not like other people: thieves, rogues, adulterers, or even like this tax collector. 12I fast twice a week; I give a tenth of all my income.' 13But the tax collector, standing far off, would not even look up to heaven, but was beating his breast and saying, 'God, be merciful to me, a sinner!' 14I tell you, this man went down to his home justified rather than the other; for all who exalt themselves will be humbled, but all who humble themselves will be exalted."

Jesus Blesses Little Children

15 People were bringing even infants to him that he might touch them; and when the disciples saw it, they sternly ordered them not to do it. 16But Jesus called for them and said, "Let the little children come to me, and do not stop them; for it is to such as these that the kingdom of God belongs. 17Truly I tell you, whoever does not receive the kingdom of God as a little child will never enter it."

The Rich Ruler

18 A certain ruler asked him, "Good Teacher, what must I do to inherit eternal life?" 19Jesus said to him, "Why do you call me good? No one is good but God alone. 20You know the commandments: 'You shall not commit adultery; You shall not murder; You shall not steal; You shall not bear false witness; Honor your father and mother.'" 21He replied, "I have kept all these since my youth." 22When Jesus heard this, he said to him, "There is still one thing lacking. Sell all that you own and distribute the money[h] to the poor, and you will have treasure in heaven; then come, follow me." 23But when he heard this, he became sad; for he was very rich. 24Jesus looked at him and said, "How hard it is for those who have wealth to enter the kingdom of God! 25Indeed, it is easier for a camel to go through the eye of a needle than for someone who is rich to enter the kingdom of God."

26 Those who heard it said, "Then who can be saved?" 27He replied, "What is impossible for mortals is possible for God."

28 Then Peter said, "Look, we have left our homes and followed you." 29And he said to them, "Truly I tell you, there is no one who has left house or wife or brothers or parents or children, for the sake of the kingdom of God, 30who will not get back very much more in this age, and in the age to come eternal life."

A Third Time Jesus Foretells His Death and Resurrection

31 Then he took the twelve aside and said to them, "See, we are going up to Jerusalem, and everything that is written about the Son of Man by the prophets will be accomplished. 32For he will be handed over to the Gentiles; and he will be mocked and insulted and spat upon. 33After they have flogged him, they will kill him, and on the third day he will rise again." 34But they understood nothing about all these things; in fact, what he said was hidden from them, and they did not grasp what was said.

Jesus Heals a Blind Beggar Near Jericho

35 As he approached Jericho, a blind man was sitting by the roadside begging. 36When he heard a crowd going by, he asked what was happening. 37They told him, "Jesus of Nazareth[i] is passing by." 38Then he shouted, "Jesus, Son of David, have mercy on me!" 39Those who were in front sternly ordered him to be quiet; but he shouted even more loudly, "Son of David, have mercy on me!" 40Jesus stood still and ordered the man to be brought to him; and when he came near, he asked him, 41"What do you want me to do for you?" He said, "Lord, let me see again." 42Jesus said to him, "Receive your sight; your faith has saved you." 43Immediately he regained his sight and followed him, glorifying God; and all the people, when they saw it, praised God.

Jesus and Zacchaeus

19 He entered Jericho and was passing through it. 2A man was there named Zacchaeus; he was a chief tax collector and was rich. 3He was trying to see who Jesus was, but on account of the crowd he could not, because he was short in stature. 4So he ran ahead and climbed a sycamore tree to see him, because he was going to pass that way. 5When Jesus came to the place, he looked up and said to him, "Zacchaeus, hurry and come down; for I

[h] Gk lacks *the money* [i] Gk *the Nazorean*

18.12 Mt 9.14; Lk 11.42

18.13 Lk 23.48

18.14 Mt 23.12; Lk 14.11; 1 Pet 5.6

18.17 Mt 18.3

18.18 Lk 10.25

18.20 Ex 20.12-16; Deut 5.16-20; Rom 13.9

18.22 Lk 12.33; Mt 19.21

18.24 Prov 11.28

18.27 Gen 18.14; Job 42.2; Jer 32.17; Lk 1.37

18.28 Lk 5.11

18.30 Mt 12.32

18.31 Lk 9.51; Ps 22

18.32 Mt 16.21; 27.2; Lk 23.1

18.34 Mk 9.32; Lk 9.45

18.38 Mt 9.27

18.39 ver 38

18.42 Mt 9.22; Mk 5.34; Lk 17.19

18.43 Mt 9.8; Lk 13.17

19.1 Lk 18.35

19.4 1 Kings 10.27; 1 Chr 27.28; Isa 9.10

must stay at your house today." 6 So he hurried down and was happy to welcome him. 7 All who saw it began to grumble and said, "He has gone to be the guest of one who is a sinner." 8 Zacchaeus stood there and said to the Lord, "Look, half of my possessions, Lord, I will give to the poor; and if I have defrauded anyone of anything, I will pay back four times as much." 9 Then Jesus said to him, "Today salvation has come to this house, because he too is a son of Abraham. 10 For the Son of Man came to seek out and to save the lost."

The Parable of the Ten Pounds

11 As they were listening to this, he went on to tell a parable, because he was near Jerusalem, and because they supposed that the kingdom of God was to appear immediately. 12 So he said, "A nobleman went to a distant country to get royal power for himself and then return. 13 He summoned ten of his slaves, and gave them ten pounds,[j] and said to them, 'Do business with these until I come back.' 14 But the citizens of his country hated him and sent a delegation after him, saying, 'We do not want this man to rule over us.' 15 When he returned, having received royal power, he ordered these slaves, to whom he had given the money, to be summoned so that he might find out what they had gained by trading. 16 The first came forward and said, 'Lord, your pound has made ten more pounds.' 17 He said to him, 'Well done, good slave! Because you have been trustworthy in a very small thing, take charge of ten cities.' 18 Then the second came, saying, 'Lord, your pound has made five pounds.' 19 He said to him, 'And you, rule over five cities.' 20 Then the other came, saying, 'Lord, here is your pound. I wrapped it up in a piece of cloth, 21 for I was afraid of you, because you are a harsh man; you take what you did not deposit, and reap what you did not sow.' 22 He said to him, 'I will judge you by your own words, you wicked slave! You knew, did you, that I was a harsh man, taking what I did not deposit and reaping what I did not sow? 23 Why then did you not put my money into the bank? Then when I returned, I could have collected it with interest.' 24 He said to the bystanders, 'Take the pound from him and give it to the one who has ten pounds.' 25 (And they said to him, 'Lord, he has ten pounds!') 26 'I tell you, to all those who have, more will be given; but from those who have nothing, even what they have will be taken away. 27 But as for these enemies of mine who did not want me to be king over them—bring them here and slaughter them in my presence.'"

Jesus' Triumphal Entry into Jerusalem

28 After he had said this, he went on ahead, going up to Jerusalem.

29 When he had come near Bethphage and Bethany, at the place called the Mount of Olives, he sent two of the disciples, 30 saying, "Go into the village ahead of you, and as you enter it you will find tied there a colt that has never been ridden. Untie it and bring it here. 31 If anyone asks you, 'Why are you untying it?' just say this, 'The Lord needs it.' " 32 So those who were sent departed and found it as he had told them. 33 As they were untying the colt, its owners asked them, "Why are you untying the colt?" 34 They said, "The Lord needs it." 35 Then they brought it to Jesus; and after throwing their cloaks on the colt, they set Jesus on it. 36 As he rode along, people kept spreading their cloaks on the road. 37 As he was now approaching the path down from the Mount of Olives, the whole multitude of the disciples began to praise God joyfully with a loud voice for all the deeds of power that they had seen, 38 saying,

"Blessed is the king
  who comes in the name of the Lord!
Peace in heaven,
  and glory in the highest heaven!"

39 Some of the Pharisees in the crowd said to him, "Teacher, order your disciples to stop." 40 He answered, "I tell you, if these were silent, the stones would shout out."

Jesus Weeps over Jerusalem

41 As he came near and saw the city, he wept over it, 42 saying, "If you, even you, had only recognized on this day the things that make for peace! But now they are hidden from your eyes. 43 Indeed, the days will come upon you, when your enemies will set up ramparts around you and surround you, and hem you in on every side. 44 They will crush you to the ground, you and your children within you, and they will

[j] The mina, rendered here by *pound*, was about three months' wages for a laborer

19.11-27 Jesus' *parable* of the *pounds* (a monetary unit worth only a fraction of the *talent* which appears in Matthew's different form of this parable in Mt 25.14-30) has three major points to make: (1) that in spite of the seeming delay, Jesus will return as king; (2) that during his absence his followers are to be *faithful* in fulfilling their assigned responsibilities (symbolized by the *pounds* given to them for use in *trading*); (3) that those who reject his kingship are going to be punished.
19.28-24.53 The Confrontation with the Religious and Civil Authorities and the Commissioning of the Apostles in Jerusalem.
19.28-44 *Bethphage* and *Bethany* are villages on the side of the *Mount of Olives*, a mountain ridge just east of Jerusalem, and on the route which leads there from *Jericho* in the Jordan Valley. The ride into the city on the *colt* is in fulfillment of Zech 9.9, as Mt 21.5 makes explicit, and the acclaim of him as king by *the multitude of the disciples* is a quotation of Ps 118.25-26. To the objection of the Pharisees at this identification of him Jesus responds by predicting the destruction of Jerusalem for the failure of its people to recognize him as God's agent, quoting Ps 137.9.

19.7 Mt 9.11; Lk 5.30
19.8 Lk 7.13; 3.14; Ex 22.1; Lev 6.5; Num 5.7; 2 Sam 12.6
19.9 Lk 3.8; 13.16; Rom 4.16; Gal 3.7
19.10 Mt 18.11
19.11 Acts 1.6
19.12 Mt 25.14-30; Mk 13.34
19.17 Lk 16.10
19.21 Mt 25.24
19.22 2 Sam 1.16; Job 15.6; Mt 25.26
19.26 Mt 13.12; Lk 8.18
19.28 Mk 10.32; Mt 21.17; Lk 21.37
19.32 Lk 22.13
19.36 2 Kings 9.13
19.38 Ps 118.26; Lk 13.35; 2.14
19.39 Mt 21.15,16
19.40 Hab 2.11
19.41 Lk 13.34,35
19.43 Isa 29.3; Jer 6.6; Ezek 4.2; Lk 21.20
19.44 Mt 13.2; Mk 13.2; Lk 21.6; 1 Pet 2.12

19.45-48 Jesus justifies his disruption of the sale of sacrificial animals in the *temple* courts by an appeal to Isa 56.7 and Jer 7.11 concerning the corruption of *the house of prayer*. The determination of the religious leaders to destroy Jesus is matched by the keen interest in him among the *people*.
20.1-8 The opponents of Jesus (*priests, scribes, elders*) demand to know the source of his *authority*, which he counters with a question about the authority of John the Baptist, which was popularly recognized as coming from God. The leaders refuse to answer his question, and he does not answer theirs.
20.9-19 The parable of the tenants, which builds on the prophet's picture of Israel as God's unfruitful vineyard (Isa 5), portrays Israel's continuing rejection of God's agents and now of his *beloved son*. This will result in the destruction of the tenants and the giving of the vineyard to the new community (*others*), in fulfillment of Ps 118.22-23, with the result that those who remain within the traditional people will be crushed, as the leaders perceive.
20.20-26 To the Markan account (Mk 12.13-17) Luke adds that the Jewish leaders' plot aimed at turning Jesus over to the Roman *governor*, and that their plan was thwarted by continuing popular support of him.
20.27-40 Luke has a more complete version of Jesus' debate about the resurrection (see Mk 12.18-27), in which he makes more frequent reference to the event of the resurrection, and particularly to those who are *worthy* to share in it. He also notes how impressed and put to silence were the official interpreters of the law, *the scribes*.

not leave within you one stone upon another; because you did not recognize the time of your visitation from God."[k]

Jesus Cleanses the Temple

45 Then he entered the temple and began to drive out those who were selling things there; 46and he said, "It is written,

'My house shall be a house of prayer';
but you have made it a den of robbers."

47 Every day he was teaching in the temple. The chief priests, the scribes, and the leaders of the people kept looking for a way to kill him; 48but they did not find anything they could do, for all the people were spellbound by what they heard.

The Authority of Jesus Questioned

20 One day, as he was teaching the people in the temple and telling the good news, the chief priests and the scribes came with the elders 2and said to him, "Tell us, by what authority are you doing these things? Who is it who gave you this authority?" 3He answered them, "I will also ask you a question, and you tell me: 4Did the baptism of John come from heaven, or was it of human origin?" 5They discussed it with one another, saying, "If we say, 'From heaven,' he will say, 'Why did you not believe him?' 6But if we say, 'Of human origin,' all the people will stone us; for they are convinced that John was a prophet." 7So they answered that they did not know where it came from. 8Then Jesus said to them, "Neither will I tell you by what authority I am doing these things."

The Parable of the Wicked Tenants

9 He began to tell the people this parable: "A man planted a vineyard, and leased it to tenants, and went to another country for a long time. 10When the season came, he sent a slave to the tenants in order that they might give him his share of the produce of the vineyard; but the tenants beat him and sent him away empty-handed. 11Next he sent another slave; that one also they beat and insulted and sent away empty-handed. 12And he sent still a third; this one also they wounded and threw out. 13Then the owner of the vineyard said, 'What shall I do? I will send my beloved son; perhaps they will respect him.' 14But when the tenants saw him, they discussed it among themselves and said, 'This is the heir; let us kill him so that the inheritance may be ours.' 15So they threw him out of the vineyard and killed him. What then will the owner of the vineyard do to them? 16He will come and destroy those tenants and give the vineyard to others." When they heard this, they said, "Heaven forbid!" 17But he looked at them and said, "What then does this text mean:

'The stone that the builders rejected
has become the cornerstone'?[l]

18Everyone who falls on that stone will be broken to pieces; and it will crush anyone on whom it falls." 19When the scribes and chief priests realized that he had told this parable against them, they wanted to lay hands on him at that very hour, but they feared the people.

The Question about Paying Taxes

20 So they watched him and sent spies who pretended to be honest, in order to trap him by what he said, so as to hand him over to the jurisdiction and authority of the governor. 21So they asked him, "Teacher, we know that you are right in what you say and teach, and you show deference to no one, but teach the way of God in accordance with truth. 22Is it lawful for us to pay taxes to the emperor, or not?" 23But he perceived their craftiness and said to them, 24"Show me a denarius. Whose head and whose title does it bear?" They said, "The emperor's." 25He said to them, "Then give to the emperor the things that are the emperor's, and to God the things that are God's." 26And they were not able in the presence of the people to trap him by what he said; and being amazed by his answer, they became silent.

The Question about the Resurrection

27 Some Sadducees, those who say there is no resurrection, came to him 28and asked him a question, "Teacher, Moses wrote for us that if a man's brother dies, leaving a wife but no children, the man[m] shall marry the widow and raise up children for his brother. 29Now there were seven brothers; the first married, and died childless; 30then

19.46 Isa 56.7
19.47 Mt 26.55; Mk 11.18; Jn 7.19
20.1 Mt 26.55; Lk 8.1
20.2 Jn 2.18; Acts 4.7; 7.27
20.6 Mt 14.5; Lk 7.29
20.9 Isa 5.1-7; Mt 25.14
20.16 Lk 19.27; Rom 3.4,6,31
20.17 Ps 118.22,23; 1 Pet 2.6
20.18 Isa 8.14,15
20.19 Lk 19.47
20.21 Jn 3.2
20.25 Rom 13.7; Lk 23.2
20.27 Acts 23.6,8
20.28 Deut 25.5

[k] Gk lacks *from God* [l] Or *keystone* [m] Gk *his brother*

the second [31]and the third married her, and
so in the same way all seven died childless.
[32]Finally the woman also died. [33]In the
resurrection, therefore, whose wife will the
woman be? For the seven had married her."
34 Jesus said to them, "Those who belong to this age marry and are given in
marriage; [35]but those who are considered
worthy of a place in that age and in the
resurrection from the dead neither marry
nor are given in marriage. [36]Indeed they
cannot die anymore, because they are like
angels and are children of God, being children of the resurrection. [37]And the fact that
the dead are raised Moses himself showed,
in the story about the bush, where he
speaks of the Lord as the God of Abraham,
the God of Isaac, and the God of Jacob.
[38]Now he is God not of the dead, but of the
living; for to him all of them are alive."
[39]Then some of the scribes answered,
"Teacher, you have spoken well." [40]For they
no longer dared to ask him another question.

The Question about David's Son

41 Then he said to them, "How can they
say that the Messiah[n] is David's son? [42]For
David himself says in the book of Psalms,
'The Lord said to my Lord,
"Sit at my right hand,
43 until I make your enemies your footstool."'
[44]David thus calls him Lord; so how can he
be his son?"

Jesus Denounces the Scribes

45 In the hearing of all the people he
said to the[o] disciples, [46]"Beware of the scribes,
who like to walk around in long robes, and
love to be greeted with respect in the
marketplaces, and to have the best seats in
the synagogues and places of honor at
banquets. [47]They devour widows' houses
and for the sake of appearance say long
prayers. They will receive the greater condemnation."

The Widow's Offering

21 He looked up and saw rich people
putting their gifts into the treasury; [2]he also saw a poor widow put in two
small copper coins. [3]He said, "Truly I tell
you, this poor widow has put in more than
all of them; [4]for all of them have contributed out of their abundance, but she out of
her poverty has put in all she had to live
on."

The Destruction of the Temple Foretold

5 When some were speaking about the
temple, how it was adorned with beautiful
stones and gifts dedicated to God, he said,
[6]"As for these things that you see, the days
will come when not one stone will be left
upon another; all will be thrown down."

Signs and Persecutions

7 They asked him, "Teacher, when will
this be, and what will be the sign that this
is about to take place?" [8]And he said, "Beware that you are not led astray; for many
will come in my name and say, 'I am he!'[p]
and, 'The time is near!'[q] Do not go after
them.
9 "When you hear of wars and insurrec-
tions, do not be terrified; for these things
must take place first, but the end will not
follow immediately." [10]Then he said to them,
"Nation will rise against nation, and kingdom against kingdom; [11]there will be great
earthquakes, and in various places famines
and plagues; and there will be dreadful
portents and great signs from heaven.
12 "But before all this occurs, they will
arrest you and persecute you; they will
hand you over to synagogues and prisons,
and you will be brought before kings and
governors because of my name. [13]This will
give you an opportunity to testify. [14]So
make up your minds not to prepare your
defense in advance; [15]for I will give you
words[r] and a wisdom that none of your
opponents will be able to withstand or
contradict. [16]You will be betrayed even by
parents and brothers, by relatives and friends;
and they will put some of you to death.
[17]You will be hated by all because of my
name. [18]But not a hair of your head will
perish. [19]By your endurance you will gain
your souls.

The Destruction of Jerusalem Foretold

20 "When you see Jerusalem surrounded
by armies, then know that its desolation
has come near.[s] [21]Then those in Judea must

[n] Or *the Christ* [o] Other ancient authorities read *his* [p] Gk *I am* [q] Or *at hand* [r] Gk *a mouth* [s] Or *is at hand*

20.36 Rom 8.16,17; 1 Jn 3.1,2
20.37 Ex 3.6
20.38 Rom 6.10,11
20.40 Mt 22.46; Mk 12.34
20.42 Ps 110.1; Acts 2.34
20.46 Lk 11.43
21.1 Mk 12.41-44
21.2 Mk 12.42
21.5 Mk 13.1
21.6 Lk 19.44
21.8 Mk 13.21; Lk 17.23
21.10 2 Chr 15.6; Isa 19.2
21.12 Jn 16.2
21.13 Phil 1.12
21.14 Lk 12.11,12
21.15 Lk 12.12
21.16 Lk 12.52,53
21.17 Mt 10.22
21.18 Mt 10.30; Lk 12.7
21.19 Rev 2.7
21.20 Lk 19.43
21.21 Lk 17.31

20.45-47 Luke's account of Jesus' rebuke of the Pharisees for their ostentatious piety matches closely Mk 12.37-40, in contrast to the greatly extended version in Mt 23.1-36.
21.1-6 The story of the gift of two *small copper coins* to the temple treasury fits well Luke's emphasis on God's special concern for the *poor*. In contrast, the splendid temple buildings and the *dedicated gifts* are all to be destroyed (*thrown down*).
21.7-36 In response to the question when the temple's destruction will occur, Luke (following Mk 13.5-37, with some omissions and additions) reports Jesus as describing the cosmic disturbances that will precede the end of the age (21.8-11), the persecutions and trials at the hands of religious and civil leadership that the community will suffer, including hatred and betrayal within families (21.12-19), the military attack on Jerusalem, the flight of God's people, and the Roman (Gentiles') occupation of the city, which will continue until God's purpose for the Gentiles (*times of the Gentiles*) is *fulfilled* (21.20-24). Also depicted are the cosmic disturbances and the perplexity of *the nations* until the *Son of Man* comes in triumph. Then God's people will know that their deliverance *is drawing near* (21.25-28); for them the fig tree about to *sprout leaves* is the symbol of the nearness of *the kingdom*. The certainty of its coming for *this generation* (either Jesus' or the writer's) is affirmed, but there is a final call to avoid *dissipation* and preoccupation with everyday matters and instead to be ever *alert*.

21.37-38 Luke pictures Jesus as daily involved in the affairs of his people (*in the temple*) but as nightly withdrawing to *the Mount of Olives*, which was the setting for God's final judgment on Jerusalem, according to the prophetic tradition (Zech 14.2-5).
22.1-13 For the link between the feasts of *Passover* and *Unleavened Bread* see note on 2.41. The religious leaders are seeking to destroy Jesus, aided by Judas, whom *Satan* has *entered* for this purpose. The description of the preparation for the meal follows Mk 14.12-16.
22.14-38 The sequence and details of the supper itself differ from those in Mk 14.17-25. Jesus' followers are now identified as *apostles*. He begins by declaring he will not *eat the Passover* (according to some ancient texts of Luke), which fits with the description of this meal in John 13.21-30 as taking place the night before the Passover. The meal will find its fulfilled meaning when the *Kingdom of God* has fully come.

flee to the mountains, and those inside the city must leave it, and those out in the country must not enter it; [22]for these are days of vengeance, as a fulfillment of all that is written. [23]Woe to those who are pregnant and to those who are nursing infants in those days! For there will be great distress on the earth and wrath against this people; [24]they will fall by the edge of the sword and be taken away as captives among all nations; and Jerusalem will be trampled on by the Gentiles, until the times of the Gentiles are fulfilled.

The Coming of the Son of Man

25 "There will be signs in the sun, the moon, and the stars, and on the earth distress among nations confused by the roaring of the sea and the waves. [26]People will faint from fear and foreboding of what is coming upon the world, for the powers of the heavens will be shaken. [27]Then they will see 'the Son of Man coming in a cloud' with power and great glory. [28]Now when these things begin to take place, stand up and raise your heads, because your redemption is drawing near."

The Lesson of the Fig Tree

29 Then he told them a parable: "Look at the fig tree and all the trees; [30]as soon as they sprout leaves you can see for yourselves and know that summer is already near. [31]So also, when you see these things taking place, you know that the kingdom of God is near. [32]Truly I tell you, this generation will not pass away until all things have taken place. [33]Heaven and earth will pass away, but my words will not pass away.

Exhortation to Watch

34 "Be on guard so that your hearts are not weighed down with dissipation and drunkenness and the worries of this life, and that day catch you unexpectedly, [35]like a trap. For it will come upon all who live on the face of the whole earth. [36]Be alert at all times, praying that you may have the strength to escape all these things that will take place, and to stand before the Son of Man."

37 Every day he was teaching in the temple, and at night he would go out and spend the night on the Mount of Olives, as it was called. [38]And all the people would get up early in the morning to listen to him in the temple.

The Plot to Kill Jesus

22 Now the festival of Unleavened Bread, which is called the Passover, was near. [2]The chief priests and the scribes were looking for a way to put Jesus[t] to death, for they were afraid of the people.

3 Then Satan entered into Judas called Iscariot, who was one of the twelve; [4]he went away and conferred with the chief priests and officers of the temple police about how he might betray him to them. [5]They were greatly pleased and agreed to give him money. [6]So he consented and began to look for an opportunity to betray him to them when no crowd was present.

The Preparation of the Passover

7 Then came the day of Unleavened Bread, on which the Passover lamb had to be sacrificed. [8]So Jesus[u] sent Peter and John, saying, "Go and prepare the Passover meal for us that we may eat it." [9]They asked him, "Where do you want us to make preparations for it?" [10]"Listen," he said to them, "when you have entered the city, a man carrying a jar of water will meet you; follow him into the house he enters [11]and say to the owner of the house, 'The teacher asks you, "Where is the guest room, where I may eat the Passover with my disciples?"' [12]He will show you a large room upstairs, already furnished. Make preparations for us there." [13]So they went and found everything as he had told them; and they prepared the Passover meal.

The Institution of the Lord's Supper

14 When the hour came, he took his place at the table, and the apostles with him. [15]He said to them, "I have eagerly desired to eat this Passover with you before I suffer; [16]for I tell you, I will not eat it[v] until it is fulfilled in the kingdom of God." [17]Then he took a cup, and after giving thanks he said, "Take this and divide it among yourselves; [18]for I tell you that from now on I will not drink of the fruit of the vine until

[t] Gk *him* [u] Gk *he* [v] Other ancient authorities read *never eat it again*

21.22 Isa 63.4; Dan 9.24-27; Zech 11.1
21.24 Isa 63.18; Dan 8.13; 9.27; 12.7; Rom 11.25; Rev 11.2
21.25 2 Pet 3.10,12
21.27 Rev 1.7; 14.14
21.28 Lk 18.7
21.31 Mt 3.2
21.33 Lk 16.17
21.34 Mk 4.19; Lk 12.45; 1 Thess 5.6,7
21.36 Lk 18.1
21.37 Lk 19.47; Mk 11.19
22.1 Jn 11.47-53
22.2 Mt 12.14
22.3 Jn 13.2
22.5 Zech 11.12
22.7 Ex 12.18-20; Deut 16.5-8
22.8 Lk 19.29; Acts 3.1
22.16 Lk 14.15; Rev 19.9

the kingdom of God comes." [19]Then he took a loaf of bread, and when he had given thanks, he broke it and gave it to them, saying, "This is my body, which is given for you. Do this in remembrance of me." [20]And he did the same with the cup after supper, saying, "This cup that is poured out for you is the new covenant in my blood.[w] [21]But see, the one who betrays me is with me, and his hand is on the table. [22]For the Son of Man is going as it has been determined, but woe to that one by whom he is betrayed!" [23]Then they began to ask one another, which one of them it could be who would do this.

The Dispute about Greatness

24 A dispute also arose among them as to which one of them was to be regarded as the greatest. [25]But he said to them, "The kings of the Gentiles lord it over them; and those in authority over them are called benefactors. [26]But not so with you; rather the greatest among you must become like the youngest, and the leader like one who serves. [27]For who is greater, the one who is at the table or the one who serves? Is it not the one at the table? But I am among you as one who serves.

28 "You are those who have stood by me in my trials; [29]and I confer on you, just as my Father has conferred on me, a kingdom, [30]so that you may eat and drink at my table in my kingdom, and you will sit on thrones judging the twelve tribes of Israel.

Jesus Predicts Peter's Denial

31 "Simon, Simon, listen! Satan has demanded[x] to sift all of you like wheat, [32]but I have prayed for you that your own faith may not fail; and you, when once you have turned back, strengthen your brothers." [33]And he said to him, "Lord, I am ready to go with you to prison and to death!" [34]Jesus[y] said, "I tell you, Peter, the cock will not crow this day, until you have denied three times that you know me."

Purse, Bag, and Sword

35 He said to them, "When I sent you out without a purse, bag, or sandals, did you lack anything?" They said, "No, not a thing." [36]He said to them, "But now, the one who has a purse must take it, and likewise a bag. And the one who has no sword must sell his cloak and buy one. [37]For I tell you, this scripture must be fulfilled in me, 'And he was counted among the lawless'; and indeed what is written about me is being fulfilled." [38]They said, "Lord, look, here are two swords." He replied, "It is enough."

Jesus Prays on the Mount of Olives

39 He came out and went, as was his custom, to the Mount of Olives; and the disciples followed him. [40]When he reached the place, he said to them, "Pray that you may not come into the time of trial."[z] [41]Then he withdrew from them about a stone's throw, knelt down, and prayed, [42]"Father, if you are willing, remove this cup from me; yet, not my will but yours be done." [[43]Then an angel from heaven appeared to him and gave him strength. [44]In his anguish he prayed more earnestly, and his sweat became like great drops of blood falling down on the ground.][a] [45]When he got up from prayer, he came to the disciples and found them sleeping because of grief, [46]and he said to them, "Why are you sleeping? Get up and pray that you may not come into the time of trial."[z]

The Betrayal and Arrest of Jesus

47 While he was still speaking, suddenly a crowd came, and the one called Judas, one of the twelve, was leading them. He approached Jesus to kiss him; [48]but Jesus said to him, "Judas, is it with a kiss that you are betraying the Son of Man?" [49]When those who were around him saw what was coming, they asked, "Lord, should we strike with the sword?" [50]Then one of them struck the slave of the high priest and cut off his right ear. [51]But Jesus said, "No more of this!" And he touched his ear and healed him. [52]Then Jesus said to the chief priests, the officers of the temple police, and the elders who had come for him, "Have you come out with swords and clubs as if I were a bandit? [53]When I was with you day after day in the temple, you did not lay hands on me. But this is your hour, and the power of darkness!"

[w] Other ancient authorities lack, in whole or in part, verses 19b-20 (*which is given ... in my blood*) [x] Or *has obtained permission* [y] Gk *He* [z] Or *into temptation* [a] Other ancient authorities lack verses 43 and 44

22.21 Mt 26.21-24; Mk 14.18-21; Jn 13.21-30
22.22 Acts 2.23; 4.28
22.24 Mk 9.34; Lk 9.46
22.25 Mt 20.25-28; Mk 10.42-45
22.26 Lk 9.48; 1 Pet 5.5
22.27 Lk 12.37
22.28 Heb 2.18; 4.15
22.29 Lk 12.32; 2 Tim 2.12
22.30 Lk 14.15; Rev 19.9; Mt 19.28; Rev 3.21
22.31 Job 1.6-12; Am 9.9
22.32 Jn 17.9,15; 21.15-17
22.35 Mt 10.9; Lk 9.3; 10.4
22.37 Isa 53.12; Mk 15.28
22.39 Lk 21.37
22.40 Mt 6.13
22.42 Mk 10.38; Jn 5.30; 18.11
22.43 Mt 4.11
22.44 Heb 5.7
22.46 ver 40
22.49 ver 38
22.52 ver 4.37
22.53 Jn 12.27

22.27-30 adds material in which Jesus calls his followers to the present role of those who *serve*, but promises them places in the *kingdom* and *thrones* as those who will *judge* Israel. Jesus predicts Peter's denial of him, as in Mark 14.26-31, but with the added details of Satan's demand to control him and Jesus' prayer in his behalf (22.31-34). Jesus' advice to the disciples to acquire basic equipment, including a *sword*, symbolizes that they must be prepared for the persecution and death that they will experience, not that they are to take up arms (see vv. 49-51).
22.39-46 Luke omits reference to Jesus' *sorrow* and the weakness of his *flesh*, as well as the three accounts of the disciples' sleeping (Mk 14.34-42), but some ancient manuscripts add a description of his bloody *sweat* and the angelic visitor.
22.47-53 Those who come to seize Jesus are identified simply as *a crowd*, although the religious leaders are mentioned later (v. 52). Here Jesus highlights the irony of Judas' having *betrayed* him to the mob by *a kiss*. Jesus' compassion is evident in his healing the *ear* of the high priest's *slave* whom one of his followers struck. Jesus challenges the officers' treating him like a *bandit* (a professional thief or disturber of the peace) when they could have seized him while he was worshiping in the *temple*.

22.54-23.1 Luke reports Peter's denial that he knows Jesus as occurring during the night after his arrest (see Mk 14.66-72). The sequence of events differs from Mark's account, but the substance is similar, except for details: the charge that Jesus threatened to destroy the temple (Mk 14.57-60) is omitted; Jesus is asked if he is the *Son of God*, which implies his unique relationship with God (22.70). The group that interrogates Jesus is the *council* (as in Mk 14.55), but it is also defined as the *assembly of elders* (in Greek, *presbyterion*). This group of religious officials turns him over to the Roman civil ruler, Pilate.
23.2-5 The charges raised against Jesus here involve violations of Roman law and order: *perverting* the Jewish nation, forbidding the payment of *taxes to Caesar*, and claiming to be *king*. Pilate finds no ground for any of these accusations. The leaders and the Jewish crowd shift the charge and accuse him of stirring up the people by his *teaching*.
23.6-16 Throughout his gospel and Acts, Luke pictures Jesus and Paul as engaged with the civil authorities, and always exonerated. Pilate then offers to release Jesus.
23.17-25 The crowds call for Pilate to release from prison *Barabbas*, a Jewish insurrectionist and murderer, but to *crucify* Jesus. Crucifixion was a death penalty for capital crimes under Roman law. Pilate again affirms Jesus' innocence, but yields to the demands of the crowd.

Peter Denies Jesus

54 Then they seized him and led him away, bringing him into the high priest's house. But Peter was following at a distance. 55 When they had kindled a fire in the middle of the courtyard and sat down together, Peter sat among them. 56 Then a servant-girl, seeing him in the firelight, stared at him and said, "This man also was with him." 57 But he denied it, saying, "Woman, I do not know him." 58 A little later someone else, on seeing him, said, "You also are one of them." But Peter said, "Man, I am not!" 59 Then about an hour later still another kept insisting, "Surely this man also was with him; for he is a Galilean." 60 But Peter said, "Man, I do not know what you are talking about!" At that moment, while he was still speaking, the cock crowed. 61 The Lord turned and looked at Peter. Then Peter remembered the word of the Lord, how he had said to him, "Before the cock crows today, you will deny me three times." 62 And he went out and wept bitterly.

The Mocking and Beating of Jesus

63 Now the men who were holding Jesus began to mock him and beat him; 64 they also blindfolded him and kept asking him, "Prophesy! Who is it that struck you?" 65 They kept heaping many other insults on him.

Jesus before the Council

66 When day came, the assembly of the elders of the people, both chief priests and scribes, gathered together, and they brought him to their council. 67 They said, "If you are the Messiah,[b] tell us." He replied, "If I tell you, you will not believe; 68 and if I question you, you will not answer. 69 But from now on the Son of Man will be seated at the right hand of the power of God." 70 All of them asked, "Are you, then, the Son of God?" He said to them, "You say that I am." 71 Then they said, "What further testimony do we need? We have heard it ourselves from his own lips!"

Jesus before Pilate

23 Then the assembly rose as a body and brought Jesus[c] before Pilate. 2 They began to accuse him, saying, "We found this man perverting our nation, forbidding us to pay taxes to the emperor, and saying that he himself is the Messiah, a king."[d] 3 Then Pilate asked him, "Are you the king of the Jews?" He answered, "You say so." 4 Then Pilate said to the chief priests and the crowds, "I find no basis for an accusation against this man." 5 But they were insistent and said, "He stirs up the people by teaching throughout all Judea, from Galilee where he began even to this place."

Jesus before Herod

6 When Pilate heard this, he asked whether the man was a Galilean. 7 And when he learned that he was under Herod's jurisdiction, he sent him off to Herod, who was himself in Jerusalem at that time. 8 When Herod saw Jesus, he was very glad, for he had been wanting to see him for a long time, because he had heard about him and was hoping to see him perform some sign. 9 He questioned him at some length, but Jesus[e] gave him no answer. 10 The chief priests and the scribes stood by, vehemently accusing him. 11 Even Herod with his soldiers treated him with contempt and mocked him; then he put an elegant robe on him, and sent him back to Pilate. 12 That same day Herod and Pilate became friends with each other; before this they had been enemies.

Jesus Sentenced to Death

13 Pilate then called together the chief priests, the leaders, and the people, 14 and said to them, "You brought me this man as one who was perverting the people; and here I have examined him in your presence and have not found this man guilty of any of your charges against him. 15 Neither has Herod, for he sent him back to us. Indeed, he has done nothing to deserve death. 16 I will therefore have him flogged and release him."[f]

18 Then they all shouted out together, "Away with this fellow! Release Barabbas for us!" 19 (This was a man who had been put in prison for an insurrection that had taken place in the city, and for murder.) 20 Pilate, wanting to release Jesus, addressed them again; 21 but they kept shouting,

[b] Or *the Christ* [c] Gk *him* [d] Or *is an anointed king* [e] Gk *he* [f] Here, or after verse 19, other ancient authorities add verse 17, *Now he was obliged to release someone for them at the festival*

22.54 Mt 26.58; Mk 14.54
22.61 ver 34
22.63 Mt 26.67,68; Mk 14.65; Jn 18.22,23
22.66 Mt 27.1; Mk 15.1
22.67 Mt 26.63-66; Mk 14.61-63; Jn 18.19-21
22.70 Mt 27.11; Lk 23.3
23.1 Mt 27.2; Mk 15.1; Jn 18.28
23.2 Lk 20.22; Jn 19.12
23.3 Lk 22.70; 1 Tim 6.13
23.4 1 Pet 2.22
23.7 Lk 3.1
23.8 Lk 9.9; Mt 14.1; Mk 6.14
23.11 Mk 15.17-19; Jn 19.2,3
23.12 Acts 4.27
23.14 ver 2,4
23.16 Mt 27.26; Mk 15.15; Jn 19.1
23.18 Mt 27.20-23; Mk 15.11-14; Jn 18.38-40; 19.14,15; Acts 3.13,14

"Crucify, crucify him!" 22A third time he
said to them, "Why, what evil has he done?
I have found in him no ground for the
sentence of death; I will therefore have him
flogged and then release him." 23But they
kept urgently demanding with loud shouts
that he should be crucified; and their voices
prevailed. 24So Pilate gave his verdict that
their demand should be granted. 25He released the man they asked for, the one who
had been put in prison for insurrection and
murder, and he handed Jesus over as they
wished.

The Crucifixion of Jesus

26 As they led him away, they seized a
man, Simon of Cyrene, who was coming
from the country, and they laid the cross on
him, and made him carry it behind Jesus.
27A great number of the people followed
him, and among them were women who
were beating their breasts and wailing for
him. 28But Jesus turned to them and said,
"Daughters of Jerusalem, do not weep for
me, but weep for yourselves and for your
children. 29For the days are surely coming
when they will say, 'Blessed are the barren,
and the wombs that never bore, and the
breasts that never nursed.' 30Then they will
begin to say to the mountains, 'Fall on us';
and to the hills, 'Cover us.' 31For if they do
this when the wood is green, what will
happen when it is dry?"
32 Two others also, who were criminals,
were led away to be put to death with him.
33When they came to the place that is called
The Skull, they crucified Jesus[g] there with
the criminals, one on his right and one on
his left. [34Then Jesus said, "Father, forgive
them; for they do not know what they are
doing."][h] And they cast lots to divide his
clothing. 35And the people stood by, watching; but the leaders scoffed at him, saying,
"He saved others; let him save himself if he
is the Messiah[i] of God, his chosen one!"
36The soldiers also mocked him, coming up
and offering him sour wine, 37and saying,
"If you are the King of the Jews, save
yourself!" 38There was also an inscription
over him,[j] "This is the King of the Jews."
39 One of the criminals who were hanged
there kept deriding[k] him and saying, "Are
you not the Messiah?[i] Save yourself and
us!" 40But the other rebuked him, saying,
"Do you not fear God, since you are under
the same sentence of condemnation? 41And
we indeed have been condemned justly, for
we are getting what we deserve for our
deeds, but this man has done nothing
wrong." 42Then he said, "Jesus, remember
me when you come into[l] your kingdom."
43He replied, "Truly I tell you, today you
will be with me in Paradise."

The Death of Jesus

44 It was now about noon, and darkness
came over the whole land[m] until three in
the afternoon, 45while the sun's light failed;[n]
and the curtain of the temple was torn in
two. 46Then Jesus, crying with a loud voice,
said, "Father, into your hands I commend
my spirit." Having said this, he breathed his
last. 47When the centurion saw what had
taken place, he praised God and said, "Certainly this man was innocent."[o] 48And when
all the crowds who had gathered there for
this spectacle saw what had taken place,
they returned home, beating their breasts.
49But all his acquaintances, including the
women who had followed him from Galilee,
stood at a distance, watching these things.

The Burial of Jesus

50 Now there was a good and righteous
man named Joseph, who, though a member
of the council, 51had not agreed to their
plan and action. He came from the Jewish
town of Arimathea, and he was waiting
expectantly for the kingdom of God. 52This
man went to Pilate and asked for the body
of Jesus. 53Then he took it down, wrapped
it in a linen cloth, and laid it in a rock-hewn
tomb where no one had ever been laid. 54It
was the day of Preparation, and the sabbath
was beginning.[p] 55The women who had
come with him from Galilee followed, and
they saw the tomb and how his body was
laid. 56Then they returned, and prepared
spices and ointments.

On the sabbath they rested according to
the commandment.

[g] Gk *him* [h] Other ancient authorities lack the sentence *Then Jesus ... what they are doing"* [i] Or *the Christ* [j] Other ancient authorities add *written in Greek and Latin and Hebrew* (that is, *Aramaic*) [k] Or *blaspheming* [l] Other ancient authorities read *in* [m] Or *earth* [n] Or *the sun was eclipsed.* Other ancient authorities read *the sun was darkened* [o] Or *righteous* [p] Gk *was dawning*

23.26-32 Instead of reporting the mocking of Jesus by the Roman soldiers (Mk 13.16-20), Luke tells of the mourning for Jesus by the *daughters of Jerusalem*, to whom he utters a warning of the dire calamities that will befall the city in the coming days of divine judgment, with phrases drawn from the prophets (Hos 10.8) and Proverbs (11.31).
23.33-43 Crucified between the two *criminals*, Jesus calls for God's forgiveness of his persecutors. *The soldiers* join in mocking Jesus as a pretender to kingship, but Luke reports scorn from one of the criminals while the other affirms the innocence of Jesus and asks for his intercession. Jesus promises to see him in *Paradise*, a term of Persian origin used in the Greek version of the Jewish scriptures for Eden, the garden of the Lord (Gen 2.8; 13.10).
23.44-49 Instead of a cry of despair (Mk 15.34), Jesus commits himself into the *hands* of the *Father*. The *centurion* in charge of the Roman soldiers also pronounces Jesus' innocence, and the crowds leave overcome with lamentation, while the *women* from Galilee watch from a distance.
23.50-56 *Joseph of Arimathea* (a Jewish city on the coastal plain), here described as a *good and righteous* member of the regional council (*synedrion*) set up by the Romans, is permitted to take Jesus' body and bury it in his tomb late in the afternoon as the *preparation* for the Sabbath begins. Having seen the place of burial, the *women* gather spices in readiness for preparing the corpse properly after the day of rest has passed.

23.22 ver 16
23.26 Jn 19.17
23.27 Lk 8.52
23.28 Lk 19.41-44; 21.23,24
23.30 Isa 2.19; Hos 10.8; Rev 6.16
23.31 Ezek 20.47
23.32 Isa 53.12
23.34 Ps 22.18; Acts 7.60
23.35 Ps 22.17
23.36 Ps 69.21; Mt 27.48
23.39 ver 35,37
23.41 ver 4,14,22
23.43 2 Cor 12.3,4; Rev 2.7
23.45 Ex 26.31-35; Heb 9.8; 10.19
23.46 Ps 31.5; 1 Pet 2.23
23.47 Mt 27.54
23.49 Ps 38.11; Lk 8.2
23.51 Lk 2.25
23.54 Mt 27.62
23.55 ver 49
23.56 Mk 16.1; Ex 12.16; 20.10

24.1-12 On the women approaching the tomb, now open, *two men in dazzling clothes* ask why they seek *the living among the dead*. Jesus has told them *in Galilee* of his death and resurrection. The women report their experience *to the eleven*, who receive this as *an idle tale*. Some ancient manuscripts of Luke add that Peter also saw the empty tomb and was puzzled.
24.13-35 Two of the disciples (one unnamed, but later [vs.34] identified as Simon Peter; the other Cleopas), while walking to *Emmaus* to the west of Jerusalem, are met by Jesus, whom they do not recognize and who asks them about their conversation concerning the recent seizure and death of this *prophet*, the disappearance of his body, and the reports of angelic messengers. Jesus' interpretation of the *prophets* and of the law of *Moses* shows that they foretold his suffering and *entering into glory*. After a meal with them, in which the features of the eucharist are evident (*took, blessed, broke, gave*), he *vanished*. Through the *opening of the scriptures* and *the breaking of bread* Jesus had become known to them.
24.36-52 In another appearance to his followers Jesus confirms that he has been raised, and is not merely a vision, by inviting them to examine and touch his wounded body, and by partaking of food with them. His final commissioning of them is based on his claim of fulfillment of all three parts of the Jewish Bible (*law, prophets, writings*), and his charge to them is to proclaim the message of *forgiveness* among *all the nations*. Meanwhile, they are to await in Jerusalem their enduement with *power from on high*. This event will be described in Acts 2 in the outpouring of the Holy Spirit. Then Jesus is taken from them up into heaven.

The Resurrection of Jesus

24 But on the first day of the week,
at early dawn, they came to the
tomb, taking the spices that they had prepared. 2They found the stone rolled away
from the tomb, 3but when they went in,
they did not find the body.[q] 4While they
were perplexed about this, suddenly two
men in dazzling clothes stood beside them.
5The women[r] were terrified and bowed their
faces to the ground, but the men[s] said to
them, "Why do you look for the living
among the dead? He is not here, but has
risen.[t] 6Remember how he told you, while
he was still in Galilee, 7that the Son of Man
must be handed over to sinners, and be
crucified, and on the third day rise again."
8Then they remembered his words, 9and
returning from the tomb, they told all this
to the eleven and to all the rest. 10Now it
was Mary Magdalene, Joanna, Mary the
mother of James, and the other women
with them who told this to the apostles.
11But these words seemed to them an idle
tale, and they did not believe them. 12But
Peter got up and ran to the tomb; stooping
and looking in, he saw the linen cloths by
themselves; then he went home, amazed at
what had happened.[u]

The Walk to Emmaus

13 Now on that same day two of them
were going to a village called Emmaus,
about seven miles[v] from Jerusalem, 14and
talking with each other about all these
things that had happened. 15While they
were talking and discussing, Jesus himself
came near and went with them, 16but their
eyes were kept from recognizing him. 17And
he said to them, "What are you discussing
with each other while you walk along?"
They stood still, looking sad.[w] 18Then one of
them, whose name was Cleopas, answered
him, "Are you the only stranger in Jerusalem who does not know the things that
have taken place there in these days?" 19He
asked them, "What things?" They replied,
"The things about Jesus of Nazareth,[x] who
was a prophet mighty in deed and word
before God and all the people, 20and how
our chief priests and leaders handed him
over to be condemned to death and crucified him. 21But we had hoped that he was
the one to redeem Israel.[y] Yes, and besides
all this, it is now the third day since these
things took place. 22Moreover, some women
of our group astounded us. They were at
the tomb early this morning, 23and when
they did not find his body there, they came
back and told us that they had indeed seen
a vision of angels who said that he was
alive. 24Some of those who were with us
went to the tomb and found it just as the
women had said; but they did not see him."
25Then he said to them, "Oh, how foolish
you are, and how slow of heart to believe
all that the prophets have declared! 26Was
it not necessary that the Messiah[z] should
suffer these things and then enter into his
glory?" 27Then beginning with Moses and
all the prophets, he interpreted to them the
things about himself in all the scriptures.
28 As they came near the village to
which they were going, he walked ahead as
if he were going on. 29But they urged him
strongly, saying, "Stay with us, because it
is almost evening and the day is now nearly
over." So he went in to stay with them.
30When he was at the table with them, he
took bread, blessed and broke it, and gave
it to them. 31Then their eyes were opened,
and they recognized him; and he vanished
from their sight. 32They said to each other,
"Were not our hearts burning within us[a]
while he was talking to us on the road,
while he was opening the scriptures to us?"
33That same hour they got up and returned
to Jerusalem; and they found the eleven and
their companions gathered together. 34They
were saying, "The Lord has risen indeed,
and he has appeared to Simon!" 35Then
they told what had happened on the road,
and how he had been made known to them
in the breaking of the bread.

Jesus Appears to His Disciples

36 While they were talking about this,
Jesus himself stood among them and said to
them, "Peace be with you."[b] 37They were
startled and terrified, and thought that they
were seeing a ghost. 38He said to them,
"Why are you frightened, and why do doubts

[q] Other ancient authorities add *of the Lord Jesus* [r] Gk *They* [s] Gk *but they* [t] Other ancient authorities lack *He is not here, but has risen* [u] Other ancient authorities lack verse 12 [v] Gk *sixty stadia;* other ancient authorities read *a hundred sixty stadia* [w] Other ancient authorities read *walk along, looking sad?"* [x] Other ancient authorities read *Jesus the Nazorean* [y] Or *to set Israel free* [z] Or *the Christ* [a] Other ancient authorities lack *within us* [b] Other ancient authorities lack *and said to them, "Peace be with you."*

24.1 Lk 23.56
24.4 Acts 1.10; 12.7
24.6 Mt 17.22,23; Mk 9.30,31; Lk 9.22
24.8 Jn 2.22
24.9 ver 46
24.10 Lk 8.1-3
24.11 ver 35
24.15 ver 36
24.18 Jn 19.25
24.19 Mt 21.11; Lk 7.16; 13.33; Acts 3.22; 24.20; Lk 23.13
24.21 Lk 1.68
24.22 ver 9,10
24.24 ver 12
24.26 Heb 2.10; 1 Pet 1.11
24.27 Gen 3.15; Num 21.9; Deut 18.15; Isa 7.14; 9.6; 40.10,11; 53; Ezek 34.23; Dan 9.24; Mic 7.20; Mal 3.1
24.28 Mk 6.48
24.30 Mt 14.19
24.33 Acts 1.14
24.34 1 Cor 15.5
24.37 Mk 6.49

24.39 Jn 20.27
24.41 Jn 21.5
24.43 Acts 10.41
24.44 Mt 16.21; Mk 8.31; Lk 9.22; 18.31
24.46 Isa 50.6; Hos 6.2; 1 Cor 15.3,4
24.47 Acts 5.31; 13.38; Mt 28.19
24.48 Acts 1.8
24.49 Jn 14.16; Acts 1.4
24.50 Acts 1.12
24.51 1 Kings 2.11
24.53 Acts 2.46

arise in your hearts? [39]Look at my hands
and my feet; see that it is I myself. Touch
me and see; for a ghost does not have flesh
and bones as you see that I have." [40]And
when he had said this, he showed them his
hands and his feet.[c] [41]While in their joy they
were disbelieving and still wondering, he
said to them, "Have you anything here to
eat?" [42]They gave him a piece of broiled fish,
[43]and he took it and ate in their presence.
44 Then he said to them, "These are my
words that I spoke to you while I was still
with you—that everything written about
me in the law of Moses, the prophets, and
the psalms must be fulfilled." [45]Then he
opened their minds to understand the scriptures, [46]and he said to them, "Thus it is
written, that the Messiah[d] is to suffer and
to rise from the dead on the third day, [47]and
that repentance and forgiveness of sins is to
be proclaimed in his name to all nations,[e]
beginning from Jerusalem. [48]You are witnesses of these things. [49]And see, I am
sending upon you what my Father promised; so stay here in the city until you have
been clothed with power from on high."

The Ascension of Jesus

50 Then he led them out as far as
Bethany, and, lifting up his hands, he blessed
them. [51]While he was blessing them, he
withdrew from them and was carried up
into heaven.[f] [52]And they worshiped him,
and[g] returned to Jerusalem with great joy;
[53]and they were continually in the temple
blessing God.[h]

[c] Other ancient authorities lack verse 40 [d] Or *the Christ* [e] Or *nations. Beginning from Jerusalem you are witnesses* [f] Other ancient authorities lack *and was carried up into heaven* [g] Other ancient authorities lack *worshiped him, and* [h] Other ancient authorities add *Amen*

The Gospel According to JOHN

1.1 Col. 1.17; 1 Jn 1.1; Phil 2.6
1.3 Col 1.16; Heb 1.2
1.4 Jn 5.26; 11.25; 14.6
1.9 Isa 49.6; 1 Jn 2.8
1.10 Col 1.16; Heb 1.2
1.12 Gal 3.26; Jn 5.13
1.13 Jn 3.5,6; Jas 1.18; 1 Pet 1.23
1.14 Rom 1.3; Gal 4.4; 1 Tim 3.16; Heb 2.14

The Word Became Flesh

1 In the beginning was the Word, and
the Word was with God, and the
Word was God. [2]He was in the beginning
with God. [3]All things came into being
through him, and without him not one
thing came into being. What has come into
being [4]in him was life,[a] and the life was the
light of all people. [5]The light shines in the
darkness, and the darkness did not overcome it.
6 There was a man sent from God, whose
name was John. [7]He came as a witness to
testify to the light, so that all might believe
through him. [8]He himself was not the light,
but he came to testify to the light. [9]The true
light, which enlightens everyone, was coming into the world.[b]
10 He was in the world, and the world
came into being through him; yet the world
did not know him. [11]He came to what was
his own,[c] and his own people did not accept
him. [12]But to all who received him, who
believed in his name, he gave power to
become children of God, [13]who were born,
not of blood or of the will of the flesh or of
the will of man, but of God.
14 And the Word became flesh and lived
among us, and we have seen his glory, the
glory as of a father's only son,[d] full of grace
and truth. [15](John testified to him and cried
out, "This was he of whom I said, 'He who

[a] Or [3]*through him. And without him not one thing came into being that has come into being.* [4]*In him was life* [b] Or *He was the true light that enlightens everyone coming into the world* [c] Or *to his own home* [d] Or *the Father's only Son*

See the Introductions, pp. 7–8 and 80–81 above.

1.1-18 The Prologue: The Word.

1.1-5 *In the beginning* echoes the opening phrase of Gen 1.1 in the Septuagint (ancient Greek version), as well as the account of creation of the world through God's speaking (*and God said...*), which is here personified in the Word. In the Old Testament, God's agent in creation is Wisdom (Prov 8.22-23; Wis 7.22-30). The light which the Word brings is for *all people*, and cannot be overcome by the powers of *darkness*.
1.6-9 Alternating with the description of *the Word* is a series of contrasts between Jesus and John the Baptist, who here is distinguished from *the true light* who is about to come into the world and who will enlighten *everyone*.
1.10-18 Neither the world which *came into being* through the Word nor his own people (Israel) recognize or accept *the Word*, but all who receive him – not because of their ethnic links (*blood*) or the sexual activity of their fathers – are given authority (*power*) to become God's children. *The Word* has come in human form (*flesh*), and through him the marvelous nature (*glory*) of God, his father, is revealed, especially God's generosity (*grace*) and dependability (*truth*). In contrast to John, who acknowledges the superiority of the Word, and to Moses, through whom the *law* was given, the Word in human form makes *known* God himself.

comes after me ranks ahead of me because he was before me.' ") [16]From his fullness we have all received, grace upon grace. [17]The law indeed was given through Moses; grace and truth came through Jesus Christ. [18]No one has ever seen God. It is God the only Son,[e] who is close to the Father's heart,[f] who has made him known.

The Testimony of John the Baptist

19 This is the testimony given by John when the Jews sent priests and Levites from Jerusalem to ask him, "Who are you?" [20]He confessed and did not deny it, but confessed, "I am not the Messiah."[g] [21]And they asked him, "What then? Are you Elijah?" He said, "I am not." "Are you the prophet?" He answered, "No." [22]Then they said to him, "Who are you? Let us have an answer for those who sent us. What do you say about yourself?" [23]He said,

"I am the voice of one crying out in the
wilderness,
'Make straight the way of the Lord,' "

as the prophet Isaiah said.

24 Now they had been sent from the Pharisees. [25]They asked him, "Why then are you baptizing if you are neither the Messiah,[g] nor Elijah, nor the prophet?" [26]John answered them, "I baptize with water. Among you stands one whom you do not know, [27]the one who is coming after me; I am not worthy to untie the thong of his sandal." [28]This took place in Bethany across the Jordan where John was baptizing.

The Lamb of God

29 The next day he saw Jesus coming toward him and declared, "Here is the Lamb of God who takes away the sin of the world! [30]This is he of whom I said, 'After me comes a man who ranks ahead of me because he was before me.' [31]I myself did not know him; but I came baptizing with water for this reason, that he might be revealed to Israel." [32]And John testified, "I saw the Spirit descending from heaven like a dove, and it remained on him. [33]I myself did not know him, but the one who sent me to baptize with water said to me, 'He on whom you see the Spirit descend and remain is the one who baptizes with the Holy Spirit.' [34]And I myself have seen and have testified that this is the Son of God."[h]

The First Disciples of Jesus

35 The next day John again was standing with two of his disciples, [36]and as he watched Jesus walk by, he exclaimed, "Look, here is the Lamb of God!" [37]The two disciples heard him say this, and they followed Jesus. [38]When Jesus turned and saw them following, he said to them, "What are you looking for?" They said to him, "Rabbi" (which translated means Teacher), "where are you staying?" [39]He said to them, "Come and see." They came and saw where he was staying, and they remained with him that day. It was about four o'clock in the afternoon. [40]One of the two who heard John speak and followed him was Andrew, Simon Peter's brother. [41]He first found his brother Simon and said to him, "We have found the Messiah" (which is translated Anointed[i]). [42]He brought Simon[j] to Jesus, who looked at him and said, "You are Simon son of John. You are to be called Cephas" (which is translated Peter[k]).

Jesus Calls Philip and Nathanael

43 The next day Jesus decided to go to Galilee. He found Philip and said to him, "Follow me." [44]Now Philip was from Bethsaida, the city of Andrew and Peter. [45]Philip found Nathanael and said to him, "We have found him about whom Moses in the law and also the prophets wrote, Jesus son of Joseph from Nazareth." [46]Nathanael said to him, "Can anything good come out of Nazareth?" Philip said to him, "Come and see." [47]When Jesus saw Nathanael coming toward him, he said of him, "Here is truly an Israelite in whom there is no deceit!" [48]Nathanael asked him, "Where did you get to know me?" Jesus answered, "I saw you under the fig tree before Philip called you." [49]Nathanael replied, "Rabbi, you are the Son of God! You are the King of Israel!" [50]Jesus answered, "Do you believe because I told you that I saw you under the fig tree? You will see greater things than these." [51]And he said to him, "Very truly, I tell

[e] Other ancient authorities read *It is an only Son, God,* or *It is the only Son* [f] Gk *bosom* [g] Or *the Christ* [h] Other ancient authorities read *is God's chosen one* [i] Or *Christ* [j] Gk *him* [k] From the word for *rock* in Aramaic (*kepha*) and Greek (*petra*), respectively

1.19-34 John's Testimony concerning Jesus.
1.19-28 In response to questions from the *priests* and the attendants in the temple (*Levites*), John denies that he is any of the three figures who are expected in the Jewish scriptures to come and establish the new age for God's people: *the Messiah* (Ps 2), *Elijah* (Mal 4.5-6), or *the prophet* (Deut 18.15-18). Instead, he is the preparatory agent for the coming of *the Lord* (Isa 40.3), and he declares that there already is among them someone far superior to him. In preparation, he carries on his baptizing activity on the eastern side of the Jordan.
1.29-34 Jesus on his arrival at the Jordan is acclaimed by John as *the Lamb of God*, which could refer to the suffering servant of God in the prophets (Jer 11.19; Isa 42.1-9; 52.13-53.12), or to the conquering lamb of apocalyptic thought (1 Enoch; Testament of Joseph; Rev 17.14). The *Spirit descending from heaven like a dove* matches the accounts of Jesus' baptism in the other gospels (Mk 1.10; Mt 3.16; Lk 3.22) as well as the prophecy about David's royal heir for Israel's renewal in Isa 11.1-2. He will pour out the Spirit on his people, and John acclaims him as *the Son of God* (Ps 2.7), or, in some manuscripts, as God's *Chosen One* (Isa 42.1).
1.35-51 Jesus' Call of his Disciples.
1.35-42 The first two of Jesus' disciples were followers of John the Baptist: Andrew, brother of Simon Peter, and one who is not named. Their invitation to *Come and see* and their *staying* with Jesus have symbolic meaning: they are inquiring about Jesus' program and they want to continue with him in this new relationship. Simon acclaims Jesus as *Messiah* and Jesus gives Simon his nickname, the Rock (*Cephas*).
1.43-51 Back in Galilee, Philip is drawn to Jesus because he sees in him the fulfilment of *the law and the prophets*, but the more skeptical Nathaniel is convinced only when he learns that Jesus has been observing him before they ever met. He acclaims Jesus as Messiah, and is told that he will see the accomplishment of God's purpose through the triumphant *Son of Man* (Dan 7.13-14). The *angels of God ascending and descending* recall the story of the father of Israel, Jacob, in Gen 28.12. Here Jesus is the founder of the New Israel.

1.16 Eph 1.23; Col 1.19
1.17 Rom 3.24
1.18 Ex 33.20; Jn 6.46; 1 Jn 4.9
1.20 Jn 3.28; Lk 3.15,16
1.21 Mt 11.14; 16.14; Deut 18.15
1.23 Mt 3.1; Mk 1.3; Lk 3.4; Isa 40.3
1.29 Isa 53.7; 1 Pet 1.19
1.32 Mt 3.16; Mk 1.10; Lk 3.22
1.33 Mt 3.11; Acts 1.5
1.36 ver 29
1.38 ver 49
1.40 Mt 4.18-22; Mk 1.16-20; Lk 5.2-11
1.41 Dan 9.25; Jn 4.25
1.42 Jn 21.15-17; 1 Cor 15.5; Mt 16.18
1.43 Mt 10.3; Jn 6.5,7; 12.21,22; 14.8,9
1.44 Jn 12.21
1.45 Jn 21.2; Lk 24.27; Mt 2.23; Lk 2.4
1.46 Jn 7.41,42
1.47 Ps 32.2; 73.1; Rom 9.4,6
1.49 ver 38,34; Mt 2.2; Mk 15.32; Jn 12.13
1.51 Gen 28.12; Mt 3.16; Lk 3.21; Mt 8.20

you,[l] you will see heaven opened and the angels of God ascending and descending upon the Son of Man.”

The Wedding at Cana

2 On the third day there was a wedding in Cana of Galilee, and the mother of Jesus was there. 2 Jesus and his disciples had also been invited to the wedding. 3 When the wine gave out, the mother of Jesus said to him, “They have no wine.” 4 And Jesus said to her, “Woman, what concern is that to you and to me? My hour has not yet come.” 5 His mother said to the servants, “Do whatever he tells you.” 6 Now standing there were six stone water jars for the Jewish rites of purification, each holding twenty or thirty gallons. 7 Jesus said to them, “Fill the jars with water.” And they filled them up to the brim. 8 He said to them, “Now draw some out, and take it to the chief steward.” So they took it. 9 When the steward tasted the water that had become wine, and did not know where it came from (though the servants who had drawn the water knew), the steward called the bridegroom 10 and said to him, “Everyone serves the good wine first, and then the inferior wine after the guests have become drunk. But you have kept the good wine until now.” 11 Jesus did this, the first of his signs, in Cana of Galilee, and revealed his glory; and his disciples believed in him.

12 After this he went down to Capernaum with his mother, his brothers, and his disciples; and they remained there a few days.

Jesus Cleanses the Temple

13 The Passover of the Jews was near, and Jesus went up to Jerusalem. 14 In the temple he found people selling cattle, sheep, and doves, and the money changers seated at their tables. 15 Making a whip of cords, he drove all of them out of the temple, both the sheep and the cattle. He also poured out the coins of the money changers and overturned their tables. 16 He told those who were selling the doves, “Take these things out of here! Stop making my Father’s house a marketplace!” 17 His disciples remembered that it was written, “Zeal for your house will consume me.” 18 The Jews then said to him, “What sign can you show us for doing this?” 19 Jesus answered them, “Destroy this temple, and in three days I will raise it up.” 20 The Jews then said, “This temple has been under construction for forty-six years, and will you raise it up in three days?” 21 But he was speaking of the temple of his body. 22 After he was raised from the dead, his disciples remembered that he had said this; and they believed the scripture and the word that Jesus had spoken.

23 When he was in Jerusalem during the Passover festival, many believed in his name because they saw the signs that he was doing. 24 But Jesus on his part would not entrust himself to them, because he knew all people 25 and needed no one to testify about anyone; for he himself knew what was in everyone.

Nicodemus Visits Jesus

3 Now there was a Pharisee named Nicodemus, a leader of the Jews. 2 He came to Jesus[m] by night and said to him, “Rabbi, we know that you are a teacher who has come from God; for no one can do these signs that you do apart from the presence of God.” 3 Jesus answered him, “Very truly, I tell you, no one can see the kingdom of God without being born from above.”[n] 4 Nicodemus said to him, “How can anyone be born after having grown old? Can one enter a second time into the mother’s womb and be born?” 5 Jesus answered, “Very truly, I tell you, no one can enter the kingdom of God without being born of water and Spirit. 6 What is born of the flesh is flesh, and what is born of the Spirit is spirit.[o] 7 Do not be astonished that I said to you, ‘You[p] must be born from above.’[q] 8 The wind[o] blows where it chooses, and you hear the sound of it, but you do not know where it comes from or where it goes. So it is with everyone who is born of the Spirit.” 9 Nicodemus said to him, “How can these things be?” 10 Jesus answered him, “Are you a teacher of Israel, and yet you do not understand these things?

11 “Very truly, I tell you, we speak of what we know and testify to what we have seen; yet you[r] do not receive our testimony. 12 If I have told you about earthly things and you do not believe, how can you believe if I tell you about heavenly things? 13 No one

[l] Both instances of the Greek word for *you* in this verse are plural [m] Gk *him* [n] Or *born anew* [o] The same Greek word means both *wind* and *spirit* [p] The Greek word for *you* here is plural [q] Or *anew* [r] The Greek word for *you* here and in verse 12 is plural

2.1 Jn 4.46; 21.2
2.4 Jn 19.26; 7.6,30; 8.20
2.6 Mk 7.3,4; Jn 3.25
2.11 Jn 1.14
2.12 Mt 4.13; 12.46
2.13 Jn 6.4; 11.55; Deut 16.1-6; Lk 2.41
2.16 Lk 2.49
2.17 Ps 69.9
2.18 Mt 12.38
2.19 Mt 26.61; 27.40; Mk 14.58
2.21 1 Cor 6.19
2.25 Jn 6.61,64; 13.11
3.2 Jn 9.16,33; Acts 2.22; 10.38
3.3 Titus 3.5; Jas 1.18; 1 Pet 1.23; 1 Jn 3.9
3.5 Eph 5.26; Titus 3.5
3.8 1 Cor 2.11
3.9 Jn 6.52,60
3.11 Jn 7.16,17
3.13 Prov 30.4; Acts 2.34; Rom 10.6; Eph 4.9

2.1-12 The First of Jesus' Signs: Water Changed into Wine.
The miracles of Jesus as John describes them are told not only to report the amazing results of Jesus' powers but to present them as *signs* which point to symbolic meanings that stand over these events. The aim of them all is to portray Jesus as *Messiah, Son of God* and to evoke trust in him (Jn 20.30-31). The site of the wedding is Cana, probably a small village north of Nazareth. The *wedding* is a symbol in prophetic tradition for the time of fulfillment of God's purpose for his people (Isa 54.4-8; 62.4-5), just as an abundance of wine symbolizes the joy that accompanies that event (Am 9.11-14; Hos 14.4-7; Jer 31.12-14). The use of the *stone water jars* indicates the inadequacy of the *Jewish rites of purification.* The good wine kept until now signifies that the consummation of God's plan is only now being disclosed. What is revealed by this act of Jesus is the very nature (*glory*) of God, in which his followers now begin to trust.

2.12 In contrast to the other gospels, which report Jesus' family as based in Nazareth but coming to Capernaum to see him (Mk 3.21-34; Mt 12.46), John describes them as living there with him.

2.13-25 Jesus Cleanses the Temple.
The annual pilgrimage of Jews to Jerusalem from all over the world recalled God's great act of deliverance of his people from slavery in Egypt in the time of Moses (Ex 14-15). Now the place of their celebration, the temple, has become a major center of commerce in religious commodities (sacrifices and money-changing). The call of Jesus to *destroy this temple* and the prediction that it will be raised up in three days is heard as a literal prediction of reconstructing a building that has been in process for nearly half a century. But Jesus is pointing to his own resurrection, which will be the basis for the new *body*, his people, as they later recall and understand. Since many of the onlookers are drawn to Jesus by his extraordinary powers (*believe in his name*) without understanding the purpose of these signs in the larger plan of God, he will not place confidence in them.

3.1-21 Jesus and Nicodemus.
The Jewish *leader*, Nicodemus, is one of those who recognize that Jesus' powers come from God, but fail to see the revolutionary program that God has launched through him, which Jesus here depicts in terms of a new birth (*from above*, or *again*) through the transforming power of the *Spirit.* Like the unseen but powerful *wind*, the Spirit of God operates in ways which humans cannot predict or fully comprehend. These insights are available only through the one who brought them from heaven, *the Son of Man*, God's agent for renewal of his people (Dan 7.13-14). Like the *serpent* placed on a pole by Moses to free Israel from the deadly consequences of their disobedience in the wilderness (Num 21.4-8), Jesus will be *lifted up* on the cross for the deliverance from death of all who look to him in faith. The *judgment* is not a future time of God's evaluating humanity but a present moment of decision for the whole world, which God loves and to which the invitation to trust in his remedy for human sin is extended.

has ascended into heaven except the one who descended from heaven, the Son of Man.[s] 14 And just as Moses lifted up the serpent in the wilderness, so must the Son of Man be lifted up, 15 that whoever believes in him may have eternal life.[t]

16 "For God so loved the world that he gave his only Son, so that everyone who believes in him may not perish but may have eternal life.

17 "Indeed, God did not send the Son into the world to condemn the world, but in order that the world might be saved through him. 18 Those who believe in him are not condemned; but those who do not believe are condemned already, because they have not believed in the name of the only Son of God. 19 And this is the judgment, that the light has come into the world, and people loved darkness rather than light because their deeds were evil. 20 For all who do evil hate the light and do not come to the light, so that their deeds may not be exposed. 21 But those who do what is true come to the light, so that it may be clearly seen that their deeds have been done in God."[t]

Jesus and John the Baptist

22 After this Jesus and his disciples went into the Judean countryside, and he spent some time there with them and baptized. 23 John also was baptizing at Aenon near Salim because water was abundant there; and people kept coming and were being baptized 24 —John, of course, had not yet been thrown into prison.

25 Now a discussion about purification arose between John's disciples and a Jew.[u] 26 They came to John and said to him, "Rabbi, the one who was with you across the Jordan, to whom you testified, here he is baptizing, and all are going to him." 27 John answered, "No one can receive anything except what has been given from heaven. 28 You yourselves are my witnesses that I said, 'I am not the Messiah,[v] but I have been sent ahead of him.' 29 He who has the bride is the bridegroom. The friend of the bridegroom, who stands and hears him, rejoices greatly at the bridegroom's voice. For this reason my joy has been fulfilled. 30 He must increase, but I must decrease."[w]

The One Who Comes from Heaven

31 The one who comes from above is above all; the one who is of the earth belongs to the earth and speaks about earthly things. The one who comes from heaven is above all. 32 He testifies to what he has seen and heard, yet no one accepts his testimony. 33 Whoever has accepted his testimony has certified[x] this, that God is true. 34 He whom God has sent speaks the words of God, for he gives the Spirit without measure. 35 The Father loves the Son and has placed all things in his hands. 36 Whoever believes in the Son has eternal life; whoever disobeys the Son will not see life, but must endure God's wrath.

Jesus and the Woman of Samaria

4 Now when Jesus[y] learned that the Pharisees had heard, "Jesus is making and baptizing more disciples than John" 2 —although it was not Jesus himself but his disciples who baptized— 3 he left Judea and started back to Galilee. 4 But he had to go through Samaria. 5 So he came to a Samaritan city called Sychar, near the plot of ground that Jacob had given to his son Joseph. 6 Jacob's well was there, and Jesus, tired out by his journey, was sitting by the well. It was about noon.

7 A Samaritan woman came to draw water, and Jesus said to her, "Give me a drink." 8 (His disciples had gone to the city to buy food.) 9 The Samaritan woman said to him, "How is it that you, a Jew, ask a drink of me, a woman of Samaria?" (Jews do not share things in common with Samaritans.)[z] 10 Jesus answered her, "If you knew the gift of God, and who it is that is saying to you, 'Give me a drink,' you would have asked him, and he would have given you living water." 11 The woman said to him, "Sir, you have no bucket, and the well is deep. Where do you get that living water? 12 Are you greater than our ancestor Jacob, who gave us the well, and with his sons and his flocks drank from it?" 13 Jesus said to her, "Everyone who drinks of this water will be thirsty again, 14 but those who drink

[s] Other ancient authorities add *who is in heaven* [t] Some interpreters hold that the quotation concludes with verse 15 [u] Other ancient authorities read *the Jews* [v] Or *the Christ* [w] Some interpreters hold that the quotation continues through verse 36 [x] Gk *set a seal to* [y] Other ancient authorities read *the Lord* [z] Other ancient authorities lack this sentence

3.22-4.3 The Differences between Jesus and John the Baptist. **3.22-30** Jesus and his disciples share in the baptizing activity of John, which is now said to be located not only by the Jordan but also at springs (*Aenon*) near Salim, east of Shechem. A debate about who can effect purification of God's people leads John to reaffirm his role as subsidiary to that of Jesus, the Messiah and *bridegroom*, who will restore and renew Israel, God's unfaithful *wife* (Hos 2; Ezek 16.30-43). **2.31-36** The only source of truth is God, who is transmitting it through Jesus, *the one from above*. Response to him is the sole criterion for receiving the life of the age to come (*eternal life*) and for escaping the *wrath* of God's judgment. **4.1-4** On learning that the religious leaders know that the success of his movement is greater than that of John's, Jesus sets out for Galilee by way of Samaria, the district north of Jerusalem where descendants of some of the tribes of Israel have established their own temple and priesthood on Mt. Gerizim. **4.5-42** Jesus and the Woman of Samaria. **4.5-26** *Sychar* refers to Shechem, the place where Abraham stayed on his arrival in Palestine (Canaan; Gen 12.6), and where Jacob purchased some land (Gen 33.18-20), and where his bones were later buried (Josh 24.32). The well outside Shechem still exists. The woman's coming for water at *noon* suggests that her bad reputation led her to avoid meeting other women who would have come for water early in the day. Puzzled that an Israelite would ask a Samaritan (whom he should regard as unclean and untouchable) for water, Jesus invites her to ask him for a drink of *living water*. This was also a term for running water, but Jesus is offering her the water of *eternal life*. When Jesus comments on her deplorable marital state, she acclaims him as a prophet and notes the difference between Jews and Samaritans as to where one should worship. When he denies that God is really to be worshiped in either of these shrines, but *in spirit and in truth*, she declares her belief in the coming of *the Messiah*. He responds by identifying himself as *Messiah*.

3.14 Num 21.9; Jn 8.28; 12.34
3.15 ver 36; Jn 20.21; 1 Jn 5.11-13
3.16 Rom 5.8; 1 Jn 4.9
3.17 Jn 5.36,38; 8.15; 12.47; 1 Jn 4.14
3.18 Jn 5.24; 1 Jn 4.9
3.19 Jn 1.4; 8.12
3.20 Eph 5.11,13
3.21 1 Jn 1.6
3.24 Mt 4.12; 14.3
3.26 Jn 1.7,28
3.27 1 Cor 4.7; Heb 5.4
3.28 Jn 1.20,23
3.29 Mk 2.19,20; Mt 25.1; Jn 15.11; 16.24
3.31 Jn 8.23; 1 Jn 4.5
3.32 ver 11; Jn 8.26; 15.15
3.33 Rom 4.11; 15.28; Eph 1.13; 4.30
3.34 Mt 12.18; Lk 4.18
3.35 Mt 28.18; Jn 5.20,22; 17.2
3.36 Jn 5.24; 6.47
4.1 Jn 3.22,26
4.5 Gen 33.19; 48.22; Josh 24.32
4.9 Mt 10.5; Lk 9.52,53; Jn 8.48
4.10 Isa 44.3; Jn 7.37; Rev 21.6; 22.17
4.14 Jn 6.35; 7.38

of the water that I will give them will never be thirsty. The water that I will give will become in them a spring of water gushing up to eternal life." 15The woman said to him, "Sir, give me this water, so that I may never be thirsty or have to keep coming here to draw water."

16 Jesus said to her, "Go, call your husband, and come back." 17The woman answered him, "I have no husband." Jesus said to her, "You are right in saying, 'I have no husband'; 18for you have had five husbands, and the one you have now is not your husband. What you have said is true!" 19The woman said to him, "Sir, I see that you are a prophet. 20Our ancestors worshiped on this mountain, but you[a] say that the place where people must worship is in Jerusalem." 21Jesus said to her, "Woman, believe me, the hour is coming when you will worship the Father neither on this mountain nor in Jerusalem. 22You worship what you do not know; we worship what we know, for salvation is from the Jews. 23But the hour is coming, and is now here, when the true worshipers will worship the Father in spirit and truth, for the Father seeks such as these to worship him. 24God is spirit, and those who worship him must worship in spirit and truth." 25The woman said to him, "I know that Messiah is coming" (who is called Christ). "When he comes, he will proclaim all things to us." 26Jesus said to her, "I am he,[b] the one who is speaking to you."

27 Just then his disciples came. They were astonished that he was speaking with a woman, but no one said, "What do you want?" or, "Why are you speaking with her?" 28Then the woman left her water jar and went back to the city. She said to the people, 29"Come and see a man who told me everything I have ever done! He cannot be the Messiah,[c] can he?" 30They left the city and were on their way to him.

31 Meanwhile the disciples were urging him, "Rabbi, eat something." 32But he said to them, "I have food to eat that you do not know about." 33So the disciples said to one another, "Surely no one has brought him something to eat?" 34Jesus said to them, "My food is to do the will of him who sent me and to complete his work. 35Do you not say, 'Four months more, then comes the harvest'? But I tell you, look around you, and see how the fields are ripe for harvesting. 36The reaper is already receiving[d] wages and is gathering fruit for eternal life, so that sower and reaper may rejoice together. 37For here the saying holds true, 'One sows and another reaps.' 38I sent you to reap that for which you did not labor. Others have labored, and you have entered into their labor."

39 Many Samaritans from that city believed in him because of the woman's testimony, "He told me everything I have ever done." 40So when the Samaritans came to him, they asked him to stay with them; and he stayed there two days. 41And many more believed because of his word. 42They said to the woman, "It is no longer because of what you said that we believe, for we have heard for ourselves, and we know that this is truly the Savior of the world."

Jesus Returns to Galilee

43 When the two days were over, he went from that place to Galilee 44(for Jesus himself had testified that a prophet has no honor in the prophet's own country). 45When he came to Galilee, the Galileans welcomed him, since they had seen all that he had done in Jerusalem at the festival; for they too had gone to the festival.

Jesus Heals an Official's Son

46 Then he came again to Cana in Galilee where he had changed the water into wine. Now there was a royal official whose son lay ill in Capernaum. 47When he heard that Jesus had come from Judea to Galilee, he went and begged him to come down and heal his son, for he was at the point of death. 48Then Jesus said to him, "Unless you[e] see signs and wonders you will not believe." 49The official said to him, "Sir, come down before my little boy dies." 50Jesus said to him, "Go; your son will live." The man believed the word that Jesus spoke to him and started on his way. 51As he was going down, his slaves met him and told him that his child was alive. 52So he asked them the hour when he began to recover, and they said to him, "Yesterday at one in the afternoon the fever left him." 53The father realized that this was the hour when

[a] The Greek word for *you* here and in verses 21 and 22 is plural [b] Gk *I am* [c] Or *the Christ* [d] Or 35... *the fields are already ripe for harvesting.* 36*The reaper is receiving* [e] Both instances of the Greek word for *you* in this verse are plural

4.27-42 On arrival, the disciples are puzzled at his conversing with the woman, who goes off to the city to report her encounter with Jesus and to raise the question if he is the Messiah. Meanwhile Jesus explains that his desire is not for ordinary food but for his own basis for life (*food*), which is to perform God's will. Evidence of the *harvest* of this food is already visible in this non-Israelite woman's response in faith. The effectiveness of her testimony to Jesus is seen in the *many* Samaritans who trust in him as *the savior of the world*.
4.43-54 Returning to Galilee, Jesus is *welcomed* by those who have observed what he did in Jerusalem at the Passover *festival*. Again in Cana (2.1), he is visited by *a royal official* serving Herod Antipas, who ruled Galilee and Peraea (east of the Jordan). His insistent request that Jesus should come to Capernaum (on the shore of the Lake of Galilee) and *heal* his son is met by Jesus' instruction to return to his home and by the promise that the child will live. This *second sign* of Jesus points to the power of his word and the inclusion of those despised by pious Jews in the benefits of God's grace.

4.15 Jn 6.34
4.20 Deut 11.29; Josh 8.33; Lk 9.53
4.21 Mal 1.11; 1 Tim 2.8
4.22 2 Kings 17.28-41; Isa 2.3; Rom 3.1,2; 9.4,5
4.23 Jn 5.25; Phil 3.3
4.24 Phil 3.3
4.25 Jn 1.41; Mt 1.16
4.26 Mt 26.63,64; Mk 14.61,62; Jn 8.24
4.29 ver 17,18; Jn 7.26,31
4.34 Jn 5.30; 6.38; 17.4; 19.30
4.35 Mt 9.37; Lk 10.2
4.36 Rom 1.13; ver 14
4.37 Job 31.8; Mic 6.15
4.39 ver 29
4.42 1 Jn 4.14; 1 Tim 4.10; 2 Tim 1.10
4.43 ver 40
4.44 Mt 13.57; Mk 6.4; Lk 4.24
4.45 Jn 2.23
4.46 Jn 2.1-11
4.47 ver 3,54
4.48 Dan 4.2; Mk 13.22; Acts 2.19,22,43; 4.30; Rom 15.19; Heb 2.4
4.53 Acts 11.14

Jesus had said to him, "Your son will live." So he himself believed, along with his whole household. 54 Now this was the second sign that Jesus did after coming from Judea to Galilee.

Jesus Heals on the Sabbath

5 After this there was a festival of the Jews, and Jesus went up to Jerusalem.

2 Now in Jerusalem by the Sheep Gate there is a pool, called in Hebrew[f] Beth-zatha,[g] which has five porticoes. 3 In these lay many invalids—blind, lame, and paralyzed.[h] 5 One man was there who had been ill for thirty-eight years. 6 When Jesus saw him lying there and knew that he had been there a long time, he said to him, "Do you want to be made well?" 7 The sick man answered him, "Sir, I have no one to put me into the pool when the water is stirred up; and while I am making my way, someone else steps down ahead of me." 8 Jesus said to him, "Stand up, take your mat and walk." 9 At once the man was made well, and he took up his mat and began to walk.

Now that day was a sabbath. 10 So the Jews said to the man who had been cured, "It is the sabbath; it is not lawful for you to carry your mat." 11 But he answered them, "The man who made me well said to me, 'Take up your mat and walk.' " 12 They asked him, "Who is the man who said to you, 'Take it up and walk'?" 13 Now the man who had been healed did not know who it was, for Jesus had disappeared in[i] the crowd that was there. 14 Later Jesus found him in the temple and said to him, "See, you have been made well! Do not sin any more, so that nothing worse happens to you." 15 The man went away and told the Jews that it was Jesus who had made him well. 16 Therefore the Jews started persecuting Jesus, because he was doing such things on the sabbath. 17 But Jesus answered them, "My Father is still working, and I also am working." 18 For this reason the Jews were seeking all the more to kill him, because he was not only breaking the sabbath, but was also calling God his own Father, thereby making himself equal to God.

The Authority of the Son

19 Jesus said to them, "Very truly, I tell you, the Son can do nothing on his own, but only what he sees the Father doing; for whatever the Father[j] does, the Son does likewise. 20 The Father loves the Son and shows him all that he himself is doing; and he will show him greater works than these, so that you will be astonished. 21 Indeed, just as the Father raises the dead and gives them life, so also the Son gives life to whomever he wishes. 22 The Father judges no one but has given all judgment to the Son, 23 so that all may honor the Son just as they honor the Father. Anyone who does not honor the Son does not honor the Father who sent him. 24 Very truly, I tell you, anyone who hears my word and believes him who sent me has eternal life, and does not come under judgment, but has passed from death to life.

25 "Very truly, I tell you, the hour is coming, and is now here, when the dead will hear the voice of the Son of God, and those who hear will live. 26 For just as the Father has life in himself, so he has granted the Son also to have life in himself; 27 and he has given him authority to execute judgment, because he is the Son of Man. 28 Do not be astonished at this; for the hour is coming when all who are in their graves will hear his voice 29 and will come out—those who have done good, to the resurrection of life, and those who have done evil, to the resurrection of condemnation.

Witnesses to Jesus

30 "I can do nothing on my own. As I hear, I judge; and my judgment is just, because I seek to do not my own will but the will of him who sent me.

31 "If I testify about myself, my testimony is not true. 32 There is another who testifies on my behalf, and I know that his testimony to me is true. 33 You sent messengers to John, and he testified to the truth. 34 Not that I accept such human testimony, but I say these things so that you may be saved. 35 He was a burning and shining lamp, and you were willing to rejoice for a

[f] That is, *Aramaic* [g] Other ancient authorities read *Bethesda*, others *Bethsaida* [h] Other ancient authorities add, wholly or in part, *waiting for the stirring of the water; 4for an angel of the Lord went down at certain seasons into the pool, and stirred up the water; whoever stepped in first after the stirring of the water was made well from whatever disease that person had.* [i] Or *had left because of* [j] Gk *that one*

5.1-10.21 Jesus Challenges the Piety of Judaism on its Holy Days. Beginning with the story of the healing of the lame man on the sabbath, the next major section locates Jesus' public actions on the festival days of Israel: Sabbath (5.1-47); Passover (6.1-71); Tabernacles (7.1-8.52). 7.53-8.11 is a later interpolation and does not fit the series, but the theme of the true understanding of covenant relationship to God prevails from 8.12 to 10.21: the issue is, Who are the true people of God?

5.1-18 Jesus Heals on the Sabbath.
The *festival* is not named, but may have been Pentecost, on which was celebrated the giving of the law through Moses. The pool, which was north of the temple area, was probably named Bethesda, which is confirmed by mention of such a pool in the copper scroll found among the Dead Sea documents from this period. A pool has been found which fits this description (*five porticoes*). The sick man assumes that he can be healed only by entering the pool when *the water is stirred up*, like intermittent springs elsewhere which were thought to bring healing. At Jesus' word of command, he is healed. On learning that it was Jesus who healed him, the *Jews* are enraged because he did this on the sabbath. Jesus defends his action on the ground that his work is God's work, which rouses the Jews to get rid of him as a blasphemer.

5.19-29 Jesus Claims to Be the Son of God.
All of Jesus' power to heal, to give life, and to judge comes to him from God. How one reacts to him determines how one responds to God. To trust in him as God's agent is to enter already into eternal life, and to be assured of sharing in the resurrection of the dead in the future.

5.30-47 The Testimony Supporting his Claim to Be Son of God.
The source of Jesus' authority is God, and his sole purpose is to do the will of God. John the Baptist bore testimony to Jesus' role in the purpose of God, as do the works of God that Jesus has performed and the scriptures that foretold his coming. If they do not accept Jesus as having come in the *name* (authority) of God, they will stand condemned by the testimony of Moses concerning him.

4.54 Jn 2.11

5.2 Neh 3.1; 12.39

5.8 Mt 9.6; Mk 2.11; Lk 5.24

5.9 Jn 9.14

5.10 ver 15,16; Neh 13.19; Jer 17.21; Mt 12.2; Mk 2.24; Jn 7.23; 9.16

5.14 Mk 2.5; Jn 8.11

5.17 Jn 9.4; 14.10

5.18 Jn 7.1,19; 10.30,33

5.19 Jn 8.28; 12.49; 14.10

5.20 Jn 3.35; 14.12

5.21 Rom 4.17; 8.11; Jn 11.25

5.22 Jn 9.39; Acts 17.31

5.23 Lk 10.16; 1 Jn 2.23

5.24 Jn 3.18; 12.44; 20.31; 1 Jn 5.13; 3.14

5.25 Jn 4.21; 6.60; 8.43,47

5.27 Acts 10.42; 17.31

5.29 Dan 12.2; Acts 24.15; Mt 25.46

5.30 Jn 8.16; 4.34; 6.38

5.31 Jn 8.14

5.32 Jn 8.18

5.33 Jn 1.7,15,19,27, 32

5.35 2 Pet 1.19; Mt 21.26

5.36 1 Jn 5.9; Jn 10.25; 14.11; 15.24
5.37 Jn 8.18; Deut 4.12; 1 Tim 1.17
5.38 Jn 3.17
5.39 Lk 24.25,27; Acts 13.27
5.44 Rom 2.29
5.45 Jn 9.28; Rom 2.17
5.46 Gen 3.15; Lk 24.27; Acts 26.22
6.5 Jn 1.43
6.11 ver 23; Mt 15.36
6.14 Gen 49.10; Deut 18.15,18; Mt 11.3; 21.11
6.15 Jn 18.36
6.22 ver 2; 15-21
6.23 ver 1,11
6.24 Mt 14.34; Mk 6.53
6.26 ver 24,30
6.27 Isa 55.2; ver 54; Jn 4.14; 3.35

while in his light. 36 But I have a testimony greater than John's. The works that the Father has given me to complete, the very works that I am doing, testify on my behalf that the Father has sent me. 37 And the Father who sent me has himself testified on my behalf. You have never heard his voice or seen his form, 38 and you do not have his word abiding in you, because you do not believe him whom he has sent.

39 "You search the scriptures because you think that in them you have eternal life; and it is they that testify on my behalf. 40 Yet you refuse to come to me to have life. 41 I do not accept glory from human beings. 42 But I know that you do not have the love of God in[k] you. 43 I have come in my Father's name, and you do not accept me; if another comes in his own name, you will accept him. 44 How can you believe when you accept glory from one another and do not seek the glory that comes from the one who alone is God? 45 Do not think that I will accuse you before the Father; your accuser is Moses, on whom you have set your hope. 46 If you believed Moses, you would believe me, for he wrote about me. 47 But if you do not believe what he wrote, how will you believe what I say?"

Feeding the Five Thousand

6 After this Jesus went to the other side of the Sea of Galilee, also called the Sea of Tiberias.[l] 2 A large crowd kept following him, because they saw the signs that he was doing for the sick. 3 Jesus went up the mountain and sat down there with his disciples. 4 Now the Passover, the festival of the Jews, was near. 5 When he looked up and saw a large crowd coming toward him, Jesus said to Philip, "Where are we to buy bread for these people to eat?" 6 He said this to test him, for he himself knew what he was going to do. 7 Philip answered him, "Six months' wages[m] would not buy enough bread for each of them to get a little." 8 One of his disciples, Andrew, Simon Peter's brother, said to him, 9 "There is a boy here who has five barley loaves and two fish. But what are they among so many people?" 10 Jesus said, "Make the people sit down." Now there was a great deal of grass in the place; so they[n] sat down, about five thousand in all. 11 Then Jesus took the loaves, and when he had given thanks, he distributed them to those who were seated; so also the fish, as much as they wanted. 12 When they were satisfied, he told his disciples, "Gather up the fragments left over, so that nothing may be lost." 13 So they gathered them up, and from the fragments of the five barley loaves, left by those who had eaten, they filled twelve baskets. 14 When the people saw the sign that he had done, they began to say, "This is indeed the prophet who is to come into the world."

15 When Jesus realized that they were about to come and take him by force to make him king, he withdrew again to the mountain by himself.

Jesus Walks on the Water

16 When evening came, his disciples went down to the sea, 17 got into a boat, and started across the sea to Capernaum. It was now dark, and Jesus had not yet come to them. 18 The sea became rough because a strong wind was blowing. 19 When they had rowed about three or four miles,[o] they saw Jesus walking on the sea and coming near the boat, and they were terrified. 20 But he said to them, "It is I;[p] do not be afraid." 21 Then they wanted to take him into the boat, and immediately the boat reached the land toward which they were going.

The Bread from Heaven

22 The next day the crowd that had stayed on the other side of the sea saw that there had been only one boat there. They also saw that Jesus had not got into the boat with his disciples, but that his disciples had gone away alone. 23 Then some boats from Tiberias came near the place where they had eaten the bread after the Lord had given thanks.[q] 24 So when the crowd saw that neither Jesus nor his disciples were there, they themselves got into the boats and went to Capernaum looking for Jesus.

25 When they found him on the other side of the sea, they said to him, "Rabbi, when did you come here?" 26 Jesus answered them, "Very truly, I tell you, you are looking for me, not because you saw signs, but because you ate your fill of the loaves. 27 Do

[k] Or *among* [l] Gk *of Galilee of Tiberius* [m] Gk *Two hundred denarii*; the denarius was the usual day's wage for a laborer [n] Gk *the men* [o] Gk *about twenty-five or thirty stadia* [p] Gk *I am* [q] Other ancient authorities lack *after the Lord had given thanks*

6.1-15 Jesus Supplies Food to God's People at Passover Time. The inability of the disciples to provide food for the crowds and Jesus' miraculous provision of food recall the supply of *manna* to Israel in the wilderness, described in Ex 16 and Num 11. The boy's offer of *barley loaves* and fish and the amazing results of supplying food for a crowd resemble an incident in the story of Elisha (2 Kings 4.42-44). The terms used to describe the distribution – *took, gave thanks, distributed* – and the details of the partakers being *satisfied*, as well as the collection of *fragments*, are reflected in the subsequent eucharistic language of the church (1 Cor 11.23-26; Lk 22.14-20; Didache 9). The misinterpretation of this act of Jesus is seen when the crowd wants to *force* Jesus into the political role of *king*.
6.16-21 Jesus walking on the water in the midst of a storm at sea and his identification of himself as *I Am* (which is the Greek translation for Yahweh, the God of the covenant) recall God's control of the waters in the act of creation (Gen 1.1-10) and the deliverance of Israel from slavery in Egypt by the miraculous crossing of the sea (Ex 14-15). Similar themes are found in Ps 107; Isa 51.10-11.
6.22-40 Jesus offers *bread from heaven* to the *crowd* which comes seeking more free food. The *food* which Jesus provides enables the partaker to share in *eternal life*, and is a gift through the one whom God has approved (*set his seal*). When the crowd asks how it can perform similar miracles, the answer is, to trust in the one whom God has *sent*: Jesus. The request for more miracles evokes Jesus' declaration that he is the *bread* which sustains God's people, enabling them to share in *eternal life* and in the resurrection *on the last day*.

6.41-59 The Jewish listeners object to this claim from one whose parents are known. Jesus replies that only those who have been *drawn* by God will come to him, hearing his word and trusting in him as God's agent, but that those who do trust in him will *live forever*. His giving them his *flesh* to eat carries a two-fold symbolism: sharing in his life of power and obedience, as well as his death; sharing in the Lord's Supper in which his death and his continuing presence with his own are represented.
6.60-71 The basis of this continuing relationship to God through Jesus is *difficult* for his hearers to grasp, but he compounds the problem of comprehension by referring to his coming ascension to God (*where he was before*), to the need to rely on the spirit rather than human capacities (*flesh*), and to the fact that to come to him is not a human achievement but is *granted* by God. Many followers are offended and leave, but Simon Peter affirms the truth of Jesus' words and his identity as God's *Holy One*. Of the inner circle of twelve, one is a *devil*: Judas.

not work for the food that perishes, but for the food that endures for eternal life, which the Son of Man will give you. For it is on him that God the Father has set his seal." [28]Then they said to him, "What must we do to perform the works of God?" [29]Jesus answered them, "This is the work of God, that you believe in him whom he has sent." [30]So they said to him, "What sign are you going to give us then, so that we may see it and believe you? What work are you performing? [31]Our ancestors ate the manna in the wilderness; as it is written, 'He gave them bread from heaven to eat.'" [32]Then Jesus said to them, "Very truly, I tell you, it was not Moses who gave you the bread from heaven, but it is my Father who gives you the true bread from heaven. [33]For the bread of God is that which[r] comes down from heaven and gives life to the world." [34]They said to him, "Sir, give us this bread always."

35 Jesus said to them, "I am the bread of life. Whoever comes to me will never be hungry, and whoever believes in me will never be thirsty. [36]But I said to you that you have seen me and yet do not believe. [37]Everything that the Father gives me will come to me, and anyone who comes to me I will never drive away; [38]for I have come down from heaven, not to do my own will, but the will of him who sent me. [39]And this is the will of him who sent me, that I should lose nothing of all that he has given me, but raise it up on the last day. [40]This is indeed the will of my Father, that all who see the Son and believe in him may have eternal life; and I will raise them up on the last day."

41 Then the Jews began to complain about him because he said, "I am the bread that came down from heaven." [42]They were saying, "Is not this Jesus, the son of Joseph, whose father and mother we know? How can he now say, 'I have come down from heaven'?" [43]Jesus answered them, "Do not complain among yourselves. [44]No one can come to me unless drawn by the Father who sent me; and I will raise that person up on the last day. [45]It is written in the prophets, 'And they shall all be taught by God.' Everyone who has heard and learned from the Father comes to me. [46]Not that anyone has seen the Father except the one who is from God; he has seen the Father. [47]Very truly, I tell you, whoever believes has eternal life. [48]I am the bread of life. [49]Your ancestors ate the manna in the wilderness, and they died. [50]This is the bread that comes down from heaven, so that one may eat of it and not die. [51]I am the living bread that came down from heaven. Whoever eats of this bread will live forever; and the bread that I will give for the life of the world is my flesh."

52 The Jews then disputed among themselves, saying, "How can this man give us his flesh to eat?" [53]So Jesus said to them, "Very truly, I tell you, unless you eat the flesh of the Son of Man and drink his blood, you have no life in you. [54]Those who eat my flesh and drink my blood have eternal life, and I will raise them up on the last day; [55]for my flesh is true food and my blood is true drink. [56]Those who eat my flesh and drink my blood abide in me, and I in them. [57]Just as the living Father sent me, and I live because of the Father, so whoever eats me will live because of me. [58]This is the bread that came down from heaven, not like that which your ancestors ate, and they died. But the one who eats this bread will live forever." [59]He said these things while he was teaching in the synagogue at Capernaum.

The Words of Eternal Life

60 When many of his disciples heard it, they said, "This teaching is difficult; who can accept it?" [61]But Jesus, being aware that his disciples were complaining about it, said to them, "Does this offend you? [62]Then what if you were to see the Son of Man ascending to where he was before? [63]It is the spirit that gives life; the flesh is useless. The words that I have spoken to you are spirit and life. [64]But among you there are some who do not believe." For Jesus knew from the first who were the ones that did not believe, and who was the one that would betray him. [65]And he said, "For this reason I have told you that no one can come to me unless it is granted by the Father."

66 Because of this many of his disciples turned back and no longer went about with him. [67]So Jesus asked the twelve, "Do you also wish to go away?" [68]Simon Peter answered him, "Lord, to whom can we go? You have the words of eternal life. [69]We have come to believe and know that you are the Holy One of God."[s] [70]Jesus answered

[r] Or *he who* [s] Other ancient authorities read *the Christ, the Son of the living God*

6.29 1 Jn 3.23; Jn 3.17
6.30 Mt 12.38; Mk 8.11
6.31 Ex 16.15; Num 11.8; Neh 9.15; Ps 78.24
6.33 ver 50
6.34 Jn 4.15
6.35 ver 48,51; Jn 4.14
6.36 ver 26
6.37 ver 39; Jn 17.2
6.38 Jn 4.34; 5.30
6.39 Jn 10.28; 17.12; 18.9
6.40 ver 27.47,54; Jn 3.15,16
6.42 Lk 4.22; Jn 7.27,28; ver 38,62
6.44 Jer 31.3; Hos 11.4; Jn 12.32
6.45 Isa 54.13; Jer 31.34; Heb 8.10; 10.16
6.46 Jn 1.18; 5.37; 7.29; 8.19
6.47 Jn 3.16,18,36; 5.24; 11.26
6.51 Heb 10.10
6.52 Jn 9.16; 10.19
6.53 Mt 26.26,28
6.54 Jn 4.14
6.56 Jn 15.4; 1 Jn 3.24; 4.15,16
6.61 Mt 11.6
6.62 Jn 3.13; 17.5
6.64 Jn 2.25
6.65 ver 37,44; Jn 3.27
6.69 Mk 8.29; Lk 9.20
6.70 Jn 15.16,19; 13.27

them, "Did I not choose you, the twelve? Yet one of you is a devil." [71]He was speaking of Judas son of Simon Iscariot,[t] for he, though one of the twelve, was going to betray him.

The Unbelief of Jesus' Brothers

7 After this Jesus went about in Galilee. He did not wish[u] to go about in Judea because the Jews were looking for an opportunity to kill him. [2]Now the Jewish festival of Booths[v] was near. [3]So his brothers said to him, "Leave here and go to Judea so that your disciples also may see the works you are doing; [4]for no one who wants[w] to be widely known acts in secret. If you do these things, show yourself to the world." [5](For not even his brothers believed in him.) [6]Jesus said to them, "My time has not yet come, but your time is always here. [7]The world cannot hate you, but it hates me because I testify against it that its works are evil. [8]Go to the festival yourselves. I am not[x] going to this festival, for my time has not yet fully come." [9]After saying this, he remained in Galilee.

Jesus at the Festival of Booths

10 But after his brothers had gone to the festival, then he also went, not publicly but as it were[y] in secret. [11]The Jews were looking for him at the festival and saying, "Where is he?" [12]And there was considerable complaining about him among the crowds. While some were saying, "He is a good man," others were saying, "No, he is deceiving the crowd." [13]Yet no one would speak openly about him for fear of the Jews.

14 About the middle of the festival Jesus went up into the temple and began to teach. [15]The Jews were astonished at it, saying, "How does this man have such learning,[z] when he has never been taught?" [16]Then Jesus answered them, "My teaching is not mine but his who sent me. [17]Anyone who resolves to do the will of God will know whether the teaching is from God or whether I am speaking on my own. [18]Those who speak on their own seek their own glory; but the one who seeks the glory of him who sent him is true, and there is nothing false in him.

19 "Did not Moses give you the law? Yet none of you keeps the law. Why are you looking for an opportunity to kill me?" [20]The crowd answered, "You have a demon! Who is trying to kill you?" [21]Jesus answered them, "I performed one work, and all of you are astonished. [22]Moses gave you circumcision (it is, of course, not from Moses, but from the patriarchs), and you circumcise a man on the sabbath. [23]If a man receives circumcision on the sabbath in order that the law of Moses may not be broken, are you angry with me because I healed a man's whole body on the sabbath? [24]Do not judge by appearances, but judge with right judgment."

Is This the Christ?

25 Now some of the people of Jerusalem were saying, "Is not this the man whom they are trying to kill? [26]And here he is, speaking openly, but they say nothing to him! Can it be that the authorities really know that this is the Messiah?[a] [27]Yet we know where this man is from; but when the Messiah[a] comes, no one will know where he is from." [28]Then Jesus cried out as he was teaching in the temple, "You know me, and you know where I am from. I have not come on my own. But the one who sent me is true, and you do not know him. [29]I know him, because I am from him, and he sent me." [30]Then they tried to arrest him, but no one laid hands on him, because his hour had not yet come. [31]Yet many in the crowd believed in him and were saying, "When the Messiah[a] comes, will he do more signs than this man has done?"[b]

Officers Are Sent to Arrest Jesus

32 The Pharisees heard the crowd muttering such things about him, and the chief priests and Pharisees sent temple police to arrest him. [33]Jesus then said, "I will be with you a little while longer, and then I am going to him who sent me. [34]You will search for me, but you will not find me; and where I am, you cannot come." [35]The Jews said to one another, "Where does this man intend to go that we will not find him? Does he intend to go to the Dispersion among the Greeks and teach the Greeks? [36]What does

[t] Other ancient authorities read *Judas Iscariot son of Simon;* others, *Judas son of Simon from Karyot* (Kerioth) [u] Other ancient authorities read *was not at liberty* [v] Or *Tabernacles* [w] Other ancient authorities read *wants it* [x] Other ancient authorities add *yet* [y] Other ancient authorities lack *as it were* [z] Or *this man know his letters* [a] Or *the Christ* [b] Other ancient authorities read *is doing*

7.1 Jn 5.18
7.2 Lev 23.34; Deut 16.16
7.3 Mt 12.46; Mk 3.31
7.5 Mk 3.21
7.6 Mt 26.18
7.7 Jn 15.18,19; 3.19,20
7.12 ver 40-43
7.13 Jn 9.22; 12.42; 19.38
7.15 Mt 13.54; Mk 6.2; Lk 4.22
7.16 Jn 3.11; 8.28; 12.49
7.17 Jn 8.43
7.18 Jn 5.41; 8.50
7.19 Ex 24.3; Jn 1.17; 11.53
7.20 Jn 8.48; 10.20
7.22 Lev 12.3; Gen 17.10
7.23 Mk 3.5
7.24 Lev 19.15; Jn 8.15
7.27 Mt 13.55; Mk 6.3; Lk 4.22
7.28 Jn 8.14,26; 1.18
7.29 Mt 11.27; Jn 10.15
7.30 Mt 21.46; Jn 8.20
7.31 Jn 8.30; Mt 12.23
7.33 Jn 13.33; 16.16-19
7.34 Jn 8.21; 13.33
7.35 Jas 1.1; 1 Pet 1.1

7.1-10.21 Jesus at the Festival of Booths Discloses Who He Is. **7.1-10** Aware of the plot in Jerusalem to kill him, Jesus seemingly resists the urging of his *brothers* to go with them to Jerusalem and to demonstrate his powers at the *Feast of Booths*, an eight day autumnal celebration of the vineyard harvest when the workers lived in temporary shelters (*booths*), which served as a symbol of Israel's years of nomadic life in transit from slavery in Egypt to new life in Canaan (Lev 23.33-43). Reminding his disciples of the hatred that his words and works have evoked, he remains behind, but then goes to Jerusalem *in secret*. **7.11-24** The questions raised about Jesus (whether he is *good* or *leading the people astray*) focus on the source of his *teaching* and the ground of his *authority*. The one who *sent* Jesus is God; those who do the will of God will know who Jesus is. The opposition to him arose when he healed the man at the pool on the sabbath day (5.1-18), yet the Jews will circumcize someone on the sabbath, since the law which arose before the time of Moses (Gen 17.9-14) required this to take place on the eighth day after birth (Lev 12.3). He has made well a man's whole body. Their values (*judgments*) are based on externals, not on what is *right*. **7.25-31** The opponents in Jerusalem deny that Jesus is the Messiah because they think they know *where he comes from*. Yet they do not know that God is *the one who sent me*. Supporters note that the Messiah will not do more *signs* than Jesus has done. **7.32-36** The coalition of *priests and Pharisees* intends to arrest Jesus and sends *officers* to seize him. His statement about going to God – *the one who sent me* – and their inability to find him puzzle his hearers. Their proposal that he may go to Jews living out of Palestine (*the Dispersion*) and *teach* them is an ironically accurate prediction of what his followers later did.

7.37-44 On the eighth (*last*) day of the feast Jesus invites his hearers to *come and drink*, promising that from their inner being (*heart*) will flow springs of water, which is said to be a promise from scripture. The reference could be to Ps 78.15-16 (God's provision of water for Israel in the wilderness; also Ex 17.6; Num 20.2-13; or Isa 43.20; 48.21) or to the outpouring of God's *Spirit* (Isa 44.3-4; Joel 2.28).
7.45-52 The reluctance of the *temple police* to seize Jesus is challenged by the religious authorities, who insist that he and his followers violate the law. Nicodemus' plea for a *hearing* for Jesus is met by the declaration that there will be no prophets from Galilee, although in fact Jonah's hometown was there (2 Kings 14.25).
7.53-8.11 This story of the woman caught in adultery is not found in the oldest manuscripts and versions of the New Testament, nor does its literary style match that of the rest of John. Those devoted to the interpretation of the law (*scribes*) and members of the group who interpret it strictly (*Pharisees*) seize the woman guilty of violation of her marriage relationship (*adultery*) and use her as a test case to show that Jesus encourages violation of the law. His reference to throwing *the first stone* recalls the law about the mode of execution in Deut 22.21, and the death penalty is required for an adulteress in Lev 20.10 and Ezek 16.38-40. The witnesses who are required to carry this out (Deut 17.7) are not forthcoming, so Jesus scribbles on the ground until the accusers leave, at which point Jesus also refuses to accuse her, while urging her not to *sin again*.
8.12-20 Jesus' next pronouncement of his identity (*I am*) is his claim to be *the light of the world*. His testimony is valid, since he meets the legal requirement of *two witnesses* (Deut 17.6): God's (*the Father's*) testimony and his own, neither of which his opponents recognize.

he mean by saying, 'You will search for me and you will not find me' and 'Where I am, you cannot come'?"

Rivers of Living Water

37 On the last day of the festival, the great day, while Jesus was standing there, he cried out, "Let anyone who is thirsty come to me, [38]and let the one who believes in me drink. As[c] the scripture has said, 'Out of the believer's heart[d] shall flow rivers of living water.' " [39]Now he said this about the Spirit, which believers in him were to receive; for as yet there was no Spirit,[e] because Jesus was not yet glorified.

Division among the People

40 When they heard these words, some in the crowd said, "This is really the prophet." [41]Others said, "This is the Messiah."[f] But some asked, "Surely the Messiah[f] does not come from Galilee, does he? [42]Has not the scripture said that the Messiah[f] is descended from David and comes from Bethlehem, the village where David lived?" [43]So there was a division in the crowd because of him. [44]Some of them wanted to arrest him, but no one laid hands on him.

The Unbelief of Those in Authority

45 Then the temple police went back to the chief priests and Pharisees, who asked them, "Why did you not arrest him?" [46]The police answered, "Never has anyone spoken like this!" [47]Then the Pharisees replied, "Surely you have not been deceived too, have you? [48]Has any one of the authorities or of the Pharisees believed in him? [49]But this crowd, which does not know the law—they are accursed." [50]Nicodemus, who had gone to Jesus[g] before, and who was one of them, asked, [51]"Our law does not judge people without first giving them a hearing to find out what they are doing, does it?" [52]They replied, "Surely you are not also from Galilee, are you? Search and you will see that no prophet is to arise from Galilee."

The Woman Caught in Adultery

8 [[53]Then each of them went home, [1]while Jesus went to the Mount of Olives. [2]Early in the morning he came again to the temple. All the people came to him and he sat down and began to teach them. [3]The scribes and the Pharisees brought a woman who had been caught in adultery; and making her stand before all of them, [4]they said to him, "Teacher, this woman was caught in the very act of committing adultery. [5]Now in the law Moses commanded us to stone such women. Now what do you say?" [6]They said this to test him, so that they might have some charge to bring against him. Jesus bent down and wrote with his finger on the ground. [7]When they kept on questioning him, he straightened up and said to them, "Let anyone among you who is without sin be the first to throw a stone at her." [8]And once again he bent down and wrote on the ground.[h] [9]When they heard it, they went away, one by one, beginning with the elders; and Jesus was left alone with the woman standing before him. [10]Jesus straightened up and said to her, "Woman, where are they? Has no one condemned you?" [11]She said, "No one, sir."[i] And Jesus said, "Neither do I condemn you. Go your way, and from now on do not sin again."][j]

Jesus the Light of the World

12 Again Jesus spoke to them, saying, "I am the light of the world. Whoever follows me will never walk in darkness but will have the light of life." [13]Then the Pharisees said to him, "You are testifying on your own behalf; your testimony is not valid." [14]Jesus answered, "Even if I testify on my own behalf, my testimony is valid because I know where I have come from and where I am going, but you do not know where I come from or where I am going. [15]You judge by human standards;[k] I judge no one. [16]Yet even if I do judge, my judgment is valid; for it is not I alone who judge, but I and the Father[l] who sent me. [17]In your law it is written that the testimony of two

7.37 Lev 23.36; Isa 55.1; Rev 22.17
7.38 Isa 12.3; Jn 4.10,14
7.39 Joel 2.28; Acts 2.17,33; Jn 20.22; 12.23
7.41 Jn 1.46
7.42 Jer 23.5; Mic 5.2; Mt 2.5; Lk 2.4
7.48 Jn 12.42
7.51 Deut 17.6; 19.15
8.5 Lev 20.10; Deut 22.22
8.7 Deut 17.7; Rom 2.1,22
8.9 Rom 2.22
8.11 Jn 3.18; 5.14
8.12 Jn 1.4; 9.5; 12.35
8.17 Deut 17.6; Mt 8.16

[c] Or *come to me and drink.* [38]*The one who believes in me, as* [d] Gk *out of his belly* [e] Other ancient authorities read *for as yet the Spirit* (others, *Holy Spirit*) *had not been given* [f] Or *the Christ* [g] Gk *him* [h] Other ancient authorities add *the sins of each of them* [i] Or *Lord* [j] The most ancient authorities lack 7.53—8.11; other authorities add the passage here or after 7.36 or after 21.25 or after Luke 21.38, with variations of text; some mark the passage as doubtful. [k] Gk *according to the flesh* [l] Other ancient authorities read *he*

witnesses is valid. [18]I testify on my own
behalf, and the Father who sent me testifies
on my behalf." [19]Then they said to him,
"Where is your Father?" Jesus answered,
"You know neither me nor my Father. If
you knew me, you would know my Father
also." [20]He spoke these words while he was
teaching in the treasury of the temple, but
no one arrested him, because his hour had
not yet come.

Jesus Foretells His Death

21 Again he said to them, "I am going
away, and you will search for me, but you
will die in your sin. Where I am going, you
cannot come." [22]Then the Jews said, "Is he
going to kill himself? Is that what he means
by saying, 'Where I am going, you cannot
come'?" [23]He said to them, "You are from
below, I am from above; you are of this
world, I am not of this world. [24]I told you
that you would die in your sins, for you will
die in your sins unless you believe that I am
he."[m] [25]They said to him, "Who are you?"
Jesus said to them, "Why do I speak to you
at all?[n] [26]I have much to say about you and
much to condemn; but the one who sent
me is true, and I declare to the world what
I have heard from him." [27]They did not
understand that he was speaking to them
about the Father. [28]So Jesus said, "When
you have lifted up the Son of Man, then you
will realize that I am he,[v] and that I do
nothing on my own, but I speak these
things as the Father instructed me. [29]And
the one who sent me is with me; he has not
left me alone, for I always do what is
pleasing to him." [30]As he was saying these
things, many believed in him.

True Disciples

31 Then Jesus said to the Jews who had
believed in him, "If you continue in my
word, you are truly my disciples; [32]and you
will know the truth, and the truth will
make you free." [33]They answered him, "We
are descendants of Abraham and have never
been slaves to anyone. What do you mean
by saying, 'You will be made free'?"

34 Jesus answered them, "Very truly, I
tell you, everyone who commits sin is a
slave to sin. [35]The slave does not have a
permanent place in the household; the son
has a place there forever. [36]So if the Son
makes you free, you will be free indeed. [37]I
know that you are descendants of Abraham;
yet you look for an opportunity to kill me,
because there is no place in you for my
word. [38]I declare what I have seen in the
Father's presence; as for you, you should do
what you have heard from the Father."[o]

Jesus and Abraham

39 They answered him, "Abraham is our
father." Jesus said to them, "If you were
Abraham's children, you would be doing[p]
what Abraham did, [40]but now you are
trying to kill me, a man who has told you
the truth that I heard from God. This is not
what Abraham did. [41]You are indeed doing
what your father does." They said to him,
"We are not illegitimate children; we have
one father, God himself." [42]Jesus said to
them, "If God were your Father, you would
love me, for I came from God and now I am
here. I did not come on my own, but he
sent me. [43]Why do you not understand
what I say? It is because you cannot accept
my word. [44]You are from your father the
devil, and you choose to do your father's
desires. He was a murderer from the beginning and does not stand in the truth, because there is no truth in him. When he
lies, he speaks according to his own nature,
for he is a liar and the father of lies. [45]But
because I tell the truth, you do not believe
me. [46]Which of you convicts me of sin? If
I tell the truth, why do you not believe me?
[47]Whoever is from God hears the words of
God. The reason you do not hear them is
that you are not from God."

48 The Jews answered him, "Are we not
right in saying that you are a Samaritan
and have a demon?" [49]Jesus answered, "I do
not have a demon; but I honor my Father,
and you dishonor me. [50]Yet I do not seek
my own glory; there is one who seeks it and
he is the judge. [51]Very truly, I tell you,
whoever keeps my word will never see
death." [52]The Jews said to him, "Now we
know that you have a demon. Abraham
died, and so did the prophets; yet you say,
'Whoever keeps my word will never taste
death.' [53]Are you greater than our father
Abraham, who died? The prophets also died.
Who do you claim to be?" [54]Jesus answered,
"If I glorify myself, my glory is nothing. It

[m] Gk *I am* [n] Or *What I have told you from the beginning* [o] Other ancient authorities read *you do what you have heard from your father* [p] Other ancient authorities read *If you are Abraham's children, then do*

8.18 Jn 5.37
8.19 Jn 14.7; 16.3
8.20 Mk 12.41; Jn 7.30
8.21 Jn 7.34
8.23 Jn 3.31; 17.14
8.24 Mk 13.6; Jn 4.26; 13.19
8.26 Jn 7.28; 3.32; 15.15
8.28 Jn 3.14; 12.32; 5.19; 3.11
8.29 Jn 4.34; 5.30; 6.38
8.32 Rom 8.2; Jas 2.12
8.33 Mt 3.9
8.34 Rom 6.16; 2 Pet 2.19
8.35 Gal 4.30
8.38 Jn 5.19,30; 14.10,24
8.39 Rom 9.7; Gal 3.7
8.41 Isa 63.16; 64.8
8.42 1 Jn 5.1; Jn 16.17,28; 17.8; 7.28
8.44 1 Jn 3.8; ver 38,41; 1 Jn 2.4; Mt 12.34
8.47 1 Jn 4.6
8.48 ver 52; Jn 7.20; 10.20
8.50 Jn 5.41
8.51 Jn 14.23; 15.20; 17.6; Mt 16.28; Heb 11.5
8.52 Jn 7.20; 14.23; 15.20; 17.6
8.53 Jn 4.12
8.54 ver 50; Jn 16.14

8.21-30 Announcing his impending *going away* (death and ascension to God) and declaring that his origin is not from within the present order (*world*), he insists that they must believe that *I am*: one with God. But only when they have *lifted up* Jesus (symbolizing both his crucifixion and his exaltation to God) will they recognize that *I am*, and that God has sent him.
8.31-59 Continuing commitment to Jesus' teaching (*word*) will free them for knowledge of *the truth* and from *sin*. His hostile listeners claim to be God's people (*descendants of Abraham*), and oppose him and seek to kill him, even though he conveys to them the truth which he received from God. Their failure to *love* Jesus proves that they are not heirs of the promise to Abraham but are children of *the devil*. His claim to free his followers from death implies that he is greater than Abraham and the prophets, all of whom *died*. His response is that it is God who *glorifies* him, and that before Abraham came into existence (*was*), Jesus is: *I am*.

9.1-12 The bringing of a man born blind to Jesus is the occasion for raising the old question whether physical disability is a sign of divine punishment for moral failure. Jesus claims that his coming is a symbolic opportunity to bring the light of God into the world: *I am the light of the world.* Sent to the pool to wash, as Naaman was sent by Elisha in 2 Kings 5.10-13, the man returns able to see.

9.13-34 Interrogated by the Pharisees about what happened, since Jesus did this on the *sabbath*, the man will only affirm that it took place through Jesus, whom he regards as *a prophet*. His parents confirm that he has been blind from birth, but shift the inquiry back to their son, since the Jewish leaders have decided that those who *confessed Jesus to be the Messiah* are to be *put out of the synagogue*. The man insists that Jesus must be from God, since not *since the world began* has such a healing taken place, although sight to the blind is promised in the prophets (Isa 29.18; 35.5), and especially in Isa 42.6-7, where it is linked with renewal of the covenant.

is my Father who glorifies me, he of whom
you say, 'He is our God,' 55 though you do
not know him. But I know him; if I would
say that I do not know him, I would be a
liar like you. But I do know him and I keep
his word. 56 Your ancestor Abraham rejoiced
that he would see my day; he saw it and
was glad." 57 Then the Jews said to him,
"You are not yet fifty years old, and have
you seen Abraham?"[q] 58 Jesus said to them,
"Very truly, I tell you, before Abraham was,
I am." 59 So they picked up stones to throw
at him, but Jesus hid himself and went out
of the temple.

A Man Born Blind Receives Sight

9 As he walked along, he saw a man
blind from birth. 2 His disciples asked
him, "Rabbi, who sinned, this man or his
parents, that he was born blind?" 3 Jesus
answered, "Neither this man nor his parents sinned; he was born blind so that God's
works might be revealed in him. 4 We[r] must
work the works of him who sent me[s] while
it is day; night is coming when no one can
work. 5 As long as I am in the world, I am
the light of the world." 6 When he had said
this, he spat on the ground and made mud
with the saliva and spread the mud on the
man's eyes, 7 saying to him, "Go, wash in
the pool of Siloam" (which means Sent).
Then he went and washed and came back
able to see. 8 The neighbors and those who
had seen him before as a beggar began to
ask, "Is this not the man who used to sit
and beg?" 9 Some were saying, "It is he."
Others were saying, "No, but it is someone
like him." He kept saying, "I am the man."
10 But they kept asking him, "Then how
were your eyes opened?" 11 He answered,
"The man called Jesus made mud, spread it
on my eyes, and said to me, 'Go to Siloam
and wash.' Then I went and washed and
received my sight." 12 They said to him,
"Where is he?" He said, "I do not know."

The Pharisees Investigate the Healing

13 They brought to the Pharisees the
man who had formerly been blind. 14 Now
it was a sabbath day when Jesus made the
mud and opened his eyes. 15 Then the Pharisees also began to ask him how he had
received his sight. He said to them, "He put
mud on my eyes. Then I washed, and now
I see." 16 Some of the Pharisees said, "This
man is not from God, for he does not
observe the sabbath." But others said, "How
can a man who is a sinner perform such
signs?" And they were divided. 17 So they
said again to the blind man, "What do you
say about him? It was your eyes he opened."
He said, "He is a prophet."

18 The Jews did not believe that he had
been blind and had received his sight until
they called the parents of the man who had
received his sight 19 and asked them, "Is this
your son, who you say was born blind?
How then does he now see?" 20 His parents
answered, "We know that this is our son,
and that he was born blind; 21 but we do not
know how it is that now he sees, nor do
we know who opened his eyes. Ask him; he
is of age. He will speak for himself." 22 His
parents said this because they were afraid
of the Jews; for the Jews had already agreed
that anyone who confessed Jesus[t] to be the
Messiah[u] would be put out of the synagogue. 23 Therefore his parents said, "He is
of age; ask him."

24 So for the second time they called the
man who had been blind, and they said to
him, "Give glory to God! We know that this
man is a sinner." 25 He answered, "I do not
know whether he is a sinner. One thing I
do know, that though I was blind, now I
see." 26 They said to him, "What did he do
to you? How did he open your eyes?" 27 He
answered them, "I have told you already,
and you would not listen. Why do you
want to hear it again? Do you also want to
become his disciples?" 28 Then they reviled
him, saying, "You are his disciple, but we
are disciples of Moses. 29 We know that God
has spoken to Moses, but as for this man,
we do not know where he comes from."
30 The man answered, "Here is an astonishing thing! You do not know where he
comes from, and yet he opened my eyes.
31 We know that God does not listen to
sinners, but he does listen to one who
worships him and obeys his will. 32 Never
since the world began has it been heard
that anyone opened the eyes of a person
born blind. 33 If this man were not from God,
he could do nothing." 34 They answered him,
"You were born entirely in sins, and are
you trying to teach us?" And they drove
him out.

[q] Other ancient authorities read *has Abraham seen you?* [r] Other ancient authorities read *I* [s] Other ancient authorities read *us* [t] Gk *him* [u] Or *the Christ*

8.55 Jn 7.28,29; 15.10
8.56 Mt 13.17; Heb 11.13
8.58 Jn 1.1; 17.5,24; Rev 1.8
8.59 Jn 10.31; 11.8; 12.36
9.3 Jn 11.4
9.4 Jn 11.9; 12.35
9.5 Jn 1.4; 8.12; 12.46
9.6 Mk 7.33; 8.23
9.7 ver 11; Lk 13.4; Jn 11.37
9.14 Jn 5.9
9.16 Mt 12.2; Jn 7.32; 10.19
9.17 ver 15; Mt 21.11
9.22 Jn 7.13; 12.42; ver 34; Lk 6.22
9.24 Josh 7.19; 1 Sam 6.5; ver 16
9.28 Jn 5.45
9.29 Jn 8.14
9.31 Job 27.8,9; Ps 34.15; 66.18; Prov 15.29; 28.9; Isa 1.15; Jer 11.11; Zech 7.13

Spiritual Blindness

35 Jesus heard that they had driven him out, and when he found him, he said, "Do you believe in the Son of Man?"[v] 36He answered, "And who is he, sir?[w] Tell me, so that I may believe in him." 37Jesus said to him, "You have seen him, and the one speaking with you is he." 38He said, "Lord,[w] I believe." And he worshiped him. 39Jesus said, "I came into this world for judgment so that those who do not see may see, and those who do see may become blind." 40Some of the Pharisees near him heard this and said to him, "Surely we are not blind, are we?" 41Jesus said to them, "If you were blind, you would not have sin. But now that you say, 'We see,' your sin remains.

Jesus the Good Shepherd

10 "Very truly, I tell you, anyone who does not enter the sheepfold by the gate but climbs in by another way is a thief and a bandit. 2The one who enters by the gate is the shepherd of the sheep. 3The gatekeeper opens the gate for him, and the sheep hear his voice. He calls his own sheep by name and leads them out. 4When he has brought out all his own, he goes ahead of them, and the sheep follow him because they know his voice. 5They will not follow a stranger, but they will run from him because they do not know the voice of strangers." 6Jesus used this figure of speech with them, but they did not understand what he was saying to them.

7 So again Jesus said to them, "Very truly, I tell you, I am the gate for the sheep. 8All who came before me are thieves and bandits; but the sheep did not listen to them. 9I am the gate. Whoever enters by me will be saved, and will come in and go out and find pasture. 10The thief comes only to steal and kill and destroy. I came that they may have life, and have it abundantly.

11 "I am the good shepherd. The good shepherd lays down his life for the sheep. 12The hired hand, who is not the shepherd and does not own the sheep, sees the wolf coming and leaves the sheep and runs away—and the wolf snatches them and scatters them. 13The hired hand runs away because a hired hand does not care for the sheep. 14I am the good shepherd. I know my own and my own know me, 15just as the Father knows me and I know the Father. And I lay down my life for the sheep. 16I have other sheep that do not belong to this fold. I must bring them also, and they will listen to my voice. So there will be one flock, one shepherd. 17For this reason the Father loves me, because I lay down my life in order to take it up again. 18No one takes[x] it from me, but I lay it down of my own accord. I have power to lay it down, and I have power to take it up again. I have received this command from my Father."

19 Again the Jews were divided because of these words. 20Many of them were saying, "He has a demon and is out of his mind. Why listen to him?" 21Others were saying, "These are not the words of one who has a demon. Can a demon open the eyes of the blind?"

Jesus Is Rejected by the Jews

22 At that time the festival of the Dedication took place in Jerusalem. It was winter, 23and Jesus was walking in the temple, in the portico of Solomon. 24So the Jews gathered around him and said to him, "How long will you keep us in suspense? If you are the Messiah,[y] tell us plainly." 25Jesus answered, "I have told you, and you do not believe. The works that I do in my Father's name testify to me; 26but you do not believe, because you do not belong to my sheep. 27My sheep hear my voice. I know them, and they follow me. 28I give them eternal life, and they will never perish. No one will snatch them out of my hand. 29What my Father has given me is greater than all else, and no one can snatch it out of the Father's hand.[z] 30The Father and I are one."

31 The Jews took up stones again to stone him. 32Jesus replied, "I have shown you many good works from the Father. For which of these are you going to stone me?" 33The Jews answered, "It is not for a good work that we are going to stone you, but for blasphemy, because you, though only a human being, are making yourself God." 34Jesus answered, "Is it not written in your law,[a] 'I said, you are gods'? 35If those to whom the word of God came were called

[v] Other ancient authorities read *the Son of God* [w] *Sir* and *Lord* translate the same Greek word [x] Other ancient authorities read *has taken* [y] Or *the Christ* [z] Other ancient authorities read *My Father who has given them to me is greater than all, and no one can snatch them out of the Father's hand* [a] Other ancient authorities read *in the law*

9.35-41 In conversation with the man cured of blindness, Jesus discloses himself as *the Son of Man* and the man believes. In sharp contrast, the Pharisees, who disputed Jesus' ability to restore sight, show themselves to be the ones who are truly *blind*.
10.1-21 Expanding on the biblical metaphor of the covenant people as God's flock (Ps 23; Isa 40.11) and of their straying from God (Isa 53.6), Jesus declares, *I am the gate*, inasmuch as he determines who are to be admitted to his people (*own sheep*) and gives them fullness of *life*. Then the image shifts (10.7) to his role as shepherd (*I am the good shepherd*) who protects his sheep, even at the risk of his own life, and to whose *voice* they respond. Even when he *lays down his life* for them, God grants him power to *take it up again* in the resurrection. The response of his hearers is divided between those who assign his powers to demons and those who acknowledge his ability to *open the eyes of the blind*.
10.22-12.50 Mounting Opposition to Jesus.
10.22-41 The Feast of Dedication celebrated the rededication of the temple by the Maccabees in 165 BCE, following their leading of the successful Jewish revolt against Antiochus Epiphanes (who had erected a statue of himself as Olympian Zeus in the temple; 1 Macc 4.41-61). Jesus is confronted in the temple *portico* by Jews who want a clear answer to the claim that he is *the Messiah*. In response, Jesus claims that he and the Father *are one*, that he is doing God's works, and that the Father is in him and he in the Father. Escaping their attempt to arrest him, he returns to the setting for the first scene in John 1.28, beyond the Jordan.

9.35 Mt 14.33; 16.16; Mk 1.1; Jn 10.36
9.36 Rom 10.14
9.37 Jn 4.26
9.39 Jn 5.22,27; 3.19; Mt 13.13; 15.14
9.40 Rom 2.19
9.41 Jn 15.22,24
10.2 Mk 6.34; ver 11,12
10.10 Jn 5.40
10.11 Isa 40.11; Ezek 34.11-16,23; Heb 13.20; 1 Pet 5.4; Jn 15.13; Rev 7.17
10.12 Zech 11.16,17
10.16 Isa 56.8; Jn 11.52; Eph 2.14; 1 Pet 2.25
10.19 Jn 7.43; 9.16
10.20 Jn 7.20; 8.48; Mk 3.21
10.21 Jn 9.32,33; Ex 4.11
10.23 Acts 3.11; 5.12
10.25 Jn 5.36
10.26 Jn 8.47
10.27 ver 4,14
10.28 Jn 17.2,3; 1 Jn 2.25; Jn 6.37,39
10.29 Jn 14.28; 17.2,6ff
10.33 Jn 5.18
10.34 Ps 82.6

11.1-44 Jesus' delay in coming in response to the news of Lazarus' illness provides the occasion for a fuller manifestation of his powers, resulting in glory to God and to *the Son of Man*. Returning to Judea in spite of the warning from his followers, he announces his intention to *awaken* Lazarus, but on his arrival at Bethany (a few miles east of Jerusalem on the road to Jericho), Lazarus is already dead and in the tomb. Instead of merely affirming the belief of many Jews in the resurrection *on the last day*, Jesus once again identifies himself: *I am the resurrection and the life* (as God intended the life of his people to be). On reaching the town and the tomb, Jesus *weeps* at the inability of his followers to understand God's purpose through him, and then calls the dead man to *come out*. Released from the grave wrappings, he resumes his former life.

'gods'—and the scripture cannot be annulled— 36can you say that the one whom the Father has sanctified and sent into the world is blaspheming because I said, 'I am God's Son'? 37If I am not doing the works of my Father, then do not believe me. 38But if I do them, even though you do not believe me, believe the works, so that you may know and understand[b] that the Father is in me and I am in the Father." 39Then they tried to arrest him again, but he escaped from their hands.

40 He went away again across the Jordan to the place where John had been baptizing earlier, and he remained there. 41Many came to him, and they were saying, "John performed no sign, but everything that John said about this man was true." 42And many believed in him there.

The Death of Lazarus

11 Now a certain man was ill, Lazarus of Bethany, the village of Mary and her sister Martha. 2Mary was the one who anointed the Lord with perfume and wiped his feet with her hair; her brother Lazarus was ill. 3So the sisters sent a message to Jesus,[c] "Lord, he whom you love is ill." 4But when Jesus heard it, he said, "This illness does not lead to death; rather it is for God's glory, so that the Son of God may be glorified through it." 5Accordingly, though Jesus loved Martha and her sister and Lazarus, 6after having heard that Lazarus[d] was ill, he stayed two days longer in the place where he was.

7 Then after this he said to the disciples, "Let us go to Judea again." 8The disciples said to him, "Rabbi, the Jews were just now trying to stone you, and are you going there again?" 9Jesus answered, "Are there not twelve hours of daylight? Those who walk during the day do not stumble, because they see the light of this world. 10But those who walk at night stumble, because the light is not in them." 11After saying this, he told them, "Our friend Lazarus has fallen asleep, but I am going there to awaken him." 12The disciples said to him, "Lord, if he has fallen asleep, he will be all right." 13Jesus, however, had been speaking about his death, but they thought that he was referring merely to sleep. 14Then Jesus told them plainly, "Lazarus is dead. 15For your sake I am glad I was not there, so that you may believe. But let us go to him." 16Thomas, who was called the Twin,[e] said to his fellow disciples, "Let us also go, that we may die with him."

Jesus the Resurrection and the Life

17 When Jesus arrived, he found that Lazarus[d] had already been in the tomb four days. 18Now Bethany was near Jerusalem, some two miles[f] away, 19and many of the Jews had come to Martha and Mary to console them about their brother. 20When Martha heard that Jesus was coming, she went and met him, while Mary stayed at home. 21Martha said to Jesus, "Lord, if you had been here, my brother would not have died. 22But even now I know that God will give you whatever you ask of him." 23Jesus said to her, "Your brother will rise again." 24Martha said to him, "I know that he will rise again in the resurrection on the last day." 25Jesus said to her, "I am the resurrection and the life.[g] Those who believe in me, even though they die, will live, 26and everyone who lives and believes in me will never die. Do you believe this?" 27She said to him, "Yes, Lord, I believe that you are the Messiah,[h] the Son of God, the one coming into the world."

Jesus Weeps

28 When she had said this, she went back and called her sister Mary, and told her privately, "The Teacher is here and is calling for you." 29And when she heard it, she got up quickly and went to him. 30Now Jesus had not yet come to the village, but was still at the place where Martha had met him. 31The Jews who were with her in the house, consoling her, saw Mary get up quickly and go out. They followed her because they thought that she was going to the tomb to weep there. 32When Mary came where Jesus was and saw him, she knelt at his feet and said to him, "Lord, if you had been here, my brother would not have died." 33When Jesus saw her weeping, and the Jews who came with her also weeping, he was greatly disturbed in spirit and deeply moved. 34He said, "Where have you laid him?" They said to him, "Lord, come and see." 35Jesus began to weep. 36So the Jews

[b] Other ancient authorities lack *and understand*; others read *and believe* [c] Gk *him* [d] Gk *he* [e] Gk *Didymus* [f] Gk *fifteen stadia* [g] Other ancient authorities lack *and the life* [h] Or *the Christ*

10.36 Jn 6.69; 3.17; Jn 5.17,18
10.37 Jn 15.24
10.38 Jn 14.10,11; 17.21
10.39 Jn 7.30; 8.59
10.41 Jn 2.11; 3.30
10.42 Jn 7.31; 11.45
11.1 Mk 11.1; Lk 10.38
11.2 Mk 14.3; Lk 7.38; Jn 12.3
11.4 ver 40; Jn 9.3
11.7 Jn 10.40
11.8 Jn 10.31
11.19 Job 2.11
11.22 Jn 9.31
11.24 Dan 12.2; Jn 5.28,29; Acts 24.15
11.25 Jn 1.4; 5.26; 14.6; 3.36
11.27 Mt 16.16; Jn 6.14
11.32 ver 21
11.35 Lk 19.41

said, "See how he loved him!" [37]But some of them said, "Could not he who opened the eyes of the blind man have kept this man from dying?"

Jesus Raises Lazarus to Life

38 Then Jesus, again greatly disturbed, came to the tomb. It was a cave, and a stone was lying against it. [39]Jesus said, "Take away the stone." Martha, the sister of the dead man, said to him, "Lord, already there is a stench because he has been dead four days." [40]Jesus said to her, "Did I not tell you that if you believed, you would see the glory of God?" [41]So they took away the stone. And Jesus looked upward and said, "Father, I thank you for having heard me. [42]I knew that you always hear me, but I have said this for the sake of the crowd standing here, so that they may believe that you sent me." [43]When he had said this, he cried with a loud voice, "Lazarus, come out!" [44]The dead man came out, his hands and feet bound with strips of cloth, and his face wrapped in a cloth. Jesus said to them, "Unbind him, and let him go."

The Plot to Kill Jesus

45 Many of the Jews therefore, who had come with Mary and had seen what Jesus did, believed in him. [46]But some of them went to the Pharisees and told them what he had done. [47]So the chief priests and the Pharisees called a meeting of the council, and said, "What are we to do? This man is performing many signs. [48]If we let him go on like this, everyone will believe in him, and the Romans will come and destroy both our holy place[i] and our nation." [49]But one of them, Caiaphas, who was high priest that year, said to them, "You know nothing at all! [50]You do not understand that it is better for you to have one man die for the people than to have the whole nation destroyed." [51]He did not say this on his own, but being high priest that year he prophesied that Jesus was about to die for the nation, [52]and not for the nation only, but to gather into one the dispersed children of God. [53]So from that day on they planned to put him to death.

54 Jesus therefore no longer walked about openly among the Jews, but went from there to a town called Ephraim in the region near the wilderness; and he remained there with the disciples.

55 Now the Passover of the Jews was near, and many went up from the country to Jerusalem before the Passover to purify themselves. [56]They were looking for Jesus and were asking one another as they stood in the temple, "What do you think? Surely he will not come to the festival, will he?" [57]Now the chief priests and the Pharisees had given orders that anyone who knew where Jesus[j] was should let them know, so that they might arrest him.

Mary Anoints Jesus

12 Six days before the Passover Jesus came to Bethany, the home of Lazarus, whom he had raised from the dead. [2]There they gave a dinner for him. Martha served, and Lazarus was one of those at the table with him. [3]Mary took a pound of costly perfume made of pure nard, anointed Jesus' feet, and wiped them[k] with her hair. The house was filled with the fragrance of the perfume. [4]But Judas Iscariot, one of his disciples (the one who was about to betray him), said, [5]"Why was this perfume not sold for three hundred denarii[l] and the money given to the poor?" [6](He said this not because he cared about the poor, but because he was a thief; he kept the common purse and used to steal what was put into it.) [7]Jesus said, "Leave her alone. She bought it[m] so that she might keep it for the day of my burial. [8]You always have the poor with you, but you do not always have me."

The Plot to Kill Lazarus

9 When the great crowd of the Jews learned that he was there, they came not only because of Jesus but also to see Lazarus, whom he had raised from the dead. [10]So the chief priests planned to put Lazarus to death as well, [11]since it was on account of him that many of the Jews were deserting and were believing in Jesus.

Jesus' Triumphal Entry into Jerusalem

12 The next day the great crowd that had come to the festival heard that Jesus

[i] Or *our temple*; Greek *our place* [j] Gk *he* [k] Gk *his feet* [l] Three hundred denarii would be nearly a year's wages for a laborer [m] Gk lacks *She bought it*

11.37 Jn 9.6,7
11.38 ver 33; Mt 27.60; Mk 15.46; Lk 24.2; Jn 20.1
11.39 ver 17
11.40 ver 4.23
11.41 Jn 17.1; Mt 11.25
11.42 Jn 12.30; 3.17
11.44 Jn 19.40; 20.7
11.45 ver 19; Jn 2.23
11.47 ver 57; Mt 26.3
11.49 Mt 26.3; Jn 18.13,14
11.50 ver 21
11.53 Mt 26.4
11.54 Jn 7.1; 2 Chr 13.19
11.55 Mt 26.1,2; Mk 14.1; Lk 22.1; Jn 12.1; Num 9.10; 2 Chr 30.17,18
12.1 Lk 7.37-39; Jn 11.55
12.2 Lk 10.38
12.3 Jn 11.2; Mk 14.3
12.7 Jn 19.40
12.8 Mt 26.11; Mk 14.7
12.11 ver 18; Jn 11.45

11.45-57 Some observers of Jesus' powers put their trust in him, while others join the plot to destroy him, on the ground that his program will result in the destruction of *the whole nation* of Israel. John sees this as foretelling Jesus' sacrificial death and the reconstituting of God's *children*, now dispersed across the world. Once more Jesus retreats to Ephraim, probably a village north of Jerusalem on the border of the Judean desert toward the Jordan Valley. Meanwhile the authorities in Jerusalem await his return at *Passover* in order to *arrest him*.
12.1-8 Coming to Jerusalem by way of Bethany, Jesus is anointed for burial with costly ointment by Mary. Judas complains on the ground that this is a waste of money. Jesus' response notes the uniqueness of his impending death and *burial*, in contrast to the constant needs of the *poor*.
12.9-19 The mixed response to Jesus is evident in the huge crowds that come to see him and the one he has raised from the dead, and in the plot of the religious authorities to kill Lazarus. Jesus' entry into the city is acclaimed as fulfilling the prophecies of the coming to Jerusalem of God's future king (Ps 118.26; Zech 9.9). The Pharisees are disgusted at the attention he has attracted.

12.20-26 When the message is relayed to Jesus that *Greeks* (Gentiles) want to see him, he responds by pointing to his impending death and resurrection under the image of a seed that is buried and rises from the ground to new life. Each of his followers must be willing to follow his example in giving up the old way of life if he or she is truly to *keep* it.

12.27-43 Struggling in the face of his impending death, Jesus first asks God to spare (*save*) him from this experience, and then affirms that his death is central to his mission under God. That is confirmed by a *voice from heaven* which the crowd hears but does not comprehend. He explains that his death will effect *judgment* on this world and expel its *ruler* (Satan). The outcome will be to draw all humanity to himself. The crowd expects the Messiah to remain *forever* in power, and questions why he must first be crucified (*lifted up*), to which he answers that they must trust the *light* of knowledge of God's purpose which he has brought, or walk *in darkness*. The refusal of the crowd to accept his explanation, in spite of his many *signs*, is seen as in fulfillment of the prophetic word about the disbelief of those who hear God's word (Isa 53.1; 6.9-10). Even many who secretly trust in him refuse to acknowledge it publicly for fear of expulsion from the *synagogue*, the gatherings of pious Jews for study and prayer that were developing in the first century.

12.44-50 To trust in Jesus is to trust in the God who sent him as *light* into the world. God will deal with those who fail to keep his word or who reject him, since his purpose and his authority derive from God. At stake is a share in *eternal life*. What Jesus speaks is what God told him to say.

was coming to Jerusalem. 13So they took
branches of palm trees and went out to
meet him, shouting,

"Hosanna!
Blessed is the one who comes in the
name of the Lord—
the King of Israel!"

14Jesus found a young donkey and sat on
it; as it is written:

15 "Do not be afraid, daughter of Zion.
Look, your king is coming,
sitting on a donkey's colt!"

16His disciples did not understand these things
at first; but when Jesus was glorified, then
they remembered that these things had been
written of him and had been done to him.
17So the crowd that had been with him
when he called Lazarus out of the tomb and
raised him from the dead continued to testify.[n]
18It was also because they heard that he
had performed this sign that the crowd
went to meet him. 19The Pharisees then said
to one another, "You see, you can do nothing.
Look, the world has gone after him!"

Some Greeks Wish to See Jesus

20 Now among those who went up to
worship at the festival were some Greeks.
21They came to Philip, who was from
Bethsaida in Galilee, and said to him, "Sir,
we wish to see Jesus." 22Philip went and
told Andrew; then Andrew and Philip went
and told Jesus. 23Jesus answered them, "The
hour has come for the Son of Man to be
glorified. 24Very truly, I tell you, unless a
grain of wheat falls into the earth and dies,
it remains just a single grain; but if it dies,
it bears much fruit. 25Those who love their
life lose it, and those who hate their life in
this world will keep it for eternal life. 26Whoever
serves me must follow me, and where
I am, there will my servant be also. Whoever
serves me, the Father will honor.

Jesus Speaks about His Death

27 "Now my soul is troubled. And what
should I say—'Father, save me from this
hour'? No, it is for this reason that I have
come to this hour. 28Father, glorify your
name." Then a voice came from heaven, "I
have glorified it, and I will glorify it again."
29The crowd standing there heard it and
said that it was thunder. Others said, "An
angel has spoken to him." 30Jesus answered,
"This voice has come for your sake, not for
mine. 31Now is the judgment of this world;
now the ruler of this world will be driven
out. 32And I, when I am lifted up from the
earth, will draw all people[o] to myself." 33He
said this to indicate the kind of death he
was to die. 34The crowd answered him, "We
have heard from the law that the Messiah[p]
remains forever. How can you say that the
Son of Man must be lifted up? Who is this
Son of Man?" 35Jesus said to them, "The
light is with you for a little longer. Walk
while you have the light, so that the darkness
may not overtake you. If you walk in
the darkness, you do not know where you
are going. 36While you have the light, believe
in the light, so that you may become
children of light."

The Unbelief of the People

After Jesus had said this, he departed and
hid from them. 37Although he had performed
so many signs in their presence,
they did not believe in him. 38This was to
fulfill the word spoken by the prophet Isaiah:

"Lord, who has believed our message,
and to whom has the arm of the Lord
been revealed?"

39And so they could not believe, because
Isaiah also said,

40 "He has blinded their eyes
and hardened their heart,
so that they might not look with their
eyes,
and understand with their heart and
turn—
and I would heal them."

41Isaiah said this because[q] he saw his glory
and spoke about him. 42Nevertheless many,
even of the authorities, believed in him. But
because of the Pharisees they did not confess
it, for fear that they would be put out
of the synagogue; 43for they loved human
glory more than the glory that comes from
God.

Summary of Jesus' Teaching

44 Then Jesus cried aloud: "Whoever
believes in me believes not in me but in him
who sent me. 45And whoever sees me sees
him who sent me. 46I have come as light
into the world, so that everyone who

[n] Other ancient authorities read *with him began to testify that he had called ... from the dead* [o] Other ancient authorities read *all things* [p] Or *the Christ* [q] Other ancient witnesses read *when*

12.13 Ps 118.25,26; Jn 1.49
12.15 Zech 9.9
12.16 Mk 9.32; Jn 2.22; 14.26; 7.39
12.19 Jn 11.48
12.20 Jn 7.35; Acts 11.20
12.23 Jn 13.1,32; 17.1; Mk 14.35,41; 12.24; 1 Cor 15.36
12.25 Mt 10.39; Mk 8.35; Lk 9.24; 14.26
12.26 Jn 14.3; 17.24; 1 Thess 4.17
12.27 Mt 26.38,39; Mk 14.34; Jn 11.33
12.28 Mt 3.17; 17.5; Mk 1.11; 9.7; Lk 3.22; 9.35
12.31 Jn 16.11; 14.30; 2 Cor 4.4; Eph 2.2
12.32 Jn 3.14; 8.28; 6.44
12.34 Ps 110.4; Isa 9.7; Ezek 37.25; Dan 7.14
12.36 Lk 16.8; Jn 8.59
12.38 Isa 53.1; Rom 10.16
12.40 Isa 6.9,10; Mt 13.14
12.41 Isa 6.1
12.42 Jn 7.13,48; 9.22
12.44 Mt 10.40; Jn 5.24
12.45 Jn 14.9
12.46 Jn 1.4; 3.19; 8.12; 9.5

believes in me should not remain in the darkness. 47 I do not judge anyone who hears my words and does not keep them, for I came not to judge the world, but to save the world. 48 The one who rejects me and does not receive my word has a judge; on the last day the word that I have spoken will serve as judge, 49 for I have not spoken on my own, but the Father who sent me has himself given me a commandment about what to say and what to speak. 50 And I know that his commandment is eternal life. What I speak, therefore, I speak just as the Father has told me."

Jesus Washes the Disciples' Feet

13 Now before the festival of the Passover, Jesus knew that his hour had come to depart from this world and go to the Father. Having loved his own who were in the world, he loved them to the end. 2 The devil had already put it into the heart of Judas son of Simon Iscariot to betray him. And during supper 3 Jesus, knowing that the Father had given all things into his hands, and that he had come from God and was going to God, 4 got up from the table,[r] took off his outer robe, and tied a towel around himself. 5 Then he poured water into a basin and began to wash the disciples' feet and to wipe them with the towel that was tied around him. 6 He came to Simon Peter, who said to him, "Lord, are you going to wash my feet?" 7 Jesus answered, "You do not know now what I am doing, but later you will understand." 8 Peter said to him, "You will never wash my feet." Jesus answered, "Unless I wash you, you have no share with me." 9 Simon Peter said to him, "Lord, not my feet only but also my hands and my head!" 10 Jesus said to him, "One who has bathed does not need to wash, except for the feet,[s] but is entirely clean. And you[t] are clean, though not all of you." 11 For he knew who was to betray him; for this reason he said, "Not all of you are clean."

12 After he had washed their feet, had put on his robe, and had returned to the table, he said to them, "Do you know what I have done to you? 13 You call me Teacher and Lord—and you are right, for that is what I am. 14 So if I, your Lord and Teacher, have washed your feet, you also ought to wash one another's feet. 15 For I have set you an example, that you also should do as I have done to you. 16 Very truly, I tell you, servants[u] are not greater than their master, nor are messengers greater than the one who sent them. 17 If you know these things, you are blessed if you do them. 18 I am not speaking of all of you; I know whom I have chosen. But it is to fulfill the scripture, 'The one who ate my bread[v] has lifted his heel against me.' 19 I tell you this now, before it occurs, so that when it does occur, you may believe that I am he.[w] 20 Very truly, I tell you, whoever receives one whom I send receives me; and whoever receives me receives him who sent me."

Jesus Foretells His Betrayal

21 After saying this Jesus was troubled in spirit, and declared, "Very truly, I tell you, one of you will betray me." 22 The disciples looked at one another, uncertain of whom he was speaking. 23 One of his disciples—the one whom Jesus loved—was reclining next to him; 24 Simon Peter therefore motioned to him to ask Jesus of whom he was speaking. 25 So while reclining next to Jesus, he asked him, "Lord, who is it?" 26 Jesus answered, "It is the one to whom I give this piece of bread when I have dipped it in the dish."[x] So when he had dipped the piece of bread, he gave it to Judas son of Simon Iscariot.[y] 27 After he received the piece of bread,[z] Satan entered into him. Jesus said to him, "Do quickly what you are going to do." 28 Now no one at the table knew why he said this to him. 29 Some thought that, because Judas had the common purse, Jesus was telling him, "Buy what we need for the festival"; or, that he should give something to the poor. 30 So, after receiving the piece of bread, he immediately went out. And it was night.

The New Commandment

31 When he had gone out, Jesus said, "Now the Son of Man has been glorified, and God has been glorified in him. 32 If God has been glorified in him,[a] God will also

[r] Gk *from supper* [s] Other ancient authorities lack *except for the feet* [t] The Greek word for *you* here is plural [u] Gk *slaves* [v] Other ancient authorities read *ate bread with me* [w] Gk *I am* [x] Gk *dipped it* [y] Other ancient authorities read *Judas Iscariot son of Simon*; others, *Judas son of Simon from Karyot* (Kerioth) [z] Gk *After the piece of bread* [a] Other ancient authorities lack *If God has been glorified in him*

12.47 Jn 3.17
12.48 Lk 10.16; Mt 10.15
13.1 Jn 11.55; 12.23; 16.28
13.2 Jn 6.70,71; Mk 14.10
13.3 Mt 28.18; Heb 2.8; Jn 8.42; 16.28
13.4 Lk 22.27
13.8 Jn 3.5; 9.7
13.11 Jn 6.64
13.13 Lk 6.46; Phil 2.11
13.14 1 Pet 5.5
13.15 1 Pet 2.21
13.16 Mt 10.24; Lk 6.40; Jn 15.20
13.18 Ps 41.9; Mt 26.23
13.19 Jn 14.29; 16.4; 8.24
13.20 Mt 10.40; Lk 10.16
13.21 Jn 12.27
13.23 Jn 19.26; 20.2; 21.7.20
13.25 Jn 21.20
13.26 Jn 6.71
13.27 Lk 22.3
13.31 Jn 7.39; 14.13; 1 Pet 4.11

13.1-17.26 Jesus Prepares his Followers for his Departure.
13.1-20 Jesus' washing the feet of his followers is a sign of his humility and his love for them, but is also a symbol of his cleansing them. Peter's objections show that he does not yet understand this, as does his request to be *bathed*, since Jesus' sacrifice will have cleansed him. They are to imitate him through mutual cleansing within the community. Jesus' quote from Ps 41.9 shows that even Judas' betrayal of him and his coming death are within the purpose of God.
13.21-30 The identity of his betrayer is disclosed to Peter. Ironically, Judas' accepting the *bread* from Jesus is not a form of communion but the occasion for *Satan* to enter this unworthy and unfaithful follower. Jesus urges him to fulfill his wicked task *quickly*, and he leaves symbolically into the *night*.
13.31-35 With certainty that beyond his impending suffering and death he will be *glorified*, Jesus tells his disciples of his departure and commands them to *love one another*. This advice for those within the group contrasts with his instruction in Mt 5.43-46 to *love your enemies*.

13.36-38 In spite of Peter's declared intention to *follow* Jesus, even though he does not know where he is going, Jesus predicts that Peter will deny him three times before morning, when *the cock crows*.
14.1-14 The purpose for Jesus' going to be with the *Father* is to *prepare a place* for his followers, and he promises to return and take them there. Yet in seeing him, they have already *seen the Father*, since God is at work through him, just as he will be at work through those who follow Jesus. In his absence they will do even *greater works* than his, and this will bring glory to God through him.
14.15-31 Although he will be gone from them in ordinary human terms, his and God's continuing presence will be with them through the *Spirit of truth* (the *Advocate*, or one who comes alongside to help and counsel) and through his disclosure of himself to the community, where he and God will *make our home*. In spite of the conflict that is about to take place, they will have *peace*. But now the power of evil (*ruler of this world*) is about to carry out his plan to destroy Jesus. But God's *power* will triumph and his love will be manifest to *the world*.

glorify him in himself and will glorify him at once. 33Little children, I am with you only a little longer. You will look for me; and as I said to the Jews so now I say to you, 'Where I am going, you cannot come.' 34I give you a new commandment, that you love one another. Just as I have loved you, you also should love one another. 35By this everyone will know that you are my disciples, if you have love for one another."

Jesus Foretells Peter's Denial

36 Simon Peter said to him, "Lord, where are you going?" Jesus answered, "Where I am going, you cannot follow me now; but you will follow afterward." 37Peter said to him, "Lord, why can I not follow you now? I will lay down my life for you." 38Jesus answered, "Will you lay down your life for me? Very truly, I tell you, before the cock crows, you will have denied me three times.

Jesus the Way to the Father

14 "Do not let your hearts be troubled. Believe[b] in God, believe also in me. 2In my Father's house there are many dwelling places. If it were not so, would I have told you that I go to prepare a place for you?[c] 3And if I go and prepare a place for you, I will come again and will take you to myself, so that where I am, there you may be also. 4And you know the way to the place where I am going."[d] 5Thomas said to him, "Lord, we do not know where you are going. How can we know the way?" 6Jesus said to him, "I am the way, and the truth, and the life. No one comes to the Father except through me. 7If you know me, you will know[e] my Father also. From now on you do know him and have seen him."

8 Philip said to him, "Lord, show us the Father, and we will be satisfied." 9Jesus said to him, "Have I been with you all this time, Philip, and you still do not know me? Whoever has seen me has seen the Father. How can you say, 'Show us the Father'? 10Do you not believe that I am in the Father and the Father is in me? The words that I say to you I do not speak on my own; but the Father who dwells in me does his works. 11Believe me that I am in the Father and the Father is in me; but if you do not, then believe me because of the works themselves. 12Very truly, I tell you, the one who believes in me will also do the works that I do and, in fact, will do greater works than these, because I am going to the Father. 13I will do whatever you ask in my name, so that the Father may be glorified in the Son. 14If in my name you ask me[f] for anything, I will do it.

The Promise of the Holy Spirit

15 "If you love me, you will keep[g] my commandments. 16And I will ask the Father, and he will give you another Advocate,[h] to be with you forever. 17This is the Spirit of truth, whom the world cannot receive, because it neither sees him nor knows him. You know him, because he abides with you, and he will be in[i] you.

18 "I will not leave you orphaned; I am coming to you. 19In a little while the world will no longer see me, but you will see me; because I live, you also will live. 20On that day you will know that I am in my Father, and you in me, and I in you. 21They who have my commandments and keep them are those who love me; and those who love me will be loved by my Father, and I will love them and reveal myself to them." 22Judas (not Iscariot) said to him, "Lord, how is it that you will reveal yourself to us, and not to the world?" 23Jesus answered him, "Those who love me will keep my word, and my Father will love them, and we will come to them and make our home with them. 24Whoever does not love me does not keep my words; and the word that you hear is not mine, but is from the Father who sent me.

25 "I have said these things to you while I am still with you. 26But the Advocate,[h] the Holy Spirit, whom the Father will send in my name, will teach you everything, and remind you of all that I have said to you. 27Peace I leave with you; my peace I give to you. I do not give to you as the world gives. Do not let your hearts be troubled, and do not let them be afraid. 28You heard me say to you, 'I am going away, and I am coming to you.' If you loved me, you would

[b] Or *You believe* [c] Or *If it were not so, I would have told you; for I go to prepare a place for you* [d] Other ancient authorities read *Where I am going you know, and the way you know* [e] Other ancient authorities read *If you had known me, you would have known* [f] Other ancient authorities lack *me* [g] Other ancient authorities read *me, keep* [h] Or *Helper* [i] Or *among*

13.33 Jn 7.33,34
13.34 Lev 19.18; Jn 15.12; 1 Pet 1.22; 1 Jn 2.7; 3.11; 4.10
13.35 1 Jn 3.14; 4.20
13.36 Jn 21.18; 2 Pet 1.14
13.37 Mt 26.33-35; Mk 14.29-31; Lk 22.33,34
14.1 Jn 16.23,24
14.3 Jn 12.26
14.6 Jn 10.9; 8.32; 1.4; 11.25
14.9 Jn 12.45
14.10 Jn 10.38; 5.19; 12.49
14.11 Jn 5.36; 10.38
14.15 Jn 15.10; 1 Jn 5.3
14.16 Jn 15.26; 16.7; 1 Jn 2.1
14.17 Jn 16.13; 1 Jn 4.6; 1 Cor 2.14
14.20 Jn 10.38
14.21 1 Jn 2.5; 5.3
14.23 1 Jn 2.24; Rev 3.20
14.24 Jn 7.16; 8.28; 12.49
14.26 Jn 15.26; 16.7,13; 1 Jn 2.20,27
14.27 Jn 16.33; Phil 4.7; Col 3.15
14.28 ver 3.18; Jn 5.18; 10.29,30; Phil 2.6

rejoice that I am going to the Father, because the Father is greater than I. [29]And now I have told you this before it occurs, so that when it does occur, you may believe. [30]I will no longer talk much with you, for the ruler of this world is coming. He has no power over me; [31]but I do as the Father has commanded me, so that the world may know that I love the Father. Rise, let us be on our way.

Jesus the True Vine

15 "I am the true vine, and my Father is the vinegrower. [2]He removes every branch in me that bears no fruit. Every branch that bears fruit he prunes[j] to make it bear more fruit. [3]You have already been cleansed[j] by the word that I have spoken to you. [4]Abide in me as I abide in you. Just as the branch cannot bear fruit by itself unless it abides in the vine, neither can you unless you abide in me. [5]I am the vine, you are the branches. Those who abide in me and I in them bear much fruit, because apart from me you can do nothing. [6]Whoever does not abide in me is thrown away like a branch and withers; such branches are gathered, thrown into the fire, and burned. [7]If you abide in me, and my words abide in you, ask for whatever you wish, and it will be done for you. [8]My Father is glorified by this, that you bear much fruit and become[k] my disciples. [9]As the Father has loved me, so I have loved you; abide in my love. [10]If you keep my commandments, you will abide in my love, just as I have kept my Father's commandments and abide in his love. [11]I have said these things to you so that my joy may be in you, and that your joy may be complete.

12 "This is my commandment, that you love one another as I have loved you. [13]No one has greater love than this, to lay down one's life for one's friends. [14]You are my friends if you do what I command you. [15]I do not call you servants[l] any longer, because the servant[m] does not know what the master is doing; but I have called you friends, because I have made known to you everything that I have heard from my Father. [16]You did not choose me but I chose you. And I appointed you to go and bear fruit, fruit that will last, so that the Father will give you whatever you ask him in my name. [17]I am giving you these commands so that you may love one another.

The World's Hatred

18 "If the world hates you, be aware that it hated me before it hated you. [19]If you belonged to the world,[n] the world would love you as its own. Because you do not belong to the world, but I have chosen you out of the world—therefore the world hates you. [20]Remember the word that I said to you, 'Servants[o] are not greater than their master.' If they persecuted me, they will persecute you; if they kept my word, they will keep yours also. [21]But they will do all these things to you on account of my name, because they do not know him who sent me. [22]If I had not come and spoken to them, they would not have sin; but now they have no excuse for their sin. [23]Whoever hates me hates my Father also. [24]If I had not done among them the works that no one else did, they would not have sin. But now they have seen and hated both me and my Father. [25]It was to fulfill the word that is written in their law, 'They hated me without a cause.'

26 "When the Advocate[p] comes, whom I will send to you from the Father, the Spirit of truth who comes from the Father, he will testify on my behalf. [27]You also are to testify because you have been with me from the beginning.

16 "I have said these things to you to keep you from stumbling. [2]They will put you out of the synagogues. Indeed, an hour is coming when those who kill you will think that by doing so they are offering worship to God. [3]And they will do this because they have not known the Father or me. [4]But I have said these things to you so that when their hour comes you may remember that I told you about them.

The Work of the Spirit

"I did not say these things to you from the beginning, because I was with you. [5]But now I am going to him who sent me; yet none of you asks me, 'Where are you going?' [6]But because I have said these things to you, sorrow has filled your hearts. [7]Nevertheless I tell you the truth: it is to your advantage that I go away, for if I do not go

[j] The same Greek root refers to pruning and cleansing [k] Or *be* [l] Gk *slaves* [m] Gk *slave* [n] Gk *were of the world* [o] Gk *Slaves* [p] Or *Helper*

14.30 Jn 12.31
14.31 Jn 10.18; 12.49; 18.1
15.3 Jn 13.10; 17.17; Eph 5.26
15.4 1 Jn 2.6
15.7 Jn 14.13; 16.23
15.8 Mt 5.16; Jn 8.31
15.10 Jn 14.15-23
15.11 Jn 17.13
15.12 Jn 13.34
15.13 Rom 5.7,8; Jn 10.11
15.14 Mt 12.50
15.16 Jn 6.70; 14.13
15.18 1 Jn 3.13
15.20 Mt 10.24; Lk 6.40; Jn 13.16
15.21 Mt 12.24; Lk 6.40; Jn 13.16
15.22 Jn 9.41; Rom 1.20
15.23 1 Jn 2.23
15.24 Jn 5.36
15.25 Ps 35.19; 69.4
15.26 Jn 14.16,17,26; 1 Jn 2.1; 5.7
15.27 Lk 24.48; Acts 2.32; 3.15; 5.32; 10.39; 13.31; 1 Jn 4.14
16.1 Jn 15.18-27; Mt 11.6
16.2 Jn 9.22; Acts 26.9,10; Isa 66.5; Rev 6.9
16.3 Jn 15.21; 17.25; 1 Jn 3.1
16.5 Jn 7.33

15.1-17 Jesus is the Vine: his people are the branches. Developing the image of Israel as the unproductive vineyard of God in Isa 5, Jesus pictures God as the owner, himself as the vine, from which life and productivity will now flow out to the *branches*, who are the members of the new community. God is glorified when they obey the commandment of love and live fruitful lives as his people.
15.18-16.4 Just as Jesus met fierce opposition, so they must expect hatred. His works and his words of rebuke have aroused this hatred, even though it is ultimately *without a cause* (Ps 35.19). They will have the support of the Spirit (*Advocate*) who will confirm Jesus' testimony and theirs in his behalf. The opposition will take the form of expulsion from *the synagogues* and even martyrdom, as he warns them.
16.5-15 Returning to the theme of the presence and support of the Spirit during his absence, Jesus declares that the role of the *Advocate* (Spirit) in his absence will be to set the world straight about *sin* (their denial of who he is), about the *righteousness* of his death (because he has been taken to be with the Father), and about *judgment*, since the power of evil in this world has already been *condemned*. Other instruction of God's people will be provided through the *Spirit of truth*.

16.16-33 While he is gone, their present sorrow at his death will be turned into joy, their prayers will be heard, and even in the midst of their being *scattered* and persecuted, God will give them peace.
17.1-25 Jesus' prayer is that God will glorify him for the *work* he has completed on earth, that his people will understand everything that he has given to them, and that he will protect them during the time of difficulty that they are to undergo, except for the traitor, Judas, who deserves to be lost, in accord with the scripture cited in 13.18 (Ps 41.9). Both those who are now his followers and those who will believe through their witness are to be *protected*, made holy (*sanctified*), unified (*all may be one*), and will see him in his *glory*.

away, the Advocate[q] will not come to you;
but if I go, I will send him to you. [8]And
when he comes, he will prove the world
wrong about[r] sin and righteousness and
judgment: [9]about sin, because they do not
believe in me; [10]about righteousness, because I am going to the Father and you will
see me no longer; [11]about judgment, because the ruler of this world has been condemned.
12 "I still have many things to say to
you, but you cannot bear them now. [13]When
the Spirit of truth comes, he will guide you
into all the truth; for he will not speak on
his own, but will speak whatever he hears,
and he will declare to you the things that
are to come. [14]He will glorify me, because
he will take what is mine and declare it to
you. [15]All that the Father has is mine. For
this reason I said that he will take what is
mine and declare it to you.

Sorrow Will Turn into Joy

16 "A little while, and you will no longer
see me, and again a little while, and you
will see me." [17]Then some of his disciples
said to one another, "What does he mean
by saying to us, 'A little while, and you will
no longer see me, and again a little while,
and you will see me'; and 'Because I am
going to the Father'?" [18]They said, "What
does he mean by this 'a little while'? We do
not know what he is talking about." [19]Jesus
knew that they wanted to ask him, so he
said to them, "Are you discussing among
yourselves what I meant when I said, 'A
little while, and you will no longer see me,
and again a little while, and you will see
me'? [20]Very truly, I tell you, you will weep
and mourn, but the world will rejoice; you
will have pain, but your pain will turn into
joy. [21]When a woman is in labor, she has
pain, because her hour has come. But when
her child is born, she no longer remembers
the anguish because of the joy of having
brought a human being into the world. [22]So
you have pain now; but I will see you
again, and your hearts will rejoice, and no
one will take your joy from you. [23]On that
day you will ask nothing of me.[s] Very truly,
I tell you, if you ask anything of the Father
in my name, he will give it to you.[t] [24]Until
now you have not asked for anything in my
name. Ask and you will receive, so that
your joy may be complete.

Peace for the Disciples

25 "I have said these things to you in
figures of speech. The hour is coming when
I will no longer speak to you in figures, but
will tell you plainly of the Father. [26]On that
day you will ask in my name. I do not say
to you that I will ask the Father on your
behalf; [27]for the Father himself loves you,
because you have loved me and have believed that I came from God.[u] [28]I came from
the Father and have come into the world;
again, I am leaving the world and am going
to the Father."
29 His disciples said, "Yes, now you are
speaking plainly, not in any figure of speech!
[30]Now we know that you know all things,
and do not need to have anyone question
you; by this we believe that you came from
God." [31]Jesus answered them, "Do you now
believe? [32]The hour is coming, indeed it has
come, when you will be scattered, each one
to his home, and you will leave me alone.
Yet I am not alone because the Father is
with me. [33]I have said this to you, so that
in me you may have peace. In the world
you face persecution. But take courage; I
have conquered the world!"

Jesus Prays for His Disciples

17 After Jesus had spoken these words,
he looked up to heaven and said,
"Father, the hour has come; glorify your
Son so that the Son may glorify you, [2]since
you have given him authority over all
people,[v] to give eternal life to all whom you
have given him. [3]And this is eternal life,
that they may know you, the only true God,
and Jesus Christ whom you have sent. [4]I
glorified you on earth by finishing the work
that you gave me to do. [5]So now, Father,
glorify me in your own presence with the
glory that I had in your presence before the
world existed.
6 "I have made your name known to
those whom you gave me from the world.
They were yours, and you gave them to me,
and they have kept your word. [7]Now they
know that everything you have given me
is from you; [8]for the words that you gave
to me I have given to them, and they have
received them and know in truth that I
came from you; and they have believed that
you sent me. [9]I am asking on their behalf;
I am not asking on behalf of the world, but

[q] Or *Helper* [r] Or *convict the world of* [s] Or *will ask me no question* [t] Other ancient authorities read *Father, he will give it to you in my name* [u] Other ancient authorities read *the Father* [v] Gk *flesh*

16.11 Jn 12.31
16.12 Mk 4.33
16.13 Jn 14.17,26
16.15 Jn 17.10
16.16 Jn 7.33; 14.18-24; 13.3
16.21 1 Thess 5.3
16.22 ver 6,16
16.24 Jn 15.11
16.27 Jn 14.21,23
16.28 Jn 13.3
16.30 Jn 8.42
16.32 Mt 26.31; Mk 14.27
16.33 Jn 14.27; Col 1.20; Rom 8.37; Rev 3.21
17.1 Jn 12.23; 13.32
17.2 Dan 7.14; Heb 2.8; Jn 6.37
17.3 Jn 5.44; 3.34; 6.29,57
17.4 Jn 13.31; 4.34; 14.31
17.5 Jn 1.1; Phil 2.6
17.6 Jn 6.37,39
17.8 Jn 8.28; 16.27
17.9 Lk 22.32; Jn 14.16

on behalf of those whom you gave me, because they are yours. 10 All mine are yours, and yours are mine; and I have been glorified in them. 11 And now I am no longer in the world, but they are in the world, and I am coming to you. Holy Father, protect them in your name that you have given me, so that they may be one, as we are one. 12 While I was with them, I protected them in your name that[w] you have given me. I guarded them, and not one of them was lost except the one destined to be lost,[x] so that the scripture might be fulfilled. 13 But now I am coming to you, and I speak these things in the world so that they may have my joy made complete in themselves.[y] 14 I have given them your word, and the world has hated them because they do not belong to the world, just as I do not belong to the world. 15 I am not asking you to take them out of the world, but I ask you to protect them from the evil one.[z] 16 They do not belong to the world, just as I do not belong to the world. 17 Sanctify them in the truth; your word is truth. 18 As you have sent me into the world, so I have sent them into the world. 19 And for their sakes I sanctify myself, so that they also may be sanctified in truth.

20 "I ask not only on behalf of these, but also on behalf of those who will believe in me through their word, 21 that they may all be one. As you, Father, are in me and I am in you, may they also be in us,[a] so that the world may believe that you have sent me. 22 The glory that you have given me I have given them, so that they may be one, as we are one, 23 I in them and you in me, that they may become completely one, so that the world may know that you have sent me and have loved them even as you have loved me. 24 Father, I desire that those also, whom you have given me, may be with me where I am, to see my glory, which you have given me because you loved me before the foundation of the world.

25 "Righteous Father, the world does not know you, but I know you; and these know that you have sent me. 26 I made your name known to them, and I will make it known, so that the love with which you have loved me may be in them, and I in them."

The Betrayal and Arrest of Jesus

18 After Jesus had spoken these words, he went out with his disciples across the Kidron valley to a place where there was a garden, which he and his disciples entered. 2 Now Judas, who betrayed him, also knew the place, because Jesus often met there with his disciples. 3 So Judas brought a detachment of soldiers together with police from the chief priests and the Pharisees, and they came there with lanterns and torches and weapons. 4 Then Jesus, knowing all that was to happen to him, came forward and asked them, "Whom are you looking for?" 5 They answered, "Jesus of Nazareth."[b] Jesus replied, "I am he."[c] Judas, who betrayed him, was standing with them. 6 When Jesus[d] said to them, "I am he,"[c] they stepped back and fell to the ground. 7 Again he asked them, "Whom are you looking for?" And they said, "Jesus of Nazareth."[b] 8 Jesus answered, "I told you that I am he.[c] So if you are looking for me, let these men go." 9 This was to fulfill the word that he had spoken, "I did not lose a single one of those whom you gave me." 10 Then Simon Peter, who had a sword, drew it, struck the high priest's slave, and cut off his right ear. The slave's name was Malchus. 11 Jesus said to Peter, "Put your sword back into its sheath. Am I not to drink the cup that the Father has given me?"

Jesus before the High Priest

12 So the soldiers, their officer, and the Jewish police arrested Jesus and bound him. 13 First they took him to Annas, who was the father-in-law of Caiaphas, the high priest that year. 14 Caiaphas was the one who had advised the Jews that it was better to have one person die for the people.

Peter Denies Jesus

15 Simon Peter and another disciple followed Jesus. Since that disciple was known to the high priest, he went with Jesus into the courtyard of the high priest, 16 but Peter was standing outside at the gate. So the other disciple, who was known to the high priest, went out, spoke to the woman who

17.10 Jn 16.15
17.11 Jn 13.1; 7.33; Rev 19.12; Jn 10.30
17.12 Heb 2.13; Jn 6.39; 18.9; 6.70
17.14 Jn 15.19; 8.23
17.15 Mt 6.13
17.18 Jn 20.21
17.21 Jn 10.38
17.22 Jn 14.20
17.24 Jn 12.26; Mt 25.34; ver 5
17.25 Jn 15.21; 16.3; 7.29; Jn 16.27
17.26 ver 6; Jn 15.9
18.2 Lk 21.37; 22.39
18.3 Acts 1.16
18.4 Jn 6.64; 13.1,11; ver 7
18.7 ver 4
18.9 Jn 17.12
18.11 Mt 20.22
18.13 Mt 26.57; Mk 14.53; Lk 22.54
18.14 Jn 11.49-51
18.15 Mt 26.58; Mk 14.54; Lk 22.54

18.1-19.42 The Arrest, Crucifixion and Burial of Jesus.
18.1-18 Although the story as a whole matches the one found in Matthew 26, there are several distinctive features: Jesus' declaration of himself as *I am* and the resultant falling to the ground of those who came to seize him; the cutting off and restoration of the ear of the high priest's slave; the detail of Peter's warming his hands at the fire of the *slaves and the police*.

[w] Other ancient authorities read *protected in your name those whom* [x] Gk *except the son of destruction* [y] Or *among themselves* [z] Or *from evil* [a] Other ancient authorities read *be one in us* [b] Gk *the Nazorean* [c] Gk *I am* [d] Gk *he*

18.19-27 Jesus asks why the authorities have arrested him now, when he has proclaimed his message in *synagogues and the temple* without being seized. Peter's second and third denials of Jesus are told as in the other gospels (Mk 14.69-72).
18.28-19.16 In his description of the hearing before Pilate, unique among the gospel accounts are (1) mention of the Jewish leaders' avoiding ritual pollution by not entering the official seat of Roman power, the praetorium (*headquarters*); (2) their denial that they had the right to execute him, which resulted in his dying by a Roman mode (crucifixion) rather than the Jewish form of execution (stoning), which would have crushed his bones (perhaps a reference to Ps 34.20, *not one of his bones is broken*, as in Jn 19.36). Jesus defines his *kingdom* as not of this world and declares that he came into the world to *testify to the truth*. Pilate says he finds *no case against* Jesus, and this is repeated when he has been *flogged* and brought out to be crucified. The Jews invoke a law which specifies death for any who call themselves *Son of God*, which intimidates Pilate and leads him to propose once more the *release* of Jesus. When the issue of Jesus as a political insurrectionist (*claiming to be king*) is raised by the Jewish leaders, Pilate orders his crucifixion.

guarded the gate, and brought Peter in. 17 The woman said to Peter, "You are not also one of this man's disciples, are you?" He said, "I am not." 18 Now the slaves and the police had made a charcoal fire because it was cold, and they were standing around it and warming themselves. Peter also was standing with them and warming himself.

The High Priest Questions Jesus

19 Then the high priest questioned Jesus about his disciples and about his teaching. 20 Jesus answered, "I have spoken openly to the world; I have always taught in synagogues and in the temple, where all the Jews come together. I have said nothing in secret. 21 Why do you ask me? Ask those who heard what I said to them; they know what I said." 22 When he had said this, one of the police standing nearby struck Jesus on the face, saying, "Is that how you answer the high priest?" 23 Jesus answered, "If I have spoken wrongly, testify to the wrong. But if I have spoken rightly, why do you strike me?" 24 Then Annas sent him bound to Caiaphas the high priest.

Peter Denies Jesus Again

25 Now Simon Peter was standing and warming himself. They asked him, "You are not also one of his disciples, are you?" He denied it and said, "I am not." 26 One of the slaves of the high priest, a relative of the man whose ear Peter had cut off, asked, "Did I not see you in the garden with him?" 27 Again Peter denied it, and at that moment the cock crowed.

Jesus before Pilate

28 Then they took Jesus from Caiaphas to Pilate's headquarters.[e] It was early in the morning. They themselves did not enter the headquarters,[e] so as to avoid ritual defilement and to be able to eat the Passover. 29 So Pilate went out to them and said, "What accusation do you bring against this man?" 30 They answered, "If this man were not a criminal, we would not have handed him over to you." 31 Pilate said to them, "Take him yourselves and judge him according to your law." The Jews replied, "We are not permitted to put anyone to death." 32 (This was to fulfill what Jesus had said when he indicated the kind of death he was to die.)

33 Then Pilate entered the headquarters[e] again, summoned Jesus, and asked him, "Are you the King of the Jews?" 34 Jesus answered, "Do you ask this on your own, or did others tell you about me?" 35 Pilate replied, "I am not a Jew, am I? Your own nation and the chief priests have handed you over to me. What have you done?" 36 Jesus answered, "My kingdom is not from this world. If my kingdom were from this world, my followers would be fighting to keep me from being handed over to the Jews. But as it is, my kingdom is not from here." 37 Pilate asked him, "So you are a king?" Jesus answered, "You say that I am a king. For this I was born, and for this I came into the world, to testify to the truth. Everyone who belongs to the truth listens to my voice." 38 Pilate asked him, "What is truth?"

Jesus Sentenced to Death

After he had said this, he went out to the Jews again and told them, "I find no case against him. 39 But you have a custom that I release someone for you at the Passover. Do you want me to release for you the King of the Jews?" 40 They shouted in reply, "Not this man, but Barabbas!" Now Barabbas was a bandit.

19 Then Pilate took Jesus and had him flogged. 2 And the soldiers wove a crown of thorns and put it on his head, and they dressed him in a purple robe. 3 They kept coming up to him, saying, "Hail, King of the Jews!" and striking him on the face. 4 Pilate went out again and said to them, "Look, I am bringing him out to you to let you know that I find no case against him." 5 So Jesus came out, wearing the crown of thorns and the purple robe. Pilate said to them, "Here is the man!" 6 When the chief priests and the police saw him, they shouted, "Crucify him! Crucify him!" Pilate said to them, "Take him yourselves and crucify him; I find no case against him." 7 The Jews answered him, "We have a law, and according to that law he ought to die because he has claimed to be the Son of God."

8 Now when Pilate heard this, he was more afraid than ever. 9 He entered his headquarters[e] again and asked Jesus, "Where are you from?" But Jesus gave him no

18.17 ver 25
18.18 Mk 14.54,67; Jn 21.9
18.19 Mt 26.59-68; Mk 14.55-65; Lk 22.63-71
18.22 ver 3; Jn 19.3
18.23 Mt 5.39; Acts 23.2-5
18.24 ver 13
18.25 ver 18
18.26 ver 10
18.27 Jn 13.38
18.28 Mt 27.1,2; Mk 15.1; Lk 23.1; Jn 11.55; Acts 11.3
18.32 Mt 20.19; Jn 12.32,33
18.33 ver 28.29; Jn 19.9
18.36 Mt 26.53; Lk 17.21; Jn 6.15
18.37 Jn 8.47; 1 Jn 3.19; 4.6
18.38 Jn 19.4,6
18.39 Mt 27.15-18, 20-23; Mk 15.6-15; Lk 23.18-25
18.40 Acts 3.14
19.1 Mt 27.26
19.2 Mt 27.27-30; Mk 15.16-19
19.3 Jn 18.22
19.4 ver 6; Jn 18.38
19.5 ver 2
19.6 Acts 3.13
19.7 Lev 24.16; Mt 26.63-66; Jn 5.18; 10.33
19.9 Isa 53.7; Mt 27.12,14

[e] Gk *the praetorium*

answer. 10Pilate therefore said to him, "Do you refuse to speak to me? Do you not know that I have power to release you, and power to crucify you?" 11Jesus answered him, "You would have no power over me unless it had been given you from above; therefore the one who handed me over to you is guilty of a greater sin." 12From then on Pilate tried to release him, but the Jews cried out, "If you release this man, you are no friend of the emperor. Everyone who claims to be a king sets himself against the emperor."

13 When Pilate heard these words, he brought Jesus outside and sat[f] on the judge's bench at a place called The Stone Pavement, or in Hebrew[g] Gabbatha. 14Now it was the day of Preparation for the Passover; and it was about noon. He said to the Jews, "Here is your King!" 15They cried out, "Away with him! Away with him! Crucify him!" Pilate asked them, "Shall I crucify your King?" The chief priests answered, "We have no king but the emperor." 16Then he handed him over to them to be crucified.

The Crucifixion of Jesus

So they took Jesus; 17and carrying the cross by himself, he went out to what is called The Place of the Skull, which in Hebrew[g] is called Golgotha. 18There they crucified him, and with him two others, one on either side, with Jesus between them. 19Pilate also had an inscription written and put on the cross. It read, "Jesus of Nazareth,[h] the King of the Jews." 20Many of the Jews read this inscription, because the place where Jesus was crucified was near the city; and it was written in Hebrew,[g] in Latin, and in Greek. 21Then the chief priests of the Jews said to Pilate, "Do not write, 'The King of the Jews,' but, 'This man said, I am King of the Jews.'" 22Pilate answered, "What I have written I have written." 23When the soldiers had crucified Jesus, they took his clothes and divided them into four parts, one for each soldier. They also took his tunic; now the tunic was seamless, woven in one piece from the top. 24So they said to one another, "Let us not tear it, but cast lots for it to see who will get it." This was to fulfill what the scripture says,

"They divided my clothes among themselves,
and for my clothing they cast lots."

25And that is what the soldiers did.

Meanwhile, standing near the cross of Jesus were his mother, and his mother's sister, Mary the wife of Clopas, and Mary Magdalene. 26When Jesus saw his mother and the disciple whom he loved standing beside her, he said to his mother, "Woman, here is your son." 27Then he said to the disciple, "Here is your mother." And from that hour the disciple took her into his own home.

28 After this, when Jesus knew that all was now finished, he said (in order to fulfill the scripture), "I am thirsty." 29A jar full of sour wine was standing there. So they put a sponge full of the wine on a branch of hyssop and held it to his mouth. 30When Jesus had received the wine, he said, "It is finished." Then he bowed his head and gave up his spirit.

Jesus' Side Is Pierced

31 Since it was the day of Preparation, the Jews did not want the bodies left on the cross during the sabbath, especially because that sabbath was a day of great solemnity. So they asked Pilate to have the legs of the crucified men broken and the bodies removed. 32Then the soldiers came and broke the legs of the first and of the other who had been crucified with him. 33But when they came to Jesus and saw that he was already dead, they did not break his legs. 34Instead, one of the soldiers pierced his side with a spear, and at once blood and water came out. 35(He who saw this has testified so that you also may believe. His testimony is true, and he knows[i] that he tells the truth.) 36These things occurred so that the scripture might be fulfilled, "None of his bones shall be broken." 37And again another passage of scripture says, "They will look on the one whom they have pierced."

The Burial of Jesus

38 After these things, Joseph of Arimathea, who was a disciple of Jesus, though a secret one because of his fear of the Jews, asked Pilate to let him take away the body of Jesus. Pilate gave him permission; so he came and removed his body. 39Nicodemus, who had at first come to Jesus by night, also came, bringing a mixture of myrrh and aloes, weighing about a hundred pounds.

[f] Or *seated him* [g] That is, *Aramaic* [h] Gk *the Nazorean* [i] Or *there is one who knows*

19.11 Rom 13.11; Jn 18.28ff
19.12 Lk 23.2
19.13 Mt 27.19
19.14 Mt 27.62; Mk 15.25; ver 19.21
19.16 Mt 27.26; Mk 15.15; Lk 23.25
19.17 Lk 23.26
19.21 ver 14
19.24 Ex 28.32; Ps 22.18
19.25 Mt 27.55,56; Mk 15.40,41; Lk 23.49; 24.18; Jn 20.1,18
19.26 Jn 13.23; 20.2; 21.20; 2.4
19.28 Jn 13.1; 17.4; Ps 69.21
19.30 Jn 17.4
19.31 Deut 21.23; Ex 12.16
19.32 ver 18
19.34 1 Jn 5.6,8
19.35 Jn 15.27; 21.24
19.36 Ex 12.46; Num 9.12; Ps 34.20
19.37 Zech 12.10
19.39 Jn 3.1; 7.50; 19.26; 21.7,20,24

19.17-37 Special details in this account of the crucifixion of Jesus include (1) that the *King of the Jews* inscription was written in *Hebrew, Latin and Greek* (reaching out symbolically to most of the Roman world); (2) that the dividing of Jesus' clothes and the preservation of his *seamless tunic* (perhaps a priestly garment; Ex 39.27-29) were in fulfillment of scripture (Ps 22.16-18); (3) that the beloved disciple is to care for Mary. Unique also is Jesus' cry at the moment of death, *It is finished*, rather than a note of despair, as in Mk 15.34; Mt 27.46. Following his interest in the Jewish holy days (notes on 5.1-10.21), John observes that Jesus' burial is on the *day of Preparation* for the Passover, which would have coincided with the sabbath. Giving vinegar to Jesus, as well as the decision not to break his legs and the *piercing of his side* in order to hasten his death, are all seen as fulfilling scripture (Ps 69.21; Ex 12.46; Ps 34.20; Zech 12.10). That Joseph of Arimathea is joined by Nicodemus (Jn 3) in preparing Jesus' body for burial, and the huge amount (the equivalent of seventy-five pounds) and cost of the spices for embalming are distinctive details in John's gospel.

20.1-31 Jesus' Resurrection and his Meeting with his Disciples.
20.1-18 The discovery of the empty tomb, first by Mary Magdalene and then by Peter and *the other disciple* (see 13.23-26; 19.26-27), leads to the belief that Jesus is gone, but not yet to the awareness of his resurrection in fulfillment of scripture (possibly Ps 16.9-10 or Hos 6.2). As in the later addition to Mark (16.9-11), Jesus first appears to Mary Magdalene. Jesus is yet to *ascend to the Father* and instructs her to report his resurrection to the *disciples*.
20.19-23 Jesus' first appearance to the disciples brings his bestowal of *peace* and of the *Spirit*, with assurance of his commissioning them to carry forward the work God gave to him, and the right to *forgive* or *retain* (hold them blameworthy for) the sins of members of the community.
20.24-29 Thomas, the absentee among the disciples, is first dubious about the resurrection claim, but then through a second appearance to the disciples he is shown the pierced *hands and side* of Jesus, and acclaims him as *Lord* and *God*.

[40]They took the body of Jesus and wrapped it with the spices in linen cloths, according to the burial custom of the Jews. [41]Now there was a garden in the place where he was crucified, and in the garden there was a new tomb in which no one had ever been laid. [42]And so, because it was the Jewish day of Preparation, and the tomb was nearby, they laid Jesus there.

The Resurrection of Jesus

20 Early on the first day of the week, while it was still dark, Mary Magdalene came to the tomb and saw that the stone had been removed from the tomb. [2]So she ran and went to Simon Peter and the other disciple, the one whom Jesus loved, and said to them, "They have taken the Lord out of the tomb, and we do not know where they have laid him." [3]Then Peter and the other disciple set out and went toward the tomb. [4]The two were running together, but the other disciple outran Peter and reached the tomb first. [5]He bent down to look in and saw the linen wrappings lying there, but he did not go in. [6]Then Simon Peter came, following him, and went into the tomb. He saw the linen wrappings lying there, [7]and the cloth that had been on Jesus' head, not lying with the linen wrappings but rolled up in a place by itself. [8]Then the other disciple, who reached the tomb first, also went in, and he saw and believed; [9]for as yet they did not understand the scripture, that he must rise from the dead. [10]Then the disciples returned to their homes.

Jesus Appears to Mary Magdalene

11 But Mary stood weeping outside the tomb. As she wept, she bent over to look[j] into the tomb; [12]and she saw two angels in white, sitting where the body of Jesus had been lying, one at the head and the other at the feet. [13]They said to her, "Woman, why are you weeping?" She said to them, "They have taken away my Lord, and I do not know where they have laid him." [14]When she had said this, she turned around and saw Jesus standing there, but she did not know that it was Jesus. [15]Jesus said to her, "Woman, why are you weeping? Whom are you looking for?" Supposing him to be the gardener, she said to him, "Sir, if you have carried him away, tell me where you have laid him, and I will take him away." [16]Jesus said to her, "Mary!" She turned and said to him in Hebrew,[k] "Rabbouni!" (which means Teacher). [17]Jesus said to her, "Do not hold on to me, because I have not yet ascended to the Father. But go to my brothers and say to them, 'I am ascending to my Father and your Father, to my God and your God.'" [18]Mary Magdalene went and announced to the disciples, "I have seen the Lord"; and she told them that he had said these things to her.

Jesus Appears to the Disciples

19 When it was evening on that day, the first day of the week, and the doors of the house where the disciples had met were locked for fear of the Jews, Jesus came and stood among them and said, "Peace be with you." [20]After he said this, he showed them his hands and his side. Then the disciples rejoiced when they saw the Lord. [21]Jesus said to them again, "Peace be with you. As the Father has sent me, so I send you." [22]When he had said this, he breathed on them and said to them, "Receive the Holy Spirit. [23]If you forgive the sins of any, they are forgiven them; if you retain the sins of any, they are retained."

Jesus and Thomas

24 But Thomas (who was called the Twin[l]), one of the twelve, was not with them when Jesus came. [25]So the other disciples told him, "We have seen the Lord." But he said to them, "Unless I see the mark of the nails in his hands, and put my finger in the mark of the nails and my hand in his side, I will not believe."

26 A week later his disciples were again in the house, and Thomas was with them. Although the doors were shut, Jesus came and stood among them and said, "Peace be with you." [27]Then he said to Thomas, "Put your finger here and see my hands. Reach out your hand and put it in my side. Do not doubt but believe." [28]Thomas answered him, "My Lord and my God!" [29]Jesus said to him, "Have you believed because you have seen me? Blessed are those who have not seen and yet have come to believe."

[j] Gk lacks *to look* [k] That is, *Aramaic* [l] Gk *Didymus*

19.40 Jn 11.44; Mt 26.12; Jn 20.5,7; Lk 24.12
20.1 Mt 27.60,66
20.2 Jn 13.23; 19.26; 21.7,20,24
20.3 Lk 24.12
20.5 Jn 19.40
20.8 ver 4
20.9 Mt 22.29; Lk 24.26,46
20.11 Mk 16.5; ver 5
20.12 Mt 28.2,3; Mk 16.5; Lk 24.4
20.13 ver 2
20.15 ver 13
20.17 Mt 28.10; ver 27; Jn 7.33
20.18 Lk 24.10,13
20.19 Lk 24.36-39; ver 21,26
20.20 Lk 24.39,40; Jn 16.20,22
20.21 Mt 28.19; Jn 17.18,19
20.23 Mt 16.19; 18.18
20.24 Jn 11.16
20.25 ver 20
20.26 ver 21
20.27 ver 25; Lk 24.40
20.29 1 Pet 1.8

The Purpose of This Book

30 Now Jesus did many other signs in the presence of his disciples, which are not written in this book. [31]But these are written so that you may come to believe[m] that Jesus is the Messiah,[n] the Son of God, and that through believing you may have life in his name.

Jesus Appears to Seven Disciples

21 After these things Jesus showed himself again to the disciples by the Sea of Tiberias; and he showed himself in this way. [2]Gathered there together were Simon Peter, Thomas called the Twin,[o] Nathanael of Cana in Galilee, the sons of Zebedee, and two others of his disciples. [3]Simon Peter said to them, "I am going fishing." They said to him, "We will go with you." They went out and got into the boat, but that night they caught nothing.

4 Just after daybreak, Jesus stood on the beach; but the disciples did not know that it was Jesus. [5]Jesus said to them, "Children, you have no fish, have you?" They answered him, "No." [6]He said to them, "Cast the net to the right side of the boat, and you will find some." So they cast it, and now they were not able to haul it in because there were so many fish. [7]That disciple whom Jesus loved said to Peter, "It is the Lord!" When Simon Peter heard that it was the Lord, he put on some clothes, for he was naked, and jumped into the sea. [8]But the other disciples came in the boat, dragging the net full of fish, for they were not far from the land, only about a hundred yards[p] off.

9 When they had gone ashore, they saw a charcoal fire there, with fish on it, and bread. [10]Jesus said to them, "Bring some of the fish that you have just caught." [11]So Simon Peter went aboard and hauled the net ashore, full of large fish, a hundred fifty-three of them; and though there were so many, the net was not torn. [12]Jesus said to them, "Come and have breakfast." Now none of the disciples dared to ask him, "Who are you?" because they knew it was the Lord. [13]Jesus came and took the bread and gave it to them, and did the same with the fish. [14]This was now the third time that Jesus appeared to the disciples after he was raised from the dead.

Jesus and Peter

15 When they had finished breakfast, Jesus said to Simon Peter, "Simon son of John, do you love me more than these?" He said to him, "Yes, Lord; you know that I love you." Jesus said to him, "Feed my lambs." [16]A second time he said to him, "Simon son of John, do you love me?" He said to him, "Yes, Lord; you know that I love you." Jesus said to him, "Tend my sheep." [17]He said to him the third time, "Simon son of John, do you love me?" Peter felt hurt because he said to him the third time, "Do you love me?" And he said to him, "Lord, you know everything; you know that I love you." Jesus said to him, "Feed my sheep. [18]Very truly, I tell you, when you were younger, you used to fasten your own belt and to go wherever you wished. But when you grow old, you will stretch out your hands, and someone else will fasten a belt around you and take you where you do not wish to go." [19](He said this to indicate the kind of death by which he would glorify God.) After this he said to him, "Follow me."

Jesus and the Beloved Disciple

20 Peter turned and saw the disciple whom Jesus loved following them; he was the one who had reclined next to Jesus at the supper and had said, "Lord, who is it that is going to betray you?" [21]When Peter saw him, he said to Jesus, "Lord, what about him?" [22]Jesus said to him, "If it is my will that he remain until I come, what is that to you? Follow me!" [23]So the rumor spread in the community[q] that this disciple would not die. Yet Jesus did not say to him that he would not die, but, "If it is my will that he remain until I come, what is that to you?"[r]

24 This is the disciple who is testifying to these things and has written them, and we know that his testimony is true. [25]But there are also many other things that Jesus did; if every one of them were written down, I suppose that the world itself could not contain the books that would be written.

20.31 Jn 19.35; 3.15
21.1 Jn 20.19,26; 6.1
21.2 Jn 11.16; 1.45; Mt 4.21; Mk 1.19; Lk 5.10
21.3 Lk 5.5
21.4 Jn 20.14
21.5 Lk 24.41
21.6 Lk 5.4,6,7
21.7 Jn 13.23; 20.2; ver 20
21.9 ver 10,13
21.13 ver 9
21.14 Jn 20.19,26
21.15 Jn 13.37; Mt 26.33; Mk 14.29
21.16 Mt 2.6; Acts 20.28; 1 Pet 5.2; Rev 7.17
21.17 Jn 16.30; ver 16
21.19 2 Pet 1.14
21.20 ver 7; Jn 13.25
21.22 Mt 16.27,28; 25.31; 1 Cor 4.5; 11.26; Rev 2.25; 3.11; 22.7,20
21.23 Acts 1.15
21.24 Jn 15.27; 19.35
21.25 Jn 20.30

20.30-31 The Original Conclusion of John's Gospel. The author indicates that he has chosen to report this group of Jesus' *signs* in order to persuade his readers that Jesus is the *Messiah* and to show them that through trust in him they may obtain *life* as God intended it to be.

21.1-25 Epilogue: the Final Appearances of Jesus to his Followers.

21.1-14 This account of the *third* appearance of the risen Jesus to a group of his disciples resembles Luke's version of the miraculous catch of fish (Lk 5.4-11, expanded from Mk 1.16-20; Mt 4.18-22) which like this story anticipates the mission of the disciples and implies God's blessing in the form of unexpectedly rich results. The meal (here called *breakfast*) is described in language which reflects the eucharistic liturgy in the church: *took the bread, gave it to them.*

21.15-19 The final conversation of Jesus with Peter indicates that his declaration of love for the *Lord* must be matched by care for the *sheep* who are the flock of God. He is warned that in his later years he will be seized by the authorities and put to death. It is with this in mind that Jesus calls him to *follow me.*

21.20-25 Peter raises the question whether the beloved disciple (still not named, but traditionally identified as John) may survive until Jesus' return, but is told that this should be no concern of his. The concluding lines identify the writer of this gospel as that disciple *whom Jesus loved.* He acknowledges that he has made a selection of the things that Jesus did, since a complete record would fill the world.

[m] Other ancient authorities read *may continue to believe* [n] Or *the Christ* [o] Gk *Didymus* [p] Gk *two hundred cubits* [q] Gk *among the brothers* [r] Other ancient authorities lack *what is that to you*

THE ACTS OF THE APOSTLES

See the Introductions, pp. 14–15 and 81–82 above.

1.1-2 The brief introduction echoes the opening of the first volume (Lk 1.1-4) and ties the narrative to the conclusion of the gospel by referring to Jesus' ascension (Lk 24.50-53), here described in greater detail.
1.3-5.42 Preparation in Jerusalem for the Apostles' Mission.
1.3-11 Jesus' appearances to the *apostles* serve as *proofs* that he has been raised from the dead. They are to remain in Jerusalem until they are *baptized with the Holy Spirit*, as both John the Baptist (Lk 3.16) and Jesus (Lk 24.48-49) have promised earlier. His followers are still expecting a renewal of ethnic Israel as God's *kingdom*, and want him to set a date for it. He refuses and tells them that with the *power* of the Spirit they are to bear witness to Jesus from Jerusalem *to the ends of the earth*. The *two men in white* who appear at his ascension promise that he will return *in the same way*.
1.12-25 To complete the sacred number, twelve, for the circle of leaders of the new community (on the model of the twelve tribes of Israel), a replacement must be chosen for *Judas*, the traitor. Membership in the new people of God includes the eleven apostles, *certain women*, the mother and brothers of Jesus, and a total of *about one hundred twenty*. Judas' death occurs here when his abdomen bursts in a field he has purchased with the *blood* money, rather than by hanging himself (as in Mt 27.5). The pollution of this *Field of Blood* as well as his being replaced as apostle are seen as in fulfillment of scripture (Ps 69.25; 109.8, in the Greek version). The candidates to replace him must have been *witnesses* of the entire career of Jesus; through a sacred *lot*, the choice is *Matthias*.

The Promise of the Holy Spirit

1 In the first book, Theophilus, I wrote about all that Jesus did and taught from the beginning [2]until the day when he was taken up to heaven, after giving instructions through the Holy Spirit to the apostles whom he had chosen. [3]After his suffering he presented himself alive to them by many convincing proofs, appearing to them during forty days and speaking about the kingdom of God. [4]While staying[a] with them, he ordered them not to leave Jerusalem, but to wait there for the promise of the Father. "This," he said, "is what you have heard from me; [5]for John baptized with water, but you will be baptized with[b] the Holy Spirit not many days from now."

The Ascension of Jesus

6 So when they had come together, they asked him, "Lord, is this the time when you will restore the kingdom to Israel?" [7]He replied, "It is not for you to know the times or periods that the Father has set by his own authority. [8]But you will receive power when the Holy Spirit has come upon you; and you will be my witnesses in Jerusalem, in all Judea and Samaria, and to the ends of the earth." [9]When he had said this, as they were watching, he was lifted up, and a cloud took him out of their sight. [10]While he was going and they were gazing up toward heaven, suddenly two men in white robes stood by them. [11]They said, "Men of Galilee, why do you stand looking up toward heaven? This Jesus, who has been taken up from you into heaven, will come in the same way as you saw him go into heaven."

Matthias Chosen to Replace Judas

12 Then they returned to Jerusalem from the mount called Olivet, which is near Jerusalem, a sabbath day's journey away. [13]When they had entered the city, they went to the room upstairs where they were staying, Peter, and John, and James, and Andrew, Philip and Thomas, Bartholomew and Matthew, James son of Alphaeus, and Simon the Zealot, and Judas son of[c] James. [14]All these were constantly devoting themselves to prayer, together with certain women, including Mary the mother of Jesus, as well as his brothers.

15 In those days Peter stood up among the believers[d] (together the crowd numbered about one hundred twenty persons) and said, [16]"Friends,[e] the scripture had to be fulfilled, which the Holy Spirit through David foretold concerning Judas, who became a guide for those who arrested Jesus— [17]for he was numbered among us and was allotted his share in this ministry." [18](Now this man acquired a field with the reward of his wickedness; and falling headlong,[f] he burst open in the middle and all his bowels gushed out. [19]This became known to all the residents of Jerusalem, so that the field was called in their language Hakeldama, that is, Field of Blood.) [20]"For it is written in the book of Psalms,

'Let his homestead become desolate,
and let there be no one to live in it';

and

'Let another take his position of
overseer.'

[21]So one of the men who have accompanied us during all the time that the Lord Jesus went in and out among us, [22]beginning from the baptism of John until the day when he was taken up from us—one of these must become a witness with us to his resurrection." [23]So they proposed two, Joseph called Barsabbas, who was also known as Justus, and Matthias. [24]Then they prayed and said, "Lord, you know everyone's heart. Show us which one of these two you have chosen [25]to take the place[g] in this ministry and apostleship from which Judas turned aside to go to his own place." [26]And they cast lots for them, and the lot fell on Matthias; and he was added to the eleven apostles.

[a] Or *eating* [b] Or *by* [c] Or *the brother of* [d] Gk *brothers* [e] Gk *Men, brothers* [f] Or *swelling up* [g] Other ancient authorities read *the share*

1.1 Lk 1.1-4
1.2 Mt 28.19
1.3 Mt 27.17; Lk 24.34,38; 1 Cor 15.5-7
1.4 Lk 24.49; Jn 14.16
1.5 Acts 11.16
1.6 Mt 24.3
1.7 Mt 24.36; Mk 13.32
1.8 Acts 2.1-4; Lk 24.48; Jn 15.27
1.9 Lk 24.51; ver 2
1.10 Lk 24.4; Jn 20.12
1.11 Mt 24.30; Mk 13.26; Jn 14.3
1.13 Acts 9.37,39; 20.8; Mt 10.2-4; Mk 3.16-19; Lk 6.14-16
1.14 Acts 2.1,46; Lk 23.49,55; Mt 12.46
1.16 Jn 13.18
1.17 Jn 6.70,71; ver 25; Acts 20.24; 21.19
1.18 Mt 27.3-10; 26.14,15
1.20 Ps 69.25; 109.8
1.22 Mk 1.1; ver 8; Acts 2.32
1.24 1 Sam 16.7; Jer 17.10; Acts 15.8; Rom 8.27

The Coming of the Holy Spirit

2 When the day of Pentecost had come, they were all together in one place. 2 And suddenly from heaven there came a sound like the rush of a violent wind, and it filled the entire house where they were sitting. 3 Divided tongues, as of fire, appeared among them, and a tongue rested on each of them. 4 All of them were filled with the Holy Spirit and began to speak in other languages, as the Spirit gave them ability.

5 Now there were devout Jews from every nation under heaven living in Jerusalem. 6 And at this sound the crowd gathered and was bewildered, because each one heard them speaking in the native language of each. 7 Amazed and astonished, they asked, "Are not all these who are speaking Galileans? 8 And how is it that we hear, each of us, in our own native language? 9 Parthians, Medes, Elamites, and residents of Mesopotamia, Judea and Cappadocia, Pontus and Asia, 10 Phrygia and Pamphylia, Egypt and the parts of Libya belonging to Cyrene, and visitors from Rome, both Jews and proselytes, 11 Cretans and Arabs—in our own languages we hear them speaking about God's deeds of power." 12 All were amazed and perplexed, saying to one another, "What does this mean?" 13 But others sneered and said, "They are filled with new wine."

Peter Addresses the Crowd

14 But Peter, standing with the eleven, raised his voice and addressed them, "Men of Judea and all who live in Jerusalem, let this be known to you, and listen to what I say. 15 Indeed, these are not drunk, as you suppose, for it is only nine o'clock in the morning. 16 No, this is what was spoken through the prophet Joel:

17 'In the last days it will be, God declares,
that I will pour out my Spirit upon all flesh,
and your sons and your daughters shall prophesy,
and your young men shall see visions,
and your old men shall dream dreams.
18 Even upon my slaves, both men and women,
in those days I will pour out my Spirit;
and they shall prophesy.
19 And I will show portents in the heaven above
and signs on the earth below,
blood, and fire, and smoky mist.
20 The sun shall be turned to darkness
and the moon to blood,
before the coming of the Lord's great and glorious day.
21 Then everyone who calls on the name of the Lord shall be saved.'

22 "You that are Israelites,[h] listen to what I have to say: Jesus of Nazareth,[i] a man attested to you by God with deeds of power, wonders, and signs that God did through him among you, as you yourselves know— 23 this man, handed over to you according to the definite plan and foreknowledge of God, you crucified and killed by the hands of those outside the law. 24 But God raised him up, having freed him from death,[j] because it was impossible for him to be held in its power. 25 For David says concerning him,

'I saw the Lord always before me,
for he is at my right hand so that I will not be shaken;
26 therefore my heart was glad, and my tongue rejoiced;
moreover my flesh will live in hope.
27 For you will not abandon my soul to Hades,
or let your Holy One experience corruption.
28 You have made known to me the ways of life;
you will make me full of gladness with your presence.'

29 "Fellow Israelites,[k] I may say to you confidently of our ancestor David that he both died and was buried, and his tomb is with us to this day. 30 Since he was a prophet, he knew that God had sworn with an oath to him that he would put one of his descendants on his throne. 31 Foreseeing this, David[l] spoke of the resurrection of the Messiah,[m] saying,

'He was not abandoned to Hades,
nor did his flesh experience corruption.'

32 This Jesus God raised up, and of that all of us are witnesses. 33 Being therefore exalted at[n] the right hand of God, and having received from the Father the promise of the Holy Spirit, he has poured out this that you both see and hear. 34 For David did not ascend into the heavens, but he himself says,

[h] Gk *Men, Israelites* [i] Gk *the Nazorean* [j] Gk *the pains of death* [k] Gk *Men, brothers* [l] Gk *he* [m] Or *the Christ* [n] Or *by*

2.1 Lev 23.15; Deut 16.9; Acts 1.14
2.2 Acts 4.31
2.4 Acts 4.8,31; 9.17; 13.9,52; 1 Cor 12.10,11; 14.21
2.15 1 Thess 5.7
2.17 Joel 2.28-32; Zech 12.10; Jn 7.38; Acts 10.45; 21.9
2.18 Acts 21.4,9,10
2.20 Mt 24.29; Mk 13.24; Lk 21.25
2.21 Rom 10.13
2.22 Jn 3.2; Acts 10.38; Jn 4.48
2.23 Mt 26.24; Lk 22.22; Acts 3.18; 4.28; 3.13
2.24 Acts 3.15; Rom 4.24; 2 Cor 4.14; Eph 1.20; Col 2.12; Heb 13.20; 1 Pet 1.21
2.25 Ps 16.8-11
2.27 Mt 11.23; Acts 13.35
2.29 Acts 7.8,9; 13.36; 1 Kings 2.10; Neh 3.16
2.30 2 Sam 7.12,13; Ps 132.11; Rom 1.3
2.31 Ps 16.10
2.32 ver 24; Acts 1.8
2.33 Acts 5.31; 1.4; Jn 7.39; 14.26; 15.26; Acts 10.45
2.34 Ps 110.1; Mt 22.44

2.1-13 The outpouring of the Spirit on the apostles, which takes place on *the day of Pentecost* (fifty days after Passover, when the giving of the law through Moses was commemorated), is accompanied by a *rushing wind* from heaven and *tongues of fire* on each of the twelve. The Spirit enabled them to *speak in other languages*, so that each of the pious visitors *from every nation* heard them speak in *our own native languages* concerning God's *deeds of power*.

2.14-36 Peter's address to interpret what has happened is based on Joel 2.28-32, where it is predicted that *everyone* has opportunity to *call on the name of the Lord* Jesus, whose deeds were signs of God's empowering him, and whose death and resurrection were in accord with God's plan and foreseen by the psalmist (Ps 16.8-11), as were his exaltation to *the right hand of God* (Ps 110.1). All *Israel* should know that God has made the crucified Jesus to be *Messiah and Lord*.

2.37-42 Peter tells the inquiring listeners that if they repent and are baptized, they will receive *forgiveness of sins* and *the gift of the Holy Spirit*, and that this opportunity is open to *everyone*. On accepting baptism, the three thousand begin to take part in instruction and the *fellowship* of the new community.
2.43-47 This summary view of the community in Jerusalem includes the *many wonders* performed by the apostles, the sharing of possessions and meals, their daily presence in the temple, the *goodwill* they evoked, and the growing numbers of members.
3.1-10 Peter's healing the crippled beggar by the *Beautiful Gate* of the temple (probably on the south, giving access from the older part of the city) attracted wide attention, since the lame man was a familiar figure.
3.11-26 Peter explains to the throng gathered in the great colonnade built by Herod but popularly attributed to *Solomon* that it is not the *power or piety* of the apostles that has wrought this dramatic healing, but the *name* (authority) of Jesus, whose sufferings were foretold by the prophets and whom the God of Israel has honored by raising him from the dead. This *Messiah appointed by God* is in heaven and will remain there until God's time of *universal restoration* has come. Jesus is the prophet whose coming Moses foretold (Deut 18.15-22) and through him the covenant blessing will be open to *all the families of the earth*, as promised to Abraham (Gen 22.18). But it is the people of Israel who are *first* to hear about Jesus and the call to repentance from their *wicked ways*.

'The Lord said to my Lord,
"Sit at my right hand,
35 until I make your enemies your
footstool." '
36Therefore let the entire house of Israel
know with certainty that God has made
him both Lord and Messiah,[o] this Jesus
whom you crucified."

The First Converts

37 Now when they heard this, they were
cut to the heart and said to Peter and to the
other apostles, "Brothers,[p] what should we
do?" 38Peter said to them, "Repent, and be
baptized every one of you in the name of
Jesus Christ so that your sins may be forgiven; and you will receive the gift of the
Holy Spirit. 39For the promise is for you, for
your children, and for all who are far away,
everyone whom the Lord our God calls to
him." 40And he testified with many other
arguments and exhorted them, saying, "Save
yourselves from this corrupt generation."
41So those who welcomed his message were
baptized, and that day about three thousand persons were added. 42They devoted
themselves to the apostles' teaching and
fellowship, to the breaking of bread and the
prayers.

Life among the Believers

43 Awe came upon everyone, because
many wonders and signs were being done
by the apostles. 44All who believed were
together and had all things in common;
45they would sell their possessions and goods
and distribute the proceeds[q] to all, as any
had need. 46Day by day, as they spent much
time together in the temple, they broke
bread at home[r] and ate their food with glad
and generous[s] hearts, 47praising God and
having the goodwill of all the people. And
day by day the Lord added to their number
those who were being saved.

Peter Heals a Crippled Beggar

3 One day Peter and John were going
up to the temple at the hour of prayer,
at three o'clock in the afternoon. 2And a
man lame from birth was being carried in.
People would lay him daily at the gate of
the temple called the Beautiful Gate so that
he could ask for alms from those entering
the temple. 3When he saw Peter and John
about to go into the temple, he asked them
for alms. 4Peter looked intently at him, as
did John, and said, "Look at us." 5And he
fixed his attention on them, expecting to
receive something from them. 6But Peter
said, "I have no silver or gold, but what I
have I give you; in the name of Jesus Christ
of Nazareth,[t] stand up and walk." 7And he
took him by the right hand and raised him
up; and immediately his feet and ankles
were made strong. 8Jumping up, he stood
and began to walk, and he entered the
temple with them, walking and leaping and
praising God. 9All the people saw him
walking and praising God, 10and they recognized him as the one who used to sit and
ask for alms at the Beautiful Gate of the
temple; and they were filled with wonder
and amazement at what had happened to
him.

Peter Speaks in Solomon's Portico

11 While he clung to Peter and John, all
the people ran together to them in the
portico called Solomon's Portico, utterly
astonished. 12When Peter saw it, he addressed the people, "You Israelites,[u] why do
you wonder at this, or why do you stare at
us, as though by our own power or piety
we had made him walk? 13The God of
Abraham, the God of Isaac, and the God of
Jacob, the God of our ancestors has glorified
his servant[v] Jesus, whom you handed over
and rejected in the presence of Pilate, though
he had decided to release him. 14But you
rejected the Holy and Righteous One and
asked to have a murderer given to you,
15and you killed the Author of life, whom
God raised from the dead. To this we are
witnesses. 16And by faith in his name, his
name itself has made this man strong, whom
you see and know; and the faith that is
through Jesus[w] has given him this perfect
health in the presence of all of you.
17 "And now, friends,[x] I know that you
acted in ignorance, as did also your rulers.
18In this way God fulfilled what he had
foretold through all the prophets, that his
Messiah[y] would suffer. 19Repent therefore,
and turn to God so that your sins may be
wiped out, 20so that times of refreshing may
come from the presence of the Lord, and

2.37 Lk 3.10; Acts 9.6; 16.30
2.38 Lk 24.47; Acts 3.19; 5.31; 8.12,16; 22.16
2.39 Isa 57.19; Joel 2.32; Acts 10.45; Eph 2.13
2.43 Acts 5.12
2.44 Acts 4.32,34
2.46 Acts 5.42; 20.7; 1 Cor 10.16
2.47 Acts 4.33; Rom 14.18; Acts 5.14; 11.24
3.1 Acts 2.46; Ps 55.17
3.2 Acts 14.8; Lk 16.20; ver 10
3.6 Acts 4.10
3.9 Acts 4.16,21
3.11 Lk 22.8; Jn 10.23; Acts 5.12
3.13 Isa 52.13; Acts 5.30; Mt 27.2; Acts 2.23; Lk 23.4
3.14 Mk 1.24; Acts 4.27; 7.52; Mk 15.11; Lk 23.18-25
3.15 Acts 5.31; 2.24,32
3.17 Lk 23.34; Acts 13.27
3.18 Acts 2.23; Lk 24.27; Acts 17.3; 26.23

[o] Or *Christ* [p] Gk *Men, brothers* [q] Gk *them* [r] Or *from house to house* [s] Or *sincere* [t] Gk *the Nazorean* [u] Gk *Men, Israelites* [v] Or *child* [w] Gk *him* [x] Gk *brothers* [y] Or *his Christ*

that he may send the Messiah[z] appointed for
you, that is, Jesus, 21who must remain in
heaven until the time of universal restoration that God announced long ago through
his holy prophets. 22Moses said, 'The Lord
your God will raise up for you from your
own people[a] a prophet like me. You must
listen to whatever he tells you. 23And it will
be that everyone who does not listen to that
prophet will be utterly rooted out of the
people.' 24And all the prophets, as many as
have spoken, from Samuel and those after
him, also predicted these days. 25You are
the descendants of the prophets and of the
covenant that God gave to your ancestors,
saying to Abraham, 'And in your descendants all the families of the earth shall be
blessed.' 26When God raised up his servant,[b]
he sent him first to you, to bless you by
turning each of you from your wicked ways."

Peter and John before the Council

4 While Peter and John[c] were speaking
to the people, the priests, the captain
of the temple, and the Sadducees came to
them, 2much annoyed because they were
teaching the people and proclaiming that in
Jesus there is the resurrection of the dead.
3So they arrested them and put them in
custody until the next day, for it was already evening. 4But many of those who
heard the word believed; and they numbered about five thousand.
5 The next day their rulers, elders, and
scribes assembled in Jerusalem, 6with Annas
the high priest, Caiaphas, John,[d] and Alexander, and all who were of the high-priestly
family. 7When they had made the prisoners[e]
stand in their midst, they inquired, "By
what power or by what name did you do
this?" 8Then Peter, filled with the Holy Spirit,
said to them, "Rulers of the people and
elders, 9if we are questioned today because
of a good deed done to someone who was
sick and are asked how this man has been
healed, 10let it be known to all of you, and
to all the people of Israel, that this man is
standing before you in good health by the
name of Jesus Christ of Nazareth,[f] whom
you crucified, whom God raised from the
dead. 11This Jesus[g] is
'the stone that was rejected by you,
the builders;
it has become the cornerstone.'[h]
12There is salvation in no one else, for there
is no other name under heaven given among
mortals by which we must be saved."
13 Now when they saw the boldness of
Peter and John and realized that they were
uneducated and ordinary men, they were
amazed and recognized them as companions of Jesus. 14When they saw the man
who had been cured standing beside them,
they had nothing to say in opposition. 15So
they ordered them to leave the council
while they discussed the matter with one
another. 16They said, "What will we do
with them? For it is obvious to all who live
in Jerusalem that a notable sign has been
done through them; we cannot deny it.
17But to keep it from spreading further among
the people, let us warn them to speak no
more to anyone in this name." 18So they
called them and ordered them not to speak
or teach at all in the name of Jesus. 19But
Peter and John answered them, "Whether
it is right in God's sight to listen to you
rather than to God, you must judge; 20for
we cannot keep from speaking about what
we have seen and heard." 21After threatening them again, they let them go, finding
no way to punish them because of the
people, for all of them praised God for what
had happened. 22For the man on whom this
sign of healing had been performed was
more than forty years old.

The Believers Pray for Boldness

23 After they were released, they went
to their friends[i] and reported what the chief
priests and the elders had said to them.
24When they heard it, they raised their
voices together to God and said, "Sovereign
Lord, who made the heaven and the earth,
the sea, and everything in them, 25it is you
who said by the Holy Spirit through our
ancestor David, your servant:[j]
'Why did the Gentiles rage,
and the peoples imagine vain things?
26 The kings of the earth took their stand,
and the rulers have gathered together
against the Lord and against his
Messiah.'[k]
27For in this city, in fact, both Herod and
Pontius Pilate, with the Gentiles and the
peoples of Israel, gathered together against
your holy servant[j] Jesus, whom you
anointed, 28to do whatever your hand and

[z] Or *the Christ* [a] Gk *brothers* [b] Or *child* [c] Gk *While they* [d] Other ancient authorities read *Jonathan* [e] Gk *them* [f] Gk *the Nazorean* [g] Gk *This* [h] Or *keystone* [i] Gk *their own* [j] Or *child* [k] Or *his Christ*

3.21 Acts 1.11; Mt 17.11; Lk 1.70 **3.22** Deut 18.15; Acts 7.37 **3.25** Acts 2.39; Rom 9.4,8; Gen 12.3; 28.14 **3.26** Acts 13.46; 2.24; ver 22 **4.1** Lk 22.4; Mt 3.7; Acts 6.12 **4.2** Acts 7.18; 23.8 **4.3** Acts 5.18 **4.4** Acts 2.41 **4.5** Lk 23.13 **4.6** Lk 3.2; Mt 26.3 **4.8** Acts 13.9; Lk 23.13; ver 5 **4.10** Acts 3.6; 2.24 **4.11** Ps 118.22; Isa 28.16; Mt 21.42 **4.12** Mt 1.21; Acts 10.43; 1 Tim 2.5,6 **4.13** ver 31; Mt 11.25; 1 Cor 1.27 **4.15** Mt 5.22 **4.16** Jn 11.47; Acts 3.7-10 **4.18** Acts 5.40 **4.19** Acts 5.28,29 **4.20** Acts 1.8; 2.32 **4.21** Acts 5.26; 3.7,8 **4.24** 2 Kings 19.15 **4.25** Ps 2.1; Acts 1.16 **4.26** Heb 1.9 **4.27** ver 30; Lk 4.18; Jn 10.36; Mt 14.1; Lk 23.12

4.1-22 Led by the *Sadducees* (an aristocratic, traditionalist segment of Jews allied with the priests), who did not believe in resurrection (Mk 12.18), the religious authorities seized *Peter and John*, but the number of believers increased to five thousand. At the meeting of the *council* led by the high priest and his associates, Peter repeats the claim that the Jesus whom they have rejected is God's agent (*cornerstone*) to rebuild God's people, quoting Ps 118.22. While acknowledging that *a notable sign* has taken place through these men, the council enjoins them to say nothing more in the *name* of Jesus, but can find no basis for punishing them. The apostles acknowledge that they will continue to bear witness to what they have seen and heard through Jesus.
4.23-31 The prayer of the rejoicing community following the apostles' release builds on Ps 2.1-2, which they see as fulfilled through Jesus, and asks for courage to speak and act in his name.

4.32-5.11 Following another summary description of the community's pooling resources in order to meet the needs of all members, there is a vivid contrast between *Barnabas*, a generous *Levite* (claiming descent from Levi, the son of Jacob, the Levites served as attendants in the temple) and a deceitful pair whose holding back funds from the common pool resulted in their being struck dead. A native of *Cyprus*, an island southwest of Paul's city, Tarsus, Barnabas later appears as a supporter and associate of Paul (9.27; 11.19-30).
5.12-16 This summary account of the community highlights the *signs and wonders* performed by them, the large numbers of converts, the reluctance of many to join them, and the mounting interest among those who brought the sick and the demon-possessed to the apostles for healing.
5.17-42 The attempt of the *high priest* and his Sadduceean supporters to silence the apostles by imprisoning them fails as a result of angelic intervention to set them free, and they return to preaching in the courts of the temple. A reminder of the earlier prohibition against preaching about Jesus as the crucified Messiah is followed by a threat to kill the apostles, which is countered by the warning of one of their number, *Gamaliel, a teacher of the law* (pictured in later rabbinic tradition as a liberal interpreter of it), that by so doing they might be *fighting against God*. The apostles are beaten, but do not cease to *proclaim Jesus as the Messiah* in the temple and in meetings in *homes*.

your plan had predestined to take place. [29]And now, Lord, look at their threats, and grant to your servants[l] to speak your word with all boldness, [30]while you stretch out your hand to heal, and signs and wonders are performed through the name of your holy servant[m] Jesus." [31]When they had prayed, the place in which they were gathered together was shaken; and they were all filled with the Holy Spirit and spoke the word of God with boldness.

The Believers Share Their Possessions

32 Now the whole group of those who believed were of one heart and soul, and no one claimed private ownership of any possessions, but everything they owned was held in common. [33]With great power the apostles gave their testimony to the resurrection of the Lord Jesus, and great grace was upon them all. [34]There was not a needy person among them, for as many as owned lands or houses sold them and brought the proceeds of what was sold. [35]They laid it at the apostles' feet, and it was distributed to each as any had need. [36]There was a Levite, a native of Cyprus, Joseph, to whom the apostles gave the name Barnabas (which means "son of encouragement"). [37]He sold a field that belonged to him, then brought the money, and laid it at the apostles' feet.

Ananias and Sapphira

5 But a man named Ananias, with the consent of his wife Sapphira, sold a piece of property; [2]with his wife's knowledge, he kept back some of the proceeds, and brought only a part and laid it at the apostles' feet. [3]"Ananias," Peter asked, "why has Satan filled your heart to lie to the Holy Spirit and to keep back part of the proceeds of the land? [4]While it remained unsold, did it not remain your own? And after it was sold, were not the proceeds at your disposal? How is it that you have contrived this deed in your heart? You did not lie to us[n] but to God!" [5]Now when Ananias heard these words, he fell down and died. And great fear seized all who heard of it. [6]The young men came and wrapped up his body,[o] then carried him out and buried him.

7 After an interval of about three hours his wife came in, not knowing what had happened. [8]Peter said to her, "Tell me whether you and your husband sold the land for such and such a price." And she said, "Yes, that was the price." [9]Then Peter said to her, "How is it that you have agreed together to put the Spirit of the Lord to the test? Look, the feet of those who have buried your husband are at the door, and they will carry you out." [10]Immediately she fell down at his feet and died. When the young men came in they found her dead, so they carried her out and buried her beside her husband. [11]And great fear seized the whole church and all who heard of these things.

The Apostles Heal Many

12 Now many signs and wonders were done among the people through the apostles. And they were all together in Solomon's Portico. [13]None of the rest dared to join them, but the people held them in high esteem. [14]Yet more than ever believers were added to the Lord, great numbers of both men and women, [15]so that they even carried out the sick into the streets, and laid them on cots and mats, in order that Peter's shadow might fall on some of them as he came by. [16]A great number of people would also gather from the towns around Jerusalem, bringing the sick and those tormented by unclean spirits, and they were all cured.

The Apostles Are Persecuted

17 Then the high priest took action; he and all who were with him (that is, the sect of the Sadducees), being filled with jealousy, [18]arrested the apostles and put them in the public prison. [19]But during the night an angel of the Lord opened the prison doors, brought them out, and said, [20]"Go, stand in the temple and tell the people the whole message about this life." [21]When they heard this, they entered the temple at daybreak and went on with their teaching.

When the high priest and those with him arrived, they called together the council and the whole body of the elders of Israel, and sent to the prison to have them brought. [22]But when the temple police went there, they did not find them in the prison; so they returned and reported, [23]"We found the prison securely locked and the guards standing at the doors, but when we opened them, we found no one inside." [24]Now when the captain of the temple and the chief priests

[l] Gk *slaves* [m] Or *child* [n] Gk *to men* [o] Meaning of Gk uncertain

4.29 ver 13.31; Acts 9.27; 13.46; 28.31
4.30 Acts 2.43; 5.12; 3.6,16; ver 27
4.31 Acts 2.2,4; ver 29
4.32 Acts 5.12; 2.44
4.33 Acts 1.8; 1.22
4.34 Acts 2.45
4.35 ver 37; Acts 5.2; 2.45; 6.1
4.37 ver 35; Acts 5.2
5.2 Acts 4.37
5.3 Deut 23.21; Lk 22.3; Jn 13.2,7; ver 9
5.6 Jn 19.40
5.9 ver 3
5.11 ver 5; Acts 19.17
5.12 Acts 2.43; 3.11; 4.32
5.13 Acts 2.47; 4.21
5.15 Mt 9.21; 14.36; Acts 19.12
5.18 Acts 4.3
5.19 Acts 12.7; 16.26
5.20 Jn 6.63,68
5.21 Acts 4.5,6; ver 27,34,41
5.24 Acts 4.1

heard these words, they were perplexed about them, wondering what might be going on. 25Then someone arrived and announced, "Look, the men whom you put in prison are standing in the temple and teaching the people!" 26Then the captain went with the temple police and brought them, but without violence, for they were afraid of being stoned by the people.

27 When they had brought them, they had them stand before the council. The high priest questioned them, 28saying, "We gave you strict orders not to teach in this name,[p] yet here you have filled Jerusalem with your teaching and you are determined to bring this man's blood on us." 29But Peter and the apostles answered, "We must obey God rather than any human authority.[q] 30The God of our ancestors raised up Jesus, whom you had killed by hanging him on a tree. 31God exalted him at his right hand as Leader and Savior that he might give repentance to Israel and forgiveness of sins. 32And we are witnesses to these things, and so is the Holy Spirit whom God has given to those who obey him."

33 When they heard this, they were enraged and wanted to kill them. 34But a Pharisee in the council named Gamaliel, a teacher of the law, respected by all the people, stood up and ordered the men to be put outside for a short time. 35Then he said to them, "Fellow Israelites,[r] consider carefully what you propose to do to these men. 36For some time ago Theudas rose up, claiming to be somebody, and a number of men, about four hundred, joined him; but he was killed, and all who followed him were dispersed and disappeared. 37After him Judas the Galilean rose up at the time of the census and got people to follow him; he also perished, and all who followed him were scattered. 38So in the present case, I tell you, keep away from these men and let them alone; because if this plan or this undertaking is of human origin, it will fail; 39but if it is of God, you will not be able to overthrow them—in that case you may even be found fighting against God!"

They were convinced by him, 40and when they had called in the apostles, they had them flogged. Then they ordered them not to speak in the name of Jesus, and let them go. 41As they left the council, they rejoiced that they were considered worthy to suffer dishonor for the sake of the name. 42And every day in the temple and at home[s] they did not cease to teach and proclaim Jesus as the Messiah.[t]

Seven Chosen to Serve

6 Now during those days, when the disciples were increasing in number, the Hellenists complained against the Hebrews because their widows were being neglected in the daily distribution of food. 2And the twelve called together the whole community of the disciples and said, "It is not right that we should neglect the word of God in order to wait on tables.[u] 3Therefore, friends,[v] select from among yourselves seven men of good standing, full of the Spirit and of wisdom, whom we may appoint to this task, 4while we, for our part, will devote ourselves to prayer and to serving the word." 5What they said pleased the whole community, and they chose Stephen, a man full of faith and the Holy Spirit, together with Philip, Prochorus, Nicanor, Timon, Parmenas, and Nicolaus, a proselyte of Antioch. 6They had these men stand before the apostles, who prayed and laid their hands on them.

7 The word of God continued to spread; the number of the disciples increased greatly in Jerusalem, and a great many of the priests became obedient to the faith.

The Arrest of Stephen

8 Stephen, full of grace and power, did great wonders and signs among the people. 9Then some of those who belonged to the synagogue of the Freedmen (as it was called), Cyrenians, Alexandrians, and others of those from Cilicia and Asia, stood up and argued with Stephen. 10But they could not withstand the wisdom and the Spirit[w] with which he spoke. 11Then they secretly instigated some men to say, "We have heard him speak blasphemous words against Moses and God." 12They stirred up the people as well as the elders and the scribes; then they suddenly confronted him, seized him, and brought him before the council. 13They set up false witnesses who said, "This man never stops saying things against this holy

[p] Other ancient authorities read *Did we not give you strict orders not to teach in this name?* [q] Gk *than men* [r] Gk *Men, Israelites* [s] Or *from house to house* [t] Or *the Christ* [u] Or *keep accounts* [v] Gk *brothers* [w] Or *spirit*

5.26 Acts 4.21
5.28 Acts 4.18; 2.33,36; 3.15; 7.52; Mt 23.35; 27.25
5.29 Acts 4.19
5.30 Acts 3.13,15; 22.14; 10.39; 13.29; Gal 3.13; 1 Pet 2.24
5.31 Acts 2.33; Heb 2.10; Acts 3.15
5.32 Lk 24.48; Jn 15.26; Rom 8.16
5.33 Acts 2.37; 7.54
5.38 Mt 15.13
5.39 Acts 7.51; 9.5; 11.17
5.40 Mt 10.17; Mk 13.9
5.41 1 Pet 4.13,16; Jn 15.21
5.42 Acts 2.46; 8.35; 11.20; 17.18; Gal 1.16
6.1 Acts 2.41,47; 9.29; 11.20; 4.35
6.3 Jn 21.23; Acts 1.15
6.5 Acts 11.19,24; 8.5,26; 21.8
6.6 Acts 1.24; 8.17; 9.17; 13.3; 1 Tim 4.14; 5.22; 2 Tim 1.6
6.7 Acts 12.24; 19.20; Acts 13.8; 14.22; Gal 1.23; 6.10
6.10 Lk 21.15; Acts 5.39
6.11 Mt 26.59,60
6.13 Acts 7.58; 21.28

6.1-12.25 Preparation for Reaching Out to the Wider World. **6.1-7** The division of labor within the community leadership is pictured here as deriving from a linguistic or cultural difference between two kinds of Jews: *Hebrews* (those oriented toward more traditional Semitic speech and culture) and *Hellenists* (those whose first language and cultural orientation are Greek). The decision is to assign to *seven* of the latter the administrative roles in the community (*wait on table* or *keep accounts*; the Greek verb for *serving* corresponds to the noun, *deacon*).
6.8-15 *Stephen,* one of the seven, is soon performing *signs* and preaching in public, which leads some Jews from other parts of the eastern Mediterranean to bring charges against him of opposing the law and the temple and of announcing that Jesus would destroy it. With visible evidence of divine support (his angelic *face*), Stephen begins his defense before the council.

7.1-53 Stephen's address traces the history of God's dealings with his people from the time of *Abraham*'s call in the *land of the Chaldeans* (Babylonia; modern Iraq) through the days of Isaac, Jacob and Joseph to the *time of fulfillment of God's promise to Abraham* which was to be achieved through *Moses*. This agent of God, *rejected* by his own people in spite of the *wonders and signs he performed*, led them out of Egypt, but they turned back to the worship of animals and *the works of their own hands*, as the prophets noted (vv. 42-43 quoted from Am 5.25-27). He told them that God would raise up a prophet like him (vs. 37; Deut 18.15-22). Although Israelites took pride in God's dwelling-place among them (vv. 44-47), humans cannot build God a *house* (vv. 49-50, from Isa 66.1-2). Their rejection of Jesus matches their ancestors' rejection of the *prophets* who *foretold* the coming of Jesus, as he informs his *stiff-necked* hearers, who have failed to keep God's law.

place and the law; 14for we have heard him
say that this Jesus of Nazareth[x] will destroy
this place and will change the customs that
Moses handed on to us." 15And all who sat
in the council looked intently at him, and
they saw that his face was like the face of
an angel.

Stephen's Speech to the Council

7 Then the high priest asked him, "Are
these things so?" 2And Stephen replied:
"Brothers[y] and fathers, listen to me. The
God of glory appeared to our ancestor
Abraham when he was in Mesopotamia,
before he lived in Haran, 3and said to him,
'Leave your country and your relatives and
go to the land that I will show you.' 4Then
he left the country of the Chaldeans and
settled in Haran. After his father died, God
had him move from there to this country
in which you are now living. 5He did not
give him any of it as a heritage, not even
a foot's length, but promised to give it to
him as his possession and to his descendants after him, even though he had no
child. 6And God spoke in these terms, that
his descendants would be resident aliens in
a country belonging to others, who would
enslave them and mistreat them during
four hundred years. 7'But I will judge the
nation that they serve,' said God, 'and after
that they shall come out and worship me
in this place.' 8Then he gave him the covenant of circumcision. And so Abraham[z]
became the father of Isaac and circumcised
him on the eighth day; and Isaac became
the father of Jacob, and Jacob of the twelve
patriarchs.
9 "The patriarchs, jealous of Joseph, sold
him into Egypt; but God was with him,
10and rescued him from all his afflictions,
and enabled him to win favor and to show
wisdom when he stood before Pharaoh,
king of Egypt, who appointed him ruler over
Egypt and over all his household. 11Now
there came a famine throughout Egypt and
Canaan, and great suffering, and our ancestors could find no food. 12But when Jacob
heard that there was grain in Egypt, he sent
our ancestors there on their first visit. 13On
the second visit Joseph made himself known
to his brothers, and Joseph's family became
known to Pharaoh. 14Then Joseph sent and
invited his father Jacob and all his relatives
to come to him, seventy-five in all; 15so
Jacob went down to Egypt. He himself died
there as well as our ancestors, 16and their
bodies[a] were brought back to Shechem and
laid in the tomb that Abraham had bought
for a sum of silver from the sons of Hamor
in Shechem.
17 "But as the time drew near for the
fulfillment of the promise that God had
made to Abraham, our people in Egypt
increased and multiplied 18until another king
who had not known Joseph ruled over Egypt.
19He dealt craftily with our race and forced
our ancestors to abandon their infants so
that they would die. 20At this time Moses
was born, and he was beautiful before God.
For three months he was brought up in his
father's house; 21and when he was abandoned, Pharaoh's daughter adopted him and
brought him up as her own son. 22So Moses
was instructed in all the wisdom of the
Egyptians and was powerful in his words
and deeds.
23 "When he was forty years old, it
came into his heart to visit his relatives, the
Israelites.[b] 24When he saw one of them
being wronged, he defended the oppressed
man and avenged him by striking down the
Egyptian. 25He supposed that his kinsfolk
would understand that God through him
was rescuing them, but they did not understand. 26The next day he came to some of
them as they were quarreling and tried to
reconcile them, saying, 'Men, you are brothers; why do you wrong each other?' 27But
the man who was wronging his neighbor
pushed Moses[c] aside, saying, 'Who made
you a ruler and a judge over us? 28Do you
want to kill me as you killed the Egyptian
yesterday?' 29When he heard this, Moses
fled and became a resident alien in the land
of Midian. There he became the father of
two sons.
30 "Now when forty years had passed,
an angel appeared to him in the wilderness
of Mount Sinai, in the flame of a burning
bush. 31When Moses saw it, he was amazed
at the sight; and as he approached to look,
there came the voice of the Lord: 32'I am the
God of your ancestors, the God of Abraham,
Isaac, and Jacob.' Moses began to tremble
and did not dare to look. 33Then the Lord
said to him, 'Take off the sandals from your
feet, for the place where you are standing
is holy ground. 34I have surely seen the
mistreatment of my people who are in Egypt

[x] Gk *the Nazorean* [y] Gk *Men, brothers* [z] Gk *he* [a] Gk *they* [b] Gk *his brothers, the sons of Israel* [c] Gk *him*

6.14 Mt 26.61; 15.1; 21.21; 26.3; 28.17
7.2 Acts 22.1; Ps 29.3; Gen 11.31; 15.7
7.3 Gen 12.1
7.4 Gen 12.5
7.5 Gen 12.7; 17.8; 26.3
7.6 Gen 15.13,14; Ex 12.40
7.7 Ex 3.12
7.8 Gen 17.9-11; 21.2-4; 25.26; 29.31ff
7.9 Gen 37.4; 11.28; 39.2,21,23
7.10 Gen 41.37; 42.6
7.11 Gen 41.54
7.12 Gen 42.1,2
7.13 Gen 45.1-4
7.14 Gen 45.9,10; 46.26,27; Deut 10.22
7.15 Gen 46.5; 49.33; Ex 1.6
7.16 Gen 23.16; 33.19; Josh 24.32
7.17 Ex 1.7-9; Ps 105.24,25
7.19 Ex 1.10,11, 15,22
7.22 1 Kings 4.30; Isa 19.11
7.23 Ex 2.11,12
7.32 Ex 3.6
7.33 Ex 3.5; Josh 5.15
7.34 Ex 3.7

and have heard their groaning, and I have
come down to rescue them. Come now, I
will send you to Egypt.'
35 "It was this Moses whom they rejected when they said, 'Who made you a
ruler and a judge?' and whom God now
sent as both ruler and liberator through the
angel who appeared to him in the bush.
[36]He led them out, having performed wonders and signs in Egypt, at the Red Sea, and
in the wilderness for forty years. [37]This is
the Moses who said to the Israelites, 'God
will raise up a prophet for you from your
own people[d] as he raised me up.' [38]He is the
one who was in the congregation in the
wilderness with the angel who spoke to him
at Mount Sinai, and with our ancestors;
and he received living oracles to give to us.
[39]Our ancestors were unwilling to obey him;
instead, they pushed him aside, and in their
hearts they turned back to Egypt, [40]saying
to Aaron, 'Make gods for us who will lead
the way for us; as for this Moses who led
us out from the land of Egypt, we do not
know what has happened to him.' [41]At that
time they made a calf, offered a sacrifice to
the idol, and reveled in the works of their
hands. [42]But God turned away from them
and handed them over to worship the host
of heaven, as it is written in the book of the
prophets:
'Did you offer to me slain victims and
sacrifices
forty years in the wilderness, O
house of Israel?
[43] No; you took along the tent of Moloch,
and the star of your god Rephan,
the images that you made to
worship;
so I will remove you beyond Babylon.'
44 "Our ancestors had the tent of testimony in the wilderness, as God[e] directed
when he spoke to Moses, ordering him to
make it according to the pattern he had
seen. [45]Our ancestors in turn brought it in
with Joshua when they dispossessed the
nations that God drove out before our
ancestors. And it was there until the time
of David, [46]who found favor with God and
asked that he might find a dwelling place
for the house of Jacob.[f] [47]But it was Solomon who built a house for him. [48]Yet the
Most High does not dwell in houses made
with human hands;[g] as the prophet says,
[49] 'Heaven is my throne,
and the earth is my footstool.
What kind of house will you build for
me, says the Lord,
or what is the place of my rest?
[50] Did not my hand make all these things?'
51 "You stiff-necked people, uncircumcised in heart and ears, you are forever
opposing the Holy Spirit, just as your ancestors used to do. [52]Which of the prophets
did your ancestors not persecute? They killed
those who foretold the coming of the Righteous One, and now you have become his
betrayers and murderers. [53]You are the ones
that received the law as ordained by angels,
and yet you have not kept it."

The Stoning of Stephen

54 When they heard these things, they
became enraged and ground their teeth at
Stephen.[h] [55]But filled with the Holy Spirit,
he gazed into heaven and saw the glory of
God and Jesus standing at the right hand
of God. [56]"Look," he said, "I see the heavens
opened and the Son of Man standing at the
right hand of God!" [57]But they covered their
ears, and with a loud shout all rushed
together against him. [58]Then they dragged
him out of the city and began to stone him;
and the witnesses laid their coats at the feet
of a young man named Saul. [59]While they
were stoning Stephen, he prayed, "Lord
Jesus, receive my spirit." [60]Then he knelt
down and cried out in a loud voice, "Lord,
do not hold this sin against them." When
8 he had said this, he died.[i] [1]And Saul
approved of their killing him.

Saul Persecutes the Church

That day a severe persecution began
against the church in Jerusalem, and all
except the apostles were scattered throughout the countryside of Judea and Samaria.
[2]Devout men buried Stephen and made loud
lamentation over him. [3]But Saul was rav-
aging the church by entering house after
house; dragging off both men and women,
he committed them to prison.

Philip Preaches in Samaria

4 Now those who were scattered went
from place to place, proclaiming the word.
[5]Philip went down to the city[k] of Samaria

[d] Gk *your brothers* [e] Gk *he* [f] Other ancient authorities read *for the God of Jacob* [g] Gk *with hands* [h] Gk *him* [i] Gk *fell asleep* [j] Other ancient authorities read *a city*

7.35 Ex 14.19
7.36 Ex 12.41; 14.21
7.37 Deut 18.15,18; Acts 3.22
7.38 Ex 19.17; Isa 63.9; Rom 3.2; Heb 5.12; 1 Pet 4.11
7.40 Ex 32.1,23
7.41 Ex 32.4,6; Ps 106.19
7.42 Ezek 20.25,39; Am 5.25,26
7.44 Ex 25.9,40
7.45 Josh 3.14-17; Ps 44.2
7.46 2 Sam 7.8-16; Ps 132.1-5
7.48 1 Kings 8.27; 2 Chr 2.6
7.49 Isa 66.1,2; Mt 5.34,35
7.51 Lev 26.41; Jer 6.10; 9.26
7.52 2 Chr 36.16; Mt 23.31,37; Acts 3.14
7.53 Ex 20.1; Heb 2.2
7.55 Acts 6.5
7.56 Mt 3.16; Dan 7.13
7.58 Lk 4.29; Lev 24.16; Deut 13.9,10
7.59 Acts 9.14
7.60 Acts 9.40
8.1 Acts 7.58; 11.19
8.2 Gen 23.2; 50.10; 2 Sam 3.31
8.3 Acts 7.58; 22.4; 26.10,11; 1 Cor 15.9; Gal 1.13; Phil 3.6; 1 Tim 1.13
8.4 ver 1; Acts 15.35
8.5 Acts 6.5

7.54-8.1 While the attack on Stephen is being mounted, he receives confirmation of his insights through the vision of Christ exalted at God's *right hand.* Dragged outside the city for *stoning* by the mob (victims were pushed over a ledge, to be crushed and buried under heavy stones thrown down on them), Stephen intercedes for his murderers, while the man safeguarding the *garments* of the attackers is *Saul,* who makes his first appearance here in Acts.
8.2-3 *Saul* (later to be known by his Greek name, Paul) is seen as trying to destroy the gatherings of followers of Jesus in homes, with authority to imprison the members. The *church* exists outside Jerusalem only in *Judea and Samaria.*
8.4-25 The outreach to the Samaritans (residents of the territory north of Judea who claimed to be the true heirs of the covenant and to have the true version of the Law of Moses and the true temple, which was on Mt. Gerizim) began with the *scattering* of the Hellenists, particularly of *Philip.* In addition to the crowds attracted by the *signs* worked by Philip, there came a professional magician, *Simon,* who was baptized into the new community. When the apostles came to inspect these developments, Simon at first offered to buy the power to transmit the Holy Spirit, but submitted to Peter's rebuke of him. The outreach is approved.

8.26-40 Philip's wider outreach for the gospel is evident in his conversation with the pilgrim to Jerusalem from Ethiopia, a *eunuch* who was a *court official* there. The scripture he is reading (Isa 53.7-9) is explained to him as fulfilled by Jesus' death. He believes and is baptized, whereupon Philip is transported by *the Spirit* to Azotus (Ashdod), a coastal city involved in manufacture and commerce with the wider Roman world.

and proclaimed the Messiah[k] to them. [6]The crowds with one accord listened eagerly to what was said by Philip, hearing and seeing the signs that he did, [7]for unclean spirits, crying with loud shrieks, came out of many who were possessed; and many others who were paralyzed or lame were cured. [8]So there was great joy in that city.

9 Now a certain man named Simon had previously practiced magic in the city and amazed the people of Samaria, saying that he was someone great. [10]All of them, from the least to the greatest, listened to him eagerly, saying, "This man is the power of God that is called Great." [11]And they listened eagerly to him because for a long time he had amazed them with his magic. [12]But when they believed Philip, who was proclaiming the good news about the kingdom of God and the name of Jesus Christ, they were baptized, both men and women. [13]Even Simon himself believed. After being baptized, he stayed constantly with Philip and was amazed when he saw the signs and great miracles that took place.

14 Now when the apostles at Jerusalem heard that Samaria had accepted the word of God, they sent Peter and John to them. [15]The two went down and prayed for them that they might receive the Holy Spirit [16](for as yet the Spirit had not come[l] upon any of them; they had only been baptized in the name of the Lord Jesus). [17]Then Peter and John[m] laid their hands on them, and they received the Holy Spirit. [18]Now when Simon saw that the Spirit was given through the laying on of the apostles' hands, he offered them money, [19]saying, "Give me also this power so that anyone on whom I lay my hands may receive the Holy Spirit." [20]But Peter said to him, "May your silver perish with you, because you thought you could obtain God's gift with money! [21]You have no part or share in this, for your heart is not right before God. [22]Repent therefore of this wickedness of yours, and pray to the Lord that, if possible, the intent of your heart may be forgiven you. [23]For I see that you are in the gall of bitterness and the chains of wickedness." [24]Simon answered, "Pray for me to the Lord, that nothing of what you[n] have said may happen to me."

25 Now after Peter and John[o] had testified and spoken the word of the Lord, they returned to Jerusalem, proclaiming the good news to many villages of the Samaritans.

Philip and the Ethiopian Eunuch

26 Then an angel of the Lord said to Philip, "Get up and go toward the south[p] to the road that goes down from Jerusalem to Gaza." (This is a wilderness road.) [27]So he got up and went. Now there was an Ethiopian eunuch, a court official of the Candace, queen of the Ethiopians, in charge of her entire treasury. He had come to Jerusalem to worship [28]and was returning home; seated in his chariot, he was reading the prophet Isaiah. [29]Then the Spirit said to Philip, "Go over to this chariot and join it." [30]So Philip ran up to it and heard him reading the prophet Isaiah. He asked, "Do you understand what you are reading?" [31]He replied, "How can I, unless someone guides me?" And he invited Philip to get in and sit beside him. [32]Now the passage of the scripture that he was reading was this:

"Like a sheep he was led to the slaughter,
  and like a lamb silent before its shearer,
    so he does not open his mouth.
[33] In his humiliation justice was denied him.
  Who can describe his generation?
    For his life is taken away from the earth."

[34]The eunuch asked Philip, "About whom, may I ask you, does the prophet say this, about himself or about someone else?" [35]Then Philip began to speak, and starting with this scripture, he proclaimed to him the good news about Jesus. [36]As they were going along the road, they came to some water; and the eunuch said, "Look, here is water! What is to prevent me from being baptized?"[q] [38]He commanded the chariot to stop, and both of them, Philip and the eunuch, went down into the water, and Philip[r] baptized him. [39]When they came up out of the water, the Spirit of the Lord snatched Philip away; the eunuch saw him no more, and went on his way rejoicing. [40]But Philip found himself at Azotus, and as he was passing through the region, he proclaimed the good news to all the towns until he came to Caesarea.

[k] Or *the Christ* [l] Gk *fallen* [m] Gk *they* [n] The Greek word for *you* and the verb *pray* are plural [o] Gk *after they* [p] Or *go at noon* [q] Other ancient authorities add all or most of verse 37, *And Philip said, "If you believe with all your heart, you may." And he replied, "I believe that Jesus Christ is the Son of God."* [r] Gk *he*

8.7 Mt 4.24
8.9 Acts 13.6; 5.36
8.10 Acts 14.11; 28.6
8.12 Acts 1.3; 2.38
8.13 ver 6; Acts 19.11
8.14 ver 1
8.15 Acts 2.38
8.16 Acts 19.2; Mt 28.19; Acts 10.48; 19.5
8.17 Acts 6.6; 2.4
8.20 Acts 2.38; Mt 10.8; 2 Kings 5.16
8.21 Ps 78.37
8.23 Isa 58.6; Heb 12.15
8.25 Lk 16.28; ver 40
8.26 Acts 5.19; ver 5
8.27 Ps 68.31; Zeph 3.10; Jn 12.20
8.29 Acts 10.19; 11.12; 13.2; 20.23; 21.11
8.32 Isa 53.7,8
8.35 Mt 5.2; Lk 24.27; Acts 17.2; 18.28; 5.42
8.36 Acts 10.47
8.39 1 Kings 18.12; 2 Kings 2.16; Ezek 3.12,14

9.1 Acts 8.3; 22.4-16; 26.9-18
9.3 Acts 22.6; 26.12; 1 Cor 15.8
9.4 Acts 22.7; 26.14
9.7 Acts 22.9; 26.13,14
9.10 Acts 22.12
9.11 Acts 21.39; 22.3
9.14 ver 21; Acts 7.59; 1 Cor 1.2; 2 Tim 2.22
9.15 Acts 13.2; Eph 3.7,8; Gal 2.7,8; Acts 25.22,23; 26.1
9.16 Acts 20.23; 21.11; 2 Cor 11.23
9.17 Acts 22.12,13; 8.17; 2.4; 4.31
9.19 Acts 26.20
9.21 Acts 8.3; Gal 1.13,23
9.22 Acts 18.28
9.23 Acts 23.12; 25.3
9.24 2 Cor 11.32,33
9.26 Acts 22.17; Gal 1.17,18
9.27 Acts 4.36; ver 20.22
9.29 Acts 6.1; 11.20; 2 Cor 11.26
9.31 Acts 8.1
9.32 ver 13
9.34 Acts 3.6,16; 4.10

The Conversion of Saul

9 Meanwhile Saul, still breathing threats and murder against the disciples of the Lord, went to the high priest 2 and asked him for letters to the synagogues at Damascus, so that if he found any who belonged to the Way, men or women, he might bring them bound to Jerusalem. 3 Now as he was going along and approaching Damascus, suddenly a light from heaven flashed around him. 4 He fell to the ground and heard a voice saying to him, "Saul, Saul, why do you persecute me?" 5 He asked, "Who are you, Lord?" The reply came, "I am Jesus, whom you are persecuting. 6 But get up and enter the city, and you will be told what you are to do." 7 The men who were traveling with him stood speechless because they heard the voice but saw no one. 8 Saul got up from the ground, and though his eyes were open, he could see nothing; so they led him by the hand and brought him into Damascus. 9 For three days he was without sight, and neither ate nor drank.

10 Now there was a disciple in Damascus named Ananias. The Lord said to him in a vision, "Ananias." He answered, "Here I am, Lord." 11 The Lord said to him, "Get up and go to the street called Straight, and at the house of Judas look for a man of Tarsus named Saul. At this moment he is praying, 12 and he has seen in a vision[s] a man named Ananias come in and lay his hands on him so that he might regain his sight." 13 But Ananias answered, "Lord, I have heard from many about this man, how much evil he has done to your saints in Jerusalem; 14 and here he has authority from the chief priests to bind all who invoke your name." 15 But the Lord said to him, "Go, for he is an instrument whom I have chosen to bring my name before Gentiles and kings and before the people of Israel; 16 I myself will show him how much he must suffer for the sake of my name." 17 So Ananias went and entered the house. He laid his hands on Saul[t] and said, "Brother Saul, the Lord Jesus, who appeared to you on your way here, has sent me so that you may regain your sight and be filled with the Holy Spirit." 18 And immediately something like scales fell from his eyes, and his sight was restored. Then he got up and was baptized, 19 and after taking some food, he regained his strength.

Saul Preaches in Damascus

For several days he was with the disciples in Damascus, 20 and immediately he began to proclaim Jesus in the synagogues, saying, "He is the Son of God." 21 All who heard him were amazed and said, "Is not this the man who made havoc in Jerusalem among those who invoked this name? And has he not come here for the purpose of bringing them bound before the chief priests?" 22 Saul became increasingly more powerful and confounded the Jews who lived in Damascus by proving that Jesus[u] was the Messiah.[v]

Saul Escapes from the Jews

23 After some time had passed, the Jews plotted to kill him, 24 but their plot became known to Saul. They were watching the gates day and night so that they might kill him; 25 but his disciples took him by night and let him down through an opening in the wall,[w] lowering him in a basket.

Saul in Jerusalem

26 When he had come to Jerusalem, he attempted to join the disciples; and they were all afraid of him, for they did not believe that he was a disciple. 27 But Barnabas took him, brought him to the apostles, and described for them how on the road he had seen the Lord, who had spoken to him, and how in Damascus he had spoken boldly in the name of Jesus. 28 So he went in and out among them in Jerusalem, speaking boldly in the name of the Lord. 29 He spoke and argued with the Hellenists; but they were attempting to kill him. 30 When the believers[x] learned of it, they brought him down to Caesarea and sent him off to Tarsus.

31 Meanwhile the church throughout Judea, Galilee, and Samaria had peace and was built up. Living in the fear of the Lord and in the comfort of the Holy Spirit, it increased in numbers.

The Healing of Aeneas

32 Now as Peter went here and there among all the believers,[y] he came down also to the saints living in Lydda. 33 There he found a man named Aeneas, who had been bedridden for eight years, for he was paralyzed. 34 Peter said to him, "Aeneas,

[s] Other ancient authorities lack *in a vision* [t] Gk *him* [u] Gk *that this* [v] Or *the Christ* [w] Gk *through the wall* [x] Gk *brothers* [y] Gk *all of them*

9.1-22 *Saul*, while in the midst of his efforts to seize and take off to prison those within the synagogues of *Damascus* who are acclaiming Jesus as Messiah, is confronted by *the Lord*. *A disciple* there named *Ananias* is told to commission Saul and to restore his sight so that he can launch his mission to *Gentiles, kings and Israel*. His symbolic regaining of sight is followed by baptism, and *Saul* launches his mission in the *synagogues*, effctively proclaiming Jesus as the *Messiah*.
9.23-30 Saul escapes over the wall of Damascus from a Jewish plot to kill him (see 2 Cor 11.32-33) and goes to Jerusalem, where *Barnabas* presents him to the apostles and where he begins his mission among those oriented toward Greek culture (*Hellenists*). Escaping a plot on his life, he returns by way of *Caesarea* on the sea coast to *Tarsus*. In his letters, Paul never mentions Tarsus.
9.32-43 Peter extends his mission to cities along the coastal plain, including *Lydda* and *Joppa*. A healing and a restoration to life of a dead woman demonstrate God's power with Peter and lead *many* to trust in *the Lord*.

10.1-33 A vision granted to a Roman military officer (*centurion*), who, with his *household*, is called *devout* (meaning that he revered the God of Israel), tells him to send for *Simon Peter*. Next day Peter is puzzled by a vision of a sheet filled with various kinds of animal. Three times he is invited to eat this meat, with the declaration that *God has made clean* what Peter as a pious Jew has regarded as unclean. When the messengers arrive from Cornelius, whom they describe as well regarded *by the whole Jewish nation*, Peter invites them in, which would be contrary to ritual laws prohibiting direct associations with impure Gentiles, and then accompanies them to the house of Cornelius, since he now understands that the point of the vision was for him to be open to association with non-Jews in the new community.

Jesus Christ heals you; get up and make
your bed!" And immediately he got up.
[35]And all the residents of Lydda and Sharon
saw him and turned to the Lord.

Peter in Lydda and Joppa

36 Now in Joppa there was a disciple
whose name was Tabitha, which in Greek
is Dorcas.[z] She was devoted to good works
and acts of charity. [37]At that time she
became ill and died. When they had washed
her, they laid her in a room upstairs. [38]Since
Lydda was near Joppa, the disciples, who
heard that Peter was there, sent two men
to him with the request, "Please come to us
without delay." [39]So Peter got up and went
with them; and when he arrived, they took
him to the room upstairs. All the widows
stood beside him, weeping and showing
tunics and other clothing that Dorcas had
made while she was with them. [40]Peter put
all of them outside, and then he knelt down
and prayed. He turned to the body and said,
"Tabitha, get up." Then she opened her
eyes and, seeing Peter, she sat up. [41]He gave
her his hand and helped her up. Then
calling the saints and widows, he showed
her to be alive. [42]This became known
throughout Joppa, and many believed in
the Lord. [43]Meanwhile he stayed in Joppa
for some time with a certain Simon, a
tanner.

Peter and Cornelius

10 In Caesarea there was a man
named Cornelius, a centurion of
the Italian Cohort, as it was called. [2]He was
a devout man who feared God with all his
household; he gave alms generously to the
people and prayed constantly to God. [3]One
afternoon at about three o'clock he had a
vision in which he clearly saw an angel of
God coming in and saying to him, "Cornelius." [4]He stared at him in terror and said,
"What is it, Lord?" He answered, "Your
prayers and your alms have ascended as a
memorial before God. [5]Now send men to
Joppa for a certain Simon who is called
Peter; [6]he is lodging with Simon, a tanner,
whose house is by the seaside." [7]When the
angel who spoke to him had left, he called
two of his slaves and a devout soldier from
the ranks of those who served him, [8]and
after telling them everything, he sent them
to Joppa.

9 About noon the next day, as they were
on their journey and approaching the city,
Peter went up on the roof to pray. [10]He
became hungry and wanted something to
eat; and while it was being prepared, he fell
into a trance. [11]He saw the heaven opened
and something like a large sheet coming
down, being lowered to the ground by its
four corners. [12]In it were all kinds of four-
footed creatures and reptiles and birds of the
air. [13]Then he heard a voice saying, "Get
up, Peter; kill and eat." [14]But Peter said, "By
no means, Lord; for I have never eaten
anything that is profane or unclean." [15]The
voice said to him again, a second time,
"What God has made clean, you must not
call profane." [16]This happened three times,
and the thing was suddenly taken up to
heaven.

17 Now while Peter was greatly puzzled
about what to make of the vision that he
had seen, suddenly the men sent by Cornelius
appeared. They were asking for Simon's
house and were standing by the gate. [18]They
called out to ask whether Simon, who was
called Peter, was staying there. [19]While Peter
was still thinking about the vision, the Spirit
said to him, "Look, three[a] men are searching for you. [20]Now get up, go down, and go
with them without hesitation; for I have
sent them." [21]So Peter went down to the
men and said, "I am the one you are
looking for; what is the reason for your
coming?" [22]They answered, "Cornelius, a
centurion, an upright and God-fearing man,
who is well spoken of by the whole Jewish
nation, was directed by a holy angel to send
for you to come to his house and to hear
what you have to say." [23]So Peter[b] invited
them in and gave them lodging.

The next day he got up and went with
them, and some of the believers[c] from Joppa
accompanied him. [24]The following day they
came to Caesarea. Cornelius was expecting
them and had called together his relatives
and close friends. [25]On Peter's arrival
Cornelius met him, and falling at his feet,
worshiped him. [26]But Peter made him get
up, saying, "Stand up; I am only a mortal."
[27]And as he talked with him, he went in
and found that many had assembled; [28]and
he said to them, "You yourselves know that
it is unlawful for a Jew to associate with or

[z] The name Tabitha in Aramaic and the name Dorcas in Greek mean *a gazelle* [a] One ancient authority reads *two*; others lack the word [b] Gk *he* [c] Gk *brothers*

9.35 1 Chr 5.16; Acts 11.21
9.36 Jon 1.3; 1 Tim 2.10; Titus 3.8
9.37 Acts 1.13
9.38 Acts 11.26
9.39 Acts 6.1
9.40 Mt 9.25; Acts 7.60; Mk 5.41,42
9.41 ver 13
9.43 Acts 10.6
10.2 ver 22.35
10.3 Acts 9.10; 3.1; 5.19
10.4 Acts 3.4; Rev 8.4; Mt 26.13
10.6 Acts 9.43
10.9 Acts 11.5-14; Mt 24.17
10.10 Acts 22.17
10.11 Acts 7.56; Rev 19.11
10.14 Acts 9.5; Lev 11.4; 20.25; Deut 14.3,7; Ezek 4.14
10.15 ver 28; Mt 15.11; Rom 14.14,17,20; 1 Cor 10.25; 1 Tim 4.4; Titus 1.15
10.17 ver 3
10.19 Acts 11.12
10.22 ver 2; Acts 11.14
10.23 ver 45; Acts 11.12
10.26 Acts 24.14,15; Rev 19.10
10.28 Jn 4.9; 18.28; Acts 11.3; 15.8,9

to visit a Gentile; but God has shown me
that I should not call anyone profane or
unclean. [29]So when I was sent for, I came
without objection. Now may I ask why you
sent for me?"
30 Cornelius replied, "Four days ago at
this very hour, at three o'clock, I was praying in my house when suddenly a man in
dazzling clothes stood before me. [31]He said,
'Cornelius, your prayer has been heard and
your alms have been remembered before
God. [32]Send therefore to Joppa and ask for
Simon, who is called Peter; he is staying in
the home of Simon, a tanner, by the sea.'
[33]Therefore I sent for you immediately, and
you have been kind enough to come. So
now all of us are here in the presence of
God to listen to all that the Lord has commanded you to say."

Gentiles Hear the Good News

34 Then Peter began to speak to them:
"I truly understand that God shows no
partiality, [35]but in every nation anyone who
fears him and does what is right is acceptable to him. [36]You know the message he
sent to the people of Israel, preaching peace
by Jesus Christ—he is Lord of all. [37]That
message spread throughout Judea, beginning in Galilee after the baptism that John
announced: [38]how God anointed Jesus of
Nazareth with the Holy Spirit and with
power; how he went about doing good and
healing all who were oppressed by the devil,
for God was with him. [39]We are witnesses
to all that he did both in Judea and in
Jerusalem. They put him to death by hanging him on a tree; [40]but God raised him on
the third day and allowed him to appear,
[41]not to all the people but to us who were
chosen by God as witnesses, and who ate
and drank with him after he rose from the
dead. [42]He commanded us to preach to the
people and to testify that he is the one
ordained by God as judge of the living and
the dead. [43]All the prophets testify about
him that everyone who believes in him
receives forgiveness of sins through his
name."

Gentiles Receive the Holy Spirit

44 While Peter was still speaking, the
Holy Spirit fell upon all who heard the
word. [45]The circumcised believers who had
come with Peter were astounded that the
gift of the Holy Spirit had been poured out
even on the Gentiles, [46]for they heard them
speaking in tongues and extolling God. Then
Peter said, [47]"Can anyone withhold the water
for baptizing these people who have received the Holy Spirit just as we have?" [48]So
he ordered them to be baptized in the name
of Jesus Christ. Then they invited him to
stay for several days.

Peter's Report to the Church at Jerusalem

11 Now the apostles and the believers[d]
who were in Judea heard that the
Gentiles had also accepted the word of God.
[2]So when Peter went up to Jerusalem, the
circumcised believers[e] criticized him, [3]say-
ing, "Why did you go to uncircumcised
men and eat with them?" [4]Then Peter began to explain it to them, step by step,
saying, [5]"I was in the city of Joppa praying,
and in a trance I saw a vision. There was
something like a large sheet coming down
from heaven, being lowered by its four
corners; and it came close to me. [6]As I
looked at it closely I saw four-footed animals, beasts of prey, reptiles, and birds of
the air. [7]I also heard a voice saying to me,
'Get up, Peter; kill and eat.' [8]But I replied,
'By no means, Lord; for nothing profane or
unclean has ever entered my mouth.' [9]But
a second time the voice answered from
heaven, 'What God has made clean, you
must not call profane.' [10]This happened three
times; then everything was pulled up again
to heaven. [11]At that very moment three
men, sent to me from Caesarea, arrived at
the house where we were. [12]The Spirit told
me to go with them and not to make a
distinction between them and us.[f] These six
brothers also accompanied me, and we
entered the man's house. [13]He told us how
he had seen the angel standing in his house
and saying, 'Send to Joppa and bring Simon,
who is called Peter; [14]he will give you a
message by which you and your entire
household will be saved.' [15]And as I began
to speak, the Holy Spirit fell upon them just
as it had upon us at the beginning. [16]And
I remembered the word of the Lord, how he
had said, 'John baptized with water, but
you will be baptized with the Holy Spirit.'
[17]If then God gave them the same gift that
he gave us when we believed in the Lord
Jesus Christ, who was I that I could hinder

[d] Gk *brothers* [e] Gk lacks *believers* [f] Or *not to hesitate*

10.34 Deut 10.17; Rom 2.11; Eph 6.9; Col 3.25; 1 Pet 1.17
10.35 Acts 15.9
10.36 Isa 57.19; Mt 28.18; Rom 10.12; Eph 1.20,22
10.38 Acts 2.22; Jn 3.2
10.39 Lk 24.48; Acts 5.30
10.40 Acts 2.24
10.41 Jn 14.17,22; Jn 21.13
10.42 Mt 28.19,20; Rom 14.9; 2 Cor 5.10; 1 Pet 4.5
10.43 Isa 53.11; Acts 26.22; 15.9; Rom 10.11; Gal 3.22
10.44 Acts 4.31; 8.15,16; 11.15; 15.8
10.45 ver 23; Acts 11.18
10.47 Acts 8.36; 11.17
10.48 1 Cor 1.17; Acts 2.38; 8.16; 19.5
11.2 Acts 10.45
11.3 Acts 10.28; Gal 2.12
11.5 Acts 10.9-32
11.12 Acts 8.29; 15.9; 10.23
11.13 Acts 10.30
11.15 Acts 10.44; 2.4
11.16 Mt 3.11; Jn 1.26,33; Acts 1.5; Joel 2.28; 3.18
11.17 Acts 10.45,47

10.34-48 Peter's message about Jesus' death, resurrection, and appearance to *chosen witnesses* concludes with his future role as judge and restorer of all humanity, which Peter declares to be in fulfillment of the prophets (Isa 2.2; 40.5; Joel 2.32). Confirmation for opening the invitation to non-Jews comes with the outpouring of the Spirit on the Gentile hearers. The community's acceptance of them is given through baptism *in the name of Jesus.*

11.1-18 The issue of admitting the uncircumcised to the fellowship is raised again by circumcised members in Jerusalem, which gives Peter the occasion for recounting his vision of inclusive participation and its confirmation by God's outpouring of the Spirit on the believing Gentiles.

11.19-26 *Barnabas* was sent by the Jerusalem leaders to investigate the report that *the Lord Jesus* had been preached to Gentiles (*Hellenists* or Greeks) who in large numbers had joined the community. After instructing these new converts, Barnabas sought out *Saul* in Tarsus, who accompanied him back to Antioch to carry on the program of instruction of the *disciples*, who are now called *Christians*, meaning *those who identify with Christ*.
11.27-30 The famine predicted by *Agabus* (21.10) in the reign of the emperor *Claudius* (from 41-54 CE) is also described by the Jewish historian Josephus (*Antiquities* 20) as occurring in Palestine (*All the world* = the whole land). The disciples in Antioch send relief through *Barnabas and Saul*.
12.1-25 Both the Christian's conflict with the political authorities and God's way of dealing with it are evident in the stories (1) of the execution by Herod (Agrippa I) of *James*, son of Zebedee and brother of John (Lk 5.10), who was leader of the Jerusalem apostles, and (2) of the imprisonment of Peter by Herod, his liberation by *an angel of the Lord*, and his reuniting with the astonished community gathered in the *house of Mary*, mother of John Mark. Mark later travels with Paul and Barnabas (Acts 12.25; 13.5, 13; 15.37-40). God's punishment of Agrippa comes in reaction to the king's seeking acclaim as divine.

God?" 18When they heard this, they were
silenced. And they praised God, saying, "Then
God has given even to the Gentiles the
repentance that leads to life."

The Church in Antioch

19 Now those who were scattered because of the persecution that took place
over Stephen traveled as far as Phoenicia,
Cyprus, and Antioch, and they spoke the
word to no one except Jews. 20But among
them were some men of Cyprus and Cyrene
who, on coming to Antioch, spoke to the
Hellenists[g] also, proclaiming the Lord Jesus.
21The hand of the Lord was with them, and
a great number became believers and turned
to the Lord. 22News of this came to the ears
of the church in Jerusalem, and they sent
Barnabas to Antioch. 23When he came and
saw the grace of God, he rejoiced, and he
exhorted them all to remain faithful to the
Lord with steadfast devotion; 24for he was
a good man, full of the Holy Spirit and of
faith. And a great many people were brought
to the Lord. 25Then Barnabas went to Tarsus to look for Saul, 26and when he had
found him, he brought him to Antioch. So
it was that for an entire year they met with[h]
the church and taught a great many
people, and it was in Antioch that the
disciples were first called "Christians."
27 At that time prophets came down
from Jerusalem to Antioch. 28One of them
named Agabus stood up and predicted by
the Spirit that there would be a severe
famine over all the world; and this took
place during the reign of Claudius. 29The
disciples determined that according to their
ability, each would send relief to the believers[i]
living in Judea; 30this they did, sending it to
the elders by Barnabas and Saul.

James Killed and Peter Imprisoned

12 About that time King Herod laid
violent hands upon some who
belonged to the church. 2He had James, the
brother of John, killed with the sword. 3After
he saw that it pleased the Jews, he proceeded to arrest Peter also. (This was during
the festival of Unleavened Bread.) 4When he
had seized him, he put him in prison and
handed him over to four squads of soldiers
to guard him, intending to bring him out
to the people after the Passover. 5While
Peter was kept in prison, the church prayed
fervently to God for him.

Peter Delivered from Prison

6 The very night before Herod was going
to bring him out, Peter, bound with two
chains, was sleeping between two soldiers,
while guards in front of the door were
keeping watch over the prison. 7Suddenly
an angel of the Lord appeared and a light
shone in the cell. He tapped Peter on the
side and woke him, saying, "Get up quickly."
And the chains fell off his wrists. 8The angel
said to him, "Fasten your belt and put on
your sandals." He did so. Then he said to
him, "Wrap your cloak around you and
follow me." 9Peter[j] went out and followed
him; he did not realize that what was
happening with the angel's help was real;
he thought he was seeing a vision. 10After
they had passed the first and the second
guard, they came before the iron gate leading into the city. It opened for them of its
own accord, and they went outside and
walked along a lane, when suddenly the
angel left him. 11Then Peter came to himself
and said, "Now I am sure that the Lord has
sent his angel and rescued me from the
hands of Herod and from all that the Jewish
people were expecting."
12 As soon as he realized this, he went
to the house of Mary, the mother of John
whose other name was Mark, where many
had gathered and were praying. 13When he
knocked at the outer gate, a maid named
Rhoda came to answer. 14On recognizing
Peter's voice, she was so overjoyed that,
instead of opening the gate, she ran in and
announced that Peter was standing at the
gate. 15They said to her, "You are out of
your mind!" But she insisted that it was so.
They said, "It is his angel." 16Meanwhile
Peter continued knocking; and when they
opened the gate, they saw him and were
amazed. 17He motioned to them with his
hand to be silent, and described for them
how the Lord had brought him out of the
prison. And he added, "Tell this to James
and to the believers."[i] Then he left and
went to another place.
18 When morning came, there was no
small commotion among the soldiers over
what had become of Peter. 19When Herod
had searched for him and could not find
him, he examined the guards and ordered

[g] Other ancient authorities read *Greeks* [h] Or *were guests of* [i] Gk *brothers* [j] Gk *He*

11.18 Rom 10.12,13; 2 Cor 7.10
11.19 Acts 8.1,4
11.20 Acts 4.36; 6.5; 13.1; 5.42
11.21 Lk 1.66; Acts 2.47; 9.35
11.23 Acts 13.43; 14.22
11.24 Acts 6.4; ver 21; Acts 5.14
11.25 Acts 9.11,30
11.26 Acts 26.28
11.27 Acts 18.22; 1 Cor 12.28
11.28 Acts 21.10
11.29 Rom 15.26; 1 Cor 16.1; 2 Cor 9.1
11.30 Acts 12.25; 14.23
12.2 Mt 4.21; 20.23
12.3 Acts 24.27; Ex 12.15; 23.15
12.5 Eph 6.18; 1 Thess 5.17
12.6 Acts 21.33
12.7 Acts 5.19; 16.26
12.9 Acts 9.10
12.10 Acts 16.26
12.11 Lk 15.17; Dan 3.28; 6.22; 2 Cor 1.10; 2 Pet 2.9
12.12 Acts 15.37; ver 5
12.13 Jn 18.16,17
12.14 Lk 24.41
12.15 Gen 48.16; Mt 18.10
12.17 Acts 13.16; 19.33; 21.40
12.19 Acts 16.27; 27.42

them to be put to death. Then Peter went down from Judea to Caesarea and stayed there.

The Death of Herod

20 Now Herod[k] was angry with the people of Tyre and Sidon. So they came to him in a body; and after winning over Blastus, the king's chamberlain, they asked for a reconciliation, because their country depended on the king's country for food. [21]On an appointed day Herod put on his royal robes, took his seat on the platform, and delivered a public address to them. [22]The people kept shouting, "The voice of a god, and not of a mortal!" [23]And immediately, because he had not given the glory to God, an angel of the Lord struck him down, and he was eaten by worms and died.

24 But the word of God continued to advance and gain adherents. [25]Then after completing their mission Barnabas and Saul returned to[l] Jerusalem and brought with them John, whose other name was Mark.

Barnabas and Saul Commissioned

13 Now in the church at Antioch there were prophets and teachers: Barnabas, Simeon who was called Niger, Lucius of Cyrene, Manaen a member of the court of Herod the ruler,[m] and Saul. [2]While they were worshiping the Lord and fasting, the Holy Spirit said, "Set apart for me Barnabas and Saul for the work to which I have called them." [3]Then after fasting and praying they laid their hands on them and sent them off.

The Apostles Preach in Cyprus

4 So, being sent out by the Holy Spirit, they went down to Seleucia; and from there they sailed to Cyprus. [5]When they arrived at Salamis, they proclaimed the word of God in the synagogues of the Jews. And they had John also to assist them. [6]When they had gone through the whole island as far as Paphos, they met a certain magician, a Jewish false prophet, named Bar-Jesus. [7]He was with the proconsul, Sergius Paulus, an intelligent man, who summoned Barnabas and Saul and wanted to hear the word of God. [8]But the magician Elymas (for that is the translation of his name) opposed them and tried to turn the proconsul away from the faith. [9]But Saul, also known as Paul, filled with the Holy Spirit, looked intently at him [10]and said, "You son of the devil, you enemy of all righteousness, full of all deceit and villainy, will you not stop making crooked the straight paths of the Lord? [11]And now listen—the hand of the Lord is against you, and you will be blind for a while, unable to see the sun." Immediately mist and darkness came over him, and he went about groping for someone to lead him by the hand. [12]When the proconsul saw what had happened, he believed, for he was astonished at the teaching about the Lord.

Paul and Barnabas in Antioch of Pisidia

13 Then Paul and his companions set sail from Paphos and came to Perga in Pamphylia. John, however, left them and returned to Jerusalem; [14]but they went on from Perga and came to Antioch in Pisidia. And on the sabbath day they went into the synagogue and sat down. [15]After the reading of the law and the prophets, the officials of the synagogue sent them a message, saying, "Brothers, if you have any word of exhortation for the people, give it." [16]So Paul stood up and with a gesture began to speak:

"You Israelites,[n] and others who fear God, listen. [17]The God of this people Israel chose our ancestors and made the people great during their stay in the land of Egypt, and with uplifted arm he led them out of it. [18]For about forty years he put up with[o] them in the wilderness. [19]After he had destroyed seven nations in the land of Canaan, he gave them their land as an inheritance [20]for about four hundred fifty years. After that he gave them judges until the time of the prophet Samuel. [21]Then they asked for a king; and God gave them Saul son of Kish, a man of the tribe of Benjamin, who reigned for forty years. [22]When he had removed him, he made David their king. In his testimony about him he said, 'I have found David, son of Jesse, to be a man after my heart, who will carry out all my wishes.' [23]Of this man's posterity God has brought to Israel a Savior, Jesus, as he promised; [24]before his coming John had already proclaimed a baptism of repentance to all the

[k] Gk *he* [l] Other ancient authorities read *from* [m] Gk *tetrarch* [n] Gk *Men, Israelites* [o] Other ancient authorities read *cared for*

12.20 Mt 11.21; 1 Kings 5.9,11; Ezek 27.17
12.23 1 Sam 25.38; 2 Sam 24.17
12.24 Acts 6.7; 19.20
12.25 Acts 13.5,13; 15.37
13.1 Acts 11.22-26
13.2 Acts 9.15; 22.21; 14.26
13.3 Acts 6.6; 14.26
13.4 ver 2,3; Acts 4.36
13.5 Acts 9.20
13.6 Acts 8.9
13.7 ver 8.12
13.8 Acts 8.9; ver 7,12; Acts 6.7
13.9 Acts 4.8
13.10 Mt 13.38; Jn 8.44; Hos 14.9
13.11 Ex 9.3
13.13 Acts 15.38
13.14 Acts 14.19,21; 16.13
13.17 Deut 7.6-8
13.18 Ex 16.35; Deut 1.31
13.19 Deut 7.1; Josh 19.51
13.20 Judg 2.16; 1 Sam 3.20
13.21 1 Sam 8.5; 10.1
13.22 1 Sam 15.23,26; 13.14
13.23 Isa 11.1; Mt 1.21; Rom 11.26
13.24 Mt 3.1; Lk 3.3

13.1-20.38 The Outreach from Syria to the Greek World. **13.1-3** The roles of the leaders of the church in *Antioch* include *prophets* (who orient the community toward present and future) and *teachers* (who carry on instruction). In addition to Barnabas and Saul, who are sent out on the mission, their names include *Simeon Niger* (local and a black, or a man with dark complexion), *Lucius of Cyrene* (from north Africa, identified by some scholars as Luke), and *Manaen* (who had a position of honor at the court of Herod Agrippa). In each place that they go there are certain common features (usually an encounter in a synagogue), but also others which point up distinct challenges that they met as they journeyed. **13.4-12** From *Seleucia*, the port of Antioch near the mouth of the Orontes River, they travelled to *Cyprus*, the large island in the northeast corner of the Mediterranean Sea, which they crossed from *Salamis* in the east to *Paphos* in the west. Those they encountered ranged from the *proconsul* (Roman governor of a region), who became a believer, to the *magician*, whose opposition led to his being struck *blind*. **13.13-52** Crossing to the mainland of Asia Minor, *Paul*, who has become the dominant figure (13.9), and *his companions* went through *Perga*, which may have had a harbor at this time, in *Pamphylia*, a small district between the mountains and the sea. Passing on into the district known as Galatia (from the Celtic [or Gallic] settlers who came there from northern Europe), they reached another *Antioch* in the district to the west called *Pisidia*. At the synagogue meeting there Paul sketches the history of the covenant people down to David, of whose *posterity* Jesus came to Israel as *Savior*. Confirmed by John the Baptist, he was rejected by the people who asked Pilate to put him to death, but God raised him from the dead and exalted him, in fulfillment of scripture (13.33 = Ps 2.7; vs. 34 = Isa 55.3; vs. 35 = Ps 16.10). Even the rejection that he met from his own people fulfills the warning of the prophet Habakkuk (13.41 = Hab 1.5). The large numbers that *follow* Paul and Barnabas arouse resentment among the Jewish leaders, who seek to refute their message. Again, this is seen as in accord with scripture, in that God's purpose is to bring *light to the Gentiles* and good news *to the ends of the earth* (13.47 = Isa 49.6). The Jewish opposition is joined by male and female leaders of the city, and the apostles move on to *Iconium*.

14.1-7 At Iconium, a major city on the central plateau of Asia Minor, the same pattern prevails: they have notable success in persuading many Jews and Gentiles to trust in Jesus as Lord, but the threat of persecution moves Paul and Barnabas to travel south to *Lystra and Derbe*.

people of Israel. 25 And as John was finishing his work, he said, 'What do you suppose that I am? I am not he. No, but one is coming after me; I am not worthy to untie the thong of the sandals[p] on his feet.'

26 "My brothers, you descendants of Abraham's family, and others who fear God, to us[q] the message of this salvation has been sent. 27 Because the residents of Jerusalem and their leaders did not recognize him or understand the words of the prophets that are read every sabbath, they fulfilled those words by condemning him. 28 Even though they found no cause for a sentence of death, they asked Pilate to have him killed. 29 When they had carried out everything that was written about him, they took him down from the tree and laid him in a tomb. 30 But God raised him from the dead; 31 and for many days he appeared to those who came up with him from Galilee to Jerusalem, and they are now his witnesses to the people. 32 And we bring you the good news that what God promised to our ancestors 33 he has fulfilled for us, their children, by raising Jesus; as also it is written in the second psalm,

'You are my Son;
today I have begotten you.'

34 As to his raising him from the dead, no more to return to corruption, he has spoken in this way,

'I will give you the holy promises
made to David.'

35 Therefore he has also said in another psalm,

'You will not let your Holy One
experience corruption.'

36 For David, after he had served the purpose of God in his own generation, died,[r] was laid beside his ancestors, and experienced corruption; 37 but he whom God raised up experienced no corruption. 38 Let it be known to you therefore, my brothers, that through this man forgiveness of sins is proclaimed to you; 39 by this Jesus[s] everyone who believes is set free from all those sins[t] from which you could not be freed by the law of Moses. 40 Beware, therefore, that what the prophets said does not happen to you:

41 'Look, you scoffers!
Be amazed and perish,
for in your days I am doing a work,
a work that you will never believe,
even if someone tells you.'"

42 As Paul and Barnabas[u] were going out, the people urged them to speak about these things again the next sabbath. 43 When the meeting of the synagogue broke up, many Jews and devout converts to Judaism followed Paul and Barnabas, who spoke to them and urged them to continue in the grace of God.

44 The next sabbath almost the whole city gathered to hear the word of the Lord.[v] 45 But when the Jews saw the crowds, they were filled with jealousy; and blaspheming, they contradicted what was spoken by Paul. 46 Then both Paul and Barnabas spoke out boldly, saying, "It was necessary that the word of God should be spoken first to you. Since you reject it and judge yourselves to be unworthy of eternal life, we are now turning to the Gentiles. 47 For so the Lord has commanded us, saying,

'I have set you to be a light for the
Gentiles,
so that you may bring salvation to
the ends of the earth.'"

48 When the Gentiles heard this, they were glad and praised the word of the Lord; and as many as had been destined for eternal life became believers. 49 Thus the word of the Lord spread throughout the region. 50 But the Jews incited the devout women of high standing and the leading men of the city, and stirred up persecution against Paul and Barnabas, and drove them out of their region. 51 So they shook the dust off their feet in protest against them, and went to Iconium. 52 And the disciples were filled with joy and with the Holy Spirit.

Paul and Barnabas in Iconium

14 The same thing occurred in Iconium, where Paul and Barnabas[u] went into the Jewish synagogue and spoke in such a way that a great number of both Jews and Greeks became believers. 2 But the unbelieving Jews stirred up the Gentiles and poisoned their minds against the brothers. 3 So they remained for a long time, speaking boldly for the Lord, who testified to the word of his grace by granting signs and wonders to be done through them. 4 But the residents of the city were divided; some sided with the Jews, and some with the apostles. 5 And when an attempt was made by both Gentiles and Jews, with their

[p] Gk *untie the sandals* [q] Other ancient authorities read *you* [r] Gk *fell asleep* [s] Gk *this* [t] Gk *all* [u] Gk *they* [v] Other ancient authorities read *God*

13.25 Mt 3.11; Lk 3.16
13.27 Lk 23.13; Acts 3.17; Lk 24.27
13.28 Mt 27.22
13.29 Lk 18.31; Mt 27.59
13.30 Mt 28.6
13.31 Mt 28.16; Lk 24.48
13.32 Gen 3.15; Rom 4.13
13.33 Ps 2.7
13.34 Isa 55.3
13.35 Ps 16.10; Acts 2.27
13.36 Acts 2.29; 1 Kings 2.10
13.38 Lk 24.47
13.39 Rom 3.28; Acts 10.43
13.40 Jn 6.45
13.43 Acts 11.23; 14.22
13.45 Acts 18.6; 1 Pet 4.4; Jude 10
13.46 ver 26; Acts 3.26; 18.6; 28.28
13.47 Isa 49.6; Lk 2.32
13.51 Mt 10.14; Mk 6.11; Lk 9.5; Acts 18.6
13.52 Acts 2.4
14.3 Heb 2.4; Jn 4.48
14.4 Acts 17.4,5; ver 14
14.5 2 Tim 3.11

rulers, to mistreat them and to stone them, 6 the apostles[w] learned of it and fled to Lystra and Derbe, cities of Lycaonia, and to the surrounding country; 7 and there they continued proclaiming the good news.

Paul and Barnabas in Lystra and Derbe

8 In Lystra there was a man sitting who could not use his feet and had never walked, for he had been crippled from birth. 9 He listened to Paul as he was speaking. And Paul, looking at him intently and seeing that he had faith to be healed, 10 said in a loud voice, "Stand upright on your feet." And the man[x] sprang up and began to walk. 11 When the crowds saw what Paul had done, they shouted in the Lycaonian language, "The gods have come down to us in human form!" 12 Barnabas they called Zeus, and Paul they called Hermes, because he was the chief speaker. 13 The priest of Zeus, whose temple was just outside the city,[y] brought oxen and garlands to the gates; he and the crowds wanted to offer sacrifice. 14 When the apostles Barnabas and Paul heard of it, they tore their clothes and rushed out into the crowd, shouting, 15 "Friends,[z] why are you doing this? We are mortals just like you, and we bring you good news, that you should turn from these worthless things to the living God, who made the heaven and the earth and the sea and all that is in them. 16 In past generations he allowed all the nations to follow their own ways; 17 yet he has not left himself without a witness in doing good—giving you rains from heaven and fruitful seasons, and filling you with food and your hearts with joy." 18 Even with these words, they scarcely restrained the crowds from offering sacrifice to them.

19 But Jews came there from Antioch and Iconium and won over the crowds. Then they stoned Paul and dragged him out of the city, supposing that he was dead. 20 But when the disciples surrounded him, he got up and went into the city. The next day he went on with Barnabas to Derbe.

The Return to Antioch in Syria

21 After they had proclaimed the good news to that city and had made many disciples, they returned to Lystra, then on to Iconium and Antioch. 22 There they strengthened the souls of the disciples and encouraged them to continue in the faith, saying, "It is through many persecutions that we must enter the kingdom of God." 23 And after they had appointed elders for them in each church, with prayer and fasting they entrusted them to the Lord in whom they had come to believe.

24 Then they passed through Pisidia and came to Pamphylia. 25 When they had spoken the word in Perga, they went down to Attalia. 26 From there they sailed back to Antioch, where they had been commended to the grace of God for the work[a] that they had completed. 27 When they arrived, they called the church together and related all that God had done with them, and how he had opened a door of faith for the Gentiles. 28 And they stayed there with the disciples for some time.

The Council at Jerusalem

15 Then certain individuals came down from Judea and were teaching the brothers, "Unless you are circumcised according to the custom of Moses, you cannot be saved." 2 And after Paul and Barnabas had no small dissension and debate with them, Paul and Barnabas and some of the others were appointed to go up to Jerusalem to discuss this question with the apostles and the elders. 3 So they were sent on their way by the church, and as they passed through both Phoenicia and Samaria, they reported the conversion of the Gentiles, and brought great joy to all the believers.[b] 4 When they came to Jerusalem, they were welcomed by the church and the apostles and the elders, and they reported all that God had done with them. 5 But some believers who belonged to the sect of the Pharisees stood up and said, "It is necessary for them to be circumcised and ordered to keep the law of Moses."

6 The apostles and the elders met together to consider this matter. 7 After there had been much debate, Peter stood up and said to them, "My brothers,[c] you know that in the early days God made a choice among you, that I should be the one through whom the Gentiles would hear the message of the good news and become believers. 8 And God, who knows the human heart,

[w] Gk *they* [x] Gk *he* [y] Or *The priest of Zeus-Outside-the-City* [z] Gk *Men* [a] Or *committed in the grace of God to the work* [b] Gk *brothers* [c] Gk *Men, brothers*

14.6 Mt 10.23
14.8 Acts 3.2
14.9 Acts 3.4; 10.4; Mt 9.28,29
14.11 Acts 8.10; 28.6
14.15 Acts 10.26; Jas 5.17; 1 Sam 12.21; Jer 14.22; 1 Cor 8.4; Gen 1.1; Ps 146.6; Rev 14.7
14.16 Ps 81.12; Acts 17.30; 1 Pet 4.3
14.17 Acts 17.27; Rom 1.20; Deut 11.14; Job 5.10; Ps 65.10
14.19 Acts 13.45; 2 Cor 11.25; 2 Tim 3.11
14.20 ver 22,28
14.22 Acts 11.23; 13.43; Jn 16.33; 1 Thess 3.3; 2 Tim 3.12
14.23 Titus 1.5; Acts 11.30; 13.3; 20.32
14.26 Acts 11.19; 13.1,3; 15.40
15.1 ver 24; Gal 2.12; ver 5; Gal 5.2; Acts 6.14
15.2 ver 7; Gal 2.2; Acts 11.30
15.3 Acts 20.38; Rom 15.24; 1 Cor 16.6,11; Acts 14.27
15.4 ver 12; Acts 14.27
15.7 Acts 10.19,20; 20.24
15.8 Acts 1.24; 10.44,47

14.8-20 The healing of a cripple effected by Paul leads the crowds to acclaim him in their local language (*Lycaonian*) as *Hermes*, messenger of the Greek gods, and Barnabas as *Zeus*, the chief of their gods. Paul's response, with its description of God's providential ordering of the universe, simply confirms the crowd's belief that the gods have come among them. Opposition arises from Jews out of Antioch and results in Paul's being stoned (a form of capital punishment prescribed by the Jewish law, especially for blasphemy; Lev 20.2; 24.16; Deut 13.10; 17.5-7). **14.21-27** After a mixture of success in Derbe, with strengthening the new members in Lystra, Iconium and Antioch-in-Pisidia, Paul and Barnabas return to Antioch-in-Syria with their report to the church of the results of their mission among the Gentiles. **15.1-21** Members of the Judean church declare in Antioch that all males in the new community must undergo circumcision. *Paul and Barnabas* are designated to report to the apostles in Jerusalem the results of their outreach to the Gentile world. In spite of objections from some community members of Pharisaic background, Peter is able to persuade the *apostles and elders* that the opening to Gentile participation took place through him, and that ritual laws should not be required for membership in the community. Following the report from Paul and Barnabas, *James* (the brother of Jesus), quoting scripture (15.16-17 = Jer 12.15; Am 9.11-12; Isa 45.21), declares that the Gentile converts are not to be bound by the law. But there are a few requirements: abstinence from contact (including eating) with what has been offered to idols; from *fornication* (irresponsible sexual acts), from what has been *strangled* and from *blood* (eating meat from animals not properly slaughtered or drained of blood; Lev 7.26). Thus minimal ritual requirements were to be observed, in contrast to the decisions of this council (reported by Paul in Gal 2.10) to place no such obligations.

15.22-35 The decision of the Jerusalem apostles is transmitted by letter to the church in Antioch, with two representatives (*Judas called Barsabbas*, perhaps meaning born on the sabbath, and *Silas*, who may be the Silvanus mentioned in the letters of Paul: 1 Thess 1.1; 2 Cor 1.19). Once their role is completed (to confirm that this communication is the policy of the Jerusalem apostles), they return there, while *Paul and Barnabas* remain in Antioch.
15.36-41 Paul and Barnabas, divided over whether to take *Mark* along with them, go separate ways: Barnabas and Mark to *Cyprus*; Paul and *Silas* across *Syria and Cilicia* en route to the cities in southern Asia Minor where Paul has worked earlier.

testified to them by giving them the Holy
Spirit, just as he did to us; 9and in cleansing
their hearts by faith he has made no distinction between them and us. 10Now therefore
why are you putting God to the test by
placing on the neck of the disciples a yoke
that neither our ancestors nor we have
been able to bear? 11On the contrary, we
believe that we will be saved through the
grace of the Lord Jesus, just as they will."
12 The whole assembly kept silence, and
listened to Barnabas and Paul as they told
of all the signs and wonders that God had
done through them among the Gentiles.
13After they finished speaking, James replied, "My brothers,[d] listen to me. 14Simeon
has related how God first looked favorably
on the Gentiles, to take from among them
a people for his name. 15This agrees with
the words of the prophets, as it is written,
16 'After this I will return,
and I will rebuild the dwelling of
David, which has fallen;
from its ruins I will rebuild it,
and I will set it up,
17 so that all other peoples may seek the
Lord—
even all the Gentiles over whom my
name has been called.
Thus says the Lord, who has been
making these things 18known from
long ago.'[e]
19Therefore I have reached the decision that
we should not trouble those Gentiles who
are turning to God, 20but we should write
to them to abstain only from things polluted
by idols and from fornication and from
whatever has been strangled[f] and from blood.
21For in every city, for generations past,
Moses has had those who proclaim him, for
he has been read aloud every sabbath in the
synagogues."

The Council's Letter to Gentile Believers

22 Then the apostles and the elders, with
the consent of the whole church, decided to
choose men from among their members[g]
and to send them to Antioch with Paul and
Barnabas. They sent Judas called Barsabbas,
and Silas, leaders among the brothers, 23with
the following letter: "The brothers, both the
apostles and the elders, to the believers[h] of
Gentile origin in Antioch and Syria and
Cilicia, greetings. 24Since we have heard
that certain persons who have gone out
from us, though with no instructions from
us, have said things to disturb you and
have unsettled your minds,[i] 25we have decided unanimously to choose representatives[j]
and send them to you, along with our
beloved Barnabas and Paul, 26who have
risked their lives for the sake of our Lord
Jesus Christ. 27We have therefore sent Judas
and Silas, who themselves will tell you the
same things by word of mouth. 28For it has
seemed good to the Holy Spirit and to us to
impose on you no further burden than
these essentials: 29that you abstain from
what has been sacrificed to idols and from
blood and from what is strangled[k] and from
fornication. If you keep yourselves from
these, you will do well. Farewell."
30 So they were sent off and went down
to Antioch. When they gathered the congregation together, they delivered the letter.
31When its members[l] read it, they rejoiced
at the exhortation. 32Judas and Silas, who
were themselves prophets, said much to
encourage and strengthen the believers.[h]
33After they had been there for some time,
they were sent off in peace by the believers[h]
to those who had sent them.[m] 35But Paul
and Barnabas remained in Antioch, and
there, with many others, they taught and
proclaimed the word of the Lord.

Paul and Barnabas Separate

36 After some days Paul said to Barnabas,
"Come, let us return and visit the believers[h]
in every city where we proclaimed the word
of the Lord and see how they are doing."
37Barnabas wanted to take with them John
called Mark. 38But Paul decided not to take
with them one who had deserted them in
Pamphylia and had not accompanied them
in the work. 39The disagreement became so
sharp that they parted company; Barnabas
took Mark with him and sailed away to
Cyprus. 40But Paul chose Silas and set out,
the believers[h] commending him to the grace
of the Lord. 41He went through Syria and
Cilicia, strengthening the churches.

[d] Gk *Men, brothers* [e] Other ancient authorities read *things. 18Known to God from of old are all his works.'* [f] Other ancient authorities lack *and from whatever has been strangled* [g] Gk *from among them* [h] Gk *brothers* [i] Other ancient authorities add *saying, 'You must be circumcised and keep the law,'* [j] Gk *men* [k] Other ancient authorities lack *and from what is strangled* [l] Gk *When they* [m] Other ancient authorities add verse 34, *But it seemed good to Silas to remain there*

15.9 Acts 10.28,34,43; 11.12
15.10 Mt 23.4; Gal 5.1
15.11 Rom 3.24; Eph 2.5-8; Titus 2.11; 3.4,5
15.12 Jn 4.48; Acts 14.27
15.13 Acts 12.17
15.16 Am 9.11,12; Jer 12.15
15.20 ver 29; 1 Cor 10.7,8,14,20; Gen 9.4; Lev 3.17; Deut 12.16,23
15.21 Acts 13.15; 2 Cor 3.14,15
15.24 ver 1; Gal 1.7; 5.10
15.26 Acts 14.19; 1 Cor 15.30
15.29 ver 20; Acts 21.25; Lev 17.14
15.33 Acts 16.36; 1 Cor 16.11; Heb 11.31
15.36 Acts 13.4,13,14, 51; 14.1,6,24,25
15.37 Acts 12.12
15.38 Acts 13.13
15.41 Acts 16.5

Timothy Joins Paul and Silas

16 Paul[n] went on also to Derbe and to Lystra, where there was a disciple named Timothy, the son of a Jewish woman who was a believer; but his father was a Greek. [2]He was well spoken of by the believers[o] in Lystra and Iconium. [3]Paul wanted Timothy to accompany him; and he took him and had him circumcised because of the Jews who were in those places, for they all knew that his father was a Greek. [4]As they went from town to town, they delivered to them for observance the decisions that had been reached by the apostles and elders who were in Jerusalem. [5]So the churches were strengthened in the faith and increased in numbers daily.

Paul's Vision of the Man of Macedonia

6 They went through the region of Phrygia and Galatia, having been forbidden by the Holy Spirit to speak the word in Asia. [7]When they had come opposite Mysia, they attempted to go into Bithynia, but the Spirit of Jesus did not allow them; [8]so, passing by Mysia, they went down to Troas. [9]During the night Paul had a vision: there stood a man of Macedonia pleading with him and saying, "Come over to Macedonia and help us." [10]When he had seen the vision, we immediately tried to cross over to Macedonia, being convinced that God had called us to proclaim the good news to them.

The Conversion of Lydia

11 We set sail from Troas and took a straight course to Samothrace, the following day to Neapolis, [12]and from there to Philippi, which is a leading city of the district[p] of Macedonia and a Roman colony. We remained in this city for some days. [13]On the sabbath day we went outside the gate by the river, where we supposed there was a place of prayer; and we sat down and spoke to the women who had gathered there. [14]A certain woman named Lydia, a worshiper of God, was listening to us; she was from the city of Thyatira and a dealer in purple cloth. The Lord opened her heart to listen eagerly to what was said by Paul. [15]When she and her household were baptized, she urged us, saying,"If you have judged me to be faithful to the Lord, come and stay at my home." And she prevailed upon us.

Paul and Silas in Prison

16 One day, as we were going to the place of prayer, we met a slave-girl who had a spirit of divination and brought her owners a great deal of money by fortune-telling. [17]While she followed Paul and us, she would cry out, "These men are slaves of the Most High God, who proclaim to you[q] a way of salvation." [18]She kept doing this for many days. But Paul, very much annoyed, turned and said to the spirit, "I order you in the name of Jesus Christ to come out of her." And it came out that very hour.

19 But when her owners saw that their hope of making money was gone, they seized Paul and Silas and dragged them into the marketplace before the authorities. [20]When they had brought them before the magistrates, they said,"These men are disturbing our city; they are Jews [21]and are advocating customs that are not lawful for us as Romans to adopt or observe." [22]The crowd joined in attacking them, and the magistrates had them stripped of their clothing and ordered them to be beaten with rods. [23]After they had given them a severe flogging, they threw them into prison and ordered the jailer to keep them securely. [24]Following these instructions, he put them in the innermost cell and fastened their feet in the stocks.

25 About midnight Paul and Silas were praying and singing hymns to God, and the prisoners were listening to them. [26]Suddenly there was an earthquake, so violent that the foundations of the prison were shaken; and immediately all the doors were opened and everyone's chains were unfastened. [27]When the jailer woke up and saw the prison doors wide open, he drew his sword and was about to kill himself, since he supposed that the prisoners had escaped. [28]But Paul shouted in a loud voice, "Do not harm yourself, for we are all here." [29]The jailer[n] called for lights, and rushing in, he fell down trembling before Paul and Silas. [30]Then he brought them outside and said, "Sirs, what must I do to be saved?" [31]They answered, "Believe on the Lord Jesus, and you will be saved, you and your household." [32]They spoke the word of the Lord[r]

[n] Gk *He* [o] Gk *brothers* [p] Other authorities read *a city of the first district* [q] Other ancient authorities read *to us* [r] Other ancient authorities read *word of God*

16.1 Acts 14.6; 19.22; Rom 16.21; 1 Cor 4.17; 2 Tim 1.2,5
16.3 Gal 2.3
16.4 Acts 15.28,29; 15.2; 11.30
16.5 Acts 15.41
16.6 Acts 18.23; 2.9
16.7 ver 8; Lk 24.49; Rom 8.9; Gal 4.6
16.8 ver 11; 2 Cor 2.12; 2 Tim 4.13
16.9 Acts 9.10; 18.5; 20.1,3; 27.2
16.10 2 Cor 2.13
16.11 ver 8; 2 Tim 4.13
16.12 Phil 1.1; Acts 18.5; 19.21,22,29; 20.1,3; 27.2
16.15 Acts 11.14; Lk 24.29
16.16 Deut 18.11; 1 Sam 28.3,7
16.17 Mk 5.7
16.19 Acts 19.25,26; 15.40; 17.6,7; Jas 2.6
16.20 Acts 17.6
16.22 2 Cor 11.23,25; 1 Thess 2.2
16.23 ver 27,36
16.24 Jer 20.2,3
16.25 Eph 5.19
16.26 Acts 4.31; 5.19; 12.7,10
16.27 Acts 12.19
16.30 Acts 2.37; 9.6; 22.10
16.31 Jn 3.16,36; 6.47; 1 Jn 5.10

16.1-5 At *Lystra* Paul chose *Timothy* (whose father was *Greek*) to join his team, taking care to have him *circumcised* as a concession to the Jewish Christians, even though he was also conveying the decision of the Jerusalem apostles freeing Gentile Christians from obligation to obey the Jewish law.
16.6-10 Paul's vision of the *man of Macedonia* urging him to come there marks a major turning point in the Acts account: the gospel is to be proclaimed on the mainland of Europe, initially in northern Greece. The attempt of Paul and his companions to go through the province of *Mysia* to the northern province of *Bithynia* (an area associated with Peter, according to 1 Pet 1.1) was hindered by *the Spirit of Jesus*, perhaps because it had already been evangelized.
16.11-15 Crossing from *Troas* (a major port in Asia Minor near the site of Homer's Troy) by way of the island of *Samothrace* to *Neapolis* (the terminus of the major Roman road, Via Egnatia, crucial for military and commercial transport across the northern Greek peninsula), Paul reached *Philippi*, the town developed by Philip, father of Alexander the Great, as fortress and capital of his expanding realm, in the later fourth century BCE. The *place of prayer* was a typical feature of towns throughout the Roman empire, where Jews resident in each area gathered for social, commercial and religious purposes. *Lydia*, a common name in the Greco-Roman world, was from *Thyatira*, a major commercial city in Asia Minor. Her *purple cloth* was a luxury item, the dye for which was obtained from a type of sea snail along the coast of Syria and Palestine. Persuaded by Paul, she and her entire *household* are converted and baptized.
16.16-40 When the evil *spirit* is expelled from a slave girl who is able to tell fortunes (*divination*), her owners are furious and accuse Paul and Silas before the civic authorities of disturbing the peace. Imprisoned, they are released when an *earthquake* opens the doors and unfastens their shackles, freeing all the prisoners. Ready to commit suicide, the jailer is addressed by Paul and invited to trust in *the Lord Jesus*. He and his household are converted and baptized, and receive Paul as a guest and friend. When the order comes for their release, Paul complains that he has not been treated as a *Roman citizen*: they were protected by law from flogging and entitled to appeal against charges made against them.

17.1-8 Travelling west to *Thessalonica*, a major port city, Paul once again successfully engaged Jews in the city with the message about Jesus as *Messiah*, but those who rejected his message gathered a mob of protesters before the city authorities.
17.10-15 In *Beroea*, southwest of Thessalonica, the same approach to the Jews meets with a more positive response, and among those who join the new community are some *Greek women and men of high standing*. Troublemakers from Thessalonica cause Paul to move on south alone to Athens.
17.16-34 First in the *synagogue* and then in the *civic center*, Paul challenges the Athenians with his strange message, and as a result is called before the civic group responsibile for cultural and moral order: the Areopagites, who convened on a small hill (named for Aries or Mars, the god of war) adjacent to the civic center and below the Acropolis, where the Parthenon (temple of Athena) was located. He decries the many idols, and declares that the creator God does not live in houses or images, but intends to unify the human race and to order its existence. In defense of his position he alludes to Stoic thinkers and their concepts of God's presence and activity among all humans, as well as their belief in the coming day when all will be called to account for their deeds on earth. His hearers follow him until he declares that the model by which all will be judged is *a man* whom God raised from the dead. Only a few are persuaded, among whom is a member of the council, *Dionysius* (named for the Greek god of wine) and *Damaris*, an otherwise unknown woman.

to him and to all who were in his house. [33]At the same hour of the night he took them and washed their wounds; then he and his entire family were baptized without delay. [34]He brought them up into the house and set food before them; and he and his entire household rejoiced that he had become a believer in God.

35 When morning came, the magistrates sent the police, saying,"Let those men go." [36]And the jailer reported the message to Paul, saying, "The magistrates sent word to let you go; therefore come out now and go in peace." [37]But Paul replied, "They have beaten us in public, uncondemned, men who are Roman citizens, and have thrown us into prison; and now are they going to discharge us in secret? Certainly not! Let them come and take us out themselves." [38]The police reported these words to the magistrates, and they were afraid when they heard that they were Roman citizens; [39]so they came and apologized to them. And they took them out and asked them to leave the city. [40]After leaving the prison they went to Lydia's home; and when they had seen and encouraged the brothers and sisters[s] there, they departed.

The Uproar in Thessalonica

17 After Paul and Silas[t] had passed through Amphipolis and Apollonia, they came to Thessalonica, where there was a synagogue of the Jews. [2]And Paul went in, as was his custom, and on three sabbath days argued with them from the scriptures, [3]explaining and proving that it was necessary for the Messiah[u] to suffer and to rise from the dead, and saying, "This is the Messiah,[u] Jesus whom I am proclaiming to you." [4]Some of them were persuaded and joined Paul and Silas, as did a great many of the devout Greeks and not a few of the leading women. [5]But the Jews became jealous, and with the help of some ruffians in the marketplaces they formed a mob and set the city in an uproar. While they were searching for Paul and Silas to bring them out to the assembly, they attacked Jason's house. [6]When they could not find them, they dragged Jason and some believers[s] before the city authorities,[v] shouting, "These people who have been turning the world upside down have come here also, [7]and Jason has entertained them as guests. They are all acting contrary to the decrees of the emperor, saying that there is another king named Jesus." [8]The people and the city officials were disturbed when they heard this, [9]and after they had taken bail from Jason and the others, they let them go.

Paul and Silas in Beroea

10 That very night the believers[s] sent Paul and Silas off to Beroea; and when they arrived, they went to the Jewish synagogue. [11]These Jews were more receptive than those in Thessalonica, for they welcomed the message very eagerly and examined the scriptures every day to see whether these things were so. [12]Many of them therefore believed, including not a few Greek women and men of high standing. [13]But when the Jews of Thessalonica learned that the word of God had been proclaimed by Paul in Beroea as well, they came there too, to stir up and incite the crowds. [14]Then the believers[s] immediately sent Paul away to the coast, but Silas and Timothy remained behind. [15]Those who conducted Paul brought him as far as Athens; and after receiving instructions to have Silas and Timothy join him as soon as possible, they left him.

Paul in Athens

16 While Paul was waiting for them in Athens, he was deeply distressed to see that the city was full of idols. [17]So he argued in the synagogue with the Jews and the devout persons, and also in the marketplace[w] every day with those who happened to be there. [18]Also some Epicurean and Stoic philosophers debated with him. Some said, "What does this babbler want to say?" Others said,"He seems to be a proclaimer of foreign divinities." (This was because he was telling the good news about Jesus and the resurrection.) [19]So they took him and brought him to the Areopagus and asked him,"May we know what this new teaching is that you are presenting? [20]It sounds rather strange to us, so we would like to know what it means." [21]Now all the Athenians and the foreigners living there would spend their time in nothing but telling or hearing something new.

22 Then Paul stood in front of the Areopagus and said, "Athenians, I see how extremely religious you are in every way.

[s] Gk *brothers* [t] Gk *they* [u] Or *the Christ* [v] Gk *politarchs* [w] Or *civic center*; Gk *agora*

16.34 Acts 11.14
16.36 ver 23,27
16.37 Acts 22.25-27
16.38 Acts 22.29
16.39 Mt 8.34
16.40 ver 14
17.1 Acts 27.2; 1 Thess 1.1; 2 Thess 1.1
17.2 Acts 9.20; 13.14; 16.13; 19.8
17.3 Lk 24.26,46; Acts 18.28; Gal 3.1
17.4 Acts 15.22,27,32, 40
17.5 ver 13; Rom 16.21
17.6 Acts 16.19,20
17.7 Lk 23.2; Jn 19.12
17.10 ver 14; Acts 20.4; ver 2
17.11 Isa 34.16; Lk 16.29; Jn 5.39
17.15 Acts 15.3; ver 16,21,22; Acts 18.5
17.16 2 Pet 2.8

23 For as I went through the city and looked carefully at the objects of your worship, I found among them an altar with the inscription, 'To an unknown god.' What therefore you worship as unknown, this I proclaim to you. 24 The God who made the world and everything in it, he who is Lord of heaven and earth, does not live in shrines made by human hands, 25 nor is he served by human hands, as though he needed anything, since he himself gives to all mortals life and breath and all things. 26 From one ancestor[x] he made all nations to inhabit the whole earth, and he allotted the times of their existence and the boundaries of the places where they would live, 27 so that they would search for God[y] and perhaps grope for him and find him—though indeed he is not far from each one of us. 28 For 'In him we live and move and have our being'; as even some of your own poets have said,

'For we too are his offspring.'

29 Since we are God's offspring, we ought not to think that the deity is like gold, or silver, or stone, an image formed by the art and imagination of mortals. 30 While God has overlooked the times of human ignorance, now he commands all people everywhere to repent, 31 because he has fixed a day on which he will have the world judged in righteousness by a man whom he has appointed, and of this he has given assurance to all by raising him from the dead."

32 When they heard of the resurrection of the dead, some scoffed; but others said, "We will hear you again about this." 33 At that point Paul left them. 34 But some of them joined him and became believers, including Dionysius the Areopagite and a woman named Damaris, and others with them.

Paul in Corinth

18 After this Paul[z] left Athens and went to Corinth. 2 There he found a Jew named Aquila, a native of Pontus, who had recently come from Italy with his wife Priscilla, because Claudius had ordered all Jews to leave Rome. Paul[a] went to see them, 3 and, because he was of the same trade, he stayed with them, and they worked together—by trade they were tentmakers. 4 Every sabbath he would argue in the synagogue and would try to convince Jews and Greeks.

5 When Silas and Timothy arrived from Macedonia, Paul was occupied with proclaiming the word,[b] testifying to the Jews that the Messiah[c] was Jesus. 6 When they opposed and reviled him, in protest he shook the dust from his clothes[d] and said to them, "Your blood be on your own heads! I am innocent. From now on I will go to the Gentiles." 7 Then he left the synagogue[e] and went to the house of a man named Titius[f] Justus, a worshiper of God; his house was next door to the synagogue. 8 Crispus, the official of the synagogue, became a believer in the Lord, together with all his household; and many of the Corinthians who heard Paul became believers and were baptized. 9 One night the Lord said to Paul in a vision, "Do not be afraid, but speak and do not be silent; 10 for I am with you, and no one will lay a hand on you to harm you, for there are many in this city who are my people." 11 He stayed there a year and six months, teaching the word of God among them.

12 But when Gallio was proconsul of Achaia, the Jews made a united attack on Paul and brought him before the tribunal. 13 They said, "This man is persuading people to worship God in ways that are contrary to the law." 14 Just as Paul was about to speak, Gallio said to the Jews, "If it were a matter of crime or serious villainy, I would be justified in accepting the complaint of you Jews; 15 but since it is a matter of questions about words and names and your own law, see to it yourselves; I do not wish to be a judge of these matters." 16 And he dismissed them from the tribunal. 17 Then all of them[g] seized Sosthenes, the official of the synagogue, and beat him in front of the tribunal. But Gallio paid no attention to any of these things.

Paul's Return to Antioch

18 After staying there for a considerable time, Paul said farewell to the believers[h] and sailed for Syria, accompanied by Priscilla and Aquila. At Cenchreae he had his hair cut, for he was under a vow. 19 When they reached Ephesus, he left them there, but first he himself went into the synagogue and had a discussion with the Jews. 20 When

[x] Gk *From one*; other ancient authorities read *From one blood* [y] Other ancient authorities read *the Lord* [z] Gk *he* [a] Gk *He* [b] Gk *with the word* [c] Or *the Christ* [d] Gk *reviled him, he shook out his clothes* [e] Gk *left there* [f] Other ancient authorities read *Titus* [g] Other ancient authorities read *all the Greeks* [h] Gk *brothers*

17.24 Isa 42.5; Acts 14.15; Mt 11.25; Acts 7.48
17.25 Ps 50.10-12; Isa 42.5; 57.16; Zech 12.1
17.26 Mal 2.10; Deut 32.8
17.27 Rom 1.20; Acts 14.17
17.28 Col 1.17; Heb 1.3
17.29 Isa 40.18ff
17.30 ver 23; Acts 14.16; Rom 3.25; Lk 24.47; Titus 2.11,12; 1 Pet 1.14
17.31 Mt 10.15; Acts 10.42; Lk 22.22; Acts 2.24
18.1 Acts 17.15; 1 Cor 1.2
18.2 Rom 16.3; 1 Cor 16.19; 2 Tim 4.19; Acts 11.28
18.3 Acts 20.34; 1 Cor 4.12; 1 Thess 2.9; 2 Thess 3.8
18.4 Acts 17.2
18.5 Acts 17.14,15; 16.9; 20.21; ver 28; Acts 17.3
18.6 Acts 13.45; 13.51; 2 Sam 1.16; Ezek 18.13; Acts 20.26; 13.46
18.7 Acts 16.14
18.8 1 Cor 1.14
18.9 Acts 23.11
18.10 Mt 28.20
18.14 Acts 23.29; 25.11,19
18.17 1 Cor 1.1
18.18 Num 6.18; Acts 21.24; Rom 16.1

18.1-17 Moving south to *Corinth*, an important commercial city on the narrow isthmus which joins the large southern peninsula of Greece to the mainland, Paul again encounters the Jews. Among them are a couple, *Priscilla and Aquila* (whose business was leather-working, like Paul's), recently come from Rome, where the whole Jewish community had been expelled by the emperor Claudius (ruled 41-54). The Roman historian Suetonius reports that the Jews in Rome were in turmoil because of one *Chrestos*, which may be a mistake for the division among the Jews in Rome that came when the message of Jesus (*Christos*) reached them. So many of the Jews in Corinth were persuaded, including the *official of the synagogue*, that Paul was forced out and set up operations in the house next door. After an effective year and a half of Paul's work, the Jewish opponents brought charges against him before the local governor, *Gallio*. This was probably about the year 49, but he exonerated Paul.
18.18-22 Before departing for Antioch-in-Syria by way of *Ephesus*, *Caesarea* (on the Palestinian coast) and *Jerusalem*, Paul took an ascetic vow resembling that of the Nazirites (Num 6), whose hair was cut as a sign of special purity. *Cenchreae*, his port of departure, was the eastern port of two that served Corinth. From Antioch he returned westward across Asia Minor, visiting regions he had previously evangelized: *Galatia and Phrygia*.

18.24-28 Before Paul's arrival in *Ephesus*, the learned *Apollos*, who had been instructed in *the way* of Christ but who needed more *accurate* information, was taught by *Priscilla and Aquila*, who had moved there from Corinth.
19.1-10 On mainland Greece (*Achaia*), Apollos proved effective in persuading Jews about Jesus, but he had not yet received *the Holy Spirit*. Through instruction from Paul, Apollos received the Spirit and spoke in *tongues* and *prophesied* as evidence of the gift. Driven out of the synagogue meeting, Paul set up operations in a hired *lecture hall*, where he was able over a period of *two years* to reach with the *word of the Lord* the entire populace of the province.
19.11-20 Unlike the magical names and formulas used by exorcists and magicians of this period, *the name of Jesus* and the power of healing linked with it are not available for use by those outside the community. The outburst of evil power terrifies the observers, with the result that many magicians destroyed their books with the secret formulas.
19.21-41 Planning to return to Jerusalem after visiting the communities in Greece, Paul's successful efforts in *Ephesus* drew many away from the worship of *Artemis*, the fertility goodess worshiped there, and caused a severe decline in business for the silversmiths who produced images of her for sale to pious vistors to her shrine, which was one of the wonders of the ancient world. The mob gathered in the theater will not allow the Jews to bring accusations against Paul, and the *town clerk* declares that any charges against him must be brought in the courts.

they asked him to stay longer, he declined;
[21]but on taking leave of them, he said, "I[i]
will return to you, if God wills." Then he
set sail from Ephesus.
22 When he had landed at Caesarea, he
went up to Jerusalem[j] and greeted the
church, and then went down to Antioch.
[23]After spending some time there he departed and went from place to place through
the region of Galatia[k] and Phrygia, strengthening all the disciples.

Ministry of Apollos

24 Now there came to Ephesus a Jew
named Apollos, a native of Alexandria. He
was an eloquent man, well-versed in the
scriptures. [25]He had been instructed in the
Way of the Lord; and he spoke with burning enthusiasm and taught accurately the
things concerning Jesus, though he knew
only the baptism of John. [26]He began to
speak boldly in the synagogue; but when
Priscilla and Aquila heard him, they took
him aside and explained the Way of God to
him more accurately. [27]And when he wished
to cross over to Achaia, the believers[l] encouraged him and wrote to the disciples to
welcome him. On his arrival he greatly
helped those who through grace had become believers, [28]for he powerfully refuted
the Jews in public, showing by the scriptures that the Messiah[m] is Jesus.

Paul in Ephesus

19 While Apollos was in Corinth, Paul
passed through the interior regions
and came to Ephesus, where he found some
disciples. [2]He said to them, "Did you receive
the Holy Spirit when you became believers?" They replied, "No, we have not even
heard that there is a Holy Spirit." [3]Then he
said, "Into what then were you baptized?"
They answered, "Into John's baptism." [4]Paul
said, "John baptized with the baptism of
repentance, telling the people to believe in
the one who was to come after him, that
is, in Jesus." [5]On hearing this, they were
baptized in the name of the Lord Jesus.
[6]When Paul had laid his hands on them,
the Holy Spirit came upon them, and they
spoke in tongues and prophesied—[7]altogether
there were about twelve of them.
8 He entered the synagogue and for three
months spoke out boldly, and argued per-
suasively about the kingdom of God. [9]When
some stubbornly refused to believe and spoke
evil of the Way before the congregation, he
left them, taking the disciples with him, and
argued daily in the lecture hall of Tyrannus.[n]
[10]This continued for two years, so that all
the residents of Asia, both Jews and Greeks,
heard the word of the Lord.

The Sons of Sceva

11 God did extraordinary miracles
through Paul, [12]so that when the handker-
chiefs or aprons that had touched his skin
were brought to the sick, their diseases left
them, and the evil spirits came out of them.
[13]Then some itinerant Jewish exorcists tried
to use the name of the Lord Jesus over those
who had evil spirits, saying, "I adjure you
by the Jesus whom Paul proclaims." [14]Seven
sons of a Jewish high priest named Sceva
were doing this. [15]But the evil spirit said to
them in reply, "Jesus I know, and Paul I
know; but who are you?" [16]Then the man
with the evil spirit leaped on them, mas-
tered them all, and so overpowered them
that they fled out of the house naked and
wounded. [17]When this became known to all
residents of Ephesus, both Jews and Greeks,
everyone was awestruck; and the name of
the Lord Jesus was praised. [18]Also many of
those who became believers confessed and
disclosed their practices. [19]A number of those
who practiced magic collected their books
and burned them publicly; when the value
of these books[o] was calculated, it was found
to come to fifty thousand silver coins. [20]So
the word of the Lord grew mightily and
prevailed.

The Riot in Ephesus

21 Now after these things had been
accomplished, Paul resolved in the Spirit to
go through Macedonia and Achaia, and
then to go on to Jerusalem. He said,"After
I have gone there, I must also see Rome."
[22]So he sent two of his helpers, Timothy and
Erastus, to Macedonia, while he himself
stayed for some time longer in Asia.
23 About that time no little disturbance
broke out concerning the Way. [24]A man

[i] Other ancient authorities read *I must at all costs keep the approaching festival in Jerusalem, but I* [j] Gk *went up* [k] Gk *the Galatian region* [l] Gk *brothers* [m] Or *the Christ* [n] Other ancient authorities read *of a certain Tyrannus, from eleven o'clock in the morning to four in the afternoon* [o] Gk *them*

18.21 1 Cor 4.19
18.22 Acts 11.19
18.23 Acts 16.6; 14.22; 15.32,41
18.24 Acts 19.1; 1 Cor 1.12; 3.5,6; 4.6; Titus 3.13
18.25 Rom 12.11; Acts 19.3
18.27 ver 12,18
18.28 Acts 9.22; 17.3; ver 5
19.1 1 Cor 1.12; 3.5,6; Acts 18.1,19-24
19.3 Acts 18.25
19.4 Mt 3.11; Acts 13.24,25
19.6 Acts 6.6; 8.17; 2.4; 10.46
19.8 Acts 17.2; 18.4; 1.3; 28.23
19.9 Acts 14.4; 2 Tim 1.15; Acts 9.2; ver 30
19.10 Acts 20.31; ver 22,26,27; Acts 13.12
19.11 Acts 8.13
19.12 Acts 5.15
19.13 Mt 12.27; Mk 9.38; Lk 9.49
19.17 Acts 2.43; 5.5,11
19.20 Acts 6.7; 12.24
19.21 Rom 15.24-28
19.22 Acts 13.5; Rom 16.23; 2 Tim 4.20; ver 10
19.23 ver 9
19.24 Acts 16.16,19

named Demetrius, a silversmith who made silver shrines of Artemis, brought no little business to the artisans. [25]These he gathered together, with the workers of the same trade, and said, "Men, you know that we get our wealth from this business. [26]You also see and hear that not only in Ephesus but in almost the whole of Asia this Paul has persuaded and drawn away a considerable number of people by saying that gods made with hands are not gods. [27]And there is danger not only that this trade of ours may come into disrepute but also that the temple of the great goddess Artemis will be scorned, and she will be deprived of her majesty that brought all Asia and the world to worship her."

28 When they heard this, they were enraged and shouted, "Great is Artemis of the Ephesians!" [29]The city was filled with the confusion; and people[p] rushed together to the theater, dragging with them Gaius and Aristarchus, Macedonians who were Paul's travel companions. [30]Paul wished to go into the crowd, but the disciples would not let him; [31]even some officials of the province of Asia,[q] who were friendly to him, sent him a message urging him not to venture into the theater. [32]Meanwhile, some were shouting one thing, some another; for the assembly was in confusion, and most of them did not know why they had come together. [33]Some of the crowd gave instructions to Alexander, whom the Jews had pushed forward. And Alexander motioned for silence and tried to make a defense before the people. [34]But when they recognized that he was a Jew, for about two hours all of them shouted in unison, "Great is Artemis of the Ephesians!" [35]But when the town clerk had quieted the crowd, he said,"Citizens of Ephesus, who is there that does not know that the city of the Ephesians is the temple keeper of the great Artemis and of the statue that fell from heaven?[r] [36]Since these things cannot be denied, you ought to be quiet and do nothing rash. [37]You have brought these men here who are neither temple robbers nor blasphemers of our[s] goddess. [38]If therefore Demetrius and the artisans with him have a complaint against anyone, the courts are open, and there are proconsuls; let them bring charges there against one another. [39]If there is anything further[t] you want to know, it must be settled in the regular assembly. [40]For we are in danger of being charged with rioting today, since there is no cause that we can give to justify this commotion." [41]When he had said this, he dismissed the assembly.

Paul Goes to Macedonia and Greece

20 After the uproar had ceased, Paul sent for the disciples; and after encouraging them and saying farewell, he left for Macedonia. [2]When he had gone through those regions and had given the believers[u] much encouragement, he came to Greece, [3]where he stayed for three months. He was about to set sail for Syria when a plot was made against him by the Jews, and so he decided to return through Macedonia. [4]He was accompanied by Sopater son of Pyrrhus from Beroea, by Aristarchus and Secundus from Thessalonica, by Gaius from Derbe, and by Timothy, as well as by Tychicus and Trophimus from Asia. [5]They went ahead and were waiting for us in Troas; [6]but we sailed from Philippi after the days of Unleavened Bread, and in five days we joined them in Troas, where we stayed for seven days.

Paul's Farewell Visit to Troas

7 On the first day of the week, when we met to break bread, Paul was holding a discussion with them; since he intended to leave the next day, he continued speaking until midnight. [8]There were many lamps in the room upstairs where we were meeting. [9]A young man named Eutychus, who was sitting in the window, began to sink off into a deep sleep while Paul talked still longer. Overcome by sleep, he fell to the ground three floors below and was picked up dead. [10]But Paul went down, and bending over him took him in his arms, and said, "Do not be alarmed, for his life is in him." [11]Then Paul went upstairs, and after he had broken bread and eaten, he continued to converse with them until dawn; then he left. [12]Meanwhile they had taken the boy away alive and were not a little comforted.

The Voyage from Troas to Miletus

13 We went ahead to the ship and set sail for Assos, intending to take Paul on

19.26 Ps 115.4; Isa 44.10-20; Jer 10.3; Acts 17.29

19.28 Acts 18.19

19.29 Rom 16.23; 1 Cor 1.4; Acts 20.4; 27.2; Col 4.10; Philem 24

19.32 Acts 21.34

19.33 1 Tim 1.20; 2 Tim 4.14; Acts 12.17

19.35 Acts 18.19

19.37 Rom 2.22

19.38 Acts 13.7

20.1 Acts 11.26; 1 Cor 16.5; 1 Tim 1.3

20.3 ver 19; Acts 23.12; 25.3; 2 Cor 11.26

20.4 Acts 19.29; 27.2; 16.1; Eph 6.21; Col 4.7; 2 Tim 4.12; Titus 3.12; Acts 21.29; 2 Tim 4.20

20.6 Acts 16.8; 2 Cor 2.12; 2 Tim 4.13

20.7 1 Cor 16.2; Rev 1.10

20.10 1 Kings 17.21; Mt 9.23,24

20.1-16 Paul revisits the churches in Macedonia and Greece, including a stay at *Troas*, where his protracted speech during the night puts a young man to sleep (his name, *Eutychus*, ironically means *good luck*); Eutychus falls out of a window to his death. Paul restores him to life, and moves on down the coast of Asia Minor to *Miletus*, a port city not far from Ephesus. On *Pentecost*, see notes on Acts 2.

[p] Gk *they* [q] Gk *some of the Asiarchs* [r] Meaning of Gk uncertain [s] Other ancient authorities read *your* [t] Other ancient authorities read *about other matters* [u] Gk *given them*

20.17-38 Paul's farewell to the Ephesian elders serves as a concluding address of the apostle to all the readers of Acts. He reviews his audacity in *proclaiming the message* of Jesus throughout the whole region, and declares that he is aware of the perils that face him on his return to Jerusalem. He indicates that he is willing to die in the process of completing his mission. The elders (whom he describes as *overseers – episkopoi*, often translated *bishops*) are to watch over *the flock* in their charge. He reminds them that he has supported himself financially, and quotes an otherwise unknown saying of Jesus. The elders realize that they will not see Paul again.

21.1-28.31 The Outreach to Rome, Center of the Gentile World.

21.1-16 Passing between the coasts of Asia Minor and the islands of the sea, Paul reached *Tyre* and then *Caesarea*, in both of which cities he visited the communities of believers, and was warned through *the Spirit* of the difficulties he would experience in Jerusalem. His response was to indicate his readiness to die there *for the name of the Lord Jesus*.

board there; for he had made this arrangement, intending to go by land himself. [14]When he met us in Assos, we took him on board and went to Mitylene. [15]We sailed from there, and on the following day we arrived opposite Chios. The next day we touched at Samos, and[v] the day after that we came to Miletus. [16]For Paul had decided to sail past Ephesus, so that he might not have to spend time in Asia; he was eager to be in Jerusalem, if possible, on the day of Pentecost.

Paul Speaks to the Ephesian Elders

17 From Miletus he sent a message to Ephesus, asking the elders of the church to meet him. [18]When they came to him, he said to them:

"You yourselves know how I lived among you the entire time from the first day that I set foot in Asia, [19]serving the Lord with all humility and with tears, enduring the trials that came to me through the plots of the Jews. [20]I did not shrink from doing anything helpful, proclaiming the message to you and teaching you publicly and from house to house, [21]as I testified to both Jews and Greeks about repentance toward God and faith toward our Lord Jesus. [22]And now, as a captive to the Spirit,[w] I am on my way to Jerusalem, not knowing what will happen to me there, [23]except that the Holy Spirit testifies to me in every city that imprisonment and persecutions are waiting for me. [24]But I do not count my life of any value to myself, if only I may finish my course and the ministry that I received from the Lord Jesus, to testify to the good news of God's grace.

25 "And now I know that none of you, among whom I have gone about proclaiming the kingdom, will ever see my face again. [26]Therefore I declare to you this day that I am not responsible for the blood of any of you, [27]for I did not shrink from declaring to you the whole purpose of God. [28]Keep watch over yourselves and over all the flock, of which the Holy Spirit has made you overseers, to shepherd the church of God[x] that he obtained with the blood of his own Son.[y] [29]I know that after I have gone, savage wolves will come in among you, not sparing the flock. [30]Some even from your own group will come distorting the truth in order to entice the disciples to follow them. [31]Therefore be alert, remembering that for three years I did not cease night or day to warn everyone with tears. [32]And now I commend you to God and to the message of his grace, a message that is able to build you up and to give you the inheritance among all who are sanctified. [33]I coveted no one's silver or gold or clothing. [34]You know for yourselves that I worked with my own hands to support myself and my companions. [35]In all this I have given you an example that by such work we must support the weak, remembering the words of the Lord Jesus, for he himself said, 'It is more blessed to give than to receive.'"

36 When he had finished speaking, he knelt down with them all and prayed. [37]There was much weeping among them all; they embraced Paul and kissed him, [38]grieving especially because of what he had said, that they would not see him again. Then they brought him to the ship.

Paul's Journey to Jerusalem

21 When we had parted from them and set sail, we came by a straight course to Cos, and the next day to Rhodes, and from there to Patara.[z] [2]When we found a ship bound for Phoenicia, we went on board and set sail. [3]We came in sight of Cyprus; and leaving it on our left, we sailed to Syria and landed at Tyre, because the ship was to unload its cargo there. [4]We looked up the disciples and stayed there for seven days. Through the Spirit they told Paul not to go on to Jerusalem. [5]When our days there were ended, we left and proceeded on our journey; and all of them, with wives and children, escorted us outside the city. There we knelt down on the beach and prayed [6]and said farewell to one another. Then we went on board the ship, and they returned home.

7 When we had finished[a] the voyage from Tyre, we arrived at Ptolemais; and we greeted the believers[b] and stayed with them for one day. [8]The next day we left and came to Caesarea; and we went into the house of Philip the evangelist, one of the seven, and stayed with him. [9]He had four unmarried daughters[c] who had the gift of prophecy.

[v] Other ancient authorities add *after remaining at Trogyllium* [w] Or *And now, bound in the spirit* [x] Other ancient authorities read *of the Lord* [y] Or *with his own blood*; Gk *with the blood of his Own* [z] Other ancient authorities add *and Myra* [a] Or *continued* [b] Gk *brothers* [c] Gk *four daughters, virgins,*

20.16 Acts 18.19; 21.4,12; 19.21; 2.1; 1 Cor 16.8
20.17 Acts 11.30
20.18 Acts 18.19; 19.1,10
20.20 ver 27
20.21 Acts 18.5; 2.38; 24.24; 26.18
20.22 ver 16
20.23 Acts 21.4,11
20.24 Acts 21.13; 2 Cor 4.16; Acts 1.17; 2 Cor 4.1; Gal 1.1; Titus 1.3
20.25 ver 38
20.26 Acts 18.6; 2 Cor 7.2
20.27 ver 20; Acts 13.36
20.28 1 Tim 4.16; 1 Pet 5.2; 1 Cor 12.28; 1 Pet 1.19; 20.29; Mt 7.15
20.31 Acts 19.10
20.32 Acts 14.23; 9.31; 26.18; Eph 1.18; Col 1.12; 3.24; 1 Pet 1.4
20.33 1 Cor 9.12; 2 Cor 7.2; 11.9; 12.17
20.34 Acts 18.3
20.35 Rom 15.1
20.36 Acts 9.40; 21.5
20.37 Gen 45.14
20.38 ver 25; Acts 15.3
21.2 Acts 11.19
21.4 ver 11; Acts 20.23
21.5 Acts 20.36
21.7 Acts 12.20; 1.15
21.8 Eph 4.11; 2 Tim 4.5; Acts 6.5; 8.26,40
21.9 Acts 2.17; Lk 2.36

21.10 Acts 11.28 [10]While we were staying there for several
days, a prophet named Agabus came down
21.11 ver 33; Acts 20.23 from Judea. [11]He came to us and took Paul's
belt, bound his own feet and hands with
it, and said, "Thus says the Holy Spirit,
'This is the way the Jews in Jerusalem will
21.13 Acts 20.24 bind the man who owns this belt and will
hand him over to the Gentiles.'" [12]When we
21.14 Mt 26.42; Lk 22.42 heard this, we and the people there urged
him not to go up to Jerusalem. [13]Then Paul
answered, "What are you doing, weeping
21.16 ver 3.4 and breaking my heart? For I am ready not
only to be bound but even to die in Jeru-
21.17 Acts 15.4 salem for the name of the Lord Jesus."
[14]Since he would not be persuaded, we
remained silent except to say, "The Lord's
21.18 Acts 12.17; 15.13 will be done."
15 After these days we got ready and
started to go up to Jerusalem. [16]Some of the
21.19 Acts 14.27; 1.17; 20.24 disciples from Caesarea also came along and
brought us to the house of Mnason of
Cyprus, an early disciple, with whom we
21.20 Acts 22.3; Rom 10.2; Gal 1.14 were to stay.

Paul Visits James at Jerusalem

21.23 Acts 18.18 17 When we arrived in Jerusalem, the
brothers welcomed us warmly. [18]The next
day Paul went with us to visit James; and
21.24 ver 26; Acts 24.18 all the elders were present. [19]After greeting
them, he related one by one the things that
God had done among the Gentiles through
21.25 Acts 15.20,29 his ministry. [20]When they heard it, they
praised God. Then they said to him,"You
see, brother, how many thousands of be-
21.26 Num 6.13; Acts 24.18 lievers there are among the Jews, and they
are all zealous for the law. [21]They have been
told about you that you teach all the Jews
21.27 Acts 24.18; 26.21 living among the Gentiles to forsake Moses,
and that you tell them not to circumcise
their children or observe the customs. [22]What
then is to be done? They will certainly hear
21.28 Acts 24.5,6 that you have come. [23]So do what we tell
you. We have four men who are under a
21.29 Acts 20.4; 18.19 vow. [24]Join these men, go through the rite
of purification with them, and pay for the
shaving of their heads. Thus all will know
21.30 Acts 26.21; 16.19 that there is nothing in what they have
been told about you, but that you yourself
observe and guard the law. [25]But as for the
21.32 Acts 23.27 Gentiles who have become believers, we
have sent a letter with our judgment that
they should abstain from what has been
21.33 Acts 20.23; ver 11 sacrificed to idols and from blood and from
what is strangled[d] and from fornication."
[26]Then Paul took the men, and the next
day, having purified himself, he entered the
temple with them, making public the completion of the days of purification when the
sacrifice would be made for each of them.

Paul Arrested in the Temple

27 When the seven days were almost
completed, the Jews from Asia, who had
seen him in the temple, stirred up the whole
crowd. They seized him, [28]shouting, "Fellow
Israelites, help! This is the man who is
teaching everyone everywhere against our
people, our law, and this place; more than
that, he has actually brought Greeks into
the temple and has defiled this holy place."
[29]For they had previously seen Trophimus
the Ephesian with him in the city, and they
supposed that Paul had brought him into
the temple. [30]Then all the city was aroused,
and the people rushed together. They seized
Paul and dragged him out of the temple,
and immediately the doors were shut. [31]While
they were trying to kill him, word came to
the tribune of the cohort that all Jerusalem
was in an uproar. [32]Immediately he took
soldiers and centurions and ran down to
them. When they saw the tribune and the
soldiers, they stopped beating Paul. [33]Then
the tribune came, arrested him, and ordered
him to be bound with two chains; he inquired who he was and what he had done.
[34]Some in the crowd shouted one thing,
some another; and as he could not learn the
facts because of the uproar, he ordered him
to be brought into the barracks. [35]When
Paul[e] came to the steps, the violence of the
mob was so great that he had to be carried
by the soldiers. [36]The crowd that followed
kept shouting, "Away with him!"

Paul Defends Himself

37 Just as Paul was about to be brought
into the barracks, he said to the tribune,
"May I say something to you?" The tribune[f]
replied, "Do you know Greek? [38]Then you
are not the Egyptian who recently stirred
up a revolt and led the four thousand as-
sassins out into the wilderness?" [39]Paul
replied, "I am a Jew, from Tarsus in Cilicia,
a citizen of an important city; I beg you, let
me speak to the people." [40]When he had
given him permission, Paul stood on the
steps and motioned to the people for silence;
and when there was a great hush, he

21.34 Acts 19.32; ver 37

21.36 Lk 23.18; Jn 19.15; Acts 22.22

21.38 Acts 5.36; Mt 24.26

21.39 Acts 9.11; 22.3

21.40 Acts 12.17; 22.2; 26.14

[d] Other ancient authorities lack *and from what is strangled* [e] Gk *he* [f] Gk *He*

21.17-26 In Jerusalem Paul agreed to the suggestion that he counter the attack on him by Jewish leaders, that he was subverting their traditions, by participating with a group of men in a Nazirite-like *rite of purification* (Num 8) similar to that reported in Acts 18.18. The freedom of Gentile converts from obligation to fulfill all but the minimal requirements of the Jewish law (Acts 15.23-29) is reaffirmed, however.
21.27-36 Paul is seized in the temple courts and charged with defiling the place by allowing Gentiles to enter. He is saved from being beaten to death through the intervention of *the tribune*, a local Roman military official in charge of one thousand soldiers.
21.37-22.29 Once Paul is differentiated from a revolutionary reportedly active in the region, he is permitted to offer his defense, speaking in Greek, in the presence of the tribune but also in the hearing of the local crowd. He emphasizes his Jewish origins and training, and describes his conversion and acceptance by the community of believers in Damascus, and his commissioning by Jesus to launch a mission to *the Gentiles*. When he is about to be beaten by the Roman authorities in an effort to determine what his crime is, he calls attention to his Roman citizenship and is turned over to the local *council*, consisting of the religious leaders, since the charge against him concerns Jewish, not Roman, law.

22.30-23.10 The members of the council treat Paul unjustly and then are divided when he brings into the discussion his belief in the future *resurrection*, which the Pharisees expected but others rejected. The ensuing split within the Jewish leadership group leads to chaos, from which Paul is rescued by the *tribune*.

addressed them in the Hebrew[g] language,
saying:
22 "Brothers and fathers, listen to
the defense that I now make before you."
2 When they heard him addressing them
in Hebrew,[g] they became even more quiet.
Then he said:
3 "I am a Jew, born in Tarsus in Cilicia,
but brought up in this city at the feet of
Gamaliel, educated strictly according to our
ancestral law, being zealous for God, just as
all of you are today. 4I persecuted this Way
up to the point of death by binding both
men and women and putting them in prison,
5as the high priest and the whole council
of elders can testify about me. From them
I also received letters to the brothers in
Damascus, and I went there in order to bind
those who were there and to bring them
back to Jerusalem for punishment.

Paul Tells of His Conversion

6 "While I was on my way and approaching Damascus, about noon a great
light from heaven suddenly shone about
me. 7I fell to the ground and heard a voice
saying to me, 'Saul, Saul, why are you
persecuting me?' 8I answered, 'Who are
you, Lord?' Then he said to me, 'I am Jesus
of Nazareth[h] whom you are persecuting.'
9Now those who were with me saw the
light but did not hear the voice of the one
who was speaking to me. 10I asked, 'What
am I to do, Lord?' The Lord said to me, 'Get
up and go to Damascus; there you will be
told everything that has been assigned to
you to do.' 11Since I could not see because
of the brightness of that light, those who
were with me took my hand and led me to
Damascus.
12 "A certain Ananias, who was a devout man according to the law and well
spoken of by all the Jews living there, 13came
to me; and standing beside me, he said,
'Brother Saul, regain your sight!' In that
very hour I regained my sight and saw him.
14Then he said, 'The God of our ancestors
has chosen you to know his will, to see the
Righteous One and to hear his own voice;
15for you will be his witness to all the world
of what you have seen and heard. 16And
now why do you delay? Get up, be baptized,
and have your sins washed away, calling
on his name.'

Paul Sent to the Gentiles

17 "After I had returned to Jerusalem
and while I was praying in the temple, I fell
into a trance 18and saw Jesus[i] saying to me,
'Hurry and get out of Jerusalem quickly,
because they will not accept your testimony
about me.' 19And I said, 'Lord, they themselves know that in every synagogue I
imprisoned and beat those who believed in
you. 20And while the blood of your witness
Stephen was shed, I myself was standing
by, approving and keeping the coats of
those who killed him.' 21Then he said to me,
'Go, for I will send you far away to the
Gentiles.' "

Paul and the Roman Tribune

22 Up to this point they listened to him,
but then they shouted,"Away with such a
fellow from the earth! For he should not be
allowed to live." 23And while they were
shouting, throwing off their cloaks, and
tossing dust into the air, 24the tribune directed that he was to be brought into the
barracks, and ordered him to be examined
by flogging, to find out the reason for this
outcry against him. 25But when they had
tied him up with thongs,[j] Paul said to the
centurion who was standing by, "Is it legal
for you to flog a Roman citizen who is
uncondemned?" 26When the centurion heard
that, he went to the tribune and said to
him, "What are you about to do? This man
is a Roman citizen." 27The tribune came
and asked Paul,[i] "Tell me, are you a Roman
citizen?" And he said,. "Yes." 28The tribune
answered, "It cost me a large sum of money
to get my citizenship." Paul said, "But I was
born a citizen." 29Immediately those who
were about to examine him drew back from
him; and the tribune also was afraid, for he
realized that Paul was a Roman citizen and
that he had bound him.

Paul before the Council

30 Since he wanted to find out what
Paul[k] was being accused of by the Jews, the
next day he released him and ordered the
chief priests and the entire council to meet.
He brought Paul down and had him stand
before them.
23 While Paul was looking intently at
the council he said,"Brothers,[l] up
to this day I have lived my life with a clear

[g] That is, *Aramaic* [h] Gk *the Nazorean* [i] Gk *him* [j] Or *up for the lashes* [k] Gk *he* [l] Gk *Men, brothers*

22.1 Acts 7.2
22.2 Acts 21.40
22.3 Acts 21.39; 20.4; Deut 33.3; 2 Kings 4.37,38; Lk 10.39; Acts 26.5; 21.20
22.4 Acts 8.3; 26.9-11; Phil 3.6; 1 Tim 1.13
22.5 Lk 22.66; Acts 4.5; 9.2; 26.10,12
22.6 Acts 9.3; 26.12,13
22.9 Acts 9.7; 26.13
22.10 Acts 16.30
22.11 Acts 9.8
22.12 Acts 9.17; 10.22
22.14 Acts 3.13; 5.30; 9.15; 26.16; 1 Cor 9.1; 15.8; Acts 7.52
22.15 Acts 23.11; 26.16
22.16 Acts 2.38; Heb 10.22; Acts 9.14; Rom 10.13
22.17 Acts 9.26; 10.10
22.19 ver 4; Acts 8.3; 26.11; Mt 10.17
22.20 Lk 11.48; Acts 8.1; Rom 1.32
22.21 Acts 9.15
22.23 Acts 7.58; 2 Sam 16.13
22.25 Acts 16.37
22.30 Acts 23.28; 21.33
23.1 Acts 22.30; 24.16; 2 Cor 1.12; 2 Tim 1.3

conscience before God." [2]Then the high priest Ananias ordered those standing near him to strike him on the mouth. [3]At this Paul said to him, "God will strike you, you whitewashed wall! Are you sitting there to judge me according to the law, and yet in violation of the law you order me to be struck?" [4]Those standing nearby said, "Do you dare to insult God's high priest?" [5]And Paul said, "I did not realize, brothers, that he was high priest; for it is written, 'You shall not speak evil of a leader of your people.'"

6 When Paul noticed that some were Sadducees and others were Pharisees, he called out in the council, "Brothers, I am a Pharisee, a son of Pharisees. I am on trial concerning the hope of the resurrection[m] of the dead." [7]When he said this, a dissension began between the Pharisees and the Sadducees, and the assembly was divided. [8](The Sadducees say that there is no resurrection, or angel, or spirit; but the Pharisees acknowledge all three.) [9]Then a great clamor arose, and certain scribes of the Pharisees' group stood up and contended, "We find nothing wrong with this man. What if a spirit or an angel has spoken to him?" [10]When the dissension became violent, the tribune, fearing that they would tear Paul to pieces, ordered the soldiers to go down, take him by force, and bring him into the barracks.

11 That night the Lord stood near him and said, "Keep up your courage! For just as you have testified for me in Jerusalem, so you must bear witness also in Rome."

The Plot to Kill Paul

12 In the morning the Jews joined in a conspiracy and bound themselves by an oath neither to eat nor drink until they had killed Paul. [13]There were more than forty who joined in this conspiracy. [14]They went to the chief priests and elders and said, "We have strictly bound ourselves by an oath to taste no food until we have killed Paul. [15]Now then, you and the council must notify the tribune to bring him down to you, on the pretext that you want to make a more thorough examination of his case. And we are ready to do away with him before he arrives."

16 Now the son of Paul's sister heard about the ambush; so he went and gained entrance to the barracks and told Paul. [17]Paul called one of the centurions and said, "Take this young man to the tribune, for he has something to report to him." [18]So he took him, brought him to the tribune, and said, "The prisoner Paul called me and asked me to bring this young man to you; he has something to tell you." [19]The tribune took him by the hand, drew him aside privately, and asked, "What is it that you have to report to me?" [20]He answered, "The Jews have agreed to ask you to bring Paul down to the council tomorrow, as though they were going to inquire more thoroughly into his case. [21]But do not be persuaded by them, for more than forty of their men are lying in ambush for him. They have bound themselves by an oath neither to eat nor drink until they kill him. They are ready now and are waiting for your consent." [22]So the tribune dismissed the young man, ordering him, "Tell no one that you have informed me of this."

Paul Sent to Felix the Governor

23 Then he summoned two of the centurions and said, "Get ready to leave by nine o'clock tonight for Caesarea with two hundred soldiers, seventy horsemen, and two hundred spearmen. [24]Also provide mounts for Paul to ride, and take him safely to Felix the governor." [25]He wrote a letter to this effect:

26 "Claudius Lysias to his Excellency the governor Felix, greetings. [27]This man was seized by the Jews and was about to be killed by them, but when I had learned that he was a Roman citizen, I came with the guard and rescued him. [28]Since I wanted to know the charge for which they accused him, I had him brought to their council. [29]I found that he was accused concerning questions of their law, but was charged with nothing deserving death or imprisonment. [30]When I was informed that there would be a plot against the man, I sent him to you at once, ordering his accusers also to state before you what they have against him.[n]"

31 So the soldiers, according to their instructions, took Paul and brought him during the night to Antipatris. [32]The next day they let the horsemen go on with him, while they returned to the barracks. [33]When they came to Caesarea and delivered the letter to the governor, they presented Paul

[m] Gk *concerning hope and resurrection* [n] Other ancient authorities add *Farewell*

23.2 Jn 18.22
23.3 Mt 23.17; Lev 19.35; Deut 25.1,2; Jn 7.51
23.5 Ex 22.28
23.6 Acts 26.5; Phil 3.5; Acts 24.15,16; 26.8
23.8 Mt 22.23; Mk 12.18; Lk 20.27
23.9 Acts 25.25; 26.31; 22.7,17,18
23.10 Acts 21.34
23.11 Acts 18.9; 19.21; 28.23
23.12 ver 21,30; Acts 25.3
23.14 ver 21
23.15 Acts 22.30
23.16 Acts 21.34; ver 10
23.18 Eph 3.1
23.20 ver 14,15
23.21 ver 12,14
23.23 ver 33
23.24 Acts 24.1,3,10; 25.14
23.26 Acts 24.3; 15.23
23.27 Acts 21.32,33; 22.25-29
23.28 Acts 22.30
23.29 Acts 18.15; 25.19; 26.31
23.30 ver 20,21; Acts 24.19; 25.16
23.32 ver 23
23.33 ver 23,24,26

23.11-22 Learning of a plot by the Jewish leaders to kill Paul when he is brought back again before the *council*, the tribune decides to shift Paul to the jurisdiction of another Roman official at the provincial capital of *Caesarea*.

23.23-34 In his message to the Roman governor, *Felix*, the tribune indicates his opinion that Paul is innocent. Arriving in Caesarea under the protection of the Roman soldiers, Paul is asked the place of his origin, which is the district of *Cilicia*, within the larger province of Syria (including Palestine), over which Felix the governor has authority. A hearing is promised. Ironically, the place where Paul is guarded from attack is in the *headquarters* of Herod Agrippa, the puppet ruler with mixed Jewish ancestry.

24.1-9 At the hearing, the Jewish authorities charge Paul with troublemaking, with leadership of a renegade sect (*the Nazarenes* could derive from Nazareth, the insignificant home-town of Jesus, or from the Nazirite tradition of dedicating someone to God from birth, such as Samson; Judg 13.2-9), and with having profaned the temple.
24.10-27 Paul's defense again emphasizes his fidelity to Jewish traditions, including his belief in the resurrection and his recent participation in the purification rite. Felix defers a decision, pending the arrival of *Lysias the tribune*, and Paul is again placed under protective custody. In private conversation with Paul, Felix is so intrigued by his message (which includes the commonplaces of Stoic philosophy: justice, self-control, coming judgment) and so eager to receive a bribe for his release that he keeps talking with him over a period of *two years*.
25.1-12 Felix's replacement as governor, *Festus*, insists on keeping Paul in his own seat of authority, Caesarea. During the interrogation, Paul denies any violation of Jewish or Roman law and exercises his right as a Roman citizen to have his case heard by the emperor himself. His request is granted by Festus.

also before him. 34 On reading the letter, he asked what province he belonged to, and when he learned that he was from Cilicia, 35 he said, "I will give you a hearing when your accusers arrive." Then he ordered that he be kept under guard in Herod's headquarters.[o]

Paul before Felix at Caesarea

24 Five days later the high priest Ananias came down with some elders and an attorney, a certain Tertullus, and they reported their case against Paul to the governor. 2 When Paul[p] had been summoned, Tertullus began to accuse him, saying:

"Your Excellency,[q] because of you we have long enjoyed peace, and reforms have been made for this people because of your foresight. 3 We welcome this in every way and everywhere with utmost gratitude. 4 But, to detain you no further, I beg you to hear us briefly with your customary graciousness. 5 We have, in fact, found this man a pestilent fellow, an agitator among all the Jews throughout the world, and a ringleader of the sect of the Nazarenes.[r] 6 He even tried to profane the temple, and so we seized him.[s] 8 By examining him yourself you will be able to learn from him concerning everything of which we accuse him."

9 The Jews also joined in the charge by asserting that all this was true.

Paul's Defense before Felix

10 When the governor motioned to him to speak, Paul replied:

"I cheerfully make my defense, knowing that for many years you have been a judge over this nation. 11 As you can find out, it is not more than twelve days since I went up to worship in Jerusalem. 12 They did not find me disputing with anyone in the temple or stirring up a crowd either in the synagogues or throughout the city. 13 Neither can they prove to you the charge that they now bring against me. 14 But this I admit to you, that according to the Way, which they call a sect, I worship the God of our ancestors, believing everything laid down according to the law or written in the prophets. 15 I have a hope in God—a hope that they themselves also accept—that there will be a resurrection of both[t] the righteous and the unrighteous. 16 Therefore I do my best always to have a clear conscience toward God and all people. 17 Now after some years I came to bring alms to my nation and to offer sacrifices. 18 While I was doing this, they found me in the temple, completing the rite of purification, without any crowd or disturbance. 19 But there were some Jews from Asia—they ought to be here before you to make an accusation, if they have anything against me. 20 Or let these men here tell what crime they had found when I stood before the council, 21 unless it was this one sentence that I called out while standing before them, 'It is about the resurrection of the dead that I am on trial before you today.'"

22 But Felix, who was rather well informed about the Way, adjourned the hearing with the comment, "When Lysias the tribune comes down, I will decide your case." 23 Then he ordered the centurion to keep him in custody, but to let him have some liberty and not to prevent any of his friends from taking care of his needs.

Paul Held in Custody

24 Some days later when Felix came with his wife Drusilla, who was Jewish, he sent for Paul and heard him speak concerning faith in Christ Jesus. 25 And as he discussed justice, self-control, and the coming judgment, Felix became frightened and said, "Go away for the present; when I have an opportunity, I will send for you." 26 At the same time he hoped that money would be given him by Paul, and for that reason he used to send for him very often and converse with him.

27 After two years had passed, Felix was succeeded by Porcius Festus; and since he wanted to grant the Jews a favor, Felix left Paul in prison.

Paul Appeals to the Emperor

25 Three days after Festus had arrived in the province, he went up from Caesarea to Jerusalem 2 where the chief

[o] Gk *praetorium* [p] Gk *he* [q] Gk lacks *Your Excellency* [r] Gk *Nazoreans* [s] Other ancient authorities add *and we would have judged him according to our law. 7 But the chief captain Lysias came and with great violence took him out of our hands, 8 commanding his accusers to come before you.* [t] Other ancient authorities read *of the dead, both of*

23.34 Acts 21.39
23.35 Acts 24.19; 25.16; 24.27
24.1 Acts 23.2,30,35
24.3 Acts 23.26; 26.25
24.5 Acts 16.20; 17.6; 21.28
24.6 Acts 21.28
24.9 1 Thess 2.16
24.10 Acts 23.24
24.11 Acts 21.26
24.12 Acts 25.8; 28.17
24.13 Acts 25.7
24.14 Acts 9.2; ver 5; Acts 3.13; 26.22; 28.23
24.15 Acts 23.6; 28.20; Dan 12.2; Jn 5.28,29
24.16 Acts 23.1
24.17 Acts 11.29,30; Rom 15.25-28; 2 Cor 8.1-4; Gal 2.10
24.18 Acts 21.26,27
24.19 Acts 23.30
24.21 Acts 23.6
24.23 Acts 23.35; 28.16; 23.16; 27.3
24.25 Gal 5.23; Acts 10.42
24.27 Acts 25.1,4,9,14; 12.3; 23.35
25.2 Acts 24.1; ver 15

priests and the leaders of the Jews gave him a report against Paul. They appealed to him [3]and requested, as a favor to them against Paul,[u] to have him transferred to Jerusalem. They were, in fact, planning an ambush to kill him along the way. [4]Festus replied that Paul was being kept at Caesarea, and that he himself intended to go there shortly. [5]"So," he said, "let those of you who have the authority come down with me, and if there is anything wrong about the man, let them accuse him."

6 After he had stayed among them not more than eight or ten days, he went down to Caesarea; the next day he took his seat on the tribunal and ordered Paul to be brought. [7]When he arrived, the Jews who had gone down from Jerusalem surrounded him, bringing many serious charges against him, which they could not prove. [8]Paul said in his defense, "I have in no way committed an offense against the law of the Jews, or against the temple, or against the emperor." [9]But Festus, wishing to do the Jews a favor, asked Paul, "Do you wish to go up to Jerusalem and be tried there before me on these charges?" [10]Paul said, "I am appealing to the emperor's tribunal; this is where I should be tried. I have done no wrong to the Jews, as you very well know. [11]Now if I am in the wrong and have committed something for which I deserve to die, I am not trying to escape death; but if there is nothing to their charges against me, no one can turn me over to them. I appeal to the emperor." [12]Then Festus, after he had conferred with his council, replied,"You have appealed to the emperor; to the emperor you will go."

Festus Consults King Agrippa

13 After several days had passed, King Agrippa and Bernice arrived at Caesarea to welcome Festus. [14]Since they were staying there several days, Festus laid Paul's case before the king, saying, "There is a man here who was left in prison by Felix. [15]When I was in Jerusalem, the chief priests and the elders of the Jews informed me about him and asked for a sentence against him. [16]I told them that it was not the custom of the Romans to hand over anyone before the accused had met the accusers face to face and had been given an opportunity to make a defense against the charge. [17]So when they met here, I lost no time, but on the next day took my seat on the tribunal and ordered the man to be brought. [18]When the accusers stood up, they did not charge him with any of the crimes[v] that I was expecting. [19]Instead they had certain points of disagreement with him about their own religion and about a certain Jesus, who had died, but whom Paul asserted to be alive. [20]Since I was at a loss how to investigate these questions, I asked whether he wished to go to Jerusalem and be tried there on these charges.[w] [21]But when Paul had appealed to be kept in custody for the decision of his Imperial Majesty, I ordered him to be held until I could send him to the emperor." [22]Agrippa said to Festus, "I would like to hear the man myself.""Tomorrow," he said, "you will hear him."

Paul Brought before Agrippa

23 So on the next day Agrippa and Bernice came with great pomp, and they entered the audience hall with the military tribunes and the prominent men of the city. Then Festus gave the order and Paul was brought in. [24]And Festus said, "King Agrippa and all here present with us, you see this man about whom the whole Jewish community petitioned me, both in Jerusalem and here, shouting that he ought not to live any longer. [25]But I found that he had done nothing deserving death; and when he appealed to his Imperial Majesty, I decided to send him. [26]But I have nothing definite to write to our sovereign about him. Therefore I have brought him before all of you, and especially before you, King Agrippa, so that, after we have examined him, I may have something to write— [27]for it seems to me unreasonable to send a prisoner without indicating the charges against him."

Paul Defends Himself before Agrippa

26 Agrippa said to Paul, "You have permission to speak for yourself." Then Paul stretched out his hand and began to defend himself:

2 "I consider myself fortunate that it is before you, King Agrippa, I am to make my defense today against all the accusations of the Jews, [3]because you are especially familiar with all the customs and controversies of the Jews; therefore I beg of you to listen to me patiently.

[u] Gk *him* [v] Other ancient authorities read *with anything* [w] Gk *on them*

25.3 Acts 23.12,15
25.4 Acts 24.23
25.7 Mk 15.3; Lk 23.2,10; Acts 24.5,13
25.8 Acts 6.13; 24.12; 28.17
25.9 Acts 24,27; ver 20
25.11 ver 25; Acts 26.32; 28.19
25.14 Acts 24.27
25.15 Acts 24.1; ver 2
25.16 ver 4,5
25.17 ver 6,10
25.19 Acts 18.15; 23.29
25.20 ver 9
25.21 ver 11,12
25.22 Acts 9.15
25.23 ver 13; Acts 26.30
25.24 ver 2,3,7; Acts 22.22
25.25 Acts 23.9,29; 26.31,32
26.1 Acts 9.15; 25.22
26.3 Acts 6.14; 25.19; ver 7

25.13-27 Meanwhile, Festus invites King Herod *Agrippa* to hear Paul's case, which he does, along with his wife, *Bernice*. Festus repeats his judgment that Paul is not guilty of legal violations but is involved in an intra-Jewish controversy about the resurrection of Jesus, and asks the help of Agrippa in formulating the charges against Paul that are to be reported to the emperor.

26.1-32 After expressing appreciation for Agrippa's knowledge of Jewish matters, Paul describes his earlier commitment as a Pharisee, his oppposition to the followers of Jesus, his encounter with the risen Christ and his commissioning to bear the message of Jesus to *the Gentiles*. His efforts to carry out that assignment have infuriated the Jews, as has his call to them to repent and to see in Jesus the fulfillment of *the prophets and Moses*. Noting the public nature of these events (*not done in a corner*), he appeals to Agrippa and all his hearers to put their trust in Jesus. Agrippa, who resists Paul's invitation, confirms that he does not find Paul to be a law-breaker, and says that he could have been freed, had he not appealed to Caesar.

27.1-12 Along with other prisoners assigned to the Roman *centurion* (officer in charge of one hundred soldiers), Paul starts his journey along the coast of southern *Asia* Minor. Transferring to another ship at *Myra in Lycia* on the mainland of Asia Minor, they took the normal route for shipping from Egypt or Syria to Rome, following the coast and touching at the islands of Cyprus and Crete. Since they were setting out late in the year, cross winds held them back or threatened to drive them on land, but they hoped to reach a safe harbor in western Crete where they could *spend the winter*. A northeast wind seemed as if it would drive them across the Mediterranean to *Syrtis*, quicksands off the coast of North Africa. Stripping the ship of much of its equipment, they *took measures to undergird the ship*, by strengthening its frame with ropes or trusses. Drifting across the lower *Adriatic Sea*, they were driven in darkness by the winds. Paul, regretting that the crew had not followed his advice to spend the winter in Crete, reports an angelic message that they will all be safe, although the ship will run *aground*. While the crew and passengers are urged to strengthen themselves by taking food, the cargo of *wheat* is thrown over in preparation for beaching the ship. Finally all jump into the sea to reach the shore by swimming or floating on planks, and all arrive safely.

4 "All the Jews know my way of life from
my youth, a life spent from the beginning
among my own people and in Jerusalem.
5They have known for a long time, if they
are willing to testify, that I have belonged
to the strictest sect of our religion and lived
as a Pharisee. 6And now I stand here on
trial on account of my hope in the promise
made by God to our ancestors, 7a promise
that our twelve tribes hope to attain, as
they earnestly worship day and night. It is
for this hope, your Excellency,[x] that I am
accused by Jews! 8Why is it thought incredible by any of you that God raises the dead?
9 "Indeed, I myself was convinced that I
ought to do many things against the name
of Jesus of Nazareth.[y] 10And that is what I
did in Jerusalem; with authority received
from the chief priests, I not only locked up
many of the saints in prison, but I also cast
my vote against them when they were
being condemned to death. 11By punishing
them often in all the synagogues I tried to
force them to blaspheme; and since I was
so furiously enraged at them, I pursued
them even to foreign cities.

Paul Tells of His Conversion

12 "With this in mind, I was traveling to
Damascus with the authority and commission of the chief priests, 13when at midday
along the road, your Excellency,[x] I saw a
light from heaven, brighter than the sun,
shining around me and my companions.
14When we had all fallen to the ground, I
heard a voice saying to me in the Hebrew[z]
language, 'Saul, Saul, why are you persecuting me? It hurts you to kick against the
goads.' 15I asked, 'Who are you, Lord?' The
Lord answered, 'I am Jesus whom you are
persecuting. 16But get up and stand on your
feet; for I have appeared to you for this
purpose, to appoint you to serve and testify
to the things in which you have seen me[a]
and to those in which I will appear to you.
17I will rescue you from your people and
from the Gentiles—to whom I am sending
you 18to open their eyes so that they may
turn from darkness to light and from the
power of Satan to God, so that they may
receive forgiveness of sins and a place among
those who are sanctified by faith in me.'

Paul Tells of His Preaching

19 "After that, King Agrippa, I was not
disobedient to the heavenly vision, 20but
declared first to those in Damascus, then in
Jerusalem and throughout the countryside
of Judea, and also to the Gentiles, that they
should repent and turn to God and do deeds
consistent with repentance. 21For this reason the Jews seized me in the temple and
tried to kill me. 22To this day I have had
help from God, and so I stand here, testifying to both small and great, saying nothing but what the prophets and Moses said
would take place: 23that the Messiah[b] must
suffer, and that, by being the first to rise
from the dead, he would proclaim light both
to our people and to the Gentiles."

Paul Appeals to Agrippa to Believe

24 While he was making this defense,
Festus exclaimed, "You are out of your
mind, Paul! Too much learning is driving
you insane!" 25But Paul said, "I am not out
of my mind, most excellent Festus, but I am
speaking the sober truth. 26Indeed the king
knows about these things, and to him I
speak freely; for I am certain that none of
these things has escaped his notice, for this
was not done in a corner. 27King Agrippa,
do you believe the prophets? I know that
you believe." 28Agrippa said to Paul, "Are
you so quickly persuading me to become a
Christian?"[c] 29Paul replied, "Whether quickly
or not, I pray to God that not only you but
also all who are listening to me today might
become such as I am—except for these
chains."
30 Then the king got up, and with him
the governor and Bernice and those who
had been seated with them; 31and as they
were leaving, they said to one another,
"This man is doing nothing to deserve death
or imprisonment." 32Agrippa said to Festus,
"This man could have been set free if he
had not appealed to the emperor."

Paul Sails for Rome

27 When it was decided that we were
to sail for Italy, they transferred
Paul and some other prisoners to a centurion
of the Augustan Cohort, named Julius. 2Em-

[x] Gk *O king* [y] Gk *the Nazorean* [z] That is, *Aramaic* [a] Other ancient authorities read *the things that you have seen* [b] Or *the Christ* [c] Or *Quickly you will persuade me to play the Christian*

26.4 Gal 1.13,14; Phil 3.5
26.5 Acts 22.3; 23.6; Phil 3.5
26.6 Acts 23.6; 13.32; Rom 15.8; Titus 2.13
26.7 Jas 1.1; 1 Thess 3.10; 1 Tim 5.5
26.8 Acts 23.6
26.9 Jn 16.2; 1 Tim 1.13; Jn 15.21
26.10 Acts 8.3; Gal 1.13; Acts 9.14,21
26.11 Acts 22.19
26.12 Acts 9.3; 22.6
26.14 Acts 9.7; 21.40
26.16 Ezek 2.1; Dan 10.11; Acts 22.14,15
26.17 Jer 1.8,19; Acts 22.21
26.18 Isa 35.5; 42.7; Eph 5.8; Col 1.13; 1 Pet 2.9; Lk 24.47; Acts 2.38; 20.32
26.20 Acts 9.19-29; 22.17-20; 13.46; 9.15; 3.19; Mt 3.8; Lk 3.8
26.21 Acts 21.30,31
26.22 Lk 24.27,44; Acts 24.14
26.23 Mt 26.24; 1 Cor 15.20; Col 1.18; Rev 1.5; Lk 2.32
26.24 2 Kings 9.11; Jn 10.20; 1 Cor 1.23
26.25 Acts 23.26; 24.3
26.28 Acts 11.26
26.29 Acts 21.33
26.30 Acts 25.33
26.31 Acts 23.29
26.32 Acts 28.18; 25.11
27.1 Acts 25.12,25; 10.1
27.2 Acts 19.29; 16.9; 17.1

barking on a ship of Adramyttium that was
about to set sail to the ports along the coast
of Asia, we put to sea, accompanied by
Aristarchus, a Macedonian from Thessalonica. [3]The next day we put in at Sidon;
and Julius treated Paul kindly, and allowed
him to go to his friends to be cared for.
[4]Putting out to sea from there, we sailed
under the lee of Cyprus, because the winds
were against us. [5]After we had sailed across
the sea that is off Cilicia and Pamphylia, we
came to Myra in Lycia. [6]There the centurion
found an Alexandrian ship bound for Italy
and put us on board. [7]We sailed slowly for
a number of days and arrived with difficulty
off Cnidus, and as the wind was against us,
we sailed under the lee of Crete off Salmone.
[8]Sailing past it with difficulty, we came to
a place called Fair Havens, near the city of
Lasea.

9 Since much time had been lost and
sailing was now dangerous, because even
the Fast had already gone by, Paul advised
them, [10]saying, "Sirs, I can see that the
voyage will be with danger and much heavy
loss, not only of the cargo and the ship, but
also of our lives." [11]But the centurion paid
more attention to the pilot and to the owner
of the ship than to what Paul said. [12]Since
the harbor was not suitable for spending
the winter, the majority was in favor of
putting to sea from there, on the chance
that somehow they could reach Phoenix,
where they could spend the winter. It was
a harbor of Crete, facing southwest and
northwest.

The Storm at Sea

13 When a moderate south wind began
to blow, they thought they could achieve
their purpose; so they weighed anchor and
began to sail past Crete, close to the shore.
[14]But soon a violent wind, called the north-
easter, rushed down from Crete.[d] [15]Since the
ship was caught and could not be turned
head-on into the wind, we gave way to it
and were driven. [16]By running under the
lee of a small island called Cauda[e] we were
scarcely able to get the ship's boat under
control. [17]After hoisting it up they took
measures[f] to undergird the ship; then, fearing that they would run on the Syrtis, they
lowered the sea anchor and so were driven.
[18]We were being pounded by the storm so
violently that on the next day they began
to throw the cargo overboard, [19]and on the
third day with their own hands they threw
the ship's tackle overboard. [20]When neither
sun nor stars appeared for many days, and
no small tempest raged, all hope of our
being saved was at last abandoned.

21 Since they had been without food for
a long time, Paul then stood up among
them and said, "Men, you should have
listened to me and not have set sail from
Crete and thereby avoided this damage and
loss. [22]I urge you now to keep up your
courage, for there will be no loss of life
among you, but only of the ship. [23]For last
night there stood by me an angel of the God
to whom I belong and whom I worship,
[24]and he said, 'Do not be afraid, Paul; you
must stand before the emperor; and indeed,
God has granted safety to all those who are
sailing with you.' [25]So keep up your courage, men, for I have faith in God that it will
be exactly as I have been told. [26]But we will
have to run aground on some island."

27 When the fourteenth night had come,
as we were drifting across the sea of Adria,
about midnight the sailors suspected that
they were nearing land. [28]So they took
soundings and found twenty fathoms; a
little farther on they took soundings again
and found fifteen fathoms. [29]Fearing that
we might run on the rocks, they let down
four anchors from the stern and prayed for
day to come. [30]But when the sailors tried to
escape from the ship and had lowered the
boat into the sea, on the pretext of putting
out anchors from the bow, [31]Paul said to
the centurion and the soldiers, "Unless these
men stay in the ship, you cannot be saved."
[32]Then the soldiers cut away the ropes of
the boat and set it adrift.

33 Just before daybreak, Paul urged all of
them to take some food, saying, "Today is
the fourteenth day that you have been in
suspense and remaining without food, having eaten nothing. [34]Therefore I urge you to
take some food, for it will help you survive;
for none of you will lose a hair from your
heads." [35]After he had said this, he took
bread; and giving thanks to God in the
presence of all, he broke it and began to eat.
[36]Then all of them were encouraged and
took food for themselves. [37](We were in all
two hundred seventy-six[g] persons in the
ship.) [38]After they had satisfied their hun-

27.3 Acts 24.23; 28.16
27.5 Acts 6.9; 13.13
27.6 Acts 6.9; 13.13; 28.11; ver 1
27.9 Lev 23.27-29
27.14 Mk 4.37
27.17 ver 26,29
27.18 Jon 1.5; ver 38
27.21 ver 10,7,12,13
27.22 ver 25,36
27.23 Acts 23.11; 5.19; Rom 1.9
27.24 Acts 23.11; ver 44
27.25 ver 22,36; Rom 4.20,21
27.26 Acts 28.1
27.30 ver 16
27.34 1 Kings 1.52; Mt 10.30; Lk 12.7; 21.18
27.35 1 Sam 9.13; Mt 15.36; Mk 8.6; Jn 6.11; 1 Tim 4.3,4
27.36 ver 22,25
27.38 ver 18

[d] Gk *it* [e] Other ancient authorities read *Clauda* [f] Gk *helps* [g] Other ancient authorities read *seventy-six*; others, *about seventy-six*

28.1-10 The land where they beached was the island of *Malta*. God's continuing protection of Paul and his fellow-travelers is evident in his surviving an attack by a deadly *viper*, and in the healing of the father of the chief man of the island and then of many of his subjects.
28.11-16 Sailing toward southern Italy, they came first to *Syracuse* on the island of Sicily, then to *Rhegium* at the southern tip of Italy, and finally to *Puteoli*, a major port south of Rome. On the main highway north to Rome, the Appian Way, Paul and his companions are met by members of the new community from Rome and escorted to the city. There Paul lives under house arrest, where he is visited by Jews, who have not heard of the disputes that have arisen in Jerusalem and are eager to hear from him more about the movement (*sect*) which has aroused so much opposition. In his extended conversation with them, he builds his case on Jesus as the fulfillment of *Moses and the prophets*, concluding with the observation that even the opposition to this message on the part of some Jews is according to the prophet (28.26-27 = Isa 6.9-10). He declares that the Gentiles will listen, and spends the next *two years* engaged in preaching and teaching about Jesus, boldly and *without hindrance*. The message which Paul was called to preach is now sounding forth in the political and cultural center of the Gentile world.

ger, they lightened the ship by throwing the wheat into the sea.

The Shipwreck

39 In the morning they did not recognize the land, but they noticed a bay with a beach, on which they planned to run the ship ashore, if they could. 40 So they cast off the anchors and left them in the sea. At the same time they loosened the ropes that tied the steering-oars; then hoisting the foresail to the wind, they made for the beach. 41 But striking a reef,[h] they ran the ship aground; the bow stuck and remained immovable, but the stern was being broken up by the force of the waves. 42 The soldiers' plan was to kill the prisoners, so that none might swim away and escape; 43 but the centurion, wishing to save Paul, kept them from carrying out their plan. He ordered those who could swim to jump overboard first and make for the land, 44 and the rest to follow, some on planks and others on pieces of the ship. And so it was that all were brought safely to land.

Paul on the Island of Malta

28 After we had reached safety, we then learned that the island was called Malta. 2 The natives showed us unusual kindness. Since it had begun to rain and was cold, they kindled a fire and welcomed all of us around it. 3 Paul had gathered a bundle of brushwood and was putting it on the fire, when a viper, driven out by the heat, fastened itself on his hand. 4 When the natives saw the creature hanging from his hand, they said to one another, "This man must be a murderer; though he has escaped from the sea, justice has not allowed him to live." 5 He, however, shook off the creature into the fire and suffered no harm. 6 They were expecting him to swell up or drop dead, but after they had waited a long time and saw that nothing unusual had happened to him, they changed their minds and began to say that he was a god.

7 Now in the neighborhood of that place were lands belonging to the leading man of the island, named Publius, who received us and entertained us hospitably for three days. 8 It so happened that the father of Publius lay sick in bed with fever and dysentery. Paul visited him and cured him by praying and putting his hands on him. 9 After this happened, the rest of the people on the island who had diseases also came and were cured. 10 They bestowed many honors on us, and when we were about to sail, they put on board all the provisions we needed.

Paul Arrives at Rome

11 Three months later we set sail on a ship that had wintered at the island, an Alexandrian ship with the Twin Brothers as its figurehead. 12 We put in at Syracuse and stayed there for three days; 13 then we weighed anchor and came to Rhegium. After one day there a south wind sprang up, and on the second day we came to Puteoli. 14 There we found believers[i] and were invited to stay with them for seven days. And so we came to Rome. 15 The believers[i] from there, when they heard of us, came as far as the Forum of Appius and Three Taverns to meet us. On seeing them, Paul thanked God and took courage.

16 When we came into Rome, Paul was allowed to live by himself, with the soldier who was guarding him.

Paul and Jewish Leaders in Rome

17 Three days later he called together the local leaders of the Jews. When they had assembled, he said to them, "Brothers, though I had done nothing against our people or the customs of our ancestors, yet I was arrested in Jerusalem and handed over to the Romans. 18 When they had examined me, the Romans[j] wanted to release me, because there was no reason for the death penalty in my case. 19 But when the Jews objected, I was compelled to appeal to the emperor—even though I had no charge to bring against my nation. 20 For this reason therefore I have asked to see you and speak with you,[k] since it is for the sake of the hope of Israel that I am bound with this chain." 21 They replied, "We have received no letters from Judea about you, and none of the brothers coming here has reported or spoken anything evil about you. 22 But we would like to hear from you what you think, for with regard to this sect we know that everywhere it is spoken against."

[h] Gk *place of two seas* [i] Gk *brothers* [j] Gk *they* [k] Or *I have asked you to see me and speak with me*

27.39 Acts 28.1
27.40 ver 29
27.41 2 Cor 11.25
27.42 Acts 12.19
27.43 ver 3
27.44 ver 22,31
28.1 Acts 27.26,39
28.2 Rom 1.14; 1 Cor 14.11; Col 3.11
28.4 Lk 13.2,4
28.5 Lk 10.19
28.6 Acts 14.11
28.8 Jas 5.14,15; Mk 5.23
28.11 Acts 27.6
28.14 Acts 1.15
28.16 Acts 24.23; 27.3
28.17 Acts 13.50; 25.8; 6.14
28.18 Acts 22.24; 26.31,32; 23.29
28.19 Acts 25.11
28.20 Acts 26.6,7,29; Eph 3.1; 4.1; 6.20; 2 Tim 1.16
28.21 Acts 22.5
28.22 Acts 24.14; 1 Pet 2.12; 4.14

Paul Preaches in Rome
23 After they had set a day to meet with
him, they came to him at his lodgings in
great numbers. From morning until evening
he explained the matter to them, testifying
to the kingdom of God and trying to convince them about Jesus both from the law
of Moses and from the prophets. [24]Some
were convinced by what he had said, while
others refused to believe. [25]So they disagreed with each other; and as they were
leaving, Paul made one further statement:
"The Holy Spirit was right in saying to your
ancestors through the prophet Isaiah,
[26] 'Go to this people and say,
You will indeed listen, but never
understand,
and you will indeed look, but never
perceive.
[27] For this people's heart has grown dull,
and their ears are hard of hearing,
and they have shut their eyes;
so that they might not look with
their eyes,
and listen with their ears,
and understand with their heart and
turn—
and I would heal them.'
[28]Let it be known to you then that this
salvation of God has been sent to the Gentiles; they will listen."[l]
30 He lived there two whole years at his
own expense[m] and welcomed all who came
to him, [31]proclaiming the kingdom of God
and teaching about the Lord Jesus Christ
with all boldness and without hindrance.

[l] Other ancient authorities add verse 29, *And when he had said these words, the Jews departed, arguing vigorously among themselves* [m] Or *in his own hired dwelling*

THE LETTER OF PAUL TO THE

ROMANS

1.2 Acts 26.6; Gal 3.8 *Salutation*
1 Paul, a servant[a] of Jesus Christ, called
to be an apostle, set apart for the
1.3 Jn 1.14 gospel of God, [2]which he promised beforehand through his prophets in the holy scrip-
1.4 Acts 13.33; Heb 9.14 tures, [3]the gospel concerning his Son, who
was descended from David according to the
flesh [4]and was declared to be Son of God
1.5 Gal 1.16; Acts 6.7; 9.15 with power according to the spirit[b] of holiness by resurrection from the dead, Jesus
Christ our Lord, [5]through whom we have
received grace and apostleship to bring about
1.7 1 Cor 1.2,3; Gal 1.3; Eph 1.2 the obedience of faith among all the Gentiles for the sake of his name, [6]including
yourselves who are called to belong to Jesus
Christ,
1.8 Phil 1.3; Acts 16.19 7 To all God's beloved in Rome, who are
called to be saints:
Grace to you and peace from God our
Father and the Lord Jesus Christ.
1.9 Phil 1.8; Acts 24.14; Eph 1.16

Prayer of Thanksgiving
8 First, I thank my God through Jesus
Christ for all of you, because your faith is
proclaimed throughout the world. [9]For God,
whom I serve with my spirit by announcing
the gospel[c] of his Son, is my witness that
without ceasing I remember you always in
my prayers, [10]asking that by God's will I
may somehow at last succeed in coming to
you. [11]For I am longing to see you so that
I may share with you some spiritual gift to
strengthen you— [12]or rather so that we
may be mutually encouraged by each other's faith, both yours and mine. [13]I want
you to know, brothers and sisters,[d] that I
have often intended to come to you (but
thus far have been prevented), in order that
I may reap some harvest among you as I
have among the rest of the Gentiles. [14]I am
a debtor both to Greeks and to barbarians,

[a] Gk *slave* [b] Or *Spirit* [c] Gk *my spirit in the gospel* [d] Gk *brothers*

See the Introductions, pp. 8–9 and 82–83 above.

1.1-7 The Introduction.
1.1 *Paul.* Formal Greek letter writing style of the first century CE placed the author's name first, followed by the name of the addressees and a greeting. Paul's letters exhibit a further structure, comprised of (1) a thanksgiving (e.g. 1.8-15), (2) the main body of the letter (e.g. 1.16-11.36), and (3) a section of admonitions and encouragement regarding Christian living (e.g. 12.1-15.33). Only Galatians lacks a formal thanksgiving (see note on Gal 1.1-5). *Servant.* Literally, "slave"; *cf.* footnote *a*, 2 Cor 4.5. *Called to be an apostle.* Concerning Paul's call see Gal 1.15-16; 2 Cor 4.5-6; also Acts 9.1-9; 22.6-11; 26.12-28. The word "apostle" means "one who is sent with a special mission"; for Paul this term is not limited to the Twelve (see 1 Cor 15.5,7), but to anyone sent out by the risen Christ to do his mission (see 1 Cor 12.28; 2 Cor 12.11). *Set apart for the gospel of God. Cf.* Gal 1.15.
1.2 *cf.* Gal 3.8.
1.3-4 These two verses contain a pre-Pauline Christological formula. *Descended from David.* A prerequisite for Messiahship; *cf.* Isa 11.1-10; 2 Sam 7.11-14. *According to the flesh.* Here this regards Messiah's human descent (see Rom 4.1; 9.3,5; 1 Cor 10.18); in other contexts the phrase can carry negative connotations (see Rom 8.4,5,12,13; 2 Cor 1.17; 10.2-3; 11.18; Gal 4.23). *Son of God. Cf.* Gal 4.4; Rom 8.3; Mark 1.1,11; 9.7; 15.39. *With power.* See the configuration of these terms in Luke 1.35. *Spirit of holiness.* I.e. the Holy Spirit. *Jesus Christ our Lord. Cf.* 10.4; Phil 2.11.
1.5 *The obedience of faith.* I.e. that obedience which is faith. For Paul faith is obedience to the gospel (see 6.17; 16.26; 2 Cor 9.13). *Among all the Gentiles.* Paul understood his calling as an apostle to have sent him out to witness particularly to non-Jews; *cf.* 1.13; 11.15; Gal 1.15-16; 2.7-9.
1.7 *Rome.* The capital and major city of the Roman empire; see introductory notes. The Christian message had reached Rome already in the 40s CE, since under the edict of Claudius in 49 CE Christians were expelled from Rome along with Jews (see Acts 18.2). The edict was lifted under Nero, who came to power in 54 CE. *Saints.* Paul uses this term of Christians in general, to designate that they belong to God and are set apart for God's work in the world; *cf.* 12.13; 1 Cor 1.2; Phil 4.21; Philem 7; also Eph 2.19; 5.3; 1 Tim 5.10. *Grace to you and peace...* The standard salutation in all of Paul's letters (plus 1 & 2 Pet; Rev), it joins the Christian concept of (God's) grace with the Jewish concept of (God's) peace. "Grace" refers to God's free and unmerited offer of mercy and love toward all people, while "peace" (= *shalom*) expresses all the benefits of a right relationship with God, namely a partnership of reconciliation, eternal well-being, and wholeness of life.
1.8-15 This section comprises the Thanksgiving portion of the letter. For similar Pauline thanksgivings see 1 Cor 1.4-9; 2 Cor 1.3-7; Phil 1.3-11; 1 Thess 1.2-10; Philem 4-7. By comparison, Rom 1.8-15 lacks the usual specific references to the life of the congregation, because Paul has not yet visited Rome (see 1.10; 15.22).
1.8 Paul recognizes the fact that he knows that a church exists in Rome, and he will later say that he has no intention of making his own demands on that church (15.20). However, in the following verses he wishes to enlist their support for his mission to the west (see 1.11-12; 15.23-24).
1.9 *With all my spirit.* I.e. wholeheartedly; Paul has invested his entire being in the work of the gospel. *In my prayers.* 2 Cor 11.28; Phil 1.3-5; 1 Thess 1.2, Philem 4-5; also Col 1.3; Eph 1.16; 2 Thess 1.3.
1.10 See note on 1.8-15.
1.11-12 See note on 1.8.
1.13 See 15.22-24. *The rest of the Gentiles.* This indicates that Paul envisions primarily, yet not exclusively, a Gentile readership in Rome.
1.14 *A debtor.* The same thought is expressed in 1 Cor 9.16, here in that he is under obligation to preach the gospel to Gentiles. *To Greeks and to barbarians.* I.e. to non-Jews, both cultured and otherwise. *To the wise and to the foolish. Cf.* 1 Cor 1.18-31.

both to the wise and to the foolish 15— hence
my eagerness to proclaim the gospel to you
also who are in Rome.

The Power of the Gospel

16 For I am not ashamed of the gospel;
it is the power of God for salvation to
everyone who has faith, to the Jew first and
also to the Greek. 17 For in it the righteousness of God is revealed through faith for
faith; as it is written, "The one who is
righteous will live by faith."[e]

The Guilt of Humankind

18 For the wrath of God is revealed from
heaven against all ungodliness and wickedness of those who by their wickedness suppress the truth. 19 For what can be known
about God is plain to them, because God
has shown it to them. 20 Ever since the
creation of the world his eternal power and
divine nature, invisible though they are,
have been understood and seen through the
things he has made. So they are without
excuse; 21 for though they knew God, they
did not honor him as God or give thanks
to him, but they became futile in their
thinking, and their senseless minds were
darkened. 22 Claiming to be wise, they became fools; 23 and they exchanged the glory
of the immortal God for images resembling
a mortal human being or birds or four-
footed animals or reptiles.
24 Therefore God gave them up in the
lusts of their hearts to impurity, to the
degrading of their bodies among themselves,
25 because they exchanged the truth about
God for a lie and worshiped and served the
creature rather than the Creator, who is
blessed forever! Amen.
26 For this reason God gave them up to
degrading passions. Their women exchanged
natural intercourse for unnatural, 27 and in
the same way also the men, giving up
natural intercourse with women, were consumed with passion for one another. Men
committed shameless acts with men and
received in their own persons the due penalty for their error.
28 And since they did not see fit to
acknowledge God, God gave them up to a
debased mind and to things that should not
be done. 29 They were filled with every kind
of wickedness, evil, covetousness, malice.
Full of envy, murder, strife, deceit, craftiness, they are gossips, 30 slanderers, God-
haters,[f] insolent, haughty, boastful, inven-
tors of evil, rebellious toward parents, 31 foolish, faithless, heartless, ruthless. 32 They know
God's decree, that those who practice such
things deserve to die—yet they not only do
them but even applaud others who practice
them.

The Righteous Judgment of God

2 Therefore you have no excuse, whoever you are, when you judge others;
for in passing judgment on another you
condemn yourself, because you, the judge,
are doing the very same things. 2 You say,[g]
"We know that God's judgment on those
who do such things is in accordance with
truth." 3 Do you imagine, whoever you are,
that when you judge those who do such
things and yet do them yourself, you will
escape the judgment of God? 4 Or do you
despise the riches of his kindness and forbearance and patience? Do you not realize
that God's kindness is meant to lead you to
repentance? 5 But by your hard and impenitent heart you are storing up wrath for
yourself on the day of wrath, when God's
righteous judgment will be revealed. 6 For he
will repay according to each one's deeds: 7 to
those who by patiently doing good seek for
glory and honor and immortality, he will
give eternal life; 8 while for those who are
self-seeking and who obey not the truth but
wickedness, there will be wrath and fury.
9 There will be anguish and distress for
everyone who does evil, the Jew first and
also the Greek, 10 but glory and honor and
peace for everyone who does good, the Jew
first and also the Greek. 11 For God shows no
partiality.
12 All who have sinned apart from the
law will also perish apart from the law, and
all who have sinned under the law will be
judged by the law. 13 For it is not the hearers
of the law who are righteous in God's sight,
but the doers of the law who will be justified. 14 When Gentiles, who do not possess
the law, do instinctively what the law requires, these, though not having the law,
are a law to themselves. 15 They show that
what the law requires is written on their
hearts, to which their own conscience also
bears witness; and their conflicting thoughts
will accuse or perhaps excuse them 16 on the

[e] Or *The one who is righteous through faith will live* [f] Or *God-hated* [g] Gk lacks *You say*

1.16-11.36 This larger section comprises the main body of the letter; see note on 1.1.
1.16-17 This section comprises a summary statement of Paul's understanding of the gospel and his own proclamation of it.
1.16 *Power of God. Cf.* 1 Cor 1.18. *Salvation.* I.e. deliverance from the power of sin into God's present and future realm; *cf.* 10.1; 11.11; 13.11; 2 Cor 6.1,12; 7.10; Gal 1.4; Phil 1.28; 1 Thess 5.8-9; also Isa 25.9; Wis 5.2; Ps 10.8; 12.7. *Faith.* Paul uses this term without institutional connotations; for Paul Christian believing is understanding that we are recipients of God's grace and, as obedience (see note on 1.5), living daily in accordance with that understanding. *To the Jew first and also to the Greek.* The gospel was first proclaimed to Israel (see Gal 3.8) and only afterward to Gentiles (*cf.* Rom 11.1,11,25-26).
1.17 *The righteousness of God.* The way God places people in a right relationship with him. This is the theme of Romans, addressed specifically in 3.21-31. The Greek word for "righteousness" is also the word for "justice" (3.5) and "justification" (5.21), and its verb is translated "justify" (3.24,26,28). *Through faith for faith.* I.e. from one person's witness to another (10.14-17). *As it is written.* Throughout Romans Paul quotes from the Hebrew scriptures, primarily from the Septuagint (the Greek translation of the Old Testament) version known to him. The quotation which follows here is from Hab 2.4.
1.18-3.20 This section deals with the revelation of God's wrath, and explains the need for God's kind of righteousness (see note on 1.17). Here Paul deals with the reality of God's judgment, to which all people, Jews and non-Jews, are accountable.
1.18 *The wrath of God.* This term has less to do with God's feelings than with his act of judgment against those whose sinful and evil actions have made a mockery of God's commands.
1.19 No one can claim ignorance of God and God's will for humanity.
1.20-21 Unbelief is placing God at human disposal.
1.21 *They did not honor him as God or give thanks to him.* Giving God honor (literally, "glory") or thanking God cannot be done when God is placed at human disposal and shaped according to human standards (see 1.23).
1.23 See note on 1.21.
1.24 *God gave them up.* Repeated in 1.26,28, this phrase builds on the ancient notion that God allows stubborn human beings to pursue their folly to the point of experiencing the full consequences of their actions; *cf.* Wis 11.16; Mt 7.2. *Degrading of their bodies.* Paul views sexual immorality as a result of placing human standards over God's; those who place God at their disposal will exploit others as well.
1.25 Self-serving possessiveness is the result of inability to understand the created world as God's gift.
1.26 *God gave them up.* See note on 1.24. *Degrading passions.* See note on 1.24. *Natural intercourse for unnatural.* Some Greek thinkers considered same sex love as more "natural" than opposite sex love; Paul, as did Judaism in general, would base his thinking on Gen 2-3 and would consider heterosexual love as "natural," i.e. as God from the beginning intended it to be.
1.27 *Shameless acts.* The language here concerns social propriety; heterosexuality remains standard. *The due penalty.* What is meant, whether addiction, acquired behavioral traits, disease, or other results, is not clear.
1.28 *God gave them up.* See note on 1.24.
1.29-31 These verses contain a "list of vices," the longest in Paul's letters (*cf.* 1 Cor 5.10; 6.9 [see note]; Gal 5.19-21). Such lists were in common use in Paul's time for ethical instruction within popular philosophical movements, such as Stoicism. For "lists of virtues" see Phil 4.8 and Gal 5.22-23.
1.32 *God's decree. Cf.* 2.15.
2.1 *Whoever you are.* This evidently indicates a shift in Paul's attention from Gentile to Jewish readers. *Passing judgment. Cf.* 14.1-23; Col 2.16-19. The idea in this verse is that Jewish aversion to Gentile morality should not lead Jews to overlook their own moral lapses.
2.4 God's covenant does not mean that God should be taken for granted.
2.6 *Deeds.* These are explained in what follows (see notes on 2.7 and 2.8).
2.7 *Eternal life.* This awaits those whose deeds are grounded in God's giving. Paul uses the term *"eternal life"* rather infrequently, and when he does he indicates that he understands it generally in terms of God's future, the world to come (*cf.* 5.21; 6.22-23; Gal 6.8).
2.8 *Wrath and fury.* This awaits those whose deeds are grounded in human achievement
2.9 *cf.* 3.9,23.
2.10 *Does good. Cf.* 3.24; Gal 2.20.

1.16 2 Tim 2.9; 1 Cor 1.18; Acts 3.26; Rom 2.9
1.17 Rom 3.21; Gal 3.11; Heb 10.38
1.18 Eph 5.6; Col 3.6
1.20 Ps 19.1-6
1.21 Jer 2.5; Eph 4.17,18
1.23 Ps 106.20; Jer 2.11; Acts 17.29
1.24 Eph 4.18,19; 1 Pet 4.3
1.25 Isa 44.20; Jer 10.14; Rom 9.5
1.26 Lev 18.22; Eph 4.19; 1 Thess 4.5
1.27 Lev 18.22; 20.13
1.28 Eph 4.19
1.30 Ps 5.5; 2 Tim 3.2
1.31 2 Tim 3.3
1.32 Rom 6.21; Acts 8.1; 22.20
2.1 Rom 1.20; 2 Sam 12.5-7; Mt 7.1,2
2.4 Eph 1.7; 2.7; Rom 11.22; 3.25; Ex 34.6; 2 Pet 3.9
2.5 Deut 32.34; Jude 6
2.6 Mt 16.27; 1 Cor 3.8; 2 Cor 5.10
2.8 Gal 5.20; 2 Thess 2.12
2.9 1 Pet 4.17
2.11 Deut 10.17; Gal 2.6; Eph 6.9
2.13 Jas 1.22,23,25
2.16 Eccl 12.14; 1 Cor 4.5; Acts 10.42; 1 Tim 1.11

day when, according to my gospel, God, through Jesus Christ, will judge the secret thoughts of all.

The Jews and the Law

17 But if you call yourself a Jew and rely on the law and boast of your relation to God [18]and know his will and determine what is best because you are instructed in the law, [19]and if you are sure that you are a guide to the blind, a light to those who are in darkness, [20]a corrector of the foolish, a teacher of children, having in the law the embodiment of knowledge and truth, [21]you, then, that teach others, will you not teach yourself? While you preach against stealing, do you steal? [22]You that forbid adultery, do you commit adultery? You that abhor idols, do you rob temples? [23]You that boast in the law, do you dishonor God by breaking the law? [24]For, as it is written, "The name of God is blasphemed among the Gentiles because of you."

25 Circumcision indeed is of value if you obey the law; but if you break the law, your circumcision has become uncircumcision. [26]So, if those who are uncircumcised keep the requirements of the law, will not their uncircumcision be regarded as circumcision? [27]Then those who are physically uncircumcised but keep the law will condemn you that have the written code and circumcision but break the law. [28]For a person is not a Jew who is one outwardly, nor is true circumcision something external and physical. [29]Rather, a person is a Jew who is one inwardly, and real circumcision is a matter of the heart—it is spiritual and not literal. Such a person receives praise not from others but from God.

3 Then what advantage has the Jew? Or what is the value of circumcision? [2]Much, in every way. For in the first place the Jews[h] were entrusted with the oracles of God. [3]What if some were unfaithful? Will their faithlessness nullify the faithfulness of God? [4]By no means! Although everyone is a liar, let God be proved true, as it is written,

"So that you may be justified in your words,
and prevail in your judging."[i]

[5]But if our injustice serves to confirm the justice of God, what should we say? That God is unjust to inflict wrath on us? (I speak in a human way.) [6]By no means! For then how could God judge the world? [7]But if through my falsehood God's truthfulness abounds to his glory, why am I still being condemned as a sinner? [8]And why not say (as some people slander us by saying that we say), "Let us do evil so that good may come"? Their condemnation is deserved!

None Is Righteous

9 What then? Are we any better off?[j] No, not at all; for we have already charged that all, both Jews and Greeks, are under the power of sin, [10]as it is written:

"There is no one who is righteous, not even one;
11 there is no one who has understanding,
there is no one who seeks God.
12 All have turned aside, together they have become worthless;
there is no one who shows kindness, there is not even one."
13 "Their throats are opened graves;
they use their tongues to deceive."
"The venom of vipers is under their lips."
14 "Their mouths are full of cursing and bitterness."
15 "Their feet are swift to shed blood;
16 ruin and misery are in their paths,
17 and the way of peace they have not known."
18 "There is no fear of God before their eyes."

19 Now we know that whatever the law says, it speaks to those who are under the law, so that every mouth may be silenced, and the whole world may be held accountable to God. [20]For "no human being will be justified in his sight" by deeds prescribed by the law, for through the law comes the knowledge of sin.

Righteousness through Faith

21 But now, apart from law, the righteousness of God has been disclosed, and is attested by the law and the prophets, [22]the righteousness of God through faith in Jesus Christ[k] for all who believe. For there is no distinction, [23]since all have sinned and fall short of the glory of God; [24]they are now justified by his grace as a gift, through the redemption that is in Christ Jesus, [25]whom God put forward as a sacrifice of

[h] Gk *they* [i] Gk *when you are being judged* [j] Or *at any disadvantage?* [k] Or *through the faith of Jesus Christ*

2.17 ver 23; Mic 3.11; Rom 9.4
2.20 Rom 6.17; 2 Tim 1.13
2.21 Mt 23.3,4
2.24 Isa 52.5
2.25 Gal 5.3
2.28 Mt 3.9; Jn 8.39; Rom 9.6; Gal 6.15
2.29 Col 2.11; 2 Cor 10.18; 1 Pet 3.4
3.2 Deut 4.8; Ps 147.19
3.3 Heb 4.2; 2 Tim 2.13
3.4 Jn 3.33; Ps 116.11; 51.4
3.5 Rom 6.19; Gal 3.15
3.8 Rom 6.1
3.9 Gal 3.22
3.10 Ps 14.1-3
3.13 Ps 5.9
3.15 Isa 59.7,8
3.19 Jn 10.34; Rom 2.12; Col 2.11; 2 Cor 10.18; 1 Pet 3.4
3.20 Ps 143.2; Acts 13.39; Gal 2.16; Rom 7.7
3.21 Rom 1.17; 9.30; 1.2; Acts 10.43
3.22 Rom 10.12; Gal 3.28; Col 3.11
3.23 Gal 3.22
3.24 Rom 4.16; Eph 1.7; 2.8; Col 1.14; Heb 9.12,15
3.25 1 Jn 2.2; Heb 9.14,28; 1 Pet 1.19

2.11 *cf.* Gal 2.6; Eph 6.9; Col 3.25; Acts 10.34.
2.12 A continuation of 2.9. *The law.* I.e. the Law of Moses, the Torah. Gentiles who do not have the Law of Moses are still subject to God's judgment, as are Jews who have that Law.
2.13 *cf.* Jas 1.22-25.
2.15 *What the law requires.* Literally, "the work of the law." *Conscience. Cf.* 9.1; 13.5; 1 Cor 8.7; 2 Cor 4.2.
2.16 *cf.* 14.12.

2.17 *cf.* 2.4.
2.19 *Guide to the blind. Cf.* Isa 42.7. *A light to those who are in darkness. Cf.* Isa 42.6; 49.6; Wis 18.4. Paul affirms these high assessments of what Jews are to be.
2.24 The quotation is from Isa 52.5 (Septuagint).
2.25 *Circumcision.* This was commanded by God as a sign of the covenant (see Gen 17.9-14). Paul's point in the verse is that, after circumcision, the breaking of the Law is a fracturing of the covenant relationship. *Cf.* also 1 Cor 7.19.
2.29 *Real circumcision is a matter of the heart. Cf.* Lev 26.41; Deut 10.16; 30.6; Jer 4.4; 9.26, Rom 6.17; Gal 6.15.
3.1-20 This section indicates Paul's method of debate: he anticipates questions which might come from his readers, puts them into expression, and proceeds to answer them (see vv. 1,3,5,7,8,9). This form of rhetoric, developed in Greek philosophical debate, was called "diatribe."
3.1 The question has to do with the identifying marks of Judaism.
3.2 The answer to 3.1 is that Israel was granted the Law as God's gift to God's people.
3.3 The question asks whether human acts fracturing the covenant (see note on 2.25) releases God from God's covenant commitment.
3.4 The answer to 3.3 is a resounding negative. God remains true to God's covenant promises; *cf.* 11.26,29. The quotation is from Ps 51.4 (Septuagint). Paul's point is that that is God's glory: God gives grace and peace precisely to the sinner (see 3.23-24; 5.6-11).
3.5 The question asks whether, if God remained true to God's covenantal promises, God would ever inflict judgment on God's people.
3.6 The answer to 3.5 is that God's work of judging the entire world cannot be relinquished; *cf.* Gen 18.25; Deut 32.4; Job 8.3; 34.10-30.
3.7 Paul's point is that it is precisely acts of human unfaithfulness which prove God's glory, in that God forgives the sinner who relies on God's grace (see 3.23-24; 5.6-11). So Paul anticipates his opponents' question: *"why am I still being condemned as a sinner?"* I.e. if God forgives, then why should Paul condemn Israel as he did in 2.17-24?
3.8 The question asked in this verse is more fully answered in chapter 6 (see 6.1,15). The final sentence of this verse evidently means that those people deserve the condemnation of God's law who willfully practise evil in order that the good of God's forgiveness may occur; the point of 2.17-24 is that God is not to be taken for granted.
3.9 *Are we any better off?* The "we" here refers to Jews. The answer given in this verse recalls 2.11 and looks forward to the theme "there is no distinction" (3.22-23).
3.10 *As it is written.* The scripture references in the following verses are cited by Paul as support for his statement in 3.9 that both Jews and Greeks are under the power of sin. The quotation in this verse is based on Ps 14.1,3 and 53.1,3.
3.11 The quotation is based on Ps 14.2 and 53.2.
3.12 The quotation is based on Ps 14.3 and 53.3.
3.13 The first quotation is from Ps 5.9. The second quotation is from Ps 140.3.
3.14 The quotation is from Ps 10.7.
3.15-17 This quotation is based on Isa 59.7-8 (*cf.* Prov 1.16).
3.18 The quotation is from Ps 36.1.
3.19 See note on 3.6. Scripture is there to tell Israel that the whole world, including Israel, is accountable to God.
3.20 The quotation is from Ps 143.2. *Through the law comes knowledge of sin. Cf.* 5.13; 7.7-8; this statement will be developed more fully in chapter 7.
3.21-31 This section deals with the revelation of God's righteousness (see note on 1.18-3.20).
3.21 *Apart from law.* God's judgment now, in view of 3.20, is carried out on grounds other than the Law. *The righteousness of God.* The way God places people in a right relationship with him; see note on 1.17. *Attested by the law and prophets.* Important for Paul is the witness of Scripture to what he is saying; *cf.* 3.31; 4.1-25.
3.22 The way God has chosen to place all people in a right

atonement[l] by his blood, effective through
faith. He did this to show his righteousness,
because in his divine forbearance he had
passed over the sins previously committed;
26 it was to prove at the present time that
he himself is righteous and that he justifies
the one who has faith in Jesus.[m]
27 Then what becomes of boasting? It is
excluded. By what law? By that of works?
No, but by the law of faith. 28 For we hold
that a person is justified by faith apart from
works prescribed by the law. 29 Or is God the
God of Jews only? Is he not the God of
Gentiles also? Yes, of Gentiles also, 30 since
God is one; and he will justify the circumcised on the ground of faith and the
uncircumcised through that same faith. 31 Do
we then overthrow the law by this faith? By
no means! On the contrary, we uphold the
law.

The Example of Abraham

4 What then are we to say was gained
by[n] Abraham, our ancestor according
to the flesh? 2 For if Abraham was justified
by works, he has something to boast about,
but not before God. 3 For what does the
scripture say? "Abraham believed God, and
it was reckoned to him as righteousness."
4 Now to one who works, wages are not
reckoned as a gift but as something due.
5 But to one who without works trusts him
who justifies the ungodly, such faith is
reckoned as righteousness. 6 So also David
speaks of the blessedness of those to whom
God reckons righteousness apart from works:
7 "Blessed are those whose iniquities are
forgiven,
and whose sins are covered;
8 blessed is the one against whom the
Lord will not reckon sin."
9 Is this blessedness, then, pronounced
only on the circumcised, or also on the
uncircumcised? We say, "Faith was reckoned to Abraham as righteousness." 10 How
then was it reckoned to him? Was it before
or after he had been circumcised? It was not
after, but before he was circumcised. 11 He
received the sign of circumcision as a seal
of the righteousness that he had by faith
while he was still uncircumcised. The purpose was to make him the ancestor of all
who believe without being circumcised and
who thus have righteousness reckoned to
them, 12 and likewise the ancestor of the
circumcised who are not only circumcised
but who also follow the example of the faith
that our ancestor Abraham had before he
was circumcised.

God's Promise Realized through Faith

13 For the promise that he would inherit
the world did not come to Abraham or to
his descendants through the law but through
the righteousness of faith. 14 If it is the adherents of the law who are to be the heirs,
faith is null and the promise is void. 15 For
the law brings wrath; but where there is no
law, neither is there violation.
16 For this reason it depends on faith, in
order that the promise may rest on grace
and be guaranteed to all his descendants,
not only to the adherents of the law but
also to those who share the faith of Abraham
(for he is the father of all of us, 17 as it is
written, "I have made you the father of
many nations")—in the presence of the God
in whom he believed, who gives life to the
dead and calls into existence the things that
do not exist. 18 Hoping against hope, he
believed that he would become "the father
of many nations," according to what was
said, "So numerous shall your descendants
be." 19 He did not weaken in faith when he
considered his own body, which was already[o]
as good as dead (for he was about a hundred years old), or when he considered the
barrenness of Sarah's womb. 20 No distrust
made him waver concerning the promise of
God, but he grew strong in his faith as he
gave glory to God, 21 being fully convinced
that God was able to do what he had
promised. 22 Therefore his faith[p] "was reckoned to him as righteousness." 23 Now the
words, "it was reckoned to him," were
written not for his sake alone, 24 but for ours
also. It will be reckoned to us who believe
in him who raised Jesus our Lord from the
dead, 25 who was handed over to death for
our trespasses and was raised for our justification.

Results of Justification

5 Therefore, since we are justified by
faith, we[q] have peace with God
through our Lord Jesus Christ, 2 through

[l] Or *a place of atonement* [m] Or *who has the faith of Jesus* [n] Other ancient authorities read *say about* [o] Other ancient authorities lack *already* [p] Gk *Therefore it* [q] Other ancient authorities read *let us*

relationship with him is through faith in Jesus Christ. *There is no distinction.* This is a major theme in Romans; *cf.* 10.12; 3.9; also Gal 3.28.
3.23 *cf.* 2.9; 3.9.
3.24 *Justified.* I.e. placed in a right relationship with God. See note on 1.17. *As a gift.* The right relationship with God has never rested on human merit anyway, which is the point of chapter 4; see also 5.6-11. *Redemption.* The Greek word means "deliverance," applied here to deliverance from the power of sin as mentioned in 3.9; *cf.* Isa 43.22-28; 44.21-22; Dan 4.34; Col 1.14; Eph 1.7. The word was also used in the Septuagint of Israel's deliverance from bondage in Egypt (Ex 6.6; 5.13,16; Deut 7.8; 9.26; 13.5), and was in general Greek usage regarding the purchase of a slave's freedom.
3.25 *Sacrifice of atonement.* This translates one Greek word, *hilasterion*, which is the Greek word used in the Septuagint for the "mercy-seat" atop the ark of the covenant, where annually on the Day of Atonement (Yom Kippur) the blood of the sacrificial animal was sprinkled by the high priest (see Lev 16.14-16) to repair the fracturing of the covenant relationship brought about by the people's sins. The use of this term in the New Testament (*cf.* also Heb 9.3-5) is to state that Christ's cross is the *hilasterion*, or mercy-seat, which is the point at which the sins of humanity meet with the forgiveness of God. *Cf.* also footnote *l*.

3.27 *Boasting.* For Paul this is the worst possible sin, since it uses human achievement, rather than God's mercy, as the basis for a right relationship with God: 4.2; 1 Cor 1.29-2.2; Eph 2.8-9.
3.28 *cf.* Gal 3.11,18,22; Eph 2.8-9.
3.30 *Since God is one. Cf.* Deut 6.4, the basic confession of Judaism, which Paul uses to affirm that Israel's God is God of all people as well; *cf.* also Rom 8.9,17. *That same faith.* I.e. the faith that understands that all people are recipients of God's grace.
3.31 *cf.* 3.21.
4.1-25 This section of the letter deals with Abraham, revered as the father of Israel. As in Gal 3.1-18, Paul's treatment of Abraham is to show that the constituent element of God's covenant is God's promise.
4.1 *Gained.* The Greek word literally means "found," and recalls Gen 18.3 (Septuagint): *Abraham found favor with God.* The Greek word for "favor" in Gen 18.3 is *charis*, the New Testament word for "grace." *Our ancestor.* Abraham was generally understood to be the progenitor of Israel.
4.3 The quotation is from Gen 15.6; *cf.* Gal 3.8; Jas 2.23.
4.5 *Him who justifies the ungodly.* God's justifying comes precisely to those who need it, who on the basis of their achievement cannot boast; *cf.* 5.6-11. *Such faith is reckoned as righteousness.* That faith by which one understands oneself as a recipient of God's giving enables a right relationship with God. *Righteousness.* See note on 1.17.
4.7-8 The quotation is from Ps 32.1-2 (Septuagint).
4.9 The question here is whether God's covenantal promise is valid only for those who are circumcised, i.e. only for Israel. The repeated quotation of Gen 15.6 refers to a time before the command for circumcision in Gen 17.9-14.
4.10 That God's promise to Abraham preceded the command for circumcision is the point made also in Gal 3.8.
4.11 The point of this verse is that Abraham, since he was accepted by God by virtue of his faith before he was circumcised, is also the father of the Gentiles.
4.12 Abraham is Israel's father as well because of the faith which he shares with his descendants.
4.13 *Inherit the world.* In Genesis the justification of Abraham stands in close connection with God's promise of many descendants (see Gen 15.5), including a "multitude of nations" (17.4).
4.14 *cf.* Gal 3.17-18.
4.15 Law brings knowledge of sin (3.20; 7.7), of sin as that abstract power under which we are sold (7.13), and that those under sin's power are subject to God's wrath (1.18-3.20). But where there is no Law no concrete acts of transgression can be counted, through which we know that we are under the power of sin (see 7.8,13). *Violation.* Literally, "transgression."
4.16 *For this reason it depends on faith.* I.e. because the Law brings only wrath (4.15).
4.17 The quotation is from Gen 17.5. *Who gives life to the dead and calls into existence the things that do not exist.* The idea of God's creating the world out of nothing is applied here both to Abraham's faith and to his and Sarah's ostensibly infertile physical condition.

3.27 Rom 2.17,23; 4.2; 1 Cor 1.29-31; Eph 2.9
3.28 Acts 13.39; Eph 2.9
3.30 Gal 3.8
4.2 1 Cor 1.31
4.3 Gen 15.6; Gal 3.6; Jas 2.23
4.4 Rom 11.6
4.7 Ps 32.1,2
4.11 Gen 17.10; Lk 19.9
4.13 Gen 17.4-6; Gal 3.29
4.15 Rom 3.20; 7.8,10,11; Gal 3.10
4.16 Rom 3.24; 9.8; 15.8
4.17 Gen 17.5; 1 Cor 1.28
4.19 Gen 17.17; Heb 11.11,12
4.21 Gen 18.14; Heb 11.19
4.23 Rom 15.4; 1 Cor 9.10; 10.11
4.24 Rom 10.9; Acts 2.24
4.25 Isa 53.5,6; 2 Cor 5.21; 1 Cor 15.17
5.1 Rom 3.28
5.2 Eph 2.18; 1 Cor 15.1; Heb 3.6

whom we have obtained access[r] to this grace in which we stand; and we[s] boast in our hope of sharing the glory of God. 3 And not only that, but we[s] also boast in our sufferings, knowing that suffering produces endurance, 4 and endurance produces character, and character produces hope, 5 and hope does not disappoint us, because God's love has been poured into our hearts through the Holy Spirit that has been given to us.

6 For while we were still weak, at the right time Christ died for the ungodly. 7 Indeed, rarely will anyone die for a righteous person—though perhaps for a good person someone might actually dare to die. 8 But God proves his love for us in that while we still were sinners Christ died for us. 9 Much more surely then, now that we have been justified by his blood, will we be saved through him from the wrath of God.[t] 10 For if while we were enemies, we were reconciled to God through the death of his Son, much more surely, having been reconciled, will we be saved by his life. 11 But more than that, we even boast in God through our Lord Jesus Christ, through whom we have now received reconciliation.

Adam and Christ

12 Therefore, just as sin came into the world through one man, and death came through sin, and so death spread to all because all have sinned— 13 sin was indeed in the world before the law, but sin is not reckoned when there is no law. 14 Yet death exercised dominion from Adam to Moses, even over those whose sins were not like the transgression of Adam, who is a type of the one who was to come.

15 But the free gift is not like the trespass. For if the many died through the one man's trespass, much more surely have the grace of God and the free gift in the grace of the one man, Jesus Christ, abounded for the many. 16 And the free gift is not like the effect of the one man's sin. For the judgment following one trespass brought condemnation, but the free gift following many trespasses brings justification. 17 If, because of the one man's trespass, death exercised dominion through that one, much more surely will those who receive the abundance of grace and the free gift of righteousness exercise dominion in life through the one man, Jesus Christ.

18 Therefore just as one man's trespass led to condemnation for all, so one man's act of righteousness leads to justification and life for all. 19 For just as by the one man's disobedience the many were made sinners, so by the one man's obedience the many will be made righteous. 20 But law came in, with the result that the trespass multiplied; but where sin increased, grace abounded all the more, 21 so that, just as sin exercised dominion in death, so grace might also exercise dominion through justification[u] leading to eternal life through Jesus Christ our Lord.

Dying and Rising with Christ

6 What then are we to say? Should we continue in sin in order that grace may abound? 2 By no means! How can we who died to sin go on living in it? 3 Do you not know that all of us who have been baptized into Christ Jesus were baptized into his death? 4 Therefore we have been buried with him by baptism into death, so that, just as Christ was raised from the dead by the glory of the Father, so we too might walk in newness of life.

5 For if we have been united with him in a death like his, we will certainly be united with him in a resurrection like his. 6 We know that our old self was crucified with him so that the body of sin might be destroyed, and we might no longer be enslaved to sin. 7 For whoever has died is freed from sin. 8 But if we have died with Christ, we believe that we will also live with him. 9 We know that Christ, being raised from the dead, will never die again; death no longer has dominion over him. 10 The death he died, he died to sin, once for all; but the life he lives, he lives to God. 11 So you also must consider yourselves dead to sin and alive to God in Christ Jesus.

12 Therefore, do not let sin exercise dominion in your mortal bodies, to make you obey their passions. 13 No longer present your members to sin as instruments[v] of wickedness, but present yourselves to God as those who have been brought from death to life, and present your members to God as instruments[v] of righteousness. 14 For sin will have no dominion over you, since you are not under law but under grace.

[r] Other ancient authorities add *by faith* [s] Or *let us* [t] Gk *the wrath* [u] Or *righteousness* [v] Or *weapons*

5.3 2 Cor 12.10; Jas 1.2,3
5.5 Phil 1.20; Eph 1.13
5.6 Gal 4.25
5.8 Jn 15.13; 1 Pet 3.18; 1 Jn 3.16
5.9 Rom 3.5,25; Heb 9.14; 1 Thess 1.10
5.10 Rom 11.28; Col 1.21,22; 2 Cor 5.18; Rom 8.34
5.12 Gen 2.17; 3.6,19; 1 Cor 15.21; Rom 6.23
5.14 1 Cor 15.22,45
5.20 Rom 7.7,8; Gal 3.19; 1 Tim 1.14
6.1 Rom 3.5,8; ver 15
6.2 Rom 7.4,6; Gal 2.19; Col 3.3; 1 Pet 2.24
6.3 Acts 2.38; 8.16; 19.5
6.4 Col 2.12; Gal 6.15; Eph 4.22-24; Col 3.10
6.6 Eph 4.22; Col 3.9; Gal 2.20; Rom 7.24
6.9 Rev 1.18
6.10 Heb 7.27
6.11 ver 2; Gal 2.19
6.12 ver 14
6.13 Rom 7.5; Col 3.5; Rom 12.1
6.14 Rom 8.2; Gal 5.18

4.18 This verse combines statements from God's promise to Abraham in Gen 17.5 and Gen 15.5.
4.19 See note on 4.17.
4.20 *He gave glory to God.* According to 1.21 this is something unbelievers cannot do.
4.22 The quotation is from Gen 15.6.
4.24 The same God who brought creation out of nothing (4.17), who gave life to Sarah's barren womb (4.19), who gave life to the crucified Jesus, is the God who justifies the ungodly (4.5), i.e. through faith sets them in a right relationship with him (*cf.* 5.6-11).
5.1-11 This section is a summary and conclusion to what began in 1.17.
5.1 *Therefore.* This indicates a conclusion to the foregoing. *We are justified by faith.* The theme of 3.21-31. *We have peace.* The wrath of God, the theme of 1.17-3.20, is resolved: peace with God is attained by God's grace through Christ, and reconciliation with God is now in effect (see 5.11). For a definition of *"peace"* see note on 1.7.
5.2 *Grace.* See note on 1.7. *We boast.* This is in contrast to the kind of boasting mentioned in 2.17 and 3.27. *Glory of God.* This is God's eschatological gift; *cf.* 2.7,10.
5.3 *We boast in our sufferings. Cf.* 2 Cor 11.30; 12.9; also 1 Cor 1.31; 3.21, 2 Cor 10.17; Gal 6.13; Phil 3.3. *Boast.* See note on 5.2. *Endurance.* The Greek word carries with it the sense of patience in testing; *cf.* 8.25; 15.4-5.
5.4 *Character.* The Greek word indicates a quality of provenness under testing. *Hope.* This means openness for God's future.
5.6-11 This section, frequently alluded to in the previous notes, emphasizes that reconciliation with God is the result of God's action. A progression of terms indicates that the human being was in no position to bring about that reconciliation: we were "weak" (v. 6), "sinners" (v. 8), "enemies" (v. 10).
5.6 *Christ died for the ungodly. Cf.* 4.5.
5.7 The first half of this verse is to be taken with v. 6, the second half with v. 8.
5.9 *Justified by his blood.* A restatement of 3.24-25.
5.10 *cf.* Gal 2.20.
5.11 *cf.* 1 Cor 1.31.
5.12-21 This section deals with Adam and Christ as inaugurators of two different aeons; *cf.* 1 Cor 15.45-49.
5.12 *Sin.* This word is used here as an abstraction, rather than as a concrete act; the words "transgression" (5.14) and "trespass" (5.15) are used to express concrete acts of sinning. *One man.* I.e. Adam (see Gen 3.1-24). *Death through sin. Cf.* Wis 2.24. *Because all have sinned.* See note on 3.23; all sinning is at once the result of and participation in Adam's sinning.
5.13 *cf.* Gal 3.17; Rom 3.20; 7.7-8.
5.14 *Transgression.* I.e. the particular sinful action; see note on 5.12.
5.15-17 This section includes various Greek terms to underscore the free gift of God's grace in Christ.
5.15 *Free gift.* I.e. Christ. *The trespass.* I.e. Adam. The relationship with God broken by Adam's sinning is restored again by God's grace in Christ, offered freely to everyone.
5.17 *Dominion in life.* This theme is developed in 6.12-23.
5.18-21 The conclusion to the Adam-Christ comparison: the results of what Adam and Christ have inaugurated are drawn out.
5.19 *cf.* 1.5; Heb 12.2.
5.20 *cf.* Gal 3.19.
5.21 *Dominion. Cf.* 6.14.
6.1-14 This section deals with baptism and the new life in Christ.
6.1 See note on 3.1-20, and *cf.* 3.5; 4.1; 7.7; 9.14,30. The second question in this verse is raised repeatedly (*cf.* 3.8; 6.15), which indicates a real misunderstanding of Paul's theology by his dialogue partners.
6.2 For Paul God's grace has consequences for daily living.
6.3 *Do you not know...?* A frequent phrase in Paul, usually indicating something his readers very well know; see notes on 1 Cor 3.16; 6.2; 9.24. *Baptized into his death.* See Gal 2.20; 2 Cor 4.10.
6.4 The basic Christian confession transmitted from the earliest traditions of the church (see 1 Cor 15.3-4) was that Jesus died, was buried, and was raised. At baptism that confession and its contents become viable in the life of the believer: at baptism Christians become participants in Jesus' death, burial, and resurrection. *Cf.* Gal 3.17; Col 2.12. *Newness of life. Cf.* Gal 2.20; 2 Cor 5.17.
6.5 *Resurrection.* For Paul the resurrection is still a future event, promised in baptism, but the renewal of the Christian life is a present reality.
6.6 *No longer enslaved to sin.* This is the "newness of life" of 6.4. *Cf.* Gal

Slaves of Righteousness

15 What then? Should we sin because we are not under law but under grace? By no means! [16]Do you not know that if you present yourselves to anyone as obedient slaves, you are slaves of the one whom you obey, either of sin, which leads to death, or of obedience, which leads to righteousness? [17]But thanks be to God that you, having once been slaves of sin, have become obedient from the heart to the form of teaching to which you were entrusted, [18]and that you, having been set free from sin, have become slaves of righteousness. [19]I am speaking in human terms because of your natural limitations.[w] For just as you once presented your members as slaves to impurity and to greater and greater iniquity, so now present your members as slaves to righteousness for sanctification.

20 When you were slaves of sin, you were free in regard to righteousness. [21]So what advantage did you then get from the things of which you now are ashamed? The end of those things is death. [22]But now that you have been freed from sin and enslaved to God, the advantage you get is sanctification. The end is eternal life. [23]For the wages of sin is death, but the free gift of God is eternal life in Christ Jesus our Lord.

An Analogy from Marriage

7 Do you not know, brothers and sisters[x]—for I am speaking to those who know the law—that the law is binding on a person only during that person's lifetime? [2]Thus a married woman is bound by the law to her husband as long as he lives; but if her husband dies, she is discharged from the law concerning the husband. [3]Accordingly, she will be called an adulteress if she lives with another man while her husband is alive. But if her husband dies, she is free from that law, and if she marries another man, she is not an adulteress.

4 In the same way, my friends,[x] you have died to the law through the body of Christ, so that you may belong to another, to him who has been raised from the dead in order that we may bear fruit for God. [5]While we were living in the flesh, our sinful passions, aroused by the law, were at work in our members to bear fruit for death. [6]But now we are discharged from the law, dead to that which held us captive, so that we are slaves not under the old written code but in the new life of the Spirit.

The Law and Sin

7 What then should we say? That the law is sin? By no means! Yet, if it had not been for the law, I would not have known sin. I would not have known what it is to covet if the law had not said, "You shall not covet." [8]But sin, seizing an opportunity in the commandment, produced in me all kinds of covetousness. Apart from the law sin lies dead. [9]I was once alive apart from the law, but when the commandment came, sin revived [10]and I died, and the very commandment that promised life proved to be death to me. [11]For sin, seizing an opportunity in the commandment, deceived me and through it killed me. [12]So the law is holy, and the commandment is holy and just and good.

13 Did what is good, then, bring death to me? By no means! It was sin, working death in me through what is good, in order that sin might be shown to be sin, and through the commandment might become sinful beyond measure.

The Inner Conflict

14 For we know that the law is spiritual; but I am of the flesh, sold into slavery under sin.[y] [15]I do not understand my own actions. For I do not do what I want, but I do the very thing I hate. [16]Now if I do what I do not want, I agree that the law is good. [17]But in fact it is no longer I that do it, but sin that dwells within me. [18]For I know that nothing good dwells within me, that is, in my flesh. I can will what is right, but I cannot do it. [19]For I do not do the good I want, but the evil I do not want is what I do. [20]Now if I do what I do not want, it is no longer I that do it, but sin that dwells within me.

21 So I find it to be a law that when I want to do what is good, evil lies close at hand. [22]For I delight in the law of God in my inmost self, [23]but I see in my members another law at war with the law of my mind, making me captive to the law of sin that dwells in my members. [24]Wretched man that I am! Who will rescue me from this body of death? [25]Thanks be to God through Jesus Christ our Lord!

[w] Gk *the weakness of your flesh* [x] Gk *brothers* [y] Gk *sold under sin*

2.20; 2 Cor 5.17.
6.11 *In Christ Jesus.* See note on 2 Cor 5.17.
6.12 Freed in baptism from the power of sin, the believer is not to allow sin to regain its dominion.
6.14 God's act of grace toward the sinner enables the sinner to live in grace, i.e. no longer to be under the dominion of sin.

6.17 *Form of teaching.* Literally, to the original pattern of teaching; that pattern, transmitted to the believer in baptism, is Christ crucified and risen; *cf.* 6.4; Gal 2.20; 1 Cor 2.2; 11.26.
6.22 *Eternal life.* See note on 2.7.
6.23 *cf.* 5.12; 6.16,21.
7.1-6 This section deals with the fact that the law's authority is limited; death frees from law.
7.1 *Do you now know...?* See note on 6.3.
7.4 Dying with Christ frees us from obligations under the law (of Moses); *cf.* 10.4; Gal 3.23-26.
7.5 *Sinful passions, aroused by the law. Cf.* 5.20; 7.13; Gal 2.19.
7.6 *cf.* 10.4; Gal 3.23-26; 2 Cor 3.6.
7.7-25 This section deals with the topic of the function of the Law.
7.7 Paul's partners in dialogue have accused him of making the Law of Moses, the Torah, less than noble, indeed evil, itself the manifestation of sin. Paul's response has to do with the real purpose of the Law. *I would not have known sin. Cf.* 3.20; 5.13; 7.8 This means that the law exists to demonstrate that humanity is under the power of sin (see 3.9), the word "sin" here being understood as an abstraction, as Paul will later say, something under which we are "sold" (7.14). The quotation is from Ex 20.17 and Deut 5.21. Paul may be using the commandment against coveting as a summary of the entire Ten Commandments, since all have to do with coveting another's place or property.
7.8 The power of sin in the abstract is now brought out into concrete actions; see note on 5.12. *All kinds of covetousness.* I.e. concrete acts of sinning; *cf.* 7.13. *Apart from the law sin lies dead. Cf.* 3.20; 5.13; 7.7.
7.11 See note on 7.8.
7.12 The question raised in 7.7 is answered.
7.13 A summary of 7.7-13. See note on 5.12.
7.14 *The law is spiritual.* I.e. the law is of heavenly origin and nature, inasmuch as it expresses the will of God. *I am of the flesh, sold into slavery under sin.* I.e. human beings, fallen under sin's power (see 3.9), are focused only on their own will and desires; *cf.* 7.25.
7.15 What a person wants is peace with God; what that person creates is estrangement from God. Peace with God comes only as God's gift (see 5.1-11; 8.3).
7.17 See note on 5.12.
7.18 *What is right.* See note on 7.15.
7.19 *The good I want* is a right relationship with God (*cf.* 7.22), which comes not by human doing but by God's free gift in Christ (see 8.3).
7.21 Precisely when we think we have achieved by our doing a right relationship with God, we have lost it, because that right relationship is God's gift.
7.22-23 To achieve the right relationship with God is impossible for human beings, who know that they are under the power of sin.
7.24 Once the law has functioned to bring the power of sin out into the open into concrete acts of transgression (see note on 5.12), the human being is free to ask the question of recipiency: *"Who will rescue me...?"* The answer follows.
7.25 Only recipients, not achievers, are able to offer thanks to God (*cf.* 1.21; 2 Cor 4.15; 1 Cor 4.7).

6.16 Rom 11.2; Mt 6.24; Jn 8.34; 2 Pet 2.19
6.17 Rom 1.8; 2 Tim 1.13
6.18 Jn 8.32; Rom 8.2
6.19 Rom 3.5; 6.13; 12.1
6.20 Mt 6.24; Jn 8.34
6.21 Rom 7.5; 8.6,13,21
6.22 Jn 8.32; 1 Cor 7.22; 1 Pet 2.16
6.23 Rom 5.12,21; Gal 6.7,8
7.2 1 Cor 7.39
7.3 Mt 5.32
7.4 Rom 6.2,11; Gal 2.19; Col 1.22
7.5 Rom 6.13,21; Gal 5.19; Jas 1.15
7.6 Rom 2.29; 2 Cor 3.6
7.7 Ex 20.17; Deut 5.21; Rom 3.20; 5.20
7.8 ver 11; 1 Cor 15.56
7.10 Lev 18.5; Rom 10.5; Gal 3.12
7.12 1 Tim 1.8
7.15 Gal 5.17
7.18 ver 25
7.22 Ps 1.2; 2 Cor 4.16; Eph 3.16
7.23 Gal 5.17

So then, with my mind I am a slave to
the law of God, but with my flesh I am a
slave to the law of sin.

Life in the Spirit

8 There is therefore now no condemnation for those who are in Christ Jesus.
[2]For the law of the Spirit[z] of life in Christ
Jesus has set you[a] free from the law of sin
and of death. [3]For God has done what the
law, weakened by the flesh, could not do:
by sending his own Son in the likeness of
sinful flesh, and to deal with sin,[b] he condemned sin in the flesh, [4]so that the just
requirement of the law might be fulfilled in
us, who walk not according to the flesh but
according to the Spirit.[z] [5]For those who live
according to the flesh set their minds on the
things of the flesh, but those who live according to the Spirit[z] set their minds on the
things of the Spirit.[z] [6]To set the mind on the
flesh is death, but to set the mind on the
Spirit[z] is life and peace. [7]For this reason the
mind that is set on the flesh is hostile to
God; it does not submit to God's law—
indeed it cannot, [8]and those who are in the
flesh cannot please God.
9 But you are not in the flesh; you are
in the Spirit,[z] since the Spirit of God dwells
in you. Anyone who does not have the
Spirit of Christ does not belong to him. [10]But
if Christ is in you, though the body is dead
because of sin, the Spirit[z] is life because of
righteousness. [11]If the Spirit of him who
raised Jesus from the dead dwells in you, he
who raised Christ[c] from the dead will give
life to your mortal bodies also through[d] his
Spirit that dwells in you.
12 So then, brothers and sisters,[e] we are
debtors, not to the flesh, to live according
to the flesh— [13]for if you live according to
the flesh, you will die; but if by the Spirit
you put to death the deeds of the body, you
will live. [14]For all who are led by the Spirit
of God are children of God. [15]For you did not
receive a spirit of slavery to fall back into
fear, but you have received a spirit of adoption. When we cry, "Abba![f] Father!" [16]it is
that very Spirit bearing witness[g] with our
spirit that we are children of God, [17]and if
children, then heirs, heirs of God and joint
heirs with Christ—if, in fact, we suffer with
him so that we may also be glorified with
him.

Future Glory

18 I consider that the sufferings of this
present time are not worth comparing with
the glory about to be revealed to us. [19]For
the creation waits with eager longing for
the revealing of the children of God; [20]for
the creation was subjected to futility, not of
its own will but by the will of the one who
subjected it, in hope [21]that the creation itself
will be set free from its bondage to decay
and will obtain the freedom of the glory of
the children of God. [22]We know that the
whole creation has been groaning in labor
pains until now; [23]and not only the creation, but we ourselves, who have the first
fruits of the Spirit, groan inwardly while we
wait for adoption, the redemption of our
bodies. [24]For in[h] hope we were saved. Now
hope that is seen is not hope. For who
hopes[i] for what is seen? [25]But if we hope for
what we do not see, we wait for it with
patience.
26 Likewise the Spirit helps us in our
weakness; for we do not know how to pray
as we ought, but that very Spirit intercedes[j]
with sighs too deep for words. [27]And God,[k]
who searches the heart, knows what is the
mind of the Spirit, because the Spirit[l] intercedes for the saints according to the will of
God.[m]
28 We know that all things work together for good[n] for those who love God,
who are called according to his purpose.
[29]For those whom he foreknew he also
predestined to be conformed to the image of
his Son, in order that he might be the
firstborn within a large family.[o] [30]And those
whom he predestined he also called; and
those whom he called he also justified; and
those whom he justified he also glorified.

God's Love in Christ Jesus

31 What then are we to say about these
things? If God is for us, who is against us?

[z] Or *spirit* [a] Here the Greek word *you* is singular number; other ancient authorities read *me* or *us* [b] Or *and as a sin offering* [c] Other ancient authorities read *the Christ* or *Christ Jesus* or *Jesus Christ* [d] Other ancient authorities read *on account of* [e] Gk *brothers* [f] Aramaic for *Father* [g] Or [15]*a spirit of adoption, by which we cry, "Abba! Father!"* [16]*The Spirit itself bears witness* [h] Or *by* [i] Other ancient authorities read *awaits* [j] Other ancient authorities add *for us* [k] Gk *the one* [l] Gk *he* or *it* [m] Gk *according to God* [n] Other ancient authorities read *God makes all things work together for good, or in all things God works for good* [o] Gk *among many brothers*

8.1 Rom 5.16
8.2 1 Cor 15.45; Rom 6.14,18; Jn 8.32,36
8.3 Acts 13.39; Heb 7.18; Phil 2.7; Heb 2.14
8.4 Gal 5.16,25
8.5 Gal 5.19-25
8.6 Rom 6.21; Gal 6.8
8.7 Jas 4.4
8.9 1 Cor 3.16; Gal 4.6; Phil 1.19; 1 Jn 4.13
8.11 Acts 2.24; Jn 5.21; 1 Cor 6.14
8.13 Gal 6.8; Col 3.5
8.14 Gal 5.18
8.15 2 Tim 1.7; Heb 2.15; Gal 4.5,6
8.16 2 Cor 1.22; Eph 1.13
8.17 Gal 4.7; 2 Tim 2.12; 1 Pet 4.13
8.23 2 Cor 1.22; 5.2,4; Gal 5.5
8.26 Mt 20.22; Eph 6.18
8.27 Ps 139.1,2; Lk 16.15; Rev 2.23
8.28 ver 32
8.29 Rom 11.2; 1 Pet 1.2,20; Eph 1.5,11; Phil 3.21; Heb 1.6
8.30 Eph 1.5,11; Rom 9.24; 1 Cor 6.11
8.31 Rom 4.1; Ps 118.6

8.1-11 This section deals with the results of liberation from the power of sin: the freedom of life in the Spirit. **8.1** *Therefore* signals a conclusion to the foregoing section (7.7-25). *No condemnation.* I.e. both now and at the final judgment. *In Christ Jesus.* See note on 2 Cor 5.17. **8.2** Beginning with this verse all that follows has to do with liberation. *The law of the Spirit of life in Christ Jesus. Cf.* Gal 6.2. **8.3** *cf.* 7.15,19. *The law, weakened by the flesh.* Human desire for achievement has employed the law in order to make claims on God, but freedom from the powers of sin and death is accomplished not by human achievement but by God's own gift in Christ; see note on 8.5. *In the likeness of sinful flesh.* For Paul Jesus was fully human, but the wording here, influenced by the hymnic, doxological tradition behind Phil 2.7, indicates early Christian belief that there was more to Jesus than merely the human. **8.4** *The just requirement of the law.* I.e. to live in a right relationship with God. *According to the flesh.* I.e. life lived only out of human resources; see note on 1 Cor 5.16. *According to the Spirit.* I.e. life lived out of God's resources. Only God's gracious work of liberation transfers the believer from life in the flesh to life in the Spirit. **8.5-8** These verses constitute an explanation and enlargement of 8.4. **8.7** *Hostile to God. Cf.* 5.10. *God's law.* I.e. God's will. **8.8** *cf.* 12.1-2; 14.18; 1 Cor 7.32; 2 Cor 5.9; Phil 4.18; 1 Thess 4.1. **8.9** *cf.* 8.11; 1 Cor 3.16; also Gal 5.25. **8.10** *cf.* Eph 2.5. **8.11** *cf.* 1 Cor 6.14; 15.20,23; 2 Cor 4.14; Phil 3.21; 1 Thess 4.14.

8.12-39 This section deals with life in the Spirit and its benefits: it means receiving adoption as God's own children (8.12-17), hope for God's future (8.18-25), help in times of weakness (8.26-27), and refuge and strength in daily life (28-39). **8.12** *Debtors.* The sense is that of obligation; those who are "in the Spirit" (8.9) are under obligation to God alone. **8.13** *cf.* 6.12; Col 3.5. *Put to death. Cf.* Gal 5.24. **8.14** *Are led.* God's action continues in the life of the believer; *cf.* 2.4; Gal 5.18; 1 Cor 12.2. *Children of God. Cf.* Gal 4.5. **8.15** *cf.* Gal 4.6; Jn 15.15. *Adoption.* This word is used also in 8.23; 9.4; Gal 4.5; Eph 1.5. While legal adoption was a common practice in Greco-Roman society, and not unknown among Jews, Paul's use of it in 9.4 (see note there) suggests an allusion to God's election of Israel; *cf.* Hos 11.1. *When we cry.* This expression is used throughout the Psalms with reference to urgent prayer (see e.g. Ps 3.4; 4.3; 18.6; 22.2,5; 34.6). *Abba, Father. Cf.* Mk 14.36; Gal 4.6. **8.16** Even engagement in prayer is being led by the Spirit (see 8.14). **8.17** *cf.* Gal 4.6-7. *Heirs.* The promise to Abraham (see chapter 4) that he would be the "father of many nations" (4.17) is fulfilled. *Suffer...glorified. Cf.* Phil 3.8-11. **8.18-39** The theme of 5.24 is renewed and enlarged. **8.18** It is important for Paul to emphasize that Christian believing includes firm hope in the future of God; *cf.* 1 Cor 1.7; Phil 3.14, 20,21. **8.19** *The creation.* I.e. the entire created universe participates in the brokenness of the fall into sin (*cf.* Gen 3.14-19). *Waits with eager longing.* I.e. the entire creation exhibits impatience, straining for release from its malaise. *The revealing of the children of God.* In God's new world the obscurities of the old will be done away with. **8.20-21** Paul's view of the world is marked by neither resignation nor contempt for it, but is one of liberation for it. God's creation, while "in bondage to decay," is not left without hope for liberation. **8.22** The idea is one of growth toward productive fulfillment; *cf.* Gal 4.19. **8.23** Christian existence is not without the ambiguities and obscurities of the old creation. **8.26** Existing within a fallen world, Christians themselves do not yet know what perfect prayer is. *Sighs too deep for words.* Literally, "wordless sighing," which in prayer is an expression of the need for liberation from a world so fallen that its praise of God is not what it will be. **8.27** *cf.* 1 Cor 2.16; Rom 8.16. **8.28** Christian hope is grounded in the eternal purpose of God. **8.29** *Foreknew...predestined.* These words, uncommon in Paul's letters, are not to be taken in an exclusive sense, but rather related to the concept in 8.29 of God's eternal plan. *Conformed to the image of his Son.* With this phrase Paul is most likely thinking of the crucified Jesus, as so many other statements indicate (see 6.3-4,17; 8.17; 1 Cor 2.2; 2 Cor 4.19-21; Gal 2.20; Phil 3.10). *Firstborn. Cf.* 1 Cor 15.20; Col 1.18.

[32]He who did not withhold his own Son, but
gave him up for all of us, will he not with
him also give us everything else? [33]Who will
bring any charge against God's elect? It is
God who justifies. [34]Who is to condemn? It
is Christ Jesus, who died, yes, who was
raised, who is at the right hand of God, who
indeed intercedes for us.[p] [35]Who will separate us from the love of Christ? Will hardship, or distress, or persecution, or famine,
or nakedness, or peril, or sword? [36]As it is
written,

"For your sake we are being killed all
day long;
we are accounted as sheep to be
slaughtered."

[37]No, in all these things we are more than
conquerors through him who loved us. [38]For
I am convinced that neither death, nor life,
nor angels, nor rulers, nor things present,
nor things to come, nor powers, [39]nor height,
nor depth, nor anything else in all creation,
will be able to separate us from the love of
God in Christ Jesus our Lord.

God's Election of Israel

9 I am speaking the truth in Christ—I
am not lying; my conscience confirms
it by the Holy Spirit— [2]I have great sorrow
and unceasing anguish in my heart. [3]For I
could wish that I myself were accursed and
cut off from Christ for the sake of my own
people,[q] my kindred according to the flesh.
[4]They are Israelites, and to them belong the
adoption, the glory, the covenants, the giving of the law, the worship, and the promises; [5]to them belong the patriarchs, and
from them, according to the flesh, comes
the Messiah,[r] who is over all, God blessed
forever.[s] Amen.

6 It is not as though the word of God had
failed. For not all Israelites truly belong to
Israel, [7]and not all of Abraham's children
are his true descendants; but "It is through
Isaac that descendants shall be named for
you." [8]This means that it is not the children
of the flesh who are the children of God, but
the children of the promise are counted as
descendants. [9]For this is what the promise
said, "About this time I will return and
Sarah shall have a son." [10]Nor is that all;
something similar happened to Rebecca
when she had conceived children by one
husband, our ancestor Isaac. [11]Even before
they had been born or had done anything
good or bad (so that God's purpose of election might continue, [12]not by works but by
his call) she was told, "The elder shall serve
the younger." [13]As it is written,

"I have loved Jacob,
but I have hated Esau."

14 What then are we to say? Is there
injustice on God's part? By no means! [15]For
he says to Moses,

"I will have mercy on whom I have
mercy,
and I will have compassion on
whom I have compassion."

[16]So it depends not on human will or ex-
ertion, but on God who shows mercy. [17]For
the scripture says to Pharaoh, "I have raised
you up for the very purpose of showing my
power in you, so that my name may be
proclaimed in all the earth." [18]So then he
has mercy on whomever he chooses, and
he hardens the heart of whomever he
chooses.

God's Wrath and Mercy

19 You will say to me then, "Why then
does he still find fault? For who can resist
his will?" [20]But who indeed are you, a
human being, to argue with God? Will what
is molded say to the one who molds it,
"Why have you made me like this?" [21]Has
the potter no right over the clay, to make
out of the same lump one object for special
use and another for ordinary use? [22]What
if God, desiring to show his wrath and to
make known his power, has endured with
much patience the objects of wrath that are
made for destruction; [23]and what if he has
done so in order to make known the riches
of his glory for the objects of mercy, which
he has prepared beforehand for glory—
[24]including us whom he has called, not
from the Jews only but also from the Gentiles? [25]As indeed he says in Hosea,

"Those who were not my people I will
call 'my people,'
and her who was not beloved I will
call 'beloved.'"
[26] "And in the very place where it was said
to them, 'You are not my people,'
there they shall be called children of
the living God."

27 And Isaiah cries out concerning Israel, "Though the number of the children

[p] Or *Is it Christ Jesus . . . for us?* [q] Gk *my brothers* [r] Or *the Christ* [s] Or *Messiah, who is God over all, blessed forever*; or *Messiah. May he who is God over all be blessed forever*

8.31-39 This section articulates the strength of Christian hope in view of an open future.
8.31 *cf.* 8.1.

8.32 *cf.* Gen 22.12,16; Isa 53.12; 1 Cor 3.21-23; 4.7.
8.33 *cf.* Isa 50.8.
8.34 *Right hand of God.* The place of power and authority; *cf.* Ps 110.1; Eph 1.20. *Who intercedes for us. Cf.* Heb 7.25; 1 Jn 2.1.
8.35 *Love of Christ. Cf.* 2 Cor 5.14; Gal 2.20; Eph 3.19. The ordeals listed in the second part of this verse all grow out of Paul's own experience: *hardship* (2 Cor 1.4,8; 2.4; 4.17), *distress* (2 Cor 6.4; 12.10), *persecution* (1 Cor 4.12; 2 Cor 4.9; 12.10; Gal 5.11), *famine* (1 Cor 4.11, 2 Cor 11.27), *nakedness* (1 Cor 4.11; 2 Cor 11.27), *peril* (1 Cor 15.30; 2 Cor 11.26), *sword* (2 Cor 11.26).
8.36 The quotation is from Ps 44.22.
8.37 *More than conquerors. Cf.* Rev 2.7,11,17,28; 3.5,12,21.
8.38-39 This is one of the most stirring affirmations of Christian hope.
9.1-11.36 This section of the letter deals with Israel's history, with the validity of God's promises to Israel, and with God's faithfulness to the covenant. If God justifies the sinner by God's grace through faith in Jesus Christ, then of what consequence are God's ancient promises to Israel?
9.4 *The adoption.* A reference to God's election of Israel; *cf.* Ex 4.22-23; Jer 31.9; Hos 11.1; also Deut 1.31; 8.5; Isa 1.2. *The glory. Cf.* Ex 16.7,10; 24.16-17; 40.34-35; Lev 9.6,23; Num 14.10,21; 16.19. *The covenants. Cf.* Gen 15.17-21; Ex 19.5; Deut 29.1; 2 Sam 4.7-29; 23.5. *The giving of the law. Cf.* Ex 20.1-17; Deut 5.1-33. *The worship.* I.e. the Temple and its services; *cf.* 1 Kings 8.22-30. *The promises. Cf.* Gen 12.3-7; 13.14-17; 15.6; 17.4-8; 22.16-18; 26.3-4; 28.13-14; Gal 3.16.
9.5 *The patriarchs.* I.e Abraham, Isaac, and Jacob, and possibly also the sons of Jacob – and possibly also David (*cf.* Mk 11.10; Acts 2.29).
9.6-7 The reason is given why it cannot be said that God's promises have failed; it is the same point made in Gal 4.21-31.
9.7 The quotation is from Gen 21.12.
9.8 The child of the promise is not Ishmael, but Isaac; *cf.* Gal 4.21-31.
9.9 The quotation is from Gen 18.10,14.
9.10 Rebecca gave birth to twins when her husband was also advanced in years: Jacob, not Esau, was the twin in the line of the promise; see Gen 25.20-25.
9.12 The quotation is from Gen 25.23.
9.13 The quotation is from Mal 1.2-3.
9.15 The quotation is from Ex 33.19.
9.17 The quotation is based on Ex 9.16.
9.18 The point of this verse is that Israel's election, just like God's justification of the ungodly, rests in the sovereign will of God and in God's freedom toward his creation.
9.19 *cf.* Job 16.8; 32.12.
9.20-21 The analogy of the potter is used often in the Old Testament for various purposes: Job 10.9; Ps 2.9; Isa 29.16; 41.25; 45.9; Jer 18.1-12; Wis 15.7-17; Eccl 27.5; 33.13; 38.29-30.
9.25-26 The quotation in these verses is a combination of Hos 2.23 and 1.10; *cf.* also Isa 2.2-4; 60.1-22; Mic 4.1-3; Zech 8.20-23.
9.27-28 The quotation in these verses is based on Isa 10.22-23.

8.33 Lk 18.7; Isa 50.8,9
8.34 Col 3.1; Heb 1.3; 7.25; 9.24; 1 Jn 2.1
8.36 Ps 44.22; 2 Cor 4.11
8.37 1 Cor 15.57; Rev 1.5
8.38 Eph 1.21; 1 Pet 3.22
9.1 2 Cor 1.23; 11.10; 1 Tim 2.7
9.3 Ex 32.32
9.4 Acts 3.25; Ps 147.19; Heb 9.1
9.5 Col 1.16-19; Jn 1.1; Rom 1.25
9.6 Num 23.19; Rom 2.28,29; Gal 6.16
9.7 Gal 4.23; Heb 11.18
9.9 Gen 18.10
9.10 Gen 25.21
9.12 Gen 25.23
9.13 Mal 1.2,3
9.14 2 Chr 19.7
9.15 Ex 33.19
9.17 Ex 9.16
9.19 2 Chr 20.6; Job 23.13; Dan 4.35
9.20 Isa 29.16; 64.8
9.21 2 Tim 2.20
9.22 Rom 2.4
9.25 Hos 2.23; 1 Pet 2.10
9.26 Hos 1.10
9.27 Isa 10.22,23; Gen 22.17; Hos 1.10

9.29 Isa 1.4; 13.19; Jer 50.40
9.30 Rom 10.6; Gal 2.16; Heb 11.7
9.31 Rom 10.2,3; Gal 5.4
9.32 1 Pet 2.6,8
9.33 Isa 28.16; Mt 21.42; Rom 10.11
10.2 Acts 21.20
10.3 Rom 1.17; Phil 3.9
10.4 Gal 3.24; Rom 7.1-4
10.5 Neh 9.29; Ezek 20.11; 13.21; Rom 7.10
10.8 Deut 30.14
10.9 Mt 10.32; Lk 12.8; Acts 16.31
10.11 Isa 28.16; Rom 9.33
10.12 Rom 3.22,29; Gal 3.28; Acts 10.36
10.13 Joel 2.32; Acts 2.21
10.15 Isa 52.7
10.16 Heb 4.2; Isa 53.1; Jn 12.38
10.18 Ps 19.4; Col 1.6,23; 1 Thess 1.8
10.19 Deut 32.21; Rom 11.11
10.20 Isa 65.1; Rom 9.30
10.21 Isa 65.2
11.1 1 Sam 12.22; Jer 31.37; 2 Cor 11.22; Phil 3.5
11.2 Ps 94.19; 1 Kings 19.10; Rom 8.29

of Israel were like the sand of the sea, only a remnant of them will be saved; 28for the Lord will execute his sentence on the earth quickly and decisively."[t] 29And as Isaiah predicted,

"If the Lord of hosts had not left
survivors[u] to us,
we would have fared like Sodom
and been made like Gomorrah."

Israel's Unbelief

30 What then are we to say? Gentiles, who did not strive for righteousness, have attained it, that is, righteousness through faith; 31but Israel, who did strive for the righteousness that is based on the law, did not succeed in fulfilling that law. 32Why not? Because they did not strive for it on the basis of faith, but as if it were based on works. They have stumbled over the stumbling stone, 33as it is written,

"See, I am laying in Zion a stone that will
make people stumble, a rock that
will make them fall,
and whoever believes in him[v] will not
be put to shame."

10 Brothers and sisters,[w] my heart's desire and prayer to God for them is that they may be saved. 2I can testify that they have a zeal for God, but it is not enlightened. 3For, being ignorant of the righteousness that comes from God, and seeking to establish their own, they have not submitted to God's righteousness. 4For Christ is the end of the law so that there may be righteousness for everyone who believes.

Salvation Is for All

5 Moses writes concerning the righteousness that comes from the law, that "the person who does these things will live by them." 6But the righteousness that comes from faith says, "Do not say in your heart, 'Who will ascend into heaven?' " (that is, to bring Christ down) 7"or, 'Who will descend into the abyss?' " (that is, to bring Christ up from the dead). 8But what does it say?

"The word is near you,
on your lips and in your heart"

(that is, the word of faith that we proclaim); 9because[x] if you confess with your lips that Jesus is Lord and believe in your heart that God raised him from the dead, you will be saved. 10For one believes with the heart and so is justified, and one confesses with the mouth and so is saved. 11The scripture says, "No one who believes in him will be put to shame." 12For there is no distinction between Jew and Greek; the same Lord is Lord of all and is generous to all who call on him. 13For, "Everyone who calls on the name of the Lord shall be saved."

14 But how are they to call on one in whom they have not believed? And how are they to believe in one of whom they have never heard? And how are they to hear without someone to proclaim him? 15And how are they to proclaim him unless they are sent? As it is written, "How beautiful are the feet of those who bring good news!" 16But not all have obeyed the good news;[y] for Isaiah says, "Lord, who has believed our message?" 17So faith comes from what is heard, and what is heard comes through the word of Christ.[z]

18 But I ask, have they not heard? Indeed they have; for

"Their voice has gone out to all the
earth,
and their words to the ends of the
world."

19Again I ask, did Israel not understand? First Moses says,

"I will make you jealous of those who
are not a nation;
with a foolish nation I will make
you angry."

20Then Isaiah is so bold as to say,

"I have been found by those who did
not seek me;
I have shown myself to those who
did not ask for me."

21But of Israel he says, "All day long I have held out my hands to a disobedient and contrary people."

Israel's Rejection Is Not Final

11 I ask, then, has God rejected his people? By no means! I myself am an Israelite, a descendant of Abraham, a member of the tribe of Benjamin. 2God has not rejected his people whom he foreknew. Do you not know what the scripture says

[t] Other ancient authorities read *for he will finish his work and cut it short in righteousness, because the Lord will make the sentence shortened on the earth* [u] Or *descendants*; Gk *seed* [v] Or *trusts in it* [w] Gk *Brothers* [x] Or *namely, that* [y] Or *gospel* [z] Or *about Christ*; other ancient authorities read *of God*

9.29 The quotation is from Isa 1.9. **9.30** *Righteousness.* The same Greek word can be translated "justification"; see note on 1.17. **9.33** The quotation is a combination of Isa 28.16 and 8.14; *cf.* also 1 Pet 2.6-8; Mk 12.10 (= Mt 21.42; Lk 20.17); Acts 4.11. **10.1** Paul can offer this prayer and still know that Israel will indeed be saved; see 11.26. *Zeal for God. Cf.* Acts 21.20; 22.3; Gal 1.14; Phil 3.6; also Jn 2.17 (=Ps 69.9). **10.3** This is Paul's criticism. **10.4** This statement can have several meanings: (a) that the law of Moses, with its demands and consequences, is no longer in effect for the believer (*cf.* Gal 3.23-26); (b) that in Christ the law is brought to its proper completion and fulfillment (*cf.* Mt 5.17); (c) that the law has as its function to drive people to the point of asking for deliverance, a deliverance offered in Christ (*cf.* Rom 7.25-26). It is possible that in this verse Paul may have all these meanings in mind. **10.5** The quotation is from Lev 18.5; as in Gal 3.12, the emphasis is on the word "does." **10.6** *Do not say in your heart.* This is a quotation of Deut 8.17 and 9.4 (Septuagint), both passages issuing a warning against trust in one's own achievement before God. *Who will ascend into heaven?* This is a quotation from Deut 30.12. *(That is, to bring Christ down).* I.e. to bring into effect God's salvation. **10.7** *Who will descend into the abyss?* This quotation is based on Ps 107.26. *The abyss.* The watery depths, which Ps 71.20 referred to as the underworld, the place of the dead, where the disobedient spirits await judgment; *cf.* Rev 9.1. *(That is, to bring Christ up from the dead).* I.e. to bring about the final stage of God's salvation. *Cf.* 1 Pet 3.19. **10.8** This verse answers the biblical questions cited in 10.6-7 by means of another biblical quotation, this time from Deut 30.14. *The word is near you.* God's word of grace and justification is God's gift, not something humanly achieved. *The word of faith.* I.e. the message of justification. **10.9** *cf.* 2 Cor 4.5; 1 Cor 8.6; 12.3; Phil 2.11; also Rom 6.17; 2.29. **10.10** The two phrases in this verse express the same idea: both *justified* and *saved* refer to that right relationship with God which ensures eschatological salvation. **10.11** The quotation is from Isa 28.16; see note on Rom 9.33. **10.12** *There is no distinction.* This theme, a major one in Romans, has been heard in 3.22; *cf.* also 3.9; Gal 3.28. *The same Lord is Lord of all. Cf.* 3.29. **10.13** The quotation is from Joel 2.32. **10.15** The quotation from Isa 52.7 is given in answer to the series of questions in 10.14-15a. The quotation refers to the preaching of the gospel. **10.16** *Not all.* I.e. not all of Israel. The quotation in this verse is from Isa 53.1; *cf.* Jn 12.38. **10.17** *cf.* Gal 3.2,5. **10.18** The quotation is from Ps 19.4. **10.19** The quotation is from Deut 32.21. *Jealous.* This anticipates the reason Paul gives for the Gentile mission in 11.11-32. **10.20** The quotation is from Isa 65.1. **10.21** The quotation is from Isa 65.2. **11.1** *cf.* Phil 3.5. **11.2** *Elijah.* An Israelite prophet who lived during the reigns of Kings Ahab and Ahaziah in the first half of the ninth century BCE.

of Elijah, how he pleads with God against Israel? 3"Lord, they have killed your prophets, they have demolished your altars; I alone am left, and they are seeking my life." 4But what is the divine reply to him? "I have kept for myself seven thousand who have not bowed the knee to Baal." 5So too at the present time there is a remnant, chosen by grace. 6But if it is by grace, it is no longer on the basis of works, otherwise grace would no longer be grace.[a]

7 What then? Israel failed to obtain what it was seeking. The elect obtained it, but the rest were hardened, 8as it is written,

"God gave them a sluggish spirit,
eyes that would not see
and ears that would not hear,
down to this very day."

9And David says,

"Let their table become a snare and a trap,
a stumbling block and a retribution for them;
10 let their eyes be darkened so that they cannot see,
and keep their backs forever bent."

The Salvation of the Gentiles

11 So I ask, have they stumbled so as to fall? By no means! But through their stumbling[b] salvation has come to the Gentiles, so as to make Israel[c] jealous. 12Now if their stumbling[b] means riches for the world, and if their defeat means riches for Gentiles, how much more will their full inclusion mean!

13 Now I am speaking to you Gentiles. Inasmuch then as I am an apostle to the Gentiles, I glorify my ministry 14in order to make my own people[d] jealous, and thus save some of them. 15For if their rejection is the reconciliation of the world, what will their acceptance be but life from the dead! 16If the part of the dough offered as first fruits is holy, then the whole batch is holy; and if the root is holy, then the branches also are holy.

17 But if some of the branches were broken off, and you, a wild olive shoot, were grafted in their place to share the rich root[e] of the olive tree, 18do not boast over the branches. If you do boast, remember that it is not you that support the root, but the root that supports you. 19You will say, "Branches were broken off so that I might be grafted in." 20That is true. They were broken off because of their unbelief, but you stand only through faith. So do not become proud, but stand in awe. 21For if God did not spare the natural branches, perhaps he will not spare you.[f] 22Note then the kindness and the severity of God: severity toward those who have fallen, but God's kindness toward you, provided you continue in his kindness; otherwise you also will be cut off. 23And even those of Israel,[g] if they do not persist in unbelief, will be grafted in, for God has the power to graft them in again. 24For if you have been cut from what is by nature a wild olive tree and grafted, contrary to nature, into a cultivated olive tree, how much more will these natural branches be grafted back into their own olive tree.

All Israel Will Be Saved

25 So that you may not claim to be wiser than you are, brothers and sisters,[h] I want you to understand this mystery: a hardening has come upon part of Israel, until the full number of the Gentiles has come in. 26And so all Israel will be saved; as it is written,

"Out of Zion will come the Deliverer;
he will banish ungodliness from Jacob."
27 "And this is my covenant with them,
when I take away their sins."

28As regards the gospel they are enemies of God[i] for your sake; but as regards election they are beloved, for the sake of their ancestors; 29for the gifts and the calling of God are irrevocable. 30Just as you were once disobedient to God but have now received mercy because of their disobedience, 31so they have now been disobedient in order that, by the mercy shown to you, they too may now[j] receive mercy. 32For God has imprisoned all in disobedience so that he may be merciful to all.

33 O the depth of the riches and wisdom and knowledge of God! How unsearchable are his judgments and how inscrutable his ways!

34 "For who has known the mind of the Lord?

[a] Other ancient authorities add *But if it is by works, it is no longer on the basis of grace, otherwise work would no longer be work* [b] Gk *transgression* [c] Gk *them* [d] Gk *my flesh* [e] Other ancient authorities read *the richness* [f] Other ancient authorities read *neither will he spare you* [g] Gk lacks *of Israel* [h] Gk *brothers* [i] Gk lacks *of God* [j] Other ancient authorities lack *now*

11.4 1 Kings 19.18
11.6 Rom 4.4
11.7 Rom 9.18,31
11.8 Isa 29.10; Deut 29.4; Mt 13.13,14
11.9 Ps 69.22,23
11.11 Acts 13.46; Rom 10.19
11.13 Acts 9.15; Rom 15.16
11.14 Rom 10.19; 1 Cor 7.16; 9.22
11.20 Rom 12.16; 2 Cor 1.24
11.22 1 Cor 15.2; Heb 3.6; Jn 15.2
11.23 2 Cor 3.16
11.25 1 Cor 2.7-10; Eph 3.3-5,9; Rom 9.18
11.26 Isa 59.20,21
11.27 Isa 27.9
11.30 Eph 2.2
11.32 Rom 3.9; Gal 3.22,23
11.33 Eph 3.8; Ps 92.5
11.34 Isa 40.13,14; 1 Cor 2.16; Job 36.22

11.3 The quotation is based on 1 Kings 19.10,14.
11.4 The quotation is based on 1 Kings 19.18. The point of this passage is to answer the question posed in 11.1. God will not reject his people, because God is faithful to his promise.
11.8 The quotation is from Deut 29.4.
11.9-10 The quotation is from Ps 69.22-23.
11.11 *Salvation has come to the Gentiles.* The idea that the nations will share with Israel in God's salvation is an Old Testament idea; *cf.* Isa 2.2-4; 25.6-10; 60.3-7; Jer 16.19; Mic 4.1-4; Zech 14.16; Ps 22.27-29. *So as to make Israel jealous.* This carries forward the point of the quotation in 10.19 of Deut 32.21. When Israel sees that the Gentiles' right relationship with God exists through God's grace alone, they will desire that right relationship, based on God's grace, for themselves.
11.12 *Their full inclusion.* The Christian mission to the Gentiles will finally result in Israel's full inclusion in God's eschatological salvation; *cf.* 11.25-26; see notes on Mt 26.64; Mk 4.12; 11.14; 14.62.
11.13-14 In this verse Paul states his pride in his ministry to the Gentiles in that it will bring greater glory to Israel. If God's salvation is by God's grace, as a gift, apart from works of law, then the gospel's rapid success among the Gentiles will encourage its rapid acceptance among Jews as well.
11.16 The same principle is at work in 1 Cor 7.14. Israel will always remain God's covenant people not because all Israel has been faithful but because of the remnant of believers within it, be these Abraham and the seed of promise (*cf.* 9.6-13) or the Jewish Christian community itself (*cf.* 9.27; 11.5,7).
11.17-24 This section warns against Gentile pride, and especially against contempt for Israel, on the grounds that Gentiles are now included in the covenant promises. Using the image of the olive tree, Paul indicates that the tree can be pruned of unfruitful branches, and that Gentiles will prove unfruitful if they come to believe that their inclusion is based on their own merit.
11.17 *You, a wild olive shoot.* The Gentiles are being addressed (see 11.13).
11.18 *You stand only through faith.* Gentile inclusion in the covenant promises is not based on merit.
11.21 God is the pruner of unfruitful branches.
11.22 *Provided you continue in his kindness.* God's kindness toward Gentiles means that they are recipients of God's grace; they are to continue to understand themselves as recipients, not as achievers before God.
11.23 God is not only the pruner of the unfruitful branches (see note on 11.21), but also the one who grafts new branches into the tree. Inclusion remains the work of God.
11.24 See notes on 11.21,22,23.
11.25-32 Will Israel be included in God's salvation? This section answers in the affirmative.
11.25 *The full number of the Gentiles.* The notion that at the end of time the nations will join Israel in God's promised salvation (see note on 11.11) is given a new rendition here: Israel's salvation will not be secure until the Gentiles have come to share in it. *Cf.* notes on Mt 26.64; Mk 4.12; 11.14; 14.62.
11.26-27 The quotation used to support Paul's statement that *all Israel will be saved* is taken from Isa 59.20-21 and 27.9; *cf.* also Ps 14.7; 53.6; 110.2.
11.28 *Enemies of God. Cf.* 5.10.
11.29 This verse articulates the basis for Paul's statements in 11.26 and in the last half of 11.28; *cf.* also 3.3-4.
11.32 The same thought is expressed in Gal 3.22.
11.33-36 A doxology concludes chapters 9-11. God's faithfulness to his covenant promises, in spite of human unfaithfulness, is reason for grateful wonder and unceasing praise.
11.34 The quotation is from Isa 40.13; *cf.* also 1 Cor 2.16.

Or who has been his counselor?"
35 "Or who has given a gift to him,
to receive a gift in return?"
36For from him and through him and to him are all things. To him be the glory forever. Amen.

The New Life in Christ

12 I appeal to you therefore, brothers and sisters,[k] by the mercies of God, to present your bodies as a living sacrifice, holy and acceptable to God, which is your spiritual[l] worship. 2Do not be conformed to this world,[m] but be transformed by the renewing of your minds, so that you may discern what is the will of God—what is good and acceptable and perfect.[n]

3 For by the grace given to me I say to everyone among you not to think of yourself more highly than you ought to think, but to think with sober judgment, each according to the measure of faith that God has assigned. 4For as in one body we have many members, and not all the members have the same function, 5so we, who are many, are one body in Christ, and individually we are members one of another. 6We have gifts that differ according to the grace given to us: prophecy, in proportion to faith; 7ministry, in ministering; the teacher, in teaching; 8the exhorter, in exhortation; the giver, in generosity; the leader, in diligence; the compassionate, in cheerfulness.

Marks of the True Christian

9 Let love be genuine; hate what is evil, hold fast to what is good; 10love one another with mutual affection; outdo one another in showing honor. 11Do not lag in zeal, be ardent in spirit, serve the Lord.[o] 12Rejoice in hope, be patient in suffering, persevere in prayer. 13Contribute to the needs of the saints; extend hospitality to strangers.

14 Bless those who persecute you; bless and do not curse them. 15Rejoice with those who rejoice, weep with those who weep. 16Live in harmony with one another; do not be haughty, but associate with the lowly;[p] do not claim to be wiser than you are. 17Do not repay anyone evil for evil, but take thought for what is noble in the sight of all. 18If it is possible, so far as it depends on you, live peaceably with all. 19Beloved, never avenge yourselves, but leave room for the wrath of God;[q] for it is written, "Vengeance is mine, I will repay, says the Lord." 20No, "if your enemies are hungry, feed them; if they are thirsty, give them something to drink; for by doing this you will heap burning coals on their heads." 21Do not be overcome by evil, but overcome evil with good.

Being Subject to Authorities

13 Let every person be subject to the governing authorities; for there is no authority except from God, and those authorities that exist have been instituted by God. 2Therefore whoever resists authority resists what God has appointed, and those who resist will incur judgment. 3For rulers are not a terror to good conduct, but to bad. Do you wish to have no fear of the authority? Then do what is good, and you will receive its approval; 4for it is God's servant for your good. But if you do what is wrong, you should be afraid, for the authority[r] does not bear the sword in vain! It is the servant of God to execute wrath on the wrongdoer. 5Therefore one must be subject, not only because of wrath but also because of conscience. 6For the same reason you also pay taxes, for the authorities are God's servants, busy with this very thing. 7Pay to all what is due them—taxes to whom taxes are due, revenue to whom revenue is due, respect to whom respect is due, honor to whom honor is due.

Love for One Another

8 Owe no one anything, except to love one another; for the one who loves another has fulfilled the law. 9The commandments, "You shall not commit adultery; You shall not murder; You shall not steal; You shall not covet"; and any other commandment, are summed up in this word, "Love your neighbor as yourself." 10Love does no wrong to a neighbor; therefore, love is the fulfilling of the law.

An Urgent Appeal

11 Besides this, you know what time it is, how it is now the moment for you to

[k] Gk *brothers* [l] Or *reasonable* [m] Gk *age* [n] Or *what is the good and acceptable and perfect will of God* [o] Other ancient authorities read *serve the opportune time* [p] Or *give yourselves to humble tasks* [q] Gk *the wrath* [r] Gk *it*

11.35 The quotation is from Job 41.11, this time more closely following the Hebrew text.
11.36 *cf.* 1 Cor 8.6.
12.1-15.33 This section of the letter contains pastoral admonitions and encouragement for Christian living, a regular feature of each of Paul's letters. See note on 1.1.
12.1-2 These two verses represent the theme for what follows: Christian life, as encouraged in 12.3-15.33, is to be done in terms of the worship of God, by means of the appointed structures of earthly existence, but Christians are not to make such structures the object of their worship.
12.1 *To present your bodies.* I.e. to present your entire selves, your whole being; *cf.* 1 Cor 6.19-20. *Spiritual worship.* The Greek phrase may be translated several ways (see footnote *k*), and is taken from the popular Greek philosophical usage, where it is employed to state that *spiritual* (or *reasonable*) *worship* is not confined to any given sacred space or sacred time, but involves the whole person at every moment of his or her life.
12.2 *Conformed.* Christian existence is not determined by the structures of earthly existence; this is exemplified and elaborated in 12.3-13; *cf.* 1 Cor 7.29-31. *Transformed by the renewal of your mind.* This is explained in 12.14-21; *cf.* 1 Cor 5.17.
12.3 *cf.* 1 Cor 4.19; 5.2; 8.1-2; 12.14-26; 13.4.
12.4-5 *Cf.* 1 Cor 12.12.
12.6 *Gifts that differ. Cf.* 1 Cor 12.4-11. *Prophecy.* I.e. intelligible preaching; *cf.* 1 Cor 14.1-5. *In proportion to faith.* The particular Greek wording indicates that Christian preaching is accountable to accepted theological standards observed within the prophetic community; see 1 Cor 14.29.
12.7 *Ministry.* The Greek word is *diakonia,* usually translated "service" or, as here, "ministry"; it can relate to official functions of office, as in 11.13; 2 Cor 4.1; 5.18; 6.3, or to specific tasks, such as the contribution for the poor among the saints in Jerusalem – Rom 15.31; 1 Cor 16.13; 2 Cor 8.4; 9.1,12,13. *The teacher. Cf.* 1 Cor 12.28.
12.8 The gifts listed in this verse have less to do with specific office bearers, and more with life and work within the congregation, perhaps distinctly among lay leaders.
12.9 Previously to this verse Paul's use of the word "love" in this letter has referred to God's love (*cf.* 5.5,8; 8.35), which now places Christians in the position to extend that love to others; *cf.* 13.8-10; 1 Cor 13; Gal 5.14,22; 1 Jn 4.19.
12.10 *Mutual affection.* The same Greek word, *philadelphia,* is used in 1 Thess 4.9; Heb 13.1; 1 Pet 1.22; 2 Pet 1.7.
12.12 *Rejoice in hope. Cf.* 5.2-5; 1 Pet 1.3-9. *Patient in suffering. Cf.* 5.2-4; 8.24-25; 1 Cor 13.7; 1 Thess 1.3. *Persevere in prayer. Cf.* 1 Thess 5.17; Col 4.2; Acts 1.14; 2.42; 6.4.
12.13 *cf.* 15.26-27; 1 Cor 16.1.
12.14 *cf.* Mt 5.44; Lk 6.27-28; 1 Cor 4.12; Jas 3.9-12; 1 Pet 2.23.
12.15 *cf.* Phil 1.19; 3.1; 4.4.
12.16 *cf.* 15.5; 2 Cor 13.11; Phil 2.2; 4.2.
12.17 *cf.* Prov 20.22; 24.29; Ex 23.4-5; 2 Chr 28.8-15; Mt 5.38-39,44; Lk 6.29,35; 1 Thess 5.15; 1 Pet 3.9. *Take thought for what is noble in the sight of all. Cf.* 1 Cor 10.32; 1 Tim 5.14; 1 Pet 2.12,15; 3.16.
12.18 *cf.* Mk 9.50; Mt 5.9; 1 Tim 2.1-2.
12.19 The quotation is from Deut 32.35. *Cf.* Lev 19.18; Prov 20.22; 24.29; 2 Chr 28.8-15.
12.20 The quotation is from Prov 25.21-22.
12.21 A summary of 12.14-21.
13.1-7 A section on the Christian's position toward the secular powers. God is the creator, who constructs avenues by which people in their daily lives may worship God; see note on 12.1-2. *Cf.* also 1 Pet 2.13-17.
13.1 *Governing authorities.* The political powers which govern society. *Instituted by God.* As Creator, God has ordered the world in such a way as to offer means for God's people to perform their "spiritual worship" (12.1).
13.3 The idea expressed here is based on the governing authorities' role as "God's servants" (see 13.4,6).
13.4 An ordered society is in place to enable God's people daily to carry out their "spiritual worship" (12.1). *God's servant.* This term is used of the one through whom such "spiritual worship" of God can be carried out; "God's servant" is not the object of worship, but the means through which God is worshiped. *Cf.* 1 Pet 2.13-14.
13.5 *Conscience. Cf.* 2.15.
13.6 *God's servants.* See note on 13.4.
13.7 *cf.* Mk 12.17 (= Mt 22.21; Lk 20.25); 1 Pet 2.17.
13.8-10 This section on love expands on 12.9-13.
13.8 *cf.* Gal 5.14.
13.9 The quotations of four of the

11.36 1 Cor 8.6; Heb 2.10; Rom 16.27; Heb 13.21
12.1 2 Cor 10.1,2; Rom 6.13; 16.19; 1 Pet 2.5
12.2 1 Pet 1.14; 1 Jn 2.15; Eph 4.23; 5.10
12.3 Rom 15.15; 2 Cor 10.13; Eph 4.7
12.4 1 Cor 12.12-14; Eph 4.4,16
12.6 1 Cor 7.7; 12.4,10; 1 Pet 4.10,11
12.7 1 Cor 12.28; 14.26
12.8 Acts 15.32; Mt 6.1-3; 1 Tim 5.17; 2 Cor 9.7
12.12 Heb 10.32,36; Acts 1.14
12.13 Rom 15.25; Heb 13.2
12.14 Mt 5.44; Lk 6.28
12.16 Rom 11.25; 15.5
12.17 Prov 20.22; 2 Cor 8.21
12.18 Mk 9.50; Rom 14.19
12.19 Lev 19.18; Heb 10.30
13.1 Titus 3.1; 1 Pet 2.13; Jn 19.11; Dan 2.21
13.3 1 Pet 2.14
13.5 Eccl 8.2; 1 Pet 2.19
13.8 Gal 5.14; Col 3.14; Jas 2.8
13.9 Ex 20.13,14; Mt 19.19
13.10 Mt 22.39,40
13.11 1 Cor 7.29,30; 15.34; Eph 5.14; 1 Thess 5.5,6

wake from sleep. For salvation is nearer to us now than when we became believers; [12]the night is far gone, the day is near. Let us then lay aside the works of darkness and put on the armor of light; [13]let us live honorably as in the day, not in reveling and drunkenness, not in debauchery and licentiousness, not in quarreling and jealousy. [14]Instead, put on the Lord Jesus Christ, and make no provision for the flesh, to gratify its desires.

Do Not Judge Another

14 Welcome those who are weak in faith,[s] but not for the purpose of quarreling over opinions. [2]Some believe in eating anything, while the weak eat only vegetables. [3]Those who eat must not despise those who abstain, and those who abstain must not pass judgment on those who eat; for God has welcomed them. [4]Who are you to pass judgment on servants of another? It is before their own lord that they stand or fall. And they will be upheld, for the Lord[t] is able to make them stand.

5 Some judge one day to be better than another, while others judge all days to be alike. Let all be fully convinced in their own minds. [6]Those who observe the day, observe it in honor of the Lord. Also those who eat, eat in honor of the Lord, since they give thanks to God; while those who abstain, abstain in honor of the Lord and give thanks to God.

7 We do not live to ourselves, and we do not die to ourselves. [8]If we live, we live to the Lord, and if we die, we die to the Lord; so then, whether we live or whether we die, we are the Lord's. [9]For to this end Christ died and lived again, so that he might be Lord of both the dead and the living.

10 Why do you pass judgment on your brother or sister?[u] Or you, why do you despise your brother or sister?[u] For we will all stand before the judgment seat of God.[v] [11]For it is written,

"As I live, says the Lord, every knee shall
bow to me,
and every tongue shall give praise to[w]
God."

[12]So then, each of us will be accountable to God.[x]

Do Not Make Another Stumble

13 Let us therefore no longer pass judgment on one another, but resolve instead never to put a stumbling block or hindrance in the way of another.[y] [14]I know and am persuaded in the Lord Jesus that nothing is unclean in itself; but it is unclean for anyone who thinks it unclean. [15]If your brother or sister[u] is being injured by what you eat, you are no longer walking in love. Do not let what you eat cause the ruin of one for whom Christ died. [16]So do not let your good be spoken of as evil. [17]For the kingdom of God is not food and drink but righteousness and peace and joy in the Holy Spirit. [18]The one who thus serves Christ is acceptable to God and has human approval. [19]Let us then pursue what makes for peace and for mutual upbuilding. [20]Do not, for the sake of food, destroy the work of God. Everything is indeed clean, but it is wrong for you to make others fall by what you eat; [21]it is good not to eat meat or drink wine or do anything that makes your brother or sister[u] stumble.[z] [22]The faith that you have, have as your own conviction before God. Blessed are those who have no reason to condemn themselves because of what they approve. [23]But those who have doubts are condemned if they eat, because they do not act from faith;[s] for whatever does not proceed from faith[s] is sin.[a]

Please Others, Not Yourselves

15 We who are strong ought to put up with the failings of the weak, and not to please ourselves. [2]Each of us must please our neighbor for the good purpose of building up the neighbor. [3]For Christ did not please himself; but, as it is written, "The insults of those who insult you have fallen on me." [4]For whatever was written in former days was written for our instruction, so that by steadfastness and by the encouragement of the scriptures we might have hope. [5]May the God of steadfastness and encouragement grant you to live in harmony with one another, in accordance with Christ Jesus, [6]so that together you may with one voice glorify the God and Father of our Lord Jesus Christ.

[s] Or *conviction* [t] Other ancient authorities read *for God* [u] Gk *brother* [v] Other ancient authorities read *of Christ* [w] Or *confess* [x] Other ancient authorities lack *to God* [y] Gk *of a brother* [z] Other ancient authorities add *or be upset or be weakened* [a] Other authorities, some ancient, add here 16.25–27

13.12 1 Jn 2.8; Eph 5.11; 1 Thess 5.8
13.13 1 Thess 4.12; Gal 5.21; Eph 5.18
13.14 Gal 3.27; Eph 4.24; Gal 5.16
14.1 1 Cor 8.9; 9.22
14.2 1 Tim 4.4; Titus 1.15
14.6 1 Cor 10.31; 1 Tim 4.3
14.7 2 Cor 5.15; Gal 2.20; Phil 1.20,21
14.9 2 Cor 5.15; Acts 10.36
14.10 2 Cor 5.10
14.11 Isa 45.23; Phil 2.10,11
14.12 Mt 12.36; 1 Pet 4.5
14.13 Mt 7.1; 1 Cor 8.13
14.14 Acts 10.15; 1 Cor 8.7
14.17 1 Cor 8.8; Rom 15.13
14.18 2 Cor 8.21
14.19 Ps 34.14; Heb 12.14; Rom 15.2
14.21 1 Cor 8.13
15.1 Rom 14.1; Gal 6.1,2
15.2 1 Cor 10.33; Rom 14.19
15.4 Rom 4.23,24; 2 Tim 3.16,17
15.5 Rom 12.16; 1 Cor 1.10

Ten Commandments are from Ex 20.13-15,17 and Deut 5.17-19,21; *cf.* Mt 19.18-19. *Love your neighbor as yourself. Cf.* Lev 19.18; Mt 5.43; 19.19; Mk 12.31 (= Mt 22.39); Mk 12.33; Lk 10.27; Gal 5.14; Jas 2.8.
13.10 *cf.* 1 Cor 13.6; Gal 6.2.
13.11-14 A section on encouragement in view of the end of time.
13.11 Eschatology and morality are often connected; *cf.* Phil 4.4-7; 1 Thess 5.1-11,23; Heb 10.24-25; Jas 5.7-11; 1 Pet 4.7-11; Mt 25.31-46; Mk 13.33-37. *Time.* The Greek word is *kairos,* i.e. the critical time, the moment before the End; see note on 1 Cor 7.29. *Wake from sleep. Cf.* Eph 5.14; 1 Thess 5.6-8.

13.12 *Lay aside the works of darkness and put on the armor of light. Cf.* Eph 4.22-25; Col 3.8-12; 1 Thess 5.8; 1 Pet 2.1; Jas 1.21.
13.14 *Put on the Lord Jesus Christ. Cf.* Gal 3.27.
14.1-15.13 This section deals with the balance between unity in the church on the one hand and the freedom of the individual believer on the other.
14.1 *Welcome.* This word has the sense of full inclusion in the Christian community with all rights and privileges of partnership. *Weak in faith.* These are defined in the verses following as those who abstain from eating meat (14.2-3) and from drinking wine (14.21). *Quarreling over opinions.* The apostle's concern is that his readers understand how important for him are harmony and unity in the church; *cf.* 15.5-6; 1 Cor 1.11; 11.18; Titus 3.9.
14.2 It is unclear whether the reference is to a strict vegetarianism or to an abstention from eating meat only on certain occasions. *Cf.* 1 Cor 8.1-13; 10.23-33.
14.3 *cf.* Col 2.16-19.
14.4 The analogy here is with etiquette in the Roman household; guests are not to address an erring servant but are to leave that up to the master. The last sentence in the verse shows the quick transition from the lord of the household to the Lord of the church.
14.5 *cf.* Gal 4.10-11; Col 2.16-20. *Convinced in his own mind.* See 14.14; 1 Cor 8.7.
14.6 *Give thanks to God. Cf.* 1 Cor 10.26,30.
14.8 *cf.* Phil 1.21.
14.11 The quotation is a combination of Isa 49.18 and 45.23; *cf.* Phil 2.10-11.
14.12 Since God has welcomed us into the company of God's people, we are finally accountable to God; *cf.* 14.3,8.
14.13 *Stumbling block.* I.e. something which would make someone fall away from Christ; *cf.* Mk 9.42 (=Mt 18.6; Lk 17.1).
14.14 *cf.* Acts 10.9-16; 1 Cor 8.7; Rom 14.5.
14.15 *Ruin.* I.e. falling away from Christ; as in 14.13.
14.16 Christian freedom should not become the reason why someone has fallen away from Christ.
14.17 *The kingdom of God.* One of the infrequent occurrences of this term in Paul; see also 1 Cor 4.20; 6.9-10; 15.24,50; Gal 5.21; 1 Thess 2.12; and Col 1.13. In this verse it applies to life in the present, rather than God's kingdom of the future time.
14.19 The same idea is expressed when Paul deals with the topic of food offered to idols in 1 Cor 8.1-2.
14.21 See notes on 14.13,15.
14.22 *The faith that you have.* This refers to the extent of one's freedom under God's grace, which remains a matter of personal conscience (see 14.5,14; 1 Cor 8.7). The beatitude in this verse commends a consistency between the believer's sense of freedom and his or her daily actions.
14.23 See note on previous verse. Faithful Christian action may proceed under the realm of God's grace, or it may proceed under the power of sin (*cf.* 3.9; 7.16-17). The final phrase means, for both the "strong" and the "weak," that to make one's own practice of the faith mandatory for others is to usurp God's place, which is sin. Perhaps Paul has the incident of Gal 2.12-13 in mind.
15.1 This follows the thought of 14.23.
15.2 *cf.* 8.1-2.
15.3 The quotation is from Ps 69.9.
15.4 *cf.* 1 Cor 9.10; 10.11.
15.5-6 This is a benediction which also is a prayer-wish. See note on 14.1.

15.8 Mt 15.24; Acts 3.25,26; Rom 3.3; 2 Cor 1.20
15.9 Ps 18.49; 2 Sam 22.50
15.12 Isa 11.10; Mt 12.21; Rev 5.5; 22.16
15.13 Rom 14.17; 1 Thess 1.5
15.14 2 Pet 1.12; 1 Cor 8.1,7,10
15.15 Rom 12.3; Eph 3.7,8
15.16 Acts 9.15; Rom 11.13; Phil 2.17
15.19 Acts 19.11; 2 Cor 12.12
15.20 2 Cor 10.15,16
15.21 Isa 52.15
15.23 Acts 19.21; Rom 1.11
15.25 Acts 19.21; 24.27
15.26 2 Cor 8.1; 9.2; 1 Thess 1.7,8
15.27 1 Cor 9.11
15.30 Gal 5.22; 2 Cor 1.11; Col 4.12
15.32 Rom 1.10; Acts 18.21; 1 Cor 16.18
15.33 Rom 16.20; 2 Cor 13.11; Phil 4.9; Heb 13.20
16.1 Acts 18.18
16.3 Acts 18.2; 2 Tim 4.19

The Gospel for Jews and Gentiles Alike

7 Welcome one another, therefore, just as Christ has welcomed you, for the glory of God. 8 For I tell you that Christ has become a servant of the circumcised on behalf of the truth of God in order that he might confirm the promises given to the patriarchs, 9 and in order that the Gentiles might glorify God for his mercy. As it is written,

"Therefore I will confess[b] you among
the Gentiles,
and sing praises to your name";

10 and again he says,

"Rejoice, O Gentiles, with his people";

11 and again,

"Praise the Lord, all you Gentiles,
and let all the peoples praise him";

12 and again Isaiah says,

"The root of Jesse shall come,
the one who rises to rule the Gentiles;
in him the Gentiles shall hope."

13 May the God of hope fill you with all joy and peace in believing, so that you may abound in hope by the power of the Holy Spirit.

Paul's Reason for Writing So Boldly

14 I myself feel confident about you, my brothers and sisters,[c] that you yourselves are full of goodness, filled with all knowledge, and able to instruct one another. 15 Nevertheless on some points I have written to you rather boldly by way of reminder, because of the grace given me by God 16 to be a minister of Christ Jesus to the Gentiles in the priestly service of the gospel of God, so that the offering of the Gentiles may be acceptable, sanctified by the Holy Spirit. 17 In Christ Jesus, then, I have reason to boast of my work for God. 18 For I will not venture to speak of anything except what Christ has accomplished[d] through me to win obedience from the Gentiles, by word and deed, 19 by the power of signs and wonders, by the power of the Spirit of God,[e] so that from Jerusalem and as far around as Illyricum I have fully proclaimed the good news[f] of Christ. 20 Thus I make it my ambition to proclaim the good news,[f] not where Christ has already been named, so that I do not build on someone else's foundation, 21 but as it is written,

"Those who have never been told of
him shall see,
and those who have never heard of
him shall understand."

Paul's Plan to Visit Rome

22 This is the reason that I have so often been hindered from coming to you. 23 But now, with no further place for me in these regions, I desire, as I have for many years, to come to you 24 when I go to Spain. For I do hope to see you on my journey and to be sent on by you, once I have enjoyed your company for a little while. 25 At present, however, I am going to Jerusalem in a ministry to the saints; 26 for Macedonia and Achaia have been pleased to share their resources with the poor among the saints at Jerusalem. 27 They were pleased to do this, and indeed they owe it to them; for if the Gentiles have come to share in their spiritual blessings, they ought also to be of service to them in material things. 28 So, when I have completed this, and have delivered to them what has been collected,[g] I will set out by way of you to Spain; 29 and I know that when I come to you, I will come in the fullness of the blessing[h] of Christ.

30 I appeal to you, brothers and sisters,[c] by our Lord Jesus Christ and by the love of the Spirit, to join me in earnest prayer to God on my behalf, 31 that I may be rescued from the unbelievers in Judea, and that my ministry[i] to Jerusalem may be acceptable to the saints, 32 so that by God's will I may come to you with joy and be refreshed in your company. 33 The God of peace be with all of you.[j] Amen.

Personal Greetings

16 I commend to you our sister Phoebe, a deacon[k] of the church at Cenchreae, 2 so that you may welcome her in the Lord as is fitting for the saints, and help her in whatever she may require from you, for she has been a benefactor of many and of myself as well.

3 Greet Prisca and Aquila, who work with me in Christ Jesus, 4 and who risked

[b] Or *thank* [c] Gk *brothers* [d] Gk *speak of those things that Christ has not accomplished* [e] Other ancient authorities read *of the Spirit* or *of the Holy Spirit* [f] Or *gospel* [g] Gk *have sealed to them this fruit* [h] Other ancient authorities add *of the gospel* [i] Other ancient authorities read *my bringing of a gift* [j] One ancient authority adds 16.25–27 here [k] Or *minister*

15.7 A continuation of what has begun in 14.1.
15.8 *cf.* 9.1-5; Mt 15.24; Jn 4.22.
15.9 The quotation is from Ps 18.49.
15.10 The quotation is from Deut 32.43.
15.11 The quotation is from Ps 117.1.
15.12 The quotation is from Isa 11.10; *cf.* Rev 5.5.
15.13 A benediction which is also a prayer-wish, as in 5.5.
15.14-33 This section explains Paul's intentions for the working partnership he envisions with the Roman church. There are three parts to this section: 15.14-21 relates to Paul's missionary principle, 15.22-29 concerns his plans to visit Rome, and 15.30-33 asks for his readers' prayers regarding his trip to Jerusalem.
15.15 *The grace given me by God. Cf.* 1.5; 12.3; Gal 1.15-16.
15.17-18 These two verses must be taken together: Paul's pride in his work is in what Christ has accomplished through him.
15.19 *cf.* 2 Cor 12.12; Gal 3.2-5. *Illyricum.* Today's Yugoslavia and Albania, this word in Paul's day could refer to "the land of the Illyrians," which may have included territories reached by Paul's Macedonian mission (*cf.* 2 Cor 8-9). There is no evidence that he himself traveled that far, but his activity in Macedonia may have brought him in touch with Illyrians living there, who then extended his mission further to the northwest of Macedonia.
15.20 Paul's missionary principle is that he establishes communities, rather than building on what other missionaries have already established; *cf.* 1 Cor 3.9-17.
15.21 The quotation is from Isa 52.15.
15.23-24 Paul expresses his desire that the Roman congregation support his mission to the west, to Spain.
15.25 *Ministry.* I.e. the collection (see Gal 2.10; 1 Cor 16.1). Paul must go to Jerusalem because his own ministry is at stake in the carrying out of the collection; *cf.* 15.31.
15.26 *Macedonia.* I.e. the territory of the Philippian and Thessalonican churches. *Achaia.* I.e. the territory of the Corinthian churches. Galatia is missing from this list; *cf.* 1 Cor 16.1. *Share their resources with the poor among the saints at Jerusalem.* This refers to Paul's collection, the effort of "remembering the poor" (Gal 2.10) to which Paul was committed after his meeting with the "pillars" of the Jerusalem church (see Gal 2.1-10); see also 2 Cor 8.1-24; 9.1-15.
15.27 *cf.* 11.17-24.
15.28 See notes on 15.23,26.
15.31 Paul reckons on hostility from *unbelievers* in Jerusalem, probably non-Christian Jews, who may try to do to him what he initially tried to do to Christians before he became one of them (*cf.* Gal 1.13). This verse also indicates that not all Christians in Jerusalem were convinced that his ministry was legitimate.
15.33 *cf.* Phil 4.9.
16.1-23 This section consists of a series of commendations and greetings, including the longest list of personal names in all of Paul's letters.
16.1 *Phoebe.* Phoebe is not mentioned elsewhere in the New Testament. Her mention here, and the information given about her, may suggest that she is the bearer of this letter. *Deacon.* The Greek word is *diakonos*, the usual term for "minister" (see footnote *j*); *cf.* 13.6; 15.8,16; 2 Cor 3.6; Eph 3.7; Col 1.7,23; 1 Tim 4.6. *Cenchreae.* A seaport of Corinth, seven miles east of the city, on the Saronic Gulf; *cf.* Acts 18.18.
16.2 *Benefactor.* The Greek word signifies a person of position, perhaps wealth, and influence; the word can be translated "presider," and is used in that sense in second-century Christian writings. A different form of the same word in 12.8 is translated "leader."
16.3 *Prisca and Aquila.* The same Priscilla and Aquila mentioned in 1 Cor 16.19 and Acts 18.2,18,26; *cf.* 2 Tim 4.19.

their necks for my life, to whom not only
I give thanks, but also all the churches of
the Gentiles. 5 Greet also the church in their
house. Greet my beloved Epaenetus, who
was the first convert[l] in Asia for Christ.
6 Greet Mary, who has worked very hard
among you. 7 Greet Andronicus and Junia,[m]
my relatives[n] who were in prison with me;
they are prominent among the apostles,
and they were in Christ before I was. 8 Greet
Ampliatus, my beloved in the Lord. 9 Greet
Urbanus, our co-worker in Christ, and my
beloved Stachys. 10 Greet Apelles, who is
approved in Christ. Greet those who belong
to the family of Aristobulus. 11 Greet my
relative[o] Herodion. Greet those in the Lord
who belong to the family of Narcissus. 12 Greet
those workers in the Lord, Tryphaena and
Tryphosa. Greet the beloved Persis, who has
worked hard in the Lord. 13 Greet Rufus,
chosen in the Lord; and greet his mother—
a mother to me also. 14 Greet Asyncritus,
Phlegon, Hermes, Patrobas, Hermas, and
the brothers and sisters[p] who are with them.
15 Greet Philologus, Julia, Nereus and his
sister, and Olympas, and all the saints who
are with them. 16 Greet one another with a
holy kiss. All the churches of Christ greet
you.

Final Instructions

17 I urge you, brothers and sisters,[p] to
keep an eye on those who cause dissensions
and offenses, in opposition to the teaching
that you have learned; avoid them. 18 For
such people do not serve our Lord Christ,
but their own appetites,[q] and by smooth
talk and flattery they deceive the hearts of
the simple-minded. 19 For while your obedience is known to all, so that I rejoice over
you, I want you to be wise in what is good
and guileless in what is evil. 20 The God of
peace will shortly crush Satan under your
feet. The grace of our Lord Jesus Christ be
with you.[r]
21 Timothy, my co-worker, greets you;
so do Lucius and Jason and Sosipater, my
relatives.[n]
22 I Tertius, the writer of this letter,
greet you in the Lord.[s]
23 Gaius, who is host to me and to the
whole church, greets you. Erastus, the city
treasurer, and our brother Quartus, greet
you.[t]

Final Doxology

25 Now to God[u] who is able to strengthen
you according to my gospel and the proclamation of Jesus Christ, according to the
revelation of the mystery that was kept
secret for long ages 26 but is now disclosed,
and through the prophetic writings is made
known to all the Gentiles, according to the
command of the eternal God, to bring about
the obedience of faith— 27 to the only wise
God, through Jesus Christ, to whom[v] be the
glory forever! Amen.[w]

[l] Gk *first fruits* [m] Or *Junias*; other ancient authorities read *Julia* [n] Or *compatriots* [o] *compatriot* [p] Gk *brothers* [q] Gk *their own belly* [r] Other ancient authorities lack this sentence [s] Or *I Tertius, writing this letter in the Lord, greet you* [t] Other ancient authorities add verse 24, *The grace of our Lord Jesus Christ be with all of you. Amen.* [u] Gk *the one* [v] Other ancient authorities lack *to whom*. The verse then reads, *to the only wise God be the glory through Jesus Christ forever. Amen.* [w] Other ancient authorities lack 16.25–27 or include it after 14.23 or 15.33; others put verse 24 after verse 27

16.5 *Epaenetus*. Mentioned only here in the New Testament.
16.6 *Mary*. She cannot be identified with any other Mary in the New Testament.
16.7 *Andronicus and Junia*. Mentioned only here in the New Testament. Junia is a common Roman name for a woman, while "Junias" (see footnote *l*) as a man's name apparently is completely unknown. *My relatives*. I.e. fellow-Jews, as in 9.3. *Prominent among the apostles*. This phrase can mean that this man and this woman were counted to be among those who were called "apostles."
16.8-15 No other mention is made in the New Testament of the names of the people listed in these verses. Of these names, *Tryphaena* (15.12), *Tryphosa* (15.12), *Persis* (15.12), and *Julia* are women.
16.16 *A holy kiss*. A liturgical gesture mentioned in 1 Cor 16.20; 2 Cor 13.21; 1 Thess 5.26. See note on 1 Cor 16.19-20.
16.17 *cf.* 1 Cor 16.22; Gal 6.12-13; Phil 3.18-19; Titus 3.9-11.
16.18 *cf.* Phil 3.19.
16.19 *cf.* 1 Cor 14.20; Mt 10.16.
16.20 *cf.* Gen 3.15.
16.21 *Timothy*. See note on 1 Tim 1.2. *Lucius*. A name mentioned in Acts 13.1. *Jason*. A name mentioned in Acts 17.5-9. *Sosipater*. Possibly a variant of the name Sopater, mentioned in Acts 20.4.
16.22 *Tertius, the writer*. Mentioned nowhere else in the New Testament, this man evidently served Paul as the one to whom the apostle dictated the letter to the Romans.
16.23 *Gaius*. This name occurs in 1 Cor 1.14; Acts 19.29; 20.4; and 3 Jn 1, but evidently not with reference to the same person in each case. *Host to me and to the whole church*. Paul stayed with Gaius, whose house was also the site of a local house church (*cf.* Philem 2).
16.25-27 This concluding doxology was attached after chapter 14 in one manuscript tradition and after chapter 15 in another.
16.25 *The revelation of the mystery which was kept secret*. *Cf.* Col 1.26-27; Eph 1.9-10; 3.9-11; 2 Tim 1.9-10; Titus 1.2-3; 1 Pet 1.20; *cf.* also 1 Cor 2.6-10.
16.26 *cf.* 1.5.
16.27 *cf.* 1 Tim 1.17; Jude 25.

16.5 1 Cor 16.15,19; Col 4.15
16.9 2 Cor 5.17
16.15 ver 2.14
16.16 1 Cor 16.20; 2 Cor 13.12; 1 Thess 5.26
16.17 1 Tim 1.3; 6.3; Gal 1.8,9; 2 Thess 3.6,14; 2 Jn 10
16.18 Phil 3.19; Col 2.4
16.19 Rom 1.8; Mt 10.16; 1 Cor 14.20
16.20 Rom 15.33; Gen 3.15; 1 Cor 16.23; 1 Thess 5.28
16.21 Acts 16.1; 13.1; 17.5; 20.4; ver 7.11
16.23 1 Cor 1.14; Acts 19.22
16.25 Eph 3.20; Rom 2.16; Eph 1.9
16.26 Eph 1.9; Rom 1.5

THE FIRST LETTER OF PAUL TO THE

CORINTHIANS

Salutation

1 Paul, called to be an apostle of Christ
Jesus by the will of God, and our
brother Sosthenes,
2 To the church of God that is in Corinth, to those who are sanctified in Christ
Jesus, called to be saints, together with all
those who in every place call on the name
of our Lord Jesus Christ, both their Lord[a]
and ours:
3 Grace to you and peace from God our
Father and the Lord Jesus Christ.
4 I give thanks to my[b] God always for
you because of the grace of God that has
been given you in Christ Jesus, 5for in every
way you have been enriched in him, in
speech and knowledge of every kind— 6just
as the testimony of[c] Christ has been strengthened among you— 7so that you are not
lacking in any spiritual gift as you wait for
the revealing of our Lord Jesus Christ. 8He
will also strengthen you to the end, so that
you may be blameless on the day of our
Lord Jesus Christ. 9God is faithful; by him
you were called into the fellowship of his
Son, Jesus Christ our Lord.

Divisions in the Church

10 Now I appeal to you, brothers and
sisters,[d] by the name of our Lord Jesus
Christ, that all of you be in agreement and
that there be no divisions among you, but
that you be united in the same mind and
the same purpose. 11For it has been reported
to me by Chloe's people that there are
quarrels among you, my brothers and sisters.[e]
12What I mean is that each of you says, "I
belong to Paul," or "I belong to Apollos,"
or "I belong to Cephas," or "I belong to
Christ." 13Has Christ been divided? Was Paul
crucified for you? Or were you baptized in
the name of Paul? 14I thank God[f] that I
baptized none of you except Crispus and
Gaius, 15so that no one can say that you
were baptized in my name. 16(I did baptize
also the household of Stephanas; beyond
that, I do not know whether I baptized
anyone else.) 17For Christ did not send me
to baptize but to proclaim the gospel, and
not with eloquent wisdom, so that the cross
of Christ might not be emptied of its power.

Christ the Power and Wisdom of God

18 For the message about the cross is
foolishness to those who are perishing, but
to us who are being saved it is the power
of God. 19For it is written,

"I will destroy the wisdom of the wise,
and the discernment of the
discerning I will thwart."

20Where is the one who is wise? Where is
the scribe? Where is the debater of this age?
Has not God made foolish the wisdom of the
world? 21For since, in the wisdom of God,
the world did not know God through wisdom, God decided, through the foolishness
of our proclamation, to save those who
believe. 22For Jews demand signs and Greeks
desire wisdom, 23but we proclaim Christ
crucified, a stumbling block to Jews and
foolishness to Gentiles, 24but to those who
are the called, both Jews and Greeks, Christ
the power of God and the wisdom of God.
25For God's foolishness is wiser than human
wisdom, and God's weakness is stronger
than human strength.
26 Consider your own call, brothers and
sisters:[d] not many of you were wise by
human standards,[g] not many were powerful, not many were of noble birth. 27But God
chose what is foolish in the world to shame
the wise; God chose what is weak in the
world to shame the strong; 28God chose
what is low and despised in the world,
things that are not, to reduce to nothing
things that are, 29so that no one[h] might
boast in the presence of God. 30He is the
source of your life in Christ Jesus, who
became for us wisdom from God, and righteousness and sanctification and redemption,
31in order that, as it is written, "Let the one
who boasts, boast in[i] the Lord."

[a] Gk *theirs* [b] Other ancient authorities lack *my* [c] Or *to* [d] Gk *brothers* [e] Gk *my brothers* [f] Other ancient authorities read *I am thankful* [g] Gk *according to the flesh* [h] Gk *no flesh* [i] Or *of*

1.2 Acts 18.1; Rom 1.7; Acts 7.59
1.3 Rom 1.7
1.6 2 Tim 1.8; Rev 1.2
1.7 Phil 3.20; Titus 2.13; 2 Pet 3.12
1.9 Isa 49.7; 1 Jn 1.3
1.10 2 Cor 13.11; Rom 12.16
1.13 2 Cor 11.4; Mt 28.19; Acts 2.38
1.14 Acts 18.8; Rom 16.23
1.16 1 Cor 16.15
1.17 Jn 4.2; Acts 10.48; 1 Cor 2.1; 4.13
1.18 Acts 17.18; 1 Cor 15.2; Rom 1.16
1.20 Isa 33.18; Rom 1.22
1.21 Gal 1.15; 1 Tim 4.16; Heb 7.25
1.23 Gal 5.11; 1 Cor 2.14
1.26 Rom 11.29
1.27 Jas 2.5
1.29 Eph 2.9
1.30 1 Cor 6.11; 1 Thess 5.23; Eph 1.7,14; Rom 3.24
1.31 Jer 9.23,24; 2 Cor 10.17

See the Introductions, pp. 8–9 and 84–85 above.

1.1-9 Paul addresses the church in Corinth.
1.1-3 Paul uses the formal Greek style for writing letters: the writer's name first, then the addressees, and a word of greeting. For details on letter style, see note on Rom 1.1. On apostleship, see note on Rom 1.5. Sosthenes was a synagogue official in Corinth, according to Acts 18.17. On the origins of the church there, see Acts 18.1-17. *Saints* are those set apart for God's work in the world.
1.4-9 This formal thanksgiving centers on God's gifts (special abilities and roles given to individuals through the Spirit) for the church there, and calls for careful use of them to avoid divisions in the church. These *gifts* are Paul's major concern in 1 Cor 12-14, where they are defined and rules are given for using them. Proper use of the gifts is essential for the shared life of the community of faith (*fellowship*) if they are to be *blameless* on the *day* when God calls to account all his people.
1.10-17 Differing Roles in Tension within a Unified Community.
Here Paul lays the groundwork for his answers to the questions sent him by the Corinthians. He seeks first to call them to a unity which will transcend the different roles that members have been empowered by the Spirit to fulfill. *Divisions* are his major concern.
1.11 *Chloe's people* may refer to the church which meets in her home, or to the members of her household, including slaves, or to her leadership role in the church (see Phil 4.2-3 and Rom 16.1-2).
1.12 *Apollos*, a leader in the church at Corinth, was with Paul when he wrote. According to Acts 18.24-19.1, he was an Alexandrine Jew, who became a follower of John the Baptist, and was instructed in faith in Christ by Priscilla and Aquila (Rom 16.3). *Cephas* is the Aramaic nickname meaning rock, and is equivalent to Peter (in Greek, *Petros*; Mt 16.18).
1.13-16 *Christ* is here the representative figure for the whole people of God (see 12.12 and Gal 3.16). He is the important figure, not the one that baptized them into the fellowship (*Paul, Cephas, Apollos*). *Crispus* is mentioned in Acts 18.8 as a synagogue officer, and *Gaius* is named in Rom 16.23. *Stephanas* and his household were Paul's first converts in Achaia, a central section of Greece (1 Cor 16.17).
1.17-2.5 The Centrality of the Cross and Resurrection of Jesus Christ.
1.17-19 The power of Paul's message and work is the cross of Christ (1.23; 1.29; 2.2), not his skill in preaching or his own wisdom, even though that message sounds like *foolishness* in human terms, as Isaiah 29.14 quotes God as affirming.
1.20-25 Proud, self-centered humans want God to be at their disposal, but God's way of dealing with human sin through the cross of Christ stands in contrast to human power and wisdom. Those who have been *called* by the message of the cross find in it God's *power* and *wisdom*.
1.26-29 The question is raised whether the Corinthian Christians had any prior accomplishments which commended them to God, but there is no basis for any of them to *boast* (quoting Jer 9.24).

2.1-5 Paul insists that the cross is central for Christian life and faith (1 Cor 11.25; 2 Cor 4.10; Phil 3.18; Gal 3.13; Rom 3.25; 6.3). The power of the cross is evident through the work of the Spirit (2 Cor 11.6; 1 Thess 1.13; Gal 3.2,5), and manifests its perfection through human *weakness.*
2.6-16 The Debate over Human and Divine Wisdom.
Paul uses the Greek debating method, called diatribe, in which one first quotes the arguments of the opponent and then answers them, as he does in 3.1-23. He argues that he came to them in human weakness, with no effort to be rationally persuasive in human terms, since he wanted their acceptance of truth to rest on God's *power* and not on human wisdom. Spiritual maturity in Corinth is not mere intellectual accomplishment but eternal wisdom given by God. *The rulers of this age* (either political or demonic powers) did not understand what God was doing through the cross, or they would not have put him to death. Human inability to grasp God's purposes was known from the Jewish scriptures, as Paul declares in a mixed quotation (2.9), probably from Isa 64.4 and Ps 31.19, and in a rhetorical question (2.16) from Isa 40.13.
3.1-4.19 Working for the Growth and Building Up of the Church.
3.1-5 Contradicting the Corinthians' claim to spiritual maturity is the fact that they cause divisions within the community, which is a sign that they are weak (*of the flesh*) and infantile. Their leaders are to consider themselves as *servants* of the other members.
3.6-23 Paul depicts the community under two metaphors: (1) that of a plant which needs care and nurturing, and that of a building in process of construction. Each of the leaders has a specific role to fulfill: Paul planted, Apollos watered, but the growth came from *God* alone. (2) Paul *laid a foundation* of the church in Corinth; others have built it up. But the true foundation is Christ: human contributions to this growing structure will be evaluated by God in *the Day* of universal judgment. The community comprises the true *temple* of God, where God dwells among his people, as in ancient Israel (*cf.* 2 Chr 6.20-23; Ps 18.6). Compared with God's wisdom, human wisdom is *foolishness* (quoting Job 5.13 and Ps 94.11). God has given them leaders (*Paul, Apollos, Cephas*) and in Christ they have been granted understanding of *all things*: life, death, present and future.

Proclaiming Christ Crucified

2 When I came to you, brothers and sisters,[j] I did not come proclaiming the mystery[k] of God to you in lofty words or wisdom. 2For I decided to know nothing among you except Jesus Christ, and him crucified. 3And I came to you in weakness and in fear and in much trembling. 4My speech and my proclamation were not with plausible words of wisdom,[l] but with a demonstration of the Spirit and of power, 5so that your faith might rest not on human wisdom but on the power of God.

The True Wisdom of God

6 Yet among the mature we do speak wisdom, though it is not a wisdom of this age or of the rulers of this age, who are doomed to perish. 7But we speak God's wisdom, secret and hidden, which God decreed before the ages for our glory. 8None of the rulers of this age understood this; for if they had, they would not have crucified the Lord of glory. 9But, as it is written,

"What no eye has seen, nor ear heard,
nor the human heart conceived,
what God has prepared for those who love him"—

10these things God has revealed to us through the Spirit; for the Spirit searches everything, even the depths of God. 11For what human being knows what is truly human except the human spirit that is within? So also no one comprehends what is truly God's except the Spirit of God. 12Now we have received not the spirit of the world, but the Spirit that is from God, so that we may understand the gifts bestowed on us by God. 13And we speak of these things in words not taught by human wisdom but taught by the Spirit, interpreting spiritual things to those who are spiritual.[m]

14 Those who are unspiritual[n] do not receive the gifts of God's Spirit, for they are foolishness to them, and they are unable to understand them because they are spiritually discerned. 15Those who are spiritual discern all things, and they are themselves subject to no one else's scrutiny.

16 "For who has known the mind of the Lord
so as to instruct him?"
But we have the mind of Christ.

On Divisions in the Corinthian Church

3 And so, brothers and sisters,[j] I could not speak to you as spiritual people, but rather as people of the flesh, as infants in Christ. 2I fed you with milk, not solid food, for you were not ready for solid food. Even now you are still not ready, 3for you are still of the flesh. For as long as there is jealousy and quarreling among you, are you not of the flesh, and behaving according to human inclinations? 4For when one says, "I belong to Paul," and another, "I belong to Apollos," are you not merely human?

5 What then is Apollos? What is Paul? Servants through whom you came to believe, as the Lord assigned to each. 6I planted, Apollos watered, but God gave the growth. 7So neither the one who plants nor the one who waters is anything, but only God who gives the growth. 8The one who plants and the one who waters have a common purpose, and each will receive wages according to the labor of each. 9For we are God's servants, working together; you are God's field, God's building.

10 According to the grace of God given to me, like a skilled master builder I laid a foundation, and someone else is building on it. Each builder must choose with care how to build on it. 11For no one can lay any foundation other than the one that has been laid; that foundation is Jesus Christ. 12Now if anyone builds on the foundation with gold, silver, precious stones, wood, hay, straw— 13the work of each builder will become visible, for the Day will disclose it, because it will be revealed with fire, and the fire will test what sort of work each has done. 14If what has been built on the foundation survives, the builder will receive a reward. 15If the work is burned up, the builder will suffer loss; the builder will be saved, but only as through fire.

16 Do you not know that you are God's temple and that God's Spirit dwells in you?[o] 17If anyone destroys God's temple, God will destroy that person. For God's temple is holy, and you are that temple.

18 Do not deceive yourselves. If you think that you are wise in this age, you should become fools so that you may become wise. 19For the wisdom of this world is foolishness with God. For it is written,

[j] Gk *brothers* [k] Other ancient authorities read *testimony* [l] Other ancient authorities read *the persuasiveness of wisdom* [m] Or *interpreting spiritual things in spiritual language,* or *comparing spiritual things with spiritual* [n] Or *natural* [o] In verses 16 and 17 the Greek word for *you* is plural

2.1
1 Cor 1.17
2.4
Rom 15.19; 1 Cor 4.20
2.6
Eph 4.13; Phil 3.15; 1 Cor 1.20; 1.28
2.9
Isa 64.4; 65.17
2.10
Mt 16.17; Eph 3.3,5; Jn 14.26
2.11
Prov 20.27; Jer 17.9
2.13
1 Cor 1.17
2.14
1 Cor 1.18; Jas 3.15
2.16
Isa 40.13; Jn 15.15
3.1
1 Cor 2.15; Rom 7.14; 1 Cor 2.14; Heb 5.13
3.2
Heb 5.12,13; 1 Pet 2.2
3.3
1 Cor 1.11; Gal 5.20; Jas 3.16
3.4
1 Cor 1.12
3.8
Ps 62.12; Gal 6.4,5
3.9
2 Cor 6.1; Isa 61.3; Eph 2.20-22; 1 Pet 2.5
3.10
Rom 12.3; 15.20; 1 Cor 15.10
3.11
Isa 28.6; Eph 2.20
3.13
1 Cor 4.5; 2 Thess 1.8
3.16
1 Cor 6.19; 2 Cor 6.16
3.18
Isa 5.21; 1 Cor 8.2; Gal 6.3
3.19
Job 5.13; 1 Cor 1.20

"He catches the wise in their craftiness," 20and again,

"The Lord knows the thoughts of the wise,
that they are futile."

21So let no one boast about human leaders. For all things are yours, 22whether Paul or Apollos or Cephas or the world or life or death or the present or the future—all belong to you, 23and you belong to Christ, and Christ belongs to God.

The Ministry of the Apostles

4 Think of us in this way, as servants of Christ and stewards of God's mysteries. 2Moreover, it is required of stewards that they be found trustworthy. 3But with me it is a very small thing that I should be judged by you or by any human court. I do not even judge myself. 4I am not aware of anything against myself, but I am not thereby acquitted. It is the Lord who judges me. 5Therefore do not pronounce judgment before the time, before the Lord comes, who will bring to light the things now hidden in darkness and will disclose the purposes of the heart. Then each one will receive commendation from God.

6 I have applied all this to Apollos and myself for your benefit, brothers and sisters,[p] so that you may learn through us the meaning of the saying, "Nothing beyond what is written," so that none of you will be puffed up in favor of one against another. 7For who sees anything different in you?[q] What do you have that you did not receive? And if you received it, why do you boast as if it were not a gift?

8 Already you have all you want! Already you have become rich! Quite apart from us you have become kings! Indeed, I wish that you had become kings, so that we might be kings with you! 9For I think that God has exhibited us apostles as last of all, as though sentenced to death, because we have become a spectacle to the world, to angels and to mortals. 10We are fools for the sake of Christ, but you are wise in Christ. We are weak, but you are strong. You are held in honor, but we in disrepute. 11To the present hour we are hungry and thirsty, we are poorly clothed and beaten and homeless, 12and we grow weary from the work of our own hands. When reviled, we bless; when persecuted, we endure; 13when slandered, we speak kindly. We have become like the rubbish of the world, the dregs of all things, to this very day.

Fatherly Admonition

14 I am not writing this to make you ashamed, but to admonish you as my beloved children. 15For though you might have ten thousand guardians in Christ, you do not have many fathers. Indeed, in Christ Jesus I became your father through the gospel. 16I appeal to you, then, be imitators of me. 17For this reason I sent[r] you Timothy, who is my beloved and faithful child in the Lord, to remind you of my ways in Christ Jesus, as I teach them everywhere in every church. 18But some of you, thinking that I am not coming to you, have become arrogant. 19But I will come to you soon, if the Lord wills, and I will find out not the talk of these arrogant people but their power. 20For the kingdom of God depends not on talk but on power. 21What would you prefer? Am I to come to you with a stick, or with love in a spirit of gentleness?

Sexual Immorality Defiles the Church

5 It is actually reported that there is sexual immorality among you, and of a kind that is not found even among pagans; for a man is living with his father's wife. 2And you are arrogant! Should you not rather have mourned, so that he who has done this would have been removed from among you?

3 For though absent in body, I am present in spirit; and as if present I have already pronounced judgment 4in the name of the Lord Jesus on the man who has done such a thing.[s] When you are assembled, and my spirit is present with the power of our Lord Jesus, 5you are to hand this man over to Satan for the destruction of the flesh, so that his spirit may be saved in the day of the Lord.[t]

6 Your boasting is not a good thing. Do you not know that a little yeast leavens the whole batch of dough? 7Clean out the old yeast so that you may be a new batch, as you really are unleavened. For our paschal lamb, Christ, has been sacrificed. 8Therefore, let us celebrate the festival, not with the old yeast, the yeast of malice and evil, but with the unleavened bread of sincerity and truth.

[p] Gk *brothers* [q] Or *Who makes you different from another?* [r] Or *am sending* [s] Or *on the man who has done such a thing in the name of the Lord Jesus* [t] Other ancient authorities add *Jesus*

3.21 1 Cor 4.6; Rom 8.32
3.23 1 Cor 15.23; 2 Cor 10.7; Gal 3.29
4.1 2 Cor 6.4; 1 Cor 9.17; Rom 11.25; 16.25
4.5 Rom 2.1; 2 Cor 10.18; Rom 2.29
4.7 Rom 12.3,6
4.9 1 Cor 15.31; 2 Cor 11.23; Rom 8.36; Heb 10.33
4.10 1 Cor 1.18; Acts 17.18; 1 Cor 3.18
4.11 Rom 8.35; 2 Cor 11.23-27
4.12 Acts 18.3; 1 Pet 3.9; Jn 15.20; Rom 8.35
4.15 1 Cor 1.30; Philem 10
4.16 Phil 3.17; 1 Thess 1.6; 2 Thess 3.9
4.19 Acts 19.21; 2 Cor 1.15; Rom 15.32
4.21 2 Cor 1.23; 13.10
5.1 Lev 18.8; Deut 22.30; 2 Cor 7.12
5.4 2 Thess 3.6; 2 Cor 2.10
5.5 1 Tim 1.20
5.6 Jas 4.16; Gal 5.9
5.7 1 Pet 1.19
5.8 Deut 16.3; Mk 8.15

4.1-13 The fidelity of the apostles to their call by God will be determined in the day of judgment. *Cf.* Rom 9.3; 14.4,12. *"Nothing beyond what is written"* is a saying from an unknown source, quoted to discourage rivalry among the church leaders in Corinth. *Cf.* Rom 3.24-28; Eph 2.8-9. Paul caricatures the Corinthians' claims of spiritual maturity and of being above the earthly order, which negate the power of the cross of Christ that stands at the center of apostolic ministry (1.17,23,29; 2.2). **4.14-21** Paul as spiritual father of the Corinthians (Philem 10; Gal 4.19), appeals to them to imitate him (11.1; Gal 4.12; Phil 3.17; 4.9; 1 Thess 1.6). Timothy was sent as Paul's personal emissary and representative (16.10). But the role of apostle involves confrontation (2 Cor 13.1,10). **5.1-6.20** The Falsity of the Corinthians' Claim to Spiritual Maturity.

This section is a transition to the rest of the letter in which Paul answers the questions the Corinthians raised in their letter to him. First he points to their behavior which contradicts their claim to spiritual maturity and superiority.

5.1-8 The report of incest within the community: *a man is living with his father's wife.* It is not clear whether the father is still living, or whether the parents are divorced, or whether the son and the father's wife are married. But such behavior is condemned by both Jewish (Lev 18.8; 20.11) and Roman law (Cicero, *Pro Cluentio* 6.15), which forbids marriage of stepson and stepmother. Some in the community are boasting of their freedom instead of mourning their misdeeds. What is required is corporate action by the community, with input from Paul's *spirit* and the *power of our Lord Jesus,* which will result in the expulsion of this member. He will be vulnerable to the attack of *Satan* and will be judged on *the day of the Lord.* Their misguided moral judgments are permeating and corrupting the whole of the community like leaven in a loaf of bread. By contrast, the Feast of Passover, which is a symbol of the sacrificial death of Christ in behalf of his people (Jn 1.29,36; 1 Pet 1.19; Rev 5.6,9,12; 12.11), is celebrated with unleavened bread (Ex 13.3-10). The *new* leaven is probably an indication that at Easter Christians had their own *new* version of the Jewish feast of Passover (see 16.8).

Sexual Immorality Must Be Judged

9 I wrote to you in my letter not to associate with sexually immoral persons— 10not at all meaning the immoral of this world, or the greedy and robbers, or idolaters, since you would then need to go out of the world. 11But now I am writing to you not to associate with anyone who bears the name of brother or sister[u] who is sexually immoral or greedy, or is an idolater, reviler, drunkard, or robber. Do not even eat with such a one. 12For what have I to do with judging those outside? Is it not those who are inside that you are to judge? 13God will judge those outside. "Drive out the wicked person from among you."

Lawsuits among Believers

6 When any of you has a grievance against another, do you dare to take it to court before the unrighteous, instead of taking it before the saints? 2Do you not know that the saints will judge the world? And if the world is to be judged by you, are you incompetent to try trivial cases? 3Do you not know that we are to judge angels— to say nothing of ordinary matters? 4If you have ordinary cases, then, do you appoint as judges those who have no standing in the church? 5I say this to your shame. Can it be that there is no one among you wise enough to decide between one believer[u] and another, 6but a believer[u] goes to court against a believer[u]—and before unbelievers at that?

7 In fact, to have lawsuits at all with one another is already a defeat for you. Why not rather be wronged? Why not rather be defrauded? 8But you yourselves wrong and defraud—and believers[v] at that.

9 Do you not know that wrongdoers will not inherit the kingdom of God? Do not be deceived! Fornicators, idolaters, adulterers, male prostitutes, sodomites, 10thieves, the greedy, drunkards, revilers, robbers—none of these will inherit the kingdom of God. 11And this is what some of you used to be. But you were washed, you were sanctified, you were justified in the name of the Lord Jesus Christ and in the Spirit of our God.

Glorify God in Body and Spirit

12 "All things are lawful for me," but not all things are beneficial. "All things are lawful for me," but I will not be dominated by anything. 13"Food is meant for the stomach and the stomach for food,"[w] and God will destroy both one and the other. The body is meant not for fornication but for the Lord, and the Lord for the body. 14And God raised the Lord and will also raise us by his power. 15Do you not know that your bodies are members of Christ? Should I therefore take the members of Christ and make them members of a prostitute? Never! 16Do you not know that whoever is united to a prostitute becomes one body with her? For it is said, "The two shall be one flesh." 17But anyone united to the Lord becomes one spirit with him. 18Shun fornication! Every sin that a person commits is outside the body; but the fornicator sins against the body itself. 19Or do you not know that your body is a temple[x] of the Holy Spirit within you, which you have from God, and that you are not your own? 20For you were bought with a price; therefore glorify God in your body.

Directions concerning Marriage

7 Now concerning the matters about which you wrote: "It is well for a man not to touch a woman." 2But because of cases of sexual immorality, each man should have his own wife and each woman her own husband. 3The husband should give to his wife her conjugal rights, and likewise the wife to her husband. 4For the wife does not have authority over her own body, but the husband does; likewise the husband does not have authority over his own body, but the wife does. 5Do not deprive one another except perhaps by agreement for a set time, to devote yourselves to prayer, and then come together again, so that Satan may not tempt you because of your lack of self-control. 6This I say by way of concession, not of command. 7I wish that all were as I myself am. But each has a particular gift from God, one having one kind and another a different kind.

8 To the unmarried and the widows I say that it is well for them to remain unmarried as I am. 9But if they are not practicing self-control, they should marry. For it is better to marry than to be aflame with passion.

10 To the married I give this command— not I but the Lord—that the wife should not separate from her husband 11(but if she does

[u] Gk *brother* [v] Gk *brothers* [w] The quotation may extend to the word *other* [x] Or *sanctuary*

5.9-13 Paul has exchanged correspondence with the Corinthian community (see 7.1). He does not call them to separate themselves from the world, but to break off from committing vices, some of which are listed here. Those who perform such wicked acts are to be excluded from the community common meals. They are to concentrate on purifying their own group, as the scriptures teach (Deut 17.7), rather than merely on denouncing wicked outsiders.
6.1-11 In spite of their claim to spiritual maturity, the Corinthians are going to civil courts to settle disputes among members, which shows how immature they really are.
6.12-19 The proper stance of the community toward moral responsibility is not a matter of individual behavior ("*All things are lawful for me*"), but must be based on an awareness of the new community as the "body of Christ," which is the new *temple* where God has chosen to dwell. In light of this, quarreling over dietary laws is of no consequence, but abstinence from sexual misdeeds is a serious issue. The Lord is concerned about bodily behavior, because all members of the community share as *members* in the [risen] body *of Christ*. Since creation (Gen 2.24) sexual activity has involved bodily union, so it is essential for members of the community to avoid sexual activity that is contrary to the law, and thus to preserve the purity of the bodily *temple of the Holy Spirit*, and thereby to *glorify God*.
7.1-40 Problems of Sexual Relationships and Marriage. This is the first of the series of responses by Paul to the questions which had been raised with him by the Corinthian community. Each topic is introduced by *concerning...* (7.25; 8.1; 12.1; 16.1).
7.1-7 Paul affirms the sanctity of monogamous marriage over against the Corinthian tendency to depreciate it as a passing feature of earthly life. He rejects the notion that avoidance of sexual activity shows higher spirituality, and asserts that sexual rights should be honored, although sexual abstinence for a mutually agreed upon time is acceptable. God gives different gifts to the members, and they must not impose their own position on others.
7.8-10 Paul indicates the range of possibilities for marital behavior by the members of the community. He was *unmarried*, probably a widower, but recognizes that others will not be able to control their sexual urges, since self-control is a gift of God. If members of the community have spouses who are not converted, they should follow the teaching of Jesus (*the Lord*; Mk 10.11-12) and not seek divorce. In Deut 24.1-4 (followed in Mt 5.32; 19.9), the husband alone can initiate divorce, but in Greek law either partner could instigate it.
7.11-16 Jesus offered no rule about divorcing a marital partner who is not a member of the community, so Paul gives his own rule in his apostolic role: divorce should not be sought, since the other partner and the offspring are *made holy* in such a marriage (*cf.* Col 2.15,20), and may decide to enter the community of faith.

5.10 1 Cor 10.27
5.12 Mk 4.11; 1 Cor 6.1-4
5.13 Deut 13.5; 21.21
6.2 Dan 7.22; Mt 19.28; Lk 22.30
6.6 2 Cor 6.14,15
6.7 Mt 5.39,40; Rom 12.17
6.9 Gal 5.21; 1 Tim 1.10; Rev 22.15
6.11 Eph 2.2; Col 3.7; Titus 3.3
6.13 Mt 15.17; Eph 5.23
6.14 Rom 6.5,8; 8.11; 2 Cor 4.14; Eph 1.19
6.15 Rom 12.5; 1 Cor 12.27
6.16 Gen 2.4; Mt 19.5; Eph 5.31
6.17 Jn 17.21-23; Gal 2.20
6.18 Rom 6.12; Heb 13.4; 1 Thess 4.4
6.19 Jn 2.21; Rom 14.7,8
6.20 1 Cor 7.23; 1 Pet 1.18,19; Rev 5.9
7.3 1 Pet 3.7
7.5 Ex 19.15; 1 Sam 21.4,5; 1 Thess 3.5
7.6 2 Cor 8.8
7.7 ver 8; 1 Cor 9.5; 12.11; Mt 19.12
7.8 ver 1.26
7.9 1 Tim 5.14
7.10 Mal 2.14; Mt 5.32; 19.3-9 Mk 10.11; Lk 16.18

7.12 ver 6; 2 Cor 11.17
7.14 Mal 2.15
7.15 Rom 14.19; 1 Cor 14.33
7.16 1 Pet 3.1
7.17 Rom 12.3; 1 Cor 4.17; 14.33; 2 Cor 8.18; 11.28
7.18 Acts 15.1,2
7.19 Gal 5.6; 6.15; Rom 2.25
7.20 ver 24
7.22 Jn 8.32,36; Philem 16; Eph 6.6
7.23 1 Cor 6.20
7.25 2 Cor 8.8,10; 1 Tim 1.13,16
7.26 ver 1.8
7.29 Rom 13.11,12; ver 31
7.31 1 Cor 9.18; 1 Jn 2.17
7.32 1 Tim 5.5
7.34 Lk 10.40
7.39 Rom 7.2; 2 Cor 6.14
8.1 Acts 15.20; Rom 15.14; 14.3,10

separate, let her remain unmarried or else be reconciled to her husband), and that the husband should not divorce his wife.

12 To the rest I say—I and not the Lord—that if any believer[y] has a wife who is an unbeliever, and she consents to live with him, he should not divorce her. 13And if any woman has a husband who is an unbeliever, and he consents to live with her, she should not divorce him. 14For the unbelieving husband is made holy through his wife, and the unbelieving wife is made holy through her husband. Otherwise, your children would be unclean, but as it is, they are holy. 15But if the unbelieving partner separates, let it be so; in such a case the brother or sister is not bound. It is to peace that God has called you.[z] 16Wife, for all you know, you might save your husband. Husband, for all you know, you might save your wife.

The Life That the Lord Has Assigned

17 However that may be, let each of you lead the life that the Lord has assigned, to which God called you. This is my rule in all the churches. 18Was anyone at the time of his call already circumcised? Let him not seek to remove the marks of circumcision. Was anyone at the time of his call uncircumcised? Let him not seek circumcision. 19Circumcision is nothing, and uncircumcision is nothing; but obeying the commandments of God is everything. 20Let each of you remain in the condition in which you were called.

21 Were you a slave when called? Do not be concerned about it. Even if you can gain your freedom, make use of your present condition now more than ever.[a] 22For whoever was called in the Lord as a slave is a freed person belonging to the Lord, just as whoever was free when called is a slave of Christ. 23You were bought with a price; do not become slaves of human masters. 24In whatever condition you were called, brothers and sisters,[b] there remain with God.

The Unmarried and the Widows

25 Now concerning virgins, I have no command of the Lord, but I give my opinion as one who by the Lord's mercy is trustworthy. 26I think that, in view of the impending[c] crisis, it is well for you to remain as you are. 27Are you bound to a wife? Do not seek to be free. Are you free from a wife? Do not seek a wife. 28But if you marry, you do not sin, and if a virgin marries, she does not sin. Yet those who marry will experience distress in this life,[d] and I would spare you that. 29I mean, brothers and sisters,[b] the appointed time has grown short; from now on, let even those who have wives be as though they had none, 30and those who mourn as though they were not mourning, and those who rejoice as though they were not rejoicing, and those who buy as though they had no possessions, 31and those who deal with the world as though they had no dealings with it. For the present form of this world is passing away.

32 I want you to be free from anxieties. The unmarried man is anxious about the affairs of the Lord, how to please the Lord; 33but the married man is anxious about the affairs of the world, how to please his wife, 34and his interests are divided. And the unmarried woman and the virgin are anxious about the affairs of the Lord, so that they may be holy in body and spirit; but the married woman is anxious about the affairs of the world, how to please her husband. 35I say this for your own benefit, not to put any restraint upon you, but to promote good order and unhindered devotion to the Lord.

36 If anyone thinks that he is not behaving properly toward his fiancée,[e] if his passions are strong, and so it has to be, let him marry as he wishes; it is no sin. Let them marry. 37But if someone stands firm in his resolve, being under no necessity but having his own desire under control, and has determined in his own mind to keep her as his fiancée,[e] he will do well. 38So then, he who marries his fiancée[e] does well; and he who refrains from marriage will do better.

39 A wife is bound as long as her husband lives. But if the husband dies,[f] she is free to marry anyone she wishes, only in the Lord. 40But in my judgment she is more blessed if she remains as she is. And I think that I too have the Spirit of God.

Food Offered to Idols

8 Now concerning food sacrificed to idols: we know that "all of us possess knowledge." Knowledge puffs up, but love builds

[y] Gk *brother* [z] Other ancient authorities read *us* [a] Or *avail yourself of the opportunity* [b] Gk *brothers* [c] Or *present* [d] Gk *in the flesh* [e] Gk *virgin* [f] Gk *falls asleep*

7.17-24 Social status (such as slavery) and religious condition (such as circumcision) are of no significance for those who are among the people of God, and they should not seek to heighten their status in the new community.
7.25-40 Paul's advice for the unmarried and widows is that, in view of the shortness of time and urgency of proclaiming the gospel before the end of the present age (*appointed time*), it is better for members not to change marital status. They will then be free to devote themselves to *the affairs of the Lord* rather than family or marital matters. Those obsessed by sexual urges had better marry, but Paul admires those who can focus their energies on the Lord's work, as in the case of widows who do not remarry, and believes God's *Spirit* supports his point of view.
8.1-11.1 Freedom and Authority within the Christian Community.
8.1-13 Meat purchased in Greco-Roman cities was nearly always linked in some way with pagan religious practices, such as having been offered to an idol. Some members of the new community prided themselves in knowing that the gods thus honored did not *exist*, while others could not ignore the connection of most meat with idol worship. Paul rebukes those who take such pride in their superior *knowledge*, and (building on Israel's confession in Deut 6.4) affirms the uniqueness of God and the Lord Jesus Christ. But he warns those who agree and thus consider themselves to be at *liberty* not to be insensitive toward those *weak believers* who cannot free themselves from the association of such food with idols and may *fall* back into idolatry.

9.1-18 Paul declares his freedom from dietary and other restrictions and points to his readers as evidence of the effectiveness of his role as *apostle*. After citing the issues on which he is free (on dietary and marital matters), he notes that he and Barnabas have chosen not to claim material support from the Corinthian community. That Peter (*Cephas*) was married is attested in Mk 1.29-31, and the other apostles seek and obtain financial support, based on a symbolic interpretation of Deut 25.4, and the precedent of priestly support (Num 18). Acts 18.3 reports Paul working as a tentmaker to support himself *cf.* Gal 6.6; 2 Cor 11.7-9; but he accepted support from the Philippians (Phil 4.15-16). The saying of Jesus quoted here (9.14) is not found in the gospel tradition, but may be based on Lk 10.7; Mt 10.10. Paul does not *boast* of his freedom, but is guided by his *commission* to preach the gospel as effectively as possible.
9.19-27 Paul has chosen not to make full use of his *rights* and to adjust his tactics in each place of his work as is appropriate to increase the effectiveness of his proclamation of the gospel, whether to Jews or to *those outside the law*. The imagery of self-control by athletes was appropriate for Corinth, since it was the site of the famous Isthmian games, of which the modern Olympics are an imitation.

up. 2 Anyone who claims to know something does not yet have the necessary knowledge; 3 but anyone who loves God is known
by him.
4 Hence, as to the eating of food offered
to idols, we know that "no idol in the world
really exists," and that "there is no God but
one." 5 Indeed, even though there may be
so-called gods in heaven or on earth—as in
fact there are many gods and many lords—
6 yet for us there is one God, the Father,
from whom are all things and for whom we
exist, and one Lord, Jesus Christ, through
whom are all things and through whom we
exist.
7 It is not everyone, however, who has
this knowledge. Since some have become so
accustomed to idols until now, they still
think of the food they eat as food offered to
an idol; and their conscience, being weak,
is defiled. 8 "Food will not bring us close to
God."[g] We are no worse off if we do not eat,
and no better off if we do. 9 But take care
that this liberty of yours does not somehow
become a stumbling block to the weak.
10 For if others see you, who possess knowledge, eating in the temple of an idol, might
they not, since their conscience is weak, be
encouraged to the point of eating food sacrificed to idols? 11 So by your knowledge
those weak believers for whom Christ died
are destroyed.[h] 12 But when you thus sin
against members of your family,[i] and wound
their conscience when it is weak, you sin
against Christ. 13 Therefore, if food is a cause
of their falling,[j] I will never eat meat, so
that I may not cause one of them[k] to fall.

The Rights of an Apostle

9 Am I not free? Am I not an apostle?
Have I not seen Jesus our Lord? Are
you not my work in the Lord? 2 If I am not
an apostle to others, at least I am to you;
for you are the seal of my apostleship in the
Lord.
3 This is my defense to those who would
examine me. 4 Do we not have the right to
our food and drink? 5 Do we not have the
right to be accompanied by a believing wife,[l]
as do the other apostles and the brothers of
the Lord and Cephas? 6 Or is it only Barnabas
and I who have no right to refrain from
working for a living? 7 Who at any time pays
the expenses for doing military service? Who
plants a vineyard and does not eat any of
its fruit? Or who tends a flock and does not
get any of its milk?
8 Do I say this on human authority?
Does not the law also say the same? 9 For
it is written in the law of Moses, "You shall
not muzzle an ox while it is treading out the
grain." Is it for oxen that God is concerned?
10 Or does he not speak entirely for our sake?
It was indeed written for our sake, for
whoever plows should plow in hope and
whoever threshes should thresh in hope of
a share in the crop. 11 If we have sown
spiritual good among you, is it too much if
we reap your material benefits? 12 If others
share this rightful claim on you, do not we
still more?
Nevertheless, we have not made use of
this right, but we endure anything rather
than put an obstacle in the way of the
gospel of Christ. 13 Do you not know that
those who are employed in the temple service get their food from the temple, and those
who serve at the altar share in what is
sacrificed on the altar? 14 In the same way,
the Lord commanded that those who proclaim the gospel should get their living by
the gospel.
15 But I have made no use of any of
these rights, nor am I writing this so that
they may be applied in my case. Indeed, I
would rather die than that—no one will
deprive me of my ground for boasting! 16 If
I proclaim the gospel, this gives me no
ground for boasting, for an obligation is laid
on me, and woe to me if I do not proclaim
the gospel! 17 For if I do this of my own will,
I have a reward; but if not of my own will,
I am entrusted with a commission. 18 What
then is my reward? Just this: that in my
proclamation I may make the gospel free of
charge, so as not to make full use of my
rights in the gospel.
19 For though I am free with respect to
all, I have made myself a slave to all, so that
I might win more of them. 20 To the Jews I
became as a Jew, in order to win Jews. To
those under the law I became as one under
the law (though I myself am not under the
law) so that I might win those under the
law. 21 To those outside the law I became as
one outside the law (though I am not free
from God's law but am under Christ's law)
so that I might win those outside the law.
22 To the weak I became weak, so that I

[g] The quotation may extend to the end of the verse [h] Gk *the weak brother . . . is destroyed* [i] Gk *against the brothers* [j] Gk *my brother's falling* [k] Gk *cause my brother* [l] Gk *a sister as wife*

8.2 1 Cor 3.18; 13.8,9,12; 1 Tim 6.4
8.3 Gal 4.9; Rom 8.29
8.4 1 Cor 10.19; Deut 6.4; Eph 4.6
8.6 Mal 2.10; Rom 11.36; Phil 2.11
8.7 1 Cor 10.28; Rom 14.14
8.8 Rom 14.17
8.9 Gal 5.13; Rom 14.1,13,20
8.11 Rom 14.15,20
8.13 Rom 14.21; 2 Cor 11.29
9.1 2 Cor 12.12; Acts 9.3,17; 18.9; 22.14,18; 23.11; 1 Cor 3.6; 4.15
9.2 2 Cor 3.2,3
9.4 1 Thess 2.6; 2 Thess 3.8,9
9.5 1 Cor 7.7,8; Mt 12.46; Mt 8.14
9.6 Acts 4.36
9.7 2 Cor 10.4; 1 Tim 1.18; Deut 20.6; Prov 27.18
9.9 Deut 25.4; 1 Tim 5.18
9.11 Rom 15.27
9.12 2 Cor 6.3; 11.12
9.13 Lev 6.16; Deut 18.1
9.14 Mt 10.10; Lk 10.7
9.17 1 Cor 3.8,14; Gal 2.7; Phil 1.16,17; Col 1.25
9.19 Gal 5.13; Mt 18.15; 1 Pet 3.1
9.21 Rom 2.12,14; Gal 3.2; 1 Cor 7.22

might win the weak. I have become all
things to all people, that I might by all
means save some. [23]I do it all for the sake
of the gospel, so that I may share in its
blessings.

24 Do you not know that in a race the
runners all compete, but only one receives
the prize? Run in such a way that you may
win it. [25]Athletes exercise self-control in all
things; they do it to receive a perishable
wreath, but we an imperishable one. [26]So I
do not run aimlessly, nor do I box as though
beating the air; [27]but I punish my body and
enslave it, so that after proclaiming to others I myself should not be disqualified.

Warnings from Israel's History

10 I do not want you to be unaware,
brothers and sisters,[m] that our
ancestors were all under the cloud, and all
passed through the sea, [2]and all were baptized into Moses in the cloud and in the sea,
[3]and all ate the same spiritual food, [4]and all
drank the same spiritual drink. For they
drank from the spiritual rock that followed
them, and the rock was Christ. [5]Neverthe-
less, God was not pleased with most of
them, and they were struck down in the
wilderness.

6 Now these things occurred as examples
for us, so that we might not desire evil as
they did. [7]Do not become idolaters as some
of them did; as it is written, "The people sat
down to eat and drink, and they rose up to
play." [8]We must not indulge in sexual
immorality as some of them did, and twenty-
three thousand fell in a single day. [9]We
must not put Christ[n] to the test, as some of
them did, and were destroyed by serpents.
[10]And do not complain as some of them did,
and were destroyed by the destroyer. [11]These
things happened to them to serve as an
example, and they were written down to
instruct us, on whom the ends of the ages
have come. [12]So if you think you are standing, watch out that you do not fall. [13]No
testing has overtaken you that is not common to everyone. God is faithful, and he
will not let you be tested beyond your
strength, but with the testing he will also
provide the way out so that you may be
able to endure it.

14 Therefore, my dear friends,[o] flee from
the worship of idols. [15]I speak as to sensible
people; judge for yourselves what I say.
[16]The cup of blessing that we bless, is it not
a sharing in the blood of Christ? The bread
that we break, is it not a sharing in the
body of Christ? [17]Because there is one bread,
we who are many are one body, for we all
partake of the one bread. [18]Consider the
people of Israel;[p] are not those who eat the
sacrifices partners in the altar? [19]What do
I imply then? That food sacrificed to idols
is anything, or that an idol is anything?
[20]No, I imply that what pagans sacrifice,
they sacrifice to demons and not to God. I
do not want you to be partners with demons. [21]You cannot drink the cup of the
Lord and the cup of demons. You cannot
partake of the table of the Lord and the
table of demons. [22]Or are we provoking the
Lord to jealousy? Are we stronger than he?

Do All to the Glory of God

23 "All things are lawful," but not all
things are beneficial. "All things are lawful," but not all things build up. [24]Do not
seek your own advantage, but that of the
other. [25]Eat whatever is sold in the meat
market without raising any question on the
ground of conscience, [26]for "the earth and
its fullness are the Lord's." [27]If an unbeliever
invites you to a meal and you are disposed
to go, eat whatever is set before you without raising any question on the ground of
conscience. [28]But if someone says to you,
"This has been offered in sacrifice," then do
not eat it, out of consideration for the one
who informed you, and for the sake of
conscience— [29]I mean the other's conscience,
not your own. For why should my liberty
be subject to the judgment of someone else's
conscience? [30]If I partake with thankfulness,
why should I be denounced because of that
for which I give thanks?

31 So, whether you eat or drink, or
whatever you do, do everything for the
glory of God. [32]Give no offense to Jews or
to Greeks or to the church of God, [33]just as
I try to please everyone in everything I do,
not seeking my own advantage, but that
of many, so that they may be saved. [1]Be
11 imitators of me, as I am of Christ.

Head Coverings

2 I commend you because you remember
me in everything and maintain the traditions just as I handed them on to you. [3]But

[m] Gk *brothers* [n] Other ancient authorities read *the Lord* [o] Gk *my beloved* [p] Gk *Israel according to the flesh*

9.24 2 Tim 4.7; Heb 12.1
9.25 Eph 6.12; 1 Tim 6.12
9.27 Rom 8.13; Col 3.5; Rom 6.18
10.1 Ex 13.21; 14.22,29; Rom 1.13
10.3 Ex 16.4,35
10.4 Ex 17.6; Num 20.11
10.5 Num 14.29,30; Heb 3.17
10.6 Num 11.4,34; Ps 106.14
10.7 Ex 32.4,6
10.8 Num 25.1ff
10.9 Num 21.5,6
10.10 Num 16.41,49; Ex 12.23
10.11 Rom 13.11; Phil 4.5
10.13 2 Pet 2.9
10.14 2 Cor 6.17
10.17 Rom 12.5; 1 Cor 12.27
10.18 Lev 7.6
10.20 Deut 32.17; Ps 106.37; Rev 9.20
10.21 2 Cor 6.15,16
10.22 Deut 32.21; Eccl 6.10; Isa 45.9
10.24 ver 33; Rom 15.1,2; Phil 2.4,21
10.26 Ps 24.1
10.29 Rom 14.16
10.30 Rom 14.6; 1 Tim 4.3,4
10.31 Col 3.17; 1 Pet 4.11
10.32 1 Cor 8.13
10.33 Rom 15.2; 1 Cor 9.22; 13.5
11.1 1 Cor 4.16

10.1-22 Paul now turns to the experiences of the exodus of Israel (*our ancestors*) from Promised land as the base for his moral appeal (Ex 13.21-22; 14.19-20,21-22,26-30; 16.4,14-18; 17.6; 32.6; Num 20.7-13). The new community is the fulfillment of the older covenant promises (*cf.* Gal 6.16, *the Israel of God*), and the experiences of water from the rock (Ex 17.6; Num 20.7-11) and manna (*spiritual food*, 10.3; Ex 16.4; Deut 8.3) correspond to the sacraments of baptism and eucharist. Just as disobedient Israel was punished (Num 14.26-38), so the Corinthians will be punished if they engage in idolatry or *immorality*. They will be *tested* by God to determine the extent of their fidelity and obedience. **10.23-11.1** Decisions about behavior are to be made on the basis of what *builds up* the community, not on the ground that for God's people, "*All things are lawful.*" The *conscience* of others in the community and what works for *the glory of God*, who is *Lord of the earth and its fulness* (Ps 24.1) must be the basis for behavior of God's new people, as Paul himself seeks to exemplify in his imitation of Christ. **11.2-34** The Shared Life of the New Community. Two issues are described which have caused major divisions in the church at Corinth: (1) headdress for church leaders, and (2) behavior of those who preside at the eucharistic meals. (1) The order of human creation (men in God's image; women formed from men; Gen 1.26-27; 2.18-25) is to prevail in church leadership, with men bareheaded as they pray or prophesy, and women veiled as they do so. Those who prophesy declare God's message for his people in the community. The veil is a *symbol of authority*, a sign of acceptance of rank in the order of creation, in contrast to prostitutes and other women who cut off their hair. Yet in 7.1-16 and Gal 3.28 Paul affirms the equality of men and women in the church. (2) In 11.17-34 instruction is given as to the proper observance of the *Lord's supper*, which took place as part of a communal meal. The purpose of the meal is to celebrate the unity of God's people, not the occasion for a display of the affluence and indulgence (*drunk*) of some members and the poverty of others. The earliest tradition of the first supper, *on the night* [Jesus] *was betrayed*, finds echoes in the gospel accounts, which were written later (Mt 26.26-28; Mk 14.22-24; Lk 22.17-20). As Paul *received* this tradition, so he is passing it on, as he does the tradition about Jesus' death and resurrection (15.3). *Remembrance*, which is not mentioned in the gospel tradition of the covenant, recalls Ex 12.14. The celebration of the meal is also a proclamation of the fact and significance of *the Lord's death*, and will be so until his return. Thus it is essential that the partakers will understand and affirm the meaning of the events which the eucharist celebrates, and so *unworthy* participants must be excluded. Otherwise God's punitive judgment may fall on the community in the form of sickness and death. The meal must symbolize the unity and common concerns of the community.

12.1-14.40 The Gifts of the Spirit.
As at 7.1; 7.25; 8.1; and 16.1, Paul addresses an issue raised by the Corinthians in an earlier letter to him. This one deals with the ways in which the Spirit of God enables members of the community to fulfill special roles for the benefit of all.
12.1-3 The presence and power of the Spirit in the lives of members of the community are evident in their public testimony that "*Jesus is Lord*" (*cf.* 1 Cor 1.18; Gal 3.13; Rom 10.9; Phil 2.11). Previously, as *pagan* worshipers they might have *cursed* Jesus in ecstatic speech.

I want you to understand that Christ is the
head of every man, and the husband[q] is the
head of his wife,[r] and God is the head of
Christ. [4]Any man who prays or prophesies
with something on his head disgraces his
head, [5]but any woman who prays or prophesies with her head unveiled disgraces her
head—it is one and the same thing as
having her head shaved. [6]For if a woman
will not veil herself, then she should cut off
her hair; but if it is disgraceful for a woman
to have her hair cut off or to be shaved, she
should wear a veil. [7]For a man ought not
to have his head veiled, since he is the
image and reflection[s] of God; but woman is
the reflection[s] of man. [8]Indeed, man was
not made from woman, but woman from
man. [9]Neither was man created for the sake
of woman, but woman for the sake of man.
[10]For this reason a woman ought to have
a symbol of[t] authority on her head,[u] because of the angels. [11]Nevertheless, in the
Lord woman is not independent of man or
man independent of woman. [12]For just as
woman came from man, so man comes
through woman; but all things come from
God. [13]Judge for yourselves: is it proper for
a woman to pray to God with her head
unveiled? [14]Does not nature itself teach you
that if a man wears long hair, it is degrading to him, [15]but if a woman has long hair,
it is her glory? For her hair is given to her
for a covering. [16]But if anyone is disposed
to be contentious—we have no such custom, nor do the churches of God.

Abuses at the Lord's Supper

17 Now in the following instructions I do
not commend you, because when you come
together it is not for the better but for the
worse. [18]For, to begin with, when you come
together as a church, I hear that there are
divisions among you; and to some extent I
believe it. [19]Indeed, there have to be factions
among you, for only so will it become clear
who among you are genuine. [20]When you
come together, it is not really to eat the
Lord's supper. [21]For when the time comes
to eat, each of you goes ahead with your
own supper, and one goes hungry and
another becomes drunk. [22]What! Do you
not have homes to eat and drink in? Or do
you show contempt for the church of God
and humiliate those who have nothing?
What should I say to you? Should I commend you? In this matter I do not commend
you!

The Institution of the Lord's Supper

23 For I received from the Lord what I
also handed on to you, that the Lord Jesus
on the night when he was betrayed took a
loaf of bread, [24]and when he had given
thanks, he broke it and said, "This is my
body that is for[v] you. Do this in remembrance of me." [25]In the same way he took
the cup also, after supper, saying, "This cup
is the new covenant in my blood. Do this,
as often as you drink it, in remembrance of
me." [26]For as often as you eat this bread
and drink the cup, you proclaim the Lord's
death until he comes.

Partaking of the Supper Unworthily

27 Whoever, therefore, eats the bread or
drinks the cup of the Lord in an unworthy
manner will be answerable for the body and
blood of the Lord. [28]Examine yourselves,
and only then eat of the bread and drink
of the cup. [29]For all who eat and drink[w]
without discerning the body,[x] eat and drink
judgment against themselves. [30]For this
reason many of you are weak and ill, and
some have died.[y] [31]But if we judged ourselves, we would not be judged. [32]But when
we are judged by the Lord, we are disciplined[z]
so that we may not be condemned along
with the world.
33 So then, my brothers and sisters,[a]
when you come together to eat, wait for
one another. [34]If you are hungry, eat at
home, so that when you come together, it
will not be for your condemnation. About
the other things I will give instructions
when I come.

Spiritual Gifts

12 Now concerning spiritual gifts,[b]
brothers and sisters,[a] I do not want
you to be uninformed. [2]You know that
when you were pagans, you were enticed
and led astray to idols that could not speak.

[q] The same Greek word means *man* or *husband* [r] Or *head of the woman* [s] Or *glory* [t] Gk lacks *a symbol of* [u] Or *have freedom of choice regarding her head* [v] Other ancient authorities read *is broken for* [w] Other ancient authorities add *in an unworthy manner,* [x] Other ancient authorities read *the Lord's body* [y] Gk *fallen asleep* [z] Or *When we are judged, we are being disciplined by the Lord* [a] Gk *brothers* [b] Or *spiritual persons*

11.2 1 Cor 4.17; 2 Thess 2.15
11.3 Eph 1.22; 4.15; 5.23; 1 Cor 3.23
11.4 Acts 13.1; 1 Thess 5.20
11.7 Gen 1.26
11.8 Gen 2.21-23
11.9 Gen 2.18
11.10 Gen 24.65
11.16 1 Cor 7.17
11.18 1 Cor 1.10-12
11.19 Mt 18.7; Lk 17.1; 1 Tim 4.1; Deut 13.3; 1 Jn 2.19
11.23 1 Cor 15.3; Mt 26.26-28; Mk 14.22-24; Lk 22.17-20
11.26 1 Cor 4.5; Jn 14.3; Acts 1.11; Rev 1.7
11.27 Heb 10.29
11.28 2 Cor 13.5
11.31 Ps 32.5; 1 Jn 1.9
11.32 Ps 94.12; Heb 12.7-10; 1 Cor 1.20
11.34 ver 21.22; 1 Cor 4.19
12.1 1 Cor 14.1,37; Rom 1.13
12.2 Eph 2.11,12; 1 Pet 4.3; 1 Thess 1.9; Ps 115.5

12.3 1 Jn 4.2,3; Rom 9.3; 10.9
12.4 Rom 12.4-7; Heb 2.4
12.5 Eph 4.11
12.7 Eph 4.7
12.8 1 Cor 2.6,7; Rom 15.4; 2 Cor 8.7
12.9 Mt 17.19,20; 2 Cor 4.13; ver 28,30
12.10 Gal 3.5; Rom 12.6; 1 Jn 4.1; Acts 2.4; 1 Cor 13.1
12.11 2 Cor 10.13; Heb 2.4
12.12 Rom 12.4; Gal 3.16
12.13 Eph 2.18; Gal 3.28; Col 3.11; Jn 7.37-39
12.27 Eph 1.23; 4.12; Col 1.18,24; Eph 5.30; Rom 12.5
12.28 Eph 4.11; 2.30; 3.5; Rom 12.6,8; ver 9,10
12.30 ver 10
12.31 1 Cor 14.1,39
13.2 Acts 13.1; 1 Cor 14.1; Mt 7.22; 1 Cor 12.9; Mt 17.20; 21.21
13.3 Mt 6.2
13.4 Prov 10.12; 1 Pet 4.8
13.5 1 Cor 10.24; 2 Cor 5.19
13.6 2 Jn 4
13.7 Rom 15.1; 1 Cor 9.12
13.12 2 Cor 5.7; Phil 3.12; 1 Jn 3.2; 1 Cor 8.3

[3]Therefore I want you to understand that no one speaking by the Spirit of God ever says "Let Jesus be cursed!" and no one can say "Jesus is Lord" except by the Holy Spirit.

4 Now there are varieties of gifts, but the same Spirit; [5]and there are varieties of services, but the same Lord; [6]and there are varieties of activities, but it is the same God who activates all of them in everyone. [7]To each is given the manifestation of the Spirit for the common good. [8]To one is given through the Spirit the utterance of wisdom, and to another the utterance of knowledge according to the same Spirit, [9]to another faith by the same Spirit, to another gifts of healing by the one Spirit, [10]to another the working of miracles, to another prophecy, to another the discernment of spirits, to another various kinds of tongues, to another the interpretation of tongues. [11]All these are activated by one and the same Spirit, who allots to each one individually just as the Spirit chooses.

One Body with Many Members

12 For just as the body is one and has many members, and all the members of the body, though many, are one body, so it is with Christ. [13]For in the one Spirit we were all baptized into one body—Jews or Greeks, slaves or free—and we were all made to drink of one Spirit.

14 Indeed, the body does not consist of one member but of many. [15]If the foot would say, "Because I am not a hand, I do not belong to the body," that would not make it any less a part of the body. [16]And if the ear would say, "Because I am not an eye, I do not belong to the body," that would not make it any less a part of the body. [17]If the whole body were an eye, where would the hearing be? If the whole body were hearing, where would the sense of smell be? [18]But as it is, God arranged the members in the body, each one of them, as he chose. [19]If all were a single member, where would the body be? [20]As it is, there are many members, yet one body. [21]The eye cannot say to the hand, "I have no need of you," nor again the head to the feet, "I have no need of you." [22]On the contrary, the members of the body that seem to be weaker are indispensable, [23]and those members of the body that we think less honorable we clothe with greater honor, and our less respectable members are treated with greater respect; [24]whereas our more respectable members do not need this. But God has so arranged the body, giving the greater honor to the inferior member, [25]that there may be no dissension within the body, but the members may have the same care for one another. [26]If one member suffers, all suffer together with it; if one member is honored, all rejoice together with it.

27 Now you are the body of Christ and individually members of it. [28]And God has appointed in the church first apostles, second prophets, third teachers; then deeds of power, then gifts of healing, forms of assistance, forms of leadership, various kinds of tongues. [29]Are all apostles? Are all prophets? Are all teachers? Do all work miracles? [30]Do all possess gifts of healing? Do all speak in tongues? Do all interpret? [31]But strive for the greater gifts. And I will show you a still more excellent way.

The Gift of Love

13 If I speak in the tongues of mortals and of angels, but do not have love, I am a noisy gong or a clanging cymbal. [2]And if I have prophetic powers, and understand all mysteries and all knowledge, and if I have all faith, so as to remove mountains, but do not have love, I am nothing. [3]If I give away all my possessions, and if I hand over my body so that I may boast,[c] but do not have love, I gain nothing.

4 Love is patient; love is kind; love is not envious or boastful or arrogant [5]or rude. It does not insist on its own way; it is not irritable or resentful; [6]it does not rejoice in wrongdoing, but rejoices in the truth. [7]It bears all things, believes all things, hopes all things, endures all things.

8 Love never ends. But as for prophecies, they will come to an end; as for tongues, they will cease; as for knowledge, it will come to an end. [9]For we know only in part, and we prophesy only in part; [10]but when the complete comes, the partial will come to an end. [11]When I was a child, I spoke like a child, I thought like a child, I reasoned like a child; when I became an adult, I put an end to childish ways. [12]For now we see in a mirror, dimly,[d] but then we will see face to face. Now I know only in part; then I will know fully, even as I have been fully known. [13]And now faith, hope, and love abide, these three; and the greatest of these is love.

[c] Other ancient authorities read *body to be burned* [d] Gk *in a riddle*

12.4-11 The *varieties of gifts...* and *services* are the result of the Spirit's work in the lives of members of the community and serve the purpose of building the church. This is *for the common good*, rather than to draw attention to the individual through whom the Spirit is active. The range of gifts by the Spirit includes not only *wisdom, knowledge, healing, working miracles*, and *prophecy*, but also ecstatic speech (*tongues*) and the ability to interpret such utterances.
12.12-30 The community (*body*) is composed of people from a range of ethnic and social backgrounds (*Jews, Greeks; slaves, free*), but all are empowered by the *one Spirit* for the benefit of the whole, just as the *body* needs different parts to function in different ways for the welfare of the whole (*common good*).
12.27-30 Here Paul enumerates the roles that are essential for the ongoing life of the church and the range of tasks that they are empowered to perform for the benefit of the whole. Each one has a role *appointed* by God.
12.31-13.13 The *more excellent way* than boastfully demonstrating one's spiritual gifts is the transforming power of *love* within the community. This *love* (in Greek, *agape*) is not self-seeking, but builds on the love of God (Rom 5.3; 8.39) which is demonstrated in his sending Christ to die for our sins (Rom 5.8). Love is evident in actions rather than merely in feelings: fifteen verbs here show concretely what love accomplishes for the upbuilding of the community. Such activity is useless when it is not motivated by love, which exceeds in importance and power even *faith* and *hope*.

Gifts of Prophecy and Tongues

14 Pursue love and strive for the spiritual gifts, and especially that you may prophesy. 2For those who speak in a tongue do not speak to other people but to God; for nobody understands them, since they are speaking mysteries in the Spirit. 3On the other hand, those who prophesy speak to other people for their upbuilding and encouragement and consolation. 4Those who speak in a tongue build up themselves, but those who prophesy build up the church. 5Now I would like all of you to speak in tongues, but even more to prophesy. One who prophesies is greater than one who speaks in tongues, unless someone interprets, so that the church may be built up.

6 Now, brothers and sisters,[e] if I come to you speaking in tongues, how will I benefit you unless I speak to you in some revelation or knowledge or prophecy or teaching? 7It is the same way with lifeless instruments that produce sound, such as the flute or the harp. If they do not give distinct notes, how will anyone know what is being played? 8And if the bugle gives an indistinct sound, who will get ready for battle? 9So with yourselves; if in a tongue you utter speech that is not intelligible, how will anyone know what is being said? For you will be speaking into the air. 10There are doubtless many different kinds of sounds in the world, and nothing is without sound. 11If then I do not know the meaning of a sound, I will be a foreigner to the speaker and the speaker a foreigner to me. 12So with yourselves; since you are eager for spiritual gifts, strive to excel in them for building up the church.

13 Therefore, one who speaks in a tongue should pray for the power to interpret. 14For if I pray in a tongue, my spirit prays but my mind is unproductive. 15What should I do then? I will pray with the spirit, but I will pray with the mind also; I will sing praise with the spirit, but I will sing praise with the mind also. 16Otherwise, if you say a blessing with the spirit, how can anyone in the position of an outsider say the "Amen" to your thanksgiving, since the outsider does not know what you are saying? 17For you may give thanks well enough, but the other person is not built up. 18I thank God that I speak in tongues more than all of you; 19nevertheless, in church I would rather speak five words with my mind, in order to instruct others also, than ten thousand words in a tongue.

20 Brothers and sisters,[e] do not be children in your thinking; rather, be infants in evil, but in thinking be adults. 21In the law it is written,

"By people of strange tongues
and by the lips of foreigners
I will speak to this people;
yet even then they will not listen to me,"

says the Lord. 22Tongues, then, are a sign not for believers but for unbelievers, while prophecy is not for unbelievers but for believers. 23If, therefore, the whole church comes together and all speak in tongues, and outsiders or unbelievers enter, will they not say that you are out of your mind? 24But if all prophesy, an unbeliever or outsider who enters is reproved by all and called to account by all. 25After the secrets of the unbeliever's heart are disclosed, that person will bow down before God and worship him, declaring, "God is really among you."

Orderly Worship

26 What should be done then, my friends?[e] When you come together, each one has a hymn, a lesson, a revelation, a tongue, or an interpretation. Let all things be done for building up. 27If anyone speaks in a tongue, let there be only two or at most three, and each in turn; and let one interpret. 28But if there is no one to interpret, let them be silent in church and speak to themselves and to God. 29Let two or three prophets speak, and let the others weigh what is said. 30If a revelation is made to someone else sitting nearby, let the first person be silent. 31For you can all prophesy one by one, so that all may learn and all be encouraged. 32And the spirits of prophets are subject to the prophets, 33for God is a God not of disorder but of peace.

(As in all the churches of the saints, 34women should be silent in the churches. For they are not permitted to speak, but should be subordinate, as the law also says. 35If there is anything they desire to know, let them ask their husbands at home. For it is shameful for a woman to speak in church.[f] 36Or did the word of God originate with you? Or are you the only ones it has reached?)

37 Anyone who claims to be a prophet,

[e] Gk *brothers* [f] Other ancient authorities put verses 34–35 after verse 40

14.1-19 Paul is especially eager that the gift of *prophecy* will be given high priority among the Corinthians, since it is the means by which God conveys his message and purpose to his people. *Tongues* are useless to the community, unless someone can interpret the message, which is also a gift of the Spirit. Paul has the gift of *tongues* in abundance (*more than all of you*), but though it is gratifying to the one who has it, the most important role for the community as a whole is *to instruct others*.
14.20-25 Although the gift of ecstatic speech was foreseen by the prophet Isaiah (28.11-12), it fascinates outsiders but does not lead them to trust in God (*bow down*) as *prophecy* does when it speaks to the *heart* of the unbeliever.
14.26-40 The spiritual gifts — singing, reading, *revelation*, ecstatic speech, interpretation — are to be exercized in the meetings of the community solely for the purpose of building up the members and in an orderly fashion. Verses 25-26, which restrict the role of women in the community, are placed in parentheses because some scholars think they are not part of the original letter. They may have been inserted later by those who shared the viewpoint of the pseudo-Pauline 1 Tim 2.11-12. Paul honors the place of women in the church in Phil 4.2-3 and Rom 16.1-2. The instruction to emphasize preaching (prophecy) rather than ecstatic speech is reiterated in 14.37-40.

14.1 1 Cor 16.14; 12.31; 12.1; 13.2
14.2 Acts 10.46; 1 Cor 12.10,28,30; 13.1
14.3 ver 5,12,17,26; Acts 4.36
14.5 Num 11.29
14.6 ver 26; 1 Cor 12.8; Rom 6.17
14.8 Num 10.9
14.9 1 Cor 9.26
14.11 Acts 28.2
14.15 Eph 5.19; Col 3.16
14.16 1 Chr 16.36; Ps 106.48; Mt 15.36; 1 Cor 11.24
14.17 Rom 14.19
14.20 Eph 4.14; Heb 5.12,13; Ps 131.2; Rom 16.19; 1 Pet 2.2
14.21 Jn 10.34; Isa 28.11,12
14.23 Acts 2.13
14.26 1 Cor 12.7-10; 2 Cor 12.19; Eph 4.12
14.34 1 Tim 2.11,12; 1 Pet 3.1; Gen 3.16
14.37 2 Cor 10.7; 1 Jn 4.6

or to have spiritual powers, must acknowledge that what I am writing to you is a
command of the Lord. [38]Anyone who does
not recognize this is not to be recognized.
[39]So, my friends,[g] be eager to prophesy, and
do not forbid speaking in tongues; [40]but
all things should be done decently and in
order.

The Resurrection of Christ

15 Now I would remind you, brothers
and sisters,[h] of the good news[i] that
I proclaimed to you, which you in turn
received, in which also you stand, [2]through
which also you are being saved, if you hold
firmly to the message that I proclaimed to
you—unless you have come to believe in
vain.
3 For I handed on to you as of first
importance what I in turn had received:
that Christ died for our sins in accordance
with the scriptures, [4]and that he was buried, and that he was raised on the third day
in accordance with the scriptures, [5]and that
he appeared to Cephas, then to the twelve.
[6]Then he appeared to more than five hundred brothers and sisters[h] at one time, most
of whom are still alive, though some have
died.[j] [7]Then he appeared to James, then to
all the apostles. [8]Last of all, as to one untimely born, he appeared also to me. [9]For
I am the least of the apostles, unfit to be
called an apostle, because I persecuted the
church of God. [10]But by the grace of God
I am what I am, and his grace toward me
has not been in vain. On the contrary, I
worked harder than any of them—though
it was not I, but the grace of God that is
with me. [11]Whether then it was I or they,
so we proclaim and so you have come to
believe.

The Resurrection of the Dead

12 Now if Christ is proclaimed as raised
from the dead, how can some of you say
there is no resurrection of the dead? [13]If
there is no resurrection of the dead, then
Christ has not been raised; [14]and if Christ
has not been raised, then our proclamation
has been in vain and your faith has been
in vain. [15]We are even found to be misrep-
resenting God, because we testified of God
that he raised Christ—whom he did not
raise if it is true that the dead are not raised.
[16]For if the dead are not raised, then Christ
has not been raised. [17]If Christ has not been
raised, your faith is futile and you are still
in your sins. [18]Then those also who have
died[j] in Christ have perished. [19]If for this life
only we have hoped in Christ, we are of all
people most to be pitied.
20 But in fact Christ has been raised
from the dead, the first fruits of those who
have died.[j] [21]For since death came through
a human being, the resurrection of the dead
has also come through a human being;
[22]for as all die in Adam, so all will be made
alive in Christ. [23]But each in his own order:
Christ the first fruits, then at his coming
those who belong to Christ. [24]Then comes
the end,[k] when he hands over the kingdom
to God the Father, after he has destroyed
every ruler and every authority and power.
[25]For he must reign until he has put all his
enemies under his feet. [26]The last enemy to
be destroyed is death. [27]For "God[l] has put
all things in subjection under his feet." But
when it says, "All things are put in subjection," it is plain that this does not include
the one who put all things in subjection
under him. [28]When all things are subjected
to him, then the Son himself will also be
subjected to the one who put all things in
subjection under him, so that God may be
all in all.
29 Otherwise, what will those people do
who receive baptism on behalf of the dead?
If the dead are not raised at all, why are
people baptized on their behalf?
30 And why are we putting ourselves in
danger every hour? [31]I die every day! That
is as certain, brothers and sisters,[h] as my
boasting of you—a boast that I make in
Christ Jesus our Lord. [32]If with merely human
hopes I fought with wild animals at Ephesus,
what would I have gained by it? If the dead
are not raised,
"Let us eat and drink,
for tomorrow we die."
[33]Do not be deceived:
"Bad company ruins good morals."
[34]Come to a sober and right mind, and sin
no more; for some people have no knowledge of God. I say this to your shame.

The Resurrection Body

35 But someone will ask, "How are the
dead raised? With what kind of body do
they come?" [36]Fool! What you sow does not

[g] Gk *my brothers* [h] Gk *brothers* [i] Or *gospel* [j] Gk *fallen asleep* [k] Or *Then come the rest* [l] Gk *he*

14.39 1 Cor 12.31
15.1 Gal 1.11; Rom 2.16; 5.2
15.2 Rom 1.16; 11.22; Gal 3.4
15.3 1 Cor 11.23; 1 Pet 2.24; Isa 53.5-12; Lk 24.25-27; Acts 26.22,23
15.4 Mt 16.8-10; Acts 2.24,25
15.5 Lk 24.34; 1 Cor 1.12; Mt 28.17
15.7 Lk 24.33,36,37; Acts 1.3,4
15.8 Acts 9.3-8; 1 Cor 9.1; Gal 1.16
15.9 Eph 3.8; 1 Tim 1.15; Acts 8.3
15.10 Eph 3.7,8; 2 Cor 11.23; 2 Cor 3.5; Gal 2.8; Phil 2.13
15.15 Acts 2.24
15.20 1 Pet 1.3; ver 23; Acts 26.23; Rev 1.5
15.21 Rom 5.12
15.24 Dan 7.14,27
15.25 Ps 110.1
15.26 2 Tim 1.10; Rev 20.14
15.27 Ps 8.6; Mt 28.18; Heb 2.8
15.28 Phil 3.21; 1 Cor 3.23
15.30 2 Cor 11.26
15.31 Rom 8.36; 2 Cor 4.10; 11.23
15.32 2 Cor 1.8; Lk 12.19
15.34 1 Thess 4.5; 1 Cor 6.5
15.36 Jn 12.24

15.1-58 The Resurrection of Christ and of God's Faithful People.
15.1-11 Central to the *message* which Paul has *handed on* to the Corinthians and which he shared with the other apostles, in spite of their differences with him, are the death, burial and resurrection of Jesus, which occurred *in accordance with the scriptures*. Here are combined a credal formula and the claim that all that happened to and through Jesus is in fulfillment of God's promises to Israel as reported in the scriptures. The initial witness to Jesus' resurrection was *Cephas* (Peter; Mk 16.7; Lk 24.34; see also Lk 22.31-32; 1 Pet 2.25), followed by *the twelve*, which became a technical term for the inner circle of Jesus' disciples (Mt 10.2-4), who are already called *apostles* in the gospels (Mk 3.16-19; Lk 6.14-16). The appearance of the risen Christ to *five hundred* is not directly reported in the gospels or Acts. Some have already died. The "James" mentioned here is Jesus' brother (Mk 6.3; Mt 13.55; Gal 1.19; Acts 12.17; 15.13; 21.18). The *apostles* are those commissioned by the risen Christ. Paul's strange path to conversion and commissioning is here compared to an *untimely* birth, yet his zeal for spreading the gospel exceeds that of Jesus' original disciples.
15.12-19 The very idea of bodily resurrection was denied by many in Corinth and the wider Greco-Roman world, since they believed that the soul alone was immortal. Paul insists that by denying resurrection, they reject the message of Christ and the apostles who proclaim it, and abandon the basis of their faith.
15.20-28 Paul depicts the resurrection of Jesus as the initial event in a series of God's actions which will culminate in the final triumph of his purpose for the whole of the creation. Jesus' being raised from the dead was the *first fruits*, on the analogy of the initial produce of the fields and offspring of the flocks which were dedicated to God (Ex 23.19; Lev 23.10; Deut 26.1-11; Num 18.16-18; Ezek 44.30). Jesus is the prototype of the new creation as *Adam* was of the old (Rom 5.12-21). The subjection of everything to God is announced in Ps 110.1 and Ps 8.7 (*cf.* Eph 1.20-22; Heb 2.8-10), including Christ as God's Son.
15.29-34 *Baptism on behalf of the dead* (being baptized vicariously for the benefit of those who had died) would be foolish if there was no resurrection of the dead, and so would be risking one's life for the sake of the gospel (fighting *wild animals*). *Ephesus* is where Paul was when he wrote. He quotes the declaration of the libertine about enjoying life while it lasts (Isa 22.13), and then quotes from a Greek play (*Thais*, by Menander) to warn against associating with the wrong people.
15.35-49 The question about the kind of body one will have in the resurrection is answered by contrasting a *seed* with the plant it produces, and by noting the great differences among various kinds of *body*, including humans, animals, and the stars and planets. The *spiritual body* is a transformed mode of being, not merely the resuscitation of the physical corpse: those who bore the flawed human image of Adam (*man of dust*; Gen 2.7) will one day bear the transforming image of Christ (*man of heaven*).

15.50-58 Human weakness (*flesh and blood*) cannot take part in (*inherit*) the kingdom of God, but when the *trumpet* signals the end of the present age (1 Thess 4.16; Mt 24.31; Rev 8.2-11,19; 2 Esd 6.23), God's people — living and dead — will be transformed and their bodies will share in *immortality*. All this will be achieved through Christ, in whose *work* the Corinthians are called to engage with diligence and confidence.
16.1-20 Paul's Final Messages to his Corinthian Readers.
16.1-4 The *collection for the saints* was the contribution by Gentile churches to the community in Jerusalem, which Paul had agreed upon with the apostles there (Gal 2.1-10). Also mentioned in 2 Cor 8.1-24; 9.1-15; Rom 15.26. *The first day of every week* was the Christian equivalent of the sabbath, in commemoration of Jesus' resurrection on *the third day* (15.4) after his death on the afternoon before the sabbath (that is, on Friday). *Cf.* Rev 1.10. The community designates in writing who will take it to Jerusalem, probably in company with Paul.
16.5-9 Paul's travel plans include an extended stay in Ephesus *until Pentecost*, probably calculated as 50 days after Passover, and thus in late spring, after which he will cross the Aegean to Macedonia on his way to Corinth by land.
16.10-12 A plea for encouragement toward *Timothy* (see 4.17) and an explanation that *Apollos* (see 1.12; 3.5-9; 4.6) has chosen to delay visiting them.
16.13-21 Personal greetings to members of the church in Corinth include those to *the household of Stephanas*, which implies that not merely individuals were converted. Greeting from members in Ephesus and other *churches of* [the province of] *Asia* known to those in Corinth. *Aquila and Prisca* (Priscilla) are mentioned in Acts 18.2 as formerly from Rome, then resident in Corinth. Paul apparently dictated letters and then concluded them in his own handwriting (*cf.* Gal 6.11; Rom 16.22). The final greetings are in liturgical style, with a warning for lack of love to Christ, a prayer for his return (the Aramaic phrase is *Maran atha*), and an expression of *love* for all in the community.

come to life unless it dies. [37]And as for what
you sow, you do not sow the body that is
to be, but a bare seed, perhaps of wheat or
of some other grain. [38]But God gives it a
body as he has chosen, and to each kind of
seed its own body. [39]Not all flesh is alike,
but there is one flesh for human beings,
another for animals, another for birds, and
another for fish. [40]There are both heavenly
bodies and earthly bodies, but the glory of
the heavenly is one thing, and that of the
earthly is another. [41]There is one glory of
the sun, and another glory of the moon,
and another glory of the stars; indeed, star
differs from star in glory.
42 So it is with the resurrection of the
dead. What is sown is perishable, what is
raised is imperishable. [43]It is sown in
dishonor, it is raised in glory. It is sown in
weakness, it is raised in power. [44]It is sown
a physical body, it is raised a spiritual body.
If there is a physical body, there is also a
spiritual body. [45]Thus it is written, "The first
man, Adam, became a living being"; the
last Adam became a life-giving spirit. [46]But
it is not the spiritual that is first, but the
physical, and then the spiritual. [47]The first
man was from the earth, a man of dust; the
second man is[m] from heaven. [48]As was the
man of dust, so are those who are of the
dust; and as is the man of heaven, so are
those who are of heaven. [49]Just as we have
borne the image of the man of dust, we
will[n] also bear the image of the man of
heaven.
50 What I am saying, brothers and
sisters,[o] is this: flesh and blood cannot inherit the kingdom of God, nor does the
perishable inherit the imperishable. [51]Listen,
I will tell you a mystery! We will not all die,[p]
but we will all be changed, [52]in a moment,
in the twinkling of an eye, at the last
trumpet. For the trumpet will sound, and
the dead will be raised imperishable, and we
will be changed. [53]For this perishable body
must put on imperishability, and this mortal body must put on immortality. [54]When
this perishable body puts on imperishability,
and this mortal body puts on immortality,
then the saying that is written will be fulfilled:
"Death has been swallowed up in
victory."
[55] "Where, O death, is your victory?
Where, O death, is your sting?"
[56]The sting of death is sin, and the power
of sin is the law. [57]But thanks be to God,
who gives us the victory through our Lord
Jesus Christ.
58 Therefore, my beloved,[q] be steadfast,
immovable, always excelling in the work of
the Lord, because you know that in the
Lord your labor is not in vain.

The Collection for the Saints

16 Now concerning the collection for
the saints: you should follow the
directions I gave to the churches of Galatia.
[2]On the first day of every week, each of you
is to put aside and save whatever extra you
earn, so that collections need not be taken
when I come. [3]And when I arrive, I will
send any whom you approve with letters to
take your gift to Jerusalem. [4]If it seems
advisable that I should go also, they will
accompany me.

Plans for Travel

5 I will visit you after passing through
Macedonia—for I intend to pass through
Macedonia— [6]and perhaps I will stay with
you or even spend the winter, so that you
may send me on my way, wherever I go.
[7]I do not want to see you now just in
passing, for I hope to spend some time with
you, if the Lord permits. [8]But I will stay in
Ephesus until Pentecost, [9]for a wide door for
effective work has opened to me, and there
are many adversaries.
10 If Timothy comes, see that he has
nothing to fear among you, for he is doing
the work of the Lord just as I am; [11]there-
fore let no one despise him. Send him on his
way in peace, so that he may come to me;
for I am expecting him with the brothers.
12 Now concerning our brother Apollos,
I strongly urged him to visit you with the
other brothers, but he was not at all willing[r]
to come now. He will come when he has
the opportunity.

Final Messages and Greetings

13 Keep alert, stand firm in your faith,
be courageous, be strong. [14]Let all that you
do be done in love.
15 Now, brothers and sisters,[o] you know
that members of the household of Stephanas

[m] Other ancient authorities add *the Lord* [n] Other ancient authorities read *let us* [o] Gk *brothers* [p] Gk *fall asleep* [q] Gk *beloved brothers* [r] Or *it was not at all God's will for him*

15.43 Phil 3.21
15.45 Gen 2.7; Rom 5.14; 8.2
15.47 Jn 3.31; Gen 2.7; 3.19
15.49 Gen 5.3; Rom 8.29; 1 Jn 3.2
15.50 Mt 16.17; Jn 3.3,5
15.51 1 Thess 4.15-17; Phil 3.21
15.52 Mt 24.31; Jn 5.25; 1 Thess 4.16
15.54 Isa 25.8; Heb 2.14; Rev 20.14
15.56 Rom 5.12; 4.15; 5.13
15.58 2 Pet 3.14; 1 Cor 16.10
16.1 Acts 24.17; 9.13; 16.6
16.2 Acts 20.7; 2 Cor 9.4,5
16.5 Acts 19.21
16.10 Acts 16.1; 19.22; 1 Cor 15.58
16.11 1 Tim 4.12; Acts 15.33
16.12 Acts 18.24; 1 Cor 1.12; 3.5,6
16.13 Phil 1.27; 1 Thess 2.15; Eph 6.10
16.14 1 Cor 14.1
16.15 Rom 16.5; 2 Cor 8.4; Heb 6.10

were the first converts in Achaia, and they have devoted themselves to the service of the saints; 16 I urge you to put yourselves at the service of such people, and of everyone who works and toils with them. 17 I rejoice at the coming of Stephanas and Fortunatus and Achaicus, because they have made up for your absence; 18 for they refreshed my spirit as well as yours. So give recognition to such persons.

19 The churches of Asia send greetings. Aquila and Prisca, together with the church in their house, greet you warmly in the Lord. 20 All the brothers and sisters[s] send greetings. Greet one another with a holy kiss.

21 I, Paul, write this greeting with my own hand. 22 Let anyone be accursed who has no love for the Lord. Our Lord, come![t] 23 The grace of the Lord Jesus be with you. 24 My love be with all of you in Christ Jesus.[u]

16.16 Heb 13.1
16.17 2 Cor 7.6,7; 11.9
16.18 2 Cor 7.13; Phil 2.29
16.19 Acts 16.6; Rom 16.5
16.22 Eph 6.24; Rom 9.3

[s] Gk *brothers* [t] Gk *Marana tha*. These Aramaic words can also be read *Maran atha*, meaning *Our Lord has come* [u] Other ancient authorities add *Amen*

THE SECOND LETTER OF PAUL TO THE

CORINTHIANS

Salutation

1 Paul, an apostle of Christ Jesus by the will of God, and Timothy our brother,
To the church of God that is in Corinth, including all the saints throughout Achaia:
2 Grace to you and peace from God our Father and the Lord Jesus Christ.

Paul's Thanksgiving after Affliction

3 Blessed be the God and Father of our Lord Jesus Christ, the Father of mercies and the God of all consolation, 4 who consoles us in all our affliction, so that we may be able to console those who are in any affliction with the consolation with which we ourselves are consoled by God. 5 For just as the sufferings of Christ are abundant for us, so also our consolation is abundant through Christ. 6 If we are being afflicted, it is for your consolation and salvation; if we are being consoled, it is for your consolation, which you experience when you patiently endure the same sufferings that we are also suffering. 7 Our hope for you is unshaken; for we know that as you share in our sufferings, so also you share in our consolation.

8 We do not want you to be unaware, brothers and sisters,[a] of the affliction we experienced in Asia; for we were so utterly, unbearably crushed that we despaired of life itself. 9 Indeed, we felt that we had received the sentence of death so that we would rely not on ourselves but on God who raises the dead. 10 He who rescued us from so deadly a peril will continue to rescue us; on him we have set our hope that he will rescue us again, 11 as you also join in helping us by your prayers, so that many will give thanks on our[b] behalf for the blessing granted us through the prayers of many.

The Postponement of Paul's Visit

12 Indeed, this is our boast, the testimony of our conscience: we have behaved in the world with frankness[c] and godly sincerity, not by earthly wisdom but by the grace of God—and all the more toward you. 13 For we write you nothing other than what you can read and also understand; I hope you will understand until the end— 14 as you have already understood us in part—that on the day of the Lord Jesus we are your boast even as you are our boast.

1.1 Col 1.1; 1 Tim 1.1; 1 Cor 1.1
1.2 Rom 1.7; 1 Cor 1.3; Gal 1.3
1.3 Eph 1.3; 1 Pet 1.3; Rom 15.5
1.5 2 Cor 4.10; Col 1.24
1.8 Acts 19.23; 1 Cor 15.32
1.10 2 Pet 2.9
1.11 Rom 15.30; Phil 1.19; 2 Cor 4.15
1.12 2 Cor 2.17; 1 Cor 2.4,13
1.14 1 Cor 1.8

[a] Gk *brothers* [b] Other ancient authorities read *your* [c] Other ancient authorities read *holiness*

See the Introductions, pp. 8–9 and 85 above.

1.1-2 Formal introductory letter-writing style, for which see note on Rom 1.1. On the probably composite origins of what is now 2 Corinthians, see introduction to this book. On *apostle* see note at Rom 1.5. *Timothy* is again with Paul (1 Cor 4.17; 1 Tim 1.1). *Achaia*, the southern part of Greece, was a senatorial province after 27 CE, and Corinth was its capital (Acts 18.12).
1.3-11 The formal thanksgiving is found in all Paul's letters (note on Rom 1.7), except Galatians, which was written in anger and protest. *Blessed* means thanking and honoring God, not conferring benefits on him. God's *consolation* is referred to ten times in 1.3-7, and points to the reconciliation that has developed in the Corinthian community, replacing its earlier divisive state. God has given this gift, just as he gave Paul the ministry of reconciliation (5.18). The *sufferings* Paul experienced recall those of Christ (Mk 8.31; Mt 16.21; Lk 9.22; 1 Pet 1.11; 4.13; 5.1; Heb 2.9-10), and likewise have beneficial effects on the community. The suffering Paul *experienced in Asia* (at Ephesus) included imprisonment (Phil 1.12-13,17) and led him to despair of surviving.
1.12-2.4 Why Paul Had to Delay his Visit to Corinth.
1.12-14 Using terms from Stoic philosophy, *conscience...godly sincerity*, Paul claims that his awareness of God's purpose for his people led him to write so sharply to the Corinthians in order to correct their misunderstandings.

1.15-2.4 His failure to visit them as promised was not the result of vacillation, since *God's promises* are always clear and definite, and he has given his people his Spirit as a *seal* (Rom 4.11; 15.28; 1 Cor 9.2) and *first installment* (or downpayment; Eph 1.13) on the blessing that is ultimately to come to them. Instead, he refrained from coming, as he had promised (12.14; 13.1-2,5-6,11) in order to avoid the *pain* they would have brought to each other because of the conflicts within their community which he would have sought to resolve. The letter filled with *distress and anguish* was not the one known as 1 Corinthians.
2.5-13 Paul Urges Reconciliation. The unnamed attacker of Paul was rebuked by *majority* vote of the community, and Paul forgives him and prays for him to be consoled and forgiven by the church as well. Blame for the trouble is placed on *Satan*; 11.14; 12.7; 1 Cor 5.5; 7.5.
2.12-13 Paul reports some success in *Troas*, an important port city in northwest Asia Minor (Acts 16.8-10). He was deeply concerned for *Titus*, a Gentile converted by Paul (Gal 2.1,3) and a negotiator in Corinth (7.6-7,13-15; 8.16,23; 12.18). Failing to find him in Troas, Paul sailed across the sea to *Macedonia*. The line of thought is interrupted here, and resumes in 7.5.
2.14-7.1 Images of Ministry.
2.14-17 The ministry is depicted in terms of a *triumphal procession* in which God has assured fine results, and then as a fragrant *aroma* which permeates the world, spreading the knowledge of Christ which brings life, but the odor of *death* to those who reject the good news.
3.1-6 The community in Corinth serves as a letter *of recommendation* for all to read. It was written by the Spirit on *human hearts*, like the new covenant announced by Jeremiah (Jer 31.31-33; Prov 3.3; 7.3) rather than on *tablets of stone*, as the old covenant with Israel was (Ex 24.12; 31.18; Deut 9.10-11). *Cf.* Rom 2.29. The ministry of the new covenant is the gift of God, and is effective through the power of the *Spirit*.
3.7-18 The radiant cloud of glory that came down when the law was given through Moses (Ex 34.39) was too bright for the people to behold (Ex 34.29-35). Failure to obey the law brought a curse (Deut 27.26). But the greater glory disclosed through the Spirit sets God's people right with him (*justification*). The temporary covenant of law has now been *set aside* through Christ, so that by the Spirit God's people can behold his glory and are transformed into his glorious *image* through the work of the *Spirit*.

15 Since I was sure of this, I wanted to
come to you first, so that you might have
a double favor;[d] 16I wanted to visit you on
my way to Macedonia, and to come back
to you from Macedonia and have you send
me on to Judea. 17Was I vacillating when
I wanted to do this? Do I make my plans
according to ordinary human standards,[e]
ready to say "Yes, yes" and "No, no" at the
same time? 18As surely as God is faithful,
our word to you has not been "Yes and
No." 19For the Son of God, Jesus Christ,
whom we proclaimed among you, Silvanus
and Timothy and I, was not "Yes and No";
but in him it is always "Yes." 20For in him
every one of God's promises is a "Yes." For
this reason it is through him that we say
the "Amen," to the glory of God. 21But it is
God who establishes us with you in Christ
and has anointed us, 22by putting his seal
on us and giving us his Spirit in our hearts
as a first installment.
23 But I call on God as witness against
me: it was to spare you that I did not come
again to Corinth. 24I do not mean to imply
that we lord it over your faith; rather, we
are workers with you for your joy, because
you stand firm in the faith.
2 So I made up my mind not to make
you another painful visit. 2For if I
cause you pain, who is there to make me
glad but the one whom I have pained? 3And
I wrote as I did, so that when I came, I
might not suffer pain from those who should
have made me rejoice; for I am confident
about all of you, that my joy would be the
joy of all of you. 4For I wrote you out of
much distress and anguish of heart and
with many tears, not to cause you pain, but
to let you know the abundant love that I
have for you.

Forgiveness for the Offender

5 But if anyone has caused pain, he has
caused it not to me, but to some extent—
not to exaggerate it—to all of you. 6This
punishment by the majority is enough for
such a person; 7so now instead you should
forgive and console him, so that he may not
be overwhelmed by excessive sorrow. 8So I
urge you to reaffirm your love for him. 9I
wrote for this reason: to test you and to
know whether you are obedient in everything. 10Anyone whom you forgive, I also
forgive. What I have forgiven, if I have
forgiven anything, has been for your sake
in the presence of Christ. 11And we do this
so that we may not be outwitted by Satan;
for we are not ignorant of his designs.

Paul's Anxiety in Troas

12 When I came to Troas to proclaim
the good news of Christ, a door was opened
for me in the Lord; 13but my mind could not
rest because I did not find my brother Titus
there. So I said farewell to them and went
on to Macedonia.
14 But thanks be to God, who in Christ
always leads us in triumphal procession,
and through us spreads in every place the
fragrance that comes from knowing him.
15For we are the aroma of Christ to God
among those who are being saved and
among those who are perishing; 16to the
one a fragrance from death to death, to the
other a fragrance from life to life. Who is
sufficient for these things? 17For we are not
peddlers of God's word like so many;[f] but
in Christ we speak as persons of sincerity,
as persons sent from God and standing in
his presence.

Ministers of the New Covenant

3 Are we beginning to commend ourselves again? Surely we do not need,
as some do, letters of recommendation to
you or from you, do we? 2You yourselves
are our letter, written on our[g] hearts, to be
known and read by all; 3and you show that
you are a letter of Christ, prepared by us,
written not with ink but with the Spirit of
the living God, not on tablets of stone but
on tablets of human hearts.
4 Such is the confidence that we have
through Christ toward God. 5Not that we
are competent of ourselves to claim anything as coming from us; our competence
is from God, 6who has made us competent
to be ministers of a new covenant, not of
letter but of spirit; for the letter kills, but the
Spirit gives life.
7 Now if the ministry of death, chiseled
in letters on stone tablets,[h] came in glory so
that the people of Israel could not gaze at
Moses' face because of the glory of his face,
a glory now set aside, 8how much more will
the ministry of the Spirit come in glory?

[d] Other ancient authorities read *pleasure* [e] Gk *according to the flesh* [f] Other ancient authorities read *like the others* [g] Other ancient authorities read *your* [h] Gk *on stones*

1.15 1 Cor 4.19; Rom 1.11; 15.29
1.16 1 Cor 16.6-7
1.19 Mt 16.16; 1 Thess 1.1; Heb 13.8
1.20 Rom 15.8,9; 1 Cor 14.16
1.21 1 Cor 1.8; 1 Jn 2.20,27
1.22 Eph 1.13
1.23 Gal 1.20; 1 Cor 4.21; 2 Cor 2.3
1.24 1 Pet 5.3; Rom 11.20; 1 Cor 15.1
2.1 2 Cor 1.23
2.3 2 Cor 12.21; 7.16; 8.22
2.6 1 Cor 5.4,5
2.9 Phil 2.22; 2 Cor 7.15; 10.6
2.12 Acts 16.8; 1 Cor 16.9
2.15 Eph 5.2; Phil 4.18; 2 Cor 4.3
2.16 Jn 9.39; 1 Pet 2.7
2.17 2 Cor 4.2; 1.12; 12.19
3.1 2 Cor 5.12; 12.11; Acts 18.27
3.3 Jer 31.33; Ezek 11.19
3.5 2 Cor 2.16; 1 Cor 15.10
3.6 Heb 8.6,8; Gal 3.10; Jn 6.63
3.7 Ex 34.29-35

3.9 ver 7; Rom 1.17; 3.21
3.12 2 Cor 7.4; Eph 6.19
3.13 ver 7; Ex 34.33
3.14 Rom 11.7; Acts 13.15; ver 6
3.16 Rom 11.23
3.17 1 Cor 15.45; Isa 61.1,2; Jn 8.32
3.18 1 Cor 13.12; 2 Cor 4.4,6; Rom 8.29
4.1 2 Cor 3.6; 1 Cor 7.25
4.2 2 Cor 2.17
4.3 2 Cor 2.12; 3.14; 1 Cor 1.18
4.4 Jn 12.31; Col 1.15; Jn 1.18
4.5 1 Cor 1.13,23; 9.19
4.6 Gen 1.3; 2 Pet 1.19
4.7 2 Cor 5.1; 1 Cor 2.5
4.10 Gal 6.17; Rom 8.17
4.13 Ps 116.10
4.14 1 Thess 4.14
4.16 Rom 7.22; Col 3.10
4.17 Rom 8.18; 1 Pet 1.6
4.18 Rom 8.24; Heb 11.1
5.1 2 Pet 1.13,14
5.4 1 Cor 15.53,54
5.5 Rom 8.23; 2 Cor 1.22
5.7 1 Cor 13.12
5.10 Rom 14.10; Eph 6.8

9For if there was glory in the ministry of condemnation, much more does the ministry of justification abound in glory! 10Indeed, what once had glory has lost its glory because of the greater glory; 11for if what was set aside came through glory, much more has the permanent come in glory!

12 Since, then, we have such a hope, we act with great boldness, 13not like Moses, who put a veil over his face to keep the people of Israel from gazing at the end of the glory that[i] was being set aside. 14But their minds were hardened. Indeed, to this very day, when they hear the reading of the old covenant, that same veil is still there, since only in Christ is it set aside. 15Indeed, to this very day whenever Moses is read, a veil lies over their minds; 16but when one turns to the Lord, the veil is removed. 17Now the Lord is the Spirit, and where the Spirit of the Lord is, there is freedom. 18And all of us, with unveiled faces, seeing the glory of the Lord as though reflected in a mirror, are being transformed into the same image from one degree of glory to another; for this comes from the Lord, the Spirit.

Treasure in Clay Jars

4 Therefore, since it is by God's mercy that we are engaged in this ministry, we do not lose heart. 2We have renounced the shameful things that one hides; we refuse to practice cunning or to falsify God's word; but by the open statement of the truth we commend ourselves to the conscience of everyone in the sight of God. 3And even if our gospel is veiled, it is veiled to those who are perishing. 4In their case the god of this world has blinded the minds of the unbelievers, to keep them from seeing the light of the gospel of the glory of Christ, who is the image of God. 5For we do not proclaim ourselves; we proclaim Jesus Christ as Lord and ourselves as your slaves for Jesus' sake. 6For it is the God who said, "Let light shine out of darkness," who has shone in our hearts to give the light of the knowledge of the glory of God in the face of Jesus Christ.

7 But we have this treasure in clay jars, so that it may be made clear that this extraordinary power belongs to God and does not come from us. 8We are afflicted in every way, but not crushed; perplexed, but not driven to despair; 9persecuted, but not forsaken; struck down, but not destroyed; 10always carrying in the body the death of Jesus, so that the life of Jesus may also be made visible in our bodies. 11For while we live, we are always being given up to death for Jesus' sake, so that the life of Jesus may be made visible in our mortal flesh. 12So death is at work in us, but life in you.

13 But just as we have the same spirit of faith that is in accordance with scripture—"I believed, and so I spoke"—we also believe, and so we speak, 14because we know that the one who raised the Lord Jesus will raise us also with Jesus, and will bring us with you into his presence. 15Yes, everything is for your sake, so that grace, as it extends to more and more people, may increase thanksgiving, to the glory of God.

Living by Faith

16 So we do not lose heart. Even though our outer nature is wasting away, our inner nature is being renewed day by day. 17For this slight momentary affliction is preparing us for an eternal weight of glory beyond all measure, 18because we look not at what can be seen but at what cannot be seen; for what can be seen is temporary, but what cannot be seen is eternal.

5 For we know that if the earthly tent we live in is destroyed, we have a building from God, a house not made with hands, eternal in the heavens. 2For in this tent we groan, longing to be clothed with our heavenly dwelling— 3if indeed, when we have taken it off[j] we will not be found naked. 4For while we are still in this tent, we groan under our burden, because we wish not to be unclothed but to be further clothed, so that what is mortal may be swallowed up by life. 5He who has prepared us for this very thing is God, who has given us the Spirit as a guarantee.

6 So we are always confident; even though we know that while we are at home in the body we are away from the Lord— 7for we walk by faith, not by sight. 8Yes, we do have confidence, and we would rather be away from the body and at home with the Lord. 9So whether we are at home or away, we make it our aim to please him. 10For all of us must appear before the judgment seat of Christ, so that each may receive recompense for what has been done in the body, whether good or evil.

[i] Gk *of what* [j] Other ancient authorities read *put it on*

4.1-15 The ministry gives courage to those who carry it out, so that they do not deceive or *falsify*. Those who reject their message are already *perishing*, since they have been blinded by *the god of this world* (or age; 1 Cor 1.20; 2.6,8; 3.18; Rom 12.2; Eph 2.2; Jn 12.31; 14.30; 16.11; see note on Mt 12.24). Those who reflect the glory of Christ through proclaiming the gospel are *slaves* of those who receive the message. Elsewhere, Paul calls himself a "servant of Jesus Christ" (Rom 1.1; 1 Cor 3.5; 4.1; 2 Cor 6.4; Gal 1.10; Phil 1.1; Titus 1.1). The quotation about light shining out of darkness recalls Gen 1.3, as well as Isa 9.2; 42.6-7; 49.6; 60.1-2, where the light goes forth to the Gentile nations. The light *in our hearts* recalls Paul's own experience of conversion as described in Acts 9.3. The power is from God, but the human instruments or vessels are fragile as *clay jars*. Constant opposition and persecution of Paul and the other apostles recalls the cross of Jesus, where death is overcome by the resurrection life, which will vindicate and renew the life of God's faithful messengers.
4.16-5.10 The temporary and afflicted manner of life of Paul and the ministers of the gospel (*earthly tent*) is contrasted with the permanent *heavenly dwelling* prepared by God for his people. Assurance is provided by the presence of the *Spirit*. Whether in bodily existence away from the Lord or ultimate dwelling in God's presence, Paul's aim is to please God, knowing that all his people will be called to account by Christ as judge for what they have done *in the body* (Rom 14.12).

The Ministry of Reconciliation

11 Therefore, knowing the fear of the Lord, we try to persuade others; but we ourselves are well known to God, and I hope that we are also well known to your consciences. 12 We are not commending ourselves to you again, but giving you an opportunity to boast about us, so that you may be able to answer those who boast in outward appearance and not in the heart. 13 For if we are beside ourselves, it is for God; if we are in our right mind, it is for you. 14 For the love of Christ urges us on, because we are convinced that one has died for all; therefore all have died. 15 And he died for all, so that those who live might live no longer for themselves, but for him who died and was raised for them.

16 From now on, therefore, we regard no one from a human point of view;[k] even though we once knew Christ from a human point of view,[k] we know him no longer in that way. 17 So if anyone is in Christ, there is a new creation: everything old has passed away; see, everything has become new! 18 All this is from God, who reconciled us to himself through Christ, and has given us the ministry of reconciliation; 19 that is, in Christ God was reconciling the world to himself,[l] not counting their trespasses against them, and entrusting the message of reconciliation to us. 20 So we are ambassadors for Christ, since God is making his appeal through us; we entreat you on behalf of Christ, be reconciled to God. 21 For our sake he made him to be sin who knew no sin, so that in him we might become the righteousness of God.

6 As we work together with him,[m] we urge you also not to accept the grace of God in vain. 2 For he says,

"At an acceptable time I have listened to you,
and on a day of salvation I have helped you."

See, now is the acceptable time; see, now is the day of salvation! 3 We are putting no obstacle in anyone's way, so that no fault may be found with our ministry, 4 but as servants of God we have commended ourselves in every way: through great endurance, in afflictions, hardships, calamities, 5 beatings, imprisonments, riots, labors, sleepless nights, hunger; 6 by purity, knowledge, patience, kindness, holiness of spirit, genuine love, 7 truthful speech, and the power of God; with the weapons of righteousness for the right hand and for the left; 8 in honor and dishonor, in ill repute and good repute. We are treated as impostors, and yet are true; 9 as unknown, and yet are well known; as dying, and see—we are alive; as punished, and yet not killed; 10 as sorrowful, yet always rejoicing; as poor, yet making many rich; as having nothing, and yet possessing everything.

11 We have spoken frankly to you Corinthians; our heart is wide open to you. 12 There is no restriction in our affections, but only in yours. 13 In return—I speak as to children—open wide your hearts also.

The Temple of the Living God

14 Do not be mismatched with unbelievers. For what partnership is there between righteousness and lawlessness? Or what fellowship is there between light and darkness? 15 What agreement does Christ have with Beliar? Or what does a believer share with an unbeliever? 16 What agreement has the temple of God with idols? For we[n] are the temple of the living God; as God said,

"I will live in them and walk among them,
and I will be their God,
and they shall be my people.
17 Therefore come out from them,
and be separate from them, says the Lord,
and touch nothing unclean;
then I will welcome you,
18 and I will be your father,
and you shall be my sons and daughters,
says the Lord Almighty."

7 Since we have these promises, beloved, let us cleanse ourselves from every defilement of body and of spirit, making holiness perfect in the fear of God.

Paul's Joy at the Church's Repentance

2 Make room in your hearts[o] for us; we have wronged no one, we have corrupted no one, we have taken advantage of no one. 3 I do not say this to condemn you, for I said before that you are in our hearts, to die together and to live together. 4 I often boast about you; I have great pride in you;

[k] Gk *according to the flesh* [l] Or *God was in Christ reconciling the world to himself* [m] Gk *As we work together* [n] Other ancient authorities read *you* [o] Gk lacks *in your hearts*

5.11-6.12 The Ministry of Reconciliation.
5.11-15 Paul responds to criticism of ineffectiveness in persuasion of others: he is not promoting himself and he is not *beside* himself. His sole motive is based on *the love of Christ* for his people as evident in giving his life *for all* (1 Cor 15.3; Rom 8.5; 11.24; Gal 2.20; 3.13; 1 Thess 5.10).
5.16-17 *From a human point of view* is literally, "according to the flesh," a term which can mean human existence (Rom 1.3; 4.1; 9.3,5; 1 Cor 10.18), but more often implies humanity in its weakness, temporality, and inclination to self-seeking (Rom 8.4-5,12; Gal 4.23,29) or actions according to purely human standards (1 Cor 1.26; 2 Cor 1.17; 10.2-3; 11.18). By contrast, life *in Christ* is the new sphere of existence, a totally transformed way of looking at life and the world, into which one enters through trusting in Christ. It is a *new creation*, transforming God's people and the whole creation (1 Cor 1.16; 2 Cor 1.17; 10.2-3; 11.18).
5.18-6.2 God took the initiative in *reconciling the world to himself*, by placing the wholly obedient Jesus under the power of sin so that through him sinful humans might come into right relationship with God. This message is proclaimed by Paul in his ministry as ambassador for Christ, appealing to his hearers to enter this community of those reconciled to God, and to do so today, quoting Isa 49.8.
6.3-13 Paul's ministry is characterized, not by spectacular success according to human standards, but by all sorts of hardship and abuse, as well as by the virtues (*purity, knowledge, holiness of spirit, love*, and truthfulness) which God bestows through his *power* at work in the apostles. In his state of deprivation, humanly speaking, he makes others *rich* and possesses *everything* of real value (2 Cor 13.11; Rom 12.12; Phil 2.18). He now seeks reconciliation with the Corinthians. This line of argument continues in 7.2.
6.14-7.1 This section breaks the flow of thought and conveys more of a separatist attitude than one finds elsewhere in Paul's letters. It may come from one of the groups in Corinth or from a later editor (see introduction to 2 Cor). *Mismatched with unbelievers* is not found elsewhere in Paul's letters, nor is there elsewhere a Pauline reference to *Beliar*, a name for Satan, the chief of the powers of darkness as found in the Dead Sea Scrolls. The Old Testament texts here quoted (6.16=Lev 26.12 and Ezek 37.27; 6.17=Isa 52.11 and Ezek 20.34; 6.18=2 Sam 7.14 and Isa 43.6) are not used in other Pauline letters. The appeal to believers to *cleanse ourselves* is here only in the New Testament. The image for the new community is the *temple of God*, and the whole section uses priestly imagery of ceremonial cleansing.
7.2-16 Paul's Joy over Reconciliation with the Church at Corinth.
Through *Titus* Paul has learned that his critical letter to the Corinthians evoked *repentance* (change of heart) and a desire by them to correct the problems within their community of faith. *The one who did wrong* is not identified here, nor was he in 2.6-8. By contrast, *Titus* has served effectively and returned to Paul with joy over the change among the Corinthians, evident in their *obedience* and their sense of awe (*fear and trembling*, Ps 2.11; Phil 2.12; Eph 6.5) in realizing what God is doing among them through the apostles and their aides.

5.11 Heb 10.31; Jude 23; 2 Cor 4.2
5.12 2 Cor 3.1; 1.14
5.13 2 Cor 11.1,16,17
5.14 Acts 18.5; Rom 5.15; Gal 2.20
5.16 2 Cor 11.18; Phil 3.4; Jn 8.15
5.17 Rom 16.7; Gal 5.6; Rev 21.4,5
5.18 Col 1.20; Rom 5.10
5.19 Rom 3.24,25
5.20 2 Cor 3.6; Eph 6.20; 2 Cor 6.1
5.21 1 Pet 2.22; 1 Jn 3.5; Gal 3.13
6.1 1 Cor 3.9; 2 Cor 5.20; Heb 12.15
6.2 Isa 49.8
6.3 Rom 14.13; 1 Cor 9.12; 10.32
6.5 2 Cor 11.23
6.7 2 Cor 4.2; 10.4; Eph 6.11,13
6.9 Rom 8.36; 2 Cor 1.8-10; 4.10,11
6.13 1 Cor 4.14
6.14 Deut 7.2,3; 1 Cor 5.9,10; Eph 5.7,11; 1 Jn 1.6
6.16 1 Cor 3.16; Jer 31.1; Ezek 27.37
6.17 Isa 52.11; Rev 18.4
6.18 Hos 1.10; Isa 43.6
7.1 2 Cor 6.17,18
7.2 2 Cor 6.12,13
7.3 2 Cor 6.11,12
7.4 2 Cor 1.4,14; 3.12

I am filled with consolation; I am overjoyed
in all our affliction.
5 For even when we came into Macedonia, our bodies had no rest, but we were
afflicted in every way—disputes without and
fears within. [6]But God, who consoles the
downcast, consoled us by the arrival of
Titus, [7]and not only by his coming, but also
by the consolation with which he was
consoled about you, as he told us of your
longing, your mourning, your zeal for me,
so that I rejoiced still more. [8]For even if I
made you sorry with my letter, I do not
regret it (though I did regret it, for I see that
I grieved you with that letter, though only
briefly). [9]Now I rejoice, not because you
were grieved, but because your grief led to
repentance; for you felt a godly grief, so that
you were not harmed in any way by us.
[10]For godly grief produces a repentance that
leads to salvation and brings no regret, but
worldly grief produces death. [11]For see what
earnestness this godly grief has produced in
you, what eagerness to clear yourselves,
what indignation, what alarm, what longing, what zeal, what punishment! At every
point you have proved yourselves guiltless
in the matter. [12]So although I wrote to you,
it was not on account of the one who did
the wrong, nor on account of the one who
was wronged, but in order that your zeal
for us might be made known to you before
God. [13]In this we find comfort.
In addition to our own consolation, we
rejoiced still more at the joy of Titus, because his mind has been set at rest by all
of you. [14]For if I have been somewhat boastful
about you to him, I was not disgraced; but
just as everything we said to you was true,
so our boasting to Titus has proved true as
well. [15]And his heart goes out all the more
to you, as he remembers the obedience of
all of you, and how you welcomed him with
fear and trembling. [16]I rejoice, because I
have complete confidence in you.

Encouragement to Be Generous

8 We want you to know, brothers and
sisters,[p] about the grace of God that
has been granted to the churches of Macedonia; [2]for during a severe ordeal of affliction, their abundant joy and their extreme
poverty have overflowed in a wealth of
generosity on their part. [3]For, as I can
testify, they voluntarily gave according to
their means, and even beyond their means,
[4]begging us earnestly for the privilege[q] of
sharing in this ministry to the saints— [5]and
this, not merely as we expected; they gave
themselves first to the Lord and, by the will
of God, to us, [6]so that we might urge Titus
that, as he had already made a beginning,
so he should also complete this generous
undertaking[r] among you. [7]Now as you excel
in everything—in faith, in speech, in knowledge, in utmost eagerness, and in our love
for you[s]—so we want you to excel also in
this generous undertaking.[r]
8 I do not say this as a command, but
I am testing the genuineness of your love
against the earnestness of others. [9]For you
know the generous act[t] of our Lord Jesus
Christ, that though he was rich, yet for
your sakes he became poor, so that by his
poverty you might become rich. [10]And in
this matter I am giving my advice: it is
appropriate for you who began last year not
only to do something but even to desire to
do something— [11]now finish doing it, so
that your eagerness may be matched by
completing it according to your means. [12]For
if the eagerness is there, the gift is acceptable according to what one has—not according to what one does not have. [13]I do
not mean that there should be relief for
others and pressure on you, but it is a
question of a fair balance between [14]your
present abundance and their need, so that
their abundance may be for your need, in
order that there may be a fair balance. [15]As
it is written,
"The one who had much did not have
too much,
and the one who had little did not
have too little."

Commendation of Titus

16 But thanks be to God who put in the
heart of Titus the same eagerness for you
that I myself have. [17]For he not only accepted our appeal, but since he is more
eager than ever, he is going to you of his
own accord. [18]With him we are sending the
brother who is famous among all the
churches for his proclaiming the good news;[u]
[19]and not only that, but he has also been
appointed by the churches to travel with us
while we are administering this generous

[p] Gk *brothers* [q] Gk *grace* [r] Gk *this grace* [s] Other ancient authorities read *your love for us* [t] Gk *the grace* [u] Or *the gospel*

8.1-9.15 The Corinthians' Contribution to the Church in Jerusalem.
The collection is also mentioned in 1 Cor 16.1; Rom 15.26; Gal 2.20.
8.1-7 God's *grace* in bestowing salvation through Christ and the gifts of the Spirit on the Macedonian community (see note on Rom 15.26) led to their generous contribution in spite of their ordeal of affliction (Phil 1.29-30; 1 Thess 1.6; 2.14; 3.3-4; Acts 17.1-11). *Sharing* (in Greek *koinonia*) means mutual participation and is called a *ministry to the saints* in Jerusalem (1 Cor 16.15; 2 Cor 9.1,12,13; Rom 15.25,31). *Titus* is to return to Corinth to complete the process of collecting their gift. Paul hopes that their generosity will match their display of spiritual gifts (*faith, speech, knowledge, love*).
8.8-15 Paul is urging them to give, not handing down an apostolic *command*. The model for their gift is the self-giving of Jesus Christ, who gave up his special relationship with God to assume human form (*became poor*), to suffer and die so that disobedient humanity might be transformed into God's new people (*become rich*). Sharing possessions is described in Acts 2.44-45 as operative from the beginning of the church. The quotation is from Ex 16.18.
8.16-24 *Titus* and an unnamed but renowned companion are coming to get the collection. Both are wholly trustworthy, and Titus was designated (*appointed*) by a whole group of *the churches* to handle the collection and to serve as a witness to the honesty and faithfulness of the entire enterprise. The only one who will receive *glory* for this enterprise is *the Lord*, but he urges the Corinthians by their generosity to give concrete *proof* of their love.

7.5 2 Cor 2.13; 4.8; Deut 32.35
7.6 2 Cor 1.3,4; ver 13; 2 Cor 2.13
7.10 Acts 11.18
7.12 ver 8; 2 Cor 2.3,9; 1 Cor 5.1,2
7.13 ver 6; 1 Cor 16.18
7.14 ver 4.6
7.15 2 Cor 2.9; Phil 2.12
7.16 2 Thess 3.4
8.4 Acts 24.17; Rom 15.25; 26.31; 2 Cor 9.1
8.6 ver 17; 2 Cor 12.18; ver 16,23,10
8.7 2 Cor 9.8; 1 Cor 1.5; 12.13
8.8 1 Cor 7.6
8.9 2 Cor 13.14; Phil 2.6,7
8.10 1 Cor 7.25; 2 Cor 9.2; 1 Cor 16.2,3
8.11 2 Cor 9.2
8.12 Mk 12.43,44; Lk 21.3
8.15 Ex 16.18
8.18 2 Cor 12.18
8.19 1 Cor 16.3,4; ver 4,6,11

9.1-15 The arrangements for the collection are repeated, or perhaps another fragment of a letter from Paul is included here. He reminds them that he has reported in Macedonia the generosity of the Corinthians, and urges them to live up to their reputation. That is why he has sent *the brothers* to prepare in advance for the collection. The gift is not compulsory, but *the brothers* whom Paul is sending to Corinth have been told of the generosity of the church there, so Paul is eager for the Corinthians to have a generous collection on hand when these members from *Macedonia* arrive. The generosity of God's people will be matched by God's showering benefits on them, as is stated in the quotation from Ps 112.9. That one reaps what one sows was proverbial among Greeks and Jews as well (Prov 11.21,24,26,30; 22.8; Job 4.8; Sir 7.3). Their gift of sharing with other believers confirms their faithful *obedience to the confession of the gospel of Christ* (Rom 1.5; 16.16) and is a form of partnership (*koinonia, cf.* 8.4).
10.1-13.13 Paul Answers his Accusers.
This section of 2 Corinthians may come from a separate letter of Paul, possibly the *distress and anguish* letter mentioned in 2.3-4. The profile of his opponents is drawn in this section: they are of Israelite origin (11.22-23); they *boast* of their achievements in the ministry of the gospel.
10.1-18 Paul feels drawn into a competitive game with these *super-apostles*, while acknowledging his own limitations: weak *bodily presence* and *contemptible* speech (10.10). But the *weapons* which he uses in behalf of the gospel are not of human origin, and can *destroy* any force which opposes the knowledge of God (10.3-6). The power of his letters will be matched by his action when *present* among them. He has been *the first* to reach them effectively with the gospel, and as the scope of his work among them expands, he expects to move on to a wider *sphere of action* in the world. Self-commendation is useless, but God *commends* his agents through significant results, so that one dare *boast* only in *the Lord* (Jer 9.24).

undertaking[v] for the glory of the Lord himself[w] and to show our goodwill. 20We intend that no one should blame us about this generous gift that we are administering, 21for we intend to do what is right not only in the Lord's sight but also in the sight of others. 22And with them we are sending our brother whom we have often tested and found eager in many matters, but who is now more eager than ever because of his great confidence in you. 23As for Titus, he is my partner and co-worker in your service; as for our brothers, they are messengers[x] of the churches, the glory of Christ. 24Therefore openly before the churches, show them the proof of your love and of our reason for boasting about you.

The Collection for Christians at Jerusalem

9 Now it is not necessary for me to write you about the ministry to the saints, 2for I know your eagerness, which is the subject of my boasting about you to the people of Macedonia, saying that Achaia has been ready since last year; and your zeal has stirred up most of them. 3But I am sending the brothers in order that our boasting about you may not prove to have been empty in this case, so that you may be ready, as I said you would be; 4otherwise, if some Macedonians come with me and find that you are not ready, we would be humiliated—to say nothing of you—in this undertaking.[y] 5So I thought it necessary to urge the brothers to go on ahead to you, and arrange in advance for this bountiful gift that you have promised, so that it may be ready as a voluntary gift and not as an extortion.

6 The point is this: the one who sows sparingly will also reap sparingly, and the one who sows bountifully will also reap bountifully. 7Each of you must give as you have made up your mind, not reluctantly or under compulsion, for God loves a cheerful giver. 8And God is able to provide you with every blessing in abundance, so that by always having enough of everything, you may share abundantly in every good work. 9As it is written,

"He scatters abroad, he gives to the poor;
his righteousness[z] endures forever."

10He who supplies seed to the sower and bread for food will supply and multiply your seed for sowing and increase the harvest of your righteousness.[z] 11You will be enriched in every way for your great generosity, which will produce thanksgiving to God through us; 12for the rendering of this ministry not only supplies the needs of the saints but also overflows with many thanksgivings to God. 13Through the testing of this ministry you glorify God by your obedience to the confession of the gospel of Christ and by the generosity of your sharing with them and with all others, 14while they long for you and pray for you because of the surpassing grace of God that he has given you. 15Thanks be to God for his indescribable gift!

Paul Defends His Ministry

10 I myself, Paul, appeal to you by the meekness and gentleness of Christ—I who am humble when face to face with you, but bold toward you when I am away!— 2I ask that when I am present I need not show boldness by daring to oppose those who think we are acting according to human standards.[a] 3Indeed, we live as human beings,[b] but we do not wage war according to human standards;[a] 4for the weapons of our warfare are not merely human,[c] but they have divine power to destroy strongholds. We destroy arguments 5and every proud obstacle raised up against the knowledge of God, and we take every thought captive to obey Christ. 6We are ready to punish every disobedience when your obedience is complete.

7 Look at what is before your eyes. If you are confident that you belong to Christ, remind yourself of this, that just as you belong to Christ, so also do we. 8Now, even if I boast a little too much of our authority, which the Lord gave for building you up and not for tearing you down, I will not be ashamed of it. 9I do not want to seem as though I am trying to frighten you with my letters. 10For they say, "His letters are weighty and strong, but his bodily presence is weak, and his speech contemptible." 11Let such people understand that what we say by letter when absent, we will also do when present.

12 We do not dare to classify or compare ourselves with some of those who commend themselves. But when they measure themselves by one another, and compare

[v] Gk *this grace* [w] Other ancient authorities lack *himself* [x] Gk *apostles* [y] Other ancient authorities add *of boasting* [z] Or *benevolence* [a] Gk *according to the flesh* [b] Gk *in the flesh* [c] Gk *fleshly*

8.21 Rom 12.17; 14.18
8.23 Phil 2.25
8.24 2 Cor 7.14; 9.2
9.2 2 Cor 7.4; Rom 15.26; Acts 18.12; 2 Cor 8.10
9.3 1 Cor 16.2
9.6 Gal 6.7,9
9.7 Deut 15.7,10; Ex 25.2; Rom 12.8; 2 Cor 8.12
9.8 Eph 3.20; Phil 4.19
9.9 Ps 112.9
9.13 2 Cor 8.4; Rom 15.31; Mt 9.8; 2 Cor 2.12
9.15 2 Cor 2.14; Rom 5.15,16
10.1 Gal 5.2; Rom 12.1
10.2 1 Cor 4.21; 2 Cor 13.2,10
10.4 1 Tim 1.18; 2 Tim 2.3; Acts 7.22; 1 Cor 2.5; Je[r] 1.10
10.5 1 Cor 1.19; Isa 2.11,12; 2 Cor 9.13
10.6 2 Cor 2.9
10.7 Jn 7.24; 1 Cor 1.12; 14.37
10.8 2 Cor 7.4; 13.10
10.10 1 Cor 2.3; Gal 4.13,14; 1 Cor 1.17
10.12 2 Cor 3.1; 5.12

themselves with one another, they do not show good sense. 13We, however, will not boast beyond limits, but will keep within the field that God has assigned to us, to reach out even as far as you. 14For we were not overstepping our limits when we reached you; we were the first to come all the way to you with the good news[d] of Christ. 15We do not boast beyond limits, that is, in the labors of others; but our hope is that, as your faith increases, our sphere of action among you may be greatly enlarged, 16so that we may proclaim the good news[d] in lands beyond you, without boasting of work already done in someone else's sphere of action. 17"Let the one who boasts, boast in the Lord." 18For it is not those who commend themselves that are approved, but those whom the Lord commends.

Paul and the False Apostles

11 I wish you would bear with me in a little foolishness. Do bear with me! 2I feel a divine jealousy for you, for I promised you in marriage to one husband, to present you as a chaste virgin to Christ. 3But I am afraid that as the serpent deceived Eve by its cunning, your thoughts will be led astray from a sincere and pure[e] devotion to Christ. 4For if someone comes and proclaims another Jesus than the one we proclaimed, or if you receive a different spirit from the one you received, or a different gospel from the one you accepted, you submit to it readily enough. 5I think that I am not in the least inferior to these super-apostles. 6I may be untrained in speech, but not in knowledge; certainly in every way and in all things we have made this evident to you.

7 Did I commit a sin by humbling myself so that you might be exalted, because I proclaimed God's good news[f] to you free of charge? 8I robbed other churches by accepting support from them in order to serve you. 9And when I was with you and was in need, I did not burden anyone, for my needs were supplied by the friends[g] who came from Macedonia. So I refrained and will continue to refrain from burdening you in any way. 10As the truth of Christ is in me, this boast of mine will not be silenced in the regions of Achaia. 11And why? Because I do not love you? God knows I do!

12 And what I do I will also continue to do, in order to deny an opportunity to those who want an opportunity to be recognized as our equals in what they boast about. 13For such boasters are false apostles, deceitful workers, disguising themselves as apostles of Christ. 14And no wonder! Even Satan disguises himself as an angel of light. 15So it is not strange if his ministers also disguise themselves as ministers of righteousness. Their end will match their deeds.

Paul's Sufferings as an Apostle

16 I repeat, let no one think that I am a fool; but if you do, then accept me as a fool, so that I too may boast a little. 17What I am saying in regard to this boastful confidence, I am saying not with the Lord's authority, but as a fool; 18since many boast according to human standards,[h] I will also boast. 19For you gladly put up with fools, being wise yourselves! 20For you put up with it when someone makes slaves of you, or preys upon you, or takes advantage of you, or puts on airs, or gives you a slap in the face. 21To my shame, I must say, we were too weak for that!

But whatever anyone dares to boast of—I am speaking as a fool—I also dare to boast of that. 22Are they Hebrews? So am I. Are they Israelites? So am I. Are they descendants of Abraham? So am I. 23Are they ministers of Christ? I am talking like a madman—I am a better one: with far greater labors, far more imprisonments, with countless floggings, and often near death. 24Five times I have received from the Jews the forty lashes minus one. 25Three times I was beaten with rods. Once I received a stoning. Three times I was shipwrecked; for a night and a day I was adrift at sea; 26on frequent journeys, in danger from rivers, danger from bandits, danger from my own people, danger from Gentiles, danger in the city, danger in the wilderness, danger at sea, danger from false brothers and sisters;[g] 27in toil and hardship, through many a sleepless night, hungry and thirsty, often without food, cold and naked. 28And, besides other things, I am under daily pressure because of my anxiety for all the churches. 29Who is weak, and I am not weak? Who is made to stumble, and I am not indignant?

30 If I must boast, I will boast of the things that show my weakness. 31The God

10.14 2 Cor 2.12
10.17 Jer 9.24; 1 Cor 1.31
10.18 Rom 2.29; 1 Cor 4.5
11.1 ver 16,17,21; 2 Cor 5.13
11.2 Hos 2.19; Eph 5.26,27; 2 Cor 4.14
11.3 Gen 3.4; Jn 8.44
11.4 1 Cor 3.11; Rom 8.15; Gal 1.6-8
11.5 2 Cor 12.11; Gal 2.6
11.6 1 Cor 1.17; Eph 3.4; 2 Cor 4.2
11.7 2 Cor 12.13; 1 Cor 9.18
11.9 2 Cor 12.13,14
11.10 Rom 9.1; 1 Cor 9.15; Acts 18.12
11.11 2 Cor 12.15
11.13 Gal 1.7; 2 Pet 2.1; Phil 3.2
11.15 Phil 3.19
11.17 1 Cor 7.6,12,25
11.21 2 Cor 10.10; Phil 3.4
11.22 Acts 6.1; Phil 3.5; Rom 9.4
11.23 1 Cor 15.10; Acts 16.23; 2 Cor 6.5
11.24 Deut 25.3
11.25 Acts 16.22; 14.19
11.26 Acts 9.23; 14.5; 21.31; Gal 2.4
11.27 1 Thess 2.9; 1 Cor 4.11; 2 Cor 6.5
11.29 1 Cor 9.22
11.30 1 Cor 2.3
11.31 Gal 1.20; Rom 9.5

11.1-15 Paul's *foolishness* is a satirical critique of his critics. He shares God's *jealousy* (Ps 78.58) toward those who have turned to other leaders (2 Cor 11.4), who portray a different *Jesus*, rely on a *different spirit*, and proclaim *a different gospel*. He asks in irony if his refusal to demand financial support from them was a sin. Instead, he is determined to maintain his independence in order to expose the self-seeking of these boastful *false apostles*, who are in fact ministers of *Satan* and will be punished accordingly.
11.16-30 Paul feels drawn into the competition with his opponents who insist that he offer proof that he is the agent of Christ. He lists his credentials: Israelite ethnic descent; persecution at the hands of the Roman and Jewish authorities (Acts 16.23-40), beatings (Acts 16.22; *cf.* Deut 25.1-3, one short of the limit); dangerous voyages and travels, in the city and on highways (Acts 18.5-17; 19.23-41). Most pressing of all is his *anxiety* for the churches which he has founded or in which he has labored. But God has protected him, as in his escape from Damascus (Acts 9.23-25).

[d] Or *the gospel* [e] Other ancient authorities lack *and pure* [f] Gk *the gospel of God* [g] Gk *brothers* [h] Gk *according to the flesh*

and Father of the Lord Jesus (blessed be he forever!) knows that I do not lie. [32]In Damascus, the governor[i] under King Aretas guarded the city of Damascus in order to[j] seize me, [33]but I was let down in a basket through a window in the wall,[k] and escaped from his hands.

Paul's Visions and Revelations

12 It is necessary to boast; nothing is to be gained by it, but I will go on to visions and revelations of the Lord. [2]I know a person in Christ who fourteen years ago was caught up to the third heaven—whether in the body or out of the body I do not know; God knows. [3]And I know that such a person—whether in the body or out of the body I do not know; God knows—[4]was caught up into Paradise and heard things that are not to be told, that no mortal is permitted to repeat. [5]On behalf of such a one I will boast, but on my own behalf I will not boast, except of my weaknesses. [6]But if I wish to boast, I will not be a fool, for I will be speaking the truth. But I refrain from it, so that no one may think better of me than what is seen in me or heard from me, [7]even considering the exceptional character of the revelations. Therefore, to keep[l] me from being too elated, a thorn was given me in the flesh, a messenger of Satan to torment me, to keep me from being too elated.[m] [8]Three times I appealed to the Lord about this, that it would leave me, [9]but he said to me, "My grace is sufficient for you, for power[n] is made perfect in weakness." So, I will boast all the more gladly of my weaknesses, so that the power of Christ may dwell in me. [10]Therefore I am content with weaknesses, insults, hardships, persecutions, and calamities for the sake of Christ; for whenever I am weak, then I am strong.

Paul's Concern for the Corinthian Church

11 I have been a fool! You forced me to it. Indeed you should have been the ones commending me, for I am not at all inferior to these super-apostles, even though I am nothing. [12]The signs of a true apostle were performed among you with utmost patience, signs and wonders and mighty works. [13]How have you been worse off than the other churches, except that I myself did not burden you? Forgive me this wrong!

14 Here I am, ready to come to you this third time. And I will not be a burden, because I do not want what is yours but you; for children ought not to lay up for their parents, but parents for their children. [15]I will most gladly spend and be spent for you. If I love you more, am I to be loved less? [16]Let it be assumed that I did not burden you. Nevertheless (you say) since I was crafty, I took you in by deceit. [17]Did I take advantage of you through any of those whom I sent to you? [18]I urged Titus to go, and sent the brother with him. Titus did not take advantage of you, did he? Did we not conduct ourselves with the same spirit? Did we not take the same steps?

19 Have you been thinking all along that we have been defending ourselves before you? We are speaking in Christ before God. Everything we do, beloved, is for the sake of building you up. [20]For I fear that when I come, I may find you not as I wish, and that you may find me not as you wish; I fear that there may perhaps be quarreling, jealousy, anger, selfishness, slander, gossip, conceit, and disorder. [21]I fear that when I come again, my God may humble me before you, and that I may have to mourn over many who previously sinned and have not repented of the impurity, sexual immorality, and licentiousness that they have practiced.

Further Warning

13 This is the third time I am coming to you. "Any charge must be sustained by the evidence of two or three witnesses." [2]I warned those who sinned previously and all the others, and I warn them now while absent, as I did when present on my second visit, that if I come again, I will not be lenient— [3]since you desire proof that Christ is speaking in me. He is not weak in dealing with you, but is powerful in you. [4]For he was crucified in weakness, but lives by the power of God. For we are weak in him,[o] but in dealing with you we will live with him by the power of God.

5 Examine yourselves to see whether you are living in the faith. Test yourselves. Do

[i] Gk *ethnarch* [j] Other ancient authorities read *and wanted to* [k] Gk *through the wall* [l] Other ancient authorities read *To keep* [m] Other ancient authorities lack *to keep me from being too elated* [n] Other ancient authorities read *my power* [o] Other ancient authorities read *with him*

12.1-10 Paul reluctantly reports a vision to match the claims of his critics about *visions and revelations* (Lk 1.22; 24.23; Acts 26.19; 2 Cor 12.7; singular *revelation* is more frequent, in Rom 2.5; 8.19; 1 Cor 1.7; Gal 1.12; 2.2; 1 Cor 14.6,26; 1 Pet 1.7; Rev 1.1; 15.4). At first Paul does not disclose that this *person in Christ* was himself; see 12.7. Speculation about the number of levels of the heavens varied, ranging from three to seventy-two. Some heroes were taken up bodily into heaven (Gen 5.24; 2 Kings 2.11), while Greek thought conceived of the flight of the disembodied soul. *Paradise* is a heavenly realm mentioned often in Jewish apocalyptic. What Paul was told cannot be repeated (Dan 12.4; Rev 10.4; 13.2-3). He will not *boast* of his visions, but only of his *weaknesses* (12.9; *cf.* 1 Cor 1.22-2.2). The *thorn...in the flesh* he received is not specified, but may have been a chronic physical ailment (Gal 4.13-14), bouts of anxiety (2 Cor 11.28), harassments and persecution (Gal 5.11). This tormenting instrument of *Satan* was intended to keep him from undue elation, reminding him of his own weakness and of the *power of Christ* at work through him. **12.11-21** The *signs of a true apostle* include the performance of signs and wonders, as in Mt 10.1,8. *Cf.* Rom 15.19; 1 Cor 12.20,28-29; Gal 3.5; Acts 2.22; 8.13; 2 Thess 2.9; Heb 2.4. Paul mentions again his refusal to accept financial support in Corinth, as in 1 Cor 9. His initial visit was when he founded the church (Acts 18.1-17); the second was the *painful visit* (2 Cor 2.1). Neither Paul nor Titus took *advantage* of the Corinthians. Rather, his sole objective is to "build up" the community, freeing them from the disruptive experience of internal conflict and from *immorality*, which means flagrant, immoral sexual activity, such as is mentioned in 1 Cor 5. *Cf.* Rom 13.13; Gal 5.19; Mk 7.22; 1 Pet 4.3; 2 Pet 2.1,7,18. **13.1-10** On *third time* see note on 12.4. Multiple witnesses are required according to Deut 19.15 (in the Septuagint). *Cf.* Mt 18.16; 1 Tim 5.19; Mk 15.56; Jn 8.17; Heb 10.28; 1 Jn 5.8. The weakness/strength terminology may have been used by the Corinthians. Paul compares those features in the death and vindication of Christ with their presence in his own ministry. He hopes not to have to exercize severely the *authority* that Christ has given him.

11.32 Acts 9.24,25
12.2 Rom 16.7; Eph 4.10; 2 Cor 11.11
12.6 2 Cor 10.8; 11.16
12.8 Mt 26.44
12.9 Phil 4.13; 2 Cor 11.30; 1 Pet 4.14
12.10 Rom 5.3; 2 Cor 6.4; 2 Thess 1.4
12.11 2 Cor 11.1,5
12.12 Rom 15.18,19
12.13 1 Cor 9.12,18; 2 Cor 11.7
12.14 2 Cor 13.1; 1 Cor 10.24,33; 4.14,15; Prov 19.14
12.15 Phil 2.17; 1 Thess 2.8
12.18 2 Cor 8.6,16,18
12.19 Rom 9.1; 2 Cor 10.8
12.20 2 Cor 2.1-4; 1 Cor 1.11; 3.3
12.21 2 Cor 2.1,4; 13.2; Gal 5.19
13.1 2 Cor 12.14; Deut 9.15; Mt 18.16
13.3 Mt 10.20; 1 Cor 5.4; 2 Cor 9.8; 10.4
13.4 Phil 2.7,8; 1 Pet 3.18; Rom 6.4,8; ver 9
13.5 Jn 6.6; 1 Cor 11.28; 9.27

13.9 2 Cor 11.30; 12.10 you not realize that Jesus Christ is in you?—
unless, indeed, you fail to meet the test! [6]I
hope you will find out that we have not
13.10 2 Cor 2.3; Titus 1.13; 2 Cor 10.8 failed. [7]But we pray to God that you may
not do anything wrong—not that we may
appear to have met the test, but that you
may do what is right, though we may seem
13.11 Rom 15.33; Eph 6.23 to have failed. [8]For we cannot do anything
against the truth, but only for the truth.
[9]For we rejoice when we are weak and you
13.12 Rom 16.16 are strong. This is what we pray for, that
you may become perfect. [10]So I write these
13.13 Rom 16.20 things while I am away from you, so that
when I come, I may not have to be severe
in using the authority that the Lord has
given me for building up and not for tearing
down.

Final Greetings and Benediction

11 Finally, brothers and sisters,[p] farewell.[q]
Put things in order, listen to my appeal,[r]
agree with one another, live in peace; and
the God of love and peace will be with you.
[12]Greet one another with a holy kiss. All the
saints greet you.
13 The grace of the Lord Jesus Christ, the
love of God, and the communion of[s] the
Holy Spirit be with all of you.

[p] Gk *brothers* [q] Or *rejoice* [r] Or *encourage one another* [s] Or *and the sharing in*

THE LETTER OF PAUL TO THE

GALATIANS

1.2 Phil 4.21; 1 Cor 16.1 *Salutation*

1 Paul an apostle—sent neither by
human commission nor from human
1.4 Rom 4.25; Gal 2.20; 2 Cor 4.4 authorities, but through Jesus Christ and
God the Father, who raised him from the
dead— [2]and all the members of God's family[a]
who are with me,
1.7 Acts 15.24; Gal 5.10 To the churches of Galatia:
3 Grace to you and peace from God our
Father and the Lord Jesus Christ, [4]who gave
1.8 2 Cor 11.4,14; Rom 9.3 himself for our sins to set us free from the
present evil age, according to the will of our
God and Father, [5]to whom be the glory
forever and ever. Amen.

1.10 1 Thess 2.4

There Is No Other Gospel

1.11 1 Cor 15.1 6 I am astonished that you are so quickly
deserting the one who called you in the
1.13 Acts 8.3; 9.21 grace of Christ and are turning to a different
gospel— [7]not that there is another gospel,
but there are some who are confusing you
1.14 Acts 22.3; Col 2.8 and want to pervert the gospel of Christ.
[8]But even if we or an angel[b] from heaven
should proclaim to you a gospel contrary to
what we proclaimed to you, let that one be
accursed! [9]As we have said before, so now
I repeat, if anyone proclaims to you a gospel
contrary to what you received, let that one
be accursed!
10 Am I now seeking human approval,
or God's approval? Or am I trying to please
people? If I were still pleasing people, I
would not be a servant[c] of Christ.

Paul's Vindication of His Apostleship

11 For I want you to know, brothers and
sisters,[d] that the gospel that was proclaimed
by me is not of human origin; [12]for I did not
receive it from a human source, nor was I
taught it, but I received it through a revelation of Jesus Christ.
13 You have heard, no doubt, of my
earlier life in Judaism. I was violently persecuting the church of God and was trying
to destroy it. [14]I advanced in Judaism beyond many among my people of the same

[a] Gk *all the brothers* [b] Or *a messenger* [c] Gk *slave* [d] Gk *brothers*

13.11-13 Paul's final injunction calls for order, heeding his *appeal*, peace within the community, and the presence of God among them. Greeting one another *with a holy kiss* occurs in Rom 16.16; 1 Cor 16.20; 1 Thess 5.16; and in 1 Pet 5.14. In the second century CE this was a formal liturgical action in Christian eucharist celebrations, and may have originated in the Pauline churches. *The grace of our Lord Jesus Christ*, *cf.* Rom 16.20; 1 Cor 6.18; Phil 4.23; 1 Thess 5.28; Philem 25. *The love of God*, *cf.* Rom 5.51, 8.39. *Communion of* [or common participation in] *the Holy Spirit*, *cf.* Phil 2.1.

See the Introductions, pp. 8–9 and 85–86 above.

1.1-5 For the form of the Pauline letter see note on Rom 1.1. Galatians lacks the formal thanksgiving section with which Paul usually begins his letters.
1.1 *Paul an apostle – sent neither by human commission nor from human authorities.* *Cf.* 1 Cor 1.17; 9.1-2; 15.8-9; see notes on Acts 9.3-6.
1.2 *All the members of God's family who are with me.* Paul generally includes greetings from those accompanying him (see 1 & 2 Cor, Phil, Col, 1 & 2 Thess, Philem). *Galatia.* It has long been debated whether this term refers to ethnic Galatia, in north-central Asia Minor, or to the Roman province of Galatia which extended southward to include Pisidian Antioch, Iconium, Lystra, and Derbe.
1.3 *Grace and peace.* See note on Rom 1.7.
1.4 *The present evil age.* A distinction commonly made in Judaism was that between the "present age" and the "age to come." Rev 21.1; 2 Pet 3.11-13.
1.5 *Cf.* Rom 9.5.
1.6-7 The theme of the gospel is introduced here and will continue to dominate the letter; *cf.* 2.14.
1.6 *The one who called you.* It was Paul's preaching which called the Galatians to faith; *cf.* 4.13-14. *A different gospel*, i.e. different from the gospel that Paul proclaimed; *cf.* 3.3; 4.12-20.
1.7 Paul understands that people have come into the Galatian churches with a view of the gospel which contrasts markedly with his own; *cf.* 4.12-20; 5.2-12.
1.8 *Let that one be accursed.* The Greek word for "accursed" is *anathema*, with the sense of being cut off from God forever; *cf.* Rom 9.3.
1.9 The fate of accursedness is the result of a "gospel" which leads away from the liberating grace of God.
1.10 These words indicate that Paul has been accused of being a "people-pleaser," most likely because he has not mandated circumcision for his Gentile converts.
1.11-2.21 Paul's answer to charges that he should not be considered an apostle because he was not officially commissioned by the leadership of the church.
1.11-12 Paul's authority cannot rest on human approval since the gospel of Christ, which he received, was not from a human source. In 1 Cor 1.17 he states that he was "sent by Christ"; *cf.* also 1 Cor 9.1-2; 15.8-9.
1.12 *A revelation.* For Paul God is always the source of a *"revelation,"* even though it may be mediated by a human agent; *cf.* 1 Cor 14.6,26; Rev 1.1. *Cf.* also Luke's presentations of Paul's experience of the risen Lord in Acts 9.3-9; 22.6-11; 26.12-18. *Nor was I taught it.* As a student of Torah Paul had no need for theological instruction; he needed to know that Jesus was under God's blessing and not under God's curse (see note on 3.13). Jews who became Christians were not joining a new religion, but understood the gospel as the fulfillment of God's promises to Israel. "Conversion" cannot really be applied to the coming to faith in Christ by Jews in the first Christian generation.
1.13 *Earlier life in Judaism.* *Cf.* Phil 3.4-6; Acts 22.3. *Violently persecuting the church of God and was trying to destroy it.* *Cf.* 1 Cor 15.9; Acts 9.1-2; 22.4-5,9-11.
1.14 *Zealous for the traditions of my ancestors.* The targets of his persecution were Jewish Christians who, in his mind, had fallen away from those traditions.

age, for I was far more zealous for the traditions of my ancestors. [15]But when God, who had set me apart before I was born and called me through his grace, was pleased [16]to reveal his Son to me,[e] so that I might proclaim him among the Gentiles, I did not confer with any human being, [17]nor did I go up to Jerusalem to those who were already apostles before me, but I went away at once into Arabia, and afterwards I returned to Damascus.

18 Then after three years I did go up to Jerusalem to visit Cephas and stayed with him fifteen days; [19]but I did not see any other apostle except James the Lord's brother. [20]In what I am writing to you, before God, I do not lie! [21]Then I went into the regions of Syria and Cilicia, [22]and I was still unknown by sight to the churches of Judea that are in Christ; [23]they only heard it said, "The one who formerly was persecuting us is now proclaiming the faith he once tried to destroy." [24]And they glorified God because of me.

Paul and the Other Apostles

2 Then after fourteen years I went up again to Jerusalem with Barnabas, taking Titus along with me. [2]I went up in response to a revelation. Then I laid before them (though only in a private meeting with the acknowledged leaders) the gospel that I proclaim among the Gentiles, in order to make sure that I was not running, or had not run, in vain. [3]But even Titus, who was with me, was not compelled to be circumcised, though he was a Greek. [4]But because of false believers[f] secretly brought in, who slipped in to spy on the freedom we have in Christ Jesus, so that they might enslave us— [5]we did not submit to them even for a moment, so that the truth of the gospel might always remain with you. [6]And from those who were supposed to be acknowledged leaders (what they actually were makes no difference to me; God shows no partiality)—those leaders contributed nothing to me. [7]On the contrary, when they saw that I had been entrusted with the gospel for the uncircumcised, just as Peter had been entrusted with the gospel for the circumcised [8](for he who worked through Peter making him an apostle to the circumcised also worked through me in sending me to the Gentiles), [9]and when James and Cephas and John, who were acknowledged pillars, recognized the grace that had been given to me, they gave to Barnabas and me the right hand of fellowship, agreeing that we should go to the Gentiles and they to the circumcised. [10]They asked only one thing, that we remember the poor, which was actually what I was[g] eager to do.

Paul Rebukes Peter at Antioch

11 But when Cephas came to Antioch, I opposed him to his face, because he stood self-condemned; [12]for until certain people came from James, he used to eat with the Gentiles. But after they came, he drew back and kept himself separate for fear of the circumcision faction. [13]And the other Jews joined him in this hypocrisy, so that even Barnabas was led astray by their hypocrisy. [14]But when I saw that they were not acting consistently with the truth of the gospel, I said to Cephas before them all, "If you, though a Jew, live like a Gentile and not like a Jew, how can you compel the Gentiles to live like Jews?"[h]

Jews and Gentiles Are Saved by Faith

15 We ourselves are Jews by birth and not Gentile sinners; [16]yet we know that a person is justified[i] not by the works of the law but through faith in Jesus Christ.[j] And we have come to believe in Christ Jesus, so that we might be justified by faith in Christ,[k] and not by doing the works of the law, because no one will be justified by the works of the law. [17]But if, in our effort to be justified in Christ, we ourselves have been found to be sinners, is Christ then a servant of sin? Certainly not! [18]But if I build up again the very things that I once tore down, then I demonstrate that I am a transgressor. [19]For through the law I died to the law, so that I might live to God. I have been crucified with Christ; [20]and it is no longer I who live, but it is Christ who lives in me. And the life I now live in the flesh I live by faith in the Son of God,[l] who loved me and gave himself for me. [21]I do not nullify the grace of God; for if justification[m] comes through the law, then Christ died for nothing.

[e] Gk *in me* [f] Gk *false brothers* [g] Or *had been* [h] Some interpreters hold that the quotation extends into the following paragraph [i] Or *reckoned as righteous*; and so elsewhere [j] Or *the faith of Jesus Christ* [k] Or *the faith of Christ* [l] Or *by the faith of the Son of God* [m] Or *righteousness*

1.15 Paul understood himself precisely as a theologian in Judaism, set apart before he was born and called through God's grace; *cf.* Isa 49.1-6; Jer 1.5.
1.16 Paul understands the moment of God's revelation to be the moment of his calling as an apostle to the Gentiles. *I did not confer with any human being.* Luke's presentation, written decades after Paul, indicates Paul's baptism by Ananias (Acts 9.10-19).
1.17 *Cf.* Acts 9.26-30. *Arabia.* The Nabataean kingdom which surrounded Damascus and stretched southward. The king was Aretas IV (9 BCE-40 CE); *cf.* 2 Cor 11.32-33. *Damascus.* One of the oldest continuously inhabited cities of the world, under Roman rule one of the cities of the Decapolis (see note on Mt 4.25), administered by Nabataean governors. Paul's return was to the areas of his persecuting activity.
1.18 *After three years.* I.e. most likely three years after his coming to faith in Christ, as described in 1.15-16. *Cephas.* The Aramaic equivalent of the name "Peter," now the leading figure among the Jerusalem apostles.
1.19 *James, the Lord's brother.* Jesus' brother James is mentioned in Mk 6.3 (=Mt 13.55). 1 Cor 15.7 lists him among those to whom the risen Jesus appeared. In Acts 1.14 Jesus' brothers are among the first Christian community, where James was a leader (see Acts 15.13-21 and 21.18). Paul seems to list James among the "apostles," a word which is not yet limited to "the Twelve" (see 1 Cor 15.5-7).
1.20 This sentence functions as an oath, and indicates the seriousness with which Paul speaks here; *cf.* 1 Thess 2.5; 2 Cor 1.23; 11.31; Phil 1.8.
1.21 *Syria and Cilicia.* At the time Syria and Eastern Cilicia comprised one Roman province. Tarsus, Paul's birthplace according to Acts 22.3, was the capital of Cilicia.
1.22 *Cf.* Acts 9.1-2; 24.5; 26.9-11.
2.1 *Barnabas.* See notes on Acts 4.36-37 and 1 Cor 9.6. According to Acts 13.1-14.28, Barnabas accompanied Paul on Paul's first missionary journey. *Titus.* Paul's close co-worker (see 2 Cor 8.6,16). See notes on 2 Cor 2.12-13 and Titus 1.1.
2.2 *Revelation.* See note on Gal 1.12. *Acknowledged leaders.* Most probably the ones named in 2.9. *Not running...in vain.* Paul was willing to allow the church's leadership in Jerusalem to judge his ministry.
2.3 Titus was a convert of Paul's among Gentiles. That he was not compelled to be circumcised was a major victory for Paul, which eventually meant that Christianity could no longer be viewed as a sect within Judaism.
2.4 *False believers.* A reference to those who advocated mandatory circumcision for all Gentile converts to Christianity; *cf.* 2.12.
2.6 *What they actually were.* The precise wording in Greek suggests the apostles' former standing as disciples of Jesus was a criterion for apostleship (see Acts 1; 21) which may have been used against Paul to disqualify him as an "apostle." *Contributed nothing to me.* The wording in Greek may suggest that the Jerusalem leadership affirmed his ministry and message, without anything (such as circumcision) added to it.
2.7-8 Paul understood there to be a clear division: that Peter's mission was to be to Jews (the *circumcised*) and his own to Gentiles (the *uncircumcised*).
2.9 See note on 2.2.
2.10 *Remember the poor.* This is the origin of Paul's collection, or offering, which he took up from his churches for "the poor among the saints in Jerusalem" (Rom 15.26); see 1 Cor 16.1-3; 2 Cor 8-9. Rom 15.26 suggests that Galatia chose not to participate.
2.11 *Antioch.* Capital of the province of Syria and third largest city in the Roman Empire. According to Acts 11.19-26, Christians came to Antioch from Jerusalem after the persecution of Stephen (*ca.* 40 CE), and received the name "Christians." The church in Antioch consisted of both Jews and Gentiles. It was (Acts 13.1-3) the starting-point for Paul's first missionary journey. Its later bishop, Ignatius, was martyred in Rome.
2.12 *Certain people came from James.* This is the first indication of divided opinion in the Jerusalem church about observance of Old Testament laws. *The circumcision faction.* Christians who insisted that Gentile converts observe circumcision and dietary laws of the Old Testament. On circumcision see Gen 17.9-14; on dietary observance see Lev 3.17. See also Acts 15.22-29, which speaks of an apostolic letter sent to Antioch releasing Gentiles from circumcision, but maintaining certain dietary and moral

1.15 Isa 49.1,5; Jer 1.5; Acts 9.15; Rom 1.1
1.16 Acts 9.20; Eph 6.12
1.18 Acts 9.22,23,26, 27
1.19 Mt 13.55
1.21 Acts 9.30
1.22 1 Thess 2.14; Rom 16.7
2.1 Acts 15.2
2.2 Acts 15.12; Gal 1.6; Phil 2.16
2.3 2 Cor 2.13; Acts 16.3; 1 Cor 9.21
2.4 Acts 15.1; 2 Cor 11.26
2.5 ver 14; Col 1.5
2.6 Gal 6.3; Rom 2.11; 2 Cor 12.11
2.7 1 Thess 2.4; Acts 13.46
2.9 Rom 12.3; Gal 1.16
2.10 Acts 11.29,30; 24.17
2.11 Acts 11.10
2.12 Acts 11.2,3
2.14 Ver 5,9,11
2.16 Acts 13.39; Rom 1.17; 3.20
2.19 Rom 8.2; 6.14; 2 Cor 5.15; 1 Thes 5.10
2.20 1 Pet 4.2; Eph 5.2; Titus 2.14

Law or Faith

3 You foolish Galatians! Who has be-
witched you? It was before your eyes
that Jesus Christ was publicly exhibited as
crucified! 2The only thing I want to learn
from you is this: Did you receive the Spirit
by doing the works of the law or by believing what you heard? 3Are you so foolish?
Having started with the Spirit, are you now
ending with the flesh? 4Did you experience
so much for nothing?—if it really was for
nothing. 5Well then, does God[n] supply you
with the Spirit and work miracles among
you by your doing the works of the law, or
by your believing what you heard?

6 Just as Abraham "believed God, and it
was reckoned to him as righteousness," 7so,
you see, those who believe are the descendants of Abraham. 8And the scripture, foreseeing that God would justify the Gentiles
by faith, declared the gospel beforehand to
Abraham, saying, "All the Gentiles shall be
blessed in you." 9For this reason, those who
believe are blessed with Abraham who
believed.

10 For all who rely on the works of the
law are under a curse; for it is written,
"Cursed is everyone who does not observe
and obey all the things written in the book
of the law." 11Now it is evident that no one
is justified before God by the law; for "The
one who is righteous will live by faith."[o]
12But the law does not rest on faith; on the
contrary, "Whoever does the works of the
law[p] will live by them." 13Christ redeemed
us from the curse of the law by becoming
a curse for us—for it is written, "Cursed is
everyone who hangs on a tree"— 14in order
that in Christ Jesus the blessing of Abraham
might come to the Gentiles, so that we
might receive the promise of the Spirit
through faith.

The Promise to Abraham

15 Brothers and sisters,[q] I give an example from daily life: once a person's will[r] has
been ratified, no one adds to it or annuls it.
16Now the promises were made to Abraham
and to his offspring;[s] it does not say, "And
to offsprings,"[t] as of many; but it says, "And
to your offspring,"[s] that is, to one person,
who is Christ. 17My point is this: the law,
which came four hundred thirty years later,
does not annul a covenant previously ratified by God, so as to nullify the promise.
18For if the inheritance comes from the law,
it no longer comes from the promise; but
God granted it to Abraham through the
promise.

The Purpose of the Law

19 Why then the law? It was added
because of transgressions, until the offspring[s]
would come to whom the promise had been
made; and it was ordained through angels
by a mediator. 20Now a mediator involves
more than one party; but God is one.

21 Is the law then opposed to the promises of God? Certainly not! For if a law had
been given that could make alive, then
righteousness would indeed come through
the law. 22But the scripture has imprisoned
all things under the power of sin, so that
what was promised through faith in Jesus
Christ[u] might be given to those who believe.

23 Now before faith came, we were
imprisoned and guarded under the law until
faith would be revealed. 24Therefore the law
was our disciplinarian until Christ came, so
that we might be justified by faith. 25But
now that faith has come, we are no longer
subject to a disciplinarian, 26for in Christ
Jesus you are all children of God through
faith. 27As many of you as were baptized
into Christ have clothed yourselves with
Christ. 28There is no longer Jew or Greek,
there is no longer slave or free, there is no
longer male and female; for all of you are
one in Christ Jesus. 29And if you belong to
Christ, then you are Abraham's offspring,[s]
heirs according to the promise.

4 My point is this: heirs, as long as they
are minors, are no better than slaves,
though they are the owners of all the property; 2but they remain under guardians and
trustees until the date set by the father. 3So
with us; while we were minors, we were
enslaved to the elemental spirits[v] of the
world. 4But when the fullness of time had
come, God sent his Son, born of a woman,
born under the law, 5in order to redeem
those who were under the law, so that we
might receive adoption as children. 6And
because you are children, God has sent the
Spirit of his Son into our[w] hearts, crying,
"Abba![x] Father!" 7So you are no longer a

[n] Gk *he* [o] Or *The one who is righteous through faith will live* [p] Gk *does them* [q] Gk *Brothers* [r] Or *covenant* (as in verse 17) [s] Gk *seed* [t] Gk *seeds* [u] Or *through the faith of Jesus Christ* [v] Or *the rudiments* [w] Other ancient authorities read *your* [x] Aramaic for *Father*

3.1 Gal 1.2; 5.7; 1 Cor 1.23
3.2 Acts 2.38; Rom 10.16,17
3.3 Gal 4.9; Heb 7.16
3.4 1 Cor 15.2
3.6 Gen 15.6; Rom 4.3; Jas 2.23
3.8 Gen 12.3; Acts 3.25
3.10 Deut 27.26
3.11 Gal 2.16; Hab 2.4; Heb 10.38
3.12 Lev 18.5; Rom 10.5
3.13 Gal 4.5; Acts 5.30; Deut 21.23
3.14 Rom 4.9; Joel 2.28; Acts 2.33
3.15 Heb 9.17
3.16 Gen 12.3; 13.15; Acts 3.25
3.17 Ex 12.40; Rom 4.13
3.18 Rom 4.14; 8.17
3.19 Acts 7.53; Deut 5.5
3.20 Heb 8.6; 9.15; 12.24
3.22 Rom 3.9-19; 11.32
3.24 Rom 10.4; 1 Cor 4.15; Gal 2.16
3.26 Jn 1.12; Rom 8.14
3.27 Rom 6.3; 13.14
3.28 Col 3.11; Jn 10.16; Eph 2.14,15
3.29 1 Cor 3.23; Gal 4.28
4.3 Col 2.8,20; Heb 5.12
4.4 Eph 1.10; Mt 5.17
4.5 Eph 1.7; Jn 1.12; Eph 1.5
4.6 Rom 5.5; 8.15

restrictions.
2.13 *Barnabas was led astray.* The dispute, which left Peter and Barnabas on one side and Paul on the other, had to do with table fellowship with Gentiles (see 1 Cor 11.17-34). *Hypocrisy.* Withdrawing from fellowship now would be an act of hypocrisy.
2.14 *The truth of the gospel.* Paul clearly understands that it is the gospel of Christ which frees people from observance of the laws of the Old Testament.
2.15 *Justified.* This word means "to be put right with God," i.e. into a right relationship with God. See notes on Rom 2.13 and 3.21-26.
2.16 *Cf.* Ps 143.2.
2.17 *Is Christ...a servant of sin?* Paul's argument is that Cephas has engaged in table fellowship and to withdraw from it would mean that Christ had led him to act wrongfully and therefore to sin. *Cf.* Acts 10.1-11.18.
2.19-21 These verses indicate the centrality of the cross of Christ for Paul's theology; see also 1 Cor 2.2; 11.26.
2.19 *I through the law died to the law.* The word "law" refers to the Torah; i.e. the Old Testament.
2.20 *Cf.* Rom 3.28; 5.1.
2.21 *Justification.* This word can also be translated "righteousness" and in Paul it means God's act of restoring people to a right relationship with God. *Cf.* Rom 3.24; 4.2.

3.1-29 Paul's interpretation of the biblical texts which underlie the debate in Galatia. For Paul's opponents it is God's command which establishes the covenant between God and God's people; for Paul it is God's promise which does so.
3.1 *Foolish.* The Greek word refers to the failure to use one's thinking capacity. *Publicly exhibited.* A reference to a visual portrayal of the crucified Christ used in Galatian worship assemblies.
3.2 *Did you receive the Spirit.* The Galatians first became believers through Paul's preaching (see 4.13-14).
3.3 *Ending with the flesh.* A reference to circumcision; *cf.* 5.2.
3.5 *Cf.* 2 Cor 12.12.
3.6 The quotation is from Gen 15.6. *Righteousness.* In Paul's writing this word refers to God's act of putting someone into a right relationship with God. See notes on 2.15; 2.21; 3.21-22; Rom 4.3-4.
3.7 *Descendants of Abraham.* The topic governing the discussion in Galatia. If God's promises were to Abraham and his descendants (see 3.16), how did one become a descendant of Abraham? Paul's opponents, drawing upon Gen 17.9-14, answered: by circumcision.
3.8 *The scripture.* Paul uses the singular to refer to the totality of the scriptural tradition (*cf.* 3.22; 4.30; Rom 4.3). *Declared the gospel beforehand.* Paul's answer to his opponents is that God's promise existed before the command for circumcision. The quotation is from Gen 12.3. God established his relationship with Abraham through promise, and those who receive that promise, i.e. that gospel, through faith are the descendants of Abraham. See also Rom 4.
3.10 *Under a curse.* The point is that the principle of the law rests on observing and obeying it: the quotation is from Deut 27.26. Those who do not are under a curse; *cf.* Rom 2.13.
3.11 *Cf.* Ps 143.2. The quotation is from Hab 2.4; *cf.* Rom 3.28.
3.12 Again, the principle of the law is in the doing. The quotation is from Lev 18.5. *Cf.* Rom 10.5; Lk 10.28.
3.13 *Redeemed.* The word is used here in the sense that Christ "secured release" of those retained under the law, an idea developed in 3.23-4.11. The quotation is from Deut 21.23, which indicates that this passage was used to argue against Jesus' Messiahship: Messiah could not have been crucified, because Messiah could not be under God's curse. At the moment of his "conversion" the only thing Paul had to know was that the crucified Jesus was not under God's curse but under God's blessing; at that moment Paul's understanding of the law changed as well (see 2.19-21; Rom 7).
3.14 *Cf.* Rom 4.11-13.
3.16 *The promises.* The promises to Abraham (see Gen 17.4-8). *Offsprings.* In both Hebrew and Greek the term *"offspring"* (or "seed") is a collective term. But Paul makes the point that, whereas Abraham had more than one son (see 4.22), only one was the child of the promise. *Christ.* Also the church (see 1 Cor 1.13; 12.12).
3.17 *The law.* Here Paul refers to the holiest part of Torah, the Decalogue; or the Ten Commandments given at Mt. Sinai. *Four hundred thirty years later.* This was the length (in Ex 12.40) of Israel's sojourn in Egypt. Paul's point is that Israel existed,

slave but a child, and if a child then also
an heir, through God.[y]

Paul Reproves the Galatians

8 Formerly, when you did not know God,
you were enslaved to beings that by nature
are not gods. [9]Now, however, that you have
come to know God, or rather to be known
by God, how can you turn back again to
the weak and beggarly elemental spirits?[z]
How can you want to be enslaved to them
again? [10]You are observing special days,
and months, and seasons, and years. [11]I am
afraid that my work for you may have been
wasted.

12 Friends,[a] I beg you, become as I am,
for I also have become as you are. You have
done me no wrong. [13]You know that it was
because of a physical infirmity that I first
announced the gospel to you; [14]though my
condition put you to the test, you did not
scorn or despise me, but welcomed me as
an angel of God, as Christ Jesus. [15]What has
become of the goodwill you felt? For I testify
that, had it been possible, you would have
torn out your eyes and given them to me.
[16]Have I now become your enemy by telling
you the truth? [17]They make much of you,
but for no good purpose; they want to
exclude you, so that you may make much
of them. [18]It is good to be made much of
for a good purpose at all times, and not only
when I am present with you. [19]My little
children, for whom I am again in the pain
of childbirth until Christ is formed in you,
[20]I wish I were present with you now and
could change my tone, for I am perplexed
about you.

The Allegory of Hagar and Sarah

21 Tell me, you who desire to be subject
to the law, will you not listen to the law?
[22]For it is written that Abraham had two
sons, one by a slave woman and the other
by a free woman. [23]One, the child of the
slave, was born according to the flesh; the
other, the child of the free woman, was
born through the promise. [24]Now this is an
allegory: these women are two covenants.
One woman, in fact, is Hagar, from Mount
Sinai, bearing children for slavery. [25]Now
Hagar is Mount Sinai in Arabia[b] and corresponds to the present Jerusalem, for she
is in slavery with her children. [26]But the
other woman corresponds to the Jerusalem
above; she is free, and she is our mother.
[27]For it is written,

"Rejoice, you childless one, you who bear
no children,
burst into song and shout, you who
endure no birth pangs;
for the children of the desolate woman
are more numerous
than the children of the one who is
married."

[28]Now you,[c] my friends,[d] are children of the
promise, like Isaac. [29]But just as at that time
the child who was born according to the
flesh persecuted the child who was born
according to the Spirit, so it is now also.
[30]But what does the scripture say? "Drive
out the slave and her child; for the child of
the slave will not share the inheritance with
the child of the free woman." [31]So then,
friends,[d] we are children, not of the slave
but of the free woman.

5 For freedom Christ has set us free.
Stand firm, therefore, and do not
submit again to a yoke of slavery.

The Nature of Christian Freedom

2 Listen! I, Paul, am telling you that if
you let yourselves be circumcised, Christ
will be of no benefit to you. [3]Once again I
testify to every man who lets himself be
circumcised that he is obliged to obey the
entire law. [4]You who want to be justified
by the law have cut yourselves off from
Christ; you have fallen away from grace.
[5]For through the Spirit, by faith, we eagerly
wait for the hope of righteousness. [6]For in
Christ Jesus neither circumcision nor
uncircumcision counts for anything; the only
thing that counts is faith working[e] through
love.

7 You were running well; who prevented
you from obeying the truth? [8]Such persuasion does not come from the one who calls
you. [9]A little yeast leavens the whole batch
of dough. [10]I am confident about you in the
Lord that you will not think otherwise. But
whoever it is that is confusing you will pay
the penalty. [11]But my friends,[d] why am I
still being persecuted if I am still preaching
circumcision? In that case the offense of the

[y] Other ancient authorities read *an heir of God through Christ* [z] Or *beggarly rudiments* [a] Gk *Brothers*
[b] Other ancient authorities read *For Sinai is a mountain in Arabia* [c] Other ancient authorities read *we*
[d] Gk *brothers* [e] Or *made effective*

4.8 Eph 2.12; 1 Thess 4.5; Rom 1.25; 1 Cor 12.2
4.9 1 Cor 8.3; Col 2.20
4.19 1 Jn 2.1; 1 Cor 4.15; Eph 4.13
4.22 Gen 16.15; 21.2,9
4.23 Rom 9.7; Gen 18.10; Heb 11.11
4.26 Isa 2.2; Heb 12.22; Rev 3.12
4.27 Isa 54.1
4.29 Gen 21.9
4.30 Gen 21.10-12
5.1 Jn 8.32; Acts 15.10
5.4 Heb 12.15; 2 Pet 3.17
5.5 Rom 8.23,24; 2 Tim 4.8
5.6 1 Cor 7.19; Jas 2.18
5.7 1 Cor 9.24; Gal 3.1
5.10 2 Cor 2.3; Gal 1.7

from Abraham to Sinai, on the basis of God's covenantal promise, without any written law at all.
3.18 Between law and promise Paul sees no both-and but only an either-or.
3.19 *It was added.* The law came later than the promise (see 3.1-18). *Because of transgressions.* See notes on Rom 5.20 and 7.12-13. *Ordained.* Literally, "ordered" or "directed." *Through angels.* In Jewish tradition angels played a role in the giving of the law at Sinai (see Deut 33.2; Heb 2.2; Acts 7.38,52-53). *A mediator.* I.e. Moses.
3.20 The law did not come directly from God to the people, as did the promise from God to Abraham.
3.21 *Righteousness.* God's act of placing a person in a right relationship with God. See note on 3.6.
3.22 *The scripture.* Again, as in 3.8, the singular is used to emphasize that the entire biblical tradition speaks with one voice. *All things are under the power of sin.* Escape from the power of sin can come only as God's free gift; see notes on Rom 3.9; 7.14; and 11.32.
3.23 *Before faith came.* I.e. before faith in Jesus Christ, the fulfillment of God's promises. *Imprisoned and guarded.* The sense here is of restriction: the law prevented our full development to maturity (see note on 1 Cor 15.7).
3.24 *Disciplinarian.* The Greek word is *paidagogos,* the household slave assigned to supervise the behavior of children.
3.26 In Rom 6.3-11 Paul develops the connection between baptism into Christ and its implications for daily living.
3.27 *Clothed yourselves with Christ. Cf.* Col 3.9-10; Eph 4.22-24; also Ps 132.9; Isa 61.10; 64.6; Zech 3.3.
3.28 *Cf.* Col 3.11.
4.1-7 This section really concludes 3.23-29, extending the imagery of growth.
4.2 *Guardians and trustees.* Roman legal custom. The *guardian* was entrusted with the general care of the child up to fourteen, the *trustee* with the financial affairs of the young man up to twenty-five (*cf.* Rom 16.23; Lk 12.42; 16.1). *The date set by the father.* Under Roman law the father was able to set limits to the time of a trusteeship. The Galatians came out from under their period of supervision at a definitely appointed time.
4.3 *The elemental spirits of the world.* Any created thing which assumes divine authority over human beings; see notes on Col 2.8-23. The law, the Torah, has assumed this authority, even though its history can be traced.
4.4 *The fullness of time.* The time of Christ's coming was fixed in the purpose of God (*cf.* Mk 1.14; Jn 2.4; 7.8,30). *Born of a woman.* I.e. as a human being; *cf.* Mt 11.11 (Lk 7.28). *Born under the law.* I.e. as a Jew.
4.5 *Redeem.* See note on 3.13. *Those under the law.* Christ's death and resurrection is an act of redemption for Jews as well as Gentiles (see Rom 1.16-17; 3.30). *Adoption.* In Greco-Roman law an adopted child received full status. Paul's language may be influenced by Israel's release from bondage in Egypt, expressed in Hosea 11.1; "Out of Egypt have I called my son" (*cf.* Mt 2.15); *cf.* also Rom 15.8,23.
4.6 *Cf.* Rom 8.15-17.

4.8-21 The Galatians, freed from slavery by Christ, want to return to slavery by falling back under the law.
4.9 *Weak and beggarly elemental spirits.* See note on 4.3. They are "*weak and beggarly*" because they are not able to bring life and salvation (see 4.21).
4.10 The freedom to observe or not has been won in Christ, and the decision regarding observance should now be left to everyone's own conscience.
4.13 *Physical infirmity.* Paul's initial preaching to the Galatians was probably not in a planned journey there, but during a time of recuperation from his unspecified infirmity.
4.14 *Put you to the test.* The Galatians had to decide whether Paul visited them as a messenger from God. *Angel of God, as Christ Jesus.* They chose to welcome Paul as God's agent, indeed as Christ himself appearing in the person of his apostle.
4.15 *Torn out your eyes.* Some view this as indicating the location of Paul's illness; all attempts to identify Paul's ailment remain speculative.
4.17 *They.* I.e. Paul's opponents, calling his apostleship into question and insisting on mandatory circumcision for Gentile converts. *They want to exclude you.* Paul's opponents wish to exclude those who are not circumcised. *That you may make much of them.* Paul sees his opponents' ambitious hope that the Galatians would vest them

cross has been removed. [12]I wish those who unsettle you would castrate themselves!

13 For you were called to freedom, brothers and sisters;[f] only do not use your freedom as an opportunity for self-indulgence,[g] but through love become slaves to one another. [14]For the whole law is summed up in a single commandment, "You shall love your neighbor as yourself." [15]If, however, you bite and devour one another, take care that you are not consumed by one another.

The Works of the Flesh

16 Live by the Spirit, I say, and do not gratify the desires of the flesh. [17]For what the flesh desires is opposed to the Spirit, and what the Spirit desires is opposed to the flesh; for these are opposed to each other, to prevent you from doing what you want. [18]But if you are led by the Spirit, you are not subject to the law. [19]Now the works of the flesh are obvious: fornication, impurity, licentiousness, [20]idolatry, sorcery, enmities, strife, jealousy, anger, quarrels, dissensions, factions, [21]envy,[h] drunkenness, carousing, and things like these. I am warning you, as I warned you before: those who do such things will not inherit the kingdom of God.

The Fruit of the Spirit

22 By contrast, the fruit of the Spirit is love, joy, peace, patience, kindness, generosity, faithfulness, [23]gentleness, and self-control. There is no law against such things. [24]And those who belong to Christ Jesus have crucified the flesh with its passions and desires. [25]If we live by the Spirit, let us also be guided by the Spirit. [26]Let us not become conceited, competing against one another, envying one another.

Bear One Another's Burdens

6 My friends,[i] if anyone is detected in a transgression, you who have received the Spirit should restore such a one in a spirit of gentleness. Take care that you yourselves are not tempted. [2]Bear one another's burdens, and in this way you will fulfill[j] the law of Christ. [3]For if those who are nothing think they are something, they deceive themselves. [4]All must test their own work; then that work, rather than their neighbor's work, will become a cause for pride. [5]For all must carry their own loads.

6 Those who are taught the word must share in all good things with their teacher.

7 Do not be deceived; God is not mocked, for you reap whatever you sow. [8]If you sow to your own flesh, you will reap corruption from the flesh; but if you sow to the Spirit, you will reap eternal life from the Spirit. [9]So let us not grow weary in doing what is right, for we will reap at harvest time, if we do not give up. [10]So then, whenever we have an opportunity, let us work for the good of all, and especially for those of the family of faith.

Final Admonitions and Benediction

11 See what large letters I make when I am writing in my own hand! [12]It is those who want to make a good showing in the flesh that try to compel you to be circumcised—only that they may not be persecuted for the cross of Christ. [13]Even the circumcised do not themselves obey the law, but they want you to be circumcised so that they may boast about your flesh. [14]May I never boast of anything except the cross of our Lord Jesus Christ, by which[k] the world has been crucified to me, and I to the world. [15]For[l] neither circumcision nor uncircumcision is anything; but a new creation is everything! [16]As for those who will follow this rule—peace be upon them, and mercy, and upon the Israel of God.

17 From now on, let no one make trouble for me; for I carry the marks of Jesus branded on my body.

18 May the grace of our Lord Jesus Christ be with your spirit, brothers and sisters.[f] Amen.

5.13 1 Cor 8.9; 1 Pet 2.16; 1 Cor 9.19
5.14 Lev 19.18; Mt 7.12; 22.39; Rom 13.8
5.16 Rom 8.4; ver 24,25; Eph 2.3
5.17 Rom 7.15-23
5.18 Rom 6.14
5.19 Eph 5.3; Col 3.5
5.21 1 Cor 6.9
5.22 Eph 5.9; Col 3.12-15; 1 Cor 13.7
5.24 Rom 6.6
6.2 Rom 15.1; Jas 2.8
6.3 Rom 12.3; 1 Cor 8.2; 2 Cor 3.5
6.4 1 Cor 11.28; Phil 1.26
6.6 1 Cor 9.11
6.7 1 Cor 6.9; Job 13.9
6.8 Hos 8.7; Jas 3.18
6.9 1 Cor 15.58; Heb 3.6; Rev 2.10
6.10 Jn 9.4; Titus [.].8; Eph 2.19
6.12 Mt 23.27,28; Acts 15.1; Gal 5.11
6.14 Gal 2.20; Rom 6.2,6
6.15 2 Cor 5.17
6.17 2 Cor 1.5

[f] Gk *brothers* [g] Gk *the flesh* [h] Other ancient authorities add *murder* [i] Gk *Brothers* [j] Other ancient authorities read *in this way fulfill* [k] Or *through whom* [l] Other ancient authorities add *in Christ Jesus*

with the power to determine the rules of fellowship.
4.19 *My little children.* Those whom Paul has brought into the Christian community; *cf.* Philem 1.10; 1 Cor 4.15. *I am again in the pain of childbirth. Cf.* 1 Thess 2.7. *Until Christ is formed in you. Cf.* 1 Cor 15.8.
4.21-5.1 The law itself teaches freedom.
4.21 See note on 2.19.
4.22 Paul refers to Gen 16.5 and 21.2,9 to recall that not every child of Abraham was the child of the promise; *cf.* Rom 9.6-13.
4.23 *Born according to the flesh.* I.e. according to the human desire to force God's promise into reality. *Born through the promise.* See Gen 15.4; 17.16,19; 18.10.
4.24 *Allegory.* Paul uses the word *"allegory"* here in the sense that the scriptural words prefigure what is to come. *Hagar.* Sarah's handmaid Hagar gave birth to Ishmael (see Gen 16.15). *Mount Sinai.* Where the law was delivered to Moses (see Ex 31.18; 34.19,32; Lev 26.46; 27.34; Neh 9.13); in the south-central part of the Sinai Peninsula, its exact location cannot be determined. *Bearing children for slavery.* The point of Gal 3-4 is now concluded: the law keeps people in bondage.
4.26 *The other woman.* I.e. Sarah, Abraham's wife, the mother of Isaac, the child of the promise. *The Jerusalem above.* This is God's city, free from earthly barriers, the city of God's future; *cf.* Rev 3.12; 21.1-22.5.
4.27 The quotation is from Isa 54.1. The *"desolate woman"* is barren Sarah, who now has more children than her handmaid by Abraham.
4.28 See note on Gal 3.16.
4.29 *So it is now.* The kind of persecution Paul carried on before he received his own freedom in Christ; *cf.* 1.13,23; 1 Cor 15.9; also Gal 5.11; 6.12.
4.30 The quotation is from Gen 21.10.
5.2 *I, Paul.* Paul's own journey from bondage under law to freedom in Christ.
5.3 *Cf.* Rom 2.25; Jas 2.10.
5.4 See note on 3.18.
5.5 For Paul God always remains the promising God, whose future judgment will come; *cf.* 5.18; Rom 2.5-16.
5.6 *Cf.* 6.15; 1 Cor 7.19; also Rom 14.13-21.
5.9 *Cf.* 1 Cor 5.6; Mt 16.1 (Lk 12.1); Mt 13.33 (Lk 13.20).
5.11 *If I am still preaching circumcision.* Evidently Paul's opponents were saying that he still would uphold the command for circumcision. *Stumbling block of the cross. Cf.* 1 Cor 1.22.

5.12 A rather strong statement. In Galatia castration was ritually practised in the Attis and Cybele cults.
5.13 Freedom from the law must not be understood as rank libertinism.
5.14 The quotation is from Lev 19.18. *Cf.* Rom 13.8-10; Mt 22.34-40 (Mk 12.28-34; Lk 10.25-28).
5.16 Christians no longer live according to worldly standards (=*the flesh*), but by God's standards (=*the Spirit*). See 5.5,18; Rom 6.12; 8.1-8.
5.17 Lists of vices were used in Paul's time, especially in Greco-Roman moral instruction. *Cf.* the lists in Rom 1.29-31; 1 Cor 5.9-11; 6.9-10.
5.21 *Cf.* 1 Cor 6.10.
5.22 *Fruit of the Spirit.* This is defined by a list which indicates the results of life in the Spirit, beginning with love (*cf.* 1 Cor 13.13); *cf.* Phil 4.8.
5.24 *Cf.* 2.19-20.
5.26 *Cf.* 2 Cor 10.12; Phil 2.3.
6.1 *Cf.* Mt 5.23-24; 18.15.
6.2 *Bear one another's burdens. Cf.* Rom 15.1-2. *Law of Christ; Cf.* Rom 8.2; 1 Cor 9.21; also Jn 13.34; 1 Jn 2.7-11; 3.11,23; 4.10-21; 2 Jn 5.
6.4 The standard for oneself is not found simply in comparison with others.
6.6 *Cf.* 1 Cor 9.13-14; Phil 4.15-16; 1 Tim 5.17-18. *All good things.* The Greek suggests the inclusion of material goods (see Lk 12.18-19).
6.7 *Cf.* 1 Cor 15.33.
6.11 *Cf.* 1 Cor 16.21; 2 Thess 3.17; Philem 19; *cf.* Rom 16.22.
6.12 *Cf.* 5.11.
6.13 *Cf.* Rom 2.17-24.
6.14 *Cf.* 1 Cor 1.23-29; 2.2; Gal 2.19-20.
6.15 *Cf.* 5.6; 1 Cor 7.19; also Rom 14.13-21.
6.17 *The marks of Jesus.* The Greek word is *stigmata,* and is most likely a reference to the beatings and stonings Paul experienced for his preaching the Gospel; *cf.* 2 Cor 11.23-25.
6.18 *Cf.* Phil 4.23; Philem 25.

THE LETTER OF PAUL TO THE EPHESIANS

See the Introductions, pp. 8–9 and 86–87 above.

Salutation

1 Paul, an apostle of Christ Jesus by the
will of God,
To the saints who are in Ephesus and are
faithful[a] in Christ Jesus:
2 Grace to you and peace from God our
Father and the Lord Jesus Christ.

Spiritual Blessings in Christ

3 Blessed be the God and Father of our
Lord Jesus Christ, who has blessed us in
Christ with every spiritual blessing in the
heavenly places, 4 just as he chose us in
Christ[b] before the foundation of the world
to be holy and blameless before him in love.
5 He destined us for adoption as his children
through Jesus Christ, according to the good
pleasure of his will, 6 to the praise of his
glorious grace that he freely bestowed on us
in the Beloved. 7 In him we have redemption
through his blood, the forgiveness of our
trespasses, according to the riches of his
grace 8 that he lavished on us. With all
wisdom and insight 9 he has made known
to us the mystery of his will, according to
his good pleasure that he set forth in Christ,
10 as a plan for the fullness of time, to gather
up all things in him, things in heaven and
things on earth. 11 In Christ we have also
obtained an inheritance,[c] having been destined according to the purpose of him who
accomplishes all things according to his
counsel and will, 12 so that we, who were
the first to set our hope on Christ, might live
for the praise of his glory. 13 In him you also,
when you had heard the word of truth, the
gospel of your salvation, and had believed
in him, were marked with the seal of the
promised Holy Spirit; 14 this[d] is the pledge of
our inheritance toward redemption as God's
own people, to the praise of his glory.

Paul's Prayer

15 I have heard of your faith in the Lord
Jesus and your love[e] toward all the saints,
and for this reason 16 I do not cease to give
thanks for you as I remember you in my
prayers. 17 I pray that the God of our Lord
Jesus Christ, the Father of glory, may give
you a spirit of wisdom and revelation as you
come to know him, 18 so that, with the eyes
of your heart enlightened, you may know
what is the hope to which he has called
you, what are the riches of his glorious
inheritance among the saints, 19 and what is
the immeasurable greatness of his power for
us who believe, according to the working of
his great power. 20 God[f] put this power to
work in Christ when he raised him from the
dead and seated him at his right hand in
the heavenly places, 21 far above all rule and
authority and power and dominion, and
above every name that is named, not only
in this age but also in the age to come.
22 And he has put all things under his feet
and has made him the head over all things
for the church, 23 which is his body, the
fullness of him who fills all in all.

From Death to Life

2 You were dead through the trespasses
and sins 2 in which you once lived,
following the course of this world, following
the ruler of the power of the air, the spirit
that is now at work among those who are
disobedient. 3 All of us once lived among
them in the passions of our flesh, following
the desires of flesh and senses, and we were
by nature children of wrath, like everyone
else. 4 But God, who is rich in mercy, out of
the great love with which he loved us 5 even
when we were dead through our trespasses,
made us alive together with Christ[g]—by
grace you have been saved— 6 and raised us
up with him and seated us with him in the
heavenly places in Christ Jesus, 7 so that in
the ages to come he might show the immeasurable riches of his grace in kindness
toward us in Christ Jesus. 8 For by grace you
have been saved through faith, and this is
not your own doing; it is the gift of God—
9 not the result of works, so that no one may
boast. 10 For we are what he has made us,

[a] Other ancient authorities lack *in Ephesus*, reading *saints who are also faithful* [b] Gk *in him* [c] Or *been made a heritage* [d] Other ancient authorities read *who* [e] Other ancient authorities lack *and your love* [f] Gk *He* [g] Other ancient authorities read *in Christ*

1.3 2 Cor 1.3; Eph 2.6; 3.10; 6.12
1.4 Eph 5.27; Col 1.22; Eph 4.2,15,16
1.5 Rom 8.29ff
1.7 Col 1.14
1.9 Rom 16.25
1.10 Gal 4.4; Col 1.16,20
1.11 Eph 3.11; Rom 9.11; Heb 6.17
1.13 Col 1.5; Eph 4.30
1.14 2 Cor 1.22; Acts 20.32
1.16 Rom 1.8,9; Col 1.3,9
1.17 Jn 20.17; Co 1.9
1.20 Acts 2.24; Heb 1.3
1.21 Phil 2.9,10
1.22 Mt 28.18; Eph 4.15; 5.23
1.23 Rom 12.5; Col 2.17
2.2 Eph 6.12; 5.
2.3 Gal 5.16,17; Rom 2.14; 5.10
2.4 Rom 10.12
2.10 Eph 4.24; Titus 2.14

1.1 The introductory wording is identical to that of Col 1.1. *Paul, an apostle.* Paul's letters often begin with his claim of apostleship (Rom 1.1; 1 Cor 1.1; 2 Cor 1.1; Gal 1.1; *cf.* Col 1.1; 1 & 2 Tim), a claim some had questioned (see 1 Cor 9.2; 2 Cor 13.3). *The saints.* See note on 1 Cor 1.2. *In Ephesus.* These words do not appear in the oldest known manuscript of Ephesians or in some other manuscripts (see footnote *a*); the contents of the letter lack reference to any one situation or occasion, and suggest a wider readership than that of one given location (see introductory notes). **1.2** *Grace to you and peace...* An initial greeting found in every one of the Pauline letters, as well as in other New Testament letters; *cf.* Rom 1.7; 1 Cor 1.3; 2 Cor 1.2; Gal 1.3; Phil 1.2; Col 1.2; 2 Thess 1.2; 1 Tim 1.2; 2 Tim 1.2; Titus 1.4; Philem 3; see also 1 Pet 1.2; 2 Pet 2.2; 2 Jn 3; Rev 1.4. **1.3-23** This section comprises the thanksgiving (see note on Rom 1.1 on the structure of the Pauline letter), written after the form of a traditional Jewish eulogy praising God (*cf.* Gen 9.26; Ps 31.21; 72.18-19; 144.1; 1 Kings 1.48; 2 Chr 6.4; Tob 13.1; 1 Macc 4.30). This section includes the first in a series of long, wordy sentences: in the Greek text 1.15-23 is one sentence, as are 3.1-7 and 4.11-16, unusual for Paul's writing style. Throughout Ephesians there are forty words not found elsewhere in Paul's letters. **1.3** *In Christ.* This term occurs several times in the immediately following verses and elsewhere throughout Ephesians; it retains Paul's sense of the Christian community (see 1 Cor 1.13; 12.12; Gal 3.16), i.e. the fellowship of those whose faith in Christ gives them mutual benefits and sets common standards. *The heavenly places.* Found elsewhere in Ephesians with different nuances in meaning (*cf.* 1.20; 2.6; 3.10; 6.12), this term refers here to the realm of God from which the entire created order is governed. **1.4** *He chose us.* The concept of God's choosing, with reference to the Christian community, is mentioned relatively seldom in the New Testament (Mk 13.30; 1 Cor 1.27-28; Jas 2.5), but becomes stronger in later Christian writings; it rests on Old Testament precedent (see Deut 14.2). *From the foundation of the world. Cf.* Mt 25.34; Lk 11.50; Jn 17.24; 1 Pet 1.20; Heb 4.3; 9.26; Rev 13.8; 17.8. *Holy and blameless. Cf.* Col 1.22, also Eph 5.27. **1.5** *He destined us for adoption.* The idea is that salvation is made possible solely through God's initiative and authority; *cf.* 1.11; Rom 8.29-30; Acts 4.28; 1 Cor 2.7. The Greek word for adoption is a legal term employed in the New Testament to designate all the rights and privileges of natural birth; it is used of Israel in Rom 9.4, and of all believers in Christ in Rom 8.15,23 and Gal 4.5. **1.6** *Grace.* I.e. unmerited favor; God's initiative for our salvation is through God's free gift of unmerited acceptance (*cf.* 1.7; 2.5,8). *The Beloved.* I.e., Christ; the Greek Old Testament uses this term of Israel (Deut 32.15; 33.5,26; Isa 44.2), of Abraham (Dan 3.35; 2 Chr 20.7), of Moses (Eccl 45.1), of Samuel (46.13), and of others (Ps 28.6); *cf.* also its application to Jesus in Mk 1.11 (pars. Mt 3.17; Lk 3.22) and Mk 9.7 (pars. Mt 17.5; Lk 9.35). **1.7** *Redemption.* The act of liberation; *cf.* 1.14; 4.30; Rom 3.24; 8.23; Col 1.14. *Through his blood.* I.e. through the cross of Christ. *The forgiveness of our trespasses.* This defines the act of liberation; *cf.* Col 1.14. **1.9** *The mystery of his will. Cf.* Rom 16.25; 1 Cor 2.1; 4.1; Col 1.26. **1.10** *Fullness of time. Cf.* Gal 4.4, where the phrase has to do with chronological time; here the phrase refers to the gatherings of all the times (*cf.* Tob 14.5; 2 Esd 4.37; Acts 1.7). *To gather up all things in him. Cf.* 1.20-23; Phil 2.9-11. **1.11** *Cf.* Num 26.55; Col 1.12. *Having been destined.* See note on 1.5. **1.13** *Marked with the seal.* The sense is that of a stamp of ownership; *cf.* 4.30; 2 Cor 1.22; Rev 7.3-4. *The promised Holy Spirit. Cf.* Joel 2.28-32; Acts 2.14-21. **1.14** *Pledge.* The Greek word, translated "guarantee" in 2 Cor 5.5, has the sense of a down payment, a first installment, as translated in 2 Cor 1.22. *Inheritance. cf.* 1.18. **1.15** *cf.* Col 1.4; Philem 5.

created in Christ Jesus for good works, which God prepared beforehand to be our way of life.

One in Christ

11 So then, remember that at one time you Gentiles by birth,[h] called "the uncircumcision" by those who are called "the circumcision"—a physical circumcision made in the flesh by human hands— [12]remember that you were at that time without Christ, being aliens from the commonwealth of Israel, and strangers to the covenants of promise, having no hope and without God in the world. [13]But now in Christ Jesus you who once were far off have been brought near by the blood of Christ. [14]For he is our peace; in his flesh he has made both groups into one and has broken down the dividing wall, that is, the hostility between us. [15]He has abolished the law with its commandments and ordinances, that he might create in himself one new humanity in place of the two, thus making peace, [16]and might reconcile both groups to God in one body[i] through the cross, thus putting to death that hostility through it.[j] [17]So he came and proclaimed peace to you who were far off and peace to those who were near; [18]for through him both of us have access in one Spirit to the Father. [19]So then you are no longer strangers and aliens, but you are citizens with the saints and also members of the household of God, [20]built upon the foundation of the apostles and prophets, with Christ Jesus himself as the cornerstone.[k] [21]In him the whole structure is joined together and grows into a holy temple in the Lord; [22]in whom you also are built together spiritually[l] into a dwelling place for God.

Paul's Ministry to the Gentiles

3 This is the reason that I Paul am a prisoner for[m] Christ Jesus for the sake of you Gentiles— [2]for surely you have already heard of the commission of God's grace that was given me for you, [3]and how the mystery was made known to me by revelation, as I wrote above in a few words, [4]a reading of which will enable you to perceive my understanding of the mystery of Christ. [5]In former generations this mystery[n] was not made known to humankind, as it has now been revealed to his holy apostles and prophets by the Spirit: [6]that is, the Gentiles have become fellow heirs, members of the same body, and sharers in the promise in Christ Jesus through the gospel.

7 Of this gospel I have become a servant according to the gift of God's grace that was given me by the working of his power. [8]Although I am the very least of all the saints, this grace was given to me to bring to the Gentiles the news of the boundless riches of Christ, [9]and to make everyone see[o] what is the plan of the mystery hidden for ages in[p] God who created all things; [10]so that through the church the wisdom of God in its rich variety might now be made known to the rulers and authorities in the heavenly places. [11]This was in accordance with the eternal purpose that he has carried out in Christ Jesus our Lord, [12]in whom we have access to God in boldness and confidence through faith in him.[q] [13]I pray therefore that you[r] may not lose heart over my sufferings for you; they are your glory.

Prayer for the Readers

14 For this reason I bow my knees before the Father,[s] [15]from whom every family[t] in heaven and on earth takes its name. [16]I pray that, according to the riches of his glory, he may grant that you may be strengthened in your inner being with power through his Spirit, [17]and that Christ may dwell in your hearts through faith, as you are being rooted and grounded in love. [18]I pray that you may have the power to comprehend, with all the saints, what is the breadth and length and height and depth, [19]and to know the love of Christ that surpasses knowledge, so that you may be filled with all the fullness of God.

20 Now to him who by the power at work within us is able to accomplish abundantly far more than all we can ask or imagine, [21]to him be glory in the church and in Christ Jesus to all generations, forever and ever. Amen.

Unity in the Body of Christ

4 I therefore, the prisoner in the Lord, beg you to lead a life worthy of the calling to which you have been called, [2]with all humility and gentleness, with patience,

[h] Gk *in the flesh* [i] Or *reconcile both of us in one body for God* [j] Or *in him*, or *in himself* [k] Or *keystone* [l] Gk *in the Spirit* [m] Or *of* [n] Gk *it* [o] Other ancient authorities read *to bring to light* [p] Or *by* [q] Or *the faith of him* [r] Or *I* [s] Other ancient authorities add *of our Lord Jesus Christ* [t] Gk *fatherhood*

2.11 Rom 2.28; Col 2.11
2.12 1 Thess 4.5; Gal 4.8
2.13 Acts 2.39; Col 1.20
2.14 Col 3.15; 1 Cor 12.13
2.15 Col 1.21,22; Gal 6.15
2.16 Col 1.20,22
2.18 Eph 3.12; 1 Cor 12.13; Col 1.12
2.19 Phil 3.20; Gal 6.10
2.20 Mt 16.18; Rev 21.14
2.21 1 Cor 3.16,17
3.3 Acts 22.17; Gal 1.12; Rom 16.25
3.4 1 Cor 4.1
3.5 Rom 16.26
3.6 al 3.29; Eph 2.15,16
3.8 1 Cor 15.9; Gal 1.16; Col 1.27
3.9 Col 1.26,27
3.10 1 Pet 1.12; 1 Cor 2.7; Eph 1.21
3.12 Heb 4.16; Eph 2.18
3.16 ph 1.18; Col 1.11; Rom 7.22
3.18 ph 1.18; Job 11.8,9
3.19 ol 2.10; Eph 1.23
3.20 Rom 16.25
4.1 Eph 3.1; Col 1.10
4.2 ol 3.12; Eph 1.4

2.11 This verse indicates that the author is Jewish and that Gentile readers are envisioned. This verse also reflects a Jewish categorization of world humanity into Gentiles (=*the uncircumcision*) and Jews (=*the circumcision*); *cf.* Rom 3.39; 9.24.
2.13 It is through Christ that non-Jews have the same benefits as Jews (see 2.12): they have membership in the people of God (*cf.* Gal 6.16), access to the covenants of promise (*cf.* Gal 3.14), and are recipients of the gift of hope.
2.14-16 This section recites a hymn about the person and work of Christ; several New Testament authors incorporate such Christological hymns into their writings (see Phil 2.6-11; Col 1.15-20; 1 Pet 3.18-19.22; Jn 1.1-18; Heb 1.3; 1 Tim 3.16). This hymn speaks of the unity and reconciliation between Jew and Gentile which the work of Christ has made possible.
2.14 *He is our peace.* The point is that in Christ the hostility and division between Jew and Gentile are abolished; *cf.* Rom 1.16; Gal 3.28. The word *peace* is used here and in the following three verses with regard to the unity which Jew and Gentile can now find in the church.
2.15 *He has abolished the law*, so that no dividing wall exists between Jew and Gentile; *cf.* Col 3.6-15.
2.16 *cf.* Col 1.20.
2.17 *You who were far off.* I.e. the Gentiles. *Those who were near.* I.e. the Jews.
2.18 *Both of us.* I.e. both Gentiles and Jews.
2.19 In the church of Christ there are no *strangers and aliens*; all are united in Christ.
2.20 *cf.* Rev 21.9-14. *Cornerstone. Cf.* Isa 28.16; Ps 188.22; also Mt 21.42.
2.21 *Structure.* The imagery has shifted from body (vs. 16) to household (vs. 19) to building (vs. 20) to a structure which is growing into a *holy temple in the Lord, a dwelling place for God* (vs. 22). *Grows.* The church of Christ is marked by constant spiritual growing.
3.1-13 In this section the life and ministry of Paul are accented, and his accomplishments are reviewed as cause for further theological reflection. The readers envisioned are Gentiles (3.1).
3.1 *Prisoner.* An imprisonment in Ephesus is never mentioned by Paul, but it is hinted at in 1 Cor 15.32.
3.2 *cf.* 3.8; Rom 1.5; Gal 1.1; 2.8.
3.3 *Mystery. Cf.* the uses of this word in Rom 11.25; 1 Cor 4.1; 13.2; 14.2; 15.51; see note on Col 1.26. *Revelation. Cf.* the uses of this word in Rom 16.25; 1 Cor 14.6,26; 2 Cor 12.7; Gal 1.12. For the writer of Ephesians the content of the mystery which has now been revealed is mentioned in 3.6.
3.4 *The mystery of Christ.* A phrase found in Paul's letters only here and in Col 4.3.
3.6 The content of the mystery, now revealed, is that the Gentiles have become fellow heirs with Jews in the people of God. This notion is not present in the undisputedly Pauline letters.

1.16 *cf.* Rom 1.9; Col 1.3; Philem 4.
1.20 *The heavenly places.* See note on 1.3.
1.21 *cf.* Phil 2.9-11; 1 Cor 15.24; Col 1.16. *Rule and authority. Cf.* 3.10; 6.12; Col 1.16; 2.10,15; also Rom 8.38.
1.22 *cf.* Ps 8.7; 1 Cor 15.27-28; Heb 2.8; Phil 3.21. *The church.* In Ephesians "the church" refers to the church throughout the world, the universal church, rather than to a local congregation.
1.23 *Cf.* 3.19; 4.13.
2.2 *The ruler of the power of the air.* I.e. the one named elsewhere as the devil (6.11) and the evil one (6.16). *At work among those who are disobedient.* Christians are no longer subservient to these powers.
2.3 *Passions of our flesh ... desires of flesh.* This is not a reference to sexual desires, but a general reference to the human being as he exists in his own selfish nature, apart from God's redemptive power; *cf.* also 2.11,14; 5.29,31; 6.5,12. *By nature children of wrath.* I.e. in our natural condition as descendants of Adam, as in Rom 5.12.
2.6 The believer participates in Christ's exaltation; *cf.* 1.3,20-21.
2.8-9 A formula summarizing Paul's theology. *Cf.* Rom 3.21-28; 1 Cor 1.22-29.
2.8 *cf.* Rom 5.1; 11.6; Gal 3.18; 3.21-22; 5.4.
2.9 *Boast.* See notes on Rom 2.27; 4.2; 1 Cor 1.29.
2.10 The consequence of God's justifying grace is that the old life described in 2.2-3 is transformed into the new life in Christ, a way of life producing good works; *cf.* 1 Cor 5.17; Gal 6.15.

bearing with one another in love, 3making
every effort to maintain the unity of the
Spirit in the bond of peace. 4There is one
body and one Spirit, just as you were called
to the one hope of your calling, 5one Lord,
one faith, one baptism, 6one God and Father
of all, who is above all and through all and
in all.
7 But each of us was given grace according to the measure of Christ's gift. 8There-
fore it is said,
"When he ascended on high he made
captivity itself a captive;
he gave gifts to his people."
9(When it says, "He ascended," what does
it mean but that he had also descended[u]
into the lower parts of the earth? 10He who
descended is the same one who ascended
far above all the heavens, so that he might
fill all things.) 11The gifts he gave were that
some would be apostles, some prophets,
some evangelists, some pastors and teachers, 12to equip the saints for the work of
ministry, for building up the body of Christ,
13until all of us come to the unity of the
faith and of the knowledge of the Son of
God, to maturity, to the measure of the full
stature of Christ. 14We must no longer be
children, tossed to and fro and blown about
by every wind of doctrine, by people's trickery, by their craftiness in deceitful scheming. 15But speaking the truth in love, we
must grow up in every way into him who
is the head, into Christ, 16from whom the
whole body, joined and knit together by
every ligament with which it is equipped, as
each part is working properly, promotes the
body's growth in building itself up in love.

The Old Life and the New

17 Now this I affirm and insist on in the
Lord: you must no longer live as the Gentiles live, in the futility of their minds. 18They
are darkened in their understanding, alienated from the life of God because of their
ignorance and hardness of heart. 19They
have lost all sensitivity and have abandoned
themselves to licentiousness, greedy to practice every kind of impurity. 20That is not the
way you learned Christ! 21For surely you
have heard about him and were taught in
him, as truth is in Jesus. 22You were taught
to put away your former way of life, your
old self, corrupt and deluded by its lusts,
23and to be renewed in the spirit of your
minds, 24and to clothe yourselves with the
new self, created according to the likeness
of God in true righteousness and holiness.

Rules for the New Life

25 So then, putting away falsehood, let
all of us speak the truth to our neighbors,
for we are members of one another. 26Be
angry but do not sin; do not let the sun go
down on your anger, 27and do not make
room for the devil. 28Thieves must give up
stealing; rather let them labor and work
honestly with their own hands, so as to
have something to share with the needy.
29Let no evil talk come out of your mouths,
but only what is useful for building up,[v] as
there is need, so that your words may give
grace to those who hear. 30And do not
grieve the Holy Spirit of God, with which
you were marked with a seal for the day of
redemption. 31Put away from you all bitterness and wrath and anger and wrangling
and slander, together with all malice, 32and
be kind to one another, tenderhearted, forgiving one another, as God in Christ has
forgiven you.[w]

5 Therefore be imitators of God, as beloved children, 2and live in love, as
Christ loved us[x] and gave himself up for us,
a fragrant offering and sacrifice to God.

Renounce Pagan Ways

3 But fornication and impurity of any
kind, or greed, must not even be mentioned
among you, as is proper among saints.
4Entirely out of place is obscene, silly, and
vulgar talk; but instead, let there be thanksgiving. 5Be sure of this, that no fornicator
or impure person, or one who is greedy
(that is, an idolater), has any inheritance in
the kingdom of Christ and of God.
6 Let no one deceive you with empty
words, for because of these things the wrath
of God comes on those who are disobedient.
7Therefore do not be associated with them.
8For once you were darkness, but now in
the Lord you are light. Live as children of
light— 9for the fruit of the light is found in
all that is good and right and true. 10Try to
find out what is pleasing to the Lord. 11Take
no part in the unfruitful works of darkness,
but instead expose them. 12For it is shameful

[u] Other ancient authorities add *first* [v] Other ancient authorities read *building up faith* [w] Other ancient authorities read *us* [x] Other ancient authorities read *you*

3.8 *The very least of all the saints. Cf.* 1 Cor 15.9.
3.10 *The wisdom of God. Cf.* 1 Cor 1.21-31.
3.12 An echo of 2.12-13.
3.13 *My sufferings for you.* In 2 Cor 1.6 Paul's sufferings are for his readers' benefit; elsewhere his sufferings are for Christ (Phil 1.13), in the Pastorals "for the gospel" (2 Tim 1.8); otherwise it is not said that Paul's sufferings are his readers' "glory"; *cf.* Gal 6.14.
3.14-21 This section comprises a prayer for the church, concluding in vv. 20-21 with a doxology.
3.14 *I bow my knees. Cf.* Rom 14.11; 11.4; Phil 2.10.
3.16 *Your inner being. Cf.* 2 Cor 4.16.
3.20 *cf.* 1.19; 2.7; 2 Cor 3.10; 9.14; Phil 4.7.
4.1-6 This section speaks of the necessary unity of the church. Unity was an important theme in Paul's letters, but his emphasis remained on the unity within the individual local congregation (see 1 Cor 1.11-15; Phil 2.1-2). In Ephesians the theme of unity is extended to the body of Christian believers throughout the world.
4.1 *A life worthy of the calling. Cf.* Phil 1.27; 1 Thess 2.12; Col 1.10.
4.2 This verse gives a list of virtues comparable to Col 3.12; *cf.* also Gal 5.22-23; Phil 2.1-3.

4.3 Here peace is the bond for Christian unity; in Col 3.14 love is. *Cf.* Eph 2.14-15.
4.4 This verse begins a sevenfold unity formula: *one body...., one Spirit...., one hope* refers to the church.
4.5 This verse continues the sevenfold unity formula: *one Lord, one faith, one baptism* refers to those factors which have established the unity of the church.
4.6 The seventh piece in the unity formula is the *one God and Father of all,* who is responsible for the previous six pieces, whose working is *above all and through all and in all; cf.* Rom 3.30; 1 Cor 8.4-6; Gal 3.20; 1 Tim 2.5; Jas 2.19
4.7 This verse begins a discussion of the grace, gifts, and ministries given by the exalted Christ to his church.
4.8 The quotation is from Ps 68.18.
4.9 *cf.* Acts 2.33.
4.11 *cf.* 1 Cor 12.28. *Apostles and prophets* comprise the foundation of the church (see Eph 2.20) and were the recipients of the revelation of Christ (see 3.5). *Evangelists* included Philip (Acts 21.8) and Timothy (2 Tim 4.5). *Pastors.* The Greek word is "shepherds," a title given in the New Testament only to Jesus (1 Pet 2.25; Heb 13.20; Jn 10.2; Mk 6.34; 14.27; Mt 25.32), who passed on pastoral tasks to others (*cf.* Jn 21.15-17; Lk 22.31). *Teachers* are mentioned as a group in 1 Cor 12.28; Acts 13.1; Jas 3.1.
4.12 The gifts, namely the offices mentioned in the previous verse, are given in order that all believers may be *equipped for the work of ministry,* for the purpose of *building up the body of Christ.*
4.13 Unity and maturity have not yet been achieved.
4.14 *cf.* Col 2.8-23.
4.15-16 A recapitulation of the foregoing: Christ, the head, with the church, his body, is made up of many gifts, and continues to grow (*cf.* 2.21). *Cf.* Col 2.19.
4.17-32 This section comprises an exhortation to ethical conduct.
4.17 *Futility of their minds. Cf.* Rom 1.18-32.
4.18 *cf.* 2.3; Col 1.21; also Rom 1.28; 2.15.
4.20 Learning about Christ has direct implications for daily living.
4.22 *cf.* 2 Cor 5.17.
4.24 *cf.* Gal 3.27; Rom 6.1-14.
4.25 *cf.* Col 3.9; 1 Tim 1.10.
4.26 *cf.* Ps 4.4 (see footnote); Col 3.8.
4.30 *Do not grieve the Holy Spirit of God. cf.* Isa 63.10; 1 Thess 5.19.
4.31 *cf.* Jas 1.19-20; 1 Tim 2.8.
4.32 *cf.* Mt 6.12; 18.23-35.
5.1 *Imitators of God.* This idea, as developed in the following verse, is closer to Mt 5.43-48 than to Paul, who speaks not of imitating God but of imitating Christ and himself (see 1 Cor 11.1; 4.16; Gal 4.12; 1 Thess 1.6; Phil 3.17).
5.3-5 A listing of vices comparable to that of Col 3.5; *cf.* also 1 Cor 5.9-11; 6.9-10; Gal 5.19-21; Rom 1.29-32.
5.7 *cf.* 1 Cor 5.9.
5.8 *cf.* 2 Cor 6.14; 1 Thess 5.5; Phil 2.15.

4.4 1 Cor 12.12; Eph 2.16; 1.18
4.7 Rom 12.3
4.8 Ps 68.18; Judg 5.12; Col 2.15
4.11 1 Cor 12.28
4.12 2 Cor 13.9; Eph 1.23; 1 Cor 12.27
4.13 Col 2.2; 1 Cor 14.20; Col 1.28
4.14 1 Cor 14.20; Jas 1.6; Eph 6.11
4.15 2 Cor 4.2; Eph 1.22; Co 1.18
4.17 Col 3.7; 1 Pe 4.3; Rom 1.21
4.18 Eph 2.1,12; 2 Cor 3.14
4.22 1 Pet 2.1; Rom 6.6
4.24 Rom 6.4; 2 Cor 5.17
4.25 Zech 8.16; Rom 12.5
4.30 1 Thess 5.1 Rom 8.23
4.31 Col 3.8; Titu 3.3
4.32 2 Cor 2.10; Mt 6.14,15
5.1 Lk 6.36
5.2 1 Thess 4.9; Gal 1.4; 2 Cor 2.15
5.3 Rom 6.13; 1 Cor 5.1
5.5 1 Cor 6.9; Col 3.5
5.6 Jer 29.8; Rom 1.18
5.8 Jn 8.12; Lk 16.8
5.11 1 Cor 5.9; Rom 6.21

5.14 Isa 60.1; Jn 5.25
5.16 Col 4.5; Eph 6.13
5.17 Rom 12.2; 1 Thess 4.3
5.18 Prov 20.1; Lk 1.15
5.19 Col 3.16; Acts 16.25
5.20 Ps 34.1; Heb 13.15
5.22 Gen 3.16; Eph 6.5
5.23 1 Cor 11.3; Col 1.18; Eph 1.23
5.27 Col 1.22; Eph 1.4
5.30 1 Cor 6.15; Eph 1.23
5.31 Gen 2.24; Mt 19.5; 1 Cor 6.16
6.2 Deut 5.16
6.4 Col 3.21; Gen 18.19
6.5 Col 3.22; 1 Tim 6.1; Phil 2.21; 1 Chr 29.17
6.9 Lev 25.43; Jn 13.13; Col 3.25
6.12 1 Cor 9.25; Rom 8.38
6.13 2 Cor 10.4; Eph 5.16
6.14 Isa 11.5; 59.17
6.16 1 Jn 5.4
6.17 Isa 59.17; Heb 4.12

even to mention what such people do secretly; [13]but everything exposed by the light
becomes visible, [14]for everything that becomes visible is light. Therefore it says,

"Sleeper, awake!
Rise from the dead,
and Christ will shine on you."

15 Be careful then how you live, not as
unwise people but as wise, [16]making the
most of the time, because the days are evil.
[17]So do not be foolish, but understand what
the will of the Lord is. [18]Do not get drunk
with wine, for that is debauchery; but be
filled with the Spirit, [19]as you sing psalms
and hymns and spiritual songs among
yourselves, singing and making melody to
the Lord in your hearts, [20]giving thanks to
God the Father at all times and for everything in the name of our Lord Jesus Christ.

The Christian Household

21 Be subject to one another out of reverence for Christ.
22 Wives, be subject to your husbands
as you are to the Lord. [23]For the husband
is the head of the wife just as Christ is the
head of the church, the body of which he
is the Savior. [24]Just as the church is subject
to Christ, so also wives ought to be, in
everything, to their husbands.
25 Husbands, love your wives, just as
Christ loved the church and gave himself up
for her, [26]in order to make her holy by
cleansing her with the washing of water by
the word, [27]so as to present the church to
himself in splendor, without a spot or wrin-
kle or anything of the kind—yes, so that she
may be holy and without blemish. [28]In the
same way, husbands should love their wives
as they do their own bodies. He who loves
his wife loves himself. [29]For no one ever
hates his own body, but he nourishes and
tenderly cares for it, just as Christ does for
the church, [30]because we are members of
his body.[y] [31]"For this reason a man will
leave his father and mother and be joined
to his wife, and the two will become one
flesh." [32]This is a great mystery, and I am
applying it to Christ and the church. [33]Each
of you, however, should love his wife as
himself, and a wife should respect her
husband.

Children and Parents

6 Children, obey your parents in the
Lord,[z] for this is right. [2]"Honor your
father and mother"—this is the first commandment with a promise: [3]"so that it may
be well with you and you may live long on
the earth."
4 And, fathers, do not provoke your
children to anger, but bring them up in the
discipline and instruction of the Lord.

Slaves and Masters

5 Slaves, obey your earthly masters with
fear and trembling, in singleness of heart,
as you obey Christ; [6]not only while being
watched, and in order to please them, but
as slaves of Christ, doing the will of God
from the heart. [7]Render service with enthusiasm, as to the Lord and not to men and
women, [8]knowing that whatever good we
do, we will receive the same again from the
Lord, whether we are slaves or free.
9 And, masters, do the same to them.
Stop threatening them, for you know that
both of you have the same Master in heaven,
and with him there is no partiality.

The Whole Armor of God

10 Finally, be strong in the Lord and in
the strength of his power. [11]Put on the
whole armor of God, so that you may be
able to stand against the wiles of the devil.
[12]For our[a] struggle is not against enemies of
blood and flesh, but against the rulers,
against the authorities, against the cosmic
powers of this present darkness, against the
spiritual forces of evil in the heavenly places.
[13]Therefore take up the whole armor of God,
so that you may be able to withstand on
that evil day, and having done everything,
to stand firm. [14]Stand therefore, and fasten
the belt of truth around your waist, and put
on the breastplate of righteousness. [15]As
shoes for your feet put on whatever will
make you ready to proclaim the gospel of
peace. [16]With all of these,[b] take the shield
of faith, with which you will be able to
quench all the flaming arrows of the evil
one. [17]Take the helmet of salvation, and the
sword of the Spirit, which is the word of
God.

[y] Other ancient authorities add *of his flesh and of his bones* [z] Other ancient authorities lack *in the Lord* [a] Other ancient authorities read *your* [b] Or *In all circumstances*

5.14 The closest biblical texts to the quotation given here are Isa 26.19; 60.1; and Jon 1.6. The quotation may be a combination of these, used in an early Christian hymn or in a baptismal liturgy.
5.15 *cf.* Col 4.5.
5.18 *Do not get drunk with wine.* Prov 22.20; 23.31-35.
5.19 *Psalms and hymns and spiritual songs. cf.* Col 3.18.
5.20 *cf.* Col. 3.16-17.
5.21-6.9 This section is known as a "household code," a formal admonition listing the categories of the average middle-class Hellenistic household: wives/husbands, children/parents, slaves/masters. A closely similar household code is given in Col 3.18-4.1, and a partial one in 1 Pet 3.1-9. Such household codes were already present in pre-Christian Hellenism, and were taught in order to promote obedience to the head of the household, namely the husband-father-master. In the Christian adaptation of the code each member of the household is subject first and foremost to the Lord Christ.
5.23 *The husband is the head of the wife.* In 1 Cor 11.3 Paul bases this same notion on the narrative in Gen 2.21-24. See note on 1 Cor 11.3 on the meaning of the word "head" in that context. *Christ is the head of the church. Cf.* Eph 1.22-23; 4.15-16; Col 1.18; 2.19.
5.25 *cf.* Col 3.19. Christ's self-giving love is the pattern for the husband's love for his wife.
5.26 *The washing of water with the word.* The language is that of baptismal theology (see also Titus 2.14).
5.27 *cf.* Rev 21.2; Ezek 16.6-14.
5.31 The quotation is from Gen 2.24. This passage is used to continue the pattern of relationship: Christ + church = one body; husband + wife = one body, i.e. "one flesh."
6.1 *cf.* Col 3.20-21.
6.2 The quotation is from Deut 5.16; *cf.* Ex 20.12.
6.3 The quotation of Deut 5.16 continues, but with the broadening of the "land (of Israel)" to "the earth."
6.4 *cf.* Col 3.21.
6.5-8 The admonitions to slaves have a parallel in Col 3.22-25.
6.9 *cf.* Col 4.1. *Do the same.* The implication is that Christian masters are to show to their slaves the same honest and considerate attitude that Christian slaves are to show their masters. *The same Master.* I.e. Christ; again, a Christian head of a household is subject to the same authority, namely the Lord Christ, as everyone else in that household.
6.10 *cf.* 1 Cor 16.13.
6.11 *cf.* Lk 11.21-22; 2 Cor 10.3-4.
6.12 *cf.* 1.21; 2.2; 3.10; Col 2.15; also 1 Cor 2.6,8.
6.13-17 This section is rich in warfare imagery for use in the Christian's battle against the evil powers; literary precedent can be found in Isa 59.17; Wis 5.17-20. *Cf.* also 1 Thess 5.8.
6.17 *The sword of the Spirit* is the only weapon of attack given in this list of warfare imagery. It is identified as *the word of God,* the same identification behind the symbol in Rev 19.15 (see note there).

6.18-20 This section has a close parallel in Col 4.2-5.
6.18 *cf.* 1 Thess 5.17.
6.19 *Mystery of the gospel. Cf.* 3.4,9.
6.20 *cf.* Philem 9 (see note).
6.21 *Tychicus.* Very likely the bearer of this letter; see Col 4.7-8.
6.23 *Peace.* A word common in the conclusions of Paul's letters; *cf.* Rom 15.33; 2 Cor 13.11; Gal 6.16; Phil 4.9; 1 Thess 3.16.
6.24 *Grace.* As in Col 4.18, a standard word in the conclusions to Paul's letters.

18 Pray in the Spirit at all times in every
prayer and supplication. To that end keep
alert and always persevere in supplication
for all the saints. [19]Pray also for me, so that
when I speak, a message may be given to
me to make known with boldness the
mystery of the gospel,[c] [20]for which I am an
ambassador in chains. Pray that I may
declare it boldly, as I must speak.

Personal Matters and Benediction

21 So that you also may know how I am
and what I am doing, Tychicus will tell you
everything. He is a dear brother and a
faithful minister in the Lord. [22]I am sending
him to you for this very purpose, to let you
know how we are, and to encourage your
hearts.

23 Peace be to the whole community,[d]
and love with faith, from God the Father
and the Lord Jesus Christ. [24]Grace be with
all who have an undying love for our Lord
Jesus Christ.[e]

[c] Other ancient authorities lack *of the gospel* [d] Gk *to the brothers* [e] Other ancient authorities add *Amen*

6.18 Lk 18.1; Mt 26.41; Phil 1.4
6.19 Acts 4.29; 2 Cor 3.12
6.20 2 Cor 5.20; Phil 1.20
6.21 Acts 20.4
6.23 1 Pet 5.14; Gal 5.6

See the Introductions, pp. 8–9 and 87–88 above.

1.1-2 Formal Greek letter-writing style began with an introductory section giving the sender's name, the names of the addressees, and a brief greeting. See note on Romans 1.1 for additional comments on the structure of Paul's letters.
1.1 *Timothy.* Often listed as a co-sender with Paul of other letters (see 2 Cor 1.1; Col 1.1; 1 Thess 1.1; 2 Thess 1.1; Philem 1), Timothy was evidently one of Paul's converts (1 Cor 4.17), and became one of Paul's closest co-workers (2 Cor 1.19) and a trusted emissary (1 Cor 16.10; Phil 2.19). See note on 1 Timothy 1.1.
1.1 *Servants.* See footnote *a* and Rom 1.1; 1 Cor 3.5; 4.1; 2 Cor 6.4; Gal 1.10; Phil 1.1; *cf.* Titus 1.1. See also note on 2 Cor 4.5. *Christ Jesus.* The word "Christ" is a title meaning "Messiah," which can therefore be placed before or after Jesus' name. See 1 Cor 1.1. *Saints.* Paul often calls Christians "saints," a word which means a people set apart for God's work in the world; *cf.* 1 Cor 1.2. *Philippi.* See introductory notes. *Bishops.* Not to be associated with the office of bishop later developed in the church; the plural does suggest that several leaders in Philippi were appointed to fulfill supervisory roles in the congregation. The Greek word for bishop means "overseer," and has roots in the Septuagint (*cf.* Job 20.29; Num 4.16; 31.14; 2 Kings 11.18; 12.11; Neh 11.9; 1 Macc 1.51). *Deacons.* More frequently used in the New Testament than "bishop," the word "deacon" evidently refers here to those leaders who had a more direct service function, including contact with the members of the congregations to care for their daily needs.
1.2 *Grace and peace.* See note on Rom 1.7.
1.3-11 This section comprises the thanksgiving, a formal part of every letter of Paul with the exception of Galatians. This thanksgiving is marked by a particular closeness to his readers in Philippi, no doubt because of their consistent support of Paul in his ministry (see 2.25-30; 4.15-19). See note on Rom 1.1 on the structure of the Pauline letter.
1.5 *Sharing.* The Greek word is *koinonia*, meaning partnership, a word used frequently in this letter, indicating the close relationship between Paul and his readers (*cf.* 1.7; 2.1; 3.10; 4.15).
1.6 *The one.* I.e. God. The idea is that God will complete what he began when the gospel was first proclaimed among the Philippians; *cf.* 1 Cor 1.7. *The day of Jesus Christ.* See notes on 1 Cor 1.8; 15.20-28; and 1 Thess 4.13-18.
1.7 *My imprisonment.* Paul writes this letter in prison. See note on 1.13.
1.8 *Compassion.* The Greek word refers to the emotions, and is here a term of deep affection.
1.10 *Day of Christ.* See note on 1 Cor 1.8.
1.12 *What has happened to me.* I.e. Paul's imprisonment. Evidently the complaint heard in Philippi is that Paul's imprisonment has brought shame to Christian believing.
1.13 *Imperial guard.* Literally, "the whole praetorium" (see note *g*). The particular military unit in question refers to guards specially assigned to protect the emperor or other high dignitaries at official points of residence outside Rome. *My imprisonment is for Christ.* Paul wants to make it clear that he has not been imprisoned for any other crime (see note on 1.17).
1.15 *From envy and rivalry.* Paul knows of some Christian leaders who have challenged him by setting up barriers of competition (see 3.2-6), much in the same manner as Paul had to face in Corinth (see 2 Cor 10.12; 11.21-22; 13.3).
1.17 Paul's accusers must have been asserting that Paul's message was in error because it threatened the authorities, that it was not the gospel itself but Paul's way of presenting it which was dangerous. See note on 1.27-30.
1.18 *Rejoice.* This theme of "rejoice" begins here and continues to the end of chapter 2.

THE LETTER OF PAUL TO THE

PHILIPPIANS

Salutation

1 Paul and Timothy, servants[a] of Christ
Jesus,
To all the saints in Christ Jesus who are
in Philippi, with the bishops[b] and deacons:[c]
2 Grace to you and peace from God our
Father and the Lord Jesus Christ.

Paul's Prayer for the Philippians

3 I thank my God every time I remember
you, [4]constantly praying with joy in every
one of my prayers for all of you, [5]because
of your sharing in the gospel from the first
day until now. [6]I am confident of this, that
the one who began a good work among
you will bring it to completion by the day
of Jesus Christ. [7]It is right for me to think
this way about all of you, because you hold
me in your heart,[d] for all of you share in
God's grace[e] with me, both in my imprisonment and in the defense and confirmation of the gospel. [8]For God is my witness,
how I long for all of you with the compassion of Christ Jesus. [9]And this is my prayer,
that your love may overflow more and
more with knowledge and full insight [10]to
help you to determine what is best, so that
in the day of Christ you may be pure and
blameless, [11]having produced the harvest of
righteousness that comes through Jesus
Christ for the glory and praise of God.

Paul's Present Circumstances

12 I want you to know, beloved,[f] that
what has happened to me has actually
helped to spread the gospel, [13]so that it has
become known throughout the whole imperial guard[g] and to everyone else that my
imprisonment is for Christ; [14]and most of
the brothers and sisters,[f] having been made
confident in the Lord by my imprisonment,
dare to speak the word[h] with greater boldness and without fear.

15 Some proclaim Christ from envy and
rivalry, but others from goodwill. [16]These
proclaim Christ out of love, knowing that I
have been put here for the defense of the
gospel; [17]the others proclaim Christ out of
selfish ambition, not sincerely but intending
to increase my suffering in my imprisonment. [18]What does it matter? Just this, that
Christ is proclaimed in every way, whether
out of false motives or true; and in that I
rejoice.

[a] Gk *slaves* [b] Or *overseers* [c] Or *overseers and helpers* [d] Or *because I hold you in my heart* [e] Gk *in grace* [f] Gk *brothers* [g] Gk *whole praetorium* [h] Other ancient authorities read *word of God*

1.2 1 Pet 1.2
1.5 Acts 2.42; 16.17
1.7 2 Pet 1.13; 2 Cor 7.3; ver 13,14,17
1.8 Rom 1.9; Gal 1.20
1.9 1 Thess 3.12; Col 1.9

Yes, and I will continue to rejoice, 19for
I know that through your prayers and the
help of the Spirit of Jesus Christ this will
turn out for my deliverance. 20It is my eager
expectation and hope that I will not be put
to shame in any way, but that by my
speaking with all boldness, Christ will be
exalted now as always in my body, whether
by life or by death. 21For to me, living is
Christ and dying is gain. 22If I am to live in
the flesh, that means fruitful labor for me;
and I do not know which I prefer. 23I am
hard pressed between the two: my desire is
to depart and be with Christ, for that is far
better; 24but to remain in the flesh is more
necessary for you. 25Since I am convinced
of this, I know that I will remain and
continue with all of you for your progress
and joy in faith, 26so that I may share
abundantly in your boasting in Christ Jesus
when I come to you again.
27 Only, live your life in a manner worthy
of the gospel of Christ, so that, whether I
come and see you or am absent and hear
about you, I will know that you are standing firm in one spirit, striving side by side
with one mind for the faith of the gospel,
28and are in no way intimidated by your
opponents. For them this is evidence of their
destruction, but of your salvation. And this
is God's doing. 29For he has graciously
granted you the privilege not only of believing in Christ, but of suffering for him as
well— 30since you are having the same
struggle that you saw I had and now hear
that I still have.

Imitating Christ's Humility

2 If then there is any encouragement in
Christ, any consolation from love, any
sharing in the Spirit, any compassion and
sympathy, 2make my joy complete: be of the
same mind, having the same love, being in
full accord and of one mind. 3Do nothing
from selfish ambition or conceit, but in
humility regard others as better than yourselves. 4Let each of you look not to your
own interests, but to the interests of others.
5Let the same mind be in you that was[i] in
Christ Jesus,

6 who, though he was in the form of God,
did not regard equality with God
as something to be exploited,
7 but emptied himself,
taking the form of a slave,
being born in human likeness.
And being found in human form,
8 he humbled himself
and became obedient to the point of death—
even death on a cross.

9 Therefore God also highly exalted him
and gave him the name
that is above every name,
10 so that at the name of Jesus
every knee should bend,
in heaven and on earth and under the earth,
11 and every tongue should confess
that Jesus Christ is Lord,
to the glory of God the Father.

Shining as Lights in the World

12 Therefore, my beloved, just as you
have always obeyed me, not only in my
presence, but much more now in my absence, work out your own salvation with
fear and trembling; 13for it is God who is at
work in you, enabling you both to will and
to work for his good pleasure.
14 Do all things without murmuring and
arguing, 15so that you may be blameless
and innocent, children of God without blemish in the midst of a crooked and perverse
generation, in which you shine like stars in
the world. 16It is by your holding fast to the
word of life that I can boast on the day of
Christ that I did not run in vain or labor
in vain. 17But even if I am being poured out
as a libation over the sacrifice and the
offering of your faith, I am glad and rejoice
with all of you— 18and in the same way
you also must be glad and rejoice with me.

Timothy and Epaphroditus

19 I hope in the Lord Jesus to send Timothy to you soon, so that I may be cheered
by news of you. 20I have no one like him
who will be genuinely concerned for your
welfare. 21All of them are seeking their own
interests, not those of Jesus Christ. 22But
Timothy's[j] worth you know, how like a son
with a father he has served with me in the
work of the gospel. 23I hope therefore to
send him as soon as I see how things go
with me; 24and I trust in the Lord that I will
also come soon.
25 Still, I think it necessary to send to

[i] Or *that you have* [j] Gk *his*

1.19 2 Cor 1.11
1.20 Rom 8.19; 5.5; Eph 6.19
1.23 2 Cor 5.8; 2 Tim 4.6
1.26 2 Cor 1.14; 5.12
1.28 2 Thess 1.5; Rom 8.17
1.29 Mt 5.12; Acts 14.22
1.30 1 Thess 2.2; Col 2.1; Acts 16.19
2.1 2 Cor 13.14; Col 3.12
2.2 Jn 3.29; Rom 12.16; 1 Pet 3.8
2.3 Gal 5.26; Rom 12.10; 1 Pet 5.5
2.4 Rom 15.1,2
2.5 Mt 11.29; 1 Pet 2.21
2.6 Jn 1.1; 2 Cor 4.4; Jn 5.18
2.7 Jn 1.14; Gal 4.4; Heb 2.17
2.8 Mt 26.39; Jn 10.18; Heb 5.8
2.9 Acts 2.33; Heb 2.9; Eph 1.20,21
2.10 Mt 28.18; Rom 14.11
2.11 Jn 13.13; Acts 2.36
2.12 Phil 1.5; Eph 6.5
2.14 1 Cor 10.10; Rom 14.1
2.15 Mt 5.45; Eph 5.1,8
2.16 2 Cor 1.14; 1 Thess 2.19
2.17 2 Tim 4.6; Rom 15.16; Col 1.24
2.21 1 Cor 10.24; 13.5
2.22 1 Cor 4.17; 1 Tim 1.2
2.25 Phil 4.18; Philem 2

1.19 *This will turn out for my deliverance.* A quotation from the Greek text of Job 13.16.
1.20 Paul's point is evident now, that his eventual release will mean vindication not only for him but for the Christian gospel as well, and will indicate that the gospel is not a subversive political message pointed against the Roman government.
1.21 For Paul Christ has given meaning and purpose to existence, and even beyond it.
1.22 Paul still must reckon with the possibility of his death at the hands of his captors.
1.24 *To remain in the flesh.* I.e. to remain alive; Paul's point is that there is still much he is able to accomplish in Christian mission, especially at Philippi.
1.26 *Your boasting in Christ Jesus.* The focal point of Christian rejoicing is in Christ, to whom alone will belong praise when Paul is delivered (see 1.19).
1.27 *Live your life in a manner worthy of the gospel of Christ.* Paul's immediate concern is that the Philippian congregation should exhibit unity in their proclamation of the gospel.
1.28 *Opponents.* Those who attempt to disturb the unity of the congregation are termed "opponents." They may be the ones who are described in 3.2.
1.29 *The privilege...of suffering.* The "opponents" (1.28) have evidently argued that Paul's imprisonment is proof that his proclamation of the gospel is in error. In response, Paul states that suffering for one's faith in Christ is a privilege.
2.1-2 If suffering for Christ is a privilege (see note on 1.29), then Paul's imprisonment should become reason for unity rather than controversy.
2.5 The unity Paul desires for the Philippian church is to be grounded in Christ's own action.
2.6-11 These verses represent an early Christian hymn, very likely known to the Philippians, which Paul uses to express Christ's own willingness to endure suffering and God's exaltation of the crucified one. Much of the wording of the hymn consists of terms which are not part of Paul's own general vocabulary. The last phrase in verse 8, however, may well have been added by Paul, since it expands the three-line symmetry of the rest of the hymn. The first part of the hymn (vv. 6-8) speaks of Christ's humiliation, i.e. of his emptying himself of his divinity, while the second part of the hymn (vv. 9-11) speaks of Christ's exaltation. See note on Heb 12.2, which is a striking summary of what is expressed in this hymn. Other passages representing fragments of early Christian hymnody on the subject of Christ's work are Col 1.15-20; Eph 2.14-16; 1 Tim 3.16; 1 Pet 3.18-19.22; and Heb 1.3.
2.6 The concept of Christ's existence prior to his humanity is expressed in John 1.1-18; Col 1.15-20; see also 1 Cor 8.6; Rom 8.3; Gal 4.4. *Form of God.* A difficult concept, in view of God's being without physical form, the Greek word is used here to express Christ's sharing in God's very nature. *Exploited.* The Greek word has to do with grasping and holding onto for one's own purposes.
2.7 See Gal 4.4.
2.8 The final phrase was very likely added by Paul himself in order to fix Christ's humiliation and obedience specifically at the moment of his death on the cross.
2.9 *God also exalted him.* With this verse God becomes the acting subject in the hymn; it is God who exalted Jesus, in Jesus' resurrection and ascension (*cf.* Acts 2.32-33; 5.30-31; Eph 1.20-21). *Gave him the name.* I.e. the name (or title) of "Lord" (see 2.11).
2.10 *Every knee should bend.* I.e. in worship.
2.11 *cf.* Rom 10.9; 2 Cor 9.13.
2.12-13 The pattern of Christ's action which led to God's vindication should now be followed in Christian living. The concept of obedience (vs. 12) is related to the living out of the Gospel of Christ as expressed in the hymn (vv. 6-11). As Christ's action reveals God's action, so also will the Philippians' selfless giving (vs. 12) reveal God at work in their community (vs. 13).
2.12 *With fear and trembling.* I.e. with respect and reverence.
2.14 *Murmuring and arguing.* These words refer to divisive actions which break down the unity of the church.
2.15 *cf.* Deut 32.5.
2.16 *Word of life.* Another term for the gospel of Christ, expressed in Paul's preaching and in the hymn he has just quoted (2.6-11). By holding fast to this "word of life" the Philippians will maintain their unity. *That I did not run in vain or labor in vain.* *Cf.* Gal 2.2; 1 Cor 9.1-2.
2.17 *Poured out as a libation.* A "libation" is a cup of wine poured out on top of the sacrifice or at the altar in honor of the deity (*cf.* 2 Kings 16.13; Jer 7.18; Hos 9.4). Paul's point is that his present

you Epaphroditus—my brother and co-worker and fellow soldier, your messenger[k] and minister to my need; [26]for he has been longing for[l] all of you, and has been distressed because you heard that he was ill. [27]He was indeed so ill that he nearly died. But God had mercy on him, and not only on him but on me also, so that I would not have one sorrow after another. [28]I am the more eager to send him, therefore, in order that you may rejoice at seeing him again, and that I may be less anxious. [29]Welcome him then in the Lord with all joy, and honor such people, [30]because he came close to death for the work of Christ,[m] risking his life to make up for those services that you could not give me.

3 Finally, my brothers and sisters,[n] rejoice[o] in the Lord.

Breaking with the Past

To write the same things to you is not troublesome to me, and for you it is a safeguard.

2 Beware of the dogs, beware of the evil workers, beware of those who mutilate the flesh![p] [3]For it is we who are the circumcision, who worship in the Spirit of God[q] and boast in Christ Jesus and have no confidence in the flesh— [4]even though I, too, have reason for confidence in the flesh.

If anyone else has reason to be confident in the flesh, I have more: [5]circumcised on the eighth day, a member of the people of Israel, of the tribe of Benjamin, a Hebrew born of Hebrews; as to the law, a Pharisee; [6]as to zeal, a persecutor of the church; as to righteousness under the law, blameless.

7 Yet whatever gains I had, these I have come to regard as loss because of Christ. [8]More than that, I regard everything as loss because of the surpassing value of knowing Christ Jesus my Lord. For his sake I have suffered the loss of all things, and I regard them as rubbish, in order that I may gain Christ [9]and be found in him, not having a righteousness of my own that comes from the law, but one that comes through faith in Christ,[r] the righteousness from God based on faith. [10]I want to know Christ[s] and the power of his resurrection and the sharing of his sufferings by becoming like him in his death, [11]if somehow I may attain the resurrection from the dead.

Pressing toward the Goal

12 Not that I have already obtained this or have already reached the goal;[t] but I press on to make it my own, because Christ Jesus has made me his own. [13]Beloved,[u] I do not consider that I have made it my own;[v] but this one thing I do: forgetting what lies behind and straining forward to what lies ahead, [14]I press on toward the goal for the prize of the heavenly[w] call of God in Christ Jesus. [15]Let those of us then who are mature be of the same mind; and if you think differently about anything, this too God will reveal to you. [16]Only let us hold fast to what we have attained.

17 Brothers and sisters,[u] join in imitating me, and observe those who live according to the example you have in us. [18]For many live as enemies of the cross of Christ; I have often told you of them, and now I tell you even with tears. [19]Their end is destruction; their god is the belly; and their glory is in their shame; their minds are set on earthly things. [20]But our citizenship[x] is in heaven, and it is from there that we are expecting a Savior, the Lord Jesus Christ. [21]He will transform the body of our humiliation[y] that it may be conformed to the body of his glory,[z] by the power that also enables him to make all things subject to himself.

4 Therefore, my brothers and sisters,[a] whom I love and long for, my joy and crown, stand firm in the Lord in this way, my beloved.

Exhortations

2 I urge Euodia and I urge Syntyche to be of the same mind in the Lord. [3]Yes, and I ask you also, my loyal companion,[b] help these women, for they have struggled beside me in the work of the gospel, together with Clement and the rest of my co-workers, whose names are in the book of life.

4 Rejoice[c] in the Lord always; again I

[k] Gk *apostle* [l] Other ancient authorities read *longing to see* [m] Other ancient authorities read *of the Lord* [n] Gk *my brothers* [o] Or *farewell* [p] Gk *the mutilation* [q] Other ancient authorities read *worship God in spirit* [r] Or *through the faith of Christ* [s] Gk *him* [t] Or *have already been made perfect* [u] Gk *Brothers* [v] Other ancient authorities read *my own yet* [w] Gk *upward* [x] Or *commonwealth* [y] Or *our humble bodies* [z] Or *his glorious body* [a] Gk *my brothers* [b] Or *loyal Syzygus* [c] Or *Farewell*

2.29 1 Cor 16.18; 1 Tim 5.17
3.2 Gal 5.15; 2 Cor 11.13
3.3 Rom 2.28,29; Gal 6.14,15
3.5 Rom 11.1; 2 Cor 11.22
3.7 Mt 13.44; Lk 14.33
3.8 Eph 4.13; 2 Pet 1.3
3.9 Rom 10.5; 9.30
3.11 Acts 26.7
3.12 1 Tim 6.12; 1 Cor 13.10; Acts 9.5,6
3.13 Lk 9.62; 1 Cor 9.24
3.14 Heb 6.1; 2 Tim 1.9
3.15 1 Cor 2.6; Gal 5.10
3.16 Rom 12.16; Gal 6.16
3.17 1 Cor 4.16; 1 Pet 5.3
3.18 Acts 20.31; Gal 6.14
3.19 2 Cor 11.15; Rom 16.18; 6.21; 8.5,6
3.21 1 Cor 15.43; Col 3.4; Eph 1.19
4.3 Rom 16.3; Lk 10.20; Rev 3.5
4.4 Rom 12.12; Phil 3.1

imprisonment, along with all his hardships and sufferings for the sake of the gospel, are joyful moments in honor of his Lord, and that therefore he can ask the Philippians to remain confident and rejoice (2.18; *cf.* also 1.12-18; 2.29-3.1a).
2.19 *Timothy.* See notes on 1.1 and 1 Tim 1.1.
2.22 *Like a son with a father. Cf.* 1 Cor 4.17. Paul uses parent-child terminology regarding those he has brought into the church (*cf.* 1 Cor 4.15; Gal 4.19; Philem 10).
2.25 *Epaphroditus.* The description of Epaphroditus in this verse indicates that he was a member of the Philippian church who was commissioned to work with Paul and to be of service to Paul on behalf of the Philippian church. See also 4.18.

2.26-28 Evidently Epaphroditus became ill during the time when he was visiting Paul and spent a period of convalescence with Paul before returning to Philippi. Vs. 27 indicates the seriousness of his illness and implies a lengthy period of convalescence.
3.1 In the middle of this verse there is an abrupt change in tone, which has led many scholars to view Philippians as a collection of shorter letters which a later editor has joined into one, as is the case with 2 Corinthians. Very possibly, then, with the second sentence in 3.1, a separate letter begins, with a different tone and with a different theme.
3.2 Paul's tone escalates into harsher designations. He now knows the source of the disunity at Philippi: those who, as in Galatia (see Gal 5.2-12), insist on mandatory circumcision for Christian converts, according to the command in Gen 17.9-14. Evidently these are the ones to whom Paul refers in 1.15,17 and 2.21, and he regards their message as antithetical to the gospel (2.27-28); he employs the same language here as he does in Gal 5.12.
3.3 *The circumcision.* In Col 4.11 the Greek word refers to Jews in general, as distinct from Gentiles; here it refers to authentic Jews (*cf.* Gal 6.15). In this verse the Greek term for "the circumcision" forms a contrasting play on words with the term "the mutilation" (see footnote *p*), i.e. inauthentic Jews. *No confidence in the flesh.* See notes on Rom 2.28-29, where Paul insists that "real circumcision is a matter of the heart," in obvious reflection on passages such as Jer 4.4; 31.31-34; and Deut 10.16.
3.5-6 Paul lists the elements in his own background in order to counter any accusation that he never really was an authentic Jew; *cf.* Gal 1.14-15.
3.9 *cf.* Rom 3.21-31. For Paul any claim that one has fulfilled the law is a "righteousness of one's own"; Rom 10.3. Actual righteousness comes from God, as a gift, and is received through faith (*cf.* Gen 15.6, which Paul cites in Rom 4.3 and Gal 3.6).
3.10 *I want to know Christ.* This stands in contrast to taking confidence from one's own pedigree or accomplishments, like the list in 3.5-6; instead the believer takes refuge in "the power of (Christ's) resurrection and the sharing of his sufferings." *Becoming like him in his death. Cf.* Rom 6.3-5.
3.11 *cf.* Rom 6.5.
3.12 *Not that I have already attained this.* Paul does not wish to claim that he has perfectly comprehended the full meaning of Christ. His "knowledge" of Christ (3.10) is still incomplete (*cf.* 1 Cor 13.9).
3.15 *Those of us who are mature.* With a touch of irony, Paul defines Christian maturity as knowing that Christians have not yet attained perfection (3.12).
3.17 *Join in imitating me.* The imitation of the apostle means a centering of Christian life in the cross of Christ (3.10,18); *cf.* 1 Cor 2.2; 4.16; 11.1.
3.18 *Enemies of the cross of Christ.* Very likely Paul is thinking of Christians who do not wish to make the cross the center of the Christian message; see note on 1 Cor 1.18. *Cf.* 1 Cor 2.2; 11.26.
3.20 *Citizenship.* This word indicates that Paul's "opponents" (see 1.28) view his imprisonment as a setback for Christians in terms of their social status within their greater communities. This would explain his emphasis on his imprisonment as in continuity with Christ's suffering, as well as his call for the Philippians' imitation of him (see 3.10). *From there we are expecting a Savior. Cf.* Acts 1.11; 2 Tim 4.1.
3.21 *cf.* 1 Cor 15.24-28.
4.2 *Euodia and...Syntyche.* The names of two women in the Philippian church. That Paul asks them to resolve their differences, for the sake of unity in the church, clearly indicates their positions of authority there.
4.3 *My loyal companion.* Some scholars understand the Greek word to be a personal name (see footnote *b*), while others view it as a general reference.

4.5 Heb 10.37; Jas 5.8,9
4.6 Mt 6.25; Eph 6.18
4.7 Jn 14.27; Col 3.15; 1 Pet 1.5
4.9 Phil 3.17; Rom 15.33
4.10 2 Cor 11.9
4.11 1 Tim 6.6
4.12 1 Cor 4.11; 2 Cor 11.9
4.13 Jn 15.5; 2 Cor 12.9
4.15 2 Cor 11.8,9
4.17 Titus 3.14
4.18 Phil 2.25; 2 Cor 2.14
4.19 Ps 23.1; 2 Cor 9.8; Eph 1.7
4.20 Gal 1.4; Rom 11.36

will say, Rejoice.[d] 5 Let your gentleness be
known to everyone. The Lord is near. 6 Do
not worry about anything, but in everything by prayer and supplication with
thanksgiving let your requests be made
known to God. 7 And the peace of God,
which surpasses all understanding, will guard
your hearts and your minds in Christ Jesus.

8 Finally, beloved,[e] whatever is true,
whatever is honorable, whatever is just,
whatever is pure, whatever is pleasing,
whatever is commendable, if there is any
excellence and if there is anything worthy
of praise, think about[f] these things. 9 Keep
on doing the things that you have learned
and received and heard and seen in me, and
the God of peace will be with you.

Acknowledgment of the Philippians' Gift

10 I rejoice[g] in the Lord greatly that now
at last you have revived your concern for
me; indeed, you were concerned for me, but
had no opportunity to show it.[h] 11 Not that
I am referring to being in need; for I have
learned to be content with whatever I have.
12 I know what it is to have little, and I
know what it is to have plenty. In any and
all circumstances I have learned the secret
of being well-fed and of going hungry, of
having plenty and of being in need. 13 I can
do all things through him who strengthens
me. 14 In any case, it was kind of you to
share my distress.

15 You Philippians indeed know that in
the early days of the gospel, when I left
Macedonia, no church shared with me in
the matter of giving and receiving, except
you alone. 16 For even when I was in
Thessalonica, you sent me help for my needs
more than once. 17 Not that I seek the gift,
but I seek the profit that accumulates to
your account. 18 I have been paid in full and
have more than enough; I am fully satisfied,
now that I have received from Epaphroditus
the gifts you sent, a fragrant offering, a
sacrifice acceptable and pleasing to God.
19 And my God will fully satisfy every need
of yours according to his riches in glory in
Christ Jesus. 20 To our God and Father be
glory forever and ever. Amen.

Final Greetings and Benediction

21 Greet every saint in Christ Jesus. The
friends[e] who are with me greet you. 22 All
the saints greet you, especially those of the
emperor's household.

23 The grace of the Lord Jesus Christ be
with your spirit.[i]

[d] Or *Farewell* [e] Gk *brothers* [f] Gk *take account of* [g] Gk *I rejoiced* [h] Gk lacks *to show it* [i] Other ancient authorities add *Amen*

THE LETTER OF PAUL TO THE

COLOSSIANS

1.3 Eph 1.16
1.4 Eph 1.15; Gal 5.6
1.5 1 Thess 5.8; 1 Pet 1.4
1.6 Mt 24.14; Jn 15.16
1.7 Philem 23; Col 4.7

Salutation

1 Paul, an apostle of Christ Jesus by the
will of God, and Timothy our brother,
2 To the saints and faithful brothers and
sisters[a] in Christ in Colossae:
Grace to you and peace from God our
Father.

Paul Thanks God for the Colossians

3 In our prayers for you we always thank
God, the Father of our Lord Jesus Christ, 4 for
we have heard of your faith in Christ Jesus
and of the love that you have for all the
saints, 5 because of the hope laid up for you
in heaven. You have heard of this hope
before in the word of the truth, the gospel
6 that has come to you. Just as it is bearing
fruit and growing in the whole world, so it
has been bearing fruit among yourselves
from the day you heard it and truly comprehended the grace of God. 7 This you
learned from Epaphras, our beloved fellow
servant.[b] He is a faithful minister of Christ
on your[c] behalf, 8 and he has made known
to us your love in the Spirit.

[a] Gk *brothers* [b] Gk *slave* [c] Other ancient authorities read *our*

4.10-20 Some scholars view these verses as Paul's thank-you note for the provisions brought from Philippi to Paul by Epaphroditus, who became ill shortly after his arrival at the prison (see notes on 2.25 and 2.26-28). If this section does constitute a separate letter, it was probably the earliest of the correspondence, placed at the end by a later editor to soften the harsh tone of chapter 3.
4.15 *Macedonia.* A province located in what is now northern Greece and southern Albania; Philippi was one of its major cities, Thessalonica its capital. For further information on Macedonia and its importance in Paul's ministry see note on Rom 15.26. *No church shared with me...except you alone; cf.* 2 Cor 11.8-9.
4.18 *cf.* 2.25-30.
4.21 *Every saint.* Paul often calls Christians "saints," a word which means a people set apart for God's work in the world (*cf.* 1 Cor 1.2).
4.22 *The emperor's household.* Most likely a reference to the soldiers of the imperial guard (see 1.13), some of whom, as this verse indicates, have become Christians.
4.23 *cf.* Gal 6.18; Philem 25; 1 Thess 5.28.

See the Introductions, pp. 8–9 and 88–89 above.

1.1 The introductory wording is identical to that of Eph 1.1. *Paul; an apostle.* Paul's letters often begin with his claim of apostleship (Rom 1.1; 1 Cor 1.1; 2 Cor 1.1; Gal 1.1; *cf.* Eph 1.1; 1 & 2 Tim); a claim some would question (see 1 Cor 9.2; 2 Cor 13.3). *Timothy.* Acts 16.1 indicates that Timothy was converted during Paul's first missionary journey and accompanied the apostle from then on; he is named as the co-author of several letters (see 2 Cor 1.1; Phil 1.1; 1 Thess 1.1; Philem 1).
1.2 *The saints.* See note on 1 Cor 1.2. *Colossae.* See introductory notes. *Grace to you and peace...* An initial greeting found in every one of the Pauline letters, as well as in other New Testament letters; *cf.* Rom 1.7; 1 Cor 1.3; 2 Cor 1.2; Gal 1.3; Eph 1.2; Phil 1.2; 2 Thess 1.2; 1 Tim 1.2; 2 Tim 1.2; Titus 1.4; Philem 3; see also 1 Pet 1.2; 2 Pet 2.2; 2 Jn 3; Jude 1.2; Rev 1.4.
1.3-8 This section comprises the thanksgiving (see note on Rom 1.1 on the structure of the Pauline letter).
1.3-4 The triad of faith, hope, and love is found in 1 Cor 13.13; 1 Thess 1.3; they are in close proximity in Rom 5.1-5; Gal 5.5-6; Eph 4.2-5; Heb 6.10-12; 10.22-24; 1 Pet 1.3-8,21-22.
1.5 *The word of truth, the gospel. Cf.* Gal 2.5,14.
1.6 *Bearing fruit.* Here, as in 1.10, this idea speaks of the power of the gospel to produce results; *cf.* Mk 4.20; Lk 8.15.
1.7 *Epaphras.* Identified here as Paul's "fellow-servant," literally "fellow-slave," and "faithful minister," Epaphras is recognized in 1.5-7 as the founder of the Colossian church. In Paul's absence (see 2.1), Epaphras is commended as the one to whom the church should pay heed in the face of the false teaching which threatens it (see 2.8-23). He is mentioned again in 4.12.

9 For this reason, since the day we heard
it, we have not ceased praying for you and
asking that you may be filled with the
knowledge of God's[d] will in all spiritual
wisdom and understanding, [10]so that you
may lead lives worthy of the Lord, fully
pleasing to him, as you bear fruit in every
good work and as you grow in the knowledge of God. [11]May you be made strong
with all the strength that comes from his
glorious power, and may you be prepared
to endure everything with patience, while
joyfully [12]giving thanks to the Father, who
has enabled[e] you[f] to share in the inheritance of the saints in the light. [13]He has
rescued us from the power of darkness and
transferred us into the kingdom of his beloved Son, [14]in whom we have redemption,
the forgiveness of sins.[g]

The Supremacy of Christ

15 He is the image of the invisible God,
the firstborn of all creation; [16]for in[h] him all
things in heaven and on earth were
created, things visible and invisible, whether
thrones or dominions or rulers or powers—
all things have been created through him
and for him. [17]He himself is before all things,
and in[h] him all things hold together. [18]He
is the head of the body, the church; he is
the beginning, the firstborn from the dead,
so that he might come to have first place
in everything. [19]For in him all the fullness
of God was pleased to dwell, [20]and through
him God was pleased to reconcile to himself
all things, whether on earth or in heaven,
by making peace through the blood of his
cross.

21 And you who were once estranged
and hostile in mind, doing evil deeds, [22]he
has now reconciled[i] in his fleshly body[j]
through death, so as to present you holy
and blameless and irreproachable before
him— [23]provided that you continue securely
established and steadfast in the faith, without shifting from the hope promised by the
gospel that you heard, which has been
proclaimed to every creature under heaven.
I, Paul, became a servant of this gospel.

Paul's Interest in the Colossians

24 I am now rejoicing in my sufferings
for your sake, and in my flesh I am completing what is lacking in Christ's afflictions
for the sake of his body, that is, the church.
[25]I became its servant according to God's
commission that was given to me for you,
to make the word of God fully known, [26]the
mystery that has been hidden throughout
the ages and generations but has now been
revealed to his saints. [27]To them God chose
to make known how great among the
Gentiles are the riches of the glory of this
mystery, which is Christ in you, the hope
of glory. [28]It is he whom we proclaim,
warning everyone and teaching everyone
in all wisdom, so that we may present
everyone mature in Christ. [29]For this I toil
and struggle with all the energy that he
powerfully inspires within me.

2 For I want you to know how much
I am struggling for you, and for those
in Laodicea, and for all who have not seen
me face to face. [2]I want their hearts to be
encouraged and united in love, so that they
may have all the riches of assured understanding and have the knowledge of God's
mystery, that is, Christ himself,[k] [3]in whom
are hidden all the treasures of wisdom and
knowledge. [4]I am saying this so that no one
may deceive you with plausible arguments.
[5]For though I am absent in body, yet I am
with you in spirit, and I rejoice to see your
morale and the firmness of your faith in
Christ.

Fullness of Life in Christ

6 As you therefore have received Christ
Jesus the Lord, continue to live your lives[l]
in him, [7]rooted and built up in him and
established in the faith, just as you were
taught, abounding in thanksgiving.

8 See to it that no one takes you captive
through philosophy and empty deceit, according to human tradition, according to
the elemental spirits of the universe,[m] and
not according to Christ. [9]For in him the
whole fullness of deity dwells bodily, [10]and

[d] Gk *his* [e] Other ancient authorities read *called* [f] Other ancient authorities read *us* [g] Other ancient authorities add *through his blood* [h] Or *by* [i] Other ancient authorities read *you have now been reconciled* [j] Gk *in the body of his flesh* [k] Other ancient authorities read *of the mystery of God, both of the Father and of Christ* [l] Gk *to walk* [m] Or *the rudiments of the world*

1.10 *cf.* Eph 4.1; Phil 1.17; 1 Thess 2.12.
1.11 This verse underscores God's power, which enables Christians to *"endure...with patience."* Coupled with Paul's references to sufferings and struggle in 1.24-2.5, the Colossians are being asked to endure in the face of an ominous false teaching which threatens them (see 2.8-23).
1.12-13 The light-darkness imagery expresses the same thought as that in Eph 1.13-14.
1.12 *Inheritance. Cf.* Eph 1.11.
1.15-20 This section comprises a hymn about the person and work of Christ; several New Testament authors incorporate such Christological hymns into their writings (see Phil 2.6-11; Eph 2.14-16; 1 Pet 3.18-19.22; Jn 1.1-18; Heb 1.3; 1 Tim 3.16). The hymn here given speaks of Christ's nature and existence (vs. 15), his participation in the creation and his sustaining of the universe (vv. 16-17), his ongoing relationship to the church through his resurrection (vs. 18), and his cross as the means by which God has brought reconciliation to the world (vv. 19-20).
1.15 *The image of the invisible God.* This lofty poetic terminology expresses the idea that in Christ the nature and being of God have been perfectly revealed; *cf.* 2 Cor 4.4; Jn 1.18; 14.9; Heb 1.3. *The firstborn of all creation; cf.* Ps 89.27; Prov 8.22-31; 2 Cor 8.9; Phil 2.6-7; Heb 1.2; 10.5-9; Rev 1.17; 2.8; 22.13,16.
1.16 *All things...were created; cf.* Jn 1.3; 1 Cor 8.6; Heb 1.2. *Whether thrones or dominions or rulers or powers.* These terms, developed in Jewish thought, refer to categories of lesser supernatural beings present in the creation; see similar lists in 2.10,15; Rom 8.38; 1 Cor 15.24; Eph 1.21; 3.10; 6.12; 1 Pet 3.22.
1.17 *cf.* Jn 1.1.
1.18 *Head of the body. Cf.* Eph 1.22-23. *The beginning.* This has the sense of "source": Christ is the source of the church's life. See note on 1 Cor 11.3. *Firstborn from the dead.* Christ's resurrection is the first of a succession of others; *cf.* Rev 1.5, also Eph 5.14.
1.19 *Fullness of God.* In this context, as seen from 1.20, the term "fullness of God" refers to the full power of divine grace which offers full reconciliation through Christ's cross; *cf.* 2.10; Jn 1.16.
1.21 *cf.* 2.1.
1.22 *cf.* Eph 1.4.
1.24 Elsewhere Paul connects his sufferings to his role as an apostle (see Rom 8.30-31; 1 Cor 4.9-13; 2 Cor 11.23-33; 12.9-10; 13.4; Gal 6.17), but only here are his sufferings for the sake of the church. Elsewhere Paul speaks of his sufferings as a participation in the death of Jesus (see 2 Cor 1.4-6; 4.8-10), but only here do his sufferings complete *what is lacking in Christ's afflictions.*
1.25 *Servant.* Literally, minister; *cf.* 1 Cor 3.5; 4.1.
1.26-28 A common theme developed in the literature of Paul's students is that the mystery hidden for long ages is now revealed to the nations by the command of God; *cf.* Rom 16.25-26; Eph 3.3-10; 1 Tim 3.16; 2 Tim 1.9; Titus 1.2-3; 1 Pet 1.20.
1.26 *Mystery.* This is the content of the *word of God* (vs. 25) that was given Paul to proclaim; but see 2.2.
1.27 *cf.* Rom 1.5; 16.26.
1.28 *cf.* 1 Cor 2.6.
2.1 *Laodicea.* A town about 12 miles west of Colossae; *cf.* 4.13; 15-16; Rev 3.14-22. *Who have not seen me face to face.* Evidently Paul had not visited either Laodicea or Colossae; *cf.* 2.5; Rom 15.20; Gal 1.22.
2.8 In this verse the negative influences opposing Christ are listed. *Philosophy.* Occurring only here in the New Testament, this word includes false religious teaching, ingredients of which are listed in the verses following: a spiritualistic flight from worldly things (2.18), abstinence from certain foods (2.16), the worship of angelic beings (2.18), claims based on visionary experiences (2.18), and other ascetic regulations (2.21). *Empty deceit. Cf.* Eph 4.22; 2 Thess 2.10; Heb 3.13; 2 Pet 2.13. *Human tradition. Cf.* Mt 15.2,3,6; Mk 7.3,5,8,9,13; Gal 1.14; 1 Pet 1.18. *Elemental spirits of the universe.* I.e. those created things which claim divine authority over human beings, many of which are listed in this and the following verses; see note on Gal 4.3.
2.9-10 In the person of Christ, crucified, resurrected, and exalted (1.19-20), the fullness of God's power resides. Within the church, which is Christ's body (1.18), Christians have access to the fullness of God's power, since all other powers are subject to him. Christians are to hold fast to their head, i.e. Christ (2.19), in contrast to all other powers and authorities which claim power over them.

1.9 Eph 1.15-17; Rom 12.2
1.10 Eph 4.1; 1 Thess 4.1; Rom 1.13
1.11 Eph 3.16; 4.2; Acts 5.41
1.13 Eph 6.12; 2 Pet 1.11
1.15 2 Cor 4.4; Rev 3.14
1.18 Eph 1.22,23; Rev 1.5
1.20 2 Cor 5.18; Eph 2.13,14
1.22 Rom 7.4; Eph 2.15; 5.27
1.23 Eph 3.17; Rom 10.18
1.25 Eph 3.2
1.26 Rom 16.25,26
1.27 2 Cor 2.14; Rom 9.23; 1 Tim 1.1
1.28 Col 3.16; 1 Cor 2.6,7
1.29 1 Cor 15.10; Col 2.1; Eph 1.19
2.2 Phil 3.8
2.3 Isa 45.3; Rom 11.33
2.5 1 Thess 2.17; 1 Cor 14.40; 1 Pet 5.9
2.7 Eph 2.21
2.8 1 Cor 8.9; 1 Tim 6.20; Gal 4.3
2.10 Eph 1.21,22

2.11 Rom 2.29; Phil 3.3; Rom 6.6; Gal 5.24
2.12 Rom 6.4,5; Acts 2.24
2.13 Eph 2.1
2.15 Gen 3.15; Isa 53.12; Eph 6.12
2.16 Rom 14.3,5,17; Gal 4.10,11
2.19 Eph 1.22; 4.16
2.20 Rom 6.3,5; Gal 4.3,9
2.22 1 Cor 6.13; Isa 29.13; Titus 1.14
3.1 Ps 110.1; Rom 8.34
3.3 Rom 6.2; 2 Cor 5.14
3.4 1 Jn 3.2; Jn 14.6
3.5 Rom 6.13; Eph 5.3,5
3.6 Rom 1.18; Eph 5.6
3.8 Eph 4.22,29
3.10 Rom 12.2; Eph 4.23; 2.10
3.11 Gal 3.28; Eph 1.23
3.12 Gal 5.22,23; Phil 2.3; 2 Cor 6.6
3.15 Phil 4.7; 1 Cor 7.15; Eph 4.4
3.16 Eph 5.19
3.17 1 Cor 10.31; Eph 5.20

you have come to fullness in him, who is the head of every ruler and authority. 11In him also you were circumcised with a spiritual circumcision,[n] by putting off the body of the flesh in the circumcision of Christ; 12when you were buried with him in baptism, you were also raised with him through faith in the power of God, who raised him from the dead. 13And when you were dead in trespasses and the uncircumcision of your flesh, God[o] made you[p] alive together with him, when he forgave us all our trespasses, 14erasing the record that stood against us with its legal demands. He set this aside, nailing it to the cross. 15He disarmed[q] the rulers and authorities and made a public example of them, triumphing over them in it.

16 Therefore do not let anyone condemn you in matters of food and drink or of observing festivals, new moons, or sabbaths. 17These are only a shadow of what is to come, but the substance belongs to Christ. 18Do not let anyone disqualify you, insisting on self-abasement and worship of angels, dwelling[r] on visions,[s] puffed up without cause by a human way of thinking,[t] 19and not holding fast to the head, from whom the whole body, nourished and held together by its ligaments and sinews, grows with a growth that is from God.

Warnings against False Teachers

20 If with Christ you died to the elemental spirits of the universe,[u] why do you live as if you still belonged to the world? Why do you submit to regulations, 21"Do not handle, Do not taste, Do not touch"? 22All these regulations refer to things that perish with use; they are simply human commands and teachings. 23These have indeed an appearance of wisdom in promoting self-imposed piety, humility, and severe treatment of the body, but they are of no value in checking self-indulgence.[v]

The New Life in Christ

3 So if you have been raised with Christ, seek the things that are above, where Christ is, seated at the right hand of God. 2Set your minds on things that are above, not on things that are on earth, 3for you have died, and your life is hidden with Christ in God. 4When Christ who is your[w] life is revealed, then you also will be revealed with him in glory.

5 Put to death, therefore, whatever in you is earthly: fornication, impurity, passion, evil desire, and greed (which is idolatry). 6On account of these the wrath of God is coming on those who are disobedient.[x] 7These are the ways you also once followed, when you were living that life.[y] 8But now you must get rid of all such things—anger, wrath, malice, slander, and abusive[z] language from your mouth. 9Do not lie to one another, seeing that you have stripped off the old self with its practices 10and have clothed yourselves with the new self, which is being renewed in knowledge according to the image of its creator. 11In that renewal[a] there is no longer Greek and Jew, circumcised and uncircumcised, barbarian, Scythian, slave and free; but Christ is all and in all!

12 As God's chosen ones, holy and beloved, clothe yourselves with compassion, kindness, humility, meekness, and patience. 13Bear with one another and, if anyone has a complaint against another, forgive each other; just as the Lord[b] has forgiven you, so you also must forgive. 14Above all, clothe yourselves with love, which binds everything together in perfect harmony. 15And let the peace of Christ rule in your hearts, to which indeed you were called in the one body. And be thankful. 16Let the word of Christ[c] dwell in you richly; teach and admonish one another in all wisdom; and with gratitude in your hearts sing psalms, hymns, and spiritual songs to God.[d] 17And whatever you do, in word or deed, do

[n] Gk *a circumcision made without hands* [o] Gk *he* [p] Other ancient authorities read *made us*; others, *made* [q] Or *divested himself of* [r] Other ancient authorities read *not dwelling* [s] Meaning of Gk uncertain [t] Gk *by the mind of his flesh* [u] Or *the rudiments of the world* [v] Or *are of no value, serving only to indulge the flesh* [w] Other authorities read *our* [x] Other ancient authorities lack *on those who are disobedient* (Gk *the children of disobedience*) [y] Or *living among such people* [z] Or *filthy* [a] Gk *its creator,* [11]*where* [b] Other ancient authorities read *just as Christ* [c] Other ancient authorities read *of God,* or *of the Lord* [d] Other ancient authorities read *to the Lord*

2.11-12 While these verses reflect the language of Rom 6.3-11, they go one step further in naming baptism the Christian circumcision; Rom 6.5 also speaks of resurrection as a future event. *Cf.* Eph 5.14.
2.13 *cf.* Rom 6.11; Eph 2.1.
2.14-15 By his cross Christ has rendered powerless all those created things which claim divine authority over us.

2.16 *Festivals, new moons, or sabbaths.* These are religious observances; *cf.* Gal 4.10; also 1 Chr 23.31; 2 Chr 31.3; Ezek 45.17; Hos 2.11.
2.17 *Shadow.* I.e. not real; *cf.* Heb 8.5; 10.1. *Substance.* Literally, "body" (Greek: *soma*); see 2.19,22.
2.18 See note on 2.8.
2.19 *The head.* I.e. Christ. *Grows.* The church of Christ is marked by constant spiritual growth; *cf.* Eph 2.21.
2.20 *You died.* I.e. in baptism; *cf.* 2.12; Rom 6.4.
3.1 *Raised with Christ.* I.e. in baptism; *cf.* 2.12; Eph 5.14.
3.3 *Hidden.* The close fellowship which exists between Christians and their Lord is not yet fully revealed, but will be only when Christ's glory is fully revealed at the end of time (see 3.4); *cf.* also 1 Cor 1.8-9.
3.4 *cf.* 1 Thess 4.16-17; Mk 13.24-27.
3.5-17 A section of pastoral admonition and encouragement which includes two sets of vices (vv. 5 and 8) and one set of virtues (vs. 12). For similar lists of vices see 1 Cor 5.10-11; 6.9-10; Gal 5.19-21; Eph 5.1-5; 1 Pet 2.1; 4.1-3.
3.5 *Fornication.* The Greek word (*porneia*) is used to refer to all forms of sexual immorality; *cf.* Rom 1.24; 2 Cor 12.21; Gal 5.19; Eph 5.3; 1 Thess 4.7. *Impurity.* In this context sexual impurity is meant. *Passion.* I.e. lust. *Evil desire.* I.e. self-centered covetousness, which is the basis of all sins; see note on Rom 7.7. *Greed (which is idolatry).* The two are connected in Eph 5.5; *cf.* Mt 6.24.
3.6 *cf.* Rom 1.18-32.
3.7 *cf.* Eph 2.1-2.
3.8 *Anger. Cf.* Ps 4.4 (see footnote); Eph 4.26. *Abusive language. Cf.* Eph 5.4; Jas 3.5-12.
3.9-10 *cf.* 2 Cor 5.17; also 1 Cor 15.45-49.
3.11 *cf.* Gal 3.28.
3.12 In contrast to the catalog of vices given in vv. 5 + 8, a catalog of virtues is presented; *cf.* Gal 5.22-23; 1 Tim 6.11; 2 Pet 1.5-7. *Compassion.* Sympathy for the needs of others; *cf.* Mk 8.2. *Kindness. Cf.* 2 Cor 6.6; Gal 5.22; Eph 2.7. *Humility. Cf.* 2.18,23; Phil 2.3. *Meekness.* The word has the sense of gentleness, considerateness toward others; *cf.* Gal 6.1; 2 Tim 2.25. *Patience. Cf.* 2 Cor 6.6; Gal 5.22; Eph 4.2; 2 Tim 3.10; 4.2.
3.13 *cf.* 2 Cor 11.19; Gal 6.6; Rom 9.19; 15.7; Heb 8.8; Mt 6.14-15; Eph 4.32.
3.14 *Love.* The primary Christian virtue, born out of God's love; Rom 13.8-10; 1 Cor 12.31-13.13; 1 Jn 4.19.
3.15 *Peace of Christ. Cf.* Jn 14.27; Eph 2.14; 2 Thess 3.16.
3.17 *cf.* 1 Cor 10.31.

everything in the name of the Lord Jesus,
giving thanks to God the Father through
him.

Rules for Christian Households

18 Wives, be subject to your husbands,
as is fitting in the Lord. [19]Husbands, love
your wives and never treat them harshly.
20 Children, obey your parents in everything, for this is your acceptable duty in the
Lord. [21]Fathers, do not provoke your children, or they may lose heart. [22]Slaves, obey
your earthly masters[e] in everything, not
only while being watched and in order to
please them, but wholeheartedly, fearing
the Lord.[e] [23]Whatever your task, put yourselves into it, as done for the Lord and not
for your masters,[f] [24]since you know that
from the Lord you will receive the inheritance as your reward; you serve[g] the Lord
Christ. [25]For the wrongdoer will be paid
back for whatever wrong has been done,
and there is no partiality.

4 Masters, treat your slaves justly and
fairly, for you know that you also
have a Master in heaven.

Further Instructions

2 Devote yourselves to prayer, keeping
alert in it with thanksgiving. [3]At the same
time pray for us as well that God will open
to us a door for the word, that we may
declare the mystery of Christ, for which I
am in prison, [4]so that I may reveal it
clearly, as I should.
5 Conduct yourselves wisely toward outsiders, making the most of the time.[h] [6]Let
your speech always be gracious, seasoned
with salt, so that you may know how you
ought to answer everyone.
7 Tychicus will tell you all the news
about me; he is a beloved brother, a faithful
minister, and a fellow servant[i] in the Lord.
[8]I have sent him to you for this very purpose, so that you may know how we are[j]
and that he may encourage your hearts;
[9]he is coming with Onesimus, the faithful
and beloved brother, who is one of you.
They will tell you about everything here.
10 Aristarchus my fellow prisoner greets
you, as does Mark the cousin of Barnabas,
concerning whom you have received instructions—if he comes to you, welcome
him. [11]And Jesus who is called Justus greets
you. These are the only ones of the circumcision among my co-workers for the kingdom of God, and they have been a comfort
to me. [12]Epaphras, who is one of you, a
servant[i] of Christ Jesus, greets you. He is
always wrestling in his prayers on your
behalf, so that you may stand mature and
fully assured in everything that God wills.
[13]For I testify for him that he has worked
hard for you and for those in Laodicea and
in Hierapolis. [14]Luke, the beloved physician,
and Demas greet you. [15]Give my greetings
to the brothers and sisters[k] in Laodicea, and
to Nympha and the church in her house.
[16]And when this letter has been read among
you, have it read also in the church of the
Laodiceans; and see that you read also the
letter from Laodicea. [17]And say to Archippus,
"See that you complete the task that you
have received in the Lord."

18 I, Paul, write this greeting with my
own hand. Remember my chains. Grace be
with you.[l]

[e] In Greek the same word is used for *master* and *Lord* [f] Gk *not for men* [g] Or *you are slaves of*, or *be slaves of* [h] Or *opportunity* [i] Gk *slave* [j] Other authorities read *that I may know how you are* [k] Gk *brothers* [l] Other ancient authorities add *Amen*

3.18-4.1 This section is known as a "household code," a formal admonition listing the categories of the average middle-class Hellenistic household: wives/husbands, children/parents, slaves/masters. A closely similar household code is given in Eph 5.21-6.9, and a partial one in 1 Pet 3.1-9; see also 1 Tim 2.8-15; 6.1-2; Titus 2.1-10. Such household codes were already present in pre-Christian Hellenistic culture, and were taught in order to promote obedience to the head of the household, namely the husband-father-master. In the Christian adaptation of the code, each member of the household is subject first and foremost to the Lord Christ. Such codes also give support to the concept of marriage and family, a concept which some in the early church were questioning (see 1 Cor 7).
3.18 This verse acknowledges the husband's leadership role in the Christian marriage and family, as was common in first-century Jewish and Hellenistic culture.
3.19 *cf.* Eph 5.25.
3.20 *cf.* Ex 20.12; Deut 5.16; Eph 6.1-3.
3.21 *Lose heart.* I.e. become discouraged and cease trying; *cf.* Eph 6.4.
3.22 *cf.* Eph 6.6.
3.24 *cf.* Eph 6.8.
3.25 *cf.* Eph 6.9.
4.1 *cf.* Eph 6.9. *Masters*, as heads of their households, are subject to the same authority, namely *the Master in heaven*, as everyone else in the household. This would be the specific Christian contribution to the typical Hellenistic moral instruction within these household codes.
4.2 *cf.* Eph 6.18.
4.3 *Mystery of Christ.* This has now become virtually a technical term for the message of the Gospel; *cf.* 1.26-27; 2.2.
4.3 *In prison.* This is the first mention in this letter of Paul's being in prison; *cf.* 1.24; 2.1; also Phil 1.13; Philem 1; 1 Cor 15.32.
4.4 *cf.* 1.26.
4.5 *Outsiders.* I.e. non-Christians; *cf.* 1 Thess 4.12; 1 Cor 5.12-13; 1 Pet 2.7-8; Titus 2.7-8; 3.1-2.
4.7-8 *Tychicus* is perhaps the bearer of this letter (see note on Eph 6.21); according to Acts 20.4 he is from the province of Asia, and elsewhere he is named as a fellow-traveler with Paul (see 2 Tim 4.12; Titus 3.12). *Fellow-servant.* The same designation as for Epaphras in 1.7.
4.9 *Onesimus.* The name of the runaway slave on whose behalf Paul wrote his letter to Philemon.
4.10 *Aristarchus.* Among the names listed in Philem 24, an Aristarchus is also mentioned in Acts 19.29 and again in Acts 20.4 as one of Paul's travel companions. *Mark. Cf.* Acts 12.12,25; 13.5,13; 15.57,39; 2 Tim 4.11; 1 Pet 5.13. Only here do we learn Mark's relationship to *Barnabas*, Paul's travel companion on the first missionary journey in Acts 13.3-15.35; they parted company over traveling with "John called Mark" (Acts 15.36-41; see also Gal 2.13).
4.11 *Jesus who is called Justus.* A name mentioned nowhere else in the New Testament.
4.12 *Epaphras.* See note on 1.7.
4.13 *Laodicea.* See note on 2.1. *Hierapolis.* A sister-city of Laodicea, six miles away in the upper Lycus valley; it is mentioned only here in the New Testament.
4.14 *Luke.* Also mentioned in Philem 24 and 2 Tim 4.11, only here is Luke identified as a physician; in Christian tradition it is the name traditionally associated with the third New Testament Gospel and the Acts of the Apostles. *Demas.* The name is mentioned in Philem 24 and 2 Tim 4.10, in the latter case with comment critical of him.
4.15 *Nympha and the church in her house.* The author knows of a house-church led by a woman named Nympha; see references to other house-churches in Rom 16.5; 1 Cor 16.19; Philem 2; *cf.* also 1 Cor 1.11. On the leadership of women in the Pauline churches, see notes on Rom 16.1-2,3-16; Phil 4.2-3.
4.16 This is the first indication that the letters of Paul were being read in the assemblies of the churches. *The letter from Laodicea.* I.e. the letter of Paul to Laodicea, now lost, was to have been passed on to the Colossians, as the letter to the Colossians was to have been passed on to the Laodiceans.
4.17 *Archippus.* Mentioned in Philem 2 as one of the recipients of that letter.
4.18 *cf.* 1 Cor 16.21; Gal 6.11; 2 Thess 3.17.

3.18 Eph 5.22-6.9
3.20 Eph 6.1
3.22 Eph 6.5,6; Philem 16
3.24 Eph 6.28; 1 Cor 7.22
3.25 Eph 6.8,9; Acts 10.34
4.2 Rom 12.12; Eph 6.18; Phil 2.7
4.3 Eph 6.19; 1 Cor 16.9; Eph 6.20
4.5 Eph 5.15,16
4.6 Eph 4.29; Mk 9.50; 1 Pet 3.15
4.7 Eph 6.21,22
4.9 Philem 10
4.10 Acts 19.29; 15.37; 4.36
4.12 Col 1.7; Rom 15.30; Phil 3.15
4.14 2 Tim 4.10,11; Philem 24
4.15 Rom 16.5
4.17 Philem 2; 2 Tim 4.5
4.18 1 Cor 16.21; Heb 13.3; 13.25

THE FIRST LETTER OF PAUL TO THE

THESSALONIANS

Salutation

1 Paul, Silvanus, and Timothy,
To the church of the Thessalonians in
God the Father and the Lord Jesus Christ:
Grace to you and peace.

The Thessalonians' Faith and Example

2 We always give thanks to God for all
of you and mention you in our prayers,
constantly [3]remembering before our God
and Father your work of faith and labor of
love and steadfastness of hope in our Lord
Jesus Christ. [4]For we know, brothers and
sisters[a] beloved by God, that he has chosen
you, [5]because our message of the gospel
came to you not in word only, but also in
power and in the Holy Spirit and with full
conviction; just as you know what kind of
persons we proved to be among you for
your sake. [6]And you became imitators of us
and of the Lord, for in spite of persecution
you received the word with joy inspired by
the Holy Spirit, [7]so that you became an
example to all the believers in Macedonia
and in Achaia. [8]For the word of the Lord
has sounded forth from you not only in
Macedonia and Achaia, but in every place
your faith in God has become known, so
that we have no need to speak about it. [9]For
the people of those regions[b] report about us
what kind of welcome we had among you,
and how you turned to God from idols, to
serve a living and true God, [10]and to wait
for his Son from heaven, whom he raised
from the dead—Jesus, who rescues us from
the wrath that is coming.

Paul's Ministry in Thessalonica

2 You yourselves know, brothers and
sisters,[a] that our coming to you was
not in vain, [2]but though we had already
suffered and been shamefully mistreated at
Philippi, as you know, we had courage in
our God to declare to you the gospel of God
in spite of great opposition. [3]For our appeal
does not spring from deceit or impure motives
or trickery, [4]but just as we have been approved by God to be entrusted with the
message of the gospel, even so we speak,
not to please mortals, but to please God who
tests our hearts. [5]As you know and as God
is our witness, we never came with words
of flattery or with a pretext for greed; [6]nor
did we seek praise from mortals, whether
from you or from others, [7]though we might
have made demands as apostles of Christ.
But we were gentle[c] among you, like a
nurse tenderly caring for her own children.
[8]So deeply do we care for you that we are
determined to share with you not only the
gospel of God but also our own selves,
because you have become very dear to us.
9 You remember our labor and toil, brothers and sisters;[a] we worked night and day,
so that we might not burden any of you
while we proclaimed to you the gospel of
God. [10]You are witnesses, and God also,
how pure, upright, and blameless our conduct was toward you believers. [11]As you
know, we dealt with each one of you like
a father with his children, [12]urging and
encouraging you and pleading that you
lead a life worthy of God, who calls you into
his own kingdom and glory.
13 We also constantly give thanks to
God for this, that when you received the
word of God that you heard from us, you
accepted it not as a human word but as
what it really is, God's word, which is also
at work in you believers. [14]For you, brothers
and sisters,[a] became imitators of the churches
of God in Christ Jesus that are in Judea, for
you suffered the same things from your
own compatriots as they did from the Jews,
[15]who killed both the Lord Jesus and the
prophets,[d] and drove us out; they displease
God and oppose everyone [16]by hindering us
from speaking to the Gentiles so that they
may be saved. Thus they have constantly
been filling up the measure of their sins; but
God's wrath has overtaken them at last.[e]

[a] Gk *brothers* [b] Gk *For they* [c] Other ancient authorities read *infants* [d] Other ancient authorities read *their own prophets* [e] Or *completely* or *forever*

1.2 2 Thess 1.3; Rom 1.8,9
1.5 2 Thess 2.14; Col 2.2; 2 Thess 3.7
1.6 1 Cor 4.16; 11.1; Acts 17.5-10; 13.52
1.8 Rom 10.18; 1.8; 2 Thess 1.4
1.9 1 Cor 12.2; Gal 4.8
1.10 2 Pet 3.12; Acts 2.24; Rom 5.9
2.2 Acts 16.22; 1 Thess 1.5; Phil 1.30
2.4 2 Cor 2.17; Gal 2.7; 1.10
2.5 Acts 20.33; Rom 1.9
2.6 2 Cor 4.5; 1 Cor 9.1,2
2.9 Acts 20.34; 2 Thess 3.8; 2 Cor 12.13
2.10 1 Thess 1.5; 2 Cor 1.12
2.12 Eph 4.1; 1 Pet 5.10
2.13 1 Thess 1.2; Gal 4.14
2.14 Acts 17.5; 2 Thess 1.4
2.15 Acts 2.23; 7.52
2.16 Acts 9.23; 13.45,50ff; Mt 23.32

See the Introductions, pp. 8–9 and 89–90 above.

1.1 This salutation comprises the normal introduction to the Greek letter in general and the Pauline letters in particular; see notes on 1 & 2 Cor, Gal, Eph, Phil, Col; 2 Thess, Philem, 1 & 2 Tim and Titus. For comments on the structure of the Pauline letter see note on Rom 1.1. *Paul.* The Greek letter is structured so that the author's name is given first, along with those with him who are participating in the writing of the letter, followed by the names of the addressees and a word of greeting. *Silvanus.* It is generally thought that Silvanus is the Silas of Acts, who worked with Paul and Timothy in the evangelization of Thessalonica (Acts 17.1-9) as well as Corinth (Acts 18.5; see also 1 Cor 1.19). It is less clear that he is the same Silvanus mentioned in 1 Peter 5.12. Both Silvanus and Timothy are named in the salutation of 2 Thess. *Timothy* A co-worker upon whom Paul relied heavily at times; see 3.2; 1 Cor 4.17; 16.10; Phil 2.19-22. See note on 1 Tim 1.2. *Thessalonians.* The city of Thessalonica was founded in 315 BCE, and in 167 BCE became capital of one of the districts of the Roman province of Macedonia. Acts 17.1-13 reports a positive response there to Paul's message from both Jews and Gentiles, but also that his preaching and its response eventually resulted in hostilities against the apostle; see also Acts 20.4; 27.2; Phil 4.16; 2 Tim 4.10. *Grace to you and peace.* An initial greeting found in every one of the Pauline letters, as well as in other New Testament letters; *cf.* Rom 1.7; 1 Cor 1.3; 2 Cor 1.2; Gal 1.3; Eph 1.2; Phil 1.2; Col 1.2; 2 Thess 1.2; 1 Tim 1.2; 2 Tim 1.2; Titus 1.4; Philem 3; see also 1 Pet 1.2; 2 Pet 2.2; 2 Jn 3; Jude 1.2; Rev 1.4.
1.2-10 This section comprises the thanksgiving, a section found in all Paul's letters except Galatians; see note on Rom 1.1.
1.3 *...faith...love...hope.* This triad is mentioned in 5.8; Rom 5.1-5; 1 Cor 13.13; Gal 5.5-6; Col 1.4-5; Heb 10.22-24; 1 Pet 1.21-22. *Work of faith and labor of love. Cf.* Gal 5.6. *Steadfastness of hope. Cf.* Rom 5.5.
1.4 *We know.* Paul has received news about the Thessalonian church from Timothy, who has just returned to Paul from Thessalonica (see 3.6). *Chosen. Cf.* Eph 1.4.
1.5 *cf.* 1 Cor 2.4; 2 Cor 12.12. *You know what kind of persons we proved to be.* This is amplified in 2.1-12.
1.6 *Imitators.* See notes on 1 Cor 11.1; Gal 4.12; Phil 3.17; 4.9. *Persecution. Cf.* 2.14; Acts 17.1-9; 2 Thess 2.4.
1.7 *cf.* 2 Cor 8.1-2. *Macedonia.* A territory in the northeastern part of the Greek peninsula which included both Thessalonica and Philippi. *Achaia.* The southern half of the Greek peninsula whose capital city is Corinth; see note on Rom 15.26.
1.9 *You turned to God from idols.* Paul has Gentile readers in mind; *cf.* Acts 14.15.
1.10 *cf.* 2.19; 3.13; 4.13-18; 5.1-11; Rom 2.5,16; 8.23; 1 Cor 1.7; Phil 3.20; Gal 5.5.
2.1 *Not in vain. Cf.* 3.5; 1 Cor 15.10,14; Gal 2.2; 4.11; Phil 2.16; also 1 Cor 15.14,58; 2 Cor 6.1.
2.2 See Acts 16.11-17.15.
2.3 *Our appeal. Cf.* 2 Cor 5.20. *Deceit or impure motives or trickery. Cf.* 2 Cor 2.17; 4.2, 10.12; 11.12-13,20.
2.4 *Not to please mortals. Cf.* Gal 1.10.
2.5 *cf.* 2 Cor 2.1-5; 11.7.
2.6 *cf.* 3.7-9; 1 Cor 9.3-18; 2 Cor 11.7-11.
2.7 *Cf.* Gal 4.19.
2.9 *Our labor and toil.* According to Acts 18.3, Paul worked as a tentmaker in order to provide for himself without burdening his churches for material support; *cf.* also 1 Cor 4.12 and Acts 19.12; 20.34.
2.11 *cf.* 1 Cor 4.15; Philem 10.
2.12 *cf.* Rom 16.2; Phil 1.27; Eph 4.1; Col 1.10.
2.13 *cf.* Gal 1.11-12.
2.14 *Churches of God in Christ Jesus that are in Judea. Cf.* Gal 1.22; 1 Cor 15.9. *You suffered...from your compatriots.* While Acts 17.5 reports action from Jewish opponents in Thessalonica, this verse indicates that opposition came also from Gentiles.

Paul's Desire to Visit the Thessalonians Again

17 As for us, brothers and sisters,[f] when, for a short time, we were made orphans by being separated from you—in person, not in heart—we longed with great eagerness to see you face to face. [18]For we wanted to come to you—certainly I, Paul, wanted to again and again—but Satan blocked our way. [19]For what is our hope or joy or crown of boasting before our Lord Jesus at his coming? Is it not you? [20]Yes, you are our glory and joy!

3 Therefore when we could bear it no longer, we decided to be left alone in Athens; [2]and we sent Timothy, our brother and co-worker for God in proclaiming[g] the gospel of Christ, to strengthen and encourage you for the sake of your faith, [3]so that no one would be shaken by these persecutions. Indeed, you yourselves know that this is what we are destined for. [4]In fact, when we were with you, we told you beforehand that we were to suffer persecution; so it turned out, as you know. [5]For this reason, when I could bear it no longer, I sent to find out about your faith; I was afraid that somehow the tempter had tempted you and that our labor had been in vain.

Timothy's Encouraging Report

6 But Timothy has just now come to us from you, and has brought us the good news of your faith and love. He has told us also that you always remember us kindly and long to see us—just as we long to see you. [7]For this reason, brothers and sisters,[f] during all our distress and persecution we have been encouraged about you through your faith. [8]For we now live, if you continue to stand firm in the Lord. [9]How can we thank God enough for you in return for all the joy that we feel before our God because of you? [10]Night and day we pray most earnestly that we may see you face to face and restore whatever is lacking in your faith.

11 Now may our God and Father himself and our Lord Jesus direct our way to you. [12]And may the Lord make you increase and abound in love for one another and for all, just as we abound in love for you. [13]And may he so strengthen your hearts in holiness that you may be blameless before our God and Father at the coming of our Lord Jesus with all his saints.

A Life Pleasing to God

4 Finally, brothers and sisters,[f] we ask and urge you in the Lord Jesus that, as you learned from us how you ought to live and to please God (as, in fact, you are doing), you should do so more and more. [2]For you know what instructions we gave you through the Lord Jesus. [3]For this is the will of God, your sanctification: that you abstain from fornication; [4]that each one of you know how to control your own body[h] in holiness and honor, [5]not with lustful passion, like the Gentiles who do not know God; [6]that no one wrong or exploit a brother or sister[i] in this matter, because the Lord is an avenger in all these things, just as we have already told you beforehand and solemnly warned you. [7]For God did not call us to impurity but in holiness. [8]Therefore whoever rejects this rejects not human authority but God, who also gives his Holy Spirit to you.

9 Now concerning love of the brothers and sisters,[f] you do not need to have anyone write to you, for you yourselves have been taught by God to love one another; [10]and indeed you do love all the brothers and sisters[f] throughout Macedonia. But we urge you, beloved,[f] to do so more and more, [11]to aspire to live quietly, to mind your own affairs, and to work with your hands, as we directed you, [12]so that you may behave properly toward outsiders and be dependent on no one.

The Coming of the Lord

13 But we do not want you to be uninformed, brothers and sisters,[f] about those who have died,[j] so that you may not grieve as others do who have no hope. [14]For since we believe that Jesus died and rose again, even so, through Jesus, God will bring with him those who have died.[j] [15]For this we declare to you by the word of the Lord, that we who are alive, who are left until the coming of the Lord, will by no means precede those who have died.[j] [16]For the Lord himself, with a cry of command, with the archangel's call and with the sound of God's trumpet, will descend from heaven, and the

[f] Gk *brothers* [g] Gk lacks *proclaiming* [h] Or *how to take a wife for himself* [i] Gk *brother* [j] Gk *fallen asleep*

2.16 *God's wrath has overtaken them at last.* This phrase may refer to a specific incident, such as the expulsion of Jews from Rome (see Acts 18.2) in 49 CE.

2.18 *Satan.* See note on Mt 4.10; *cf.* 1 Cor 5.5.
2.19 *cf.* 1 Cor 9.2; 2 Cor 9.2; Phil 4.1.
3.1 *Athens.* See Acts 17.16-34.
3.2 *Timothy.* See note on 1.1.
3.3 *Persecutions.* See notes on 1.1,6; 2.2; 2.14.
3.4 *cf.* Rom 8.17; Phil 1.29.
3.5 *The tempter.* I.e. Satan; see 1.18; 2 Cor 2.11.
3.13 See 4.13-17.
4.1 *As you learned from us.* This is Paul's reference to his founding of the Thessalonian church; *cf.* Acts 17.1-9.
4.2 *Through the Lord Jesus.* Apostolic tradition is grounded in the authority of Christ: 4.15; 1 Cor 11.17; 2 Cor 13.3; Mt 28.20.
4.3 *Sanctification.* Here the Greek word refers to the process of becoming holy, i.e. of becoming set apart distinctly for God's purposes in the world. One result of this process is outlined in what follows. *Abstain from fornication; cf.* Acts 15.20,29; 21.25; 1 Cor 5.1; Gal 5.19; Eph 5.3; Col 3.5. The Greek word for "fornication" refers to any kind of illicit sexual activity. In Thessalonica certain pagan religions practised ritual fornication.
4.4 *Your own body.* The control over one's own body is what is meant here, in preference to the traditional wording (see footnote *i*).
4.6 *The Lord is an avenger. Cf.* 3.13; 1 Cor 4.5; 2 Thess 1.8; Eph 5.6; Col 3.5,6; Rev 16.15; 22.12.
4.7 *cf.* 3.13; 5.23,24; Rom 1.7; 1 Cor 1.2; 2 Thess 2.13,14; 2 Tim 1.9; 1 Pet 1.2,15; also 1 Cor 7.15; Gal 5.13; Eph 2.10; 2 Tim 2.14.
4.9 *Love of the brothers and sister. Cf.* Rom 12.10; Heb 13.1; 1 Pet 1.22; 2 Pet 1.7.
4.11 *To live quietly.* A probable reference to the agitation which some have brought to the discussion about the end of the world (see 4.18; 5.11; *cf.* 2 Thess 2.2). *Work with your own hands. Cf.* 2.9; 2 Thess 3.7-10.
4.12 *cf.* Col 4.5; 1 Tim 3.7.
4.13-18 This section addresses the question of the fate of the Christian dead. Perhaps the Thessalonians, believing that Jesus would return during their lifetime (see note on Acts 1.11), expressed their fears to Paul that their loved ones would not be able to participate in the joys of Jesus' return. Paul is not interested in describing here a general resurrection of all people; rather his focus is on the fate of the Christian dead: they have a future (see also 1 Cor 15.12-28).
4.13 *Who have died.* The Greek word is literally "who have fallen asleep" (see note *j*), a reference to the Christian hope of resurrection.
4.14 *Jesus died and rose again.* The basic proclamation about Jesus forms the basis for further theological development.
4.15 *The word of the Lord.* See note on 4.2. *Cf.* also Mk 13.27 (par Mt 24.31); Mt 25.31-46; Lk 14.14; Jn 5.28,29. *We who are alive, who are left until the coming of the Lord.* When Paul writes this letter, he shares the belief that Jesus' return will occur within the lifetime of the first Christian generation. This would indicate an earlier date for the writing of this letter than for Philippians, when Paul must reckon with his death before Jesus' return (see Phil 1.22-23).
4.16 *With a cry of command. Cf.* Mt 25.6; Rev 16.15; 22.12. *With the archangel's call. Cf.* Jude 9. *With the sound of God's trumpet. Cf.* Isa 27.13; Joel 2.1,15; Zech 9.14; 1 Cor 15.52; Mt 24.31; Rev 11.15. *Will descend from heaven. Cf.* Mk 13.26; Lk 17.24. *The dead in Christ. Cf.* 1 Cor 15.18. *Will rise first. Cf.* the resurrection hope as expressed in 1 Cor 15.12-28.

2.17 1 Cor 5.3; 1 Thess 3.10
2.18 Rom 15.22; 1.13
2.19 2 Cor 1.14; Phil 4.1; 1 Thess 3.13
3.1 ver 5; Acts 17.15
3.2 2 Cor 1.1; Col 1.1
3.3 Acts 9.16; 14.22
3.5 1 Cor 11.3; Gal 2.2
3.6 Acts 18.5; 1 Thess 1.3
3.10 2 Tim 1.3; 2 Cor 13.9
3.12 1 Thess 4.1.10
3.13 1 Cor 1.8; 1 Thess 2.19; 4.17
4.1 Phil 1.27; 1 Thess 2.12; Col 1.10
4.3 1 Cor 6.18; Col 3.5
4.6 1 Cor 6.8; Heb 13.4
4.9 Rom 12.10; 1 Thess 5.1
4.11 Eph 4.28; 2 Thess 3.10-12
4.12 Rom 13.12
4.14 1 Cor 15.13,23
4.16 Mt 24.31; 1 Cor 15.23; 2 Thess 2.1

dead in Christ will rise first. [17]Then we who are alive, who are left, will be caught up in the clouds together with them to meet the Lord in the air; and so we will be with the Lord forever. [18]Therefore encourage one another with these words.

5 Now concerning the times and the seasons, brothers and sisters,[k] you do not need to have anything written to you. [2]For you yourselves know very well that the day of the Lord will come like a thief in the night. [3]When they say, "There is peace and security," then sudden destruction will come upon them, as labor pains come upon a pregnant woman, and there will be no escape! [4]But you, beloved,[k] are not in darkness, for that day to surprise you like a thief; [5]for you are all children of light and children of the day; we are not of the night or of darkness. [6]So then let us not fall asleep as others do, but let us keep awake and be sober; [7]for those who sleep sleep at night, and those who are drunk get drunk at night. [8]But since we belong to the day, let us be sober, and put on the breastplate of faith and love, and for a helmet the hope of salvation. [9]For God has destined us not for wrath but for obtaining salvation through our Lord Jesus Christ, [10]who died for us, so that whether we are awake or asleep we may live with him. [11]Therefore encourage one another and build up each other, as indeed you are doing.

Final Exhortations, Greetings, and Benediction

12 But we appeal to you, brothers and sisters,[k] to respect those who labor among you, and have charge of you in the Lord and admonish you; [13]esteem them very highly in love because of their work. Be at peace among yourselves. [14]And we urge you, beloved,[k] to admonish the idlers, encourage the faint hearted, help the weak, be patient with all of them. [15]See that none of you repays evil for evil, but always seek to do good to one another and to all. [16]Rejoice always, [17]pray without ceasing, [18]give thanks in all circumstances; for this is the will of God in Christ Jesus for you. [19]Do not quench the Spirit. [20]Do not despise the words of prophets,[l] [21]but test everything; hold fast to what is good; [22]abstain from every form of evil.

23 May the God of peace himself sanctify you entirely; and may your spirit and soul and body be kept sound[m] and blameless at the coming of our Lord Jesus Christ. [24]The one who calls you is faithful, and he will do this.

25 Beloved,[n] pray for us.

26 Greet all the brothers and sisters[k] with a holy kiss. [27]I solemnly command you by the Lord that this letter be read to all of them.[o]

28 The grace of our Lord Jesus Christ be with you.[p]

[k] Gk *brothers* [l] Gk *despise prophecies* [m] Or *complete* [n] Gk *Brothers* [o] Gk *to all the brothers* [p] Other ancient authorities add *Amen*

4.17 1 Cor 15.52; Jn 12.26
5.1 Acts 1.7; 1 Thess 4.9
5.2 1 Cor 1.8; 2 Pet 3.10
5.3 Hos 13.13
5.4 Acts 26.18; 1 Jn 2.8
5.6 Rom 13.11; 1 Pet 1.13
5.7 Acts 2.15; 2 Pet 2.13
5.8 Eph 6.14,23.17
5.9 2 Thess 2.13,14; Rom 14.9
5.10 2 Cor 5.15
5.12 1 Tim 5.17; Heb 13.17
5.14 2 Thess 3.11; Rom 14.1
5.15 Rom 12.17; 1 Pet 3.9; Gal 6.10
5.21 1 Cor 14.29; 1 Jn 4.1
5.23 Rom 15.33
5.24 1 Cor 1.9
5.25 Eph 6.19
5.27 Col 4.16

4.17 *Then.* As in 1 Cor 15.23, the resurrection is described in terms of a sequence of events. *Will be caught up. Cf.* Acts 8.39; 2 Cor 12.2-3; Rev 12.5. *In the clouds.* Clouds are a regular component of biblical theophanies; *cf.* Ex 19.16; 24.15-18; 40.34; Dan 7.13; Mk 9.7; Acts 1.9; Rev. 1.7; 11.12; 14.14. *With the Lord forever. Cf.* Mt 25.46; 2 Cor 5.8; Phil 1.23.
4.18 The purpose of 4.13-17 is to encourage and comfort Christian believers; *cf.* 5.11.
5.1 *Times and season.* The day(s) when the things mentioned in 4.13-17 will happen; *cf.* Acts 1.7.
5.2 *The day of the Lord.* An Old Testament concept, "the day of the Lord" was the day when God would vindicate his cause and execute judgment (see Am 5.18; Joel 2.31; Mal 4.5). In the New Testament that "day" generally referred to the last day at the end of the world, and Jesus was "the Lord" whose day it was (see Acts 17.31; 1 Cor 1.8; 5.5; 2 Cor 1.14; Phil 1.6,10; 2.16; 2 Thess 2.2; 2 Pet 3.10); an exception is Rev 1.10, where the term "the Lord's day" can refer simply to Sunday, the first day of the week (*cf.* 1 Cor 16.2) and consequently the primary day of the week for Christian worship. *Like a thief in the night. Cf.* Mt 24.43 (par Lk 12.39); 2 Pet 3.10; Rev 3.3; 16.15.
5.3 *Sudden destruction. Cf.* Lk 21.34-36. *As labor pains come upon a pregnant woman. Cf.* Isa 13.8; 21.3; 37.3; Jer 6.24; Mk 13.8.
5.4 *cf.* Rom 13.12.
5.5 *Children of light and children of the day. Cf.* Jn 12.36; Eph 5.8; 1 Jn 1.5-6.
5.6 *cf.* Mt 24.43 (par Lk 12.39); Mt 24.49 (par. Lk 21.45); Mk 13.35-36.
5.8 *cf.* Eph 6.11-18. Regarding the metaphor of armor, see Isa 59.17. Regarding the triad of "faith, hope, and love," see note on 1.3.
5.9 *Salvation.* As in 5.8, this word refers to all the benefits of life in Christ, present and future.
5.11 Again, as in 4.18, the purpose of the foregoing is for the encouragement and comfort of believers.
5.12-13 *cf.* Rom 12.8; 16.2; Gal 6.6; 1 Tim 3.4,5,12; Titus 3.8,14; 1 Tim 5.17.
5.14 *Idlers.* The Greek word refers to undisciplined and disorderly people who neglect their daily duties; *cf.* 2 Thess 3.6-12.
5.15 *cf.* Mt 5.44-48 (par Lk 6.27-36); Rom 12.17.
5.16 *cf.* Phil 4.4.
5.17 *cf.* Lk 18.1.
5.18 *cf.* Phil 4.6; Col 2.7.
5.19 *cf.* Jer 20.9; Rom 12.11.
5.20 *cf.* 1 Cor 14.1.
5.23 *The God of peace. Cf.* Rom 15.33; 16.20; 2 Cor 13.11; Phil 4.9; Heb 13.20.
5.26 *Holy kiss.* See note on 1 Cor 16.19-20; *cf.* also Rom 16.16; 2 Cor 13.12; 1 Pet 5.14.
5.27 See note on 1 Cor 16.19-20; *cf.* also Col 4.16; Rev 1.3.
5.28 This is the customary Pauline benediction, generally opening and closing his letters.

THE SECOND LETTER OF PAUL TO THE
THESSALONIANS

See the Introductions, pp. 8–9 and 90 above.

Salutation

1 Paul, Silvanus, and Timothy,
To the church of the Thessalonians
in God our Father and the Lord Jesus Christ:
2 Grace to you and peace from God our[a]
Father and the Lord Jesus Christ.

Thanksgiving

3 We must always give thanks to God for
you, brothers and sisters,[b] as is right, because your faith is growing abundantly,
and the love of everyone of you for one
another is increasing. 4 Therefore we ourselves boast of you among the churches of
God for your steadfastness and faith during
all your persecutions and the afflictions that
you are enduring.

The Judgment at Christ's Coming

5 This is evidence of the righteous judgment of God, and is intended to make you
worthy of the kingdom of God, for which
you are also suffering. 6 For it is indeed just
of God to repay with affliction those who
afflict you, 7 and to give relief to the afflicted
as well as to us, when the Lord Jesus is
revealed from heaven with his mighty angels 8 in flaming fire, inflicting vengeance on
those who do not know God and on those
who do not obey the gospel of our Lord
Jesus. 9 These will suffer the punishment of
eternal destruction, separated from the presence of the Lord and from the glory of his
might, 10 when he comes to be glorified by
his saints and to be marveled at on that day
among all who have believed, because our
testimony to you was believed. 11 To this end
we always pray for you, asking that our
God will make you worthy of his call and
will fulfill by his power every good resolve
and work of faith, 12 so that the name of our
Lord Jesus may be glorified in you, and you
in him, according to the grace of our God
and the Lord Jesus Christ.

The Man of Lawlessness

2 As to the coming of our Lord Jesus
Christ and our being gathered together
to him, we beg you, brothers and sisters,[b]
2 not to be quickly shaken in mind or alarmed,
either by spirit or by word or by letter, as
though from us, to the effect that the day
of the Lord is already here. 3 Let no one
deceive you in any way; for that day will
not come unless the rebellion comes first
and the lawless one[c] is revealed, the one
destined for destruction.[d] 4 He opposes and
exalts himself above every so-called god or
object of worship, so that he takes his seat
in the temple of God, declaring himself to
be God. 5 Do you not remember that I told
you these things when I was still with you?
6 And you know what is now restraining
him, so that he may be revealed when his
time comes. 7 For the mystery of lawlessness
is already at work, but only until the one
who now restrains it is removed. 8 And then
the lawless one will be revealed, whom the
Lord Jesus[e] will destroy[f] with the breath of
his mouth, annihilating him by the manifestation of his coming. 9 The coming of the
lawless one is apparent in the working of
Satan, who uses all power, signs, lying
wonders, 10 and every kind of wicked deception for those who are perishing, because
they refused to love the truth and so be
saved. 11 For this reason God sends them a
powerful delusion, leading them to believe
what is false, 12 so that all who have not
believed the truth but took pleasure in
unrighteousness will be condemned.

Chosen for Salvation

13 But we must always give thanks to
God for you, brothers and sisters[b] beloved
by the Lord, because God chose you as the
first fruits[g] for salvation through sanctification by the Spirit and through belief in the
truth. 14 For this purpose he called you
through our proclamation of the good news,[h]

[a] Other ancient authorities read *the* [b] Gk *brothers* [c] Gk *the man of lawlessness*; other ancient authorities read *the man of sin* [d] Gk *the son of destruction* [e] Other ancient authorities lack *Jesus* [f] Other ancient authorities read *consume* [g] Other ancient authorities read *from the beginning* [h] Or *through our gospel*

1.1 *Paul, Silvanus, and Timothy.* See note on 1 Thess 1.1. *Thessalonians.* See introductory note and note on 1 Thess 1.1.
1.2 *Grace to you and peace.* See note on 1 Thess 1.1.
1.3-4 This section comprises the formal thanksgiving which begins every letter of Paul with the exception of Galatians; for comments on the structure of the Pauline letter see Rom 1.1.
1.3 In Gal 5.6 Paul says that faith works itself out in love. *Cf.* 1 Thess 4.9-10.
1.4 *We ourselves boast of you. Cf.* 2 Cor 8.1-5.
1.5-11 This section is a working out of Paul's principle articulated in Rom 12.14-21, especially the admonition, "never avenge yourselves, but leave it to the wrath of God, for it is written, 'Vengeance is mine, I will repay, says the Lord'" (Rom 14.19). In 2 Thess 1.5-11 traditional apocalyptic imagery is used to portray when and how God's vengeance on the unjust oppressor will occur. *Cf.* also Phil 1.28.
1.5 *cf.* 1 Pet 4.17-18. *Kingdom of God, for which you are suffering.* To suffer for the kingdom of God is the same idea as suffering for Christ (*cf.* Phil 1.29); the idea is not that Christians suffer in order to inherit the kingdom of God.
1.6 *Just of God to repay.* This is based on Old Testament concepts of God's sovereign right to punish the wicked; *cf.* Isa 66.6; Ps 137.8.
1.7 The recompense spoken of in 2 Thess 1.6 is reserved for the end-time judgment (see also Rom 8.18). *When the Lord Jesus is revealed. Cf.* 1 Thess 4.16; 1 Cor 1.7.
1.8 *In flaming fire. Cf.* Isa 66.15-16. Fire is a common ingredient in Old Testament theophanies: Ex 3.2 (see Acts 7.30); Deut 33.2; Ps 18.8; Ezek 1.13,37; Hab 3.4. *Those who do not know God. Cf.* Ps 79.6. *Those who do not obey the gospel. Cf.* Rom 1.5; 2 Cor 9.13.
1.9 *Eternal destruction.* The alternative to eternal life; *cf.* Rom 2.7; 5.21; 6.22-23; Gal 6.8; 1 Thess 5.3. *Separated from the presence of the Lord. Cf.* Mt 25.41,16; Lk 13.27.
1.11 *cf.* Phil 1.17; 3.14.
2.1 *The coming of our Lord Jesus.* I.e. the return of Christ at the end of time, as in 1 Thess 4.13-17. *Our being gathered together to him. Cf.* 1 Thess 4.17.
2.2 Ideas about when the return of Christ and the consequent resurrection of the dead would happen, in the future or already in the present, evidently circulated in the church; *cf.* 2 Tim 2.18. *By spirit.* I.e. by prophetic utterance; *cf.* 1 Cor 14.12,32; 1 Jn 4.1-3; 1 Thess 5.19,20 (see note on Rev. 1.10). *By word.* I.e. a spoken word, in distinction from a prophetic utterance. *By letter, as though from us.* This may be a reference to the fact that written communication was circulating bearing Paul's name but not written by him.
2.3-12 A common feature of apocalyptic writing about the end-time is the positing of a timetable of events; *cf.* 1 Cor 15.23-28. The lengthy scenario given here contrasts with 1 Thess 4.13-17, in which Paul expects the End to come within his own lifetime.
2.3 *That day.* I.e. the last day at the end of the world; see note on 1 Thess 5.2. *The rebellion.* Inter-testamental Jewish literature (see Jubilees 23.14-23) used this word to refer to a general revolt by Israel against God's law, to occur at the end of time; the Jewish historian Josephus (Vita 43) used this word to refer to the Jewish revolt against Rome in 66-70 CE. Consistent with apocalyptic thought in general, the word is used in this verse to refer to the end-time upheaval, which will have religious, political, and cosmic consequences. *The lawless one.* The Greek Old Testament uses this word, along with the word for "rebellion," to translate the Hebrew word "Belial," a figure associated with the forces of darkness and often a name for the devil (see note on 2 Cor 6.15); *cf.* 2.9. *The one destined for destruction.* In apocalyptic writings the ultimate future of the devil, after he is allowed free rein for a period, is destruction; *cf.* Rev 20.7-10.
2.4 A common feature of apocalyptic texts is that, immediately preceding the end of time and God's final victory, the demonic forces will attempt to

1.3 1 Thess 1.2; 3.12
1.4 2 Cor 7.14; 1 Thess 1.3; 2.14
1.5 Phil 1.28; 1 Thess 2.14
1.7 1 Thess 4.16; Jude 14
1.8 Gal 4.8; Rom 2.8
1.9 Phil 3.19; 2 Pet 3.7; 2 Thess 2.8
1.12 Phil 2.9ff
2.1 1 Thess 4.15-17; Mk 13.27
2.2 Eph 5.6; 2 Thess 3.17; 1 Cor 1.8
2.3 Eph 5.6-8; Dan 7.25; 8.25; 11.36; Rev 13.5ff; Jn 17.12
2.4 1 Cor 8.5; Isa 14.13,14; Ezek 28.2
2.7 Rev 17.5,7
2.8 Dan 7.10; Rev 19.15
2.9 Mt 24.24; Jn 4.48
2.10 1 Cor 1.18
2.11 Rom 1.28; Mt 24.5; 1 Tim 4.1
2.12 Rom 1.32
2.13 Eph 1.4; 1 Pet 1.2
2.14 1 Pet 5.10

2.15 1 Cor 16.13; 11.2
2.17 1 Thess 3.2; 2 Thess 3.3
3.1 1 Thess 4.1; 5.25; 1.8
3.3 1 Cor 1.9; 1 Thess 5.24; 2 Pet 2.9
3.4 2 Cor 2.3; Gal 5.10
3.6 1 Cor 5.4,11; 2 Thess 2.15
3.7 1 Thess 1.6
3.8 1 Thess 2.9; Acts 18.3; Eph 4.28
3.9 1 Cor 9.4ff
3.11 1 Tim 5.13
3.12 1 Thess 4.1,11; Eph 4.28
3.14 Mt 18.17

so that you may obtain the glory of our Lord Jesus Christ. 15 So then, brothers and sisters,[i] stand firm and hold fast to the traditions that you were taught by us, either by word of mouth or by our letter.

16 Now may our Lord Jesus Christ himself and God our Father, who loved us and through grace gave us eternal comfort and good hope, 17 comfort your hearts and strengthen them in every good work and word.

Request for Prayer

3 Finally, brothers and sisters,[i] pray for us, so that the word of the Lord may spread rapidly and be glorified everywhere, just as it is among you, 2 and that we may be rescued from wicked and evil people; for not all have faith. 3 But the Lord is faithful; he will strengthen you and guard you from the evil one.[j] 4 And we have confidence in the Lord concerning you, that you are doing and will go on doing the things that we command. 5 May the Lord direct your hearts to the love of God and to the steadfastness of Christ.

Warning against Idleness

6 Now we command you, beloved,[i] in the name of our Lord Jesus Christ, to keep away from believers who are[k] living in idleness and not according to the tradition that they[l] received from us. 7 For you yourselves know how you ought to imitate us; we were not idle when we were with you, 8 and we did not eat anyone's bread without paying for it; but with toil and labor we worked night and day, so that we might not burden any of you. 9 This was not because we do not have that right, but in order to give you an example to imitate. 10 For even when we were with you, we gave you this command: Anyone unwilling to work should not eat. 11 For we hear that some of you are living in idleness, mere busybodies, not doing any work. 12 Now such persons we command and exhort in the Lord Jesus Christ to do their work quietly and to earn their own living. 13 Brothers and sisters,[m] do not be weary in doing what is right.

14 Take note of those who do not obey what we say in this letter; have nothing to do with them, so that they may be ashamed. 15 Do not regard them as enemies, but warn them as believers.[n]

Final Greetings and Benediction

16 Now may the Lord of peace himself give you peace at all times in all ways. The Lord be with all of you.

17 I, Paul, write this greeting with my own hand. This is the mark in every letter of mine; it is the way I write. 18 The grace of our Lord Jesus Christ be with all of you.[o]

[i] Gk *brothers* [j] Or *from evil* [k] Gk *from every brother who is* [l] Other ancient authorities read *you* [m] Gk *Brothers* [n] Gk *a brother* [o] Other ancient authorities add *Amen*

usurp God's authority. God's people will resist that attempt and be vindicated.
2.5 *cf.* 1 Thess 1.9-10; 5.27.
2.6 *When his time comes.* This is explained further in 2.7-8.
2.8 *The breath of his mouth. Cf.* Isa 11.4; Job 4.9; Rev 19.15.
2.9 *Powers, signs, lying wonders. Cf.* Mk 13.22 (par Mt 24.24); Acts 2.22; 1 Cor 12.12.
2.11 *cf.* Rom 1.24,26,28; 11.8 (=Isa 29.10).
2.13 *First fruits. Cf.* Jas 1.18; Rev 14.4. *Sanctification.* See note on 1 Thess 4.3.
2.14 *He called you. Cf.* 1 Thess 2.12; 4.7; 5.24.

2.15 *cf.* 1 Thess 3.8; 1 Cor 11.2; 15.1-2.
2.17 *cf.* 2 Cor 1.4.
3.1 Paul frequently requests his readers to pray for him; *cf.* Rom 15.30; 2 Cor 1.11; Eph 6.19; Phil 1.19; Col 4.3-4; 1 Thess 5.25. *That the word of the Lord may spread rapidly; cf.* Ps 147.15.
3.2 *cf.* Rom 15.31.
3.3 *The Lord is faithful. Cf.* 1 Cor 1.9; 10.13; 2 Cor 1.18; 1 Thess 5.24. *He will strengthen you. Cf.* 2.17; 1 Thess 3.13.
3.6 A stronger admonition is given here than in 1 Thess 4.9-12 and 5.14. *According to the tradition. Cf.* 1 Cor 11.2.
3.7 *Imitate us.* See notes on 1 Cor 11.1; Gal 4.12; Phil 3.17; 4.9; 1 Thess 1.6. *Not idle. Cf.* 1 Thess 2.9; Acts 18.3.
3.8 *With toil and labor we worked night and day.* Note parallel wording in 1 Thess 2.9.
3.9 *cf.* 1 Cor 9.4-5. *An example to imitate.* In 1 Cor 9 Paul does not insist on imitating him in his decision to give up his right to support at Corinth.
3.10 *Cf.* Gen 3.19.
3.11 *Busybodies.* I.e. meddlers in other people's affairs; *cf.* 1 Thess 4.11; 1 Pet 4.15.
3.13 *cf.* Gal 6.9; Eph 4.28.
3.14 *Have nothing to do with them. Cf.* Rom 16.17.
3.15 *cf.* 1 Thess 5.14.
3.16 *The Lord of peace.* A variation on a theme: *cf.* Rom 15.33; 16.20; 2 Cor 13.11; Phil 4.9; 1 Thess 5.23; Heb 13.20.
3.17 *With my own hand. Cf.* 1 Cor 16.21; Gal 6.11; Col 4.18; Philem 19.
3.18 The final benediction is equivalent to that in 1 Thess 5.28; see also the footnote on Rom 16.24.

THE FIRST LETTER OF PAUL TO

TIMOTHY

See the Introductions, pp. 8–9 and 90–91 above.

Salutation

1 Paul, an apostle of Christ Jesus by the command of God our Savior and of Christ Jesus our hope,

2 To Timothy, my loyal child in the faith:

Grace, mercy, and peace from God the Father and Christ Jesus our Lord.

Warning against False Teachers

3 I urge you, as I did when I was on my way to Macedonia, to remain in Ephesus so that you may instruct certain people not to teach any different doctrine, [4]and not to occupy themselves with myths and endless genealogies that promote speculations rather than the divine training[a] that is known by faith. [5]But the aim of such instruction is love that comes from a pure heart, a good conscience, and sincere faith. [6]Some people have deviated from these and turned to meaningless talk, [7]desiring to be teachers of the law, without understanding either what they are saying or the things about which they make assertions.

8 Now we know that the law is good, if one uses it legitimately. [9]This means understanding that the law is laid down not for the innocent but for the lawless and disobedient, for the godless and sinful, for the unholy and profane, for those who kill their father or mother, for murderers, [10]fornicators, sodomites, slave traders, liars, perjurers, and whatever else is contrary to the sound teaching [11]that conforms to the glorious gospel of the blessed God, which he entrusted to me.

Gratitude for Mercy

12 I am grateful to Christ Jesus our Lord, who has strengthened me, because he judged me faithful and appointed me to his service, [13]even though I was formerly a blasphemer, a persecutor, and a man of violence. But I received mercy because I had acted ignorantly in unbelief, [14]and the grace of our Lord overflowed for me with the faith and love that are in Christ Jesus. [15]The saying is sure and worthy of full acceptance, that Christ Jesus came into the world to save sinners—of whom I am the foremost. [16]But for that very reason I received mercy, so that in me, as the foremost, Jesus Christ might display the utmost patience, making me an example to those who would come to believe in him for eternal life. [17]To the King of the ages, immortal, invisible, the only God, be honor and glory forever and ever.[b] Amen.

18 I am giving you these instructions, Timothy, my child, in accordance with the prophecies made earlier about you, so that by following them you may fight the good fight, [19]having faith and a good conscience. By rejecting conscience, certain persons have suffered shipwreck in the faith; [20]among them are Hymenaeus and Alexander, whom I have turned over to Satan, so that they may learn not to blaspheme.

Instructions concerning Prayer

2 First of all, then, I urge that supplications, prayers, intercessions, and thanksgivings be made for everyone, [2]for kings and all who are in high positions, so that we may lead a quiet and peaceable life in all godliness and dignity. [3]This is right and is acceptable in the sight of God our Savior, [4]who desires everyone to be saved and to come to the knowledge of the truth. [5]For

there is one God;
there is also one mediator between
God and humankind,
Christ Jesus, himself human,
[6] who gave himself a ransom for all

—this was attested at the right time. [7]For this I was appointed a herald and an apostle (I am telling the truth,[c] I am not lying), a teacher of the Gentiles in faith and truth.

8 I desire, then, that in every place the men should pray, lifting up holy hands without anger or argument; [9]also that the women should dress themselves modestly and decently in suitable clothing, not with their hair braided, or with gold, pearls, or expensive clothes, [10]but with good works, as is proper for women who profess reverence

[a] Or *plan* [b] Gk *to the ages of the ages* [c] Other ancient authorities add *in Christ*

1.1 Acts 9.15; Col 1.27
1.2 Acts 16.1; 2 Tim 1.2
1.3 Acts 20.1; Gal 1.6,7
1.4 Titus 1.14; 1 Tim 6.4
1.5 2 Tim 2.2
1.9 Gal 3.19; 1 Pet 4.18
1.10 2 Tim 4.3; Titus 1.9
1.12 2 Cor 12.9; Col 1.25
1.13 Acts 8.3
1.14 Rom 5.20; 2 Tim 1.13
1.15 2 Tim 2.11; Titus 3.8
1.17 Col 1.15; Rom 11.36
1.18 1 Tim 4.14; 2 Tim 2.2,3
1.19 1 Tim 6.12, 21
1.20 2 Tim 2.17, 4.14
2.2 Ezra 6.10; Rom 13.1
2.3 Rom 12.2; 1 Tim 4.10
2.4 Jn 3.16; 2 Tim 2.25
2.5 Gal 3.20; Heb 9.15
2.6 Mk 10.45; 1 Cor 1.6; Gal 4.4
2.7 Eph 3.7,8; Gal 1.16

1.1 *Paul, an apostle.* Paul's letters often begin with his claim of apostleship (Rom 1.1; 1 Cor 1.1; 2 Cor 1.1; Gal 1.1; *cf.* Eph 1.1; Col 1.1; 2 Tim 1.1), a claim some would question (see 1 Cor 9.2; 2 Cor 13.3). *By the command of God. Cf.* Rom 1.1; Gal 1.15.
1.2 *Timothy.* According to Acts 16.1 Timothy was the son of a Jewish Christian woman and a Gentile father from Lystra, and evidently became a Christian under Paul's influence (see 1 Cor 4.17). He served on various occasions as Paul's personal messenger (e.g. 1 Cor 16.10), and is mentioned as the joint sender with Paul of 1 Thess; Phil; 2 Cor, Philem, Col, and 2 Thess. Later church tradition reports that he became bishop of Ephesus, and in this letter he is understood to be in the position of a teacher (*cf.* 3.2; 4.6,11; 5.7; 6.2). *Grace, mercy, and peace...* An initial greeting found, with minor variations, in every one of the Pauline letters, as well as in other New Testament letters; *cf.* Rom 1.7; 1 Cor 1.3; 2 Cor 1.2; Gal 1.3; Eph 1.2; Phil 1.2; Col 1.2; 1 Thess 1.1; 2 Thess 1.2; 2 Tim 1.2; Titus 1.4; Philem 3; see also 1 Pet 1.2; 2 Pet 2.2; 2 Jn 3; Jude 1.2; Rev 1.4.
1.3-20 This section, in the place where Paul's letters usually offer a thanksgiving, consists of a warning against false teaching.
1.3 *Macedonia.* A Roman province equivalent to what is now northern Greece; its capital is Thessalonica. *Ephesus.* The capital city of the Roman province of Asia; *cf.* 1 Cor 16.8. *That you may instruct.* Timothy's ministry is envisioned as a teacher who is to safeguard and promote apostolic teaching; see note on 6.20.
1.4 *Myths and endless genealogies. Cf.* 4.7; 2 Tim 4.4; Titus 1.13-14; 3.9; 2 Pet 1.16. Various ancient texts, some recently discovered, indicate fascination with the genealogies of Genesis (see note 1.7), in order to promote esoteric cosmological and anthropological teaching.
1.5 *Pure heart. Cf.* 1.19; 3.9; 2 Tim 1.3; 1 Cor 14.1; Ps 51.12; Heb 10.22; 1 Pet 3.21. *Clear conscience. Cf.* 4.2; 2 Tim 1.3; Rom 2.15; 9.1; 1 Cor 8.7; 2 Cor 4.2; Acts 24.16; 1 Pt 3.16.
1.6 *Deviated from these*, i.e. the triad mentioned in the previous verse: a pure heart, a good conscience, and sincere faith. *Meaningless talk.* Literally, "useless words," which result when the triad of the previous verse is missing.
1.7 *Teachers of the law.* The opponents envisioned here evidently have presented themselves as experts on the Torah, specifically Mosaic law, the first five books of the Old Testament.
1.8 *cf.* Rom 7.12.
1.9 Since love is the fulfilling of the Law (see Rom 13.10; Gal 5.6,14), and those in Christ are no longer under it (Rom 10.4; Gal 3.24-25), the Law is meant only for those who do not know the love of Christ.
1.9-10 The attention given to vice-lists in the Pastoral Letters (see also 1 Tim 6.4-5; 2 Tim 3.2-5; Titus 3.3) indicates a special emphasis on morality; the lists are broadened beyond the normal Pauline lists (see 1 Cor 5.11; 6.9-10; Gal 5.18-21; Rom 1.29-31).
1.12-17 This section repeats the story of Paul's conversion and commissioning as an apostle. While Paul makes brief mention of his calling to apostleship (see 1 Cor 15.8-11; Gal 1.13-16), references to Paul's past become more frequent in the post-Pauline literature; see Col 1.13-29; Eph 3.1-11; 1 Tim 2.7; 3.14-15; 2 Tim 1.3-4,11,15-18; *cf.* also Acts 9.1-22; 22.1-16; 26.9-18.
1.14 In the Pastoral Letters love and faith have become virtual synonyms; *cf.* 1.14; 2.15; 4.12; 6.11; 2 Tim 1.13; 2.22; Titus 2.2.
1.15 *cf.* Lk 5.32; 19.10.
1.18 *The prophecies made earlier about you.* Probably a reference to the homilies made at Timothy's ordination, *cf.* 4.14; 6.12. *Fight the good fight.* In this context this refers to Timothy's ministry to preserve and promote apostolic teaching; see notes on 1.3; 6.20.
1.20 *Hymenaeus.* Mentioned in 2 Tim 2.17, where he is not yet *turned over to Satan*, i.e. expelled from the fellowship (*cf.* 1 Cor 5.5). *Alexander* is mentioned in 2 Tim 4.14.
2.1-2 Prayer for secular authorities will result in respect for Christianity among those outside the faith, and will lessen the risk of persecution.

for God. [11]Let a woman[d] learn in silence with full submission. [12]I permit no woman[d] to teach or to have authority over a man;[e] she is to keep silent. [13]For Adam was formed first, then Eve; [14]and Adam was not deceived, but the woman was deceived and became a transgressor. [15]Yet she will be saved through childbearing, provided they continue in faith and love and holiness, with modesty.

Qualifications of Bishops

3 The saying is sure:[f] whoever aspires to the office of bishop[g] desires a noble task. [2]Now a bishop[h] must be above reproach, married only once,[i] temperate, sensible, respectable, hospitable, an apt teacher, [3]not a drunkard, not violent but gentle, not quarrelsome, and not a lover of money. [4]He must manage his own household well, keeping his children submissive and respectful in every way— [5]for if someone does not know how to manage his own household, how can he take care of God's church? [6]He must not be a recent convert, or he may be puffed up with conceit and fall into the condemnation of the devil. [7]Moreover, he must be well thought of by outsiders, so that he may not fall into disgrace and the snare of the devil.

Qualifications of Deacons

8 Deacons likewise must be serious, not double-tongued, not indulging in much wine, not greedy for money; [9]they must hold fast to the mystery of the faith with a clear conscience. [10]And let them first be tested; then, if they prove themselves blameless, let them serve as deacons. [11]Women[j] likewise must be serious, not slanderers, but temperate, faithful in all things. [12]Let deacons be married only once,[k] and let them manage their children and their households well; [13]for those who serve well as deacons gain a good standing for themselves and great boldness in the faith that is in Christ Jesus.

The Mystery of Our Religion

14 I hope to come to you soon, but I am writing these instructions to you so that, [15]if I am delayed, you may know how one ought to behave in the household of God, which is the church of the living God, the pillar and bulwark of the truth. [16]Without any doubt, the mystery of our religion is great:

He[l] was revealed in flesh,
vindicated[m] in spirit,[n]
seen by angels,
proclaimed among Gentiles,
believed in throughout the world,
taken up in glory.

False Asceticism

4 Now the Spirit expressly says that in later[o] times some will renounce the faith by paying attention to deceitful spirits and teachings of demons, [2]through the hypocrisy of liars whose consciences are seared with a hot iron. [3]They forbid marriage and demand abstinence from foods, which God created to be received with thanksgiving by those who believe and know the truth. [4]For everything created by God is good, and nothing is to be rejected, provided it is received with thanksgiving; [5]for it is sanctified by God's word and by prayer.

A Good Minister of Jesus Christ

6 If you put these instructions before the brothers and sisters,[p] you will be a good servant[q] of Christ Jesus, nourished on the words of the faith and of the sound teaching that you have followed. [7]Have nothing to do with profane myths and old wives' tales. Train yourself in godliness, [8]for, while physical training is of some value, godliness is valuable in every way, holding promise for both the present life and the life to come. [9]The saying is sure and worthy of full acceptance. [10]For to this end we toil and struggle,[r] because we have our hope set on the living God, who is the Savior of all people, especially of those who believe.

11 These are the things you must insist on and teach. [12]Let no one despise your youth, but set the believers an example in speech and conduct, in love, in faith, in purity. [13]Until I arrive, give attention to the public reading of scripture,[s] to exhorting, to

2.13 Gen 1.27; 1 Cor 11.8
2.14 Gen 3.6; 2 Cor 11.3
3.1 1 Tim 1.15; Acts 20.28
3.2 Titus 1.6-8; 2 Tim 2.24
3.3 2 Tim 2.24; 1 Pet 5.2
3.7 1 Cor 5.12; 2 Tim 2.26
3.8 Acts 6.3; Titus 2.3
3.15 Eph 2.21; ver 5; 1 Tim 4.10; Gal 2.9
3.16 Jn 1.14; 1 Pet 3.18; Acts 1.9
4.1 Jn 16.13; 2 Thess 2.3; 2 Tim 3.1; 3.13; Rev 9.20
4.3 1 Cor 7.28; Heb 13.4; Gen 1.29; Rom 14.6
4.4 Rom 14.14
4.6 2 Cor 11.23; 1 Tim 1.10; 2 Tim 3.10
4.7 2 Tim 2.16; Heb 5.14
4.8 1 Tim 6.6; Ps 37.4; Rom 8.28
4.10 1 Cor 4.11; 1 Tim 2.4
4.11 1 Tim 5.7; 6.2
4.12 Titus 2.7; 1 Pet 5.3; 1 Tim 1.14

[d] Or *wife* [e] Or *her husband* [f] Some interpreters place these words at the end of the previous paragraph. Other ancient authorities read *The saying is commonly accepted* [g] Or *overseer* [h] Or *an overseer* [i] Gk *the husband of one wife* [j] Or *Their wives,* or *Women deacons* [k] Gk *be husbands of one wife* [l] Gk *Who*; other ancient authorities read *God*; others, *Which* [m] Or *justified* [n] Or *by the Spirit* [o] Or *the last* [p] Gk *brothers* [q] Or *deacon* [r] Other ancient authorities read *suffer reproach* [s] Gk *to the reading*

2.5-6 Very like a hymn or confession spoken in a worship setting; *cf.* Col 1.15-20; Eph 1.15-23; 4.5-6.
2.5 *Mediator. Cf.* Heb 9.15; 12.24.
2.6 *Ransom.* The price paid for someone's freedom; *cf.* Mk 10.35 (Mt 20.28).
2.7 See note on 1.12-17.
2.8 Instruction for men in the worship assemblies. *In every place.* I.e. in the worship assemblies. *Lift up holy hands.* I.e. in prayer (see Ps 141.2; 143.6).
2.9 Instruction for women in the worship assemblies; *cf.* also 1 Cor 11.2-16.
2.10 *Good works. Cf.* 5.10,25; 6.18; Titus 2.7,14; 3.8,14; Eph 2.10.

2.11-15 This section offers a thought-structure and wording similar to 1 Cor 14.33-36 (see note there).
2.13 The story in Gen 2.18-25 is used to substantiate the notion of the primary role of the male in God's creation (*cf.* 1 Cor 11.7-12).
2.14 The interpretation of the story in Gen 3.1-21 to identify the woman as the cause of the Fall into Sin can be seen in Sir 25.24. *Cf.* the contrasting treatment of the Fall in Rom 5.12-21; 7.7-25.
2.15 This verse builds on Gen 3.16.
3.1-16 This section deals with the ordained ministry, exhibiting an ordered set of offices and the qualifications for those who hold these offices. That this discussion of ordained ministry precedes a section on false teaching (chapter 4) indicates that the offices of ministry function as safeguards against heresy.

3.1 *Bishop.* The Greek for bishop is *episkopos,* which means "overseer"; *cf.* Phil 1.1; Titus 1.5,7. By the time of this writing a singular "bishop" has become the chief leader of the local church; in Phil 1.1 they were still in the plural.
3.2 The qualifications for a bishop listed here have to do with morality. *Above reproach.* I.e. of highly respectable reputation; *cf.* 5.7; 6.14. *Married only once* (see footnote *i*). The Greek phrase itself is unclear, and could mean that a bishop (1) must have only one wife at a time (i.e. be monogamous, not polygamous); (2) cannot remarry after divorce; (3) cannot remarry after the death of his spouse. *Temperate. Cf.* 5.23. *Hospitable. Cf.* Titus 1.8; Rom 12.13; 1 Pet 4.9; Heb 13.2; Mt 10.11; Acts 16.15,21. 7.17; 28.14; 3 Jn 8; Philem 22.
3.6 *cf.* 5.14; 6.1; Titus 2.5,8,10.
3.7 The concern for the outsiders is a frequent theme in the Pastoral Letters; *cf.* Titus 2.7-8; 3.1-2; see also 1 Pet 2.11-17.
3.8 *Deacons.* Closely connected to the "bishops" in Phil 1.1, they seem here to have their own ranking office in the church. *Not double-tongued.* I.e. sincere, truthful.
3.9 *Mystery of the faith. Cf.* 3.16. Developing a concept present in Paul's letters (see 1 Cor 2.7, 4.1; Rom 16.25-27), Paul's followers understood the *"mystery of the faith"* to refer to Christ, present at the beginning and active in the creation, whose glory is hidden but is to be revealed at the end of time (see Col 2.2; 4.3; Eph 1.9; 3.4); this "mystery" is known only to Christian believers, and in this context the knowledge of this "mystery" has implications for Christian behavior. *Cf.* also 2 Tim 1.9; Titus 1.2-3; Eph 3.3-10; Col 1.26-28; 1 Pet 1.20.
3.11 This abrupt entry about women in this context suggests a category of female deacons (see Rom 16.1-2), in spite of 2.11-12.
3.12 *cf.* 3.2. *Married only once.* See note on 3.2.
3.15 *Household of God.* I.e. the church; *cf.* 3.5; Gal 6.10. *Pillar. Cf.* Rev 3.12.
3.16 This verse contains a hymn comparable to the other New Testament Christological hymns; see Phil 2.6-11; Col 1.15-20; Eph 2.14-16; 1 Pet 3.18-19,22; Heb 1.3; Jn 1.1-18.
4.1 *The Spirit.* I.e. prophetic witness; *cf.* 2 Pet 3.2; Jude 17. *In later times.* Various later New Testament writings identify false teaching and apostasy as a phenomenon of the time before the end of the world: 2 Tim 3.1-9; 4.3; 2 Pet 3.3; Jude 18; *cf.* 2 Thess 2.3. *Renounce the faith. Cf.* 2 Tim 3.1; Mt 24.12; Jude 17-18; 2 Pet 3.3-7. *Deceitful spirits and the teachings of demons. Cf.* 2 Cor 4.4; 11.3,13-14.
4.2 *Hypocrisy.* This author describes the false teachers as unconscionably promoting their teachings for personal gain; *cf.* 1.19; 6.5; 2 Tim 3.5; Titus 1.11.
4.3 *They forbid marriage.* See note on 1 Cor 7.1; *cf.* Rev 14.4. *Demand abstinence. Cf.* Rom 14.2-3; 1 Cor 10.25,30; Col 2.16-18.
4.4-5 *cf.* Gen 1.29-31; 9.2-3; Mk 7.19; Acts 10.15; Rom 14.14; 1 Cor 10.25-26.

teaching. [14]Do not neglect the gift that is in
you, which was given to you through prophecy with the laying on of hands by the
council of elders.[t] [15]Put these things into
practice, devote yourself to them, so that all
may see your progress. [16]Pay close attention
to yourself and to your teaching; continue
in these things, for in doing this you will
save both yourself and your hearers.

Duties toward Believers

5 Do not speak harshly to an older
man,[u] but speak to him as to a father,
to younger men as brothers, [2]to older women
as mothers, to younger women as sisters—
with absolute purity.
3 Honor widows who are really widows.
[4]If a widow has children or grandchildren,
they should first learn their religious duty
to their own family and make some repayment to their parents; for this is pleasing in
God's sight. [5]The real widow, left alone, has
set her hope on God and continues in supplications and prayers night and day; [6]but
the widow[v] who lives for pleasure is dead
even while she lives. [7]Give these commands
as well, so that they may be above reproach. [8]And whoever does not provide for
relatives, and especially for family members,
has denied the faith and is worse than an
unbeliever.
9 Let a widow be put on the list if she
is not less than sixty years old and has been
married only once;[w] [10]she must be well
attested for her good works, as one who has
brought up children, shown hospitality,
washed the saints' feet, helped the afflicted,
and devoted herself to doing good in every
way. [11]But refuse to put younger widows on
the list; for when their sensual desires alienate them from Christ, they want to marry,
[12]and so they incur condemnation for having violated their first pledge. [13]Besides that,
they learn to be idle, gadding about from
house to house; and they are not merely
idle, but also gossips and busybodies, saying
what they should not say. [14]So I would
have younger widows marry, bear children,
and manage their households, so as to give
the adversary no occasion to revile us. [15]For
some have already turned away to follow
Satan. [16]If any believing woman[x] has relatives who are really widows, let her assist
them; let the church not be burdened, so
that it can assist those who are real widows.
17 Let the elders who rule well be considered worthy of double honor,[y] especially
those who labor in preaching and teaching;
[18]for the scripture says, "You shall not muzzle
an ox while it is treading out the grain,"
and, "The laborer deserves to be paid."
[19]Never accept any accusation against an
elder except on the evidence of two or three
witnesses. [20]As for those who persist in sin,
rebuke them in the presence of all, so that
the rest also may stand in fear. [21]In the
presence of God and of Christ Jesus and of
the elect angels, I warn you to keep these
instructions without prejudice, doing nothing on the basis of partiality. [22]Do not ordain[z]
anyone hastily, and do not participate in
the sins of others; keep yourself pure.
23 No longer drink only water, but take
a little wine for the sake of your stomach
and your frequent ailments.
24 The sins of some people are conspicuous and precede them to judgment, while
the sins of others follow them there. [25]So
also good works are conspicuous; and even
when they are not, they cannot remain
hidden.

6 Let all who are under the yoke of
slavery regard their masters as worthy of all honor, so that the name of God
and the teaching may not be blasphemed.
[2]Those who have believing masters must
not be disrespectful to them on the ground
that they are members of the church;[a] rather
they must serve them all the more, since
those who benefit by their service are believers and beloved.[b]

False Teaching and True Riches

Teach and urge these duties. [3]Whoever
teaches otherwise and does not agree with
the sound words of our Lord Jesus Christ
and the teaching that is in accordance with
godliness, [4]is conceited, understanding nothing, and has a morbid craving for controversy and for disputes about words. From
these come envy, dissension, slander, base
suspicions, [5]and wrangling among those
who are depraved in mind and bereft of the

[t] Gk *by the presbytery* [u] Or *an elder*, or *a presbyter* [v] Gk *she* [w] Gk *the wife of one husband* [x] Other ancient authorities read *believing man or woman*; others, *believing man* [y] Or *compensation* [z] Gk *Do not lay hands on* [a] Gk *are brothers* [b] Or *since they are believers and beloved, who devote themselves to good deeds*

4.7 See note on 1.4.
4.8 *cf.* Titus 1.2.
4.12 *Let no one despise your youth. Cf.* Jer 1.6-8.
4.13 *Public reading of scripture. Cf.* 2 Cor 3.14; Col 4.16; Rev 1.3. *Exhorting.* I.e. the act of preaching in the public worship services; see Acts 13.15; Heb 13.22; *cf.* also 1 Tim 1.10; 4.1,6; 5.17; 6.1,3; 2 Tim 3.10.

4.14 *Gift...given...through prophecy. Cf.* 1.18; 6.12. *Laying on of hands. Cf.* Deut 34.9; Num 27.18-23; Acts 13.1-3; 2 Tim 1.6-7. *The council of elders.* A term of respect which includes the whole circle of church leaders present at Timothy's ordination; see 5.17-20; *cf.* Acts 11.30; 14.23; 15.2,4,6; Titus 1.5-6; Jas 5.14; 1 Pet 5.1.
4.15 Bearers of the office of ministry are to take seriously their responsibility for the safeguarding and transmission of true teaching (*cf.* 1.11,18; 6.20; 2 Tim 1.14), for this has to do with salvation (*cf.* 2.4; 2 Tim 1.8-9; 4.18).
5.1 Ancient tradition demands respect for elders (*cf.* Lev 19.32; Prov 16.31); but if Christian office bearers are meant here (see footnote *u*), then respect is due to them in no lesser measure than to younger office bearers (see 4.12).
5.2 The biblical tradition demands care and concern for widows (*cf.* Ex 22.22; Deut 24.17,19-21; Job 29.13; Ps 68.5; Isa 1.17; Acts 6.1-6; 9.36,39,41; Jas 1.27). *Really widows.* See following verses.
5.4 *cf.* 5.16.
5.5 *Real widow.* I.e. the one who has no family to offer support. *Continues in supplications and prayers night and day. Cf.* Lk 2.37.
5.8 *cf.* 2.2; 3.1-7; 5.14; 6.1.
5.9-10 These verses indicate a category in the church for widows, with criteria for inclusion in this category: age, previous marital history, and demeanor.
5.10 *Hospitality. Cf.* 3.2; Rom 12.13; Mt 25.35; Heb 13.2; 3 Jn 5-8. *Washed the saints' feet. Cf.* Jn 13.14-17. *Helped the afflicted. Cf.* 1 Thess 3.4; 2 Cor 1.6; 7.7.
5.11 But *cf.* 1 Cor 7.39.
5.12 *First pledge.* This may refer to one of the following: (1) a pledge to the church to remain single (*cf.* vs. 5); (2) a pledge of eternal matrimony to her first husband (*cf.* vs. 9); (3) a pledge to remain a Christian (*cf.* vs. 15).
5.16 *cf.* 5.4-5.
5.17 *Elders.* I.e. the presbyters, i.e. those who hold ordained office in the church, including bishops; *cf.* 4.14.
5.18 The first quotation is from Deut 25.4 and is also quoted in 1 Cor 9.9. The second quotation is a saying of Jesus in Lk 10.7 = Mt 10.10, and is alluded to in 1 Cor 9.14.
5.19 *cf.* Deut 19.15; 2 Cor 13.1.
5.20 *cf.* Mt 18.17.
5.22 *cf.* 4.14; 2 Tim 1.6; Acts 6.6; 13.3.
5.23 Christian office bearers are not to be ascetics. *A little wine. Cf.* 3.8; Ps 60.3; 104.15; Lk 7.33-34.
5.24-25 *cf.* Mt 25.34-40.
6.1-2 *cf.* Col 3.22-25; Eph 6.5-8; 1 Pet 2.18-25; Titus 2.9-10; also 1 Cor 7.21-24; Philem 10-17.
6.3 For example, the second quotation in 5.18 (see note there).
6.4 There is a vice-list here; see note on Col 3.5-17. *Conceited. Cf.* 3.6. *Controversy and disputes about words. Cf.* 1.4; Titus 3.9. *Slander. Cf.* 2 Tim 3.2; Titus 3.2; Mk 7.22; Col 3.8; Eph 4.31.
6.5 *cf.* 2.4; 4.3; 2 Tim 2.15; 3.7-8.

4.14 2 Tim 1.6; 1 Tim 1.18; 5.22; Acts 6.6
4.16 Acts 20.28; Ezek 33.9
5.1 Lev 19.32
5.4 Eph 6.1,2
5.5 ver 3,16; 1 Cor 7.32; Lk 2.37
5.6 Jas 5.5
5.7 1 Tim 4.11
5.8 Gal 6.10; Titus 1.16
5.10 Acts 16.15; Heb 13.2; Lk 7.44; ver 16
5.13 2 Thess 3.11; Titus 1.11
5.14 1 Cor 7.9; Titus 2.5
5.17 Phil 2.29; Rom 12.8; Acts 28.10
5.18 1 Cor 9.9; Lev 19.13; Deut 24.14,15; Mt 10.10
5.20 Titus 1.13; Deut 13.11
5.21 1 Tim 6.13; 2 Tim 2.14
5.22 Acts 6.6; 2 Tim 1.6; Eph 5.11
6.1 Titus 2.9; 1 Pet 2.18; Titus 2.5,8
6.2 Gal 3.28; Philem 16; 1 Tim 4.11
6.3 2 Tim 1.13; Titus 1.1
6.4 1 Cor 8.2; 2 Tim 2.14
6.5 1 Cor 11.16; Titus 1.11; 2 Pet 2.3

6.6 Phil 4.11; Heb 13.5
6.9 1 Tim 3.7; 1.19
6.12 1 Cor 9.25,26; 1 Tim 1.18; Heb 13.23
6.13 1 Tim 5.21; Jn 18.37
6.14 Phil 1.6; 2 Thess 2.8
6.15 1 Tim 1.11,17; Rev 17.14; 19.16
6.16 1 Tim 1.17; Jn 1.18; Eph 3.21
6.17 Lk 12.20,21; 1 Tim 4.10; Acts 14.17
6.18 1 Tim 5.10; Rom 12.8,13
6.20 2 Tim 1.14; 2.16

truth, imagining that godliness is a means
of gain.[c] [6]Of course, there is great gain in
godliness combined with contentment; [7]for
we brought nothing into the world, so that[d]
we can take nothing out of it; [8]but if we
have food and clothing, we will be content
with these. [9]But those who want to be rich
fall into temptation and are trapped by
many senseless and harmful desires that
plunge people into ruin and destruction.
[10]For the love of money is a root of all kinds
of evil, and in their eagerness to be rich
some have wandered away from the faith
and pierced themselves with many pains.

The Good Fight of Faith

11 But as for you, man of God, shun all
this; pursue righteousness, godliness, faith,
love, endurance, gentleness. [12]Fight the good
fight of the faith; take hold of the eternal
life, to which you were called and for which
you made[e] the good confession in the presence of many witnesses. [13]In the presence
of God, who gives life to all things, and of
Christ Jesus, who in his testimony before
Pontius Pilate made the good confession, I
charge you [14]to keep the commandment
without spot or blame until the manifestation of our Lord Jesus Christ, [15]which he
will bring about at the right time—he who
is the blessed and only Sovereign, the King
of kings and Lord of lords. [16]It is he alone
who has immortality and dwells in unap-
proachable light, whom no one has ever
seen or can see; to him be honor and
eternal dominion. Amen.

17 As for those who in the present age
are rich, command them not to be haughty,
or to set their hopes on the uncertainty of
riches, but rather on God who richly provides us with everything for our enjoyment.
[18]They are to do good, to be rich in good
works, generous, and ready to share, [19]thus
storing up for themselves the treasure of a
good foundation for the future, so that they
may take hold of the life that really is life.

Personal Instructions and Benediction

20 Timothy, guard what has been entrusted to you. Avoid the profane chatter
and contradictions of what is falsely called
knowledge; [21]by professing it some have
missed the mark as regards the faith.

Grace be with you.[f]

[c] Other ancient authorities add *Withdraw yourself from such people* [d] Other ancient authorities read *world—it is certain that* [e] Gk *confessed* [f] The Greek word for *you* here is plural; in other ancient authorities it is singular. Other ancient authorities add *Amen*

THE SECOND LETTER OF PAUL TO TIMOTHY

1.3 Rom 1.8,9; 1 Thess 1.2,21; Acts 20.37
1.5 1 Tim 1.5; Acts 16.1
1.7 Rom 18.15; Jn 14.27
1.8 Rom 1.16; Eph 3.1; 2 Tim 2.3,9; 4.5
1.9 Heb 3.1; Rom 16.25

Salutation

1 Paul, an apostle of Christ Jesus by the
will of God, for the sake of the promise
of life that is in Christ Jesus,

2 To Timothy, my beloved child:

Grace, mercy, and peace from God the
Father and Christ Jesus our Lord.

Thanksgiving and Encouragement

3 I am grateful to God—whom I worship
with a clear conscience, as my ancestors
did—when I remember you constantly in
my prayers night and day. [4]Recalling your
tears, I long to see you so that I may be
filled with joy. [5]I am reminded of your
sincere faith, a faith that lived first in your
grandmother Lois and your mother Eunice
and now, I am sure, lives in you. [6]For this
reason I remind you to rekindle the gift of
God that is within you through the laying
on of my hands; [7]for God did not give us
a spirit of cowardice, but rather a spirit of
power and of love and of self-discipline.

8 Do not be ashamed, then, of the testimony about our Lord or of me his prisoner,
but join with me in suffering for the gospel,
relying on the power of God, [9]who saved us

6.7 *cf.* Job 1.21; Eccl 5.14; Wis 7.6.
6.8 *cf.* Gen 28.20; Deut 10.18; Sir 29.21; 1 Cor 9.15-17; Phil 4.11; Jas 2.15.
6.9 *cf.* Mk 10.25; 1 Jn 2.15-17; Jas 1.13-18.
6.10 *Love of money is a root of all kinds of evil.* This is a common proverb found in various Greek popular philosophical writers. *Wandered away from the faith. Cf.* 4.1; 5.8.
6.11 A list of virtues; see note on Col 3.12.
6.12 *cf.* 1.18; 1 Cor 9.24-27; Phil 3.12-15; 2 Tim 4.7. *The good confession in the presence of many witnesses.* I.e. at Timothy's ordination; *cf.* 1.18; 4.14; 2 Tim 2.2.
6.13 *cf.* 2 Tim 2.8-10; 3.10-11; Mk 13.9; 15.1-5.
6.14 *Commandment.* I.e. the charge given Timothy at his ordination (*cf.* 4.14).
6.15 *King of kings and Lord of lords. Cf.* Ezek 26.7; Dan 2.37; Deut 10.17; Ps 136.3; Rev 17.14; 19.16.
6.16 *cf.* Ex 13.18-23; 1 Jn 1.5; Rev 1.6.
6.18 *Do good. Cf.* 2.10; 5.10,25; 2 Tim 2.21; 3.17; Titus 1.14; 1.16; 2.7; 3.1.
6.19 *cf.* Lk 12.16-21.
6.20 *Guard what has been entrusted to you.* In the Pastoral Letters the function of ministry is to safeguard the traditions handed down about Jesus and the apostles; *cf.* 1.3,18; 2 Tim 1.13-14; 2.2,14-15,24-25; 3.14; 4.2; Titus 1.13; 2.1. *Profane chatter. Cf.* 2 Tim 2.16. *What is falsely called knowledge.* This suggests that the false teaching combatted in this letter is a form of Gnosticism.

See the Introductions, pp. 8–9 and 91 above.

1.1 *Paul, an apostle.* Paul's letters often begin with his claim of apostleship (Rom 1.1; 1 Cor 1.1; 2 Cor 1.1; Gal 1.1; *cf.* Eph 1.1; Col 1.1; 1 Tim 1.1), a claim some would question (see 1 Cor 9.2; 2 Cor 13.3). *By the will of God. Cf.* Rom 1.1; Gal 1.15.
1.2 *Timothy.* See note on 1 Tim 1.2. *My beloved child.* Paul's usual designation for those whom he brought into Christianity; *cf.* 1 Cor 4.15; Gal 4.19; Philem 10. *Grace, mercy, and peace...* An initial greeting found, with minor variations, in every one of the Pauline letters, as well as in other New Testament letters; *cf.* Rom 1.7; 1 Cor 1.3; 2 Cor 1.2; Gal 1.3; Eph 1.2; Phil 1.2; Col 1.2; 1 Thess 1.1; 2 Thess 1.2; 1 Tim 1.2; Titus 1.4; Philem 3; see also 1 Pet 1.2; 2 Pet 2.2; 2 Jn 3; Jude 1.2; Rev 1.4.
1.3-7 This section comprises the thanksgiving, following the common Pauline pattern. See note on Rom 1.1 on the structure of the Pauline letter, and *cf.* especially Phil 1.3-11 and Col 1.4-9.
1.3 *Clear conscience. Cf.* 1 Tim 1.5; 4.2; Rom 2.15; 9.1; 2 Cor 4.2; 1 Pet 3.16; Acts 24.16. *As my ancestors did.* A phrase not found in Paul's letters, it accords with the emphasis in 2 Timothy on Christianity's continuity with its Old Testament roots (see 1.9-10; 2.8,19; 3.8,14-17).
1.5 Implied is that Timothy's mother and grandmother were Christians; see Acts 16.1.
1.6 See notes on 1 Tim 4.14; 6.12,14. *My hands.* This indicates that Paul was present at Timothy's ordination.
1.8 In the Pastoral Letters the function of ministry is to safeguard the traditions handed down about Jesus and the apostles; *cf.* 1.13-14; 2.2,14-15,24-25; 3.14; 4.2; 1 Tim 6.20. *The testimony about our Lord.* This could mean the actual teachings of Jesus (as in 1 Tim 6.3) or the preaching about him (as in 1 Tim 4.13).
1.9 *Saved us. Cf.* 1 Tim 1.15; 2.3-4; 4.10; Titus 1.3; 2.10; 3.4-5. *Not according to our works. Cf.* Eph 2.8-9; Titus 3.5. *Before the ages began. Cf.* Titus 1.2.

1.10 *Appearing. Cf.* Titus 2.11,13; 3.4; 1 Tim 6.14.
1.11 *cf.* 1 Tim 2.7.
1.13-14 See note on 1.8.
1.15 No details are available concerning the precise controversy alluded to here, but perhaps this is a residue of the hint about difficulties in Asia mentioned in 2 Cor 1.8. *Cf.* also 2 Tim 4.16. *Phygelus and Hermogenes.* Mentioned only here in the New Testament.
1.16-17 These verses suggest that Paul's imprisonment was in Rome; *cf.* Acts 28.30-31.
1.16 *Onesiphorus.* Mentioned in the New Testament only here and in 4.19. In both cases the reference is to his household, which may suggest that he is deceased.
1.18 *Ephesus.* Paul and Timothy were together in Ephesus (see 1 Cor 16.8).
2.2 Again, the function of Timothy's office is to pass on apostolic teaching; *cf.* 1.8; 2.14-15,24-25.
2.3 *cf.* 2 Cor 10.3-5; Philem 2; Eph 6.10-17.
2.5 *cf.* 4.8; 1 Tim 1.18; 6.12; 1 Cor 9.24-27.
2.8 *Remember. Cf.* 1.4-6; 3.14-15. *Descendant of David. Cf.* Rom 1.3-4.
2.11 *Saying.* What follows is a poem or a hymn. *If we have died with him, we will also live with him. Cf.* Rom 6.8; Col 2.20; 3.1.
2.12 *cf.* Rom 12.12; 1 Cor 4.8; Rev 3.21.
2.13 *cf.* Rom 3.3.
2.14-3.9 This section focuses on the negative behavior of the false teachers and how Timothy should act in view of it.
2.14 *Remind...and warn.* As stated previously (1.8; 2.2), the function of Timothy's office is to safeguard the tradition, to pass it on, and to admonish when others do not abide by it; *cf.* also 3.14; 4.2. *Wrangling over words. Cf.* 1 Tim 6.4.
2.15 See note on 1.8.
2.16 *cf.* 1 Tim 6.20.
2.17 *Hymenaeus.* Here it seems as if he still belongs to the fellowship, whereas in 1 Tim 1.20 he has been "turned over to Satan," i.e. expelled. *Philetus.* Mentioned only here.
2.18 This teaching is based on the idea that resurrection is only a spiritual event which occurs at baptism or at the moment of faith; *cf.* 2 Thess 2.2; 1 Cor 15.12.
2.19 See Num 16.5; Lev 24.16; Isa 26.13; Ps 34.14; Prov 3.7.
2.20 *cf.* Jer 18.1-11; Wis 15.7; Rom 9.19-24.
2.22 *Passions. Cf.* 4.3; 1 Tim 6.9. This may be an allusion to the negative actions listed previously in vv. 14-16 and subsequently in vs. 23.
2.23 *cf.* 1 Tim 1.4,7; 4.7; 6.4,20.
2.24-25 See note on 1.8.

and called us with a holy calling, not according to our works but according to his own purpose and grace. This grace was given to us in Christ Jesus before the ages began, 10but it has now been revealed through the appearing of our Savior Christ Jesus, who abolished death and brought life and immortality to light through the gospel. 11For this gospel I was appointed a herald and an apostle and a teacher,[a] 12and for this reason I suffer as I do. But I am not ashamed, for I know the one in whom I have put my trust, and I am sure that he is able to guard until that day what I have entrusted to him.[b] 13Hold to the standard of sound teaching that you have heard from me, in the faith and love that are in Christ Jesus. 14Guard the good treasure entrusted to you, with the help of the Holy Spirit living in us.

15 You are aware that all who are in Asia have turned away from me, including Phygelus and Hermogenes. 16May the Lord grant mercy to the household of Onesiphorus, because he often refreshed me and was not ashamed of my chain; 17when he arrived in Rome, he eagerly[c] searched for me and found me 18—may the Lord grant that he will find mercy from the Lord on that day! And you know very well how much service he rendered in Ephesus.

A Good Soldier of Christ Jesus

2 You then, my child, be strong in the grace that is in Christ Jesus; 2and what you have heard from me through many witnesses entrust to faithful people who will be able to teach others as well. 3Share in suffering like a good soldier of Christ Jesus. 4No one serving in the army gets entangled in everyday affairs; the soldier's aim is to please the enlisting officer. 5And in the case of an athlete, no one is crowned without competing according to the rules. 6It is the farmer who does the work who ought to have the first share of the crops. 7Think over what I say, for the Lord will give you understanding in all things.

8 Remember Jesus Christ, raised from the dead, a descendant of David—that is my gospel, 9for which I suffer hardship, even to the point of being chained like a criminal. But the word of God is not chained. 10Therefore I endure everything for the sake of the elect, so that they may also obtain the salvation that is in Christ Jesus, with eternal glory. 11The saying is sure:

If we have died with him, we will also
live with him;
12 if we endure, we will also reign with
him;
if we deny him, he will also deny us;
13 if we are faithless, he remains
faithful—
for he cannot deny himself.

A Worker Approved by God

14 Remind them of this, and warn them before God[d] that they are to avoid wrangling over words, which does no good but only ruins those who are listening. 15Do your best to present yourself to God as one approved by him, a worker who has no need to be ashamed, rightly explaining the word of truth. 16Avoid profane chatter, for it will lead people into more and more impiety, 17and their talk will spread like gangrene. Among them are Hymenaeus and Philetus, 18who have swerved from the truth by claiming that the resurrection has already taken place. They are upsetting the faith of some. 19But God's firm foundation stands, bearing this inscription: "The Lord knows those who are his," and, "Let everyone who calls on the name of the Lord turn away from wickedness."

20 In a large house there are utensils not only of gold and silver but also of wood and clay, some for special use, some for ordinary. 21All who cleanse themselves of the things I have mentioned[e] will become special utensils, dedicated and useful to the owner of the house, ready for every good work. 22Shun youthful passions and pursue righteousness, faith, love, and peace, along with those who call on the Lord from a pure heart. 23Have nothing to do with stupid and senseless controversies; you know that they breed quarrels. 24And the Lord's servant[f] must not be quarrelsome but kindly to everyone, an apt teacher, patient, 25correcting opponents with gentleness. God may perhaps grant that they will repent and come to know the truth, 26and that they

[a] Other ancient authorities add *of the Gentiles* [b] Or *what has been entrusted to me* [c] Or *promptly* [d] Other ancient authorities read *the Lord* [e] Gk *of these things* [f] Gk *slave*

1.10 Eph 1.9; 1 Cor 15.24
1.11 1 Tim 2.7
1.12 Titus 3.8; 1 Tim 6.20
1.13 Titus 1.9; Rom 2.20; 1 Tim 1.14
1.16 2 Tim 4.19
1.18 2 Thess 1.10; Heb 6.10
2.2 2 Tim 1.13; 1 Tim 6.12; 1.18; 1.12
2.5 1 Cor 9.25
2.9 Acts 9.16; Phil 1.7; Acts 28.31
2.10 Eph 3.13; 2 Cor 1.6
2.12 1 Pet 4.13; Mt 10.33
2.13 Rom 3.3; Num 23.19
2.14 1 Tim 5.21; 6.4
2.16 1 Tim 4.7
2.17 1 Tim 1.20
2.18 1 Cor 15.12
2.19 Isa 28.16,17; 1 Tim 3.15; Jn 10.14; 1 Cor 1.2
2.20 Rom 9.21
2.21 Isa 52.11; 2 Tim 3.17
2.22 1 Tim 6.11; 1.14; 1.5
2.23 1 Tim 6.4; Titus 3.9
2.24 1 Tim 3.3; Titus 1.7; 1 Tim 3.2
2.25 Gal 6.1; 1 Pet 3.15

3.2 2 Pet 2.3; Rom 1.30
3.3 Rom 1.31; Titus 1.8
3.4 2 Pet 2.10; Phil 3.19
3.6 Titus 1.11
3.8 Ex 7.11; Acts 13.8; 1 Tim 6.5
3.10 1 Tim 4.6; Phil 2.22
3.11 Acts 13.45; 14.2,19
3.12 Ps 34.19; Mt 16.24; 1 Thess 3.3
3.13 2 Tim 2.16; Titus 3.3
3.16 Rom 15.4; 2 Pet 1.20,21
3.17 1 Tim 6.11; 2 Tim 2.21
4.1 1 Tim 5.21; Acts 10.42
4.2 1 Tim 5.20; Titus 1.13; 1 Tim 4.13
4.3 2 Tim 3.1,6; 1 Tim 1.10
4.5 Acts 21.8
4.6 Phil 2.17; 1.23
4.7 Phil 3.14; 1 Tim 6.12
4.8 Jas 1.12; 1 Pet 5.4; 2 Tim 1.12
4.10 Col 4.14; 1 Jn 2.15
4.11 2 Tim 1.15; Col 4.14; Acts 12.12
4.14 Acts 19.33; Rom 12.19; Ps 119.98,99
4.17 Acts 23.11; 2 Pet 2.9
4.18 Ps 121.7; Rom 11.36

may escape from the snare of the devil,
having been held captive by him to do his
will.[g]

Godlessness in the Last Days

3 You must understand this, that in the
last days distressing times will come.
[2]For people will be lovers of themselves,
lovers of money, boasters, arrogant, abusive, disobedient to their parents, ungrateful, unholy, [3]inhuman, implacable, slanderers, profligates, brutes, haters of good,
[4]treacherous, reckless, swollen with conceit,
lovers of pleasure rather than lovers of God,
[5]holding to the outward form of godliness
but denying its power. Avoid them! [6]For
among them are those who make their way
into households and captivate silly women,
overwhelmed by their sins and swayed by
all kinds of desires, [7]who are always being
instructed and can never arrive at a knowledge of the truth. [8]As Jannes and Jambres
opposed Moses, so these people, of corrupt
mind and counterfeit faith, also oppose the
truth. [9]But they will not make much
progress, because, as in the case of those
two men,[h] their folly will become plain to
everyone.

Paul's Charge to Timothy

10 Now you have observed my teaching,
my conduct, my aim in life, my faith, my
patience, my love, my steadfastness, [11]my
persecutions and suffering the things that
happened to me in Antioch, Iconium, and
Lystra. What persecutions I endured! Yet
the Lord rescued me from all of them. [12]In-
deed, all who want to live a godly life in
Christ Jesus will be persecuted. [13]But wicked
people and impostors will go from bad to
worse, deceiving others and being deceived.
[14]But as for you, continue in what you have
learned and firmly believed, knowing from
whom you learned it, [15]and how from
childhood you have known the sacred
writings that are able to instruct you for
salvation through faith in Christ Jesus. [16]All
scripture is inspired by God and is[i] useful for
teaching, for reproof, for correction, and for
training in righteousness, [17]so that everyone who belongs to God may be proficient,
equipped for every good work.

4 In the presence of God and of Christ
Jesus, who is to judge the living and
the dead, and in view of his appearing and
his kingdom, I solemnly urge you: [2]pro-
claim the message; be persistent whether
the time is favorable or unfavorable; convince, rebuke, and encourage, with the
utmost patience in teaching. [3]For the time
is coming when people will not put up with
sound doctrine, but having itching ears,
they will accumulate for themselves teachers to suit their own desires, [4]and will turn
away from listening to the truth and wander away to myths. [5]As for you, always be
sober, endure suffering, do the work of an
evangelist, carry out your ministry fully.
6 As for me, I am already being poured
out as a libation, and the time of my departure has come. [7]I have fought the good
fight, I have finished the race, I have kept
the faith. [8]From now on there is reserved for
me the crown of righteousness, which the
Lord, the righteous judge, will give me on
that day, and not only to me but also to all
who have longed for his appearing.

Personal Instructions

9 Do your best to come to me soon, [10]for
Demas, in love with this present world, has
deserted me and gone to Thessalonica;
Crescens has gone to Galatia,[j] Titus to
Dalmatia. [11]Only Luke is with me. Get Mark
and bring him with you, for he is useful in
my ministry. [12]I have sent Tychicus to
Ephesus. [13]When you come, bring the cloak
that I left with Carpus at Troas, also the
books, and above all the parchments. [14]Al-
exander the coppersmith did me great harm;
the Lord will pay him back for his deeds.
[15]You also must beware of him, for he
strongly opposed our message.
16 At my first defense no one came to
my support, but all deserted me. May it not
be counted against them! [17]But the Lord
stood by me and gave me strength, so that
through me the message might be fully
proclaimed and all the Gentiles might hear
it. So I was rescued from the lion's mouth.
[18]The Lord will rescue me from every evil
attack and save me for his heavenly kingdom. To him be the glory forever and ever.
Amen.

3.1 See note on 1 Tim 4.1.
3.2-5 See note on 1 Tim 1.9-10.
3.5 *cf.* Col 2.23.
3.6-7 Evidently a goal of the false teachers has been to influence the women in the congregation.
3.8 *Jannes and Jambres.* These represent names given in later Jewish tradition to Egyptian magicians who opposed Moses (see Ex 7.22; 9.11).
3.10 The impetus and example for Timothy is Paul himself.
3.11 *Antioch. Cf.* Acts 13.50. *Iconium. Cf.* Acts 14.2-6. *Lystra. Cf.* Acts 14.19-20.
3.12 *cf.* Gal 4.29; Phil 1.29; 1 Thess 3.4.
3.13 *cf.* 3.6-9; 4.5; 1 Tim 4.12.
3.14 See notes on 1.8; 2.14.
3.15 *The sacred writings.* I.e. the Hebrew scriptures, namely the Old Testament.
3.16 *All scripture.* As in the previous verse, the Hebrew scriptures, namely the Old Testament. *Inspired by God.* This phrase translates one Greek adjective, which literally means that the Hebrew scriptures were "produced by power of God's own breath."
4.2 See notes on 1.8; 2.14.
4.3-4 *cf.* 3.1-5; 1 Tim 4.1-2.
4.6 *Libation. Cf.* Phil 2.17; this term reflects ancient custom (see Num 13.5,7,10; 28.7; Ps 16.4).
4.7 *cf.* 2.5; 1 Tim 1.10; 6.12; 1 Cor 9.24-27; Phil 3.12-14.
4.8 *Crown of righteousness. Cf.* 2.5; 1 Cor 9.25; Rev 2.10.
4.10 *Demas. Cf.* Col 4.12; Philem 24. *Dalmatia.* The coast of ancient Illyricum, now in Yugoslavia; *cf.* Rom 15.9.
4.11 *Luke. Cf.* Col 4.14; Philem 24. *Mark. Cf.* Col 4.10; Philem 24; also Acts 12.12,25; 13.13; 15.37-39.
4.12 *Tychicus. Cf.* Titus 3.12; Col 4.7; Eph 6.21-22; Acts 20.4.
4.13 *The cloak.* Winter is coming (see 4.21). *Carpus.* Mentioned only here. *Troas.* An Aegean port city on the west coast of Asia Minor. *Books.* Papyrus scrolls. *Parchments.* Scrolls made out of animal skin, usually sheep or goat.
4.14 *Alexander the coppersmith.* It is uncertain whether this Alexander is the one mentioned elsewhere (*cf.* 1 Tim 1.19-20; Acts 19.33-34). *The Lord will pay him back for his deeds. Cf.* Ps 28.4; 62.12; Prov 24.12; Rom 2.6.
4.17 *cf.* Ps 22.19.
4.18 *cf.* 1 Tim 1.17; 6.16; Phil 4.20.

[g] *Or by him, to do his* (that is, *God's*) *will* [h] Gk lacks *two men* [i] Or *Every scripture inspired by God is also* [j] Other ancient authorities read *Gaul*

4.19 *Prisca and Aquila.* See note on Acts 18.2. *The household of Onesiphorus.* See note on 1.16.
4.20 *Erastus. Cf.* Rom 16.23; Acts 19.22. *Trophimus. Cf.* Acts 20.4; 21.29. *Miletus.* An Aegean port city south of Ephesus; *cf.* Acts 20.17.
4.21 *Before winter. Cf.* 4.13. The names in this verse are mentioned only here.
4.22 *cf.* Philem 25; 1 Tim 6.21.

Final Greetings and Benediction

19 Greet Prisca and Aquila, and the household of Onesiphorus. 20 Erastus remained in Corinth; Trophimus I left ill in Miletus. 21 Do your best to come before winter. Eubulus sends greetings to you, as do Pudens and Linus and Claudia and all the brothers and sisters.[k]

22 The Lord be with your spirit. Grace be with you.[l]

[k] Gk *all the brothers* [l] The Greek word for *you* here is plural. Other ancient authorities add *Amen*

See the Introductions, pp. 8–9 and 91–92 above.

THE LETTER OF PAUL TO TITUS

Salutation

1 Paul, a servant[a] of God and an apostle of Jesus Christ, for the sake of the faith of God's elect and the knowledge of the truth that is in accordance with godliness, 2 in the hope of eternal life that God, who never lies, promised before the ages began— 3 in due time he revealed his word through the proclamation with which I have been entrusted by the command of God our Savior,

4 To Titus, my loyal child in the faith we share:

Grace[b] and peace from God the Father and Christ Jesus our Savior.

Titus in Crete

5 I left you behind in Crete for this reason, so that you should put in order what remained to be done, and should appoint elders in every town, as I directed you: 6 someone who is blameless, married only once,[c] whose children are believers, not accused of debauchery and not rebellious. 7 For a bishop,[d] as God's steward, must be blameless; he must not be arrogant or quick-tempered or addicted to wine or violent or greedy for gain; 8 but he must be hospitable, a lover of goodness, prudent, upright, devout, and self-controlled. 9 He must have a firm grasp of the word that is trustworthy in accordance with the teaching, so that he may be able both to preach with sound doctrine and to refute those who contradict it.

10 There are also many rebellious people, idle talkers and deceivers, especially those of the circumcision; 11 they must be silenced, since they are upsetting whole families by teaching for sordid gain what it is not right to teach. 12 It was one of them, their very own prophet, who said,

"Cretans are always liars, vicious
brutes, lazy gluttons."

13 That testimony is true. For this reason rebuke them sharply, so that they may become sound in the faith, 14 not paying attention to Jewish myths or to commandments of those who reject the truth. 15 To the pure all things are pure, but to the corrupt and unbelieving nothing is pure. Their very minds and consciences are corrupted. 16 They profess to know God, but they deny him by their actions. They are detestable, disobedient, unfit for any good work.

Teach Sound Doctrine

2 But as for you, teach what is consistent with sound doctrine. 2 Tell the older men to be temperate, serious, prudent, and sound in faith, in love, and in endurance.

3 Likewise, tell the older women to be reverent in behavior, not to be slanderers or slaves to drink; they are to teach what is good, 4 so that they may encourage the young women to love their husbands, to love their children, 5 to be self-controlled, chaste, good managers of the household, kind, being submissive to their husbands, so

[a] Gk *slave* [b] Other ancient authorities read *Grace, mercy,* [c] Gk *husband of one wife* [d] Or *an overseer*

1.2 2 Tim 1.1; Rom 16.25
1.3 2 Tim 1.10; 1 Thess 2.4
1.4 2 Cor 2.13; Eph 1.2; 1 Tim 1.2
1.5 Acts 27.7; 14.23; 11.30
1.6 1 Tim 3.2-4
1.7 1 Cor 4.1; Eph 5.18
1.10 1 Tim 1.6; Acts 11.2
1.11 2 Tim 3.6; 1 Tim 6.5
1.13 2 Cor 13.10; Titus 2.2
1.14 1 Tim 1.4; Isa 29.13
1.15 Lk 11.39,41; Rom 14.23
1.16 1 Jn 2.4; 2 Tim 3.5,8
2.3 1 Tim 3.8
2.5 1 Cor 14.34; Eph 5.22; 1 Tim 6.1

1.1 See notes on 1 Tim 1.1; 2 Tim 1.1. *Servant.* Literally, "slave" (see footnote *a*); *cf.* 2 Cor 4.5. *God's elect. Cf.* 2 Tim 2.10. *Knowledge of the truth. Cf.* 1 Tim 2.4.
1.2 *Before the ages began. Cf.* 2 Tim 1.9.
1.3 *cf.* 1 Tim 1.1; 1.11; 2.6; 3.16; 2 Tim 1.10-11.
1.4 *Titus.* According to Gal 2.3, *Titus* was a Gentile Christian who was instrumental in the church's decision not to require circumcision of Gentile converts. An important co-worker of Paul's, Titus played an effective negotiating role at Corinth (see 2 Cor 2.12-13; 7.5-16). Later church tradition reports that he became bishop of Crete, where he is said to have died at Gortyna at the age of 94. *Child.* Paul's usual designation for those he converted to Christianity; *cf.* 2 Tim 1.2; 1 Cor 4.15; Gal 4.19; Philem 10.
1.5-9 A description of the ministry expected of bishops in the church, with an emphasis on guarding against false teaching and upholding sound doctrine.
1.5 *Crete.* The fifth largest island in the Mediterranean, located southeast of Greece. *Cf.* Acts 27.7-13. *Elders.* See notes on 1 Tim 4.14; 5.17.
1.6 *cf.* 1 Tim 3.2,10.
1.7 *cf.* 1 Tim 3.1-8.
1.10 *cf.* 1 Tim 1.6. *Those of the circumcision.* I.e. Jews who had become Christians; *cf.* Gal 2.12; Acts 11.12.
1.11 *Upsetting whole families. Cf.* 2 Tim 2.18.
1.12 The quotation is attributed to the Cretan philosopher and poet Epimenides (*ca.* 600 BCE).
1.14 *cf.* 1 Tim 1.4; 4.7; 6.5; 2 Tim 4.4; Isa 29.13.
1.15 *To the pure all things are pure. Cf.* Rom 14.14,20; 1 Tim 4.3.
1.16 *cf.* Rom 2.17-18.
2.1-10 This section resembles a household code, much like the ones presented in Col 3.18-4.1; Eph 5.21-6.9; *cf.* also 1 Pet 3.1-9; 1 Tim 2.8-15; 6.1-2.
2.1 This verse restates the function of ministry in the Pastoral Letters; see note on 2 Tim 1.8.
2.2 *Temperate. Cf.* 1 Tim 3.2,11. *Serious. Cf.* 1 Tim 3.8,11. *Prudent. Cf.* 1 Tim 3.2. *Sound in faith, in love, and in endurance. Cf.* 1 Tim 6.11; 2 Tim 3.10.
2.3 *cf.* 1 Tim 2.10; 3.8,11.
2.4-5 *cf.* 1 Tim 2.9-15; 5.11-14; also Col 3.18; Eph 5.21-23; 1 Pet 3.1.
2.5 *So that the word of God may not be discredited.* A frequent theme in the Pastoral Letters is good conduct for the sake of nonbelievers (*cf.* 1.6; 2.8,10,11,14; 3.2,8,14; 1 Tim 2.1-2; see also 1 Pet 2.11-17).

2.8 1 Tim 6.3
2.9 Eph 6.5
2.11 Rom 5.15; 1 Tim 2.4
2.12 Titus 3.3; 2 Tim 3.12
2.13 2 Thess 2.8; 2 Pet 1.1
2.14 1 Tim 2.6; Heb 9.14; Ex 19.5; Eph 2.10
3.1 Rom 13.1; 2 Tim 2.21
3.2 Eph 4.31; 2 Tim 2.24,25
3.3 1 Cor 6.11; 1 Pet 4.3
3.4 Titus 2.11; 1 Tim 2.3
3.5 Rom 3.20; Eph 5.26; Rom 12.2
3.7 Rom 3.24; 8.17,24
3.8 1 Tim 2.14
3.9 1 Tim 1.4; 2 Tim 2.14
3.10 Rom 16.17
3.12 Acts 20.4; 2 Tim 4.9,10

that the word of God may not be discredited.

6 Likewise, urge the younger men to be self-controlled. [7]Show yourself in all respects a model of good works, and in your teaching show integrity, gravity, [8]and sound speech that cannot be censured; then any opponent will be put to shame, having nothing evil to say of us.

9 Tell slaves to be submissive to their masters and to give satisfaction in every respect; they are not to talk back, [10]not to pilfer, but to show complete and perfect fidelity, so that in everything they may be an ornament to the doctrine of God our Savior.

11 For the grace of God has appeared, bringing salvation to all,[e] [12]training us to renounce impiety and worldly passions, and in the present age to live lives that are self-controlled, upright, and godly, [13]while we wait for the blessed hope and the manifestation of the glory of our great God and Savior,[f] Jesus Christ. [14]He it is who gave himself for us that he might redeem us from all iniquity and purify for himself a people of his own who are zealous for good deeds.

15 Declare these things; exhort and reprove with all authority.[g] Let no one look down on you.

Maintain Good Deeds

3 Remind them to be subject to rulers and authorities, to be obedient, to be ready for every good work, [2]to speak evil of no one, to avoid quarreling, to be gentle, and to show every courtesy to everyone. [3]For we ourselves were once foolish, disobedient, led astray, slaves to various passions and pleasures, passing our days in malice and envy, despicable, hating one another. [4]But when the goodness and loving kindness of God our Savior appeared, [5]he saved us, not because of any works of righteousness that we had done, but according to his mercy, through the water[h] of rebirth and renewal by the Holy Spirit. [6]This Spirit he poured out on us richly through Jesus Christ our Savior, [7]so that, having been justified by his grace, we might become heirs according to the hope of eternal life. [8]The saying is sure.

I desire that you insist on these things, so that those who have come to believe in God may be careful to devote themselves to good works; these things are excellent and profitable to everyone. [9]But avoid stupid controversies, genealogies, dissensions, and quarrels about the law, for they are unprofitable and worthless. [10]After a first and second admonition, have nothing more to do with anyone who causes divisions, [11]since you know that such a person is perverted and sinful, being self-condemned.

Final Messages and Benediction

12 When I send Artemas to you, or Tychicus, do your best to come to me at Nicopolis, for I have decided to spend the winter there. [13]Make every effort to send Zenas the lawyer and Apollos on their way, and see that they lack nothing. [14]And let people learn to devote themselves to good works in order to meet urgent needs, so that they may not be unproductive.

15 All who are with me send greetings to you. Greet those who love us in the faith.

Grace be with all of you.[i]

2.9-10 The instruction for Christian slaves is reminiscent of Col 3.22-25; Eph 6.5-8; 1 Tim 6.1-2.
2.11 *cf.* 1 Tim 2.5-6; Col 1.15-20; Eph 1.15-23; 4.5-6.
2.12 *cf.* Rom 1.18; Gal 5.16,24.
2.13 *cf.* 1 Cor 1.7; 2 Cor 4.4,6; 1 Tim 1.11.
2.14 *cf.* Gal 1.4; Rev 1.5; Mk 10.45.
2.15 See note on 2 Tim 1.8.
3.1 *cf.* Rom 13.1-7; 1 Pet 2.13-17.
3.3 *cf.* 2 Tim 3.13; Gal 4.3.
3.4 *Appeared.* I.e. when Jesus came into the world.
3.5 *Not because of any works. Cf.* Eph 2.8-9. *Water.* Literally, "washing" (see footnote *h*); *cf.* especially Eph 5.26; 1 Pet 3.21. *Rebirth and renewal. Cf.* Jn 3.3-7; 1 Pet 1.3. *By the Holy Spirit. Cf.* Mk 1.8; Acts 1.5.
3.6 *Poured out. Cf.* Acts 2.17-18 (*cf.* Joel 2.28-29); Acts 2.33.
3.7 *cf.* Rom 3.24,28; 5.1; 1 Tim 3.16.
3.8 See note on 2 Tim 1.8.
3.9 *cf.* 2 Tim 2.16,23; 1 Tim 1.4,7-8; 6.4; Titus 1.10,14.
3.10 *cf.* Mt 18.15-17; 1 Tim 4.7; 2 Tim 2.23.
3.11 *cf.* 1 Tim 5.24.
3.12 *Artemas.* Mentioned only here. *Tychicus.* See 2 Tim 4.12; Col 4.7; Eph 6.21-22; Acts 20.4. *Nicopolis.* Probably the Nicopolis located in southern Greece on the shore of the Adriatic. *Winter.* See 2 Tim 4.21.
3.13 *Zenas the lawyer.* Mentioned only here. *Apollos.* It is not known whether this refers to Paul's co-worker mentioned in 1 Cor 3.1-9; Acts 18.24; 19.1.
3.14 *Not be unproductive. Cf.* 2 Thess 3.6-12.
3.15 *cf.* 2 Tim 4.19,21; also 1 Tim 6.21; 2 Tim 4.22.

[e] Or *has appeared to all, bringing salvation* [f] Or *of the great God and our Savior* [g] Gk *commandment* [h] Gk *washing* [i] Other ancient authorities add *Amen*

THE LETTER OF PAUL TO

PHILEMON

See the Introductions, pp. 8–9 and 92 above.

Salutation
1 Paul, a prisoner of Christ Jesus, and
Timothy our brother,[a]
To Philemon our dear friend and co-
worker, 2to Apphia our sister,[b] to Archippus
our fellow soldier, and to the church in
your house:
3 Grace to you and peace from God our
Father and the Lord Jesus Christ.

Philemon's Love and Faith
4 When I remember you[c] in my prayers,
I always thank my God 5because I hear of
your love for all the saints and your faith
toward the Lord Jesus. 6I pray that the
sharing of your faith may become effective
when you perceive all the good that we[d]
may do for Christ. 7I have indeed received
much joy and encouragement from your
love, because the hearts of the saints have
been refreshed through you, my brother.

Paul's Plea for Onesimus
8 For this reason, though I am bold
enough in Christ to command you to do
your duty, 9yet I would rather appeal to you
on the basis of love—and I, Paul, do this as
an old man, and now also as a prisoner of
Christ Jesus.[e] 10I am appealing to you for my
child, Onesimus, whose father I have become during my imprisonment. 11Formerly
he was useless to you, but now he is indeed
useful[f] both to you and to me. 12I am
sending him, that is, my own heart, back
to you. 13I wanted to keep him with me, so
that he might be of service to me in your
place during my imprisonment for the gospel; 14but I preferred to do nothing without
your consent, in order that your good deed
might be voluntary and not something
forced. 15Perhaps this is the reason he was
separated from you for a while, so that you
might have him back forever, 16no longer as
a slave but more than a slave, a beloved
brother—especially to me but how much
more to you, both in the flesh and in the
Lord.
17 So if you consider me your partner,
welcome him as you would welcome me.
18If he has wronged you in any way, or
owes you anything, charge that to my
account. 19I, Paul, am writing this with my
own hand: I will repay it. I say nothing
about your owing me even your own self.
20Yes, brother, let me have this benefit from
you in the Lord! Refresh my heart in Christ.
21Confident of your obedience, I am writing
to you, knowing that you will do even more
than I say.
22 One thing more—prepare a guest room
for me, for I am hoping through your prayers
to be restored to you.

Final Greetings and Benediction
23 Epaphras, my fellow prisoner in Christ
Jesus, sends greetings to you,[g] 24and so do
Mark, Aristarchus, Demas, and Luke, my
fellow workers.
25 The grace of the Lord Jesus Christ be
with your spirit.[h]

1 Eph 3.1; 2 Cor 1.1; Phil 2.25
2 Col 4.17; Phil 2.25; Rom 16.5
4 Rom 1.8,9
5 Eph 1.15; Col 1.4
7 ver 20; 2 Cor 7.13
10 Col 4.9; 1 Cor 4.14,15
13 Phil 1.7
14 1 Pet 5.2; 2 Cor 9.7
16 Mt 23.8; 1 Tim 6.2; Col 3.22
17 2 Cor 8.23
21 2 Cor 2.3
22 Acts 28.23; Phil 1.25; 2.24; 2 Cor 1.11
23 Col 1.7
24 Acts 12.12; Col 4.10
25 2 Tim 4.22

[a] Gk *the brother* [b] Gk *the sister* [c] From verse 4 through verse 21, *you* is singular [d] Other ancient authorities read *you* (plural) [e] Or *as an ambassador of Christ Jesus, and now also his prisoner* [f] The name *Onesimus* means *useful* or (compare verse 20) *beneficial* [g] Here *you* is singular [h] Other ancient authorities add *Amen*

1 *Prisoner.* The location of Paul's imprisonment is not mentioned. For comments on Paul's imprisonment see note on Phil 1.13. For the structure of a letter, see note on Rom 1.1. *Timothy.* Regarding Timothy see notes on Acts 16.1 and Rom 16.21. Timothy is mentioned by Paul as a co-sender of 2 Corinthians, Philippians, Colossians, and 1 and 2 Thessalonians. Timothy was Paul's emissary from Ephesus to Corinth concerning the collection (*cf.* 1 Cor 16.1-10) and from the place of Paul's imprisonment to Philippi (*cf.* Phil 2.19).
2 *The church in your house.* Before larger church structures were built, the earliest Christians assembled in homes large enough to serve as gathering places for preaching and teaching, for worship, and for social and eucharist table-sharing. Modeled after the synagogues, such meeting places were called "house churches." People of means, then, were part of the Christian movement, such as Philemon, who was a home-owner as well as a slave-owner. Other leaders of house churches included Chloe (1 Cor 1.11), Aquila and Priscilla (1 Cor 16.19; Rom 16.5), Stephanus (1 Cor 1.16; 16.15), Nympha (Col 4.15), Gaius (Rom 16.23), and most likely also Phoebe (Rom 16.1-2).
3 *Grace and peace.* See note on Rom 1.7. This formal-liturgical greeting indicates the use to be made of this letter, namely as a communication to be read to the assembled church in Philemon's house.
4 *I always thank my God.* Paul begins, as in all his letters except Galatians, with a thanksgiving. See notes on Rom 1.8-15 and 1 Cor 1.4-7.
5 *The saints.* Paul typically refers to all Christians, whether living or dead, as "the saints." See note on Rom 1.7; *cf.* also Rom 15.26; Phil 4.21; Eph 2.19; Col 1.12; 1 Thess 3.13. Literally the word means "those set apart for God's work in the world."
10 *My child...whose father I have become.* Paul uses this language of those who have become Christians under his tutelage (*cf.* 1 Cor 4.15; Gal 4.19).
13 *Of service to me in your place.* Paul is raising the question whether or not Onesimus might serve in the Pauline mission as the representative of the church in Philemon's house. The question must be raised delicately, since runaway slaves were subject to the death penalty. Verse 11 states that Onesimus, a name which means *the useful one*, can now be useful to both Philemon and Paul. *Cf.* the role of Epaphroditus as the Philippians' emissary to Paul (Phil 2.25-30).
17 *Partner.* Paul calls for Philemon to treat Onesimus as Philemon would treat Paul: they are partners in the work of the gospel.
18 *If he has wronged you...or owes you anything.* Perhaps Onesimus had stolen something as he fled Philemon's custody.
19 *I, Paul, am writing this with my own hand.* Paul's signature here is his promise to make reparation, if any is required. Paul adds comments in his own hand in 1 Cor 16.21-24 and Gal 6.11-18. *Your owing me even your own self.* This wording suggests that Philemon himself became a Christian under Paul's tutelage.
21 *Knowing that you will do even more than I say.* This wording suggests the delicacy with which Paul is treating the subject of Philemon's acceptance of Onesimus and of his releasing the runaway slave for work in the Pauline mission. Paul knows that Philemon must answer to his fellow slave-owners for not inflicting the required punishment on Onesimus.
23-24 The names listed occur also in Col 4.10-14.

THE LETTER TO THE

HEBREWS

1.2 Gal 4.4; Heb 2.3; Ps 2.8; Jn 1.3; 1 Cor 8.6

1.3 Jn 1.14; Col 1.17; Heb 7.27; 8.1

1.4 Eph 1.21; Phil 2.9,10

1.5 Ps 2.7

1.7 Ps 104.4

1.8 Ps 45.6,7

1.9 Phil 2.9; Isa 61.1,3

1.10 Ps 102.25

1.11 Isa 34.4

1.13 Ps 110.1; Heb 10.13

1.14 Ps 103.20; Heb 5.9

2.2 Heb 1.1; Acts 7.53; Heb 10.28,35

2.3 Heb 10.29; 1.1; Lk 1.2

2.4 Jn 4.48; 1 Cor 12.4; Eph 1.5

2.5 Heb 6.5

2.6 Ps 8.4-6

God Has Spoken by His Son

1 Long ago God spoke to our ancestors
in many and various ways by the
prophets, 2 but in these last days he has
spoken to us by a Son,[a] whom he appointed
heir of all things, through whom he also
created the worlds. 3 He is the reflection of
God's glory and the exact imprint of God's
very being, and he sustains[b] all things by
his powerful word. When he had made
purification for sins, he sat down at the
right hand of the Majesty on high, 4 having
become as much superior to angels as the
name he has inherited is more excellent
than theirs.

The Son Is Superior to Angels

5 For to which of the angels did God ever
say,

"You are my Son;
today I have begotten you"?

Or again,

"I will be his Father,
and he will be my Son"?

6 And again, when he brings the firstborn
into the world, he says,

"Let all God's angels worship him."

7 Of the angels he says,

"He makes his angels winds,
and his servants flames of fire."

8 But of the Son he says,

"Your throne, O God,[c] is forever and
ever,
and the righteous scepter is the
scepter of your[d] kingdom.
9 You have loved righteousness and
hated wickedness;
therefore God, your God, has anointed
you
with the oil of gladness beyond your
companions."

10 And,

"In the beginning, Lord, you founded
the earth,
and the heavens are the work of
your hands;
11 they will perish, but you remain;
they will all wear out like clothing;
12 like a cloak you will roll them up,
and like clothing[e] they will be
changed.
But you are the same,
and your years will never end."

13 But to which of the angels has he ever
said,

"Sit at my right hand
until I make your enemies a
footstool for your feet"?

14 Are not all angels[f] spirits in the divine
service, sent to serve for the sake of those
who are to inherit salvation?

Warning to Pay Attention

2 Therefore we must pay greater attention to what we have heard, so that
we do not drift away from it. 2 For if the
message declared through angels was valid,
and every transgression or disobedience
received a just penalty, 3 how can we escape
if we neglect so great a salvation? It was
declared at first through the Lord, and it
was attested to us by those who heard him,
4 while God added his testimony by signs
and wonders and various miracles, and by
gifts of the Holy Spirit, distributed according
to his will.

Exaltation through Abasement

5 Now God[g] did not subject the coming
world, about which we are speaking, to
angels. 6 But someone has testified somewhere,

"What are human beings that you are
mindful of them,[h]
or mortals, that you care for them?[i]
7 You have made them for a little while
lower[j] than the angels;

[a] Or *the Son* [b] Or *bears along* [c] Or *God is your throne* [d] Other ancient authorities read *his* [e] Other ancient authorities lack *like clothing* [f] Gk *all of them* [g] Gk *he* [h] Gk *What is man that you are mindful of him?* [i] Gk *or the son of man that you care for him?* In the Hebrew of Psalm 8.4–6 both *man* and *son of man* refer to all humankind [j] Or *them only a little lower*

See the Introductions, pp. 9–10 and 93–94 above.

1.1-14 Jesus as Ultimate Revelation and Agent of God.
1.1-2 The God who over the centuries addressed his people through the *prophets* of Israel has now spoken to his people through his *Son*, who is to take control of the universe and through whom the course of history (*worlds*) was created.
1.2-4 God was believed by ancient Israel to be present visibly in a radiant cloud of *glory* in the inner court of the temple, but now he is revealed through Jesus, who manifests his nature (the Greek means literally, *who bears the imprint of God's basic being*) and who on completion of his act of *purification* of human *sins* is now enthroned at the side of God in heaven. There he is exalted far above all the *angels* of God, since his role and rank (*name*) in God's purpose exceed theirs.
1.5-14 In an extended series of quotations from the Jewish scriptures (in the Greek translation, or Septuagint), the author shows how God had long planned what has now occurred through Jesus. He has been established and acclaimed as God's *Son* (Ps 2.7; 2 Sam 7.14; 1 Chr 17.13). In what follows, the superiority of Jesus to the angels of God is detailed. The angels worship him and are the *servants* to do God's work (Deut 32.43; Ps 104.4), but the *Son* is established *forever* on the *throne*, where he is the agent through whom God's rule is maintained. His reign is characterized by justice and hatred of human *wickedness*, but also by unmatched joy as God's chosen instrument (Ps 45.6-7). This work of God is in keeping with his eternal purpose to create and sustain the world (Ps 102.25-27), and it is through Christ that God's triumph over evil (*your enemies*) will be accomplished (Ps 110.1). The angels' task is to serve the purpose of God in behalf of his new people, who will now *inherit* [enter the new life of] *salvation*.
2.1-4 Exhortation. The first of the series of exhortations indicates that the problem addressed by the writer is a decline of interest and commitment on the part of the members of the community. God has always held his people accountable for what has been disclosed to them, and there is no way out for those who *neglect* this great plan of human deliverance and renewal, announced by Jesus through his words and attested further by his miracles. These evidences of God's *Spirit* are still manifest among his people as God wills.
2.5-3.6 Jesus' Identification with Human Suffering and Death.
2.5-9 The Hebrew text of Ps 8.4-6 speaks of the humiliation and exaltation of human beings, but the Greek version quoted here is understood as referring to Jesus, whose experience of human limits of suffering and death has led to his being assigned a unique place of honor and power over *all things*, for which *Son of Man* is his title. His acceptance of these human limits is God's way of dealing with *death*, and its benefits are potentially available for *everyone*.

2.10-18 This was God's remedy for human evil, sin and death, and Jesus was the prototype (*pioneer*) of this divine deliverance and transformation of those who now accept their role as God's people. Jesus shared the flesh and blood limitations of human existence, and the faithful now share in the defeat of evil and death which he has accomplished. He was both *high priest* and ultimate *sacrifice* in making *atonement for the sins of the people*. Having experienced suffering and death, he can help those passing through the same human trials.
3.1-6 The community which Christ has brought into being is the true *house* of God. *Moses* performed his role faithfully in an earthly house – the mobile tent of meeting where Israel gathered of old before the temple was built – but the life of the new community is *heavenly* in its orientation and is presided over by Christ as God's Son. The possibility of sharing in that eternal *house* is contingent on the steadfastness and *pride* with which they face this future *hope* of the completion of God's purpose for his new people.
3.7-4.16 Exhortation.
3.7-19 The second exhortation is also concerned about fidelity of the members of the community in matters of both faith and practice. Again the appeal is to the Jewish scriptures, warning against putting God to the test and as a result experiencing his *anger* (Ps 95.7-11), as Israel did during the exodus from Egypt to the land of promise (Deut 6.16; Num 14.21-23). To persist in their rebellious or indifferent ways will exclude them from ever entering the place of heavenly rest which Christ has opened for them, just as the disobedient within Israel never reached the new land.

you have crowned them with glory
and honor,[k]
8 subjecting all things under their
feet."
Now in subjecting all things to them, God[l]
left nothing outside their control. As it is,
we do not yet see everything in subjection
to them, 9but we do see Jesus, who for a
little while was made lower[m] than the
angels, now crowned with glory and honor
because of the suffering of death, so that by
the grace of God[n] he might taste death for
everyone.
10 It was fitting that God,[l] for whom and
through whom all things exist, in bringing
many children to glory, should make the
pioneer of their salvation perfect through
sufferings. 11For the one who sanctifies and
those who are sanctified all have one Father.[o]
For this reason Jesus[l] is not ashamed to call
them brothers and sisters,[p] 12saying,
"I will proclaim your name to my
brothers and sisters,[p]
in the midst of the congregation I
will praise you."
13And again,
"I will put my trust in him."
And again,
"Here am I and the children whom
God has given me."
14 Since, therefore, the children share
flesh and blood, he himself likewise shared
the same things, so that through death he
might destroy the one who has the power
of death, that is, the devil, 15and free those
who all their lives were held in slavery by
the fear of death. 16For it is clear that he did
not come to help angels, but the descendants of Abraham. 17Therefore he had to
become like his brothers and sisters[p] in
every respect, so that he might be a merciful
and faithful high priest in the service of
God, to make a sacrifice of atonement for
the sins of the people. 18Because he himself
was tested by what he suffered, he is able
to help those who are being tested.

Moses a Servant, Christ a Son

3 Therefore, brothers and sisters,[p] holy
partners in a heavenly calling, consider that Jesus, the apostle and high priest
of our confession, 2was faithful to the one
who appointed him, just as Moses also "was
faithful in all[q] God's[r] house." 3Yet Jesus[s] is
worthy of more glory than Moses, just as
the builder of a house has more honor than
the house itself. 4(For every house is built
by someone, but the builder of all things is
God.) 5Now Moses was faithful in all God's[r]
house as a servant, to testify to the things
that would be spoken later. 6Christ, however, was faithful over God's[r] house as a
son, and we are his house if we hold firm[t]
the confidence and the pride that belong to
hope.

Warning against Unbelief

7 Therefore, as the Holy Spirit says,
"Today, if you hear his voice,
8 do not harden your hearts as in the
rebellion,
as on the day of testing in the
wilderness,
9 where your ancestors put me to the
test,
though they had seen my works
10for forty years.
Therefore I was angry with that
generation,
and I said, 'They always go astray in
their hearts,
and they have not known my
ways.'
11 As in my anger I swore,
'They will not enter my rest.'"
12Take care, brothers and sisters,[p] that none
of you may have an evil, unbelieving heart
that turns away from the living God. 13But
exhort one another every day, as long as it
is called "today," so that none of you may
be hardened by the deceitfulness of sin.
14For we have become partners of Christ, if
only we hold our first confidence firm to the
end. 15As it is said,
"Today, if you hear his voice,
do not harden your hearts as in the
rebellion."
16Now who were they who heard and yet
were rebellious? Was it not all those who
left Egypt under the leadership of Moses?
17But with whom was he angry forty years?
Was it not those who sinned, whose bodies
fell in the wilderness? 18And to whom did
he swear that they would not enter his rest,
if not to those who were disobedient? 19So
we see that they were unable to enter
because of unbelief.

[k] Other ancient authorities add *and set them over the works of your hands* [l] Gk *he* [m] Or *who was made a little lower* [n] Other ancient authorities read *apart from God* [o] Gk *are all of one* [p] Gk *brothers* [q] Other ancient authorities lack *all* [r] Gk *his* [s] Gk *this one* [t] Other ancient authorities add *to the end*

2.8 Mt 28.18; 1 Cor 15.27; 15.25
2.9 Phil 2.7-9; Acts 2.33; Jn 3.16; 1 Jn 2.2
2.10 Lk 24.46; Rom 11.36; Acts 3.15; 5.31; Lk 13.32
2.11 Heb 10.10; Acts 17.26; Jn 20.17
2.12 Ps 22.22
2.13 Isa 8.17,18; Jn 10.29
2.14 Mt 16.17; Jn 1.14; 1 Cor 15.54-57; 1 Jn 3.8
2.15 Rom 8.15; 2 Tim 1.7
2.17 Phil 2.7; Heb 4.15; 5.1,2; 1 Jn 2.2; 4.10
2.18 Heb 4.15
3.1 Heb 2.11; Phil 3.14; Rom 15.8; Heb 10.21
3.3 2 Cor 3.7-11
3.4 Eph 2.10; Heb 1.2
3.5 Num 12.7; Ex 14.31; Deut 18.18,19
3.6 Heb 1.2; 1 Cor 3.16; Rom 5.2; Col 1.23
3.7 Heb 9.8; Ps 95.7
3.15 ver 7
3.16 Num 14.2
3.17 Num 14.29; Ps 106.26
3.18 Num 14.23; Heb 4.6
3.19 Jn 3.36

4.1 Heb 12.15
4.2 1 Thess 2.13
4.4 Gen 2.2; Ex 20.11
4.7 Ps 95.7,8; Heb 3.7,8
4.12 Jer 23.29; Eph 6.17; 1 Cor 14.24,25
4.13 Ps 33.13-15; Job 26.6
4.14 Heb 3.1; 7.26; 10-23
4.15 Heb 2.18; 2 Cor 5.21; 1 Pet 2.22
5.2 Heb 2.18; Jas 5.19; Heb 7.28
5.4 2 Chr 26.18; Ex 28.1
5.5 Jn 8.54; Ps 2.7; Heb 1.1,5
5.6 Ps 110.4; Heb 7.17
5.7 Mt 26.39,53; 27-46; Mk 14.36; 15.34
5.8 Heb 3.6; Phil 2.8
5.9 Heb 2.10
5.12 Gal 4.3; Heb 6.1; Acts 7.38; 1 Cor 3.2
5.14 Isa 7.15
6.1 Phil 3.12-14; Heb 5.12; 9.14

The Rest That God Promised

4 Therefore, while the promise of entering his rest is still open, let us take
care that none of you should seem to have
failed to reach it. 2For indeed the good news
came to us just as to them; but the message
they heard did not benefit them, because
they were not united by faith with those
who listened.[u] 3For we who have believed
enter that rest, just as God[v] has said,

"As in my anger I swore,
'They shall not enter my rest,'"

though his works were finished at the foundation of the world. 4For in one place it
speaks about the seventh day as follows,
"And God rested on the seventh day from
all his works." 5And again in this place it
says, "They shall not enter my rest." 6Since
therefore it remains open for some to enter
it, and those who formerly received the
good news failed to enter because of disobedience, 7again he sets a certain day—
"today"—saying through David much later,
in the words already quoted,

"Today, if you hear his voice,
do not harden your hearts."

8For if Joshua had given them rest, God[v]
would not speak later about another day.
9So then, a sabbath rest still remains for the
people of God; 10for those who enter God's
rest also cease from their labors as God did
from his. 11Let us therefore make every
effort to enter that rest, so that no one may
fall through such disobedience as theirs.

12 Indeed, the word of God is living and
active, sharper than any two-edged sword,
piercing until it divides soul from spirit,
joints from marrow; it is able to judge the
thoughts and intentions of the heart. 13And
before him no creature is hidden, but all are
naked and laid bare to the eyes of the one
to whom we must render an account.

Jesus the Great High Priest

14 Since, then, we have a great high
priest who has passed through the heavens,
Jesus, the Son of God, let us hold fast to our
confession. 15For we do not have a high
priest who is unable to sympathize with our
weaknesses, but we have one who in every
respect has been tested[w] as we are, yet
without sin. 16Let us therefore approach the
throne of grace with boldness, so that we
may receive mercy and find grace to help
in time of need.

5 Every high priest chosen from among
mortals is put in charge of things
pertaining to God on their behalf, to offer
gifts and sacrifices for sins. 2He is able to
deal gently with the ignorant and wayward, since he himself is subject to weakness; 3and because of this he must offer
sacrifice for his own sins as well as for those
of the people. 4And one does not presume
to take this honor, but takes it only when
called by God, just as Aaron was.

5 So also Christ did not glorify himself in
becoming a high priest, but was appointed
by the one who said to him,

"You are my Son,
today I have begotten you";

6as he says also in another place,

"You are a priest forever,
according to the order of
Melchizedek."

7 In the days of his flesh, Jesus[v] offered
up prayers and supplications, with loud
cries and tears, to the one who was able to
save him from death, and he was heard
because of his reverent submission. 8Al-
though he was a Son, he learned obedience
through what he suffered; 9and having been
made perfect, he became the source of eternal salvation for all who obey him, 10having
been designated by God a high priest according to the order of Melchizedek.

Warning against Falling Away

11 About this[x] we have much to say
that is hard to explain, since you have
become dull in understanding. 12For though
by this time you ought to be teachers, you
need someone to teach you again the basic
elements of the oracles of God. You need
milk, not solid food; 13for everyone who
lives on milk, being still an infant, is un-
skilled in the word of righteousness. 14But
solid food is for the mature, for those whose
faculties have been trained by practice to
distinguish good from evil.

The Peril of Falling Away

6 Therefore let us go on toward perfection,[y] leaving behind the basic teaching about Christ, and not laying again the

[u] Other ancient authorities read *it did not meet with faith in those who listened* [v] Gk *he* [w] Or *tempted* [x] Or *him* [y] Or *toward maturity*

4.1-11 The prospect of missing out on entering God's *rest* that is intended for his people is developed by showing the lack of trust (*faith*) in God's promise and God's punitive response, with the repeated quotation from Ps 95.11 about the people's failure to enter (Heb 4.3,5). The same psalm is quoted again to express God's continued appeal to open one's heart to his message. But the ultimate *rest* did not come even through *Joshua*, who led the people into the land of Canaan (Deut 31.7; Josh 22.4). God had intended a final *rest*, for which the *sabbath rest* was the symbol and which has been achieved through Jesus. The readers of Hebrews are appealed to, so that they will heed the call and not fail to enter the *rest*.

4.12-16 The depiction of God's word (*logos*) as a sword recalls the angel placed by God at the entrance to the Garden of Eden to keep out evildoers (Gen 3.24), and especially the word of God as a sword bringing death to all disobedient humanity (Wis 18.14-18), from which there is no escape. God calls everyone to account (*logos*) for their behavior. Yet God has also provided a remedy for human sin through the *great High Priest*, Jesus, who experienced temptations and sufferings as a human being, and through whom access to the merciful God is now available.

5.1-10 Christ the Superior High Priest (Part One).

5.1-3 The similarity between Jesus as high priest and those who served in the tradition of the Jewish cultic system is that he too can sympathize with their difficulties, but unlike Jesus, the priests descended from Aaron must offer sacrifices for their own misdeeds.

5.4-6 Like the traditional priests, Jesus is called of God for this role, but unlike theirs, his priesthood continues *forever*, as promised in the psalms (Ps 2.7; 110.4).

5.7-10 During his earthly life (*days of his flesh*), Jesus prayed to God and learned to obey God through his suffering. He was *reverent* and confident that God could deliver him even *from death*. When God raised him from the dead and installed him on his heavenly throne, Jesus' work of salvation was completed (*made perfect*), and all who *obey him* may now share in the benefits wrought by this great High Priest.

5.11-6.12 Exhortation. The third of the extended exhortations gives the reader a vivid picture of the problems and conditions within the Christian communities that are being addressed.

5.11-14 The leaders have not matured and taken on the task of instruction. Using images that are found in Greek and Latin discourses of this period on how education should be developed, the simple level of teaching is compared to *milk* and contrasted with *solid food*. The members are like infants, untrained to tell good from evil.

6.1-8 The call is for them to move toward *maturity*, in contrast to the basic initial instruction they received about repentance, resurrection and baptism. *Laying on of hands* probably refers to the formal act of the leader when a convert has been baptized and is accepted into the community. At the same time, those who have shared in the benefits of the community – enlightenment, the gifts from heaven, the Holy Spirit's presence and power – but who have abandoned it are beyond hope of restoration. They have now identified themselves with the enemies of Jesus who put him to death, and are doomed to an eternal curse.

6.9-12 The writer is confident that his readers do not fall into this group who have fallen away from their commitment, and expects that their *love* and service will continue and will be rewarded by God. Yet he urges them again to enter more fully into the *promises*, so that they will not be *sluggish*, but fully assured of the hope that is theirs in Christ.
6.13-10.18 Christ the Superior High Priest (Part Two).
6.13-20 Entering the Land of Promise. God's promise to childless Abraham recorded in Gen 22.15-18 is that he will have a son and numerous descendants. Undergirding that promise is God's oath, which is given in a technical formula. The *promise* and the *oath* are the two *unchangeable things* which provided assurance to Abraham, and now to his spiritual heirs in the new community of faith. Abraham's historical descendants were established in Canaan, the land of promise, but the new people of God now have assurance of a heavenly land (*city* or *rest*), since Christ has already entered that sacred place.
7.1-10 Melchizedek as the Prototype of Christ's Priestly Role. Here the author expands the theme of Melchizedek as the priest who did not fit the human requirements for that role as set out in the law of Moses, since neither his ancestry nor his posterity is reported (Gen 14.18-20) and he was not descended from Levi, the son of Jacob and descendant of Abraham to whom God assigned the priestly task (Heb 6.20; Num 18.1-20). Abraham demonstrated the superiority of Melchizedek by paying tithes to him (Gen 14.18-20), while later the other tribes of Israel continued to pay tithes to the sons of Levi (Num 18.21-32).
7.11-19 *Perfection* here means the fulfillment of God's purpose to form a holy and obedient covenant people. This was not accomplished through the priestly work performed by *Aaron* and the descendants of Levi, but is now being achieved through Jesus, whose ancestry is from the non-priestly, royal line of *Judah* (Micah 5.2). Like Melchizedek's, Christ's priesthood is not dependent on physical ancestry, but instead arches over time (7.3), enduring *forever* as promised (7.17). The priestly system under the law of Moses was *ineffectual*, but a sure *hope* is now made certain for the followers of Jesus through his having been exalted to God's right hand.

foundation: repentance from dead works
and faith toward God, 2instruction about
baptisms, laying on of hands, resurrection
of the dead, and eternal judgment. 3And we
will do[z] this, if God permits. 4For it is impossible to restore again to repentance those
who have once been enlightened, and have
tasted the heavenly gift, and have shared in
the Holy Spirit, 5and have tasted the goodness of the word of God and the powers of
the age to come, 6and then have fallen
away, since on their own they are crucify-
ing again the Son of God and are holding
him up to contempt. 7Ground that drinks
up the rain falling on it repeatedly, and that
produces a crop useful to those for whom
it is cultivated, receives a blessing from God.
8But if it produces thorns and thistles, it is
worthless and on the verge of being cursed;
its end is to be burned over.
9 Even though we speak in this way,
beloved, we are confident of better things in
your case, things that belong to salvation.
10For God is not unjust; he will not overlook
your work and the love that you showed for
his sake[a] in serving the saints, as you still
do. 11And we want each one of you to show
the same diligence so as to realize the full
assurance of hope to the very end, 12so that
you may not become sluggish, but imitators
of those who through faith and patience
inherit the promises.

The Certainty of God's Promise

13 When God made a promise to
Abraham, because he had no one greater
by whom to swear, he swore by himself,
14saying, "I will surely bless you and multiply you." 15And thus Abraham,[b] having
patiently endured, obtained the promise.
16Human beings, of course, swear by someone greater than themselves, and an oath
given as confirmation puts an end to all
dispute. 17In the same way, when God desired
to show even more clearly to the heirs of
the promise the unchangeable character of
his purpose, he guaranteed it by an oath,
18so that through two unchangeable things,
in which it is impossible that God would
prove false, we who have taken refuge might
be strongly encouraged to seize the hope set
before us. 19We have this hope, a sure and
steadfast anchor of the soul, a hope that
enters the inner shrine behind the curtain,
20where Jesus, a forerunner on our behalf,
has entered, having become a high priest
forever according to the order of Melchizedek.

The Priestly Order of Melchizedek

7 This "King Melchizedek of Salem, priest
of the Most High God, met Abraham
as he was returning from defeating the
kings and blessed him"; 2and to him
Abraham apportioned "one-tenth of everything." His name, in the first place, means
"king of righteousness"; next he is also king
of Salem, that is, "king of peace." 3Without
father, without mother, without genealogy,
having neither beginning of days nor end
of life, but resembling the Son of God, he
remains a priest forever.
4 See how great he is! Even[c] Abraham
the patriarch gave him a tenth of the spoils.
5And those descendants of Levi who receive
the priestly office have a commandment in
the law to collect tithes[d] from the people,
that is, from their kindred,[e] though these
also are descended from Abraham. 6But this
man, who does not belong to their ancestry,
collected tithes[d] from Abraham and blessed
him who had received the promises. 7It is
beyond dispute that the inferior is blessed by
the superior. 8In the one case, tithes are
received by those who are mortal; in the
other, by one of whom it is testified that he
lives. 9One might even say that Levi himself,
who receives tithes, paid tithes through
Abraham, 10for he was still in the loins of
his ancestor when Melchizedek met him.

Another Priest, Like Melchizedek

11 Now if perfection had been attainable
through the levitical priesthood—for the
people received the law under this priesthood—what further need would there have
been to speak of another priest arising according to the order of Melchizedek, rather
than one according to the order of Aaron?
12For when there is a change in the priesthood, there is necessarily a change in the
law as well. 13Now the one of whom these
things are spoken belonged to another tribe,
from which no one has ever served at the
altar. 14For it is evident that our Lord was
descended from Judah, and in connection
with that tribe Moses said nothing about
priests.

[z] Other ancient authorities read *let us do* [a] Gk *for his name* [b] Gk *he* [c] Other ancient authorities lack *Even* [d] Or *a tenth* [e] Gk *brothers*

6.2 Acts 19.3,4; 6.6; 17.31,32
6.4 Heb 10.26; 10.32; Eph 2.8; Gal 3.2,5
6.5 Heb 2.5
6.6 Heb 10.26-29
6.7 Ps 65.10
6.8 Gen 3.17,18
6.10 Mt 10.42; 25.40; 2 Thess 1.6,7; 1 Thess 1.3; Rom 15.25
6.11 Heb 3.6,14; Col 2.2
6.12 Heb 10.36
6.13 Gen 22.16,17; Lk 1.73
6.16 Gal 3.15; Ex 22.11
6.17 Heb 11.9; Ps 110.4
6.18 Titus 1.2; Heb 7.19
6.19 Lev 16.2; Heb 9.7
6.20 Heb 4.14; 5.6
7.1 Gen 14.18-20
7.3 ver 6.28
7.4 Gen 14.20
7.5 Num 18.21,26
7.6 Gen 14.19; Rom 4.13
7.8 Heb 5.6; 6.20
7.11 ver 18,19; Heb 8.7; 10.1; ver 17
7.14 Isa 11.1; Mt 1.3; Lk 3.33; Rom 1.3; Rev 5.5

15 It is even more obvious when another priest arises, resembling Melchizedek, [16]one who has become a priest, not through a legal requirement concerning physical descent, but through the power of an indestructible life. [17]For it is attested of him,

"You are a priest forever,
according to the order of
Melchizedek."

[18]There is, on the one hand, the abrogation of an earlier commandment because it was weak and ineffectual [19](for the law made nothing perfect); there is, on the other hand, the introduction of a better hope, through which we approach God.

20 This was confirmed with an oath; for others who became priests took their office without an oath, [21]but this one became a priest with an oath, because of the one who said to him,

"The Lord has sworn
and will not change his mind,
'You are a priest forever' "—

[22]accordingly Jesus has also become the guarantee of a better covenant.

23 Furthermore, the former priests were many in number, because they were prevented by death from continuing in office; [24]but he holds his priesthood permanently, because he continues forever. [25]Consequently he is able for all time to save[f] those who approach God through him, since he always lives to make intercession for them.

26 For it was fitting that we should have such a high priest, holy, blameless, undefiled, separated from sinners, and exalted above the heavens. [27]Unlike the other[g] high priests, he has no need to offer sacrifices day after day, first for his own sins, and then for those of the people; this he did once for all when he offered himself. [28]For the law appoints as high priests those who are subject to weakness, but the word of the oath, which came later than the law, appoints a Son who has been made perfect forever.

Mediator of a Better Covenant

8 Now the main point in what we are saying is this: we have such a high priest, one who is seated at the right hand of the throne of the Majesty in the heavens, [2]a minister in the sanctuary and the true tent[h] that the Lord, and not any mortal, has set up. [3]For every high priest is appointed to offer gifts and sacrifices; hence it is necessary for this priest also to have something to offer. [4]Now if he were on earth, he would not be a priest at all, since there are priests who offer gifts according to the law. [5]They offer worship in a sanctuary that is a sketch and shadow of the heavenly one; for Moses, when he was about to erect the tent,[h] was warned, "See that you make everything according to the pattern that was shown you on the mountain." [6]But Jesus[i] has now obtained a more excellent ministry, and to that degree he is the mediator of a better covenant, which has been enacted through better promises. [7]For if that first covenant had been faultless, there would have been no need to look for a second one.

8 God[j] finds fault with them when he says:

"The days are surely coming, says the
Lord,
when I will establish a new
covenant with the house of
Israel
and with the house of Judah;
9 not like the covenant that I made
with their ancestors,
on the day when I took them by
the hand to lead them out of
the land of Egypt;
for they did not continue in my
covenant,
and so I had no concern for them,
says the Lord.
10 This is the covenant that I will make
with the house of Israel
after those days, says the Lord:
I will put my laws in their minds,
and write them on their hearts,
and I will be their God,
and they shall be my people.
11 And they shall not teach one another
or say to each other, 'Know the
Lord,'
for they shall all know me,
from the least of them to the
greatest.
12 For I will be merciful toward their
iniquities,
and I will remember their sins no
more."

[13]In speaking of "a new covenant," he has made the first one obsolete. And what is obsolete and growing old will soon disappear.

7.16 Heb 9.10; 9.14
7.17 Ps 110.4; Heb 5.6; 6.20; ver 21
7.18 Rom 8.3; Gal 4.9
7.19 Acts 13.39; Rom 3.20; Gal 2.16; Heb 9.9; 6.18; 8.6; 4.16
7.21 Ps 110.4
7.22 Heb 8.6; 9.15; 12.24
7.25 ver 19; Rom 8.34; Heb 9.24
7.26 Heb 4.15; 8.1
7.27 Heb 5.1,3; 9.12; Eph 5.2; Heb 9.14,28
7.28 Heb 5.2; 1.2; 2.10
8.1 Heb 2.17; 1.3
8.2 Heb 9.11,24
8.3 Heb 5.1; 9.14
8.5 Col 2.17; Heb 9.23; 10.1; Ex 25.40; Heb 11.7; 12.25
8.6 1 Tim 2.5; Heb 7.22
8.7 Heb 7.11,18
8.8 Jer 31.31-34
8.10 Heb 10.16; 2 Cor 3.3; Zech 8.8
8.11 Isa 54.13; Jn 6.45; 1 Jn 2.27
8.12 Heb 10.17
8.13 2 Cor 5.17

7.20-22 Christ's eternal priesthood and the covenant he has established rest on the highest possible certainty: God's own *oath* (Ps 110.4).
7.23-28 Apparent here is the influence of the Platonic philosophical distinction between (1) a single, eternal form or ideal of all earthly objects and experiences, and (2) the multiple, transitory copies of these items that are present in everyday life. Here in Hebrews the contrast is between the *many* priests and the one eternal priesthood of Christ. The sacrifice of himself which Jesus offered, unlike the repeated offerings of the traditional priests (which included offerings for their *own sins*), is *once for all*. Its eternal potency shows him to be the ideal (*perfect*) Son of God.
8.1-13 The Platonic contrast between the many copies and the single eternal model continues. Jesus' sacrifice has been presented in the eternal, archetypal temple in heaven, while the Israelite priests offered theirs repeatedly in what was merely a copy (*shadow*) of the true sanctuary. Moses himself is said to have contrasted the heavenly original and the earthly imitation (8.5 = Ex 25.40). The limitations of the Jerusalem temple are evident in that God has now acted to replace it and to confirm a superior covenant, as promised through Jeremiah the prophet (Heb 8.8-12 = Jer 31.31-33). The useless copies *will soon disappear*, as they did historically when the Romans conquered Jerusalem in 67-70 CE.

[f] Or *able to save completely* [g] Gk lacks *other* [h] Or *tabernacle* [i] Gk *he* [j] Gk *He*

9.1-10 The imperfections of the earthly copy of the sanctuary are further specified: it is a portable *tent* (or tabernacle), as decribed in Ex 25-26 and Num 9.15-23, rather than the more permanent temple built by Solomon (1 Kings 6-9). The outer space within the tent contained the *lampstand* (symbolizing the light of the knowledge of God), the table and the *bread of the Presence,* which was always kept as a reminder of the people's continuing dependence on, and association with, the God of the covenant (Num 24.5-9; Ex 25.23-30). The inner part of the tent was the Most Holy Place (*Holy of Holies*) where *the altar of incense* (Ex 30.6-10) symbolized the prayers of the people ascending to God, and where the *ark* or sacred box (Ex 25) containing the *manna* (Ex 16.31-35), Aaron's rod (Num 17.1-11) and the stone *tablets of the covenant* (Ex 24.1-18; Deut 10.1-5) recalled the powerful presence of God with Israel during the exodus from Egypt into the promised land. *The cherubim of glory* were images of winged creatures that hovered over the cover of the sacred box as symbols of God's eternal presence at *the mercy seat,* where the ultimate annual sacrifice was offered on the Day of Atonement (Lev 16.1-34, especially vs. 14). This offering was for the forgiveness of the sins of all Israel, symbolized by the scapegoat driven out into the desert, bearing away the sins of the people (Lev 16.20-22). The annual repetition of this ceremony showed that neither entrance to the true and eternal *sanctuary* nor the ultimate perfection of God's people was possible under the traditional cultic system set out in the law of Moses.
9.11-14 Christ's sacrifice of himself and his entrance into the true *Holy Place* has achieved, not a temporal but an *eternal redemption.* His blood, through the power of God's *Spirit,* transforms his new people inwardly (*conscience*) and enables them fully and truly to *worship God.*
9.15-10.18 Christ's death as the sacrifice ratifies forever the new *covenant,* replacing the elaborate but temporary system of purification decreed under the law of ancient Israel. The latter dealt with sin at the earthly level and on a repeated, temporal basis, but Christ's sacrifice is *once for all* and has eternal effects. The new community now awaits his reappearance from heaven, when he will take them forever into God's presence. This radical change was anticipated in scripture: Heb 10.5-7 = Isa 40.7-9; Heb 10.16 = Jer 31.33-34. No further offering for human sin is necessary.

The Earthly and the Heavenly Sanctuaries

9 Now even the first covenant had regulations for worship and an earthly
sanctuary. 2 For a tent[k] was constructed, the
first one, in which were the lampstand, the
table, and the bread of the Presence;[l] this
is called the Holy Place. 3 Behind the second
curtain was a tent[k] called the Holy of Holies.
4 In it stood the golden altar of incense and
the ark of the covenant overlaid on all sides
with gold, in which there were a golden urn
holding the manna, and Aaron's rod that
budded, and the tablets of the covenant;
5 above it were the cherubim of glory overshadowing the mercy seat.[m] Of these things
we cannot speak now in detail.
6 Such preparations having been made,
the priests go continually into the first tent[k]
to carry out their ritual duties; 7 but only the
high priest goes into the second, and he but
once a year, and not without taking the
blood that he offers for himself and for the
sins committed unintentionally by the people. 8 By this the Holy Spirit indicates that
the way into the sanctuary has not yet been
disclosed as long as the first tent[k] is still
standing. 9 This is a symbol[n] of the present
time, during which gifts and sacrifices are
offered that cannot perfect the conscience of
the worshiper, 10 but deal only with food and
drink and various baptisms, regulations for
the body imposed until the time comes to
set things right.
11 But when Christ came as a high priest
of the good things that have come,[o] then
through the greater and perfect[p] tent[k] (not
made with hands, that is, not of this creation), 12 he entered once for all into the Holy
Place, not with the blood of goats and
calves, but with his own blood, thus obtaining eternal redemption. 13 For if the blood of
goats and bulls, with the sprinkling of the
ashes of a heifer, sanctifies those who have
been defiled so that their flesh is purified,
14 how much more will the blood of Christ,
who through the eternal Spirit[q] offered himself without blemish to God, purify our[r]
conscience from dead works to worship the
living God!
15 For this reason he is the mediator of
a new covenant, so that those who are
called may receive the promised eternal
inheritance, because a death has occurred
that redeems them from the transgressions
under the first covenant.[s] 16 Where a will[s] is
involved, the death of the one who made it
must be established. 17 For a will[s] takes effect
only at death, since it is not in force as long
as the one who made it is alive. 18 Hence not
even the first covenant was inaugurated
without blood. 19 For when every commandment had been told to all the people by
Moses in accordance with the law, he took
the blood of calves and goats,[t] with water
and scarlet wool and hyssop, and sprinkled
both the scroll itself and all the people,
20 saying, "This is the blood of the covenant
that God has ordained for you." 21 And in
the same way he sprinkled with the blood
both the tent[k] and all the vessels used in
worship. 22 Indeed, under the law almost
everything is purified with blood, and without the shedding of blood there is no forgiveness of sins.

Christ's Sacrifice Takes Away Sin

23 Thus it was necessary for the sketches
of the heavenly things to be purified with
these rites, but the heavenly things themselves need better sacrifices than these. 24 For
Christ did not enter a sanctuary made by
human hands, a mere copy of the true one,
but he entered into heaven itself, now to
appear in the presence of God on our behalf.
25 Nor was it to offer himself again and
again, as the high priest enters the Holy
Place year after year with blood that is not
his own; 26 for then he would have had to
suffer again and again since the foundation
of the world. But as it is, he has appeared
once for all at the end of the age to remove
sin by the sacrifice of himself. 27 And just as
it is appointed for mortals to die once, and
after that the judgment, 28 so Christ, having
been offered once to bear the sins of many,
will appear a second time, not to deal with
sin, but to save those who are eagerly
waiting for him.

Christ's Sacrifice Once for All

10 Since the law has only a shadow
of the good things to come and not
the true form of these realities, it[u] can never,
by the same sacrifices that are continually

[k] Or *tabernacle* [l] Gk *the presentation of the loaves* [m] Or *the place of atonement* [n] Gk *parable* [o] Other ancient authorities read *good things to come* [p] Gk *more perfect* [q] Other ancient authorities read *Holy Spirit* [r] Other ancient authorities read *your* [s] The Greek word used here means both *covenant* and *will* [t] Other ancient authorities lack *and goats* [u] Other ancient authorities read *they*

9.2 Ex 25.8,9; 25.23-39
9.3 Ex 26.31-33
9.4 Ex 30.1-5; 25.10ff; 16.32,33; Num 17.10
9.5 Ex 25.17ff
9.7 Lev 16.11ff; Ex 30.10; Heb 5.2,3
9.8 Heb 10.19,20; Jn 14.6
9.9 Heb 11.19; 5.1; Gal 3.21
9.10 Lev 11.2ff; Col 2.16; Heb 7.16
9.11 Heb 2.17; 10.1; 8.2
9.12 Heb 7.27; 10.4
9.13 Num 19.9,17,18
9.14 1 Jn 1.7; 1 Pet 3.18; Titus 2.14
9.15 1 Tim 2.5; Heb 3.1; 7.22
9.18 Ex 24.6
9.19 Ex 24.6ff; Lev 14.4,7
9.21 Lev 8.15
9.22 Lev 17.11
9.24 Heb 6.20; 8.2; 7.25; 1 Jn 2.1
9.26 Heb 4.3; 7.27; 1.2
9.27 Gen 3.19; 2 Cor 5.10
9.28 Rom 6.10; 1 Pet 2.24; Titus 2.13
10.1 Heb 9.9,11,23

10.3 Heb 9.7
10.4 Mic 6.6,7
10.5 Ps 40.6-8; Heb 1.6; 1 Pet 2.24
10.7 Jer 36.2
10.10 Jn 17.19; Heb 7.27; 1 Pet 2.24
10.11 Heb 5.1; ver 4
10.13 Ps 110.1; Heb 1.13
10.16 Jer 31.33,34
10.19 Eph 2.18; Heb 9.8,12
10.20 Heb 9.8; 9.3
10.21 Heb 2.17; 1 Tim 3.15
10.22 Heb 4.16; Eph 3.12; Heb 9.14; Ezek 36.25
10.23 Heb 4.14; 1 Cor 1.9
10.25 Acts 2.42; Heb 3.13; Phil 4.5
10.26 Num 15.30; 2 Pet 2.20
10.27 Heb 9.27; Isa 26.11
10.28 Deut 17.2-6; Heb 2.2
10.29 Heb 2.3; 6.6; 13.20; Eph 4.30; Heb 6.4
10.30 Deut 32.35,36; Rom 12.19
10.32 Heb 6.4; Phil 1.29,30
10.33 1 Cor 4.9; 1 Thess 2.14
10.34 Heb 9.15
10.36 Lk 21.19; Col 3.24
10.37 Hab 2.3,4; Lk 18.8

offered year after year, make perfect those
who approach. [2]Otherwise, would they not
have ceased being offered, since the
worshipers, cleansed once for all, would no
longer have any consciousness of sin? [3]But
in these sacrifices there is a reminder of sin
year after year. [4]For it is impossible for the
blood of bulls and goats to take away sins.
[5]Consequently, when Christ[v] came into the
world, he said,

"Sacrifices and offerings you have not
desired,
but a body you have prepared for
me;
[6] in burnt offerings and sin offerings
you have taken no pleasure.
[7] Then I said, 'See, God, I have come to
do your will, O God'
(in the scroll of the book[w] it is
written of me)."

[8]When he said above, "You have neither
desired nor taken pleasure in sacrifices and
offerings and burnt offerings and sin offerings" (these are offered according to the
law), [9]then he added, "See, I have come to
do your will." He abolishes the first in order
to establish the second. [10]And it is by God's
will[x] that we have been sanctified through
the offering of the body of Jesus Christ once
for all.

11 And every priest stands day after day
at his service, offering again and again the
same sacrifices that can never take away
sins. [12]But when Christ[y] had offered for all
time a single sacrifice for sins, "he sat down
at the right hand of God," [13]and since then
has been waiting "until his enemies would
be made a footstool for his feet." [14]For by
a single offering he has perfected for all time
those who are sanctified. [15]And the Holy
Spirit also testifies to us, for after saying,

[16] "This is the covenant that I will make
with them
after those days, says the Lord:
I will put my laws in their hearts,
and I will write them on their
minds,"

[17]he also adds,

"I will remember[z] their sins and their
lawless deeds no more."

[18]Where there is forgiveness of these, there
is no longer any offering for sin.

A Call to Persevere

19 Therefore, my friends,[a] since we have
confidence to enter the sanctuary by the
blood of Jesus, [20]by the new and living way
that he opened for us through the curtain
(that is, through his flesh), [21]and since we
have a great priest over the house of God,
[22]let us approach with a true heart in full
assurance of faith, with our hearts sprinkled
clean from an evil conscience and our bodies
washed with pure water. [23]Let us hold fast
to the confession of our hope without
wavering, for he who has promised is faithful. [24]And let us consider how to provoke
one another to love and good deeds, [25]not
neglecting to meet together, as is the habit
of some, but encouraging one another, and
all the more as you see the Day approaching.

26 For if we willfully persist in sin after
having received the knowledge of the truth,
there no longer remains a sacrifice for sins,
[27]but a fearful prospect of judgment, and a
fury of fire that will consume the adversaries. [28]Anyone who has violated the law of
Moses dies without mercy "on the testimony of two or three witnesses." [29]How
much worse punishment do you think will
be deserved by those who have spurned the
Son of God, profaned the blood of the covenant by which they were sanctified, and
outraged the Spirit of grace? [30]For we know
the one who said, "Vengeance is mine, I
will repay." And again, "The Lord will judge
his people." [31]It is a fearful thing to fall into
the hands of the living God.

32 But recall those earlier days when,
after you had been enlightened, you endured a hard struggle with sufferings, [33]some-
times being publicly exposed to abuse and
persecution, and sometimes being partners
with those so treated. [34]For you had compassion for those who were in prison, and
you cheerfully accepted the plundering of
your possessions, knowing that you yourselves possessed something better and more
lasting. [35]Do not, therefore, abandon that
confidence of yours; it brings a great reward. [36]For you need endurance, so that
when you have done the will of God, you
may receive what was promised.

[37] For yet "in a very little while,

10.19-39 Exhortation. In contrast to the waverers and apostates mentioned in the previous exhortation (5.11-6.12), the writer calls the people to show *confidence* in approaching God through the new and eternal access that Jesus has opened. They have been cleansed inwardly (*conscience*) and outwardly through baptism. Mutual support among the members is essential, through works of *love*, and faithful attendance at the group meetings. Persistence in sin among those who have come to know *the truth* has no remedy, but leads instead to God's certain judgment on those who, having previously professed allegiance to Christ, have now *spurned the Son of God*. The writer recalls the suffering that the faithful members have endured, their *compassion* for those of their number in prison, and their quiet acceptance of the Roman authorities' seizure of their possessions. The ground of their confidence (*faith*) concerning the future was – and must remain – the fulfillment of God's promise conveyed through the prophets who spoke of the speedy deliverance of his people, expressed here (10.37-38) in a combination of Isa 26.20 and Hab 2.3. The biblical precedents for this confidence, but also the relative limits of it in the experience of men and women of faith before the coming of Christ, are spelled out in 11.1-40.

[v] Gk *he* [w] Meaning of Gk uncertain [x] Gk *by that will* [y] Gk *this one* [z] Gk *on their minds and I will remember* [a] Gk *Therefore, brothers*

the one who is coming will come
and will not delay;
38 but my righteous one will live by
faith.
My soul takes no pleasure in
anyone who shrinks back."

39 But we are not among those who shrink back and so are lost, but among those who have faith and so are saved.

The Meaning of Faith

11 Now faith is the assurance of things hoped for, the conviction of things not seen. 2 Indeed, by faith[b] our ancestors received approval. 3 By faith we understand that the worlds were prepared by the word of God, so that what is seen was made from things that are not visible.[c]

The Examples of Abel, Enoch, and Noah

4 By faith Abel offered to God a more acceptable[d] sacrifice than Cain's. Through this he received approval as righteous, God himself giving approval to his gifts; he died, but through his faith[e] he still speaks. 5 By faith Enoch was taken so that he did not experience death; and "he was not found, because God had taken him." For it was attested before he was taken away that "he had pleased God." 6 And without faith it is impossible to please God, for whoever would approach him must believe that he exists and that he rewards those who seek him. 7 By faith Noah, warned by God about events as yet unseen, respected the warning and built an ark to save his household; by this he condemned the world and became an heir to the righteousness that is in accordance with faith.

The Faith of Abraham

8 By faith Abraham obeyed when he was called to set out for a place that he was to receive as an inheritance; and he set out, not knowing where he was going. 9 By faith he stayed for a time in the land he had been promised, as in a foreign land, living in tents, as did Isaac and Jacob, who were heirs with him of the same promise. 10 For he looked forward to the city that has foundations, whose architect and builder is God. 11 By faith he received power of procreation, even though he was too old—and Sarah herself was barren—because he considered him faithful who had promised.[f] 12 Therefore from one person, and this one as good as dead, descendants were born, "as many as the stars of heaven and as the innumerable grains of sand by the seashore."

13 All of these died in faith without having received the promises, but from a distance they saw and greeted them. They confessed that they were strangers and foreigners on the earth, 14 for people who speak in this way make it clear that they are seeking a homeland. 15 If they had been thinking of the land that they had left behind, they would have had opportunity to return. 16 But as it is, they desire a better country, that is, a heavenly one. Therefore God is not ashamed to be called their God; indeed, he has prepared a city for them.

17 By faith Abraham, when put to the test, offered up Isaac. He who had received the promises was ready to offer up his only son, 18 of whom he had been told, "It is through Isaac that descendants shall be named for you." 19 He considered the fact that God is able even to raise someone from the dead—and figuratively speaking, he did receive him back. 20 By faith Isaac invoked blessings for the future on Jacob and Esau. 21 By faith Jacob, when dying, blessed each of the sons of Joseph, "bowing in worship over the top of his staff." 22 By faith Joseph, at the end of his life, made mention of the exodus of the Israelites and gave instructions about his burial.[g]

The Faith of Moses

23 By faith Moses was hidden by his parents for three months after his birth, because they saw that the child was beautiful; and they were not afraid of the king's edict.[h] 24 By faith Moses, when he was grown up, refused to be called a son of Pharaoh's daughter, 25 choosing rather to share ill-treatment with the people of God than to enjoy the fleeting pleasures of sin. 26 He considered abuse suffered for the Christ[i] to

[b] Gk *by this* [c] Or *was not made out of visible things* [d] Gk *greater* [e] Gk *through it* [f] Other ancient authorities read *By faith Sarah herself, though barren, received power to conceive, even when she was too old, because she considered him faithful who had promised.* [g] Gk *his bones* [h] Other ancient authorities add *By faith Moses, when he was grown up, killed the Egyptian, because he observed the humiliation of his people* (Gk *brothers*) [i] Or *the Messiah*

11.1-40 The Exemplars of Faith Prior to the Coming of Christ. **11.1-3** The explanation of *faith* given here conforms in style to definitions in Greek philosophical writings, and the crucial terms, *conviction* and *assurance*, carry philosophical meaning as to how ultimate reality can be known. But the writer has made a crucial addition: *faith* is also oriented toward the future and is grounded in the hope of fulfillment of God's purpose. The *assurance* is that the heavenly realities, which humans have not yet *seen*, will be revealed to God's faithful people, just as the *ancestors* looked forward to this reality. God's *word*, which was the instrument for shaping the creation (Gen 1.3; Ps 33.6; Wis 9.1) and the ages of history (*worlds*), is here seen as disclosing an eternal world which exists in the heavens but is *not visible* as yet to humans. **11.4-7** Early exemplars of the people of *faith* are (1) *Abel*, the superiority of whose sacrifice was attested by his receiving God's approval, in contrast to his brother Cain (Gen 4.1-7); and (2) *Enoch*, whose having pleased God was rewarded by God's taking him into his presence without having to experience *death* (Gen 5.24). Confidence that the invisible God *exists* and assurance concerning the future reward echo the definition of faith in 11.1. (3) The next example of faith, *Noah*, expressed his confidence in the *unseen* future when, warned by God, he acted in *righteousness* by building the *ark*, which saved his family, and at the same time renounced the evil *world* of his contemporaries. **11.8-16** (4) The *faith* of Abraham and Sarah, of Isaac and Jacob, is more directly linked with confidence about the future and the realm of the unseen, here symbolically indicated by the *place that he was to receive, the land he had been promised, a homeland*, and *a better country*. As a result of their reliance in his promise, God is pleased to fulfill it, and has established through Christ the new community, whose membership is *innumerable*, as Abraham was told it would be (Gen 22.15-18). **11.17-22** True faith enabled the ancestors to see beyond death. (1) Abraham was willing to sacrifice Isaac, without giving up hope of the *descendants* who were promised through Isaac (Gen 21.12); (2) Isaac was confident about the *future* of his posterity through *Jacob and Esau* (Gen 27-28); (3) Jacob, so old that he had to lean on *the top of his staff* (Gen 47.31), died with assurance of God's blessing on his sons (Gen 48.8-22); (4) Joseph died in confidence that his people would escape from slavery in Egypt and that he would be buried in the land of promise (Gen 50.24-26). **11.23-28** The future orientation of faith is seen in Moses' parents' defiance of Pharaoh's decree about killing all male Hebrew children (Ex 1.15-21) when they schemed successfully to preserve him (Ex 2.1-10). Moses decided to identify with his own people rather than with the Egyptian royalty and the *fleeting pleasures* enjoyed by the Egyptians. He preferred the *abuse* he suffered as the one chosen by God (*anointed;* in Greek, *christos*) for leadership of his people to the wealth and prestige of the royal household which he abandoned. His focus was on the future promise, seeing the God *who is invisible*, and by observing the Passover (the symbolic feast commemorating God's preservation of his people through their time of suffering; Ex 12.1-13.43-49; Deut 16.1-8; Num 9.1-14) he was able to keep his people free of the plague that God sent on all the *firstborn* in Egypt (Ex 11.1-10; 12.29-32).

10.38 Rom 1.17; Gal 3.11
10.39 2 Pet 2.20; Acts 16.30
11.1 Rom 8.24; 2 Cor 4.18; 5.7
11.3 Gen 1.1; Jn 1.3; Heb 6.5
11.4 Gen 4.4,10; 1 Jn 3.12; Heb 12.24
11.5 Gen 5.21-24
11.7 Gen 6.13-22
11.8 Gen 12.1-4; Acts 7.2-4
11.9 Gen 12.8; 18.1,9; Heb 6.17
11.10 Heb 12.22; 13.14; Rev 21.2
11.11 Gen 17.19; 18.11-14; 21.2
11.12 Rom 4.19; Gen 22.17; 32.12
11.13 Gen 23.4; Ps 39.12
11.16 Ex 3.6,15; Phil 3.20; Heb 13.14
11.17 Gen 22.1-10 Jas 2.21
11.18 Gen 21.12; Rom 9.7
11.19 Rom 4.21
11.21 Gen 48.5,16,20
11.22 Gen 50.24,25; Ex 13.19
11.23 Ex 2.2; 1.16

be greater wealth than the treasures of Egypt, for he was looking ahead to the reward. [27]By faith he left Egypt, unafraid of the king's anger; for he persevered as though[j] he saw him who is invisible. [28]By faith he kept the Passover and the sprinkling of blood, so that the destroyer of the firstborn would not touch the firstborn of Israel.[k]

The Faith of Other Israelite Heroes

29 By faith the people passed through the Red Sea as if it were dry land, but when the Egyptians attempted to do so they were drowned. [30]By faith the walls of Jericho fell after they had been encircled for seven days. [31]By faith Rahab the prostitute did not perish with those who were disobedient,[l] because she had received the spies in peace.

32 And what more should I say? For time would fail me to tell of Gideon, Barak, Samson, Jephthah, of David and Samuel and the prophets—[33]who through faith conquered kingdoms, administered justice, obtained promises, shut the mouths of lions, [34]quenched raging fire, escaped the edge of the sword, won strength out of weakness, became mighty in war, put foreign armies to flight. [35]Women received their dead by resurrection. Others were tortured, refusing to accept release, in order to obtain a better resurrection. [36]Others suffered mocking and flogging, and even chains and imprisonment. [37]They were stoned to death, they were sawn in two,[m] they were killed by the sword; they went about in skins of sheep and goats, destitute, persecuted, tormented—[38]of whom the world was not worthy. They wandered in deserts and mountains, and in caves and holes in the ground.

39 Yet all these, though they were commended for their faith, did not receive what was promised, [40]since God had provided something better so that they would not, apart from us, be made perfect.

The Example of Jesus

12 Therefore, since we are surrounded by so great a cloud of witnesses, let us also lay aside every weight and the sin that clings so closely,[n] and let us run with perseverance the race that is set before us, [2]looking to Jesus the pioneer and perfecter of our faith, who for the sake of[o] the joy that was set before him endured the cross, disregarding its shame, and has taken his seat at the right hand of the throne of God.

3 Consider him who endured such hostility against himself from sinners,[p] so that you may not grow weary or lose heart. [4]In your struggle against sin you have not yet resisted to the point of shedding your blood. [5]And you have forgotten the exhortation that addresses you as children—

"My child, do not regard lightly the
discipline of the Lord,
or lose heart when you are
punished by him;
[6] for the Lord disciplines those whom he
loves,
and chastises every child whom he
accepts."

[7]Endure trials for the sake of discipline. God is treating you as children; for what child is there whom a parent does not discipline? [8]If you do not have that discipline in which all children share, then you are illegitimate and not his children. [9]Moreover, we had human parents to discipline us, and we respected them. Should we not be even more willing to be subject to the Father of spirits and live? [10]For they disciplined us for a short time as seemed best to them, but he disciplines us for our good, in order that we may share his holiness. [11]Now, discipline always seems painful rather than pleasant at the time, but later it yields the peaceful fruit of righteousness to those who have been trained by it.

12 Therefore lift your drooping hands and strengthen your weak knees, [13]and make straight paths for your feet, so that what is lame may not be put out of joint, but rather be healed.

Warnings against Rejecting God's Grace

14 Pursue peace with everyone, and the holiness without which no one will see the Lord. [15]See to it that no one fails to obtain the grace of God; that no root of bitterness springs up and causes trouble, and through it many become defiled. [16]See to it that no one becomes like Esau, an immoral and godless person, who sold his birthright for a single meal. [17]You know that later, when

[j] Or *because* [k] Gk *would not touch them* [l] Or *unbelieving* [m] Other ancient authorities add *they were tempted* [n] Other ancient authorities read *sin that easily distracts* [o] Or *who instead of* [p] Other ancient authorities read *such hostility from sinners against themselves*

11.28 Ex 12.21
11.29 Ex 14.21-31
11.30 Josh 6.12-21
11.31 Josh 2.9ff; 6.23; Jas 2.25
11.33 2 Sam 7.11; Judg 14.5; 1 Sam 17.34; Dan 6.22
11.34 2 Kings 20.7; Judg 15.8
11.35 1 Kings 17.22; Acts 22.25
11.36 Jer 20.2
11.37 1 Kings 21.13; Acts 7.58; 2 Kings 1.8
11.38 1 Kings 18.4
11.40 Heb 5.9
12.1 1 Cor 9.24; Heb 10.36
12.2 Phil 2.8,9; Heb 1.3,13; 1 Pet 3.22
12.3 Mt 10.24; Gal 6.9
12.5 Prov 3.11,12
12.6 Ps 94.12; Jas 1.12
12.7 Deut 8.5
12.8 1 Pet 5.9
12.10 2 Pet 1.4
12.11 1 Pet 1.6; Jas 3.17,18
12.12 Isa 35.3
12.13 Prov 4.26; Gal 6.1
12.15 Gal 5.4; Deut 29.18; Heb 3.12
12.16 Gen 25.33
12.17 Gen 27.30-40

11.29-38 God's preservation of the faithful who relied on his promise for the future was evident in their safe passage through the Red Sea (Ex 13.17; 14.22), in the fall of the walls of Jericho (Josh 2.1-4; 6.22-25), and in the safety of a *prostitute* who had hidden the Israelite spies and thus helped them to capture the city of Jericho (Josh 2.1-4; 6.22-25). The list of those who accomplished great things *through faith* includes judges of ancient Israel (Gideon, Barak, Jephtha, and Samuel; Judg 4-16; 1 Sam 1) and a king (David; 1 Sam 16). The faith experiences of these and others include military, political and personal triumphs, as well as tragedies and deprivations accepted in fidelity to their commitments to God and the future of his people. The technical term for *torment* (vs. 37) – being stretched on a rack or a wheel – fits the experiences of the martyrs in the time of the Maccabean revolt against the Syrian rulers in the second century BCE (2 Macc 5-7).
11.39-40 Though all these faithful ones lived in confidence and hope of future divine deliverance, they died without seeing such fulfillment of God's promise (*being made perfect*), which has now begun to be disclosed to the present generation through the death of Jesus and his exaltation into the presence of God.
12.1-29 Exhortation.
12.1-2 Using the image of an athletic contest, with the faithful of the past as a horde (*cloud*) of spectators (*witnesses*), the faithful in the present are called to strip off all impediments (*sin that clings*) and to devote themselves solely to the contest of faith. Their prime model is Jesus, who is both forerunner (*pioneer*) and achiever (*perfected*) of the race of faith. These two last terms also carry the philosophical meanings of prototype and consummator of God's purpose for his people. Jesus' contest was *to endure the cross*; his victory was his exaltation before God's *throne*.
12.3-13 What is required of those in this contest is *discipline*, as Jesus demonstrated and as scripture affirms (12.5 = Prov 3.11), and as children reared by responsible parents have experienced. Through athletic-like *training*, discipline now leads to a future *peace* and the reward of *righteousness*. There is no place for moral lameness or flabbiness in the demanding life of the faithful.
12.14-17 The faithful are to live in *peace* with everyone and in *holiness* toward God. If they tolerate *bitterness* or moral *defilement*, they will forfeit their inheritance, just as Esau did (Gen 27.1-45).

12.18-24 Based on the imagery of God's encounter with Israel at Sinai through Moses (Ex 19), who trembled with fear (Deut 9.19), there is a contrast between (1) the awe and terror that filled the Israelites in the past, and the prospect of death for those who desecrated the divine presence, and (2) the present prospect of seeing the true *Mount Zion*, the heavenly *city*, where there are already gathered in *festal* spirit not only angels but also the first representatives of the new community (in Greek, *ekklesia*), who have entered the presence of God, the *judge*, and who are the first wave of *the righteous* for whom God's purpose is being completed (*made perfect*). *Jesus*, through whose mediation this *new covenant* is being established, is the primary figure there: *Abel's blood* called out for vengeance; Jesus' blood has achieved reconciliation of God and his new people. **12.25-29** Those who failed to obey when God spoke through Moses and the prophets did not *escape* his judgment. The prophet's prediction of shaking heaven and earth (Hag 2.6,21) is now past, but the unshakable *kingdom* which Christ has brought can still be missed by those who *reject* him. **13.1-24** Final Advice to the Community. **13.1-5** The virtues called for here involve the shared life of the community: love of brothers and sisters; caring for the needs of strangers, just as in the time of the old covenant hospitality was extended even to *angel* visitors (Gen 18.2-15; 19.1-14; Judg 6.11-18; 13.3-22); concern for imprisoned members; avoidance of marital irresponsibility and of greed, both of which can corrupt the community. Instead, there is to be gratitude for what *the Lord* has provided (13.6 = Ps 117.6). **13.6-17** Responsibilities within the community include support for the *leaders* and emulation of their *way of life*; avoidance of false *teachings*, such as adopting dietary restrictions; acceptance of opposition from the civil authorities or even martyrdom for the sake of Christ. Their focus is to be on *the city that is to come*, in expectation of which gratitude is to offered to God, generous support is to be given to the community, and obedience is to be paid to the *leaders*, who care for their *souls*. **13.18-24** Concluding remarks include a request for prayerful support for the writer and for his restoration (perhaps from prison), and a final word about the release of *Timothy*, the writer's companion. Greetings are extended to *the leaders* from *those from Italy*, which may refer to local residents of Rome or to expatriates at the place of the writer's imprisonment.

he wanted to inherit the blessing, he was
rejected, for he found no chance to repent,[q]
even though he sought the blessing[r] with
tears.
18 You have not come to something[s]
that can be touched, a blazing fire, and
darkness, and gloom, and a tempest, [19]and
the sound of a trumpet, and a voice whose
words made the hearers beg that not another word be spoken to them. [20](For they
could not endure the order that was given,
"If even an animal touches the mountain,
it shall be stoned to death." [21]Indeed, so
terrifying was the sight that Moses said, "I
tremble with fear.") [22]But you have come to
Mount Zion and to the city of the living
God, the heavenly Jerusalem, and to innumerable angels in festal gathering, [23]and to
the assembly[t] of the firstborn who are enrolled in heaven, and to God the judge of
all, and to the spirits of the righteous made
perfect, [24]and to Jesus, the mediator of a
new covenant, and to the sprinkled blood
that speaks a better word than the blood of
Abel.
25 See that you do not refuse the one
who is speaking; for if they did not escape
when they refused the one who warned
them on earth, how much less will we
escape if we reject the one who warns from
heaven! [26]At that time his voice shook the
earth; but now he has promised, "Yet once
more I will shake not only the earth but
also the heaven." [27]This phrase, "Yet once
more," indicates the removal of what is
shaken—that is, created things—so that
what cannot be shaken may remain. [28]There-
fore, since we are receiving a kingdom that
cannot be shaken, let us give thanks, by
which we offer to God an acceptable worship with reverence and awe; [29]for indeed
our God is a consuming fire.

Service Well-Pleasing to God

13 Let mutual love continue. [2]Do not
neglect to show hospitality to strangers, for by doing that some have entertained angels without knowing it. [3]Remem-
ber those who are in prison, as though you
were in prison with them; those who are
being tortured, as though you yourselves
were being tortured.[u] [4]Let marriage be held
in honor by all, and let the marriage bed
be kept undefiled; for God will judge fornicators and adulterers. [5]Keep your lives free
from the love of money, and be content
with what you have; for he has said, "I will
never leave you or forsake you." [6]So we can
say with confidence,

"The Lord is my helper;
I will not be afraid.
What can anyone do to me?"

7 Remember your leaders, those who
spoke the word of God to you; consider the
outcome of their way of life, and imitate
their faith. [8]Jesus Christ is the same yesterday and today and forever. [9]Do not be
carried away by all kinds of strange teachings; for it is well for the heart to be strengthened by grace, not by regulations about
food,[v] which have not benefited those who
observe them. [10]We have an altar from
which those who officiate in the tent[w] have
no right to eat. [11]For the bodies of those
animals whose blood is brought into the
sanctuary by the high priest as a sacrifice
for sin are burned outside the camp. [12]There-
fore Jesus also suffered outside the city gate
in order to sanctify the people by his own
blood. [13]Let us then go to him outside the
camp and bear the abuse he endured. [14]For
here we have no lasting city, but we are
looking for the city that is to come. [15]Through
him, then, let us continually offer a sacrifice
of praise to God, that is, the fruit of lips that
confess his name. [16]Do not neglect to do
good and to share what you have, for such
sacrifices are pleasing to God.
17 Obey your leaders and submit to them,
for they are keeping watch over your souls
and will give an account. Let them do this
with joy and not with sighing—for that
would be harmful to you.
18 Pray for us; we are sure that we have
a clear conscience, desiring to act honorably
in all things. [19]I urge you all the more to
do this, so that I may be restored to you
very soon.

Benediction

20 Now may the God of peace, who
brought back from the dead our Lord Jesus,
the great shepherd of the sheep, by the
blood of the eternal covenant, [21]make you
complete in everything good so that you
may do his will, working among us[x] that

[q] Or *no chance to change his father's mind* [r] Gk *it* [s] Other ancient authorities read *a mountain* [t] Or *angels, and to the festal gathering* [23]*and assembly* [u] Gk *were in the body* [v] Gk *not by foods* [w] Or *tabernacle* [x] Other ancient authorities read *you*

12.18 Ex 19.12-22; Deut 4.11
12.19 Ex 20.19; Deut 5.5
12.20 Ex 19.12,13
12.21 Ex 19.16
12.22 Phil 3.20; Gal 4.26
12.23 Lk 10.20; Phil 3.12
12.24 1 Tim 2.5; Gen 4.10; Heb 11.4
12.25 Heb 2.2,3; 8.5; 11.7
12.26 Ex 19.18; Hag 2.6
12.27 1 Cor 7.31; 2 Pet 3.10
12.29 Deut 4.24
13.2 1 Pet 4.9; Gen 18.3
13.4 1 Cor 6.9; Rev 22.15
13.5 Phil 4.11; Deut 31.6,8; Josh 1.5
13.9 Eph 4.14; Col 2.7,16
13.10 1 Cor 9.13; 10.18
13.11 Ex 29.14; Lev 16.27
13.12 Jn 19.17
13.14 Phil 3.20; Heb 10.34; 12.22
13.15 1 Pet 2.5; Isa 57.9; Hos 14.2
13.17 Isa 62.6; Acts 20.28
13.18 1 Thess 5.25; Acts 24.16
13.20 Rom 15.33; Zech 9.11
13.21 1 Pet 5.10; Phil 2.13

13.23 1 Thess 3.2; 1 Tim 6.12
13.25 Col 4.18; Titus 3.15

which is pleasing in his sight, through Jesus Christ, to whom be the glory forever and ever. Amen.

Final Exhortation and Greetings

22 I appeal to you, brothers and sisters,[y] bear with my word of exhortation, for I have written to you briefly. [23]I want you to know that our brother Timothy has been set free; and if he comes in time, he will be with me when I see you. [24]Greet all your leaders and all the saints. Those from Italy send you greetings. [25]Grace be with all of you.[z]

[y] Gk *brothers* [z] Other ancient authorities add *Amen*

THE LETTER OF

JAMES

1.2 Mt 5.12; Heb 10.34; 1 Pet 1.6
1.5 1 Kings 3.9; Prov 2.3; 1 Jn 5.14
1.6 Mk 11.24
1.10 1 Cor 7.31; 1 Pet 1.24
1.12 Heb 12.5; Jas 2.5
1.15 Job 15.35; Ps 7.14; Rom 6.21,23
1.17 Jn 3.27; Mal 3.6
1.18 Jn 1.13; Eph 1.12; Rev 14.4

Salutation

1 James, a servant[a] of God and of the Lord Jesus Christ,

To the twelve tribes in the Dispersion: Greetings.

Faith and Wisdom

2 My brothers and sisters,[b] whenever you face trials of any kind, consider it nothing but joy, [3]because you know that the testing of your faith produces endurance; [4]and let endurance have its full effect, so that you may be mature and complete, lacking in nothing.

5 If any of you is lacking in wisdom, ask God, who gives to all generously and ungrudgingly, and it will be given you. [6]But ask in faith, never doubting, for the one who doubts is like a wave of the sea, driven and tossed by the wind; [7,8]for the doubter, being double-minded and unstable in every way, must not expect to receive anything from the Lord.

Poverty and Riches

9 Let the believer[c] who is lowly boast in being raised up, [10]and the rich in being brought low, because the rich will disappear like a flower in the field. [11]For the sun rises with its scorching heat and withers the field; its flower falls, and its beauty perishes. It is the same way with the rich; in the midst of a busy life, they will wither away.

Trial and Temptation

12 Blessed is anyone who endures temptation. Such a one has stood the test and will receive the crown of life that the Lord[d] has promised to those who love him. [13]No one, when tempted, should say, "I am being tempted by God"; for God cannot be tempted by evil and he himself tempts no one. [14]But one is tempted by one's own desire, being lured and enticed by it; [15]then, when that desire has conceived, it gives birth to sin, and that sin, when it is fully grown, gives birth to death. [16]Do not be deceived, my beloved.[e]

17 Every generous act of giving, with every perfect gift, is from above, coming down from the Father of lights, with whom there is no variation or shadow due to change.[f] [18]In fulfillment of his own purpose he gave us birth by the word of truth, so that we would become a kind of first fruits of his creatures.

[a] Gk *slave* [b] Gk *brothers* [c] Gk *brother* [d] Gk *he*; other ancient authorities read *God* [e] Gk *my beloved brothers* [f] Other ancient authorities read *variation due to a shadow of turning*

See the Introductions, pp. 9–10 and 94–95 above.

1.1-2 The introduction to the letter follows the typical Greek letter-writing style by placing the author's name first, followed by those of the addressees, and a word of greeting.
1.1 *James.* Traditionally viewed as James the brother of Jesus and leader of the Jerusalem church, the author gives no further information which could lead to certainty about his identity; *cf.* Mk 6.3; Acts 15.13; Gal 1.19. *The twelve tribes in the Dispersion.* Literally, to Jews living outside Palestine; but this address may well be figurative, namely to Christians throughout the world. The Greek word for "Dispersion" is *Diaspora*, a word used to refer to Jews who after the Babylonian captivity in the sixth century BCE continued to live in countries outside Palestine. *Greetings.* The normal greeting issued in letters; *cf.* Acts 15.23.
1.2 *Trials.* The sense of the word is that of temptations designed to make believers fall away from their faith; *cf.* 1.12. *Joy. Cf.* 1 Thess 1.6; Heb 12.1; 1 Pet 1.6; Mt 5.11-12 (= Lk 6.23).
1.3 *cf.* Rom 5.3.
1.4 *Mature.* See note on Mt 5.48.
1.5 *cf.* Mt 7.7 = Lk 11.9.
1.6 *cf.* Mt 21.21; Mk 11.23-24.
1.8 *Double-minded.* The Greek word is not known in Greek literature previous to James, but its background in Old Testament theology has to do with those who cannot commit themselves wholly to God; *cf.* 4.8.
1.9-11 The first of a series concerning rich and poor; see also 2.1-7; 5.1-6.
1.10 *Disappear like a flower in the field. Cf.* 4.14; Isa 40.6-7; 1 Pet 1.24.
1.11 Isa 40.7.
1.12 *cf.* Dan 12.12; Mt 10.22. *Crown of life. Cf.* Rev 2.10.
1.14 *One's own desire.* I.e. one's own covetousness.
1.17 *Every gift...is from above. Cf.* Mt 7.11 (= Lk 11.13). *Father of lights.* This designation of God is a reference to God's creation of the heavenly bodies.
1.18 *Word of truth.* I.e. the gospel; *cf.* 1 Pet 1.23.

Hearing and Doing the Word

19 You must understand this, my
beloved:[g] let everyone be quick to listen,
slow to speak, slow to anger; 20for your
anger does not produce God's righteousness. 21Therefore rid yourselves of all sordid-
ness and rank growth of wickedness, and
welcome with meekness the implanted word
that has the power to save your souls.
22 But be doers of the word, and not
merely hearers who deceive themselves. 23For
if any are hearers of the word and not
doers, they are like those who look at
themselves[h] in a mirror; 24for they look at
themselves and, on going away, immediately forget what they were like. 25But those
who look into the perfect law, the law of
liberty, and persevere, being not hearers
who forget but doers who act—they will be
blessed in their doing.
26 If any think they are religious, and do
not bridle their tongues but deceive their
hearts, their religion is worthless. 27Religion
that is pure and undefiled before God, the
Father, is this: to care for orphans and
widows in their distress, and to keep oneself
unstained by the world.

Warning against Partiality

2 My brothers and sisters,[i] do you with
your acts of favoritism really believe
in our glorious Lord Jesus Christ?[j] 2For if a
person with gold rings and in fine clothes
comes into your assembly, and if a poor
person in dirty clothes also comes in, 3and
if you take notice of the one wearing the
fine clothes and say, "Have a seat here,
please," while to the one who is poor you
say, "Stand there," or, "Sit at my feet,"[k]
4have you not made distinctions among
yourselves, and become judges with evil
thoughts? 5Listen, my beloved brothers and
sisters.[l] Has not God chosen the poor in the
world to be rich in faith and to be heirs of
the kingdom that he has promised to those
who love him? 6But you have dishonored
the poor. Is it not the rich who oppress you?
Is it not they who drag you into court? 7Is
it not they who blaspheme the excellent
name that was invoked over you?
8 You do well if you really fulfill the
royal law according to the scripture, "You
shall love your neighbor as yourself." 9But
if you show partiality, you commit sin and
are convicted by the law as transgressors.
10For whoever keeps the whole law but fails
in one point has become accountable for all
of it. 11For the one who said, "You shall not
commit adultery," also said, "You shall not
murder." Now if you do not commit adultery but if you murder, you have become
a transgressor of the law. 12So speak and so
act as those who are to be judged by the
law of liberty. 13For judgment will be without mercy to anyone who has shown no
mercy; mercy triumphs over judgment.

Faith without Works Is Dead

14 What good is it, my brothers and
sisters,[l] if you say you have faith but do not
have works? Can faith save you? 15If a
brother or sister is naked and lacks daily
food, 16and one of you says to them, "Go in
peace; keep warm and eat your fill," and yet
you do not supply their bodily needs, what
is the good of that? 17So faith by itself, if it
has no works, is dead.
18 But someone will say, "You have faith
and I have works." Show me your faith
apart from your works, and I by my works
will show you my faith. 19You believe that
God is one; you do well. Even the demons
believe—and shudder. 20Do you want to be
shown, you senseless person, that faith apart
from works is barren? 21Was not our ancestor Abraham justified by works when he
offered his son Isaac on the altar? 22You see
that faith was active along with his works,
and faith was brought to completion by the
works. 23Thus the scripture was fulfilled
that says, "Abraham believed God, and it
was reckoned to him as righteousness," and
he was called the friend of God. 24You see
that a person is justified by works and not
by faith alone. 25Likewise, was not Rahab
the prostitute also justified by works when
she welcomed the messengers and sent them
out by another road? 26For just as the body
without the spirit is dead, so faith without
works is also dead.

Taming the Tongue

3 Not many of you should become teachers, my brothers and sisters,[l] for you
know that we who teach will be judged
with greater strictness. 2For all of us make
many mistakes. Anyone who makes no

[g] Gk *my beloved brothers* [h] Gk *at the face of his birth* [i] Gk *My brothers* [j] Or *hold the faith of our glorious Lord Jesus Christ without acts of favoritism* [k] Gk *Sit under my footstool* [l] Gk *brothers*

1.19 A traditional Jewish exhortation; *cf.* Eccl 7.9; Sir 5.11; Mt 5.22; Eph 4.26.
1.21 *The implanted word.* The imagery recalls Lk 8.8,11-12.
1.22 *Doers. Cf.* 1.23,25; Rom 2.13; Mt 7.21.
1.23 *cf.* Mt 7.26 = Lk 6.49.
1.25 *The perfect law, the law of liberty. Cf.* Rom 8.2; 1 Cor 9.21; Gal 5.13-14; 6.2.
1.26-27 These verses constitute a summary of 1.19-25, stating that religion which has no practical ethical results is worthless.
2.1 *Favoritism. Cf.* Job 32.21; Lk 20.21 (=Mk 12.14; Mt 22.16); Acts 10.34; Rom 2.11; Eph 6.9.
2.3 *cf.* Mt 23.39.
2.4 *Distinctions. Cf.* Rom 3.22-25; 14.4,10-13.
2.5 *The poor in the world.* This may be a reference to God's choice of Israel among the nations, or to the general idea of God's constant concern for the poor; *cf.* Job 30.25; Ps 34.6; 113.7; Isa 25.4. *Heirs of the kingdom. Cf.* Lk 6.20 (= Mt 5.3); Lk 7.22 (= Mt 11.5).
2.6 *Drag you into court. Cf.* Mk 13.9.
2.7 *The excellent name.* I.e. either God's (*cf.* Deut 16.2) or Christ's (1 Pet 4.14). *Was invoked over you.* This could be a reference to baptism; Acts 2.38 refers to baptism as being baptized "in the name of Jesus Christ."
2.8 *The royal law.* I.e. the commandment which follows; Jesus said it was the greatest commandment, *cf.* Mk 12.31 (= Mt 22.38; Lk 10.27), and Paul said it was the fulfilling of the law, *cf.* Gal 5.14; Rom 13.9. The quotation is from Lev 19.18.
2.9 *cf.* 2.1-7.
2.10 *cf.* Rom 2.25; Gal 5.3; 3.10; Mt 5.19. *Accountable.* Literally, "guilty."
2.11 The quotations are from Ex 20.14 and Ex 20.13.
2.12 See note on 1.25.
2.13 *cf.* Mt 18.23-35.
2.14 Rom 5.1; 6.1.
2.15-16 *cf.* 1 Jn 3.17; Gal 5.13.
2.17 *cf.* Gal 5.6.
2.18 The same point is made by Paul in Gal 5.6,13.
2.19 *God is one.* This basic affirmation of Israel's faith is recorded in Deut 6.4.
2.21 *cf.* Rom 4.2-6,14,17-22; Gal 3.6-9,14; Heb 11.17-19.
2.23 The quotation is from Gen 15.6. *Cf.* the treatment of this same verse in Rom 4.3,9,22; Gal 3.6. *Friend of God. Cf.* Isa 41.8; 2 Chr 20.7.
2.24 *cf.* Rom 3.23-25; 4.13,22; 5.1; Gal 3.8,25; Phil 3.9.
2.25 *Rahab the prostitute.* See Josh 2.1-21; Heb 11.31.
3.1 *Teachers.* The office of teacher was a position of great honor in the early church; *cf.* 1 Cor 12.28; Rom 12.7; Acts 13.1. *We who teach.* James holds the position of teacher in his church, which explains the style of this letter, namely that of an ethical treatise. *Judged with greater strictness. Cf.* Mt 12.26-27; 15.11,18.
3.2 The admonition concerning the loose tongue is common in Judaism and Christianity; *cf.* Ps 120.2; Prov 10.19; 19.19; 21.23; Sir 19.16; 25.8; Rom 1.29; 2 Cor 12.20; 1 Tim 5.13.

1.19 Prov 5.1,2; 10.19
1.21 Eph 4.22; 1 Pet 2.1; Eph 1.13; Titus 2.11
1.22 Mt 7.21; Rom 2.13; 1 Jn 3.7
1.23 Lk 6.47; 1 Cor 13.12
1.25 2 Cor 3.18; Jas 2.12; Jn 13.17
1.26 Ps 34.13; 1 Pet 3.10
1.27 Mt 25.36; Rom 12.2; 1 Jn 5.18

2.1 Prov 24.23; Mt 22.16; 1 Cor 2.8
2.3 ver 2
2.5 1 Cor 1.26-28; 12.21; Jas 1.12
2.6 1 Cor 11.22; Acts 8.3
2.8 Lev 19.18; Mt 22.39
2.10 Mt 5.19; Gal 3.10
2.11 Ex 20.13,14; Deut 5.17,18
2.12 Jas 1.25
2.13 Mt 5.7; 18.32-35
2.14 Mt 7.26; Jas 1.22ff
2.15 Lk 3.11
2.18 Jas 3.13
2.19 Deut 6.4; Mt 8.29; Lk 4.34
2.21 Gen 22.9
2.22 Heb 11.17
2.23 Gen 15.6; Rom 4.3; 2 Chr 20.7; Isa 41.8
2.25 Josh 2.1ff; Heb 11.31

3.1 Mt 23.8; Lk 6.37
3.2 1 Kings 8.46; 1 Pet 3.10; Mt 12.37; Jas 1.26

mistakes in speaking is perfect, able to keep the whole body in check with a bridle. [3]If we put bits into the mouths of horses to make them obey us, we guide their whole bodies. [4]Or look at ships: though they are so large that it takes strong winds to drive them, yet they are guided by a very small rudder wherever the will of the pilot directs. [5]So also the tongue is a small member, yet it boasts of great exploits.

How great a forest is set ablaze by a small fire! [6]And the tongue is a fire. The tongue is placed among our members as a world of iniquity; it stains the whole body, sets on fire the cycle of nature,[m] and is itself set on fire by hell.[n] [7]For every species of beast and bird, of reptile and sea creature, can be tamed and has been tamed by the human species, [8]but no one can tame the tongue—a restless evil, full of deadly poison. [9]With it we bless the Lord and Father, and with it we curse those who are made in the likeness of God. [10]From the same mouth come blessing and cursing. My brothers and sisters,[o] this ought not to be so. [11]Does a spring pour forth from the same opening both fresh and brackish water? [12]Can a fig tree, my brothers and sisters,[p] yield olives, or a grapevine figs? No more can salt water yield fresh.

Two Kinds of Wisdom

13 Who is wise and understanding among you? Show by your good life that your works are done with gentleness born of wisdom. [14]But if you have bitter envy and selfish ambition in your hearts, do not be boastful and false to the truth. [15]Such wisdom does not come down from above, but is earthly, unspiritual, devilish. [16]For where there is envy and selfish ambition, there will also be disorder and wickedness of every kind. [17]But the wisdom from above is first pure, then peaceable, gentle, willing to yield, full of mercy and good fruits, without a trace of partiality or hypocrisy. [18]And a harvest of righteousness is sown in peace for[q] those who make peace.

Friendship with the World

4 Those conflicts and disputes among you, where do they come from? Do they not come from your cravings that are at war within you? [2]You want something and do not have it; so you commit murder. And you covet[r] something and cannot obtain it; so you engage in disputes and conflicts. You do not have, because you do not ask. [3]You ask and do not receive, because you ask wrongly, in order to spend what you get on your pleasures. [4]Adulterers! Do you not know that friendship with the world is enmity with God? Therefore whoever wishes to be a friend of the world becomes an enemy of God. [5]Or do you suppose that it is for nothing that the scripture says, "God[s] yearns jealously for the spirit that he has made to dwell in us"? [6]But he gives all the more grace; therefore it says,

"God opposes the proud,
but gives grace to the humble."

[7]Submit yourselves therefore to God. Resist the devil, and he will flee from you. [8]Draw near to God, and he will draw near to you. Cleanse your hands, you sinners, and purify your hearts, you double-minded. [9]Lament and mourn and weep. Let your laughter be turned into mourning and your joy into dejection. [10]Humble yourselves before the Lord, and he will exalt you.

Warning against Judging Another

11 Do not speak evil against one another, brothers and sisters.[t] Whoever speaks evil against another or judges another, speaks evil against the law and judges the law; but if you judge the law, you are not a doer of the law but a judge. [12]There is one lawgiver and judge who is able to save and to destroy. So who, then, are you to judge your neighbor?

Boasting about Tomorrow

13 Come now, you who say, "Today or tomorrow we will go to such and such a town and spend a year there, doing business and making money." [14]Yet you do not even know what tomorrow will bring. What is your life? For you are a mist that appears for a little while and then vanishes. [15]Instead you ought to say, "If the Lord wishes, we will live and do this or that." [16]As it is, you boast in your arrogance; all such boasting is evil. [17]Anyone, then, who knows the right thing to do and fails to do it, commits sin.

[m] Or *wheel of birth* [n] Gk *Gehenna* [o] Gk *My brothers* [p] Gk *my brothers* [q] Or *by* [r] Or *you murder and you covet* [s] Gk *He* [t] Gk *brothers*

3.5 Prov 12.18; Ps 12.3
3.6 Prov 16.27; Mt 15.11,18,19
3.8 Ps 140.3; Rom 3.13
3.9 Gen 1.26
3.13 Gal 6.4; Jas 2.18
3.15 Jas 1.17; 1 Tim 4.1
3.16 Gal 5.20
3.17 1 Cor 2.6; Rom 12.9; 1 Pet 1.22
3.18 Prov 11.18; Isa 32.17
4.3 Ps 18.41; 1 Jn 3.22; 5.14
4.4 Jas 1.27; 1 Jn 2.15; Jn 15.19
4.5 Gen 6.5; Num 11.29
4.6 Ps 138.6; Prov 3.34
4.7 1 Pet 5.6-9
4.8 2 Chr 15.2; Isa 1.16; Jas 1.8
4.10 Mt 23.12
4.11 1 Pet 2.1
4.12 Mt 10.28; Rom 14.4
4.13 Prov 27.1
4.14 Job 7.7; Ps 102.3
4.15 Acts 18.21
4.17 Lk 12.47; Jn 9.41

3.4 *Ships. Cf.* 1.6. The analogy here is with the human body. *Very small rudder.* The *rudder* is to the ship what the tongue is to the body.
3.5 James' concern is with the teacher who is boastful; *cf.* Sir 20.7.
3.6 *The tongue is a fire. Cf.* Ps 39.3; Prov 16.27; 26.21.
3.7 *cf.* Gen 1.26.
3.8 *Deadly poison. Cf.* Ps 140.3; Rom 3.13.
3.9 *Likeness of God. Cf.* Gen 1.26.
3.12 *cf.* Mt 7.16 (= Lk 6.44-45).
3.13 *Gentleness. Cf.* Gal 6.1; Eph 4.2; 2 Tim 2.25; Titus 3.2; 1 Pet 3.15.
3.14 *cf.* 2 Cor 4.7.
3.15-16 *cf.* 1 Cor 3.1-3. *Envy and selfish ambition.* The Greek terms appear in the vice-lists of 2 Cor 12.20 (translated "selfishness") and Gal 5.20 (translated "quarrels").
3.17 After describing false wisdom (vv. 15-16), the author now describes true wisdom.
3.18 *Harvest of righteousness. Cf.* Isa 32.16-18; Am 6.12; Prov 11.30; 2 Cor 9.10; Phil 1.11; Heb 12.11. *Those who make peace. Cf.* Mt 5.9.
4.1 *Conflicts and disputes.* These words refer most probably to the human situation in general, rather than to specific controversies within the Christian church. *Cf.* 1 Pet 2.11.
4.2 *You do not ask.* Prayer corrects envious desires, centering instead on actual needs.
4.3 *cf.* Mt 7.7-11 (= Lk 11.9-13).
4.4 *cf.* Mt 6.24 (= Lk 16.13).
4.5 The exact wording of the quotation is not to be found elsewhere in Scripture. There may be an allusion to Ex 20.5.
4.6 The quotation is from Prov 3.34 (*cf.* 1 Pet 5.5).
4.7 *Submit yourselves...to God. Cf.* 1 Pet 5.6. *Resist the devil. Cf.* 1 Pet 5.9.
4.8 *Double-minded.* See note on 1.8 and *cf.* Mt 6.22.
4.9 *cf.* Lk 6.25.
4.10 A common scriptural theme: *cf.* Job 5.11; 22.29; Ps 149.4; Prov 3.34; 29.25; Mt 23.12 (= Lk 14.11); 18.14; 1 Pet 5.6.
4.11 *Do not speak evil against one another. Cf.* Lev 19.16; Ps 50.20; Prov 20.13; Rom 1.30; 2 Cor 12.20; 1 Pet 2.1. *Judges. Cf.* Mt 7.1 (= Lk 6.37); Rom 14.4; 1 Cor 4.5; 5.12; Col 2.16-23.
4.12 *cf.* Rom 14.4.
4.13-14 *cf.* Mt 6.34.
4.16 *Boasting. Cf.* 1 Cor 1.29; 5.6; Gal 6.13; Rom 3.27; 4.2.
4.17 *cf.* Lk 12.47.

Warning to Rich Oppressors

5 Come now, you rich people, weep and
wail for the miseries that are coming
to you. [2]Your riches have rotted, and your
clothes are moth-eaten. [3]Your gold and silver
have rusted, and their rust will be evidence
against you, and it will eat your flesh like
fire. You have laid up treasure[u] for the last
days. [4]Listen! The wages of the laborers
who mowed your fields, which you kept
back by fraud, cry out, and the cries of the
harvesters have reached the ears of the Lord
of hosts. [5]You have lived on the earth in
luxury and in pleasure; you have fattened
your hearts in a day of slaughter. [6]You
have condemned and murdered the righteous one, who does not resist you.

Patience in Suffering

7 Be patient, therefore, beloved,[v] until the
coming of the Lord. The farmer waits for
the precious crop from the earth, being
patient with it until it receives the early and
the late rains. [8]You also must be patient.
Strengthen your hearts, for the coming of
the Lord is near.[w] [9]Beloved,[x] do not grumble
against one another, so that you may not
be judged. See, the Judge is standing at the
doors! [10]As an example of suffering and
patience, beloved,[v] take the prophets who
spoke in the name of the Lord. [11]Indeed we
call blessed those who showed endurance.
You have heard of the endurance of Job,
and you have seen the purpose of the Lord,
how the Lord is compassionate and merciful.

12 Above all, my beloved,[v] do not swear,
either by heaven or by earth or by any
other oath, but let your "Yes" be yes and
your "No" be no, so that you may not fall
under condemnation.

The Prayer of Faith

13 Are any among you suffering? They
should pray. Are any cheerful? They should
sing songs of praise. [14]Are any among you
sick? They should call for the elders of the
church and have them pray over them,
anointing them with oil in the name of the
Lord. [15]The prayer of faith will save the sick,
and the Lord will raise them up; and anyone who has committed sins will be forgiven. [16]Therefore confess your sins to one
another, and pray for one another, so that
you may be healed. The prayer of the righteous is powerful and effective. [17]Elijah was
a human being like us, and he prayed
fervently that it might not rain, and for
three years and six months it did not rain
on the earth. [18]Then he prayed again, and
the heaven gave rain and the earth yielded
its harvest.

19 My brothers and sisters,[y] if anyone
among you wanders from the truth and is
brought back by another, [20]you should know
that whoever brings back a sinner from
wandering will save the sinner's[z] soul from
death and will cover a multitude of sins.

[u] Or *will eat your flesh, since you have stored up fire* [v] Gk *brothers* [w] Or *is at hand* [x] Gk *Brothers* [y] Gk *My brothers* [z] Gk *his*

5.1 *cf.* Am 8.4-6; Lk 6.24-25.
5.2-3 *cf.* Mt 6.19-20 (= Lk 6.37); 12.33.
5.3 *Laid up treasure. Cf.* Lk 12.21.
5.4 *cf.* Lev 19.13; Deut 24.14-15; Ps 12.5; Jer 22.13.
5.7 *cf.* 1 Cor 1.7-8; Rom 8.25.
5.9 *cf.* Mt 5.22; 7.1; 24.33; Mk 13.29.
5.10 *cf.* Mt 5.11-12.
5.11 Job is a common example; *cf.* Ezek 14.14,20
5.12 *cf.* Mt 5.34-37.
5.13 *cf.* Ps 30; 50.15; 91.15.
5.14 *Elders.* See note on 1 Tim 4.14; *cf.* Acts 5.6,10; 1 Pet 5.1-5. *Anointing them with oil.* The use of oil as a healing agent was common in the ancient world; *cf.* Isa 1.6; Jer 8.22; Mk 6.13; Lk 10.34.
5.15 *cf.* 1 Jn 5.14-17.
5.17-18 According to 1 Kings 17.1, the prophet Elijah prophesied that it would not rain, but his praying is not mentioned until 1 Kings 17.20-22; later Jewish tradition sees Elijah as a strong example of the one who prays. *Cf.* Lk 4.25.
5.18 *cf.* 1 Kings 18.1,45.
5.20 *cf.* 1 Pet 4.8.

5.2 Job 13.28; Mt 6.20

5.4 Lev 19.13; Deut 24.15; Rom 9.29

5.5 Am 6.1; Jer 12.3; 25.34

5.7 Deut 11.14; Jer 5.24

5.8 1 Pet 4.7

5.9 Jas 4.11,12; Mt 24.33

5.11 Mt 5.10; Job 1.21,22; 42.10; Num 14.18

5.13 ver 101; Ps 50.15; Col 3.16

5.14 Mk 6.13

5.16 Mt 3.6; 1 Pet 2.24; Jn 9.31

5.17 Acts 14.15; 1 Kings 17.1; Lk 4.25

5.18 1 Kings 18.42,45

5.20 Rom 11.14; 1 Pet 4.8

THE FIRST LETTER OF

PETER

Salutation

1 Peter, an apostle of Jesus Christ,

To the exiles of the Dispersion in Pontus, Galatia, Cappadocia, Asia, and Bithynia, [2]who have been chosen and destined by God the Father and sanctified by the Spirit to be obedient to Jesus Christ and to be sprinkled with his blood:

May grace and peace be yours in abundance.

A Living Hope

3 Blessed be the God and Father of our Lord Jesus Christ! By his great mercy he has given us a new birth into a living hope through the resurrection of Jesus Christ from the dead, [4]and into an inheritance that is imperishable, undefiled, and unfading, kept in heaven for you, [5]who are being protected by the power of God through faith for a salvation ready to be revealed in the last time. [6]In this you rejoice,[a] even if now for a little while you have had to suffer various trials, [7]so that the genuineness of your faith—being more precious than gold that, though perishable, is tested by fire—may be found to result in praise and glory and honor when Jesus Christ is revealed. [8]Although you have not seen[b] him, you love him; and even though you do not see him now, you believe in him and rejoice with an indescribable and glorious joy, [9]for you are receiving the outcome of your faith, the salvation of your souls.

10 Concerning this salvation, the prophets who prophesied of the grace that was to be yours made careful search and inquiry, [11]inquiring about the person or time that the Spirit of Christ within them indicated when it testified in advance to the sufferings destined for Christ and the subsequent glory. [12]It was revealed to them that they were serving not themselves but you, in regard to the things that have now been announced to you through those who brought you good news by the Holy Spirit sent from heaven—things into which angels long to look!

A Call to Holy Living

13 Therefore prepare your minds for action;[c] discipline yourselves; set all your hope on the grace that Jesus Christ will bring you when he is revealed. [14]Like obedient children, do not be conformed to the desires that you formerly had in ignorance. [15]Instead, as he who called you is holy, be holy yourselves in all your conduct; [16]for it is written, "You shall be holy, for I am holy."

17 If you invoke as Father the one who judges all people impartially according to their deeds, live in reverent fear during the time of your exile. [18]You know that you were ransomed from the futile ways inherited from your ancestors, not with perishable things like silver or gold, [19]but with the precious blood of Christ, like that of a lamb without defect or blemish. [20]He was destined before the foundation of the world, but was revealed at the end of the ages for your sake. [21]Through him you have come to trust in God, who raised him from the dead and gave him glory, so that your faith and hope are set on God.

22 Now that you have purified your souls by your obedience to the truth[d] so that you have genuine mutual love, love one another deeply[e] from the heart.[f] [23]You have been born anew, not of perishable but of imperishable seed, through the living and enduring word of God.[g] [24]For

"All flesh is like grass
  and all its glory like the flower of grass.
The grass withers,
  and the flower falls,
[25] but the word of the Lord endures forever."

That word is the good news that was announced to you.

The Living Stone and a Chosen People

2 Rid yourselves, therefore, of all malice, and all guile, insincerity, envy, and all slander. [2]Like newborn infants, long for the pure, spiritual milk, so that by it you

[a] Or *Rejoice in this* [b] Other ancient authorities read *known* [c] Gk *gird up the loins of your mind* [d] Other ancient authorities add *through the Spirit* [e] Or *constantly* [f] Other ancient authorities read *a pure heart* [g] Or *through the word of the living and enduring God*

1.2 2 Thess 2.13; Heb 10.22; 2 Pet 1.21
1.3 2 Cor 1.3; Jas 1.18; 1 Cor 15.20
1.5 Jn 10.28
1.6 Rom 5.2; 1 Pet 5.10; Jas 1.2
1.7 Jas 1.3; Ps 66.10; Rom 2.7
1.8 1 Jn 4.20; Jn 20.29
1.10 Mt 13.17; Mt 26.24
1.11 2 Pet 1.21; Isa 53
1.12 Dan 9.24; Eph 3.10
1.13 Eph 6.14; 1 Thess 5.6
1.15 2 Cor 7.1
1.16 Lev 11.44
1.17 Deut 10.17; Heb 12.28
1.19 Ex 12.5
1.20 Eph 1.4; Heb 9.26
1.22 Jas 4.8; Heb 13.1
1.23 Jn 3.3; 1.13; Heb 4.12
1.24 Isa 40.6-9; Jas 1.10,11
1.25 Jn 1.1
2.1 Eph 4.22; Jas 1.21; 4.11
2.2 Mk 10.15; 1 Cor 3.2

See the Introductions, pp. 9–10 and 95–96 above.

1.1-2 The customary introduction for Greek letter-writing places the author's name first, followed by those of the addressees, and a usual brief word of greeting. See notes on Rom 1.1.
1.1 *Peter.* This word renders the Greek equivalent of the Aramaic name "Cephas," which Jesus gave to Simon Bar-Jona (*cf.* Mt 16.18; Mk 3.16); both "Cephas" and "Peter" mean "rock." See introductory notes for the question of authorship. *Apostle.* Literally, "one who is sent," and, in early Christian usage, sent by the risen Christ. See note on 1 Cor 15.5. *Dispersion.* Technical term for those living outside their homeland and hoping to return; this term has primary reference to Jews (*cf.* Deut 30.4; Neh 1.9; Ps 147.2), but it can be understood figuratively to refer to all Christians, as the following word suggests. *Exiles.* Used figuratively, this word refers to all believers, whose true home is not this world (*cf.* 1.17; 2.11; Eph 2.19; Phil 3.20; Heb 11.13; 13.14).
1.2 *Chosen.* New Testament Christians understood themselves to be the continuation of God's chosen people Israel; *cf.* 2.4,9; Deut 7.6; Isa 49.7; Gal 6.16; Col 3.12; Rev 17.14. *Destined.* When God "destines" something it means both that God knows it beforehand and that God brings it to pass; *cf.* Rom 8.29-30; 11.2; Eph 1.4,11-12; 2 Thess 2.13. *Obedient to Jesus Christ. Cf.* Rom 1.5; 16.26; 2 Cor 9.13. *Sprinkled with his blood. Cf.* Ex 29.19-21; Heb 9.15-22; 1 Jn 1.7.
1.3-12 This section is a prayer of thanksgiving.
1.3 *Blessed be...* This is a traditional Jewish prayer-form (*cf.* Ps 68.19; 72.18; 2 Cor 1.3; Eph 1.3; Lk 1.68). *New birth. Cf.* Jn 3.3,5; Rom 6.3-11; 2 Cor 5.17; Gal 4.19; Titus 3.5; 1 Jn 3.9).
1.4 *Inheritance. Cf.* Rom 8.17; Gal 4.7.
1.6 *In this.* I.e. to all that is mentioned in vv. 3-5.
1.7 *The genuineness of your faith.* Suffering (see vs. 6) brings this out; "faith" here has to do with faithfulness toward God (see Jas 1.2-3). *Gold...tested by fire. Cf.* Prov 17.3; 27.21; Ps 66.10; Jer 9.7; Mal 3.3.
1.8 *cf.* Jn 20.29.
1.9 *cf.* Acts 16.31; Eph 2.8; 2 Thess 2.13; 2 Tim 3.15; Heb 10.39.
1.11 *The Spirit of Christ.* See note on Col 1.15-20; *cf.* also 1 Cor 10.4; 2 Cor 3.17-18.
1.12 *cf.* Rom 15.4; 1 Cor 9.10; 19.11.
1.16 The quotation comes from Lev 11.44; 19.2; 20.7.
1.17 To address God as Father is not unknown in the Old Testament (*cf.* Ps 82.6; Jer 3.19), but is more frequent in early Christianity, which followed Jesus' example (*cf.* Mt 6.9,32; 11.25; Lk 22.42; 23.34; Jn 5.17; Rom 1.7; 8.15; Gal 4.6). *Live in reverent fear.* Addressing God as Father has implications for conduct; see Mt 5.44-48.
1.18 *Ransomed.* This word is used with reference to payment made for freeing slaves or prisoners of war, or for the redemption of property; *cf.* Ex 13.12-13; Lev 25.26,48-49. It can also refer to the Israelites' release from slavery in Egypt; *cf.* Ex 6.6; Isa 44.22-23; 51.2,10-11; 52.3; Deut 7.8). In the New Testament it is used of Jesus and his work; *cf.* Mk 10.45; Titus 2.14; Heb 9.12. *Futile ways inherited from your ancestors.* This is a reference to the readers' pre-Christian Gentile past.
1.19 *cf.* 1 Jn 1.7.
1.20 *Destined. Cf.* Isa 37.26; Rom 16.25-26; 1 Cor 2.7; Eph 3.9; Col 1.26; Titus 1.2-3. *Before the foundation of the world. Cf.* Phil 2.6-7; Gal 4.4; Col 1.18; Jn 1.1-14; 17.24. *Revealed at the end of the ages. Cf.* Mk 14.62; 1 Cor 1.7; Jude 18.
1.22 *Having purified your souls.* This is probably a reference to the rite of baptism; *cf.* Eph 5.26; Heb 10.22. *Obedience to the truth.* The act of confession connected with baptism; *cf.* Heb 10.22-23.
1.23 *Born anew.* Again, a reference to baptism; see notes on 1.3,22.
1.24-25 The quotation is from Isa 40.6-9. It is quoted here to support what is said in the previous verse. The final sentence in vs. 25 is further interpretation:

may grow into salvation— 3 if indeed you have tasted that the Lord is good.

4 Come to him, a living stone, though rejected by mortals yet chosen and precious in God's sight, and 5 like living stones, let yourselves be built[h] into a spiritual house, to be a holy priesthood, to offer spiritual sacrifices acceptable to God through Jesus Christ. 6 For it stands in scripture:

"See, I am laying in Zion a stone,
a cornerstone chosen and precious;
and whoever believes in him[i] will not
be put to shame."

7 To you then who believe, he is precious; but for those who do not believe,

"The stone that the builders rejected
has become the very head of the
corner,"

8 and

"A stone that makes them stumble,
and a rock that makes them fall."

They stumble because they disobey the word, as they were destined to do.

9 But you are a chosen race, a royal priesthood, a holy nation, God's own people,[j] in order that you may proclaim the mighty acts of him who called you out of darkness into his marvelous light.

10 Once you were not a people,
but now you are God's people;
once you had not received mercy,
but now you have received mercy.

Live as Servants of God

11 Beloved, I urge you as aliens and exiles to abstain from the desires of the flesh that wage war against the soul. 12 Conduct yourselves honorably among the Gentiles, so that, though they malign you as evildoers, they may see your honorable deeds and glorify God when he comes to judge.[k]

13 For the Lord's sake accept the authority of every human institution,[l] whether of the emperor as supreme, 14 or of governors, as sent by him to punish those who do wrong and to praise those who do right. 15 For it is God's will that by doing right you should silence the ignorance of the foolish. 16 As servants[m] of God, live as free people, yet do not use your freedom as a pretext for evil. 17 Honor everyone. Love the family of believers.[n] Fear God. Honor the emperor.

The Example of Christ's Suffering

18 Slaves, accept the authority of your masters with all deference, not only those who are kind and gentle but also those who are harsh. 19 For it is a credit to you if, being aware of God, you endure pain while suffering unjustly. 20 If you endure when you are beaten for doing wrong, what credit is that? But if you endure when you do right and suffer for it, you have God's approval. 21 For to this you have been called, because Christ also suffered for you, leaving you an example, so that you should follow in his steps.

22 "He committed no sin,
and no deceit was found in his
mouth."

23 When he was abused, he did not return abuse; when he suffered, he did not threaten; but he entrusted himself to the one who judges justly. 24 He himself bore our sins in his body on the cross,[o] so that, free from sins, we might live for righteousness; by his wounds[p] you have been healed. 25 For you were going astray like sheep, but now you have returned to the shepherd and guardian of your souls.

Wives and Husbands

3 Wives, in the same way, accept the authority of your husbands, so that, even if some of them do not obey the word, they may be won over without a word by their wives' conduct, 2 when they see the purity and reverence of your lives. 3 Do not adorn yourselves outwardly by braiding your hair, and by wearing gold ornaments or fine clothing; 4 rather, let your adornment be the inner self with the lasting beauty of a gentle and quiet spirit, which is very precious in God's sight. 5 It was in this way long ago that the holy women who hoped in God used to adorn themselves by accepting the authority of their husbands. 6 Thus Sarah obeyed Abraham and called him lord. You have become her daughters as long as you do what is good and never let fears alarm you.

7 Husbands, in the same way, show consideration for your wives in your life together, paying honor to the woman as the weaker sex,[q] since they too are also

[h] Or *you yourselves are being built* [i] Or *it* [j] Gk *a people for his possession* [k] Gk *God on the day of visitation* [l] Or *every institution ordained for human beings* [m] Gk *slaves* [n] Gk *Love the brotherhood* [o] Or *carried up our sins in his body to the tree* [p] Gk *bruise* [q] Gk *vessel*

the Isaiah quotation is fulfilled by the preaching of the Gospel of Christ.
2.1 *cf.* Eph 4.25; Heb 12.1; Jas 1.21.
2.2 *Newborn infants. Cf.* 1.3,23; also 1 Cor 3.1-2; Heb 5.12-14. *Grow into salvation.* This process of growth is reflected also in Eph 2.21; 4.13.

2.3 This verse quotes Ps 34.8.
2.4 *Him, a living stone.* I.e. Christ; *cf.* 1 Cor 10.4. *Chosen and precious. Cf.* Lk 9.35; 23.35; Jn 1.34.
2.5 *Living stones...yourselves. Cf.* Mt 16.18. *Spiritual house.* The image of the church as God's building, or temple, is common in the New Testament; see 1 Cor 3.16; Eph 2.19-22; 1 Tim 3.15; Heb 12.18-24; Rev 3.12; 11.1. *A holy priesthood.* The metaphor shifts from believers as living stones composing God's building to believers as those who serve within God's building; *cf.* Ex 19.6; Rev 1.6; 5.10; also Rom 15.16; Heb 13.10.
2.6 The quotation is from Isa 28.16, with the same variation as in Rom 9.33.
2.7 The quotation is from Ps 118.22; *cf.* Mk 12.10-11 (=Mt 21.42; Lk 20.17); Acts 4.11.
2.8 The quotation is from Isa 8.14-15. *As they were destined to do. Cf.* 1 Thess 5.9; Rom 8.28-30; Eph 1.12; Jude 4.
2.9 The language of this verse is drawn from Isa 43.20-21 and Ex 19.6. *Royal priesthood. Cf.* Rev 1.6; 5.10. *Holy nation. Cf.* Deut 7.6; 14.2,21. *God's own people. Cf.* Mal 3.17; Acts 20.28; Titus 2.14. *Called out of darkness into his marvelous light.* The change from unbelief to faith is often described as the transition from darkness to light; see Mt 4.16; 6.22-23; Lk 1.79; Acts 26.18; 2 Cor 4.6; 6.14; 1 Thess 5.4-5; Eph 5.8; Col 1.12-13; 1 Jn 1.6-7.
2.10 The quotation is a composite of phrases from Hos 3.23; 1.6,9; 2.1; *cf.* Rom 9.25.
2.11-12 This section expresses concern for the reputation of Christians among those outside the church; *cf.* 3.16; Titus 2.7-8; 3.1-2.
2.13-17 Continuing the theme of concern for Christian reputation outside the church, this section has to do with respect for secular government; *cf.* Rom 13.1-7; 1 Tim 2.1-3; Titus 3.1-3,8.
2.16 A combination of ideas from 1 Cor 7.22-23 and Gal 5.1.
2.18-3.7 This section contains a household code, similar to Eph 5.22-6.9; Col 3.18-4.1; 1 Tim 6.1-2; Titus 2.9-10.
2.22 The quotation is from Isa 53.9.
2.23 *cf.* Mk 15.29-32; 14.65; 15.16-20; Lk 23.11,36-37; Jn 19.1-5.
2.24 *Bore our sins. Cf.* Isa 53.4,11,12; Heb 9.28. *By his wounds you have been healed. Cf.* Isa 53.5.
2.25 *Going astray like sheep. Cf.* Isa 53.6. *Shepherd and guardian.* I.e. Jesus. A common biblical theme is the shepherd-flock imagery, used for God and his people (Ps 23; Isa 40.11; Jer 23.4-5; Ezek 34.11-16) and for Jesus and his followers (Mt 18.10-14; Lk 15-47; Jn 10.1-16; Heb 13.20), as well as for Christian leaders and the people to whom they minister (Jn 21.15-17; Acts 20.28; 1 Pet 5.2-3).
3.1 *cf.* 1 Cor 7.14.
3.3 *cf.* 1 Tim 2.9.

2.3 Heb 6.5; Titus 3.4
2.5 Heb 3.15; Phil 4.18
2.6 Isa 28.16; Eph 2.20
2.7 Ps 118.22; Mt 21.42
2.8 Isa 8.14; 1 Cor 1.23; Rom 9.22
2.9 Deut 10.15; Acts 26.18
2.10 Hos 1.9,10
2.11 Rom 12.1; Ps 39.12; Gal 5.16; Jas 4.1
2.12 Phil 2.15; 1 Pet 3.16; Mt 5.16
2.13 Rom 13.1
2.16 Gal 5.1; 1 Cor 7.22
2.17 Rom 12.10; Heb 13.1
2.20 1 Pet 3.17
2.21 Mt 16.24; Acts 14.22
2.23 Isa 53.7; Heb 12.3; Lk 23.46
2.24 Heb 9.28; Rom 6.2; Isa 53.5
2.25 Isa 53.6; 1 Pet 5.4
3.1 Eph 5.22; 1 Cor 7.16
3.3 1 Tim 2.9; Isa 3.18-23
3.4 Rom 7.22
3.6 Gen 18.12
3.7 Eph 5.25; 1 Thess 4.4; Mt 5.23ff

heirs of the gracious gift of life—so that nothing may hinder your prayers.

Suffering for Doing Right

8 Finally, all of you, have unity of spirit, sympathy, love for one another, a tender heart, and a humble mind. [9]Do not repay evil for evil or abuse for abuse; but, on the contrary, repay with a blessing. It is for this that you were called—that you might inherit a blessing. [10]For

"Those who desire life
and desire to see good days,
let them keep their tongues from evil
and their lips from speaking deceit;
[11] let them turn away from evil and do good;
let them seek peace and pursue it.
[12] For the eyes of the Lord are on the righteous,
and his ears are open to their prayer.
But the face of the Lord is against those who do evil."

13 Now who will harm you if you are eager to do what is good? [14]But even if you do suffer for doing what is right, you are blessed. Do not fear what they fear,[r] and do not be intimidated, [15]but in your hearts sanctify Christ as Lord. Always be ready to make your defense to anyone who demands from you an accounting for the hope that is in you; [16]yet do it with gentleness and reverence.[s] Keep your conscience clear, so that, when you are maligned, those who abuse you for your good conduct in Christ may be put to shame. [17]For it is better to suffer for doing good, if suffering should be God's will, than to suffer for doing evil. [18]For Christ also suffered[t] for sins once for all, the righteous for the unrighteous, in order to bring you[u] to God. He was put to death in the flesh, but made alive in the spirit, [19]in which also he went and made a proclamation to the spirits in prison, [20]who in former times did not obey, when God waited patiently in the days of Noah, during the building of the ark, in which a few, that is, eight persons, were saved through water. [21]And baptism, which this prefigured, now saves you—not as a removal of dirt from the body, but as an appeal to God for[v] a good conscience, through the resurrection of Jesus Christ, [22]who has gone into heaven and is at the right hand of God, with angels, authorities, and powers made subject to him.

Good Stewards of God's Grace

4 Since therefore Christ suffered in the flesh,[w] arm yourselves also with the same intention (for whoever has suffered in the flesh has finished with sin), [2]so as to live for the rest of your earthly life[x] no longer by human desires but by the will of God. [3]You have already spent enough time in doing what the Gentiles like to do, living in licentiousness, passions, drunkenness, revels, carousing, and lawless idolatry. [4]They are surprised that you no longer join them in the same excesses of dissipation, and so they blaspheme.[y] [5]But they will have to give an accounting to him who stands ready to judge the living and the dead. [6]For this is the reason the gospel was proclaimed even to the dead, so that, though they had been judged in the flesh as everyone is judged, they might live in the spirit as God does.

7 The end of all things is near;[z] therefore be serious and discipline yourselves for the sake of your prayers. [8]Above all, maintain constant love for one another, for love covers a multitude of sins. [9]Be hospitable to one another without complaining. [10]Like good stewards of the manifold grace of God, serve one another with whatever gift each of you has received. [11]Whoever speaks must do so as one speaking the very words of God; whoever serves must do so with the strength that God supplies, so that God may be glorified in all things through Jesus Christ. To him belong the glory and the power forever and ever. Amen.

Suffering as a Christian

12 Beloved, do not be surprised at the fiery ordeal that is taking place among you to test you, as though something strange were happening to you. [13]But rejoice insofar as you are sharing Christ's sufferings, so that you may also be glad and shout for joy when his glory is revealed. [14]If you are reviled for the name of Christ, you are blessed, because the spirit of glory,[a] which

[r] Gk *their fear* [s] Or *respect* [t] Other ancient authorities read *died* [u] Other ancient authorities read *us* [v] Or *a pledge to God from* [w] Other ancient authorities add *for us*; others, *for you* [x] Gk *rest of the time in the flesh* [y] Or *they malign you* [z] Or *is at hand* [a] Other ancient authorities add *and of power*

3.8 Phil 2.3; 1 Pet 5.5
3.9 Rom 12.17; Heb 6.14
3.14 1 Pet 2.19ff; Isa 8.12,13
3.15 Col 4.6; 1 Pet 1.3; 1.17
3.16 Heb 13.18; 1 Pet 2.12,15
3.18 1 Pet 2.21; 2 Cor 13.4; Eph 3.12; 1 Pet 4.1; 4.6
3.20 Gen 6.3,5; Heb 11.7; Gen 8.18
3.21 Titus 3.5; Heb 9.14; 1 Pet 1.3
3.22 Rom 8.34; 8.38
4.1 1 Pet 3.18; Gal 5.24
4.2 Gal 2.20; Rom 6.11
4.3 Eph 4.17
4.4 1 Pet 3.16
4.5 Acts 10.42; 2 Tim 4.1
4.7 Rom 13.11; 1 Pet 1.13
4.8 Heb 13.1; 1 Cor 13.7
4.10 Rom 12.6,7; 1 Cor 4.1
4.11 Eph 6.10; 5.20; 1 Tim 6.16
4.13 Phil 3.10; Rom 8.17
4.14 Mt 5.11

3.8-12 This section comprises an exhortation to all Christians; *cf.* Rom 12.9-12; Col 3.8-15; 1 Thess 5.13-22. **3.9** *cf.* Mt 5.43-44; Lk 6.27-28; Rom 12.14; 1 Thess 5.15. **3.10-12** The quotation comes from Ps 34.12-16, with some variations. **3.13-17** This section discusses the conduct of Christians under persecution (*cf.* 1.6; 2.12,19; 4.12-19). **3.14** This verse indicates that the readers have suffered for no other reason than that they are Christians; *cf.* 4.16; Mt 5.11-12; Jas 1.12; Rev 6.9; 14.13. *Do not fear. Cf.* Isa 8.12. **3.15** *Sanctify Christ as Lord. Cf.* Isa 8.13. *The hope that is in you.* I.e. your faith (see 1.13,21; 3.5). **3.18-22** This section has to do with Christ's example in suffering and his consequent victory. Verses 18-19 and 22 contain fragments of a hymn comparable to the other New Testament Christological hymns; *cf.* Phil 2.6-11; Col 1.15-20; Eph 2.14-16; Heb 1.3; Jn 1.1-18. **3.18** *Righteous.* A description frequently used of Jesus; *cf.* Acts 7.52; 3.14; 1 Jn 2.1,29; 3.7. *In order to bring you to God. Cf.* Rom 5.2; Eph 2.18; 3.12. *Put to death in the flesh, but made alive in the spirit; cf.* Rom 1.3-4; 1 Tim 3.16. **3.19** *The spirits in prison.* It is unclear who is meant by this term, whether fallen angels (see Jude 6; 2 Pet 2.4), Satan himself (Rev 20.3), or those who had died in the flood (see next verse). *Cf.* Jn 5.25; Phil 2.10. **3.20** See Gen 6-8. Noah frequently appears as a great hero of the past in both Jewish (see Ezek 14.14,20; Wis 10.4; Sir 44.17) and Christian (Mt 24.37-38; Heb 11.7; 2 Pet 2.5) literature. **3.21** In 1 Cor 10.1-2 the passage through the Red Sea is a prefigurement for baptism; here baptism is prefigured by the flood. God's saving acts in the past occur again in the present, and in baptism God's salvation is available to everyone. Baptism opens the way for the believers' *appeal to God for a clear conscience.* For the connection between Jesus' resurrection and baptism *cf.* also Rom 6.1-11. **3.22** *cf.* Rom 8.38; 1 Cor 15.24-25; Gal 4.3,9; Col 2.8; Eph 1.21; 6.12; Phil 3.21. **4.1** The imitation of Christ is the basis for Christian ethics, specifically his suffering. **4.3-4** The negative assessment of Gentile morality is inherited by the early church from traditional Judaism (see Wis 13-15; Rom 1.18-32; Eph 4.17-19). Early Christian preaching demanded a clean break from such unconscionably immoral ways. **4.5** *The living and the dead.* I.e. all people. **4.7-11** This section deals with the nature of Christian fellowship, reflecting traditional Christian material. Eschatological considerations underlie the exhortation to Christian behavior; *cf.* Mt 24.45-25.13; Mk 13.33-37; Rom 13.11-14; Heb 10.25; 1 Jn 2.28-29. **4.7** *The end of all things is near. Cf.* 1.5-6; 4.13,17; 5.1,10; 1 Thess 5.1-11; 2 Thess 2.2. **4.8** *cf.* Prov 10.12; Jas 5.20; Gal 5.14. **4.9** *cf.* Rom 12.13; 15.7; 1 Tim 3.2; Titus 1.8; Heb 13.2; 3 Jn 5-8. **4.10** *cf.* Rom 12.3-8; 1 Cor 12.4-31. **4.12-19** This section repeats the theme of persecution, but with one different emphasis. Up to this point in this writing the author has spoken of the persecution of Christians as a possibility still to come. Now the writer refers to the persecution as a present, ongoing occurrence. **4.13** *Share Christ's sufferings; cf.* 2 Cor 1.5; Phil 3.10; Col 1.24. **4.14** *Reviled for the name of Christ.* This verse, along with 4.16, indicates that Christians known to the author are being persecuted for their faith. *The Spirit of God...resting upon you. Cf.* Num 11.25; Isa 11.2; Mk 13.11; Mt 10.20; Lk 12.11-12.

is the Spirit of God, is resting on you.[b] [15]But
let none of you suffer as a murderer, a thief,
a criminal, or even as a mischief maker.
[16]Yet if any of you suffers as a Christian, do
not consider it a disgrace, but glorify God
because you bear this name. [17]For the time
has come for judgment to begin with the
household of God; if it begins with us, what
will be the end for those who do not obey
the gospel of God? [18]And

"If it is hard for the righteous to be
saved,
what will become of the ungodly
and the sinners?"

[19]Therefore, let those suffering in accordance with God's will entrust themselves to
a faithful Creator, while continuing to do
good.

Tending the Flock of God

5 Now as an elder myself and a witness
of the sufferings of Christ, as well as
one who shares in the glory to be revealed,
I exhort the elders among you [2]to tend the
flock of God that is in your charge, exercising the oversight,[c] not under compulsion
but willingly, as God would have you do
it[d]—not for sordid gain but eagerly. [3]Do not
lord it over those in your charge, but be
examples to the flock. [4]And when the chief
shepherd appears, you will win the crown
of glory that never fades away. [5]In the same
way, you who are younger must accept the
authority of the elders.[e] And all of you must
clothe yourselves with humility in your
dealings with one another, for

"God opposes the proud,
but gives grace to the humble."

6 Humble yourselves therefore under the
mighty hand of God, so that he may exalt
you in due time. [7]Cast all your anxiety on
him, because he cares for you. [8]Discipline
yourselves, keep alert.[f] Like a roaring lion
your adversary the devil prowls around,
looking for someone to devour. [9]Resist him,
steadfast in your faith, for you know that
your brothers and sisters[g] in all the world
are undergoing the same kinds of suffering.
[10]And after you have suffered for a little
while, the God of all grace, who has called
you to his eternal glory in Christ, will himself restore, support, strengthen, and establish you. [11]To him be the power forever and
ever. Amen.

Final Greetings and Benediction

12 Through Silvanus, whom I consider a
faithful brother, I have written this short
letter to encourage you and to testify that
this is the true grace of God. Stand fast in
it. [13]Your sister church[h] in Babylon, chosen
together with you, sends you greetings; and
so does my son Mark. [14]Greet one another
with a kiss of love.

Peace to all of you who are in Christ.[i]

[b] Other ancient authorities add *On their part he is blasphemed, but on your part he is glorified* [c] Other ancient authorities lack *exercising the oversight* [d] Other ancient authorities lack *as God would have you do it* [e] Or *of those who are older* [f] Or *be vigilant* [g] Gk *your brotherhood* [h] Gk *She who is* [i] Other ancient authorities add *Amen*

4.16 *Christian.* This term is first used by non-Christians to describe Jesus' followers (see Acts 11.26).
4.17 A frequent theme in the Old Testament is that God's judgment begins first with God's people; *cf.* Mal 3.1-5; Jer 25.29; Ezek 9.6; Isa 10.12; Zech 13.7-9.
4.18 The quotation is from Prov 11.31.
5.1 *cf.* 1.1, where Peter is called an apostle; here the term "elder" seems to imply ministerial office (see 5.2).
5.2 See note on 2.25.
5.4 *The chief shepherd.* I.e. Jesus.
5.5 The quotation is from Prov 3.34.
5.6-11 This section is a closing admonition to remain faithful.
5.7 *cf.* Ps 55.22; Mt 6.25-34; Lk 21.18.
5.8 *Your adversary the devil.* See note on Mt 4.10.
5.12-14 A section of greetings is given in conclusion.
5.12 *Silvanus.* A Silvanus is mentioned in 2 Cor 1.19; 1 Thess 1.1; and 2 Thess 1.1, and is probably the same person who accompanied Paul after the Apostolic Council in Acts 15 (see Acts 15.22,27,32,40; 18.5). The wording of the present verse leaves open the possibility that Silvanus is either the bearer of this letter, or the one to whom it was dictated, or its actual author.
5.13 *Babylon.* This could be a code name for Rome; *cf.* 2 Bar 11.1-2; 67.7; 2 Esd 3.1-2,28; Rev 14.8; 16.19; 17.5; 18.2,10,21. *Mark.* A travel companion of Paul before the Apostolic Council in Acts 15 (see Acts 12.12; 13.4-13; 15.37-39; Philem 24; Col 4.10; 2 Tim 4.11).
5.14 *Kiss of love.* See note on 2 Cor 13.12.

4.15 1 Thess 4.11
4.17 Jer 25.29; Mal 3.5
5.1 Lk 24.28; 1 Pet 1.5,7; Rev 1.9
5.2 Jn 21.16; 1 Cor 9.17; 1 Tim 3.3,8; Titus 1.7
5.3 Ezek 34.4; Phil 3.17
5.4 Heb 13.20; 2 Tim 4.8
5.5 Jas 4.6; Isa 57.15
5.7 Ps 37.5; Mt 6.25; Heb 13.5
5.8 Lk 21.34; Job 1.7
5.9 Jas 4.7; Col 2.5; Acts 14.22
5.10 Heb 13.21; 2 Thess 2.17
5.12 2 Cor 1.19; Heb 13.22
5.14 Rom 16.16; Eph 6.23

THE SECOND LETTER OF

PETER

Salutation

1 Simeon[a] Peter, a servant[b] and apostle of Jesus Christ,

To those who have received a faith as precious as ours through the righteousness of our God and Savior Jesus Christ:[c]

2 May grace and peace be yours in abundance in the knowledge of God and of Jesus our Lord.

The Christian's Call and Election

3 His divine power has given us everything needed for life and godliness, through the knowledge of him who called us by[d] his own glory and goodness. [4]Thus he has given us, through these things, his precious and very great promises, so that through them you may escape from the corruption that is in the world because of lust, and may become participants of the divine nature. [5]For this very reason, you must make every effort to support your faith with goodness, and goodness with knowledge, [6]and knowledge with self-control, and self-control with endurance, and endurance with godliness, [7]and godliness with mutual[e] affection, and mutual[e] affection with love. [8]For if these things are yours and are increasing among you, they keep you from being ineffective and unfruitful in the knowledge of our Lord Jesus Christ. [9]For anyone who lacks these things is nearsighted and blind, and is forgetful of the cleansing of past sins. [10]Therefore, brothers and sisters,[f] be all the more eager to confirm your call and election, for if you do this, you will never stumble. [11]For in this way, entry into the eternal kingdom of our Lord and Savior Jesus Christ will be richly provided for you.

12 Therefore I intend to keep on reminding you of these things, though you know them already and are established in the truth that has come to you. [13]I think it right, as long as I am in this body,[g] to refresh your memory, [14]since I know that my death[h] will come soon, as indeed our Lord Jesus Christ has made clear to me. [15]And I will make every effort so that after my departure you may be able at any time to recall these things.

Eyewitnesses of Christ's Glory

16 For we did not follow cleverly devised myths when we made known to you the power and coming of our Lord Jesus Christ, but we had been eyewitnesses of his majesty. [17]For he received honor and glory from God the Father when that voice was conveyed to him by the Majestic Glory, saying, "This is my Son, my Beloved,[i] with whom I am well pleased." [18]We ourselves heard this voice come from heaven, while we were with him on the holy mountain.

19 So we have the prophetic message more fully confirmed. You will do well to be attentive to this as to a lamp shining in a dark place, until the day dawns and the morning star rises in your hearts. [20]First of all you must understand this, that no prophecy of scripture is a matter of one's own interpretation, [21]because no prophecy ever came by human will, but men and women moved by the Holy Spirit spoke from God.[j]

False Prophets and Their Punishment

2 But false prophets also arose among the people, just as there will be false teachers among you, who will secretly bring in destructive opinions. They will even deny the Master who bought them—bringing swift destruction on themselves. [2]Even so, many will follow their licentious ways, and because of these teachers[k] the way of truth will be maligned. [3]And in their greed they will exploit you with deceptive words. Their condemnation, pronounced against them long ago, has not been idle, and their destruction is not asleep.

4 For if God did not spare the angels when they sinned, but cast them into hell[l]

[a] Other ancient authorities read *Simon* [b] Gk *slave* [c] Or *of our God and the Savior Jesus Christ* [d] Other ancient authorities read *through* [e] Gk *brotherly* [f] Gk *brothers* [g] Gk *tent* [h] Gk *the putting off of my tent* [i] Other ancient authorities read *my beloved Son* [j] Other ancient authorities read *but moved by the Holy Spirit saints of God spoke* [k] Gk *because of them* [l] Gk *Tartaros*

1.3 1 Pet 1.5; 1 Thess 2.12
1.4 2 Cor 7.1; Eph 4.24; 1 Jn 3.2; 2 Pet 2.18-20
1.5 2 Pet 3.18; Col 2.3
1.8 Jn 15.2; Titus 3.14
1.9 1 Jn 2.11; Eph 5.26; 1 Jn 1.7
1.12 1 Jn 2.21
1.13 2 Cor 5.1
1.14 2 Tim 4.6; Jn 21.18,19
1.16 1 Tim 1.4; Mt 17.1; Mk 9.2
1.17 Mt 3.17; Lk 9.35
1.18 Mt 17.6
1.19 1 Pet 1.10,11; Ps 119.105; Rev 22.16
1.21 2 Tim 3.16; 1 Pet 1.11; Acts 1.16
2.1 1 Tim 4.1; Jude 18; 1 Cor 6.20
2.3 1 Tim 6.5; 2 Cor 2.17; Deut 32.25
2.4 Jude 6; Jn 8.44; Rev 20.1,2

See the Introductions, pp. 9–10 and 96 above.

1.1 *Simeon.* A Hebraized version of the name "Simon," the spelling more common in Greek circles; *cf.* Lk 2.25,34; 3.30; Acts 13.1; 15.14; Rev 7.7.
1.2 *cf.* 1 Pet 1.2; Jude 2.
1.3 *Him who called us.* I.e. Christ; see 1 Pet 2.9.
1.4 *Participants of the divine nature.* A famous phrase which has no real parallels in the New Testament; with a strong Hellenistic religious background, this phrase probably echoes a goal of the author's opponents, who, as the rest of the letter shows, are still caught up in the corruption caused by lust.
1.5 *Knowledge.* Here this word refers to morality; *cf.* 2 Cor 6.6. 8.7.
1.6 *Self-control. Cf.* 1 Cor 7.9; 9.25; Gal 5.23. *Endurance. Cf.* Rom 5.3-4; 1 Tim 6.11; 2 Tim 3.10; Titus 2.2; Rev 2.19. *Godliness. Cf.* 1 Tim 6.11.
1.7 *Mutual affection. Cf.* Rom 12.10; 1 Thess 4.9; Heb 13.1; 1 Pet 1.22; 3.8. *Love. Cf.* 1 Cor 13; 2 Cor 6.6; Gal 5.22; Eph 4.2; Col 3.14; 1 Tim 4.12; 6.11; 2 Tim 2.22; 3.10; Titus 2.2; Rev. 2.19.
1.9 *The cleansing of past sins.* I.e. in baptism; *cf.* Acts 22.16; 1 Cor 6.11; Eph 5.26; Titus 3.5.
1.10 *Your call and election. Cf.* 1 Cor 1.26-27; 1 Pet 2.9.
1.14 *As indeed our Lord Jesus Christ has made clear to me.* Perhaps this is a reference to Jn 21.18-19.
1.16 *cf.* 1 Tim 1.4; 4.7; 2 Tim 4.4; Titus 1.14. *Eyewitnesses of his majesty.* As the next two verses will show, this is a reference to Jesus' transfiguration (see Mk 9.2-8).
1.17 The quotation is from Mk 9.7 (Mt 17.5; Lk 9.35).
1.18 *The holy mountain.* I.e. of Jesus' transfiguration (see Mk 9.2-8; pars. Mt 17.1-8 and Lk 9.28-36).
1.19 *The prophetic word.* Most likely the author is thinking of the Old Testament scriptures in general. *Lamp shining in a dark place. Cf.* Mk 4.21; Jn 5.35. *Morning star. Cf.* Num 24.17.
1.20 This verse rejects the notion that biblical interpretation is a private matter; it is properly done in community, as the next verse says, under the guidance of the Spirit; *cf.* 1 Cor 14.29.
1.21 This verse rejects the notion that the Old Testament prophets were the originating source of their message; they do not speak on their own initiative, but are empowered by the Holy Spirit; *cf.* 2.1.
2.1-3.3 This section paraphrases most of the Letter of Jude, using largely the same terminology. Most commentators have suggested that Jude was written first, primarily because the author of 2 Peter displays an interest in the developing Christian canon (1.16-18; 3.1,15-16) as a communal process (1.19-21), which has led him to omit the direct references in Jude to the non-canonical Jewish pseudepigraphal writings (see notes on Jude 6, 9, and 14-16).
2.1-3 *cf.* Jude 4.
2.1 The phenomenon of false prophets in Old Testament times is itself a prototype of false prophets in New Testament times; *cf.* Jer 14.14; 23.14; Mt 24.11,24.
2.4 *cf.* Jude 6. *Angels.* The fallen angels are a frequent theme in Jewish and Christian literature of the period; see note on Jude 6.

and committed them to chains[m] of deepest
darkness to be kept until the judgment;
5and if he did not spare the ancient world,
even though he saved Noah, a herald of
righteousness, with seven others, when he
brought a flood on a world of the ungodly;
6and if by turning the cities of Sodom and
Gomorrah to ashes he condemned them to
extinction[n] and made them an example of
what is coming to the ungodly;[o] 7and if he
rescued Lot, a righteous man greatly distressed by the licentiousness of the lawless
8(for that righteous man, living among them
day after day, was tormented in his righteous soul by their lawless deeds that he saw
and heard), 9then the Lord knows how to
rescue the godly from trial, and to keep the
unrighteous under punishment until the
day of judgment 10—especially those who
indulge their flesh in depraved lust, and
who despise authority.

Bold and willful, they are not afraid to
slander the glorious ones,[p] 11whereas angels, though greater in might and power, do
not bring against them a slanderous judgment from the Lord.[q] 12These people, however, are like irrational animals, mere creatures of instinct, born to be caught and
killed. They slander what they do not understand, and when those creatures are
destroyed,[r] they also will be destroyed,
13suffering[s] the penalty for doing wrong.
They count it a pleasure to revel in the
daytime. They are blots and blemishes,
reveling in their dissipation[t] while they feast
with you. 14They have eyes full of adultery,
insatiable for sin. They entice unsteady souls.
They have hearts trained in greed. Accursed children! 15They have left the straight
road and have gone astray, following the
road of Balaam son of Bosor,[u] who loved the
wages of doing wrong, 16but was rebuked
for his own transgression; a speechless
donkey spoke with a human voice and
restrained the prophet's madness.

17 These are waterless springs and mists
driven by a storm; for them the deepest
darkness has been reserved. 18For they speak
bombastic nonsense, and with licentious
desires of the flesh they entice people who
have just[v] escaped from those who live in
error. 19They promise them freedom, but
they themselves are slaves of corruption; for
people are slaves to whatever masters them.
20For if, after they have escaped the defile-
ments of the world through the knowledge
of our Lord and Savior Jesus Christ, they are
again entangled in them and overpowered,
the last state has become worse for them
than the first. 21For it would have been
better for them never to have known the
way of righteousness than, after knowing it,
to turn back from the holy commandment
that was passed on to them. 22It has happened to them according to the true proverb,

"The dog turns back to its own
vomit,"

and,

"The sow is washed only to wallow in
the mud."

The Promise of the Lord's Coming

3 This is now, beloved, the second letter
I am writing to you; in them I am
trying to arouse your sincere intention by
reminding you 2that you should remember
the words spoken in the past by the holy
prophets, and the commandment of the
Lord and Savior spoken through your apostles. 3First of all you must understand this,
that in the last days scoffers will come,
scoffing and indulging their own lusts 4and
saying, "Where is the promise of his coming? For ever since our ancestors died,[w] all
things continue as they were from the
beginning of creation!" 5They deliberately
ignore this fact, that by the word of God
heavens existed long ago and an earth was
formed out of water and by means of water,
6through which the world of that time was
deluged with water and perished. 7But by
the same word the present heavens and
earth have been reserved for fire, being kept
until the day of judgment and destruction
of the godless.

8 But do not ignore this one fact, beloved, that with the Lord one day is like a
thousand years, and a thousand years are
like one day. 9The Lord is not slow about
his promise, as some think of slowness, but
is patient with you,[x] not wanting any to

[m] Other ancient authorities read *pits* [n] Other ancient authorities lack *to extinction* [o] Other ancient authorities read *an example to those who were to be ungodly* [p] Or *angels*; Gk *glories* [q] Other ancient authorities read *before the Lord*; others lack the phrase [r] Gk *in their destruction* [s] Other ancient authorities read *receiving* [t] Other ancient authorities read *love feasts* [u] Other ancient authorities read *Beor* [v] Other ancient authorities read *actually* [w] Gk *our fathers fell asleep* [x] Other ancient authorities read *on your account*

2.5 *cf.* 1 Pet 3.20.
2.6 *cf.* Jude 7, and see note there.
2.7 *Lot.* Abraham's nephew; see Gen 19.
2.9-11 *cf.* Jude 8-9.
2.12 *cf.* Jude 10.
2.13 *cf.* Jude 12.
2.15 *cf.* Jude 11, and see note there.
2.16 *Speechless donkey.* See Num 22.28.
2.17 *cf.* Jude 12-13. See note on Jude 13.
2.18 *cf.* Jude 16.
2.22 The first quotation is from Prov 26.11; the second is from a well-known story in the ancient world called *The Story of Ahikar* (8.18).
3.1 *The second letter.* This author knows that 1 Peter has circulated in the church.
3.2 *cf.* Jude 17. *Holy prophets.* As in 1.19, Old Testament prophets are probably meant here.; *cf.* Am 9.10; Mal 2.17; Zeph 1.12.
3.3 *cf.* Jude 18. This verse expresses a commonly accepted general teaching that the last days would be featured by the appearance of false prophets; *cf.* Mt 7.15; 24.11,24; Mk 13.22; Acts 20.29-30; 1 Tim 4.1-3; 2 Tim 3.1-9; 4.3-4; 1 Jn 2.8; 4.1-3.
3.4 The false prophets' position is quoted here. They have called into question the promise of Christ's return. *Our ancestors* may refer to the first Christian generation.
3.5-7 A theme current in Jewish speculative religious literature of the time was that the earlier destruction of the world by the flood was a prototype of the coming destruction of the world by fire.
3.8 *A thousand years are like one day. Cf.* Ps 90.4.
3.9 The delay of the End of time is a sign of God's patience, to give people more time to repent; *cf.* Joel 2.12-13; Jon 4.2; Rom 2.4,4; Ezra 3.30; 7.33; 9.21; 7.14.

2.5 Gen 7.1; Heb 11.7; 1 Pet 3.20
2.7 Gen 19.16; 2 Pet 3.17
2.9 1 Cor 10.13; Jude 6
2.10 2 Pet 3.3; Jude 8; Titus 1.7
2.13 Rom 13.13; Jude 12; 1 Cor 11.20,21
2.15 Num 22.5,7; Jude 11
2.17 Jude 12,13
2.19 Jn 8.34; Rom 6.16
2.20 Mt 12.45; Lk 11.26; 2 Pet 1.2
2.21 Heb 6.4ff; 2 Pet 3.2; Jude 3
2.22 Prov 26.11
3.3 1 Tim 4.1; Jude 18; 2 Pet 2.10
3.4 Jer 17.15; Ezek 12.22; Mt 24.48; Acts 7.60; Mt 10.6
3.5 Gen 1.6,9; Heb 11.3; Ps 24.2; Col 1.17
3.6 Gen 7.21,22
3.7 ver 10; 2 Thess 1.7; 1 Cor 3.13
3.8 Ps 90.4
3.9 Heb 10.37; Isa 30.18; 1 Pet 3.20; Rom 2.4

3.10 Mt 24.43; 1 Thess 5.2; Mt 24.35; Rev 21.1,12; 1 Cor 1.7; Titus 2.13; Ps 50.3; Isa 34.4; ver 10
3.13 Isa 65.17; 66.22; Rev 21.1
3.14 2 Pet 1.10; 1 Cor 15.58; Phil 2.15
3.15 ver 9; 1 Cor 3.10; Eph 3.3
3.17 1 Cor 10.12; 2 Pet 2.18; Rev 2.5

perish, but all to come to repentance. [10]But
the day of the Lord will come like a thief,
and then the heavens will pass away with
a loud noise, and the elements will be
dissolved with fire, and the earth and
everything that is done on it will be disclosed.[y]
11 Since all these things are to be dissolved in this way, what sort of persons
ought you to be in leading lives of holiness
and godliness, [12]waiting for and hastening[z]
the coming of the day of God, because of
which the heavens will be set ablaze and
dissolved, and the elements will melt with
fire? [13]But, in accordance with his promise,
we wait for new heavens and a new earth,
where righteousness is at home.

Final Exhortation and Doxology

14 Therefore, beloved, while you are
waiting for these things, strive to be found
by him at peace, without spot or blemish;
[15]and regard the patience of our Lord as
salvation. So also our beloved brother Paul
wrote to you according to the wisdom given
him, [16]speaking of this as he does in all his
letters. There are some things in them hard
to understand, which the ignorant and
unstable twist to their own destruction, as
they do the other scriptures. [17]You therefore, beloved, since you are forewarned,
beware that you are not carried away with
the error of the lawless and lose your own
stability. [18]But grow in the grace and knowledge of our Lord and Savior Jesus Christ. To
him be the glory both now and to the day
of eternity. Amen.[a]

[y] Other ancient authorities read *will be burned up* [z] Or *earnestly desiring* [a] Other ancient authorities lack *Amen*

THE FIRST LETTER OF
JOHN

See the Introductions, pp. 9–10 and 97 above.

1.1 Jn 1.1,14; 2 Pet 1.16; Jn 20.27
1.2 Jn 1.1-4; Rom 16.26; Jn 21.24
1.3 Acts 4.20; 1 Cor 1.9
1.5 1 Jn 3.11
1.7 Heb 9.14; 1 Pet 1.19; Rev 1.5
1.9 Ps 51.2
1.10 1 Jn 5.10; 2.14
2.1 Rom 8.34; Heb 7.25
2.2 Rom 3.25; Jn 1.29

The Word of Life

1 We declare to you what was from the
beginning, what we have heard, what
we have seen with our eyes, what we have
looked at and touched with our hands,
concerning the word of life— [2]this life was
revealed, and we have seen it and testify to
it, and declare to you the eternal life that
was with the Father and was revealed to
us— [3]we declare to you what we have seen
and heard so that you also may have fellowship with us; and truly our fellowship is
with the Father and with his Son Jesus
Christ. [4]We are writing these things so that
our[a] joy may be complete.

God Is Light

5 This is the message we have heard
from him and proclaim to you, that God is
light and in him there is no darkness at all.
[6]If we say that we have fellowship with him
while we are walking in darkness, we lie
and do not do what is true; [7]but if we walk
in the light as he himself is in the light, we
have fellowship with one another, and the
blood of Jesus his Son cleanses us from all
sin. [8]If we say that we have no sin, we
deceive ourselves, and the truth is not in us.
[9]If we confess our sins, he who is faithful
and just will forgive us our sins and cleanse
us from all unrighteousness. [10]If we say that
we have not sinned, we make him a liar,
and his word is not in us.

Christ Our Advocate

2 My little children, I am writing these
things to you so that you may not sin.
But if anyone does sin, we have an advocate with the Father, Jesus Christ the righteous; [2]and he is the atoning sacrifice for our
sins, and not for ours only but also for the
sins of the whole world.

[a] Other ancient authorities read *your*

1.1-4 The basis of faith for the community is the Jesus who lived, and was seen, touched and heard: the incarnate *word of life*. The meaning of this life has been experienced by the writer and his community (*us*) through God's having revealed it to them. He invites them to share in these insights and this life, so that they may participate in the common life (*fellowship*) which *the Father* has made possible through *his Son* and which brings true *joy* to those who participate.
1.5-10 Since *God is light*, those who share in this community must walk in light and truth, experiencing the cleansing that God has provided through the death (*blood*) of Jesus for those who acknowledge their sins.
2.1-5 While the ideal is to avoid sin, those who commit sins must rely on the one who presents *the Father* with a case in their behalf: Christ is both *advocate* and *sacrifice for sins*. The *whole world* has this resource potentially, even though it does not avail itself of access to God through Christ. Those who do are to keep his commandments, which will be evident in the transforming power of love in their lives. This has as its model how Christ *walked* through life.

2.7-17 Life in the Light of God's Love.
2.7-11 The commandment to love is familiar and therefore *old,* but it constantly renews human relations within the community, and is therefore ever *new.* To fail to live by this command is to *walk in darkness.*
2.12-14 This insight has implications for every level of the members: the *little children* are to recognize that they are forgiven because of Jesus (*his name*); the *fathers* are reminded that they have known Christ *from the beginning*; the *children* know *the Father*; the *young people* are commended for their strength and their victory over the power of *evil.*
2.15-17 Their values and their devotion must be for the *Father* and his eternal purpose rather than for the transitory pleasures and accomplishments of this *world.*
2.18-28 Living Faithfully before the Coming End of the Age.
2.18-25 The crisis that will precede the end of the present age is already upon the community, as is evident in the withdrawal from membership of those who deny *that Jesus is the Christ* and hence deny what the *Father* has said and done through him. The faithful know the truth, and they formally, publicly acknowledge (*confess*) both the Father and the Son, and hence stand firm (*abide*) in that relationship which endures to *eternal life.*
2.26-28 They are kept from error by *the anointing* of the Spirit of God, which instructs and sustains them in the truth. Thus they can be confident that they will be vindicated at Jesus' *coming.*
2.29-3.10 Differentiating God's Children from Those of the Devil. Jesus is the model of obedience, and God's children follow his example. He was not understood by *the world,* and neither are they. Their future is to become like him, and to become pure as he is.

3 Now by this we may be sure that we
know him, if we obey his commandments.
[4]Whoever says, "I have come to know him,"
but does not obey his commandments, is a
liar, and in such a person the truth does not
exist; [5]but whoever obeys his word, truly in
this person the love of God has reached
perfection. By this we may be sure that we
are in him: [6]whoever says, "I abide in him,"
ought to walk just as he walked.

A New Commandment

7 Beloved, I am writing you no new
commandment, but an old commandment
that you have had from the beginning; the
old commandment is the word that you
have heard. [8]Yet I am writing you a new
commandment that is true in him and in
you, because[b] the darkness is passing away
and the true light is already shining. [9]Who-
ever says, "I am in the light," while hating
a brother or sister,[c] is still in the darkness.
[10]Whoever loves a brother or sister[d] lives in
the light, and in such a person[e] there is no
cause for stumbling. [11]But whoever hates
another believer[f] is in the darkness, walks
in the darkness, and does not know the way
to go, because the darkness has brought on
blindness.

12 I am writing to you, little children,
because your sins are forgiven on
account of his name.
13 I am writing to you, fathers,
because you know him who is from
the beginning.
I am writing to you, young people,
because you have conquered the
evil one.
14 I write to you, children,
because you know the Father.
I write to you, fathers,
because you know him who is from
the beginning.
I write to you, young people,
because you are strong
and the word of God abides in you,
and you have overcome the evil
one.

15 Do not love the world or the things
in the world. The love of the Father is not
in those who love the world; [16]for all that
is in the world—the desire of the flesh, the
desire of the eyes, the pride in riches—
comes not from the Father but from the
world. [17]And the world and its desire[g] are
passing away, but those who do the will of
God live forever.

Warning against Antichrists

18 Children, it is the last hour! As you
have heard that antichrist is coming, so
now many antichrists have come. From this
we know that it is the last hour. [19]They
went out from us, but they did not belong
to us; for if they had belonged to us, they
would have remained with us. But by going
out they made it plain that none of them
belongs to us. [20]But you have been anointed
by the Holy One, and all of you have
knowledge.[h] [21]I write to you, not because
you do not know the truth, but because you
know it, and you know that no lie comes
from the truth. [22]Who is the liar but the one
who denies that Jesus is the Christ?[i] This is
the antichrist, the one who denies the Father and the Son. [23]No one who denies the
Son has the Father; everyone who confesses
the Son has the Father also. [24]Let what you
heard from the beginning abide in you. If
what you heard from the beginning abides
in you, then you will abide in the Son and
in the Father. [25]And this is what he has
promised us,[j] eternal life.

26 I write these things to you concerning those who would deceive you. [27]As for
you, the anointing that you received from
him abides in you, and so you do not need
anyone to teach you. But as his anointing
teaches you about all things, and is true
and is not a lie, and just as it has taught
you, abide in him.[k]

28 And now, little children, abide in him,
so that when he is revealed we may have
confidence and not be put to shame before
him at his coming.

Children of God

29 If you know that he is righteous, you
may be sure that everyone who does right
has been born of him.

3 See what love the Father has given
us, that we should be called children
of God; and that is what we are. The reason
the world does not know us is that it did
not know him. [2]Beloved, we are God's

[b] Or *that* [c] Gk *hating a brother* [d] Gk *loves a brother* [e] Or *in it* [f] Gk *hates a brother* [g] Or *the desire for it* [h] Other ancient authorities read *you know all things* [i] Or *the Messiah* [j] Other ancient authorities read *you* [k] Or *it*

2.5 Jn 14.23; 1 Jn 4.12,13
2.6 Jn 15.4; 1 Pet 2.21
2.8 Eph 5.8; 1 Thess 5.5; Jn 1.9
2.9 2 Pet 1.9
2.11 Jn 12.35
2.12 Lk 24.47
2.14 1 Jn 1.1; Eph 6.10; Jn 5.38
2.15 Rom 12.2; Mt 6.24; Jas 4.4
2.17 1 Cor 7.31
2.18 1 Pet 4.7; 1 Jn 4.1,3
2.19 Acts 20.30; Mt 24.24; 1 Cor 11.19
2.20 2 Cor 1.21; Acts 3.14; Jn 14.26
2.23 Jn 14.7
2.24 2 Jn 6; Jn 14.23
2.25 Jn 17.3
2.27 Jn 14.26; 14.17
2.28 1 Jn 3.2; 3.21; 4.17; Mk 8.38; 1 Thess 2.19
2.29 1 Jn 3.7,9; 4.7
3.1 1 Jn 1.12; 16.3
3.2 Rom 8.15; 2 Cor 4.17; Rom 8.29; 2 Pet 1.4; 2 Cor 3.18

3.4 Rom 4.15; 1 Jn 5.17
3.5 Isa 53.5,6; 2 Cor 5.21
3.8 Jn 8.44; 16.11; Heb 3.14
3.9 1 Jn 5.18; 1 Pet 1.23
3.10 1 Jn 2.29
3.11 1 Jn 1.5; Jn 13.34,35; 2 Jn 5
3.13 Jn 15.18
3.14 Jn 5.24; 1 Jn 2.9,11
3.15 Mt 5.21,22; Jn 8.44; Gal 5.20,21
3.16 Jn 3.16; 13.1; 15.13
3.17 Deut 15.7; 1 Jn 4.20
3.18 Rom 12.9; Jas 1.22
3.19 1 Jn 2.21
3.22 Mt 7.7; 21.22; 1 Jn 2.3
3.23 1 Jn 2.8
3.24 Rom 8.9; 1 Jn 4.13
4.1 Mt 24.4; 2 Pet 2.1; 1 Jn 2.18
4.3 2 Jn 7; 1 Jn 2.22; 2 Thess 2.7; 1 Jn 5.4
4.6 Jn 8.47; 1 Cor 14.37; Jn 14.17; 1 Tim 4.1
4.7 1 Jn 3.10,11
4.9 Jn 3.16; 1 Jn 5.11
4.10 Rom 5.8,10; 1 Jn 2.2
4.11 Jn 3.16; 15.12
4.12 Jn 1.18; 1 Tim 6.16; 1 Jn 2.5

children now; what we will be has not yet been revealed. What we do know is this: when he[l] is revealed, we will be like him, for we will see him as he is. 3And all who have this hope in him purify themselves, just as he is pure.

4 Everyone who commits sin is guilty of lawlessness; sin is lawlessness. 5You know that he was revealed to take away sins, and in him there is no sin. 6No one who abides in him sins; no one who sins has either seen him or known him. 7Little children, let no one deceive you. Everyone who does what is right is righteous, just as he is righteous. 8Everyone who commits sin is a child of the devil; for the devil has been sinning from the beginning. The Son of God was revealed for this purpose, to destroy the works of the devil. 9Those who have been born of God do not sin, because God's seed abides in them;[m] they cannot sin, because they have been born of God. 10The children of God and the children of the devil are revealed in this way: all who do not do what is right are not from God, nor are those who do not love their brothers and sisters.[n]

Love One Another

11 For this is the message you have heard from the beginning, that we should love one another. 12We must not be like Cain who was from the evil one and murdered his brother. And why did he murder him? Because his own deeds were evil and his brother's righteous. 13Do not be astonished, brothers and sisters,[o] that the world hates you. 14We know that we have passed from death to life because we love one another. Whoever does not love abides in death. 15All who hate a brother or sister[n] are murderers, and you know that murderers do not have eternal life abiding in them. 16We know love by this, that he laid down his life for us—and we ought to lay down our lives for one another. 17How does God's love abide in anyone who has the world's goods and sees a brother or sister[p] in need and yet refuses help?

18 Little children, let us love, not in word or speech, but in truth and action. 19And by this we will know that we are from the truth and will reassure our hearts before him 20whenever our hearts condemn us; for God is greater than our hearts, and he knows everything. 21Beloved, if our hearts do not condemn us, we have boldness before God; 22and we receive from him whatever we ask, because we obey his commandments and do what pleases him.

23 And this is his commandment, that we should believe in the name of his Son Jesus Christ and love one another, just as he has commanded us. 24All who obey his commandments abide in him, and he abides in them. And by this we know that he abides in us, by the Spirit that he has given us.

Testing the Spirits

4 Beloved, do not believe every spirit, but test the spirits to see whether they are from God; for many false prophets have gone out into the world. 2By this you know the Spirit of God: every spirit that confesses that Jesus Christ has come in the flesh is from God, 3and every spirit that does not confess Jesus[q] is not from God. And this is the spirit of the antichrist, of which you have heard that it is coming; and now it is already in the world. 4Little children, you are from God, and have conquered them; for the one who is in you is greater than the one who is in the world. 5They are from the world; therefore what they say is from the world, and the world listens to them. 6We are from God. Whoever knows God listens to us, and whoever is not from God does not listen to us. From this we know the spirit of truth and the spirit of error.

God Is Love

7 Beloved, let us love one another, because love is from God; everyone who loves is born of God and knows God. 8Whoever does not love does not know God, for God is love. 9God's love was revealed among us in this way: God sent his only Son into the world so that we might live through him. 10In this is love, not that we loved God but that he loved us and sent his Son to be the atoning sacrifice for our sins. 11Beloved, since God loved us so much, we also ought to love one another. 12No one has ever seen God; if we love one another, God lives in us, and his love is perfected in us.

13 By this we know that we abide in him and he in us, because he has given us of

[l] Or *it* [m] Or *because the children of God abide in him* [n] Gk *his brother* [o] Gk *brothers* [p] Gk *brother* [q] Other ancient authorities read *does away with Jesus* (Gk *dissolves Jesus*)

3.11-24 True Love in Action. Love of the other members of the community is basic, and stands in contrast to *Cain's* murder of his brother and to the hatred that the contemporary world pours out on the community of faith. Love is exemplified by Jesus in his having laid down his life for his new people (*us*), and should become the way of life of the members, manifesting itself in fidelity to the *truth* and in direct *action.* Reassurance comes in the midst of guilt and doubt if the commandments are obeyed and there is trust in the power and authority (*name*) of Jesus Christ.
4.1-6 For the present the *spirit of error* is active in the world, since false teachers (*prophets*) are denying that Jesus was a real human being (*come in the flesh*), and thus are moved by *the spirit of the antichrist.* The community must accept that *the world* will not listen to them, but those who belong to *God* will listen to him through his people.
4.7-5.5 The Ground of Confidence for the Community.
4.7-12 The very nature of God is *love,* as is primarily evident in his having *sent his Son* as a sacrifice for the sins of his people. The only fitting response is for them to love one another.
4.13-16 This commitment is confirmed by the presence of God's *Spirit,* through whom his abiding presence is experienced by those who *confess* Jesus as God's Son.

4.17-21 The enduring reality of love among God's people enables them to be confident in *the day of judgment*, since the love they manifest is the response to God's demonstrated love for them.
5.1-12 Love Confirmed by Faith. The mutual support of love and obedience to God's commandment is further reinforced by the confidence (*faith*) which this experience produces. The content of that faith – that *Jesus is the Son of God* – is confirmed by three additional factors: the *Spirit* at work within the community; the *water* of baptism by which public testimony to their commitment to Christ was given; and the *blood*, which may refer to the death of Jesus on the cross, or the eucharist by which that death is celebrated, or both of these factors. The ultimate guarantor of faith is God, who has made all this possible, and thereby divided humanity into two groups: those who trust God's work and are given *life* in its fulness, and those who reject that word of divine *testimony*.
5.13-21 Epilogue.
The assurance of *eternal life* produces *boldness* in making requests to God, especially in interceding with God in behalf of an erring member of the community. Yet some sins are *mortal* (for which the penalty is death) and hence are beyond the possibility of forgiveness and restoration through the prayers of others. The lives of God's people are not to be characterized by *sin*, but are protected from the power of Satan (*the evil one*). Through the coming of *the Son of God*, the truth of God is now known and embodied in him. A final warning is to avoid the worship of any worldly objects (*idols*).

his Spirit. 14 And we have seen and do testify
that the Father has sent his Son as the
Savior of the world. 15 God abides in those
who confess that Jesus is the Son of God,
and they abide in God. 16 So we have known
and believe the love that God has for us.
God is love, and those who abide in love
abide in God, and God abides in them.
17 Love has been perfected among us in this:
that we may have boldness on the day of
judgment, because as he is, so are we in this
world. 18 There is no fear in love, but perfect
love casts out fear; for fear has to do with
punishment, and whoever fears has not
reached perfection in love. 19 We love[r] because he first loved us. 20 Those who say, "I
love God," and hate their brothers or sisters,[s]
are liars; for those who do not love a brother
or sister[t] whom they have seen, cannot love
God whom they have not seen. 21 The commandment we have from him is this: those
who love God must love their brothers and
sisters[s] also.

Faith Conquers the World

5 Everyone who believes that Jesus is
the Christ[u] has been born of God, and
everyone who loves the parent loves the
child. 2 By this we know that we love the
children of God, when we love God and
obey his commandments. 3 For the love of
God is this, that we obey his commandments. And his commandments are not
burdensome, 4 for whatever is born of God
conquers the world. And this is the victory
that conquers the world, our faith. 5 Who is
it that conquers the world but the one who
believes that Jesus is the Son of God?

Testimony concerning the Son of God

6 This is the one who came by water and
blood, Jesus Christ, not with the water only
but with the water and the blood. And the
Spirit is the one that testifies, for the Spirit
is the truth. 7 There are three that testify:[v]
8 the Spirit and the water and the blood, and
these three agree. 9 If we receive human
testimony, the testimony of God is greater;
for this is the testimony of God that he has
testified to his Son. 10 Those who believe in
the Son of God have the testimony in their
hearts. Those who do not believe in God[w]
have made him a liar by not believing in
the testimony that God has given concerning his Son. 11 And this is the testimony: God
gave us eternal life, and this life is in his
Son. 12 Whoever has the Son has life; whoever does not have the Son of God does not
have life.

Epilogue

13 I write these things to you who believe in the name of the Son of God, so that
you may know that you have eternal life.
14 And this is the boldness we have in
him, that if we ask anything according to
his will, he hears us. 15 And if we know that
he hears us in whatever we ask, we know
that we have obtained the requests made of
him. 16 If you see your brother or sister[x]
committing what is not a mortal sin, you
will ask, and God[y] will give life to such a
one—to those whose sin is not mortal.
There is sin that is mortal; I do not say that
you should pray about that. 17 All wrongdoing is sin, but there is sin that is not mortal.
18 We know that those who are born of
God do not sin, but the one who was born
of God protects them, and the evil one does
not touch them. 19 We know that we are
God's children, and that the whole world
lies under the power of the evil one. 20 And
we know that the Son of God has come and
has given us understanding so that we may
know him who is true;[z] and we are in him
who is true, in his Son Jesus Christ. He is
the true God and eternal life.
21 Little children, keep yourselves from
idols.[a]

4.15 Rom 10.9
4.17 1 Jn 2.28
4.20 1 Jn 2.4; 1.6; 3.17
5.1 Jn 1.12; 1 Jn 2.22,23; Jn 1.13; 8.42
5.3 Jn 14.15; 1 Jn 2.5; 2 Jn 6
5.4 Jn 16.33
5.5 1 Jn 4.15
5.6 Jn 19.34
5.7 Jn 15.26
5.9 Jn 8.17,18; Mt 3.16,17
5.10 Rom 8.16; Gal 4.6; Jn 3.33
5.12 Jn 3.36
5.13 Jn 20.31; 1 Jn 1.1,2
5.16 Jas 5.15; Heb 6.4,6
5.18 1 Jn 3.9; Jn 14.30
5.19 1 Jn 4.6; Gal 1.4
5.20 Lk 24.45; Jn 17.3; Rev 3.7

[r] Other ancient authorities add *him*; others add *God* [s] Gk *brothers* [t] Gk *brother* [u] Or *the Messiah* [v] A few other authorities read (with variations) *7There are three that testify in heaven, the Father, the Word, and the Holy Spirit, and these three are one. 8And there are three that testify on earth:* [w] Other ancient authorities read *in the Son* [x] Gk *your brother* [y] Gk *he* [z] Other ancient authorities read *know the true God* [a] Other ancient authorities add *Amen*

THE SECOND LETTER OF

JOHN

See the Introductions, pp. 9–10 and 98 above.

1 3 Jn 3.18; Jn 8.32
3 1 Tim 1.2
5 1 Jn 2.7; 3.11
6 1 Jn 2.5; 2.24
7 1 Jn 4.1-3; 2.22
8 Mk 13.9; 1 Cor 3.8; Heb 10.32
9 1 Jn 2.23
10 Rom 16.17
11 1 Tim 5.22
12 3 Jn 13.14; 1 Jn 1.4

Salutation

1 The elder to the elect lady and her
children, whom I love in the truth, and not
only I but also all who know the truth,
2because of the truth that abides in us and
will be with us forever:
3 Grace, mercy, and peace will be with
us from God the Father and from[a] Jesus
Christ, the Father's Son, in truth and love.

Truth and Love

4 I was overjoyed to find some of your
children walking in the truth, just as we
have been commanded by the Father. 5But
now, dear lady, I ask you, not as though
I were writing you a new commandment,
but one we have had from the beginning,
let us love one another. 6And this is love,
that we walk according to his commandments; this is the commandment just as you
have heard it from the beginning—you must
walk in it.
7 Many deceivers have gone out into the
world, those who do not confess that Jesus
Christ has come in the flesh; any such
person is the deceiver and the antichrist!
8Be on your guard, so that you do not lose
what we[b] have worked for, but may receive
a full reward. 9Everyone who does not abide
in the teaching of Christ, but goes beyond
it, does not have God; whoever abides in the
teaching has both the Father and the Son.
10Do not receive into the house or welcome
anyone who comes to you and does not
bring this teaching; 11for to welcome is to
participate in the evil deeds of such a person.

Final Greetings

12 Although I have much to write to
you, I would rather not use paper and ink;
instead I hope to come to you and talk with
you face to face, so that our joy may be
complete.
13 The children of your elect sister send
you their greetings.[c]

[a] Other ancient authorities add *the Lord* [b] Other ancient authorities read *you* [c] Other ancient authorities add *Amen*

1-2 The title *elder* (*presbyteros*) is an indication of the authority role of the writer in relation to the community here addressed. *The elect lady* could be an individual, but is more likely a term for the community (the Greek word for church, *ekklesia*, is feminine). *Her children* could be her family or the members of the community. Emphasis on *the truth* is an indication that correct doctrine has become an issue for this community, although there is also concern for right behavior by the members.
3 The qualities that are to characterize the group are reflections of the nature of God and Christ.
4-11 The commandment to love is repeated here, as in 1 John, but there is the added note of living (*walking*) in accord with the *truth*. The false alternative is the denial that Jesus was truly human (*come in the flesh*), but the faithful must continue in the correct *teaching* about Christ. Those who do not share in this belief are not to be offered hospitality by any member of the community. The writer hopes to confirm his message in person.

THE THIRD LETTER OF
JOHN

See the Introductions, pp. 9–10 and 98 above.

1-4 *The elder*, as in 2 John, addresses an individual, *Gaius*, offering congratulations, since the report has reached the elder of Gaius' fidelity to *the truth*, both in what he believes and how he lives (*walks*).
5-8 Advice is offered about providing material support for certain *friends* (probably travelling preachers or teachers), since thereby Gaius' community can participate as *co-workers with the truth*.
9-12 Exercising a supervisory role, the elder denounces *Diotrephes*, who fails to submit to the authority of the elder, and is making *false charges* against the elder and expelling from the community those who want to support the elder's *friends*. On the other hand there is commendation for *Demetrius*, whose fine reputation is confirmed by *the truth* which he teaches.
13-15 A personal visit is promised, as in 2 Jn 12, and communications of *peace* are to be exchanged between the elder's associates (*friends*) and the faithful members of Gaius' community.

Salutation

1 The elder to the beloved Gaius, whom
I love in truth.

Gaius Commended for His Hospitality

2 Beloved, I pray that all may go well
with you and that you may be in good
health, just as it is well with your soul. 3I
was overjoyed when some of the friends[a]
arrived and testified to your faithfulness to
the truth, namely how you walk in the
truth. 4I have no greater joy than this, to
hear that my children are walking in the
truth.
5 Beloved, you do faithfully whatever you
do for the friends,[a] even though they are
strangers to you; 6they have testified to
your love before the church. You will do
well to send them on in a manner worthy
of God; 7for they began their journey for the
sake of Christ,[b] accepting no support from
non-believers.[c] 8Therefore we ought to support such people, so that we may become
co-workers with the truth.

Diotrephes and Demetrius

9 I have written something to the church;
but Diotrephes, who likes to put himself
first, does not acknowledge our authority.
10So if I come, I will call attention to what
he is doing in spreading false charges against
us. And not content with those charges, he
refuses to welcome the friends,[a] and even
prevents those who want to do so and
expels them from the church.
11 Beloved, do not imitate what is evil
but imitate what is good. Whoever does
good is from God; whoever does evil has not
seen God. 12Everyone has testified favorably
about Demetrius, and so has the truth itself.
We also testify for him,[d] and you know that
our testimony is true.

Final Greetings

13 I have much to write to you, but I
would rather not write with pen and ink;
14instead I hope to see you soon, and we
will talk together face to face.
15 Peace to you. The friends send you
their greetings. Greet the friends there, each
by name.

[a] Gk *brothers* [b] Gk *for the sake of the name* [c] Gk *the Gentiles* [d] Gk lacks *for him*

3 2 Jn 4; ver 5,10
4 1 Cor 4.15; Philem 10
5 Rom 12.13; Heb 13.2
6 Acts 15.3; Titus 3.13
7 Acts 5.41; 20.33,35
10 2 Jn 12; ver 5; Jn 9.34
11 Ps 37.27; 1 Jn 2.2.9; 3.6,9
12 1 Tim 3.7; Jn 21.24
13 2 Jn 12
15 1 Pet 5.14

THE LETTER OF

JUDE

Salutation

1 Jude,[a] a servant[b] of Jesus Christ and brother of James,

To those who are called, who are beloved[c] in[d] God the Father and kept safe for[d] Jesus Christ:

2 May mercy, peace, and love be yours in abundance.

Occasion of the Letter

3 Beloved, while eagerly preparing to write to you about the salvation we share, I find it necessary to write and appeal to you to contend for the faith that was once for all entrusted to the saints. 4 For certain intruders have stolen in among you, people who long ago were designated for this condemnation as ungodly, who pervert the grace of our God into licentiousness and deny our only Master and Lord, Jesus Christ.[e]

Judgment on False Teachers

5 Now I desire to remind you, though you are fully informed, that the Lord, who once for all saved[f] a people out of the land of Egypt, afterward destroyed those who did not believe. 6 And the angels who did not keep their own position, but left their proper dwelling, he has kept in eternal chains in deepest darkness for the judgment of the great Day. 7 Likewise, Sodom and Gomorrah and the surrounding cities, which, in the same manner as they, indulged in sexual immorality and pursued unnatural lust,[g] serve as an example by undergoing a punishment of eternal fire.

8 Yet in the same way these dreamers also defile the flesh, reject authority, and slander the glorious ones.[h] 9 But when the archangel Michael contended with the devil and disputed about the body of Moses, he did not dare to bring a condemnation of slander[i] against him, but said, "The Lord rebuke you!" 10 But these people slander whatever they do not understand, and they are destroyed by those things that, like irrational animals, they know by instinct. 11 Woe to them! For they go the way of Cain, and abandon themselves to Balaam's error for the sake of gain, and perish in Korah's rebellion. 12 These are blemishes[j] on your love-feasts, while they feast with you without fear, feeding themselves.[k] They are waterless clouds carried along by the winds; autumn trees without fruit, twice dead, uprooted; 13 wild waves of the sea, casting up the foam of their own shame; wandering stars, for whom the deepest darkness has been reserved forever.

14 It was also about these that Enoch, in the seventh generation from Adam, prophesied, saying, "See, the Lord is coming[l] with ten thousands of his holy ones, 15 to execute judgment on all, and to convict everyone of all the deeds of ungodliness that they have committed in such an ungodly way, and of all the harsh things that ungodly sinners have spoken against him." 16 These are grumblers and malcontents; they indulge their own lusts; they are bombastic in speech, flattering people to their own advantage.

Warnings and Exhortations

17 But you, beloved, must remember the predictions of the apostles of our Lord Jesus Christ; 18 for they said to you, "In the last time there will be scoffers, indulging their own ungodly lusts." 19 It is these worldly people, devoid of the Spirit, who are causing divisions. 20 But you, beloved, build yourselves up on your most holy faith; pray in the Holy Spirit; 21 keep yourselves in the love of God; look forward to the mercy of our Lord Jesus Christ that leads to[m] eternal life. 22 And have mercy on some who are wavering; 23 save others by snatching them out of the fire; and have mercy on still others with fear, hating even the tunic defiled by their bodies.[n]

Benediction

24 Now to him who is able to keep you from falling, and to make you stand without blemish in the presence of his glory with rejoicing, 25 to the only God our Savior, through Jesus Christ our Lord, be glory, majesty, power, and authority, before all time now and forever. Amen

[a] Gk *Judas* [b] Gk *slave* [c] Other ancient authorities read *sanctified* [d] Or *by* [e] Or *the only Master and our Lord Jesus Christ* [f] Other ancient authorities read *though you were once for all fully informed, that Jesus* (or *Joshua*) *who saved* [g] Gk *went after other flesh* [h] Or *angels*; Gk *glories* [i] Or *condemnation for blasphemy* [j] Or *reefs* [k] Or *without fear. They are shepherds who care only for themselves* [l] Gk *came* [m] Gk *Christ to* [n] Gk *by the flesh.* The Greek text of verses 22–23 is uncertain at several points

1 Acts 1.13; 1 Pet 1.5
3 Titus 1.4; 1 Tim 6.12
4 Gal 2.4; 2 Pet 2.1; Rom 9.22; 2 Pet 2.1
5 Num 14.29; Ps 106.26
6 Jn 8.44; 2 Pet 2.4; Rev 20.10
7 2 Pet 2.6; Gen 19.24
8 2 Pet 2.10
9 Dan 10.13; Zech 3.2
11 Gen 4.3-8; 1 Jn 3.12; Num 22.7; 2 Pet 2.15; Num 16.1-3,31-35
12 2 Pet 2.13; 1 Cor 11.20ff; Eph 4.14; Mt 15.13
13 Isa 57.20; Phil 3.19; 2 Pet 2.17
14 Gen 5.18; Deut 33.2; Dan 7.10
16 2 Pet 2.18
18 1 Tim 4.1; 2 Pet 2.1
20 Col 2.7; Eph 6.18
21 Titus 2.13; 2 Pet 3.12
23 Am 4.11; Zech 3.2-5
24 Rom 16.25; Eph 3.20; Col 1.22
25 1 Tim 1.17; Rom 11.36

See the Introductions, pp. 9–10 and 98–99 above.

1-2 The typical introduction to the Hellenistic letter with the normal Christian modifications; see note on Rom 1.1.
1 *Jude.* For information on authorship see introductory notes. *Those who are called.* A designation for Christians in general, used mostly by Paul; *cf.* Rom 1.6-7; 8.28; 1 Cor 1.2,24; Gal 1.15; Rev 17.14.
3-17 This section indicates the purpose of this letter.
3 *Contend.* This indicates a situation of confrontation. *The faith.* The term as used here clearly indicates a body of doctrine and practice meant for all Christians to hold.
4 *Intruders.* The false teachers have not simply come from within, but have come from outside the church; *cf.* 2 Cor 11.4. *Long ago were designated.* In keeping with vv. 14 and 18 (see notes there), the notion here is that the last days of the world will be featured by the emergence of false teachers who sway people from the truth. *Pervert the grace of God into licentiousness.* Paul also knew of those who, freed from Law, would advocate uncontrolled immorality; *cf.* Rom 3.8; 6.1,15; 1 Cor 6.12-20; Gal 5.13. *Who deny our only Master and Lord, Jesus Christ. Cf.* 1 Jn 2.22-23; 3.1-10; 2 Jn 7.
5 The purpose of this verse is to state that membership in the people of God does not ensure salvation. The argument here is similar to that of Paul in 1 Cor 10.5; the incident referred to is reported in Num 14.1-45; 26.64-65. *Cf.* also Deut 1.32; 9.23; Ps 95.7-9; 106.24; Heb 3.19; 4.6,11.
6 *Angels who did not keep their own position.* Probably a reference to Gen 6.1-4. Many commentators believe that the latter half of Jude 6 represents ideas derived from the Jewish pseudepigraphal writing 1 Enoch (10.12-13; 22.11); see note on Jude 14-16.
7 *Sodom and Gomorrah.* See Gen 19. In later Jewish literature these two cities represent total moral depravity. *Surrounding cities. Cf.* Gen 19.22; Deut 29.23; Hos 11.8. *Punishment of eternal fire. Cf.* Mt 5.22; 13.42,50; 18.8; 25.41; Rev 20.14-15.
8 *These dreamers.* I.e. the false teachers in the church.
9 This verse rests on traditional Jewish literary presentations of Satanic struggles against the people of God, with Moses as a special target. Jude envisions one last attempt of Satan to gain power over Moses. *The archangel Michael. Cf.* Dan 10.13,21; 12.1; Rev 12.7. *"The Lord rebuke you!" Cf.* Zech 3.2.
11 *Cain.* The first murderer (see Gen 4.1-16). *Balaam.* A Canaanite prophet mentioned in Num 22-24, remembered in postbiblical Jewish literature as the one who enticed Israel into apostasy (Num 25.1-3); *cf.* Rev 2.14. *Korah.* According to Num 16.11; 16.9, *Korah* led a rebellion against God.
12 *Love-feasts.* These were the community meals eaten in connection with early Christian Eucharistic observances; *cf.* 1 Cor 11.17-32.
13 *Wandering stars...reserved forever.* This entire phrase reflects language from 1 Enoch 18.13-16, 21.1-6; 90.24 (see note on Jude 6). *Cf.* also 2 Pet 2.17.
14-16 The author formally quotes from 1 Enoch, applying the words of the prophecy to the false teachers. 1 Enoch is a Jewish pseudepigraphal writing containing a collection of visionary and revelatory writings composed in the first two centuries BCE.
14 *The seventh generation from Adam. Cf.* Gen 5.3-19.
14-15 The quotation is from 1 Enoch 1.9.
16 *Grumblers and malcontents.* Probably a reference to those who complained against God in the wilderness; *cf.* Ex 15.24; 17.3; Num 14.29. These designations are transferred to the false teachers Jude envisions.
17-23 In this section Jude turns from the predictions of Enoch to the predictions of the apostles.
17 *The apostles.* This term is used here of the apostles as a group in the past to which the author looks back.
18 The quotation has no direct source, but rather comprises a commonly accepted general teaching that the last days would be featured by the appearance of false prophets; *cf.* Mt 7.15; 24.11,24; Mk 13.22; Acts 20.29-30; 1 Tim 4.1-3; 2 Tim 3.1-9; 4.3-4; 1 Jn 2.8; 4.1-3.
19 *cf.* Rom 16.17; 1 Cor 2.14; 15.44; Jas 3.15.
20 *cf.* Eph 2.19-21.
23 *cf.* Zech 3.2.
24-25 The conclusion is a doxology. *Cf.* Rom 9.5; 16.25-27; Eph 3.20; 1 Tim 1.17; 6.15-16; 1 Pet 4.11.

THE REVELATION TO JOHN

Introduction and Salutation

1 The revelation of Jesus Christ, which God gave him to show his servants[a] what must soon take place; he made[b] it known by sending his angel to his servant[c] John, [2]who testified to the word of God and to the testimony of Jesus Christ, even to all that he saw.

3 Blessed is the one who reads aloud the words of the prophecy, and blessed are those who hear and who keep what is written in it; for the time is near.

4 John to the seven churches that are in Asia:

Grace to you and peace from him who is and who was and who is to come, and from the seven spirits who are before his throne, [5]and from Jesus Christ, the faithful witness, the firstborn of the dead, and the ruler of the kings of the earth.

To him who loves us and freed[d] us from our sins by his blood, [6]and made[b] us to be a kingdom, priests serving[e] his God and Father, to him be glory and dominion forever and ever. Amen.

7 Look! He is coming with the clouds;
every eye will see him,
even those who pierced him;
and on his account all the tribes of the earth will wail.

So it is to be. Amen.

8 "I am the Alpha and the Omega," says the Lord God, who is and who was and who is to come, the Almighty.

A Vision of Christ

9 I, John, your brother who share with you in Jesus the persecution and the kingdom and the patient endurance, was on the island called Patmos because of the word of God and the testimony of Jesus.[f] [10]I was in the spirit[g] on the Lord's day, and I heard behind me a loud voice like a trumpet [11]saying, "Write in a book what you see and send it to the seven churches, to Ephesus, to Smyrna, to Pergamum, to Thyatira, to Sardis, to Philadelphia, and to Laodicea."

12 Then I turned to see whose voice it was that spoke to me, and on turning I saw seven golden lampstands, [13]and in the midst of the lampstands I saw one like the Son of Man, clothed with a long robe and with a golden sash across his chest. [14]His head and his hair were white as white wool, white as snow; his eyes were like a flame of fire, [15]his feet were like burnished bronze, refined as in a furnace, and his voice was like the sound of many waters. [16]In his right hand he held seven stars, and from his mouth came a sharp, two-edged sword, and his face was like the sun shining with full force.

17 When I saw him, I fell at his feet as though dead. But he placed his right hand on me, saying, "Do not be afraid; I am the first and the last, [18]and the living one. I was dead, and see, I am alive forever and ever; and I have the keys of Death and of Hades. [19]Now write what you have seen, what is, and what is to take place after this. [20]As for the mystery of the seven stars that you saw in my right hand, and the seven golden lampstands: the seven stars are the angels of the seven churches, and the seven lampstands are the seven churches.

The Message to Ephesus

2 "To the angel of the church in Ephesus write: These are the words of him who holds the seven stars in his right hand, who walks among the seven golden lampstands:

2 "I know your works, your toil and your patient endurance. I know that you cannot tolerate evildoers; you have tested those who claim to be apostles but are not, and have found them to be false. [3]I also know that you are enduring patiently and bearing up for the sake of my name, and that you have not grown weary. [4]But I

[a] Gk *slaves* [b] Gk *and he made* [c] Gk *slave* [d] Other ancient authorities read *washed* [e] Gk *priests to* [f] Or *testimony to Jesus* [g] Or *in the Spirit*

See the Introductions, pp. 10 and 99–100 above.

1.1-8 The Prologue. This section contains an introduction (1.1-2), a beatitude (1.3), a salutation (1.4-5c), a doxology (5d-6), a promise (1.7), and a theme (1.8). *Cf.* the Epilogue to Rev (22.6-21).
1.1 *Revelation.* This is the heading to the entire writing, naming it as a *"revelation,"* the same word Paul used of a spoken presentation given in the worship assembly (*cf.* 1 Cor 14.6,26). It is used interchangeably with the word "prophecy" (1.3), the New Testament word for "preaching"; it is to be read in the worship services (1.3), and in the writer's absence (1.9) is to function as a sermon. *John.* Church tradition has identified this writer as Jesus' disciple John, son of Zebedee; however, nowhere does this author identify himself as an apostle, even though he mentions the "Twelve" (21.14). He identifies himself to his readers as their "brother" exiled on the island of Patmos (1.9). The message he has to give them is sent from God (1.11).
1.2 *Word of God and the testimony of Jesus.* These terms are used frequently together as interchangeable descriptions of Christian preaching; *cf.* 1.9.
1.3 *Blessed.* This is the first of seven beatitudes in this book; *cf.* 14.13; 16.15; 19.9; 20.6; 22.7,14. This beatitude pronounces a blessing on those who read this book in church and upon those who listen to it and obey its contents; *cf.* Lk 11.28. Reading scripture in worship assemblies is a practice the church inherited from Judaism; *cf.* Neh 8.2; Lk 4.16; Acts 13.15; Col 4.16; 1 Thess 5.27.
1.4 *John.* See note on 1.9. *To the seven churches.* This epistolary introduction gives this book the form of a letter, a means of communication between people who are geographically separated from each other (see 1.9,11). *Grace and peace...* The salutation used in all the Pauline letters, by now a traditional greeting used among Christians (*cf.* 1 & 2 Pet 1.2). *Seven spirits. Cf.* 3.1; 4.5. *Who is and who was and who is to come.* I.e. God; *cf.* 1.8; 4.8; Ex 3.14-15.
1.5 *The faithful witness. Cf.* 1 Tim 6.13. *The firstborn from the dead. Cf.* 1 Cor 15.20; Col 1.15. *Ruler of the kings of the earth. Cf.* 11.15; 19.16. *Freed us from our sins by his own blood. Cf.* 6.9; 7.14; 12.11; 17.14; 19.13; Rom 5.10,16; 1 Jn 1.7.
1.6 *Kingdom, priests. Cf.* 6.10; Ex 19.5-6; Isa 61.6. *Amen.* Literally, "it is true"; throughout the Old Testament and in Judaism, *"amen"* acknowledges that which is valid and binding.
1.7 *cf.* Dan 7.13; Zech 12.10; also Ex 13.21; 16.10; Acts 1.9.
1.8 Throughout Rev, only here and in 21.5-8 is God the speaker. *Alpha and Omega.* The first and last letters in the Greek alphabet – a comprehensive term encompassing all others in between: God is sovereign over all that takes place in human history.
1.9-20 This section comprises the call of the prophet to write and send to his churches the message he receives from the risen Christ.
1.9 *I, John.* See notes on 1.1 and 1.4. Traditionally thought to have been Jesus' disciple John, the son of Zebedee, the author nowhere identifies himself as an apostle and does not seem to include himself in the apostolic circle (see 21.14). He understands himself to be someone with the authority to preach in the church (19.10; 22.9), and the lack of further identification would indicate that he is well known to his readers. *Your brother.* I.e. fellow-Christian. *Share with you in Jesus the persecution.* The author has experienced the hostility and oppression faced by his readers. *Patmos.* The author's place of exile is a small island in the Aegean Sea about forty miles southwest of Miletus, a city on the western coast of Asia Minor. *Word of God and the testimony of Jesus.* See note on 1.2.
1.10 *In the spirit.* Most likely this means that John was at worship, in a place of worship; see footnote *g*. *On the Lord's day.* I.e. Sunday.
1.11 *Send it to the seven churches.* Geographically these churches lie in a semi-circle around Ephesus, which might indicate the author's territorial responsibility; it is also the area of the Pauline mission. In biblical writings the number seven is a symbol for completeness, which also may be used by the author to address all Christians. At least, each of the seven churches is to listen to what is said to all of them.
1.12 *Lampstands* stood in Israel's temple; *cf.* Ex 25.31-40; 1 Kings 7.49; Zech 4.1-6.
1.13 *In the midst of the lampstands.* The image is that of Christ among the churches (see 1.20). *Son of Man. Cf.* Dan 7.9,13; Ezek 1.7; and note on Mt 8.20. *Long robe and...golden sash.* The attire of the high priest (*cf.* Ex 28.4; 29.5; 39.29).
1.14 *White wool. Cf.* Dan 7.9; Isa 1.18. *Flame of fire. Cf.* 2.18; 19.12.
1.15 *Many waters. Cf.* 14.2; 19.6; Ezek 43.2.

1.1 Jn 12.49; Rev 22.16
1.2 1 Cor 1.6; Rev 12.17
1.4 Jn 1.1; Rev 3.1; 4.5
1.6 1 Pet 2.5; Rev 5.10; Rom 11.36
1.7 Zech 12.10; Lk 23.28
1.8 Rev 21.6; 4.8; 16.7
1.9 Phil 4.14; 2 Tim 2.12
1.10 Rev 4.1,2
1.12 Ex 25.27; Zech 4.2
1.13 Ezek 1.26; Dan 7.13; 10.5
1.14 Dan 7.9; 10.6; Rev 19.12
1.15 Dan 10.6; Ezek 43.2
1.16 Rev 2.1; 3.1; Heb 4.12; Rev 2.12,16
1.17 Ezek 1.28; Dan 8.18; 10.10; Isa 41.4
1.18 Rom 6.9; Rev 4.9; 20.1
1.20 Zech 4.2
2.2 Rev 3.1,8; 1 Jn 4.1; 2 Cor 11.13
2.3 Jn 15.21

have this against you, that you have abandoned the love you had at first. [5]Remember
then from what you have fallen; repent,
and do the works you did at first. If not, I
will come to you and remove your lampstand
from its place, unless you repent. [6]Yet this
is to your credit: you hate the works of the
Nicolaitans, which I also hate. [7]Let anyone
who has an ear listen to what the Spirit is
saying to the churches. To everyone who
conquers, I will give permission to eat from
the tree of life that is in the paradise of God.

The Message to Smyrna

8 "And to the angel of the church in
Smyrna write: These are the words of the
first and the last, who was dead and came
to life:
9 "I know your affliction and your poverty, even though you are rich. I know the
slander on the part of those who say that
they are Jews and are not, but are a synagogue of Satan. [10]Do not fear what you are
about to suffer. Beware, the devil is about
to throw some of you into prison so that
you may be tested, and for ten days you will
have affliction. Be faithful until death, and
I will give you the crown of life. [11]Let
anyone who has an ear listen to what the
Spirit is saying to the churches. Whoever
conquers will not be harmed by the second
death.

The Message to Pergamum

12 "And to the angel of the church in
Pergamum write: These are the words of
him who has the sharp two-edged sword:
13 "I know where you are living, where
Satan's throne is. Yet you are holding fast
to my name, and you did not deny your
faith in me[h] even in the days of Antipas my
witness, my faithful one, who was killed
among you, where Satan lives. [14]But I have
a few things against you: you have some
there who hold to the teaching of Balaam,
who taught Balak to put a stumbling block
before the people of Israel, so that they
would eat food sacrificed to idols and practice fornication. [15]So you also have some
who hold to the teaching of the Nicolaitans.
[16]Repent then. If not, I will come to you
soon and make war against them with the
sword of my mouth. [17]Let anyone who has
an ear listen to what the Spirit is saying to
the churches. To everyone who conquers I
will give some of the hidden manna, and I
will give a white stone, and on the white
stone is written a new name that no one
knows except the one who receives it.

The Message to Thyatira

18 "And to the angel of the church in
Thyatira write: These are the words of the
Son of God, who has eyes like a flame of
fire, and whose feet are like burnished bronze:
19 "I know your works—your love, faith,
service, and patient endurance. I know that
your last works are greater than the first.
[20]But I have this against you: you tolerate
that woman Jezebel, who calls herself a
prophet and is teaching and beguiling my
servants[i] to practice fornication and to eat
food sacrificed to idols. [21]I gave her time to
repent, but she refuses to repent of her
fornication. [22]Beware, I am throwing her on
a bed, and those who commit adultery with
her I am throwing into great distress, unless
they repent of her doings; [23]and I will strike
her children dead. And all the churches will
know that I am the one who searches
minds and hearts, and I will give to each
of you as your works deserve. [24]But to the
rest of you in Thyatira, who do not hold
this teaching, who have not learned what
some call 'the deep things of Satan,' to you
I say, I do not lay on you any other burden;
[25]only hold fast to what you have until I
come. [26]To everyone who conquers and
continues to do my works to the end,
I will give authority over the nations;
[27] to rule[j] them with an iron rod,
as when clay pots are shattered—
[28]even as I also received authority from my
Father. To the one who conquers I will also
give the morning star. [29]Let anyone who
has an ear listen to what the Spirit is saying
to the churches.

The Message to Sardis

3 "And to the angel of the church in
Sardis write: These are the words of
him who has the seven spirits of God and
the seven stars:
"I know your works; you have a name
of being alive, but you are dead. [2]Wake up,
and strengthen what remains and is on the
point of death, for I have not found your
works perfect in the sight of my God. [3]Re-

[h] Or *deny my faith* [i] Gk *slaves* [j] Or *to shepherd*

2.7 Mt 11.15; Rev 3.6,13; 22.2,14; Gen 2.9
2.8 Rev 1.11,17,18
2.9 Rev 1.9; Jas 2.5; Rev 3.9
2.10 Rev 3.10; Dan 1.12
2.11 Rev 20.14; 21.8
2.12 Rev 1.11,16
2.14 Num 24.14; 2 Pet 2.15; Jude 11; 1 Cor 8.9; 10.19,20; 6.13
2.16 2 Thess 2.8; Rev 1.16
2.17 Jn 6.49,50; Isa 62.2; Rev 19.12
2.18 Rev 1.11; 14.15
2.20 1 Kings 16.31; 21.25; 2 Kings 9.7; Acts 15.20
2.21 Rom 2.4; Rev 9.20
2.23 Jer 11.20; Acts 1.24; Rom 8.27; Ps 62.12
2.24 Acts 15.28
2.26 Heb 3.6; Ps 2.8; Rev 3.21
2.27 Rev 12.5; Isa 30.14; Jer 19.11
2.28 Rev 22.16
3.1 Rev 1.4,16; 2.2; 1 Tim 5.6
3.3 1 Thess 5.2,6; 2 Pet 3.10

1.16 *Seven stars.* See 1.20. *Two-edged sword. Cf.* 2.12,16; 6.8; 19.15,21; this identifies the one in John's vision as Christ. *His face was like the sun shining in full force. Cf.* Mt 17.2.
1.17 *Fell at his feet. Cf.* Josh 5.14; Isa 6.5; Ezek 1.28; Dan 8.17; Mt 17.6; Acts 26.14. *First and the last.* See note on 1.8.
1.18 *Hades.* Always joined with death in Rev (see 6.8; 20.13-14). "Hades" is the Greek equivalent of the Hebrew Sheol, the place of departed spirits. According to Jewish tradition only God has power over death and Hades, and here that power resides now with the crucified and risen Christ.
2.1-3.22 This section contains the letters to the seven churches (see introductory notes).
2.1 *To the angel.* The formula which opens each of the letters to the seven churches (*cf.* 2.8,12,18; 3.1,7,14). Perhaps based on the ancient idea that God has given responsibility to his angels for the administration of the nations (*cf.* Deut 32.8; Dan 10.20-21; 12.1), the term here functions as a reference to the leader of each congregation, who may be the one who would read it aloud in the worship services (see Rev 1.3). *Ephesus.* The most important city of Asia at the time, it was situated on a gulf of the Aegean Sea, and was an important center for the mission work of Paul (see 1 Cor 16.8). *These are the words...* A part of the formula opening each letter, identifying the speaker as Christ, using a piece of the description of the risen Christ in 1.12-16; *cf.* 2.8,12,18; 3.1,7,14. *Seven stars...golden lampstands. Cf.* 1.13,16.
2.2 Ephesus is an active, zealous church.
2.3 An allusion to the persecution mentioned in 1.9.
2.4 In its zeal to purge itself of false teachers, it has succumbed to lovelessness (*cf.* 2.2).

2.5 *Remove your lampstand from its place.* I.e. the church at Ephesus will not be allowed by its Lord to continue if it cannot be a loving church.
2.6 *Hate the works.* I.e. hate deeds, not people. *The Nicolaitans.* See note on 2.15.
2.7 The same formula concludes each of the letters to the seven churches (see 2.11,17,29; 3.6,13,22). It means that Rev is to be read in the worship assemblies (see 1.3) and is to be received as the Word of God. *Tree of life. Cf.* Gen 2.9; 3.22-24.
2.8 *To the angel...* See note on 2.1. *Smyrna.* Modern Izmir, thirty-five miles north of Ephesus on the west coast of the Aegean Sea. *First and last...came to life. Cf.* 1.17-18.
2.9 *Poverty.* The church in Smyrna is under economic stress. *Who say they are Jews...* This may indicate that the Christians of Smyrna were originally Jews who were excommunicated from the synagogue because of their belief in Jesus as Messiah; the issue was then over who was and who was not truly Jewish.
2.10 As late as 155 CE Polycarp, bishop of Smyrna, was martyred.
2.11 See note on 2.7. *The second death.* This could be a reference, well known in previous rabbinic teaching, to the death of the wicked in the next world; *cf.* 20.14; 21.8.
2.12 *To the angel...* See note on 2.1. *Pergamum.* Fifty miles north of Smyrna and ten miles inland from the Aegean Sea, this was a city of great wealth and splendor and an important center for emperor-worship. *Him who had the sharp two-edged sword. Cf.* 1.16.
2.13 *Satan's throne.* A probable reference to the imperial cult and to the temple built in 29 BCE in honor of Caesar Augustus. *Antipas.* One of the members of the Pergamum church who was executed for his faith in Christ, and, most probably, because he refused to participate in acts of emperor-worship.
2.14 *Balaam. Cf.* Num 25.1-3; 31.16. *Food sacrificed to idols and practice fornication.* This could mean the same act of religious idolatry, or it could be taken as two separate acts (see Num 25.1-3).
2.15 *Nicolaitans.* In this context this group, whose origin is unknown, evidently was willing to make compromises with the local imperial religion, by allowing Christians to participate in worship at the pagan shrines; *cf.* 1 Cor 8.1-13; 6.12-20.
2.16 *Sword of my mouth. Cf.* 1.16; 19.15,21.
2.17 *Hidden manna.* According to Jewish tradition, the pot of manna placed in the ark of the covenant (see Ex 16.32-34) was later hidden by the prophet Jeremiah during the siege of Solomon's temple (2 Macc 2.4-7). *White stone.* A symbol of victory.
2.18 *To the angel...* See note on 2.1. *Thyatira.* On the banks of the Lycus river, this was a prospering industrial city known especially for its flourishing trade guilds. *Cf.*

member then what you received and heard;
obey it, and repent. If you do not wake up,
I will come like a thief, and you will not
know at what hour I will come to you. [4]Yet
you have still a few persons in Sardis who
have not soiled their clothes; they will walk
with me, dressed in white, for they are
worthy. [5]If you conquer, you will be clothed
like them in white robes, and I will not blot
your name out of the book of life; I will
confess your name before my Father and
before his angels. [6]Let anyone who has an
ear listen to what the Spirit is saying to the
churches.

The Message to Philadelphia

7 "And to the angel of the church in
Philadelphia write:
These are the words of the holy one,
the true one,
who has the key of David,
who opens and no one will shut,
who shuts and no one opens:
8 "I know your works. Look, I have set
before you an open door, which no one is
able to shut. I know that you have but little
power, and yet you have kept my word and
have not denied my name. [9]I will make
those of the synagogue of Satan who say
that they are Jews and are not, but are
lying—I will make them come and bow
down before your feet, and they will learn
that I have loved you. [10]Because you have
kept my word of patient endurance, I will
keep you from the hour of trial that is
coming on the whole world to test the
inhabitants of the earth. [11]I am coming
soon; hold fast to what you have, so that
no one may seize your crown. [12]If you
conquer, I will make you a pillar in the
temple of my God; you will never go out of
it. I will write on you the name of my God,
and the name of the city of my God, the
new Jerusalem that comes down from my
God out of heaven, and my own new name.
[13]Let anyone who has an ear listen to what
the Spirit is saying to the churches.

The Message to Laodicea

14 "And to the angel of the church in
Laodicea write: The words of the Amen, the
faithful and true witness, the origin[k] of
God's creation:
15 "I know your works; you are neither
cold nor hot. I wish that you were either
cold or hot. [16]So, because you are luke-
warm, and neither cold nor hot, I am about
to spit you out of my mouth. [17]For you say,
'I am rich, I have prospered, and I need
nothing.' You do not realize that you are
wretched, pitiable, poor, blind, and naked.
[18]Therefore I counsel you to buy from me
gold refined by fire so that you may be rich;
and white robes to clothe you and to keep
the shame of your nakedness from being
seen; and salve to anoint your eyes so that
you may see. [19]I reprove and discipline
those whom I love. Be earnest, therefore,
and repent. [20]Listen! I am standing at the
door, knocking; if you hear my voice and
open the door, I will come in to you and
eat with you, and you with me. [21]To the
one who conquers I will give a place with
me on my throne, just as I myself conquered and sat down with my Father on his
throne. [22]Let anyone who has an ear listen
to what the Spirit is saying to the churches."

The Heavenly Worship

4 After this I looked, and there in heaven
a door stood open! And the first voice,
which I had heard speaking to me like a
trumpet, said, "Come up here, and I will
show you what must take place after this."
[2]At once I was in the spirit,[l] and there in
heaven stood a throne, with one seated on
the throne! [3]And the one seated there looks
like jasper and carnelian, and around the
throne is a rainbow that looks like an
emerald. [4]Around the throne are twenty-
four thrones, and seated on the thrones are
twenty-four elders, dressed in white robes,
with golden crowns on their heads. [5]Com-
ing from the throne are flashes of lightning,
and rumblings and peals of thunder, and in
front of the throne burn seven flaming
torches, which are the seven spirits of God;
[6]and in front of the throne there is something like a sea of glass, like crystal.
Around the throne, and on each side of
the throne, are four living creatures, full of
eyes in front and behind: [7]the first living
creature like a lion, the second living creature like an ox, the third living creature
with a face like a human face, and the
fourth living creature like a flying eagle.
[8]And the four living creatures, each of them
with six wings, are full of eyes all around
and inside. Day and night without ceasing

[k] Or *beginning* [l] Or *in the Spirit*

Acts 16.14-15. *Flame of fire...burnished bronze. Cf.* 1.14-15.
2.20 *Jezebel.* A local prophet who advocated compromise with the worship practices in the trade guilds. *Practice fornication and to eat food sacrificed to idols.* See note on 2.14.
2.24 *The deep things of Satan. Cf.* 1 Cor 2.10.
2.26-27 *cf.* Ps 2.8-9.
2.29 See note on 2.7.
3.1 *To the angel...* See note on 2.1. *Sardis.* Fifty miles east of Ephesus. *Seven spirits of God and the seven stars. Cf.* 1.4,16; 4.5. *Name of being alive, but you are dead.* A church with a good external reputation but with a moribund internal condition.
3.3 *Come like a thief.* As Sardis experienced the stealthy attacks at night by the Persians (546 BCE) and the Syrians (218 BCE).

3.5 *Book of life. Cf.* Ex 32.32-33; Ps 69.28; Dan 12.1; Phil 4.3. *Confess your name. Cf.* Mt 10.32; Mk 8.38 = Lk 9.26.
3.6 See note on 2.7.
3.7 *To the angel...* See note on 2.1. *Philadelphia.* Modern Aleshehir, this was a prosperous city with an economy based on agriculture, industry, and commerce. Located at the eastern end of a valley leading down to the Aegean Sea, the city was an important link on trade routes leading eastward to the provinces of Lydia and Phrygia. Founded as a conduit for the spread of Greek culture, it was known as "the gateway to the East."
3.8 *Open door.* This reflects the location of the city (see note on 3.7).
3.9 See note on 2.9.
3.12 See 21.1-2.
3.13 See note on 2.7.
3.14 *To the angel...* See note on 2.1. *Laodicea.* Modern Eski-hisar, this was a prosperous city, a banking center with a flourishing textile industry renowned for the clothing and carpeting manufactured from the soft, rich black wool produced in the region. Its medical school had produced effective medicinal compounds, including an eye-salve made from oil and "Phrygian powder." *The words of the Amen. Cf.* Isa 65.16; 1.6,7; 22.20-21. *The origin of God's creation. Cf.* Col 1.15,18.
3.16 *Neither cold nor hot.* The church at Laodicea had lost its ability to heal; it could neither invigorate nor soothe.
3.20 *Eat with you.* The particular Greek word used here alludes to the Christian eucharistic meal.
3.22 See note on 2.7.
4.1-5.14 This section relates John's vision of God's throne and the heavenly scene around it, with the praises that are sung there.
4.1 *Like a trumpet. Cf.* 1.10.
4.2 *In the spirit.* See note on 1.10 and footnote *l*.
4.3 *Jasper and carnelian. Cf.* Ezek 28.13; Ex 28.17-21. *Rainbow. Cf.* Ezek 1.26-28; *cf.* also Gen 9.16-17, where the *rainbow* indicates God's mercy toward humanity.
4.4 *Twenty-four elders* recalls the idea of the heavenly council (see Job 1-2; Ps 82), but here their function is solely to praise God. *Lightning, and ... thunder. Cf.* Ex 19.16; Ps 18.12-15.
4.5 *Seven spirits of God.* See 1.4; 3.1.
4.7 Late in the second century the equation was made between these living creatures and the four New Testament Gospels: Jn the lion, Lk the ox, Mt the human face, Mk the eagle.
4.8 *Six wings. Cf.* Isa 6.2. *Holy, holy, holy, the Lord God the Almighty. Cf.* Isa 6.3. *Who was and is and is to come.* See note on 1.4.

3.4 Acts 1.15; Jude 23; Rev 6.11; 7.9,13
3.5 Mt 10.32
3.7 Acts 3.14; 1 Jn 5.20; Isa 22.22
3.8 Acts 14.27; Rev 2.13
3.9 Rev 2.9; Isa 49.23; 43.4
3.10 2 Pet 2.9; Rev 16.14; 6.10; 17.8
3.12 Gal 2.9; Rev 22.4; 21.2
3.14 Isa 65.16
3.17 Hos 12.8; Zech 11.5; 1 Cor 4.8
3.18 Isa 55.1; Mt 13.44; Rev 7.13
3.19 Prov 3.11; Heb 12.5,6; Rev 2.5
3.20 Mt 24.33; Lk 12.36; Jn 14.23
3.21 Rev 2.7; Mt 19.28; Rev 5.5
4.1 Rev 1.10; 11.12; 1.19
4.2 Rev 1.10; Isa 6.1; Ezek 1.26-28; Dan 7.9
4.4 Rev 11.16; 3.4,5
4.5 Rev 8.5; 16.18; 1.4; Zech 4.2
4.6 Rev 15.2; Ezek 1.5
4.7 Ezek 1.10; 10.14
4.8 Isa 6.2,3; Rev 1.8; 1.4

they sing,

"Holy, holy, holy,
the Lord God the Almighty,
who was and is and is to come."

9 And whenever the living creatures give glory and honor and thanks to the one who is seated on the throne, who lives forever and ever, 10 the twenty-four elders fall before the one who is seated on the throne and worship the one who lives forever and ever; they cast their crowns before the throne, singing,

11 "You are worthy, our Lord and God,
to receive glory and honor and power,
for you created all things,
and by your will they existed and were created."

The Scroll and the Lamb

5 Then I saw in the right hand of the one seated on the throne a scroll written on the inside and on the back, sealed[m] with seven seals; 2 and I saw a mighty angel proclaiming with a loud voice, "Who is worthy to open the scroll and break its seals?" 3 And no one in heaven or on earth or under the earth was able to open the scroll or to look into it. 4 And I began to weep bitterly because no one was found worthy to open the scroll or to look into it. 5 Then one of the elders said to me, "Do not weep. See, the Lion of the tribe of Judah, the Root of David, has conquered, so that he can open the scroll and its seven seals."

6 Then I saw between the throne and the four living creatures and among the elders a Lamb standing as if it had been slaughtered, having seven horns and seven eyes, which are the seven spirits of God sent out into all the earth. 7 He went and took the scroll from the right hand of the one who was seated on the throne. 8 When he had taken the scroll, the four living creatures and the twenty-four elders fell before the Lamb, each holding a harp and golden bowls full of incense, which are the prayers of the saints. 9 They sing a new song:

"You are worthy to take the scroll
and to open its seals,
for you were slaughtered and by your blood you ransomed for God
saints from[n] every tribe and language and people and nation;
10 you have made them to be a kingdom and priests serving[o] our God,
and they will reign on earth."

11 Then I looked, and I heard the voice of many angels surrounding the throne and the living creatures and the elders; they numbered myriads of myriads and thousands of thousands, 12 singing with full voice,

"Worthy is the Lamb that was slaughtered
to receive power and wealth and wisdom and might
and honor and glory and blessing!"

13 Then I heard every creature in heaven and on earth and under the earth and in the sea, and all that is in them, singing,

"To the one seated on the throne and to the Lamb
be blessing and honor and glory and might
forever and ever!"

14 And the four living creatures said, "Amen!" And the elders fell down and worshiped.

The Seven Seals

6 Then I saw the Lamb open one of the seven seals, and I heard one of the four living creatures call out, as with a voice of thunder, "Come!"[p] 2 I looked, and there was a white horse! Its rider had a bow; a crown was given to him, and he came out conquering and to conquer.

3 When he opened the second seal, I heard the second living creature call out, "Come!"[p] 4 And out came[q] another horse, bright red; its rider was permitted to take peace from the earth, so that people would slaughter one another; and he was given a great sword.

5 When he opened the third seal, I heard the third living creature call out, "Come!"[p] I looked, and there was a black horse! Its rider held a pair of scales in his hand, 6 and I heard what seemed to be a voice in the midst of the four living creatures saying, "A quart of wheat for a day's pay,[r] and three quarts of barley for a day's pay,[r] but do not damage the olive oil and the wine!"

7 When he opened the fourth seal, I heard the voice of the fourth living creature call out, "Come!"[p] 8 I looked and there was a pale green horse! Its rider's name was Death, and Hades followed with him; they were given authority over a fourth of the

[m] Or *written on the inside, and sealed on the back* [n] Gk *ransomed for God from* [o] Gk *priests to* [p] Or *"Go!"* [q] Or *went* [r] Gk *a denarius*

4.9 Ps 47.8; Rev 10.6; 15.7
4.10 Rev 5.8,14; ver 2,9,4
4.11 Rev 5.12; Gen 1.1; Eph 3.9; Rev 10.6
5.1 ver 7,13; Ezek 2.9,10; Isa 29.11; Dan 12.4
5.5 Gen 49.9; Heb 7.14; Isa 11.1,10; Rom 15.12; Rev 22.16
5.6 Rev 4.6; Isa 53.7; Rev 13.8; Zech 3.9; 4.10; Rev 4.5
5.8 Rev 14.2; Ps 141.2
5.9 Ps 40.3; Rev 4.11; 1 Cor 6.20; Heb 9.12
5.10 Ex 19.6; Isa 61.6
5.11 Dan 7.10; Heb 12.22
5.13 Phil 2.10; ver 3; 1 Tim 6.16; Rev 1.6; 6.16; 7.10
6.1 Rev 5.5-7; 5.1; Rev 14.2; 19.6
6.2 Zech 6.3; Rev 19.11; Zech 6.11; Rev 14.14
6.4 Zech 6.2
6.5 Rev 4.7; Zech 6.2
6.8 Zech 6.3; Hos 13.14; Ezek 5.12

5.1 The symbol of the scroll in God's right hand is that all of world history is subject to the will and power of God.
5.5 *The Lion of the tribe of Judah. Cf.* Gen 49.9-10. *The Root of David. Cf.* Isa 11.1,10.
5.6 *A lamb...as if it had been slaughtered. Cf.* Isa 53.7; 1 Cor 5.7; 1 Pet 1.18-19; Acts 8.32.
5.9 The identification of this Lamb is now clear: Jesus the Crucified; *cf.* also 5.12; Jn 1.29. The title *"Lamb who was slaughtered"* is used of Jesus twenty-eight times in Rev.
5.10 *cf.* 1.5-6.
5.12 Elsewhere in the New Testament Jesus is ascribed the words of praise offered here: *power* (1 Cor 1.24), *wealth* (2 Cor 8.9; Eph 3.8), *wisdom* (1 Cor 1.24), *might* (Lk 11.22), *honor* (Phil 2.11), *glory* (Jn 1.14), *blessing* (Rom 15.29).
5.14 *Amen.* See note on 1.6.
6.1-7.17 This section depicts the opening of the scroll with the seven seals.
6.1-8 The vision of the Four Horsemen.
6.2 The first rider represents military conquest.
6.3-4 The second rider represents deadly internal conflict.
6.5-6 The third rider represents famine. The cost of the amount of wheat and barley in 6.6 would have equaled ten to twelve times normal cost. The restriction at the end of 6.6 means that famine will not have the final word.
6.7-8 The fourth rider represents death.
6.8 *Hades.* See note on 1.18. The means of destruction listed in 6.8 recall Ezek 14.21.

earth, to kill with sword, famine, and pestilence, and by the wild animals of the earth.

9 When he opened the fifth seal, I saw under the altar the souls of those who had been slaughtered for the word of God and for the testimony they had given; [10]they cried out with a loud voice, "Sovereign Lord, holy and true, how long will it be before you judge and avenge our blood on the inhabitants of the earth?" [11]They were each given a white robe and told to rest a little longer, until the number would be complete both of their fellow servants[s] and of their brothers and sisters,[t] who were soon to be killed as they themselves had been killed.

12 When he opened the sixth seal, I looked, and there came a great earthquake; the sun became black as sackcloth, the full moon became like blood, [13]and the stars of the sky fell to the earth as the fig tree drops its winter fruit when shaken by a gale. [14]The sky vanished like a scroll rolling itself up, and every mountain and island was removed from its place. [15]Then the kings of the earth and the magnates and the generals and the rich and the powerful, and everyone, slave and free, hid in the caves and among the rocks of the mountains, [16]calling to the mountains and rocks, "Fall on us and hide us from the face of the one seated on the throne and from the wrath of the Lamb; [17]for the great day of their wrath has come, and who is able to stand?"

The 144,000 of Israel Sealed

7 After this I saw four angels standing at the four corners of the earth, holding back the four winds of the earth so that no wind could blow on earth or sea or against any tree. [2]I saw another angel ascending from the rising of the sun, having the seal of the living God, and he called with a loud voice to the four angels who had been given power to damage earth and sea, [3]saying, "Do not damage the earth or the sea or the trees, until we have marked the servants[s] of our God with a seal on their foreheads."

4 And I heard the number of those who were sealed, one hundred forty-four thousand, sealed out of every tribe of the people of Israel:

5 From the tribe of Judah twelve
thousand sealed,
from the tribe of Reuben twelve
thousand,
from the tribe of Gad twelve thousand,
6 from the tribe of Asher twelve
thousand,
from the tribe of Naphtali twelve
thousand,
from the tribe of Manasseh twelve
thousand,
7 from the tribe of Simeon twelve
thousand,
from the tribe of Levi twelve thousand,
from the tribe of Issachar twelve
thousand,
8 from the tribe of Zebulun twelve
thousand,
from the tribe of Joseph twelve
thousand,
from the tribe of Benjamin twelve
thousand sealed.

The Multitude from Every Nation

9 After this I looked, and there was a great multitude that no one could count, from every nation, from all tribes and peoples and languages, standing before the throne and before the Lamb, robed in white, with palm branches in their hands. [10]They cried out in a loud voice, saying,

"Salvation belongs to our God who is
seated on the throne, and to
the Lamb!"

[11]And all the angels stood around the throne and around the elders and the four living creatures, and they fell on their faces before the throne and worshiped God, [12]singing,

"Amen! Blessing and glory and
wisdom
and thanksgiving and honor
and power and might
be to our God forever and ever!
Amen."

13 Then one of the elders addressed me, saying, "Who are these, robed in white, and where have they come from?" [14]I said to him, "Sir, you are the one that knows." Then he said to me, "These are they who have come out of the great ordeal; they have washed their robes and made them white in the blood of the Lamb.

[15] For this reason they are before the
throne of God,

[s] Gk *slaves* [t] Gk *brothers*

6.9-11 This section deals with the pain of those whose lives were cut short because of their faithfulness to Christ.
6.9 The author knows of martyrs slain for their faith in Christ; *cf.* 20.4. *Under the altar. Cf.* Lev 4.7; Ex 29.12.
6.10 The cry of the martyrs is less a cry of revenge than a cry for God to exercise his power in the face of oppression.
6.11 The author knows that the oppression is not yet over; *cf.* 1.9.
6.12-17 This section speaks of the great earthquake.
6.12 In the Old Testament great cosmic disturbances are a sign of God's power and intervention (see Ex 19.18; Joel 2.31; Isa 2.17-19; 13.9-10).
6.16 *Fall on us. Cf.* Hos 10.8; Lk 22.30.
6.17 *The great day of their wrath has come. Cf.* Joel 2.11; Zeph 1.14-18. *Who is able to stand? Cf.* Nahum 1.6.
7.1-17 This section answers the question "Who is able to stand?" (6.17). The answer: the faithful people of God. Two pictures are presented of God's people, emphasizing the continuity between Israel and the Christian church: the 144,000 sealed (7.4-8) and the countless multitude (7.9-17).
7.1 In apocalyptic literature angels are given charge over the forces of nature; *cf.* 16.5; 14.18.
7.2 *The seal.* Most likely a signet ring used to authenticate or protect official documents.
7.3 *A seal on their foreheads. Cf.* 3.12; 14.1; 22.4; Ezek 9.4; also Rev 13.16-17; 14.9-11; 16.2; 19.20.
7.4-8 The first of two pictures portraying the people of God; here the fullness of Israel.
7.9-17 The second of two pictures portraying the people of God in all its fullness: "a great multitude that no one could count, from every nation..." (7.9).
7.11 *cf.* 4.4,6; 5.11.
7.14 *The great ordeal.* I.e. the catastrophes which will precede the end of the world; *cf.* 3.10; Dan 12.1; Mk 13.19; Jn 16.33; 2 Tim 3.12. *Washed their robes and made them white in the blood of the Lamb; cf.* 5.9; Isa 1.18.
7.15 *cf.* Isa 4.5-6.

6.9 Rev 14.18; 16.7; 20.4; 1.9; 12.17
6.10 Zech 1.12; Ps 79.5; Rev 3.7; 19.2
6.11 Rev 3.5; 7.9; 14.13; Heb 11.40
6.12 Rev 16.18; Mt 24.29; Joel 2.31; Acts 2.20
6.13 Rev 8.10; 9.1; Isa 34.4
6.14 Isa 34.4; Jer 3.23; 4.24; Rev 16.10
6.15 Isa 2.10,19
6.16 Hos 10.8; Lk 23.30; Rev 9.6
6.17 Zeph 1.14; Rev 16.14; Ps 76.7
7.1 Rev 9.4
7.3 Rev 6.6; Ezek 9.4; Rev 22.4
7.4 Rev 9.16; 14.1
7.9 Rom 11.25; Rev 5.9; 3.5,18; 4.4; 6.11
7.10 Ps 3.8; Rev 12.10; 19.1; 5.13
7.12 Rev 5.12-14
7.14 Mt 24.21; Zech 3.3-5; Heb 9.14; 1 Jn 1.7
7.15 Isa 4.5,6; Rev 21.3

and worship him day and night
within his temple,
and the one who is seated on the
throne will shelter them.
16 They will hunger no more, and thirst
no more;
the sun will not strike them,
nor any scorching heat;
17 for the Lamb at the center of the
throne will be their shepherd,
and he will guide them to springs
of the water of life,
and God will wipe away every tear
from their eyes."

The Seventh Seal and the Golden Censer

8 When the Lamb opened the seventh seal, there was silence in heaven for about half an hour. 2 And I saw the seven angels who stand before God, and seven trumpets were given to them.

3 Another angel with a golden censer came and stood at the altar; he was given a great quantity of incense to offer with the prayers of all the saints on the golden altar that is before the throne. 4 And the smoke of the incense, with the prayers of the saints, rose before God from the hand of the angel. 5 Then the angel took the censer and filled it with fire from the altar and threw it on the earth; and there were peals of thunder, rumblings, flashes of lightning, and an earthquake.

The Seven Trumpets

6 Now the seven angels who had the seven trumpets made ready to blow them.

7 The first angel blew his trumpet, and there came hail and fire, mixed with blood, and they were hurled to the earth; and a third of the earth was burned up, and a third of the trees were burned up, and all green grass was burned up.

8 The second angel blew his trumpet, and something like a great mountain, burning with fire, was thrown into the sea. 9 A third of the sea became blood, a third of the living creatures in the sea died, and a third of the ships were destroyed.

10 The third angel blew his trumpet, and a great star fell from heaven, blazing like a torch, and it fell on a third of the rivers and on the springs of water. 11 The name of the star is Wormwood. A third of the waters became wormwood, and many died from the water, because it was made bitter.

12 The fourth angel blew his trumpet, and a third of the sun was struck, and a third of the moon, and a third of the stars, so that a third of their light was darkened; a third of the day was kept from shining, and likewise the night.

13 Then I looked, and I heard an eagle crying with a loud voice as it flew in midheaven, "Woe, woe, woe to the inhabitants of the earth, at the blasts of the other trumpets that the three angels are about to blow!"

9 And the fifth angel blew his trumpet, and I saw a star that had fallen from heaven to earth, and he was given the key to the shaft of the bottomless pit; 2 he opened the shaft of the bottomless pit, and from the shaft rose smoke like the smoke of a great furnace, and the sun and the air were darkened with the smoke from the shaft. 3 Then from the smoke came locusts on the earth, and they were given authority like the authority of scorpions of the earth. 4 They were told not to damage the grass of the earth or any green growth or any tree, but only those people who do not have the seal of God on their foreheads. 5 They were allowed to torture them for five months, but not to kill them, and their torture was like the torture of a scorpion when it stings someone. 6 And in those days people will seek death but will not find it; they will long to die, but death will flee from them.

7 In appearance the locusts were like horses equipped for battle. On their heads were what looked like crowns of gold; their faces were like human faces, 8 their hair like women's hair, and their teeth like lions' teeth; 9 they had scales like iron breastplates, and the noise of their wings was like the noise of many chariots with horses rushing into battle. 10 They have tails like scorpions, with stingers, and in their tails is their power to harm people for five months. 11 They have as king over them the angel of the bottomless pit; his name in Hebrew is Abaddon,[u] and in Greek he is called Apollyon.[v]

12 The first woe has passed. There are still two woes to come.

13 Then the sixth angel blew his trumpet, and I heard a voice from the four[w] horns of the golden altar before God, 14 saying to the sixth angel who had the trumpet,

[u] That is, *Destruction* [v] That is, *Destroyer* [w] Other ancient authorities lack *four*

7.16 Isa 49.10; Ps 121.5,6; Rev 21.4
7.17 Ps 23.1; Jn 10.11,14; Isa 25.8
8.1 Rev 6.1
8.2 1 Cor 15.52; 1 Thess 4.16
8.3 Rev 7.2; 5.8; Ex 30.1; Rev 6.9
8.4 Ps 141.2
8.5 Lev 16.12; Rev 4.5; 6.12
8.7 Ezek 38.22; Rev 9.4
8.8 Jer 51.25; Rev 16.3
8.10 Isa 14.12; Rev 9.1; 16.4
8.11 Jer 9.15; 23.15
8.12 Rev 6.12,13
8.13 Rev 14.6; 19.17; 9.12; 11.14
9.1 Rev 8.10; Lk 8.31; Rev 17.8; 20.1
9.2 Gen 19.28; Ex 19.18; Joel 2.2,10
9.3 Ex 10.12-15; ver 10
9.4 Rev 6.6; 8.7; 7.2,3
9.5 ver 10,3
9.6 Job 3.21; Jer 8.3; Rev 6.16
9.7 Joel 2.4; Nah 3.17; Dan 7.8
9.8 Joel 1.8
9.9 Joel 2.5
9.11 Eph 2.2
9.12 Rev 8.13
9.13 Ex 30.1-3; Rev 8.3
9.14 Rev 16.12

7.16 *cf.* Isa 49.10.
7.17 *cf.* Jn 10.1-30; 21.15-17; Ps 23.1; Isa 40.11.
8.1-9.21 The seven trumpets, a cycle set in motion by the opening of the seventh seal.
8.1 *Silence in heaven. Cf.* Zeph 1.7; Zech 2.13; Hab 2.20.
8.2 *Trumpets* are used to gather God's people to celebrate the great festivals (Num 10.3,10; 29.1), or the beginning of the reign of the new king (*cf.* 1 Kings 1.34,39; 2 Kings 9.13).
8.3 *cf.* 8.4; Heb 5.7; Eph 5.2. *Incense.* For its ingredients see Ex 30.34-35; incense and prayer are connected in Ps 141.2.
8.5 A purification process begins; *cf.* Isa 6.6-7.
8.7-13 The refiner's fire which purifies is cast toward the earth, and no part of it remains unaffected: the food we eat (8.7-8), the water we drink (8.10-11), the celestial bodies (8.12). The power of each one is limited, so that none can become a god.
8.11 *Wormwood.* This reverses the miracle at Marah, where bitter water became sweet (see Ex 15.25).
8.13 *Eagle.* The Greek word can also mean "vulture," as in Lk 17.37.
9.1 *Bottomless pit.* Literally, "the abyss." This was the watery depths, the place of the underworld, thought of in terms of a vast subterranean cavern where the evil and disobedient spirits awaited judgment (see 20.1-3; Lk 8.31; Jude 6). In Rev it is the place from which the beast will ascend (Rev 11.7; 17.8).
9.3 *Locusts.* Throughout the Old Testament locusts are a symbol of destruction; *cf.* Ex 10.1-20; Joel 1.2-2.11.
9.5 The damage the locusts can do is limited, as in the episodes of the first four trumpets (8.7-13); God is the one whose power limits catastrophes.
9.7 *cf.* Joel 2.4-5.
9.8 *cf.* Joel 1.6.
9.11 *Abaddon.* Jewish Christians would recognize this Hebrew word as an allusion to the underworld, already personified in Job 28.22. *Apollyon.* Greek Christians would recognize this word as meaning "Destroyer" and as a cryptic reference to the Greek god Apollo, whose symbol was the locust and whose name the emperor Domitian, the persecutor of the church, used of himself.
9.14 *Euphrates.* This river marked the eastern boundary of the land promised to Abram (see Gen 15.18; Deut 11.24; Josh 1.4; Isa 8.5-8).

"Release the four angels who are bound at
the great river Euphrates." 15So the four
angels were released, who had been held
ready for the hour, the day, the month, and
the year, to kill a third of humankind. 16The
number of the troops of cavalry was two
hundred million; I heard their number. 17And
this was how I saw the horses in my vision:
the riders wore breastplates the color of fire
and of sapphire[x] and of sulfur; the heads of
the horses were like lions' heads, and fire
and smoke and sulfur came out of their
mouths. 18By these three plagues a third of
humankind was killed, by the fire and smoke
and sulfur coming out of their mouths.
19For the power of the horses is in their
mouths and in their tails; their tails are like
serpents, having heads; and with them they
inflict harm.
20 The rest of humankind, who were not
killed by these plagues, did not repent of the
works of their hands or give up worshiping
demons and idols of gold and silver and
bronze and stone and wood, which cannot
see or hear or walk. 21And they did not
repent of their murders or their sorceries or
their fornication or their thefts.

The Angel with the Little Scroll

10 And I saw another mighty angel
coming down from heaven,
wrapped in a cloud, with a rainbow over
his head; his face was like the sun, and his
legs like pillars of fire. 2He held a little scroll
open in his hand. Setting his right foot on
the sea and his left foot on the land, 3he
gave a great shout, like a lion roaring. And
when he shouted, the seven thunders
sounded. 4And when the seven thunders
had sounded, I was about to write, but I
heard a voice from heaven saying, "Seal up
what the seven thunders have said, and do
not write it down." 5Then the angel whom
I saw standing on the sea and the land
raised his right hand to heaven
6 and swore by him who lives forever
and ever,
who created heaven and what is in it, the
earth and what is in it, and the sea and
what is in it: "There will be no more delay,
7but in the days when the seventh angel is
to blow his trumpet, the mystery of God will
be fulfilled, as he announced to his servants[y]
the prophets."

8 Then the voice that I had heard from
heaven spoke to me again, saying, "Go, take
the scroll that is open in the hand of the
angel who is standing on the sea and on the
land." 9So I went to the angel and told him
to give me the little scroll; and he said to
me, "Take it, and eat; it will be bitter to
your stomach, but sweet as honey in your
mouth." 10So I took the little scroll from the
hand of the angel and ate it; it was sweet
as honey in my mouth, but when I had
eaten it, my stomach was made bitter.
11 Then they said to me, "You must
prophesy again about many peoples and
nations and languages and kings."

The Two Witnesses

11 Then I was given a measuring rod
like a staff, and I was told, "Come
and measure the temple of God and the
altar and those who worship there, 2but do
not measure the court outside the temple;
leave that out, for it is given over to the
nations, and they will trample over the holy
city for forty-two months. 3And I will grant
my two witnesses authority to prophesy for
one thousand two hundred sixty days,
wearing sackcloth."
4 These are the two olive trees and the
two lampstands that stand before the Lord
of the earth. 5And if anyone wants to harm
them, fire pours from their mouth and
consumes their foes; anyone who wants to
harm them must be killed in this manner.
6They have authority to shut the sky, so
that no rain may fall during the days of
their prophesying, and they have authority
over the waters to turn them into blood,
and to strike the earth with every kind of
plague, as often as they desire.
7 When they have finished their testimony, the beast that comes up from the
bottomless pit will make war on them and
conquer them and kill them, 8and their
dead bodies will lie in the street of the great
city that is prophetically[z] called Sodom and
Egypt, where also their Lord was crucified.
9For three and a half days members of the
peoples and tribes and languages and nations will gaze at their dead bodies and
refuse to let them be placed in a tomb; 10and
the inhabitants of the earth will gloat over
them and celebrate and exchange presents,
because these two prophets had been a

[x] Gk *hyacinth* [y] Gk *slaves* [z] Or *allegorically*; Gk *spiritually*

9.17 *My vision.* The only indication in Rev that John's revelations have the form of visions.
9.18 *cf.* Gen 19.24; Jude 7.
10.1-11.19 A section dealing with the role of the prophet, the prophet's witness in the world, and the struggle with the worldly powers because of that witness.
10.1 *cf.* Ezek 1.26-28; Ex 13.21-22; 14.19,24.
10.2 *A little scroll. Cf.* Ezek 2.8-3.3.
10.4 *Seal up...and do not write it down. Cf.* Dan 12.4; this is in contrast to the instructions given in Rev 1.1 and 22.10.
10.6 *There will be no more delay.* This answers the question raised in 6.10.
10.9-10 *cf.* Ezek 2.8-3.3; Ps 119.103; Jer 15.16. The message John and his churches are given to speak comes from God, sweet at first but not easy to digest. We welcome its message of freedom and hope, but it challenges our values and our entanglements in the world.
10.11 The prophet's scope of interest is not narrowly fixed on only one nation's welfare; *cf.* 11.10.
11.1-3 The prophet's task is to measure, to assess the people of God. This section recalls the measuring of the temple in Ezek 40-42.
11.4 *Two olive trees and the two lampstands. Cf.* Zech 4.10-12.
11.5-6 *cf.* 1 Kings 17.1-8; 2 Kings 1.9-12.
11.7 *The beast.* The first time this enemy of the church is mentioned; see note on 13.1. *Bottomless pit.* See note on 9.1. *Make war on them and kill them.* Christian prophets and witnesses will be engaged in struggles with the world, resulting at times in the death of some of them.
11.8 *Sodom.* A symbol of moral degeneration (see Gen 19.4-11). *Egypt.* A symbol of oppression and slavery. *Where also their Lord was crucified.* The worldly powers prevailed for a time also over Christ.

9.16 Rev 5.11; 7.4
9.17 ver 18; Rev 11.5
9.20 Deut 31.29; 1 Cor 10.20; Ps 115.4; 135.15; Dan 5.23
10.1 Rev 5.2; Mt 17.2; Rev 1.16; 1.15
10.3 Isa 31.4; Rev 4.5
10.4 Dan 8.26; 12.4,9; Rev 22.10
10.5 Ex 6.8; Dan 12.7
10.6 Rev 4.11; 14.7; 16.17
10.7 Rev 11.15; Rom 16.25
10.9 Jer 15.16; Ezek 2.8
10.10 Ezek 3.3
11.1 Ezek 40.3; Rev 21.15
11.2 Ezek 40.17; Lk 21.24; Rev 13.5
11.3 Rev 19.10; 12.6
11.4 Ps 52.8; Jer 11.16; Zech 4.3,11,14
11.5 2 Kings 1.10 Jer 5.14; Num 16.29
11.6 1 Kings 17.1 Ex 7.17,19
11.7 Rev 13.1; 9.1,2; Dan 7.21
11.8 Rev 14.8; Isa 1.9; Heb 13.12
11.10 Rev 3.10; Esth 9.19,22

torment to the inhabitants of the earth.

11 But after the three and a half days, the breath[a] of life from God entered them, and they stood on their feet, and those who saw them were terrified. [12]Then they[b] heard a loud voice from heaven saying to them, "Come up here!" And they went up to heaven in a cloud while their enemies watched them. [13]At that moment there was a great earthquake, and a tenth of the city fell; seven thousand people were killed in the earthquake, and the rest were terrified and gave glory to the God of heaven.

14 The second woe has passed. The third woe is coming very soon.

The Seventh Trumpet

15 Then the seventh angel blew his trumpet, and there were loud voices in heaven, saying,

"The kingdom of the world has
become the kingdom of our
Lord
and of his Messiah,[c]
and he will reign forever and ever."

16 Then the twenty-four elders who sit on their thrones before God fell on their faces and worshiped God, [17]singing,

"We give you thanks, Lord God
Almighty,
who are and who were,
for you have taken your great power
and begun to reign.
[18] The nations raged,
but your wrath has come,
and the time for judging the dead,
for rewarding your servants,[d] the
prophets
and saints and all who fear your
name,
both small and great,
and for destroying those who destroy
the earth."

19 Then God's temple in heaven was opened, and the ark of his covenant was seen within his temple; and there were flashes of lightning, rumblings, peals of thunder, an earthquake, and heavy hail.

The Woman and the Dragon

12 A great portent appeared in heaven: a woman clothed with the sun, with the moon under her feet, and on her head a crown of twelve stars. [2]She was pregnant and was crying out in birth pangs, in the agony of giving birth. [3]Then another portent appeared in heaven: a great red dragon, with seven heads and ten horns, and seven diadems on his heads. [4]His tail swept down a third of the stars of heaven and threw them to the earth. Then the dragon stood before the woman who was about to bear a child, so that he might devour her child as soon as it was born. [5]And she gave birth to a son, a male child, who is to rule[e] all the nations with a rod of iron. But her child was snatched away and taken to God and to his throne; [6]and the woman fled into the wilderness, where she has a place prepared by God, so that there she can be nourished for one thousand two hundred sixty days.

Michael Defeats the Dragon

7 And war broke out in heaven; Michael and his angels fought against the dragon. The dragon and his angels fought back, [8]but they were defeated, and there was no longer any place for them in heaven. [9]The great dragon was thrown down, that ancient serpent, who is called the Devil and Satan, the deceiver of the whole world—he was thrown down to the earth, and his angels were thrown down with him.

10 Then I heard a loud voice in heaven, proclaiming,

"Now have come the salvation and
the power
and the kingdom of our God
and the authority of his Messiah,[c]
for the accuser of our comrades[f] has
been thrown down,
who accuses them day and night
before our God.
[11] But they have conquered him by the
blood of the Lamb
and by the word of their testimony,
for they did not cling to life even in
the face of death.
[12] Rejoice then, you heavens
and those who dwell in them!
But woe to the earth and the sea,
for the devil has come down to you
with great wrath,
because he knows that his time is
short!"

[a] Or *the spirit* [b] Other ancient authorities read *I* [c] Gk *Christ* [d] Gk *slaves* [e] Or *to shepherd* [f] Gk *brothers*

11.11 God's act of resurrection reverses the brief victory of the worldly powers mentioned in 11.7-8. The language here is reminiscent of Ezek 37.1-10.
11.12 *cf.* 2 Kings 2.11; Mt 24.27; 1 Thess 4.17.
11.13 *Earthquake. Cf.* Ezek 38.19-20; Zech 14.15; Hag 2.6-7.
11.15 *cf.* Dan 12.10; 19.16.
11.18 *cf.* Ps 2.2; 46.6.
11.19 *Ark of the covenant.* See Deut 10.1-8; 2 Kings 25.8-10; 2 Macc 2.4-8.
12.1-14.20 This section depicts the church's conflict with the worldly powers.
12.1 *Portent.* I.e. a sign, pointing beyond itself to the deeper meaning of the world's history; *cf.* 12.3; 15.1. *A woman.* The woman is the mother of God's people (*cf.* Isa 54.1), whose offspring is Israel and the Christian church (see note on 12.7). *Crown of twelve stars.* This may allude to the twelve tribes of Israel (see 21.12) or to the twelve apostles (see 21.14), or both.
12.2 *Birthpangs. Cf.* Isa 26.17.
12.3 *Great red dragon.* The identification of this dragon is given in 12.9. *Ten horns. Cf.* Dan 7.7,24.
12.5 *Rod of iron. Cf.* 19.15; Ps 2.9.
12.7 *Michael.* In Jewish thought, Michael is an archangel who is the protector of Israel and who in the last days will deliver Israel from destruction (see Dan 12.1).
12.9 *That ancient serpent. Cf.* Gen 3.1-21. *Devil.* The word means "slanderer," the deceiver of the whole world (see Rev 20.8). *Satan.* The word means "adversary," the one who accuses people of wrongdoing before God (see Job 1.6-11; Zech 3.1-10).
12.10 *cf.* Rom 8.33-34.
12.11 The defeat of Satan is accomplished by Christ's cross.
12.12 *Woe. Cf.* 8.13; 9.12; 11.14. *The devil has come down to you. Cf.* Lk 10.18.

11.11 Ezek 37.5,9,10,14
11.12 Rev 4.1; 2 Kings 2.11; Acts 1.9
11.13 Rev 6.12; 14.7; 16.11
11.14 Rev 9.12
11.15 Rev 10.7; 16.17; 19.1; 12.10; Dan 2.44; 7.14,27
11.16 Rev 4.4; 5.8
11.17 Rev 1.8; 19.6
11.18 Ps 2.1; Dan 7.9,10; Rev 10.7; 19.5
11.19 Rev 15.5,8; 8.5; 16.21
12.2 Isa 66.7; Gal 4.19
12.3 Rev 13.1; Dan 7.7; Rev 19.12
12.4 Rev 8.7,12; Dan 8.10
12.5 Ps 2.27; 2 Cor 12.2
12.6 Rev 11.3
12.7 Dan 10.13; Rev 20.2
12.9 Gen 3.1,4; Rev 20.2; 20.3,8,10; Jn 12.31
12.10 Rev 11.15; Job 1.9-11; Zech 3.1
12.11 Rom 16.20; Lk 14.26
12.12 Ps 96.11; Isa 49.13; Rev 18.20; 8.13; 10.6

12.14 *cf.* Deut 32.10-11.
12.17 *Her children.* See note on 12.1.
12.18 *Took his stand.* I.e. called his lieutenants into action. *On the seashore.* See note on 13.1.
13.1 *Beast rising out of the sea.* The Roman armies attacked Asia Minor from the sea. The portrait of the beast suggests total, radical evil.
13.2 The description of the beast is a composite of the four beasts of Dan 7. *The dragon gave it its power.* I.e. behind Rome is the power of Satan.
13.3 That this verse refers to a historical figure is conjecture; more likely it depicts the resilience of Rome as a world power.
13.5 *Mouth uttering haughty and blasphemous words. Cf.* Dan 7.8,20,25; 11.36.
13.7-8 The oppression of the church by the Roman government is depicted here (*cf.* 2.13; 13.16-17).
13.9 *cf.* 2.7,11,17,19; 3.6,13,22.
13.10 This verse is a statement of early Christian pacifism; the Christian is not to return violence for violence. *Cf.* Mt 5.38-42; 26.52; see note on 19.21. *Here is a call... Cf.* 14.12.
13.11-18 This section speaks of a second beast, whose duty is to ensure that the authority of the first beast (13.1-10) is carried out. This most likely depicts a provincial governor, a puppet ruler who demands allegiance to Rome and seeks out those who refuse to participate in the imperial cult (see 13.16-17). It has a number for its name: 666 (13.18).
13.18 *Six hundred sixty-six.* In contrast to the number seven, which for John of Patmos symbolizes perfection, this number suggests imperfection in triplicate.
14.1 *Mount Zion.* A term of majesty and triumph referring to Jerusalem, but to its heavenly, eternal shape (see Joel 2.32; Gal 4.26; Heb 12.22). *One hundred forty-four thousand.* See notes on 7.1-17 and 7.4-8. *Name...written on their foreheads.* See note on 7.3.

The Dragon Fights Again on Earth

13 So when the dragon saw that he had been thrown down to the earth, he pursued[g] the woman who had given birth to the male child. 14 But the woman was given the two wings of the great eagle, so that she could fly from the serpent into the wilderness, to her place where she is nourished for a time, and times, and half a time. 15 Then from his mouth the serpent poured water like a river after the woman, to sweep her away with the flood. 16 But the earth came to the help of the woman; it opened its mouth and swallowed the river that the dragon had poured from his mouth. 17 Then the dragon was angry with the woman, and went off to make war on the rest of her children, those who keep the commandments of God and hold the testimony of Jesus.

The First Beast

18 Then the dragon[h] took his stand on the sand of the seashore. 1 And I saw a beast

13 rising out of the sea, having ten horns and seven heads; and on its horns were ten diadems, and on its heads were blasphemous names. 2 And the beast that I saw was like a leopard, its feet were like a bear's, and its mouth was like a lion's mouth. And the dragon gave it his power and his throne and great authority. 3 One of its heads seemed to have received a death-blow, but its mortal wound[i] had been healed. In amazement the whole earth followed the beast. 4 They worshiped the dragon, for he had given his authority to the beast, and they worshiped the beast, saying, "Who is like the beast, and who can fight against it?"

5 The beast was given a mouth uttering haughty and blasphemous words, and it was allowed to exercise authority for forty-two months. 6 It opened its mouth to utter blasphemies against God, blaspheming his name and his dwelling, that is, those who dwell in heaven. 7 Also it was allowed to make war on the saints and to conquer them.[j] It was given authority over every tribe and people and language and nation, 8 and all the inhabitants of the earth will worship it, everyone whose name has not been written from the foundation of the world in the book of life of the Lamb that was slaughtered.[k]

9 Let anyone who has an ear listen:
10 If you are to be taken captive,
into captivity you go;
if you kill with the sword,
with the sword you must be killed.
Here is a call for the endurance and faith of the saints.

The Second Beast

11 Then I saw another beast that rose out of the earth; it had two horns like a lamb and it spoke like a dragon. 12 It exercises all the authority of the first beast on its behalf, and it makes the earth and its inhabitants worship the first beast, whose mortal wound[l] had been healed. 13 It performs great signs, even making fire come down from heaven to earth in the sight of all; 14 and by the signs that it is allowed to perform on behalf of the beast, it deceives the inhabitants of earth, telling them to make an image for the beast that had been wounded by the sword[m] and yet lived; 15 and it was allowed to give breath[n] to the image of the beast so that the image of the beast could even speak and cause those who would not worship the image of the beast to be killed. 16 Also it causes all, both small and great, both rich and poor, both free and slave, to be marked on the right hand or the forehead, 17 so that no one can buy or sell who does not have the mark, that is, the name of the beast or the number of its name. 18 This calls for wisdom: let anyone with understanding calculate the number of the beast, for it is the number of a person. Its number is six hundred sixty-six.[o]

The Lamb and the 144,000

14 Then I looked, and there was the Lamb, standing on Mount Zion! And with him were one hundred forty-four thousand who had his name and his Father's name written on their foreheads. 2 And I heard a voice from heaven like the sound of many waters and like the sound of loud thunder; the voice I heard was like the sound of harpists playing on their harps,

[g] Or *persecuted* [h] Gk *Then he*; other ancient authorities read *Then I stood* [i] Gk *the plague of its death* [j] Other ancient authorities lack this sentence [k] Or *written in the book of life of the Lamb that was slaughtered from the foundation of the world* [l] Gk *whose plague of its death* [m] Or *that had received the plague of the sword* [n] Or *spirit* [o] Other ancient authorities read *six hundred sixteen*

12.14 Ex 19.4; Dan 7.25; 12.7
12.15 Isa 59.19
12.17 Gen 3.15; Rev 11.7; 14.12; 1.2,9
13.1 Dan 7.1-6; Rev 17.3
13.2 Rev 16.10
13.3 Rev 17.8
13.4 Rev 18.18
13.5 Dan 7.8,11,25; Rev 11.2
13.7 Dan 7.21; Rev 11.7; 5.9
13.8 Phil 4.3; Rev 3.5; 17.8; 5.6
13.10 Isa 33.1; Mt 26.52; Rev 14.12
13.13 Mt 24.24; Rev 16.14; 1 Kings 18.38; Rev 20.9
13.14 Rev 12.9; 2 Thess 2.9,10
13.16 Rev 11.18; 19.5,18; 14.9
13.17 Rev 14.9; 14.11; 15.2
13.18 Rev 17.9; 15.2; 21.17
14.1 Rev 5.6; Ps 2.6; Rev 3.12; 7.3
14.2 Rev 1.15; 5.8

3and they sing a new song before the throne
and before the four living creatures and
before the elders. No one could learn that
song except the one hundred forty-four
thousand who have been redeemed from
the earth. 4It is these who have not defiled
themselves with women, for they are virgins; these follow the Lamb wherever he
goes. They have been redeemed from humankind as first fruits for God and the
Lamb, 5and in their mouth no lie was found;
they are blameless.

The Messages of the Three Angels

6 Then I saw another angel flying in
midheaven, with an eternal gospel to proclaim to those who live[p] on the earth—to
every nation and tribe and language and
people. 7He said in a loud voice, "Fear God
and give him glory, for the hour of his
judgment has come; and worship him who
made heaven and earth, the sea and the
springs of water."

8 Then another angel, a second, followed,
saying, "Fallen, fallen is Babylon the great!
She has made all nations drink of the wine
of the wrath of her fornication."

9 Then another angel, a third, followed
them, crying with a loud voice, "Those who
worship the beast and its image, and receive
a mark on their foreheads or on their hands,
10they will also drink the wine of God's
wrath, poured unmixed into the cup of his
anger, and they will be tormented with fire
and sulfur in the presence of the holy angels
and in the presence of the Lamb. 11And the
smoke of their torment goes up forever and
ever. There is no rest day or night for those
who worship the beast and its image and
for anyone who receives the mark of its
name."

12 Here is a call for the endurance of the
saints, those who keep the commandments
of God and hold fast to the faith of[q] Jesus.

13 And I heard a voice from heaven
saying, "Write this: Blessed are the dead
who from now on die in the Lord." "Yes,"
says the Spirit, "they will rest from their
labors, for their deeds follow them."

Reaping the Earth's Harvest

14 Then I looked, and there was a white
cloud, and seated on the cloud was one like
the Son of Man, with a golden crown on
his head, and a sharp sickle in his hand!
15Another angel came out of the temple,
calling with a loud voice to the one who sat
on the cloud, "Use your sickle and reap, for
the hour to reap has come, because the
harvest of the earth is fully ripe." 16So the
one who sat on the cloud swung his sickle
over the earth, and the earth was reaped.

17 Then another angel came out of the
temple in heaven, and he too had a sharp
sickle. 18Then another angel came out from
the altar, the angel who has authority over
fire, and he called with a loud voice to him
who had the sharp sickle, "Use your sharp
sickle and gather the clusters of the vine of
the earth, for its grapes are ripe." 19So the
angel swung his sickle over the earth and
gathered the vintage of the earth, and he
threw it into the great wine press of the
wrath of God. 20And the wine press was
trodden outside the city, and blood flowed
from the wine press, as high as a horse's
bridle, for a distance of about two hundred
miles.[r]

The Angels with the Seven Last Plagues

15 Then I saw another portent in
heaven, great and amazing: seven
angels with seven plagues, which are the
last, for with them the wrath of God is
ended.

2 And I saw what appeared to be a sea
of glass mixed with fire, and those who had
conquered the beast and its image and the
number of its name, standing beside the sea
of glass with harps of God in their hands.
3And they sing the song of Moses, the
servant[s] of God, and the song of the Lamb:

"Great and amazing are your deeds,
Lord God the Almighty!
Just and true are your ways,
King of the nations![t]
4 Lord, who will not fear
and glorify your name?
For you alone are holy.
All nations will come
and worship before you,
for your judgments have been
revealed."

5 After this I looked, and the temple of
the tent[u] of witness in heaven was opened,
6and out of the temple came the seven

[p] Gk *sit* [q] Or *to their faith in* [r] Gk *one thousand six hundred stadia* [s] Gk *slave* [t] Other ancient authorities read *the ages* [u] Or *tabernacle*

14.4 2 Cor 11.2; Rev 3.4; 5.9; Jas 1.18
14.5 Ps 32.2; Zeph 3.13; Eph 5.27
14.6 Rev 8.13; 3.10; 5.9
14.7 Rev 15.4; 11.13; 4.11; 8.10
14.8 Isa 21.9; Jer 51.8; Rev 18.2; 17.5; 18.10
14.9 Rev 13.14-16
14.10 Isa 51.17; Jer 25.15; Rev 18.6; 20.10; 19.20
14.11 Isa 34.10; Rev 19.3; 4.8; Rev 13.17
14.12 Rev 13.10; 12.17
14.13 Rev 20.6; 1 Cor 15.18; 1 Thess 4.16
14.14 Dan 7.13; Rev 1.13; 6.2
14.15 Joel 3.13; Jer 51.33; Rev 13.12
14.18 Rev 16.8; Joel 3.13
14.20 Isa 63.3; Heb 13.12; Rev 11.8
15.1 Rev 12.1,3; 16.1; Lev 26.21; Rev 14.10
15.2 Rev 4.6; 13.14,15; 5.8
15.3 Deut 32.3,4; Ps 111.2; 145.17; Hos 14.9
15.4 Jer 10.7; Isa 66.23

14.3 *Sound of many waters. Cf.* Ezek 1.24; 43.2; 6.1; 19.6.
14.4-5 The highest degree of spiritual perfection is symbolized; *cf.* 2 Kings 19.21; Lam 2.13; Jer 18.13; Am 5.2.
14.5 *cf.* 22.15.
14.8 *"Fallen, fallen..." Cf.* Am 5.2. *Babylon the great.* I.e. Rome.
14.9 *Mark on their foreheads. Cf.* 13.17-18; 16.2; 20.4. This is in contrast to the mark on the foreheads of God's people (see 3.12; 7.3).
14.10 *Wine of God's wrath. Cf.* Job 21.20; Ps 75.8; Isa 51.17; Jer 25.15-38. *Fire and sulfur. Cf.* 19.20; 20.10; 21.8; Gen 19.28; Lk 17.29.
14.12 *Here is a call. Cf.* 13.10.
14.13 *Blessed...* See note on 1.3.
14.14 This verse gives a picture of the exalted Christ. *Son of Man. Cf.* Dan 7.13-14. See note on Mt 8.20; Rev 1.3.
14.15 The language of harvest is used frequently with regard to the final judgment; *cf.* Joel 3.13; Mt 9.37-38; Mk 4.29; Lk 10.2; Jn 4.35-38.
14.18 *cf.* 8.3-5.
14.19 *cf.* 19.15,17-18.
14.20 *cf.* Joel 3.12-14; Zech 14.1-4; Heb 13.12; Jn 19.20.
15.1-16.15 This section is John's vision of the seven bowls of God's wrath.
15.1 *Portent.* I.e. a sign, pointing beyond itself to the deeper meaning of the world's history; *cf.* 12.1.3.
15.2 *Sea of glass. Cf.* 4.6. *Harps of God in their hands.* I.e. ready to join in the song of praise; *cf.* Ps 82.2.
15.3 *cf.* Ps 139.14; Deut 32.4.
15.4 *cf.* Ps 86.9; 144.17; Mal 1.11.
15.5 *Tent of witness.* I.e. the tabernacle (see Num 17.7; 18.2) which contained the two tablets which Moses brought down from Mount Sinai (see Ex 32.15; Deut 10.5).

angels with the seven plagues, robed in
pure bright linen,[v] with golden sashes across
their chests. [7]Then one of the four living
creatures gave the seven angels seven golden
bowls full of the wrath of God, who lives
forever and ever; [8]and the temple was filled
with smoke from the glory of God and from
his power, and no one could enter the
temple until the seven plagues of the seven
angels were ended.

The Bowls of God's Wrath

16 Then I heard a loud voice from the
temple telling the seven angels,
"Go and pour out on the earth the seven
bowls of the wrath of God."
2 So the first angel went and poured his
bowl on the earth, and a foul and painful
sore came on those who had the mark of
the beast and who worshiped its image.
3 The second angel poured his bowl into
the sea, and it became like the blood of a
corpse, and every living thing in the sea
died.
4 The third angel poured his bowl into
the rivers and the springs of water, and
they became blood. [5]And I heard the angel
of the waters say,

"You are just, O Holy One, who are
and were,
for you have judged these things;
6 because they shed the blood of saints
and prophets,
you have given them blood to
drink.
It is what they deserve!"

[7]And I heard the altar respond,

"Yes, O Lord God, the Almighty,
your judgments are true and just!"

8 The fourth angel poured his bowl on
the sun, and it was allowed to scorch them
with fire; [9]they were scorched by the fierce
heat, but they cursed the name of God, who
had authority over these plagues, and they
did not repent and give him glory.
10 The fifth angel poured his bowl on
the throne of the beast, and its kingdom
was plunged into darkness; people gnawed
their tongues in agony, [11]and cursed the
God of heaven because of their pains and
sores, and they did not repent of their deeds.
12 The sixth angel poured his bowl on
the great river Euphrates, and its water was
dried up in order to prepare the way for the
kings from the east. [13]And I saw three foul
spirits like frogs coming from the mouth of
the dragon, from the mouth of the beast,
and from the mouth of the false prophet.
[14]These are demonic spirits, performing signs,
who go abroad to the kings of the whole
world, to assemble them for battle on the
great day of God the Almighty. [15]("See, I am
coming like a thief! Blessed is the one who
stays awake and is clothed,[w] not going about
naked and exposed to shame.") [16]And they
assembled them at the place that in Hebrew
is called Harmagedon.
17 The seventh angel poured his bowl
into the air, and a loud voice came out of
the temple, from the throne, saying, "It is
done!" [18]And there came flashes of lightning, rumblings, peals of thunder, and a
violent earthquake, such as had not occurred since people were upon the earth, so
violent was that earthquake. [19]The great
city was split into three parts, and the cities
of the nations fell. God remembered great
Babylon and gave her the wine-cup of the
fury of his wrath. [20]And every island fled
away, and no mountains were to be found;
[21]and huge hailstones, each weighing about
a hundred pounds,[x] dropped from heaven
on people, until they cursed God for the
plague of the hail, so fearful was that plague.

The Great Whore and the Beast

17 Then one of the seven angels who
had the seven bowls came and
said to me, "Come, I will show you the
judgment of the great whore who is seated
on many waters, [2]with whom the kings of
the earth have committed fornication, and
with the wine of whose fornication the
inhabitants of the earth have become drunk."
[3]So he carried me away in the spirit[y] into
a wilderness, and I saw a woman sitting on
a scarlet beast that was full of blasphemous
names, and it had seven heads and ten
horns. [4]The woman was clothed in purple
and scarlet, and adorned with gold and
jewels and pearls, holding in her hand a
golden cup full of abominations and the
impurities of her fornication; [5]and on her
forehead was written a name, a mystery:
"Babylon the great, mother of whores and
of earth's abominations." [6]And I saw that
the woman was drunk with the blood of the
saints and the blood of the witnesses to
Jesus.

[v] Other ancient authorities read *stone* [w] Gk *and keeps his robes* [x] Gk *weighing about a talent* [y] Or *in the Spirit*

15.7 *The four living creatures. Cf.* 4.6; 5.6; 6.1; 7.11; 14.3; 15.7; 19.4.
15.8 *cf.* Ex 19.18.
16.1 *cf.* Isa 66.6.
16.2 *Sore. Cf.* Ex 9.9-11.
16.3 *cf.* Ex 7.20-21.
16.4 *cf.* 8.10-11; Ps 78.44.
16.5 *cf.* 15.4-5.
16.6 *cf.* Isa 49.26; Wis 11.16.
16.7 *The speaking altar. Cf.* 6.9; 8.3-5.
16.11 *Cursed the God of heaven. Cf.* 13.1,5-6; 17.3.
16.12 *Euphrates.* See note on 9.14.
16.13 *The dragon. Cf.* 12.3. *The beast. Cf.* 13.1. *The false prophet.* I.e. probably the beast from the earth (see 13.11).
16.14 *Demonic spirits, performing signs. Cf.* Mt 24.24. *Battle. Cf.* 19.11-21.
16.15 *"See, I am coming like a thief!" Cf.* Mt 24.42-44; 1 Thess 5.2. *Blessed...* The third beatitude of seven in Rev; *cf.* 1.3; 14.13; 19.9; 20.6; 22.7,14.
16.16 *Harmagedon.* Possibly an allusion to Mt. Megiddo, the site of many historic battles. The Hebrew word "har" means mountain.
16.19 *The great city.* Probably a reference to Rome.
16.20 *Cursed God. Cf.* 13.1,5-6; 16.11; 17.3.
17.1-18.24 This section deals with the coming fall of "Babylon," a code-name for imperial Rome (see also 1 Pet 5.13). The use of a code-name enables John to speak of the Roman state as itself symbolic of all those worldly powers hostile to the people of God. The picture given is full of Old Testament imagery, beginning with the role of Babylon during Israel's exile there in the 6th century BCE.
17.1 *The great whore.* I.e. Rome (see 17.18). In the Old Testament Israel's idolatry is often spoken of in terms of harlotry (see Isa 1.21; Jer 2.24; 13.27; Ezek 16.15-17; Hos 2.5. *Seated on many waters.* The identity of the *many waters* is explained in 17.15; *cf.* Jer 51.13.
17.2 The imagery of this verse, fornication and drunkenness, is used to depict the collusion of the nations with the Roman government.
17.3 *A scarlet beast.* A reference to the beast of 13.1. *Purple* symbolizes royalty (*cf.* Judg 8.26; Dan 5.7); *scarlet* is a color of dramatic splendor (*cf.* Nahum 2.3).
17.4 Rome's lavish life-style is meant to attract everyone.
17.5 By now the sign of the mark on the forehead is common. It can be the mark of the beast (13.16; 14.19; 20.4), or it can be God's own mark (3.12; 7.3; 9.4; 14.1; 22.4).
17.6 Isa 49.26 describes the oppressors of Israel in terms of drunkenness. That the woman here is *drunk with the blood of the saints and the blood of the witnesses to Jesus* indicates Rome's oppression of the Christian church; *cf.* 2.13; 6.9.

15.7 Rev 4.6,9; 10.6
15.8 Ex 40.34; 1 Kings 8.10; Isa 6.4
16.1 Rev 15.1
16.2 Rev 8.7; Ex 9.9-11; Rev 13.15-17
16.3 Rev 8.8,9; Ex 17.17-21
16.4 Rev 8.10; Ex 7.17-21
16.5 Rev 15.3; 11.17; 15.4
16.7 Rev 6.9; 14.18; 15.3; 19.2
16.9 Rev 2.21; 11.13
16.10 Rev 13.2; 9.2; 11.10
16.12 Rev 9.14; Isa 41.2
16.13 Rev 12.3; 13.1; 19.20
16.14 1 Tim 4.1; Rev 13.13; 3.10; 17.14
16.15 1 Thess 5.2; 2 Cor 5.3
16.18 Rev 4.5; 6.12; Dan 12.1
16.19 Rev 17.18; 14.8; 18.5; 14.10
16.21 Rev 11.19; Ex 9.23
17.1 Rev 21.9; 16.19; 19.2; Jer 51.13
17.2 Rev 18.3; 14.8
17.3 Rev 12.3,6,14
17.4 Jer 51.7; Rev 18.16; 18.6
17.5 2 Thess 2.7; Rev 14.8; 16.19; 18.9
17.6 Rev 18.24; 13.15; 12.11

When I saw her, I was greatly amazed. 7 But the angel said to me, "Why are you so amazed? I will tell you the mystery of the woman, and of the beast with seven heads and ten horns that carries her. 8 The beast that you saw was, and is not, and is about to ascend from the bottomless pit and go to destruction. And the inhabitants of the earth, whose names have not been written in the book of life from the foundation of the world, will be amazed when they see the beast, because it was and is not and is to come.

9 "This calls for a mind that has wisdom: the seven heads are seven mountains on which the woman is seated; also, they are seven kings, 10 of whom five have fallen, one is living, and the other has not yet come; and when he comes, he must remain only a little while. 11 As for the beast that was and is not, it is an eighth but it belongs to the seven, and it goes to destruction. 12 And the ten horns that you saw are ten kings who have not yet received a kingdom, but they are to receive authority as kings for one hour, together with the beast. 13 These are united in yielding their power and authority to the beast; 14 they will make war on the Lamb, and the Lamb will conquer them, for he is Lord of lords and King of kings, and those with him are called and chosen and faithful."

15 And he said to me, "The waters that you saw, where the whore is seated, are peoples and multitudes and nations and languages. 16 And the ten horns that you saw, they and the beast will hate the whore; they will make her desolate and naked; they will devour her flesh and burn her up with fire. 17 For God has put it into their hearts to carry out his purpose by agreeing to give their kingdom to the beast, until the words of God will be fulfilled. 18 The woman you saw is the great city that rules over the kings of the earth."

The Fall of Babylon

18 After this I saw another angel coming down from heaven, having great authority; and the earth was made bright with his splendor. 2 He called out with a mighty voice,

"Fallen, fallen is Babylon the great!
It has become a dwelling place of demons,
a haunt of every foul spirit,
a haunt of every foul bird,
a haunt of every foul and hateful beast.[z]
3 For all the nations have drunk[a]
of the wine of the wrath of her fornication,
and the kings of the earth have committed fornication with her,
and the merchants of the earth have grown rich from the power[b] of her luxury."

4 Then I heard another voice from heaven saying,

"Come out of her, my people,
so that you do not take part in her sins,
and so that you do not share in her plagues;
5 for her sins are heaped high as heaven,
and God has remembered her iniquities.
6 Render to her as she herself has rendered,
and repay her double for her deeds;
mix a double draught for her in the cup she mixed.
7 As she glorified herself and lived luxuriously,
so give her a like measure of torment and grief.
Since in her heart she says,
'I rule as a queen;
I am no widow,
and I will never see grief,'
8 therefore her plagues will come in a single day—
pestilence and mourning and famine—
and she will be burned with fire;
for mighty is the Lord God who judges her."

9 And the kings of the earth, who committed fornication and lived in luxury with her, will weep and wail over her when they see the smoke of her burning; 10 they will stand far off, in fear of her torment, and say,

"Alas, alas, the great city,
Babylon, the mighty city!
For in one hour your judgment has come."

[z] Some ancient authorities lack the words *a haunt of every foul and hateful beast* and attach the words *and hateful* to the previous line so as to read *a haunt of every foul and hateful bird* [a] Other ancient authorities read *she has made all nations drink* [b] Or *resources*

17.8 Rev 11.7; 13.10; 3.10; 13.3; 13.8
17.9 Rev 13.18
17.12 Dan 7.20; Rev 13.1; 18.10,17,19
17.14 Rev 16.14; 1 Tim 6.15; Rev 19.16; Mt 22.14
17.15 Isa 8.7; Rev 5.9; 13.7
17.16 Rev 18.17,19; Ezek 16.37,39; Rev 19.18; 18.8
17.17 2 Thess 2.11; Rev 10.7
17.18 Rev 14.8
18.1 Rev 17.1; 10.1; Ezek 43.2
18.2 Rev 14.8; Isa 13.21,22; Jer 50.39
18.3 Rev 14.8; Jer 25.15,27
18.4 Isa 48.20; Jer 50.8; 2 Cor 6.17
18.5 Jer 51.9; Rev 16.19
18.6 Ps 137.8; Jer 50.15; Rev 14.10; 16.19
18.7 Ezek 28.2-8; Isa 47.7,8; Zeph 2.15
18.8 Isa 47.9; Rev 17.16; Jer 50.34; Rev 11.17
18.9 Rev 17.2; Jer 50.46; ver 18; Rev 19.3
18.10 ver 15,17,16,19

17.8-18 The imagery depicts the situation in which John's churches find themselves. **17.8** *Was, is not, and is about to ascend.* This is a parody on Roman rulers' claims to divine authority in language reminiscent of God's own self-description (see 1.4,8; 4.8). Rome has become a false standard, in contrast to the true God. **17.9** *Seven mountains.* Rome was built on seven hills. *Seven kings.* Their fate is described in the next verse; their identity has been the subject of much unresolved speculation; perhaps the imagery is meant to describe the power of Rome as a whole, which for John is in process of disintegration (see 18.10). **17.11** *Eighth but it belongs to the seven.* This means that the church will always have to face the hostility of the worldly powers. It gives an indication that John's symbolic depiction of Rome is not exhaustive, but serves as a model for future church-world conflicts. **17.13** The nations are willing collaborators with Rome. **17.14** *War on the Lamb.* This conflict is described in 19.11-21. The Lamb is Christ; *cf.* 5.8-14 and see note on 5.9. **17.15** *Waters. Cf.* 17.1. **17.16** Finally the allies of Rome will turn on Rome: the power of evil is always self-destructive. **17.18** The identification of the whore of Babylon is clear: it is Rome. **18.1-24** This section comprises an eloquent funeral dirge in which John combines elements from various Old Testament songs of lament, flavored with irony and humor; *cf.* Jer 51.59-64. **18.2** *Fallen, fallen. Cf.* Isa 21.9; Am 5.2. *Dwelling place of demons...and...hateful beast. Cf.* Isa 13.20-22. **18.3** *Fornication.* I.e. the rejection of God and the collusion with the powers of evil; *cf.* Hos 4.10; Jer 3.2. **18.4** Up to the last minute God's gracious invitation is still given. **18.5** *cf.* Jer 51.9. **18.6** *Double for her deeds.* This expresses full retribution; *cf.* Isa 40.2; Jer 16.18; 17.18. **18.7-8** For all its glory Rome's fall will occur suddenly, "in a single day" (*cf.* 18.10,17,19). **18.7** *I am no widow. Cf.* Isa 47.8. **18.9** *cf.* 17.2; Jer 51.25.

18.11-19 In this section the fall of Rome is lamented by the merchants of the earth; the language reveals the scope of Rome's consumer interests.
18.20 The fall of imperial Rome is the result of God's action.
18.21-24 Arts and festival will cease in Rome.
18.22 *cf.* Isa 24.8; 30.29.
19.1-20.15 This section speaks of the final victory.
19.1-4 A hymn of praise is heard in heaven over the fall of imperial Rome.
19.1 *A great multitude. Cf.* 7.9-10,13-17. *Salvation.* This belongs to God; it is God's proper work.
19.2 Rome's offenses are specified: the corruption of the nations (17.2,5; 18.9) and the oppression of the servants of God (2.13; 6.9-10; 18.23-24).
19.3 *cf.* Jer 51.25,59-64.
19.6 *Sound of many waters. Cf.* 1.15; 14.2. *Thunderpeals. Cf.* 6.1; 10.3.
19.7 *Marriage of the Lamb.* Marriage is used as symbolic of the relationship between God and God's people (Hos 2.19; Isa 54.5-7), and it was applied to the relationship between Christ and the church (Eph 5.32).

11 And the merchants of the earth weep
and mourn for her, since no one buys their
cargo any more, 12 cargo of gold, silver,
jewels and pearls, fine linen, purple, silk and
scarlet, all kinds of scented wood, all articles
of ivory, all articles of costly wood, bronze,
iron, and marble, 13 cinnamon, spice, incense, myrrh, frankincense, wine, olive oil,
choice flour and wheat, cattle and sheep,
horses and chariots, slaves—and human
lives.[c]

14 "The fruit for which your soul longed
has gone from you,
and all your dainties and your
splendor
are lost to you,
never to be found again!"

15 The merchants of these wares, who gained
wealth from her, will stand far off, in fear
of her torment, weeping and mourning
aloud,

16 "Alas, alas, the great city,
clothed in fine linen,
in purple and scarlet,
adorned with gold,
with jewels, and with pearls!
17 For in one hour all this wealth has
been laid waste!"

And all shipmasters and seafarers, sailors
and all whose trade is on the sea, stood far
off 18 and cried out as they saw the smoke
of her burning,

"What city was like the great city?"

19 And they threw dust on their heads, as
they wept and mourned, crying out,

"Alas, alas, the great city,
where all who had ships at sea
grew rich by her wealth!
For in one hour she has been laid
waste.
20 Rejoice over her, O heaven,
you saints and apostles and
prophets!
For God has given judgment for you
against her."

21 Then a mighty angel took up a stone
like a great millstone and threw it into the
sea, saying,

"With such violence Babylon the great
city
will be thrown down,
and will be found no more;
22 and the sound of harpists and
minstrels and of flutists and
trumpeters
will be heard in you no more;
and an artisan of any trade
will be found in you no more;
and the sound of the millstone
will be heard in you no more;
23 and the light of a lamp
will shine in you no more;
and the voice of bridegroom and bride
will be heard in you no more;
for your merchants were the magnates
of the earth,
and all nations were deceived by
your sorcery.
24 And in you[d] was found the blood of
prophets and of saints,
and of all who have been
slaughtered on earth."

The Rejoicing in Heaven

19 After this I heard what seemed to
be the loud voice of a great multitude in heaven, saying,

"Hallelujah!
Salvation and glory and power to our
God,
2 for his judgments are true and just;
he has judged the great whore
who corrupted the earth with her
fornication,
and he has avenged on her the blood
of his servants."[e]

3 Once more they said,

"Hallelujah!
The smoke goes up from her forever
and ever."

4 And the twenty-four elders and the four
living creatures fell down and worshiped
God who is seated on the throne, saying,

"Amen. Hallelujah!"

5 And from the throne came a voice
saying,

"Praise our God,
all you his servants,[e]
and all who fear him,
small and great."

6 Then I heard what seemed to be the voice
of a great multitude, like the sound of many
waters and like the sound of mighty
thunderpeals, crying out,

"Hallelujah!
For the Lord our God
the Almighty reigns.
7 Let us rejoice and exult
and give him the glory,
for the marriage of the Lamb has
come,

[c] Or *chariots, and human bodies and souls* [d] Gk *her* [e] Gk *slaves*

18.12
Rev 17.4

18.13
Ezek 17.13

18.15
Ezek 27.36,31

18.16
Rev 17.4

18.17
Rev 17.16; Isa 23.14; Ezek 27.29

18.18
Ezek 27.30; Rev 13.4

18.19
Josh 7.6; Job 2.12; Ezek 27.30

18.20
Isa 44.23; Jer 51.48; Rev 19.2

18.21
Jer 51.63; Rev 12.8

18.22
Isa 24.8; Ezek 26.13; Jer 25.10

18.23
Jer 25.10; 7.34; 16.9; Isa 23.8; Nah 3.4

18.24
Rev 17.6; Jer 51.49

19.1
Rev 11.15; 4.11; 7.10,12; 12.10

19.2
Deut 32.43; Rev 6.10

19.3
Isa 34.10; Rev 14.11

19.4
Rev 4.4,6; 5.14

19.5
Ps 134.1; Rev 11.18; 20.12

19.6
Rev 11.15,17; 14.2

19.7
Mt 22.2; 25.10; 2 Cor 11.2; Eph 5.32; Rev 21.2,9

19.8 Rev 15.4
19.9 ver 10; Rev 1.19; Lk 14.15; Rev 21.5
19.10 Rev 22.8; Acts 10.26; Rev 22.9; 12.17
19.11 Rev 15.5; 6.2; 3.14; Isa 11.4
19.12 Rev 1.14; 6.2; 2.17
19.13 Isa 63.2,3; Jn 1.1
19.15 Isa 11.4; 2 Thess 2.8; Ps 2.9; Rev 2.27; 14.19,20
19.16 Dan 2.47; Rev 17.14
19.17 Rev 8.13; Ezek 39.17
19.18 Ezek 39.18-20; Rev 11.18
19.19 Rev 11.7; 16.14,16
20.2 2 Pet 2.4; Jude 6; Rev 12.9
20.3 Dan 6.17; Rev 12.9
20.4 Dan 7.9,22,27; Rev 6.9; 13.12,15,16
20.6 Rev 14.13; 2.11; Rev 21.8; 1.6
20.8 Ezek 38.2; 39.1; Rev 16.14; Heb 11.12
20.9 Ezek 38.9; 38.22; 39.6

and his bride has made herself
ready;
8 to her it has been granted to be
clothed
with fine linen, bright and pure"—
for the fine linen is the righteous deeds of the saints.

9 And the angel said[f] to me, "Write this: Blessed are those who are invited to the marriage supper of the Lamb." And he said to me, "These are true words of God." 10 Then I fell down at his feet to worship him, but he said to me, "You must not do that! I am a fellow servant[g] with you and your comrades[h] who hold the testimony of Jesus.[i] Worship God! For the testimony of Jesus[i] is the spirit of prophecy."

The Rider on the White Horse

11 Then I saw heaven opened, and there was a white horse! Its rider is called Faithful and True, and in righteousness he judges and makes war. 12 His eyes are like a flame of fire, and on his head are many diadems; and he has a name inscribed that no one knows but himself. 13 He is clothed in a robe dipped in[j] blood, and his name is called The Word of God. 14 And the armies of heaven, wearing fine linen, white and pure, were following him on white horses. 15 From his mouth comes a sharp sword with which to strike down the nations, and he will rule[k] them with a rod of iron; he will tread the wine press of the fury of the wrath of God the Almighty. 16 On his robe and on his thigh he has a name inscribed, "King of kings and Lord of lords."

The Beast and Its Armies Defeated

17 Then I saw an angel standing in the sun, and with a loud voice he called to all the birds that fly in midheaven, "Come, gather for the great supper of God, 18 to eat the flesh of kings, the flesh of captains, the flesh of the mighty, the flesh of horses and their riders—flesh of all, both free and slave, both small and great." 19 Then I saw the beast and the kings of the earth with their armies gathered to make war against the rider on the horse and against his army. 20 And the beast was captured, and with it the false prophet who had performed in its presence the signs by which he deceived those who had received the mark of the beast and those who worshiped its image. These two were thrown alive into the lake of fire that burns with sulfur. 21 And the rest were killed by the sword of the rider on the horse, the sword that came from his mouth; and all the birds were gorged with their flesh.

The Thousand Years

20 Then I saw an angel coming down from heaven, holding in his hand the key to the bottomless pit and a great chain. 2 He seized the dragon, that ancient serpent, who is the Devil and Satan, and bound him for a thousand years, 3 and threw him into the pit, and locked and sealed it over him, so that he would deceive the nations no more, until the thousand years were ended. After that he must be let out for a little while.

4 Then I saw thrones, and those seated on them were given authority to judge. I also saw the souls of those who had been beheaded for their testimony to Jesus[l] and for the word of God. They had not worshiped the beast or its image and had not received its mark on their foreheads or their hands. They came to life and reigned with Christ a thousand years. 5 (The rest of the dead did not come to life until the thousand years were ended.) This is the first resurrection. 6 Blessed and holy are those who share in the first resurrection. Over these the second death has no power, but they will be priests of God and of Christ, and they will reign with him a thousand years.

Satan's Doom

7 When the thousand years are ended, Satan will be released from his prison 8 and will come out to deceive the nations at the four corners of the earth, Gog and Magog, in order to gather them for battle; they are as numerous as the sands of the sea. 9 They marched up over the breadth of the earth and surrounded the camp of the saints and the beloved city. And fire came down from heaven[m] and consumed them. 10 And the devil who had deceived them was thrown into the lake of fire and sulfur, where the

[f] Gk *he said* [g] Gk *slave* [h] Gk *brothers* [i] Or *to Jesus* [j] Other ancient authorities read *sprinkled with* [k] Or *will shepherd* [l] Or *for the testimony of Jesus* [m] Other ancient authorities read *from God, out of heaven,* or *out of heaven from God*

19.9 *Blessed...* The fourth of the seven beatitudes of Rev; *cf.* 1.3; 14.13; 16.15; 20.6; 22.7,14.
19.11-21 A word-picture of Christ himself.
19.11 *Faithful and true. Cf.* 3.14.
19.12 Diadems. *Cf.* 12.3; 13.1.
19.13 *Robe dipped in blood.* I.e. his own blood; *cf.* 8.13; 7.14; 12.11. *The Word of God. Cf.* Jn 1.1-14; Heb 4.12.
19.15 *Sharp sword. Cf.* 1.16; 2.12,16; 19.21; Isa 11.4. *Rod of iron. Cf.* Ps 2.9. *Winepress. Cf.* 14.19-20; Isa 63.3; Lam 1.15; Joel 3.13.
19.16 *King of kings and Lord of lords. Cf.* 17.14; Deut 10.17; 1 Tim 6.15; Dan 2.47.
19.17-21 To stress the finality of the conflict, John uses imagery drawn from the Old Testament, especially Ezek 39.17-20.
19.19 *The beast.* Obviously the beast of 13.1-10. *The kings of the earth: cf.* 17.2.
19.20 *The false prophet.* I.e. the second beast of 13.11-18. *The lake of fire.* An image used only in Rev, it is the final destination of all that is evil in the world, here the beast and the false prophet, later the devil (20.10), Death and Hades (20.14), and all evil people (21.8).
19.21 *The sword* with which the rider is victorious is *"the sword that came from his mouth."* This image is part of the author's pacifism: the church will conquer its persecutors, not by direct retaliatory violence, but by patient and persistent witness (*cf.* 13.10).
20.1 *Bottomless pit.* See note on 9.1.
20.2 *Ancient serpent.* Only here and in 12.9 is the serpent of Gen 3 identified as *the Devil and Satan;* see note on 12.9. *A thousand years.* Like all the other numbers, this is to be taken symbolically: John's readers are not to expect the final victory of Satan, Death, and Hades to come immediately, even within their own lifetimes (20.5). The "thousand years" are God's own time, not like ours (see Ps 90.4; 2 Pet 3.8). It is a time for the martyrs (Rev 20.4), free from Satan's working (20.3).
20.4 *Souls...beheaded. Cf.* 6.9; Mk 13.16-18.
20.5 *The rest of the dead. Cf.* 20.12. The consequences of death continue during these thousand years. *First resurrection.* This refers to the reign of the martyrs in 20.4.
20.6 *Blessed...* The fifth of the seven beatitudes in Rev; *cf.* 1.3; 14.13; 16.15; 19.9; 22.7,14. *The second death.* See 20.14; 21.8. *Priests of God. Cf.* 1.6; 5.10; Ex 19.6; 1 Pet 2.5.
20.7-15 Satan is released for the final battle and for his final destiny.
20.8 *Four corners of the earth.* Idiomatic of universality. *Cf.* 12.9; 20.3; 13.14; 19.20. *Gog and Magog.* According to Ezek 38.2,15, these two figures represent invading hordes from the north, poised to attack Israel.
20.9 *cf.* 2 Esd 13.1-12.
20.10 See note on 19.20.

beast and the false prophet were, and they will be tormented day and night forever and ever.

The Dead Are Judged

11 Then I saw a great white throne and the one who sat on it; the earth and the heaven fled from his presence, and no place was found for them. 12 And I saw the dead, great and small, standing before the throne, and books were opened. Also another book was opened, the book of life. And the dead were judged according to their works, as recorded in the books. 13 And the sea gave up the dead that were in it, Death and Hades gave up the dead that were in them, and all were judged according to what they had done. 14 Then Death and Hades were thrown into the lake of fire. This is the second death, the lake of fire; 15 and anyone whose name was not found written in the book of life was thrown into the lake of fire.

The New Heaven and the New Earth

21 Then I saw a new heaven and a new earth; for the first heaven and the first earth had passed away, and the sea was no more. 2 And I saw the holy city, the new Jerusalem, coming down out of heaven from God, prepared as a bride adorned for her husband. 3 And I heard a loud voice from the throne saying,

"See, the home[n] of God is among
mortals.
He will dwell[n] with them as their
God;[o]
they will be his peoples,[p]
and God himself will be with them;[q]
4 he will wipe every tear from their
eyes.
Death will be no more;
mourning and crying and pain will be
no more,
for the first things have passed away."

5 And the one who was seated on the throne said, "See, I am making all things new." Also he said, "Write this, for these words are trustworthy and true." 6 Then he said to me, "It is done! I am the Alpha and the Omega, the beginning and the end. To the thirsty I will give water as a gift from the spring of the water of life. 7 Those who conquer will inherit these things, and I will be their God and they will be my children. 8 But as for the cowardly, the faithless,[r] the polluted, the murderers, the fornicators, the sorcerers, the idolaters, and all liars, their place will be in the lake that burns with fire and sulfur, which is the second death."

Vision of the New Jerusalem

9 Then one of the seven angels who had the seven bowls full of the seven last plagues came and said to me, "Come, I will show you the bride, the wife of the Lamb." 10 And in the spirit[s] he carried me away to a great, high mountain and showed me the holy city Jerusalem coming down out of heaven from God. 11 It has the glory of God and a radiance like a very rare jewel, like jasper, clear as crystal. 12 It has a great, high wall with twelve gates, and at the gates twelve angels, and on the gates are inscribed the names of the twelve tribes of the Israelites; 13 on the east three gates, on the north three gates, on the south three gates, and on the west three gates. 14 And the wall of the city has twelve foundations, and on them are the twelve names of the twelve apostles of the Lamb.

15 The angel[t] who talked to me had a measuring rod of gold to measure the city and its gates and walls. 16 The city lies foursquare, its length the same as its width; and he measured the city with his rod, fifteen hundred miles;[u] its length and width and height are equal. 17 He also measured its wall, one hundred forty-four cubits[v] by human measurement, which the angel was using. 18 The wall is built of jasper, while the city is pure gold, clear as glass. 19 The foundations of the wall of the city are adorned with every jewel; the first was jasper, the second sapphire, the third agate, the fourth emerald, 20 the fifth onyx, the sixth carnelian, the seventh chrysolite, the eighth beryl, the ninth topaz, the tenth chrysoprase, the eleventh jacinth, the twelfth amethyst. 21 And the twelve gates are twelve pearls, each of the gates is a single pearl, and the street of the city is pure gold, transparent as glass.

22 I saw no temple in the city, for its temple is the Lord God the Almighty and the Lamb. 23 And the city has no need of sun or moon to shine on it, for the glory of God

[n] Gk *tabernacle* [o] Other ancient authorities lack *as their God* [p] Other ancient authorities read *people* [q] Other ancient authorities add *and be their God* [r] Or *the unbelieving* [s] Or *in the Spirit* [t] Gk *He* [u] Gk *twelve thousand stadia* [v] That is, almost seventy-five yards

20.11-15 A brief picture of the final judgment.
20.11 *The one who sat on it.* In Rev this is God the Father (see 4.2,9; 5.1,7,13; 6.16; 7.10,15; 19.4; 21.5); *cf.* Rom 14.10.
20.12 *The dead, both great and small. Cf.* 20.5. *The books were opened.* The ledgers on which people's deeds during their lifetimes were recorded. *The book of life. Cf.* 3.5; 17.8; 21.27; Isa 4.3; Dan 12.1; Mal 3.6. *Judged according to their works. Cf.* Jer 17.10; Rom 2.6; 1 Pet 1.17; Jas 2.18.
20.13 The point here is that no one will escape the judgment, no matter where they are.
20.14 See note on 19.20. *The second death.* Probably a reference to the fact that those who are banished to eternal punishment are temporarily resurrected from their first death.
20.15 *The book of life. Cf.* 3.5; 17.8; 21.27; Isa 4.3; Dan 12.1; Mal 3.6.
21.1-22.5 This section is John's vision of the new heaven and the new earth. Throughout apocalyptic literature, the conflagration of the old, corrupt world will be followed by a new creation. John's description of the new city of God contrasts with the old corrupt city described in Rev 17-18.
21.1 *The sea was no more.* From the sea had come the evil oppressors (see 13.1).
21.2 *Holy city.* I.e. a city set apart for God's use in the world. *The new Jerusalem. Cf.* Gal 4.26; Heb 11.10. *Coming down out of heaven.* God comes to his people (*cf.* 21.3). *As a bride adorned for her husband.* This city contrasts with the old, impure city, Babylon = Rome, which was described in terms of harlotry and drunkenness (17.2).
21.3 *cf.* Lev 26.12; 21.7; 2 Sam 7.14. *He will dwell with them.* The Greek word for "dwell" is "tabernacle" (see footnote *p*), the same word used in Jn 1.14: "The Word became flesh and tabernacled among us."
21.4 *cf.* 7.16-17; Isa 35.10. In contrast to the old city, which brought pain and death to its victims (18.24), God's new city will provide healing for the nations (*cf.* 21.4; 22.2).
21.5 See note on 20.11.
21.6 *The Alpha and the Omega.* See note on 1.8. *To the thirsty I will give water. Cf.* Ps 42.1; Isa 55.1; Jer 2.13; Jn 4.14; 7.37-38.
21.7 *Those who conquer. Cf.* 2.7,11,17,26; 3.5,12,21. *I will be their God and they will be my children. Cf.* Gen 17.7; 2 Sam 7.14.
21.8 *The second death.* See notes on 19.20 and 20.14.
21.10 *In the spirit.* See note on 1.10.
21.11 *The glory of God. Cf.* Isa 60.1,2,19; Ezek 43.5; Lk 2.9. *Clear as crystal.* Note the element of transparency; *cf.* 21.18,21.
21.12 *cf.* Ezek 48.30-34.
21.14 *cf.* Eph 2.20.
21.15-21 This section reflects the measuring of the temple in Ezek 40-41.
21.16-17 *Fifteen hundred miles* is the size of the city; *one hundred forty-four cubits,* i.e. about seventy-five yards (see footnote *v*), is the size of the city wall.
21.18 *Jasper* is a transparent gem; *cf.* 21.19. *Clear as glass. Cf.* 21.11,21.
21.21 *Transparent as glass. Cf.* 21.11,18.
21.22 There is no temple at all in the new city of God; God is fully present in the city, and is thus its *temple. The Lamb.* See note on 5.9.
21.23 *The Lamb.* See note on 5.9. Christ is the light of the new city of God. *Cf.* also 2 Cor 5.17.

20.11 Rev 4.2; Dan 2.35; Rev 12.8
20.12 Mt 16.27; Rev 2.3; 22.12
20.13 Rev 6.8; Isa 26.19; Rev 2.23
20.14 1 Cor 15.26; Rev 6.8
21.1 Isa 65.17; 2 Pet 3.13; Rev 20.11
21.2 Heb 11.10; 12.22; Rev 3.12
21.3 Ezek 37.27; 2 Cor 6.16; Rev 7.15
21.4 Rev 7.17; 1 Cor 15.26; Rev 20.14; Isa 35.10; 65.19
21.5 Rev 4.9; 20.11; Isa 43.19; Rev 19.9
21.6 Rev 16.17; 1.8; 22.13; Jn 4.10
21.8 Heb 12.14; Rev 22.15; 19.20; 2.11
21.9 Rev 15.1,6,7; 20.14ff
21.10 Rev 1.10; Ezek 40.2; Rev 17.3
21.11 Rev 15.8; 22.5; Rev 4.6
21.12 Ezek 48.31-34
21.14 Mt 16.18; Eph 2.20
21.15 Rev 11.1
21.23 Isa 24.23; 60.19,20; Rev 22.5

21.24 Isa 60.3,5
21.25 Isa 60.11; Zech 14.7; Rev 22.5
21.27 Isa 52.1; Joel 3.17; Rev 22.14; 3.5
22.1 Ezek 47.1; Zech 14.8; Rev 4.6
22.2 Gen 2.9; Rev 2.7; Ezek 47.12
22.3 Zech 14.11; Rev 7.15
22.4 Mt 5.8; Rev 14.1
22.5 Rev 21.25; 21.23; Dan 7.27
22.6 Rev 1.1; 19.19,21-5
22.7 Rev 3.11; 1.3
22.11 Dan 12.10; Ezek 3.27
22.12 Isa 40.10; Jer 17.10; Rev 2.23
22.15 Gal 5.19ff; Col 3.6; Phil 3.2
22.16 Rev 1.1; 5.5; Zech 6.12; 2 Pet 1.19; Rev 2.28
22.17 Rev 2.7; 21.2; Isa 55.1; Rev 21.6
22.18 Deut 4.2; Prov 30.6; Rev 15.6-16.21
22.20 Rev 1.2; 2 Tim 4.8; Rom 16.20; 2 Thess 3.18

is its light, and its lamp is the Lamb. 24 The
nations will walk by its light, and the kings
of the earth will bring their glory into it.
25 Its gates will never be shut by day—and
there will be no night there. 26 People will
bring into it the glory and the honor of the
nations. 27 But nothing unclean will enter it,
nor anyone who practices abomination or
falsehood, but only those who are written
in the Lamb's book of life.

The River of Life

22 Then the angel[w] showed me the
river of the water of life, bright as
crystal, flowing from the throne of God and
of the Lamb 2 through the middle of the
street of the city. On either side of the river
is the tree of life[x] with its twelve kinds of
fruit, producing its fruit each month; and
the leaves of the tree are for the healing of
the nations. 3 Nothing accursed will be found
there any more. But the throne of God and
of the Lamb will be in it, and his servants[y]
will worship him; 4 they will see his face,
and his name will be on their foreheads.
5 And there will be no more night; they need
no light of lamp or sun, for the Lord God
will be their light, and they will reign forever and ever.
6 And he said to me, "These words are
trustworthy and true, for the Lord, the God
of the spirits of the prophets, has sent his
angel to show his servants[y] what must soon
take place."
7 "See, I am coming soon! Blessed is the
one who keeps the words of the prophecy
of this book."

Epilogue and Benediction

8 I, John, am the one who heard and
saw these things. And when I heard and
saw them, I fell down to worship at the feet
of the angel who showed them to me; 9 but
he said to me, "You must not do that! I am
a fellow servant[z] with you and your
comrades[a] the prophets, and with those
who keep the words of this book. Worship
God!"
10 And he said to me, "Do not seal up
the words of the prophecy of this book, for
the time is near. 11 Let the evildoer still do
evil, and the filthy still be filthy, and the
righteous still do right, and the holy still be
holy."

12 "See, I am coming soon; my reward
is with me, to repay according to everyone's
work. 13 I am the Alpha and the Omega, the
first and the last, the beginning and the
end."
14 Blessed are those who wash their
robes,[b] so that they will have the right to
the tree of life and may enter the city by the
gates. 15 Outside are the dogs and sorcerers
and fornicators and murderers and idolaters, and everyone who loves and practices
falsehood.
16 "It is I, Jesus, who sent my angel to
you with this testimony for the churches. I
am the root and the descendant of David,
the bright morning star."
17 The Spirit and the bride say, "Come."
And let everyone who hears say,
"Come."
And let everyone who is thirsty come.
Let anyone who wishes take the water
of life as a gift.
18 I warn everyone who hears the words
of the prophecy of this book: if anyone adds
to them, God will add to that person the
plagues described in this book; 19 if anyone
takes away from the words of the book of
this prophecy, God will take away that
person's share in the tree of life and in the
holy city, which are described in this book.
20 The one who testifies to these things
says, "Surely I am coming soon."
Amen. Come, Lord Jesus!
21 The grace of the Lord Jesus be with
all the saints. Amen.[c]

[w] Gk *he* [x] Or *the Lamb.* [2]*In the middle of the street of the city, and on either side of the river, is the tree of life* [y] Gk *slaves* [z] Gk *slave* [a] Gk *brothers* [b] Other ancient authorities read *do his commandments* [c] Other ancient authorities lack *all*; others lack *the saints*; others lack *Amen*

21.24 See notes on previous two verses; Christ is the light of the nations (*cf.* Jn 8.12).
21.25 Everyone will have free access to this city at all times.
21.26-27 There are no racial or ethnic barriers: those who come to the city are one with those who dwell there.
21.27 *Book of life.* See note on 20.15.
22.2 *cf.* Ezek 47.1-12. *The healing of the nations.* This is the goal and the result of God's new creation.
22.4 *They will see his face.* The old warning of death at the sight of God is repealed (see Ex 33.20; Isa 6.5); in God's new city God's people will see God (*cf.* Mt 5.8; 1 Jn 3.2). *His name will be on their foreheads. Cf.* 3.12.
22.6-21 The Epilogue. This section comprises various statements whose specific speakers are often difficult to determine. There are many similarities to the Prologue (1.1-8), as well as to the section on the prophet's call (1.9-20).
22.6 *cf.* 1.1.
22.7 *Blessed...* The sixth of the seven beatitudes of Rev (*cf.* 1.3; 14.13; 16.15; 19.9; 20.6; 22.14). *Keeps the words of the prophecy. Cf.* 1.3.
22.8 The author is a duly commissioned prophet (*cf.* 1.1,9-10). *I, John. Cf.* 1.9.
22.10 This writing is a genuine prophecy (*cf.* 1.3) to be read in the assemblies of the churches (*cf.* 1.3; 22.16,18).
22.12 *cf.* 22.7.
22.13 *The Alpha and the Omega.* See note on 1.8.
22.14 *Blessed...* The last of the seven beatitudes of Rev (*cf.* 1.3; 14.13; 16.15; 19.9; 20.6; 22.7).
22.16 *cf.* 1.1,3; 22.18. *The root and descendant of David. Cf.* 5.5; Isa 11.1,10. *The bright morning star. Cf.* Num 24.17.
22.17 *The bride.* I.e. the city = the church (21.2,9). *Everyone who is thirsty. Cf.* Isa 55.1; Jn 7.37. *Water of life. Cf.* 22.1.
22.18-19 The author's warning against revision of his work.
22.19 *This prophecy...this book.* I.e. Rev itself.
22.20 *cf.* 22.7,12. *Amen. Come, Lord Jesus! Cf.* 1 Cor 16.22.
22.21 The normal closing benediction for New Testament letters (*cf.* 1 Cor 16.23; Eph 6.24). Rev began as a letter to the churches, to be read in the churches, and concludes with a blessing on all those who hear what has been read.

GLOSSARY

Entries for place names include, where possible, modern equivalent forms of the name – in italics after the Bible cross reference.

Aaron The elder brother of Moses who assisted him in the work of freeing the Israelites from slavery in Egypt, and whose family became hereditary priests. Ex 4.10–5.13; 6.20–27; 24.1–15; 28.1–29.35; 32; Num 20.22–29; Acts 7.40; Heb 5.4; 9.4.

Abana A river of Damascus. 2 Kings 5.10–12. *Nahr Barada.*

abba An Aramaic term of affection for father. Mk 14.36; Rom 8.15; Gal 4.6.

Abed-nego A companion of Daniel cast into the fire for refusing to worship Nebuchadnezzar's image. Dan 1.7; 3.8–30.

Abel The son of Adam, murdered by his brother Cain. Gen 4.1–16; Mt 23.35; Lk 11.51; Heb 11.4.

Abiathar The high priest, descended from Eli, in office during David's reign, who conspired against Solomon. 1 Sam 22.20–23; 23.6; 2 Sam 15; 17.15–16; 1 Kings 1.7–2.27.

Abigail The widow of Nabal whom David married. 1 Sam 25.2–43; 30.1–18.

Abijah The successor to Jeroboam as king of Judah. 1 Kings 15; 2 Chr 13. Others of the same name. 1 Sam 8; 1 Kings 14; 2 Chr 29; Neh 12.

Abilene A district in the E mountain range, roughly parallel to the Lebanon in N Syria, under the rule of Lysanias. Its chief town was Abila. Lk 3.1. *Sûq Wâdi Baradā.*

Abimelech (1) The Philistine king of Gerar who made a covenant with Abraham. Gen 20. (2) The son of Gideon. Judg 9.

Abishai The nephew of David, and his devoted and loyal follower. 1 Sam 26.4–12; 2 Sam 2.17–24; 18.1–13.

Abner Saul's cousin and commander-in-chief. 1 Sam 14.51; 17.55–58; 2 Sam 2.8–9; 3.6–34.

Abomination Gen 43.32; Lev 7.18; 11.13; 18.22; 19.7; 20.13; 1 Kings 11.5; 11.7; 2 Kings 23.13; Prov 3.32; 6.16; 8.7; 11.1; 12.22; 15.8,9; 15.26; 16.5; 16.12; 20.10; 20.23; 21.27; 24.9; 28.9; 29.27; Isa 1.13; 41.24; 44.19; Jer 2.7; 6.15; 8.12; 32.35; Ezek 18.12; 22.11; Mal 2.11; Lk 16.15; Rev 21.27.

Abomination of Desolation Dan 11.31; 12.11.

Abraham The son of Terah and the founder of the Hebrew nation. At God's call he emigrated, with his wife Sarah and nephew Lot, from Ur to Canaan (via Haran) where God made a covenant with him and promised that he would be the ancestor of a great nation. Gen ch. 11–25; Mt 3.9; 8.11; Mk 12.26; Lk 13.16; Jn 8.31–59; Rom 4; Gal ch. 3–4; Jas 2.21–24.

Absalom David's third and favorite son, who plotted against him. 2 Sam ch. 13–18.

acacia A tree, found in the Jordan valley, especially valued for its durability and much used in construction work. Ex 25.10; 26.26–28; Isa 41.19.

Accad A city in the land of Shinar or Babylonia which became the capital of Sargon I and gave its name to the whole of N Babylonia. Gen 10.10.

Achaia The Roman province, which included Greece, with its headquarters at Corinth. Acts 18.12; 19.21; 1 Cor 16.15–16; 2 Cor 9.2.

Achan An Israelite who broke Joshua's ban on looting after the fall of Jericho. Josh 7.

Achish The Philistine king of Gath who protected David from Saul. 1 Sam ch. 21; 27–29.

Acts of the Apostles *See* the Introductions, pp. 81–82 above.

Adam The Hebrew word for "man" or "mankind"; the name of the first creature made in the image and likeness of God. Gen 1.26–3.24.

Adder Any of a number of heavy bodied, poisonous snakes of the family Viperidae. Ps 91.13; Prov 23.32.

Adonijah The fourth son of David who conspired to seize the throne in rivalry to Solomon. 1 Kings 1.5–2.25.

adoption The act of taking officially the child of another as one's own. Ex 2.10; Esth 2.7. In the NT, sonship is not man's by nature but comes as the gift of God through Christ who is Son in his own right. Rom 8.14–23; 9.4; Gal 4.4–7; Eph 1.5.

Adramyttium A seaport in Mysia in Asia Minor. Acts 27.2. *Edremit.*

Adullam An ancient Canaanite city in the low country SW of Jerusalem. Nearby was the limestone cave where David hid from Saul. 1 Sam ch. 22–23. *Tell esh-Sheikh-Madhkûr*.

adultery In the OT unconditional faithfulness in marriage is demanded. Ex 20.14; Lev 20.10. In the NT Jesus goes beyond this in his teaching. Mt 5.27–32; 19.9. "Adultery" is also used metaphorically for the worship of false gods. Jer 3.8–9; Ezek 23.37; Hos ch. 1–3.

Adummim A place on the road between Jericho and Jerusalem. Josh 15.7; 18.17. *Tal'at ed-Damm*.

Advocate Found only in the writings of John, and used of the Holy Spirit in the sense of one who not only consoles but who, with authority, strengthens. Jn ch. 14–16.

Aeneas A paralytic healed by Peter at Lydda. Acts 9.32–35.

Agabus A Jerusalem prophet who foretold a famine and predicted Paul's imprisonment. Acts 11.27–28; 21.8–14.

Agag The king of Amalek, captured by Saul and killed by Samuel. 1 Sam 15.

agriculture The excavation of OT Jericho has shown that Palestine was one of the earliest agricultural countries with an irrigation culture existing around 7500 BCE. The principal crops were wheat and barley with a secondary crop of lentils, peas and beans. Vegetables, especially onions and garlic, were widely grown. The heavy winter rains gave the crops their major moisture, but the rains of March–April were needed to bring the grain to head. The cultivation of grapes, cucumbers and melons was made possible by the heavy summer dews in many parts of the country.

Agrippa (1) Herod Agrippa I who put James to death. Acts 12.1–23. (2) Herod Agrippa II before whom Paul made his defence. Acts 25.13–26.1.

Ahab Son of Omri and seventh king of Israel. His foreign-born wife, Jezebel, introduced the worship of the Tyrian Baal and she was denounced by Elijah. 1 Kings 16.28–31; 18; 20.34; 21; 22.

Ahasuerus Traditionally the Persian king Xerxes I. Ezra 4.6; Esth 1.1.

Ahaz The king of Judah who, when attacked by Syria and Israel, appealed for help to Assyria against the advice of Isaiah. 2 Kings 16.1–20; Isa 7.1–25; 14.28.

Ahaziah (1) The king of Israel, denounced by Elijah for continuing idolatrous worship, who died from an accident after a brief reign. 1 Kings 22.51–2 Kings 1.18. (2) A king of Judah who followed the pagan religious policy of the house of Ahab. 2 Kings 9.16–28; 2 Chr 22.1–12.

Ahijah There are nine of this name in the OT, the most important being (1) The great-grandson of Eli. 1 Sam 14.18. (2) The prophet of Shiloh who foretold the division of the kingdom. 1 Kings 11.29–39; 2 Chr 9.29.

Ahikam The son of Shaphan the secretary and one of the deputation sent by Josiah to the prophetess Huldah. Later, he was the protector of Jeremiah and the father of Gedaliah. 2 Kings 22.12–14; Jer 26.24.

Ahimelech Saul's high priest who assisted David at the cost of his life. 1 Sam ch. 21–22.

Ahithophel The politically skilled, but unprincipled, counsellor of David who committed suicide after the failure of Absalom's revolt. 2 Sam ch. 15–17.

Ai A royal city of central Canaan, close to Bethel, which strongly resisted Joshua's assault. Josh 7.2–5; 8.1–28. Excavations made at *Et-Tell* by Mme J. Marquet-Krause 1933–5.

Alexander (1) The son of Simon of Cyrene. Mk 15.21. (2) A kinsman of Annas the high priest. Acts 4.6. (3) A coppersmith who opposed Paul. 2 Tim 4.14.

Alexandria The city founded on the N coast of Egypt by Alexander the Great which became famous as an intellectual center and wealthy as a seaport. It attracted a large Jewish community, and the Septuagint was made here. It early became a strong center of Christianity. Acts 6.9; 18.24; 27.6; 28.11.

alien (1) People who put themselves under the protection of Israel and Israel's God, submitting to the requirements of the law, were given certain privileges. Ex 20.10; 22.21; Num 15.14–16; Deut 24.19. (2) Foreigners who did not share cultus-fellowship with Israel. Ezek 44.7–9. (3) People different from and hostile to Israel. Isa 1.7.

algum A cone-shaped tree which grows on the mountains of Lebanon and Gilead. Probably a red sandalwood. 2 Chr 2.8; 9.10–11.

almond A tree, growing wild in Palestine, but also cultivated for its fruit from which oil is produced. It grows to over 15 feet. Gen 43.11; Num 17.6–8; Eccl 12.5. Used figuratively Jer 1.11.

alms Something given freely to the needy; an act of charity. The Bible constantly insists that it is one of the duties of the religious person. Mt 6.1–4.

almug *See* algum. 1 Kings 10.11–12.

aloes A plant with thick, fleshy leaves from which hang bell-shaped flowers. A substance known as aloin, used in the making of spices, was taken from its leaves. Not to be confused with the succulent, aloe. Ps 45.8; Prov 7.17; Jn 19.38–40.

Alphaeus (1) The father of James the Less. Mt 10.3. (2) The father of Levi (Matthew). Mk 2.14.

altar Any raised structure on which sacrifices and incense were burnt and thus offered to God. The shape, size and material used varied widely. 1 Sam 14.33–35; 1 Kings 18.30–32. In the Tabernacle were two altars. Ex ch. 27; 30. New altars were made in Solomon's Temple. 1 Kings 8.64; 2 Chr 4.1, 19.

Amalekites Nomadic wanderers of the Sinai peninsula and desert regions in S Palestine from the times of Abraham to Hezekiah. Descendants of Esau, they were fierce enemies of the Israelites. Ex 17.8–16; Num 14.43–45; Deut 25.17–19; 1 Sam ch. 15; 30.

Amasa Nephew of David and commander-in-chief of Absalom's troops during his revolt. 2 Sam 17.25–20.12.

Amaziah A king of Judah who defeated the Edomites but was unsuccessful against the Israelites. After a long reign he was assassinated. 2 Kings 14.1–21.

amen A transliteration of a Hebrew word from a root meaning "to be firm, steady, trustworthy." Deut 27.15–26. It is used in the NT to express agreement with an act of praise or blessing. Rom 1.25; 1 Cor 14.16.

Ammonites Traditionally descended from Ben-ammi, they lived E of the Jordan and NE of the Dead Sea. Notorious for their cruelty, they worshiped the god Kemosh. Frequently at war with the Israelites, they were friendly for a time during the reign of Solomon. Gen 19.38; Judg 3.13; 1 Sam 11; 2 Sam 10; 1 Kings 11.7; Jer 49; Am 1.13–15.

Amorites A Semitic people who migrated to Canaan before the Israelites and inhabited mainly the hilly regions. After fiercely resisting the Israelite invasion, they became menials and were gradually absorbed when the land was settled. Ex 3.8; Num 21; Josh 12; Judg 3; 1 Kings 9.20.

Amos A shepherd from Tekoa in Judah who prophesied at the northern shrine of Bethel in the time of Jeroboam. Am 1.1.

Amos, Book of The theme is that religion divorced from morality is no religion at all. No idea of geographical limits to God's power is accepted. Jehovah is the God of all nations 9.7. Israel has been chosen by him and is therefore subjected to the greater judgment which goes with greater privilege and responsibility 3.2; 4.11–12. Since Jehovah is a God of justice, the Israelites cannot please him with sacrifices while continuing to practise injustice 5.21–27. Hence the urgent call to repentance; and the promise of prosperity if the call is heard and obeyed 9.14.

Amphipolis An important town on a bend of the river Strymon in Macedonia. Acts 17.1.

Anakim A race of very tall people living in S Palestine, driven from the Hebron district by Caleb. Remnants were left in the Gaza area. Deut 1.28. *See also* Num 13.22; Judg 1.20.

Ananias (1) A Jerusalem Christian who lied to the apostles. Acts 5.1–12. (2) The high priest presiding at Paul's trial before the Council. Acts ch. 23–24. (3) A Christian Jew of Damascus who baptized Saul. Acts 1–19.

Anathoth Personal name and also the name of a city of Benjamin allocated to the priests. It was the birthplace of Jeremiah. Josh 21.18; 1 Chr 6.60; Jer 1.1; 32.7–15. Excavations by A. Bergman of the American Schools of Oriental Research 1936. *Râs el-Kharrûbeh.*

Andrew One of the twelve apostles and the brother of Peter. A fisherman from Bethsaida, he lived in Capernaum and was first a disciple of John the Baptist. Mt 10.2; Mk 1.16–18; Jn 1.35–42; 6.8; 12.22.

Andronicus A Jewish believer, once a fellow-prisoner of Paul. Rom 16.7.

angel A heavenly being, attendant on God. Belief in angels was widespread in OT times, and was accepted by Jesus in his teaching. Gen 22.15–18; 1 Sam 29.9; 2 Sam 24.16; Ps 148.2–5; Isa 63.9; Dan 3.28; Mt 18.10; 22.30; 26.53; 28.5–7; Lk 1.26–38; 12.8; Acts 5.19; Col 2.18; Heb 1.4–7; 2 Pet 2.11.

angel of the Lord The messenger of God, sent by him to deal with men as his personal agent and spokesman. Ex 3.2; 1 Kings 19.5–8; 2 Kings 19.35; Ps 35.5; Zech 1.7–6.8; Mt 1.20; Lk 1.11.

Anna A widowed prophetess who, in the Temple, recognized the infant Jesus as the Messiah. Lk 2.36–38.

Annas High priest at Jerusalem from 6 CE until deposed by the Romans in 15 CE. His influence continued during the high-priesthood of his son-in-law, Caiaphas. Lk 3.2; Jn 18.12–24; Acts 4.6.

anoint Persons and places were anointed in both the OT and NT as a sign of holiness or setting apart for God. Ex 28.41; 30.22–33; Judg 9.8; 1 Sam 10.1–7; 16.13; 2 Sam 2.4; 1 Kings 19.16; Acts 10.38. *See also* 1 Jn 2.20, 27. In the NT anointing is also referred to as a sign of hospitality Lk 7.46. In connection with burial Jn 12.3; and spiritual healing Mk 6.13; Jas 5.14.

ant This insect is referred to only twice in the Bible, as an example of industry and wisdom. The most likely species is the Harvester Ant. Prov 6.6; 30.24–25.

Antichrist Used in the NT by John, to identify those who deny the deity of Christ. 1 Jn 2.18–22; 4.3; 2 Jn 7. The idea of a great power hostile to God appears elsewhere. Ezek 38; Dan 11; 2 Thess 2; Rev ch. 13; 17; 20.

Antioch (1) A Syrian city on the Orontes some 300 miles N of Jerusalem intimately connected with the spread of Christianity. Acts 11.19–30; 13; 14.26; 15.22–35; 18.22; Gal 2.11. *Antâkiyeh.* (2) A Roman colony and the administrative center of Galatia. It had a synagogue and was visited by Paul and Barnabas. Acts 13.14–52; 14.19–15.2; 2 Tim 3.11. *Yahaç.*

Antiochus Kings of the Seleucid dynasty who ruled over the western regions of Alexander's eastern empire: (1) Antiochus I who was compelled to replace his wife, Laodice, by Ptolemy's daughter, Berenice. *See* Dan 11.6. (2) Antiochus III, the Great, who annexed Palestine in 198 BCE. Dan 11.11–19.

Antipas A martyr of the church at Pergamum. Rev 2.13.

Antipatris The town founded by Herod the Great on the road between Jerusalem and Caesarea on the site of the Canaanite city, Aphek. Acts 23.12–31. *Râs el-'Ain.*

apes These are mentioned only among the animal imports made by Solomon, and the genus depends on the origin of the cargo. If it came from India these were probably langurs; if from Egypt, then baboons or vervet monkeys. 1 Kings 10.22.

Apollonia A town, standing between the rivers Strymon and Axino, through which Paul passed on his way from Philippi to Macedonia. Acts 17.1. *Pollina.*

Apollos A Christian Jew of Alexandria, famous for his oratory, who taught in Ephesus and Corinth. Acts 18.24–28; 1 Cor 1.10–17; 3.1–9.

apostle A commissioned envoy. (1) The Twelve chosen by Jesus to be eyewitnesses of the events of his life and his resurrection, and hearers of his teaching. Mt 10.2–4; Mk 3.16–19; Lk 6.14–16; Jn 20.21–29; Acts 1. (2) In later usage, Christian messengers accredited by a community. Acts 14.4,14; Rom 16.7; 1 Cor 12.28; 2 Cor 11.13; Eph 4.11.

Appius Forum A town on the Appian Way 40 miles from Rome. Acts 28.15.

apple A difficult tree to grow in Palestine, and the fruit is usually of poor quality. It is seldom cultivated today. Joel 1.12.

Aquila A Jew, banished from Rome, who settled with his wife Priscilla in Corinth, where Paul met them. Later they settled in Ephesus where their house became a Christian center. Acts 18.1–4,24–26; Rom 16.3–5; 2 Tim 4.19.

Arabah The rift running, mostly below sea-level, from the Sea of Galilee to the Gulf of Aqabah. Much of it is desert but copper was mined in the south. Josh 18.18; 2 Sam 2.29; 2 Kings 14.25; Jer 39.4.

Arabia Originally the N part of the peninsula between the Red Sea and the Persian Gulf, but later the whole of it. 1 Kings 10.15; 2 Chr 9.14; Ezek 27.21.

Aram A person, a people and a region: (1) The son of Shem, ancestor of the Semitic Arameans. Gen 10.22. (2) The area, largely NNE of Palestine, extending from Haran (E of the Euphrates) to Hauran (E of Galilee). Gen 24.10; Num 23.7; 2 Sam 8.5; 10.16; 1 Kings 15.18.

Aram-naharaim *See* Mesopotamia.

Ararat The mountainous area in the northern part of modern Armenia; one source of the Euphrates. Gen 8.4; 2 Kings 19.37; Jer 51.27.

Araunah A Jebusite whose threshing-floor was bought by David. It became the site of Solomon's Temple. 2 Sam 24.18–25. *See also* 2 Chr 3.2.

archaeology Biblical archaeology contributes enormously to our understanding of the Bible, and to our knowledge of the background against which it was written. It is detective work in the service of history which tries to fill up the gaps in our knowledge by reconstructing what happened from the clues which have been left behind. Archaeology gives us perspective and enables us to understand much more fully practices, circumstances and allusions in the Bible which were so familiar to the writer and his circle that there was no need to explain them.

Many of the interesting things which have been found in Palestine by archaeologists can be seen in museums. In the USA, the Brooklyn Museum, the University of Chicago, the Oriental Institute and the Boston Museum of Fine Arts have especially good collections.

The principal excavated sites are at Ai,

Anathoth, Ashkelon, Bethel, Bethlehem, Beth-shan, Beth-shemesh, Beth-zur, Capernaum, Carmel, Debir, Dibon, Dothan, Eglon, Ezion-geber, Gaza, Gerasa, Gezer, Gibeah, Gibeon, Hazor, Jericho, Jerusalem, Lachish, Megiddo, Mizpah, Qumran, Rabbath-Ammon, Samaria, Sela, Shechem, Shiloh, Succoth, Taanach, Tirza.

Areopagus A rocky hill opposite the Acropolis, and the meeting-place of the supreme court of Athens. Acts 17.16–34.

Aretas The name of four Nabataean (Arab) rulers, of whom one is mentioned in the Bible: Aretas IV who tried unsuccessfully to capture Paul in Damascus. 2 Cor 11.32–33.

Ariel A name for Jerusalem, probably meaning "altar-hearth." It is found on the Moabite Stone. Isa 29.1–8. *See also* Ezek 43.15.

Arimathea The town NW of Jerusalem from which came the Joseph who buried the body of Jesus. Mt 27.57–60.

Aristarchus A Jew from Thessalonica who was a fellow-worker with Paul. Acts 19.29; 20.4; 27.2; Col 4.10; Philem 24.

Aristobulus A Roman Christian. Rom 16.10.

Ark The name of the sacred chest, dating from the wilderness period, containing the tables of the law. In early times it was regarded as a symbol of the presence of God. Ex 25.10–22; Num 10.33–35; Deut 10.1–9; 2 Sam 6; 1 Kings 8.

Arnon A river flowing into the Dead Sea from the east, forming the boundaries of Moab and the Amorites. Num 21.13; Judg 11.18.

Aroer A town on the N bank of the Arnon where David's census began. It is mentioned on the Moabite Stone. Josh 12.1–3; 2 Sam 24.1–5; Jer 48.16–19. *'Arâ'ir.*

art Because of the commandment against representational art, Israel did little with painting and sculpture, but music was a familiar part of Hebrew life from early times. Ex 20.4.

Artaxerxes The Persian king who allowed the Jews to return to Jerusalem from exile and to rebuild the Temple. Ezra 7; Neh 2.

Artemis The Asiatic goddess of fertility, also known as Diana. Acts 19.24.

arts and crafts The Jews had a high regard for manual labor, and every boy had to learn a trade. The more skilled artisans lived in special quarters of the towns and formed guilds. Ezra 2.42. Artisans included boat-builders 2 Chr 9.21; brickmakers Gen 11.3; Ex 5.14; carpenters 2 Sam 5.11; Isa 44.13–17; Mk 6.3; embroiderers Ex 35.35; fullers 2 Kings 18.17; masons 2 Chr 24.12; metal-workers Ex 26.37; 35.32; 38.3; Num 33.52; 1 Kings 7.23; miners Job 28.1–11; potters Isa 30.14; Jer 18.6; smiths 1 Sam 13.19; Isa 44.12; spinners Ex 35.25–26; stonemasons 1 Kings 5.17–18; 6.36; tanners Acts 9.43; tentmakers Acts 18.3; timber-cutters 1 Kings 5.6,18; weavers Ex 35.35.

Asa The third king of Judah, known for his piety and religious zeal. His long reign was a time of prosperity. 1 Kings 15.8–24; 2 Chr ch. 14–16.

ascension The last post-resurrection appearance of Jesus to his disciples. Mk 16.19; Lk 24.50; Acts 1.1–11.

Ashdod A Philistine city commanding the entrance to Palestine from Egypt; the center of Dagon worship to which the captured Ark was taken. Josh 13.3; 1 Sam ch. 5-6; 2 Chr 26.6; Isa 20.1; Neh 4.7; 13.23. *Esdûd.*

Asherah A Canaanite fertility goddess sometimes worshiped in Israel. 1 Kings 18.19–40; 2 Kings 23.4–7.

Ashkelon A Philistine city on the coast between Joppa and Gaza, and the birthplace of Herod the Great. Josh 13.3; Judg 14.19; 1 Sam 6.17; Jer 47.7. Excavations 1920–2 by J. Garstang. *Khirbet 'Asqalân.*

Asia The rich and important Roman province in Asia Minor which comprised Mysia, Lydia, Phrygia and Caria, with its capital at Ephesus. Acts 19.10, 22; 20.18–19; 1 Cor 16.19; 2 Cor 1.8; 2 Tim 1.15.

Astarte The principal name for the Semitic goddess of love and fertility. Judg 2.13; 10.6; 1 Sam 31.10; 1 Kings 11.5,33; 2 Kings 23.13.

Assos A seaport of Mysia, where Paul embarked after going by land from Troas. Acts 20.13–14. *Berhamköy.*

Assyria, Assyrians The country E of the Tigris which took its name from its ancient capital, Asshur. Its rise and fall in the first half of the first millennium BCE played an important part in international affairs in the OT period. At its greatest extent the empire, centered on Nineveh, stretched from the Persian Gulf to the Mediterranean. Prophets like Isaiah saw in Assyrian aggression an instrument used by God to punish national unfaithfulness. 2 Kings 15.17–20,27–29; 16.15–18; 17.1–6,24–29; Ezra 4.2; Isa 10.5–12.6; ch. 36–37.

astrologer(s) Wise men who interpreted the messages of the gods and dreams from astronomical observations. The usage broadens to include all who practised magic arts. Mt 2.

1–12. *See also* Dan 1.20; 2.27; 5.15; Acts 8.9; 13.6.

Athaliah Daughter of Ahab and Jezebel, and the only woman to occupy the throne of Judah. 2 Kings 8.18,25–28; 11.1–20; 2 Chr 22.1–23.21; 24.7.

Athens The center of Greek culture where Paul preached. Acts 17.14–34; 1 Thess 3.1.

atonement God's appointed way of dealing with the problem posed by the sin of man and of reconciling sinners into a right relationship with God. In the OT *see* Ex 29.36; 30.10; Lev 16.17. In the NT *see* Jn 1.29; Rom 5.8–11; 2 Cor 5.18–19; Gal 1.4; 1 Tim 2.5–6; Heb 2.9–18; 9.11–10.25; 1 Pet 2.24; 1 Jn 2.2; 4.10.

Atonement, Day of Celebrated annually on 10th day of Tishri (September–October), and known today as Yom Kippur, it was the most solemn holy day of Israel and a strict fast. No work was done and, in addition to the regular sacrifices, the blood of an animal was shed to expiate the sins of both priests and people. Lev 23.27–32. *See also* Ex 30.10; Lev 16; Num 29.7–11.

Attalia The seaport of Pamphylia from which Paul and Barnabas sailed during the first missionary journey. Acts 14.25–26. *Adalia.*

Augustus The first Roman emperor. He ruled from 31 BCE to 14 CE and ordered the census of Lk 2.1.

avenger of blood One who carried out on a murderer the law of a life for a life. *See* Num 35.11–34; 2 Kings 14.5–7; Mt 5.38–48.

Azariah A common name among Hebrew families, especially among priests. Among the more important were: (1) The son of Ahimaaz. 1 Chr 6.9. (2) The king of Judah, also called Uzziah. 2 Kings 14.21. (3) The son of Oded, a prophet. 2 Chr 15.1.

Azotus The Greek form of Ashdod found in the NT. It was sacked on several occasions. Acts 8.40.

Baal (= "master" or "husband") A Canaanite agricultural god, who controlled the weather and fertility of man, beast and crops. Each locality had its own Baal which was worshiped at a hill-shrine, but these were gradually amalgamated into a single divinity. The Baal cult affected and challenged the worship of Jehovah and was denounced by the prophets for three centuries. Judg 2.12; 6.25–32; 1 Kings 16.31; 2 Kings 10.18–28; 23.4–7; 2 Chr 17.3; Jer 7.1–13; 19.5; Hos 2.8. It also occurs in place-names.

Baal-hamon (= Baal of abundance) The site of Solomon's vineyard. Song 8.11.

Baalis The king of Ammon who instigated the murder of Gedaliah. Jer 40.14.

Baal-zebub (Beelzebul) (= Lord of the flies) A Philistine god worshiped at Ekron. 2 Kings 1.1–16. *See also* Mt 12.22–28.

Baanah A Benjamite who killed Saul's son, Ishbosheth. 2 Sam 4.

Baasha A plundering king of Israel. 1 Kings 15.16–16.14.

Babel A city of Nimrod's kingdom where the tower was built. Gen 10.10; 11.2–9.

Babylon, Babylonia The country, and capital city, of the area bounded by the Tigris and Euphrates (Mesopotamia) which reached its peak under Nebuchadnezzar. As the place of Jewish exile in the 6th century BCE, it strongly influenced later Jewish thought, business and worship. The Bible is filled with prophecies against it. Isa ch. 13; 14; 21; 46; 47; Jer ch. 29; 50; 51. In the NT it refers to Rome in Rev 14.8; 16.19; 17.5; 18.1–24.

bags These were usually of leather, cloth or skin, sometimes fastened with a cord for carrying money or weights. Deut 25.13; 2 Kings 5.23.

baker, baking This was usually done by the housewife, but professionals existed in towns and were attached to royal households. Gen 40.2; Jer 37.21.

Balaam An occultist hired by Balak, king of Moab, to put a curse on the Israelites. Num ch. 22–24; Rev 2.14.

Balak A Moabite king. *See* Balaam.

balance (scales) A simple form was a crossbar with two hooks on slings hanging down. The word is used of mental or moral attitudes Dan 5.27. The prophets frequently stressed the necessity for just balances and true weights. *See* Lev 19.36; Am 8.5; Mic 6.11.

balm An evergreen shrub, reaching a height of 12–14 feet with white blossom and apple-like fruit, growing freely today around the Dead Sea. Gum resin from its bark was used for medicinal purposes. Gen 37.25; Jer 8.22; 46.11; 51.8.

balsam Probably the Mecca balsam (Balm of Gilead). 2 Sam 5.23; 1 Chr 14–15.

banquet (feast) Because of the eastern belief that a common meal establishes a close bond, these were usually (though not invariably: Esth 1; Dan 5) held on special occasions such as: weddings Gen 29.22; Jn 2; birthdays Gen 40.20; Mk 6.21; sheep-shearing 1 Sam 25.4, 36; vintage Judg 9.27; laying of foundations

Prov 9.1–5; weaning of a child Gen 21.8; offering a sacrifice Ex 34.15; Judg 16.23–25; the establishing of a covenant Gen 26.30. *See also* Mt 22.2–14; Lk 14.7–12. Also used in a literal and symbolic way in connection with the occasion when God would deliver his people. Isa 25.6; Mt 8.11.

baptism Ceremonial washing with water is often mentioned in the OT Ex 29.4; 30.17–21; Lev 11.25; 15; and converts from paganism to Judaism underwent a ceremony which included a bath of purification. A fuller meaning was given to the baptism which was characteristic of John the Baptist's ministry. Mt 3; Mk 1.1–13; Lk 3.15–17. Baptism by Jesus' disciples. Mt 28.19; Jn 3.22; 4.2. Baptism in the early church. Acts 2.38–41; 8.35–38; 9.18; 10.47–48; 19.1–6; Rom 6.3–4; 1 Cor 1.14–17; 12.13; Gal 3.27. *See also* Eph 5.26; Heb 10.22.

Bar An Aramaic word meaning "son," often prefixed to proper names. Mt 27.16; Acts 13.6.

Barabbas A bandit arrested for political terrorism. Mt 27.15–26; Mk 15.6–15.

Barak The son of Abinoam summoned by the prophetess, Deborah, to lead the Israelites against the confederate Canaanite forces under Sisera. Judg ch. 4–5.

barbarian Originally one who did not speak Greek, and therefore a foreigner. Col 3.11. *See also* Acts 28.2–4; Rom 1.14; 1 Cor 14.11.

Bar-Jesus A false prophet at the court of Sergius Paulus who opposed Paul in Cyprus. Acts 13.4–12.

barley A staple cereal cultivated universally from ancient times. Ex 9.31; Deut 8.8; Ruth 2.15–17; 2 Kings 7.1; Jn 6.3–13.

Barnabas A Levite convert from Cyprus who commended Paul to the Jerusalem church and became his fellow-worker. Acts 4.36; 11.19–30; ch. 13–15; 1 Cor 9.6; Gal 2.

Barsabbas The surname of the Joseph who was nominated to succeed Judas Iscariot. Acts 1.23.

Bartholomew One of the twelve apostles. Mt 10.3; Mk 3.18; Lk 6.14; Acts 1.13. On the grounds that this is a family name he has been identified by some with Nathanael. Jn 1.44–50.

Bartimaeus A blind man of Jericho healed by Jesus. Mk 10.46–52.

Baruch The aristocratic friend and secretary of Jeremiah associated with his prophetic work for over 20 years. Jer 36.4–20; 43.1–7.

Barzillai A wealthy Gileadite who befriended David when he fled from Absalom. 2 Sam 17.27–29; 19.31–40; 1 Kings 2.7.

Bashan A hilly, fertile region SE of the Sea of Galilee. Num 21.33; Deut 3.1; 29.7; Ps 68.15.

bat Several species of this animal, which thrives in hot climates, have been identified in Palestine. By the Law of Moses they were unclean, and not fit for food. Lev 11.19; Isa 2.20.

bathe, bathing Generally used in the Bible in connection with the ceremonial washing of the body in water. Travelers and guests were always offered this facility. Jn 13.10. *See also* Gen 18.4; Ex 30.17–21; Mt 6.17; Mk 7.1–8. *See* washing.

Bathsheba The wife of Uriah the Hittite. David married her after causing the death of her husband. She was the mother of Solomon. 2 Sam 11.2–12.25.

bear In biblical times the Syrian bear was found over most of the hilly, wooded parts of Palestine where the rock formation gave it good cover. It is now extinct. 1 Sam 17.34–36; Prov 17.12; 28.15; Hos 13.8.

beard To the Jews it was a mark of manly dignity, and was shaved off as a sign of mourning. To mutilate another's beard was to cause great humiliation. 2 Sam 10.4; 19.24; Ps 133.2; Isa 15.2; Jer 48.37.

Beatitudes The word, meaning "blessedness," is not scriptural, but is universally associated with Jesus' sayings in Mt 5.3–12; Lk 6.20–23.

Beautiful Gate A gate of the Temple, which was the scene of a healing by Peter and John, probably the bronze gate leading into the Court of Women. Acts 3.1–10.

bed (couch) In early times the poor slept on the ground using their outer garments as both mattress and cover; or sometimes a rug or straw-filled sack. Bedsteads were known quite early, and in elaborate form for the wealthy. 2 Sam 4.7; Am 6.4. *See also* Ex 22.26–27; Esth 1.6.

bee The Palestinian bee is small and plentiful, and the honey has been cultivated from biblical times. The name "Deborah" = bee. Deut 1.44; Judg 14.5–9; Isa 7.18.

Beer (1) A stopping-place in the wilderness wanderings between the Arnon and Jordan. Num 21.16. (2) The place to which Jotham fled. Judg 9.21.

Beer-lahai-roi A well where Hagar was met by an angel. Isaac also met Rebecca here. Gen 16.5–14; 24.62–67.

Beersheba The most southerly town of Judah, with many patriarchal associations; important because of its excellent water supply. Gen 21.14–20; 26.23–25; 28.10; Judg 20.1; 1 Kings 19.3; Neh 11.25–30; Am 8.14. *Tell es-Seba`*.

Bel The Babylonian equivalent to Baal, used as both a proper name and a title. Isa 46.1; Jer 50.2.

Beliar Used by Paul as a synonym for Satan. 2 Cor 6.15.

bellows The Egyptians especially, but the Middle East in general, knew the use of these for stimulating fire. Jer 6.29. *See also* Isa 54.16.

bells Small tinkling bells were worn as ornaments on women's ankles. They were also attached to the bottom of the high priest's robe, and to the harness of war-horses. Ex 28.33–34; Isa 3.16–17; Zech 14.20.

Belshazzar According to the book of Daniel the last king of Babylon, at the time of its capture in 539 BCE. Dan 5.

Belteshazzar The name given to Daniel in Babylon. Dan 1.7; 2.26; 5.12.

Benaiah The captain of David's body-guard who succeeded Joab as commander-in-chief of the army. 2 Sam 8.18; 23.20–22; 1 Kings 1.38; 2.35.

Ben-hadad A religious title of the kings of Damascus. Three of this name are mentioned in the OT. (1) 1 Kings 15.17–20. (2) 1 Kings 20; 2 Kings 8.7–15. (3) 2 Kings 13.24; Jer 49.27; Am 1.4.

Ben-hinnom A valley SW of Jerusalem associated with the worship of Molech. It was desecrated by Josiah and used for burning refuse. 2 Kings 23.10; Jer 7.31; 32.35.

Benjamin (1) The youngest son of Jacob and Rachel. Gen 35.16–18; ch. 42–44. (2) The tribe settled in Palestine between Ephraim and Judah. Josh 18.11–28; Judg ch. 19–21; 1 Sam 9. 1–2; Rom 11.1.

Bernice The daughter of Herod Agrippa I who was present with her brother, Agrippa II, at Paul's defence before Festus. Acts 25.23–26.32.

Beroea A town in Macedonia where Paul preached. Acts 17.10–13; 20.4. *Verria*.

Bethany A village less than 2 miles from Jerusalem on the road to Jericho, and the home of Lazarus and his family. Christ's ascension took place here. Mt 26.6–13; Mk 11.11; Lk 19.29; 24.50; Jn 11.1–46. *el-`Azariyeh*.

Bethel The Canaanite town of Luz 12 miles N of Jerusalem, renamed Bethel by Jacob. When the kingdom was divided it became a royal shrine for the north and a center of idolatry; and as such it was denounced by the prophets. Gen 28.10–19; 1 Kings 12.25–13.32; 2 Kings 10.29; Am 3.14; 5.5–6. Excavations by W. F. Albright and J. L. Kelso of the American Schools of Oriental Research 1935–8. *Tell Beitin*.

Bethlehem (= house of bread) A town 5 miles S of Jerusalem called Ephratha in Jacob's time, and the home of Naomi and Boaz. David was anointed here, and Micah's prophecy was fulfilled by the birth of Jesus. Ruth ch. 1–4; 1 Sam 16.1–13; Mic 5.2; Mt 2.1–2; Lk 2.1–16. Excavations by E. W. Garner 1934–6 and H. Richmond 1935. *Beit Lahm*.

Beth-peor One of Israel's last camp sites and the place where Moses was buried. Deut 3.29; 4.46; 34.6. *Khirbet esh-Sheikh-Jâyil*.

Bethphage A village close to Bethany on the Mt. of Olives from which came the colt used for the triumphal entry into Jerusalem. Lk 19.28–36. *Kefr et-Tûr*.

Bethsaida The village on the NE shore of the Sea of Galilee from which Philip, Andrew and Peter came. Mt 11.21; Lk 9.10–11; Jn 1.44; 12.21. *Khirbet el'Araj*.

Bethzatha A pool in Jerusalem, otherwise called Bethesda, where Jesus healed a cripple. Jn 5.1–7.

Beth-zur (= house of the rock) A city in the hill-country of Judah, fortified by Rehoboam. Josh 15.58; 2 Chr 11.7. *Khirbet et-Tubeiqah*. Excavations by the American Schools of Oriental Research 1931, 1957.

betrothal *See* bride, bridegroom.

Bible The work of many writers over a period of more than a thousand years. There are two collections of writings (Scriptures) in the Bible. In the OT (written almost entirely in Hebrew) are the remains of the literature of the Jewish people, the books of which took their final shape between the 8th and 2nd centuries BCE. In the NT are the writings of the Christian church during about the first half-century of its existence.

The central message of the Bible is the story of salvation in which three strands can be distinguished: the bringer of salvation, the way of salvation, and the heirs of salvation. God's message to all people has been communicated by his chosen spokespersons, and finally by Jesus Christ. *See* Heb 1.1–2.

Bildad One of the three friends of Job. Job 2.11; ch. 8; 18; 25; 42.7–9.

Bilhah Rachel's slave-girl who became the mother of Dan and Naphtali. Gen 29.29; 30.1–8; 46.25.

birds Palestine is a land very rich in birds

because of its wide range of climates varying from semi-tropical to true desert. Moreover, one of the main migration routes from Africa into Europe and W Asia runs from the northern point of the Red Sea through the whole length of the country, and there is some movement in progress almost every month.

birthright The special privilege and position belonging to the first-born son in the family who inherited the headship of the household and a double portion of his father's wealth. Gen 25.21–34. *See also* Deut 21.15–17; 25.5–10.

Bithynia The Roman province in NW Asia Minor bordering on the Black Sea which early attracted the attention of Paul. Acts 16.6–10; 1 Pet 1.1.

bitter herbs Salads eaten at Passover time. Ex 12.8; Num 9.11.

bitumen Mineral pitch with waterproofing properties found especially near the Dead Sea. Gen 11.3; 14.10. *See also* Gen 6.14; Ex 2.3.

Black Obelisk A black limestone pillar, about $6\frac{1}{2}$ feet high, found by a young English excavator, A. H. Layard, in 1846 at Nimrud, about 25 miles S of Nineveh where Shalmaneser III of Assyria had his palace. It is now in the British Museum. One of its carved panels in bas-relief shows Jehu offering Israel's tribute: the only known portrayal of an Israelite king.

blasphemy In the OT this was any attack on the majesty, honor or authority of God. Ex 20.7; Lev 24.10–16. The meaning is extended in the NT where God is blasphemed in his representatives. Acts 6.11.

bless, blessing In very early times this was a magical utterance or act, charged with power to bring about some desired good, often material, to a person. Only gradually was it understood in the fully religious sense as an act of God. Gen 27.7–40; 39.5–6; 48.12–20; Num 6.22–27; Deut 28.1–8; 1 Kings 8.54–61; Prov 10.22. The NT takes up and develops the idea and practice. Lk 6.28; Rom 12.14; 1 Cor 4.13; 1 Pet 3.9.

blight A fungus disease caused by damp. Deut 28.22; 1 Kings 8.37; Am 4.9; Hag 2.17.

blind, blindness A common condition in the Middle East, but also the result of old age. The Mosaic law commanded kindness to the blind; and by healing the blind Jesus fulfilled messianic prophecies. Lev 19.14; 21.18; Deut 27.18; Isa 29.18; 35.5; 42.7; Mt 20.30; Mk 8.22–25. *See also* Gen 27.1; 1 Sam 3.2.

blood Its use for food was forbidden. Gen 9.3–6; Lev 3.17; Acts 15.19–29. In the OT ritual it played a significant part. Ex 24.3–8; Lev 1.5; 4.6–7; 17.10–14; Deut 12.15–28. In the NT it is also used as a sacrificial term. Mk 14.24; Col 1.20; Heb 9.11–28; 1 Pet 1.19; 1 Jn 5.6. *See also* Rom 3.25; 5.9; Heb 10.5–14.

Boanerges The nickname (= sons of thunder) given to the brothers James and John. Mk 3.17.

boar The wild boar was plentiful in Palestine in biblical times, especially in the Jordan valley where it still survives. It is unclean to both Muslim and Jew. Ps 80.13.

boats The Israelites were not a seafaring people, and the Phoenicians held the best coastal harbors, but boats were used for inshore and lake fishing. Lk 5.1–11; Jn 6.16–24.

Boaz (1) A wealthy Benjamite who married Ruth. Ruth ch. 2–4; Mt 1.5. (2) The pillar on the N side of the entrance to Solomon's Temple. 1 Kings 7.21.

body of Christ Mt 26.26; Rom 12.5; 1 Cor 12.12–27; Eph 1.23; 4.1–16. *See also* Jn 2.21; Heb 2.14; 1 Jn 4.2–4.

boil A common term used in the OT to denote different kinds of local inflammation. Ex 9.9; Deut 28.27; 2 Kings 20.7. *See also* Lev 13.18–44; Job 2.7; Rev 16.2.

book The first writings were inscriptions on plaster and stone; but later materials were leather and papyrus which were kept rolled. *See* Deut 27.2–3; Isa 30.8; Jer 36.2; Ezek 2.9; 2 Tim 4.13; 2 Jn 12.

booths A simple shelter made of branches featured especially in the Feast of Booths (Tabernacles). Lev 23.35–43; Neh 8.15. *See also* Job 27.18; Isa 1.8.

Booths, Festival of The third most important of the great annual festivals. Kept from 15th to 22nd Tishri (September-October), it marked the completion of the fruit, wine and oil harvests and also commemorated the beginnings of the wilderness wanderings. Everyone born an Israelite had to live in an arbor made from branches during the festival. Lev 23.34–36,39–44; Deut 16.13–15; 31.10–13; Jn 7.2. *See also* Ex 23.16; 34.22; Num 29.12–39.

bottles These were usually made from complete animals' skins, most often goat, softened and tanned and used to hold wine, water, milk and other liquids. *See* Gen 21.14; Josh 9.4,13; Judg 4.19; Lk 5.37–38.

boundary A landmark between property, the removal of which was punishable by law. Deut 19.14; 27.17; Job 24.2; Prov 22.28; 23.10; Hos 5.10.

bow A weapon used for hunting and war, bent by either hand or foot, and made of wood with ox or camel gut string, and using arrows tipped with stone, bronze or iron according to period. Gen 27.3; Job 6.4; Isa 49.2; Lam 3.13; Ezek 39.9. *See also* Gen 21.20.

Bozrah (1) A city of Edom frequently mentioned in prophecy. Isa 34.6; 63.1; Jer 49.13,22; Am 1.12. (2) A city of Moab. Jer 48.24.

bracelet Worn by both men and women on the wrist or upper arm. Gen 24.22; Ezek 16.11. *See also* 2 Sam 1.10; Isa 3.20.

brazier Used for carrying hot charcoal. Jer 36.22. *See also* Ex 27.3; Lev 10.1; 1 Kings 7.50.

breastpiece (1) Part of the high priest's sacred vestments. Ex 28.3–30; 39.8–21; Lev 8.8. (2) Part of a soldier's defensive armor, generally of leather for the ordinary soldier and of metal for officers. *See* 1 Sam 17.5. Used figuratively. *See* Isa 59.17; Eph 6.14; 1 Thess 5.8.

bribe, bribery Strictly forbidden by the law. Ex 23.8; 1 Sam 8.3; 2 Chr 19.7.

bricks These were usually made of mud and straw and sun-dried. Gen 11.3; Ex 1.11–14; 5.6–19; 2 Sam 12.31; Isa 9.10; 65.3.

bride, bridegroom Betrothal and marriage customs. Gen 29.27; Judg 14.12; Ps 45.15; Isa 61.10; Ezek 16.8–12; Mt 25.1–12. Used metaphorically Mk 2.19; Jn 3.29; Rev 19.7–8; 21.2. *See also* 2 Cor 11.2; Eph 5.22.

bronze Much use of this brown-colored alloy of copper and tin, which was known to the patriarchs, was made in the Tabernacle. Ex 38. Other uses included the making of armor, chains, cymbals and idols. Num 16.39; 21.9; 1 Sam 17.5; 1 Kings 7.15–22; 1 Chr 15.19; Ps 107.16; Rev. 9.20.

broom A flowering desert tree highly valued as fuel. Its flowers and fruit resemble those of a pea. 1 Kings 19.4; Job 30.4.

burial It was customary for the Israelites to bury their dead. Gen 23.3–20; 25.9–10; 35.8; Deut 21.22; 1 Sam 31.11–13; 2 Sam 3.32; 1 Kings 13.22; Jer 14.16; Mk 15.46; Jn 19.40; Acts 5.6.

burning bush The scene of Moses' call. Ex 3.2; Mk 12.26.

burnt-offering *See* offerings.

butter Thickened or hardened milk; curds obtained by long churning in a goatskin bag. Ps 55.21. *See also* Gen 18.8; Job 20.17.

Caesar The official title of all Roman emperors. Those referred to in the Bible are: Augustus Lk 2.1; Tiberius Mk 12.14; Lk 3.1; Claudius Acts 17.7; 18.2; Nero Acts 25.11.

Caesarea The coastal city 60 miles NW of Jerusalem, built by Herod the Great and the residence of the Roman Governor of Palestine. Acts 8.40; 9.30; 18.22; 21.8–16; 23.23–25.14. *Qaisâriyeh.*

Caesarea Philippi A city at the southern tip of Mt. Hermon where the Jordan rises, built by Philip the tetrarch. Previously known as Paneas, it was near here that Antiochus III defeated Egypt and brought Palestine under Seleucid rule. Mt 16.13; Mk 8.27. *Bāniyās.*

Caiaphas The son-in-law of Annas and high priest 18–36 CE. Mt 26.3,57–66; Lk 3.2; Jn 11.49–53; 18.24; Acts 4.5–6.

Cain The first son of Adam and Eve. Gen 4.1–25; Heb 11.4.

cakes Various kinds are mentioned in the Bible, some being used in the sanctuary as offerings. Gen 18.6; Lev 2.4–7; Num 11.7–8; 2 Sam 6.19; Jer 7.18.

Calah A city of Assyria, on the banks of the Tigris, founded by Nimrod. Gen 10.11. Excavations by the British School. Giant alabaster slabs from the site are in the collections of Philadelphia, Boston and New York museums. *Nimrûd.*

calamus Sweet flag root yielding flavoring and perfume oil. Song 4.14.

Caleb One of the spies sent into Canaan by Joshua. Num ch. 13–14; Josh 14.6–14.

Calf, Golden The image made for the rebellious Israelites by Aaron during Moses' absence. Similar idols were set up by Jeroboam. Ex 32; 1 Kings 12.25–33.

camel The Arabian, one-humped camel, mostly used in ancient Palestine, can carry 400 pounds at an average of 28 miles a day and go for three or four days without water. Although its meat was forbidden by Mosaic law, its rich but not very sweet milk could be drunk or made into butter or cheese. Gen 37.25; Judg 6.5; 1 Kings 10.2; 1 Chr 27.30; Isa 30.6; 60.6; Mt 3.4. Used figuratively Mt 19.24.

Cana A Galilean village near Capernaum. Jn 2.1–11; 4.46–54; 21.2. *Khirbet Qana.*

Canaan, Canaanites All the land between the Jordan and the Mediterranean from Egypt into Syria. Its inhabitants were Semites. Gen 10.15–19; 17.8. *See also* Deut 34.1–4. Numerous excavations. *See* archaeology.

Candace The title of the rulers of Ethiopia. Acts 8.26–27.

candle, candlestick *See* lamp.

Capernaum A Roman garrison town and fishing center on the NW shore of the Sea of Galilee, used by Jesus as his headquarters. Mt 4.13; 8.5–17; 11.23; 17.24; Mk 1.21–2.12; 9.33; Lk 4.31–37; 10.15; Jn 4.46–53; 6.59. *Tell Hûm.* Excavations 1905–14 by the Deutsche Orient-Gesellschaft.

Caphtor The land (probably Crete) from which the Philistines originally came. Jer 47.4; Am 9.7.

Cappadocia The Roman province in E Asia Minor known as good grain country. Acts 2.9; 1 Pet 1.1.

Captivity (1) Of the northern kingdom of Israel in 722 BCE after a series of invasions by the Assyrians. 2 Kings 15.29; 17.3–6. (2) Of Judah in 586 BCE by Nebuchadnezzar. 2 Kings 24.14–16; 25.2–21; 2 Chr 36.2–7; Dan 1.1–4.

caravan A group of merchants traveling together for safety. Gen 37.25; Job 6.18.

Carchemish The capital of the Hittite empire, guarding the main ford of the Euphrates. 2 Chr 35.20; Isa 10.9; Jer 46.2. *Jerablus.*

Carmel A range of well-wooded hills between Samaria and the Mediterranean some 30 miles long and rising to 1700 feet in the NW. It had rich pasture land and was renowned for its beauty. 1 Sam 15.12; 1 Kings 18; 2 Kings 4.25; Song 7.5; Isa 35.2; Am 1.2. *Jebel Mâr Elyâs.*

carpenter A skilled woodworker capable of undertaking all carpentry tasks required in building. 1 Chr 22.15; Mt 13.55; Mk 6.3. *See also* Isa 10.15; 44.13–17; Jer 10.3–4.

Carpus A man of Troas. 2 Tim 4.13.

cassia Similar to the cinnamon-tree, it had many uses. A substance made from the pods and leaves was an important article of commerce; its bark was used as a spice, and its buds as a food-seasoning. Ex 30.22–25; Ezek 27.19.

castanets These take their name from the two chestnuts which in ancient times were attached to the fingers and beaten together to make music. Later, they were made from small spoon-shaped cymbals of wood or bone. 2 Sam 6.4–5.

Castor and Pollux Two gods (twin brothers) regarded as the special protectors of sailors in Greek mythology. Acts 28.11.

cattle Human wealth and the sacrificial worship of God in OT times centered around cattle which included oxen, bullocks, heifers, goats and sheep. Gen 13.2; Ex 34.19. *See also* 1 Kings 1.19.

Cauda A small island in the Mediterranean off Crete. Acts 27.16–17. *Gaudho.*

caves These were abundant in the soft limestone hills of Palestine and were sometimes enlarged for shelter and defense. Gen 19.30; 23; Josh 10.16–27; 1 Sam 22.1; 24; 1 Kings 18.4.

cedar A stately evergreen tree growing on the high mountains of the Lebanon and often reaching a height of 120 feet. It has a distinctive resinous smell, and its great durability made it a great favorite for use in furniture and boats. 1 Kings 5.6; 6.2–7.12; 9.11; Ezek 27.5. It is a symbol of strength, beauty, nobility, goodness, and of the Messiah. Ezek 17.22–24.

Cenchreae The eastern harbor of Corinth. Acts 18.18–21; Rom 16.1. *Kichries.*

censer An incense burner. 2 Chr 26.19; Ezek 8.11; Rev 8.3–5.

census The numbering or registering of the population. Acts 5.37. *See also* Ex 30.11–15; Num 1.1–45; 2 Sam 24.1–15; Lk 2.1–5.

centurion The commander of 100 soldiers in the Roman army. Mt 8.5–13; 27.54; Lk 7.2–10; Acts 22.25; 23.17; 27.1–43.

Cephas The name given by Jesus to Peter. Jn 1.42.

chain(s) Used as a mark of distinction Gen 41.41–43; Dan 5.7; for ornaments in the Tabernacle Ex 28.14; for fetters Ps 149.8; Isa 45.14; Lam 3.7.

Chaldaea(ns) Strictly S Babylonia and its semi-nomadic inhabitants, but later used for Babylonia as a whole. Gen 11.28–31; 2 Kings 24.2; 25; Jer 37.1–16; 39.1–14.

chameleon A lizard-like reptile flourishing especially in the Jordan valley where its effective camouflage makes it hard to see. It is famous for its ability to change its color to match its surroundings, and for its muscular tongue which can flick out to almost the length of its body when catching an insect. Lev 11.30.

chariot A two-wheeled vehicle used for war and state processions. In common use by their enemies, it only became a main arm of the Israelite army from the time of Solomon. Gen 41.43; 46.29; Ex ch. 14–15; 1 Sam 8.11; 2 Sam 8.4; 1 Kings 7.33; 9.19; 10.26.

chastity *See* Ex 20.14; Prov 5.3–6; 6.25–26; 7; Mt 5.28; 1 Cor 7.1–9; Gal 5.19–21; Eph 5.3; 1 Thess 4.2–8; Heb 13.4; Rev 22.14–15.

Chebar A river in Babylonia where a colony of exiles lived, and the scene of Ezekiel's visions. Ezek ch. 1; 3.23; 10.15–22; 43.1–3.

Chedorlaomer The king of Elam defeated by Abraham. Gen 14.1–7.

Chemosh The god of the Moabites whose worship was introduced into Jerusalem by Solomon. Num 21.29; 1 Kings 11.7,33; 2 Kings 23.13; Jer 48.13. *See also* 2 Kings 3.27.

Cherethites Mercenaries who formed the core of David's standing army. 1 Sam 30.14; 2 Sam 8.18; 20.7,23.

Cherith The brook, E of the Jordan, where Elijah lived. 1 Kings 17.1–7. *Wâdi Yâbis.*

cherub, cherubim Heavenly beings represented as winged creatures having hands and feet. Ex 25.16–21; 1 Kings 6.21–35; Ezek 10. *See also* Rev 4.6–8.

child, children *See* Ex 20.12; 21.17; Num 3.40–51; Prov 13.24; 20.11; 22.6; 23.13; 29.15; Mt 11.25; 18.3; Mk 9.33–37; 10.13–16; Eph 6.1–4; 2 Tim 3.15.

Chinnereth, Sea of *See* Galilee, Sea of.

Chinnereth A city in Naphtali which gave its name (which means "harp") to the sea of Chinnereth (Galilee). Num 34.10–12; Josh 19.35.

Chios An Aegean island in the Mediterranean. Acts 20.15.

Chloe A woman of Corinth. 1 Cor 1.11.

Chorazin A town near Capernaum which Jesus denounced. Mt 11.21; Lk 10.13. *Khirbet Kerâzeh.*

Chosen The thought expressed is present everywhere in the Scriptures. It is associated with the sovereignty of God in carrying out his purposes. See Gen 17.1–21; Deut 4.37; 7.7; Isa 42.1; 45.4; Jer 1.5; Mt 5.13–16; Lk 9.35; 10.20; 17.1–21; Acts 9.15; Rom 8.28–30; 9.11–16; 11.5; Eph 1.4–10; 1 Thess 1.4; 2 Thess 2.13; Titus 1.1; 1 Pet 2.9.

Christ The Greek equivalent of the Hebrew "Messiah" (= the anointed one). Jn 4.21–25; 20.30–31; Acts 3.12–4.12. *See also* Mk 8.27–30; 14.60–62; Lk 2.8–18,22–32; Jn 7.40–42; Acts 5.42; 9.22.

Christian The name for a follower of Jesus, first used at Antioch. Acts 11.25–26; 26.28; Gal 1.2; 1 Pet 4.16.

church The congregation of God represented by Christians meeting in community as God's people, wherever they may be. Mt 16.18; Acts 5.11–16; 9.31; 12.17; 18.22; 1 Cor 14.26; Eph 1.22; 5.25–29; 1 Tim 3.15.

Chuza The steward of Herod. Lk 8.3.

Cilicia The territory in SE Asia Minor whose capital was Tarsus. Acts 15.23,41; 21.39; 22.3; Gal 1.21.

cinnamon A spice obtained from the inner bark of the tree which grows in Arabia and Ceylon. Ex 30.22–25; Rev 18.13. Used as a figure of speech Song 4.14.

circumcision Commanded by God as the sign of his covenant with Abraham. Gen 17.9–14; Lev 12.3; Lk 1.59; 2.21. Insistence on it as an essential condition for membership of the church caused serious dispute. Acts 10.28–11.18; 15.1–29. Used figuratively Deut 10.16; Jer 6.10; Rom 2.29; Gal 5.6.

cistern An underground tank dug in the rock or earth for collecting rain-water. Lev 11.36; Deut 6.11; 2 Kings 18.31; Prov 5.15; Isa 36.16.

city, cities These are distinguished as places surrounded by a wall rather than by size. Lev 25.29; Josh 2.15; Jer 17.19. The prophets denounced their corrupting influence. Isa 1.21–23; Ezek 9.9; 24.6. The heavenly city. Rev ch. 21.

city of refuge A place of asylum set apart for those who had committed accidental manslaughter. Ex 21.12–14; Num 35.9–34.

Claudius The Roman emperor who expelled the Jews from Rome. Acts 11.28; 18.2. Reigned 41–54 CE.

Claudius Lysias The Roman officer who arrested Paul in the Temple. Acts 21.30–23.30.

clay Found especially in the Jordan valley and widely used in Israel. Job 4.19; 10.9; Dan 2.33.

clean, uncleanness Much of the Mosaic law was directed to securing the ritual purity of Israel. Lev 20.25; Deut 14.

Cleopas One of the two disciples met by the risen Jesus. Lk 24.13–35.

clouds Often used figuratively by biblical writers. Gen 9.13; Job 3.5; Isa 19.1; 44.22; Ezek 30.3. A symbol of God's presence. Ex 13.21; 19.9; 33.9; 40.34; Mt 17.1–7.

Cnidus A coastal port in SW Asia Minor. Acts 27.7.

coastland(s) In the OT this usually means "habitable land" or unknown territory at the end of the earth. Isa 41.5; 66.19; Jer 31.10; Ezek 27.15. It is used to emphasize God's rule. Ps 97.1; Isa 51.5.

cock By NT times it had become economically important and was regularly eaten by the Romans. It had long been used to indicate time and was carried on camel caravans as an "alarm clock." Mt 26.34; Mk 13.35.

cohort A subdivision of a Roman legion or the more lightly-armed auxiliary infantry. Acts 10.1; 21.30–33; 27.1.

colony An organized group of Roman citizen-soldiers with special privileges, settled at strategic points in conquered territory. Acts 16.12.

Colossae An ancient Phrygian city on the river Lycus, on the trade route from Ephesus to the Euphrates. Col 1.2. *See also* Col 2.1; 4.12.

Coming of Christ Mt ch. 24–25; Lk 21.27; Acts 1.11; 1 Cor 15.23; Phil 3.20; 1 Thess 3.13; 5.2; 2 Thess 2.1–12; Heb 9.28.

Commandments God's laws for his people given to Moses on Mt. Sinai. Ex 20.1–17; 34.28; Deut ch. 5–6; Mt 22.34–40.

commerce Until the time of the monarchy, the Israelites farmed and left trade to the Canaanites. After the exile they became engaged more and more in commerce, and this had become an accepted way of life by NT times. *See* 1 Kings 9.26–10.29; Prov 31.24; Isa 23; Ezek 27; Hos 12.7; Jas 4.13.

compassion A divine as well as a human quality, and synonymous with pity and mercy. Zech 7.8–10. *See also* Deut 14.29; 24.19; Ps 146.9; Prov 19.17; Jer 22.3; Mt 9.36; 11.28; Lk 7.13; Jn 11.33; 2 Cor 11.29; Gal 6.2; 1 Pet 3.8–12; 1 Jn 3.17.

conduit A channel, usually cut through rock, to bring water from its source. 2 Kings 20.20; Isa 7.3.

confess, confession Either an acknowledgement of sin before God. Lev 5.5; 26.40; Num 5.7; Mk 1.4–5; Acts 19.18; Jas 5.16. *See also* Ps 51. Or a profession of faith before men. Rom 10.9; Phil 2.11. *See also* Ps 48.13; Jn 9.22; 1 Jn 4.3, 14.

congregation Ex 12.6; 35.1; Lev 4.13; Num 10.7; 16.3; 1 Kings 8.14,65; Heb 2.12.

conquest of Canaan The biblical accounts show this to have been a complex operation, consisting partly of guerrilla warfare, well-planned campaigns and peaceful infiltration.

conscience Among Stoics, the human capacity to recognize the laws of nature. For some Jews, and for Paul, it became the awareness of what God reveals as right. Acts 23.1; 24.16; Rom 9.1; 1 Cor 8.7–13; 1 Tim 1.5,19; Heb 9.14.

consecration The setting apart of men or things for the service of God. Ex 13.2; 28.3, 41; 29.36; Lev 8.11; Num 3.13; 1 Kings 9.3.

contentment *See* Ps 37.16; 1 Tim 6.6–10; Heb 13.5–6.

conversion A turning to God. Acts 15.3. *See also* Mt 18.3; Jn 6.44; Acts 3.19–20; 11.21; 26.20.

cook, cooking Boiling was the most usual method but sometimes meat was roasted. *See* Gen 25.29; Ex 12.8–10; 23.19; 2 Kings 4.38. Professional cooks existed. 1 Sam 8.13; 9.23.

copper The most important metal in OT times. It was mined in Palestine and put to a variety of uses. *See also* bronze; Deut 8.9; Job 28.2.

Corban An offering dedicated to God and therefore not free to be used for other purposes. Mk 7.11–13. *See also* Lev 1.2; Num 7.3.

coriander A member of the carrot family, with leaves like parsley, which grows wild in Palestine. It has white or pinkish flowers and a round seed often used for flavoring bread and cakes. Ex 16.31; Num 11.6–8.

Corinth The capital of the Roman province of Achaia, situated on the Isthmus. Acts 18.1–8; 19.1.

cormorant A large fish-eating bird, regarded as unclean, commonly seen along the Jordan and the Sea of Galilee. Lev 11.17; Deut 14.17.

Cornelius A Roman centurion of Caesarea who was converted to Christianity. Acts 10.1–48.

Corner Gate A gate in the wall of Jerusalem. 2 Kings 14.13; 2 Chr 26.9; Jer 31.38.

corner-stone An important stone specially cut to hold together the sides of a building at the bottom, or the top. Ps 118.22; Isa 28.16. Used figuratively Mt 21.42; 1 Pet 2.5–7. *See also* Eph 2.20.

Cos A small island in the Aegean. Acts 21.1.

cosmetics Beautifying applications were valued by all peoples in the Near and Middle East. *See* Ex 30.25; 1 Sam 8.13; 2 Kings 9.30; Neh 3.8; Esth 2.3; Ps 45.8; Prov 7.17; Isa 3.24; Jer 4.30; Ezek 23.40; Am 6.6; Rev 18.13.

Council As depicted in the Mishnah and the Talmud (second–fifth centuries CE), this was the Sanhedrin, the highest court of justice of the Jewish people. Its origins are uncertain, but it was said to have been reorganized by Ezra after the exile. The number of members varied but its full size was seventy or seventy-one, and a quorum was twenty-three. Both Pharisees and Sadducees were members, and in NT times the influence of the former was strongest. The Council's president was the high priest, and when in session it sat in a semicircle. It had its own police force, authority to arrest and to inflict all penalties except the death sentence. In the NT, the Council, *synedrion*, was a group composed of leading figures in each district of the hellenistic and Roman empires. In Palestine it consisted of wealthy and priestly members. Mk 14.55; Acts 5.21; 6.8–15; 22.5,30.

covenant, new covenant An agreement between individuals, or between God and individuals or people, usually accompanied by symbolic actions. Gen 9.8–17; 17.1–14; Ex 34.10–28; Deut 29.1. *See also* Gen 31.44–54. The new covenant. Jer 31.31–34; Ezek 37.21–28; Mt 26.26–29; 1 Cor 11.25.

creation In Scripture always the act of God. It is used specifically of the creation of the world and all that is in, on and around it. Gen 1.1–2.4; 2.5–25; Ps 104.

Crescens A companion of Paul's sent to Galatia. 2 Tim 4.10.

Crete A large island S of Greece and once the center of Minoan culture. Acts 2.11; 27.6–15; Titus 1.5–14.

crime and punishment Actual crimes, civil and religious, were catalogued with their penalties in the several law codes. Ex ch. 20–23; Lev ch. 17–26; Deut ch. 12–28.

Crispus The chief ruler of the Jewish synagogue in Corinth. Acts 18.8; 1 Cor 1.14.

crocodile In ancient times the only species around the E Mediterranean was the Nile crocodile. It is a carnivore, largely aquatic, coming ashore only to bask in the sun and lay its eggs. Job 40.15–41.34.

cross, crucify The Roman method of execution for slaves and rebels. Mt 27.32–54. The theological significance of the cross. Mk 8.34; Rom 6.5; 1 Cor 1.17–24; Gal 2.20; 5.24–25; 6.14; Eph 2.16; Phil 2.5–11; Col 2.13–15. *See also* 1 Pet 4.13.

crown, crown of thorns A symbol of authority of one kind or another, worn on the head. 2 Sam 1.10; 12.30; Ps 21.3; Zech 6.11; Mk 15.17. Used symbolically Prov 12.4; 16.31. *See also* 1 Cor 9.25.

cucumber A common variety, smaller than the western species, is indigenous to NW India and spread to the Mediterranean area in quite early times. Num 11.5; Isa 1.8.

cummin A small, delicate plant whose fruit had medicinal uses and whose seed is used as a spice. Isa 28.25–27; Mt 23.23.

cup(s) These were of many materials, shapes and sizes, and for both secular and religious use, but the commonest form was a bowl, wider and shallower than the modern tea cup and made of pottery. 2 Sam 12.3; 1 Kings 7.26; 2 Kings 12.13; Mt 26.27. Used symbolically Mt 23.25; 26.39; Rev 17.4.

cupbearer A palace official of high trust. 1 Kings 10.5; 2 Chr 9.4; Neh 2.1. *See also* Gen 40.1–23.

curds A substance made from milk by churning in a goatskin bag, similar to yoghurt. Gen 18.8; Job 20.17.

curse On the human level to wish harm to someone; on the divine to impose judgment. Gen 3; Num 22.4–12; Deut 11.26–28; 27; Josh 6.26; Jer 17.5; Mt 25.41; Lk 6.28; Rom 12.14; Gal 3.10–14. *See also* Ex 20.7; 21.17; 22.28; Lev 24.11.

curtain The curtain separating the holy place from the holy of holies in the Temple. Ex 26.31–35. *See also* Mt 27.50–51; Heb 6.19–20; 10.19–20.

cymbals These were used especially in OT times at festivals and ceremonies. Some were concave plates of brass or bronze clanged together. Others were a neat conical shape with handles and were beaten together vertically. 2 Sam 6.5; 1 Chr 15.19; Ezra 3.10; Ps 150.5; 1 Cor 13.1.

Cyprus A large island in the Mediterranean. A contingent of troops from here were in the Seleucid army, and Nicanor was governor of the island. Acts 4.36; 11.19–20; 13.4–12; 15.39; 21.16.

Cyrene A city of Libya in N Africa. Mt 27.32; Acts 2.10; 6.9; 11.20; 13.1.

Cyrus "The Mede" and founder of the Persian empire who permitted the Jews to return home to Palestine from exile to rebuild the Temple 2 Chr 36.22–23; Ezra 1.1–11; Dan 1.21; 6.28; 10.1.

Cyrus Cylinder During extensive excavations in Babylon carried out by Hormuzd Rassam 1879–82 a clay, barrel-shaped inscription in cuneiform writing was found. It is now in the British Museum. It gives Cyrus the Mede's own account of his overthrow of the Babylonian empire in 539 BCE, and scholars date it about 536 BCE. It also records the release of the Jews and their return to Jerusalem. *See* 2 Chr 36.23; Ezra 1.1,5; Ps 137.

Dagon A Philistine god with a temple at Ashdod. Judg 16.23; 1 Sam 5.1–5; 1 Chr 10.10.

Dalmanutha On the W coast of the Sea of Galilee. Mk 8.10.

Dalmatia A district on the E coast of the Adriatic. 2 Tim 4.10.

Damascus The capital of Syria, strategically placed at a road terminus some 130 miles NE of Jerusalem. Gen 14.15; 15.2; 2 Sam 8.5; 1 Kings 20.34; 2 Kings 16.10–11; Isa 8.4. In NT times it had a large colony of Jews. Acts 9; 22.5–16.

Dan (1) The territory occupied by this tribe. Josh 19.40–48; Judg 1.34. (2) The city, formerly Laish, occupied by the Danites. Judg

18.29; 20.1; 1 Kings 12.25–30. *Tell el Qâdi.* (3) The son of Jacob by Bilhah. Gen 30.1–6.

dancing There are occasional references to secular dancing in the Bible, but generally it had a religious or ritualistic function. Ex 15.20–21; 32.19; Judg 21.21; 1 Sam 18.6; 2 Sam 6.13–16; Eccl 3.4; Mk 6.22; Lk 7.32; 15.25.

Daniel (1) A post-exilic priest. Ezra 8.2; Neh 10.6. (2) A son of David 1 Chr 3.1. (3) The central figure of the book of Daniel.

Darius (1) The Great, who reorganized the Persian empire and assisted in the restoration of the Temple at Jerusalem after the exile. Ezra 4.5; 5.6; Hag 1.1; 2.10; Zech 1.1,7. (2) The Mede. Dan 5.31–6.9. (3) Darius III, the Persian. Neh 12.22.

David The youngest son of Jesse and the second king of Israel. His conquest of Edom and Syria gave him an opportunity to develop profitable commercial activities, but these were not exploited until the time of his son, Solomon. 1 Sam ch. 16–31; 2 Sam ch. 1–24; 1 Kings ch. 1–2.

David, City of (1) The former Jebusite stronghold and most ancient part of Jerusalem, southeast of the temple site. 2 Sam 5.6–8. Excavations by the Palestine Exploration Fund 1924. (2) Bethlehem, his ancestral home. Lk 2.4,11.

day The Israelites counted their day from one sunset to another. Ex 12.18; Lev 23.32.

Day of the Lord This was popularly regarded as the time when God would destroy Israel's enemies. Amos declared that it would involve the certainty of judgment for all peoples, including Israel. Am 5.18–20; Joel ch. 1–2. In the NT it is the second coming of Christ. 1 Cor 1.8; 5.5; Phil 1.6–11; 1 Thess 5.2; 2 Thess 2.1–12; 2 Pet 3.2–14.

deacon Phil 1.1; 1 Tim 3.8–13. *See also* Acts 6.2–6.

Dead Sea The lowest stretch of water in the world, into which the Jordan flows. It has no outlet, and its waters are so salty that no fish can live in them. Gen 14.3; Num 34.3; Deut 3.17.

Dead Sea Scrolls The popular name given to the collection of biblical and sectarian manuscripts found at Qumran and other regions W of the Dead Sea in 1947 and following years. Fragments of every book in the OT except Esther have been found in the caves, and are now housed at the Hebrew University of Jerusalem. Many readings from the Scrolls, especially in the book of Isaiah, have been included in recent translations of the Bible.

death The lot of all men and the result of sin, but conquered by Christ. 2 Sam 14.14; Rom 5.12; 6.23; 1 Cor 15.12–29; 2 Tim 1.10.

Debir (1) City in the hill-country of Judah. Josh 11.21; 15.15. *Tell Beit Mirsim.* Excavations by Albright and Kyle of the American Schools of Oriental Research 1926–32. (2) The king of Eglon. Josh 10.1–10.

Deborah The prophetess who inspired Barak to deliver Israel. Judg ch. 4–5.

debt Regarded as a misfortune. Usury was forbidden by the Mosaic law, and the poor were protected. *See* Ex 22.25–27; Lev 25.25–55; Deut 28.12.

Decapolis *See* Ten Towns.

deceit 1 Pet 3.10. *See also* Ps 5.6; 36.3; Prov 24.28; Isa 53.9; Mk 7.22; Rom 1.28–32; 3.13; 1 Thess 2.3–4; 1 Pet. 2.21–22.

Decision, Valley of The place of God's judgment on the nations. Joel 3.14.

Dedication, Feast of A festival kept on 25th Kislev (November–December) in honor of the purifying of the Temple by Judas Maccabaeus in 164 BCE after its desecration by Antiochus Epiphanes. It was also known as the Feast of Lights since each evening for eight days the Temple and houses were specially lit with lamps. It is known today as Hanukkah. Jn 10.22.

Delilah The Philistine woman who outwitted Samson. Judg 16.4–22.

Demas A companion of Paul in prison. Col 4.14; 2 Tim 4.10; Philem 24.

Demetrius A silversmith of Ephesus. Acts 19.23–41.

denarius A Roman silver coin reckoned as a day's wage. *See* Mt 20.9; Mk 12.13–17.

Derbe A city in the Roman province of Galatia. Acts 14.6–7; 16.1. *Kerti Hüyük.*

Devil The personification of all evil and all that is against God. Mt 4.1–11; 13.39; Jn 8.44; 13.2; Eph 6.11; 1 Tim 3.6; Heb 2.14; 1 Jn 3.8; Rev 2.10; 12.9; 20.2,10.

dew Plentiful in Palestine at certain seasons and a great help in growing fruit and vegetables. It is used figuratively of the word and power of God. Deut 32.2; Isa 26.19.

Dibon A city E of the Dead Sea and N of the Arnon. The Moabite Stone was found here. Num 21.29–30; Josh 13.8–9. Excavations by the American Schools of Oriental Research 1950–57 have shown occupation from the Early Bronze to Arab time with a gap from *c.* 1850 to 1300 BCE. *Dhībān*

dill A flower, also grown in Europe, with grey-green foliage and upright yellow flowers whose leaves and seeds were used for flavoring and medicinal purposes. Isa 28.25–27; Mt 23.23.

Dinah The daughter of Jacob by Leah. Gen 30.21; 34.

Dionysius A member of the Court of Areopagus. Acts 17.34.

Diotrephes An unworthy member of the church. 3 Jn 9–10.

disciples Literally "learners": the followers of a religious leader. Isa 8.16; Mt 10.1; Mk 2.18; Lk 6.17; Jn 1.35; 6.66; Acts 6.1–7.

disease In biblical times this was regarded as closely connected with sin or some breach of the law. *See* Gen 12.17; Num 12.9; 2 Sam 12.15; Mt 9.2,35; Lk 13.16; Jn 9.1–3; 2 Cor 12.7.

disobedience *See* Gen 3.1–7; Isa 3.8–9; Jer 9.12–16; 12.17; 18.8–10; Eph 5.6–17; Titus 1.16; 3.3.

Dispersion Forecast as the penalty for the breaking of the law. *See* Lev 26.14–33; Deut 28.58–68. Many Jews did not return from the exile, and settlements outside Palestine continued to spread widely throughout the Graeco-Roman world. These communities, known as the Dispersion or Diaspora, retained their faith and worship, and provided the Christians with their first opportunities of preaching the gospel.

divination Attempts to foretell the future by abnormal means. Gen 44.5,15; Ezek 13.6–7. *See also* 1 Sam 28.8; Isa 47.13; Ezek 21.21; Acts 16.16.

divisions Condemned in the church as contrary to the mind of Christ. 1 Cor 1.10–13. *See also* Mt 12.25–27; Jn 10.16–17; 17.20–23; Rom 16.17; 1 Cor 3.1–9; 11.17–22.

divorce In the OT Deut 24.1–4. In the NT Mt 5.31–32; 19.3–9; Mk 10.2–12; 1 Cor 7.10–16.

doctors of the law Mk 7.1; Acts 6.12. *See* lawyers.

Doeg An Edomite herdsman of Saul. 1 Sam 21.7; 22.7–23.

dog Although highly valued in Egypt and Mesopotamia, in Palestine the dog was mainly a pariah and scavenger, and did in the larger towns what the hyenas helped to do outside the walls. Ex 22.31; 1 Sam 17.43; 2 Sam 16.9; 2 Kings 8.13; 9.30–37; Job 30.1; Ps 59.6; Isa 56.10; Mt 7.6; Lk 16.21.

donkey The donkey is mentioned over one hundred times in the Bible. The secret of its success in Mediterranean countries is that it is both sure-footed and is able to manage on poor forage. The Hebrews were one of the few people who rode donkeys. Ex 21.33; Isa 1.3; 30.24; Zech 9.9.

Dorcas A Christian woman of Joppa, also called Tabitha. Acts 9.36–41.

Dothan A city N of Shechem associated with Joseph, Elijah and Holophernes. Gen 37.12–35; 2 Kings 6.8–19; *Tell Dôthā.* Excavations have revealed continuous occupation from the early Bronze Age to the time of the Assyrian invasion *c.* 725 BCE. Areas of the Iron Age town have been cleared to show the narrow streets and small houses of Elisha's day.

dove, turtle-dove The poetic name for pigeons of which there are several varieties in Palestine. It was used as a sacrifice by the poorer people. Lev 1.14; Ps 55.6; Song 2.12; Isa 38.14; 60.8; Jer 48.28; Lk 2.22–24. Christian artists have used it as a symbol for peace, hope and the Holy Spirit. Lk 3.21–22.

dreams One of the means by which God communicates with men. Gen ch. 40–41; Num 12.6; Job 33.15–18; Dan 2.24–30; Mt 1.20; 2.12–13; 27.19.

dress Originally animal skins were worn. Gen 3.21; 2 Kings 1.8; Mt 3.4. Then came the use of wool or linen. Prov 31.13. Apart from the veil, women's dress differed little basically from men's, consisting of a long shirt or tunic reaching to the ankles and close-fitting at the neck, with a belt. Ex 28.4; Job 30.18; Jer 13.1. An outer garment or cloak was protection against cold. Ex 22.26. Workmen wore loincloths. Isa 3.24.

dromedary A thoroughbred camel used for riding and racing, and longer in the leg than the freight camel. Isa 66.20.

drunkenness Lk 21.34; Gal 5.16–21; Eph 5.15–18. *See also* Isa 5.11; 28.7; Hos 4.18.

Drusilla The wife of Felix. Acts 24.24.

dung Used in the Middle East today, as in biblical times, both for fuel and manure. Ezek 4.12,15. *See also* Lk 13.8.

Dung Gate One of the eleven gates of Jerusalem. Neh 3.14.

Dura The plain where Nebuchadnezzar set up his image. Dan 3.1.

dust Used literally and in simile for multitude Gen 13.16; Isa 29.5; smallness Deut 9.21; poverty 1 Sam 2.8; abasement Gen 18.27; sorrow Job 2.12; Rev 18.19; contrition Josh 7.6; lowliness Gen 2.7; 3.19; Job 4.19; 42.6; judgment Mt 10.14; Acts 13.51.

eagle There are several species of this bird in Palestine. Though not strictly a scavenger, its flesh was forbidden as food. It is often used as a figure of speech because of its graceful flight and skill in caring for its young. Deut 28.49; 32.11; 2 Sam 1.23; Job 39.27; Prov 23.5; Mic 1.16; Rev 4.7.

ear(s) Hearing, for the Hebrews, involved the whole personality. "Ear" and "to hear" signify attention resulting in obedience. Ex 29.20; Ps 40.6; Isa 6.10; Jer 6.10; Mt 11.15.

earrings Worn more often by women. Ex 32.2. Rings were also worn in the nose. Gen 24.22; Isa 3.20; Ezek 16.12.

earthquake In the biblical record, earthquakes are recorded at various periods. 1 Sam 14.15; 1 Kings 19.11; Ps 18.7; Mt 27.51–54; Acts 16.26. Used in prophetic imagery. Isa 29.6; Mk 13.8; Rev 6.12; 8.5; 11.13.

Ebal The mountain near Shechem where Joshua erected a copy of the law on stones. Deut 11.29; 27.4,13; Josh 8.30–35. *Jebel Eslāmîyeh.*

Ebed-melech The Ethiopian or Cushite who rescued Jeremiah. Jer 38.7–13; 39.15–18.

Eben-ezer (1) The scene of two battles with the Philistines and the loss of the Ark 1 Sam 4.1–11; 5.1. (2) A stone erected by Samuel. 1 Sam 7.12.

Ecbatana The capital of Media where the decree of Cyrus was found. Ezra 6.2.

Eden The first home of Adam and Eve. Gen 2.8–17; 3.24; Isa 51.3; Ezek 28.13; 36.35.

Edom The hill country S of the Dead Sea. Gen 32.3; Num 20.14–21; 24.18; 1 Sam 14.47; 2 Kings 3.8.

Edomites Descendants of Esau but hostile to the Israelites. Deut 23.7.

education This was pre-eminently religious and children were taught at home in early times. Deut 6.20–25; Prov 1.7. After the exile, the Book of the Law became the textbook and the synagogue the place of instruction. Neh 8.1–8.

Eglon A city destroyed by Joshua. Josh 10.3–10,34; 12.12. Excavations in 1890 by W. F. Petrie brought to light pottery and weapons.

Egypt The Nile basin from the Mediterranean to the first cataract. The Hebrew settlement there. Gen ch. 42–50; Ex ch. 1–2. Later relations between it and Israel and Judah. 1 Kings 3.1; 14.25–26; 2 Kings 23.28–29; Isa 36.4–6; Jer 37.3–8; Mt 2.13. After the death of Alexander the Great, Egypt came under the rule of the Ptolemies for more than a century until the time of Antiochus III.

Egyptian The terrorist for whom Paul was mistaken in Jerusalem. Acts 21.38.

Ekron The northernmost of the five great Philistine cities. Josh 13.3; 1 Sam 5.1–12; 2 Kings 1.2–6; Am 1.8.

Elam The country E of Babylonia whose capital was Susa. Gen 14.1–16; Neh 1.1; Isa 21.2; Jer 49.34–39; Ezek 32.24; Dan 8.2.

Eldad One of Moses' elders. Num 11.26–29.

elder One of the older men of a community appointed to take decisions. Ex 3.16; 24.1; Num 11.25; Deut 19.12; 21.2; 25.7; 1 Sam 8.4; 2 Sam 5.3; 1 Kings 8.1; 2 Kings 23.1; Ezek 8.1; Mt 27.12; Acts 14.23; 20.17; Jas 5.14; 1 Pet 5.1–5.

Eleazar (1) Aaron's third son who succeeded him as high priest. Num 20.25–28. (2) One of David's heroes. 2 Sam 23.9.

Elephantine Papyri These are Aramaic documents and letters, now in the Brooklyn Museum, USA, which have gradually come to light since 1893, all dating from the 5th century BCE when the Jewish colony on the island of Elephantine in the Nile opposite Aswan acted as a military garrison for the Persian conquerors of Egypt.

Eli The priest of Shiloh who judged Israel for forty years, and who brought up Samuel. 1 Sam 1.9–4.18.

Eliakim The overseer of Hezekiah's household was sent to negotiate with Sennacherib. 2 Kings 18.18; Isa 22.20–25.

Eliezer (1) Abraham's servant. Gen 15.2. (2) The second son of Moses. Ex 18.4.

Elihu (1) An ancestor of Samuel. 1 Sam 1.1. (2) A friend and adviser of Job. Job ch. 32–37.

Elijah The prophet from Tishbe in Gilead who opposed the cult of the god Baal during the reigns of Ahab and Ahaziah. 1 Kings 17.1–19.21; 2 Kings 1.1–2.11; Mt 11.14; 17.11; Mk 6.14–15; 8.27–28.

Elim A camp site in the wilderness wanderings. Ex 15.27; Num 33.9.

Elimelech The husband of Naomi. Ruth 1.1–3; 2.1; 4.1–10.

Eliphaz (1) The son of Esau. Gen 36.4. (2) One of Job's three friends. Job 2.11; 4; 15; 22; 42.7–9.

Elisha The prophet from Abel-meholah who succeeded Elijah. 1 Kings 19.16–21; 2 Kings 2.1–9.10; 13.14–20.

Elizabeth The wife of Zechariah and mother of John the Baptist. Lk 1.5–25,57–66.

Elkanah The husband of Hannah and father of Samuel. 1 Sam 1.1; 2.11,20.

Elymas *See* Bar-Jesus.

embalming The Egyptian method of preserving dead bodies from decay. Gen 50.1–3.

Emmanuel *See* Immanuel.

Emmaus The village, some 7 miles from Jerusalem, where Jesus appeared after his resurrection. Lk 24.13–32.

En-dor A town, 6 miles SE of Nazareth, where a medium lived. Josh 17.11; 1 Sam 28; Ps 83.10.

En-gedi A place in Judah on the W shore of the Dead Sea. 1 Sam 23.29–24. 2; 2 Chr 20.2. *Tell el-Jurn.*

Enoch (1) The son of Cain and father of Irad. Gen 4.17. (2) The father of Methuselah. Gen 5.18–24; Lk 3.37; Heb 11.5.

Epaenetus The first convert in the Roman province of Asia. Rom 16.5.

Epaphras A fellow-prisoner of Paul. Col 1.7; 4.12; Philem 23.

Epaphroditus A fellow-worker with Paul sent by him to Philippi. Phil 2.25–30; 4.18.

Ephes-dammim The site of the battle in which Goliath was killed. 1 Sam 17.1.

Ephesus The capital of the province of Asia on the left bank of the Cayster. Acts 18.24–28; 19.1–20.1; 20.16; 1 Cor 16.8; 1 Tim 1.3; 2 Tim 4.12; Rev 1.11; 2.1–7.

ephod A vestment worn by the high priest when ministering before the LORD. Ex 28.4–35; 39.2–26.

Ephphatha The word of command used by Christ when healing a man with a speech impediment. Mk 7.31–35.

Ephraim (1) The son of Joseph. Gen 41.50–53; 48.1–21. (2) The hill-country of W Palestine occupied by the tribe. Josh 17.14–18; 21.20; 2 Sam 18.6.

Ephron The Hittite from whom Abraham bought the cave and plot of land for Sarah's burial. Gen 23.1–20.

Epicureans Greek philosophers who advocated the achievement of happiness through the pursuit of pleasure. Acts 17.16–33.

Erastus (1) The city treasurer of Corinth. Rom 16.23. (2) An assistant of Paul. Acts 19.22; 2 Tim 4.20.

Esarhaddon The successor of Sennacherib. 2 Kings 19.37; Ezra 4.2.

Esau The son of Isaac called Edom. Gen 25.25–34; 27; 33.

Esther The Jewish queen of Ahasuerus, also called Hadassah, who succeeded Vashti as his wife. Esth 2.1–23; 3.12–9.32.

Ethiopia The region bordering on Egypt and the Red Sea, called Cush in Hebrew. Esth 1.1; 8.9; Acts 8.26–39. *See also* Isa 45.14; Ezek 30.1–32.32.

Eunice The mother of Timothy. Acts 16.1; 2 Tim 1.5.

Euodia A Christian woman of Philippi. Phil 4.2–3.

Euphrates The longest river in Asia, rising in Armenia and joined by the Tigris before reaching the Persian Gulf. Under the Persians, the country W of the Euphrates formed an administrative province, and under the Seleucid monarch, Antiochus IV, Lysias was left in charge of the same area. Gen 2.14; Ex 23.31; 1 Kings 4.24; Ezra 4.9–10; Rev 9.14; 16.12.

Eutychus A young man brought back to life by Paul. Acts 20.6–12.

evangelist One who proclaims the good news about Jesus Christ. Acts 21.8; Eph 4.11. *See also* 2 Tim 4.5.

Eve The first woman and the wife of Adam. Gen 2.18–3.24; 2 Cor 11.3.

Evil-merodach The son and successor of Nebuchadnezzar who freed Jehoiachin. Jer 52.31–34.

evil spirits Called "unclean" because they produced evil effects. Mt 10.1; 12.43–45; Mk 1.23–27; 5.8; 7.25; Lk 8.26–39; 11.24–26; Acts 5.16; 8.7; Rev 16.13–14.

excommunication Disciplinary exclusion from church fellowship. *See* Mt 18.15–17; Lk 6.22; Jn 9.34; 1 Cor 5.13; 2 Cor 2.5–11; 1 Tim 1.20; Titus 3.10.

Exile The period, lasting until 538 BCE, when many of the people of Israel and Judah were in captivity in Babylonia. *See* Captivity.

exodus The journey of Israel from Egypt into Canaan. Ex ch. 1–15; Num ch. 10–33. It was commemorated at the Feast of the Passover.

exorcism The driving out of an evil spirit by the invocation of a holy name. Acts 19.13–20. Christ commanded on his own authority. Mt 8.16; 10.1. The apostles commanded in Christ's name. Acts 16.18.

expiation *See* Atonement, Day of.

Ezekiel The son of the priest Buzi, he was taken into captivity in Babylon where he received his call as a prophet. Ezek 1.1–3. *See also* 2 Kings 24.8–17.

Ezion-geber A settlement at the NE end of the Gulf of Aqabah Elath, and a terminal port for Solomon's Red Sea trading fleet. Num 33.35; 1 Kings 9.26; 22.48. *Tell el-Kheleifeh.* Excavations by N. Glueck of the American Schools of Oriental Research 1937–40 uncovered 5th and 4th century BCE Aramaic ostraca and 7th century BCE Edomite sealings.

Ezra The priest and scribe authorized by King Artaxerxes to lead a party of Jewish exiles back to Jerusalem. Ezra 7.10–27; Neh 8.1–8.

face Used literally, figuratively and idiomatically. Ex 3.6; 33.20; Num 6.25; 12.14; Ps 13.1; 27.9; Prov 21.29; Jer 21.10; Lk 9.51; Rev 22.4.

Fair Havens A harbor on the S coast of Crete. Acts 27.8. *Kali Limenes*.

faith, faithful In the OT the idea is more frequently expressed by "belief," "trust," "hope" and by example. It is man's response of trustful acceptance of the revelation and promise of God. Hab 2.4; Mk 11.22; Lk 7.50; Rom 5.1; Gal 3.6–26; 5.6; Heb 11.8–12.2; Jas 2.14–26. *See also* Eph 2.8.

falcon Palestine has a wide range of the smaller birds which catch their prey by sheer speed. Job 28.7.

Fall, The Theological term applied to the story told in Gen 3.1–20. *See also* Rom 5.12–21; 1 Cor 15.21–26; 1 Tim 2.13.

falsehood Prov 12.13. *See also* Prov 19.1 and "lie, lying."

family *See* household.

famine Caused by lack of rain Gen 41; Jer 14.1–9; by war and siege 2 Kings 6.25; Deut 28.45–57. Sometimes depicted as a judgment of God. Lev 26.19; 1 Kings 17.1; Am 4.6.

farming The chief occupation of the Israelites after the settlement in Canaan. *See* Gen 26.12; Ex 23.10–11; Lev 27.16; Deut 8.7–10; 19.14; Ruth 2; Isa 28.24–28. Used in parables. Mt 3.12; 13.24–30; Mk 4.26–32.

fast, fasting This was practised mainly for religious reasons and was also associated with mourning. 1 Sam 7.6; 2 Sam 1.12; Zech 8.19; Mt 4.2; 6.16–18; Mk 2.18–20; Lk 2.37; 18.12; Acts 13.2; 14.23.

father His authority over his children was almost complete in biblical times. *See* Gen 24.4; Ex 21.7; Heb 12.7–10. Used of God. Mal 2.10; Lk 11.1–13; Jn 8.41–47.

fathom A measure of depth, equal to 6 feet. Acts 27.28.

fear The awe and reverence due to God. Deut 10.12; Ps 34.11; Prov 1.7. The fear which has to do with punishment as the result of sin. Rom 8.15; Heb 2.15; 1 Jn 4.18.

feast *See* festivals.

Felix, Antoninus The Roman Governor of Judaea. Acts 23.23–24.27.

fellowship The sharing of something in common. 1 Cor 15.18; 2 Cor 13.13. *See also* Jn 15.4; Acts 2.42–47; 1 Cor 1.9; Gal 2.9; 3.28; 6.2; Phil 2.1–5,14–15; 3.10; 1 Jn 1.3.

Fertile Crescent A modern description of the well-watered territory reaching NW from the Persian Gulf through Mesopotamia, then W to the N of Syria and Palestine.

festivals There were three main pilgrimage festivals in the Jewish calendar. These were: the Passover, Pentecost or Weeks, and Tabernacles. Another important feast was Purim.

Festus, Porcius The successor of Felix as Governor of Judaea. Acts 24.27–26.32.

fig The fig is referred to at least fifty times in the Bible; and the tree is a common sight in Palestine where its edible fruit is seen on the branches for about ten months of the year. Gen 3.7; Judg 9.7–15; 2 Kings 20.7; Song 2.13; Jer 8.13; Joel 2.22; Mt 7.16; Mk 11.12–14; Jn 1.47–50.

fine(s) These were originally compensation paid to the injured party. *See* Ex ch. 21–22; Lev 6.2–7.

fire Frequently used symbolically in the Bible record. Ex 3.2; 13.21; 19.16–18; 2 Kings 6.17; Isa 9.18; 66.5–16; Jer 6.29; Ezek 1.4, 13; Mt 3.11; Lk 12.49–50; Acts 2.3; 1 Cor 3.13; Heb 12.29.

first-born The Jews attached special value to the elder son. Ex 13.1; Deut 15.19–20; 21.17. *See also* Gen 25.29–34. Used figuratively. Ex 4.22; Rom 8.29; Heb 1.6.

firstfruits These were to be offered to God on the three great annual festivals of Passover, Pentecost and Tabernacles. Lev 2.14; Deut 18.4. Used of Christ. 1 Cor 15.20–26.

fish, fishing Fish was plentiful, especially in the Sea of Galilee, and was eaten salted and dried, as well as fresh. Lev 11.9–12; Neh 13.16; Job 41.7; Isa 19.8; Mt 4.18–22; 47; Jn 21.1–13.

Fish Gate One of the eleven gates of Jerusalem on the N side of the city. 2 Chr 33.14; Neh 3.3; 12.39; Zeph 1.10.

flax An important plant in Palestine and Egypt from the inner stem of which linen was made. Ex 9.31; Josh 2.1–6; Prov 31.13.

flea The dry countries of the Middle East are notorious for the flea, a small parasitic insect infesting both mammals and birds. 1 Sam 24.14; 26.20.

fleece The shorn wool of a sheep. Deut 18.4; Judg 6.37–40.

flesh Used in opposition to mental and spiritual qualities. Mt 26.41. *See also* Rom 8.1–8; Gal 5.16–21.

flogging A recognized form of punishment, in which no more than 40 strokes were allowed. Deut 25.2–3; Mt 10.17; 20.19; Jn 19.1; Acts 5.40; 16.22; 22.19–29.

Flood The deluge of water sent by God in Noah's time to destroy all but a selected few from the earth. Gen ch. 6–8; 9.11,28; 10.1, 32; Mt 24.38; Lk 17.27; 2 Pet 2.5.

flour This was made by crushing wheat or barley. Gen 18.6; Lev 6.15; Deut 32.14; 1 Kings 4.22. *See also* Lev 2.14–16.

fly, flies In the Near and Middle East these are present in great numbers, and are carriers of eye and other diseases. Ex 8.21–25; Ps 78.45; 105.31; Eccl 10.1.

food The basic food of the people was wheat and barley, beans and lentils eaten either as bread or stew. This was supplemented by vegetables such as onions, cucumbers, melons, radishes, garlic and various herbs; possibly also various nuts and fruit. Eggs were a useful addition to the diet, as was the milk of the domestic cattle, goats and sheep, which was usually preserved by turning it into curds, a form of yogurt. Meat, usually goat, was a luxury; but small birds could be trapped at any time of the year. And by the Persian period, poultry and pigeons were kept for food. Fish was preserved by drying and salting. *See* Ex 12.8; Lev 11.1–45; Num 6.3; 11.5; Deut 14.4–21; 32.13–14; Judg 7.13; Ruth 2.14; 1 Sam 17.18; 25.18; 2 Chr 31.5; Prov 15.17; Isa 10.14; Ezek 44.30; Lk 15.29; Jn 21.9–13.

fool One in whom there is no wisdom or judgment. Prov 12.15; 18.2; 20.3; Eccl 7.6; Lk 12.20. *See also* Prov 14.16; 17.24; 18.6.

foot Often used figuratively in the Bible. Footwashing was a sign of hospitality and humility. Gen 18.4; Josh 10.24; 1 Sam 25.24,41; Ps 73.2; Jer 18.22; Ezek 24.17; Lk 7.36–38; Jn 13.3–9; Acts 4.35; 1 Cor 15.25. *See also* Ex 3.5.

footstool Used literally 2 Chr 9.18; Jas 2.3. Used figuratively 1 Chr 28.2; Ps 99.5; 132.7; Isa 66.1; Lam 2.1; Mt 5.35; Acts 2.35.

ford A shallow place for crossing a river or stream. Gen 32.22; Josh 2.7; Judg 12.5; Isa 16.2.

foreigner, stranger (1) One passing through. *See* Gen 31.15; Deut 23.20; Job 31.32. (2) A permanent refugee (alien). *See* Lev 24.22; Judg 17.8; 2 Sam 1.13; Jer 7.6.

forerunner A herald or courier. Heb 6.20. *See also* Isa 40.3; Mt 11.10.

forest In OT times Palestine was extensively wooded. Josh 17.15; 2 Sam 18.6; Isa 10.18.

forget, forgetfulness The Bible draws a contrast between God and man in this respect. 1 Sam 12.9; Ps 78.11; Isa 49.14–16; Jer 18.15; Hos 8.14. *See also* Jer 31.34; Lk 12.6; Heb 8.12.

forgive, forgiveness This is not regarded in the OT as inherent in the nature of things, but something to be received with gratitude and only because God is compassionate. Ex 34.6–7; Deut 29.20; 1 Kings 8.35–40; Neh 9.17; Ps 86.5; 130.4; Jer 5.7; 31.34; 36.3; Dan 9.9. *See also* Gen 45; Lev 17.11; 19.18; Mic 7.18–20. It is an essential part of the teaching of the NT where a readiness to forgive others is an indication of true repentance. Mt 6.9–15; 18.21–35; 26.28; Mk 1.4; 2.10; Lk 23.34; Acts 2.38; 5.31; 13.38; Eph 1.7; Col 1.14; 1 Jn 1.9. *See also* Rom 3.25.

Fortunatus A Christian of Corinth. 1 Cor 16.17.

Foundation Gate A gate of Jerusalem leading from the royal palace to the Temple. 2 Chr 23.5.

fountain A spring of fresh water. Used literally and figuratively. Ps 36.9; Prov 13.14; 14.27; Hos 13.15. *See also* Ex 15.27; Prov 25.26; Jn 4.14.

fox Three species are found in Palestine and Egypt: the Red, the Desert and the Fennec fox. They are solitary hunters, living in the drier parts of the country and taking a wide range of prey. Neh 4.3; Mt 8.20; Lk 13.32.

frankincense This hardwood tree grows mainly in India and N Arabia. The juice or resin of the tree is used as incense. Ex 30.34; Lev 5.11; Num 5.15; Isa 60.6; Jer 6.20; Mt 2.11.

frog The commonest kind in Palestine is the edible frog which spends most of its time in the water. The tree-frog is also found in the Jordan valley. Ex 8.2–13; Ps 78.45; 105.30; Rev 16.13.

fruit Those most often mentioned are grape, pomegranate, fig, olive, and apple. Used metaphorically Deut 7.13; Prov 1.31. *See also* Jn 4.36; Gal 5.22.

fuel This was usually dried grass, branches of bushes and trees, and dung. Ezek 4.12,15; 15.4–5; 21.32. *See also* Mt 6.30.

fulfil This is most notably used in connection with the correspondence between the events of the Old and New Testaments. Mt 1.22; 2.15; Jn 19.36; Acts 13.27. *See also* Jn 19.24; Acts 1.16.

fuller One who washed, bleached, and sometimes dyed cloth. Mal 3.2. *See also* Mk 9.3. The Fuller's Field was the name of a place outside the walls of Jerusalem. 2 Kings 18.17; Isa 7.3; 36.2.

furnace smelter Used both literally and figuratively. Deut 4.20; 1 Kings 8.51; Dan 3; Isa 31.9; 48.10; Jer 11.4; Mt 13.36–42; Rev 9.2.

Gabbatha The place in Jerusalem where Jesus was tried by Pilate. Jn 19.13.

Gabriel The archangel and messenger of God. Dan 8.16–26; 9.21–27; Lk 1.11–38.

Gad The son of Jacob and ancestor of the tribe. Gen 30.11; Num 32; 1 Chr 5.18–22.

Gadara, Gadarenes *See Gerasa, Gerasenes.*

Gaddi One of Joshua's twelve spies. Num 13.11.

Gaius A common Roman name appearing frequently in the NT. Acts 19.29; 20.4; Rom 16.23; 1 Cor 1.14; 3 Jn 1.

Galatia The Roman province in central Asia Minor. Acts 16.6; 18.23; 1 Cor 16.1; Gal 1.2; 2 Tim 4.10; 1 Pet 1.1.

Galilee Originally the fertile territory in N Palestine W of the Jordan, but in NT times a Roman province. 1 Kings 9.11; Isa 9.1; Mt 4.12–16; 26.69; Lk 23.5–7; Jn 7.52.

Galilee, Sea of A large fresh-water lake in N Palestine some 18 miles long by 8 miles wide; 650 feet below sea level, and subject to sudden and violent storms. Mt 4.18; Mk 4.35–41. *See also* Num 34.11; Josh 12.3; Lk 5.2; Jn 6.1. *Bahr Tabarîyeh.* See also Chinnereth.

gall Possibly the juice of the opium poppy and a kind of narcotic which could render a person unconscious. Mt 27.34.

Gallio The Roman proconsul of Achaia and the brother of the philosopher Seneca. Acts 18.12–17.

Gamaliel A great Jewish rabbi: a Pharisee, member of the Council and Paul's former tutor. Acts 5.34–40; 22.3.

garden The term is used of ground, usually enclosed and under cultivation of vegetables, fruit or flowers. Gen 2.10; 1 Kings 21.2; 2 Kings 21.26; Isa 1.30; Jer 31.12; Jn 19.41. *See also* Prov 24.31.

garlic Many species are known in Palestine and, as today, it was used for flavoring. Num 11.5.

gate(s) These were made of wood, bronze or iron. The city gates were the recognized places for meeting and conducting business. Deut 21.18–19; Ruth 4.1; Neh 2.17; 3.1–32; Esth 4.1–2. Used figuratively Gen 28.17; Ps 87.2; Mt 16.18.

Gath This was the nearest Philistine city to Israelite territory. 1 Sam 5.8–9; 17.4; 21.10; 1 Kings 2.39; 2 Kings 12.17; 1 Chr 18.1.

Gaza A Philistine city and a great trade center. Josh 13.3; Judg 1.18; 16.1–3; 2 Kings 18.8; Am 1.6–7; Acts 8.26. Flinders Petrie excavated the site 1930–34, uncovering five occupation levels from the Middle Bronze to the Late Bronze Age.

gazelle A medium-sized antelope like the South African springbok. They are common and widespread in Palestine and there are several families of this graceful species. Both sexes have horns. Deut 12.22; 1 Kings 4.23; Prov 6.5; Acts 9.36.

gecko This small, nocturnal lizard is most frequently seen in the desert, where it lives among the rocky outcrops. Other species are closely connected with buildings due to their ability to cling to smooth surfaces. Lev 11.30.

Gedaliah The son of Ahikam, appointed Governor of the remnant left behind in Judah. 2 Kings 25.22–26; Jer 40.7–41.3.

Gehazi The servant of the prophet Elisha. 2 Kings 4.8–37; 5; 8.1–6.

Gehenna *See* Hell.

Gemariah (1) The son of Shaphan. Jer 36.10–26. (2) A messenger of Zedekiah. Jer 29.3.

genealogy For details of ancestors, descendants, and other lists of people and tribes *see* Gen 5; 10; 11.10–32; 35.23–36.43; 46.8–27; 1 Chr ch. 1–9; Ezra 2.1–67; 8.1–20; Neh 7.5–69; Mt 1.1–17; Lk 3.23–38.

Gennesaret Lk 5.1. *See* Galilee, Sea of.

Gentiles Originally any non-Israelite people, but after the exile exclusiveness, based solely on religion, developed. However, converts to Judaism were welcomed; and the Christian church admitted both Jewish and non-Jewish converts without distinction. Acts 10; 15.22–29; Gal 3.8. *See also* Isa 2.2–3; 42.6.

Gerasenes Inhabitants of Gerasa, a city of the Decapolis some 6 miles SE of the Sea of Galilee. Mk 5.1–20. Excavations by the American Schools of Oriental Research 1928–34.

Gerizim A mountain near Shechem facing Mt. Ebal, on which the Samaritans built a temple in the fourth century BCE. Deut 11.29; Judg 9.7–21. *See also* Jn 4.19–22. *Jebel et-Tôr.*

Gethsemane The place on the western slope of the Mt. of Olives where Christ was betrayed. Mt 26.36–56; Mk 14.32–52. *See also* Lk 22.39–53; Jn 18.1–11.

Gezer A Canaanite city 18 miles NW of Jerusalem. Josh 10.33; 1 Kings 9.15–16. *Tell Jezer.* Extensive excavations by R. A. S. Macalister, 1902–5, 1907–9, were carried out here and important discoveries made, including the Gezer Calendar, a schoolboy's mnemonic rhyme describing the agricultural year.

Gibeah A military stronghold 4 miles N of Jerusalem. Judg 20.5; 1 Sam 10.26–11.4. *Tell* *el-Fûl.* Excavations by W. F. Albright 1922–3 show it to have been inhabited and fortified early in the Iron Age. There is good reason to identify its destruction with Judg ch. 19–20. The second level dates from the time of Saul, and pottery and an iron plow-tip have been found in the rebuilt fortress. It lost its importance after David's reign and was deserted until about the 9th century BCE when the fortress was rebuilt on a smaller scale.

Gibeon A hill town 5 miles NW of Jerusalem. Josh 9.3–11.19; 2 Sam 21.1–9; 1 Kings 3.4–15. *el Jîb.* Excavations by the University Museum, Philadelphia, 1956–7 have revealed remains, including a pit and tunnel, of the Early and Middle II Bronze Age and of the Iron Age from its beginning to the Persian period. An extensive wine-making industry was located here in the 7th century BCE.

Gideon One of the Judges, who delivered the Israelites from the Midianites. Judg ch. 6–8; Heb 11.32.

gifts, giving In the OT these are recorded as having been given with many and mixed motives. Gen 34.12; 1 Chr 29.14; Ps 45.12; 72.10; Prov 18.16; Dan 2.48; Mt 5.23; Phil 4.17. In the NT the word is used primarily of God's gift to people. Rom 6.23; 8.32; 11.35; Eph 4.7–13. *See also* Jn 3.16; 14.16; 16.7; Gal 5.22.

Gihon The place near Jerusalem, and the site of a spring, where Solomon was anointed king. 1 Kings 1.33–40; 2 Chr 32.30. *'Ain Sittî Maryam.*

Gilboa A ridge of hills W of the Jordan where Saul fought his last battle. 1 Sam 28.4; 31.1–6. *Jebel Fuqqû'ah.*

Gilead Mountainous country E of the Jordan. Josh 13.24–25; Judg ch. 10–11; 1 Kings 17.1; Jer 8.22.

Gilgal (1) A place some 5 miles N of where the Jordan enters the Dead Sea. Josh 4.19–24; 1 Sam 11.14; Hos 4.15; Am 4.4. *Khirbet el-Mefjer.* (2) A village of Bethel. 2 Kings 2.1–2; 4.38.

glass This was made at an early date by the Phoenicians, but is used figuratively in the NT. Rev 4.6; 15.2; 21.18.

glean The custom of allowing the poor to follow the harvesters and collect the remnants. Lev 19.9; Ruth 2; Isa 17.6.

glory What is of real, as opposed to reputed, worth and its visible appearance. Ex 16.6–10; 24.13–17; 33.19–23; 40.34; Lev 9.5–7; 1 Kings 8.11; 2 Chr 7.1–3; Isa 40.5; 60.1–3; Ezek 1.28; Mt 16.27; Jn 1.14; 2.11; 17.5; Rom 2.7–10; Rev 21.10–22.5. *See also* Ex 34.29–35; Mt 17.2; Lk 2.9; 2 Cor 3.7–18; Phil 3.21.

goad A long spiked pole used for urging on cattle, and sometimes as a weapon. 1 Sam 13.21; Judg 3.31; Eccl 12.11; Acts 26.14.

goat The earliest accepted evidence for its domestication is from the New Stone Age pre-pottery levels of Jericho 6000–7000 BCE. Varieties were distinguished by their color and horn-shapes, corkscrew and scimitar. At first they were kept as milk-producers, but the kid was very edible and was the standard meal prepared for strangers. Their skin was used especially to make containers for water and wine. Gen 30.32; Lev 4.27–28; 1 Sam 25.2; Prov 27.27; Ezek 43.22–25; Mt 25.31–33.

God The supreme power in the universe and the source of all existence Isa 40.28; Mk 13.19; controller of history Isa 10.5–6; Am 9.7; eternal Rev 4.8–11; immortal 1 Tim 6.16; omnipotent Gen 17.1; omnipresent Jer 23.23–24; omniscient Ps 139.1–18; Prov 5.21; unchanging Jas 1.17; invisible Jn 5.37; 1 Tim 1.17; spirit Jn 4.24; perfect Job 11.7; one Deut 6.4; only wise Rom 16.27; holy Ps 99.9; Isa 6.3; good Mt 5.48; faithful 1 Cor 1.9; just Rom 3.25; truthful Titus 1.2; gracious Rom 5.15; electing Eph 1.4; saving Ex 14.30; 1 Cor 1.18; patient Num 14.18; compassionate Ex 34.6; Ps 86.5; Jas 5.11; father Mal 2.10; Jn 8.41–47; loving 1 Jn 4.9; known by his acts and fully revealed in Jesus Christ Jn 1.14,18; Heb 1.1–2.4.

Gog A prince of Meshech and Tubal, and the leader of the hosts of evil against God and his people. Ezek 38.1–39.16. He is associated with Satan in Rev 20.8.

gold The precious metal which was found at Havilah, Sheba and Ophir and used in the furnishings of the Tabernacle. Gen 2.11–12; Ex 37; 1 Kings 10.2; 22.48. It serves as a symbol of worth and value. Lam 4.1–2; Rev 21.18–21.

Golgotha The place where Jesus was crucified. Mt 27.33; Mk 15.22; Jn 19.17–30.

Goliath The champion of Gath killed by David. 1 Sam 17.4,23–58.

Gomorrah One of the cities of the Plain. Gen 14.2–11; 18.20–21; Isa 1.9; Jer 50.40; Mt 10.15; Rom 9.29; 2 Pet 2.6.

Goshen (1) The region of Egypt on the Nile delta where Jacob and his family settled. Gen 45.9–13; 46.28–47.11; Ex 8.22; 9.26. (2) A place in the Judaean highlands. Josh 15.51.

Gospel The good news about Jesus Christ and

the kingdom. Mt 4.23; Mk 1.1; Rom 1 1,16; 15.19; 2 Cor 4.4; 10.14. *See also* Mt 9.35; 1 Thess 2.2,9.

Gospels, the Four The post-biblical name given to the writings attributed to Matthew, Mark, Luke and John, each of which contains a record of the life of Jesus.

grace That attitude of God towards sinful man which moves him to help rather than to condemn him. Jn 1.17; Acts 15.11; Rom 3.24; 5.21; 11.5; 1 Cor 15.10; 2 Cor 12.9; Gal 1.15; 5.4; Eph 2.4–10; 6.24; 2 Thess 2.16; 2 Tim 1.9; Heb 4.16; 2 Pet 3.18. *See also* Deut 7.7–10; 9.4–5; Jn 3.16; Rom 5.8; 2 Cor 8.9.

Greece The land in the SE corner of Europe known as Javan in the OT. Isa 66.19; Ezek 27.13; Zech 9.13. After its conquest by Rome in 146 BCE it became the province of Achaia. Acts 18.12; 20.2.

Greek language The language of the ancient Greeks which spread over the Mediterranean world in a simplified form, and in which the NT is written. The spread of Christianity was greatly helped by the existence of this common language. Acts 21.37.

Hadad (1) The supreme Syrian god. Zech 12.11. (2) The grandson of Abraham. Gen 25.15.

Hadadezer The king of Zobah. 2 Sam 8.3–12; 10.16–19; 1 Kings 11.23.

Hadassah The Jewish name of Esther. Esth 2.7.

Hades *See* "hell" and "Sheol."

Hagar The Egyptian slave-girl of Sarah. Gen 16; 21.14–20.

hair Usually worn long, though kept trimmed. Baldness was despised. Lev 14.8; 19.27; 21.5; Num 6.5; Judg 16.13; 20.16; 1 Sam 14.45; 2 Sam 14.26; Ps 40.12; Ezek 44.20; Mt 10.29. *See also* 2 Kings 2.23; 1 Cor 11.14.

Hakeldama The piece of land bought with the money received by Judas for betraying Christ. Acts 1.18–19.

Ham The son of Noah. Gen 6.10; 9.18–19; 10.6.

Haman The chief official of Ahasuerus and a bitter enemy of the Jews. Esth ch. 3–7.

Hamath A city on the Orontes in Syria which gave its name to the region of which it was the capital. Jonathan marched there against Demetrius. 2 Sam 8.9–12; 2 Kings 14.28; 17.24–33; 25.21; 2 Chr 8.4; Jer 39.5; 52.9, 27; Zech 9.2. *Hamā.*

hamlet *See* village.

hammer The ordinary hammer Judg 4.21; 1 Kings 6.7; Isa 44.12; Jer 10.4; and one used for breaking rocks Jer 23.29.

hand(s) Used in many figurative senses. For power Ps 31.15; 1 Pet 5.6; anger Num 24.10; protection Ps 63.8; Isa 49.2; punishment 1 Sam 5.6; supplication Ex 9.33; 17.11; Ps 28.2; ratifying an agreement 24.9; communicating authority or blessing Gen 48.14; Deut 34.9.

hands, laying on A symbolical act associated with (1) sacrifice Lev 1.4; 3.2; 4.4; (2) blessing Gen 48.14–20; Mt 19.13; (3) healing Mk 6.5; Lk 4.40; 13.13; (4) appointment Num 27.18–23; Acts 6.6; 1 Tim 5.22; (5) the gift of the Holy Spirit Acts 8.17; 9.17; 19.6; 1 Tim 4.14; 2 Tim 1.6.

hands, washing This was an action intended to convey innocence and also ceremonial cleanness. Deut 21.6; Ps 26.6; Mt 15.1–9; 27.24; Mk 7.1–8.

Hannah The wife of Elkanah and the mother of Samuel. 1 Sam 1.1–2.10.

Haran The brother of Abraham. Gen 11. 27–30.

hare The hare of Palestine is a sub-species of the European variety and is smaller, paler and has shorter ears. It appears in the Bible only as an unclean animal, possibly because of its habit of "refection." Lev 11.6; Deut 14.7.

Harmagedon The final battleground between the forces of good and evil. Rev 16.16.

harp, lyre Made of wood, usually cypress or almug, it was stringed, and played with the fingers or a plectrum; and small enough to be carried about. Gen 4.21; 1 Sam 16.16; 1 Kings 10.12; Ps 71.22; Neh 12.27.

Harran An important commercial city in N Mesopotamia, strategically located on the main route from Nineveh to the river Euphrates and Aleppo. Gen 11.31–12.6; 27.43; Isa 37.12; Ezek 27.23. Excavations since 1951 have shown that it was inhabited from at least as early as the third millennium BCE.

harvest There were three each year. First the barley reaping, followed by the wheat and vine. The main religious festivals (Passover, Pentecost and Booths) fitted respectively into this agricultural economy. Ex 23.16–17; 34.22.

hate, hatred Condemned in the OT between fellow-Israelites. Ex 23.5; Lev 19.17; Prov 10.12; 15.17. In the NT. it is shown to be utterly contrary to the teaching of Christ. Mt 5.43–48; 1 Jn 2.9–11; 3.15; 4.20. *See also* Gal 5.20; Col 3.8.

hawk A common bird of prey in Palestine whose flesh was forbidden by the law. Lev 11.16; Deut 14.15; Job 39.26.

Hazael The Syrian who murdered Ben-hadad and seized his throne. 1 Kings 19.15; 2 Kings 8.7–15; 12.17.

Hazor A Canaanite city in N Palestine. Josh 11.1–13; Judg 4.2; 1 Kings 9.15; 2 Kings 15. 29. *Tell el-Qebah.* Excavations by J. Garstang 1926–8 and Y. Yadin 1955–8 have disclosed its size and importance, and its destruction in the period of the Israelite settlement. Among the discoveries in the lower city were a pottery jug with the earliest known inscription scratched on it, a Canaanite temple and a shrine. Evidence from the later Israelite period includes a city gate from the time of Solomon and a pillared public building of Ahab's time.

head Regarded by the Hebrews as the seat of life rather than of the intellect, and often used with a figurative meaning. Gen 48.14–19; Lev 16.21; Josh 2.19; Judg 8.28; 2 Sam 1.2; 15.30; Job 20.6; Ps 27.6; 83.2; Mt 5.36; Rom 12.20; Eph 1.22; 5.23; Col 2.19.

heart The physical organ, also regarded as the seat of the mind and the governing center which makes a person what they are. Gen 6.6; Deut 8.5; 1 Sam 2.35; 2 Kings 9.24; Ps 51.10; Prov 4.23; 23.7; Ezek 36.26; Mt 5.8; 13.19; Lk 8.15; 24.32; Rom 5.5; 2 Cor 1.22; Eph 3.17.

Heber The Kenite husband of Jael. Judg 4.11–24.

Hebrew(s) The word is used of Abraham and his descendants. Gen 14.13; 1 Sam 13.19; Phil 3.5. *See also* Israel, Israelite.

Hebrew language The NW branch of the Semitic language family in which almost all of the OT is written.

Hebron An ancient Canaanite city 20 miles SW of Jerusalem. Later, it was taken by Jonathan after being re-occupied by the Edomites. Gen 13.18; 23.1–19; Num 13.22; Josh 10.1–10; 14.13–15; 20.1–7; 2 Sam 2.1–4; 15.7–12. *el-Khalîl.*

heifer A young, unmated cow, sometimes used for threshing or plowing, but also for sacrificial purposes. Deut 21.3; Judg 14.18. Used figuratively Jer 46.20; Hos 10.11.

heir The principle of inheritance and the concept play a great part in the Bible story. Gen 15.3; Mk 12.7; Rom 8.16; Heb 1.2. *See also* Gen 21.10; Num 27.1–11; Deut 21.17; Job 42.15; Jn 1.12; Heb 9.15.

Heli The father of Joseph. Lk 3.23.

hell A common translation of the OT "Sheol" and the NT "Hades." Originally the place of departed spirits, it came to be thought of as the place of punishment for the wicked. Mt 18.9; Mk 9.45; 2 Pet 2.4. *See also* 2 Sam 22.6; Job 26.6; Ps 16.10; 139.8; Lk 16.23; Rev 20.14.

Heman The musician and grandson of Samuel. 1 Chr 6.33; 15.16–21.

hen By Jesus' day eggs, as well as the bird, were established as a food in Palestine. Used figuratively of Jerusalem. Mt 23.37; Lk 13.34. *See also* Lk 11.12.

henna A shrub originating in N India and widely used there and in the Middle East as a cosmetic and orange hair dye. It grows wild in Palestine and has spiny branches tipped with clusters of white flowers. Song 1.14.

Hermas A Christian of Rome. Rom 16.14.

Hermes In Greek mythology, the messenger of the gods. Known as Mercury in Roman mythology. Acts 14.8–18.

Hermon The snow-clad mountain in Syria, over 9000 feet high, marking the limit of Israel's conquests. Deut 3.9; 4.48; Josh 12.1–5; 13.11; Ps 133.3. *Jebel esh-Sheikh.*

Herod Agrippa *See* Agrippa.

Herod Antipas The son of Herod the Great and the ruler of Galilee and Perea. Mt 14.1–11; Lk 3.1; 13.31–32; 23.7–12.

Herod the Great The ruler of Judaea at the time of Christ's birth. Mt 2.1–19.

Herodians An influential group of Jews supporting the dynasty of Herod and so, indirectly, Rome. It was largely through them that Greek influences entered the life of Israel. *See* Mt 22.16.

Herodias The half-sister of Herod Agrippa I. She married her uncle, Philip. Mt 14.3–11.

Heshbon A Moabite city 20 miles E of Jordan with an excellent spring. Num 21.26; Josh 13.26; 21.39; Isa 15.4; 16.8; Jer 48.34. *Hesbân.*

Hezekiah The king of Judah who, in his long and prosperous reign, reformed religious worship. 2 Kings ch. 18–20; 2 Chr ch. 29–32; Isa ch. 36–39; Jer 26.17–19.

Hierapolis A city in the Lycus valley where Epaphras ministered. Col 4.13. *Pambuk Kalesi.*

high places Usually consisting of a level platform with an altar and standing stones, these were used for the sacrificial worship of pagan gods. They were bitterly denounced by the prophets, and destroyed by Hezekiah and Josiah. 1 Sam 9.12–14; 10.5; 1 Kings 3.2–3; 11.7; 14.23; 2 Kings 23.1–8; 2 Chr 33; Isa 36.7. *See also* Num 22.41; Deut 12.13; Jer 19.5.

high priest The man who spoke for the nation to God, and who reported God's will to the nation. Mk 14.53–65. *See also* Ex ch. 28–29; Lev 4; 16; 21.16–23; Num 27.21.

Hilkiah (1) The father of Eliakim. 2 Kings 18.18–37; Isa 22.20–25. (2) The high priest under Josiah. 2 Kings 22.3–23.4.

hill-country Generally applied to the uplands of Judaea in the NT (*see* Lk 1.39, 65); and in the OT to the southern part of Lebanon E of Sidon. Josh 13.6.

hinge Used figuratively Prov 26.14.

Hinnom, Valley of *See* Ben-hinnom.

Hiram (1) King of Tyre. 2 Sam 5.11; 1 Kings 5.1–18; 9.10–14. (2) A craftsman. 1 Kings 7.13.

Hittites An ethnic group living in Palestine from patriarchal times until after the Israelite settlement. Gen 15.20; 23.1–20; 26.34; Deut 7.1; Judg 3.5.

Hivites Early inhabitants of Syria and Palestine. Gen 10.17; Ex 3.8; Judg 3.3; 1 Kings 9.20.

holy, holiness The root idea is separateness. It originates in the revealed character of God and is communicated to things, places, times and persons engaged in his service. Ex 19.6; 20.8; Lev 19.2; Ps 2.6; 24.3–4; 65.4; Isa 41.14; Mk 1.24; Acts 4.30; Heb 12.10; 1 Pet 1.15. *See also* Heb 7.26.

Holy Spirit In the OT the term is used twice Ps 51.11; Isa 63.10; but the meaning is simply that God deals with men by his spirit which is holy because it is the spirit of God who is himself holy.

This tradition continues in the NT Mt 3.1–17; 4.1; 12.28; Lk 4.16–21; but it also develops a much deeper meaning. The turning-point in the usage is largely provided by the events of Pentecost when the prophecies of both Joel and Christ himself are fulfilled Acts 2.1–39. With the coming of Christ, and faith in him as savior, there developed a fuller knowledge of the nature of God which remained with men even after Christ's ascension. Thus, the Holy Spirit is called the Spirit of Truth and regarded as a personal reality, "God-with-man," because he would lead man to the Truth itself. In this work Father, Son and Spirit are each involved: a work which would not be possible unless each did his own part, though not working in the same way. *See* Jn 14.15–17; 16.12–15; Rom 5.5; 8.9; 14; 15.16; 1 Cor 3.16; 6.11. *See also* Spirit.

homicide *See* avenger of blood.

honey Prized as food and delicacy, and for sweetening since sugar was unknown. Gen 43.11; Ex 3.8; 16.31; Lev 2.11; Deut 32.13; Judg 14.8; Ps 19.10; Mk 1.6.

hook Used for various purposes. Ex 26.32, 37; 27.10,17; Job 41.2; Joel 3.10; Mt 17.27.

hoopoe A bird, seen in Palestine in spring and summer, which has a long, curved beak and a crest on its head which it can spread out as a fan. Lev 11.19; Deut 14.18.

hope In the later OT books true hope is linked with faith in God. Ps 39.7; 71.5; 119.74; 146.5. In the NT it is based on the resurrection. Rom 4.18; 5.3–5; 15.4,13; 1 Cor 13.13; 15.19; Eph 2.12; Col 1.27; 1 Thess 1.3; 5.8; 1 Tim 1.1; Titus 1.2; Heb 6.19; 11.1; 1 Jn 3.3.

Hophni One of the wicked sons of Eli 1 Sam 1.3; 2.13–4.18.

Hor The mountain, on the borders of Edom, where Aaron died. Num 20.22–29; 33.37–39.

Horeb The "mountain of God" situated between Canaan and Egypt, also known as Sinai. Ex 3.1–6; 17.5–7; 19.1–21; 31.18–32.15; Deut 1.2–8; 4.10–19; 9.8–19.

horn A simple curved wind instrument, first made from a ram's horn but later also of metal. Josh 6.4–5; Ps 98.6; Dan 3.4–5.

horns The projections at the corners of altars. Ex 29.12; 1 Kings 1.50; Ps 118.27. Also used to signify strength. Ps 75.4; Jer 48.25; Rev 17.7–14.

horse A symbol of war because it was used for chariots; but it seems that they were not widely used by the Israelites until the times of David and Solomon when they became an integral part of Israel's armed forces. Deut 17.14–16; Josh 11.4–9; 2 Sam 8.4; 1 Kings 10.25,28–29; Job 39.19; Ps 33.16–17. Used symbolically Zech 1.8; 6.1–7; Rev 6.2–8.

Horse Gate One of the eleven gates of Jerusalem. Neh 3.28; Jer 31.40.

hosanna The Greek transliteration of the Hebrew word meaning "save now." Mt 21.9. *See also* Ps 118.25.

Hosea (= salvation) The son of Beri, a prophet of Israel, contemporary with Isaiah, Amos and Micah.

Hoshea (1) The last king of the northern kingdom of Israel. 2 Kings 15.30; 17.1–6; 18.1. (2) Joshua's early name. Num 13.8.

hospitality A necessity among nomads, and counted a major virtue throughout the Bible. Rom 12.13; 1 Tim 3.2; Titus 1.8; 1 Pet 4.9. *See also* Gen 18.1–8; Ex 2.20; Deut 23.4; 1 Kings 17.10–16; 2 Kings 4.8–15; Ps 41.9; Mt 10.11; 25.35–45; Lk 7.44–46; Col 4.10; 2 Jn 10; 3 Jn 5–8.

hour The Jews reckoned days from sunrise to sunset, dividing them into 12 lengths differing according to season. Mt 20.1–16; 24.36; Mk 14.37; 15.25; Jn 11.9; Acts 5.7; 19.34; 23.23; Rev 17.12. *See also* Jn 4.52.

house(s) Construction and design Ex 12.27; Deut 6.8; 20.5; 22.8; 2 Sam 17.18; 1 Kings 6; 2 Chr 8.16; Ezra 6.16; Job 4.19; Hos 13.3; Lk 5.19. Furnishings and utensils Gen 24.15; 2 Sam 4.7; 17.28; 1 Kings 17.12; Job 37.18; Jer 36.22; Am 3.12; Jn 2.6.

household Everyone who lived beneath the roof, including servants and slaves. Gen 7.1.

household gods *See* teraphim.

Huldah A prophetess in the time of Josiah. 2 Kings 22.14–20.

humility Praised in the OT. *See* Num 12.3; Prov 15.33; 18.12; 22.4. It is not defined in the NT but is taught and exemplified by Christ. *See* Mt 11.29; 18.4; 23.12; Lk 14.11; 18.14; Jn 13.3–9; Acts 20.19; 1 Cor 13.4; 2 Cor 8.9; Phil 2.3; 1 Pet 5.5.

hunter, hunting A necessity rather than a pastime. Gen 10.9; 25.27; 27.3. *See also* Gen 21.20; Ex 23.29; Deut 12.15; 15.22; Judg 14.5; 1 Sam 17.34.

Hur (1) An attendant on Moses at Rephidim. Ex 17.10–13; 24.14. (2) A king of Midian. Num 31.8.

hyena This is the striped hyena which ranges from India through SW Asia to E Africa. It has a body length of about 40 inches with a massive head and jaws. Its main food is carrion. Jer 12.9.

hypocrite One who pretends to be what he is not. Mt 6.1–6,16–18; 7.5; 23.13–32; Mk 7.6; Lk 12.56; 13.15. *See also* Rom 2.17–29.

hyssop A small shrubby perennial growing up to 2 feet. Originally cultivated as a medicinal herb. Ex 12.21–23; Lev 14.4; 1 Kings 4.33; Ps 51.7.

I AM The name by which God revealed himself to Moses showing that he is faithful and unchangeable. Ex 3.14. It can also mean "I cause to be."

Ibleam A Canaanite town SE of Megiddo. Judg 1.27.

Ibzan The Judge who succeeded Jephthah. Judg 12.8–10.

Ichabod The grandson of Eli whose mother died in childbirth. 1 Sam 4.19–21.

Iconium An important center of missionary activity in the Roman province of Galatia, situated on the trade route linking Ephesus and Syria. Acts ch. 14; 2 Tim 3.11.

idleness The effects of idleness illustrated. Prov 10.4; 19.15; 24.30–34; 2 Thess 3.11–12; 1 Tim 5.13. *See also* Prov 12.27; 13.4; 18.9; 20.4; 13; 26.14–16; Mt 25.14–30; Heb 6.12.

idol, idolatry Common in the ancient world where it was believed that the god represented lived in the idol. *See* Judg 6.25–32; 1 Sam 5.1–5. It was prohibited by Israelite laws and denounced by the prophets. Lev 26.1; Isa 10.10–11; 44.9–20. *See also* Ex 20.4; Isa 40.18–20. The NT continues with and emphasizes this teaching. 1 Cor 10.19–21; Eph 5.5; Col 3.5; 1 Thess 1.9. *See also* Rom 1.22; 1 Cor 8.4; 1 Jn 5.21.

Ignorance In the OT inadvertence is regarded as a mitigating feature of sinful acts. *See* Num 15.22–29; Lev ch. 4–5. This is reflected in NT use. Acts 17.30; Eph 4.18; 1 Tim 1.13; 1 Pet 1.14; 2.15.

illness For the Israelites, this was sometimes divine punishment caused by sin. *See* Ex 4.11; Deut 7.15; 28.22; Job 2.7; 7.20; Jn 5.14; 9.2. Specific illnesses mentioned. Lev 13.1–46; 26.16; Num 5.2; Deut 28.22,27; 1 Sam 25.37; 1 Kings 15.23; Isa 32.4; Mt 9.20; 17.15; Mk 7.32; Lk 5.12; 6.6; 8.27; 13.11; 14.2; Jn 5.3; Acts 12.23.

Illyricum The Roman province on the E side of the Adriatic. Rom 15.19.

image The mental and moral attributes in which man resembles God. Blurred through sin, the image is restored in the redemption of Christ. Gen 1.26–27; Col 1.15; 3.10. *See also* Gen 5.1; Rom 8.29; Eph 4.24; Heb 1.3; Jas 3.9. For man-made images *see* idol.

Immanuel (Emmanuel) (= God is with us) the symbolic name given by Isaiah to the child whose birth he predicted. In the NT it is applied to Jesus. Isa 7.14; Mt 1.21–24.

immortality No direct equivalent in the OT. In the NT God alone is immortal; but death has been overcome through Christ, and "immortality" is given to man as a gift. Rom 2.7; 1 Cor 15.50–57; 1 Tim 1.17; 6.16; 2 Tim 1.10.

incense (frankincense) Aromatic resins and spices burned in ceremonial worship and regarded as a symbol of prayer rising to God. Ex 30.1–9,34; Ps 141.2; Isa 43.23; Jer 6.20; Mt 2.11; Rev 5.8; 8.3.

India That part of the country watered by the river Indus, and the E boundary of the empires of Ahasuerus, Artaxerxes and Darius. Esth 1.1; 8.9; Add Esth 13.1; 16.1.

industry Commended in both OT and NT. *See*

Prov 6.6–11; 31.10–28; Eph 4.28; 1 Thess 2.9; 4.11–12.

ingratitude A characteristic of the wicked. *See* Job 19.13–16; Ps 35.12; 38.20; Prov 17.13; Jer 18.20; 2 Cor 12.15; 2 Tim 3.2.

inheritance This is chiefly used in the OT in connection with the patrimony of Canaan. *See* Josh 13.33; Ps 105.8–45. Later the concept becomes broadened. Ps 2.8; 16.5–11; 73.26; Isa 19.25. In the NT it is spiritualized and connected with the person and work of Christ. Heb 6.12; 1 Pet 1.4. *See also* Rom 8.14–17; Gal 3.29; 4.7; Eph 1.13–14; Col 1.12; 3.24; Heb 1.2; Rev 21.7. *See* heir.

ink This was made from carbon-black mixed with a gum solution to which water was added. Jer 36.18; 2 Cor 3.3; 3 Jn 13. *See also* Num 5.23.

inn A night resting-place, usually consisting of a number of small unfurnished rooms opening at one side on to a court and well. Lk 10.34. *See also* Jer 9.2; Lk 2.7.

innocent, innocence The word conveys the idea of being "clean from guilt." Job 4.7; 9.28; Ps 19.13; 26.6; Jer 2.34; Mt 10.16; 27.4.

inspire, inspiration The action of the Holy Spirit enabling men to give their witness to what God has revealed. 2 Tim 3.16. *See also* Mt 16.17; Jn 16.13; 2 Pet 1.21; 1 Jn 1.1–7.

intercession The duty of all Christians, and practiced throughout the biblical record. *See* Gen 18.20–34; Ex 32.30–32; 1 Sam 7.7–9; Ps 122.6–9; Isa 53.12; Lk 23.24; Jn 17; 1 Tim 2.1–8; Jas 5.16.

interest *See* usury.

iron Most OT history falls within the Iron Age. Originally almost a Philistine monopoly, iron became available for ordinary purposes after David's conquests. Judg 1.19; 4.13; 2 Sam 23.7; 2 Kings 6.6; Ps 105.18. *See also* 1 Sam 13.19–22.

irrigation This was not easy in Palestine because of the scarcity of wells. Deut 11.10. *See also* Isa 58.11.

Isaac The only son of Abraham by Sarah and one of three patriarchs who were the ancestors of the Hebrews. Gen 17.19; 21.13; ch. 22; 24–27; 35.28.

Isaiah The great prophet who received his call in the last year of Uzziah's reign and prophesied throughout those of Ahaz and Hezekiah. He called primarily for the people to trust God and his purpose for his people. In this alone, and not in any political maneuverings, lay Judah's safety. Isa 1.1; 6.1; 7.1–4; 8.3; ch. 37–39.

Ishbosheth The son of Saul who succeeded him until he was murdered. 2 Sam ch. 2–4.

Ishmael The son of Abraham by Hagar. Gen 16.15; 17.23–27; 25.17; 28.9. *See also* Gen 21.14–21.

Ishmaelites A nomadic N Arabian people of mixed blood descended from Ishmael. Gen 37.25–28.

Israel, Israelite (1) The name given to Jacob. Gen 32.28. (2) The nation made up of his descendants Ex 3.16; and in a narrower sense the northern tribes 2 Sam 19.39–43; 1 Kings 12; 2 Kings 17; Ezra 4. (3) Used in the NT of Christians as descendants of Abraham by faith. Rom ch. 9–11; Gal 6.16. *See also* Gal 3.29.

Issachar The son of Jacob by Leah and the founder of the tribe. Gen 30.18; 35.23; 49.14; Josh 19.17.

Italy, Italian The country between the Alps and Messina of which Rome was the capital. Acts 10.1; 18.2; 27.1–2; Heb 13.24. *See also* Acts 28.12–31.

Ittai The Gittite who supported David against Absalom. 2 Sam 15.18–23; 18.2.

Ituraea The mountainous country NE of the Sea of Galilee. Lk 3.1.

ivory An imported source of wealth and a sign of luxury. 1 Kings 10.22; 22.39; 2 Chr 9.17; Ps 45.8; Song 5.14; Ezek 27.15; Am 6.4; Rev 18.12.

Jabbok The river flowing into the Jordan 20 miles N of the Dead Sea. Gen 32.22–30; Judg 11.12–13. *Nahr ez-Zerqâ.*

Jabesh-gilead A town in the highlands E of the Jordan. Judg 21.8–14; 1 Sam 11.1–11; 31.12; 2 Sam 2.4–7. *Tell Abū Kharâz.*

Jabin A Canaanite king defeated by Joshua. Josh 11.1–9; Judg 4.1–2,23–24.

Jachin One of the two symbolic pillars in the porch of Solomon's Temple. 1 Kings 7.13–22. *See also* 2 Kings 25.13–17.

jackal Basically a night scavenger about the size of the fox, with a dirty-yellow coat, which travels in packs. It is more typical of dry and desolate places than the fox, which likes some cover. Ps 63.10; Lam 5.18. Used figuratively Isa 13.22.

Jacob The younger son of Isaac and Rebecca who received the promise of God that the covenant would continue in him and was given the name Israel. Gen 25.19–50.13.

Jacob's Well A mile E of Shechem on the slope of Mt. Ebal. Jn 4.3–15. *See also* Gen 33.18–20.

Jael The wife of Heber who murdered Sisera. Judg 4.15–22; 5.24–27.

James (1) The son of Zebedee. Mt 4.21; Mk 5.37; 9.2; 10.35–40; Lk 9.54; Acts 12.2. (2) The son of Alphaeus. Mt 10.3; Mk 15.40; Acts 1.13. (3) The brother of Jesus. Mt 13.55; Mk 6.3; Acts 12.17; Gal 1.19; 2.9. *See also* Mk 3.21,31; Jn 7.5.

Japheth One of the sons of Noah. Gen 6.10; 9.18–10.5.

Jashar, Book of Probably a collection of ballads. Josh 10.13; 2 Sam 1.18.

Jason Paul's host at Thessalonica. Acts 17.5–9.

jealousy Mainly used in the Bible to express zeal or intense devotion and linked to God's choice of Israel. Ex 20.5; Num 25.10; Josh 24.19; 1 Kings 14.22; 2 Cor 11.2. *See also* Joel 2.18.

Jebus The old name for the fortress of Jerusalem taken by David. Josh 15.63; 18.28; Judg 19.10.

Jebusite(s) A Canaanite tribe. Gen 10.16; Josh 18.28; Judg 19.11; 2 Sam 5.6–8; 24.16–24.

Jeconiah *See* Jehoiachin.

Jedidiah The name given to Solomon by Nathan. 2 Sam 12.24–25.

Jegar-sahadutha The monument built by Laban in the N highlands of Gilead. Gen 31.45–48.

Jehoahaz (1) The son and successor of Jehu who had to face Syrian attacks on Israel. 2 Kings 13.1–9. (2) The son of Josiah, made king of Judah on his father's death but deposed by Pharaoh Necho and taken to Egypt. 2 Kings 23.30–34. Also called Shallum Jer 22.11.

Jehoash The son and successor of Jehoahaz as king of Israel who stemmed the tide of Syrian aggression. 2 Kings 13.10–14.17.

Jehoiachin The son and successor of Jehoiakim as king of Judah, taken prisoner to Babylon after a reign of only three months. 2 Kings 24.8–15; 25.27–30. He is also called Jeconiah Esth 2.6; and Coniah Jer 22.24–28.

Jehoiada A priest in Jerusalem at the time of Athaliah and Joash. 2 Kings 11.13–20; 12.4–16; 2 Chr 24.15–22.

Jehoiakim The son of Josiah, originally named Eliakim, who was placed on the throne by Pharaoh Neco. 2 Kings 23.34–24.6; Jer 22.18–19; 26.20–24; 36.13–32.

Jehonadab The founder of the Rechabites and an ally of Jehu. 2 Kings 10.15–29.

Jehoram The son of Ahab who succeeded his brother, Ahaziah, as king of Israel, in whose reign there were hostilities with Edom and Syria. 2 Kings 3.1–25; 9.14–26.

Jehoshaphat (1) The father of Jehu. 2 Kings 9.2,14. (2) The son and successor of Asa as king of Judah who made an alliance with Israel. 1 Kings 22.2–50; 2 Chr 19.1–21.1.

Jehovah The English rendering of the four Hebrew consonants YHWH, one of the names of God. Ex 3.15. Because of the commandment in Ex 20.7 the name was not pronounced on normal occasions but replaced in reading by Adonay (= my lord). The word Jehovah arose from the combination of the vowels of Adonay with the consonants YHWH.

Jehovah-jireh The name given by Abraham to the place where he prepared to sacrifice Isaac. Gen 22.14.

Jehu (1) One who prophesied against Baasha. 1 Kings 16.1–7; 2 Chr 19.1–3. (2) The founder of a dynasty of kings of Israel who seized the throne by violence. 2 Kings 9.1–10.36.

Jephthah One of the most important Judges of Israel. Judg 11.1–12.7; Heb 11.32.

Jeremiah The young priest of Anathoth called to prophesy in the reign of Josiah. A contemporary of Zephaniah and Habbakuk, he was a devoted patriot, but was persecuted for his unwelcome message about the impending captivity. After the fall of Jerusalem he chose, voluntarily, not to go to Babylon but to remain in Judah with the remnant. Against his will he was taken to Egypt after the murder of Gedaliah. Jer ch. 1; 11; 25–26; 37–39; 43.

Jericho An ancient city 17 miles ENE of Jerusalem and 6 miles from the Dead Sea, standing in a key position defending the Jordan valley. Its capture was essential for any further penetration into Canaan. Josh 2.1–21; 5.10–6. 26; 1 Kings 16.34; 2 Kings 2.4–22; Mk 10.46–52; Lk 10.30–37; 19.1–10. OT site *Tell es-Sultân*. NT site *Tulûl Abû el-'Alayiq*. Excavations by J. Garstang 1930–36 and K. Kenyon 1952–58 have uncovered remains which throw light on Abraham's Canaanite and Amorite town-dwelling neighbors. Splendid pottery, wooden tables, stools and beds, trinket boxes with bone inlay, basketry, metal daggers and bracelets have been found. The remains of the Jericho of the 9th to 6th centuries BCE are fragmentary but quite definite.

Jeroboam (1) Jeroboam I, the leader of the discontent against Solomon, crowned king over the ten northern tribes. He made the shrines of Bethel and Dan into royal sanctuaries. 1 Kings 11.26–40; 12.20–13.10; 13.33–14.20,30. (2) Jeroboam II, the son of Joash, in whose reign Israel prospered but the accompanying social and religious evils were denounced by the prophets. 2 Kings 14.23–29; Hos 1.1; Am 1.1.

Jerusalem On a rocky plateau 2723 feet above sea level, 30 miles E of the Mediterranean and 14 miles W of the Dead Sea; access to the city on the E, S and W is hampered by deep ravines. The original site was called Ophel (Jebus) and occupied by the Jebusites. From the time of its occupation by David, it became the heart of the history and religion of the OT. 2 Sam 5.6–12; 1 Kings ch. 5–9; Ps 122; 125; 128; 137; 147; Isa 52.1–2; 62.1–11; 65.18–25; Mt 5.35; 23.37–39; Lk 21.20–24; 24.44–49; Acts 1.8; Rom 15.19; Gal 4.26; Rev 21.2. *See also* Ps 48; 87.

Jeshua The son of Jozadak and high priest in Jerusalem after the exile. Ezra 3.1–13.

Jesse The father of David. Ruth 4.17; 1 Sam 16; Isa 11.1–10; Rom 15.12.

Jesus The Greek form of the Hebrew "Joshua" (= God saves). Mt 1.1–25; Lk 1.26–38; 2.21–40; Jn 20.31.

Jethro The priest-shepherd of a Midianite tribe, and father-in-law of Moses. Ex 3.1; 18.1–27. *See also* Ex 2.16–22.

Jew(s) A member of the Hebrew race. The word was used especially, during and after the exile, of those who had gone from and returned to Judaea. Jn 4.22; Rom 1.16; 1 Thess 2.14.

jewel, jewellery This was used for personal adornment, especially in connection with marriage ceremonies and religious festivals. *See* Gen 24.22–23; Ex 32.3; Prov 25.11–12; Isa 3.18–23; Ezek 16.11–13.

Jezebel The daughter of Ethbaal of Sidon who married Ahab and promoted Baal worship in Israel. 1 Kings 16.31; 18.4; 19.1–2; 21.5–15,23–25; 2 Kings 9.30–37; Rev 2.20.

Jezreel (1) A city on a spur of Mt. Gilboa. 1 Kings 18.45; 21.1; 2 Kings 9.15–26. (2) Hosea's eldest son. Hos 1.4.

Jezreel, Valley of The only break of any size in the range of hills running the length of Palestine to the W of the Jordan, and the key to the whole area. Also known as the Plain of Esdraelon. Josh 17.16.

Joab The son of Zeruiah and David's ruthless commander-in-chief who murdered Abner and had Absalom killed. 2 Sam 2.12–32; 3.22–32; 8.16; 11.6–25; 12.26–29; 18.5–19.3; 1 Kings 2.5,28–34.

Joash The son and successor of Ahaziah as king of Judah who reigned for forty years. 2 Kings 11.1–3; 12.1–21.

Job The central figure of the book of Job. A pious and prosperous man who was accused by Satan of being pious because it paid. He is put to incredible tests but bears them all with patience, denying the accusations of his three friends that he has brought his sufferings on himself. Job ch. 1; 2; 3–31; 32; 38; 42; Ezek 14.14,20; Jas 5.11.

John, the Apostle The son of Zebedee and the brother of James. Mt 4.21; 17.1; Mk 3.16–19; 14.33; Lk 8.51; Acts 3.1–4.31; 8.14–25. *See also* Jn 13.23; 19.26; 20.1–9; 21.1–24.

John the Baptist The cousin and forerunner of Jesus. Mt 3.1–15; 11.2–19; 14.1–12; Lk 1.5–25,57–80; Jn 1.19–37; Acts 18.25; 19.3.

Jonadab David's nephew. 2 Sam 13.1–5; 32–33.

Jonah (1) The prophet, son of Amittai, who was sent to Nineveh much against his will and, after being shipwrecked, converted the city. Jon ch. 1–4. (2) The father of Simon Peter. Mt 16.17.

Jonathan The son of Saul who became a close friend of David. 1 Sam 14.1–15,24–46; 18.1–4; 19.1–7; 20; 31.2; 2 Sam 1.17–27.

Joppa The chief harbor of SW Palestine. Josh 19.46; Jon 1.3; Acts 9.36–43; 10.4–11.17. *Jaffa.*

Joram The son and successor of Jehoshaphat as king of Judah who married Athaliah. 2 Kings 8.16–24; 2 Chr 21.12–20.

Jordan (= the descender) The longest river in Palestine. Rising 1200 feet above sea level near Caesarea Philippi, it flows through the Sea of Galilee to the Dead Sea, much of its course below sea level. Josh 3.9–17; Judg 12.5–6; 2 Kings 2.4–14; 5.9–14; Jer 12.5; Mt 3.4–6; Lk 4.1.

Joseph (1) The eleventh son of Jacob and Rachel, through whom the whole of his father's clan came to settle in Egypt. Gen 30.22–24; ch. 37–50. (2) The husband of Mary. Mt 1.18–2.22; Lk 2.1–16; 3.23. *See also* Mt 13.55. (3) The brother of Jesus. Mt 13.55; Mk 6.3. (4) The son of Mary. Mt 27.56; Mk 15.40.

Joseph Barsabbas One of the two proposed to fill the place of Judas Iscariot. Acts 1.23–26.

Joseph of Arimathaea The secret disciple of Jesus who buried his body. Mt 27.57–60; Lk 23.50–53.

Joshua The successor to Moses who led the

Israelites into the Promised Land. Ex 17.9; Num 27.18–23; Josh ch. 1–24.

Josiah The son and successor of Amon as king of Judah whose reign was marked by religious reforms. 2 Kings 21.24; 22.3–23.30; 2 Chr 33.24–35.27.

Jotham (1) The youngest son of Gideon (Jerubaal). Judg 9.5–21. (2) The regent in the reign of Uzziah and his successor as king of Judah. 2 Kings 15.5,32–38; 2 Chr 27.1–9.

Journey, Sabbath Day's *See* Sabbath Day's Journey.

joy In both the OT and the NT it is a quality grounded on and derived from God himself, and it is consistently the mark of both the individual believer and the corporate fellowship. Ps 16.11; 104.34; 137.6; Isa 35.2; 51.11; Zeph 3.17; Lk 2.10; 15.10; Jn 15.11; Acts 2.42–47; Rom 14.17; Gal 5.22.

jubilee The fiftieth year, or the one after seven "sabbaths of years." It was a year of freedom and deliverance to the poor and rest for all Israel. Lev 25.8–55; 27.17; Num 36.4.

Judea The Greek and Roman name for Judah. Used for the whole country but more commonly for the southern region of Palestine. Lk 23.5.

Judah (1) The fourth son of Leah and Joseph and founder of the tribe. Gen 29.35; 49.8; 1 Chr 5.2. (2) The kingdom formed when the monarchy divided and to which the exiles returned. Though small, some fifty miles by fifty, its capital was Jerusalem and it was the scene of the most important events in Christ's ministry.

Judas (1) An apostle. Lk 6.16; Jn 14.22. (2) The brother of Jesus. Mt 13.55. (3) A Galilean rebel leader. Acts 5.37. (4) A Damascus Jew with whom Paul stayed. Acts 9.11. (5) Barsabbas. Acts 15.22–33.

Judas Iscariot The treasurer of the Twelve and the traitor who betrayed Jesus. Mt 26.14–25; 27.3–10; Jn 6.71; 12.4–8; 13.21–30; 18.1–6; Acts 1.15–20. *See also* Lk 22.21–23; Jn 13.10–11.

Judgment Day From the conviction that everything is subject to God's rule and control, the OT prophets proclaimed that one day the whole world would show the perfection of God's rule. The judgment of God would mean the demonstration of God's might and glory; salvation for the faithful; and condemnation for the wicked. *See* Isa 2.12–22; Dan 12.1–4; Joel 1.15; 2.1–14; Am 5.18–20; 9.11. The NT says that it will come "at the end of the age" and that Christ will be the judge. Mt 13.36–43; 25.31–46; Mk 13.14–36; Jn 5.22; 2 Cor 5.10; Rev 20.11–15.

Judges Local hero-leaders who sprang into prominence in the early days of the settlement in Canaan because of their military skill and their ability to rally the Israelite forces when a crisis arose. The exploits of 13 of them are described in the book of Judges.

justice One aspect of the righteousness of God who is completely fair and impartial. Gen 18.25; Isa 30.18; Jas 1.17. As the source of all human justice Ex 20.1–17; Ps 25.8; 86.11, he demands that people shall practice it in dealings with each other. Isa 1.17,27; Am 5.24; Mic 6.8. An even higher standard is demanded in the NT, and this is made possible by the new relationship with God established for all by Christ. Mt 5.20–48; Jn 1.17.

justification, justify This relates to man's status as a sinner before God, and the right relationship he may enter into with him through Christ. *See* Rom ch. 3–5; Gal ch. 2–3.

Kabzeel A town in S Judah and the birthplace of Benaiah. 2 Sam 23.20–21.

Kadesh, Kadesh-barnea An oasis in the wilderness of Zin 70 miles E of Hebron where Miriam died. Num 13.26; 20.1–22; 27.14; Deut 1.19–24. *'Ain Qedeirât.*

Karkor The place, in Ammonite territory, where Gideon defeated Zebah and Zalmunna. Judg 8.10–12.

Kedar (1) The son of Ishmael. Gen 25.13. (2) The Bedouin tribe descended from him. Ps 120.5; Song 1.5; Isa 42.11; 60.7; Ezek 27.21.

Kedesh A fortified Canaanite town. Josh 20.7; 21.32; Judg 4.6–10; 2 Kings 15.29. *Tell Qades.*

Keilah A town in the lowland of Judah. 1 Sam 23.1–13.

Kenites A Midianite tribe closely connected with Judah and the Rechabites. Judg 1.16; 4.11; 1 Chr 2.55.

Keturah The wife Abraham married after Sarah's death. Gen 25.1–4.

key(s) In OT times a piece of wood with pins fixed along the side. Judg 3.25. Used figuratively as a symbol of authority. Isa 22.22; Mt 16.19; Rev 1.18.

Keziah The daughter of Job. Job 42.14.

Kibroth-hattaavah A stopping-place in the wilderness where the people were punished by a plague. Num 11.31–34; Deut 9.22.

kid Gen 27.9; 1 Sam 16.20; Isa 11.6. *See* goat.

kidnap The kidnapping of an Israelite was punishable by death. Ex 21.16; Deut 24.7.

kidney Regarded as the most precious part of the sacrificed animal and, therefore, reserved for God in burnt-offerings. Ex 29.13; Lev 3.4; 4.9; 7.4.

Kidron The torrent valley running along the E side of Jerusalem and extending to the Dead Sea. 2 Sam 15.23; 1 Kings 15.13; 2 Kings 23.4–6. *See also* Jn 18.1. *Wâdis el-Jawz, Sitti Maryam, el-Qeini.*

kin, kinsman One who shares the same race or family and so has certain privileges and obligations. Lev 25.25–28; Num 35.9–12; Ruth ch. 2–4; Jer 32.8–10.

kingdom of God, kingdom of Heaven That condition of human life in which the will of God as revealed in Jesus Christ is in complete control. It is the theme of Jesus' teaching and the subject of many parables. Mt 13.1–52; Mk 1.15. Entry is by the new birth, and men share in it if they accept and obey him. Mt 12.28; Mk 10.15; Lk 6.20; 17.20–37. Yet in its fulness it is still in the future. Mt 8.11; Mk 14.25; Lk 18.28–30.

kings The need for centralized government was felt only after the nomadic tribes settled in Canaan and had to withstand attacks. Saul was the first king. Besides being the chief general, the king was supreme judge, leader of worship, and was regarded as God's representative, though still subject to his laws. 1 Sam 8.4–22; 10.1,24; 11.12–15; 2 Sam 2.1–4; 5.1–5; 12.1–12.

King's Garden An open space in Jerusalem close to the Pool of Siloam. 2 Kings 25.4; Neh 3.15; Jer 39.4; 52.7.

King's Highway An ancient caravan route, marked by Early Bronze Age settlements and Roman milestones, running from the Gulf of Aqaba to Syria, passing through the hill-country E of the Jordan valley. Num 20.17; 21.22; Deut 2.27.

Kiriath-jearim (= city of forests) A Gibeonite frontier town. Josh 9.17; 15.9; 18.14; Judg 18.12; 1 Sam 6.21–7.2; Neh 7.29; Jer 26.20–22.

Kish The father of Saul. 1 Sam 9.1; 14.51; Acts 13.21.

Kishon A seasonal river flowing through the plain of Esdraelon to enter the Mediterranean near Haifa. Judg 4.7,13; 5.21; 1 Kings 18.40. *Nahr el-Mukatta'.*

kiss The customary salutation of affection or respect given on the cheek or neck, or the feet as a mark of the greatest reverence. Gen 27.26; 29.13; 48.10; Ruth 1.14; 2 Sam 15.5; Mt 26.49; Lk 7.38; Acts 20.37; Rom 16.16; 1 Pet 5.14.

kitchen In an Israelite house meals were prepared outside in the courtyard or in its single room. Kitchens are mentioned only in the Temple. Ezek 46.24.

kite Both black and red species of this bird are known in Palestine, and they are said to have remarkably keen vision. Lev 11.14; Deut 14.13.

Kittim The son of Javan whose descendants settled in Cyprus and whose name came to apply to the islands and coastlands of the E Mediterranean. Gen 10.4; Num 24.24; Isa 23.1,12; Jer 2.10; Ezek 27.6.

kneading-trough A large shallow bowl of pottery or wood in which dough was prepared. Ex 8.3; 12.34; Deut 28.5,17.

knee, kneel An action expressing homage, worship or prayer. 1 Kings 19.18; 2 Kings 1.13; Dan 6.10; Mk 1.40; 10.17; 15.19; Acts 7.60; 9.40; 21.5; Rom 11.4; 14.11; Eph 3.14; Phil 2.10.

knife Excavations have revealed many sharp-edged cutting-instruments made of flint and metal. Gen 22.6; Josh 5.2; Jer 36.23.

know, knowledge Conceived by the Hebrews as making demands on the will as well as on the understanding. Ps 139; Jer 1.5; 8.7; 24.7; 31.34; Hos 13.4; 1 Cor 13.12; 1 Tim 2.4; 2 Tim 2.19; 3.7; Titus 1.1. *See also* Job 28.20–28.

Kohath, Kohathites The son of Levi who gave his name to a section of the Levites. Gen 46.11; Ex 6.16–18; 2 Chr 20.19.

Korah (1) The son of Esau. Gen 36.4–5. (2) The leader of a revolt against Moses. Num 16.1–33.

Laban Rebecca's brother. Gen ch. 29–31.

labor Regarded as honorable in Hebrew society, and idleness was condemned. Gen 3.17; Ex 20.8; Ps 104.23; 128.2; Prov 10.16. *See also* Deut 24.14; Prov 6.6; 1 Thess 4.11.

Lachish A stronghold 30 miles SW of Jerusalem dominating the Palestine-Egypt route. 2 Kings 14.19; 18.14–17; 2 Chr 11.9; Neh 11.30; Isa 36.2; 37.8. *Tell ed-Duweir.* Excavations by the Wellcome-Marston expedition (J. Starkey) 1932–38 showed that the site had been occupied from at least the Early Bronze Age and had become a military fortress by about 1650 BCE. Fortifications dating from the time of Rehoboam or earlier have been uncovered.

Lachish Letters In 1935 eighteen ostraca inscribed in Hebrew of the time of Jeremiah were found in a small guardroom under the gate-tower of Lachish. As well as being the earliest known copies of documents in classical Hebrew yet discovered, they shed light on the conditions prevailing during the Babylonian attack made at the time of the siege of Jerusalem 589–587 BCE..

Laish The original name of Dan. Judg 18.7–10. *See also* Josh 19.47.

lamb Frequently referred to from earliest times in connection with sacrifice. In fact no Hebrew festival took place without the offering of a lamb. Ex 12.3–10; Deut 32.14; Am 6.4. *See also* Ex 29.38–42; Lev 4.32–35. Used of Christ in the NT. Jn 1.29–36; Acts 8.32; Rev 5.6–12.

Lamb of God The title given to Jesus by John the Baptist. Jn 1.29–36. *See also* Isa 53.7; 1 Cor 5.7; Rev 5.6; 12.11; 17.14.

Lamech (1) A descendant of Cain. Gen 4.19–24. (2) The father of Noah. Gen 5.25–31.

lameness A common affliction and a bar from the priesthood. Lev 21.18; 2 Sam 4.4; 9.13. Jesus healed many cripples. Mt 11.5; 15.30, Lk 14.13. Used figuratively Job 29.15; Isa 35.6; Mt 18.8.

lamp Originally a clay saucer containing oil which fed a flax or rush wick, it developed into a closed bowl with a hole for the oil, a spout for the wick, and a handle. It was used both domestically and in worship. Ex 27.20; 30.7; Lev 24.2–4; 2 Kings 4.10; Prov 31.18; Mt 5.15; Lk 11.33; 15.8. Used figuratively Ps 119.105; Mt 6.22; Lk 12.35; Rev 21.23; 22.5.

lamp-stand Ex 25.31–40; 1 Kings 7.49; 1 Chr 28.15; 2 Chr 4.20; Zech 4.2; Mt 5.15; Mk 4.21.

language(s) The family of Semitic languages spoken in OT Palestine were as numerous as the various resident peoples. The Israelites originally spoke Hebrew which remained the literary language, but in everyday conversation Aramaic later replaced it. Gen 11.1–9; Ezra 4.7; Acts 2.5–11.

Laodicea An important commercial center in the Lycus valley in Asia Minor. Col 2.1; 4.13; Rev 3.14–22. *Eski Hisar*.

Lappidoth The husband of Deborah. Judg 4.4.

Lasea A town in Crete. Acts 27.8.

Latin The official language of Roman-occupied Palestine. Jn 19.20.

laugh Sometimes mentioned in a purely joyful sense. Ps 126.2; Eccl 3.4; Lk 6.21. More generally, however, it is associated with scorn or skepticism. Gen 18.11–15; Ps 2.4; 37.13; Mk 5.40.

law Specifically the Pentateuch containing the Mosaic codes. Ex 20.1–17; ch. 21–23; 25.1–31.17; ch. 35–40; Lev ch. 17–26; Deut ch. 12–26. For the NT teaching on the law Mt 5.17–48; 22.35–40; Jn 13.34; Rom 2.14; 7.22; 8.3; 13.7–10; Gal 2.16–3.25; 6.2; Heb 10.1–18; Jas 2.8–13.

lawyers In pre-exilic times, primarily priests by profession, they served as secretaries handling correspondence and book-keeping for the king. *See* 2 Kings 12.10. Later, they began copying the law and various sacred writings. Ezra 7.11. Gradually they separated themselves from the priestly class and became official interpreters of both the written and oral law. They are also called "scribes." Mt 23.1–32; Lk 7.30; 10.25; 11.43–54.

laying on of hands A symbolic act of dedication transferring blessing, power or authority. Gen 48.14; Deut 34.9; Mt 9.18; Mk 6.5; 10.16; 16.18; Lk 13.13; Acts 6.6; 8.17; 13.3; 19.6; 1 Tim 4.14; 2 Tim 1.6.

Lazarus (1) The brother of Martha and Mary. Jn 11.1–44. (2) The beggar in a parable. Lk 16.19–31.

lead The main sources of this metal were the Sinai peninsula, Egypt and Tarshish. Num 31.22–23; Job 19.24; Jer 6.29; Ezek 27.12; Zech 5.7. Used figuratively Ezek 22.18.

Leah The elder daughter of Laban. Gen 29.16–30.21; 49.31.

leather The skin of animals prepared for use as clothing. 2 Kings 1.8; Mt 3.4. Also used as a writing material. *See* Dead Sea Scrolls.

leaven A substance which causes fermentation when added to dough. Ex 12.14–20; 23.18; Lev 2.11. Used figuratively Mt 13.33; Mk 8.15; 1 Cor 5.6.

Lebanon The mountain mass, 100 miles long and averaging 7000 feet in height, of N Palestine; famed for its snowy peaks and cedars, and the source of the Jordan. Josh 13.6; 1 Kings 5.9; 2 Chr 2.8; Ps 92.12; Song 4.8,15; Jer 18.14.

Lebbaeus An apostle, also known as Thaddaeus and Judas. Mt 10.4; Mk 3.18; Lk 6.16; Acts 1.13.

leech This blood-sucking and tenacious worm, which fastens on to the skin, was abundant in Palestine before the swamps were drained. Prov 30.15.

leek A common and popular vegetable, of the onion genus, which is also used for medicinal purposes. Num 11.5.

legion A division of the Roman army totalling 6000 men. It is used in the NT for any very large number. Mt 26.53; Mk 5.1–17.

Lemuel The king of Massa. Prov 31.1–9.

lentil A cereal which grows freely in Palestine. Gen 25.34; 2 Sam 23.11; Ezek 4.9.

leopard Well known over most of Palestine in biblical times, this large spotted carnivore can reach a body length of up to 5 feet. Its ability to hide in the scantiest cover has helped it to survive in the Fertile Crescent. Song 4.8; Jer 5.6; 13.23; Hos 13.7. Used symbolically Isa 11.6; Dan 7.6; Rev 13.2.

leper, leprosy Used in the Bible to describe skin diseases which are deep-seated, spreading or chronic and require isolation. 2 Kings 5.1–14; 7.3; 2 Chr 26.19; Mt 8.2–4; Lk 17.11–19.

Levi (1) The son of Jacob and Leah, and ancestor of the priestly tribe. Gen 29.34; 49.5; Ex 6.16; Deut 33.8–10. (2) An ancestor of Jesus. Lk 3.24. (3) Another name for Matthew. Mk 2.14.

Leviathan A transliteration of a Hebrew root (= gathering itself in folds). The context of its use in the OT suggests some form of water creature. Job 41.1; Ps 74.12–14; Isa 27.1.

levirate marriage *See* Deut 25.5–10; Mt 22.23–30.

Levites Descendants of Levi who became the priestly tribe. Num 1.47–53; Judg 17.7–13. After the exile, those not descended from Aaron became an inferior order. Ezek 44.10–45.5.

liberty The essence of Christian liberty, found in Christ, lies in its *freedom* from the bondage of sin. 2 Cor 3.17; Gal 2.4. *See also* Lk 4.18; Jn 8.31–36; Rom 6.20–23; 8.3–17; Gal 5.1,13; 1 Pet 2.16; 2 Pet 2.19; Jas 2.12.

Libnah A Canaanite city near Lachish. Josh 10.29–31; 12.15; 15.42.

lie, lying God is, above all, a God of truth, and any attempts to veil or suppress the truth are unworthy of the people of God. Num 23.19; Prov 19.22; 21.28; 30.8; Jer 14.14; Hos 7.13; Mic 6.12; Jn 8.44; Acts 5.3; Col 3.9. *See also* Lev 19.11; Deut 19.16–19; Jn 17.17.

life Presented in the OT as the gift of God and linked essentially with the blood. Gen 2.7; Ps 27.1; 36.9; 91.16. In the NT it has a spiritual meaning and is shown to be the true life lived in fellowship with God now, and not interrupted by death; though its perfection is in the life to come. Mt 6.25; Jn 1.4; 3.36; 5.24–26; 14.6; 17.3; 20.31; Rom 2.7; 8.6; 2 Pet 1.3; 1 Jn 3.14; 5.12.

light The OT associates it closely with God. Gen 1.3; Ps 104.2; Isa 2.5; 10.17. In the NT Jesus is called the "light of the world," as are also his followers. Mt 5.14; Jn 1.4; 8.12.

lightning Associated in the Bible as a symbol of God's power. Ex 19.16; 20.18; Job 38.35; Ps 18.14; 144.6; Ezek 1.13; Dan 10.6; Nah 2.4; Zech 9.14; Mt 28.3; Lk 10.18; Rev 4.5; 8.5; 16.18.

Lights, Feast of *See* Dedication.

likeness Used by biblical writers as almost identical with "image." Gen 1.26; 2 Cor 3.18. *See also* Eph 4.24; Col 3.10.

lilies Bulbous plants abounding in Palestine in numerous varieties, but not specified in the Bible. They probably included the iris and lotus, and possibly the anemone. Song 2.1; Mt 6.28.

limestone Abundant in Palestine and burned to produce lime for plastering. *See* Deut 27.2; Dan 5.5; Am 2.1; Mt 23.27.

linen A material prepared from the fiber of flax, well known in the ancient world and a mark of quality. The dead were usually wrapped in it. Ex 28.4–8; 35.25; 2 Chr 3.14; 5.12; Mt 27.59; Mk 14.51; Lk 16.19; Jn 20.3–7; Rev 19.8,14.

lintel The horizontal beam above a doorway. Ex 12.21–23.

Linus A Christian at Rome. 2 Tim 4.21.

lion Throughout OT times these were widespread in Palestine, and common enough to be some danger to both humans and their stock. They are mentioned over one hundred times. Judg 14.5–6; 1 Sam 17.34–36; 1 Kings 13.23–26; Job 38.38–40; Dan 6.1–24; Heb 11.33. Used figuratively Ps 7.2; 10.9; 22.13, 21; Prov 26.13; 2 Tim 4.17; Rev 5.5.

lizard The most conspicuous vertebrates in Palestine, other than birds, numbering some 40 species and ranging in size from 2 feet down to about 2 inches. Lev 11.29–30; Prov 30.28.

loaf(ves) Mt 15.32–38; Mk 8.1–9; Cor 10.17.

Lo-ammi The symbolic name given to Hosea's third child. Hos 1.9; 2.23.

loan In early times these were made only for personal need. Interest was forbidden until trading methods changed in NT times. Lev 25.35–38; Deut 24.10–13. *See also* Ex 22.25; Deut 28.12; Ps 15.5; 37.21; Mt 25.27; Lk 19.23.

locust One of the most important insects in the Bible with over fifty mentions. It breeds in the Middle East and swarms can form clouds large enough to obscure the sun and strip trees and crops of all their leaves. Some species were, and are, eaten as a great delicacy and source of protein. Ex 10.3–5; Lev 11.20–22; Isa 33.4; Joel 1.4; Mt 3.4.

Lo-debar A town in Gilead E of Jordan. 2 Sam 9.1–5; 17.27.

Lois The grandmother of Timothy. 2 Tim 1.5.

LORD *See* Jehovah.

LORD of hosts A title for God, used especially by the prophets, showing that he is at all times the savior and protector of his people. 1 Sam 1.3; 17.45; Ps 24.10; 46.7,11; Jas 5.4.

Lord's Day, the The occasion when the Christian community met together for worship. Rev 1.10. *See also* Acts 20.7; 1 Cor 16.2.

Lord's Prayer The pattern prayer taught to his disciples by Christ. Mt 6.7–13; Lk 11.1–4.

Lord's Supper The name used for the commemoration of the last supper of Christ. *See* Mt 26.26–29; Mk 14.22–24; 1 Cor 11.17–26. It is also referred to as the "breaking of bread." Acts 20.7; 1 Cor 10.16.

Lo-ruhamah The name given to Hosea's daughter. Hos 1.6; 2.1; 2.23.

Lot The nephew of Abraham. Gen 11.31; 12.4; 13.1–13; 19.1–30; Lk 17.28–30; 2 Pet 2.7.

lots, casting of A popular method of divination in the OT, and used to make choices. Num 26.55; Ps 22.18; Jon 1.7; Mt 27.35; Acts 1.26. *See also* Urim.

love Although in the OT Hebrew the word has as wide a range of meanings as in English, it comes to stand for the chief quality of the ideal character because it is the very nature of God himself. Lev 19.18; Deut 6.4; Hos 3.1; 11.1. The NT is mainly concerned with the love of God as shown in Christ and the Christian love it awakens and commands in believers. Mt 5.44–48; 22.37–40; Jn 13.34–35; Rom 5.5; 1 Cor 13.4–13; 2 Cor 5.14–17; 1 Jn 3.13–24; 4.7–21.

Lucius A Christian of Cyrene. Acts 13.1.

Luke The traditional author of the third Gospel and of the Acts, a physician and companion of Paul on some of his missionary journeys. Col 4.14; 2 Tim 4.11; Philem 24. *See also* Acts 20.6–28.31.

Luz A Canaanite town N of Jerusalem. Gen 28.19; 35.6; Josh 18.13.

LXX The Roman form of the number 70, used for the Greek (Septuagint) translation of the OT and Apocrypha, which was reputedly done by seventy translators.

Lycia A fertile region in SW Asia Minor almost opposite Alexandria. Acts 27.5.

Lysanias The governor of a territory on the N side of Mt. Hermon. Lk 3.1.

Lystra A city some 25 miles SSW of Iconium on the "imperial road" to Pisidian Antioch. Acts 14.5–20; 16.1–3. *Zoldera.*

Maacah (1) The mother of Absalom. 2 Sam 3.3. (2) The favorite wife of Rehoboam. 2 Chr 11.20.

Macedonia The region in the Balkan peninsula where Paul first preached in Europe. Acts 16.9–17.14; 18.5.

Machir (1) The grandson of Joseph. Num 27.1. (2) A man who helped Mephibosheth. 2 Sam 9.1–6; 17.27.

madness In early times a disorder of the mind was thought to be caused by evil spirits. Later it was recognized that the Spirit of the Lord might cause a man to prophesy and at the same time show signs of "madness." *See* 1 Sam 10.5–7; 18.10; Mt 4.24; Jn 7.20; 10.20.

Magdala A town on the edge of the Sea of Galilee some 3 miles N of Tiberias. Mk 15.40; Lk 8.2; Jn 20.1.

magic All processes designed to tap and use supernatural powers to influence events, including divination, necromancy, sorcery, exorcism, soothsaying and witchcraft; all of which were forbidden to the Israelites. *See* Ex 22.18; Lev 19.26; 20.27; Deut 18.10–11; 1 Sam 28.8; Isa 47.9; Jer 27.9; Ezek 21.21; Acts 8.9; 13.6–8; 19.13–16.

magistrate The civil authority in a Roman colony. Acts 16.20–40.

Magog (1) The son of Japheth. Gen 10.2. (2) A land in the far north. Ezek 38.2; 39.6. Used symbolically Rev 20.8.

Mahalath (1) The wife of Esau. Gen 28.9. (2) The first wife of Rehoboam. 2 Chr 11.18.

Mahanaim An important site E of the Jordan on the frontier of Gad and Manasseh. Gen 32.2; Josh 13.24–30; 21.38–40; 2 Sam 2.8; 17.24–27; 1 Kings 4.14.

Maher-shalal-hash-baz The symbolic name Isaiah gave to his second son. Isa 8.1–4.

Mahli (= weak, sickly) The founder of a prominent levitical family. Num 3.20,33; Ezra 8.18.

Mahlon The first husband of Ruth. Ruth 1.2–5; 4.9–10.

Makkedah A Canaanite royal city in the Shephelah. Josh 10.10–30.

Malchus The servant of the high priest, Caiaphas. Jn 18.10. *See also* Lk 22.50.

Malta The rocky Mediterranean island of about 100 square miles colonized by the

Phoenicians and Greeks before its Roman conquest. Acts 27.39–28.10.

Mamre A place in the Hebron district. Gen 18.1; 23.17–19; 49.29–31.

Manaen A Christian at Antioch. Acts 13.1.

Manasseh (1) Joseph's son and the ancestor of the tribe. Gen 41.51; 48.1–20. (2) The king of Judah after Hezekiah. 2 Kings 20.21–21.18; 2 Chr 33.1–20.

mandrake A stemless perennial of the nightshade family which grows wild in Palestine, and has emetic, purgative and narcotic qualities. Gen 30.14–16; Song 7.13.

manger The feeding-trough for animals in a stall or stable which, in Palestine, would be attached to the owner's house. Lk 2.7–16; 13.15.

manna The food miraculously supplied to the Israelites during their wanderings in the desert. Ex 16.11–36; Josh 5.12. Throughout the Bible it is regarded as an example of God's blessing to man. Ps 78.24; Jn 6.31; Rev 2.17.

Manoah The father of Samson. Judg 13.2–24; 16.31.

mantle A loose cloak, usually of good quality. Josh 7.21; 2 Kings 2.13.

Maon A place in the hill-country of Judah, the home of Nabal. 1 Sam 25.2–42. *Tell Ma'în.*

Mara The name Naomi gave to herself. Ruth 1.20.

Marah (= bitter) The first camp of the Israelites after crossing the Red Sea. Ex 15.22–26.

Marana tha An Aramaic expression used by Paul meaning "Our Lord [has] come." 1 Cor 16.22.

marble Recrystallized limestone which can be highly polished. 1 Chr 29.2; Song 5.15; Rev 18.12.

Mark The Roman name for the cousin of Barnabas who finally became Paul's trusted helper in spite of an earlier disagreement. Acts 12.12,25; 13.5,13; 15.37–40; Col 4.10; 2 Tim 4.11; Philem 24; 1 Pet 5.13. Traditionally, the author of the earliest gospel.

market, market-place This was used also for recreation, public business, and for a court room. Mt 11.16; 20.3; Mk 7.4; Lk 11.43. *See also* Acts 16.19; 17.17.

marriage One wife was the ideal; and though polygamy was not expressly forbidden it is shown to be more likely to cause strife. *See* Gen 2.24; 16.2–3; 1 Sam 1.1–7; 1 Kings 11.1–4; Ps 128; Prov 31.10–31. Marriages were arranged and certain unions were forbidden or actively discouraged. Gen 21.21; 24.45–58; 29.17–19; 34.1–12; Lev 18.6–8; Josh 15.16; Judg 14.1–3; 1 Cor 7.39. Used symbolically of God and Israel, and of Christ and his church. Isa 54.5–8; Hos 2.2–20; 2 Cor 11.2; Eph 5.25–32; Rev 19.7–8; 21.2.

marriage ceremonies Special clothes were worn; there were bridesmaids and a "best man"; a procession with music and dancing to the bride's house; and a wedding feast. Judg 14.20; Isa 61.10; Jer 2.32; 7.34; Mt 25.1–13; Jn 2.1–10.

marriage customs Betrothal was almost as binding as marriage itself. Deut 22.23–24; Mt 1.18–19. Gifts were exchanged. Gen 34.12; Ex 22.16–17; 1 Kings 9.16. A public declaration of the relationship was followed by a written contract. Mal 2.14.

marrow The heart of the bone. Job 21.24; Heb 4.12.

Mars' Hill *See* Areopagus.

Martha The sister of Lazarus and Mary. Lk 10.38–42; Jn 11.1–45.

Mary (1) The mother of Jesus. Lk 1.26–56; 2.1–35; 8.19–21; Jn 19.26–27; Acts 1.14. (2) The sister of Martha. Lk 10.38–42; Jn 11.1–45; 12.1–7. (3) Mary of Magdala (Mary Magdalene). Mk 15.40; 16.1–7; Lk 8.2; Jn 20.11–18. (4) The mother of James and Joseph. Mt 27.55–56. (5) The mother of John Mark. Acts 12.12.

mason The simple Palestinian house was built by craftsmen who were stoneshapers, masons and carpenters. Skilled masons were employed in specialized work on fortifications, palaces and the Temple. 2 Sam 5.11; 2 Kings 12.11; 22.6.

Massah (= testing) The scene of the miraculous gift of water to the thirsty Israelites in the wilderness. Ex 17.1–7; Ps 95.8.

Mattaniah The original name of king Zedekiah. 2 Kings 24.17.

Matthan The grandfather of Joseph. Mt 1.15.

Matthew (= gift of God) One of the Twelve, also known as Levi. Mt 10.3; Lk 5.27–29; 6.15; Acts 1.13.

Matthias The disciple chosen to fill Judas' place. Acts 1.15–26.

mattock A more robust agricultural implement than the wooden Egyptian hoe. 1 Sam 13.20; Isa 2.4.

Media, Medes The ancient names for NW Iran and its steppe dwellers. Overrun by the Assyrians, they later founded the Persian empire in alliance with the Chaldaeans but were finally merged into it as a province. 2 Kings 17.6; 18.11; Dan 5.28,31; 6.8.

mediator, mediation An intermediary who brings together two or more estranged people. Christ is the mediator of the new covenant between God and man. 1 Tim 2.5; Heb 8.6; 9.15; 12.24. *See also* 1 Sam 2.25; Job 9.33; Rom 8.34.

medicine Doctors were known from earliest times, and although scientific medical knowledge was limited, basic laws of hygiene existed. Lev ch. 11–25; Deut 23.9–14. Forms of treatment. Isa 1.6; 38.21; Lk 10.34.

Megiddo An important fortress on the Carmel range 20 miles SSE of Haifa, guarding the crossing place of the great commercial and military highway between Egypt and Syria. Josh 17.11–13; Judg 5.19; 1 Kings 9.15; 2 Kings 9.27; 23.29; Zech 12.11. *Tell el-Mutesillim.* A major excavation site which has shown the formidable civilization facing the Israelites when they invaded Canaan; and has yielded many treasures from its twenty main occupation levels, including examples of carved ivory of the Later Bronze Age now in the Oriental Institute of the University of Chicago.

Melchizedek The priest-king of Salem. Gen 14.18–20. And, in this dual role, regarded as the forerunner and type of Christ. Ps 110.4; Heb 5.6; 6.20–7.28.

Memphis The capital of ancient Egypt, a few miles S of Cairo. Isa 19.13; Jer 2.16; 44.1; 46.14, 19; Ezek 30.13; Hos 9.6. *Mît Rahîneh.*

Menahem (= comforter) The son of Gadi who seized the throne of Israel. 2 Kings 15.14–22.

Mene mene tekel parsin The Aramaic inscription interpreted by Daniel during Belshazzar's feast. Dan 5.1–31.

Mephibosheth Jonathan's lame son. 2 Sam 4.4; 9.1–13.

Merab Saul's eldest daughter. 1 Sam 14.49; 18.17–20.

Merari The third and youngest son of Levi and ancestor of a division of the Levites. Num 3.16–20,33–37; Josh 21.34–40; 1 Chr 15.16–21.

Merathaim The region where the Tigris and Euphrates enter the sea. Used symbolically of Babylon. Jer 50.21.

mercy, merciful The basic idea is compassion to one in need or distress who has no claim to favorable treatment. Deut 4.31; Mt 5.7; Eph 2.4; 1 Tim 1.2; Titus 3.5; Jas 2.13. *See also* Ex 34.6; Ps 103.8; Lk 6.36.

Meribah The place where the Israelites rebelled against Moses. Ex 17.1–7; Ps 106.32.

Merodach-baladan The leader of the Chaldaeans who seized the throne of Babylon and tried to persuade Hezekiah to join an alliance against Assyria. 2 Kings 20.12–19.

Merom, Waters of The scene of Joshua's victory over his allies. Josh 11.1–9.

Mesha The king of Moab who rebelled against Israel and offered his son as a human sacrifice. 2 Kings 3.4–27.

Meshach The name given to Mishael, one of Daniel's three companions. Dan 1.6–3.30.

Meshech The grandson of Noah and the ancestor of a warlike people inhabiting what is now E Anatolia. 1 Chr 1.5; Ps 120.5; Ezek 27.13; 39.1–6.

Mesopotamia A rendering of the Hebrew Aram-naharaim. The whole area between the rivers Euphrates and Tigris, but often restricted to the western portion. The home of Abraham. Acts 2.9; 7.2. *See also* Gen 24.10; Judg 3.8; 1 Chr 19.6.

Messiah The Hebrew for "anointed one." This Israelite way of making a king became specially applied to the line of David, from which the prophets looked for a deliverer who would bring in a rule of universal peace and justice. *See* 2 Sam 22.51; Isa 9.2–7; 11.1–11; Jer 23.5–6; Ezek 34.23–24. The NT concept of the Messiah follows from that in the OT but includes more directly the concept of suffering for others. Isa ch. 53. Jesus claims to be the Messiah and is acknowledged as such by his disciples. Mt 1.18; Lk 4.14–21; 24.26; Acts 4.27. *See* Christ.

Methuselah The grandfather of Noah who lived to a great age. Gen 5.21–27.

Micah (1) A prophet of Judah contemporary with Hosea and Isaiah. Jer 26.18. (2) An Ephraimite who set up a shrine in his house and persuaded a wandering Levite to be its priest. Judg 17.1–18.26.

Micaiah The son of Imlah, and the prophet who advised Ahab and Jehoshaphat on their proposed attack on Ramoth-gilead. 1 Kings 22.1–38.

Michael The guardian of the Jews. Dan 10.13; 11.1; 12.1. An archangel. Jude 9; Rev 12.7–9.

Michal Saul's youngest daughter, and the wife of David. 1 Sam 18.17–29; 19.11–17; 25.44; 2 Sam 3.12–15; 6.20–23.

Michmash A city on the pass from Bethel to Jericho and 7 miles N of Jerusalem. 1 Sam 13.2–14.31; Neh 11.31. *Mukhmâs.*

Midian, Midianites The son of Abraham and Keturah and ancestor of the Bedouin tribe living in N Arabia opposite the Sinai peninsula. Their relations with the Israelites varied from time to time. Gen 25.1–6; 37.28; Ex 2.15–22; Num 31.1–10; Judg 6.1–8.28.

midwife A person who assists women in childbirth. Gen 35.17; 38.28; Num 31.1–10; Ex 1.15–21. *See also* Ezek 16.4.

Milcah Rebecca's grandmother. Gen 11.29; 24.15.

Milcom The national god of the Ammonites. 1 Kings 11.5; 2 Kings 23.13–14.

mile The Roman mile of about 1000 double paces or 1620 yards. Mt 5.41.

milk The staple diet of the Hebrews, obtained from sheep, goats, cows and camels and often churned into curds. Gen 32.15; Deut 32.14; Prov 27.27. Jewish dietary law forbade the cooking of meat in milk. Deut 14.21. Used as a symbol of prosperity and fertility. Ex 3.8; Joel 3.18.

mill, millstones A combination of two stones, one resting on the other. The upper was moved, usually by hand, to grind the grain put between them. Deut 24.6; Job 41.24; Jer 25.10; Mk 9.42. *See also* Judg 16.21.

millennium The Latin for a thousand years; the period given in Rev 20.1–15 for the reign of Christ and his resurrected saints. *See also* Acts 3.20; 1 Cor 15.3–28.

millet Used only as an ingredient of bread, and not as a substitute for flour. Ezek 4.9.

Millo An ancient fortification or bastion of Jerusalem. 2 Sam 5.9; 1 Kings 11.27; 2 Chr 32.5.

mines, mining Excavations for various mineral ores were known to have existed in Palestine from an early date. Job 28.1–11. *See also* Gen 4.22; Num 31.22; Deut 8.9.

ministry The Greek word used, found mainly in the Acts and Letters of Paul, applies generally to work for Christ in the church. 2 Cor 4.1; Eph 4.11–12.

mint There are three varieties in Palestine growing wild on banks and in ditches. It was commonly used medicinally, and as a perfume and flavoring. Mt 23.23; Lk 11.42.

miracle(s) A number of Greek and Hebrew words are used in the Bible to refer to the personal activity in nature and history of a loving God. These characterize it as distinctive, powerful and meaningful; and are variously translated as "miracle," "portent," "sign." Miracles in the Gospels:

Found only in Matthew

Two blind men cured	Mt 9.27–31
A mute man cured	9.32–33
The temple-tax money	17.24–27

Found only in Mark

Deaf and mute man cured	Mk 7.31–37
Blind man cured	8.22–26

Found only in Luke

The big catch of fish	Lk 5.1–11
The widow of Nain's son raised	7.11–17
A crippled woman cured	13.11–17
Dropsy cured	14.1–6
Ten lepers cured	17.11–19
Malchus' ear restored	22.50–51

Found only in John

Water made wine at Cana	Jn 2.1–11
Roman officer's son cured of fever	4.46–54
A cripple healed at Jerusalem	5.1–9
A man born blind cured	9.1–7
Lazarus raised from the dead	11.38–44
The catch of large fish	21.1–14

Common to Matthew and Mark

Canaanite woman's daughter cured	Mt 15.28; Mk 7.24
Four thousand fed	Mt 15.32; Mk 8.1
Fig-tree cursed	Mt 21.19; Mk 11.13

Common to Matthew and Luke

Centurion's paralysed servant cured	Mt 8.5; Lk 7.1
Blind and mute man cured	Mt 12.22; Lk 11.14

Common to Mark and Luke

Possessed man cured in synagogue	Mk 1.23; Lk 4.33

Common to Matthew, Mark, Luke

Leper cured	Mt 8.2; Mk 1.40; Lk 5.12
Peter's mother-in-law cured	Mt 8.14; Mk 1.30; Lk 4.38
Storm calmed	Mt 8.23; Mk 4.37; Lk 8.22
Possessed men cured	Mt 8.28; Mk 5.1; Lk 8.26
Paralysed man cured	Mt 9.2; Mk 2.3; Lk 5.18
Jairus' daughter raised	Mt 9.23; Mk 5.23;

	Lk 8.41
Woman with hemorrhages cured	Mt 9.20; Mk 5.25; Lk 8.43
Man's withered hand cured	Mt 12.10; Mk 3.1; Lk 6.6
Epileptic boy cured	Mt 17.14; Mk 9.17; Lk 9.37
Blind man cured	Mt 20.30; Mk 10.46; Lk 18.35
Common to Matthew, Mark, John	
Christ walks on the lake	Mt 14.25; Mk 6.48; Jn 6.19
Common to All	
Five thousand fed	Mt 14.15; Mk 6.34; Lk 9.10; Jn 6.3

Miriam The eldest sister of Moses and Aaron. Ex 15.20–21; Num 12.1–15; 20.1. *See also* Ex 2.4–8.

Mirror(s) These consisted of round or oval polished metal surfaces, usually of bronze. Ex 38.8; Job 37.18; 1 Cor 13.12; Jas 1.23.

Mishael *See* Meshach.

Mithredath The treasurer of Cyrus of Persia. Ezra 1.7–8.

Mizpah (= watchpost) (1) Where Jacob and Laban made a covenant. Gen 31.44–54. (2) The home of Jephthah E of the Jordan. Judg 11.11,29–39. (3) A town of Benjamin near Gibeon and Ramah. 1 Sam 7.11; 1 Kings 15.22; 2 Kings 25.23–25; Jer 40.6–15.

Mnason A Christian from Cyprus. Acts 21.16.

Moab, Moabites The ancient kingdom and people in the highlands E of the Jordan opposite Bethlehem. Though probably kinsmen of the Israelites, they opposed their entry into Palestine and there was constant war between them. Judg 3.12–30; 11.15–18; 2 Sam 8.2; Isa ch. 15–16; Ezek 25.8–11; Zeph 2.8–10.

Moabite Stone Slabs of black basalt discovered at *Dhibhan* in Transjordan in 1863, now in the Louvre. Dated about 830 BCE the inscription, left by Mesha, king of Moab, commemorates his revolt against Israel and supplements the OT narrative of the events and the reigns of Omri and Ahab.

Molech (Moloch) An Amorite god whose worship was associated with the sacrifice of children in the fire. Lev 20.1–5; 1 Kings 11.6–8; 2 Kings 23.10; Acts 7.40–43. *See also* 2 Kings 16.2–3; Jer 7.30–31.

money There was no coined money in Israel until after the exile. Before this, payment was made by barter. Later it took the form of paying out an agreed quantity of precious metal. *See* Gen 13.2; 23.16. Until the Maccabean period the Jews used the coinage of their conquerors. The NT emphasizes the spiritual dangers that money can bring. Mk 10.23–25; 1 Tim 6.10,17–19.

money-changers Since only Jewish money could be offered in the Temple, these dealers changed, at a commission, all currencies for the Jews of the Dispersion. Mt 21.12; Jn 2.15.

monkeys *See* apes.

month There were twelve months of 29 or 30 days running from one new moon to the next. In order to keep the lunar and solar year synchronized it was necessary from time to time to add a supplementary month. Names, of Canaanite origin, were given according to the season. Ex 13.4; 1 Kings 6.37–38; 8.2. After the exile, numbers were used until the Babylonian calendar was adopted. Neh 1.1; 2.1; Zech 1.7.

moon The object of pagan worship, forbidden to the Israelites. Deut 4.19; 17.2–5; 2 Kings 23.5. It was associated with the coming of the Messiah and the Day of the Lord. Joel 2.10,31; Mk 13.24; Rev 21.23.

Mordecai A Jewish exile and the deliverer of his countrymen from Persian persecution. Esth 2.5–10.3.

Moriah The place where God tested Abraham, and the site of Solomon's Temple. Gen 22.2; 2 Chr 3.1.

Moses The great political and religious leader of the Israelites from slavery in Egypt to a developed nationhood. He was the instrument of God's revelation by which Israel was called to be the people of God. Ex 2.1–40.38; Lev ch. 1–27; Num ch. 1–36; Deut ch. 1–34; Mt 17.1–5; Lk 24.44.

moth An insect larva common to all parts of the world which damages and destroys cloth. Isa 50.9; Mt 6.19–20.

mother Both the OT and NT refer to motherhood as a privilege and joy. Gen 3.20; Prov 31.1; Jn 16.21. She was to be honored equally with the father. Ex 20.12. Also used of the earthly and heavenly Jerusalem. Isa 66.7–13; Gal 4.26.

mount, mountain Like most ancient people,

the Israelites thought of mountains as the dwelling-place of God. Deut 33.2; Ps 74.2. Their own worship became contaminated by the hill-shrines of the Canaanites. 2 Kings 23.13–20. Mountains also served as refuges, landmarks, look-outs, assembly-places and cemeteries. Josh 8.33; Judg 6.2; Isa 18.3.

mountain-goat This is the Nubian Ibex or Rock Goat which stands about 34 inches at the shoulder with slender, clearly-ridged horns sweeping back in a wide curve. The general color is grey, and the species is confined to the mountains E of the Nile. Deut 14.5; Job 39.1; Ps 104.18.

mourning The Israelites had elaborate and varied ways of showing sorrow. Deut 14.1; 1 Sam 31.13; 2 Sam 1.2; 3.31; 2 Chr 35.25; Jer 16.5–7; Mt 9.23. The period of mourning also varied. Gen 50.4; Num 20.29; 1 Sam 31.13.

mulberry The tree was cultivated in biblical times for its fruit, though it is rather rare in Palestine today. Lk 17.6.

mule There was an implicit ban on breeding this cross between a donkey stallion and a horse mare, but they appear to have been imported for load-carrying (being sure-footed in hilly country). Their use for riding seems to have been confined to the nobility. 2 Sam 13.29; 1 Kings 1.33; 10.25; Ps 32.9; Ezek 27.14. *See also* Lev 19.19.

murder, murderer Premeditated murder is punishable by death in all OT law codes, and an obligation was on the nearest relative to see that the death sentence was carried out. Ex 21.12–14; Num 35.16–21; Deut 19.11–13. When the murderer could not be found, a special atonement service had to be offered. Deut 21.1–9.

music, musician Both instrumental and vocal music were a familiar part of Israelite life from early times in ceremonial, military exercises and as recreation. The Levites provided a choir and orchestra for the Temple worship which kept together right through the exile. *See* Gen 4.21; 31.27; 1 Sam 10.5; 16.23; 2 Kings 3.15; 1 Chr 6.31–32; 15.16; 2 Chr 5.12–14; 7.6; Neh 12.27,45; Ps 68.25; 150; Eccl 2.8. Music played an important part in the Christian life. Eph 5.19; Col 3.16.

mustard Both the black and white varieties of this plant are known in Palestine. While the leaves were used as vegetables, the seeds provided powder for seasoning. In NT times the black mustard-seed was also cultivated for its oil. Mt 13.31–32; 17.20.

muzzle The Mosaic law had specific and humane regulations about oxen. Deut 25.4.

Myra A town in Asia Minor. Acts 27.5. *Dembre.*

myrrh The resin of a thorny bush with a thin, papery bark which was used as a spice and in the making of cosmetics, in the preparation of the holy oil for anointing, and for embalming. It is a native of Arabia and Africa. Ex 30.23–25; Song 1.13; Mt 2.11; Jn 19.39–40.

myrtle An evergreen shrub well known in Palestine and used for making the arbors used at the Festival of Booths. Neh 8.15; Isa 41.19; 55.13; Zech 1.8–11. Esther's Hebrew name "Hadassah" = "myrtle." Esth 2.7.

Mysia A region in NW Asia Minor. Acts 16.6–8.

mystery In NT times it was widely used of the "secret knowledge" given to initiates into certain pagan religions. NT writers contrast with it God's eternal purpose for the world which is made known through Christ. 1 Cor 15.51. *See also* 1 Cor 2.6–10; Eph 1.9; Col 1.26.

Naamah (1) Tubal-cain's sister. Gen 4.22. (2) Solomon's wife. 1 Kings 14.21.

Naaman The commander-in-chief of Ben-hadad, king of Damascus. 2 Kings 5.1–19; Lk 4.27.

Nabal A wealthy sheep-farmer who refused to pay tribute to David. 1 Sam 25.2–42.

Naboth A citizen of Jezreel who refused to sell his vineyard to Ahab. 1 Kings 21.1–25. *See also* Lev 25.23; 2 Kings 9.30–37.

Nadab (1) The eldest son of Aaron. Ex 6.23; Lev 10.1–7. (2) The son and successor of Jeroboam, king of Judah. 1 Kings 15.25–32.

Nahash An Ammonite king who tried to humiliate the Israelites. 1 Sam 11.1–11.

Nahor (1) The grandfather of Abraham. Gen 11.22-27. (2) The brother of Abraham who stayed in Harran, and was the ancestor of the Aramaean tribes. Gen 22.20–24.

Nahum (= full of comfort) A prophet of Elkosh, contemporary with Jeremiah.

nail Small metal spike, usually used for fastening wood. Isa 41.7; Jn 20.25.

nails To leave the nails untrimmed was a sign of mourning. Deut 21.12.

Nain A town SE of Nazareth where Jesus performed a miracle. Lk 7.11–17.

name In the biblical record a person's name was important both to himself and to others. Names are seen as indicators of character, function, relationship or destiny. The choice of a name often has special significance. To give a new name was to signify a new character. Gen 17.5–8; 25.25–26; 32.24–30; 35.18; Deut 28.9–10; 1 Sam 4.21; Isa 8.3; Hos 1.4; Mt 28.19; Acts 2.38.

Naomi The wife of Elimelech who immigrated to Moab. Ruth ch. 1–4.

Naphtali (1) The sixth son of Jacob and ancestor of the tribe. Gen 30.7–8; Num 1.42–43; Josh 19.32–39; 2 Kings 15.29. (2) The territory which in NT times was included in Galilee, and so became the cradle of the Christian faith. Mt 4.13–16.

Narcissus A Roman whose family was greeted by Paul. Rom 16.11.

nard *See* spikenard.

Nathan A notable prophet in the reigns of David and Solomon. 2 Sam 7.1–17; 12.1–25; 1 Kings 1.5–45.

Nathanael One of Christ's disciples from Cana in Galilee. Jn 1.44–51; 21.2.

nations Refers to the non-Israelite nations in the sense of "outsiders" or "heathen." Isa 43.9; Ezek 5.6. *See also* Lk 12.30.

Nazarene, Nazorean (= one from Nazareth) A term often applied to Christ, at first with some condescension. Mt 2.23. Later used as a popular name for the early Christians. Acts 24.5.

Nazareth A village in the hills of Galilee overlooking the caravan routes through Palestine, and the boyhood home of Jesus. Mt 2.23; Lk 1.26; 2.4,51; 4.16–30. *En Nâsirah.*

Nazirite One who put himself completely at the disposal of God by vow for a certain period, and undertook strict self-discipline. Num 6.1–21; Am 2.11–12. *See also* Lk 1.15; Acts 18.18; 21.23–24.

Neapolis The port of Philippi. Acts 16.11. *Kavalla.*

Nebo (1) The mountain in Moab where Moses died. Deut 34.1–5. *Jebel en-Nebā.* (2) The Babylonian god of literature and science. Isa 46.1.

Nebuchadnezzar (Nebuchadrezzar) The son of Nabopolassar, founder of the neo-Babylonian empire. He made Judah a vassal state, and on three occasions deported Jews to Babylon. He went out of his mind and died in 562 BCE. 2 Kings 24.1–25.22; 2 Chr 36.5–13; Jer 39.1–12; 46.2–28; Dan ch. 2–4.

Nebuzaradan The captain of Nebuchadnezzar's bodyguard. 2 Kings 25.8–12; Jer 39.11–14; 52.12–30.

Neco The Pharaoh of Egypt who supported Assyria against Babylon. He defeated the forces of Judah under Josiah at Megiddo and made it a vassal state. 2 Chr 35.20–36.5.

needle Many have been found in Bible lands made of bone, bronze and iron. Mt 19.24. *See also* Gen 3.7; Job 16.15.

Negeb An area of semi-desert country S of Judah, E of the coastal plain and W of the Dead Sea. Gen 12.9; Num 13.17–29; Judg 1.9; 1 Sam 27.10–11; Zech 7.7.

Nehemiah A Jewish exile who reached high rank at the court of Artaxerxes of Persia, and obtained permission to return as governor of Judah to supervise the task of reconstruction. Neh 1.1–2.18; 6.15.

Nehushtan The bronze serpent made by Moses as a symbol of deliverance which became an object of idolatrous worship. 2 Kings 18.4.

neighbor Normally a fellow-Israelite, but foreigners taking up permanent residence came within the range of neighborly conduct. In the NT the scope is widened to include any person whom one is able to help. Ex 20.16–17; Lev 19.18,33–34; Lk 10.25–27.

Nereus A Roman Christian greeted by Paul. Rom 16.15.

Nergal A Babylonian deity worshiped as the god of storm, war, pestilence and hunting. 2 Kings 17.30.

Nergal-sharezer The Babylonian general who released Jeremiah from prison. Jer 39.13–14.

Nero The Roman emperor to whom Paul appealed. *See* Acts 25.10–12.

net Used for catching birds and fish in OT times. Prov 1.17; Isa 19.8. The NT mentions three methods of fishing with nets. Mt 4.18; 13.47; Lk 5.4. Used metaphorically of the plots of the wicked. Ps 10.9; 141.10.

new moon This marked the opening of a new month and was celebrated with sacrifices, social gatherings and recreation. 2 Kings 4.22–23; Isa 66.23; Hos 2.11; Am 8.5. *See also* Num 10.10.

New Testament About one-third the size of the OT, it contains twenty-seven short books, the Scriptures of the Christians and the record of a new covenant made through Jesus Christ. Written over a period of some 75 years, it contains accounts of the life and works of Jesus Christ, the beginnings of the Christian church and the essentials of Christian teaching.

New Year Originally it was kept at the end of the harvest (September–October). *See* Ex 23.16. During the exile the Babylonian spring

New Year was adopted (March–April). After the exile the emphasis came back to the original date. *See* Lev 23.23–25; Num 29.1–6.

Nicanor (1) One of those chosen to distribute relief to the poor. Acts 6.1–6.

Nicodemus A wealthy Pharisee who, from a cautious inquirer, became an open disciple of Christ. Jn 3.1–12; 7.50–52; 19.38–42.

Nicolaitans A sect which arose in the churches of Ephesus and Pergamum. Rev 2.6, 15–16. *See also* Acts 15.28–29.

Nicolaus One of those chosen to distribute relief to the poor. Acts 6.1–6.

Nicopolis A city in Epirus where Paul invited Titus to spend the winter with him. Titus 3.12. *Paleoprevaza.*

Niger The surname of Simeon of Antioch. Acts 13.1.

Nile The great river of Egypt whose annual flooding renewed the fertility of the land. Gen 41.1; Ex 1.22–2.3; 7.17–21; Isa 18.2; 19.5–7; Jer 46.7; Am 8.8.

Nimrod The great-grandson of Noah who lived in Babylonia. Gen 10.8–12.

Nimshi The father of Jehu. 1 Kings 19.16.

Nineveh The capital of the Assyrian empire, on the E bank of the Tigris defended by a great wall and moat, which fell about 612 BCE. 2 Kings 19.36; Jon 1.2; 3; 4.11; Nah 3.7; Zeph 2.13–15. *Tell Quyunjiq* and *Tell Nebi Yûnus.*

Nisroch An Assyrian god worshiped in Nineveh. 2 Kings 19.37.

Noah The grandson of Methuselah who appears as the first cultivator, and the hero of the Flood. Gen 5.28–32; 6.5–9.17; Mt 24.37–38; Heb 11.7.

Nob A city of priests, near Anathoth, whose inhabitants were massacred by Saul after Ahimelech had assisted the fugitive David. 1 Sam ch. 21–22.

Nod The land of Cain's exile. Gen 4.16.

Nun The father of Joshua. Ex 33.11.

nurse Generally, Hebrew women nursed their own children, but wet nurses were employed and regarded as an important member of the household. Gen 24.59; Ex 2.7–9; 2 Kings 11.2. "Nurse" in the sense of "attendant" is used in 2 Sam 4.4; Ruth 4.16.

Nympha The owner of a house in Laodicea where a church met. Col 4.15.

oak Many species of this tree grow in Palestine and it is frequently mentioned in the Bible. Gen 35.8; 2 Sam 18.9–10; Ezek 27.6; Zech 11.2. In some religions it was considered sacred. Isa 1.29. Also used to symbolize power and strength. Isa 2.13; Am 2.9.

oath A method of calling God to witness that one is telling the truth, and therefore that one's declaration is absolutely binding. Gen 21.23; Num 5.20–24; ch. 30; Deut 6.13; Ruth 1.17; Mt 5.33–37; Heb 6.16; Jas 5.12. *See also* Ex 22.10; Ps 63.11; Zech 5.3.

Obadiah Ahab's minister who protected the prophets. 1 Kings 18.2–16.

Obed The grandfather of David and the ancestor of Jesus. Ruth 4.17–21.

Obed-edom The man in whose house David left the Ark for safe keeping. 2 Sam 6.9–12.

obedience, obey The supreme test of faith in God, and the response which he looks for in people. Gen 22.18; Jn 14.15; Rom 5.19; 6.17; Phil 2.8; Heb 5.8; 1 Pet 1.14; 1 Jn 2.3–5. People must also discharge their obligations to those in lawful authority over them. *See* Prov 5.12; Mt 22.21; Rom 13.1–7; Eph 6.1; Col 3.20; 1 Pet 2.18.

offerings Making offerings to God was a very ancient practice. Gen 4.3–4; 8.20; Ex 10.25. The detailed form and order laid down in Lev ch. 1–7 arose from the need for purification from sin and the desire to enter into fellowship with God. *See* sacrifice.

Og A king of the Amorites. Deut 3.1–11; 31.4; Ps 135.10–11.

Oholah, Oholibah Symbolic names for Samaria and Jerusalem. Ezek ch. 23.

Oholibamah The wife of Esau. Gen 36.2–25.

oil Obtained mainly from the fruit of the olive-tree by crushing the olives. It was an important element in the economy of the people. Num 18.12; Ezra 3.7; Neh 5.11. It was used for cooking 1 Kings 17.12–16; lighting Ex 27.20; Mt 25.1–4; anointing kings, priests, sacred objects, guests and the sick Ex 30.25–33; 1 Sam 10.1; Isa 1.6; Mk 6.13; Lk 7.46; and for personal use 2 Sam 12.20; Dan 10.3.

ointment Used medicinally, for personal use and in embalming. The base was olive oil with various spices added. Mt. 26.6–13.

Old Testament This consists of those books in Hebrew (and Aramaic) which tell how God made a covenant with his chosen people, and how that special relationship was worked out in history. The Jews make a threefold division into Law, Prophets and Writings, the historical books being included under the Prophets. It is more usual among Christians to class the books as Law, Histories, Prophets, Poetical Books and Wisdom Literature. *See* Mt 5.17; Lk 24.44–47.

olive A slow-growing, but long-lived tree which grows best in the dry, stony soil of the Middle East. It was greatly valued for its fruit, used as a food, and for the oil made from it which was used in cooking and as a fuel for lamps. Used as a common figure of speech in the Bible for prosperity and joy. Gen 8.10–11; Deut 24.20; 1 Chr 27.28; Ps 52.8; Jer 11.16; Hos 14.6; Mt 26.30; Rom 11.17–18.

Olives, Mount of (Olivet) A ridge of hills running for about a mile on the E of Jerusalem and separated from it by the Kidron gorge. It had deep religious associations. 2 Sam 15.30; Zech 14.4; Mt 21.1; 26.30; Lk 19.37; 21.37; 22.39; Acts 1.12. *See also* Ezek 11.23. *Jebel et Tûr*.

Olympas A Roman Christian. Rom 16.15.

omega The last letter of the Greek alphabet. Used with "alpha," the first letter, as a symbol of the inclusiveness of God. Rev 1.8; 21.6; 22.13.

omer A Hebrew dry measure containing about 2.25 liters.

Omri One of the most important of Israel's kings, who seized the throne and established his dynasty by a military coup. He is the first to be mentioned in non-biblical records: the Moabite Stone. 1 Kings 16.8–28.

On An ancient city of Lower Egypt near Memphis. Associated with sun worship, it was called Heliopolis by the Greeks. Gen. 41.45; Ezek 30.17.

Onesimus (= profitable) The slave of Philemon of Colossae who ran away from his master. *See* Philemon, Letter to.

Onesiphorus A Christian of Ephesus. 2 Tim 1.16–18; 4.19.

Ophel Part of the E hill of Jerusalem. 2 Chr 27.3; Neh 3.27.

Ophir The country from which gold, precious stones and almug wood were imported into Judah. 1 Kings 9.26–28; 10.11.

Ophrah The home of Gideon in Manasseh. Judg 6.11–24; 8.27,32.

oracle(s) Pronouncements that come from a deity. Used for the entire OT, or a specific part of it; and for God's final revelation through Jesus Christ. Num 23; 24; Rom 3.2; Heb 5.12; 1 Pet 4.11.

Oreb A Midianite chief who invaded Israel. Judg 7.24–25; Isa 10.26.

Orion A group of fixed stars visible for the greater part of the year. Job 38.31.

ornaments Many examples of personal ornaments have been found in excavations, perhaps the most outstanding being those at Ur. Although the wearing of ornaments at such special occasions as weddings was considered fit and proper, the excessive wearing of ornaments is condemned in both the OT and NT. Details of ornaments commonly worn are given in Gen 24.22–23; Ex 32.3; 33.5; Prov 25.11–12; Isa 3.18–23; 61.10; Ezek 16.11–13; 1 Tim 2.9.

Orpah The sister-in-law of Ruth. Ruth 1.4–14.

orphan(s) From earliest times their care was to be the concern of Israelites. Deut 10.18; 24.17; 26.12; 27.19. *See also* Ex 22.22–24. However, there was a general failure to do this. Job 24.3; Isa 1.23; Jer 5.28.

Osnapper The Assyrian king who the Samaritans claimed had brought men from Susa and Elam to their city. Ezra 4.9–10.

ostrich A very large bird which can run at great speeds. It was much more common in Palestine in biblical times than it is today. Job 39.13; Isa 43.20; Lam 4.3.

Othniel The nephew of Caleb and the first of the Judges. Judg 1.13; 3.8–11.

oven Originally a hole in the ground with the sides coated in clay; later made of stone or well-baked bricks. Ex 8.3. Used figuratively. Hos 7.7.

owl Many species of this nocturnal bird live in Palestine, building their nests in areas near villages, preferably in olive-trees. It is listed among the unclean birds. Lev 11.16–18; Deut 14.15–17; Ps 102.6; 34.11; Zeph 2.14.

ox, oxen By the beginning of the Bronze Age, before the patriarchs settled in Palestine, the ox was part of the farming scene in the Nile valley. Several distinct types were known around 4500 BCE in Mesopotamia; and biblical records show that cattle were widely kept. Num 7.3; Deut 22.10; 1 Kings 1.9; Ezek 1.10; Lk 14.3–6.

Ozni The son of Gad and founder of a clan. Num 26.16.

Paddan-aram The region in Mesopotamia where Laban lived. Gen 28.2–7; 46.15.

paint Used with powder by Egyptian women as it is today, but the practice was frowned on by the Hebrews. 2 Kings 9.30. *See also* Jer 4.30.

palace The royal residence, often fortified. 1 Kings 21.1; 2 Kings 20.18; Dan 4.4. *See also* 1 Kings 7.1–12; 22.39. Archaeological excavation has shown that those in Palestine differed little from palaces in neighboring countries.

Palestine A form of the name "Philistine," at

first assigned to the coastal plain. Ps 60.8. Later, it was used of the whole country which the Bible calls "Canaan" Gen 11.31, or of the land of Israel 1 Sam 3.20; 13.19. Only about 150 miles long and 75 miles wide, it has a great variety of altitude and temperature. Geographically, it consists of four zones running from north to south. The coastal plain with the foothills (Shephelah); the western highlands stretching from the Lebanon to Judah, broken only by the plain of Esdraelon; the Jordan valley, with the Dead Sea (deeper than the Grand Canyon) at its extremity; and the central plateau consisting of the highlands E of the Jordan. As the strategic highway between Egypt and Mesopotamia it was an area of military conflict throughout its history.

palm The only species of this tree which flourishes in Palestine is the date-palm. Its fruit is not directly mentioned but reference is made to the beauty of the tree and the use of its branches. Num 33.9; 2 Chr 28.15; Jn 12.12–13; Rev 7.9.

Palti The man to whom Saul gave David's wife. 1 Sam 25.44.

Pamphylia The coastal region of Asia Minor between Cilicia and Lycia, walled in on the N by the Taurus mountains. Its chief town was Perga. Acts 2.10; 13.13; 14.24; 15.37–38.

Paphos The name of two settlements in Cyprus. The old Phoenician one and the Roman. It was the latter at which Paul first presented the Christian faith before the Roman authorities. Acts 13.6–12. *Baffo.*

papyrus A tall aquatic plant common in the rivers of Egypt and Palestine from which a writing-paper was made. The outer layer of the stem was removed and the inner pith was thinly sliced lengthwise, shaped and squared, and laid edge to edge. Sheets were pressed together into rolls. Papyrus, however, becomes brittle with age and decays easily in damp conditions. It was used for many of the Bible manuscripts.

parable(s) (= putting things side by side) A short descriptive story told as an interesting illustration to enable the reader to discover for himself a moral and religious truth. The form was known before the time of Christ, but examples in the OT are few. 2 Sam 12.1–6; Isa 5.1–7. Only in his teaching was the parable used to its fullest and highest effect. Parables in the Gospels:

Found only in Matthew

The weeds	Mt 13.24–30
The hidden treasure	13.44
The pearl of great value	13.45–46
The fishing-net	13.47–48
The unforgiving servant	Mt 18.23–34
Laborers in the vineyard	20.1–16
The man with two sons	21.28–32
The wedding banquet	22.1–14
The ten bridesmaids	25.1–13
The talents	25.14–30
The sheep and the goats	25.31–46

Found only in Mark

The growing seed	Mk 4.26–29
Keep awake!	13.34–36

Found only in Luke

The two debtors	Lk 7.36–50
The good Samaritan	10.25–37
The friend in the middle of the night	11.5–8
The rich fool	12.16–21
The watchful slaves	12.35–40
The faithful manager	12.42–48
The barren fig-tree	13.6–9
The great dinner	14.16–24
The tower and its cost	14.28–33
The lost sheep	15.3–7
The lost piece of silver	15.8–10
The prodigal son	15.11–32
The dishonest manager	16.1–13
The rich man and Lazarus	16.19–31
The master and the servant	17.7–10
The persistent widow	18.1–8
The Pharisee and the tax collector	18.9–14
The pounds	19.12–27

Common to Matthew and Luke

The house with foundations on rock	Mt 7.24–27; Lk 6.48–49
The yeast	Mt 13.33; Lk 13.20–21
The lost sheep	Mt 18.12–14; Lk 15.3–7

Common to Matthew, Mark, Luke

The lamp under the bushel	Mt 5.14–16; Mk 4.21–22; Lk 8.16–17
The new patch on the old coat	Mt 9.16; Mk 2.21; Lk 5.36
New wine and old wineskins	Mt 9.17; Mk 2.22; Lk 5.37–38
The weed among the wheat	Mt 13.24–30; Mk 4.3–20;

	Lk 8.4–15
The mustard seed	Mt 13.31–32; Mk 4.31–32; Lk 13.18–19
The vineyard tenants	Mt 21.33–41; Mk 12.1–9; Lk 20.9–16
The leaves on the fig-tree	Mt 24.32–35; Mk 13.28–31; Lk 21.29–33

paradise Of Persian origin, meaning a walled garden. Used by Jesus for the place where the souls of God's people go immediately after death. Lk 23.43. *See also* Lk 16.19–31; 2 Cor 12.2–4; Rev 2.7.

Paran An area of wild country in the central part of the Sinai peninsula. Gen 21.21; Num 10.12; 13.1–3; 1 Sam 25.1; 1 Kings 11.18.

parched grain Roasted grain as in certain modern breakfast cereals. Lev 23.14.

parchment A specially prepared skin of animals (mainly sheep, pigs and goats) which came into use as a writing material in the later OT period.

Parmenas One of those chosen to distribute relief to the poor. Acts 6.5.

Parthians A warlike people, originally inhabiting a region SE of the Caspian Sea, who established a considerable empire under Mithridates out of the ruins of the Persian empire. They invaded Judaea and placed Antigonus on the throne. Acts 2.9.

partridge A common bird in the deserts of Palestine and around the Dead Sea. There are several species varying in size and color. 1 Sam 26.20; Jer 17.11.

Passover The most important of the Israelite festivals kept annually on 14th Nisan or Abib (March–April) to commemorate their deliverance from the last plague and slavery in Egypt. Also known as the Feast of Unleavened Bread. Ex 12.1–36; Lev 23.4–8; Num 9.2–4; 28.16–25; Deut 16.1–8. In NT times there were always big crowds in Jerusalem at Passover time. Mk 14.1–2; Lk 2.41.

Patara A seaport near the mouth of the Zanthus, convenient for ships sailing for Phoenicia and Egypt. Acts 21.1–2. *Gelemish*.

Pathros An area of Upper Egypt between Cairo and Aswan where ancient texts show that a colony of Jews lived. Isa 11.11; Jer 44.1–30; Ezek 29.14.

patience, patient A characteristic of God's nature and a quality which he values highly in his people. Isa 48.9; Rom 2.4; 1 Cor 13.4; Eph 4.2; Col 1.11; 3.12; 2 Tim 4.2; Jas 5.7; 1 Pet 3.9.

Patmos A small island of the Dodecanese to which John was exiled. Rev 1.9.

patriarch(s) The word is usually applied to the male head of a long family line as in Gen 5.3–31; but especially to the three great ancestors of Israel, Abraham, Isaac, and Jacob, and Jacob's twelve sons. Acts 7.8; Rom 9.1–5.

Patrobas A Roman Christian. Rom 16.14.

Paul Formerly Saul, according to Acts he was born in Tarsus with the full privileges of a Roman citizen, though educated in Jerusalem as a Pharisee. At first he was violently anti-Christian, but after his conversion he became a great missionary who took the faith to Europe. He was imprisoned and executed in Rome. A number of his letters are preserved in the NT.

Paulus, Sergius The Roman Governor of Cyprus at the time of Paul's visit. Acts 13.4–12.

peace offering *See* offering.

pearl Highly valued gems known from the time of Solomon. Mt 7.6; 13.45; 1 Tim 2.9; Rev 21.21.

Pekah A revolutionary who seized the throne of Israel and attempted to organize an anti-Assyrian faction. 2 Kings 15.25–31.

Pekahiah The son and successor of Menahem as king of Israel, assassinated by Pekah. 2 Kings 15.22–26.

Pekod An Aramaean tribe living near the mouth of the Tigris. Jer 50.21; Ezek 23.23.

Pelethites Members of David's bodyguard, of Philistine ancestry. 2 Sam 15.18; 20.7.

pen These were specially cut with a penknife for writing on papyrus or parchment. Ps 45.1; Jer 8.8; 36.23; 3 Jn 13.

Peniel The place near the Jabbok where Jacob wrestled with the angel. Gen 32.24–32.

Pentateuch The Greek name for the first five books of the OT, the traditional five books of Moses. They are also called the Books of the Law, and contain the early history of the Israelites and the Mosaic Law.

Pentecost Derived from the Greek word for "fiftieth" since the festival was kept fifty days after the beginning of the Passover on 5th Sivan (May–June), and marked the end of the harvest. It was the second in importance of Jewish festivals and was also called the Festival of Weeks, the Festival of Harvest, and the Day of First-fruits. Ex 23.16; Num 28.26; Deut 16.10. *See also* Lev 23.15–21. It was at this time that the Holy Spirit came upon the apostles. Acts 1.5; 2.1–4. *See also* 1 Cor 16.8.

Peor A mountain N of the Dead Sea and opposite Jericho. Num 23.25–24.25. *Khirbet Faghûr.*

perfume(s) Used from early times in worship, on the person and in connection with burial. Ex 30.25,34–38; Esth 2.12; Song 1.3; 4.10; Lk 23.56.

Perga The civil capital and center of the worship of Diana in Pamphylia. Acts 13.13–14; 14.24–25. *Murtana.*

Pergamum The administrative capital of the Roman province of Asia in what is now W Turkey; famous for its great library and as a center of pagan worship. Rev 1.11; 2.12–17. *Bergama.*

Perizzites One of the original Canaanite tribes who intermarried with the Israelites. Gen 15.20; Judg 3.5.

persecute, persecution This persistent hostility, directed against sincere and god-fearing people, was known in OT days. *See* 1 Kings 19; Jer 20.1; Dan 3.8–30. In the NT Christ predicts it for his followers. Mt 5.10–12; 10.17–23; Acts 8.1. *See also* Mt 24.9–14; Acts 12.1–2; 19.23–40; 1 Pet 4.12–16; Rev 2.10.

Persia The Iranian plateau bounded on the W and S by the Tigris and Indus valleys and on the E and N by the Armenian ranges and the Caspian Sea, and inhabited by Indo-European peoples. It was the greatest empire in biblical times and, under a succession of very able leaders such as Cyrus and Darius, it dominated the Middle East for nearly 200 years. Its religion was Zoroastrianism. In the Hellenistic period it was claimed by the Seleucids, but their control was far from secure. Ezra 1.1–11; 4.1–6.15; 7.1–26.

Persis A Christian convert in Rome. Rom 16.12.

pestilence Usually mentioned in the OT as a general epidemic. 2 Sam 24.15. The prophets class it with sword and famine as punishments laid on a disobedient people. Jer 14.12; 21.7; 24.10; Ezek 7.15; 12.16.

Peter The nickname of one of the three disciples closest to Jesus, and the leader of the Twelve. His actual name was Simon. He was the first to recognize Jesus as the Messiah and to welcome Gentiles into the church. Mt 4.18–20; 16.13–19; 17.1–4; Mk 14.53–72; Jn 20.1–9; 21.1–22; Acts 1.12–22; 2.1–41; 9.31–11.18; 15.1–12.

Pethor A city in N Mesopotamia S of Carchemish. Num 22.2–24.25.

Phanuel The father of the prophetess Anna. Lk 2.36.

Pharaoh The Egyptian royal title. Several are mentioned in the OT but few by their individual names. Gen 12.10–20; 39.1–41.55; Ex 1.8–2.10; 5.1–21; 1 Kings 3.1; 9.16; 11.18; 14.25 (Shishak); 2 Kings 23.29 (Neco); Jer 44.30 (Hophra). *See also* 2 Kings 18.21; 19.9.

Pharisee(s) (= separated ones) A sect of Judaism which arose about a century before the birth of Christ in protest against laxity in keeping the law and the introduction of foreign customs into Palestine. Their emphasis on the exact observance of dietary and ritual rules led to the movement known as rabbinic Judaism. In Matthew they are charged with observing the letter rather than the spirit of the law. Mt 5.17–20; 15.1–9; 16.5–12; 23.1–32; Acts 5.34; 23.1–9.

Pharpar One of the two rivers of Damascus. 2 Kings 5.1–14.

Philadelphia (= brotherly love) A commercial center of Lydia in Asia Minor situated in a fertile but seismic area. Rev 1.11; 3.7–13. *Alashehir.*

Philemon A convert of Paul who lived in Colossae. Philem 1–2.

Philetus A teacher accused of undermining the true doctrine of the resurrection. 2 Tim 2.17. *See also* 1 Cor ch. 15.

Philip (= lover of horses) (1) The apostle. Mt 10.3; Jn 1.43–50; 12.20–22; 14.7–9; Acts 1.13. (2) The evangelist. Acts 6.1–6; 8.1–40; 21.8–15. (3) The son of Herod the Great and ruler of Ituraea from 4 BCE to 34 CE. Lk 3.1.

Philippi An important city on the E border of Macedonia about 10 miles inland, where the gospel was first preached in Europe. Acts 16.11–40; 20.6. *See also* 2 Cor 2.13–14; Phil 4.10–20.

Philistines The people who invaded Canaan from the south about the same time as the Israelites crossed the Jordan, and who settled in the coastal plain. Although not Semites, they gave their name in a modified form to the whole country. When they tried to extend their power into central Palestine they came into conflict with the Israelites. In early clashes they were victorious; and although David finally defeated them, they continued to be a thorn in the side of Israel. Judg ch. 13–16; 1 Sam ch. 4–6; 13–14; 17.1–18.7; 28–29; 31; 2 Sam 5.17–25; 8.1; Isa 9.12; Am 1.6–8; Zech 9.5–6.

Phinehas (= mouth of brass) (1) The grandson of Aaron. Ex 6.25; Num 25.1–13; Judg 20.28. (2) The younger of Eli's evil sons. 1 Sam 1.4; 2.12–17; 4.17.

Phoebe A woman who held office in the church at Cenchreae. Rom 16.1.

Phoenicia The narrow coastal strip along the E Mediterranean, the modern Lebanon. Its Semitic population were seafarers and merchants with their chief towns at Tyre and Sidon. Acts 11.19; 15.3; 21.2–3. *See also* 1 Kings 5.1–14; 16.31; 18.19; Mt 15.21.

Phrygia An inland region in W Asia Minor forming part of the Roman province of Asia which was extensively evangelized by Paul. Acts 2.10; 16.6; 18.23. *See also* Acts 13.14–14.24; 19.1.

Phygelus One of the Asiatic Christians who deserted Paul. 2 Tim 1.15.

phylacteries (= safeguard) Small boxes or pouches fastened to leather straps and worn either on the forehead or the left arm by Jewish males over thirteen. They contained small pieces of parchment on which were written certain passages from the law (Ex 13.1–10, 11–16; Deut 6.4–9; 11.13–21). Deut 6.8; Mt 23.5.

physician(s) Men skilled in the art of healing practised in Bible lands from an early date. Gen 50.2; 2 Chr 16.12; Jer 8.22; Lk 4.23. *See also* Eccl 38.1; Mt 9.12; Mk 5.26; Col 4.14.

piety The spirit represented by this word in Judaism and Christianity is present everywhere in Scripture. The basic idea is the love and loyalty that are the duties required by the relationships of family, society and God. *See* Gen 47.29; 2 Sam 16.17–19; Ps 30.4; 85.8; 1 Tim 5.4.

pig One of the earliest domesticated animals, dated back to the neolithic period. An omnivorous eater and scavenger, all five OT references reflect its unclean character. Lev 11.7; Deut 14.8; Prov 11.22; Isa 66.3,17; Mk 5.1–13; Lk 15.11–24.

Pi-hahiroth A place in NE Egypt where the Israelites were overtaken by the pursuing Egyptians. Ex 14.1–20.

Pilate The fifth Roman Governor of Judaea from about 26 to 36 CE, appointed by Tiberius Caesar. Mt 27.11–26; Lk 13.1; 23.1–25; Jn 18.28–19.16,38; Acts 3.13; 4.27; 13.28; 1 Tim 6.13.

pilgrimage Special journeys to sacred places were a feature of the ancient world, and by NT times Jerusalem was well established as such a center for the main festivals. Lk 2.41–50. *See also* Ps 122. For the figurative sense *see* 1 Chr 29.15; Heb 11.13; 1 Pet 2.11.

pillar(s) The pillars of cloud and fire in the wilderness were regarded as signs of God's presence. Ex 13.21–22. Heaps of stones commemorated important and sacred happenings. Gen 28.18; 31.45; 35.14. Two great pillars stood at the entrance to Solomon's Temple. 1 Kings 7.15–22. In OT times pillars were associated with pagan worship. Deut 12.3; Hos 10.2. Used symbolically of the church and the apostles. Gal 2.9; 1 Tim 3.15.

pipe(s) Some were simple, straight tubes with holes, others had two parallel tubes to provide melody and a kind of accompaniment; some were more like the modern flute. Gen 4.21; Job 21.12; Ps 150.4; Dan 3.5.

Pisgah A headland in the Abarim range of Moab W of the Jordan. Num 21.20; 23.13–14; Deut 3.27; 34.1–5.

Pisidia A mountainous region at the W end of the Taurus range. Acts 13.14; 14.24.

pit Although used literally Gen 14.10; 37.22; it also refers to death, the grave, or to Sheol. Job 33.18; Ps 16.10. *See also* Num 16.30–33.

pitch A resinous product of petroleum, used for caulking. Gen 6.14; Isa 34.9. *See also* Gen 14.10; Ex 2.3.

Pithom A city in Egypt in the valley between the Nile and Lake Timsâh, dedicated to the sun-god Atum. Ex 1.11.

plague No indication is given of its exact nature, but the bubonic plague was endemic in Bible lands. Num 11.33; 14.37; 16.46–47; 25.8. *See also* 2 Kings 19.35.

Plagues, The Ten The catastrophic events by which Pharaoh was persuaded to let the Israelites leave their slavery in Egypt. *See* Ex 7.14–12.36; Ps 78.42–51.

plane-tree A tree, greatly valued for the shade of its vine-like leaves, which grows particularly well in Syria and along the Mediterranean coast. The bark peels annually. Gen 30.37; Isa 41.19; 60.13; Ezek 31.8.

plants It is not always possible to identify these with absolute correctness, partly owing to the fact that for the original writers present-day standards of accuracy in botanical matters did not exist, and also because their terminology was not so precise and comprehensive as that of the modern botanist.

plaster The inner, and sometimes the outer, walls of buildings were coated with a covering mixture of clay, or clay and straw in the case of the poor. Deut 27.2; Dan 5.5.

pledge The taking of a pledge from a debtor as guarantee for the repayment of a debt was allowed by the law, but with certain humane provisos. Deut 24.6,10–13,17.

Pleiades A constellation of seven stars. Job 9.9; 38.31.

plow, plowshare This was simple and light, made of wood with a point tipped with iron. It scratched the soil rather than turned it. Deut 22.10; 1 Sam 13.20; Lk 9.62.

plumb-line, plummet A simple instrument consisting of a cord, with a stone or other weight attached, for testing whether a wall was straight. 2 Kings 21.13; Am 7.7–8.

poetry Associated with music and dancing from the earliest times, the teaching of the wise and the oracles of the prophets were delivered in poetic form. The structure of Hebrew poetry, in general, consists of parallelism (lines are in pairs and the second resembles the first but is not exactly the same) and metre (the number of stressed or emphasized words in each line). Over 35 per cent of the OT consists of poetry.

Pollux *See* Castor and Pollux.

polygamy Under the earlier system of polygamy a secondary and inferior wife could be taken to ensure the continuation of the family. However, the practice was discouraged and monogamy advocated. *See* Gen 16.1–16; Deut 17.17; Prov 31.10–31; Eph 5.22–33.

pomegranate A shrub with spreading branches and dark-green, shiny leaves which grows wild in Persia and Syria. Its fruit, dark-red in colour and about the size of an orange, has a juicy pulp and many seeds. The blossoms were used in treating dysentery. Ex 28.31–34; Num 13.23; 1 Sam 14.2; Song 7.12.

Pontus The coastal strip in NE Asia Minor bordering on the Black Sea administered with Bithynia as a Roman province. Acts 2.9; 18.2; 1 Pet 1.1.

pool A natural or artificial reservoir to collect rainfall or water from springs. Neh 3.15; Eccl 2.6; Isa 22.9; Jn 9.7.

poplar This tree, which grows to a height of between 30 and 60 feet, is a native of Syria and Palestine. Its green leaves are white on the underside. Gen 30.37; Hos 4.13.

portico A covered walk, like cloisters. Jn 10.23.

Potiphar The captain of Pharaoh's guard. Gen 39.1–20.

Potiphera An Egyptian priest of On. Gen 41.45; 46.20.

potter The clay and water were trodden into a mixture of the right consistency and then molded on a flat wheel turned by hand. Isa 41.25; Jer 18.1–6.

Potter's Field A piece of land in or near Jerusalem where foreigners are buried. Mt 27.3–10. *See also* Acts 1.15–20.

prayer A devout petition, or spiritual communication with God. Among the most noteworthy prayers in the OT are: 1 Kings 8.15–53; Jer 15.15–18; 17.14–18; 20.7–18; Dan 9.3–19. NT prayer differs from that in the OT because of the teaching and example of Christ. Mt 6.5–13; Jn 17; 1 Cor 14.13–15.

preach, proclaim The proclamation of the good news of the coming of God's kingdom. 1 Cor 9.16; 1 Tim 5.17. *See also* Mt 4.17; 10.7; Acts 5.42; 8.35–36; 28.31; Rom 1.15–17; Eph 4.11; 1 Tim 4.13.

precious stones There are four principal lists of gem stones recorded in the Bible. These are (1) The 12 precious stones of Aaron's breast-piece, each stone representing a tribe of Israel. Ex 28.17–20; 39.10–13. (2) The wisdom list of Job. Job 28.16–19. (3) The gems of the king of Tyre. Ezek 28.13. (4) The precious stones of the holy city, Rev 21.18–21, with one for each of the 12 foundations.

The stones named in these lists are: agate, amethyst, beryl, carnelian, chrysolite, chrysoprase, emerald, jacinth, jasper, moonstone, onyx, pearls, sapphire, topaz, turquoise.

pride There is a constant condemnation of human arrogance throughout the Bible. Ps 10.2; Prov 8.13; 16.18; Isa 14.11; 1 Cor 4.6. *See also* Ex 5.2; 2 Kings 5.10–13; Dan 4.28–32; Mt 23.1–12; Mk 10.45; Lk 18.11–12; Jn 13.12–17; Jas 4.6; 1 Pet 5.5.

priest(s) In early Israel any man could present an offering to God. Gen 12.8; but at Sinai, Aaron and his descendants were nominated as priests. Ex 28.1–2. They had to meet very rigid requirements and to wear special vestments when they performed the ritual in the sanctuary, which became elaborate. Ex 28.40–43; 29.36–42; Lev 21.16–23; Num 18.1–7; 1 Chr 24.1–19. Other functions Lev 7.29–36; ch. 13–14; Num 10.1–10; 18.8–20. In the NT Christ is described as a high priest after the order of Melchizedek and Christians as sharing in his priestly activity. Heb 4.14–15; 5.1–10; 1 Pet 2.9; Rev 1.6; 5.10; 20.6.

Prisca, Priscilla The wife of a Jewish Christian tent-maker. Acts 18.24–26; Rom 16.3; 1 Cor 16.19.

prison(s) These were usually sordid, often consisting of natural pits or cave-like dungeons. Gen 37.22–24; 39.20–23; Judg 16.21; Ps 79.11; Jer 37.15–16; Mt 14.3; Acts 12.5–10; 16.16–40.

Prochorus One of those chosen to see to the needs of Christian widows. Acts 6.5.

proconsul The chief official of provinces which were administered by the Roman Senate. Acts 18.12. *See also* Acts 13.7.

prophecy, prophets This arose and developed in Israel against a background of prophecy in the Near East; but in Israel it became something unique. 1 Sam 9.1–14; 19.20–24; 1 Kings 18.17–29. The true prophet was the spokesman of God and his messages to the people were consistent with the character of God as revealed in the law. The great prophets denounced every denial of Israel's special relationship with Yahweh. Isa 1.10–17; Hos 6.4–6; Am 5.21–24; Mic 6.6–8. They were not, however, pessimistic, but believed that there was a core of the nation which, as the Remnant, would inherit the promises of God, and that there would be a brighter age when the will of God would be perfectly done. Isa 1.9; 2.2–4; 9.6–7; 11.1–10; Jer 23.5–6; 38.14–28; Ezek 34.22–31.

prophetess A woman called by God to the work of prophecy. Ex 15.20 (Miriam); Judg 4.4 (Deborah); 2 Kings 22.14 (Huldah); Neh 6.14 (Noadiah). *See also* Isa 8.3; Rev 2.20.

prophets, false The OT mentions prophets of heathen gods 1 Kings 18.19; but there were also prophets in Israel who spoke falsely in the LORD's name. Various explanations for this are given, as are also the distinguishing marks of true prophecy. Deut 18.21–22; 1 Kings 22.1–28; Jer 14.14–15; 23.12–22,25–32; Ezek 13.1–10.

proverbs The name given by the Israelites to short, forceful sentences containing valuable truths in familiar language. Job 14.19; Jer 13.23; Ezek 16.44; Jn 4.37.

province An administrative unit of the Roman empire. Those presenting no special problems were ruled by a pro-consul appointed by the Senate. Provinces on the frontier were under the control of a legate or procurator appointed by the emperor.

Publius The chief magistrate of Malta at the time of Paul's shipwreck. Acts 28.1–10.

Pul Tiglath-pileser III of Assyria. 2 Kings 15.19; 1 Chr 5.26.

punishment(s) The two forms laid down in the OT for wrongdoing are retaliation Ex 21.23–25; Lev 24.14–22; and restitution Ex 21.19–22,26–34; 22.1–4,5–15. The underlying principle was that the evil was punished rather than the wrongdoer. Deut 17.12–13. The NT further extends this in stressing that the aim is for the offender to recognize his guilt and to repent. 1 Cor 5.5.

Pur, Purim A Jewish festival kept on 14th and 15th Adar (February–March) celebrating their deliverance from the pogrom planned by Haman. Gifts were exchanged and given to the poor. Esth 3.7; 9.1–32.

purification, purify The OT laws lay down rules for purifying persons and objects which have become "ritually" unclean. Lev ch. 12–25 (Lk 2.22–24); Num 19. In the NT, although there is a movement from the outer to the inner, there is no relaxation in the basic requirement of purity itself. *See* Mt 5.8,27; 19.3–9; Mk 7.14–23; Lk 11.37–41; 1 Cor 5.9–13; 6.12–20.

purple A famous Tyrian dye obtained from a species of shellfish. Its use in clothing was a sign of rank and wealth. Ex 28.1–8; Judg 8.26; 2 Chr 3.14; Esth 1.6; Mk 15.17–20; Lk 16.19.

Puteoli An important harbor on the W coast of Italy. Acts 28.13. *Pozzuoli.*

quail One of the smallest game birds. They breed in many parts of Europe and go south in the winter to the Mediterranean areas, many reaching Africa. Ex 16.13; Num 11.31–32; Ps 105.40.

Quartus A Corinthian Christian who sent greetings to the Roman church. Rom 16.23.

queen(s) The most influential in the biblical records were dowager queens or queen mothers. Jezebel 1 Kings 16.29–2 Kings 9.37; Athaliah 2 Kings 11.1–16; Bathsheba 1 Kings 1. Among foreign queens are Vashti Esth 1; Esther Esth 2.17; the Queen of Sheba 1 Kings 10.1–13; Bernice Acts 25.13–23; Drusilla Acts 24.24.

Queen of Heaven The female fertility goddess, possibly Astarte. Jer 7.18; 44.15–30.

Quirinius The Governor of Syria at the time of Jesus' birth. Lk 2.2.

quiver A case for carrying arrows, worn either on the back or at the side. Isa 49.2; Lam 3.13.

Qumran The name of a wadi and an ancient ruin in its vicinity NW of the Dead Sea. Excavations by G. L. Harding and R. de Vaux 1948–58 have shown that the site was inhabited during the time of the Hamonean monarchy in the two centuries before Christ and the first century after. The complex of buildings uncovered formed the headquarters of the community (possibly Essenes) which produced the Qumran manuscripts. *'Ain Feshka. See* Scrolls, Dead Sea.

quotations There are some 250 direct citations of the OT in the NT. If indirect or partial quotations and allusions are added, then the total exceeds a thousand. Quotations are sometimes taken from the Hebrew text, but more often from the Greek (Septuagint) translation. The minor verbal differences which occur show that the biblical writers' concern was with the meaning rather than with the words in themselves.

Raamah A region and its people in SW Arabia. Gen 10.7; Ezek 27.22.

Rabbah The capital city of Ammon 22 miles E of the Jordan. Deut 3.11; 2 Sam 12.26–30; Ezek 21.18–21; Am 1.14. *See also* Jer 49.1–3. In the Hellenistic period it was called Philadelphia and became one of the cities of the Decapolis. *'Ammân.*

Rabbi A title of respect (= my master) which, after 70 CE, became the name for the authorized Jewish teachers. Mt 23.1–12; Jn 1.35–39; 3.1–2,26.

Rabbouni My lord, my master. Jn 20.16.

race This pastime was apparently known to the Israelites, and Paul uses it as a symbol of competition. Eccl 9.11; 1 Cor 9.24; 2 Tim 4.7.

Rachel The younger daughter of Laban. Gen ch. 29–33; 35.16–20.

Rahab (1) The woman of Jericho who hid Joshua's spies. Josh 2.1–24; 6.22–25; Mt 1.5; Heb 11.31; Jas 2.25. (2) A poetical name for the Egypt of the Exodus. Ps 89.10; Isa 51.9–10.

rain There are two periods of rainfall in the Palestinian area, the light rains which fall about the end of October before the sowing, and the heavier rains about March. Annual rainfall varies considerably from zero in the Negeb desert to 60 inches in the Lebanon range. Jerusalem has an average of 25 inches.

rainbow The outward appearance of the glory of the Lord in the visions of Ezekiel and John. Ezek 1.28; Rev 4.3; 10.1. *See also* Gen 9.13–15, where God's bow in the clouds is the sign of his covenant with Noah.

ram(s) The male sheep, sometimes used for sacrifice. Gen 22.13. Their skins were used in the Tabernacle and their heat-flattened horns as trumpets. Ex 36.19; Josh 6.6.

Ramah (1) A town near Bethel N of Gibeah, fortified by Baasha. Judg 4.5; 1 Kings 15.16–22; Jer 40.1–2; Mt 2.18. (2) The birthplace of Samuel in Ephraim. 1 Sam 1.19–20; 7.15–17; 8.4–22; 19.18–24.

Rameses A district and town in NE Egypt. Gen 47.1–12; Ex 1.11; 12.37.

Ramoth-gilead A walled city in Gilead near the Syrian border. Deut 4.41–43; Josh 21.38; 1 Kings 4.13; 22.1–38; 2 Kings 9.1–6.

ransom The price paid for injury or damage. Lev 19.20. For other laws about restitution *see* Ex 21.26–22.15; Lev ch. 25; 27. As applied to Christ in the NT. Mk 10.45. *See also* redeem, redemption.

Ras Shamra The modern name for the ancient city of Ugarit on the Syrian coast opposite Cyprus where clay tablets were found (1929–36) which throw great light on Canaanite culture and religion, and the world in which Israel developed.

raven Palestine has six species of this bird which shares the scavenging habits of many birds of prey. Gen 8.6–7; 1 Kings 17.2–6; Lev 11.15; Deut 14.14; Job 38.41; Isa 34.11; Lk 12.24.

razor The razor, used for shaving, was in common use in Israel from ancient times. Num 6.5; Judg 13.5; 16.17; 1 Sam 1.11. *See also* Num 8.7. Used metaphorically Ps 52.2; Isa 7.20; Ezek 5.1.

reaping In ancient times the grain was pulled up by the roots or cut with a sickle, and the stalks collected into bundles for threshing. Strict rules were laid down. Lev 19.9; 23.10–11; 25.11; 1 Sam 8.12. Used figuratively Prov 22.8; Hos 8.7; Gal 6.7–8.

Rebecca The sister of Laban and the wife of Isaac. Gen 24; 25.20–26.11; 27.1–28.3.

Rechab, Rechabites (1) A Kenite who helped Jehu stamp out Baal worship. His descendants followed the nomadic life as in the wilderness period to show their loyalty to Jehovah and, in particular, took no intoxicating drink. 2 Kings 10.15–28; Jer 35.1–19. (2) One of the murderers of Ishbosheth. 2 Sam 4.5–12.

redeem, redemption The basic idea has two parts. Deliverance *from* the penalty of the law (including the price paid); and as a metaphor in the NT for deliverance *to* a new freedom from sin, a new relationship with God and a new life in Christ. *See* Rom 3.21–26; 6.1–4; 1 Cor 6.20; Gal 3.13–14; Eph 1.4–10; 1 Pet 1.18–19; 3.18; Rev 5.9.

redemption of land Any land forfeited by economic distress could be bought back by the nearest relation. Lev 25.23–34. *See also* Lev 27.16–25.

Red Sea The thousand-mile stretch of water separating Africa from Arabia, part of the great Rift Valley. In the OT it refers to the Bitter Lakes region in the Egyptian Delta north of Suez Ex 10.19; 13.17–15.22; and also to the Gulfs of Suez and Aqabah 1 Kings 9.26.

reeds Several varieties of reed grow along the river banks and the lake edges in Palestine and

Egypt. They were used for making pens, paper (papyrus) and boats. Job 40.21; Isa 18.2.

refiner, refining The process of separating metal from alloy and dross was known by the Canaanites and Philistines from early times. Isa 1.25; Jer 6.29. Used figuratively of God purifying Israel in the furnace of suffering. *See* Prov 17.3; 27.21; Isa 48.10; Zech 13.9; Mal 3.2–3.

regeneration The new birth of the Christian. *See* Ezek 36.26–27; Jn 1.12–13; 3.5; Rom 6.4; 12.2; Eph 2.4–6; Titus 3.4–7; 1 Pet 1.23; 2 Pet 1.3–4; 1 Jn 3.9.

Rehob The northern limit to which Joshua's spies went. Num 13.21.

Rehoboam The son of Solomon who succeeded only to the territory of Judah and Benjamin. 1 Kings 12.1–24; 14.21–31.

Rehoboth Wells restored by Isaac's servants. Gen 26.16–22.

Rehum The high commissioner of the Samaritans whose complaints to Artaxerxes delayed the rebuilding of Jerusalem's walls. Ezra 4.6–24.

Rekem One of the kings of Midian killed by Moses' army. Num 31.8; Josh 13.21.

Remaliah The father of king Pekah. 2 Kings 15.25.

remnant The spiritual nucleus of Israel who would survive God's judgment and become the means through which he continues his work in the world. Isa 1.9; 10.20–23; 11.11–12; Rom 9.27–29; 11.5–7. *See also* Gen 6.7–8; 7.1; Jer 32.36–40; Ezek 36.22–29; Zeph 3.11–13; Zech 8.7–13; Heb 8.8–12.

repent, repentance In the Bible this always means something much deeper than man's regret for sin or his resolution to do better. It is a complete turning to God, made possible only by him, which must be sincere and must show itself in appropriate action. Mt 4.17; Lk 3.3–9; Acts 20.20–21; 2 Pet 3.9.

Rephaim The name of a people tall in stature, who were in Canaan before Abraham's time. Gen 14.5; 15.20; Deut 2.10–11; Josh 12.4.

Rephaim, Valley of A fertile plain between Jerusalem and Bethlehem. 1 Chr 11.15–19; 14.8–17.

Rephan A pagan god worshiped by the Israelites in the wilderness. Acts 7.39–43.

Rephidim A camping site in the wilderness where the Amalekites were defeated. Ex 17.1–13.

resurrection Literally, the return of the dead to life; a belief which is apparent in later OT times but was not accepted by all Jews. The Christian hope is based on the resurrection of Christ. Mt 22.23–33; Lk 20.34–38; Jn 11.21–26; Acts 23.6–8; 24.14–15; 1 Cor 15.20–27; Rev 20.4–15. *See also* Job 19.25–27; Ps 16.9–11; Isa 26.19; Dan 12.2; Jn 5.25–29; 2 Cor 5.1; Phil 3.20–21; 1 Thess 4.13–17. The resurrection of Christ Mt 27.57–28.20; Mk 15.42–16.14; Lk 23.50–24.49; Jn 19.38–21.14.

Reuben, Reubenites The first child of Jacob and Leah whose descendants formed the tribe. Gen 29.15–32; 37.12–30; 42.18–38; 46.9; 49.1–4; Num 26.5–11; 32.1–38; Josh 13.15–23.

Reuel The priest of Midian and father-in-law of Moses. Ex 2.16–22. *See* Jethro.

revelation The various means by which God makes himself, his character and his will known to men. *See* Gen 28.10–16; Ps 19.1; Jer 1.4–10; Ezek 37.1–6; Am 7.7–8; Lk 10.22; Jn 1.1–18; 7.15–17; 14.9; 15.15; 16.13; 17.6; 1 Cor 12.3; Heb 1.1–3.

revenge *See* avenger of blood.

reverence The respect that man should show in the presence of God, inspired by his goodness. Lev 19.30; Eph 5.21; Heb 12.28; 1 Pet 3.15. *See also* Ex 3.5; Ps 95.6; Isa 6.5.

Rezin The last king of Samaria to reign in Damascus. 2 Kings 15.37; 16.5–9; Isa 7.1–9.

Rezon A guerrilla leader who made himself king of Damascus. 1 Kings 11.23–24.

Rhegium A safe and strategically important harbor in SW Italy opposite Messina. Acts 28.13. *Reggio.*

Rhoda The maid of John Mark's mother. Acts 12.6–17.

Rhodes An important Greek city on the island of the same name. Ezek 27.15; Acts 21.1.

Riblah An important town on the E bank of the river Orontes. 2 Kings 25.1–7; Jer 39.1–8; 52.26–27. *Ribleh.*

riddle A form of hidden saying. Judg 14.5–19; Ps 49.4; Dan 5.12.

righteous, righteousness The OT teaches that behavior which is just and good agrees with the will of God, and this teaching is continued and developed in the NT, where God in Christ takes the initiative in setting his people in right relationship with himself. Isa 45.8; Ezek 18.5–9; Mal 4.2. *See also* Ex 20.1–17; Deut 6.25; Mt 5.6–10; Jn 16.8–11; 1 Jn 1.6–10.

Rimmon A Syrian storm god worshiped at Damascus. 2 Kings 5.18–19.

ring A popular form of jewellery worn by both men and women. Ex 35.22. Rulers had signet-rings to seal official documents. Gen 41.42; Esth 3.10; 8.2.

river(s) With the exception of the Jordan, the rivers of Palestine are mostly small streams or wadis, often seasonal, and important only for irrigation. In the OT the word is used chiefly of foreign rivers. Gen 2.10; 15.18; 2 Kings 5.12. Used symbolically Ps 46.4; Isa 43.2; Rev 22.1–2.

roads As a buffer state between Egypt and the great empires of the north, Palestine was crossed by military and commercial highways serviceable for chariots. Secondary roads were simple trails. Isa 40.3; 62.10; Jer 31.21. *See also* Num 20.17; Isa 57.14; Mt 13.4.

robbery Such illegal seizure of another's property, although forbidden by law, still persisted. Judg 9.25; Isa 10.2; Ezek 22.29; Hos 6.9; Lk 10.30–37; Jn 10.1; 2 Cor 11.26.

rock A natural fortress. Judg 20.45–47. Used figuratively 2 Sam 22.2–3; Ps 18.2; 71.3; Mt 16.18.

rock-badger, coney A form of the Syrian Rock Hyrax. Round-backed and with no visible tail, it has short, sturdy legs and feet with flexible soles. The general color is gray-brown and it is roughly rabbit-sized. Lev 11.5; Ps 104.18; Prov 30.26.

Rocks of the Wild Goats The place where David saved Saul's life. 1 Sam 24.1–22.

rodents Mice, rats and other small rodents are found in Palestine. The black rat, host to the flea which carries bubonic plague, had made its way into Mesopotamia from the East well before Israel's entry into Canaan. Isa 5.6–6.5; Isa 66.17.

roebuck This is a small deer, standing only some 30 inches, with short upright antlers. It stays mostly in cover, coming out only to graze. Deut 14.5; 1 Kings 4.23.

Roman(s) (1) Inhabitants of Rome. Acts 2.10. (2) Officials representing the Roman authority. Jn 11.48; Acts 25.16. (3) Citizens of the empire who enjoyed important privileges. Acts 16.16–39; 22.22–29.

Rome The capital of the ancient world from the first century BCE, situated on the left bank of the Tiber some 15 miles from the sea. Jews were expelled by Claudius (reigned 41–54 CE), but the city soon became a center of Christianity. Acts 2.10; 18.2; 19.21; 28.14–16,30–31; Rom 1.15; 2 Tim 1.15–18. By the second century CE it had become, like Babylon, a symbol of organized paganism and opposition to Christianity. *See* Rev ch. 17–18.

rudder In biblical times these were, in effect, steering oars at the stern of the ship on the port or starboard side which could be lifted and fixed to the side of the ship in rough weather. Used figuratively Jas 3.3–5.

rue A plant, growing up to 5 feet tall, with clusters of bright yellow flowers at the top of its stems. It was in great use medicinally as an antiseptic, and in cooking. Lk 11.42.

Rufus The son of Simon of Cyrene who carried Christ's cross. Mk 15.21.

rush The rush grows along the edges of Palestinian streams or rivers and its grasslike leaves are used for basket-making. Isa 19.6; 35.7.

Ruth A Moabite, the widow of Mahlon, who married Boaz. Ruth ch. 1–4; Mt 1.5.

sabbath (= ceasing) Usually applied to the seventh day of the week, it lasted from sunset on Friday to the appearance of the first stars on Saturday. It was observed as a memorial of the creation, of the deliverance from Egypt, a humane provision of rest for man and beast, and a day to worship the LORD. Ex 20.8–11; Lev 23.3; Deut 5.15. During and after the exile its observance became an important mark distinguishing the Jews from their heathen neighbors. Neh 10.31; Mk 2.3–3.5; Lk 4.16–21; Jn 7.19–24. For other NT teaching *see* Acts 15.28–29; 20.7; Rom 14.5; 1 Cor 16.1–2; Col 2.16–17; Rev 1.10.

Sabbath Day's Journey The distance that could be traveled on that day without breaking the law, worked out by the scribes on the basis of Ex 16.29; Josh 3.3–4. Acts 1.12.

Sabbatical Year Special legislation was provided in the OT governing every seventh year. Behind this lay an awareness that land, like people, needed rest and that human dignity is entitled to land, liberty and the pursuit of happiness. Ex 21.2–6; 23.10–11; Lev 25.1–55; Deut 15.1–3.

sackcloth A coarse material, often made from goat hair, usually associated with mourning, humiliation and penitence. Gen 37.34; 2 Sam 3.31; 1 Kings 20.31–32; 21.27; 2 Kings 6.30; Job 16.15; Isa 3.24; Mt 11.21; Rev 11.3.

sacrifice The OT writers saw sacrifice as a means which God had given men to enable them to have fellowship with him. The fundamental underlying belief was the idea of the covenant. At bottom, sacrifice was always a prayer to which was added the idea of giving, of real offering. Other elements mingled with this. First, the search for a sure and exclusive relationship with God through blood. Then sacrifice became an accepted punishment, a sort of penance. Finally, there came the idea of at-one-ment effected by a restitution sacrifice.

The origin of sacrifice goes back further than Moses, Jer 7.22; but food offerings were seldom involved before the settlement in Canaan, and even then they were considered of less value than sacrifices of domestic animals. During the early monarchy, sacrifices were first presented to God and then burnt; and they could be offered almost anywhere and even without the help of a priest, but the worshiper must be ritually pure. Gen 35.2; 1 Sam 16.5–6; 20.26. All the circumstances of life could be the occasion of a sacrifice, but most were associated with gratitude for the harvests.

When worship became centralized at Jerusalem, regular sacrifices began to be made on behalf of the community rather than the individual, in which the priests became necessary intermediaries between the people and God. This led to a detailed organization of the sacrificial ritual; but it is noticeable that the evolution and development of the cult of sacrifice marked a time of spiritual cooling-off in Israel. After the return from the exile, these meticulous details were extended to concern the choice of offerings.

The NT speaks of the death of Christ in words that recall OT sacrifices. In Rom 3.25 Paul speaks of atonement as that which removes human sin as a barrier between God and his people. Also in 2 Cor 5.9; Eph 5.1–2; Heb 9.11–28. The sacrifice which Christians offer is essentially that of themselves in God's service. Rom 12.1; Phil 2.17; Heb 13.15–16; 1 Pet 2.4–5. *See* offerings.

Sadducees A Jewish party which took its name from Zadok. 1 Kings 1.34. From about 200 BCE it consisted chiefly of the aristocratic priestly and lay families. They were conservative in religion, rejecting the oral traditions of the elders as well as belief in the resurrection of the dead. Politically, they were concerned primarily in maintaining good relations with the Roman occupying power. Little is heard of them after the destruction of Jerusalem in 70 CE. Mt 3.7–8; 22.23–34; Acts. 5.17; 23.6–8.

saffron A substance, produced from the dried stigma of several species of crocus native to Greece and Asia Minor, which was used for flavoring and coloring food. Song 4.14.

saints (= holy ones) God's people, who are called to reflect his holiness in their own lives. Rom 1.7; 1 Cor 1.2; 16.1; Phil 1.1.

Salamis An important city on the SE coast of Cyprus. Acts 13.4–5. *Famagusta.*

Salem The city of the priest-king Melchizedek, traditionally associated with Jerusalem. Gen 14.18–19; Ps 76.2; Heb 7.1–2.

Salim A place near Aenon on the Jordan. Jn 3.23.

Salome (1) The wife of Zebedee and the mother of James and John. Mt 27.56; Mk 15.40; 16.1. (2) The daughter of Herodias who danced before Herod. *See* Mt 14.3–11.

salt There are two special uses in the Bible. It was an accompaniment of all sacrifices Lev 2.13; Ezek 43.23–24; and the word acquired a symbolic significance for permanence since salt preserves from decay Num 18.19; Mt 5.13; Mk 9.49–50. It also stands for barrenness because of the extreme sterility of the land surrounding the Dead (Salt) Sea. *See* Deut 29.23; Judg 9.45.

Salt, Valley of The scene of David's, and also Amaziah's, victories over the Edomites. 2 Sam 8.13; 2 Kings 14.7. *Wâdi el-Milh.*

salutation(s) These played, and still do, an important function in the East, and were laid down in detail for observance at every kind of social occasion. They could be time-consuming. *See* Gen 33.3–4; 1 Sam 20.41–42; 25.6; 2 Kings 4.29; Esth 3.1–6; Mt 5.47; Lk 10.5–6; 15.20; Rom 16.16; 1 Pet 5.14.

salvation, save Basically, it implies "deliverance" from any kind of evil. From defeat in battle Ex 15.1–18; trouble Ps 34.6; violence 2 Sam 22.1–51; reproach Ps 57.1–3; exile Ps 106.47; death Ps 6.4; sin Ezek 36.22–31. At first, the conception of salvation was primarily national, but the prophet's horizon gradually widened to include the Gentiles. Isa 49.5–6; 55.1–55. There is also increasing stress on the righteous remnant and the individual rather than the whole nation; and deliverance is from sin itself as well as from the consequences of it. *See* Ps 51; Jer 31.31–34; Ezek 36.24–28.

In the OT the most important human conditions necessary for salvation are complete trust in God, obedience to his moral law, and repentance accompanied by the required ritual sacrifice. The central theme of the NT is the salvation brought by Christ, through which a new covenant people is established for all who will to enter by faith. *See* Mt 1.18–21; Lk 19.9–10; Acts 4.12; 13.26; Rom 5.6–11; Eph 1.11–14.

Samaria (1) Built by Omri as the capital of the northern kingdom of Israel on a hill 7 miles NW of Shechem which commanded the main trade routes through the plain of Esdraelon. Captured by the Assyrians about 721 BCE, many non-Jews were settled there. 1 Kings 16.24,29–32; 20.1–34; 2 Kings 3.1–6; 6.24–7.16; 10.1–7,17–28; 17.1–6,24–33; Am 4.1. *See also* 1 Kings 22.39. *Sebastiyeh.* Excavations by G. A. Reisner 1908–10 and J. W. Crowfoot 1931–5 have shown that the site was unoccupied from the Early Bronze Age until the Israelite kingdom. Fortifications and palaces dating from the time of Omri until its fall have been uncovered in the 16 levels of occupation. Particularly fine remains, including buildings, coins, stamped jar-handles, pottery and papyri, of the Hellenistic period have been found. (2) The administrative area and district in the center of Palestine, and another name for the kingdom of Israel, which extended from Bethel to Dan and from the Mediterranean to Syria. 1 Kings 18.1–6; Jer 31.5; Hos 8.1–13; Am 3.1–12; Lk 17.11; Jn 4.3–4; Acts 1.8; 8.1; 9.31; 15.3.

Samaritans The people of the region of Samaria, between whom and the Jews of Judaea hostility increasingly developed in post-exilic times. The breach was completed with the establishment of a rival Temple at Mt. Gerizim. Some of their descendants still live at *Nablus* (the new city, Neapolis), which replaced Samaria as the center of Samaritan life and worship. Ezra 4; Lk 10.30–37; Jn 4.3–26,39–42; Acts 8.4–25.

Samos A rocky island in the Mediterranean, only about a mile off the mainland of Asia Minor. Acts 20.15.

Samothrace A small Aegean island between Asia and Macedonia. Acts 16.11.

Samson An Israelite hero of the tribe of Dan famous for his one-man guerrilla war against the Philistines. Judg ch. 13–16.

Samuel The last of the great Judges and the first of the prophets after Moses, who created the kingship in Israel by anointing Saul as the first king. He played a vital role in the transition of the Israelite tribes into a nation; and no other OT figure combined in himself so many different functions. 1 Sam ch. 1–3; 7.1–17; 8.6–22; ch. 9–12; 13.8–15; ch. 15–16; 19.18–24; 25.1.

Sanballat The Governor of Samaria in the time of Nehemiah, and his bitterest enemy. Neh 2.10,19–20; 4.1–9; 6.1–9; 13.28.

sanctuary A place set aside for worship; but in the Bible the place where Jehovah was worshiped. At first this was the Tabernacle, built after the occupation of Canaan, Solomon built the Temple in Jerusalem as a permanent sanctuary. 1 Chr 22.19; Ps 114.2; Ezek 23.39; 28.18; Zeph 3.4. In the NT the earthly sanctuary is shown to be only a type of the true heavenly one. Heb 8.1–2; 9.1–12; 10.19.

sandal The normal outdoor footwear, consisting of a plain sole of leather or wood held to the foot by a leather thong, though the poor went barefoot. For various customs concerning sandals: Ex 3.5; Deut 25.7–10; Ruth 4.7–8; 2 Sam 15.30.

Sanhedrin Acts 5.21. *See* Council.

Sarah The wife of Abraham, first called Sarai. Gen 11.29; 12.10–20; 16.1–6; 17.15–22; 20.1–21.13; 23.1–2,19.

Sardis A city in Asia Minor, capital of the kingdom of Sardis. Rev 1.11; 3.1–6. *Sarta.*

Sargon A usurper who succeeded to the throne of Assyria (772–705 BCE) after the murder of Shalmaneser V. He completed the siege of Samaria and, after the conquest of Israel, settled the city with other peoples. Isa 20.1.

Satan (= adversary) The personification of evil power that stands in opposition to God, but which is subject to his will in the end. 1 Chr 21.1; Job 1.6–12; Zech 3.1–2; Mk 1.12; 3.22–26; Lk 10.17–18; Acts 26.12–18; Rev 20.1–3.

Saul (1) The son of Kish and the first king of Israel, who set up his capital at Gibeah. He led Israel to victory against her enemies, especially the Philistines. In later life he became moody and suspicious, quarrelled with his advisers and drove his son-in-law, David, out of the kingdom. After his defeat at Mt. Gilboa he committed suicide. 1 Sam 8.1–2 Sam 1.27. (2) Saul of Tarsus. *See* Paul.

savior It is a basic OT concept that people cannot save themselves and that God alone is the deliverer of his people. Isa 43.11; Jer 14.8–9. In the NT the term is used of God the Father, the author of salvation, and God the Son through whom it comes. Mt 1.18–21; Lk 1.47; 2 Tim 1.9–10; 2 Pet 3.2,18.

saw(s) In prehistoric times these were made of flint. Later, small metal handsaws which, because of the set of the teeth, were pulled and not pushed against the wood, came into use. 2 Sam 12.31; 1 Kings 7.9; Isa 10.15; Heb 11.37.

scales Instruments for weighing. Prov 16.11; 20.23. *See* balance.

scarlet A bright red color obtained from the eggs of the cochineal insect. As a material it was expensive and was used as a mark of distinction. Ex 28.3–6; 2 Sam 1.24; Mt 27.28. Its bright color is sometimes associated with wickedness. Isa 1.18; Rev 17.3–4.

sceptre A rod or staff held in the hand as a symbol of authority. Gen 49.10; Esth 4.11; Ps 45.6; Am 1.5; Heb 1.8.

school In early times education was given at home and was mainly concerned with religion. *See* Gen 18.19; Deut 6.6–7; 2 Tim 3.14–15. In Greek culture, language, literature and history were taught in schools. Acts 19.9.

scorpion About 5 of the world's 500 or more known varieties of this carnivore are found in parts of Palestine. Although differing in size and color, their outline – almost that of a lobster or crayfish – is unmistakable. Their sting is painful but seldom fatal. Deut 8.15; Ezek 2.6; Lk 10.19.

scribes Learned laymen who, after the exile, took over from the priests the task of applying the Mosaic law to the conditions of changing times.Ezra 7.12. *See* "lawyers" and "doctors of the law."

Scripture(s) (= writings) Used of the writings of the OT. When the OT revelation is considered as a whole it is used in the singular Jn 7.42; Gal 3.22; and in the plural when the thought is of a number of separate passages, or of the OT as made up of a number of books Lk 24.27; Rom 1.2.

scroll Documents in biblical times were on papyrus or parchment, sewn into long strips and wound around sticks at both ends. Isa 34.4; Jer 36.21–23; Ezek 2.9–10; Lk 4.16–20; Rev. 5.1; 10.1–10.

Scrolls, Dead Sea Manuscripts discovered in and around Qumran, NW of the Dead Sea, since 1947, which were probably written between 170 and 34 BCE and between 4 BCE and 70 CE; and formed part of the library of a strict Jewish community. Among the 500 scrolls and fragments found are about 100, representing all books of the OT in Hebrew except Esther, which are some 1000 years earlier than any other existing OT manuscripts.

Scythians A nomadic people living between the Danube and the Don whose name became a general term for barbarians. Col 3.11.

sea Although created and controlled by God, the Israelites disliked and feared it as the home of horrible monsters. Ex 20.11; Job 38.8–11; Isa 27.1; Rev 21.1. The word is used of the Red Sea Ex 13.18; the Mediterranean Num 34.6; Acts 10.6; the sea of Galilee (Chinnereth) Num 34.11; Mt 4.18; the Dead Sea Num 34.12; Deut 3.17.

Sea of Bronze The great basin in Solomon's Temple where the priests ceremonially washed their hands and feet. 1 Chr 18.8; 2 Chr 4.2–6.

seal, signet An implement, often made of a hard semi-precious stone, engraved with a recognizable design or name which could be used to stamp its impression on clay or wax as a mark of authority or authenticity. Among the Hebrews, these were usually oval and could be set in a ring or worn on a chain around the neck. Gen 38.18; 41.42; 1 Kings 21.8; Isa 29.11; Jer 32.10–14; Dan 6.17; Mt 27.66. Used figuratively Job 14.17; Jn 6.27; Rom 15.28; 2 Cor 1.22; Eph 1.13; 4.30. One of the greatest collections of cylinder seals in the world is in the Pierpont Morgan Library, New York.

sect (= choosing) In the NT the basic idea is of a party within the parent community. Acts 24.5. *See also* Acts 5.17; 15.5; 1 Cor 11.19; Gal 5.20.

Seir A mountainous district S of the Dead Sea originally inhabited by Horites. Gen 36.9,21; Deut 2.1–5.

Sela (= rock) The Edomite capital, 50 miles S of the Dead Sea, captured by Amaziah. 2 Kings 14.7; 2 Chr 25.11–14; Isa 42.11. It has been identified as *Umm el-Bayâra* on the massive rocky plateau 1000 feet above Petra and 3700 above sea level. Excavations by N. Glueck 1933 and W. H. Morton 1955 established the existence of an Iron Age Edomite settlement here.

Sennacherib The son of Sargon, whom he succeeded as king of Assyria in 705 BCE, and a contemporary of Hezekiah who rebelled against him. 2 Kings 18.7,13–19.37.

Septuagint The most important Greek translation of the Hebrew OT, traditionally made by 70 (LXX) Jewish elders in the third century BCE for the Greek-speaking colony of Jews around Alexandria. It became the Bible of the early church and most OT quotations in the NT come from it. Because the manuscripts are so ancient the LXX is a valuable companion to the Hebrew Bible.

seraphs (=burning ones) Heavenly beings described in the prophet Isaiah's vision. Isa 6.1–8.

Sermon on the Mount, The The name commonly given to Christ's teaching in Mt ch. 5–7 about the character and conduct of the one who is truly obedient to God. *See also* Lk 6.20–49.

serpent Used both literally and figuratively. Its character traits are thought of as those of the Devil: deceptive, crawling, poisonous and cunning. Gen 3.1–7; Ex 7.8–13; Num 21.6.

Serpent, Bronze The image made by Moses to remind the Israelites that the LORD was able to heal and protect them. It later became an object of worship in Jerusalem. Num 21.4–9; 2 Kings 18.1–4; Jn 3.14.

servant A general term used of anyone working for another, from slaves to trusted officials. It is also used of a man's relationship to God and his fellow men. Gen 32.16; Ex 32.13; 2 Kings 5.2; Ps 31.16; 105.6; Jer 25.9; Lk 15.17; Jn 13.12–17; Acts 16.17.

Servant of the LORD The title is notably used in Isa ch. 40–55, especially 42.1–7 and 53. In these passages the Servant is at times to be understood as the people of Israel, at times as the faithful remnant; but, in the end, the Servant is that one individual, the Messiah, in whom the full destiny of Israel is summed up and achieved. Mt 12.15–21; Acts 3.26; 4.23–30.

Seventy, The (1) Those appointed by Moses to assist him in taking care of the people. Num 11.16–17,24–26. (2) The seventy-two followers sent out by Jesus on an evangelistic tour. Lk 10.1–20.

shadow, shade Used as a metaphor referring to the protection of the weak by the strong, or of people by God, Job 7.1–2; Ps 63.6–8; as a passing thing, like a person's life compared with God, 1 Chr 29.15; Job 8.8–9; Jas 1.16–17; as insubstantial compared with the real. Col 2.16–17; Heb 8.1–6; 10.1–18.

Shadrach The Babylonian name given to Daniel's companion, Hananiah. Dan 1.7; 3.8–30.

Shallum (1) The assassin of Zechariah who ruled Israel for one month. 2 Kings 15.13. (2) A king of Judah also called Jehoahaz. Jer 22.10–12.

Shalmaneser The name of several kings of Assyria. That Shalmaneser III fought Ahab and Jehu is recorded on the Black Obelisk of Nimrûd, a copy of which is in the Museum of the Oriental Institute, Chicago. It was Shalmaneser V (727–722 BCE) who besieged Samaria, and to whom Hoshea became a vassal. 2 Kings 17.1–6.

shame Often used in the Bible of the human feeling of humiliation or self-condemnation. 2 Sam 19.1–5; Ezra 9.7; Ps 97.7; Jer 6.15; Joel 2.27.

Shamgar An Israelite champion who killed 600 Philistines. Judg 3.31; 5.6.

Shaphan The adjutant-general of King Josiah of Judah when the book of the law was found in the Temple. 2 Kings 22.3–20; 2 Chr 34.8–28.

Sharon The most fertile part of the coastal plain, stretching from Mt. Carmel to Joppa, on the caravan route to Egypt. Song 2.1; Isa 35.1–2.

Sheba, Queen of The ruler of a district in Arabia, corresponding roughly with the modern Yemen, which controlled the trade in precious spices. 1 Kings 10.1–13.

Shechem A town in the central hill-country of Palestine 41 miles N of Jerusalem between Mt. Ebal and Mt. Gerizim. Originally a Canaanite town, it was both a religious and political center, and became the first capital of the northern kingdom of Israel. Gen 12.6; 33.18; 35.4; Josh 20.1–7; 24.1–27,32; Judg 9.1–49; 1 Kings 12.1,25; Jer 41.2–10.

sheep Most commonly the fat-tailed variety which were kept for their meat, milk and wool. 1 Sam 14.32–34; 25.2–8. *See also* Deut 32.14. They were used in sacrifice. Lev 4.32; 22.21.

shekel The fundamental unit of both weight and money. Ex 38.25; 1 Kings 10.16.

Shem The second son of Noah and the ancestor of the Semitic people. Gen 5.32; 9.26; 10.21–31.

Shemaiah (=Jah has heard) The prophet who stopped Rehoboam from making war on the 10 tribes of Israel after their secession. 1 Kings 12.21–24; 2 Chr 12.2–10. (2) A false prophet during the exile. Jer 29.24–32.

Sheol The OT counterpart of the Greek and Roman gloomy underworld (Hades) of the departed spirits. Ps 18.5; 86.13; Isa 14.15.

Shephelah A geographical term for the low hill tract between the coastal plain of Palestine and the high central ranges. 1 Kings 10.27.

shepherd Since the Palestinian shepherd leads, rather than drives, his sheep to water and pasture, the word is aptly applied to God and Christ. Ps 23; Jn 10.2–17; 1 Pet 5.4.

Sheshbazzar The Persian name of the Jewish governor appointed by Cyrus to take back to Jerusalem the sacred vessels looted from the Temple by Nebuchadnezzar. Ezra 1.7–11; 5.13–17.

shibboleth (= ears of corn) A word used by Jephthah to test whether or not fugitives belonged to his own people. Judg 12.4–6.

shield These were of two kinds: the smaller, round shield; and the heavy shield covering the whole body. 1 Kings 10.16–17; 14.27; 1 Chr 12.8. Used metaphorically for God's protection. Ps 5.12; 18.2; Eph 6.16.

Shiloh A town 12 miles N and E of Bethel where the Tent of the Presence was kept, and which became the central sanctuary. Josh 18.1; 1 Sam 1.1–4; 1 Kings 11.29–37; 14.1–18; Ps 78.60; Jer 7.11–15; 26.4–9. *Seilûn.* Excavations by Danish expeditions 1926–9 and 1932 suggest that it was destroyed about 1050 BCE and not reoccupied until Hellenistic times.

Shimei (1) The grandfather of Mordecai. Esth 2.5. (2) The Benjamite who opposed David and was executed by Solomon. 2 Sam 16.5–14; 19.15–23; 1 Kings 2.36–46.

ship(s) Although the Israelites were not a seafaring people, there are a number of detailed references to foreign ships in the Bible. Solomon's ships were manned by Phoenician crews. The Egyptians used papyrus boats; and the general design of ships in the OT would be similar to that of the modern dhow with square sails. 1 Kings 9.26–28; 2 Chr 20.35–37; Ps 107.23–27; Isa 18.1–2; Ezek 27.1–9,25–29. There is frequent mention of ships in the NT since several apostles were fishermen. Paul and other missionaries traveled extensively by boat. Acts 27. *See* boat.

Shishak An Egyptian king who invaded Judah in Jeroboam's reign. 1 Kings 11.40; 14.25–26.

Shittim The last camp site of Israel, in the plains of Moab E of the NE end of the Dead Sea opposite Jericho, before they crossed the Jordan. Num ch. 25–36; Josh 2.1; 3.1. *Tell el-Hammâm.*

Shunem, Shunammite A border town of Issachar near Mt. Gilboa. 1 Sam 28.4; 1 Kings 1.1–4; 2 Kings 4.8–37. *Sôlem.*

Sidon A seaport of Phoenicia and its oldest city, 22 miles N of Tyre, whose inhabitants were skilled metal-workers and which provided timber for the Temple. Gen 10.19; 49.13; Josh 11.8; 1 Kings 17.9; Isa 23.1–4, 11–12; Ezek 28.20–23; Mk 7.31; Lk 4.26; Acts 27.3–4. *Saidā.*

sign(s) Something visible and remarkable which serves as a witness to God or the will of God. The rainbow, the rite of circumcision, the plagues of Egypt were signs. Gen 9.12; 17.11; Ex 10.1–2. Gideon and Saul were granted signs. Judg 6.11–24; 1 Sam 10.1–8. And the Jews demanded miracles from Jesus as signs. Mt 16.1–4. They are to precede the end of the age. Mt 24.29–31; 2 Thess 2.9–10. In John, Jesus' miracles are called signs. Jn 2.11; 20.30–31.

Sihon The king of the Amorites in Transjordan who refused to let the Israelites through his territory. Num 21.21–30; 32.33.

Silas A prophet of the Jerusalem church who went with Paul on his second missionary journey. Acts 15.22–41; 16.19–17.15; 18.5. *See* Silvanus.

silk A fine cloth woven from the threads produced by the silkworm but little known in ancient Palestine. Rev 18.12.

Siloam A reservoir, still existing, constructed within the walls of Jerusalem by Hezekiah. Jn 9.1–8. In 1880 the tunnel, 1700 feet long, was found with a Hebrew inscription (now in Istanbul) describing the method of construction.

Silvanus Generally identified as the Latin form of Silas. 2 Cor 1.19; 1 Thess 1.1; 2 Thess 1.1; 1 Pet 5.12. *See* Silas.

silver, silversmith Used from very early times for vessels, ornaments, and, by weight, as a form of money. Num 7.13; 10.2; Judg 17.1–4; 1 Kings 10.27; Acts 19.23–27. It was mined in Middle East countries. 2 Chr. 9.14; Jer 10.9. Used figuratively Ps 12.6.

Simeon (1) The second son of Jacob by Leah and ancestor of one of the tribes of Israel. Gen 29.32–33; 34.25–31; 49.5–7. (2) The devout man who recognized the infant Jesus as the Messiah. Lk 2.25–35.

Simon (1) One of the twelve apostles who had been a member of the Jewish extremist group, the Zealots. Mk 3.16. (2) A brother of Jesus. Mt 13.55; Mk 6.1–3. (3) Simon the Leper. Mk 14.3–9. (4) A Pharisee who entertained Jesus. Lk 7.36–47. (5) The father of Judas Iscariot. Jn 13.2. (6) A man from Cyrene who carried Christ's cross. Mk 15.21. (7) A magician of Samaria. Acts 8.9–24. (8) A tanner of Joppa. Acts 9.43. (9) *See* Peter.

sin The Bible recognizes the power of evil as everywhere present in the whole of human existence. It is a fact which has to be accepted and overcome in the power of God.

Three different Hebrew words are used. The first means "rebellion": a wrong attitude taken up by man towards a personal God who is his father and creator. The second word means a deliberate turning towards what a man knows to be evil and contrary to the will of God. The third means "missing the mark"; and it stands for that element of wickedness in man's nature which seems to drive him into sinful acts, even when he knows how disastrous the consequences will be.

Since sinful man cannot enter into the presence of the holy God, a great part of Israel's sacrificial system was directed to the means by which the impurity could be removed. But throughout, the emphasis is on man's inability to cleanse himself.

In later times, especially during the exile when no sacrifice could be offered, the sense of sin deepened in Israel. Ezek 33.10–20. Some realized that even sacrifice could not really meet the need of men; and there arose a growing hope and faith in the forgiveness of God. Ps 130.

The NT takes over the OT understanding of the nature of sin, but deepens both it and the meaning of forgiveness. In the teaching of Jesus, the emphasis is not so much on the action as on the motives behind the action. Mt ch. 5. The social consequences of sin are emphasized, as is the fact that failure to act rightly may be as serious as committing wrong acts. Mt 18.5–7; 25.31–46. Finally, it is the dishonesty or "hypocrisy" involved in refusing to face the human situation which makes it impossible for man to be reconciled with God. Lk 18.9–14.

With this deepened sense of sin comes also a new emphasis on forgiveness, associated with the death of Christ who has broken the power of sin, making possible reconciliation with God. Rom ch. 7; Mt 1.21; Acts 2.37–38; 10.38–43; Col 2.13–15. Indeed, God is the agent of reconciliation of the world. 2 Cor 5.18–19.

Sinai The volcanic mountain in the south of the Sinai peninsula, also known as Horeb, where Jehovah gave the law to Moses. Ex 19.1–21; 31.18. *See also* Deut 5.1–23.

sin-offering Like the guilt-offering, this kind of sacrifice was offered to cover faults committed in ignorance but, unlike the other which was rather for restitution, this was to expiate both moral and ritual offenses. Lev 4.1–5.13.

sins In general, the Bible distinguishes between "sin," the state of alienation from God in which natural man lives, and "sins," which are the specific acts that give outward expression of this condition. *See* Jn 1.29; Gal 5.19–21.

Sisera The commander-in-chief of the Canaanite king, Jabin, defeated by Deborah and killed by Jael. Judg ch. 4–5.

slander Malicious gossip is condemned throughout the Bible. Lev 19.16; 1 Tim 5.13. *See also* Ex 23.1; Deut 5.20; Prov 6.16,19; 2 Cor 12.20; 1 Tim 3.11; Jas 4.11.

slave, slavery In the OT slaves were in law the property of their master; and were obtained in war, from the slave-trade, as prisoners undergoing punishment, or native Israelites who had sold themselves owing to poverty or debt. Ex 20.17. However, they still had various rights and privileges and could rise to a position of responsibility in a household. Gen 15.3; Ex 12.44; 20.10,17; 21.20–21,26–27; Lev 25.39–55; Deut 15.12–18; Prov 17.2.

sleep A gift of God who himself never sleeps. Ps 121.4. While men sleep God can speak to them in dreams. Gen 28.10–16; Mt 1.18–21; 2.19–20.

sling The common form of the weapon was a narrow strip of leather with two thongs attached, in which a stone was laid. When this was whirled round the head and one thong released, the stone could be flung with great force and accuracy. Judg 20.16; 1 Sam 17.40–50; 2 Kings 3.25. Flint slingstones have been excavated at Megiddo weighing about $2\frac{1}{4}$ pounds and about 4 inches in diameter.

smith(s) These seem to have been unknown in the pastoral period and emerged with the general use of metal about the 11th century BCE. 1 Sam 13.19–22; Isa 41.7; 54.16. *See also* 1 Kings 6.20; 2 Chr 34.3.

Smyrna An important city on the W coast of Asia Minor, a center of worship of the Asian goddess Cybele, it became one of the seven churches of Asia. Rev 1.11; 2.8–11. *Izmir*.

snakes These are used both literally and figuratively. One or two species are mentioned, but often they are referred to in general terms. Their characteristics are usually seen as deceptive, crawling, poisonous and cunning. Ex 4.1–5. *See also* serpent.

snow Not a common sight on the hills of Palestine even in winter, though the summit of Mt. Hermon was always snow-capped. 2 Sam 23.20; Prov 31.21; Jer 18.14. Used symbolically for purity. Isa 1.18; Dan 7.9; Mt 28.3; Rev 1.14.

soap A solution of potash and soda obtained from vegetable ash and sometimes mixed with oil. Job 9.30; Jer 2.22; Mal 3.2.

Sodom One of the five cities of the plain of the Jordan in what is now the southern part of the Dead Sea, where Lot chose to settle. Its wickedness was proverbial, and it was destroyed. Gen 13.1–13; 18.16–19.29; Isa 3.9; Jer 23.14; Ezek 16.49–50; Mt 10.15.

Solomon David's son by Bathsheba and his successor. Famous for his wisdom and wealth, he exploited the trading and commercial possibilities of the territory won by David, built the Temple and a chain of defense cities. 1 Kings ch. 1–11.

Solomon's Portico A covered walk or cloister on the S side of Herod's Temple where the scribes taught and money-changers had their tables. Jn 10.23; Acts 3.11; 5.12. *See also* Lk 2.46; Jn 2.14–16.

Son of God In the OT the term is used of those who stand in any special relationship with God, including the whole people of God. Hos 11.1. In the NT it signifies the very special relationship between God and Jesus which the apostles affirmed in their preaching. Mt 3.16–17; 11.26–27; 17.1–5; 26.63–64; Jn 1.14–18; 10.36; Acts 9.20; Rom 1.4; Heb 1.5–14.

Son of Man In Ps 8.4 human beings ("mortals") are referred to literally as "Son of man." In Dan 7.13 "one like a human being," literally "one like a son of man," is made ruler of God's kingdom. The title is used 78 times in the Gospels but only by Christ about himself in connection with both his early mission and his future glory. Mt 8.20; 9.1–7; 12.1–8; 16.27–28; 25.31–32. Elsewhere in the NT it occurs only once, used by Stephen. Acts 7.56.

Sosthenes The ruler of the synagogue at Corinth who was beaten as a result of Paul's preaching. Acts 18.13–17.

Spain Unknown in OT times, it was regarded as the limit of the world to the west, which may explain Paul's great desire to take the gospel there. Rom 15.22–29.

sparrow Many varieties (House, Spanish, Dead Sea) of this bird are to be found in all parts of Palestine, and an even greater number of Palestinian birds are sparrow-like in their appearance and behavior. Ps 84.3; Prov 26.2; Lk 12.6–7.

spear(s) Long, sharp-pointed instruments of varying shapes and sizes, but all designed for thrusting or throwing. 1 Sam 17.7; 18.11; 26.7. When stuck into the ground it indicated the king's headquarters. 1 Sam 17.7; 18.11; 26.7. *See also* Judg 5.8.

speechlessness, mute This was sometimes regarded as the sign of God's judgment and the healing of it as a sign of the coming of his kingdom. Isa 35.6; Ezek 3.22–27; Mt 9.32–33; 12.22; Mk 7.31–37; Lk 1.20; 11.14–15.

spelt A grain resembling wheat which grows in very poor soil. Ex 9.32; Isa 28.25; Ezek 4.9.

spices Fragrant, vegetable substances used in making incense, preparing bodies for burial, and in flavoring food and wine. Ex 30.34–35; 2 Chr 16.13–14; Song 4.10; Jn 19.40.

spider Used figuratively and only in Job 8.14.

spies A person or persons employed to gain secret information or intelligence. Gen 42.5–17; Josh 2.1–23; 2 Sam 10.1–3.

spikenard This small plant from N India was the source of one of the costliest perfumes of biblical times. Song 1.12; 4.14; Mk 14.3; Jn 12.3.

spirit In the OT it stands for a life-giving power that comes from God. Gen 6.17; Num 11.25; 1 Sam 10.10; Eccl 12.7; Ezek 37.1–14. In the NT it more frequently refers to the nonmaterial side of human personality and that part of a person which survives death. Acts 7.59; 2 Cor 7.1; Col 2.5; 1 Pet 3.18–19. The underlying Greek and Hebrew words also mean "breath" or "wind."

star(s) Created by God and carefully ordered by him. Gen 1.16; Ps 8.3; Isa 13.10; Jer 31.35. *See also* Am 5.8. Worship of them was forbidden. Deut 4.19.

Stephanas The first man to be baptized in Achaia (Greece) by Paul. 1 Cor 1.16.

Stephen One from the Greek-speaking section of the Jewish church appointed to assist the apostles by taking over responsibility for the worldly affairs of the Jerusalem Christians. His bold proclamation of the gospel led to his martyrdom which was a factor in Paul's conversion. Acts ch. 6–7.

Stoics Philosophers who believed in conscience as the human capacity to perceive and obey natural law, which would bring peace of mind and confidence in the ultimate triumph of justice. Acts 17.18; Rom 2.14–15.

stone(s) Extremely common in Palestine and used for many purposes: pillow Gen 28.18; seat Ex 17.12; cover or door Gen 29.2–3; Josh 10.18; Mt 27.60; building 1 Kings 5.17–18; Neh 4.2–3; Am 5.11; memorials Gen 31.45–48; weapons 1 Sam 17.40. Used metaphorically Ps 118.22; Mk 12.10.

stoning In earliest times a simple but violent expression of anger, it became the normal method of capital punishment in Israel. Ex 17.4; Num 15.32–36; Deut 17.2–7; Acts 7.58.

stork Two kinds of stork, the white and slightly smaller black, migrate through Palestine every year. They are mixed feeders but the large concentrations tend to settle in Upper Galilee. Lev 11.19; Deut 14.18; Ps 104.17; Jer 8.7; Zech 5.9.

stumble, stumbling-block Anything that trips up or is a hindrance materially or spiritually. Jer 18.15; Mt 16.23; Rom 9.33; 11.9; 14.13; 1 Pet 2.8. *See also* 1 Cor 8.7–13.

Succoth A town E of the Jordan and W of Penuel. Gen 33.17; Judg 8.4–17; 1 Kings 7.40–46. Excavations by H. Francken of the Nederlands Inst. 1961. *Tell Deir`alla.*

suffering A part of human life on earth and a sign of mortality and imperfection. It is represented in the Bible as the direct consequence of sin Deut 28.15–68; Judg 2.16–23; Hos 8.7; Gal 6.7–8; or as a divine testing Ps 66.10–12; Jas 1.12; 1 Pet 1.6–7; or as educative Prov 3.12; Rom 5.3–4. It may result from persecution, even undeserved as in Job's case. Dan 7.25; Job 1.1–2.10. Christ accepted his share of it and told his followers of the redemptive power of the way of the cross. Mk 8.30–31; Heb 2.14–18. Christians are to share in Christ's sufferings and endure them without resentment that they may live with him. Mt 5.11–12; Rom 8.17; 2 Cor 1.5–7; Phil 3.10–11; 2 Tim 2.3–13; 1 Pet 3.13–18; 4.12–19.

sun Regarded as the greatest and most important of the heavenly bodies. Job 9.7; Ps 19.4–6; 74.16. The day was divided according to its light and heat. Gen 43.16; 1 Sam 11.9; Ps 50.1. *See also* 2 Kings 20.8–11. Eclipses were taken as a sign of God's judgment. Joel 2.30–31; Rev 6.12. Sun-worship, though forbidden, was practiced at Jerusalem at certain periods. Deut 17.2–5; 2 Kings 23.5,11; Ezek 8.16. Used metaphorically Isa 30.26; Mal 4.2; Mt 13.43; Rev 21.23.

Susa The capital of Elam in SW Persia. Ezra 4.8–10; Neh 1.1; Esth 1.1–2; Dan 8.1–2.

swallow Several members of this family, which take their food in the air and nest in man-made situations, are found in Palestine. Ps 84.3; Prov 26.2; Isa 38.14.

swear *See* oath.

sweet-cane Not native to Palestine but imported from India and Arabia. A strong-smelling oil was taken from its root. Isa 43.24; Ezek 27.19.

swine Isa 65.4. *See* pig.

sword Usually made of iron with a fairly short, straight blade, sometimes with two edges. It was worn sheathed, hanging from a belt. Gen 3.24; Ex 17.13; Judg 7.20; 2 Sam 20.8; Ps 149.6. Used symbolically Deut 32.25; Mt 10.34; Rom 13.4; Heb 4.12.

sycamore Unlike the sycamore of the west, this is a tree producing yellowish fig-like fruit, resembling the mulberry in its greenery, with branches growing close to the ground. 1 Kings 10.27; Isa 9.10; Am 7.14; Lk 19.1–4.

Sychar A village of Samaria on the main road from Jerusalem to Galilee. Jn 4.3–6.

Syene A fortress town on the border of Egypt and Ethiopia opposite the island of Elephantine. Ezek 29.10; 30.6. Aramaic papyri found in 1903 show that a Jewish military colony existed there in the 5th century BCE with its own Temple. *Aswân.*

synagogue (= gathering together) The form of worship which grew up during the exile when it was impossible to sacrifice at the Temple, consisting of readings from the scriptures, an address, prayers and psalms. Originally meeting in homes and public places (Neh 8.1–8), synagogues later became places of more formal worship. The buildings also served as schools and meeting-houses. Lk 4.15–30; 13.10–17; Jn 12.42–43; 16.1–3; Acts 13.13–15; 14.1; 15.21; 17.1–3.

synoptic The name usually given to the first three Gospels, because, by and large, they tell the same story in the same way; and although differing in details, each is complementary to the other since it was written for different readers. *See* Matthew, Mark, Luke, John, Gospel of.

Syracuse On the E coast of Sicily, it was the most important and prosperous Greek city on the island. Acts 28.12. *Siracusa.*

Syria (Aram) A continuation of Palestine with no well-defined natural frontier, it was more a political than a geographical unit. It was peopled by Arameans whose small kingdoms seem to have formed some sort of federation under the king of Damascus. The Syrians were great traders and carried their language (Aramaic) well beyond Asia Minor. Both Israel and Judah had close relations with Syria, and its influence was always strong until it was absorbed into the Assyrian empire in 732 BCE. *See* 2 Sam 8.3–6; 10.16–19; 1 Kings 11.23–24; 15.16–20; 2 Kings 6.8–7.20; 9.14–16; 10.32–33. From the time of Alexander the Great, it was controlled by Greeks and Romans. *See* Aram and Damascus.

Syrtis Treacherous sandbanks on the N coast of Africa between the headlands of Tunis and Barce. Acts 27.17.

Taanach A Canaanite royal city whose king was defeated by Joshua. Josh 12.21; 21.25; Judg 1.27; 5.19; 1 Kings 4.12. *Tell Ta`annak.* Excavations by E. Sellin of the Vienna Academy 1902–4 revealed a strong Late Bronze Age defensive system. Finds included 12 cuneiform tablets of about 1450 BCE and an earthenware incense-altar of the Iron Age.

Tabernacle The portable sanctuary set up to

shelter the Ark of the Covenant in the desert which served the Israelites as a place of worship and their appointed meeting-place with God. It was used long after the entry into Canaan. Under the Judges it was at Shiloh, in Saul's reign at Nob and later at Gibeon; and eventually Solomon replaced it by the Temple. *See* Josh. 18.1; 1 Sam 21; 1 Kings 8.1–13; 1 Chr 16.39. The detailed instructions for its construction are in Ex ch. 25–27; 30–31; 35–40. The whole ritual of the service and method of approach to God are laid down in Lev ch. 1–10.

Tabitha *see* Dorcas.

Tabor (1) The place where Gideon's brothers were killed. Judg 8.13–21. (2) An isolated mountain over 1800 feet high in the NE of the plain of Esdraelon and 7 miles E of Nazareth. Josh 19.17–22; Judg 4.4–7; Ps 89.12; Jer 46.18; Hos 5.1.

Tahpanhes A city in Egypt to which Jeremiah was taken. Jer 43.1–44.30. *Tel Defneh.*

Tahpenes The queen of Egypt whose sister married Hadad. 1 Kings 11.14–20.

Tamar (1) A Canaanite woman who married into the family of Judah. Gen 38.6–30. (2) Absalom's sister. 2 Sam 13.1–22. (3) A daughter of Absalom. 2 Sam 14.27. (4) A city in the wilderness built by Solomon. 1 Kings 9.18.

tamarisk Many varieties of this tree with its graceful, curved branches, small leaves and pink flowers grow in the Mediterranean area; some to a considerable size. It was regarded as sacred in OT times. 1 Sam 22.6; 31.13; Isa 44.4.

tambourine, timbrel This resembled a tom-tom and consisted of a wooden hoop with skins pulled across the frame. Its use is particularly associated with merrymaking. Ex 15.20; Judg 11.34; Ps 68.25.

Tammuz A Mesopotamian fertility god, the counterpart of the Egyptian Osiris and the Greek Adonis, who gave his name to the fourth Jewish month (June–July). Ezek 8.14.

Tarshish Its occurrence in the OT in association with ships and ports suggests that it may have been a land in the W Mediterranean where deposits of minerals existed. Ps 72.10; Isa 23.1–7; 66.18–19; Jer 10.9; Ezek 27.12; 38.13; Jon 1.1–3; 4.1–2.

Tarsus The capital city of the Roman province of Cilicia on the river Cnidus and some 10 miles inland. The birthplace of Paul according to Acts, it was a center of Greek learning which revolted with Mallus against Antiochus Epiphanes. Acts 9.11,28–30; 21.39; 22.1–3. *Tarsous.*

Tattenai The Governor of the province of Beyond-the-Euphrates under King Darius. Ezra 5.1–6.14.

taxes Civil taxation, as opposed to money for the support of Israel's central worship, began under David to provide for administrative costs, and was in kind rather than cash. *See* Ex 30.13; 1 Kings 4.7–28. Special taxes were imposed to meet emergencies. 2 Kings 23.35. In the Persian empire each territory had its quota of tolls to meet. Neh 5.15. Under the Romans the system varied, but it was usual for them to be farmed out and the right to collect the taxes of a district sold to the highest bidder. After the exile, each Israelite over twenty had to pay an annual Temple tax. Mt 17.24–25; 22.17–21.

Taylor Prism One of the hexagonal prisms found at Nineveh, and now in the British Museum, on which Sennacherib of Assyria gave his account of his invasion of Judah. It is dated about 691 BCE. Isa 37.36–37.

teacher, teaching At the time of the settlement of Canaan there were no schools as such, and instruction, which concerned the traditions and faith of the nation, came through parents, prophets, priests and wise men. After the exile, instruction was entirely in the hands of the scribes or official teachers of the law. Prov 4.2; 13.14; Isa 8.16; Lk 5.17. *See also* Prov 1.8; Mic 3.11; Mal 2.7. The Jews were amazed that Jesus should presume to teach. Mk 1.27; Jn 7.14–18. In the early church, teaching was a recognized occupation. Eph 4.11.

Tekoa A fortified town on the edge of the wilderness 12 miles S of Jerusalem and the same distance NE of Hebron. It was the home of Amos, and the place where Jonathan and Simon hid. 2 Sam 14.1–20; 2 Chr 11.6; Am 1.1.

Tell An Arabic word for a flat-topped mound with steeply-sloping sides. It almost always indicates the site of an ancient city, and its distinctive shape results from using the same site for city after city.

Tell el-Amarna Tablets These were found accidentally in 1877 at a site about 200 miles S of Cairo. They consist of ancient Egyptian diplomatic files dealing with correspondence between the kings of small city states in W Asia and the Pharaoh Akhen-aten and his father between 1400 and 1360 BCE. They tell a great deal about the state of affairs in Canaan before the Exodus.

Teman A region of Edom and its people, descendants of Esau, who were famous for their wisdom. Gen 36.10–11; Job 2.11; Jer 49.7; Ezek 25.12–13.

Temple The name given to the complex of buildings in Jerusalem on Mt. Moriah which was the center of the sacrificial worship of Israel. The first, built by Solomon, consisted of three parts and was the royal chapel as well as the central sanctuary of the people. *See* 1 Kings 6.1–38; 7.13–51. A model is on display in modern Jerusalem.

Solomon's Temple was burned by the Babylonians, and a second was built by the returned exiles after 520 BCE. It was less elaborate in design and construction, but tended to keep the laity at an ever-increasing distance from the inner shrine. This Temple was pillaged and desecrated in 168 BCE by Antiochus Epiphanes. Ezra 6.

About 19 BCE Herod the Great began to rebuild and enlarge it with a whole series of surrounding covered courts. This is the building referred to in the NT, which was destroyed by the Romans in 70 CE.

tempt, temptation (= "testing," "trial," "prove") When God tests man it is to teach him something or to strengthen his character. Mt 4.1–11; 1 Thess 3.4–5; Jas 1.12–15. *See also* Gen 22.1–18; Ex 20.18–20; Deut 8.16; Mt 6.13; Heb 2.18; 4.14–15; 1 Pet 1.7.

Ten Commandments These were the laws given orally to Moses by God on Sinai and engraved on the two stone tablets which were placed in the Ark. They set out plainly and briefly the way in which people must live together in society before God. In the Roman Catholic and Lutheran churches, the first and second commandment in the usual English numbering are treated as one, and the last is divided into two. Ex 19.17–20.17; 24.3; 1 Kings 8.9.

Ten Towns, The The territory at the mouth of the Jordan on the plain of Esdraelon occupied by Greek settlers, also known as Decapolis. Mt 4.25; Mk 5.20; 7.31.

tent The normal dwelling of the desert nomad which differed little from those used today by the Bedouin of the Negeb. Although stone houses were built after the settlement, it seems that the poorer people continued to live in tents on the outskirts of towns throughout the OT period. Gen 9.27; Job 8.22; Isa 54.2.

Tent of the Meeting Ex 40.1–2. *See* Tabernacle.

Terah The father of Abraham. Gen 11.26–32.

teraphim Idols in the form of small human statues, used as household gods and consulted for oracles. They fell into disuse after the exile. Judg 17.5; Ezek 21.21. *See also* Gen 31.19–35; 1 Sam 15.23; 19.11–17; 2 Kings 23.24; Hos 3.4; Zech 10.2. Archaeology has shown that, among some peoples, possession of these by the woman's husband ensured for him the succession to the father-in-law's property.

Teresh A eunuch of King Ahasuerus who plotted against him. Esth 2.21–23.

Tertius The Christian who wrote down Paul's letter to the Romans. Rom 16.22.

Tertullus The attorney for the prosecution in Paul's trial before Felix. Acts 24.1–8.

Thaddaeus One of the twelve apostles. Mt 10.3; Mk 3.18. His name is replaced by "Judas son of James" in Lk 6.16; Acts 1.13.

thanks, thanksgiving Gratitude to God as the mark of all true worship. Ps 95.2; 100.4; 107.8–31; Mt 26.27–29; Lk 22.17–19; 1 Cor 1.4–5; Eph 5.20; Phil 1.3–5.

theater These were built in most parts of the ancient world where Greek civilization had penetrated, and were used for meetings as well as dramatic performances. They were usually in the open air: a semi-circular excavation in a hill-side, cut into steps for seats. Acts 19.29.

Thebes Chief city of Upper Egypt, built on both sides of the Nile. Jer 46.25; Ezek 30.14; Nah 3.8.

Theophilus The person to whom Luke dedicated both his Gospel and the Acts. Lk 1.1; Acts 1.1.

Thessalonica An important city on the Gulf of Salonika, originally called Therme. Situated where the road from Italy to the east joined the sea route from the Aegean to the Danube, it was a key to the spread of Christianity both west and east and to its establishment as a world religion. Acts 17.1–10; 20.4; 27.2; Phil 4.16; 2 Tim 4.10. *Salonika.*

Theudas A Jewish nationalist leader who led a revolt against Rome. Acts 5.35–36.

thief Stealing is forbidden in the OT and special restitution had to be made. Ex 20.15; 22.1–13; Prov 6.30–31; Jer 2.26; Jn 10.10; 12.3–6; 1 Pet 4.15. *See also* Mt 27.38.

thistle A tall weed with mauve or yellow flowers and a spiny stem. Varieties known on the shore of the Sea of Galilee grow up to thirteen feet. Hos 10.8; Mt 7.16.

Thomas One of the twelve apostles, known as "the Twin." Although devoted to Jesus, he was pessimistic and rather slow to believe. Mt 10.3; Jn 11.16; 14.1–6; 20.24–29; 21.2.

thorn Several species are found in Palestine of which the buck-thorn and camel-thorn seem to have been the most common. It was used for hedging and fuel. Judg 9.14–15; Ps 58.9; Hos 10.8; Mk 15.16–18. It is constantly referred to figuratively. Ezek 28.24; Hos 2.6.

Three Taverns A village on the Appian Way about 33 miles from Rome. Acts 28.15.

threshing The process of separating grain from chaff which was done with a stick on a windy day in ancient times. Later, an ox-drawn sledge with a heavy curved base was used on a specially prepared hard floor. 2 Sam 24.22; Isa 41.15; Am 1.3.

throne(s) (1) The chair of state occupied by one in authority. 1 Kings 10.18–20. (2) The throne of God or Christ. Ps 93.2; Isa 6.1; Heb 12.2. (3) The unseen powers of good and evil which are finally brought under the authority of Christ. Col 1.16.

thunder This commonly occurs in storms at the beginning and end of the rainy season. In both the OT and NT it is associated with the presence and activity of God. Ex 9.22–23; 19.14–16; 1 Sam 7.10; Ps 104.7; Jn 12.28–30; Rev 4.5; 10.3.

Thyatira A city in the Roman province of Asia on the road from Pergamum to Laodicea. It was a center for dyeing, cloth manufacture, pottery, brass-working and other trades. Acts 16.12–15; Rev 1.11; 2.18–29. *Akhisar.*

Tiberias A town on the W shore of the Sea of Galilee built by Herod Antipas about 20 CE in honor of Tiberius. Jn 6.23. *Tabariyeh.* The name is also given to the Sea of Galilee Jn 6.1.

Tiberius The second Roman emperor (14–37 CE) who followed Augustus. With the exception of Lk 2.1 he is the "Caesar" of the Gospels. *See* Mt 22.17; Mk 12.14; Lk 3.1; Jn 19.12.

Tiglath-pileser The king of Assyria, also known as "Pul," from about 745 to 727 BCE, who revitalized the empire. He made successful attacks on Israel, carrying off captives from the northern cities, and made all the petty kingdoms of Palestine and Syria his vassals. *See* 2 Kings 15.17–20; 16.5–18.

Tigris A river of Asia which joins the Euphrates 40 miles N of the Persian Gulf. Gen 2.14; Dan 10.

time This was marked in the early biblical period by sunrise and sunset and by phases of the moon. Num 9.3; Ps 104.19; Eccl 3.1–8. In particular, it refers to the times appointed by God and the opportunities given by him. Lk 19.41–44; Acts 1.6–7; Titus 1.2–3; 1 Pet 1.11. *See also* Deut 11.11–15; Ps 145.15; Isa 49.8; Jer 18.23; Mk 13.29–32; Acts 17.26.

Timnah The place where Samson's first wife came from. Judg 14.1–18. *Khirbet Tibnah.*

Timothy The son of a Gentile father and Jewish mother who became Paul's trusted companion and official representative. Acts 16.1–17.15; 18.5–19.22; Rom 16.21; 1 Cor 4.17; 16.10–11; 2 Cor 1.1,19; 1 Thess 1.1; 2 Thess 1.1; Philem 1.

tin A metal essential to the making of bronze and well known to the Israelites. Num 31.22; Ezek 22.18; 27.12–13.

Tirhakah King of Ethiopia or Cush who became the ruler of Egypt. He is mentioned in connection with Sennacherib's campaign against Hezekiah. 2 Kings 19.8–13.

Tirzah A Canaanite city which Jeroboam I made the capital of the northern kingdom until Omri moved it to Samaria. Josh 12.24; 1 Kings 14.17; 16.6–24; Song 6.4. *Tell el-Fâr'ah.* Excavations by de Vaux of the Ecole Biblique, Jerusalem, 1946–7, 50–, have shown it to be a city which flourished in the 9th century BCE but later sank to the status of an ordinary provincial town.

tithe The custom of giving to God one tenth of one's possessions in recognition of him as lord of the land and in thankfulness for his blessings. This was used for the support of the Levites. Lev 27.30–33; Num 18.20–32; Deut 14.22–29. *See also* Gen 28.20–22.

titles and names of Christ *See* Mt 1.23; Mk 1.24; Lk 1.76; 9.20; Jn 1.9,29; 5.27; 6.35; 8.12; 10.14; 11.25; 15.1; Rom 11.26; 22.16; 1 Cor 10.4; 15.45; Eph 2.20; 5.23; 1 Thess 1.10; 1 Tim 2.5; Heb 4.14; 6.20; Jas 4.12; 1 Pet 5.4; 2 Pet 2.20; 1 Jn 1.1; 5.20; Rev 1.5; 13.8.

Titus (1) A Greek convert and one of Paul's most reliable companions and trusted helpers who is associated particularly with the Corinthian church. 2 Cor 7.5–7; 13–16; 8.1–24; 12.14–18; Gal 2.1; 2 Tim 4.10. (2) Roman emperor who destroyed Jerusalem in 70 CE.

Tob A region S of Damascus where Jephthah lived when an outlaw. Judg 11.2–5.

Tobiah An Ammonite governor, partly Jewish, who, with Sanballat, opposed Nehemiah's efforts to rebuild the walls of Jerusalem after the exile. Neh 2.9–20; 4.1–9; 6.1–19; 13.1–9.

tomb Any burial place, from a modest hole in

the ground or cave to a beehive-vault or one cut from the rock itself. The stone door to the latter could weigh up to three tons. 2 Sam 2.32; Lk 23.55–24.2; Jn 11.38–41. *See also* Gen 50.12–13.

tongues A spiritual gift, the ability to speak in a language other than one's own, regarded by some early Christians, especially the Corinthians, as the highest of the gifts of the Spirit. Paul stresses that it is, in fact, a lesser gift than love or even prophecy. Its value is to be judged by the extent to which it results in the increase of Christian charity in those who claim the gift. Acts 10.44–46; 19.1–7; 1 Cor 13.8; 14.1–33,39–40. *See also* Acts 2.1–4; 1 Cor 13.1.

Topheth A place near Jerusalem where Molech worship, which included human sacrifice, was practiced in the times of Ahaz and Manasseh. 2 Kings 23.10; Jer 19.1–15.

tower(s) Cities were usually fortified; and towers built into the walls, especially near the gates, were an important part of the defense. Watch, or siege, towers were often built by attacking armies; and defense chains of towers or forts were built in desert areas. 2 Chr 26.9–10; Ezek 21.22.

town clerk An official of Graeco-Roman cities in the empire whose many duties included responsibility for law and order. Acts 19.35–41.

Trachonitis A region SE of Damascus governed by Herod Philip. Lk 3.1. *Lejā.*

tradition (1) The interpretation of the law handed down by word of mouth to the Jewish elders which the Pharisees tended to make of even greater authority than the scriptures. Mk 7.1–13; Gal 1.14. (2) The gospel truths and the behavior which those who accept them must show. 2 Thess 2.15; 3.6.

trance A half-conscious state, between sleeping and waking, in which ability to function voluntarily may be suspended. Acts 11.5–11; 22.17–21.

Transfiguration The occasion in the life of Jesus (probably on Mt. Hermon) when, in the presence of his three closest disciples, his visible appearance was changed as a sign of divine approval. Mt 17.1–13; Mk 9.2–13; Lk 9.28–36.

treasury A place where valuables are kept, generally attached to a sanctuary or belonging to a king. Josh 6.19,24; Esth 3.9. In the NT it refers to the thirteen trumpet-shaped boxes for money offerings in the Court of the Women. Lk 21.1.

tree In ancient times Palestine must have been extensively wooded. There are more than 300 references to over 20 varieties in the Bible. They were associated with heathen worship. Deut 12.2; 16.21; 1 Kings 14.23.

Trial of Jesus After his arrest Jesus was informally examined by the high priest. At dawn the Council condemned him for blasphemy. It had the power to inflict the death-sentence for a major violation of Jewish law, but they sent Jesus to Pilate charged with insurrection. Unwilling to condemn an innocent man, Pilate tried to get Herod to try the prisoner. When this failed, Pilate tried to save Jesus at the expense of Barabbas but finally yielded and condemned him. Mt 26.57–27.31; Mk 14.53–15.20; Lk 22.54–23.25; Jn 18.12–19.16.

Tribes of Israel The twelve sons of Jacob and their households who settled in Egypt and became tribes by the end of the period of slavery. Gen 49.1–28; Num 1.20–44; 26.5–51; Josh 13.1–22.8.

Tribes, the Ten Those who rebelled against Rehoboam on Solomon's death and formed the kingdom of Israel. Conquered by the Assyrians in 722 BCE, many of its inhabitants were deported. Those left behind formed the nucleus of the people later known as Samaritans. 1 Kings 11.29–39. *See also* 1 Kings 12.16–20; 2 Kings 17.4–6.

tribute Enforced contributions, either of money or labor, imposed on subject peoples. 2 Kings 17.1–6. *See also* Josh 16.10; 1 Kings 20.1–7; 2 Kings 23.33; Ezra 4.13; Lk 20.21–26.

triumph In Rome, victorious generals were granted "triumphs" which were official celebrations of a victory. They included a procession in which foreign prisoners were shown to the people, and this thought lies behind 2 Cor 2.14; Col 2.15.

Troas A city in Asia Minor on the Aegean shore about 10 miles from ancient Troy. Acts 16.6–11; 20.5–12; 2 Cor 2.12–13; 2 Tim 4.13. *Eskistanbul.*

Trophimus A Christian from Ephesus who went with Paul on missionary work to Asia and Jerusalem. Acts 20.3–4; 21.18–29; 2 Tim 4.20.

trumpet(s) Those used for signals in war were usually made from rams' horns. Those used as musical instruments in worship were long and made of metal. Num 10.1–10; Josh 6.4; Judg 3.27; 7.15–22; 1 Kings 1.34; 2 Kings 12.13; Hos 5.8; 1 Thess 4.16; Rev 8.2.

Trumpets, Festival of This celebration

marked the beginning of the seventh month, in which fell the Day of Atonement and the Feast of Booths. It was set aside as a day of rest. Today, it is known as Rosh Hashanah, marking the beginning of the Jewish year. Num 29.1–6. *See also* Lev 23.24–25.

truth Basically the meaning as understood today, but especially God's will as made known to men in the gospel of Jesus Christ: God's reality as contrasted with what is false or merely seems to be true. Prov 12.17; Jn 8.40–47; 14.6; Rom 1.18; 2 Cor 4.1–2; Gal 2.1–5; 5.7.

Tubal A region of Asia Minor whose people, though traders, were warlike. Isa 66.19; Ezek 27.13; 38.1–9.

Tubal-cain The son of Lamech and a skilled metal-worker. His descendants were probably Kenites who worked the copper and iron mines SE of the Dead Sea. Gen 4.19–22.

Twelve, The Those disciples chosen by Jesus to be his constant companions and to proclaim the gospel. They were called apostles, and their number corresponded to that of the tribes of Israel. Mk 3.13–19; Lk 6.13–16. *See also* Acts 1.15–26.

Tychicus An Asian Christian who accompanied Paul to Jerusalem and, at various times, acted as his trusted messenger. Acts 20.4; Eph 6.21–22; Col 4.7–8; 2 Tim 4.12; Titus 3.12.

Tyrannus A Greek teacher in Ephesus in whose lecture-hall Paul held discussions. Acts 19.8–11.

Tyre An important and wealthy Phoenician city built on a rocky island 22 miles S of Sidon and 35 miles N of Carmel. 2 Sam 5.11; 1 Kings 5.1–18; Ezek ch. 26–28; 29.18; Mk 7.24–31; Acts 12.20–21; 21.3–7. *Sûr.*

Ulai A river of Elam beside which Daniel saw a vision. Dan 8.1–2,16.

unclean, uncleanness The eating of certain kinds of animal was forbidden to the Israelites. The only clean animals were cattle, sheep, goats and the deer family. All beasts of prey, carrion, bats; all insects except the locust; water creatures without both fins and scales; anything strangled or that had died of itself was unclean. Lev 11.1–47. The NT shows that God requires moral rather than outward purity, and that Christians should deal gently with others' scrupulous convictions. Mk 7.14–23; Acts 10.9–16; Rom 14.13–15; Col 2.16–22.

universe, Hebrew Allowing for poetic imagery, some idea of the concept held in OT times may be traced from these verses. The foundations of the earth Ps 18.15 support it and stand in the springs of a great abyss Gen 7.11; 49.25. The vault of heaven Gen 1.14; Ps 104.2; Job 37.18 holds the sun, moon and stars Gen 15.5. The earth is surrounded by sea Gen 1.7; and Sheol, the abode of the dead, is like a great chasm Num 16.30. When the windows of the sky Gen 7.11 are opened, the water above the vault pours through them and falls as rain on the earth Job 38.37. The LORD's throne is in highest heaven Deut 10.14; Ps 148.4; above the earth Gen 1.14.

Unleavened Bread, Festival of A festival which was very closely connected with the Passover in time, lasting from 15th to 21st Nisan or Abib (March–April); and at some periods in Jewish history was kept simultaneously with it. Ex 23.14–15; Deut 16.3–8; Mk 14.1.

Ur of the Chaldeans The city in S Iraq from which Abraham began his journey to Canaan via Haran. Gen 11.28–31; 15.6–7; Neh 9.7. *el-Muqaiyar*. Spectacular discoveries of many remarkable and beautiful objects now in the British Museum were made on the site by C. L. Woolley 1922–34.

Urbanus A Roman Christian greeted by Paul. Rom 16.9.

Uriah (1) The Hittite husband of Bathsheba. 2 Sam 11.2–12.14. (2) A prophet in the reign of Jehoiakim. Jer 26.20–24. (3) High priest in the reign of Ahaz. 2 Kings 16.10–16.

Urim and Thummim Sacred symbols kept in the breast-piece of the high priest's vestments. They were used to discover God's will on important matters. Ex 28.30; Num 27.18–21; 1 Sam 14.36–42.

usury The Israelites were allowed to charge interest only on loans made to foreigners. This was because they were shepherds and farmers, not traders. In NT times when conditions were different, traders expected interest on loans but Jews were still bound not to have such dealings among themselves. *See* Ex 22.25; Lev 25.35–37; Deut 23.19–20; Mt 25.27; Lk 19.23.

Uz The homeland of Job which may have been in the area of Edom. Job 1.1; Jer 25.20; Lam 4.21.

Uzza, Garden of The place, adjoining the palace of Manasseh, where both he and King Amon were buried. 2 Kings 21.18,26.

Uzzah A driver of the cart which took the Ark from Abinadab's house to Obededom. 2 Sam 6.1–11.

Uzziah The son and successor of Amaziah, also known as Azariah, who made Judah strong externally and prosperous at home. 2 Kings 14.21; 2 Chr 26.1–23.

valley Fertile areas, common in Palestine, fed by water running into them in the rainy season. Gen 26.17; 1 Sam 6.13; Ps 65.13.

Vashti The Persian queen of Ahasuerus (Xerxes I) whom he divorced. Esth 1.1–2.4.

veil A covering for the face or head. Gen 24.62–65; Ex 34.34–35; Ezek 13.17–23.

vengeance Any punishment inflicted for retribution. Deut 32.40–41; Isa 34.8; Jer 20.12. *See also* Ex 21.23–25; Judg 15.7. In the NT Christ substitutes the law of forgiveness. *See* Mt 6.14; 18.21; Mk 11.25; 1 Thess 5.15; 1 Pet 3.9.

Versions of the Bible As the Christian church became more and more centered on Rome, the need was found for a translation into Latin as well as the existing Greek. The most widely used was that made by Jerome in the 4th century CE, which was known as the Vulgate and was *the* Bible for a thousand years in western Europe.

John Wycliffe and others made the first complete Bible into English (1380–4) from the Vulgate, but the real "father" of our present English Bible is William Tyndale who worked direct from the *original* languages. Eighty per cent of the words in even the Revised Version of 1881 stand precisely as they did in Tyndale's NT.

Coverdale produced the first English Bible entirely by one man (1535); and other versions such as the Great Bible (1539), the Geneva Bible (1560), the Bishop's Bible (1568) were based on Tyndale's and Coverdale's work.

The King James (or Authorized) Version of 1611 was an attempt to provide a Bible without any theological notes, which would therefore be acceptable to all shades of Protestant thought. It was not so much a new translation as the careful revision of the best existing versions.

The Revised Version of 1881 (American Standard Version 1901) was a conservative revision intended to introduce changes in the KJ Bible only where newly discovered knowledge and manuscripts showed the need for correction.

The Revised Standard Version 1937–57 was yet a further revision, aimed primarily at removing out-of-date usages. It has been said that the RSV kept what it could and changed what it must, and so lacks a certain unity.

During the past one hundred years many entirely new translations have been made, intended to supplement the KJ Bible by making the meaning clearer in modern idiom. Among these are the New English Bible, the New American Standard Bible, the New International Version, the Revised English Bible and the New Revised Standard Version. This glossary is based on the New Revised Standard Version published in 1989.

vestments The garments worn by Aaron and the priests when officiating in the sanctuary. Ex 28.2–43.

village(s) These were usually grouped around a walled town into which the people could retreat in time of war. Num 21.25; Neh 11.25. *See also* Lev 25.31.

vine, vineyard The soil and climate of Palestine are well suited to the grape-vine, which was grown to make wine and provide raisins for food. 1 Sam 25.18; 1 Kings 4.25; Isa 5.1–10; Mk 12.1. In the OT Israel is pictured as the vine of God. Ps 80.8–15; Ezek 17.5–10. And in the NT Jesus uses it in parables about the kingdom, and to show the relationship between himself and his church. Mt 21.33–43; Jn 15.1–8.

vinegar The name given to the light wine of Palestine after it has gone sour. Ps 69.21; Prov 10.26. *See also* Ruth 2.14; Jn 19.28–30.

viper, asp There are several species in the Palestinian area, all poisonous. Gen 49.17; Isa 11.8; 30.6; Acts 28.1–6. Used figuratively Mt 12.34–35.

virgin A woman who has not had sexual intercourse. Gen 24.16. Used figuratively of a country. 2 Kings 19.21; Isa 47.1; Am 5.2; Mt 1.23; Lk. 1.27.

vision An experience of special awareness of God. In many cases what is heard is as important as what is seen. 1 Sam 3.1–18; Ps 89.19; Isa 1.1; Ezek 1.1–3.14; 12.26–28; Dan 2.19–23; Ob 1–4; Lk 1.5–22; Acts 9.10–16; 10.9–23. *See also* Isa 6.1–13; Jer 1.4–19; Acts 9.1–9.

vow A promise made either to give something to God, or to honor and thank him by worship and self-denial. Gen 28.20–22; Num 6.2; Deut 23.21–23; 1 Sam 1.11; Ps 66.13–14; Jon 1.15–16.

vulture A large bird of prey, not unlike the eagle, of which several varieties were known in Palestine. Lev 11.13; Deut 14.12.

wadi A small stream which usually flows only in the rainy season. 1 Kings 17.2–7.

wafer A thin cake made of flour, sometimes mixed with honey. Ex 16.31.

wages In a subsistence agricultural community there was not much room for the hired hand. Wages, which were not high, had to be paid daily. Lev 19.13; Deut 24.14–15; Jer 22.13. Used figuratively Rom 6.23. *See also* Lk 3.14; 1 Tim 5.18.

wagon In Old Testament times, this was usually a vehicle with a low wooden body with one pair of wooden wheels with 6 or 8 spokes. It was drawn by a pair of oxen yoked to a pole which passed between them. Gen 45.19; Num 7.3; 1 Sam 6.7.

wail In funeral processions wailing relatives, often accompanied by hired professional women mourners and musicians, preceded the body to the grave. Jer 9.17–21; Am 5.16. *See also* Mt 9.23.

wait Both the OT and NT teach that those who trust in God's character and promises must wait in hope and patience. Ps 27.14; Isa 30.18; Lk 2.25; Acts 1.4; Rom 8.19; 1 Thess 1.9–10.

wall(s) Those of houses were usually made of mud or rough brick; stone being kept for the fortifications of towns, which were often double and could be very formidable. Excavations at Gibeon (*Tell el-Fûl)* have shown walls 8–10 feet thick. Num 32.17; Deut 3.5; Josh 2.15; Neh 12.37–39. *See also* Deut 1.28; 22.8. Used symbolically Isa 26.1; Jer 15.20; Zech 2.4–5; Eph 2.14; Rev 21.10–21.

Walls, Gate between the Two The way by which Zedekiah escaped from Jerusalem. 2 Kings 25.4.

wanderings The books of Exodus, Numbers and Deuteronomy tell of the wanderings of the tribes of Israel in the wilderness S of Judah, before they entered the promised land.

war, warfare Palestine, situated in a position of great strategic importance, and the natural highway for trading caravans, was an area of constant conflict. Every aspect of Israel's existence, including war, was bound up with her God, and the rules governing it were meant not only to restrain savagery and self-enrichment but to keep Israel a holy nation. Num 21.14; Joel 3.9. *See also* Deut 7.1–6; 20.2–9; Josh 6.17; 1 Sam 23.1–2.

Spring was the best season, and the usual methods and weapons were used. *See* Josh 8; Judg 7.8–25; 11; 20; 1 Sam 14; 17; 2 Sam 11.1; 1 Kings 20; 2 Kings 3.25; 2 Chr 14.8–17; Ezek 4.2–3.

Originally people's wars; the concept of a standing army was introduced by David and extended by Solomon. 1 Sam 11.6–7. *See also* Deut 20.5–8; 1 Kings 4.26–27. Israel thus entered on a career as a nation involved in alliances and balances of power which was consistently denounced by the prophets.

In the NT the soldier is neither condemned nor commended. However, the teaching of Jesus brought an almost wholly new idea into the world. *See* Mt 24.6–7; 26.51–52; Lk 3.14; Jn 18.36. Spiritual warfare is referred to in 2 Cor 10.3–6; Eph 6.11–18; Rev 12.7–9.

Wars of the Lord, Book of the A lost book quoted in Numbers, and evidently a collection of poems about Israelite victories. Num 21.14–15.

washing Frequent washing is necessary in hot climates to preserve health, but the OT law contained rules which also covered ceremonial cleanness. Ex 19.10; 30.17–21; Lev 14.8; 15.1–31; Num 19.11–22. Used symbolically Ps 51.2; Jer 4.14. In the NT Christ condemns the Pharisees for neglecting the inner cleanliness of which washing is supposed to be the outward sign. Mk 7.1–8,14–23; Lk 11.37–42.

watch A division into which the twelve hours of the night were made. The Jews, like the Babylonians, had three watches. Judg 7.19; 1 Sam 11.11; Lam 2.19.

watchman A guard for a city who kept his lookout from the walls; or a night watchman. 2 Sam 18.24–27; Song 5.7; Isa 21.11–12; Jer 31.6.

water Because of its scarcity in the dry season (May–October) when springs failed, great efforts were made to store it in cisterns and reservoirs. 1 Kings 17.1–11; 18.1–6; Jer 38.6. It is often used figuratively of the life-giving power of God. Jer 2.13; Jn 4.13–15.

Water Gate On the E side of Jerusalem. Ezra read the law in the square in front of it. Neh 3.26; 8.1–4; 12.37.

way In addition to its literal meaning of path, it is used in both OT and NT in a moral and religious sense: (1) A person's character or conduct. Prov 2.8; Jer 18.11. (2) The moral order which God has established in the world. Ps 18.30. (3) The earliest name for the Christian church. Acts 9.2; 18.25; 19.9 (4) Christ speaks of himself as "the Way." Jn 14.5–6; Heb 10.19–22.

weave, weaving The ancient process of preparing sheep's wool, camels' and goats' hair, flax and hemp into material for clothes, tents and curtains. The wooden loom on which the work was done could be either horizontal or upright. Judg 16.13–15; Isa 19.9. *See also* Ex 26.1–13; Lev 13.47–49; 1 Sam 17.7; Acts 18.3.

week A period of seven days, probably first used as a measurement of time because it is a quarter of the moon. *See* Gen 29.27.

Weeks, Festival of One of the three great annual festivals. It marked the completion of the barley harvest, and was named after the seven-week period from the offering of the barley sheaf at the beginning of the Passover to this festival. It was also known as Pentecost. Ex 34.22; Lev 23.9–21; Deut 16.16–17.

well A pit or hole dug down to the water table and filled through seepage. Water was hauled up by a bucket on a rope. Gen 21.30–31; 29.1–3; Ex 21.33; Jn 4.3–15. Be'er = well is found in a number of place-names. Gen 21.31.

Western Sea A name for the Mediterranean as contrasted with the Eastern (Dead) Sea. Deut 11.24; Zech 14.8.

wheat A cereal grown in Palestine from early times. Gen 30.14; Judg 6.11; Ezek 4.9. Used in metaphor. Mt 3.12; 13.29–30; Jn 12.24–25.

wheels These were probably at first just a disc of wood cut from a log, but quite early they developed into something resembling the modern device. Metal wheels were being made in Solomon's time. Ex 14.24–25; 1 Kings 7.30–33.

whole-offering *See* offering.

wicked Although used in the general moral or judicial sense of "wrong" (Ps 18.21), it more commonly means active mischief in the Bible. Num 16.26; Ps 10.1–11; 37.35; Prov 21.10. *See also* Gen 6.5; Mt 13.19; Mk 7.21–23; Rom 1.28–32.

widow They wore distinctive dress, and from early times it was laid down that they should be treated with special consideration. Ex 22.22–24; Deut 24.17–22; Ps 68.4–5; Prov 15.25; Isa 47.8; Jer 7.6; Acts 6.1–4; 1 Tim 5.3–6; Jas 1.27.

wife Legally a wife was owned by her husband. *See* Gen 3.16; Ex 20.17. And although polygamy was practiced from early times, both the OT and NT show God intending husband and wife to be equal partners. Gen 2.18–24; 30.1–13; Prov 31.10–31; Mk 10.2–9.

wilderness A wild, treeless area with little vegetation other than thorn and tamarisk bushes, except when the rains provided temporary pasturage. In addition to the wilderness of the wanderings in the Sinai peninsula under Moses, others are named in Gen 21.14; Deut 2.8; Josh 18.12; Judg 1.16; 1 Sam 23.24; 1 Kings 19.15. It was thought of as God's meeting-place with man. Jer 2.2; Mt 3.1–3; 4.1–11.

wild ox This is the Aurochs, and ancestor of domestic cattle. The bulls were enormous, over 6 feet at the shoulder with long, forward-pointing horns. Remains dating from the Pleistocene period have been found in Palestine, but it had disappeared well before NT times. OT references to it are in more or less figurative contexts. Num 23.22; Deut 33.17; Job 39.9; Ps 29.6; 92.10; Isa 34.6–7.

willow A tree common to almost every country, growing near water and having a long, narrow leaf, green on top and white underneath. Lev 23.40; Ps 137.2; Ezek 17.5.

wind The Hebrews thought of the wind as an instrument of God and a sign of his presence. Gen 8.1; Ex 10.13; Ps 18.10; 104.3. In Palestine the winds affect climate and vegetation. During the dry season, May–October, they blow mainly from the N and temper the heat. From September–October dry E winds blow from across the desert, followed by hot S winds. Then W winds bring the rain. 1 Kings 18.41–45; Song 4.16; Ezek 17.10; Lk 12.55.

window(s) Only large dwellings had windows, usually upstairs and closed with lattice work. In the ordinary house, light came in through the door. Judg 5.28; 1 Sam 19.12; 2 Kings 1.2; 13.17.

wine An everyday drink in Palestine, though forbidden to priests on duty in the sanctuary. Although in general it was considered as a food, the dangers of excess were recognized and some abstained completely. Gen 49.11; Lev 10.9; Num 6.1–4; Ps 104.15; Jer 35.3–7; Jn 2.1–10; Rom 14.20–22. *See also* Isa 5.22; Mk 14.25; Eph 5.18; 1 Tim 3.8.

winepress This was in two parts: the press vat where the grapes were trampled, and the wine vat into which the juice ran and remained for the beginning of fermentation. Judg 6.11; Neh 13.15; Isa 63.2–3; Mt 21.33. Used figuratively of the anger of God. Lam 1.15; Rev 14.19–20; 19.15.

winnow After harvesting, the grain was threshed or beaten to strip the chaff from the ears of corn. It was then all tossed into the air with a fork for the wind to blow away the straw. Ruth 3.3; Isa 30.24. Used as a picture of God's judgment. Mt 3.12.

winter Usually short and mild in Palestine, but the hilly regions have hail and snow. Gen 8.22; Ps 74.17; Zech 14.8.

wisdom In the Bible it is both religious and

practical. Stemming from the fear of the LORD who is the source of all wisdom, it branches out to touch all life, taking insights from the knowledge of God's ways and applying them to daily living. Only in humble trust in God and in obedience to his will can a man attain this wisdom. Job 28.12–28; Ps 111.10; Prov ch. 1–5; 8–9. The NT stands in the same traditions as the OT, that all wisdom has ultimately to do with God. 1 Cor 1.30; 2.6–15.

Wisdom Literature A literary form, common in the ancient Near East, in which instructions for successful living are given. The traditional form is a crisp, popular saying expressed in a short couplet. 1 Kings 20.11; Jer 31.29. The deposit of Israel's oral wisdom is recorded in the books of Proverbs, Job and Ecclesiastes in the OT.

witch, witchcraft The attempt by man to use supernatural powers through charms and spells to secure his ends. Though practiced by Israel's neighbors, it was forbidden in the law and condemned by the prophets. Ex 22.18. *See also* Lev 19.26; Deut 18.9–11; 1 Sam 28.3–8; Jer 27.9.

witness One who can state the truth about a debatable matter because he was present. 1 Sam 12.1–6; Job 16.19; Rom 1.9; 2 Cor 1.23. These were necessary in legal business. Num 35.30; Deut 19.16–19; Jer 32.10. Even a material thing such as a stone may be described as a "witness." Gen 31.44; Josh 24.27. The word is especially used of those who tell what God has done. Isa 43.10–12; Lk 24.45–48; Acts 2.32; 22.14–15; Heb 12.1–2. *See also* Rev 17.6.

wolf A familiar beast of prey in biblical times but referred to figuratively in the Bible; often for someone in authority who is misusing his position. Gen 49.27; Isa 65.25; Ezek 22.27; Mt 7.15; Jn 10.12; Acts 20.29.

woman Although the creation story shows woman created by God as an equal partner with man (Gen 2.18–24; 3.16), in Hebrew society a woman "belonged" to her father or husband. *See* Ex 21.7. However, some women reached positions of leadership. *See* Ex 15.20–21; Judg 4.4–10. In the NT Jesus treats women with respect and gives them a new freedom. Mt 15.21–28; Mk 14.3–9; 15.40–41; Lk 8.1–3; 10.38–42; Jn 4.7–30; Acts 16.12–15; 18.26. *See also* Mk 12.41–44; Jn 20.11–18; Gal 3.28.

wood-offering Special arrangements were made for the provision of wood for burning on the altar of the Temple. Neh 10.34–35; 13.31.

wool The soft hair of sheep or goats widely used in making clothes, though not to be woven together with linen. Lev 13.47; Deut 22.11. It was a valuable article of trade. 2 Kings 3.4; Ezek 27.21. Used as a symbol of purity. Isa 1.18; Rev 1.14.

word Apart from its literal meaning, it contains and carries something of the speaker's own self, character and purpose in it. Thus, God created the world by his "word" which stands for ever and must be fulfilled. Ps 33.6; Isa 9.8; 40.8; 55.11. It comes to men through the prophets. Isa 8.11; Jer 17.19; Ezek 21.18; Am 3.1. In the NT it is often applied to the Christian gospel. Lk 8.11; Acts 8.4. In Jn 1.1–18 the "Word" is Jesus Christ; the OT idea of the "word of the LORD" has developed to mean a unique Person who shares the very being of God.

work Used of God's work in creation and in saving, guiding and correcting his people. Gen 2.2; Ps 111.7; Jn 5.17; Eph 1.11. Man was made to find satisfaction in his own daily work which is also his duty. Ps 104.23; Eccl 3.22; 2 Cor 6.1; 2 Thess 3.10. *See also* Gen 2.15.

world In the Bible this generally stands for the created "universe" or the inhabited earth. Mt 25.34; Mk 8.36; Acts 17.24. Through the entry of sin, this world of human beings has become disordered and is in rebellion against God, but Christ has also entered it to reconcile man with God. Rom 5.12; 2 Cor 5.13–21. The characteristics of "this" (secular) worldliness are pride and covetousness which lead to idolatry.

wormwood Several species of this tree grow in Palestine. Its leaves were used medicinally, and a bitter juice obtained from its roots. It is associated with pain and sorrow. Prov 5.4; Jer 9.15; Rev 8.11.

worship Four elements seem to have been continuously present in Israel's worship: (1) The recitation of the way God had delivered his people and made them a nation. Josh 24.14–27. *See also* Ps 105; 106. (2) Sacrifice and daily offerings, which were a perpetual reminder of God's covenant with his people. (3) The offering of praise to God for what he is, king and creator, as well as for what he does. (4) The annual festivals in which the early events of the farmer's year, brought into relationship with God's great acts, were made occasions for the renewed dedication of the people to God.

Worship in the sanctuary at Jerusalem became very elaborate, but the prophets seem to object less to the cult of sacrifice itself than to the magic-working ideas borrowed from the fertility cults which became associated with it, and to the fact that much worship was outward only.

In the NT the church seems to have taken over much of its form of worship from the post-exilic synagogue, though everything assumed a new character since it was centered in Jesus Christ. Its unique feature, however, was the Lord's Supper. *See* Acts 2.42–47; 1 Cor 11.17–29; 14.26–40.

writing In early times inscriptions were made on stones; but later, clay tiles or tablets, pieces of pottery (shards or ostraca), wood with an inlaid wax surface, leather, papyrus and parchment were used.

In the earliest forms of writing, evolved before 3000 BCE, each word or syllable was represented by a picture sign and later by a conventional, stylized form of it. Shortly before the Israelites entered Canaan there developed in the Palestinian–Phoenician–Syrian area a partly alphabetic form with only 22 letters, all consonants, which was adopted by them and in which the OT was written. The first complete alphabet (24 letters, including vowels) was perfected by the Greeks about 850 BCE. The NT is written in this.

Xerxes A Greek form of the Hebrew name, Ahasuerus.

YHWH The four consonants standing for the Hebrew name for God, usually referred to as "Jehovah" or "Yahweh," meaning "I am," or "I cause to be." YHWH was considered too sacred to be pronounced, so Adonay (= my lord) was substituted in reading.

yoke A wooden frame fitted on the necks of two animals when plowing. Num 19.2. Used as a figure of the subjection of one person to another. Gen 27.40; 1 Kings 12.14; Mt 11.29–30.

Zacchaeus A citizen of Jericho, and a superintendent of taxes, converted by Jesus. Lk 19.1–10.

Zadok A descendant of Aaron and a priest in Jerusalem under David and Solomon. A guardian of the Ark during Absalom's rebellion, he became sole high priest; and the office remained in his family until the 2nd century BCE. 2 Sam 8.15–17; 15.16–29; 1 Kings 1.5–8,32–40; 2.35.

Zalmunna *See* Zebah.

Zarephath A town belonging to Sidon where Elijah stayed during the famine. 1 Kings 17.8–24. *See also* Lk 4.25–26. *Sarafand*.

Zarethan A town in the Jordan valley near the spot where the Israelites crossed the river. Josh 3.15–16.

Zealot(s) A Jewish nationalist party formed during the reign of Nero (54–68 CE) which for a time (66–70) achieved Jewish independence. Simon the Zealot (= enthusiast) was one of the Twelve. Mk 3.13–18.

Zebah A Midianite king who, with Zalmunna, had oppressed Israel. Both were defeated and killed by Gideon. Judg 8.4–27.

Zeboiim One of the five cities in the Dead Sea area destroyed with Sodom and Gomorrah. Abraham rescued Lot from its king. Gen 14.1–16; Deut 29.22–23; Hos 11.8.

Zebulun The son of Jacob and Leah and ancestor of the tribe. Gen 30.20. It occupied the fertile area of southern and central Galilee. Deut 33.18–19; Josh 19.10–16; Judg 4.10. Many of its people were deported by the Assyrians in 721 BCE. *See* 2 Kings 15.29.

Zechariah (1) The father of John the Baptist. Lk 1.5–25,57–79. (2) The son of Jehoiada the priest who was stoned to death. 2 Chr 24.17–22; Lk 11.51. (3) The prophet who returned from Babylon in 537 BCE with Haggai. Ezra 5.1; 6.14.

Zedekiah The last of the kings of Judah, placed on the throne as a puppet king by Nebuchadnezzar in 597 BCE. His advisers plotted with Egypt against the advice of Jeremiah, and their rebellion led to the fall of Jerusalem in 586 BCE. 2 Kings 24.10–25.7; Jer 27; 38.14–28.

Zelophedad A man of Manasseh who died in the wilderness wanderings leaving five daughters but no son. His daughters successfully made their claim to the inheritance, and the precedent of female succession was established provided that the heiress married within the tribe. Num 27.1–11; 36.1–12.

Zephaniah The great-grandson of Hezekiah, who lived and prophesied about the same time as Jeremiah.

Zerubbabel A grandson of Jehoiachin of Judah and a direct ancestor of Jesus. One of the leaders of the first groups returning from the Babylonian captivity, he became Governor of Judah and took a leading part, with Joshua the high priest, in rebuilding the Temple. Ezra 2.1–2; 5.1–2; Neh 7.6–7; Hag 1.1–15; Zech 4.6–10.

Ziba A member of Saul's household staff, appointed by David to work for Mephibosheth who, by slandering his master, obtained his property. 2 Sam 9.1–13; 16.1–4; 19.24–30.

ziggurat An artificial brick platform built in terraces to give the effect of a stepped pyramid. Outer staircases led to a temple at the top. The tower of Babel may have been the ziggurat at Babylon. *See* Gen 11.2–4.

Ziklag A town in S Judah assigned to Simeon, which was taken by the Philistines and later given by them to David to use as his headquarters in his guerrilla warfare with Saul. Josh 19.5; 1 Sam 27.1–6; 30.1–4; 2 Sam 1.1–16.

Zilpah The servant whom Laban gave to his daughter Leah, and later, through Jacob, the mother of Gad and Asher. Gen 30.9–13.

Zimri (1) An army officer who seized the throne of Israel after a military revolt and reigned for one week. 1 Kings 16.9–20; 2 Kings 9.31–34. (2) A Simeonite prince who defied Moses. Num 25.6–15.

Zion The Jebusite hill fortress captured by David and made his royal city of Jerusalem. 2 Sam 5.6–7; 1 Kings 8.1. From early times it stands for God's choice of the place where he dwells and where his power is operative. Ps 2.4–6; 48.2; Isa 24.23. In the NT it is the invisible city of God, the new Jerusalem. Heb 12.22–24.

Zipporah The daughter of Jethro, or Reuel, the priest of Midian, who became Moses' first wife. Ex 2.16–22; 18.1–4.

Zoan A city in the NE delta of Egypt and a royal residence of the Pharaohs, Set I and Rameses II. It continued to be important in later times. Num 13.23; Ps 78.12,43; Isa 19.11–18; Ezek 30.14. *Sân el-Hagar.*

Zoar One of the cities SE of the Dead Sea to which Lot escaped when Sodom and Gomorrah were destroyed. Gen 19.12–26.

Zobah An Aramaean kingdom whose king, Hadadezer, took a leading part in Syrian attacks on David, but was finally defeated. 2 Sam 8.3–12; 10.6–19.

Zoheleth The place where Adonijah, David's fourth son, gathered his conspirators before his father's death. 1 Kings 1.9–10.

Zorah A city about 15 miles W of Jerusalem on the borders of Judah and Dan; Samson's family home near which he was buried. Judg 13.2; 16.31.

CHRONOLOGICAL TABLES

OLD TESTAMENT CHRONOLOGY

There was no uniform chronological system in the ancient Near East, and writers often sought to glorify the subjects about whom they were writing by grossly exaggerating their length of life (one king in an ancient document is said to have reigned for 36,000 years). Dates of earlier epochs can sometimes be derived in general terms from inscriptions and writings found in Egypt and Mesopotamia, and in more precise terms in later periods from Syria, Greece and Asia Minor. The dates offered below reflect the changing results from analysis of the ancient sources.

The most likely time of the events just prior to and during the Exodus of Israel from Egypt is the nineteenth Egyptian dynasty: *ca.* 1350–1200 BCE. The following probable dates may be inferred from this chronological base:

2500–2000 BCE	Patriarchal period
1700–1300	Sojourn of the tribes of Israel in Egypt
1250–1200	The Exodus and the period in the Sinai
1200–1100	Entry and occupation of the land of Canaan
1050–1000	Reign of Saul

The first reasonably firm dates in Israel's history begin with the reign of David:

1000–962 BCE	Reign of David
962–922	Reign of Solomon

The division of Israel into the northern kingdom and the southern kingdom (based in Jerusalem) begins in 924 BCE.

	Judah		Israel
924–907 BCE	Rehoboam	924–903 BCE	Jeroboam I
907–906	Abijah		
905–874	Asa		
		903–902	Nadab
		902–886	Baasha
		886	Elah
		885	Zimri
		885–873	Omri
874–850	Jehoshaphat		
		873–851	Ahab
850–843	Joram	851–849	Ahaziah
		849–843	Jehoram
843	Ahaziah		
843–837	Athaliah	843–816	Jehu

	Judah		Israel
837–? BCE	Joash	816–800 BCE	Jehoahaz
?	Amaziah		
?	Azariah or Uzziah		
		800–785	Jehoash
?–742	Jotham	785–745	Jeroboam II
		745	Zechariah
		745	Shallum
742–727	Ahaz	745–736	Menahem
		736–735	Pekahiah
		735–732	Pekah
727–698	Hezekiah	732–723	Hoshea
		722	*Fall of Israel (Samaria)*
697–642	Manasseh		
642–640	Amon		
639–609	Josiah		
609	Jehoahaz		
608–598	Jehoiakim		
597	Jehoiachin		
597	*Babylonian Conquest of Jerusalem*		
597–586	Zedekiah		
586	*Destruction of Jerusalem*		

The exile of Israel in Assyria after the fall of Samaria in 722, and the exile of Judah in Babylon after the fall of Jerusalem in 586, came to an end over a period of time when the Persians allowed the Israelites to return to their land. This seems to have been a protracted process, which took place in four stages:

(1) A return under Cyrus about 538; work began on the Temple.
(2) A return under Darius I around 500; Temple completed; support from the prophets Haggai and Zechariah.
(3) A return under Artaxerxes I, led by Nehemiah, around 440.
(4) A return under Artaxerxes II, led by Ezra after 400.

After the invasion of the Middle East by Alexander the Great (334–330), followed by the dividing up of the region by his successors, Palestine was alternately controlled by the Syria-based Seleucids and the Egypt-based Ptolemies. The Jewish priests continued to preside over the Temple in Jerusalem until the Seleucid ruler, Antiochus IV Epiphanes, intervened to convert the temple to a shrine in his own honor, and began to designate the high-priest.

175 BCE	Onias deposed by Antiochus, Jason high-priest.
172	Menelaus, Jason's brother, nominated high-priest.
172	Onias III murdered about this time.
169	Jason seizes Jerusalem, which Antiochus attacks on his return from Egypt and pollutes the Temple.
168	Daily sacrifice interrupted.
166	Battle of Emmaus. Victory of Judas Maccabaeus.
165	Dedication of the Temple.
163	Lysias defeated by Judas at Bethsura. Alcimus, high-priest. Menelaus put to death.
161	Nicanor defeated at Capharsalama. Death of Judas Maccabaeus at Eleasa.
160	Decree of the Roman Senate in favor of the Jews.
159	Death of Alcimus.
156	Jonathan, brother of Judas, ruler of Judaea.
153	Jonathan made high-priest by Balas.
150	Jonathan honored by Philometor and Balas.
143	Jonathan put to death by Trypho. Simon, high-priest.
142	Simon, "Prince of the Jews." Jews allowed to coin money.
135	Murder of Simon. John Hyrcanus, high-priest.
109 BCE	Hyrcanus wars on Samaria and destroys the temple on Gerizim.
106	Hyrcanus dies. Aristobulus (his son), first king of the Jews.
105	Alexander Jannaeus made king of the Jews.
94	The Pharisees hostile to Jannaeus.
93	War of Jannaeus in Gilead and Moab.
88	Jannaeus defeated at Shechem.
78	Death of Jannaeus. Alexandra, his widow, rules after him. Hyrcanus II, high-priest.
69	Aristobulus II seizes the government.
64	Disputes between Aristobulus and Hyrcanus.
63	Jerusalem taken by Pompey. Hyrcanus again high-priest.
54	Palestine divided into five districts.
51	Crassus plunders the Temple.
48	Antipater made procurator of Judaea.
44	Hyrcanus, "Prince of the Jews."
41	Herod and Phasael, joint tetrarchs of Judaea.
40	Herod flees to Rome. Antigonus set up in his stead.
38	Herod marries Mariamne.
37	Herod takes Jerusalem.
29	Mariamne put to death.
25	Herod rebuilds Samaria.
17	Herod restores the Temple.
6	Alexander and Aristobulus put to death.

NEW TESTAMENT CHRONOLOGY

BCE	Christian history	Jewish history
4	Birth of Jesus Christ.	Death of Herod the Great.
CE		
6		Banishment of Archelaus.
7		Coponius procurator of Judaea; Annas high-priest.
8	Jesus at Jerusalem in the Temple.	Cyrenius completes "the taxing" commenced 4 BCE
17		Caiaphas, high-priest.
26	Beginning of the ministry of the Baptist.	Pontius Pilate, procurator.
30	The Crucifixion.	
33		Death of Herod Philip.
35	Conversion of Paul.	Pontius Pilate exiled.
37		Jonathan, high-priest. Herod Agrippa obtains the tetrarchy of Herod Philip. Marcellus, procurator.
38		Josephus born.
39	The Churches have rest.	Antipas deposed. Agrippa made tetrarch of Galilee.
41		Agrippa receives Judaea.
44	Death of James the brother of John.	Death of Herod Agrippa I. Cuspius Fadus, procurator.
45	Paul's first Missionary Tour.	
46		Tiberius Alexander, procurator.
48		Ventidius Cumanus, procurator.
49	Council of Jerusalem.	
50	1 and 2 Thessalonians written.	
51		Claudius [*or* Antoninus (?)] Felix, procurator.
55	1 and 2 Corinthians, Galatians, Romans.	
57	Paul a prisoner at Caesarea.	
58	Paul sent to Rome.	Porcius Festus, procurator.
59	Paul leaves Melita for Rome,	Joseph, son of Simon, high-priest.
60	Philippians, Colossians, Ephesians, Philemon.	Albinus, procurator.
61	Close of the history of the Acts of the Apostles.	
62		Gessius Florus, procurator. Completion of the Temple.
64	Titus, 1 and 2 Timothy.	Jewish war commences.
65	Martyrdom of Peter and Paul.	Capture of Jotapata by Vespasian.
70	Christians retire to Pella.	Siege and capture of Jerusalem.
95	Persecution of Christians by Domitian.	
96	John probably still alive.	

WEIGHTS, MEASURES, AND VALUES

No precise modern equivalents can be given for the units of measurement, weight, and value used in the ancient world, which themselves varied at different times, in different places, and in different contexts of use. The approximate equivalents given below may be helpful as an indication of the order of magnitude implied by a particular term.

LENGTH

Unit	*Approx. equivalent in metres*	*As read at*
handsbreadth	0.075	Ezek 40.5
span	0.225	1 Sam 17.4
cubit (short) = 6 handsbreadths	0.45	Judg 3.16
cubit (long) = 7 handsbreadths	0.525	2 Chr 3.3

WEIGHTS AND VALUES

Unit	*Approx. equivalent in grams*	*As read at*
gerah	0.6	Ezek 45.12
shekel (sacred) = 20 gerahs	12	Lev 27.25
mina = 50 shekels	600	1 Kings 10.17
mina = 60 shekels	720	Ezek 45.12
talent:3000 shekels	36000	Ex 38.25

Mention is made (Gen 23.16) of a shekel of "the standard recognized by merchants"; its relationship to the sacred standard is uncertain.

The "pound" of the New Testament (Jn 12.3) may be referred to the Roman standard of about 317 grams.

Related to gold or silver, the weights tabulated above are frequently used as measures of value. In the Old Testament "beka" (*lit.* half) is used to signify a half-shekel (Ex 38.26). The "talent" of the New Testament (Mt 18.24) evidently signifies a large but not precise monetary value.

COINS

The "daric" (1 Chr 29.7) was a gold coin weighing just over 8 grams, said to have been equivalent to a month's pay for a soldier in the Persian army. What is referred to as a "drachma" (Neh 7.70) may have been a silver coin of about 4.4 grams.

The "denarius" of the New Testament (Mk 14.5) is said to have been the equivalent of a day's wage for a laborer.

MEASURES OF CAPACITY
DRY MEASURES

Unit	*Approx. equivalent in litres*	*As read at*
kab	2.5	2 Kings 6.25
omer	4.5	Ex 16.32
seah	15	1 Sam 25.18
ephah = 10 omers	45	Ex 16.36
kor = 10 ephahs	450	1 Kings 4.22
homer = 10 ephahs	450	Ezek 45.11

LIQUID MEASURES

Unit	*Approx. equivalent in litres*	*As read at*
log	1	Lev 14.10
hin = 12 log	12	Num 15.7
bath = 6 hin	72	Ezek 45.14
kor = 10 bath	720	Ezek 45.14

SYNOPSIS OF THE GOSPELS

PART I
THE NATIVITY AND EARLY YEARS

		Matthew	Mark	Luke	John
1.	The Preface of John	—	—	—	1.1-13[a]
2.	The Preface of Luke	—	—	1.1-4[b]	—
3.	The Birth of John the Baptist announced	—	—	1.5-25	—
4.	The Annunciation to Mary	—	—	1.26-38	—
5.	The Salutation of Mary. The Magnificat	—	—	1.39-56	—
6.	Birth of John the Baptist. The Benedictus	—	—	1.57-80	—
7.	Appearance of an Angel to Joseph in a dream	1.18-25a[c]	—	—	—
8.	The Nativity of Jesus	1.25b[d]	—	2.1-7[d]	1.14[d]
9.	The Genealogies	1.1-17e	—	3.23-38e	—
10.	The Announcement to the Shepherds	—	—	2.8-20	—
11.	The Circumcision and Presentation in the Temple	—	—	2.21-38	—
12.	The Visit of the Magi	2.1-12[f]	—	—	—
13.	The Flight into Egypt	2.13-15	—	—	—
14.	The Children slain at Bethlehem	2.16-18	—	—	—
15.	The Return to Nazareth	2.19-23	—	2.39,40	—
16.	Jesus, 12 years of age, goes up to Jerusalem	—	—	2.41-52	—

[a] This Preface, peculiar to John, indicates the scope of his Gospel. (1) The life and work of Christ are viewed as a revelation in part of an eternal fact. (2) The later date of the Gospel is implied by a statement of positive truth against growing error. [b] This Preface is most valuable (1) as indicating the existence of many oral or written Gospels; (2) as throwing light on the sources and origin of Luke's Gospel. The language and style exhibit scholarship and literary skill. [c] Note the citation of prophecy in this passage in accordance with Matthew's plan. [d] The birth of Jesus is now placed by most scholars in the year 4 BCE. The determining points are: (1) The first rule of Quirinius (Lk 2.2); (2) the accession of Tiberius; (3) the death of Herod. [e] Matthew traces from Abraham, the father of Israel, Luke (the Gentile Evangelist) from Adam, the father of the human race. [f] The insertion of this and the following incidents (13,14) by Matthew again connects the NT with OT prophecy (see Num 24.17; Hos 11.1; Jer 31.15).

		Matthew	Mark	Luke	John

PART II
THE MINISTRY

		Matthew	Mark	Luke	John
17.	John the Baptist	3.1-12	1.1-8	3.1-18	1.15-18
18.	The Baptism of Jesus	3.13-17	1.9-11	3.21-3	1.32-4
19.	The Temptation of Jesus	4.1-11	1.12,13	4.1-13	—
20.	The Testimony of John the Baptist	—	—	—	1.19-34
21.	The first Call of Disciples: Andrew and another [? John], Simon Peter, Philip, Nathanael [? Bartholomew]	—	—	—	1.35-51[a]
22.	The Marriage in Cana	—	—	—	2.1-11[b]
23.	Jesus goes to Capernaum	—	—	—	2.12
24.	The Passover. Jerusalem. The cleansing of the Temple	—	—	—	2.13-25
25.	Interview with Nicodemus	—	—	—	3.1-21
26.	Jesus in Judaea baptizing. John also baptizing	—	—	—	3.22-36
27.	Jesus passes through Samaria into Galilee. The Woman of Samaria	—	—	—	4.4-44
28.	Cure of the nobleman's son	—	—	—	4.45-54
29.	Return to Jerusalem: Cure of an impotent man at the Pool of Bethesda	—	—	—	5
30*a*.	The Imprisonment of John the Baptist	14.3-5	6.17-20	3.19,20	—
31.	Jesus preaches in Galilee	4.12-17	1.14,15	4.14,15	—
32.	Teaches in Nazareth; is rejected. *Cf.* sec. 63	—	—	4.16-30	*Cf.* 4.44
33.	Dwells in Capernaum	4.13-16[c]	—	4.31,32[c]	—
34.	The (second) Call of Peter, Andrew, James and John: the first group of four disciples	4.18-22	1.16-20	5.1-11	—
35.	Heals a Demoniac in the Synagogue	—	1.21-8	4.33-7	—
36.	Heals Peter's wife's mother and other sick folk	8.14-17	1.29-34	4.38-41	—
37.	The Retirement of Jesus	—	1.35-7	4.42,43	—

[a] It is characteristic of John to choose for his narrative the inner, spiritual, first call of the Apostles. The synoptists relate the second, external call of four. [b] Narrated by John as a typical manifestation of power. [c] Matthew proving that Jesus is the Christ points out the prophetic significance of this sojourn in Galilee. Luke, true to his motive, sees in rejection at Nazareth and acceptance at Capernaum a forecast of the Christ rejected by Jews, accepted by Gentiles, and a fulfilment of the OT instances cited by Jews. This connection is an instance of what is meant by "in order," Lk 1.3.

		Matthew	Mark	Luke	John
38.	A Second Circuit in Galilee	4.23-5	1.38,39	4.44	—
39*a*.	The Sermon on the Mount. [Matthew's order]	5.1-7.29	—	—	—
40.	Heals a Leper	8.1-4	1.40-5	5.12-16	—
41.	Heals a Paralytic Man. Discourse thereupon	9.1-8	2.1-12	5.17-26	—
42.	The Call of Levi or Matthew	9.9-13	2.13-17	5.27-32	—
43.	Discourse on Fasting	9.14-17	2.18-22	5.33-9	—
44.	The Disciples pluck ears of corn. Discourse on the Sabbath	12.1-8	2.23-8	6.1-5	—
45.	Restores the withered hand on the Sabbath	12.9-13	3.1-5	6.6-10	—
46.	The Plot against Jesus	12.14	3.6	6.11	—
47.	Retirement of Jesus: many follow: He heals many	4.24,25; 12.15-23	3.7-12	6.12,17-19	—
48.	The Appointment of the Twelve	10.2-4	3.13-19	6.13-16	—
39*b*.	The Sermon on a level place on the Mount. [Luke's order: see 39*a*]	—	—	6.20-49	—
49.	The Mission of the Twelve	10.5-11.1	*Cf.* 3.14*b*,15	—	—
50.	Jesus heals the Centurion's Slave	8.5-13	—	7.1-10	—
51.	Raises the Widow's Son to life	—	—	7.11-17	—
52.	The Messengers of John the Baptist. Discourse about John	11.2-19	—	7.18-35	—
53.	Jesus upbraids the Cities of Galilee	11.20-30	—	*Cf.* 10.13-15	—
54.	(*a*) The Supper in the house of Simon the Pharisee; (*b*) Parable of the Two Debtors	—	—	7.36-50	—
55.	Circuit of Galilee with the Twelve	—	—	8.1-3	—
56.	(*a*) A Demoniac healed	9.32-4	3.19-30	11.14-36; 12.10	—
	(*b*) Charge of casting out through Beelzebub	12.22-8			
	Discourse thereon	12.22-45			
57.	The true Kinsfolk of the Lord	12.46-50	3.31-5	8.19-21	—

PARABLES

		Matthew	Mark	Luke	John
58.	(*a*) The Sower	13.1-23	4.1-20	8.4-15	—
	(*b*) The Candle under the Bushel	5.14-16, *cf.* 7.2; 13.12	4.21-5	8.16-18, *cf.* 6.38	—
	(*c*) The Seed growing secretly	—	4.26-9	—	—

		Matthew	Mark	Luke	John
	(*d*) The Tares	13.24–30 and 36–52	—	—	—
	(*e*) The Grain of Mustard-seed	13.31,32	4.30-2	13.18,19	—
	(*f*) The Hidden Leaven and other parables	13.33-5	4.33,34	—	—
59.	The Stilling of the Tempest on Sea of Galilee	8.18,23-7	4.35-41	8.22-5	—
60.	The Gadarene Demoniacs	8.28-34	5.1-20	8.26-39	—
61.	(*a*) Healing of the Woman with Issue. (*b*) The Daughter of Jairus	9.18-26	5.21-43	8.40-56	—
62.	The Cure of Two Blind Men	9.27-31	—	—	—
63.	A Second Rejection at Nazareth	13, 54-8	6.1-6*a*	—	—
64.	Third Circuit in Galilee. [*Cf.* Mt 4.23 and 10.1]	9.35-8	6.6*b*	13.22	—
65.	The Mission of the Twelve	10.1,5-42	6.7-11	9.1-5	—
66.	Their work described	—	6.12,13	9.6	—
67.	Jesus preaches alone	11.1	—	—	—
68.	What Herod thought of Jesus	14.1,2	6.14-16	9.7-9	—
30*b*.	The story of John the Baptist; a retrospect. See 30*a*	14.3-12	6.17-20	—	—
69.	The Feeding of the Five Thousand	14.13-21	6.30-44	9.10-17	6.1-14
70.	Jesus walks upon the Sea	14.22-33	6.45-52	—	6.15-22
71.	Heals Sick Folk at Gennesaret	14.34-6	6.53-6	—	—
72.	Discourse concerning the Bread of Life	—	—	—	6.23-65
73.	Jesus reproves the Scribes and Pharisees	15.1-20	7.1-23	—	—
74.	(*a*) The Syrophoenician Woman; (*b*) Cure of Sick Folk	15.21-31	7.24-37	—	—
75.	The Feeding of the Four Thousand	15.32-9*a*	8.1-9	—	—
76.	The Pharisees seek a sign	15.39*b*-16.4; 12.38,39	8.10-13	*Cf.* 11.16-29	—
77.	The Leaven of the Pharisees	16.5-12	8.14-21	12.1	—
78.	Cure of a Blind Man at Bethsaida	—	8.22-6	—	—
79.	Caesarea Philippi. The Confession of Peter	16.13-16[a]	8.27-9[a]	9.18-20[a]	6.66-71[a]
80.	The Church of Christ. The First Prediction of the Passion	16.17-28[b]	8.30-9.1[b]	9.21-7[b]	—

[a] We notice here a marked instance of close correspondence in a crucial incident. [b] The whole of this section is closely similar in the synoptic accounts, a note of its deep importance. Luke omits the rebuke of Peter, and the important words of Mt 16.17-20 belong to that Gospel alone.

	Matthew	Mark	Luke	John
81. The Transfiguration	17.1-13	9.2-13	9.28-36	—
82. Jesus heals a Lunatic Boy	17.14-21	9.14-29	9.37-43*a*	—
83. (*a*) The Second Prediction of the Passion. (*b*) The Poll-tax demanded. (*c*) Dispute who should be greatest	17.22-18.5	9.30-7	9.43*b*-8	—
84. A certain one casts out Devils in the Name of Jesus, and follows not with Him	*Cf.* 10.40	9.38-40	9.49,50	—
85. A Discourse on Offenses	10.42; 18.6-9; 5.13	9.41-50	17.1,2; 14.34	—
86. The Lost Sheep	18.10-14	—	15.3-7	—
87. (*a*) Of Forgiveness. (*b*) Parable of the Unforgiving Servant	18.15-35	—	17.3,4	—
88. (*a*) Jesus goes to the Feast of Tabernacles in Jerusalem	—	—	—	7.1-10
(*b*) Incident on the way	—	—	9.51-6	—
89. Types of Discipleship	8.19-22	—	9.57-62	—
90. Mission of the Seventy	—	—	10.1-16	—
91. Jesus teaches at the Feast	—	—	—	7.11-8.59
92. The Man born Blind	—	—	—	9.1-41
93. Jesus teaches of Himself as the Door and the Good Shepherd	—	—	—	10.1-21
94. Return of the Seventy	[11.25-7]	—	10.17-24	—
95. The Parable of the Good Samaritan	—	—	10.25-37	—
96. Martha and Mary	—	—	10.38-42	—
97. Jesus teaches His Disciples how to pray	6.9–13; 7.7-11	—	11.1–13	—
98. Discourses of the Pharisees, Scribes and Lawyers	—	—	11.37-54	—
99. Teaches of Hypocrisy, and of Courage in Persecution	—	—	12.1-12	—
100. Parable of the Rich Fool	—	—	12.13-21	—
101. Worldly Anxiety	—	—	12.22-32	—
102. Of Alms and the Treasures in Heaven	[6.19,20]	—	12.33,34	—
103. Of watching for the Master's coming	[24.43-51]	—	12.35-48	—
104. Some effects of Christ's Coming	[10.34-6; 16.2,3; 5.25,26]	—	12.49-59	—
105. Pilate's Cruelty. The Tower of Siloam	—	—	13.1-5	—
106. The Parable of the Barren Fig-tree	—	—	13.6–9	—

	Matthew	Mark	Luke	John
107. The Healing of a Woman with an Infirmity	—	—	13.10-17	—
108. The Feast of the Dedication. Retreat to the Jordan	? 19.1,2	? 10.1	—	10.22-42
109. Of being saved. Are there few that be saved?	—	—	13.22-30	—
110. Jesus speaks of Herod	—	—	13.31-3	—
111. Lamentation over Jerusalem	[23.37-9]	—	13.34,35	—
112. Jesus heals one sick of the Dropsy	—	—	14.1-6	—
113. Jesus teaches of Humility	—	—	14.7-14	—
114. The Supper of the Kingdom	—	—	14.15-24[a]	—
115. The Cost of following Jesus	—	—	14.25-35	—
116. Parables (1) Addressed to Scribes and Pharisees. *a.* The Lost Sheep. *b.* The Lost Coin. *c.* The Lost Son. (2) Addressed to His Disciples. *d.* The Unjust Steward	—	—	15.1-16.13	—
117. (*a*) Reproof of the Pharisees. (*b*) Dives and Lazarus	—	—	16.14-31	—
118. Of Offenses. See 85				
119. Of Faith and Duty	—	—	17.5-10	—
120. The Raising of Lazarus	—	—	—	11.1-45[b]
121. A Council of the Chief Priests and Pharisees about Christ	—	—	—	11.46-54
122. Jesus goes up to Jerusalem to the Last Passover	? 19.1,2[c]	? 10.1[c]	17.11[c]	—
123. Ten Lepers cleansed	—	—	17.12-19	—
124. Discourse on the Coming of the Kingdom	—	—	17.20-37	—
125. The Importunate Widow: God the Judge	—	—	18.1-5	—
126. The Pharisee and the Publican	—	—	18.9-14	—

[a] This parable is similar to one related Mt 22.1-10, the framework in parts is verbally parallel, but the incidents and teaching differ materially. [b] Placed by several authorities after Lk 19.27. [c] Scholars differ as to whether the passages in Matthew and Mark refer to this or to a previous journey to Jerusalem for the feast of the Dedication. Matthew's report however seems to unite and reconcile the other two.

	Matthew	Mark	Luke	John
127. Question of Divorce	19.3-12[a]	10.2-12[a]	*Cf.* 16.18[a]	—
128. Young Children brought to Christ	19.13-15[b]	10.13-16[b]	18.15-17[b]	—
129. The Rich Young Ruler. Discourse on Riches and Sacrifice	19.16-29	10.17-30	18.18-30	—
130. The Laborers in the Vineyard	19.30-20.16[c]	10.31[c]	—	—
131. The Third Prediction of the Passion	20.17-19[d]	10.32-4[d]	18.31-4[d]	—
132. (*a*) The prayer of the Sons of Zebedee. (*b*) Dispute as to the greatest	20.20-8	10.35-45	[*Cf.* 22.24-7]	—
133. Cure of the Blind at Jericho	20.29-34	10.46-52	18.35-43	—
134. Zacchaeus	—	—	19.1-10	—
135. The Ten Minae (Luke) and the Ten Talents (Matthew)	[25.14-30]	—	19.11-28	—
136. The approach of the Passover. Orders to betray Jesus	—	—	—	11.55-7

PART III
THE PASSION

	Matthew	Mark	Luke	John
137. The Supper at Bethany	26.6-13	14.3-9	[7.36-50]	12.1-11
138. The triumph of Palm Sunday	21.1-11[e]	11.1-11[e]	19.29-44[e]	12.12-19[e]
139. (i) The Curse on the Fig-tree (ii) The (second) Cleansing of the Temple (iii) Other incidents the same day	21.12-18	11.12-19	19.45,46	—
140. The lesson of the Fig-tree	21.19-22	11.20-6	—	—
141. The Authority of Christ questioned	21.23-7	11.27-33	20.1-8	—
142. (*a*) The Two Sons	21.28-32	—	—	—
(*b*) The Unthankful Husbandmen	21.33-46	12.1-12	20.9-19	—

[a] The very close correspondence here shows the importance of this weighty judgment. [b] Once more the synoptic correspondence becomes very close, Matthew contains a slight addition, and Mark has two special points of interest. The identity of this record marks how highly treasured the words were. [c] Mark has only the words which introduce the parable. [d] This prediction is more definite and detailed than those which precede. Luke, by omitting all mention of the chief priests and scribes, throws into prominence the share of the Gentiles in the Passion: an instance of the manner in which the Evangelists adapted their narrative to their special readers. [e] Here there is the great interest of a fourfold comparison. In the synoptics the same sequence is observed, and the points of contact are numerous; yet each Evangelist has characteristic points of separate description. John connects the joyous recognition of the crowd from Jerusalem with the raising of Lazarus.

	Matthew	Mark	Luke	John
(*c*) The Royal Marriage Feast. The Wedding Garment	22.1-14	—	—	—
143. Tribute to Caesar	22.15-22	12.13-17	20.20-6	—
144. The Sadducees confuted	22.23-33	12.18-27	20.27-39	—
145. The First and Great Commandment	22.34-40	12.28-34*a*	Cf. 10.25-8	—
146. (*a*) The Pharisees confuted. (*b*) Their practices rebuked	22.41–6 23.1-39	12.34*b*–40	20.40–7	—
147. The Widow's Mites	—	12.41-4	21.1-4	—
148. The Greeks desire to see Jesus. Teaching of Jesus in the Temple	—	—	—	12.20-50
149. The Destruction of the Temple foretold. The End of the World	24.1-42	13.1-37	21.5-36	—
150. Parables of Passion-tide				
(*a*) The Ten Virgins	25.1-13	—	—	—
(*b*) The Talents	25.14-30	—	—	—
151. The Last Judgment	25.31-46	—	—	—
152. The Council convenes to destroy Jesus	26.1-5	14.1,2	22.1-6	—
153. The Covenant with Judas	26.14-16	14.10,11	22.3-6	—
154. The Passover	26.17-19	14.12-16	22.7-13	13.1
155. (*a*) The Last Supper	26.20-5	14.17-21	22.14 [15-19]–23	13.21-38
(*b*) The Strife among the Apostles	—	—	22.24-30	—
(*c*) Jesus washes the Disciples' feet	—	—	—	13.2-20
(*d*) Institution of the Eucharist	26.26-9[a]	14.22-5[a]	22.15-20[a]	—
156. The Last Discourses of Jesus and Prayer of Intercession	—	—	—	14.1-17.26
157. Crossing to the Mount of Olives. Discourse of Jesus. Confidence of Peter	26.30-5	14.26-31	22.29,31-4,38	13.36-8
158. The Agony in the Garden of Gethsemane	26.36-46	14.32-42	22.41-6	—
159. The Betrayal	26.47-56	14.43-52	22.47-53	18.3-11
160. Jesus taken to Annas	—	—	—	18.12-14
161. (*a*) Thence to Caiaphas [the first informal Trial]. (*b*) Denials of Peter	26.57-75	14.53-72	22.54,63-5	18.15-18, 25-7
162. The formal Trial before the Council	27.1	15.1*a*	22.66-71	—
163. Jesus taken to Pilate	27.2[3-10]-14	15.1*b*	23.1	18.28
164. The End of Judas	27.3-10	—	—	—

[a] In this deeply important parallel Matthew and Mark are in close, almost identical correspondence. Luke has additional matter, and (according to the best reading) omits important words found in the other synoptics and paralleled in 1 Cor 11.25.

	Matthew	Mark	Luke	John
165. The Trial before Pilate	27.11-14[a]	15.2-5[a]	23.2-5[a]	18.33-8[a]
166. Remission to Herod	—	—	23.6-12	—
167. Jesus delivered by Pilate to be crucified	27.15[19]-31[b]	15.6-20[b]	23.13-25[b]	18.39-19.16[b]
168. The Dream of Pilate's wife	27.19	—	—	—
169. The Crucifixion				
(*a*) Simon compelled to bear the Cross	27.32	15.21	23.26	—
(*b*) The Women of Jerusalem	—	—	23.27-31[c]	—
(*c*) The Scene at Golgotha	27.33-8	15.22-7	23.33,34	19.17-24
(*d*) The Mockery	27.39-44	15.29-32	23.35-43	—
(*e*) Jesus commends His Mother to John	—	—	—	19.25-7
(*f*) The Death of Jesus	27.45-56	15.33-41	23.44-9	—
(*g*) Piercing of the Side	—	—	—	19.31-7
170. The Burial	27.57-61	15.42-7	23.50-6	19.38-42
171. The Sepulchre made sure by Seal and Watch	27.62-6	—	—	—
172. The Resurrection	28.1-10[d]	16.1-11[d]	24.1-12[d]	20.1-18[d]
173. The Soldiers bribed to give false evidence	28.11-15[e]	—	—	—
174. The Journey to Emmaus	—	16.12,13[f]	24.13-35[f]	—
175. Appearance to the Apostles in the absence of Thomas	—	16.14[g]	24.36-43[g]	20.19-25[g]
176. Appearance to the Apostles, Thomas being present	—	—	—	20.26-9
177. The Eleven go to Galilee	28.16*a*	—	—	—
178. Appearance to six Disciples at the Sea of Tiberias	—	—	—	21.1-24
179. Appearance on a Mountain in Galilee	28.16*b*-20[h]	16.15-18[h]	—	—
180. The Ascension	—	16.19[i]	24.44-53	*Cf.* Acts 1.1-12

[a] All agree in the report of Pilate's opening words. Matthew and Mark agree throughout. Luke has a general agreement but a fuller report; the definite statement of the charge belongs to him alone. John's account is the most special and of the deepest interest. [b] Luke (having alone narrated the mockery by Herod's soldiers) omits the mockery in the Praetorium where the other synoptists agree closely. The synoptic accounts have much in common, but Luke as before shows independent sources. [c] This incident, peculiar to Luke, is characteristic of his research and of his pathos. [d] The mode of narration varies, and the peculiar points are unusually numerous. The angel's message of the Resurrection is the same. In the rest of the message Matthew and Mark are agreed. John gives a detailed account of the appearance to Mary Magdalene. After Mk 16.8 the report is thought to be not that of the Evangelist. [e] An incident which would naturally come before Matthew who was writing for Jews and was therefore bound to face Jewish objections. [f] The brief notice in Mark follows a different report. [g] The three Evangelists here follow independent evidence. Luke and John have each special and important particulars. [h] The two reports are independent. [i] The short notice in this appendix to Mark is clearly from an independent source.

CAMBRIDGE BIBLE MAPS AND GAZETTEER

CAMBRIDGE
BIBLE MAPS

Followed by a Gazetteer

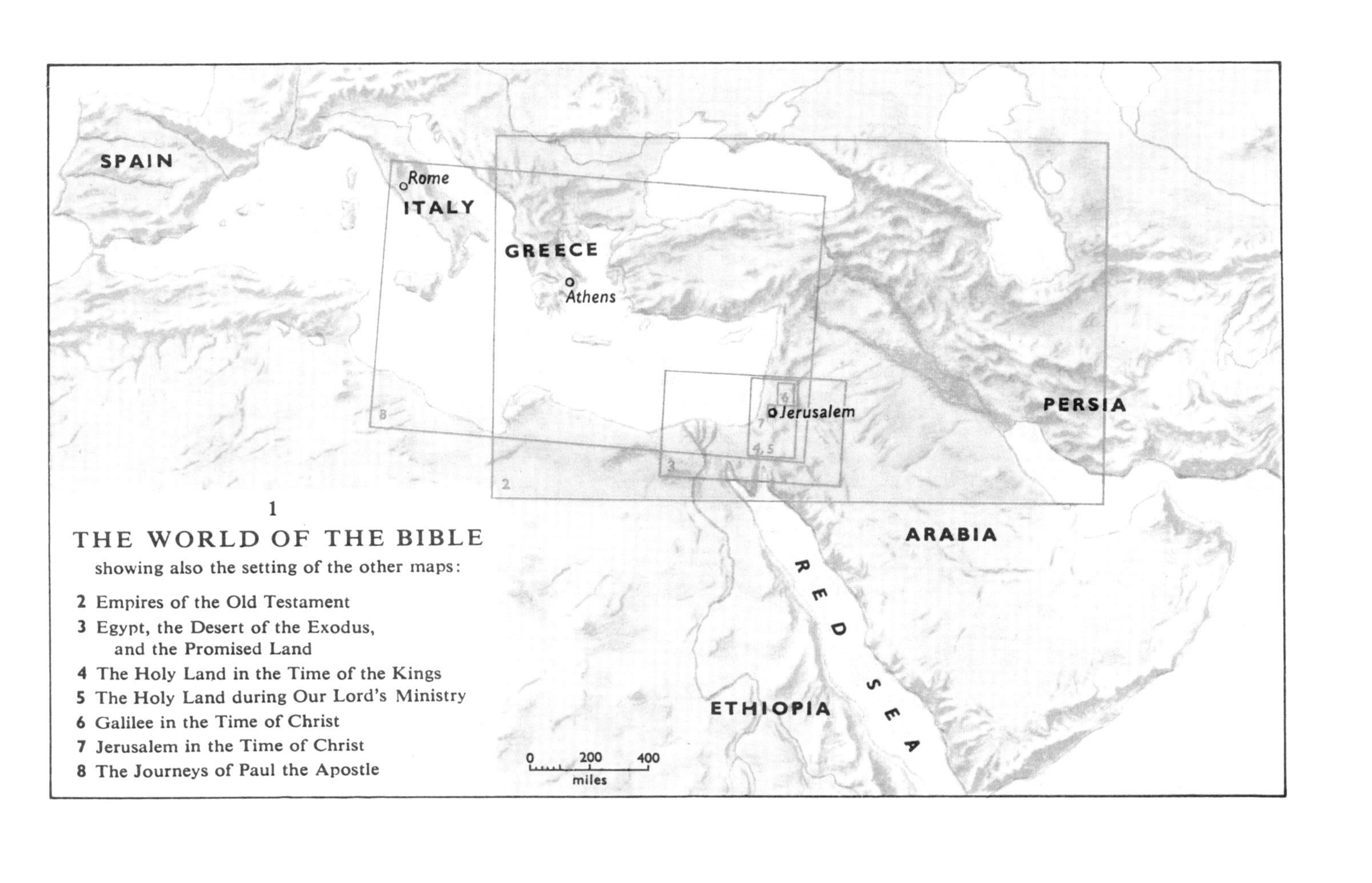
SPAIN
Rome
ITALY
GREECE
Athens
Jerusalem
PERSIA
ARABIA
RED SEA
ETHIOPIA
0 200 400
miles
1 THE WORLD OF THE BIBLE
showing also the setting of the other maps:
2 Empires of the Old Testament
3 Egypt, the Desert of the Exodus, and the Promised Land
4 The Holy Land in the Time of the Kings
5 The Holy Land during Our Lord's Ministry
6 Galilee in the Time of Christ
7 Jerusalem in the Time of Christ
8 The Journeys of Paul the Apostle

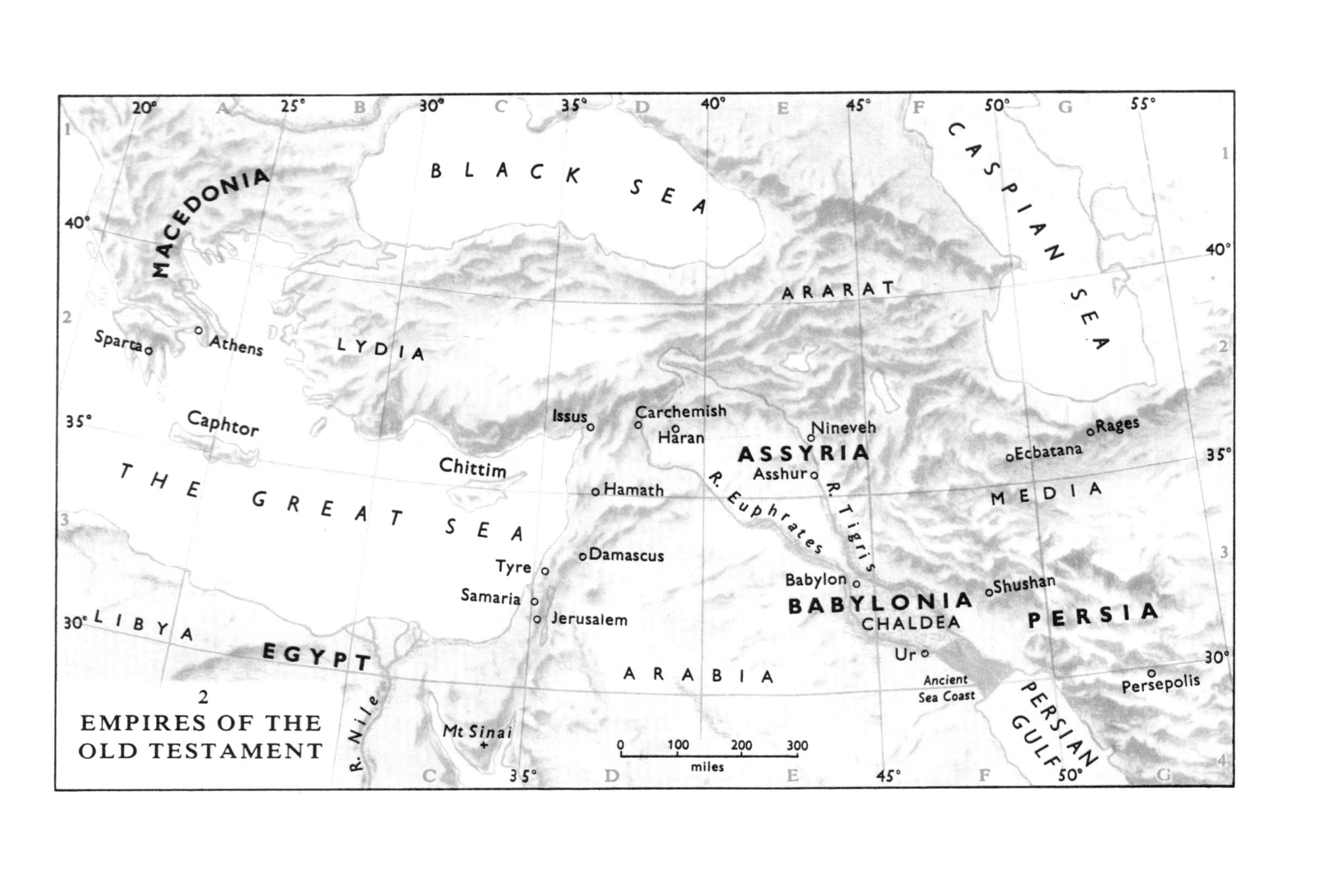

2

EMPIRES OF THE OLD TESTAMENT

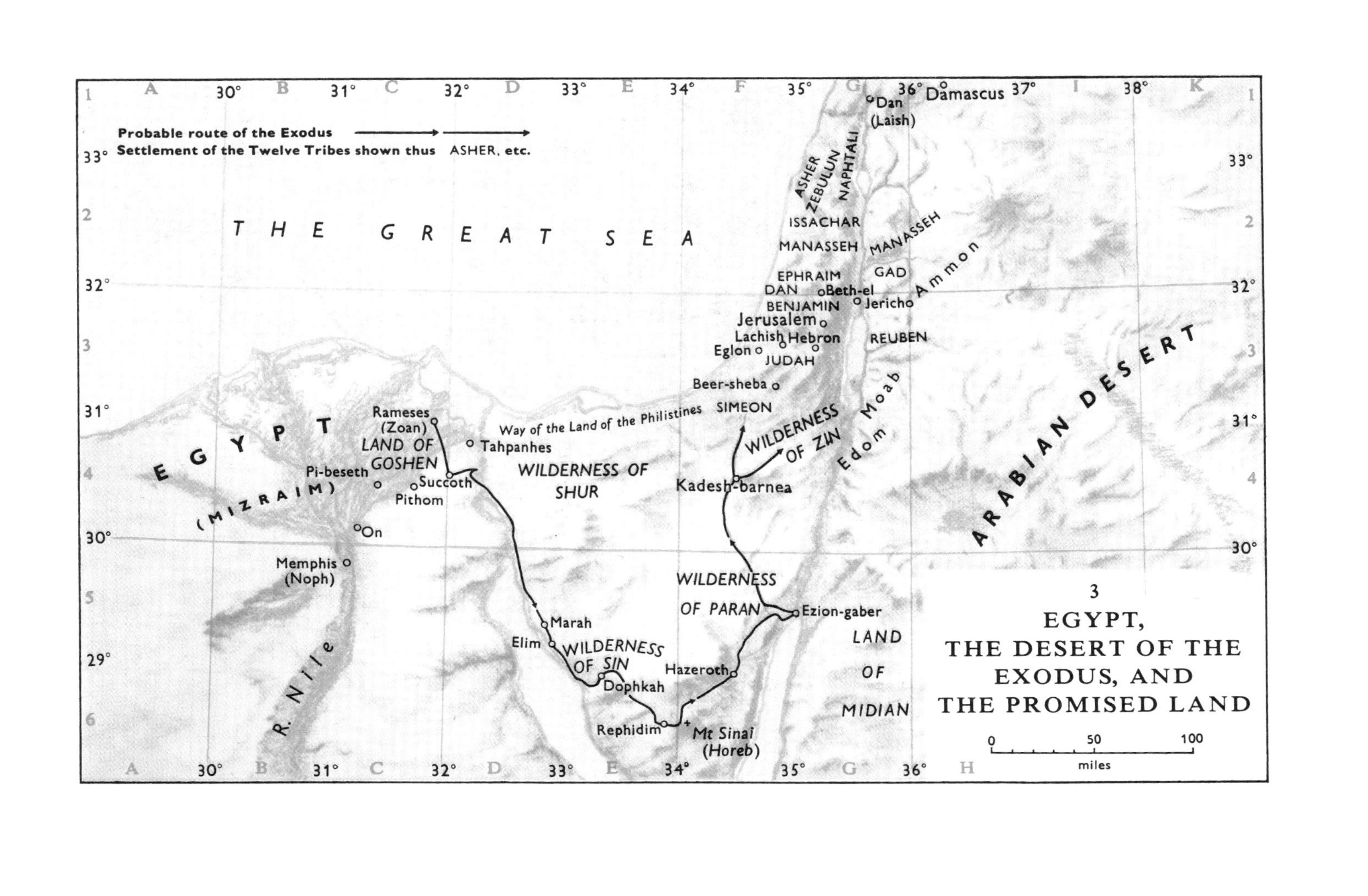

3

EGYPT,
THE DESERT OF THE
EXODUS, AND
THE PROMISED LAND

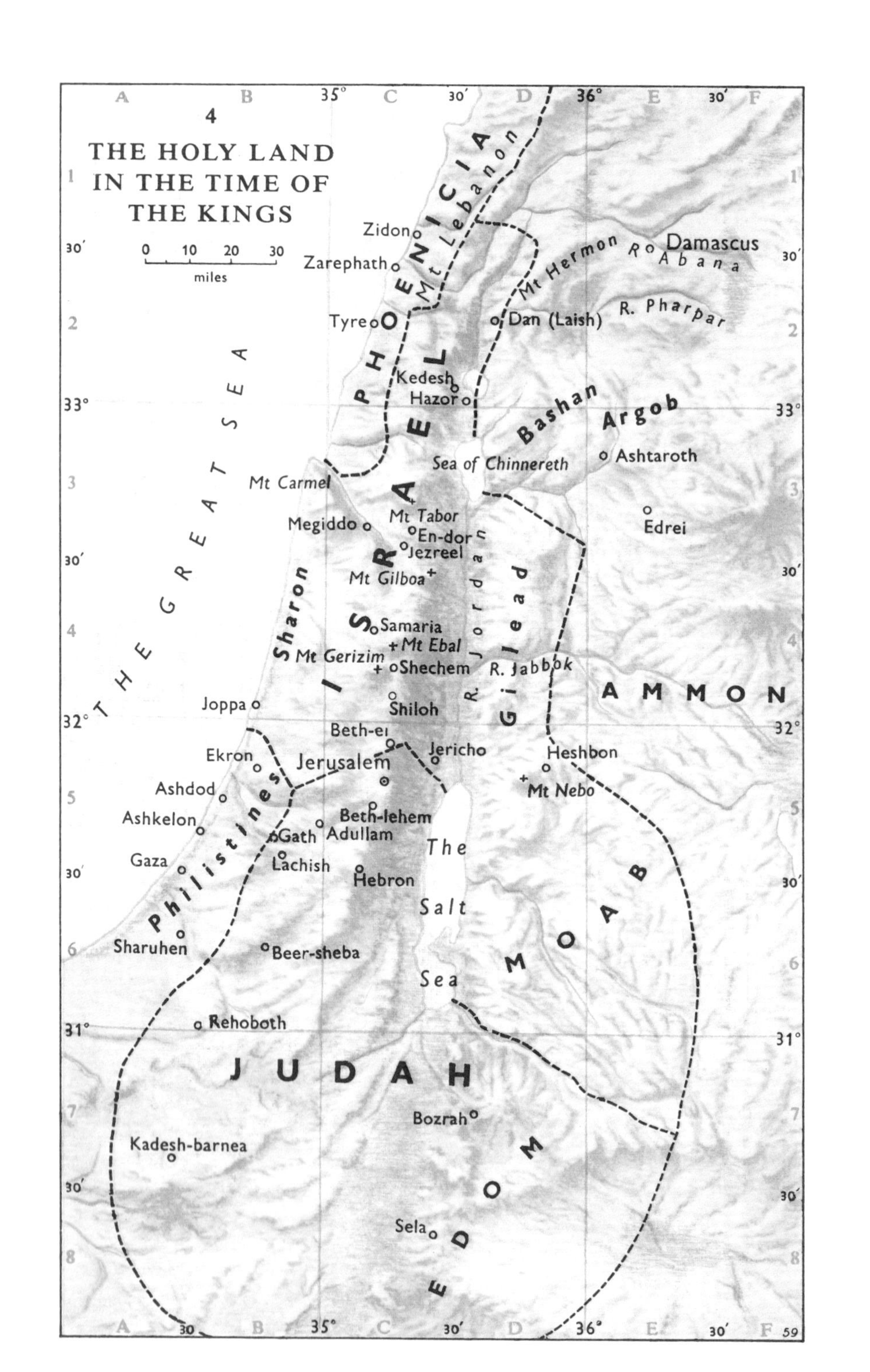
4
THE HOLY LAND IN THE TIME OF THE KINGS
0 10 20 30
miles
THE GREAT SEA
PHOENICIA
Mt Lebanon
Zidon
Zarephath
Tyre
Mt Hermon
Damascus
R. Abana
R. Pharpar
Dan (Laish)
Kedesh
Hazor
Bashan
Argob
ISRAEL
Sea of Chinnereth
Ashtaroth
Mt Carmel
Megiddo
Mt Tabor
En-dor
Jezreel
Edrei
Mt Gilboa
Sharon
R. Jordan
Gilead
Samaria
Mt Ebal
Mt Gerizim
Shechem
R. Jabbok
AMMON
Joppa
Shiloh
Beth-el
Ekron
Jerusalem
Jericho
Heshbon
Ashdod
Mt Nebo
Ashkelon
Beth-lehem
Gath
Adullam
Philistines
Gaza
Lachish
Hebron
The Salt Sea
MOAB
Sharuhen
Beer-sheba
Rehoboth
JUDAH
Bozrah
Kadesh-barnea
EDOM
Sela
59

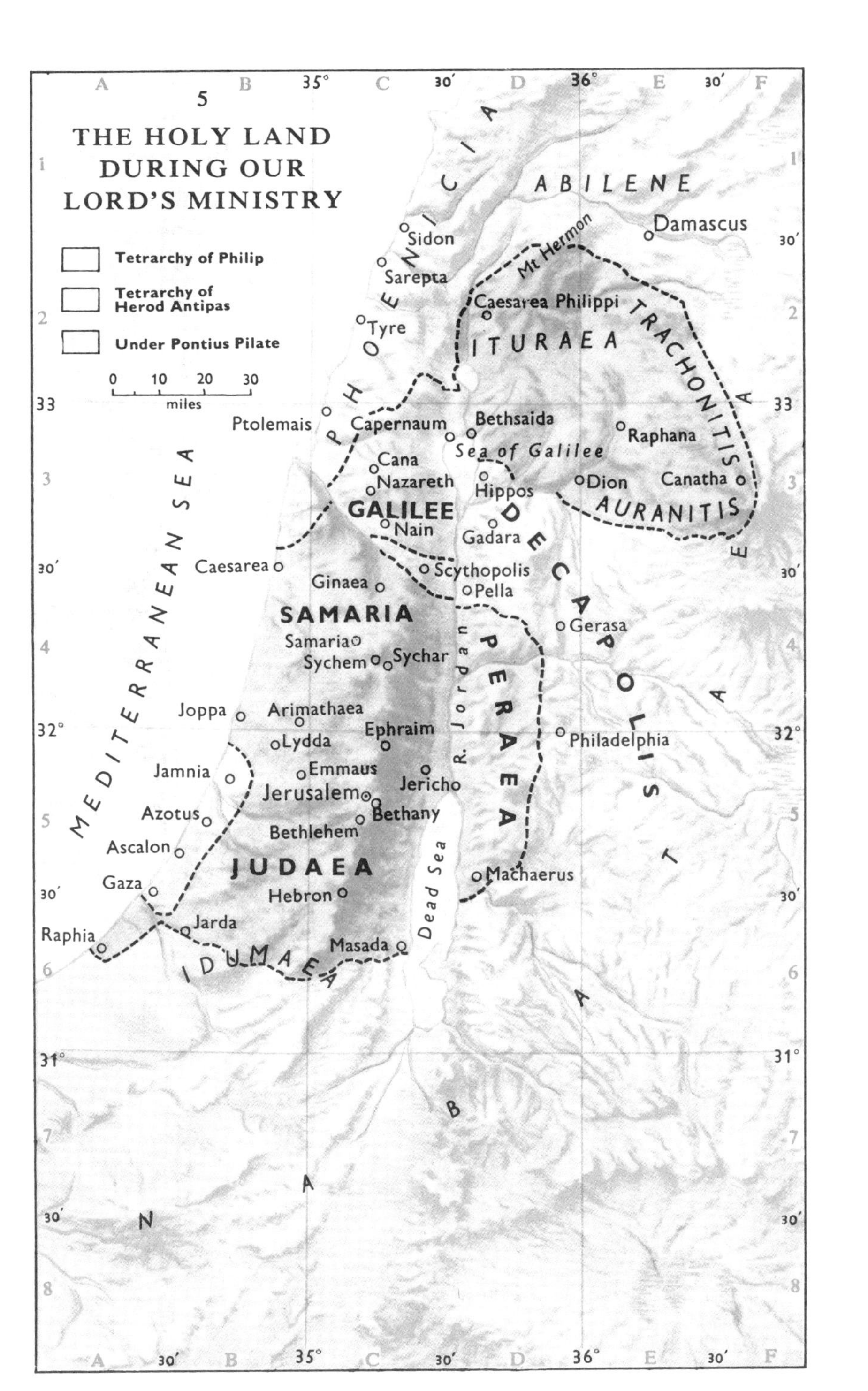

5
THE HOLY LAND DURING OUR LORD'S MINISTRY
Tetrarchy of Philip
Tetrarchy of Herod Antipas
Under Pontius Pilate
0 10 20 30
miles
PHOENICIA
ABILENE
Sidon
Damascus
Sarepta
Mt Hermon
Caesarea Philippi
Tyre
ITURAEA
TRACHONITIS
Ptolemais
Capernaum
Bethsaida
Raphana
Sea of Galilee
Cana
Nazareth
Hippos
Dion
Canatha
GALILEE
AURANITIS
Nain
Gadara
DECAPOLIS
Caesarea
Scythopolis
Ginaea
Pella
SAMARIA
Gerasa
Samaria
Sychem
Sychar
PERAEA
R. Jordan
Joppa
Arimathaea
Ephraim
Lydda
Philadelphia
Emmaus
Jamnia
Jericho
Jerusalem
Bethany
Azotus
Bethlehem
Ascalon
JUDAEA
Dead Sea
Machaerus
Gaza
Hebron
Jarda
Raphia
Masada
IDUMAEA
MEDITERRANEAN SEA
ARABIA
NABATAEA
35°
30′
36°
31°
32°
33

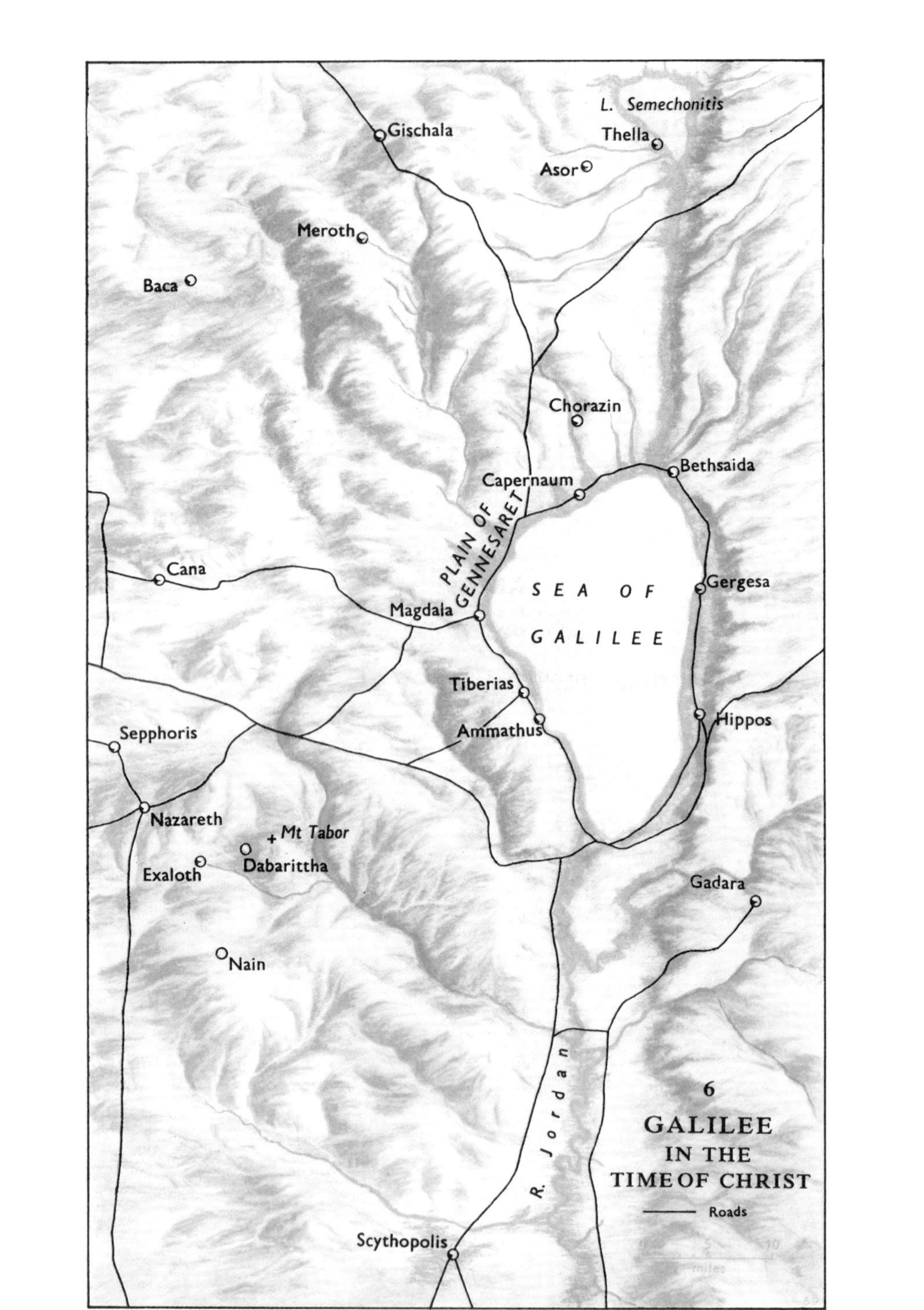

6

GALILEE IN THE TIME OF CHRIST

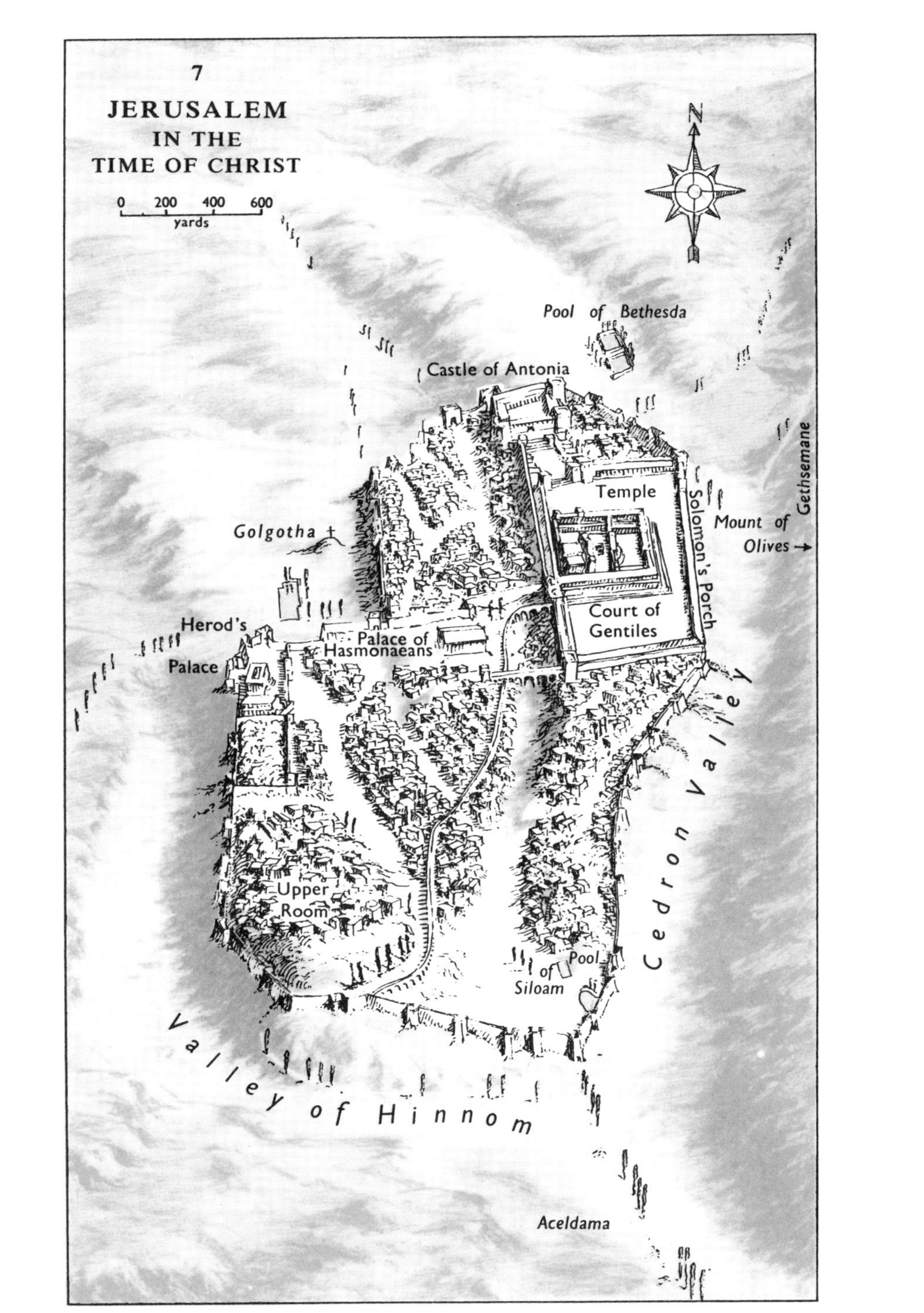

7
JERUSALEM
IN THE
TIME OF CHRIST
0 200 400 600
yards
N
Pool of Bethesda
Castle of Antonia
Temple
Solomon's Porch
Gethsemane
Mount of
Olives →
Golgotha
Herod's
Palace
Palace of
Hasmonaeans
Court of
Gentiles
Cedron Valley
Upper
Room
Pool
of
Siloam
Valley of Hinnom
Aceldama

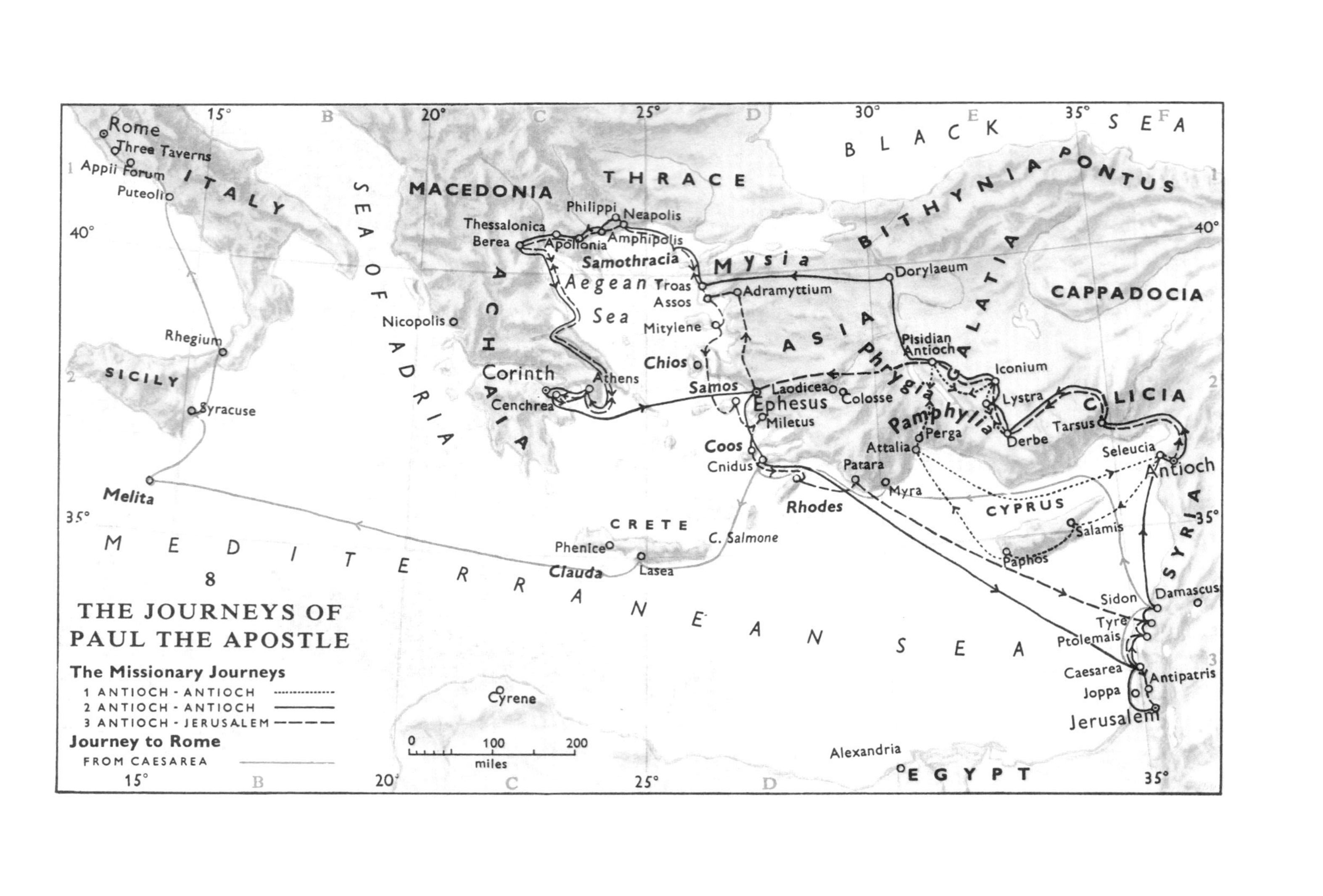
8
THE JOURNEYS OF PAUL THE APOSTLE
The Missionary Journeys
1 ANTIOCH - ANTIOCH
2 ANTIOCH - ANTIOCH
3 ANTIOCH - JERUSALEM
Journey to Rome
FROM CAESAREA
0 100 200
miles
BLACK SEA
MEDITERRANEAN SEA
SEA OF ADRIA
Aegean Sea
ITALY
SICILY
MACEDONIA
THRACE
ACHAIA
Mysia
ASIA
Phrygia
BITHYNIA
PONTUS
GALATIA
CAPPADOCIA
Pamphylia
CILICIA
SYRIA
CYPRUS
CRETE
EGYPT
Rome
Three Taverns
Appii Forum
Puteoli
Rhegium
Syracuse
Melita
Nicopolis
Thessalonica
Berea
Apollonia
Philippi
Neapolis
Amphipolis
Samothracia
Troas
Assos
Adramyttium
Dorylaeum
Mitylene
Chios
Samos
Corinth
Cenchrea
Athens
Ephesus
Laodicea
Colosse
Miletus
Coos
Cnidus
Rhodes
Patara
Myra
Attalia
Perga
Pisidian Antioch
Iconium
Lystra
Derbe
Tarsus
Seleucia
Antioch
Salamis
Paphos
Sidon
Damascus
Tyre
Ptolemais
Caesarea
Antipatris
Joppa
Jerusalem
C. Salmone
Phenice
Claudа
Lasea
Cyrene
Alexandria
15°
20°
25°
30°
35°
40°

GAZETTEER

The figure in bold type denotes the number of the map. Where a letter and second figure follow, these denote the square on which the item will be found.

The gazetteer includes not only the names that appear on the maps but also some alternative Biblical names and spellings, with cross-references. If an item appears with another name elsewhere in the set of maps, this other name is given after the words *and see*.

The sites of some places are still disputed by Biblical scholars, and in such cases the site shown on the map is necessarily conjectural.

GAZETTEER